Oxbridge Directory of Newsletters

1996

...ensive guide to U.S.
...sletters available.

Oxbridge Communications, Inc.
150 Fifth Avenue, Suite 302, New York, NY 10011

Editorial & Sales Office: Oxbridge Communications, Inc.
150 Fifth Avenue, Suite 302
New York, NY 10011
Phone: (212) 741-0231
Fax: (212) 633-2938

Database Media Management: Deborah Striplin

Editors: Bino Alves
Joy Goldstein
Mayerline Joseph
Craig Schwartzberg

Sales & Marketing: Ken Njenga

Multimedia Sales & Marketing: Ira Wexler

Account Management: Tracy Grimsley
Paula Rozier
Andrew Thiani

Information Technologies: Jake Richter

Subscription & Fulfillment: Craig Schwartzberg
Mayerline Joseph

Administrative Assistant: Frances Donato

Cover Design: Smallkaps, Port Washington, NY

President: Patricia Hagood, PhD.
Chief Executive Officer: Louis Hagood
Publisher: Fay Shapiro

Department Extensions
Editorial: Ext. 212
Sales: Ext. 200
Customer Service: Ext. 214, 211

ISBN 0-917460-65-0
ISSN 0163-7010

Printed in the United States of America by Port City Press, Baltimore, MD.
© Copyright 1995. **Oxbridge Communications, Inc.** 150 Fifth Avenue, Suite 302, New York, NY 10011

Preface

What communications media is growing yearly, involves many who might be termed non-conformists, serves dedicated and informed audiences worldwide, and is increasing its impact through technological advances? Did you say "The Internet?" How about newsletters? That's right, and they are also a part of the Information Superhighway. There are newsletters available only online such as *Digital Dispatch* and the real estate industry's *ALQ Executive Report,* as well as those that are in both print and electronic formats--*Internet Marketing & Technology* and *PETA News* for animal rights activists. The growth of the Online Index in the 1996 edition of the **Oxbridge Directory of Newsletters** reflects this trend as does the increase in publications that are available by FAX. Still, the majority are delivered in print. This year's directory contains over 20,000 publications including Newsletters along with Looseleafs, Bulletins, Proceedings and Indexes.

Oxbridge remains the leading source for information about newsletters published in the United States and Canada, produced in print and any electronic format. We know you'll find a wide range sources in these pages. Please give us your comments and suggestions so that we can further support your needs.

Deborah Striplin
Dir. DB Media Management

Industry Phone Numbers

Associations

American Advertising Federation . . . .(202) 898-0089
American Association of Advertising Agencies . . . .(212) 682-2500
American Library Association . . . .(312) 944-6780
American Society for Association Publishing . . . .(708) 577-5772
American Society for Information Science . . . .(301) 495-0900
Canadian Magazine Publishers Association . . . .(908) 775-7524
Comics Magazine Association of America . . . .(212) 661-4261
COSMEP . . . .(415) 922-9490
Council for Periodical Distributors . . . .(212) 818-0234
Direct Marketing Association . . . .(202) 347-1222
Magazine Publishers Association . . . .(212) 872-3700
National Association of Printers & Lithographers . . . .(201) 342-0707
Newsletter Publishers Association . . . .(703) 527-2333
North American Graphic Arts Association (NAGASA) . . . .(202) 328-8441
Paper Industry Management Association . . . .(708) 956-0250
Printing Industries of America . . . .(703) 519-8100
Public Relations Society of America . . . .(212) 995-2230
Special Library Association . . . .(202) 234-4700

Conventions/Shows

American Soc. for Information Science Conf., Fall . . . .(301) 495-0900
American Library Association Convention, June . . . .(312) 944-6780
COSMEP Conf., Sept. . . . .(415) 922-9490
Circulation Management Conf. & Expo, Sept. . . . .(212) 979-0730
Direct Marketing Day, May . . . .(202) 347-1222
Folio Metro, July . . . .(203) 358-9900
Folio Midwest, March . . . .(203) 358-9900
Folio Show, October . . . .(203) 358-9900
Folio Spring, May . . . .(203) 358-9900
Graphic Arts Expo . . . .(703) 264-7200
Magazine Publishers Association Conf., Fall . . . .(212) 872-3700
Masthead Trade Show, June . . . .(905) 625-7070
NAGASA Dealer/Manufacturer FORUM, Spring . . . .(202) 328-8441
NAGASA DBX Dealer Business Exchange, Sept. . . . .(202) 328-8441
National Online Convention, May . . . .(609) 654-6266
Newsletter Publishers Association Conf., June . . . .(703) 527-2333
Public Relations Society Conv., June . . . .(212) 995-2230
Special Library Association Conv., June . . . .(202) 234-4700

THE NEWSLETTER WORLD TODAY

Newsletter Publishers Association

1401 Wilson Boulevard, Suite 207, Arlington, VA 22209

Welcome to the *Oxbridge Directory of Newsletters* and the world of the 20000+ newsletters featured on these pages. Some newsletters are published by associations as a member benefit, some by corporations as an in-house organ to communicate the company's activities, some by publishing companies as a for-profit venture, and many other variations. In view of my role as the executive director of the Newsletter Publishers Association, a non-profit trade association with 750+ members publishing over 2200 for-profit, subscription newsletters, the focus of this introduction is on subscription newsletters.

Over the past 20 years since the Newsletter Publishers Association was formed, the industry has changed from a cottage industry with many members publishing from their kitchen tables to today's professional publishing companies. A recent study produced by Northwestern University and funded by the Newsletter Publishers Foundation indicates that the subscription newsletter industry's revenues exceed the billion-dollar level and its employees number in the tens of thousands. This research report also finds that two-thirds of the newsletters have been started since 1980.

While newsletters are published on a wide variety of topics—from *Soups Cheap or Almost Free* (about, of course, soup) to *Nutz and Boltz* (covering auto maintenance)—the one thing they tend to have in common is that they each deliver a message to a niche market. Newsletters have typically been delivered via the mail on 4-16 pages of copy.

Times are changing and the industry is changing along with it. When we pick up the newspaper each day, or read our favorite magazines and newsletters, it's nearly impossible to get through an issue without reading something about the Internet or the World Wide Web. As we prepare to enter the 21st century, most of us are asking ourselves how this popular electronic vehicle will change the newsletter business as it exists today.

While many newsletter publishers are investing in a home page, "surfing the Net" for editorial purposes, using it as a delivery mechanism and using e-mail to communicate with subscribers, we haven't heard from publishers who are getting rich from the Internet. In fact, many newsletter publishers and looseleaf providers have products created by gathering information from government agencies via the FOIA (Freedom of Information Act) and repackaging and selling these products for substantial sums. Many government agencies are now providing this same information FREE to the public via the Internet which may put some of the newsletters out of business, if they aren't prepared to add value.

Newsletter publishers are facing new challenges as we enter the next millenium. Subscription newsletters have been highly regarded for their journalistic integrity because thay generally contain no advertising. Today, subscription-based newsletters are competing with Internet newsletters that provide the newsletter free of charge to the user, while generating their income from advertrisers rather than subscribers. Considering all the free information available on the Internet, newsletter publishers are questionning the future of selling high-priced newsletters on a system that is inexpensive, if not free, to users.

For many years newsletter publishers have attempted to educate the public on copyright laws—stressing that it is illegal to do cover-to-cover photocopying. In today's world of high technology, we need to re-educate the public on what's legal and what's not. It's so easy to scan a newsletter into your computer and have it available to everyone via the network—but it's not legal. Many publishers today deliver their publications on disk or via the Internet. Again, it's so easy to push a button and the information could be on the Internet free to anyone who wants it. Newsletter publishers will be challenged in the coming years to protect their copyrighted information—their bread and butter.

Again, welcome to the world of newsletters. I hope you find this fast-paced, lucrative industry as exciting as I do. I am sure that the *Oxbridge Directory of Newsletters* will prove to be as invaluable a resource to you as it is to NPA.

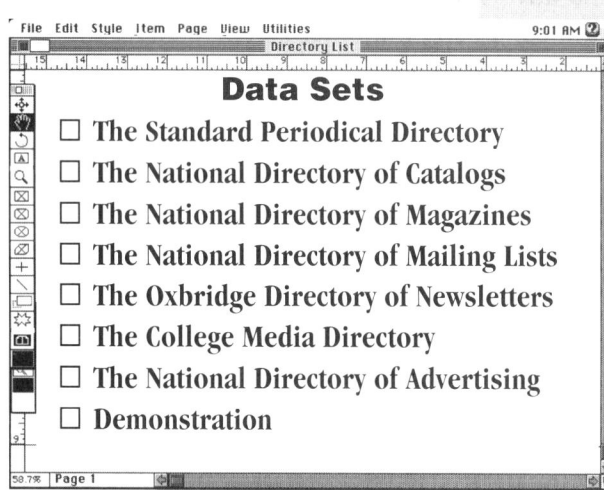

Digital Frontiers

Web Site Creation • Interactive Design • Web Marketing

Digital Frontiers *integrates all of the elements of a successful web presence. We offer cutting-edge design, the latest marketing techniques and a keen business sense – all of which we mold to fit your company's unique business goals. Clients include Time Warner, Inc., Phillips Business Information, Inc., Oxbridge Communications, Inc. and TosoHaas (a joint venture of Rohm and Haas and Toso).*

How To Use The Oxbridge Directory of Newsletters

The listings have been designed to be self-explanatory. A sample listing is shown below. If you have any questions or suggestions for further clarification please call the Database Department at (800) 955-0231, ext. 212.

9. Target Audience

1. Title – **bold** indicates publication has advertising and/or rents its list.

2. Name, address, phone and fax of the publisher

3. Names of key staff

4. Description of editorial content

5. General information and production data including printing method, paper and binding type

6. Subscription rates

7. Circulation figures

8. Printing company information

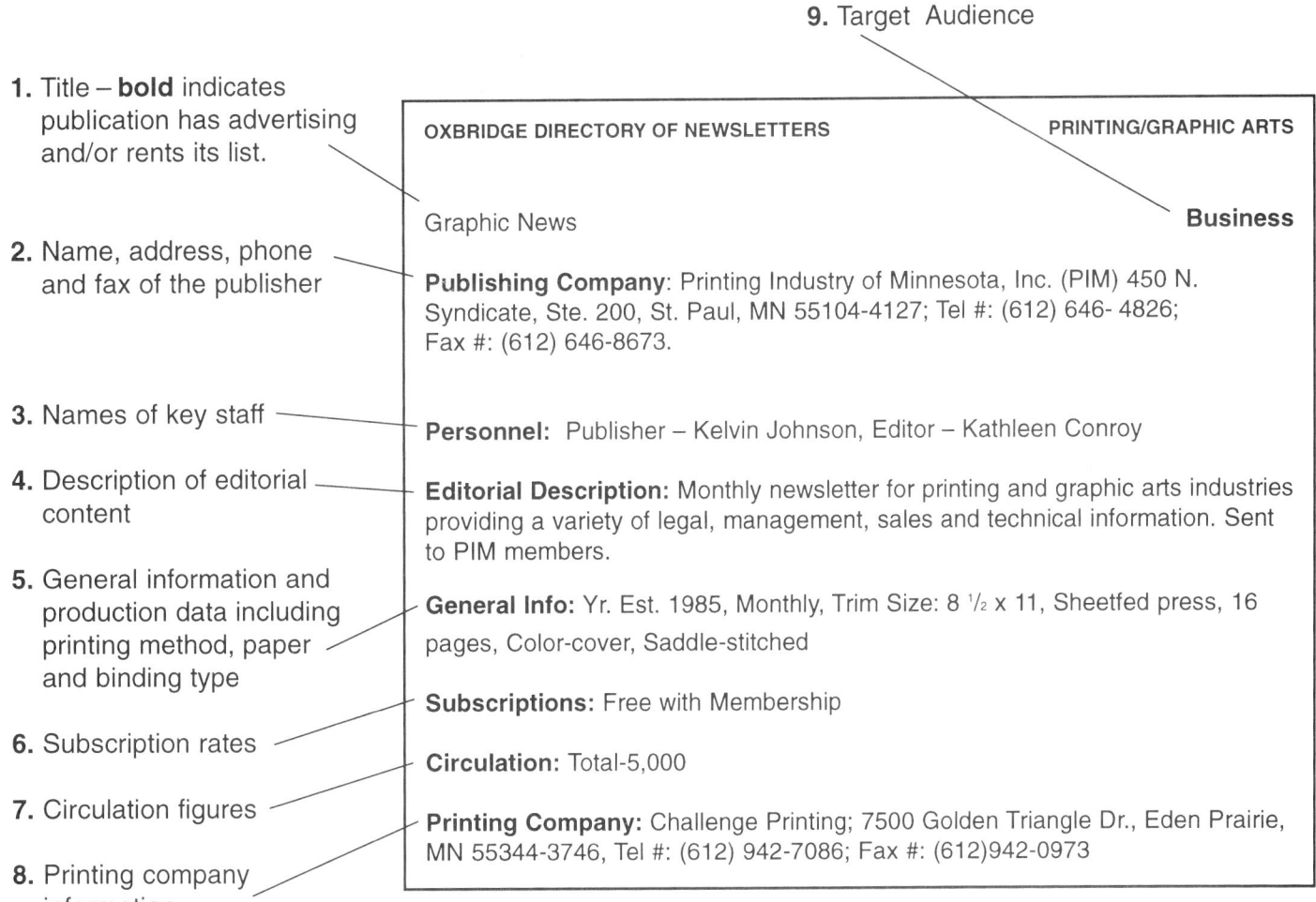

OXBRIDGE DIRECTORY OF NEWSLETTERS   PRINTING/GRAPHIC ARTS

Graphic News

Business

Publishing Company: Printing Industry of Minnesota, Inc. (PIM) 450 N. Syndicate, Ste. 200, St. Paul, MN 55104-4127; Tel #: (612) 646- 4826; Fax #: (612) 646-8673.

Personnel: Publisher – Kelvin Johnson, Editor – Kathleen Conroy

Editorial Description: Monthly newsletter for printing and graphic arts industries providing a variety of legal, management, sales and technical information. Sent to PIM members.

General Info: Yr. Est. 1985, Monthly, Trim Size: 8 ½ x 11, Sheetfed press, 16 pages, Color-cover, Saddle-stitched

Subscriptions: Free with Membership

Circulation: Total-5,000

Printing Company: Challenge Printing; 7500 Golden Triangle Dr., Eden Prairie, MN 55344-3746, Tel #: (612) 942-7086; Fax #: (612)942-0973

TABLE OF CONTENTS

Listings

ACCOUNTING

AICPA Audit and Accounting Manual — *Business*

Publishing Co: CCH, Inc., 2700 Lake Cook Rd., Riverwoods, IL 60015 Parent Co.-Kluwer Law & Taxation Publishers, Cambridge; Title Tel # (847) 267-7000 Title Fax # (800) 224-8299
Editorial Description: Provides a set of nonauthoritative audit tools & illustrations provided by the staff of the AICPA for continuing reference.
General Info: Irregular, Looseleaf
Subscriptions: Indv. $135

AICPA Financial Statement Prepartion Manual

Publishing Co: CCH, Inc., 2700 Lake Cook Rd., Riverwoods, IL 60015 Parent Co.-Kluwer Law & Taxation Publishers, Cambridge; Title Tel # (847) 267-7000 Title Fax # (800) 224-8299
Editorial Description: This service is designed as a nonauthoritative set of audit tools, time-saving examples & practice aids offering choices & alternatives to help in the prepartion of financial statements & reports.
General Info: Quarterly, Trim Size-8$\frac{1}{2}$ x 11, 288 pages, Looseleaf
Subscriptions: Indv. $186

AICPA Peer Review Program Manual

Publishing Co: CCH, Inc., 2700 Lake Cook Rd., Riverwoods, IL 60015 Parent Co.-Kluwer Law & Taxation Publishers, Cambridge; Title Tel # (847) 267-7000 Title Fax # (800) 224-8299
Editorial Description: This manual reproduces the AICPA's Peer Review Divison's booklet, 'Standards for Performing & Reporting on Peer Reviews', plus policies, procedures, checklists & programs for use in administering, arranging for & carrying out peer reviews.
General Info: (Formerly AICPA Quality Review Program Manual), Quarterly, Looseleaf
Subscriptions: Indv. $193

AICPA Professional Standards — *Business*

Publishing Co: CCH, Inc., 2700 Lake Cook Rd., Riverwoods, IL 60015 Parent Co.-Kluwer Law & Taxation Publishers, Cambridge; Title Tel # (847) 267-7000 Title Fax # (800) 224-8299
Editorial Description: Provides currently effective pronouncements on professional standards issued by the AICPA.
General Info: Yr. Est. 1982, Irregular, 192 pages, Looseleaf
Subscriptions: Indv. $171

AICPA Technical Practice Aids — *Business*

Publishing Co: CCH, Inc., 2700 Lake Cook Rd., Riverwoods, IL 60015 Fax # (800) 224-8299 Parent Co.-Kluwer Law & Taxation Publishers, Cambridge; Title Tel # (847) 267-7000 Title Fax # (800) 244-8299
Editorial Description: Reporter furnishes for continuing reference selected Technical Information Service Inquiries & Replies & Statements of Position of the AICPA's Auditing & Accounting Standards Divisions.
General Info: Yr. Est. 1975, Irregular, 160 pages, Looseleaf
Subscriptions: Indv. $135

API Account — *Association*

Publishing Co: Accountants for the Public Interest, 1012 14th St. NW, Ste. 906, Washington, DC 20005-3406; Title Tel # (202) 347-1668 Title Fax # (202) 347-1663
Personnel: Editor-Desmond Ross
Editorial Description: Current events in public interest accounting.
General Info: Yr. Est. 1974, Quarterly, Trim Size-8$\frac{1}{2}$ x 11, Sheetfed press, 6 pages, ISSN: 0883-2102, No Color, Newsprint
Subscriptions: Indv. $35, $3/copy
Circulation: Total-3,000

AWSCPA Newsletter — *Business, Association*

Publishing Co: American Woman's Society of Certified Public Accountants, 401 N. Michigan Ave., Chicago, IL 60611-4212; Title Tel # (312) 644-6610
Personnel: Editor-Maggie Yost, Production Mgr.-Art Dir.-Marlene McGrath
Editorial Description: For members only of AWSCPA. (Women CPA's).
General Info: Yr. Est. 1954, Bi-monthly

AWTAO Bulletin
See: BUSINESS & INDUSTRY

Abstract of Management Services Analysis
See: MANAGEMENT

Accountancy Law Reports — *Business*

Publishing Co: CCH, Inc., 2700 Lake Cook Rd., Riverwoods, IL 60015 Parent Co.-Kluwer Law & Taxation Publishers, Cambridge; Title Tel # (847) 267-7000 Title Fax # (800) 224-8299
Editorial Description: Spans law and rules regulating practice of public accounting in the fifty states and other jurisdictions. Includes law texts, regulations, forms, court decisions and attorney general opinions.
General Info: Yr. Est. 1938, Monthly, Trim Size-6 x 9, Web press, 20 pages, No Color, Looseleaf
Subscriptions: Indv. $686

Accountant, The

Publishing Co: Lafferty Publications, 420 Lexington Ave., Ste. 1745, New York, NY 10170 Tel # (212) 557-6729 Fax # (212) 557-7266; Title Tel # (404) 636-6610 Title Fax # (404) 636-6422
Personnel: Publisher-Frank Lawson, Editor in Chief-Michael Lafferty, Editor-Ciaran Hancock
Editorial Description: The Accountant is a monthly newsletter which reports on the events & personalities of the United Kingdom's accounting profession. Its insert, European Accountant keeps readers abreast of matters in Continental Europe.
General Info: Yr. Est. 1874, Monthly
Subscriptions: Indv. $599

Accountants SEC Practice Manual — *Business*

Publishing Co: CCH, Inc., 2700 Lake Cook Rd., Riverwoods, IL 60015 Parent Co.-Kluwer Law & Taxation Publishers, Cambridge; Title Tel # (847) 267-7000 Title Fax # (800) 224-8299
Editorial Description: Summarizes securities laws, regulation S-X, SEC accounting series releases and staff accounting bulletins to help those who prepare and file financial statements with the SEC.
General Info: Yr. Est. 1976, Monthly, Trim Size-6 x 9, Web press, 30 pages, No Color, Looseleaf
Subscriptions: Indv. $616

Accounting & Auditing Update Service

Publishing Co: Warren, Gorham & Lamont, 31 Saint James Ave., Boston, MA 02116-4112 Parent Co.-Thomson Professional Publications, Stamford; Title Tel # (617) 423-2020 Title Fax # (617) 423-1914
Personnel: Publisher-Andrew Boden, Production Mgr.-Ed Novack, Mktg. Dir.-Sandra Fox
Editorial Description: Current information & developments from FASB & other accounting authorities.
General Info: Yr. Est. 1984, Offset press, 2 Color, Newsprint, Looseleaf
Subscriptions: Indv. $270
List Rental: List Management Co.: Manager: Seena Benedek; WG & L List Management, 1 Penn Plz Fl 42, New York, NY 10119-0002 Tel # (212) 971-5000

Accounting Articles — *Business*

Publishing Co: CCH, Inc., 2700 Lake Cook Rd., Riverwoods, IL 60015 Parent Co.-Kluwer Law & Taxation Publishers, Cambridge; Title Tel # (847) 267-7000 Title Fax # (800) 224-8299
Editorial Description: Describes and indexes articles on accounting and management services appearing in accounting, business, economic, management and other pertinent journals.
General Info: Yr. Est. 1965, Monthly, Trim Size-6 x 9, Web press, 25 pages, No Color, Looseleaf
Subscriptions: Indv. $593

Accounting for Banks — *Business*

Publishing Co: Matthew Bender & Co., 11 Penn Plaza, New York, NY 10001-2006 Tel # (212) 967-7707 Fax # (212) 244-3188
Editorial Description: A comprehensive guidebook featuring numerous computational examples illustrations, flowcharts, sample financial reports & other valuable practice aids throughtout the text.
General Info: Yr. Est. 1982, Irregular, Looseleaf

Accounting Education News — *Business, Association*

Publishing Co: American Accounting Assn, 5717 Bessie Dr, Sarasota, FL 34233-2399 Fax # (813) 923-4093; Title Tel # (813) 921-7747
Personnel: Editor-Paul Gerhardt
Editorial Description: News items within the AAA, information within the profession.
General Info: Bi-monthly, Trim Size-8$\frac{1}{2}$ x 11, 12 pages, 5% ads, No Color, Newsprint, Saddle-stitched
Subscriptions: Indv. $15
Circulation: Total-13,500
Advertising: Inquire for rates.

Accounting for Law Firms

Publishing Co: Leader Publications, Inc., 345 Park Avenue South, New York, NY 10010 Parent Co.-New York Law Publishing Co., New York; Title Tel # (212) 545-6170 Title Fax # (212) 696-1848
Personnel: Publisher-Stuart Wise, Editor-Mark Hopkins, Circ. Mgr.-Kerry Kyle, Promotion Dir.-Rose-Ann Morangelli
Editorial Description: Tax & accounting strategies for lawyers & their firms.
General Info: Yr. Est. 1988, Monthly, Trim Size-8$\frac{1}{2}$ x 11, Offset press, 8 pages, ISSN: 0898-8102, Color, Matte, Saddle-stitched
Subscriptions: Indv. $185, $15/copy
Printing Co: Columbus Bookbinding, 1343 Belfast Ave, Columbus, OH 31904 Tel # (206) 323-9313, Fax # (206) 323-2987

Accounting for Public Utilities — *Business*

Publishing Co: Matthew Bender & Co., 11 Penn Plaza, New York, NY 10001-2006 Tel # (212) 967-7707 Fax # (212) 244-3188
Editorial Description: A thorough analysis of public utility accounting for anyone involved in rate-making & utility accounting.
General Info: Yr. Est. 1983, Irregular, Looseleaf

Accounting Systems for Law Offices
See: LAW

Accreditation Council for Accountancy & Taxation-Action Letter *Business, Association*

Publishing Co: Accreditation Council for Accountancy & Taxation, 1010 N Fairfax St, Alexandria, VA 22314-1504; Title Tel # (703) 549-6400
Editorial Description: To raise professional standards for the practice of accountancy and taxation and foster increased awareness of accredited practitioners in the public, private and educational sectors.
General Info: Yr. Est. 1982, Quarterly
Subscriptions: Free With Membership

American Accounting Assn. Newsletter *Business, Association*

Publishing Co: American Accounting Assn, 5717 Bessie Dr, Sarasota, FL 34233-2399 Fax # (813) 923-4093; Title Tel # (813) 921-7747
Editorial Description: Covers Association news and industry developments.
General Info: Irregular

Applying Government Accounting Principles *Business*

Publishing Co: Matthew Bender & Co., 11 Penn Plaza, New York, NY 10001-2006 Tel # (212) 967-7707 Fax # (212) 244-3188
Editorial Description: Covers virtually every aspect of accounting & financial reporting for state & local governments, as well as federal government programs.
General Info: Irregular, Looseleaf

Applying Government Auditing Standards *Business*

Publishing Co: Matthew Bender & Co., 11 Penn Plaza, New York, NY 10001-2006 Tel # (212) 967-7707 Fax # (212) 244-3188
Editorial Description: Comprehensive coverage of both independent government audits by CPA firms & government auditors, & internal audits of federal, state, & local government finances & programs.
General Info: Yr. Est. 1990, Irregular, Looseleaf

Arthur Young Tax Guide *Business*

Publishing Co: Arthur Young, 277 Park Ave., New York, NY 10172-0269; Title Tel # (212) 407-1500
General Info: Annually, Trim Size-8½ x 11, 29 pages
Circulation: (100% controlled), Total-15,000

Asian American Certified Public Accountants-Newsletter

Publishing Co: Asian American Certified Public Accountants, 1 Embarcadero Ctr., #610, San Francisco, CA 94111-3671; Title Tel # (415) 433-6396
Personnel: Editor-Art Louie
Editorial Description: Newsletter covering assn. activities & events.
General Info: Bi-monthly
Subscriptions: Indv. $40

Assets Protection *Business*

Publishing Co: Assets Protection Publishing, P.O. Box 5323, Madison, WI 53705-0323 Parent Co.-Assets Protection Publishing, Madison; Title Tel # (608) 877-1409
Personnel: Publisher, Editor-Paul Shaw
Editorial Description: Internal controls, audits & investigations for protecting company assets from fraud, abuse & waste.
General Info: Yr. Est. 1975, Bi-monthly, Trim Size-8½ x 11, Sheetfed press, 22 pages, ISSN: 0098-9169, Color-cover, Newsprint, Perfect bound, Looseleaf
Subscriptions: Indv. $56, Can. $68, For. $88, $10/copy
Circulation: Total-2,500
List Rental: Actives: $75/M

Associated Accounting Firms International *Business, Association*

Publishing Co: Associated Accounting Firms Intl., 1000 Connecticut Ave NW Ste, 1006, Washington, DC 20036-5302; Title Tel # (202) 463-7900
Personnel: Publisher-Robert Taylor, Ph.D., CPA, Editor-Michael Platt
Editorial Description: Provides summary of AAFI activities and timely accounting topics.
General Info: Yr. Est. 1969, Semi-annually, Trim Size-8½ x 11, 16 pages, 2 Color
Circulation: (100% controlled), Total-3,500

Association of Insolvency Accountants Newsletter *Business, Association*

Publishing Co: Assn. of Insolvency Accountants, 31332 Via Colinas Ste 112, Westlake Village, CA 91362-3910; Title Tel # (818) 889-8317 Title Fax # (213) 456-4758
Personnel: Circ. Mgr.-Karen Whitney
Editorial Description: Presents Association and industry news and developments.
General Info: Quarterly

Attorney-CPA
See: LAW

Attorney's Handbook of Accounting *Business*

Publishing Co: Matthew Bender & Co., 11 Penn Plaza, New York, NY 10001-2006 Fax # (212) 244-3188; Title Tel # (212) 967-7707
Personnel: Editor-A. Sarakin
Editorial Description: Written specifically for attorneys by practicing CPAs. Covers accounting principles and practices, from financial statement analysis to accounting procedures for businesses and non-profit organizations.
General Info: (Formerly Attorney's Practical Guide to Accounting), Yr. Est. 1965, Irregular, Looseleaf
Subscriptions: $100/copy

Best of Your Money Matters with Ric Edelman, The
See: INVESTMENT

Beta Alpha Psi Newsletter *Association*

Publishing Co: Beta Alpha Psi, Dept. of Accounting, Univ. NE, Lincoln, NE 68588-0001; Title Tel # (402) 472-2337
Editorial Description: Honorary, professional accounting fraternity.
General Info: Yr. Est. 1919

Board of Examiners Newsletter

Publishing Co: American Institute of CPA's, Harborside Financial Center, 201 Plaza Three, Jersey City, NJ 07311-3881 Tel # (201) 938-3283; Title Tel # (201) 938-3000 Title Fax # (201) 938-3329
Personnel: Publisher-Robert Rainer, Editor-Mary Moore, Mktg. Dir.-Charles Cohn
General Info: Irregular, Trim Size-8½ x 11, Offset press, 2 Color, Matte
Subscriptions: Free With Membership
Circulation: Total-1,000, Readership-1,000

Bookkeeping & Accounting Service Profit/Growth *Business*

Publishing Co: Jayhill's, PO Box 5362, Little Rock, AR 72215-5362; Title Tel # (501) 664-7064
Personnel: Publisher, Editor-J. Bush Williams
General Info: Yr. Est. 1985, Bi-monthly
Subscriptions: Indv. $96

Bottom Line *Business, Association*

Publishing Co: Kentucky Society of Certified Public Accountants, 310 W. Liberty, Louisville, KY 40202-3074; Title Tel # (502) 589-9239
Personnel: Editor-Diana Ott
General Info: (Formerly Kentucky Accountant), Monthly, Web press, 12 pages, 3% ads, 2 Color, Newsprint
Circulation: Total-3,000
Advertising: Inquire for rates.
Printing Co: Hamilton Printing Co., 1703 S Brook St, Louisville, KY 40208-1926 Tel # (502) 635-7465

Bottom Line's Canadian Internal Auditing Letter

Publishing Co: T.B.L. Communications, Inc., 75 Clegg Rd., Ste. #200, Markham, ON L6G 1A9 Canada; Title Tel # (416) 474-9532 Title Fax # (905) 474-9803
Personnel: Editor-John Sayers
General Info: Yr. Est. 1987, Monthly
Subscriptions: Indv. $225

Bowman's Accounting Report *Business*

Publishing Co: Hudson Sawyer Professional Services Marketing, 950 E Paces Ferry Rd NE, Ste. 2425, Atlanta, GA 30326-9868; Title Tel # (404) 264-9977 Title Fax # (404) 264-9968
Personnel: Publisher-Martha H. Sawyer, Editor-Arthur Bowman, Calendar Ed.-Tamara Coan, Circ. Mgr.-Gunter Schmidt
Editorial Description: Reporting & analyzing the news, strategies, trends, & politics that effect the accounting profession firms and accountants.
General Info: Yr. Est. 1987, Monthly, Trim Size-8½ x 11, Offset press, 16 pages, ISSN: 0897-3482, Saddle-stitched
Subscriptions: Indv. $215, Can. $275, For. $275, $25/copy
Advertising: Accepts Inserts.
Printing Co: Wilcox Graphics, 6364 Warren Dr, Norcross, GA 30093 Tel # (770) 449-7744

Boycott Law Bulletin
See: INTERNATIONAL TRADE

Business Accounting for Lawyers Newsletter

Publishing Co: Practising Law Institute, 810 7th Ave., New York, NY 10019-5856 Tel # (212) 765-5700; Title Tel # (212) 824-5700 Title Fax # (800) 321-0093
Personnel: Editor-Samuel Gunther, Mktg. Dir.-Arlene Bein
Editorial Description: For attorneys who must understand & apply accounting principles in practice of law.
General Info: Yr. Est. 1984, 8x/yr., 12 pages
Subscriptions: Indv. $110, $15/copy
Circulation: Total-300
List Rental: List Management Co.: Manager: Audrey Campbell; A.H. Direct Marketing, Inc., 360 W. 22nd St., New York, NY 10011 Tel # (212) 242-6652, Fax # (212) 463-8526, Actives: $90/M

Business Matters
See: BUSINESS & INDUSTRY

CCH Tax Day Report
See: TAXES

CFO & Controller Alert   *Business*

Publishing Co: Progressive Business Publications, 370 Technology Dr., #3019, Malverne, PA 19355-9863 Parent Co.-American Future Systems, Inc., Bryn Mawr; Title Tel # (610) 695-8600 Title Fax # (610) 647-8089
Personnel: Publisher-Edward M. Satell, Editor-John T. Hiatt, Editorial Dir.-Stephen Meyer, Mktg. Dir.-Ed Moore
Editorial Description: Advisory report to help financial executives boost cash flow, control expenses and manage resources.
General Info: Yr. Est. 1995, Bi-weekly, 8 pages
Subscriptions: Indv. $299
List Rental: List Management Co.: Manager: Philip Ahr; Mail Marketing, Inc., 171 Terrace St., Haworth, NJ 07641-1899 Tel # (201) 387-1023, Fax # (201) 387-2976

CICA Handbook/Manuel de l'ICCA   *Association*

Publishing Co: Canadian Institute of Chartered Accountants, 277 Wellington Street West, Toronto, ON M5V 3H2 Canada Tel # (416) 977-3222 Fax # (414) 204-3416; Title Tel # (416) 962-1242
Personnel: Production Mgr.-A. Wootton
Editorial Description: Recommendations from the CICA accounting research & auditing standards committees on generally accepted accounting, auditing & financial reporting standards.
General Info: Yr. Est. 1968, Trim Size-$6\frac{1}{4}$ x $9\frac{1}{4}$, Offset press, 800 pages, No Color, Looseleaf
Subscriptions: Indv. $48, Can. $48, Free With Membership
Circulation: Total-75,005
Printing Co: General Printers, 1001 Ritson Rd., S., Oshawa, ON L1H 4G5 Canada Tel # (416) 490-6000, Fax # (905) 436-0813

C.I.C.A./I.C.C.A. Dialogue   *Association*

Publishing Co: Canadian Institute of Chartered Accountants, 277 Wellington Street West, Toronto, ON M5V 3H2 Canada Tel # (416) 977-3222 Fax # (414) 204-3416; Title Tel # (416) 962-1242 Title Fax # (416) 062-3375
Personnel: Editor-Mary Stobbe
Editorial Description: Brief articles on developments of interest to Canadian chartered accountants.
General Info: Yr. Est. 1968, Bi-monthly, Trim Size-$8\frac{1}{8}$ x $10\frac{7}{8}$, 4 pages, No Color
Circulation: Total-50,000
Advertising: Inquire for rates.

CMA Update

Publishing Co: Society of Management Accountants of B.C., 1575-650 W. Georgia St., Box 11548, Vancouver, BC V6B 4W7 Canada; Title Tel # (604) 687-5891 Title Fax # (604) 687-6688
Personnel: Editor-D. Folka, Art Dir.-J. Brown
Editorial Description: News and information of interest to certified management accountants.
General Info: Yr. Est. 1978, Semi-monthly, Trim Size-$8\frac{1}{2}$ x 11, 6 pages
Circulation: Total-6,500
Printing Co: College Printers, 865 Terminal Avenue, Vancouver, BC V6A 2N3 Canada Tel # (604) 685-6322, Fax # (604) 685-0743

CPA Administrative Report   *Business*

Publishing Co: Harcourt Brace Professional Publishing, 6277 Sea Harbor Dr, Orlando, FL 32887-0001 Tel # (407) 345-2000 Fax # (800) 874-6418; Title Tel # (414) 797-9999 Title Fax # (414) 782-7997
Personnel: Publisher-Jerry Huss, Editor-JoAnn Petaschnick
General Info: Yr. Est. 1981, Monthly, Trim Size-$8\frac{1}{2}$ x 11, Sheetfed press, 8 pages, Matte, Other
Subscriptions: Indv. $198, $19/copy
Acquistions: Publication Bought
Advertising: Accepts Inserts.
List Rental: Actives: $125/M

CPA Client Bulletin   *Business, Consumer*

Publishing Co: American Institute of CPA's, Harborside Financial Center, 201 Plaza Three, Jersey City, NJ 07311-3881 Tel # (201) 938-3283 Fax # (201) 938-3329; Title Tel # (201) 938-3301 Title Fax # (201) 938-3780
Personnel: Publisher-Robert Rainier, Editor-Anne Wagenbrenner, Production Mgr.-Peter Touhy, Mktg. Dir.-Charles Cohn
Editorial Description: Financial management news and information for small businesses and individuals.
General Info: Yr. Est. 1978, Monthly, Trim Size-$8\frac{1}{2}$ x 11, Web press, 4 pages, 2 Color, Matte
Subscriptions: Indv. $160, Can. $182, Free With Membership
Circulation: Total-471,000, Readership-471,000
Printing Co: Clarkwood Corp., 690 Union Blvd, Totowa, NJ 07512-2208 Tel # (201) 256-2456

CPA Client Health Care Letter   *Business*

Publishing Co: American Institute of CPA's, Harborside Financial Center, 201 Plaza Three, Jersey City, NJ 07311-3881 Tel # (201) 938-3283 Fax # (201) 938-3329; Title Tel # (201) 938-3301 Title Fax # (201) 938-3780
Personnel: Publisher-Robert Rainer, Editor-Anne Wagenbrenner, Mktg. Dir.-Charles Cohn
Editorial Description: Practice management news for doctors.
General Info: Yr. Est. 1994, Quarterly, Trim Size-$8\frac{1}{2}$ x 11, 6 pages, 2 Color, Matte
Subscriptions: Indv. $44
Circulation: Total-21,872, Readership-21,872
Printing Co: Clarkwood Corp., 690 Union Blvd, Totowa, NJ 07512-2208 Tel # (201) 256-2456

CPA Client Tax Letter   *Business*

Publishing Co: American Institute of CPA's, Harborside Financial Center, 201 Plaza Three, Jersey City, NJ 07311-3881 Tel # (201) 938-3283 Fax # (201) 938-3329; Title Tel # (201) 938-3301 Title Fax # (201) 938-3788
Personnel: Publisher-Robert Rainer, Editor-Anne Wagenbrenner, Production Mgr.-Peter Tuohy, Mktg. Dir.-Charles Cohn
Editorial Description: Tax nmews & information for business individuals.
General Info: Yr. Est. 1989, Quarterly, Trim Size-$8\frac{1}{2}$ x 11, Offset press, 6 pages, 2 Color, Matte
Subscriptions: Indv. $111
Circulation: Total-324,053

CPA Construction Niche Builder   *Business*

Publishing Co: Harcourt Brace Professional Publishing, 6277 Sea Harbor Dr, Orlando, FL 32887-0001 Tel # (407) 345-2000 Fax # (800) 874-6418; Title Fax # (800) 336-7377
Personnel: Publisher-Jerry Huss, Editor-JoAnn Kegel
Editorial Description: Facts, strategies & techniques relevant to CPA's in the construction specialty.
General Info: Yr. Est. 1989, Monthly
Subscriptions: Indv. $179, $25/copy
Acquisitions: Publication Bought
List Rental: Actives: $125/M

CPA Digest   *Business*

Publishing Co: Harcourt Brace Professional Publishing, 6277 Sea Harbor Dr, Orlando, FL 32887-0001 Tel # (407) 345-2000 Fax # (800) 874-6418; Title Fax # (800) 336-7377
Personnel: Publisher-Jerry Huss, Editor-Dan Hounsell, Circ. Mgr.-Mary Hartzell, Promotion Dir.-Shelley Brannan
Editorial Description: Concise reporting of developments useful to CPAs.
General Info: Yr. Est. 1980, Monthly, Trim Size-$8\frac{1}{2}$ x 11, Offset press, 8 pages, 2 Color, Newsprint, Saddle-stitched
Subscriptions: Indv. $185, $25/copy
Acquistions: Publication Bought
Advertising: Accepts Inserts.
List Rental: Actives: $25/M

CPA Expert   *Business*

Publishing Co: American Institute of CPA's, Harborside Financial Center, 201 Plaza Three, Jersey City, NJ 07311-3881 Tel # (201) 938-3283; Title Tel # (201) 938-3000 Title Fax # (201) 938-3329
Personnel: Publisher-Robert Rainer, Editor-Bill Moran, Mktg. Dir.-Charles Cohen
Editorial Description: Litigation consulting news.
General Info: Yr. Est. 1995, Quarterly, Trim Size-$8\frac{1}{2}$ x 11, Offset press, 12 pages, 2 Color, Matte, Saddle-stitched
Subscriptions: Indv. $72
Circulation: Total-2,500, Readership-2,500
Printing Co: Cunningham Graphics, Inc., 629 Grove Street, Jersey City, NJ 07319 Tel # (201) 217-1990

CPA Health Niche Advisor   *Business*

Publishing Co: Harcourt Brace Professional Publishing, 6277 Sea Harbor Dr, Orlando, FL 32887-0001 Tel # (407) 345-2000 Fax # (800) 874-6418; Title Tel # (619) 699-6526 Title Fax # (800) 336-7377
Personnel: Publisher-Jerry Huss, Editor-Brian Peters, Promotion Dir.-S. Brannan
Editorial Description: To help CPA's obtain & service healthcare clients.
General Info: Yr. Est. 1988, Monthly, 8 pages
Subscriptions: Indv. $195, $25/copy
Advertising: Accepts Inserts.
List Rental: Actives: $125/M

CPA Letter   *Association*

Publishing Co: American Institute of CPA's, Harborside Financial Center, 201 Plaza Three, Jersey City, NJ 07311-3881 Tel # (201) 938-3283 Fax # (201) 938-3329; Title Tel # (212) 596-6112 Title Fax # (212) 596-6213
Personnel: Publisher-Robert Rainer, Editor-Ellen Goldstein, Production Mgr.-Peter Tuohy, Mktg. Dir.-Charles Cohn
Editorial Description: News on developments in accounting, auditing, management advisory services, etc.
General Info: Yr. Est. 1973, Monthly, Trim Size-$8\frac{1}{2}$ x 11, Web press, 8 pages, ISSN: 0094-792x, 2 Color, Matte, Saddle-stitched
Subscriptions: Indv. $40, Free With Membership
Circulation: Total-327,000, Readership-327,000
Printing Co: Clarkwood Corp., 690 Union Blvd, Totowa, NJ 07512-2208 Tel # (201) 256-2456

CPA Litigation Service Counselor   *Business*

Publishing Co: Harcourt Brace Professional Publishing, 6277 Sea Harbor Dr, Orlando, FL 32887-0001 Tel # (407) 345-2000 Fax # (800) 874-6418; Title Fax # (800) 336-7377
Personnel: Publisher-Jerry Huss, Editor-Corine Anshus, Circ. Mgr.-Mary Hartzell
Editorial Description: Information pertinent to CPA's in the legal niche field.
General Info: Yr. Est. 1989, Monthly
Subscriptions: Indv. $196, $25/copy
Acquistions: Publication Bought
List Rental: Actives: $125/M

CPA Management
Consultant
Business

Publishing Co: American Institute of CPA's, Harborside Financial Center, 201 Plaza Three, Jersey City, NJ 07311-3881 Tel # (201) 938-3283; Title Tel # (201) 938-3000 Title Fax # (201) 938-3329
Personnel: Publisher-Robert Rainer, Editor-Bill Moran, Mktg. Dir.-Charles Cohn
Editorial Description: Articles and information for CPA's who offer management consulting services.
General Info: Quarterly, Trim Size-8$\frac{1}{2}$ x 11, Offset press, 12 pages, 2 Color, Matte, Saddle-stitched
Subscriptions: Indv. $48
Circulation: Total-5,200, Readership-5,200
Printing Co: Clarkwood Corp., 690 Union Blvd, Totowa, NJ 07512-2208 Tel # (201) 256-2456

CPA Marketing Report
Business

Publishing Co: Strafford Pubs., Inc., 590 Dutch Valley Rd., N.E., Postal Drawer 13729, Atlanta, GA 30324-0729; Title Tel # (404) 881-1141 Title Fax # (404) 881-0074
Personnel: Publisher-Richard M. Ossoff, Editor-Suzanne Verity, Circ. Mgr., Mktg. Mgr.-Marianne Mueller, Mktg. Mgr.-Marla Rawls Hill
Editorial Description: Helps public accounting firms design, implement and evaluate effective programs to attract new clients, enhance the firm's image improve client relations and build sound practices.
General Info: Yr. Est. 1981, 12x/yr., Sheetfed press, 8 pages, ISSN: 0279-1021, 1% ads, No Color
Subscriptions: Indv. $247, Can. $227, For. $292, $20/copy
Acquistions: Publication Bought, Publication Sold
List Rental: Rents Lists

CPA Personnel Report
See: EMPLOYMENT

CPA Profitability Monthly
Business

Publishing Co: Harcourt Brace Professional Publishing, 6277 Sea Harbor Dr, Orlando, FL 32887-0001 Tel # (407) 345-2000 Fax # (800) 874-6418; Title Fax # (800) 336-7377
Personnel: Publisher-Jerry Huss, Editor-Betsy Morris, Promotion Dir.-Shelley Brannan
Editorial Description: Contains practical techniques for maximum positive client impact.
General Info: (Formerly Quality Client Service), Yr. Est. 1988, Monthly, 4 pages
Subscriptions: Indv. $185, $25/copy
Advertising: Accepts Inserts.
List Rental: Actives: $125/M

CPA Technology Advisor
See: COMPUTERS & AUTOMATION

Canadian Accounting
Education and
Research News
Business, Association

Publishing Co: Canadian Academic Accounting Association, 850-120 King St, W., P.O. Box 176, Hamilton, ON L8N 3C3 Canada Tel # (905) 525-1884 Fax # (905) 525-3046
Personnel: Editor-Paul E. Roy
Editorial Description: Reports on association events, research opportunities, professional activities, and more.
General Info: Quarterly, Trim Size-8$\frac{1}{2}$ x 11, Desktop press, 18 pages, ISSN: 1196-5991, Color-cover, Coated, Saddle-stitched
Subscriptions: Indv. $75, Inst. $100, Can. $75, For. $75, Free With Membership
Circulation: Readership-700
Advertising: $350. Accepts Inserts.

Canadian Current Income Tax Proposals
See: TAXES

Canadian Tax Forms
See: TAXES

Canadian Tax Objection & Appeal Procedures
See: TAXES

Caveat Emptor
See: PURCHASING

Certified General
Accountants' Assn. of
British Columbia,
Newsletter

Publishing Co: Certified General Accountants' Assn. of B.C., 1555 W. 8th Ave., Vancouver, BC V6J 1T5 Canada; Title Tel # (604) 732-1211
Personnel: Editor-Maureen Sydor
General Info: Quarterly, 16 pages
Circulation: Total-7,000

Certified General
Accountants Assn. of
Manitoba Newsletter
Business, Association

Publishing Co: Certified General Accountants Assn. of Manitoba, 4 Donald St. S., Winnipeg, MB R3L 2T7 Canada; Title Tel # (204) 477-1256 Title Fax # (204) 453-7176
General Info: Yr. Est. 1973, Monthly, Trim Size-8$\frac{1}{2}$ x 11, Mimeo press, 1 pages
Circulation: (100% controlled), Total-2,000
Advertising: Inquire for rates.

Church Treasurer Alert
See: TAXES

Client Advisory
Business

Publishing Co: WPI Communications, Inc., 55 Morris Ave, Springfield, NJ 07081-1496; Title Tel # (201) 467-8700 Title Fax # (201) 467-0368
Personnel: Publisher-S. Klinghoffer, Editor-K. Berry, Circ. Mgr.-M. Lang, Production Mgr.-J. Petino
Editorial Description: Sold in bulk to accountants for redistribution to clients.
General Info: Yr. Est. 1986, Monthly, 4 pages
List Rental: Actives: $55/M

Client Information Bulletin
Business

Publishing Co: WPI Communications, Inc., 55 Morris Ave, Springfield, NJ 07081-1496; Title Tel # (201) 467-8700 Title Fax # (201) 467-0368
Personnel: Publisher-S.H. Klinghoffer, Editor-K. Berry, Circ. Mgr.-M. Lang, Production Mgr.-J. Petino
Editorial Description: Sold in bulk to accounting and law firms to keep clients up to date on tax matters.
General Info: Yr. Est. 1951, Monthly, Trim Size-8$\frac{1}{2}$ x 11, 4 pages
Acquistions: Publication Bought
List Rental: List Management Co.: WMI/Worldata, 5200 Town Center Circle, Boca Raton, FL 33486 Tel # (407) 393-8200, Fax # (407) 368-8345, Actives: $55/M

Commodity Futures Law Reports
See: INVESTMENT

Corporate Accounting
International
Business, Association

Publishing Co: Lafferty Publications, 420 Lexington Ave., Ste. 1745, New York, NY 10170 Tel # (212) 557-6729 Fax # (212) 557-7266; Title Tel # (404) 636-6610 Title Fax # (404) 636-6422
Personnel: Publisher-Frank Lawson, Editor in Chief-Michael Lafferty, Editor-Ciaran Hancock
Editorial Description: Reports & analyzes trends in corporate financial reporting & the laws & regulations which affect it. The journal tracks steps toward the attainment of international accounting standards.
General Info: Yr. Est. 1989, 10x/yr.
Subscriptions: Indv. $979

Corporate Compliance: Internal Reviews, Audits, and Investigations
See: BUSINESS & INDUSTRY

Cost Accounting Standards
Guide
Business

Publishing Co: CCH, Inc., 2700 Lake Cook Rd., Riverwoods, IL 60015 Parent Co.-Kluwer Law & Taxation Publishers, Cambridge; Title Tel # (847) 267-7000 Title Fax # (800) 224-8299
Editorial Description: Help for government contractors and subcontractors who must disclose their cost accounting practices in writing to the Cost Accounting Standards Board and follow its standards.
General Info: Yr. Est. 1972, Monthly, Trim Size-6 x 9, Web press, 40 pages, No Color, Looseleaf
Subscriptions: Indv. $320

Cost Management
Insiders Report
Business

Publishing Co: Warren, Gorham & Lamont, 31 Saint James Ave., Boston, MA 02116-4112 Parent Co.-Thomson Professional Publications, Stamford; Title Tel # (617) 423-2020 Title Fax # (617) 423-1914
Personnel: Publisher-Andrew Boden, Production Mgr.-Ed Novack, Mktg. Dir.-Sandra Fox
General Info: Yr. Est. 1994, Monthly
Subscriptions: Indv. $98
List Rental: List Management Co.: Manager: Seena Benedek; WG & L List Management, 1 Penn Plz Fl 42, New York, NY 10119-0002 Tel # (212) 971-5000

Credit Manager
Business

Publishing Co: Warren, Gorham & Lamont, 31 Saint James Ave., Boston, MA 02116-4112 Fax # (617) 423-1914 Parent Co.-Thomson Professional Publications, Stamford; Title Tel # (617) 423-2020 Title Fax # (617) 402-1914
Personnel: Publisher-Andrew Boden, Editor-Basil Mavrovitis, Production Mgr.-Ed Novack, Mktg. Dir.-Sandra Fox
General Info: Yr. Est. 1993, Monthly
Subscriptions: Indv. $125
Advertising: Inquire for rates.
List Rental: List Management Co.: Manager: Seena Benedek; WG & L List Management, 1 Penn Plz Fl 42, New York, NY 10119-0002 Tel # (212) 971-5000

Credit Union Accountant
See: BANKING & FINANCE

Directions
Association

Publishing Co: Youth Society of Management Accountants, 70 University Ave., Ste. 300, Toronto, ON M5J 2M4 Canada Parent Co.-Society of Management Accountants, Hamilton, Canada; Title Tel # (416) 204-3103 Title Fax # (416) 977-6079
Personnel: Editor-John Karapita
Editorial Description: Information and news for Accounting students and new accountants.
General Info: Quarterly
Subscriptions: Free With Membership

EDP Auditing
See: COMPUTERS & AUTOMATION

E.F.T.A., A Service Mark   *Association*

Publishing Co: Natl. Assn. of Enrolled Fedl. Tax Accountants, 6108 N Harding Ave, Chicago, IL 60659-3108; Title Tel # (312) 463-5577
Personnel: Editor, Circ. Mgr.-S.A. Rish
Editorial Description: Seeks to obtain greater public recognition for taxpayers representatives and our designation,which is a service mark.
General Info: Quarterly

Electronic Payment Journal
See: COMPUTERS & AUTOMATION

European Accountant

Publishing Co: Lafferty Publications, 420 Lexington Ave., Ste. 1745, New York, NY 10170
  Tel # (212) 557-6729 Fax # (212) 557-7266; Title Tel # (404) 636-6610 Title Fax # (404) 636-6422
Personnel: Publisher-Frank Lawson, Editor-Ciaran Hancock
Editorial Description: European Accountant asesses, monitors and reports on the emerging European market for accounting services.
General Info: 10x/yr.
Subscriptions: Indv. $899

Farm and Ranch Tax Letter
See: AGRICULTURE

Federal Audit Guides   *Business*

Publishing Co: CCH, Inc., 2700 Lake Cook Rd., Riverwoods, IL 60015 Parent Co.-Kluwer Law & Taxation Publishers, Cambridge; Title Tel # (847) 267-7000 Title Fax # (800) 224-8299
Editorial Description: Provides current texts of federal agency guides for external audits of state and local governments and other recipients of federally assisted programs.
General Info: Yr. Est. 1977, Irregular, Trim Size-6 x 9, Web press, No Color, Looseleaf
Subscriptions: Indv. $593

Federal Auditing Information Service for Higher Education   *Business*

Publishing Co: Atlantic Information Svcs., Inc., 1100 17th St. NW, Ste. 300, Washington, DC 20036-5503; Title Tel # (202) 775-9008 Title Fax # (202) 331-9542
Personnel: Publisher-Richard Biehl, Editor-Steve Goodwin, Circ. Mgr.-Gwen Arnold, Production Dir.-Gary Peteisor, Mktg. Mgr.-Christine Burdell
Editorial Description: Valuable hands-on guidance for colleges and universities with $100,000 or more in federal funds, including student aid.
General Info: Monthly
Subscriptions: Indv. $403

Federal Securities Law Reports
See: LAW

Fiduciary Tax Guide
See: TAXES

General Ledger, The   *Business*

Publishing Co: American Institute of Professional Bookkeepers, 6001 Montrose Rd., Ste. 207, Rockville, MD 20852-4874 Fax # (800) 541-0066; Title Tel # (301) 770-7300
Personnel: Publisher-Stanley Hartman, Editor-Carolee Brady, Circ. Mgr.-Liz Reeves, Production Mgr.-Nancy Giddings, Adv. Dir.-Nicholas Bibby, Promotion Dir.-William Barth
Editorial Description: For bookkeepers about bookkeeping & taxes.
General Info: Yr. Est. 1984, Monthly, Trim Size-8½ x 11, Sheetfed press, 4 pages, Color, Newsprint
Subscriptions: Indv. $65, $5/copy
Circulation: Total-4,500
Advertising: Inquire for rates.
List Rental: Rents Lists
Printing Co: Newsletter Services, Inc., 9700 Philadelphia Court, Lanham, MD 20706
  Tel # (301) 731-5200, Fax # (301) 731-5201

Government Accounting and Auditing Update   *Business*

Publishing Co: Warren, Gorham & Lamont, 31 Saint James Ave., Boston, MA 02116-4112 Parent Co.-Thomson Professional Publications, Stamford; Title Tel # (617) 423-2020
  Title Fax # (617) 423-1914
Personnel: Publisher-Andrew Boden, Production Mgr.-Ed Novack, Mktg. Dir.-Sandra Fox
Editorial Description: Up-to-date information on all the changes taking place in government accounting and financial reporting.
General Info: Yr. Est. 1990, Monthly
Subscriptions: Indv. $172
List Rental: List Management Co.: Manager: Seena Benedek; WG & L List Management, 1 Penn Plz Fl 42, New York, NY 10119-0002 Tel # (212) 971-5000

Government Contract Costs Pricing & Accounting Report
See: LAW

Governmental Accounting Standards Board-Action Report   *Business*

Publishing Co: Governmental Accounting Standards Board, 401 Merritt 7, PO Box 5116, Norwalk, CT 06856-5116; Title Tel # (203) 847-0700 Title Fax # (203) 849-9714
Editorial Description: Action report newsletter.
General Info: Yr. Est. 1984, Monthly, 4 pages, No Color
Circulation: Total-11,000

Granite State CPA Newsletter   *Business, Association*

Publishing Co: New Hampshire Society for CPAs, 3 Executive Park Dr., Bedford, NH 03110-6918; Title Tel # (603) 622-1999
Personnel: Editor-Monique Manna
General Info: (Formerly NHCPA Account), Monthly, Trim Size-8½ x 11, Sheetfed press, 8 pages, 4% ads, No Color
Subscriptions: Indv. $20
Circulation: Total-700
Advertising: Inquire for rates.

Guidelines on Auditing, Education, Ethics, & Management Accounting

Publishing Co: International Federation of Accountants (IFAC), 114 West 47th St., Ste. 2410, New York, NY 10036-1510; Title Tel # (212) 486-2446
Editorial Description: Series of technical announcements regarding the profession.

HARA: Hospital Accounts Receivable Analysis
See: HOSPITALS & NURSING HOMES

Handbook for Internal Auditors   *Business*

Publishing Co: Matthew Bender & Co., 11 Penn Plaza, New York, NY 10001-2006
  Fax # (212) 244-3188; Title Tel # (212) 967-7707
Editorial Description: Guidance on every aspect of internal auditing--from establishing an internal auditing function within a company, to managing an internal auditing department, to performing audit fieldwork.
General Info: Yr. Est. 1985, Irregular, Looseleaf

Horizons

Publishing Co: Institute of Chartered Accountants of Saskatchewan, 1867 Hamilton St., #530, Regina, SK S4P 2C2 Canada; Title Tel # (306) 359-1010
Personnel: Editor-Jodi Brandt
General Info: (Formerly Chaff), 5x/yr.

Hospital Cost Management & Accounting
See: HOSPITALS & NURSING HOMES

IIA Today   *Business, Association*

Publishing Co: Institute of Internal Auditors, Inc., 249 Maitland Ave., Altamonte Springs, FL 32701-4201; Title Tel # (407) 830-7600 Title Fax # (407) 831-5171
Personnel: Editor-Lisa Krist, Art Dir.-Parry Dolle
Editorial Description: Assn. & internal auditing news, activities, member & chapter news, etc.
General Info: (Formerly Inter-Nos), Yr. Est. 1976, Bi-monthly, Trim Size-8½ x 11, Offset press, 20 pages, ISSN: 0744-1223, Color, Saddle-stitched
Circulation: Total-30,000
List Rental: Actives: $75/M

IMA Focus   *Association*

Publishing Co: Institute of Management Accountants, 10 Paragon Dr., Montvale, NJ 07645-1760; Title Tel # (201) 573-9000 Title Fax # (201) 573-8601
Personnel: Publisher-Gary Scopes, Editor-Kathryn Hogan
Editorial Description: Membership and profession News
General Info: Yr. Est. 1993, Bi-monthly, Trim Size-8 x 10¾, 8 pages, 2 Color, Saddle-stitched
Circulation: Total-87,000
List Rental: List Management Co.: Aggressive List Management, 18-2 E Dundee Rd Ste 101, Barrington, IL 60010-5273 Tel # (708) 304-4030, Fax # (708) 304-4032, Actives: $100/M
Printing Co: Pendell Printing, 1700 James Savage Rd., Midland, MI 48642 Fax # (517) 496-3700

Information Interchange
See: OFFICE METHODS & EQUIPMENT

Infotech Update   *Business*

Publishing Co: American Institute of CPA's, Harborside Financial Center, 201 Plaza Three, Jersey City, NJ 07311-3881 Tel # (201) 938-3283; Title Tel # (201) 938-3000 Title Fax # (201) 938-3329
Personnel: Publisher-Robert Reiner, Editor-Andrew Kiuseffi, Mktg. Dir.-Charles Cohn
General Info: Quarterly, Trim Size-8½ x 11, Offset press, 12 pages, 2 Color, Matte, Saddle-stitched
Subscriptions: Free With Membership
Circulation: Total-3,700, Readership-3,700

Inside Nonprofit Accountability   *Business*

Publishing Co: Aspen Publishers, Inc., 200 Orchard Ridge Dr., Ste 200, Gaithersburg, MD 20878-5440 Tel # (301) 417-7500 Fax # (301) 417-7655 Parent Co.-Wolters Kluwer US Corporation, New York
Editorial Description: Reports on what's happening in the nonprofit sector as far as accountabilty, and keeps nonprofits up-to-date on activities on federal and state levels.
General Info: (Formerly Nonprofit Regulation & Accountability), Yr. Est. 1995
Subscriptions: Indv. $89, For. $107, $9/copy

Insight   *Business, Consumer*

Publishing Co: Certified General Accountants' Assn. of Alberta, 555 Fourth Ave., S.W., #1410, Calgary, AB T2P 3E7 Canada; Title Tel # (403) 299-1300
Personnel: Editor-Corinne Wilkinson
General Info: Quarterly

Institute of Chartered Accountants of Alberta, Monthly Statement *Association*

Publishing Co: Institute of Chartered Accountants of Alberta, Manu Life Place, Suite 580, 10180 101st Street, Edmonton, AB T5J 4R2 Canada; Title Tel # (403) 424-7391 Title Fax # (403) 425-8766
Personnel: Editor-Dianne Bennett
Editorial Description: Member news, institute activities, proposed rule changes & significant federal and provincial accounting legislation.
General Info: Yr. Est. 1960, Monthly, Trim Size-8½ x 11, Offset press, 12 pages, 2 Color, Recycled
Subscriptions: Free With Membership
Circulation: Total-6,500

Insurance Accountant
See: INSURANCE

Internal Auditing Alert *Business*

Publishing Co: Warren, Gorham & Lamont, 31 Saint James Ave., Boston, MA 02116-4112 Parent Co.-Thomson Professional Publications, Stamford; Title Tel # (617) 423-2020 Title Fax # (617) 423-1914
Personnel: Publisher-Andrew Boden, Production Mgr.-Ed Novack, Mktg. Dir.-Sandra Fox
Editorial Description: Covers key developments in the field of internal auditing.
General Info: Yr. Est. 1981, Monthly, Offset press
Subscriptions: Indv. $140
Circulation: Total-2,692
Advertising: Inquire for rates.
List Rental: List Management Co.: Manager: Seena Benedek; WG & L List Management, 1 Penn Plz Fl 42, New York, NY 10119-0002 Tel # (212) 971-5000

Internal Revenue Manual-Audit and Administration
See: TAXES

International Accounting Bulletin

Publishing Co: Lafferty Publications, 420 Lexington Ave., Ste. 1745, New York, NY 10170 Tel # (212) 557-6729 Fax # (212) 557-7266; Title Tel # (404) 636-6610 Title Fax # (404) 636-6422
Personnel: Publisher-Frank Lawson, Editor in Chief-Michael Lafferty, Editor-Ciaran Hancock
Editorial Description: An international business briefing for the management of public accounting firms, this journal reports & analyzes the competitive environment.
General Info: Yr. Est. 1983, 23x/yr.
Subscriptions: Indv. $1,099

International Affiliation of Independent Accounting Firms-Update *Business, Association*

Publishing Co: International Affiliation of Independent Accounting Firms, 9200 S Dadeland Blvd Ste 510, Miami, FL 33156-2713; Title Tel # (305) 670-0580 Title Fax # (305) 670-3818
Personnel: Editor-Ellen Atkins
Editorial Description: International accounting news.
General Info: (Formerly Update), Yr. Est. 1978, Monthly, Web press
Subscriptions: Free With Membership
Circulation: Total-800

International Federation of Accountants-Newsletter

Publishing Co: International Federation of Accountants (IFAC), 114 West 47th St., Ste. 2410, New York, NY 10036-1510; Title Tel # (212) 486-2446
Personnel: Editor-Robert Sempier
Editorial Description: Covering worldwide meetings & activities.
General Info: Quarterly
Circulation: Total-2,500

Interpreter *Business*

Publishing Co: Insurance Accounting & Systems Assn., PO Box 51340, Durham, NC 27717-1340; Title Tel # (919) 489-0991 Title Fax # (919) 489-1994
Personnel: Editor-Charles Fucks
Editorial Description: Reporting on research, theory, & procedures concerning the accounting & statistical functions of insurance companies.
General Info: Yr. Est. 1941, Bi-monthly
Subscriptions: Indv. $15, Inst. $15, Can. $15, For. $15
Circulation: Total-6,500

Keep Up to Date on Payroll *Business*

Publishing Co: Progressive Business Publications, 370 Technology Dr., #3019, Malverne, PA 19355-9863 Parent Co.-American Future Systems, Inc., Bryn Mawr; Title Tel # (610) 695-8600 Title Fax # (610) 647-8089
Personnel: Publisher-Edward M. Satell, Editorial Dir.-Steve Meyer, Editor-Kelly Wiessner, Mktg. Dir.-Ed Moore
Editorial Description: Business-to-business newsletter to keep payroll administrators abreast of legal developments and payroll management strategies.
General Info: Yr. Est. 1994, Bi-weekly, 8 pages
Subscriptions: Indv. $230
List Rental: List Management Co.: Mail Marketing, Inc., 171 Terrace St., Haworth, NJ 07641-1899 Tel # (201) 387-1023, Fax # (201) 387-2976

LLC Advisor
See: TAXES

Ledger Quarterly
See: REAL ESTATE

Limited Liability Company Guide
See: TAXES

Management Accounter *Association*

Publishing Co: Society of Management Accountants of Alberta, 1800-125 Ninth Ave., S.E., Calgary, AB T2G 0P6 Canada; Title Tel # (403) 269-5341 Title Fax # (403) 262-5477
Personnel: Publisher-Jan Fisher
Editorial Description: Features Society news as well as articles covering the accounting field in Alberta province.
General Info: (Formerly Accounter), Tri-annually, 8 pages
Subscriptions: Free To Qualified Recipient
Circulation: (100% controlled), Total-6,500
Advertising: Inquire for rates. Accepts Inserts.

Managing International Credit & Collections *Business*

Publishing Co: IOMA, 29 W. 35th St., 5th Fl., New York, NY 10001-2299; Title Tel # (212) 244-0360 Title Fax # (212) 564-0465
Personnel: Publisher-Perry Patterson, Editor-Mary Ludwig, Mktg. Dir.-Claudia Levine
Editorial Description: To help credit and receivables managers at companies that do business internationally set credit policies and accelerate receivables.
General Info: Yr. Est. 1996, Monthly, ISSN: 1085-9764
Subscriptions: Indv. $199, Can. $199, For. $223
List Rental: List Management Co.: Manager: Debra Goldfarb; Institute Lists, 29 W. 35th St., 5th Fl., New York, NY 10001-2299 Tel # (212) 244-0360, Fax # (212) 564-0465, Actives: $125/M

MicroView
See: COMPUTERS & AUTOMATION

Modern Accounting and Auditing Checklists *Business*

Publishing Co: Warren, Gorham & Lamont, 31 Saint James Ave., Boston, MA 02116-4112 Parent Co.-Thomson Professional Publications, Stamford; Title Tel # (617) 423-2020 Title Fax # (617) 423-1914
Personnel: Publisher-Andrew Boden, Production Mgr.-Ed Novack, Mktg. Dir.-Sandra Fox
Editorial Description: Practical guides for operating and reporting-kept current through supplements.
General Info: Irregular, Looseleaf
Subscriptions: Indv. $155
List Rental: List Management Co.: Manager: Seena Benedek; WG & L List Management, 1 Penn Plz Fl 42, New York, NY 10119-0002 Tel # (212) 971-5000

Money and Family Law *Business*

Publishing Co: Carswell, 2075 Kennedy Road, One Corporate Plaza, Scarborough, ON M1T 3V4 Canada Tel # (416) 609-8000 Fax # (416) 298-5094; Title Tel # (416) 445-4940 Title Fax # (416) 445-5352
Personnel: Publisher-Barry Garnet, Editor-Lorne Wolfson, Circ. Mgr.-Mike Moore, Production Mgr.-Barry Corbin, Adv. Dir.-Melanie Causton
Editorial Description: Covers comestic contracts, settlement negotiations, pensions & life insurance, valuation & more.
General Info: Yr. Est. 1986, Monthly, Trim Size-8½ x 11, 8 pages, ISSN: 0832-7653
Subscriptions: Indv. $180

NABCA Bulletin *Business, Association*

Publishing Co: Natl. Assn. for Bank Cost & Management Accounting, PO Box 458, Northbrook, IL 60065-0458; Title Tel # (708) 272-4233
Personnel: Publisher-Nancy Basinger, Circ. Mgr.-Linda Feldman
Editorial Description: Information on association-sponsored educational programs.
General Info: Yr. Est. 1981, Quarterly, Trim Size-8½ x 11, Sheetfed press, 8 pages, 2 Color, Coated
Circulation: (100% controlled), Total-700

NOSA Newsletter

Publishing Co: National One-Write Systems Association, PO Box 8187, Silver Spring, MD 20907-8187 Tel # (201) 589-8125; Title Tel # (301) 589-8125
Personnel: Editor-Kathleen Barker
General Info: Quarterly

NSPA Washington Reporter *Association*

Publishing Co: Natl. Soc. of Public Accountants, 1010 N Fairfax St, Alexandria, VA 22314-1504; Title Tel # (703) 549-6400 Title Fax # (703) 549-2984
Personnel: Editor-Susan Cappitelli
Editorial Description: Contains news of members in the various states: coverage of NSPA activity with the government (Treasury, Internal Revenue, The Congress, etc.).
General Info: Yr. Est. 1960, Monthly, Sheetfed press, 32 pages, 2 Color, Newsprint, Saddle-stitched
Circulation: Total-23,000
List Rental: Rents Lists
Printing Co: Corporate Press, 403 Brightseat Rd., Landover, MD 20785-4706 Tel # (301) 499-9200, Fax # (301) 499-5435

National Property Tax Manual
See: TAXES

National Sales Tax Manual
See: TAXES

National Sales Tax Rate Directory
See: TAXES

News Plus
Business, Association

Publishing Co: Natl. Assn. of Black Accountants, New York, NY; Title Tel # (212) 969-0560
Personnel: Editor-Beverly Everson-Tores, Adv. Dir.-Linda Gaston, Production Mgr., Art Dir.-Denise Lane
Editorial Description: National, regional, chapter, members news; updates on accounting regulations & proposals.
General Info: Bi-monthly, Trim Size-8½ x 11, Sheetfed press, 8 pages, 2 Color, Matte
Subscriptions: Indv. $20
Circulation: Total-3,000
Advertising: Inquire for rates.

NewsAccount
Business, Association

Publishing Co: Colorado Society of Certified Public Accountants, 7979 East Tufts Avenue, Suite 500, Denver, CO 80237-2845; Title Tel # (303) 773-2877 Title Fax # (303) 773-6344
Personnel: Editor-Kelli Dyer
Editorial Description: News of interest to CPA's.
General Info: 8x/yr., Trim Size-8½ x 11, Offset press, 28 pages, 3% ads, 2 Color, Coated, Saddle-stitched
Subscriptions: Free With Membership
Circulation: Total-7,900
Advertising: Inquire for rates.
Printing Co: Precision Graphics, 2021 S. Platte River Drive, Denver, CO 80233 Tel # (303) 922-7545

Nonprofit Financial Advisor

Publishing Co: Aspen Publishers, Inc., 200 Orchard Ridge Dr., Ste 200, Gaithersburg, MD 20878-5440 Tel # (301) 417-7500 Fax # (301) 417-7655 Parent Co.-Wolters Kluwer US Corporation, New York
Editorial Description: Kepps executive directors on top of current issues and trends in financial management. Regular special inserts, forms, or checklists.
General Info: Yr. Est. 1994, ISSN: 1074-6331
Subscriptions: Indv. $129, For. $155, $14/copy

Nonprofit Report: Accounting, Taxation, & Management
Business

Publishing Co: Warren, Gorham & Lamont, 31 Saint James Ave., Boston, MA 02116-4112 Parent Co.-Thomson Professional Publications, Stamford; Title Tel # (617) 423-2020 Title Fax # (617) 423-1914
Personnel: Publisher-Andrew Boden, Production Mgr.-Ed Novack, Mktg. Dir.-Sandra Fox
Editorial Description: Offers CPAs with nonprofit clients--and professionals working in the nonprofit sector--a practical, timely look at today's key nonprofit issues.
General Info: Yr. Est. 1991, Monthly
Subscriptions: Indv. $118
List Rental: List Management Co.: Manager: Seena Benedek; WG & L List Management, 1 Penn Plz Fl 42, New York, NY 10119-0002 Tel # (212) 971-5000

Outlook (CPA)

Publishing Co: CPA Associates, 201 Rte. 17 N, 4th fl., Rutherford, NJ 07070; Title Tel # (201) 804-8686
General Info: Yr. Est. 1957, Quarterly

Pacioli Society News
Association

Publishing Co: Pacioli Society, Albers School of Business, Seattle University, Seattle, WA 98122; Title Tel # (206) 296-5723 Title Fax # (206) 296-5795
Editorial Description: Newsletter about the Fra Luca Pacioli Society - the father of accounting.
General Info: Quarterly, Trim Size-8½ x 11, 8 pages

Partnership Tax Planning & Practice
See: TAXES

Payroll Administration Guide
See: INDUSTRIAL RELATIONS/PERSONNEL

Perspectives on the Construction Industry
See: CONSTRUCTION & BUILDING

Peyron Tax Accountants Communique
See: TAXES

Peyron Tax Letter & Social Security Report
See: TAXES

Planner , The
Business

Publishing Co: American Institute of CPA's, Harborside Financial Center, 201 Plaza Three, Jersey City, NJ 07311-3881 Tel # (201) 938-3283; Title Tel # (201) 938-3000 Title Fax # (201) 938-3329
Personnel: Publisher-Robert Rainer, Editor-Murray Schwartzberg, Mktg. Dir.-Charles Cohn
Editorial Description: Articles for personal financial planning , professionals - management & services.
General Info: Bi-monthly, Trim Size-8½ x 11, Offset press, 8 pages, 2 Color, Matte, Saddle-stitched
Subscriptions: Free With Membership
Circulation: Total-8,200, Readership-8,200
Printing Co: Clarkwood Corp., 690 Union Blvd, Totowa, NJ 07512-2208 Tel # (201) 256-2456

Practicing CPA
Business, Association

Publishing Co: American Institute of CPA's, Harborside Financial Center, 201 Plaza Three, Jersey City, NJ 07311-3881 Tel # (201) 938-3283 Fax # (201) 938-3329; Title Tel # (201) 938-3796 Title Fax # (201) 938-3780
Personnel: Publisher-Robert Rainier, Editor-Graham Godard, Mktg. Dir.-Charles Cohn
Editorial Description: Articles on administration development and management of CPA firms.
General Info: (Formerly CPA Practitioner), Yr. Est. 1977, Monthly, Trim Size-8½ x 11, Web press, 8 pages, ISSN: 0885*-693, 2 Color, Matte, Saddle-stitched
Subscriptions: Free With Membership
Circulation: Total-64,000, Readership-64,000
Printing Co: Clarkwood Corp., 690 Union Blvd, Totowa, NJ 07512-2208 Tel # (201) 256-2456

Public Accounting Report
Business

Publishing Co: Strafford Pubs., Inc., 590 Dutch Valley Rd., N.E., Postal Drawer 13729, Atlanta, GA 30324-0729; Title Tel # (404) 881-1141 Title Fax # (404) 881-0074
Personnel: Publisher-Richard M. Ossoff, Editor-Suzanne Verity, Circ. Mgr., Mktg. Dir.-Marianne Mueller, Mktg. Mgr.-Marla Rawls Hill
Editorial Description: Provides public accounting firms (& others interested) with authoritative news & analysis of developments in the accounting profession today and emerging trends for the future; also reports mergers, acquisitions, auditor changes & related events.
General Info: Yr. Est. 1978, 23x/yr., Trim Size-8½ x 11, Sheetfed press, 8 pages, ISSN: 0161-309X, 3% ads, No Color
Subscriptions: Indv. $247, Can. $277, For. $297, $14/copy
Acquistions: Publication Bought, Publication Sold
List Rental: Rents Lists

Receivables Report
Business

Publishing Co: Zimmerman & Associates, Inc., 5307 South 92nd St., Hales Corners, WI 53130-1677 Parent Co.-Aspen Publishers, Inc., Gaithersburg; Title Tel # (414) 425-2189 Title Fax # (414) 425-4807
Personnel: Publisher-David Zimmerman, Editor-Bruce Nelson
Editorial Description: Published for healthcare financial managers.
General Info: Yr. Est. 1984, Monthly, Sheetfed press, 8 pages, Color, Coated
Subscriptions: Indv. $197, Inst. $197
Circulation: Total-2,000
Printing Co: Marek Lithographics, PO Box 904, Muskego, WI 53150-0904

Retirement & Tax Planning with 1-2-3
Business

Publishing Co: Research Press Inc., 4500 W 72nd Ter, Prairie Village, KS 66208-2824 Fax # (913) 362-4922; Title Tel # (913) 362-9667
Personnel: Publisher, Editor-Vernon Jacobs, Circ. Mgr., Production Mgr.-Alan Lehman
Editorial Description: Tax advising software news.
General Info: (Formerly CATPLAN Report), Monthly, Trim Size-8½ x 11, Letrpr. press, 4 pages, No Color
Subscriptions: Free To Qualified Recipient
Circulation: (100% controlled), Total-250

S Corporations Guide
See: TAXES

SEC Accounting & Reporting Update Service
Business

Publishing Co: Warren, Gorham & Lamont, 31 Saint James Ave., Boston, MA 02116-4112 Parent Co.-Thomson Professional Publications, Stamford; Title Tel # (617) 423-2020 Title Fax # (617) 423-1914
Personnel: Publisher-Andrew Boden, Editor-Allen Afterman, Production Mgr.-Ed Novack, Mktg. Dir.-Sandra Fox
Editorial Description: Contains current information & developments from SEC & other authorities.
General Info: (Formerly SEC Accounting Report), Yr. Est. 1985, Irregular, Trim Size-7½ x 10, Offset press, 8 pages, ISSN: 0146-485X, No Color
Subscriptions: Indv. $345
Circulation: Total-958
List Rental: List Management Co.: Manager: Seena Benedek; WG & L List Management, 1 Penn Plz Fl 42, New York, NY 10119-0002 Tel # (212) 971-5000

SEC Accounting Report
Business

Publishing Co: Warren, Gorham & Lamont, 31 Saint James Ave., Boston, MA 02116-4112 Parent Co.-Thomson Professional Publications, Stamford; Title Tel # (617) 423-2020 Title Fax # (617) 423-1914
Personnel: Publisher-Andrew Boden, Production Mgr.-Ed Novack, Mktg. Dir.-Sandra Fox
General Info: Yr. Est. 1974, Monthly
Subscriptions: Indv. $228
List Rental: List Management Co.: Manager: Seena Benedek; WG & L List Management, 1 Penn Plz Fl 42, New York, NY 10119-0002 Tel # (212) 971-5000

SEC Accounting Rules

Publishing Co: CCH, Inc., 2700 Lake Cook Rd., Riverwoods, IL 60015 Parent Co.-Kluwer Law & Taxation Publishers, Cambridge; Title Tel # (847) 267-7000 Title Fax # (800) 224-8299
Editorial Description: Focuses on accounting requirements prescribed by the Securities and Exchange Commission and provides texts of Regulations S-X and S-K, Financial Reporting Releases, the Codification of Financial Reporting Policies.
General Info: Irregular, Looseleaf
Subscriptions: Indv. $378

SEC Docket
See: INVESTMENT

Small Firm Profit Report - CPA Edition *Business*

Publishing Co: Professional Newsletters, Inc, State Taxation Institute, PO Box 81143, Atlanta, GA 30366-1143; Title Tel # (770) 457-1000
Personnel: Publisher-Robert Palmer
Editorial Description: Practice management and marketing help for small CPA firms and sole practioners.
General Info: Yr. Est. 1995, Monthly
Subscriptions: Indv. $69

Software Connection *Business*

Publishing Co: American Institute of CPA's, Harborside Financial Center, 201 Plaza Three, Jersey City, NJ 07311-3881 Tel # (201) 938-3283; Title Tel # (201) 938-3000 Title Fax # (201) 938-3329
Personnel: Publisher-Robert Rainer, Editor-Tracy Monaghan, Production Mgr.-Peter Tuohy, Mktg. Dir.-Charles Cohn
Editorial Description: Update & information for CPA's who previously purchased AICPA software.
General Info: Yr. Est. 1994, Quarterly, Trim Size-8½ x 11, Offset press, 6 pages, 2 Color, Matte, Saddle-stitched
Subscriptions: Free With Membership
Circulation: Total-11,000, Readership-11,000
Printing Co: Clarkwood Corp., 690 Union Blvd, Totowa, NJ 07512-2208 Tel # (201) 256-2456

State Board Report *Association*

Publishing Co: National Association of State Boards of Accountancy, 380 Lexington Ave, New York, NY 10168-0002; Title Tel # (212) 490-3868 Title Fax # (212) 490-5841
Personnel: Editor-James Thomashower, Assoc. Ed.-Louise Haberman, Production Mgr.-Angela Willenbring
Editorial Description: Association news as well as features on trends and current developments in state regulations of the accounting profession.
General Info: Yr. Est. 1972, Monthly, 4 pages
Subscriptions: Indv. $40, Inst. $40, Can. $40, For. $40, Free In Designated Area
Circulation: Total-1,200

State Legislative Matters
See: LAW

Strategic Governance for Nonprofit Executives and Boards *Business*

Publishing Co: Aspen Publishers, Inc., 200 Orchard Ridge Dr., Ste 200, Gaithersburg, MD 20878-5440 Tel # (301) 417-7500 Fax # (301) 417-7655 Parent Co.-Wolters Kluwer US Corporation, New York
Editorial Description: Assists nonprofit executives and boards to tackle tough issues facing today's nonprofit.
General Info: Yr. Est. 1995, Monthly, ISSN: 1080-4706
Subscriptions: Indv. $109, For. $131, $11/copy

Sum Monthly News *Association, Business* CPM: $125

Publishing Co: Massachusetts Society of Certified Public Accountants Inc., 105 Chauncy St., 10th Floor, Boston, MA 02111-1726; Title Tel # (617) 556-4000 Title Fax # (617) 556-4126
Personnel: Editor-Cheryl McCloud, Adv. Dir.-Wendy Devine
Editorial Description: Analyzes various business topics for association members.
General Info: Yr. Est. 1940, Bi-monthly, Trim Size-8½ x 11, 12 pages, 5% ads, 2 Color, Coated, Other
Subscriptions: Free With Membership
Circulation: Total-7,800
Advertising: $980. Accepts Inserts.
Printing Co: Graphlex, 173 Harvey St., Cambridge, MA 09140 Tel # (617) 547-1370, Fax # (617) 868-4171

Tax & Business Adviser *Business*

Publishing Co: Grant Thornton, One Prudential Plz., 130 E. Randolph Dr., Ste. 700, Chicago, IL 60601; Title Tel # (312) 856-0001 Title Fax # (312) 861-1340
Personnel: Editor-Mary Jaspers, Circ. Mgr., Production Mgr.-Beth Rose, Art Dir.-Marilyn Markle
Editorial Description: Current developments in accounting and auditing, taxation, business management, and securities regulation of interest to a general business audience.
General Info: (Formerly Business Scan/Tax Planner), Yr. Est. 1972, Bi-monthly, Sheetfed press, 8 pages, 2 Color, Matte
Circulation: Total-58,550
Printing Co: Darwill Press, 11900 Roosevelt Rd, Hillside, IL 60162-2070 Tel # (708) 449-7770

Tax Accounting
See: TAXES

Tax Division Newsletter *Business*

Publishing Co: American Institute of CPA's, Harborside Financial Center, 201 Plaza Three, Jersey City, NJ 07311-3881 Tel # (201) 938-3283; Title Tel # (201) 938-3000 Title Fax # (201) 938-3329
Personnel: Publisher-Robert Rainer, Editor-NJ Fiore, Mktg. Dir.-Charles Cohn
Editorial Description: Divisional news & information for Tax Division members.
General Info: Irregular, Trim Size-8½ x 11, Offset press, 6 pages, 2 Color, Matte, Saddle-stitched
Subscriptions: Free With Membership
Circulation: Total-25,000, Readership-25,000
Printing Co: Clarkwood Corp., 690 Union Blvd, Totowa, NJ 07512-2208 Tel # (201) 256-2456

Taxes on Parade
See: TAXES

Treasury Manager's Report *Business*

Publishing Co: Phillips Business Information, Inc., 1201 Seven Locks Rd., Ste 300, Potomac, MD 20854-2958 Tel # (301) 340-1520 Fax # (301) 424-4297
General Info: Bi-weekly, ISSN: 1071-8532
Subscriptions: Indv. $595, For. $630

U.S. International Practice & Procedure
See: TAXES

Wendell's Report to Controllers *Business*

Publishing Co: Warren, Gorham & Lamont, 31 Saint James Ave., Boston, MA 02116-4112 Parent Co.-Thomson Professional Publications, Stamford; Title Tel # (617) 423-2020 Title Fax # (617) 423-1914
Personnel: Publisher-Andrew Boden, Editor-Paul Wendell, Production Mgr.-Ed Novack, Mktg. Dir.-Sandra Fox
Editorial Description: Information on: New accounting rules and proposals; what's new in corporate financing; major tax changes and proposals; what's happening in compensation trends; risk management.
General Info: (Formerly CFO Alert), Yr. Est. 1979, Monthly
Subscriptions: Indv. $135
List Rental: List Management Co.: Manager: Seena Benedek; WG & L List Management, 1 Penn Plz Fl 42, New York, NY 10119-0002 Tel # (212) 971-5000

What's Working in Credit & Collection *Business*

Publishing Co: Progressive Business Publications, 370 Technology Dr., #3019, Malverne, PA 19355-9863 Parent Co.-American Future Systems, Inc., Bryn Mawr; Title Tel # (610) 695-8600 Title Fax # (610) 647-8089
Personnel: Publisher-Edward M. Satell, Editor-Russell Case, Editorial Dir.-Stephen Meyer, Mktg. Dir.-Ed Moore
Editorial Description: Helps credit and collection professionals avoid losses and build credit sales for their companies.
General Info: Bi-weekly, 8 pages
Subscriptions: Indv. $253
List Rental: List Management Co.: Mail Marketing, Inc., 171 Terrace St., Haworth, NJ 07641-1899 Tel # (201) 387-1023, Fax # (201) 387-2976

World Accounting
See: INTERNATIONAL TRADE

ADVERTISING & MARKETING

2 Minute Break *Business*

Publishing Co: Alan Lawrence Co., 279 E. 44th Street, New York, NY 10017; Title Tel # (212) 697-4015 Title Fax # (212) 697-4827
Personnel: Publisher-Martha Gargle, Editor-Alan Lawrence
Editorial Description: Small Business marketing tool.
General Info: Yr. Est. 1988, Monthly, Trim Size-11 x 8, Desktop press, 4 pages, Other
Subscriptions: Free To Qualified Recipient
List Rental: Rents Lists
Printing Co: Man Art, 111 8th Ave, New York, NY 10011 Tel # (212) 691-1010

AAPOR News *Association*

Publishing Co: American Association for Public Opinion Research, PO Box 1248, Ann Arbor, MI 48106-1248; Title Tel # (313) 764-1555 Title Fax # (313) 764-3341
Personnel: Editor-Janice Bailey
Editorial Description: Members are individuals concerned with public opinion research and the application of its results to advertising, marketing, scholarship and public affairs.
General Info: Tri-annually, Trim Size-8½ x 11, Offset press, 8 pages, No Color, Newsprint
Circulation: (100% controlled), Total-1,450

ABC NewsBulletin
See: MEDIA & COMMUNICATIONS

ACME Newsletter
See: HOTEL INDUSTRY

AD-PR Agency Report

Publishing Co: AD-PR Agency Report, Box 715, San Rafael, CA 94914-0715; Title Tel # (415) 461-2588 Title Fax # (415) 461-6526
Personnel: Publisher, Editor-Len Gross
Editorial Description: Contains information for small advertising & PR agencies.
General Info: Yr. Est. 1977, Bi-monthly
Subscriptions: Indv. $54

ADM Flash *Business, Association*

Publishing Co: Association of Directory Marketing, One Thorn Run Ctr., Ste. 202, 1187 Thorn Run Rd., Moon Township, PA 15108-3198 Tel # (412) 268-0663 Fax # (412) 269-0655
Personnel: Mktg. Dir.-Stu Hayes
Editorial Description: Association news, information and calendar.
General Info: Monthly, Trim Size-8½ x 11, 8 pages, Matte

A/E Marketing Journal
See: CONSTRUCTION & BUILDING

AIM Newsletter — *Association*

Publishing Co: Natl. Premium Sales Executives, 1600 Rt. 22, Union, NJ 07083-3478; Title Tel # (908) 687-3090
Personnel: Editor-Andy Bopp
Editorial Description: Assn. news including general incentive field information.
General Info: (Formerly NPSE Newsletter), Yr. Est. 1957, Monthly, Sheetfed press, 4 pages, No Color, Newsprint
Circulation: (100% controlled), Total-400

APNY Newsletter
See: PHOTOGRAPHY

ARF Quarterly Report — *Association*

Publishing Co: Advertising Research Foundation, 641 Lexington Ave Fl 11, New York, NY 10022-4503 Fax # (212) 319-5265; Title Tel # (212) 751-5656
Editorial Description: Reports on activities of the foundation, meetings, new members, etc.

ASCOT News — *Association, Business*

Publishing Co: Advertising & Sales Club of Toronto, Box 237, Sta. K, Toronto, ON M4P 2G5 Canada; Title Tel # (416) 363-5886

AWNY Matters — *Business, Association*

Publishing Co: Advertising Women of New York, 153 E 57th St Fl 3a, New York, NY 10022-2121; Title Tel # (212) 593-1950
Editorial Description: Covers activities of membership.
General Info: Irregular

AWNY Roster — *Business, Association*

Publishing Co: Advertising Women of New York, 153 E 57th St Fl 3a, New York, NY 10022-2121; Title Tel # (212) 593-1950
General Info: Annually

About Marketing to Women — *Business*

Publishing Co: About Women Inc., 33 Broad St., Boston, MA 02109; Title Tel # (617) 723-4337 Title Fax # (617) 723-7107
Personnel: Publisher, Editor, Mng. Editor, Technology Ed.-E. Janice Leeming, Fashion Ed.-Cynthia Tripp, Bk. Rev. Ed.-Judith Dorato, Mktg. Dir.-Emilie Antonetti
Editorial Description: Current research studies on women are analyzed and summarized to provide reader with an understanding of what women want, what their buying behaviors and shopping habits are.
General Info: (Formerly Marketing to Women), Yr. Est. 1987, Monthly, Trim Size-8$\frac{1}{2}$ x 11, Offset press, 16 pages, ISSN: 10471677, Ind/Abs/Online: Information Access, 2 Color, Matte
Subscriptions: Indv. $289, Inst. $145, Can. $300, For. $335, $25/copy
Circulation: Total-2,500
List Rental: Rents Lists

Academia

Publishing Co: Academy of Hospital Public Relations, 33 Irving Pl., New York, NY 10003-2332; Title Tel # (212) 826-1750
General Info: Monthly
Circulation: Total-2,500

Ad Business Report — *Business*

Publishing Co: Executive Communications, Inc., 185 E 85th St Ste 11c, New York, NY 10028-2148; Title Tel # (212) 831-3147
Personnel: Publisher-G. Buxton, Editor-Sue Fulton
Editorial Description: Covers advertising agency new business development and management issues, as well as marketing trends in major industries.
General Info: Yr. Est. 1978, Monthly, 10 pages
Subscriptions: Indv. $75

Ad Club Directory — *Association*

Publishing Co: Advertising Club of Greater Boston, 38 Newbury St., #7, Boston, MA 02116-3210; Title Tel # (617) 262-1100
Editorial Description: Listings of membership and guide to agencies and services in the area.
General Info: Annually, Trim Size-4$\frac{1}{4}$ x 9, Offset press, 280 pages, 4% ads, Coated
Subscriptions: $30/copy
Circulation: Total-2,200
Advertising: Inquire for rates.

Ad Club of Greater Hartford Newsletter — *Business*

Publishing Co: Ad Club, B.K. Hensey Assoc., 18 Stirrup Trl, Pawling, NY 12564-2222
Editorial Description: Ad club news.
General Info: Bi-monthly, Trim Size-8$\frac{1}{2}$ x 11, 4 pages, No Color
Subscriptions: Indv. $60
Circulation: Total-550

Ad Clubber — *Association, Business*

Publishing Co: Advertising Club of Metropolitan Washington, Inc., The, 7200 Wisconsin Ave Ste 200, Bethesda, MD 20814-4811; Title Tel # (301) 656-2582
Personnel: Editor-Gene Reynolds
Editorial Description: News of and for the advertising profession, the Ad Club, and the community in Metro Washington.
General Info: Yr. Est. 1918, Monthly, Trim Size-8$\frac{1}{2}$ x 11, Offset press, 8 pages, No Color
Circulation: Total-650
Advertising: Inquire for rates.

Ad News — *Business, Association* CPM: $735

Publishing Co: Philadelphia Advertising Club, PO Box 12923, Philadelphia, PA 19108-0923 Tel # (215) 627-2862; Title Tel # (609) 234-7930 Title Fax # (609) 234-7930
Personnel: Editor-Thomas J. Quigley, Circ. Mgr.-Bernardine Steinmetz, Adv. Dir.-Daryl Ann Merenich, Art Dir.-Beth Megelsh
Editorial Description: News and features about the people and programs which comprise the Delaware Valley's advertising industry (southeastern Pennsylvania, southern New Jersey and Delaware).
General Info: (Formerly Philadelphia Ad Club News), Yr. Est. 1964, Monthly, Sheetfed press, 24 pages, 4% ads, 2 Color, Coated, Saddle-stitched
Subscriptions: $5/copy
Acquistions: Publication Bought
Circulation: Total-1,000
Advertising: $735.

Ad News

Publishing Co: Ad Club of New Hampshire, PO Box 4448, Manchester, NH 03108-4448; Title Tel # (603) 898-6332
Personnel: Publisher-Maureen Anderson
Editorial Description: News on New Hampshire advertising, marketing, public relations, related industries.
General Info: Monthly, 12 pages, No Color, Coated
Subscriptions: Indv. $20
Circulation: Total-300
Advertising: Inquire for rates.
Printing Co: Kopy Korner, 85 Cilley Rd, Manchester, NH 03103-5636 Tel # (603) 669-8800

Ad Trends — *Business*

Publishing Co: National Research Bureau, 150 N. Wacher Drive, Chicago, IL 60601 Tel # (312) 541-0100 Fax # (312) 541-1492 Parent Co.-Reed Reference Publishing, New Providence; Title Tel # (319) 752-5415 Title Fax # (319) 752-3421
Personnel: Publisher-Michael Darnall
Editorial Description: A monthly report of advertising and merchandising ideas covering home, food, and shopping centers. Actual reproductions of ad ideas from leading stores.
General Info: Yr. Est. 1933, Monthly, Trim Size-8$\frac{1}{2}$ x 11, 26 pages, Color-cover, Looseleaf
Subscriptions: Indv. $52

AdMarks — *Business, Association*

Publishing Co: Chicago Assn. of Direct Marketing, 200 N. Michigan Ave. #300, Chicago, IL 60601-5909; Title Tel # (312) 541-1272 Title Fax # (312) 541-1271
Personnel: Editor-Jean Nelson
General Info: Yr. Est. 1954, Monthly, 8 pages, 3% ads, 2 Color, Coated
Circulation: Total-2,700
Advertising: Inquire for rates.

AdVantage Point — *Business*

Publishing Co: AdVantage Point Press, 17 Paul Dr, San Rafael, CA 94903-2043; Title Tel # (415) 485-6969 Title Fax # (415) 485-0143
Personnel: Publisher, Editor-Binnie Perper, Production Mgr.-Inna Jane Ray
Editorial Description: News, information, how-to techniques of marketing and advertising for business owners, marketing and advertising executives.
General Info: Yr. Est. 1987, Bi-monthly, Trim Size-8$\frac{1}{2}$ x 11, Offset press, 4 pages, 2 Color, Matte
Subscriptions: Indv. $59
Circulation: Total-5,000

Adcrafter — *Business* CPM: $118

Publishing Co: Adcraft Club of Detroit, 2630 Book Tower, Detroit, MI 48226; Title Tel # (313) 962-7225 Title Fax # (313) 962-3599
Personnel: Publisher-S.M. Roberts, Editor-Lee H. Wilson
Editorial Description: News on advertising, marketing and club activities.
General Info: Yr. Est. 1923, Weekly, Trim Size-8$\frac{3}{8}$ x 10$\frac{7}{8}$, Web press, 20 pages, ISSN: 0001-8066, 4% ads, 4 Color, Coated, Saddle-stitched
Subscriptions: Indv. $35, $1/copy
Circulation: Total-4,600
Advertising: $546. Accepts Inserts.
Printing Co: Brookes Printing Co., 7600 Chrysler Dr, Detroit, MI 48211-1900 Tel # (313) 871-3357

Admetrics — *Business*

Publishing Co: C Systems Ltd., Box 708, 1006 Plume St., Winnsboro, TX 75494; Title Tel # (903) 342-5284 Title Fax # (903) 342-5803
Personnel: Publisher-James Callan, Editor-D. Bailey, Art Dir.-S. Bassham
Editorial Description: Analysis of hi-tech advertising in trade and business publications.
General Info: (Formerly Advantages), Yr. Est. 1983, Monthly, Offset press, 4 pages, 2 Color, Newsprint
Subscriptions: Indv. $125, $15/copy
Circulation: (83% controlled), Total-600

Advertising Age Daily Fax
Edition **Business**
Publishing Co: Crain Communications, Inc., 220 E. 42nd St., New York, NY 10017-5806
 Tel # (212) 210-0100 Fax # (212) 210-0114 Parent Co.-Crain Communications Inc, Chicago
Editorial Description: Daily faxed news about the advertising community.
General Info: Daily
Subscriptions: Indv. $179

Advertising Creativity
Newsletter
Publishing Co: Prosperity & Profits Unlimited, PO Box 416, Denver, CO 80201-0416;
 Title Tel # (303) 575-5676
Personnel: Publisher, Editor-A.C. Doyle
Editorial Description: Ideas on creative advertising.
General Info: Yr. Est. 1990, Annually
Subscriptions: Indv. $5, Inst. $5, Can. $11, For. $13, $5/copy

Advertising Marketing
Bulletin **Business**
Publishing Co: Special Library Association, 1014 Manoa Rd, Wynnewood, PA 19096-4032
Editorial Description: Information from the Special Library Association's Advertising/Marketing
 division.
General Info: Quarterly, Trim Size-8$\frac{1}{2}$ x 11, 10 pages, No Color, Matte, Saddle-stitched
Advertising: Inquire for rates.

Advertising Topics **Business**
Publishing Co: Council of Better Business Bureaus, 4200 Wilson Blvd Ste 800, Arlington, VA
 22203-1800; Title Tel # (703) 276-0100
Editorial Description: Analysis and interpretation of advertising issues.
General Info: Yr. Est. 1949, Monthly, 8 pages, Color
Subscriptions: Indv. $96

Advertising Via Telemarketing Script Presentations Newsletter
 See: BUSINESS & INDUSTRY

Advertising Wildfire **Business**
Publishing Co: West, Adams, Christopher & Associates, 1000 W. McNab Rd., Suite 158, Pompano,
 FL 33069-9871 Tel # (305) 384-8500 Fax # (305) 578-4200
Editorial Description: Reviews techniques and technologies in advertising and promotion.
General Info: Weekly

Adweek Special Report **Business**
Publishing Co: Adweek, Inc., 1515 Broadway, New York, NY 10036 Parent Co.-BPI
 Communications, Nashville; Title Tel # (212) 536-5336
Personnel: Editor-Mike Winkeleman, Circ. Mgr.-Mark Dolliver, Production Mgr.-Jane Ceccarelli, Art
 Dir.-Keith Lepkowski, Promotion Dir.-Thomas Forbes
Editorial Description: Covers magazine business events & people.
General Info: Trim Size-8$\frac{1}{2}$ x 11
Subscriptions: $3/copy

Affiliated Advertising
Agencies Intl. News
Publishing Co: Affiliated Advertising Agencies Intl., 2280 S Xanadu Way Ste 300, Aurora, CO
 80014-1374; Title Tel # (303) 671-8551 Title Fax # (303) 337-9576
General Info: Bi-monthly

Aging America Resources
 See: SENIOR CITIZENS

Akron Daily Digest
 See: HOUSE ORGANS

American Academy of
Advertising Newsletter **Association, Business**
Publishing Co: American Academy of Advertising, Michigan State Univ., c/o Prof. Keith Adler, E.
 Lansing, MI 48824; Title Tel # (216) 742-1870
Personnel: Editor-Jane Reid
General Info: (Formerly AAA Newsletter), Yr. Est. 1958, Quarterly
Circulation: Total-600

American Marketplace **Business**
Publishing Co: Business Publishers, Inc., 951 Pershing Dr., Silver Spring, MD 20910-4464
 Tel # (301) 589-5103 Fax # (301) 589-8493; Title Tel # (301) 587-6300 Title Fax # (301) 587-1081
Personnel: Publisher-Eric Easton, Editor-David Speights, Circ. Mgr.-Kathleen Harrow, Promotion Dir.-
 Pat Nussman
Editorial Description: Covers all the latest news on consumer trends, population shifts. employment
 gains and losses and more.
General Info: (Formerly U.S. Census Report), Yr. Est. 1980, Bi-weekly, Trim Size-8$\frac{1}{2}$ x 11, Desktop
 press, 8 pages, ISSN: 0276-2900, Ind/Abs/Online: NewsNet, DIALOG, No Color, Recycled
Subscriptions: Indv. $364, Can. $364, For. $377
Advertising: Accepts Inserts.
List Rental: List Management Co.: Manager: Donald Peterson; BPI Direct, 951 Pershing Dr., Silver
 Spring, MD 20910-4464 Tel # (301) 585-5976, Fax # (301) 587-4530

American Society of
Association Executives-
Associate Member
Update **Association**
Publishing Co: American Society of Association Executives, 1575 'I' St., N.W., 11th Fl., Washington,
 DC 20005-1168 Tel # (202) 626-2711 Fax # (202) 408-9633; Title Tel # (202) 626-2739
Personnel: Editor-Joseph Cavarretta
Editorial Description: Newsletter for supplier members of ASAE; covers marketing opportunities, etc.
General Info: Semi-annually
Subscriptions: Free With Membership
Circulation: Total-4,500, Readership-6,000
List Rental: Actives: 3,519, $175/M

Antin Marketing Letter **Business**
Publishing Co: Antin Marketing Group, 9204 W. 71st Street, Merriam, KS 66204
 Tel # (913) 677-3999 Fax # (913) 677-2223
Personnel: Editor-Brad Antin
Editorial Description: Marketing tips for business professionals.
General Info: Yr. Est. 1992, Monthly
Subscriptions: Indv. $177

Art of Self Promotion, The **Business**
Publishing Co: Creative Marketing & Management, 303 Park Ave, Hoboken, NJ 07030-3805;
 Title Tel # (201) 653-0783 Title Fax # (201) 222-2494
Personnel: Publisher, Editor-Ilise Benun
Editorial Description: Bite size nuts and bolts for manageable marketing for the serlf employed.
General Info: Yr. Est. 1989, Quarterly, Trim Size-8$\frac{1}{2}$ x 11, Offset press, 6 pages, ISSN: 1068-9753,
 2 Color
Subscriptions: Indv. $30, $7/copy
Circulation: Total-4,000
Advertising: Accepts Inserts.

ArtSource Quarterly **Business, Consumer**
Publishing Co: Art Network, 18757 Wildflower Dr., P.O. Box 1268, Penn Valley, CA 95946-9717
 Tel # (916) 432-7630 Fax # (916) 432-7633; Title Tel # (916) 692-1355 Title Fax # (916) 692-1370
Personnel: Editor-C. Smith, Circ. Mgr.-S. Meyers
Editorial Description: Focuses on the latest marketing information, including interviews with art
 professionals, sales strategies, and more. Guide to Fine Art Marketing.
General Info: Yr. Est. 1992, Quarterly, ISSN: 1064-6620
Subscriptions: Indv. $19, Inst. $19, Can. $24, For. $29, $6/copy

Artworld Hotline **Business, Consumer**
Publishing Co: Art Network, 18757 Wildflower Dr., P.O. Box 1268, Penn Valley, CA 95946-9717;
 Title Tel # (916) 432-7630 Title Fax # (916) 432-7633
Personnel: Editor-C. Smith, Circ. Mgr.-Sarah Meyers
Editorial Description: Concise and timely information on the most current opportunities in the art
 world.
General Info: Yr. Est. 1990, Monthly, Trim Size-8$\frac{1}{2}$ x 11, 4 pages, ISSN: 1057-5413
Subscriptions: Indv. $26, Inst. $26, Can. $26, For. $36, $3/copy
Advertising: Inquire for rates.

Association of New Gay & Lesbian Entrepreneurs
 See: GAY & LESBIAN INTEREST

BOMI Newsletter: Annual Conference Edition
 See: REGIONAL INTEREST

Bank Marketing International
 See: BANKING & FINANCE

Barnard's Retail Marketing Report
 See: DEPARTMENT STORE & RETAIL

Beverage Alcohol Market Report
 See: BEVERAGES - BREWING

Bill Nelson Newsletter
 See: COLLECTIBLES

Blueprints **Business**
Publishing Co: Proteus Publishing, P.O. Box 2940, Ann Arbor, MI 48106 Tel # (313) 668-2743
 Fax # (313) 668-8535
Personnel: Mng. Editor-Sara Korte
Editorial Description: Information and news about trade show marketing.

Board Report for Graphic Artists
 See: PRINTING/GRAPHIC ARTS

Book Marketing Update
 See: BOOKS & BOOK TRADE

Book Promotion Hotline   *Business, Association*

Publishing Co: Ad-Lib Publications, 51 1/2 W. Adams, PO Box 1102, Fairfield, IA 52556-1102; Title Tel # (515) 472-6617 Title Fax # (515) 472-3186
Personnel: Editor-Marie Kiefer, Circ. Mgr.-Jeanette Beasley
Editorial Description: Key contacts at magazines, newspapers, radio, TV, book wholesalers, book clubs, mail order catalogs, etc.
General Info: Yr. Est. 1990, Bi-weekly, Trim Size-8½ x 11, Sheetfed press, 8 pages, No Color
Subscriptions: Indv. $150, $3/copy
Circulation: Total-1,000
List Rental: Actives: 16,000, $80/M
Printing Co: Tribune Printing, 111 W Briggs Ave, Fairfield, IA 52556-2825

Boomer Report
See: BANKING & FINANCE

Boomer Report, The   *Business*

Publishing Co: InfoCom Group, 1250 45th St., Ste 200, Emeryville, CA 94608-2924 Tel # (510) 596-9300 Fax # (510) 596-9331
Personnel: Publisher-Andrew Garvin, Editor-Susan Mitchell, Mng. Editor-Margaret Nichols, Exec. Ed.-Cheryl Russell, Circ. Dir.-Michael Shor
Editorial Description: Monitors the 'Baby-boom generation'--what it's buying, thinking, feeling--and doing next.
General Info: Monthly
Subscriptions: Indv. $195

Bottom Line Exhibit
Marketing   *Business*

Publishing Co: Giltspur Inc., 500 Park Blvd., Itasca, IL 60143-1267; Title Tel # (708) 250-3930 Title Fax # (708) 250-3929
Personnel: Editor-Pat Friedlander
Editorial Description: Tips for exhibit and conference sales from this custom exhibit manufacturer.
General Info: Yr. Est. 1990, Quarterly, Trim Size-8½ x 11, 4 pages, 2 Color, Matte
Subscriptions: Free To Qualified Recipient
Circulation: Total-35,000

Briefings

Publishing Co: Advertising Specialty Institute, 1120 Wheeler Way, Langhorne, PA 19047-1785; Title Tel # (215) 752-4200
Personnel: Publisher-Marvin Spike, Editor-Christine Finley, Adv. Dir.-Ron Ball, Art Dir.-Jim Lang
Editorial Description: Address changes, other relevant information for specialty advertising businesses.
General Info: Bi-weekly, Sheetfed press, 4 pages, 2 Color, Newsprint
Subscriptions: Indv. $36
Circulation: (100% controlled), Total-6,000

Bulldog Reporter: Eastern
Edition   *Business*

Publishing Co: InfoCom Group, 1250 45th St., Ste 200, Emeryville, CA 94608-2924; Title Tel # (510) 596-9300 Title Fax # (510) 596-9331
Personnel: Publisher-James Sinkinson, Editor-Chris Kent, Production Mgr.-Suzi Geiger, Art Dir.-Cynthia Levitas
Editorial Description: Media placement newsletter for PR professionals; media profiles; editor/reporter changes.
General Info: Semi-monthly
Subscriptions: Indv. $389, $20/copy
Circulation: Total-2,000
Advertising: Inquire for rates.

Bulldog Reporter:
Western Edition   *Business*

Publishing Co: InfoCom Group, 1250 45th St., Ste 200, Emeryville, CA 94608-2924; Title Tel # (510) 596-9300 Title Fax # (510) 596-9331
Personnel: Publisher-James Sinkinson, Editor-Carolyn Huffman, Circ. Dir.-Peter Klehm, Production Mgr.-Suzi Geiger, Art Dir.-Cynthia Levitas
Editorial Description: Media placement newsletter for PR professionals; media profiles; editor/reporter changes; agency news.
General Info: (Formerly Bulldog Reporter), Yr. Est. 1990, Semi-monthly, Offset press, 8 pages, No Color
Subscriptions: Indv. $389, $10/copy
Acquistions: Publication Bought, Publication Sold
Circulation: Total-850
Advertising: Inquire for rates. Accepts Inserts.
List Rental: Rents Lists

Business Marketing
Notepad   *Business*

Publishing Co: Direct Marketing Publishers, 1304 University Dr, Yardley, PA 19067-2829; Title Tel # (215) 321-3068 Title Fax # (215) 321-9647
Personnel: Publisher-Bernie Goldberg, Editor-Marie Smith
Editorial Description: Marketing information for telemarketing and direct mail.
General Info: Yr. Est. 1991, Monthly, Trim Size-8½ x 11, 8 pages, No Color, Matte, Saddle-stitched
Subscriptions: $15/copy

Business Review
See: BUSINESS & INDUSTRY

Cable TV Advertising
See: TELEVISION & VIDEO

Cable TV Marketing Letter   *Business*

Publishing Co: Kerner Group, 3231 Forks St, Easton, PA 18045-5970; Title Tel # (610) 253-3054
Editorial Description: Practical advice for businesses who advertise on cable.
General Info: Yr. Est. 1993, Monthly
Subscriptions: Indv. $145

Campus Market Report   *Business, Consumer*

Publishing Co: Natl. Assn. of College Stores, 500 E Lorain St, Oberlin, OH 44074-1238 Fax # (216) 775-4769; Title Tel # (216) 775-7777
Personnel: Publisher-Mavis Clark, Editor-Ron Stevens, Circ. Mgr.-Elaine Smith, Production Mgr.-Ben Ryba, Adv. Dir.-Chip Wigton, Art Dir.-David Russell
General Info: Yr. Est. 1986, Monthly
Subscriptions: Indv. $60
Circulation: Total-1,000

Canadian Direct Marketing
Notes

Publishing Co: Mailing List Systems, 711 Directors Dr, Arlington, TX 76011-5103; Title Tel # (817) 640-7007 Title Fax # (817) 633-8008
Editorial Description: Direct mail information and news.
General Info: Yr. Est. 1992, Quarterly, Trim Size-8½ x 11, 4 pages, No Color, Matte, Saddle-stitched
Subscriptions: Free
Circulation: Readership-900

Capell's Circulation
Report   *Business*

Publishing Co: Vos, Gruppo, Capell, 60 E 42nd St Rm 3810, New York, NY 10165-0006; Title Tel # (212) 697-5753 Title Fax # (212) 949-7294
Personnel: Publisher, Editor, Circ. Mgr., Adv. Dir.-Dan Capell
Editorial Description: Information on the magazine circulation industry.
General Info: Yr. Est. 1982, 20x/yr., Trim Size-8½ x 11, Desktop press, 8 pages, ISSN: 0736-9077, No Color, Newsprint
Subscriptions: Indv. $345, Can. $425, For. $425, $20/copy
List Rental: Actives: 500

Catalog Marketer, The   *Business*

Publishing Co: Maxwell Sroge Publishing, Inc., 522 Forest Ave, Evanston, IL 60202-3005; Title Tel # (847) 866-1890 Title Fax # (847) 866-1899
Personnel: Publisher-Maxwell Sroge, Editor-Ann Meyer, Circ. Mgr.-Rachell Hamill
Editorial Description: Designed for those in catalog marketing and production. Covers industry news, new developments, & all areas involved in catalog operations.
General Info: Yr. Est. 1981, Bi-weekly, Trim Size-8½ x 11, Sheetfed press, 8 pages, ISSN: 0730-9937, No Color, Matte
Subscriptions: Indv. $199, Can. $244, For. $244, $15/copy

Category Report:
Household, Pets, &
Miscellaneous

Publishing Co: Marketing Intelligence Service, Ltd., 6473D Route 64, Naples, NY 14512; Title Tel # (716) 374-6326 Title Fax # (716) 374-5217
Personnel: Publisher-Richard Lawrence, Production Mgr.-Patricia Peck
Editorial Description: Combines domestic & foreign new product reviews. Each review typically includes detailed product & packaging descriptions, with illustrations, important manufacturing & marketing innovations, emerging trends, & other background information.
General Info: Monthly, Trim Size-8½ x 11, Mimeo press, No Color, Newsprint
Subscriptions: Indv. $1,000

Change
See: DIRECT MAIL

Channelmarker Letter
See: COMPUTERS & AUTOMATION

Channels
See: MEDIA & COMMUNICATIONS

Cheap Relief   *Business*

Publishing Co: Jean Lawrence, 3217 Connecticut Ave NW Apt 78, Washington, DC 20008-2504; Title Tel # (202) 362-8585 Title Fax # (202) 537-2980
Personnel: Publisher, Editor-Jean Lawrence
Editorial Description: Time & moneysavers for professional communicators.
General Info: Yr. Est. 1988, Monthly, Trim Size-8½ x 11, Other press, 4 pages, ISSN: 1062-9548, No Color, Matte
Subscriptions: Indv. $48, $4/copy
Advertising: Accepts Inserts.

Circulation Council Newsletter
See: DIRECT MAIL

Classified Advertising
Report

Publishing Co: Cowles Magazine, Inc., 4 High Ridge Park, Stamford, CT 06905
Tel # (203) 322-2900 Fax # (203) 322-1966; Title Tel # (914) 833-0600 Title Fax # (914) 833-0558
Personnel: Publisher, Editor-Efrem Sigel
Editorial Description: For publishers involved in classified ad sales in newspapers, yellow pages, magazines and electronic media.
General Info: Yr. Est. 1986, Monthly, Trim Size-8$\frac{1}{2}$ x 11, 10 pages
Subscriptions: Indv. $396, $33/copy

Classified Communication
Newsletter   *Business, Association*

Publishing Co: Classified Communiucation, Inc., PO Box 4242, Prescott, AZ 86302-4242
Fax # (602) 445-0517; Title Tel # (602) 778-6788
Personnel: Publisher, Editor-Agnes Franz, Copy Editor-Magda Gregory, Technology Ed.-Joseph Kasmer, Production Dir.-Kathy Humphrey, Eastern Adv. Mgr.-Karen Grossman
Editorial Description: Monthly newsletter providing advertising and promotions tips in a sharp, easy to understand format.
General Info: Yr. Est. 1985, Monthly, Trim Size-8$\frac{1}{2}$ x 11, Letrpr. press, 8 pages, No Color, Matte
Subscriptions: Indv. $29, Can. $35, $3/copy
Acquistions: Publication Bought
Circulation: Total-1,500
Printing Co: Fornara Printing & Graphics Co., 555 White Spar Rd, Prescott, AZ 86303-4627
Tel # (602) 445-3534

Client Line   *Business*

Publishing Co: Newkirk Products, Inc., 15 Corporate Cir, Albany, NY 12203-5154
Tel # (518) 452-1000
Editorial Description: Custom publication designed for distribution to clients by professionals with finance, tax or accounting practices. Available in monthly, bimonthly, and quarterly editions.
General Info: Monthly, Trim Size-8$\frac{1}{2}$ x 11, 4 pages, Color

Clipnotes   *Business*

Publishing Co: Gardner, Carton & Douglas, Quaker Twr., 321 N. Clark St., Chicago, IL 60610;
Title Tel # (312) 644-3000
Personnel: Editor-Priscilla Walter
General Info: Yr. Est. 1988, Monthly

Collegiate Trends   *Business*

Publishing Co: Strategic Marketing Communications, 550 N Maple Ave, Ridgewood, NJ 07450-1632;
Title Tel # (201) 612-8100 Title Fax # (201) 612-1444
Personnel: Publisher-Eric Weil, Editor-Christine Canning, Mktg. Dir.-Robert Doran
Editorial Description: Marketing & media data for those targeting students as consumers.
General Info: Yr. Est. 1987, Quarterly, Trim Size-8 x 10$\frac{1}{2}$, Sheetfed press, 14 pages, ISSN: 1065-0296, 2 Color, Matte, Saddle-stitched
Subscriptions: Indv. $86, Inst. $48, Can. $100, For. $100, $25/copy
Printing Co: Midland Press, 69 Washington St, West Orange, NJ 07052-5585 Tel # (201) 325-2242, Fax # (201) 325-3697

Color Q Connection
See: ART & SCULPTURE

Communication News   *Association*

Publishing Co: American Society of Association Executives, 1575 'I' St., N.W., 11th Fl., Washington, DC 20005-1168 Tel # (202) 626-2711 Fax # (202) 408-9633; Title Tel # (202) 626-2739
Personnel: Editor-Joseph Cavarretta
Editorial Description: Membership newsletter for communications section of non-profits.
General Info: (Formerly Editor's News), Monthly
Subscriptions: Free With Membership
Circulation: Total-1,900, Readership-4,000
List Rental: Actives: 1,974, $175/M

Communications Insights
See: MANAGEMENT

Communicator

Publishing Co: American Advertising Federation, 1101 Vermont Ave NW Ste 500, Washington, DC 20005-3521; Title Tel # (202) 898-0089
Personnel: Editor-Peter Allen
Editorial Description: Newsletter of college/univ. advertising education & service programs.
General Info: Monthly
Circulation: Total-4,500

Communicator   *Business, Association*   **CPM: $172**

Publishing Co: Canadian Direct Marketing Assn., 1 Concorde Gate, Suite 607, Don Mills, ON M3C 3N6 Canada; Title Tel # (416) 391-2362 Title Fax # (416) 441-4062
Personnel: Editor-Scott McClellan, Adv. Dir.-Katherine Brasch
Editorial Description: Editorial focus is on direct marketing activities in the Canadian marketplace.
General Info: Yr. Est. 1970, Quarterly, Desktop press, 16 pages, 2 Color, Coated, Saddle-stitched
Subscriptions: Indv. $30, Free With Membership
Circulation: Total-4,200
Advertising: $725. Accepts Inserts.
List Rental: Rents Lists

Communique

Publishing Co: Advertising & Sales Executives Club of Montreal, Suite 369, Queen Elizabeth Hot, Montreal, PQ H3B 4A5 Canada; Title Tel # (503) 866-1668
Personnel: Publisher, Editor-Bruce Riley
Editorial Description: Industry news-club internal news.
General Info: Monthly, Trim Size-8$\frac{1}{2}$ x 11, Web press, 8 pages, 4 Color, Coated
Circulation: Total-3,000
Advertising: Inquire for rates.

Communique   *Association*   **CPM$1235**

Publishing Co: Canadian Association of Exposition Managers, 6900 Airport Road, Suite 239A, Box 82, Mississauga, ON L4V 1E8 Canada; Title Tel # (905) 678-9377 Title Fax # (905) 678-9578
Personnel: Editor, Mng. Editor-Carol Ann Burrell
Editorial Description: Association newsletter for trade and consumer show managers and exposition contractors belonging to the Canadian Association of Exposition Managers.
General Info: (Formerly Caemeo), 8x/yr., 25% ads
Circulation: Total-425
Advertising: $525.

Competitive Advantage
See: SALESMANSHIP & SELLING

Computer Publishing & Advertising Report
See: PERIODICAL INDUSTRY

Connections to Mail
Order/World Trade and
Homebased Business
Info.   *Business, Consumer*   **CPM: $75**

Publishing Co: Four Winds Publishing, 4729 Amelia Dr, Fair Oaks, CA 95628-5517;
Title Fax # (916) 966-9325
Personnel: Publisher, Editor-Robert R. Soucy
Editorial Description: Offers how-to and other printed material dealing with mail order, import-export and homebased business information. Accepts and contains int'l advertising.
General Info: Yr. Est. 1994, Daily, Trim Size-8$\frac{1}{2}$ x 11, Offset press, 14 pages
Subscriptions: Free
Circulation: Total-1,200
Advertising: $90. Accepts Inserts.
List Rental: Actives: $70/M

Construction Market Data
See: CONSTRUCTION & BUILDING

Contacts: The Media
Pipeline for P.R. People   *Business*

Publishing Co: Cap Communications, 3520 Broadway, Astoria, NY 11106-1114;
Title Tel # (718) 721-0508 Title Fax # (718) 274-3387
Personnel: Publisher-Michael Smith, Editor-Madeleine Gillis
Editorial Description: Meets information needs of editors, columnists & producers of consumer & trade magazines, newspapers, TV & radio.
General Info: Yr. Est. 1970, Weekly, 4 pages, No Color, Newsprint
Subscriptions: Indv. $287
Circulation: Total-5,000
Advertising: Inquire for rates.

Corporate Community Relations Letter
See: BUSINESS & INDUSTRY

Counselor
See: RELIGIOUS & THEOLOGICAL

Cowles Report on
Database Marketing   *Business*

Publishing Co: Cowles Magazine, Inc., 4 High Ridge Park, Stamford, CT 06905
Tel # (203) 322-2900 Fax # (203) 322-1966; Title Tel # (203) 358-9900 Title Fax # (203) 357-9014
Personnel: Editor in Chief-Toni Apgar, Mng. Editor-Holly Wallinger
Editorial Description: Reliable and useful database marketing tips and information.
General Info: Yr. Est. 1992, Monthly, Trim Size-8$\frac{1}{2}$ x 11, 12 pages, 2 Color, Matte
Subscriptions: Indv. $299

Creative Marketing
Newsletter   *Business, Association*

Publishing Co: Association of Retail Marketing Services, 3 Caro Ct, Red Bank, NJ 07701-2315;
Title Tel # (908) 842-5070 Title Fax # (908) 219-1938
Personnel: Editor-George Meredith
Editorial Description: The only publication aimed at incentive marketing at the retail level. Focuses on the Grocery Field -- yet encompasses all promotion at the retail level.
General Info: Yr. Est. 1980, Quarterly, Trim Size-8$\frac{1}{2}$ x 11, Letrpr. press, 4 pages, 2 Color
Circulation: (100% controlled), Total-4,200
Printing Co: Union Graphics, 1634 East Elizabeth Avenue, Linden, NJ 07036 Tel # (908) 486-0300, Fax # (908) 486-7640

Culpepper Letter: Software Intelligence for Growth and Profits
See: COMPUTERS & AUTOMATION

Customer Service Report
See: MANAGEMENT

Cybernautics Digest
See: MEDIA & COMMUNICATIONS

Cyberspace PR Newsletter *Business, Association*

Publishing Co: Public Relations Society of America, Inc., 33 Irving Place, New York, NY 10003-2376
Tel # (212) 460-1428 Fax # (212) 460-1424
Editorial Description: Presents ways electronic media can be used by PR professionals.
General Info: Yr. Est. 1995, 22x/yr.
Subscriptions: Indv. $395

DFISA Reporter

Publishing Co: Dairy & Food Industries Supply Assn., Inc., 1451 Dolley Madison Blvd., McLean, VA 22101-3811; Title Tel # (301) 984-1444 Title Fax # (301) 881-7832
Personnel: Editor-Lori Bellavia
Editorial Description: Trend for Food & Dairy. . . Member activity. . . Happenings in the industry.
General Info: (Formerly Your Market), Yr. Est. 1958, Monthly, Trim Size-8½ x 11, Letrpr. press, 8 pages, 2 Color, Newsprint
Circulation: Total-2,000

DMA Catalog Council
Newsletter *Business, Association*

Publishing Co: DMA Catalog Council, 11 W 42nd St Fl 25, New York, NY 10036-8002 Parent Co.-Direct Marketing Association, Annapolis Junction; Title Tel # (212) 768-7277
Title Fax # (212) 768-4546
Personnel: Editor-Donald Mokrynski, Mng. Editor-Maureen Blake, Mng. Editor-Janet Morelli, Co-Editor-Susan-Jane Zuniga, Production-Carrissa Buenafe
General Info: Quarterly
Advertising: $450.

DMA Circulation Council
Newsletter *Business, Consumer*

Publishing Co: DMA Catalog Council, 11 W 42nd St Fl 25, New York, NY 10036-8002 Parent Co.-Direct Marketing Association, Annapolis Junction; Title Tel # (212) 768-7277
Personnel: Co-Editor-Leslie Grossman, Co-Editor-Lisa M. Merizio, Circ. Dir.-Cary Castle
General Info: Trim Size-8½ x 11, 10 pages, No Color, Matte, Saddle-stitched

DMAW Marketing Advents *Business, Association* CPM: $563

Publishing Co: Sponsor-Direct Mktg. Assn. of Washington, DC, Direct Marketing Association of Washington, 8229 Boone Blvd Ste 740, Vienna, VA 22182-2623; Title Tel # (703) 821-3629
Title Fax # (703) 821-3694
Personnel: Editor-John Jay Daly
Editorial Description: Newsletter for 1,650 members of Direct Marketing Assn. of Washington, DC. It does accept space ads; rate card on request.
General Info: Yr. Est. 1956, Monthly, Trim Size-8½ x 11, Offset press, 24 pages, 2 Color
Subscriptions: Free With Membership
Circulation: Total-1,650
Advertising: $930.
List Rental: List Management Co.: Manager: Anna Hargroove; Pinnacle List Company, 2800 Shirlington Rd Ste 405b, Arlington, VA 22206-3601 Tel # (703) 379-4394, Fax # (703) 379-5312, Actives: 1,650, $200/M, Expires: 730, $150/M
Printing Co: DMAW, 8229 Boone Blvd. #740, Vienna, VA 22182-2623 Tel # (703) 821-3629, Fax # (703) 821-3694

Database Marketing
Newsletter *Business*

Publishing Co: Lloydmedia, 1200 Markham Rd., Suite 301, Scarborough, ON M1H 3C3 Canada Fax # (416) 439-4086; Title Tel # (416) 439-4083
Personnel: Editor-Steve Lloyd
Editorial Description: Covers companies that use and profit from database marketing.
General Info: Yr. Est. 1992, Monthly
Subscriptions: Indv. $349

Day Break
See: DIRECT MAIL

DeLay Letter *Business*

Publishing Co: DeLay Letter, PO Box 58, Jamaica, NY 11426-0058; Title Tel # (212) 688-7559
Title Fax # (212) 753-6439
Personnel: Editor-Robert DeLay, Production Mgr.-Bernadette Lee
Editorial Description: Direct marketing trends, news, perspective in D.M. for top management.
General Info: Yr. Est. 1985, Semi-monthly, Trim Size-8½ x 11, Offset press, 4 pages, 2 Color, Newsprint
Subscriptions: Indv. $145, For. $185
Circulation: Total-750
Printing Co: Tyme Graphics, 250 Hudson St, New York, NY 10013-1471 Tel # (212) 691-4444

DecoMarketing

Publishing Co: National Decorating Products Assn., Inc., 1050 N Lindbergh Blvd, Saint Louis, MO 63132-2912; Title Tel # (314) 991-3470 Title Fax # (314) 991-5039
Personnel: Editor-Ernie Stewart
Editorial Description: Market Trends.
General Info: (Formerly Italics), Quarterly
Subscriptions: Indv. $100, Free With Membership
Circulation: Total-4,000

Delaney Report *Business*

Publishing Co: Delaney Report, 149 Fifth Ave., Ste. 725, New York, NY 10010-6801;
Title Tel # (212) 979-7881 Title Fax # (212) 979-7874
Personnel: Publisher-Thomas Delaney, Mng. Editor-Julia Igoe
Editorial Description: International newsletter for marketing, advertising, and media executives.
General Info: Yr. Est. 1990, Weekly, Trim Size-8½ x 11½, 4 pages, No Color, Matte
Subscriptions: Indv. $245, Inst. $245, Can. $295, For. $295, $10/copy

Development Director's Letter
See: PHILANTHROPY

Direct Line
See: DIRECT MAIL

Direct Marketing Optimization Letter
See: DIRECT MAIL

Direct Marketing Success Letter
See: DIRECT MAIL

Direct Marketing Tips and Targets
See: DIRECT MAIL

Direct Response
See: DIRECT MAIL

Direct Response Specialist
See: DIRECT MAIL

Direct Success Ideas
See: DIRECT MAIL

Doctor's Office, The
See: MANAGEMENT

Do's and Don'ts In
Advertising *Business*

Publishing Co: Council of Better Business Bureaus, 4200 Wilson Blvd Ste 800, Arlington, VA 22203-1800; Title Tel # (703) 276-0100
Personnel: Editor, Adv. Dir.-Roger Campbell
Editorial Description: An authoritative newsletter providing in-depth analysis & interpretation of current advertising issues, court decisions, FTC rulings, opinions & policy statements. Includes timely interviews with ad professionals; coverage of conferences & noteworthy spe ches.
General Info: (Formerly Advertising Topics), Yr. Est. 1949, Monthly, Desktop press, 8 pages, Color, Looseleaf
Subscriptions: Indv. $325
Circulation: Total-680

Downtown Promotion
Reporter *Business*

Publishing Co: Alexander Research & Communications, Inc., 215 Park Ave S., Ste. 1301, New York, NY 10003-1603; Title Tel # (212) 228-0246 Title Fax # (212) 228-0376
Personnel: Publisher-Shirley Alexander, Editor-Laurence Alexander, Circ. Mgr.-Mary Pagliaroli, Mktg. Dir.-Margaret DeWitt
Editorial Description: Presents case studies and how-to-do-it articles reports, typical issues focus on: raising funds,new promotional ideas and concepts, marketing facts and trends, image building campaiigns, organizing events, building downtown support, parking and transit, and more.
General Info: Yr. Est. 1976, Monthly, Trim Size-8½ x 11, 12 pages, ISSN: 0363-2830
Subscriptions: Indv. $115, Can. $115, For. $145, $10/copy
Acquistions: Publication Bought, Publication Sold
Advertising: Accepts Inserts.
List Rental: Rents Lists

Drop Shipping News *Business*

Publishing Co: Consolidated Marketing Services , inc, Box 1361, New York, NY 10017;
Title Tel # (212) 688-8797
Personnel: Publisher, Editor-Nicholas Scheel
Editorial Description: Focuses on sources that drop ship single units of products for mail order firms, publishers and other middlemen.
General Info: Yr. Est. 1974, Monthly, Sheetfed press, Saddle-stitched
Subscriptions: Indv. $27
Acquistions: Publication Bought

EDK Forecast: Women Consumers
See: WOMEN'S

EPS Decisions
See: PRINTING/GRAPHIC ARTS

Early Warning Forecast
See: BUSINESS & INDUSTRY

Eco, The
See: PRINTING/GRAPHIC ARTS

Educational Marketer   *Business*

Publishing Co: Simba Information, Inc., 213 Danbury Rd. PO Box 7430, Wilton, CT 06897-7430
Parent Co.-Cowles Business Media, New York; Title Tel # (203) 834-0033
Title Fax # (203) 834-1771
Personnel: Publisher-Chris Elwell, Editor-Patrick Quinn, Editorial Dir.-Claire Schoen, Adv. Mgr.-Rosalind Flans, Mktg. Dir.-Michael Genero
Editorial Description: Reports on the market for educational publishing and marketing from elementary to high schools to college. Regular reports include demographics and enrollment trends, legislative issues, funding and industry meetings.
General Info: Yr. Est. 1968, 36x/yr., ISSN: 0013-1806, Ind/Abs/Online: DIALOG, NewsNet, Predicasts
Subscriptions: Indv. $349, Can. $349, For. $399
List Rental: Rents Lists

Effective Telephone Techniques
See: SALESMANSHIP & SELLING

Electrical Sales Builder
See: SALESMANSHIP & SELLING

Electronic Business
Forecast   *Business*

Publishing Co: Cahners Publishing Co., 275 Washington St., Newton, MA 02158-1630
Tel # (617) 964-3030 Fax # (617) 558-4470 Parent Co.-Reed Elsevier, New York;
Title Tel # (617) 630-2119 Title Fax # (617) 630-2100
Personnel: Publisher-Jim Haughey, Co-Editor-Maddy Franehi, Circ. Mgr.-Sandra Coburn, Product Mgr.-Julie Handelman-Sagan, Mktg. Dir.-Wendy Chambers
Editorial Description: Forecasts & analysis of the computer, components, communications equipment & instrumentation markets. Discussions of prices & leadtimes for key components & parts.
General Info: Yr. Est. 1983, Bi-weekly, Trim Size-$8\frac{1}{2}$ x 11, Desktop press, 6 pages, ISSN: 0741-3629, Newsprint
Subscriptions: Indv. $337, Can. $337, For. $387, $20/copy
Circulation: Total-1,000
List Rental: Rents Lists
Printing Co: Ben Franklin Smith, 320 Stuart St, Boston, MA 02116-5290 Tel # (617) 426-1160

Emerging Media Report
See: MEDIA & COMMUNICATIONS

Euromarketing   *Business*

Publishing Co: Crain Communications, Inc., 220 E. 42nd St., New York, NY 10017-5806
Tel # (212) 210-0100 Fax # (212) 210-0114 Parent Co.-Crain Communications Inc, Chicago
Editorial Description: Weekly European news bulletin which is designed to complement Advertsing Age. Contains brief articles on the industry's most current news, agency business and people.
General Info: Weekly
Subscriptions: Indv. $350
List Rental: List Management Co.: Mail Marketing, Inc., 171 Terrace St., Haworth, NJ 07641-1899
Tel # (201) 387-1023, Fax # (201) 387-2976, Actives: 950

Executive's Business Digest
See: BUSINESS & INDUSTRY

Exhibit Mexico   *Business*

Publishing Co: Proteus Publishing, P.O. Box 2940, Ann Arbor, MI 48106 Tel # (313) 668-2743
Fax # (313) 668-8535
Personnel: Publisher, Editor-Wendell R. Deaton, Mng. Editor-Sara Korte
Editorial Description: Information on trade show marketing in Mexico. Written in English for associations, exhibitors, show organizers, and suppliers from U.S. and Canada. Includes show calendar.
General Info: Yr. Est. 1995, Monthly, Trim Size-$8\frac{1}{2}$ x 11, 8 pages, ISSN: 1080-4072, Matte
Subscriptions: Indv. $135
Circulation: Readership-1,772
Advertising: Inquire for rates. Accepts Inserts.

Exhibitor   *Business, Association*

Publishing Co: Material Handling Industry of America, 8720 Red Oak Blvd Ste 201, Charlotte, NC 28217-3990; Title Tel # (704) 522-8644
Personnel: Editor-Lisa Woodie
Editorial Description: Newsletter updates trade show space sales & gives exhibitors advice on improving their trade show efforts.
General Info: Yr. Est. 1986, 9x/yr., Trim Size-$8\frac{1}{2}$ x 11, Sheetfed press, 8 pages, 2 Color, Matte, Saddle-stitched
Circulation: Total-5,000

Exhibitor Extra
See: BUSINESS & INDUSTRY

Export Marketing Insights   *Business*

Publishing Co: West, Adams, Christopher & Associates, 1000 W. McNab Rd., Suite 158, Pompano, FL 33069-9871 Tel # (305) 384-8500 Fax # (305) 578-4200
Editorial Description: Focuses on ways manufacturers, wholesalers and retailers sell their products and services internationally.
General Info: Weekly

FDA Advertising and Promotion Manual
See: LAW

Fed/Direct   *Business*

Publishing Co: Amtower & Co., PO Box 339, Ashton, MD 20861-0339; Title Tel # (301) 924-0058
Title Fax # (301) 924-1565
Personnel: Publisher, Editor, Circ. Mgr.-Mark Amtower
Editorial Description: Fed/Direct reviews trends in direct marketing to the Federal Government, discusses publications by & about the Federal Government, publishes a calendar of trade shows, & offers in-depth information of interest to those marketing products & services to the Federal Govt.
General Info: (Formerly Fedinfo Update), Yr. Est. 1989, Monthly, Trim Size-$8\frac{1}{2}$ x 11, 8 pages
Subscriptions: Indv. $149, $30/copy
Advertising: Accepts Inserts.

Food Marketing Briefs   *Business*

Publishing Co: Newsletters, Inc., P.O. Box 342730, Bethesda, MD 20827-2730 Tel # (301) 469-8507
Fax # (301) 469-7271
Personnel: Publisher-Ellis Meredith, Editor-Ray Marsili, Circ. Mgr.-Alice Foley
Editorial Description: National digest of food marketing information.
General Info: Yr. Est. 1987, Monthly, Trim Size-$8\frac{1}{2}$ x 11, 8 pages, ISSN: 0896-4203
Subscriptions: Indv. $97, Inst. $97, Can. $97, For. $97
Printing Co: Plymouth Printing, 1200 Cushing Pl SE, Washington, DC 20003-3599
Tel # (202) 488-7777, Fax # (202) 863-1078

Foodservice Planning
See: RESTAURANTS & CATERING

Foundation & Corporate Funding Advantage
See: BUSINESS & INDUSTRY

Frame, The   *Business*

Publishing Co: Survey Sampling, Inc., 1 Post Rd., Fairfield, CT 06430-6215;
Title Tel # (203) 255-4200 Title Fax # (203) 254-0372
Personnel: Editor-Diane Chagares Urso
Editorial Description: Published for survey researchers.
General Info: Yr. Est. 1977, Quarterly, Trim Size-$8\frac{1}{2}$ x 11, Offset press, 4 pages, 2 Color, Matte
Subscriptions: Free
Circulation: Total-35,000
List Rental: Rents Lists
Printing Co: LeFebvre Intergraphics, 1701 Winthrop Dr, Des Plaines, IL 60018-1993
Tel # (708) 299-2250, Fax # (708) 299-2413

Franchise Wise (Quarterly newsletter of the intl gay & lesbian franchise assoc.)
See: GAY & LESBIAN INTEREST

Fred Goss's What's
Working   *Business*

Publishing Co: United Communications Group, 11300 Rockville Pike, Ste. 1100, Rockville, MD 20852-3030; Title Tel # (301) 816-8950 Title Fax # (301) 816-8945
Personnel: Publisher-Fred Goss
Editorial Description: How to increase results & cut costs in direct marketing & fulfillment.
General Info: (Formerly What's Working in DM & Fulfillment), Yr. Est. 1985, Bi-weekly, 6 pages
Subscriptions: Indv. $242, Can. $202, For. $212, $7/copy
Acquistions: Publication Bought
List Rental: Actives: $125/M

Friday Report   *Business*

Publishing Co: Hoke Communications, Inc., 224 Seventh St., Garden City, NY 11530-5771;
Title Tel # (516) 746-6700 Title Fax # (516) 294-8141
Personnel: Publisher-Henry Hoke, III, City Ed.-Stu Boysen, Entertainment Ed.-Rosemarie Varonier, Bk. Rev. Ed.-Mollie Neal, Promotion Dir.-Liz Gabriel
Editorial Description: Newsletter of direct marketing, including mail, telemarketing, catalogs, databases, etc.
General Info: Yr. Est. 1961, Weekly, Trim Size-$8\frac{1}{2}$ x 11, Offset press, 8 pages, No Color
Subscriptions: Indv. $165, $5/copy
Circulation: Total-800

Frohlinger's Marketing
Report   *Business*

Publishing Co: Frohlinger's Marketing Report, 7 Coppel Dr, Tenafly, NJ 07670-2903;
Title Tel # (201) 567-4447 Title Fax # (201) 568-8538
Personnel: Publisher, Editor-Joseph Frohlinger, Assoc. Ed.-Margery Weinstein, Circulation-Randy Tom
Editorial Description: Covers advertising, marketing and media with focus on leading multi-national organizations. Contains detailed analysis of key trends and news pertinent to advertisers.
General Info: Yr. Est. 1987, Bi-weekly, Trim Size-8 x 11, Offset press, 6 pages, ISSN: 1057-5316, Ind/Abs/Online: Predicast; Newsnet, No Color
Subscriptions: Indv. $2, Can. $205, For. $225, $10/copy
Circulation: Total-5,000
List Rental: Rents Lists

Front and Center   *Business, Scholarly*

Publishing Co: JW Hartman Center for Sales, Advertising and Mktg. History, Special Collections Library, Duke University, Durham, NC 27708-0185; Title Tel # (919) 660-5827
Title Fax # (919) 684-2855
Editorial Description: Through preserving historical records and archives and through related programs, the Center stimulates interest in and study of the roles of sales, advertising, and marketing in society.
General Info: Yr. Est. 1994, Semi-annually, 4 pages, 2 Color, Matte
Subscriptions: Free
Circulation: Total-1,400

FutureScan
Business, Association

Publishing Co: Future Scan, 2118 Wilshire Blvd # 826, Santa Monica, CA 90403-5704; Title Tel # (310) 451-2990 Title Fax # (310) 828-0427
Personnel: Publisher, Editor-Roger Selbert
Editorial Description: FutureScan covers economic, social, political, technological, demographic, lifestyle, consumer, business, management, workforce & marketing trends.
General Info: Yr. Est. 1981, Bi-weekly, Trim Size-11 x 17, 4 pages
Subscriptions: Indv. $95, Can. $146, For. $146, $5/copy
Circulation: Total-550
Printing Co: Exec U Mail, 1650 21st St, Santa Monica, CA 90404-3941 Tel # (310) 453-0371

GA-SK Newsletter
See: DEAF

Gary Halbert Letter

Publishing Co: Gary Halbert Letter, 820 Ocean Dr. #308, Miami Beach, FL 33139-5809; Title Tel # (305) 294-8425 Title Fax # (305) 296-2296
General Info: Yr. Est. 1985, Monthly
Subscriptions: Indv. $195

Gauge, The
See: MEDIA & COMMUNICATIONS

George Whalin's Retail Management Letter
Business

Publishing Co: Retail Management Consultants, 1635 South Rancho Santa Fe Rd., Suite 206, San Marcos, CA 92069; Title Tel # (619) 471-0207 Title Fax # (619) 471-0263
Personnel: Publisher-George Whzlin, Editor-Terri Pilot
Editorial Description: Exclusively for retailers and suppliers to the retail industry. Includes effective ways to beat the competition, marketing strategies and more.
General Info: Yr. Est. 1992, Monthly
Subscriptions: Indv. $148

Global Packaging & Brand Identity
See: PACKAGING

Golf Update Newsletter
See: GOLF

Government Report
Business, Association

Publishing Co: American Advertising Federation, 1101 Vermont Ave NW Ste 500, Washington, DC 20005-3521; Title Tel # (202) 898-0089
Personnel: Editor-Peter Allen
Editorial Description: Supports the advertising political action committee.
General Info: (Formerly Washington Report), Yr. Est. 1905, Monthly

Grayson Report
Business

Publishing Co: Grayson Associates, Inc., 108 Loma Media Rd, Santa Barbara, CA 93103-2178; Title Tel # (805) 564-1313 Title Fax # (805) 564-8800
Personnel: Editor-Suzanne Grayson, Circ. Mgr.-Betty Lloyd
Editorial Description: Marketing analysis of packaged good industry with particular attention to cosmetics & toiletries.
General Info: Yr. Est. 1970, Bi-monthly, 4 pages
Subscriptions: Indv. $45, $4/copy

Grindline
Business

Publishing Co: Cincinnati Milacron, 4701 Marburg Ave, Cincinnati, OH 45209-1025
Personnel: Editor-Richard Lawlor
General Info: Yr. Est. 1989, Bi-monthly, Trim Size-8½ x 11, Sheetfed press, 10 pages, Color-cover, Matte
Circulation: Total-2,000
Printing Co: Cincinnati Milacron Marketing Co., 4701 Marburg Ave, Cincinnati, OH 45209-1025 Tel # (513) 841-8100

Guerrilla Marketing
Business

Publishing Co: Cascade Seaview Corp., PO Box 1336, Mill Valley, CA 94942-1336
Personnel: Editor-Jay Levinson
Editorial Description: Information for marketers with new approaches for marketing profits.
General Info: Yr. Est. 1989, Bi-monthly, Trim Size-8½ x 11, 8 pages
Subscriptions: Indv. $49

Guide to U.S. Food Labeling Law
Business

Publishing Co: Thompson Publishing Group, 747 Third Ave., New York, NY 10017 Tel # (212) 888-7220 Fax # (212) 486-3400; Title Tel # (212) 888-1245 Title Fax # (800) 949-2320
Personnel: Publisher-Kenneth P. Gesser, Editor-Judy Pokras, Art Dir.-Kevin Mahon, Promotion Dir.-R.D. Whitney
Editorial Description: The latest developments in United States food labeling law. Subcription includes updates and monthly newsletter.
General Info: Monthly, 8 pages, 2 Color, Looseleaf
Subscriptions: Indv. $547

Hard Hat Times
See: MEDIA & COMMUNICATIONS

Healthcare Marketing Abstracts
See: HOSPITALS & NURSING HOMES

Healthcare PR & Marketing News
See: HEALTH

High-Tech Hot Sheet
See: MEDIA & COMMUNICATIONS

High-Tech Hot Wire
See: MEDIA & COMMUNICATIONS

Holography News
See: PRINTING/GRAPHIC ARTS

Home Advantage
Business

Publishing Co: Carney Marketing Resources, Inc., 12 Burnham Rd., Andover, MA 01810-3104 Tel # (508) 475-2096 Fax # (508) 475-8476
Personnel: Publisher-Karen Carney
Editorial Description: Covers marketing and public relations for the home health care and home care industry.
General Info: Yr. Est. 1994, Monthly
Subscriptions: Indv. $165
Circulation: Total-2,500
Advertising: Inquire for rates. Accepts Inserts.
List Rental: Hotline: 1,500

Home Business Idea Possibility Newsletter
See: BUSINESS & INDUSTRY

Home Income Quarterly
Consumer

Publishing Co: Home Income Quarterly, PO Box 424, Morganville, NJ 07751-0424
Editorial Description: Discusses home based mail order and marketing plans.
General Info: Quarterly

IAA World News
Business, Association

Publishing Co: International Advertising Association, 521 5th Ave., Rm. 1807, New York, NY 10175; Title Tel # (212) 557-1133 Title Fax # (212) 983-0455
Personnel: Publisher-Norman Vale, Editor-Ellen Corey
Editorial Description: For international executives in advertising, public relations, marketing, marketing research.
General Info: (Formerly International Marketing Report), Yr. Est. 1960, Bi-monthly, Trim Size-8⅛ x 10⅞, Desktop press, 8 pages, ISSN: 0198-6228, 4% ads, 4 Color, Coated, Saddle-stitched
Subscriptions: Indv. $80, $15/copy
Circulation: (ABC, 100% controlled), Total-4,500, Readership-15,000
List Rental: Actives: $175/M

ICSA News
Association   **CPM: $866**

Publishing Co: Intl. Customer Service Assn., 401 N. Michigan Ave., Chicago, IL 60611-4267; Title Tel # (312) 321-6800
Personnel: Editor-Kathleen Keenan
Editorial Description: Develop the theory of total quality service and service management.
General Info: Yr. Est. 1981, Bi-monthly, 6 pages
Subscriptions: Free With Membership
Circulation: Total-1,500
Advertising: $1,300.
List Rental: Actives: 3,600

I'm Too Busy To Read Marketing Report Service
Business

Publishing Co: Win-Win Marketing, 662 Crestview Dr., San Jose, CA 95117-1105; Title Tel # (408) 247-0122 Title Fax # (408) 249-5754
Personnel: Editor-Frankie Kangas
Editorial Description: Marketing info for small business owners and executives.
General Info: (Formerly Win-Win Marketing Newsletter for Small Business), Yr. Est. 1992, Monthly, Trim Size-8½ x 11, 12 pages, ISSN: 1063-5904, No Color, Matte, Saddle-stitched
Subscriptions: Indv. $149, Can. $169, For. $169, $15/copy

Impressions
See: PRINTING/GRAPHIC ARTS

In Control

Publishing Co: Brock Control Systems, 2859 Paces Ferry Rd., Overlook III, Suite 1000, Atlanta, GA 30339 Tel # (770) 431-1200; Title Tel # (770) 431-1200 Title Fax # (770) 431-1201
Editorial Description: Explores critical sales and marketing issues.
General Info: Quarterly, Desktop press, 2 Color, Matte, Other
Circulation: Total-12,000
Advertising: Inquire for rates.
List Rental: Rents Lists

In House Graphics   *Business*

Publishing Co: United Communications Group, 11300 Rockville Pike, Ste. 1100, Rockville, MD 20852-3030; Title Tel # (301) 816-8950 Title Fax # (301) 816-8945
Personnel: Circ. Mgr.-Monica Brown, Publisher, Editor, Art Dir.-Ronnie Lipton, Mktg. Dir.-Barbara Kaplowitz
Editorial Description: For producers of newsletters, brochures, prmos, ads, etc. How-to information and resource information.
General Info: Yr. Est. 1984, Monthly, Trim Size-8½ x 11, Sheetfed press, 12 pages, ISSN: 0883-6973, 2 Color, Other, Saddle-stitched
Subscriptions: Indv. $117, Can. $97, $10/copy
Circulation: Total-2,500
List Rental: List Management Co.: Manager: Diane Turner; PBI List Marketing, 1201 Seven Locks Rd., Potomac, MD 20854 Tel # (301) 340-7788, Fax # (301) 738-7581, Actives: $125/M

Industrial Controls Intelligence   *Business*

Publishing Co: Carefree Communications, PO Box 5268, Carefree, AZ 85377-5268; Title Tel # (602) 488-1462 Title Fax # (602) 488-5376
Personnel: Publisher-Jack Grenard
Editorial Description: Produces 12 monthly issues each year pills 3-4 special reports on forums and trade shows for high-level execs and marketing people who make and sell industrial computers and related software.
General Info: (Formerly The PLC Insiders Newsletter), Yr. Est. 1981, Monthly, Trim Size-8.5 x 11, 12 pages, ISSN: 1040-9718
Subscriptions: Indv. $195
Acquistions: Publication Sold

InfoAge Marketing   *Business*

Publishing Co: Crain Communications Inc, 740 N. Rush St., Chicago, IL 60611-2590 Tel # (312) 649-5200 Fax # (312) 649-5462
Editorial Description: Weekly faxed newsletter covering media, telecommunications and computer interaction.
General Info: Weekly
Subscriptions: Indv. $44
Advertising: Inquire for rates.

Infomercial Marketing Report   *Business*   **CPM: $995**

Publishing Co: Infomercial Marketing Report, 11533 Thurston Cir, Los Angeles, CA 90049-2426; Title Tel # (310) 472-5253 Title Fax # (310) 472-6004
Personnel: Editor-Steven Dworman
Editorial Description: Marketing and production information on television infomercials.
General Info: Monthly, Desktop press, 16 pages
Subscriptions: Indv. $395
Circulation: Total-1,000
Advertising: $995.

Information Advisor
See: LIBRARY

Information Marketing News

Publishing Co: Publishers Media, 116 E Main St # 546, El Cajon, CA 92020-3910
Personnel: Publisher, Editor-Russ Von Hoelscher
General Info: Bi-monthly
Subscriptions: Indv. $36

Information Solutions: A newsletter of ideas & techniques on how to profit from info.
See: MANAGEMENT

Ink! Ink! Ink!
See: BUSINESS & INDUSTRY

Insurance Marketing Insider
See: INSURANCE

Interactive Marketing News
See: DIRECT MAIL

Interactive Marketing Newsletter   *Business*

Publishing Co: Interactive Marketing Newsletter, 2200 Pacific Coast Hwy Ste 318, Hermosa Beach, CA 90254-2702; Title Tel # (310) 798-0433
Personnel: Editor-George Kopp
Editorial Description: Covers new technologies and ideas in the interactive media/marketing industry.
General Info: Monthly
Subscriptions: Indv. $395

Interactive Public Relations   *Business*

Publishing Co: Lawrence Ragan Communications, Inc., 212 W.Superior St,Ste 200, Chicago, IL 60610-3533 Tel # (312) 335-0037 Fax # (312) 335-9583
Editorial Description: Covers using electronic media in public relations.
General Info: Yr. Est. 1995, Monthly

International Marketing Newsletter

Publishing Co: Miller Freeman, Inc., 411 Borel Avenue, Suite 100, San Mateo, CA 94402 Tel # (415) 358-9500 Fax # (415) 358-9749
General Info: Monthly

International News   *Association*

Publishing Co: American Society of Association Executives, 1575 'I' St., N.W., 11th Fl., Washington, DC 20005-1168 Tel # (202) 626-2711; Title Tel # (202) 626-2823 Title Fax # (202) 408-9633
Personnel: Editor-Joseph Cavarretta
Editorial Description: Newsletter for association executives who deal in international affairs.
General Info: Yr. Est. 1986, Bi-monthly, Trim Size-8½ x 11, 8 pages
Subscriptions: Free With Membership
Circulation: Total-900, Readership-1,000
List Rental: Actives: 799, $175/M

International Pet Industry News
See: ANIMALS

International Product Alert   *Business*

Publishing Co: Marketing Intelligence Service, Ltd., 6473D Route 64, Naples, NY 14512; Title Tel # (716) 374-6326 Title Fax # (716) 374-5217
Personnel: Publisher-Richard Lawrence, Editor-Sherie Meeker-Barton, Production Mgr.-Patricia Peck
Editorial Description: Reports product introductions from Europe, the United Kingdom, Japan, South Africa & Australia with commercial potential for N. American marketers. Product descriptions include detailed packaging information, key ingredients, other label copy & retail pr ce.
General Info: Yr. Est. 1982, Semi-monthly, Trim Size-8½ x 11, Mimeo press, 60 pages, Ind/Abs/Online: Data-Star, DIALOG, No Color, Newsprint, Perfect bound
Subscriptions: Indv. $600, $15/copy

Issues & Policy   *Business, Association*

Publishing Co: InfoCom Group, 1250 45th St., Ste 200, Emeryville, CA 94608-2924 Tel # (510) 596-9300 Fax # (510) 596-9331; Title Tel # (510) 596-9332
Personnel: Publisher-James Sinkinson, Editor-Michael Horowitz, Circ. Mgr.-Peter Klehm, Art Dir.-Cynthia Levitas
Editorial Description: Communication strategies for public affairs advocates.
General Info: Yr. Est. 1994, Semi-monthly
Subscriptions: Indv. $367
Circulation: Total-600
List Rental: Rents Lists

JEG Sponsorship Report   *Business*

Publishing Co: Intl. Events Group, 215 W. Institute Pl., Ste. 303, Chicago, IL 60610-3125; Title Tel # (312) 944-1727 Title Fax # (312) 944-1897
Personnel: Publisher-Jon Ukman, Asst. Pub.-Jim Ryscamp, Editorial Dir.-Jim Andrews, Exec. Ed.-Lesa Ukman, Art Dir.-Steve Liska
Editorial Description: Covers the 3 Billion-a-year corporate sponsorship event marketing industry. Focuses on what companies sponsor & why.
General Info: (Formerly Special Events Report), Yr. Est. 1982, Bi-weekly, Trim Size-8.5 in. x 11 in., Sheetfed press, 8 pages, 2 Color, Newsprint
Subscriptions: Indv. $340, Can. $350, For. $360
Acquistions: Publication Bought
Circulation: Readership-25,000
Advertising: Inquire for rates.
List Rental: Rents Lists
Printing Co: Active Graphics, Chicago, IL

Jack O'Dwyer's Newsletter
See: MEDIA & COMMUNICATIONS

JonesReport   *Business*   **CPM$1119**

Publishing Co: Report Communications, 9595 Whitley Dr Ste 100, Indianapolis, IN 46240-1308; Title Tel # (317) 844-9024 Title Fax # (317) 848-6953
Personnel: Publisher-Lawrence Stillerman, Editor-Maureen Gilmer, Circ. Mgr.-Patty Williams, Production Mgr.-Bridget Gurtowsky, Adv. Dir.-Marsha Davis
Editorial Description: For shopping center marketing directors.
General Info: Yr. Est. 1978, Monthly, Trim Size-8½ x 11, Offset press, 16 pages, ISSN: 0889-485X, 25% ads, 2 Color, Coated, Saddle-stitched
Subscriptions: Indv. $125, Inst. $125, Can. $145, $16/copy
Acquistions: Publication Bought
Circulation: Total-1,782, Readership-6,000
Advertising: $1,995. Accepts Inserts.
List Rental: Rents Lists
Printing Co: Corporate Printing, 5220 W 79th St, Indianapolis, IN 46268-1604 Tel # (317) 872-8480, Fax # (317) 875-5939

Just Classified Catalog
See: DIRECT MAIL

Kettle Care-Pure Herbal Body Care   *Consumer, Association*

Publishing Co: Kettle Care, 710 Trap Road, Columbia Falls, MT 59912; Title Tel # (406) 892-3294
Editorial Description: Kettle Care is a small family business operated from our hone. It has all natural skin care products made of herbs and flowers, which we grow, harvest, dry and carefully hand blend.
General Info: Annually, Looseleaf
Advertising: Inquire for rates.
List Rental: Rents Lists

Language Matters
See: LITERATURE & LINGUISTICS

Laser Focus World Bulletin
See: COMPUTERS & AUTOMATION

Laser Report
See: ENERGY

Laughter Works
See: HUMOR & SATIRE

Law of Advertising
See: LAW

Levison Letter
Business, Consumer

Publishing Co: Ivan Levison & Associates, 14 Los Cerros Dr, Greenbrae, CA 94904-1157; Title Tel # (415) 461-0672 Title Fax # (415) 461-7738
Personnel: Editor-Ivan Levison
Editorial Description: Marketing information for technology companies.
General Info: Monthly
Subscriptions: Indv. $50

Lewis & Clark Research Notes
See: MANAGEMENT

Liaison
Business

Publishing Co: Bean & Petrie, Inc., 1636 Club Trail Dr., Westerville, OH 43081; Title Tel # (614) 965-4080
Personnel: Publisher-Melody Borchers, Editor-Cynthia Petrie
Editorial Description: Corporate contribution programming ideas for positive community relations
General Info: Yr. Est. 1983, Monthly
Subscriptions: Indv. $55

Licensing Letter, The
Business

Publishing Co: EPM Communications, Inc., 160 Mercer St., 3rd Floor, New York, NY 10012-3212; Title Tel # (212) 941-0099 Title Fax # (212) 941-1622
Personnel: Publisher-Ira Mayer, Editor-Karen Raugust, Circ. Mgr.-Riva Bennett, VP Mktng.-Michele Jensen
Editorial Description: Information on licensed properties, agents, and licensees as well as survey analyses.
General Info: Yr. Est. 1977, Monthly, Trim Size-8$\frac{1}{2}$ x 11, Sheetfed press, 12 pages, Color-cover, Newsprint
Subscriptions: Indv. $325, Can. $325, For. $355, $35/copy
List Rental: Actives: $250/M, Hotline: $250/M, Expires: $250/M

Lifestyle Media-Relations Reporter
See: MEDIA & COMMUNICATIONS

List News
See: DIRECT MAIL

Living Music
See: MUSIC & MUSIC TRADES

Lookout Foods
Business

Publishing Co: Marketing Intelligence Service, Ltd., 6473D Route 64, Naples, NY 14512; Title Tel # (716) 374-6326 Title Fax # (716) 374-5217
Personnel: Publisher-Richard Lawrence, Editor-Tom Vierhile, Production Mgr.-Patricia Peck
Editorial Description: Reviews potentially influential new products. Each product is reviewed in the context of its marketer's history, product line & current market trends.
General Info: Semi-monthly, Trim Size-8$\frac{1}{2}$ x 11, Mimeo press, 70 pages, No Color, Newsprint, Perfect bound
Subscriptions: Indv. $600, $15/copy

Lookout Non-Foods
Consumer

Publishing Co: Marketing Intelligence Service, Ltd., 6473D Route 64, Naples, NY 14512; Title Tel # (716) 374-6326 Title Fax # (716) 374-5217
Personnel: Publisher-Richard Lawrence, Editor-T. Vierhele, Production Mgr.-Patricia Peck
Editorial Description: Reviews potentially influential new products. Each product is reviewed in the context of its marketer's history, product line & current market trends.
General Info: Yr. Est. 1975, Semi-monthly, Trim Size-8$\frac{1}{2}$ x 11, Mimeo press, 70 pages, No Color, Newsprint
Subscriptions: Indv. $600, $15/copy

Luce Media Report
Business

Publishing Co: Luce Press Clippings, 42 S Center, Mesa, AZ 85210-1306; Title Tel # (602) 834-4884 Title Fax # (602) 834-3821
Editorial Description: Media information for PR firms.
General Info: Yr. Est. 1993, Monthly

MAFSI News
Business

Publishing Co: Marketing Agents for Food Service Industry, 401 N. Michagan Ave., Chicago, IL 60611-4212; Title Tel # (312) 644-6610
Personnel: Editor-Jodi O'Neill
General Info: Yr. Est. 1982, Quarterly, 10 pages
Circulation: Total-700

MLS-Marketing Library Services
See: LIBRARY

MPA Circulation Marketing

Publishing Co: Magazine Publishers of America, 919 3rd Avenue, 22nd Floor, New York, NY 10022-3801; Title Tel # (212) 872-3700
Personnel: Editor-Robert Cohn
General Info: 6 pages

Magnet Marketing
Business

Publishing Co: Graham Communications, 40 Oval Rd, Quincy, MA 02170-3813; Title Tel # (617) 328-0069 Title Fax # (617) 471-1504
Personnel: Publisher-John Graham, Editor-Cindy Cantrell, Circ. Dir., Circ. Mgr.-Paul Graham, Art Dir.-Robert Downs, Art Dir.-Bob Jankowski
Editorial Description: A marketing, public relations & advertising newsletter published by Graham Communications (Newsletter of John R. Graham, Inc.).
General Info: (Formerly Good Impressions), Yr. Est. 1976, Quarterly, Trim Size-8$\frac{1}{2}$ x 11, Offset press, 12 pages, 2 Color, Coated, Saddle-stitched
Subscriptions: Free To Qualified Recipient
Circulation: Total-5,000, Readership-5,000
List Rental: Rents Lists
Printing Co: Account Manager: Mary Weafer; Ink Spot, The, 40 Oval Rd, Quincy, MA 02170-3813 Tel # (617) 273-7605, Fax # (617) 471-8810

Mail Order Digest
See: DIRECT MAIL

Mainly Marketing
Business

Publishing Co: Schoonmaker Assocs., PO Box 973, Coram, NY 11727-0973; Title Tel # (516) 473-8741
Personnel: Publisher-W. K. Schoonmaker, Editor-D. Schoonmaker, Circ. Mgr.-D. Wayne
Editorial Description: Surveys and tutorial articles on methods of marketing high technology products.
General Info: Yr. Est. 1962, Monthly, Trim Size-8$\frac{1}{2}$ x 11, Sheetfed press, 12 pages, ISSN: 0464-591X, No Color, Newsprint
Subscriptions: Indv. $200, Can. $260, For. $250
Circulation: Total-750

Managed Care & Health Care Marketing
See: HEALTH

Management Focus
Business

Publishing Co: Dartnell Corp., 4660 N. Ravenswood Ave., Chicago, IL 60640-4510 Fax # (312) 561-3801; Title Tel # (312) 561-4000 Title Fax # (312) 561-4842
Personnel: Sales Rep.-Christopher D. Ackley
Editorial Description: Prepared for businesses to use with their customers as a marketing tool. Frequency of publication (m, b-m, or q) decided by sponsoring orgainization.
General Info: Trim Size-8$\frac{1}{2}$ x 11, 2 Color, Matte
Advertising: Inquire for rates.

Market
Business

Publishing Co: Advertising Specialty Institute, 1120 Wheeler Way, Langhorne, PA 19047-1785; Title Tel # (215) 752-4200

Market: Asia Pacific
Business

Publishing Co: W-Two Publications, 202 The Commons, #401, Ithaca, NY 14850-5578; Title Tel # (607) 277-0934 Title Fax # (607) 277-0935
Personnel: Publisher-Doris Walsh, Circ. Dir.-Marjorie Waldman, Production Mgr.-Margaret Nichols
Editorial Description: Explores demographic and lifestyle trends in the Asia/Pacific region and the opportunities they create for business.
General Info: Yr. Est. 1992, Monthly, Trim Size-8$\frac{1}{2}$ x 11, Sheetfed press, 12 pages, ISSN: 1059-275X, Ind/Abs/Online: Predicasts, 2 Color, Recycled, Saddle-stitched
Subscriptions: Indv. $295, Inst. $175, Can. $295, For. $295, $32/copy
Circulation: Total-300
List Rental: Rents Lists
Printing Co: Graphics Printing Plus, 3736 Kellogg Rd, Cortland, NY 13045-8818 Tel # (607) 753-9815

Market: Europe
See: INTERNATIONAL TRADE

Market: Latin America
See: INTERNATIONAL TRADE

Marketing Communications Report
Business

Publishing Co: Pete Silver Assn., PO Box 432152, Miami, FL 33243-2152; Title Tel # (305) 595-0063 Title Fax # (305) 595-5953
Personnel: Publisher, Editor-Pete Silver
Editorial Description: Covers direct mail, audio-visual, and newsletters.
General Info: Yr. Est. 1982, Monthly, Trim Size-8$\frac{1}{2}$ x 11, Color

Marketing Higher Education
See: EDUCATION

Marketing Insights   *Business*

Publishing Co: WPI Communications, Inc., 55 Morris Ave, Springfield, NJ 07081-1496;
Title Tel # (201) 467-8700 Title Fax # (201) 467-0368
Personnel: Editor-Ken Berry
General Info: Bi-monthly

Marketing International   *Association, Business*

Publishing Co: Miller Freeman, Inc., 1 Penn Plaza, 10th Fl., New York, NY 10119-1198;
Title Tel # (415) 358-9500 Title Fax # (415) 358-9739
Personnel: Publisher-Jennifer Meighan, Production Dir.-Carrie Hechtman, Art Dir.-Amy Brokering
General Info: Yr. Est. 1985, Monthly, Trim Size-$8\frac{1}{2}$ x 11, 12 pages, 2 Color, Matte, Saddle-stitched
Subscriptions: Indv. $395, For. $450
Circulation: Total-300
Advertising: Inquire for rates.
List Rental: Rents Lists

Marketing to Kids   *Business*

Publishing Co: Marketing to Kids, 3364 Country Rose Cir, Encinitas, CA 92024-5709;
Title Tel # (619) 942-1046 Title Fax # (619) 436-8775
Editorial Description: International newsletter on the youth market.
General Info: Monthly

Marketing Law Reporting Service   *Business*

Publishing Co: Businesstek Publishing, Inc., Box 250, Carleton Place, ON K7C 3P4 Canada;
Title Tel # (613) 253-2833 Title Fax # (613) 253-2834
Personnel: Publisher, Editor-Shaun McLaughlin
Editorial Description: Canadian marketing, advertising, labelling and packaging law - federal and provincial.
General Info: Yr. Est. 1974, Monthly, Trim Size-$8\frac{1}{2}$ x 11, Desktop press, 34 pages, ISSN: 0827-2115, Looseleaf
Subscriptions: Inst. $295, Can. $335

Marketing Manager, The   *Business*

Publishing Co: West, Adams, Christopher & Associates, 1000 W. McNab Rd., Suite 158, Pompano, FL 33069-9871 Fax # (305) 578-4200; Title Tel # (305) 384-8500 Title Fax # (305) 384-9700
Editorial Description: Information and ideas for senior level marketing managers developing marketing plans and strategies.
General Info: Yr. Est. 1994, Weekly

Marketing Report, The   *Business*

Publishing Co: Progressive Business Publications, 370 Technology Dr., #3019, Malverne, PA 19355-9863 Parent Co.-American Future Systems, Inc., Bryn Mawr; Title Tel # (610) 695-8600 Title Fax # (610) 647-8089
Personnel: Publisher-Edward M. Satell, Editorial Dir.-Steve Meyer, Editor-Aimee Stern, Mktg. Dir.-Ed Moore
Editorial Description: Business-to-business newsletter with information in a fast, easy to read format for marketing and sales professionals.
General Info: Yr. Est. 1991, Bi-weekly, Trim Size-$8\frac{1}{2}$ x 11, 8 pages, ISSN: 1064-3893
Subscriptions: Indv. $264
List Rental: List Management Co.: Mail Marketing, Inc., 171 Terrace St., Haworth, NJ 07641-1899 Tel # (201) 387-1023, Fax # (201) 387-2976, Actives: 21,090, $125/M

Marketing Science Institute Newsletter

Publishing Co: Marketing Science Inst, 1000 Massachusetts Ave, Cambridge, MA 02138-5379;
Title Tel # (617) 491-2060 Title Fax # (617) 991-2065
Personnel: Editor-Marni Clippinger
Editorial Description: Focuses on the people, events & research of MSI.
General Info: Yr. Est. 1975, Quarterly
Subscriptions: Free
Circulation: Total-7,000

Marketing Shorts   *Business*

Publishing Co: Marketing Works! Publishing, 1031 Sterling Rd Ste 204, Herndon, VA 22070-3834;
Title Tel # (703) 742-3640 Title Fax # (703) 742-6280
Editorial Description: Marketing news briefs summarizing highlights from top marketing publications, seminars and books.
General Info: Monthly
Subscriptions: Indv. $179

Marketing Technology   *Business*

Publishing Co: Zhivago Marketing Partners, 70 Princeton Rd, Menlo Park, CA 94025-5327;
Title Tel # (415) 328-6000 Title Fax # (415) 322-9149
Personnel: Publisher, Production Mgr., Art Dir.-Philip Zhivago, Editor, Circ. Dir., Promotion Dir.-Kristin Zhivago
Editorial Description: Advises marketers of technical products; covers advertising, PR, shows, literature, seminars, direct mail, media and the politics of marketing. Uses current examples to show what works, what doesn't, and why. Also predicts and analyzes interactive marketing trends and techniques.
General Info: Yr. Est. 1991, Monthly, Trim Size-$8\frac{1}{2}$ x 11, Sheetfed press, 10 pages, No Color, Matte
Subscriptions: Indv. $269, Can. $299, For. $299, $25/copy
Printing Co: Scribner Graphic Press, 3925 Bohannon Dr, Menlo Park, CA 94025-1037 Tel # (415) 327-2424

Marketing Treasures   *Business*

Publishing Co: Chris Olson & Associates, 857 Twin Harbor Dr, Arnold, MD 21012-1027;
Title Tel # (410) 647-6708 Title Fax # (410) 647-0415
Personnel: Publisher-Christine Olson, Editor-Suzanne Peake, Circ. Mgr.-Todd M. Olson
Editorial Description: Ideas and pointers on how to promote library and information services. Includes sheets of original library dip art. Annual index and binder.
General Info: Yr. Est. 1987, Bi-monthly, Trim Size-$8\frac{1}{2}$ x 11, Desktop press, 6 pages, ISSN: 0895-1799, No Color, Other
Subscriptions: Indv. $54, Can. $59, For. $66, $20/copy
Circulation: Total-1,000
List Rental: Rents Lists

Marketing Update
See: BANKING & FINANCE

Markets Abroad   *Business*

Publishing Co: Strawberry Media, Inc., 2460 Lexington, Owosso, MI 48867-1015;
Title Tel # (517) 725-9072
Personnel: Publisher, Editor-Michael Sledge
Editorial Description: Regional marketing information.
General Info: Quarterly
Subscriptions: Indv. $25

Matthews Revelations

Publishing Co: Courtesy Graphics Inc., 940 N Milwaukee Ave, Libertyville, IL 60048-1934;
Title Tel # (708) 367-8710
Personnel: Publisher-Jack Matthews
General Info: Monthly

Mature Market Report
See: SENIOR CITIZENS

McKone
See: HOUSE ORGANS

Media Matters
See: MEDIA & COMMUNICATIONS

Media Update
See: MEDIA & COMMUNICATIONS

Media Update Environment
See: MEDIA & COMMUNICATIONS

Media Update Minority
See: MEDIA & COMMUNICATIONS

Media Update Outdoors
See: MEDIA & COMMUNICATIONS

MediaScope (year) Atlanta
Market & Media Planner   *Business*

Publishing Co: Standard Rate & Data Service, 1700 Higgins Rd., Des Plaines, IL 60018 Tel # (708) 375-5000 Fax # (708) 375-5008 Parent Co.-VNU Business Publications, Hasbrouck Heights
General Info: Yr. Est. 1992
Advertising: Inquire for rates.

Medical Business Letter, The
See: HEALTH

Meetings & Expositions   *Business, Association*

Publishing Co: American Society of Association Executives, 1575 'I' St., N.W., 11th Fl., Washington, DC 20005-1168 Tel # (202) 626-2711 Fax # (202) 408-9633; Title Tel # (202) 626-2739
Personnel: Editor-Joseph Cavarretta
Editorial Description: Newsletter for association meeting planners, suppliers, and related professions.
General Info: (Formerly Conventions & Expositions), Monthly
Subscriptions: Free With Membership
Circulation: Total-3,700, Readership-5,000
List Rental: Actives: 3,704, $175/M

Membership Developments   *Business, Association*

Publishing Co: American Society of Association Executives, 1575 'I' St., N.W., 11th Fl., Washington, DC 20005-1168 Tel # (202) 626-2711 Fax # (202) 408-9633; Title Tel # (202) 626-2739
Personnel: Editor-Joe Cavarretta
Editorial Description: For membership marketers--covers recruitment, retention, and other member services
General Info: (Formerly Membership Marketer), Monthly, 4 pages
Subscriptions: Free With Membership
Circulation: Total-2,700, Readership-4,500
List Rental: Actives: 4,100, $175/M

Memo to Mailers
Business

Publishing Co: U.S. Postal Service, 475 L'Enfant Plz SW, Rm 10541, Washington, DC 20260-0004; Title Tel # (202) 268-2197 Title Fax # (202) 268-5685
Personnel: Editor-Jim Quirk
Editorial Description: Reporting on postal news programs, rates, rules, mail management.
General Info: Yr. Est. 1966, Monthly, Trim Size-8½ x 11, Desktop press, 8 pages, 2 Color, Recycled, Perfect bound
Subscriptions: Free
Circulation: (100% controlled), Total-114,000
Printing Co: McDonald & Eudy Printers, Inc., 4509 Beech Rd, Temple Hills, MD 20748-6705

Men's Art Service

Publishing Co: Retail Reporting Corp., 302 5th Ave Fl 11, New York, NY 10001-3604 Tel # (212) 279-7000 Fax # (212) 279-7014; Title Tel # (212) 255-9595
General Info: Quarterly, ISSN: 0025-942X

Metro Scene
See: COLLECTIBLES

Micro Software Marketing
See: COMPUTERS & AUTOMATION

Minority Markets Alert
Business

Publishing Co: EPM Communications, Inc., 160 Mercer St., 3rd Floor, New York, NY 10012-3212 Fax # (212) 941-1622; Title Tel # (212) 941-0099 Title Fax # (212) 941-1633
Personnel: Publisher-Ira Mayer, Editor-Micheal Schau, VP Mktng.-Michele Jensen
Editorial Description: Coverage of research, trends, lifestyles of all U.S. Minority Markets.
General Info: Yr. Est. 1989, Monthly, Trim Size-8½ x 11, Sheetfed press, 8 pages, ISSN: 1041-7524, Color-cover, Newsprint
Subscriptions: Indv. $295, Can. $295, For. $325, $35/copy
List Rental: Actives: $250/M, Hotline: $250/M, Expires: $250/M

Monthly Magazine Advertising Summary

Publishing Co: Leading Natl. Advertisers, 1200 Bay St., #405, Toronto, ON M5R 2A5 Canada; Title Tel # (416) 961-2840
Personnel: Promotion Dir.-Carole MacDonald
General Info: (Formerly Par), 12x/yr., Trim Size-8½ x 11, Looseleaf
Subscriptions: Indv. $450

Moskowitz Jacobs Inc.
Business

Publishing Co: Moskowitz Jacobs Inc., 14 Madison Ave, Valhalla, NY 10595-1940; Title Tel # (914) 428-9204 Title Fax # (914) 428-8364
Editorial Description: Information about market research techniques.
General Info: Monthly

Motorsports Marketing Sponsorship News
Business, Consumer   CPM: $200

Publishing Co: Ernie Saxon Communications, 1448 Hollywood Ave, Langhorne, PA 19047-7417 Fax # (215) 762-1518; Title Tel # (215) 752-7797 Title Fax # (215) 752-1518
Personnel: Publisher-Ernie Saxton, Editor-Marilyn Saxton, Adv. Dir.-Joe McHugh
Editorial Description: Directed to those involved in motorsports marketing, sponsorships, & promotion.
General Info: Yr. Est. 1985, Monthly, Trim Size-8½ x 11, Letrpr. press, 8 pages, No Color, Newsprint
Subscriptions: Indv. $70, Can. $90, $10/copy
Circulation: Total-1,000
Advertising: $200. Accepts Inserts.
List Rental: Actives: $100/M
Printing Co: Bill's Printing, 2829 S Broad St, Trenton, NJ 08610-3603 Tel # (609) 888-1841

Mouser Report, The
Business

Publishing Co: CAMCO, 124 E Carolina Ave, Crewe, VA 23930-1802; Title Tel # (804) 645-8200 Title Fax # (804) 645-8232
Personnel: Publisher, Editor-Charles Mouser, Circ. Mgr.-Dina Newbert, Production Mgr.-Brenda DeLuca
Editorial Description: Newsletter contains useful facts, pointers, tips & trade information, & keeps publishers & professional sales-people up-to-date on advertising trends.
General Info: Yr. Est. 1980, Monthly
Subscriptions: Indv. $96, Can. $96, For. $96
Circulation: Total-1,809

Multinational PR Report
Business

Publishing Co: Pigafetta Press, PO Box 39244, Washington, DC 20016-9244; Title Tel # (202) 244-2580 Title Fax # (202) 244-2581
Personnel: Editor-John M. Reed
General Info: Yr. Est. 1984, Monthly
Subscriptions: Indv. $95

NAW Report
Business, Association

Publishing Co: National Association of Wholesaler-Distributors, 1725 K St. NW, Washington, DC 20006-1401; Title Tel # (202) 872-0885 Title Fax # (202) 785-0586
Personnel: Editor-Philip Jaffa
Editorial Description: Covers federal legislation, regulation, industry research & data, service programs for wholesaler-distributors.
General Info: (Formerly Channels), Yr. Est. 1972, Monthly, 2 Color, Newsprint
Circulation: Total-10,000

National Association of Marketing Officials, Bulletin

Publishing Co: Maryland State Dept. of Agriculture, c/o S.C. Miller, Dept. of Agri, Annapolis, MD 24101; Title Tel # (301) 269-2181

National Executive/ Commercial Traveller
Business, Consumer

Publishing Co: North West Commercial Travellers' Assn. of Canada, 291 Garry St., Box 336, Winnipeg, MB R3C 2H6 Canada; Title Tel # (204) 957-1442 Title Fax # (204) 957-0115
General Info: 5x/yr.
Subscriptions: Indv. $45
Circulation: Total-12,500

National Newsline
See: SECURITY & SURVEILLANCE

New Product News
See: GROCERY

Newsletter Consultant, The
Business

Publishing Co: Laughing Bear Press, PO Box 36159, Denver, CO 80236-0159; Title Tel # (303) 744-3624
Personnel: Editor-Tom Person
Editorial Description: The Newsletter Consultant is an integrated program of a monthly newsletter and personal consultation to turn your office newsletter into your most effective marketing tool.
General Info: Yr. Est. 1993, Monthly, Trim Size-8½ x 11, Desktop press, 8 pages, Matte
Subscriptions: Indv. $200, Can. $220, For. $300

Nido Qubein Letter
Business

Publishing Co: Creative Services Inc., PO Box 6008, High Point, NC 27262-6008; Title Tel # (910) 889-3010 Title Fax # (910) 885-3001
Personnel: Publisher-Nido Qubein
General Info: Yr. Est. 1982, 9x/yr.
Subscriptions: Indv. $64

Nobis Marketing Letter
Business

Publishing Co: Empire Communications, 5818 N 7th St Ste 103, Phoenix, AZ 85014-5810; Title Tel # (602) 269-3111 Title Fax # (602) 269-3113
Personnel: Publisher-Dan Kennedy
Editorial Description: Direct mail and response information.
General Info: (Formerly No B.S. Marketing Letter), Monthly
Subscriptions: Indv. $100

Non-Store Marketing Report
Business

Publishing Co: Maxwell Sroge Publishing, Inc., 522 Forest Ave, Evanston, IL 60202-3005; Title Tel # (847) 866-1890 Title Fax # (847) 866-1899
Personnel: Publisher-Maxwell Sroge, Editor-Ann Meyer, Circ. Mgr.-R. Hamill, Promotion Dir.-Ann Keeton
Editorial Description: Industry news & statistical information for the mail order/interactive shopping industry. Supplements include 2 company profiles, NSM trendwatch, special reports.
General Info: Yr. Est. 1977, Bi-weekly, Trim Size-8½ x 11, Sheetfed press, 6 pages, ISSN: 0279-2893, No Color, Matte
Subscriptions: Indv. $245, Can. $320, For. $320, $15/copy

Nonprofit Marketing Insider

Publishing Co: Wordsworth Communications, Inc., PO Box 5311, Evanston, IL 60204-5311 Fax # (708) 835-5540; Title Tel # (708) 475-5855
Personnel: Publisher, Editor-Albert Copeland
General Info: Semi-monthly
Subscriptions: Indv. $189

Numbers News
Business

Publishing Co: American Demographics, PO Box 68, Ithaca, NY 14851 Fax # (607) 273-3190; Title Tel # (607) 273-6343 Title Fax # (607) 273-3196
Personnel: Publisher-Peter Francese, Editor-Diane Crispell, Circ. Mgr.-Mike Edmondson, Production Mgr.-Patricia Driscoll
Editorial Description: Examines new demographic data & analyses population, housing, income and other consumer related trends.
General Info: Yr. Est. 1980, Monthly, Trim Size-8½ x 11, Sheetfed press, 12 pages, ISSN: 0732-1597, Recycled, Saddle-stitched
Subscriptions: Indv. $149
Circulation: Total-1,400
List Rental: Actives: 1,300, $250/M
Printing Co: East Hill Printers, 370 Snyder Hill Rd, Ithaca, NY 14850-6356 Tel # (607) 277-8153

O'Dwyer PR Marketplace
See: EMPLOYMENT

O'Dwyer's Washington Report
Business

Publishing Co: J.R. O'Dwyer Company, Inc., 271 Madison Ave Ste 600, New York, NY 10016-1001; Title Tel # (212) 679-2471 Title Fax # (212) 683-2750
Personnel: Publisher-Jack O'Dwyer
Editorial Description: D.C. area public relations news.
General Info: Yr. Est. 1991, Bi-weekly
Subscriptions: Indv. $125

Off the Shelf
Business

Publishing Co: Gerstman+Meyers, 111 W. 57th St., New York, NY 10019-2211 Tel # (212) 586-2535 Fax # (212) 307-5473
Editorial Description: Covers brand identity and package design.
General Info: Yr. Est. 1992, Tri-annually
Subscriptions: Free To Qualified Recipient
Circulation: Readership-4,000

On Achieving Excellence
Business

Publishing Co: InfoCom Group, 1250 45th St., Ste 200, Emeryville, CA 94608-2924 Tel # (510) 596-9300 Fax # (510) 596-9331; Title Tel # (415) 549-4300 Title Fax # (415) 549-4331
Subscriptions: Indv. $342

On-Line
Business, Consumer

Publishing Co: AUS Consultants, ICR Survey Research Group, 605 W. State St., Media, PA 19063 Tel # (215) 565-9280
Personnel: Publisher-Carolyn Williams, Editor-Gregory Moore
Editorial Description: Reports on market research and consumer trends.
General Info: Quarterly, Trim Size-8½ x 11, 4 pages, Matte
Subscriptions: Free To Qualified Recipient

Online Tactics
See: COMPUTERS & AUTOMATION

PMA Newsletter
See: BOOKS & BOOK TRADE

PMC NY Newsletter
Association

Publishing Co: Premium Merchandising Club of America, 1600 Rt. 22, Union, NJ 07083-3410; Title Tel # (201) 687-3090
Personnel: Editor-John Kalemkerian
General Info: Monthly, Offset press, 4 pages, No Color, Newsprint
Circulation: Total-300

PR Activity Report
See: LIBRARY

P.R. Clock
Business

Publishing Co: Norma A. Lee Co., 220 E. 54th St., Apt. 4H, New York, NY 10022-4839; Title Tel # (212) 221-0410 Title Fax # (212) 768-3746
Personnel: Publisher, Editor-Norma Lee
General Info: Yr. Est. 1985, Bi-weekly
Subscriptions: Indv. $95

PR Marcom Jobs East
See: EMPLOYMENT

PR Marcom Jobs West-No. Calif./Pacific Nothwest
See: EMPLOYMENT

PR Marcom Jobs West-So. Calif.
See: EMPLOYMENT

PR News
Business

Publishing Co: Phillips Business Information, Inc., 1201 Seven Locks Rd., Ste 300, Potomac, MD 20854-2958 Tel # (301) 340-1520 Fax # (301) 424-4297
Personnel: Editor-Thomas Moore
Editorial Description: Newsletter covering trends and news of the public relations profession, worldwide. Regular features include case studies and a series of guides: media relations services, PR software, PR executive recruiters, and a 50-state report on legislative issues and developments.
General Info: Yr. Est. 1944, Weekly, Trim Size-8½ x 11, 8 pages, ISSN: 0003-3697, No Color
Subscriptions: Indv. $347, For. $410
Advertising: Inquire for rates.

PR Watch
Business, Consumer

Publishing Co: John C. Stauber, 3318 Gregory St, Madison, WI 53711; Title Tel # (608) 233-3346 Title Fax # (608) 238-2236
Personnel: Editor-John Stauber
Editorial Description: Created to help wrestle decision-making powers away from corporations and lobbies and into hands of people.
General Info: Yr. Est. 1993, Quarterly, Trim Size-8½ x 11, 12 pages, No Color, Matte
Subscriptions: Indv. $35, Inst. $200
Circulation: Total-3,000

Park Avenue South
Business

Publishing Co: Park Avenue South Publications, 165 W. 46th St., New York, NY 10036-2501
General Info: Yr. Est. 1987, 10x/yr.
Subscriptions: Indv. $12

Partyline, Public Relations Media Newsletter
Association, Business

Publishing Co: Partyline Publishing, 35 Sutton Pl, New York, NY 10022-2464; Title Tel # (212) 755-3487 Title Fax # (212) 755-3488
Personnel: Editor-Morton Yarmon
Editorial Description: Media placement opportunities for the PR trade.
General Info: Yr. Est. 1960, Weekly, Trim Size-8½ x 10
Subscriptions: Indv. $175
Circulation: Total-1,250
List Rental: Actives: $75/M

Perspective
Business

Publishing Co: Noble Group, PO Box 491, Bellevue, WA 98009-0491; Title Tel # (206) 867-9100
Personnel: Editor-C. Norman Noble, Art Dir.-Robert Daniel
Editorial Description: Information on marketing and communication for corporations.
General Info: Yr. Est. 1993, Quarterly, Trim Size-17 x 11, 4 pages, 2 Color, Coated
Subscriptions: Indv. $16, Inst. $16, $5/copy
Circulation: Total-550
Printing Co: Western Press, 10621 NE 8th St., Bellevue, WA 98004 Tel # (206) 455-9237, Fax # (206) 453-3177

Perspectives on the Construction Industry
See: CONSTRUCTION & BUILDING

Perspectives on Employee Benefits
See: INDUSTRIAL RELATIONS/PERSONNEL

Perspectives on Family Business
See: BUSINESS & INDUSTRY

Perspectives on Law Firm Management
See: MANAGEMENT

Perspectives on Litigation Support Services
See: LAW

Perspectives on Medical Practice Management
See: MANAGEMENT

Perspectives on Not-for-Profit Organizations
See: PHILANTHROPY

Phone Sales Presentations for Service Type Businesses - A Newsletter
See: BUSINESS & INDUSTRY

Plastics Brief Newsletter
See: PLASTICS

Plus Business
Business, Association

Publishing Co: Metro Creative Graphics, 33 W 34th St, New York, NY 10001-3098; Title Tel # (212) 947-5100 Title Fax # (212) 714-9139
Personnel: Editor-Maria Manliclic
Editorial Description: Emphasis is strictly on newspaper advertising promotions, contests and techniques on how to increase ad linage.
General Info: Yr. Est. 1937, Monthly, Trim Size-8½ x 11, Desktop press, 12 pages, 2 Color, Coated
Subscriptions: Indv. $30, $1/copy
Circulation: (100% controlled), Total-7,000
Printing Co: Major Press, E. 16th St., New York, NY

Prespectives on Esatate and Financial Planning
See: BANKING & FINANCE

Pricing Advisor, The
Business

Publishing Co: Pricing Advisor, 3277 Roswell Rd NE Ste 620, Atlanta, GA 30305-1840; Title Tel # (404) 252-5708 Title Fax # (404) 252-0637
Personnel: Publisher, Editor-Eric Mitchell, Circ. Mgr.-Anita Farley
Editorial Description: Pricing strategy/tactics for corporate & marketing executives.
General Info: Yr. Est. 1983, Monthly, Sheetfed press, 8 pages, Color
Subscriptions: Indv. $195, For. $295, $20/copy
Circulation: Total-4,000
List Rental: List Management Co.: Manager: Anita Farley; List Emporium, 2000 Shawnee Mission Pky Ste, 235, Westwood, KS 66205-3601 Tel # (913) 236-6830, Fax # (913) 236-4842, Actives: 14,442, $90/M

Printips
See: PRINTING/GRAPHIC ARTS

Prisoners of Advertising
Association

Publishing Co: San Francisco Advertising Club, 150 Post St Ste 325, San Francisco, CA 94108-4707; Title Tel # (415) 986-3878 Title Fax # (415) 986-7457
General Info: (Formerly Ad Age/Adword), Yr. Est. 1915, Monthly, Trim Size-7¼ x 10, Offset press, 4 pages, No Color
Subscriptions: Free With Membership
Circulation: Total-1,200
Advertising: Inquire for rates.

Pro-Motion
See: RESTAURANTS & CATERING

Product Alert
Publishing Co: Marketing Intelligence Service, Ltd., 6473D Route 64, Naples, NY 14512; Title Tel # (716) 374-6326 Title Fax # (716) 374-5217
Personnel: Publisher-Richard Lawrence, Editor-Diane Beach, Production Mgr.-Patricia Peck
Editorial Description: The definitive illustrated twice a month briefing on N. American packaged goods introductions. Product descriptions include detailed packaging information, key ingredients, other label copy & retail price.
General Info: Yr. Est. 1970, Semi-monthly, Trim Size-8½ x 11, Mimeo press, 40 pages, Ind/Abs/Online: Data-Star, DIALOG, Predicasts, No Color, Newsprint, Perfect bound
Subscriptions: Indv. $600, $15/copy

Professional Apartment Management
See: REAL ESTATE

Profile Briefings *Business*
Publishing Co: Advertising Specialty Institute, 1120 Wheeler Way, Langhorne, PA 19047-1785; Title Tel # (215) 752-4200
Personnel: Editor-Jeanne Woldenberg, Art Dir.-Jim Lang
General Info: Monthly, Sheetfed press, 2 Color, Newsprint
Circulation: Total-1,000

Promotion Idea File
Publishing Co: Promotion Idea File, 19 Joslin Street, Providence, RI 02909-2599; Title Tel # (401) 751-6217
Personnel: Publisher, Editor-Thomas J. Lopatosky
Editorial Description: Ideas for Promoting the objectives of non-profit organizations.
General Info: Yr. Est. 1993, Bi-monthly, Trim Size-8½ x 11, Sheetfed press, 10 pages, No Color
Subscriptions: Indv. $12, Inst. $12, Can. $12, For. $12

Promotional Links
Publishing Co: Strawberry Media, Inc., 2460 Lexington, Owosso, MI 48867-1015; Title Tel # (517) 725-9027
Personnel: Publisher, Editor-Michael Sedge, Circ. Mgr.-H.R. Sedge
General Info: Yr. Est. 1990, Semi-monthly, Trim Size-8½ x 11, Sheetfed press, No Color, Matte
Subscriptions: Indv. $50, For. $65, $10/copy
Circulation: Total-200
List Rental: Actives: $100/M

Publicity & Marketing Ideas *Business*
Publishing Co: International Features, Inc., 8 South J St., Ste. 3, Box 1349, Lake Worth, FL 33460-3742 Tel # (407) 582-8320 Fax # (407) 582-8320
Personnel: Publisher-William Bates, Editor-Byron Lutz
Editorial Description: Low-cost publicity, public relations & marketing ideas for large & small businesses.
General Info: Yr. Est. 1992, Quarterly, Trim Size-8½ x 11, Web press, 12 pages, 2 Color, Saddle-stitched
Subscriptions: Indv. $42
Circulation: Total-3,258, Readership-6,000
Advertising: Inquire for rates.

Publishers Information Bureau-Reports *Business*
Publishing Co: Publishers Information Bureau, 919 Third Ave., 22nd Fl., New York, NY 10022; Title Tel # (212) 872-3700
Editorial Description: Reports advertising space & revenue in about 179 general magazines & 4 newspaper supplements.
General Info: Yr. Est. 1948, Monthly, No Color, Looseleaf

Publisher's Multinational Direct *Business*
Publishing Co: Direct International, 1501 Third Ave., New York, NY 10028-2101; Title Tel # (212) 861-4188 Title Fax # (212) 986-3757
Personnel: Publisher, Editor-Alfred Goodloe
Editorial Description: Monthly newsletter for publishers who seek to increase sales in foreign markets.
General Info: Yr. Est. 1986, Monthly
Subscriptions: Indv. $195
List Rental: Rents Lists

Publisher's Report
See: BOOKS & BOOK TRADE

Quarterly Report *Association*
Publishing Co: Assn. of Natl. Advertisers, Inc., 155 E. 44th St., New York, NY 10017-4201 Fax # (212) 683-1296; Title Tel # (212) 697-5950
Personnel: Publisher-DeWitt Helm, Jr., Editor-Dick Shahan
Editorial Description: News of events relating to the assn. & the advertising business.
General Info: (Formerly A.N.A. Newsletter), Yr. Est. 1982, Quarterly, Offset press, 8 pages, 2 Color, Newsprint
Circulation: (100% controlled), Total-4,200

Quarterly Review of Doublespeak
See: EDUCATION

RAB Instant Background
See: BROADCASTING

Radio Promotion Bulletin
See: BROADCASTING

Ray's Adlet *Business*
Publishing Co: Ray Gillem, Rr 2 Box 210, Fort Atkinson, IA 52144-9771
General Info: Quarterly
Circulation: Total-1,000
Advertising: Inquire for rates.

Real Estate Marketing Management Alert
See: REAL ESTATE

Really, a Free Newsletter
See: BOOKS & BOOK TRADE

Remarks: Trademark News for Business
See: PATENTS/COPYRIGHTS/TRADE MARKS

Representative *Association*
Publishing Co: National Association General Merchandise Representatives, 401 N. Michigan Ave., Chicago, IL 60611-4212; Title Tel # (312) 644-6610 Title Fax # (312) 321-5144
Personnel: Publisher-Jack Springer, Editor-Barbara Wolf
Editorial Description: Addressing the problems & opportunities available to consumer product brokers.
General Info: Yr. Est. 1978, Monthly, Trim Size-8½ x 11, Letrpr. press, 8 pages
Circulation: Total-500

Research Alert *Business*
Publishing Co: EPM Communications, Inc., 160 Mercer St., 3rd Floor, New York, NY 10012-3212; Title Tel # (212) 941-0099 Title Fax # (212) 941-1622
Personnel: Publisher-Ira Mayer, Editor-Michael Schau, Circ. Mgr.-Riva Bennett, VP Mktng.-Michele Jensen
Editorial Description: Information service for consumer marketing research.
General Info: Yr. Est. 1983, Bi-weekly, Trim Size-8½ x 11, Sheetfed press, 10 pages, ISSN: 0739-358X, Color-cover, Newsprint
Subscriptions: Indv. $369, Can. $369, For. $429, $25/copy
List Rental: Actives: $250/M, Hotline: $250/M, Expires: $250/M

Retiree Roundup
See: HOUSE ORGANS

SHOWFAX *Business*
Publishing Co: Maclean Hunter Publishing Ltd., Maclean Hunter Building, 777 Bay St., Toronto, ON M5W 1A7 Canada Tel # (416) 596-5000 Fax # (416) 596-5526
Personnel: Publisher-Henry Beckman
Editorial Description: Covers the latest news on people, events, facilities, and exhibitors at Canadian trade shows.
General Info: 10x/yr.

SMT Trends
See: MANUFACTURING

SOURCEfile *Business*
Publishing Co: Applied Computer Research, PO Box 82266, Phoenix, AZ 85071-2266; Title Tel # (602) 995-5929
Personnel: Publisher-Phillip Howard, Editor-David Wendland
Editorial Description: Reports on resources useful to computer-related marketers.
General Info: (Formerly Sources), Yr. Est. 1980, Bi-monthly, Trim Size-8½ x 11, Sheetfed press, 12 pages, ISSN: 0897-4128, Ind/Abs/Online: CmLI, 2 Color, Coated, Saddle-stitched
Subscriptions: Indv. $95, $22/copy

SPAN Connection
See: BOOKS & BOOK TRADE

Sales & Marketing Executive Report
See: MANAGEMENT

Sales Letter *Business* CPM: $20
Publishing Co: G & B Records, PO Box 10150, Terra Bella, CA 93270-0150 Tel # (209) 535-5722
Editorial Description: Provides advertising opportunities for small businesses.
General Info: Irregular, Trim Size-11½ x 17, 8 pages, Newsprint
Circulation: Total-5,000
Advertising: $100.

Sales Managers Idea Letter
See: SALESMANSHIP & SELLING

Sales Pro, The
See: SALESMANSHIP & SELLING

Salesman's Insider   *Business*

Publishing Co: Marv. Q. Modell Assocs., 6009 Montgomery Cor, San Jose, CA 95135-1431; Title Tel # (408) 270-4526
Personnel: Publisher, Editor-M.Q. Modell
General Info: Yr. Est. 1981, Monthly, Trim Size-8½ x 11, Desktop press, 4 pages, ISSN: 0738-6362
Subscriptions: Indv. $48, Can. $48, For. $54
Circulation: Total-1,600

Sarah Stambler's Marketing with Technology News   *Business*

Publishing Co: TechProse, Inc., 370 Central Park W., Apt 210, New York, NY 10025-6517; Title Tel # (212) 222-1765 Title Fax # (212) 678-6357
Personnel: Publisher, Editor-Sarah Stambler, Production Mgr.-Shlomo Bar-Ayal, Production Mgr.-Don Croll
Editorial Description: Available only by fax, covers how businesses can use electronics media to market and deliver their products
General Info: (Formerly Marketing with Technology News), Yr. Est. 1991, Monthly, ISSN: 1070-809X
Subscriptions: Indv. $149, For. $249, $10/copy
Circulation: Total-5,000

School Marketing Newsletter   *Business*

Publishing Co: School Market Research Institute, 1721 Saybrook Rd, P.O. Box 10, Haddam, CT 06438-1324 Tel # (203) 345-8183; Title Tel # (203) 345-4018 Title Fax # (203) 345-3985
Personnel: Publisher-Robert Stimolo, Editor-Lynn Vosburgh, Circ. Mgr., Production Dir.-Kathleen Bill
Editorial Description: How to improve direct marketing to schools/some original research.
General Info: (Formerly Direct Response Mktg. to Schls. Newsletter), Yr. Est. 1981, Monthly, Trim Size-8½ x 11, Letrpr. press, 12 pages, ISSN: 0882-701X, No Color, Matte
Subscriptions: Indv. $119, Can. $129, For. $129, $13/copy
Circulation: Total-500
List Rental: List Management Co.: Manager: Kathleen Bill; School market Research, 1721 Saybrook Road, P.O. Box 10, Haddam, CT 06438 Tel # (203) 345-8183, Fax # (203) 345-3985, Actives: 500, $100/M, Expires: 600, $100/M
Printing Co: Shannon Printing, 500 Main St., Box 899, Deep River, CT 06417 Tel # (203) 526-4937

Science Marketing Newsletter

Publishing Co: Scherago Associates, Inc., 11 Penn Plz Rm 1003, New York, NY 10001-2006; Title Tel # (212) 730-1050
Personnel: Editor-Dave Hackler
General Info: Monthly, 8 pages
Circulation: Total-200,000

Se Habla Espanol Newsletter
See: MEDIA & COMMUNICATIONS

Searching Dialogue: A Complete Guide   *Business*

Publishing Co: Dialog Information Services, Inc., 3460 Hillview Ave, Palo Alto, CA 94304-1338; Title Tel # (415) 858-3782
Personnel: Editor-Barbara Anderson

Self Employment Update - Business Idea Letters Edition
See: BUSINESS & INDUSTRY

Self Publishing Update - How to Basics Edition
See: BOOKS & BOOK TRADE

Selling to Seniors   *Business*

Publishing Co: CD Publications, 8204 Fenton St., Silver Spring, MD 20910-4571; Title Tel # (301) 588-6380 Title Fax # (301) 588-6385
Personnel: Publisher-Mike Gerecht, Editor-Frank Cavaliere, Editor-Leah Thayer, Circ. Mgr.-Kurt Eisentraut, Mktg. Dir.-Joyce Meals
Editorial Description: Practical advice on ways to reach the senior market.
General Info: Yr. Est. 1987, Monthly, Trim Size-8½ x 11, Sheetfed press, 14 pages, ISSN: 1050-382X, No Color, Matte
Subscriptions: Indv. $185, Can. $195, For. $225, $15/copy
List Rental: List Management Co.: Manager: Amy Seyler; Washington Advertising Service, 8204 Fenton St., Silver Spring, MD 20910 Tel # (301) 588-7920, Fax # (301) 588-6385, Actives: 3,326, $150/M, Expires: 3,001, $150/M

Selling Space   *Business*

Publishing Co: JB & ME Publishing, Manhattan Beach, CA 90266; Title Tel # (310) 546-1255
Personnel: Editor-Marilyn Elkind
General Info: Yr. Est. 1986, Bi-monthly
Subscriptions: Indv. $25

Service that Sells!
See: MANAGEMENT

Shelf Presence
See: PACKAGING

Siedlecki on Business   *Business*

Publishing Co: Richard Siedlecki Marketing & Management, 4767 Lake Forrest Drive, NE, Atlanta, GA 30342-2539; Title Tel # (404) 816-4040
Editorial Description: News on management and marketing, aimed at small and medium sized businesses.
General Info: Yr. Est. 1988, Bi-monthly
Subscriptions: Indv. $10

Signals
See: ELECTRIC & ELECTRONIC EQUIPMENT

Small Business & Direct Response=Success   *Business*   CPM: $800

Publishing Co: Noevir Consultant, 6817 Rainier Ave. #1742, Gig Harbor, WA 98335-1920
Personnel: Publisher-Jack Reid, Editor, Circ. Mgr.-Sammie L. Davis, Art Dir.-Jane Fraser
Editorial Description: Tactics for using low cost direct response marketing for the small business owner.
General Info: Yr. Est. 1991, Bi-monthly, Trim Size-8½ x 11, Letrpr. press, 4 pages, 50% ads, No Color, Matte
Subscriptions: Indv. $24, Inst. $48, $4/copy
Acquistions: Publication Bought
Circulation: Total-500
Advertising: $400.
List Rental: Actives $100/M, Expires: $100/M
Printing Co: Reid Printing, PO Box 1910, Tacoma, WA 98401-1910

Small Business Builder
See: BUSINESS & INDUSTRY

Small Market Radio Newsletter
See: BROADCASTING

Sound Thinking
See: MANAGEMENT

Soundview Executive Book Summaries
See: BUSINESS & INDUSTRY

Spare on Sales and Marketing   *Business*

Publishing Co: S. Todd Spare & Assoc., P.O. Box 344, Leola, PA 17540 Tel # (717) 656-7402
Editorial Description: Covers sales performance and marketing topics.
General Info: Quarterly

Special Events Report   *Business*

Publishing Co: Intl. Events Group, 215 W. Institute Pl., Ste. 303, Chicago, IL 60610-3125; Title Tel # (312) 944-1727 Title Fax # (312) 944-1897
General Info: Yr. Est. 1982, 24x/yr.
Subscriptions: Indv. $340

Specialty Lab Update
See: PHOTOGRAPHY

Sports Industry News
See: SPORTS & SPORTING GOODS

Starch Tested Copy   *Business*

Publishing Co: Roper Starch Worldwide, 566 E Boston Post Rd, Mamaroneck, NY 10543-3705; Title Tel # (914) 698-0800 Title Fax # (914) 698-0485
Personnel: Editor-Philip Sawyer, Circ. Mgr.-Rosemary Hughes
Editorial Description: A newsletter based on the largest print ad database in the world, Tested Copy offers guidance - using current examples - on what works in print advertising and what doesn't.
General Info: Yr. Est. 1938, Quarterly, Trim Size-8½ x 11, 6 pages
Subscriptions: $35/copy
Circulation: Total-800
List Rental: Rents Lists

Starting Smart Newsletter   *Business*

Publishing Co: David Bruce, PO Box 7109, Mount Jewett, PA 16740-7109; Title Tel # (814) 837-1096 Title Fax # (814) 837-7906
Personnel: Publisher, Editor-Bruce David
Editorial Description: Geared to small businesses. Promotes low-cost, effective resources
General Info: Yr. Est. 1987, Bi-monthly, Trim Size-8½ x 11, Desktop press, 12 pages, 2 Color, Newsprint
Subscriptions: Indv. $55, Inst. $55, Can. $60, For. $70, $5/copy
Acquistions: Publication Bought
Circulation: Total-600, Readership-800
Advertising: Accepts Inserts.
List Rental: Actives: $60/M
Printing Co: Walker Printing Co., 224 Chase St, Kane, PA 16735-1376 Tel # (814) 837-9520

Strategic Health Care Marketing
See: HEALTH

Subscription Marketing
See: PERIODICAL INDUSTRY

Subway Entertainment Guide
See: MUSIC & MUSIC TRADES

Success Ads   *Business*

Publishing Co: Success Concepts International, PO Box 3840, Humble, TX 77347-3840;
Title Tel # (713) 443-9067
Editorial Description: For the home-based small business advertiser.
General Info: Monthly, Desktop press, 4 pages
Subscriptions: Inst. $7, Can. $9, For. $12, $1/copy
Circulation: Total-3,000
Advertising: Inquire for rates.
List Rental: Actives: $60/M

Success Orientation
See: MANAGEMENT

Successful Fund Raising   *Business*

Publishing Co: Stevenson Consultants, Inc, 417 Eton Court, PO Box 4528, Sioux City, IA 51104
Editorial Description: Reports and ideas on successful fundraising techniques.
General Info: Yr. Est. 1993, Monthly, ISSN: 1070-9061
Subscriptions: Indv. $120, Can. $130, For. $130

Supermarket Strategic Alert
See: GROCERY

TDC Letterspace   *Association*

Publishing Co: Advertising Production Club of New York, 60 E 42nd St Rm 721, New York, NY
10165-0799; Title Tel # (212) 983-6042 Title Fax # (212) 983-6043
Editorial Description: Newsletter informing club members of new technology & techniques in
advertising production.
General Info: (Formerly APC Newsletter), Yr. Est. 1986, Quarterly
Circulation: Total-1,500

Tag's Channel Compass
See: COMPUTERS & AUTOMATION

Tax Report
See: TAXES

Team Marketing Report
See: SPORTS & SPORTING GOODS

Technology Transfer Week
See: MILITARY & NAVAL

Telecom Advertising Report
See: TELECOMMUNICATIONS

Telemarketing Tips, Tactics & Techniques
See: SALESMANSHIP & SELLING

Telemarketing Update-
Answering Service
Business Script
Presentations   *Business*

Publishing Co: Prosperity & Profits Unlimited, PO Box 416, Denver, CO 80201-0416;
Title Tel # (303) 575-5676
Personnel: Publisher-A. Doyle
Editorial Description: Telemarketing script presentations.
General Info: Yr. Est. 1983, Irregular, Trim Size-8½ x 11, 4 pages, ISSN: 0736-167x, No Color,
Looseleaf
Subscriptions: Indv. $10, Inst. $10, Can. $12, For. $14, $10/copy

Telemarketing Update-
Catering Service
Business Script
Presentations   *Business*

Publishing Co: Prosperity & Profits Unlimited, PO Box 416, Denver, CO 80201-0416;
Title Tel # (303) 575-5676
Personnel: Publisher-A. Doyle
Editorial Description: Telemarketing script presentations for catering services.
General Info: Yr. Est. 1983, Irregular, Trim Size-8½ x 11, 8 pages, Looseleaf
Subscriptions: Indv. $7, Inst. $7, Can. $9, For. $10, $7/copy

Telemarketing Update-
Copier Service Business
Script Presentations   *Business*

Publishing Co: Prosperity & Profits Unlimited, PO Box 416, Denver, CO 80201-0416;
Title Tel # (303) 575-5676
Personnel: Publisher, Editor-A. Doyle
General Info: Yr. Est. 1983, Irregular, Trim Size-8½ x 11, 8 pages, Looseleaf
Subscriptions: Indv. $7, Inst. $7, Can. $9, For. $10, $7/copy

Telemarketing Update-
Secretarial Business
Script Presentations   *Business*

Publishing Co: Prosperity & Profits Unlimited, PO Box 416, Denver, CO 80201-0416;
Title Tel # (303) 575-5676
Personnel: Publisher, Editor-A.C. Doyle, Promotion Dir.-B. Asheyr
Editorial Description: Telemarketing script presentations, news, etc. for secretarial businesses.
General Info: Yr. Est. 1983, Irregular, Trim Size-8½ x 11, Desktop press, 8 pages, No Color
Subscriptions: Can. $9, For. $10, $7/copy
Circulation: Total-5,000

Telephone Selling Report   *Business*

Publishing Co: Business By Phone, Inc., 13254 Stevens St, Omaha, NE 68137-1728;
Title Tel # (402) 895-9399 Title Fax # (402) 896-3353
Personnel: Publisher, Editor-Art Sobczak
Editorial Description: How-to ideas, tips & techniques for more profitable telephone selling,
prospecting, & setting appointments.
General Info: Yr. Est. 1984, Monthly, Trim Size-8.5 x 11, 8 pages, ISSN: 0882-1461, 2 Color
Subscriptions: Indv. $109, Can. $109, For. $127
Advertising: Accepts Inserts.
List Rental: Actives: $175/M

Test Patterns   *Business*

Publishing Co: Bloom & Gelb, 232 Madison Ave Rm 1106, New York, NY 10016-2901;
Title Fax # (212) 906-3880
Personnel: Publisher, Editor-Carl Bloom, Production Mgr.-Beverly Cohen, Art Dir.-Rafi Billig
Editorial Description: Reports, results and ideas for direct marketing and fundraising executives.
General Info: Yr. Est. 1983, Quarterly, Trim Size-8½ x 11, 8 pages
Acquistions: Publication Bought
Circulation: (100% controlled), Total-10,000

Torch   *Association*

Publishing Co: Milwaukee Adv. Club, 231 W Wisconsin Ave Ste 701, Milwaukee, WI 53203-2306
Tel # (412) 226-8999; Title Tel # (414) 271-7351
General Info: 9x/yr.
Circulation: Total-500

Towers Club Information
Marketing Report   *Business, Association*

Publishing Co: Towers Club Press, Inc., 9107 NW 11th Ave, Vancouver, WA 98665-6801
Tel # (206) 524-3081 Fax # (206) 576-8969; Title Tel # (206) 574-3084
Personnel: Publisher, Editor-Jerry Buchanan, Circ. Mgr.-Pamela Powers
Editorial Description: News, tips & sources for direct response marketing of self-published works.
General Info: (Formerly Towers Club USA Newsletter), Yr. Est. 1974, 10x/yr., Trim Size-8½ x 11,
Sheetfed press, 8 pages, ISSN: 1070-3179, 1% ads, No Color, Coated
Subscriptions: Indv. $95, Can. $72, For. $78, $6/copy
Circulation: Total-6,500
Printing Co: Premier Press, 510 NW 15th Ave, Portland, OR 97209-2204

Trademark Trends
See: PATENTS/COPYRIGHTS/TRADE MARKS

Travel & Tourism Executive Report
See: TRAVEL

Travel Publicity Leads
See: TRAVEL

Travel Sales & Marketing Newsletter
See: TRAVEL

Trend/Wire
See: FOOD

UAMR Confidential
Bulletin

Publishing Co: United Assn. of Manufacturers Representatives, 34071 La Plaza, PO Box 986, Dana
Point, CA 92629; Title Tel # (714) 240-4966 Title Fax # (714) 240-4966
Personnel: Editor-H. Keith Kittrell
Editorial Description: Information on lines available for representation.
General Info: Yr. Est. 1956, Monthly, Web press
Subscriptions: Indv. $48, $5/copy
Circulation: Total-1,200
Advertising: Inquire for rates.
Printing Co: Howard Johnson Printing, 127 Terrace Trl W, Lake Quivira, KS 66106-9504
Tel # (913) 631-7781

Washington Alert

Publishing Co: Direct Marketing Association, PMDS Book Distribution Co., PO Box 391, Annapolis
Junction, MD 20701-0391 Tel # (301) 604-0187 Fax # (301) 206-9789; Title Tel # (212) 689-4977
Personnel: Editor-Elizabeth Scanlon

Washington Newsletter   *Business, Association*

Publishing Co: National Mail Order Association, 2807 Polk St. NE., Minneapolis, MN 55418-2954 Fax # (612) 788-1147; Title Tel # (612) 788-1673
Personnel: Publisher, Editor-John Schulte
Editorial Description: Changes in rates, regulations, procedure, FTC, legislation of concern to mail order marketers.
General Info: Yr. Est. 1972, Monthly, Trim Size-8½ x 11, Sheetfed press, 2 pages, Newsprint
Subscriptions: Indv. $75, Can. $90, For. $150

Washington Report   *Association*

Publishing Co: Direct Marketing Association, PMDS Book Distribution Co., PO Box 391, Annapolis Junction, MD 20701-0391 Tel # (301) 604-0187 Fax # (301) 206-9789; Title Tel # (202) 347-1222
Personnel: Editor-Kay Pauley
General Info: Yr. Est. 1917, Semi-monthly

What's Ahead Report   *Consumer*   CPM: $22

Publishing Co: Events/USA Publishing Co., 136 E 57th St Ste 1001, New York, NY 10022-2707; Title Tel # (212) 758-8303
Personnel: Editor-Charles Monaghan
Editorial Description: Advanced reports on investments, new business opportunities, health, technology, and lifestyle enhancements.
General Info: (Formerly Events USA), Yr. Est. 1993, Monthly
Subscriptions: Indv. $48, $3/copy
Circulation: Total-250,000
Advertising: $5,595.

What's Working in Non-Profit Fundraising   *Business*

Publishing Co: Progressive Business Publications, 370 Technology Dr., #3019, Malverne, PA 19355-9863 Tel # (610) 695-8600 Fax # (610) 647-8089 Parent Co.-American Future Systems, Inc., Bryn Mawr
Personnel: Publisher-Edward Satell, Editorial Dir.-Steve Meyer, Editor-Susan E. Wade
Editorial Description: Actionable information to help nonprofits improve fundraising tactics and increase funding.
General Info: (Formerly Non-Profit Marketing Report, The), Yr. Est. 1991, Monthly, 8 pages
Subscriptions: Indv. $240
List Rental: List Management Co.: Mail Marketing, Inc., 171 Terrace St., Haworth, NJ 07641-1899 Tel # (201) 387-1023, Fax # (201) 387-2976

Who's Mailing What!
See: DIRECT MAIL

Winning Sweepstakes Newsletter
See: HOBBY

Winning in Washington-NAW Annual Report

Publishing Co: National Association of Wholesaler-Distributors, 1725 K St. NW, Washington, DC 20006-1401; Title Tel # (202) 872-0885 Title Fax # (202) 785-0586
Personnel: Editor-Philip Jaffa
Editorial Description: Encompasses the activities of the National Assn. of Wholesaler-Distributors (NAW), & its component organizations: The Wholesaler-Distributor Political Action Committee (WDPAC), The Distribution Research & Education Foundation (DREF), & The NAW Service Corporation (SC).
General Info: Annually

WorldWide Business Exchange
See: BUSINESS & INDUSTRY

Yellow Sheet, The   *Business*

Publishing Co: Communications Management, Inc., 13523 Barrett Parkway Dr., Suite 221, Ballwin, MO 63021-3800; Title Tel # (314) 822-0555 Title Fax # (314) 822-0555
Personnel: Editor-George Johnson, Circ. Mgr.-Lori Marks, Production Mgr.-Dana Koehler
Editorial Description: The practical newsletter on agency management for smaller agencies. Ideas & techniques which you can use immediately to serve your clients better, get properly paid, survive, grow, make money, and get the psychic rewards you are looking for.
General Info: Yr. Est. 1984, Monthly, Trim Size-8½ x 11, Desktop press, 4 pages, Color
Subscriptions: Indv. $119, Can. $124, $10/copy
Circulation: Total-704
Advertising: Inquire for rates.
List Rental: Actives: 8,725, $145/M
Printing Co: Dale Printing Company, Inc., 7610 Dale Avenue, St. Louis, MO 63117 Tel # (314) 781-1404, Fax # (314) 781-1759

Young Adult/Teen Market Report   *Business*

Publishing Co: Charles Oliver Co., 20 Oak Neck Rd., Hyanas, MA 02601; Title Tel # (508) 771-9636
Personnel: Publisher, Editor-Charles Oliver
Editorial Description: Advises advertisers, agencies, & communicators about specific youth trends. Includes descriptions of new youth media with advertising rates, circulation, demographics, etc. Numerous sources of information are provided for young adult, teenage and, particularly, student marketers. Subscribers include big corporations, agencies & libraries.
General Info: Yr. Est. 1988, Monthly, Trim Size-8½ x 11, Desktop press, 4 pages, No Color, Matte
Subscriptions: Indv. $60, Inst. $96, Can. $96, For. $126
Advertising: Accepts Inserts.

Your Clipping Analyst

Publishing Co: Burrelle's Information Services, 75 E. Northfield Rd., Livingston, NJ 07039-4501 Tel # (201) 992-6600 Fax # (800) 898-6677; Title Tel # (212) 227-5570
Editorial Description: A promotion newsletter for Burelle's which includes helpful advice and other articles of interest to publicists.
General Info: Monthly

Youth Market Alert   *Business*

Publishing Co: EPM Communications, Inc., 160 Mercer St., 3rd Floor, New York, NY 10012-3212; Title Tel # (212) 941-0099 Title Fax # (212) 941-1622
Personnel: Publisher-Ira Mayer, Editor-Michael Schau, Circ. Mgr.-Riva Bennett, VP Mktng.-Michele Jensen
Editorial Description: Coverage & analysis of all research, trends and lifestyle involving the different youth markets.
General Info: Yr. Est. 1989, Monthly, Trim Size-8½ x 11, Sheetfed press, 8 pages, ISSN: 1041-7516, Color-cover
Subscriptions: Indv. $235, Can. $295, For. $325, $35/copy
List Rental: Actives: $250/M, Hotline: $250/M, Expires: $250/M

Zandl/Slant   *Business*

Publishing Co: Xtreme, 270 Lafayette St Ste 612, New York, NY 10012-3327; Title Tel # (212) 473-4674 Title Fax # (212) 473-4750
General Info: Yr. Est. 1987, 3x/yr.
Subscriptions: Indv. $100

ADVERTISING SHOPPING GUIDES

Old Saybrook, Connecticut

Penny Saver

Publishing Co: Penny Saver, PO Box 628, Old Saybrook, CT 06475-0628; Title Tel # (203) 388-9793
General Info: Yr. Est. 1949, Weekly

Vernon, Connecticut

Rockville Reminder

Publishing Co: Rockville Reminder, 130 Old Town Rd., Box 27, Vernon, CT 06066-2362; Title Tel # (203) 875-3366
General Info: Yr. Est. 1949, Weekly
Circulation: Total-12,207

Suburban Reminder

Publishing Co: Suburban Reminder, 130 Old Town Rd., Box 27, Vernon, CT 06066-2322; Title Tel # (203) 643-8374
General Info: Yr. Est. 1962, Weekly
Circulation: Total-6,700

Sandwich, Illinois
Rusty Iron Monthly
See: ANTIQUES & ART GOODS

South Holland, Illinois

Shopper

Publishing Co: Shopper, 924 E 162nd St, South Holland, IL 60473-2442; Title Tel # (708) 333-5901
Personnel: Publisher-Alonzo Kallemeyn, Editor-Antoinette Schilling, Circ. Mgr.-Ronald Schaap, Adv. Dir.-Andrew Rietueld, Art Dir.-David Kallemeyn
Editorial Description: Display advertising limited local news.
General Info: Yr. Est. 1957, Weekly, Trim Size-11 x 17, Web press, 225 pages, 2 Color
Circulation: Total-32,000

Potomac, Maryland
Bank Securities Report
See: BANKING & FINANCE

Liberty, Missouri

Liberty Shopper News

Publishing Co: Liberty Shopper News, 12 N Main St, Liberty, MO 64068-1698 Tel # (816) 781-1044
General Info: Yr. Est. 1961, Weekly
Circulation: Total-11,473

Columbia Falls, Montana
Kettle Care-Pure Herbal Body Care
See: ADVERTISING & MARKETING

Englewood Cliffs, New Jersey

Advertising Manager's Handbook   *Business*

Publishing Co: Prentice-Hall Business and Professional Publishing, 113 Sylvan Ave., Englewood Cliffs, NJ 07632 Parent Co.-Simon & Schuster, Inc., New York; Title Fax # (515) 284-2607
Editorial Description: Tackle any type of advertising task with confidence. This handbook shows different strategies for advertising successfully.

Cazenovia, New York

Hi, Neighbour

Publishing Co: Hi, Neighbour, PO Box 324, Cazenovia, NY 13035-0324; Title Tel # (315) 655-9431
General Info: Yr. Est. 1957, Weekly
Circulation: Total-5,200

Owego, New York

Owego Pennysaver Press

Publishing Co: Towanda Printing, PO Box 149, Owego, NY 13827-0149; Title Tel # (607) 687-2434
General Info: Yr. Est. 1936, Weekly, 48 pages
Subscriptions: Indv. $12
Circulation: Total-12,400

Chapel Hill, North Carolina

Village Advocate   *Consumer*

Publishing Co: Village Publishing Co., PO Box 2777, Chapel Hill, NC 27515-2777; Title Tel # (919) 929-7121
Personnel: Publisher-R. Louden, Circ. Mgr.-Mary Price, Art Dir.-P. Tomolonius
Editorial Description: Free circulation shopping guide.
General Info: Yr. Est. 1969, Semi-weekly, Trim Size-11⅛ x 15, Offset press, 80 pages, Color
Subscriptions: Indv. $20, Free
Circulation: Total-30,000

Dayton, Tennessee

Rhea County Shopper

Publishing Co: Rhea County Publishing Co, Inc, 3687 Rhea County Highway, P.O. Box 286, Dayton, TN 37321-0286 Tel # (615) 775-6111 Fax # (615) 775-8218 Parent Co.-Greenville Sun, The, Greenville
Personnel: Publisher-Ed Emens, Circ. Mgr.-Cary Clark, Adv. Dir.-Sara Locke
General Info: Web press, 10 pages, 4 Color, Looseleaf
Circulation: (100% controlled), Total-8,479
Advertising: Inquire for rates.

Dodgeville, Wisconsin

Dodgeville Reminder

Publishing Co: Dodgeville Reminder, 1O8 E. Merrimac St., Dodgeville, WI 53533; Title Tel # (668) 935-3643
General Info: Yr. Est. 1934, Weekly
Circulation: Total-6,500

Evansville, Wisconsin

Leader, The

Publishing Co: Leader, The, 116 E Main St, Evansville, WI 53536-1124
General Info: Yr. Est. 1949, Weekly
Circulation: Total-3,700

CANADA

Dartmouth, Nova Scotia

Network
See: MANAGEMENT

AERONAUTICS/ASTRONAUTICS

AN Equipment Forecast   *Business, Consumer*

Publishing Co: Forecast International/DMS, Inc., 22 Commerce Rd., Newtown, CT 06470-1643 Fax # (203) 426-1964; Title Tel # (203) 426-0800 Title Fax # (203) 426-4262
General Info: Monthly, Ind/Abs/Online: Army & defense agencies are covered. Includes descriptions, No Color, Looseleaf
Subscriptions: Indv. $1,295
List Rental: Rents Lists

AWA Newsletter   *Association, Business*

Publishing Co: Aviation/Space Writers Assn., 6540 50th St. N, Oakdale, MN 55128-1708; Title Tel # (614) 221-1900
General Info: Yr. Est. 1938, Bi-monthly
Circulation: (100% controlled), Total-1,300

Abbotsford International Airshow Newsletter   *Association*

Publishing Co: Abbotsford Intl. Airshow Society, Box 361, Abbotsford, BC V2S 4N9 Canada; Title Tel # (604) 852-8511
Personnel: Editor-Debbie Nielsen
Editorial Description: Annual event the Abbotsford International Airshow.
General Info: Yr. Est. 1962, Quarterly, Trim Size-8½ x 11, Mimeo press, 2 pages, No Color
Circulation: Total-900

Advanced Composites Monthly   *Business*

Publishing Co: Composite Market Reports, 1345 E. Main St., Suite 100, Mesa, AZ 85203-8950; Title Tel # (602) 461-9445 Title Fax # (602) 461-8177
Personnel: Publisher, Editor-Bill Benjamin
Editorial Description: Market and technology intelligence for fabricators, users, prime & sub-contractors, universities, government and others. Covers advanced composite materials, processes, markets, applications, and acquisition/divestiture information in the sectors of aircraft, missiles, and spacecraft structures.
General Info: Yr. Est. 1972, Monthly, Offset press, 8 pages, ISSN: 1058-899X, No Color, Matte
Subscriptions: Inst. $2,535

Aerolog

Publishing Co: National Aviation Club, PO Box 2717, Arlington, VA 22202-0717 Tel # (703) 521-1991; Title Tel # (703) 522-7718
Editorial Description: Newsletter of interest to club members.
General Info: Bi-monthly
Circulation: Total-1,000

Aerospace Daily   *Business*

Publishing Co: McGraw-Hill Aviation Group, 1200 G St NW Ste 200, Washington, DC 20005-3814 Tel # (202) 383-2350; Title Tel # (202) 383-2378 Title Fax # (202) 293-7482
Personnel: Publisher-Pat Ryan, Editor-William Hall, Circ. Mgr.-Dale Sleppy, Production Mgr.-Bill Orchard, Art Dir.-Mahin Kooros, Promotion Dir.-Margaret Davis
Editorial Description: Daily intelligence on the defense & space industries, including aircraft, weapons, space systems & the Government Agencies they serve.
General Info: Yr. Est. 1963, Daily, Trim Size-8¼ x 10¾, Sheetfed press, 8 pages, Ind/Abs/Online: BRS, DIALOG, Dow Jones, FT Profile, NewsNet, Nexis, 4 Color, Newsprint, Saddle-stitched
Subscriptions: Indv. $1,340
Acquistions: Publication Bought
Circulation: Total-25,000
Advertising: Inquire for rates.
List Rental: List Management Co.: Manager: Bill DenHardt; The Lake Group, 411 Theodore Freund Ave., Rye, NY 10580-1497 Tel # (914) 925-2400, Fax # (914) 925-2499, Actives: $90/M

Aerospace Facts
See: HOUSE ORGANS

Aerospace Industries Assn. Newsletter

Publishing Co: Aerospace Industries Assn of America, 1250 Eye St., NW, #1100, Washington, DC 20005-3922; Title Tel # (202) 371-8400
Personnel: Editor-Lynn Dudinsky

Aerospace News

Publishing Co: Aerospace Industries Assn. of Canada, 60 Queens St., #1200, Ottawa, ON K1P 5Y7 Canada; Title Tel # (613) 232-4297 Title Fax # (613) 232-1142
Personnel: Editor-Denise Faguy
Editorial Description: Contains general information about the aerospace industry in Canada, as well as articles on specific member company activities.
General Info: Bi-monthly, Matte, Saddle-stitched
Circulation: (100% controlled), Total-1,500

Aerospace Newsletter
See: SAFETY

Aerospace Propulsion

Publishing Co: McGraw-Hill Aviation Group, 1200 G St NW Ste 200, Washington, DC 20005-3814; Title Tel # (202) 383-2350 Title Fax # (202) 293-2682
Personnel: Publisher-Pat Ryan, Editor-Jim Mathews, Circ. Mgr.-Dale Sleppy, Adv. Dir.-Carol Byrne
Editorial Description: Covers power plants found on commercial & military aircraft, business jets, helicopters, missiles, and space launch vehicles.
General Info: Yr. Est. 1990, Bi-weekly, Ind/Abs/Online: Dialog, Dow Jones, NewsNet, Nexis
Subscriptions: Indv. $550
Advertising: Inquire for rates. Accepts Inserts.
List Rental: List Management Co.: The Lake Group, 411 Theodore Freund Ave., Rye, NY 10580-1497 Tel # (914) 925-2400, Fax # (914) 925-2499

Aerostatical Notes

Publishing Co: ECCE Clampsus Vitos, Drawer 2247, Menlo Park, CA 94026-2247
  Tel # (415) 326-7679; Title Tel # (415) 324-2385
Personnel: Publisher-F. Krakutnyoi, Editor-Deke Sonnichsen, Art Dir.-Jose Boyer, III
Editorial Description: Documents unusual/exotic/bizarre balloon achievements by members,
  planetwide. Esp at Whiskey Hill, Atherton, Menlo Oaks Ballooning & Sporting Society balloon
  rallies.
General Info: Yr. Est. 1965

Air Safety Week
See: SAFETY

Air Transport Newsletter
See: SAFETY

Airborne Electronics
Forecast   *Business*

Publishing Co: Forecast International/DMS, Inc., 22 Commerce Rd., Newtown, CT 06470-1643
  Fax # (203) 426-1964; Title Tel # (203) 426-0800 Title Fax # (203) 426-4262
General Info: Monthly, Looseleaf
Subscriptions: Indv. $1,295

Airborne R&M Systems
Forecast   *Business*

Publishing Co: Forecast International/DMS, Inc., 22 Commerce Rd., Newtown, CT 06470-1643
  Fax # (203) 426-1964; Title Tel # (203) 426-0800 Title Fax # (203) 426-4262
General Info: Monthly, Looseleaf
Subscriptions: Indv. $1,295

Aircraft Engine Inventory
Database License   *Business*

Publishing Co: Forecast International/DMS, Inc., 22 Commerce Rd., Newtown, CT 06470-1643
  Fax # (203) 426-1964; Title Tel # (203) 426-0800 Title Fax # (203) 426-4262
General Info: Quarterly, Looseleaf
Subscriptions: Indv. $6,900

Aircraft Forecast   *Business*

Publishing Co: Forecast International/DMS, Inc., 22 Commerce Rd., Newtown, CT 06470-1643
  Fax # (203) 426-1964; Title Tel # (203) 426-0800 Title Fax # (203) 426-4262
General Info: Monthly
Subscriptions: Indv. $1,395

Aircraft Value Newsletter   *Business*

Publishing Co: Phillips Business Information, Inc., 1201 Seven Locks Rd., Ste 300, Potomac, MD
  20854-2958 Tel # (301) 340-1520 Fax # (301) 424-4297; Title Tel # (301) 424-3338
  Title Fax # (301) 309-3847
General Info: Yr. Est. 1992, Bi-weekly, ISSN: 1071-0655
Subscriptions: Indv. $695, For. $730
List Rental: Rents Lists

Airline Financial News   *Business, Association*

Publishing Co: Phillips Business Information, Inc., 1201 Seven Locks Rd., Ste 300, Potomac, MD
  20854-2958 Tel # (301) 340-1520 Fax # (301) 424-4297; Title Tel # (703) 522-8333
  Title Fax # (703) 522-8334
Personnel: Publisher-Joseph Murphy, Editor-Steven Nearman
General Info: Yr. Est. 1986, 50x/yr., Trim Size-8½ x 11, Sheetfed press, 16 pages, ISSN: 1040-5410,
  Ind/Abs/Online: NewsNet, 1% ads, No Color, Newsprint
Subscriptions: Indv. $695, For. $760
Circulation: Total-300
Advertising: Inquire for rates. Accepts Inserts.
Printing Co: Twin Towers Printing, 1000 Wilson Blvd, Arlington, VA 22209-3902
  Tel # (703) 276-1996

Airline Marketing News   *Business*

Publishing Co: Phillips Business Information, Inc., 1201 Seven Locks Rd., Ste 300, Potomac, MD
  20854-2958 Tel # (301) 340-1520 Fax # (301) 424-4297
Personnel: Sales Mgr.-Susan Incarnato
Editorial Description: Information for airline marketing professionals./
General Info: Yr. Est. 1994, Bi-weekly, ISSN: 1071-1325
Subscriptions: Indv. $695, For. $630
List Rental: Rents Lists

Airliners Monthly News   *Business*   **CPM: $195**

Publishing Co: World Transport Press Inc., Box 52-1238, Miami, FL 33152;
  Title Tel # (305) 477-7163 Title Fax # (305) 599-1995
Personnel: Editor-Tom Norwood, Editor-John Wegg, Circ. Mgr.-Pauline Drum, Production Mgr.-Keith
  Armes, Adv. Dir.-Bryant Petitt
Editorial Description: Monthly news of airline fleet changes, route news - airline capsules, airliner
  accidents, industry update. Over 40 B/W photos of latest airline liveries.
General Info: Yr. Est. 1987, Monthly, 24 pages, 1% ads, 2 Color, Saddle-stitched
Subscriptions: Indv. $40, Can. $49, For. $55, $4/copy
Circulation: Total-3,200
Advertising: $625.
Printing Co: Colonial Press, 3690 NW 50th St, Miami, FL 33142-3987 Tel # (305) 633-1581

Airport Highlights   *Association*

Publishing Co: Airport Council Intl. - North America, 1775 K St. NW Ste 500, Washington, DC
  20006-1502 Fax # (202) 831-1362; Title Tel # (202) 293-8500 Title Fax # (202) 331-1362
Personnel: Editor-N. Hasanian, Mktg. Dir.-Victoria Pannell
Editorial Description: Covers government actions, airport construction and expansion programs,
  technological developments,significant legal cases, and other subjects of interest to airport
  executives.
General Info: Yr. Est. 1965, Bi-weekly, Trim Size-8½ x 11, Desktop press, 8 pages, 2 Color, Coated
Subscriptions: Free With Membership
Acquistions: Publication Bought
Circulation: Total-1,600
Printing Co: Huff Duplicating, 1100 17th St NW Ste 8b, Washington, DC 20036-4601
  Tel # (202) 833-2000, Fax # (202) 452-1307

Airport Operation Bulletin   *Business*

Publishing Co: Flight Safety Foundation, 2200 Wilson Blvd Ste 500, Arlington, VA 22201-3369;
  Title Tel # (703) 522-8300 Title Fax # (703) 525-6047
Personnel: Publications Director-Roger Rozelle, Art Dir.-Karen Bostick, Promotion Dir.-Ed Peery
Editorial Description: Newsletter examines safety issues that involve aircraft, air traffic control,
  airport personnel and ground operations.
General Info: (Formerly FSF Airport Operation Safety Bulletin), Yr. Est. 1974, Bi-monthly, Trim Size-
  8½ x 10, Letrpr. press, 6 pages, ISSN: 1057-5537, Color-cover, Matte, Other
Subscriptions: Indv. $50, Inst. $60, Can. $60, For. $65, $10/copy
Printing Co: Master Print, Inc., 8401-A Terminal Rd., Box 1467, Newington, VA 22122
  Tel # (703) 550-9555

Airport Report   *Business, Association*

Publishing Co: American Assn. of Airport Executives, 4212 King St, Alexandria, VA 22302-1507;
  Title Tel # (703) 824-0500
Personnel: Editor-Ellen Horton, Adv. Dir.-Maureen Dysart
Editorial Description: Information on federal, national & regional issues facing professional airport
  managers.
General Info: Bi-weekly, Desktop press, 12 pages, No Color
Subscriptions: Indv. $175
Circulation: Total-3,500
List Rental: Rents Lists

Airports   *Business*

Publishing Co: McGraw-Hill Aviation Group, 1200 G St NW Ste 200, Washington, DC 20005-3814;
  Title Tel # (202) 383-2350
Personnel: Publisher-Pat Ryan, Editor-Avery Vise, Circ. Mgr.-Dale Sleppy, Adv. Dir.-Carol Byrne
Editorial Description: Airport business issues/intelligence for airport managers, users, suppliers,
  regulators & financial & concessionaires.
General Info: Yr. Est. 1985, Weekly, 8 pages, Ind/Abs/Online: Dow Jones, Dialog, FT Profile,
  NewsNet, Nexis
Subscriptions: Indv. $525
List Rental: List Management Co.: The Lake Group, 411 Theodore Freund Ave., Rye, NY
  10580-1497 Tel # (914) 925-2400, Fax # (914) 925-2499

American Star   *Consumer, Association*

Publishing Co: American Yankee Association, PO Box 1531, Cameron Park, CA 95682-1531;
  Title Tel # (916) 676-4292 Title Fax # (916) 676-4292
Editorial Description: Association newsletter for enthusisats, owners, and pilots of Grumman,
  Gulfstream, and American light aircraft.
General Info: Bi-monthly

Asian Aviation News   *Business*

Publishing Co: Phillips Business Information, Inc., 1201 Seven Locks Rd., Ste 300, Potomac, MD
  20854-2958 Tel # (301) 340-1520 Fax # (301) 424-4297
General Info: Bi-weekly, ISSN: 1071-0663
Subscriptions: Indv. $695, For. $730

Astro News   *Consumer, Association*

Publishing Co: Young Astronaut Council, 1308 19th St NW, Washington, DC 20036-1602
  Tel # (202) 682-1984 Fax # (202) 775-1773; Title Tel # (202) 682-1985
Personnel: Editor-Cecelia Blalock
Editorial Description: Published for Young Astronaut Council members. Contains program
  information and space news.
General Info: (Formerly Astrobits), Yr. Est. 1985, Bi-monthly
Circulation: Total-5,000

Atlantic Inflight
See: HOBBY

Aviation Accident Law   *Business*

Publishing Co: Matthew Bender & Co., 11 Penn Plaza, New York, NY 10001-2006
  Fax # (212) 244-3188; Title Tel # (212) 967-7707
Personnel: Editor-R. Kaye
Editorial Description: Provides a full combination of domestic and international law.
General Info: Yr. Est. 1963, Irregular, Looseleaf
Subscriptions: $230/copy

Aviation Consumer · *Consumer*

Publishing Co: Belvoir Pubs., 75 Holly Hill Lane, Greenwich, CT 06836; Title Tel # (203) 661-6111
Personnel: Publisher-Robert Englander, Editor-Richard Weeghman
General Info: Semi-monthly
Subscriptions: Indv. $60
Circulation: Total-32,000
List Rental: List Management Co.: Kleid Company, Inc., 530 5th Ave., 17 Floor, New York, NY 10036-5101 Tel # (212) 819-3406, Fax # (212) 719-9788, Actives: 27,678, $80/M, Expires: 7,251, $55/M

Aviation Daily · *Business*

Publishing Co: McGraw-Hill Aviation Group, 1200 G St NW Ste 200, Washington, DC 20005-3814; Title Tel # (202) 383-2350 Title Fax # (202) 293-2682
Personnel: Publisher-Pat Ryan, Editor-Ed Pinto, Circ. Mgr.-Dale Sleppy, Production Mgr.-Bill Orchard, Adv. Dir.-Carol Byrne, Art Dir.-Mahin Kooros
Editorial Description: Daily intelligence of the commercial air transportation & commercial aviation industry worldwide.
General Info: Yr. Est. 1938, Daily, Trim Size-$8\frac{1}{4}$ x $10\frac{3}{4}$, Sheetfed press, 8 pages, Ind/Abs/Online: Dow Jones, Dialog, FT Profile, NewsNet, Nexis, 4 Color
Subscriptions: Indv. $1,340
Acquistions: Publication Bought
Circulation: Total-22,000
Advertising: Inquire for rates. Accepts Inserts.
List Rental: List Management Co.: The Lake Group, 411 Theodore Freund Ave., Rye, NY 10580-1497 Tel # (914) 925-2400, Fax # (914) 925-2499, Actives: $90/M

Aviation Disaster Management

Publishing Co: Interests Ltd., 8512 Cedar St, Silver Spring, MD 20910-4347 Fax # (301) 588-2009; Title Tel # (301) 588-7916 Title Fax # (310) 588-2085
General Info: Yr. Est. 1992, Bi-monthly

Aviation Europe · *Business*

Publishing Co: McGraw-Hill Aviation Group, 1200 G St NW Ste 200, Washington, DC 20005-3814; Title Tel # (202) 383-2350
Personnel: Publisher-Pat Ryan, Editor-Ed Pinto, Circ. Mgr.-Dale Sleppy, Adv. Dir.-Carol Byrne
General Info: Weekly, Ind/Abs/Online: Dialog, Dow Jones, NewsNet, Nexis
Subscriptions: Indv. $625
List Rental: Rents Lists

Aviation Law Reports · *Business*

Publishing Co: CCH, Inc., 2700 Lake Cook Rd., Riverwoods, IL 60015 Parent Co.-Kluwer Law & Taxation Publishers, Cambridge; Title Tel # (847) 267-7000 Title Fax # (800) 224-8299
Editorial Description: Covers federal aviation laws, regulations, decisions, plus air liabilities.
General Info: Yr. Est. 1931, Semi-monthly, Trim Size-6 x 9, Web press, 150 pages, No Color, Looseleaf
Subscriptions: Indv. $1,970

Aviation Litigation Reporter · *Business*

Publishing Co: Andrews Publications, Inc., 1646 West Chester Pike, PO Box 1000, Westtown, PA 19395; Title Tel # (610) 399-6600 Title Fax # (610) 399-6610
Personnel: Publisher-John E. Backe, Editor-Nick Sullivan, Mktg. Dir.-Andrew Katz
Editorial Description: Provides the latest information on aviation crash and defect suits and other legal issues in the field of aviation.
General Info: Yr. Est. 1983, Bi-monthly, Trim Size-$8\frac{1}{2}$ x 11, Mimeo press, 70 pages, ISSN: 0737-7746, Ind/Abs/Online: News Net, No Color, Newsprint
Subscriptions: Indv. $825, $39/copy
List Rental: Actives: 990, $110/M

Aviation Mechanics Bulletin

Publishing Co: Flight Safety Foundation, 2200 Wilson Blvd Ste 500, Arlington, VA 22201-3369; Title Tel # (703) 522-8300 Title Fax # (703) 525-6047
Personnel: Publications Director-Roger Rozelle, Feature Ed.-Robert Feeler, Art Dir.-Karen Bostick, Promotion Dir.-Ed Peery
Editorial Description: Booklet written and edited for ground crewmen, A & D information for new products and methods.
General Info: Yr. Est. 1972, Bi-monthly, Trim Size-$5\frac{1}{4}$ x $7\frac{1}{2}$, Letrpr. press, 20 pages, ISSN: 0005-2140, Color-cover, Matte, Other
Subscriptions: Indv. $35, Inst. $35, Can. $35, For. $40, $10/copy
Circulation: Total-2,500
Printing Co: Master Print, Inc., 8401-A Terminal Rd., Box 1467, Newington, VA 22122 Tel # (703) 550-9555

Aviation Medical Bulletin

Publishing Co: Aviation Insurance Agency, Box 20787, Atlanta Airport, Atlanta, GA 30320-0787; Title Tel # (404) 767-7501
Personnel: Publisher-Harvey Watt, Editor-Bill Maness
Editorial Description: Promotes health education for the professional airline pilot.
General Info: Yr. Est. 1969, Monthly, Trim Size-$8\frac{1}{2}$ x 11, Web press, 6 pages, 2 Color
Subscriptions: Indv. $8
Circulation: Total-38,000

Aviation Monthly · *Business*

Publishing Co: Peter Katz Productions, PO Box 831, White Plains, NY 10602-0831; Title Tel # (914) 949-7443
Personnel: Publisher, Editor-Peter Katz
Editorial Description: Aviation safety report & accident summary.
General Info: Yr. Est. 1972, Monthly, Trim Size-$8\frac{1}{2}$ x 11, Sheetfed press, 8 pages, ISSN: 0145-1014, 2 Color
Subscriptions: Indv. $36, Can. $46, For. $56, $3/copy
Circulation: Total-11,000
List Rental: Rents Lists

Aviation News of South Florida · *Business, Association*

Publishing Co: Aviation News from South Florida, 1711 N Anhinga Ln, Homestead, FL 33035-1001
General Info: Yr. Est. 1990, Bi-monthly, ISSN: 1058-1014

Aviation Safety · *Business*

Publishing Co: Belvoir Pubs., 75 Holly Hill Lane, Greenwich, CT 06836; Title Tel # (203) 661-6111
Personnel: Publisher-Robert Englander, Editor-Andrew Douglas, Circ. Mgr.-Nancy Dreyer
General Info: Semi-monthly
Subscriptions: Indv. $48
List Rental: List Management Co.: Kleid Company, Inc., 530 5th Ave., 17 Floor, New York, NY 10036-5101 Tel # (212) 819-3406, Fax # (212) 719-9788, Actives: 40,738, $80/M, Expires: 10,096, $55/M

Aviation Safety Monitor · *Business*

Publishing Co: Aviation Safety Institute, 6797 N. High St., Worthington, OH 43085-2533; Title Tel # (614) 885-1597 Title Fax # (614) 885-5891
Personnel: Publisher, Editor-Mike Overly, Circ. Mgr.-Judith Lowe
Editorial Description: Safety information for aviation professionals, private pilots, & passengers.
General Info: Yr. Est. 1976, Monthly, Sheetfed press, 8 pages, No Color, Newsprint
Subscriptions: Indv. $60, $4/copy
Circulation: Total-1,000

Aviation Safety, Ultralight and Balloon · *Business, Consumer*

Publishing Co: Transport Canada, 200 Kent St., Ottawa, ON K1A 0N8 Canada; Title Tel # (613) 996-4006
Editorial Description: Cover aviation and safety issues.
General Info: Yr. Est. 1990, Semi-annually

Aviation/Space Writers Association News · *Business, Association*

Publishing Co: Aviation/Space Writers Assn., 6540 50th St. N, Oakdale, MN 55128-1708; Title Tel # (614) 221-1900
Personnel: Editor-Bob Searles
Editorial Description: News & book reviews of interest to the members of the association.
General Info: Yr. Est. 1938, 10x/yr., Trim Size-$8\frac{1}{2}$ x 11, 12 pages, No Color
Circulation: (100% controlled), Total-1,400

Aviators Hot Line · CPM: $6

Publishing Co: Heartland Communications Group, 1003 Central Ave., PO Box 1115, Fort Dodge, IA 50501 Fax # (800) 247-2000; Title Tel # (515) 955-1600
Personnel: Circ. Mgr.-Andrea Peterson, Production Mgr.-Sheila Davis, Adv. Dir.-Cindy Benton, Mktg. Dir.-Denise McLellan
Editorial Description: News of aircraft and related products for sale. National marketplace for active buyers and sellers of corporate and general aircraft, parts and service.
General Info: Yr. Est. 1979, Monthly, Trim Size-$7\frac{3}{4}$ x $10\frac{3}{4}$, Web press, 72 pages, ISSN: 0195-0347, 4 Color, Coated, Saddle-stitched
Subscriptions: Indv. $22, $2/copy
Acquistions: Publication Bought
Circulation: Total-95,000
Advertising: $600. Accepts Inserts.
List Rental: Actives: $75/M
Printing Co: Allen Printing Co., 215 S Main St, Clarion, IA 50525-1417 Tel # (515) 532-2105

B.C Contact! · *Consumer, Association*

Publishing Co: Airdance Inc, PO Box 708, Brookfield, WI 53008-0708 Tel # (414) 783-2565; Title Tel # (414) 783-6559 Title Fax # (414) 783-6558
Personnel: Editor-Lawrence D'Attilio, Production Mgr.-Scott Thomas, Adv. Dir.-Pamela Foard
Editorial Description: Newsletter containing technical information on Bellanca and Champion aircraft.
General Info: (Formerly Bellanca Contact), Yr. Est. 1980, Quarterly, Trim Size-$8\frac{1}{2}$ x 11, Offset press, 20 pages, ISSN: 0899-6954, Matte, Saddle-stitched
Subscriptions: Indv. $34, Can. $40, For. $40, $5/copy
Circulation: Total-1,300, Readership-1,300
Advertising: Inquire for rates.
Printing Co: Leesburg Printing Co., 1100 North Blvd E, Leesburg, FL 34748-5350 Tel # (904) 787-3348, Fax # (904) 787-2210

Basha Blabber · *Association*

Publishing Co: First Air Commandos Assn., PO Box 466, Broderick, CA 95605-0466; Title Tel # (916) 372-6705
Circulation: Total-350

Buckeye Pietenpol Association Newsletter *Association*

Publishing Co: Buckeye Pietenpol Association, 6364 Franks Rd., Byrnes Mill, MO 63051-1103; Title Tel # (314) 677-1669
Personnel: Publisher, Editor-Grant MacLaren
Editorial Description: Promotes Pietenpol airplanes, acknowledges Bernard H. Pietenpol's contribution to the world of amateur-built aircraft.
General Info: Yr. Est. 1981, Quarterly, Trim Size-8$\frac{1}{2}$ x 11, Offset press, 12 pages, ISSN: 1059-3977, Coated, Saddle-stitched
Subscriptions: Indv. $10, Inst. $12, Can. $12, For. $15, $3/copy
Circulation: Total-900

Business Aviation *Business, Association*

Publishing Co: McGraw-Hill Aviation Group, 1200 G St NW Ste 200, Washington, DC 20005-3814; Title Tel # (202) 383-2350
Personnel: Publisher-Pat Ryan, Editor-Dave Collogan, Circ. Mgr.-Dale Sleppy
Editorial Description: Corporate flight depts., fixed-base operators, aircraft & component manufacturers & related vendors.
General Info: Yr. Est. 1965, Weekly, Trim Size-8$\frac{1}{4}$ x 10$\frac{3}{4}$, Sheetfed press, 8 pages, Ind/Abs/Online: Dow Jones, Dialog, FT Profile, NewsNet, Nexis, 3% ads, 4 Color, Newsprint, Saddle-stitched
Subscriptions: Indv. $470
Acquistions: Publication Bought
Circulation: Total-8,000
Advertising: Accepts Inserts.
List Rental: List Management Co.: Information Marketing Services, 8130 Boone Blvd., Ste 310, Vienna, VA 22182-2640 Tel # (703) 821-8130, Fax # (703) 821-8243, Actives: $100/M

CAL/NX211 Collectors Society Newsletter
See: HISTORY

CBAA NEWS BRIEF *Business, Association*

Publishing Co: CDN Business Aircraft Association, 1317-50 O'Connor St., Ottawa, ON K1P 6L2 Canada; Title Tel # (613) 236-5611 Title Fax # (613) 236-2361
Personnel: Publisher-J.D. Lyon, Editor-Darrell Eagles
Editorial Description: Timely information regarding activities in business aviation.
General Info: (Formerly Newsletter), Yr. Est. 1989, Monthly
Subscriptions: Free With Membership
Circulation: Total-515

CNS Outlook *Business*

Publishing Co: Phillips Business Information, Inc., 1201 Seven Locks Rd., Ste 300, Potomac, MD 20854-2958 Fax # (301) 424-4297; Title Tel # (301) 340-1520
Personnel: Publisher-Heather Treat, Editor-Damon Hart, Editorial Dir.-Dexter Hutchins, Mng. Editor-Seth Arenstein, Asst. Ed.-Peter S. Kelly, Mktg. Mgr.-Kelly Ebbs, Natl. Sales Mgr.-Jim Snyder
Editorial Description: Market opportunities, policy, and technology for aviation and air traffic management.
General Info: Yr. Est. 1992, Bi-weekly, Trim Size-8$\frac{1}{2}$ x 11, 8 pages, ISSN: 1072-5393, Matte
Subscriptions: Indv. $497, Can. $497, For. $560

CPIA Bulletin *Business* CPM: $37

Publishing Co: Johns Hopkins University/Chemical Propulsion Info Agency, 10630 Little Patuxent Pky Ste, 202, Columbia, MD 21044-3204 Parent Co.-Johns Hopkins Univ. Whiting School of Engineering, Baltimore; Title Tel # (410) 992-7307 Title Fax # (410) 730-4969
Personnel: Editor-Catherine McDermott
Editorial Description: News within the missile, space, and gun propulsion community.
General Info: Yr. Est. 1974, Bi-monthly, 16 pages, 20% ads, 2 Color
Subscriptions: Free To Qualified Recipient
Circulation: (89% controlled), Total-10,600
Advertising: $400.

Cabin Crew Safety

Publishing Co: Flight Safety Foundation, 2200 Wilson Blvd Ste 500, Arlington, VA 22201-3369; Title Tel # (703) 522-8300
Personnel: Publications Director-Roger Rozelle, Art Dir.-Karen Bostick, Promotion Dir.-Ed Peery
Editorial Description: Newsletter written & edited for aviation cabin crew personnel.
General Info: Yr. Est. 1965, Bi-monthly, Trim Size-8$\frac{1}{2}$ x 10, Letrpr. press, 6 pages, ISSN: 0898-5758, Color-cover, Newsprint, Other
Subscriptions: Indv. $60, Inst. $60, Can. $60, For. $65, $10/copy
Circulation: Total-2,100
Printing Co: Master Print, Inc., 8401-A Terminal Rd., Box 1467, Newington, VA 22122 Tel # (703) 550-9555

Canadian Museum Of Flight And Transportation

Publishing Co: Canadian Museum of Flight and Transportation, 13527 Crescent Rd, Surrey, BC V4A 1S5 Canada Fax # (604) 535-3292; Title Tel # (604) 535-1115
General Info: Yr. Est. 1990, ISSN: 1184-065x

Cardinal Club Newsletter *Consumer, Association*

Publishing Co: Cardinal Club, 1701 Saint Andrews Dr, Lawrence, KS 66047-1703; Title Tel # (913) 842-7016 Title Fax # (913) 842-1777
Editorial Description: Association newsletter for owners of Cessna Cardinal series aircraft.
General Info: Yr. Est. 1982, Bi-monthly, Trim Size-8$\frac{1}{2}$ x 11, Offset press, 16 pages, No Color, Saddle-stitched
Subscriptions: Indv. $27, Inst. $27, Can. $30, For. $34, $5/copy
Circulation: Total-1,200
Advertising: Inquire for rates. Accepts Inserts.
Printing Co: Lawrence Printing, Lawrence, KS 66047 Tel # (913) 843-4600

ChapterGram

Publishing Co: Experimental Aircraft Association, Inc., EAA Aviation Center, 3000 Poberezny Rd., Oshkosh, WI 54903-3086; Title Tel # (414) 426-4800 Title Fax # (414) 426-4828
Personnel: Editor-Bob Mackey
General Info: (Formerly EAA Headquarters Chapter Bulletin), Yr. Est. 1969, Trim Size-8$\frac{1}{2}$ x 11, Offset press, 4 pages, No Color, Newsprint
Acquistions: Publication Bought
Circulation: Total-800

Civil Aircraft Forecast *Business, Consumer*

Publishing Co: Forecast International/DMS, Inc., 22 Commerce Rd., Newtown, CT 06470-1643 Fax # (203) 426-1964; Title Tel # (203) 426-0800 Title Fax # (203) 426-4262
Editorial Description: Reports on U.S. and foreign civil aircraft programs, including proposed designs still in concept stage.
General Info: Yr. Est. 1960, Monthly, No Color, Looseleaf
Subscriptions: Indv. $1,295

Civil Aircraft Inventory Database License *Business*

Publishing Co: Forecast International/DMS, Inc., 22 Commerce Rd., Newtown, CT 06470-1643 Fax # (203) 426-1964; Title Tel # (203) 426-0800 Title Fax # (203) 426-4262
General Info: Quarterly, Looseleaf
Subscriptions: Indv. $6,900

Civil Penalty Case Digest Service *Business*

Publishing Co: Hawkins Publishing Co., Inc., 1207 B Central Avenue, Box 480, Mayo, MD 21106; Title Tel # (410) 798-1677 Title Fax # (410) 798-1098
Personnel: Editor-C.R. Eyler
Editorial Description: Indexed summaries & analyses of the decisions of the FAA dealing with civil penalty actions relative to aviation safety enforcement matters.
General Info: Yr. Est. 1992, Monthly, Trim Size-8$\frac{1}{2}$ x 11, Sheetfed press, No Color, Matte, Looseleaf
Subscriptions: $320/copy

Commuter Regional Airline News *Business*

Publishing Co: Phillips Business Information, Inc., 1201 Seven Locks Rd., Ste 300, Potomac, MD 20854-2958 Fax # (301) 424-4297; Title Tel # (301) 340-1520
Personnel: Publisher-Joseph Murphy, Editor-Kelly Murphy
Editorial Description: A weekly management newsletter written for & about the regional airlines of the U.S. & Canada.
General Info: Yr. Est. 1982, Weekly, Sheetfed press, 18 pages, ISSN: 1040-5402, 1% ads
Subscriptions: Indv. $695, For. $760
Circulation: Total-300
Advertising: Accepts Inserts.
Printing Co: Twin Towers Printing, 1000 Wilson Blvd, Arlington, VA 22209-3902 Tel # (703) 276-1996

Commuter Regional Airline News Intl. *Business*

Publishing Co: Phillips Business Information, Inc., 1201 Seven Locks Rd., Ste 300, Potomac, MD 20854-2958 Tel # (301) 340-1520 Fax # (301) 424-4297
Personnel: Publisher-Craig Bourne, Editor-Alison Chambers
General Info: Yr. Est. 1988, Weekly, ISSN: 1056-0254, Ind/Abs/Online: NewsNet, Predicasts
Subscriptions: Indv. $595
List Rental: Rents Lists

Confidential Air Letter

Publishing Co: Air Incident Research, PO Box 4745, East Lansing, MI 48826-4745; Title Tel # (517) 336-9375 Title Fax # (517) 336-9375
Personnel: Editor-Maureen Maclaughlin
Editorial Description: Newsletter on unlawful interference and untoward events in civil and V-I-P aviation.
General Info: Yr. Est. 1992, 10x/yr., Trim Size-8$\frac{1}{2}$ x 11, Desktop press, 6 pages, ISSN: 1065-9455, 2 Color, Matte, Other
Subscriptions: Indv. $45
Circulation: Readership-1,000

Connections
See: SHIPS & SHIPPING

Defense & Aerospace Companies, Volume I *Business*

Publishing Co: Forecast International/DMS, Inc., 22 Commerce Rd., Newtown, CT 06470-1643; Title Tel # (203) 426-0800 Title Fax # (203) 426-1964
Editorial Description: Includes reports on the top 67 aerospace/defense companies-activities, programs, organizations, sales forecasts, R&D efforts, plus other key information. Monthly updates.
General Info: (Formerly Aerospace Companies), Yr. Est. 1960, Monthly, Trim Size-8.5 x 11, Offset press, 1,200 pages, Color-cover, Matte, Looseleaf
Subscriptions: Indv. $1,295
Acquistions: Publication Sold
List Rental: Rents Lists

Defense Acquisition Report   *Business*

Publishing Co: Callahan Pubs., PO Box 1173, McLean, VA 22101-1173; Title Tel # (703) 356-1925
Title Fax # (703) 356-9614
Personnel: Publisher, Editor-Vincent Callahan, Jr.
Editorial Description: Contract and procurement data for suppliers to Department of Defense's missile and rocket programs.
General Info: (Formerly Missile Ordinance Letter), Yr. Est. 1958, Semi-monthly, Trim Size-8½ x 11, Offset press, 8 pages, ISSN: 0026-5993, No Color
Subscriptions: Indv. $190, For. $200

E Clampsus Vitus Balloon
Corps News

Publishing Co: Sponsor-E. Clampus Vitus, ECCE Clampus Vitos, Drawer 2247, Menlo Park, CA 94026-2247; Title Tel # (415) 326-7679
Personnel: Publisher-Dynamite Deke, Editor-J.J. Saxon-Gomez, Art Dir.-Comtesse De Rosiers
Editorial Description: Reports on ballooning activities by ECV Organs, Allied Affiliates records Anvil firing World Record attempts & keeps records.
General Info: Yr. Est. 1949, Monthly, Web press, 4 Color
Subscriptions: $63/copy

Electro Optical Systems
Forecast   *Business*

Publishing Co: Forecast International/DMS, Inc., 22 Commerce Rd., Newtown, CT 06470-1643; Title Tel # (203) 426-0800 Title Fax # (203) 426-1964
General Info: Yr. Est. 1995, Monthly, Looseleaf

Extraterrestrial Society   *Association*

Publishing Co: Space Settlement Studies Project, Niagara Univ., Sociology Dept., New York, NY 14109 Tel # (716) 826-8094; Title Tel # (716) 285-1212 Title Fax # (716) 286-8581
Personnel: Editor-Stewart Whitney
General Info: Yr. Est. 1976, Semi-annually
Circulation: Total-1,000

Fairfax Newsletter

Publishing Co: Dulles Intl. Airport, 2203 Burgee Ct, Reston, VA 22091-4705; Title Tel # (703) 860-2666
Personnel: Editor-Mary Klein
General Info: Yr. Est. 1956, Weekly

Federal Air Surgeon's
Medical Bulletin

Publishing Co: U.S. Federal Aviation Adm./Dept. of Transportation Warehouse, Publications Dept., 3341Q 75th Ave., Landover, MD 20785 Tel # (301) 322-4961
General Info: Bi-monthly

Flight Test News   *Business, Association*

Publishing Co: Society of Flight Test Engineers, PO Box 4047, Lancaster, CA 93539-4047; Title Tel # (805) 538-9715 Title Fax # (805) 538-9715
Personnel: Editor-Roger Counts
Editorial Description: News and information for and about Society members including convention proceedings.
General Info: Yr. Est. 1968, Monthly
Subscriptions: Indv. $48, Free With Membership
Advertising: Inquire for rates.

Flying Engineers Newsletter

Publishing Co: Flying Engineers Intl., 507 NW 60th St Ste C, Gainesville, FL 32607-2055; Title Tel # (904) 376-3157
Personnel: Editor-William Kessler
General Info: Semi-annually

For the Record   *Consumer, Association*   CPM: $81

Publishing Co: National Aeronautic Assn., 1815 Fort Myer Dr Ste 700, Arlington, VA 22209-1805; Title Tel # (703) 527-0226 Title Fax # (703) 527-0229
Personnel: Publisher-Jack Cole, Editor-Matt Farina
Editorial Description: Membership consists of corporations, sporting aviation organizations. Interests include promoting aviation & space activities to encourage US aerospace development & technology.
General Info: (Formerly Natl. Aeronautic Assn. of the USA Newsletter), Yr. Est. 1905, Bi-monthly, Trim Size-8½ x 11, 8 pages, 2 Color
Circulation: Total-5,500
Advertising: $450.

Foreign Military Markets
Latin American &
Australasia

Publishing Co: Forecast International DMS, Inc., 22 Commerce Road, Newtown, CT 06470-1643; Title Tel # (203) 426-0800 Title Fax # (203) 426-1964
Editorial Description: An analysis of the military requirements & market opportunities in Latin America & Australasia.
General Info: (Formerly Latin American & Australasia), Monthly, Trim Size-8½ x 11, 1,200 pages, Color-cover, Matte, Other, Looseleaf
Subscriptions: Indv. $1,200
List Rental: Rents Lists

Foreign Military Markets Middle East & Africa
See: INTERNATIONAL AFFAIRS

Foreign Military Markets
NATO & Europe   *Business*

Publishing Co: Forecast International/DMS, Inc., 22 Commerce Rd., Newtown, CT 06470-1643; Title Tel # (203) 426-0800 Title Fax # (203) 426-1964
Editorial Description: A country-by-country examination of the military capabilities, equipment requirements, & current inovatores for 16 Nato & 6 European nations.
General Info: (Formerly NATO & Europe), Monthly, No Color, Looseleaf
Subscriptions: Indv. $1,295
List Rental: Rents Lists

Gas Turbine Engines/Markets
See: MACHINERY

Gay Airline & Travel Club Newsletter, The
See: TRAVEL

General Aviation/Helicopter Accident Report
See: LAW

GraFiber News   *Business*

Publishing Co: Composite Market Reports, 1345 E. Main St., Suite 100, Mesa, AZ 85203-8950; Title Tel # (602) 461-9445 Title Fax # (602) 461-8177
Personnel: Publisher, Editor-Bill Benjamin
Editorial Description: Market and technology intelligence for materials suppliers. Covers advanced composite materials, processes, applications and acquisition/divestiture information in the sectors of aircraft, missiles, and spacecraft structures.
General Info: Yr. Est. 1971, Monthly, Offset press, 8 pages, ISSN: 1058-9023, No Color
Subscriptions: Inst. $2,325

HAC Techline

Publishing Co: Historical Aircraft Corp., 536 Star Ln, South Saint Paul, MN 55075-1511; Title Tel # (612) 451-3283 Title Fax # (612) 457-8280
Personnel: Publisher, Editor, Adv. Dir.-Warren Eberspacher
Editorial Description: How-to information for people who build replica fighter sport aircraft.
General Info: Yr. Est. 1981, Quarterly, Trim Size-8½ x 11, Mimeo press, 10 pages, 10% ads, No Color
Subscriptions: Indv. $10
Circulation: Total-150
Advertising: Inquire for rates. Accepts Inserts.
List Rental: Rents Lists
Printing Co: Local Biz Mart

Hansen Planetarium-
Update

Publishing Co: Hansen Planetarium, 15 S State St, Salt Lake City, UT 84111-1590; Title Tel # (801) 538-2104
Personnel: Circ. Mgr.-Joseph Bennett, Editor, Adv. Dir.-Doug Lowe
General Info: Yr. Est. 1984, Quarterly, 4 pages
Circulation: Total-10,000

Hawkins Chief Counsel's
Interpretations   *Business*

Publishing Co: Hawkins Publishing Co., Inc., 1207 B Central Avenue, Box 480, Mayo, MD 21106; Title Tel # (410) 798-1677 Title Fax # (410) 798-1098
Personnel: Editor-C.R. Eyler
Editorial Description: Index and text of the interpretations of the Federal Aviation Administration Chief Counsel relative to application of FAA regulations.
General Info: Yr. Est. 1992, Monthly, Trim Size-8½ x 11, No Color, Matte, Looseleaf
Subscriptions: $320/copy

Helicopter News   *Business*

Publishing Co: Phillips Business Information, Inc., 1201 Seven Locks Rd., Ste 300, Potomac, MD 20854-2958 Tel # (301) 340-1520; Title Tel # (301) 340-2100 Title Fax # (301) 424-4297
Personnel: Publisher-Thomas Phillips, Editor-Bill Carey, Mng. Editor-Kathleen Kocks, Circ. Mgr.-Vanessa Henderson, Production Mgr.-Bill Wynne, Adv. Dir., Promotion Dir.-Mark Ziebarth
Editorial Description: Provides latest information on rapidly changing helicopter industry.
General Info: Yr. Est. 1975, Bi-weekly, Sheetfed press, 8 pages, ISSN: 0363-8227, Ind/Abs/Online: NewsNet, DIALOG, Predicasts, No Color, Newsprint
Subscriptions: Indv. $495, For. $530
Advertising: Inquire for rates. Accepts Inserts.
List Rental: Actives: $95/M

Helicopter Safety   *Business*

Publishing Co: Flight Safety Foundation, 2200 Wilson Blvd Ste 500, Arlington, VA 22201-3369; Title Tel # (703) 522-8300 Title Fax # (703) 525-6047
Personnel: Editor-Roger Rozelle, Art Dir.-Karen Bostick, Promotion Dir.-Ed Peery
Editorial Description: Newsletter writter for votary-wing aircraft pilots and operations personnel.
General Info: (Formerly FSF Helicopter Safety Bulletin), Yr. Est. 1974, Bi-monthly, Trim Size-8½ x 10, Letrpr. press, 6 pages, ISSN: 0898-8145, Color-cover, Matte, Other
Subscriptions: Indv. $60, Inst. $60, Can. $60, For. $65, $10/copy
Circulation: Total-1,800
Printing Co: Master Print, Inc., 8401-A Terminal Rd., Box 1467, Newington, VA 22122 Tel # (703) 550-9555

Hotline

Publishing Co: Aeronautical Repair Station Association, 121 N Henry St, Alexandria, VA 22314-2903; Title Tel # (202) 293-2511
General Info: Bi-monthly

Hovernews   *Association*   CPM: $433

Publishing Co: Hoverclub of America, PO Box 908, Foley, AL 36536-0908 Fax # (233) 443-3279; Title Tel # (334) 943-3279 Title Fax # (334) 943-3279
Personnel: Editor-David Galka
General Info: (Formerly Hoverclub of America-Newsletter), Yr. Est. 1974, Bi-monthly, Trim Size-8½ x 11, Offset press, 24 pages, 5% ads, No Color, Matte, Perfect bound
Subscriptions: Indv. $25, Can. $35, For. $40, $3/copy
Circulation: Total-750
Advertising: $325.
List Rental: Actives: 750, $9/M
Printing Co: Strider Inc., PO Box 909, Foley, AL 36535-1308 Tel # (334) 943-3279, Fax # (334) 943-3279

Human Factors and Aviation Medicine

Publishing Co: Flight Safety Foundation, 2200 Wilson Blvd Ste 500, Arlington, VA 22201-3369; Title Tel # (703) 522-8300 Title Fax # (703) 525-6047
Personnel: Publications Director-Roger Rozelle, Art Dir.-Karen Bostick, Promotion Dir.-Ed Peery
Editorial Description: Newsletter addresses issues in crew resource management and the physiological and psychological health of aviation professionals.
General Info: (Formerly Human Factors Bulletin), Yr. Est. 1953, Bi-monthly, Trim Size-8½ x 10, Letrpr. press, 6 pages, ISSN: 0898-5723, Color-cover, Matte, Other
Subscriptions: Indv. $60, Inst. $60, Can. $60, For. $65, $10/copy
Circulation: Total-2,175
Printing Co: Master Print, Inc., 8401-A Terminal Rd., Box 1467, Newington, VA 22122 Tel # (703) 550-9555

IAAF Newsletter   *Business*   CPM$1464

Publishing Co: AG Pilot International, PO Box 1607, Mount Vernon, WA 98273-1607 Fax # (206) 336-2506; Title Tel # (206) 336-9737 Title Fax # (360) 336-2506
Personnel: Publisher-P.J. Anderson, Editor-Tom Wood, Production Mgr.-Tamara Pugh
Editorial Description: Published for the professional agriculture aviator.
General Info: Yr. Est. 1982, Monthly, Trim Size-8½ x 11, Sheetfed press, 4 pages, No Color, Matte, Saddle-stitched
Subscriptions: Indv. $60, $5/copy
Circulation: Total-1,280
Advertising: $1,874. Accepts Inserts.

IE News: Aerospace & Defense   *Association*   CPM: $287

Publishing Co: Institute of Industrial Engineers, 25 Technology Park/Atlanta, Norcross, GA 30092-2988 Tel # (770) 449-0461; Title Tel # (404) 449-0460 Title Fax # (770) 263-8532
Personnel: Production Mgr.-Dona Brown
Editorial Description: Newsletter for IIE Aerospace & Defense Division.
General Info: (Formerly IE News: Aerospace), Quarterly, Trim Size-8½ x 11, Sheetfed press, 4 pages, 2 Color, Matte, Saddle-stitched
Circulation: (100% controlled), Total-1,650
Advertising: $475. Accepts Inserts.
List Rental: Rents Lists

IEEE Vehicular Technology Society News See: ENGINEERING

IFR   *Business*

Publishing Co: Belvoir Pubs., 75 Holly Hill Lane, Greenwich, CT 06836; Title Tel # (203) 661-6111
Personnel: Editor-Kas Thomas
Editorial Description: Instrument flight rated.
General Info: Bi-monthly, 8 pages
Circulation: Total-1,980
List Rental: List Management Co.: Kleid Company, Inc., 530 5th Ave., 17 Floor, New York, NY 10036-5101 Tel # (212) 819-3406, Fax # (212) 719-9788, Actives: 12,000, $80/M

Industry News   *Association*

Publishing Co: Aviation Maintenance Foundation Intl., PO Box 2826, Redmond, WA 98073-2826; Title Tel # (206) 828-3917 Title Fax # (206) 827-6895
Personnel: Publisher-Richard Kost, Circ. Mgr.-Edith Nystrom, Editor, Adv. Dir.-Gilbert Hendrix, Production Mgr., Art Dir.-Gary Mosely
Editorial Description: Focuses on membership services, activities, & industry news.
General Info: (Formerly Aviation Maintenance Foundation Inc. Newsletter), Yr. Est. 1971, Bi-monthly, Trim Size-5¼ x 7½, Offset press, 18 pages, 2% ads, No Color, Newsprint, Saddle-stitched
Circulation: (100% controlled), Total-6,000

Inside Flyer   *Consumer*

Publishing Co: Frequent Flyer Services, 4715C Town Center Dr., Colorado Springs, CO 80916-4701; Title Tel # (719) 597-8889 Title Fax # (719) 597-6855
Personnel: Publisher, Editor-Randy Peterson
Editorial Description: Discusses frequent flyer and airplane travel information. Presents over 9000 ways frequent flyer miles can be earned.
General Info: Monthly
Subscriptions: Indv. $33
Circulation: Total-79,000
List Rental: List Management Co.: TCI Direct, 5511 Laurel Canyon Blvd, North Hollywood, CA 91607-2116 Tel # (818) 752-1800, Fax # (818) 752-1808

International Airline Review   *Consumer*

Publishing Co: Enterprises Unlimited, 400 E 59th St., Apt 9F, New York, NY 10022-2344 Tel # (212) 755-4363
Personnel: Publisher-Tom Weston, Editor-John Edwards
Editorial Description: Reviews and rates airline equipment, service and accomodations.
General Info: Yr. Est. 1993, Monthly, Trim Size-8½ x 11, 6 pages, No Color, Looseleaf
Subscriptions: Indv. $50
Circulation: Total-20,000

International Business Aviation Council-News Brief   *Business, Association*

Publishing Co: National Business Aviation Assn., 1200 18th St., NW, Washington, DC 20036-2506; Title Tel # (202) 783-9005
Personnel: Editor-Edmond Stohr
Editorial Description: Covers business and corporate aviation news of interest to member associations of IBAC.
General Info: (Formerly International Business Aviation Council-News Release), Irregular

International Contractors, Volume I   *Business*

Publishing Co: Forecast International/DMS, Inc., 22 Commerce Rd., Newtown, CT 06470-1643 Fax # (203) 426-1964; Title Tel # (203) 426-0800 Title Fax # (203) 426-4262
Editorial Description: Covers aircraft, retrofit, & engines.
General Info: Monthly, Looseleaf
Subscriptions: Indv. $945

International Women Pilots   *Business, Association*

Publishing Co: Ninety-Nines Inc., The, Box 965, Will Rogers Airport, Oklahoma City, OK 73159-0008 Tel # (405) 615-7969; Title Tel # (405) 685-7969 Title Fax # (405) 685-7985
Personnel: Editor-Robyn Sclair, Circ. Mgr.-L. Gragg, Production Mgr.-Marie Christensen, Adv. Dir.-Dave Sclair
Editorial Description: For licensed women pilots. Organization news, aviation safety and education, aviation industry and government affairs, and the advancement of women in aerospace careers.
General Info: (Formerly 99s News, The), Yr. Est. 1929, 10x/yr., Trim Size-8⅜ x 10⅞, Offset press, 32 pages, Color
Subscriptions: Indv. $20, Can. $28, For. $34, $2/copy
Circulation: Total-7,000
Advertising: Inquire for rates.

Iowa Aviation Bulletin   *Association*

Publishing Co: Iowa State Dept. of Transportation, Air & Transit Div. State, Capitol, Des Moines, IA 50319-0001; Title Tel # (515) 244-9124
Personnel: Editor, Circ. Mgr.-Kathleen Robinson
Editorial Description: Aviation safety & information.
General Info: Quarterly, 8 pages, No Color
Circulation: (100% controlled), Total-3,000

JAL Newsletter   *Consumer*

Publishing Co: Japan Airlines, 655 5th Ave, New York, NY 10022-5347; Title Tel # (212) 310-1221 Title Fax # (212) 310-1230
Personnel: Editor-Irene Jackson
Editorial Description: Company information for customers and employees along with information on goings on in Japan.
General Info: Yr. Est. 1989, Bi-monthly, Trim Size-8½ x 11, 8 pages, No Color, Matte, Saddle-stitched
Subscriptions: Free

Light Aircraft Manufacturers Assn. - Newsletter   *Business, Association*

Publishing Co: Light Aircraft Manufacturers Assn., 22 Deer Oaks Ct, Pleasanton, CA 94588-8233; Title Tel # (510) 426-0771 Title Fax # (510) 426-0771
General Info: Yr. Est. 1984, Annually
Acquistions: Publication Bought
Circulation: Total-400
Advertising: Inquire for rates.

Light Plane Maintenance   *Business*

Publishing Co: Belvoir Pubs., 75 Holly Hill Lane, Greenwich, CT 06836; Title Tel # (203) 661-6111
Personnel: Editor-Chris Maida
Editorial Description: Articles of interest to aircraft owners & pilots containing maintenance tips, source information for parts, product evaluations, news items, etc.
General Info: Monthly, ISSN: 0278-8950
Circulation: Total-15,000
List Rental: List Management Co.: Kleid Company, Inc., 530 5th Ave., 17 Floor, New York, NY 10036-5101 Tel # (212) 819-3406, Fax # (212) 719-9788, Actives: 10,308, $80/M

Lockheed Reports

Publishing Co: Lockheed Aircraft Svc. Co., PO Box 33, Ontario, CA 91761-0033 Tel # (909) 395-2411; Title Tel # (213) 847-2465
General Info: Yr. Est. 1948, Monthly
Circulation: Total-8,000

Maintenance & Operations Bulletin — *Association*

Publishing Co: National Business Aircraft Association, 1200 18th St. NW, Ste. 400, Washington, DC 20036-2506; Title Tel # (202) 783-9000 Title Fax # (202) 331-8364
General Info: Irregular, Trim Size-8½ x 11, 40 pages
Subscriptions: Free To Qualified Recipient
Printing Co: Corporate Press, 403 Brightseat Rd., Landover, MD 20785-4706 Tel # (301) 499-9200, Fax # (301) 499-5435

Many Happy Returns - U.S. Boomerang Assn. Newsletter
See: SPORTS & SPORTING GOODS

Membergram — *Association*

Publishing Co: American Helicopter Society, Inc., 217 N Washington St, Alexandria, VA 22314-2538 Fax # (703) 739-9279; Title Tel # (703) 684-6777
Personnel: Publisher-John Zugschwert, Circ. Mgr.-Penny Dudley, Editor, Production Mgr.-Mark Paris
Editorial Description: Contains information on the Society's membership activities.
General Info: Yr. Est. 1982, Bi-monthly, Trim Size-8½ x 11, Sheetfed press, 4 pages, No Color, Newsprint
Circulation: (100% controlled), Total-8,000

Meteor News
See: SCIENCE

Metropolitan Air Post Society Bulletin — *Association*

Publishing Co: Metropolitan Air Post Society, c/o Steven Rinehard, Box 110, Mineola, NY 11501
General Info: Monthly
Subscriptions: Indv. $2

Michigan Aviation — *Business*

Publishing Co: Aeronautics Commission, Capital City Airport, Lansing, MI 48906; Title Tel # (517) 373-1834 Title Fax # (517) 886-0366
Personnel: Editor-Kenneth Schaschl, Circ. Mgr.-Norma Dietz, Art Dir.-Bill Spaqnuolo
Editorial Description: Communication between the Michigan Aeronautics Commission and the pilots in the state, on policy, legislation, safety, and other matters.
General Info: Bi-monthly, Letrpr. press, 8 pages, 2 Color, Coated
Circulation: Total-1,700
Printing Co: Speaker-Hines & Thomas, Inc., 3366 Remy Dr, Lansing, MI 48906-2727 Tel # (517) 321-0740

Military Aircraft Forecast
See: MILITARY & NAVAL

Military Aircraft Inventory Database License
See: MILITARY & NAVAL

Missile Forecast — *Business, Consumer*

Publishing Co: Forecast International/DMS, Inc., 22 Commerce Rd., Newtown, CT 06470-1643; Title Tel # (203) 426-0800 Title Fax # (203) 426-1964
Editorial Description: Contains reports on all DOD & rockets, missiles & spacecraft under development or in production.
General Info: Yr. Est. 1960, Monthly, Trim Size-8.8 x 11, Offset press, 1,200 pages, Color-cover, Matte, Saddle-stitched, Looseleaf
Subscriptions: Indv. $1,295
List Rental: Rents Lists

Montana and the Sky — *Business, Association*

Publishing Co: Aeronautics Div., PO Box 5178, Helena, MT 59604-5178; Title Tel # (406) 444-2506
Personnel: Editor-Debbie Alke
Editorial Description: To promote, encourage and inform those interested in aeronautics in the state of Montana.
General Info: Yr. Est. 1949, Monthly, Trim Size-8½ x 11, Offset press, 8 pages, No Color
Subscriptions: Indv. $5
Circulation: Total-3,200

Monthly Gram

Publishing Co: Experimental Aircraft Association, Inc., EAA Aviation Center, 3000 Poberezny Rd., Oshkosh, WI 54903-3086; Title Tel # (414) 426-4800 Title Fax # (414) 426-4828
Personnel: Editor-Stephanie Brown
General Info: Yr. Est. 1987, Monthly, Trim Size-8½ x 11, 4 pages, No Color
Acquistions: Publication Bought
Circulation: Total-1,500

Museum of Flight News
See: MUSEUM PUBLICATIONS

Museum Newsletter
See: MUSEUM PUBLICATIONS

NASA STI Bulletin — *Business, Association*

Publishing Co: Sponsor-RMS Assocs., NASA Center for AeroSpace Information, 800 Elkridge Landing Road, Linthicum Heights, MD 21090-2934 Tel # (301) 621-0390 Fax # (301) 621-0134; Title Tel # (301) 621-0105
Personnel: Editor-Robert Ferris
Editorial Description: Covers NASA events, also search strategies for NASA RECONselect.
General Info: (Formerly NASA STI-Recon Bulletin & Tech Info News), Yr. Est. 1970, Semi-monthly, Trim Size-8½ x 11, Web press, 4 pages, Matte
Subscriptions: Free
Circulation: (100% controlled), Total-8,200

NBAA Digest — *Business, Association*

Publishing Co: National Business Aircraft Association, 1200 18th St. NW, Ste. 400, Washington, DC 20036-2506; Title Tel # (202) 783-9000 Title Fax # (202) 331-8364
Personnel: Publisher, Editor, Circ. Mgr.-Cassandra Bosco
Editorial Description: Business aviation information on legislative and regulatory activity.
General Info: (Formerly Business Aviation Digest), Yr. Est. 1988, Semi-monthly, Trim Size-8½ x 11, Desktop press, 6 pages, 2 Color
Subscriptions: Free With Membership
Circulation: Total-15,000
Printing Co: Corporate Press, 403 Brightseat Rd., Landover, MD 20785-4706 Tel # (301) 499-9200, Fax # (301) 499-5435

NBAA Maintenance Operation Bulletin — *Business*

Publishing Co: National Business Aviation Assn., 1200 18th St., NW, Washington, DC 20036-2506; Title Tel # (202) 783-9000
Personnel: Editor-William Stine, II
Editorial Description: Operational flight information for intl. business aircraft crews.
General Info: Yr. Est. 1982, Quarterly, 16 pages, No Color, Coated, Saddle-stitched
Printing Co: Corporate Press, 403 Brightseat Rd., Landover, MD 20785-4706 Tel # (301) 499-9200, Fax # (301) 499-5435

NTSB Reporter — *Business*

Publishing Co: Peter Katz Productions, PO Box 831, White Plains, NY 10602-0831; Title Tel # (914) 949-7443
Personnel: Publisher, Editor-Peter Katz
Editorial Description: Aviation safety and accident monthly update.
General Info: Yr. Est. 1981, Monthly, Trim Size-8½ x 11, Sheetfed press, ISSN: 0745-9874, No Color, Newsprint, Saddle-stitched
Subscriptions: Indv. $39, Can. $49, For. $59, $3/copy
Circulation: Total-25,000

National Transportation Safety Board Digest Service — *Business*

Publishing Co: Hawkins Publishing Co., Inc., 1207 B Central Avenue, Box 480, Mayo, MD 21106; Title Tel # (410) 798-1677 Title Fax # (410) 798-1098
Personnel: Editor-C.R. Eyler
Editorial Description: A loose-leaf indexed-digested-analysis of the decisions of the National Transportation Safety Board and its predecssor (the C.A.B.), dealing with aviation safety enforcement matters.
General Info: Yr. Est. 1972, Monthly, Trim Size-8½ x 11, Sheetfed press, No Color, Matte, Looseleaf
Subscriptions: $320/copy
Circulation: Total-150

Navigator Newsletter — *Association*

Publishing Co: Aeronautical Navigator Assn., 640 Brumbaugh Dr, New Carlisle, OH 45344-2523; Title Tel # (513) 849-6082
General Info: Yr. Est. 1974, Monthly

Negro Airmen International Newsletter — *Association*

Publishing Co: Negro Airmen International, Inc., PO Box 1340, Tuskegee Institute, AL 36087-1340; Title Tel # (205) 727-0721
Personnel: Publisher-Solomon Hamilton, Editor-Leslie Morris, Production Mgr.-Barbara Childs
General Info: Yr. Est. 1967, Monthly, 10 pages, No Color, Newsprint
Circulation: Total-1,000
Advertising: Inquire for rates.
Printing Co: McCray Printing, 203 N Main St, Tuskegee, AL 36083-1721 Tel # (205) 727-7656

New Jersey Aviation News — *Consumer*

Publishing Co: NJDOT-Office of Aviation, 1035 Parkway Ave., CN 610, Trenton, NJ 08625-0610 Tel # (609) 530-2900; Title Tel # (609) 530-2914 Title Fax # (609) 530-5719
Personnel: Editor-Emmett O'Hare, Art Dir.-Gerald Guarnieri
Editorial Description: Flight safety information. Current state legislation, policy, & aviation news.
General Info: (Formerly New Jersey Flight Log), Yr. Est. 1962, Quarterly, Trim Size-8 x 11, Sheetfed press, 4 pages, No Color
Circulation: (100% controlled), Total-2,000

News from ACAP — *Association*

Publishing Co: Aviation Consumer Action Project, PO Box 19029, Washington, DC 20036-9029; Title Tel # (202) 293-9142
Editorial Description: Current measures for reform of airline practices.
General Info: Quarterly, 6 pages
Subscriptions: Indv. $15

Newsline
See: TRAFFIC & TRANSPORTATION

PAMA News
Business, Association CPM: $130

Publishing Co: Professional Aviation Maintenance Association, 500 Northwest Plaza, Suite 1016, Saint Ann, MO 63074-2225; Title Tel # (301) 424-6757
Personnel: Publisher, Editor-Peter Rohrbach, Adv. Dir.-Jan Grumke
Editorial Description: Professional pub. for members in Aviation maintenance.
General Info: Yr. Est. 1978, Monthly, Trim Size-8½ x 11, Web press, 16 pages, ISSN: 0896-8926, 5% ads, 2 Color, Coated, Saddle-stitched
Subscriptions: Indv. $35, Free With Membership
Circulation: Total-6,500
Advertising: $850.

PIREPS
Association

Publishing Co: Nebraska Department of Aeronautics, PO Box 82088, Lincoln, NE 68501-2088; Title Tel # (402) 471-2371 Title Fax # (402) 471-2906
Editorial Description: New aviation developments, rules & regulations, safety, announcements of events & available materials.
General Info: Yr. Est. 1946, Monthly, Trim Size-8½ x 11, Offset press, 4 pages, No Color
Subscriptions: Free
Circulation: (100% controlled), Total-6,000

Palmetto Aviation
Association

Publishing Co: South Carolina Aeronautics Commission, PO Box 280068, Columbia, SC 29220-0068; Title Tel # (803) 822-5400
Personnel: Editor-Helen Munnerlyn
Editorial Description: Covers news interesting to and concerning aviators; emphasis on South Carolina.
General Info: (Formerly South Carolina Aviation Newsletter), Yr. Est. 1947, Monthly, Trim Size-8½ x 11, Letrpr. press, 8 pages, 2 Color, Newsprint
Acquistions: Publication Bought
Circulation: (100% controlled)
Printing Co: Dependable Printing Co., 5349 46th Ave, Hyattsville, MD 20781-2309 Tel # (301) 779-9200

Performance Materials
Business

Publishing Co: Garrett Communications, 210 North Adams Street, Suite 1000, Rockville, MD 20850 Tel # (301) 738-7927 Fax # (301) 738-7896; Title Tel # (415) 896-5988 Title Fax # (415) 896-5989
Personnel: Publisher-Thomas Woodall, Editor-Richard Piellisch
Editorial Description: Information on composites, advanced ceramics, resins, and fibers.
General Info: Yr. Est. 1987, Bi-weekly, ISSN: 0888-3467, Ind/Abs/Online: NewsNet
Subscriptions: Indv. $577, For. $597, $20/copy
Advertising: Inquire for rates. Accepts Inserts.
List Rental: List Management Co.: Performance Marketing, P.O Box 32699, Laughlin, NV 89028 Tel # (702) 299-0011, Fax # (702) 299-0224

Plane Talk
Consumer

Publishing Co: Southwest Airlines, PO Box 36662, Southwest Company Club, Dallas, TX 75235-1662; Title Tel # (214) 263-1717
Personnel: Mktg. Dir.-Susan Parker
Editorial Description: Frequent traveler newsletter for Southwest Airlines passengers.
General Info: Quarterly

Poly Probe
See: METALS & METALWORKING

RUPA Newsletter
Association

Publishing Co: Retired United Pilots Association, 218 Highland Ave, Piedmont, CA 94611-3710
Editorial Description: Commentaries by and for retired United pilots and dispatchers.
General Info: Bi-monthly, Trim Size-5½ x 8½, 60 pages

Radar Forecast
Business, Consumer

Publishing Co: Forecast International/DMS, Inc., 22 Commerce Rd., Newtown, CT 06470-1643; Title Tel # (203) 426-0800 Title Fax # (203) 426-1964
Personnel: Editor-K. Chaisson
Editorial Description: Covers technology, airborne, sea-based, ground-based radar systems and sonar systems.
General Info: Monthly, No Color, Looseleaf
Subscriptions: Indv. $1,295
List Rental: Rents Lists

Robot Explorer
See: COMPUTERS & AUTOMATION

Rockwell News
See: HOUSE ORGANS

Rotor Breeze
Consumer

Publishing Co: Bell Helicopter Textron, Inc., 600 E Hurst St, Hurst, TX 76053 Tel # (817) 280-2011; Title Tel # (817) 280-3847
Personnel: Editor-Susan Green
Editorial Description: Briefs readers on the commercial helicopter business at Bell Helicopter Textron, Inc.
General Info: Yr. Est. 1951, Bi-monthly, Trim Size-8½ x 11, 8 pages, 2 Color
Circulation: Total-4,000
Printing Co: Global Group, Inc., 4901 N Beach St, Fort Worth, TX 76137-3404 Tel # (817) 831-2631

Rotornews

Publishing Co: Rotornews, 1333 H St NW Ste 410, Washington, DC 20005-4707; Title Tel # (202) 898-8300
Personnel: Editor-Keith Stafford
General Info: Yr. Est. 1948, Bi-monthly, 8 pages
Circulation: Total-2,100

Rudder Flutter
Business, Consumer

Publishing Co: Division of Aeronautics, PO Box 7129, Boise, ID 83707-1129; Title Tel # (208) 334-8775 Title Fax # (208) 334-8789
Editorial Description: Schedule of events, safety articles, legislation, articles of interest to the flying public.
General Info: (Formerly Idaho Aviation Report), Quarterly, Trim Size-8½ x 11, Desktop press, 8 pages, 2 Color
Subscriptions: Free With Membership
Circulation: Total-3,300

Russia Desk
Consumer

Publishing Co: Commerce Publishing International, 4001 9th St N Suite 904, Arlington, VA 22203-1962 Tel # (703) 524-7750 Fax # (703) 524-1630
Personnel: Publisher-Ed Hazelwood
Editorial Description: Covers the aviation and aerospace industry in the former Soviet Union and Eastern Europe.
General Info: Yr. Est. 1993, Bi-weekly, 8 pages, ISSN: 1068-7963
Subscriptions: Indv. $695
Circulation: Readership-450
Advertising: $800. Accepts Inserts.

Russian Tech Briefs
Business

Publishing Co: Associated Business Publications Co., Ltd., 41 E. 42nd St., Ste. 921, New York, NY 10017-5301 Fax # (212) 986-7864; Title Tel # (212) 490-3999
Editorial Description: For the Russian Space Agency.
General Info: Yr. Est. 1994, Monthly, Trim Size-8½ x 11, 16 pages
Subscriptions: Indv. $195

SSI Update

Publishing Co: Space Studies Institute, PO Box 82, Princeton, NJ 08542-0082; Title Tel # (609) 921-0377
Personnel: Editor-Bettie Greber
General Info: Yr. Est. 1977, Bi-monthly
Circulation: Total-5,000

Sea-Tac Forum
See: TRAFFIC & TRANSPORTATION

Select Hostile Actions Against Civil Aviation
See: LAW ENFORCEMENT & PENOLOGY

Sermatech Review
See: POWER & POWER PLANTS

Space Age Times
Association CPM: $75

Publishing Co: U.S. Space Education Assn., Global Operations Center, 231 School Lane, Box 249, Rheems, PA 17570-0249; Title Tel # (717) 367-3265 Title Fax # (717) 367-5196
Personnel: Publisher-Robert Preston, Editor-Stephen Cobaugh
Editorial Description: Devoted to worldwide space exploration news for professionals & lay people.
General Info: (Formerly LCSEA Takes Up Space), Yr. Est. 1974, Bi-monthly, Sheetfed press, 50 pages, ISSN: 0738-0968, 1% ads, No Color, Newsprint
Subscriptions: Indv. $24, For. $30, $4/copy
Acquistions: Publication Bought
Circulation: Total-1,000
Advertising: $75.

Space Autograph News
Consumer CPM: $500

Publishing Co: Michael E. Johnson, 862 Thomas Ave, San Diego, CA 92109-3940; Title Tel # (619) 483-8632
Personnel: Publisher-Michael E. Johnson
Editorial Description: Newsletter designed for people who collect the autographs of astronauts and cosmonauts, covering who's who and why, authenticity, addresses, availability, values, fakes and forgeries, and market trends.
General Info: Yr. Est. 1993, Bi-monthly, Trim Size-8½ x 11, Desktop press, 8 pages, ISSN: 1069-6016
Subscriptions: Indv. $15, Can. $20, For. $20, $3/copy
Circulation: Total-200
Advertising: $100.

Space Business News
Business

Publishing Co: Phillips Business Information, Inc., 1201 Seven Locks Rd., Ste 300, Potomac, MD 20854-2958 Tel # (301) 340-1520 Fax # (301) 424-4297
Personnel: Publisher-Harry Baisden, Editor-Melinda Gipson, Circ. Mgr.-Kathy Thorne, Production Mgr.-Steve Baisden, Promotion Dir.-Katrine Hellaver
Editorial Description: Business, political & trends in the commercial space industry.
General Info: (Formerly SpaceCommerceWeek; Space Exploration Tech; SpaceStation News), Bi-weekly, Web press, 8 pages, ISSN: 0738-9884, Ind/Abs/Online: NewsNet, DIALOG
Subscriptions: Indv. $595, For. $502, $19/copy
Acquistions: Publication Bought
List Rental: Rents Lists

Space Calendar   *Business*

Publishing Co: Space Age Publishing Company, 75-5751 Kuakini Hwy., Ste. 209, Kailua-Kona, HI 96740-1705; Title Fax # (808) 326-2014 Title Fax # (808) 326-1825
Personnel: Publisher, Editor-Steve Durst
Editorial Description: Publication about the space industry & space sciences.
General Info: Yr. Est. 1982, Weekly, Trim Size-8½ x 11, Web press, 8 pages, ISSN: 0741-1731, No Color, Coated
Subscriptions: Indv. $79, Inst. $139, $3/copy
Circulation: Total-1,000
List Rental: Rents Lists

Space Fax Daily   *Business*

Publishing Co: Space Age Publishing Company, 75-5751 Kuakini Hwy., Ste. 209, Kailua-Kona, HI 96740-1705; Title Tel # (408) 996-9210 Title Fax # (408) 996-2125
Personnel: Publisher, Editor-Steve Durst
General Info: (Formerly Space Daily), Yr. Est. 1984, Daily, Trim Size-8½ x 14, Mimeo press, 1 pages, ISSN: 1048-2652, Ind/Abs/Online: NewsNet, No Color, Newsprint
Subscriptions: Indv. $195, Inst. $295
Advertising: Inquire for rates.

Space Letter   *Business*

Publishing Co: Callahan Pubs., PO Box 1173, McLean, VA 22101-1173; Title Tel # (703) 356-1925 Title Fax # (703) 356-9614
Personnel: Publisher, Editor-Vincent F. Callahan, Jr.
Editorial Description: Contract and procurement data for contractors and subcontractors to National Aeronautics and Space Administration.
General Info: Yr. Est. 1958, Semi-monthly, Trim Size-8½ x 11, Offset press, 8 pages, ISSN: 0038-6278, No Color
Subscriptions: Indv. $190, For. $200

Space Shuttle Orbiter Newsletter

Publishing Co: Ramey Aerospace, PO Box 39, Carmel Valley, CA 93924-0039; Title Tel # (408) 655-2772 Title Fax # (408) 655-4858
Personnel: Publisher-Tom Ramey
Editorial Description: Comprehensive indepth technical coverage of vehicles, crews, missions, experiments & payloads. Short courses on Orbiter aerodynamics, computers, guidance naviagaton, control & other major systems.
General Info: Yr. Est. 1985, Monthly, Trim Size-8½ x 11, Sheetfed press, 32 pages, ISSN: 0882-0902, 2 Color, Matte, Saddle-stitched
Subscriptions: Indv. $55, Can. $55, For. $90
Acquistions: Publication Bought

Space Systems Forecast   *Business, Consumer*

Publishing Co: Forecast International/DMS, Inc., 22 Commerce Rd., Newtown, CT 06470-1643; Title Tel # (203) 426-0800 Title Fax # (203) 426-1964
Editorial Description: Info on major U.S. and non-U. S. space systems.
General Info: Monthly, No Color, Looseleaf
Subscriptions: Indv. $1,295
List Rental: Rents Lists

Space Trends Update   *Business*

Publishing Co: QW Communications, Co., PO Box 6591, Concord, NH 03303-6591; Title Tel # (603) 648-2629
General Info: (Formerly Space Information Guidebook), Yr. Est. 1984, 24x/yr.
Subscriptions: Indv. $249
Circulation: Total-18,275
List Rental: Actives: $100/M

Spacewatch   *Business*   CPM: $516

Publishing Co: U.S. Space Foundation, 2860 S Circle Dr Ste 2301, Colorado Springs, CO 80906-4184; Title Tel # (719) 576-8000 Title Fax # (719) 576-8801
Personnel: Publisher-Richard MacLeod, Editor-Laurie Johnson, Promotion Dir.-Jack Flannery
Editorial Description: A concise synopsis of current civil, military and commercial space activities and emerging policy.
General Info: Yr. Est. 1984, Monthly, Trim Size-8½ x 11, Web press, 20 pages, 2 Color, Coated, Saddle-stitched
Subscriptions: Free With Membership
Acquistions: Publication Bought
Circulation: Total-1,550
Advertising: $800.
Printing Co: Gowdy-Printcraft Press Inc., 22 N Sierra Madre St, Colorado Springs, CO 80903-3311 Tel # (719) 634-1593

Sport Marketry   *Association*

Publishing Co: Natl. Assn of Rocketry, 1311 Edgewood Dr, Altoona, WI 54720-2528 Tel # (715) 834-8074
Personnel: Editor-Steve Weaver
Editorial Description: Photos, plans, & articles dealing with the hobby of model rocketry.
General Info: (Formerly American Space Modeling), Yr. Est. 1958, Monthly, Trim Size-8½ x 11, Sheetfed press, 20 pages, ISSN: 0190-1060, 2% ads, 4 Color, Coated
Subscriptions: Indv. $15, $2/copy
Circulation: Total-6,000

Texas Aeronautics Commission Newsletter   *Association*

Publishing Co: Texas Aeronautics Commission, 125 E. 11th St., Austin, TX 78701-2409; Title Tel # (512) 416-4500
Personnel: Editor-Nona Gold
Editorial Description: Items of interest to pilots, as well as news of current activities of the Commission.
General Info: Yr. Est. 1950, Quarterly, Trim Size-8½ x 14, Sheetfed press, 2 pages, No Color
Circulation: (100% controlled), Total-2,000

Travel Safety Alert   *Consumer, Association*

Publishing Co: International Airline Passenger Association, 5335 Wisconsin Ave NW Ste 440, Washington, DC 20015-2030 Tel # (202) 686-2870
Editorial Description: Covers airline passenger safety issues.
General Info: Bi-monthly

USAir Frequent Traveler Program News   *Consumer*

Publishing Co: USAir Frequent Traveler Program, Box 5, Winston-Salem, NC 27102-0005
Editorial Description: News to all USAir frequent fliers about services and offers.
General Info: Bi-monthly, Trim Size-8½ x 11, 4 pages, 4 Color

United States Space Law: Natl. & Intl. Regulation
See: LAW

Utah Aviation News

Publishing Co: State Aeronautics Commission, 135 N 2400 W, Salt Lake City, UT 84116-2931; Title Tel # (801) 328-2066

Warships Forecast   *Business*

Publishing Co: Forecast International/DMS, Inc., 22 Commerce Rd., Newtown, CT 06470-1643; Title Tel # (203) 426-0800 Title Fax # (203) 426-1964
Editorial Description: Reports on major ship, programs being developed or produced by DOD.
General Info: Monthly, Looseleaf
Subscriptions: Indv. $1,295
List Rental: Rents Lists

Washington Remote Sensing Letter   *Business, Consumer*

Publishing Co: Murray Felsher, 1057-B Natl. Press Bldg., Washington, DC 20045; Title Tel # (202) 393-3640 Title Fax # (202) 393-3640
Personnel: Publisher, Editor-Murray Felsher
Editorial Description: All applications of photography of the earth from space, including monitoring, & surveillance by satellite, including US & foreign govt. activities, programs, & solicitations.
General Info: Yr. Est. 1981, Semi-monthly, Offset press, 4 pages, ISSN: 0739-6538, 2 Color, Newsprint
Subscriptions: Indv. $410, Inst. $410, Can. $410, For. $500

World Aerospace & Defense Intelligence   *Business*

Publishing Co: Forecast International/DMS, Inc., 22 Commerce Rd., Newtown, CT 06470-1643; Title Tel # (203) 426-0800 Title Fax # (203) 426-1964
Personnel: Publisher-Edward Nebinger, Editor-Ray Peterson, Adv. Dir.-Inez Johnson
Editorial Description: Authoritative source for world aerospace developments.
General Info: (Formerly World Aerospace Weekly), Yr. Est. 1981, Weekly, Trim Size-11 x 8.50, Sheetfed press, 20 pages, Ind/Abs/Online: DIALOG, 2 Color, Newsprint
Subscriptions: Indv. $495
List Rental: Rents Lists

World Airline Maintenance Forecast   *Business*

Publishing Co: Forecast International/DMS, Inc., 22 Commerce Rd., Newtown, CT 06470-1643 Fax # (203) 426-1964; Title Tel # (203) 426-0800 Title Fax # (203) 426-4262
General Info: Quarterly, Looseleaf
Subscriptions: Indv. $2,495

World Airline News   *Business*

Publishing Co: Phillips Business Information, Inc., 1201 Seven Locks Rd., Ste 300, Potomac, MD 20854-2958 Tel # (301) 340-1520 Fax # (301) 424-4297
Personnel: Sales Mgr.-Susan Incarnato
Editorial Description: Covers the international airline industry.
General Info: Weekly, ISSN: 1059-4183
Subscriptions: Indv. $595, For. $595
List Rental: Rents Lists

World Commerical Aircraft/Engines Orders & Options *Business*

Publishing Co: Forecast International/DMS, Inc., 22 Commerce Rd., Newtown, CT 06470-1643; Title Tel # (203) 426-0800 Title Fax # (203) 426-1964
General Info: Quarterly, Looseleaf
Subscriptions: Indv. $945
List Rental: Rents Lists

World Power Systems Intelligence *Business, Consumer*

Publishing Co: Forecast International/DMS, Inc., 22 Commerce Rd., Newtown, CT 06470-1643; Title Tel # (203) 426-0800 Title Fax # (203) 426-1964
Editorial Description: Covers weekly developments, contracts, innovations, personnel & other news of the worldwide gas turbine engine market.
General Info: (Formerly Power Letter), Yr. Est. 1979, Bi-weekly, Ind/Abs/Online: DIALOG, No Color
Subscriptions: Indv. $395
List Rental: Rents Lists

World Retrofit & Modernization Forecast Airborne Systems

Publishing Co: Forecast International/DMS, Inc., 22 Commerce Rd., Newtown, CT 06470-1643; Title Tel # (203) 426-0800 Title Fax # (203) 426-1964
Editorial Description: Using our platform-oriented analysis, retrofit & modernizations programs are identified. This service covers planned anticipated & speculative programs which will be needed to keep aircraft operational through 2003. Updated monthly.
General Info: (Formerly Intl. Defense Budgets), Monthly, Looseleaf
Subscriptions: Indv. $1,700

Wright Flyer

Publishing Co: First Flight Society, PO Box 1903, Kitty Hawk, NC 27949-1903; Title Tel # (919) 441-3761
Personnel: Editor-Gene O'Bleness
General Info: Quarterly
Circulation: Total-650

Wyoming Aviation News

Publishing Co: Wyoming Department of Transportation, Aeronautics Division Box 1708, Cheyenne, WY 82002-0001; Title Tel # (307) 777-4880
Personnel: Editor-Edward Pew
General Info: Yr. Est. 1958, Quarterly, 8 pages
Circulation: Total-800

AFRICAN-AMERICAN INTEREST

African-American Family History Assn. Newsletter
See: GENEALOGY

African-American Traveler
See: TRAVEL

Africana Libraries Newsletter
See: LIBRARY

Best of Health
See: HEALTH

Black Camera
See: FILM

Black Child Advocate
See: CHILDREN

Black History News & Notes
See: HISTORY

Black Literary Players
See: BOOKS & BOOK TRADE

Black Student Union Newsletter
See: COLLEGE STUDENT

Black Vet
See: MILITARY & NAVAL

Book Newsletter & Catalog
See: BOOKS & BOOK TRADE

CBMR Digest
See: MUSIC & MUSIC TRADES

Caribbean Newsletter
See: INTERNATIONAL AFFAIRS

Civil Rights/State Capitals
See: CIVIL RIGHTS

Creative Escapes
See: HEALTH

Education Program Calendar
See: MUSEUM PUBLICATIONS

Fight Back

Publishing Co: Attica Brigade of Richmond College, Stuyvesant Pl., Staten Island, NY 10301
Editorial Description: Black underground.
General Info: Yr. Est. 1974, Monthly

Focus
See: POLITICS

IBW Monthly Report

Publishing Co: Institute of the Black World, 1275 Capitol Ave SW, Atlanta, GA 30315-2707; Title Tel # (404) 330-4120
Personnel: Editor-Betty Chaney
Editorial Description: Explores issues of importance to the African American community.
General Info: Yr. Est. 1971, Monthly
Circulation: Total-6,300

Interracial Club of Buffalo Newsletter
See: ETHNIC

JULUKA Newsletter
See: ETHNIC

Lead Belly Letter
See: MUSIC & MUSIC TRADES

Lion
See: COLLEGE ALUMNI

Mamaroots
See: WOMEN'S

Minorities in Business Insider
See: BUSINESS & INDUSTRY

Morehouse Update
See: COLLEGE STUDENT

Multicultural Publishing and Education Council Newsletter
See: BOOKS & BOOK TRADE

NCBL Notes
See: LAW

NOMMO; Power of the Word
See: ETHNIC

Negro Airmen International Newsletter
See: AERONAUTICS/ASTRONAUTICS

News Plus
See: ACCOUNTING

Newsletter of the Afro-American Religious History Group
See: RELIGIOUS & THEOLOGICAL

Nubian Exchange News *Business*

Publishing Co: Nubian Exchange, 154 Patrick St. #175, Vienna, VA 22182
Personnel: Publisher-Claudette Brown
Editorial Description: The newsletter for and about the African-American business community, showcasing today's business and trends.
General Info: Quarterly, Trim Size-8½ x 11, 8 pages, No Color
Subscriptions: Indv. $15, For. $18
Circulation: Total-1,500

Operation Big Vote Newsletter
See: GOVERNMENT

Oracle
See: CLUBS

Overground
See: APPAREL & ACCESSORIES

Pepper Bird Pathways
See: TRAVEL

Program and Legislative Action
See: POLITICS

Psych Discourse
  See: PSYCHOLOGY

Responsibility
  See: WOMEN'S

Routes
  See: ENTERTAINMENT

Sisterhood Newsletter
  See: WOMEN'S

Viking Import House, Inc.
  See: COLLECTIBLES

Voices in Black Studies
  See: EDUCATION

AGRICULTURAL SUPPLIES

AgriBioScan — Business

Publishing Co: Oryx Press, The, 4041 N. Central Ave., Ste. 700, Indian School Rd., Phoenix, AZ 85012-3397; Title Tel # (602) 265-2651 Title Fax # (602) 265-6250
Editorial Description: Provides hard facts, such as locations & R&D personnel, as well as data on finances, partnerships, & products awaiting FDA approval. Successfully meets the demand for data on those companies specifically involved in plant & seed genetic engineering, veterinary medicine, animal genetic engineering, food processing, bio-pesticides, & aquaculture.
General Info: Yr. Est. 1995, Tri-annually, Trim Size-8$\frac{1}{2}$ x 11, 320 pages, ISSN: 1079-9060
Subscriptions: Indv. $395, For. $445

Chek-Chart Tractor Digest

Publishing Co: H.M. Gousha, Simon & Schuster, Inc., 320 Soquel Way, Sunnyvale, CA 94086-4101; Title Tel # (408) 296-1060
Personnel: Editor-Terry Collings
General Info: Yr. Est. 1982, Quarterly, 2 pages
Subscriptions: Indv. $9

Fertilizer Markets — Business

Publishing Co: CRU International, 7500 Greenway Center Dr., Suite 480, Greenbelt, MD 20770-4430 Tel # (301) 441-8997 Fax # (301) 441-9091; Title Tel # (301) 441-4724 Title Fax # (301) 441-4726
General Info: Yr. Est. 1990, Weekly, ISSN: 1051-9130
Subscriptions: Indv. $849, For. $849

In Good Tilth
  See: AGRICULTURE

Land Letter

Publishing Co: Huber Farm Management, PO Box 1616, Greenville, MS 38702-1616; Title Tel # (601) 335-0792
Personnel: Editor-Marty Tubbs
General Info: Bi-monthly, Desktop press, 4 pages, No Color, Newsprint
Printing Co: Burford Bros., 726 Seventh Broadway, Greenville, MS 38701 Tel # (601) 332-5429

Nebraska Pest Control Association Newsletter — Business, Association

Publishing Co: Nebraska State Pest Control Assn., Inc., 1111 Lincoln Mall, Ste. 308, Lincoln, NE 68508-2882 Tel # (402) 476-1525; Title Tel # (402) 476-1528 Title Fax # (402) 476-1259
Personnel: Publisher, Circ. Mgr.-Robert Anderson, Production Mgr.-Alice Licht, Adv. Dir.-Rebecca Barker
Editorial Description: Confidential membership newsletter for the Nebraska State Pest Control Association.
General Info: Yr. Est. 1992, Quarterly, Trim Size-8$\frac{1}{2}$ x 11, Other press, 10 pages, No Color, Matte, Other
Subscriptions: Free With Membership
Advertising: $200.
List Rental: Rents Lists

Prairie Agricultural Machinery Institute, Evaluation Report — Scholarly, Association

Publishing Co: Prairie Agricultural Machinery Institute, Box 1900, Humboldt, SK S0K 2A0 Canada; Title Tel # (306) 682-2555 Title Fax # (306) 682-5080
Personnel: Circ. Mgr.-Barrie Broad, Editor, Product Mgr.-Dan Dyck
Editorial Description: Contractual design & testing services available. Latest information on research and agricultural innovation projects on the prairies.
General Info: Yr. Est. 1974, Semi-annually, Trim Size-8$\frac{1}{2}$ x 11, Desktop press, 6 pages, ISSN: 0383-0445, Matte, Saddle-stitched, Looseleaf
Subscriptions: Indv. $20, Can. $10, For. $25, $1/copy
Advertising: Accepts Inserts.

Representative — Business

Publishing Co: Agricultural & Industrial Mfgs. Representatives Assn. (AIMRA, 5818 Reeds Rd, Mission, KS 66202-2740; Title Tel # (913) 262-0317
Personnel: Editor-Betchie Bistrom
Editorial Description: Newsletter providing marketing information for representatives of agricultural & industrial manufacturers.
General Info: Yr. Est. 1970, Monthly
Circulation: Total-300

Shortliner — Association

Publishing Co: Farm Equipment Mfrs. Assn., 243 N. Lindbergh, St. Louis, MO 63141-7851; Title Tel # (314) 991-0702
Personnel: Editor-Robert Schnell
Editorial Description: A newsletter published for FEMA members about Shortline Industry happenings.
General Info: Yr. Est. 1957, Bi-weekly, Trim Size-8$\frac{1}{2}$ x 11, Sheetfed press, 8 pages, No Color, Newsprint, Perfect bound
Circulation: Total-1,000

TIPS — Association

Publishing Co: Farm Equipment Wholesalers Assn. (FEWA), 611 Southgate Ave., Iowa City, IA 52240-4443; Title Tel # (319) 354-5156 Title Fax # (319) 354-5157
General Info: Yr. Est. 1945, Monthly
Subscriptions: Free With Membership

Widespread

Publishing Co: Farm Equipment Dealers Assn. of Alberta-BC, #2921, 15th St., NE, Calgary, AB T2E 7L8 Canada; Title Tel # (403) 250-7581 Title Fax # (403) 291-5138
Personnel: Publisher, Editor, Art Dir.-William Lipsey, Production Mgr., Adv. Dir., Promotion Dir.-Carol Wieland
General Info: Yr. Est. 1966, Monthly, Trim Size-8$\frac{1}{2}$ x 11, Sheetfed press, 20 pages, 1% ads, 2 Color, Coated
Circulation: Total-875
Advertising: Inquire for rates. Accepts Inserts.

AGRICULTURE

4-H Child Care
  See: CHILDREN

4-H Club News

Publishing Co: Nova Scotia Department of Agriculture, Box 550, Truro, NS B2N 2E3 Canada Fax # (902) 895-7693; Title Tel # (902) 893-6585
Personnel: Editor, Adv. Dir.-Elizabeth Crouse
General Info: Quarterly, Trim Size-8$\frac{1}{2}$ x 11, 8 pages, 2 Color
Circulation: Total-8,000

AALS Newsletter — Association

Publishing Co: Association for Arid Land Studies, Texas Tech. University, Box 41036, Lubbock, TX 79409-1036; Title Tel # (806) 742-2218 Title Fax # (806) 742-1954
Personnel: Editor-Idris Traylor
Editorial Description: Professional, scholarly newsletter reporting activities of AALS.
General Info: Yr. Est. 1978, Annually, No Color
Subscriptions: Free With Membership
Circulation: (100% controlled), Total-250

AAPA Bulletin

Publishing Co: American Alfalfa Processors Association, 9948 Santa Fe Dr., SE, Overland Park, KS 66212-4744; Title Tel # (913) 648-6800
Personnel: Editor-Wanda Cobb
Editorial Description: Alfalfa processors & suppliers to alfalfa processing industry.
General Info: (Formerly American Dehydrators Assn. Bulletin), Yr. Est. 1941, Weekly, Trim Size-8$\frac{1}{2}$ x 11, 4 pages, No Color
Circulation: Total-220

AASCO Newsletter — Association

Publishing Co: Michigan Dept. of Agriculture, PO Box 30017, Lansing, MI 48909-7517 Tel # (517) 373-1087; Title Tel # (503) 378-3774
Personnel: Editor-Ken Rauscher
Editorial Description: Official paper of U.S. federal and state seed laws and Canadian seed laws.
General Info: (Formerly Association of American Seed Control Officials Bulletin), Quarterly, Trim Size-8$\frac{1}{2}$ x 11, 2 pages

ACT Newsletter — Association

Publishing Co: American Assn. of Agricultural Communicators of Tomorrow, 67 Mumford Hall, 1301 W. Gregory, Urbana, IL 61801; Title Tel # (217) 333-4782
Editorial Description: For college students with professional interest in agricultural communications.
General Info: Yr. Est. 1970, Bi-monthly, Desktop press, 4 pages, No Color, Newsprint
Circulation: (100% controlled), Total-400

AFIA Safetygram
Association

Publishing Co: American Feed Industry Assn., 1501 Wilson Blvd # 1100, Arlington, VA 22209-2403; Title Tel # (703) 524-0810 Title Fax # (703) 524-1921
Personnel: Editor-Janice Clover
Editorial Description: Covers the latest in feed industry safety practices, preventative measures & government regulations.
General Info: Monthly
Subscriptions: Indv. $30

ANR Educator
See: EDUCATION

ARClight
Association

Publishing Co: Agricultural Relations Council (ARC), 1629 K St NW Ste 1100, Washington, DC 20006-1602; Title Tel # (202) 785-6710
Personnel: Editor-Paul Weller
Editorial Description: Newsletter of interest to ARC members who are involved in agricultural public relations.
General Info: Monthly
Circulation: Total-300

ARI Newsletter
Business, Association

Publishing Co: Agricultural Research Institute, 9650 Rockville Pike, Bethesda, MD 20814-3998; Title Tel # (301) 530-7122
Personnel: Publisher, Editor-Stan Cath
Editorial Description: Reports activities of ARI committees/panels & relevant agricultural research matters.
General Info: Bi-monthly, Trim Size-8½ x 11, Offset press, 6 pages, No Color, Newsprint
Subscriptions: Indv. $12
Circulation: Total-250
Printing Co: FCS Communications Corp., 255 N Stonestreet Ave, Rockville, MD 20850-1654 Tel # (301) 762-1475

Abundant Life Seed Foundation Newsletter
See: GARDENING & HORTICULTURE

Ag Executive
Business

Publishing Co: Ag Executive, Inc., 115 E. Twyman, PO Box 180, Bushnell, IL 61422; Title Tel # (309) 772-2168 Title Fax # (309) 772-2167
Personnel: Publisher, Editor-Darrell L. Dunteman
Editorial Description: Issues affecting management of farming and ranching operations.
General Info: Yr. Est. 1986, Monthly, Trim Size-8½ x 11, Sheetfed press, 8 pages, ISSN: 1053-2692, 2 Color, Matte, Saddle-stitched
Subscriptions: Indv. $78
Acquistions: Publication Sold
Circulation: Readership-3,100
Advertising: Inquire for rates. Accepts Inserts.
List Rental: Actives: 3,100, $75/M, Expires: 7,800, $70/M

Ag Focus
Business

Publishing Co: Orange County Cooperative Extension, Agricultural Division, 239 Wisner Ave, Middletown, NY 10940-2400; Title Tel # (914) 343-1105 Title Fax # (914) 343-7471
Personnel: Editor-Lucy Joyce, Adv. Dir.-Dorothy Constable, Art Dir.-Jill O'Grodnick
Editorial Description: Information of interaction of interest to all commercial farms in Orange County (dairy, poultry, vegetable, horticultural and fruit crop producers).
General Info: Yr. Est. 1917, Monthly, Trim Size-8½ x 11, Offset press, 20 pages, ISSN: 0899-7535, 2 Color
Subscriptions: Indv. $10
Circulation: (100% controlled)
Advertising: Inquire for rates.

Ag Industry Watch
Business

Publishing Co: Johnson Hill Press, Inc., 1233 Janesville Ave., PO Box 803, Ft. Atkinson, WI 53538-0803 Tel # (414) 563-6388 Fax # (414) 563-1699 Parent Co.-PTN Publishing Co., Melville
Editorial Description: Covers news and events in the Ag equipment industry.
General Info: Yr. Est. 1994, Monthly
Subscriptions: Indv. $285, Can. $325, For. $325

AgBioTech Stock Letter
Business, Consumer

Publishing Co: Piedmont Venture Group, PO Box 40460, Berkeley, CA 94704-4460; Title Tel # (510) 843-1842 Title Fax # (510) 843-0901
Personnel: Editor-Jim McCamant
Editorial Description: News and information for investors regarding agricultural biotechnology.
General Info: Yr. Est. 1988, Monthly, 8 pages, ISSN: 1066-0569
Subscriptions: Indv. $165, For. $185

Ag/Innovator
Business

Publishing Co: Ag/Innovator, PO Box 1, Linn Grove, IA 51033-0001; Title Tel # (712) 296-3615
Personnel: Publisher, Editor-Grant Mangold
Editorial Description: Agricultural computing technology information.
General Info: Monthly
Subscriptions: Indv. $48
Circulation: Total-10,000

Agrarian Advocate
See: ENVIRONMENT & ECOLOGY

Agri-Naturalist
Business, Consumer

Publishing Co: Ohio State University, College of Agriculture, 204 Agriculture Admin. Bldg., 2120 Fyffe Rd., Columbus, OH 43210; Title Tel # (614) 292-0202
Personnel: Editor-Susan Jenkins
Editorial Description: Provides the college community with information about forthcoming events and activities of interest.
General Info: Yr. Est. 1893
Subscriptions: Indv. $10
Circulation: Total-2,500

Agri-News
Business, Association

Publishing Co: Iowa Agricultural Statistics, 833 Federal Bldg., 210 Walnut St., Des Moines, IA 50309-2195; Title Tel # (515) 284-4340
Personnel: Editor-Duane Skow
Editorial Description: Highlights prices of various farm products reported by the US Dept. of Agriculture Crop Reporting Board.
General Info: (Formerly Agricultural Prices), 12x/yr., 4 pages
Subscriptions: Indv. $11

AgriBioScan
See: AGRICULTURAL SUPPLIES

Agricultural & Forestry Experiment Station Bulletin

Publishing Co: West Virginia Univ. Printing Services, 112 Communications Bldg., Evansville, WV 26690; Title Tel # (304) 293-6366 Title Fax # (304) 293-3740
Editorial Description: Covers research conducted at the Experiment Station.
General Info: Yr. Est. 1888

Agricultural Chemical Newsletter
Business

Publishing Co: Thomson Publications, 1118 W Stuart Ave, Fresno, CA 93711-2039; Title Tel # (209) 435-2163
General Info: Yr. Est. 1979, Monthly, Trim Size-8½ x 11

Agricultural Credit Conditions Survey

Publishing Co: Federal Reserve Bank of Minneapolis, 250 Marquette Ave, Minneapolis, MN 55401-2117; Title Tel # (612) 340-2446 Title Fax # (612) 340-7757
Personnel: Editor-Ed Lotterman
Editorial Description: Surveys rural bankers in Ninth Federal Reserve District about agricultural credit conditions.
General Info: Yr. Est. 1968, Quarterly, Trim Size-17 x 11, Web press, 4 pages, ISSN: 0737-948X, Ind/Abs/Online: Woodrow, 2 Color, Newsprint
Subscriptions: Free
Circulation: Total-5,000

Agricultural Digest

Publishing Co: Salt Institute, 700 N Fairfax St Ste 600, Alexandria, VA 22314-2040; Title Tel # (703) 549-4648
Editorial Description: Contains information on animal nutrition, with special emphasis on salt and trace minerals.
General Info: Yr. Est. 1966, Trim Size-8½ x 11, Offset press, 4 pages, 2 Color
Circulation: Total-14,000

Agricultural Estate, Tax & Business Planning
See: TAXES

Agricultural Genetics Report

Publishing Co: Mary Ann Liebert, Inc., 1651 3rd Ave, New York, NY 10128-3649; Title Tel # (212) 289-2300
Personnel: Publisher-Mary Ann Liebert
Editorial Description: Considers the impact of biotechnology in its agriculture & food processing.
General Info: Yr. Est. 1980, Bi-monthly, Trim Size-8½ x 11, 12 pages, ISSN: 0278-9736, Newsprint, Saddle-stitched
Subscriptions: Indv. $115, Can. $148, For. $178
Circulation: Total-600

Agricultural Law Update
See: LAW

Agricultural Letter
Business

Publishing Co: Fedl. Reserve Bank of Chicago, Public Information Center, Box 834, Chicago, IL 60690; Title Tel # (312) 322-5112
Personnel: Editor-Gary Benjamin
General Info: Yr. Est. 1949, Bi-weekly, 2 pages, ISSN: 0002-1512
Circulation: Total-15,000

Agricultural Market Review
Business

Publishing Co: California Dept. of Food & Agriculture, Communications Dept., 1220 N St. Rm. 100, Sacramento, CA 95814 Tel # (916) 654-0466
Editorial Description: Weekly and yearly comparisons of commodities prices for California.
General Info: Weekly
Subscriptions: Indv. $54, Can. $54, For. $108, $5/copy

Agriculture & Food — *Business*

Publishing Co: National Technical Information Service U.S., 5285 Port Royal Rd., Springfield, VA 22161-0001 Fax # (703) 487-4630; Title Tel # (703) 487-4630
Editorial Description: Subject-specific newsletter produced weekly from NTIS scientific/technical database.
General Info: Weekly, Trim Size-8$\frac{1}{2}$ x 11, Offset press, 10 pages, ISSN: 0364-7994, No Color
Subscriptions: Indv. $135, Can. $135, For. $195

Agriculture Council of America — *Business, Association*

Publishing Co: Agriculture Council of America Education Foundation, 927 15th St NW Ste 800, Washington, DC 20005-2304; Title Tel # (202) 682-9200 Title Fax # (202) 289-6648
Personnel: Editor-Brian King
General Info: (Formerly Agriculture Council of America, the Forum), Yr. Est. 1969, Quarterly, 6 pages
Circulation: Total-16,000

Agriculture News Bulletin — *Business, Association*

Publishing Co: Pennsylvania Dept. of Agriculture, 2301 N Cameron St, Harrisburg, PA 17110-9405; Title Tel # (717) 787-5085
Personnel: Editor-Diane Yingst
Editorial Description: Events, issues, regulatory programs concerning Pennsylvania agriculture, livestock, crops, and animal and plant health.
General Info: Yr. Est. 1915, Bi-weekly, Trim Size-8$\frac{1}{2}$ x 14, Sheetfed press, 2 pages, Color, Coated
Circulation: Total-5,600

Agriview

Publishing Co: Vermont Dept. of Agriculture, Food & Markets, 116 State St. Drawer 20, Montpelier, VT 05620-2901; Title Tel # (802) 828-2500 Title Fax # (802) 828-2361
Personnel: Publisher-Jeffrey B. Cook, Editor-Jennifer Grahovac
Editorial Description: Contains agriculture news about Vermont and of interest to the Vermont farm community.
General Info: Yr. Est. 1940, Bi-weekly, Trim Size-11 x 14, Offset press, 8 pages, 5% ads
Subscriptions: Indv. $7
Circulation: Total-4,500
Advertising: Inquire for rates.
Printing Co: B.D. Press, Box 138, Rt. #104A, Fairfax, VT 05454 Tel # (802) 893-4002

Agriweek

Publishing Co: Century Publishing Co., 167 Lombard Ave., Ste. 143, Winnipeg, MB R3B 0T4 Canada; Title Tel # (204) 943-8861 Title Fax # (802) 828-2361
Personnel: Publisher-Morris Dorosh
Editorial Description: Developments and news in the agricultural industry.
General Info: Yr. Est. 1967, Weekly
Subscriptions: Indv. $127

Agronomy News — *Association*

Publishing Co: American Soc. of Agronomy, 677 S Segoe Rd, Madison, WI 53711-1048; Title Tel # (608) 273-8080 Title Fax # (608) 273-2021
Editorial Description: Covers recent happenings in the Society and the field of agronomy in general.
General Info: Monthly

Agrotechnology Transfer — *Consumer*

Publishing Co: IBSNAT Project, 2500 Dole St., Krauss Hall 23, Honolulu, HI 96822-2332; Title Tel # (808) 948-8858
Personnel: Editor-Jeri-Lynn Palacio, Production Mgr.-Victoria Pecsok
Editorial Description: Uses systems analysis & crop simulation models for agrotechnology transfer.
General Info: (Formerly Benchmark Sites News + Soil Taxonomy), Yr. Est. 1985, 20 pages, ISSN: 0883-8631
Circulation: Total-3,000

Agrow World Crop Protection News — *Business, Association*

Publishing Co: Pharmabooks, 1775 Broadway Ste 511, New York, NY 10019-1903 Fax # (212) 262-8234; Title Tel # (212) 262-8230 Title Fax # (212) 262-8236
Personnel: Publisher-Philip Brown, Editor-Jane Sackett, Adv. Dir.-Peter Coltart
General Info: Bi-weekly, Trim Size-209mm x 294mm, Offset press, 28 pages, 2 Color, Newsprint, Saddle-stitched
Subscriptions: Indv. $520
Circulation: Total-1,341
Advertising: Accepts Inserts.

Al Hanson's Economic Newsletter
See: BUSINESS & INDUSTRY

Alberta Agrologist — *Association* — CPM: $192

Publishing Co: Alberta Institute of Agrologists, 8506 104th St., Edmonton, AB T6E 4G4 Canada; Title Tel # (403) 432-0663 Title Fax # (403) 439-8414
Personnel: Editor-Bob Burden
Editorial Description: Information for and on professional agrologists in Alberta.
General Info: Yr. Est. 1947, 5x/yr., Trim Size-8$\frac{1}{2}$ x 11, Offset press, 8 pages, 20% ads, 2 Color, Other
Subscriptions: Indv. $25, Inst. $25, Can. $25, For. $25
Circulation: (92% controlled), Total-1,300, Readership-2,000
Advertising: $250. Accepts Inserts.

Alternative Agriculture News

Publishing Co: Henry A. Wallace Institute for Alternative Agriculture, Inc., 9200 Edmonston Rd Ste 117, Greenbelt, MD 20770-1506; Title Tel # (301) 441-8777
Personnel: Editor-Garth Youngberg
Editorial Description: This monthly newsletter informs Institute members of scientific, legislative, & other developments involving alternative agriculture. It includes reports on activities of other organizations & actions taken by Congress & federal agencies.
General Info: Yr. Est. 1983, Monthly, 4 pages
Subscriptions: Indv. $15
Circulation: Total-1,300

Alternative Aquaculture Network
See: FISH & FISHERIES

American Bamboo Society-Newsletter
See: GARDENING & HORTICULTURE

American Beekeeping Federation Newsletter — *Business, Association*

Publishing Co: American Beekeeping Fed., PO Box 1038, Jesup, GA 31588-1038; Title Tel # (912) 427-8447 Title Fax # (912) 427-4018
Personnel: Publisher, Editor-Troy Fore, Circ. Mgr.-Christina Wright, Adv. Dir.-Donna Poythress
Editorial Description: A newsletter for members of the American Beekeeping Federation. Covers topics of interest to those in the beekeeping and honey industry.
General Info: Yr. Est. 1943, Bi-monthly, Trim Size-8.5 x 11, Sheetfed press, 16 pages, No Color
Subscriptions: Indv. $25, Can. $27, For. $30, $1/copy
Advertising: $175. Accepts Inserts.
Printing Co: Palmer's Printing, Jesup, GA 31545

American CattleWoman
See: LIVESTOCK

American Farm Bureau Official Newsletter — *Business*

Publishing Co: American Farm Bureau, 225 Puhy Ave., Parker Ridge, IL 60068; Title Tel # (312) 399-5700 Title Fax # (312) 399-5896
Editorial Description: Devoted to the interests of ranchers and farmers nationwide.
Advertising: Inquire for rates.

American Society of Agricultural Consultants Newsletter — *Association*

Publishing Co: American Society for Agricultural Consultants, 950 S Cherry St Ste 508, Denver, CO 80222-2664; Title Tel # (303) 758-3513
General Info: Yr. Est. 1963, Bi-monthly

Animal Welfare Information Center Newsletter
See: ANIMALS

Apple Newsletter — *Business*

Publishing Co: New Brunswick Dept. of Agriculture, Box 6000, Fredericton, NB E3B 5H1 Canada Tel # (506) 457-7244 Fax # (506) 457-7267; Title Tel # (506) 453-3476 Title Fax # (506) 453-7978
Personnel: Editor-Shirley Stuible
General Info: Quarterly, Trim Size-8$\frac{1}{2}$ x 11, Mimeo press, 6 pages
Circulation: Total-200

Aquaculture Newsletter International
See: FISH & FISHERIES

Atlanta Wholesale Fruit
See: PRODUCE

Bang Board, The
See: HOBBY

Beale's Industry Letter

Publishing Co: Beale's Industry Letter, Box 48651, Bentall Ctr. 111, Vancouver, BC V7X 1A3 Canada; Title Tel # (604) 984-0958
Personnel: Publisher-Colin Beale
Editorial Description: Covers a variety of agricultural industry related topics.
General Info: Yr. Est. 1971, Bi-weekly
Subscriptions: Indv. $237

Bean Market News — *Business*

Publishing Co: U.S. Dept. of Agriculture, 711 O St., Greeley, CO 80631-9540; Title Tel # (970) 353-9750 Title Fax # (970) 353-9790
Editorial Description: Dealer-shipper selling prices F.O.B. warehouse.
General Info: Yr. Est. 1954, Weekly, Trim Size-8$\frac{1}{2}$ x 11, Mimeo press, 4 pages
Subscriptions: Indv. $55, Can. $60, For. $90

Bean Market News - Sacramento   *Business*

Publishing Co: California Dept. of Food & Agriculture, Communications Dept., 1220 N St. Rm. 100, Sacramento, CA 95814 Tel # (916) 654-0466; Title Tel # (916) 654-0298
Title Fax # (916) 654-1046
Editorial Description: Dry bean prices to growers and at wholesale; market situation and exports.
General Info: Weekly, Trim Size-8½ x 11, 3 pages, No Color
Subscriptions: Indv. $150, Can. $150, $5/copy

Beefalo News
See: MEAT & MEAT PROVISIONS

Beefalo Nickel
See: MEAT & MEAT PROVISIONS

Beekeeping Notes
See: GARDENING & HORTICULTURE

Bluebook Update Newsletter   *Business, Association*

Publishing Co: Soyatech, Inc., 318 Main St, P.O. Box 84, Bar Harbor, ME 04609-1637;
Title Tel # (207) 288-4969 Title Fax # (207) 288-5264
Personnel: Publisher-Peter Golbitz, Circ. Mgr.-Joy Froding, Editor, Production Mgr.-Keri Hayes, Mktg. Dir.-Jot Froding
Editorial Description: Current information on the soybean, corn, canola, cottonseed, rapeseed, sunflower and palm industries.
General Info: (Formerly Bluebook Update), Yr. Est. 1994, Quarterly, 4 pages, ISSN: 1081-5228
Subscriptions: Free To Qualified Recipient
Circulation: Total-4,000

Border Connections
See: EDUCATION

Breaking New Ground
See: DISABILITY

Broadwater Market Letter   *Business*

Publishing Co: DePutter Publishing Ltd., 190 Wortley Road Suite #200, London, ON N6C 4Y7 Canada; Title Tel # (519) 663-2224 Title Fax # (519) 663-9124
Personnel: Publisher-John De Putter, Editor, Editorial Page Ed., Circ. Mgr.-Ruth C. Belcher
Editorial Description: Market analysis, news and insight. All main Canadian markets covered. Profit oriented and practical. For farmers, agribuiness and goverment subcribers.
General Info: Yr. Est. 1975, Weekly, Trim Size-8½ x 11, Desktop press, 6 pages, ISSN: 0711-7590, 2 Color
Subscriptions: Indv. $149, Can. $149
Printing Co: Mac Top Publishing, 152 Wharncliffe Rd. S., London, ON N6J 2K6 Canada
Tel # (519) 433-1603, Fax # (519) 439-5830

Browse   *Association*   CPM: $100

Publishing Co: Ontario Goat Breeders' Assn., Box 2776, Sta. A., Sudbury, ON P3A 5J3 Canada;
Title Tel # (705) 694-5686
Personnel: Circ. Mgr.-Manon Whitman, Publisher, Editor, Production Mgr.-Pat Marcotte
Editorial Description: Promotes the goat industry within Ontario: articles, advertising & current events. Provides up-to-date management advice & information about products of the goat.
General Info: Yr. Est. 1951, Bi-monthly, Trim Size-8½ x 11, Offset press, 24 pages, 25% ads, No Color, Newsprint, Other
Subscriptions: Indv. $20, Can. $20, $3/copy
Circulation: Total-250
Advertising: $25.

Bulletin-Association for Living Historical farms and Agricultural Museums
See: MUSEUM PUBLICATIONS

California Fruit Fax Report   *Business*

Publishing Co: California Dept. of Food & Agriculture, Communications Dept., 1220 N St. Rm. 100, Sacramento, CA 95814 Tel # (916) 654-0466; Title Tel # (916) 654-0298
Title Fax # (916) 654-1046
Editorial Description: California fruit shipping point prices, volume, market situation and selected wholesale markets.
General Info: (Formerly California Fruit Report), Daily
Subscriptions: Indv. $1,080, Can. $1,080, $15/copy

California Fruit Fax Report Weekly   *Business*

Publishing Co: California Dept. of Food & Agriculture, Communications Dept., 1220 N St. Rm. 100, Sacramento, CA 95814 Tel # (916) 654-0466; Title Tel # (916) 654-0298
Title Fax # (916) 654-1046
Editorial Description: California Fruit shipping point prices, volume, market situation and selected wholesale markets.
General Info: (Formerly California Fruit Report Weekly), Weekly, Trim Size-8½ x 14, 4 pages, No Color
Subscriptions: Indv. $204, Can. $204, $8/copy

California Macadamia Society Yearbook
See: PRODUCE

California Ornamental Crops Report
See: FLORIST

California Prune News
See: FOOD

California Strawberry Report   *Business*

Publishing Co: USDA-AMS-F&V. Div., 630 Sansome St Ste 727, San Francisco, CA 94111-2215;
Title Tel # (415) 705-1300 Title Fax # (415) 705-1301
Personnel: Editor-Frederick Teensma
Editorial Description: Latest marketing information on strawberries. Provides price and volume information for California strawberries by shipping districts and information for competing areas. Also included are prices at the major U.S. produce markets, an arrival summary at 22 major citites, and daily arrivals at Los Angeles and San Francisco areas. Similar information is provided for raspberries.
General Info: Semi-weekly, Trim Size-8½ x 14, 4 pages, No Color, Matte
Subscriptions: Indv. $135, Can. $135, For. $270

California Tender Vegetables, Asparagus & Sweet Potatoes

Publishing Co: U.S. Dept. of Agriculture, 711 O St., Greeley, CO 80631-9540;
Title Tel # (209) 466-0881 Title Fax # (209) 466-0616
Personnel: Editor-Melvin Ries
Editorial Description: F.O.R. Shipping point markets for northern San Joaquin Valley Cal.
General Info: Yr. Est. 1954, Semi-weekly, Trim Size-8½ x 14, Mimeo press, 4 pages, No Color
Subscriptions: Indv. $132, Can. $132, For. $264, $2/copy

California Wool Growers Newsletter
See: LIVESTOCK

Canadian Nursery Trades Association Newsbrief   *Association*

Publishing Co: Canadian Nursery Trades Assn., 7856 Fifth Line S., RR 4 Stn. Main, Milton, ON L9T 2X8 Canada; Title Tel # (905) 875-1399
General Info: Monthly
Subscriptions: Free With Membership
Circulation: (100% controlled), Total-1,300

Canola Digest
See: FEED, GRAIN & MILLING

Caretaker Gazette, The
See: EMPLOYMENT

Center for Rural Affairs Newsletter   *Consumer*

Publishing Co: Center for Rural Affairs, 101 South Taliman, Box 406, Walthill, NE 68067-0406;
Title Tel # (402) 846-5428 Title Fax # (402) 846-5420
Personnel: Publisher-Marty Strange, Editor-Marie Powell
Editorial Description: Provides information for agriculture and rural communities, including topics such as farm legislation, rural development, environmental concerns.
General Info: Yr. Est. 1973, Monthly, Trim Size-8 x 10, Offset press, 4 pages, ISSN: 1085-4975, 2 Color
Subscriptions: Free
Circulation: Total-7,000
Printing Co: West Point News, 134 Grove St., West Point, NB 68788 Tel # (402) 372-2461

Changing Horizons   *Business*

Publishing Co: Montgomery County Cooperative Extension, Annex Bldg., Box 1500, Ithaca, NY 12068; Title Tel # (518) 853-3471
Personnel: Editor-T. Burbins, Adv. Dir.-Mary Guzior
Editorial Description: New and improved techniques in agriculture.
General Info: (Formerly Montgomery County Agricultural News), Yr. Est. 1922, Monthly, Trim Size-8½ x 11½, Letrpr. press, 16 pages, 2 Color
Subscriptions: Indv. $7
Circulation: Total-450
Advertising: Inquire for rates.

Collier Farm Bankruptcy
See: LAW

Commercial Cattle Issue
See: LIVESTOCK

Composting News
See: ENVIRONMENT & ECOLOGY

Connecticut Weekly Agricultural Report — *Business*

Publishing Co: Connecticut Dept. of Agriculture, 165 Capitol Ave., #263, State Office Bldg., Hartford, CT 06106-1630; Title Tel # (203) 566-4845 Title Fax # (203) 566-6094
Personnel: Editor-Jane Murdock
Editorial Description: Reports farm commodity wholesale prices, agricultural meeting notices. Agricultural advertisements.
General Info: (Formerly Connecticut Market Bulletin), Yr. Est. 1920, Weekly, Trim Size-8½ x 11, Desktop press, 4 pages, No Color
Subscriptions: Indv. $10
Circulation: Total-2,400
Advertising: Inquire for rates.

Cooperative News Intl.

Publishing Co: Agricultural Cooperative Development Intl., 50 F St NW Ste 900, Washington, DC 20001-1530; Title Tel # (202) 638-4661 Title Fax # (202) 626-8726
Personnel: Editor, Production Mgr.-Suzanne Rucker
Editorial Description: News of interest to intl. audience, mostly cooperative. Innovations in cooperative management & training. Agricultural news, i.e. agricultural practices. News of projects in agricultural developing countries.
General Info: Yr. Est. 1965, Quarterly, 4 pages
Subscriptions: Indv. $10
Circulation: Total-2,300

Corn/Bean Profit Alert

Publishing Co: Oster Communications, Inc., 219 Parkade, PO Box 6, Cedar Falls, IA 50613 Fax # (319) 277-7982; Title Tel # (319) 277-1278
Personnel: Publisher-Merrill Oster, Editor-Ron Michaelsen, Circ. Mgr.-Sandy Golz, Art Dir.-Pete Cornell, Promotion Dir.-John Heidersbach
Editorial Description: Cash, futures & options strategies for corn & soybean growers.
General Info: Weekly, Sheetfed press, 6 pages, Coated
Subscriptions: Indv. $74
Circulation: Total-4,475
List Rental: List Management Co.: Venture Communications, 60 Madison Avenue, 3rd fl., New York, NY 10010 Tel # (212) 684-4800, Fax # (212) 545-1680
Printing Co: Woolverton Printing Co., 115 E 4th St, Cedar Falls, IA 50613-2825 Tel # (319) 277-2616, Fax # (319) 277-8136

Cotton Exchange News

Publishing Co: New York Cotton Exchange, 4 World Trade Ctr., S.E. Plz., New York, NY 10048-0137 Tel # (212) 742-5070; Title Tel # (212) 938-2650
General Info: Yr. Est. 1984, Trim Size-8½ x 11, 4 pages, 2 Color
Circulation: (100% controlled), Total-10,000

Cotton Grower — *Business* — CPM: $76

Publishing Co: Meister Publishing Co., 37733 Euclid Ave., Willoughby, OH 44094-5925; Title Tel # (216) 942-2000 Title Fax # (216) 975-3447
Personnel: Publisher-William J. Miller, II, Editor-William Spencer, Circ. Mgr.-Brad M. Mitchell, Asst. Circ. Mgr.-Luana Y. Smith, Production Mgr.-Angela Riffle, Adv. Dir.-Alan C. Strohmaier, Art Dir.-William Rigo, Jr., Mktg. Dir.-Judi Widgren, Promotion Dir.-Kelly Schupska
Editorial Description: Published for cotton growers and ginners throughout the U.S.
General Info: Yr. Est. 1901, 9x/yr., Trim Size-8 x 10¾, Web press, ISSN: 0194-9772, 4 Color, Coated, Saddle-stitched, Looseleaf
Subscriptions: Indv. $14, Can. $14, For. $20, Free To Qualified Recipient
Circulation: (BPA, 96% controlled As of 06/30/95), Total-58,309
Advertising: $4,445.
List Rental: Rents Lists
Printing Co: R.R. Donnelley & Sons, 121 Matthews Dr., Senatobia, MS 38668-2304 Tel # (601) 562-5252, Fax # (601) 562-9939

Cotton Talks — *Association*

Publishing Co: Plains Cotton Growers, Inc., 4510 Englewood Ave, Lubbock, TX 79414-1227; Title Tel # (806) 792-4904 Title Fax # (806) 792-4906
Personnel: Editor-Cotton Fanning
Editorial Description: Cotton production legislation consumption, marketing, taxation, regulation and similar information.
General Info: Yr. Est. 1964, Weekly, Mimeo press, 2 pages
Circulation: Total-350

Cranberry Vine — *Consumer, Association*

Publishing Co: Washington State Univ.-Long Beach, Research & Extension Unit, Rt. 1, Box 570, Long Beach, WA 98631; Title Tel # (206) 642-2031
Personnel: Editor-Beverly Rolfe, Mng. Editor-Kim Patten
General Info: Yr. Est. 1965, Quarterly, Trim Size-8½ x 11, Mimeo press, 4 pages
Subscriptions: Free To Qualified Recipient
Circulation: Total-240

Cream Separator and Dairy Newsletter
See: DAIRY

Crop Weather Report

Publishing Co: U.S. Department of Agriculture, California Ag. Stat. Service, PO Box 1258, Sacramento, CA 95812
Editorial Description: Weather's affect on crops; planting & harvesting information; weekly & accumulated precipitation data & temperatures by station.
General Info: Weekly
Subscriptions: Indv. $30, For. $60

Cultivar: Newsletter of the UCSC Center for Agroecology & Sustainable Food Systems — *Business, Consumer*

Publishing Co: University of California, CASFS, 1156 High St., Santa Cruz, CA 95064-1077; Title Tel # (408) 459-4140 Title Fax # (408) 459-2799
Editorial Description: Devoted to farmers, researchers and others interested in agro-ecological approaches to farming and cultivation. Reports on research and issues in sustainable agriculture.
General Info: Yr. Est. 1982, Semi-annually, ISSN: 1065-1691
Subscriptions: Free
Circulation: Total-4,000

Curran's Ginseng Farmer

Publishing Co: Curran Productions, PO Box 3141, Missoula, MT 59806-3141
Personnel: Publisher, Editor-Dave Curran, Circ. Mgr., Production Mgr.-Pat Curran
Editorial Description: Contains information about the growing & selling of American Ginseng.
General Info: Yr. Est. 1981, Monthly, Trim Size-8½ x 11, Offset press, 8 pages, ISSN: 0735-9322, Color
Subscriptions: Indv. $63, Can. $74, $6/copy
Advertising: Inquire for rates.

Dakota Counsel
See: ENERGY

Divining Rod
See: ENVIRONMENT & ECOLOGY

Doane's Agricultural Report

Publishing Co: Doane Agricultural Services Co., 11701 Borman Dr., Ste. 100, St. Louis, MO 63146-4199 Fax # (314) 569-1083; Title Tel # (314) 569-2700
Personnel: Publisher, Editor-Paul Justis, Circ. Mgr.-Marilyn Wind, Promotion Dir.-Gene Ross
Editorial Description: Contains farm market forecasts, farm management information, crop and livestock production facts, plus items on government regulations, taxes, and farm real estate.
General Info: Yr. Est. 1938, Weekly, Trim Size-8½ x 11, Offset press, 6 pages, ISSN: 0093-5271, No Color, Matte
Subscriptions: Indv. $92
Circulation: Total-21,700
List Rental: Actives: $85/M

Durum Kernels — *Association*

Publishing Co: U.S. Durum Growers Assn., 824 Thompson St, Bottineau, ND 58318-1726; Title Tel # (701) 228-3057
Personnel: Editor-Diane Scheflo
General Info: Yr. Est. 1957, Monthly, Trim Size-8½ x 11, Offset press, 24 pages, Color
Subscriptions: Indv. $10
Advertising: Inquire for rates.

Earthkeeping Ontario

Publishing Co: Jubilee Centre for Agricultural Research, 115 Woolwich St., 2nd Floor, Guelph, ON N1H 3V1 Canada Parent Co.-Christian Farmers Fed. of Ontario, Guelph, Canada; Title Tel # (519) 837-1620 Title Fax # (519) 824-1835
Personnel: Editor-Elbert Van Donkersgoed, Assoc. Ed.-Nellie Van Donkersgoed, Mng. Editor, Circ. Mgr.-Cathy Pater, Art Dir.-Nellie van Donkersgoed
Editorial Description: A letter on faith and agriculture.
General Info: (Formerly Earthkeeping), Yr. Est. 1985, Bi-monthly, Trim Size-8 x 11, Web press, 6 pages, ISSN: 1183-630X, No Color
Subscriptions: Indv. $15, Can. $20, For. $25, $3/copy
Advertising: $304. Accepts Inserts.
Printing Co: Graphic Services, 32-24 Essex St, Guelph, ON N1H 3K8 Canada

Egg & Poultry National Weekly Review

Publishing Co: Edison Market News Office, 103 Metroplex Dr, Edison, NJ 08817-2683; Title Tel # (908) 985-8880 Title Fax # (908) 985-3732
General Info: Weekly
Subscriptions: Indv. $110

Egg Market News
See: POULTRY & POULTRY PRODUCTS

Egg Producer
See: POULTRY & POULTRY PRODUCTS

Entomological Society of Canada, Bulletin
See: ENTOMOLOGY

Exclaimer — *Business, Association*

Publishing Co: University of Missouri-University Extension, 822 Clark Hall, Columbia, MO 65211-0001; Title Tel # (314) 882-0604
Personnel: Editor-Eileen Bennett
Editorial Description: Reports on extension and continuing education activities of the University of Missouri system, Lincoln University, and University Extension field specialists.
General Info: Yr. Est. 1973, Bi-monthly, Trim Size-11 x 17, Sheetfed press, 4 pages, 2 Color, Matte
Subscriptions: Free
Circulation: Total-10,000

Extension News-Albany, Rensselaer, Saratoga, Washington Counties

Publishing Co: Cooperative Extension Assn. of Albany County, Agricultural D, Martin Rd., Voorheesville, NY 12186; Title Tel # (518) 765-3510
General Info: Monthly
Circulation: Total-5,000

FAO Plant Protection Bulletin

Publishing Co: Sponsor-FAO, UNIPUB, 4611-F Assembly Dr, Lanham, MD 20706-4370; Title Tel # (301) 459-7666 Title Fax # (301) 459-0056
Editorial Description: Contains information received by the World Reporting Service on plant diseases & pests.
General Info: Quarterly
Subscriptions: $6/copy

FFA Update   *Association*

Publishing Co: National FFA Organization, PO Box 15160, 5632 Mt. Vernon Memorial Hwy., Alexandria, VA 22309-0160 Fax # (703) 360-5524; Title Tel # (703) 360-3600
Personnel: Editor-Bill Stagg
Editorial Description: Monthly newsletter to state and national agriculture education/FFA leadership.
General Info: Yr. Est. 1928, Monthly, 4 pages, Newsprint, Saddle-stitched
Circulation: (100% controlled), Total-250

FMRA News   *Business, Association*

Publishing Co: American Society of Farm Managers & Rural Appraisers, 950 S. Cherry St., Ste. 508, Denver, CO 80222-2664; Title Tel # (303) 758-3513 Title Fax # (303) 758-0190
Personnel: Editor-Alan Yoder
Editorial Description: Discusses topics of interest to farm managers rural appraisers, agricultural consultants,and other agricultural professionals.
General Info: Bi-monthly, Trim Size-8$\frac{1}{2}$ x 11, Sheetfed press, 16 pages, Color, Coated, Saddle-stitched
Subscriptions: Free To Qualified Recipient
Circulation: Total-3,500, Readership-3,500
List Rental: Actives: $100/M

Farm Broadcasters Letter   *Association*

Publishing Co: USDA Radio & TV Div., Off. Of Public Affairs #410-A, Washington, DC 20250-0001; Title Tel # (202) 720-4330 Title Fax # (202) 690-2165
Personnel: Editor-Vic Powell
Editorial Description: USDA Radio & TV's 4-page newsletter highlights recent developments at USDA & in agriculture. Includes news tips & news services. R-TV programming included. Mailed weekly. Also available on USDA's CID.
General Info: Weekly, Trim Size-8$\frac{1}{2}$ x 11, Sheetfed press, 4 pages, ISSN: 0364-5444, Coated
Subscriptions: Free To Qualified Recipient
Acquistions: Publication Bought
Circulation: (100% controlled), Total-2,300

Farm City Week Newsletter   *Association*

Publishing Co: Natl. Farm-City Council, Inc., 3636 Woodview Trce, Indianapolis, IN 46268-1168; Title Tel # (317) 875-8755
Personnel: Publisher, Editor-J. McGehee
Editorial Description: Members of Natl. City Council & agri-business addresses.
General Info: Yr. Est. 1954, Monthly, Mimeo press, 6 pages, No Color
Circulation: Total-2,000

Farm Economics   *Business, Association*

Publishing Co: Pennsylvania State Univ, Agriculture, Economics & Rural Dev., 201 Armsby Building, ., University Park, PA 16802; Title Tel # (814) 865-7656
Personnel: Editor-Dr. Blair Smith
Editorial Description: Topics pertaining to Pennsylvania agribusiness, public affairs, rural development and national farm & food policy.
General Info: Yr. Est. 1955, Monthly, Trim Size-8$\frac{1}{2}$ x 11, Offset press, 4 pages
Circulation: Total-17,000

Farm Economics Facts & Opinions

Publishing Co: Univ. of Illinois at Urbana Champaign, 227 Illini Union, 1401 W. Green Street, Urbana, IL 61801 Tel # (217) 333-1477 Fax # (217) 333-7803; Title Tel # (217) 333-2666 Title Fax # (217) 333-1952
Personnel: Publisher-Richard Kesler
Editorial Description: Economic principles applied to farm problems such as marketing strategies, crop & livestock production decisions, government & institutional policies.
General Info: 18x/yr.
Subscriptions: Indv. $15

Farm and Ranch Tax Letter   *Business*

Publishing Co: Ag Executive, Inc., 115 E. Twyman, PO Box 180, Bushnell, IL 61422
Tel # (309) 772-2168; Title Tel # (309) 372-2168 Title Fax # (309) 772-2167
Personnel: Publisher-Darrell L. Dunteman
Editorial Description: Issues affecting agriculture taxation; includes both income and estate tax.
General Info: Yr. Est. 1993, Monthly, Trim Size-8$\frac{1}{2}$ x 11, Web press, 4 pages, 2 Color, Matte, Looseleaf
Subscriptions: Indv. $35
Circulation: Total-1,100, Readership-1,100
Advertising: Inquire for rates. Accepts Inserts.
List Rental: Actives: 1,000, $75/M, Expires: 1,000, $70/M

Farm Tax Saver   *Business*

Publishing Co: Farm Progress Publications, 191 S Gary Ave, Carol Stream, IL 60188-2095
Fax # (708) 462-4656 Parent Co.-Capital Cities/ABC, Inc., New York; Title Tel # (708) 690-5600
Personnel: Publisher-Alan Johnson, Editor-Trenna Grabowski, Circ. Mgr.-Jan Ciolino, Adv. Dir.-Steve Joss
Editorial Description: Tips for income tax & estate planning.
General Info: Yr. Est. 1976, Monthly, Trim Size-8$\frac{1}{2}$ x 11, Sheetfed press, 4 pages, 2 Color, Newsprint
Subscriptions: Indv. $20
Acquistions: Publication Bought
Circulation: Total-45,000
List Rental: List Management Co.: Direct Marketing Resources, 301 Duck Rd., Grandview, MO 64030-1664 Tel # (816) 767-9700, Fax # (816) 767-0770, Actives: $130/M
Printing Co: Plain Talk Publishing, 511 6th Ave, Des Moines, IA 50309-2402 Tel # (515) 282-0485

Farmers Federal Tax Alert
See: TAXES

Farmers Grain & Livestock Corp. -Viewpoint

Publishing Co: Farmers Grain & Livestock Corp., 1400 50th St., #400, Box 65537, W. Des Moines, IA 50265-0914; Title Tel # (515) 223-2200
General Info: Yr. Est. 1974, Weekly, 6 pages
Subscriptions: Indv. $125
Circulation: Total-5,000

Farming for Profit   *Business*

Publishing Co: Doane Agricultural Services Co., 11701 Borman Dr., Ste. 100, St. Louis, MO 63146-4199 Fax # (314) 569-1083; Title Tel # (314) 569-2700
Personnel: Publisher-Lynn Henerson, Editor-Irving Smith, Circ. Mgr.-Marilyn Wind, Promotion Dir.-Cecil King
Editorial Description: News, government action, financial advice geared to farmers.
General Info: Yr. Est. 1948, Monthly, Trim Size-8$\frac{1}{2}$ x 13$\frac{3}{4}$, 2 pages, No Color, Matte
Circulation: Total-55,500

Feed Facts
See: LIVESTOCK

Feedgram   *Business, Association*

Publishing Co: American Feed Industry Assn., 1501 Wilson Blvd # 1100, Arlington, VA 22209-2403; Title Tel # (703) 524-0810 Title Fax # (703) 524-1921
Editorial Description: Covers current industry & association news. Focuses on legislative, regulatory & feed control items; also USDA news & membership happenings.
General Info: Monthly
Subscriptions: Free With Membership

Fertilizer and Agricultural Chemical Newsletter
See: SAFETY

Field Crop Reporting Series   *Business, Association*

Publishing Co: Statistics Canada, Holland Ave/RH Coats, Holland Ave/Tunney's Pasture, Ottawa, ON K1A O26 Canada Tel # (613) 951-8116 Fax # (613) 951-0581; Title Tel # (613) 990-8116
Editorial Description: Text in English or French. Acreage, seeding, growth, harvesting for 8 crops. 22-002.
General Info: Yr. Est. 1922, 8x/yr., 11 pages, ISSN: 0575-8548
Subscriptions: Indv. $14, Can. $12, For. $16, $14/copy

Food & Fiber Letter

Publishing Co: Sparks Companies Inc., 6708 Whittier Ave, Mc Lean, VA 22101-4529
Tel # (703) 734-8787 Fax # (703) 893-1065
Personnel: Editor-James Webster
Editorial Description: Agricultural policy, politics, markets & trade.
General Info: Yr. Est. 1981, Weekly, Trim Size-8$\frac{1}{2}$ x 11, Sheetfed press, 6 pages, ISSN: 0739-6791, Newsprint
Subscriptions: Indv. $445
Acquistions: Publication Bought
List Rental: Rents Lists

Food Industry Futures-A Strategy Service
See: FOOD

Foodland Alert

Publishing Co: Jesuit Farm Project, Box 1238, 5 Douglas St., Guelph, ON N1H 6N6 Canada
Personnel: Editor-Diane Baltaz
Editorial Description: Editorial comment & news on the urban on prime foodland, locally & abroad.
General Info: Yr. Est. 1986, Quarterly, Trim Size-8½ x 11, Sheetfed press, 6 pages, No Color, Newsprint
Subscriptions: Indv. $10
Circulation: Total-400
Printing Co: Kwik Kopy, 27 Wyndham St., Guelph, ON N1H 4E4 Canada Tel # (519) 837-2220

Forage Seed News   *Association*

Publishing Co: Saskatchewan Dept. of Agriculture & Food, Box 3003, Prince Albert, SK S6V 6G1 Canada; Title Tel # (306) 953-2770 Title Fax # (306) 953-2440
Personnel: Editor-Dorothy Murrell
General Info: (Formerly Alfalo Seed News), Yr. Est. 1992, Semi-annually, Trim Size-8½ x 11, Desktop press, 30 pages, ISSN: 1188-6358, Color-cover, Other
Subscriptions: Free
Circulation: (100% controlled), Total-850
Printing Co: Action Printing, 129 15th Street East, Prince Albert, SK S6V 1G1 Canada Tel # (306) 922-2322, Fax # (306) 922-2313

Forefront

Publishing Co: Agricultural Communication Service, Purdue University, 1143 Agricultural Adm. Bldg., W. Lafayette, IN 47907-1143 Tel # (317) 494-6946; Title Tel # (317) 494-8396 Title Fax # (317) 496-1117
Editorial Description: A report in layman's terms of the research taking place in Purdue's School of Agriculture through the Agricultural Experiment Station.
General Info: (Formerly Purdue Ag Report), Yr. Est. 1989, Sheetfed press, 4 pages, 4 Color, Matte
Subscriptions: Free
Circulation: (100% controlled), Total-6,000
Printing Co: Moeller Printing Company, 4401 E New York St, Indianapolis, IN 46201-3646

Fruit & Nut Review   *Business*

Publishing Co: U.S. Department of Agriculture, California Ag. Stat. Service, PO Box 1258, Sacramento, CA 95812
Editorial Description: Grape, citrus, deciduous, & nut acreage, production, price & utilization.
General Info: Monthly
Subscriptions: Indv. $15, For. $30

Fruit & Vegetable Truck Rate Report   *Business*

Publishing Co: USDA-AMS-F&V. Div., 630 Sansome St Ste 727, San Francisco, CA 94111-2215 Tel # (415) 705-1300 Fax # (415) 705-1301
Editorial Description: Covers rates for shipping select produce items.
General Info: Monthly
Subscriptions: Indv. $120

Fruit and Vegetable Truck Rate Report
See: PRODUCE

Good Earth Times
See: MUSEUM PUBLICATIONS

Grain & Feed Market News   *Business, Consumer*

Publishing Co: Agricultural Marketing Service, U.S. Dept. of Agriculture, South Bldg., Rm. 2613, Washington, DC 20090-6456; Title Tel # (202) 720-8054 Title Fax # (202) 690-3732
Personnel: Editor-Kim Harmon
Editorial Description: News and statistics in the grain and feed industry.
General Info: Yr. Est. 1932, Weekly, Trim Size-5 x 8½, 30 pages, No Color, Saddle-stitched
Subscriptions: Indv. $70, Can. $75, For. $105, $2/copy
Circulation: (91% controlled), Total-548
List Rental: Rents Lists
Printing Co: U.S. Government Printing Office, Superintendent Of Documents, Washington, DC 20402-0001 Tel # (202) 512-1800, Fax # (202) 512-2233

Grain and Livestock Market News
See: LIVESTOCK

Grain Price Outlook

Publishing Co: Univ. of Illinois at Urbana Champaign, 227 Illini Union, 1401 W. Green Street, Urbana, IL 61801 Tel # (217) 333-1477 Fax # (217) 333-7803; Title Tel # (217) 333-2666 Title Fax # (217) 333-1952
Personnel: Publisher-Darrel Good
Editorial Description: Issues on corn & soybeans. In-depth analysis of supply, demand & price outlook. Also discussion of storage & pricing strategies for producers.
General Info: 8x/yr.
Subscriptions: Indv. $12

Grain Shipments   *Business*

Publishing Co: California Dept. of Food & Agriculture, Communications Dept., 1220 N St. Rm. 100, Sacramento, CA 95814 Tel # (916) 654-0466
General Info: Monthly
Subscriptions: Indv. $24, Can. $24, For. $48, $2/copy

Grange Advocate   *Association*

Publishing Co: Pennsylvania State Grange, 1604 N 2nd St, Harrisburg, PA 17102-2447; Title Tel # (717) 234-5001 Title Fax # (717) 234-7654
Personnel: Publisher-Gordon Hiller, Circ. Mgr.-Nancy Cole, Editor, Promotion Dir.-James Mentzer
Editorial Description: Rural and agricultural news, Grange activities.
General Info: (Formerly PA Grange News, The), Yr. Est. 1904, Monthly, Trim Size-9½ x 12½, Web press, 4 pages, ISSN: 0279-9391, No Color, Newsprint
Acquistions: Publication Bought
Circulation: Total-26,000
Printing Co: The Sentinel, 375 6th St, Lewistown, PA 17044-1214

Grape Acreage   *Business*

Publishing Co: U.S. Department of Agriculture, California Ag. Stat. Service, PO Box 1258, Sacramento, CA 95812
Editorial Description: Acreages of grapes by year planted, variety, & county; removal data.
General Info: Annually
Subscriptions: Indv. $10, For. $15

Grape Crush Report   *Business*

Publishing Co: U.S. Department of Agriculture, California Ag. Stat. Service, PO Box 1258, Sacramento, CA 95812
Editorial Description: Tons purchased, crushed, Brix factors, & price per ton by variety, by district, preliminary & final.
General Info: Semi-annually
Subscriptions: Indv. $20, For. $30

Green Markets Dealer Reports   *Business*

Publishing Co: Pike & Fischer Inc., 4600 East-West Hwy., Ste. 200, Bethesda, MD 20814-1438 Parent Co.-Bureau of National Affairs, Inc., Washington; Title Tel # (301) 652-6262 Title Fax # (301) 654-6297
Personnel: Editor in Chief-Kimberly Shepherd, Mng. Editor-Carolyn Rhodes, Circ. Mgr.-Kristin Strickland, Mktg. Dir.-Zachary Wheat
Editorial Description: Serves retailers of fertilizers & ag chemicals.
General Info: Yr. Est. 1987, Weekly
Subscriptions: Indv. $267, $8/copy
List Rental: Rents Lists

Green Markets Newsletter   *Business*

Publishing Co: Pike & Fischer Inc., 4600 East-West Hwy., Ste. 200, Bethesda, MD 20814-1438 Parent Co.-Bureau of National Affairs, Inc., Washington; Title Tel # (301) 652-6262 Title Fax # (301) 654-6297
Personnel: Editor-James Wilson, Circ. Mgr.-Kristin Strickland, Mktg. Dir.-Zarchary Wheat
Editorial Description: Covers chemical fertilizer industry, with emphasis in markets.
General Info: Yr. Est. 1977, Weekly, 10 pages, ISSN: 0149-5669
Subscriptions: Indv. $699, Can. $699, For. $953, $17/copy
Acquistions: Publication Bought, Publication Sold
List Rental: Actives: $175/M

Growing for Market   *Business*   **CPM: $90**

Publishing Co: Fairplain Publications, PO Box 3747, Lawrence, KS 66046; Title Tel # (913) 841-2559 Title Fax # (913) 841-2559
Personnel: Publisher, Editor-Lynn Byczynski, Assoc. Ed.-Daniel Nagengast, Adv. Dir.-Faye Jones
Editorial Description: News and ideas for market gardeners interested in sustainable practices.
General Info: Yr. Est. 1992, Monthly, Trim Size-8½ x 11, Offset press, 16 pages, ISSN: 1060-9296, 25% ads, No Color, Matte, Saddle-stitched
Subscriptions: Indv. $27, Inst. $27, Can. $30, For. $36, $3/copy
Circulation: Total-2,200
Advertising: $200.
List Rental: Actives: 2,200, $80/M, Expires: 1,300, $70/M
Printing Co: T.K. Printing, 1000 SW 6th Ave, Topeka, KS 66606-1494 Tel # (913) 233-9117

Harvest Times
See: ENVIRONMENT & ECOLOGY

Hawaii Weekly Weather   *Business, Association*

Publishing Co: Hawaii Agricultural Statistics Service, 1428 S King St # 22159, Honolulu, HI 96814-2512; Title Tel # (808) 548-7155
Personnel: Editor-Homer Rowley
General Info: Weekly, Offset press, 2 pages
Circulation: Total-670

Hay Market News   *Business, Association*

Publishing Co: USDA, Market News Svc., 225 Livestock Exchange Bldg., Box 2437, Sioux City, IA 51107; Title Tel # (712) 252-3286 Title Fax # (712) 252-2542
Personnel: Editor-James McElhany
Editorial Description: Nationwide hay market conditions & prices.
General Info: Yr. Est. 1948, Weekly, 20 pages, No Color
Subscriptions: Indv. $35
Circulation: Total-190

Hay Market News - Sacramento   *Business*

Publishing Co: California Dept. of Food & Agriculture, Communications Dept., 1220 N St. Rm. 100, Sacramento, CA 95814 Tel # (916) 654-0466; Title Tel # (916) 654-0298 Title Fax # (916) 654-1046
Editorial Description: California, Arizona, Utah, and Nevada hay prices and market situation.
General Info: Weekly, Trim Size-8½ x 14, 2 pages, No Color
Subscriptions: Indv. $99, Can. $99, $4/copy

Hay There! *Association*

Publishing Co: National Hay Association, Inc., 102 Treasure Island Causeway, St. Petersburg, FL 33706-4716; Title Tel # (813) 367-9702 Title Fax # (813) 367-9608
Personnel: Publisher-John Wilson, Editor, Adv. Dir.-Don Kieffer
Editorial Description: A publication for Assn. members dealing with hay & forage production & marketing.
General Info: Yr. Est. 1895, Monthly, 28 pages, No Color, Newsprint
Subscriptions: Indv. $260, Free With Membership
Acquistions: Publication Bought
Circulation: (100% controlled), Total-500, Readership-500
Advertising: Inquire for rates. Accepts Inserts.
Printing Co: Free Press Publishing Co., 1010 W Cass St, Tampa, FL 33606-1307 Tel # (813) 254-5888

Holistic Resource Management Quarterly
See: ENVIRONMENT & ECOLOGY

Home, Yard & Garden Pest Newsletter

Publishing Co: Univ. of Illinois at Urbana Champaign, 227 Illini Union, 1401 W. Green Street, Urbana, IL 61801 Tel # (217) 333-1477 Fax # (217) 333-7803; Title Tel # (217) 333-2666 Title Fax # (217) 333-1952
Personnel: Publisher-Roscoe Randell
Editorial Description: Insect, weed & plant disease pests of yard & garden. Current controls, application equipment & methods, storage & disposal of pesticides, plus other topics.
General Info: Weekly
Subscriptions: Indv. $15

Horizons

Publishing Co: Virginia Cooperative Extension Svce., Dept. of Agri. & Applied Econ, Blacksburg, VA 24061; Title Tel # (540) 231-9443
Personnel: Editor-Karen Mundy
Editorial Description: Horizons is a bi-monthly newsletter that deals with issues relating to agriculture & rural Virginia. It is the official publication of the Rural Economic Analysis Program (REAP).
General Info: (Formerly Virginia Agriculture Economics), Yr. Est. 1989, Bi-monthly, Trim Size-8$\frac{1}{2}$ x 11, Sheetfed press, 4 pages, 2 Color, Coated, Saddle-stitched
Subscriptions: Free
Circulation: Total-3,500
Printing Co: Virginia Tech Printing Dept., Virginia Tech, Blacksburg, VA 24061

IAAF Newsletter
See: AERONAUTICS/ASTRONAUTICS

ICASALS Newletter *Association*

Publishing Co: International Center for Arid Lands, PO Box 41036, Lubbock, TX 79409-1036 Tel # (816) 742-2218; Title Tel # (806) 742-2218 Title Fax # (806) 742-1954
Personnel: Editor-Dr. Idris Traylor, Jr., Mng. Editor-Sonia Moore
Editorial Description: Arid and semi-arid lands, plant and animal life, in arid environments.
General Info: Yr. Est. 1967, Trim Size-8$\frac{1}{2}$ x 11$\frac{1}{2}$, Letrpr. press, 12 pages, No Color, Newsprint, Saddle-stitched
Subscriptions: Free
Circulation: Total-4,000

IFPRI Report
See: INTERNATIONAL AFFAIRS

Idaho Wool Growers Association
See: LIVESTOCK

Illinois Dairy Digest

Publishing Co: Univ. of Illinois at Urbana Champaign, 227 Illini Union, 1401 W. Green Street, Urbana, IL 61801 Tel # (217) 333-1477 Fax # (217) 333-7803; Title Tel # (217) 333-2666 Title Fax # (217) 333-1952
Personnel: Publisher-Mike Hutjens
Editorial Description: Latest dairy information from Vol. 1 & other sources; practical tips to help dairy producers make management decisions.
General Info: Quarterly
Subscriptions: Indv. $5

Illinois Farmers' Outlook Letter

Publishing Co: Univ. of Illinois at Urbana-Champaign Foreign Lang. Dept., G70 Foreign Languages Bldg., 707 S. Mathews Ave., Urbana, IL 61801 Tel # (217) 333-9776

Illinois Grain & Livestock Market News

Publishing Co: Illinois Department of Agriculture, State Fairgrounds, Springfield, IL 62706-0001; Title Tel # (217) 782-2172
General Info: Yr. Est. 1970, Monthly
Subscriptions: Free
Circulation: Total-2,600

Illinois Soybean Farmer Leader Newsletter *Association*

Publishing Co: Illinois Soybean Checkoff Board, 2422 E. Washington, Bloomington, IL 61704; Title Tel # (309) 662-3373
Personnel: Editor-Claudine Wargel
General Info: Monthly, Trim Size-8$\frac{1}{2}$ x 11, 4 pages, 2 Color
Circulation: Total-6,500
Advertising: Inquire for rates. Accepts Inserts.

Illinois Vegetable Farmers' Letter

Publishing Co: Univ. of Illinois at Urbana Champaign, 227 Illini Union, 1401 W. Green Street, Urbana, IL 61801 Tel # (217) 333-1477 Fax # (217) 333-7803; Title Tel # (217) 333-2666 Title Fax # (217) 333-1952
Personnel: Publisher-Charles Voigt
Editorial Description: Production, harvest, handling & marketing advice for commercial producers.
General Info: Quarterly
Subscriptions: Indv. $5

In Good Tilth *Consumer* **CPM: $110**

Publishing Co: Oregon Tilth, Inc., PO Box 218, Tualatin, OR 97062-0218; Title Tel # (503) 692-4877 Title Fax # (503) 691-2514
Editorial Description: Promoting sustainable and organic agriculture in the Pacific Northwest.
General Info: Yr. Est. 1990, Monthly, Trim Size-11 x 17, Web press, 12 pages, ISSN: 1065-1527, 25% ads, 2 Color, Newsprint
Subscriptions: Indv. $35, Free With Membership
Circulation: Total-4,000, Readership-12,000
Advertising: $440.
Printing Co: Corvallis Web Press, 435 S.W. 2nd St., Corvallis, OR 97333 Tel # (503) 752-7043

Infoletter

Publishing Co: Oregon State Univ. Intl. Plant Protection Ctr., Publications, Corvallis, OR 97331; Title Tel # (503) 754-3541
Personnel: Editor-Allan Deutsch
Editorial Description: Concerned with crop pest & pesticide management.
General Info: Yr. Est. 1970, Semi-annually, Trim Size-11 x 21$\frac{3}{4}$, Sheetfed press, 2 pages, ISSN: 0145-6288, No Color, Newsprint
Circulation: Total-8,851
Printing Co: Oregon State Univ. Printing, Covallis, OR 97331 Tel # (503) 754-0123

International Association of Agriculture Economists- Proceedings of Conferences *Business, Association*

Publishing Co: International Association of Agriculture Economists, 1211 W. 22nd St., Oak Brook, IL 60521-2109; Title Tel # (708) 571-9393 Title Fax # (708) 571-9580
Personnel: Editor-George Peters
Editorial Description: Proceedings from IAAE conferences.
General Info: Tri-annually
Subscriptions: Free With Membership

Iowa Crop Report *Business, Association*

Publishing Co: Iowa Agricultural Statistics, 833 Federal Bldg., 210 Walnut St., Des Moines, IA 50309-2195; Title Tel # (515) 284-4340
Personnel: Editor-Duane Skow
Editorial Description: Highlights all major acreage, production & stock reports of concern to Iowa producers.
General Info: 10x/yr.
Subscriptions: Indv. $11

Iowa Crops & Weather

Publishing Co: Iowa Agricultural Statistics, 833 Federal Bldg., 210 Walnut St., Des Moines, IA 50309-2195; Title Tel # (514) 284-4340
Editorial Description: Weekly report on growing conditions giving stage of crop growth resume of weeks weather & accumulated precipitation & growing degree data. Published during the growing season only (April through November).
General Info: 36x/yr.
Subscriptions: Indv. $13

Journal *Association*

Publishing Co: New York State Dept. of Agriculture, 1 Winners Circle, Albany, NY 12235-0001; Title Tel # (518) 457-2747
Personnel: Editor-Louis Van Dyck, Circ. Mgr.-Angela Rootes
Editorial Description: Department programs, employee activities.
General Info: (Formerly A&M Sun), Yr. Est. 1957, Bi-monthly, Offset press, 4 pages, No Color
Circulation: (100% controlled), Total-1,400

Kentucky Agri-News *Business, Consumer*

Publishing Co: Kentucky Dept. of Agriculture, PO Box 1120, Louisville, KY 40201-1120; Title Tel # (502) 582-5293
Personnel: Editor-David Williamson
Editorial Description: Summary of our statistical reports on crop acreage & production, inventory numbers, egg & milk production & monthly price information, etc.
General Info: Yr. Est. 1982, Semi-monthly, Trim Size-8$\frac{1}{2}$ x 11, Letrpr. press, 4 pages, ISSN: 8750-9792
Subscriptions: Indv. $10
Circulation: Total-2,327

King's Gulf Grain Guide

Publishing Co: King Publishing Corp., 6914 Office Park Cir # 52210, Knoxville, TN 37909-1161
Tel # (619) 584-6214; Title Tel # (615) 584-6294 Title Fax # (615) 558-6101
Editorial Description: Features information relating to a variety of grains.
General Info: Weekly
Subscriptions: Indv. $547

Kiplinger Agricultural
Letter   *Business, Consumer*

Publishing Co: Kiplinger Washington Editors, Inc., 1729 H Street N.W., Washington, DC 20006-3924; Title Tel # (202) 887-6400
Personnel: Publisher-Austin H. Kiplinger, Editor-Melisa Bristow
Editorial Description: Forecasts and judgements of legislative and USDA policy, farm labor supply, wages, income, crops, new food packaging and processing and marketing techniques.
General Info: Yr. Est. 1929, Bi-weekly, Trim Size-8½ x 11, 4 pages, ISSN: 0023-1746
Subscriptions: Indv. $42
Circulation: Total-41,000
List Rental: List Management Co.: Kleid Company, Inc., 530 5th Ave., 17 Floor, New York, NY 10036-5101 Tel # (212) 819-3406, Fax # (212) 719-9788, Actives: 19,787, $90/M

Kiwifruit Growers of
California-Newsletter

Publishing Co: I S G A, 2205 Dixon St., Chico, CA 95926-2179; Title Tel # (916) 427-1544
Personnel: Editor-Dave Locklin
General Info: Yr. Est. 1975, Bi-monthly, Trim Size-8½ x 11, Sheetfed press, 20 pages, 2 Color, Coated, Saddle-stitched
Circulation: Total-500
Advertising: Inquire for rates.
Printing Co: Capital Printing, 1103 North B St., Sacramento, CA 95814 Tel # (916) 442-2947

Living Off the Land,
Subtropic Newsletter

Publishing Co: Geraventure Corp., PO Box 2131, Melbourne, FL 32902-2131; Title Tel # (305) 723-5554
Personnel: Editor-Marian Van Atta, Art Dir.-Kathleen Wilcox
Editorial Description: Obtaining better food in warm areas.Includes raising tropical fruit, vegetables, foraging, seed exchange.
General Info: Yr. Est. 1975, 5x/yr., Trim Size-8½ x 11, Letrpr. press, 6 pages, No Color, Newsprint
Subscriptions: Indv. $14, For. $15, $3/copy
Circulation: Total-500
Printing Co: Kwik Kopy, 749 S Apollo Blvd, Melbourne, FL 32901-1457 Tel # (407) 725-6434

Maine Agriculture

Publishing Co: Maine Dept of Agriculture, State House Station #28, Augusta, ME 04333-0001; Title Tel # (207) 289-3871
Editorial Description: Features news and developments relating to the agricultural industry in Maine.
General Info: Yr. Est. 1976
Subscriptions: Indv. $10

Maine-Ly Agriculture

Publishing Co: Maine Dept of Agriculture, State House Station #28, Augusta, ME 04333-0001; Title Tel # (207) 289-3871
Personnel: Editor-Rod McCormick
Editorial Description: Agriculture.
General Info: Yr. Est. 1976, Weekly, Trim Size-8½ x 11, Sheetfed press, 6 pages, 2% ads, No Color, Newsprint
Subscriptions: Indv. $10
Circulation: Total-2,300
Printing Co: Atkins Printing, 155 Main St, PO Box 1169, Waterville, ME 04901-6623 Tel # (207) 872-5565, Fax # (207) 872-0792

Making A Difference   *Business, Association*

Publishing Co: National FFA Organization, PO Box 15160, 5632 Mt. Vernon Memorial Hwy., Alexandria, VA 22309-0160; Title Tel # (703) 360-3600 Title Fax # (703) 360-5524
Personnel: Editor, Circ. Mgr.-Jack Pitzer
Editorial Description: Serves high school school agriculture educators and those state educators and university educators who support them.
General Info: (Formerly Between Issues), Yr. Est. 1965, Bi-monthly, Trim Size-8½ x 11, Sheetfed press, 16 pages, 2 Color, Newsprint, Saddle-stitched
Acquistions: Publication Bought
Circulation: Total-10,000
List Rental: Rents Lists

Malcriado/Voice of the Farm Worker
See: LABOR UNION

McLean County Farm
Bureau News

Publishing Co: McLean County Farm Bureau, 402 N Hershey Rd, Bloomington, IL 61704-3512
Personnel: Editor-Howard M. Dagley
Editorial Description: News of sponsoring organization, affiliated companies, state and national organizations and new developments in agriculture.
General Info: Yr. Est. 1920, Monthly
Subscriptions: Indv. $1
Circulation: Total-6,000
Advertising: Inquire for rates.

Meat Sheet
See: MEAT & MEAT PROVISIONS

Minnesota Agricultural
Economist   *Business*

Publishing Co: Minnesota Extension Service, 231 ClassRm. Office Bldg., 1994 Buford Avenue., St. Paul, MN 55108-6040; Title Tel # (612) 625-5733
Personnel: Editor-Steven Taff
Editorial Description: To inform agribusiness persons and public officials about key policy issues facing agriculture and rural communities.
General Info: (Formerly Minnesota Farm Business Notes), Yr. Est. 1924, Quarterly, Trim Size-8½ x 11, Offset press, 8 pages, No Color
Subscriptions: Free
Circulation: Total-3,800

Minnesota Pest Report   *Business, Association*

Publishing Co: Minnesota Dept. of Ag. Plant Protection Div., 90 Plato Blvd W, Saint Paul, MN 55107-2004; Title Tel # (612) 296-8387 Title Fax # (612) 296-7386
Personnel: Editor-Neville Wilson, Production Dir.-Karen Whiting
Editorial Description: Current economic pest conditions by regions in Minnesota. Based on field surveys, published summer only.
General Info: Yr. Est. 1968, Weekly, Trim Size-8½ x 11, Offset press, 4 pages, Color
Subscriptions: Free
Circulation: Total-2,000

NCAE Newsletter

Publishing Co: Natl. Council of Agricultural Employers (NCAE), 1735 I St. NW, Ste. 704, Washington, DC 20006-2402; Title Tel # (202) 728-0300 Title Fax # (202) 728-0303
Personnel: Editor-Sharon Hughes
Editorial Description: Newsletter for National Council of Agricultural Employers members.
General Info: Irregular, Trim Size-8½ x 11, Other press, 4 pages, Color-cover, Matte, Other
Subscriptions: Indv. $75
Circulation: Total-650
Printing Co: Huff Duplicating, 1100 17th St NW Ste 8b, Washington, DC 20036-4601 Tel # (202) 833-2000, Fax # (202) 452-1307

NCAMP's Technical Report
See: ENVIRONMENT & ECOLOGY

NCPA Newsletter   *Association*

Publishing Co: National Cottonseed Products Association, PO Box 172267, Memphis, TN 38187-2267; Title Tel # (901) 682-0800 Title Fax # (901) 682-2856
Personnel: Editor-Ben Morgan
Editorial Description: Current events of trade association
General Info: Yr. Est. 1897, Bi-weekly, Sheetfed press, 4 pages, No Color
Subscriptions: Indv. $200, Inst. $200, For. $200
Circulation: (100% controlled), Total-400

National Agricultural
Marketing Officials-
Newsletter

Publishing Co: Natl. Agricultural Marketing Officials, VA Dept. Ag. & Consumer Svcs., Box 1163, Richmond, VA 23209; Title Tel # (804) 786-3944
Personnel: Editor-Thomas Yates
Editorial Description: Newsletter of interest to marketing officials.

National Farm Workers
Minority Newsletter

Publishing Co: National Farm Workers Minority Newsletter, 1109 Cass St, Deland, FL 32720-6510; Title Tel # (813) 223-2141
Personnel: Editor-Connie Caldwell
General Info: Yr. Est. 1938, Quarterly, Trim Size-8½ x 11, Mimeo press, 2 pages
Circulation: Total-2,000

National Farmers Union
Newsletter   *Association*

Publishing Co: National Farmers Union/Canada, 250-C 2nd Ave., S., Saskatoon, SK S7K 2M1 Canada Fax # (306) 664-6226; Title Tel # (306) 652-9465
General Info: Monthly, 4 pages
Subscriptions: Indv. $10

National Farmers Union
Washington Newsletter

Publishing Co: National Farmers Union, 12025 E. 45th Ave., Denver, CO 80251-0001; Title Tel # (202) 554-1600 Title Fax # (202) 463-2785
Personnel: Editor-Milton Hakel
Editorial Description: News and developments in the Union and the agricultural industry in general.
General Info: Yr. Est. 1948, 18x/yr.
Subscriptions: Indv. $10

National Honey Market
News   *Business*

Publishing Co: U.S. Dept. of Agriculture, 2015 S 1st St Rm 4, Yakima, WA 98903-2231; Title Tel # (509) 575-2494 Title Fax # (509) 457-7132
Personnel: Publisher-Linda Verstrate
Editorial Description: General information on beekeeping conditions in the U.S. by state. Price information on bulk honey.
General Info: Yr. Est. 1916, Monthly, Trim Size-8½ x 11, Offset press, 20 pages, ISSN: 0364-2054
Subscriptions: Indv. $36, Can. $36, For. $72, $2/copy
Circulation: Total-200

Nebraska Union Farmer   *Business*

Publishing Co: Nebraska Farmers Union, 1305 Plum St, Lincoln, NE 68502-2343; Title Tel # (402) 476-8815
Personnel: Editor-John Hansen
General Info: Yr. Est. 1914, Monthly
Subscriptions: Indv. $1
Circulation: (100% controlled), Total-4,000

New England Farm
Bulletin & Garden
Gazette   *Consumer*

Publishing Co: Jacob's Meadow, Inc., PO Box 67, Taunton, MA 02780-0067; Title Tel # (508) 998-5424
Personnel: Publisher-V. A. Lipsett, Editor, Adv. Dir., Art Dir.-M. Maire
Editorial Description: Articles for small-scale farmers, gardeners.
General Info: (Formerly Massachusetts Farm Bulletin), Yr. Est. 1976, Monthly, Trim Size-8½ x 11, Offset press, 8 pages, No Color, Other
Subscriptions: Indv. $17, $2/copy
Circulation: Total-11,000
Advertising: Inquire for rates.
List Rental: Actives: $60/M, Expires: $60/M

New Hampshire Agricultural
Experiment Station
Bulletin   *Business, Association*

Publishing Co: Univ. of New Hampshire Agriculture Dept., Agricultural Experiment Stn., Durham, NH 03824; Title Tel # (603) 862-1234
Editorial Description: Covers current research and activities of the Agricultural Experiment Station.
General Info: Yr. Est. 1961, ISSN: 0077-832X

News & Views   *Consumer*   CPM: $150

Publishing Co: Allegany County Cooperative Extension, 5435A County Road 48, Belmont, NY 14813-9758; Title Tel # (716) 268-7644
Personnel: Editor-Paul Westfall, Adv. Dir.-Kay Fanton
Editorial Description: Agricultural, rural youth, consumer economics.
General Info: (Formerly Allegany County Cooperative Extension News), Yr. Est. 1914, Monthly, Trim Size-1 x 8½, Sheetfed press, 16 pages, 1% ads, 2 Color, Newsprint
Subscriptions: Indv. $6, $1/copy
Circulation: Total-400
Advertising: $60.
Printing Co: Media Services, Cornell Univ., Ithaca, NY 14853 Tel # (607) 255-2000

News from CAST   *Consumer, Association*

Publishing Co: Council for Agricultural Science & Technology, 4420 W. Lincoln Way, Ames, IA 50014-3447; Title Tel # (515) 292-2125 Title Fax # (515) 292-4512
Personnel: Publisher-Stanely Wilson, Editor-Robert Ver Streten
Editorial Description: CAST activities related to the science of food & agriculture.
General Info: (Formerly News from Cast), Yr. Est. 1974, Quarterly, Trim Size-8½ x 11, Sheetfed press, 14 pages, ISSN: 0194-1763, 2 Color, Coated, Saddle-stitched
Circulation: Total-5,500

News Spreader

Publishing Co: Quebec Young Farmers Federation, Box 80, S.A. de Bellevue, PQ H9X 3L4 Canada; Title Tel # (514) 457-2010 Title Fax # (514) 398-7972
Personnel: Editor-Lynn Adnerson-Arthur
General Info: Yr. Est. 1983, Monthly, Desktop press, 4 pages
Acquistions: Publication Bought
Circulation: Total-5,000

No-Till Farmer   *Business*

Publishing Co: Lessiter Publications, PO Box 624, Brookfield, WI 53008-0624 Fax # (414) 782-4252; Title Tel # (414) 782-4480 Title Fax # (414) 782-1252
Personnel: Editor-Frank Lessiter
Editorial Description: Devoted to farmers interested in reduced tillage.
General Info: Yr. Est. 1972, 17x/yr., Trim Size-8½ x 11, Sheetfed press, 8 pages, ISSN: 0091-9993, 2 Color, Coated, Saddle-stitched
Subscriptions: Indv. $35
Circulation: Total-11,000
Advertising: Accepts Inserts.
List Rental: Rents Lists

North American Bull Buyers Guide
See: LIVESTOCK

North-West Farmer-
Rancher

Publishing Co: Mcintosh Publishing Co., 1219 100 St., Box 430, North Battleford, SK S9A 2Y5 Canada; Title Tel # (306) 455-4401
Personnel: Publisher-Rod McDonald
Editorial Description: Y.
General Info: Yr. Est. 1905, Quarterly, Web press, 36 pages, 6% ads
Acquistions: Publication Bought
Circulation: Total-14,612

Nova Scotia Institute of
Agrologists Newsletter   *Business, Scholarly*

Publishing Co: Nova Scotia Institute of Agrologists, Box 550, Truro, NS B2N 5E3 Canada; Title Tel # (902) 893-6520 Title Fax # (902) 893-6393
Personnel: Editor-David Livingstone
Editorial Description: Information on research and development in agriculture.
General Info: Quarterly, 10 pages, ISSN: 0833-8485
Circulation: Total-250

Nut Kernel, The
See: PRODUCE

Nutshell The   *Association*   CPM: $71

Publishing Co: Northern Nut Growers Association, 654 Beinhower Rd, Etters, PA 17319-9774; Title Tel # (717) 938-6090 Title Fax # (717) 938-6090
Personnel: Editor-Tucker Hill
Editorial Description: Covers association activities and industry developments. Plus culture breeding pist control, grafting, and other topics related to nuts and nut trees.
General Info: Yr. Est. 1910, Quarterly, Trim Size-8½ x 11, Mimeo press, 16 pages, No Color, Other, Saddle-stitched
Subscriptions: Indv. $20, Can. $22, For. $25, $5/copy
Circulation: Total-1,400, Readership-1,400
Advertising: $100.
Printing Co: Penns Valley Printers, 1807 Market St, Camp Hill, PA 17011-4800 Tel # (717) 737-6769, Fax # (717) 737-1836

OFA Members' Digest   *Association*

Publishing Co: Ontario Federation of Agriculture, 491 W. Eglinton, #500, Toronto, ON M5N 3A2 Canada; Title Tel # (416) 485-3333 Title Fax # (416) 485-9027
Personnel: Editor-Gary Johnson
General Info: (Formerly Management Digest), Yr. Est. 1970, Monthly, Trim Size-8½ x 11, 8 pages, ISSN: 0255-0985, Newsprint, Saddle-stitched
Subscriptions: Indv. $2
Acquistions: Publication Bought
Circulation: Total-22,500

OIA Newsletter

Publishing Co: Ontario Inst. of Agrologists, 173 Wollwich Street, Suite 203, Guelph, ON N1H 3V4 Canada; Title Tel # (519) 837-2820 Title Fax # (519) 837-2820
Personnel: Editor-Don McAlpine
General Info: Bi-monthly, 4 pages, 2 Color
Circulation: (100% controlled), Total-1,300

Officer-In-Charge

Publishing Co: AMS, F&V Division, USDA, Federal Building, 550 Main St., Rm. 9522, Cincinnati, OH 45202-3222; Title Tel # (513) 684-3194
Personnel: Publisher-Bradford Porter
Editorial Description: Marketing & price information on fruits & vegetables.
General Info: Weekly, Trim Size-8½ x 14, 2 pages
Subscriptions: Indv. $96, Can. $96, For. $192, $2/copy
Acquistions: Publication Sold
Printing Co: Group Sales Assocs., 550 Main St., Cincinnati, OH 45202 Tel # (513) 651-1330

Orange County Ag Focus

Publishing Co: Orange County Agricultural Co-Op Extension Service, Community Campus, Dillion Drive, Middletown, NY 10940; Title Tel # (914) 343-1105
Personnel: Editor-Charles Boynton
Editorial Description: Organization news, as well as general interest items relating to the agricultural industry.
General Info: Monthly
Circulation: Total-1,050

Ornamental Crops National Market Trends
See: FLORIST

Ostriches
See: LIVESTOCK

PEPI Update
See: LABOR

Pest Management & Crop Development Bulletin   *Business*

Publishing Co: Univ. of Illinois at Urbana Champaign, 227 Illini Union, 1401 W. Green Street, Urbana, IL 61801 Tel # (217) 333-1477 Fax # (217) 333-7803; Title Tel # (217) 333-2666 Title Fax # (217) 333-1952
Personnel: Publisher-Kevin Steffey
Editorial Description: Weekly reports include the current agricultural insect, weed & plant disease situation with advice on control methods new developments in pesticide application techniques.
General Info: 20x/yr.
Subscriptions: Indv. $20

Pesticide & Toxic Chemical News Guide   *Business*

Publishing Co: Food Chemical News, 1101 Pennsylvania Ave SE, Washington, DC 20003-2229 Parent Co.-CRC Press, Inc., Boca Raton; Title Tel # (202) 544-1980 Title Fax # (202) 546-3890
Personnel: Publisher-Marjorie Weiner, Mktg. Dir.-Jill Casasola
Editorial Description: Complete in one volume - The only reference service listing all tolerances, administrative guidelines or exemptions for pesticide residues in food or feed. Indexed by both chemical and by crop. Updated monthly with the latest U.S. pesticide tolerances, proposals and pending petitions.
General Info: Yr. Est. 1974, Monthly, No Color, Looseleaf
Subscriptions: Indv. $742

Pigletter
See: LIVESTOCK

Plant Pathology Circular, Entomology Arcular, Hematology Arcular, Botany Circular
See: BOTANY

Pool People

Publishing Co: Saskatchewan Wheat Pool, 2625 Victoria Ave., Regina, SK S4T 7T9 Canada Tel # (306) 569-4411
Personnel: Editor-Marj Strandlund
Editorial Description: Staff newsletter.
General Info: (Formerly In Touch), Yr. Est. 1976, 10x/yr., Web press, 12 pages, Matte
Circulation: (100% controlled), Total-5,000
Printing Co: MC Graphics, 1048 Fleury St., Regina, SK S4N 4W8 Canada

Pool Today

Publishing Co: Saskatchewan Wheat Pool, 2625 Victoria Ave., Regina, SK S4T 7T9 Canada; Title Tel # (306) 569-4411
Personnel: Publisher-Don O'Neill, Editor-Pieter Van Der Breggen
Editorial Description: Directed to member owners of the co-operative.
General Info: Yr. Est. 1988, Quarterly, Web press, 8 pages, 4 Color, Matte
Circulation: (100% controlled), Total-70,000
Printing Co: MC Graphics, Inc., 2310 Millar Ave., Saskatoon, SK Canada Tel # (306) 665-3500

Potato Newsletter   *Business, Association*

Publishing Co: New Brunswick Dept. of Agriculture, Box 6000, Fredericton, NB E3B 5H1 Canada Tel # (506) 457-7244 Fax # (506) 457-7267; Title Tel # (506) 392-5100 Title Fax # (503) 392-5102
Personnel: Editor-Robert Hinds
Editorial Description: Designed for Potato Producers in NB - to provide technical information on potato production, trends in the potato industry & appropriate marketing information.
General Info: (Formerly Agricultural Report-Potatoes), Yr. Est. 1979, Bi-monthly, Trim Size-8½ x 11, Offset press, 8 pages, 2 Color, Other, Saddle-stitched
Subscriptions: Free
Circulation: Total-1,100
Printing Co: New Brunswick Dept. of Agriculture Print Shop, NB Agriculture, Box 6000, Fredericton, NB E3B 5H1 Canada Tel # (506) 453-3448, Fax # (506) 453-7978

Poultry Market News Report
See: POULTRY & POULTRY PRODUCTS

Prayer Letter   *Business*

Publishing Co: FARMS Intl., Inc., PO Box 270, Knife River, MN 55609-0270 Tel # (218) 834-2676 Fax # (218) 834-2676
Editorial Description: Agriculture Evangelism.
General Info: Monthly
Circulation: Total-1,500

Pro Farmer

Publishing Co: Oster Communications, Inc., 219 Parkade, PO Box 6, Cedar Falls, IA 50613 Fax # (319) 277-7982; Title Tel # (319) 277-1278
Personnel: Publisher-Merrill Oster, Editor-Dan Manternach, Circ. Mgr.-Sandy Golz, Adv. Dir.-John Heidersbach, Art Dir.-Pete Cornell
Editorial Description: Farm related market news & analysis. Also recommendations & management advice.
General Info: Yr. Est. 1973, Weekly, Sheetfed press, 8 pages, Coated
Subscriptions: Indv. $99
Circulation: Total-25,000
List Rental: List Management Co.: Venture Communications, 60 Madison Avenue, 3rd fl., New York, NY 10010 Tel # (212) 684-4800, Fax # (212) 545-1680
Printing Co: Congdon Printing Co., 115 E 2nd St, Cedar Falls, IA 50613-3357 Tel # (319) 266-7578

Pulse Crop Newsletter

Publishing Co: Saskatchewan Pulse Crop Growers' Development Bd., 101-2515 Victoria Ave., Regina, SK S4P 0T2 Canada; Title Tel # (306) 781-7475 Title Fax # (306) 525-4173
Personnel: Editor-Donald Jaques
General Info: Yr. Est. 1985, Bi-monthly, 16 pages, 2 Color
Subscriptions: Indv. $20
Circulation: (100% controlled), Total-6,000

Q-Weather Forecast & Commodities Outlook
See: INVESTMENT

Quate's Grain/Weather Forecast

Publishing Co: Quate Assocs., PO Box 7065, Suffolk, VA 23437-0065; Title Tel # (804) 657-6531
Personnel: Publisher, Editor-Boyd Quate, Promotion Dir.-Lois White
Editorial Description: Long Range Weather Forecast & its likely effects on the commodity market.
General Info: Yr. Est. 1962, Bi-monthly, Trim Size-8½ x 11, Mimeo press, 20 pages, No Color, Newsprint
Subscriptions: Indv. $75, $25/copy
Circulation: (95% controlled)

R.N.R. Reports

Publishing Co: Univ. of Nevada, Las Vegas, 4505 S Maryland Pky, Las Vegas, NV 89154-9900 Tel # (702) 739-3011; Title Tel # (702) 739-3443
General Info: Yr. Est. 1972, 2 pages, No Color
Circulation: (100% controlled), Total-200

Ram's Horn   *Consumer*

Publishing Co: The Ram's Horn, 125 Highfield Rd., Toronto, ON M4L 2T9 Canada; Title Tel # (416) 469-8414 Title Fax # (416) 469-8414
Personnel: Publisher-Brewster Kneen, Editor-Cathleen Kneen
Editorial Description: Analysis of the food system, agricultural policy, corporate structure, from farm to supermarket: information & radical critique.
General Info: Yr. Est. 1980, 11x/yr., Trim Size-8½ x 11, Offset press, 8 pages, ISSN: 0827-4053, Matte
Subscriptions: Indv. $20, Inst. $30, Can. $15, For. $20
Circulation: (83% controlled), Total-600, International-100

Research

Publishing Co: Cook College, Rutgers Univ., Nichol Ave., New Brunswick, NJ 08901; Title Tel # (201) 247-1766
Editorial Description: Reports and descriptions of research and related matters of Agricultural Experiment Station.
General Info: Yr. Est. 1968, Quarterly, Trim Size-8½ x 11, Offset press, 16 pages, Color
Circulation: Total-12,000

Resource Development Newsletter

Publishing Co: University of Tennessee Agricultural Extensions, PO Box 1071, Knoxville, TN 37901-1071; Title Tel # (615) 974-7306
Editorial Description: Items related to community development.
General Info: (Formerly Community Resource Development Newsletter), Yr. Est. 1945, Quarterly, Trim Size-8½ x 11½, Sheetfed press, 4 pages, No Color
Circulation: Total-5,000

Rice Price Advisory

Publishing Co: Rice Journal Enterprises, Inc., Box 14260, Ben Franklin Sta., Washington, DC 20044-4260; Title Tel # (202) 547-5633 Title Fax # (202) 546-3890
Personnel: Publisher-C.B. Morrison, Editor-David Morrison
Editorial Description: Information for rice farmers, millers & traders.
General Info: Yr. Est. 1989, Weekly, Sheetfed press, 2 pages, No Color, Matte
Subscriptions: Indv. $135, For. $150

Ridge Till HotLine   *Business, Consumer*

Publishing Co: Lessiter Publications, PO Box 624, Brookfield, WI 53008-0624 Fax # (414) 782-4252; Title Tel # (414) 782-4480 Title Fax # (414) 782-1252
Personnel: Publisher-Frank Lessiter
Editorial Description: For farmers interested in any aspect of ridge till farming.
General Info: Yr. Est. 1991, Monthly, Trim Size-8½ x 11, Letrpr. press, 8 pages, No Color, Recycled, Saddle-stitched
Subscriptions: Indv. $35, Can. $42, For. $52, $3/copy
Circulation: Total-1,500
Advertising: Accepts Inserts.
List Rental: Actives: 1,500, Expires: 1,400

Rural Advance

Publishing Co: Rural Advancement Fund, 2124 Commonwealth Ave, Charlotte, NC 28205-5126; Title Tel # (704) 334-3051
Personnel: Editor-Cary Fowler

Rusty Iron Monthly
See: ANTIQUES & ART GOODS

SAGA   *Association*

Publishing Co: Saskatchewan Agricultural Graduates Assn., Inc., Box 320, Sub. PO 6, Saskatoon, SK S7N 0W0 Canada; Title Tel # (306) 933-1257
Personnel: Editor-Jack Braider
Editorial Description: Informational & humorous.
General Info: (Formerly Ag. Grad. Newsletter), Yr. Est. 1940, Trim Size-8½ x 11, 16 pages, No Color
Subscriptions: Indv. $10, Free With Membership
Circulation: (95% controlled), Total-2,000

San Francisco Wholesale Fruit & Vegetable Report
See: PRODUCE

San Francisco Wholesale Ornamental Crops Report
See: GARDENING & HORTICULTURE

Saskatchewan Alfalfa Seed Producers Assn. Newsletter

Publishing Co: Saskatchewan Alfalfa Seed Producers Assn., 107 Science Crescent, Saskatoon, SK S7N 0X2 Canada; Title Tel # (306) 975-7014 Title Fax # (306) 242-1839
Personnel: Publisher, Editor-W. Goerzen
General Info: Yr. Est. 1988, Quarterly, Letrpr. press, 20 pages, No Color
Circulation: (33% controlled), Total-375, Subscriptions-200
Advertising: Inquire for rates.
Printing Co: University of Saskatoon Printing Svc., Univ. of Saskatoon, Saskatoon, SK S7N 0W0 Canada Tel # (306) 966-6639

Saskatchewan Institute of Agrologists Newsletter   *Business, Association*

Publishing Co: Saskatchewan Institute of Agrologists, #7-3012 Louise St., Saskatoon, SK S7J 3L8 Canada; Title Tel # (306) 242-2606 Title Fax # (306) 955-5561
Personnel: Editor-Wayne Gamble
General Info: Yr. Est. 1975, Bi-monthly, Desktop press, 6 pages, 1% ads
Circulation: Total-1,300
Advertising: Inquire for rates. Accepts Inserts.

Schenectady County Cooperative Extension News

Publishing Co: Cooperative Extension of Schenectady County, 620 State St, Schenectady, NY 12305-2114; Title Tel # (518) 377-2271
Personnel: Editor-W. Durniak
Editorial Description: Continuous adult education as related to family and home.
General Info: Yr. Est. 1918, Monthly
Subscriptions: Indv. $3
Circulation: Total-1,400
Advertising: Inquire for rates.

Scientists Center for Animal Welfare's Newsletter
See: ANIMALS

Seed Scoop   *Business, Association*

Publishing Co: Canadian Seed Growers Assn, CPO Box 8455, Ottawa, ON K1G 3T1 Canada; Title Tel # (613) 236-0497
Personnel: Editor-O.M. Clayton
Editorial Description: Activities of the association; instructions to growers on production of pedigreed seed crops.
General Info: Yr. Est. 1954, Quarterly, Trim Size-8½ x 11, Web press, 8 pages, ISSN: 0049-0040, 2 Color
Circulation: (100% controlled), Total-12,000

Seed Technologist News   *Business, Association*

Publishing Co: Society of Commercial Seed Technologists, PO Box 1393, Saint Joseph, MO 64502-1393; Title Tel # (816) 238-7333 Title Fax # (816) 238-7849
Editorial Description: Personal news of Registered Seed Technologists; research in seed technology--reports of meetings; book reviews concerning seed technology.
General Info: Quarterly
Subscriptions: Indv. $25
Printing Co: Omnipress, 2600 Anderson St., Madison, WI 53704-3132

Seedhead News   *Business, Consumer*

Publishing Co: Native Seeds/SEARCH, 2509 N Campbell Ave # 325, Tucson, AZ 85719-3304; Title Tel # (520) 327-9123 Title Fax # (520) 327-5821
Personnel: Editor-Kevin Dahl
Editorial Description: Information and developments relating to seeds and Native American agriculture.
General Info: Yr. Est. 1983, Quarterly, Sheetfed press, 12 pages, No Color, Newsprint
Subscriptions: Indv. $20
Circulation: (11% controlled)

Sharecropper

Publishing Co: National Sharecropper's Fund/Rual Advancement Fund, PO Box 18217, Charlotte, NC 28218-0217; Title Tel # (704) 334-3051
Editorial Description: News relating to the activities of the Sharecroppers Fund and farm issues.
General Info: Bi-monthly

Small Scale Agriculture Today   *Consumer, Association*

Publishing Co: H.W. 'Bud' Kerr, Dir. of Office for Small Scale Argriculture, Ag Box 2244, Washington, DC 20250-2244; Title Tel # (202) 720-5245 Title Fax # (202) 205-2448
Editorial Description: Cat. A1:125.
General Info: Yr. Est. 1979, Monthly

Sodus News, The
See: REGIONAL INTEREST

Soilless Grower   *Association*   CPM: $106

Publishing Co: Leesburg Printing Co., 1100 North Blvd. East, Leesburg, FL 34748 Fax # (904) 787-2210; Title Tel # (510) 743-9605 Title Fax # (510) 743-9302
Personnel: Editor-Maynard Bates, Circ. Mgr., Adv. Dir.-Patty Bates
Editorial Description: Association & industry newsletter concerning hydroponics.
General Info: Yr. Est. 1979, Bi-monthly, Trim Size-8½ x 11½, Mimeo press, 24 pages, Color-cover, Perfect bound
Subscriptions: Indv. $40, For. $60
Circulation: Total-800
Advertising: $85. Accepts Inserts.

Song News   *Association*

Publishing Co: Society of Ontario Nut Growers, C/o G.R. Hambleton, RR2, 1540 Concession 6 Rd., Niagara on the Lake, ON L0S 1J0 Canada
Personnel: Editor-R. Douglas Campbell
General Info: Yr. Est. 1972, Semi-annually, Trim Size-8½ x 11, 12 pages, ISSN: 0704-5859
Subscriptions: Indv. $12, Free With Membership
Circulation: Total-600
Advertising: Inquire for rates.

Spudletter   *Business, Consumer*

Publishing Co: Natl. Potato Council, 5690 DTC Blvd., Ste. 230-E, Englewood, CO 80111-3200; Title Tel # (303) 773-9295
General Info: Bi-monthly, 8 pages, No Color
Circulation: Total-11,000

Supima Association of America Newsletter   *Association*

Publishing Co: Supima Assn. of America, 4141 E. Broadway Rd., Phoenix, AZ 85040-8803; Title Tel # (602) 437-1364 Title Fax # (602) 437-0143
Personnel: Publisher, Editor-Matt Laughlin
Editorial Description: Information on pima cotton growers, acres to be planted, market for cotton, promotional activities of association.
General Info: Yr. Est. 1954, Monthly, 4 pages, Coated
Circulation: Total-3,000
Printing Co: Printing Center, 2227 S. 48th St. C-D, Tempe, AZ 85282

Tater News

Publishing Co: Natl. Potato Promotion Board, 7555 E Hampden Ave Ste 412, Denver, CO 80231-4835; Title Tel # (303) 758-7783 Title Fax # (303) 756-9256
Personnel: Publisher-Larry Brooks, Editor, Circ. Mgr., Promotion Dir.-Andrea Merriman
Editorial Description: Provides information to the potato industry updating Board efforts and programs along with other miscellaneous industry information.
General Info: Yr. Est. 1973, Bi-monthly, Letrpr. press, 4 pages
Circulation: (100% controlled), Total-17,000
Advertising: Accepts Inserts.
Printing Co: Moser Printing, 3900 S Mariposa St, Englewood, CO 80110-4424

TechAgra News   *Business*   CPM: $31

Publishing Co: Clark Consulting International, Inc., 14n921 Lac Du Beatrice, Dundee, IL 60118-3115; Title Tel # (708) 843-9952 Title Fax # (708) 843-8793
Personnel: Publisher, Editor, Adv. Dir.-Warren Clark
Editorial Description: Latest management and production developments affecting the largest 90,000 computerized farmers who produce 75% of all the food and fiber grown in the U.S.
General Info: (Formerly Ag Technology News), Yr. Est. 1988, Irregular, Trim Size-8½ x 11, 2 Color, Matte, Saddle-stitched
Subscriptions: Free To Qualified Recipient
Acquistions: Publication Bought
Circulation: Total-90,000
Advertising: $2,800. Accepts Inserts.
List Rental: Actives: 90,000, $55/M

Tiger on Spreads
See: INVESTMENT

Tomato Club, The
See: GARDENING & HORTICULTURE

Tri-Ology Technical Report
See: BIOLOGY

University of Illinois At Urbana-Champaign, College of Agriculture, Current Affairs
See: COLLEGE STUDENT

Vegan News, The
See: ENVIRONMENT & ECOLOGY

Virginia Agriculture
Commodity Newsletter — *Association, Business*

Publishing Co: Virginia Department of Agriculture and Consumer Services, 1100 Bank St Ste 805, Richmond, VA 23219-3638; Title Tel # (804) 786-3947 Title Fax # (804) 371-7787
Personnel: Editor-J.P. Welch, Production Mgr.-Diane Kendall
Editorial Description: Weekly summary of grain, feedstuffs, cotton, tobacco, peanut and livestock prices and trends.
General Info: (Formerly Market Report Weekly), Yr. Est. 1981, Weekly, Trim Size-8½ x 11, Offset press, 4 pages, ISSN: 1064-4067, No Color
Subscriptions: Free In Designated Area
Circulation: Total-2,600

Virginia Fruit & Vegetable
Bulletin — *Business, Association*

Publishing Co: Virginia Department of Agriculture and Consumer Services, 1100 Bank St Ste 805, Richmond, VA 23219-3638; Title Tel # (804) 786-3947 Title Fax # (804) 371-7787
Personnel: Editor-J.P. Welch, Production Mgr.-Nancy Waller
Editorial Description: Summary of fruit and vegetable prices and trends.
General Info: Yr. Est. 1917, Weekly, Trim Size-8½ x 14, Offset press, 2 pages, ISSN: 1064-4075
Subscriptions: Free In Designated Area
Circulation: Total-600

Virginia Hay Clearing
House — *Business*

Publishing Co: Virginia Department of Agriculture and Consumer Services, 1100 Bank St Ste 805, Richmond, VA 23219-3638; Title Tel # (804) 786-3947 Title Fax # (804) 371-7787
Personnel: Editor-J.P. Welch, Production Mgr.-Diane Kendall
Editorial Description: Monthly listing of hay to buy and sell.
General Info: Yr. Est. 1985, Quarterly, Trim Size-8½ x 14, Offset press, 2 pages, ISSN: 1065-5948
Subscriptions: Free In Designated Area
Circulation: Total-700

Visitor — *Association*

Publishing Co: Univ. of Minnesota, Dept. of Agricultural Education, St. Paul Campus, St. Paul, MN 55108; Title Tel # (612) 373-1021
Editorial Description: Education-agriculture and vocational.
General Info: Quarterly, Trim Size-4 x 6, 4 pages
Circulation: Total-500

Voice of the American Agri-
Woman — *Business, Association*

Publishing Co: American Agri-Women, 6835 Road Two, Kanorado, KS 67741-9400; Title Tel # (913) 399-2204 Title Fax # (913) 399-2205
Personnel: Publisher-Jeanne Pettibone
Editorial Description: News and information for farm & ranch women.
General Info: Bi-monthly
Circulation: Total-5,000

WACA News — *Business, Association*

Publishing Co: Western Agricultural Chemicals Assn., 3835 N Freeway Blvd Ste 140, Sacramento, CA 95834-1954 Tel # (916) 568-3660; Title Tel # (916) 446-9222 Title Fax # (916) 565-0113
Personnel: Editor, Adv. Dir., Art Dir.-Gregory P. Hurner
Editorial Description: Membership newsletter of assn. activities.
General Info: Yr. Est. 1921, Quarterly, Trim Size-8½ x 11, Sheetfed press, 12 pages, 70% ads, 2 Color, Coated, Saddle-stitched
Subscriptions: Free To Qualified Recipient
Circulation: (50% controlled), Total-3,000, Single Copy/Newsstand-1,500, Readership-3,500, Source-IS

Washington Agricultural
Record

Publishing Co: Agro/Info., PO Box 25001, Washington, DC 20007-8001; Title Tel # (202) 659-6599
Personnel: Publisher, Editor-Mark Pyle
Editorial Description: Weekly review of Washington National & International agricultureal events. Fee vials available.
General Info: Weekly, Letrpr. press, 1 pages, Ind/Abs/Online: PMLA, SSCI, 2 Color
Subscriptions: Indv. $65, For. $85

Washington Aquafarm
Letter

Publishing Co: Rice Journal Enterprises, Inc., Box 14260, Ben Franklin Sta., Washington, DC 20044-4260; Title Tel # (202) 547-5633
Personnel: Publisher-C.B. Morrison, Editor-David Morrison
Editorial Description: News of interest to commercial producers of fish & shellfish natl. & state aquaculture policy.
General Info: Yr. Est. 1984, Bi-weekly, Sheetfed press, 4 pages, Newsprint
Subscriptions: Indv. $70

Washington Bakery Report
See: BAKING

Water: Protection,
Conservation,
Management

Publishing Co: University of Tennessee Agricultural Extensions, PO Box 1071, Knoxville, TN 37901-1071; Title Tel # (615) 974-7306
Personnel: Editor-George Smith
Editorial Description: Items related to the protection, conservation & management of water resources.
General Info: Yr. Est. 1988, Quarterly, Sheetfed press, 4 pages
Circulation: Total-5,500

Webster Agricultural
Letter — *Business*

Publishing Co: Webster Communications Corp., 1530 Key Blvd., PH 2, Arlington, VA 22209-1532; Title Tel # (703) 525-4512 Title Fax # (703) 525-4917
Personnel: Publisher-James Webster, Editor-James C. Webster
Editorial Description: Federal/state/private actions in the farm/rural policy area.
General Info: (Formerly Agricultural Credit Letter), Yr. Est. 1985, Semi-monthly, Trim Size-8½ x 11, Sheetfed press, 6 pages, ISSN: 1073-4813, No Color
Subscriptions: Indv. $295, Can. $295, For. $325, $12/copy
List Rental: Rents Lists

Weekly Market Summary — *Business*

Publishing Co: Missouri Department of Agriculture, PO Box 630, Jefferson City, MO 65102-0630; Title Tel # (314) 751-4211 Title Fax # (314) 751-2868
Personnel: Editor-Sam Shelton
Editorial Description: Weekly prices of livestock, grain, futures, wholesale meat, slaughter & comments.
General Info: Yr. Est. 1981, Weekly, Sheetfed press, 1 pages
Subscriptions: Indv. $15
Circulation: Total-2,000

Weekly Weather & Crop
Bulletin

Publishing Co: NOAA/USDA Joint Agricultural Weather Facility, Usda S. Bldg., Rm. 5844, Washington, DC 20250-0001; Title Tel # (202) 720-7917
Personnel: Editor-Douglas Le Comte
Editorial Description: Presents maps, tables, & text describing the weekly weather over the US & other major crop-producing countries. Also contains international monthly temperature & precipitation data, & US seasonal summaries. Includes state & national agricultural summaries.
General Info: Yr. Est. 1872, Weekly, ISSN: 0043-1974
Subscriptions: Indv. $45, For. $55, $1/copy
Circulation: Total-1,600

West Virginia Department
of Agriculture Market
Bulletin — *Business*

Publishing Co: West Virginia State Dept. of Agriculture, 1900 Kanawha Blvd E, Charleston, WV 25305-0002 Tel # (304) 558-3708; Title Tel # (304) 348-3708 Title Fax # (304) 558-2203
Personnel: Publisher-Howard T. Knotts
Editorial Description: Ad-type market paper for West Virginia farmers.
General Info: Yr. Est. 1921, Monthly, Trim Size-8½ x 11, Offset press, 16 pages, No Color, Saddle-stitched
Subscriptions: Free In Designated Area
Circulation: Total-60,000

Western Barley Growers
Assn. Newsletter

Publishing Co: Western Barley Growers Assn., 2116 27th Ave., NE, Ste. 232, Calgary, AB T2E 7A6 Canada
General Info: Monthly
Circulation: Total-1,400

Western Canada Fertilizer
Assn. Newsletter

Publishing Co: Western Canada Fertilizer Assn., 12202G 86th Ave., Surrey, BC V3W 3H7 Canada; Title Tel # (604) 572-7775 Title Fax # (604) 591-7743
Personnel: Publisher, Editor-D.C. McLean
Editorial Description: Promotes the safe handling and use of fertilizer and the environmentally responsive use of fertilizer. Features government regulatory news and fertilizer agronomics.
General Info: Yr. Est. 1964, Quarterly, 6 pages, 2 Color, Newsprint
Subscriptions: Free
Circulation: Total-200
Advertising: Accepts Inserts.
Printing Co: Whalley Printers, 10715 King George Hwy., Surrey, BC V3T 2X6 Canada Tel # (604) 588-3533

Western Melon and
Vegetable Report — *Business*

Publishing Co: AMS, F&V Division, USDA-Market News Dept., 522 N Central Ave Ste 245, Phoenix, AZ 85004-2168; Title Tel # (602) 379-3066 Title Fax # (602) 379-3160
Editorial Description: Marketing and pricing information on fruits and vegetables.
General Info: Daily, Looseleaf
Subscriptions: Indv. $240, For. $480

Western Stock Growers
Newsletter

Publishing Co: Western Stock Growers Assn., 2116 27th Ave., NE, Ste. 101, Calgary, AB T2E 7A6 Canada; Title Tel # (403) 250-9117
Personnel: Editor-Garth Cochran
General Info: Yr. Est. 1976, Monthly
Circulation: Total-1,900
Advertising: Inquire for rates.

Wheat Briefs *Business*

Publishing Co: Wheat Quality Council, PO Box 966, Pierre, SD 57501-0966; Title Tel # (605) 224-5187 Title Fax # (605) 224-0517
Personnel: Publisher, Editor-Ben Handcock
Editorial Description: Current information on wheat quality.
General Info: (Formerly Wheat Quality Notes), Yr. Est. 1938, Irregular, Trim Size-8½ x 14, Mimeo press, 1 pages
Circulation: (100% controlled), Total-1,100

Windmillers' Gazette *Business, Consumer*

Publishing Co: Windmillers' Gazette, PO Box 507, Rio Vista, TX 76093-0507
Personnel: Publisher, Editor-T. Lindsay Baker
Editorial Description: Journal of wind power history and water-pumping windmills.
General Info: Yr. Est. 1982, Quarterly, Trim Size-8½ x 11, Offset press, 12 pages, ISSN: 0736-7287, Ind/Abs/Online: 1982-91 index, 10% ads, No Color, Matte, Other
Subscriptions: Indv. $15, Inst. $15, Can. $15, For. $15, $5/copy
Circulation: Total-1,000
Advertising: Inquire for rates.

ALMANACS

Aunt Caroline's Almanac

Publishing Co: Aunt Caroline, Inc., 3806 Alisa Ann Dr, Corpus Christi, TX 78418-3002; Title Tel # (512) 937-4303
Personnel: Publisher, Editor-Caroline Lane
General Info: Yr. Est. 1984, Monthly

Crusader's Almanac *Association*

Publishing Co: Commissariat of the Holy Land, 1400 Quincy St NE, Washington, DC 20017-3041; Title Tel # (202) 526-6800
Personnel: Editor-Fr. Drew McGeehan
Editorial Description: Catholic pub. News from the Holy Land, Rome & Washington, DC.
General Info: Yr. Est. 1892, Semi-annually, Trim Size-5¼ x 8, 16 pages, Color
Circulation: Total-80,000

Miniature Book News
See: BOOKS & BOOK TRADE

Washington Aquafarm Letter
See: AGRICULTURE

ANIMALS

AMC CenterScope
See: VETERINARY

Aardvarks in the News

Publishing Co: Natl. Assn. for the Advancement of Aardvarks in America, 947 Perkins Ave, Waukesha, WI 53186-5247
General Info: Semi-annually
Circulation: Total-172

Alert, National Service Dog Center Newsletter
See: DOGS

American Standard
Chinchilla Rabbit Assn.
News

Publishing Co: American Standard Chinchilla Rabbit Assn., 1607 9th St W, Palmetto, FL 34221-4465; Title Tel # (813) 729-1184
Editorial Description: Reports on shows & natl. sweepstake standings for breeders of Chinchilla Rabbit.
General Info: Yr. Est. 1952, Bi-monthly

Animal Defence League of
Canada News Bulletin *Association*

Publishing Co: Animal Defence League of Canada, Box 3880, STN C, Ottawa, ON K1Y 4M5 Canada; Title Tel # (613) 233-6117
Editorial Description: Information on immediate problems, general progress & activities of ADLC & other animal welfare/rights organizations.
General Info: Yr. Est. 1958, Semi-annually, Trim Size-8½ x 14, Mimeo press, 4 pages, ISSN: 0044-829X, No Color
Subscriptions: Free
Acquistions: Publication Bought
Circulation: Total-3,500

Animal News
See: VETERINARY

Animal Review

Publishing Co: Nell Zink, 81 Grand ST #4, Jersey City, NJ 07302
Editorial Description: Full of obscure animal trivia, review animals & wonderful reviews of unusual zoos and roadside attractions.
General Info: Trim Size-5 x 7, 22 pages
Subscriptions: Indv. $2

Animal Sheltering
Magazine

Publishing Co: Humane Society of the United States, 2100 L St., NW, Washington, DC 20037-1525; Title Tel # (202) 452-1100
Personnel: Editor-Geoffrey L. Handy, Asst. Ed.-Jill Shepherd, Production Mgr.-Ron Vaget
Editorial Description: The community animal care, control, and protection resource. Provides news & information on a variety of companion animal issues, including pet overpopulation, humane society & animal control management, animal cruelty, legislation & pet owner education.
General Info: (Formerly Shelter Sense), Yr. Est. 1978, Bi-monthly, Trim Size-8½ x 11, Sheetfed press, 32 pages, ISSN: 0734-3078, 2 Color, Recycled, Saddle-stitched
Subscriptions: Indv. $8, Inst. $8, Can. $8, For. $8, $1/copy
Circulation: Total-4,000, Readership-10,000
Advertising: Inquire for rates.
Printing Co: Artison Printing, 7905 Fernham Ln, Forestville, MD 20747-4544 Tel # (301) 736-6905

Animal Transportation
Association Newsletter CPM$1285

Publishing Co: Animal Transportation Association, 5521 Greenville Ave., Suite 104-310, Dallas, TX 75206 Tel # (903) 769-2267; Title Tel # (903) 725-6553 Title Fax # (903) 769-2867
Personnel: Publisher-Cherie Derouin
Editorial Description: For those concerned with the humane transportation and handling of animals.
General Info: Yr. Est. 1976, Quarterly, Trim Size-8½ x 11, Sheetfed press, 24 pages, 8% ads, 2 Color, Matte, Saddle-stitched
Subscriptions: Indv. $150, Inst. $125, Free With Membership
Circulation: Total-350
Advertising: $450. Accepts Inserts.

Animal Welfare Information
Center Newsletter *Consumer, Association*

Publishing Co: Sponsor-Natl. Agricultural Library, US Dept. of Agriculture, Animal Welfare Information Center, Nat. Agricultural Library, 10301 Baltimore Blvd., Beltsville, MD 20705-2351; Title Tel # (301) 504-6212 Title Fax # (301) 504-7125
Personnel: Editor-Tim Allen, Production Mgr.-D'anna Jensen
Editorial Description: Designed to provide information relevont to the regulated research, testing and teaching communities on alternatives to painful procedures used on animals.
General Info: Yr. Est. 1990, Quarterly, ISSN: 1050-561X
Subscriptions: Free
Circulation: (96% controlled), Total-6,000, International-200

Animaldom

Publishing Co: Pennsylvania SPCA, 350 E Erie Ave, Philadelphia, PA 19134-1013; Title Tel # (215) 426-6300 Title Fax # (215) 426-5848
Personnel: Editor-Charlene Peters
Editorial Description: Activities of Pennsylvania SPCA, animal welfare, conservation, pet care, legislation.
General Info: Yr. Est. 1930, Monthly, Trim Size-8½ x 11, Offset press, 4 pages, No Color
Subscriptions: Indv. $2
Circulation: Total-38,000
Printing Co: Waldman Graphics, 9100 Pennsauken Hwy, Pennsauken, NJ 08110-1293 Tel # (609) 662-9111, Fax # (609) 665-1789

Animals & Us

Publishing Co: Human-Animal Bond Association of Canada, P.O. Box 71012, Maplehurst Postal Outlet, Burlington, ON L7T 4J8 Canada; Title Tel # (416) 410-2026
General Info: Yr. Est. 1987, Quarterly, Trim Size-8½ x 11, 8 pages, 2 Color, Matte, Perfect bound
Subscriptions: Indv. $25

Animals' Advocate

Publishing Co: Animal Legal Defense Fund, 1363 Lincoln Ave Ste 7, San Rafael, CA 94901-2124; Title Tel # (415) 459-0885
Personnel: Editor-Joyce Tischler
General Info: Quarterly, 4 pages, No Color
Circulation: (100% controlled), Total-50,000
List Rental: Actives: $65/M, Expires: 9,400, $55/M

Animals International   *Consumer, Association*

Publishing Co: Sponsor-W.S.P.A., World Society for the Protection of Animals, 29 Perkins St # 190, Boston, MA 02130-1114; Title Tel # (617) 522-7000
Personnel: Editor-John Walsh
Editorial Description: International animal protection news reports.
General Info: Yr. Est. 1961, Quarterly, Trim Size-8½ x 11, 12 pages, 2 Color, Coated
Subscriptions: Indv. $10, Inst. $25
Circulation: (100% controlled), Total-22,000

Association for Biomedical Research-Regulatory Alert

Publishing Co: Association for Biomedical Research, 818 Connecticut Ave NW Ste 303, Washington, DC 20006-2702; Title Tel # (202) 371-6606
Personnel: Editor-Barbara Rich
Editorial Description: Summarizes news concerning the use of laboratory animals in biomedical research & testing.
General Info: (Formerly Research Animal Alliance Regulatory Alert), 2 pages
Circulation: Total-500

Bide-A-Wee News

Publishing Co: Bide-A-Wee Home Assn., 410 E 38th St, New York, NY 10016-2702; Title Tel # (212) 532-4455
Editorial Description: News & information for supporters of Bide-A-Wee.
General Info: Quarterly, 2 Color, Coated

Big Cat Sculpture Association
See: CATS

Breeder's Registry Newsletter   *Consumer, Association*

Publishing Co: Breeder's Registry, PO Box 255373, Sacramento, CA 95865-5373
Editorial Description: For those who captively breed tropical fish.
General Info: Quarterly, Trim Size-8½ x 11

Brief Paws   *Association*

Publishing Co: Tacoma-Pierce County Humane Society, 2608 S Center St, Tacoma, WA 98409-7602; Title Tel # (206) 383-7069
Personnel: Editor-Dian Douglas
Editorial Description: Animal welfare; pet care information.
General Info: (Formerly Paw Prints), Trim Size-8½ x 11, Offset press, 16 pages, 2 Color
Subscriptions: Indv. $25
Circulation: Total-6,000
Advertising: Inquire for rates.

Buffalo!

Publishing Co: Natl. Buffalo Assn., 10 Main St., Box 580, Ft. Pierre, SD 57532; Title Tel # (605) 223-2829
Personnel: Editor-Kimberly Dowling
Editorial Description: Dedicated to promotion & propagation of American Buffalo & its products.
General Info: Yr. Est. 1966, Bi-monthly, Trim Size-8½ x 11, Web press, 28 pages, ISSN: 0196-9137, 2% ads, 2 Color, Newsprint
Subscriptions: Indv. $15, $3/copy
Circulation: Total-1,000
Advertising: Inquire for rates.
List Rental: Actives: $50/M
Printing Co: State Publishing Co., 303 E Sioux Ave, Pierre, SD 57501-3138 Tel # (605) 224-9999

CATsumer Report
See: CATS

CHAI Lights

Publishing Co: Concern for Helping Animals in Israel, PO Box 3341, Alexandria, VA 22302-0341; Title Tel # (703) 658-9650 Title Fax # (703) 941-6132
Personnel: Editor-Nina Natelson
Editorial Description: Problems for domestic animals in Israel & CHAI's efforts to improve the situation.
General Info: Yr. Est. 1984, Semi-annually, Offset press, 8 pages, Color, Saddle-stitched
Subscriptions: Indv. $18
Circulation: Total-3,000
Printing Co: Welsh Printing Co., 439 S Washington St, Falls Church, VA 22046-4477 Tel # (703) 534-0232

Cat Industry Newsletter
See: CATS

Civil Abolitionist
See: HEALTH

Connecticut Humane Bulletin   *Association*

Publishing Co: Connecticut Humane Society, 701 Russell Rd, Newington, CT 06111-1527; Title Tel # (203) 666-3337
General Info: Quarterly, Trim Size-6¼ x 9
Subscriptions: Indv. $25
Circulation: Total-6,000

Cornell Animal Health Newsletter
See: VETERINARY

Cornell University Animal Health Newsletter

Publishing Co: W.H. White Publications, Inc., 53 Park Pl, New York, NY 10007-2407
Personnel: Publisher-Deborah White, Editor-Katherine Houpt, Circ. Mgr.-Scott Accatino, Promotion Dir.-Dottie Saliski
Editorial Description: Covers animal health.
General Info: Yr. Est. 1983, Monthly, ISSN: 0884-092X
Subscriptions: Indv. $45, $4/copy
List Rental: List Management Co.: Kleid Company, Inc., 530 5th Ave., 17 Floor, New York, NY 10036-5101 Tel # (212) 819-3406, Fax # (212) 719-9788, Actives: 15,325, $70/M
Printing Co: News Type Service, PO Box 1806, Glendale, CA 91209-1806

Dog Industry Newsletter
See: DOGS

DogGone
See: TRAVEL

Harlequin Happenings

Publishing Co: American Harlequin Rabbit Club, Star Route Box 235F, Leopold, IN 47551; Title Tel # (812) 843-5460
Personnel: Editor-Pam Granderson
Editorial Description: Carries items concerning the Harlequin rabbit.
General Info: Yr. Est. 1974, Bi-monthly
Circulation: Total-150

Humane News   *Association*   CPM: $12

Publishing Co: Associated Humane Societies, 124 Evergreen Ave, Newark, NJ 07114-2133; Title Tel # (201) 824-7084 Title Fax # (201) 824-2720
Personnel: Publisher-Lee Bernstein, Circ. Mgr.-Douglas Barnes, Editor, Adv. Dir.-Roseann Trezza, Promotion Dir.-Jeanne Balsam
Editorial Description: Imparting news concerning animal welfare on a local, state, national & international level & reporting on incidents of cruelty, abuse & animal welfare legislation.
General Info: Yr. Est. 1969, Monthly, Trim Size-8½ x 11, Web press, 24 pages, 1% ads, 2 Color, Newsprint
Subscriptions: For. $20, $1/copy
Acquistions: Publication Bought
Circulation: Total-120,500
Advertising: $1,500.
Printing Co: Vanguard Offset Printers, 470 Mundet Place, Hillside, NJ 07205-1115 Tel # (908) 851-2222

Humane Society of New York News   *Association*

Publishing Co: Humane Society of New York, 306 E 59th St, New York, NY 10022-2006

International Bear News
See: ZOOLOGY

International Ferret Review   *Business, Association*   CPM: $24

Publishing Co: Ferret Fanciers Club, 711 Chautauqua Ct, Pittsburgh, PA 15214-3537; Title Tel # (412) 322-1161
Personnel: Publisher, Editor, Adv. Dir.-Mary Field, Art Dir.-Terri Scripko, Production Mgr., Mktg. Dir., Promotion Dir.-Daniel Huber
Editorial Description: Contains educational information on ferrets for breeders, owners, & health care professionals.
General Info: (Formerly Ferret News), Yr. Est. 1984, Bi-monthly, Trim Size-8½ x 11, Web press, 8 pages, No Color, Newsprint
Subscriptions: Indv. $20, For. $30, Free With Membership
Acquistions: Publication Bought
Circulation: Total-7,000
Advertising: $170. Accepts Inserts.

International Pet Industry News   *Business*

Publishing Co: Good Communications, Inc., PO Box 10069, Austin, TX 78766; Title Tel # (512) 454-6090 Title Fax # (512) 454-3420
Personnel: Publisher, Editor-Ross Becker, Circ. Mgr.-Lynn McQueen
Editorial Description: For executives in the international pet products industries. Covers new products, marketing, pet food business and supplies. Provides sensitive business information about competitors.
General Info: Yr. Est. 1993, Monthly, Trim Size-8½ x 11, 10 pages, ISSN: 1074-780x
Subscriptions: Indv. $295

International Society for Animal Rights Report
See: ENVIRONMENT & ECOLOGY

Latham Letter

Publishing Co: Latham Foundation, Latham Plaza Bldg., 1826 Clement Ave., Alameda, CA 94501; Title Tel # (510) 521-0920 Title Fax # (510) 521-9861
Personnel: Editor-Judy Johns
General Info: Yr. Est. 1979, Quarterly, 24 pages
Subscriptions: Indv. $12, Can. $15, For. $24
Circulation: Total-2,500

Love of Animals
Consumer

Publishing Co: Phillips Publishing, Inc., 7811 Montrose Rd., Potomac, MD 20854-3394
Tel # (301) 340-2100 Fax # (301) 294-1307 Parent Co.-Phillips Business Information, Inc., Potomac
Personnel: Co-Editor-Bob Goldstein, Co-Editor-Susan Goldstein
General Info: Monthly
Subscriptions: Indv. $40
Circulation: Total-10,000
List Rental: List Management Co.: Phillips Publishing List Marketing, 7811 Montrose Rd., Potomac, MD 20854-3394 Tel # (301) 340-2100, Fax # (301) 294-1307, Actives: 10,000

NYCA News
Association, Consumer

Publishing Co: New Yorkers for Companion Animals, 1324 Lexington Ave. #2, New York, NY 10128
Tel # (212) 427-8273
Personnel: Editor-Livi French
Editorial Description: Information on how to become foster care or adoptive 'Parents' for abondoned pets.
General Info: Quarterly, Trim Size-8½ x 11, 4 pages, No Color

National Ferret Fancier's Club
Consumer, Association

Publishing Co: FFC, 711 Chautauqua Ct, Pittsburgh, PA 15214-3537; Title Tel # (412) 322-1161
Personnel: Editor-Daniel Hober, Production Mgr.-Daniel Huber, Publisher, Adv. Dir.-Mary Field
Editorial Description: News and information of interest to fanciers of ferrets.
General Info: Yr. Est. 1985, Bi-monthly, Trim Size-8½ x 11, 8 pages, 1% ads
Subscriptions: Indv. $20, Can. $30
Acquistions: Publication Bought
Circulation: Total-7,700
Advertising: Inquire for rates. Accepts Inserts.
List Rental: Rents Lists

Official Rules and Judging Standards
Association

Publishing Co: International Fancy Guppy Assn. (IFGA), 20935 Golden Springs Rd., Walnut, CA 91789
General Info: (Formerly American Guppy Assoicaton News), Monthly

Pet Gazette

Publishing Co: Town of Hempstead Office of Communication & Public Affairs, 1 Washington St, Hempstead, NY 11550-4921; Title Tel # (516) 489-5000
Personnel: Editor-Alexandra Trias
Editorial Description: Care of pets, humane education programs in schools, pet therapy programs for nursing home residents, & adoption programs.
General Info: Semi-annually
Circulation: Total-10,000

Pet Gazette

Publishing Co: Gazette Publishing, 1309 N Halifax Ave, Daytona Beach, FL 32118-3658;
Title Tel # (904) 255-6935
Personnel: Publisher, Editor-Faith Senior, Adv. Dir.-Joanne Kash
Editorial Description: For animal lovers.
General Info: Yr. Est. 1984, Quarterly, Trim Size-8½ x 11, Offset press, 24 pages, ISSN: 0888-1995, No Color, Newsprint, Saddle-stitched
Subscriptions: Indv. $13, $3/copy
Circulation: Total-350
Advertising: Accepts Inserts.
Printing Co: Independent Printing Co., 500 Mason Ave, Daytona Beach, FL 32117-4887
Tel # (904) 252-7351

Pet News
Business

Publishing Co: World Wide Pet Supply Assn., Inc., 406 S 1st Ave, Arcadia, CA 91006-3829;
Title Tel # (818) 447-2222 Title Fax # (818) 447-8350
Personnel: Editor-Thomas McLaughlin
Editorial Description: News about our pet industry association's activities & trade shows.
General Info: Yr. Est. 1982, Quarterly, Trim Size-8½ x 11, Web press, 8 pages, No Color, Matte, Saddle-stitched
Subscriptions: Free To Qualified Recipient
Circulation: Total-20,000
Printing Co: Licher Direct Mail, 980 Seco St, Pasadena, CA 91103-2897 Tel # (818) 792-7000

Pet Partners Newsletter
Consumer

Publishing Co: Delta Society, 289 Perimeter Rd. E., Renton, WA 98055-1329;
Title Tel # (206) 226-7357 Title Fax # (206) 235-1076
Personnel: Editor-Maureen Fredrikson, Production Mgr.-Terry Albert
Editorial Description: Practical tips for registered Delta Society Pet Partners & those interested in learning more about providing effective animal assisted activities.
General Info: (Formerly Pet Partners Program), Yr. Est. 1990, Bi-monthly, Trim Size-8½ x 14, Offset press, 2 pages, ISSN: 1069-0735, 2 Color
Subscriptions: Indv. $6, Inst. $6, Can. $9, For. $9

Pigletter
See: LIVESTOCK

Plastron Papers
See: ZOOLOGY

Pointer Points
Consumer

Publishing Co: American Pointer Club, 5430 N. Camino Escuela, Tucson, AZ 85718-5021
General Info: Quarterly, Trim Size-8½ x 11, Offset press, 15 pages, No Color
Subscriptions: Indv. $8
Circulation: Total-250

Saskatchewan Humanitarian

Publishing Co: Saskatchewan Soc. for Prevention of Cruelty to Animals, Box 37, Saskatoon, SK S7N 3K1 Canada; Title Tel # (306) 382-7722
Personnel: Editor-D.L. Thornton
General Info: Quarterly
Circulation: Total-150
Advertising: Inquire for rates.

Scientists Center for Animal Welfare's Newsletter
Business, Association

Publishing Co: Scientists Center for Animal Welfare, 7833 Walker Dr Ste 340, Greenbelt, MD 20770-3211; Title Tel # (301) 345-3500 Title Fax # (301) 345-3503
Personnel: Editor-Lee Krulisch, Asst. Ed.-Jane Zimmerman, Circ. Mgr.-Linda Tockey
Editorial Description: Animal experimentation; legislation on laboratory animals; research institutional oversight of animal experiments; bioethics; animals in education, agricutaral, 300 aquarium animal research.
General Info: Yr. Est. 1978, Quarterly, Trim Size-8½ x 11, Offset press, 16 pages, ISSN: 1052-7559, Ind/Abs/Online: NLM, 2 Color, Other
Subscriptions: Indv. $40, Inst. $500, Can. $50, For. $50, Free With Membership
Circulation: Total-3,000
Printing Co: Daystar Press, 151315 Lawn Ln., Rockville, MD 20850 Tel # (301) 424-0686

SeaScope
Business, Consumer

Publishing Co: Aquarium Systems, Inc., 8141 Tyler Blvd., Mentor, OH 44060;
Title Tel # (216) 255-1997 Title Fax # (216) 255-8994
Editorial Description: Fish aquarium info - free for dealers and $2.00 for owners.
General Info: Quarterly, Trim Size-8½ x 11, 4 pages, ISSN: 1045-3520, 4 Color, Coated
Subscriptions: Indv. $2, Free To Qualified Recipient

Shoptalk
Association

Publishing Co: American Humane Association, 63 Inverness Dr. E., Englewood, CO 80112-5117;
Title Tel # (303) 792-9900 Title Fax # (303) 792-5333
Personnel: Editor-Jane Ehrhardt, Art Dir.-Karon Harolds
Editorial Description: Newsletter for animal care & control professionals.
General Info: Yr. Est. 1983, Quarterly, Trim Size-7 x 10, Offset press, 12 pages, ISSN: 1066-4890, 2 Color, Coated, Saddle-stitched
Subscriptions: Indv. $10, For. $20, $3/copy
Circulation: (63% controlled), Total-6,600, Single Copy/Newsstand-400, Subscriptions-200
List Rental: Rents Lists
Printing Co: Mido, 6845 E 48th Ave, Denver, CO 80216-5310

Tatoo-A-Pet News

Publishing Co: Pet Services Unlimited, 1625 Emmons Ave., Brooklyn, NY 11235-2758;
Title Tel # (718) 646-8200
Personnel: Publisher, Editor-Julie Moscove
Editorial Description: Co. news to companies over 2,000 authorized agents & participating veterinarians who offer our service.
General Info: Quarterly, Offset press, 14 pages
List Rental: Actives: $50/M

Veterinary Industry Newsletter
See: VETERINARY

Voice (for the animals), The

Publishing Co: David Lee Riley, Voice For Animals, P.O. Box 120095, San Antonio, TX 78212
Editorial Description: A radical vegan political group that seems to take a vary pragmatic approach to eliminating animal abuse.
General Info: Trim Size-8.5 x 11, 8 pages
Subscriptions: Indv. $12

Wolf Park News
Association

Publishing Co: North American Wildlife Park Foundation Inc., Wolf Park, Rt 1, Battle Ground, IN 47920 Tel # (312) 567-2265 Fax # (317) 567-2084; Title Tel # (317) 567-2265
Personnel: Publisher, Editor-Erich Klinghammer, Production Mgr.-Holly Jaycox DiMaio
Editorial Description: Covers events at Wolf Park, an education and research facility dealing with wolves and bison.
General Info: Quarterly, 8 pages
Subscriptions: Indv. $20, Free With Membership
Circulation: Total-6,000
Printing Co: White Arts, Inc., 1203 E Saint Clair St, Lafayette, IN 46202-3590 Tel # (317) 356-9970

Worm Digest

Publishing Co: Worm Digst, P.O. Box 544, Eugene, OR 97440
Editorial Description: A publiction by and for worms. An informative newsletter promoting the importance of worm composting.
General Info: Trim Size-8.5 x 11, 24 pages
Subscriptions: Indv. $3

ANTHROPOLOGY

American Paleontologist
See: GEOLOGY

Anthropology Newsletter   *Association*

Publishing Co: American Anthropological Assn., 4350 N. Fairfax Drive, Suite 640, Arlington, VA 22203-1621; Title Tel # (703) 528-1902 Title Fax # (703) 528-3546
Personnel: Publisher-John M. Comman, Editor-Susan Skomal, Circ. Mgr.-Donna McHugh, Production Mgr.-Rick Custer, Adv. Dir.-Theresa Clifford
Editorial Description: Covers Assn. news & developments in the field of anthropology.
General Info: Yr. Est. 1959, 9x/yr., Trim Size-11½ x 15, Web press, 32 pages, ISSN: 0098-1605, Color-cover, Newsprint
Subscriptions: Indv. $55, Inst. $55, $5/copy
Circulation: Total-11,500
Advertising: Inquire for rates.
List Rental: Actives: $130/M
Printing Co: Suburban Record/Record Printing Co., 7676 Fenton St, Silver Spring, MD 20910-4903

Anthropology Northwest   *Association*

Publishing Co: David Braynen, Oregon State, Dept. of Anthropology, Corvallis, OR 97331; Title Tel # (503) 737-4515
Personnel: Editor-David Brauner
Editorial Description: Short articles, job opportunities, conservation, archaeology, changes in federal legislation, regulation and policy concerning cultural resource management.
General Info: Yr. Est. 1974, Bi-monthly, Trim Size-8½ x 11, 20 pages, No Color
Subscriptions: Indv. $10
Circulation: Total-400

Archaeoastronomy & Ethnoastronomy News
See: ASTRONOMY

Archaeology on Kaua'i
See: ARCHAEOLOGY

Arkansas Amateur
See: ARCHAEOLOGY

Association for the Study of Play Newsletter   *Consumer, Association*

Publishing Co: Assn. for the Study of Play, Box 6375, Southwestern Univ., Georgetown, TX 78626; Title Tel # (512) 863-1392
Personnel: Publisher, Editor-Dan Hilliard
Editorial Description: Contains brief articles, book reviews, & news notices concerning the academic study of play & related issues.
General Info: Yr. Est. 1974, Desktop press, 15 pages, ISSN: 0887-140X
Subscriptions: Indv. $9, Inst. $15, $2/copy
Circulation: Total-230

Bishop Museum Bulletins in Anthropology

Publishing Co: Bishop Museum, 1525 Bernice St # 19000-A, Honolulu, HI 96817-2704; Title Tel # (808) 848-4135
General Info: ISSN: 0005-9439, Ind/Abs/Online: BioA, GeoRef
Circulation: Total-300

Communicator   *Association*

Publishing Co: American Anthropological Assn., 4350 N. Fairfax Drive, Suite 640, Arlington, VA 22203-1621; Title Tel # (703) 528-1902 Title Fax # (703) 528-3546
Personnel: Editor-Gerladine Moreno-Black
Editorial Description: Official newsletter of the council on nutritional anthropology.
General Info: Yr. Est. 1976, Semi-annually, Trim Size-8½ x 11, 16 pages, No Color, Newsprint
Subscriptions: Indv. $10
Circulation: Total-250
List Rental: Rents Lists

Connection
See: PSYCHOLOGY

Cornell Modern Indonesia Project:
See: INTERNATIONAL AFFAIRS

Gypsy Lore Society Newsletter   *Association*   **CPM: $200**

Publishing Co: Gypsy Lore Society, 5607 Greenleaf Rd, Cheverly, MD 20785-1110; Title Tel # (301) 341-1261 Title Fax # (301) 341-1261
Personnel: Editor-David Nemeth
Editorial Description: Covers current scholarly research in Gypsy Studies (history, folklore, etc.).
General Info: Yr. Est. 1978, Quarterly, Offset press, 8 pages, ISSN: 1070-4604, No Color, Matte, Case bound
Subscriptions: Indv. $30, Inst. $35, For. $35
Circulation: Total-250
Advertising: $50.

History of Anthropology Newsletter

Publishing Co: History of Anthropology Newsletter, George W. Stocking, 1126 E. 59th, Univ. of Chicago, Chicago, IL 60637-1539; Title Tel # (312) 962-7702
Personnel: Editor-Goerge Stocking, Jr.
Editorial Description: Research notes, bibliography and source material in history of anthropology.
General Info: Yr. Est. 1973, Semi-annually, Trim Size-8½ x 11, Mimeo press, 20 pages, Ind/Abs/Online: Isis., No Color
Subscriptions: Indv. $5, Inst. $6, For. $6
Circulation: Total-330

Information North
See: SCIENCE

Institute of Human Origins

Publishing Co: Institute of Human Origins, 2700 Bancroft Way, Berkeley, CA 94704-1719; Title Tel # (415) 845-0333

Institute for the Study of Earth and Man Newsletter   *Association*

Publishing Co: Southern Methodist Univ, Inst for the Study of Earth and Man, Heroy Science Hall, 3225 D, Dallas, TX 75203 Tel # (214) 768-3762 Fax # (214) 768-4289; Title Tel # (214) 692-2000
Personnel: Editor-Susan Liepins
Editorial Description: Reports activities in departments of anthropology and geological sciences.
General Info: Yr. Est. 1974, Semi-annually, Trim Size-8½ x 11, Letrpr. press, 6 pages, Color
Subscriptions: Free
Circulation: Total-2,100
Printing Co: SMU Printing Dept., Southern Methodist Univ., Dallas, TX 75275-0001 Tel # (214) 692-2000

International Newsletter on Migration   *Association*

Publishing Co: Center for Migration Studies of New York, Inc., 209 Flagg Pl, Staten Island, NY 10304-1199; Title Tel # (718) 351-8800 Title Fax # (718) 667-4598
Personnel: Publisher-Lydio Tomasi, Editor-Catherine De Wenden
Editorial Description: Published and prepared by the research committee on migration.
General Info: Quarterly, Trim Size-4½ x 7½, Sheetfed press, 10 pages, Ind/Abs/Online: ISA.', No Color, Newsprint
Subscriptions: Indv. $25, Inst. $38, $9/copy
Circulation: Total-2,500
Printing Co: Sheridan Press, 450 Fame Avenue, Hanover, PA 17331-9581 Tel # (717) 632-3535, Fax # (717) 633-8900

Kansas Anthropological Association Newsletter   *Association*

Publishing Co: Kansas Anthropological Association, 6425 SW 6th Ave, Topeka, KS 66615-1099 Fax # (913) 272-8682; Title Tel # (913) 272-8681 Title Fax # (272) 868-2005
Personnel: Editor-Virginia A. Wulfkuhle
Editorial Description: Association news, announcements, current research notes, brief articles.
General Info: Yr. Est. 1955, Bi-monthly, Trim Size-8½ x 11, 8 pages, ISSN: 1069-0360, No Color, Saddle-stitched
Subscriptions: Indv. $22, Inst. $25, Free With Membership
Circulation: Total-450

Margaretologist, The
See: JEWELRY & HOROLOGY

Newsletter of the Society Farsarotul
See: ETHNIC

Oklahoma Anthropological Society, Newsletter   *Scholarly*

Publishing Co: Oklahoma Anthropological Society, RR 1 Box 62B, Cheyenne, OK 73628-9729 Tel # (405) 497-2566; Title Tel # (405) 497-2662 Title Fax # (405) 497-2662
Personnel: Circ. Mgr.-R.W. Bellamy, Circ. Mgr.-Linda Penderson, Publisher, Editor, Production Mgr.-Frieda Odell
Editorial Description: Information on statewide archeological investigations. Brief contributed articles on Oklahoma history & prehistory. Reviews of recent publications pertaining to Oklahoma archaeology, anthropology & history.
General Info: Yr. Est. 1952, 6x/yr., Trim Size-8½ x 11, Web press, 15 pages, ISSN: 0078-4338, Ind/Abs/Online: Bk.Rev.Abstr., Anthropol., No Color, Matte
Subscriptions: Indv. $12, Inst. $17, Can. $20, For. $20, $25/copy
Circulation: Total-530
Advertising: Accepts Inserts.
Printing Co: Pruett Printing, Norman, OK 73019-0001 Tel # (405) 299-0303

Poppin' Zits!
See: SOCIOLOGY

Prehistoric Times
See: ARCHAEOLOGY

Russia and Her Neighbors, Facts & Views on Daily Life
See: INTERNATIONAL AFFAIRS

SAVICOM *Consumer, Association*

Publishing Co: Society for the Anthropology of Visual Communication, Suny/Brockport, Anthrop. Dept., Brockport, NY 14420; Title Tel # (215) 242-1678
Personnel: Editor-Jack Rollwagen
Editorial Description: Contains verbal and visual material describing and analyzing research in the areas of interest of the Society.
General Info: Yr. Est. 1984, Quarterly, Trim Size-8½ x 11, Offset press, 14 pages, No Color
Subscriptions: Indv. $10, $5/copy
Circulation: Total-1,000

SMRC Newsletter

Publishing Co: Southwestern Mission Research Center, Arizona State Museum Univ. Of, Arizona, Tucson, AZ 85721-0001; Title Tel # (602) 621-4898 Title Fax # (602) 621-2976
Personnel: Editor-Thomas Sheridan
Editorial Description: News & bibliography related to research in Spanish Borderlands.
General Info: Yr. Est. 1967, Quarterly, Trim Size-8½ x 11, Offset press, 32 pages, No Color, Perfect bound
Subscriptions: Indv. $10
Circulation: Total-900
Printing Co: Univ. of Arizona Printing & Publishing, Univ. Of Arizona, Tucson, AZ 85721-0001 Tel # (602) 621-2571

San Bernardino County Museum Association Newsletter
See: MUSEUM PUBLICATIONS

Southeast Asia Program Series: Monographs, Translations, Bibliographies
See: INTERNATIONAL AFFAIRS

Strecker Museum News
See: MUSEUM PUBLICATIONS

Tennessee Anthropological
Assn. Newsletter

Publishing Co: University of Tennessee Department of Anthropology, Publications, 252 South Stadium Hall, Knoxville, TN 37996-0720 Tel # (615) 974-4408
Editorial Description: Covers Association news & events, recent developments in research in the field of anthropology.
General Info: Yr. Est. 1976, Bi-monthly, ISSN: 0196-0377

Textile Museum Bulletin
See: MUSEUM PUBLICATIONS

University of South
Dakota Bulletin *Association*

Publishing Co: Institute of American Indian Studies, Univ. of South Dakota, Vermillion, SD 57069; Title Tel # (605) 677-5209 Title Fax # (605) 677-5073
Personnel: Publisher-Leonard R. Brugvier, Editor-Margaret Quintal, Art Dir.-Marty Two Bulls
Editorial Description: News items concerning the activities of the Institute and information of general interest to the Native American people of South Dakota and across the nation.
General Info: (Formerly News Report), Yr. Est. 1955, Semi-annually, Trim Size-8½ x 11, 20 pages, ISSN: 0042-0069, Color
Acquistions: Publication Bought
Circulation: Total-2,500
List Rental: Rents Lists

ANTIQUES & ART GOODS

ABAA Newsletter *Association*

Publishing Co: Antiquarian Booksellers Assn. of America, 50 Rockefeller Plaza, New York, NY 10020; Title Tel # (212) 757-9395 Title Fax # (212) 459-0307
Personnel: Editor-Robert Rulon-Miller
Editorial Description: For the Antiquarian Booksellers Association members.
General Info: Quarterly
Subscriptions: Indv. $20

ATHA Newsletter
See: HOBBY

American Lock Collectors Association Newsletter
See: COLLECTIBLES

Antique Comb Collector *Scholarly, Association*

Publishing Co: Sponsor-Antique Comb Collectors Club Int'l, Pet Project, 3748 Sunray Dr, Holiday, FL 34691-3239; Title Tel # (813) 942-7354
Personnel: Publisher, Editor-Belva Green
Editorial Description: Collectors share pertinent information about ancient and antique hair ornaments for future enjoyment & knowledge. Newsletter prints itiems covering all aspects of ornamental comb collecting, updates member and club news, indexed annually
General Info: (Formerly Antique Fancy Comb Collector; Combs & Hair Accessories), Yr. Est. 1985, Bi-monthly, Trim Size-8½ x 11, 4 pages, ISSN: 0892-7162
Subscriptions: Indv. $23, For. $27, $2/copy
Advertising: Inquire for rates.

Appraiser, The *Consumer, Association*

Publishing Co: Appraisers Association of America, 386 Park Avenue South, New York, NY 10016-8804; Title Tel # (212) 889-5404 Title Fax # (212) 889-5503
Personnel: Editor-Louis Zara, Assoc. Ed.-Helaine Fendelman, Assoc. Ed.-Victor Wiener
General Info: Yr. Est. 1980, Quarterly, Letrpr. press, 8 pages, No Color, Matte
Subscriptions: Indv. $65
Acquistions: Publication Bought
Circulation: Total-2,000

Appraisers Standard *Association*

Publishing Co: NEAA, 5 Gill Ter, Ludlow, VT 05149-1003 Tel # (804) 228-7444; Title Tel # (802) 228-7444
Personnel: Publisher, Editor, Adv. Dir.-Linda Tucker, Circ. Mgr., Production Mgr., Promotion Dir.-Janeea Tucker
Editorial Description: Covers all articles on antiques, fine arts, collectibles, coins, stamps, and auctions. Geared towards appraisers and collectors.
General Info: (Formerly NEAA News), Yr. Est. 1980, Bi-monthly, 12 pages, No Color
Subscriptions: Indv. $20, Inst. $15, Can. $25, For. $30, $3/copy
Circulation: Total-1,000
Advertising: Inquire for rates. Accepts Inserts.
List Rental: Actives: 1,000, $200/M
Printing Co: Rutland Printing, Lincoln Avenue, Rutland, VT 05149 Tel # (802) 775-1948

Art in Wisconsin
See: ART & SCULPTURE

Artistic Opportunities
See: EDUCATION

Auction Bulletin *Business*

Publishing Co: Salvage Bids, PO Box 5, Laconia, NH 03247-0005; Title Tel # (603) 524-4121
Personnel: Publisher, Editor-John Tamke
Editorial Description: International industrial & commercial auction data.
General Info: Yr. Est. 1965, Bi-weekly, Looseleaf
Subscriptions: Indv. $500
Circulation: Total-1,600

Auction News from Christie's
See: ART & SCULPTURE

Bridal Collectors News
See: BRIDE

Butterfly Net *Association*

Publishing Co: Fenton Art Glass Collectors of America, Inc., PO Box 384, Williamstown, WV 26187-0384; Title Tel # (304) 375-6196
Personnel: Editor-Ferill Rice
Editorial Description: Articles & pictures designed for study of Fenton Art Glass.
General Info: Yr. Est. 1977, Bi-monthly, Trim Size-8½ x 11, Offset press, 30 pages
Subscriptions: Indv. $15
Circulation: Total-2,500
Advertising: Inquire for rates.

Cartomania
See: GEOGRAPHY

Coin-Op Newsletter   CPM: $133

Publishing Co: Coin-Op Newsletter, 909 26th St NW, Washington, DC 20037-2029; Title Tel # (202) 338-1342
Personnel: Publisher-Ken Durham
Editorial Description: For collectors of antique slot machines, jukeboxes, gumball machines, etc.
General Info: Yr. Est. 1985, Bi-monthly, Trim Size-8½ x 11, 14 pages
Subscriptions: Indv. $24, $5/copy
Circulation: Total-225
Advertising: $30.

Cream Separator and Dairy Newsletter
See: DAIRY

Creative Outlets

Publishing Co: Country Press, PO Box 5024, Durango, CO 81301-6813
Editorial Description: If you have an art or craft related business you will be interested in Creative Outlets. A directory for the craftsperson & small manufacturer.
General Info: Annually, Trim Size-8½ x 11, Desktop press
Subscriptions: Indv. $5
Advertising: Accepts Inserts.

Decorative Arts Trust-
Newsletter

Publishing Co: Decorative Arts Trust, 106 Bainbridge St, Philadelphia, PA 19147-2402; Title Tel # (215) 627-2859 Title Fax # (215) 925-1144
Personnel: Editor-Penny McCaskill Hunt
Editorial Description: Encourages and promotes study of decorative arts.
General Info: Yr. Est. 1977, Quarterly, Trim Size-8½ x 11, Letrpr. press, 8 pages, No Color
Subscriptions: Indv. $25
Circulation: Total-2,000

Dollmasters, The   *Consumer*

Publishing Co: Gold Horse Publishing/Theriault's, PO Box 151, Annapolis, MD 21404-0151;
Title Tel # (410) 224-3655 Title Fax # (410) 224-2515
Personnel: Publisher-George Theriault, Editor-Florence Theriault, Circ. Mgr.-Angela Rutherford, Art Dir.-Susan Robinson, Mktg. Dir.-Stuart Holbrook, Promotion Dir.-Cynthia Gaskill
Editorial Description: Theriault's is an international auction house that specializes in the sale of antique dolls and toys.
General Info: Yr. Est. 1975, Monthly, 10 pages, 4 Color, Coated, Saddle-stitched
Subscriptions: Free
Circulation: Total-14,000

Doorknob Collector, The
See: HOBBY

ETCetera   *Association*

Publishing Co: Early Typewriter Collectors Assn., 2591 Military Ave, Los Angeles, CA 90064-1933 Tel # (310) 477-5229
Personnel: Editor-Darryl Rehr
Editorial Description: Devoted to the history of the typewriter and office machines. Encourages collection preservation. Includes buy-sell trade ads.
General Info: Yr. Est. 1987, Quarterly, Trim Size-8½ x 11, Sheetfed press, 12 pages, ISSN: 1062-9645, 15% ads, Matte
Subscriptions: Indv. $20, Inst. $20, Can. $20, For. $25
Advertising: Inquire for rates.

Egg Cup Collectors Corner
See: HOBBY

Evaluator, The   *Business, Association*

Publishing Co: International Society of Fine Arts Appraisers Ltd., 701 S. Euclid Ave., Oak Park, IL 60304-1205; Title Tel # (708) 848-3340
Personnel: Publisher, Editor-Elizabeth Carr
General Info: Yr. Est. 1979, Quarterly, Web press, 8 pages, ISSN: 8756-775X, 2 Color
Subscriptions: Free With Membership
Circulation: Total-1,000
Advertising: Accepts Inserts.
Printing Co: Complemetary Colours, Ltd., 113 S Marion St, Oak Park, IL 60302-2808 Tel # (708) 848-5330

Game Researcher's Notes
See: COLLECTIBLES

Game Times
See: COLLECTIBLES

Harrison Fisher Society
Newsletter   *Consumer, Association*

Publishing Co: Harrison Fisher Society, The, PO Box 8188, Redlands, CA 92375-1388 Tel # (714) 633-5206; Title Tel # (909) 794-8348 Title Fax # (909) 794-8348
Personnel: Publisher, Editor-Deena Zachritz
Editorial Description: Publicizes the art of Harrison Fisher, turn-of-the-century artist and illustrator (1877-1934.)
General Info: (Formerly Exchange Letter), Yr. Est. 1977, 3x/yr., Desktop press, 8 pages, No Color, Matte, Saddle-stitched
Subscriptions: $6/copy
Circulation: Total-325
Advertising: Inquire for rates.
List Rental: Rents Lists

Historicalog
See: HISTORY

IFARreports   *Association*

Publishing Co: Intl. Foundation for Art Research, 46 E 70th St, New York, NY 10021-4928; Title Tel # (212) 879-1780
Personnel: Editor-Anna Kisluk
Editorial Description: Listing of stolen works of art, & authentication service articles, & news of legal developments in art recovery.
General Info: (Formerly Stolen Art Alert & Art Research News), Yr. Est. 1977, 10x/yr., 24 pages, ISSN: 8756-7172, Coated
Subscriptions: Indv. $50, Inst. $65, $5/copy
Circulation: Total-1,200
Printing Co: Grand Central Letter, 14 Jay St., New York, NY 10013 Tel # (212) 966-1270

ISA Newsletter
See: FURNITURE & HOME FURNISHINGS

Illustrator Collector's News, The
See: COLLECTIBLES

Illustrator Magazine & Paper Collector's News
See: COLLECTIBLES

Illustratotor's Swap incl JW Anglund Collectors News
See: CHILDREN

In the Groove
See: COLLECTIBLES

JPR
See: JEWELRY & HOROLOGY

Kovels on Antiques &
Collectibles   *Business, Consumer*

Publishing Co: Kovels on Antiques and Collectibles, 30799 Pinetree Rd., Pepper Pike, OH 44124; Title Tel # (216) 752-2252 Title Fax # (216) 752-3115
Personnel: Publisher-Ralph Kovel, Editor-Terry Kovel, Circ. Mgr.-Gloria Pearlman
Editorial Description: For dealers, collectors & investors.
General Info: Yr. Est. 1974, Monthly, Trim Size-8½ x 10½, 12 pages, ISSN: 0741-6091, No Color
Subscriptions: Indv. $36, $3/copy
List Rental: List Management Co.: Kleid Company, Inc., 530 5th Ave., 17 Floor, New York, NY 10036-5101 Tel # (212) 819-3406, Fax # (212) 719-9788, Actives: 168,000, $75/M, Hotline: 81,171, $80/M

Marble Mania
See: HOBBY

Margaretologist, The
See: JEWELRY & HOROLOGY

Mechanical Banker, The   *Association*

Publishing Co: Mechanical Bank Collectors of America, PO Box 128, Allegan, MI 49010-0128; Title Tel # (616) 673-4509
Personnel: Editor-Tim Anderson
Editorial Description: Concerned with antique mechanical banks.
General Info: Yr. Est. 1958, 24 pages
Circulation: Total-250

Miniature Book News
See: BOOKS & BOOK TRADE

Mobilia
See: AUTOMOTIVE

Motif   *Association*   CPM: $66

Publishing Co: Art Deco Society of Boston, 1 Murdock Ter, Brighton, MA 02135-2817; Title Tel # (617) 787-2637
Personnel: Editor-Helene Linne
Editorial Description: Official newsletter of the Art Deco Society of Boston containing information and announcements of interest to collectors & preservationists of Art Deco and related styles.
General Info: Yr. Est. 1989, Quarterly, Trim Size-8½ x 11, 8 pages, Matte, Saddle-stitched
Subscriptions: Indv. $20, $5/copy
Circulation: Total-1,500
Advertising: $100. Accepts Inserts.
List Rental: List Management Co.: Twin Peaks Press, PO Box 129, Vancouver, WA 98666-0129 Tel # (206) 694-2462, Fax # (206) 696-3210, Actives: 500, Expires: 500

National Association of
Dealers in Antiques-
Bulletin

Publishing Co: Natl. Assn. of Dealers in Antiques, PO Box 421, Barrington, IL 60011-0421; Title Tel # (708) 312-7096
Personnel: Editor-Shirley Kowing
Editorial Description: Bulletin providing educational & assn. news.
General Info: Yr. Est. 1962, Monthly
Acquistions: Publication Bought
Advertising: Inquire for rates.

National Association of
Dealers in Antiques,
Membership Roster

Publishing Co: Natl. Assn. of Dealers in Antiques, PO Box 421, Barrington, IL 60011-0421; Title Tel # (815) 877-4282
Personnel: Editor-Shirley Oler-Kowing
General Info: Annually

Newsletter East Asian Art & Archaeology
See: ART & SCULPTURE

Northern Lights
(Minneapolis)

Publishing Co: Antique Automobile Club of America, Minnesota Region, 621 E. 61st St., Minneapolis, MN 55417; Title Tel # (612) 869-1710
Personnel: Editor-Priscilla Johansen, Editor-Paul M. Remfer
General Info: Yr. Est. 1957

Opaque News   *Association*

Publishing Co: National Milk Glass Collectors Society, 80 Crestview Dr, Newington, CT 06111-2405
Personnel: Co-Editor-Claudia Schultz, Co-Editor-Frank Schultz
Editorial Description: A quarterly newsletter of the National Milk Glass Collectors Society. Informative articles written by members.
General Info: Quarterly
Subscriptions: Indv. $15

PATINAGRAM
Business, Association

Publishing Co: Potomac Antique Tools & Industries Assn., 13004 Clarion Rd, Fort Washington, MD 20744-2816; Title Tel # (301) 292-1606
Personnel: Editor-Dale Bultman
Editorial Description: Concentrates on antique tools.
General Info: Yr. Est. 1978, Bi-monthly, Trim Size-8½ x 11, Mimeo press, 6 pages, No Color
Subscriptions: Free To Qualified Recipient
Circulation: Total-300
Printing Co: Allen's Copy Center, 3410 Wilson Blvd, Arlington, VA 22201-2231 Tel # (703) 524-2020

Project Salvador Crafts
See: CRAFTS

Rusty Iron Monthly
Consumer, Association

Publishing Co: Rusty Iron Monthly, PO Box 342, Sandwich, IL 60548-0342; Title Tel # (815) 496-9267
Personnel: Publisher, Editor-Shawn Rogers
Editorial Description: A shopping guide for antique mechanical equipment including gas engines, steam engines, antique tractors, literature, windmills, farm advertising items, magazines , etc.
General Info: Yr. Est. 1983, Monthly
Subscriptions: Indv. $14, Can. $20, For. $28
Circulation: Total-1,500
Advertising: Inquire for rates.
List Rental: Rents Lists

Snow Biz
Consumer   **CPM: $76**

Publishing Co: Snow Biz, PO Box 53262, Washington, DC 20009-9262
Personnel: Publisher, Editor, Adv. Dir.-Nancy McMichael
Editorial Description: Aims to enhance the knowledge, enjoyment and collections of snowdome (waterglobe) collectors. Provides practical and historical information and manufacturers' information and ads, plus an exchange column for trading, buying and selling among subscribers.
General Info: Yr. Est. 1990, Quarterly, 25% ads
Subscriptions: Indv. $10, Inst. $10, Can. $13, For. $15, $3/copy
Circulation: Total-1,300
Advertising: $100.

Sotheby's Newsletter

Publishing Co: Sotheby's, 980 Madison Ave., New York, NY 10021; Title Tel # (212) 606-7138
Personnel: Editor-Lynn Pearson
Editorial Description: Auction schedules for all Sotheby's locations, worldwide, plus exhibition dates & catalogue prices. Articles on upcoming sales.
General Info: Yr. Est. 1972, 7x/yr., Trim Size-11 x 17, Web press, 8 pages, 4 Color, Coated, Saddle-stitched
Subscriptions: Indv. $15, For. $20
Circulation: Total-55,000

Sound Waves
See: HOBBY

Stained Finger, The
See: COLLECTIBLES

Stove Parts Needed
Business, Association

Publishing Co: Antique Stove Assn., 417 N Main St, Monticello, IN 47960-1932; Title Tel # (219) 583-6465
Personnel: Editor-Clifford Boram
Editorial Description: News of interest to antique stove owners, restorers, dealers, users.
General Info: Yr. Est. 1984, Quarterly, Trim Size-8½ x 14, Sheetfed press, 10 pages, 2% ads, No Color, Newsprint
Subscriptions: Free With Membership
Advertising: Inquire for rates. Accepts Inserts.
Printing Co: Blasted Works, 214 N Main St, Monticello, IN 47960-2131 Tel # (219) 583-3211

Streamline
See: INTERIOR DESIGN & DECORATION

Stumpwork Society Chronicle
Consumer, Association

Publishing Co: Stumpwork Society, 1315 Anderson Ave. #23, Fort Lee, NJ 07024-1702; Title Tel # (201) 224-3622 Title Fax # (201) 224-3075
Personnel: Circ. Mgr.-Lillian Peterkin, Production Mgr.-Bernard Fishman, Publisher, Editor, Adv. Dir., Art Dir., Promotion Dir.-Sylvia Fishman
Editorial Description: Information about the art of stumpwork--raised embroidery.
General Info: Yr. Est. 1979, Quarterly, Letrpr. press, 8 pages, ISSN: 0194-4193, No Color
Subscriptions: Indv. $15, $3/copy

Thimbletter
See: COLLECTIBLES

Tiffin Glassmasters
See: GLASS, STONE & CLAY

Toothpick Bulletin
See: HOBBY

Underground Lamp Post
Consumer

Publishing Co: Henry A. Pohs, Ed., 4537 Quitman St, Denver, CO 80212-2535; Title Tel # (303) 455-3922
Editorial Description: Informal exchange of information for collectors of pre-electric underground illuminating devices, ie, old mine lamps and miner's candleholders.
General Info: Yr. Est. 1967, Semi-annually, Trim Size-8½ x 11, Mimeo press, 6 pages, No Color
Subscriptions: Free
Circulation: Total-400

WAAC Newsletter
See: ART & SCULPTURE

William Hardash Auction Newsletter
See: ART & SCULPTURE

Windmillers' Gazette
See: AGRICULTURE

World Fine Art

Publishing Co: Art Baron Management Corp., PO Box 5365, Scottsdale, AZ 85261-5365; Title Tel # (602) 954-2400
Personnel: Publisher-Jeffrey Coffin, Editor-Steve Shipp
Editorial Description: An art investment pub. uniquely blending art history, values, & projections.
General Info: Yr. Est. 1982, Bi-monthly, Trim Size-8½ x 11, 12 pages, No Color
Subscriptions: Indv. $75, $5/copy

Worldwide Treasure Bureau Newsletter
See: NUMISMATICS

APPAREL & ACCESSORIES

AAMA Washington Newsletter
See: LAW

American Apparel Manufacturers Association Newsletter
Business

Publishing Co: American Apparel Manufacturers Assn., 2500 Wilson Blvd Ste 301, Arlington, VA 22201-3834; Title Tel # (703) 524-1864 Title Fax # (703) 522-6741
Personnel: Editor-Joan McNeal
Editorial Description: Provides important information on developments and changes in the apparel industry for American Apparel Manufacturers Association members and associate members.
General Info: Bi-monthly, 8 pages
Circulation: Total-2,400
Printing Co: Corporate Press, 403 Brightseat Rd., Landover, MD 20785-4706 Tel # (301) 499-9200, Fax # (301) 499-5435

Apparel Research Notes
Business

Publishing Co: American Apparel Manufacturers Assn., 2500 Wilson Blvd Ste 301, Arlington, VA 22201-3834; Title Tel # (703) 524-1864 Title Fax # (703) 522-6741
Editorial Description: Explores current apparel technology & manufacturing systems.
General Info: Quarterly, 4 pages
Circulation: Total-4,500

Apparel Sourcing Analysis
Business

Publishing Co: Werner International Apparel Marketing, 111 W. 40th St., New York, NY 10018-2564; Title Tel # (212) 642-6000
Editorial Description: Analysis of potential off-shore manufacturing opportunities for the Tex-Apparel producers.
General Info: Annually, Looseleaf
Subscriptions: $3,500/copy

Apparel Strategist
Business

Publishing Co: TAWCO Inc., 200 Katonah Ave., Katonah, NY 10536; Title Tel # (914) 232-2200 Title Fax # (914) 241-3794
General Info: Yr. Est. 1987, Monthly
Subscriptions: Indv. $375

Barbara's Report/Shoes and. . .
Business

Publishing Co: Barbara's View, PO Box 531006, Miami, FL 33153-1006; Title Tel # (305) 757-7638 Title Fax # (305) 756-5353
Personnel: Publisher, Editor-Barbara W. Levy, Art Dir.-Lauren Hughes
Editorial Description: Report on shoes, fashion, and where to purchase them.
General Info: Yr. Est. 1974, Irregular, Looseleaf
Subscriptions: For. $13, $8/copy

Barbara's View: Paris
See: TRAVEL

Business Newsletter   *Association*

Publishing Co: Menswear Retailers of America, 325 7th St. NW, Ste. 1000, Washington, DC 20004-2801; Title Tel # (202) 347-1932
Personnel: Editor-Walter Raymond, Adv. Dir.-Mr. Jan Walker
Editorial Description: Men's wear specialty store business trends and proven promotional ideas.
General Info: Yr. Est. 1914, Weekly, Trim Size-8½ x 11, Offset press, 4 pages, No Color
Subscriptions: Indv. $25
Circulation: Total-4,500
Advertising: Inquire for rates.

CSA News   *Association*

Publishing Co: Costume Society of America, 55 Edgewater Dr # 73, Earleville, MD 21919-2226; Title Tel # (410) 275-2329 Title Fax # (410) 275-8936
Personnel: Editor-R. Lester
Editorial Description: Society news; calendar of events, exhibits; membership exchange of information.
General Info: Yr. Est. 1973, Quarterly, Trim Size-8½ x 11, 12 pages, ISSN: 0361-2112, No Color
Subscriptions: Indv. $55, Inst. $85, $2/copy
Circulation: (9% controlled), Total-16,000, International-144
List Rental: Rents Lists

FIA Executive Digest   *Business, Association*

Publishing Co: Footwear Industries of America, 1420 K St. NW, Ste. 600, Washington, DC 20005-2505 Fax # (202) 789-4058; Title Tel # (202) 789-1420 Title Fax # (202) 789-1425
Personnel: Editor-Barb Singer
General Info: (Formerly American Footwear Industries Assn. -Newsletter), Yr. Est. 1982, Monthly
Subscriptions: Indv. $60, Inst. $60, $10/copy
Circulation: Total-850

Fashion Calendar   *Business*

Publishing Co: FI Publishing, Inc., 153 E. 87th St., New York, NY 10128; Title Tel # (212) 289-0420
Personnel: Publisher, Editor-Ruth Finley
Editorial Description: Lists openings, fashion shows and activities.
General Info: Yr. Est. 1941, Bi-weekly
Subscriptions: Indv. $350, $40/copy

Fashion International
See: DEPARTMENT STORE & RETAIL

Fashion Newsletter   *Business*

Publishing Co: Newsletter Services, Inc., 9700 Philadelphia Ct., Lanham, MD 20706-4405; Title Tel # (301) 731-5202 Title Fax # (301) 731-5203
Personnel: Publisher-Lisa A. Anthony, Exec. VP/Group Publisher-Michael Nagan, Editor-Alice Meyer, Circ. Mgr.-Priscilla Arenas, Mktg. Mgr.-Susan Pangman
Editorial Description: Monthly forecasts of the best looks for manufacturers, designers, buyers and merchandisers to create, buy and sell. Reports from the world's most important fashion centers plus a spotlight on the secondary market. Numbers on who is spending what and where make it easy to compare with your sales figures.
General Info: Yr. Est. 1963, 11x/yr., Trim Size-8½ x 11, Offset press, 8 pages, 2 Color, Matte
Subscriptions: Indv. $179, Can. $179, For. $199
Acquisitions: Publication Bought, Publication Sold
List Rental: List Management Co.: Manager: Alice Meyer; Taybi Direct East, Inc., 13321 New Hampshire Ave., Ste. 202, Silver Spring, MD 20904-3450 Tel # (301) 680-3633, Fax # (301) 680-3635

Fashion Retail Intelligence
Newsletter   *Association, Business*

Publishing Co: CSG Information Services, 3922 Coconut Palm Drive, Tampa, FL 33619-8321; Title Fax # (800) 846-8047
Editorial Description: Covers business events and information in the fashion industry.
General Info: Bi-monthly, Trim Size-8½ x 11, 4 pages, No Color

Financial   *Association*

Publishing Co: Clothing Manufacturers Assn. of the U.S.A., 730 Broadway, 9th Floor, New York, NY 10003; Title Tel # (212) 757-6664
Personnel: Editor-Robert A. Kaplan
Editorial Description: Contains vital statistics on financial & economic trends in men's & boys' tailored clothing industry, including profit, sales, production (by wholesale price range, fabric), surveys of retail clothing sales by price bracket.
General Info: Yr. Est. 1960, Annually, Trim Size-8½ x 11½, Mimeo press, 24 pages, No Color
Subscriptions: For. $28, $25/copy
List Rental: Rents Lists

Formalwords   *Association*

Publishing Co: International Formalwear Association, 401 N. Michigan Ave., Chicago, IL 60611-4212; Title Tel # (312) 644-6610 Title Fax # (312) 321-6869
Personnel: Publisher-Jack Springer, Editor-Annette Claussen
Editorial Description: Update on formal wear & formal wear specialists.
General Info: (Formerly Formalwear News Bureau), Yr. Est. 1973, Bi-monthly, Trim Size-8½ x 11, Letrpr. press, 8 pages, Saddle-stitched
Subscriptions: Free With Membership
Circulation: (90% controlled), Total-500, International-50
Advertising: Inquire for rates. Accepts Inserts.
List Rental: Rents Lists

Kid News   *Business*

Publishing Co: Kid News, PO Box 797, Forest Hills, NY 11375-0797; Title Tel # (718) 520-8829
Personnel: Publisher-Sue Robinson, Editor-Lori Frank, Feature Ed.-Susan Robinson, Adv. Dir.-Fred Robinson, Jr.
Editorial Description: Tells parents where to get bargains on designer children's clothing across the USA. Children's consumer reporting guide for parents.
General Info: Yr. Est. 1988, Bi-monthly
Subscriptions: $27/copy
Advertising: Inquire for rates.

Ladies' & Girls Wear   *Business*

Publishing Co: Prent Thomas Textile Consultants, PO Box 7005, Columbus, GA 31908-7005; Title Tel # (706) 568-1386
Editorial Description: Supplement to USA Textiles/Apparel Newsletter.
General Info: Semi-monthly
Subscriptions: Indv. $90

Members News Bulletin   *Business*

Publishing Co: Clothing Manufacturers Assn. of the U.S.A., 730 Broadway, 9th Floor, New York, NY 10003 Tel # (212) 757-6664
Editorial Description: Presents industry and Association news and developments.
General Info: Yr. Est. 1933, Bi-weekly, Trim Size-8 x 10, 4 pages
Subscriptions: Free With Membership

Men's & Boys Wear   *Business*

Publishing Co: Prent Thomas Textile Consultants, PO Box 7005, Columbus, GA 31908-7005; Title Tel # (706) 568-1386
Editorial Description: Supplement to USA Textiles/Apparel Newsletter.
General Info: Semi-monthly, 2 pages
Subscriptions: Indv. $90

Monthly Imports of Down
Filled Outerwear

Publishing Co: American Down Assn. (ADA), 3728 Canna Ct, Sacramento, CA 95821-3101; Title Tel # (916) 971-1135
Personnel: Editor-Howard Winslow
Editorial Description: Statistical report covering imports of downfill outerwear by source & cost.
General Info: Monthly

NAMSB News

Publishing Co: Natl. Assn. of Men's Sportswear Buyers, Inc., 500 5th Ave Fl 1425, New York, NY 10110-0002 Fax # (212) 837-0166; Title Tel # (212) 391-8580
Personnel: Editor-Jack Herschlag
Editorial Description: Men's fashions newsletter.
General Info: Yr. Est. 1953, Monthly, Trim Size-8½ x 11, Sheetfed press, 8 pages, 2 Color, Coated, Saddle-stitched
Subscriptions: Free With Membership
Circulation: Total-1,500
Printing Co: Fleetwood Litho & Letter, 304 Hudson St, New York, NY 10013-1079 Tel # (212) 924-4422

NAUMD Newsletter   *Association*

Publishing Co: Natl. Assn. of Uniform Manufacturers, 1156 Ave. of Americas, New York, NY 10036-2702; Title Tel # (212) 869-0670 Title Fax # (212) 575-2847
Personnel: Editor-Jackei Rosselli
General Info: Quarterly, 8 pages, No Color, Coated
Circulation: Total-1,000

Overground   *Consumer*

Publishing Co: Bandele Communications, P.O. Box 050410, Brooklyn, NY 11205-0008
Editorial Description: Fashion news of and for the African American community.

RTW Review   *Business*   CPM: $299

Publishing Co: Danielle Consultants, PO Box 27688, Milwaukee, WI 53227-0688; Title Tel # (414) 425-5503 Title Fax # (414) 425-2501
Personnel: Publisher, Editor-Lauren Daniel-Falk, Circ. Dir.-Florence Davidsavor, Art Dir.-Susan Marie, Art Dir.-Michelle Whalen, Mktg. Dir.-Renee Voit, Adv. Dir., Promotion Dir.-Patricia Biese
Editorial Description: The fashion business news source that brings you the perfect blend of comprehensive fashion coverage, merchandising strategies & emerging industry trends.
General Info: (Formerly Ready-To-Wear Review), Yr. Est. 1985, Bi-monthly, Trim Size-8½ x 11, 12 pages, ISSN: 0887-3003, 15% ads, 2 Color, Coated, Saddle-stitched
Subscriptions: Indv. $149, Can. $169, For. $199, $25/copy
Circulation: Total-5,000
Advertising: $1,495. Accepts Inserts.
List Rental: Actives: $125/M, Expires: $75/M
Printing Co: Wisconsin Graphics, Pewaukee, WI 53072 Tel # (414) 521-3200

Retail News Fashion
Merchandising Report

Publishing Co: Retail Reporting Corp., 302 5th Ave Fl 11, New York, NY 10001-3604 Tel # (212) 279-7000 Fax # (212) 279-7014; Title Tel # (212) 255-9595
Personnel: Publisher-Larry Fuersich
Editorial Description: Analysis of current fashion trends from U.S. & Europe.
General Info: Weekly, 25 pages, Looseleaf
Subscriptions: Indv. $420

S&B Report
Business, Consumer

Publishing Co: S&B Report, 108 East 38th Street, New York, NY 10016; Title Tel # (212) 683-7612
Personnel: Publisher, Editor-Elysa Lazar
Editorial Description: A guide to unadvertised manufacturer & designer showroom sales in NY, where clothing, jewelry, accessories & furniture can be purchased at wholesale prices.
General Info: Monthly
Subscriptions: Indv. $32
Circulation: Total-5,000

STA Newsletter
Association

Publishing Co: Shoe Tester's Association, 660 Spartan Blvd Ste 9, Spartanburg, SC 29301-1300 Tel # (803) 587-1719 Fax # (803) 576-0110
Editorial Description: Newsletter of the Shoe Tester's Association.
General Info: Monthly, Trim Size-8½ x 11, 4 pages, 2 Color

Seidman News Bulletin

Publishing Co: Seidman News Bulletin, 51 Pine Mountain Rd., West Redding, CT 06896-2717; Title Tel # (203) 544-8249
Personnel: Editor-Seymour Seidman
Editorial Description: Reports on trends, sales, developments, new items in linens & domestics, reviews all sheet, towel, blanket, bedspread, pillow, table linen, rug manufacturers.
General Info: Yr. Est. 1954, Weekly, Trim Size-8½ x 11, Web press, 2 pages
Subscriptions: Indv. $68, Can. $68

Sunglass Association of America-Newsletter
Association

Publishing Co: Sunglass Association of America, 49 East Ave., Norwalk, CT 06851; Title Tel # (203) 845-9015 Title Fax # (203) 847-1304
Editorial Description: Membership activities newsletter.
General Info: Yr. Est. 1974, Quarterly
Subscriptions: Free With Membership

T-Shirt Business Info Mapping Newsletter--How To & Ideas Edition
See: PRINTING/GRAPHIC ARTS

Tourist Outfitter

Publishing Co: Northern Ontario Tourist Outfitters Assn., Box 1140, North Bay, ON P1B 8K4 Canada
General Info: Monthly, 22 pages
Circulation: Total-1,200
Advertising: Inquire for rates.

Trouser Institute of America Bulletin
Association

Publishing Co: Mens Fashion Assn., 475 Park Ave S Fl 17, New York, NY 10016-6901; Title Tel # (212) 686-3440
General Info: Bi-weekly

Two/Ten International Footwear Foundation-Two/Ten Today

Publishing Co: Two/Ten International Footwear Foundation, 56 Main St, Watertown, MA 02172-4413; Title Tel # (617) 923-4500 Title Fax # (617) 926-6037
Editorial Description: Membership activities newsletter for members of the shoe, leather, & allied industries.
General Info: (Formerly Two/Ten Foundation -Update), Quarterly, Desktop press, 2 Color, Matte
Circulation: Total-12,000

USA Textiles/Apparel Newsletter
See: TEXTILES

Western Industry Report International
See: BUSINESS & INDUSTRY

Woman to Woman
Business, Consumer

Publishing Co: Donna Karan Company, The, 550 Seventh Avenue, New York, NY 10018
Personnel: Pres. /Exec. Publ.-Donna Karan
Editorial Description: A professional and personal fashion update from Donna Karan on the latest styles and trends impacting the world of fashion.
General Info: Yr. Est. 1995, Quarterly, Trim Size-11 x 14, 8 pages, No Color, Coated, Saddle-stitched
Advertising: Inquire for rates.

APPLIANCES

Dateline AHAM
Business, Association

Publishing Co: Assn. of Home Appliance Manufacturers (AHAM), 20 N Wacker Dr Ste 1500, Chicago, IL 60606-2903 Fax # (312) 984-5823; Title Tel # (312) 984-5800
Personnel: Mng. Editor-Tracy Haak
Editorial Description: Assn. newsletter for AHAM executives. Information on home appliances.
General Info: (Formerly Exec-U-Letter), Quarterly
Subscriptions: Free With Membership
Circulation: Total-1,500

Energy News Exchange
Business

Publishing Co: Kentucky Utilities Co., 1 Quality St, Lexington, KY 40507-1462; Title Tel # (606) 255-2100 Title Fax # (606) 288-1165
Personnel: Editor-Joy Barr
Editorial Description: Provides information concerning developments in appliance retailing & building industry. Also current trends in electric energy industry.
General Info: Yr. Est. 1946, Bi-monthly, Trim Size-8½ x 11, Sheetfed press, 6 pages, 2 Color, Coated
Circulation: (100% controlled), Total-3,500
Printing Co: Post Printing Co., 1033 Trotwood Dr., Lexington, KY 40511 Tel # (606) 254-7714

Kitchen & Collectible News
Consumer

Publishing Co: Kitchen & Collectible News, 4645 Laurel Ridge Dr, Harrisburg, PA 17110-3446; Title Tel # (717) 545-7320
Subscriptions: $3/copy

MACAP Statistical Report
Business, Association

Publishing Co: Sponsor-Major Appliance Consumer Action Panel, Assn. of Home Appliance Manufacturers (AHAM), 20 N Wacker Dr Ste 1500, Chicago, IL 60606-2903 Fax # (312) 984-5823; Title Tel # (312) 984-5858
Personnel: Editor-Marian Stamos
Editorial Description: Detailed annual statistical report of complaints received by MACAP about kitchen & household appliances.
General Info: Annually, Looseleaf
Circulation: Total-700

Major Appliance Factory Shipment Report
Association

Publishing Co: Assn. of Home Appliance Manufacturers (AHAM), 20 N Wacker Dr Ste 1500, Chicago, IL 60606-2903 Fax # (312) 984-5823; Title Tel # (312) 984-5800
Personnel: Editor-Joyce Biso
Editorial Description: Statistical report of factory shipments of major appliances. Also trends & forecast tables.
General Info: (Formerly AHAM Major Appliance Indicators), Yr. Est. 1972, Monthly
Subscriptions: Indv. $50
Circulation: Total-330

Obsolete & Excess Inventory Program

Publishing Co: Air-Conditioning & Refrigeration Wholesalers, 10251 W Sample Rd # B, Coral Springs, FL 33065-3939; Title Tel # (305) 771-1000
Personnel: Publisher-David Kellough, Editor-Charles Willets
Editorial Description: Listing of excess inventory items offered at discount.
General Info: Annually
Circulation: Total-150

Specified Domestic Electrical Appliances
Business

Publishing Co: Statistics Canada, Holland Ave/RH Coats, Holland Ave/Tunney's Pasture, Ottawa, ON K1A O26 Canada Tel # (613) 951-8116 Fax # (613) 951-0581; Title Tel # (613) 951-1581 Title Fax # (613) 951-1584
Editorial Description: Monthly production, shipments, and month-end stocks. Cat. #43-003.
General Info: Yr. Est. 1958, Monthly, Trim Size-8½ x 11½, Offset press, 4 pages, ISSN: 0410-5907
Subscriptions: Indv. $6, Can. $5, For. $7, $6/copy

Sylvania News

Publishing Co: GTE-Sylvania, 500 Frank W Burr Blvd., Teaneck, NJ 07666-6802; Title Tel # (212) 288-9484
Personnel: Editor-D. James McCue
Editorial Description: Innovations in electronics featuring company products.
General Info: Yr. Est. 1930, Bi-monthly
Circulation: Total-130,000

Trends & Forecasts

Publishing Co: Assn. of Home Appliance Manufacturers (AHAM), 20 N Wacker Dr Ste 1500, Chicago, IL 60606-2903 Fax # (312) 984-5823; Title Tel # (312) 984-5800
Personnel: Editor-Paul Roman
Editorial Description: Statistical report giving trends & forecasts of domestic & export shipments of major appliances.
General Info: Quarterly

ARCHAEOLOGY

ASOR Newsletter

Publishing Co: Scholars Press, PO Box 15399, Atlanta, GA 30333-0399 Tel # (404) 727-2320 Fax # (404) 727-2348; Title Tel # (404) 727-2345
Personnel: Editor-Eric Meyers
General Info: Quarterly, Trim Size-8½ x 11, 16 pages, ISSN: 0361-6029, 2 Color, Coated, Saddle-stitched
Subscriptions: $4/copy

Advances in Computer Archaelogy

Publishing Co: Arizona State University, Department of Anthropology, Publications, Tempe, AZ 85281; Title Tel # (602) 965-7516
General Info: (Formerly Newsletter of Computer Archaelogy), Yr. Est. 1965, Semi-annually, Trim Size-5½ x 8, Offset press
Circulation: Total-200

Albuquerque Archaeological Society-Newsletter

Publishing Co: Albuquerque Archaeological Society, PO Box 4029, Albuquerque, NM 87196-4029
Personnel: Editor-Dolores Sundt
General Info: Yr. Est. 1966, Monthly, Trim Size-8½ x 11, Offset press, 8 pages, ISSN: 0002-4953, No Color, Newsprint
Subscriptions: Indv. $5
Circulation: Total-275

Arch Notes   *Association*   CPM: $93

Publishing Co: Ontario Archaeological Society, 126 Willowdale Ave., #4, North York, ON M2N 4Y2 Canada Fax # (416) 730-0797; Title Tel # (416) 730-0797
Personnel: Publisher-Charles Garrad, Editor-Michael Kirby
Editorial Description: Newsletter of the Ontario Archaeological Society.
General Info: Yr. Est. 1956, Bi-monthly, Trim Size-5½ x 8½, Sheetfed press, 40 pages, ISSN: 0068-1742, No Color, Newsprint, Saddle-stitched
Subscriptions: Indv. $28, Inst. $55
Circulation: Total-750
Advertising: $70. Accepts Inserts.
Printing Co: Sunrise Printing, 5580 Yonge St., North York, ON M2N 5S2 Canada Tel # (416) 221-1484

Archaeoastronomy & Ethnoastronomy News
See: ASTRONOMY

Archaeological Conservancy-Newsletter   *Association*

Publishing Co: Archaeological Conservancy, 5301 Central Ave. N.E., Ste. 12181, Albuquerque, NM 87108-1517; Title Tel # (505) 266-1540
Personnel: Mktg. Dir.-Theresa Oderman
Editorial Description: Reports on conservation projects, research and archaeological tours.
General Info: Yr. Est. 1980, Quarterly, Trim Size-8½ x 11, Web press, 8 pages, Color-cover, Matte
Subscriptions: Indv. $25, Free With Membership
Circulation: Total-12,500
List Rental: List Management Co.: Names in the News-California, 1 Bush St Bsmt 3, San Francisco, CA 94104-4425 Tel # (415) 989-3350, Fax # (415) 433-7796, Actives: 8,880, $65/M
Printing Co: Quik Print, 5000e Menaul Blvd NE, Albuquerque, NM 87110-3044 Tel # (505) 881-2927

Archaeological Newsletter   *Association*

Publishing Co: Royal Ontario Museum, 100 Queen's Park, Toronto, ON M5S 2C6 Canada Tel # (416) 586-5549; Title Tel # (416) 586-5698 Title Fax # (416) 586-5863
Personnel: Editor-D.M. Pendergast, Circ. Mgr., Production Mgr.-Imogene Friedman
Editorial Description: Newsletter on current archaeological excavations under the direction of the Royal Ontario Museum.
General Info: Yr. Est. 1965, Bi-monthly, Trim Size-8½ x 11, Offset press, 4 pages, No Color, Matte
Subscriptions: Free
Circulation: Total-4,600

Archaeological Society of New Jersey Newsletter

Publishing Co: Archeological Society of New Jersey, Seton Hall Univ. Museum, South Orange, NJ 07079; Title Tel # (201) 761-9543
Editorial Description: Notes of current interest to Society members. Distributed without charge to members.
General Info: Quarterly, 12 pages
Circulation: Total-700

Archaeology on Kaua'i

Publishing Co: Sponsor-Anthropology Club, Kaua'i Community College, 3-1901 Kaumualii Hwy., Anthrop, Lihue, HI 96766-9591 Tel # (808) 245-8218; Title Tel # (808) 245-8311 Title Fax # (808) 245-8220
Personnel: Editor-Dr. William Kikuchi
Editorial Description: Archaeology and anthropology of Kauai Island, Hawaiian Islands.
General Info: Yr. Est. 1973, Semi-annually, Trim Size-8½ x 11, 14 pages, ISSN: 0190-7730, No Color
Subscriptions: Free
Circulation: Total-450, Readership-450

Archeological Society of New Jersey, Bulletin   *Association*

Publishing Co: Archeological Society of New Jersey, Seton Hall Univ. Museum, South Orange, NJ 07079; Title Tel # (201) 761-9543
Personnel: Editor-Charles Bello
Editorial Description: Articles on archeology in the Northeast, particularly New Jersey. Distributed without charge to Society members.
General Info: Yr. Est. 1931, Annually, Trim Size-8½ x 11, Offset press, 75 pages, ISSN: 0196-8319, No Color
Subscriptions: Indv. $12, Inst. $15
Circulation: Total-700

Arkansas Amateur   *Association*

Publishing Co: Sponsor-Northwest, Arkansas Archaeological Society, Inc., Northwest Arkansas Archaeological Society, Inc., PO Box 1154, Fayetteville, AR 72702-1154; Title Tel # (501) 855-1970
Personnel: Publisher, Editor in Chief-Larry Swaim, Circulation-Virginia Swaim
Editorial Description: News of archaeology and anthropology.
General Info: Yr. Est. 1962, Bi-monthly, Trim Size-8 x 11, Mimeo press, 12 pages, ISSN: 0518-6617, Color-cover, Newspaper
Subscriptions: Indv. $15, Can. $15, For. $15, $1/copy
Circulation: (28% controlled)
Printing Co: Northwest Printing Co., 1903 S. Walcon Blvd., Bentonville, AR 72712 Tel # (501) 273-5010

Backdirt

Publishing Co: UCLA Institute of Archaeology, A222 Fowler, 405 Hilgard, Los Angeles, CA 90024-1510; Title Tel # (213) 825-7411 Title Fax # (213) 206-4723
Personnel: Editor-Ernastien Elster, Production Mgr.-Carol Leyba
Editorial Description: Newsletter of the UCLA Institute of Archaeology, reporting on excavations, lectures, & other programs.
General Info: Yr. Est. 1986, Semi-annually, Sheetfed press, 12 pages, No Color, Coated, Saddle-stitched
Circulation: Total-1,400

Cahokian   *Association*

Publishing Co: Cahokia Mounds Museum Society, PO Box 382, Collinsville, IL 62234-0382; Title Tel # (618) 344-7316
Personnel: Editor-Chris Pallozola
Editorial Description: Covers activities, programs, etc. at Cahokia Mounds Historic Site, & current archaeology in area.
General Info: Yr. Est. 1974, Quarterly, Trim Size-8½ x 11, Sheetfed press, 16 pages, Color-cover, Matte, Saddle-stitched
Subscriptions: $2/copy
Circulation: Total-500
Printing Co: Graham-Pierce, 1607 W. Hwy. 50, Fairview Heights, IL 62269 Tel # (618) 632-5600

Coastal Research
See: SCIENCE

Connecticut News   *Association*

Publishing Co: Archaeological Society of Connecticut, C/O Joseph Parkos, 60 Bashan Rd., East Haddam, CT 06423
Personnel: Editor-E. Wiegand, Circ. Mgr.-Roger Moeller
Editorial Description: Activities of the various organizations.
General Info: Quarterly, Mimeo press, 6 pages
Subscriptions: Indv. $13
Circulation: Total-800

Conservation: The Getty Conservation Institute Newsletter
See: MUSEUM PUBLICATIONS

Expedition News
See: OUTDOORS

Field Notes, Newsletter of the Arkansas Archeological Society   *Scholarly, Association*

Publishing Co: Arkansas Archeological Society, PO Box 1222, Fayetteville, AR 72702-1222; Title Tel # (501) 575-3556
Personnel: Editor-Hester Davis, Circ. Mgr.-Russell Scheibel
Editorial Description: Articles about archeology in general and on Arkansas in particular.
General Info: Yr. Est. 1965, Bi-monthly, Trim Size-8½ x 11, Offset press, 15 pages, ISSN: 0015-0711, Ind/Abs/Online: Hist.Abs., No Color
Subscriptions: Indv. $20, Inst. $25, Can. $30, For. $30, $1/copy
Circulation: Total-750

Information North
See: SCIENCE

Kansas Anthropological Association Newsletter
See: ANTHROPOLOGY

Missouri Archeological Society Quarterly   *Association*

Publishing Co: Missouri Archaeological Society, PO Box 958, 101A Museum Support Center, Columbia, MO 65205-0958 Fax # (314) 882-9410; Title Tel # (314) 882-3544
Personnel: Editor-Michael O'Brien, Circ. Mgr., Production Mgr.-Melody Galen
Editorial Description: Contains articles on archaeology of Missouri & related areas, membership information, chapter information, book reviews, & interviews with prominent archaeologists.
General Info: (Formerly Missouri Archeological Society Newsletter), Yr. Est. 1984, Quarterly, Trim Size-8½ x 11, Offset press, 24 pages, ISSN: 0743-7641, No Color, Saddle-stitched
Subscriptions: Indv. $15, Inst. $15, Can. $15, For. $15, $2/copy
Circulation: Total-900
Printing Co: University of Misouri Printing and Records Management, 2800 Maguire, Columbia, MO 65211-0001 Tel # (314) 882-7801, Fax # (314) 882-1413

NEA Newsletter   *Association*   CPM: $178

Publishing Co: New England Archivists, Massachusetts Archives, 220 Morrissey Blvd., Boston, MA 02125; Title Tel # (617) 727-2816
Personnel: Editor-Kim Brookes, Editor-Bridget Carr, Bk. Rev. Ed.-Frank Wheeler
Editorial Description: Newsletter for New England Archivists members.
General Info: Yr. Est. 1973, Quarterly, Trim Size-8½ x 11, Desktop press, 32 pages, Matte
Subscriptions: Indv. $15, Inst. $25, Free With Membership
Circulation: Total-700
Advertising: $125.
List Rental: Actives: 718, $25/M
Printing Co: Ink Spot, The, 40 Oval Rd, Quincy, MA 02170-3813 Tel # (617) 273-7605, Fax # (617) 471-8810

NETOP, The   *Association*

Publishing Co: American Indian Archaeological Institute, PO Box 1260, Curtis Road, Washington, CT 06793-0260
Editorial Description: News for the American Indian Archaeological Institute.
General Info: Semi-monthly

Nestor
See: LITERATURE & LINGUISTICS

Newsletter
See: LITERATURE & LINGUISTICS

Newsletter East Asian Art & Archaeology
See: ART & SCULPTURE

Newsletter of the Massachusetts Archaeological Society, Inc.   *Association*   CPM: $105

Publishing Co: Massachusetts Archaeological Society, PO Box 700, Middleboro, MA 02346-0700; Title Tel # (508) 947-9005
Personnel: Production Dir.-Lisa Dufer, Publisher, Editor, Adv. Dir.-Thomas Lux
Editorial Description: Featuring society news, items of interest in archaeology, & book notes.
General Info: (Formerly Newsletter), Tri-annually, Trim Size-8½ x 11, Offset press, 6 pages, No Color, Other
Subscriptions: Indv. $18, Inst. $30, Can. $35, For. $35, Free
Circulation: Total-850
Advertising: $90.

Newsletter of the Society of Maine Archivists
See: HISTORY

Newsletter/Journal

Publishing Co: Iowa Archeological Society, IAS Office of Newsletter, Box 27, Highlandville, IA 52149; Title Tel # (319) 335-2394
Personnel: Editor-Sheila Hainlin
Editorial Description: Iowa archeology, geology & history for interested amateur archeologists.
General Info: Yr. Est. 1951, Quarterly, Desktop press, 8 pages
Subscriptions: Indv. $10
Acquistions: Publication Bought
Circulation: Total-500
Printing Co: University of Iowa, Printing Service, Iowa City, IA 52242 Tel # (319) 353-2121

OHS Bulletin
See: HISTORY

Oklahoma Anthropological Society, Newsletter
See: ANTHROPOLOGY

Over the Edge
See: HISTORY

PCAS Newsletter   *Association*

Publishing Co: Pacific Coast Archaeological Society, Inc., PO Box 10926, Costa Mesa, CA 92627-0926; Title Tel # (714) 646-1314
Personnel: Editor-Beth Padon, Circ. Mgr.-Cory Smith
Editorial Description: Activities of Society, progress reports on archaeology locally, legislation.
General Info: (Formerly Smoke Signals), Yr. Est. 1961, Monthly, Trim Size-8½ x 11, Letrpr. press, 6 pages, ISSN: 0270-6776, No Color
Subscriptions: Indv. $6, For. $9
Circulation: Total-350

Pottery Southwest

Publishing Co: Albuquerque Archaeological Society, PO Box 4029, Albuquerque, NM 87196-4029; Title Tel # (505) 881-1675
Personnel: Editor-William Sundt
Editorial Description: News, queries & views on archaeological ceramics by southwesternists.
General Info: Yr. Est. 1974, Quarterly, Trim Size-8½ x 11, Sheetfed press, 7 pages, ISSN: 0738-8020, No Color
Subscriptions: Indv. $3
Circulation: Total-160

Prehistoric Times   *Scholarly, Association*

Publishing Co: Center for American Archaeology, PO Box 22, Kampsville, IL 62053-0022; Title Tel # (618) 655-4532
Personnel: Publisher-Center for American Archeology, Editor-Cynthia Sutton, Product Mgr.-Mary Gilman
General Info: Semi-annually
Subscriptions: Free With Membership

Saskatchewan Archaeological Society Newsletter   *Association*

Publishing Co: Saskatchewan Archaeological Society, #5-816 1st Ave., N., Saskatoon, SK S7K 1Y3 Canada Fax # (306) 665-1928; Title Tel # (306) 664-4124
Personnel: Editor-Jim Finnigan, Circ. Mgr.-Tim Jones
Editorial Description: News items and short articles on archaeology in Saskatchewan and nearby.
General Info: (Formerly Saskatchewan Archaeology Newsletter), Yr. Est. 1963, Bi-monthly, Trim Size-8½ x 11, Offset press, 20 pages, ISSN: 0227-7514, No Color
Subscriptions: Indv. $15, Inst. $21, $2/copy
Circulation: Total-657

Ships & Shipwrecks: The Newsletter of Nautical History & Discovery   *Consumer*   CPM: $625

Publishing Co: Riderwood Publishing Co., 5049 Smith Rd, Rohrersville, MD 21779-1039; Title Tel # (301) 296-3990
Personnel: Publisher/President/Advisor-David P. Robson, Publisher, Editor-Lynn K. Sibley, Mktg. Dir.-John L. Sibley
Editorial Description: Focuses on maritime history and related subjects.
General Info: Yr. Est. 1990, Bi-monthly, Trim Size-8½ x 11, Sheetfed press, 8 pages, ISSN: 1052-6862, 2 Color, Recycled
Subscriptions: Indv. $36, Inst. $36, Can. $36, For. $36, $5/copy
Circulation: Total-400
Advertising: $250.
List Rental: Rents Lists
Printing Co: Printing Service Inc., 107 York Rd., Towson, MD 21204

Society for American Archaeology Bulletin   *Business, Association*   CPM: $67

Publishing Co: Society for American Archaeology, 900 2nd St NE Ste 12, Washington, DC 20002-3557 Fax # (202) 789-0284; Title Tel # (202) 789-8200
Personnel: Publisher-Jerome Miller, Editor-Alan Downer, Production Mgr., Adv. Dir.-Ralph Johnson
Editorial Description: American archaeology news and views.
General Info: Yr. Est. 1983, 5x/yr., Trim Size-8½ x 11, Offset press, 8 pages, ISSN: 0741-5672, Newsprint
Subscriptions: Indv. $30
Circulation: Total-5,400
Advertising: $365.
List Rental: Actives: 5,200, $75/M
Printing Co: Newsletter Services, Inc., 9700 Philadelphia Court, Lanham, MD 20706 Tel # (301) 731-5200, Fax # (301) 731-5201

Society for Historical Archaeology-Newsletter

Publishing Co: Society for Historical Archaeology, Dept. Anthropology, Box 8795, College of William & Mary, Williamsburg, VA 23187-8795; Title Tel # (804) 221-1059
Personnel: Editor-Norman Barka
Editorial Description: Official organ for the dissemination of news about historical archaeology in North America.
General Info: Yr. Est. 1968, Quarterly, Trim Size-8½ x 11, Sheetfed press, 48 pages, No Color, Saddle-stitched
Subscriptions: Indv. $50, Inst. $65
Circulation: Total-2,000

Society for Industrial Archeology Newsletter   *Association*

Publishing Co: Society for Industrial Archeology, Houghton, MI 49931; Title Tel # (906) 487-2070
Personnel: Editor-Robert Frame
Editorial Description: History of industry & technology based on physical survivals.
General Info: Yr. Est. 1972, Quarterly, Trim Size-8½ x 11, Offset press, 16 pages, ISSN: 0160-1067, Ind/Abs/Online: ABC-CLIO; Avery Arch. Ind., No Color, Coated
Subscriptions: Indv. $35, Inst. $40, Free With Membership
Circulation: Total-1,600
Printing Co: M&M Printers, 631 8th Ave N, Minneapolis, MN 55411-4317 Tel # (612) 338-8545

Stones and Bones Newsletter   *Association*

Publishing Co: Alabama Archaeological Society, Moundville Archaeological Park, Moundville, AL 35474 Fax # (205) 371-2494; Title Tel # (205) 371-2266 Title Fax # (201) 371-2494
Personnel: Editor-Dorothy P. Luke
Editorial Description: Current news & activities concerning archaeology in the southeast, especially in Alabama.
General Info: Yr. Est. 1957, Monthly, Trim Size-8½ x 11, Offset press, 8 pages, No Color, Coated
Subscriptions: Indv. $9, Inst. $13, $1/copy
Acquistions: Publication Bought
Circulation: (100% controlled), Total-550
List Rental: Actives: $100/M

Strecker Museum News
See: MUSEUM PUBLICATIONS

VAS Newsletter   *Association*

Publishing Co: Vermont Archaeological Society, Inc., C/O Victor R. Rolando, RR 1 Box 1521-3, Manchester Center, VT 05255; Title Tel # (802) 362-4382
Personnel: Editor-Victor R. Rolando
Editorial Description: All activities related to Vermont archaeology (prehistoric and historic) reviews.
General Info: Yr. Est. 1968, Quarterly, Trim Size-8½ x 11, Offset press, 8 pages, ISSN: 1043-1918, No Color
Subscriptions: Indv. $12, Inst. $50, Can. $12, For. $12, Free With Membership
Printing Co: Sharp Offset Printing, 10 Cleveland Ave., Rutland, VT 05701-2712 Tel # (802) 773-9194

W.A.S. Newsletter   *Scholarly, Association*

Publishing Co: World Archaeological Society, 120 Lakewood Dr, Hollister, MO 65672-5176; Title Tel # (417) 334-2377
Personnel: Editor-Ron Miller
Editorial Description: Covers all areas of archaeology, anthropology and art history, scientific.
General Info: Yr. Est. 1971, Irregular, Trim Size-8½ x 11, Mimeo press, 10 pages, ISSN: 0738-8063, No Color
Subscriptions: Indv. $12, For. $16, $1/copy
Acquistions: Publication Bought, Publication Sold
Advertising: $75. Accepts Inserts.

Wisconsin Preservation
See: HISTORY

ARCHITECTURE

A-E-C Automation Newsletter
See: COMPUTERS & AUTOMATION

AAHE Newsletter

Publishing Co: American Assn. of Housing Educators, Texas A&M Univ., College of Architecture, College Station, TX 77843-0001; Title Tel # (409) 845-0986 Title Fax # (409) 845-4491
Personnel: Editor-Paul Woods
Editorial Description: Publishes Association bulletins, dead-lines, etc., plus position announcements & information relative to the Association's interests.
General Info: Quarterly, 10 pages, No Color
List Rental: Rents Lists

AAMA Quarterly Review

Publishing Co: American Architectural Manufacturers Association, 1540 E Dundee Rd Ste 310, Palatine, IL 60067-8321; Title Tel # (847) 202-1350
Personnel: Editor-Tony Coorlim
Circulation: Total-30,000

AAMA Update

Publishing Co: Architectural Aluminum Mfgrs. Assn., 1540 E Dundee Rd Ste 310, Palatine, IL 60067-8321; Title Tel # (708) 699-7310
Personnel: Editor-Tony Coorlim
Editorial Description: Current assn. news & developments & meetings.
General Info: 4 pages
Circulation: (100% controlled), Total-1,200

ACSA News   *Association*   CPM: $237

Publishing Co: Association of Collegiate Schools of Architecture, Inc., 1735 New York Ave., Washington, DC 20006-5209; Title Tel # (202) 785-2324
Personnel: Editor-Karen Eldridge, Circ. Mgr.-Emily Cole, Adv. Dir.-John Edwards
General Info: Yr. Est. 1969, Monthly, Trim Size-9 x 12, Web press, 24 pages, ISSN: 0149-2446, Saddle-stitched
Subscriptions: Indv. $50, Inst. $50, Can. $50, For. $60
Circulation: Total-4,000
Advertising: $950.

ADPSR News
See: POLITICS

A.E. Legal Newsletter
See: LAW

AGSA Newsletter
See: GLASS, STONE & CLAY

AIAS News   *Association*

Publishing Co: AIA Press, 1735 New York Ave. NW, Washington, DC 20006-5292 Tel # (202) 626-7300; Title Tel # (202) 626-7472 Title Fax # (202) 626-7421
Personnel: Editor-Lee Chatham Hubbard, Circ. Mgr., Adv. Dir., Promotion Dir.-Carl Costello
Editorial Description: Student newsletter for architecture, describing, promoting, & reporting on natl. student programs & issues of architectural education & practice.
General Info: (Formerly AIAS News-Concepts), Quarterly, Trim Size-8½ x 11, Desktop press, 12 pages, Color, Newsprint
Circulation: Total-15,000
Advertising: Inquire for rates.
List Rental: Actives: $250/M

APVA Newsletter   *Association*

Publishing Co: Association for the Preservation of Virginia Antiquities, 2300 E Grace St, Richmond, VA 23223-7152; Title Tel # (804) 648-1889
Personnel: Editor-Catherine Long
Editorial Description: Preservation-related articles; activities announcements; contributors acknowledgments; branch reports.
General Info: Yr. Est. 1983, Trim Size-8½ x 11, Offset press, 12 pages, ISSN: 0890-2518, No Color, Newsprint
Subscriptions: Indv. $20
Circulation: (100% controlled), Total-4,600
Printing Co: Satterwhite Printing Co., 3413 Carlton St, Richmond, VA 23230-4301 Tel # (804) 359-6100

American Institute of Architects Memo   *Association*

Publishing Co: American Institute of Architects, 1735 New York Ave., NW, Washington, DC 20006-5209 Tel # (202) 626-7300; Title Tel # (202) 626-7465
Personnel: Editor-Peter McCall
Editorial Description: General member news.
General Info: Yr. Est. 1947, Monthly
Subscriptions: Indv. $50
Circulation: Total-54,000

Arkansas Preservation Digest
See: HISTORY

Association for Preservation Technology International Communique   *Association*

Publishing Co: Association for Preservation Technology, PO Box 3511, Williamsburg, VA 23187-3511; Title Tel # (703) 373-1621 Title Fax # (703) 373-6050
Personnel: Editor-Susan Ford Johnson
Editorial Description: Meeting Course announcement & reports; publications; articles; extension listing of annotated periodicals, job openings, advertising.
General Info: (Formerly APT Newsletter), Yr. Est. 1972, Quarterly, Trim Size-8½ x 11, Offset press, 12 pages, ISSN: 0319-4558, No Color
Subscriptions: Indv. $8, $2/copy
Circulation: (100% controlled), Total-2,000
Advertising: Inquire for rates.

Columns   *Association*

Publishing Co: Saskatchewan Assn. of Architects, 200-642 Broadway Avenue, Saskatoon, SK S7N 1A9 Canada; Title Tel # (306) 242-0733 Title Fax # (306) 664-2598
General Info: (Formerly Saskatchewan Assoication of Architects Newsletter), Monthly
Circulation: Total-200

Construction Market Data   *Business*

Publishing Co: Construction Market Data, 4126 Pleasantdale Rd, Atlanta, GA 30340-3516; Title Tel # (770) 447-6633 Title Fax # (770) 449-9687
Personnel: Editor-Calvin Oren
General Info: Yr. Est. 1981, Semi-weekly
Subscriptions: Indv. $750

Construction Marketing Research
See: CONSTRUCTION & BUILDING

Design Drafting News
See: ENGINEERING

Design Line   *Business*

Publishing Co: American Institute of Building Design, 991 Post Road East, Westport, CT 06880; Title Tel # (203) 227-3640 Title Fax # (203) 227-8624
Personnel: Editor-Tammy Crosby, Circ. Mgr.-Bobbi Currie
Editorial Description: Designed for residential/light frame building designers. Emphasizes custom residential design and information related to the building design profession.
General Info: Yr. Est. 1960, Quarterly, Trim Size-7½ x 10½, 4 Color
Subscriptions: Indv. $28
Circulation: Total-1,500
Advertising: Inquire for rates.
List Rental: Rents Lists

Downtown Idea Exchange
See: PUBLIC MANAGEMENT & PLANNING

Eagle   *Association*

Publishing Co: Alabama Council American Institute of Architects, 1521 Mulberry St, Montgomery, AL 36106-1519; Title Tel # (205) 264-3037
Personnel: Publisher-J.R. Ortega
Editorial Description: Current activities of organizations and items of interest.
General Info: Yr. Est. 1973, Bi-monthly, Offset press, 6 pages, 2 Color, Newsprint
Circulation: (100% controlled)

Energy Exchange
See: PETROLEUM & NATURAL GAS

Friends Newsletter

Publishing Co: Sleepy Hollow Restorations, 150 White Plains Rd., Tarrytown, NY 10591-5521
General Info: Quarterly

Guidelines for Improving Practice: Architects and Engineers Professional Liability *Business, Scholarly*

Publishing Co: Victor O. Schinnerer, 2 Wisconsin Cir., Chevy Chase, MD 20815-7022; Title Tel # (301) 961-9800
General Info: Yr. Est. 1971, Bi-monthly, Trim Size-8½ x 11, Sheetfed press, 4 pages, ISSN: 0091-8245, 2 Color, Matte, Looseleaf
Subscriptions: Indv. $110
Circulation: Total-17,000
Printing Co: Linemark Printing, Inc., 1220 Caraway Ct., Landover, MD 20785 Tel # (301) 925-9000

Guidelines Letter *Business*

Publishing Co: Guidelines, PO Box 456, Orinda, CA 94563-0456; Title Tel # (510) 254-9393 Title Fax # (510) 254-9397
Personnel: Editor-Fred Stitt
Editorial Description: Technical and business information for design professionals (architects, engineers); aspects of office management; articles on production methods.
General Info: Yr. Est. 1969, Monthly, Trim Size-8½ x 11, Offset press, 4 pages
Subscriptions: Indv. $56, For. $66, $5/copy
Circulation: Total-3,000

Heritage Newsletter *Association*

Publishing Co: Foundation for San Francisco's Architectural Heritage, 2007 Franklin St, San Francisco, CA 94109-2909; Title Tel # (415) 441-3000 Title Fax # (415) 441-3015
Personnel: Editor-Donald Andreini
Editorial Description: Presents local planning & historic preservation issues, activities & programs.
General Info: Yr. Est. 1973, Bi-monthly, Trim Size-8½ x 11, Sheetfed press, 12 pages, 1% ads, No Color, Newsprint, Saddle-stitched
Subscriptions: $1/copy
Circulation: (100% controlled), Total-4,000
Advertising: Inquire for rates.
Printing Co: Smythe & Son, 30 Harriet St, San Francisco, CA 94103-4006 Tel # (415) 864-0943

Historic House News
See: HISTORY

IDP

Publishing Co: Natl. Council of Architectural Registration Boards, 1735 NY Ave., NW, Ste. 700, Washington, DC 20006; Title Tel # (202) 783-6500
Personnel: Editor-Kathleen Butler
Editorial Description: For participants in the Intern Development Program.
General Info: Quarterly
Circulation: Total-50,000

IFMA News
See: CONSTRUCTION & BUILDING

IFRAA Quarterly
See: RELIGIOUS & THEOLOGICAL

Indoor Air Bulletin
See: ENVIRONMENT & ECOLOGY

Interior Concerns Newsletter
See: ENVIRONMENT & ECOLOGY

LAND: Landscape Architectural News Digest *Association*

Publishing Co: American Society of Landscape Architects, 4401 Connecticut Ave., NW, Washington, DC 20008; Title Tel # (202) 686-2752
Personnel: Editor-Andy Brown, Production Mgr.-Ellen Harrington
General Info: 8x/yr., ISSN: 0023-754X
Subscriptions: Indv. $32, Inst. $32
Circulation: Total-8,000

Landmarks Observer
See: HISTORY

Liability Update
See: LAW

Log Cabin News
See: HISTORY

MSA Bulletin *Association*

Publishing Co: AIA Michigan, 553 E Jefferson Ave, Detroit, MI 48226-4324; Title Tel # (313) 965-4100 Title Fax # (313) 965-1501
Personnel: Editor-Rae Dumkie
Circulation: Total-1,800

Making Cities Livable Newsletter
See: PUBLIC MANAGEMENT & PLANNING

Metropolitan Historic Structures Assn. News

Publishing Co: Metropolitan Historic Structures Assn., Dyckman House Museum, 4881 Broadway, New York, NY 10034
Personnel: Editor-Jane Crowley
Editorial Description: Covers Association news. Features on historic buildings in Metropolitan New York.
General Info: Yr. Est. 1976, Quarterly
Subscriptions: Indv. $5
Circulation: Total-2,000
Advertising: Inquire for rates.

Motif
See: ANTIQUES & ART GOODS

NCARB Bulletin

Publishing Co: Natl. Council of Architectural Registration Boards, 1735 NY Ave., NW, Ste. 700, Washington, DC 20006
General Info: Yr. Est. 1965, Semi-annually
Circulation: Total-7,200

Nari Focus
See: CONSTRUCTION & BUILDING

Neon News
See: LIGHTING

Newfoundland Assn. of Architects Newsletter

Publishing Co: Newfoundland Assn. of Architects, Box 5204, St. Johns, NF A1C 5V5 Canada; Title Tel # (709) 726-8550
General Info: Monthly

Nouvelles O.A.Q. *Business*

Publishing Co: Ordre des Architectes du Quebec, 1825 Blvd. Rene-Levesque Ouest, Montreal, PQ H3H 1R4 Canada Fax # (614) 933-0242; Title Tel # (514) 937-6168 Title Fax # (514) 933-0242
Personnel: Production Mgr., Adv. Dir.-Madeleine Lanoix
Editorial Description: Architecture, professional problems, general information to members, committee reports, in French and English.
General Info: (Formerly Esquisses), Yr. Est. 1990, Monthly, Offset press, 16 pages, 2% ads
Acquisitions: Publication Bought
Circulation: Total-3,500
Advertising: Inquire for rates. Accepts Inserts.

Nova Scotia Assn. of Architects Newsletter

Publishing Co: Nova Scotia Assn. of Architects, 1361 Barrington St., Halifax, NS B3J 1Y9 Canada; Title Tel # (902) 423-7607
Personnel: Publisher, Editor-Diane Scott-Stewart
General Info: Monthly

OALA News

Publishing Co: Ontario Assn. of Landscape Architects, 75 The Donway W., Ste. 302, Don Mills, ON M3C 2E9 Canada; Title Tel # (416) 443-1785 Title Fax # (416) 443-1418
Personnel: Editor-Mark Inglis, Production Mgr.-Josee Ouellet
General Info: (Formerly Newspreader), Bi-monthly, 16 pages, ISSN: 0847-3030
Subscriptions: Can. $32
Circulation: Total-1,300

Ordre des Architectes du Quebec Bulletin/Order of Architects of Quebec Bulletin *Association* CPM: $175

Publishing Co: Ordre des Architectes du Quebec, 1825 Blvd. Rene-Levesque Ouest, Montreal, PQ H3H 1R4 Canada Fax # (614) 933-0242; Title Tel # (514) 937-6168 Title Fax # (514) 933-0242
Personnel: Editor-Madeleine Lynoix
Editorial Description: Text in English and French.
General Info: (Formerly Association des Architects de la Province de Quebec Bulletin), Yr. Est. 1966, Monthly, Trim Size-8.5 x 11, Offset press, 8 pages, Matte, Saddle-stitched
Subscriptions: Can. $50, Free With Membership
Circulation: Total-4,000
Advertising: $700. Accepts Inserts.
List Rental: List Management Co.: Ordre des Prchitectes du Quebec, 1825 Rene - Levesque Quest, Montreal, PQ H34 1R4 Canada Tel # (514) 937-6168, Fax # (514) 933-0242

PEB Exchange
See: EDUCATION

Preservation Law Reporter
See: LAW

Preservation New York
See: HISTORY

Preservation Perspective   *Consumer*

Publishing Co: Preservation New Jersey, Inc., 149 Kearny Ave., Perth Amboy, NJ 08861-4700; Title Tel # (908) 442-1100 Title Fax # (908) 442-2442
Personnel: Editor-Suzanne Rose
General Info: Yr. Est. 1981, Quarterly, Offset press, 8 pages, Matte
Subscriptions: Indv. $20, Inst. $35, Can. $45, For. $45
Circulation: Total-3,000
Advertising: Inquire for rates.

Preservation Progress   *Association*

Publishing Co: Preservation Society of Charleston, PO Box 521, Charleston, SC 29402-0521; Title Tel # (803) 722-4630
Editorial Description: Historic preservation news & features relating to Charleston SC.
General Info: Yr. Est. 1956, Bi-monthly, Desktop press, 14 pages, No Color, Recycled
Subscriptions: Indv. $25, Inst. $15
Circulation: Total-1,700
Advertising: Inquire for rates.

Redwood News   *Business*

Publishing Co: California Redwood Association, 405 Enfrente Rd # 200, Novato, CA 94949-7206; Title Tel # (415) 382-0662 Title Fax # (415) 382-8531
Personnel: Editor-Christopher Grover, Production Mgr.-Cecile Batchelor
Editorial Description: Recent notable applications of redwood in building and landscape.
General Info: Yr. Est. 1916, Semi-annually, Trim Size-8 x 9, Sheetfed press, 8 pages, 2 Color, Saddle-stitched
Circulation: (100% controlled), Total-22,000
Printing Co: GRI Tony Masood, 487 Bryant St, San Francisco, CA 94107-1316 Tel # (415) 227-0698, Fax # (415) 442-0208

Royal Architectural Institute of Canada Update

Publishing Co: Royal Architectural Institute of Canada, 55 Murray - Suite 330, Ottawa, ON M5W 1A7 Canada; Title Tel # (613) 232-7165
Personnel: Editor-Alex Fitzgerald
General Info: Quarterly

SARAScope   *Association*

Publishing Co: Society of American Registered Architects, 1245 S. Highland Ave., Lombard, IL 60148-4543; Title Tel # (708) 932-4622
Personnel: Publisher, Editor-Stanley Banash
Editorial Description: Publishes information about Society activities, including annual convention, chapter & council meetings, member achievements, student & professional design competitions, committees, issues affecting the architectural profession, etc.
General Info: (Formerly ARAScope), Yr. Est. 1973, Bi-monthly, Trim Size-8½ x 11, Sheetfed press, 4 pages, No Color, Newsprint
Subscriptions: Free With Membership
Circulation: Total-800
Printing Co: Sir Speedy Printing, 6707 Northwest Hwy., Chicago, IL 60631 Tel # (312) 763-7450

SPEC-DATA Program
See: CONSTRUCTION & BUILDING

SPNEA News   *Association*

Publishing Co: Soc. for the Preservation of New England Antiquities, 141 Cambridge St, Boston, MA 02114-2702; Title Tel # (617) 227-3956
Personnel: Editor-Nancy Curtis
Editorial Description: Covers activities of SPNEA, a museum & presentation organization, focussing on New England architecture, furnishings, & domestic life.
General Info: Trim Size-8½ x 11, Offset press, 8 pages, No Color, Newsprint

Society of Architectural Historians Newsletter   *Association*   CPM: $65

Publishing Co: Society of Architectural Historians, 1365 N. Astor St., Chicago, IL 60610-2144 Fax # (312) 573-1144; Title Tel # (312) 573-1365 Title Fax # (312) 573-1141
Editorial Description: Focuses on architecture, preservation, study tours, meetings, publications.
General Info: Bi-monthly, Trim Size-8½ x 11, 8 pages, No Color
Subscriptions: Indv. $60
Circulation: Total-4,200
Advertising: $275.
List Rental: Rents Lists
Printing Co: Constable-Hodgins, 550 Stanley Rd, Kansas City, KS 66115-1277

Spotlight

Publishing Co: Waterfront Center, 1536 44th St NW, Washington, DC 20007-2066; Title Tel # (202) 337-0356 Title Fax # (202) 625-1654
Personnel: Publisher-Dick Rigby, Editor-Ann Breen, Circ. Mgr., Adv. Dir.-Virginia Murphy, Promotion Dir.-Susan Kirk
Editorial Description: Covers full range of subjects affecting urban waterfront planning, development & culture. Audience consists of municipal, developer, boating, preservationist, design & citizen's groups interested in waterfront developments.
General Info: (Formerly Waterfront World), Yr. Est. 1981, Quarterly, Trim Size-8½ x 11, Sheetfed press, 36 pages, ISSN: 0733-0677, 2% ads, 2 Color, Newsprint, Saddle-stitched
Subscriptions: Indv. $60, Inst. $95, Can. $105, For. $125, $6/copy
Circulation: Readership-8,300, Source-I
Advertising: $450.
Printing Co: Beacon Printing, 1150 17th St NW, Washington, DC 20036-4669 Tel # (202) 293-7160

Streamline
See: INTERIOR DESIGN & DECORATION

Times (Bethlehem)   *Association*

Publishing Co: Council on Tall Buildings & Urban Habitat, Lehigh University, 13 East Packer Avenue, Bethlehem, PA 18015-3044; Title Tel # (610) 758-3515 Title Fax # (610) 758-4522
Personnel: Editor-Lynn Beedle, Circ. Mgr.-Geri Kery, Art Ed., Production Mgr., Mktg. Dir., Promotion Dir.-Dolores Rice
Editorial Description: Explores research news, items of special interest on the architecture of tall buildings and their surrounding urban environment.
General Info: Yr. Est. 1969, Quarterly, Trim Size-8½ x 11, Desktop press, 4 pages, ISSN: 1061-5121, 2 Color, Coated
Subscriptions: Indv. $75, Free With Membership
Circulation: Total-1,500
Advertising: Accepts Inserts.
List Rental: Actives: 3,600, $350/M

TransitPulse
See: TRAFFIC & TRANSPORTATION

Wisconsin Preservation
See: HISTORY

World Monuments Fund   *Business, Association*

Publishing Co: World Monument Funds, 949 Park Ave., New York, NY 10028-0307; Title Tel # (212) 517-9367
Personnel: Editor-Rebecca Anderson
General Info: 3x/yr., 8 pages, 2 Color
Circulation: Total-5,000

ART & SCULPTURE

AGS Quarterly: Bulletin of the Association for Gravestone Studies
See: HISTORY

AGSA Newsletter
See: GLASS, STONE & CLAY

AHA! Hispanic Arts News

Publishing Co: Association of Hispanic Arts, Inc., 173 E 116th St Fl 2, New York, NY 10029-1352; Title Tel # (212) 860-5445 Title Fax # (212) 427-2787
Personnel: Editor-Dolores Prida
Editorial Description: Promotes Hispanic arts & cultural activities as well as announces grant/competition awards.
General Info: (Formerly Hispanic Arts News), Yr. Est. 1976, Monthly, Trim Size-8½ x 11, Web press, 16 pages, No Color, Matte, Saddle-stitched
Subscriptions: Indv. $20, Inst. $40, $4/copy
Acquisitions: Publication Bought, Publication Sold
Advertising: $500.
Printing Co: Globe Mail Agency, Inc., 541 W 25th St, New York, NY 10001-5501 Tel # (212) 675-4600

AIC Newsletter   *Association*

Publishing Co: Am. Inst. for the Conservation of Historic & Artistic Works, 1717 K St NW Ste 301, Washington, DC 20006-1501; Title Tel # (202) 452-9545 Title Fax # (202) 452-9328
Personnel: Editor in Chief-Sarah Rosenberg, Editor-Carol Christensen, Product Mgr.-Marcia Anderson
Editorial Description: Focuses on conservation of artisitic and historically significant works.
General Info: Bi-monthly
Subscriptions: Free With Membership
Circulation: Total-3,000
Advertising: Inquire for rates.
List Rental: Rents Lists

ARLIS/NA Update
See: LIBRARY

ART Ideas

Publishing Co: American Renaissance for the Twenty-first Century, Inc., FDR Station, P.O. Box 8379, New York, NY 10150; Title Tel # (212) 759-7765
Personnel: Publisher, Editor-Alexandra York, Circ. Mgr.-Irene Pierpont
Editorial Description: Feature short stories, poetry, photos of new art work and all manner of worthy art endeavors as well as a calendar of notable upcoming events in all of the arts.
General Info: Quarterly, Trim Size-8½ x 11, 15 pages, Color-cover, Coated, Perfect bound
Subscriptions: Indv. $25, Can. $30, For. $10

ARTnewsletter   *Business, Consumer*

Publishing Co: ARTnews Associates, 48 W. 38th St., New York, NY 10018-6238; Title Tel # (212) 398-1690 Title Fax # (212) 819-0394
Personnel: Publisher-Milton Esterow, Editor-Bonnie Barrett Stretch
Editorial Description: The most authoritative, complete bi-weekly report on the world art market. Thorough reporting of public & private art sales. Indispensable for museum directors, gallery owners, investment advisors, & art collectors.
General Info: Yr. Est. 1975, Bi-weekly, Trim Size-8½ x 11, Offset press, 8 pages, ISSN: 0145-7241, No Color, Newsprint
Subscriptions: Indv. $249, Can. $277, For. $277, $10/copy
Circulation: Total-1,500
Printing Co: Globe Mail Agency, Inc., 541 W 25th St, New York, NY 10001-5501 Tel # (212) 675-4600

ASMA News · *Association*

Publishing Co: American Society of Marine Artists, PO Box 90, Ambler, PA 19002-0090
Personnel: Editor-Jack Kennedy, Editor-John Kennedy
Editorial Description: Covers Society news and general interests pieces relating to marine art.
General Info: Yr. Est. 1978, Quarterly, Trim Size-8½ x 11, Offset press, 20 pages, 2 Color, Coated, Saddle-stitched
Subscriptions: Indv. $25, Free With Membership
Circulation: Total-450
Advertising: Accepts Inserts.

ATHA Newsletter
See: HOBBY

Academy Bulletin

Publishing Co: National Academy of Design, 1083 5th Ave, New York, NY 10128-0114; Title Tel # (212) 360-6794
General Info: Quarterly

Alaska State Council on the Arts Bulletin

Publishing Co: Alaska State Council on the Arts, 411 W. 4th Ave., #1E, Ste. 220, Anchorage, AK 99501-2302; Title Tel # (907) 279-1558
Editorial Description: Covers Council news as well as recent developments in the arts in the state of Alaska.
General Info: (Formerly Arts in Alaska), Monthly

AmAcademy · *Consumer, Association*

Publishing Co: American Academy in Rome, 7 E 60th St, New York, NY 10022-1030; Title Tel # (212) 517-4200
Personnel: Editor-Elizabeth Klise
Editorial Description: Newsletter describing annual activities of the Academy, a center for advanced study in the arts & humanities.
General Info: Annually

American Art Therapy Assn. -Newsletter · *Association* · **CPM: $66**

Publishing Co: American Art Therapy Assn., Inc., 1202 Allanson Rd, Mundelein, IL 60060-3808 Fax # (708) 949-5645; Title Tel # (708) 949-6064 Title Fax # (708) 566-4580
Personnel: Editor-Polly Cullen, Production Mgr.-Karen Savage
General Info: Yr. Est. 1974, Quarterly, Trim Size-8½ x 11, Web press, 30 pages, ISSN: 1066-4076, Matte, Saddle-stitched
Subscriptions: Indv. $26, For. $38, $7/copy
Circulation: Total-4,500, Readership-4,500
Advertising: $300.
List Rental: List Management Co.: American Art Therapy Association, Inc., 1202 Allanson Road, Mundelein, IL 60060 Tel # (708) 949-6064, Fax # (708) 566-4580, Actives: $100/M

American Physicians Art Association Newsletter

Publishing Co: American Physicians Art Association, 1130 N Cabrillo Ave, San Pedro, CA 90731-1316 Fax # (310) 436-7119; Title Tel # (310) 832-7024
Personnel: Editor-James Benedict
General Info: Yr. Est. 1937, Quarterly, Trim Size-8½ x 11, Letrpr. press, 20 pages, Matte
Circulation: Total-800

American Watercolor Society Newsletter · *Association*

Publishing Co: American Watercolor Society, 47 5th Ave., New York, NY 10003-4322; Title Tel # (212) 206-8986
Personnel: Editor-Kent Day Coes
Editorial Description: Coverage of juries, awards, exhibitions, societies, etc., concerned with watercolor. Reports on shipping photographing, and preserving art works.
General Info: Yr. Est. 1961, Semi-annually, Trim Size-8½ x 11, Sheetfed press, 12 pages, 2 Color, Newsprint
Subscriptions: Free
Circulation: Total-2,500

Appraiser, The
See: ANTIQUES & ART GOODS

Appraisers Standard
See: ANTIQUES & ART GOODS

Art & Artists

Publishing Co: Foundation for the Community of Artists, 280 Broadway Ste 412, New York, NY 10007-1809; Title Tel # (212) 227-3770
General Info: Yr. Est. 1971, Bi-monthly, ISSN: 0740-5723
Subscriptions: Indv. $18

Art & Crafts Catalyst · *Business, Consumer*

Publishing Co: Art & Crafts Catalyst, PO Box 159, Bogalusa, LA 70429-0159; Title Tel # (219) 344-1174
Personnel: Publisher, Editor-Ann Porter
Editorial Description: For the amateur-professional artist & craftsperson, who actively participate as exhibitors & sell their creations at art & craft shows & festivals.
General Info: (Formerly National Calendar Indoor/Outdoor Art Fairs), Yr. Est. 1969, Bi-monthly, Trim Size-8½ x 11, Sheetfed press, 24 pages, ISSN: 0731-2989, Color-cover, Newsprint, Saddle-stitched
Subscriptions: Indv. $17, $5/copy
Circulation: Total-700
Advertising: Inquire for rates.
List Rental: Actives: $55/M

Art Alliance Bulletin

Publishing Co: Philadelphia Art Alliance, 251 S 18th St, Philadelphia, PA 19103-6118
General Info: Quarterly
Subscriptions: Indv. $6
Circulation: Total-2,500

Art Hazards Newsletter
See: SAFETY

Art Lover's Art and Craft Fair Bulletin · *Consumer*

Publishing Co: American Society of Artists, Inc., PO Box 1326, Palatine, IL 60078-1326; Title Tel # (312) 751-2500
Editorial Description: Lists arts/crafts shows in Illinois. Society sponsors arts/crafts festivals & lectures.
General Info: Yr. Est. 1972, Quarterly, ISSN: 0892-102
Subscriptions: Indv. $12

Art: The Newsletter of the American Federation of Arts

Publishing Co: American Federation of Arts, 41 E 65th St, New York, NY 10021-6508 Fax # (212) 861-2487; Title Tel # (212) 988-7700
General Info: (Formerly American Federation of Arts Newsletter), Tri-annually
Subscriptions: Free With Membership
Circulation: Total-5,000

Art on Screen · *Business, Association*

Publishing Co: Program for Art on Film, 2875 Broadway, 2nd Fl., New York, NY 10025-7805; Title Tel # (212) 854-9570 Title Fax # (212) 854-9577
Editorial Description: Free newsletter on the intersecting fields of media and the arts.
General Info: Yr. Est. 1992, Semi-annually, ISSN: 1062-9459
Subscriptions: Free To Qualified Recipient
Circulation: Total-10,000

Art in Wisconsin · *Business, Association* · **CPM: $167**

Publishing Co: Sponsor-Wisconsin Painters&Sculptors/Wisconsin Artists in All Media, Wisconsin Painters, 323 E Allouez Ave, Green Bay, WI 54301-2105; Title Tel # (414) 432-1481
Personnel: Publisher, Editor-Kathleen Barlament
Editorial Description: Report of events, exhibitions, and legislation affecting Wisconsin artists as well as technical articles on the arts.
General Info: Yr. Est. 1978, Bi-monthly, Trim Size-8½ x 11, Offset press, 3 pages, Newsprint
Subscriptions: Indv. $25, Free To Qualified Recipient
Circulation: (54% controlled), Total-1,098, Subscriptions-498
Advertising: $184. Accepts Inserts.
List Rental: Rents Lists
Printing Co: Journal Publishing, 126 S Broadway, De Pere, WI 54115-2598 Tel # (414) 336-4221

Art Works

Publishing Co: Labor Heritage Foundation, 815 16th St NW Ste 301, Washington, DC 20006-4104; Title Tel # (202) 842-7880
Personnel: Editor-Larry Rubin
General Info: Yr. Est. 1983, 6 pages
Subscriptions: Indv. $10

Art/Antiques Investment Report

Publishing Co: The Art/Antiques Investment Report, 99 Wall St., New York, NY 10005-4301; Title Tel # (212) 747-9500
Editorial Description: Published for art collectors, curators, and dealers.
General Info: Yr. Est. 1973, Bi-weekly

ArtSource Quarterly
See: ADVERTISING & MARKETING

Arterra

Publishing Co: CARFAC Manitoba, 221-100 Arthur St., Winnipeg, MB R3B 1H3 Canada
Fax # (204) 942-1555; Title Tel # (204) 943-7211
Personnel: Publisher-C. Asmundson, Editor, Production Mgr.-Tyrrell Mendis
General Info: Yr. Est. 1978, Monthly, Trim Size-8½ x 11, Desktop press, 20 pages, 1% ads, Color-cover, Newsprint, Saddle-stitched
Subscriptions: $2/copy
Acquistions: Publication Bought
Circulation: (50% controlled), Total-1,000, Subscriptions-475
Advertising: Inquire for rates. Accepts Inserts.
Printing Co: Dave's Quick Print, 603 Roseberry, Winnipeg, MB R3H 0T3 Canada
Tel # (204) 985-9625

Artistamp News · *Scholarly* · CPM: $800

Publishing Co: Banana Productions, Box 2480, Sechelt, BC V0N 3AC Canada;
Title Tel # (604) 885-7156 Title Fax # (604) 885-7183
Personnel: Publisher, Editor, Circ. Mgr., Adv. Dir., Mktg. Dir., Promotion Dir.-Anna Banana
Editorial Description: ASN is a 12-page newsletter about postage-like stamps by artists, with generously illustrated listings of new editions, artist profiles, reviews of books, periodicals and exhibitions featuring this miniature art form. Each issue has several actual stamps tipped in.
General Info: Yr. Est. 1991, Irregular, Trim Size-8½ x 11, Sheetfed press, 12 pages, ISSN: 1181-9456, No Color, Other, Saddle-stitched
Subscriptions: Indv. $12, Inst. $25, Can. $15, $4/copy
Circulation: Total-500
Advertising: $400. Accepts Inserts.
List Rental: Rents Lists

Artists Equity Fund-Newsletter

Publishing Co: Artists Equity Fund, Inc., Box 28068, Central Sta., Washington, DC 20038-8068;
Title Tel # (202) 628-9633
Personnel: Editor-Jim Minden
General Info: Yr. Est. 1983, Quarterly
Circulation: Total-8,000

Artists in Stained Glass Bulletin · *Association*

Publishing Co: Ontario Crafts Council, 35 McCaul St., Toronto, ON M5T 1V7 Canada;
Title Tel # (416) 977-3551
Personnel: Editor-Susan Higgins, Circ. Mgr.-Ettore Del Aquila
Editorial Description: Stained glass & architectural glass, Canadian viewpoint.
General Info: Yr. Est. 1976, Bi-monthly, Offset press, 6 pages, ISSN: 0705-6931, Coated
Subscriptions: $2/copy
Advertising: Inquire for rates.
Printing Co: King Print, 38 Lisgar St., Toronto, ON M6J 3T3 Canada Tel # (416) 588-6468

Arts Center News
See: MUSEUM PUBLICATIONS

Arts Partners Newsletter

Publishing Co: NYC Board of Ed.; Div. of Instruction & Professional Dev., 131 Livingston St Rm 410, Brooklyn, NY 11201-5181; Title Tel # (718) 935-4225 Title Fax # (718) 935-3802
Editorial Description: Citywide arts program for NYC public schools & arts agencies.
General Info: Yr. Est. 1984, Annually, Offset press, 8 pages
Circulation: Total-7,000

Artspace

Publishing Co: Ohio Arts Council, 727 E Main St, Columbus, OH 43205-1796;
Title Tel # (614) 466-2613
Personnel: Publisher-Beth Fisher, Editor-Charles Fenton
Editorial Description: Features and timely news on arts related topics.
General Info: (Formerly OAC Newsletter), Yr. Est. 1968, Quarterly, Offset press, 12 pages, Color, Matte
Subscriptions: Free
Circulation: Total-7,500

Artworld Hotline
See: ADVERTISING & MARKETING

Association of Medical Illustrators Newsletter · *Association*

Publishing Co: Association of Medical Illustrators, 1819 Peachtree St. N.E., Atlanta, GA 30309-1848
Fax # (404) 351-3348; Title Tel # (404) 350-7900
Personnel: Editor-Linda Warren
Editorial Description: Current news of interest to medical and health sciences illustrators.
General Info: Yr. Est. 1946, Bi-monthly, Desktop press, 8 pages, 1% ads, No Color, Coated
Subscriptions: Indv. $25, $7/copy
Advertising: Inquire for rates.
List Rental: Actives: $175/M
Printing Co: Alpha Printing Co., 716 Spring St NW, Atlanta, GA 30308-1081 Tel # (404) 881-8202

Auction News from Christie's

Publishing Co: Christie's Publications Dept., 502 Park Avenue, New York, NY 10022-1196;
Title Tel # (718) 784-1480
Personnel: Editor-R. Starr Collins, Circ. Mgr.-Diane Abbaetecola, Art Dir.-Linda Stillman
Editorial Description: Domestic newsletter devoted to the promotion of Christie's Fine Art Auctions in U.S. Emphasis on fine and decorative arts, collectibles, photographs, stamps, coins, wine, etc. Cultural features of interest.
General Info: Yr. Est. 1980, Monthly, Sheetfed press, 12 pages, 4 Color, Coated, Saddle-stitched
Subscriptions: Indv. $15, Can. $15, For. $20
Circulation: Total-50,000
Printing Co: Allied Printing, 280 Midland Ave, Saddle Brook, NJ 07663-6404 Tel # (201) 794-0400

BCA News · *Business*

Publishing Co: Business Committee for the Arts, Inc., 1775 Broadway Ste 510, New York, NY 10019-1903; Title Tel # (212) 664-0600 Title Fax # (212) 956-5980
Personnel: Editor-Jenna Fried
Editorial Description: Focuses on alliances between business and the arts. Includes profiles, case studies and interviews with business leaders.
General Info: Yr. Est. 1967, Quarterly, Trim Size-8½ x 11, 12 pages, Color
Subscriptions: Indv. $55, Inst. $55, Can. $65, For. $65
Circulation: Total-1,000

BVAU News

Publishing Co: Boston Visual Artists Union, Art Institute of Boston, 700 Beacon St., Boston, MA 02215; Title Tel # (617) 266-1101
Personnel: Editor-Laurie Poklop
Editorial Description: A wide array of information and features of interest to professional visual artists.
General Info: Yr. Est. 1973, Monthly
Subscriptions: Indv. $15
Circulation: Total-1,500

Beaverbrook Art Gallery · *Business, Association*

Publishing Co: Beaverbrook Art Gallery, Box 605, Fredericton, NB E3B 5A6 Canada;
Title Tel # (506) 458-8545 Title Fax # (506) 459-7450
Personnel: Editor-Caroline Walker
Editorial Description: Calendar of exhibitions and Gallery programme and acquisitions.
General Info: Yr. Est. 1970, Semi-monthly, Trim Size-8½ x 11, Letrpr. press, 20 pages, ISSN: 0845-8081, No Color, Matte
Subscriptions: Free With Membership
Circulation: Total-1,500
Advertising: Inquire for rates.
Printing Co: Ronalds Printing, Box 1373, Fredericton, NB E3B 5E3 Canada Tel # (506) 453-9909

Berks Arts

Publishing Co: Berks Arts Council, The Pagoda, P.O. Box 854, Reading, PA 19603;
Title Tel # (610) 655-6374 Title Fax # (610) 655-6378
Editorial Description: Provides information on events at Berks Arts in Pennsylvania.
General Info: Monthly, Trim Size-8½ x 11, 8 pages, No Color, Matte

Big Cat Sculpture Association
See: CATS

Board Report for Graphic Artists
See: PRINTING/GRAPHIC ARTS

Bulletin of the Caucus on Social Theory & Art Education

Publishing Co: Caucus on Social Theory & Art Education, Florida State Univ., 123 Carothers Hall, B-171, Tallahassee, FL 32306-3014; Title Tel # (904) 644-5473
Personnel: Editor-Tom Anderson
General Info: Yr. Est. 1980, Annually

Burlington Fine Arts Association Newsletter · *Business, Association*

Publishing Co: Burlington Fine Arts Association, 425 Brock Ave., Burlington, ON L7S 1M8 Canada;
Title Tel # (905) 632-7796
Personnel: Editor-Sibya O'PI
Editorial Description: Information on coming events of the Burlington Fine Arts Association and of its members.
General Info: Yr. Est. 1966, Monthly, Trim Size-8½ x 14, 4 pages, No Color
Subscriptions: Indv. $10
Circulation: (100% controlled), Total-200

CAA News   *Association*

Publishing Co: College Art Assn., 275 7th Ave Frnt 5, New York, NY 10001-6708;
   Title Tel # (212) 691-1051 Title Fax # (212) 627-2381
Personnel: Publisher-Virginia Wageman, Editor-Renee Ramirez
Editorial Description: Reports on Association activities, placement trends, fellowships, conferences,
   etc.
General Info: (Formerly CAA Newsletter), Yr. Est. 1976, Bi-monthly, Trim Size-8½ x 11, Sheetfed
   press, 24 pages, No Color, Matte
Subscriptions: Free
Circulation: (71% controlled), Total-14,000
Advertising: Inquire for rates.
List Rental: Rents Lists
Printing Co: John S. Swift, Rte 46 W., Teterboro, NJ 07608 Tel # (201) 288-2056,
   Fax # (201) 288-4061

CWAO News   *Association*

Publishing Co: Sponsor-Coalition of Women's Art Org., Coalition of Women's Art Organizations, 123
   E. Beutel Rd., Port Washington, WI 53074-1103 Fax # (414) 284-8878; Title Tel # (414) 284-4458
   Title Fax # (414) 284-8875
Personnel: Editor-Dorothy Provis
Editorial Description: Federal and state arts legislation information to effect member participation.
   Events, issues, announcements of interest to membership.
General Info: Yr. Est. 1982, Monthly, Trim Size-8½ x 14, Desktop press, 1 pages, No Color,
   Newsprint
Subscriptions: Indv. $10, Inst. $25, Free With Membership
Circulation: (100% controlled), Total-300

Calendar

Publishing Co: Grand Rapids Art Museum, 155 Division, N., Grand Rapids, MI 49503-3126;
   Title Tel # (616) 459-4677 Title Fax # (616) 459-8491
Personnel: Editor-Paula Wilkerson
General Info: Yr. Est. 1979, Bi-monthly, Trim Size-11½ x 17, 4 pages, No Color
Circulation: Total-5,000
Printing Co: Commercial Printing Co., 90 Market Ave SW, Grand Rapids, MI 49503-4082
   Tel # (616) 454-9334

China Institute in America Bulletin
   See: CULTURE & HUMANITIES

Color Q Connection   *Business, Consumer*

Publishing Co: Color Q Inc., Art Education Division, 2651 S Kearney St, Denver, CO 80222-6327;
   Title Fax # (303) 758-6204
Personnel: Editor-Sue Viders
Editorial Description: Marketing ideas for artists who create art prints. Also includes information
   about Color Q Printing Co.
General Info: Quarterly, 6 pages, 4 Color
Circulation: Total-10,000
Advertising: Inquire for rates.
Printing Co: Color Q, 2710 Dryden Rd, Dayton, OH 45439-1683

Conservation: The Getty Conservation Institute Newsletter
   See: MUSEUM PUBLICATIONS

Crafts News   *Association*   **CPM: $40**

Publishing Co: Crafts Center, 1001 Connecticut Ave NW Ste, 1138, Washington, DC 20036-5504;
   Title Tel # (202) 728-9603 Title Fax # (202) 457-0540
Personnel: Editor-Sheila Mooney, Editor-Caroline Ramsay
Editorial Description: Profiles artisans, crafts organizations sources of credit, schools, and
   conferences worldwide.
General Info: Yr. Est. 1988, Quarterly, Trim Size-8½ x 11, 10 pages
Subscriptions: Indv. $35, Free With Membership
Circulation: Total-5,000
Advertising: $200. Accepts Inserts.
List Rental: Actives: 6,000, $1,500/M

DOE
   See: SCIENCE FICTION & FANTASY

Edna Hibel Society
   Newsletter   *Association*

Publishing Co: Edna Hibel Society, PO Box 9721, Coral Springs, FL 33075-9721;
   Title Tel # (305) 731-6699
Personnel: Editor-Ralph Burg
Editorial Description: Newsletter about Edna Hibel, a painter and porcelain artist, for society
   members.
General Info: Quarterly
Subscriptions: Free With Membership
Circulation: Total-7,000

Egger's Journal

Publishing Co: Treasure Chest, 400 E. Dover St., Apt. 308, Easton, MD 21601-3605;
   Title Tel # (410) 820-7739
Personnel: Editor-Kit Stansbury
Editorial Description: Includes information on egg decor. Shows instruction (when available), news
   with egg artists and activities.
General Info: Yr. Est. 1972, Quarterly, Web press, 34 pages, Looseleaf
Subscriptions: Indv. $25, Can. $29, For. $35
Circulation: Total-600
Printing Co: Harmony Press, 717 Berwick Street, Easton, PA 18042 Tel # (610) 559-9800,
   Fax # (610) 559-9857

Express Exchange
   See: FILM

Folk Art Finder   *Business, Association*

Publishing Co: Gallery Press, One River Road, Essex, CT 06426-1071; Title Tel # (203) 767-0313
Personnel: Publisher-Julius Laffal, Editor-Florence Laffal, Circ. Mgr., Adv. Dir.-Fran Schultz
Editorial Description: Features new folk artists, reader exchange, book reviews, exhibitions and
   events country wide.
General Info: Yr. Est. 1980, Quarterly, Trim Size-5½ x 8½, Offset press, 24 pages, ISSN: 0738-
   8357, No Color
Subscriptions: Indv. $14, Can. $18, For. $22, $6/copy
Advertising: $225.
Printing Co: K & G Graphics, 540 E. Main St., Branford, CT 06405

Folk Art Messenger   *Business, Association*

Publishing Co: Folk Art Society of America, PO Box 17041, Richmond, VA 23226-7041;
   Title Tel # (804) 285-4532 Title Fax # (804) 285-4532
Personnel: Publisher, Editor-Ann Oppenhimer, Art Dir.-Ann Henderson, Promotion Dir.-Laura Peery
Editorial Description: Newsletter devoted to contemporary folk art. Contains feature articles, book &
   exhibition reviews, calendar, photographs & museum profiles.
General Info: Yr. Est. 1987, Quarterly, Trim Size-8½ x 11, 12 pages, ISSN: 1043-5026, No Color,
   Coated
Subscriptions: Indv. $25, Can. $35, For. $35, $7/copy
Printing Co: Bisco Printers, 2904 W Clay St, Richmond, VA 23230-4807 Tel # (804) 353-7292,
   Fax # (804) 353-0390

Folk Arts Quarterly   *Consumer, Association*

Publishing Co: Folk Arts Quarterly, 686 Old Homestead Hwy, Richmond, NH 03470-5012;
   Title Tel # (603) 239-6231
Personnel: Editor-Barbara Rogers
General Info: Yr. Est. 1983, Quarterly, 12 pages

Fort Wayne Museum of Art-
   Newsletter

Publishing Co: Fort Wayne Museum of Art, 311 E Main St, Fort Wayne, IN 46802-1997;
   Title Tel # (219) 422-6467
Personnel: Publisher-Emily Kass, Editor-September McConnell
Editorial Description: Devoted to the events & activities of the Museum & news of interest to the
   membership.
General Info: Yr. Est. 1924, Bi-monthly, Sheetfed press, 6 pages, 2 Color, Newsprint
Circulation: Total-2,000

Genuine Article, The
   See: MEN'S

Gift Basket Idea Newsletter
   See: GIFTS, GAMES, TOYS

Harvard University Art
   Museums Review

Publishing Co: Harvard Univ., 32 Quincy St., Cambridge, MA 02138-3804;
   Title Tel # (617) 495-4336 Title Fax # (617) 495-9936
Personnel: Editor-Evelyn Rosenthal
Editorial Description: News and features from the Fogg Art Museum, Arthur M. Sackler Museum.
   and Busch-Reisinger Museum.
General Info: (Formerly Harvard University Art Museums Newsletter), Yr. Est. 1992, 3x/yr., Trim Size-
   11 x 17, Web press, 8 pages, ISSN: 1065-819x, 2 Color, Matte
Circulation: Total-6,000

Highland Highlights
   See: HOBBY

Huntington Calendar
   See: MUSEUM PUBLICATIONS

IFRAA Quarterly
   See: RELIGIOUS & THEOLOGICAL

ISA Newsletter
   See: FURNITURE & HOME FURNISHINGS

In Brief   *Association*

Publishing Co: Artists in Print, Inc., 665 Third St., #530, San Francisco, CA 94107-1901;
   Title Tel # (415) 243-8244 Title Fax # (415) 495-3155
Personnel: Publisher-Joel Blum, Editor-Patti Mangan
Editorial Description: Journal dedicated to information & issues in contemporary or historical graphic
   arts since 1974.
General Info: (Formerly Graphiti), Yr. Est. 1974, Quarterly, Web press, 12 pages, Ind/Abs/Online:
   Tr.Lit., 3% ads, 2 Color, Coated
Subscriptions: Indv. $8, Inst. $8, For. $12
Circulation: (3% controlled), Total-3,000
List Rental: Actives: $100/M

Innervisions

Publishing Co: Tyuonyi, PO Box 23266, Santa Fe, NM 87502-3266 Tel # (505) 982-9468;
   Title Tel # (505) 988-6603
Editorial Description: Student newsletter of the Institute of American Indian Arts.
General Info: Monthly

International Porcelain Artists/Teachers News

Publishing Co: International Porcelain Artists/Teachers, 4125 NW 57th St, Oklahoma City, OK 73112-1505; Title Tel # (405) 946-7121
General Info: Yr. Est. 1956, Monthly
Advertising: Inquire for rates.

Joan Walsh Anglund Collector's News
See: CHILDREN

Journal   *Association*

Publishing Co: University of Guelph Department of Fine Art, Publications, Guelph, ON N1G 2W1 Canada; Title Tel # (306) 584-4880
Personnel: Publisher, Editor-Chandler Kirwin
Editorial Description: To announce and request information regarding research and conferences. To inform members of current and relevent information about UAAC members and list job vacancies.
General Info: Yr. Est. 1972, Quarterly, Trim Size-8½ x 11, Offset press, 6 pages, 4 Color
Subscriptions: Indv. $15
Circulation: (100% controlled), Total-325

Kendall College of Art and Design
See: COLLEGE STUDENT

Letters from Abraham
Lincoln   *Business, Association*

Publishing Co: Whiz Bang Graphics, 43 Ankara Ave # 98, Brookville, OH 45309-1207; Title Tel # (513) 833-3078 Title Fax # (513) 833-3078
Editorial Description: Covers handwriting, calligraphy, related products and book reviews, also covers alphabets, how to use basic writing skills for pleasure and profit. Also articles hearkening back to eras when humans lived in closer harmony with the environment.
General Info: Monthly, Trim Size-8½ x 11, 6 pages, ISSN: 1065-2256, Matte
Subscriptions: Indv. $27, Inst. $20, Can. $30, For. $30
Advertising: Inquire for rates.

Limited Edition   *Association*   **CPM: $277**

Publishing Co: Michigan Guild of Artists & Artisans, 118 N 4th Ave, Ann Arbor, MI 48104-1402; Title Tel # (313) 662-3382 Title Fax # (313) 662-0339
Personnel: Publisher-Mary Strope, Editor-Sara Wheeler
Editorial Description: The Limited Edition is a bi-monthly publication used to inform the membership of the Michigan Guild of Artists & Artisans of membership benefits, exhibition possibilities. Art Fair listings & written articles that would interest the working artist.
General Info: (Formerly Michigan Guild of Artists & Artisans Newsletter), Yr. Est. 1970, Bi-monthly, Trim Size-8½ x 11, Sheetfed press, 16 pages, 4% ads, No Color, Matte, Saddle-stitched
Subscriptions: Free With Membership
Acquistions: Publication Bought
Circulation: Total-1,800
Advertising: $500.
Printing Co: Kimcraft Printers Inc., 11705 Levan Rd, Livonia, MI 48150-1401 Fax # (313) 591-3446

Log of the Bridgetender
See: BLIND

Magnes News
See: MUSEUM PUBLICATIONS

Magnifier, The   *Business, Association*

Publishing Co: Ray Olszewski, 8080 Counselor Rd, Manassas, VA 22111-4752 Tel # (703) 791-5538; Title Tel # (703) 590-5400
Personnel: Publisher, Editor-Ray Olszewski
Editorial Description: Information on Robert Olszewski, creator and master artist and goebel miniature bronze figurines.
General Info: (Formerly Goebel Miniatures Newsletter), Yr. Est. 1985, Semi-annually, Trim Size-8½ x 11, Desktop press, 6 pages, No Color, Recycled, Other
Subscriptions: Free To Qualified Recipient
Circulation: Total-1,000
Advertising: Accepts Inserts.
List Rental: Rents Lists

Members Exchange   *Association*

Publishing Co: American Medallic Sculpture Assn., 22 N. Main St. #356, New City, NY 10956-3720; Title Tel # (914) 634-4751
Personnel: Editor-Beverly Mazze
Editorial Description: Members Exchange disseminates information of interest to members, & serves as a networking tool whereby members express views, ask questions, or provide advice on numerous areas related to medallic sculpture.
General Info: Yr. Est. 1983, Quarterly, Trim Size-8½ x 11, Offset press, 25 pages, No Color
Subscriptions: Inst. $35, Can. $40, For. $45
Circulation: Total-300
Advertising: Accepts Inserts.

Memphis Brooks Museum
of Art Newsletter   *Consumer, Association*

Publishing Co: Memphis Brooks Museum of Art, Overton Park, Memphis, TN 38104; Title Tel # (901) 722-3500 Title Fax # (601) 722-3522
Editorial Description: Releases concerning the museum including acquisitions, art openings, etc.
General Info: Yr. Est. 1955, Quarterly, 16 pages, 4 Color, Coated
Subscriptions: Free To Qualified Recipient
Circulation: Total-24,000
Printing Co: Harding Associates, 2500 Lamar Ave, Memphis, TN 38114-4347 Tel # (901) 743-4444

Michigan Association of
Calligraphers-Newsletter   *Association*

Publishing Co: Michigan Assn. of Calligraphers, PO Box 55, Royal Oak, MI 48068-0055
Editorial Description: Features workshop reviews, upcoming events and other items of calligraphic interest.
General Info: Yr. Est. 1978, Monthly, 8 pages, No Color, Newsprint
Subscriptions: Indv. $25, Free With Membership
Circulation: Total-350

Mixed Media

Publishing Co: Maine Art Education Assn., PO Box 10463, Portland, ME 04104-0463; Title Tel # (207) 675-3235
Personnel: Circ. Mgr.-Chris Chapman, Adv. Dir.-Tony Tyler-Millar, Editor, Production Mgr., Art Dir.-Diane Noble
Editorial Description: Art education. Contact between teachers, events, opportunities and news.
General Info: (Formerly MAEA Newsletter), Yr. Est. 1977, Quarterly, 8 pages, 2 Color, Newsprint
Circulation: Total-900
Advertising: Inquire for rates.
Printing Co: Journal Tribune, Alfred Road, Biddeford, ME 04005 Tel # (207) 282-1535

Municipal Art Society
Newsletter   *Association*

Publishing Co: Municipal Art Society, 457 Madison Ave, New York, NY 10022-6879; Title Tel # (212) 935-3960
General Info: Monthly, 4 pages

Musea

Publishing Co: Tom Hendricks, 4000 Hawthorne #5, Dallas, TX 75219
Editorial Description: The only media source that Opposes the LA/NY Monopolies in Art.
General Info: Trim Size-5 x 7, 8 pages

Museum Archivist
See: MUSEUM PUBLICATIONS

Museum Insights
See: MUSEUM PUBLICATIONS

Museum Matters
See: MUSEUM PUBLICATIONS

NACLites   *Association*

Publishing Co: The National Arts Club, 15 Gramercy Park S, New York, NY 10003-1796 Tel # (212) 475-3427; Title Tel # (212) 475-3424 Title Fax # (212) 475-3692
Editorial Description: Newsletter of the National Arts Club of NY.
General Info: Quarterly, Trim Size-8½ x 11, 10 pages, 2 Color, Matte

NAMTA News & Views   *Association*   **CPM: $166**

Publishing Co: Natl. Art Materials Trade Assn, 178 Lakeview Ave, Clifton, NJ 07011-4019; Title Tel # (201) 546-6400
Personnel: Editor-Hope Crawley
Editorial Description: News of art materials industry.
General Info: Yr. Est. 1950, Monthly, Trim Size-8½ x 11, Sheetfed press, 8 pages, 2 Color, Newsprint
Acquistions: Publication Sold
Circulation: Total-3,000
Advertising: $500.

National Arts Club
Member's Bulletin, The   *Association*

Publishing Co: The National Arts Club, 15 Gramercy Park S, New York, NY 10003-1796; Title Tel # (212) 475-3427 Title Fax # (212) 475-3692
Editorial Description: Newsletter of the National Arts Club.
General Info: Quarterly, Trim Size-8½ x 11, 28 pages, No Color, Matte, Saddle-stitched

National Association of
Women Artists
Newsletter   *Association*

Publishing Co: National Association of Women Artists, 41 Union Square W, New York, NY 10003-3208
Personnel: Editor-Mary Anna Goetz
Editorial Description: Contains member information and president's letter.
General Info: Semi-annually

National Cartoonist Society
Newsletter: 'The
Cartoonist'   *Association*

Publishing Co: Natl. Cartoonists Society, PO Box 20267, New York, NY 10023-1484; Title Tel # (704) 358-5180
General Info: Yr. Est. 1977, Trim Size-8½ x 11, Offset press, 16 pages, Color
Circulation: (100% controlled), Total-1,000

National Jewish Arts Newsletter — *Consumer*

Publishing Co: Martin Steinberg Ctr. for Jewish Artists, 15 E 84th St, New York, NY 10028-0458; Title Tel # (212) 879-4500
Personnel: Publisher-Chava Miller
Editorial Description: News and features relating to Jewish arts and artists.
General Info: Yr. Est. 1981, Quarterly
Subscriptions: Indv. $18
Circulation: Total-3,000

National Sculpture Society Newsletter — *Association*

Publishing Co: Natl. Sculpture Society, 1177 6th Avenue, 15 Floor, New York, NY 10036-2705; Title Tel # (212) 889-6960
General Info: Quarterly, 5% ads, No Color
Advertising: Inquire for rates. Accepts Inserts.

Native Arts Update — *Business, Association*

Publishing Co: Atlatl, 2303 N Central Ave Ste 104, Phoenix, AZ 85004-1323; Title Tel # (602) 253-2731 Title Fax # (602) 256-6385
Personnel: Editor-Wendy Weston
Editorial Description: Current information contemporary Native American arts: issues, regional highlights, interviews, exhibitions, and opportunities.
General Info: (Formerly Atlatl Newsletter), Yr. Est. 1985, Quarterly, Trim Size-8½ x 11, 12 pages, 2 Color
Subscriptions: Indv. $25, Inst. $25, Can. $30, For. $35, Free With Membership
Circulation: Total-2,000
List Rental: Rents Lists

Neon News
See: LIGHTING

News & Events — *Association*

Publishing Co: Art Institute of Chicago, S. Michigan Ave. & Adams St., Chicago, IL 60603; Title Tel # (312) 443-3600
Personnel: Circ. Mgr.-Susan Anderson, Design Director-Virginia Voedisch
Editorial Description: Exhibition schedule & description, museum news & programs, calendar of events. Exclusively related to The Art Institute of Chicago.
General Info: (Formerly Bulletin), Yr. Est. 1907, Bi-monthly, Trim Size-8½ x 11, Sheetfed press, 32 pages, ISSN: 0094-3312, Color-cover, Recycled, Saddle-stitched
Circulation: (100% controlled), Total-100,000
Printing Co: Wicklander Printing Co., 1550 S State St, Chicago, IL 60605-2805 Tel # (312) 225-1300

Newsletter East Asian Art & Archaeology — *Consumer, Association* CPM: $312

Publishing Co: Sponsor-Center for Japanese Studies, Univ. of Michigan, Dept. of the History of Art, Tappan Hall, Rm. 50, Ann Arbor, MI 48109-1357; Title Tel # (313) 936-2539 Title Fax # (313) 747-4121
Personnel: Editor-Jonathan Reynolds, Mag. Ed.-Wendy Holden
Editorial Description: Lists current exhibitions, pubs., symposia & lectures relating to East Asian art and archaeology in U.S. & abroad. Museum news, research & individual news, dissertation news, jobs & grants also included. Provides information on new books, book and print dealers, and museum publications.
General Info: Trim Size-8½ x 11, 40 pages, ISSN: 8755-4593, 4% ads
Subscriptions: Indv. $12, Inst. $12, Can. $15, For. $15, $4/copy
Circulation: Total-400
Advertising: $125.

Newsletter for Leonardisti — *Scholarly*

Publishing Co: Newsletter for Leonardisti, Western Kentucky Univ., Dept. of Art, Bowling Green, KY 42101-3576; Title Tel # (502) 745-3944 Title Fax # (502) 745-5932
Personnel: Publisher, Editor, Circ. Mgr.-Patricia Trutty-Coohill, Art Dir.-Veronica Koss
Editorial Description: Newsletter for specialists in Leonardo da Vinci studies.
General Info: Yr. Est. 1982, Semi-annually, Trim Size-8½ x 11, Sheetfed press, 6 pages, ISSN: 0741-9597, Color-cover
Circulation: Total-150
Printing Co: Western Kentucky Univ., Services and Supply Bldg., Bowling Green, KY 42101 Tel # (502) 745-4949

Omega Arts Network News — *Consumer*

Publishing Co: Omega Arts Network News, PO Box 1227, Jamaica Plain, MA 02130-0011; Title Tel # (617) 522-8300
Editorial Description: Links 'tranformational, visionary, and sacred artist' from around the world who are working together to use their art to offer visions of a positive future.
General Info: Semi-annually
Subscriptions: Indv. $20

Original Art Report, The (TOAR) — *Business, Consumer*

Publishing Co: FS Original, 3024 Sunnyside Dr, Rockford, IL 61114-6025
Personnel: Publisher-June Salantrie, Editor-Frank Salantrie
Editorial Description: Commentary & analysis of economic, political, & socio-philosophical conditions in the visual arts.
General Info: Yr. Est. 1967, Irregular, Trim Size-8½ x 11, Offset press, 6 pages, ISSN: 0030-5529
Subscriptions: Indv. $16, Inst. $16, Can. $21, For. $27, $2/copy

Painted Monkey — *Association*

Publishing Co: California Art Education Assn., 1836 Walnut Ave, Carmichael, CA 95608-5417; Title Tel # (916) 482-7789
Personnel: Editor-Majorie Sahs
Editorial Description: News related to art education in state. Relays national, international.
General Info: Yr. Est. 1974, 8x/yr., Trim Size-8½ x 11, Sheetfed press, 12 pages, 2% ads, 2 Color, Newsprint
Subscriptions: Indv. $30, $2/copy
Circulation: Total-14,500
Advertising: Inquire for rates.
List Rental: Actives: $10/M

Pen and Ink
See: EDUCATION

Photograph Collector
See: PHOTOGRAPHY

Portfolio
See: POETRY & CREATIVE WRITING

Portland Art Museum Newsletter — *Association*

Publishing Co: Portland Art Museum, 1219 SW Park Ave, Portland, OR 97205-2486; Title Tel # (503) 226-2811
Personnel: Editor Diane Kantor
Editorial Description: Forthcoming exhibitions, programs & events sponsored by the Portland Art Museum.
General Info: (Formerly Oregon Art Institute Newsletter), Yr. Est. 1949, Bi-monthly, Trim Size-22 x 17, Web press, 8 pages, 2 Color, Coated
Acquistions: Publication Bought
Circulation: (100% controlled), Total-16,000
Printing Co: Daily Journal of Commerce, 2014 NW 24th Ave, Portland, OR 97210-2345 Tel # (503) 226-1311

Portraits — *Business*

Publishing Co: Holland & Edwards Publishing, Inc., 250 Mercer St., Apt. A-203, New York, NY 10012-1144 Fax # (212) 966-1203; Title Tel # (212) 431-1652
Personnel: Publisher-Edward Holland, Editor-Christopher Holland, Editorial Asst.-Craig Houser, Assoc. Ed.-Clare Cannon, Circ. Mgr.-Gina Dilillo, Production Mgr.-Gina DiLillo, Art Dir.-Karen Holland
Editorial Description: Each issue profiles one artist with examples of his/her work.
General Info: Yr. Est. 1991, Monthly, Trim Size-8.5 x 11, 12 pages, 4 Color, Coated, Saddle-stitched
Subscriptions: Indv. $47, Can. $55, For. $55
Circulation: (100% controlled), Total-48,500
Advertising: Inquire for rates.
Printing Co: Strathmore Printing, 200 Gary Lane, Geneva, IL 60134 Tel # (708) 232-9677, Fax # (708) 232-0198

Public Domain Report — *Consumer*

Publishing Co: Public Domain Report, PO Box 3102, Margate, NJ 08402; Title Fax # (609) 822-9445
Personnel: Publisher-James Colaianni, Editor in Chief-E. Scott Johnson
Editorial Description: Covers issues and events in the arts and entertainment.
General Info: Monthly, ISSN: 1070-2555
Subscriptions: Indv. $395

Quill
See: PRINTING/GRAPHIC ARTS

Records of Early English Drama Newsletter
See: LITERATURE & LINGUISTICS

Rotkin Review
See: PHOTOGRAPHY

SPACES; Notes on America's Folk Art Environments — *Association*

Publishing Co: Saving & Preserving Arts & Cultural Environments, 1804 N Van Ness Ave, Los Angeles, CA 90028-5615; Title Tel # (213) 463-1629
Editorial Description: Concerned with the identification & preservation of monumental folk art environments.
General Info: Yr. Est. 1982, Irregular, 8 pages, ISSN: 0748-8378, No Color, Coated
Subscriptions: Indv. $15, Inst. $25
Circulation: Total-1,000

The Salmagundian — *Association*

Publishing Co: Salmagundi Club, 47 5th Ave, New York, NY 10003-4396; Title Tel # (212) 255-7740
Editorial Description: Newsletter of the Salmagundi Club of New York.
General Info: Semi-annually, Trim Size-8½ x 11, 12 pages, No Color, Matte, Saddle-stitched

Sharing Memories
See: HOBBY

Sirius
See: MUSEUM PUBLICATIONS

Society of Animal Artists
Newsletter   *Association*

Publishing Co: Society of Animal Artists, 151 Carroll St # 24, Bronx, NY 10464-1430; Title Tel # (212) 885-2181
Personnel: Editor, Circ. Mgr.-Patricia Bott
Editorial Description: News of members, exhibitions of art by Society new books by members educational information.
General Info: Yr. Est. 1960, Quarterly, Offset press, 6 pages, 4 Color
Circulation: (100% controlled), Total-300
Advertising: Inquire for rates.

Step-By-Step Electronic Design
See: COMPUTERS & AUTOMATION

Studio Link   *Consumer*

Publishing Co: Osmundsen & Rains, PO Box 321450, Cocoa Beach, FL 32932-1450; Title Tel # (407) 722-4099
Editorial Description: Newsletter from the Osmundsen & Rains art gallery.
General Info: Quarterly, Trim Size-8½ x 11, 8 pages, No Color, Matte
Circulation: Total-600
Advertising: Inquire for rates.

Success Now! for Artists   *Business, Consumer*

Publishing Co: Renee Phillips Assocs., 200 E 72nd St Apt 26l, New York, NY 10021-4546; Title Tel # (212) 472-1660
Editorial Description: Advice, listings and services for career management and success for artists.
General Info: Yr. Est. 1989, Monthly, Trim Size-8½ x 11, 8 pages
Subscriptions: Indv. $18, $4/copy
Circulation: Total-2,500
Advertising: Inquire for rates. Accepts Inserts.

Sumi-E Notes

Publishing Co: Sumi-E Society of America, c/o Nippon Club, 4200 Kings Mill Ln, Annandale, VA 22003-2033

Tennessee Arts Report
See: CULTURE & HUMANITIES

Textile Museum Bulletin
See: MUSEUM PUBLICATIONS

To The Point   *Consumer, Association*

Publishing Co: Colored Pencil Society of America, 17006 106th Ave. SE, Renton, WA 98055-5431; Title Tel # (206) 271-6628 Title Fax # (206) 271-6628
Editorial Description: Newsletter of the Colored Pencil Society of America. Published exclusively for society members.
General Info: (Formerly The Point), Yr. Est. 1990, ISSN: 1058-5303

Travelling Exhibition
Information Service
Newsletter

Publishing Co: Humanities Exchange Inc., PO Box 1608, Largo, FL 34649-1608 Fax # (813) 585-6398; Title Tel # (813) 581-7328
Personnel: Publisher, Editor-Shirley Howarth, Art Dir.-Joseph Eustace
Editorial Description: Information on art, science, history exhibits by museums, libraries and other non-profit groups.
General Info: Yr. Est. 1981, Bi-monthly, Trim Size-8½ x 11, Offset press, 12 pages, ISSN: 0733-463X, 3% ads, No Color, Newsprint
Subscriptions: Indv. $30, $5/copy
Circulation: Total-600
Advertising: Inquire for rates.
List Rental: Actives: $60/M

Umbrella   *Consumer*

Publishing Co: Umbrella Assocs., Box 3692, Pasadena, CA 91114; Title Tel # (818) 797-0514 Title Fax # (818) 794-5445
Personnel: Publisher, Editor-Judith Hoffberg
Editorial Description: Contemporary art views & reviews, including artists' books, and artists' publications.
General Info: Yr. Est. 1978, Semi-annually, Trim Size-8¼ x 10½, Web press, 28 pages, ISSN: 0160-0699, No Color, Newsprint, Saddle-stitched
Subscriptions: Indv. $15, Inst. $25, Can. $30, For. $30, $8/copy
Circulation: Total-500
Advertising: Inquire for rates.
Printing Co: Glendale Printing Service, 640 W Broadway, Glendale, CA 91204-1008 Tel # (818) 247-7033

Universities Art Association
of Canada Journal

Publishing Co: Universities Art Association of Canada, c/o D. Burnett, 5163 Duke St., Halifax, NS B3J 3J6 Canada; Title Tel # (204) 786-9362
General Info: Yr. Est. 1972, ISSN: 0315-940X
Circulation: Total-400

Univ. Art Museum Newsletter
See: MUSEUM PUBLICATIONS

University of Illinois, School
of Art and Design, Alumni
Newsletter   *Consumer*

Publishing Co: Univ. of Illinois School of Art & Design, Art & Design Bldg., 408 E. Peabody Dr., Champaign, IL 61820; Title Tel # (217) 333-0418
Personnel: Editor-Carol Fisher, Circ. Mgr.-Ken McWilliams, Art Dir.-David Colley
Editorial Description: Recent developments and events in the University of Illinois School of Art & Design of interest to alumni.
General Info: (Formerly University of Illinois, Department of Art, Alumni Newsletter), Yr. Est. 1951, Annually, Trim Size-8½ x 11, Offset press, 16 pages, No Color
Subscriptions: Free
Circulation: (51% controlled), Total-6,000

Update, The
See: LABOR UNION

Valley Calligraphy Guild
Newsletter   *Association*

Publishing Co: Valley Calligraphy Guild, 2352 Van Ness St, Eugene, OR 97403-1862; Title Tel # (503) 345-8129
Personnel: Editor-Myra Miller-Smith
Editorial Description: Promotion of calligraphy & related activities.
General Info: Yr. Est. 1976, Bi-monthly, Sheetfed press, 32 pages, 1% ads, No Color, Newsprint
Subscriptions: Indv. $15, $3/copy
Circulation: (100% controlled), Total-850
Advertising: Inquire for rates.

Viewpoints   *Association*

Publishing Co: Canadian Society for Education Through Art, 1487 Parish Ln., Oakville, ON L6M 2Z6 Canada; Title Tel # (905) 847-0975 Title Fax # (905) 847-0975
Personnel: Editor-B. Sunday
Editorial Description: Current information or resources, methods, curriculum in art education. Newsletters-journals-reviews, three different publications included at one price.
General Info: (Formerly Canadian Society for Education Through Art Newsletter), Yr. Est. 1956, 5x/yr., Trim Size-8½ x 11, 20 pages, ISSN: 1200-2151
Subscriptions: Indv. $65, Can. $65, For. $65, Free With Membership
Circulation: Total-600
Advertising: Inquire for rates. Accepts Inserts.

Vista   *Association*

Publishing Co: MacKenzie Art Gallery, 3475 Albert St., Regina, SK S4S 6X6 Canada; Title Tel # (306) 522-4242 Title Fax # (306) 569-8191
Personnel: Editor-Bonnie Schaffer
Editorial Description: Gallery exhibition and program information, art education, etc.
General Info: (Formerly NMAG), Yr. Est. 1965, Quarterly, Trim Size-11 x 17½, Web press, 8 pages, ISSN: 0712-9238, Color, Saddle-stitched
Subscriptions: $3/copy
Circulation: (100% controlled), Total-5,000
Printing Co: Merit Printing, 1759 McAra St., Regina, SK S4N 6H5 Canada Tel # (306) 569-1660, Fax # (306) 359-1488

Volunteer Committees of
Art Museums-Newsletter

Publishing Co: Volunteer Committees of Art Museums, 6121 N 22nd St, Phoenix, AZ 85016-2033; Title Tel # (602) 956-3036
Personnel: Editor-Suzanne Hamblin
General Info: Yr. Est. 1952, Quarterly

WAAC Newsletter   *Consumer, Association*

Publishing Co: Western Association for Art Conservation, Conservation Ctr., 5905 Wilshire Blvd., Los Angeles, CA 90036; Title Tel # (213) 857-6000
Personnel: Editor-Elizabeth Welsh
Editorial Description: Devoted to the exchange of ideas, information and news pertaining to the conservation of cultural property.
General Info: Yr. Est. 1979, 3x/yr., Trim Size-8½ x 11, Sheetfed press, 36 pages, ISSN: 1052-0066, No Color, Saddle-stitched
Subscriptions: Indv. $30, Inst. $35, Can. $35, For. $35, $10/copy
Circulation: Total-500
Printing Co: Mr. Printer, Thomas & Central, Phoenix, AZ 85026

Westbridge Art Market
Report   *Business, Consumer*

Publishing Co: Westbridge Publications, Ltd., 2339 Granville St., Vancouver, BC V6H 3G4 Canada Fax # (604) 734-4944; Title Tel # (604) 736-1014 Title Fax # (604) 731-4576
Personnel: Publisher, Editor-Anthony Westbridge, Circ. Mgr.-Rowena Westbridge
Editorial Description: National & international fine art auction results & analysis.
General Info: (Formerly Fine Art & Auction Review), Yr. Est. 1974, Bi-monthly, Trim Size-8½ x 11, Offset press, 12 pages, ISSN: 1191-3371, No Color, Saddle-stitched
Subscriptions: Indv. $66
Circulation: Total-300
Advertising: Inquire for rates.

William Hardash Auction
Newsletter   *Consumer*

Publishing Co: William Hardash Communications, 249 N Brand Blvd # 530, Glendale, CA 91203-2609; Title Tel # (818) 953-8564 Title Fax # (818) 240-0256
General Info: Yr. Est. 1989, Monthly, ISSN: 1047-7500
Subscriptions: Indv. $52

World Fine Art
  See: ANTIQUES & ART GOODS

World Monuments Fund
  See: ARCHITECTURE

ASTROLOGY

Astro-Analytics   *Consumer, Association*

Publishing Co: Astro Analytics Productions, PO Box 16927, Encino, CA 91416-6927;
  Title Tel # (818) 997-8684
Personnel: Publisher-Harry Whitaker, Mktg. Dir.-Craig Green
General Info: Yr. Est. 1978, Quarterly, 10 pages
Subscriptions: Indv. $5, $1/copy

Astroflash   *Consumer*

Publishing Co: ACS Publications, PO Box 34487, San Diego, CA 92163-4487;
  Title Tel # (619) 492-9919 Title Fax # (619) 492-9917
Personnel: Editor-Maritha Pottenger, Production Mgr.-Daryl Fuller, Publisher, Art Dir.-Maria Kay
  Simms
Editorial Description: Feature articles devoted to astrology professionals, students, and all those
  interested in New Age topics.
General Info: Yr. Est. 1979, Quarterly, Trim Size-5$\frac{3}{8}$ x 8$\frac{3}{8}$, Desktop press, 32 pages, 2 Color, Matte,
  Saddle-stitched
Subscriptions: Indv. $6, $2/copy
Circulation: Total-8,000
List Rental: List Management Co.: ACS, 5521 Ruffin Road, San Diego, CA 92123-1314
  Tel # (619) 492-9919, Fax # (619) 492-9917, Actives: $90/M

Astrotalk

Publishing Co: Matrix Software, 315 Marion Ave, Big Rapids, MI 49307-1345;
  Title Tel # (616) 796-2483
General Info: Bi-monthly

Coffee News Break

Publishing Co: Tea & Coffee Assn. of Canada, 885 Don Mills Rd., Ste. 301, Don Mills, ON M3C 1V9
  Canada
General Info: (Formerly Tea & Coffee Assn. of Canada Bulletin), 10x/yr.

Constellation

Publishing Co: Middle Atlantic Planetarium Society, Vanderbilt Planetarium, Centerport, NY 11721;
  Title Tel # (516) 757-7502
Personnel: Editor-Tom Cargy
General Info: Yr. Est. 1965, Quarterly, 8 pages
Circulation: Total-175

Crawford Perspectives
  See: INVESTMENT

Four Elements   *Consumer, Association*

Publishing Co: Madison Astrological Society, 302 S Brooks St, Madison, WI 53715-1502;
  Title Tel # (608) 251-6738
Personnel: Editor-Dennis Murray
General Info: Monthly, 3 pages
Subscriptions: Indv. $3

International Investor
  See: INVESTMENT

Iridis
  See: PARAPSYCHOLOGY

Memberletter   *Association*

Publishing Co: National Council for Geocosmic Research, Inc., PO Box 1220, Dunkirk, MD
  20754-1220 Fax # (410) 257-2824; Title Tel # (301) 855-2747 Title Fax # (201) 818-2871
Personnel: Editor-Madalyn Hillis, Editorial Page Ed.-Lorraine Welsh, Circ. Mgr.-Margaret Meister,
  Publisher, Bk. Rev. Ed., Production Mgr.-Mary B. Downing, Adv. Dir.-Arlene Nimark
Editorial Description: Current association news and articles of interest to the membership of NCGR.
General Info: Yr. Est. 1984, Monthly, Trim Size-8$\frac{1}{2}$ x 11, Sheetfed press, 16 pages, No Color,
  Newsprint, Other
Subscriptions: Indv. $35, Can. $45, For. $45, $8/copy
Circulation: Total-3,500
Advertising: Inquire for rates. Accepts Inserts.
List Rental: Actives: 3,500, $175/M
Printing Co: John Everson, 3 River View Rd, Westport, CT 06880-4925

North Florida Astrology
Assn. Newsletter   *Association*

Publishing Co: North Florida Astrology Assn., PO Box 1741, Jacksonville, FL 32201-1741;
  Title Tel # (904) 355-8753
Personnel: Editor-Joan Johns
Editorial Description: Informative newsletter on various astrological subjects & bulletins.
General Info: Yr. Est. 1973, Monthly, Trim Size-8$\frac{1}{2}$ x 11, Letrpr. press, 4 pages
Subscriptions: Indv. $15
Advertising: Inquire for rates.
Printing Co: Fast Print, 1506 King St, Jacksonville, FL 32204-4514 Tel # (904) 387-0243

Seventh House, The
  See: LIFESTYLE

Star Beacon
  See: UNIDENTIFIED FLYING OBJECTS

Winged Chariot, The   *Consumer*

Publishing Co: Moon Star Enterprises, PO Box 1718, Milwaukee, WI 53201-1718;
  Title Tel # (414) 871-1490
Personnel: Publisher, Editor-Tracey Hoover
Editorial Description: Newsletter devoted to the Tarot Discipline.
General Info: Yr. Est. 1981, Bi-monthly, Trim Size-4$\frac{1}{4}$ x 5$\frac{1}{2}$, Desktop press, 22 pages, 5% ads,
  Matte, Other
Subscriptions: Indv. $10, Inst. $15, Can. $18, $3/copy
Advertising: Inquire for rates.

ASTRONOMY

AAVSO Bulletin   *Consumer, Association*

Publishing Co: American Association of Variable Star Observers, 25 Birch St, Cambridge, MA
  02138-1205; Title Tel # (617) 354-0484 Title Fax # (617) 354-0665
Personnel: Editor-Janet Mattei
Editorial Description: Annual predicted dates of maxima and minima of 600 long period variables.
General Info: Yr. Est. 1911, Annually, Trim Size-8$\frac{1}{2}$ x 11, Ind/Abs/Online: Ast&AA, No Color, Matte
Subscriptions: Indv. $25, Inst. $40, For. $30
Circulation: Total-1,000

AAVSO Circular   *Association*

Publishing Co: American Association of Variable Star Observers, 25 Birch St, Cambridge, MA
  02138-1205; Title Tel # (617) 354-0484 Title Fax # (617) 354-0665
Personnel: Editor-John Bortle
Editorial Description: Preliminary observations of some eruptive and other interesting variables.
General Info: Trim Size-8$\frac{1}{5}$ x 11, 4 pages, No Color, Matte, Other
Subscriptions: Indv. $15, Inst. $30, For. $25
Circulation: Total-300

Academy Newsletter
  See: MUSEUM PUBLICATIONS

Archaeoastronomy &
Ethnoastronomy News   *Consumer*

Publishing Co: Center for Archaeoastronomy, PO Box X, College Park, MD 20741-3022
  Fax # (301) 399-5337; Title Tel # (301) 864-6637 Title Fax # (301) 699-5337
Editorial Description: The journal 'Archaeoastronomy' is included with the subscription package.
General Info: Quarterly
Subscriptions: Indv. $36, Inst. $60, Can. $42, For. $42

Cassiopeia   *Association*

Publishing Co: Canadian Astronomical Society, Mount Royal College, 4825 Richard Road S.W,
  Calgary, AB T3E 6K6 Canada; Title Tel # (403) 240-6029 Title Fax # (403) 240-6505
Personnel: Editor-Dr. Jack Penfold
Editorial Description: Quarterly newsletter of Canadian Astronomical Society.
General Info: Yr. Est. 1973, Quarterly, Trim Size-8$\frac{1}{2}$ x 11, 30 pages, ISSN: 0715-7747
Circulation: (100% controlled), Total-400

Cosmic Quarterly   *Association, Consumer*

Publishing Co: Chicago Astronomical Society, PO Box 30287, Chicago, IL 60630-0287;
  Title Tel # (312) 725-5618
Personnel: Editor-William Becker
Editorial Description: Informs and educates on the study of astronomy.
General Info: Quarterly

David Dunlap Doings   *Business, Association*

Publishing Co: David Dunlap Observatory, Box 360, Richmond Hill, ON L4C 4Y6 Canada;
  Title Tel # (905) 884-9562 Title Fax # (905) 884-2672
Personnel: Editor-C.T. Bolton
Editorial Description: Internal newsletter for current employees, faculty & students as well as former
  employees, students, & faculty.
General Info: Yr. Est. 1968, Bi-monthly, Trim Size-8$\frac{1}{2}$ x 11, 10 pages, ISSN: 0713-5904, No Color
List Rental: Rents Lists

Eyepiece   *Association*

Publishing Co: Amateur Astronomers Association, 1010 Park Ave, New York, NY 10028-0903;
  Title Tel # (212) 535-2922
Personnel: Editor-Jack Dittrick
Editorial Description: Activities of NY astronomers, news from the profession, observations,
  meetings, local exhibits & lectures, stargazing, celestial events.
General Info: Yr. Est. 1954, Monthly, Trim Size-8$\frac{1}{2}$ x 11, Offset press, 10 pages, ISSN: 0146-7662,
  Ind/Abs/Online: On bulletin bds. timed to RIME, Intelect, FIDO & Space Factor, Color-cover, Other,
  Other
Subscriptions: Indv. $36, Can. $44, For. $44, Free To Qualified Recipient
Circulation: Total-600

MIRA Newsletter

Publishing Co: Monterey Institute for Research in Astronomy, 900 Major Sherman Ln, Monterey, CA 93940-4633; Title # (408) 375-3220
Personnel: Editor-Tom Logan
General Info: Yr. Est. 1978, Quarterly, 8 pages, No Color, Matte
Subscriptions: Indv. $30
Circulation: Total-1,000

Mawewi
See: GENERAL INTEREST

Meteor News
See: SCIENCE

NASA STI Bulletin
See: AERONAUTICS/ASTRONAUTICS

National Amateur Astronomy News

Publishing Co: Scott Publishing Co., Rr 14 Box 394-A, Tyler, TX 75707-9814
Editorial Description: Covers astronimical news & research of interest to amateur astronomers.
General Info: Yr. Est. 1989, Monthly, ISSN: 1044-7059
Subscriptions: Indv. $18

News Letter of the Astronomical Society of NY
Consumer

Publishing Co: L. Davis Press, Inc., 1125 Oxford Pl, Schenectady, NY 12308-2913; Title Tel # (518) 374-5636 Title Fax # (518) 346-5781
Personnel: Publisher, Editor-A. G. Davis Philip
Editorial Description: Articles on astronomy.
General Info: Yr. Est. 1976, Semi-annually, Offset press, 30 pages, No Color
Subscriptions: Indv. $12

Occultation Newsletter
Association

Publishing Co: Intl. Occultation Timing Assn., 2760 SW Jewell Ave, Topeka, KS 66611-1614; Title Tel # (913) 232-3693
Personnel: Editor-Joan Dunham
Editorial Description: News & information concerning lunar occultations, asteroidal occultations, eclipses & the methods used to observe them.
General Info: Yr. Est. 1974, Irregular, Trim Size-$8\frac{1}{2}$ x 11, Mimeo press, 26 pages, ISSN: 0737-6766, Other
Subscriptions: Indv. $25, Can. $25, For. $30, $6/copy
Circulation: Total-300

Sky Calendar
See: EDUCATION

Solar Bulletin
Consumer, Association

Publishing Co: American Association of Variable Star Observers, 25 Birch St, Cambridge, MA 02138-1205; Title Tel # (617) 354-0484 Title Fax # (617) 354-0665
Personnel: Editor-Peter Taylor
Editorial Description: American and international sunspot numbers and sudden ionospheric disturbance data.
General Info: Yr. Est. 1944, Monthly, Trim Size-$8\frac{1}{2}$ x 11, 2 pages, Ind/Abs/Online: Ast&AA, No Color, Matte
Subscriptions: Indv. $25, Inst. $40, For. $30
Circulation: Total-400

Space Autograph News
See: AERONAUTICS/ASTRONAUTICS

Universe in the Classroom
See: EDUCATION

AUDIO

ARSC Newsletter
See: SOUND ENGINEERING

B.A.S. Speaker
See: SOUND ENGINEERING

Efficient Auditor
See: PSYCHOLOGY

Home Automation News
See: ELECTRIC & ELECTRONIC EQUIPMENT

Voice Coil Newsletter
See: SOUND ENGINEERING

AUTOMOTIVE

300 Star Letter

Publishing Co: Gullwing Group Intl., 2229 Via Cerritos, Palos Verdes, CA 90274-2141; Title Tel # (213) 375-8630
General Info: Monthly
Circulation: Total-900

510 Again Newsletter
Consumer, Association

Publishing Co: National Datsun 510 Club, PO Box 150, Pacific Grove, CA 93950-0150 Tel # (408) 655-0510
Personnel: Publisher, Editor-Ray Johns
Editorial Description: Information and club activities for owners of 1968-1973 Datsun 510s.
General Info: Yr. Est. 1992, Monthly, Trim Size-$8\frac{1}{4}$ x $10\frac{3}{4}$, 16 pages, No Color, Matte, Saddle-stitched
Subscriptions: Can. $31, For. $31, $3/copy
Circulation: Total-1,015
Advertising: Inquire for rates.

1949-50-51 Mercury Owners Newsletter
Consumer

Publishing Co: ShoeBox Ford Enterprises, Box 30647, Midwest City, OK 73140-3647 Tel # (405) 737-6027 Fax # (405) 737-0058; Title Tel # (405) 737-6021
Personnel: Publisher, Editor-Mike McCarville
General Info: Yr. Est. 1987, Monthly
Subscriptions: Indv. $14
Circulation: Total-835

AAMVA Bulletin
Association

Publishing Co: American Assn. of Motor Vehicle Administrators, 4301 Wilson Blvd Ste 400, Arlington, VA 22203-1800; Title Tel # (703) 522-4200 Title Fax # (703) 522-1553
Personnel: Editor-Jamie Lacey, Editor-Jennifer Thompson, Production Mgr.-Kate Wernersbach
Editorial Description: Bi-monthly newsletter covering issues of interest to motor vehicle administrators & traffic law enforcement officials in the U.S. & Canada.
General Info: Yr. Est. 1923, Bi-monthly, Trim Size-$8\frac{1}{2}$ x 11, Sheetfed press, 12 pages, 4 Color, Matte, Saddle-stitched
Subscriptions: Indv. $25, Can. $35, For. $40
Circulation: (100% controlled), Total-2,000

ACM Monthly
See: PLASTICS

Accelerator

Publishing Co: Auburn-Cord-Duesenberg Club, 9n089 Corron Rd, Elgin, IL 60123-8304; Title Tel # (219) 925-1444 Title Fax # (219) 925-6266
Personnel: Editor-Sharon Vick, Circ. Mgr.-Jan Schippers, Circ. Mgr.-Jan Schippeus, Production Mgr.-Jay Engler
Editorial Description: Activities of the ACD Museum, historical reprints, automobile features.
General Info: Yr. Est. 1974, Quarterly, Trim Size-$8\frac{1}{2}$ x 11, Offset press, 16 pages, Color-cover, Matte
Circulation: Total-1,600
Advertising: Inquire for rates. Accepts Inserts.
Printing Co: Engler Printing Co., 808 W State St, Fremont, OH 43420-2538 Tel # (419) 332-2181

Advanced Transportation Technology News
See: TRAFFIC & TRANSPORTATION

Aftermarket Distribution
Association

Publishing Co: Automotive Warehouse Distributors Association, 9140 Ward Pky Ste 200, Kansas City, MO 64114-3313; Title Tel # (816) 444-3500 Title Fax # (816) 444-0330
Personnel: Editor-Robert Stewart
Editorial Description: News of AWDA and automotive aftermarket industry.
General Info: (Formerly AWDA News), Yr. Est. 1977, 10x/yr., Offset press, 8 pages, 2 Color, Matte
Subscriptions: Free With Membership

Aftermarket Update
Business, Association

Publishing Co: Automobile Industries Assn., 1272 Wellington St., Ottawa, ON K1Y 3A7 Canada Fax # (613) 728-6021; Title Tel # (613) 728-5821
Personnel: Editor-Denise Faguy
General Info: 10x/yr.
Circulation: Total-4,500

Aftermarket Watch
Business, Association

Publishing Co: Automobile Industries Assn., 1272 Wellington St., Ottawa, ON K1Y 3A7 Canada Fax # (613) 728-6021; Title Tel # (613) 728-5821
Personnel: Editor-Denise Faguy
General Info: Bi-monthly
Circulation: (100% controlled), Total-4,500

Akron Daily Digest
See: HOUSE ORGANS

Alldata News
See: COMPUTERS & AUTOMATION

American Association for Fuel Cells Newsletter
See: ENERGY

Asia/Pacific Automotive Bulletin
Business

Publishing Co: Forecast International/DMS, Inc., 22 Commerce Rd., Newtown, CT 06470-1643
Fax # (203) 426-1964; Title Tel # (203) 426-0800 Title Fax # (203) 426-4262
General Info: Monthly
Subscriptions: Indv. $595

Auburn-Cord-Duesenberg Club Newsletter
See: HOBBY

Auto Dealer Law Reporter
See: LAW

Auto Fax
Business, Association

Publishing Co: Automotive Parts and Accessories Assn., 4600 E.W. Hwy., Ste. 300, Bethesda, MD 20814; Title Tel # (301) 654-6664 Title Fax # (301) 654-3299
Personnel: Editor-John Reilly
Editorial Description: Newsletter reporting the news & enents of automotive parts & accessories aftermarket.
General Info: (Formerly International Report), Yr. Est. 1984, Weekly
Subscriptions: Free With Membership
Circulation: Total-1,850

Auto Financing Update
See: BANKING & FINANCE

Auto Free Press
Consumer

Publishing Co: Auto-Free New York Committee of Transportation Alternatives, 92 St. Marks Place, New York, NY 10009-5840; Title Tel # (212) 941-4600
General Info: Bi-monthly
Subscriptions: Indv. $20

Auto Insurance Report
See: INSURANCE

Auto Mi$er
Consumer

Publishing Co: JAX Mobile Auto Service, 1308 Walnut Ave., Manhattan Beach, CA 90266-5051; Title Tel # (310) 545-4756
Editorial Description: Automotive letter for consumers.
General Info: Monthly, Trim Size-$8\frac{1}{2}$ x 11, 8 pages, No Color, Matte
Subscriptions: Indv. $12, $1/copy

Auto Retail Report

Publishing Co: United Communications Group, 11300 Rockville Pike, Ste. 1100, Rockville, MD 20852-3030 Tel # (301) 816-8950 Fax # (301) 816-8945
Editorial Description: Reports on sales of cars and trucks by new car dealers.
General Info: Yr. Est. 1990, Bi-weekly
List Rental: Rents Lists

Auto Service Insider
Business, Consumer

Publishing Co: United Communications Group, 11300 Rockville Pike, Ste. 1100, Rockville, MD 20852-3030 Tel # (301) 816-8950 Fax # (301) 816-8945; Title Tel # (212) 873-5900 Title Fax # (212) 799-1728
Personnel: Publisher-Beverly Walker, Editor-Steven Byers, Circ. Mgr.-Pamela Ortiz, Production Mgr.-Eladia Orellna, Art Dir.-Rise Cappadonna, Promotion Dir.-Ann Cheevers
Editorial Description: For professionals involved in all aspects of car & truck service, repair, & reconditioning.
General Info: Yr. Est. 1989, Bi-weekly, Sheetfed press, 8 pages, ISSN: 1042-7414
Subscriptions: Indv. $195, Can. $195, For. $230, $10/copy
Acquistions: Publication Bought, Publication Sold
Circulation: Total-300
List Rental: List Management Co.: George Mann & Associates, 569 Abbington Dr., PO Box 930, Hightstown, NJ 08520-9990 Tel # (609) 443-1330, Fax # (609) 443-0397, Actives: $85/M, Expires: $75/M

Automobile Accident Law and Practice
See: LAW

Automotive Engine Rebuilders Assn. - Service Bulletin
Association

Publishing Co: Automotive Engine Rebuilders Assn., 330 Lexington Dr, Buffalo Grove, IL 60089-6933; Title Tel # (708) 541-6550 Title Fax # (708) 541-5808
Personnel: Editor-Joe Polich
Editorial Description: Provides information about automotive engines.
General Info: Yr. Est. 1971, Monthly, Looseleaf
Circulation: Total-3,500

Automotive Engine Rebuilders Assn. - Technical Bulletin
Association

Publishing Co: Automotive Engine Rebuilders Assn., 330 Lexington Dr, Buffalo Grove, IL 60089-6933; Title Tel # (708) 541-6550 Title Fax # (708) 541-5808
Personnel: Editor-Joe Polich
Editorial Description: Provides technical changes in specification of engines.
General Info: (Formerly Engineering Bulletin), Yr. Est. 1968, Monthly, Looseleaf
Circulation: Total-3,500

Automotive Engine Rebuilders Association, Administrative Bulletin
Association

Publishing Co: Automotive Engine Rebuilders Assn., 330 Lexington Dr, Buffalo Grove, IL 60089-6933; Title Tel # (708) 541-6550 Title Fax # (708) 541-5808

Automotive Engine Rebuilders Association, Monthly Bulletin
Business

Publishing Co: Automotive Engine Rebuilders Assn., 330 Lexington Dr, Buffalo Grove, IL 60089-6933; Title Tel # (708) 541-6550 Title Fax # (708) 541-5808
General Info: Monthly, Offset press, Looseleaf
Circulation: (100% controlled), Total-4,200

Automotive Investor
Business

Publishing Co: Mary Ann Liebert, Inc., 1651 3rd Ave, New York, NY 10128-3649; Title Tel # (212) 289-2300
Personnel: Editor-Richard Langworth
Editorial Description: For buyers, sellers and collectors of vintage, classic, and special-interest cars, 1925-1975. Reports current market activities and trends and analyzes future investment opportunities by make.
General Info: Yr. Est. 1987, Monthly, ISSN: 0898-2155, Coated, Saddle-stitched
Subscriptions: Indv. $79, Can. $275, For. $335

Automotive Litigation Reporter

Publishing Co: Andrews Publications, Inc., 1646 West Chester Pike, PO Box 1000, Westtown, PA 19395; Title Tel # (610) 399-6600 Title Fax # (610) 399-6610
Personnel: Publisher-John Backe, Editor-Nick Sullivan, Mktg. Dir.-Andrew Katz
Editorial Description: Provides up-to-date information on developments in automotive product liability suits from around the country.
General Info: Yr. Est. 1981, Bi-monthly, Trim Size-$8\frac{1}{2}$ x 11, Mimeo press, 70 pages, ISSN: 0278-4726, Ind/Abs/Online: News Net, No Color, Newsprint
Subscriptions: Indv. $850, $40/copy
Advertising: Inquire for rates.
List Rental: Actives: 2,182, $110/M

Automotive Newsletter
Association

Publishing Co: IADA, PO Box 1288, Elmhurst, IL 60126-8288; Title Tel # (414) 541-7550
Personnel: Publisher, Editor-Norm Wetzel
Editorial Description: Activities in association with regards to automotive damage and repair.
General Info: Quarterly, 8 pages
Circulation: Total-7,000

Automotive Week
Business

Publishing Co: Automotive Week Publishing, 573 Valley Road, PO Box 3495, Wayne, NJ 07470-3495; Title Tel # (201) 694-7792 Title Fax # (201) 694-2817
Personnel: Publisher, Editor-Chuck Laverty
Editorial Description: Marketing & merchandising of auto parts, accessories, chemicals & services to traditional retail markets & specialty service installers.
General Info: (Formerly Automotive Buyer), Yr. Est. 1975, Weekly, Trim Size-$8\frac{1}{2}$ x 11, Letrpr. press, 4 pages, No Color, Newsprint
Subscriptions: Indv. $120, $10/copy
Advertising: Inquire for rates. Accepts Inserts.
Printing Co: A V Printing and Mailing, 356 Union Ave, Paterson, NJ 07502-1932 Tel # (201) 790-1155

Autoparts Reports
Business

Publishing Co: International Trade Services, PO Box 5950, Bethesda, MD 20824-5950 Fax # (202) 229-3995; Title Tel # (202) 857-8454 Title Fax # (301) 229-3995
Personnel: Publisher-Ronald DeMarines, Editor-Fred Donovan, Circ. Mgr.-Gloria Fenton
Editorial Description: Reporting on int'l investment & trade in the automotive industry. Provides information on supplier/manufacturer relationships, joint ventures, & impact of gov't action on industry.
General Info: (Formerly Automotive Parts International), Yr. Est. 1986, Bi-weekly, Trim Size-$8\frac{1}{2}$ x 11, Sheetfed press, 8 pages, ISSN: 0896-3614, 2 Color, Coated
Subscriptions: Indv. $340, Can. $340, For. $405, $13/copy
Acquistions: Publication Bought
Printing Co: Print-A-Copy, 7315 Wisconsin Ave., Bethesda, MD 20814 Tel # (301) 656-4456

BMW Vintage/Classic Bulletin

Publishing Co: BMW Vintage Club of America, Inc., PO Box S, San Rafael, CA 94913-4358; Title Tel # (415) 897-0220 Title Fax # (415) 898-0831
Personnel: Publisher, Editor-Thomas Graham
General Info: Yr. Est. 1974, Quarterly, 20 pages
Circulation: Total-150

Battery & EV Technology
See: ENGINEERING, ELECTRICAL

Big Bird

Publishing Co: Thunderbirds of America, PO Box 2766, Cedar Rapids, IA 52406-2766;
Title Tel # (319) 364-6859
Personnel: Editor-Bob Peterson
Editorial Description: Assists owners with the restoration & preservation of 1967 and later model Ford Thunderbirds.
General Info: Yr. Est. 1980, Bi-monthly, Trim Size-8½ x 11, 12 pages, 3% ads, No Color, Newsprint
Subscriptions: Indv. $20
Circulation: Total-400
Advertising: Accepts Inserts.

Blue Seal

Publishing Co: National Institute for Automotive Service Excellence, 13505 Dulles Technology Dr, Herndon, VA 22071-3413; Title Tel # (703) 713-1113
Personnel: Editor-Martin Lawson
Editorial Description: For ASE-certified technicians (mechanics) & their employers.
General Info: (Formerly Gear/Excelsior), Yr. Est. 1984, Semi-annually, Trim Size-8½ x 11, Sheetfed press, 12 pages, ISSN: 0897-9421, 2 Color, Newsprint
Circulation: Total-350,000

Body Language   *Association*

Publishing Co: Sarco Management & Pubs., 2900 Wilcrest Dr Ste 122, Houston, TX 77042-3355; Title Tel # (713) 977-5551 Title Fax # (713) 531-9411
Personnel: Publisher, Editor-Stan Rodman
Editorial Description: For companies that distribute recycled & new auto body parts to auto dealers & garages & who are members &/or subscribers. Sold in conjunction with Collision Parts Journal.
General Info: Yr. Est. 1981, Monthly, Trim Size-8½ x 11, Sheetfed press, 8 pages, No Color, Matte
Subscriptions: Indv. $70, $6/copy
Circulation: Total-600
List Rental: Actives: $60/M
Printing Co: Downtown Duplicating, 2012 Baldwin St, Houston, TX 77002-8594 Tel # (713) 659-8295

Booster News: Topics   *Association*

Publishing Co: Automotive Booster Clubs International, 1806 Johns Dr, Glenview, IL 60025-1657; Title Tel # (708) 729-2227 Title Fax # (708) 729-3670
Editorial Description: For automotive aftermarket salespersons.
General Info: Yr. Est. 1921, Quarterly, Trim Size-8½ x 11, 6 pages, 2 Color
Circulation: (100% controlled), Total-3,100

Borgward-Owners' Club-Newsletter   *Consumer, Association*

Publishing Co: Borgward-Owners' Club, 77 New Hampshire Ave, Bay Shore, NY 11706-2520; Title Tel # (516) 273-0458
Personnel: Editor-Dyck Livant
Editorial Description: Club works for the preservation of all Borgward, Goliath & Lloyd vehicles. Parts bought & sold.
General Info: Yr. Est. 1974, Quarterly, Sheetfed press, 12 pages, Matte
Subscriptions: Indv. $20
Advertising: Inquire for rates.

CASI Lubricator   *Business*

Publishing Co: Convenient Automotive Services Institute, PO Box 34595, Bethesda, MD 20827-0595; Title Tel # (301) 897-3191
Personnel: Editor-Larry Northrup
General Info: Yr. Est. 1986, Monthly

CMI News (Complete Mercury Interest)

Publishing Co: Sponsor-American Comet Club-United Spoilers of America, Auto Craft, Rr 4 Box 116, Alexandria, IN 46001-9413; Title Tel # (317) 724-7601
Personnel: Publisher, Editor-L.C. Wilson, Circ. Mgr., Adv. Dir.-S.E. Werline, Promotion Dir.-Susie Wilson
Editorial Description: Interest of the Mercury Automobile from 1939-1978.
General Info: (Formerly Comet, Meteor, Spoiler News), Yr. Est. 1982, Bi-monthly, Trim Size-8½ x 11, Mimeo press, 24 pages, 2% ads, Color, Coated
Subscriptions: Indv. $20, $4/copy
Circulation: Total-697
Advertising: Accepts Inserts.

Cabrioletter, The   *Association*

Publishing Co: Model A Ford Cabriolet Club, PO Box 515, Porter, TX 77365-0515 Tel # (713) 429-2505; Title Tel # (713) 572-2505
Personnel: Editor-Gwyn Machacek
Editorial Description: A network for the exchange of information & automotive parts among owners & enthusiasts of the Cabriolet, a rare style of the Model A Ford manufactured from 1929-1931.
General Info: Yr. Est. 1980, Quarterly, Trim Size-8½ x 11, Offset press, 12 pages, 1% ads, No Color
Subscriptions: Indv. $10, Can. $10, For. $12
Circulation: Total-400
Advertising: Inquire for rates. Accepts Inserts.
List Rental: Rents Lists
Printing Co: Jiffy Printing, 515 North Belt, E., #160, Houston, TX 77060 Tel # (713) 445-7970

Car & Truck Rental / Leasing Insider   *Business*

Publishing Co: Atcom, Inc., 140 Riverside Dr Ste 14h, New York, NY 10024-2605 Tel # (212) 799-2294 Fax # (212) 799-2294; Title Tel # (212) 873-5900 Title Fax # (212) 799-1728
Personnel: Publisher-Beverly Walker, Editor-James Koscs, Circ. Mgr.-Pamela Ortiz, Production Mgr.-Eladia Orellana, Art Dir.-Rise Cappadonna, Promotion Dir.-Anne Cheevers
Editorial Description: Newsletter for automobile rental and leasing professionals.
General Info: Yr. Est. 1963, Weekly, Trim Size-8½ x 11, Sheetfed press, 6 pages, ISSN: 0008-6053, 3% ads, No Color, Newsprint
Subscriptions: Indv. $230, Can. $230, For. $265, $10/copy
Acquistions: Publication Bought, Publication Sold
Circulation: Total-2,000
List Rental: List Management Co.: George Mann & Associates, 569 Abbington Dr., PO Box 930, Hightstown, NJ 08520-9990 Tel # (609) 443-1330, Fax # (609) 443-0397, Actives: $85/M, Expires: $75/M

Car Dealer Insider   *Business*

Publishing Co: United Communications Group, 11300 Rockville Pike, Ste. 1100, Rockville, MD 20852-3030 Tel # (301) 816-8950 Fax # (301) 816-8945; Title Tel # (212) 873-5900 Title Fax # (212) 799-1728
Personnel: Editor-Al Burns
General Info: Yr. Est. 1966, Weekly
Subscriptions: Indv. $229
List Rental: Rents Lists

Car Rental/Leasing Insider

Publishing Co: United Communications Group, 11300 Rockville Pike, Ste. 1100, Rockville, MD 20852-3030 Tel # (301) 816-8950 Fax # (301) 816-8945; Title Tel # (212) 873-5900 Title Fax # (212) 799-1728
Personnel: Editor-James Koscs
General Info: Yr. Est. 1964, Weekly
Subscriptions: Indv. $229
List Rental: Rents Lists

Cars & Comments

Publishing Co: Automotive Information Council, 13505 Dulles Technology Dr, Herndon, VA 22071-3413; Title Tel # (313) 559-5922
Personnel: Editor-Charles Charpie
Editorial Description: Covers consumer oriented auto news & tips.
General Info: Weekly

Chauffeurs' Badges and Transportation Badges of the World
See: HOBBY

Checkerboard News

Publishing Co: Checker Car Club of America, 469 Tremaine Ave, Kenmore, NY 14217-2537; Title Tel # (716) 877-3358
Personnel: Editor-Donald McHenry
Circulation: Total-700

Chek-Chart Service Bulletin   *Business*

Publishing Co: Chek-Chart, H. M. Gousha Co., 320 Soquel Way, Sunnyvale, CA 94086-4101 Tel # (408) 739-2435; Title Tel # (408) 739-2436 Title Fax # (408) 739-2475
Personnel: Editor-Rick Dupuy
Editorial Description: Up-to-date information on all the new automotive developments from the car manufacturers. An information bulletin for service station dealers, mechanics, and instructors.
General Info: Yr. Est. 1929, Monthly, Trim Size-8½ x 11, Offset press, 8 pages, 2 Color
Subscriptions: Indv. $16
Circulation: (100% controlled), Total-25,000

Chrysler 300 Club News   *Association*

Publishing Co: Chrysler 300 Club Intl., 4900 Jonesville Rd, Jonesville, MI 49250-9439; Title Tel # (517) 849-2783 Title Fax # (517) 849-7445
Personnel: Editor-Eleanor Riehl
Editorial Description: News, history, and parts information on the 300 series by Chrysler built 1955-1965.
General Info: Yr. Est. 1970, Quarterly, Trim Size-5½ x 8½, Sheetfed press, 40 pages, 3% ads, No Color, Newsprint, Saddle-stitched
Subscriptions: Indv. $17, Can. $20, For. $20, $1/copy
Circulation: Total-850
Advertising: Inquire for rates.

Classic Chevrolet Memories   *Consumer*

Publishing Co: Entertainment Art Co., The, 1200 High Ridge Road, Stamford, CT 06905-1202; Title Fax # (203) 353-9304
Personnel: Publisher-Bruce Kasanoff
Editorial Description: Newsletter for fans of Chevrolets from 1950 to 1969. Features articles, plus wonderful Chevy memorabilia, much of it not available in stores or catalogs.
General Info: Yr. Est. 1993, Quarterly
Subscriptions: Indv. $15, $4/copy

Cormorant News Bulletin   *Association*   **CPM: $44**

Publishing Co: Packard Automobile Classics, 84 Hoy Ave, Fords, NJ 08863-1938;
Title Tel # (908) 738-7859 Title Fax # (908) 738-7625
Personnel: Editor-Stuart Blond
Editorial Description: Emphasis on Packard automobiles and regions of the Packard club.
General Info: Yr. Est. 1953, Monthly, Trim Size-8½ x 11, Web press, 36 pages, ISSN: 0045-8554,
50% ads, No Color, Coated
Subscriptions: $1/copy
Circulation: Total-3,700, Readership-5,000
Advertising: $165.

Crosley Automobile Club-
Quarterly

Publishing Co: Crosley Automobile Club, 217 N Gilbert St, Iowa City, IA 52245-2125;
Title Tel # (414) 542-1787
Personnel: Editor-J. Friday
General Info: Yr. Est. 1970, Quarterly
Circulation: Total-800

DeSoto Days

Publishing Co: DeSoto Club of America, 105 East 96, Kansas City, MO 64114-1827;
Title Tel # (816) 421-6006
Personnel: Editor-Walter O'Kelly
General Info: Yr. Est. 1970, Bi-monthly, Trim Size-8½ x 11, Sheetfed press, 10 pages, No Color,
Newsprint
Subscriptions: Indv. $15
Acquistions: Publication Bought
Circulation: Total-600
Advertising: Accepts Inserts.

Dealers Edge   *Business*

Publishing Co: WD&S Publishing, 20 Highland Ave, Metuchen, NJ 08840-1949;
Title Tel # (908) 548-4440 Title Fax # (908) 603-0690
Personnel: Publisher-James Muntz, Editor-Russ La Due, Editorial Page Ed.-Coriann Fell, Promotion
Mgr.-Ted Epstein
Editorial Description: The auto dealers profit division
General Info: (Formerly Front End), Yr. Est. 1994, Semi-monthly, Trim Size-8.5 x 11, 8 pages, 2
Color
Subscriptions: Indv. $259
List Rental: Actives: 3,400, $135/M, Hotline: 10,500, $95/M, Expires: 2,400, $110/M

Dealership Management
Review

Publishing Co: Auto Polish, PO Box 9505, Mc Lean, VA 22102-0505; Title Fax # (703) 356-8008
General Info: Yr. Est. 1990, 24x/yr.
Subscriptions: Indv. $295

Directory of Automotive
Related Business Pubs.   *Association*

Publishing Co: MEMA-Motor & Equipment Manufacturers Assn., PO Box 13966, Rtp, NC
27709-3966; Title Tel # (919) 549-4800 Title Fax # (919) 549-4824
Personnel: Publisher-J. J. Conner
Editorial Description: Listing & pubs. serving all segments of the automotive industry.
General Info: (Formerly Directory of Automotive), Trim Size-5½ x 8½, Sheetfed press, 125 pages,
No Color, Looseleaf
Circulation: Total-1,000

Double Clutch

Publishing Co: Antique Truck Club of America, Inc., PO Box 291, Hershey, PA 17033-0291;
Title Tel # (717) 533-9032
Personnel: Publisher-Robert Gallagher, Editor-Hope Emerich, Adv. Dir., Promotion Dir.-Cy Kranick
Editorial Description: Magazine for antique truck enthusiasts, dis. to club members only; included
history, restoration articles, articles about members' trucks, or members in trucking in
General Info: Yr. Est. 1971, Bi-monthly, Sheetfed press, 32 pages, 1% ads, Color-cover, Coated
Subscriptions: $3/copy
List Rental: Rents Lists
Printing Co: Gallagher Printing Co., 616 E Main St, Palmyra, PA 17078-1833 Tel # (717) 838-1527

Electric Vehicle Digest   *Business*

Publishing Co: Electric Vehicle Digest, 301 Seola Road, Brookhaven, PA 19015;
Title Tel # (610) 872-6727
Personnel: Publisher, Editor-Illy Sobel, Copy Editor-Robert Goldberg, Asst. Ed.-Irene Evangelista, Art
Dir.-Karl Sobel
Editorial Description: Electric vehicles--technical and marketing.
General Info: Yr. Est. 1993, Monthly

Electric Vehicle News
See: TRAFFIC & TRANSPORTATION

Electric Vehicle Progress   *Business*

Publishing Co: Alexander Research & Communications, Inc., 215 Park Ave S., Ste. 1301, New York,
NY 10003-1603; Title Tel # (212) 228-0246 Title Fax # (212) 228-0376
Personnel: Publisher-Shirley Alexander, Editor-Laurence Alexander, Mng. Editor-Paul Braus, Circ.
Mgr.-Mary Pagliaroli, Mktg. Dir.-Margaret DeWitt
Editorial Description: Provides in-depth news, data and information on worldwide electric vehicle
commercialization. Not only is EV & hybrid news covered in EVP but detail specifications are
presented along with news of research & development, demonstration projects, new vehicles, news
of component manufactures, interviews, on-the-spot reports & analyses, technical news & project
developments & news of business and governmen
General Info: Yr. Est. 1979, Semi-monthly, 8 pages, ISSN: 0190-4175
Subscriptions: Indv. $397, Can. $397, For. $427, $17/copy
List Rental: Rents Lists

Employment Trends
See: EMPLOYMENT

English Channel   *Association, Consumer*

Publishing Co: Vintage Triumph Register Inc., 15218 W Warren Ave, Dearborn, MI 48126-1356
Personnel: Circ. Mgr.-Don Kennedy, Publisher, Editor, Production Mgr.-Linda Sohl, Adv. Dir.-Bill Sohl
Editorial Description: Dedicated to the history, preservation and enjoyment of Triumph automobiles.
General Info: Yr. Est. 1974, Bi-monthly, Trim Size-8½ x 11, Offset press, 8 pages, 4% ads, No
Color, Newsprint
Subscriptions: Indv. $20, $3/copy
Circulation: (55% controlled), Total-14,000, Subscriptions-4,000, International-200
Advertising: Inquire for rates.
Printing Co: Lloyd Waters & Assoc., 15218 W Warren Ave, Dearborn, MI 48126-1356
Tel # (313) 584-2777

Enviro-Compliance
Update   *Business*

Publishing Co: WD&S Publishing, 20 Highland Ave, Metuchen, NJ 08840-1949 Tel # (908) 548-4440
Fax # (908) 603-0690
Personnel: Publisher-James Muntz, Editor-Loriann Fell, Circ. Mgr.-Mary Ruchalski
Editorial Description: Environmental regulation and enforcement for vehicle repair facilities.
General Info: Yr. Est. 1990, Monthly, Trim Size-8½ x 11, 4 pages, 2 Color, Matte
Subscriptions: Indv. $148
List Rental: Actives: 3,000, $125/M, Expires: 2,200, $115/M

European Automotive
Bulletin   *Business*

Publishing Co: Forecast International/DMS, Inc., 22 Commerce Rd., Newtown, CT 06470-1643
Tel # (203) 426-0800 Fax # (203) 426-1964; Title Tel # (203) 426-1964 Title Fax # (203) 426-4262
General Info: Monthly
Subscriptions: Indv. $595

FDA Newsletter   *Business, Association*

Publishing Co: Ford Dealers Alliance, Continental Plaza, 401 Hackensack Ave., Hackensack, NJ
07601; Title Tel # (201) 342-4542 Title Fax # (201) 342-3997
Editorial Description: Info for Ford and Lincoln-Continental dealers.
General Info: Monthly
Circulation: Total-6,000

Fast Track News -
Automotive Sales &
Production   *Business*

Publishing Co: Integrated Automotive Resources, 4 Polly Drummond Hill Rd, Newark, DE
19711-5703; Title Tel # (302) 368-2700 Title Fax # (302) 368-6099
Personnel: Publisher-Thomas O'Grady, Production Mgr.-Hitomi Matsuda, Mktg. Dir.-Ann Lake
Editorial Description: Comprehensive, detailed, sales and production statistics. Analysis based on
developing events in the automotive industry.
General Info: Yr. Est. 1989, 60x/yr.
Subscriptions: Indv. $448, $15/copy

Financial Insight   *Association*

Publishing Co: MEMA-Motor & Equipment Manufacturers Assn., PO Box 13966, Rtp, NC
27709-3966 Tel # (919) 549-4800 Fax # (919) 549-4824
Personnel: Publisher-J. J. Conner
Editorial Description: Financial & customer credit information & analysis for automotive
manufacturers.
General Info: Monthly, Trim Size-8½ x 11, Sheetfed press, 4 pages, Color-cover, Newsprint
Circulation: (100% controlled), Total-1,000

Fish Facts

Publishing Co: Marlin Owners Club, Box 187, RD 5, Coatesville, PA 19320-4142;
Title Tel # (215) 383-4664
Personnel: Editor-Donald Siver, Circ. Mgr.-Don Siver
General Info: Quarterly
Circulation: Total-300

Fixed Coverage - Parts & Service Profit Report   *Business*

Publishing Co: WD&S Publishing, 20 Highland Ave, Metuchen, NJ 08840-1949 Tel # (908) 548-4440 Fax # (908) 603-0690
Personnel: Publisher-James Muntz, Editor-Loriann Fell, Circ. Mgr.-Mary Ruchalski, Production Mgr.-Ruth Grose
Editorial Description: Management/marketing reports for the service director at new car dealerships.
General Info: Yr. Est. 1985, Monthly, Trim Size-8½ x 11, 8 pages, ISSN: 1084-3272, 2 Color
Subscriptions: Indv. $207
Circulation: Total-3,000
List Rental: Actives: 3,400, $135/M, Hotline: $110/M, Expires: 2,400, $1,100/M

For Vettes Only

Publishing Co: Natl. Corvette Owner's Assn., Box 777-A, Falls Church, VA 22046-9860; Title Tel # (703) 533-7222 Title Fax # (703) 533-1153
Editorial Description: Membership 12,000. Dues 35.00 per year. Publishes monthly newsletter. Recognizes 1953 to present Corvettes only. Purpose is to bring Corvette owners together to qualify for group benefits.
General Info: (Formerly National Corvette Owners Assn. Newsletter), Yr. Est. 1975, Monthly, Trim Size-11 x 8.5, 12 pages, ISSN: 124-890
Acquistions: Publication Bought
Circulation: Total-12,000
List Rental: Rents Lists

Galaxie Gazette   *Consumer, Association*

Publishing Co: Ford Galaxie Club of America, PO Box 360, Salkum, WA 98582-0360; Title Tel # (360) 985-7675
Editorial Description: Encourages the enjoyment of the Galaxie (Ford) auto.
General Info: 8x/yr.
Circulation: Total-593

Good Guys, The

Publishing Co: Automatic Transmission Rebuilders Assn., 2472 Eastman Ave Ste 23, Ventura, CA 93003-5776; Title Tel # (805) 654-1700
Personnel: Editor-Garnet Lewis
Editorial Description: Articles of interest to the transmission rebuilding industry, featuring technical and management issues.
General Info: Yr. Est. 1972, Monthly, 8 pages
Circulation: Total-3,200
List Rental: List Management Co.: Name-Finders Lists, Inc., 3180 18th St Fl 2, San Francisco, CA 94110-2028 Tel # (510) 533-4177, Fax # (510) 553-8677, Actives: 1,850,951, $65/M

H.A.C. News   *Consumer, Association*   **CPM: $28**

Publishing Co: Hamilton Automobile Club, 393 Main St. E., Hamilton, ON L8N 3T7 Canada; Title Tel # (905) 525-1210
Personnel: Publisher-Richard Congdon, Editor-Leo Laviolette
Editorial Description: Reports on club activities as well as taking positions on matters of legistlation & taxation, giving consumer, technical and legal advice, providing tips & advice on auto and travel agency activities.
General Info: Yr. Est. 1956, Bi-monthly, Trim Size-8½ x 11, Web press, 12 pages, 4 Color, Coated, Saddle-stitched
Circulation: (100% controlled), Total-110,000
Advertising: $3,125. Accepts Inserts.

IEEE Vehicular Technology Society News
See: ENGINEERING

Impact: A Journal of Safety Litigation and News   *Business, Scholarly*

Publishing Co: Center for Auto Safety, 2001 S St NW Ste 410, Washington, DC 20009-1160; Title Tel # (202) 328-7700
Personnel: Editor-Irene Nagaraj
Editorial Description: Reports on auto and highway safety projects. Also covers recalls, federal investigations, secret warranties, Lemon Laws, defects, litigation, and more.
General Info: Yr. Est. 1975, Bi-monthly, ISSN: 0162-4989
Subscriptions: Indv. $75, Inst. $75, Can. $90, For. $90, $10/copy

Imported Car Reports   *Business, Consumer*

Publishing Co: United Communications Group, 11300 Rockville Pike, Ste. 1100, Rockville, MD 20852-3030 Tel # (301) 816-8950 Fax # (301) 816-8945; Title Tel # (313) 851-1377
Personnel: Publisher, Editor-Maynard Gordon
General Info: Yr. Est. 1945, Weekly
Subscriptions: Indv. $85
List Rental: Rents Lists

In Brief   *Business, Association*

Publishing Co: Automotive Parts and Accessories Assn., 4600 E.W. Hwy., Ste. 300, Bethesda, MD 20814; Title Tel # (301) 654-6664 Title Fax # (301) 654-3299
Personnel: Editor-John Reilly
Editorial Description: Newsletter summarizing events in the automotive after market.
General Info: (Formerly APAA Government Affairs Report), Quarterly
Subscriptions: Free With Membership
Circulation: Total-1,850

In the Fast Lane

Publishing Co: International Camaro Club, 2001 Pittston Ave, Scranton, PA 18505-3233; Title Tel # (717) 585-4082
Personnel: Editor-D.M. Crispino, Adv. Dir.-Bob DeSandis
Editorial Description: For all Camaro Enthusiasts. Camaro History-Tech-How-To's-etc. Pace car registry. We have noe added a registry for all big block 1967-69 camaros.
General Info: Yr. Est. 1984, Bi-monthly, Trim Size-8½ x 11, 20 pages
Subscriptions: Indv. $20, Can. $25, For. $35
Circulation: Total-2,000
Advertising: Inquire for rates. Accepts Inserts.

Inside IVHS: Intelligent Vehicle/Highway Systems Update
See: TRAFFIC & TRANSPORTATION

Intelligent Highway, The
See: TRAFFIC & TRANSPORTATION

International Ford Retractable Club, Inc.   *Association*

Publishing Co: Intl. Ford Retractable Club, Inc., PO Box 389, Marlborough, MA 01752-0389
Personnel: Editor, Adv. Dir.-Joyce Moore
Editorial Description: Information relating to the preservation and restoration of '57-'59 Ford retractable hardtop automobiles.
General Info: Yr. Est. 1971, Monthly, Trim Size-8½ x 11, Sheetfed press, 28 pages, 1% ads, 2 Color
Subscriptions: Indv. $22, $2/copy
Circulation: Total-1,500
Advertising: Inquire for rates.

International Insight   *Association*

Publishing Co: MEMA-Motor & Equipment Manufacturers Assn., PO Box 13966, Rtp, NC 27709-3966 Tel # (919) 549-4800 Fax # (919) 549-4824
Personnel: Publisher-J. J. Conner
Editorial Description: International marketing information for automotive manufacturers.
General Info: Trim Size-8½ x 11, Offset press, 2 Color
Circulation: Total-1,000

Japan Automotive Insights   *Business, Association*

Publishing Co: MEMA-Motor & Equipment Manufacturers Assn., PO Box 13966, Rtp, NC 27709-3966 Tel # (919) 549-4800 Fax # (919) 549-4824
Personnel: Publisher-James Conner, Editor-John Creamer
Editorial Description: Summary of marketing, technical/production developments and plans relating to Japanese vehicle builders and parts manufacturers. Economic and political developments which may impact U.S. manufacturers of automotive products. Prepared by MEMA administered U.S. automotive parts industry, Japan Office.
General Info: Yr. Est. 1986, Monthly, Trim Size-8½ x 11, Sheetfed press, 2 Color, Matte
Subscriptions: Indv. $350, Can. $375, For. $375
Circulation: Total-2,400

Japan Transportation Scan

Publishing Co: Kyodo News Intl., 50 Rockefeller Plaza #803, New York, NY 10020-1605; Title Tel # (212) 397-3723 Title Fax # (212) 397-3721
Editorial Description: Information on the automotive industry of Japan as well as other transportation news.
General Info: Yr. Est. 1988, Weekly

Leaf, The   *Business, Association*

Publishing Co: Suspension Specialists Assn., 4015 Marks Rd., Ste. 2B, Median, OH 44256 Fax # (216) 723-7359; Title Tel # (216) 725-7160
Editorial Description: Published by & for members of SSA.
General Info: Yr. Est. 1981, Monthly
Circulation: Total-500

Lemon Times   *Consumer*

Publishing Co: Center for Auto Safety, 2001 S St NW Ste 410, Washington, DC 20009-1160; Title Tel # (202) 328-7700
Personnel: Editor-Irene Nagaraj
Editorial Description: Newsletter covering automobile safety and other consumer issues.
General Info: Quarterly, Trim Size-8½ x 11, 4 pages, Matte
Subscriptions: Indv. $15, Inst. $15, $1/copy
Circulation: (100% controlled), Total-14,000

Lindens Lines

Publishing Co: General Motors Corp. Linden Assembly, 1016 W Edgar Rd, Linden, NJ 07036-6522; Title Tel # (908) 474-4877
Personnel: Editor-Paul Makuch
Editorial Description: A comprehensive publication covering the auto industry on a corporate level.
General Info: (Formerly Newsmobile), Yr. Est. 1985, Bi-monthly, Trim Size-8½ x 11, Web press, 12 pages, 4 Color, Coated, Saddle-stitched
Circulation: (100% controlled), Total-6,500
Printing Co: Quality Graphics, 262 W 1st Ave, Roselle, NJ 07203-1102 Tel # (908) 245-7300

MACS ACTION!   *Association*

Publishing Co: Mobile Air Conditioning Society, Inc., PO Box 97, East Greenville, PA 18041-0097; Title Tel # (215) 679-2220 Title Fax # (215) 541-4635
Personnel: Editor-Elvis Hoffpauir, Asst. Ed.-Amy Kline
General Info: Yr. Est. 1985, Bi-monthly, Trim Size-8½ x 11, Desktop press, 8 pages, 2 Color, Saddle-stitched
Subscriptions: Free
Circulation: Total-1,300

MACS Service Reports   *Association*

Publishing Co: Mobile Air Conditioning Society, Inc., PO Box 97, East Greenville, PA 18041-0097; Title Tel # (215) 679-2220 Title Fax # (215) 541-4635
Personnel: Editor-Elvis Hoffpauir, Asst. Ed.-Amy Kline
General Info: Yr. Est. 1981, Monthly, Trim Size-8½ x 11, Desktop press, 8 pages, Saddle-stitched
Subscriptions: Indv. $70, Free
Circulation: Total-1,300

Market Analysis   *Association*

Publishing Co: MEMA-Motor & Equipment Manufacturers Assn., PO Box 13966, Rtp, NC 27709-3966; Title Tel # (919) 549-4800 Title Fax # (919) 549-4824
Editorial Description: Items & interest on the automotive products market: Consumers, distribution channels, Etc. Most taken from more extensive market Studies.
General Info: Yr. Est. 1983, Bi-monthly, Letrpr. press, 16 pages, 2 Color
Subscriptions: Free With Membership
List Rental: Rents Lists

Marketing Insight   *Association*

Publishing Co: MEMA-Motor & Equipment Manufacturers Assn., PO Box 13966, Rtp, NC 27709-3966 Fax # (919) 549-4824; Title Tel # (919) 549-4800 Title Fax # (919) 549-4810
Personnel: Publisher-J. J. Conner
Editorial Description: Marketing developments, ideas and research for automotive and truck product manufacturers.
General Info: Trim Size-8½ x 11, Sheetfed press, Color

Maryland Motorist   *Association*

Publishing Co: American Automobile Association of Maryland, 1401 W Mt Royal Ave, Baltimore, MD 21217-4245; Title Tel # (410) 462-4000
Personnel: Publisher-Wm. Bass, Jr., Editor-William Zorzi
Editorial Description: Contains information on economical operation, safety and legislative events affecting the motorist.
General Info: Yr. Est. 1910, 7x/yr., Web press, 4 pages, 2 Color
Subscriptions: Indv. $1
Circulation: Total-210,000

Megazine

Publishing Co: J.D. Power & Assocs., 30401 Agoura Rd., Agoura Hills, CA 91301-2084; Title Tel # (818) 889-6330 Title Fax # (818) 889-3719
Personnel: Publisher-David Whiteside, Editor-John Rettie
General Info: Yr. Est. 1987, Monthly
Subscriptions: Indv. $495

Mighty Mopars   *Consumer, Association*   CPM: $266

Publishing Co: MOPAR Scat Pack Club, PO Box 2303, Dearborn, MI 48123-2303 Tel # (313) 278-2240; Title Tel # (313) 563-5974
Personnel: Editor-Jim Bielenda
Editorial Description: Covers recreation and preservation of Chrysler high performance vehicles.
General Info: (Formerly News from Scat City), Yr. Est. 1981, Bi-monthly, Trim Size-8½ x 11, 10 pages, 10% ads, Matte
Subscriptions: Indv. $25
Circulation: Total-750, Readership-750
Advertising: $200. Accepts Inserts.

Mile Post
See: HOBBY

Minor News   *Association*   CPM: $133

Publishing Co: Morris Minor Registry of North America, 318 Hampton Park, Westerville, OH 43081-5723; Title Tel # (614) 899-2394 Title Fax # (614) 899-2394
Personnel: Editor-Tony Burgess
Editorial Description: Morris Minor automobile use and restoration.
General Info: (Formerly Morris Minor Gram), Yr. Est. 1975, Bi-monthly, Trim Size-8½ x 11, Sheetfed press, 12 pages, 8% ads, No Color, Coated
Subscriptions: Indv. $20, Can. $20, For. $30
Circulation: Total-750, Readership-1,500
Advertising: $100.

Mobilia   *Consumer*

Publishing Co: Hyatt Research Corp., PO Box 575, Middlebury, VT 05753-0575; Title Tel # (802) 545-2510 Title Fax # (802) 545-2543
Editorial Description: Covers the full range of auto art and collectibles.
General Info: Yr. Est. 1993, Monthly, Trim Size-8½ x 11, Web press, 80 pages, 40% ads, Color-cover, Coated, Saddle-stitched
Subscriptions: Indv. $29, Can. $67, For. $67, $4/copy
Advertising: Inquire for rates.

Motor News Analysis   *Business*

Publishing Co: United Communications Group, 11300 Rockville Pike, Ste. 1100, Rockville, MD 20852-3030 Tel # (301) 816-8950 Fax # (301) 816-8945; Title Tel # (301) 961-8700 Title Fax # (301) 961-8666
Personnel: Publisher-David Rhode, Editor-Maynard Gordon, Circ. Mgr.-Sharon Welch
Editorial Description: Newsletter interpreting automotive marketing and product developments U.S. and worldwide.
General Info: Yr. Est. 1945, Bi-weekly, Trim Size-8½ x 11, Offset press, 4 pages, ISSN: 0027-1942, 2 Color, Newsprint
Subscriptions: Indv. $145, $4/copy
Circulation: Total-3,000
Advertising: Inquire for rates.
List Rental: Rents Lists
Printing Co: Zip Printing, Inc., 28631 Southfield Rd, Lathrup Village, MI 48076-2795 Tel # (313) 559-2230

Motor Vehicle & Traffic Laws of New Jersey

Publishing Co: Gould Publications, Inc, 1333 N US Highway 17-92, Longwood, FL 32750-3724 Tel # (407) 695-9500 Fax # (407) 695-2906; Title Tel # (607) 724-3000
Editorial Description: Book. Supplemented annually at additional cost. Presentation of Title 39 of the New Jersey Statutes.
General Info: Annually, Trim Size-5½ x 8½, Sheetfed press, 400 pages, No Color, Looseleaf
Subscriptions: $17/copy

Motor Vehicle Regulation/ State Capitals   *Business, Consumer*

Publishing Co: Wakeman/Walworth, 300 N. Washington St., Alexandria, VA 22314-2530; Title Tel # (703) 549-8606 Title Fax # (703) 549-1372
Personnel: Publisher-Keyes Walworth
Editorial Description: Roundup of state laws & regulations regarding vehicle safety, inspections, licensing, etc.
General Info: (Formerly Motor Vehicle Regulation from the State Capitals), Yr. Est. 1946, Weekly, 4 pages, ISSN: 0016-1810
Subscriptions: Indv. $265, Inst. $212, Can. $235, For. $255

Motorcycle Business Newsletter
See: CYCLING-BICYCLE & MOTOR

Motorist's Advocate, The

Publishing Co: Canadian Automobile Association, 1775 Courtwood Cr., Ottawa, ON K2C 3J2 Canada; Title Tel # (613) 226-7631 Title Fax # (613) 225-7383
Personnel: Editor-David Leonhardt
Editorial Description: Each edition focuses on a timely topic of import to motorists across Canada, including the presentation of facts, options & CAA views.
General Info: (Formerly Public Policy), Yr. Est. 1981, Semi-annually, 12 pages, Color-cover

Motorsports Marketing Sponsorship News
See: ADVERTISING & MARKETING

NAFA Fleet Focus   *Association*

Publishing Co: National Association of Fleet Administrators, Inc, 120 Wood Ave S Ste 615, Iselin, NJ 08830-2709; Title Tel # (908) 494-8100 Title Fax # (908) 494-6789
Personnel: Editor-Denise Rucci, Production Mgr.-Josephine Tropeano
Editorial Description: Current events pertaining to fleet managers.
General Info: (Formerly NAFA Newsletter), Yr. Est. 1962, Monthly, Trim Size-8½ x 11, Web press, 6 pages, 2 Color, Matte, Saddle-stitched
Subscriptions: Free With Membership
Circulation: Total-4,000
Printing Co: B & R Photo Offset Printers, 211 Stokes Ave, Trenton, NJ 08638-3729 Tel # (609) 882-9270, Fax # (609) 882-9660

NAPA News   *Association*

Publishing Co: National Automotive Parts Assn., 2999 Circle 75 Pky. NW, Atlanta, GA 30339-3050; Title Tel # (404) 956-2200 Title Fax # (770) 956-2212
Personnel: Editor-Kathy Randall
Editorial Description: Repair, maintenance, installation, diagnostics how-to-do-it articles for the professional service repairman & do-it-yourselfer.
General Info: Yr. Est. 1962, Trim Size-11 x 13½, Offset press, 12 pages, No Color, Newsprint
Circulation: (100% controlled), Total-400,000

NTDRA Hotline   *Association*

Publishing Co: National Tire Dealers and Retreaders Assn., 1250 I St NW Ste 400, Washington, DC 20005-3922; Title Tel # (202) 789-2300 Title Fax # (202) 682-3999
General Info: Monthly

NTDRA Membergram   *Association*

Publishing Co: National Tire Dealers and Retreaders Assn., 1250 I St NW Ste 400, Washington, DC 20005-3922; Title Tel # (202) 789-2300 Title Fax # (202) 682-3999
Personnel: Editor-C.D. Hylton
Editorial Description: Assn. newsletter.
General Info: Monthly, ISSN: 0744-5676

Neckarsulm News

Publishing Co: NSU Enthusiasts USA, 11192 Prouty Rd, Concord, OH 44077-2318; Title Tel # (216) 354-4403 Title Fax # (216) 354-4403
Personnel: Publisher, Editor-Terry Stuchlik
Editorial Description: Member news. Includes technical tips and meet information.
General Info: Yr. Est. 1971, Quarterly, Sheetfed press, 10 pages, 2% ads, No Color
Advertising: Inquire for rates.

Newsletter

Publishing Co: General Motors Corp., Boxwood & Dodson Rds., Wilmington, DE 19899
Personnel: Editor-Alice Petitt
General Info: Trim Size-8½ x 11, Color-cover, Coated
Acquistions: Publication Bought

Newsletter of Engineering Analysis Software
See: ENGINEERING

No-Fault and Uninsured Motorist Automobile Insurance
See: LAW

Northeastern Limousine Operators Association Nor'Easter Newsletter
See: TRAFFIC & TRANSPORTATION

Northern Lights (Minneapolis)
See: ANTIQUES & ART GOODS

Nutz & Boltz   *Consumer*

Publishing Co: Nutz & Boltz, PO Box 123, Butler, MD 21023-0123; Title Tel # (410) 584-7574 Title Fax # (410) 584-1054
Personnel: Publisher-David Solomon, Editor, Exec. Ed.-Alan Elman, Photo Ed.-Bonnie Buddie, Circ. Mgr.-Vernon D. Duff, Production Mgr.-Susan Snyder, Art Dir.-William Schwartz
Editorial Description: Information on auto maintenance, repair, purchase, ripoffs, and trends.
General Info: Yr. Est. 1988, Monthly, Trim Size-8½ x 11, Offset press, 16 pages, ISSN: 1076-514X, 2 Color, Matte, Saddle-stitched
Subscriptions: Indv. $25, Can. $35, For. $45, $3/copy
Circulation: Total-5,000

Octane Week
See: PETROLEUM & NATURAL GAS

PBC Auto Briefs   *Business, Consumer*

Publishing Co: Publishing & Business Consultants, 101 W. 64th St. Unit #3, Inglewood, CA 90302-1255 Tel # (213) 732-3477 Fax # (213) 732-3477
Personnel: Publisher, Editor-Andeson Atia
General Info: Quarterly, ISSN: 1059-2983
Subscriptions: Indv. $180
Advertising: Inquire for rates.

Performance Warehouse
Association Newsletter   *Business*

Publishing Co: Performance Warehouse Association, 21311 Hawthorne Blvd., Torrance, CA 90503-5610; Title Tel # (619) 943-9500
Personnel: Circ. Mgr.-Jamie Boldt, Publisher, Editor, Adv. Dir.-John Duke, Art Dir.-Willie Loman
Editorial Description: Information pertaining to the wholesale distribution of automotive aftermarket products.
General Info: Monthly, Trim Size-8½ x 11, Offset press, 20 pages, No Color
Subscriptions: Indv. $15, $1/copy
Circulation: Total-425
Advertising: Inquire for rates.

Pierce-Arrow Service
Bulletin   *Association*

Publishing Co: Pierce-Arrow Society, Inc., 135 Edgerton St, Rochester, NY 14607-2945
Personnel: Editor-Bernard Weis
Editorial Description: Technical information relating to restoration & operation of Pierce-Arrows.
General Info: Yr. Est. 1966, Bi-monthly, Trim Size-8½ x 11, Mimeo press, 10 pages, No Color
Subscriptions: Indv. $25, $1/copy
Circulation: Total-1,100

Poly Probe
See: METALS & METALWORKING

Porsche Market Letter   *Business*

Publishing Co: Porsche Market Letter, PO Box 54679, Oklahoma City, OK 73154-1679; Title Tel # (405) 524-7880 Title Fax # (405) 524-8193
Personnel: Publisher-John Hoke, Editor-Kevin Barnes
Editorial Description: An intl. pub. listing Porsche automobiles (new & used) for sale in the U.S. Also offers recommendations for medels most likely to appreciate in value, current market conditions & much more.
General Info: Yr. Est. 1982, Monthly, Trim Size-8½ x 11, Sheetfed press, 12 pages, No Color
Subscriptions: Indv. $40, $5/copy
Advertising: $100.

Porsche Uber Alles

Publishing Co: Porsche Club of America, Western Michigan Region, 1503 43rd St SW, Wyoming, MI 49509-4342 Tel # (616) 942-8577
Personnel: Editor-Bob Clark
General Info: 10x/yr.
Subscriptions: Indv. $5

Power Builders   *Business*

Publishing Co: General Motors Corp., G3248 Van Slyke Rd, Flint, MI 48552-0001; Title Tel # (313) 236-4300
Personnel: Editor-Pete Ternes
Editorial Description: Flint Engine Plant newsletter for employees.
General Info: Semi-weekly, Trim Size-8½ x 11, Mimeo press, 2 pages
Circulation: Total-1,000

Power Report on
Automotive Marketing   *Business*

Publishing Co: J.D. Power & Assocs., 30401 Agoura Rd., Agoura Hills, CA 91301-2084; Title Tel # (818) 889-6330 Title Fax # (818) 889-3719
Personnel: Publisher-J.D. Power, III, Editor-Rita Pulaski
General Info: Yr. Est. 1979, Weekly, Trim Size-8½ x 11, Offset press, 4 pages
Subscriptions: Indv. $295
Circulation: Total-300

RADAR   *Consumer*

Publishing Co: R.A.D.A.R., 4949 S. 25A, Tipp City, OH 45371; Title Tel # (513) 667-5472
Personnel: Editor-Janice Lee
Editorial Description: Drivers' rights. Informs members of radar, radar detector & transportation issues.
General Info: Monthly
Subscriptions: Indv. $29, Can. $39, For. $39
Circulation: Total-16,000

RepTalk   *Business, Association*

Publishing Co: Automotive Parts and Accessories Assn., 4600 E.W. Hwy., Ste. 300, Bethesda, MD 20814; Title Tel # (301) 654-6664 Title Fax # (301) 654-3299
Personnel: Publisher-Susan Medick, Editor-John Reilly
General Info: (Formerly APAA Report; APAA Newsletter), Monthly
Subscriptions: Free To Qualified Recipient
Circulation: Total-500

Research Insight   *Association*

Publishing Co: MEMA-Motor & Equipment Manufacturers Assn., PO Box 13966, Rtp, NC 27709-3966 Tel # (919) 549-4800 Fax # (919) 549-4824
Editorial Description: Management research and survey information for automotive manufacturers.
General Info: Trim Size-8½ x 11, Offset press, Color

Retiree Roundup
See: HOUSE ORGANS

Roadrunner

Publishing Co: General Motors Corp., Box 10100, GM Desert Proving Ground, Mesa, AZ 85216-0100; Title Tel # (602) 827-5348
Personnel: Editor-Phyllis Typer
General Info: Bi-monthly, Trim Size-8½ x 11, 8 pages
Circulation: Total-500

Rolling   CPM: $116

Publishing Co: Volvo Club of America, PO Box 16, Afton, NY 13730-0016; Title Tel # (607) 639-2279 Title Fax # (607) 639-2279
Personnel: Editor-William Van Allen, Adv. Dir.-Mark Downing
Editorial Description: Provides historical & technical items about Volvo autos from 1930's to present.
General Info: Yr. Est. 1983, Bi-monthly, Trim Size-8½ x 11, Web press, 24 pages, 1% ads, Color-cover, Coated, Saddle-stitched
Subscriptions: Indv. $25, $5/copy
Circulation: Total-3,000
Advertising: $350.
List Rental: Actives: $100/M
Printing Co: C.R. Waldman Graphic Communications, 9100 Pennsauken Highway, CN-90239, Pennsauken, NJ Tel # (609) 662-9111, Fax # (609) 665-1789

Rolls-Royce/Bentley
Marketletter

Publishing Co: Mary Ann Liebert, Inc., 1651 3rd Ave, New York, NY 10128-3649; Title Tel # (212) 289-2300
Editorial Description: Extensive listings of cars for sale or trade. It meets the need expressed by hundreds of buyers, sellers, & collectors of Rolls-Royce & Bentley automobiles.
General Info: Yr. Est. 1987, Monthly, ISSN: 1041-1127
Subscriptions: Indv. $53

Rough Rider

Publishing Co: Morgan Car Club of Washington DC, Inc., 616 Gist Ave., Silver Spring, MO 20910-5232; Title Tel # (301) 585-0121
Personnel: Editor-Ed Zielinski
Editorial Description: Provides news & info for those who own Morgan Cars.
General Info: Yr. Est. 1959, Monthly
Subscriptions: Indv. $25
Circulation: Total-350, Readership-600

Runzheimer on Cars & Living Costs
See: ECONOMICS

SAE Update   *Business*

Publishing Co: Society of Automotive Engineers, Inc., 400 Commonwealth Dr., Warrendale, PA 15096-0001 Fax # (412) 776-4026; Title Tel # (412) 776-4841 Title Fax # (412) 776-2103
Personnel: Editor-Martha B. Swiss
General Info: Yr. Est. 1984, Monthly, Trim Size-11½ x 15, Web press, 12 pages, ISSN: 0742-972X, Newsprint
Subscriptions: Indv. $2
Circulation: Total-51,000
Advertising: Inquire for rates.
Printing Co: Gateway Press Co., 610 Beatty Rd, Monroeville, PA 15146-1502 Tel # (412) 321-4209

Self-Starter, The   *Association*

Publishing Co: Cadillac la Salle Club, Inc., 223 S. Fairfield Rd., Devon, PA 19333-1630
Personnel: Editor-Ansel Sackett
Editorial Description: Contains general and technical information about Cadillac and laSalle autos.
General Info: Yr. Est. 1958, Monthly, Trim Size-8½ x 11, 28 pages
Subscriptions: Indv. $25, Can. $33, For. $35, $3/copy
Circulation: Total-5,000
Printing Co: Oakland Publishing, 1100 N. Opdyke, Auburn Hills, MI 48057 Tel # (313) 373-8400

Shop Management Handbook

Publishing Co: Automotive Engine Rebuilders Assn., 330 Lexington Dr, Buffalo Grove, IL 60089-6933; Title Tel # (708) 541-6550 Title Fax # (708) 541-5808
Personnel: Editor-Joe Polich
Editorial Description: Management handbook for machine shop operators.
General Info: (Formerly Shop Management Bulletin), Monthly, ISSN: 0318-6237, Looseleaf
Subscriptions: Indv. $54
Circulation: Total-3,500

Shop Procedure Bulletin

Publishing Co: Automotive Engine Rebuilders Assn., 330 Lexington Dr, Buffalo Grove, IL 60089-6933; Title Tel # (708) 541-6550 Title Fax # (708) 541-5808
Personnel: Editor-Joe Polich
Editorial Description: Bulletin for machinists & shop managers describing machining of engine components.
General Info: Yr. Est. 1971, Monthly, Looseleaf

Shop Talk   *Association*

Publishing Co: Automotive Engine Rebuilders Assn., 330 Lexington Dr, Buffalo Grove, IL 60089-6933; Title Tel # (708) 541-6550 Title Fax # (708) 541-5808
Personnel: Editor-Jennifer Holton, Art Dir.-Angela Dunn
Editorial Description: Assn. & industry newsletter.
General Info: (Formerly AERA News Bulletin), Monthly, Offset press, 8 pages, 2 Color
Circulation: Total-4,300

ShopTalk   *Business*

Publishing Co: Modine Mfg. Co., 1500 De Koven Ave, Racine, WI 53403-2540; Title Tel # (414) 636-1200 Title Fax # (414) 636-1424
Personnel: Publisher-Dale Roble, Editor-Cynthia Mackin
Editorial Description: Newsletter for radiator repair professionals who work in radiator shops or service stations. Car & truck radiator repair tips, techniques and new products features in each issue.
General Info: Yr. Est. 1970, Quarterly, Sheetfed press, 4 pages, Saddle-stitched
Circulation: Total-16,000
Printing Co: Account Manager: Jim Dobvzynski; Crossmark Graphics, 6009 S Kingan Ave, Cudahy, WI 53110-3036

Show Stopper

Publishing Co: International Show Car Assn., 8667 Georgia Ave, Silver Spring, MD 20910-3475; Title Tel # (313) 588-5568 Title Fax # (810) 588-6007
Personnel: Editor-Bill Bosman, Publisher, Circ. Mgr.-Hayne Dominick, Art Dir.-Bill Bozman, Adv. Dir., Promotion Dir.-Kim Nye
Editorial Description: A car association report, with stories on shows, cars competing, technology, officials and current point standings.
General Info: Monthly, Trim Size-8⅜ x 10⅞, Web press, 32 pages, ISSN: 1053-9964, 2% ads, Coated, Saddle-stitched
Subscriptions: $3/copy
Circulation: Total-12,106
Advertising: Inquire for rates. Accepts Inserts.
List Rental: Rents Lists

Sign of the Cat

Publishing Co: Cougar Club of America, 5810 142nd Place SE, Bellevue, WA 98006-4318; Title Tel # (216) 356-1291
Editorial Description: Contains info about Cougar autos from 1967-1973.
General Info: Quarterly
Circulation: Total-700

Stark's Component Ledger   *Business*

Publishing Co: Stark Communications, Inc., 176 W. Adams St., Ste. 1932, Chicago, IL 60603-3610; Title Tel # (312) 236-5122 Title Fax # (312) 236-3297
Personnel: Publisher, Editor-John Stark, Circ. Mgr.-Mary H. Bieszk
Editorial Description: Production sales and inventories of gasoline engines, diesel engines, transmissions and axles for automotive industries.
General Info: Yr. Est. 1992, 24x/yr., 6 pages
Subscriptions: Indv. $570, Can. $570, For. $620

Sunbeam Tiger Owners Association -Newsletter

Publishing Co: Sunbeam Alpine Club, 1752 Oswald Pl, Santa Clara, CA 95051-3026; Title Tel # (408) 984-1474
General Info: Monthly
Circulation: Total-600

TADRA Newsbreak   *Association*   CPM: $440

Publishing Co: Texas Automotive Dismantlers & Recyclers Assn., 823 Congress Ave. #1300, Austin, TX 78701-2429; Title Tel # (512) 479-0425
Personnel: Editor-Lisa Fry
Editorial Description: Official publication of the Texas Automotive Dismantlers & Recyclers Assn. TADRA is an association of firms whose primary business is the dismantling of automobiles and/or trucks and the sale of parts from these vehicles.
General Info: (Formerly TATPA Newsbreak), Bi-monthly, Letrpr. press, 8 pages, 10% ads, No Color, Matte
Subscriptions: Free With Membership
Circulation: Total-250
Advertising: $110.
Printing Co: Austex Printing Co., 501 W 3rd St, Austin, TX 78701-3807 Tel # (512) 476-7581

TARA News & Topics   *Business, Association*

Publishing Co: Truck-Frame & Axle Repair Association, P.O Box 122, Adelphia, NJ 07710-0122 Tel # (908) 577-8485 Fax # (908) 577-9474; Title Tel # (718) 257-6133 Title Fax # (718) 272-9198
Personnel: Editor-Silvie Licitra
Editorial Description: Update in technical & management functions.
General Info: Yr. Est. 1966, Monthly, Trim Size-8½ x 11, Sheetfed press, 4 pages, No Color, Newsprint
Subscriptions: Free To Qualified Recipient
Circulation: Total-1,000

TMDA Newsletter   *Business, Association*   CPM: $550

Publishing Co: Texas Motorcycle Dealers Assn., 1601 Rio Grande St Ste 440, Austin, TX 78701-1149; Title Tel # (512) 479-0425
Personnel: Publisher, Editor-Lisa Fry
Editorial Description: Official publication of the Texas Motorcycle Dealers Association.
General Info: Bi-monthly, Letrpr. press, 8 pages, No Color, Matte
Subscriptions: Free With Membership
Circulation: Total-200
Advertising: $110.
Printing Co: Austex Printing Co., 501 W 3rd St, Austin, TX 78701-3807 Tel # (512) 476-7581

TP Plus   *Business*

Publishing Co: Trans 21, Fields Corner Station, Box 249, Boston, MA 02122; Title Tel # (617) 825-2318 Title Fax # (617) 482-7417
Personnel: Publisher, Editor-Lawrence J. Fabian
Editorial Description: Faxed notice of new projects and industry news.
General Info: Yr. Est. 1990, Bi-weekly, Trim Size-8½ x 11, 2 pages, No Color
Subscriptions: Indv. $375, Inst. $375, Can. $375, For. $425
Circulation: Total-504

Tadra Newsbreak   *Association*   CPM: $612

Publishing Co: Texas Automotive Dismantlers & Recyclers Assn., 823 Congress Ave. #1300, Austin, TX 78701-2429; Title Tel # (512) 479-0425
Personnel: Editor-Lisa Fry
Editorial Description: Official organ of Texas Automotive Dismantlers Recycler Association.
General Info: (Formerly Texas Journal), Bi-monthly, Trim Size-8½ x 11, Offset press, 8 pages, 20% ads, 2 Color, Matte
Subscriptions: Indv. $15, Free With Membership
Circulation: Total-400
Advertising: $245. Accepts Inserts.
Printing Co: Austex Printing Co., 501 W 3rd St, Austin, TX 78701-3807 Tel # (512) 476-7581

Today's Parts Manager   *Business*

Publishing Co: Management Computer Systems, 2790 Fisher Rd, Columbus, OH 43204-3581; Title Tel # (614) 272-0202
Editorial Description: Management topics for General Motors parts managers.
General Info: Bi-monthly

Torsion Bar

Publishing Co: Chrysler Product Owners Club, 5203 Edmonson Ave., Baltimore, MD 21229-2305
Personnel: Editor-Brian Scott
General Info: Monthly, Trim Size-8 x 11, 4 pages
Subscriptions: Indv. $8, For. $12
Circulation: Total-200

Traders' Horn
See: GIFTS, GAMES, TOYS

Tread Tips *Association*

Publishing Co: National Tire Dealers and Retreaders Assn., 1250 I St NW Ste 400, Washington, DC 20005-3922; Title Tel # (202) 638-6650 Title Fax # (202) 682-3999
General Info: Bi-monthly

Tucker Topics *Consumer*

Publishing Co: Sponsor-Tucker Automobile Club of America, Inc, PAF Associates, 8080 Dagger Street, San Diego, CA 92071-2326 Tel # (619) 576-3227; Title Tel # (619) 562-9644 Title Fax # (619) 573-0196
Personnel: Editor-Patricia Fortin, Circ. Mgr.-Richard Fortin, Editor, Adv. Dir., Promotion Dir.-William Pommering
General Info: Yr. Est. 1973, Monthly, Web press, 8 pages, ISSN: 0882-3782, No Color, Newsprint
Subscriptions: Indv. $25, $3/copy
Circulation: Total-750
Advertising: Inquire for rates. Accepts Inserts.
List Rental: Rents Lists
Printing Co: Rainier Press, 8057 16th Ave NE, Seattle, WA 98115-4365 Tel # (206) 526-1791, Fax # (206) 526-8921

Urban Transport News
See: TRAFFIC & TRANSPORTATION

Used Cars Insider *Business*

Publishing Co: United Communications Group, 11300 Rockville Pike, Ste. 1100, Rockville, MD 20852-3030 Tel # (301) 816-8950 Fax # (301) 816-8945; Title Tel # (212) 873-5900 Title Fax # (212) 799-1728
Personnel: Publisher-Beverley Walker, Editor-Tom Sullivan, Circ. Mgr.-Pamela Ortiz, Production Mgr.-Eladia Orellana, Art Dir.-Romeo Cloma, Promotion Dir.-Charles Antin
Editorial Description: Fortnightly newsletter for professionals in the used car sales business.
General Info: Yr. Est. 1983, Bi-weekly, Trim Size-7$\frac{1}{4}$ x 11, Sheetfed press, 8 pages, ISSN: 0148-6721, Newsprint
Subscriptions: Indv. $175, Can. $175, For. $205, $10/copy
Acquistions: Publication Bought
Circulation: Total-900
List Rental: Actives: $75/M, Hotline: $85/M

VVWCA Newsletter

Publishing Co: Vintage Volkswagen Club of America, 818 Main St, Portage, PA 15946-1717; Title Tel # (814) 736-4343
Personnel: Editor-Terry Shuler
Editorial Description: For those interested in Volkswagen automobiles.
General Info: Yr. Est. 1976, Monthly, 12 pages, No Color
Subscriptions: Indv. $20, Can. $25, For. $35
Circulation: Total-2,500
Advertising: Inquire for rates.

Wagons of Steel *Consumer*

Publishing Co: Wagons of Steel, PO Box 1435, Vashon, WA 98070-1435; Title Tel # (206) 463-5947
Personnel: Publisher-Gaffo Jones, Editor in Chief-Christopher Barnes, Circ. Dir.-Benjamin Barnes, Adv. Dir.-Spewy Smith, Art Dir.-Natalie Barnes
Editorial Description: Consumer advice, photographs, anecdotes, cartoons, relating to station wagons.
General Info: Yr. Est. 1991, Quarterly, Trim Size-4$\frac{1}{4}$ x 6, Desktop press, 60 pages, Color-cover
Subscriptions: Indv. $7, Inst. $50, Can. $8, For. $13, $2/copy

Ward's Automotive International *Business*

Publishing Co: Ward's Communications, 3000 Town Center, Ste. 2750, Southfield, MI 48075-1212 Tel # (810) 357-0800 Fax # (810) 357-0810 Parent Co.-Intertec Publishing Corporation, Overland Park; Title Tel # (313) 962-4433 Title Fax # (313) 962-4532
Personnel: Publisher-David Smith, Exec. VP/Group Publisher-Roger Powers, Editor-Dave Zola, Mng. Editor-Mark Phelan, Art Dir.-Dick Mayer
Editorial Description: Covers international automotive technology news and statistics for OEM executives, engineers, and suppliers.
General Info: Yr. Est. 1986, Bi-weekly, Trim Size-8$\frac{1}{2}$ x 11
Subscriptions: Indv. $430, Inst. $430, Can. $460, For. $460
Advertising: Inquire for rates.

Ward's Automotive Reports *Business*

Publishing Co: Ward's Communications, 3000 Town Center, Ste. 2750, Southfield, MI 48075-1212 Tel # (810) 357-0800 Fax # (810) 357-0810 Parent Co.-Intertec Publishing Corporation, Overland Park; Title Tel # (313) 962-4433 Title Fax # (313) 962-4532
Personnel: Publisher-David Smith, Editor-David Zola, Mng. Editor-Haig Stoddard
Editorial Description: Provides complete statistics and exclusive weekly news on the automotive industry.
General Info: Yr. Est. 1924, Weekly, 8 pages
Subscriptions: Indv. $950, Inst. $9,500, Can. $1,017, For. $1,000

Ward's Engine & Vehicle Technology Update *Business*

Publishing Co: Ward's Communications, 3000 Town Center, Ste. 2750, Southfield, MI 48075-1212 Parent Co.-Intertec Publishing Corporation, Overland Park; Title Tel # (810) 357-0800 Title Fax # (810) 357-0810
Personnel: Publisher-David Smith, Editor-David Zola, Mng. Editor-Bill Ulsnic, Art Dir.-Dick Mayer
Editorial Description: Covers the latest developments in engine design, powertrains, materials, chassis, electronics, and manufacturing.
General Info: (Formerly Ward's Wankel Report; Ward's Engine Update), Yr. Est. 1975, Bi-weekly, Trim Size-8$\frac{1}{2}$ x 10$\frac{1}{2}$, Sheetfed press, 8 pages, No Color
Subscriptions: Indv. $675, Inst. $675, Can. $722, For. $700

Warranty Dollars & Sense *Business*

Publishing Co: WD&S Publishing, 20 Highland Ave, Metuchen, NJ 08840-1949 Tel # (908) 548-4440; Title Fax # (908) 603-0690
Personnel: Publisher-James Muntz, Editor-Loriann Fell, Circ. Mgr.-Mary Ruchalski, Production Mgr.-Ruth Grose
Editorial Description: Issues and developments affecting GM & Ford dealers relations with the manufacturers.
General Info: Yr. Est. 1980, Semi-monthly, Trim Size-8$\frac{1}{2}$ x 11, 4 pages, 2 Color, Matte
Subscriptions: Indv. $297
List Rental: Actives: 3,000, $125/M, Expires: 2,200, $115/M

Washington Digest *Association*

Publishing Co: MEMA-Motor & Equipment Manufacturers Assn., PO Box 13966, Rtp, NC 27709-3966; Title Tel # (919) 549-4800 Title Fax # (919) 549-4824
Personnel: Publisher-J. J. Conner
Editorial Description: Contains legislative updates & late breaking Capitol Hill news for automotive product manufacturers.
General Info: Yr. Est. 1978, Bi-weekly, Trim Size-8$\frac{1}{2}$ x 11, Sheetfed press, 4 pages, Color, Newsprint

Western Automotive Report *Business*

Publishing Co: Sunset Publishing Corp., 80 Willow Rd, Menlo Park, CA 94025-3661 Fax # (415) 328-6215 Parent Co.-Time Inc. Ventures, New York; Title Tel # (415) 321-3600 Title Fax # (415) 321-0551
Personnel: Editor-Mark Hickling
Editorial Description: Circulated to new-car dealers in the 13 Western states.
General Info: Quarterly
Subscriptions: Free To Qualified Recipient
Circulation: (100% controlled), Total-4,700

Wild Rumpus

Publishing Co: Alana Kumbier, P.O. Box 4988, Springfield, MO 65808-4988
Editorial Description: The main feature here is Tim Manus' long and brutal apreciation of '60s -era muscle cars.
General Info: Trim Size-8.5 x 11, 14 pages
Subscriptions: Indv. $2

William Hardash Auction Newsletter
See: ART & SCULPTURE

Wiretapper *Business*

Publishing Co: General Motors Corp., PO Box 260, Clinton, MS 39060-0260; Title Tel # (601) 924-8109
Personnel: Editor-Danny Greene
Editorial Description: News relating to local plant, division, General Motors & auto industry.
General Info: Yr. Est. 1975, Monthly, Trim Size-10 x 14, Sheetfed press, 8 pages, 2 Color, Coated
Circulation: Total-1,800
Printing Co: Graphic Reproductions, 663 N State St, Jackson, MS 39202-3304 Tel # (601) 948-6478

Women with Wheels
See: WOMEN'S

World Automotive Alternative Energy & Fuels Bulletin *Business*

Publishing Co: Forecast International/DMS, Inc., 22 Commerce Rd., Newtown, CT 06470-1643 Fax # (203) 426-1964; Title Tel # (203) 426-0800 Title Fax # (203) 426-4262
General Info: Monthly
Subscriptions: Indv. $475

World Automotive Environment & Safety Bulletin
See: ENVIRONMENT & ECOLOGY

World Automotive Industry Weekly *Business*

Publishing Co: Forecast International/DMS, Inc., 22 Commerce Rd., Newtown, CT 06470-1643 Fax # (203) 426-1964; Title Tel # (203) 426-0800 Title Fax # (203) 426-4262
General Info: Weekly
Subscriptions: Indv. $995

World Automotive Materials & Components Bulletin
Business

Publishing Co: Forecast International/DMS, Inc., 22 Commerce Rd., Newtown, CT 06470-1643 Fax # (203) 426-1964; Title Tel # (203) 426-0800 Title Fax # (203) 426-4262
General Info: Monthly
Subscriptions: Indv. $475

World Automotive Technology Tracking
Business

Publishing Co: Forecast International/DMS, Inc., 22 Commerce Rd., Newtown, CT 06470-1643 Fax # (203) 426-1964; Title Tel # (203) 426-0800 Title Fax # (203) 426-4262
General Info: Monthly
Subscriptions: Indv. $475

BABY

ABDC Newsletter
See: HEALTH

Birth to Three
Consumer

Publishing Co: Birth to Three, 3875 Kincaid St # 15, Eugene, OR 97405-4554; Title Tel # (541) 484-4401 Title Fax # (541) 484-1449
Personnel: Editor-Sylvia Lee Hanley
Editorial Description: For parents of children birth to three.
General Info: (Formerly Birth to Three Newsletter), Yr. Est. 1978, Bi-monthly, Trim Size-8½ x 11, 20 pages, ISSN: 0895-6669, No Color
Subscriptions: Indv. $15, Inst. $20, $2/copy
Acquistions: Publication Bought
Circulation: Total-2,900
Advertising: Inquire for rates.
Printing Co: McKenzie-Williamette Hosp., 1460 G St, Springfield, OR 97477-4190 Tel # (503) 726-4400

Brown University Child and Adolescent Behavior Letter, The
See: CHILDREN

Bulletin of the NPA
Consumer, Association

Publishing Co: National Perinatal Assn., 3500 E. Flecher Ave. #209, Tampa, FL 33613-4712; Title Tel # (813) 971-1008 Title Fax # (913) 971-9306
Editorial Description: Health care issues involving pregnant women, fetus, & newborn.
General Info: (Formerly National Perinatal Association Newsletter), Yr. Est. 1977, Quarterly, Offset press, 12 pages, Saddle-stitched
Subscriptions: Indv. $15
Circulation: Total-1,300
List Rental: Actives: 1,300

CWPEA-Memo
Association

Publishing Co: Childbirth Without Pain Education Assn, 20134 Snowden St, Detroit, MI 48235-1170; Title Tel # (313) 341-3816
Personnel: Editor-Debrah Haddad
Editorial Description: Promotes, practical and teaches the Lamaze Method of Psycho-Prophalaxis for a painless and joyful childbirth to expectant parents.
General Info: Yr. Est. 1958, Bi-monthly, Offset press, 16 pages, No Color
Subscriptions: Indv. $25
Circulation: Total-2,000
Advertising: Inquire for rates.

Canadian Childbirth Educator
See: HEALTH

Early Intervention
Business, Consumer

Publishing Co: Illinois Early Childhood Intervention Clearinghouse, 840 S Spring St, Springfield, IL 62704-2652; Title Tel # (217) 785-1364 Title Fax # (217) 524-5339
Personnel: Editor-Chet Brandt
Editorial Description: Carries feature articles, a calendar of professional meetings, reviews of materials received by the Clearinghouse & other items of special interest to people involved in early intervention services for children with special needs.
General Info: Yr. Est. 1985, Quarterly, 7 pages, ISSN: 1058-8396, Saddle-stitched
Subscriptions: Free
Circulation: Total-4,000
Printing Co: Ink Expressions, 1905 S 10 1/2 St, Springfield, IL 62703-3202 Tel # (217) 522-8921

ICEA Review

Publishing Co: ICEA, PO Box 20048, Minneapolis, MN 55420-0048; Title Tel # (612) 854-8660
Personnel: Editor-Rebecca Scott
Editorial Description: Topics of current interest within childbearing field; includes literature abstracts.
General Info: Yr. Est. 1977, Trim Size-8½ x 11, Sheetfed press, 8 pages, Color
Subscriptions: Indv. $3, $2/copy
Circulation: (100% controlled), Total-4,800

NAPSAC News
See: FAMILY

NPA Bulletin
Association

Publishing Co: National Perinatal Association, 3500 E Fletcher Ave Ste 525, Tampa, FL 33613-4711; Title Tel # (813) 971-1008 Title Fax # (813) 971-9306
Personnel: Editor-Julie Leachman
Editorial Description: Health care for pregnant women, fetus and newborn.
General Info: Quarterly, 25 pages, 3% ads, No Color
Subscriptions: $15/copy
Circulation: Total-2,500
Advertising: Inquire for rates.
List Rental: Actives: 2,500, $250/M
Printing Co: Print Shack, 7538 N Dale Mabry Hwy, Tampa, FL 33614-3226 Tel # (813) 885-7279, Fax # (813) 882-3040

New Beginnings
Association

Publishing Co: Sponsor-LaLeche League, La Leche League International, Inc., 1400 N. Meacham Rd., Schaumburg, IL 60173; Title Tel # (847) 519-7730
Personnel: Publisher-Sally Murphy, Editor-Judy Torgus, Circ. Mgr.-Diana Grinvalds, Production Mgr.-Elayne Shpak, Adv. Dir.-Susan Huml
Editorial Description: Support & information for breast feeding mothers; book reviews; columns; letters from mothers, fathers.
General Info: (Formerly LLL News), Yr. Est. 1985, Bi-monthly, Trim Size-8½ x 11, Web press, 30 pages, ISSN: 8756-9981, 4 Color, Matte, Saddle-stitched
Subscriptions: Indv. $15, $3/copy
Circulation: Total-35,000
Advertising: Inquire for rates.
Printing Co: Bawden Printing, 400 S 14th Ave, Eldridge, IA 52748-9789 Tel # (319) 285-4800, Fax # (319) 285-4828

PR Marcom Jobs Mid-America
See: EMPLOYMENT

Parent Care News Brief
Business, Consumer

Publishing Co: Sponsor-Parent Care, Parent Care, Inc., 9041 Colgate St, Indianapolis, IN 46268-1210; Title Tel # (317) 872-9913 Title Fax # (317) 872-0795
Personnel: Editor-Sarah Killion
Editorial Description: For parents of premature & high risk infants, families, professionals.
General Info: (Formerly Support Lines), Yr. Est. 1985, Quarterly, Trim Size-8½ x 11, Desktop press, 24 pages, 2 Color, Saddle-stitched
Subscriptions: Indv. $40, Inst. $125
Circulation: (93% controlled), Total-750
List Rental: Rents Lists

Six Months to Six Years
See: EDUCATION

Topline
Business

Publishing Co: McCollum Spielman Worldwide, 235 Great Neck Rd., Great Neck, NY 11021-3343; Title Tel # (516) 482-0310 Title Fax # (516) 482-3228
Personnel: Editor-Paula Kay Pierce
Editorial Description: Market research findings, observations, guidelines.
General Info: Yr. Est. 1978, Quarterly, Offset press, 4 pages, 2 Color
Subscriptions: Free To Qualified Recipient
Circulation: Total-15,000

Twin Services Reporter
Consumer

Publishing Co: Twinline, PO Box 10066, Berkeley, CA 94709-5066 Tel # (510) 524-0863 Fax # (510) 524-0869; Title Tel # (570) 524-0863 Title Fax # (510) 524-0894
Editorial Description: Muliple birth news and information.
General Info: (Formerly Twinline Newsletter), Yr. Est. 1983, Semi-annually
Subscriptions: Free With Membership
Advertising: Inquire for rates.

Washington Watch

Publishing Co: Family Research Council, 700 13th St NW Ste 500, Washington, DC 20005-3960; Title Tel # (202) 393-2100 Title Fax # (202) 393-2134
Personnel: Publisher-Gary Baver, Editor-Robert Morrison
Editorial Description: Covers the news of nations capital that has an impact on American families.
General Info: Monthly
Circulation: Total-79,000
Advertising: Inquire for rates.
Printing Co: EU Services, 649 N Horners Ln, Rockville, MD 20850-1299 Tel # (301) 424-3300

Your Baby
Consumer

Publishing Co: Today's Parent Magazine Group, 269 Richmond St., W., Toronto, ON M5V 1X1 Canada Parent Co.-Maclean Hunter Publishing Ltd., Toronto, Canada; Title Tel # (416) 596-5230 Title Fax # (416) 593-3197
Personnel: Editor-Helen Keeler
Editorial Description: Info for new mothers.
General Info: Yr. Est. 1989, Monthly
Subscriptions: Indv. $24
Advertising: Inquire for rates.

Your Child's Wellness
Consumer

Publishing Co: Your Child's Wellness, 244 Madison Ave Apt 9h, New York, NY 10016-2813; Title Tel # (212) 983-6880 Title Fax # (212) 983-1220
Personnel: Publisher-Jan Kirshiner, Editor-Ruben Reiman, MD, Circ. Mgr.-Jeff Klainberg
Editorial Description: Health information for parents with young children.
General Info: Bi-monthly, Trim Size-8½ x 11, 8 pages
Subscriptions: Indv. $15, Can. $20

BAKING

American Deli-Bakery News

Publishing Co: American Deli-Bakery News, PO Box 194130, San Francisco, CA 94119-4130; Title Tel # (415) 777-0604 Title Fax # (415) 777-9590
Personnel: Editor-Larry Jenkins
Editorial Description: News and industry developments for deli and bakery professionals.
General Info: Yr. Est. 1987, 18x/yr.
Subscriptions: Indv. $145

American Institute of Baking-Technical Bulletin   *Business*

Publishing Co: American Institute of Baking, 1213 Bakers Way, Manhattan, KS 66502-4576; Title Tel # (913) 537-4750 Title Fax # (913) 537-1493
Personnel: Editor-Gur Ranhotra
Editorial Description: Technical bulletin on products ingredients, processing, equipments, nutrition & sanitation.
General Info: Yr. Est. 1979, Monthly, Trim Size-8½ x 11, 6 pages
Subscriptions: Indv. $30, Can. $30, For. $44, $3/copy
Circulation: Total-1,700

Bakers Way   *Association*

Publishing Co: American Institute of Baking, 1213 Bakers Way, Manhattan, KS 66502-4576; Title Tel # (913) 537-4750
Personnel: Editor-Martin Puntney
Editorial Description: Membership activities newsletter.
General Info: Monthly
Circulation: Total-750

Baking with the American Harvest   *Consumer*

Publishing Co: Baking with the American Harvest, 1341 Ocean Ave., #526, Santa Monica, CA 90401
Editorial Description: Articles on appreciating American baking, pastry and dessert making.
General Info: Bi-monthly

Baking Sheet, The   *Consumer*

Publishing Co: Sands, Taylor & Wood Co., PO Box 876, Norwich, VT 05055-0876 Tel # (802) 649-3881
Editorial Description: Recipes and baking tips for home bakers from the King Arthur Flour bakers.
General Info: 8x/yr., Trim Size-8 x 10, 32 pages, Matte
Subscriptions: Indv. $18, $1/copy
Circulation: Total-6,000
List Rental: Rents Lists

Bayberry Farm Peddlers
See: COLLECTIBLES

Bridal Collectors News
See: BRIDE

Cookies

Publishing Co: Cookies, 9610 Greenview Lane, Manassas, VA 22110; Title Tel # (703) 361-5898 Title Fax # (202) 687-4664
Personnel: Editor-Rosemary Henry
Editorial Description: Historical information about cookie shaping, sources of new cutters & molds, appropriate recipes, reviews of new cookie related (cook) books, cookie trivia.
General Info: Yr. Est. 1972, Bi-monthly, Offset press, 10 pages
Subscriptions: Indv. $8, $2/copy
Advertising: Inquire for rates.
List Rental: Rents Lists
Printing Co: Spee-dee-Que, 1417 27th St NW, Washington, DC 20007-3144 Tel # (202) 333-7111

Cooking on the Edge
See: FOOD

Cooks Corner, The
See: FOOD

Curmudgeon's Home Companion, The
See: FOOD

Gloria Pitzer's Secret Recipes Publications
See: FOOD

Grace Kirschenbaum's World of Cookbooks
See: FOOD

Healthy Eating
See: FOOD

Independent

Publishing Co: Independent Bakers Assn., PO Box 3731, Washington, DC 20007-0231; Title Tel # (202) 223-2325
Editorial Description: Provides legislative updates & industry news.
General Info: Annually
Circulation: Total-360

Magic Bread Letter   *Consumer*

Publishing Co: Magic Bread Letter, P.O. Box 337-KA, Moss Beach, CA 94038-0337
Personnel: Publisher-Ada Lai
Editorial Description: Information, news, and recipes especially for bread machine owners.
General Info: Bi-monthly

Pacific Bakers News

Publishing Co: Pacific Bakers News, 180 Mendell St., San Francisco, CA 94124-1740; Title Tel # (415) 826-2664 Title Fax # (415) 821-1070
Personnel: Publisher, Editor-Cliff Soward
Editorial Description: Business news of commercial baking industry in 13 far western states.
General Info: Yr. Est. 1961, Monthly, Trim Size-8½ x 11, Sheetfed press, 22 pages, 5% ads, No Color
Subscriptions: Indv. $18, Can. $28, For. $55, $2/copy
Circulation: (100% controlled), Total-3,000
Advertising: Inquire for rates.

Pennsylvania Baker   *Business, Association*

Publishing Co: Pennsylvania Baker Assn., 47 W Main St, Mechanicsburg, PA 17055-6262 Tel # (717) 790-9352; Title Tel # (717) 236-7949
Personnel: Editor-Connie Mallios
Editorial Description: News items of interest to bakers and their suppliers.
General Info: Yr. Est. 1933, Monthly, Trim Size-8½ x 11, Offset press, 10 pages, 3% ads, 2 Color, Newsprint, Saddle-stitched
Subscriptions: Indv. $15, $2/copy
Circulation: (100% controlled), Total-400
Advertising: Inquire for rates.
Printing Co: Horton Printing, 5490 Linglestown Rd, Harrisburg, PA 17112-9190 Tel # (717) 657-3220

Washington Bakery Report   *Business*

Publishing Co: Webster Communications Corp., 1530 Key Blvd., PH 2, Arlington, VA 22209-1532; Title Tel # (703) 525-4512 Title Fax # (703) 525-4917
Personnel: Publisher-James C. Webster
Editorial Description: Government and industry news of baking and baked foods.
General Info: Yr. Est. 1980, Weekly, Trim Size-8½ x 11, Sheetfed press, 4 pages, ISSN: 1064-0878, No Color
Subscriptions: Indv. $195, For. $225, $5/copy

BANKING & FINANCE

100 Highest Yields   *Consumer*

Publishing Co: Bank Rate Monitor, Inc., PO Box 88888, North Palm Beach, FL 33408-8888; Title Tel # (407) 627-7330 Title Fax # (407) 627-7335
Personnel: Publisher-Robert Heady, Editor-Hugo Ottolenghi, Circ. Mgr.-Sarah Schofield
Editorial Description: Ranking of highest-yielding, cd's & MMA federally-insured banks & thrifts nationwide.
General Info: Yr. Est. 1983, Weekly, Trim Size-8½ x 11, 8 pages
Subscriptions: Indv. $124, Can. $169, For. $234

401(k) Legislative News   *Consumer*

Publishing Co: 401(k) Association, 1 Summit Square, Doublewoods Rd. & Rte. 413, Langhorne, PA 19047 Tel # (215) 579-8830 Fax # (215) 579-8832
Personnel: Editor-R. Theodore Benna, Circ. Mgr.-Barbara A. Marano, Art Dir.-Nicole Melton
General Info: Yr. Est. 1993, Quarterly, Trim Size-8½ x 10, Desktop press, 4 pages, 2 Color, Coated
Subscriptions: Indv. $10
Circulation: Total-600
Printing Co: 3-D Printing, 15 N State St, Newtown, PA 18940-2026 Tel # (215) 968-7900, Fax # (215) 968-1770

401(k) Reporter
See: INVESTMENT

ABA Bank Security & Fraud Prevention   *Business*

Publishing Co: American Bankers Association, 1120 Connecticut Ave NW, Washington, DC 20036-3902; Title Tel # (202) 663-5000
Personnel: Publisher-Lawrence Price, Editor-Hunter Moss
Editorial Description: Current trends, issues and regulations in bank insurance and risk management.
General Info: (Formerly Bank Insurance&Protection Bulletin; Bank Security Newsletter), Yr. Est. 1994, Monthly, Trim Size-8½ x 11, Letrpr. press, 6 pages, 2 Color, Coated
Subscriptions: Indv. $36, For. $252, $23/copy
Circulation: (100% controlled), Total-10,000

ABA Trust Letter   *Business, Association*

Publishing Co: American Bankers Association, 1120 Connecticut Ave NW, Washington, DC 20036-3902 Tel # (202) 663-5000; Title Tel # (202) 663-5200
Personnel: Publisher-Lawrence Price, Editor-Susan Johnson
Editorial Description: Legal/regulatory update on trust and investment management.
General Info: Yr. Est. 1971, Monthly
Subscriptions: Indv. $210, For. $252, $23/copy
Circulation: Total-1,900

ADP Advisor　　　　　*Business, Consumer*

Publishing Co: Automatic Data Processing Inc., ADP Employer Services MS#245, One ADP Blvd., Roseland, NJ 07068
Personnel: Editor-Ronald Love
Editorial Description: ADP's newsletter to its customers giving financial and tax information.
General Info: Quarterly, Trim Size-8^{12}/ x 11, 6 pages, 2 Color

AICPA Audit and Accounting Manual
See: ACCOUNTING

AICPA Financial Statement Prepartion Manual
See: ACCOUNTING

AICPA Professional Standards
See: ACCOUNTING

AICPA Technical Practice Aids
See: ACCOUNTING

Abstract of American Economic Trend Analysis
See: ECONOMICS

Abstract of International Economic Trend Analysis
See: ECONOMICS

Accounting for Banks
See: ACCOUNTING

Ag Executive
See: AGRICULTURE

Agency Law Quarterly Real Estate Intelligence Report
See: REAL ESTATE

Agora, Inc.　　　　　*Association*

Publishing Co: The Oxford Club, 2020 Pennsylvania Ave. NW, Suite 654, Washington, DC 20006; Title Tel # (410) 234-0515 Title Fax # (410) 837-3879
Personnel: Publisher-William Bonner
Editorial Description: The Oxford Club's own views on economic trends and developments.
General Info: Monthly
Subscriptions: Indv. $67

Agricultural Credit Conditions Survey
See: AGRICULTURE

Alternative Currents

Publishing Co: Alternatives Federal Credit Union, 301 West State Street, Ithaca, NY 14850; Title Tel # (607) 273-3582 Title Fax # (607) 277-6391
Personnel: Editor-Leni Hochman, Mng. Editor-William Myers
Editorial Description: We cover Community development banking and banking services.
General Info: Monthly, Trim Size-8$\frac{1}{2}$ x 11, 4 pages, 2 Color
Subscriptions: Free
Circulation: (91% controlled), Total-6,000

American Banker's Washington Watch　　　　*Business*

Publishing Co: American Banker Newsletters, One State Plaza, New York, NY 10004-1505 Fax # (202) 843-9620; Title Tel # (212) 803-8300 Title Fax # (212) 843-9620
Personnel: Publisher-David G. Schutt, Editor-Arthur Postal, Circulation, Adv. Dir., Mktg. Dir.-Hans Winberg
Editorial Description: Policy Report on Developments at the Bank Regulatory Agencies
General Info: (Formerly Thrift Regulator; FDIC Watch; Banking Reporter), Weekly, Ind/Abs/Online: Mead Data Central, NewsNet, Predicasts/Dialog
Subscriptions: Indv. $695, Can. $695, For. $725, $20/copy
Advertising: Inquire for rates.

American Institute of Banking Leaders Letter　　　*Association*

Publishing Co: American Bankers Association, 1120 Connecticut Ave NW, Washington, DC 20036-3902; Title Tel # (202) 663-5000
Personnel: Publisher-Diane Powers, Editor-Lisa Underwood
Editorial Description: Covers educational programs and policies of the American Bankers Association for American Institute of Banking leaders.
General Info: Yr. Est. 1965, 10x/yr., Trim Size-8$\frac{1}{2}$ x 11, Sheetfed press, 8 pages, 2 Color, Matte
Subscriptions: Indv. $25, Free With Membership
Circulation: Total-7,200

American Recovery Association, Inc. News & Views　　　　*Association*

Publishing Co: American Recovery Assn., Inc., PO Box 6788, New Orleans, LA 70174-6788 Tel # (504) 367-0711; Title Tel # (407) 260-0712
Personnel: Editor-Jodi Lenz, Publisher, Circ. Mgr.-Huey Mayronne
Editorial Description: News regarding the repossession industry at an international level.
General Info: Yr. Est. 1965, Monthly, Trim Size-8$\frac{1}{2}$ x 11, Web press, 12 pages, 4 Color, Newsprint, Saddle-stitched
Acquistions: Publication Bought
Circulation: (100% controlled), Total-30,000

American Stock Exchange Guide　　　　*Business*

Publishing Co: CCH, Inc., 2700 Lake Cook Rd., Riverwoods, IL 60015 Parent Co.-Kluwer Law & Taxation Publishers, Cambridge; Title Tel # (847) 267-7000 Title Fax # (800) 224-8299
Personnel: Editor-Ed Hanlon
Editorial Description: Directory, constitution & rules of the AMEX. Published for the AMEX.
General Info: Yr. Est. 1960, Monthly, Trim Size-6 x 9, 88 pages, No Color
Subscriptions: Indv. $377

Andrews' Bank & Lender Liability Litigation Reporter
See: LAW

Antitrust Litigation Reporter
See: LAW

Asian Banker

Publishing Co: Lafferty Publications, 420 Lexington Ave., Ste. 1745, New York, NY 10170 Tel # (212) 557-6729 Fax # (212) 557-7266; Title Tel # (404) 636-6610 Title Fax # (404) 636-6422
Personnel: Publisher-Frank Lawson, Editor-Emmanuel Daniel
Editorial Description: Is a bulletin which enables you to monitor trends, initiatives and developments in the fast-moving and fast-growing Asian financial services market. Eaqch issue monitors the regulatory environment, the major players, cross-border activity and all productand service developments.
General Info: (Formerly Practice Marketing International), Yr. Est. 1994, Monthly
Subscriptions: Indv. $779

Asset Based Financing: A Transactional Guide　　　*Business*

Publishing Co: Matthew Bender & Co., 11 Penn Plaza, New York, NY 10001-2006 Tel # (212) 967-7707 Fax # (212) 244-3188
Personnel: Editor-Howard Ruda
Editorial Description: The first complete guide to asset based lending, providing a unique how-to approach to structuring the loan transaction, monitoring the security underlying the loan, and proceeding in case of default.
General Info: Yr. Est. 1985, Irregular, Looseleaf

Asset Sales Report　　　　*Business*

Publishing Co: American Banker Newsletters, One State Plaza, New York, NY 10004-1505 Tel # (212) 803-8300 Fax # (202) 843-9620; Title Tel # (212) 943-5730 Title Fax # (212) 943-2224
Personnel: Publisher-David G. Schutt, Editor-Jeanne Burke, Circulation, Adv. Dir., Mktg. Dir.-Hans Winberg
Editorial Description: Loan sales and securitization in development.
General Info: (Formerly Guarantor, The; Global Guaranty; Global Asset Backed Monitor), Yr. Est. 1987, Weekly, Ind/Abs/Online: Mead Data Central, NewsNet, Dialog and Datastar, DataTimes, Predicasts
Subscriptions: Indv. $1,250, Can. $1,250, For. $1,280, $20/copy
Advertising: Inquire for rates.

Auto Financing Update　　　*Business*

Publishing Co: Bank Lease Consultants, 2590 Merced St, San Leandro, CA 94577-4213; Title Tel # (510) 895-1900 Title Fax # (510) 895-5885
Personnel: Publisher-Randall McCathren, Editor, Circ. Mgr.-Dave Walter
Editorial Description: Practical & general interest pub. for the auto finance industry.
General Info: Yr. Est. 1986, Monthly, Trim Size-8$\frac{1}{2}$ x 11, 8 pages, ISSN: 1045-5760, No Color
Subscriptions: Indv. $295, Can. $295, For. $365
Circulation: Total-1,000
List Rental: Rents Lists

Automated Payments Update　　　*Business, Association*

Publishing Co: National Automated Clearing House Association, 607 Herndon Pky Ste 200, Herndon, VA 22070-5477; Title Tel # (703) 742-9190
Personnel: Editor-Catherine McDonald
Editorial Description: Official ACH newsletter covers new ACH applications, upcoming rule changes, legislative and regulatory developments, policy issues and the latest in ACH products and marketing.
General Info: Monthly, Trim Size-8$\frac{1}{2}$ x 11, 12 pages, 25% ads, 2 Color, Matte, Saddle-stitched
Subscriptions: Indv. $150
Advertising: $800. Accepts Inserts.

BCA Interest Rate Forecast
See: INVESTMENT

Bank & S&L Quarterly
Rating Service

Publishing Co: Sheshunoff Information Services, Inc., P.O. Box 13203, Capitol Sta., Austin, TX 78711-3203; Title Tel # (512) 472-2244
Editorial Description: Information for all federally insured banks and savings loan associations from the reports on branch office .
General Info: Quarterly

Bank Advertising News   *Business*

Publishing Co: Bank Rate Monitor, Inc., PO Box 88888, North Palm Beach, FL 33408-8888; Title Tel # (407) 627-7330 Title Fax # (407) 627-7335
Personnel: Publisher-Robert Heady, Editor-Hugo Ottolenghi, Circ. Mgr.-Sarah Schofield
Editorial Description: Independent national newspaper of financial marketing by banks, thrifts and credit unions.
General Info: Yr. Est. 1986, Bi-weekly, Trim Size-11 x 14$\frac{1}{2}$, 12 pages, 2 Color
Subscriptions: Indv. $398, Can. $443, For. $508, $45/copy

Bank Asset/Liability
Management   *Business*

Publishing Co: Warren, Gorham & Lamont, 31 Saint James Ave., Boston, MA 02116-4112 Parent Co.-Thomson Professional Publications, Stamford; Title Tel # (617) 423-2020 Title Fax # (617) 423-1914
Personnel: Publisher-Larry Selby, Mktg. Dir.-Sandra Fox
Editorial Description: Practical & general interest pub. for asset/liability managers in banks.
General Info: Yr. Est. 1985, Monthly, Trim Size-8$\frac{1}{2}$ x 11, 8 pages, No Color
Subscriptions: Indv. $193
List Rental: List Management Co.: Manager: Seena Benedek; WG & L List Management, 1 Penn Plz Fl 42, New York, NY 10119-0002 Tel # (212) 971-5000

Bank Auditing and
Accounting Report   *Business*

Publishing Co: Warren, Gorham & Lamont, 31 Saint James Ave., Boston, MA 02116-4112 Parent Co.-Thomson Professional Publications, Stamford; Title Tel # (617) 423-2020 Title Fax # (617) 423-1914
Personnel: Publisher-Andrew Boden, Production Mgr.-Ed Novack, Mktg. Mgr.-Sandra Fox
Editorial Description: Covers bank auditing, accounting, FASB, SEC, regulatory & tax issues.
General Info: Yr. Est. 1973, Monthly, Trim Size-8$\frac{1}{2}$ x 11, Offset press, 6 pages, ISSN: 0522-2478, 2 Color
Subscriptions: Indv. $160
Advertising: Inquire for rates.
List Rental: List Management Co.: Manager: Seena Benedek; WG & L List Management, 1 Penn Plz Fl 42, New York, NY 10119-0002 Tel # (212) 971-5000

Bank Automation News
See: COMPUTERS & AUTOMATION

Bank Bailout Litigation
News   *Business*

Publishing Co: LRP Publications, 747 Dresher Rd., P.O. Box 980, Horsham, PA 19044-0980 Tel # (215) 784-0910 Fax # (215) 784-0317; Title Tel # (215) 784-0860 Title Fax # (215) 784-9645
Personnel: Publisher-Ken Kahn, Editor-Vick Simon
Editorial Description: Reports on failed bank litigation, bank enforcement litigation, & regulatory and legislative developments affecting these areas. Emphasis on putting these developments into context and identifying trends in case law.
General Info: Yr. Est. 1989, Weekly, Trim Size-8$\frac{1}{2}$ x 11, Web press, 8 pages, ISSN: 1047-5133
Subscriptions: Indv. $645, For. $645

Bank Compliance Guide   *Business*

Publishing Co: CCH, Inc., 2700 Lake Cook Rd., Riverwoods, IL 60015 Parent Co.-Kluwer Law & Taxation Publishers, Cambridge; Title Tel # (847) 267-7000 Title Fax # (800) 224-8299
Editorial Description: In-depth analysis of federal consumer compliance laws & reguations applicable to financial institutions. Covers Truth-in-Lending Truth-in-Savings. Home Mortgage Disclosure, RESPA & more.
General Info: Yr. Est. 1994, Monthly, Looseleaf
Subscriptions: Indv. $389

Bank Credit Analyst   *Business*

Publishing Co: BCA Publications Ltd., 1002 Sherbrook St. W., Montreal, PQ H3A 3L6 Canada; Title Tel # (514) 499-9550 Title Fax # (514) 874-1894
Personnel: Editor-J.A. Boeckh, Circ. Mgr.-H. Paulson, Production Mgr.-E. Lankinen
Editorial Description: Analysis of trends in business conditions and major investment markets.
General Info: Yr. Est. 1949, Monthly, Trim Size-6$\frac{7}{8}$ x 9$\frac{3}{8}$, Offset press, 44 pages, ISSN: 0822-5788, Color-cover, Saddle-stitched
Subscriptions: Indv. $645, $50/copy

Bank Digest

Publishing Co: CCH Washington Service Bureau, Inc., 655 15th St NW Ste 275, Washington, DC 20005-5701; Title Tel # (202) 508-0600 Title Fax # (202) 508-0694
Personnel: Editor-Nathalie Auer, Circ. Dir.-Trent Seibert
Editorial Description: Daily summaries of every banking regulatory release from FRB, Comptroller of the Currency, OTS, RTC, RTCOB, FCA, NCUA, FDIC, Tresury, Congressional Calendar, Federal Courts (including Supreme Court), SEC and lists of pertinent filings. Full text also available.
General Info: Yr. Est. 1988, Daily, 10 pages
Subscriptions: Indv. $715

Bank Directors Briefing

Publishing Co: Simmons-Boardman Publishing Corp., 345 Hudson St., New York, NY 10014-4590 Tel # (212) 620-7200; Title Tel # (212) 620-7219 Title Fax # (212) 633-1165
Personnel: Publisher-David Bayard, Editor-Steven Cochpo
Editorial Description: News and information of particular interest to bank directors.
General Info: Yr. Est. 1979, Monthly

Bank Financial Quarterly   *Business*

Publishing Co: United Communications Group, 11300 Rockville Pike, Ste. 1100, Rockville, MD 20852-3030 Tel # (301) 816-8950 Fax # (301) 816-8945; Title Tel # (301) 961-8700 Title Fax # (301) 961-8666
Personnel: Publisher-Dan Brown, Circ. Mgr.-Sharon Welch
Editorial Description: 30 key financial indicators of more than 11,000 commercial banks.
General Info: Yr. Est. 1986, Quarterly, 200 pages
Subscriptions: Indv. $349, $87/copy
Acquistions: Publication Bought, Publication Sold
List Rental: Rents Lists

Bank Fraud Bulletin   *Business*

Publishing Co: Bank Administration Institute, One N. Franklin St., Chicago, IL 60606 Tel # (312) 553-4600 Fax # (312) 683-2426; Title Tel # (708) 228-6200
Personnel: Editor-Phyllis Van Holland
Editorial Description: Covers fraud and risk management topics.
General Info: Yr. Est. 1986, 8 pages
Subscriptions: Indv. $150
Circulation: Total-2,400
List Rental: Rents Lists

Bank Holding Company
Compliance Manual   *Business*

Publishing Co: Matthew Bender & Co., 11 Penn Plaza, New York, NY 10001-2006 Tel # (212) 967-7707 Fax # (212) 244-3188
Editorial Description: A practical, how-to guide on the day-to-day compliance responsibilities faced by bank holding company line officers.
General Info: Yr. Est. 1986, Irregular, Looseleaf

Bank Investment Product
News   *Business*

Publishing Co: Capital Cities/ABC, 488 Madison Ave., 16th Floor, New York, NY 10022-5751 Fax # (212) 224-3353 Parent Co.-Capital Cities/ABC, Inc., New York; Title Tel # (212) 224-3233 Title Fax # (212) 224-3111
General Info: Weekly, Trim Size-8$\frac{1}{2}$ x 11, Sheetfed press, 10 pages, 2 Color, Newsprint
Advertising: Inquire for rates.

Bank Lawyer Liability
See: LAW

Bank Letter   *Business*

Publishing Co: Capital Cities/ABC, 488 Madison Ave., 16th Floor, New York, NY 10022-5751 Parent Co.-Capital Cities/ABC, Inc., New York; Title Tel # (212) 224-3233 Title Fax # (212) 224-3353
Personnel: Publisher-Linda Litner, Editor-Tom Lamont, Circ. Dir.-Gladys Delgado, Production Dir.-Susan Drobney, Adv. Dir.-Pat Bertucci, Mktg. Dir.-Dahlia Weinman
Editorial Description: Featuring breaking news on the trends, issues and events that affect major U.S. commercial banks. Bank Letter is considered a key information resource for senior commercial and investment banking executives. Every Monday, Bank Letter covers retail banking, corporate lending, balance sheet strategies, marketing plans, technology and governmental regulations within the banking industry.
General Info: Yr. Est. 1977, Weekly, Trim Size-8$\frac{1}{2}$ x 11, Sheetfed press, 10 pages, Ind/Abs/Online: Lexis/Nexis news services, 2 Color, Newsprint
Subscriptions: Indv. $1,295, Can. $1,325, For. $1,370, $30/copy
Advertising: Inquire for rates.

Bank Loan Report   *Business*

Publishing Co: IDD Enterprises, 2 World Trade Ctr. 18th Fl., New York, NY 10048-0203 Fax # (212) 321-2336 Parent Co.-Dow Jones & Co., Inc., New York; Title Tel # (212) 227-1200
Personnel: Editor-Clint Winstead, Circ. Mgr.-Philip M. McGee, Production Mgr.-Maxine Margolese, Mktg. Dir.-Janice Fellagera
Editorial Description: Reports on the commercial lending marketplace. Covers theterms and progress of dozens of deals in syndication or restructuring weekly.
General Info: Yr. Est. 1986, Weekly, 12 pages
Subscriptions: Indv. $2,700
Acquistions: Publication Bought, Publication Sold
Advertising: Accepts Inserts.
Printing Co: Dealers Digest, 2 World Trade Ctr., New York, NY 10048 Tel # (212) 227-1200

Bank Marketing
International

Publishing Co: Lafferty Publications, 420 Lexington Ave., Ste. 1745, New York, NY 10170 Tel # (212) 557-6729 Fax # (212) 557-7266; Title Tel # (404) 636-6610 Title Fax # (404) 636-6422
Personnel: Publisher-Frank Lawson, Editor in Chief-Michael Lafferty, Editor-Peter Kinahan
Editorial Description: Reports & analyzes trends in bank marketing. The journal features a distinctly international outlook.
General Info: Yr. Est. 1989, 10x/yr.
Subscriptions: Indv. $790

Bank MergerFax *Business*

Publishing Co: SNL Securities, 410 E. Main St., P.O. Box 2124, Charlottesville, VA 22902 Tel # (804) 977-1600 Fax # (804) 977-4466

Personnel: Publisher-Reid Nagle, Circ. Mgr.-Pat LaBua, Editor, Production Mgr.-Kari Pitkin, Adv. Dir.-Jenn Nagaj, Mktg. Dir.-Judy Lewis

Editorial Description: Provides all the key financial data on the previous week's merger and acquisition activity including branch sales, merger conversions, RTC and FDIC transactions, and more.

General Info: Yr. Est. 1990, Weekly, Trim Size-8½ x 11, Desktop press, 10 pages, Other

Subscriptions: Indv. $1,700

Advertising: Inquire for rates.

Bank Mergers & Acquisitions *Business*

Publishing Co: SNL Securities, 410 E. Main St., P.O. Box 2124, Charlottesville, VA 22902; Title Tel # (804) 977-1600 Title Fax # (804) 977-4466

Personnel: Publisher-Reid Nagle, Circ. Mgr.-Pat LaBua, Editor, Production Mgr.-Ed Dillon, Mktg. Dir.-Judy Lewis

Editorial Description: Provides complete financial analysis of all aspects of the bank and thrift M&A market.

General Info: Yr. Est. 1986, Monthly, Trim Size-8½ x 11, Sheetfed press, 30 pages, Color, Matte, Saddle-stitched

Subscriptions: Indv. $795

Acquistions: Publication Bought, Publication Sold

Advertising: $500.

List Rental: Actives: $95/M

Printing Co: Eastern Graphics, 2 Taft St., S. Norwalk, CT 06854 Tel # (203) 853-8050

Bank Network News (Newsletter) *Business*

Publishing Co: Faulkner & Gray, Inc., 11 Penn Plz., 17th Floor, New York, NY 10001-2006 Tel # (212) 967-7000 Fax # (212) 695-8172 Parent Co.-Thomson Corp., Stamford; Title Tel # (312) 648-0261 Title Fax # (312) 648-9569

Personnel: Publisher-Kurt Peters, Editor-Lauri Giesen, Circ. Mgr.-Linda Ragusin

Editorial Description: Editorial focus on retail electronic banking--ATMs, POS & home banking.

General Info: Yr. Est. 1982, Semi-monthly, 8 pages, 2 Color

Subscriptions: Indv. $395, $20/copy

List Rental: List Management Co.: Aggressive List Management, 18-2 E Dundee Rd Ste 101, Barrington, IL 60010-5273 Tel # (708) 304-4030, Fax # (708) 304-4032, Actives: $95/M

Bank One
See: HOUSE ORGANS

Bank Operations Bulletin *Business, Association*

Publishing Co: American Bankers Association, 1120 Connecticut Ave NW, Washington, DC 20036-3902; Title Tel # (202) 663-5000

Personnel: Publisher-Lawrence Price, Editor-HUnter Moss

Editorial Description: Industry developments in bank operation techniques, systems & procedures & standards.

General Info: (Formerly Thruput), Yr. Est. 1974, Monthly, Trim Size-8½ x 11, 8 pages

Subscriptions: Indv. $16,590, For. $198, $18/copy

Circulation: (100% controlled), Total-1,986

Bank Personnel News *Business, Association*

Publishing Co: American Bankers Association, 1120 Connecticut Ave NW, Washington, DC 20036-3902 Tel # (202) 663-5000; Title Tel # (202) 663-5282

Personnel: Publisher-Larry Price, Editor-Hunter Moss

Editorial Description: Latest information on industry resources, publications, courses, expertise. Articles written by peers, competitors and experts that cover HR issues issues large and small, including legislative updates, new products and more.

General Info: Monthly, 8 pages, No Color, Coated

Subscriptions: Indv. $180, For. $216, $18/copy

Circulation: Total-1,400

Printing Co: Corporate Press, 403 Brightseat Rd., Landover, MD 20785-4706 Tel # (301) 499-9200, Fax # (301) 499-5435

Bank Rate Monitor *Business*

Publishing Co: Bank Rate Monitor, Inc., PO Box 88888, North Palm Beach, FL 33408-8888; Title Tel # (407) 627-7330 Title Fax # (407) 627-7335

Personnel: Publisher-Robert Heady, Editor-Hugo Ottolenghi, Circ. Mgr.-Sarah Schofield

Editorial Description: Average rates paid on CD's and Money Market accounts at major banks, thrifts and credit unions nationwide, and average rates charged on mortgages and loans.

General Info: Yr. Est. 1982, Weekly, Trim Size-8½ x 11, 12 pages

Subscriptions: Indv. $695, Can. $740, For. $805, $30/copy

Bank Securities Advisor *Business*

Publishing Co: Warren, Gorham & Lamont, 31 Saint James Ave., Boston, MA 02116-4112 Parent Co.-Thomson Professional Publications, Stamford; Title Tel # (617) 423-2020 Title Fax # (617) 423-1914

Personnel: Publisher-Larry Selby, Mktg. Dir.-Sandra Fox

General Info: Yr. Est. 1994, Monthly

Subscriptions: Indv. $225

List Rental: List Management Co.: Manager: Seene Benedek; WG & L List Management, 1 Penn Plz Fl 42, New York, NY 10119-0002 Tel # (212) 971-5000

Bank Securities Report *Business*

Publishing Co: Phillips Business Information, Inc., 1201 Seven Locks Rd., Ste 300, Potomac, MD 20854-2958 Tel # (301) 340-1520; Title Tel # (301) 340-2100 Title Fax # (301) 424-4297

Personnel: Publisher-Chris Scotton, Editor-Ed Bond, Production Mgr.-Teresa Fleisher, Adv. Dir.-KIm Hudak, Mktg. Dir.-Kelly Ebbs

Editorial Description: Strategies and technologies for marketing bank investment products.

General Info: Yr. Est. 1993, Bi-weekly, 8 pages, ISSN: 1068-3763, Ind/Abs/Online: NewsNet, DIALOG, Predicasts, Bloomberg, 2 Color

Subscriptions: Indv. $595, For. $630, $37/copy

List Rental: Rents Lists

Bank Security Report
See: SECURITY & SURVEILLANCE

Bank Teller's Report *Business*

Publishing Co: Warren, Gorham & Lamont, 31 Saint James Ave., Boston, MA 02116-4112 Parent Co.-Thomson Professional Publications, Stamford; Title Tel # (617) 423-2020 Title Fax # (617) 423-1914

Personnel: Publisher-Larry Selby, Mktg. Dir.-Sandra Fox

Editorial Description: Offers handy tips on all aspects of the teller's job, from customer relations and product promotion to security and compliance procedures.

General Info: Yr. Est. 1973, Monthly, Trim Size-8½ x 11, Offset press, 4 pages, ISSN: 0162-7473, No Color

Subscriptions: Indv. $105

List Rental: List Management Co.: Manager: Seena Benedek; WG & L List Management, 1 Penn Plz Fl 42, New York, NY 10119-0002 Tel # (212) 971-5000

Bankers' Letter of the Law
See: LAW

Bankers Middle Market Lending Letters

Publishing Co: Tax Institute, PO Box 191091, San Francisco, CA 94119-1091 Tel # (415) 566-5111 Parent Co.-Faulkner & Gray, Inc., New York; Title Tel # (212) 766-1251

General Info: (Formerly Middle Market Lending)

List Rental: Rents Lists

Bankers Research *Business*

Publishing Co: Bankers Research Inc., 34 Imperial Ave # 431, Westport, CT 06880-4304; Title Tel # (203) 227-1237

Personnel: Publisher, Editor-Theodore Volckhausen, Circ. Mgr.-Guillaine Dale

Editorial Description: Describes trends and developments in mortgages, consumer credit, savings and demand deposits.

General Info: Yr. Est. 1946, Semi-monthly, Trim Size-8½ x 11, Letrpr. press, 8 pages, 2 Color

Subscriptions: Indv. $196, $5/copy

Circulation: Total-2,000

Banking Attorney *Business*

Publishing Co: American Banker Newsletters, One State Plaza, New York, NY 10004-1505 Fax # (202) 843-9620; Title Tel # (212) 803-8300 Title Fax # (212) 843-9620

Personnel: Publisher-David G. Schutt, Editor-Arthur D. Postal, Circulation, Adv. Dir., Mktg. Dir.-Hans Winberg

Editorial Description: Legal trends affecting all depository institutions

General Info: Weekly

Subscriptions: Indv. $725, Can. $725, For. $755, $20/copy

Advertising: Inquire for rates.

List Rental: Rents Lists

Banking Automation
See: COMPUTERS & AUTOMATION

Banking Issues & Innovation in Products Marketing & Technology *Business*

Publishing Co: Bank Administration Institute, One N. Franklin St., Chicago, IL 60606 Tel # (312) 553-4600 Fax # (312) 683-2426; Title Tel # (708) 228-6200

Personnel: Editor-Phyllis Van Holland

General Info: Yr. Est. 1980, Monthly, 8 pages

Subscriptions: Indv. $120

Circulation: Total-1,600

List Rental: Rents Lists

Banking Law *Business*

Publishing Co: Matthew Bender & Co., 11 Penn Plaza, New York, NY 10001-2006 Tel # (212) 967-7707 Fax # (212) 244-3188

Editorial Description: Operational guidance for bank officers, with analysis of statutory law and agency regulations.

General Info: Yr. Est. 1989, Irregular, Looseleaf

Banking Law Briefs
See: LAW

Banking Law Manual: Legal Guide to Commerical Banks, Thrift Institutions and Credit Unions *Business*

Publishing Co: Matthew Bender & Co., 11 Penn Plaza, New York, NY 10001-2006 Tel # (212) 967-7707 Fax # (212) 244-3188
Editorial Description: The ideal desk reference, procedural guide, or training and management tool for the banking professional.
General Info: Yr. Est. 1983, Irregular, Looseleaf

Bankruptcy Alert
See: LAW

Bankruptcy Court Decisions
See: LAW

Bankruptcy Data Source *Business*

Publishing Co: New Generation Research, Inc., 225 Friend St Ste 801, Boston, MA 02114-1812 Fax # (617) 573-4554; Title Tel # (617) 573-9550 Title Fax # (617) 573-9554
Personnel: Publisher-George Putnam, Circ. Mgr.-Stacey Viveiros
Editorial Description: A comprehensive research product which follows public companies in bankruptcy, in default, or in financial distress which have assets greater than $50 million.
General Info: Yr. Est. 1988, Monthly
Subscriptions: Indv. $5,000, Inst. $5,000
List Rental: Rents Lists

Banks in Insurance Report
See: INSURANCE

Barrels, Bars, and BTUs *Business*

Publishing Co: New York Mercantile Exchange, 4 World Trade Center, New York, NY 10048-0137; Title Tel # (212) 748-3000
Editorial Description: Information on exchange activities and trading statistics.
General Info: (Formerly New York Mercantile Exchange News), Yr. Est. 1968, Monthly, Trim Size-8½ x 11, Offset press, 8 pages, No Color
Circulation: Total-500

Baxter Newsletter

Publishing Co: Baxter Co., 1030 E. Putnam Ave., Greenwich, CT 06836; Title Tel # (203) 637-4559
Personnel: Editor-William Banter
Editorial Description: Financial advisory newsletter.
General Info: Weekly
Subscriptions: Indv. $175

Best of Your Money Matters with Ric Edelman, The
See: INVESTMENT

Blue Chip Financial Forecasts
See: BUSINESS & INDUSTRY

Blue Chip Stocks
See: INVESTMENT

Boomer Report *Business*

Publishing Co: G.S. Schwartz & Co., Inc., 470 Park Ave S Fl 10, New York, NY 10016-6819; Title Tel # (212) 696-4744
Personnel: Publisher-Mary Ellen Ellwood, Editor-Frank Forest
Editorial Description: Reports on consumer buying trends, etc.
General Info: Yr. Est. 1989, Monthly
Subscriptions: Indv. $195

Bowne Digest for Corporate & Securities Lawyers
See: LAW

Bowne Review for CFO's & Investment Bankers 00 *Business*

Publishing Co: Brumberg Publications, Inc., 124 Harvard St., Brookline, MA 02146-6432; Title Tel # (617) 734-1979 Title Fax # (617) 734-1989
Personnel: Publisher-Bruce Brumberg, Editor-Susan Koffman, Production Mgr.-Karen Axelrod
Editorial Description: Summaries of articles on corporate finance & restructuring. Selects articles from hundreds of publications focusing on articles on trends & strategies.
General Info: Yr. Est. 1989, Monthly, Ind/Abs/Online: newsnet

Broadcast Banker/Broker *Business*

Publishing Co: Paul Kagan Associates Inc., 126 Clock Tower Pl., Carmel, CA 93923-8746; Title Tel # (408) 624-1536 Title Fax # (408) 625-3225
Personnel: Publisher-Paul Kagan, Circ. Mgr.-Judith Pinney, Adv. Dir., Adv. Dir.-Johanne Hardy
Editorial Description: Equity/debt financing for radio & TV, interest rates & cash/flow.
General Info: Yr. Est. 1984, Monthly, Trim Size-7¼ x 11, Other press, 12 pages, ISSN: 0889-2644, No Color, Other, Saddle-stitched
Subscriptions: Indv. $675
Advertising: $1,560.

Business Accounting for Lawyers Newsletter
See: ACCOUNTING

Business of Pleasure Boats *Business, Association*

Publishing Co: Natl. Marine Bankers Assn., 401 N Michigan Ave Ste 1150, Chicago, IL 60611-4205; Title Tel # (312) 836-9070
Personnel: Editor-Gregory Proteau
Editorial Description: News, statistics and trends for the recreational marine lender.
General Info: Yr. Est. 1980, Quarterly, Offset press, 4 pages, Color
Circulation: Total-2,700

Business Russia
See: INTERNATIONAL TRADE

CBA Reports *Business, Association*

Publishing Co: Consumer Bankers Assn., 1000 Wilson Blvd., 30th Fl., Arlington, VA 22209-3908; Title Tel # (703) 276-1750 Title Fax # (703) 528-1290
Personnel: Editor-Fritz Elmendorf
Editorial Description: News on retail banking for association members.
General Info: (Formerly Morris Plan Bankers Assn.), Yr. Est. 1919, Semi-monthly, Sheetfed press, 8 pages, 2 Color, Newsprint
Subscriptions: Indv. $100, Free With Membership
Circulation: (100% controlled), Total-5,200
List Rental: Actives: 13,616, $90/M
Printing Co: Lettercomm, Inc., 310 Swann Ave, Alexandria, VA 22301-1042 Tel # (703) 683-3105

CD Rate Watch *Consumer*

Publishing Co: Bauer Communications, Inc., PO Drawer 145510, 2655 LeJeune Rd PH1, Coral Gables, FL 33114-5510 Tel # (305) 445-9500 Fax # (305) 445-6775; Title Tel # (305) 441-2062 Title Fax # (305) 441-0691
Personnel: Publisher, Editor-Paul Bauer, Circ. Mgr.-Caroline Jervey
Editorial Description: Tracks the highest money market account & CD yields from federally insured, credit-worthy banks & thrifts nationwide for deposits from 100.00 up to 50,000.
General Info: (Formerly Rate Watch), Yr. Est. 1983, Monthly, Trim Size-8½ x 11, Letrpr. press, 8 pages, ISSN: 8750-3727, 2 Color, Other
Subscriptions: Indv. $99, Inst. $99, Can. $99, For. $119, $20/copy
Acquistions: Publication Bought
Circulation: (100% controlled), Total-2,500

CD Rateline

Publishing Co: United Communications Group, 11300 Rockville Pike, Ste. 1100, Rockville, MD 20852-3030 Tel # (301) 816-8950 Fax # (301) 816-8945; Title Tel # (301) 961-8700
Personnel: Publisher-Daniel Brown, Editor-Martin Zook, Circ. Mgr.-Sharon Welch
Editorial Description: Data on federally insured investments including the top 200 jumbo CD rates.
General Info: Yr. Est. 1983, Weekly, Web press, 8 pages, ISSN: 0746-5505, No Color
Subscriptions: Indv. $395, $8/copy
Acquistions: Publication Bought, Publication Sold
List Rental: Rents Lists

CFO & Controller Alert
See: ACCOUNTING

CPA Financial Planner Newsletter

Publishing Co: Practitioners Publishing Co., 3221 Collinsworth St, Fort Worth, TX 76107-6582; Title Tel # (817) 332-3709

CPA Managing Partner Report
See: LAW

CRA Bulletin (Community Reinvestment Act) *Business*

Publishing Co: Warren, Gorham & Lamont, 31 Saint James Ave., Boston, MA 02116-4112 Parent Co.-Thomson Professional Publications, Stamford; Title Tel # (617) 423-2020 Title Fax # (617) 423-1914
Personnel: Publisher-Larry Selby, Mktg. Dir.-Sandra Fox
Editorial Description: How to create cost-effective compliance procedures that satisfy federal examiners, community groups and the bank.
General Info: Yr. Est. 1991, Monthly, Trim Size-8½ x 11, Offset press, 8 pages
Subscriptions: Indv. $165
List Rental: List Management Co.: Manager: Seena Benedek; WG & L List Management, 1 Penn Plz Fl 42, New York, NY 10119-0002 Tel # (212) 971-5000

CRA/HMDA Update *Business*

Publishing Co: Inside Mortgage Finance Publications, Box 42387, Washington, DC 20015; Title Tel # (301) 951-1240 Title Fax # (301) 656-1709
Personnel: Publisher-Guy Cecala, Editor, Mng. Editor-John Lewis, Production Mgr.-Tony Cecala, Circ. Mgr., Mktg. Dir.-Didi Parks
General Info: Monthly, Trim Size-8½ x 11, 30 pages, Color
Subscriptions: Indv. $395, $50/copy

CRB Futures Chart Service
See: INVESTMENT

CSBS Examiner
Business, Association

Publishing Co: Conference of State Bank Supervisors, 1015 18th St. NW #1100, Washington, DC 20036-5275; Title Tel # (202) 296-2840
Personnel: Editor-Ellen Lamb
Editorial Description: Weekly newsletter of events affecting state banking.
General Info: Yr. Est. 1990, Weekly, Trim Size-17 x 11, Web press, 4 pages, No Color
Subscriptions: Inst. $375, Free With Membership
Circulation: Total-5,600, Readership-5,600
Printing Co: Plymouth Printing, 1200 Cushing Pl SE, Washington, DC 20003-3599
Tel # (202) 488-7777, Fax # (202) 863-1078

Cable TV Finance
See: TELEVISION & VIDEO

California Public Finance
Business

Publishing Co: American Banker Newsletters, One State Plaza, New York, NY 10004-1505
Fax # (202) 843-9620; Title Tel # (212) 803-8300 Title Fax # (212) 843-9620
Personnel: Publisher-David G. Schutt, Editor-David Calvey, Circulation-Maria Pritchett, Adv. Dir., Mktg. Dir.-Hans Winberg
Editorial Description: Municipal finance in the Golden State.
General Info: Yr. Est. 1989, Weekly, Ind/Abs/Online: Mead Data Central, NewsNet, Predicasts
Subscriptions: Indv. $595, Can. $595, For. $625, $20/copy

Callahan's Credit Union Report
Business

Publishing Co: Callahan & Assocs., Inc., 1001 Connecticut Ave NW Ste, 1022, Washington, DC 20036-5504 Tel # (202) 223-3920; Title Tel # (202) 223-3922 Title Fax # (202) 223-1311
Personnel: Editor-Brooke Stoddard, Production Mgr.-Mary Sue Farley
Editorial Description: Written by credit union managers & consultants working at the cutting edge of change. Each issue delivers data & analysis available nowhere else.
General Info: Yr. Est. 1987, Monthly, Sheetfed press, 8 pages, 2 Color, Coated
Subscriptions: $149/copy
Circulation: Total-1,000
List Rental: Rents Lists
Printing Co: Panic Press, 1656 K St NW, Washington, DC 20006-2801

Canadian Small Business Financing and Tax Planning Guide
See: TAXES

Canadian Treasury Management Review

Publishing Co: Royal Bank of Canada, 9th fl., South Tower, Royal Bank Plaza, Toronto, ON M5J 2J5 Canada; Title Tel # (416) 974-6268
Personnel: Circ. Mgr.-Anne Henry, Editor, Circ. Mgr.-Colleen Killeavy
General Info: Yr. Est. 1984, Bi-monthly, Trim Size-8½ x 11, Web press, 12 pages, ISSN: 0829-4003, 2 Color, Coated, Saddle-stitched
Subscriptions: Indv. $75

Card Fax

Publishing Co: Faulkner & Gray, Inc., 11 Penn Plz., 17th Floor, New York, NY 10001-2006
Tel # (212) 967-7000 Fax # (212) 695-8172 Parent Co.-Thomson Corp., Stamford;
Title Tel # (312) 648-0261
Editorial Description: Fax newsletter on credit card issues. 150 bulletins sent per year in addition to weekly issues.
General Info: Weekly
Subscriptions: Indv. $695

Card News
See: CREDIT AND CREDIT UNIONS

Cards International

Publishing Co: Lafferty Publications, 420 Lexington Ave., Ste. 1745, New York, NY 10170
Tel # (212) 557-6729 Fax # (212) 557-7266; Title Tel # (404) 636-6610 Title Fax # (404) 636-6422
Personnel: Publisher-Frank Lawson, Editor in Chief-Michael Lafferty, Editor-Richard Martin
Editorial Description: Reports & analyzes the latest developments in credit, debit & ATM cards & the efforts of those who market them. The coverage is global in scope.
General Info: Yr. Est. 1989, 23x/yr.
Subscriptions: Indv. $1,159

Cardtrak
See: CREDIT AND CREDIT UNIONS

Cash Manager

Publishing Co: Phillips Business Information, Inc., 1201 Seven Locks Rd., Ste 300, Potomac, MD 20854-2958 Tel # (301) 340-1520 Fax # (301) 424-4297; Title Tel # (301) 340-2100
Title Fax # (301) 340-0542
Editorial Description: Focuses on cash management and other financial topics.
General Info: Monthly
Subscriptions: Indv. $275
Acquistions: Publication Sold

Center for Rural Affairs Newsletter
See: AGRICULTURE

Chapter 11 Update
See: LAW

Cheapskate Monthly
Consumer

Publishing Co: Cheapskate Monthly, PO Box 2135, Paramount, CA 90723-8135;
Title Tel # (310) 630-8845 Title Fax # (310) 630-3433
Personnel: Editor-Ann Hunt
Editorial Description: Helps families with financial tips and advice for saving money.
General Info: Yr. Est. 1992, Monthly
Subscriptions: Indv. $13

Checks & Checking

Publishing Co: Moroney & Co., PO Box 720, Glen Echo, MD 20812-0720; Title Tel # (301) 229-4100
Title Fax # (301) 229-4102
Personnel: Publisher-William Moroney, Editor-Patti Murphy
Editorial Description: Focuses on checking and other financial subjects.
General Info: Monthly, 8 pages, No Color
Subscriptions: Indv. $295

Checks and Balances

Publishing Co: Chemical Bank, 270 Park Avenue, New York, NY 10017
Editorial Description: General information on personal finance for Chemical Bank patrons.
General Info: Quarterly, Trim Size-8½ x 11, 4 pages, 2 Color

Checks, Drafts and Notes
Business

Publishing Co: Matthew Bender & Co., 11 Penn Plaza, New York, NY 10001-2006
Tel # (212) 967-7707 Fax # (212) 244-3188
Editorial Description: Coverage of the law of checks and negotiable instruments.
General Info: Yr. Est. 1983, Irregular, Looseleaf

Chicago Stock Exchange Guide
Business

Publishing Co: CCH, Inc., 2700 Lake Cook Rd., Riverwoods, IL 60015 Parent Co.-Kluwer Law & Taxation Publishers, Cambridge; Title Tel # (847) 267-7000 Title Fax # (800) 224-8299
Editorial Description: Covers directory, officers, governors, directors, membership, constitution and rules.
General Info: (Formerly Midwest Stock Exchange Guide), Yr. Est. 1967, Monthly, Trim Size-6 x 9, Web press, 128 pages, No Color, Looseleaf
Subscriptions: Indv. $475

Chile Economic Report
See: INTERNATIONAL TRADE

Clark's Bank Deposits and Payments Monthly
Business

Publishing Co: Warren, Gorham & Lamont, 31 Saint James Ave., Boston, MA 02116-4112 Parent Co.-Thomson Professional Publications, Stamford; Title Tel # (617) 423-2020
Title Fax # (617) 423-1914
Personnel: Publisher-Larry Selby, Co-Editor-Barbara Brewer Clark, Co-Editor-Barkley Clark, Mktg. Dir.-Sandra Fox
Editorial Description: Explains new developments in the laws affecting bank deposits, collections, and credit cards.
General Info: Yr. Est. 1993, Monthly
Subscriptions: Indv. $165
List Rental: List Management Co.: Manager: Seena Benedek; WG & L List Management, 1 Penn Plz Fl 42, New York, NY 10119-0002 Tel # (212) 971-5000

Clark's Secured Transactions Monthly
Business

Publishing Co: Warren, Gorham & Lamont, 31 Saint James Ave., Boston, MA 02116-4112 Parent Co.-Thomson Professional Publications, Stamford; Title Tel # (617) 423-2020
Title Fax # (617) 423-1914
Personnel: Publisher-Larry Selby, Co-Editor-Barbara Brewer Clark, Co-Editor-Barkley Clark, Mktg. Dir.-Sandra Fox
Editorial Description: Information on the latest developments impacting the banking industry.
General Info: Yr. Est. 1985, Monthly, Trim Size-8½ x 11, 8 pages, 2 Color
Subscriptions: Indv. $150
List Rental: List Management Co.: Manager: Seena Benedek; WG & L List Management, 1 Penn Plz Fl 42, New York, NY 10119-0002 Tel # (212) 971-5000

Client Planning Advisory
See: BUSINESS & INDUSTRY

Client Quarterly

Publishing Co: WPI Communications, Inc., 55 Morris Ave, Springfield, NJ 07081-1496;
Title Tel # (201) 467-8700 Title Fax # (201) 467-0368
Personnel: Publisher-Steven Klingoffer
Editorial Description: Financial news and information.
General Info: Yr. Est. 1988, Quarterly
List Rental: Rents Lists

Coffee, Sugar & Cocoa Exchange
See: INVESTMENT

Collection Agency Report *Business*

Publishing Co: First Detroit Corp., PO Box 5025, Warren, MI 48090-5025; Title Tel # (810) 573-0045 Title Fax # (810) 573-9219
Personnel: Publisher, Editor-Albert W. Scace, Circ. Mgr.-Patricia A. Herrick
Editorial Description: News and analysis of the collection agency industry.
General Info: Yr. Est. 1990, Monthly, Trim Size-8½ x 11, Offset press, 8 pages, ISSN: 1052-4029, 2 Color, Matte, Other
Subscriptions: Indv. $231
Circulation: Total-350
List Rental: Actives: 9,000, $100/M
Printing Co: Lesnau Printing, 6025 Wall St., Sterling Heights, MI 48312 Tel # (810) 795-9200, Fax # (810) 795-5523

Collier on Bankruptcy
See: LAW

Collier Bankruptcy Compensation Guide
See: LAW

Collier Bankruptcy Exemption Guide
See: LAW

Collier Bankruptcy Practice Guide
See: LAW

Collier Family Law and the Bankruptcy Code
See: LAW

Collier Farm Bankruptcy
See: LAW

Collier Labor Law and the Bankruptcy Code
See: LAW

Collier Lending Institutions and the Bankruptcy Code
See: LAW

Collier Real Estate Transactions and the Bankruptcy Code
See: REAL ESTATE

Collier, Sarner & Associates
Doctors Newsletter *Business*

Publishing Co: Collier, Sarner & Associates, Inc, 30195 Chagrin Boulevard, #100, Cleveland, OH 44124 Tel # (212) 765-1199; Title Tel # (216) 765-1199 Title Fax # (216) 831-8279
Personnel: Publisher, Editor-Richard Collier
Editorial Description: Tax, practice management and financial advice ofr doa
General Info: Yr. Est. 1970, Semi-monthly
Subscriptions: Indv. $130

Commercial Finance *Business*

Publishing Co: Matthew Bender & Co., 11 Penn Plaza, New York, NY 10001-2006 Tel # (212) 967-7707 Fax # (212) 244-3188
Personnel: Editor in Chief-Joseph J. Norton
Editorial Description: The perfect companion to Norton's Commercial Loan Documentation Guide provides extensive coverage of commerical financial products other than basic loan agreements.
General Info: Yr. Est. 1990, Irregular, Looseleaf

Commercial Lending
Newsletter *Business*

Publishing Co: Robert Morris Associates, 1 Liberty Pl., 1650 Market St., Suite 2300, Philadelphia, PA 19103-7398 Tel # (215) 851-0585 Fax # (215) 851-9205; Title Tel # (215) 851-9100 Title Fax # (215) 851-9206
Personnel: Editor-Louis Morales
Editorial Description: Dealing exclusively with the needs of commercial bank lenders.
General Info: (Formerly RMA News), Yr. Est. 1969, Monthly, Trim Size-8½ x 11, Sheetfed press, 6 pages, 2 Color, Coated
Subscriptions: Indv. $35, $3/copy
Circulation: Total-20,200
Printing Co: George H. Buchanan Co., 23rd & Washington Ave., Philadelphia, PA 19146 Tel # (215) 545-3960

Commercial Loan
Documentation Guide *Business*

Publishing Co: Matthew Bender & Co., 11 Penn Plaza, New York, NY 10001-2006 Tel # (212) 967-7707 Fax # (212) 244-3188
Personnel: Editor-Joseph J. Norton
Editorial Description: Covers the full spectrum of loan documentation and includes forms, checklists, and useful hints for both borrowers and lenders,
General Info: Yr. Est. 1988, Irregular, Looseleaf

Commercial Mortgage
Alert *Business* CPM$2125

Publishing Co: Harrison Scott Publications, One Riverfront Plaza, Suite 1480, Newark, NJ 07102-5495; Title Tel # (201) 596-1300 Title Fax # (201) 596-0148
Personnel: Publisher, Editor-Andrew Albert, Production Mgr.-Daniel Cowles
Editorial Description: Updates on commercial mortgage securitization for lenders, investment banks, and securities attorneys.
General Info: Yr. Est. 1993, Weekly, 6 pages
Subscriptions: Indv. $1,347, Inst. $1,347, Can. $1,347, For. $1,397
Circulation: Total-400
Advertising: $850.
List Rental: Rents Lists
Printing Co: Sir Speedy, 40 Commerce St, Newark, NJ 07102-4003 Tel # (201) 242-4040

Commodex (R) System, The
See: INVESTMENT

Commodity Futures Forecast (R) Service
See: INVESTMENT

Community Bank President,
The *Business*

Publishing Co: Siefer Consultants, Inc., 525 Cayuga St., PO Box 1384, Storm Lake, IA 50588; Title Tel # (712) 732-7340 Title Fax # (712) 732-7906
Personnel: Editor-Steve Stepanek, Publisher, Circ. Mgr.-Dan Siefer
Editorial Description: Management and marketing ideas for presidents and executive officers.
General Info: Yr. Est. 1981, Semi-monthly, Sheetfed press, 8 pages, ISSN: 0276-0908, No Color
Subscriptions: Indv. $319, Can. $319, For. $350, $15/copy

Community First *Business, Consumer*

Publishing Co: Community Capital Bank, 111 Livingston St, Brooklyn, NY 11201-8111; Title Tel # (718) 802-1212
Editorial Description: Information about Community Capital Bank and its work in community development.
General Info: Quarterly
Subscriptions: Free To Qualified Recipient

Community Reinvestment
Quarterly *Business*

Publishing Co: Illinois Bankers Association, 111 N. Canal St., Chicago, IL 60606-7299; Title Tel # (312) 876-9900 Title Fax # (312) 876-3826
Editorial Description: Quarterly newsletter with practical information on complying with the challenge of the Community Reinvestment Act.
General Info: Yr. Est. 1990, Quarterly
Subscriptions: Indv. $65
Circulation: Total-250

Compliance Reporter *Business*

Publishing Co: Capital Cities/ABC, 488 Madison Ave., 16th Floor, New York, NY 10022-5751 Fax # (212) 224-3353 Parent Co.-Capital Cities/ABC, Inc., New York; Title Tel # (212) 224-3233 Title Fax # (212) 224-3111
General Info: Bi-weekly, Trim Size-8½ x 11, Sheetfed press, 14 pages, 2 Color, Newsprint
Advertising: Inquire for rates.

Conservative Speculator
See: INVESTMENT

Consumer Bankruptcy
Issues *Consumer*

Publishing Co: Consumer Bankruptcy Issues, PO Box 535, Princeton, IL 61356-0535; Title Tel # (815) 875-4078
Personnel: Publisher, Editor-Bob Throckmorton
Editorial Description: Covers bankruptcy issues for consumers.
General Info: Bi-monthly
Subscriptions: Indv. $24

Consumer Bankruptcy
News *Business*

Publishing Co: LRP Publications, 747 Dresher Rd., P.O. Box 980, Horsham, PA 19044-0980 Tel # (215) 784-0910 Fax # (215) 784-0317
Personnel: Publisher-Ken Kahn, Editor-David Light
Editorial Description: Latest news & cases involving consumer bankruptcy including summaries and practical analyses in-depth articles, commentaries and practice pointers.
General Info: Bi-weekly
Subscriptions: Indv. $255

Consumer Confidence
Survey

Publishing Co: Conference Board, Inc., 845 3rd Ave., New York, NY 10022-6679; Title Tel # (212) 759-0900 Title Fax # (212) 980-7014
Personnel: Editor-Fabian Linden
General Info: Monthly

Consumer Credit & TIL
Compliance Report   *Business*

Publishing Co: Warren, Gorham & Lamont, 31 Saint James Ave., Boston, MA 02116-4112 Parent Co.-Thomson Professional Publications, Stamford; Title Tel # (617) 423-2020 Title Fax # (617) 423-1914
Personnel: Publisher-Larry Selby, Mktg. Dir.-Sandra Fox
Editorial Description: Reports on consumer credit and related topics.
General Info: Yr. Est. 1973, Monthly
Subscriptions: Indv. $180
List Rental: List Management Co.: Manager: Seena Benedek; WG & L List Management, 1 Penn Plz Fl 42, New York, NY 10119-0002 Tel # (212) 971-5000

Consumer Credit Guide   *Business*

Publishing Co: CCH, Inc., 2700 Lake Cook Rd., Riverwoods, IL 60015 Parent Co.-Kluwer Law & Taxation Publishers, Cambridge; Title Tel # (847) 267-7000 Title Fax # (800) 224-8299
Editorial Description: Spans federal and state consumer credit, disclosure and recission rules.
General Info: Yr. Est. 1969, Bi-weekly, Trim Size-6 x 9, Web press, 150 pages, No Color, Looseleaf
Subscriptions: Indv. $1,102

Consumer Credit: Law,
Transaction and Forms   *Business*

Publishing Co: Matthew Bender & Co., 11 Penn Plaza, New York, NY 10001-2006 Tel # (212) 967-7707 Fax # (212) 244-3188
Editorial Description: Detailed treatment of the law with practical, step-by-step guidance for every stage of consumer credit transaction.
General Info: Yr. Est. 1984, Irregular, Looseleaf

Consumer Finance Law
Bulletin   *Association*

Publishing Co: American Financial Services Assn., 919 18th Street, N.W., Washington, DC 20006-5503; Title Tel # (202) 296-5544 Title Fax # (202) 223-0321
Personnel: Editor-Robert McKew
Editorial Description: Information & summaries of consumer finance legal issues.
General Info: Monthly
Subscriptions: Indv. $95

Consumer Finance
Newsletter   *Business*

Publishing Co: Financial Publishing Co., 82 Brookline Ave, Boston, MA 02215-3905; Title Tel # (617) 262-4040
Personnel: Editor-Dorothy Walter
Editorial Description: Provides information on effective & pending changes affecting the consumer finance industry.
General Info: Yr. Est. 1975, Monthly, Trim Size-8$\frac{1}{2}$ x 11, Sheetfed press, 2 pages, No Color, Newsprint
Circulation: Total-1,800
Printing Co: Financial Publishing Co., 82 Brookline Ave, Boston, MA 02215-3905 Tel # (617) 262-4040

Consumer Lending News   *Business*

Publishing Co: Siefer Consultants, Inc., 525 Cayuga St., PO Box 1384, Storm Lake, IA 50588; Title Tel # (712) 732-7340 Title Fax # (712) 732-7906
Personnel: Editor-Connie McClain
Editorial Description: Strategies to improve consumer loan portfolios for financial institutions. Ideas to improve consumer loan qualtiy, growth and collections.
General Info: Yr. Est. 1993, Monthly, ISSN: 1077-0445
Subscriptions: Indv. $249, Can. $249, For. $280, $15/copy

Consumer Trends   *Association*

Publishing Co: Intl. Credit Assn., 243 N. Lindbergh Blvd., PO Box 419057, St. Louis, MO 63141-1757; Title Tel # (314) 991-3030 Title Fax # (314) 991-3029
Personnel: Publisher-Elizabeth Miller, Adv. Dir.-William Murray, Circ. Mgr., Production Mgr., Art Dir.-Pattie Gillham, Editor, Art Dir.-Janet Lipkind
Editorial Description: Newsletter on credit & financial affairs, published by and owned by the International Credit Association. Consumer Trends is a benefit to ICA members and by subscription.
General Info: (Formerly ICA's Newsletter), Yr. Est. 1963, Monthly, Offset press, 2 Color, Matte, Other
Subscriptions: Indv. $100, $10/copy
Circulation: (100% controlled), Total-7,000
List Rental: Actives, 8,000, $100/M
Printing Co: Hadler Printing, 815 Ferguson, St. Louis, MO 63135 Tel # (314) 522-0457

Corporate Control Alert   *Business*

Publishing Co: American Lawyer Media, L.P., 600 3rd Ave., New York, NY 10016-1999 Tel # (212) 973-2800 Fax # (212) 972-6258; Title Tel # (212) 973-2816 Title Fax # (212) 973-2829
Personnel: Publisher-Karen Dillion, Editor-John Close
Editorial Description: Newsletter on takeovers and proxy fights.
General Info: Yr. Est. 1984, 11x/yr., 8 pages, ISSN: 0743-0272, No Color
Subscriptions: Indv. $1,495
Circulation: Total-475
List Rental: Rents Lists

Corporate EFT Report   *Business*

Publishing Co: Phillips Business Information, Inc., 1201 Seven Locks Rd., Ste 300, Potomac, MD 20854-2958 Tel # (301) 340-1520; Title Tel # (301) 340-2100 Title Fax # (301) 424-4297
Personnel: Publisher-Chris Scotton, Editor-Ed Bond, Production Mgr.-Teresa Fleisher, Adv. Dir.-Kim Hudak, Mktg. Dir.-Kelly Ebbs
Editorial Description: Analyzes all aspects of electronic cash management and money transfer. Covers technologies used by companies to effect sound cash and treasury management.
General Info: (Formerly Treasury Manager; Treasury Watch), Yr. Est. 1980, Bi-weekly, 8 pages, ISSN: 0272-0299, Ind/Abs/Online: NewsNet, DIALOG, Predicasts, Bloomberg., 2 Color
Subscriptions: Indv. $595, For. $630, $37/copy
Acquistions: Publication Bought, Publication Sold
List Rental: Rents Lists

Corporate Finance Letter

Publishing Co: America's Community Bankers, 900 19th St. NW, Ste. 400, Washington, DC 20006-2105 Fax # (202) 659-1134; Title Tel # (202) 857-3100
Editorial Description: Covers research on new financing & management techniques in savings industry.
General Info: Yr. Est. 1983, Monthly
Subscriptions: Indv. $295

Corporate Financing Week
See: BUSINESS & INDUSTRY

Corporate Growth Weekly Report
See: BUSINESS & INDUSTRY

Cost Control News   *Business*

Publishing Co: Siefer Consultants, Inc., 525 Cayuga St., PO Box 1384, Storm Lake, IA 50588; Title Tel # (712) 732-7340 Title Fax # (712) 732-7906
Personnel: Publisher-Dan Siefer, Editor-Steve Stepanek
Editorial Description: Cost cotrol ideas for financial institutions. Proven ways to reduce operating and interest cost.
General Info: Yr. Est. 1990, Monthly, ISSN: 1060-0677
Subscriptions: Indv. $249, Can. $249, For. $280, $15/copy

Cost Control Strategies for
Health Care Providers   *Business*

Publishing Co: Siefer Consultants, Inc., 525 Cayuga St., PO Box 1384, Storm Lake, IA 50588 Tel # (712) 732-7340 Fax # (712) 732-7906
Editorial Description: Proven strategies to reduce overhead costs.
General Info: Yr. Est. 1995
Subscriptions: Indv. $249, $15/copy

Courier

Publishing Co: Arizona Bank, PO Box 2511, Phoenix, AZ 85002-2511; Title Tel # (602) 262-2211
Personnel: Editor-Wayne Leshaune
Editorial Description: Internal newsletter, includes promotions, classified ads.
General Info: Yr. Est. 1983, Bi-weekly, Trim Size-8$\frac{1}{2}$ x 11, Offset press, 4 pages, 3% ads, No Color, Newsprint
Circulation: Total-3,000
Advertising: Inquire for rates.

Cred-Alert   *Business, Association*

Publishing Co: American Collectors Assn., Inc., 4040 W 70th St, Minneapolis, MN 55435-4104; Title Tel # (612) 926-6547 Title Fax # (612) 926-1624
Personnel: Editor-Sandra Whalen
General Info: Monthly, 4 pages
Subscriptions: Indv. $36, Free With Membership
Circulation: Total-39,000
Printing Co: Curle Printing Co., 3982 Alabama Ave S, Minneapolis, MN 55416-2877 Tel # (612) 929-0346

Credit Card Collector
See: CREDIT AND CREDIT UNIONS

Credit Risk Management Report
See: CREDIT AND CREDIT UNIONS

Credit Union Accountant   *Business*

Publishing Co: American Banker Newsletters, One State Plaza, New York, NY 10004-1505 Fax # (202) 843-9620; Title Tel # (212) 803-8300 Title Fax # (212) 843-9620
Personnel: Publisher-David G. Schutt, Editor-Melanie Waddell, Circulation-Celia Benjamin, Adv. Dir., Mktg. Dir.-Hans Winberg
Editorial Description: Developments affecting accounting for Credit Unions.
General Info: Weekly
Subscriptions: Indv. $695, Can. $695, For. $725, $20/copy
Advertising: Inquire for rates.

Credit Union Directors
Newsletter   *Business, Association*

Publishing Co: Credit Union National Association, Inc., 5710 Mineral Point, Madison, WI 53705
Tel # (608) 231-4860 Fax # (608) 231-4858; Title Tel # (608) 231-4080
Personnel: Publisher-Nancy Huepenbecker, Editor-James Hanson, Circ. Mgr.-Mark Condon, Circ. Mgr.-Philip Heckman, Adv. Dir.-Phyllis Peterson.
Editorial Description: Policy advice and trends for boards of directors.
General Info: (Formerly Board CEO Newsletter), Yr. Est. 1977, Monthly, Trim Size-8½ x 11, Letrpr. press, 4 pages, 3% ads, No Color, Newsprint
Subscriptions: Indv. $58, $10/copy
Circulation: Total-3,613

Credit Union Law Service   *Business*

Publishing Co: Matthew Bender & Co., 11 Penn Plaza, New York, NY 10001-2006
Tel # (212) 967-7707 Fax # (212) 244-3188
Editorial Description: Guide to the laws & regulation governing credit unions, with practical governing credit unions, with pracitcal analysis, explanations, forms & primary source documentation. Written in collaboration with the Credit Union National Assn. (CUNA).
General Info: Yr. Est. 1985, Monthly, Looseleaf

Credit Union Newswatch   *Business, Association*

Publishing Co: Credit Union National Association, Inc., 5710 Mineral Point, Madison, WI 53705
Tel # (608) 231-4860; Title Tel # (608) 231-4042 Title Fax # (608) 231-4858
Personnel: Publisher-Dick Williamson, Editor-Jack Blake, Circ. Mgr.-Ellie Berg, Circ. Mgr.-Lynn Kitsemble, Art Dir.-Linda Napiwocki
Editorial Description: Association and industry news and information for credit union officials.
General Info: (Formerly Leadership Letter), Yr. Est. 1973, Weekly, Trim Size-8½ x 11, Offset press, 8 pages, ISSN: 0889-5597, 2 Color
Subscriptions: Indv. $125, Free With Membership
Circulation: (100% controlled), Total-18,000

Creditors Workout Report
See: LAW

Creneau

Publishing Co: Creneau Inc., 1620 Northwest Blvd., Coeur d'Alene, ID 83814;
Title Tel # (208) 667-7844 Title Fax # (208) 667-7844
Personnel: Editor-Gretchen Berning
Editorial Description: Presents timely financial news and information.
General Info: Yr. Est. 1988, Monthly
Subscriptions: Indv. $89

Cross Roads

Publishing Co: Federal Reserve Bank of Dallas, Station K, Dallas, TX 75222;
Title Tel # (214) 651-6111

Cross Sales Report   *Business*

Publishing Co: Siefer Consultants, Inc., 525 Cayuga St., PO Box 1384, Storm Lake, IA 50588;
Title Tel # (712) 732-7340 Title Fax # (712) 732-7906
Personnel: Publisher-Dan Siefer, Editor-Joe Sheller
Editorial Description: Cross sales and customer service ideas for financial institutions. Techniques to improve sales and cross sales of bank products and services.
General Info: Yr. Est. 1992, Semi-monthly, ISSN: 1066-6419
Subscriptions: Indv. $319, Can. $319, For. $350, $15/copy

Crow's Weekly Market Report
See: LUMBER & WOOD

Currency Quarterly
See: INVESTMENT

Current Issues in Bank
Auditing   *Association*

Publishing Co: Bank Research Assocs., PO Box 7812, Boise, ID 83707-1812;
Title Tel # (208) 322-3508
General Info: Yr. Est. 1978, Monthly
Subscriptions: Indv. $58

Cuso Network

Publishing Co: Natl. Assn. of Federal Credit Unions, PO Box 3769, Washington, DC 20007-0269;
Title Tel # (703) 522-4770
Personnel: Editor-Pat Keefe
General Info: Bi-monthly, 4 pages

Daily BankFAX   *Business*

Publishing Co: SNL Securities, 410 E. Main St., P.O. Box 2124, Charlottesville, VA 22902;
Title Tel # (804) 977-1600 Title Fax # (804) 977-4466
Personnel: Publisher-Reid Nagle, Circ. Mgr.-Pat Labua, Production Mgr.-L. Todd Vencil, Adv. Dir.-Jenn Nagaj, Mktg. Dir.-Judy Lewis
Editorial Description: Summarizes the news of the previous day providing the latest filings, M & A activity, and more.
General Info: Yr. Est. 1988, Daily, Trim Size-8.5 x 11, Desktop press, 6 pages, No Color, Other
Subscriptions: Indv. $695
Advertising: $400.

Daily Thrift watch   *Business*

Publishing Co: SNL Securities, 410 E. Main St., P.O. Box 2124, Charlottesville, VA 22902;
Title Tel # (804) 977-1600 Title Fax # (804) 977-4466
Personnel: Publisher-Reid Nagle, Editor-Jenn Nagaj, Circ. Mgr.-Pat LaBua, Production Mgr.-Paul Doherty, Mktg. Dir.-Judy Lewis
Editorial Description: The Daily Thrift Watch is a fax letter that summarizes all relevant data on the thrift industry.
General Info: Yr. Est. 1988, Daily, Trim Size-8.5 x 11, Desktop press, No Color
Advertising: Inquire for rates.

Daily Treasury Statement

Publishing Co: Daily Treasury Statement, G.P.O., Washington, DC 20402-0001;
Title Tel # (202) 783-3238 Title Fax # (202) 275-0019
General Info: Daily
Subscriptions: Indv. $174, Can. $218, For. $218
List Rental: Rents Lists

Dallas Fed Roundup

Publishing Co: Federal Reserve Bank of Dallas, Station K, Dallas, TX 75222;
Title Tel # (214) 651-6111

Deposit Growth Strategies   *Business*

Publishing Co: Siefer Consultants, Inc., 525 Cayuga St., PO Box 1384, Storm Lake, IA 50588;
Title Tel # (712) 732-7340 Title Fax # (712) 732-7906
Personnel: Publisher-Dan Siefer, Editor-Joe Sheller
Editorial Description: Ideas to help financial institutions increase deposits and retain them. Proven ways to profitably increase retail deposits.
General Info: Yr. Est. 1994, Monthly, ISSN: 1082-8605
Subscriptions: Indv. $249, Can. $249, For. $280, $15/copy

Depreciation & Capital
Planning   *Business, Association*

Publishing Co: Research Institute of America, 90 5th Avenue, New York, NY 10011-7629
Tel # (212) 645-4800; Title Tel # (800) 562-0245 Title Fax # (201) 816-3484
Editorial Description: Complete planning reference to all changes in depreciation & investment credits.
General Info: Yr. Est. 1987, Semi-annually, Trim Size-7 x 9
Subscriptions: Indv. $125
List Rental: List Management Co.: WG & L List Management, 1 Penn Plz Fl 42, New York, NY 10119-0002 Tel # (212) 971-5000

Derivatives Week
See: INVESTMENT

Development Bank Business Report
See: INTERNATIONAL TRADE

Direct Delivery International   *Business*

Publishing Co: Lafferty Publications, 420 Lexington Ave., Ste. 1745, New York, NY 10170
Tel # (212) 557-6729 Fax # (212) 557-7266
Personnel: Publisher-Frank Lawson, Editor-Peter Kinahan
Editorial Description: Focuses exclusively on the new developments, strategies and growing trends associated with the direct delivery of consumer financial services. Each issue reports on new launches, new products and technology in insurance and banking. It tracks the innovative practices of the major banks as well as the non bank players. Most of all it will keep you at the cutting edge of developments in the worldwide exp
General Info: Yr. Est. 1995, Monthly
Subscriptions: Indv. $579

Direct Investment in North
America   *Business*

Publishing Co: Bureau of National Affairs, Inc., 1231 25th St. NW, Bldg. N-200, Washington, DC 20037-1157; Title Tel # (202) 452-4200 Title Fax # (202) 822-8092
Personnel: Publisher-William Beltz, Editor-Kenneth Skilling, Circ. Mgr.-Gaina Hadley
Editorial Description: Two binders housing monthly journal news & analysis & reference binder
General Info: (Formerly Direct Investment in the U.S.), Yr. Est. 1989, Monthly, Trim Size-8¼ x 11¾, ISSN: 0958-3076
Subscriptions: Indv. $660

Directors Digest   *Business*

Publishing Co: Savings & Community Bankers of America, 900 19th St. NW, Ste. 400, Washington, DC 20006-2105; Title Tel # (202) 857-3146 Title Fax # (202) 296-8716
Personnel: Publisher-Robert Bradner, Editor-William Marshall, Circ. Mgr.-Mary Ann Kiszka
Editorial Description: News & instruction for savings association outside directors.
General Info: Yr. Est. 1942, Monthly, Trim Size-8½ x 11, Sheetfed press, 4 pages, ISSN: 0279-2141, Color
Subscriptions: Indv. $28, $3/copy
Circulation: Total-23,000

EFT Report
Business

Publishing Co: Phillips Business Information, Inc., 1201 Seven Locks Rd., Ste 300, Potomac, MD 20854-2958; Title Tel # (301) 340-1520 Title Fax # (301) 424-4297
Personnel: Publisher-Chris Scotton, Editor-Claire Taylor, Production Mgr.-Teresa Fleisher, Adv. Dir.-Kim Hudak, Mktg. Dir.-Kelly Ebbs
Editorial Description: Electronic banking, ATMS & networks.
General Info: Yr. Est. 1978, Bi-weekly, 8 pages, ISSN: 0195-7287, Ind/Abs/Online: NewsN, DIALOG, Predicasts, Bloomberg, 2 Color
Subscriptions: Indv. $595, For. $630
Acquistions: Publication Bought, Publication Sold
List Rental: Rents Lists

ERISA Newsletter

Publishing Co: ERISA Newsletter, 11 Pleasant St, Berlin, MA 01503-1610; Title Tel # (508) 838-2104
Personnel: Publisher-Thomas Andrew
General Info: Yr. Est. 1975, Monthly
Subscriptions: Indv. $77

East European Banker

Publishing Co: Lafferty Publications, 420 Lexington Ave., Ste. 1745, New York, NY 10170 Tel # (212) 557-6729 Fax # (212) 557-7266; Title Tel # (404) 636-6610 Title Fax # (404) 636-6422
Personnel: Publisher-Frank Lawson, Editor in Chief-Michael Lafferty
Editorial Description: East European Banker examines and analyses developments in privatization, legislation, banking, insurance, consulting and accounting across-East and Central Europe.
General Info: 10x/yr.
Subscriptions: Indv. $899

Economic & Business Outlook

Publishing Co: Bank of America NT & SA, 555 California St., San Francisco, CA 94104-1590
General Info: (Formerly US Economic Report)

Economic Update

Publishing Co: America's Community Bankers, 900 19th St. NW, Ste. 400, Washington, DC 20006-2105 Fax # (202) 659-1134; Title Tel # (202) 857-3100
Editorial Description: Newsletter reporting on economic trends & issues affecting savings industry.
General Info: Yr. Est. 1983, Monthly
Subscriptions: Indv. $148

Econoscope, The Royal Bank of Canada
See: ECONOMICS

Educational Bulletin
Association

Publishing Co: American Safe Deposit Assn., 330 W. Main St., Greenwood, IN 46142-3130 Fax # (317) 888-1787; Title Tel # (317) 888-1118
Personnel: Publisher-Bill Lee
General Info: Yr. Est. 1924, Quarterly, Trim Size-8½ x 11, 2 pages, No Color
Circulation: Total-4,000

Electronic Banking Economics Society Newsletter

Publishing Co: Electronic Banking Economics Society, 56 Roberts Rd, Marlborough, CT 06447-1454; Title Tel # (203) 295-9788
Personnel: Editor-Linda Zimmer
Editorial Description: Covers membership proceedings, activities & upcoming speakers.
General Info: Yr. Est. 1987, Monthly, Looseleaf

Electronic Payments International

Publishing Co: Lafferty Publications, 420 Lexington Ave., Ste. 1745, New York, NY 10170 Tel # (212) 557-6729 Fax # (212) 557-7266; Title Tel # (404) 636-6610 Title Fax # (404) 636-6422
Personnel: Publisher-Frank Lawson, Editor in Chief-Michael Lafferty, Editor-Richard Martin
General Info: (Formerly EFTPOS Ltd.), 10x/yr.
Subscriptions: Indv. $1,059

Eliot Sharp's Financing News

Publishing Co: Miller Freeman, Inc., 13760 Noel Rd., Ste. 500, Dallas, TX 75240-4332 Tel # (214) 239-3060 Fax # (214) 419-7825; Title Tel # (212) 227-1200 Title Fax # (212) 321-3805
Personnel: Editor-Frank Santos
General Info: (Formerly Eliot Sharp's Corporate News), Yr. Est. 1944, Daily
Subscriptions: Indv. $4,600

Emerging Markets Analyst
Business

Publishing Co: BCA Publications Ltd., 1002 Sherbrook St. W., Montreal, PQ H3A 3L6 Canada; Title Tel # (514) 499-9550 Title Fax # (514) 874-1894
Personnel: Editor-M. Nakhjavani, Circ. Dir.-H. Paulson, Production Dir.-E. Lankinen
Editorial Description: Forecasts and developments in emerging capital markets.
General Info: Yr. Est. 1992, Monthly, Trim Size-8½ x 11, Offset press, 28 pages, Color
Subscriptions: Indv. $595, $50/copy

Emprise Investment Newsletter
See: INVESTMENT

End Point Express
Business

Publishing Co: United Communications Group, 11300 Rockville Pike, Ste. 1100, Rockville, MD 20852-3030 Fax # (301) 816-8945; Title Tel # (301) 816-8950
Personnel: Publisher-Daniel Brown, Editor-Martin Zook, Circ. Mgr.-Sharon Welch
Editorial Description: For financial operations professionals, with focus on payment systems.
General Info: (Formerly Back-Office Bulletin), Yr. Est. 1984, Bi-weekly, Web press, 4 pages, No Color
Subscriptions: Indv. $247, $8/copy
Acquistions: Publication Bought, Publication Sold
List Rental: Rents Lists

Estate & Financial Planners Alert
Business, Consumer

Publishing Co: Research Institute of America, 117 E Stevens Ave, Valhalla, NY 10595-1264; Title Tel # (212) 645-4800 Title Fax # (212) 337-4280
Personnel: Editor-Betsy McKenney
Editorial Description: News and information foe estate and financial planners.
General Info: Yr. Est. 1978, Monthly
Subscriptions: Indv. $104
List Rental: List Management Co.: WG & L List Management, 1 Penn Plz Fl 42, New York, NY 10119-0002 Tel # (212) 971-5000

Estate Planning Review
See: TAXES

Euronomics Review

Publishing Co: Euronomics, Inc., PO Box 13683, Albany, NY 12212-3683; Title Tel # (518) 783-3876 Title Fax # (518) 783-3876
Editorial Description: Covers a variety of financial and economic topics.
General Info: Yr. Est. 1990, Monthly
Subscriptions: Indv. $120

European Banker

Publishing Co: Lafferty Publications, 420 Lexington Ave., Ste. 1745, New York, NY 10170 Tel # (212) 557-6729 Fax # (212) 557-7266; Title Tel # (404) 636-6610 Title Fax # (404) 636-6422
Personnel: Publisher-Frank Lawson, Editor in Chief-Michael Lafferty, Editor-Aine Coney
Editorial Description: European Banker monitors the news, analysis the impact of the new developments and highlights emerging trends in the Europe-wide market.
General Info: 10x/yr.
Subscriptions: Indv. $1,099

Eximbank Letter

Publishing Co: International Business Affairs Corp., c/o Richard Barovick, 4938 Hampden Lane, Bethesda, MD 20814-2914; Title Tel # (301) 907-8647
Personnel: Publisher, Editor-Richard Barovick, Circ. Mgr.-Patricia Anderson
Editorial Description: Trends in Trade, Project & Investment Finance.
General Info: Yr. Est. 1986, Semi-monthly, 15 pages, ISSN: 0890-4251
Subscriptions: Indv. $288, $12/copy

FCIB Intl. Bulletin

Publishing Co: FCIB - NACM Corp., 100 Wood Ave. South, Ishlin, NJ 08830-2716; Title Tel # (212) 947-5368 Title Fax # (212) 465-8360
Personnel: Editor-Raymond Schweitzer, Production Mgr.-Michael Loprete
Editorial Description: Reports current changes affecting credit collection, & exchange conditions throughout the world. Presents forward looking economic data to assist executives in the formulation of future co. financial policy.
General Info: Yr. Est. 1919, Monthly
Subscriptions: Indv. $350

FDIC Consumer News

Publishing Co: Federal Deposit Insurance Corp., Division of Bank Supervision, 550 17th St. NW, Washington, DC 20429; Title Tel # (202) 393-8400
General Info: Bi-monthly

FEI Briefing

Publishing Co: Financial Executives Institute, 10 Madison Ave., Box 1938, Morristown, NJ 07960-6096 Tel # (201) 898-4600 Fax # (201) 898-4649; Title Tel # (201) 898-4621 Title Fax # (201) 267-4031
Personnel: Editor-Mimi Deitsch
Editorial Description: Interprets the latest technical developments of interest to CFO's, treasurers, & controllers at major corps.
General Info: (Formerly Financial Executives Institute-Bulletin), Yr. Est. 1986, Monthly, Trim Size-8½ x 11, Sheetfed press, 4 pages, No Color, Coated
Subscriptions: Free With Membership
Circulation: (100% controlled), Total-14,000
Printing Co: Science Press, 300 W Chestnut St, Ephrata, PA 17522-2002 Tel # (717) 738-9300, Fax # (717) 738-9413

FEI Canada Newsletter

Publishing Co: Financial Executive Institute Canada, 141 Adelaide St. West, Ste. 1701, Toronto, ON M5H 3L5 Canada; Title Tel # (416) 366-3007 Title Fax # (416) 366-3008
Personnel: Editor-Rita Witrylak
General Info: (Formerly Financial Executive), Bi-monthly, Trim Size-8½ x 11, 4 pages, No Color
Subscriptions: Free With Membership
Advertising: Accepts Inserts.
List Rental: Actives: 10,350, $60/M

FERC Report

Publishing Co: United Communications Group, 11300 Rockville Pike, Ste. 1100, Rockville, MD 20852-3030 Tel # (301) 816-8950 Fax # (301) 816-8945; Title Tel # (301) 961-8700 Title Fax # (301) 961-8666
Personnel: Publisher, Editor-Daniel Brown, Circ. Mgr.-Sharon Welch
Editorial Description: Covers financial enforcement, regulation & compliance.
General Info: Yr. Est. 1982, Bi-weekly, Web press, 4 pages, No Color
Subscriptions: Indv. $196
Acquistions: Publication Bought, Publication Sold
List Rental: Rents Lists

FRBSF Weekly Letter   *Business*

Publishing Co: Fedl. Reserve Bank of San Francisco, Box 7702, Public Information Department, San Francisco, CA 94120-7702; Title Tel # (415) 974-2246 Title Fax # (415) 974-3341
Personnel: Editor-Judith Goff
Editorial Description: Analysis of current economic & banking issues.
General Info: (Formerly Business & Financial Newsletter), Yr. Est. 1973, Weekly, Trim Size-10$\frac{1}{2}$ x 14, Web press, 4 pages, ISSN: us/08090-, Ind/Abs/Online: fedwest online, No Color, Newsprint
Subscriptions: For. $50, Free
Circulation: Total-17,000
Printing Co: Abbey Press, 401 Lesser St, Oakland, CA 94601-4901 Tel # (510) 261-7176, Fax # (510) 534-3767

FWANY/News   *Association*   CPM: $863

Publishing Co: Financial Women's Association of N.Y., 215 Park Ave S Ste 2010, New York, NY 10003-1603; Title Tel # (212) 533-2141
Personnel: Editor-Mary Cartwell, Adv. Dir.-Rose Marcotte
Editorial Description: Lists activities of F.W.A. description and opportunity of membership, update on careers, employment listing.
General Info: (Formerly F.W.A.N.Y. Newsletter), Monthly, Trim Size-8$\frac{1}{2}$ x 11, Offset press, 12 pages, No Color, Newsprint, Saddle-stitched
Subscriptions: Indv. $75
Circulation: Total-1,100
Advertising: $950. Accepts Inserts.

FX Week   *Business*

Publishing Co: Waters Information Services, PO Box 2248, Binghamton, NY 13902-2248 Tel # (607) 770-4075; Title Tel # (607) 770-9242 Title Fax # (607) 770-9435
Editorial Description: Covers business of currency trading in the global foreign exchange.
General Info: Yr. Est. 1990, Weekly, 14 pages, ISSN: 1050-0782
Subscriptions: Indv. $1,295, For. $1,295

Fannie Mae Investor/ Analyst Report

Publishing Co: Fannie Mae Foundation, 4000 Wisconsin Ave NW, Washington, DC 20016-2892 Tel # (202) 752-7761 Fax # (202) 752-4933
Editorial Description: Investment report on FNMA financial performance.
General Info: Quarterly, Letrpr. press, 32 pages, No Color

Farming for Profit
See: AGRICULTURE

Federal Banking Law Reports
See: LAW

Federal Banking Law Service of A.S. Pratt
See: LAW

Federal Guide   *Business*

Publishing Co: Savings & Community Bankers of America, 900 19th St. NW, Ste. 400, Washington, DC 20006-2105; Title Tel # (202) 857-3146 Title Fax # (202) 296-8716
Personnel: Publisher-Robert Bradner, Editor-Robert Wiorski
Editorial Description: Laws, regulations & commentary governing federal savings institutions.
General Info: Monthly, Trim Size-6 x 9, Web press, 208 pages, ISSN: 0190-4558, No Color, Looseleaf
Subscriptions: Indv. $680
Circulation: Total-7,300

Federal Income Taxation of Banks and Financial Institutions
See: TAXES

Federal Reserve Bulletin

Publishing Co: Board of Governors of the Fedl. Reserve System, Pub. Svcs. #m5138, Washington, DC 20551-0001; Title Tel # (202) 452-3000
Editorial Description: Summarizes business conditions, financial and business statistics (finance, banking, credit, commerce, industrial production, construction, employment, prices, etc.).
General Info: Yr. Est. 1915, Monthly, Ind/Abs/Online: DIALOG
Subscriptions: Indv. $20

Federal Reserve Notes   *Business*

Publishing Co: Federal Reserve Bank of Cleveland, E. 6th & Superior, Cleveland, OH 44114 Tel # (216) 579-2157 Fax # (216) 579-3050; Title Tel # (216) 579-2045 Title Fax # (216) 579-2477
Personnel: Editor-Julie Bjorkman, Production Mgr.-Robin Ratliff, Art Dir.-Michael Galka
Editorial Description: Contains articles of interest to employees--benefits, policy, etc.
General Info: Yr. Est. 1913, Quarterly, 7 pages, 4 Color
Subscriptions: Free
Circulation: Total-3,000
Printing Co: Watt Printing Co., 1278 W 9th St., Ste. 600, Cleveland, OH 44113-1046 Tel # (216) 696-5000

Federal Securities Act of 1933-Treatise and Primary Source Manual   *Business*

Publishing Co: Matthew Bender & Co., 11 Penn Plaza, New York, NY 10001-2006 Fax # (212) 244-3188; Title Tel # (212) 967-7707
Personnel: Editor-A.A. Sommers, Jr., Editor-Hugh L. Sowards
Editorial Description: A comprehensive, up-to-date treatise of the Securities Act of 1933 & all amendments thereto, as well as the application of the Trust Indenture Act of 1939 to offerings of debt securities. Covers civil liability & SEC enforcement. The Primary source Manual contains materials relating to the Securities Act & Trust Indenture Act.
General Info: Yr. Est. 1965, Irregular, Looseleaf
Subscriptions: $485/copy

Federal Securities Exchange Act of 1934   *Business*

Publishing Co: Matthew Bender & Co., 11 Penn Plaza, New York, NY 10001-2006 Fax # (212) 244-3188; Title Tel # (212) 967-7707
Personnel: Editor-Edward N. Gadsby, Editor-A.A. Sommer, Jr.
Editorial Description: Complements Sowards with full coverage of the 1934 Act and all amendments to date.
General Info: Yr. Est. 1967, Irregular, Looseleaf
Subscriptions: $640/copy

Federal Securities Law Reports
See: LAW

Fed Letter   *Business*

Publishing Co: Federal Reserve Bank of Kansas City, Public Affairs Dept. 925 Grand, Blvd, Kansas City, MO 64198-0001; Title Tel # (816) 881-2683 Title Fax # (816) 881-2569
Personnel: Editor-Lowell Jones
Editorial Description: Informs bankers about Federal Reserve issues and topics, primarily in the Tenth Federal Reserve District.
General Info: Yr. Est. 1980, Monthly, Trim Size-8$\frac{1}{2}$ x 11, Offset press, 4 pages, ISSN: 0739-5299, 2 Color
Subscriptions: Free
Circulation: Total-6,000

Fed Wire

Publishing Co: Fedl. Reserve Bank of Chicago, Public Information Center, Box 834, Chicago, IL 60690
General Info: Monthly

Fedwest

Publishing Co: Fedl. Reserve Bank of San Francisco, Box 7702, Public Information Department, San Francisco, CA 94120-7702 Tel # (415) 974-2246; Title Tel # (415) 974-2163 Title Fax # (415) 974-3341
Personnel: Editor-Lyndi Beale
Editorial Description: Updates on Federal Reserve services, regulations, & policies.
General Info: (Formerly FedWest), Yr. Est. 1975, Quarterly, Trim Size-11 x 17, Desktop press, 4 pages, 2 Color, Newsprint
Circulation: Total-8,500

Fee Income Report

Publishing Co: Siefer Consultants, Inc., 525 Cayuga St., PO Box 1384, Storm Lake, IA 50588; Title Tel # (712) 732-7340 Title Fax # (712) 732-7906
Personnel: Publisher-Dan Siefer, Editor-Steve Herron
Editorial Description: Fee income news and opportunities for financial institutions. Ideas to increase non-interest income from service charges and ancillary services.
General Info: Yr. Est. 1986, Semi-monthly, 8 pages, ISSN: 0892-7383
Subscriptions: Indv. $319, Can. $319, For. $350, $15/copy

Finance & Treasury
See: INTERNATIONAL TRADE

Finance Latin America
See: INTERNATIONAL TRADE

Financial & Estate Planners Quarterly   *Consumer*

Publishing Co: Lexington House, 98 Dennis Drive, Lexington, KY 40503; Title Tel # (606) 277-6135
Editorial Description: Financial & estate planning service. Two looseleaf binders, booklet format.
General Info: (Formerly Estate Planners Quarterly), Yr. Est. 1956, Quarterly, Trim Size-6 x 9, Sheetfed press, 100 pages, No Color, Looseleaf
Subscriptions: Indv. $50
Circulation: Total-5,000

Financial & Estate Planning
See: TAXES

Financial Digest   *Business*

Publishing Co: Chemical Bank, 270 Park Avenue, New York, NY 10017
Editorial Description: Analysis of business trends with selected financial indicators.
General Info: Weekly, Trim Size-8$\frac{1}{2}$ x 11, 4 pages, 2 Color, Matte

Financial Marketing
Newsletter   *Association*

Publishing Co: Sponsor-Financial Institutions Marketing Assn., Financial Instns. Mktg. Assn., 401 North Michigan Avenue, Suite 2200, Chicago, IL 60611-4206; Title Tel # (312) 644-6610 Title Fax # (312) 321-5147
Personnel: Editor-Tom Hefter
Editorial Description: Financial marketing topics.
General Info: (Formerly SIMSA News), Yr. Est. 1965, Monthly, 12 pages, 2 Color
Subscriptions: Indv. $150
Circulation: Total-2,100

Financial News

Publishing Co: Financial News Corp., 10 N. Newman St., P.O. Box 176, Jacksonville, FL 32202-3322; Title Tel # (904) 356-2466
Personnel: Publisher-James Bailey, Editor-Christopher Green, Adv. Dir.-Michael Clemento
Editorial Description: Business & Legal.
General Info: Yr. Est. 1912, Daily, Web press, 16 pages
Subscriptions: Indv. $65
Advertising: Inquire for rates.

Financial Planning
Advisory

Publishing Co: WPI Communications, Inc., 55 Morris Ave, Springfield, NJ 07081-1496; Title Tel # (201) 467-8700 Title Fax # (201) 467-0368
Personnel: Publisher-Steven Klinghoffer, Editor-Ken Berry
General Info: Yr. Est. 1988, Monthly
List Rental: Rents Lists

Financial Planning Digest   *Business*

Publishing Co: Harcourt Brace Professional Publishing, 6277 Sea Harbor Dr, Orlando, FL 32887-0001 Tel # (407) 345-2000 Fax # (800) 874-6418
Personnel: Publisher-Ken Rethmeier
Editorial Description: Up-to-the-minute coverage of issues important to a variety of financial planning institutions.
General Info: Yr. Est. 1994, Monthly
Subscriptions: Indv. $99

Financial Planning
Newsletter   *Consumer*

Publishing Co: Financial Planning Newsletter, 7665 Sun Island Dr S Apt 101, Saint Petersburg, FL 33707-4433; Title Tel # (813) 360-7423
Personnel: Publisher-Peter Olsen, Editor-Peter Olson
Editorial Description: Shows the reader how to keep what he earns and how to make sure their money is working as hard as they are.
General Info: Yr. Est. 1979, Monthly, Offset press, 4 pages, No Color
Subscriptions: Indv. $48

Financial Planning
Quarterly

Publishing Co: WPI Communications, Inc., 55 Morris Ave, Springfield, NJ 07081-1496; Title Tel # (201) 467-8700 Title Fax # (201) 467-0368
Personnel: Publisher-Steven Klinghoffer
Editorial Description: Focuses on financial planning ideas and issues.
General Info: Yr. Est. 1988, Quarterly

Financial Reading Review   *Business*

Publishing Co: Advisory Board Company, 600 New Hampshire Ave., N.W., Washington, DC 20037; Title Tel # (202) 672-5600 Title Fax # (202) 338-1715
Personnel: Exec. Ed.-Salma Hasan Ali, Production Mgr.-Janet Pfost
Editorial Description: Digest of best financial services, articles, market surveys, industry reports & government studies.
General Info: (Formerly Bank Reading Review), Yr. Est. 1984, Quarterly, Trim Size-8½ x 11, 12 pages, 2 Color, Matte, Saddle-stitched
Subscriptions: Indv. $248
Circulation: Total-4,000
Printing Co: Borrello White Printing, 14140 Park Lane Ct., Chantilly, VA 22021

Financial Services Daily
Fax   *Business*

Publishing Co: SNL Securities, 410 E. Main St., P.O. Box 2124, Charlottesville, VA 22902 Tel # (804) 977-1600 Fax # (804) 977-4466
Personnel: Publisher-Reid Nagle, Editor-Brian Hester, Circ. Mgr.-Pat LaBua, Production Mgr.-Ed Karppi, Adv. Dir.-Jenn Nagaj, Mktg. Dir.-Judy Lewis
Editorial Description: Consists of company specific and summarized industry news stories as well as information pertaining to specialized financial services for companies with publicly traded debt or equity. Includes mortgoge banks, finance companies, broker dealers, investment advisors and reits.
General Info: Yr. Est. 1992, Daily, Trim Size-8½ x 11, Desktop press, 5 pages, No Color, Other
Advertising: Inquire for rates.

Financial Services Report
See: COMPUTERS & AUTOMATION

Financial Statistics -Part 1

Publishing Co: Organization for Economic Cooperation & Development, 2001 L St NW Ste 650, Washington, DC 20036-4910; Title Tel # (202) 785-6323 Title Fax # (202) 785-0350
Editorial Description: Data on the financial markets in 16 European countries, the USA, Canada, and Japan. 'Financial Market Trends' is included with subscription price.
General Info: Yr. Est. 1970, Bi-monthly, Trim Size-7⅞ x 10⅝, Offset press, 50 pages, ISSN: 0304-3371, No Color
Subscriptions: Indv. $325

Financial Woman Today
See: WOMEN'S

First Friday

Publishing Co: ASCU, PO Box 5488, Madison, WI 53705-0488; Title Tel # (608) 238-2646
Personnel: Publisher-C. Barle, Editor-Walter Polner, Circ. Mgr.-A.L. Ferri, Promotion Dir.-Jay Allis
Editorial Description: Covers varied financial issues.
General Info: Yr. Est. 1973, Monthly, 6 pages, ISSN: 0094-0240, Color
Subscriptions: Indv. $35, $4/copy
Circulation: Total-1,400
List Rental: Rents Lists

Florida Public Finance   *Business*

Publishing Co: American Banker-Bond Buyer, 1 State Street Plz, New York, NY 10004-1549 Tel # (212) 943-4294 Parent Co.-Thomson Corp., Stamford
Personnel: Editor-Joseph Sims
General Info: Yr. Est. 1994, Monthly

Foreign Activity Report
See: INVESTMENT

Foreign Investment in
Canada   *Business*

Publishing Co: Research Institute of America, 90 5th Avenue, New York, NY 10011-7629 Tel # (212) 645-4800; Title Tel # (800) 562-0245 Title Fax # (201) 816-3484
Editorial Description: Based on Canada's Foreign Investment Review Act. Includes laws, regulations and other official material.
General Info: Yr. Est. 1974, Monthly, Trim Size-6 x 9¼, Looseleaf
Subscriptions: Indv. $341
List Rental: List Management Co.: WG & L List Management, 1 Penn Plz Fl 42, New York, NY 10119-0002 Tel # (212) 971-5000

Freidberg's Commodity & Currency Comments
See: INVESTMENT

Frohlinger's Marketing Report
See: ADVERTISING & MARKETING

Frugal Bugle, The   *Business, Consumer*

Publishing Co: Frugal Bugle, Box 60567, Dept. OC, Florence, MA 01060-0567; Title Tel # (617) 584-1854
Personnel: Publisher, Editor-Kathleen Ryan
Editorial Description: Better living for less money.
General Info: Yr. Est. 1993, Monthly, Trim Size-8½ x 11, 8 pages, No Color, Matte
Subscriptions: Indv. $12, Can. $17, For. $19, $1/copy
Circulation: Total-1,000

Funds International   *Business*

Publishing Co: Lafferty Publications, 420 Lexington Ave., Ste. 1745, New York, NY 10170 Tel # (212) 557-6729 Fax # (212) 557-7266
Personnel: Publisher-Frank Lawson, Editor-Ian Orton
Editorial Description: Funds International has become the prime source of intelligence for senior management in investment and funds- related industries worldwide. Each monthly issue reports on corporate strategy; regional trends; distribution and pricing; regulatory issues; investment management techniques and approaches; country close ups and more.
General Info: Yr. Est. 1994
Subscriptions: Indv. $979

Funds Transfer Report   *Business*

Publishing Co: Bankers Research Inc., 34 Imperial Ave # 431, Westport, CT 06880-4304; Title Tel # (203) 227-1237
Personnel: Editor-Theodore Volckhausen
Editorial Description: Information of interest to banking professionals.
General Info: Semi-monthly, 8 pages
Subscriptions: Indv. $194
Circulation: Total-700

Futures Market Alert

Publishing Co: Robbins Trading Co., 222 S. Riverside Plz., Chicago, IL 60606-5808; Title Tel # (312) 454-5335
Editorial Description: Covers futures trading.
General Info: Yr. Est. 1984, Monthly
Subscriptions: Indv. $100

Futures and Options Factors
See: INVESTMENT

Futures and Options News
See: INVESTMENT

Gateway
See: INTERNATIONAL TRADE

Global Economic Outlook
Publishing Co: Bank of Nova Scotia, Public & Corporate Affairs, 44 King St. W., 8th Fl., Scotia Plz., Toronto, ON M5H 1H1 Canada; Title Tel # (416) 866-6253 Title Fax # (416) 866-2829
Editorial Description: Economic & financial outlook for major industrial economics with emphasis on Canad & U.S. Provincial forecasts & the outlook for several major Canadian industries are aslo included.
General Info: Yr. Est. 1983

Global Financial Institutions Weekly
Publishing Co: Merrill Lynch, North Tower, World Trade Center, New York, NY 10281-1215 Tel # (212) 637-1960; Title Tel # (212) 766-5868
General Info: Weekly

Global Investment Technology
Business   **CPM$1536**
Publishing Co: Investment Media Inc., 909 3rd Ave., 6th Fl., New York, NY 10022-4731; Title Tel # (212) 888-5810 Title Fax # (212) 888-6145
Personnel: Publisher-Michael Horton, Editor-Pavan Sahgal
Editorial Description: Focuses exclusively on strategic business trends, operations, & automation issues facing US & non-US investment institutions & banks. Offers reports on software, systems, & innovative applications of technology for pension fund sponsors, money managers, & sell-side professionals.
General Info: Yr. Est. 1991, Bi-weekly, Trim Size-$8\frac{1}{2}$ x 11, Sheetfed press, 12 pages, ISSN: 1058-3920, 25% ads, 4 Color, Matte, Saddle-stitched
Subscriptions: Indv. $595, Inst. $595, Can. $595, For. $675, $25/copy
Circulation: Total-1,800
Advertising: $2,765.

Global Private Banking - International Investment Outlook
Business
Publishing Co: Sponsor-Royal Bank of Canada, Ariad Custom Publishing, 119 Spadina Ave., #1005, Toronto, ON M5V 2L1 Canada Tel # (416) 971-9294
Editorial Description: Covers developments and past performances of international markets including stocks, currency, and interest rates.
General Info: Yr. Est. 1991, Quarterly

Going Public: The IPO Reporter
See: INVESTMENT

Gold Standard Review
Publishing Co: Gold Standard Review, c/o Thomas, Box 1311, Germantown, MD 20875-1311; Title Tel # (301) 963-3103
Personnel: Publisher, Editor-H. Thomas
Editorial Description: Gold standard news, financial information.
General Info: Yr. Est. 1982, Quarterly
Subscriptions: Indv. $13

Ground Floor
Business
Publishing Co: Hirsch Organization, 6 Deer Trl, Old Tappan, NJ 07675-7125; Title Tel # (201) 664-3400
Personnel: Editor-Yale Hirsch
General Info: Yr. Est. 1981, Monthly, 4 pages, No Color
Subscriptions: Indv. $144
Circulation: Total-5,000
List Rental: List Management Co.: Name-Finders Lists, Inc., 3180 18th St Fl 2, San Francisco, CA 94110-2028 Tel # (510) 533-4177, Fax # (510) 553-8677, Actives: 6,143, $430/M

Guide to Export & Project Financing
See: INTERNATIONAL TRADE

Handbook of Modern Finance
Business
Publishing Co: Warren, Gorham & Lamont, 31 Saint James Ave., Boston, MA 02116-4112 Tel # (617) 423-2020 Fax # (617) 423-1914 Parent Co.-Thomson Professional Publications, Stamford
Personnel: Publisher-Andrew Boden, Production Mgr.-Seena Beneder, Mktg. Dir.-Sandra Fox
General Info: Yr. Est. 1990, Irregular, Looseleaf
Subscriptions: Indv. $150
List Rental: List Management Co.: WG & L List Management, 1 Penn Plz Fl 42, New York, NY 10119-0002 Tel # (212) 971-5000

Hedge Fund News
Business
Publishing Co: United States Offshore Funds Directory, 405 Park Ave Ste 500, New York, NY 10022-4405; Title Tel # (212) 371-5935 Title Fax # (212) 758-9032
Personnel: Publisher-Antoine Bernheim, Editor-Debra Friedman, Circ. Dir.-Gloria Phillip
Editorial Description: Covers issues and developments in the hedge funds industry.
General Info: Yr. Est. 1994, Quarterly
Subscriptions: Indv. $150

High Spots
Business
Publishing Co: Ohio Credit Union League, 1201 Dublin Rd, Columbus, OH 43215-1044; Title Tel # (614) 486-2917 Title Fax # (614) 424-3889
Editorial Description: News of credit unions on national, statewide, and local basis.
General Info: Yr. Est. 1960, Monthly, Trim Size-17 x 22, Web press, 4 pages, ISSN: 0885-2138, 2 Color, Coated
Circulation: Total-8,700

High Yield Report
See: INVESTMENT

Highlights & Documents
See: TAXES

Hotline
Business, Association   **CPM: $195**
Publishing Co: California League of Savings Institutions, 1960 E. Grand Ave., Ste. 1000, El Segundo, CA 90245 Tel # (310) 414-8300; Title Tel # (310) 670-6300 Title Fax # (310) 410-0372
Personnel: Publisher-Louis Nevins, Editor-Kathleen Wedekina
Editorial Description: Newsletter covering U.S. thrift industry.
General Info: (Formerly CA Savings & Loan), Yr. Est. 1982, Bi-weekly, Trim Size-$8\frac{1}{2}$ x 11, Offset press, 6 pages, 3% ads, No Color, Coated, Saddle-stitched
Subscriptions: Indv. $40
Circulation: (97% controlled), Total-3,700
Advertising: $725.
Printing Co: Adcraft Business Mail, 6501 Avalon Blvd, Los Angeles, CA 90003-1900

Housing Research News
Business, Consumer
Publishing Co: Fannie Mae Foundation, 4000 Wisconsin Ave NW, Washington, DC 20016-2892; Title Tel # (202) 752-7761 Title Fax # (202) 752-4933
Personnel: Editor-James H. Carr, Mag. Ed.-Kathryn McLean Bombard, Assoc. Ed.-Amy Young
Editorial Description: A periodic commentary on housing and urban issues.
General Info: Yr. Est. 1993, Bi-monthly, Trim Size-$8\frac{1}{2}$ x 11, 12 pages, ISSN: 1071-8508, 2 Color
Subscriptions: Free
Circulation: Total-7,000

How to Manage Your Money
See: CONSUMER INTERESTS

Hudson City Trends
Business, Consumer
Publishing Co: Hudson City Savings Bank, Marketing Dept., W. 80 Century Rd., Paramus, NJ 07652
Editorial Description: Banking and finance news about the bank and the industry.
General Info: Bi-monthly

Hulbert Financial Digest Almanac
Business, Consumer
Publishing Co: Hulbert Financial Digest, 316 Commerce St, Alexandria, VA 22314-2802; Title Tel # (703) 683-5905
Editorial Description: Tracks the performance of 135 financial newsletters.
General Info: Monthly

I/B/E/S Monthly Comments
Business
Publishing Co: I/B/E/S International, Inc., 345 Hudson St., New York, NY 10014-4511; Title Tel # (212) 243-3335 Title Fax # (212) 727-1386
Personnel: Publisher-Ed Keon, Editor-John Eliseo, Adv. Dir.-Dale Berman
Editorial Description: Monitors changes in global earnings estimate database.
General Info: Yr. Est. 1971, Monthly, No Color
Circulation: Total-4,000
Printing Co: Mathias & Carr, 75 Varick St., New York, NY 10013

IDA Report
Business, Association
Publishing Co: Investment Dealers Assn. of Canada, 121 King St. W, Ste. 1600, Toronto, ON M5H 3T9 Canada Fax # (416) 364-0753; Title Tel # (416) 364-6133
General Info: (Formerly Investment Dealers Assn. of Canada, Report), Quarterly

IE News: Financial Services
Association
Publishing Co: Institute of Industrial Engineers, 25 Technology Park/Atlanta, Norcross, GA 30092-2988 Tel # (770) 449-0461; Title Tel # (404) 449-0460 Title Fax # (770) 263-8532
Personnel: Production Mgr.-Dona Brown
Editorial Description: Newsletter for IIE Financial Services division.
General Info: Quarterly, Trim Size-$8\frac{1}{2}$ x 11, Sheetfed press, 8 pages, 2 Color, Matte, Saddle-stitched
Circulation: (100% controlled)
Advertising: $475. Accepts Inserts.
List Rental: Rents Lists

IMF Survey
See: ECONOMICS

IRA-Individual Retirement Account Stocks
See: INVESTMENT

IRA Reference Service
See: INVESTMENT

IRA Reporter
See: INVESTMENT

Illinois Banknews
Association   **CPM: $310**

Publishing Co: Illinois Bankers Association, 111 N. Canal St., Chicago, IL 60606-7299; Title Tel # (312) 876-9900 Title Fax # (312) 876-3826

Personnel: Publisher-William Hocter, Editor-Meg Bullock, Circ. Mgr.-Charlene Knox, Adv. Dir.-Kathleen Gill

General Info: Yr. Est. 1983, Bi-weekly, Trim Size-11 x 14, Sheetfed press, 4 pages, 2 Color, Saddle-stitched

Subscriptions: Indv. $30, Inst. $60, $3/copy

Circulation: Total-2,300

Advertising: $715.

Printing Co: Darby Graphics, 4015 N. Rockwell St., Chicago, IL 60618-3720 Tel # (312) 583-5090

Income Stocks
See: INVESTMENT

Independent Operations

Publishing Co: American Financial Services Assn., 919 18th Street, N.W., Washington, DC 20006-5503; Title Tel # (202) 296-5544 Title Fax # (202) 223-0321

Personnel: Editor-Glenn Kamp

Editorial Description: Issues & features material of interest to small finance companies.

General Info: Yr. Est. 1985, Quarterly, Trim Size-8½ x 11, 16 pages, 4% ads

Subscriptions: Indv. $12, Inst. $15

Circulation: Total-1,100

Advertising: Inquire for rates.

Index and Digest of OCC Opinion Letters
Business

Publishing Co: Legal Publication Svcs., 2008 N Emerson St., Arlington, VA 22207-1948 Tel # (703) 276-9796 Fax # (703) 243-3562

Personnel: Publisher-Ellen Smith, Editor-Tim Pryor

Editorial Description: Summarizes all Office of the Comptroller of the Currency opinion letters and no objection letters.

General Info: Yr. Est. 1992, Quarterly

Subscriptions: Indv. $260

Circulation: Total-120

Printing Co: USA Print & Copy, Wilson Blvd., Arlington, VA 22201

Individual Retirement Plans Guide-IRA, SEP, Keogh
See: U.S. (& CANADIAN) FED. GOV'T.

Information Returns Guide
See: TAXES

Inside the Economy
Business

Publishing Co: Statistical Indicator Assocs., PO Box 187, North Egremont, MA 01252-0187; Title Tel # (413) 528-3280

Personnel: Publisher, Editor-Leonard Lempert

Editorial Description: Bimonthly assessment & forecast of direction of U. S. economy.

General Info: Yr. Est. 1954, Bi-monthly

Subscriptions: Indv. $285, $55/copy

Inside Market Data
Business

Publishing Co: Waters Information Services, PO Box 2248, Binghamton, NY 13902-2248 Tel # (607) 770-4075 Fax # (607) 770-9435; Title Tel # (607) 770-9242 Title Fax # (607) 798-1692

Personnel: Publisher-Dennis Waters, Editor-Andrew Delaney, Circ. Mgr.-Beth Arnold, Production Mgr.-James Willis, Adv. Dir.-Joe Viviani, Mktg. Dir.-Betsy Martens

Editorial Description: Covers the financial quotation industry.

General Info: (Formerly Micro Ticker Report), Yr. Est. 1985, Bi-weekly, Offset press, 14 pages, ISSN: 1047-2908, Ind/Abs/Online: Newsnet, Predicasts, DIALOG, No Color, Newsprint

Subscriptions: Indv. $795, For. $945

Printing Co: Carr Printing, PO Box 7, Endicott, NY 13761-0007 Tel # (607) 748-0481

Inside Mortgage Finance
Business

Publishing Co: Inside Mortgage Finance Publications, Box 42387, Washington, DC 20015; Title Tel # (301) 951-1240 Title Fax # (301) 656-1709

Personnel: Publisher-Guy Cecala, Editor, Mng. Editor-John Lewis, Production Mgr.-Tony Cecala, Circ. Mgr., Mktg. Dir.-Didi Parks

Editorial Description: A weekly publication focusing on the primary mortgage market.

General Info: Yr. Est. 1984, Weekly, 13 pages, No Color, Saddle-stitched

Subscriptions: Indv. $595, $50/copy

Acquistions: Publication Bought

Inside Mortgage Securities
Business

Publishing Co: Inside Mortgage Finance Publications, Box 42387, Washington, DC 20015; Title Tel # (301) 951-1240 Title Fax # (301) 656-1709

Personnel: Publisher-Guy Cecala, Editor, Mng. Editor-John Lewis, Production Mgr.-Tony Cecala, Circ. Mgr., Mktg. Dir.-Didi Parks

Editorial Description: A weekly newsletter focusing on the secondary mortgage market.

General Info: (Formerly Inside Mortgage Capital Markets), Yr. Est. 1985, Weekly, Trim Size-8½ x 11, Sheetfed press, 13 pages, No Color

Subscriptions: Indv. $895, $50/copy

Acquistions: Publication Bought

Inside Strategy
Business

Publishing Co: Strategy Research Corp., 100 NW 37th Ave., Miami, FL 33125-4844 Fax # (305) 649-6312; Title Tel # (305) 649-5400

Personnel: Publisher-Richard Tobin, Editor-Andrew Yap

General Info: Yr. Est. 1988, Bi-monthly

Circulation: Total-5,000

Insider, The

Publishing Co: Farm Credit Council, 50 F St NW Ste 900, Washington, DC 20001-1530; Title Tel # (202) 626-8710

General Info: Yr. Est. 1983, Bi-monthly

International Bank Credit Analyst
Business

Publishing Co: BCA Publications Ltd., 1002 Sherbrook St. W., Montreal, PQ H3A 3L6 Canada; Title Tel # (514) 499-9550

Personnel: Editor-Francis Scotland, Circ. Mgr.-Helen Paulson, Production Mgr.-E. Lankinen

Editorial Description: Forecast & analysis of currency movements, interest rates, & stock market developments in the principal countries.

General Info: Yr. Est. 1962, Monthly, Trim Size-8½ x 11, 80 pages, Color-cover, Saddle-stitched

Subscriptions: Indv. $695, $50/copy

International Banking Regulator
Business

Publishing Co: American Banker Newsletters, One State Plaza, New York, NY 10004-1505 Fax # (202) 843-9620; Title Tel # (212) 803-8300 Title Fax # (212) 843-9620

Personnel: Publisher-David G. Schutt, Editor-William Acworth, Circ. Dir., Adv. Dir., Mktg. Dir.-Hans Winberg

Editorial Description: Global regulatory & legislative developments, worldwide banking news and data.

General Info: Weekly, Ind/Abs/Online: Mead Data Central, NewsNet, Predicasts/Dialog

Subscriptions: Indv. $925, Can. $925, For. $955, $20/copy

Advertising: $1,400.

International Country Risk Guide
Business

Publishing Co: Political Risk Services, 6320 Fly Road Suite #102, PO Box 248, East Syracuse, NY 13057-0248 Tel # (315) 431-0511 Fax # (315) 431-0200 Parent Co.-International Business Communications, Ashland; Title Tel # (315) 472-1224 Title Fax # (315) 472-1235

Personnel: Publisher-Mary Lou Walsh, Editor-Thomas Sealy, Circ. Mgr.-P. Davis

Editorial Description: Political and economic risk in all regions of the world. Statistical report section on factors involved in assessing risks.

General Info: Yr. Est. 1979, Monthly, Trim Size-8½ x 11, Sheetfed press, 120 pages, ISSN: 0278-6680, Color-cover, Matte, Perfect bound

Subscriptions: $3,150/copy

Circulation: Total-200

List Rental: List Management Co.: PRS List Management, 222 Teal Ave., POB 6482, Syracuse, NY 13217-6482 Tel # (315) 472-1224, Fax # (315) 472-1235, Actives: $250/M

International Currency Report
Business

Publishing Co: International Business Information, Inc., PO Box 8312, Cincinnati, OH 45208-0312; Title Tel # (513) 871-5501 Title Fax # (513) 871-5458

Personnel: Publisher, Editor-Walter Lynch

Editorial Description: Independent analysis of the foreign exchange markets examining the forces that affect the long-term value of major world currencies.

General Info: Yr. Est. 1978, Semi-monthly, Trim Size-8½ x 11, Web press, 8 pages, ISSN: 0738-8888, 2 Color

Subscriptions: Indv. $797, $35/copy

Acquistions: Publication Bought

List Rental: Actives: $250/M

International Financier
Business, Association   **CPM$2000**

Publishing Co: International Society of Financiers, PO Box 18508, Asheville, NC 28814-0508; Title Tel # (704) 252-5907 Title Fax # (704) 851-5061

Personnel: Publisher-Ronald Gershen

Editorial Description: A professional society for brokers, consultants, investors, and corporate lenders.

General Info: Yr. Est. 1979, Monthly, Trim Size-8½ x 11, 8 pages, No Color, Newsprint

Subscriptions: Free With Membership

Circulation: Total-500

Advertising: $1,000.

International Market Alert
See: INTERNATIONAL TRADE

International Regulation of Finance and Investment
See: LAW

International Reports Newsletter
See: INTERNATIONAL TRADE

Investment Horizons
See: INVESTMENT

Investment Management Weekly
See: INVESTMENT

Investor Relations
Newsletter — *Business*

Publishing Co: Remy Publishing Co., 350 W Hubbard St # 440, Chicago, IL 60610-4011; Title Tel # (312) 464-0300 Title Fax # (312) 464-0166
Personnel: Publisher-Robert Root, Editor-Gerald Murray, Circ. Mgr.-Trish Bissell
Editorial Description: Newsletter covering all facets of investor relations, offering practical information to corporate financial officers and top management.
General Info: Yr. Est. 1964, Monthly, Trim Size-8½ x 11, 4 pages, No Color
Subscriptions: Indv. $195, Inst. $195, Can. $195, For. $215

Irving's Interest Rate Spectator
See: INVESTMENT

Item Processing Report — *Business*

Publishing Co: Phillips Business Information, Inc., 1201 Seven Locks Rd., Ste 300, Potomac, MD 20854-2958 Tel # (301) 340-1520 Fax # (301) 424-4297; Title Tel # (301) 340-2100 Title Fax # (301) 309-3847
Personnel: Publisher-Chris Scotton, Editor-Lisa Hane, Production Mgr.-Teresa Fleisher, Adv. Dir.-Kim Hudak, Mktg. Dir.-Kelly Ebbs
Editorial Description: New technologies and strategies for remittance and check processing executives.
General Info: (Formerly Powell Report), Yr. Est. 1990, Bi-weekly, 8 pages, ISSN: 1048-5120, Ind/Abs/Online: NewsNet, Dialog, Predicasts, Bloomberg, 2 Color
Subscriptions: Indv. $495, For. $530, $37/copy

John Pugsley's Journal — *Business, Consumer*

Publishing Co: John Pugsley's Journal, 23-00 Route 208, Fairlawn, NJ 07410 Tel # (201) 794-8886 Fax # (201) 794-1221 Parent Co.-Marketing & Publishing Associates, Fair Lawn
Personnel: Publisher, Editor-N.S. Hayden, Circ. Mgr., Production Mgr., Mktg. Dir.-Donald Pinto
Editorial Description: Financial information on government and economy.
Subscriptions: Indv. $95
List Rental: List Management Co.: Name Bank, 14 W. Monument St., Baltimore, MD 21201 Tel # (410) 783-8463, Fax # (410) 783-8464, Actives: 5,000, $15/M, Expires: 11,700, $100/M

John T. Reed's Real Estate Investor's Monthly
See: REAL ESTATE

Jumbo Flash Report

Publishing Co: Bank Rate Monitor, Inc., PO Box 88888, North Palm Beach, FL 33408-8888; Title Tel # (407) 627-7330 Title Fax # (407) 627-7335
Personnel: Publisher-Robert Heady, Editor-Hugo Ottolenghi, Circ. Mgr.-Sarah Sahofield
Editorial Description: Listing of highest-yielding Jumbo CD's and Money Markets from federally insured banks & thrifts nationwide.
General Info: Yr. Est. 1983, Weekly, Trim Size-8¼ x 11, 4 pages
Subscriptions: Indv. $245, Can. $291, For. $355

Jumbo Rate News — *Business*

Publishing Co: Bauer Communications, Inc., PO Drawer 145510, 2655 LeJeune Rd PH1, Coral Gables, FL 33114-5510 Tel # (305) 445-9500; Title Tel # (305) 441-2062 Title Fax # (305) 445-6775
Personnel: Publisher, Editor-Paul A. Bauer, Mng. Editor, Circ. Mgr.-Caroline P. Jervey
Editorial Description: Tracks & reports on jumbo 100.000 certificates of deposit from federally insured, credit-worthy banks & S&L's nationwide. Includes commentary on the jumbo CD market & financial data on hundreds of institutions.
General Info: (Formerly CD Investors Weekly), Yr. Est. 1983, 48x/yr., Trim Size-8½ x 11, Letrpr. press, 48 pages, ISSN: 8756-2332, 2 Color, Other
Subscriptions: Indv. $445, Inst. $445, Can. $445, For. $490, $20/copy
Acquistions: Publication Bought
Circulation: Total-4,200

Kansas City Insurance
Report

Publishing Co: Chartrand Communications, 130 N. Cherry St., #202, Olathe, KS 66061-3460; Title Tel # (913) 831-0080 Title Fax # (913) 831-2905
Personnel: Publisher, Editor-David Chartrand
Editorial Description: News and information of interest to insurance professionals.
General Info: Yr. Est. 1986, Monthly
Subscriptions: Indv. $50

Kiplinger's Retirement Report
See: SENIOR CITIZENS

LDC Debt Report — *Business*

Publishing Co: American Banker Newsletters, One State Plaza, New York, NY 10004-1505 Fax # (202) 843-9620; Title Tel # (212) 803-8300 Title Fax # (212) 843-9620
Personnel: Publisher-David G. Schutt, Editor-Mary D'Ambrosio, Circulation, Adv. Dir., Mktg. Dir.-Hans Winberg
Editorial Description: Covers debt in developing countries.
General Info: Yr. Est. 1988, Weekly, Ind/Abs/Online: Mead Data Central, NewsNet, Dialog
Subscriptions: Indv. $850, Can. $850, For. $880, $20/copy
Advertising: Inquire for rates.

Lagniape Monthly on Latin American Projects & Finance
See: INTERNATIONAL TRADE

Lagniappe Letter
See: INTERNATIONAL TRADE

Lagniappe Quarterly Monitor
See: INTERNATIONAL TRADE

Language Matters
See: LITERATURE & LINGUISTICS

Lanston Letter — *Business*

Publishing Co: Aubrey G. Lanston, 1 Chase Manhattan Plaza, 53rd Fl., New York, NY 10005; Title Tel # (212) 612-1600
Personnel: Editor-David Jones
General Info: Yr. Est. 1949, Weekly, 4 pages
Circulation: Total-2,600

Latin American Finance & Capital Markets
See: INTERNATIONAL TRADE

Law of Pooling and Unitization
See: LAW

Leaders Letter

Publishing Co: American Institute of Banking, 1120 Connecticut Ave., NW, Washington, DC 20036-3902; Title Tel # (202) 663-5391
Personnel: Editor-Hunter Moss
General Info: Yr. Est. 1956, Monthly, 8 pages, 2 Color, Coated
Subscriptions: Indv. $15
Circulation: Total-6,500

Legislative & Regulatory
Report — *Business*

Publishing Co: Assn. of Natl. Advertisers, Inc., 155 E. 44th St., New York, NY 10017-4201 Fax # (212) 683-1296; Title Tel # (212) 697-5950
Personnel: Publisher-Dewitt Helm, Jr., Editor-Dan Jaffe
Editorial Description: Updates on legislative & regulatory matters affecting advertising.
General Info: (Formerly Washington Newsletter), Yr. Est. 1973, Quarterly, Offset press, Newsprint
Circulation: (100% controlled), Total-900

Lender Liability Law and
Litigation — *Business*

Publishing Co: Matthew Bender & Co., 11 Penn Plaza, New York, NY 10001-2006 Tel # (212) 967-7707 Fax # (212) 244-3188
Personnel: Editor in Chief-Joseph J. Norton
Editorial Description: The first complete guide to the theory & practice of lender liability cases. Expert guidance for both lender & borrower includes discussions of cases of action & defenses, as well as how to litigate these often complex disputes.
General Info: Yr. Est. 1989, Irregular, Looseleaf

Lender Liability Law Report
See: LAW

Lender Liability News
See: LAW

Letter of Credit Update — *Business*

Publishing Co: Government Information Services, Inc., 4301 Fairfax Dr., Ste. 875, Arlington, VA 22203-1627; Title Tel # (703) 528-1000 Title Fax # (703) 528-6060
Personnel: Publisher-James Marshall, Editor-James Byrne, Circ. Mgr.-Thomas Wright, Promotion Dir.-Joel Drucker
Editorial Description: Each issue covers legislative & judicial developments concerning letter of credit practices of special interest to businessmen, bankers & lawyers.
General Info: Yr. Est. 1985, Monthly, 40 pages, ISSN: 0883-0487
Subscriptions: Indv. $395, For. $425
Acquistions: Publication Bought, Publication Sold
List Rental: Rents Lists
Printing Co: Newsletter Press, 76 Valley St, East Providence, RI 02914-4424 Tel # (401) 438-5352

Letter Ruling Index-Digest Bulletins
See: TAXES

Letters of Credit — *Business*

Publishing Co: Matthew Bender & Co., 11 Penn Plaza, New York, NY 10001-2006 Tel # (212) 967-7707 Fax # (212) 244-3188
Editorial Description: Shows you how to use the letter of credit to your clients' advantage.
General Info: Yr. Est. 1987, Irregular, Looseleaf

Letters of Credit Report — *Business*

Publishing Co: John Wiley & Sons, Inc., 605 Third Avenue, New York, NY 10158-0012 Tel # (212) 850-6000 Fax # (212) 850-6088; Title Tel # (212) 645-7880 Title Fax # (212) 675-4883
Personnel: Editor-Thomas Whitehill
Editorial Description: Covers latest legal & financial developments affecting letters of credit, bank acceptances, & bank guaranties, domestic & international. Contains case information for bankers & lawyers.
General Info: Yr. Est. 1986, Bi-monthly, Trim Size-8½ x 11, Sheetfed press, 16 pages, ISSN: 0886-0459, Coated, Saddle-stitched
Subscriptions: Indv. $248, Can. $248, For. $284
List Rental: Rents Lists
Printing Co: Hessey Printing, Inc., 424 Lafayette St # 100226, Nashville, TN 37203-4255 Tel # (615) 244-7180, Fax # (615) 255-6911

Leveraged Buyout & Acquisitions Litigation Reporter
See: LAW

LifeLine / Vitalite
See: INSURANCE

Liquidation Alert
See: REAL ESTATE

Louisiana Banker　　　　*Business, Association*
Publishing Co: Louisiana Bankers Assn., PO Box 2871, Baton Rouge, LA 70821-2871;
Title Tel # (504) 387-3282
Personnel: Editor-Heidi Dicard
Editorial Description: Louisiana banking.
General Info: (Formerly LBA Banker), Yr. Est. 1934, Semi-monthly, Trim Size-8½ x 11, Web press, 4 pages, 2 Color
Subscriptions: Indv. $15, $1/copy
Circulation: Total-2,000
Printing Co: Ipc Printing, 5201 Government St, Baton Rouge, LA 70806-6027 Tel # (504) 927-3496

Low Priced Stocks
See: INVESTMENT

Low Profile　　　　*Consumer*
Publishing Co: Hoisager & Laird, Inc., 101 S Jennings Ave Ste 204, Fort Worth, TX 76104-1149
Tel # (817) 335-5443 Fax # (817) 335-7909; Title Fax # (602) 943-2363
Personnel: Publisher-Sharon Holsager, Publisher-Trey Laird, Editor-Mark Nestmann
Editorial Description: Covers asset protection and financial privacy.
General Info: Yr. Est. 1992, Monthly
Subscriptions: Indv. $149, $13/copy
Circulation: Total-2,000

MHFA Update　　　　*Business*
Publishing Co: Sponsor-Massachusetts Housing Finance Agency, Massachusetts Housing Finance Agency, 1 Beacon St., Ste. 26-28, Boston, MA 02108-3106 Fax # (617) 451-3650;
Title Tel # (617) 451-3480 Title Fax # (617) 451-0859
Personnel: Editor-Samantha Selvin
Editorial Description: News and information on single and multi-family housing programs.
General Info: (Formerly MHFA Newsletter), Yr. Est. 1980, Quarterly, Trim Size-8.5 x 11, Sheetfed press, 4 pages, 2 Color, Recycled
Subscriptions: Free
Circulation: Total-1,000
Printing Co: Calgraphics, 493 C St., Boston, MA 02210

Making Ends Meet
Publishing Co: Pascit Publications, PO Box 1125, Traverse City, MI 49685-1125 Parent Co.-Corbett Communications, Traverse City; Title Tel # (616) 929-7227
Personnel: Publisher, Editor-William A. Corbett, Circ. Mgr.-C. Holden-Corbett
Editorial Description: Financial and investment news, information, etc.
General Info: Quarterly, Trim Size-8½ x 11, 8 pages, 2 Color, Recycled
Subscriptions: Indv. $25, $7/copy

Market Timing Report
See: INVESTMENT

Marketing Timing Report
See: INVESTMENT

Marketing Update　　　　*Association*
Publishing Co: Bank Marketing Assn., 1120 Connecticut Ave NW Ste, 300, Washington, DC 20036-3902 Tel # (202) 663-5378 Parent Co.-American Bankers Association, Washington; Title Tel # (202) 663-5070 Title Fax # (202) 828-4540
Personnel: Editor-Tanja Lian, Production Ed.-Jill Jones
Editorial Description: Reports on latest trends, strategies & promotions in financial services marketing as identified by members calls to BMA's Information Center.
General Info: Yr. Est. 1984, Monthly, Trim Size-8½ x 11, Sheetfed press, 4 pages, Ind/Abs/Online: FINIS, 2 Color, Newsprint
Subscriptions: $4/copy
Circulation: Total-4,000
Printing Co: North American Press, 820 S. Bartlett Rd., Streamwood, IL 60107-2407
Tel # (708) 483-1400, Fax # (708) 483-1404

Meeting Monitor
See: MANAGEMENT

Membership Bulletin
Publishing Co: U.S. League of Savings Institutions, 111 E. Wacker Dr., Chicago, IL 60601-4208;
Title Tel # (312) 644-3100
Editorial Description: Covers League news as well as current developments in the banking/savings industry.
General Info: Bi-monthly

Merchant Connections
See: CREDIT AND CREDIT UNIONS

Mergers & Acquisitions Report
See: INVESTMENT

Michigan Banker
Publishing Co: Public Relations Enterprises, Inc., PO Box 12236, Lansing, MI 48901-2236;
Title Tel # (517) 332-7800
Personnel: Publisher-Jerome H. O'Neil
General Info: Monthly, ISSN: 1044-1948

Microbanker's High-Tech Banking Strategies　　*Business*
Publishing Co: Microbanker, Inc., PO Box 708, Lake George, NY 12845-0708;
Title Tel # (518) 745-7071 Title Fax # (518) 745-7009
Personnel: Publisher-Nancy R. Davis, Editor-Lisa Valentine, Circ. Mgr.-Christine Yakush
Editorial Description: News and information for banking professionals on the use of PCs and LANs in a distributed environment.
General Info: (Formerly Microbanker Research Letter), Yr. Est. 1981, Semi-monthly, Trim Size-8½ x 11, 8 pages, 2 Color, Other
Subscriptions: Indv. $395
List Rental: Actives: 50,000, $125/M

Modern Trust Forms Checklists
Publishing Co: Warren, Gorham & Lamont, 31 Saint James Ave., Boston, MA 02116-4112 Parent Co.-Thomson Professional Publications, Stamford; Title Tel # (617) 423-2020
Title Fax # (617) 423-1914
Personnel: Publisher-Larry Selby, Mktg. Dir.-Sandra Fox
General Info: Yr. Est. 1980, Irregular, Looseleaf
Subscriptions: Indv. $185
List Rental: List Management Co.: Manager: Seena Benedek; WG & L List Management, 1 Penn Plz Fl 42, New York, NY 10119-0002 Tel # (212) 971-5000

Monetary Digest
Publishing Co: Bull & Bear Financial Newspaper, PO Box 917179, Longwood, FL 32791-7179;
Title Tel # (407) 682-6170
Personnel: Editor-David J. Robinson
General Info: Monthly

Money Laundering Alert
See: LAW

Money Laundering, Asset Forfeiture & Intl. Financial Crimes Newsletter
See: LAW

Money Laundering Law Report
See: LAW

Money Master　　　　*Business*
Publishing Co: EBA Inc./Publishing Division, 33 Bolivia St., 4th Floor, San Juan, PR 00917;
Title Tel # (809) 754-1915 Title Fax # (809) 751-1284
Editorial Description: Interactive personal finance.
General Info: Yr. Est. 1993, Monthly

Money Pro 'The Steve Crowley Report'
Publishing Co: Crowley Publishing Co., Inc., 5100 NW 33rd Ave Ste 155, Fort Lauderdale, FL 33309-6399; Title Tel # (305) 735-5222 Title Fax # (305) 735-5226
Personnel: Editor-Steve Crowley
Editorial Description: Money management information and financial news.
General Info: Yr. Est. 1990, Monthly
Subscriptions: Indv. $57

Money Talks
Publishing Co: Thomas J. Keany, 520 N Brookhurst St Ste 230, Anaheim, CA 92801-5207;
Title Tel # (714) 778-4375
Personnel: Publisher-Tom Keany, Editor-Stewart Case
Editorial Description: News of the financial planning and investment world.
General Info: Yr. Est. 1989, Quarterly, Sheetfed press, 4 pages, 2 Color, Coated
Subscriptions: Free With Membership
Circulation: Total-1,000
Advertising: Inquire for rates. Accepts Inserts.
Printing Co: Step Ahead Graphics, 222 N Crescent Way Unit E, Anaheim, CA 92801-6703
Tel # (714) 535-4826

Money Watch Bulletin　　　　*Business*
Publishing Co: International Wealth Success, Inc., 24 Canterbury Rd., Rockville Center, NY 11570-1310; Title Tel # (516) 766-5850 Title Fax # (516) 766-5919
Personnel: Editor-Tyler Hicks
Editorial Description: Provides names, addresses, phone numbers of lenders for business & real estate worldwide.
General Info: Yr. Est. 1984, Monthly, 20 pages, No Color
Subscriptions: Indv. $95, Can. $102, $8/copy
Acquistions: Publication Bought
Advertising: Accepts Inserts.

MoneyWorks for Women
See: WOMEN'S

Monthly Statistics/Open-End Investment Companies Trends
See: INVESTMENT

Mortgage-Backed Securities Letter
See: INVESTMENT

Mortgage Bank Weekly *Business*

Publishing Co: SNL Securities, 410 E. Main St., P.O. Box 2124, Charlottesville, VA 22902
Tel # (804) 977-1600 Fax # (804) 977-4466
Personnel: Publisher-Reid Nagle, Editor-Jenn Nagaj, Circ. Mgr.-Pat Liabua, Production Mgr.-Ed Karppi, Adv. Dir.-Jenn Nagle, Mktg. Dir.-Judy Lewis
Editorial Description: Includes detailed market information, research reports, and debt & equity offerings along with concise summaries of important news of the week.
General Info: Yr. Est. 1993, Weekly, Trim Size-8½ x 11, Desktop press, 6 pages, No Color, Other
Subscriptions: Indv. $295, Inst. $295
Advertising: Inquire for rates.

Mortgage Bankers Assn. of America-Washington Report

Publishing Co: Mortgage Bankers Assn. of America, 1125 15th St., NW, Washington, DC 20005-2766 Tel # (202) 861-6979 Fax # (202) 861-0736; Title Tel # (202) 861-6500
Personnel: Editor-Jim Freeman
Editorial Description: Covers legislation on housing & real estate finance.
General Info: Quarterly
Subscriptions: Indv. $25
Circulation: Total-3,500

Mortgage Marketplace *Business*

Publishing Co: American Banker Newsletters, One State Plaza, New York, NY 10004-1505
Fax # (202) 843-9620; Title Tel # (212) 803-8300 Title Fax # (212) 843-9620
Personnel: Publisher-David G. Schutt, Editor-Craig Webb, Circ. Mgr., Adv. Dir., Mktg. Dir.-Hans Winberg
Editorial Description: Developments affecting the mortgage markets.
General Info: (Formerly Mortgage Commentary), Yr. Est. 1963, Weekly, Trim Size-8½ x 11, Desktop press, 4 pages, Ind/Abs/Online: Mead Data Central, 2 Color
Subscriptions: Indv. $750, Can. $750, For. $780, $20/copy
Advertising: $1,400.

Mutual Fund Letter
See: INVESTMENT

Myers Finance & Energy *Business*

Publishing Co: Myers Finance & Energy, S. 104 Freya St., #214-A, Spokane, WA 99202;
Title Tel # (509) 534-7132 Title Fax # (509) 534-8054
Personnel: Publisher, Editor-C. Myers
Editorial Description: Intl. & domestic monetary coverage of the finance & energy fields.
General Info: Yr. Est. 1967, Monthly
Subscriptions: Indv. $149
List Rental: List Management Co.: InfoMat, 1815 W 213th St Ste 210, Torrance, CA 90501-2839 Tel # (310) 212-5944, Fax # (310) 212-5773, Actives: 9,500, $125/M

NABCA Bulletin
See: ACCOUNTING

NABS Newsletter

Publishing Co: Natl. Assn. of Bank Services, 5008-02 Pine Creek Dr., Westerville, OH 43081-4899;
Title Tel # (614) 895-1208
Personnel: Editor-Beverly Kerins
General Info: Yr. Est. 1989, Semi-annually
Subscriptions: $1/copy
Circulation: Total-700

NASACT Newsletter *Association*

Publishing Co: National Assn. of State Auditors, Comptrollers & Treasurers, 2401 Regency Rd Ste 302, Lexington, KY 40503-2914; Title Tel # (606) 276-1147 Title Fax # (606) 278-0507
General Info: (Formerly NASIS Newsletter), Monthly

NASD Manual *Association*

Publishing Co: CCH, Inc., 2700 Lake Cook Rd., Riverwoods, IL 60015 Parent Co.-Kluwer Law & Taxation Publishers, Cambridge; Title Tel # (847) 267-7000 Title Fax # (800) 224-8299
Editorial Description: Covers NASD members, activities, rules of fair practice, by-laws, procedures for handling complaints, uniform practice code, relevant SEC controls.
General Info: Yr. Est. 1967, 8x/yr., Trim Size-6 x 9, Web press, 120 pages, No Color, Looseleaf
Subscriptions: Indv. $381

NBA Today *Business, Association*

Publishing Co: National Bankers Association, Inc., 1802 T St NW, Washington, DC 20009-7126;
Title Tel # (202) 588-5432
Personnel: Editor, Production Mgr.-Lethia Kelly
General Info: Yr. Est. 1927, Quarterly, 1 pages, 2 Color
Circulation: (100% controlled), Total-3,200

NCFE Motivator
See: CONSUMER INTERESTS

NCUA Watch *Business*

Publishing Co: American Banker Newsletters, One State Plaza, New York, NY 10004-1505
Fax # (212) 843-9620; Title Tel # (212) 803-8300 Title Fax # (212) 843-9620
Personnel: Publisher-David G. Schutt, Editor-Melanie Waddell, Circ. Mgr.-Celia Benjamin, Adv. Dir., Mktg. Dir.-Hans Winberg
Editorial Description: Developments at the National Credit Union Administration.
General Info: Weekly, Trim Size-8½ x 11, Letrpr. press, 4 pages, No Color
Subscriptions: Indv. $675, Can. $675, For. $705, $20/copy
Advertising: $1,400.
List Rental: Rents Lists

NHEMA Legislative Report *Association*

Publishing Co: Natl. Second Mortgage Assn., 3833 Schaefer Ave #K, Chino, CA 91710
Fax # (909) 590-8128; Title Tel # (909) 590-8133
Personnel: Editor-Harold Rees
Editorial Description: Provides information on federal & state legislation affecting the industry.
General Info: Yr. Est. 1977, Semi-annually
Circulation: Total-500

NIBESA News *Association* CPM: $222

Publishing Co: Natl. Independent Bank Equipment & Systems Assn., 1411 Peterson, Park Ridge, IL 60068-5071; Title Tel # (708) 825-8419 Title Fax # (708) 825-8445
Personnel: Editor-Ann Walk
General Info: Yr. Est. 1978, Monthly, Trim Size-8½ x 11, 6 pages, No Color
Subscriptions: Free With Membership
Circulation: Total-450
Advertising: $100. Accepts Inserts.

NQB Pink Sheets for Equities
See: INVESTMENT

NQB Yellow Sheets for Taxable Bonds
See: INVESTMENT

NYSE-Weekly Stock Buys
See: INVESTMENT

National Association of Federal Credit Unions - Update *Association* CPM: $157

Publishing Co: Natl. Assn. of Credit Unions, PO Box 3769, Washington, DC 20007-0269;
Title Tel # (703) 522-4770 Title Fax # (703) 524-1082
Personnel: Editor-Patrick Keefe
Editorial Description: Covers legislative/regulatory events affecting federal credit unions. Reports NAFCU positions on issues.
General Info: (Formerly Washington Line), Yr. Est. 1970, Weekly, Trim Size-8½ x 11, Sheetfed press, 4 pages, No Color, Newsprint
Subscriptions: Indv. $35, Inst. $350
Circulation: (100% controlled), Total-9,500
Advertising: $1,500.
Printing Co: CLB Publishers & Lithographers, 10580 Metropolitan Ave, Kensington, MD 20895-2606 Tel # (301) 933-5220, Fax # (301) 933-2498

National Bankruptcy Litigation Reporter
See: LAW

National Council of Savings Institutions-Washington Memo *Association*

Publishing Co: America's Community Bankers, 900 19th St. NW, Ste. 400, Washington, DC 20006-2105 Tel # (202) 857-3100 Fax # (202) 659-1134; Title Tel # (202) 857-3143
Personnel: Editor-Mark Wolff, Circ. Mgr.-Jannice Hodge-Bannerman, Production Mgr.-Laura Porinchak
Editorial Description: Weekly interpretive newsletter about Washington events affecting savings institutions.
General Info: Weekly, Trim Size-8½ x 11, Letrpr. press, 4 pages, 2 Color, Newsprint
Subscriptions: Indv. $200

National Delinquency Survey

Publishing Co: Mortgage Bankers Assn. of America, 1125 15th St., NW, Washington, DC 20005-2766 Tel # (202) 861-6979 Fax # (202) 861-0736; Title Tel # (202) 861-6500
Personnel: Editor-Laura Gorman
Editorial Description: Newsletter reporting on delinquency rates of loans.
General Info: Yr. Est. 1953, Quarterly
Subscriptions: Indv. $30, $11/copy
Circulation: Total-500

National Financing Law Digest
See: LAW

New England Economic Review
See: ECONOMICS

New York Banking Law
See: LAW

New York Futures Exchange
See: INVESTMENT

New York Mercantile Exchange
See: INVESTMENT

New York State Banker   *Business*
Publishing Co: New York State Bankers Assn., 485 Lexington Ave Fl 25, New York, NY 10017-2630; Title Tel # (212) 949-1173
Personnel: Editor-Robert Cole
Editorial Description: Banking and financial news; management features on current industry problems and practices and activities of the New York State Bankers Association.
General Info: Yr. Est. 1938, Bi-weekly, Trim Size-8½ x 11, Offset press, 6 pages, No Color
Subscriptions: Indv. $24, $1/copy
Circulation: (100% controlled), Total-3,200

New York Stock Exchange Guide
See: INVESTMENT

News; New York League of Savings Institution   *Business, Association*
Publishing Co: News, 200 Park Ave. #6Fl-W, New York, NY 10166-0005
Personnel: Editor-William Foley

Nilson Report   *Business*
Publishing Co: HSN Consultants, Inc., 300 Esplanade, Suite 1790, Oxnard, CA 93030; Title Tel # (805) 983-0448 Title Fax # (805) 983-0792
Personnel: Publisher, Editor-H. Spencer Nilson
Editorial Description: Credit card newsletter.
General Info: Yr. Est. 1970, Semi-monthly, 10 pages, Color
Subscriptions: Indv. $695, Inst. $695, Can. $745, For. $745

Non-Credit Learning News
See: EDUCATION

Notice to Members   *Business, Association*
Publishing Co: Natl. Assn. of Securities Dealers, Inc., 1735 K St., N.W., Washington, DC 20006-1500 Tel # (202) 728-8000 Fax # (202) 293-6260; Title Tel # (202) 728-6900
Personnel: Publisher-Margo Porter, Editor-Jean R. Curtiss, Production Mgr.-Mark DiJulio, Adv. Dir.-Sharon Lippincott, Art Dir.-Dan McQuillen
Editorial Description: Official notice of proposed & adopted rules, regulations, interpretations, qualification requirements, fee changes, etc. to inform NASD members & to solicit their comments.
General Info: Yr. Est. 1964, Monthly, Trim Size-8½ x 11, Sheetfed press, 80 pages, 2 Color, Saddle-stitched
Subscriptions: Indv. $225, $25/copy
Circulation: (91% controlled), Total-10,000, Subscriptions-900
Printing Co: Hennage Creative Printers, 500 N Henry St, Alexandria, VA 22314-2233 Tel # (703) 683-8282

Ohio Banker   *Business*   CPM: $143
Publishing Co: Ohio Bankers Assoc., 37 W. Broad St., Ste. 1001, Columbus, OH 43215-4162 Fax # (617) 221-3421; Title Tel # (614) 221-5121 Title Fax # (614) 221-3421
Personnel: Editor-Melea Wachtman, Mng. Editor-David Finley, Staff Writer-Nancy Neptune
Editorial Description: For commercial bankers throughout Ohio. Features on banking news, financial trends, assn. news, etc.
General Info: Yr. Est. 1908, Monthly, Trim Size-8½ x 11, 16 pages, ISSN: 0030-0802, 50% ads, 2 Color, Coated, Saddle-stitched
Subscriptions: Indv. $25, Free With Membership
Circulation: Total-3,800, Readership-14,820
Advertising: $546.
Printing Co: Pony X Press, 6800 Tussing Road, Columbus, OH 43068 Tel # (614) 575-4242

Oil Buyers Guide
See: PETROLEUM & NATURAL GAS

On Reserve
Publishing Co: Fedl. Reserve Bank of Chicago, Public Information Center, Box 834, Chicago, IL 60690

Online Marketplace
See: COMPUTERS & AUTOMATION

Ontra Update
See: REAL ESTATE

Operations Management   *Business*
Publishing Co: Capital Cities/ABC, 488 Madison Ave., 16th Floor, New York, NY 10022-5751 Fax # (212) 224-3353 Parent Co.-Capital Cities/ABC, Inc., New York; Title Tel # (212) 224-3233 Title Fax # (212) 224-3111
General Info: Bi-weekly, Trim Size-8½ x 11, Sheetfed press, 14 pages, 2 Color, Newsprint
Advertising: Inquire for rates.

Outlook   *Business*
Publishing Co: Standard & Poor's Corp., 25 Broadway, New York, NY 10004 Tel # (212) 208-8000 Parent Co.-McGraw-Hill, New York; Title Tel # (212) 208-8768
Personnel: Publisher-Stephen Sanborn, Editor-Arnold Kaufman
Editorial Description: Investment advisory newsletter.
General Info: Yr. Est. 1928, Weekly
Subscriptions: Indv. $255, $5/copy
List Rental: List Management Co.: NRL Direct, 100 Union Ave, Cresskill, NJ 07626 Tel # (201) 568-0707, Actives: 30,800, $150/M, Expires: 114,000, $100/M

Output   *Business, Association*
Publishing Co: Corporate Transfer Agents Assn., 600 Grant St Ste 611, Pittsburgh, PA 15219-2703 Tel # (412) 433-4801
Editorial Description: Articles of interest to transfer security agents.
General Info: Monthly

POS News   *Business*
Publishing Co: Faulkner & Gray, Inc., 11 Penn Plz., 17th Floor, New York, NY 10001-2006 Tel # (212) 967-7000 Fax # (212) 695-8172 Parent Co.-Thomson Corp., Stamford; Title Tel # (212) 766-1251
Personnel: Publisher-John Love, Editor-Lauri Giesen, Circ. Mgr.-Cathy Klebofski
Editorial Description: News & analysis of developments in retail electronic payment.
General Info: Yr. Est. 1984, 14x/yr., 8 pages, 2 Color
Subscriptions: Indv. $245, $20/copy
List Rental: List Management Co.: Aggressive List Management, 18-2 E Dundee Rd Ste 101, Barrington, IL 60010-5273 Tel # (708) 304-4030, Fax # (708) 304-4032, Actives: $95/M

P.Q. Wall Forecast   *Business*
Publishing Co: P.Q. Wall Forecast, Inc., PO Box 15558, New Orleans, LA 70175-5558; Title Tel # (504) 895-4891 Title Fax # (504) 895-4852
Personnel: Editor-Audrey Santee, Editor-Ellen Wall
Editorial Description: Financial news and forecasts.
General Info: Yr. Est. 1989, Monthly, Trim Size-8½ x 11, Desktop press, 10 pages, ISSN: 198, No Color
Subscriptions: Indv. $198, $25/copy
Circulation: Total-4,000
List Rental: Rents Lists

Pacific Stock Exchange Guide   *Business*
Publishing Co: CCH, Inc., 2700 Lake Cook Rd., Riverwoods, IL 60015 Parent Co.-Kluwer Law & Taxation Publishers, Cambridge; Title Tel # (847) 267-7000 Title Fax # (800) 224-8299
Editorial Description: Covers directory, constitution, rules. Published for the Pacific Stock Exchange.
General Info: Yr. Est. 1967, Monthly, Trim Size-6 x 9, Web press, 50 pages, No Color, Looseleaf
Subscriptions: Indv. $437

Payment Systems Newsletter
Publishing Co: Tax Institute, PO Box 191091, San Francisco, CA 94119-1091 Tel # (415) 566-5111 Parent Co.-Faulkner & Gray, Inc., New York; Title Tel # (212) 766-1251

Payments Monthly   *Business*
Publishing Co: Moroney & Co., PO Box 720, Glen Echo, MD 20812-0720; Title Tel # (301) 229-4100 Title Fax # (301) 229-4102
Personnel: Publisher-William Moroney, Editor-Patricia Murphy
Editorial Description: Covers all elements of multi-billion-dollar payment industry: from credit cards to wire transfers, automated teller machines to cash management systems, & paper checks to home banking.
General Info: Yr. Est. 1989, Monthly, Trim Size-8½ x 11, 8 pages, ISSN: 1042-8879, 2 Color, Matte
Subscriptions: Indv. $345, Can. $345, For. $425, $30/copy
Acquistions: Publication Bought
List Rental: Rents Lists
Printing Co: Newsletter Services, Inc., 9700 Philadelphia Court, Lanham, MD 20706 Tel # (301) 731-5200, Fax # (301) 731-5201

Pension Actuary, The
See: INSURANCE

Personal Financial Planning Letter
Publishing Co: ECC Financial Group, 67 Yonge St., #1200, Toronto, ON M5E 1J8 Canada; Title Tel # (416) 364-0181
Editorial Description: News and ideas on financial planning.
General Info: Yr. Est. 1980, Monthly
Subscriptions: Indv. $147

Philadelphia Stock Exchange Guide   *Business*
Publishing Co: CCH, Inc., 2700 Lake Cook Rd., Riverwoods, IL 60015 Parent Co.-Kluwer Law & Taxation Publishers, Cambridge; Title Tel # (847) 267-7000 Title Fax # (800) 224-8299
Editorial Description: Covers directory & constitution rules. Published for the Exchange & available to others.
General Info: Yr. Est. 1965, Monthly, Trim Size-6 x 9, Web press, 64 pages, No Color, Looseleaf
Subscriptions: Indv. $378

Pocket Change Investor, The
See: CONSUMER INTERESTS

Pointer
See: HOUSE ORGANS

Positive Economist Bulletin
See: ECONOMICS

Post
See: HOUSE ORGANS

Practical Cash Management
Publishing Co: Bankers Research Inc., 34 Imperial Ave # 431, Westport, CT 06880-4304; Title Tel # (203) 227-1237
Personnel: Publisher-Ted Volckhausen, Editor-Ted Volckhausen, Jr.
General Info: Yr. Est. 1946, Monthly
Subscriptions: Indv. $242

Pratt's Letter   *Business*
Publishing Co: A.S. Pratt & Sons, 1911 Fort Myer Dr., Ste 308, Arlington, VA 22209-1603 Tel # (703) 528-1045; Title Tel # (703) 528-0145
Personnel: Publisher, Editor-Alan Rice
Editorial Description: News and commentary on banking and monetary developments, regulation and legislation.
General Info: Yr. Est. 1933, Weekly, Trim Size-8½ x 11, Offset press, 4 pages, No Color
Subscriptions: Indv. $138

Prespectives on Esatate and Financial Planning   *Business, Consumer*
Publishing Co: Newkirk Products, Inc., 15 Corporate Cir, Albany, NY 12203-5154 Tel # (518) 452-1000
Editorial Description: Custom publication designed for distribution to clients by professionals.
General Info: Quarterly, Trim Size-8½ x 11, 4 pages, 2 Color

Privacy & American Business
See: BUSINESS & INDUSTRY

Private Banker International
Publishing Co: Lafferty Publications, 420 Lexington Ave., Ste. 1745, New York, NY 10170 Tel # (212) 557-6729 Fax # (212) 557-7266; Title Tel # (404) 636-6610 Title Fax # (404) 636-6422
Personnel: Publisher-Frank Lawson, Editor in Chief-Michael Lafferty, Editor-Ian Orton
Editorial Description: Private Banker Intl. is an informative mix of news, comments, analysis, case studies, interviews, country surveys and statistics designed to meet the needs of all who service the private banking customer.
General Info: 10x/yr.
Subscriptions: Indv. $1,059

Private Investors Abroad   *Business*
Publishing Co: Matthew Bender & Co., 11 Penn Plaza, New York, NY 10001-2006 Tel # (212) 967-7707 Fax # (212) 244-3188; Title Tel # (518) 487-3000
Personnel: Editor-Carol Holgren
Editorial Description: An annual symposium that pinpoints worthwhile private investment opportunities abroad & explains the best methods of transacting international business by integrating professional knowledge from the fields of law, economics & business management.
General Info: Yr. Est. 1967, Annually, Looseleaf
Subscriptions: Indv. $75, $90/copy

Private Placement Letter
See: INVESTMENT

Private Placement Reporter
See: INVESTMENT

Productivity Views: Newsletter of Service Quality
See: BUSINESS & INDUSTRY

Products Marketing & Technology (PMT) Issues & Innovations
Publishing Co: Bank Administration Institute, One N. Franklin St., Chicago, IL 60606 Tel # (312) 553-4600 Fax # (312) 683-2426; Title Tel # (708) 228-2302
Personnel: Editor-Phyllis van Holland
Editorial Description: Information of interest to bank administration professionals.
General Info: Monthly
Subscriptions: Indv. $120
List Rental: Rents Lists

Professional Corporation Advisor
Publishing Co: W.H. White Publications, Inc., 53 Park Pl, New York, NY 10007-2407; Title Tel # (212) 608-6516
Personnel: Publisher-William White, Editor-Viola Roth, Circ. Mgr.-Dottie Saliski
Editorial Description: Professional corporation financial & legal advice.
General Info: Monthly
Subscriptions: Indv. $72
List Rental: List Management Co.: GMI Uni-Mail, 352 Park Ave. South, New York, NY 10010-1709 Tel # (212) 679-7655, Actives: 3,000, $25/M

Qualified Plan Reference Service   *Business*
Publishing Co: Universal Pensions Inc., PO Box 979, Brainerd, MN 56401-0979 Tel # (218) 829-4781; Title Tel # (218) 824-4781 Title Fax # (218) 829-2106
Personnel: Editor-Jennifer Norquist
Editorial Description: Issues relating to defined contributions plans. For financial organizations.
General Info: Yr. Est. 1991, Quarterly, Trim Size-8.5 x 11, Offset press, 600 pages, Other, Other, Looseleaf
Subscriptions: Indv. $119, Inst. $119
Printing Co: Universal Printing of Brainerd, 213 NW 4th St, Brainerd, MN 56401-3219 Tel # (218) 829-1982

Quality Customer Service   *Business*
Publishing Co: Siefer Consultants, Inc., 525 Cayuga St., PO Box 1384, Storm Lake, IA 50588; Title Tel # (712) 732-7340 Title Fax # (712) 732-7906
Editorial Description: Strategies and tips to improve customer service and account retention.
General Info: Yr. Est. 1995, Monthly
Subscriptions: Indv. $319, $15/copy

RTC Report   *Business*
Publishing Co: Land Development Law Reporter, 1401 16th St NW, Washington, DC 20036-2201; Title Tel # (202) 232-2144 Title Fax # (202) 232-4757
Editorial Description: Covers enforcement & regulatory activities of the RTC, the FDIC & office of Thrift Supervision. Highlights the latest on federal thrift resolutions & asset dispositions.
General Info: Yr. Est. 1984, Weekly, Trim Size-8½ x 11, 6 pages, Color-cover, Matte
Subscriptions: Indv. $425, Can. $245, For. $245
Circulation: (50% controlled)
Printing Co: Plymouth Printing, 1200 Cushing Pl SE, Washington, DC 20003-3599 Tel # (202) 488-7777, Fax # (202) 863-1078

RTC Resource Book
See: LAW

Refunding Makes Cents   *Consumer*
Publishing Co: Refunding Makes Cents, PO Box R-FB, Farmington, UT 84025
Editorial Description: Information on coupon offers, refunds, free offers and many other sources for families to save money.
General Info: Monthly, Trim Size-8½ x 11, 88 pages, No Color, Matte, Saddle-stitched

Regulatory Compliance Watch   *Business*
Publishing Co: American Banker Newsletters, One State Plaza, New York, NY 10004-1505 Fax # (202) 843-9620; Title Tel # (212) 803-8300 Title Fax # (212) 843-9620
Personnel: Publisher-David G. Schutt, Editor-Patricia Cinelli, Circ. Dir.-Celia Benjamin, Adv. Dir.-, Mktg. Dir.-Hans Winberg
Editorial Description: Enforcement and supervision by financial regulators.
General Info: Weekly, Ind/Abs/Online: Mead Data Central, NewsNet, Predicasts/Dialog
Subscriptions: Indv. $675, Can. $675, For. $705, $20/copy
Advertising: $1,400.
List Rental: Rents Lists

Regulatory Report
Publishing Co: Savings & Community Bankers of America, 900 19th St. NW, Ste. 400, Washington, DC 20006-2105; Title Tel # (202) 857-3146 Title Fax # (202) 296-8716
Personnel: Editor-Bob Bartlett, Production Mgr.-Betsy Pavichevich
Editorial Description: Information & analysis on savings institution regulatory developments.
General Info: Yr. Est. 1988, Monthly, 24 pages
Subscriptions: Indv. $410, $25/copy
Circulation: Total-3,200

Remnant Review   *Business*
Publishing Co: Hoisager & Laird, Inc., 101 S Jennings Ave Ste 204, Fort Worth, TX 76104-1149 Tel # (817) 335-5443 Fax # (817) 335-7909
Personnel: Editor-Gary North, Ph.D
Editorial Description: Financial news and developments.
General Info: 22x/yr.
Subscriptions: Indv. $95
List Rental: List Management Co.: Carnegie Marketing Assocs., Koll Executive Plaza, 3878 Carson St., Suite 220, Torrance, CA 90503 Tel # (310) 540-4757, Fax # (310) 540-7407, Actives: 26,397, $150/M

Resort Management Report
See: BUSINESS & INDUSTRY

Retail Banker International
Publishing Co: Lafferty Publications, 420 Lexington Ave., Ste. 1745, New York, NY 10170 Tel # (212) 557-6729 Fax # (212) 557-7266; Title Tel # (404) 636-6610 Title Fax # (404) 636-6422
Personnel: Publisher-Frank Lawson, Editor in Chief-Michael Lafferty, Editor-Peter Kinahan
Editorial Description: Reports & analyzes the activities of the world's largest retail banks, focusing on marketing trends & operational improvements.
General Info: 23x/yr.
Subscriptions: Indv. $1,159

Retail Banking Digest
Business, Association

Publishing Co: American Bankers Association, 1120 Connecticut Ave NW, Washington, DC 20036-3902 Tel # (202) 663-5000; Title Tel # (202) 663-5094 Title Fax # (202) 828-4544
Personnel: Publisher-Craig Sablosky, Editor-Allyn Buzzell, Production Mgr.-Stephanie Hill
Editorial Description: In-depth treatment of key consumer banking issues.Summarizes current legislative and regulatory developments affecting retail banking in every other issue.
General Info: (Formerly ABA Consumer Banking Digest/Consumer Banking Digest), Yr. Est. 1980, Bimonthly, Trim Size-8½ x 11, 24 pages, 2 Color, Coated
Subscriptions: Indv. $115
Circulation: Total-900
List Rental: Rents Lists

Review for CFOs & Investment Bankers
Business

Publishing Co: Brumberg Publications, Inc., 124 Harvard St., Brookline, MA 02146-6432; Title Tel # (617) 734-1979 Title Fax # (617) 734-1989
Personnel: Publisher-Bruce Brumberg, Editor-Susan Koffman, Mktg. Dir.-Karen Axelrod
Editorial Description: Analysis of current events, discusses strategies and trends related to capital raising and financial restructuring.
General Info: Yr. Est. 1989, Monthly, Offset press, 8 pages, 2 Color, Newsprint
Subscriptions: Indv. $125

Risk Management News/Risk Management Manual
See: INSURANCE

Risk Report
See: INSURANCE

Ron Paul Survival Report
See: INVESTMENT

Rundt's Weekly Intelligence
See: INTERNATIONAL TRADE

S & L Financial Quarterly

Publishing Co: United Communications Group, 11300 Rockville Pike, Ste. 1100, Rockville, MD 20852-3030 Tel # (301) 816-8950 Fax # (301) 816-8945; Title Tel # (301) 961-8700 Title Fax # (301) 961-8666
Editorial Description: Focuses on news and developments in the savings & loan industry.
General Info: Yr. Est. 1986, Quarterly
Subscriptions: Indv. $349
List Rental: Rents Lists

SBANE Enterprise
See: BUSINESS & INDUSTRY

SCOR Report

Publishing Co: SCOR Report, PO Box 781992, Dallas, TX 75378-1992; Title Tel # (214) 620-2489 Title Fax # (214) 406-0213
Personnel: Publisher, Editor-Tom S. Gordon, Circ. Mgr.-Malcolm Gatto, Mktg. Dir.-Delton Simmons
Editorial Description: Capital formation alternativesfor small business target audience small business, their lawyers and accountants.
General Info: Yr. Est. 1993, ISSN: 1074-6498
Subscriptions: Indv. $200

SEC Compliance

Publishing Co: Research Institute of America, 90 5th Avenue, New York, NY 10011-7629 Tel # (212) 645-4800; Title Tel # (800) 562-0245 Title Fax # (201) 816-3484
Editorial Description: Five volume service containing practical & procedural information for SEC Compliance for
General Info: Quarterly, Looseleaf
Subscriptions: Indv. $681
List Rental: List Management Co.: WG & L List Management, 1 Penn Plz Fl 42, New York, NY 10119-0002 Tel # (212) 971-5000

SEC New Registrations Report
See: LAW

SEC Today
See: LAW

S.I. Reports
Business

Publishing Co: Statistical Indicator Assocs., PO Box 187, North Egremont, MA 01252-0187; Title Tel # (413) 528-3280
Personnel: Publisher, Editor-Leonard Lempert
Editorial Description: Weekly assessment and forecast of direction of U.S. economy.
General Info: Yr. Est. 1954, Weekly, 4 pages, Color
Subscriptions: Indv. $210, $4/copy

SNL Conversion Watch
See: INVESTMENT

SNL Finance Company Weekly
Business

Publishing Co: SNL Securities, 410 E. Main St., P.O. Box 2124, Charlottesville, VA 22902 Tel # (804) 977-1600 Fax # (804) 977-4466
Personnel: Publisher-Reid Nagle, Circ. Mgr.-Pat Labua, Product Mgr.-Chandler Spears, Adv. Dir.-Jenn Nagaj, Mktg. Dir.-Judy Lewis
Editorial Description: Provides a summary of all the week's news and market information that effects finance companies and related industries.
General Info: Weekly, Trim Size-8½ x 11, Desktop press, 10 pages, No Color, Other
Subscriptions: Indv. $296

SNL REIT Weekly
See: REAL ESTATE

SNL Weekly BankFAX
Business

Publishing Co: SNL Securities, 410 E. Main St., P.O. Box 2124, Charlottesville, VA 22902; Title Tel # (804) 977-1600 Title Fax # (804) 977-4466
Personnel: Publisher-Reid Nagle, Circ. Mgr.-Pat LaBua, Adv. Dir.-Jenn Nagaj, Mktg. Dir.-Judy Lewis
Editorial Description: Provides concise coverage of news, stock prices, merger activity and more for each week.
General Info: Yr. Est. 1988, Weekly, Trim Size-8½ x 11, 12 pages, No Color, Other
Subscriptions: Indv. $220
Advertising: $400.

SNL Weekly ComplianceFax
Business

Publishing Co: SNL Securities, 410 E. Main St., P.O. Box 2124, Charlottesville, VA 22902; Title Tel # (804) 977-1600 Title Fax # (804) 977-4466
Personnel: Publisher-Reid Nagle, Editor-Jenn Nagaj, Circ. Mgr.-Pat LaBua, Production Mgr.-Paul Wanner, Mktg. Dir.-Judy Lewis
Editorial Description: Summarizes recent news stories and regulatory releases affecting the bank and thrift industries.
General Info: Yr. Est. 1993, Weekly, Trim Size-8.5 x 11, Desktop press, 5 pages, No Color
Subscriptions: Indv. $97, Inst. $97
Advertising: Inquire for rates.

SWAAA Newsletter
See: INSURANCE

Scope
Business, Association

Publishing Co: American Commercial Collectors Assn., 4040 W 70th St, Minneapolis, MN 55435-4104; Title Tel # (612) 925-0760
Personnel: Editor-Ted Smith, Promotion Dir.-David Peterson
Editorial Description: Specialists in the collection of commercial accounts receivable.
General Info: Yr. Est. 1969, Monthly, Trim Size-11 x 17, Sheetfed press, 5 pages, No Color, Newsprint
Circulation: Total-250

Second District Member Activity Report

Publishing Co: Fed. Home Loan Bank of New York, 1 World Trade Ctr Fl 103, New York, NY 10048-0202; Title Tel # (212) 912-4833
General Info: Quarterly

Secondary Mortgage Market Guide
Business

Publishing Co: Matthew Bender & Co., 11 Penn Plaza, New York, NY 10001-2006 Tel # (212) 967-7707 Fax # (212) 244-3188
Editorial Description: Focuses on business, tax and legal considerations.
General Info: Yr. Est. 1985, Irregular, Looseleaf

Secured Transaction Guide
Business

Publishing Co: CCH, Inc., 2700 Lake Cook Rd., Riverwoods, IL 60015 Parent Co.-Kluwer Law & Taxation Publishers, Cambridge; Title Tel # (847) 267-7000 Title Fax # (800) 224-8299
Editorial Description: Covers, explains state rules for creating, filing, perfecting and enforcing security interests in personal property.
General Info: Yr. Est. 1969, Bi-weekly, Trim Size-6 x 9, Web press, 75 pages, No Color, Looseleaf
Subscriptions: Indv. $1,053

Securities Industry Trends
See: INVESTMENT

Securities Regulation and Law Report
See: LAW

Security Investing
See: INVESTMENT

Seller/Servicer Update

Publishing Co: Inside Mortgage Finance Publications, Box 42387, Washington, DC 20015; Title Tel # (301) 951-1240 Title Fax # (301) 656-1709
Personnel: Publisher-Guy Cecala, Editor, Mng. Editor-John Lewis, Production Mgr.-Tony Cecala, Circ. Mgr., Mktg. Dir.-Didi Parks
Editorial Description: Financial and investment news and developments.
General Info: Yr. Est. 1988, Monthly, Trim Size-8½ x 11, 30 pages, Color
Subscriptions: Indv. $395, $50/copy

The Small Business Advisor
See: BUSINESS & INDUSTRY

Smart's Insurance Bulletin
See: INSURANCE

Society Now
See: HOUSE ORGANS

Sourceletter
Publishing Co: Sourceletter, Inc., PO Box 7282, Arlington, VA 22207-0282;
Title Tel # (703) 533-7939
Editorial Description: Financial news and information.
General Info: Yr. Est. 1988, Monthly
Subscriptions: Indv. $59

Standard & Poor's Semi-Weekly Called Bond Record
Publishing Co: Standard & Poor's Corp., 25 Broadway, New York, NY 10004 Tel # (212) 208-8000
Parent Co.-McGraw-Hill, New York
General Info: Semi-weekly, ISSN: 073-7299X, Looseleaf

Statistical Indicator Reports
See: INVESTMENT

Statistics on Banking
Publishing Co: Statistics on Banking, 550 17th St NW, Washington, DC 20429-0001;
Title Tel # (202) 389-4602

Straight Talk on Your Money *Consumer*
Publishing Co: Phillips Publishing, Inc., 7811 Montrose Rd., Potomac, MD 20854-3394
Tel # (301) 340-2100 Fax # (301) 294-1307 Parent Co.-Phillips Business Information, Inc.,
Potomac; Title Tel # (301) 340-1520 Title Fax # (301) 340-0542
Personnel: Publisher-Thomas L. Phillips, Co-Editor-Daria Dolan, Co-Editor-Ken Dolan, Mktg. Dir.-Nancy Cathey
Editorial Description: Finance information for families on everything from loans and travel to taxes and investment.
General Info: Monthly
Subscriptions: Indv. $40
List Rental: List Management Co.: Manager: John Baldwin; Phillips Publishing List Marketing, 7811 Montrose Rd., Potomac, MD 20854-3394 Tel # (301) 340-2100, Fax # (301) 294-1307, Actives: 171,557, $195/M, Expires: 109,622, $95/M

Sum Monthly News
See: ACCOUNTING

Superfund Report
See: LAW

Szabo Collective Wisdom
See: CREDIT AND CREDIT UNIONS

TD Notes
Publishing Co: Toronto-Dominion Bank, Toronto Dominion Center, Box 1, Toronto, ON M5K 1A2 Canada Tel # (416) 866-5696
Personnel: Editor-Casandra Sanders
General Info: Monthly, Trim Size-11 x 17, 8 pages
Circulation: Total-16,350

TJFR Business News Reporter
See: MEDIA & COMMUNICATIONS

Tax Avoidance Digest
See: INVESTMENT

Tax, Estate and Financial Planning for the Elderly *Business*
Publishing Co: Matthew Bender & Co., 11 Penn Plaza, New York, NY 10001-2006
Tel # (212) 967-7707 Fax # (212) 244-3188
Editorial Description: A handy how-to guide that covers a broad spectrum of planning areas of special concern to the elderly and their families.
General Info: Yr. Est. 1985, Irregular, Looseleaf

Taxation of Securities Transactions
See: TAXES

Technology News and Trends *Business*
Publishing Co: Siefer Consultants, Inc., 525 Cayuga St., PO Box 1384, Storm Lake, IA 50588;
Title Tel # (712) 732-7340 Title Fax # (712) 732-7906
Editorial Description: Real life examples of how bankers are using technology to improve their profitability.
General Info: Yr. Est. 1995
Subscriptions: Indv. $319, $15/copy

Teller Vision *Business, Association*
Publishing Co: Bureau of Business Practice, 24 Rope Ferry Rd, Waterford, CT 06386-0001
Tel # (806) 442-4365 Fax # (860) 434-3341 Parent Co.-Prentice Hall, Waterford;
Title Tel # (860) 442-4365 Title Fax # (860) 434-3078
Personnel: Editor-Maria Marquis, Adv. Dir.-Ruth Nagle, Art Dir.-D. Fedeli
Editorial Description: On the job skills and security into for financial institution personnel.
General Info: Yr. Est. 1981, Semi-monthly, Trim Size-8½ x 11, Offset press, 4 pages, ISSN: 0895-1039, 2 Color
Subscriptions: Indv. $47
Circulation: Total-13,000

Texas Finance Report *Business*
Publishing Co: Report Publications, Inc., PO Box 12368, Austin, TX 78711-2368;
Title Tel # (512) 478-5663
Personnel: Editor-Bill Kidd, Circ. Mgr.-Shirl Scott
Editorial Description: Detailed account of orders and action by the state finance-related agencies. Reports on finance-related legislation, court decisions and politics.
General Info: Yr. Est. 1957, Weekly, Trim Size-7 x 9, Offset press, 4 pages, No Color
Subscriptions: Indv. $65, $2/copy
Circulation: Total-300

Texas Leaguer *Association*
Publishing Co: Texas Credit Union League, 4455 LBJ Frwy., Box 225147, Dallas, TX 75244-5992;
Title Tel # (214) 980-5517
Personnel: Editor-Virginia Robertson
Editorial Description: Keeps Texas credit unions informed about C.U. activities.
General Info: Yr. Est. 1970, Weekly, Trim Size-8½ x 11, Sheetfed press, 6 pages, 2 Color, Coated
Subscriptions: Indv. $100
Circulation: (100% controlled), Total-2,000

Tiger on Spreads
See: INVESTMENT

Trading Systems Technology *Business*
Publishing Co: Waters Information Services, PO Box 2248, Binghamton, NY 13902-2248
Tel # (607) 770-4075; Title Tel # (607) 770-9242 Title Fax # (607) 770-9435
Personnel: Publisher-Dennis Waters, Editor-Andrew Delaney, Circ. Mgr.-Beth Arnold, Production Mgr.-James Willis, Adv. Dir.-Joe Viviani, Mktg. Dir.-Betsy Martens
Editorial Description: Covers applications of advanced information technology in the financial markets.
General Info: Yr. Est. 1987, Bi-weekly, 16 pages, ISSN: 0892-5542, Ind/Abs/Online: NewsNet, Predicasts, DIALOG, No Color, Newsprint
Subscriptions: Indv. $795, For. $945
Printing Co: C & L Lettershop, 216 Court St, Binghamton, NY 13901-3697 Tel # (607) 724-1318

Treasury Pro *Business*
Publishing Co: Phoenix-Hecht, 68 T.W. Alexander Dr., Box 13628, Reseach Triangle Pk., NC 27709;
Title Tel # (919) 541-9339 Title Fax # (919) 541-9026
Personnel: Editor-Kenneth Parkinson
General Info: Yr. Est. 1988, Monthly
Subscriptions: Indv. $245

Trends & Projections
See: ECONOMICS

Trust Department Administration and Operations *Business*
Publishing Co: Matthew Bender & Co., 11 Penn Plaza, New York, NY 10001-2006
Tel # (212) 967-7707 Fax # (212) 244-3188
Personnel: Editor-Victor P. Whitney
Editorial Description: Covers every aspect of setting up a trust department, day-to-day administration, asset management, operations, marketing, and internal management.
General Info: Yr. Est. 1981, Irregular, Looseleaf

Trustees & Directors Letter
Publishing Co: America's Community Bankers, 900 19th St. NW, Ste. 400, Washington, DC 20006-2105 Fax # (202) 659-1134; Title Tel # (202) 857-3100
Editorial Description: Covers current legislative, regulatory and economic issues targeted to directors and trustees of savings institutions.

Truth-In Lending Manual *Business*
Publishing Co: Warren, Gorham & Lamont, 31 Saint James Ave., Boston, MA 02116-4112
Fax # (617) 423-1914 Parent Co.-Thomson Professional Publications, Stamford;
Title Tel # (617) 423-2020
Personnel: Publisher-Laurence Selby, Mktg. Dir.-Sandra Fox
Editorial Description: Coverage and guidance in compliance to the Truth-in-Lending Act.
General Info: Yr. Est. 1976, Semi-annually, Looseleaf
Subscriptions: Indv. $175, $72/copy
List Rental: List Management Co.: American List Counsel, 88 Orchard Cir # Cn-5219, Princeton, NJ 08540-3026 Tel # (908) 874-4300, Fax # (908) 874-4433

Twin Ports Financial Record
Publishing Co: Odegaard Printing Co., 2502 W 3rd St, Duluth, MN 55806-1839; Title Tel # (218) 722-2598
Personnel: Editor-Knute Odegaard
Editorial Description: Business and financial news.
General Info: Yr. Est. 1883, Semi-weekly
Subscriptions: Indv. $15
Circulation: Total-816
Advertising: Inquire for rates.

UPBeat
See: HOUSE ORGANS

United Student Aid Funds Newsletter
See: EDUCATION

Unlimited Editions Preview   *Business*   CPM: $83
Publishing Co: Noble Publishing Co., PO Box 1509, Candler, NC 28715-1509 Parent Co.-Unlimited Editions International, Candler; Title Tel # (704) 696-3269
Personnel: Publisher, Editor-Gregory Hugh Leng
Editorial Description: Financial and tax strategies, investment opportunities, real estate and stock advice.
General Info: Yr. Est. 1990, Quarterly, Trim Size-8½ x 11, Web press, 16 pages, No Color, Matte
Subscriptions: Indv. $60, $15/copy
Acquistions: Publication Bought
Circulation: Total-18,000
Advertising: $1,500.
List Rental: Actives: $45/M, Hotline: $90/M

Wasatch Letter
See: INVESTMENT

Washington Bond & Money Market Report   *Business*
Publishing Co: Newsletter Services, Inc., 9700 Philadelphia Ct., Lanham, MD 20706-4405; Title Tel # (301) 731-5202 Title Fax # (301) 731-5203
Personnel: Publisher-Lisa A. Anthony, Exec. VP/Group Publisher-Michael Nagan, Editor-Joesph R. Slevin, Circ. Dir.-Priscilla Arenas, Mktg. Mgr.-Susan Pangman
Editorial Description: Analyses of Federal Reserve and market thinking on the course of the economy and money supply; Fed reations to market events; the impact of events abroad on Fed policy; and the interest rate outlook. Four pages plus quarterly interest rate forecasts.
General Info: (Formerly ROG/Bond & Money Market Letter), Yr. Est. 1936, Bi-weekly, Trim Size-8½ x 11, Letrpr. press, 4 pages, ISSN: 1059-017X, No Color, Matte
Subscriptions: Indv. $385
List Rental: List Management Co.: Taybi Direct East, Inc., 13321 New Hampshire Ave., Ste. 202, Silver Spring, MD 20904-3450 Tel # (301) 680-3633, Fax # (301) 680-3635

Washington Notes   *Association*
Publishing Co: Savings & Community Bankers of America, 900 19th St. NW, Ste. 400, Washington, DC 20006-2105; Title Tel # (202) 857-3146 Title Fax # (202) 296-8716
Personnel: Editor-James Eberle
Editorial Description: Legislative & regulatory news for savings institution managers.
General Info: Weekly
Subscriptions: Indv. $220
Circulation: Total-10,000

Washington Weekly Report   *Business, Association*
Publishing Co: Independent Bankers Assn. of America, 1 Thomas Cir NW Ste 950, Washington, DC 20005-5802; Title Tel # (202) 659-8111 Title Fax # (202) 659-9216
Personnel: Publisher-Kenneth Guenther, Editor-Elmer Ramos
Editorial Description: Covers banking legislation & regulation of interest to community banks.
General Info: (Formerly Independent Bankers Association Newsletter), Yr. Est. 1962, Weekly, Trim Size-8⁹⁄₁₆ x 11¼, 4 pages, ISSN: 0274-5127, No Color
Subscriptions: Indv. $20, Free With Membership
Circulation: Total-8,100

Webster Agricultural Letter
See: AGRICULTURE

Weekly Financial Statistics   *Business*
Publishing Co: Bank of Canada, Public Distribution, 234 Wellington St, Ottawa, ON K1A 0G9 Canada; Title Tel # (613) 782-8248 Title Fax # (613) 782-8874
Editorial Description: Weekly update of financial & economic data on chartered banks, trust & mortgage loan cos., interest & exchange rates, financial markets, government finance & credit.
General Info: Yr. Est. 1954, Weekly, Trim Size-8½ x 14, Mimeo press, 12 pages, ISSN: 0005-5158, No Color
Subscriptions: Indv. $70, Inst. $55, Can. $55, For. $110, $2/copy
Circulation: Total-1,800

Weekly International Market Alert
See: INTERNATIONAL TRADE

Wendell's Report to Controllers
See: ACCOUNTING

Women's Market Share
See: WOMEN'S

Working Capital
Publishing Co: John Hancock Financial Services, Inc., John Hancock Pl., Box 111, Boston, MA 02117
General Info: Quarterly

World Bank News   *Business*
Publishing Co: World Bank, 1818 H St., NW N-9023, Washington, DC 20433-0001; Title Tel # (202) 477-1234 Title Fax # (202) 477-6391
Personnel: Editor-Leandro Coronel
General Info: Yr. Est. 1981, Weekly, 6 pages, ISSN: 0254-6353
Circulation: Total-6,000

WorldWide Business Exchange
See: BUSINESS & INDUSTRY

Wrap Fee Advisor   *Business*
Publishing Co: AMR Publishing, 122 E 42nd St Rm 1605, New York, NY 10168-0002 Tel # (212) 541-3923
Editorial Description: For fee wrap money managers with investment ↓vice.
General Info: (Formerly Wrap Fee Newsletter), Yr. Est. 1993, Monthly
Subscriptions: Indv. $295

Wright Investment Advice and Analysis   *Business*
Publishing Co: Wright Investors' Service, 1000 Lafayette Blvd, Bridgeport, CT 06604-4720; Title Tel # (203) 333-6666
Personnel: Editor-John Winthrop
General Info: (Formerly Wright Advisory Report, Wright Bankers' Service), Yr. Est. 1962, Weekly

BARBER & BEAUTICIAN

Club Natural   *Consumer*
Publishing Co: Club Natural, P.O. Box 14088, Baltimore, MD 21268
Editorial Description: Contain beauty tips and special offers for users of Clairol hair coloring.
Subscriptions: Free

Dragoco Report
Publishing Co: Conrad Heinrichs, Dragoco, Inc., King Road, Totowa, NJ 07512
Personnel: Editor-Conrad Heinrichs
Editorial Description: Editions in French, English, German, Italian and Spanish.
General Info: Yr. Est. 1956, Monthly
Circulation: Total-16,000

Forecast
Publishing Co: Natl. Beauty Culturists' League, 25 Logan Cir NW, Washington, DC 20005-3725 Tel # (202) 332-2695; Title Tel # (212) 332-2695
General Info: Semi-annually

Monthly Report for Hairstylists & Salon Owners
Publishing Co: Ken Lange Inc., 7112 N 15th Pl # 1, Phoenix, AZ 85020-5416; Title Tel # (602) 944-1483 Title Fax # (602) 997-1103
Personnel: Publisher, Editor-Ken Lange
Editorial Description: Features ideas to help hairstylists and salon owners increase their income. Includes promotion ideas, successful techniques, etc.
General Info: Yr. Est. 1981, 11x/yr., Trim Size-8½ x 11, Desktop press, 8 pages, ISSN: 0277-0334, Coated, Saddle-stitched
Subscriptions: Indv. $50, Can. $65, For. $65
Circulation: Total-1,000
List Rental: Actives: 75,000, $65/M

NABS Weekly
Publishing Co: Natl. Assn. of Barber Styling Schools, 304 S 11th St, Lincoln, NE 68508-2102; Title Tel # (402) 474-4244
Personnel: Editor-Alyce Howard
General Info: Quarterly, 4 pages

BASEBALL

Baseball Coach   *Association*
Publishing Co: Baseball Coach, 76 N Maple Ave Ste 172, Ridgewood, NJ 07450-3212
Editorial Description: Information for High School basball coaches.
General Info: 10x/yr.

Baseball Forecaster — *Consumer*

Publishing Co: Shandler Enterprises Co., PO Box 20503, Roanoke, VA 24018 Tel # (540) 777-6315 Fax # (540) 777-6315; Title Tel # (603) 424-1669 Title Fax # (603) 424-1669
Personnel: Publisher-Ron Shandler, Assoc. Publ.-Susan Shandler
Editorial Description: Baseball Forecaster tracks statistical trends; supported by charts, essays and commentary.
General Info: Yr. Est. 1986, Monthly, Trim Size-8½ x 11, Desktop press, 24 pages, Matte, Saddle-stitched
Subscriptions: Indv. $79
Circulation: Total-1,200
List Rental: Actives: 1,500, $100/M, Hotline: 500, $125/M, Expires: 1,500, $85/M

Baseball Insight — *Consumer*

Publishing Co: Parrish Pubs., PO Box 23205, Portland, OR 97281-3205; Title Tel # (503) 244-8975
Personnel: Publisher-Perry Parrish, Editor-Phil Erwin
Editorial Description: Team & pitching statistics, analysis & interpretation, book reviews & commentary.
General Info: Yr. Est. 1982, Weekly, 12 pages
Subscriptions: Indv. $139, $7/copy
Circulation: Total-750

Baseball News — *Consumer, Association*

Publishing Co: National Association of Professional Baseball Leagues, PO Box A, Saint Petersburg, FL 33731-1950; Title Tel # (813) 822-6937 Title Fax # (813) 821-5819
Personnel: Editor-Bob Sparks
Editorial Description: Oversees the activity of minor league baseball.
General Info: (Formerly Baseball), Yr. Est. 1901, Annually
Subscriptions: Indv. $10
Circulation: Total-550

Baseball Perspective — *Consumer*

Publishing Co: Baseball Perspective, PO Box 12212, La Jolla, CA 92039-2212 Tel # (619) 450-0375
Personnel: Publisher-Steve Fall
Editorial Description: News and information about baseball.
General Info: Yr. Est. 1993, Bi-monthly
Subscriptions: Indv. $12

Baseball's Active Leaders — *Consumer*

Publishing Co: Baseball's Active Leaders, 1263 Paso Fino Dr, Warrington, PA 18976-1928; Title Tel # (215) 343-6033
Personnel: Publisher, Editor-Dan Heisman
Editorial Description: Statistics and articles on leaders in sport of baseball.
General Info: Yr. Est. 1990, 4x/yr., Trim Size-8½ x 11, 14 pages
Subscriptions: Indv. $12

Batter Up! — *Consumer*

Publishing Co: John Skipper, 707 6th St. SE, Mason City, IA 50401-4155 Tel # (515) 423-2283
Editorial Description: Baseball facts and anecdotes.
General Info: Yr. Est. 1993, Monthly
Subscriptions: Indv. $25

Benson's Baseball Monthly — *Consumer*

Publishing Co: Diamond Analytics, PO Box 7302, Wilton, CT 06897-7302 Tel # (203) 834-0812
Editorial Description: Covers baseball with stats and info.
General Info: Monthly, Trim Size-8½ x 11, 2 Color
Subscriptions: Indv. $59
Advertising: Inquire for rates.

Between the Lines

Publishing Co: Stephen Wolf Publishers, 247 Arlington Ave, Syracuse, NY 13207-1603; Title Tel # (315) 478-0351
Personnel: Editor-Stephen Wolf
General Info: Yr. Est. 1989, Monthly
Subscriptions: Indv. $15

By the Numbers
See: MATHEMATICS

Current Baseball Publications — *Consumer, Association*

Publishing Co: Society for American Baseball Research, PO Box 93183, Cleveland, OH 44101-5183 Fax # (216) 575-0502; Title Tel # (216) 575-0500
Editorial Description: Lists newly published baseball books, magazines and newsletters.
General Info: Quarterly, Looseleaf
Subscriptions: Indv. $8

Diamond Duds — *Consumer*

Publishing Co: Diamond Duds, PO Box 10153, Silver Spring, MD 20914-0153
Editorial Description: For collectors of baseball paraphenalia.
General Info: Quarterly

Fielder's Choice — *Consumer*

Publishing Co: Fielder's Choice, PO Box 456, Waite Park, MN 56387-0456; Title Fax # (612) 252-3913
Personnel: Editor-Jason Gabbert
Editorial Description: Covers high school and college baseball in Minnesota.
General Info: Monthly
Subscriptions: Indv. $13

Here's the Pitch

Publishing Co: W.L. Johnson, 205 W 66th Ter, Kansas City, MO 64113-1854; Title Tel # (816) 822-1740
General Info: Quarterly

International Baseball Rundown — *Consumer*

Publishing Co: International Baseball Rundown, PO Box 608, Glen Ellyn, IL 60138-0608; Title Tel # (708) 668-8341 Title Fax # (708) 668-2148
Personnel: Editor-Jeff Elijah, Adv. Dir.-Lori McCaffrey, Art Dir.-Brian Willse
Editorial Description: Covers international baseball information and world baseball directory.
General Info: Yr. Est. 1992, Monthly, Trim Size-8½ x 11, Offset press, 22 pages, 20% ads, No Color, Coated, Saddle-stitched
Subscriptions: Indv. $18, Can. $20, For. $29
Circulation: Total-4,000, Readership-5,000

Milestones and Memories — *Business, Consumer*

Publishing Co: Milestones and Memories, PO Box 679, Jessup, MD 20794-0679 Tel # (410) 761-7191
Personnel: Editor-Jim Fredlund
Editorial Description: Puts current baseball accomplishments and achievements into historical perspective.
General Info: Yr. Est. 1992, Monthly, Trim Size-8½ x 11, Desktop press, 8 pages, 2 Color
Subscriptions: Indv. $15, $2/copy

National Softball Hall of Fame Newsletter
See: SPORTS & SPORTING GOODS

Old Tyme Baseball News — *Consumer*

Publishing Co: McKinstry Bros. Publishing Group, Inc., PO Box 833, Petoskey, MI 49770-0833; Title Tel # (616) 348-3982
Personnel: Publisher-Mike McKinstry, Editor-Scott McKinstry, Photo Ed.-George Brace, Art Dir.-Bob Carroll, Asst. Ed., Promotion Dir.-Chuck Hershberger
Editorial Description: Articles and recollections of old time baseball greats.
General Info: Yr. Est. 1988, Bi-monthly
Subscriptions: Indv. $24, $4/copy
Circulation: Total-1,500
Advertising: Inquire for rates.

People to People Sports Newsletter
See: SPORTS & SPORTING GOODS

Prospects Report — *Consumer*

Publishing Co: Prospects Report, PO Box 6193, Evanston, IL 60204-6193
Personnel: Editor-Thorn Henninger
Editorial Description: Covers up and coming minor league and high school/college baseball players.
General Info: Quarterly
Subscriptions: Indv. $15

RBI Newsletter — *Consumer*

Publishing Co: Canadian Fed. of Amateur Baseball, 1600 James Naismith Dr., Gloucester, ON K1B 5N4 Canada Fax # (613) 748-5767; Title Tel # (613) 748-5606 Title Fax # (613) 748-5706
Editorial Description: Annual yearbook covering amateur & professional baseball, national & international championships.
General Info: (Formerly Baseball Canada/Hit & Run), Yr. Est. 1989, Bi-monthly, 4 pages, ISSN: 0829-6782
Subscriptions: Indv. $6
Circulation: Total-500
Advertising: Inquire for rates.

Sports Weekly Newsletter-Baseball

Publishing Co: R.W. Livingston, Publishing, PO Box 60008, North Charleston, SC 29419-0008; Title Tel # (803) 797-6173
Personnel: Publisher, Editor-R. W. Livingston
General Info: Yr. Est. 1968, Weekly, Trim Size-14 x 17, Offset press, 2 pages
Circulation: Total-1,000

Stadium Newsletter — *Consumer*

Publishing Co: J & J Postcards, 213 E Lilac St, Elburn, IL 60119-8948
Personnel: Publisher-Mike Cervenka
General Info: Monthly
Subscriptions: Indv. $9

Tournament News

Publishing Co: Natl. Amateur Baseball Fed., 12406 Keynote Ln, Bowie, MD 20715-2739; Title Tel # (517) 685-2990
Personnel: Editor-Ronald McMinn
General Info: Yr. Est. 1967, Annually, Trim Size-16½ x 22, 4 pages
Circulation: Total-10,000
List Rental: Rents Lists

Tuff Stuff's Baseball Bulletin *Business*

Publishing Co: Cadmus Communications, 1974 E Parham Rd, Richmond, VA 23228-2206
Tel # (804) 264-4263
Personnel: Publisher, Editor-Larry Canale
Editorial Description: Covers the effects of the baseball strike on the baseball card collecting industry.
General Info: Yr. Est. 1994, Weekly
Subscriptions: Free To Qualified Recipient

Your Season Ticket   CPM: $23

Publishing Co: Baseball Cards Unlimited, 106 Liberty Rd., Woodsboro, MD 21798; Title Tel # (301) 845-6076
Personnel: Editor-Richard M. Toms, Jr., Adv. Dir.-Pamela Toms, Production Mgr., Art Dir.-Ron Soule, Publisher, Circ. Dir., Promotion Dir.-Rick Toms
Editorial Description: Newsletter designed for sports cards collectors with information & tips on the hobby; also has card collector show & convention information.
General Info: Yr. Est. 1991, Bi-monthly, Trim Size-8 x 11, Desktop press, 16 pages, 50% ads, 2 Color
Subscriptions: Indv. $8, Free
Circulation: (95% controlled), Total-4,000, Subscriptions-200
Advertising: $95.
Printing Co: Account Manager: Pamela Toms; Valley Web, 1299 Stowe Avenue, Medford, OR 97504 Tel # (503) 772-7039

BEVERAGES - BREWING

ASBC Newsletter   *Association*   CPM: $548

Publishing Co: American Society of Brewing Chemists, 3340 Pilot Knob Rd, Saint Paul, MN 55121-2055 Fax # (612) 454-0766; Title Tel # (612) 454-7250
Personnel: Publisher-Steven Nelson, Circ. Mgr.-Larry Hartman, Production Mgr.-Steve Kronmiller, Advertising & Sales-Amy Hope
Editorial Description: Organization news.
General Info: Yr. Est. 1941, Quarterly, Trim Size-8½ x 11, Sheetfed press, 25 pages, ISSN: 0149-7308, Color, Newsprint, Saddle-stitched
Subscriptions: Indv. $25, For. $31, $10/copy
Circulation: Total-820
Advertising: $450.

Alcohol Issues Insights   *Business*

Publishing Co: Beer Marketer's Insights, Inc., 51 Virginia Ave., West Nyack, NY 10994-2005
Fax # (914) 258-7860; Title Tel # (914) 358-7751
Personnel: Publisher-Benjamin Steinman, Editor-Eric Shepard, Circ. Mgr.-Irene Steinman
Editorial Description: Covers sociological & legislative developments concerning alcohol issues.
General Info: Yr. Est. 1984, Monthly, Trim Size-8½ x 11, Sheetfed press, 4 pages, No Color
Subscriptions: Indv. $215, For. $227
Acquistions: Publication Bought
Printing Co: Mid-Atlantic Litho Sales, 300 Corporate Dr Ste 6, Blauvelt, NY 10913-1144

Alcoholic Beverage Control/ State Capitals   *Business, Association*

Publishing Co: Wakeman/Walworth, 300 N. Washington St., Alexandria, VA 22314-2530; Title Tel # (703) 549-8606 Title Fax # (703) 549-1372
Personnel: Publisher-Keyes Walworth
Editorial Description: Fast, concise, accurate reports on state liquor laws and regulations. Covers privatization, advertising, taxes, bottle bills, Sunday sales laws, drunk driving laws, legal drinking ages, and other laws affecting wine, beer, and liquor distribution.
General Info: (Formerly Alcoholic Beverage Control from the State Capitals), Yr. Est. 1946, Weekly, Trim Size-8½ x 11, Sheetfed press, 4 pages, ISSN: 0734-0842, No Color
Subscriptions: Indv. $265, Can. $235, For. $255

Alcoholic Beverage Executive's Newsletter   *Business*

Publishing Co: Alcoholic Beverage Executive's Newsletter, PO Box 3188, Omaha, NE 68103-0188; Title Tel # (402) 397-5514 Title Fax # (402) 397-3843
Personnel: Publisher, Editor-Patricia Kennedy
Editorial Description: News of beer, wine & liquor industries.
General Info: Yr. Est. 1940, Weekly, 6 pages
Subscriptions: Indv. $250, Inst. $250, Can. $250, For. $275, $10/copy

BSR On Tap
See: SPORTS & SPORTING GOODS

Beer Marketer's Insights   *Business*

Publishing Co: Beer Marketer's Insights, Inc., 51 Virginia Ave., West Nyack, NY 10994-2005
Fax # (914) 258-7860; Title Tel # (914) 358-7751 Title Fax # (914) 358-7860
Personnel: Publisher, Editor-Jerry Steinman, Circ. Mgr.-Irene Steinman
Editorial Description: Developments in beer industry concerning competitive battles, wholesaler relationships, brewers shipments in various regions; and other legislative and government actions.
General Info: 23x/yr., Trim Size-9 x 12, Offset press, 4 pages, ISSN: 0300-7480, 2 Color
Subscriptions: Indv. $335, For. $360
Acquistions: Publication Bought

Beer Statistics News   *Business*

Publishing Co: Beer Marketer's Insights, Inc., 51 Virginia Ave., West Nyack, NY 10994-2005
Fax # (914) 258-7860; Title Tel # (914) 358-7751
Personnel: Publisher-Jerry Steinman, Editor-Eric Shepard, Circ. Mgr.-Irene Steinman
Editorial Description: Beer industry statistics showing major brewery shipments each month in 39 states where two-thirds of beer is sold. Also changing trends, market share on each state, and listing of each brewer's record.
General Info: Yr. Est. 1975, Semi-monthly, Trim Size-7¾ x 10, Sheetfed press, 32 pages, 2 Color, Saddle-stitched, Looseleaf
Subscriptions: Indv. $280, For. $305

Best Bottles Wineletter   *Consumer*

Publishing Co: Best Bottles Inc., PO Box 21011, Stratford, ON N5A 7V4 Canada; Title Tel # (519) 273-5517
Personnel: Publisher, Adv. Dir., Promotion Dir.-William Munnelly
General Info: Yr. Est. 1983, Bi-monthly, Trim Size-8½ x 11, Desktop press, 12 pages, 2 Color, Newsprint
Subscriptions: Indv. $35
Circulation: Total-3,500
Printing Co: Commercial Printers, 205 Griffiths Rd., Stratford, ON N5A 6S4 Canada
Tel # (519) 271-0316

Beverage Alcohol Market
Report   *Business*   CPM: $323

Publishing Co: Peregrine Communications, 160 E 48th St, New York, NY 10017-1225; Title Tel # (212) 371-5237
Personnel: Publisher, Editor-Perry Luntz, Circ. Mgr.-Carol Rinzler
Editorial Description: Newsletter for executives; Beer/Wine/Spirits Industry Internationally.
General Info: Yr. Est. 1982, Bi-weekly, Trim Size-8½ x 11, Offset press, 8 pages, ISSN: 0736-220X, 2 Color, Newsprint
Subscriptions: Indv. $195, Can. $215, For. $215
Acquistions: Publication Bought
Circulation: Total-3,000
Advertising: $970. Accepts Inserts.
Printing Co: Pushcart Printing, 123-17 18th Rd., College Pt., NY 11356 Tel # (718) 358-6658

Beverage Digest   *Business, Consumer*

Publishing Co: Beverage Digest Co, Inc., PO Box 238, Old Greenwich, CT 06870-0238; Title Tel # (203) 358-8198 Title Fax # (203) 327-9761
Personnel: Publisher, Editor-Jesse Meyers & John Sicher, Circ. Mgr.-Anna Nilson
Editorial Description: World's largest, most widely quoted perspective on the non-alcoholic beverage market.
General Info: Yr. Est. 1982, Bi-weekly, ISSN: 0738-8853
Subscriptions: Indv. $525, Can. $525, For. $595, $50/copy
Circulation: Readership-3,000

Brewers Association of America Bulletin

Publishing Co: Brewers Assn. of America, PO Box 6296, Harrisburg, PA 17112-0296; Title Tel # (717) 939-7722 Title Fax # (717) 939-7722
Personnel: Editor-John Burton
General Info: Monthly
Circulation: (100% controlled), Total-2,000

California Beverage
Hotline   *Consumer*

Publishing Co: Paul Gillette Enterprises, 3284 Barham Blvd Apt 201, Los Angeles, CA 90068-1454; Title Tel # (213) 876-7590 Title Fax # (213) 876-4090
Personnel: Publisher-Paul Gillette, Editor-Jennifer O'Rourke, Adv. Dir.-Roger Zeidman
Editorial Description: Recent news and developments in the beverage industry.
General Info: Yr. Est. 1983, Monthly
Subscriptions: Indv. $120, For. $150
Advertising: Inquire for rates. Accepts Inserts.

California Grapevine   *Consumer*

Publishing Co: California Grapevine, PO Box 22152, San Diego, CA 92192-2152; Title Tel # (619) 457-4818 Title Fax # (619) 457-3676
Personnel: Publisher, Editor-Nicholas Ponomareff
General Info: Yr. Est. 1973, Bi-monthly
Subscriptions: Indv. $24

California Wine Merchant's Gazette

Publishing Co: Evento Pubs., PO Box 77291, San Francisco, CA 94107-0291; Title Tel # (415) 285-7333
Personnel: Publisher-Anna Del Vento Everett, Editor-Ed Everett
General Info: Yr. Est. 1982, Monthly

Canada Dry Crown
Association

Publishing Co: Natl. Assn. of Canada Dry Franchise Bottlers, 1535 Southbrook Dr, South Bend, IN 46614-1549; Title Tel # (219) 287-9097 Title Fax # (219) 232-4252
Personnel: Editor-Clement Haines
Editorial Description: News of soft drink business, parent co. & member bottlers.
General Info: Yr. Est. 1957, Bi-monthly, Trim Size-8½ x 11, Sheetfed press, 4 pages, No Color, Newsprint
Circulation: (100% controlled), Total-400
Printing Co: Instant Copy of Indiana, 129 N Main St, South Bend, IN 46601-1608 Tel # (219) 234-9484

Casa Nuestra Journal

Publishing Co: Casa Nuestra Vineyards, 3473 Silverado Trl N, Saint Helena, CA 94574-9662; Title Tel # (707) 963-4684
Personnel: Editor-George Kirkham
General Info: Yr. Est. 1984
Circulation: Total-1,000

Case Club News

Publishing Co: Poplar Ridge Vineyards, 9782 Rt 414, Valois, NY 14888; Title Tel # (800) 227-0504
Editorial Description: Information on wine industry with specific information on Poplar Ridge Vineyard's best releases.
General Info: 2 pages

Category Report: Beverages
Consumer

Publishing Co: Marketing Intelligence Service, Ltd., 6473D Route 64, Naples, NY 14512; Title Tel # (716) 374-6326 Title Fax # (716) 374-5217
Personnel: Publisher-Richard Lawrence, Production Mgr.-Patricia Peck
Editorial Description: Combines domestic & foreign new product reviews. Each review typically includes detailed product & packaging descriptions, with illustrations, important manufacturing & marketing innovations, emerging trends, & other background information.
General Info: Yr. Est. 1984, Monthly, Trim Size-8½ x 11, Mimeo press, No Color, Newsprint
Subscriptions: Indv. $1,000

Coffee Matters
Consumer

Publishing Co: Starbucks Coffee Co., 2203 Airport Way South, P.O. Box 34510, Seattle, WA 98124-1510
Editorial Description: Information about coffee and coffee drinking.
General Info: Bi-monthly

Connoisseurs' Guide to California Wine
Consumer

Publishing Co: Connoisseurs' Guide to California Wine, PO Box V, Alameda, CA 94501-0265; Title Tel # (510) 865-3150 Title Fax # (510) 865-3150
Personnel: Editor-Charles Olken
General Info: Yr. Est. 1974, Monthly, 12 pages, ISSN: 0161-6668, No Color
Subscriptions: Indv. $45, Can. $45, For. $70, $5/copy

Fine Wine Folio
Business

Publishing Co: Holland & Edwards Publishing, Inc., 250 Mercer St., Apt. A-203, New York, NY 10012-1144 Tel # (212) 431-1652; Title Tel # (212) 431-1659 Title Fax # (212) 966-1203
Personnel: Publisher-Edward Holland, Editor-Christopher Holland, Editorial Asst.-Craig Hauser, Assoc. Ed.-Clare Cannon, Production Mgr.-Gina Dilillo, Art Dir.-Karen Holland
Editorial Description: Each issues is a profile on one wine-producing area the top ten producers & the previous ten years vintage assessed-also a menu with recipes from a noted restaurant to go with the wine.
General Info: Yr. Est. 1987, Monthly, Trim Size-8.5 x 11, Web press, 16 pages, ISSN: 1045-0921, 4 Color, Coated, Saddle-stitched
Subscriptions: Indv. $47, Can. $52, For. $55
Circulation: Total-100,000, Readership-240,000
Advertising: Inquire for rates.
List Rental: Rents Lists
Printing Co: Account Manager: Chang Park; Strathmore Printing, 200 Gary Lane, Geneva, IL 60134 Tel # (708) 232-9677, Fax # (708) 232-0198

Flavour of Mid-Atlantic Living
Business

Publishing Co: Wine Industry News Inc., PO Box 19502, Washington, DC 20036-0502; Title Tel # (202) 223-9744
Personnel: Publisher-Ruth Pursglove, Editor-Ruth T. Pursglove, Promotion Dir.-Vanessa Pursglove
Editorial Description: Food & beverage upscale consumer segment studies & forecasts.
General Info: Yr. Est. 1968, Quarterly
Subscriptions: Indv. $36
Circulation: Total-3,600
Advertising: Inquire for rates.

Food & Beverage Newsletter
See: SAFETY

Food & Drink Daily
See: FOOD

Food Industry Futures-A Strategy Service
See: FOOD

Food Labeling & Nutrition News
See: FOOD

Frick Winery Information Letter
Consumer

Publishing Co: Frick Winery, 23072 Walling Rd., Geyserville, CA 95441-9676; Title Tel # (415) 362-1911
Personnel: Editor-Bill Frick
Editorial Description: Wine & food subject matter.
General Info: Yr. Est. 1984, Semi-annually, Trim Size-8½ x 11, 4 pages, No Color, Newsprint
Subscriptions: Free
Circulation: Total-3,000

Gomberg-Fredrikson Report
Consumer

Publishing Co: Gomberg Fredrikson & Assocs., 703 Market St., Ste. 2101, San Francisco, CA 94103-2131; Title Tel # (415) 957-5071
Personnel: Editor-John Fredrikson
General Info: (Formerly Gomberg Report, The), Yr. Est. 1981, Monthly
Subscriptions: Indv. $350
Circulation: Total-350

Healthy Eating
See: FOOD

Hennessey's Wines & Spirits
Business, Consumer

Publishing Co: Hennessey's Wines & Spirits, 3600 16th, San Francisco, CA 94114-1566; Title Tel # (415) 864-6677 Title Fax # (415) 626-3791
Personnel: Publisher-Les Hennessy, Production Mgr.-Jim Shuck, Art Dir.-Bennett King
Editorial Description: Features an assortment of wines and spirits.
General Info: Quarterly, Trim Size-8½ x 11, 4 pages, No Color, Matte
List Rental: List Management Co.: Name-Finders Lists, Inc., 3180 18th St Fl 2, San Francisco, CA 94110-2028 Tel # (510) 533-4177, Fax # (510) 553-8677, Actives: 14,552, $85/M

Hops USA

Publishing Co: Hop Growers of America, PO Box 9218, Yakima, WA 98909-0218; Title Tel # (509) 248-7043 Title Fax # (509) 248-7044
Personnel: Editor-William Elkins, Production Mgr.-Carolyn Cullier
General Info: Yr. Est. 1956, Monthly, 4 pages, 2 Color, Newsprint
Subscriptions: Indv. $100
Circulation: Total-500
Advertising: Inquire for rates.

IBWA Newsletter
Association

Publishing Co: International Bottled Water Association, 113 N Henry St, Alexandria, VA 22314-2903; Title Tel # (703) 683-5213 Title Fax # (703) 683-4074
Personnel: Publisher-William Deal, Editor-Geary Campbell
General Info: Yr. Est. 1958, Bi-monthly, Sheetfed press, 6 pages
Circulation: (36% controlled), Total-2,500
List Rental: Rents Lists

Impact International
Consumer

Publishing Co: M. Shanken Communications, Inc., 387 Park Ave S., 8th Floor, New York, NY 10016-8810; Title Tel # (212) 684-4224 Title Fax # (212) 684-5424
Personnel: Publisher, Editor-Marvin Shanken, Circ. Mgr.-Laura Richter, Adv. Dir.-Jeff Diskin, Art Dir.-Debra Trisler
General Info: Yr. Est. 1986, Bi-weekly, Trim Size-8½ x 11, Sheetfed press, 24 pages, ISSN: 0268-8212, 4 Color, Newsprint
Subscriptions: Indv. $345, Can. $345, For. $345, $15/copy
Advertising: $4,900. Accepts Inserts.

Impact Newsletter (Wine, Spirits & Beer)
Consumer

Publishing Co: M. Shanken Communications, Inc., 387 Park Ave S., 8th Floor, New York, NY 10016-8810; Title Tel # (212) 684-4224 Title Fax # (212) 684-5424
Personnel: Publisher, Editor-Marvin Shanken, Circ. Mgr.-Laura Richter, Adv. Dir.-Jeff Diskin, Art Dir.-Debra Trisler
Editorial Description: Marketing & economic data for the U.S. alcoholic beverage executive.
General Info: Yr. Est. 1970, Bi-weekly, Trim Size-8½ x 11, Sheetfed press, ISSN: 0363-9444, Ind/Abs/Online: Impact, 4 Color, Newsprint, Saddle-stitched
Subscriptions: Indv. $300, Can. $315, For. $330, $13/copy
Advertising: $4,000.

Import Report

Publishing Co: Natl. Assn. of Beverage Importers, Inc., 1025 Vermont Ave NW Ste 1205, Washington, DC 20005-3516; Title Tel # (202) 638-1617

Import Statistics

Publishing Co: Natl. Assn. of Beverage Importers, Inc., 1025 Vermont Ave NW Ste 1205, Washington, DC 20005-3516; Title Tel # (202) 638-1617
General Info: Monthly

Industry World

Publishing Co: Women's Association of Alcohol Beverage Industries, 1250 Eye Street NW, Suite 900, Washington, DC 20005; Title Tel # (202) 628-3544
Personnel: Editor-Duncan Cameron
General Info: (Formerly Industry Woman), Yr. Est. 1940, Quarterly, Trim Size-8½ x 11, 8 pages, 2 Color
Circulation: Total-2,600
Advertising: Inquire for rates.

Inside Spirit   *Association*

Publishing Co: Virginia Dept. of Alcoholic Beverage Control, 2901 Hermitage Rd, Richmond, VA 23220-1010; Title Tel # (804) 367-0651 Title Fax # (804) 367-2009
Personnel: Editor-William Gee
Editorial Description: Employee publication which chronicles policies, legislation, programs, personnel and other activities relating to the Virginia Department of Alcoholic Beverage Control.
General Info: (Formerly ABC News), Yr. Est. 1973, Quarterly, Trim Size-8½ x 11, Sheetfed press, 8 pages, No Color
Circulation: Total-2,500

Jesse Meyers' Beverage
Digest   *Business*

Publishing Co: Beverage Digest, PO Box 238, Old Greenwich, CT 06870-0238; Title Tel # (203) 358-8198 Title Fax # (203) 327-9761
Personnel: Publisher, Editor-Jesse Meyers, Assoc. Ed.-Thomas Fine, Circ. Dir.-Lola Meyers, Circ. Dir.-Lynn Richardson
Editorial Description: Soft drink market, especially marketing, technology, sales, legal & regulatory developments, plant ownership.
General Info: Yr. Est. 1982, Bi-monthly, ISSN: 0738-8853
Subscriptions: Indv. $470, Inst. $435, Can. $435, For. $530, $50/copy
Printing Co: Holly Press, 823 Main Street, Stamford, CT 06902 Tel # (203) 324-5779

Kamora Culinary Trends
See: FOOD

Kane's Beverage Week   *Business*

Publishing Co: Whitaker Newsletters, 313 South Ave., Box 340, Fanwood, NJ 07023-1350; Title Tel # (908) 889-6336 Title Fax # (908) 889-6339
Personnel: Publisher, Editor-Joel Whitaker, Circ. Mgr.-Sandra Smith
Editorial Description: Marketing, legislative news for beverage alcohol industry.
General Info: (Formerly Kane Report), Yr. Est. 1938, Weekly, Trim Size-8½ x 11, Desktop press, 8 pages, ISSN: 0882-2573, No Color
Subscriptions: Indv. $399, Can. $449, For. $449, $15/copy
Acquistions: Publication Bought, Publication Sold
List Rental: List Management Co.: The Lake Group, 411 Theodore Freund Ave., Rye, NY 10580-1497 Tel # (914) 925-2400, Fax # (914) 925-2499, Actives: 29,196, $70/M

Legislative & Regulatory
Issues Alert

Publishing Co: Natl. Beer Wholesalers Assn., 1100 S Washington St, Falls Church, VA 22046-4023; Title Tel # (703) 578-4300
Editorial Description: Examines current regulatory and legislative issues having an impact on the brewing and beer wholesale industries.

Leisure Beverage Insider   *Business*

Publishing Co: Whitaker Newsletters, 313 South Ave., Box 340, Fanwood, NJ 07023-1350; Title Tel # (908) 889-6336 Title Fax # (908) 889-6339
Personnel: Publisher-Joel Whitaker, Editor-Ann Bittner, Circ. Dir.-Sandra Smith
Editorial Description: For owners & managers of soft drink & juice bottling operations.
General Info: (Formerly Soft Drink Newsletter), Yr. Est. 1966, Bi-weekly, Trim Size-8½ x 11, Desktop press, 6 pages, ISSN: 1040-3736
Subscriptions: Indv. $299, Inst. $299, Can. $349, For. $349, $15/copy
Acquistions: Publication Bought, Publication Sold
List Rental: List Management Co.: The Lake Group, 411 Theodore Freund Ave., Rye, NY 10580-1497 Tel # (914) 925-2400, Fax # (914) 925-2499, Actives: 29,196, $70/M

Liquid Assets   *Consumer*

Publishing Co: Liquid Assets, 169 Nassau St, Princeton, NJ 08542-7007; Title Tel # (609) 683-0565
General Info: 2x/yr.
Subscriptions: Indv. $30

Liquor Control Law Reports   *Business*

Publishing Co: CCH, Inc., 2700 Lake Cook Rd., Riverwoods, IL 60015 Parent Co.-Kluwer Law & Taxation Publishers, Cambridge; Title Tel # (847) 267-7000 Title Fax # (800) 224-8299
Editorial Description: Federal & state regulation & taxation of alcoholic beverages, with current developments, regulations, topical digests.
General Info: Yr. Est. 1934, Semi-monthly, Trim Size-6 x 9, Web press, No Color, Looseleaf
Subscriptions: Indv. $3,042

Master Brewers Association
of America
Communications

Publishing Co: Master Brewers Assn of America, 2421 N. Mayfair Rd., #310, Wauwatosa, WI 53226-1407; Title Tel # (608) 231-3446
General Info: Yr. Est. 1975, Bi-monthly
Subscriptions: Indv. $60

Matter World Times-
'International Beer
Newsletter, The'   *Business, Association*   CPM: $90

Publishing Co: Matter World Times, P.O. Box 275, White Plains, NY 10601; Title Tel # (914) 633-2973 Title Fax # (914) 681-2924
Editorial Description: Information about beer and brewing for connoisseurs.
General Info: Yr. Est. 1992, Quarterly, Trim Size-8½ x 11½, Desktop press, 8 pages, No Color
Subscriptions: Free
Circulation: Total-10,000, Readership-12,000
Advertising: $900. Accepts Inserts.

Miller Management Briefing   *Business*

Publishing Co: Miller Brewing Co., 3939 W Highland Blvd, Milwaukee, WI 53208-2866
Personnel: Editor-Elizabeth Conlisk
General Info: Monthly, Trim Size-8½ x 11, Offset press, 4 pages, 2 Color
Circulation: Total-500

Mixin'

Publishing Co: American Bartenders' Assn., PO Box D, Plant City, FL 33564-9004; Title Tel # (941) 922-3316
Personnel: Publisher, Editor-Douglas Ferguson
Editorial Description: Newsletter for industry. Bookstore division offers catalog featuring over 40 training guides & references for restaurant/bar management.
General Info: Yr. Est. 1983, Monthly, Web press, 8 pages, 2 Color, Matte
Subscriptions: Indv. $25, $1/copy
Acquistions: Publication Bought
Circulation: Total-4,000

Monthly Brewing Industry
Commentary Including
State Beer Statistics   *Business*

Publishing Co: C.J. Lawrence/Deutsche Bank Securities, 1290 Ave. of the Americas, New York, NY 10104-0051; Title Tel # (212) 468-5000
Personnel: Editor-A. J. Brenner
Editorial Description: Analysis of industry developments & forecasts; company outlooks; statistics on beer shipments for 26 states.
General Info: Yr. Est. 1975, Monthly, Offset press, 18 pages
Subscriptions: Indv. $100, $10/copy

NSDA Dateline   *Association*

Publishing Co: Natl. Soft Drink Assn., 1101 16th St NW, Washington, DC 20036-4877; Title Tel # (202) 463-6773
Editorial Description: Member newsletter.
General Info: (Formerly NSDA Bulletin), Bi-weekly, 4 pages
Circulation: Total-3,700

National Association of
Alcoholic Beverage
Importers Bulletin

Publishing Co: Natl. Assn. of Alcoholic Beverage Importers, 1025 Vermont Ave., N.W., Suite, Washington, DC 20005-3516; Title Tel # (202) 638-1617 Title Fax # (202) 638-3122

National Association of
Beverage Importers-
Member Letter

Publishing Co: Natl. Assn. of Beverage Importers, Inc., 1025 Vermont Ave NW Ste 1205, Washington, DC 20005-3516; Title Tel # (202) 638-1617
Personnel: Editor-Bob Maxwell
Editorial Description: Newsletter covering legislative & regulatory changes in imported beverage industry.

National Coffee Association
of U.S.A., Inc.,
Newsletter   *Business, Association*

Publishing Co: National Coffee Association of U.S.A., Inc., 110 Wall St Fl 13, New York, NY 10005-3801; Title Tel # (212) 344-5596
Personnel: Editor-D.M. Brennan
Editorial Description: Weekly newsletter covering topics of interest to coffee industry.
General Info: Weekly, Web press, 4 pages, No Color
Subscriptions: Indv. $25
Circulation: (100% controlled), Total-600

National Liquor Stores
Association News &
Views

Publishing Co: National Liquor Stores Assn., 5101 River Rd Apt 108, Bethesda, MD 20816-1560; Title Tel # (301) 656-1494
Editorial Description: Covers Association news and opinions as well as news of the alcoholic beverage industry in general.
General Info: Quarterly

New York Wine Cellar

Publishing Co: Tanzer Business Communications, Inc., Box 392, Prince Station, New York, NY 10012; Title Tel # (212) 777-1006
Personnel: Editor-Stephen Tanzer
General Info: Bi-monthly
Subscriptions: Indv. $35
Circulation: Total-500

Parducci Wine Press

Publishing Co: Parducci Wine Cellars, 501 Parducci Rd, Ukiah, CA 95482-3015; Title Tel # (707) 462-3828
Personnel: Editor-Tom Parducci
General Info: 4 pages

Peerless Coffee Company
Coffee Break *Consumer*

Publishing Co: Peerless Coffee Company, 260 Oak St, Oakland, CA 94607-4512;
Title Tel # (510) 893-3201 Title Fax # (510) 763-5026
Editorial Description: Lists coffees and teas available as well as company information and restaurant reviews.
General Info: Semi-annually

Premium Grower

Publishing Co: Napa Valley Grape Growers Assn., 4075 Solano Ave, Napa, CA 94558-2231;
Title Tel # (707) 944-8311
Personnel: Editor-Teresa Geremia-Chart
General Info: (Formerly Grower Forecast), Yr. Est. 1975, Quarterly
Circulation: Total-300

Sommelier Society of
America-Newsletter *Business, Consumer*

Publishing Co: Sommelier Society of America, 205 E. 25th St., New York, NY 10159;
Title Tel # (212) 679-4190
General Info: Bi-monthly
Subscriptions: Free To Qualified Recipient
Circulation: Total-500

Take a Bunnbreak *Consumer*

Publishing Co: Bunn Coffee Service, 51 Alpha Plaza, Hicksville, NY 11801 Tel # (516) 733-7600
Fax # (516) 433-7870
Editorial Description: Information and tips from distributor of Starbucks coffee.
General Info: Quarterly, Trim Size-8$\frac{1}{2}$ x 11, 2 pages, 2 Color, Coated

Tea Talk, A Newsletter on
the Pleasures of Tea *Consumer* CPM: $250

Publishing Co: R & R Publications, PO Box 860, Sausalito, CA 94966-0860;
Title Tel # (415) 331-1557 Title Fax # (415) 331-1557
Personnel: Publisher-Lucy Roman, Editor-Diana Rosen
Editorial Description: A newsletter on the pleasures of tea as a beverage afternoon tea as a way to entertain and the appreciation of tea ceremonies from around the world.
General Info: Yr. Est. 1989, Quarterly, Trim Size-7$\frac{1}{2}$ x 10, Offset press, 24 pages, 2 Color, Matte, Saddle-stitched
Subscriptions: Indv. $18, Can. $8, For. $8, $5/copy
Circulation: Total-3,000
Advertising: $750. Accepts Inserts.
List Rental: Rents Lists

Tea Times *Consumer*

Publishing Co: Tea Times, PO Box 841, Langley, WA 98260-0841
Personnel: Publisher, Editor-Mary Mac
Editorial Description: Discusses making, drinking, and serving tea as well as history of tea, ceremonies, and other related topics.
General Info: Bi-monthly
Subscriptions: Indv. $18, Can. $21

Technical Newsletter *Association*

Publishing Co: International Bottled Water Association, 113 N Henry St, Alexandria, VA 22314-2903;
Title Tel # (703) 683-5213 Title Fax # (703) 683-4074
Personnel: Publisher-Sylvia E. Swanson, Editor-Tyrone Wilson
Editorial Description: Technical information on the bottled water industry.
General Info: Yr. Est. 1958, Quarterly, Sheetfed press, 4 pages
Circulation: (63% controlled), Total-1,500

Uncorked *Consumer*

Publishing Co: California Wine Club, 2175 Goodyear Ave Ste 114, Ventura, CA 93003-7761
Tel # (805) 650-4330
Personnel: VP Sales & Mktg.-Bruce Boring
General Info: Monthly

Upfront *Business, Association*

Publishing Co: Wine & Spirits Wholesalers of America, Inc., 1023 15th St NW Ste 4, Washington, DC 20005-2602; Title Tel # (202) 371-9792
Personnel: Editor-David Dickerson
Editorial Description: Industry, business & assn. news to WSWA members.
General Info: (Formerly Directions-Wine), Yr. Est. 1991, Monthly, 8 pages
Circulation: Total-1,100

Vinotizie *Business, Consumer*

Publishing Co: Italian Trade Commission-Wine Center, 499 Park Avenue, New York, NY 10022;
Title Tel # (212) 980-1500 Title Fax # (212) 758-1050
Personnel: Editor-Elizabeth Kane
Editorial Description: Newsletter on Italian wine industry.
General Info: Quarterly, Trim Size-11 x 17, 8 pages, 4 Color, Coated, Saddle-stitched
Printing Co: Intelligencer Printing Co., 330 Eden Rd #1768, Lancaster, PA 17601-4218
Tel # (717) 291-3100, Fax # (717) 569-2643

WSSA Grapevine

Publishing Co: Wine & Spirits Shippers Assn., 1180 Sunrise Valley Dr., Reston, VA 22091;
Title Tel # (703) 860-2300 Title Fax # (703) 860-2422
Editorial Description: Covers Association news as well as industry developments.
General Info: Bi-monthly

Warner

Publishing Co: Warner Vineyards, PO Box 269, Paw Paw, MI 49079-0269;
Title Tel # (616) 657-3165
Personnel: Editor-Jim Warner

Washington Beverage
Insight *Business*

Publishing Co: George Wells, Publisher, 2942 S Columbus St Apt A2, Arlington, VA 22206-1444;
Title Tel # (703) 671-8140
Personnel: Publisher, Editor-George Wells
Editorial Description: Reports & interprets federal & state-level actionsaffecting the mfg., distrib. & sale of soft drinks, beer, & other beverages.
General Info: Yr. Est. 1974, Weekly, 4 pages, Ind/Abs/Online: Newsnet, Predacasts, No Color
Subscriptions: Indv. $350

What's Brewing *Association*

Publishing Co: National Coffee Service Association, 4000 Williamsburg Ct, Fairfax, VA 22032-1139;
Title Tel # (703) 273-9008
Personnel: Publisher-G. Dean Wood, Editor-Maggie Lyons
Editorial Description: News by the Natl. Coffee Service Assn. for membership, about office coffee service.
General Info: Yr. Est. 1972, Monthly, Mimeo press, 6 pages, 2 Color
Circulation: (100% controlled), Total-1,000

Wine Advocate *Consumer*

Publishing Co: Wine Advocate, PO Box 311, Monkton, MD 21111-0311; Title Tel # (410) 329-6477
Title Fax # (301) 357-4504
Personnel: Publisher, Editor-Robert Parker, Jr.
General Info: Yr. Est. 1977, Bi-monthly
Subscriptions: Indv. $35

Wine Investor-Executive
Edition, The *Business*

Publishing Co: Paul Gillette Enterprises, 3284 Barham Blvd Apt 201, Los Angeles, CA 90068-1454;
Title Tel # (213) 876-7590 Title Fax # (213) 876-4090
Personnel: Editor-Paul Gillette, Circ. Mgr.-Shelly Hoyle, Publisher, Adv. Dir.-Ursula Ziegler
Editorial Description: In depth analysis of the wine industry.
General Info: Yr. Est. 1977, Bi-weekly, 10 pages, 2% ads
Subscriptions: Indv. $300, $15/copy
Advertising: Inquire for rates.

Wine Investor/Buyer's
Guide *Consumer*

Publishing Co: Paul Gillette Enterprises, 3284 Barham Blvd Apt 201, Los Angeles, CA 90068-1454;
Title Tel # (213) 876-7590 Title Fax # (213) 876-4090
Personnel: Publisher-Paul Gillette, Editor-J.D. Kronman, Adv. Dir.-Roger Zeidman
Editorial Description: Wine consumer advice and wine tasting notes.
General Info: (Formerly Notes for the FrugalEnophile), Yr. Est. 1970, Monthly, Offset press, 12 pages, Ind/Abs/Online: CompuServe, No Color, Newsprint
Subscriptions: Indv. $75, For. $115, $5/copy
Advertising: Inquire for rates. Accepts Inserts.

Wine Letter

Publishing Co: Raymond Vineyards, 849 Zinfandel Ln, Saint Helena, CA 94574-1645;
Title Tel # (707) 963-3141
Personnel: Editor-Don Defesi
General Info: Semi-annually

Wine Newsletter *Consumer*

Publishing Co: Wine Newsletter, PO Box 22152, San Diego, CA 92192-2152;
Title Tel # (619) 457-4818
Personnel: Publisher, Editor, Circ. Mgr., Adv. Dir.-Nick Ponomareff
Editorial Description: Wine reviews (both domestic and imported).
General Info: (Formerly San Diego Grapevine), Yr. Est. 1973, Bi-monthly, Trim Size-8$\frac{1}{2}$ x 11, Web press, 20 pages, ISSN: 0273-8961, No Color
Subscriptions: $3/copy

Wine Odyssey

Publishing Co: Wine Odyssey, PO Box 5157, Hoboken, NJ 07030-1502; Title Tel # (201) 507-8989
Personnel: Publisher, Editor-John Foy
General Info: Yr. Est. 1988, 8x/yr., 4 pages
Subscriptions: Indv. $79

Wine Review for the Trade

Publishing Co: Wine Industry News Inc., PO Box 19502, Washington, DC 20036-0502;
Title Tel # (202) 223-9744
Personnel: Editor-David Pursglove, Promotion Dir.-Vanessa Pursglove
Editorial Description: Beverage industry studies & computer based forecasts.
General Info: Yr. Est. 1968, Monthly
Subscriptions: Indv. $62
Circulation: Total-3,100

Women on Wine National News   *Consumer*

Publishing Co: Women on Wine, 6110 Sunset Ranch Dr, Riverside, CA 92506-4621;
Title Tel # (909) 784-3096
Personnel: Publisher, Editor-Barbara Mader Ivey, Promotion Dir.-Carolyn Kincaid
Editorial Description: National Wine Industry news for wine enthusiasts.
General Info: Yr. Est. 1981, Quarterly, Sheetfed press, 4 pages
Acquistions: Publication Bought
Advertising: Inquire for rates. Accepts Inserts.

Working Wine Guide, The   *Consumer*

Publishing Co: Working Wine Guide, The, 414 South Craig Street, Suite #263, Pittsburgh, PA 15213
Fax # (412) 621-4150
Personnel: Publisher-David R. DeSimone
Editorial Description: Covers best buys and cellar selections in wines from around the world and Pennsylvania. Emphasis is placed on recommending good values and matching foods. No numerical ratings are used.
General Info: Yr. Est. 1994, Bi-monthly, Trim Size-4$\frac{1}{4}$ x 9, Web press, 28 pages, 2 Color, Coated, Saddle-stitched
Subscriptions: Indv. $30, Inst. $40, Can. $40, For. $50
Circulation: (28% controlled), Total-350, Subscriptions-250
Advertising: Inquire for rates.

World Beer Review   *Consumer*

Publishing Co: WBR Pubs., PO Box 71, Clemson, SC 29633-0071; Title Tel # (803) 654-3360
Personnel: Publisher, Editor-Steve Johnson, Circ. Mgr.-Lis Trayhum, Adv. Dir.-Louis Bregger
Editorial Description: Reviews & rates new beers. Articles on beer appreciation, microbreweries, brew pubs, breweriana collecting, book reviews, pubs, bars. Features industry news and developments.
General Info: Yr. Est. 1987, Bi-monthly, Sheetfed press, 20 pages, Color-cover
Subscriptions: Indv. $18, Can. $23, For. $32, $3/copy
Circulation: Total-975
List Rental: Rents Lists
Printing Co: Campus Copyshop, Rubin Sq., Clemson, SC 29631 Tel # (803) 654-3863

Written Wort

Publishing Co: New York City Homebrewers Guild, 299 Prospect Pl # 3f, Brooklyn, NY 11238-3909
Personnel: Publisher-Keith Cunningham, Editor-Matthew Manning
Editorial Description: The Wort is written to help home brewers perfect their art.
General Info: Bi-monthly, 8 pages

Zip City

Publishing Co: Zip City Brewing Co., 3 West 18th Street, New York, NY 10011;
Title Tel # (212) 366-6333
Editorial Description: News and events on Zip City's special brew beers and great tasting menus.
General Info: Bi-monthly, Trim Size-8$\frac{1}{2}$ x 11, 4 pages, 2 Color, Matte
Subscriptions: Free

BIBLIOGRAPHY

Current Library Acquisitions   *Consumer*

Publishing Co: West Virginia Institute of Technology, Publications, Montgomery, WV 25136;
Title Tel # (304) 442-3141
Personnel: Editor-Victor C. Young
Editorial Description: Complete listing of all current acquisitions.
General Info: Yr. Est. 1966, Quarterly, Trim Size-8$\frac{1}{2}$ x 11, Offset press, 20 pages, No Color
Subscriptions: Free
Circulation: Total-300

Deadly Serious
See: MYSTERY & HORROR

Eudora Welty Newsletter
See: LITERATURE & LINGUISTICS

Infomat   *Business, Association*

Publishing Co: Statistics Canada, Holland Ave/RH Coats, Holland Ave/Tunney's Pasture, Ottawa, ON K1A O26 Canada Tel # (613) 951-8116 Fax # (613) 951-0581; Title Tel # (613) 951-1581
Title Fax # (613) 951-1584
Editorial Description: Digest of major statistics Canada reports, reference papers & other releases. Catalog #11-002.
General Info: (Formerly DBS Weekly Bulletin), Yr. Est. 1932, Weekly, 4 pages, ISSN: 0380-0547
Subscriptions: Indv. $3, Can. $3, For. $4, $3/copy

Info   *Business*

Publishing Co: Tulsa City- County Library System, 400 Civic Ctr, Tulsa, OK 74103-3830;
Title Tel # (918) 596-7908 Title Fax # (918) 596-7895
Personnel: Editor-Karen Curtis
Editorial Description: Highlights library materials and services of current interest to Tulsans.
General Info: Yr. Est. 1965, Bi-monthly, Offset press, 6 pages, No Color
Subscriptions: Free
Acquistions: Publication Bought
Circulation: Total-1,200

Information Service on Latin America   *Business, Consumer*

Publishing Co: Sponsor-Information Svc. on Latin America, Third World Resources, DataCenter, 464 19th St., Oakland, CA 94612-2297 Tel # (510) 835-4692; Title Tel # (510) 835-0678
Title Fax # (510) 835-3017
Personnel: Publisher-Elizabeth Patelke, Editor-E. Patelke, Circ. Mgr.-Carrie Barclay
Editorial Description: Copies of articles on Latin America from 9 English language newspapers. Comprehensive coverage of foreign relations, diplomatic & economic news, trade & commerce, & human rights.
General Info: Yr. Est. 1970, Monthly, Trim Size-8$\frac{1}{2}$ x 11, 350 pages, ISSN: 0046-8401
Subscriptions: Indv. $580
Circulation: Total-200
List Rental: Rents Lists

Information Standards Quarterly   *Business, Association*

Publishing Co: National Information Standards Organization (NISO), 4733 Bethesda Ave, Suite 300, Bethesda, MD 20814 Tel # (301) 654-2512 Fax # (301) 654-1721
Personnel: Editor-Pat Ensor
Editorial Description: News about voluntary technical standards for libraries, publishing, information sciences.
General Info: (Formerly Voice of Z39), Yr. Est. 1989, Quarterly, Trim Size-8$\frac{1}{2}$ x 11, Desktop press, 24 pages, ISSN: 1041-0031, Color, Matte, Saddle-stitched
Subscriptions: Indv. $70, Can. $100, For. $100, $18/copy
Circulation: Total-1,200
Printing Co: Odyssey Press, 113 Crosby Rd., Forum Ct., #15, Dover, NH 03820

AIDS Literature & Law Review
See: LAW

Aquaphyte
See: SCIENCE

BOMI Newsletter: Annual Conference Edition
See: REGIONAL INTEREST

Bibliography of Technical Papers Presented At OTI Meetings   *Association*

Publishing Co: Cooling Tower Institute, 530 Wells Fargo Dr Ste 107, Houston, TX 77090-4026;
Title Tel # (713) 583-4087 Title Fax # (713) 537-1721
Editorial Description: List of technical papers presented at CTI meetings since 1950.
General Info: Yr. Est. 1970, Annually, Trim Size-8$\frac{1}{2}$ x 11, Offset press, 30 pages, Newsprint, Saddle-stitched
Circulation: Total-7,000, Readership-7,000

Bioethics Literature Review
See: MEDICINE

Books About Birds
See: BOOKS & BOOK TRADE

Canadian Bookbinders & Book Artists Guild Newsletter
See: BOOKS & BOOK TRADE

James Fenimore Cooper Society Newsletter
See: LITERATURE & LINGUISTICS

Lead Belly Letter
See: MUSIC & MUSIC TRADES

Legal Information Alert: What's New in Legal Publications
See: LAW

Library Bulletin

Publishing Co: Sponsor-Boreal Institute for Northern Studies, Boreal Institute for Northern Studies, CW 401 Bio. Sci. Bldg., Univ. of Alberta, Edmonton, AB T6G 2E9 Canada;
Title Tel # (403) 432-4409
Personnel: Editor-R. Minion
Editorial Description: Lists pubs. received by library during proceeding month; Northern orientation multi-disciplinary.
General Info: (Formerly Library Accessions List), Yr. Est. 1980, Monthly, Trim Size-8$\frac{1}{2}$ x 11, 30 pages, ISSN: 0225-4484, No Color
Subscriptions: Indv. $130
Circulation: Total-175

Linington Lineup
See: LITERARY REVIEWS

Nestor
See: LITERATURE & LINGUISTICS

New York State Library
Bibliography Bulletin

Publishing Co: New York State Library, Gift & Exchange Section, Albany, NY 12225
General Info: Yr. Est. 1895

Nook News Review of
Writers' Publications — *Business, Consumer*

Publishing Co: Writer's Nook Press, 38114 3rd St Ste 181, Willoughby, OH 44094-6140
Fax # (216) 354-6403; Title Tel # (216) 762-9128
Personnel: Editor-Eugene Ortiz
General Info: Yr. Est. 1991, Trim Size-5½ x 8½, 12 pages, Matte, Saddle-stitched
Subscriptions: Indv. $18, For. $36, $5/copy

Problem Solving
Information for State &
Local Governments — *Business*

Publishing Co: National Technical Information Service U.S., 5285 Port Royal Rd., Springfield, VA 22161-0001 Fax # (703) 487-4630; Title Tel # (703) 487-4630
Editorial Description: Bibliographic announcements produced weekly from NTIS scientific/technical database.
General Info: Weekly, Trim Size-8½ x 11, Offset press, ISSN: 0364-6459, No Color
Subscriptions: Indv. $105, Can. $105, For. $145

Proceedings in Print

Publishing Co: Proceedings in Print, Inc., PO Box 369, Halifax, MA 02338-0369; Title Tel # (617) 646-0686
Personnel: Editor-Barbara A. Spence
Editorial Description: Lists and indexes of proceedings of conferences, symposia, etc. in all subject areas, and in all languages.
General Info: Yr. Est. 1964, Bi-monthly, Trim Size-8½ x 11, 125 pages, ISSN: 0032-9568
Subscriptions: Indv. $610, $100/copy

Recycling Related Newsletters, Publications, Etc; A Reference
See: ENVIRONMENT & ECOLOGY

Recycling Update
See: ENVIRONMENT & ECOLOGY

SHARP News
See: BOOKS & BOOK TRADE

Surveillant: Acquisitions for Security & Intelligence Professionals
See: SECURITY & SURVEILLANCE

U.S. Bureau of Census,
Census and You — *Business, Consumer*

Publishing Co: U.S. Bureau of the Census - Dept. of Commerce, Data User Services Division, Customer Services, Washington, DC 20233-1900 Tel # (301) 457-4100 Fax # (301) 457-4714; Title Fax # (301) 763-4795
Editorial Description: Articles on Census Bureau programs and products, including statistical reports, computer and microcomputer files, maps, etc.; also covers local data sources and programs.
General Info: Yr. Est. 1966, Monthly, Trim Size-8½ x 11, 16 pages
Subscriptions: Indv. $21, $2/copy

Washington State
Publications — *Association*

Publishing Co: Washington State Library, Aj-11, Olympia, WA 98504-0001; Title Tel # (206) 753-4027
Personnel: Editor-Ann Bregent
Editorial Description: Monthly listing of Washington state publications for free distribution to libraries. Annual cumulations.
General Info: Yr. Est. 1965, Monthly, Trim Size-9½ x 11, Offset press, 4 pages, No Color
Circulation: (100% controlled), Total-946

BIOCHEMISTRY

AgriBioScan
See: AGRICULTURAL SUPPLIES

BioPeople — *Business*

Publishing Co: BioVenture Publishing, 32 W. 25th Ave., Ste. 203, San Mateo, CA 94403-2236
Tel # (415) 574-7128 Fax # (415) 574-8319
Personnel: Editor in Chief-Cynthia Robbins-Roth
Editorial Description: Contains articles about individuals in the biotechnology field.
General Info: Yr. Est. 1993, Quarterly
Subscriptions: Indv. $28

BioVenture Stock Report
See: INVESTMENT

BioVenture View — *Business*

Publishing Co: BioVenture Publishing, 32 W. 25th Ave., Ste. 203, San Mateo, CA 94403-2236
Tel # (415) 574-7128 Fax # (415) 574-8319
Personnel: Editor in Chief-Cynthia Robbins-Roth
Editorial Description: Provides information on biotechnology companies and products.
General Info: Yr. Est. 1986, Monthly
Subscriptions: Indv. $550

Biomedical Materials — *Business*

Publishing Co: Elsevier Science Inc., 655 Avenue of the Americas, New York, NY 10010-5107
Tel # (212) 633-3916 Fax # (212) 633-3913 Parent Co.-Reed Elsevier, New York
Personnel: Publisher-Guy Kitteringtter, Editor-Amenda Weawes
General Info: (Formerly Biomedical Polymers), Yr. Est. 1984, Monthly, Desktop press, ISSN: 0955-7717, 2 Color, Newsprint, Other
Subscriptions: Indv. $474
List Rental: Rents Lists

Biomedical Technology Information Service
See: MEDICINE

Biotechnology News
See: SCIENCE

Canadian Society for Immunology, Bulletin
See: MEDICINE

Cancer & Genetics Report
See: MEDICINE

Cell & Tissue Culture:
Laboratory Procedures — *Business, Scholarly* — CPM: $291

Publishing Co: John Wiley & Sons, Inc., 605 Third Avenue, New York, NY 10158-0012
Tel # (212) 850-6000 Fax # (212) 850-6088
Personnel: Editor in Chief-J.B. Griffiths, Editor-Michael Dixon, Production Ed.-Cliff Morgan, Circ. Mgr.-Margaret Radbourne, Mktg. Mgr.-Lesley Valentine
Editorial Description: Provides a comprehensive collection of cell and tissue culture techniques and procedures to assist scientists with the labour intensive and expensive in vitro techniques. Subscription includes four updates annually.
General Info: 5x/yr., Trim Size-8½ x 11, Sheetfed press, 4 Color, Looseleaf
Subscriptions: Indv. $595, For. $595
Circulation: Total-5,000, Readership-35,000
Advertising: $1,455.
List Rental: List Management Co.: American List Counsel, 88 Orchard Cir # Cn-5219, Princeton, NJ 08540-3026 Tel # (908) 874-4300, Fax # (908) 874-4433

Clinical Investigator News
See: DRUGS & PHARMACEUTICALS

Clinical Trials Monitor
See: DRUGS & PHARMACEUTICALS

D-J-M Enzyme Report — *Consumer*

Publishing Co: Bio Engineering News, 109 Minna St # 304, San Francisco, CA 94105-3728; Title Tel # (206) 675-1370 Title Fax # (360) 679-3084
Personnel: Publisher-Deborah Mysiewicz, Editor-Thomas Mysiewicz
Editorial Description: Scientific & business developments in the enzyme industry, Patent review. Subscription includes free co. directory & back issues on microficho.
General Info: Yr. Est. 1982, Monthly, Offset press, 8 pages, ISSN: 0731-4027
Subscriptions: Indv. $225, Can. $195, For. $207, $20/copy

Diagnostics Intelligence
See: DRUGS & PHARMACEUTICALS

DuPont Biotech Update

Publishing Co: E.I. du Pont de Nemours, 10007 Market Street, Wilmington, DE 19898-0001
Tel # (302) 774-1000; Title Tel # (302) 992-4785 Title Fax # (302) 992-4442
Personnel: Editor-Jeffrey Neumann, Circ. Mgr.-Dan Dees, Production Mgr.-Algis Rajeckas, Art Dir.-Jill Deardorff
Editorial Description: Update on new research products & applications in biotechnology research.
General Info: Yr. Est. 1986, Bi-monthly, Sheetfed press, 20 pages, 2 Color, Recycled, Saddle-stitched
Circulation: Total-30,000
Printing Co: Varies, 3600 W Market St, York, PA 17404-5894 Tel # (717) 792-3551

Emerging Pharmaceuticals
See: DRUGS & PHARMACEUTICALS

FASEB Newsletter
See: BIOLOGY

Genetic Technology News
See: GENETICS

HLB Newsletter
See: MEDICINE

Industrial Bioprocessing   *Business*

Publishing Co: Technical Insights, Inc., PO Box 1304, Fort Lee, NJ 07024-9967;
Title Tel # (201) 568-4744 Title Fax # (201) 568-8247
Personnel: Publisher/President/Advisor-Kenneth A. Kovaly, Editorial Dir.-Peter R. Savage, Circ. Mgr.-Barbara Chaffee, Mktg. Dir.-Lyn Schmiat
Editorial Description: Focuses on industrial processes involving biological routes to produce chemicals/energy; the conversion of biomaterials via fermentation, enzymatic conversion, biodegradation; advances in bioreactor design; product separation; process monitoring; bioremediation, etc. Special feature: IB Market forecasts-projections of industry segments, patents.
General Info: (Formerly Bioprocessing Technology), Yr. Est. 1979, Monthly, Trim Size-8½ x 11, Sheetfed press, 10 pages, ISSN: 1056-7194, 2 Color, Matte, Other
Subscriptions: Indv. $595, For. $655
List Rental: Actives: $180/M
Printing Co: Allied Lettercraft, 307 W. 36th St., New York, NY 10018 Tel # (212) 279-4800

Japan Medical Review
See: MEDICINE

Life Sciences & Biotechnology Update
See: BIOLOGY

Primary Probe
See: MEDICINE

Spectrum   *Business, Scholarly*

Publishing Co: Life Technologies, Inc., 8717 Grovemont Circle, P.O. Box 6009, Gaithersburg, MD 20884-9980 Tel # (301) 840-8000 Fax # (800) 331-2286
Editorial Description: Information on products for research in biochemistry.
General Info: Monthly, Trim Size-8½ x 11, 16 pages, Color, Matte, Saddle-stitched

BIOLOGY

AgriBioScan
See: AGRICULTURAL SUPPLIES

American Paleontologist
See: GEOLOGY

American Type Culture Collection-Quarterly Newsletter

Publishing Co: American Type Culture Collection, 12301 Parklawn Dr, Rockville, MD 20852-1749; Title Tel # (301) 881-2600 Title Fax # (301) 231-5826
Personnel: Editor-Harold Hatt
General Info: Yr. Est. 1981, Quarterly, Trim Size-8½ x 11, Web press, 8 pages, ISSN: 0894-9026, 2 Color, Coated, Perfect bound
Circulation: Total-20,000
Printing Co: Balmar Printing, 16780 Oakmont Ave, Gaithersburg, MD 20877-4188
Tel # (301) 258-0700

Appledore Times
See: OCEANOGRAPHY

Applied Genetics News
See: GENETICS

Assn. of Pacific Systematists Newsletter   *Association*

Publishing Co: Assn. of Pacific Systematists, PO Box 19000a, Honolulu, HI 96817-0916; Title Tel # (818) 847-3511
Personnel: Publisher, Editor-S.H. Sohmer
Editorial Description: Designed to aid communication between & among Pacific Systematists; all those engaged in the identification, classification & diversity of living organisms in the Pacific area.
General Info: Yr. Est. 1984, Annually, Desktop press, 8 pages, No Color, Newsprint
Subscriptions: Indv. $5
Circulation: Total-250
Advertising: Accepts Inserts.
Printing Co: R&W Printing, 1334 Young St., Honolulu, HI 96814 Tel # (808) 526-0361

Association of Systematics Collections Newsletter   *Association*   **CPM: $150**

Publishing Co: Assn. of Systematics Collections, 730 11th St. NW 2nd Fl., Washington, DC 20001-4521; Title Tel # (202) 347-2850 Title Fax # (202) 347-0072
Personnel: Publisher-K.E. Hoagland, Editor-Mike Schauff, Circ. Mgr.-Elizabeth Hathway
Editorial Description: Items of interest to persons working with biological collections.
General Info: Yr. Est. 1972, Bi-monthly, Trim Size-8½ x 11, Sheetfed press, 12 pages, ISSN: 0147-7889, No Color, Newsprint, Saddle-stitched
Subscriptions: Indv. $21, Inst. $35, For. $33, $2/copy
Circulation: (32% controlled), Total-2,000, Subscriptions-1,250, International-180
Advertising: $300.
List Rental: Rents Lists
Printing Co: Automated Graphic Systems, 4590 Graphics Drive, White Plains, MD 20695
Tel # (301) 843-1800, Fax # (301) 843-6339

Bio Engineering News   *Business*

Publishing Co: Bio Engineering News, 109 Minna St # 304, San Francisco, CA 94105-3728; Title Tel # (206) 928-3176
Personnel: Publisher-Deborah Mysiewicz, Editor-Thomas Mysiewicz, Production Mgr., Promotion Dir.-Sharon Thompson
Editorial Description: Commercial applications of biotechnology-all aspects including legal.
General Info: Yr. Est. 1980, Weekly, Trim Size-11 x 17, 4 pages, ISSN: 0275-4207
Subscriptions: Indv. $495, $30/copy
Acquistions: Publication Bought
List Rental: Actives: $85/M

Bio-Rad   *Business*

Publishing Co: Bio-Rad Laboratories, 1200 Alfred Nobel Dr., Hercules, CA 94547; Title Tel # (510) 741-1000

BioEngineering News

Publishing Co: Bio Engineering News, 109 Minna St # 304, San Francisco, CA 94105-3728; Title Tel # (206) 675-1370 Title Fax # (360) 679-3084
Personnel: Editor-Thomas Mysiewicz
Editorial Description: Developments in research in the fiueld of bioengineering.
General Info: Yr. Est. 1980, Weekly
Subscriptions: Indv. $495

Biological Therapies in Psychiatry Newsletter
See: PSYCHOLOGY

Biometric Bulletin   **CPM: $97**

Publishing Co: Biometric Society, 808 17th St. NW, Washington, DC 20006-3910
Tel # (202) 223-9699; Title Tel # (202) 223-9669
Personnel: Editor-G.K. Shukla
Editorial Description: Membership newsletter.
General Info: Yr. Est. 1984, Quarterly, Trim Size-7¼ x 9¾, 28 pages, ISSN: 8750-0434, Color, Coated
Subscriptions: Indv. $10, $5/copy
Circulation: (95% controlled), Total-6,500
Advertising: $635.
List Rental: Actives: $75/M

Bishop Museum Bulletins in Entomology

Publishing Co: Bishop Museum, 1525 Bernice St # 19000-A, Honolulu, HI 96817-2704; Title Tel # (808) 848-4135
General Info: ISSN: 0893-3146
Circulation: Total-300

Bishop Museum Bulletins in Zoology

Publishing Co: Bishop Museum, 1525 Bernice St # 19000-A, Honolulu, HI 96817-2704; Title Tel # (808) 848-4135
General Info: ISSN: 0893-312X
Circulation: Total-300

Briefings on Laboratory Safety and Accreditation
See: HOSPITALS & NURSING HOMES

CBE Views   *Association*

Publishing Co: Council of Biology Editors, Inc., 11 S. LaSalle St., Ste. 1400, Chicago, IL 60603-1210; Title Tel # (312) 616-0800 Title Fax # (312) 616-0223
Personnel: Publisher-Cindy Clark, Editor, Production Mgr.-Alan Brush
Editorial Description: About writing, editing, and publishing in the biological sciences.
General Info: (Formerly Council of Biology Editors Newsletter), Yr. Est. 1978, Bi-monthly, Trim Size-8½ x 11, Sheetfed press, 20 pages, ISSN: 0164-5609, 2% ads, No Color, Newsprint
Subscriptions: Indv. $38, $8/copy
Circulation: Total-1,000
Advertising: Inquire for rates.
List Rental: Rents Lists
Printing Co: District Creative Printing, 6350 Fallard Dr, Upper Marlboro, MD 20772-3885
Tel # (301) 868-8610, Fax # (301) 868-1015

CFBS Newsletter/Bulletin de la FCSB   *Association*   **CPM: $160**

Publishing Co: Canadian Fed. of Biological Societies, Inc., 104-1750 Courtwood Crescent, Ottawa, ON K2C 2B5 Canada Tel # (613) 225-8889 Fax # (613) 225-9621; Title Tel # (613) 234-9555 Title Fax # (613) 234-6667
Personnel: Publisher, Editor, Circ. Mgr.-Suzan Tuke
Editorial Description: Newsletter covering status of CFBS & constituent society issues.
General Info: Semi-annually, Trim Size-8½ x 11, 28 pages, ISSN: 0714-9956, Ind/Abs/Online: http://www.hwc.ca:8800/, 2% ads, Color
Subscriptions: Indv. $10, Can. $10, $5/copy
Circulation: Total-5,000
Advertising: $800. Accepts Inserts.
List Rental: Rents Lists

Canadian Association for Laboratory Animal Science Newsletter

Publishing Co: Canadian Assn. for Lab. Animal Science, M524 Biol. Sci. Bldg., Univ. Alberta, Edmonton, AB T6G 2E9 Canada
General Info: Bi-monthly, Trim Size-8½ x 11, Offset press, 24 pages, Color
Subscriptions: Indv. $50, Inst. $180
Circulation: (100% controlled), Total-1,000
Advertising: Inquire for rates.

Canadian Biotech News
See: DRUGS & PHARMACEUTICALS

Canadian Society of Environmental Biologists Newsletter
See: ENVIRONMENT & ECOLOGY

Carolina Tips   *Business*

Publishing Co: Carolina Biological Supply Co., 2700 York Rd, Burlington, NC 27215-3398; Title Tel # (919) 584-0381 Title Fax # (910) 584-3399
Personnel: Editor-Phillip Owens, Production Mgr.-Jennifer Armstrong, Publisher, Adv. Dir.-Harry Shoffner, Art Dir.-Bruce Anliker
Editorial Description: Life sciences with emphasis on articles that present new teaching materials and techniques.
General Info: Yr. Est. 1938, Quarterly, Trim Size-8½ x 11, Sheetfed press, 4 pages, ISSN: 0045-5865, Ind/Abs/Online: Biol.Abstr., 4 Color, Coated
Subscriptions: Free To Qualified Recipient
Circulation: Total-100,000
Printing Co: Meredith Webb, 334 N Main St, Burlington, NC 27217-3906 Tel # (919) 228-8379

Clinical Investigator News
See: DRUGS & PHARMACEUTICALS

Coral Reef Newsletter

Publishing Co: Marine Lab/Univ. of Guam, UOG Station, Mangilao, GU 96923; Title Tel # (671) 734-2421 Title Fax # (671) 734-6767
General Info: Semi-annually, Trim Size-5¾ x 8¾
Circulation: Total-1,500

Cultivar: Newsletter of the UCSC Center for Agroecology & Sustainable Food Systems
See: AGRICULTURE

Cycad Newsletter   *Association*

Publishing Co: Cycad Society, c/o David S. Mayo, 1161 Phyllis Ct., Mountain View, CA 94040; Title Tel # (415) 964-7898
Personnel: Editor, Adv. Dir.-Garrie Landry, Circ. Mgr., Promotion Dir.-David Mayo
Editorial Description: Culture, research & history of the family Cycadaceae.
General Info: Yr. Est. 1977, Quarterly, Trim Size-8 x 10, Offset press, 15 pages
Subscriptions: Indv. $15
Circulation: Total-650
Advertising: Inquire for rates. Accepts Inserts.
List Rental: Rents Lists

Diagnostic Quarterly
See: MEDICINE

Doctor's Office Lab News
See: MEDICINE

Drosophila
See: SCIENCE

Ecdipiast, The

Publishing Co: Crustacean Society, C/O Denton Belk, 840 E. Mulberry, San Antonio, TX 78212; Title Tel # (210) 732-8809 Title Fax # (210) 732-3943
Personnel: Editor-R. Bauer
Editorial Description: News for members, meeting information.
General Info: Yr. Est. 1971, Semi-annually, Trim Size-8.5 x 11, 6 pages
Subscriptions: Indv. $20, Inst. $20, Can. $20, For. $20
Circulation: Total-800

Entomological Society of Canada, Bulletin
See: ENTOMOLOGY

FASEB Newsletter   *Scholarly, Association*

Publishing Co: Fed. of American Societies for Experimental Biology, 9650 Rockville Pike, Bethesda, MD 20814-3998; Title Tel # (301) 530-7075
Editorial Description: Covers FASEB public affairs activities.
General Info: 9x/yr., Trim Size-8½ x 11, 8 pages
Subscriptions: Indv. $60, Free With Membership
Circulation: Total-36,000
Advertising: Inquire for rates.

Fill Transcript

Publishing Co: Cold Spring Harbor Laboratory, 1 Bungtown Rd, Cold Spring Harbor, NY 11724-2209 Tel # (516) 349-1930 Fax # (516) 349-1946; Title Tel # (516) 367-8455
Personnel: Publisher, Editor-Susan Cooper, Circ. Mgr.-Emily Eryou, Art Dir.-Margot Bennett
Editorial Description: A house organ reporting on all aspects of the lab: its science, public relations/development activities, & the personalities involved with its management.
General Info: Yr. Est. 1983, Quarterly, 8 pages, Coated, Saddle-stitched
Circulation: Total-4,500

Focus

Publishing Co: Life Technologies, Inc., 8717 Grovemont Circle, P.O. Box 6009, Gaithersburg, MD 20884-9980 Tel # (301) 840-8000 Fax # (800) 331-2286
Personnel: Editor-Nancy Safavage, Art Dir.-Lynn Kieffer
Editorial Description: Techniques & protocols in molecular biology & life science research.
General Info: Yr. Est. 1978, Quarterly, Trim Size-8½ x 11, Offset press, 32 pages, 2 Color, Recycled, Saddle-stitched
Circulation: Total-41,000
Printing Co: Expert Brown, 2015 W Laburnum Ave, Richmond, VA 23227-4352 Tel # (804) 358-9131, Fax # (804) 262-7759

Frontiers in Immunology & Biotechnology Scientific Newsletter
See: MICROBIOLOGY

Fungal Genetics Newsletter   *Consumer*

Publishing Co: Fungal Genetics Stock Center, U Of K Med. Ctr., Microbiology, Kansas City, KS 66160-0001; Title Fax # (913) 588-7295
Personnel: Publisher-Kevin McCluskey, Editor-Peter Russell
Editorial Description: Contains stock lists; linkage maps; and data; bibliography; covers Neurospora, Podospora, technical notes and methods; research notes; Sordaria.
General Info: (Formerly Neurospora Newsletter), Yr. Est. 1962, Annually, Trim Size-8½ x 11½, Offset press, 100 pages, ISSN: 0895-1942, No Color, Perfect bound
Subscriptions: Indv. $10
Circulation: Total-650

Hawaiian Shell News
See: NATURAL HISTORY

Herbarium News
See: BOTANY

Huntsman Marine Science News
See: FISH & FISHERIES

The ISC Newsletter
See: ZOOLOGY

International Bear News
See: ZOOLOGY

Intl. Society of Differentiation-Newsletter

Publishing Co: International Society of Differentiation, Univ. of Minnesota, Biological Sciences Ctr., St. Paul, MN 55108-1004; Title Tel # (612) 624-2244
Personnel: Editor-R.G. McKinnell
General Info: Yr. Est. 1982
Circulation: Total-700

Life Sciences & Biotechnology Update   *Business*

Publishing Co: Infoteam, Inc., PO Box 15640, Plantation, FL 33318-5640 Fax # (954) 472-0544; Title Tel # (954) 473-9560 Title Fax # (954) 473-0544
Personnel: Publisher, Editor-Merton Allen
Editorial Description: Covers research & development, technology, applications, products, processes, etc. related to for example: agriculture; food; medicine; health; biology; bioengineering; nutrition; bodilyfluids, organs & tissues; disease, medical engineering; & more.
General Info: Yr. Est. 1995, Monthly, Trim Size-8½ x 11, Web press, 18 pages, ISSN: 1081-7972, Ind/Abs/Online: Newsnet, Dialog, Predicasts, Data-Star, No Color, Newsprint, Saddle-stitched
Subscriptions: Indv. $269, Can. $309, For. $379, $25/copy

Lookdown, The
See: MUSEUM PUBLICATIONS

MIT Sea Grant Quarterly Report
See: OCEANOGRAPHY

Medical Materials Update
See: MEDICINE

Membrane & Separation Technology News   *Business*

Publishing Co: Business Communications Co., 25 Van Zant St., Ste.13, Norwalk, CT 06855-1781; Title Tel # (203) 853-4266 Title Fax # (203) 853-0348
Personnel: Publisher-Louis Naturman, Editor-Anna Crull, Editor-Karen Lindsey, Mktg. Dir.-Robert Butler
Editorial Description: Latest developments & commercial applications in membrane & separation technology.
General Info: Yr. Est. 1982, Monthly, Trim Size-8½ x 11, 12 pages, ISSN: 0720-8483, Ind/Abs/Online: DIALOG, No Color, Matte
Subscriptions: Indv. $395, Can. $445, For. $445, $40/copy
Circulation: (100% controlled), Total-300
List Rental: List Management Co.: W.I. Mail Marketing, 470 Main St. #317, Ridgefield, CT 06877-4516 Tel # (203) 438-6822, Fax # (203) 438-7756, Actives: 1,300, $250/M

Microporous Materials Technology News
See: CHEMISTRY & CHEMICALS

Microscopial Society of Canada. Bulletin
See: OPTICAL

Mycological Society of America Newsletter

Publishing Co: Mycological Society of America, SUNY College at Oswego, Biology Dept., Oswego, NY 13126; Title Tel # (315) 341-2768
Personnel: Editor-Terrence Hammill, Circ. Mgr.-F. B. Reeves
Editorial Description: Covers Society news, events, Annual Metting, etc.
General Info: Yr. Est. 1950, Semi-annually, 64 pages, ISSN: 0541-4938, Color-cover
Subscriptions: Indv. $25
Circulation: Total-1,400
Printing Co: SUNY College Publications Dept., SUNY-Oswego, Rich Hall, Oswego, NY 13126 Tel # (315) 341-3130

Nematology Newsletter

Publishing Co: Society of Nematologists, 3012 Skyview Dr, Lakeland, FL 33801-7072 Tel # (813) 665-4481 Fax # (813) 665-1297
General Info: Yr. Est. 1956, Quarterly, 20 pages
Circulation: Total-850
Advertising: Inquire for rates.

News & Views
See: EDUCATION

News from Mote
See: SCIENCE

Pacific Science Association Information Bulletin
See: SCIENCE

Physiology Canada
See: PHYSIOLOGY

Plant Pathology Circular, Entomology Arcular, Hematology Arcular, Botany Circular
See: BOTANY

Primate Library Report: Audio-Visual Acquisitions
See: ZOOLOGY

Radioassay Ligand-Assay News
See: MEDICINE

Resonance
See: BIOPHYSICS

SIGBIO Newsletter
See: MEDICINE

Scales and Tales
See: ZOOLOGY

Seiche, The
See: ENVIRONMENT & ECOLOGY

Spirit!
See: HOUSE ORGANS

Spoof Newsletter
See: OCEANOGRAPHY

Tri-Ology Technical Report   *Business, Association*

Publishing Co: Florida Department of Agriculture & Consumer Services, PO Box 147100 m, Gainesville, FL 32614-7100 Fax # (904) 955-2301; Title Tel # (904) 372-3505
Personnel: Editor, Circ. Mgr.-W.N. Dixon
Editorial Description: Summary of significant species and number of specimens found in Florida of organisms on plants in the previous two months. Provides biological, distribution and economic information on organisms of possible significance to Florida's plant industries.
General Info: Yr. Est. 1962, Bi-monthly, Trim Size-8½ x 11, Coated
Subscriptions: Free
Circulation: Total-1,000

World Biolicensing & Patent Report

Publishing Co: Bio Engineering News, 109 Minna St # 304, San Francisco, CA 94105-3728; Title Fax # (360) 679-3084
Personnel: Publisher-Deborah Mysiewicz, Editor, Circ. Mgr.-Thomas Mysiewicz
Editorial Description: Licensing opportunities offered in biotechnology, listings of patent applications worldwide. Free bonus to bioengineering news subscription.
General Info: Yr. Est. 1985, 10x/yr., Trim Size-8½ x 11, 8 pages, ISSN: 0883-5527, No Color

Worldwide Biotech   *Business*

Publishing Co: Worldwide Videotex Co., PO Box 3273, Boynton Beach, FL 33424-3273 Fax # (407) 738-2276; Title Tel # (407) 738-2276 Title Fax # (407) 738-2275
Editorial Description: News and information on the biotechnology industry.
General Info: Yr. Est. 1990, Monthly
Subscriptions: Indv. $150, Inst. $150, Can. $150, For. $165

BIOPHYSICS

Details

Publishing Co: Association of Biotechnology Companies, 1625 K St NW Ste 1100, Washington, DC 20006-1604; Title Tel # (202) 234-3330 Title Fax # (202) 234-3565
Personnel: Editor-Jeffrey Gibbs, Production Mgr.-Derek Koecher
Editorial Description: Assn. & industry newsletter.
General Info: Yr. Est. 1985, Bi-monthly
Circulation: (ABC), Total-473,625
Advertising: Inquire for rates.

Electrical Sensitivity News
See: ENVIRONMENT & ECOLOGY

HLB Newsletter
See: MEDICINE

Physiology Canada
See: PHYSIOLOGY

Resonance   *Consumer, Scholarly*   CPM: $125

Publishing Co: Judy Wall, 684 County Rd. #535, Sumterville, FL 33585 Tel # (904) 793-8748; Title Tel # (352) 793-8748
Personnel: Editor-Judy Wall
Editorial Description: Reviews scientific literature dealing with the subject of bioelectromagnetics; that is, the interaction between electric and/or magnetic fields and living organisms and related topics.
General Info: Yr. Est. 1985, Quarterly, Trim Size-5½ x 8½, 48 pages, Saddle-stitched
Subscriptions: Indv. $15, For. $20, $3/copy
Circulation: Total-200
Advertising: $25.

BLIND

AER Report

Publishing Co: Assn. for Education & Rehabilatation of the Blind & Visually, 206 N Washington St Ste 320, Alexandria, VA 22314-2528; Title Tel # (703) 548-1884
General Info: Yr. Est. 1984, Bi-monthly
Circulation: Total-5,200
Advertising: Inquire for rates.

AFB News   *Consumer*

Publishing Co: American Foundation for the Blind, 11 Penn Plz., Ste. 300, New York, NY 10001-2018 Tel # (212) 502-7600 Fax # (212) 502-7777; Title Tel # (212) 502-7674 Title Fax # (212) 502-7765
Editorial Description: Reports on AFB activities.
General Info: (Formerly AFB Newsletter), Yr. Est. 1966, Semi-annually, Web press, 12 pages, No Color, Coated
Circulation: Total-7,500
Printing Co: Jersey Printing Company, 111 Linnett St # 79, Bayonne, NJ 07002-4321 Tel # (201) 436-4200, Fax # (201) 436-0116

Badger Informer

Publishing Co: Badger Assocs. of the Blind, 912 N. Hawley Rd., Milwaukee, WI 53213-3298; Title Tel # (414) 258-9200 Title Fax # (414) 256-8744
General Info: Quarterly

Blind Bowler, The   *Association*

Publishing Co: American Blind Bowling Assn., 3500 Terry Dr, Norfolk, VA 23518-5731;
Title Tel # (412) 662-5748
Personnel: Editor-Alice Hoover
General Info: Yr. Est. 1953, 16 pages
Circulation: Total-2,600

Braille Institute-Outlook

Publishing Co: Braille Institute of America, 741 N Vermont Ave, Los Angeles, CA 90029-3514;
Title Tel # (213) 663-1111
Personnel: Editor-Julie Juliusson
Editorial Description: Information pertinent to students attending the Braille Institute.
General Info: Yr. Est. 1950, Monthly

Deaf Blind News Summary   *Consumer*

Publishing Co: Xavier Society for the Blind, 154 E. 23rd St., New York, NY 10010-4501;
Title Tel # (212) 473-7800 Title Fax # (212) 473-7801
Personnel: Publisher-Alfred Caruana, Editor-Jeanette Scott
Editorial Description: Simplified summary of current news in grade I Braille and large print.
General Info: Yr. Est. 1978, Bi-weekly
Circulation: Total-160

Deafblind Weekly   *Consumer*

Publishing Co: Xavier Society for the Blind, 154 E. 23rd St., New York, NY 10010-4501;
Title Tel # (212) 473-7800 Title Fax # (212) 473-7801
Personnel: Publisher-Alfred Caruana, Editor-Jeanette Scott
Editorial Description: Braille newsletter containing world news. (Grade 2 Braille).
General Info: Yr. Est. 1970, Weekly
Subscriptions: Free
Circulation: Total-150
Printing Co: Clovernook Printing House, 7000 Hamilton Ave, Cincinnati, OH 45231-5240
Tel # (513) 522-3860

Disability Funding News
    See: PHILANTHROPY

Division on Visual
    Handicaps Quarterly   *Association*

Publishing Co: Council for Exceptional Children, 1920 Association Dr., Reston, VA 22091-1589
Tel # (703) 620-3660 Fax # (703) 264-9494
Editorial Description: Current information on educating children who are usually impaired.
General Info: (Formerly DVH Quarterly), Yr. Est. 1956, Quarterly
Subscriptions: Indv. $15, Inst. $20
Circulation: Total-1,200
Advertising: Inquire for rates.

Federal Securities Law Reports
    See: LAW

Fighting Blindness News
    See: MEDICINE

Florida School Herald
    See: HEARING & SPEECH

Free Press   *Association*

Publishing Co: Wisconsin School for the Visually Handicapped-American Print, 1700 W State St,
Janesville, WI 53546-5344; Title Tel # (608) 755-2977
Personnel: Editor-Robert Arndt
Editorial Description: Braille, school news and alumni features.
General Info: Yr. Est. 1912, 5x/yr., Trim Size-8½ x 11½, Mimeo press, 20 pages, No Color
Circulation: (100% controlled), Total-400

Freedom Forum   *Consumer, Association*

Publishing Co: Freedom Guide Dogs, 1210 Hardscrabble Rd, Cassville, NY 13318-1304;
Title Tel # (315) 822-5132
Editorial Description: Articles and information about seeing-eye-dogs for the blind.
General Info: Quarterly, Trim Size-8½ x 11, 4 pages, No Color, Matte

Gleams
    See: MEDICINE

Guide Dog News   *Consumer*

Publishing Co: Guide Dogs for the Blind, Inc, PO Box 151200, San Rafael, CA 94915-1200
Fax # (415) 449-4023; Title Tel # (415) 499-4000 Title Fax # (415) 499-4023
Personnel: Editor-Joanne Ritter
Editorial Description: Guide Dog News is the informational publication of Guide Dogs for the Blind, Inc.
General Info: Yr. Est. 1942, Quarterly, Web press, 6 pages, 4 Color, Coated, Saddle-stitched
Subscriptions: Free
Acquistions: Publication Bought
Circulation: Total-50,000
Printing Co: Typestylers, P.O Box 1152, Zaphyr Cove, NV 89448 Tel # (702) 588-8301

Illinois Braille Messenger   *Consumer, Association*

Publishing Co: Illinois Council of the Blind, PO Box 1336, Springfield, IL 62705-1336
Tel # (217) 523-4967; Title Tel # (212) 523-4967
Personnel: Editor-Clyde Forth
Editorial Description: For the visually impaired in Illinois.
General Info: Yr. Est. 1930, Quarterly
Subscriptions: Indv. $5
Circulation: Total-2,000

Insight   *Association*

Publishing Co: Helen Keller Intl., 90 Washington St Fl 15, New York, NY 10006-2214;
Title Tel # (212) 807-5800
Personnel: Editor-Ron Texley
Editorial Description: Worldwide blindness prevention, education and rehabilitation programs, and
international efforts to restore sight in developing countries.
General Info: (Formerly HKI Report), Yr. Est. 1978, Trim Size-8½ x 11, Offset press, 6 pages, 2
Color, Newsprint
Circulation: (100% controlled)

Insight Newsletter   *Association*

Publishing Co: U.S. Assn. for Blind Athletes, 33 N Institute St, Colorado Springs, CO 80903-3508;
Title Tel # (719) 630-0422 Title Fax # (719) 630-0616
Personnel: Asst. Pub.-Mark Lucas
Editorial Description: Organization activities, stories about athletes & events, nutrition information,
plus other information for the blind.
General Info: (Formerly USABA Agenda; USABA Newsletter; SportsScoop), Yr. Est. 1977, Monthly,
Sheetfed press, 2 pages, 2 Color, Saddle-stitched
Subscriptions: Indv. $30, Inst. $40
Printing Co: Ink Spot, 9 East Vermigo Ave., Colorado Spgs., CO 80903 Tel # (719) 578-1955

Insights

Publishing Co: Western Pennsylvania School for Blind Children, 201 N Bellefield Ave, Pittsburgh, PA
15213-1458; Title Tel # (412) 621-0100
Personnel: Editor-Barbara Paull
General Info: Trim Size-8½ x 11, Offset press, 8 pages, 2 Color, Newsprint
Circulation: Total-8,000

Jewish Guild for the Blind
    Newsletter   *Association*

Publishing Co: Jewish Guild for the Blind, 15 W 65th St, New York, NY 10023-6694;
Title Tel # (212) 769-6200 Title Fax # (212) 769-6266
Personnel: Editor-Peter Williamson
Editorial Description: Coverage of programs, people and events at the Guild and its affiliates.
General Info: Yr. Est. 1960, Quarterly
Subscriptions: Free
Circulation: Total-22,000

Jottings   *Consumer*

Publishing Co: Gospel Assn. for the Blind, Inc., PO Box 62, Delray Beach, FL 33447-0062;
Title Tel # (407) 274-9700 Title Fax # (407) 274-4288
Personnel: Editor-Beatrice Montanus
General Info: Yr. Est. 1955, Monthly, 4 pages, 2 Color
Subscriptions: Free
Circulation: Total-8,000

Log of the Bridgetender

Publishing Co: Friends in Art of ACB, 166 Little Deer Rd, Bridgeport, CT 06606-1750;
Title Tel # (203) 374-3865
Personnel: Editor-Donald Coleman
Editorial Description: Articles of interest to blind artists, musicians, poets and museum lovers.
General Info: Yr. Est. 1979, Quarterly, Trim Size-8½ x 11, Mimeo press, 20 pages, No Color,
Newsprint
Subscriptions: Indv. $12

Lutheran Braille Evangelism
    Bulletin   *Consumer, Association*

Publishing Co: Lutheran Braille Evangelism Association, 1740 Eugene St, White Bear Lake, MN
55110-3312; Title Tel # (612) 426-0469
Personnel: Editor-Dennis Hawkinson
Editorial Description: Quarterly informational & update of ministry.
General Info: Yr. Est. 1952, Quarterly, Offset press, 2 pages, No Color
Subscriptions: Free
Circulation: (100% controlled), Total-1,100

Minnesota Bulletin

Publishing Co: Minnesota State Services for the Blind, 2200 University Ave., W., St. Paul, MN 55114
Tel # (612) 642-0500
General Info: Bi-monthly

NAPH National Newsletter
    See: DISABILITY

NFADB Newsletter
    See: DEAF

National Braille Association Bulletin
    See: EDUCATION

National Federation of the Blind, Legislative Bulletin
See: LAW

News About Library Services for the Blind

Publishing Co: South Carolina State Library, 1500 Senate St. #11469, Columbia, SC 29211-3815 Fax # (803) 734-8676; Title Tel # (803) 737-9970
Personnel: Editor-Naomi Bradey
Editorial Description: Information for print-handicapped users of library service.
General Info: Yr. Est. 1975, Quarterly, Trim Size-8½ x 11½, 4 pages, ISSN: 0883-5845
Subscriptions: Free
Circulation: (84% controlled), Total-7,300

Opportunity   *Consumer, Association*

Publishing Co: National Industries for the Blind, 1901 N. Beauregard St., Ste. 200, Alexandria, VA 22311-1727; Title Tel # (201) 595-9200 Title Fax # (201) 595-9122
Personnel: Editor-Jill L. Cregar
Editorial Description: A publication of National Industries for the Blind describing its program & activities as well as those of its associated agencies.
General Info: Quarterly, Trim Size-11 x 16, 4 pages, 2 Color
Subscriptions: Free To Qualified Recipient

Prevent Blindness   *Consumer*

Publishing Co: Natl. Society for the Prevention of Blindness, 500 E. Remington Rd., Schaumburg, IL 60173-4557 Tel # (708) 843-2020 Fax # (708) 843-8458
Personnel: Editor-Patricia Dahlberg, Mktg. Dir.-Suzanne Gedance
Editorial Description: Information about preventing loss of vision and maintaining sight.
General Info: Irregular, Trim Size-11 x 17, 8 pages, 2 Color, Matte

Projections

Publishing Co: Protestant Guild for the Blind, Inc., 441 Waverley Oaks Rd, Waltham, MA 02154-8405; Title Tel # (617) 484-7700
Personnel: Editor-Linda Flint
General Info: (Formerly Protestant Guild for the Blind-Newsletter), Yr. Est. 1970, Quarterly
Circulation: Total-5,000

RFB News
See: DISABILITY

Rehabilitation Technology Newsletter
See: SOCIAL SERVICES & WELFARE

Scene

Publishing Co: Braille Institute of America, 741 N Vermont Ave, Los Angeles, CA 90029-3514; Title Tel # (213) 663-1111
Personnel: Editor-Paul Porrelli
Editorial Description: Programs and training, offered by Braille Institute.
General Info: Yr. Est. 1974, Quarterly, Trim Size-8½ x 11, 8 pages
Circulation: Total-180,000

Seeing Eye Guide, The   *Business, Association*

Publishing Co: Seeing Eye, Inc., The, PO Box 375, Morristown, NJ 07963-0375; Title Tel # (201) 539-4425 Title Fax # (201) 539-0922
Personnel: Editor, Production Mgr.-Carol Gray
Editorial Description: Concerns activities at The Seeing Eye, Inc. Also published in braille, audio tape.
General Info: Yr. Est. 1936, Quarterly, Trim Size-8½ x 11, Offset press, 8 pages, ISSN: 0037-0819, 4 Color, Coated
Subscriptions: Free
Circulation: Total-25,000

TAC Newsletter   *Association*

Publishing Co: Helen Keller Technical Assistance Center, 111 Middle Neck Rd, Sands Point, NY 11050-1298 Tel # (516) 944-8900 Fax # (516) 944-7302
Personnel: Editor-Theresa Carr
Editorial Description: News and developments relating to the Technical Assistance Center, a national project to provide technical assistance to agencies and programs offering school-to-adult-life transition services to deaf/blind youth.
General Info: Yr. Est. 1985, 3x/yr.
Circulation: Total-5,000

Towers   *Association*

Publishing Co: Overbrook School for the Blind, 6333 Malvern Ave, Philadelphia, PA 19151-2529; Title Tel # (215) 877-0313
Personnel: Editor-William Reynolds
Editorial Description: News of students, alumni, staff, & friends of the school.
General Info: Yr. Est. 1946, Quarterly, Trim Size-17 x 11, Offset press, 4 pages, 2 Color, Matte
Subscriptions: Free To Qualified Recipient
Circulation: Total-7,500
Printing Co: Reynolds & Schaeffer Association, PO Box 265, Haddonfield, NJ 08033-0219 Tel # (609) 428-6700

Understanding and Living with Glaucoma
See: HEALTH

U.S. Library of Congress, National Library for the Blind and Physically Handicapped News

Publishing Co: Natl. Library Service for the Blind & Physically Handicapped, 1291 Taylor St NW, Washington, DC 20542-0001 Tel # (202) 707-5100; Title Tel # (202) 287-5100
Personnel: Editor-Vicki Fitzpatrick
Editorial Description: Program developments at NLS, in cooperating libraries & in intl. activities.
General Info: (Formerly DBPH News), Yr. Est. 1958, Quarterly, Web press, 2 Color
Circulation: (100% controlled), Total-25,000

Update   *Consumer, Association*

Publishing Co: Natl. Library Service for the Blind & Physically Handicapped, 1291 Taylor St NW, Washington, DC 20542-0001; Title Tel # (202) 707-5100
Editorial Description: Newsletter about volunteers who assist visually impaired and physically disabled readers of braille and recorded books and magazines.
General Info: Yr. Est. 1977, Quarterly, Trim Size-8½ x 11, 8 pages, ISSN: 0160-9203, Saddle-stitched
Subscriptions: Free

Utah Eagle   *Association*

Publishing Co: Sponsor-UT Schools for the Deaf and the Blind, Utah State School Deaf-Blind, 742 Harrison Blvd, Ogden, UT 84404-5231; Title Tel # (801) 399-9631
Personnel: Editor-Blaine Seamons
Editorial Description: Professional articles of interest to parents & educators of the deaf & the blind.
General Info: Yr. Est. 1889, Quarterly, Trim Size-8½ x 11, Offset press, 8 pages, No Color
Circulation: Total-1,000
Printing Co: University of Texas State Printing, 1007 State Office Building, Salt Lake City, UT 84114-1201 Tel # (801) 538-3015

Vendorscope   *Business, Association*

Publishing Co: Sponsor-Randolph-Sheppard Vendors of America, Randolph-Sheppard Vendors of America, 1527 Royal Rd, Aberdeen, SD 57401-7646 Parent Co.-American Council of the Blind, Indianapolis; Title Tel # (605) 229-4129 Title Fax # (605) 226-3141
Personnel: Editor-Dean Flewwellin
Editorial Description: Articles of interest to blind persons who operate vending stands & cafeterias, plus related support personnel of the Business Enterprise Program under the Rehabilitative Services Administration.
General Info: Yr. Est. 1969, Quarterly, Trim Size-8½ x 11, Sheetfed press, 28 pages, Color-cover, Coated, Saddle-stitched
Subscriptions: Indv. $10, Free To Qualified Recipient
Circulation: Total-4,247
Printing Co: Quality Quick Print, 112 N Main St, Aberdeen, SD 57401-3429 Tel # (605) 226-2541

Vision Resource Update

Publishing Co: Vision Foundation, 818 Mount Auburn St, Watertown, MA 02172-1567; Title Tel # (617) 926-4232
Personnel: Editor-Fran Weisse
Editorial Description: Large print & cassette bi-monthly newsletter for individuals coping with sight loss.
General Info: Bi-monthly, Trim Size-8½ x 11, Desktop press, 8 pages
Subscriptions: Indv. $20

BOATS & BOATING

ABYC News   *Association*

Publishing Co: American Boat and Yacht Council, 3069 Solomons Island Rd, Edgewater, MD 21037-1416; Title Tel # (410) 956-1050 Title Fax # (410) 956-2737
Personnel: Editor-Louise Lincoln, Production Mgr.-Jennifer Ruppert, Publisher, Mktg. Dir.-Skip Moyer
Editorial Description: News and technical information of interest to ABYC members. Primary topics about boating safety. Technical meetings schedule.
General Info: Yr. Est. 1968, Quarterly, Trim Size-8½ x 11, Offset press, 12 pages, No Color, Other
Subscriptions: Free To Qualified Recipient
Circulation: Total-3,000

Affiliate & Instructor News   *Association*

Publishing Co: American Sailing Association, 13922 Marquesas Way, Marina Del Rey, CA 90292-6000; Title Tel # (310) 822-7171 Title Fax # (310) 822-4741
Personnel: Editor-Harry Munns
Editorial Description: Business information for sailing schools & sailing instructors.
General Info: (Formerly Professional Sailing Instructor), Yr. Est. 1982, Quarterly, Trim Size-8½ x 11, Offset press, 9 pages, No Color, Newsprint
Subscriptions: Inst. $125
Circulation: Total-4,000
Advertising: Inquire for rates. Accepts Inserts.

American Boat Builders & Repairers Assn. - Newsletter

Publishing Co: American Boat Builders & Repairers Assn., PO Box 1236, Stamford, CT 06904-1236; Title Tel # (203) 967-4745
Personnel: Editor-Elizabeth Cross
Editorial Description: Membership newsletter.
General Info: Yr. Est. 1940, Monthly, Desktop press
Subscriptions: Free

America's Cup Report

Publishing Co: Belvoir Pubs., 75 Holly Hill Lane, Greenwich, CT 06836; Title Tel # (203) 661-6111
Circulation: Total-5,016
List Rental: List Management Co.: George Mann & Associates, 569 Abbington Dr., PO Box 930, Hightstown, NJ 08520-9990 Tel # (609) 443-1330, Fax # (609) 443-0397, Actives: 5,000, $100/M

Antique Outboarder, The   *Consumer, Association*   CPM: $71

Publishing Co: Antique Outboard Motor Club, Inc., PO Box 09293, Milwaukee, WI 53209-0293; Title Tel # (414) 966-3697
Editorial Description: Newsletter covering meets, outboard motor repairs and restoration, racing, and other items of interest to antique outboard motor enthusiasts.
General Info: Quarterly
Subscriptions: Free With Membership
Circulation: Total-1,260
Advertising: $90.

Ash Breeze

Publishing Co: Traditional Small Craft Assn., PO Box 350, Mystic, CT 06355-0350; Title Tel # (203) 536-6342
Personnel: Editor-Ken Steinmetz
Editorial Description: Articles on the design, construction, & use of traditional small craft for Rowing, Sail, & Paddle. Assn. business, book reviews, & news of members activities. Sent to all members.
General Info: Yr. Est. 1975, Quarterly, Sheetfed press, 24 pages, Matte
Subscriptions: $3/copy
Circulation: Total-800

BOAT/U.S. Reports   *Consumer, Association*

Publishing Co: Boat Owners Association of the U.S., 800 S Pickett St, Alexandria, VA 22304-4606 Tel # (703) 823-9550; Title Tel # (703) 461-2864 Title Fax # (703) 461-2845
Personnel: Publisher-Richard Schwartz, Editor-Michael Sciulla, Circ. Mgr.-Diane Wilson, Art Dir.-Lisa Nyce
Editorial Description: Covers legislation, regulation & consumer news of interest to recreational boaters.
General Info: (Formerly At Your Service), Yr. Est. 1966, Bi-monthly, Trim Size-11 x 14, Web press, 16 pages, 4 Color, Coated
Subscriptions: Indv. $17
Circulation: Total-510,000

Bearings

Publishing Co: Maritime Retailers Assn. of America, 150 E Huron St Apt 802, Chicago, IL 60611-2912; Title Tel # (312) 944-5080 Title Fax # (312) 944-2716
Personnel: Editor-K. Small
Editorial Description: Comprehensive coverage of news & trends in the marine retailing industry.
General Info: (Formerly MRAA Newsletter), Yr. Est. 1972, Monthly
Circulation: Total-4,500
Advertising: Inquire for rates.
List Rental: Rents Lists

Better Boat

Publishing Co: Belvoir Pubs., 75 Holly Hill Lane, Greenwich, CT 06836; Title Tel # (203) 661-6111
General Info: Monthly
Subscriptions: Indv. $34
List Rental: List Management Co.: Compuname, Inc., 411 Theodore Fremd Ave., Rye, NY 10580 Tel # (914) 925-4000, Fax # (914) 925-2499, Actives: $75/M

Boating Safety Circular   *Association*

Publishing Co: U.S. Coast Guard, 2100 2nd St SW, Washington, DC 20593-0001; Title Tel # (202) 426-7830
Editorial Description: Boating safety as it applies to manufacturers, dealers, distributors & the boating public.
General Info: (Formerly Safe Boating), Yr. Est. 1969, Quarterly, Offset press, 20 pages, No Color
Circulation: Total-26,000

Business of Pleasure Boats
See: BANKING & FINANCE

Butterflyer, The

Publishing Co: National Butterfly Association, C/o Barnett Boat Company, 534 Commercial Avenue, Green Lake, WI 54941; Title Tel # (414) 294-6351
Circulation: Total-300

Canews   *Association*

Publishing Co: Canoe Ontario, 1220 Sheppard Ave. E., Willowdale, ON M2K 2X1 Canada Fax # (416) 426-7363
Personnel: Editor-Trinela Cane
Editorial Description: Covers adventure canoe trips.
General Info: Yr. Est. 1982, Bi-monthly, Trim Size-8½ x 11, Desktop press, 36 pages, Color-cover, Recycled, Other
Subscriptions: Free To Qualified Recipient
Circulation: (80% controlled), Total-800
Advertising: Inquire for rates.

Constitution Chronicle
See: MUSEUM PUBLICATIONS

Cruisabout

Publishing Co: Richardson Boat Owners Association, C/O Chamber of Commerce, 20 Main St., Tonawanda, NY 14150-2106; Title Tel # (716) 692-5120
Personnel: Editor-Jim Nogle
General Info: Quarterly
Circulation: Total-275

Current   *Association*   CPM: $200

Publishing Co: Electric Boat Association of the Americas, PO Box 4151, Deerfield Beach, FL 33442; Title Tel # (954) 725-0640 Title Fax # (954) 725-0640
Personnel: Publisher, Editor-Ken Matthews, Production Mgr.-Tom Wilbur, Promotion Dir.-Judy Shepherd
Editorial Description: News of electric-powered boating in North America and elsewhere.
General Info: Yr. Est. 1992, Bi-monthly, Trim Size-8½ x 11, Sheetfed press, 8 pages, ISSN: 1073-158X, No Color, Matte
Subscriptions: Indv. $35, Can. $35, For. $50, $4/copy
Circulation: (30% controlled), Total-1,000, Subscriptions-500, Readership-3,000
Advertising: $200.

DOE
See: SCIENCE FICTION & FANTASY

Etchells News   *Association*

Publishing Co: International Etchells Class Association, 22 Sewall Street, Marblehead, MA 01945 Tel # (617) 631-3201; Title Tel # (617) 631-3166
General Info: Quarterly
Subscriptions: Indv. $10, Free With Membership
Advertising: Inquire for rates.

Global Positioning &
Navigation News   *Business*

Publishing Co: Phillips Business Information, Inc., 1201 Seven Locks Rd., Ste 300, Potomac, MD 20854-2958 Tel # (301) 340-1520 Fax # (301) 424-4297
Editorial Description: Covers the marine industry with news and technologies.
General Info: (Formerly Marine Technology News; GPS Report), Bi-weekly, ISSN: 1072-3080
Subscriptions: Indv. $497, For. $530

Hovernews
See: AERONAUTICS/ASTRONAUTICS

Inter-Port   *Association*

Publishing Co: Natl. Marine Manufacturers Assn., 600 Third Avenue, New York, NY 10016-1901 Tel # (212) 922-1212; Title Tel # (312) 836-4747
Personnel: Editor-Sheryl Rubel
Editorial Description: News, statistics, trends for the recreational boating industry.
General Info: (Formerly Monday Morning Report), Yr. Est. 1979, Weekly, Trim Size-8½ x 11, Offset press, 4 pages, 2 Color, Newsprint
Subscriptions: Indv. $100
Circulation: (100% controlled), Total-2,500

Interlake Sailing Class
Association Intercom   *Consumer, Association*

Publishing Co: Interlake Sailing Class Association, 1341 Frank Dr., Monroe, OH 48161-3483
General Info: Bi-monthly
Subscriptions: Free With Membership
Circulation: Total-400
Advertising: Inquire for rates.

International D.N. Ice
Yacht Racing
Association Newsletter   *Association*

Publishing Co: International D.N. Ice Yacht Racing Association, 21 Marion St, Burlington, VT 05401-4826; Title Tel # (802) 863-3208
Editorial Description: Association activities.
General Info: Quarterly
Subscriptions: Free With Membership
Circulation: Total-900
Advertising: Inquire for rates.

Lightning Flashes   *Consumer, Association*

Publishing Co: International Lightning Class Association, P O Box 586, Worthington, OH 43085 Fax # (614) 885-4219; Title Tel # (614) 885-0475
Editorial Description: Newsletter covering regattas, rules, plans, and other information pertaining to sailing Lightning Class boats.
General Info: 10x/yr., ISSN: 0746-7052
Subscriptions: Indv. $13, Free With Membership
Circulation: Total-3,500
Advertising: Inquire for rates.

Mainsheet
Association

Publishing Co: Rhodes 19 Class Assn., c/o George Gail, 22 W. Shore Dr., Marblehead, MA 01945; Title Tel # (617) 631-5229
Personnel: Editor-George Cail
Editorial Description: Quarterly newsletter for Rhodes 19 class sailboat owners assn. members.
General Info: Yr. Est. 1965, Quarterly, Trim Size-8½ x 11, Sheetfed press, 24 pages, No Color, Newsprint
Subscriptions: Indv. $30
Circulation: (100% controlled), Total-200
Advertising: Inquire for rates.

Marina Management/
Marketing

Publishing Co: Marina Management/Marketing, PO Box 24351, New Orleans, LA 70184-4351; Title Tel # (504) 282-0261
Personnel: Publisher-Ralph Lally, II, Editor-Ron Duvernet
Subscriptions: Indv. $18, $3/copy
Circulation: Total-8,752

Marine Safety Report
See: SAFETY

NAMS News
See: OCEANOGRAPHY

NMMA Boat Show News

Publishing Co: Natl. Marine Manufacturers Assn., 600 Third Avenue, New York, NY 10016-1901 Tel # (212) 922-1212
Personnel: Editor-Henry Brehm

New England Harbormaster
See: GOVERNMENT

Notice to Mariners

Publishing Co: U.S. Mariners Class Assn., C/O Raymond Gerber 56, Amityville, NY 11701; Title Tel # (516) 264-6308
General Info: Yr. Est. 1969, Quarterly
Circulation: Total-400

Powerboat Reports
Business

Publishing Co: Belvoir Pubs., 75 Holly Hill Lane, Greenwich, CT 06836; Title Tel # (203) 661-6111
Editorial Description: Evaluates equipment and gear in this Bi-Monthly newsletter for powerboat owners/users.
General Info: Monthly
Circulation: Total-27,000
List Rental: List Management Co.: Kleid Company, Inc., 530 5th Ave., 17 Floor, New York, NY 10036-5101 Tel # (212) 819-3406, Fax # (212) 719-9788, Actives: 27,311, $80/M

Running Free
Consumer, Association

Publishing Co: American Sail Training Association, PO Box 1459, Newport, RI 02840-0996; Title Tel # (401) 846-1775 Title Fax # (401) 849-5400
Editorial Description: Newsletter providing information on sail training, sea education, and tall ship activities.
General Info: Quarterly
Subscriptions: Free With Membership
Circulation: Total-1,000
Advertising: Inquire for rates.

Rusty Rudder

Publishing Co: Antique & Classic Boat Society, Inc., 234 Ridgedale Ave, Cedar Knolls, NJ 07927-2103; Title Tel # (201) 326-9484 Title Fax # (201) 326-9749
Personnel: Editor-Dan Rothwell, Production Mgr.-Robert Shubert, Adv. Dir.-Jeff Rodengen
Editorial Description: Covers the historical significance of wooden boats, educates the public as to the value of antique boats in association with 35 chapters in the U.S. and Canada. Features boat shows, workshops, and seminars.
General Info: Yr. Est. 1975, Quarterly, Trim Size-8½ x 11, Sheetfed press, 24 pages, 1% ads, 2 Color, Coated
Acquistions: Publication Bought
Circulation: (100% controlled), Total-3,500
Advertising: Inquire for rates. Accepts Inserts.
Printing Co: Triart Graphics, Box 0, Cedar Knolls, NJ 07927

Sailrite Newsletter

Publishing Co: Sailrite Enterprises, 305 W Van Buren St, Columbia City, IN 46725-2039; Title Tel # (219) 244-6715
General Info: Irregular, Trim Size-8½ x 11, 12 pages, No Color

Shipboard Cruiser, The
See: TRAVEL

Showboat Centennials
See: HISTORY

Solo

Publishing Co: U.S.A. Finn Assn., C/O John McIntosh, Jr., 208 Salisbury Road, Savannah, GA 31410-3920; Title Tel # (912) 236-5751
General Info: Bi-monthly
Circulation: Total-350

Spearhead, The
Consumer, Association

Publishing Co: Javelin Class Association, 874 Beecher's Brook Rd., Mayfield Village, OH 44143; Title Tel # (216) 461-8511
Editorial Description: Newsletter covering racing, safety, boat maintenance, and association news.
General Info: Bi-monthly, ISSN: 0279-7836
Subscriptions: Free With Membership
Circulation: Total-250

Spotlight
See: ARCHITECTURE

Standards &
Recommended Practices
for Small Craft
Association

Publishing Co: American Boat and Yacht Council, 3069 Solomons Island Rd, Edgewater, MD 21037-1416 Tel # (410) 956-1050; Title Fax # (410) 956-2737
Personnel: Editor-Jennifer Ruppers, Art Dir.-Tom Halel, Art Dir.-Jennifer Ruppert, Publisher, Mktg. Dir.-Skip Moyer
Editorial Description: Technical report for small craft, including hull, equipment, machinery, electrical & engineering standards.
General Info: Yr. Est. 1954, Offset press, No Color, Other, Looseleaf
Subscriptions: Indv. $75, Inst. $75, Can. $75, For. $75, $150/copy
Acquistions: Publication Bought, Publication Sold
Circulation: Total-3,200, Readership-3,200

Starlights
Association

Publishing Co: International Star Class Yacht Racing Assn., 1545 Waukegan Rd., Glenview, IL 60025-2185; Title Tel # (708) 729-0630
Personnel: Editor-Richard Munson
Editorial Description: Newsletter and official information organ of International Star Class YRA.
General Info: Yr. Est. 1925, Monthly, Trim Size-7½ x 9¾, 4 pages, No Color
Subscriptions: Indv. $3
Circulation: Total-3,500

Stern Words
See: SPORTS & SPORTING GOODS

Tanzer Talk Newsletter

Publishing Co: Tanzer 16 Class Assn., PO Box 26003, Raleigh, NC 27611-6003; Title Tel # (919) 469-3513
Editorial Description: Promotes family daysailing & class racing of Tanzer 16 One-Design class sailboats.
General Info: Bi-monthly
Circulation: Total-185

Tempest, The

Publishing Co: U.S. Intl. Tempest Assn., 111 Maple Dr NW, Lenoir, NC 28645-5031; Title Tel # (704) 754-9992
Personnel: Editor-Mrs. William Respres, Jr.
Editorial Description: Of interest to owners of Intl. Tempest-Class sailboats.
General Info: Yr. Est. 1968, Semi-annually
Circulation: Total-150

Thoroughbred, Quarterly
Journal

Publishing Co: Century Boat Club, 936 Jackman Ave, Pittsburgh, PA 15202-2808
Personnel: Editor-Frank Miklos, Circ. Mgr.-Chuck Miklos
Editorial Description: Antique boat club.
General Info: (Formerly C.B.C. Newsletter; Century Boat Club Quarterly), Yr. Est. 1980, Quarterly, Trim Size-8½ x 11, Offset press, 20 pages, 2 Color, Coated, Saddle-stitched
Subscriptions: $3/copy
Circulation: Total-1,500
Printing Co: Suburban Printing Co., 720 Ohio River Blvd., Pittsburgh, PA 15202-3122 Tel # (412) 766-7227, Fax # (412) 766-0914

Tidings
Association

Publishing Co: Natl. Marine Representatives Assn., PO Box 660, Camden, TN 38320-0660; Title Tel # (901) 584-0203 Title Fax # (901) 584-0420
Personnel: Editor in Chief-Richard Block, Production Mgr.-Lynn McGee
Editorial Description: Internal newsletter distributed to the members of this professional assn. of independent marine sales representatives.
General Info: (Formerly National Marines Representatives Assn. Newsletter), Yr. Est. 1960, Bi-monthly, Trim Size-8½ x 11, Sheetfed press, 6 pages, No Color, Newsprint
Acquistions: Publication Bought
Circulation: Total-430
Advertising: Inquire for rates.
List Rental: Rents Lists
Printing Co: Shoreline Graphics, 7 Nippersink Blvd, Fox Lake, IL 60020-1413 Tel # (708) 587-4804

Tropical American
Cruising   *Business, Association*

Publishing Co: Sailaway Cruising Club, PO Box 473, Puerto Real, PR 00740-0473
Personnel: Publisher, Editor-J.A. Rogers
Editorial Description: Information for people planning a small boat cruise to the tropical Americas.
General Info: (Formerly Sailaway Crusing Report), Yr. Est. 1991, Quarterly, Trim Size-8½ x 11, Desktop press, 8 pages, ISSN: 107B-1404, Ind/Abs/Online: GEnie, 2 Color, Matte
Subscriptions: Free In Designated Area
Circulation: Readership-1,000
Advertising: Accepts Inserts.

The Typhooner

Publishing Co: The Typhooner, 23311 Country Road 88, Winters, CA 95694; Title Tel # (916) 662-3364
Personnel: Publisher-Noel Peattie
General Info: Yr. Est. 1994, Irregular, Trim Size-8 x 11, 6 pages, ISSN: 680-7586
Subscriptions: Free
Circulation: Total-150

BOOKS & BOOK TRADE

ABA Newswire   *Association*

Publishing Co: American Booksellers Assn., 828 S Broadway, Tarrytown, NY 10591-6600 Tel # (914) 591-2665; Title Tel # (914) 631-7800
Personnel: Editor-Gaye Quaranta
General Info: Yr. Est. 1973, Weekly, Trim Size-8½ x 11, 6 pages, No Color, Newsprint
Circulation: Total-7,000
List Rental: Rents Lists

ABAA Newsletter
See: ANTIQUES & ART GOODS

ADM Flash
See: ADVERTISING & MARKETING

ASJA Newsletter
See: JOURNALISM

Abbey Newsletter   *Business*

Publishing Co: Abbey Publications, 7105 Geneva Dr, Austin, TX 78723-1510; Title Tel # (512) 929-3992 Title Fax # (512) 929-3995
Personnel: Publisher, Editor-Ellen McCrady, Circ. Mgr.-Renee A. Knauth
Editorial Description: Focuses on bookbinding and conservation.
General Info: Yr. Est. 1975, 8x/yr., Sheetfed press, 16 pages, ISSN: 0276-8291, No Color
Subscriptions: Indv. $40, Inst. $49
Circulation: Total-1,243
List Rental: Rents Lists
Printing Co: Wind River Press, 3403 Andtree Blvd, Austin, TX 78724-2501 Tel # (512) 929-1664

Augsburg Fortress Book
Newsletter   *Consumer*

Publishing Co: Augsburg Fortress Publishers, PO Box 1209, 426 S. Fifth St., Minneapolis, MN 55440-1209 Fax # (612) 330-3215; Title Tel # (612) 330-3300
Personnel: Editor-Roderick Olson
Editorial Description: Reviews of religious books, and other trade books which are religion-oriented.
General Info: Yr. Est. 1944, Quarterly, Trim Size-8 x 10¾, Offset press, 12 pages, ISSN: 1043-352X, No Color
Circulation: Total-37,000

BIN   *Business*

Publishing Co: Walrus Press, The, 32 Trimountain Ave., Box 280, South Range, MI 49963; Title Tel # (906) 487-9522
Personnel: Publisher, Editor-Bryan R. Johnson
Editorial Description: News, reviews, & interest to rare book librarians, antiquarian booksellers, book collectors, and to those concerned with books, printing, the allied arts, and their history.
General Info: Yr. Est. 1973, Trim Size-8½ x 11, Sheetfed press, 16 pages, ISSN: 0145-3084, No Color, Matte, Saddle-stitched
Subscriptions: Indv. $20
Circulation: Total-700

Bam! Bam!
See: PERIODICAL INDUSTRY

Bank Street Bookstore
Bookmark   *Consumer*

Publishing Co: Bank Street Bookstore, Broadway at 112th Street, New York, NY 10025; Title Tel # (212) 678-1654
Editorial Description: Bookstore's newsletter of publications and events.
General Info: Monthly, Trim Size-8½ x 11, 4 pages, No Color, Matte

BiblioExport   *Business*

Publishing Co: Assn. for the Export of Canadian Books, 1 Nicholas St., #504, Ottawa, ON K1N 7B7 Canada; Title Tel # (613) 562-2324 Title Fax # (613) 562-2329
Personnel: Editor-Sue Stewart
Editorial Description: Provides Canadian publishers with information on AECB activities, export opportunities, intl. contacts & market research results.
General Info: (Formerly BooksExport/Livres Export), Yr. Est. 1987, Quarterly, Trim Size-8½ x 11, Offset press, 20 pages, ISSN: 1196-5363, 2 Color, Coated, Saddle-stitched
Subscriptions: Free
Circulation: (100% controlled), Total-1,200

Bibliofile

Publishing Co: Borders Book Shop, 11301 Rockville Pike, Kensington, MD 20895-1021
Editorial Description: Newsletter of the Borders Book Shop. It is designed to inform customers of events and activities the shop offers for adults and children, including readings, book talks, panel discussions and storytelling hours.
General Info: Yr. Est. 1990, Bi-monthly

Binders Bulletin

Publishing Co: Binding Industries of America, 70 E. Lake St., Chicago, IL 60601-5907; Title Tel # (312) 372-7606
Personnel: Editor-James Niesen

Black Literary Players   *Business, Association*

Publishing Co: Grace Publishing Company, Box 47, Rochester Hills, MI 48308; Title Tel # (810) 650-9450 Title Fax # (810) 650-9450
Personnel: Editor-Grace Adams
Editorial Description: Black Literary Players updates The Black Authors & Published Writers Directory. Contains industry news, views, and reviews.
General Info: Yr. Est. 1990, Monthly, Trim Size-8½ x 11, Desktop press, 6 pages, Matte
Subscriptions: Indv. $28
Circulation: Total-200
Advertising: Inquire for rates. Accepts Inserts.

Bloch's Book Bulletin

Publishing Co: Bloch Publishing Co., Inc., 37 W 26th St Fl 9, New York, NY 10010-1006; Title Tel # (212) 673-7910
Personnel: Editor-Solomon Kerstein
Editorial Description: Information on books pertaining to Judaica and Hebraica with listings on recent books of Jewish interest.
General Info: Yr. Est. 1929, Quarterly
Circulation: Total-18,000
Advertising: Inquire for rates.

Boletin Informativo
Newsletter   *Consumer, Scholarly*   CPM: $266

Publishing Co: Luz Bilingual Publishing, Inc., PO Box 571062, Tarzana, CA 91357-1062; Title Tel # (818) 907-1454
Personnel: Editor-Veronica Miranda
General Info: Yr. Est. 1993, Trim Size-5½ x 8½, Desktop press, 12 pages, No Color
Subscriptions: Free To Qualified Recipient
Circulation: (66% controlled), Total-1,500, International-500, Readership-1,500
Advertising: $400.

Book Gazette
See: LITERATURE & LINGUISTICS

Book Marketing Update   *Business, Association*   CPM: $116

Publishing Co: Open Horizons, PO Box 205, Fairfield, IA 52556-0205; Title Tel # (515) 472-6130 Title Fax # (515) 472-1560
Personnel: Publisher, Editor-John Kremer, Production Mgr.-Gail Berry, Adv. Dir.-Robert Sanny, Circ. Mgr., Promotion Dir.-Paula Fritchen
Editorial Description: Update of book marketing trends, ideas, sources & resources.
General Info: Yr. Est. 1986, Monthly, Trim Size-8½ x 11, Sheetfed press, 16 pages, ISSN: 0891-8813, 10% ads, 2 Color, Matte, Saddle-stitched
Subscriptions: Indv. $60, Inst. $60, Can. $75, For. $100, $6/copy
Circulation: Total-3,000
Advertising: $350. Accepts Inserts.
List Rental: List Management Co.: HR Direct, 508 N. Second Street, Fairfield, IA 52556-2464 Tel # (515) 472-7188, Fax # (515) 472-5729, Actives: 7,000, $90/M
Printing Co: Tribune Printing, 111 W Briggs Ave, Fairfield, IA 52556-2825

Book-of-the-Month Club
News   *Consumer*

Publishing Co: Book-of-the-Month Club, Inc., 1271 Avenue of the Americas, Bsmt 3, New York, NY 10020-1302; Title Tel # (212) 522-4200
Personnel: Editor-Ralph Thompson
Editorial Description: Reviews club selections and alternate selections.
General Info: Yr. Est. 1927, 15x/yr., Trim Size-7½ x 10½, Offset press, 32 pages
Circulation: Total-3,200,000
Advertising: Inquire for rates.

Book Newsletter & Catalog   *Business, Consumer*

Publishing Co: Sponsor-International Publishers Co., The, International Publishers Co., Inc., 239 W 23rd St Fl 5, New York, NY 10011-2302; Title Tel # (212) 366-9816 Title Fax # (212) 366-9820
Personnel: Editor-Betty Smith
Editorial Description: News of new books, reprints, promotion of IP Books, listings of IP books on print.
General Info: Yr. Est. 1962, Semi-annually, Trim Size-8 x 10, Sheetfed press, 4 pages, Color, Newsprint
Subscriptions: For. $2, Free To Qualified Recipient
Circulation: (96% controlled), Total-30,000, International-1,000, Readership-125,000

Book, The: Newsletter of the Program in the History of the Book in American Culture   *Association*

Publishing Co: American Antiquarian Society, 185 Salisbury St, Worcester, MA 01609-1636; Title Tel # (508) 755-5221 Title Fax # (508) 754-9069
Personnel: Editor-John B. Hench, Co-Editor-Robert A. Gross, Asst. Ed.-Caroline Sloat
Editorial Description: Newsletter of Program in the History of the Book in American Culture of the American Antiquarian Society.
General Info: Yr. Est. 1983, Tri-annually, Trim Size-8$\frac{1}{2}$ x 11, Offset press, 8 pages, ISSN: 0740-8439, No Color, Matte
Subscriptions: Free To Qualified Recipient
Circulation: (100% controlled), Total-2,200
List Rental: Actives $100/M
Printing Co: Image Press, 76 W Boylston St, West Boylston, MA 01583-1712 Tel # (508) 835-3579

Book Peddler/der Pakn-Treger   *Business*

Publishing Co: National Yiddish Book Center, PO Box 969, Amherst, MA 01004-0969; Title Tel # (413) 256-1241
Personnel: Editor-Aaron Lansky, Art Dir.-Glenn Ruga
Editorial Description: Activities of National Yiddish Book Center and world of Yiddish.
General Info: (Formerly Der Pakn-Treger), Yr. Est. 1981, Semi-annually, Trim Size-8.5 x 11, Web press, 56 pages, 4 Color, Coated, Saddle-stitched
Subscriptions: Indv. $36, Inst. $36
Circulation: Total-20,000
List Rental: List Management Co.: Names in the News-California, 1 Bush St Bsmt 3, San Francisco, CA 94104-4425 Tel # (415) 989-3350, Fax # (415) 433-7796
Printing Co: Cummings Printing Co., 4 Peters Brook Dr., P.O. Box 16495, Hooksett, NH 03106 Tel # (603) 625-6901, Fax # (603) 623-5132

Book Promotion Hotline
See: ADVERTISING & MARKETING

Book Publishing Report   *Business*

Publishing Co: Simba Information, Inc., 213 Danbury Rd. PO Box 7430, Wilton, CT 06897-7430 Parent Co.-Cowles Business Media, New York; Title Tel # (203) 834-0033 Title Fax # (203) 834-1771
Personnel: Publisher-Chris Elwell, Editor-Linda Kopp, Editorial Dir.-Clare Schoen, Assoc. Ed.-Patrick Quinn, Circ. Mgr.-Joyce Brigish, Mktg. Dir.-Michael Genaro
Editorial Description: Provides insight into the business of book publishing including the deals, market data, legal developments, technological issues, distribution, people and more.
General Info: (Formerly BP Report), Yr. Est. 1974, Weekly, Trim Size-8$\frac{1}{2}$ x 11, Offset press, 8 pages, ISSN: 0145-9457, Ind/Abs/Online: DIALOG, NewsNet, Predicasts, 1% ads
Subscriptions: Indv. $479, Can. $479, For. $529
Acquistions: Publication Bought, Publication Sold
List Rental: Rents Lists

Book Talk   CPM: $166

Publishing Co: New Mexico Book League, 8632 Horacio Pl. NE, Albuquerque, NM 87111-3218; Title Tel # (505) 299-8940 Title Fax # (505) 294-8032
Personnel: Editor-Carol Myers
Editorial Description: Articles and reviews relevant to the Southwest.
General Info: Yr. Est. 1972, 5x/yr., Trim Size-8$\frac{1}{2}$ x 11, Offset press, 12 pages, ISSN: 0145-627X, Ind/Abs/Online: Bk.Rev.In., No Color
Subscriptions: Indv. $15, $2/copy
Circulation: Total-600
Advertising: $100.

Bookbuilders of Washington   *Business*

Publishing Co: Bookbuilders of Washington, PO Box 23805, Washington, DC 20026-3805 Tel # (301) 769-3840
Personnel: Editor-Robert Elwood
Editorial Description: News and information to book publishers in Washington, DC.
General Info: Yr. Est. 1988, Monthly

Bookplates in the News   *Association*

Publishing Co: American Society of Bookplate Collectors & Designers, 605 N Stoneman Ave Apt F, Alhambra, CA 91801-1406; Title Tel # (213) 283-1936
Personnel: Editor-Audrey Spencer Arellanes
Editorial Description: Articles about contemporary and historical bookplates and artists. News of exhibitions, events, etc.
General Info: Yr. Est. 1970, Quarterly, Trim Size-8$\frac{1}{2}$ x 11, Mimeo press, 10 pages, ISSN: 0024-2574, No Color
Subscriptions: Indv. $25, For. $25, $5/copy
Circulation: (100% controlled), Total-200

Books About Birds   *Business, Consumer*

Publishing Co: Books About Birds, Box 150106, Kew Gardens, Jamaica, NY 11415-0106; Title Tel # (718) 544-3279
Personnel: Editor-Jessie Kitching
Editorial Description: Book reviews, bibliographies, news of ornithological books.
General Info: Yr. Est. 1974, 10x/yr., No Color
Subscriptions: Indv. $9, For. $12, $1/copy

Books to Build a New Society   *Consumer*

Publishing Co: New Society Publishers, 4527 Springfield Avenue, Philadelphia, PA 19143-3708; Title Tel # (215) 382-6543
Personnel: Publisher, Editor, Circ. Mgr., Production Mgr., Adv. Dir., Art Dir., Promotion Dir.-David Albert
Editorial Description: Catalog & newsletter of New Society Publishers, the nation's only publishing house promoting fundamental social change through nonviolent action. Lists books on peace, ecology & environment, feminism, Third World studies, worker self-management, etc.
General Info: Yr. Est. 1983, Semi-annually, Trim Size-11$\frac{1}{4}$ x 17, Web press, 12 pages, 2 Color, Newsprint
Subscriptions: Free
Circulation: Total-125,000
List Rental: Actives: 80, $30,000/M
Printing Co: Pizazz, 1070 Commercial St Ste 110, San Jose, CA 95112-1420 Tel # (408) 453-1144

Books of Wonder   *Consumer*

Publishing Co: Books of Wonder, 132 7th Avenue at 18th Street, New York, NY 10011-1803 Fax # (212) 989-1203; Title Tel # (212) 989-3270
Personnel: VP Pubs.-James Carey
Editorial Description: Newsletter and catalog of children's books. Includes schedules of readings, storytellings, author appearances, and special events at the three Books of Wonder stores.
General Info: Yr. Est. 1987, Monthly, Trim Size-8$\frac{1}{2}$ x 11, Sheetfed press, 6 pages, No Color, Matte, Saddle-stitched
Printing Co: Downtown Offset, 216 W. 18th St., New York, NY 10011 Tel # (212) 807-1930

Bookseller   *Business*   CPM: $80

Publishing Co: Bookseller, PO Box 8183, Ann Arbor, MI 48107-8183; Title Tel # (313) 930-0450 Title Fax # (313) 920-0450
Personnel: Publisher-C.A. Hough, Editor-R.L. Hough
Editorial Description: Advertising and editorial medium for out-of-print book dealers and book collectors.
General Info: Yr. Est. 1970, Bi-weekly, Trim Size-8$\frac{1}{2}$ x 14, Sheetfed press, 44 pages, Newsprint
Subscriptions: Indv. $36, Inst. $36, Can. $40, For. $84, $2/copy
Acquistions: Publication Bought
Circulation: Total-1,500
Advertising: $120. Accepts Inserts.
List Rental: Actives: 6,000, $85/M

Bookviews   *Consumer*

Publishing Co: Bookviews, 9 Brookside Rd, Maplewood, NJ 07040-1201 Parent Co.-Caruba Organization, The, Maplewood; Title Tel # (201) 763-6392
Personnel: Editor-Alan Caruba
Editorial Description: Provides information to broadcast and print media to encourage coverage of books. Books on cassette, calenders, atlases, fiction and non-fiction
General Info: Yr. Est. 1990, Monthly, Trim Size-8$\frac{1}{2}$ x 14, 3 pages
Subscriptions: Free
Circulation: Readership-50,000

Bookwatch, The   *Business, Consumer*   CPM: $10

Publishing Co: Midwest Book Review, 12424 Mill Street, Petaluma, CA 94952; Title Tel # (415) 587-7009
Personnel: Editor-Diane Donovan
Editorial Description: Capsule reviews the best of large & small press pubs.
General Info: (Formerly Midwest Bookwatch), Yr. Est. 1980, Monthly, Web press, 12 pages, ISSN: 0896-4521, Color, Newsprint
Subscriptions: Indv. $12, $2/copy
Circulation: Total-50,000
Advertising: $504. Accepts Inserts.

Bookwoman   *Association*

Publishing Co: Women's National Book Association, 160 Fifth Ave., New York, NY 10010-7000 Tel # (212) 675-7805; Title Tel # (212) 675-7804
Personnel: Editor-LaVonne Taylor Pickell
Editorial Description: News about women in the book world. Also reviews women's books.
General Info: Yr. Est. 1936, Tri-annually, Trim Size-8$\frac{1}{2}$ x 11, Offset press, 16 pages, ISSN: 0163-1128, No Color, Newsprint, Saddle-stitched
Subscriptions: Indv. $10
Acquistions: Publication Bought
Circulation: Total-1,000
Advertising: Accepts Inserts.
List Rental: Rents Lists

Both Angles

Publishing Co: Random House, 201 E. 50th St., New York, NY 10022-7799 Tel # (212) 572-2855 Fax # (212) 572-4949
General Info: Yr. Est. 1971, Quarterly

Brief Chronicles
See: THEATRE

CBC Features
See: CHILDREN

Canadian Bookbinders & Book Artists Guild Newsletter

Publishing Co: Canadian Bookbinders & Book Artists Guild, 35 McCaul St., #221, Toronto, ON M5T 1V7 Canada; Title Tel # (416) 581-1071
Personnel: Circ. Mgr.-Ellen Spears, Editor, Adv. Dir., Art Dir.-Richard Miller, Promotion Dir.-Iona McCraith
Editorial Description: Vehicle for disseminating current news, opinions, and opportunities in the book arts. Book-binding, box-making, paper-making, paper decorating, fine printing and calligraphy are examined. Also covers collecting, conservation and restoration.
General Info: Yr. Est. 1983, Quarterly, Trim Size-5¹/₂ x 8¹/₂, Sheetfed press, 32 pages, ISSN: 0822-9538, 1% ads, No Color, Saddle-stitched
Subscriptions: Indv. $35, Inst. $55, Can. $35, For. $45, $5/copy
Circulation: Total-500

Children's Book Insider *Consumer*

Publishing Co: Children's Book Insider, PO Box 1030, Fairplay, CO 80440-1030; Title Tel # (719) 836-0394
Personnel: Publisher-Laura Backes, Mng. Editor-Jon Bard
Editorial Description: Features Children's writers and illustrators.
General Info: Yr. Est. 1990, Monthly, Trim Size-8¹/₂ x 11, 8 pages, ISSN: 1073-7596, No Color, Matte
Subscriptions: Indv. $33, Can. $38, $3/copy

Children's Book News
See: CHILDREN

Children's Writer *Consumer*

Publishing Co: Children's Writer, 95 Long Ridge Rd., West Redding, CT 06896-1124 Parent Co.-Institute, Inc., W. Redding; Title Tel # (203) 792-8600 Title Fax # (203) 792-8406
Personnel: Publisher-Prescott Kelly, Editor-Susan Tierney
Editorial Description: Devoted exclusively to the writing and publishing of children's literature.
General Info: Yr. Est. 1991, Monthly, Sheetfed press, 12 pages, ISSN: 1060-5274
Subscriptions: Indv. $24
Circulation: (3% controlled), Total-35,000, Subscriptions-33,700, Readership-35,000

Christian Communicator
See: RELIGIOUS & THEOLOGICAL

Computer Committee Newsletter

Publishing Co: Association of American University Presses, Inc., 584 Broadway Rm 410, New York, NY 10012-3264; Title Tel # (212) 941-6610
Personnel: Editor-Charles Creasy
Editorial Description: For reports on computer assisted publishing, especially in relation to university presses.
General Info: Yr. Est. 1987, Monthly, Trim Size-8¹/₂ x 11, 8 pages, No Color, Matte

Contrary Opinion Basic Books *Business*

Publishing Co: Fraser Management Associates, PO Box 494, Burlington, VT 05402-0494; Title Tel # (802) 658-0322 Title Fax # (802) 658-0260
Personnel: Editor-James L. Fraser
Editorial Description: Acquaints readers with the body of literature of especial interest to them. Intended as a book newsletter as well as catalog of books - not all readily available in normal book outlets.
General Info: (Formerly Contrary Opinion Library), Yr. Est. 1962, Annually, Offset press
Circulation: Total-30,000
List Rental: Rents Lists

Cookbook Review, The *Consumer*

Publishing Co: The Cookbook Review, 60 Kinnaird St, Cambridge, MA 02139-3128; Title Tel # (617) 868-8857
Personnel: Publisher, Editor-Lise Stern, Adv. Dir.-Lauren Byrne
Editorial Description: In-depth reviews of cookbooks; includes selected recipes.
General Info: Yr. Est. 1992, Bi-monthly, Trim Size-8¹/₂ x 11, 12 pages, ISSN: 1060-7765
Subscriptions: Indv. $24, Inst. $37

Copy Editor Newsletter
See: JOURNALISM

Directory Digest *Business*

Publishing Co: Directory Digest, 1713 Cedar Park Rd., Annapolis, MD 21401-3251
Personnel: Publisher-Michael Taliaferro
Editorial Description: Practical information and advice for directory and information publishers.
General Info: Yr. Est. 1995, Monthly, Trim Size-8¹/₂ x 11, 10 pages, 2 Color
Subscriptions: Indv. $195

Directory Strategies *Business, Association* CPM: $391

Publishing Co: Directory Publishing Resources, Box 19107, George Mason Sta., Alexandria, VA 22320; Title Tel # (703) 329-8206 Title Fax # (703) 960-9618
Personnel: Publisher, Editor-Dianne Johansson-Adams
Editorial Description: For mid and upper level directory professionals: directory profiles, how-to info, exploration of issues affecting directory publishers.
General Info: Yr. Est. 1991, 9x/yr., Trim Size-8¹/₂ x 11, Sheetfed press, 12 pages, No Color
Subscriptions: Indv. $99, $12/copy
Circulation: Total-3,000
Advertising: $1,175. Accepts Inserts.
Printing Co: Eco-Print, 9335 Fraser Ave, Silver Spring, MD 20910-1228 Tel # (301) 585-7077

Dollmasters, The
See: ANTIQUES & ART GOODS

ERIC/CRESS Bulletin
See: EDUCATION

Emerald City Mirror
See: CHILDREN

Exchange *Association*

Publishing Co: Association of American University Presses, Inc., 584 Broadway Rm 410, New York, NY 10012-3264; Title Tel # (212) 941-6610
Personnel: Editor-Hollis Holmes
Editorial Description: Contains articles of interest to scholarly publishers , particularly university presses.
General Info: Yr. Est. 1964, Quarterly
Subscriptions: Indv. $10, Inst. $10, For. $15, Free With Membership
Circulation: Total-2,500
List Rental: Rents Lists

Fiction Digest *Consumer*

Publishing Co: Amcan Inc., 187 Vanderbilt Ave., Ste. 3, Brooklyn, NY 11205-3305; Title Tel # (718) 643-2988 Title Fax # (718) 797-9403
Personnel: Publisher-Piotr Jagninski, Editor-Tom Jagninski
Editorial Description: A review of new novels, giving a book's 5w's- Who, What, Where, When, Why? It is distributed by postal and e-mail to bookstores, libraries, newspapers, radio and TV.
General Info: Yr. Est. 1994, Bi-weekly, Trim Size-8¹/₂ x 11, Desktop press, 8 pages, ISSN: 1078-9723, No Color, Matte
Subscriptions: Inst. $250

Fillers for Publications
See: JOURNALISM

First Impressions *Business, Association*

Publishing Co: Sponsor-Graduate School of Library Svce., University of Alabama, Box 870252, Tuscaloosa, AL 35403-1609; Title Tel # (205) 348-4610
Personnel: Editor, Circ. Mgr.-Paula Gourley
Editorial Description: Newsletter of The Institute for the Book Arts.
General Info: Yr. Est. 1984, Annually, Trim Size-7 x 8¹/₂, 12 pages
Subscriptions: Free
Circulation: Total-2,500

Flower Essence Society Newsletter
See: HEALTH

Folio: First Day
See: PERIODICAL INDUSTRY

Forum *Business, Association*

Publishing Co: Directory Publishers' Forum Northeast, 21 Greenhouse Ln, Poughkeepsie, NY 12603-3634; Title Tel # (914) 473-3719 Title Fax # (914) 473-3719
Personnel: Publisher/President/Advisor-Barry Lee, Editor-Audrey Bird
Editorial Description: Covers Directory Publishers' Forum activities and developments of interest to directory publishing professionals.
General Info: Yr. Est. 1990, Monthly, Trim Size-8¹/₂ x 11, Desktop press, 4 pages, No Color
Subscriptions: Free With Membership
Advertising: Accepts Inserts.
Printing Co: Data-Matic Systems Co., 150 S Front St, Souderton, PA 18964-1599 Tel # (215) 723-8500, Fax # (215) 721-4740

The Freelancer
See: JOURNALISM

Frommer's Travel Book Club Tips & Travel
See: TRAVEL

Globe Corner Bookstore
See: TRAVEL

Guild of Book Workers-Newsletter
See: PRINTING/GRAPHIC ARTS

Hard Row to Hoe
See: CULTURE & HUMANITIES

Heartland Critiques
See: ROMANCE

Helen Hecker's Hotline -
Marketing Strategies for
Publishers &
Entrepreneur's   *Business*

Publishing Co: Twin Peaks Press, PO Box 129, Vancouver, WA 98666-0129;
   Title Tel # (360) 694-2462 Title Fax # (360) 696-3210
Editorial Description: For small to medium size book, audio,video,cd rom and software publishers.
General Info: Yr. Est. 1993, Bi-monthly, 1% ads
Subscriptions: Free To Qualified Recipient
Circulation: Total-35,000
Advertising: Inquire for rates. Accepts Inserts.
List Rental: Actives: 27,000, $90/M

Hot News   *Business*

Publishing Co: Barricade Books, 150 Fifth Ave., Ste. 700, New York, NY 10011-4311;
   Title Tel # (212) 627-7000 Title Fax # (212) 627-7028
Personnel: Editor-Lyle Stuart
Editorial Description: News and information about the book publishing industry.
General Info: Yr. Est. 1981, Monthly
Subscriptions: Free To Qualified Recipient

How to Be Your Own
Publisher Update

Publishing Co: Prosperity & Profits Unlimited, PO Box 416, Denver, CO 80201-0416;
   Title Tel # (303) 575-5676
Personnel: Publisher-A. Doyle
Editorial Description: How to on publishing and possibilities.
General Info: Yr. Est. 1986, 10 pages, ISSN: 0738-7415
Subscriptions: Indv. $7, Inst. $7, Can. $9, For. $11, $7/copy
Circulation: (98% controlled), Total-2,000
Advertising: Inquire for rates.

Huenefeld Report, The   *Business*

Publishing Co: Huenefeld Company, The, 41 North Rd., Ste. 201, Bedford, MA 01730
Personnel: Publisher-John Huenefeld
Editorial Description: Covers new trends, techniques and ideas for manager of small to midsize book publishing houses.
General Info: Yr. Est. 1973, Bi-weekly
Subscriptions: Indv. $88

ISIS Forum   *Business, Association*

Publishing Co: ISIS, 21 Greenhouse Ln., Poughkeepsie, NY 12603-3634; Title Tel # (914) 473-3719
   Title Fax # (914) 473-3717
Personnel: Publisher, Editor-Barry Lee
General Info: Yr. Est. 1994, Monthly, Trim Size-8½ x 11, Desktop press, 8 pages, Matte
Subscriptions: Free With Membership
Advertising: Accepts Inserts.

Illustrator Collector's News, The
See: COLLECTIBLES

Illustrator Magazine & Paper Collector's News
See: COLLECTIBLES

Illustratotor's Swap incl JW Anglund Collectors News
See: CHILDREN

Independent Publishers
Trade Report   *Business*

Publishing Co: Greenfield Press, PO Box 176, Southport, CT 06490-0176;
   Title Tel # (203) 332-7629
Personnel: Publisher, Editor-Henry Berry
Editorial Description: News items and reports of interest to independent publishers.
General Info: Yr. Est. 1988, Monthly, 4 pages
Subscriptions: Indv. $48
Circulation: Total-2,000
Printing Co: Brew Printing Co., 53 Hancock St, Stratford, CT 06497-6204 Tel # (203) 375-5861

Information Standards Quarterly
See: BIBLIOGRAPHY

Jewish Book World   *Business, Consumer*

Publishing Co: JWB Jewish Book Council, 15 E. 26th St., New York, NY 10010-1505;
   Title Tel # (212) 532-4949
Personnel: Publisher-Paula Gribetz Gottlieb, Editor-Amy Gottlieb, Adv. Dir.-Elain Rosenberg, Art Dir.-Kalmon Shironi
Editorial Description: Information about Jewish books.
General Info: Tri-annually, Trim Size-8½ x 11, Sheetfed press, 28 pages, 3% ads, No Color, Matte, Saddle-stitched
Subscriptions: Indv. $20
Circulation: Total-3,500

Joan Walsh Anglund Collector's News
See: CHILDREN

Kobrin Letter, The
See: CHILDREN

Koob Stra   *Consumer, Association*

Publishing Co: Center for Book Arts, 626 Broadway Fl 5, New York, NY 10012-2601;
   Title Tel # (212) 460-9768
Personnel: Publisher, Exec. Ed.-Brian Hannon
Editorial Description: Lists news on book arts and opportunities for book artists including exhibits, call-for-entries, etc.
General Info: (Formerly Book Arts Review), Yr. Est. 1992, Quarterly
Subscriptions: Indv. $35, Free With Membership
Acquistions: Publication Sold
Circulation: Total-1,000
Advertising: Accepts Inserts.
List Rental: Rents Lists

Laughing Bear Newsletter   *Business*

Publishing Co: Laughing Bear Press, PO Box 36159, Denver, CO 80236-0159;
   Title Tel # (303) 744-3624
Personnel: Editor-Tom Person
Editorial Description: Provides information on surviving as a publisher into the 21st century with how-to articles, reviews, & information on marketing, production, growing internationally, & cutting costs. Winner of the 1992 Small Press Magazine Newsletter Awards.
General Info: Yr. Est. 1976, Monthly, Trim Size-8½ x 11, Offset press, 3 pages, ISSN: 1056-0327, Ind/Abs/Online: Copyright Clearence Center, 10% ads, No Color, Matte, Other
Subscriptions: Indv. $12, Inst. $10, Can. $14, For. $22, $1/copy
Circulation: Total-150
Advertising: Inquire for rates. Accepts Inserts.

Legal Publisher, The
See: LAW

Library Notes
See: LIBRARY

Literary Sketches
See: LITERARY REVIEWS

MFE Collectors' Bookline   *Consumer, Association*

Publishing Co: MFE Collectors' Bookline, PO Box 150119, San Rafael, CA 94915-0119;
   Title Tel # (415) 457-5463
Personnel: Editor-David Brown
Editorial Description: For collectors of modern first editions and recent fiction.
General Info: Monthly, Trim Size-8½ x 11, 12 pages, No Color
Subscriptions: Indv. $195

Manuscript Society News
See: HOBBY

Mass Media Booknotes   *Business*

Publishing Co: Temple University, Anderson Hall #921, Philadelphia, PA 19122
   Tel # (215) 204-8505; Title Tel # (614) 292-8444 Title Fax # (614) 292-2055
Personnel: Editor-Dr. Christopher Sterling
Editorial Description: A mass media publications reporting service.
General Info: Yr. Est. 1969, Monthly, No Color
Subscriptions: Indv. $5

Mazda Publishers Book
News   *Business*

Publishing Co: Mazda Publishers, 3100 Airway Ave Ste 137, Costa Mesa, CA 92626-4604;
   Title Tel # (714) 751-5252
Personnel: Publisher-Ahmad Jabbari, Editor-Abbas Daneshvari
General Info: Yr. Est. 1988, Bi-monthly, Trim Size-8½ x 11, Sheetfed press, No Color, Newsprint

Miniature Book News

Publishing Co: Julian Edison, 16 Dromara Rd, Saint Louis, MO 63124-1880;
   Title Tel # (314) 567-3533
Personnel: Publisher, Editor-Julian I. Edison
General Info: Yr. Est. 1965, Quarterly, 8 pages, No Color
Subscriptions: Indv. $10, For. $13

Minnesota Center for
Book Arts

Publishing Co: Minnesota Center for Book Arts, 24 N 3rd St, Minneapolis, MN 55401-1612;
   Title Tel # (612) 338-3634 Title Fax # (612) 338-1562
Personnel: Editor-Loring Johnson
General Info: (Formerly MCBA), Yr. Est. 1985, Quarterly, 8 pages, 2 Color, Newsprint
Circulation: Total-4,000, Readership-10,000
Advertising: Inquire for rates.
List Rental: Rents Lists

Multicultural Publishing and Education Council Newsletter
Association

Publishing Co: Multicultural Publishing and Education Council, 2280 Grass Valley Hwy., #181, Auburn, CA 95603 Tel # (916) 889-4438 Fax # (916) 889-0690
Editorial Description: Promotes marketing and distribution of African American books.
General Info: (Formerly Multicultural Publishers Exchange), Yr. Est. 1989, Bi-monthly, Trim Size-8½ x 11, 10 pages, ISSN: 1049-5428
Subscriptions: Indv. $48, Inst. $48, Can. $54, $3/copy
Advertising: $250. Accepts Inserts.
List Rental: Actives: 20,000, $65/M

Multimedia Business Report
See: COMPUTERS & AUTOMATION

NFAIS Newsletter
See: LIBRARY

NYLA Bulletin
See: LIBRARY

Nook News Review of Writers' Publications
See: BIBLIOGRAPHY

Outlines, Synopses, Proposals that Sold
Business, Consumer

Publishing Co: Science Fiction & Fantasy Workshop, 1193 S 1900 E, Salt Lake City, UT 84108-1855; Title Tel # (801) 582-2090
Personnel: Publisher, Editor-Kathleen Woodbury
Editorial Description: Contains outlines, synopses, proposals by published authors that actually led to the sale and publicaton of their books.
General Info: Yr. Est. 1993, Quarterly, Trim Size-5½ x 8½, Offset press, 6 pages
Subscriptions: Indv. $9, $3/copy

PMA Newsletter
Business, Association   CPM: $137

Publishing Co: Publishers Marketing Association, 2401 Pacific Coast Hwy Ste 102, Hermosa Beach, CA 90254-2734; Title Tel # (310) 372-2732 Title Fax # (310) 374-3342
Personnel: Publisher, Editor-Jan Nathan, Copy Editor-Robin Quinn, Advertising & Sales-Rick Stoff
Editorial Description: Produced for those who are engaged in the independent book publishing world, presenting information on cost-effective marketing opportunities & educational information for publishers.
General Info: Yr. Est. 1983, Monthly, Trim Size-8⅜ x 10⅞, Sheetfed press, 32 pages, ISSN: 1058-4102, 5% ads, 2 Color, Matte, Saddle-stitched
Subscriptions: Indv. $40, Can. $60, For. $60, $4/copy
Circulation: Total-4,000
Advertising: $550.
List Rental: Actives: 4,000, $125/M
Printing Co: Challenge Graphics, 7245 Canby Ave, Reseda, CA 91335-3003 Tel # (818) 966-3222, Fax # (818) 705-3102

Pacific Currents
Consumer

Publishing Co: Pacific Book Auction Galleries, 139 Townsend St Ste 305, San Francisco, CA 94107-1922; Title Tel # (415) 896-2665 Title Fax # (415) 896-1664
Editorial Description: The Pacific Book Auction Galleries newsletter.
General Info: Quarterly

Practical Law Books Review

Publishing Co: Library Managemental Services, 5914 Highland Hills Dr, Austin, TX 78731-4057; Title Tel # (512) 454-7229
Personnel: Publisher, Editor, Adv. Dir.-Judith Helburn
Editorial Description: A quick reference to new legal publication by field of specialization. Abstractions of reviews found in Law Reviews & Journals.
General Info: Yr. Est. 1978, Quarterly, Offset press, 24 pages, ISSN: 0160-8177, Color-cover, Newsprint, Saddle-stitched
Subscriptions: Indv. $32, $5/copy
Circulation: Total-150
Printing Co: Ginny's Copying Service, 5541 N Lamar Blvd, Austin, TX 78751-1015 Tel # (512) 452-0617

Publishers' Monthly Domestic Sales

Publishing Co: Assn. of American Publishers, Inc., 71 Fifth Avenue, New York, NY 10003-3004 Tel # (212) 255-0200 Fax # (212) 255-7007; Title Tel # (202) 232-3335
Personnel: Editor-Thomas McKee
General Info: Monthly

Publisher's Report
Association, Business

Publishing Co: National Association of Independent Publishers, PO Box 430, Highland City, FL 33846-0430; Title Tel # (941) 648-4420 Title Fax # (941) 648-4420
Personnel: Publisher, Editor-Betsy Lampe
Editorial Description: Provides a information about small press publishing and support for those in the industry, especially self-publishers.
General Info: Yr. Est. 1985, Irregular, Trim Size-8½ x 11, Desktop press, 16 pages, ISSN: 0884-3090, No Color, Other, Other
Subscriptions: Can. $100, For. $100, $15/copy
Circulation: Total-500
Advertising: Inquire for rates. Accepts Inserts.

Publishing Poynters
Business

Publishing Co: Para Publishing, Box 8206-815, Santa Barbara, CA 93140-8206; Title Tel # (805) 968-7277 Title Fax # (805) 968-1379
Personnel: Publisher, Editor-Dan Poynter, Circ. Mgr.-Monique Tihanyi, Promotion Dir.-Pat Finn
Editorial Description: Book & information marketing news & ideas.
General Info: Yr. Est. 1986, Quarterly, Trim Size-8½ x 11, Web press, 2 pages, No Color, Matte
Subscriptions: Indv. $10, Can. $10, For. $10, $1/copy
Circulation: Total-13,000
Advertising: Accepts Inserts.
List Rental: List Management Co.: Manager: Jennifer Bond; Paralists, P.O. Box 8206-815, Santa Barbara, CA 93118-8206 Tel # (805) 968-7277, Fax # (805) 968-1379, Actives: 3,600, Hotline: 8,000
Printing Co: Kimberlt Press, 5390 Overpass Rd., Santa Barbara, CA 93110 Tel # (805) 964-6469

Pubwatch Update
Business

Publishing Co: Pubwatch, 350 W. 85th Street, New York, NY 10024; Title Tel # (212) 362-6572 Title Fax # (212) 580-1099
Editorial Description: Supports book culture and alliances with Central and Eastern Europe.
General Info: Yr. Est. 1990, Semi-annually, Trim Size-8½ x 11, 6 pages, No Color

RIF Newsletter
See: EDUCATION

Read, America!
See: EDUCATION

Reader's Review, The

Publishing Co: Reader's Review, The, 2966 Diamond Street, Suite #290, San Francisco, CA 94131; Title Tel # (415) 585-2639 Title Fax # (415) 337-2064
General Info: 35x/yr., 12 pages
Subscriptions: Indv. $200
Circulation: Total-61,000

Really, a Free Newsletter
Business

Publishing Co: Bold Productions, PO Box 152281, Arlington, TX 76015-8281
Personnel: Publisher-Mary Bold
Editorial Description: Covers desktop publishing, small press publishing, and marketing.
General Info: Quarterly, ISSN: 1070-2962
Subscriptions: Free

Reporter--Your Editorial Assistant
See: JOURNALISM

Round Table Review
See: PSYCHOLOGY

SHARP News
Association

Publishing Co: Society for the History of Authorship, Reading & Publishing, Drew University, History Department, Madison, NJ 07940; Title Tel # (201) 408-3545 Title Fax # (201) 408-3768
Personnel: Editor-Jonathan Rose, Bk. Rev. Ed.-Patrick Leary, Circ. Mgr.-Linda Connors
Editorial Description: Information for book and literary historians.
General Info: Yr. Est. 1991, Quarterly, Trim Size-8½ x 11, 12 pages, No Color, Matte
Subscriptions: Indv. $15, Inst. $15, Can. $15, For. $20, Free With Membership
Circulation: Total-900
List Rental: Rents Lists

SIMBA Report on Directory Publishing
See: PERIODICAL INDUSTRY

S.L.A. Marshall Military History Collection-Newsletter
See: MILITARY & NAVAL

SPAN Connection
Association   CPM: $100

Publishing Co: Small Publishers Association of North America, P.O. Box 1306, Buena Vista, CO 81211; Title Tel # (719) 395-4790 Title Fax # (719) 395-8374
Editorial Description: Articles and tips directed toward small publishers and self-publishers to educate them to produce better books and market them more effectively.
General Info: Yr. Est. 1996, Monthly, Trim Size-8½ x 11, 16 pages, ISSN: 1087-2949
Subscriptions: Inst. $75, Can. $95, $8/copy
Circulation: Total-5,000, Readership-15,000
Advertising: $500.
List Rental: Rents Lists

SPEX: Small Publishers Exchange
Association

Publishing Co: Marin Small Publishers Assoc., PO Box E, Corte Madera, CA 94976-0867 Tel # (815) 257-8275; Title Tel # (415) 257-8275
Personnel: Editor-Margaret S. Yuan
Editorial Description: Newsletter for small & self publishers. Presents resources, articles on the business of publishing, book reviews of books published by our members.
General Info: Yr. Est. 1979, Monthly, Trim Size-8½ x 11, Offset press, 12 pages, ISSN: 0730-2223, 2% ads, No Color, Matte, Saddle-stitched
Subscriptions: Indv. $20
Circulation: Total-350
Advertising: Inquire for rates. Accepts Inserts.

SSC Booknews   *Association*

Publishing Co: Spiritual Studies Center, PO Box 1104, Rockville, MD 20849-1104; Title Tel # (301) 963-9243
Personnel: Editor-Millard Nachtwey
Editorial Description: To bring to the attention of its readers those books we feel to be more definitive and scholarly than the regular newsstand offerings.
General Info: Yr. Est. 1974, Monthly, Trim Size-7 x 8½, Offset press, 12 pages, ISSN: 0730-2371, No Color
Circulation: (100% controlled), Total-3,000

Satin Sheets
See: ROMANCE

Self Publisher Newsletter   *Business, Consumer*

Publishing Co: Parnell Publishing Co., PO Box 16432, Phoenix, AZ 85011-6432 Fax # (602) 279-2358; Title Tel # (602) 279-2358
Personnel: Publisher-Shami Maxwell, Editor-Peter Weber, Adv. Dir.-Kathryn S. Maxwell
Editorial Description: Covers book production, pricing, marketing. A platform for established authors and those wanting to write. Welcomes letters, articles, tips and ideas to help the self-publisher.
General Info: Yr. Est. 1993, Bi-monthly, ISSN: 1060-5060
Subscriptions: Indv. $50
Advertising: Inquire for rates.
List Rental: Rents Lists

Self-Publisher's Business
Letter   *Business*

Publishing Co: Self-Publisher's Business Letter, PO Box 5234, Apache Junction, AZ 85278-5234 Tel # (602) 671-0046
Personnel: Publisher, Editor-Eve Paludan
Editorial Description: Articles by and for self-publishers and small press publishers.
General Info: Yr. Est. 1993, Monthly
Subscriptions: Indv. $36

Self Publishing Update -
How to Basics Edition   *Business, Association*

Publishing Co: Update Publicare Co, P O Box 416, Denver, CO 80201 Tel # (308) 577-5567; Title Tel # (303) 575-5676
Personnel: Editor-A. Doyle
Editorial Description: Ideas, tips, basics on self publishing.
General Info: Yr. Est. 1983, Irregular, Trim Size-8.5 x 11, 4 pages, ISSN: 0736-1882
Subscriptions: Indv. $6, Inst. $6, Can. $8, For. $10, $6/copy

Shortruns
See: PRINTING/GRAPHIC ARTS

Small Press Book Review   *Consumer*

Publishing Co: Greenfield Press, PO Box 176, Southport, CT 06490-0176; Title Tel # (203) 332-7629
Personnel: Publisher, Editor-Henry Berry, Lit. Ed.-Charles Agrent, Production Mgr.-Nancy Murcko
Editorial Description: Reviews of books published by small presses.
General Info: Yr. Est. 1985, Quarterly, ISSN: 8756-7202, 3% ads
Subscriptions: Free
Circulation: Total-3,000, Readership-10,000
Advertising: Inquire for rates.

Small Press Center News   *Consumer, Association*

Publishing Co: Small Press Center, 50 W. 44th St., New York, NY 10036-6604; Title Tel # (212) 764-7021
Personnel: Editor-Mary Bertschmann, Production-Tom Tolnay
Editorial Description: Covers events and issues of importance in the small press industry.
General Info: (Formerly Small Press Center Newsletter), Quarterly, Trim Size-8½ x 11, 8 pages, 2 Color, Matte
List Rental: Rents Lists

Soundview Executive Book Summaries
See: BUSINESS & INDUSTRY

Sports Book File   *Consumer*

Publishing Co: Barry Mandell- Writing and Publishing, 1069 Alexander Dr., Rotterdam Junction, NY 12150-9708; Title Tel # (518) 887-2768
Personnel: Editor-Barry Mandell
Editorial Description: Approximately 500 word synopsis of 20 seperate new sports books each issue. Interviews with authors of 10 other annotated titles.
General Info: (Formerly Sports Book Digest), Yr. Est. 1988, Bi-monthly, 8 pages
Subscriptions: Indv. $15, $3/copy

Subrights Letter   *Business*

Publishing Co: Intellectual Properties Council, Four High Ridge Park, Stamford, CT 06905
Editorial Description: Covers buying and selling of subsidiary rights.
General Info: Yr. Est. 1996, Semi-monthly, Trim Size-8½ x 11, 2 Color, Matte
Subscriptions: Indv. $239

Subtext

Publishing Co: Open Book Publishing, Inc., PO Box 2288, 90 Holmes Avenue, Darien, CT 06820; Title Tel # (203) 316-8008 Title Fax # (203) 975-8469
Personnel: Editor-Stephanie Oda, Editor-Glenn Saniflo
Editorial Description: A bi-weekly newsletter on the book business.
General Info: Yr. Est. 1995, Bi-weekly, Trim Size-8.5 x 11, Offset press, 22 pages, Color-cover, Newsprint, Other
Subscriptions: Indv. $308, Can. $358, For. $358
Printing Co: Goodway Printing, Stanford, CT

TARC Writers Report   *Consumer, Association*

Publishing Co: The Authors Resource Center, 4725 E Sunrise Dr # 219, Tucson, AZ 85718-4534; Title Tel # (520) 577-7751
Personnel: Editor-Martha Gore
Editorial Description: Seeks to help writers understand the business and professional realities of the publishing world. Includes list of manuscripts being sought by the TARC literary agent. Announces sponsored tours for writers.
General Info: Yr. Est. 1984, Bi-monthly
Subscriptions: Indv. $60, Inst. $60, Can. $70, For. $70

Tattered Cover   *Consumer*

Publishing Co: Tattered Cover Book Store, 1628 16th Street, Denver, CO 80202; Title Tel # (303) 322-7727 Title Fax # (303) 399-2279
Personnel: Adv. Dir.-Laura Snapp, Editor, Art Dir.-Patty Miller
Editorial Description: Brief synopses of new titles that are not likely to be bestsellers but offer fine literate entertainment for the discriminating reader.
General Info: Yr. Est. 1980, Semi-annually, Trim Size-8½ x 11, 32 pages, No Color, Matte, Saddle-stitched
Circulation: Total-85,000

Tools of the Trade: Books
for Communicators   *Business, Consumer*

Publishing Co: Tools of the Trade: Books for Communicators, PO Box 23556, Lexington, KY 40523-3556
General Info: Yr. Est. 1993, Trim Size-8½ x 11, 4 pages, 2 Color, Matte

Travel Books Worldwide
See: TRAVEL

USBBY   *Association*

Publishing Co: IRA, PO Box 8139, Newark, DE 19714-8139; Title Tel # (302) 731-1600
Personnel: Editor-Alice Swinger
Editorial Description: Articles, bibliographies, listings of international children's literature; and their translation.
General Info: Yr. Est. 1976, Semi-annually, Trim Size-8½ x 11, Offset press, 18 pages, No Color
Subscriptions: Indv. $25
Circulation: (100% controlled), Total-1,000

Umbrella
See: ART & SCULPTURE

What Is to Be Read

Publishing Co: Cooperative Economics News Service, 1736 Columbia Rd NW Apt 202, Washington, DC 20009-2846; Title Tel # (202) 387-1753
Personnel: Editor-Henry Leland
Editorial Description: Review of current trade & college textbooks reflecting heterodox points of view in economic & social theory & policy; also covers books on social science research methods, statistics, forecasting, & travel, tax & good writing guides.
General Info: Yr. Est. 1984, Bi-monthly, Trim Size-8½ x 11, Mimeo press, 25 pages, ISSN: 0896-6354, No Color, Looseleaf
Subscriptions: Indv. $25, For. $35, Free To Qualified Recipient
Circulation: (20% controlled), Subscriptions-2,000

Wiley Librarians'
Newsletter, The   *Consumer*

Publishing Co: John Wiley & Sons, Inc., 605 Third Avenue, New York, NY 10158-0012 Tel # (212) 850-6000; Title Tel # (212) 850-6291 Title Fax # (212) 850-6088
Personnel: Editor-Stacy Wax, Mktg. Dir.-Jacqueline Thompson
Editorial Description: Lists new professional, scientific and technical titles published by John Wiley & Sons.
General Info: Yr. Est. 1962, Quarterly, Trim Size-8½ x 11, Offset press, 50 pages, 2 Color, Matte, Saddle-stitched
Subscriptions: Free
Circulation: Total-29,000
List Rental: List Management Co.: American List Counsel, 88 Orchard Cir # Cn-5219, Princeton, NJ 08540-3026 Tel # (908) 874-4300, Fax # (908) 874-4433, Actives: 18,300, $75/M
Printing Co: Sowers Printing Co., N. 10th & Scull St., Box 479, Lebanon, PA 17042-0479 Tel # (717) 272-6667, Fax # (717) 276-2928

Worldwide Graphics
See: INTERNATIONAL TRADE

BOTANY

AABGA Newsletter
See: GARDENING & HORTICULTURE

ASPP Newsletter   *Association*

Publishing Co: American Society of Plant Physiologists, 15501 Monona Dr., Rockville, MD 20855-2768; Title Tel # (301) 251-0560 Title Fax # (301) 279-2996
Personnel: Publisher-M. Josephs, Editor-Melinda Carlson
Editorial Description: Contains assn. news on plant physiology.
General Info: Yr. Est. 1924, Bi-monthly, Trim Size-11.0 x 8.5, Offset press, 32 pages, No Color, Matte, Saddle-stitched
Subscriptions: Indv. $2
Circulation: Total-3,800
Advertising: Inquire for rates.
List Rental: Rents Lists
Printing Co: Jarboe Printing Co., 15 Oglethorpe St NW, Washington, DC 20011-2395 Tel # (202) 291-3800

American Bamboo Society-Newsletter
See: GARDENING & HORTICULTURE

Aquaphyte
See: SCIENCE

Assn. of Pacific Systematists Newsletter
See: BIOLOGY

Bibliography of Plant Protection

Publishing Co: Springer-Verlag Inc., 175 5th Ave., New York, NY 10010-7858 Tel # (212) 460-1500 Fax # (212) 473-6272; Title Tel # (212) 679-0782
General Info: Quarterly, ISSN: 0006-1387
Subscriptions: Inst. $216

Bishop Museum Bulletins in Botany

Publishing Co: Bishop Museum, 1525 Bernice St # 19000-A, Honolulu, HI 96817-2704; Title Tel # (808) 848-4135
General Info: ISSN: 0893-3138
Circulation: Total-300

Bulletin   *Association*

Publishing Co: Board of Trustees of Missouri Botanical Garden, PO Box 299, Saint Louis, MO 63166-0299; Title Tel # (314) 577-5123 Title Fax # (314) 577-9599
Personnel: Circ. Mgr.-Linda Raming, Editor, Production Mgr., Art Dir.-Susan Wooleyhan Caine
Editorial Description: Activities of Missouri botanical garden only. Contains articles, photos re: botany, nature, gardening, science education, organization's events. No unsolicited releases or editorial accepted.
General Info: Yr. Est. 1913, Bi-monthly, Trim Size-8½ x 11, 24 pages, ISSN: 0026-6507, 2 Color, Matte, Saddle-stitched
Subscriptions: $2/copy
Circulation: Total-30,000

Canadian Botanical Association Bulletin   *Association*

Publishing Co: Canadian Botanical Assn., Dept. of Botany, Univ. of Guelph, Guelph, ON N1G 2W1 Canada; Title Tel # (519) 824-4120
Personnel: Publisher, Editor-J.F. Gerrath
Editorial Description: Items of interest to Canadian botanists, as well as activities of the Association.
General Info: Yr. Est. 1967, Quarterly, Trim Size-8½ x 11, Desktop press, 12 pages, ISSN: 0008-3046, No Color, Recycled
Subscriptions: Indv. $45, Can. $45, Free With Membership
Circulation: Total-325
Advertising: Inquire for rates. Accepts Inserts.

Clippings
See: GARDENING & HORTICULTURE

Fiddlehead Forum
See: GARDENING & HORTICULTURE

Flower Essence Society Newsletter
See: HEALTH

Growing Native Newsletter
See: GARDENING & HORTICULTURE

Heather Notes   *Consumer, Association*

Publishing Co: North East Heather Society, Box 101, Highland View, Alstead, NH 03602-0101; Title Tel # (603) 835-6165
Personnel: Editor-Walter Wornick
Editorial Description: Promotes the advancement of knowledge of the several botanical genera of heaths and heathers.
General Info: (Formerly Heather News), Yr. Est. 1982, Quarterly, Letrpr. press, 4 pages, ISSN: 1041-6838
Subscriptions: Indv. $5, Can. $5, For. $5, $2/copy
Circulation: (80% controlled), Total-500, International-50
Advertising: Inquire for rates.
Printing Co: Village Printer, Bellows Falls, VT Tel # (802) 463-9697

Herbarium News

Publishing Co: Missouri Botanical Garden, PO Box 299, Saint Louis, MO 63166-0299 Fax # (314) 577-9594; Title Tel # (314) 577-9534
Personnel: Editor-James Solomon
General Info: Yr. Est. 1980, Monthly, Trim Size-8½ x 11, Desktop press, 8 pages, ISSN: 0731-7824, No Color
Subscriptions: Indv. $9, Inst. $16, Can. $9, For. $11
Circulation: Total-500

Morris Arboretum Newsletter

Publishing Co: Univ. of Pennsylvania, 9414 Meadowbrook Ave, Philadelphia, PA 19118-2624; Title Tel # (215) 247-5777
Personnel: Editor-Sally Baldwin
Editorial Description: Newsletter of moffis Arboretum of the University of Pennsylvania.
General Info: Quarterly, 8 pages, 2 Color
Subscriptions: Indv. $15
Acquistions: Publication Bought
Circulation: Total-3,850

NEWFSletter   *Association*

Publishing Co: New England Wild Flower Society, 180 Hemenway Rd., Framingham, MA 01701-2699; Title Tel # (508) 877-7630 Title Fax # (508) 877-3658
Editorial Description: Contains information about native plants, botany, conservation, horticulture.
General Info: (Formerly Newsletter), Yr. Est. 1965, 4x/yr., Trim Size-8½ x 11, 2 Color, Recycled
Subscriptions: Indv. $35
Circulation: Total-5,000
Printing Co: Bay State, 2 Watson Pl, Framingham, MA 01701-4109 Tel # (508) 877-0116

Newsleaf   *Association*

Publishing Co: Univ. of Wisconsin, 1207 Seminole Hwy, Madison, WI 53711-3726; Title Tel # (608) 263-7888
Personnel: Editor-William Jordan, III
Editorial Description: News items, announcements, & features, management research, other research, events at arboretum.
General Info: Yr. Est. 1987, Monthly, Trim Size-7 x 10, Offset press, 4 pages, No Color
Subscriptions: Indv. $15
Circulation: (100% controlled)

Phycological Newsletter   *Consumer*

Publishing Co: Phycological Society of America, Dept. Biological Sciences, 1036 W. Belden - DePaul Univ., Chicago, IL 60614; Title Tel # (312) 362-8171 Title Fax # (312) 362-5689
Personnel: Editor-M. Dennis Hanisak
Editorial Description: Botany-biology with emphasis on algae.
General Info: Yr. Est. 1965, Trim Size-8½ x 11, 12 pages, No Color
Circulation: Total-1,200

Phytochemical Bulletin   *Association*

Publishing Co: Botanical Society of America, University of Kansas, RL McGregor Herbarium, Lawrence, KS 66047
Editorial Description: Articles relating to phytochemistry and botany.
General Info: ISSN: 0898-3437

Phytopathology News   *Association*

Publishing Co: American Phytopathological Society, 3340 Pilot Knob Rd, St. Paul, MN 55121-2055; Title Tel # (612) 454-7250 Title Fax # (612) 454-0766
Personnel: Publisher-Steven C. Nelson, Editor-C. Lee Campbell, Circ. Mgr.-Larry Hartman, Production Mgr.-Miles Wimer
Editorial Description: Organization news.
General Info: Yr. Est. 1967, Monthly, Trim Size-8½ x 11, Sheetfed press, 16 pages, ISSN: 0278-0267, No Color, Newsprint
Subscriptions: Indv. $15
Circulation: Total-4,220
Advertising: Inquire for rates.

Phytophthora Newsletter   *Association*

Publishing Co: Univ. of Wisconsin, Dept. of Plant Pathology, 1630 Linden Dr, Madison, WI 53706-1520
Editorial Description: Reports on studies of fungus and its affects.

Plant Cell

Publishing Co: American Society of Plant Physiologists, 15501 Monona Dr., Rockville, MD 20855-2768 Tel # (301) 251-0560; Title Fax # (301) 279-2996
Personnel: Editor-Robert Goldberg
Editorial Description: Scientific papers describing research on plant growth & development. Regulation of gene expression, plant-microbe interactions, & molecular aspects of plant cell organization & function.
General Info: Yr. Est. 1989, 100 pages, ISSN: 1040-4651, 4 Color, Coated
Subscriptions: Indv. $100, $50/copy
Circulation: Total-4,500

Plant Cell Reports
Consumer

Publishing Co: Springer-Verlag Inc., 175 5th Ave., New York, NY 10010-7858; Title Tel # (212) 460-1500 Title Fax # (212) 473-6272
Personnel: Publisher-J. Von Hagen, Editor-K. Hahlbrock, Production Mgr.-J. Mickelbank, Adv. Dir.-J. Foder, Circ. Mgr., Promotion Dir.-C. Deno
Editorial Description: Covers plant cell structure research.
General Info: Yr. Est. 1981, Monthly, ISSN: 0721-7714, Ind/Abs/Online: BIO. ABS. , CHEM. ABS. , PLANT BRED. ABS.
Subscriptions: Indv. $584, $18/copy

Plant Pathology Circular, Entomology Arcular, Hematology Arcular, Botany Circular
Business, Association

Publishing Co: Florida Department of Agriculture & Consumer Services, PO Box 147100 m, Gainesville, FL 32614-7100 Tel # (904) 372-3505 Fax # (904) 955-2301
Editorial Description: Covers current research & developments of interest in the area of plant pathology, entomology mematology, and botany.
General Info: (Formerly Plant Pathology Circular), Yr. Est. 1962, Bi-monthly, Trim Size-8½ x 11, 2 pages, ISSN: 0032-0870
Circulation: Total-1,000

Plant Science Bulletin
Association

Publishing Co: Sponsor-Botanical Society of America, Botanical Society of America, University of Kansas, RL McGregor Herbarium, Lawrence, KS 66407; Title Tel # (913) 864-5298
Personnel: Editor-Meredith Lane
Editorial Description: Short articles dealing with matters of interest especially to academic botanists.
General Info: Yr. Est. 1955, Quarterly, Trim Size-8½ x 11½, Offset press, 12 pages, ISSN: 0032-0919, No Color
Circulation: Total-3,000

Plants & Gardens News
See: GARDENING & HORTICULTURE

Soil-Plant Analyst
Consumer, Association

Publishing Co: Soil and Plant Analysis Council, Univ. Sta., Box 2007, Athens, GA 30612-0007; Title Tel # (706) 546-0425 Title Fax # (706) 548-4891
Personnel: Editor-J. Benton Jones, Jr.
Editorial Description: Promotes uniform soil test & plant analysis method, use, interpretation & terminology.
General Info: Yr. Est. 1970, Quarterly, Trim Size-5½ x 8½, Desktop press, 4 pages, 3% ads, 2 Color, Newsprint, Saddle-stitched
Subscriptions: Indv. $40, Inst. $150
Circulation: (100% controlled), Total-350
Advertising: Inquire for rates.
List Rental: Rents Lists

Tomato Club, The
See: GARDENING & HORTICULTURE

Tri-Ology Technical Report
See: BIOLOGY

Watergardening News
See: GARDENING & HORTICULTURE

Wood Duck
See: NATURAL HISTORY

BRIDE

ABC Dialogue
Consumer, Association   **CPM: $176**

Publishing Co: Association of Bridal Consultants, 200 Chestnut Land Rd, New Milford, CT 06776-2521; Title Tel # (203) 355-0464 Title Fax # (203) 354-1404
Personnel: Publisher, Editor-Gerard Monaghan
Editorial Description: Information related to bridal/wedding business; general business news and information about members.
General Info: (Formerly American Association of Professional Bridal Consultants), Yr. Est. 1981, Bi-monthly, Trim Size-8½ x 11, Offset press, 20 pages, ISSN: 10539107, 40% ads, No Color, Matte
Subscriptions: Indv. $24, Free With Membership
Circulation: Total-1,700
Advertising: $300. Accepts Inserts.
List Rental: Actives: 1,550, $100/M, Hotline: 4,000, $80/M, Expires: 200, $50/M
Printing Co: Oakwood Associates, 72 Newton Road, Unit 6 Suite 138, Danbury, CT 06810 Tel # (860) 354-4637, Fax # (860) 350-9435

Abstract of Marital Relationship Analysis
See: PSYCHOLOGY

Bridal Collectors News
Business, Association

Publishing Co: Bridal Collectors News, PO Box 105, Amherst, NH 03031-0105 Tel # (603) 673-1885
Personnel: Publisher-Ann Bergin
Editorial Description: For collectors of books, dolls, plates-anyitems related to brides, weddings, bridal cakes, bridal flowers etc, for wedding historians, ephemera collectors and stiguette specialists
General Info: Yr. Est. 1993, Annually, Trim Size-8.5 x 11, 6 pages
Subscriptions: Indv. $10
Circulation: Readership-100
Advertising: Accepts Inserts.

Northeastern Limousine Operators Association Nor'Easter Newsletter
See: TRAFFIC & TRANSPORTATION

BROADCASTING

AFBA Transmitter
Association

Publishing Co: Armed Forces Broadcasters Assn., 10888 La Tuna Canyon Rd #, Carnes, Sun Valley, CA 91352-2009; Title Tel # (202) 433-6069
Personnel: Editor-Robert Bubniak
General Info: Yr. Est. 1982, Quarterly
Subscriptions: Indv. $20

AM Journal
Business, Consumer

Publishing Co: Dajja Enterprises, PO Box 24, Cambridge, WI 53523-0024 Tel # (608) 423-4159 Fax # (608) 423-4355
Personnel: Publisher, Editor-Mike Knitter
Editorial Description: Listings of all broadcast stations in the US and Canada. Includes transmitter site coordinates, studi address network affiliation, antenna height, and more.
General Info: Yr. Est. 1990, Semi-annually, Trim Size-8½ x 11, 300 pages, ISSN: 1068-0322, 2 Color, Looseleaf
Subscriptions: Indv. $17
Circulation: Total-500

ANARC Newsletter
Association

Publishing Co: Assn. of North American Radio Clubs, 2216 Burkey Drive, Wyomissing, PA 19610-1553 Tel # (610) 678-0937 Fax # (341) 921-6096; Title Tel # (213) 961-8202
Personnel: Editor-Rich D'Angelo, Publisher, Circ. Mgr.-Bill Kurrasch
Editorial Description: News of member clubs, radio activities, news of radio meetings world-wide.
General Info: Yr. Est. 1964, Quarterly, Trim Size-8½ x 11, Sheetfed press, 10 pages, 4 Color, Matte, Saddle-stitched
Subscriptions: Indv. $10, Can. $10, For. $10, $2/copy
Advertising: Inquire for rates.

AWRT News and Views
Business, Association

Publishing Co: American Women in Radio, 1650 Tysons Blvd Ste 200, Mc Lean, VA 22102-3915
Personnel: Editor-Chris Murphy
Editorial Description: Covers AWRT local, regional, and national meetings and other activities.
General Info: 8x/yr., Trim Size-8½ x 11, 10 pages, 2 Color
Subscriptions: Indv. $70
Circulation: Total-3,000
Advertising: Inquire for rates.

Ad News
See: ADVERTISING & MARKETING

Associated Press Broadcasters Association News

Publishing Co: Associated Press Broadcast Services, 1825 K St NW Ste 615, Washington, DC 20006-1202; Title Tel # (202) 955-7261
General Info: Monthly

BDA Update
See: PRINTING/GRAPHIC ARTS

Better Radio and Television
Association

Publishing Co: Natl. Assn. for Better Broadcasting, 1100 Graynold Avenue, Glendale, CA 91202-2019
Editorial Description: Reports, reprints and opinions of interest to broadcast consumers - viewers. Emphasis on violence, television for children, media access.
General Info: Yr. Est. 1960, Quarterly, Trim Size-8½ x 11, Offset press, 8 pages, ISSN: 0006-0194, No Color
Subscriptions: $2/copy
Circulation: Total-2,000

Broadband Networking News
Business

Publishing Co: Phillips Business Information, Inc., 1201 Seven Locks Rd., Ste 300, Potomac, MD 20854-2958 Tel # (301) 340-1520; Title Tel # (301) 340-2100 Title Fax # (301) 424-4297
Personnel: Publisher-Chris Scotton, Editor-Patricia Brown, Production Mgr.-Teresa Lowry, Circ. Mgr., Mktg. Dir.-Ruth Zellers
Editorial Description: An Executive report on the emerging broadband technologies of ATM, B-ISDN, SMDS, frame relay and T-3. Each issue includes comprehensive product comparisons, news on standards progress and marketplace news on advanced high capacity data communications services.
General Info: (Formerly US Telecommunications), Yr. Est. 1991, Bi-weekly, Trim Size-8½ x 11, 8 pages, ISSN: 1059-0544, Ind/Abs/Online: NEWSNET, PREDICASTS
Subscriptions: Indv. $597, Inst. $497, Can. $597, For. $630, $25/copy
Advertising: Accepts Inserts.
List Rental: Rents Lists

Broadcast Investor — *Business*

Publishing Co: Paul Kagan Associates Inc., 126 Clock Tower Pl., Carmel, CA 93923-8746; Title Tel # (408) 624-1536 Title Fax # (408) 625-3225
Personnel: Publisher-Paul Kagan, Circ. Mgr.-Judith Pinney, Adv. Dir.-Johanne Hardy
Editorial Description: Investments in private radio/TV stations and public broadcast companies.
General Info: Yr. Est. 1975, Monthly, Trim Size-7¼ x 10, Other press, 10 pages, ISSN: 0146-0110, No Color, Other, Saddle-stitched
Subscriptions: Indv. $795
Advertising: $1,560.

Broadcast Investor Charts — *Business*

Publishing Co: Paul Kagan Associates Inc., 126 Clock Tower Pl., Carmel, CA 93923-8746; Title Tel # (408) 624-1536 Title Fax # (408) 625-3225
Personnel: Publisher, Editor-Paul Kagan, Circ. Mgr.-Judith Pinney, Adv. Dir.-Johanne Hardy
Editorial Description: Chart service showing stock price movements of 42 publicly held broadcast companies for the past 2 years.
General Info: Yr. Est. 1983, Monthly, Trim Size-7¼ x 10, Other press, 10 pages, ISSN: 0736-9069, No Color, Other, Saddle-stitched
Subscriptions: Indv. $450
Advertising: Inquire for rates.

Broadcast Pioneers Library Reports

Publishing Co: Library, The, 1771 N St. , N. W., Washington, DC 20036-2898; Title Tel # (202) 223-0088
General Info: Yr. Est. 1985, Quarterly

Broadcast Stats — *Business*

Publishing Co: Paul Kagan Associates Inc., 126 Clock Tower Pl., Carmel, CA 93923-8746; Title Tel # (408) 624-1536 Title Fax # (408) 625-3225
Personnel: Publisher-Paul Kagan, Circ. Mgr.-Judith Pinney, Adv. Dir.-Johanne Hardy
Editorial Description: Radio & TV market billings revenues, and station sales.
General Info: Yr. Est. 1984, Monthly, Trim Size-7¼ x 10, Other press, 12 pages, ISSN: 0749-2936, Other, Saddle-stitched
Subscriptions: Indv. $625
Advertising: $1,560.

Broadcasting & Cable's TV International — *Business*

Publishing Co: Baskerville Communications, 2455 Teller Rd, Newbury Park, CA 91320-2218 Fax # (805) 499-0871 Parent Co.-SAGE Publication, Inc., Thousand Oaks; Title Tel # (805) 499-0721
Editorial Description: Covers events and news in bradcasting/tv industries.
General Info: Yr. Est. 1994, Bi-weekly
Advertising: Inquire for rates.

Broadcasting and the Law — *Business*

Publishing Co: Broadcasting and the Law Inc., 1 SE 3rd Ave Ste 1450, Miami, FL 33131-1715; Title Tel # (305) 576-4743 Title Fax # (305) 576-7980
General Info: Yr. Est. 1970, 26x/yr.
Subscriptions: Indv. $120

Cable Re-Regulation Handbook
See: TELEVISION & VIDEO

Cable TV Law Reporter — *Business*

Publishing Co: Paul Kagan Associates Inc., 126 Clock Tower Pl., Carmel, CA 93923-8746; Title Tel # (408) 624-1536 Title Fax # (408) 625-3225
Personnel: Publisher-Paul Kagan, Circ. Mgr.-Judith Pinney, Adv. Dir.-Johanne Hardy
Editorial Description: Cable legal cases; antitrust, copyright, taxation, franchising, first amendment.
General Info: Yr. Est. 1984, Monthly, Trim Size-7¼ x 10, Other press, 12 pages, ISSN: 0749-7652, No Color, Other, Saddle-stitched
Subscriptions: Indv. $695
Advertising: $1,560.

Cable TV and New Media Law & Finance
See: TELECOMMUNICATIONS

Cable Theft Newsletter

Publishing Co: Schreff, 9 Frontier Rd, Cos Cob, CT 06807-1208; Title Tel # (312) 432-5583
Personnel: Publisher, Editor-Don Skybridge
General Info: Yr. Est. 1985, Monthly
Subscriptions: Indv. $72

Calendar — *Association*

Publishing Co: International Amateur Radio Union, Box AAA, Newington, CT 06107-0901; Title Tel # (203) 666-1541
Editorial Description: Newsletter for the union members, concerning the development and promotion of amateur radio around the world.
General Info: Yr. Est. 1925, Quarterly, Offset press, 10 pages
Circulation: Total-250

Canadian FundRaiser — *Business* — CPM: $627

Publishing Co: Hilborn Group Ltd., The, 109 Vanderhoof Ave., Ste. 200, Toronto, ON M4G 2H7 Canada; Title Tel # (416) 696-8146 Title Fax # (416) 424-3016
Personnel: Bk. Rev. Ed.-Maggie Leighead, Circ. Mgr., Production Mgr.-Les Mortimer, Editorial Page Ed., Adv. Dir.-Maggie Leithead, Publisher, Editor, Mktg. Dir.-James Hilborn
Editorial Description: News and developments affecting fundraising in Canada.
General Info: (Formerly Canadian Professional Fundraiser), Yr. Est. 1991, 30x/yr., Trim Size-8½ x 11, Desktop press, 13 pages, ISSN: 1183-8957, No Color, Recycled, Other
Subscriptions: Indv. $187, Can. $187, For. $187, $10/copy
Circulation: Total-1,275
Advertising: $800. Accepts Inserts.
List Rental: Actives: 9,000, $160/M

Celebrity Bulletin Newsletter — *Consumer*

Publishing Co: Celebrity Service Intl., 1780 Broadway Ste 300, New York, NY 10019-1414; Title Tel # (212) 757-7979 Title Fax # (212) 397-4626
Personnel: Publisher-Vicki Bagley, Editor-Bill Murray
Editorial Description: We let our subscribers know how to reach celebrities & their agents.
General Info: Yr. Est. 1939, Daily
Subscriptions: Indv. $1,650

Chats — *Business, Association*

Publishing Co: Natl. Assn. of Farm Broadcasters, 26 Exchange St E Ste 307, Saint Paul, MN 55101-2264; Title Tel # (612) 224-0508 Title Fax # (612) 224-1956
Editorial Description: For those who broadcast farm news.
General Info: Monthly
Advertising: Inquire for rates.

Communications Business & Finance — *Business*

Publishing Co: BRP (Washington DC), 1333 H St., NW, Suite 1100, West Tower, Washington, DC 20005-4707; Title Tel # (202) 842-3006 Title Fax # (202) 842-3047
Personnel: Publisher-Andrew Jacobson, Editor-Victoria Mason, Circ. Mgr.-Ellen Hartman, Mktg. Dir.-Adam Goldstein
Editorial Description: Tracks financial, investment, business, and cross-industry merger activity in the communications industries.
General Info: Yr. Est. 1994, Bi-weekly, Trim Size-8½ x 11, 18 pages
Subscriptions: Indv. $547, Inst. $547, Can. $547, For. $585, $35/copy

Community Antenna Television Assn., Inc.

Publishing Co: Community Antenna Television Assn., PO Box 1005, Fairfax, VA 22030-1005; Title Tel # (703) 691-8875
Personnel: Editor-Stephen Effros
Editorial Description: An assn. representing 2,000 systems serving 12,000,000 subscribers.
General Info: Yr. Est. 1973, Monthly

Community Radio News — *Business, Association* — CPM: $333

Publishing Co: National Federation of Community Broadcasting, 666 11th St NW Ste 805, Washington, DC 20001-4542; Title Tel # (202) 393-2355
Personnel: Editor-Lynn Chadwick, Production Mgr.-Charmaine Peters
Editorial Description: Contains a calendar of events, information on public broadcasting, NFCB, & membership. Also includes job openings & a program clearinghouse.
General Info: Yr. Est. 1976, Monthly, Trim Size-8½ x 11, Desktop press, 16 pages, No Color, Saddle-stitched
Subscriptions: Indv. $75, Inst. $75, $2/copy
Circulation: Total-450
Advertising: $150.
List Rental: Rents Lists
Printing Co: Paragraphics, 16479 Frederick Rd, Woodbine, MD 21797-8515

Connecticut Broadcasters Association Newsletter — *Association*

Publishing Co: Sponsor-Conn. Broadcasters Assn., Connecticut Broadcasters Assn., 101 Tall Timbers Ln, Glastonbury, CT 06033-3339; Title Tel # (203) 633-5031
Editorial Description: Minutes of board meetings, news of meetings, broadcast legislation.
General Info: (Formerly CBA Voice), Yr. Est. 1955, Monthly, Trim Size-8½ x 11, Offset press, 4 pages, 2 Color, Newsprint
Circulation: Total-125

DX Monitor — *Association*

Publishing Co: Intl. Radio Club of America, 6059 Essex St, Riverside, CA 92504-1544; Title Tel # (714) 687-5910
Personnel: Publisher-Ralph Sanserino, Editor, Circ. Mgr.-Donald Erickson
Editorial Description: For the broadcast band listener; emphasis on listings of members individual DX catches.
General Info: Yr. Est. 1964, 34x/yr., Trim Size-5½ x 8½, Sheetfed press, 24 pages, ISSN: 0899-9732, Color-cover, Saddle-stitched
Subscriptions: Indv. $27, Can. $29, For. $31, $1/copy
Circulation: Total-400

Dispatcher
See: FIRE PROTECTION

Dr. Free's Radio Remedies
See: COLLEGE STUDENT

Education Reporter
See: JOURNALISM

Emerging Media Report
See: MEDIA & COMMUNICATIONS

Euro Cable TV Programming
See: TELEVISION & VIDEO

European Radio   *Business*

Publishing Co: Kagan World Media Inc., 126 Clock Tower Pl., Carmel, CA 93923-8734 Parent Co.-Paul Kagan Associates Inc., Carmel; Title Tel # (408) 624-1536 Title Fax # (408) 625-3225
Personnel: Publisher-Paul Kagan, Circ. Mgr.-Judy Pinney, Adv. Dir.-Johanne Hardy
Editorial Description: Information on regulatory changes, advertiser spending, station launches, and more.
General Info: Yr. Est. 1989, Monthly, Trim Size-7$\frac{1}{4}$ x 10, Other press, 10 pages, Other, Saddle-stitched
Subscriptions: Indv. $595
Advertising: $1,560.

European Television
See: TELEVISION & VIDEO

FMedia!   *Business, Consumer*

Publishing Co: FM Atlas Publishing, PO Box 336, Esko, MN 55733-0336 Fax # (218) 879-8333; Title Tel # (218) 879-7676 Title Fax # (918) 879-8333
Personnel: Publisher, Editor-Bruce Elving
Editorial Description: Facts & opinions about FM radio and related technologies for the professional and hobbyist. List new stations and translator grants, new call letter assignations, format changes and deletions.
General Info: Yr. Est. 1987, Monthly, Trim Size-8$\frac{1}{2}$ x 11, 8 pages, ISSN: 0890-6718, 2 Color
Subscriptions: Indv. $26, Inst. $65, $5/copy
Circulation: Total-300

Fiction Digest
See: BOOKS & BOOK TRADE

Film Technology News
See: FILM

High Speed Networking Newsletter
See: COMPUTERS & AUTOMATION

IRTS News   *Business, Association*

Publishing Co: International Radio & Television Society, 420 Lexington Ave Rm 1714, New York, NY 10170-1799; Title Tel # (212) 867-6650
Personnel: Editor-Joyce Tudryn
Editorial Description: Covers activities of this broadcasting assn.
General Info: Quarterly, Letrpr. press, 7 pages, 2 Color, Newsprint
Circulation: (100% controlled), Total-2,000
Printing Co: Atwater Press, 207 W. 25th, New York, NY 10001 Tel # (212) 675-2710

Inside Radio   *Business*

Publishing Co: Inside Radio Inc., 1930 Marlton Pike E Ste S93, Cherry Hill, NJ 08003-4208; Title Tel # (609) 424-6800 Title Fax # (609) 424-2301
Personnel: Publisher-Jerry Del Colliano, Editor-Steve Butler
Editorial Description: Radio industry executives' newsletter covering the hot news & trends in ratings & sales.
General Info: Yr. Est. 1975, Daily, Trim Size-8$\frac{1}{2}$ x 14, Desktop press, 3 pages
Subscriptions: Indv. $325, Can. $255, $5/copy
Circulation: Total-5,500
Advertising: Inquire for rates.

It's Only A Movie
See: ENTERTAINMENT

Jack Benny Times
See: FAN MAGAZINES-MOVIE, RADIO, TV

Journal, The   *Consumer, Scholarly*

Publishing Co: North American Shortwave Association, 45 Wild Flower Road, Levittown, PA 19057; Title Tel # (610) 678-0937 Title Fax # (610) 921-6096
Personnel: Editor-Harold Cones, Feature Ed.-Hans Johnson, Bk. Rev. Ed.-Skip Arey, Publisher, Circ. Mgr.-Bill Oliver, Production Mgr.-Ralph Brandi
General Info: Yr. Est. 1960, Monthly, Trim Size-5$\frac{1}{2}$ x 8$\frac{1}{2}$, 64 pages, ISSN: 0160-1989, Matte, Saddle-stitched
Subscriptions: Indv. $26, Can. $26, For. $32, $3/copy
Circulation: Total-1,700, Readership-1,700

M Street Journal   *Business*

Publishing Co: M Street Corp., PO Box 1479, Madison, TN 37116-5312; Title Tel # (615) 865-1525 Title Fax # (615) 865-2598
Personnel: Publisher-Robert Unmacht, Editor-Pat McCrommen
Editorial Description: Weekly FCC Broadcast actions, station format changes & general broadcast news. Yearly directory of US & Canadian stations included with subscription.
General Info: Yr. Est. 1984, Weekly, Trim Size-8$\frac{1}{2}$ x 11, Sheetfed press, 8 pages, ISSN: 1052-7109, 2 Color, Newsprint
Subscriptions: Indv. $119, Can. $150, For. $200, $3/copy
Acquistions: Publication Bought, Publication Sold
Circulation: Total-900
Advertising: Inquire for rates. Accepts Inserts.
List Rental: Actives: $50/M

Media and the Law   *Business*

Publishing Co: Simba Information, Inc., 213 Danbury Rd. PO Box 7430, Wilton, CT 06897-7430 Tel # (203) 834-0033 Fax # (203) 834-1771 Parent Co.-Cowles Business Media, New York; Title Tel # (413) 628-3376 Title Fax # (413) 628-4647
Personnel: Publisher-Timothy Cole, Publisher-Chris Elwell, Editor in Chief-Robert Nylen, Production Mgr.-Hillary Veeder, Art Dir.-Douglas Kelly, Mktg. Dir.-Michael Genaro
Editorial Description: An insider's guide to the legal challenges that face all news media-print, grodcast and new media.
General Info: Yr. Est. 1992, Bi-weekly, Trim Size-8$\frac{1}{2}$ x 11, 8 pages, ISSN: 1065-965X, No Color
Subscriptions: Indv. $357, Inst. $357, For. $357, $25/copy
Circulation: Total-220
List Rental: Rents Lists
Printing Co: Success Printing, 10 Pearl Street, Norwalk, CT 06850 Tel # (203) 847-1112, Fax # (203) 846-2770

Media Matters
See: MEDIA & COMMUNICATIONS

NAPBC Newsletter

Publishing Co: Native American Public Broadcasting Consortium, Inc., 1800 N 33rd St # 83111, Lincoln, NE 68503-1409; Title Tel # (402) 472-3522
Personnel: Editor-Matthew Jones
General Info: Yr. Est. 1981, Quarterly, 4 pages
Circulation: Total-1,100

NATAS News
See: TELEVISION & VIDEO

National Friends of Public Broadcasting Newsletter

Publishing Co: Natl. Friends of Public Broadcasting, 620 Folcroft Ct, Indianapolis, IN 46234-2103; Title Tel # (317) 271-8404
Personnel: Editor-Sally Ouweneel
General Info: Yr. Est. 1977, Quarterly, Letrpr. press, 6 pages, 2 Color
Circulation: (100% controlled), Total-550

Ohio Network Notes   *Consumer*

Publishing Co: Ohio Educational Broadcasting Network Commission, 2470 N Star Rd, Columbus, OH 43221-3405; Title Tel # (614) 644-1714
Personnel: Editor, Circ. Mgr.-Cynthia Tinapple
Editorial Description: News & activities of Ohio's 40 public TV & radio stations & radio reading services.
General Info: Yr. Est. 1969, Bi-monthly, Trim Size-8$\frac{1}{2}$ x 11, Offset press, 4 pages, Color
Circulation: (100% controlled), Total-5,000

Ollie, The   *Business*

Publishing Co: Hollywood Radio & Television Society, 13701 Riverside Dr Ste 205, Sherman Oaks, CA 91423-2447; Title Tel # (818) 789-1182 Title Fax # (818) 789-1210
Personnel: Editor-Gene Herd
Editorial Description: To provide a forum for the exchange of ideas for persons professionally engaged in radio & TV broadcasting and its allied fields.
General Info: (Formerly Spike), Quarterly, Desktop press, 6 pages
Subscriptions: Indv. $95, Free With Membership

One to One, the Journal of Creative Broadcasting   *Business*

Publishing Co: CreeYadio Services, PO Box 9787, Fresno, CA 93794-9787; Title Tel # (209) 226-0558 Title Fax # (209) 226-7481
Personnel: Publisher, Editor-Jay Trachman, Circ. Mgr.-Debbie Marcus
Editorial Description: Topical & current humor, information, & tips for broadcast personalities, day to day calendars of history, events & activities.
General Info: (Formerly Fruitbowl), Yr. Est. 1976, Weekly, Trim Size-8$\frac{1}{2}$ x 11, Offset press, 16 pages, Ind/Abs/Online: CompuServe, No Color
Subscriptions: Indv. $150, Can. $175, For. $185, $5/copy
Circulation: Total-3,000
Advertising: Inquire for rates.

Private Cable Investor   *Business*

Publishing Co: Paul Kagan Associates Inc., 126 Clock Tower Pl., Carmel, CA 93923-8746; Title Tel # (408) 624-1536 Title Fax # (408) 625-3225
Personnel: Publisher-Paul Kagan, Circ. Mgr.-Judith Pinney, Adv. Dir.-Johanne Hardy
Editorial Description: The economic, technical, marketing & legal issues affecting SMATV, valuations of SMATV system sales; census of various SMATV offerings.
General Info: (Formerly SMATV New; Pay TV Sports), Yr. Est. 1982, Monthly, Trim Size-7$\frac{1}{4}$ x 10, Other press, 10 pages, ISSN: 0734-5399, No Color, Other, Saddle-stitched
Subscriptions: Indv. $625
Advertising: Inquire for rates.

Promotional Programming   *Business*

Publishing Co: TVC Enterprises, PO Box 1088, Easton, MA 02334-1088; Title Tel # (508) 238-1179
Personnel: Publisher-Stephen Albert, Editor-Diane Albert
Editorial Description: Published for radio station personnel at stations which have 'Oldies' shows. Aimed toward programming directors & disc jockeys.
General Info: Yr. Est. 1989, Monthly, Trim Size-8$\frac{1}{2}$ x 11, 10 pages, No Color, Matte
Subscriptions: Indv. $100, Can. $110, For. $120, $10/copy

RAB Instant Background   *Business, Association*

Publishing Co: Radio Advertising Bureau, 304 Park Ave S, New York, NY 10010-5312;
Title Tel # (212) 681-7200
Personnel: Editor-Kenneth Costa, Production Mgr.-Chuck Shepard, Art Dir.-Ruth Friedman
Editorial Description: Provides marketing information on radio clients & their products. 50 categories per issue.
General Info: Yr. Est. 1967, Semi-annually, Trim Size-8½ x 11, 110 pages, Color-cover, Saddle-stitched, Looseleaf
Subscriptions: $10/copy
Circulation: Total-6,000

RTNDA Weekly   *Association*

Publishing Co: Radio Television News Directors Assn., 1000 Connecticut Ave NW Ste, 615, Washington, DC 20036-5302; Title Tel # (202) 659-6510 Title Fax # (202) 223-4007
Personnel: Editor-Jane Rulon
Editorial Description: Publication for electronic journalists.
General Info: Weekly, Desktop press, 4 pages, ISSN: 0743-6319
Subscriptions: Free With Membership
Circulation: Total-3,600
List Rental: Rents Lists

Radio Business Report   *Business*

Publishing Co: Radio Business Report, 3208B Old Franconia Rd, Alexandria, VA 22310
Tel # (703) 719-9500 Fax # (703) 719-7910; Title Tel # (703) 866-9300 Title Fax # (703) 866-9306
Personnel: Publisher-James Carnegie, Editor-Jim Carnegie, Circ. Mgr.-Cathy Carnegie
Editorial Description: Business issues, inside news on people, and company controversies.
General Info: Yr. Est. 1983, Semi-monthly, Trim Size-11 x 8, Web press, 24 pages, ISSN: 0741-8469, 2% ads, 4 Color, Saddle-stitched
Subscriptions: Indv. $195, Inst. $186
Circulation: (100% controlled), Total-5,000
Advertising: Inquire for rates.
List Rental: Rents Lists
Printing Co: Newsletter Services, Inc., 9700 Philadelphia Court, Lanham, MD 20706
Tel # (301) 731-5200, Fax # (301) 731-5201

Radio Campaigns and Copy Service   *Business*

Publishing Co: National Research Bureau, 150 N. Wacher Drive, Chicago, IL 60601
Tel # (312) 541-0100 Fax # (312) 541-1492 Parent Co.-Reed Reference Publishing, New Providence; Title Tel # (319) 752-5415 Title Fax # (319) 752-3421
Personnel: Publisher-Michael Darnall, Editor-Teresa Levinson
Editorial Description: A sales, programming & copy service for radio broadcasters, consisting of tested case histories.
General Info: Yr. Est. 1936, Monthly, Trim Size-8½ x 11, 64 pages, Color-cover, Looseleaf
Subscriptions: Indv. $56, $56/copy
Circulation: Total-1,000

Radio Promotion Bulletin   *Business*

Publishing Co: Sullivan Company, PO Box 841002, Houston, TX 77284-1002 Tel # (713) 855-3475; Title Tel # (713) 855-2964 Title Fax # (713) 855-2964
Personnel: Publisher, Editor-Jon Sullivan, Circ. Dir.-Leslie Lawrence
Editorial Description: Ideas for innovative broadcasters.
General Info: Yr. Est. 1989, Monthly, Trim Size-8½ x 11, 8 pages, ISSN: 1044-985X, Matte
Subscriptions: Indv. $135, Can. $135, For. $145

Radio-TV Interview Report   *Business*

Publishing Co: Bradley Communications Corp., PO Box 1206, 135 East Plumstead, Lansdowne, PA 19050-8206; Title Tel # (610) 259-1070 Title Fax # (610) 284-3704
Personnel: Publisher, Editor-Lou Harrison, VP Mktng., Mktg. Dir.-Stephen Hall
Editorial Description: This is a source for finding authors and experts to interview about a wide variety of subjects. Advertising-based catalog of talk show guests--available to radio/TV stations only.
General Info: Yr. Est. 1986, Semi-monthly, Web press, 88 pages, 2 Color, Matte, Saddle-stitched
Circulation: Total-4,000
Advertising: Inquire for rates.
List Rental: Actives: $100/M

SBCA Report
See: TELEVISION & VIDEO

SPERDVAC Radiogram

Publishing Co: Society to Preserve & Encourage Radio Drama/Variety/Comedy, Box 1587, Hollywood, CA 90078; Title Tel # (213) 947-9800
Personnel: Editor-Mary Kallenberger, Promotion Dir.-Richard Glasband
General Info: Yr. Est. 1974, Monthly, 8 pages, No Color
Subscriptions: Indv. $15, $2/copy
Acquistions: Publication Bought
Circulation: Total-1,500
Advertising: Accepts Inserts.

SWL
See: HOBBY

Satellite News   *Business, Association*

Publishing Co: Phillips Business Information, Inc., 1201 Seven Locks Rd., Ste 300, Potomac, MD 20854-2958 Tel # (301) 340-1520 Fax # (301) 424-4297; Title Tel # (301) 340-2100 Title Fax # (301) 424-4247
Personnel: Publisher-Ellen Stuhlmann, Editor-Chris McConnell, Circ. Mgr.-Vanessa Henderson, Production Mgr.-William Wynne, Promotion Dir.-Mark Ziebarth
Editorial Description: Covers U.S. and international satellite telecommunications, broadcast video, data transmission & space coverage.
General Info: (Formerly DBS News), Yr. Est. 1977, Weekly, Trim Size-8½ x 11, Sheetfed press, 10 pages, ISSN: 0161-3448, Ind/Abs/Online: NewsNet, DIALOG, No Color
Subscriptions: Indv. $897, For. $960
Acquistions: Publication Bought, Publication Sold
Advertising: Accepts Inserts.
List Rental: Rents Lists

Small Market Radio Newsletter   *Business*

Publishing Co: Jay Mitchell Associates, Rte. 2, Box 1285, Fairfield, IA 52556-1285
Tel # (515) 472-4087
Personnel: Publisher, Editor-Jay Mitchell, Co-Editor-Bob Doll, Production Mgr.-Lori Morgan
General Info: Yr. Est. 1982, Weekly
Subscriptions: Indv. $109
Circulation: Total-650

Sound Thinking
See: MANAGEMENT

Sound Waves
See: HOBBY

Sports Industry News
See: SPORTS & SPORTING GOODS

TV Program Investor   *Business*

Publishing Co: Paul Kagan Associates Inc., 126 Clock Tower Pl., Carmel, CA 93923-8746; Title Tel # (408) 624-1536 Title Fax # (408) 625-3225
Personnel: Publisher-Paul Kagan, Circ. Mgr.-Judith Pinney, Adv. Dir.-Johanne Hardy
Editorial Description: Trends in TV program syndication, values of programs, public & private companies.
General Info: Yr. Est. 1985, Monthly, Trim Size-7¼ x 10, Other press, 12 pages, ISSN: 0885-2340, No Color, Other, Saddle-stitched
Subscriptions: Indv. $645
Advertising: $1,560.

TV Program Stats   *Business*

Publishing Co: Paul Kagan Associates Inc., 126 Clock Tower Pl., Carmel, CA 93923-8746; Title Tel # (408) 624-1536 Title Fax # (408) 625-3225
Personnel: Publisher-Paul Kagan, Circ. Mgr.-Judith Pinney, Adv. Dir.-Johanne Hardy
Editorial Description: Compilation of data on specific syndicated TV programs, episode license fees, cost deficits, market shares, TV household coverage.
General Info: Yr. Est. 1988, Monthly, Trim Size-7¼ x 10, Other press, 10 pages, ISSN: 1040-6123, No Color, Other, Saddle-stitched
Subscriptions: Indv. $595
Advertising: Inquire for rates.

Television & Radio Newsletter   *Business*

Publishing Co: Restivo Communications, 201 Elden St Ste 167, Herndon, VA 22070-4812
General Info: Yr. Est. 1988, Monthly, Desktop press, 12 pages, Coated
Subscriptions: Indv. $125, Can. $125
Circulation: Total-1,100

Totem Tabloid
See: CLUBS

Variety Deal Memo
See: FILM

Vermont ETV Program Guide
See: TELEVISION & VIDEO

Viewer & Listener
See: TELEVISION & VIDEO

Wireless Satellite & Broadcasting
See: TELECOMMUNICATIONS

BUSINESS & INDUSTRY

AACE Bonus Briefs
See: EDUCATION

AACE Careers Update
See: EDUCATION

ACCA News   *Association*

Publishing Co: American Corporate Counsel Assn., 1225 Connecticut Ave NW Ste, 302, Washington, DC 20036-2604; Title Tel # (202) 296-4522 Title Fax # (202) 331-7454
Personnel: Editor-Deeneen Stambone
General Info: Bi-monthly, Trim Size-8³⁄₈ x 11, 8 pages, 2 Color, Matte, Saddle-stitched
Printing Co: Fontana Lithograph, 3342 Bladensburg Rd, Brentwood, MD 20722-1802 Tel # (301) 927-3800

AFFI Letter
See: FOOD

AICPA Audit and Accounting Manual
See: ACCOUNTING

AICPA Professional Standards
See: ACCOUNTING

AICPA Technical Practice Aids
See: ACCOUNTING

AOI Business Viewpoint   CPM: $103

Publishing Co: Associated Oregon Industries, 1149 Court St., NE, PO Box 12519, Salem, OR 97309; Title Tel # (503) 588-0050 Title Fax # (503) 588-0052
Personnel: Publisher-Richard M. Butrick, Editor-Donna Lewis, Adv. Dir.-Brian Dunlevy
Editorial Description: Topics include government influence on business and how to comply with government regulations, laws, etc.
General Info: (Formerly AOI News Digest), Yr. Est. 1960, Bi-monthly, Trim Size-10¹⁄₂ x 15³⁄₄, Web press, 24 pages, 4 Color
Circulation: (1% controlled), Total-17,851, Subscriptions-17,500
Advertising: $1,850.
Printing Co: Eagle Web Press, P.O. Box 12008, Salem, OR 97305-1128 Tel # (503) 635-8811, Fax # (503) 635-8817

APEE Newsletter

Publishing Co: Association for Private Enterprise Education, Univ. Of Tenn., Martin, Martin, TN 38238-0001; Title Tel # (901) 587-7208
Personnel: Publisher-Tom Appleby, Editor-Fred Kiesner
General Info: (Formerly APEE Newsletter), 10 pages, No Color

APNY Newsletter
See: PHOTOGRAPHY

ASIS Dynamics   *Business, Association*

Publishing Co: American Society for Industrial Security, 1655 N. Fort Myer Dr., Ste. 1200, Arlington, VA 22209-3108 Fax # (703) 243-4954; Title Tel # (703) 522-5800
Personnel: Publisher-Mary Crawford, Editor-Karen Addis, Circ. Mgr.-Paul D'Addario, Production Mgr.-Suzanne Marshall, Adv. Dir.-Sandy Wade
Editorial Description: Information for and about members.
General Info: Bi-monthly, Trim Size-8¹⁄₄ x 11, Web press, 16 pages, Color-cover, Newsprint, Saddle-stitched
Circulation: (BPA), Total-25,000
Advertising: Inquire for rates.

A.T. Quarterly

Publishing Co: RESNA Technical Assistance Project, 1700 N. Moore St., Ste. 1540, Arlington, VA 22209 Tel # (703) 524-6686; Title Tel # (202) 857-1140
General Info: Quarterly

AWTAO Bulletin

Publishing Co: Association of Water Transportation Accounting Officers, Box 53, Bowling Green Sta., New York, NY 10004; Title Tel # (212) 264-1384
Editorial Description: Covers current Association news and industry developments.
General Info: Bi-monthly

Abstract of American Economic Trend Analysis
See: ECONOMICS

Abstract of American Industrial Trend Analysis   *Business, Association*

Publishing Co: Maxiplan Financial Club, Box 5255 Stn. C, 12687 52nd Ave., Montreal, PQ H1E 2H6 Canada Tel # (514) 648-2953
Personnel: Editor-Marcel Wistaff
Editorial Description: Covers winning strategies in business opportunities; productivity growth; marketing surveys; management perspectives and global operations: technology development.
General Info: Yr. Est. 1990, Quarterly
Subscriptions: Indv. $60, $25/copy

Academy of Management News
See: MANAGEMENT

Access

Publishing Co: United Communications Group, 11300 Rockville Pike, Ste. 1100, Rockville, MD 20852-3030 Tel # (301) 816-8950 Fax # (301) 816-8945; Title Tel # (301) 961-8700 Title Fax # (301) 961-8666
Personnel: Publisher, Editor-Dave Douglas
General Info: Yr. Est. 1987, Monthly
Subscriptions: Indv. $335
List Rental: Rents Lists

Accommodating Disabilities: Business Management Guide
See: DISABILITY

Accountants SEC Practice Manual
See: ACCOUNTING

Administrative Assistant
Adviser   *Business*

Publishing Co: Progressive Business Publications, 370 Technology Dr., #3019, Malverne, PA 19355-9863 Parent Co.-American Future Systems, Inc., Bryn Mawr; Title Tel # (610) 695-8600 Title Fax # (610) 647-8089
Personnel: Publisher-Edward M. Satell, Editor-Wancy L. March, Editorial Dir.-Stephen Meyer, Mktg. Dir.-Ed Moore
Editorial Description: Offers office professionals tactics for managing multiple priorities, improving job performance, organizing paperwork, planning events and making the most of technology.
General Info: Yr. Est. 1995, Bi-weekly, 8 pages
Subscriptions: Indv. $230
List Rental: List Management Co.: Mail Marketing, Inc., 171 Terrace St., Haworth, NJ 07641-1899 Tel # (201) 387-1023, Fax # (201) 387-2976

Administrative Assistant's Update
See: EMPLOYMENT

Advanced Coatings & Surface Technology
See: CHEMISTRY & CHEMICALS

Advertising Creativity Newsletter
See: ADVERTISING & MARKETING

Advertising Via
Telemarketing Script
Presentations Newsletter   *Business*

Publishing Co: Prosperity & Profits Unlimited, PO Box 416, Denver, CO 80201-0416; Title Tel # (303) 575-5676
Personnel: Publisher-A. Doyle
Editorial Description: Script presentations for various businesses.
General Info: Yr. Est. 1990, Every two years, Trim Size-8¹⁄₂ x 11
Subscriptions: Indv. $40, Inst. $40, Can. $43, For. $46, $40/copy
Circulation: Total-1,500

Agency Law Quarterly Real Estate Intelligence Report
See: REAL ESTATE

Aging America Resources
See: SENIOR CITIZENS

AgriBioScan
See: AGRICULTURAL SUPPLIES

Al Hanson's Economic
Newsletter   *Business*

Publishing Co: Al Hanson's Economic Newsletter, PO Box 9, Ottertail, MN 56571-0009; Title Tel # (218) 367-2404
Editorial Description: Economic trends of interest to businessmen and farmers.
General Info: Yr. Est. 1982, Monthly, Trim Size-11 x 17, 2 pages
Subscriptions: Indv. $40

Alabama Business   *Business*

Publishing Co: University of Alabama, CBER/Box 870221, Tuscaloosa, AL 35487; Title Tel # (205) 348-6191 Title Fax # (205) 348-2951
Personnel: Circ. Mgr.-Deborah Hamilton, Publisher, Editor, Production Mgr.-Annette Watters, Art Dir.-Sherry O'Brien
Editorial Description: Data on economic indicators including industry, construction, retail trade, finance and employment.
General Info: Yr. Est. 1930, Monthly, Trim Size-8¹⁄₂ x 11, Offset press, 4 pages, ISSN: 0002-4163, Color-cover, Matte
Subscriptions: Free In Designated Area
Circulation: Total-5,000
Printing Co: Drake Printing Co., 1925 6th St, Tuscaloosa, AL 35401-1722 Tel # (205) 472-3639

Alabama Development
News   *Association*

Publishing Co: Alabama Development Office, State Capital 401 Adams Ave., Montgomery, AL 36130-0001 Tel # (205) 242-0400 Fax # (205) 242-0486; Title Tel # (334) 242-0476
Personnel: Editor-Bebe Barefoot
General Info: Quarterly, Trim Size-8¹⁄₂ x 11, 16 pages, ISSN: 0889-7468, 4 Color, Coated, Saddle-stitched
Circulation: Total-15,000

Alabama Today
Business, Association

Publishing Co: Business Council of Alabama, PO Box 76, Montgomery, AL 36101-0076; Title Tel # (334) 834-6000
Personnel: Editor-Kathleen Healey
Editorial Description: A publication dedicated to discussing key state & federal issues as well as the activities of the Business Council of Alabama.
General Info: Yr. Est. 1985, Monthly, Trim Size-11 x 17, Desktop press, 8 pages, 4 Color, Matte, Other
Subscriptions: Free With Membership
Circulation: Total-6,200

Albert Advisor
See: INSURANCE

Alert
Business

Publishing Co: California Chamber of Commerce, 1201 K St Ste 1200, Sacramento, CA 95814-3923; Title Tel # (916) 444-6670
Personnel: Publisher-Kirk West, Exec. Ed.-Ann Amioka, Circ. Mgr., Art Dir.-Jan Harrison
Editorial Description: Report on state & federal legislation & regulations affecting business.
General Info: Yr. Est. 1922, 34x/yr., Trim Size-8½ x 11, Sheetfed press, 8 pages, ISSN: 0882-0929, 2 Color, Matte
Subscriptions: Indv. $50, $1/copy
Circulation: Total-13,000
Printing Co: Citadel Press, Inc., 3300 Business Dr, Sacramento, CA 95820-2171 Tel # (916) 732-2070, Fax # (916) 732-2070

Alert
Business

Publishing Co: General Services Admin., 18th and F Streets, Washington, DC 20406-0001; Title Tel # (202) 523-1200
Editorial Description: Provides information on selling to the federal government.
General Info: Bi-monthly

Alternative Energy Trends & Forecasts
See: ENERGY

American Textile Reporter

Publishing Co: International Society of Industrial Fabric Manufacturers, PO Box 1369, Kings Mountain, NC 28086-1369; Title Tel # (704) 861-2063
Editorial Description: For engineers, executives, technicians and salespersons in the yarn industry.
General Info: Yr. Est. 1974, Monthly

Antitrust Counseling and Litigation Techniques
See: LAW

Antitrust Counselor, The
See: LAW

Antitrust FOIA Log
See: LAW

Antitrust and Trade Regulation Report
See: LAW

Apparel Strategist
See: APPAREL & ACCESSORIES

Archivists Society of Alberta Newsletter
See: CULTURE & HUMANITIES

Arizona Business
Business

Publishing Co: Arizona State University, Center for Business Research, PO Box 874406, Tempe, AZ 85287-4406; Title Tel # (602) 965-3961 Title Fax # (602) 965-5458
Personnel: Editor-Nan Beams, Circ. Mgr.-Jeannine Paca
Editorial Description: Covers local economic, business trends in Arizona & the Phoenix MSA.
General Info: Yr. Est. 1951, Monthly, Trim Size-8½ x 11, Sheetfed press, 16 pages, ISSN: 0093-0717, Ind/Abs/Online: BPI, PAIS, MGT. CONT. , BPIA, 2 Color, Matte, Saddle-stitched
Subscriptions: Indv. $24, Can. $30, For. $30, $2/copy
Circulation: (30% controlled), Subscriptions-1,290
Printing Co: Vista Press, 411 Semini Drive, Tempe, AZ 85283 Tel # (602) 820-0910

Arizona's Economy
Business

Publishing Co: University of Arizona, 1052 North Highland Ave., Tucson, AZ 85721-0001 Tel # (602) 621-2484; Title Tel # (602) 626-2155
Personnel: Publications Director, Editor-Diana Hunter
Editorial Description: Focuses on business and economic topics as they relate to Arizona in particular; statistical data included.
General Info: Yr. Est. 1979, Quarterly, Trim Size-8½ x 11, Offset press, 20 pages, Matte, Saddle-stitched
Subscriptions: Can. $12, For. $12, Free In Designated Area
Circulation: Total-5,000

Arkansas Business Bulletin

Publishing Co: Univ. of Arkansas, College of Business Administration, Bureau of Business & Ec. Res., Fayetteville, AR 72701; Title Tel # (501) 575-4151
Editorial Description: Contains economic indicators, statistical reports, ports, and articles pertaining to Arkansas.
General Info: Quarterly

Art of Self Promotion, The
See: ADVERTISING & MARKETING

Asahi Shimbun Satellite Edition
See: INTERNATIONAL TRADE

Asian Economic News
See: INTERNATIONAL TRADE

Association of New Gay & Lesbian Entrepreneurs
See: GAY & LESBIAN INTEREST

Associations' Forum
Business, Association

Publishing Co: American Business Association, 292 Madison Ave., New York, NY 10017 Tel # (212) 949-5900 Fax # (212) 949-5910
Personnel: Editor-William Driscoll
Editorial Description: Contains business, professional, and law related articles.
General Info: Yr. Est. 1970, Quarterly, 2 Color, Perfect bound
Subscriptions: Indv. $10
Circulation: Total-15,000

Audit Bureau of Circulations

Publishing Co: International Federation of Audit Bureau of Circulations, 900 N. Meacham Road, Schaumburg, IL 60173-4968 Tel # (708) 605-0909 Fax # (708) 605-0483; Title Tel # (703) 605-0909 Title Fax # (708) 605-0783
Personnel: Editor-Colleen M. O'Grady
Editorial Description: The News Bulletin is published after Board of Director's Meeting to keep members and others informed about ABC rules, services and activities.

Australian Business News
Business, Association

Publishing Co: Australian Information Service, 630 5th Ave., New York, NY 10111-0110; Title Tel # (212) 245-4000
Personnel: Publisher-Tony Miller, Editor-Helen Ashton
Editorial Description: Round up of business news from Australia & US news with Australian links.
General Info: (Formerly Australia News RoundUp Bulletin; Business News from Australia), Yr. Est. 1979, Bi-weekly, Trim Size-8½ x 11, 4 pages
Circulation: Total-3,600
Advertising: Inquire for rates.
Printing Co: Meridien Design Group, 876 Park Ave # 4n, New York, NY 10021-1832

Authentication News
See: PACKAGING

Automated Payments Update
See: BANKING & FINANCE

Awed in Business
Business

Publishing Co: American Woman's Economic Development Co., 71 Vanderbilt Ave Fl 3, New York, NY 10169-0099; Title Tel # (212) 688-1900 Title Fax # (212) 688-2718
Editorial Description: For women in business.
General Info: (Formerly Woman Entrepreneur), Bi-monthly, 4 pages, 25% ads, 2 Color
Subscriptions: Indv. $33, Free With Membership
Circulation: Total-5,000
Advertising: Inquire for rates.

BBI Newsletter, The
See: HOSPITALS & NURSING HOMES

BBI's Monitor of Technology Assessment & Reimbursement
See: MEDICINE

BCA News
See: ART & SCULPTURE

BENS Trendline
Business

Publishing Co: Business Executives for National Security, 601 Pennsylvania Ave NW Apt, 700, Washington, DC 20004-2611
General Info: Monthly

BNA/ACCA Compliance Manual: Prevention of Corporate Liability
Business

Publishing Co: Bureau of National Affairs, Inc., 1231 25th St. NW, Bldg. N-200, Washington, DC 20037-1157; Title Tel # (202) 452-4200 Title Fax # (202) 822-8092
Personnel: Publisher-William A. Beltz, Mng. Editor-Mike Moore, Circ. Mgr.-Gary C. Seltzer
Editorial Description: Designed to help companies create & operate 'effective' compliance programs under criminal & civil liability of business organizations. Covers judicial decisions (state & federal), pre-decisonal developments in criminal prosecutions, enforcement trends, state & federal legislation, company activity, Sentencing Commission activity, & more.
General Info: Yr. Est. 1993, Monthly, Trim Size-8½ x 11, Offset press, 12 pages, Looseleaf
Subscriptions: Indv. $618

BNA's Corporate Counsel Weekly
See: LAW

BNA's Eastern Europe Reporter
See: INTERNATIONAL TRADE

BNA's Managed Care Reporter

Publishing Co: Bureau of National Affairs, Inc., 1231 25th St. NW, Bldg. N-200, Washington, DC 20037-1157 Tel # (202) 452-4200 Fax # (202) 822-8092
Personnel: Mng. Editor-Deborah Spiegelman
Editorial Description: Covering legislative, regulatory, legal & marketplace developments in the managed care industry, with an emphasis on their business implications. Supplies analysis & interpretation of the actions & policies of federal & state regulators as well as prespective on new business deals, trends, & shifts in the industry, & the strategic thinking of players.
General Info: Yr. Est. 1995, Weekly, ISSN: 1083-1622
Subscriptions: Indv. $595

BPI Newsletter *Business, Association*

Publishing Co: Business & Professional People for the Public Interest, 17 E. Monroe St., #212, Chicago, IL 60603-5609; Title Tel # (312) 641-5570
Personnel: Editor-Julie Kuzera
General Info: Quarterly, 8 pages
Subscriptions: Indv. $35
Circulation: Total-200

Ballantine and Sterling California Corporation Laws
See: LAW

Bank Automation News
See: COMPUTERS & AUTOMATION

Bank Loan Report
See: BANKING & FINANCE

Bankruptcy Data Source
See: BANKING & FINANCE

Banks in Insurance Report
See: INSURANCE

Barter Update - Barter Basics Edition *Business, Association*

Publishing Co: Update Publicare Co, P O Box 416, Denver, CO 80201 Tel # (308) 577-5567; Title Tel # (303) 575-5676
Personnel: Editor-A. Doyle
Editorial Description: How to basics & ideas for barter
General Info: Yr. Est. 1983, Irregular, Trim Size-8.5 x 11, 4 pages, ISSN: 0736-1904
Subscriptions: Indv. $3, Inst. $3, Can. $4, For. $6, $3/copy

Bates International Trade Update
See: INTERNATIONAL TRADE

Benefits Communicator
See: MANAGEMENT

Benefits Watch *Business*

Publishing Co: Applied Benefits Research, 34125 U.S. Highway 19N, Palm Harbor, FL 34684; Title Tel # (813) 785-2819 Title Fax # (813) 785-4306
Personnel: Editor-Patrick Mandberg
Editorial Description: Features information on the management of employee benefit compliance issues.
General Info: Bi-monthly
Subscriptions: Indv. $48
Circulation: Total-15,000
Advertising: Inquire for rates.

Best of Your Money Matters with Ric Edelman, The
See: INVESTMENT

Better Supervision
See: MANAGEMENT

Beyond the Bottom Line *Business*

Publishing Co: Economics Press, Inc., 12 Daniel Rd., Fairfield, NJ 07004-2565; Title Tel # (201) 227-1224 Title Fax # (201) 227-9742
Personnel: Editor-Robert Guder, Circ. Mgr.-Ann Lanahan
General Info: Yr. Est. 1989, Weekly, Trim Size-8½ x 11, 4 pages, Looseleaf
Subscriptions: Indv. $107, $3/copy
Circulation: Total-1,000
List Rental: List Management Co.: Manager: Michael Korman; Names in the News, 411 Theodore Fremd Ave., Rye, NY 10580 Tel # (914) 925-2400, Actives: 200,000, $85/M, Expires: 60,000, $60/M
Printing Co: Beckley Press, 2 Sperry Rd, Fairfield, NJ 07004-2056 Tel # (201) 227-6350

Beyond the Counter *Business*

Publishing Co: Facts & Comparisons, Inc., 111 West Port Plaza, Suite 300, St. Louis, MO 63146-3098; Title Tel # (314) 878-2515 Title Fax # (314) 878-5563
Editorial Description: Practical business information based on actual experiences of pharamcists and pharmacy managers. This 8-page monthly newsletter focuses on running your business, smarter and more competitvely. Each issue includes an insert.
General Info: Yr. Est. 1994, Monthly, ISSN: 1077-1166
Subscriptions: Indv. $89

Bill Shipp's Georgia
See: GOVERNMENT

Bill Staton's Money Advisory *Business, Consumer*

Publishing Co: Financial Training Group, The, 300 East Blvd., Suite B-4, Charlotte, NC 28203-4784; Title Tel # (704) 332-7514 Title Fax # (704) 332-0427
Personnel: Editor-Bill Staton
Editorial Description: Concise plain English overviews of the markets for stocks, bonds, real estate, gold as well as long-term economic projections. Where to invest money today for people who manage their own money.
General Info: Yr. Est. 1986, Monthly, Trim Size-8½ x 11, Offset press, 8 pages, ISSN: 0886-5078
Subscriptions: Indv. $89, $10/copy

BioVenture View
See: BIOCHEMISTRY

Biomedical Market Newsletter
See: MEDICINE

Biotech Business
See: GENETICS

Biz Law Update
See: LAW

Blue Chip Economic Indicators *Business*

Publishing Co: Capitol Publications, Inc., 1101 King St., Ste. 444, Alexandria, VA 22314-2968 Fax # (703) 739-6501; Title Tel # (703) 683-4100 Title Fax # (703) 739-6437
Personnel: Publisher-Chris Vestal, Editor-Robert Eggert, Exec. Ed.-Randell Moore, Circ. Mgr.-Liz Soper, Production Mgr.-Richard Rosethal, Art Dir.-Judy Denton, Mktg. Dir., Promotion Dir.-Richard Rosenthal
Editorial Description: Consensus forecasts from 50 economists for 14 key economic indicators.
General Info: Yr. Est. 1976, Monthly, Trim Size-8½ x 11, 8 pages, ISSN: 0193-4600, 2 Color, Newsprint
Subscriptions: Indv. $498, Can. $498, For. $510, $50/copy
Acquistions: Publication Bought, Publication Sold
List Rental: Actives: $185/M, Expires: $185/M
Printing Co: Capitol Publications, Inc., 1101 King St., Ste. 444, Alexandria, VA 22314-2968 Tel # (703) 683-4100, Fax # (703) 739-6501

Blue Chip Financial Forecasts *Business*

Publishing Co: Capitol Publications, Inc., 1101 King St., Ste. 444, Alexandria, VA 22314-2968 Fax # (703) 739-6501; Title Tel # (703) 683-4100 Title Fax # (703) 739-6437
Personnel: Publisher-Chris Vestal, Editor-Randell Moore, Circ. Mgr.-Liz Soper, Art Dir.-Judy Denton, Production Mgr., Mktg. Dir., Promotion Dir.-Richard Rosenthal
Editorial Description: Timely interest-rate forecasts from 50 top financial analysts.
General Info: Yr. Est. 1981, Monthly, Trim Size-8½ x 11, Web press, 8 pages, ISSN: 0741-8345, 2 Color, Newsprint
Subscriptions: Indv. $467, Can. $467, For. $479, $50/copy
Acquistions: Publication Bought, Publication Sold
List Rental: Actives: $185/M, Expires: $185/M
Printing Co: Capitol Publications, Inc., 1101 King St., Ste. 444, Alexandria, VA 22314-2968 Tel # (703) 683-4100, Fax # (703) 739-6501

Boomer Report
See: BANKING & FINANCE

Bootstrappin' Entrepreneur *Business, Consumer*

Publishing Co: Research Done Write!, 8726 South Sepulveda Blvd., #B261-OX, Los Angeles, CA 90045-4082; Title Tel # (310) 568-9861
Personnel: Publisher-Kimberly Stansell
Editorial Description: Helps people run a business on a small budget. Articles contain low-cost marketing strategies, business building tips & ideas, nat'l networking contacts, free products & services, bootstrappers' sucess stories, & a problem-and-solution exchange with other self-employed people.
General Info: Yr. Est. 1992, Quarterly, Trim Size-8½ x 11, Offset press, 12 pages, ISSN: 1063-3561, 2 Color, Other
Subscriptions: Indv. $30, $8/copy

Bootstrappin' Entrepreneur Bulletin *Business*

Publishing Co: Research Done Write!, 8726 South Sepulveda Blvd., #B261-OX, Los Angeles, CA 90045-4082; Title Tel # (310) 568-9861
Personnel: Publisher, Editor-Kimberly Stansell
Editorial Description: A collection of small business tips, ideas and resources researched and compiled by Kimberly Stansell, a business information specialist.
General Info: Yr. Est. 1996, Quarterly, Trim Size-8½ x 11, Letrpr. press, 3 pages, ISSN: 1082-9725, Color-cover
Printing Co: M & M Printing, 112 Pacific Ave, Long Beach, CA 90802-4410 Tel # (213) 495-0085

Bottom Line/Business   *Business*

Publishing Co: Boardroom Publishing, PO Box 2614, 55 Railroad Ave., Greenwich, CT 06836-6378
Tel # (203) 625-5216 Fax # (203) 861-7442
Personnel: Publisher-Martin Edelston
Editorial Description: Advice and information for business people.
General Info: (Formerly Boardroom Reports), Yr. Est. 1995, Semi-monthly, Trim Size-8½ x 11, 16 pages, 2 Color, Matte, Saddle-stitched
Circulation: Total-100,000

Bowman's Accounting Report
See: ACCOUNTING

Braintree Express
See: HOUSE ORGANS

Brazil Service   *Business*

Publishing Co: United Communications Group, 11300 Rockville Pike, Ste. 1100, Rockville, MD 20852-3030 Tel # (301) 816-8950 Fax # (301) 816-8945
Personnel: Publisher-Susan R. Goldberg, Editor-Jaures Mazzone, Circ. Mgr.-Loretta Netzer
Editorial Description: Information analysis and forecasts of investment opportunities and/or risk and political climate in Brazil.
General Info: Yr. Est. 1981, Bi-weekly, Mimeo press, 24 pages, ISSN: 0889-1761, Color-cover
Subscriptions: Indv. $545, Can. $545, For. $545
Circulation: Total-175
List Rental: List Management Co.: PRS List Management, 222 Teal Ave., POB 6482, Syracuse, NY 13217-6482 Tel # (315) 472-1224, Fax # (315) 472-1235, Actives: $250/M, Expires: $250/M
Printing Co: Xerox Reproduction Center, 200 Madison Ave., New York, NY 10016 Tel # (212) 685-7252

Bread Pudding Update
See: FOOD

Break, The
See: SPORTS & SPORTING GOODS

Broadcast Banker/Broker
See: BANKING & FINANCE

Broadcast Investor
See: BROADCASTING

Broadcast Investor Charts
See: BROADCASTING

Broadcast Stats
See: BROADCASTING

Broadwater Market Letter
See: AGRICULTURE

Brown's Business Reporter   *Business*

Publishing Co: Comp/Graphics Inc., PO Box 1376, Eugene, OR 97440-1376; Title Tel # (503) 345-8665
Personnel: Editor-Dennis Hunt
Editorial Description: Business incorporations, name filings, bankruptcies, management changes, new products, services, financial reports, construction starts, real estate transfers. Geographic coverage of Willamette Valley, Oregon, only.
General Info: Yr. Est. 1958, Weekly, Trim Size-5½ x 8½, Sheetfed press, 16 pages, 2% ads, 2 Color
Subscriptions: Indv. $45, $1/copy
Circulation: Total-1,300
Advertising: Inquire for rates.
Printing Co: QSL Printing, 309 W 4th Ave, Eugene, OR 97401-2581 Tel # (541) 687-1184, Fax # (541) 687-0078

Bulletin-U.S. Business & Indust. Council

Publishing Co: U.S. Business & Industrial Council, 122 C Street NW, Suite #815, Washington, DC 20001-2109; Title Tel # (202) 662-8744 Title Fax # (202) 662-8754
Personnel: Editor-Jeffry Dodt
Editorial Description: Member & staff activities; reports of board proceedings; summary of national & D.C. work on trade regulation, legislation, tort reform, energy industry, federal budget & deficit; report on press coverage.
General Info: Yr. Est. 1933, Sheetfed press, Matte
Circulation: Total-2,000

Business & Acquisition Newsletter   *Business*

Publishing Co: Newsletters International, 2600 South Gessner Rd., Houston, TX 77063-3297; Title Tel # (713) 783-0100
Personnel: Editor-Len Fox
Editorial Description: Advises readers of companies, product lines, & patents available for sale. Provides information on how to find & make good acquisitions & mergers. List names of companies looking for acquistions.
General Info: Yr. Est. 1965, Monthly, Trim Size-8½ x 11, Offset press, 6 pages, ISSN: 0738-7253, No Color
Subscriptions: Indv. $300, For. $350, $25/copy
Acquistions: Publication Bought

Business & Economics   *Business*

Publishing Co: National Technical Information Service U.S., 5285 Port Royal Rd., Springfield, VA 22161-0001 Fax # (703) 487-4630; Title Tel # (703) 487-4630
Editorial Description: R&D results, analyses and other information relevant to business and economics from the NTIS scientific/technical database.
General Info: Weekly, Trim Size-8½ x 11, Offset press, 8 pages, ISSN: 0364-7978
Subscriptions: Indv. $135, Can. $135, For. $195

Business Breakthroughs   *Business*

Publishing Co: Phillips Publishing, Inc., 7811 Montrose Rd., Potomac, MD 20854-3394 Tel # (301) 340-2100 Fax # (301) 294-1307 Parent Co.-Phillips Business Information, Inc., Potomac
Personnel: Editor-Jay Abraham
General Info: Monthly
Subscriptions: Indv. $150
Circulation: Total-9,000
List Rental: List Management Co.: Phillips Publishing List Marketing, 7811 Montrose Rd., Potomac, MD 20854-3394 Tel # (301) 340-2100, Fax # (301) 294-1307, Actives: 9,000

Business Computer Report
See: COMPUTERS & AUTOMATION

Business Counsel
See: LAW

Business Crime: Criminal Liabilty of the Business Community
See: LAW

Business and the Environment

Publishing Co: Cutter Information Corp., 37 Broadway, Ste. 1, Arlington, MA 02174-5552 Fax # (617) 648-1950; Title Tel # (617) 648-8700 Title Fax # (617) 648-8707
Personnel: Publisher-Karen Coburn, Editor-Kate Victory, Circ. Mgr.-Dennis Crowley, Production Mgr.-Laura St. Clair
Editorial Description: News of green initiatives by companies around the world; regulatory trends. News and analysis of strategic corporate environmental management initiatives worldwide; trends in policy and regulation; monthly supplement on ISO 1400 and EMS standards.
General Info: Yr. Est. 1990, Monthly, Trim Size-8½ x 11, 16 pages, ISSN: 1052-7206, Ind/Abs/ Online: NewsNet
Subscriptions: Indv. $397, Inst. $197, Can. $397, For. $497, $20/copy
Printing Co: Benjamin Franklin Smith Printers, 320 Stuart St, Boston, MA 02116-5242 Tel # (617) 426-1160

Business Europe   *Business*

Publishing Co: Economist Intelligence Unit, 111 W. 57th St., New York, NY 10019 Tel # (212) 554-0600 Fax # (212) 586-1181; Title Tel # (212) 540-0600
Personnel: Editor-Nicholas Stevenson
Editorial Description: Reports developments affecting investment & trade in European markets.
General Info: Weekly
Subscriptions: Indv. $1,150

Business Franchise Guide   *Business*

Publishing Co: CCH, Inc., 2700 Lake Cook Rd., Riverwoods, IL 60015 Parent Co.-Kluwer Law & Taxation Publishers, Cambridge; Title Tel # (847) 267-7000 Title Fax # (800) 224-8299
Editorial Description: Sets out, explains & reports on rules & developments affecting franchising - state disclosure & relationship laws; the Federal Trade Commission Franchise Rule, court decisions, & state regulations. Covers intl. franchise law issues.
General Info: Yr. Est. 1980, Monthly, Trim Size-6 x 9, Web press, ISSN: 0274-8991, No Color, Looseleaf
Subscriptions: Indv. $794

Business History Bulletin

Publishing Co: Hagley Museum & Library, PO Box 3630, Wilmington, DE 19807-0630; Title Tel # (302) 658-2400 Title Fax # (302) 658-0568
Editorial Description: Features articles & news on contemporary uses of history by business & industry & ways in which corporations benefit by using & preserving history.
General Info: Yr. Est. 1988, Letrpr. press, 10 pages, No Color
Circulation: Total-3,000

Business Ideas   *Business*

Publishing Co: Dan Newman Co., 1051 Bloomfield Ave., Clifton Lake, NJ 07012-2120; Title Tel # (201) 778-6677
Personnel: Publisher, Editor-Dan Newman, Adv. Dir.-Doris Leff
Editorial Description: Contains valuable tips for business and advertising/promotion professionals. Covers practical techniques, what's new and what works. Directed to businessman and advertising.
General Info: (Formerly Small Business World), Yr. Est. 1950, 10x/yr., Trim Size-8½ x 11, Offset press, 4 pages, ISSN: 0738-7024, No Color
Subscriptions: Indv. $60, For. $60, $4/copy
Circulation: Total-4,000

Business Information Alert:Sources,Strategies & Signposts for Information Professionals
See: LIBRARY

Business Information from Your Public Library
See: LIBRARY

Business Insurance Law and Practice Guide
See: LAW

Business and the Law
See: LAW

Business Law Europe
See: INTERNATIONAL TRADE

Business Law Update
See: LAW

Business Mailers Review   *Business*

Publishing Co: Pasha Publications, Inc, 1616 N. Fort Myer Dr., #1000, Arlington, VA 22209-3103; Title Tel # (703) 528-1244 Title Fax # (703) 528-4926
Personnel: Grp. Pub.-Harry L. Baisden, Editor-Kate Phelan, Exec. Ed.-Van H. Seagraves
Editorial Description: Monitors postal service & other carriers' activities affecting large mailers.
General Info: Yr. Est. 1980, Bi-weekly, Trim Size-8½ x 11, 4 pages
Subscriptions: Indv. $279, For. $294, $11/copy

Business Matters   *Business*

Publishing Co: Canadian Institute of Chartered Accountants, 277 Wellington Street West, Toronto, ON M5V 3H2 Canada Tel # (416) 977-3222 Fax # (414) 204-3416
Personnel: Editor-Richard Fulcher
General Info: Bi-monthly
Subscriptions: Indv. $180

Business Network   *Business*

Publishing Co: Business Network, 5420 Mayfield Rd., Lyndhurst, OH 44124-2924; Title Tel # (216) 442-5600 Title Fax # (216) 449-3227
Editorial Description: Funding for businesses from private investors.
General Info: Yr. Est. 1985
Subscriptions: Indv. $95, Inst. $75, Can. $125, For. $195, $10/copy
Circulation: Total-200

Business Newsletter   *Business*

Publishing Co: Business Newsletter, Inc., 537 E Vine St, Owatonna, MN 55060-2518; Title Tel # (507) 455-3220 Title Fax # (507) 455-3220
Personnel: Editor-Don W. Larson
General Info: Yr. Est. 1980, Semi-monthly
Subscriptions: Indv. $39
Circulation: Total-2,000

Business Organizations:
Pension and Profit-
Sharing Plans   *Business*

Publishing Co: Matthew Bender & Co., 11 Penn Plaza, New York, NY 10001-2006 Tel # (212) 967-7707 Fax # (212) 244-3188
Editorial Description: The first full treatment of the whole field of pension and profit-sharing plans-- complete with implementing forms and detailed legal analysis.
General Info: Yr. Est. 1977, Irregular, Looseleaf

Business Organizations:
Professional Corporations
and Associations   *Business*

Publishing Co: Matthew Bender & Co., 11 Penn Plaza, New York, NY 10001-2006 Tel # (212) 967-7707 Fax # (212) 244-3188
Editorial Description: Contains information on forming, operating, and changing ownership of a professional corporation or association.
General Info: Yr. Est. 1970, Irregular, Looseleaf

Business Organizations
with Tax Planning   *Business*

Publishing Co: Matthew Bender & Co., 11 Penn Plaza, New York, NY 10001-2006 Fax # (212) 244-3188; Title Tel # (212) 967-7707
Personnel: Editor-D. Schneider
Editorial Description: Provides full coverage on all business entities: corporations, partnerships, joint ventures.
General Info: Yr. Est. 1963, Quarterly, Looseleaf
Subscriptions: $1,125/copy

Business Planning Advisory   *Business*

Publishing Co: WPI Communications, Inc., 55 Morris Ave, Springfield, NJ 07081-1496; Title Tel # (201) 467-8700 Title Fax # (201) 467-0368
Personnel: Editor-Ken Berry
General Info: Monthly

Business Review

Publishing Co: Hofstra Univ., 121 Hofstra University, Hempstead, NY 11550-1090 Tel # (516) 463-5910 Fax # (516) 463-5072; Title Tel # (516) 560-5705
Personnel: Editor-Russell Moore
Editorial Description: Business conditions on Long Island.
General Info: Yr. Est. 1984, Quarterly, Trim Size-8½ x 11, 6 pages, Color
Circulation: Total-3,500
Printing Co: Ariel Graphics, PO Box 100, Sayville, NY 11782-0100 Tel # (516) 589-7447

Business Review   *Business*

Publishing Co: Cypress Publishing, PO Box 777, Cypress, TX 77429-0777 Tel # (713) 373-9142 Fax # (713) 256-1722; Title Tel # (713) 373-3535 Title Fax # (713) 373-4450
Personnel: Editor-Kevin Hill, Art Dir.-Cheryl Abts
General Info: Yr. Est. 1985, Trim Size-8½ x 11, Offset press, 4 pages, 4 Color, Coated, Other
Subscriptions: Free With Membership

Business Sales &
Acquisitions Digest   *Business*

Publishing Co: Canadian Institute of Chartered Accountants, 277 Wellington Street West, Toronto, ON M5V 3H2 Canada Tel # (416) 977-3222 Fax # (414) 204-3416; Title Tel # (416) 927-2322
Personnel: Editor-Wayne Albo, Editor-A.Randal Henderson
General Info: Yr. Est. 1987, Quarterly, Trim Size-8½ x 11, Offset press, 25 pages, No Color
Subscriptions: Indv. $195
Circulation: Total-250

Business Speaks   *Business*

Publishing Co: New York Board of Trade, PO Box 3020, New York, NY 10185-3020; Title Tel # (212) 661-6300
Personnel: Editor-William Sloboda
Editorial Description: Newsletter of Board activities, plus items of information of interest to members.
General Info: Yr. Est. 1954, Quarterly
Circulation: Total-3,000

Business Strategies   *Business*

Publishing Co: CCH, Inc., 2700 Lake Cook Rd., Riverwoods, IL 60015 Parent Co.-Kluwer Law & Taxation Publishers, Cambridge; Title Tel # (847) 267-7000 Title Fax # (800) 224-8299
Editorial Description: Continuing analyses of business strategies from accounting, tax and legal viewpoints.
General Info: Yr. Est. 1983, Semi-monthly, 96 pages, No Color, Looseleaf
Subscriptions: Indv. $707

Business Torts   *Business*

Publishing Co: Matthew Bender & Co., 11 Penn Plaza, New York, NY 10001-2006 Tel # (212) 967-7707 Fax # (212) 244-3188
Personnel: Editor in Chief-Joseph D. Zamore
Editorial Description: Covers a varity of important business torts.
General Info: Yr. Est. 1989, Irregular, Looseleaf

Business Trends   *Business*

Publishing Co: Bank of Hawaii, Economics Dept., PO Box 2900, Honolulu, HI 96846-0001; Title Tel # (808) 537-8375 Title Fax # (808) 536-9433
Personnel: Editor-Paul H. Brewbaker
Editorial Description: Economic newsletter.
General Info: (Formerly Monthly Review), Yr. Est. 1956, Bi-monthly, 6 pages, ISSN: 0893-0732
Subscriptions: Free

Business Trends Report   *Business*

Publishing Co: Business Research, 537 Newport Center Dr Ste 355, Newport Beach, CA 92660-6937 Tel # (714) 664-0818; Title Tel # (714) 644-8818 Title Fax # (714) 644-8818
Personnel: Publisher, Editor-Thomas Thompson
Editorial Description: Summarizes America's leading investment, business and travel newsletters.
General Info: Yr. Est. 1991, Monthly, Letrpr. press, 8 pages, 2 Color, Coated
Subscriptions: Indv. $35, Inst. $50, $5/copy
Circulation: Total-1,500, Readership-4,500
Advertising: Inquire for rates.

Business/Education Insider
See: EDUCATION

BusinessGram   *Business*

Publishing Co: BusinessGram Inc., PO Box 273390, Tampa, FL 33688-3390; Title Tel # (813) 968-2979 Title Fax # (813) 968-6113
Personnel: Editor-Joseph McAuliffe
General Info: Yr. Est. 1982, 11x/yr.

Businessmen's
Expectations   *Business*

Publishing Co: Dun & Bradstreet, PO Box 870, Wilton, CT 06897 Tel # (212) 593-6800; Title Tel # (212) 285-7417
General Info: Quarterly
Subscriptions: Indv. $23

Buyerism Newsletter   *Business*

Publishing Co: WWWWW/Information Services, Inc., PO Box 10046, Rochester, NY 14610-0046; Title Tel # (716) 461-1888
Personnel: Publisher, Editor-Robert A. Fowler
Editorial Description: Covers such topics as buying a business, starting a business, becoming a distributor or sales rep for a line-of-products.
General Info: Yr. Est. 1970, Monthly, Trim Size-8½ x 11, Offset press, 8 pages, No Color
Subscriptions: Indv. $39, $3/copy

CA Business Partners
See: COMPUTERS & AUTOMATION

CARD TALK
See: PRINTING/GRAPHIC ARTS

CB
See: RELIGIOUS & THEOLOGICAL

CBI Online   *Business*

Publishing Co: Equifax Inc., 1600 Peachtree St. NW, Atlanta, GA 30309; Title Tel # (404) 885-8146
Personnel: Editor-Barbara Wilkes
Editorial Description: Describes CBI's services; includes industry news and related legislative material.
General Info: Yr. Est. 1975, Semi-annually, Trim Size-10 x 14, Offset press, 7 pages, 2 Color
Circulation: Total-16,000

CCM Communicator   *Association*

Publishing Co: Council of Communication Management, 17W703/E Butterfield Rd., Oakbrook Terrace, IL 60181-4280; Title Tel # (708) 268-0707
Personnel: Editor-David Freeland
Editorial Description: Articles by members on policies, strategies and practices in organizational communication.
General Info: (Formerly ICC Newsletter), Yr. Est. 1955, Monthly, Trim Size-8½ x 11, Offset press, 8 pages, No Color
Subscriptions: Free With Membership
Circulation: Total-300

CEO Job Opportunities
Update   *Business*

Publishing Co: CEO Job Opportunities Update - ARA, 325 7th St. NW, Ste. 1000, Washington, DC 20004-2801; Title Tel # (202) 331-3828 Title Fax # (202) 457-0386
Personnel: Publisher-Don J. BeBolt
General Info: Yr. Est. 1991, Bi-weekly
Subscriptions: Indv. $300

CEP Research Report
See: ECONOMICS

CFO & Controller Alert
See: ACCOUNTING

CJA Forum   *Business*

Publishing Co: CJA, 17852 17th St Ste 209, Tustin, CA 92680-2143; Title Tel # (714) 731-0867
Personnel: Editor-Lou Adler
Editorial Description: Career management, hiring & selection process, interviewing techniques.
General Info: Yr. Est. 1984, Quarterly, Trim Size-8½ x 11, Web press, 5 pages, 2 Color, Newsprint
Subscriptions: Indv. $30
Circulation: (100% controlled), Total-4,000

CMC Report   *Business, Association*

Publishing Co: Institute of Certified Management Consultants of B.C., 1501-650 W. Georgia St., Vancouver, BC V6B 4N9 Canada; Title Tel # (604) 681-1419 Title Fax # (604) 687-6688
Personnel: Editor-Jennie Ambrose
General Info: (Formerly Inst. of Cert. Management Consultants of B. C. Newsletter), Bi-monthly
Subscriptions: Free With Membership
Circulation: Total-750

CPA Administrative Report
See: ACCOUNTING

CPIA Bulletin
See: AERONAUTICS/ASTRONAUTICS

CQSS Reporter
See: MANAGEMENT

C.S.T. Connection   *Business*

Publishing Co: C.S.T. Consultants, Inc., 200-240 Duncan Mill Road, Don Mills, ON M3B 3P1 Canada Tel # (416) 445-2597; Title Tel # (416) 445-7377 Title Fax # (416) 445-1708
Personnel: Editor-Sandra Cipriano
Editorial Description: A newsletter for CST sales representatives across Canada and Bermuda.
General Info: Yr. Est. 1988, Monthly, Trim Size-8½ x 11, Desktop press, 10 pages, Color-cover, Matte, Saddle-stitched
Subscriptions: Free To Qualified Recipient
Circulation: Total-550

Cable TV Investor
See: TELEVISION & VIDEO

Canada Corporations
Bulletin   *Business, Association*

Publishing Co: Canada Communication Group Operation, Ottawa, ON K1A 0S9 Canada; Title Tel # (613) 994-3103
General Info: Monthly
Subscriptions: Indv. $38, $3/copy

Canada Corporations Law Reporter
See: LAW

Canada Letter   *Business*

Publishing Co: S & S Press Co., Ltd., 13964 Tallon Pl., Surrey, BC V3V 5X8 Canada; Title Tel # (604) 856-1646
Personnel: Editor-Akira Shigematsu
Editorial Description: Business news in Japanese.
General Info: Yr. Est. 1975, Monthly
Subscriptions: Indv. $64

Canada-U.S. Trade   *Business*

Publishing Co: Carswell, 2075 Kennedy Road, One Corporate Plaza, Scarborough, ON M1T 3V4 Canada; Title Tel # (416) 609-8000 Title Fax # (416) 298-5094
Personnel: Publisher-Barry Garnet, Editor-R. Gottlieb, Adv. Dir.-Melanie Causton
Editorial Description: An informative newsletter written by experts in the area of international trade. Trade laws, tribunal decisions & government policy changes, in both Canada & the U.S., are examined in a journalistic style for the business & professional reader.
General Info: Monthly, Trim Size-8½ x 11, 8 pages, ISSN: 0840-6278
Subscriptions: Indv. $185

Canada's Business Climate   *Business*

Publishing Co: Toronto-Dominion Bank, Toronto Dominion Center, Box 1, Toronto, ON M5K 1A2 Canada Tel # (416) 866-5696; Title Tel # (416) 866-8061
Editorial Description: Commentary and charts depicting the Canadian economy and its outlook.
General Info: Yr. Est. 1968, Quarterly, Trim Size-5½ x 8¾, 16 pages, ISSN: 0045-4303, 2 Color
Circulation: Total-40,000

Canadian Biotech News
See: DRUGS & PHARMACEUTICALS

Canadian Commercial Law Guide
See: LAW

Canadian Co-Operative
Association News
Service   *Business*

Publishing Co: Canadian Co-Operative Assn., 400-275 Bank St., Ottawa, ON K2P 2L6 Canada; Title Tel # (613) 238-6711 Title Fax # (613) 567-0658
Personnel: Publisher-Lynden Hillier, Editor-Roy LaBerge
Editorial Description: Reports programs of Canadian Co-operative Assn. to members; reports on happenings in Canadian & intl. co-op scene, & discusses issues & trends that may affect cooperatives.
General Info: Yr. Est. 1980, Semi-monthly, Trim Size-8½ x 11, Sheetfed press, 16 pages, No Color
Subscriptions: Indv. $50, $5/copy
Circulation: (50% controlled), Total-450, Subscriptions-225

Canadian Corporate R&D
Directory   *Business, Association*

Publishing Co: Evert Communications Ltd., 1296 Carling Ave., Ottawa, ON K1Z 7K8 Canada; Title Tel # (613) 728-4621 Title Fax # (613) 728-0385
Personnel: Publisher-Gordon Hutchison, Editor-Natalie Gallimore, Circ. Mgr.-Carole Jeffrey
Editorial Description: Directory of Canadian Corporate R & D performers, continuously updated and issued currently at time of order.
General Info: Yr. Est. 1992, Monthly, Trim Size-8½ x 11, Sheetfed press, 300 pages, No Color, Matte, Other
Subscriptions: Indv. $495, Inst. $495, Can. $495, For. $495
List Rental: Rents Lists
Printing Co: Bradda Printing Services, 130 Slater Street, Ottawa, ON K1P 6E2 Canada Tel # (613) 238-5433

Canadian Corporate
Secretary's Guide   *Business*

Publishing Co: CCH Canadian Ltd., 6 Garamond Ct., North York, ON M3C 1Z5 Canada Fax # (416) 444-8011 Parent Co.-CCH, Inc., Riverwoods; Title Tel # (416) 441-2992 Title Fax # (416) 444-9011
Personnel: Editor-Lionel Goulet
Editorial Description: Reference manual for corporate secretaries and administrators. Outline of duties and responsibilities: information on incorporation, organization and corporate administration.
General Info: Monthly, Trim Size-6 x 9, Web press, No Color, Looseleaf
Subscriptions: Can. $305

Canadian Employment Benefits and Pension Guide
See: INDUSTRIAL RELATIONS/PERSONNEL

Canadian Employment Safety and Health Guide
See: SAFETY

Canadian Energy Program Reporter
See: ENERGY

Canadian Goods & Services Tax Reporter
See: TAXES

Canadian Government Programs & Services
See: U.S. (& CANADIAN) FED. GOV'T.

Canadian Health Care
Management   *Business*

Publishing Co: MPL Communications, Inc., 133 Richmond St. W., Ste. 700, Toronto, ON M5H 3M8 Canada Fax # (416) 869-0456; Title Tel # (416) 869-1177 Title Fax # (416) 869-0616
Editorial Description: A looseleaf service providing current need-to-know information for health care administrators.
General Info: Yr. Est. 1985, Monthly, 4 pages, 2 Color
Subscriptions: Indv. $349
List Rental: Rents Lists

Canadian Industrial Relations and Personnel Developments
See: INDUSTRIAL RELATIONS/PERSONNEL

Canadian Nursing
Management   *Business, Association*

Publishing Co: MPL Communications, Inc., 133 Richmond St. W., Ste. 700, Toronto, ON M5H 3M8 Canada Fax # (416) 869-0456; Title Tel # (416) 869-1177 Title Fax # (416) 869-0616
Personnel: Editor-Hayley Chandler
Editorial Description: A news service for nurse managers.
General Info: Yr. Est. 1987, Monthly, 8 pages, 2 Color, Matte
Subscriptions: Indv. $109
List Rental: Rents Lists

Canadian Real Estate Income Tax Guide
See: TAXES

Canadian Small Business
Guide   *Business, Association*

Publishing Co: CCH Canadian Ltd., 6 Garamond Ct., North York, ON M3C 1Z5 Canada Fax # (416) 444-8011 Parent Co.-CCH, Inc., Riverwoods; Title Tel # (416) 441-2992 Title Fax # (416) 444-9011
Editorial Description: A handy, practical reference for owners and administrators of small business in Canada.
General Info: Yr. Est. 1981, Monthly, Trim Size-6 x 9, Web press, Ind/Abs/Online: Topical Index, No Color, Looseleaf
Subscriptions: Can. $295

Canadian Tax Forms
See: TAXES

Canadian Tax Reporter
See: TAXES

Canadian Transportation Law Reporter
See: TRAFFIC & TRANSPORTATION

Candlelighter   *Business, Association*   CPM: $63

Publishing Co: Intl. Guild of Candle Artisans, 867 Browning Ave S, Salem, OR 97302-6112; Title Tel # (503) 364-5475
Personnel: Editor-Eleanor Wulff
Editorial Description: Sharing of information & ideas relative to candle making, annual listing of members and also suppliers of candle making ingredients & equipment.
General Info: Monthly, Trim Size-8½ x 11, Web press, 10 pages, No Color, Newsprint, Looseleaf
Subscriptions: Indv. $25
Circulation: Total-550
Advertising: $35.

Capital Changes Reports
See: TAXES

Capital Journal   *Business, Association*

Publishing Co: Business Council of New York State, 152 Washington Ave, Albany, NY 12210-2203; Title Tel # (518) 465-7511 Title Fax # (518) 465-4389
Personnel: Editor-Robert Ward
Editorial Description: Published for business lobbying organization.
General Info: Yr. Est. 1980, Weekly, Desktop press, 16 pages, Newsprint
Subscriptions: Indv. $20
Circulation: Total-5,000
Printing Co: Hipple Printing, PO Box 878, Pierre, SD 57501-0878 Tel # (605) 224-7301

Capitations Contracts: A
Guide to Negotiating   *Business*

Publishing Co: Thompson Publishing Group, 747 Third Ave., New York, NY 10017 Tel # (212) 888-7220 Fax # (212) 486-3400; Title Fax # (800) 999-2320
Personnel: Editor-Wendy Krasner, Production Mgr.-Mauro Vaisman, Mktg. Dir.-James Kavanage
General Info: (Formerly Successful Agreements), Irregular, Looseleaf
Subscriptions: Indv. $395

Card News
See: CREDIT AND CREDIT UNIONS

Career Connections
See: EDUCATION

Caribbean Update
See: INTERNATIONAL TRADE

Carlson Report for Shopping Center Management
See: REAL ESTATE

Case Evaluation/Basic
Settlement Value
Software

Publishing Co: LRP Publications, 747 Dresher Rd., P.O. Box 980, Horsham, PA 19044-0980 Tel # (215) 784-0910 Fax # (215) 784-0317
Personnel: Publisher-Virginia Herman, Editor-Don Marshall, Circ. Mgr.-David Dreimiller, Adv. Dir.-Jodi Yuhaz, Promotion Dir.-Gerda Burton
Editorial Description: Computer software with manuals for identifying personal injury settlement & verdict value.
General Info: Yr. Est. 1959, Semi-annually, Letrpr. press, No Color, Looseleaf
Subscriptions: Indv. $890
Circulation: Total-3,000

Case Study   *Business*

Publishing Co: American Productivity & Quality Center, 123 N. Post Oak Ln., Ste. 300, Houston, TX 77024-7718 Tel # (713) 685-4642 Fax # (713) 681-8578; Title Tel # (713) 681-4020
Personnel: Editor-Steve Stewart, Staff Writer-Steve Scheffler, Art Dir.-Eric Heisserer
Editorial Description: Each issue contains in-depth report on one companies productivity & quality practices.
General Info: Yr. Est. 1981, Bi-monthly, 8 pages, ISSN: 0741-6423, 2 Color, Coated, Looseleaf
Subscriptions: $13/copy
Circulation: Total-1,600
Printing Co: Brandt & Lawson, 815 Live Oak St., Houston, TX 77003-3220 Tel # (713) 227-5173

Catering Service Idea
Newsletter   *Business*

Publishing Co: Prosperity & Profits Unlimited, PO Box 416, Denver, CO 80201-0416; Title Tel # (303) 575-5676
Personnel: Editor-A.C. Doyle
Editorial Description: Ideas for catering businesses.
General Info: Yr. Est. 1990, Every two years, Trim Size-8½ x 11, Letrpr. press, 4 pages, No Color
Subscriptions: Indv. $5, Inst. $5, Can. $12, For. $15, $5/copy
Circulation: Total-2,500

Caveat Emptor
See: PURCHASING

Center for Self Sufficiency Update
See: PHILANTHROPY

Central Hudson Newsletter
See: HOUSE ORGANS

Change
See: DIRECT MAIL

Chief Economist (Straight Talk)
See: ECONOMICS

Chile Economic Report
See: INTERNATIONAL TRADE

China Business Law Guide

Publishing Co: CCH, Inc., 2700 Lake Cook Rd., Riverwoods, IL 60015 Parent Co.-Kluwer Law & Taxation Publishers, Cambridge; Title Tel # (847) 267-7000 Title Fax # (800) 224-8299
Editorial Description: Provides a discussion of all pertinent business laws, and their practical application to assist foreigners doing business in China.
General Info: Quarterly, Looseleaf
Subscriptions: Indv. $765

China Laws for Foreign Business-Business Regulation
See: LAW

Chronicle of Minority
Business   *Business, Association*

Publishing Co: Association of African American Women Business Owners, PO Box 13933, Silver Spring, MD 20911-0933; Title Tel # (301) 565-0258
Personnel: Editor-Tracy Mason
Editorial Description: Informational for African American and other minority business owners.
General Info: Quarterly, Trim Size-8½ x 11, 8 pages, No Color
Circulation: Total-2,000
Advertising: Inquire for rates.

Clean Air News
See: ENVIRONMENT & ECOLOGY

Client Newsletter   *Business*

Publishing Co: WPI Communications, Inc., 55 Morris Ave, Springfield, NJ 07081-1496; Title Tel # (201) 467-8700 Title Fax # (201) 467-0368
Personnel: Publisher-S. H. Klinghoffer, Editor-K. Berry, Circ. Mgr.-M. Lang, Production Mgr.-J. Petino
Editorial Description: Bulk NL sold camera ready to financial profs. for redistribution to clients.
General Info: Yr. Est. 1986, Quarterly, 8 pages
List Rental: Actives: $55/M

Client Planning Advisory

Publishing Co: WPI Communications, Inc., 55 Morris Ave, Springfield, NJ 07081-1496;
Title Tel # (201) 467-8700 Title Fax # (201) 467-0368
List Rental: Rents Lists

Client Quarterly
See: BANKING & FINANCE

Client Server News
See: COMPUTERS & AUTOMATION

Coffee, Sugar & Cocoa Exchange
See: INVESTMENT

Cogent Communicator, The   *Association, Business*

Publishing Co: The Cogent Communicator, 9571 E Caldwell Dr, Tucson, AZ 85747-9218;
Title Tel # (602) 574-9353 Title Fax # (602) 574-0620
Personnel: Publisher, Editor-James Patterson
Editorial Description: How-to articles for organizations to improve communication and quality/ISO 9000.
General Info: Yr. Est. 1992, Quarterly, Trim Size-8½ x 11, Desktop press, 4 pages, No Color, Matte
Subscriptions: Indv. $40, Can. $50, For. $60, Free To Qualified Recipient
Circulation: Total-7,000

Cole Papers, The
See: NEWSPAPER INDUSTRY

Color Businesss Report
See: COMPUTERS & AUTOMATION

Colorado City Retail Sales
by SIC   *Business*

Publishing Co: Univ. of Colorado, Graduate School of Business Admin., Campus Box 420, Boulder, CO 80309-0001; Title Tel # (303) 492-8227 Title Fax # (303) 492-3620
Personnel: Publisher-C.R. Goeldner, Editor-Richard Wobbekind
Editorial Description: Retail sales by standard industrial classification for 120 cities in Colorado.
General Info: Yr. Est. 1965, Quarterly, Trim Size-8½ x 11, Offset press, 37 pages, No Color
Subscriptions: Indv. $75

Commercial Cattle Issue
See: LIVESTOCK

Commercial and Consumer Warranties--Drafting, Performing and Litigating
See: LAW

Commercial Damages: A Guide To Remedies in Business Litigation
See: LAW

Commercial Law Manual
See: LAW

Commercial Paper Under the UCC
See: LAW

Commerical Law Report
See: LAW

Commodity Futures Law Reports
See: INVESTMENT

Communicate 2000

Publishing Co: Hartley Gibson Company, Ltd., 2533 Gerrard Street East, Scarborough, ON M1N 1W9 Canada; Title Tel # (416) 690-6163 Title Fax # (416) 690-6203

Communique
See: ADVERTISING & MARKETING

CompFlash
See: LABOR

Co-Op Newsletter, The   *Consumer, Association*

Publishing Co: Northcoast Arcata Fortuna Cooperative, 977 9th St, Arcata, CA 95521-6112;
Title Tel # (707) 445-3185 Title Fax # (707) 443-8792
Personnel: Publisher-Amie Haas LaBanca, Editor-Amy Haas LaBanca
Editorial Description: News of food co-ops, natural foods, lifestyles .
General Info: Bi-monthly, Trim Size-11½ x 14, Web press, 16 pages, 2 Color, Newsprint
Subscriptions: Indv. $10
Circulation: (23% controlled), Total-6,500, Subscriptions-5,000
Printing Co: Humboldt Printing, 938 Main St # 310, PO Box 690, Fortuna, CA 95540-0690
Tel # (707) 725-1171

Compensation
See: INDUSTRIAL RELATIONS/PERSONNEL

Competitive Concepts   *Business*

Publishing Co: EMS Network International, 858 Longview Rd, Burlingame, CA 94010-6974;
Title Tel # (415) 342-5259 Title Fax # (415) 344-5005
Personnel: Publisher-Nancy Shays, Editor-E. Michael Shays
General Info: Yr. Est. 1990, Monthly
Subscriptions: Indv. $36

Competitive Healthcare Market Reporter
See: HEALTH

Compliance Reporter
See: BANKING & FINANCE

Composites Industry Monthly
See: PLASTICS

Composites News: Infrastructure
See: PLASTICS

Computer Letter
See: COMPUTERS & AUTOMATION

ConnTAP Quarterly
See: ENVIRONMENT & ECOLOGY

Connections to Mail Order/World Trade and Homebased Business Info.
See: ADVERTISING & MARKETING

Conservative Speculator
See: INVESTMENT

Consolidated Index to Units 1-5 of Bender's UCC Service
See: LAW

Construction Claims Monthly
See: CONSTRUCTION & BUILDING

Consultants' & Contractors' Newsletter

Publishing Co: Fides-Vandame, Inc., 105 N. Main St., Boonton, NJ 07005-1257;
Title Tel # (201) 299-1535 Title Fax # (201) 335-4866
Personnel: Publisher-Wendy Vandame, Editor-Stephanie Ferm, Adv. Dir.-Christing Fanning
Editorial Description: Covers the data processing consulting and contracting industry.
General Info: Yr. Est. 1986, Monthly, 12 pages, 3% ads, Saddle-stitched
Subscriptions: Indv. $70, Can. $80, For. $120, $3/copy
Advertising: Inquire for rates. Accepts Inserts.
List Rental: Rents Lists

Consultants News
See: MANAGEMENT

Consulting Intelligence   *Business, Association*

Publishing Co: American Consultants League, 1290 N Palm Ave # 112, Sarasota, FL 34236-5604
Tel # (941) 952-9290 Fax # (941) 379-6024; Title Tel # (813) 952-9290 Title Fax # (813) 925-3670
Personnel: Publisher, Editor-Hubert Bermont
Editorial Description: Timely articles on current developments, new techniques, how to get new clients & keep old ones.
General Info: Yr. Est. 1986, Bi-monthly, Sheetfed press, 8 pages, ISSN: 0887-0314, Color, Newsprint
Subscriptions: Free With Membership
Circulation: Total-750
Advertising: Accepts Inserts.
Printing Co: Sir Speedy, Main St., Sarasota, FL 34236 Tel # (813) 365-0458

Consulting Opportunities
Journal   *Business*

Publishing Co: Consultants National Resource Center, PO Box 430, Clear Spring, MD 21722-0430;
Title Tel # (301) 791-9332
Personnel: Publisher, Editor-J. Stephen Lanning, Circ. Mgr.-Lynda Ramsay, Adv. Dir.-Jack Stephens
Editorial Description: Information source for the independent consultant on marketing professional services.
General Info: Yr. Est. 1981, Bi-monthly, Trim Size-8½ x 11, Web press, 8 pages, ISSN: 0273-4613, Newsprint
Subscriptions: Indv. $69, For. $97, $8/copy
Acquistions: Publication Bought
Advertising: Inquire for rates.
List Rental: Actives: $85/M
Printing Co: Mr. Print, 130 S 20th St, Purcellville, VA 22132-3301 Tel # (703) 338-5900

Contact

Publishing Co: Canadian Council for Aboriginal Business, 204 Saint George St., 2nd Fl., Toronto, ON M5R 2N5 Canada; Title Tel # (416) 961-8663 Title Fax # (416) 961-3995
Personnel: Publisher, Editor-Karen Leone
General Info: (Formerly Counciline), Yr. Est. 1985, Quarterly

Continental Franchise
Review *Business*

Publishing Co: Sparks Publishing & Reporting Corp., PO Box 260558, Littleton, CO 80163; Title Tel # (303) 450-7744 Title Fax # (303) 450-6711
Personnel: Publisher-Janet L. Sparks, Assoc. Publ.-Thomas H. Murphy, Editor-Ron Vlieger, Editor-Nancy Weingartner, Adv. Dir.-Roger Steen
Editorial Description: Coverage of legal legislative activity; franchise development; consumer, industry and economic trends affecting franchising. Published bi-weekly not including 4 special reports each year.
General Info: Yr. Est. 1967, Bi-weekly, Trim Size-8½ x 11, Offset press, 8 pages, ISSN: 0045-8376
Subscriptions: Indv. $195, Can. $195, For. $225, $6/copy

Continuous Improvement
See: MANUFACTURING

Conventionews *Business*

Publishing Co: Metropolitan Detroit Convention & Visitors Bureau, 100 Renaissance Center, Ste. 1900, Detroit, MI 48243-1006; Title Tel # (313) 259-4333
Personnel: Editor-Kathryn Usitalo
Editorial Description: Announcements, events, news for members (firms) of the Metro Detroit Convention & Visitors Bureau about the travel & meetings business in the area.
General Info: Monthly, Trim Size-8½ x 11
Circulation: Total-1,100

Converting Business Register
See: PACKAGING

Corporate Acquisitions, Mergers & Divestiture's
See: INVESTMENT

Corporate Annual Report *Business*

Publishing Co: Lawrence Ragan Communications, Inc., 212 W.Superior St,Ste 200, Chicago, IL 60610-3533 Tel # (312) 335-0037 Fax # (312) 335-9583; Title Tel # (312) 922-8245 Title Fax # (312) 922-3336
Personnel: Publisher-Lawrence Ragan, Editor-Bob Gheleardi, Circ. Mgr.-Susan Weston, Mktg. Dir.-Melissa Eckhardt, Mktg. Dir.-Gretchen Eisenfelder
Editorial Description: Tips, trends, and tactics for the producer of the annual report.
General Info: Yr. Est. 1986, Monthly
Subscriptions: Indv. $287
List Rental: List Management Co.: Taybi Direct East, Inc., 13321 New Hampshire Ave., Ste. 202, Silver Spring, MD 20904-3450 Tel # (301) 680-3633, Fax # (301) 680-3635

Corporate Community
Relations Letter *Business*

Publishing Co: Center for Corporate Community Relations at Boston College, 36 College Rd., Chestnut Hill, MA 02167-3800 Tel # (617) 552-8000 Fax # (617) 552-8499
Personnel: Editor-Lisa LaBanca, Mng. Editor-Susan Thomas, Mktg. Mgr.-Kathleen Leonara
Editorial Description: Provides corporations with information and ideas on good community relations practices.
General Info: Yr. Est. 1986, 10x/yr., Trim Size-8½ x 11, 8 pages, ISSN: 1083-7930, 2 Color
Subscriptions: Indv. $115, For. $130
Circulation: Total-1,778

Corporate Compliance:
Internal Reviews, Audits,
and Investigations *Business*

Publishing Co: Assets Protection Publishing, P.O. Box 5323, Madison, WI 53705-0323 Parent Co.-Assets Protection Publishing, Madison; Title Tel # (608) 877-1409
Personnel: Publisher, Editor-Paul Shaw
Editorial Description: Describes how to conduct prompt, efficient, and diligent internal corporate compliance reviews, audits, and investigations including practical and legal aspects.
General Info: Yr. Est. 1995, Bi-monthly, Trim Size-8½ x 11, 32 pages, 2 Color, Saddle-stitched, Looseleaf
Subscriptions: Indv. $72, Can. $84, For. $104, $10/copy
Circulation: Total-200

Corporate Control Alert
See: BANKING & FINANCE

Corporate Counsel LAWCST
See: LAW

Corporate Counsel's Commercial Law Advisor
See: LAW

Corporate Counsel's Monitor
See: LAW

Corporate Crime Reporter *Business*

Publishing Co: Corporate Crime Reporter, PO Box 18384, Washington, DC 20036-8384; Title Tel # (202) 429-6928
Personnel: Editor-Russell Mokhiber
Editorial Description: Covers all aspects of corporate crime.
General Info: Yr. Est. 1987, 48x/yr.
Subscriptions: Indv. $795, Inst. $595

Corporate EFT Report
See: BANKING & FINANCE

Corporate Examiner *Business*

Publishing Co: Interfaith Center on Corporate Responsibility, 475 Riverside Dr Ste 566, New York, NY 10115-0122; Title Tel # (212) 870-2296
Personnel: Publisher-Timothy Smith, Editor-Diane Bratcher
Editorial Description: Examines actions & policies of U.S. corps. on environment, foreign investment, minorities, women, military, energy, corporate responsibility, apartheid, infant formula.
General Info: Yr. Est. 1971, 10x/yr., Trim Size-8½ x 11, 8 pages, 2 Color, Matte, Saddle-stitched
Subscriptions: Indv. $35, Can. $40, For. $45, $4/copy
List Rental: Rents Lists
Printing Co: Natl. Council of Churches, 475 Riverside Dr Ste 552, New York, NY 10115-0122

Corporate Financing
Week *Business*

Publishing Co: Capital Cities/ABC, 488 Madison Ave., 16th Floor, New York, NY 10022-5751 Tel # (212) 224-3233 Parent Co.-Capital Cities/ABC, Inc., New York; Title Tel # (212) 303-3233 Title Fax # (212) 224-3353
Personnel: Publisher-Linda Litner, Editor-Tom Lamont, Circ. Mgr.-Gladys Delgado, Production Dir.-Susan Drobney, Adv. Dir.-Pat Bertucci, Mktg. Dir.-Dahlia Weinman
Editorial Description: Provides penetrating coverage of all aspects of corporate capital raising, including mergers and acquisitions, taxation issues, accounting and regulatory news. There is also heavy coverage of activities at investment banks. It is read by corporateCEOs, CFOs and other corporate financial executives.
General Info: Yr. Est. 1975, Weekly, Trim Size-8½ x 11, Sheetfed press, 10 pages, Ind/Abs/Online: Lexis/Nexis news review, 2 Color, Newsprint
Subscriptions: Indv. $1,295, Can. $1,325, For. $1,370, $30/copy
Advertising: Inquire for rates.

Corporate Governance
Bulletin *Business*

Publishing Co: Investor Responsibility Research Ctr., 1350 Connecticut Ave. N.W., Suite 700, Washington, DC 20036-1701 Fax # (202) 833-3555; Title Tel # (202) 833-0700
Personnel: Editor-Jim Singer, Mktg. Dir.-John McMahon
Editorial Description: Current corporate governance issues.
General Info: Bi-monthly
Subscriptions: Indv. $150

Corporate Growth Weekly
Report *Business* CPM: $333

Publishing Co: Quality Services, Inc., 5290 Overpass Rd., Ste 126, Santa Barbara, CA 93111-2042; Title Tel # (805) 964-7841 Title Fax # (805) 964-1073
Personnel: Publisher-Dr. Walter Jurek, Editor-Carl A. Shrager, Assoc. Ed.-David Jurek, Assoc. Ed.-Carmen Lodise, Circ. Dir.-Nancy Rothlein
Editorial Description: Provides financial details on current mergers and acquisitions. Also provides details on business valuations, restructuings, and methods of increasing shareholder value.
General Info: (Formerly Corporate Growth Report; Joint Venture Digest), Yr. Est. 1983, Weekly, Trim Size-8½ x 11, Offset press, 28 pages, ISSN: 1050-320X, 2 Color
Subscriptions: Indv. $795, For. $895
Circulation: Total-1,500
Advertising: $500. Accepts Inserts.
List Rental: Actives: 1,500, $500/M
Printing Co: PIP, 5733 Hollister Ave., Goleta, CA 93117

Corporate Internet Strategies
See: COMPUTERS & AUTOMATION

Corporate Philanthropy Report
See: PHILANTHROPY

Corporate Public Issues
and Their Management *Business*

Publishing Co: Issue Action Pubs. Inc., 207 Loudoun St. SE, Leesburg, VA 22075-3115; Title Tel # (703) 777-8450
Personnel: Publisher, Editor-Teresa Crane, Circ. Mgr.-Mary Jane Timpano
Editorial Description: Issue management, the executive's systems approach to policy formulation. Includes case studies, seminar coverage, commentary, reviews of relevant literature, software and other products.
General Info: Yr. Est. 1976, Semi-monthly, Trim Size-8½ x 11, 6 pages, ISSN: 0730-5192, No Color, Newsprint
Subscriptions: Indv. $215, Can. $225, For. $240, $9/copy
Circulation: (100% controlled), Total-2,500
List Rental: Rents Lists

Corporate Responsibility
Monitor *Business, Association*

Publishing Co: Third World Resources, DataCenter, 464 19th St., Oakland, CA 94612-2297; Title Tel # (510) 835-4692 Title Fax # (510) 835-3017
Personnel: Editor-Andy Kivel
General Info: Yr. Est. 1983, Bi-monthly, Desktop press, 150 pages
Subscriptions: Indv. $450, Inst. $450

Corporate Restructuring

Publishing Co: MLR Publishing Co., 229 S 18th St, Philadelphia, PA 19103-6192; Title Tel # (215) 790-7000
Personnel: Publisher-Robert Rock, Editor-Martin Sikora, Circ. Mgr.-Roxanne Christensen
Editorial Description: Contains reports on the latest restructuring techniques including financing & deal structuring & legal, accounting, & tax implications. Also contains a roster summary of over 100 noteworthy restructurings each month.
General Info: Yr. Est. 1988, Monthly, ISSN: 0896-775X
Subscriptions: Indv. $495
Acqustions: Publication Bought

Corporate Secretary's Guide

Publishing Co: CCH, Inc., 2700 Lake Cook Rd., Riverwoods, IL 60015 Tel # (847) 267-7000 Fax # (800) 224-8299 Parent Co.-Kluwer Law & Taxation Publishers, Cambridge; Title Tel # (312) 583-8500 Title Fax # (312) 866-3895
Editorial Description: Includes summaries of state business laws and state-by-state treatment of blue sky laws and major federal regulatory programs, plus pertinent forms, examples and recommendations. Includes semimonthly newsletter, 'Corporate Directions.'
General Info: Monthly, Looseleaf
Subscriptions: Indv. $545

Correctional Industries Assn. Newsletter
See: LAW ENFORCEMENT & PENOLOGY

Cost Controller, The *Business*

Publishing Co: Siefer Consultants, Inc., 525 Cayuga St., PO Box 1384, Storm Lake, IA 50588; Title Tel # (712) 732-7340 Title Fax # (712) 732-7906
Personnel: Publisher-Dan Siefer, Editor-Lynn Hardt
Editorial Description: Cost control ideas for the business and industry segment. Practical ways to reduce over read and operating costs.
General Info: Yr. Est. 1991, Monthly, ISSN: 1063-2735
Subscriptions: Indv. $249, Can. $249, For. $280, $15/copy

Council Reports *Business*

Publishing Co: New England Council, Inc., 580 Boylston St., 5th Fl., Boston, MA 02199-8001; Title Tel # (617) 437-0304
Personnel: Editor-Thomas Sommer
Editorial Description: Council activities and information on New England trends in business, economics, budget.
General Info: Monthly, 8 pages, 2 Color
Subscriptions: Indv. $15
Circulation: Total-3,000

Countertrade Outlook (CTO)
See: INTERNATIONAL TRADE

Crane Safety Report, The
See: SAFETY

Creative Leap International *Business*

Publishing Co: Scharf and Associates, 1137 Elliott St., Saskatoon, SK S7N 0V4 Canada; Title Tel # (306) 244-4164 Title Fax # (306) 652-0633
Personnel: Editor-Alan Scharf
General Info: Yr. Est. 1987, Semi-annually, ISSN: 0833=1146
Subscriptions: Indv. $50

Creative Marketing Newsletter
See: ADVERTISING & MARKETING

Credit & Collection Manager's Letter *Business*

Publishing Co: Bureau of Business Practice, 24 Rope Ferry Rd, Waterford, CT 06386-0001 Tel # (806) 442-4365 Fax # (860) 434-3341 Parent Co.-Prentice Hall, Waterford; Title Tel # (860) 444-4365 Title Fax # (860) 434-3078
Personnel: Publisher-Martin E. Kenny, Jr., Editor-Russell L. Case
Editorial Description: Experts in credit and collection management reveal their success stories and offer specific hands-on information for improving the credit and collection department.
General Info: (Formerly Credit & Collection Management Bulletin), Semi-monthly, Trim Size-8$\frac{1}{2}$ x 11, Letrpr. press, 8 pages, ISSN: 1060-2739, 2 Color, Matte, Perfect bound
Subscriptions: Indv. $143
Circulation: Total-5,000
Printing Co: Commercial Printers, 3 Hilltop Rd, Norwich, CT 06360-1554 Tel # (203) 886-0541, Fax # (203) 886-5805

Currencies & Credit Markets *Business*

Publishing Co: Investment Rarities, Inc., 7850 Metro Pky Ste 106, Minneapolis, MN 55425-1521 Tel # (612) 853-0700; Title Tel # (612) 851-8731
Personnel: Editor-Kurt Richebacher
General Info: Monthly
Subscriptions: Indv. $400

Customer Service Manager's Letter *Business*

Publishing Co: Bureau of Business Practice, 24 Rope Ferry Rd, Waterford, CT 06386-0001 Tel # (806) 442-4365 Fax # (860) 434-3341 Parent Co.-Prentice Hall, Waterford; Title Tel # (203) 444-4365 Title Fax # (203) 434-3078
Personnel: Publisher-Elaine Stattler, Editor-Christine M. Greeley, Art Dir.-Diane Smith
Editorial Description: Interview-based articles provide managers with proven methods and best practices in customer Service.
General Info: (Formerly Customer Service Management Bulletin), Yr. Est. 1987, Semi-monthly, Trim Size-8$\frac{1}{2}$ x 11, 8 pages, ISSN: 1068-154X, 4 Color
Subscriptions: Indv. $160
Circulation: Total-8,111, Readership-8,161

Customer Service Newsletter *Business*

Publishing Co: Alexander Research & Communications, Inc., 215 Park Ave S., Ste. 1301, New York, NY 10003-1603; Title Tel # (212) 228-0246 Title Fax # (212) 228-0376
Personnel: Publisher, Editor-Leslie Hansen Harps, Circ. Dir.-Mary Pagliaroti, Mktg. Dir.-Margaret DeWitt
Editorial Description: Reports on practical, action-oriented techniques & tactics for improving customer service operations. Help customer service directors, managers & supervisors improve their operations with timely information on how other managers get top management support; train & motivate their staff; measure the improvement of their operations; set standards; compile information & benchmark for greater effectiveness;
General Info: Yr. Est. 1973, Monthly, Trim Size-8$\frac{1}{2}$ x 11, Sheetfed press, 8 pages, ISSN: 0145-8422, 2 Color, Newsprint
Subscriptions: Indv. $124, Can. $124, For. $154, $10/copy
Acquistions: Publication Sold
List Rental: List Management Co.: Response Media Products Inc., 2323 Perimeter Park Dr., Ste. 200, Atlanta, GA 30341-1335 Tel # (404) 451-5478, Fax # (404) 451-4929
Printing Co: Plymouth Printing, 1200 Cushing Pl SE, Washington, DC 20003-3599 Tel # (202) 488-7777, Fax # (202) 863-1078

Customer Service Report
See: MANAGEMENT

Customer Service Report
See: MANAGEMENT

Customers First
See: SALESMANSHIP & SELLING

Data Channels
See: COMPUTERS & AUTOMATION

Dateline Winnipeg *Business*

Publishing Co: BBB of Winnipeg & Manitoba Inc., 365 Hargrave St., Suite 301, Winnipeg, MB R3B 2K3 Canada; Title Tel # (204) 942-7166 Title Fax # (204) 343-1489
Personnel: Publisher, Editor, Circ. Mgr., Adv. Dir., Art Dir.-T.S. Durham
Editorial Description: Privileged member information, news and commentary on ethical practice in area business.
General Info: Yr. Est. 1971, Quarterly, Trim Size-8$\frac{1}{2}$ x 11, Sheetfed press, 4 pages, No Color, Newsprint
Circulation: (100% controlled), Total-2,000

Dealing with Technology *Business*

Publishing Co: Waters Information Services, PO Box 2248, Binghamton, NY 13902-2248 Tel # (607) 770-4075 Fax # (607) 770-9435
Personnel: Editor-Peter Harris
Editorial Description: Reports on electronic information services.
General Info: Yr. Est. 1989, Bi-weekly, ISSN: 0955-2138
Subscriptions: Indv. $795

Debtor-Creditor law
See: LAW

Delaware Corporate Litigation Reporter
See: LAW

Delaware Corporation Law and Practice
See: LAW

Delaware Today Aware *Business*

Publishing Co: Delaware Today, Inc., PO Box 2087, Wilmington, DE 19899-2087
Personnel: Publisher-Len Quinn, Editor-Peter Mucha
General Info: Yr. Est. 1962, Monthly
Circulation: Total-7,500

Dempsey Canadian Letter *Business*

Publishing Co: John B. Dempsey, II, 1127 Euclid Ave Ste 375, Cleveland, OH 44115-1601; Title Tel # (216) 241-1160 Title Fax # (216) 566-1536
Editorial Description: Fortnightly coverage of Canadian affairs, with emphasis on impact upon & from U.S.
General Info: (Formerly Dempsey Canadian Newsletter), Yr. Est. 1952, Bi-weekly, Trim Size-8$\frac{1}{2}$ x 11, 4 pages, Matte
Subscriptions: Indv. $125, For. $125

Development Director's Letter
See: PHILANTHROPY

Diagnostic Quarterly
See: MEDICINE

Dialogue
See: ELECTRIC & ELECTRONIC EQUIPMENT

Digest of Municipal and Planning Law, The

Publishing Co: Carswell, 2075 Kennedy Road, One Corporate Plaza, Scarborough, ON M1T 3V4 Canada Fax # (416) 298-5094; Title Tel # (416) 609-8000 Title Fax # (416) 298-5063

Director's Monthly
See: MANAGEMENT

Directorship
Business

Publishing Co: Directosip Inc., 8 Sound Shore Dr Ste 254, Greenwich, CT 06830-7242; Title Tel # (203) 861-7000 Title Fax # (203) 861-7007
Personnel: Publisher-Abraham Nad, Editor-Elsa Nad, Circ. Mgr.-Carol Malone, Production Mgr.-David Calhoun, Promotion Dir.-Marlene Allen
Editorial Description: 16-pages monthly of fact - field articles written by experts for directors or virtually every issue of corporate governouce.
General Info: Yr. Est. 1975, Monthly, Trim Size-8½ x 11, Sheetfed press, 16 pages, ISSN: 0193-4279, Ind/Abs/Online: Directorship Inc., Coated, Saddle-stitched
Subscriptions: Indv. $470, $48/copy

Discount & Wholesale Printing Newsletter
See: PRINTING/GRAPHIC ARTS

Disease Management News
See: HEALTH

Distribution Center Management
Business

Publishing Co: Alexander Research & Communications, Inc., 215 Park Ave S., Ste. 1301, New York, NY 10003-1603; Title Tel # (212) 228-0246 Title Fax # (212) 228-0376
Personnel: Publisher-Shirley B. Alexander, Mng. Editor-Aniota Rosepka, Circ. Mgr.-Mary Pagliaroli, Mktg. Dir.-Margaret DeWitt
Editorial Description: Provides practical strategies for distribution center and warehouse managers Topics covered include: warehouse infrastructure, new technologies, working with employees, law and government regulations, performance measures, opeations management and more.
General Info: Monthly, Trim Size-8.5 x 11.0, 8 pages, ISSN: 0894-7651
Subscriptions: Indv. $119, Can. $119, For. $149
Advertising: Accepts Inserts.
List Rental: Rents Lists

Distributor Management Digest
See: MANAGEMENT

Distributor's & Wholesaler's Advisor, The
Business

Publishing Co: Alexander Research & Communications, Inc., 215 Park Ave S., Ste. 1301, New York, NY 10003-1603; Title Tel # (212) 228-0246 Title Fax # (212) 228-0376
Personnel: Publisher-Shirley Alexander, Editor-Laurence Alexander, Mng. Editor-Anita Rosepka, Circ. Mgr.-Mary Pagliaroli, Mktg. Dir.-Margaret DeWitt
Editorial Description: For owners and operators of wholesale distributorships. Provides timely, practical news & information in four critical areas of running a distribution company: purchasing, inventory handling, selling, & overall business management. It also provides basicinsights into wholesaling trends, economic trends, industry issues, operating strategies & more.
General Info: Yr. Est. 1989, Semi-monthly, Trim Size-8½ x 11, 8 pages, ISSN: 1043-7118
Subscriptions: Indv. $197, Can. $197, For. $227, $9/copy
Acquistions: Publication Bought
List Rental: Rents Lists

Doing Business in Asia

Publishing Co: CCH, Inc., 2700 Lake Cook Rd., Riverwoods, IL 60015 Parent Co.-Kluwer Law & Taxation Publishers, Cambridge; Title Tel # (847) 267-7000 Title Fax # (800) 224-8299
Editorial Description: Provides an itemized list of considerations and vital questions that businesses or individuals need to ask when investing in Asia, and supplies the answers to these questions and considerations, in detail, from major Asian trading nations.
General Info: Quarterly, Looseleaf
Subscriptions: Indv. $715

Doing Business in Eastern Europe

Publishing Co: CCH, Inc., 2700 Lake Cook Rd., Riverwoods, IL 60015 Parent Co.-Kluwer Law & Taxation Publishers, Cambridge; Title Tel # (847) 267-7000 Title Fax # (800) 224-8299
Editorial Description: Provides latest information on new business and tax laws, including currency, banking, import-export, land ownership, privatization, intellectual property, anti-trust, resources and regulations.
General Info: Monthly, Looseleaf
Subscriptions: Indv. $410

Doing Business in Europe
Business

Publishing Co: CCH, Inc., 2700 Lake Cook Rd., Riverwoods, IL 60015 Parent Co.-Kluwer Law & Taxation Publishers, Cambridge; Title Tel # (847) 267-7000 Title Fax # (800) 224-8299
Editorial Description: This report provides an overview of the complex company; tax, labor, and financial requirements for business operations in Europe.
General Info: Yr. Est. 1972, Monthly, Trim Size-6 x 9, Web press, 80 pages, No Color, Looseleaf
Subscriptions: Indv. $715

Doing Business in the United States
Business

Publishing Co: Matthew Bender & Co., 11 Penn Plaza, New York, NY 10001-2006 Fax # (212) 244-3188; Title Tel # (212) 967-7707
Personnel: Editor-J. O'Brien
Editorial Description: A guide in contract law, corporation law, corporate accounting, banking, etc.
General Info: Yr. Est. 1978, Irregular, Looseleaf
Subscriptions: $495/copy

Don Larson's Business Newsletter
Business

Publishing Co: Business Newsletter, Inc., 537 E Vine St, Owatonna, MN 55060-2518 Fax # (507) 455-3220; Title Tel # (507) 455-3220
Personnel: Publisher, Editor-Don Larson
General Info: Yr. Est. 1980, 22x/yr.
Subscriptions: Indv. $39

EDI News
Business

Publishing Co: Phillips Business Information, Inc., 1201 Seven Locks Rd., Ste 300, Potomac, MD 20854-2958 Tel # (301) 340-1520; Title Tel # (301) 340-2100 Title Fax # (301) 424-4297
Personnel: Publisher-Chris Scotton, Grp. Pub.-Megan St. John, Editor-John Zyskowski, Mng. Editor-Mary Crowley, Production Mgr.-Sherry Mitchell, Circ. Mgr., Mktg. Dir., Promotion Dir.-Ruth Zellers
Editorial Description: The publication of record in the electronic data interchange marketplace. It provides insightful reporting on industry news and analysis of applications & standards developments.
General Info: (Formerly Quick ResponseNews; Electronic Trade&TransportNews; EDI Exec), Yr. Est. 1989, Bi-weekly, Trim Size-8½ x 11, 8 pages, ISSN: 0894-9212, Ind/Abs/Online: NEWSNET PREDICASTS
Subscriptions: Indv. $597, For. $630
Advertising: Inquire for rates. Accepts Inserts.
List Rental: Rents Lists

EFT Report
See: BANKING & FINANCE

ETCetera
See: ANTIQUES & ART GOODS

Early Warning Forecast
Business

Publishing Co: Cahners Publishing Co., 275 Washington St., Newton, MA 02158-1630 Fax # (617) 558-4470 Parent Co.-Reed Elsevier, New York; Title Tel # (617) 964-3030 Title Fax # (617) 630-2100
Personnel: Publisher-Jim Haughey, Editor-Bill Wood, Circ. Mgr.-Michelle DeSimone, Production Mgr.-Chris Blocher, Promotion Dir.-Dan Buchan
Editorial Description: Analysis & forecasts of general economy and industrial markets. Insights for companies forecasting their own sales.
General Info: Yr. Est. 1971, Monthly, Trim Size-8½ x 11, Desktop press, 8 pages, ISSN: 0733-0138, 2 Color, Newsprint
Subscriptions: Indv. $259, Can. $259, For. $259, $35/copy
Circulation: Total-1,000
Printing Co: Ben Franklin Smith, 320 Stuart St, Boston, MA 02116-5290 Tel # (617) 426-1160

Early Warnings
Business

Publishing Co: Institute for Crisis Management, 1169 E. Broadway Street, Louisville, KY 40204-1764 Tel # (502) 584-0402 Fax # (502) 584-0207
Personnel: Publisher-Robert B. Irvine, Editor-Catherine R. Turcotte
Editorial Description: A new publication designed to keep readers aware of major news events and their subsequent impact on daily living conditions.
General Info: Yr. Est. 1993, Quarterly
Subscriptions: Indv. $75

East Asian Business Intelligence
See: INTERNATIONAL TRADE

Eco, The
See: PRINTING/GRAPHIC ARTS

Economic Development/ State Capitals
Business

Publishing Co: Wakeman/Walworth, 300 N. Washington St., Alexandria, VA 22314-2530; Title Tel # (703) 549-8606 Title Fax # (703) 549-1372
Personnel: Publisher-Keyes Walworth
Editorial Description: State and local efforts to attract new industries and expand existing plants, commerce, tourism - covers state incentives & disincentives, taxes and environmental regulations. Includes urban development programs, growth control legislation, and construction programs.
General Info: (Formerly Industrial Development from the State Capitals), Yr. Est. 1946, Weekly, Trim Size-8½ x 11, Offset press, 8 pages, ISSN: 1061-9712, No Color
Subscriptions: Indv. $265, Inst. $212, Can. $235, For. $255

Economic Issues
See: ECONOMICS

Economics Update

Publishing Co: Federal Reserve Bank of Atlanta, 104 Marietta St NW, Atlanta, GA 30303-2713 Fax # (404) 521-8050; Title Tel # (404) 521-8020
Personnel: Editor-John Marsh, Circ. Mgr.-Ellen Arth, Art Dir.-Carole Starkey
Editorial Description: Reports news affecting Federal Reserve.
General Info: (Formerly Economic Insight), Monthly
Circulation: Total-7,000

Editorials on File
See: NEWSPAPER INDUSTRY

Edmonton Report on Economic Development *Business*

Publishing Co: Economic Development Edmonton, 9797 Jasper Ave., Edmonton Convention Centre, Edmonton, AB T5J 1N9 Canada; Title Tel # (403) 424-7870 Title Fax # (403) 426-0535
Personnel: Editor-Janice Dewar
Editorial Description: Variety of economic stories in digest form to achieve awareness of city in specific market areas.
General Info: (Formerly Edmonton Report on Economic Dev.), Yr. Est. 1966, Quarterly, Trim Size-8½ x 11, Sheetfed press, 8 pages, 4 Color, Matte, Saddle-stitched
Subscriptions: Free
Acquistions: Publication Bought
Circulation: Total-14,000

EduQuest Connections *Business, Consumer*

Publishing Co: Mejia and Associates, Inc., 1047 E 29th St, Brooklyn, NY 11210-3743; Title Tel # (718) 253-5113
Personnel: Editor-Dorian Skeete, Publisher, Editorial Page Ed.-Aimee Mejia, Circ. Mgr.-Frank Mejia, Feature Ed., Bk. Rev. Ed., Production Mgr.-Danette Green, Asst. Prod. Mgr.-Amparo Mejia, City Ed., Asst. Ed., Adv. Dir.-Lenny Vigliotti, Promotion Dir.-Theodore N. Mejia
Editorial Description: Provides information for small and home-based entrepreneurs, business owners from under-represented groups, and individuals considering changing careers. Covers the education and business link. Discusses health issues, investment, job opportunities, professional development, and technology issues advice for readers.
General Info: Yr. Est. 1991, 12x/yr., Trim Size-8½ x 11, Sheetfed press, 12 pages, Ind/Abs/Online: Netcom, No Color, Matte, Saddle-stitched
Subscriptions: Indv. $25, Inst. $25, Can. $30, For. $33
Advertising: $120. Accepts Inserts.
List Rental: Actives: $60/M
Printing Co: Account Manager: N. Goldman; Far Better Printing, Hillel Place, Brooklyn, NY 11210

Electronic Filer's Report
See: TAXES

Electronic Messaging News
See: TELECOMMUNICATIONS

Empire State Development *Business*

Publishing Co: Empire State Development, One Commerce Plaza, Albany, NY 12245-0001 Fax # (516) 474-5687; Title Tel # (518) 474-6950 Title Fax # (518) 474-5687
Personnel: Publisher-Caroline Quarteraro, Editor-Brian Stratten, Art Dir.-Bill Finnerty
Editorial Description: New York State's economic development newsletter.
General Info: (Formerly Opportunity New York), Yr. Est. 1987, Quarterly, Sheetfed press, 8 pages, 2 Color, Coated, Saddle-stitched
Subscriptions: Free
Circulation: Total-20,000

Employee Benefits Alert
See: INDUSTRIAL RELATIONS/PERSONNEL

Employee Ownership Report *Business, Association*

Publishing Co: Natl. Center for Employee Ownership, 2201 Broadway Ste 807, Oakland, CA 94612-3024; Title Tel # (510) 272-9461 Title Fax # (510) 272-9510
Personnel: Publisher-Corey Rosen, Editor-Karen Young
Editorial Description: Case studies, legal tips, new resources and developments in employee ownership, media notes, substantive articles.
General Info: Yr. Est. 1981, Bi-monthly, Trim Size-8½ x 11, Offset press, 12 pages, No Color, Saddle-stitched
Subscriptions: $5/copy
Circulation: Total-1,600
List Rental: Rents Lists

Employee Relations Bulletin
See: INDUSTRIAL RELATIONS/PERSONNEL

Employee Security Connection
See: SECURITY & SURVEILLANCE

Employer's Health Benefits Bulletin
See: HEALTH

Employers' Human Rights & Equity Report *Business, Association*

Publishing Co: Carswell, 2075 Kennedy Road, One Corporate Plaza, Scarborough, ON M1T 3V4 Canada; Title Tel # (416) 609-8000 Title Fax # (416) 298-5094
Personnel: Publisher-Robert McElman, Editor-Laurie Blake
General Info: Yr. Est. 1989, 10x/yr.
Subscriptions: Indv. $175

Employment Opportunities
See: EMPLOYMENT

Emprise Investment Newsletter
See: INVESTMENT

Entrepreneur's Alert

Publishing Co: Entrepreneur's Guild, 142 Morris Ave, Mountain Lakes, NJ 07046-1127; Title Tel # (201) 263-2988
Personnel: Publisher-Berkeley Fleming, Editor-Richard Samson
Editorial Description: Advice for business owners & people who want to start businesses.
General Info: Yr. Est. 1988, Monthly, Trim Size-8½ x 11, Sheetfed press, 6 pages, 2 Color
Subscriptions: Indv. $72
Circulation: Total-240

Environment Watch: Latin America
See: ENVIRONMENT & ECOLOGY

Environment Watch: Western Europe
See: ENVIRONMENT & ECOLOGY

Environmental Compliance Alert
See: ENVIRONMENT & ECOLOGY

Environmental Control News for Southern Industry
See: ENVIRONMENT & ECOLOGY

Environmental Manager
See: ENVIRONMENT & ECOLOGY

Ethical Management
See: MANAGEMENT

Ethics in Government Reporter
See: GOVERNMENT

EuroWatch *Business*

Publishing Co: LRP Publications, 747 Dresher Rd., P.O. Box 980, Horsham, PA 19044-0980 Tel # (215) 784-0910 Fax # (215) 784-0317
Personnel: Publisher-Ken Kahn, Editor-Michael Petrovsky
Editorial Description: Reports on political, business & legal developments that are taking place in the European community including such infomation as: explanations of EC directives, regulatory guidelines, and coverage of the European FTA nations.
General Info: (Formerly External Impact of European Unification), Yr. Est. 1989, Bi-weekly, Trim Size-8½ x 11, Sheetfed press, 8 pages, ISSN: 1043-4380, 2 Color, Matte
Subscriptions: Indv. $797, For. $797
Acquistions: Publication Bought, Publication Sold

Euromarketing
See: ADVERTISING & MARKETING

Euromedia Acquisitions & Finance *Business*

Publishing Co: Kagan World Media Inc., 126 Clock Tower Pl., Carmel, CA 93923-8734 Parent Co.-Paul Kagan Associates Inc., Carmel; Title Tel # (408) 624-1536 Title Fax # (408) 625-3225
Personnel: Publisher-Paul Kagan, Circ. Mgr.-Judy Pinney, Editor, Adv. Dir.-Johanne Hardy
Editorial Description: Tracks mergers, sales, and management buyouts.
General Info: (Formerly Euromedia Acquisitions), Yr. Est. 1992, Monthly, Trim Size-7¼ x 10, Other press, 10 pages, No Color, Other, Saddle-stitched
Subscriptions: Indv. $795
Advertising: $1,560.

European Community
See: INTERNATIONAL TRADE

Executive Compensation
See: TAXES

Executive Compensation Report (ECR) *Business*

Publishing Co: DP Pubs., PO Box 7188, Fairfax Station, VA 22039-7188 Tel # (703) 452-1322; Title Tel # (703) 425-1322 Title Fax # (703) 425-7911
Personnel: Publisher-Judith Fischer, Editor-Carol Bowie
Editorial Description: Covers executive compensation at over 1000 companies.
General Info: Yr. Est. 1981, Semi-monthly, 8 pages, ISSN: 0738-6982
Subscriptions: Indv. $439, Can. $439, For. $499

Executive Report on Customer Satisfaction *Business*

Publishing Co: Alexander Research & Communications, Inc., 215 Park Ave S., Ste. 1301, New York, NY 10003-1603; Title Tel # (212) 228-0246 Title Fax # (212) 228-0376
Personnel: Publisher-Shirely Alexander, Editor-Susan Hash, Circ. Mgr.-Mary Pagliarolt, Mktg. Dir.-Margaret Dewitt
Editorial Description: Provides the latest information on such critical issues as monitoring and measuring customer satisfaction; changing to a customer-focused corporate culture; bench marking; using complaints and customer feedback to improve satisfaction; calculating the ROI on service improvements; putting vision and mission statement into action and more.
General Info: Yr. Est. 1988, Semi-monthly, Trim Size-8½ x 11, 8 pages, ISSN: 0164-862
Subscriptions: Indv. $199, Can. $199, For. $229, $9/copy
List Rental: List Management Co.: Manager: Mary Dalessandro; Response Media Products Inc., 2323 Perimeter Park Dr., Ste. 200, Atlanta, GA 30341-1335 Tel # (404) 451-5478, Fax # (404) 451-4929

Executive Report on Managed Care
See: HEALTH

Executive Solutions
See: MANAGEMENT

Executive Strategies
See: MANAGEMENT

Executive's Business Digest
Business

Publishing Co: Dartnell Corp., 4660 N. Ravenswood Ave., Chicago, IL 60640-4510 Fax # (312) 561-3801; Title Tel # (312) 561-4000 Title Fax # (312) 561-4842
Personnel: Editor-Deanne Tsoukalas, Sales Rep.-Christopher Ackley
Editorial Description: Produced to help companies maintain contact with their customers. Frequency determined by sponsoring organization.
General Info: Monthly, Trim Size-8½ x 11, Matte
Advertising: Inquire for rates.

Executives Tax Report
See: TAXES

Exhibit Mexico
See: ADVERTISING & MARKETING

Exhibitor
See: ADVERTISING & MARKETING

Exhibitor Extra
Business

Publishing Co: Exhibitor Publications, Inc., 206 S. Broadway, Ste. 745, Rochester, MN 55904-6565 Tel # (507) 289-6556; Title Tel # (507) 289-6565 Title Fax # (507) 289-5253
Personnel: Publisher-Lee Knight, Editor-Paula Marlow, Circ. Dir.-Jennifer Blink, Art Dir.-Diane Hart
Editorial Description: Tips and tactics for trade show marketing. Published as a regular section within its parent publication Exhibitor Magazine.
General Info: (Formerly Creative Exhibiting Techniques), Yr. Est. 1992, Irregular, Trim Size-8½ x 11, 8 pages, ISSN: 1070-826X, 2 Color, Matte, Saddle-stitched
Subscriptions: Indv. $89, Inst. $89, Can. $109, For. $130
Circulation: Total-1,500
Printing Co: Sulla Printing, 9-1st Street NW, Rochester, MN 55901

FCG Report

Publishing Co: Business Communications Group, 3727 N Oak Trfy, Kansas City, MO 64116-2778; Title Tel # (816) 931-0381
General Info: Yr. Est. 1991, Monthly
Subscriptions: Indv. $20

FTC FOIA Log

Publishing Co: Washington Regulatory Reporting Group, PO Box 356, Basye, VA 22810-0356; Title Tel # (703) 856-2216 Title Fax # (703) 856-8331
Personnel: Publisher-Mimi Madden, Editor-Art Amolsch
Editorial Description: Summarizes all Freedom of Information Act requests as they are received at the FTC.
General Info: Yr. Est. 1980, Weekly, Trim Size-8½ x 11, Letrpr. press, 2 pages, ISSN: 0161-7036, Ind/Abs/Online: NewsNet, DIALOG, No Color
Subscriptions: Indv. $345, For. $395
Acquistions: Publication Bought
Advertising: Accepts Inserts.

FTC WATCH
Association, Business

Publishing Co: Washington Regulatory Reporting Group, PO Box 356, Basye, VA 22810-0356 Tel # (703) 856-2216 Fax # (703) 856-8331; Title Tel # (202) 434-8222 Title Fax # (202) 347-1882
Personnel: Publisher, Editor-Art Amolsch
Editorial Description: News and information on the Federal Trade Commission and U.S. Justice Dept.'s Antitrust Division.
General Info: Yr. Est. 1976, Bi-weekly, Trim Size-8½ x 11, 16 pages, ISSN: 0196-0016, Ind/Abs/Online: NewsNet, DIALOG
Subscriptions: Indv. $632, For. $714
Acquistions: Publication Bought
Advertising: Inquire for rates. Accepts Inserts.

FYI International
See: HOUSE ORGANS

Facility Manager's Alert
See: CONSTRUCTION & BUILDING

FactSheet

Publishing Co: Empire State Development, One Commerce Plaza, Albany, NY 12245-0001 Tel # (518) 474-6950 Fax # (516) 474-5687; Title Tel # (518) 474-6005
General Info: Monthly

Facts & Trends

Publishing Co: Vancouver Board of Trade, 999 Canada Pl., #400, Vancouver, BC V6C 3C1 Canada; Title Tel # (604) 681-2111
Personnel: Publisher-Roger Young, Editor-Sandra Hochstein
General Info: Bi-weekly, Trim Size-8½ x 11, Mimeo press, 1 pages, ISSN: 0429-9949, No Color
Subscriptions: Can. $96

Facts on File World News Digest
See: INTERNATIONAL AFFAIRS

Fairfax Prospectus
Business

Publishing Co: Fairfax County Economic Development Authority, 8300 Boone Blvd Ste 450, Vienna, VA 22182-2626; Title Tel # (703) 790-0600 Title Fax # (703) 893-1269
Personnel: Publisher-Gerald Gordon, Editor, Circ. Mgr.-Elizabeth Andrews
Editorial Description: Reports on business relocation and expansion in Fairfax County, Virginia.
General Info: Yr. Est. 1969, Bi-monthly, Trim Size-8½ x 11, Offset press, 8 pages, No Color
Circulation: (100% controlled), Total-10,100

Federal Contract Disputes
See: LAW

Federal Contracts Report
Business

Publishing Co: Bureau of National Affairs, Inc., 1231 25th St. NW, Bldg. N-200, Washington, DC 20037-1157; Title Tel # (202) 452-4200 Title Fax # (202) 822-8092
Personnel: Publisher-William A. Beltz, Editor-Sheila Quigley, Mng. Editor-Melanie I. Dooley, Circ. Mgr.-Gary C. Seltzer
Editorial Description: A weekly reporting service providing comprehensive coverage of the latest significant developments affecting federal contracts & grants.
General Info: Yr. Est. 1964, Weekly, Trim Size-8½ x 11, Web press, 45 pages, ISSN: 0014-9063, Ind/Abs/Online: Lexis, WESTLAW, Mead Data Central, Nexis
Subscriptions: Indv. $1,051

Federal Ethics Report
See: GOVERNMENT

Federal Income Taxation of Corporations Filing Consolidated Returns
See: TAXES

Federal Income Taxation of Corporations and Shareholders
See: TAXES

Fiberoptics Marketing/ Intelligence
Business

Publishing Co: Kessler Marketing Intelligence, America's Cup Ave., 31 Bridge St., Newport, RI 02840; Title Tel # (401) 849-6771 Title Fax # (401) 847-5866
Personnel: Publisher-John Kessler, Editor-Richard Rube, Circ. Mgr.-Donna Rube
Editorial Description: Bi-weekly executive briefing on Fiberoptics Markets, news & Technologies.
General Info: Yr. Est. 1981, Bi-weekly, 4 pages, ISSN: 0748-9358
Subscriptions: Indv. $375, For. $395, $45/copy

Field Reports
Association

Publishing Co: Workover/Well Servicing Publications, Inc., 6060 N Central Expy Ste 428, Dallas, TX 75206-5205; Title Tel # (214) 692-0771
Personnel: Editor-Katherine Leidy
Editorial Description: Actions, activities of the industry, the Association of Oilwell Servicing Contractors, and its members.
General Info: (Formerly AOSC Newsletter), Yr. Est. 1956, Monthly, Trim Size-8½ x 11, 8 pages, No Color, Coated, Other
Subscriptions: Indv. $125, Free With Membership
Circulation: Total-1,200

Financial Observer - Canadian Financial Industry Digest, The
Business, Association

Publishing Co: CCH Canadian Ltd., 6 Garamond Ct., North York, ON M3C 1Z5 Canada Fax # (416) 444-8011 Parent Co.-CCH, Inc., Riverwoods; Title Tel # (416) 441-2992 Title Fax # (416) 444-9011
Personnel: Editor-Brad Morrison, Adv. Dir.-Michael Dyet, Mktg. Dir.-Rick Humphrey
Editorial Description: Detailed cross section of Canada's financial industry and reformss that are reshaping it. Reports on financial performance of Canada and foreign banks and other financial institutions and developments abroad are also covered.
General Info: (Formerly Canadian Financial Institutions), Yr. Est. 1992, Monthly, Trim Size-8½ x 11, Web press, 8 pages, ISSN: 1188-4649, No Color
Subscriptions: Can. $130

Financial Services Report
See: COMPUTERS & AUTOMATION

Financial Update
Business

Publishing Co: Federal Reserve Bank of Atlanta, 104 Marietta St NW, Atlanta, GA 30303-2713 Fax # (404) 521-8050; Title Tel # (404) 521-8020
Personnel: Editor-John D. Marsh, Circ. Mgr.-Ellen Arth, Art Dir.-Carole Starkey
General Info: Quarterly, ISSN: 0899-6563
Subscriptions: Free
Circulation: Total-7,000

Flash Market News
Association

Publishing Co: Natl. Writers Assn./Associated Business Writers of America, 1450 S. Havana, Ste. 424, Aurora, CO 80012; Title Tel # (303) 751-7844 Title Fax # (303) 751-8593
Personnel: Mng. Editor-Sandra Whelchel
Editorial Description: Marketing bulletin for professional members of National Writers Club & of Associated Business Writers of America.
General Info: Yr. Est. 1950, Bi-monthly, Trim Size-8½ x 11, 4 pages
Subscriptions: Indv. $60, Can. $60, For. $80, $5/copy
Circulation: Total-1,000
Printing Co: Econo Copy, 1082 Havana St., Aurora, CO 80010

Florida Market UpDate   *Business*

Publishing Co: Data Direction Inc., PO Box 1052, Port Washington, NY 11050-0204; Title Tel # (516) 741-8887 Title Fax # (616) 741-3131
Personnel: Editor-Hank Boerner
Editorial Description: Key developments, news, trends, to executive audiences.
General Info: Yr. Est. 1985, Monthly
Subscriptions: Indv. $100
Circulation: Total-3,000

Focus, the Business Continuity Planning Newsletter
See: MANAGEMENT

Fordyce Letter
See: EMPLOYMENT

Forms and Procdures Under the UCC
See: LAW

Foundation & Corporate Funding Advantage   *Business*

Publishing Co: Progressive Business Publications, 370 Technology Dr., #3019, Malverne, PA 19355-9863 Parent Co.-American Future Systems, Inc., Bryn Mawr; Title Tel # (610) 695-8600 Title Fax # (610) 647-8089
Personnel: Editorial Dir.-Steve Meyer, Editor-Susan Wade, Mktg. Dir.-Ed Moore
Editorial Description: Information to assist nonprofits in attracting funds and givers to target their philanthropic dollars effectively.
General Info: Yr. Est. 1994, Monthly, 8 pages
Subscriptions: Indv. $240
List Rental: List Management Co.: Mail Marketing, Inc., 171 Terrace St., Haworth, NJ 07641-1899 Tel # (201) 387-1023, Fax # (201) 387-2976

Franchise Wise (Quarterly newsletter of the intl gay & lesbian franchise assoc.)
See: GAY & LESBIAN INTEREST

Franchising in Canada

Publishing Co: Canadian Franchisors Association, 5054 Orbitor Dr., Building #12, Unit 201, Mississaqua, ON L4W 4Y4 Canada; Title Tel # (905) 625-2896 Title Fax # (905) 625-9076
Personnel: Publisher-Margaret Guerrier, Editor-Gordon Green
General Info: Yr. Est. 1980, Monthly, Trim Size-8½ x 11, Desktop press, 12 pages, 2% ads, 2 Color, Newsprint, Saddle-stitched
Acquistions: Publication Bought
Circulation: Total-500
Advertising: Inquire for rates.

Frohlinger's Marketing Report
See: ADVERTISING & MARKETING

Front Line Management
See: MANAGEMENT

Fulton County Daily Report
See: LAW

FutureScan
See: ADVERTISING & MARKETING

Futures and Options News
See: INVESTMENT

Futuretech
See: SCIENCE

Gateway
See: INTERNATIONAL TRADE

Gauge, The
See: MEDIA & COMMUNICATIONS

Genetic Technology News
See: GENETICS

Georgeson Report   *Business*

Publishing Co: Georgeson, Wall St. Plaza, New York, NY 10005; Title Tel # (212) 440-9800 Title Fax # (212) 440-9013
Personnel: Editor-Ernest Sando
General Info: (Formerly Trends in Management/Stockholder Relations), Yr. Est. 1952, Quarterly, Trim Size-8½ x 11, 4 pages, ISSN: 0041-2406, 2 Color
Subscriptions: Free To Qualified Recipient
Acquistions: Publication Bought
Circulation: Total-6,500
Printing Co: The Corporate Printing Co., 225 Varick St., New York, NY 10005

German American Business Council
See: INTERNATIONAL TRADE

Getting Along
See: INDUSTRIAL RELATIONS/PERSONNEL

Global Business Technology Report   *Business*

Publishing Co: Global Business Technology Report, 5100-1B, Suite 170, Concord, CA 94521; Title Tel # (510) 977-8685
Personnel: Editor-Patrice-Anne Rutledge

Global Survey
See: MILITARY & NAVAL

Going Public: The IPO Reporter
See: INVESTMENT

Goods & Services Bulletin   *Business*

Publishing Co: Commonwealth of Massachusetts, State Bookstore, State House, Rm. 116, Boston, MA 02133-1019; Title Tel # (617) 727-2834
General Info: Yr. Est. 1984, Weekly
Subscriptions: Indv. $45

Goods in Transit
See: TRAFFIC & TRANSPORTATION

Government Inventions for Licensing   *Business*

Publishing Co: National Technical Information Service U.S., 5285 Port Royal Rd., Springfield, VA 22161-0001 Fax # (703) 487-4630; Title Tel # (703) 487-4630
Personnel: Editor-Linda LaGarde
Editorial Description: Identifies government research & development inventions available for licensing. Summarizes inventions from all government agencies arranged in ten subject areas.
General Info: Yr. Est. 1972, Weekly, Trim Size-8½ x 11, Offset press, 10 pages, ISSN: 0364-6491
Subscriptions: Indv. $250, Can. $250, For. $365

Government Prime Contracts Monthly
See: U.S. (& CANADIAN) FED. GOV'T.

GraFiber News
See: AERONAUTICS/ASTRONAUTICS

Grantee's Action Alert Bulletin   *Business*

Publishing Co: Master Guide Pubs., PO Box 27203, Salt Lake City, UT 84127-0203; Title Tel # (801) 561-1556 Title Fax # (801) 561-8495
Personnel: Editor-Vince Harding
General Info: Yr. Est. 1987, Monthly
Subscriptions: Indv. $249

Grassroots Economic Organizing (GEO)
See: CONSUMER INTERESTS

Green Business Letter, The   *Business*

Publishing Co: Tilden Press, Inc., 1519 Connecticut Ave NW, Washington, DC 20036; Title Tel # (202) 332-1700 Title Fax # (202) 332-3028
Personnel: Editor-Joel Makower, Assoc. Ed.-Jamie Queoff
Editorial Description: Reports on environmental practices of corporations and provides information to help companies use more environmentally sound practices and products.
General Info: Yr. Est. 1991, Monthly, Trim Size-8½ x 11, Offset press, 8 pages, ISSN: 1056-490X, 2 Color
Subscriptions: Indv. $127, Can. $132, For. $147, $10/copy
Printing Co: Newsletter Services, Inc., 9700 Philadelphia Court, Lanham, MD 20706 Tel # (301) 731-5200, Fax # (301) 731-5201

Green MarketAlert   *Business*

Publishing Co: Bridge Group, 345 Woodcreek Rd, Bethlehem, CT 06751-1014; Title Tel # (203) 266-7209 Title Fax # (203) 266-5049
Personnel: Publisher, Editor-Carl Frankel, Circ. Mgr., Production Mgr.-Molly Barnes
Editorial Description: Tracks corporate environmentalism and green business strategies.
General Info: Yr. Est. 1990, Monthly, Trim Size-8½ x 11, Desktop press, 12 pages, ISSN: 1052-1755, 2 Color, Saddle-stitched
Subscriptions: Indv. $145, Inst. $295, Can. $295, For. $325, $20/copy
Advertising: Accepts Inserts.
List Rental: Actives: 1,000, $250/M
Printing Co: Newsletter Services, Inc., 9700 Philadelphia Court, Lanham, MD 20706 Tel # (301) 731-5200, Fax # (301) 731-5201

Green Markets Newsletter
See: AGRICULTURE

Guide
See: WOMEN'S

Guide to Computer Law

Publishing Co: CCH, Inc., 2700 Lake Cook Rd., Riverwoods, IL 60015 Parent Co.-Kluwer Law & Taxation Publishers, Cambridge; Title Tel # (847) 267-7000 Title Fax # (800) 224-8299
Editorial Description: Covers more than 20 areas of computer law, includig copyrights, trade secrets, patents, sales, and more. Also includes full-text reproduction of pertinent laws, uniform acts and more court cases.
General Info: Looseleaf
Subscriptions: Indv. $475

HR Training   *Business*

Publishing Co: Business & Legal Reports, Inc., 39 Academy St., PO Box 1513, Madison, CT 06443-2646 Tel # (860) 245-7448 Fax # (860) 245-2559; Title Tel # (203) 245-7448 Title Fax # (203) 245-2559
Editorial Description: Everything you need to run training sessions on critical personnel topics for supervisors including lesson plans reproducible handouts, quizzes, forms, permanent record and attendance sheets.
General Info: Yr. Est. 1995, Quarterly, Looseleaf
Subscriptions: Indv. $295

HVAC ProfitMaker   *Business*

Publishing Co: Tom Davies & Assocs., 3608 Linden Ln, Mobile, AL 36608-1410; Title Tel # (205) 471-2001 Title Fax # (334) 471-2001
Personnel: Publisher, Editor-Tom Davies, Sr.
Editorial Description: Publication is devoted toward increasing the net before tax profits of heating and air conditioning contractors.
General Info: Yr. Est. 1988, 10x/yr., 12 pages, ISSN: 0899-9791, 2 Color
Subscriptions: Indv. $285

Healthcare Technology & Business Opportunities
See: HOSPITALS & NURSING HOMES

Healthy Companies:
Leadership for the New
Workplace   *Business*

Publishing Co: Jossey-Bass Publishers, Inc., 350 Sansome St., Fifth Fl., San Francisco, CA 94104-1310 Tel # (415) 433-1740; Title Tel # (415) 433-1767 Title Fax # (415) 433-0499
Personnel: Publisher-Robert Rosen
Editorial Description: Created to increase business productivity and growth.
General Info: Yr. Est. 1993, Monthly
Subscriptions: Indv. $119

Healthy, Wealthy & Wise   *Consumer*

Publishing Co: TPN The Peoples Network, 2420 Courtland Dr., Arlington, TX 76017
Fax # (817) 465-6486
Editorial Description: Information on starting home based businesses as a part of The Peoples Network.
General Info: Annually

High Tech Ceramics
News   *Business*

Publishing Co: Business Communications Co., 25 Van Zant St., Ste.13, Norwalk, CT 06855-1781; Title Tel # (203) 853-4266 Title Fax # (203) 853-0348
Personnel: Publisher-Louis Naturman, Editor-Thomas Abraham, Mktg. Dir.-Robert Butler
Editorial Description: Analyzes and reports on high-tech ceramics materials, patents and industry trends.
General Info: Yr. Est. 1989, Monthly, Trim Size-8½ x 11, 12 pages, ISSN: 1045-2397, Ind/Abs/ Online: NewsNet, DIALOG, No Color, Matte
Subscriptions: Indv. $375, Can. $425, For. $425, $38/copy
List Rental: List Management Co.: W.I. Mail Marketing, 470 Main St. #317, Ridgefield, CT 06877-4516 Tel # (203) 438-6822, Fax # (203) 438-7756, Actives: 120, $175/M

High-Tech Materials Alert
See: MANUFACTURING

High Tech Separations News
See: SCIENCE

Hiring & Firing Newsletter
See: EMPLOYMENT

Hiring Compliance Update
See: LABOR

Home-Based Business
Newsletter   *Business*

Publishing Co: Home-Based Business Newsletter, PO Box 1232, Meridian, ID 83680-1232; Title Tel # (208) 887-5359
Personnel: Publisher, Editor-Pam De Pena
Editorial Description: Practical ideas on low-cost marketing and optimizing productivity. News, tax and financial information, book reviews of interest to home-based business owners.
General Info: Yr. Est. 1993, Monthly, Trim Size-8½ x 11, 8 pages, ISSN: 1072-5555, No Color, Matte, Saddle-stitched
Subscriptions: Indv. $24, $2/copy

Home Business Express   *Business*   CPM$1625

Publishing Co: Integrity Communications, PO Box 1125, Ames, IA 50014-1125 Tel # (515) 292-7154 Fax # (515) 292-7154
Personnel: Publisher-Clare Bills
Editorial Description: Newsletter for home businesses.
General Info: Yr. Est. 1994, Monthly, Trim Size-8½ x 11, 8 pages, No Color, Matte
Subscriptions: Indv. $15, $2/copy
Circulation: Total-200
Advertising: $325.
List Rental: List Management Co.: Integrity Communications, PO Box 1125, Ames, IA 50014-1125 Tel # (515) 292-7154

Home Business Idea
Possibility Newsletter

Publishing Co: Prosperity & Profits Unlimited, PO Box 416, Denver, CO 80201-0416; Title Tel # (303) 575-5676
Personnel: Publisher-A. Doyle
Editorial Description: Ideas for home businesses.
General Info: Yr. Est. 1991, Annually, Trim Size-8½ x 11, ISSN: 0738-7490
Subscriptions: Indv. $4, Inst. $4, Can. $7, For. $9, $4/copy
Circulation: Total-5,000

Home Business Report
See: MANAGEMENT

Home Inc.   *Business, Consumer*

Publishing Co: Agora, Inc., 105 W. Monoment St., Baltimore, MD 21202-4702 Tel # (410) 783-2647; Title Tel # (410) 223-2658 Title Fax # (410) 223-2662
Personnel: Editor-Sean Carton, Circ. Mgr.-Shayvonne Rounds, Production Mgr.-Anne Kelly, Adv. Dir.-Doug Cooke, Art Dir.-Laura Farnan, Publisher, Mktg. Dir., Promotion Dir.-Nina Rose
Editorial Description: Advice to business owners who run businesses from home.
General Info: Monthly, Trim Size-8½ x 11, Web press, 12 pages, 2 Color, Other, Other
Subscriptions: Indv. $49
Circulation: Total-45,000
Advertising: Accepts Inserts.
List Rental: List Management Co.: Manager: Beth Dent; Name Bank, 14 W. Monument St., Baltimore, MD 21201 Tel # (410) 783-8463, Fax # (410) 783-8464, Actives: 45,000, $85/M

Home Income Quarterly
See: ADVERTISING & MARKETING

Home Income Reporter   *Business*

Publishing Co: Red Hot Publishing Co., PO Box 7423, Trenton, NJ 08628-0423; Title Tel # (609) 835-2347 Title Fax # (609) 835-2324
Personnel: Asst. Pub.-Sonja Simpson, Publisher, Editor-Ed Durham, Sr., Circ. Mgr.-F. Henderson, Art Dir.-Ed Durham, Jr.
Editorial Description: How to start & operate a profitable home-based business. Contains profiles of successful home-based businesses, book reviews, mail order information, computer opportunities & more.
General Info: (Formerly Home Business News; Work at Home Report), Yr. Est. 1983, Bi-monthly, Trim Size-8¼ x 10¾, Web press, 8 pages, 4% ads, 2 Color, Matte
Subscriptions: Indv. $39, $4/copy
Circulation: Total-1,500
List Rental: Actives: $50/M
Printing Co: E & L Graphics, 1505 Parkway Ave, Trenton, NJ 08628-2730 Tel # (609) 882-0649

Home Office Connection
See: OFFICE METHODS & EQUIPMENT

Home Treasures Newsletter   *Business, Consumer*

Publishing Co: Home Treasures, 1250 Clark Mill Rd., Sweet Home, OR 97386-3014
Editorial Description: Success stories and information for home based entrepreneurs.
General Info: Monthly
Subscriptions: Indv. $10

Home Work

Publishing Co: Posy Collection, PO Box 394, Simsbury, CT 06070-0394; Title Tel # (203) 651-5503 Title Fax # (203) 651-5415
Personnel: Editor-Posy Lough
Editorial Description: Home business newsletter with a Christian perspective; includes feature articles on home based business topics, profiles of successful home businesses, hints and tips, etc.
General Info: Yr. Est. 1980, Bi-monthly, ISSN: 1053-3745
Subscriptions: Indv. $20, Can. $20, For. $26

HomeWorking   *Business*

Publishing Co: Essence Communications, Inc., 1500 Broadway, New York, NY 10036 Tel # (212) 642-0600 Fax # (212) 921-5173; Title Fax # (903) 367-2426
Editorial Description: Information for home-based businesses or those who plan to start one.
General Info: Yr. Est. 1994, Monthly, Trim Size-8½ x 11, 8 pages
Subscriptions: Indv. $15

Homebased   *Business*

Publishing Co: Joyce E. Francis, Publisher, 450 Lexington Ave., Grand Central P.O., Box 2614, New York, NY 10163-2614
Personnel: Publisher, Editor-Joyce E. Francis
Editorial Description: Homebased is geared towards the person who would like to operate a home-based business. It will feature other home-base business owners giving advice.
General Info: Yr. Est. 1990, Bi-monthly
Subscriptions: Indv. $18, Can. $22, $4/copy

Homebased Business News Report
Business, Consumer

Publishing Co: Home Office Management Svces., 1151 NE Todd George Rd, Lees Summit, MO 64086-5332; Title Tel # (816) 525-4484 Title Fax # (816) 525-4484
Personnel: Publisher, Editor-Beth Smith
Editorial Description: Information on starting and running a homebased business.
General Info: Yr. Est. 1992, Monthly, Trim Size-8½ x 11, Offset press, 6 pages, ISSN: 1067-0300, No Color
Subscriptions: Indv. $14, Can. $17, For. $23, $2/copy
Circulation: Total-1,000
Advertising: Inquire for rates. Accepts Inserts.
List Rental: Rents Lists

How to Be Your Own Publisher Update
See: BOOKS & BOOK TRADE

How to Succeed in Rotten Times
See: EMPLOYMENT

Human Resource Management Compensation
See: MANAGEMENT

Human Resources Equal Employment Opportunity
See: EMPLOYMENT

Human Resources Management Employee Relations
See: LABOR UNION

Human Resources Management Ideas and Trends Newsletter
See: MANAGEMENT

IBIS Briefing Service
Business

Publishing Co: Charles D. Spencer & Assocs., Inc., 250 S. Wacker Dr., Ste. 600, Chicago, IL 60606-5834; Title Tel # (312) 993-7900 Title Fax # (312) 993-7910
Personnel: Publisher, Editor-Bruce Spencer, Production Mgr.-Tracy Coyne, Adv. Dir., Promotion Dir.-Kathleen Reidy
Editorial Description: Information on international employee benefit plans & programs.
General Info: Yr. Est. 1969, Monthly, Desktop press, ISSN: 0018-8611, Looseleaf
Subscriptions: Indv. $825, Inst. $825, Can. $825, For. $825
Circulation: Total-600

IMA Focus
See: ACCOUNTING

INFOCUS
Business

Publishing Co: Business Forms Management Assn. Inc., 519 SW 3rd Ave Ste 712, Portland, OR 97204-2519; Title Tel # (503) 227-3393 Title Fax # (503) 274-7667
Personnel: Publisher-Andrew Paltaka, Editor, Circ. Mgr., Promotion Dir.-Bill Urban
Editorial Description: Technical newsletter covering products, services, people in the information resources management industry.
General Info: Yr. Est. 1988, 10x/yr., Sheetfed press, 8 pages, 2 Color, Newsprint
Subscriptions: Indv. $50, $5/copy
Acquistions: Publication Bought
Circulation: Total-2,000
Advertising: Accepts Inserts.
List Rental: Actives: $100/M

IQ Quarterly
See: COMPUTERS & AUTOMATION

ISDN News
See: COMPUTERS & AUTOMATION

Idaho Wool Growers Association
See: LIVESTOCK

Ideas Unlimited for Canadian Editors
See: JOURNALISM

Ideas Unlimited for Editors
See: MEDIA & COMMUNICATIONS

Illinois Business Review
Business, Consumer

Publishing Co: Bureau of Economic & Business Research, 428 Commerce West, 120L S. Sixth St., Champaign, IL 61820-6915 Fax # (217) 333-7410 Parent Co.-University of Illinois at Urbana-Champaign, Urbana; Title Tel # (217) 333-2332 Title Fax # (217) 244-3118
Personnel: Circ. Mgr.-Jane Wood, Editor, Production Mgr.-Janet Fitch
Editorial Description: Summary of business conditions in Illinois.
General Info: Yr. Est. 1944, Quarterly, Trim Size-8⅜ x 10⅞, Offset press, 24 pages, Ind/Abs/Online: DIALOG, Color, Newsprint
Subscriptions: Indv. $10, Inst. $10, Can. $10, For. $10, $4/copy
Circulation: (53% controlled), Total-750, Subscriptions-225

I'm Too Busy To Read Marketing Report Service
See: ADVERTISING & MARKETING

Impact!
See: THEATRE

In Business

Publishing Co: Two Ems, Inc., 786 Boston Post Rd, Madison, CT 06443-3047; Title Tel # (203) 245-8211 Title Fax # (203) 245-1805
Personnel: Publisher-Margaret M. Sprague, Production Mgr.-Paul D. Sprague, Adv. Dir.-J. Kent Sprague
Editorial Description: News magazine for and about businesses in small towns which employ local residents.
General Info: (Formerly Shoreline Business), Yr. Est. 1990, Quarterly, Sheetfed press, 16 pages, No Color, Matte, Saddle-stitched
Circulation: Total-4,000
Advertising: Inquire for rates.
List Rental: Actives: 4,000

Income Advisor
See: INVESTMENT

India Business and Investment Report
See: INTERNATIONAL TRADE

Indiana Minority Business Report

Publishing Co: Indiana Minority Business Report, 8054 Harvest Ln, Indianapolis, IN 46256-3401; Title Tel # (317) 845-0665
Personnel: Publisher-Edward Wills, Jr., Production Mgr.-Wanda Bryant
Editorial Description: This newsletter typically carries interviews with key leaders of minority & majority businesses, features successful minority & female-owned businesses, reports on laws affecting minority procurement, & much more.
General Info: Yr. Est. 1988, Bi-monthly, Sheetfed press, ISSN: 1045-7232, No Color, Matte
Subscriptions: Indv. $50, $10/copy
Printing Co: Sir Speedy, 1236 W 86th St, Indianapolis, IN 46260-2204 Tel # (317) 848-1535

Industrial Bioprocessing
See: BIOCHEMISTRY

Industrial Environment
See: ENVIRONMENT & ECOLOGY

Industries in Transition
Business

Publishing Co: Business Communications Co., 25 Van Zant St., Ste.13, Norwalk, CT 06855-1781; Title Tel # (203) 853-4266 Title Fax # (203) 853-0348
Personnel: Publisher-Louis Naturman, Editor-Betsy Duwalt, Mktg. Dir.-Robert Butler
Editorial Description: Government, business, industry, current information on research and development in government and industry manufacturing technology.
General Info: (Formerly Growth Industry News), Yr. Est. 1977, Monthly, Trim Size-8½ x 11, 10 pages, ISSN: 0085-0003, Ind/Abs/Online: DIALOG, No Color, Matte
Subscriptions: Indv. $350, Can. $400, For. $400, $35/copy
List Rental: List Management Co.: W.I. Mail Marketing, 470 Main St. #317, Ridgefield, CT 06877-4516 Tel # (203) 438-6822, Fax # (203) 438-7756, Actives: $120/M

Info
See: BIBLIOGRAPHY

Information Advisor
See: LIBRARY

Information Broker
See: MEDIA & COMMUNICATIONS

Info Franchise Newsletter
Business, Consumer

Publishing Co: Info Press, Inc., PO Box 550, Lewiston, NY 14092-0550; Title Tel # (716) 754-4669 Title Fax # (905) 688-7728
Personnel: Publisher-Ted Dixon, Asst. Ed.-Denise Muir, Circ. Mgr.-Lori Marsh
Editorial Description: Business format franchises, new franchises, recent legislation and litigation, all that is new on the franchise scene.
General Info: Yr. Est. 1977, Monthly, Desktop press, 8 pages, ISSN: 0147-5924, 2 Color
Subscriptions: Indv. $96, Can. $96, For. $120, $8/copy
Circulation: Total-4,000
Advertising: Accepts Inserts.

Information Returns Guide
See: TAXES

Information Solutions: A newsletter of ideas & techniques on how to profit from info.
See: MANAGEMENT

Ink! Ink! Ink!
Business, Consumer

Publishing Co: Cypress Publishing, PO Box 777, Cypress, TX 77429-0777; Title Tel # (713) 373-9142 Title Fax # (713) 256-1722
General Info: Yr. Est. 1994, Monthly, Trim Size-8½ x 11, Web press, 4 pages, 4 Color, Coated, Case bound
Subscriptions: Free To Qualified Recipient

Innovator's Digest
See: MANAGEMENT

Inside NAFTA
See: INTERNATIONAL TRADE

Inside R&D
  See: MANUFACTURING

Insider, The

Publishing Co: Toledo Area Chamber of Commerce, Enterprise Suite 200, 300 Madison Ave., Toledo, OH 43604-1575; Title Tel # (419) 243-8191 Title Fax # (419) 241-8302
Personnel: Publisher-J.M. Porter, Editor-Krystine Warner
Editorial Description: Regional & local business news. Chamber happenings.
General Info: (Formerly Toledo Business News/Chamber Insider), Yr. Est. 1990, Monthly, 12 pages, 2 Color, Coated, Saddle-stitched
Circulation: Total-4,500
Advertising: Inquire for rates.
List Rental: Rents Lists

Institute of Business
  Appraiser's Newsletter   *Business*

Publishing Co: IBA, PO Box 1447, Boynton Beach, FL 33425-1447; Title Tel # (407) 732-3202
Personnel: Editor-Raymond Miles
Editorial Description: Association news for members.
General Info: Yr. Est. 1978, Bi-monthly, Trim Size-8½ x 11, 4 pages
Circulation: Total-1,900

Institute of Corporate
  Directors in Canada,
  Newsletter   *Business, Association*

Publishing Co: Institute of Corporate Directors in Canada, 55 St. Claire Avenue, Suite 255, Toronto, ON M4V 2Y7 Canada; Title Tel # (416) 944-8282
Personnel: Editor-Sonita Horvikch
General Info: Yr. Est. 1981, Bi-monthly, Trim Size-8½ x 11, 8 pages
Circulation: Total-700

Integrated Health Care Delivery: Business and Legal Forms
  See: HEALTH

Inter-Americas Business Newsletter
  See: INTERNATIONAL TRADE

Interaction
  See: CHAMBER OF COMMERCE

Interactive Marketing News
  See: DIRECT MAIL

International Barometer   *Business*

Publishing Co: Issue Action Pubs. Inc., 207 Loudoun St. SE, Leesburg, VA 22075-3115; Title Tel # (703) 777-8450
Personnel: Publisher, Editor-Teresa Crane, Circ. Mgr.-M.J. Timpano
Editorial Description: Profiles activities of issue-oriented organizations; interviews, commentary.
General Info: Yr. Est. 1986, Monthly, Trim Size-8½ x 11, 4 pages, ISSN: 0882-7966, No Color, Newsprint
Subscriptions: Indv. $147, For. $175, $15/copy
Circulation: (100% controlled), Total-500

International High
  Technology Report   *Business*

Publishing Co: Amersham Associates, 1209 G St NE, Washington, DC 20002-4423; Title Tel # (202) 396-2568
Personnel: Circ. Mgr.-Frances Healey
Editorial Description: Report on significant trends in high tech activity abroad.
General Info: Yr. Est. 1984, Web press, 10 pages, Color
Subscriptions: Indv. $197
Circulation: Total-300,400
Printing Co: Frank's Duplicating, 529 14th St., N.W., Washington, DC 20045 Tel # (202) 628-7883

International Information Report
  See: INTERNATIONAL TRADE

International Labor Affairs
  See: INTERNATIONAL TRADE

International Observer
  See: INTERNATIONAL AFFAIRS

International Tax Planning- Expatriates & Migrants
  See: TAXES

International Virtual Reality Association
  See: ENTERTAINMENT

Internet Business Report   *Business*

Publishing Co: CMP Publications, Inc., 600 Community Dr., Manhasset, NY 11030-3875
Tel # (516) 562-5000 Fax # (516) 562-7013
Personnel: Publisher-Bob Evans
Editorial Description: Industry information about the Internet.
General Info: Yr. Est. 1993, Quarterly, Ind/Abs/Online: TechWeb
Subscriptions: Indv. $279

Investext Advisor
  See: INVESTMENT

Israel High-Tech Report
  See: INTERNATIONAL TRADE

Issues Bulletin
  See: GROCERY

Item Processing Report
  See: BANKING & FINANCE

JEG Sponsorship Report
  See: ADVERTISING & MARKETING

Jack Kemp's American
  Entrepreneur   *Business, Consumer*

Publishing Co: Eagle Publishing, Inc., 422 First Street SE, Suite 300, Washington, DC 20003 Tel # (202) 546-5005 Parent Co.-Phillips Business Information, Inc., Potomac; Title Tel # (301) 340-2100 Title Fax # (301) 424-4297
Editorial Description: Conservative newsletter giving guidelines for political, economic, and regulatory issues.
General Info: Monthly
Subscriptions: Indv. $99
List Rental: Rents Lists

Japan Financial Market Report
  See: INTERNATIONAL TRADE

Japan M & A Reporter
  See: INTERNATIONAL TRADE

Japan Weekly
  See: INTERNATIONAL TRADE

Job Express   *Business*

Publishing Co: Fides-Vandame, Inc., 105 N. Main St., Boonton, NJ 07005-1257
Fax # (201) 335-4866; Title Tel # (201) 299-1535 Title Fax # (201) 335-4886
Personnel: Publisher, Editor-Wendy Vandame
Editorial Description: Market survey of DP billing rates, listing of open assignments & section for readers seeking work.
General Info: Yr. Est. 1987, Bi-weekly, Saddle-stitched
Subscriptions: Indv. $42, Can. $60, For. $75, $3/copy
Advertising: Inquire for rates. Accepts Inserts.
List Rental: Rents Lists

John T. Reed's Real Estate Investor's Monthly
  See: REAL ESTATE

Joint Venture News
  See: INTERNATIONAL TRADE

JonesReport
  See: ADVERTISING & MARKETING

Jot and Jolts
  See: MANAGEMENT

Keep Up to Date on Payroll
  See: ACCOUNTING

Keeping Customers Happy

Publishing Co: Productivity Development Group, Inc., PO Box 488, Westford, MA 01886-0013; Title Tel # (508) 692-1818 Title Fax # (508) 692-5080
Editorial Description: Leaders from AT & T, LL Bean Federal Express, Wendy's and more tell how to make good service excellent. Includes dozens of how to tips and lessons.
General Info: Irregular, Looseleaf
Subscriptions: Indv. $395, For. $395

Ken Blanchard's Profiles of Success
  See: MANAGEMENT

Kennedy's Career Strategist
  See: EMPLOYMENT

Keying In   *Business, Association*

Publishing Co: National Business Education Association, 1914 Association Dr., Reston, VA 22091-1596; Title Tel # (703) 860-8300 Title Fax # (703) 620-4483
Editorial Description: Each issue features a different issue or trend of facting business education.
General Info: Yr. Est. 1991, 4x/yr.
Subscriptions: Inst. $60
List Rental: List Management Co.: MGI-Marketing General Inc., 105 Oronoco St., Alexandria, VA 22314-2015 Tel # (703) 739-1000

Kiplinger California Letter *Business*

Publishing Co: Kiplinger Washington Editors, Inc., 1729 H Street N.W., Washington, DC 20006-3924; Title Tel # (202) 887-6400
Personnel: Publisher-Austin H. Kiplinger, Editor-John Fogarty
Editorial Description: Guidance for businessmen with interests in California. Business and economic trends in the state, politics, legislation, wages, prices, tourism, farming, real estate, defense spending.
General Info: Yr. Est. 1965, Monthly, Trim Size-8½ x 11, 4 pages, ISSN: 0453-9249
Subscriptions: Indv. $68
Circulation: Total-19,000
List Rental: List Management Co.: Kleid Company, Inc., 530 5th Ave., 17 Floor, New York, NY 10036-5101 Tel # (212) 819-3406, Fax # (212) 719-9788, Actives: 19,929, $90/M

Kiplinger Florida Letter *Business*

Publishing Co: Kiplinger Washington Editors, Inc., 1729 H Street N.W., Washington, DC 20006-3924 Tel # (202) 887-6400; Title Tel # (202) 887-6408 Title Fax # (202) 778-8976
Personnel: Publisher-Austin Kiplinger, Editor-Kenneth Dalecki
Editorial Description: Information and guidance for businessmen with interests in Florida. Business and economic trends in the state, new industries, new roads, land prices, taxes, employment, prices, wages.
General Info: Yr. Est. 1955, Monthly, Trim Size-8½ x 11, 4 pages, ISSN: 0023-1754
Subscriptions: Indv. $34
Circulation: Total-22,500
List Rental: List Management Co.: Kleid Company, Inc., 530 5th Ave., 17 Floor, New York, NY 10036-5101 Tel # (212) 819-3406, Fax # (212) 719-9788, Actives: 28,000, $90/M

Kiplinger Washington Letter *Business*

Publishing Co: Kiplinger Washington Editors, Inc., 1729 H Street N.W., Washington, DC 20006-3924; Title Tel # (202) 887-6400
Personnel: Publisher, Editor-Austin H. Kiplinger
Editorial Description: Briefings for businessmen on trends and developments affecting their jobs, finances, businesses.
General Info: Yr. Est. 1923, Weekly, Trim Size-8½ x 11, 4 pages, ISSN: 0023-1770
Subscriptions: Indv. $63
Circulation: Total-450,000
Advertising: Inquire for rates.
List Rental: List Management Co.: Kleid Company, Inc., 530 5th Ave., 17 Floor, New York, NY 10036-5101 Tel # (212) 819-3406, Fax # (212) 719-9788, Actives: 328,601, $90/M, Hotline: 5,000, $105/M

Kiwanis International Foundation Newsletter
See: CLUBS

LAMA Manager
See: MANAGEMENT

LAMA's Watch on Washington *Association* CPM: $200

Publishing Co: Latin American Management Assn., 419 New Jersey Ave SE, Washington, DC 20003-4007; Title Tel # (202) 546-3803 Title Fax # (202) 546-3807
Personnel: Publisher-Marina M. Laverdy, Editor-Angela Manso
Editorial Description: Covers national minority & small business issues; including legislative updates regulatory analysis & practical advice for business owners.
General Info: (Formerly LAMA Newsletter/Washington Notes; Washington Memo), Yr. Est. 1979, Quarterly, Trim Size-8½ x 11, Offset press, 24 pages, 2 Color, Matte
Subscriptions: Free With Membership
Circulation: Total-5,000
Advertising: $1,000. Accepts Inserts.

LIDMA

Publishing Co: Long Island Direct Marketing Assn., 17 Bettina Ct, Hampton Bays, NY 11946-1229
Personnel: Publisher-Susan Soules, Editor-Cathy Grieger
Editorial Description: News briefs of interest to LIDMA members.
General Info: Monthly, No Color, Newsprint
Circulation: Total-1,500

LIVG News

Publishing Co: Hofstra Univ., 121 Hofstra University, Hempstead, NY 11550-1090 Tel # (516) 463-5910 Fax # (516) 463-5072; Title Tel # (516) 560-5705
Personnel: Editor-Russell Moore
General Info: Yr. Est. 1984, Trim Size-8½ x 11, 20 pages, No Color
Circulation: Total-150

Lagniappe Quarterly Monitor
See: INTERNATIONAL TRADE

Laughter Works
See: HUMOR & SATIRE

Lead Your Company to Quality

Publishing Co: Productivity Development Group, Inc., PO Box 488, Westford, MA 01886-0013; Title Tel # (508) 692-1818 Title Fax # (508) 692-5080
Editorial Description: Leadership lessons learned and plenty of how to's from executives at Milliken, Kodak, Shenandoah Life, IBM Citizens Utilities and more.
General Info: Irregular, Looseleaf
Subscriptions: Indv. $495, For. $495

Leadership - for the Front Lines *Business*

Publishing Co: Bureau of Business Practice, 24 Rope Ferry Rd, Waterford, CT 06386-0001 Tel # (806) 442-4365 Fax # (860) 434-3341 Parent Co.-Prentice Hall, Waterford; Title Tel # (860) 444-4365 Title Fax # (860) 434-3078
Personnel: Publisher-David Deffley, Editor-Patricia Thunberg, Art Dir.-Denise Fedeli
Editorial Description: Designed for first line supervisors. Emphasis on the role of the supervisor & solving the specific problems & situations associated with that position.
General Info: (Formerly Front Line Supervisor's Bulletin), Yr. Est. 1989, Semi-monthly
Subscriptions: Indv. $66

Leads *Business, Consumer*

Publishing Co: Leads, Box 9333, Ottawa, ON K1G 3V1 Canada; Title Tel # (613) 746-2292
Personnel: Publisher, Editor-Tom Kennedy
Editorial Description: Opportunities for second income seekers.
General Info: Yr. Est. 1981, Bi-monthly, ISSN: 0834-3586
Circulation: Total-2,000

Left Business Observer *Business, Consumer*

Publishing Co: Left Business Observer, 250 W. 85th St., New York, NY 10024-3217; Title Tel # (212) 874-4020 Title Fax # (212) 874-3137
Personnel: Publisher, Editor-Douglas Henwood, Circ. Mgr.-Christine Bratton
Editorial Description: News & analyzing economics & politics worldwide.
General Info: Yr. Est. 1986, Monthly, Trim Size-8½ x 11, Offset press, 8 pages, ISSN: 1042-0134, No Color, Matte, Other
Subscriptions: Indv. $22, Inst. $55, For. $60, $3/copy
Circulation: Total-3,000
List Rental: Actives: $35/M
Printing Co: Sheridan Printing, 1425 3rd Ave, Alpha, NJ 08865-4695 Tel # (908) 454-0700, Fax # (908) 454-2554

Legacies *Business, Consumer*

Publishing Co: Baylor Univ., P.O. Box 98011, Waco, TX 76798; Title Tel # (817) 755-2265 Title Fax # (817) 755-2271
Personnel: Editor-Nancy Upton
Editorial Description: Information for developing and continuing family businesses.
General Info: Yr. Est. 1989, Quarterly, Trim Size-8½ x 11, Offset press, 16 pages, No Color, Saddle-stitched
Subscriptions: Free
Circulation: Total-7,000
Printing Co: Baylor Printing Service, Baylor Univ., Waco, TX 76798 Tel # (817) 755-1011

Leisure Industry Report *Business*

Publishing Co: Leisure Industry/Recreation News, PO Box 43563, Washington, DC 20010-9563; Title Tel # (202) 232-7107
Personnel: Publisher-Marj Jensen
Editorial Description: Covers discretionary spending for gaming, spectator sports, movies, concerts, theme parks, etc. and economic trends.
General Info: Yr. Est. 1981, 10x/yr., ISSN: 0276-0916
Subscriptions: Indv. $65

Lesko's Info-Power Newsletter *Consumer*

Publishing Co: Information USA, Inc., PO Box E, Kensington, MD 20895-0418; Title Tel # (301) 924-0556
Personnel: Editor-Matthew Lasko, Production Mgr.-Beth Meserve, Mktg. Dir.-Toni Murray, Promotion Dir.-Debbie Samson
Editorial Description: Identifies money, help and information giveaways by the government.
General Info: Monthly
Subscriptions: Indv. $55

Letters of Credit Report
See: BANKING & FINANCE

Liaison
See: ADVERTISING & MARKETING

LifeLines
See: HEALTH

Linda Perret's Humor Files
See: HUMOR & SATIRE

Louisiana Business Survey *Business, Association*

Publishing Co: Univ. of New Orleans/Division of Business & Economic Res., Lakefront, New Orleans, LA 70148-0001; Title Tel # (504) 286-6240 Title Fax # (504) 286-6094
Personnel: Editor-Patricia Connor
General Info: (Formerly Univ. of New Orleans, Div. of Business & Economic Research), Yr. Est. 1970, Semi-annually, Trim Size-8½ x 11, Desktop press, 12 pages, ISSN: 0193-5712, No Color, Matte, Saddle-stitched
Subscriptions: Free
Circulation: Total-9,000
Printing Co: Wendel Printing, 5700 Hayne Blvd, New Orleans, LA 70126-1252 Tel # (504) 246-5757

MCI Connections Gold

Publishing Co: MCI, 1111 19th Street, Washington, DC 20036

MHI News
See: ENGINEERING

MIN: Media Industry Newsletter
See: MEDIA & COMMUNICATIONS

Make it Tasty with No/Low Salt--How To & Receipe Blends Edition
See: FOOD

Make it Tasty Spice Co. Blends Food Business Newsletter
See: FOOD

Managed Care & Health Care Marketing
See: HEALTH

Managed Dental Care
See: EMPLOYMENT

Management Consultant International
See: MANAGEMENT

Management Focus
See: ADVERTISING & MARKETING

Management Memo
See: MANAGEMENT

Management Policies & Personnel Law
See: MANAGEMENT

Management Report for Nonunion Organizations
See: LABOR

Manager/Motivator
See: MANAGEMENT

Manager's Legal Bulletin
See: MANAGEMENT

Managing Your Future
See: INVESTMENT

Managing Your Medical Practice
See: MEDICINE

Manufacturing News
See: MANUFACTURING

Marcus Report — *Business*

Publishing Co: Bedford House, 1800 Ironstone Mnr.Pickering, Toronto, ON L1W 3T9 Canada Tel # (905) 831-3000; Title Tel # (416) 340-9809 Title Fax # (416) 340-9813
Personnel: Editor-Bruce Marcus
General Info: Yr. Est. 1988, 10x/yr.
Subscriptions: Indv. $199

Market: Europe
See: INTERNATIONAL TRADE

Market: Latin America
See: INTERNATIONAL TRADE

Market Mirror
See: INVESTMENT

Market Monitor — *Association*

Publishing Co: Better Business Bureau Inc., 2217 E 9th St, Cleveland, OH 44115-1299; Title Tel # (216) 623-8964
Personnel: Editor-Barb Marinko
General Info: Yr. Est. 1967, 4 pages

Market Timing Report
See: INVESTMENT

Marketarian Letter
See: INVESTMENT

Marketing Pulse
See: MEDIA & COMMUNICATIONS

Marketing Report, The
See: ADVERTISING & MARKETING

Marketing Timing Report
See: INVESTMENT

Marple's Business Newsletter — *Business*

Publishing Co: Newsletter Publishing Corp., 117 W Mercer St Ste 200, Seattle, WA 98119-3953; Title Tel # (206) 281-9609 Title Fax # (206) 281-8035
Personnel: Publisher, Editor-Michael Parks
Editorial Description: Independent coverage of business, finance and investments in the Pacific Northwest states; covers important developments in basic industries (forest products, agriculture).
General Info: Yr. Est. 1949, Bi-weekly, Trim Size-8½ x 11, Sheetfed press, 4 pages, ISSN: 0279-960X, 2 Color
Subscriptions: Indv. $72, Can. $72, For. $72
Circulation: Total-4,000
Printing Co: Academy Press, 3210 16th Ave W, Seattle, WA 98119-1707 Tel # (206) 285-2511

Martin Brower's Orange County Report — *Business*

Publishing Co: Orange County Report, 180 Newport Center Dr., Ste. 180, Newport Beach, CA 92660-6915; Title Tel # (714) 760-0209
Personnel: Publisher, Editor-Martin Brower, Circ. Mgr.-Tamar Brower
Editorial Description: Business and development trends in Orange County, California.
General Info: Yr. Est. 1985, Monthly, Trim Size-8½ x 11, Offset press, 4 pages, ISSN: 0882-0589, No Color
Subscriptions: Indv. $235

Maryland Procurement Report — *Business*

Publishing Co: Bancroft Information Group, Inc., PO Box 65360, Baltimore, MD 21209-0560; Title Tel # (410) 358-0658 Title Fax # (410) 764-1967
Personnel: Pres. /Exec. Publ.-Bruce Bortz
Editorial Description: For those looking to tap into, or keep their share of Maryland's $4 billion a year in contracts.
General Info: Yr. Est. 1993, Bi-weekly
Subscriptions: Indv. $207

Matching Gift Notes — *Business*

Publishing Co: Case Publications, 11 Dupont Cir NW Ste 400, Washington, DC 20036-1207; Title Tel # (202) 328-5978 Title Fax # (202) 387-4973
General Info: Quarterly
Subscriptions: Indv. $52

Mature Market Report
See: SENIOR CITIZENS

Mealey's Litigation Report: Intellectual Property — *Business*

Publishing Co: Mealey Publications, Inc., PO Box 446, Wayne, PA 19087-0446; Title Tel # (610) 688-6566 Title Fax # (610) 688-7552
Personnel: Publisher-Michael Mealey, Editor-Maureen McGuire, Mktg. Dir.-Kathy Roach
Editorial Description: Covers all areas of intellectual property litigation including copyright, patent, trademark, trade secret and unfair competition disputes.
General Info: Yr. Est. 1993, Semi-monthly, ISSN: 1065-9390
Subscriptions: Indv. $795, For. $915, $50/copy

Measurement Chain, The
See: INSTRUMENTS

Measuring Improvement

Publishing Co: Productivity Development Group, Inc., PO Box 488, Westford, MA 01886-0013; Title Tel # (508) 692-1818 Title Fax # (508) 692-5080
Editorial Description: Leaders at AT & T , American Express, BancOne, federal Express, Lotus,USAA and more tell what to measure, why to measure and how to measure. Plenty of how to tips and lessons learned.
General Info: Irregular, Looseleaf
Subscriptions: Indv. $395, For. $395

Media Mergers & Acquisitions
See: MEDIA & COMMUNICATIONS

Medical Business Letter, The
See: HEALTH

Medical Industry Employment Opportunities
See: MEDICINE

Member Advantage — *Business*

Publishing Co: New York State Business Group, 180 E. Main St., Patchogue, NY 11772 Tel # (516) 654-0600 Fax # (516) 654-0840
Personnel: Editor-Marjorie Dion, Mng. Editor-Heath S. Cohen
Editorial Description: News and information for entrepreneurs in New York State.
General Info: Yr. Est. 1995, Bi-monthly, Trim Size-8½ x 11, 12 pages, 4 Color, Coated, Saddle-stitched
Advertising: Inquire for rates.

Memphis Economy
Business

Publishing Co: Bureau of Business & Economic Research, Memphis State Univ., Memphis, TN 38152-0001 Tel # (901) 454-2281; Title Tel # (901) 678-2281 Title Fax # (901) 678-4086
Personnel: Editor-Chris Lyons
Editorial Description: Monthly review of the economy of Memphis.
General Info: Monthly, Trim Size-5½ x 8½, Sheetfed press, 6 pages, 2 Color, Newsprint
Circulation: Total-2,000
List Rental: Actives: $50/M

Mercer Bulletin, The
See: INDUSTRIAL RELATIONS/PERSONNEL

Merger Management
Report
Business

Publishing Co: Securities Data Co., 40 W 57th St Ste 802, New York, NY 10019-4001; Title Tel # (212) 765-5311 Title Fax # (212) 765-6123
Personnel: Editor-Ted Weissberg, Circ. Mgr.-Patricia Pierro
Editorial Description: Interviews key merger executives on acquisitions, career ops, successes.
General Info: Yr. Est. 1983, Monthly, 14 pages, ISSN: 0885-8616
Subscriptions: Indv. $298, $25/copy

Mergers & Acquisitions Report
See: INVESTMENT

Mergers and Corporate
Policy
Business

Publishing Co: Securities Data Co., 40 W 57th St Ste 802, New York, NY 10019-4001 Tel # (212) 765-5311; Title Tel # (212) 571-2324 Title Fax # (212) 267-2391
Personnel: Editor-Evan Simonoff, Circ. Mgr.-M. Lieberman
Editorial Description: Reports on individual merges & joint ventures by industry with financial data, price/earnings ratios. Also features breaking news on the M&A business.
General Info: Yr. Est. 1977, Weekly, Trim Size-8½ x 11, Letrpr. press, 12 pages, No Color, Newsprint, Saddle-stitched
Subscriptions: Indv. $698, For. $748, $35/copy
Acquisitions: Publication Bought, Publication Sold
Advertising: Inquire for rates.

Metric Today
See: CONSUMER INTERESTS

Mexico Business Monthly
See: INTERNATIONAL TRADE

Mid American Outlook
Business

Publishing Co: AmeriTrust Co., 900 Euclid Ave, Cleveland, OH 44115-1461; Title Tel # (216) 687-5029
Editorial Description: Discussion and analysis of the business and economic affairs of the 7-state area comprising the Industrial crescent.
General Info: Yr. Est. 1978, Quarterly, 12 pages, 2 Color
Circulation: Total-23,000

Middle East Business
Intelligence
Business

Publishing Co: Intl. Executive Reports, 717 D St. NW, Ste. 300, Washington, DC 20004-2807; Title Tel # (202) 628-6900 Title Fax # (202) 628-6618
Personnel: Publisher-William Hearn, Editor-Colin MacKinnon, Circ. Mgr.-Valerie Wood, Promotion Dir.-Lloyd Gibson
Editorial Description: Provides current business information; contracting and sales leads; contact information on Middle East Business opportunities.
General Info: Yr. Est. 1982, Semi-monthly, Trim Size-8½ x 11, Sheetfed press, 8 pages, ISSN: 0731-6305, Ind/Abs/Online: Newsnet, No Color, Matte
Subscriptions: Indv. $345, Inst. $195, Can. $355, For. $355, $15/copy
Acquisitions: Publication Bought, Publication Sold
Circulation: Total-700
List Rental: List Management Co.: Manager: Lloyd Gibson; Information Marketing Services, 8130 Boone Blvd., Ste 310, Vienna, VA 22182-2640 Tel # (703) 821-8130, Fax # (703) 821-8243, Actives: 15,200, $145/M, Expires: $145/M

Midwest Transaction Guide
See: LAW

Mind Play
Business

Publishing Co: Innovative Thinking Network, 1324 State Street J-153, Santa Barbara, CA 93101-2620; Title Tel # (805) 963-9151
Editorial Description: Relating to techniques of innovation and creativity. Interviews, stories, trends, mind puzzles.
General Info: Yr. Est. 1986, Bi-monthly, Trim Size-8½ x 11, 12 pages
Subscriptions: Indv. $36, Inst. $85
Acquisitions: Publication Bought
List Rental: Actives: 500, $75/M

Mini Manager
See: MANAGEMENT

Minnesota Labor Market Review
See: LABOR

Minnesota Management
Review

Publishing Co: Carlson School of Management, Univ. of Minnesota, 271 19th Ave., S., Minneapolis, MN 55455-0100; Title Tel # (612) 625-0843
Personnel: Editor-Martha Douglas, Art Dir.-Dawn Mathers
Editorial Description: Alumni magazine containing news about management research, alumni & school.
General Info: Yr. Est. 1981, Quarterly, Trim Size-8½ x 11, Sheetfed press, 32 pages, 4 Color, Coated
Circulation: (100% controlled), Total-25,000

Minorities in Business
Insider
Business

Publishing Co: CD Publications, 8204 Fenton St., Silver Spring, MD 20910-4571; Title Tel # (301) 588-6380 Title Fax # (301) 588-6385
Personnel: Publisher-Mike Gerecht, Editor-Ken Silverstone, Circ. Mgr.-Kurt Eisentraut, Mktg. Dir.-Joyce Meals, Promotion Dir.-Keith Brody
Editorial Description: Timely coverage of issues concerning minorities in business, including affirmative action, employment, government contracts, & education.
General Info: (Formerly Minority Business Insider), Yr. Est. 1987, Semi-monthly, Trim Size-8½ x 11, Sheetfed press, 16 pages, ISSN: 1050-3463, No Color, Matte, Other
Subscriptions: Indv. $289, Can. $307, For. $337, $15/copy
List Rental: List Management Co.: Manager: Amy Seyler; Washington Advertising Service, 8204 Fenton St., Silver Spring, MD 20910 Tel # (301) 588-7920, Fax # (301) 588-6385, Actives: 6,587, $150/M, Expires: 1,540, $150/M

Modern UCC Litigation Forms
See: LAW

Monthly Product
Announcement
Business, Scholarly

Publishing Co: U.S. Bureau of the Census - Dept. of Commerce, Data User Services Division, Customer Services, Washington, DC 20233-1900; Title Tel # (301) 457-4100 Title Fax # (301) 457-4714
Personnel: Editor-Mary Killride
Editorial Description: Lists new Census Bureau reports, CD-ROMs, computer tapes, floppy disks, etc. Provides guidance on how to order the products.
General Info: (Formerly Monthly Product Announcements), Yr. Est. 1980, Monthly, Trim Size-8½ x 11, Desktop press, 12 pages, No Color, Matte
Subscriptions: Free
Circulation: Total-6,000

Morfogen Assocs.
Newsletter
Consumer

Publishing Co: Morfogen Assocs. Newsletter, Elm Rd., Box 324, Mountain Lakes, NJ 07046; Title Tel # (201) 334-0675 Title Fax # (201) 334-7458
Personnel: Publisher-Marilyn McCormick, Editor-Zachary Morfogen
Editorial Description: Listing of current and future exhibitions in museums around the world. List of some exhibitions in development.
General Info: Yr. Est. 1987, Quarterly, 5 pages
Subscriptions: Indv. $100, Can. $100, For. $120

Morningstar Japan
See: INTERNATIONAL AFFAIRS

Mortgage-Backed Securities Letter
See: INVESTMENT

NABE News
See: ECONOMICS

NABE Outlook, Industry Survey & Policy Survey
See: ECONOMICS

NAEIR Advantage
See: EDUCATION

NAP Forum
Business, Association

Publishing Co: Natl. Assn. of the Professions, 292 Madison Ave., New York, NY 10017-6307; Title Tel # (212) 949-5900
Editorial Description: Association membership newsletter on financial planning for professionals.
General Info: Yr. Est. 1975, Quarterly, Trim Size-8¾ x 11½, Sheetfed press, 4 pages, 2 Color, Newsprint
Circulation: Total-10,000

NASBIC News
Business

Publishing Co: National Association of Small Business Investment Companies, 1199 N Fairfax St Ste 200, Alexandria, VA 22314-1437; Title Tel # (703) 683-1601 Title Fax # (703) 683-1605
Personnel: Editor-Jeanette D. Smith
Editorial Description: Describes legislative and regulatory developments that affect venture capital industry: also industry and Association news.
General Info: Yr. Est. 1958, Monthly, Trim Size-8½ x 11, Mimeo press, 2 pages, No Color, Newsprint
Subscriptions: Indv. $125
Circulation: (100% controlled), Total-1,400

NAWBO Time
See: WOMEN'S

NBIA Review
Association

Publishing Co: National Business Incubation Association, 20 E. Circle Dr., Ste.190, Athens, OH 45701-3751; Title Tel # (614) 593-4331 Title Fax # (614) 593-1996
Personnel: Editor-Sally Hayhoe
Editorial Description: Assn. membership newsletter provides updates on members, legislation, conferences & other developments of interest.
General Info: Yr. Est. 1985, Bi-monthly, Trim Size-8½ x 11, Sheetfed press, 16 pages, No Color, Coated, Saddle-stitched
Subscriptions: Free With Membership
Circulation: (100% controlled), Total-900
Advertising: Inquire for rates. Accepts Inserts.
List Rental: Rents Lists

Naddum News
See: ENVIRONMENT & ECOLOGY

National Business News
Business, Association

Publishing Co: National Business Association, PO Box 700728, Dallas, TX 75370 Parent Co.-National Business Association, Dallas; Title Tel # (214) 458-0900 Title Fax # (214) 960-9149
Personnel: Publisher, Editor, Art Dir., Mktg. Dir.-Amy Bonney
Editorial Description: For effective development and productivity for the self-employed business owner.
General Info: Yr. Est. 1989, Bi-monthly, Trim Size-8½ x 11, Offset press, 20 pages, 2 Color, Coated, Saddle-stitched
Subscriptions: $2/copy
Circulation: Total-30,000, Readership-30,000
Printing Co: F & E Printing, 10657 Shady Trail, Dallas, TX 75220 Tel # (214) 350-1800

National Property Tax Manual
See: TAXES

National Review of Corporate Acquisitions

Publishing Co: Acquisition Resource Corp., 49 Main St, Tiburon, CA 94920-2507; Title Tel # (415) 435-2175
General Info: Weekly
Subscriptions: Indv. $295

National Sales Tax Manual
See: TAXES

National Sales Tax Rate Directory
See: TAXES

Nationwide Intelligence Strategic Information for US Travel
See: TRAVEL

Nebraska County Profiles
Business

Publishing Co: Bureau of Business Research - UNL, 114 CBA, Lincoln, NE 68588-0406; Title Tel # (402) 472-2334 Title Fax # (402) 472-3878
Editorial Description: Statistical profiles on each county in Nebraska.
General Info: Trim Size-8½ x 11, Looseleaf
Subscriptions: $10/copy

Netherlands News
See: INTERNATIONAL TRADE

Network
See: MANAGEMENT

Network City News
Business

Publishing Co: Network City News, 11415 Walpole Ct, Bowie, MD 20720-3425; Title Tel # (301) 464-5857
Editorial Description: A business networking publication for the D.C. area.
General Info: Weekly
Subscriptions: Indv. $50

Network News
Business, Association

Publishing Co: Network of Small Businesses, 5420 Mayfield Rd # 205, Lyndhurst, OH 44124-2924; Title Tel # (216) 442-5600 Title Fax # (216) 449-3227
Personnel: Editor-Irwin Friedman
Editorial Description: Financial assistance for new or expanding businesses. Offering 100's of new business contacts. Help with buying or selling businesses. Cost-effective insurance. Support for legal & tax advice.
General Info: Yr. Est. 1985, Monthly, Sheetfed press, Ind/Abs/Online: DIALOG, 1% ads, No Color, Coated
Subscriptions: Indv. $195, $25/copy
Circulation: Total-400
Advertising: Inquire for rates. Accepts Inserts.
List Rental: Actives: 200

Networker
Business CPM: $190

Publishing Co: Business Network, 5420 Mayfield Rd., Lyndhurst, OH 44124-2924; Title Tel # (216) 442-5600 Title Fax # (216) 449-3227
Editorial Description: Assistance for venture funding, grant writing, partner search.
General Info: Yr. Est. 1985, Monthly, Trim Size-8½ x 11, Desktop press, 4 pages, 2 Color
Subscriptions: Indv. $95, Inst. $75, Can. $125, For. $195
Circulation: Total-500
Advertising: $95.
List Rental: Rents Lists

Networker
Business

Publishing Co: David Bruce, PO Box 7109, Mount Jewett, PA 16740-7109 Tel # (814) 837-1096; Title Fax # (216) 562-2902
Personnel: Publisher, Editor-Bruce David
Editorial Description: Geared to the needs of small business owners.
General Info: Yr. Est. 1985, Monthly, Trim Size-8½ x 11, 2 pages
Subscriptions: Indv. $125

Networking-Newsletter

Publishing Co: U.S. Hispanic Chamber of Commerce, 1030 15th St NW Ste 206, Washington, DC 20005-1503; Title Tel # (816) 531-6363 Title Fax # (816) 756-0575
Personnel: Editor-Maxine Weber
General Info: Yr. Est. 1985, Quarterly, Trim Size-8½ x 11, 8 pages, Color-cover
Circulation: Total-5,000

New Account Selling
See: SALESMANSHIP & SELLING

New Leaders, The
Business

Publishing Co: Sterling & Stone, Inc., 1668 Lombard St., San Francisco, CA 94123; Title Tel # (415) 928-1473 Title Fax # (415) 928-3346
Personnel: Publisher, Editor-John Renesch
Editorial Description: Merging business with transformation and human consciousness.
General Info: Yr. Est. 1990, Bi-monthly, Trim Size-8½ x 11, Sheetfed press, 12 pages, ISSN: 1065-1306, 2 Color, Saddle-stitched
Subscriptions: Indv. $89, Can. $104, For. $104

New Orleans Board of Trade Membership Bulletin

Publishing Co: New Orleans Board of Trade, 316 Board Of Trade Pl, New Orleans, LA 70130-2431 Tel # (504) 525-3271
General Info: Monthly

New York Business Group on Health

Publishing Co: New York Business Group on Health, 622 3rd Ave Fl 34, New York, NY 10017-6707

New York Futures Exchange
See: INVESTMENT

New York Mercantile Exchange
See: INVESTMENT

New York Practice Guide: Business and Commericial
See: LAW

New York Wine Companion
Consumer

Publishing Co: NYW Publishing Ltd., 210 5th Ave., New York, NY 10010-2102; Title Tel # (212) 683-9221
Personnel: Publisher-Steven Roffwarz, Editor-Bernard Klein
Editorial Description: A classified book of over 7000 directories.
General Info: Yr. Est. 1985, 9x/yr.
Subscriptions: Indv. $36

Newsletter

Publishing Co: AM&A Meakin/Art, 402 West Taylor Avenue, Suite A-367, Round Rock, TX 78664-4237; Title Tel # (512) 343-5092
Personnel: Publisher-Art Meakin
Editorial Description: Newsletter on referral marketing and multi-level/network marketing.
General Info: 6 pages

Newsletter Consultant, The
See: ADVERTISING & MARKETING

Newsletter/Museletter
Association

Publishing Co: League of Canadian Poets, 54 Wolseley St., 3rd Floor, Toronto, ON M5T 1A5 Canada; Title Tel # (416) 504-1657 Title Fax # (416) 947-0159
General Info: (Formerly Buyline), Yr. Est. 1970, 8x/yr., Trim Size-8½ x 11, 8 pages
Subscriptions: Indv. $25, Inst. $25, Can. $20, For. $30, $2/copy

Nonprofit Board Report
See: MANAGEMENT

Nordic Network
See: SKIING & SNOWMOBILING

Nubian Exchange News
　See: AFRICAN-AMERICAN INTEREST

Oberweis Report
　See: INVESTMENT

Office Hours
　See: OFFICE METHODS & EQUIPMENT

Ohio Tax Alert
　See: TAXES

Oklahoma Business Bulletin   *Business*

Publishing Co: Univ. of Oklahoma, Ctr. for Economics, 307 W Brooks St Rm 4, Norman, OK 73019-4000; Title Tel # (405) 325-2931 Title Fax # (405) 325-7688
Personnel: Editor-John McCraw, Circ. Mgr.-Deanna Eades
Editorial Description: A survey of business conditions, with a continuing series of benchmark statistical data about the Oklahoma economy.
General Info: Yr. Est. 1928, Monthly, Trim Size-8$\frac{1}{2}$ x 11, Offset press, 6 pages, ISSN: 0030-1671
Subscriptions: Indv. $10, Can. $15, For. $15, $3/copy
Circulation: Total-1,000

On Buying or Selling a Business   *Business*

Publishing Co: F.W. Robbins & Co., 1416 W. Fletcher, Chicago, IL 60657; Title Tel # (312) 327-9393 Title Fax # (312) 327-6055
Personnel: Publisher-Frank Robbins
General Info: Yr. Est. 1991, Quarterly
Subscriptions: Free To Qualified Recipient
Circulation: Total-1,500

On Target-For Individuals Running Small & Midsize Companies

Publishing Co: William Horstman & Associates, PO Box 784, Troy, OH 45373-0784; Title Tel # (513) 339-0336
Personnel: Publisher, Editor-William Hortsman
Editorial Description: Covers strategic planning and marketing for owners, presidents and CEO's of small & midsize companies.
General Info: Yr. Est. 1989, Irregular
Subscriptions: Indv. $36

Ontario Corporations Law Guide
　See: LAW

Ontario Industrial Arts Bulletin

Publishing Co: Westminster Word Processing, 64 Smith St., Welland, ON L3C 4H4 Canada; Title Tel # (416) 734-7447
Personnel: Editor-Brian Carswell
General Info: Semi-annually
Subscriptions: Indv. $30

Organizing Corporate and Other Business Enterprises   *Business*

Publishing Co: Matthew Bender & Co., 11 Penn Plaza, New York, NY 10001-2006 Tel # (212) 967-7707 Fax # (212) 244-3188
Editorial Description: A guide to legal and tax factors to be considered in selecting a form of business organization--for the attorney who is advising proposed or exisitng small businesses.
General Info: Yr. Est. 1949, Irregular, Looseleaf

Ottawa Calendar   *Business, Association*

Publishing Co: Informetrica Limited, Box 828, Station B, Ottawa, ON K1P 5P9 Canada Fax # (613) 230-7698; Title Tel # (613) 238-4831 Title Fax # (613) 238-7698
Personnel: Editor-Steve Hall, Production Mgr.-Anne Richard
Editorial Description: Public agenda of federal cabinet ministers, conferences, announcements, etc.
General Info: Yr. Est. 1986, Weekly, Trim Size-8$\frac{1}{2}$ x 11, Desktop press, 20 pages, No Color
Subscriptions: Can. $450
List Rental: Rents Lists

Ottawa Letter
　See: LAW

Our Washington Newsletter
　See: ECONOMICS

Overseas Living
　See: INTERNATIONAL TRADE

PC Digest
　See: COMPUTERS & AUTOMATION

PCS News   *Business*

Publishing Co: Phillips Business Information, Inc., 1201 Seven Locks Rd., Ste 300, Potomac, MD 20854-2958 Tel # (301) 340-1520; Title Tel # (301) 340-2100 Title Fax # (301) 424-4297
Personnel: Publisher-Ellen Stuhlman, Editor-Andrea K. Bora, Mktg. Dir.-Kismet Gould
Editorial Description: Gives the reader in depth comparison of vendor prod early info. on new business opportunites in the US mkt.
General Info: Yr. Est. 1989, Bi-weekly, ISSN: 1070-6607
Subscriptions: Indv. $697, For. $730

PC's Mean Business   *Business, Consumer*

Publishing Co: CD Kloek & Associates, 843 E Main St Ste 100, Medford, OR 97504-7137 Fax # (503) 776-3429
Personnel: Publisher-Chris Kloek
Editorial Description: Discusses use of PC computers for home and small business applications.
General Info: Monthly, Trim Size-8$\frac{1}{2}$ x 11, 8 pages
Subscriptions: Indv. $35

PPF Survey (Personnel Policies Forum)
　See: INDUSTRIAL RELATIONS/PERSONNEL

PR Marcom Jobs East
　See: EMPLOYMENT

PR Marcom Jobs Mid-America
　See: EMPLOYMENT

PR Marcom Jobs West-No. Calif./Pacific Nothwest
　See: EMPLOYMENT

PR Marcom Jobs West-So. Calif.
　See: EMPLOYMENT

PSI Research Memo   *Business*

Publishing Co: PSI Research, 300 N Valley Dr, Grants Pass, OR 97526-8533; Title Tel # (503) 479-9464
Editorial Description: Informs readers about everday business issues.
General Info: Yr. Est. 1993, Quarterly

Partnership Tax Planning & Practice
　See: TAXES

Payments Monthly
　See: BANKING & FINANCE

Payroll Administration Guide
　See: INDUSTRIAL RELATIONS/PERSONNEL

Payroll Inserts
　See: INDUSTRIAL RELATIONS/PERSONNEL

Penny-Pinchers Periodical   *Business, Consumer*

Publishing Co: CD Kloek & Associates, 843 E Main St Ste 100, Medford, OR 97504-7137 Fax # (503) 776-3429
Personnel: Publisher-Chris Kloek
Editorial Description: Money saving, profit making tips for small and home-based businesses.
General Info: Monthly, Trim Size-8$\frac{1}{2}$ x 11, 8 pages
Subscriptions: Indv. $25

Pension and Profit-Sharing Plans Compliance Guide
　See: INDUSTRIAL RELATIONS/PERSONNEL

Pension and Profit-Sharing Plans: Forms and Practice with Tax Analysis
　See: INDUSTRIAL RELATIONS/PERSONNEL

People Trends
　See: INDUSTRIAL RELATIONS/PERSONNEL

Perryman Report
　See: ECONOMICS

Perryman Texas Letter, The
　See: ECONOMICS

Personal Report for the Professional Secretary *Business*

Publishing Co: National Institute of Business Management, 1101 King St Ste 411, Alexandria, VA 22314-2966 Parent Co.-National Information Corp., Alexandria; Title Tel # (703) 548-3885 Title Fax # (703) 549-0182
Personnel: Publisher-Steve Sturm, Editorial Dir.-Anne Cheevers, Mktg. Mgr.-Donna Houseman
Editorial Description: Career letter for secretaries and administrative assistants.
General Info: Yr. Est. 1972, Monthly, Color
Subscriptions: Indv. $36, Can. $48
Acquistions: Publication Sold
Circulation: Total-20,000
Advertising: Accepts Inserts.
List Rental: List Management Co.: Direct Media, Inc., 200 Pemberwick Rd., PO Box 4565, Greenwich, CT 06830 Tel # (203) 532-3713, Fax # (203) 531-1452, Actives: 12,798, $95/M, Expires: 3,949, $50/M

Personnel Legal Alert *Business*

Publishing Co: Alexander Hamilton Inst., 70 Hilltop Rd, Ramsey, NJ 07446-1119 Tel # (201) 825-8161 Fax # (201) 825-8696; Title Tel # (201) 825-3377 Title Fax # (201) 825-2696
Personnel: Editor-Brian Zevnik, Promotion Dir.-Christine LaCorte
Editorial Description: Guides personnel directors on latest legislation affecting the field.
General Info: (Formerly Personnel Alert), Yr. Est. 1989, Semi-monthly, 2 Color
Subscriptions: Indv. $74, $3/copy
Circulation: Total-2,300
List Rental: Rents Lists

Personnel Practices/Communications
See: INDUSTRIAL RELATIONS/PERSONNEL

Perspective *Business*

Publishing Co: Natl. Assn. of Investment Companies, 1111 14th St NW Ste 700, Washington, DC 20005-5603; Title Tel # (202) 289-4336

Perspective *Business*

Publishing Co: Catalyst, 250 Park Ave S Fl 5, New York, NY 10003-1402; Title Tel # (212) 777-8900
Personnel: Editor-Debbie Scheinholtz
Editorial Description: Features topics including leadership development, flexibility, mentoring, women on corporate boards and work and family programs. Each issue includes examples of successful solutions from America's top companies.
General Info: Trim Size-$8\frac{1}{2}$ x 11, 2 pages, ISSN: 0899-000X, 2 Color, Coated
Subscriptions: Indv. $60, Inst. $36, $2/copy
Circulation: Total-2,800
Printing Co: Associated Offset, 599 11th Ave., New York, NY 10036 Tel # (212) 924-6415

Perspectives on Family Business *Business*

Publishing Co: Newkirk Products, Inc., 15 Corporate Cir, Albany, NY 12203-5154 Tel # (518) 452-1000
Editorial Description: Custom publication designed for distribution to clients with family businesses.
General Info: Quarterly, Trim Size-$8\frac{1}{2}$ x 11, 4 pages, 2 Color

Phone Sales Presentations for Service Type Businesses - A Newsletter

Publishing Co: Prosperity & Profits Unlimited, PO Box 416, Denver, CO 80201-0416; Title Tel # (303) 575-5676
Personnel: Publisher, Editor-A. Doyle
Editorial Description: Phone Scripts for various businesses.
General Info: Yr. Est. 1991, Annually
Subscriptions: Indv. $16, Inst. $16, Can. $19, For. $21, $16/copy
Circulation: Total-1,500

Plant Prospector *Business*

Publishing Co: Beard Group, Inc., PO Box 9867, Washington, DC 20016-8867 Tel # (301) 951-6400 Fax # (301) 951-3621
Personnel: Publisher-Christopher Beard
Editorial Description: Identifies companies in flux through layoffs, cutbacks and shutdowns.
General Info: Yr. Est. 1995, Weekly
Subscriptions: Indv. $1,150, Inst. $1,150

Plant Shutdowns Monitor
See: INTERNATIONAL TRADE

Plastics Business News
See: PLASTICS

Political Risk Letter
See: INTERNATIONAL TRADE

Positive Economist Bulletin
See: ECONOMICS

Post Industrial Issues
See: GOVERNMENT

Practical Supervision
See: OFFICE METHODS & EQUIPMENT

Prairie Progress Newsletter *Business, Consumer*

Publishing Co: Westarc Group, Inc., Brandon University, Brandon, MB R7A 6A9 Canada; Title Tel # (204) 729-3450 Title Fax # (204) 727-7555
Personnel: Publisher-Robert Annis, Editor-Fred McGuinness, Editorial Asst.-Joy Dornian
Editorial Description: A 'good news' newsletter of ideas, suggestions and reports directed to those interested in rural economic development.
General Info: Yr. Est. 1991, Bi-monthly, 8 pages, ISSN: 1188-2255, Color, Matte
Subscriptions: Indv. $20, Inst. $20, Can. $20, For. $20, Free To Qualified Recipient
Circulation: (66% controlled), Total-3,000, Subscriptions-1,000
Printing Co: Leech Printing, 857 18th St., Brandon, MB R7A 5B7 Canada Tel # (204) 728-3037, Fax # (204) 727-3338

PresentFutures Report *Business*

Publishing Co: PresentFutures Group, 101 Park Washington Ct #100, Falls Church, VA 22046; Title Tel # (703) 538-6181
General Info: Yr. Est. 1991, 11x/yr.
Subscriptions: Free To Qualified Recipient

Prewritten Job Descriptions *Business*

Publishing Co: Business & Legal Reports, Inc., 39 Academy St., PO Box 1513, Madison, CT 06443-2646 Tel # (860) 245-7448 Fax # (860) 245-2559; Title Tel # (203) 245-7448 Title Fax # (203) 245-2559
Editorial Description: Over 300 pages of job descriptions, plus step by step guidelines to help you prepare, organize, and implement the job description you need.
General Info: Yr. Est. 1986, Bi-monthly, Looseleaf
Subscriptions: Indv. $160

Pricing Advisor, The
See: ADVERTISING & MARKETING

Print Business Register
See: PRINTING/GRAPHIC ARTS

Printing Sales Index
See: ECONOMICS

Privacy & American Business *Business*

Publishing Co: Center for Social & Legal Research, Two University Plaza, Suite 414, Hackensack, NJ 07601; Title Tel # (201) 996-1154 Title Fax # (201) 996-1883
Personnel: Publisher-Alan Westin, Editor-Lorrie Sherwood
Editorial Description: P&AB analyzes privacy development in financial services, insurance, health/medical, communications, electronic media, direct marketing, employment, and in the global marketplace.
General Info: Yr. Est. 1993, Bi-monthly, Trim Size-$8\frac{1}{2}$ x 11, 24 pages, ISSN: 1070-0536, 2 Color, Matte, Saddle-stitched
Subscriptions: Indv. $395

Private Placement Letter
See: INVESTMENT

Procedures Review
See: NUCLEAR ENERGY

Process Re-Engineering

Publishing Co: Productivity Development Group, Inc., PO Box 488, Westford, MA 01886-0013; Title Tel # (508) 692-1818 Title Fax # (508) 692-5080
Editorial Description: Why and how leading edge firms like AT &t , American States Insurance , First Chicago Trust and others realign jobs and automation to raise productivity, reduce managerial ratios, increase job motivation and slash service cycle times. dozens of how to tips and lessons learned.
General Info: Irregular, Looseleaf
Subscriptions: Indv. $495, For. $495

Productivity *Business*

Publishing Co: Productivity Inc., 101 Merritt 7, Norwalk, CT 06851-1059; Title Tel # (203) 846-3777 Title Fax # (203) 846-6883
Personnel: Publisher-Norman Bodek, Editor-Chet Marchwinski, Circ. Mgr.-Antoinette Saloomey
General Info: Yr. Est. 1980, Monthly, ISSN: 0275-8040
Subscriptions: Indv. $167
Circulation: Total-1,100
List Rental: List Management Co.: List Technology Systems Group, Inc., 1001 Ave. of the Americas, New York, NY 10018 Tel # (212) 719-3850, Fax # (212) 719-1878, Actives: $95/M

Productivity Views: Newsletter of Service Quality
Business

Publishing Co: Productivity Development Group, Inc., PO Box 488, Westford, MA 01886-0013; Title Tel # (508) 692-1818 Title Fax # (508) 692-5080
Personnel: Publisher, Editor-Martin Stankard, Circ. Mgr.-Kathleen Veth, Art Dir.-Debra Tarsitano
Editorial Description: Devoted exclusively to practical development in white-collar productivity and quality in service firms. Positive interviews/reports on how leading companies are saving money, speeding services, pleasing customers and reducing errors.
General Info: Yr. Est. 1983, Bi-monthly, ISSN: 0891-7167
Subscriptions: Indv. $295, For. $295
Printing Co: Casco Graphics, 79 Prospect St # 273, Somerville, MA 02143-4126 Tel # (617) 776-3400

Professional Consultant & Information Marketing Report
See: MANAGEMENT

Professional Directory of Indy Women
See: WOMEN'S

Professional Regulation News
See: HEALTH

Professional Services Management Journal
See: MANAGEMENT

Profit-Building Strategies for Business Owners
Business

Publishing Co: TRR Publishing Co., Inc., 81 Montgomery St, Scarsdale, NY 10583-5150; Title Tel # (914) 472-0366
Personnel: Publisher-John Springer, Editor-Karen Sanders, Circ. Mgr.-Helen Faulkner
Editorial Description: Ideas to help small businesses achieve greater success & profitability.
General Info: (Formerly Professional Report), Monthly, Trim Size-8½ x 11, 28 pages, Ind/Abs/Online: DIALOG
Subscriptions: Indv. $60, $8/copy
Circulation: Total-25,000

Profits

Publishing Co: Small Business Development Ctr. -Howard Univ., 2600 Sixth St. N.w., Rm. 125, Washington, DC 20059-0001 Tel # (202) 806-1550; Title Tel # (202) 636-7187
Personnel: Editor-Mary Merchant
Circulation: Total-2,000

Property Tax Alert
See: TAXES

Protector

Publishing Co: Better Business Bureau of Nova Scotia, Box 2124, Halifax, NS B3J 3B7 Canada; Title Tel # (902) 422-6583
Personnel: Editor-Marlene Moore
General Info: Yr. Est. 1980, Monthly
Circulation: Total-2,000

Pryor Report
Business

Publishing Co: Imagine, Inc., 398 Avenue, PO Box 101, Clemson, SC 29633-0101; Title Tel # (864) 654-5148 Title Fax # (864) 654-7275
Personnel: Editor-Paul Friedman
General Info: (Formerly Breakthrough Strategies), Yr. Est. 1984, Monthly
Subscriptions: Indv. $89, $10/copy
List Rental: List Management Co.: List Emporium, 2000 Shawnee Mission Pky Ste, 235, Westwood, KS 66205-3601 Tel # (913) 236-6830, Fax # (913) 236-4842, Actives: 126,970, $85/M

Publisher's Report
See: BOOKS & BOOK TRADE

Purchaser's Legal Adviser
See: PURCHASING

Purchasing Executive's Bulletin
See: PURCHASING

Quality 1st.
See: INDUSTRIAL RELATIONS/PERSONNEL

Quality Executive
See: MANAGEMENT

Quarterly Business Failures Report
Association

Publishing Co: Dun & Bradstreet, PO Box 870, Wilton, CT 06897; Title Tel # (212) 593-6800
Personnel: Editor-F.R. Brown, Circ. Mgr.-Nova Culver, Publisher, Production Mgr.-A.M. Dowden
General Info: Quarterly, Trim Size-8½ x 11, Sheetfed press, 150 pages, No Color, Newsprint, Perfect bound
Subscriptions: Indv. $40, Inst. $55
Circulation: Total-2,100
Advertising: Inquire for rates.
Printing Co: Mack Printing Group, 1991 Northampton St., Easton, PA 18042-3189 Tel # (610) 250-7261, Fax # (610) 250-7211

Quarterly Domestic & Global Forecasts of Key Economic Indicators
Business

Publishing Co: Graceway Publishing Co., Box 670159, Flushing, NY 11367-0159; Title Tel # (718) 463-3914 Title Fax # (718) 544-9086
Personnel: Editor-Dennis Ellis
Editorial Description: Covers forecasts of key economic indicators of 47 countries; 13 economic variables of U.S. economy; & industry forecasts.
General Info: Yr. Est. 1984, Quarterly, Web press, 12 pages, ISSN: 0888-787X
Subscriptions: Indv. $105, Can. $150, For. $150
Circulation: Total-500
List Rental: Actives: 4,200, $95/M
Printing Co: Crystal Clear Printing, 3621 164th St, Flushing, NY 11358-2003 Tel # (718) 445-9782

Quincy Business News
Business   CPM: $191

Publishing Co: Graham Communications, 40 Oval Rd, Quincy, MA 02170-3813; Title Tel # (617) 328-0069 Title Fax # (617) 471-1504
Personnel: Publisher-John Graham, Circ. Mgr.-Paul Graham, Editor, Adv. Dir.-Cindy Cartell, Art Dir.- Robert Jankowski
Editorial Description: QBN, distributed to nearly 3,000 Quincy businesses, is written about the residents & businesses in Quincy reaching more than 5,000 readers.
General Info: Yr. Est. 1989, Monthly, Trim Size-8½ x 11, Offset press, 12 pages, 4% ads, 2 Color, Other, Saddle-stitched
Subscriptions: Free To Qualified Recipient
Circulation: Total-3,400, Readership-5,000
Advertising: $650. Accepts Inserts.
List Rental: Rents Lists
Printing Co: Account Manager: Mary Weafer; Ink Spot, The, 40 Oval Rd, Quincy, MA 02170-3813 Tel # (617) 273-7605, Fax # (617) 471-8810

RAB Instant Background
See: BROADCASTING

RAP Session
See: EMPLOYMENT

RBA Insight
See: FOOD

RIC Insight
See: SCIENCE

Rap Session

Publishing Co: Kimberly Organization, PO Box 31011, Saint Louis, MO 63131-0011; Title Tel # (314) 965-0291
Personnel: Publisher, Editor-Paul Hawkinson
General Info: Yr. Est. 1981, Weekly, 2 pages, No Color, Newsprint
Subscriptions: Indv. $130, $3/copy
Circulation: Total-5,000

Re-Designing Customer Service

Publishing Co: Organization Development Corporation, PO Box 312, Mukwonago, WI 53149; Title Tel # (414) 363-9848 Title Fax # (414) 363-9828
Personnel: Publisher-James Logsdon
Editorial Description: A newsletter on improving customer service to maximize profit, sales and cash flow.
General Info: Yr. Est. 1994, Monthly, Trim Size-8.5 x 11, Desktop press, 8 pages, ISSN: 1083-2254, 2 Color, Matte, Saddle-stitched
Subscriptions: Indv. $144
Printing Co: TJ Printing, 14150 W National Ave # 406, New Berlin, WI 53151-4529

Reading Labor Market News Release
See: GOVERNMENT

The Real Entrepreneur
Business, Consumer

Publishing Co: Real Entrepreneur, PO Box 1, Varnell, GA 30756-0001; Title Tel # (706) 694-8441
Personnel: Publisher, Editor-Bob Riemke, Circ. Mgr.-Paul Womac
Editorial Description: Devoted to the small business owner.
General Info: Monthly, Trim Size-8½ x 11, 10 pages
Subscriptions: Indv. $40, Can. $43, For. $58
Advertising: Inquire for rates.
List Rental: List Management Co.: Bo-Mar Enterprises, P.O. Box I, Varnell, GA 30756, Actives: 200, $7.50/M

Recruiting & Search Report
See: EMPLOYMENT

Recruiting Trends
See: EMPLOYMENT

Recycling Related Newsletters, Publications, Etc; A Reference
See: ENVIRONMENT & ECOLOGY

Recycling Update
See: ENVIRONMENT & ECOLOGY

Re$earch Money — *Business*

Publishing Co: Evert Communications Ltd., 1296 Carling Ave., Ottawa, ON K1Z 7K8 Canada; Title Tel # (613) 728-4621 Title Fax # (613) 728-0385
Personnel: Publisher-Gordon Hutchison, Editor-Mark Henderson, Circ. Dir.-Carole Jeffrey
Editorial Description: The management and financing of R&D performers and entrepreneurs in Canada.
General Info: Yr. Est. 1987, 20x/yr., Trim Size-8½ x 11, Sheetfed press, 8 pages, ISSN: 0833-1677, No Color, Matte, Saddle-stitched
Subscriptions: Inst. $475, Can. $475, For. $475
List Rental: Actives: $850/M
Printing Co: Bradda Printing Services, 130 Slater Street, Ottawa, ON K1P 6E2 Canada Tel # (613) 238-5433

Reference Point
See: LIBRARY

Regional Update

Publishing Co: Federal Reserve Bank of Atlanta, 104 Marietta St NW, Atlanta, GA 30303-2713 Fax # (404) 521-8050; Title Tel # (404) 521-8020 Title Fax # (404) 521-8956
Personnel: Editor-John D. Marsh, Circ. Mgr.-Ellen Arth, Art Dir.-Carole Starkey
General Info: Quarterly, Trim Size-8½ x 11, Sheetfed press, 12 pages, ISSN: 0899-6571, 2 Color, Matte, Saddle-stitched
Circulation: (100% controlled), Total-7,000

Relocation Report
See: REAL ESTATE

Research News — *Business*

Publishing Co: Bureau of Business Research, University of Texas, 21st St. & Speedway, Austin, TX 78712-1104 Tel # (512) 471-1616; Title Tel # (512) 471-5179 Title Fax # (512) 471-1063
Editorial Description: Offers up-to-date information on faculty research activities and fundiong resources for business and economic research.
General Info: Bi-monthly
Subscriptions: Free

Research Recommendations — *Business*

Publishing Co: National Institute of Business Management, 1101 King St Ste 411, Alexandria, VA 22314-2966 Parent Co.-National Information Corp., Alexandria
Personnel: Publisher-Brian Smith, Editor-Paul Hencke
Editorial Description: Economic, political, and tax advisory letter
General Info: Yr. Est. 1937, Weekly, Trim Size-7½ x 10, 8 pages
Subscriptions: Indv. $96
Acquistions: Publication Bought, Publication Sold
Circulation: Total-100,000
Advertising: Accepts Inserts.
List Rental: List Management Co.: The Lake Group, 411 Theodore Freund Ave., Rye, NY 10580-1497 Tel # (914) 925-2400, Fax # (914) 925-2499, Actives: 46,299, $95/M, Expires: 15,925, $55/M

Resolution Trust Reporter — *Business*

Publishing Co: Faulkner & Gray, Inc., 11 Penn Plz., 17th Floor, New York, NY 10001-2006 Tel # (212) 967-7000 Fax # (212) 695-8172 Parent Co.-Thomson Corp., Stamford; Title Tel # (212) 563-4405 Title Fax # (212) 564-8877
Personnel: Publisher-John Gynn, Editor-Stan Strachan, Production Mgr.-Stephan Potter, Adv. Dir.-Brian Quasitrock, Promotion Dir.-Ralph Wegs
Editorial Description: Keeps an eye on the activities of the Resolution Trust Corporation. The focus is on regulation, disposition of assets, thrifts and real estate.
General Info: Yr. Est. 1989, Bi-weekly, Trim Size-8½ x 11, Sheetfed press, 20 pages, Color-cover
Subscriptions: Indv. $398, For. $498, $25/copy
Advertising: $1,800.
Printing Co: Globe Mail Agency, Inc., 541 W 25th St, New York, NY 10001-5501 Tel # (212) 675-4600

Resort Management Report — *Business*

Publishing Co: Rouge et Noir Inc., PO Box 1146, Midlothian, VA 23113-8146; Title Tel # (804) 230-0736 Title Fax # (804) 230-4931
Editorial Description: Financial analysis of casino gaming operations.
General Info: Yr. Est. 1976, Monthly, 100 pages, 5% ads, No Color, Saddle-stitched
Subscriptions: Indv. $495

Responsibility
See: WOMEN'S

Revenews

Publishing Co: Ministry of Revenue, 33 King Street West, Sixth Floor, Box 627, Oshawa, ON L1H 8H5 Canada; Title Tel # (416) 433-5780 Title Fax # (905) 433-6699

Rico Business Disputes Guide
See: LAW

Roanoke Valley Chamber of Commerce-Business & Professional Directory

Publishing Co: Roanoke Valley Chamber of Commerce, 212 S. Jefferson, Roanoke, VA 24011 Tel # (540) 983-0700 Fax # (540) 983-0723; Title Tel # (703) 344-5188
Personnel: Editor-Lynn Davis
Editorial Description: ABC & category listing of 1,600 businesses in Roanoke Valley.
General Info: Sheetfed press, 112 pages, Color, Coated
Subscriptions: $5/copy
Circulation: Total-10,000
Printing Co: Progress Press, 2922 Nicholas Ave NE, Roanoke, VA 24012-5651 Tel # (703) 345-1820

Robert L. Siegel Letter — *Business*

Publishing Co: Robert L. Siegel & Associates, Inc., 26 Trianon Drive, Kohner, LA 70065 Tel # (504) 471-0300 Fax # (504) 471-0526
Editorial Description: Publication covering business issues.
General Info: Yr. Est. 1980, Semi-monthly
Subscriptions: Indv. $199

Rolling Ventures
See: MOBILE HOMES

Roman Reports
See: DIRECT MAIL

Runzheimer Reports on Relocation
See: MANAGEMENT

Russian Far East Update
See: INTERNATIONAL TRADE

SAS Newsletter

Publishing Co: Society for Applied Spectroscopy, 201 B Broadway St., Frederick, MD 21701-6501 Fax # (301) 694-6860; Title Tel # (301) 694-8122
General Info: Quarterly

SBANE Enterprise — *Business* — CPM: $134

Publishing Co: Smaller Business Assn. of N.E., 204 Second Ave, Waltham, MA 02154; Title Tel # (617) 890-9070 Title Fax # (617) 890-4567
Personnel: Editor-Julie Scofield, Circ. Mgr.-Jean Peckham
Editorial Description: Focuses on association events and management aids benefiting small businesses.
General Info: (Formerly Small Business News), Yr. Est. 1984, Monthly, Trim Size-8½ x 11, 12 pages, ISSN: 8750-3158, 3% ads, 2 Color, Saddle-stitched
Subscriptions: Indv. $49, Free With Membership
Circulation: Total-6,200
Advertising: $834. Accepts Inserts.

SBDC News — *Business*

Publishing Co: Sponsor-Iowa Small Business Dev. Ctrs., Iowa State Univ., 137 Lynn, Ames, IA 50010-7126; Title Tel # (512) 292-6351
Personnel: Publisher-Jan DeYoung
Editorial Description: Describes assistance available and reports services offered to Iowa small businesses.
General Info: (Formerly SBDC Update), Yr. Est. 1982, Quarterly, Sheetfed press, 6 pages, 2 Color, Matte, Saddle-stitched
Circulation: (100% controlled), Total-4,000
Printing Co: Iowa State University, Dept. Of English Ross Hall, Ames, IA 50011-0001 Tel # (515) 292-0140

SCOR Report
See: BANKING & FINANCE

SCWEA Newsletter
See: EDUCATION

SEC Accounting Rules
See: ACCOUNTING

SEC Case Monitor
See: GOVERNMENT

SEC Docket
See: INVESTMENT

SMT Trends
See: MANUFACTURING

SORT'ing News
See: OFFICE METHODS & EQUIPMENT

SPEX: Small Publishers Exchange
See: BOOKS & BOOK TRADE

Safe Money Report
Business, Consumer

Publishing Co: Weiss Publishing & Marketing, 4176 Burns Rd., Palm Beach Gardens, FL
33410-4606 Fax # (407) 625-6685; Title Tel # (407) 627-3300 Title Fax # (407) 684-9039
Editorial Description: Financial business news on and for big and small business.
General Info: Yr. Est. 1978, Monthly, Trim Size-8.5 x 11, 12 pages, No Color, Matte
Subscriptions: Indv. $99
Circulation: Total-56,000
List Rental: Actives: 56,000, $165/M

Saint John Business Today
Business

Publishing Co: Saint John Board of Trade, 40 King Street, Box 6037, Saint John, NB E2L 4R5
Canada; Title Tel # (506) 634-8111 Title Fax # (506) 632-2008
Personnel: Editor-Darryl Goyetche, Adv. Dir.-Steve Fowler
Editorial Description: Developments in business, industry; community news in relation to business
environment.
General Info: (Formerly Saint John Today), Yr. Est. 1976, Monthly, Trim Size-8½ x 11, Sheetfed
press, 8 pages, ISSN: 1184-731X, 5% ads, 2 Color
Circulation: (77% controlled), Total-1,100
Advertising: Inquire for rates. Accepts Inserts.
List Rental: Actives: $25/M

Salary Characteristics
See: ECONOMICS

Sales & Use Tax Alert
See: TAXES

Sales and Bulk Transfers Under the UCC
See: LAW

Sales Prospector
Business

Publishing Co: Intertec International, Inc., 2472 Eastman Ave., Bldg. 33-34, Ventura, CA 93003
Tel # (805) 650-7070 Fax # (805) 650-7079; Title Tel # (617) 899-1271
Personnel: Publisher-George Rohr, VP Editorial-Sheri Levin, Mktg. Dir.-Ron Shandler
Editorial Description: Reports for 15 marketing areas in U.S. and Canada and all new manufacturing
firms, new plants, plant additions, and relocations.
General Info: Yr. Est. 1954, Bi-monthly, Trim Size-8½ x 11, Web press, 8 pages, Ind/Abs/Online:
NewsNet, DIALOG, No Color
Subscriptions: Indv. $495
Circulation: Total-5,200
List Rental: List Management Co.: Lakewood Lists, 50 S. 9th St., Minneapolis, MN 55402
Tel # (612) 333-0471, Fax # (612) 333-6526, Actives: 10,000, $125/M, Expires: 65,000, $95/M

Sales Rep's Advisor, The
See: SALESMANSHIP & SELLING

Salesmanship
See: SALESMANSHIP & SELLING

Secretary's Letter
Business

Publishing Co: Economics Press, Inc., 12 Daniel Rd., Fairfield, NJ 07004-2565 Tel # (201) 227-1224
Fax # (201) 227-9742
Editorial Description: Information and advice on work issues for secretaries.
General Info: Monthly
Subscriptions: Indv. $69

Secured Transactions Under the UCC
See: LAW

Securities and Federal Corporate Law Report
Business, Scholarly

Publishing Co: Clark Boardman Callaghan, 375 Hudson St, New York, NY 10014-3685
Fax # (212) 807-6209; Title Tel # (212) 929-7500 Title Fax # (212) 924-0460
Personnel: Publisher-Jim Fegen, Editor-John Duxbury, Adv. Dir.-Wayne Smith, Art Dir.-Gene Spinelli,
Promotion Dir.-Steve Murtha
Editorial Description: Comprehensive newsletter on securities law and regulation.
General Info: Yr. Est. 1979, 10x/yr., Trim Size-8½ x 11, Sheetfed press, 8 pages, ISSN: 0273-0685,
2 Color
Subscriptions: Indv. $225
List Rental: Rents Lists
Printing Co: Financial Press, 600 River Ave, Pittsburgh, PA 15212-5935 Tel # (412) 321-0440

Security Letter
See: SECURITY & SURVEILLANCE

Security Management Bulletin: Protecting People, Property & Assets
See: SECURITY & SURVEILLANCE

Security Technology News
See: SECURITY & SURVEILLANCE

Self-Employed America
Business, Association

Publishing Co: Sponsor-Natl. Assn. for the Self-Employed, National Association for the Self-
Employed, Inc., 2121 Precinct Line Rd, Hurst, TX 76054-3136; Title Tel # (800) 433-8004
Personnel: Editor-Karen Jones, Production Mgr.-Cheryl Springer, Art Dir.-Karen Frey
Editorial Description: Provides info on business, financial, and legislative matters of interest to small
business owners.
General Info: (Formerly Profitline; NASE Newsletter; Small Business America), Bi-monthly, Trim Size-
11 x 14, Web press, 16 pages, 4 Color, Newsprint
Subscriptions: Free With Membership
Circulation: Total-320,000
Printing Co: Account Manager: Dick Davis; Sullivan Graphics, Lufkin, TX Tel # (214) 233-4046

Self-Employment Survival Letter
Business, Consumer

Publishing Co: Barbara Brabec Prod., PO Box 2137, Naperville, IL 60567-2137;
Title Tel # (708) 717-4188 Title Fax # (708) 717-5198
Personnel: Publisher, Editor-Barbara Brabec
Editorial Description: Business Management and marketing guidance for homebased professionals.
General Info: (Formerly National Home Business Report), Yr. Est. 1981, Bi-monthly, Trim Size-8½ x
11, Sheetfed press, 8 pages, ISSN: 0741-5729, 2 Color, Matte
Subscriptions: Indv. $29, Can. $33, For. $33, $5/copy
Circulation: Total-1,000
Printing Co: Roger's Printing, 9 E Chapman St, Ely, MN 55731-1227 Tel # (218) 365-6275

Self Employment Update - Business Idea Letters Edition

Publishing Co: Prosperity & Profits Unlimited, PO Box 416, Denver, CO 80201-0416;
Title Tel # (303) 575-5676
Personnel: Publisher, Editor-A. Doyle
Editorial Description: Business idea letters for home or small business
General Info: Yr. Est. 1983, Irregular, ISSN: 0736-1912
Subscriptions: Indv. $11, Inst. $11, Can. $13, For. $16, $11/copy
Circulation: Total-2,000

Self Publishing Update - How to Basics Edition
See: BOOKS & BOOK TRADE

Selling Advantage
See: SALESMANSHIP & SELLING

Semi Standards Information Alert
Business

Publishing Co: Semiconductor Equipment & Materials Intl., 805 E Middlefield Rd, Mountain View, CA
94043-4025; Title Tel # (415) 964-5111
Personnel: Editor-Lisa Altera, Editor-Lisa Sanchez
General Info: (Formerly Standards in Review; Semi Standards), Yr. Est. 1980, Quarterly, 12 pages

Sensor Technology
See: ENGINEERING, ELECTRICAL

Set-Aside Alert
Business **CPM: $727**

Publishing Co: Small Business Press, 2000 14th St N Ste 450, Arlington, VA 22201-2573;
Title Tel # (703) 243-9868 Title Fax # (703) 243-2317
Personnel: Publisher-Leonard Chusmir, Editor-Margaret Ryan, Adv. Dir.-Mary Liston
Editorial Description: Information for small business owners and owners from under-represented
groups.
General Info: Yr. Est. 1993, Bi-weekly, 24 pages, ISSN: 1068-5715, 2 Color, Matte, Saddle-stitched
Subscriptions: Indv. $637
Circulation: Total-2,200
Advertising: $1,600.
Printing Co: Newsletter Services, Inc., 9700 Philadelphia Court, Lanham, MD 20706
Tel # (301) 731-5200, Fax # (301) 731-5201

Sid Cato's Newsletter on Annual Reports
Business

Publishing Co: Sid Cato Communications, Inc., PO Box 19850, Kalamazoo, MI 49019-0850;
Title Tel # (616) 344-2286 Title Fax # (616) 344-4145
Personnel: Publisher, Editor-Sid Cato
Editorial Description: Latest news & information on annual reports to shareholders.
General Info: Yr. Est. 1983, Monthly, 6 pages, Ind/Abs/Online: Newsnet, No Color, Newsprint
Subscriptions: Indv. $197

Siedlecki on Business
See: ADVERTISING & MARKETING

Silver Prescription
Business

Publishing Co: Silver Prescription Press Inc., 524 Camino Del Monte Sol, Santa Fe, NM
87501-2828; Title Tel # (505) 983-1815 Title Fax # (505) 983-2887
Personnel: Publisher, Editor-A.D. Silver
General Info: Yr. Est. 1987, Monthly
Subscriptions: Indv. $80

The Small Business Advisor *Business*

Publishing Co: Small Business Advisors, PO Box 436, Woodmere, NY 11598-0436; Title Tel # (516) 374-1387 Title Fax # (516) 374-1175
Personnel: Publisher-Joseph Gelb, Editor-Ann Liss, Production Mgr.-Barbara Goetz, Art Dir.-Lorraine Periconne
Editorial Description: Helps managers and owners of small businesses better manage their companies with information on taxes, finance management presented in an informative iniplementntion oriented style.
General Info: Yr. Est. 1993, Monthly, Trim Size-8½ x 11, 16 pages, ISSN: 1069-9619, 2 Color, Coated, Saddle-stitched
Subscriptions: Indv. $35, $6/copy
Circulation: (100% controlled), Total-1,000

Small Business Builder *Business*

Publishing Co: FINL-Financial Independent Network Ltd., Inc., 310 Second St., Boscobel, WI 53805-1164 Tel # (815) 356-8800 Fax # (815) 356-8804; Title Tel # (708) 658-9107 Title Fax # (708) 658-9107
Personnel: Circ. Dir.-Lois Cummuta, Art Dir.-Michael DiFrisco, Publisher, Editor, Mktg. Dir.-John Cummuta
Editorial Description: Teaching small business operators how to manage, market, use computers, operate from home, maximize profits, and how to stay motivated.
General Info: Yr. Est. 1993, Monthly, Trim Size-8½ x 11, Offset press, 8 pages, 2 Color, Matte, Saddle-stitched
Subscriptions: Indv. $120
Circulation: Total-1,500
List Rental: List Management Co.: Manager: Michael Mikrut; Macro Mark, 65 West 96th Street, New York, NY 10025 Tel # (212) 662-1170, Fax # (212) 662-1195
Printing Co: New Life, 1508 South Main St., Route 31, Algonquin, IL 60102 Tel # (708) 658-4111

Small Business Chronicle

Publishing Co: PSBC, 221 W. Germantown Pike, Plymouth Meeting, PA 19462-1444; Title Tel # (215) 540-9440 Title Fax # (215) 540-1775
Personnel: Publisher-Libby Barland, Editor-Greg Matusky
General Info: (Formerly Philadelphia Small Business Chronicle), Yr. Est. 1988, Monthly, Web press, 32 pages, Color-cover, Newsprint
Subscriptions: Indv. $18, $2/copy
Acquistions: Publication Bought, Publication Sold
Circulation: Total-35,000
Advertising: Inquire for rates. Accepts Inserts.

Small Business Computer News
See: COMPUTERS & AUTOMATION

Small Business Economic Trends *Business*

Publishing Co: Natl. Federation of Independent Business Education Fndn., 600 Maryland Ave. SW, Suite 770, Washington, DC 20024-2520 Tel # (202) 554-9000
General Info: (Formerly NFIB Quarterly Economic Report for Small Business), Yr. Est. 1974, Monthly
Subscriptions: Indv. $150

Small Business Service Bureau, Inc. Bulletin *Business, Association*

Publishing Co: Small Business Service Bureau, Inc., 554 Main St # 1441, Worcester, MA 01608-2014; Title Tel # (508) 756-3513 Title Fax # (508) 791-4709
Personnel: Publisher-Francis Carroll, Editor-Rosemary Heinold, Circ. Mgr.-Vincent Tynan, Production Mgr.-Elizabeth Gribbons, Adv. Dir.-Teresa Ceppi
Editorial Description: Small business legislation, management assistance, benefits and services.
General Info: (Formerly Small Business), Yr. Est. 1978, Bi-monthly, Trim Size-8½ x 11, Web press, 16 pages, ISSN: 0893-8326, 2 Color, Newsprint, Saddle-stitched
Subscriptions: Free With Membership
Circulation: (100% controlled), Total-35,000
Printing Co: Saltus Press, 31 Jolma Rd, Worcester, MA 01604-2009 Tel # (508) 752-1969

Small Business Tax Control *Business*

Publishing Co: Inside Mortgage Finance Publications, Box 42387, Washington, DC 20015 Tel # (301) 951-1240 Fax # (301) 656-1709
Personnel: Publisher-Guy Cecala, Editor-Larry Witner, Production Mgr.-Tony Cecala, Circ. Mgr., Mktg. Dir.-Didi Parks
Editorial Description: A monthly newsletter and 400 page tax guide for small businesses.
General Info: Monthly, Trim Size-8½ x 11, 6 pages, Looseleaf
Subscriptions: Indv. $149

Small Business Tax Saver
See: TAXES

Small Business-USA *Business*

Publishing Co: National Small Business United, 1155 15th St NW Ste 710, Washington, DC 20005-2706; Title Tel # (202) 293-8830
Personnel: Editor-Marcia Bradford
Editorial Description: For members of National Small Business Assn., describing assn's. activities in Washington on behalf of smaller companies.
General Info: Yr. Est. 1987, Monthly, Web press, 4 pages, ISSN: 0037-7198, No Color
Subscriptions: Indv. $50
Circulation: (100% controlled), Total-50,000

Small Business Wealth Builder *Business*

Publishing Co: Enterprise Publishing, 6069 Crown Royal Cir, Alexandria, VA 22310-1744; Title Tel # (302) 654-0110
Personnel: Publisher-Ted Nicholas, Editor-Ann Faccenda
General Info: Yr. Est. 1983, Monthly, 8 pages, 1% ads
Subscriptions: Indv. $96
Advertising: Inquire for rates.

Small Business Wire

Publishing Co: Business Council of New York State, 152 Washington Ave, Albany, NY 12210-2203 Fax # (518) 465-4389; Title Tel # (518) 465-7511
Personnel: Editor-Robert Ward
General Info: Yr. Est. 1986
Subscriptions: Indv. $20

Small Corporation Update *Business*

Publishing Co: TPR Publishing Co., Inc., 81 Montgomery St, Scarsdale, NY 10583-5150 Tel # (914) 472-0366 Fax # (914) 472-0379
Personnel: Publisher-John L. Springer
Editorial Description: Provides small corporations with tax, legal, and management information.
General Info: Yr. Est. 1989, Monthly
Subscriptions: Indv. $84, $10/copy
List Rental: List Management Co.: SpeciaLISTS, 1200 Harbor Blvd Ste 9, Weehawken, NJ 07087-6728 Tel # (201) 865-5800, Fax # (201) 867-2450

Small Firm Profit Report - Attorney Edition
See: LAW

Small Firm Profit Report - CPA Edition
See: ACCOUNTING

Smart Buying
See: PURCHASING

Snapshot *Association*

Publishing Co: Society of National Association Pubs., 1735 N Lynn St Ste 950, Arlington, VA 22209-2019; Title Tel # (703) 524-2000 Title Fax # (202) 333-5365
Personnel: Editor-Allison Parker
General Info: Monthly, Sheetfed press, 12 pages, 3% ads, 2 Color, Matte
Circulation: Total-550
Advertising: Inquire for rates.
List Rental: Rents Lists

Software Digest
See: COMPUTERS & AUTOMATION

Soundview Executive Book Summaries *Business*

Publishing Co: Concentrated Knowledge., 3 Pond Lane, Middlebury, VT 05753-1164 Tel # (802) 388-8910; Title Tel # (802) 388-8920 Title Fax # (802) 388-8939
Personnel: Publisher-Cynthia Folino, Editor-Jeff Olson, Production Mgr.-Sheila Knight, Mktg. Dir.-Robert Carter
Editorial Description: Soundview Summaries are concise, 8-page distillations of new business books. Editors pick the 66 best business books published each year, summarizing 30 and reviewing 36.
General Info: Yr. Est. 1978, Monthly, Trim Size-8½ x 11, Sheetfed press, 8 pages, ISSN: 0747-2196, 2 Color, Matte
Subscriptions: Indv. $90, Can. $90, For. $139, $5/copy
Acquistions: Publication Bought
Circulation: Total-49,000
Advertising: Accepts Inserts.
List Rental: List Management Co.: Direct Media, Inc., 200 Pemberwick Rd., PO Box 4565, Greenwich, CT 06830 Tel # (203) 532-3713, Fax # (203) 531-1452, Actives: 49,000, $95/M, Expires: 9,000, $50/M
Printing Co: Offset House Printers, 89 Sand Hill Rd., Essex, VT 05451

Sourcebank

Publishing Co: Financial Sourcebooks, PO Box 313, Naperville, IL 60566-0313; Title Tel # (708) 961-2161
General Info: Yr. Est. 1989, Bi-monthly
Subscriptions: Indv. $189

South Carolina Economic Indicators *Business*

Publishing Co: Univ. of South Carolina, College of Business Adm., Division of Research, Columbia, SC 29208 Fax # (803) 777-9344; Title Tel # (803) 777-2510
Personnel: Publisher-James Kane, Editor-Douglas Woodward
Editorial Description: South Carolina economic indicators in graphs, tables, and text.
General Info: Yr. Est. 1966, Monthly, Offset press, 12 pages, 2 Color, Looseleaf
Circulation: Total-2,100

South Dakota Business
Review   *Business*

Publishing Co: Business Research Bureau, 414 E. Clark, U of SD, Vermillion, SD 57069; Title Tel # (605) 677-5287
Personnel: Editor-Donald Lewis
Editorial Description: South Dakota business; numerous tables and charts comparing a variety of business series.
General Info: Yr. Est. 1942, Quarterly, Trim Size-8½ x 11, Offset press, 12 pages, ISSN: 0038-3260, 2 Color, Newsprint, Saddle-stitched, Looseleaf
Circulation: Total-1,450

Southeastern Tax Alert
See: TAXES

Southern Wholesalers
Assn. -News & Views   *Business, Association*

Publishing Co: Southern Wholesalers Assn., 3522 Habersham At Northlake, Tucker, GA 30084-4009; Title Tel # (404) 939-9832
Personnel: Editor-Frank Rizzo
General Info: Quarterly
Circulation: Total-300

Space Business News
See: AERONAUTICS/ASTRONAUTICS

Specialty Lab Update
See: PHOTOGRAPHY

Spencer's Compliance Guide for Health & Benefit Plans
See: TAXES

Spencer's Research Reports on Employee Benefits
See: INDUSTRIAL RELATIONS/PERSONNEL

Spencer's Retirement Plan Service
See: INDUSTRIAL RELATIONS/PERSONNEL

Springfield Scene, The

Publishing Co: Illinois State Chamber of Commerce, 215 E Adams St, Springfield, IL 62701-1122 Tel # (217) 522-5512 Fax # (217) 522-5518; Title Tel # (312) 372-7373 Title Fax # (312) 372-7382
Personnel: Editor-Gregg Durham, Production Mgr.-Julie Brennan
Editorial Description: The Springfield Scene is a weekly newsletter that covers business-related legislative issues on taxes, gov't regulations, human resources, health care, worker's comp., environment, and education.
General Info: Weekly, Trim Size-11 x 17, Offset press, 2 pages, 2 Color, Recycled
Subscriptions: Free To Qualified Recipient
Circulation: Total-11,000, Readership-11,000
Printing Co: Frye Williamson, 901 N Macarthur Blvd, Springfield, IL 62702-2307

Staffing Industry Report
See: EMPLOYMENT

Stanger Review: Partnership Sales
See: INVESTMENT

State Income Tax Alert
See: TAXES

Strategic Direction
Newsletter   *Business*

Publishing Co: Strategic Direction Publishers, 5352 Ashley Rd., Fairfax, VA 22030; Title Tel # (703) 830-5507 Title Fax # (703) 830-5506
General Info: Monthly
Subscriptions: Indv. $485

Success Ads
See: ADVERTISING & MARKETING

Success Orientation
See: MANAGEMENT

Success Today

Publishing Co: Stewart Associates, 12625 Frederick St., #I-5, Ste. 243, Moreno Valley, CA 92553-5216; Title Tel # (714) 247-4726
Editorial Description: Published for professionals who want to move up in their organizations.
General Info: Monthly, Trim Size-8½ x 11, Sheetfed press, 6 pages, Color
Subscriptions: Indv. $59
List Rental: Rents Lists

Successful Benefits
Communicator, The   *Business*

Publishing Co: Lawrence Ragan Communications, Inc., 212 W.Superior St,Ste 200, Chicago, IL 60610-3533; Title Tel # (312) 335-0037 Title Fax # (312) 335-9583
Personnel: Publisher-Lawrence Ragan, Editor-Forrest Cates, Circ. Mgr.-Susan Weston, Art Dir.-Sharon Giankos, Mktg. Dir.-Melissa Eckhardt, Mktg. Dir.-Gretchen Eisenfelder
Editorial Description: A monthly idea source and reporting service for all who communicate benefits information.
General Info: (Formerly Techniques for the Benefits Communicator), Yr. Est. 1994, Monthly
Subscriptions: Indv. $179
List Rental: List Management Co.: Taybi Direct East, Inc., 13321 New Hampshire Ave., Ste. 202, Silver Spring, MD 20904-3450 Tel # (301) 680-3633, Fax # (301) 680-3635

Successful Closing Techniques
See: SALESMANSHIP & SELLING

Successtrax
See: LIFESTYLE

Sum Monthly News
See: ACCOUNTING

Superinvestor Hotsheet,
The   *Consumer*

Publishing Co: The Hume Group, PO Box 105627, Atlanta, GA 30348-5627 Tel # (404) 426-1920
Personnel: Editor-Eril Kirzner, Mktg. Dir.-Suzanne Eastman
Editorial Description: A futures market, spread trading, timing advisory service based on the proprietary 'superinvestor files' futures trading system.
General Info: Weekly, 4 pages, No Color
Subscriptions: Indv. $298, $6/copy
Circulation: Total-1,000
List Rental: List Management Co.: Kleid Company, Inc., 530 5th Ave., 17 Floor, New York, NY 10036-5101 Tel # (212) 819-3406, Fax # (212) 719-9788

Supervisory Management   *Business, Association*

Publishing Co: American Management Association, 135 West 50th Street, New York, NY 10020-1201 Tel # (212) 586-8100; Title Tel # (212) 903-8075 Title Fax # (212) 903-8083
Personnel: Publisher-Rosemary Carlough, Editor-Florence Stone, Circ. Mgr.-Inez Lambert, Product Mgr.-Carole Thielman, Art Dir.-Seval Newton, Mktg. Dir.-Beverly Hart
Editorial Description: Designed to give first and second line managers nuts-and-bolts solutions to situations that come up daily. It includes skills improvement and supervisory polishing exercises, feature articles, case studies and how-to articles.
General Info: (Formerly Management Solutions), Yr. Est. 1955, Monthly, Trim Size-8½ x 11, Offset press, 1 pages, ISSN: 1045-263X, Ind/Abs/Online: BRS, DIALOG, Dow Jones/News Retrieval, 2 Color, Matte, Saddle-stitched
Subscriptions: Indv. $65, Can. $80, For. $90, $8/copy
Circulation: Total-14,451
List Rental: List Management Co.: Manager: Beverly Hart; American Management Associatin, 1121 Rue Avenue, LeeWood, KS 66211 Tel # (913) 451-2700, Fax # (913) 451-2026

T-Shirt Business Info Mapping Newsletter--How To & Ideas Edition
See: PRINTING/GRAPHIC ARTS

TJFR Business News Reporter
See: MEDIA & COMMUNICATIONS

Tadra Newsbreak
See: AUTOMOTIVE

Take-Charge Assistant,
The   *Business, Association*

Publishing Co: American Management Association, 135 West 50th Street, New York, NY 10020-1201 Tel # (212) 586-8100; Title Tel # (212) 903-8075 Title Fax # (212) 903-8083
Personnel: Publisher-Rosemary Kane Carlough, Editor-Florence Stone, Circ. Mgr.-Inez Lambert, Product Mgr.-Carole Thielman, Art Dir.-Seval Newton, Mktg. Mgr.-Beverly Hart
Editorial Description: A monthly newsletter for office professional, that helps manage stress, develop a strong professional image, build writing and math skills.
General Info: Yr. Est. 1995, Monthly, Trim Size-8.5 x 11, Offset press, 8 pages, 4 Color, Matte, Saddle-stitched
Subscriptions: Indv. $75, Can. $90, For. $100, $10/copy
List Rental: List Management Co.: American Management Associatin, 1121 Rue Avenue, LeeWood, KS 66211 Tel # (913) 451-2700, Fax # (913) 451-2026
Printing Co: Ovid Bell Press, Inc., 1201-05 Bluff St., Fulton, MO 65251-0370 Fax # (314) 642-8467

Target Washington
See: U.S. (& CANADIAN) FED. GOV'T.

Tax Planning for Corporations and Shareholders
See: TAXES

Tax Update for Business Owners
Business

Publishing Co: TPR Publishing Co., Inc., 81 Montgomery St, Scarsdale, NY 10583-5150
Fax # (914) 472-0379; Title Tel # (914) 472-0366
Personnel: Publisher-John Springer, Editor-Karen Sanders, Circ. Mgr.-Helen Faulkner
Editorial Description: Tax newsletter for small business.
General Info: Yr. Est. 1982, Monthly, Trim Size-8½ x 11, 16 pages, 2 Color
Subscriptions: Indv. $72, $10/copy
Circulation: Total-30,000
List Rental: List Management Co.: SpeciaLISTS, 1200 Harbor Blvd Ste 9, Weehawken, NJ 07087-6728 Tel # (201) 865-5800, Fax # (201) 867-2450

Tax Watch
See: TAXES

Team Leader
See: MANAGEMENT

Technicnews

Publishing Co: Technic, Inc., 1 Spectacle St, Cranston, RI 02910-1058; Title Tel # (410) 781-6100
Personnel: Editor-James Elliott
General Info: Yr. Est. 1983, Quarterly, 4 pages
Circulation: Total-3,000
Advertising: Inquire for rates.

Technology Access Report
See: SCIENCE

Technology Alert
See: MANAGEMENT

Technology Forecasts & Technology Surveys
See: SCIENCE

Technology New York Report
Business

Publishing Co: Technology New York Report, 1223 Peoples Ave., Troy, NY 12181
Fax # (518) 276-6380; Title Tel # (518) 276-8769
Personnel: Publisher-John Wallner, Editor-Kathryn Doughty
Editorial Description: Business, academic, and government news on technology development in New York.
General Info: (Formerly Technology NY Newsletter), Yr. Est. 1983, Monthly, Trim Size-8½ x 11, Desktop press, 8 pages, ISSN: 0732-7382, 2 Color, Looseleaf
Subscriptions: Indv. $87, Free With Membership
Circulation: Total-250
List Rental: Actives: $100/M

Technology Strategies Newsletter
See: SCIENCE

Telecom Newsflash, The
See: TELECOMMUNICATIONS

Telemarketing Update-Answering Service Business Script Presentations
See: ADVERTISING & MARKETING

Telemarketing Update-Catering Service Business Script Presentations
See: ADVERTISING & MARKETING

Telemarketing Update-Copier Service Business Script Presentations
See: ADVERTISING & MARKETING

Telemarketing Update-Secretarial Business Script Presentations
See: ADVERTISING & MARKETING

Texas Business Review
Business

Publishing Co: Bureau of Business Research, University of Texas, 21st St. & Speedway, Austin, TX 78712-1104 Tel # (512) 471-1616; Title Tel # (512) 471-5179 Title Fax # (512) 471-1063
Personnel: Editor-Lois Shrout, Ph.D.
Editorial Description: Comments on economic trends and developments in the state and Southwest. Focuses on issues important to industry.
General Info: Yr. Est. 1926, Bi-monthly, Trim Size-8½ x 11, Sheetfed press, 6 pages, Ind/Abs/Online: dialog, pals, sri/current issues sourcefile, Color, Coated
Subscriptions: Free
Circulation: Total-6,000

Texas Corporations--Law and Practice
See: LAW

Texas Industrial Expansion
See: REGIONAL INTEREST

Think and Grow Rich Newsletter
Business

Publishing Co: Imagine, Inc., PO Box 101, Clemson, SC 29633-0101; Title Tel # (803) 654-5148
Title Fax # (803) 654-7275
Personnel: Editor-Rives Cheney
Editorial Description: Motivational articles.
General Info: Yr. Est. 1988, Monthly, Trim Size-8½ x 11, 8 pages, ISSN: 1053-718X
Subscriptions: Indv. $47, Can. $68, For. $68, $4/copy
Circulation: Total-11,000
List Rental: List Management Co.: List Emporium, 2000 Shawnee Mission Pky Ste, 235, Westwood, KS 66205-3601 Tel # (913) 236-6830, Fax # (913) 236-4842, Actives: 33,757, $80/M
Printing Co: Martin Printing Co., 401 Powdersville Rd, Easley, SC 29642-1349 Tel # (803) 859-4032, Fax # (803) 859-8620

Think Yourself Rich

Publishing Co: Cossman International, Inc., PO Box 4480, Palm Springs, CA 92263; Title Tel # (619) 320-7717
Personnel: Publisher, Editor-E. Jos Cossman
General Info: Yr. Est. 1970, Monthly
Subscriptions: Indv. $50
Circulation: Total-28,000

Thomas Report, The
Business

Publishing Co: Thomas Associates, 335 Washington St # 154, Woburn, MA 01801-2115; Title Tel # (617) 938-5502 Title Fax # (617) 938-5504
Personnel: Publisher, Editor-Carole Copeland Thomas
General Info: Yr. Est. 1989, 4x/yr., Trim Size-8½ x 11, 20 pages, 2 Color, Matte, Saddle-stitched
Subscriptions: Indv. $25
Advertising: Inquire for rates.

TidBITS
See: COMPUTERS & AUTOMATION

Total Employee Involvement
Business

Publishing Co: Productivity Inc., 101 Merritt 7, Norwalk, CT 06851-1059 Tel # (203) 846-3777
Personnel: Publisher-Norman Bodek, Editor in Chief-Lloyd Resnick, Circ. Mgr.-Antoinette Saloomey
General Info: Yr. Est. 1980, Monthly, ISSN: 0896-7776
Subscriptions: Indv. $167
Circulation: Total-1,400
List Rental: List Management Co.: List Technology Systems Group, Inc., 1001 Ave. of the Americas, New York, NY 10018 Tel # (212) 719-3850, Fax # (212) 719-1878, Actives: $95/M

Total Productive Maintenance
Business

Publishing Co: Productivity Inc., 101 Merritt 7, Norwalk, CT 06851-1059; Title Tel # (203) 846-3777
Title Fax # (203) 846-6883
Personnel: Publisher-Norman Bodek, Editor in Chief-Lloyd Resnick, Circ. Mgr.-Antoinette Saloomey
General Info: Yr. Est. 1980, Monthly, ISSN: 1054-1233
Subscriptions: Indv. $167
Circulation: Total-1,200
List Rental: List Management Co.: List Technology Systems Group, Inc., 1001 Ave. of the Americas, New York, NY 10018 Tel # (212) 719-3850, Fax # (212) 719-1878, Actives: $95/M

Trade & Licensing Hot List
See: SCIENCE

Trade Regulations Reports
See: LAW

Trading Trends
See: INVESTMENT

Transnational Bulletin, The
See: LAW

Transport (De)Regulation Report
See: TRAFFIC & TRANSPORTATION

Travel Marketing and Agency Management Guidelines
See: TRAVEL

Travel Sales & Marketing Newsletter
See: TRAVEL

Travel Smart for Business
See: TRAVEL

Treasury Pro
See: BANKING & FINANCE

Trends & Projections
See: ECONOMICS

Troubled Company
Prospector   *Business*

Publishing Co: Beard Group, Inc., PO Box 9867, Washington, DC 20016-8867;
Title Tel # (301) 951-6400 Title Fax # (301) 951-3621
Personnel: Mktg. Dir.-Nancy Parks
Editorial Description: Profiles of companies in transition.
General Info: Yr. Est. 1992, Weekly
Subscriptions: Indv. $1,150, Inst. $1,150, $30/copy

Truck Renting & Leasing
Assn. -News Digest   *Association*   **CPM: $644**

Publishing Co: Truck Renting & Leasing Assn., 1725 Duke Street, #600, Alexandria, VA 22314-3457
Tel # (703) 299-9120 Fax # (703) 299-9115; Title Tel # (202) 775-4859
Personnel: Editor-Beverly Walker
Editorial Description: Membership newsletter.
General Info: Yr. Est. 1978, Bi-monthly
Subscriptions: Free With Membership
Circulation: Total-2,771
Advertising: $1,785.

Turnarounds & Workouts   *Business*

Publishing Co: Beard Group, Inc., PO Box 9867, Washington, DC 20016-8867;
Title Tel # (301) 951-6400 Title Fax # (301) 951-3621
Personnel: Publisher-Christopher Beard
Editorial Description: News for people tracking distressed businesses.
General Info: Yr. Est. 1986, Semi-monthly, 8 pages, ISSN: 0889-1699, 2 Color
Subscriptions: Indv. $354, Can. $379, For. $379, $25/copy
Acquistions: Publication Bought
Advertising: Inquire for rates. Accepts Inserts.
Printing Co: Newsletter Services, Inc., 9700 Philadelphia Court, Lanham, MD 20706
Tel # (301) 731-5200, Fax # (301) 731-5201

Turnarounds & Workouts -
Europe   *Business*

Publishing Co: Beard Group, Inc., PO Box 9867, Washington, DC 20016-8867;
Title Tel # (301) 951-6400 Title Fax # (301) 951-3621
Personnel: Publisher-C. Beard, Editor-Venny Brown, Mktg. Dir.-Nancy Parks
Editorial Description: Developments in bankruptcy and insolvency in Europe.
General Info: Yr. Est. 1991, Quarterly, ISSN: 10614176
Subscriptions: Indv. $195, Inst. $195, Can. $195, For. $195, $54/copy

USET Gaming
See: GAMBLING

USSR Business

Publishing Co: Stamm Publishing, Ltd., 389 - 810 West Broadway, Vancouver, BC V5Z 4C9
Canada; Title Tel # (604) 873-4347 Title Fax # (604) 873-4347
Personnel: Editor-R. Stamm
General Info: Yr. Est. 1989, Monthly
Subscriptions: Indv. $160

Ukrainian Business
Digest   *Business*

Publishing Co: International Information Systems, PO Box 3127, Westport, CT 06880-8127;
Title Tel # (203) 221-7450 Title Fax # (203) 221-7414
Personnel: Publisher-Richard Shriver, Production Mgr.-Andrew Shriver, Art Dir.-Matt Davies, Promotion Dir.-Barbara Shriver
Editorial Description: The most comprehensive analysis of important topics and issues affectin g business opportunities in the Ukraine.
General Info: Yr. Est. 1990, Monthly, Trim Size-8½ x 11, 12 pages, ISSN: 1053-4237, Matte, Saddle-stitched
Subscriptions: Indv. $245, Inst. $245, Can. $245, For. $295, $40/copy
Advertising: $2,000.
List Rental: Rents Lists

United Nations Report   *Business, Association*

Publishing Co: U.S. Council for International Business, 1212 Ave of the Americas, New York, NY 10036-1689; Title Tel # (212) 354-4480
Personnel: Editor-W. Stibravy
Editorial Description: Reports on developments in intergovernmental organizations of interest to the business world, especially the United Nations.
General Info: (Formerly U.N. Report), Monthly, Offset press, 12 pages
Subscriptions: Indv. $50
Circulation: Total-2,800

U.S. Council for
International Business
Newsletter   *Business, Association*

Publishing Co: U.S. Council for International Business, 1212 Ave of the Americas, New York, NY 10036-1689; Title Tel # (212) 354-4480
Personnel: Editor-Ann Micon
Editorial Description: Reports on U.S. Council actions and policies in international trade, finance, and investment.
General Info: Yr. Est. 1980, Monthly, 4 pages, No Color
Subscriptions: Indv. $50
Circulation: Total-2,850

U.S. ITC Update
See: GOVERNMENT

U.S. Rail News
See: RAILROADS

University of Houston,
Center for Research in
Business and Economics,
Bulletins

Publishing Co: Univ. of Houston, Center for Research in Bus., Cullen Blvd., Houston, TX 77004

Utah Economic and
Business Review   *Business*

Publishing Co: Univ. of Utah Bureau of Economic & Business Research, 401 Kendall D. Garff Bldg., Salt Lake City, UT 84112; Title Tel # (801) 581-6333 Title Fax # (801) 581-3354
Personnel: Editor-Diane Gillam, Art Dir.-James Peters
Editorial Description: Articles dealing with contemporary, Utah social or economic development shown in monthly and yearly-to-date selected business statistics.
General Info: Yr. Est. 1941, 9x/yr., Trim Size-8¼ x 10½, Offset press, 12 pages, 2 Color, Saddle-stitched
Subscriptions: Free In Designated Area
Circulation: (100% controlled), Total-4,000

Valuation Researcher   *Business*

Publishing Co: Valuation Research Corp., 411 E. Wisconsin Ave., Milwaukee, WI 53202-4495;
Title Tel # (414) 271-8662 Title Fax # (414) 271-3240
Personnel: Editor-James Marciniak
Editorial Description: Valuation news and information for use in tax planning, finance, development, and asset management.
General Info: Yr. Est. 1983, 3x/yr., Trim Size-8½ x 11, 4 pages
Subscriptions: Free To Qualified Recipient
Circulation: Total-28,000

Vietnam Business InfoTrack
See: INTERNATIONAL TRADE

Vietnam Market Watch
See: INTERNATIONAL TRADE

View, The
See: CHAMBER OF COMMERCE

Virginia Business Report   *Business*

Publishing Co: College of William & Mary, Publications, Williamsburg, VA 23185;
Title Tel # (804) 221-2930
Personnel: Editor-Roy Pearson
Editorial Description: Economic analysis of current business conditions in Virginia.
General Info: (Formerly Virginia Business Index Report), Yr. Est. 1963, Monthly, Trim Size-8½ x 11, Offset press, 4 pages, No Color
Circulation: Total-3,000

Voice of the Federal
Reserve Bank of Dallas

Publishing Co: Federal Reserve Bank of Dallas, Station K, Dallas, TX 75222;
Title Tel # (214) 651-6147
Personnel: Editor-Adrian W. Throop
Editorial Description: Commentary on current economic problems and issues and reports on research done at the Federal Reserve Bank of Dallas.
General Info: (Formerly Business Review), Yr. Est. 1916, Monthly, Trim Size-8½ x 11, Letrpr. press, 20 pages
Subscriptions: Free
Circulation: Total-10,700

WMF Newsletter   *Business*

Publishing Co: Private Effort, 90 Park Ave Fl 12, New York, NY 10016-1301;
Title Tel # (212) 370-8451 Title Fax # (414) 271-3240
General Info: Bi-monthly
Subscriptions: Indv. $50

Wacky Business Report

Publishing Co: Wacky Business, P.O. Box 373, Hohokus, NJ 07423
Editorial Description: This publication is exactly what it claims to be Unusual business ideas presented by the editors and sent in by readers.
General Info: Trim Size-8.5 x 11, 10 pages
Subscriptions: Indv. $3

Wahine Wireless
See: WOMEN'S

Wall Street Transcript   *Business*

Publishing Co: Wall Street Transcript Corp., 99 Wall St., New York, NY 10005-4393;
Title Tel # (212) 747-9500
Personnel: Publisher, Editor-R.A. Holman, Production Mgr., Adv. Dir.-Carol Blackberg
Editorial Description: Contains: company studies, industry surveys, technical analysis, presentation by corporate officers before security analyst societies.
General Info: Yr. Est. 1963, Weekly, Trim Size-11¼ x 17⅝, Web press, 80 pages, Ind/Abs/Online: VU/TEXT, No Color
Subscriptions: $50/copy
Circulation: (ABC), Total-6,900
Advertising: Inquire for rates.

Warehouse Management and Control Systems   *Business*

Publishing Co: Alexander Research & Communications, Inc., 215 Park Ave S., Ste. 1301, New York, NY 10003-1603 Tel # (212) 228-0246; Title Tel # (212) 228-0245 Title Fax # (212) 228-0376
Personnel: Publisher-Margaret DeWitt, Mng. Editor-Anita Rosepka, Circ. Mgr.-Mary Pagliaroli, Mktg. Dir.-Ann Healey
Editorial Description: Subscribers receive a loose leaf source book which contains in-depth information on warehouse management systems and monthly updates of new information, news and case studies. Subscribers also receive access to the Subcriber Helpline where the authors provide expert advice on individual programs.
General Info: Monthly, Looseleaf
Subscriptions: Indv. $240, Can. $240, For. $290

Warrens Forms of Agreement
See: LAW

Washington Business

Publishing Co: Association of Washington Business, 1414 Cherry St SE # 658, Olympia, WA 98501-2341; Title Tel # (206) 943-1600
Personnel: Editor-Bill Carter
Editorial Description: News of state government & the legislature which may impact the Washington business community.
General Info: Yr. Est. 1962, Bi-weekly, Offset press, 4 pages, ISSN: 0164-4505, Color-cover, Newsprint
Circulation: Total-4,700

Washington Economic & Policy Trends
See: MANUFACTURING

Webb Report, The   *Business*

Publishing Co: Premiere Publishing Ltd., 145 NW 85th St Ste 104, Seattle, WA 98117-3148; Title Tel # (206) 782-8310 Title Fax # (206) 782-4601
Personnel: Publisher, Editor-Susan Webb
Editorial Description: Reports on sexual harrassment.
General Info: Yr. Est. 1985, Monthly, Trim Size-8¼ x 10¾, Letrpr. press, 8 pages, ISSN: 1053-0932, Ind/Abs/Online: LibJrl, 2 Color, Matte
Subscriptions: Indv. $120, $15/copy
Circulation: Total-200

Weigand Report
See: COMPUTERS & AUTOMATION

Welland Alive

Publishing Co: Greater Welland Chamber of Commerce, 55 Main St. E., Welland, ON L3B 3W3 Canada; Title Tel # (416) 732-7515
Personnel: Editor-Dolores Faviano
General Info: Yr. Est. 1975, Monthly, 4 pages
Circulation: Total-500

West Virginia Business Index

Publishing Co: West Virginia Chamber of Commerce, PO Box 2789, Charleston, WV 25330-2789; Title Tel # (304) 342-1115
Personnel: Editor, Circ. Mgr.-Maggie Poling
General Info: Yr. Est. 1940, Monthly
Subscriptions: Indv. $300, $5/copy
Circulation: (100% controlled), Total-2,500

Western Industry Report International   *Business*

Publishing Co: Westnash Resources, PO Box 90665, Nashville, TN 37209-0665 Tel # (615) 269-6165 Fax # (615) 269-6165
Personnel: Publisher, Editor-Wes Crabbe, Circ. Dir.-Jacqueline Fox, Production Mgr.-Laura Doyle, Promotion Dir.-Beatrice Seay
Editorial Description: Information about western industry for a worldwide audience. Provides the who's, where's and how to reach the western industry key players.
General Info: Yr. Est. 1993, Monthly, Trim Size-8½ x 11, 12 pages, ISSN: 1072-9186, Coated
Subscriptions: Indv. $120, Inst. $135, Can. $135, For. $135

What Improvement Teams Are Up To

Publishing Co: Productivity Development Group, Inc., PO Box 488, Westford, MA 01886-0013; Title Tel # (508) 692-1818 Title Fax # (508) 692-5080
Editorial Description: Why and how , ITT Hartford, Mortorola, Paul Revere Insurance, Xerox and other leading firms consider teams the most rapidly expanding approach to involving employees in improving business results.
General Info: Irregular, Looseleaf
Subscriptions: Indv. $395, For. $395

What's Ahead in Human Resources
See: INDUSTRIAL RELATIONS/PERSONNEL

What's Ahead Report
See: ADVERTISING & MARKETING

What's New in Benefits & Compensation
See: INDUSTRIAL RELATIONS/PERSONNEL

What's Working in Credit & Collection
See: ACCOUNTING

What's Working in Non-Profit Fundraising
See: ADVERTISING & MARKETING

What's Working in Sales Management
See: SALESMANSHIP & SELLING

Wholesaler News   *Business*

Publishing Co: Air-Conditioning & Refrigeration Wholesalers, 10251 W Sample Rd # B, Coral Springs, FL 33065-3939; Title Tel # (305) 771-1000 Title Fax # (305) 491-8100
Personnel: Publisher-D.L. Kellough, Editor-N.F. Aramino
Editorial Description: Assn. & business news of interest to members.
General Info: Yr. Est. 1973, Trim Size-8½ x 11, Desktop press, 6 pages, 2 Color, Coated
Circulation: Total-1,000

Window on Canadian Tax
See: TAXES

Winsor Report, The

Publishing Co: WHA Enterprises, Inc., P.O. Box 164, East Glastonbury, CT 06025-0164; Title Tel # (203) 633-4301 Title Fax # (203) 633-4301
Personnel: Editor-Maryanne Sims, Mktg. Mgr.-Dave Wolf
General Info: Monthly
Subscriptions: Indv. $275

Wisconsin Environmental Law and Regulation Report
See: ENVIRONMENT & ECOLOGY

Woman Oughta Know
See: WOMEN'S

Women's Business Exclusive
See: WOMEN'S

Work in America
See: LABOR

Workers' Compensation Cost Control
See: LAW

WorldScan

Publishing Co: Allen Tech, PO Box 139, White Plains, NY 10605-0139; Title Tel # (914) 949-6364
Personnel: Publisher-Helen Hoart
General Info: Monthly
Subscriptions: Indv. $366

WorldWide Business Exchange   *Business, Consumer*

Publishing Co: Phlander Company, PO Box 5385, Cleveland, TN 37320-5385; Title Tel # (706) 259-2280 Title Fax # (706) 259-2291
Personnel: Publisher-J.F. Straw
Editorial Description: Worldwide business opportunities for individuals.
General Info: Yr. Est. 1963, Monthly, Trim Size-8½ x 11, 8 pages, ISSN: 1070-0471, No Color, Matte
Subscriptions: Indv. $48, For. $60, $5/copy
Advertising: Accepts Inserts.
List Rental: Actives: 100,000, $120/M

Worldwide Business Practices Report
See: INTERNATIONAL TRADE

Yardstick
See: COMPUTERS & AUTOMATION

CATS

Animal Sheltering Magazine
  See: ANIMALS

Big Cat Sculpture
Association
Association   **CPM: $533**

Publishing Co: Big Cat Sculpture Assn., 2765 N. Scottsdale Rd., Ste. 104-D, Scottsdale, AZ 85257 Tel # (602) 949-7848; Title Tel # (602) 649-7848 Title Fax # (602) 990-1958
Personnel: Publisher, Editor, Adv. Dir.-Thomas R. Cutler, Production Mgr., Art Dir.-Daniel Flynn
Editorial Description: Focus is on wildlife sculpture with special emphasis on female sculptor P.J. La Barge. Commissioned works as the best big cat artist alive today.
General Info: Yr. Est. 1995, Quarterly, Trim Size-8½ x 11, Web press, 16 pages, No Color
Subscriptions: Indv. $400, Inst. $400, Can. $500, For. $500
Circulation: (33% controlled), Total-1,500, Subscriptions-1,000, International-250
Advertising: $800.

CATsumer Report   *Consumer*

Publishing Co: Good Communications, Inc., PO Box 10069, Austin, TX 78766; Title Tel # (512) 454-6090 Title Fax # (512) 454-3420
Personnel: Publisher, Editor-Ross Becker, Mng. Editor-Judi Sklar, Adv. Dir.-Karen Laufer
Editorial Description: The consumer letter for cat owners. It focuses on cat products, nutrition, health and behavior. Our team of expert cats tests food, litter, toys, and more. They tell you what's best for your cat and what's a waste of your money!
General Info: Monthly, Trim Size-8½ x 1, 8 pages, ISSN: 1080-1332
Subscriptions: Indv. $18, Can. $29, For. $43
Advertising: $550.

Cat Industry Newsletter   *Business*

Publishing Co: Good Communications, Inc., PO Box 10069, Austin, TX 78766; Title Tel # (512) 454-6090 Title Fax # (512) 454-3420
Personnel: Publisher, Editor-Ross Becker, Mng. Editor-Judi Sklar
Editorial Description: Monthly newsletter for Senior Executives in the pet products industry and their advertisers and P.R. agencies. Provides sensitive information on new products, strategies, industry data, new consumer promotions, cat food business.
General Info: Yr. Est. 1992, Monthly, Trim Size-8½ x 11, 9 pages, ISSN: 1074-7788, No Color
Subscriptions: Indv. $295

Cat Mews

Publishing Co: Cat Mews Pubs., 57 Whitehall Blvd # 7, Garden City, NY 11530-4248; Title Tel # (516) 294-8275
Personnel: Publisher-Susan Behn
General Info: Yr. Est. 1986, Bi-monthly, Trim Size-8½ x 11, Letrpr. press, 5 pages, ISSN: 0889-3125, No Color, Newsprint
Subscriptions: Indv. $18, $3/copy
Printing Co: Garden City Printers, 144 Cherry Valley Ave, West Hempstead, NY 11552-1213 Tel # (516) 485-1600

Cat Talk
  See: CLUBS

Catnip   *Consumer*

Publishing Co: Tufts University School of Veterinary Medicine, 200 Westboro Rd., North Grafton, MA 01536
Editorial Description: Information for cat owners and others caring for cats.

Feline Health Topics
  See: VETERINARY

Humane News
  See: ANIMALS

International Pet Industry News
  See: ANIMALS

Linington Lineup
  See: LITERARY REVIEWS

National Birman Fanciers
News   *Association*

Publishing Co: Sponsor-Cat Fanciers Assn. (CFA), Natl. Birman Fanciers News, 8507 N Illinois St, Indianapolis, IN 46260-2321; Title Tel # (317) 251-4486
Personnel: Editor-Maribeth Echard
Editorial Description: Interesting features, history, breed standards, photos, results, pedigrees, medical findings.
General Info: (Formerly Birman Cat), Yr. Est. 1981, Quarterly, 32 pages, No Color
Subscriptions: Indv. $15
Circulation: (100% controlled), Total-250

PETA News
  See: ENVIRONMENT & ECOLOGY

Perspectives on Cats

Publishing Co: Cornell Feline Health Center, College of Veterinary Medicine, Cornell University, Ithaca, NY 14853; Title Tel # (607) 253-3414 Title Fax # (607) 253-3419
Personnel: Editor-June Tuttle, Circ. Dir.-Marsha Leonard
Editorial Description: Provides practical feline health care tips for cat owners/breeders.
General Info: (Formerly Perspectives), Yr. Est. 1980, Quarterly, Trim Size-8½ x 11, Sheetfed press, 8 pages, 2 Color, Recycled, Saddle-stitched
Subscriptions: Indv. $15, Free To Qualified Recipient
Printing Co: Cayuga Press, 1650 Hanshaw Rd, Ithaca, NY 14850-9102 Tel # (607) 257-2811

Prindletter

Publishing Co: Prindle Class Assn., 1810 E Borchard Ave, Santa Ana, CA 92705-4694; Title Tel # (714) 835-6416
Personnel: Editor-Leslie Lindeman
General Info: Yr. Est. 1974, Bi-monthly
Circulation: Total-7,500

StepAhead

Publishing Co: Nynex, 82 Brigham Street, Marlborough, MA 01752-3137
Editorial Description: A newsletter for small companies in New York, made possible by a commitment from NYNEX to provide sound business-management advice for small companies.
General Info: Yr. Est. 1979

Tatoo-A-Pet News
  See: ANIMALS

Veterinary Industry Newsletter
  See: VETERINARY

CHAMBER OF COMMERCE

Action   *Association*

Publishing Co: Cape Girardeau Chamber of Commerce, PO Box 98, Cape Girardeau, MO 63702-0098; Title Tel # (314) 335-3312
General Info: (Formerly Cape Girardeau Beacon), Yr. Est. 1962, Bi-monthly
Circulation: Total-625

Alabama Today
  See: BUSINESS & INDUSTRY

Alert
  See: BUSINESS & INDUSTRY

Asheville Report   *Association*

Publishing Co: Asheville Area Chamber of Commerce, PO Box 1010, Asheville, NC 28802-1010; Title Tel # (704) 258-6128
Personnel: Editor-John Barber
Editorial Description: Chamber programs and activities.
General Info: (Formerly Sky News), Monthly, Trim Size-8½ x 11, Offset press, 4 pages, Color
Subscriptions: Indv. $12
Circulation: (74% controlled), Total-2,700
Advertising: Inquire for rates.

Association Memo

Publishing Co: U.S. Chamber of Commerce, 1615 H St NW, Washington, DC 20062-0002 Tel # (202) 463-5600; Title Tel # (202) 463-5560
Personnel: Editor-Mills Edwards, Jr.
General Info: Monthly
Circulation: Total-1,900

BEDC Update

Publishing Co: Brooklyn Economic Development Corp., 30 Flatbush Ave, Brooklyn, NY 11217-1121; Title Tel # (718) 522-4600 Title Fax # (718) 797-9286
Personnel: Editor-Diane Adler
General Info: Yr. Est. 1979, Quarterly, 4 pages, 2 Color, Coated
Circulation: Total-35,000

Bulldog
  See: INTERNATIONAL TRADE

Business Briefs   *Business*

Publishing Co: Windsor District Chamber of Commerce, 2575 Owellette Place, Windsor, ON N8X 1L9 Canada; Title Tel # (519) 966-3696 Title Fax # (519) 966-0603
Editorial Description: Information on chamber activities -- statistics on community -- items on community progress-government action of interest to community.
General Info: Yr. Est. 1927, Monthly, Sheetfed press, 8 pages, 3% ads, Coated, Saddle-stitched
Circulation: (85% controlled), Total-1,400
Advertising: Inquire for rates.

Business Bulletin   *Business*

Publishing Co: Sponsor-KY Chamber of Commerce, Kentucky Chamber of Commerce, 452 Versailles Rd # 817, Frankfort, KY 40601-3832; Title Tel # (502) 695-4700
Personnel: Publisher-Robert Lewis, Jr., Editor-Debbie Gibson
General Info: (Formerly Strictly Business), Yr. Est. 1985, Monthly, Trim Size-8½ x 11, Sheetfed press, 6 pages, ISSN: 8750-8303, 2 Color, Newsprint, Saddle-stitched
Subscriptions: Indv. $30
Acquistions: Publication Bought
Circulation: (100% controlled), Total-6,500

Business Focus   *Business, Association*

Publishing Co: Salt Lake City Chamber of Commerce, 175 E. 400 S., Ste. 600, Salt Lake City, UT 84111-2355; Title Tel # (801) 364-3631 Title Fax # (801) 328-5005
Personnel: Editor-Alison Barnett
Editorial Description: Chamber information & events. Monthly statistical & all major economic development activities for Utah.
General Info: (Formerly Salt Lake Area Business), Yr. Est. 1920, Bi-monthly, Trim Size-8 x 12, Offset press, 12 pages, 3% ads, 2 Color, Coated, Saddle-stitched
Subscriptions: Free With Membership
Circulation: Total-3,000
Advertising: Inquire for rates.
Printing Co: Lorraine Press, 1952 W 1500 S, Salt Lake City, UT 84104-4197 Tel # (801) 972-5626

Business Guide   *Business*

Publishing Co: Greater Stockton Chamber of Commerce, 445 W Weber Ave Ste 220, Stockton, CA 95203-3148; Title Tel # (209) 547-2770 Title Fax # (209) 466-5271
Personnel: Editor, Adv. Dir.-Evenyl Roemmich
Editorial Description: Owners' names & mailing addresses as well as classified & commodity listings are included. Also staff, Board of Directors, yearly & monthly calendar and community information.
General Info: (Formerly Membership Directory and Buyers Guide), Annually, Trim Size-8½ x 11, Sheetfed press, 96 pages, 2 Color, Matte, Other, Looseleaf
Subscriptions: $35/copy
Circulation: (100% controlled), Total-2,500
Advertising: Inquire for rates.

Business Leader   *Association*

Publishing Co: Dayton Chamber of Commerce, 1 Chamber Plaza, Dayton, OH 45402-2400 Tel # (513) 226-8242; Title Tel # (513) 226-1444
Personnel: Publisher-T. Heine, Editor-K. Turner
Editorial Description: Chamber of Commerce & its activities.
General Info: Bi-monthly, Trim Size-11¼ x 15¼, Sheetfed press, 4 pages, No Color
Subscriptions: Indv. $3
Circulation: (100% controlled), Total-5,600

Business Plan, The   *Association*

Publishing Co: Charlottesville-Albemarle County Chamber of Commerce, PO Box 1564, Charlottesville, VA 22902-1564; Title Tel # (804) 295-3141 Title Fax # (804) 295-3144
General Info: (Formerly Program of Work), Yr. Est. 1984, Annually, Trim Size-8½ x 11, Offset press, 16 pages, 2 Color, Coated, Saddle-stitched
Subscriptions: Free
Circulation: Total-3,500
Advertising: Inquire for rates.

Business Today   *Association*

Publishing Co: St. Paul Area Chamber of Commerce, 55 5th St E Ste 101, Saint Paul, MN 55101-1718; Title Tel # (612) 222-5561 Title Fax # (612) 297-6879
Personnel: Publisher, Editor, Art Dir.-Margaret Wethington
Editorial Description: Communicate chamber-sponsored activities to members, chamber stance on government issues.
General Info: Monthly, Sheetfed press, 8 pages, 4% ads, 2 Color, Newsprint
Subscriptions: Indv. $20
Circulation: Total-3,800
Advertising: Inquire for rates.
List Rental: Rents Lists
Printing Co: Miller Printing, 19309 Beech Daly Rd, Redford, MI 48240-1420

C of C Newsletter   *Business, Association*

Publishing Co: Gainesville Area Chamber of Commerce, 101 S Culberson St, Gainesville, TX 76240-4756; Title Tel # (817) 665-2831
Personnel: Editor-Donna Hogan
Editorial Description: To inform members of happenings and aims of the Chamber.
General Info: Monthly, Trim Size-8½ x 11½, Sheetfed press, 4 pages, 2 Color
Circulation: Total-600

Chamber, The   *Association*

Publishing Co: Greater Portland Chamber of Commerce, 145 Middle St, Portland, ME 04101-4121; Title Tel # (207) 772-2811 Title Fax # (207) 772-1179
Personnel: Editor-Jane Glass
Editorial Description: Company publication to keep membership informed.
General Info: (Formerly Chamber Action), Monthly, Sheetfed press, 8 pages, No Color, Newsprint
Subscriptions: Indv. $6, $50/copy
Circulation: (100% controlled), Total-2,200
List Rental: Actives: $100/M

Chamber Bulletin
Soundings   *Business, Association*

Publishing Co: Cape Ann Chamber of Cmrc., 33 Commercial St., Gloucester, MA 01930-5040; Title Tel # (617) 283-1601
Personnel: Editor, Art Dir.-Michael Costello
Editorial Description: Newsletter to Chamber members.
General Info: Monthly, Trim Size-8½ x 11, Mimeo press, 8 pages, No Color
Subscriptions: Free
Circulation: Total-700

Chamber Comments   *Business, Association*

Publishing Co: Charlottesville-Albemarle County Chamber of Commerce, PO Box 1564, Charlottesville, VA 22902-1564; Title Tel # (804) 295-3141 Title Fax # (804) 295-3144
Personnel: Editor-Shanon Bickart
Editorial Description: Informs members of the internal and external activities of the Chamber of Commerce Board of Directors and committees.
General Info: (Formerly Metabusiness, Dividends), Yr. Est. 1964, Monthly, Trim Size-8½ x 11, Offset press, 12 pages, No Color, Matte, Saddle-stitched
Subscriptions: Indv. $18, Free
Circulation: (100% controlled), Total-1,600, Readership-1,600
Advertising: Inquire for rates.
List Rental: Rents Lists

Chamber Comments   *Business, Association*

Publishing Co: British Columbia Chamber of Commerce, 700 W. Pender St., Ste. 1607, Vancouver, BC V6C 1G8 Canada; Title Tel # (604) 683-0700
General Info: Quarterly

Chamber of Commerce
Bulletin   *Business, Association*

Publishing Co: Bloomfield Chamber of Commerce, 547 Bloomfield Ave, Bloomfield, NJ 07003-3301; Title Tel # (201) 748-2000
Personnel: Editor-Virginia Schmidt
Editorial Description: News of Chamber members, chamber activities, state & federal laws & bills, local affairs.
General Info: Yr. Est. 1962, Monthly, Offset press, 4 pages, No Color
Circulation: (100% controlled), Total-450
Advertising: Inquire for rates.

Chamber of Commerce
Memo

Publishing Co: Marinette Area C of C, PO Box 512, Marinette, WI 54143-0512; Title Tel # (715) 735-6681 Title Fax # (715) 735-6682
Personnel: Editor-Mary Eickman
General Info: Yr. Est. 1952, Monthly, Trim Size-8½ x 11, Mimeo press, 4 pages
Subscriptions: Indv. $5
Circulation: Total-680

Chamber of Commerce
Reports   *Association*

Publishing Co: South Salt Lake City Chamber of Commerce, 220 Morris Ave Ste 235, South Salt Lake, UT 84115-3283; Title Tel # (801) 466-3377
Personnel: Editor-D. Glissmeyer
Editorial Description: News applicable to the South Salt Lake Chamber of Commerce, civic activities, governmental programs.
General Info: Yr. Est. 1950, Monthly, Trim Size-8½ x 11, Offset press, 2 pages, No Color
Circulation: Total-400

Chamber Executive
Network   *Association*

Publishing Co: Hakes Pubs., PO Box 603, Storm Lake, IA 50588-0603; Title Tel # (712) 732-7718
Personnel: Publisher, Editor-Dick Hakes
Editorial Description: Project ideas and unmanagement techniques for Chamber of Commerce executives.
General Info: (Formerly Community Development Executive), Yr. Est. 1984, Monthly, Sheetfed press, 6 pages, Ind/Abs/Online: Index, No Color
Subscriptions: Indv. $98
Acquistions: Publication Bought
Circulation: Total-700

Chamber Forum   *Business*

Publishing Co: Calhoun County Chamber of Commerce, PO Box 1087, Anniston, AL 36202-1087; Title Tel # (205) 237-3536
Personnel: Editor-Michael Dunbar
Editorial Description: Monthly business oriented newsletter covering topics of local interest.
General Info: (Formerly Growth Index), Yr. Est. 1982, Monthly, Trim Size-8½ x 11, Sheetfed press, 8 pages, 4% ads, Color-cover, Newsprint
Circulation: Total-1,500
Printing Co: Moore Printing Co., 1025 Gurnee Ave, Anniston, AL 36201-4594

Chamber Report *Association*

Publishing Co: Greater Columbia Chamber of Commerce, 930 Richland St, Columbia, SC 29201-2329; Title Tel # (314) 874-1132
Personnel: Editor-Donald Laird
Editorial Description: Chamber of Commerce activities and programs.
General Info: Yr. Est. 1975, 10x/yr., Trim Size-8$\frac{1}{2}$ x 11, Offset press, 8 pages, 9% ads, 2 Color, Newsprint, Saddle-stitched
Subscriptions: Indv. $8
Circulation: (100% controlled), Total-1,200
Advertising: Inquire for rates.

Chamber Report *Business*

Publishing Co: Greater Manchester Chamber of Commerce, 889 Elm St., Manchester, NH 03101-2000; Title Tel # (603) 666-6600 Title Fax # (603) 626-0910
Personnel: Editor-Christine Heyssel
Editorial Description: A membership newsletter.
General Info: (Formerly Chamber News), Yr. Est. 1980, Monthly, Trim Size-8$\frac{1}{2}$ x 11, Web press, 6 pages, 4% ads, 2 Color, Coated
Subscriptions: Free With Membership
Acquistions: Publication Bought
Circulation: Total-1,500
Advertising: Inquire for rates. Accepts Inserts.
Printing Co: Keystone Press, 9 Old Falls Rd, Manchester, NH 03103-3622 Tel # (603) 622-5222

Chamber Today, The *Business*

Publishing Co: Greater San Antonio Chamber of Commerce, 602 E Commerce St, San Antonio, TX 78205-2620; Title Tel # (512) 229-2146
Personnel: Publisher-Joseph Krier, Production Mgr.-Jose Trujillo, Editor, Circ. Mgr., Art Dir.-Marti Demoss
Editorial Description: News of chamber programs & activities, calendar of events, departmental updates.
General Info: (Formerly The San Antonian), Yr. Est. 1981, Monthly, Trim Size-8$\frac{1}{2}$ x 11, Sheetfed press, 8 pages, ISSN: 0279-0785, 2 Color
Subscriptions: Indv. $3
Circulation: (100% controlled)

Clevelander *Business, Association*

Publishing Co: Greater Cleveland Growth Assn., 200 Tower City Ctr., 50 Public Square, Cleveland, OH 44113-2291; Title Tel # (216) 621-3300 Title Fax # (216) 621-6013
Personnel: Editor in Chief-Della Schutt, Editor-Denise Henry, Publisher, Adv. Dir.-William Bryant
Editorial Description: Reports Association actions/programs, business news. Gives local, state, federal legislative news.
General Info: Yr. Est. 1926, Monthly, Trim Size-8$\frac{1}{2}$ x 11, Offset press, 10 pages, ISSN: 0009-8892, 2 Color, Matte, Saddle-stitched
Subscriptions: Indv. $12, $1/copy
Circulation: Total-13,800
Advertising: Inquire for rates.
Printing Co: Schaefer Printing Co., 2817 Detroit Ave, Cleveland, OH 44113-2780 Tel # (216) 241-6306

Commerce Comments

Publishing Co: Calgary Chamber of Commerce, 517 Center St., S., Calary, AB T2G 2C4 Canada; Title Tel # (403) 263-7435

Congressional Action *Business*

Publishing Co: U.S. Chamber of Commerce, 1615 H St NW, Washington, DC 20062-0002; Title Tel # (202) 463-5600
Personnel: Editor-Kevin Meath
Editorial Description: To alert business leaders to congressional activities and help them communicate effectively with legislators on issues of importance to business.
General Info: Yr. Est. 1958, Bi-weekly, Trim Size-8$\frac{1}{2}$ x 11, Offset press, 4 pages, 2 Color
Subscriptions: Indv. $10, $1/copy
Circulation: (100% controlled), Total-45,000

Delaware County Chamber of Commerce Newsletter

Publishing Co: Delaware County Chamber of Commerce, 602 E Baltimore Pike, Media, PA 19063-1752; Title Tel # (215) 565-3677
Personnel: Editor-Anen Allcott Price
Editorial Description: Communicates to members, national, state and local events.
General Info: Yr. Est. 1971, Monthly, Trim Size-8$\frac{1}{2}$ x 11, Offset press, 2 pages
Circulation: (100% controlled), Total-2,700
Advertising: Inquire for rates. Accepts Inserts.

Detroit Business News

Publishing Co: Greater Detroit Chamber of Commerce, 600 W Lafayette Blvd, Detroit, MI 48226-3125; Title Tel # (313) 964-4000
Personnel: Editor-Louise Thomas
General Info: Yr. Est. 1903, Monthly
Subscriptions: Indv. $3
Circulation: Total-7,000

Downtown Promotion Reporter
See: ADVERTISING & MARKETING

Exec Report *Business, Association*

Publishing Co: Illinois State Chamber of Commerce, 311 S. Wacker Drive, Ste. 1500, Chicago, IL 60606-6619; Title Tel # (312) 372-7373
Personnel: Editor-Ron Polaniecki
Editorial Description: Digest of current information of interest to key business executives.
General Info: (Formerly Executive Report), Monthly, Trim Size-8$\frac{1}{2}$ x 11, Sheetfed press, 4 pages, 2 Color, Recycled, Saddle-stitched
Circulation: Total-16,000

Florida Jaycee News

Publishing Co: Florida Junior Chamber of Commerce, PO Box 90125, Lakeland, FL 33804-0125
General Info: Yr. Est. 1942, Monthly
Circulation: Total-12,000

Focal Points *Business*

Publishing Co: Greater Columbia Chamber of Commerce, 930 Richland St, Columbia, SC 29201-2329; Title Tel # (803) 733-1110 Title Fax # (803) 733-1149
Personnel: Editor-Melissa Spruse, Circ. Mgr., Production Mgr.-Sonya Chapman, Adv. Dir.-Melissa Sprouse
Editorial Description: Monthly membership newsletter.
General Info: (Formerly Update), Bi-monthly, Trim Size-11 x 17, Sheetfed press, 10 pages, 3% ads, No Color, Newsprint
Subscriptions: Free With Membership
Circulation: Total-5,000
Advertising: Inquire for rates. Accepts Inserts.
Printing Co: Wentworth Printing Corp., PO Box 4660, West Columbia, SC 29171 Tel # (803) 796-9990, Fax # (803) 739-0556

For Members Only

Publishing Co: Sponsor-Deming Luna County Chamber of Commerce, Deming-Luna County Chamber of Commerce, PO Box 8, Deming, NM 88031; Title Tel # (505) 546-2674 Title Fax # (505) 546-9569
Personnel: Editor-Linda Stevens
Editorial Description: Current projects, reports of progress, coming events, local & area in scope.
General Info: (Formerly Sun Man Reports), Yr. Est. 1965, Monthly
Subscriptions: Free With Membership
Circulation: Total-300
Advertising: Inquire for rates.

German American Commerce *Association*

Publishing Co: German-American Chamber of Commerce, 40 West 57th Street, New York, NY 10019 Tel # (212) 874-8830; Title Tel # (212) 974-8830 Title Fax # (212) 974-8830
Personnel: Circ. Mgr.-Inge Orth, Editor, Production Mgr., Adv. Dir.-Nancy O'Keefe
Editorial Description: Current news notes, facts, figures, economic analyses helpful to Americans doing business with Germany.
General Info: (Formerly German Business Weekly), Yr. Est. 1959, Bi-weekly, Offset press, 6 pages, Ind/Abs/Online: DIALOG, No Color
Subscriptions: Indv. $100
Circulation: (100% controlled), Total-1,700
Advertising: Inquire for rates.

Greater Knoxville Chamber of Commerce Membership Newsletter *Business*

Publishing Co: Greater Knoxville Chamber of Commerce, 301 E Church Ave, Knoxville, TN 37915-2502; Title Tel # (615) 637-4550 Title Fax # (615) 523-2071
Personnel: Editor-Jacquelyn McClary, Production Mgr.-Mark Freeman, Adv. Dir.-Sandra Goss
Editorial Description: Subjects which inform membership of activities and chamber programs.
General Info: (Formerly Greater Knoxville), Bi-monthly, Letrpr. press, 4 pages, 2% ads, 2 Color, Newsprint
Circulation: Total-4,200
List Rental: Actives: $25/M
Printing Co: Preston Graphics, PO Box 50035, Knoxville, TN 37950-0035 Tel # (615) 584-1195

Greater Lubbock *Business, Association* CPM: $250

Publishing Co: Lubbock Chamber of Commerce, PO Box 561, Lubbock, TX 79408-0561; Title Tel # (806) 763-4666 Title Fax # (806) 763-2311
Personnel: Editor-Connie Chapman, Mng. Editor-Grey Lewis
Editorial Description: To inform Chamber members & others of the many activities undertaken & accomplished by the Chamber, to promote the progress of Lubbock & the S. Plains. Features of community-wide interest.
General Info: Yr. Est. 1929, Monthly, Trim Size-8$\frac{1}{2}$ x 11, Offset press, 4 pages, 2 Color
Subscriptions: Indv. $10
Circulation: Total-3,000
Advertising: $750.
Printing Co: Chapparal Press, 921 E 66th St, Lubbock, TX 79404-5505 Tel # (806) 745-9292

Greater Port Huron-Marysville Chamber of Commerce, Bulletin
Business, Association   **CPM: $666**

Publishing Co: Greater Port Huron-Marysville Chamber of Commerce, 920 Pine Grove Ave, Port Huron, MI 48060-3732; Title Tel # (313) 985-7101
Editorial Description: A report to members of activities of the Chamber of Commerce and of things going on in the area. Business notes and coming events.
General Info: Yr. Est. 1987, Monthly, Trim Size-8½ x 11, Offset press, 4 pages, 12% ads, No Color, Coated
Subscriptions: Free With Membership
Circulation: Total-600
Advertising: $400.
Printing Co: Sir Speedy, 600 Huron Ave, Port Huron, MI 48060-3702 Tel # (810) 982-8202

HR Report
Business, Association   **CPM: $275**

Publishing Co: Harrisonburg Rockingham Chamber of Commerce, 800 Country Club Rd, Harrisonburg, VA 22801-5033; Title Tel # (703) 434-3862 Title Fax # (703) 434-4508
Personnel: Editor-Patricia H. Doss
General Info: Bi-monthly, Trim Size-8½ x 11, 8 pages
Subscriptions: Indv. $6, $6/copy
Circulation: Total-1,000
Advertising: $275. Accepts Inserts.

Hampton Roads Chamber of Commerce, Newsletter

Publishing Co: Hampton Roads Chamber of Commerce, 420 Bank St, Norfolk, VA 23510-2401; Title Tel # (804) 622-2312
Personnel: Publisher-Robert A. Metrakos, Editor-Andi Peck
Editorial Description: Pending national, state and local legislation.
General Info: (Formerly Portsmouth Chamber of Commerce Newsletter), Yr. Est. 1922, Monthly, Trim Size-8½ x 11, Offset press, 4 pages
Subscriptions: Indv. $1
Circulation: Total-1,200

Hellenic-American Chamber of Commerce Newsletter
Business, Consumer

Publishing Co: Hellenic-American Chamber of Commerce, 960 6th Ave., #1204, New York, NY 10001-2112 Fax # (212) 564-9281; Title Tel # (212) 629-6380
General Info: (Formerly Hellenic-American Chamber of Commerce Bulletin), Yr. Est. 1948, Semi-annually

Interaction
Business, Association   **CPM: $141**

Publishing Co: Greater O'Hare Assn., PO Box 1516, Elk Grove Village, IL 60009-1516 Tel # (708) 350-2944 Fax # (708) 350-2979
Personnel: Editor-Lisa Zeigler
Editorial Description: Membership activities and monthly meetings reports. Provides information on transportation & intl. trade, human resources, sales small business & networking to businesses serving the greater O'Hare region.
General Info: Monthly, Trim Size-8½ x 11, Web press, 16 pages, ISSN: 8750-4030, 4 Color, Coated, Saddle-stitched
Subscriptions: Free With Membership
Circulation: Total-3,000
Advertising: $425. Accepts Inserts.

Jackson Commerce
Business

Publishing Co: Jackson Chamber of Commerce, PO Box 849, Jackson, MS 39205-0849 Tel # (601) 359-2907; Title Tel # (601) 948-7575
Editorial Description: Projects and activities of interest to members.
General Info: (Formerly Building Jackson), Yr. Est. 1931, Monthly, Trim Size-8½ x 11, Letrpr. press, 4 pages, No Color, Coated
Circulation: Total-2,500
Advertising: Inquire for rates.

Jamestown Chamber of Commerce Newsletter
Business, Consumer

Publishing Co: Jamestown Area Chamber of Commerce, 101 W 5th St, Jamestown, NY 14701-5013; Title Tel # (716) 484-1101 Title Fax # (716) 487-0785
Editorial Description: Information for members and calendar of events.
General Info: Yr. Est. 1915, Semi-monthly
Subscriptions: Free With Membership
Circulation: Total-800

Kansas Citian
Business, Association

Publishing Co: Greater Kansas City Chamber of Commerce, 2600 Commerce Tower, 911 Main St., Kansas City, MO 64105-2049; Title Tel # (816) 221-2424 Title Fax # (816) 221-7440
Personnel: Editor-Pamela Kingsolver, Production Mgr.-Liz Wheeler
Editorial Description: Reports Chamber activities, issues and business, community activities of interest to chamber membership.
General Info: Yr. Est. 1924, Semi-monthly, Trim Size-8½ x 11, Sheetfed press, 12 pages, 2 Color, Matte, Saddle-stitched
Subscriptions: Indv. $50
Circulation: Total-6,000
Advertising: Inquire for rates.
Printing Co: Smith Grieves Co., 1717 Washington St # 419573, Kansas City, MO 64108-1121 Tel # (816) 421-2020, Fax # (816) 842-3475

Klamath County Chamber of Commerce Newsletter
Association

Publishing Co: Klamath County Chamber of Commerce, 507 Main St., Klamath Falls, OR 97601-6031; Title Tel # (503) 884-5193
Personnel: Publisher-David Goss, Editor, Art Dir.-Candice Richard
Editorial Description: Informs chamber membership of program, projects and news items.
General Info: (Formerly Chamber News), Yr. Est. 1938, Monthly, Sheetfed press, 4 pages, 2% ads, 2 Color, Newsprint
Subscriptions: Indv. $5
Acquistions: Publication Bought
Circulation: (100% controlled), Total-700
Advertising: Inquire for rates. Accepts Inserts.
Printing Co: PIP Printing, 830 Main St, Klamath Falls, OR 97601-6012 Tel # (503) 883-3185

Lebanon and Wilson County Chamber of Commerce Letter
Business

Publishing Co: Lebanon, 149 Public Sq, Lebanon, TN 37087-2736; Title Tel # (615) 444-5503
Personnel: Editor-Mark Davis
Editorial Description: Discussion of business and industry of interest to members.
General Info: Yr. Est. 1956, Bi-monthly, Trim Size-8½ x 11, Sheetfed press, 4 pages, No Color, Newsprint
Circulation: (100% controlled), Total-400

Legislative Report

Publishing Co: Saskatchewan Chamber of Commerce, 1920 Broad St., #1630, Regina, SK S4P 3V2 Canada; Title Tel # (306) 352-2671 Title Fax # (306) 781-7084
General Info: Yr. Est. 1974, Monthly
Subscriptions: Indv. $125, Inst. $134, Can. $127

Milwaukee Commerce Hot-Line
Association, Business

Publishing Co: Metropolitan Milwaukee Association of Commerce, 756 N. Milwaukee St., Milwaukee, WI 53202-3719; Title Tel # (414) 287-4100 Title Fax # (414) 271-7253
Personnel: Publisher-Tim Sheehy, Editor-Julie Granger
Editorial Description: Informs membership of association and business community activities.
General Info: Yr. Est. 1923, Weekly, Trim Size-8½ x 11, Offset press, 4 pages, ISSN: 0026-4342, 2 Color, Matte, Saddle-stitched
Circulation: Total-4,200

Minnesota Views
Business

Publishing Co: Minnesota Chamber of Commerce, 30 7th St E Ste 1700, Saint Paul, MN 55101-4901; Title Tel # (612) 292-4665
Personnel: Editor-Craig McHenry
General Info: (Formerly Minnesota's Business), Monthly, Offset press, 12 pages, 2 Color, Coated
Circulation: Total-9,000

Missouri Business
Business

Publishing Co: Missouri Chamber of Commerce, PO Box 149, Jefferson City, MO 65102-0149; Title Tel # (314) 634-3511
Personnel: Publisher-Jo Frappier, Editor-Nancy Sell
Editorial Description: Reports to business and industry items of interest in Missouri and the nation relative to taxes, industrial development, legislation, agriculture, water, education.
General Info: Yr. Est. 1921, Monthly, Trim Size-8½ x 11, Offset press, 48 pages, Color, Coated, Saddle-stitched
Subscriptions: Indv. $3, $1/copy
Circulation: Total-4,100

Morgantown Area Chamber of Commerce Newsletter
Business, Association

Publishing Co: Morgantown Area Chamber of Commerce, PO Box 658, Morgantown, WV 26507-0658; Title Tel # (304) 292-3311
Personnel: Editor-Terry Jones
Editorial Description: Current events, chamber activities.
General Info: Yr. Est. 1950, Monthly
Circulation: Total-800

Network
Association

Publishing Co: Ohio Chamber of Commerce, P O Box 15159, Columbus, OH 43215-0159; Title Tel # (614) 228-4201 Title Fax # (614) 228-6403
Personnel: Editor-Charlest McConville
Editorial Description: A newsletter devoted to the exchange of ideas & information among the Chambers of Commerce in Ohio.
General Info: Quarterly, Sheetfed press, 6 pages, 2 Color
Circulation: Total-500

New Horizons
Business, Association   CPM: $335

Publishing Co: Anderson Chamber of Commerce, Box 1568, Sta. A, Anderson, SC 29622-1568; Title Tel # (803) 226-3455 Title Fax # (803) 226-3300
Personnel: Publisher, Editor-Janette Mitchell, Adv. Dir.-Eddie Nail
Editorial Description: Concerns the industrial, commercial and economic growth of Anderson and discusses tbe personalities involved in same.
General Info: Yr. Est. 1952, Monthly, Trim Size-8½ x 11, 16 pages, 2 Color
Subscriptions: Free With Membership
Circulation: Total-1,600
Advertising: $536.
Printing Co: Attaway, PO Box 302, Anderson, SC 29622-0302 Tel # (803) 226-1286

New York Chamber of Commerce Bulletin

Publishing Co: New York Chamber of Commerce & Industry, 1 Battery Park Plz, New York, NY 10004-1491 Tel # (212) 493-7559 Fax # (212) 344-3344; Title Tel # (212) 766-1300
General Info: Yr. Est. 1909, Monthly

Newton-Needham Business
Business

Publishing Co: Newton-Needham Chamber of Commerce, PO Box 66028, Auburndale, MA 02166-0986; Title Tel # (617) 244-5300 Title Fax # (617) 299-5302
Personnel: Editor-Lewis B. Songer
Editorial Description: News of interest to members, civic and community leaders in Newton and Needham.
General Info: Yr. Est. 1959, Monthly, Trim Size-2 x 2, Offset press, 4 pages, Color, Coated
Subscriptions: Indv. $25
Circulation: Total-1,200
Advertising: Inquire for rates.

North Shore Business Journal
Business

Publishing Co: North Shore Chamber of Commerce, 5 Cherry Hill Dr Ste 100, Danvers, MA 01923-2500; Title Tel # (508) 774-8565 Title Fax # (508) 774-3418
Personnel: Publisher-Robert Bradford, Editor-Barclay Berry, Adv. Dir.-Kte McCormack
Editorial Description: Business news of the city plus information of interest to commerce and industry on state and federal regulations, taxes, etc.
General Info: (Formerly Beverly News Bulletin), Yr. Est. 1918, Monthly, Trim Size-8½ x 11, Mimeo press, 8 pages, 3% ads, 2 Color, Coated, Saddle-stitched
Subscriptions: Indv. $10
Acquistions: Publication Bought
Circulation: Total-1,200
Advertising: Inquire for rates. Accepts Inserts.
List Rental: Rents Lists
Printing Co: Minuteman Press, 12 Tozer Rd, Beverly, MA 01915-5588 Tel # (508) 927-8757

Northeast Business

Publishing Co: Philadelphia Chamber of Commerce, 8601 Roosevelt Blvd, Philadelphia, PA 19152-2001

Omaha Profile
Business

Publishing Co: Greater Omaha Chamber of Commerce, 1301 Harney St, Omaha, NE 68102-1832; Title Tel # (402) 346-5000 Title Fax # (402) 346-7050
Personnel: Editor, Adv. Dir.-Liz Cajka, Art Dir.-Susan Elliott
Editorial Description: Omaha business news and activities of Chamber of Commerce.
General Info: Yr. Est. 1925, Semi-monthly, Trim Size-8½ x 11, Offset press, 8 pages, No Color
Subscriptions: Indv. $20, Free To Qualified Recipient
Circulation: Total-4,200
Advertising: Inquire for rates.
Printing Co: Interstate Printing Co., 2002 N 16th St # 22, Omaha, NE 68110-2411 Tel # (402) 341-8028, Fax # (402) 341-6168

Port-O-Call
Business

Publishing Co: Greater Stockton Chamber of Commerce, 445 W Weber Ave Ste 220, Stockton, CA 95203-3148; Title Tel # (209) 547-2770 Title Fax # (209) 466-5271
Personnel: Publisher-Paula Edwards, Editor-David McCoy, Adv. Dir.-Evenyl Roemmich
Editorial Description: Business news to and about members - Government alert.
General Info: Yr. Est. 1954, Monthly, Trim Size-11½ x 16, Desktop press, 16 pages, Color-cover, Matte
Subscriptions: Indv. $60, Free With Membership
Circulation: Total-2,000
Advertising: Inquire for rates.

Prairie Progress Newsletter
See: BUSINESS & INDUSTRY

Profile
Association

Publishing Co: Los Angeles Jr. Chamber of Commerce, 404 S Bixel St, Los Angeles, CA 90017-1420; Title Tel # (213) 482-1311
Personnel: Editor-Bob Levey
Editorial Description: Official organ of the Los Angeles Junior Chamber of Commerce.
General Info: Yr. Est. 1927, Monthly, Trim Size-9¼ x 11¾, Letrpr. press, 4 pages, ISSN: 0300-7782, No Color, Coated
Subscriptions: Indv. $1
Circulation: (100% controlled), Total-1,400

Profit-The Bottom Line in Greater New Haven Business
Business   CPM: $116

Publishing Co: Greater New Haven Chamber of Commerce, 195 Church St Ste 15, New Haven, CT 06510-2009; Title Tel # (203) 787-6735
Personnel: Editor-Jeff Van Tienen
Editorial Description: Official newsletter of the Greater New Haven Chamber of Commerce.
General Info: Yr. Est. 1984, Semi-monthly, Web press, 24 pages, 7% ads, 2 Color
Subscriptions: Indv. $14, $2/copy
Circulation: (27% controlled), Total-4,300, Subscriptions-2,500
Advertising: $500. Accepts Inserts.
List Rental: Rents Lists
Printing Co: Imprint Printing, 97 Defco Park Rd., North Haven, CT 06473-1129 Tel # (203) 239-4421

Progress Report
Business

Publishing Co: Greater Providence Chamber of Commerce, Commerce Center, 30 Exchange Terrace, Providence, RI 02903; Title Tel # (401) 521-5000
Personnel: Editor-Sandi Seltzer
Editorial Description: Reports on Chamber events, legislative issues, member news & business related feature articles.
General Info: Yr. Est. 1958, 10x/yr., Trim Size-8½ x 11, Offset press, 16 pages, 3% ads, 2 Color, Newsprint, Saddle-stitched
Subscriptions: Indv. $3
Circulation: Total-3,500
Advertising: Inquire for rates.
List Rental: Rents Lists
Printing Co: Docu-Print, 1243 Mineral Spring Ave., N. Providence, RI 02914 Tel # (401) 724-6590

Results News Report
Business, Association

Publishing Co: Texas Dept. of Commerce, PO Box 12728, Austin, TX 78711-2728; Title Tel # (512) 320-9643
Personnel: Editor-O.C. Garza, Art Dir.-Virginia Dunnam
Editorial Description: Everything related to Texas tourism.
General Info: (Formerly Newsletter of Tourism), Monthly, 4 pages
Circulation: Total-3,000

St. Catharines News and Views

Publishing Co: St. Catharines Chamber of Commerce, 11 King St., Box 940, St. Catharines, ON L2R 6Z4 Canada Tel # (416) 684-2361
Personnel: Editor-R. Raws Thorne
Editorial Description: Comments on local topics of interest, local economic outlook and forecast, provincial and federal matters.
General Info: Yr. Est. 1921, Bi-monthly
Circulation: Total-800

Saint John's Edmonton Report

Publishing Co: Saint John's Edmonton Report, 17327-106A Ave., Edmonton, AB T5M 1T9 Canada; Title Tel # (403) 484-8884
Personnel: Publisher-Keith Bennett, Editor-Ted Byfield, Adv. Dir.-Robert Clarke
General Info: Yr. Est. 1975, Weekly, Offset press, Color
Subscriptions: Indv. $20
Circulation: Total-23,842

Salisbury-Rowan County in Action

Publishing Co: Salisbury-Rowan County Chamber of Commerce, PO Box 559, Salisbury, NC 28145-0559; Title Tel # (704) 633-4221
Personnel: Editor-K.V. Epting, Jr.
Editorial Description: Chamber of Commerce activities, Congressional and legislative issues, local economic data.
General Info: Yr. Est. 1961, Monthly
Subscriptions: Indv. $50
Circulation: Total-850

Sanford-Springvale Chamber of Commerce, Monthly Report

Publishing Co: Sanford-Springvale Chamber of Commerce, 261 Main St., P.O. Box 270, Sanford, ME 04073-3545; Title Tel # (207) 324-4280 Title Fax # (207) 324-8290
Personnel: Editor-Richard L. Stanley
Editorial Description: Chamber news and activities.
General Info: Yr. Est. 1954, Bi-monthly
Circulation: Total-300

Sheboygan Chamber of Commerce, Monthly Newsletter
Business

Publishing Co: Sheboygan Chamber of Commerce, 712 Riverfront Dr., #101, Sheboygan, WI 53081-4665; Title Tel # (414) 457-9491
Personnel: Editor-Gregory Borsecnik
Editorial Description: Activity of committee functions for community promotion and development.
General Info: Yr. Est. 1925, Monthly
Circulation: (100% controlled), Total-1,100

South Charleston Chamber of Commerce Newsletter

Publishing Co: South Charleston Chamber of Commerce, 411 1/2 D St, South Charleston, WV 25303-3107; Title Tel # (304) 744-0051
Personnel: Editor-Oscar Fudge
Editorial Description: Covers activities of the Chamber.
General Info: Yr. Est. 1957, Monthly, 4 pages
Circulation: Total-200

Southern Cooperator — *Business, Association*

Publishing Co: Federation of Southern Cooperatives, PO Box 95, Epes, AL 35460-0095 Tel # (205) 652-9676 Fax # (205) 652-9678
Personnel: Editor-Alice Paris
General Info: Yr. Est. 1970, Irregular
Subscriptions: Indv. $5
Circulation: Total-6,000

Spokane Affairs — *Business, Association*

Publishing Co: Sponsor-COFC, Spokane Chamber of Commerce, W. 1020 Riverside, Spokane, WA 99201; Title Tel # (509) 624-1393 Title Fax # (509) 747-0077
Personnel: Editor-C.M. Archer
Editorial Description: Economic news of the Spokane area; events, reviews, and community issues.
General Info: Yr. Est. 1924, Monthly, Sheetfed press, 4 pages, No Color, Coated, Saddle-stitched
Subscriptions: Indv. $25, $2/copy
Circulation: Total-3,400
Advertising: Inquire for rates. Accepts Inserts.
Printing Co: Litho Art Printers, S. 118 Lincoln, Spokane, WA 99204

Travel Publicity Leads
See: TRAVEL

Update — *Association*

Publishing Co: Greater LaCrosse Area C of C, PO Box 219, La Crosse, WI 54602-0219
Personnel: Publisher-Bill Sorenson, Editor-Dawn Sandy, Mktg. Dir.-Connie Knutson
Editorial Description: Deals mainly with information pertaining to chamber activities & items of interest to our membership.
General Info: (Formerly La Crosse Roads), Yr. Est. 1981, Semi-monthly, Trim Size-8½ x 11, Letrpr. press, 1 pages, No Color
Subscriptions: Free With Membership
Circulation: Total-1,350
Advertising: Accepts Inserts.

Update

Publishing Co: Louisville Magazine, 137 W. Muhammad Ali Blvd., Ste 101, Louisville, KY 40202
Personnel: Editor-Charles Springer
General Info: (Formerly Action), Yr. Est. 1968, Weekly
Circulation: Total-2,500

Valley Commerce — *Business*

Publishing Co: Roanoke Valley Chamber of Commerce, 212 S. Jefferson, Roanoke, VA 24011 Tel # (540) 983-0700 Fax # (540) 983-0723; Title Tel # (703) 344-5188
Personnel: VP Mktng.-Patti Dunbar
Editorial Description: News of Roanoke business community and chamber of commerce.
General Info: (Formerly Roanoke Record), Yr. Est. 1948, Monthly, Trim Size-8½ x 11½, Sheetfed press, 16 pages, ISSN: 0028-4629, 4% ads, Color, Coated
Subscriptions: Indv. $15
Circulation: (100% controlled), Total-1,850
Advertising: Inquire for rates.
Printing Co: Progress Press, 2922 Nicholas Ave NE, Roanoke, VA 24012-5651 Tel # (703) 345-1820

Victoria Chamber of Commerce Newsletter — *Business*

Publishing Co: Victoria Chamber, PO Box 2465, Victoria, TX 77902-2465; Title Tel # (512) 573-5277
Editorial Description: Coverage of projects important to business.
General Info: Yr. Est. 1966, Quarterly, 16 pages, 2 Color, Coated
Circulation: Total-1,000
Advertising: Inquire for rates.

Vietnam Business InfoTrack
See: INTERNATIONAL TRADE

View, The

Publishing Co: Mobile Area Chamber of Commerce, PO Box 2187, Mobile, AL 36652-2187 Tel # (334) 433-6951; Title Tel # (334) 431-8623 Title Fax # (334) 431-8646
Personnel: Publisher-Winthrop M. Hallett, Editor-Marian Reagan, Mag. Ed.-Susan R. Blanchard, Exec. Ed.-Jodi Swiderek
Editorial Description: A monthly business publication for the members of the Mobile area Chamber of Commerce.
General Info: (Formerly Mobile), Monthly, Trim Size-11 x 17, Offset press, 4,000 pages, 2 Color, Other, Other
Subscriptions: Indv. $24, Free To Qualified Recipient
Circulation: Total-3,900
Printing Co: Office Supplies Inc., 1558 S. Beltline Hwy., Mobile, AL 36693 Tel # (334) 666-7204, Fax # (334) 661-6209

WAVES

Publishing Co: South Shore Chamber of Commerce, 36 Miller Stile Rd, Quincy, MA 02169-5400; Title Tel # (617) 479-1111 Title Fax # (617) 479-9274
Personnel: Publisher, Editor-John R. Graham, Adv. Dir.-Elisabeht B. Newberry
Editorial Description: Published monthly for and about the members of the South Shore Chamber of Commerce.
General Info: Yr. Est. 1971, Monthly, Sheetfed press, 16 pages, 4% ads, 4 Color, Coated, Saddle-stitched
Circulation: Total-2,543
Advertising: Inquire for rates.
List Rental: Actives: $250/M
Printing Co: Ink Spot, The, 40 Oval Rd, Quincy, MA 02170-3813 Tel # (617) 273-7605, Fax # (617) 471-8810

Winchester — *Business, Association*

Publishing Co: Winchester-Frederick County Chamber of Commerce, Inc., 1360 S Pleasant Valley Rd, Winchester, VA 22601-4447; Title Tel # (703) 662-4118
Personnel: Editor-William Shendow
Editorial Description: Activities of local Chamber, business, National and State legislation, civic affairs, economic development.
General Info: Yr. Est. 1960, Monthly, No Color
Subscriptions: Indv. $5
Circulation: Total-1,000

Your Wharton Chamber of Commerce Newsletter

Publishing Co: Wharton Chamber of Commerce, PO Box 868, Wharton, TX 77488-0868; Title Tel # (409) 532-1862
Personnel: Editor-Billy H. Jones
Editorial Description: Community development and progress reports of Wharton.
General Info: Yr. Est. 1966, Monthly
Circulation: (100% controlled), Total-375

CHEMISTRY & CHEMICALS

21st Century Fuels
See: ENERGY

AA Newsletter — *Business*

Publishing Co: Perkin-Elmer Corp., 761 Main Ave., Norwalk, CT 06859-0105 Tel # (203) 762-6023 Fax # (203) 764-2892
Personnel: Editor-Jane Sebestyen, Production Mgr., Art Dir.-Anneliese Lust
Editorial Description: Information on analytical instrumentation and supplies for customers.
General Info: Yr. Est. 1992, Semi-annually, Trim Size-8½ x 11, Offset press, 6 pages, 2 Color, Coated, Saddle-stitched
Subscriptions: Free
Circulation: Total-38,000
Printing Co: Kenographics, Danbury Rd., Hilton, CT 06897

ACA Newsletter — *Association* — CPM: $330

Publishing Co: American Crystallographic Association, 73 High St., Buffalo, NY 14203-0096 Fax # (716) 852-4846; Title Tel # (716) 856-9600
Personnel: Circ. Mgr., Adv. Dir.-Marcia Vair
General Info: Yr. Est. 1950, Quarterly, Trim Size-8½ x 11, Letrpr. press, 28 pages, ISSN: 1058-9945, 12% ads, 2 Color, Matte, Saddle-stitched
Subscriptions: Free With Membership
Circulation: Total-2,000
Advertising: $660.
List Rental: Actives: $120/M

AIC Newsletter
See: ART & SCULPTURE

Additives for Polymers
See: PLASTICS

Advanced Battery Technology
See: ELECTRIC & ELECTRONIC EQUIPMENT

Advanced Coatings & Surface Technology — *Business*

Publishing Co: Technical Insights, Inc., PO Box 1304, Fort Lee, NJ 07024-9967; Title Tel # (201) 568-4744 Title Fax # (201) 568-8247
Personnel: Publisher-Kenneth A. Kovaly, Editorial Dir.-Peter R. Savage, Circ. Mgr.-Barbara Chaffee, Mktg. Dir.-Lyn Schmidt
Editorial Description: Reports on significant developments in coatings & surface modification of an across the board range of industries & analyzes commercial potential.
General Info: Yr. Est. 1988, Monthly, Trim Size-8½ x 11, Sheetfed press, 12 pages, ISSN: 0896-422X, 2 Color, Matte, Other
Subscriptions: Indv. $590, For. $650
List Rental: Actives: $180/M, Expires: $235/M
Printing Co: Allied Lettercraft, 307 W. 36th St., New York, NY 10018 Tel # (212) 279-4800

Amber-Hi-Lites   *Business*

Publishing Co: Rohm & Haas Co., Independence Mall West, Philadelphia, PA 19105
Tel # (215) 592-3480; Title Tel # (215) 592-3030
Personnel: Publisher-J.C. Fanelli, Editor-G. Button, Circ. Mgr.-J. Fanelli, Art Dir.-A. Ferrara
Editorial Description: Discussions of ion exchange resin use in fields of water conditioning, pharmaceutical production, waste recovery and chemical processing.
General Info: Yr. Est. 1949, Quarterly, 2 Color
Circulation: Total-12,000

Amplifications -- A Forum for PCR Users   *Business*

Publishing Co: Perkin-Elmer Corp., 761 Main Ave., Norwalk, CT 06859-0105 Tel # (203) 762-6023 Fax # (203) 764-2892
Personnel: Editor-Leslie Kelley, Mng. Editor, Production Mgr.-Anneliese Lust
Editorial Description: Amplifications brings users timely & practical information on PCR applications & methodologies based on the experience of leading scientists & PCR users worldwide.
General Info: Yr. Est. 1989, Quarterly, Trim Size-8¼ x 11, Offset press, 12 pages, 2 Color, Matte, Saddle-stitched
Subscriptions: Free
Circulation: Total-35,000
Printing Co: Wm. J. Mack Co., Box 495, New Haven, CT 06473

CPIA Bulletin
See: AERONAUTICS/ASTRONAUTICS

CSMA Executive Newswatch

Publishing Co: Chemical Specialties Manufacturers Assn., 1913 Eye St., NW, Washington, DC 20006-5103; Title Tel # (202) 872-8110 Title Fax # (202) 874-8114
Editorial Description: Covers regulatory & market information about a changing specialties industry.
General Info: Yr. Est. 1914, Weekly

Camford Chemical Report   *Business*

Publishing Co: Camford Information Services, 801 York Mills Road, Suite 201, Don Mills, ON M3B 1X7 Canada; Title Tel # (416) 291-3215 Title Fax # (416) 291-3406
Personnel: Editor-Joe Piccione, Publisher, Circ. Mgr.-Bob Douglas
Editorial Description: Chemical marketing newsletter. The emphasis is on the Canadian market.
General Info: (Formerly Corpus Chemical Report), Yr. Est. 1969, Weekly, Trim Size-8½ x 11, Sheetfed press, 6 pages, ISSN: 0313-257X, No Color
Subscriptions: Indv. $689, Can. $650, For. $689, $20/copy
Acquisitions: Publication Bought, Publication Sold
Circulation: Total-250
Advertising: Accepts Inserts.

Catalysis Society Newsletter

Publishing Co: Catalysis Soc. of North America, C/O Dupont Experimental Sta., Bldg. 402, C/O Linn, Wilmington, DE 19898-0001; Title Tel # (302) 695-4655
Personnel: Editor-William Linn
Editorial Description: News of interest to chemists & engineers in industry & academia doing research in catalysis.
General Info: Yr. Est. 1966, Quarterly, 4 pages, No Color
Circulation: Total-2,500
List Rental: Actives: $50/M
Printing Co: Joseph W. Small Assn., Marsh Rd., Wilmington, DE 19809 Tel # (302) 764-0820

ChemEcology   *Business*

Publishing Co: Chemical Manufacturers Association, 1300 Wilson Blvd., Arlington, VA 22209 Tel # (703) 741-5807 Fax # (703) 741-6095
Personnel: Editor-Rebecca Swinhart
Editorial Description: Published to promote a clean environment and healthy workplace, as well as to provide information on current issues surrounding health, safety and the environment.
General Info: Yr. Est. 1972, Monthly, Trim Size-8½ x 11, Web press, 12 pages, ISSN: 0738-7776, 4 Color, Coated, Saddle-stitched
Circulation: (98% controlled), Total-75,000

Chemical Bond   *Association*

Publishing Co: American Chemical Society, 1155 16th St. NW, Washington, DC 20036-4899 Tel # (202) 872-4600 Fax # (202) 872-6005
Personnel: Editor-Martha Rhine
Editorial Description: Covers organization activities, editorial comment, news to members, events of interest, meeting notices, member's activities (mainly professional) and member's comments.
General Info: Yr. Est. 1950, 8x/yr., Trim Size-5½ x 8½, Offset press, 10 pages, Color
Subscriptions: $1/copy
Circulation: Total-1,900

Chemical Design Automation News   *Business*

Publishing Co: Butterworth Legal Publishers, 8 Industrial Way # C, Salem, NH 03079-2837 Tel # (603) 898-9664 Fax # (603) 898-9858; Title Tel # (617) 438-8464 Title Fax # (617) 438-1479
Personnel: Production Mgr.-Becky Hale
General Info: Yr. Est. 1985, Monthly, Trim Size-8½ x 11, 44 pages, Color-cover, Coated, Saddle-stitched
Subscriptions: Inst. $300, $30/copy
Advertising: $800.
List Rental: Rents Lists

Chemical Distributors   *Association*

Publishing Co: Natl. Assn. of Chemical Dist., C/O United Technologies, 5100 Springfield Pike, #412, Dayton, OH 45431; Title Tel # (513) 228-3020
Editorial Description: Association news, news of industry, features.
General Info: Yr. Est. 1972, Monthly, Trim Size-8½ x 11, Offset press, 8 pages, 2 Color
Circulation: Total-450

Chemical Economics Handbook   *Business*

Publishing Co: SRI Intl. -Chemical Bus. Research Division, 333 Ravenswood Ave, Menlo Park, CA 94025-3453 Tel # (415) 859-3627 Fax # (415) 859-4623; Title Tel # (415) 859-3900 Title Fax # (415) 859-2182
Personnel: Editor-Thomas Gunn
Editorial Description: Provides information on the current & future supply/demand situation for major chemical derivatives.
General Info: Yr. Est. 1950, Monthly, Trim Size-8½ x 11, Offset press, No Color, Looseleaf

Chemical Industries Newsletter   *Business*

Publishing Co: SRI Intl. -Chemical Bus. Research Division, 333 Ravenswood Ave, Menlo Park, CA 94025-3453 Tel # (415) 859-3627 Fax # (415) 859-4623; Title Tel # (415) 859-3346
Personnel: Editor-Ellen Lane, Production Mgr.-Ellen Blue
Editorial Description: Discusses the activities of SRI Intl's. Chemical Industries Centers.
General Info: (Formerly Chemical Economics Newsletter), Yr. Est. 1959, Bi-monthly, Trim Size-8½ x 11, Offset press, 12 pages, Color
Circulation: (100% controlled), Total-6,000

Chemical Industry Monitor   *Business*

Publishing Co: C.J. Lawrence/Deutsche Bank Securities, 1290 Ave. of the Americas, New York, NY 10104-0051 Tel # (212) 468-5000; Title Tel # (212) 962-2200
Personnel: Editor-Don Pattison
Editorial Description: Monitors prices, technical developments, industry & company outlooks; charts, tables.
General Info: Yr. Est. 1976, Bi-weekly, Trim Size-8½ x 11, Offset press, 8 pages, No Color
Subscriptions: Indv. $200, $8/copy
Circulation: Total-2,500

Chemical Monitor   *Consumer*

Publishing Co: Chemical Monitor, PO Box 314, Lindenhurst, NY 11757-0314; Title Tel # (516) 669-8147
Personnel: Editor-Angelo Tulumello
Editorial Description: Dedicated to chemical instrumentation. Reviews trends in instrument design, new materials, studies in reliability & recent patents.
General Info: Yr. Est. 1984, Monthly, Offset press, 8 pages, Ind/Abs/Online: NewsNet, DIALOG predicasts Newsletter, 2 Color, Newsprint
Subscriptions: Indv. $95, Can. $105, For. $105, $9/copy

Chemical Newsletter
See: SAFETY

Chemical Process Alert   *Business*

Publishing Co: Technical Insights, Inc., PO Box 1304, Fort Lee, NJ 07024-9967; Title Tel # (201) 568-4744 Title Fax # (201) 568-8247
Personnel: Publisher-Kenneth A. Kovaly, Circ. Mgr.-Barbara Chaffee, Mktg. Dir.-Lyn A. Schmidt
Editorial Description: Provides advances across a broad range of disciplines including chemical, biochemical, & polymer techniques. Emphasis is on discrete technological advances & environmental technology related to process plants. Key patents listed.
General Info: Weekly, 7 pages, ISSN: 1084-4538
Subscriptions: Indv. $890, For. $990
List Rental: Actives: $185/M

Chemical Profiles

Publishing Co: Schnell Publishing Co., Inc., 80 Broad St Fl 23, New York, NY 10004-2209 Tel # (212) 298-4177
Personnel: Editor-Glenn Hess
General Info: Monthly

Chemical Regulation Reporter   *Business*

Publishing Co: Bureau of National Affairs, Inc., 1231 25th St. NW, Bldg. N-200, Washington, DC 20037-1157 Fax # (202) 822-8092; Title Tel # (202) 452-4200 Title Fax # (202) 452-4610
Personnel: Publisher-William A. Beltz, Mng. Editor-Bill Bank, Circ. Mgr.-Gary C. Seltzer
Editorial Description: A weekly notification & reference service that comprehensibly cover federal chemical regulation.
General Info: Yr. Est. 1977, Weekly, Trim Size-8½ x 11, Offset press, 64 pages, ISSN: 0148-7973, Ind/Abs/Online: Lexis, Westlaw, HRIN, Mead Data Central, Nexis, Looseleaf
Subscriptions: Indv. $1,669
Circulation: Total-3,000
Printing Co: McArdle Printing Co., 800 Commerce Dr, Upper Marlboro, MD 20772-8792 Tel # (301) 390-8500

Chemical Substances
Control *Business*

Publishing Co: Bureau of National Affairs, Inc., 1231 25th St. NW, Bldg. N-200, Washington, DC 20037-1157; Title Tel # (202) 452-4200 Title Fax # (202) 822-8092
Personnel: Publisher-William A. Beltz, Editor-Eileen Joseph, Mng. Editor-Karen Walker, Circ. Mgr.-Gary C. Seltzer
Editorial Description: A reference & advisory service on the management of chemicals from premanufacture through use & disposal.
General Info: Yr. Est. 1980, Bi-weekly, Trim Size-8½ x 11, Offset press, 4 pages, ISSN: 0271-1478, Ind/Abs/Online: HRIN
Subscriptions: Indv. $680

Chemistry

Publishing Co: National Technical Information Service U.S., 5285 Port Royal Rd., Springfield, VA 22161-0001 Tel # (703) 487-4630 Fax # (703) 487-4630; Title Tel # (703) 487-4650
Editorial Description: Covers analytical chemistry, industrial chemistry, chemical process engineering, polymer chemistry, radiation chemistry, etc.
General Info: Weekly
Subscriptions: Can. $115, For. $155

Composites News: Infrastructure
See: PLASTICS

Compressions *Association*

Publishing Co: Compressed Gas Assn., 1725 Jefferson Davis Hwy Ste, 1004, Arlington, VA 22202-4102; Title Tel # (703) 979-0900
Personnel: Editor-Owen Baker
Editorial Description: Items covered are those of timely & prime concern to the industry.
General Info: Yr. Est. 1913, Monthly, Mimeo press, 5 pages
Circulation: Total-1,100

Courtroom Toxicology
See: LAW

CryoGas International *Business* CPM: $228

Publishing Co: J.R. Campbell & Associates, Inc., 5 Militia Dr., Lexington, MA 02173; Title Tel # (617) 862-0624 Title Fax # (617) 863-9411
Personnel: Publisher-John Campbell, Editor-Linda Grant, Adv. Dir.-Lori Campbell Frieling
Editorial Description: Reports on the industrial gas industry including the cryogenic equipment business. Feature articles cover topical issues and include interviews of industry executives.
General Info: (Formerly Cryogenic Information Report), Yr. Est. 1962, 11x/yr., Trim Size-8½ x 11, Sheetfed press, 48 pages, ISSN: 1052-0139, 9% ads, No Color, Matte, Saddle-stitched
Subscriptions: Indv. $150, Can. $200, For. $200
Circulation: Total-3,500
Advertising: $800.

Cureletter
See: MANUFACTURING

Current Awareness Profile
on Quantum Chemistry

Publishing Co: Indiana University, Chemistry Dept., QCPE Creative Arts Bldg. #181, Bloomington, IN 47405; Title Tel # (812) 855-4848
Personnel: Editor-Richard Counts
General Info: Yr. Est. 1973, Bi-weekly, 10 pages, No Color
Circulation: Total-150

D&A Hazardous Waste
Hotline *Business*

Publishing Co: Deul Co., 7208 Jefferson St NE, Albuquerque, NM 87109-4309; Title Tel # (505) 345-8732
Personnel: Publisher-Robert Prindle, Editor-John D'Aloia, Jr.
Editorial Description: Hazardous waste regulations, impacts; new developments; natl. conferences.
General Info: Yr. Est. 1984, Monthly, Trim Size-8½ x 11, Offset press, 2 pages, 2 Color, Newsprint
Subscriptions: Indv. $48
Circulation: Total-250

DCAT Digest
See: DRUGS & PHARMACEUTICALS

Del-Chem Bulletin *Consumer, Association*

Publishing Co: American Chemical Society, 1155 16th St. NW, Washington, DC 20036-4899 Tel # (202) 872-4600 Fax # (202) 872-6005; Title Tel # (302) 992-4713
Personnel: Editor-Ann Moffett, Circ. Mgr.-Ed Harford, Adv. Dir.-Andrea Martin
Editorial Description: Information about local section activities; articles on subjects pertinent to chemistry.
General Info: Yr. Est. 1944, 10x/yr., 16 pages, No Color
Subscriptions: Indv. $2
Circulation: Total-3,000

Diamond Industry Week
See: SCIENCE

DuPont Biotech Update
See: BIOCHEMISTRY

Einhorn Newsletter

Publishing Co: Einhorn Assocs., Inc., 2323 N Mayfair Rd Ste 490, Milwaukee, WI 53226-1507; Title Tel # (414) 453-4488 Title Fax # (414) 453-4831
Editorial Description: Covers mergers & acquisitions in the coating, adhesives, paints, inks, sealants & chemical fields.
General Info: Yr. Est. 1988, Quarterly, 4 pages
Subscriptions: Indv. $35

Electrolysis World *Association*

Publishing Co: American Electrology Assn., 106 Oakridge Rd, Trumbull, CT 06611-5213; Title Tel # (203) 372-7119 Title Fax # (203) 372-7134
Personnel: Editor-Nancy Ledins, Adv. Dir.-Sheila Ahern
Editorial Description: Educational and informative articles pertinent to electrolysis.
General Info: Yr. Est. 1982, Bi-monthly, Trim Size-8½ x 11, Sheetfed press, 12 pages, 2 Color
Circulation: Total-2,000

Electronic Chemicals News *Business*

Publishing Co: Pasha Publications, Inc, 1616 N. Fort Myer Dr., #1000, Arlington, VA 22209-3103 Fax # (703) 528-4926; Title Tel # (703) 528-1244
Personnel: Editor-Laurence Alexander
General Info: Yr. Est. 1986, 24x/yr.
Subscriptions: Indv. $437

Endocrinology and
Metabolism *Consumer, Association*

Publishing Co: American Assn. for Clinical Chemistry, Inc., 2101 L St., NW, Ste. 202, Washington, DC 20037-1526 Fax # (202) 887-5093; Title Tel # (202) 857-0717
General Info: (Formerly American Assn. of Clinical Chemists), Yr. Est. 1982, Monthly, Offset press, 20 pages, ISSN: 0740-7734, 2 Color, Looseleaf
Subscriptions: Indv. $345, Inst. $295, Can. $295, For. $295, $25/copy

Environmental Regulatory
Advisor *Business*

Publishing Co: J.J. Keller & Assoc., Inc., PO Box 368, Neenah, WI 54957-0368; Title Tel # (414) 722-2848 Title Fax # (414) 727-7516
Personnel: Publisher-J.J. Keller, Editor-Webb Shaw, Adv. Dir.-David Szczepanik, Mktg. Dir.-Ed Sieracki
Editorial Description: Regulatory information on hazardous and toxic substances, OSHA, etc.
General Info: (Formerly Hazardous Substances Advisor), Yr. Est. 1979, Monthly, Trim Size-8 x 10¾, Offset press, 24 pages, No Color
Subscriptions: $90/copy
Circulation: Total-2,577
Printing Co: J.J. Keller & Assoc., 3003 Breezewood Ln, Neenah, WI 54956-9611 Tel # (414) 722-2848, Fax # (414) 727-7516

Forensic Forum *Business*

Publishing Co: Perkin-Elmer Corp., 761 Main Ave., Norwalk, CT 06859-0105 Tel # (203) 762-6023 Fax # (203) 764-2892
Personnel: Mng. Editor-Anneliese Lust
General Info: Quarterly

Green Markets Dealer Reports
See: AGRICULTURE

Green Markets Newsletter
See: AGRICULTURE

Hazardous Regulation
Guide *Business*

Publishing Co: J.J. Keller & Assoc., Inc., PO Box 368, Neenah, WI 54957-0368; Title Tel # (414) 722-2848 Title Fax # (414) 727-7516
Personnel: Editor-Webb Shaw, Adv. Dir.-David Szczepanik, Mktg. Dir.-Ed Sieracki
Editorial Description: A quick reference guide complete with hazardous materials regulations.
General Info: (Formerly Hazardous Materials Guide), Yr. Est. 1977, Semi-annually, Web press, 600 pages, Looseleaf
Subscriptions: $129/copy
Circulation: Total-12,326
Printing Co: J.J. Keller & Assoc., 3003 Breezewood Ln, Neenah, WI 54956-9611 Tel # (414) 722-2848, Fax # (414) 727-7516

Hazardous Waste Guide *Business*

Publishing Co: J.J. Keller & Assoc., Inc., PO Box 368, Neenah, WI 54957-0368; Title Tel # (414) 722-2848 Title Fax # (414) 727-7516
Personnel: Editor-Webb Shaw, Adv. Dir.-David Szczepanick, Mktg. Dir.-Ed Sieracki
Editorial Description: Management compliance program for identifying, monitoring, treating, disposing hazardous wastes.
General Info: (Formerly Hazardous Waste Mangement Guide), Yr. Est. 1980, Semi-annually, Web press, 800 pages, Looseleaf
Subscriptions: $109/copy
Circulation: Total-1,279
Printing Co: J.J. Keller & Assoc., 3003 Breezewood Ln, Neenah, WI 54956-9611 Tel # (414) 722-2848, Fax # (414) 727-7516

Hazardous Waste Litigation Reporter
See: LAW

Hazardous Waste
Regulatory Guide *Business*

Publishing Co: J.J. Keller & Assoc., Inc., PO Box 368, Neenah, WI 54957-0368; Title Tel # (414) 722-2848 Title Fax # (414) 727-7516
Personnel: Editor-Webb Shaw, Adv. Dir.-David Szczepanik, Mktg. Dir.-Ed Sieracki
Editorial Description: Complete requirements for generators, transporters, etc. in all states.
General Info: Yr. Est. 1982, Semi-annually, Web press, 500 pages, Looseleaf
Subscriptions: $109/copy
Circulation: Total-1,501
Printing Co: J.J. Keller & Assoc., 3003 Breezewood Ln, Neenah, WI 54956-9611 Tel # (414) 722-2848, Fax # (414) 727-7516

Hazchem Alert

Publishing Co: Van Nostrand Reinhold Co., Inc., 115 5th Ave, New York, NY 10003-1085; Title Tel # (212) 254-3232 Title Fax # (212) 673-1239
Personnel: Publisher-Sal Gelardi, Editor-Judith Douville, Circ. Mgr.-Irene Hoffman, Production Mgr.-Leeann Graham, Promotion Dir.-Judy Kessler
Editorial Description: The global communique on hazardous chemical news & information.
General Info: Yr. Est. 1985, Bi-weekly, 8 pages, ISSN: 0891-3072
Subscriptions: Indv. $260, Can. $315, For. $315, $10/copy

High Performance Plastics
See: PLASTICS

High-Tech Materials Alert
See: MANUFACTURING

ILMA Compoundings
See: PETROLEUM & NATURAL GAS

IOMA Broadcaster

Publishing Co: Independent Oxygen Manufacturers Assn, PO Box 16248, Cleveland, OH 44116-0248; Title Tel # (216) 228-2166
General Info: Monthly

IPMI News and Reviews
See: METALS & METALWORKING

Independent Liquid
Terminals Assn. -
Newsletter

Publishing Co: Independent Liquid Terminals Association, 1133 15th St NW Ste 650, Washington, DC 20005-2710; Title Tel # (202) 659-2301 Title Fax # (202) 466-4166
Personnel: Publisher, Editor-John Prokop
Editorial Description: For companies providing terminaling & above ground tank storage service for shippers, users, & carriers of bulk liquid commodities & products.
General Info: Yr. Est. 1974, Monthly, 8 pages, No Color, Newsprint
Subscriptions: Indv. $120
Circulation: Total-120

Index to Chemical
Regulations *Business*

Publishing Co: Bureau of National Affairs, Inc., 1231 25th St. NW, Bldg. N-200, Washington, DC 20037-1157; Title Tel # (202) 452-4200 Title Fax # (202) 822-8092
Personnel: Publisher-William A. Beltz, Mng. Editor-Inara Z. Apinis, Circ. Mgr.-Gary C. Seltzer
Editorial Description: Index containing more than 80,000 citations by chemical name to the code of Federal Regulations & the Federal Register.
General Info: (Formerly Index to Government Regulation), Yr. Est. 1980, Monthly, Trim Size-8½ x 11, Web press, Looseleaf
Subscriptions: Indv. $707

Indoor Pollution News *Business*

Publishing Co: Business Publishers, Inc., 951 Pershing Dr., Silver Spring, MD 20910-4464 Tel # (301) 589-5103 Fax # (301) 589-8493; Title Tel # (301) 587-6300 Title Fax # (301) 587-1081
Personnel: Publisher-Leonard Eiserer, Editor-David Veazy, Mktg. Dir.-Fay S. Gold
Editorial Description: Indoor air quality regulation, legislation, and litigation.
General Info: (Formerly Toxic Materials News), Yr. Est. 1988, Bi-weekly, Trim Size-8½ x 11, Mimeo press, 8 pages, ISSN: 0093-5891, Ind/Abs/Online: NewsNet, DIALOG, No Color
Subscriptions: Indv. $497, Inst. $497, Can. $497, For. $510
Advertising: Accepts Inserts.
List Rental: List Management Co.: BPI Direct, 951 Pershing Dr., Silver Spring, MD 20910-4464 Tel # (301) 585-5976, Fax # (301) 587-4530

Industrial Chemical
Research Association
Newsletter *Association*

Publishing Co: Industrial Chemical Research Association, 1811 Monroe St, Dearborn, MI 48124-2924 Fax # (313) 563-0360; Title Tel # (313) 563-0360 Title Fax # (313) 563-2940
Acquistions: Publication Bought
Circulation: Total-30,000

Industrial Specialties News
See: MINING & MINERALS

Inside R&D
See: MANUFACTURING

Interface *Business*

Publishing Co: Perkin-Elmer Corp., 761 Main Ave., Norwalk, CT 06859-0105 Tel # (203) 762-6023 Fax # (203) 764-2892
Personnel: Mng. Editor-Anneliese Lust
General Info: Quarterly

Kaufman Letter, The
See: SAFETY

Material Safety Data
Sheet Collection
Updating Service *Consumer*

Publishing Co: Genium Publishing Corp., 1 Genium Plz, Schenectady, NY 12304-4607; Title Tel # (518) 377-8854 Title Fax # (518) 377-1891
Personnel: Publisher, Editor, Production Mgr.-John Stuart, Promotion Dir.-Paul Hans
Editorial Description: Collection of custom written safety data sheets on industrial materials.
General Info: Yr. Est. 1979, Trim Size-8½ x 11, Sheetfed press, 60 pages, No Color, Newsprint, Looseleaf
Subscriptions: Indv. $134, Can. $134, For. $164
Circulation: Total-2,250
List Rental: Actives: $85/M

McGraw-Hill's Report on
Performance Materials

Publishing Co: McGraw-Hill, 1221 Ave. of the Americas, 36th Fl., New York, NY 10020-1095 Tel # (212) 512-2000 Fax # (212) 512-6590; Title Tel # (202) 463-1600
Personnel: Publisher-Thomas Woodal, Editor-Richard Piellischl
General Info: Yr. Est. 1987, Bi-weekly
Subscriptions: Indv. $367

Medical Materials Update
See: MEDICINE

Microporous Materials
Technology News *Business*

Publishing Co: Business Communications Co., 25 Van Zant St., Ste.13, Norwalk, CT 06855-1781; Title Tel # (203) 853-4266 Title Fax # (203) 853-0348
Personnel: Publisher-Louis Naturman, Editor-Dick Hilton, Editor-Karen Lindseys, Mktg. Dir.-Robert Butler
Editorial Description: Explores, analyzes and reports on the science, technology and business of sorbent polymers, inorganic sorbents, molecular sieves, zeolites, activated carbon, microsponges, chelates, clathrates, ion exchange resins.
General Info: Yr. Est. 1994, Monthly, Trim Size-8½ x 11, 14 pages, ISSN: 1077-6869
Subscriptions: Indv. $375, Can. $425, For. $425, $38/copy
Advertising: Inquire for rates.
List Rental: List Management Co.: W.I. Mail Marketing, 470 Main St. #317, Ridgefield, CT 06877-4516 Tel # (203) 438-6822, Fax # (203) 438-7756

Minnesota Chemist *Association*

Publishing Co: American Chemical Society, 1155 16th St. NW, Washington, DC 20036-4899 Tel # (202) 872-4600 Fax # (202) 872-6005; Title Tel # (612) 484-2435
General Info: Monthly, ISSN: 0026-5411
Subscriptions: Indv. $5
Advertising: Inquire for rates.

NASA STI Bulletin
See: AERONAUTICS/ASTRONAUTICS

NOx Report *Business*

Publishing Co: Fieldston Co., 1920 N Street, N.W., Ste. 210, Washington, DC 20036
Personnel: Publications Director-Jay Kumar, Editor-Sue Follett, Assoc. Ed.-Mike Harms, Mktg. Dir.-Laura Dowe
Editorial Description: News and analysis on NOx issues dealing with stationary and mobile sources.
General Info: Yr. Est. 1995, Irregular
Subscriptions: Indv. $415

National Agricultural
Chemicals Association
News *Association*

Publishing Co: Natl. Agricultural Chemicals Assn., 1156 15th St NW Ste 400, Washington, DC 20005-1704; Title Tel # (202) 296-1585
General Info: Bi-monthly

New Fuels Report
See: ENERGY

Octagon, The *Association*

Publishing Co: Lehigh Valley Section, American Chemical Society, 45 Charles Ave, Nazareth, PA 18064-1702; Title Tel # (215) 759-1715
Personnel: Editor-William C. Broad
Editorial Description: Meeting notices, local A.C.S. news, membership changes, meetings of other local related societies, national A.C.S. news.
General Info: Yr. Est. 1918, 8x/yr., Trim Size-5½ x 8½, Mimeo press, 8 pages, No Color
Subscriptions: Indv. $1
Circulation: (100% controlled), Total-850
Advertising: Inquire for rates.

Octane Week
See: PETROLEUM & NATURAL GAS

Pest Control Progress
See: GARDENING & HORTICULTURE

Pesticide & Toxic Chemical
News *Business*

Publishing Co: Food Chemical News, 1101 Pennsylvania Ave SE, Washington, DC 20003-2229
Parent Co.-CRC Press, Inc., Boca Raton; Title Tel # (202) 544-1980 Title Fax # (202) 546-3890
Personnel: Publisher-Marjorie Weiner, Editor-Sue Darcey, Circ. Dir.-Iris Shamaskin, Mktg. Dir.-Jill Casasola
Editorial Description: Weekly reports on hazardous wastes, pesticides, toxic substances and general issues of regulation and legislation.
General Info: (Formerly Pesticide Chemical News), Yr. Est. 1972, Weekly, Trim Size-8½ x 11, Sheetfed press, 35 pages, ISSN: 0146-0501, Ind/Abs/Online: Predicasts, 2 Color
Subscriptions: Indv. $887

Pesticide & Toxic Chemical News Guide
See: AGRICULTURE

PetroChemical News *Business*

Publishing Co: William F. Bland Co., 111 Cloister Court, Suite 114, PO Box 16666, Chapel Hill, NC 27516-6666; Title Tel # (919) 490-0700 Title Fax # (919) 490-3002
Personnel: Publisher-William Bland, Editor-Susan D. Kensil, Editor-Christopher R. Schultz, Circ. Mgr.-Mollie Sandor, Promotion Mgr.-David M. Bland
Editorial Description: Weekly report of current developments in the worldwide petrochemical business.
General Info: Yr. Est. 1963, Weekly, Trim Size-8½ x 11, Sheetfed press, 4 pages, ISSN: 0031-6342, No Color, Looseleaf
Subscriptions: Indv. $667, Can. $527, For. $527, $15/copy
List Rental: List Management Co.: Manager: Mollie Sandor; Media Marketplace, 140 Terry Drive, P.O. Box 500, Newtown, PA 18940-0500 Tel # (215) 968-5020, Fax # (215) 968-9410, Actives: 8,797, $80/M

Petrochemical Industry - Worldwide
See: PETROLEUM & NATURAL GAS

R & D Innovator
See: TELECOMMUNICATIONS

RCRA Land Disposal
Restrictions-A Guide to
Compliance *Business, Association*

Publishing Co: Elsevier Science Inc., 655 Avenue of the Americas, New York, NY 10010-5107
Tel # (212) 633-3916 Fax # (212) 633-3913 Parent Co.-Reed Elsevier, New York
Personnel: Publisher-Drew McCoy, Editor-Eric Weber, Production Dir.-Heather Nutting
Editorial Description: Instruction pertaining to EPA land disposal restrictions of hazardous waste.
General Info: Annually, Looseleaf
Subscriptions: $70/copy
Acquistions: Publication Sold

Refining & Gas Processing Worldwide
See: PETROLEUM & NATURAL GAS

Resin Review *Consumer*

Publishing Co: Rohm & Haas Co., Independence Mall West, Philadelphia, PA 19105;
Title Tel # (215) 592-3480
Personnel: Editor-Thomas Hansen, Art Dir.-J. Gary Ryan
Editorial Description: Detailed discussions of synthetic resins manufactured by Rohm & Haas.
General Info: Yr. Est. 1951, Quarterly, Trim Size-8½ x 11, Offset press, 24 pages, 2 Color
Circulation: (100% controlled), Total-20,000

Retort *Business, Association*

Publishing Co: Chemists' Club Library, 40 W 45th St, New York, NY 10036-4202;
Title Tel # (212) 532-7649
Personnel: Editor-June Rosse
General Info: (Formerly Chemist's Club News), Monthly

Risk Management Program Handbook
See: MANUFACTURING

Rohm and Haas Reporter *Consumer*

Publishing Co: Rohm & Haas Co., Independence Mall West, Philadelphia, PA 19105
Tel # (215) 592-3480; Title Tel # (215) 592-3482
Personnel: Editor-Henry Gambino, Ph. D., Art Dir.-Anthony Ferrara
Editorial Description: Articles focus on worldwide use of Rohm and Haas chemical products.
General Info: Yr. Est. 1943, Quarterly, Trim Size-8½ x 11, 32 pages, 4 Color
Circulation: Total-90,000

SARA Title III:
Regulations & Keyword
Index *Business, Association*

Publishing Co: Elsevier Science Inc., 655 Avenue of the Americas, New York, NY 10010-5107
Tel # (212) 633-3916 Fax # (212) 633-3913 Parent Co.-Reed Elsevier, New York
Personnel: Publisher-Drew McCoy, Editor-Eric Weber, Production Dir.-Heather Nutting
Editorial Description: Information on Federal EPA SARA regulations.
General Info: Annually, Looseleaf
Subscriptions: $30/copy
Acquistions: Publication Sold
List Rental: Rents Lists

SDA Newsletter

Publishing Co: Soap & Detergent Assn., 475 Park Ave S, New York, NY 10016-6947;
Title Tel # (212) 725-1262
Personnel: Editor-Mary Ansbro
Editorial Description: This newsletter is a member service & is sent to SDA member companies only.
General Info: Yr. Est. 1975, Monthly, 6 pages
Circulation: Total-1,000

SOCMA Newsletter *Business*

Publishing Co: Synthetic Organic Chemical Manufacturers Assn., Inc., 1100 New York Ave. NW, Suite 1090, Washington, DC 20005-3934; Title Tel # (202) 659-0060 Title Fax # (202) 659-1699
Personnel: Editor-Eric Christensen
Editorial Description: Regulatory and legislative information on the organic chemical industry.
General Info: Yr. Est. 1980, Bi-weekly, Trim Size-8½ x 11, Mimeo press, 6 pages, No Color
Circulation: Total-1,109

Speaking of Safety
See: SAFETY

TAPPI Technical
Information Sheets *Consumer, Association*

Publishing Co: Sponsor-Tappi, TAPPI, Box 105113, Tech Park/ATL, Atlanta, GA 30348-5113;
Title Tel # (404) 446-1400
Personnel: Publisher, Editor-Kathy Harris
General Info: Every two years, Sheetfed press, Ind/Abs/Online: ABIPC, No Color, Matte, Looseleaf
Subscriptions: Indv. $70
Circulation: Total-400

TAPPI Test Methods *Consumer, Association*

Publishing Co: Sponsor-Tappi, TAPPI, Box 105113, Tech Park/ATL, Atlanta, GA 30348-5113;
Title Tel # (404) 446-1400
Personnel: Publisher, Editor, Promotion Dir.-Kathy Harris
General Info: Yr. Est. 1950, Every two years, Sheetfed press, Ind/Abs/Online: ABIPC, No Color, Matte, Perfect bound, Looseleaf
Subscriptions: Indv. $50, $5/copy
Circulation: Total-400

Thermoanalysis News *Business*

Publishing Co: Perkin-Elmer Corp., 761 Main Ave., Norwalk, CT 06859-0105 Tel # (203) 762-6023 Fax # (203) 764-2892
Personnel: Mng. Editor-Anneliese Lust
General Info: Quarterly

Toxic Chemicals Litigation Reporter
See: LAW

U.S.I. News *Business*

Publishing Co: U.S. Industrial Chemicals Co., 11500 Northlake Dr, Cincinnati, OH 45249-1642;
Title Tel # (513) 530-7330
Personnel: Editor-T.T. Townsend
Editorial Description: Sent to customers and prospects. Articles on polyethylene, vinylacetate, sulfuric acid, ethylalcohol (general interest) and plant expansions.
General Info: Yr. Est. 1960, Quarterly, Offset press, 8 pages, 2 Color, Newsprint, Saddle-stitched
Circulation: Total-25,000

Underground Storage Tank Guide
See: ENVIRONMENT & ECOLOGY

WACA News
See: AGRICULTURE

Wasteline *Business, Association*

Publishing Co: New York State Department of Environmental Conservation, Division of Water, 50 Wolf Rd., Albany, NY 12233 Tel # (518) 457-3014 Fax # (518) 485-7786
Personnel: Editor-Brian Swinn
Editorial Description: Solid waste management issues in New York.
General Info: Yr. Est. 1987, Quarterly, Trim Size-8½ x 11, Sheetfed press, 12 pages, 2 Color, Recycled, Saddle-stitched
Subscriptions: Free
Circulation: Total-14,000

Wiley Static SIMS Library, The
Business　　CPM: **$41**

Publishing Co: John Wiley & Sons, Inc., 605 Third Avenue, New York, NY 10158-0012 Tel # (212) 850-6000 Fax # (212) 850-6088
Personnel: Editor-Jonathon Agbenyega, Production Mgr.-Cliff Morgan, Mktg. Mgr.-Sue Stewart
Editorial Description: A comprehensive collection of static SIMS spectra will enable the analyst to fully access the mass spectral power of the technique for the analysis of materials with complex surface chemistry.
General Info: Semi-annually, Looseleaf
Subscriptions: Indv. $2,250
Circulation: Total-35,000
Advertising: $1,455.

World Feedstocks
Consumer

Publishing Co: SRI Intl. -Chemical Bus. Research Division, 333 Ravenswood Ave, Menlo Park, CA 94025-3453 Tel # (415) 859-3627 Fax # (415) 859-4623; Title Tel # (415) 326-6200
Personnel: Editor-Hugh Tobin
Editorial Description: The World Petrochemicals Program is a comprehensive easy-to-use source of information on the international petrochemical industry including producers, capacities, locations, technology/feedstocks, production by process, import, exports, & consumption by end-use as well as interpretive text & many other features such as some price & production cost data.
General Info: Yr. Est. 1974, Annually, Looseleaf

CHILDREN

4-H Child Care

Publishing Co: Cornell Cooperative Extension/Clinton County, Clinton County, RFD 6, Box 16B, Plattsburgh, NY 1290; Title Tel # (518) 561-7450
Personnel: Editor-Peggy Clifford

ADHD Report
See: PSYCHOLOGY

ASDC Newsletter
See: DENTAL

Adventures for Kids-Newsletter

Publishing Co: Adventures for Kids, 3457 Telegraph Rd, Ventura, CA 93003-3314; Title Tel # (805) 650-9688 Title Fax # (805) 650-5962
Personnel: Editor-Jody Fickens
General Info: Yr. Est. 1974
Circulation: Total-24,000

Adventures in Movement
See: SOCIAL SERVICES & WELFARE

Association for Bright Children Newsmagazine
Consumer, Association

Publishing Co: Assn. for Bright Children of Ontario, 2 Bloor St. W., #100-156, Toronto, ON M4W 2G7 Canada; Title Tel # (416) 925-6136
Personnel: Editor-Margaret Tofflemire
General Info: Quarterly, Trim Size-8½ x 11, 8 pages, ISSN: 1185-362x
Subscriptions: Can. $30
Circulation: Total-2,000
Advertising: Inquire for rates. Accepts Inserts.

Association for Child Psychoanalysis Newsletter
See: PSYCHOLOGY

Black Child Advocate
Association

Publishing Co: Black Child Development Inst, 1023 15th Street NW, Suite 600, Washington, DC 20005; Title Tel # (202) 387-1281 Title Fax # (202) 234-1738
Personnel: Editor-Merlene Vassal
Editorial Description: Provides public policy and legislative updates, reports on NBCDI's local service programs for Black children, current issues reports, and more.
General Info: Yr. Est. 1973, Quarterly, 8 pages, 2 Color, Coated, Saddle-stitched
Subscriptions: Indv. $13
Acquistions: Publication Bought, Publication Sold
Circulation: Total-3,000
List Rental: Rents Lists
Printing Co: Corporate Press, 403 Brightseat Rd., Landover, MD 20785-4706 Tel # (301) 499-9200, Fax # (301) 499-5435

Books of Wonder
See: BOOKS & BOOK TRADE

Brown University Child and Adolescent Behavior Letter, The
Business

Publishing Co: Manisses Communications Group, Inc., PO Box 3357, Providence, RI 02906-0757; Title Tel # (401) 831-6020 Title Tel # (401) 861-6370
Personnel: Publisher-Fraser Lang, Editor-Lewis Lipsitt, Ph.D., Circ. Mgr.-Deb Zajas, Mktg. Dir.-Betty Lang
Editorial Description: Provides updates on news practices, policies, theories and trends on the problems of children and adolescents growing up.
General Info: (Formerly Brown University Child Behavior & Human Develop Letter), Yr. Est. 1985, Monthly, Offset press, 8 pages, ISSN: 1058-1073
Subscriptions: Indv. $97, Inst. $127, Can. $137, For. $147
Circulation: Total-3,000
List Rental: List Management Co.: Conrad Direct, Inc., 300 Knickerbocker Road, Creskill, NJ 07626 Tel # (201) 567-3200, Fax # (201) 567-4959, Actives: 2,464, $90/M, Expires: 2,020, $90/M
Printing Co: Newsletter Press, 76 Valley St, East Providence, RI 02914-4424 Tel # (401) 438-5352

CBC Features
Business, Association

Publishing Co: Children's Book Council, Inc., 568 Broadway, Ste. 404, New York, NY 10012-0000 Fax # (212) 966-2073; Title Tel # (212) 966-1990
Editorial Description: Children's books & reading--publishing, bookselling, teaching, librarian-ship.
General Info: (Formerly Calendar), Yr. Est. 1945, Semi-annually, Trim Size-5.5 x 8.5, Offset press, 16 pages, ISSN: 0008-0721, Other, Saddle-stitched
Subscriptions: Indv. $60, Inst. $60
Circulation: Total-36,500

CDF Reports
Association

Publishing Co: Children's Defense Fund, 25 E St NW, Washington, DC 20001-1591 Tel # (202) 328-8787 Fax # (202) 662-3530; Title Tel # (202) 628-8787
Personnel: Publications Director-Donna M. Jablonski, Editor-David Heffernam, Production Mgr.-Janis Johnston
Editorial Description: Teen pregnancy prevention.
General Info: Monthly, Trim Size-8½ x 11, Sheetfed press, 8 pages, ISSN: 0276-6531, 2 Color, Matte, Other
Subscriptions: Indv. $30, $4/copy
Circulation: Total-8,500
Printing Co: Doyle Printing & Offset, 6911 Old Landover Rd, Landover, MD 20785-1503 Tel # (301) 322-4800, Fax # (301) 372-2860

CIRA Bulletin
See: EDUCATION

C.S.T. Connection
See: BUSINESS & INDUSTRY

California Tomorrow
See: EDUCATION

Camps Canada
See: PARKS & RECREATION AREAS

Careers Bridge Newsletter
See: EDUCATION

Catalyst: Voices of Chicago School Reform
See: EDUCATION

Cherokee Boys Club-Newsletter & Cherokee Voice
See: ETHNIC

Chicago Union Teacher
See: LABOR UNION

Chiefline
See: SCHOOL ADMINISTRATION

Child and Adolescent Psychopharmacology News
See: PSYCHOLOGY

Child Assessment News
See: PSYCHOLOGY

Child Care ActioNews
Business, Association

Publishing Co: Child Care Action Campaign, 330 7th Ave., 17th fl., New York, NY 10001; Title Tel # (212) 239-0138 Title Fax # (212) 268-6515
Personnel: Editor-Dolores Schaefer
Editorial Description: Research, legislative reports, innovative programs, resources, calendar on child care issues across country.
General Info: Yr. Est. 1983, Bi-monthly, Trim Size-8½ x 11, 8 pages, 2 Color
Subscriptions: Indv. $25, Inst. $100, Free With Membership

Child Development Research News
See: SOCIAL SERVICES & WELFARE

Child Health Talk
See: HEALTH

Child Labor Monitor
See: CONSUMER INTERESTS

Child Protection Report   *Business*

Publishing Co: Business Publishers, Inc., 951 Pershing Dr., Silver Spring, MD 20910-4464
  Tel # (301) 589-5103 Fax # (301) 589-8493; Title Tel # (301) 587-6300 Title Fax # (301) 587-1081
Personnel: Publisher-Eric Easton, Editor-Linda Roeder, Circ. Mgr.-Kathleen Harrow, Promotion Dir.-
  Connie Arnold
Editorial Description: The only national newsletter covering programs helping children and youth in
  the U.S. Broad coverage of physical and sexual abuse, health services, juvenile justice, and
  community services.
General Info: Yr. Est. 1975, Bi-weekly, Trim Size-8½ x 11, Desktop press, 8 pages, ISSN: 0147-
  1260, Ind/Abs/Online: Newsnet and Predicasts, No Color, Recycled
Subscriptions: Indv. $221, Can. $221, For. $234
Advertising: Accepts Inserts.
List Rental: List Management Co.: Manager: Don Peterson; BPI Direct, 951 Pershing Dr., Silver
  Spring, MD 20910-4464 Tel # (301) 585-5976, Fax # (301) 587-4530
Printing Co: Newsletter Press, 930-32 Bonifant St., Silver Spring, CT 20910

Child Support Report

Publishing Co: Office of Child Support Enforcement, 370 L'enfant Promenade S.W., 4th Floor,
  Washington, DC 20447-0001; Title Tel # (202) 401-9373
Personnel: Editor-Ann Slayton
General Info: Yr. Est. 1979, Monthly, Sheetfed press, 8 pages
Circulation: Total-15,000

Child Welfare Report (CWR)
See: SOCIAL SERVICES & WELFARE

Children & Youth Funding Report
See: PHILANTHROPY

Children's Book News   *Consumer*

Publishing Co: Children's Book Center, 35 Spadina Rd., Toronto, ON M5R 2S9 Canada;
  Title Tel # (416) 975-0010
Personnel: Publisher-Debbie Rogosin, Editor-Margaret Milnes, Art Dir.-Blair Kerrigan
Editorial Description: Information on Canadian children's books, reviews, interviews, new listings,
  general information.
General Info: Yr. Est. 1978, Quarterly, Trim Size-8½ x 11, 20 pages, ISSN: 0705-0033, 2 Color,
  Newsprint, Saddle-stitched
Circulation: Total-40,000

Children's Historical Newsletter
See: HISTORY

Children's Hospice
International Newsletter   *Business, Association*

Publishing Co: Children's Hospice Intl., 1850 M. St. NW, Ste. 900, Washington, DC 20036-5803
  Fax # (703) 684-0330; Title Tel # (703) 684-0330 Title Fax # (703) 684-0226
Personnel: Publisher-Ann Armstrong, Dailey, Editor-Ann Armstrong Dailey
General Info: Yr. Est. 1983, Quarterly, Trim Size-9 x 11, 8 pages, Matte
Subscriptions: Indv. $45, Inst. $275, Free With Membership
Circulation: Total-6,000

Children's Residential Treatment News
See: PSYCHOLOGY

Children's Video Review
Newsletter

Publishing Co: Children's Video Review Newsletter, 16765 Lena Ct., Grass Valley, CA 95949-7369;
  Title Tel # (916) 273-7471 Title Fax # (916) 273-6542
Personnel: Editor, Pack. Suppl.-Eveline P. Carsman, PhD
Editorial Description: Reviews selected children's videos released within 2 months of publication
  date. Discusses educational, literary & recreational content; interest level; and age appropriateness
  among other topics. Cumulative index by vol.
General Info: Yr. Est. 1987, Bi-monthly, Trim Size-8½ x 11, Sheetfed press, 8 pages, ISSN: 0895-
  2094, Ind/Abs/Online: Media Review Index, Color-cover, Matte
Subscriptions: Indv. $36, Can. $40, For. $46, $6/copy
Circulation: Total-220
Printing Co: Account Manager: Clint Graham; Printman, 13253 Brunswick Rd, Grass Valley, CA
  95945-9388 Tel # (416) 273-7354

Children's Writer
See: BOOKS & BOOK TRADE

Communique
See: SOCIAL SERVICES & WELFARE

Compassion Today   *Consumer, Association*

Publishing Co: Compassion Canada, 99 Enterprise Dr., S., London, ON N6N 1B9 Canada;
  Title Tel # (519) 668-0224 Title Fax # (519) 685-1107
Personnel: Art Dir.-Trish Sheeler
Editorial Description: Our publication concerns itself with child development activities & programs in
  developing countries of the world in the context of Christian response to people who are in need of
  various kinds of assistance.
General Info: (Formerly CORD), Yr. Est. 1980, Quarterly, Trim Size-8½ x 11, Web press, 16 pages,
  4 Color, Coated, Saddle-stitched
Subscriptions: Free To Qualified Recipient
Circulation: Total-17,000
Printing Co: Commercial Print Craft, 1193 Dundas St., PO Box 24023, Woodstock, ON N4S 7Y5
  Canada Tel # (519) 539-4871, Fax # (519) 539-9763

Crossroads
See: HISTORY

Cryer, The
See: SOCIAL SERVICES & WELFARE

Day Care Guide   *Business*

Publishing Co: Day Care Guide, PO Box 11885, Reno, NV 89510-1885; Title Tel # (702) 333-6651
Personnel: Publisher, Editor-Mary Pat Eymann
Editorial Description: Training for those who work in child day care facilities.
General Info: Yr. Est. 1991, Monthly, 4 pages, 2 Color
Subscriptions: $18/copy

Day Care Information
Service

Publishing Co: United Communications Group, 11300 Rockville Pike, Ste. 1100, Rockville, MD
  20852-3030 Tel # (301) 816-8950 Fax # (301) 816-8945; Title Tel # (301) 961-8700
  Title Fax # (301) 961-8666
Personnel: Publisher-Richard Hadley, Editor-Charles Pekow, Circ. Mgr.-Sharon Welch
Editorial Description: Washington news on day care funding; practical guidance on organizing day
  care services.
General Info: Bi-weekly
Subscriptions: Indv. $184, $7/copy
Acquistions: Publication Bought
List Rental: List Management Co.: PRS List Management, 222 Teal Ave., POB 6482, Syracuse, NY
  13217-6482 Tel # (315) 472-1224, Fax # (315) 472-1235, Actives: $85/M

Day Care USA   *Business*

Publishing Co: United Communications Group, 11300 Rockville Pike, Ste. 1100, Rockville, MD
  20852-3030 Tel # (301) 816-8950 Fax # (301) 816-8945; Title Tel # (301) 961-8700
Personnel: Publisher-Richard Hadley
Editorial Description: Timely information for day care professionals.
General Info: Yr. Est. 1972, Bi-weekly
Subscriptions: $7/copy
Acquistions: Publication Bought
List Rental: Actives: $125/M

Dellcrest News

Publishing Co: Dellcrest Children's Centre, Community Relations, 1645 Sheppard Avenue W.,
  Downsview, ON M3M 2X4 Canada; Title Tel # (416) 633-0515 Title Fax # (416) 633-7141
Personnel: Editor-Kim Balfour
Editorial Description: Covers agency programs, services, mandate, treatment philosophy,
  fundraising, volunteer activities, client/donor/volunteer profiles.
General Info: (Formerly Dellcrest Children's Ctr. Newsletter), Yr. Est. 1966, Semi-annually, Trim Size-
  8½ x 11, Web press, 4 pages, Color, Coated
Acquistions: Publication Bought
Circulation: Total-3,500

Digital Kids Report, The
See: COMPUTERS & AUTOMATION

Discoveries

Publishing Co: Children's Ministries, 6401 The Paseo, Kansas City, MO 64131;
  Title Tel # (816) 633-3700
Personnel: Editor-Molly Mitchell
General Info: Yr. Est. 1920, Weekly, Trim Size-8½ x 11, 8 pages, 2 Color, Looseleaf
Subscriptions: Indv. $6
Circulation: Total-90,000

ERIC/EECE Newsletter
See: EDUCATION

Earth Patrol
See: ENVIRONMENT & ECOLOGY

Emerald City Mirror

Publishing Co: Royal Club of Oz, Box 714, New York, NY 10011; Title Tel # (212) 989-3270
  Title Fax # (212) 989-1203
Editorial Description: The offical newsletter of the Royal Club of Oz, the Emerald City Mirror
  stimulates young imaginations and encourages a love of reading through an exciting combination of
  Oz stories (both old and new), contests, puzzles, games, activities and news articles.
General Info: Yr. Est. 1991, Bi-monthly, Trim Size-8½ x 11, Offset press, 12 pages, No Color, Matte,
  Other
Subscriptions: Indv. $10, Free With Membership
Printing Co: Eagle Press, 75 S Church St, Pittsfield, MA 01201-6132 Tel # (413) 477-7311

Exploring 1
See: RELIGIOUS & THEOLOGICAL

Exploring 2
See: RELIGIOUS & THEOLOGICAL

Five Owls
See: LITERATURE & LINGUISTICS

Forum
See: EDUCATION

Growing Child

Publishing Co: Dunn & Hargitt, 22 N. 2nd St., Ste. 620, Lafayette, IN 47902-0620;
Title Tel # (317) 423-2624 Title Fax # (317) 423-4495
Personnel: Publisher-Dennis D. Dunn, Editor-Nancy Kleckner, Art Dir.-Bruce Graves
Editorial Description: Development newsletter for parents of children ages birth to six years of age.
General Info: Yr. Est. 1971, Monthly, Trim Size-8½ x 11, Offset press, 6 pages, 2 Color
Subscriptions: Indv. $20, Inst. $12, Can. $26, For. $50
Circulation: Total-100,000
List Rental: List Management Co.: 21st Century Marketing, 2 Dubon Ct, Farmingdale, NY 11735-1012 Tel # (516) 293-8550, Fax # (516) 293-8974, Actives: 128,112, $70/M, Hotline: 16,399, $75/M

Growing Child Research Review

Publishing Co: Dunn & Hargitt, 22 N. 2nd St., Ste. 620, Lafayette, IN 47902-0620;
Title Tel # (317) 423-2624 Title Fax # (317) 423-4495
Personnel: Publisher-Dennis Dunn, Editor-Nancy Kleckner
Editorial Description: Child research updates from over 80 journals and publications.
General Info: Yr. Est. 1983, Monthly, Trim Size-8½ x 11, Sheetfed press, 8 pages, ISSN: 0737-0318, Color, Newsprint
Subscriptions: Indv. $36, Can. $42, $3/copy
Circulation: Total-2,000

Growing Together

Publishing Co: Dunn & Hargitt, 22 N. 2nd St., Ste. 620, Lafayette, IN 47902-0620;
Title Tel # (317) 423-2624 Title Fax # (317) 423-4495
Personnel: Publisher-Dennis Dunn, Editor-Nancy Kleckner
Editorial Description: Written for parents of preschool children--covers child's growth & development, ideas for activities, reading suggestions.
General Info: Yr. Est. 1985, Monthly
Subscriptions: Indv. $30

Growing Up

Publishing Co: Dunn & Hargitt, 22 N. 2nd St., Ste. 620, Lafayette, IN 47902-0620;
Title Tel # (317) 423-2624 Title Fax # (317) 423-4495
Editorial Description: Book filled with single-page newsletters which cover an entire school year.
Subscriptions: Indv. $10

HIV - Drug Exposure & Foster Care: Network Bulletin
See: SOCIAL SERVICES & WELFARE

Happenings
Business, Association

Publishing Co: Childhaven, 316 Broadway, Seattle, WA 98122-5325; Title Tel # (206) 624-6477
Personnel: Publisher, Editor-Wendy Prescott
Editorial Description: Information, updates, and highlights of associations work and events.
General Info: (Formerly Provider), Yr. Est. 1981, Quarterly, Trim Size-8½ x 11, Web press, 6 pages, 2 Color, Newsprint
List Rental: List Management Co.: Labels & Lists, Bellevue, WA 98005
Printing Co: Thompson Printing, 401 Dexter Ave N, Seattle, WA 98109-4704

IDRA Newsletter
See: EDUCATION

Illustratotor's Swap incl JW Anglund Collectors News
Business, Association

Publishing Co: AC Bergin, P.O. Box 105, Amherst, NH 03031; Title Tel # (603) 673-1885
Title Fax # (508) 649-6905
Personnel: Publisher-Ann Bergin
Editorial Description: Bringing together collectors of the works of illustrators & designers
General Info: Yr. Est. 1995, Irregular, Trim Size-8.5 x 11, 6 pages
Circulation: Total-200, Readership-200
Advertising: Inquire for rates. Accepts Inserts.

In Contact
See: RELIGIOUS & THEOLOGICAL

Inclusion Times
See: DISABILITY

It's Our World
See: RELIGIOUS & THEOLOGICAL

Jerome Riker Intl. Study of Organized Persecution of Children Newsletter

Publishing Co: Child Development Research, 30 Soundview Ln, Sands Point, NY 11050-1341;
Title Tel # (516) 883-3850
Personnel: Publisher-Judith Kestenberg, Editor-Shirley Jucovy, Circ. Mgr.-Maria Morroco, Circ. Mgr., Art Dir., Promotion Dir.-Maria Morrocu
Editorial Description: Review books & articles on child persecution during the Holocaust.
General Info: Yr. Est. 1984, Semi-annually, Trim Size-8½ x 11, Sheetfed press, 13 pages, No Color, Newsprint
Subscriptions: Indv. $35
Acquistions: Publication Bought, Publication Sold
Circulation: Total-5,000

Joan Walsh Anglund Collector's News
Consumer, Association

Publishing Co: Joan Walsh Anglund Collector's News, PO Box 105, Amherst, NH 03031-0105;
Title Tel # (603) 673-1885
Personnel: Publisher-Ann Bergin
Editorial Description: For collectors of children's illustrator Joan Walsh Anglund's art.
General Info: Yr. Est. 1984, Annually, Trim Size-8½ x 11, 25 pages
Subscriptions: Indv. $15
Circulation: Total-300
Advertising: Inquire for rates. Accepts Inserts.

KIDStuff
See: HOSPITALS & NURSING HOMES

Kid News
See: APPAREL & ACCESSORIES

KidTECH News
See: EDUCATION

Kidfit Newsletter
Consumer

Publishing Co: LJK Wellness Corp., 130 W 30th St Fl 15, New York, NY 10001-4004
Tel # (212) 279-3001 Fax # (212) 643-8470
Personnel: Publisher, Editor-Edwin Lewis
Editorial Description: Parent's guide for giving their children ages 2-12 a healthier lifestyle.
General Info: Yr. Est. 1994, Monthly, Trim Size-8½ x 11, 6 pages, No Color
Subscriptions: Indv. $28

Kids Club News
Consumer

Publishing Co: Fox Kids Club, 6130 Sun Bay, Westerville, OH 43081; Title Tel # (614) 895-2800
Personnel: Editor-Tammy Adcock
Editorial Description: Club newsletter for kids who watch Fox television.
General Info: Bi-weekly, Trim Size-8½ x 11, 4 pages
Circulation: Total-311,000
Advertising: Inquire for rates.

Kids Rhyme Newsletter - Stories, Games & More

Publishing Co: Prosperity & Profits Unlimited, PO Box 416, Denver, CO 80201-0416;
Title Tel # (303) 575-5676
Personnel: Publisher-A. Doyle
General Info: Yr. Est. 1991, Annually, Trim Size-8½ x 11, ISSN: 0738-7431
Subscriptions: Indv. $4, Inst. $4, Can. $8, For. $10, $4/copy
Circulation: Total-1,500

Koala Club News
Association

Publishing Co: Zoological Society of San Diego, PO Box 551, San Diego, CA 92112-0551;
Title Tel # (619) 231-1515 Title Fax # (619) 557-3970
Personnel: Editor-Karen Worley
Editorial Description: For children ages 15 and under. Features stories about animals, conservation, the San Diego Zoo and the San Diego Wild Animal Park.
General Info: Yr. Est. 1974, Quarterly, 8 pages, 2 Color
Subscriptions: Free With Membership
Circulation: Total-110,000
Printing Co: Neyenesch Printers, 2750 Kettner Blvd, San Diego, CA 92101-1295
Tel # (619) 297-2281, Fax # (619) 299-7250

Kobrin Letter, The
Professional

Publishing Co: Kobrin Letter, The, 732 Greer Rd, Palo Alto, CA 94303-3022;
Title Tel # (415) 856-6658 Title Fax # (415) 856-6658
Personnel: Publisher, Editor-Beverly Kobrin
Editorial Description: Reviews children's nonfiction books for educators.
General Info: Yr. Est. 1980, 6x/yr., Trim Size-8½ x 11, Sheetfed press, 4 pages, ISSN: 0271-1990, No Color, Newsprint
Subscriptions: Indv. $12, Can. $14, For. $15, $2/copy

Last Resort

Publishing Co: End Violence Against the Next Generation, Inc., 977 Keeler Ave, Berkeley, CA 94708-1440; Title Tel # (510) 527-0454
Personnel: Editor-Adah Maurer, Ph. D., Art Dir.-Carolyn McCoy
Editorial Description: Corporal punishment of school children; research, surveys, opinions, court cases, protest, abuses, editorials, anecdotes, its relation to delinquency, vandalism, aggressive violence etc.
General Info: Yr. Est. 1972, Quarterly, Trim Size-8½ x 11, Offset press, 28 pages, Color-cover
Subscriptions: Indv. $10, $2/copy
Circulation: Total-1,000
Printing Co: P.S. Printing, 1622 Castro St, Oakland, CA 94612-1347

Link, The

Publishing Co: Intl. Society for Prevention of Child Abuse and Neglect, 1205 Oneida St, Denver, CO 80220-2944; Title Fax # (303) 329-3523

Little Times, The
See: FAMILY

Manitoba Assn. for Schooling At Home, Newsletter
See: EDUCATION

Mel Gabler's Newsletter
See: EDUCATION

Mind Garden Newsletter, The
See: FAMILY

Mother-To-Mother
See: FAMILY

Music Time
See: RELIGIOUS & THEOLOGICAL

NACHRI Newsletter
See: HOSPITALS & NURSING HOMES

NCCCC Newsletter   *Association*

Publishing Co: National Coalition for Campus Child Care, Inc., PO Box 258, Cascade, WI 53011-0258; Title Tel # (414) 528-7080 Title Fax # (414) 528-8653
General Info: Semi-annually
Subscriptions: Indv. $35, Inst. $90

NPA Bulletin
See: BABY

National Center for Children
in Poverty News & Issues   *Consumer*

Publishing Co: NCCP, 154 Haven Ave, New York, NY 10032-1180; Title Tel # (212) 927-8793
Editorial Description: Poverty issues concerning health and safety of children.
General Info: Tri-annually, Trim Size-8½ x 11, 2 Color, Matte

National Homeschool Assn. Newsletter
See: EDUCATION

National Reye's Syndrome Foundation-In the News
See: HEALTH

Native Child Advocate   *Consumer*

Publishing Co: Native American Educational Services College, 2838 W. Peterson, Chicago, IL 60659; Title Tel # (312) 761-5000
Editorial Description: A publication of the Native American Child & Family Resource Center. Sharing information about the progress of the initiative and about other programs and issues impacting on Native children.
General Info: Quarterly

New Beginnings
See: BABY

New Moon Network
See: FAMILY

News Digest
See: DISABILITY

News n' Notes
See: EDUCATION

Newsletter of the International Study of Organized Persecution of Children
See: CIVIL RIGHTS

On Location
See: PSYCHOLOGY

Parent & Preschooler
See: EDUCATION

Pennsylvania Partnerships
for Children   *Business*

Publishing Co: Sponsor-Annenberg Foundation, The, Pennsylvania Partnerships for Children, 931 N. Front St., Ste. 101, Harrisburg, PA 17102-3422; Title Tel # (717) 236-5680
Title Fax # (717) 236-7745
Personnel: Editor-Jennifer Williams
Editorial Description: A new public policy briefing paper series designed to provide background information and perspectives on current issues affecting children and families.
General Info: Quarterly, Trim Size-11 x 15½, 4 pages, 2 Color, Matte

Projects Communique
See: SOCIAL SERVICES & WELFARE

Raising Your Child's Self-
Esteem   *Consumer*

Publishing Co: JDI, Inc., PO Box 1003, North Wales, PA 19454-0003; Title Tel # (215) 699-4527
Personnel: Publisher-Deborah Connor, Publisher, Editor-Kevin Connor
Editorial Description: Parenting ideas, tips and techniques.
General Info: Monthly, Trim Size-8½ x 11, 8 pages, ISSN: 1071-8486, No Color, Matte
Subscriptions: Indv. $24

Reading Programs with
Stories that Educate,
Inform, Entertain and
Rhyme   *Consumer*

Publishing Co: Story Time Stories that Rhyme, PO Box 416, Denver, CO 80201-0416;
Tel # (303) 575-5676
Personnel: Publisher, Editor-A. Doyle
Editorial Description: Stories that educate, rhyme, entertain and inspire.
General Info: Yr. Est. 1989, Irregular, Trim Size-8½ x 11, Letrpr. press, Looseleaf
Subscriptions: Inst. $30, Can. $35, For. $35, $30/copy

Recycling Stories that Rhyme Newsletter
See: ENVIRONMENT & ECOLOGY

Reference Guide to
Counseling Children &
Adolescents   *Business*

Publishing Co: Manisses Communications Group, Inc., PO Box 3357, Providence, RI 02906-0757; Title Tel # (401) 831-6020 Title Fax # (401) 861-6370
Personnel: Publisher-Fraser Lang, Editor-Anne M. Christner, Ph.D., Circ. Mgr.-Deb Zajas, Mktg. Dir.-Betty Lang
General Info: Yr. Est. 1991, Annually, Looseleaf
Subscriptions: Indv. $198, Inst. $198, Can. $208, For. $238
Circulation: Total-1,000

Report on Preschool Programs
See: EDUCATION

Research Reports

Publishing Co: Children's Bureau, 330 Independence Ave., S.w., Washington, DC 20201-0001; Title Tel # (202) 963-6867
Personnel: Editor-Miss Dorothy E. Bradbury
Editorial Description: Reports of research on childrearing and child life.
General Info: Yr. Est. 1967
Subscriptions: $1/copy

SKOLE: The Journal of Alternative Education
See: EDUCATION

Six Months to Six Years
See: EDUCATION

Sport Scene
See: SPORTS & SPORTING GOODS

Stories that Rhyme, Every
Time Kids Pages   *Consumer*

Publishing Co: Story Time Stories that Rhyme, PO Box 416, Denver, CO 80201-0416;
Title Tel # (303) 575-5676
Personnel: Publisher-A. Doyle
Editorial Description: Stories that entertain, inspire, educate, and inform.
General Info: Yr. Est. 1992, Irregular, Trim Size-8½ x 11, 8 pages, ISSN: 1063-1380, No Color
Subscriptions: Inst. $5, Can. $7, For. $8, $5/copy

Story Rhyme Reproducible Newsletter
See: EDUCATION

Story Rhyme Word Mapping
See: CROSS-WORD PUZZLES

Story Time Stories That
Rhyme   *Consumer*

Publishing Co: Story Time Stories that Rhyme, PO Box 416, Denver, CO 80201-0416;
Title Tel # (303) 575-5676
Personnel: Publisher, Editor-A. Doyle
Editorial Description: Rhymed stories about plants, birds, & other topics.
General Info: Yr. Est. 1990, Quarterly, Trim Size-8½ x 11, Letrpr. press, 4 pages, ISSN: 1045-5515, No Color, Looseleaf
Subscriptions: Indv. $20, Inst. $20, Can. $23, For. $28, $5/copy

Teacher's PET Term Paper
See: EDUCATION

Teen Star Zine

Publishing Co: Gina Young, Box 22, 5863 Chevy Chase Pkwy NW, Washington, DC 20015
Editorial Description: A newsletter for kids 10-17 who want to pursue a career in the performing arts, put out by an aspiring 14-year old.
General Info: Trim Size-8.5 x 11, 4 pages
Subscriptions: Indv. $1

Texas Talk
Association

Publishing Co: Association for Retarded Citizens/Texas, PO Box 5368, Austin, TX 78763-5368
Tel # (517) 454-6694 Fax # (517) 454-4956; Title Tel # (512) 454-6694 Title Fax # (512) 464-4956
Personnel: Editor-Cheryl Sawyer
Editorial Description: Information regarding children & adults with mental retardation and developmental disabilities, legislation, education, employment.
General Info: Quarterly, Trim Size-17 x 11, Web press, 8 pages, Matte, Saddle-stitched
Subscriptions: Indv. $15, Free With Membership
Circulation: (100% controlled), Total-4,800

UNICEF Communique
See: SOCIAL SERVICES & WELFARE

Ultimate Early Childhood Music Resource
See: EDUCATION

Video-Rising to the Challenge
Consumer

Publishing Co: Parents Music Resource Center, 1500 Arlington Blvd, Arlington, VA 22209-3501; Title Tel # (703) 527-9466 Title Fax # (703) 527-9468
Editorial Description: Educate the public, especially parents, about the importance of learning the massages contained in popular music marketed to children and adolescents.
General Info: (Formerly Record), Quarterly, Trim Size-8$\frac{1}{2}$ x 11
Subscriptions: Indv. $25

WYO Network
See: EDUCATION

WarChild Monitor International

Publishing Co: Center on War & the Child, PO Box 487, Eureka Springs, AR 72632-0487; Title Tel # (501) 253-8900
Personnel: Publisher-Richard Parker, Editor-Samuel Hilburn
Editorial Description: Analysis of the impact of violence & war on children, news on governmental action impacting on children in war zones-research on how children are socialized to war & violence.
General Info: Quarterly, 8 pages, 2 Color
Subscriptions: Indv. $18, Inst. $23
Acquistions: Publication Bought

Washington Watch
See: BABY

YABA Framework
See: SPORTS & SPORTING GOODS

Yale Children's Health Letter
See: HEALTH

CIVIL RIGHTS

AAAA News
Association　　　　　**CPM: $333**

Publishing Co: American Association for Affirmative Action, 8335 Allison Pointe Trail, Ste. 250, Indianapolis, IN 46250-1686; Title Tel # (312) 549-1272 Title Fax # (312) 549-1271
Editorial Description: News of association activities and members. Articles of interest. Resources.
General Info: Yr. Est. 1987, Quarterly, Trim Size-8$\frac{1}{2}$ x 11, 12 pages, ISSN: 0896-8217, 15% ads, 2 Color
Subscriptions: Indv. $15, Free With Membership
Circulation: Total-1,500
Advertising: $500.
List Rental: Rents Lists

ACLU News
Association

Publishing Co: ACLU of Northern California, 1663 Mission St., San Francisco, CA 94103-2449; Title Tel # (415) 621-2493 Title Fax # (415) 255-1478
Personnel: Publisher-Dorothy Ehrlich, Circ. Mgr.-Sandy Holmes, Editor, Production Mgr., Promotion Dir.-Elaine Elinson
Editorial Description: Covers civil liberties issues; litigation, legislation & analysis.
General Info: Yr. Est. 1936, Bi-monthly, Trim Size-11 x 17, Web press, 8 pages, No Color, Newsprint, Other
Subscriptions: Indv. $20, Inst. $20, Free With Membership
Acquistions: Publication Bought
Circulation: Total-29,000
Printing Co: Howard Quinn Co., 298 Alabama St, San Francisco, CA 94103-4218
Tel # (415) 621-3750, Fax # (415) 621-0430

ADA Update
See: DISABILITY

ALMA Searchlight

Publishing Co: Adoptees Liberty Movement Assn., Box 154 Washington Bridge Sta., New York, NY 10033-0154
General Info: Semi-annually

Action Agenda
See: MEDIA & COMMUNICATIONS

Action on Colombia
Consumer

Publishing Co: Colombia Support Network, PO Box 1505, Madison, WI 53701
Editorial Description: Informs readers about the many & diverse activities of the organization, encourages involvement, & provides information missing from the coverage of most U.S. newspapers. The newsletter is a comprehensive but compact compilation of events in this part ofthe Americas & a much-needed antidote to the popular stereotype of Colombia.
General Info: 3x/yr., Trim Size-8$\frac{1}{2}$ x 11, 8 pages

Affirmative Action Compliance Manual for Federal Contractors
Business

Publishing Co: Bureau of National Affairs, Inc., 1231 25th St. NW, Bldg. N-200, Washington, DC 20037-1157; Title Tel # (202) 452-4200 Title Fax # (202) 822-8092
Personnel: Publisher-William A. Beltz, Editor-Susan Sala, Mng. Editor-Jeff Day, Circ. Mgr.-Gary C. Seltzer
Editorial Description: A two-binder service containing the official text of the office of Federal Contract Compliance Programs Manual & reports on related developments.
General Info: Yr. Est. 1975, Monthly, Trim Size-8$\frac{1}{2}$ x 11, Offset press, ISSN: 0148-8147, Looseleaf
Subscriptions: Indv. $340

Affirmative Action/EEO Update
Business, Association

Publishing Co: NYPER Publications, PO Box 662, Latham, NY 12110-0662 Fax # (518) 458-8582; Title Tel # (518) 786-1654
Personnel: Editor-Harvey Randall
Editorial Description: Summariizes important court and administrative rulings concerning civil rights, equal employment and affirmative action of interest to personnel administators and attorneys.
General Info: (Formerly Affirmative Action/EEO Personnel Notes), Yr. Est. 1985, Monthly, ISSN: 1071-7390
Subscriptions: Indv. $95, Inst. $95

Africa Fund
Association

Publishing Co: Advanstar Communications, 431 W 1st Street, Duluth, MN 55802-2065
Tel # (218) 723-9200 Fax # (218) 723-9457 Parent Co.-Advanstar Communications, Inc., Cleveland
Personnel: Editor-Rachael Kagan
General Info: Semi-annually

Agenda
Consumer, Association

Publishing Co: National Council of Laraza, 1111 19th St. NW, Washington, DC 20036-3603
Fax # (202) 289-8173; Title Tel # (202) 289-1380
Personnel: Editor-Lisa Navarrete, Editor-Martha Peredo
Editorial Description: News of interest to the Council membership and to the Latino community.
General Info: (Formerly Noticiaro), Yr. Est. 1979, Quarterly, Trim Size-8$\frac{1}{2}$ x 11, 20 pages, 2 Color
Subscriptions: Free
Circulation: Total-7,000

American Gay & Lesbian Atheist
See: GAY & LESBIAN INTEREST

Americans Before Columbus
See: ETHNIC

Anti-Sexism Newsletter

Publishing Co: Natl. Lawyers Guild-Santa Clara, 131 George St, San Jose, CA 95110-2116; Title Tel # (408) 292-0174

Association of New Gay & Lesbian Entrepreneurs
See: GAY & LESBIAN INTEREST

Bill of Rights Newsletter
Association

Publishing Co: Constitutional Rights Foundation, 601 S Kingsley Dr, Los Angeles, CA 90005-2319; Title Tel # (213) 487-5590
Editorial Description: Promotes a more meaningful teaching of the Constitution.
General Info: Yr. Est. 1971, Quarterly, Trim Size-8$\frac{1}{2}$ x 11, Web press, 24 pages, No Color
Subscriptions: $5/copy
Circulation: Total-20,000

Black Congressional Monitor
See: GOVERNMENT

Bread & Justice
Consumer, Association

Publishing Co: Interfaith Hunger Coalition of Southern California, 2449 Hyperion Ave Apt 100, Los Angeles, CA 90027-4760; Title Tel # (213) 913-7333 Title Fax # (213) 664-1725
Personnel: Editor-Jeannie Hwang
Editorial Description: Focuses on anti-poverty and anti-hunger issues with original articles, legislative updates, and general updates on relevant issues in California and the rest of the country.
General Info: Quarterly, 16 pages
Subscriptions: Indv. $20

CAA Newsletter

Publishing Co: Chinese for Affirmative Action, 17 Walter U Lum Pl, San Francisco, CA 94108-1890; Title Tel # (415) 274-6750
Personnel: Editor-Kathy Turner
General Info: Yr. Est. 1970, Monthly, Trim Size-8$\frac{1}{2}$ x 11, Offset press, 12 pages, No Color
Subscriptions: Indv. $25
Circulation: Total-2,000

CAN News
Association

Publishing Co: Cult Awareness Network, 2421 W Pratt Blvd # 1173, Chicago, IL 60645-4621; Title Tel # (312) 267-7777
Personnel: Editor-C. Kisser
Editorial Description: Summary of news on controversial groups considered cults.
General Info: Yr. Est. 1974, Monthly, Trim Size-8½ x 11, 8 pages
Subscriptions: Indv. $30, Can. $40, For. $40, $3/copy
Circulation: Total-2,000

CORAspondent
See: RELIGIOUS & THEOLOGICAL

CSI Newsletter
See: RELIGIOUS & THEOLOGICAL

Censorship News
Consumer

Publishing Co: National Coaliation Against Censorship, 275 7th Ave Fl 20, New York, NY 10001-6708; Title Tel # (212) 807-6222 Title Fax # (212) 807-6245
Editorial Description: Promotes and defends free speech, inquiry and expression.
General Info: Yr. Est. 1974, 5x/yr., Trim Size-8½ x 11, Offset press, 4 pages, ISSN: 0749-6001, 2 Color, Matte
Subscriptions: Indv. $30
Circulation: Readership-22,000
List Rental: List Management Co.: Names in the News-California, 1 Bush St Bsmt 3, San Francisco, CA 94104-4425 Tel # (415) 989-3350, Fax # (415) 433-7796

Chicago Reporter
See: PUBLIC MANAGEMENT & PLANNING

Choices
See: HEALTH

Citizens Committee for the Right to Keep & Bear Arms Newsletter
Association

Publishing Co: Citizens Committee for the Right to Keep & Bear Arms, 12500 NE 10th Pl, Bellevue, WA 98005-2538; Title Tel # (206) 454-4911
Personnel: Editor-Sam Adams

Citizen's Voice

Publishing Co: Citizens Call, PO Box 1722, Cedar City, UT 84721-1722; Title Tel # (801) 586-4808
Personnel: Editor-Mary Lou Malling
Editorial Description: Nuclear radiation action information.
General Info: Semi-annually, 4 pages

Civil Liberties
Association

Publishing Co: American Civil Liberties Union of New York, 132 West 43 St., New York, NY 10036-6599; Title Tel # (212) 944-9800
Personnel: Editor-Jean Bond
Editorial Description: Reports on ACLU litigation and legislative work involving free speech, separation of church and state, privacy, sex and race discrimination, abortion, political surveillance, etc.
General Info: Yr. Est. 1920, Quarterly, Trim Size-11½ x 17, Web press, 8 pages, ISSN: 0009-790X, No Color
Subscriptions: Indv. $20
Circulation: Total-275,000

Civil Liberties

Publishing Co: American Civil Liberties Union of Washington, 705 2nd Ave Ste 300, Seattle, WA 98104-1799; Title Tel # (206) 624-2184
Personnel: Editor-Madeline Kesten
Editorial Description: Current ACLU-W news, legal cases, civil liberty issues, events.
General Info: Yr. Est. 1969, Bi-monthly, Web press, 4 pages, ISSN: 0045-7051, No Color, Newsprint
Subscriptions: Indv. $20
Circulation: (100% controlled), Total-8,500
Printing Co: Valco Graphics, Inc., 480 Andover Park E, Seattle, WA 98188-7606 Tel # (206) 575-3500

Civil Liberties Alert
Association

Publishing Co: American Civil Liberties Union - National Prison Project, 1875 Connecticut Ave. NW, Washington, DC 20009 Tel # (202) 234-4830; Title Tel # (202) 544-1681 Title Fax # (202) 546-0738
Personnel: Publisher-Mort Halperin, Editor-Sherille Ismail, Circ. Mgr., Production Mgr.-Rachel Fischer
Editorial Description: The ACLU's legislative newsletter informs readers about important legislation concerning civil liberties.
General Info: Yr. Est. 1975, Quarterly, Desktop press, 12 pages, 2 Color, Newsprint, Saddle-stitched
Circulation: Total-4,500
List Rental: Actives: $65/M, Expires: 26,000, $50/M
Printing Co: Hundley Lithograph, Inc., 6503 Chillum Pl NW, Washington, DC 20012-2189 Tel # (202) 829-7800

Civil Rights Actions
Business

Publishing Co: Matthew Bender & Co., 11 Penn Plaza, New York, NY 10001-2006 Tel # (212) 967-7707 Fax # (212) 244-3188
Editorial Description: The most comprehensive, up-to-date treatise available on civil rights actions.
General Info: Irregular, Looseleaf

Civil Rights Monitor
Association

Publishing Co: Leadership Conference Education Fund, 1629 K St NW Ste 1010, Washington, DC 20006-1602; Title Tel # (202) 667-6243
Personnel: Editor-Karen McGill Arrington, Circ. Mgr.-Karen Arrington
Editorial Description: Reports on civil rights activities of the Federal government including court cases, Supreme Court oral arguments, and pending legislation.
General Info: Yr. Est. 1985, Bi-monthly, 12 pages
Subscriptions: Indv. $35
Circulation: Total-1,000

Civil Rights/State Capitals
Business, Association

Publishing Co: Wakeman/Walworth, 300 N. Washington St., Alexandria, VA 22314-2530; Title Tel # (703) 549-8606 Title Fax # (703) 549-1372
Personnel: Publisher-Keyes Walworth
Editorial Description: Covers ethnic, race, gender, sexual orientation, and disabilty discrimination. Includes legislation, judicial and administrative decisions across the country as well as corrective actions.
General Info: (Formerly Civil Rights from the State Capitals), Yr. Est. 1946, Weekly, Offset press, 8 pages, ISSN: 0741-353X, No Color
Subscriptions: Indv. $265, Inst. $212, Can. $235, For. $255

Commitment

Publishing Co: Natl. Catholic Conference for Interracial Justice, 3033 4th St NE, Washington, DC 20017-1102; Title Tel # (202) 529-6480
Personnel: Publisher, Editor-Jerome Ernst, Production Mgr.-Patricia Ortiz
Editorial Description: Dedicated to multi-racial multi-cultural justice.
General Info: Yr. Est. 1960, Quarterly, Trim Size-8½ x 11, Sheetfed press, 6 pages, No Color, Matte
Subscriptions: Indv. $25, Inst. $50
Circulation: Total-5,500

Committee on Native American Struggles Newsletter

Publishing Co: Natl. Lawyer's Guild, 55 6th Ave, New York, NY 10013-1679; Title Tel # (212) 966-5000
General Info: Yr. Est. 1972, Quarterly
Subscriptions: Indv. $5

Committee Report
See: LAW

Council on Battered Women Newsletter

Publishing Co: Council on Battered Women, PO Box 54383, Atlanta, GA 30308-0383; Title Tel # (404) 870-9600
General Info: Monthly, 5 pages, No Color
Circulation: Total-400

CrossCurrents
See: ETHNIC

Dallas Memorial Center for Holocaust Studies Newsletter
See: HISTORY

Dykes, Disability & Stuff
See: DISABILITY

Educators Against Racism and Apartheid
Association, Consumer

Publishing Co: Educators Against Racism and Apartheid, 625 Linden Ave, Teaneck, NJ 07666-2353; Title Tel # (201) 836-6644
Personnel: Editor-Paula Bower
General Info: Yr. Est. 1982, 10x/yr.

Employer's Guide to Controlling Sexual Harassment
See: INDUSTRIAL RELATIONS/PERSONNEL

Employment Discrimination
Association

Publishing Co: Matthew Bender & Co., 11 Penn Plaza, New York, NY 10001-2006 Fax # (212) 244-3188; Title Tel # (212) 967-7707
Personnel: Editor-M. Clements
Editorial Description: Full coverage treatise on both substantive and procedural law governing employment discrimination based on sex, age race religion, national origin, etc. Provides full analysis of employment-at-will and comparable worth.
General Info: Yr. Est. 1975, Annually, Looseleaf
Subscriptions: $560/copy

Entre Nous
See: RELIGIOUS & THEOLOGICAL

Equal Employment Compliance Update

Publishing Co: Clark Boardman Callaghan & Co., 155 Pfingsten Rd., Deerfield, IL 60015; Title Tel # (708) 948-7000 Title Fax # (708) 948-8955
Editorial Description: Summary & analysis recent cases on employment law.
General Info: Yr. Est. 1977, Monthly, 10 pages
Subscriptions: Indv. $195
Acqusitions: Publication Bought, Publication Sold

FCL Newsletter   *Consumer*

Publishing Co: Friends Committee on Legislation of California, 926 J St Ste 707, Sacramento, CA 95814-2707; Title Tel # (916) 443-3734
Personnel: Editor-Doug Thompson
Editorial Description: Analyzes legislative developments in California State Legislature with major attention to peace, welfare & criminal justice.
General Info: Yr. Est. 1952, Irregular, Trim Size-8½ x 11, Offset press, 6 pages, ISSN: 0532-7091, 2 Color, Other, Other
Subscriptions: Indv. $20, Inst. $20, Can. $30, $2/copy
Circulation: Total-3,200, Readership-4,000

F.E.A.R. Chronicles   *Association*

Publishing Co: F.E.A.R., PO Box 5424, Somerset, NJ 08875-5424; Title Tel # (415) 388-8128
Personnel: Publisher, Editor-Brenda Grantland, Circ. Mgr.-John Paff
Editorial Description: Information and case histories regarding asset forfeiture law.
General Info: Yr. Est. 1992, Irregular, Trim Size-8.5 x 11, Offset press, 12 pages, No Color, Other, Other
Subscriptions: Indv. $35
Circulation: Total-600

First Principles: National Security and Civil Liberties   *Association*

Publishing Co: Center for National Security Studies, 122 Maryland Ave NE, Washington, DC 20002-5610; Title Tel # (202) 544-1681 Title Fax # (202) 546-0738
Editorial Description: Focuses on actions taken by Congress, the administration and the courts on issues involving national security and civil liberties.
General Info: Yr. Est. 1975, Quarterly, Trim Size-8½ x 11, 16 pages
Subscriptions: Indv. $15, For. $25
Circulation: Total-2,800

Freedom Writer   *Consumer, Association*

Publishing Co: Institute for First Amendment Studies, Inc., PO Box 589, Great Barrington, MA 01230-0589; Title Tel # (413) 274-3786 Title Fax # (413) 274-0245
Personnel: Publisher-Skip Porteous, Editor-Barbara Simon
Editorial Description: Defends traditional American Freedoms, particularly the separation of church & state.
General Info: Yr. Est. 1984, Monthly, Trim Size-8½ x 11, Sheetfed press, 4 pages, ISSN: 1059-6372, No Color, Matte
Subscriptions: $2/copy
Circulation: (26% controlled), Total-25,000

Guatemala Bulletin
See: CULTURE & HUMANITIES

Guatemala Human Rights

Publishing Co: Guatemala Human Rights Commission, 3321 12th St NE, Washington, DC 20017; Title Tel # (202) 529-6599 Title Fax # (202) 526-4611
General Info: Yr. Est. 1995, Bi-monthly, ISSN: 1085-0864
Subscriptions: Indv. $30
Circulation: Total-400

Hispanic Newsletter
See: LAW

Horizons Newsletter   *Consumer, Scholarly*

Publishing Co: Horizons of Friendship, 50 Covert Street, Cobourg, ON K9A 4L1 Canada; Title Tel # (905) 372-5483 Title Fax # (905) 372-7095
Editorial Description: Newsletter addressing root causes of poverty and injustice.
General Info: Semi-annually

Human Rights Bulletin   *Association*

Publishing Co: Intl. League for Human Rights, 432 Park Ave S Ste 1103, New York, NY 10016-8013; Title Tel # (212) 684-1221 Title Fax # (212) 684-1696
Personnel: Editor-Barbara Appel
General Info: Quarterly, 10 pages
Subscriptions: Indv. $20, Inst. $50

Human Rights Perspectives   *Association*

Publishing Co: National Council of Churches, 475 Riverside Dr, New York, NY 10115-0122 Tel # (212) 870-2227; Title Tel # (212) 870-2377
General Info: Quarterly, 8 pages

Human Rights Research and Education Bulletin   *Consumer, Association*

Publishing Co: Human Rights Internet c/o Human Rights Centre, 8 York Street, Suite 202, Ottawa, ON K1N 5S6 Canada Tel # (613) 564-3492 Fax # (613) 564-4054
Editorial Description: Information, contacts, and bibliography on current human rights issues.
General Info: Quarterly
Subscriptions: Indv. $16, Inst. $23

IDRA Newsletter
See: EDUCATION

ISLA
See: INTERNATIONAL AFFAIRS

Indian Affairs
See: ETHNIC

Interfaith Impact & Preparedness
See: RELIGIOUS & THEOLOGICAL

Interracial Club of Buffalo Newsletter
See: ETHNIC

Iowa Civil Rights Communicator   *Consumer*

Publishing Co: Iowa Civil Rights Commission, 211 E. Maple St., 2nd Fl., Des Moines, IA 50319-0001; Title Tel # (515) 281-4121 Title Fax # (515) 242-5840
Personnel: Editor-Carol Anne Leach
Editorial Description: Civil rights issues; articles by experts in the field. News of agency's work & civil rights events.
General Info: Yr. Est. 1980, Semi-annually, Desktop press, 6 pages, No Color
Subscriptions: Free
Circulation: Total-3,000

Issues & Concerns

Publishing Co: Disciples of Christ, PO Box 1986, Indianapolis, IN 46206-1986; Title Tel # (317) 353-1491
Personnel: Editor-Paul Wilson
Editorial Description: Focus on International Human Rights & Torture.
General Info: Yr. Est. 1975, Quarterly, Trim Size-8 x 11, 8 pages, Color-cover, Newsprint, Saddle-stitched
Circulation: Total-2,300

Jail & Prisoner Law Bulletin
See: LAW ENFORCEMENT & PENOLOGY

Journal of the New York Institute of Legal Research
See: LAW

Kentucky Commission on Human Rights, Reports and Newsletter

Publishing Co: Kentucky Commission on Human Rights, Heyburn Bldg 7th flr, 332 W. Broadway, Louisville, KY 40202-1; Title Tel # (502) 595-4024 Title Fax # (502) 595-4801
Personnel: Publisher-Beverly Watts
Editorial Description: Newsletter about the work of the KY Commission on Human Rights in promoting civil rights in Kentucky.
General Info: Yr. Est. 1960, Quarterly, Trim Size-8.5 x 11, Sheetfed press, 8 pages, No Color, Newsprint, Saddle-stitched
Circulation: Total-2,000
Printing Co: Commonwealth of Kentucky, Frankfort, KY 40601

Klanwatch Intelligence Report

Publishing Co: Klanwatch Project Southern Poverty Law Center, 400 Washington St # 548, Montgomery, AL 36104-4344; Title Tel # (205) 264-0286
Personnel: Editor-Sara Bullard, Circ. Mgr.-JoAnn Chancellor
Editorial Description: Educational tool on Klan activity research mailed to media & law enforcement.
General Info: Yr. Est. 1981, Bi-monthly
Circulation: Total-6,000

LFL Reports: *Consumer*

Publishing Co: Libertarians for Life, 13424 Hathaway Dr., #17, Wheaton, MD 20906-3221; Title Tel # (301) 460-4141
Personnel: Publisher-Doris Gordon, Editor-John Walker
Editorial Description: Anti-abortion, pro-life, anti-draft, libertarian philosophy, children's rights.
General Info: Yr. Est. 1981, Irregular, Trim Size-8½ x 11, Desktop press, 8 pages, ISSN: 0882-116X, No Color, Matte
Subscriptions: $1/copy
Circulation: Total-1,000

Lambda Update
Consumer, Association

Publishing Co: Lambda Legal Defense & Education Fund, Inc., 666 Broadway, Suite 1200, New York, NY 10012-2317; Title Tel # (212) 995-8585 Title Fax # (212) 995-2306
Personnel: Editor-Deirdre Reznik
Editorial Description: News and updates of legal issues of interest to gay/lesbian community.
General Info: Yr. Est. 1976, Tri-annually, Trim Size-8½ x 11, Web press, 32 pages, ISSN: 1058-949X, No Color, Matte, Saddle-stitched
Subscriptions: Indv. $40, Free With Membership
Circulation: Total-20,000
Printing Co: Sowers Printing Co., N. 10th & Scull St., Box 479, Lebanon, PA 17042-0479 Tel # (717) 272-6667, Fax # (717) 276-2928

Last Resort
See: CHILDREN

Law Enforcement Liability Reporter
See: LAW ENFORCEMENT & PENOLOGY

Law Group Docket
Association

Publishing Co: Intl. Human Rights Law Group, 1601 Connecticut Ave NW Ste, 700, Washington, DC 20009-1035; Title Tel # (202) 232-8500
Editorial Description: Law Group's current and recent human rights legal advocacy.
General Info: Yr. Est. 1980, Trim Size-8½ x 11, 12 pages, No Color
Subscriptions: Indv. $15, For. $20
Circulation: Total-650

Lead Belly Letter
See: MUSIC & MUSIC TRADES

Leading Hispanics

Publishing Co: Mexican-American Legal Defense, 634 S. Spring St., 11th Fl., Los Angeles, CA 90014-1978; Title Tel # (213) 629-2512 Title Fax # (213) 629-8016
Personnel: Editor-Alicia Maldonado
Editorial Description: The newsletter of MALDEF's Leadership Development prgram, Leading Hispanics features articles on public policy & leadership as they relate to Hispanics.
General Info: Yr. Est. 1985
Circulation: Total-6,000

Lesbian/Gay Law Notes
See: GAY & LESBIAN INTEREST

Liberator, The
Association

Publishing Co: Men's Defense Assn., 17854 Lyons St NE, Forest Lake, MN 55025-8107; Title Tel # (612) 464-7663 Title Fax # (612) 464-7135
Personnel: Publisher, Editor-R.F. Doyle, Production Mgr.-Inez Doyle
Editorial Description: To restore equal rights & equal dignity to the male sex.
General Info: (Formerly Legal Beagle), Yr. Est. 1968, Monthly, Trim Size-11½ x 13½, Web press, 24 pages, ISSN: 1040-3760, No Color
Subscriptions: Indv. $24, $2/copy
Acquistions: Publication Bought, Publication Sold
Circulation: Total-2,000
Advertising: Inquire for rates.

Link, The
See: CHILDREN

MALDEF Newsletter

Publishing Co: Mexican-American Legal Defense, 634 S. Spring St., 11th Fl., Los Angeles, CA 90014-1978; Title Tel # (213) 629-2512 Title Fax # (213) 629-8016
Personnel: Editor-Alicia Maldonado
Editorial Description: National civil rights newspaper on Hispanic issues.
General Info: Yr. Est. 1969, Trim Size-8½ x 11, 8 pages, No Color
Subscriptions: Indv. $35
Circulation: Total-18,000

Michigan Civil Rights Commission Newsletter
Business

Publishing Co: Michigan Civil Rights Dept., 303 W. Kalamazoo 4th Floor, Lansing, MI 48913-0001; Title Tel # (517) 373-1189
Personnel: Editor-James Horn, II
Editorial Description: Recap of commission and department events or activities during quarter.
General Info: Yr. Est. 1971, Quarterly, Trim Size-8½ x 11, Offset press, 4 pages, No Color
Circulation: Total-7,000
Printing Co: Reproduction Svcs., Secondary Complex, Lansing, MI 48909 Tel # (517) 335-3165

Momentum
See: GAY & LESBIAN INTEREST

Mom's Apple Pie
See: GAY & LESBIAN INTEREST

Monitor

Publishing Co: Center for Democratic Renewal & Education, PO Box 50469, Atlanta, GA 30302-0469; Title Tel # (404) 221-0025
Personnel: Publisher-Lynora Williams, Editor-D. Levitas
Editorial Description: Reports on & analyzes hate group activity & community response to such activity.
General Info: (Formerly Natl. Anti-Klan Newsletter), Yr. Est. 1980, Bi-monthly, Trim Size-8½ x 11, Web press, 16 pages, 2 Color, Newsprint
Subscriptions: Indv. $15, $3/copy
Circulation: Total-11,000
Advertising: Inquire for rates.
Printing Co: Black Belt Communications Group, 1123 South Thru St., Montgomery, AL 36104 Tel # (205) 265-6753

More than a Paycheck
See: POLITICS

Municipalities in the U.S. Supreme Court

Publishing Co: Natl. Institute of Municipal Law Officers, 1000 Connecticut Ave NW Ste, 902, Washington, DC 20036-5302; Title Tel # (202) 466-5424 Title Fax # (202) 785-0152
Editorial Description: Description by states of all cases affecting municipal law, on supreme courts docket.
General Info: Yr. Est. 1985, Quarterly

NAAFA Newsletter
Consumer, Association

Publishing Co: Natl. Assn. to Advance Fat Acceptance, Inc., PO Box 188620, Sacramento, CA 95818-8620 Tel # (916) 588-6880; Title Tel # (916) 558-6880
Personnel: Editor-Sally Smith
Editorial Description: Latest news on the size acceptance movement.
General Info: Yr. Est. 1969, Bi-monthly, Trim Size-8½ x 11, Desktop press, 12 pages, 3% ads, No Color, Matte
Subscriptions: Indv. $35, Free With Membership
Circulation: Total-10,000
Advertising: Inquire for rates. Accepts Inserts.
List Rental: Actives: 5,000, $120/M, Expires: 5,000, $120/M

NARF Legal Review
See: LAW

N.Y. Civil Liberties
Association

Publishing Co: New York Civil Liberties Union, 132 W. 43rd St., New York, NY 10036-6599; Title Tel # (212) 382-0557
Personnel: Editor-John Rosenthal, Production Mgr.-Donna Liebeman
Editorial Description: Reports on work on New York Civil Liberties Union.
General Info: Yr. Est. 1953, Quarterly, 8 pages, No Color
Subscriptions: Indv. $20
Circulation: Total-30,000

National Bulletin on Police Misconduct
See: LAW ENFORCEMENT & PENOLOGY

National Campaign for A Peace Tax Fund Newsletter
See: TAXES

Neighbors
Association

Publishing Co: National Neighborhood Coalition, 1875 Connecticut Ave. NW, Ste. 710, Washington, DC 20009-5728 Tel # (202) 986-2096 Fax # (202) 986-2539; Title Tel # (202) 347-6501
Personnel: Editor-Bud Kanitz, Circ. Mgr.-Susan Learmonth
Editorial Description: Issues and subjects of interest to multiracial living.
General Info: Yr. Est. 1970, Quarterly, Trim Size-8½ x 11, 8 pages, No Color
Subscriptions: Indv. $10
Circulation: Total-3,000

New York Civil Service Update
See: EMPLOYMENT

News from Americas Watch
Consumer, Association

Publishing Co: Human Rights Watch, 485 5th Ave., New York, NY 10017-6104
Personnel: Circ. Mgr.-Suzanne Guthrie
Editorial Description: Covers Human Rights issues in the Americas.
General Info: Yr. Est. 1989, 10x/yr.

News from MCLI
Consumer, Association

Publishing Co: Meiklejohn Civil Liberties Institute, PO Box 673, Berkeley, CA 94701-0673 Tel # (510) 848-0599 Fax # (510) 848-6008; Title Tel # (415) 848-0599 Title Fax # (415) 848-6008
Editorial Description: Contains news of human rights projects of the institute.
General Info: Yr. Est. 1965, Annually, 4 pages

Newsletter of the International Study of Organized Persecution of Children

Publishing Co: Child Development Research, 30 Soundview Ln, Sands Point, NY 11050-1341; Title Tel # (516) 883-7135
Personnel: Editor-Shirley Jucovy
Editorial Description: Study of persecution of children by the Nazis during the Holocaust.
General Info: Yr. Est. 1984, Semi-annually
Subscriptions: Indv. $35

Nimmer on Feedom of Speech   *Business*

Publishing Co: Matthew Bender & Co., 11 Penn Plaza, New York, NY 10001-2006 Tel # (212) 967-7707 Fax # (212) 244-3188
Editorial Description: Thorough analysis of the reach & limitations of freedom of speech under the First Amendment, with full, clear analysis of the law, significant case precedents, & comprehensive discussion of all the prevailing issues.
General Info: Yr. Est. 1984, Irregular, Looseleaf

OCA Image
See: ETHNIC

Obscenity Law Bulletin

Publishing Co: Morality in Media, Inc., 475 Riverside Dr., New York, NY 10115-0056; Title Tel # (212) 870-3222 Title Fax # (212) 870-2765
Personnel: Editor-Paul McGeady
Editorial Description: Summarizes all U.S. Supreme and important Lower Court obscenity decisions. Specialized articles on aspects of obscenity law.
General Info: Yr. Est. 1977, Bi-monthly, 4 pages, ISSN: 0195-1696
Subscriptions: Indv. $15
Circulation: Total-800

Operation Big Vote Newsletter
See: GOVERNMENT

Organizer
See: POLITICS

Out in the Mountains
See: GAY & LESBIAN INTEREST

PCR Information   *Consumer, Association*

Publishing Co: World Council of Churches, 475 Riverside Dr., Ste 915, New York, NY 10115-0122 Fax # (212) 870-2528; Title Tel # (212) 870-3340
Editorial Description: News of program to combat racism.
General Info: Quarterly

Patients' Rights Assn. Newsletter

Publishing Co: Patients' Rights Assn., 40 Homewood Ave., Ste. 315, Toronto, ON M4Y 2K2 Canada
General Info: Quarterly

Patriots for Liberty
See: TAXES

Peace & Democracy News
See: POLITICS

Point Blank   *Association*

Publishing Co: Citizens Committee for the Right to Keep & Bear Arms, 12500 NE 10th Pl, Bellevue, WA 98005-2538; Title Tel # (206) 454-4911
Personnel: Publisher-Alan Gottlieb, Editor-John Snyder, Adv. Dir.-John Hosford
Editorial Description: Pro-gun rights newsletter, covers natl. , state & local gun legislation.
General Info: Yr. Est. 1971, Monthly, Trim Size-8½ x 11, Web press, 8 pages, 2 Color, Matte
Subscriptions: Indv. $15
Circulation: Total-102,000
List Rental: Actives: $70/M, Expires: $50/M

Police Civil Liability   *Business*

Publishing Co: Matthew Bender & Co., 11 Penn Plaza, New York, NY 10001-2006 Tel # (212) 967-7707 Fax # (212) 244-3188
Editorial Description: A comprehensive guide to the personal injury & civil rights aspects of police misconduct. An essential resource for personal injury lawyers plaintiff & defense, civil rights attorneys, government counsel, & for law enforcement officers at all levels, provides numerous practice aids & forms throughout.
General Info: Yr. Est. 1983, Irregular, Looseleaf

Police Misconduct & Civil Rights Law Report   *Business*

Publishing Co: Clark Boardman Callaghan, 375 Hudson St, New York, NY 10014-3685 Fax # (212) 807-6209; Title Tel # (212) 929-7500 Title Fax # (212) 924-0460
Personnel: Publisher-David Doughty, Art Dir.-William Rushford, Promotion Dir.-Robert Arkin
Editorial Description: Current legal developments for lawyers, police & public administrators.
General Info: Yr. Est. 1983, Bi-monthly, Trim Size-8½ x 11, Sheetfed press, 12 pages, ISSN: 0738-0623
Subscriptions: Indv. $170
List Rental: Rents Lists
Printing Co: Port City Press, 1323 Greenwood Rd, Pikesville, MD 21208-3611 Tel # (410) 486-3000, Fax # (410) 486-0706

Political Woman Hotline
See: POLITICS

Polygraph Update   *Business*

Publishing Co: Lafayette Instrument Co., PO Box 5729, Lafayette, IN 47903-5729 Parent Co.-Fred Sammons, Hinsdale; Title Tel # (317) 423-1505
Personnel: Editor-Chris Fausett
General Info: Quarterly

Poverty & Race Newsletter
See: SOCIOLOGY

Privacy Journal
See: PHILANTHROPY

Pro-Life News   *Business, Consumer*   **CPM: $14**

Publishing Co: Alliance Action, Inc., B1-90 Garry St., Winnipeg, MB R3C 4H1 Canada; Title Tel # (204) 943-5273 Title Fax # (204) 943-9283
Personnel: Editor-Mary Lamont, Adv. Dir.-Barbar Lebow
Editorial Description: Current Pro-Life, Pro-Family issues. Mostly Canadian with some international interest.
General Info: Yr. Est. 1976, 10x/yr., Trim Size-8½ x 11, Web press, 16 pages, ISSN: 0715-4356, 4 Color, Newsprint, Saddle-stitched
Subscriptions: Can. $25
Circulation: Total-50,000, Readership-110,000
Advertising: $725.
Printing Co: Derksen Printers Ltd., 377 Main St., Steinbach, MB R0A 2A0 Canada Tel # (204) 475-0494, Fax # (204) 326-4860

Program and Legislative Action
See: POLITICS

Project Equality-Update   *Business, Association*

Publishing Co: Project Equality, 6301 Rockhill Rd Ste 315, Kansas City, MO 64131-1117; Title Tel # (816) 361-9222 Title Fax # (816) 361-8997
Personnel: Publisher, Editor-Maurice Culver
Editorial Description: Provides news & information about Project Equality, new employer participants, & info on equal employment opportunity & affirmative action.
General Info: (Formerly Project Equaility Newsletter), Yr. Est. 1965, Quarterly, Trim Size-8½ x 11, 12 pages, No Color, Newsprint
Subscriptions: Free With Membership
Circulation: Total-2,000

Quaker Committee on Jails & Justice Newsletter
See: LAW

Quality of Care
See: DISABILITY

Religious Coalition for Reproductive Choice Newsletter
See: WOMEN'S

Resource Center Bulletin
See: INTERNATIONAL AFFAIRS

Right to Know & the Freedom to Act, The   *Association*

Publishing Co: National Committee Against Repressive Legislation, 3321 12th St NE, Washington, DC 20017-4008; Title Tel # (202) 529-4225 Title Fax # (202) 526-4611
Personnel: Editor-Kit Gage
Editorial Description: Monitor developments related to protection of First Amendment rights. Special focus on infringement of these rights by federal law enforcement & intelligence agencies.
General Info: Yr. Est. 1981, Semi-annually, Offset press, 6 pages, Color
Subscriptions: Indv. $15, Inst. $15
Circulation: Total-12,000, Readership-12,000
Printing Co: Agency Lithograph and Printing, 1561 Venice Blvd, Los Angeles, CA 90006-4717 Tel # (213) 383-2161

RightsLine   *Consumer, Association*

Publishing Co: New York City Commission on Human Rights, 40 Rector St Fl 10, New York, NY 10006-1705
Personnel: Editor-Keith O'Connor
Editorial Description: For and by the New York City Commission on Human Rights.
General Info: Yr. Est. 1992, Quarterly, Trim Size-8½ x 11, 6 pages

Service Committee News
See: RELIGIOUS & THEOLOGICAL

Spectrum
Association

Publishing Co: Kansas Commission on Civil Rights, 900 SW Jackson St Rm 851s, Topeka, KS 66612-1220; Title Tel # (913) 296-3206
Personnel: Editor-Steven Ramires
Editorial Description: Emphasis on commission activities and civil rights issues in the areas of employment, housing, and public accomodations.
General Info: Yr. Est. 1969, Semi-annually, Trim Size-8½ x 11, Offset press, 6 pages, No Color
Circulation: Total-6,500

Stateswoman
See: WOMEN'S

Uncommon Desires Newsletter
Consumer

Publishing Co: Uncommon Desires Newsletter, PO Box 2377, New York, NY 10185-2377
Editorial Description: Covers immoral acts of sexual abuse on all people.
General Info: Bi-monthly
Subscriptions: Indv. $25

U.S. Holocaust Memorial Museum Campaign News

Publishing Co: Sponsor-Campaign to Remember, U.S. Holocaust Memorial Council, 100 Raoul Wallenberg Pl SW, Washington, DC 20024-2126; Title Tel # (202) 653-9220
Personnel: Publisher-Richard Krieger
Editorial Description: Dedicated to prevention of state sponsored mass murder.
General Info: Quarterly

Vermont Right to Life Newsletter

Publishing Co: Vermont Right to Life, 73 Main St Rm 30, Montpelier, VT 05602-2944; Title Tel # (802) 229-4885
Editorial Description: Promotes the RTL of all born & unborn human beings.
General Info: (Formerly Vermonters for Life Newsletter), Yr. Est. 1974, Bi-monthly, Trim Size-8½ x 11, Sheetfed press, 8 pages, No Color
Subscriptions: Free With Membership
Circulation: Total-13,000

Voice of Reason Newsletter
Association

Publishing Co: Americans for Religious Liberty, PO Box 6656, Silver Spring, MD 20916-6656; Title Tel # (301) 598-2447
Personnel: Publisher, Editor-Edd Doerr
Editorial Description: Contains news & analysis of religious liberty topics. Covers school finance, public school religious neutrality, & abortion rights.
General Info: Yr. Est. 1981, Quarterly, Trim Size-8½ x 11, Offset press, 12 pages, 2 Color
Subscriptions: Indv. $10
List Rental: List Management Co.: Manager: Edd Doerr; Names in the News-California, 1 Bush St Bsmt 3, San Francisco, CA 94104-4425 Tel # (415) 989-3350, Fax # (415) 433-7796, Actives: $55/M
Printing Co: District Creative Printing, 6350 Fallard Dr, Upper Marlboro, MD 20772-3885 Tel # (301) 868-8610, Fax # (301) 868-1015

WLDF News
See: WOMEN'S

Walk Away
See: RELIGIOUS & THEOLOGICAL

Washington Memo
See: HEALTH

Waves
See: GAY & LESBIAN INTEREST

Webb Report, The
See: BUSINESS & INDUSTRY

West Coast Libertarian
See: POLITICS

Women around New York
See: WOMEN'S

Word from Washington
Association

Publishing Co: United Cerebral Palsy Assn., Inc., 7 Penn Plz Ste 804, New York, NY 10001-3900
Personnel: Editor-Dr. E. Clarke Ross
Editorial Description: Monthly review of federal govt. public policy issues, legislation, and agency rules and regulations concerning the disabled.
General Info: Yr. Est. 1969, Monthly, 14 pages, 4 Color
Circulation: (100% controlled)

World Freedom Bulletin
Association

Publishing Co: International Society for Individual Liberty, 1800 Market St, San Francisco, CA 94102-6227; Title Tel # (415) 864-0952
Personnel: Editor-Vincent Miller
Editorial Description: Articles on individual liberty and the struggle against government violations of basic human rights (personal and property).
General Info: (Formerly Individual Liberty), Yr. Est. 1969, Monthly, Trim Size-8 x 10, Offset press, 8 pages, No Color
Subscriptions: Free With Membership
Circulation: Total-5,500
Advertising: Inquire for rates.

CLUBS

510 Again Newsletter
See: AUTOMOTIVE

AAAD Bulletin
See: SPORTS & SPORTING GOODS

AMBUC Leader
Business, Association

Publishing Co: Natl. Assn. of American Business Clubs, PO Box 5127, High Point, NC 27262-5127; Title Tel # (910) 869-2166 Title Fax # (910) 887-8451
Personnel: Editor-J.J. Copeland
Editorial Description: A newsletter of information and education for AMBUC leaders.
General Info: Yr. Est. 1983, Monthly, Trim Size-8½ x 11, Offset press, 4 pages, 2 Color, Recycled
Circulation: (100% controlled), Total-625

ATO Leader

Publishing Co: ATO Fraternity, 4001 W Kirby Ave, Champaign, IL 61821-9725; Title Tel # (217) 351-1865
Personnel: Publisher-M. Thorsby, Editor-Steve Glaser, Circ. Mgr.-Laura Zuber, Production Mgr.-Beverly Arten
Editorial Description: News & information for student & alumni ATO fraternity leaders.
General Info: (Formerly ATO Letter), Semi-monthly, Trim Size-8½ x 11, Desktop press, 2 pages, 2 Color, Newsprint
Circulation: (100% controlled)

Alpha Tau Delta President's Letter
Association

Publishing Co: Alpha Tau Delta, 350 Bluemont Hall, Kansas St. Univ., Manhattan, KS 66502-5724; Title Tel # (602) 942-5934
General Info: 20x/yr.

America Italy Society Newsletter
See: ETHNIC

American Friends of Lafayette
See: HISTORY

American Italian Historical Association Newsletter
See: ETHNIC

American Veterans of Israel Newsletter
See: VETERANS

An Enduring Legacy

Publishing Co: Daughters of Utah Pioneers Museum, 300 N Main St, Salt Lake City, UT 84103-1632; Title Tel # (801) 538-1050
Personnel: Editor-Beatrice Malouf
General Info: Yr. Est. 1938, 9x/yr., Trim Size-6 x 9, 64 pages, No Color
Subscriptions: Indv. $8, $1/copy
Circulation: Total-1,400
Printing Co: Utah Printing, 2855 S West Temple, Salt Lake City, UT 84115-3551 Tel # (801) 487-8574

Arbor Newsletter, The

Publishing Co: Gleaner Life Insurance Society, 5200 W. US 223, Box 1894, Adrian, MI 49221-9461; Title Tel # (517) 263-2244 Title Fax # (517) 265-7745
Personnel: Publisher-Frank Dick, Editor, Art Dir.-Greg Warfield
Editorial Description: Society organ for lodge officers & members, provides news of lodge & member activities & awards. Fraternal office news is also reported.
General Info: (Formerly Arbor News), Yr. Est. 1970, Monthly, Sheetfed press, 8 pages, Color-cover, Saddle-stitched
Circulation: (100% controlled), Total-900
Printing Co: Q & Q Printing Co., 40 Hague St, Detroit, MI 48202-2119 Tel # (313) 872-5151

Armenian Welfare Association of New York News
See: ETHNIC

Baltimore County Muster

Publishing Co: Sons of the American Revolution, 233 Linden Ave., Towson, MD 21204-5427; Title Tel # (301) 828-0926
Personnel: Editor-John F. Burk, Co-Editor-Ray R. Potter
General Info: Yr. Est. 1987, Quarterly, Trim Size-5½ x 8½, Mimeo press, 8 pages
Circulation: (75% controlled), Total-200

Bond — *Association*

Publishing Co: Kappa Epsilon Fraternity, PO Box 870393, Stone Mountain, GA 30087-0010; Title Tel # (317) 925-0778
Personnel: Editor-Patsy Towery
Editorial Description: Information on activities of chapters and individual members as well as activities of the whole fraternity.
General Info: Yr. Est. 1921, Trim Size-8½ x 11, 10 pages, Color
Circulation: (100% controlled), Total-5,000
Advertising: Inquire for rates.
List Rental: Actives: $25/M
Printing Co: Wentworth Printing Corp., PO Box 4660, West Columbia, SC 29171 Tel # (803) 796-9990, Fax # (803) 739-0556

Boys & Girls Clubs of America Bulletin — *Association*

Publishing Co: Boys & Girls' Clubs of America, 1230 N.W. Peachtree St., Atlanta, GA 30309-3494; Title Tel # (404) 815-5700
Personnel: Editor-Joseph DelPonte, Art Dir.-Judith Olenick
Editorial Description: Activities and accomplishments of the Boys Club movement.
General Info: Yr. Est. 1965, Quarterly, Trim Size-8½ x 14, Offset press, 4 pages, Color
Circulation: (100% controlled), Total-25,000

Bulletin for Kiwanis Officers — *Association*

Publishing Co: Kiwanis International, 3636 Woodview Trce, Indianapolis, IN 46268-3196; Title Tel # (317) 875-8755
Personnel: Editor-Edward Wills, Production Mgr.-Vicki Jonak
Editorial Description: Tips on administration, service projects, and fund-raising for club leaders.
General Info: Monthly, Sheetfed press, 4 pages, No Color, Newsprint
Subscriptions: Indv. $1
Circulation: Total-44,848
Printing Co: Printing Co., 2820 N Shadeland Ave, Indianapolis, IN 46219-1127 Tel # (317) 547-4571

Bulletin for Kiwanis Officers: African Edition

Publishing Co: Kiwanis International, 3636 Woodview Trce, Indianapolis, IN 46268-3196; Title Tel # (317) 875-8755

Bulletin for Kiwanis Officers: Asian Edition

Publishing Co: Kiwanis International, 3636 Woodview Trce, Indianapolis, IN 46268-3196; Title Tel # (317) 875-8755

Bulletin for Kiwanis Officers: European Edition

Publishing Co: Kiwanis International, 3636 Woodview Trce, Indianapolis, IN 46268-3196; Title Tel # (317) 875-8755

CARD TALK
See: PRINTING/GRAPHIC ARTS

Calling All Scots
See: ETHNIC

Candlewick Collector Newsletter, The
See: GLASS, STONE & CLAY

Cardinal Club Newsletter
See: AERONAUTICS/ASTRONAUTICS

Cat Talk — *Consumer, Association*

Publishing Co: Cat Collectors, 33161 Wendy Dr, Sterling Heights, MI 48310-6473; Title Tel # (810) 264-0285
Personnel: Publisher, Editor-Marilyn Dipboye
Editorial Description: Bimonthly newsletter, 16 pages, of antique, current, museum news for an intl. readership: beginning/advanced collectors. Bimonthly, 12 pages, of catalogues of new & antique cats for sale.
General Info: Yr. Est. 1982, Bi-monthly, Trim Size-8½ x 11, Sheetfed press, 16 pages, 3% ads, Newsprint, Saddle-stitched
Subscriptions: Indv. $18, Can. $21, For. $25, $4/copy
Acquisitions: Publication Sold
Advertising: Inquire for rates. Accepts Inserts.

Cherokee Boys Club-Newsletter & Cherokee Voice
See: ETHNIC

Chips — *Association*

Publishing Co: Catholic Assn. of Foresters, 347 Commonwealth Ave, Boston, MA 02115-1999; Title Tel # (617) 536-8221
Personnel: Editor-Joseph McVeigh, Circ. Mgr.-John Anderson, Jr.
Editorial Description: Summarizes fraternal activities and annoucements of the association.
General Info: Yr. Est. 1879, Bi-monthly, Web press, 4 pages, No Color
Circulation: (100% controlled), Total-8,000

Christopher News Notes
See: RELIGIOUS & THEOLOGICAL

Chrome-Dome — *Association*

Publishing Co: Bald Headed Men of America, 102 Bald Dr, Morehead City, NC 28557-2919; Title Tel # (919) 726-1855 Title Fax # (919) 726-6061
Personnel: Editor-John Capps
Editorial Description: Promotes a positive image and acceptance of baldness.
General Info: Yr. Est. 1973, Annually, Trim Size-8½ x 11, Letrpr. press, 2 pages, No Color
Subscriptions: Free With Membership
Circulation: Total-15,000
Printing Co: Capps Printing, 3819 Bridges St, Morehead City, NC 28557-2917 Tel # (919) 726-1004

Chrysler 300 Club News
See: AUTOMOTIVE

Circle — *Association*

Publishing Co: Omicron Delta Kappa Soc., 118 Bradley Hall, Lexington, KY 40506; Title Tel # (606) 257-5000
Personnel: Editor-Dr. Dacho Dachoff
Editorial Description: Publication of Omicron Delta Kappa Society.
General Info: Quarterly, Trim Size-8½ x 11, Offset press, 4 pages, No Color
Subscriptions: Indv. $1
Circulation: Total-18,000

Cooking Contest Chronicle
See: FOOD

Cormorant News Bulletin
See: AUTOMOTIVE

Cucurbits
See: GARDENING & HORTICULTURE

Danish Odd Fellow Bulletin

Publishing Co: Berthel Thorvaldsen Lodge No. 530, IOOF, Inc., 220 E 15th St, New York, NY 10003-3901
Personnel: Editor-Svend Hansen
General Info: Yr. Est. 1917, Bi-monthly
Circulation: Total-250

Delta Kappa Gamma News — *Association*

Publishing Co: Delta Kappa Gamma Society International, 416 W 12th St, Austin, TX 78701-1817; Title Tel # (512) 478-5748 Title Fax # (512) 478-3861
Personnel: Editor-Jane Posten
Editorial Description: Disseminates information pertinent to the activities of the society.
General Info: (Formerly Delta Kappa Gamma, the News), Yr. Est. 1943, 8x/yr., Trim Size-8½ x 11, Web press, 8 pages, No Color, Matte
Circulation: Total-160,000
Printing Co: Hart Graphics, 8000 Shoal Creek Blvd., P.O. Box 968, Austin, TX 78767 Tel # (512) 454-4761

Delta Mu Delta Newsletter — *Consumer, Association*

Publishing Co: Delta Mu Delta, PO Box 48028, Niles, IL 60714-0028
General Info: Quarterly

Dickin' Around — *Business, Association*

Publishing Co: Dicks of America, PO Box 600782, San Diego, CA 92160-0782; Title Tel # (619) 286-5448
Editorial Description: Stories about Richards, with jokes and recipes. Dicks of America is an organization dedicated to making Dick the most beloved name in the world, and have a whole lot of fun doing it. Call for membership information or t-shirts, mugs, and other Dick merchandise.
General Info: Yr. Est. 1986, Quarterly, Trim Size-8½ x 11, Offset press, 4 pages, No Color, Matte, Other
Subscriptions: Indv. $15, Free With Membership
Advertising: Accepts Inserts.

Director
See: HOBBY

Ducas
See: ETHNIC

Easter Seal Communicator — *Association*

Publishing Co: Natl. Easter Seal Society, 230 W. Monroe Street, 18th Floor, Chicago, IL 60606-4703; Title Tel # (312) 726-6200
Personnel: Editor-Barbara Palombo
Editorial Description: News of Easter Seal affiliates, natl. programs, & corporate sponsors.
General Info: Yr. Est. 1972, Semi-annually, Trim Size-8½ x 11, Offset press, 8 pages, No Color, Saddle-stitched
Circulation: Total-3,000

Elbeetee

Publishing Co: Elbeetian Legion, PO Box 9127, North Bergen, NJ 07047-1327; Title Tel # (201) 945-0717
Personnel: Editor-Charles J. Merlin
Editorial Description: Perpetuation of friendships made during duration of Lone Scouts of America days (1915-1924) and publicizing news of members of the Elbeetian Legion-their activities, etc.
General Info: Yr. Est. 1927, Monthly, Trim Size-8½ x 11, Offset press, 16 pages
Circulation: Total-1,000

Equitable Reserve Guide *Association*

Publishing Co: Equitable Reserve Association, 116 S. Commercial St., Box 448, Neenah, WI 54956-3080
Personnel: Editor-Ernie Bellin
Editorial Description: Fraternal life insurance news.
General Info: Yr. Est. 1897, Bi-monthly, Desktop press, 16 pages, 4 Color, Coated, Saddle-stitched
Subscriptions: Indv. $1
Circulation: (100% controlled)
Printing Co: Ripon Community Printers, 6516 Douglas St., Box 6, Ripon, WI 54971-0006
Tel # (414) 748-3136, Fax # (414) 748-3741

FACS Newsletter

Publishing Co: Finnish American Club of Saima, Inc., PO Box 30, Fitchburg, MA 01420-0030;
Title Tel # (508) 756-9614
Personnel: Publisher, Editor-Tarmo Hannula
Editorial Description: Club news and items of interest to ethnic Finns.
General Info: Yr. Est. 1946, Monthly, Trim Size-8½ x 11, Offset press, 4 pages
Subscriptions: Indv. $5
Circulation: Total-2,500
Advertising: Inquire for rates.

FMCA Newsletter
See: INSURANCE

Fan Club Monitor
See: FAN MAGAZINES-MOVIE, RADIO, TV

Fire Bell Club News Notes
See: FIRE PROTECTION

Flame

Publishing Co: Alpha Lamba Delta, Freshman Scholastic Honor Society, PO Box 1576, Muncie, IN 47308-1576; Title Tel # (317) 282-5620
Editorial Description: Reports installations of chapters, National Council actions, chapter news, fellowship awards, articles of interest to chapters and members.
General Info: Yr. Est. 1962, Annually, Trim Size-8½ x 11, 7 pages
Circulation: Total-20,000

For Vettes Only
See: AUTOMOTIVE

Friends of Doctor Who Newsletter
See: SCIENCE FICTION & FANTASY

G.I. Joe Collectors Club
See: COLLECTIBLES

Gilligan's Island News *Consumer* CPM: $113

Publishing Co: Original Gilligan's Island Fan Club, PO Box 25311, Salt Lake City, UT 84125-0311;
Title Tel # (801) 272-5729 Title Fax # (801) 263-0585
Personnel: Feature Ed.-Pete Salisbury, News Ed.-Peter Salisbury, Entertainment Ed.-Robert Van Sile, Circ. Mgr.-Sue Rankin, Publisher, Editor, Production Mgr., Adv. Dir., Art Dir., Mktg. Dir.-Bob Rankin, Promotion Dir.-Jeff Foxwell
Editorial Description: Information for Gilligan's Island fans.
General Info: (Formerly Island News), Yr. Est. 1972, Quarterly, 20 pages, 10% ads, Newsprint, Saddle-stitched
Subscriptions: Indv. $15, Can. $20, For. $40, $3/copy
Circulation: Total-1,100
Advertising: $125.
Printing Co: Inter-Mountain Press, 3362 S. 2300 E., Holladay, UT 84109

Girth Shaking News/
Midwest *Association*

Publishing Co: Girth & Mirth, PO Box 14384, Chicago, IL 60614-0384; Title Tel # (312) 327-1585
Title Fax # (312) 549-7721
Personnel: Editor-Harold Wilke
Editorial Description: Announces activities of the club, a social club for gay men over 21 who are overweight or sympathetic to overweight men.
General Info: Yr. Est. 1980, Monthly
Subscriptions: Free With Membership
Circulation: Total-350

Gold Star Mother *Association*

Publishing Co: American Gold Star Mothers, 2128 Leroy Pl NW, Washington, DC 20008-1893;
Title Tel # (202) 265-0991
Personnel: Publisher-Winona Tucker, Editor-Marge Etense
Editorial Description: Gold star mothers and their activities, aiding patriotic works and veterans, to teach a sense of individual obligation to community, state & nation.
General Info: Yr. Est. 1928, Bi-monthly, Trim Size-11½ x 14½, Sheetfed press, 4 pages, No Color
Subscriptions: Indv. $1
Circulation: (100% controlled), Total-5,000

Golden Links *Association*

Publishing Co: Grand Lodge of Manitoba. Indep. Order of Odd Fellows, 381 Parkway Blvd., Flin Flon, MB R8A 0K5 Canada; Title Tel # (204) 687-6120
Personnel: Editor-George Dusenbury
General Info: Yr. Est. 1964, Monthly, Trim Size-8½ x 11, 6 pages, Color, Newsprint
Subscriptions: Indv. $8
Circulation: Total-500

Good and Welfare *Association*

Publishing Co: Zeta Beta Tau, 3905 Vincennes Rd., Ste. 101, Indianapolis, IN 46268-3025;
Title Tel # (212) 629-0888
Editorial Description: Fraternal publication.
General Info: (Formerly Monday), Yr. Est. 1971, Monthly, Trim Size-8 x 11, 4 pages, 2 Color
Circulation: Total-1,500
List Rental: Actives: $50/M

Grand Chapter News

Publishing Co: Iota Lambda Sigma, 305 Teachers College, Univ. Of, Cincinnati, OH 45221-0001
Personnel: Editor-Dr. Dennis H. Price

Grand Lodge *Association*

Publishing Co: Legionarios del Trabajo en America, 2154 S San Joaquin St, Stockton, CA 95206-3254; Title Tel # (209) 463-6516
Personnel: Editor, Circ. Mgr.-Ruthe Navarro
General Info: (Formerly Supreme Consistory), Mimeo press, 3 pages, Color
Subscriptions: Indv. $5
Circulation: Total-400

Guidon *Association*

Publishing Co: Miniature Figure Collectors of America, 102 Saint Pauls Rd., Ardmore, PA 19003-2811 Tel # (610) 649-4144; Title Tel # (215) 649-4144
Personnel: Editor Miko Ferguson
Editorial Description: Military miniatures, history, military art, uniforms, dioramas, painting, casting, books, prints & related.
General Info: Yr. Est. 1940, Bi-monthly, Trim Size-8½ x 11, Offset press, 4 pages, No Color, Newsprint
Subscriptions: Indv. $13
Circulation: Total-300
Advertising: Inquire for rates. Accepts Inserts.

Hall Collector's Club Newsletter
See: GLASS, STONE & CLAY

Harbor Highlights *Association*

Publishing Co: Danish Brotherhood in America, Po Box 266000, Highlands Ranch, CO 80163-6000;
Title Tel # (402) 341-5049
General Info: Monthly

Hatsofe

Publishing Co: Natl. Jewish Committee on Scouting, 1325 W Walnut Hill Ln, Irving, TX 75038-3008;
Title Tel # (214) 580-2059
Personnel: Editor-Fred Tichauer
General Info: Yr. Est. 1950, Annually, 4 pages
Circulation: Total-5,000

Highlights *Consumer, Association*

Publishing Co: New York Chapter Hadassah, 250 West 57th Street, New York, NY 10107-0230;
Title Tel # (212) 765-7050 Title Fax # (212) 765-8138
Personnel: Editor-Debbie Silverman, Sr. Ed.-Judith Marbach
Editorial Description: Features fundraising, membership, special events & education highlights of the New York Chapter Hadassah.
General Info: Monthly, Trim Size-8⅜ x 10⅞, 12 pages, 2 Color, Matte

JULUKA Newsletter
See: ETHNIC

J.W.V.A. Bulletin
See: VETERANS

Japan North American Commission on Cooperative Mission Bulletin
See: RELIGIOUS & THEOLOGICAL

Jim Smith Society-
Newsletter

Publishing Co: Jim Smith Society, Inc., 2016 Milltown Rd, Camp Hill, PA 17011-7433;
Title Tel # (717) 737-7406
Personnel: Editor-James H. Smith, Jr.
Editorial Description: Publishes news about people everywhere named Jim Smith.
General Info: Yr. Est. 1969, Quarterly, 2 pages
Subscriptions: Indv. $7
Circulation: Total-500
Advertising: Inquire for rates.

Kappa Alpha News *Association*

Publishing Co: Kappa Alpha, 317 W State St, Ithaca, NY 14850-5431; Title Tel # (607) 273-2220

Kappa Gamma Pi News   *Association*

Publishing Co: Kappa Gamma Pi, 2415 Hillcrest Dr, Stow, OH 44224-4278;
Title Tel # (216) 688-1407 Title Fax # (216) 688-3284
Personnel: Editor-Pamela Waitinas
Editorial Description: Natl. organizational news, features, articles pertaining to college graduate's interests.
General Info: Yr. Est. 1930, 5x/yr., Trim Size-8½ x 11, Offset press, 8 pages, No Color
Circulation: (100% controlled), Total-14,000
Printing Co: ESA Direct Mktg. Svces. Inc., 1890 E 40th St, Cleveland, OH 44103-3557
Tel # (216) 881-8909, Fax # (216) 881-1208

Kappa Profile   *Association*

Publishing Co: Kappa Kappa Iota, 1875 E 15th St, Tulsa, OK 74104-4610;
Title Tel # (918) 744-0389 Title Fax # (918) 744-0389
Personnel: Publisher, Editor, Mktg. Dir., Promotion Dir.-Emily Sleeth
General Info: (Formerly Kappa Kappa Iota Bulletin), Yr. Est. 1949, Semi-annually, 20 pages, 4 Color
Circulation: Total-9,000

Kappa Tau Alpha Newsletter
See: JOURNALISM

Key Reporter   *Association*

Publishing Co: Phi Beta Kappa Society, 1811 Q St NW, Washington, DC 20009-1613;
Title Tel # (202) 265-3808
Personnel: Editor-Priscilla S. Taylor
Editorial Description: Articles on the liberal arts & sciences in colleges & univ's. ; articles on activities of the society; book reviews.
General Info: Yr. Est. 1936, Quarterly, Trim Size-8½ x 11, Web press, 16 pages, ISSN: 0023-0804, 2 Color
Subscriptions: Indv. $5, $2/copy
Circulation: (100% controlled), Total-400,000
Printing Co: William Byrd Press, 2901 Byrdhill Rd, Richmond, VA 23228-5805 Tel # (804) 264-2828, Fax # (804) 262-3267

Kiwanis International Foundation Newsletter   *Business, Association*

Publishing Co: Kiwanis International, 3636 Woodview Trce, Indianapolis, IN 46268-3196;
Title Tel # (317) 875-8755
Personnel: Editor-Aubrey Irby, Adv. Dir.-Pat Hatcher
General Info: Yr. Est. 1970, Quarterly
Circulation: Total-25,000
Advertising: Inquire for rates.

Kiwanis News   *Association*

Publishing Co: Kiwanis, Western Canada, Box 581, Regina, SK S4P 3A3 Canada
Personnel: Editor-Eleanor Milton
Editorial Description: Kiwanis Club activity in Western Canada.
General Info: Yr. Est. 1958, Quarterly, Trim Size-8 x 11, Offset press, 4 pages
Subscriptions: Indv. $1
Circulation: Total-2,750

Kombatant W Ameryce

Publishing Co: Polish Veterans of W.W. II, PO Box 179, New York, NY 10116-0179
Editorial Description: Veterans organization news in Polish and English.
General Info: Yr. Est. 1956, Quarterly

Kwan Um School of Zen Newsletter
See: RELIGIOUS & THEOLOGICAL

LANSA
See: NUMISMATICS

LPA News

Publishing Co: Little People of America, Inc., 7238 Piedmont Dr, Dallas, TX 75227-9324
Tel # (212) 388-9576

LULAC News
See: ETHNIC

Last Month's Newsletter   *Association*

Publishing Co: Procrastinators' Club of America, PO Box 712, Bryn Athyn, PA 19009-0712;
Title Tel # (215) 947-9020 Title Fax # (215) 947-7007
Personnel: Editor-Les Waas
Editorial Description: News of the Procrastinators' Club; benefits of procrastination; news of chapters; humorous material; etc.
General Info: Yr. Est. 1962, Irregular, Trim Size-8½ x 11, Offset press, 4 pages, 2 Color, Newsprint
Subscriptions: Free With Membership
Circulation: (100% controlled), Total-12,000

Latvian House, Inc. Bulletin
See: ETHNIC

Legacy Newsletter
See: HISTORY

Legion News

Publishing Co: Detroit Districts Assn., Hte American Legion, 55 Victor, Highland Park, MI 48203
General Info: Yr. Est. 1928, Monthly, Offset press
Subscriptions: Indv. $1
Advertising: Inquire for rates.

Liga
See: ETHNIC

Listening Post   *Association*

Publishing Co: Intl. Listening Assn., McNeese State Univ., Comm., Box 9042, Lake Charles, LA 70609-9998; Title Tel # (318) 475-5039
Personnel: Editor-Charles Roberts
General Info: Yr. Est. 1979, Quarterly, 24 pages
Subscriptions: Indv. $20, $12/copy

Loyal Legion Historical Journal   *Consumer, Association*

Publishing Co: Military Order of the Loyal Legion of the U.S., 1805 Pine St., Philadelphia, PA 19103-6601; Title Tel # (215) 546-2425
Personnel: Editor-Thomas Curtis
Editorial Description: Promotes democratic government and informs members of current organizational projects concerning the preservation of Civil War artifacts and history. Publishes articles on Civil War history.
General Info: (Formerly Loyal Legion Bulletin), Yr. Est. 1943, Quarterly, Trim Size-8½ x 11, Offset press, 8 pages
Subscriptions: Indv. $10
Circulation: Total-1,500

Magyar Cserke'sz   *Association*

Publishing Co: Hungarian Scouts Association, PO Box 68, Garfield, NJ 07026-0068;
Title Tel # (201) 772-8810
Personnel: Editor-Julius Pap
Editorial Description: Text: Hungarian. Hungarian scout activities. Educational articles.
General Info: Yr. Est. 1951, Semi-annually, Trim Size-8½ x 11, 16 pages, No Color
Subscriptions: Indv. $5
Circulation: Total-1,500

Maltese-American Social Club of San Francisco Newsletter
See: ETHNIC

Marklin Club
See: HOBBY

Marklin Digital Club
See: HOBBY

Mazama

Publishing Co: Mazamas, 909 NW 19th Ave, Portland, OR 97209-1496
Personnel: Editor-James Miller
General Info: Yr. Est. 1918, Monthly
Subscriptions: Indv. $8
Circulation: Total-2,600

Mercury   *Association*

Publishing Co: Society of Rosicrucians, Box 192-13, Preston Hollow, NY 12469;
Title Tel # (518) 234-4349
Personnel: Editor, Circ. Mgr.-Lucia Grosch
Editorial Description: About 1,000 words concerning our Great Work.
General Info: Yr. Est. 1916, Quarterly, Mimeo press, 12 pages, No Color, Newsprint
Subscriptions: Indv. $7, Can. $8, For. $10, $2/copy

Metta   M
See: RELIGIOUS & THEOLOGICAL

Military & Police Uniform Association Newsletter   *Consumer, Association*   CPM: $10

Publishing Co: Fan Club Publishing Co. / Louis Wendruck, Box 69A04-Dept. OX, West Hollywood, CA 90069-0066; Title Tel # (213) 650-5112
Personnel: Publisher, Editor-Louis Wendrick
Editorial Description: Publication for gay men interested in military & police uniforms, personal ads & videos.
General Info: Yr. Est. 1992, Quarterly, Trim Size-8½ x 11, Offset press, 24 pages
Subscriptions: Indv. $29, Can. $39, For. $39, $8/copy
Circulation: Total-20,000
Advertising: $200. Accepts Inserts.
List Rental: Rents Lists

Moila Temple Bulletin   *Association*

Publishing Co: Moila Temple, 701 N Noyes Blvd, St. Joseph, MO 64506-2860;
Title Tel # (816) 232-5129 Title Fax # (816) 232-7739
Personnel: Publisher-Terry L. Gardner, Editor-Gail Morris
Editorial Description: A fraternal publication.
General Info: Yr. Est. 1923, Bi-monthly, Trim Size-8½ x 11, Offset press, 20 pages, 2 Color
Subscriptions: Free With Membership
Circulation: Total-5,000

Montserrat Progressive Society of New York Newsletter
See: ETHNIC

Motif
See: ANTIQUES & ART GOODS

NFLCC Gazette   *Consumer, Association*
Publishing Co: National Fishing Lure Collector's Club, 1418 E Portland St, Springfield, MO 65804-1221
Personnel: Editor-George Richey, Adv. Dir.-Steve Lumpkin
Editorial Description: High quality newsletter with 6-10 feature articles on antique fishing tackle makers, tackle discovery tales and calendarof club events. Plenty of quality photos, and illustrations. Classified advertisements of items for sale and tradew from club members.
General Info: Yr. Est. 1976, Quarterly, 32 pages, Coated, Saddle-stitched
Circulation: Total-3,200

NIAF News,The
See: ETHNIC

Nachrichten der Donauschwaben in Chicago
See: ETHNIC

National Association of College Women Bulletin
Publishing Co: National Association of College Women, 1501 11th St NW, Washington, DC 20001-3215; Title Tel # (202) 785-7700
General Info: Quarterly

National Catholic Committee on Scouting Newsletter   *Association*
Publishing Co: Natl. Catholic Committee on Scouting, 1325 W Walnut Hill Ln # 61030, Irving, TX 75038-3008; Title Tel # (218) 659-2059

National Council of Women of the United States Bulletin
Publishing Co: Natl. Council of Women of the U.S., 777 UN Plaza, New York, NY 10017; Title Tel # (212) 697-1278
Personnel: Editor-Merrinelle Sullivan, Adv. Dir.-Dorothea Hopfer
Editorial Description: Subjects of interest to organized women around the world.
General Info: Yr. Est. 1888, Quarterly, Trim Size-8½ x 11, 8 pages
Subscriptions: Indv. $10, $1/copy
Circulation: Total-1,500
Advertising: Inquire for rates.

National Grange-Newsletter   *Consumer, Association*
Publishing Co: National Grange, 1616 H St NW, Washington, DC 20006-4999; Title Tel # (202) 628-3507 Title Fax # (202) 347-1091
Personnel: Editor-Judy Massabny
General Info: Yr. Est. 1907, Bi-monthly, 6 pages, 2 Color, Newsprint
Subscriptions: Free To Qualified Recipient
Circulation: (100% controlled), Total-35,000

National League of Masonic Clubs, League News
Publishing Co: Natl. League of Masonic Clubs, 1 North Dr, Plandome, NY 11030-1416
General Info: Bi-monthly

National Society of Scabbard and Blade Newsletter
Publishing Co: Natl. Society of Scabbard, 205 Thatcher Hall, Okla State, Stillwater, OK 74078-0001; Title Tel # (405) 743-0200
General Info: Monthly

National Society, United States Daughters of 1812 News-Letter
Publishing Co: Natl. Society, U.S. Daughters of 1812, 1461 Rhode Island Ave NW, Washington, DC 20005-5402; Title Tel # (317) 736-8011
Personnel: Editor-Arthur Beineke
General Info: Semi-annually, Mimeo press
Circulation: Total-4,500
Printing Co: Franklin Printing Svc., 26 E Jefferson St, Franklin, IN 46131-2321 Tel # (317) 738-3434

Navy Wives News
Publishing Co: Navy Wives Clubs of America, 225 Euclid St, Mount Clemens, MI 48043-1723; Title Tel # (313) 463-6721
General Info: Monthly

New Era/Nova Doba   *Association*
Publishing Co: American Fraternal Union, 111 S 4th Ave E, Ely, MN 55731-1460; Title Tel # (218) 365-3143
Personnel: Editor-Ann Wognum
Editorial Description: Text in English & Slovenian.
General Info: Yr. Est. 1925, Monthly, Trim Size-15 x 21½, 4 pages, ISSN: 0028-5021, No Color
Subscriptions: Indv. $2
Circulation: (100% controlled), Total-8,250
Advertising: Inquire for rates.

News, Notes and Quotes   *Association*
Publishing Co: Phi Delta Kappa, Inc., 8th & Union, Box 789, Bloomington, IN 47402; Title Tel # (812) 339-1156
Personnel: Editor-David Rushland, Art Dir.-Vladimir Bektesh
Editorial Description: Informs members of events within the international fraternity and in its chapters.
General Info: Yr. Est. 1956, Quarterly, Trim Size-8½ x 11, Offset press, 8 pages, ISSN: 0028-923X, 2 Color
Subscriptions: Free
Circulation: (100% controlled), Total-130,000
Printing Co: Metropolitan Printing Services,Inc, 720 S Morton St, Bloomington, IN 47403-2462

News from Turkey
See: ETHNIC

Newsletter   *Association*
Publishing Co: Chesapeake Bay Girl Scout Council, 501 S College Ave, Newark, DE 19713-1301; Title Tel # (302) 658-4258
Personnel: Editor-Claudia French
Editorial Description: News pertaining to Council Girl Scout activities.
General Info: Yr. Est. 1964, 5x/yr., Trim Size-8¼ x 11, Sheetfed press, 8 pages, No Color
Circulation: Total-3,000

Ninth Manhattan Masonic News
Publishing Co: German Masonic Home Corp, 220 E 15th St, New York, NY 10003-3997; Title Tel # (212) 254-2077
Personnel: Editor-Marvin Goldsmith
Editorial Description: Group interests.
General Info: Yr. Est. 1937, Semi-monthly

Nippon Club Dayori   *Association*
Publishing Co: Nippon Club, Inc., 145 W 57th St., New York, NY 10019; Title Tel # (212) 581-2223
Editorial Description: Monthly newsletter of club events and activities.
General Info: Monthly, 12 pages, No Color
Advertising: Inquire for rates.

Notes for Now
See: WOMEN'S

Novyny z Akademii (UVAN)
See: ETHNIC

Odd Fellows News of Texas
Publishing Co: Odd Fellows News of Texas, 3324 W. 2nd Ave., Corsicana, TX 75110; Title Tel # (903) 872-7438
General Info: Yr. Est. 1944, Monthly
Subscriptions: Indv. $1
Circulation: Total-2,600
Advertising: Inquire for rates.

Ohio DeMolay Action   *Association*
Publishing Co: Meredith Graphics, 1231 E. 286th St., Euclid, OH 44132-2194; Title Tel # (216) 261-6333
Personnel: Editor-M.E. Meredith
General Info: Yr. Est. 1976, Irregular, Trim Size-8½ x 11, 4 pages, No Color, Other
Circulation: Total-12,000
Printing Co: Meredith Printing, 1231 E 286th St, Euclid, OH 44132-2194

On Campus
See: RELIGIOUS & THEOLOGICAL

Oracle   *Association*
Publishing Co: Omega Psi Phi Fraternity, Inc., 3951 Snapfinger Pky., Decatur, GA 30035-3203; Title Tel # (202) 667-7158
Personnel: Editor-Otto McClarrin
Editorial Description: Covers news, events, and activities of the second oldest fraternity founded by African American men.

Outlook
See: MANAGEMENT

Page
Association

Publishing Co: Society for Creative Anachronism, 1277 Fallen Leaf Dr, Milpitas, CA 95035-6216; Title Tel # (408) 262-5250
Editorial Description: Announcements & reports of North California SCA events.
General Info: Yr. Est. 1968, Monthly, Trim Size-8½ x 11, 20 pages
Circulation: Total-1,100

Palo Alto Jaycee Connection
Association

Publishing Co: Palo Alto Jaycees, 325a Forest Ave, Palo Alto, CA 94301-2515; Title Tel # (415) 323-7252
Personnel: Editor-Gwen Schoephoester
General Info: Quarterly, 8 pages

Peanut Papers
See: COLLECTIBLES

Perspective
See: RELIGIOUS & THEOLOGICAL

Perspectives
See: COLLEGE STUDENT LIFESTYLE

Phi Kappa Sigma News Letter
Association

Publishing Co: Phi Kappa Sigma Fraternity, PO Box 947, Valley Forge, PA 19482-0947; Title Tel # (215) 783-7222
Personnel: Editor-Ronald Siggi
Editorial Description: General news on the day to day occurences in the fraternity. Features prominent alumni, Headquarters news.
General Info: Yr. Est. 1901, Semi-annually, Trim Size-8½ x 11, Offset press, 16 pages, No Color
Circulation: Total-26,000

Phi Psi Quarterly

Publishing Co: Phi Psi, Philadelphia College of Textil, Philadelphia, PA 19144
Personnel: Editor-James H. Kennedy

Pibroch
See: ETHNIC

Plus Ultra
See: ETHNIC

Proceedings of the General Grand Chapter

Publishing Co: General Grand Chapter, 1618 New Hampshire Ave NW, Washington, DC 20009-2549

Progression
Association

Publishing Co: Canadian Progress Club, 2395 Bayview Ave., North York, ON M2L 1A2 Canada; Title Tel # (416) 446-1830
Personnel: Publisher-Roy Urbach, Editor, Circ. Mgr.-Susan Rilkoff
Editorial Description: Service club work & articles relating to the same.
General Info: Yr. Est. 1971, Quarterly, Trim Size-8½ x 11, Offset press, 24 pages, 2 Color
Circulation: (100% controlled), Total-1,200

Record

Publishing Co: Order of St. Benedict, Inc., St. John's Univ., Collegeville, MN 56321-9999; Title Tel # (612) 363-2011
Personnel: Editor-Don Maher
Editorial Description: Contents include creative journalism, picture spreads accompanying issue, regular editorials, two feature stories per issue, and special section for letters to editor.
General Info: Yr. Est. 1888, Bi-weekly
Subscriptions: Indv. $2
Circulation: Total-3,800

Rollin' Rock Club-News Letter
See: HOBBY

Royal Craftsman

Publishing Co: Royal Arch Masons of Nova Scotia, C/O L.C. Armstrong, RR #4, Shubenacadie, NS B0N 2H0 Canada; Title Tel # (902) 261-2971
Personnel: Editor-L.C. Armstrong
General Info: Quarterly, Trim Size-5½ x 8½, 4 pages
Circulation: Total-3,000

Rural Network Advocate
See: LIFESTYLE

Ruritan
Association

Publishing Co: Ruritan Natl. Inc., Ruritan Rd., PO Box 487, Dublin, VA 24084 Tel # (540) 674-5431 Fax # (540) 674-2304; Title Tel # (703) 674-5431 Title Fax # (703) 674-2304
Personnel: Editor-Ben Crawford, Production Mgr.-Mike Chrisley, Adv. Dir.-Rick Poff
Editorial Description: Quarterly magazine of a community service organization, news of general interest and community volunteer service & monthly newsletter.
General Info: (Formerly Ruritan National, Inc.), Yr. Est. 1930, 5x/yr., Trim Size-8½ x 11, Web press, 32 pages, 2% ads, Color-cover, Other
Subscriptions: Indv. $8, $2/copy
Circulation: Total-37,000
Advertising: Inquire for rates.
Printing Co: Beacon Press, Inc., 4731 Eubank Rd., P.O. Box 26905, Richmond, VA 23261 Tel # (804) 226-2120

SWL
See: HOBBY

Saenger-Zeitung
See: MUSIC & MUSIC TRADES

The Salmagundian
See: ART & SCULPTURE

Scan
See: ETHNIC

Scouter's Digest
See: YOUTH

Scrabble News
See: GIFTS, GAMES, TOYS

Scroll, The
Association

Publishing Co: Phi Delta Theta Fraternity, 2 S Campus Ave, Oxford, OH 45056-1872
Personnel: Editor-David C. Slatton, Sports Ed.-John Davis, Jr.
Editorial Description: Contains education information and news for members of Phi Delta Theta fraternity and their families.
General Info: Yr. Est. 1874, Quarterly, Trim Size-8¼ x 10⅞, 52 pages, ISSN: 00369799, 4 Color, Recycled, Saddle-stitched
Circulation: Total-80,000
Printing Co: Mack Printing Co., 20th and Northampton Streets, Easton, PA 18042

Second Penny
Association

Publishing Co: Saskatchewan Women's Inst., Univ. of Saskatchewan, 137 Kirk Hall, Saskatoon, SK S7N 0W0 Canada; Title Tel # (306) 966-5566
Personnel: Editor-Gwenyth Borsheim
Editorial Description: News, information, and activities of Saskatchewan Womens Institutes at the club, district and provincial level.
General Info: Yr. Est. 1963, Bi-monthly, Trim Size-8½ x 11, Letrpr. press, 10 pages, No Color, Matte
Subscriptions: Indv. $10
Circulation: (100% controlled), Total-1,600

Serbia
See: ETHNIC

Servo

Publishing Co: Louisiana Dept. of Veterans Affairs, Box 94095, Capitol Statio, Baton Rouge, LA 70804-9095; Title Tel # (504) 342-5863
Personnel: Editor-David Perkins
Editorial Description: Issued by LDVA for its service officers to keep them informed on matters affecting veterans.
General Info: Yr. Est. 1949, Monthly, Offset press
Circulation: Total-200
Printing Co: Louisiana Dept. Of Veterans Affairs, 4560 N. Blvd., Ste. 116, Baton Rouge, LA 70806 Tel # (504) 925-7268

Sextant
See: INSURANCE

Sharing Memories
See: HOBBY

Short Talk Bulletin
Association

Publishing Co: Masonic Service Association of the U.S., 8120 Fenton St., Silver Spring, MD 20910; Title Tel # (301) 588-4010
Personnel: Editor-Stewart M. L. Pollard, Circ. Mgr.-Robert Proudley
Editorial Description: Short pamphlets treating of Masonic philosophy, symbolism, customs, ritual, jurisprudence, history.
General Info: Yr. Est. 1923, Monthly, Trim Size-3½ x 8½, Offset press, 10 pages, No Color
Subscriptions: Indv. $2
Circulation: (100% controlled), Total-27,850

Signals

Publishing Co: Alpha Epsilon Rho, Univ. of S. Carolina, Journali, Columbia, SC 29208; Title Tel # (803) 777-3324
Personnel: Publisher-John Lopiccolo
General Info: Monthly

Signet of Theta Psi

Publishing Co: Theta Psi Fraternity, 2305 York St, Kirksville, MO 63501-2067
Editorial Description: Information concerning active chapters and the alumni.
General Info: Yr. Est. 1903, Annually, Mimeo press, 26 pages, No Color, Newsprint
Circulation: Total-600

Society of California Pioneers Newsletter

Publishing Co: Society of California Pioneers, PO Box 191850, San Francisco, CA 94119-1850; Title Tel # (415) 861-5278
General Info: Quarterly

South Carolina Committee Against Hunger
See: NUTRITION

South Dakota Legion
News   *Association*

Publishing Co: American Legion, Dept. of South Dakota, PO Box 67, Watertown, SD 57201-0067; Title Tel # (605) 886-3604
Personnel: Editor-Maynard Hemp
Editorial Description: Devoted to the doings, aims and accomplishments of American Legion Posts and Legionnaires in South Dakota.
General Info: Yr. Est. 1943, Monthly, Offset press, 8 pages, 2 Color
Subscriptions: Indv. $1
Circulation: Total-31,000
Advertising: Inquire for rates.

Southern California DX Club Bulletin

Publishing Co: Southern California DX Club, 12567 Brooklake St., Box 56292, Mar Vista, CA 90066-1809; Title Tel # (213) 397-2984
Personnel: Editor-Don Minkoff
General Info: Yr. Est. 1947, Monthly, Mimeo press, 6 pages, 1% ads, No Color, Newsprint
Subscriptions: Indv. $10
Circulation: (100% controlled)
Advertising: Inquire for rates. Accepts Inserts.
Printing Co: Copytron, 11742 W. Pico Blvd., W. Los Angeles, CA 90064 Tel # (213) 473-0773

Southwest Alliance for Latin America Bulletin
See: ETHNIC

Spokes

Publishing Co: Rotary Club of Portland, 111 SW 5th Ave., Portland, OR 97204-3604; Title Tel # (503) 228-1542
Personnel: Editor-Lisa Jane
Editorial Description: Informs membership of the program and activities of the club as a whole, news concerning the individual members, and the general activities of Rotary International.
General Info: Yr. Est. 1920, Weekly, 4 pages, No Color
Subscriptions: Indv. $15
Circulation: Total-775
Advertising: Inquire for rates.

Sri Lankan
See: ETHNIC

Svithiod Journal   *Association*

Publishing Co: Independent Order of Svithiod, 5518 W Lawrence Ave, Chicago, IL 60630-3412; Title Tel # (312) 736-1191
Personnel: Publisher-Ron Nielsen, Editor-Betty Jane Clausen
Editorial Description: Reports social & charitable activities of lodges to all members.
General Info: Yr. Est. 1898, Monthly, Trim Size-8½ x 11, Mimeo press, 8 pages, ISSN: 0300-6212, No Color, Newsprint, Saddle-stitched
Subscriptions: Indv. $1, $1/copy
Circulation: Total-1,600
Printing Co: R.M. Nielsen Printing Co., 5825 W Irving Park Rd, Chicago, IL 60634-2609 Tel # (312) 523-4300

Swiss Canadian News   *Association*

Publishing Co: Swiss Canadian News, 25 Aylesbury Road, Islington, ON M9A 2M3 Canada; Title Tel # (416) 243-1201
Personnel: Editor-A. Mettler, Adv. Dir.-E. Boxler
Editorial Description: Essentially club news bulletin with information about current events in Switzerland.
General Info: Monthly, Trim Size-8¼ x 11, 20 pages, Color
Subscriptions: Indv. $15
Circulation: Total-800
Advertising: Inquire for rates.

Symbol   *Association*

Publishing Co: Phi Theta Pi, 2103 Cortez Rd, Jacksonville, FL 32246-2313; Title Tel # (904) 641-0964
Personnel: Publisher-Richard Glover
General Info: Yr. Est. 1926, Quarterly, Trim Size-8½ x 11, 5 pages
Circulation: Total-1,500
Advertising: Inquire for rates. Accepts Inserts.
Printing Co: Hartley Press, 4056 Saint Augustine Rd, Jacksonville, FL 32207-6661 Tel # (904) 398-5141

Synagogue Council of America Analysis
See: RELIGIOUS & THEOLOGICAL

Technical Counselor
Newsletters   *Consumer, Association*

Publishing Co: EAA, PO Box 3086, Oshkosh, WI 54903-3086; Title Tel # (414) 426-4821
Personnel: Editor-Ben Owen
Editorial Description: Technical information for aircraft inspectors on the subject of building experimental aircraft.
General Info: (Formerly Designee News), Quarterly, Trim Size-8½ x 11, 12 pages, No Color, Matte
Circulation: Total-3,500

Tiesa

Publishing Co: Assn. of Lithuanian Workers, 26 N St., #42, Middletown, NY 10940
General Info: Monthly, ISSN: 0040-7372

Torchlight
See: RELIGIOUS & THEOLOGICAL

Totem Tabloid   *Association*

Publishing Co: Western Washington DX Club, Inc., PO Box 224, Mercer Island, WA 98040-0224; Title Tel # (206) 321-5671
Personnel: Editor-Jack Fleming
Editorial Description: Information for amateur radio operators who are interested in working DX.
General Info: Yr. Est. 1966, Monthly, Trim Size-8½ x 11, Mimeo press, 16 pages, No Color, Newsprint
Subscriptions: Indv. $10, For. $14
Acquisitions: Publication Bought
Advertising: $30. Accepts Inserts.
Printing Co: Professional Copy, 4200 University Way NE, Seattle, WA 98105-5807 Tel # (206) 634-2689

Triangles Bulletin   *Consumer*

Publishing Co: Lucis Publishing Co., 120 Wall Street 24th Floor, New York, NY 10005; Title Tel # (212) 292-0707
Personnel: Editor-Steve Nation
Editorial Description: The Triangles Bulletin is for men & women of good will. Triangles is a world service activity for all who believe in the power of thought. It is an activity of the Lucis Trust, a non-profit educational corporation.
General Info: Yr. Est. 1937, Quarterly, Offset press, 8 pages, 2 Color, Matte
Subscriptions: Free
Circulation: Total-5,800
Printing Co: Fort Orange Press, 31 Sand Creek Rd, Albany, NY 12205-1442 Tel # (518) 489-3233, Fax # (800) 950-7117

Turtle Bay News

Publishing Co: Turtle Bay Assn., 224 E 47th St, New York, NY 10017-2102; Title Tel # (212) 751-5465
Personnel: Editor-George Bonner, Jr., Production Mgr.-Millie Margiotta
Editorial Description: Community newsletter update on Turtle Bay news.
General Info: Yr. Est. 1971, Bi-monthly, Trim Size-11 x 17, Offset press, 4 pages, No Color
Circulation: Total-1,000

Ukrainian Professional & Business Club Bulletin

Publishing Co: Ukrainian Professional & Business Club of Winnipeg, Inc., Box 1144, Winnipeg, MB R3C 2Y1 Canada
Personnel: Editor-Myrna Tycholaz
Editorial Description: Club business; Ukrainian community events-Natl; book reviews; Issues in the Ukr. community; Articles on Ukr. culture; Achievements of club members.
General Info: Yr. Est. 1943, Monthly, Trim Size-8½ x 11, Mimeo press, 6 pages, 2 Color
Circulation: Total-250
Advertising: Accepts Inserts.

Velouchi Bulletin
See: ETHNIC

Vorwarts, Forward   *Association*

Publishing Co: Sudeten Club Forward, Toronto, 179 Durant Avenue, Toronto, ON M4J 4W5 Canada; Title Tel # (416) 425-9785
Personnel: Publisher, Editor-Ludwig Lowit, Circ. Mgr., Production Mgr.-Hermine Weisbach
Editorial Description: Political, social cultural, text in German.
General Info: Yr. Est. 1947, Bi-monthly, Trim Size-8½ x 11, Mimeo press, 28 pages, ISSN: 0380-3244, No Color
Subscriptions: Indv. $4, $2/copy
Circulation: (100% controlled), Total-400

Washington Action Reporter   *Business, Association*

Publishing Co: Veterans of Foreign Wars of the U.S., 406 W. 34th St., Kansas City, MO 64111-2736; Title Tel # (816) 756-3390
Personnel: Editor-Richard Kolb
Editorial Description: Informs membership of legislative, service, national security work done by V.F.W. in Washington, D.C.
General Info: Yr. Est. 1976, Monthly, Offset press, 12 pages, 2 Color, Newsprint
Circulation: (100% controlled), Total-10,000

West Virginia Legionnaire
See: VETERANS

Westchester Country Club News

Publishing Co: Westchester Country Club News, Westchester Country Club, Rye, NY 10580-1891; Title Tel # (914) 967-6000
Personnel: Editor-Cathy McCabe, Production Mgr.-Fred Jarvis
Editorial Description: Reports on sporting & social activities plus reports by president & committees.
General Info: Yr. Est. 1933, 7x/yr., Trim Size-8½ x 11, 40 pages, No Color
Subscriptions: Indv. $25
Circulation: (100% controlled), Total-1,600
Advertising: Inquire for rates.
Printing Co: SBS Graphics, 635 6th Ave., New York, NY 10011 Tel # (212) 564-4787

Western Catholic Union Record
See: RELIGIOUS & THEOLOGICAL

Working Class Hero Beatles Club, The
See: FAN MAGAZINES-MOVIE, RADIO, TV

Written Wort
See: BEVERAGES - BREWING

Ye Olde Bastards Bulletin *Association*

Publishing Co: Feature News Service, 9328 Sondra Avenue, St. Louis, MO 63144-1010; Title Tel # (314) 961-2300 Title Fax # (314) 961-9828
Personnel: Publisher-Susan Sonora, Editor-Robert Adams, Sr., Circ. Mgr.-Wolff White, Production Mgr.-Bat Guano, Adv. Dir.-Victor Viator, Art Dir.-Sam Sonora, Sr., Promotion Dir.-Abe Blitz
Editorial Description: Bastardy, royalty, politics, archives reports, research reports, debauchery, crime and corruption, gambling and government.
General Info: (Formerly Ye Old Bastards League of London), Yr. Est. 1863, Monthly, Web press, 24 pages, 4 Color, Coated
Subscriptions: Indv. $60, Inst. $350, $25/copy
Acquistions: Publication Bought, Publication Sold
Circulation: (VAC), Total-286,000

Young Women's Christian Assn. of Canada Newsletter

Publishing Co: Young Women's Christian Assn. of Canada, 80 Gerrard St. East, Toronto, ON M5B 1G6 Canada
General Info: Bi-monthly

COLLECTIBLES

American Fish Decoy Association
See: HOBBY

American Lock Collectors Association Newsletter *Association*

Publishing Co: American Lock Collectors Association, 36076 Grennada St, Livonia, MI 48154-5278; Title Tel # (313) 522-0920
Personnel: Publisher, Editor-Charles Chandler
Editorial Description: News about antique locks, padlocks, shackles and related collector information.
General Info: Yr. Est. 1970, Bi-monthly, Trim Size-8½ x 11, 3 pages, No Color
Subscriptions: Indv. $16, Can. $16, For. $20
Circulation: Total-350

Antique Comb Collector
See: ANTIQUES & ART GOODS

Appraisers Standard
See: ANTIQUES & ART GOODS

Ashtray Journal
See: TOBACCO

Autograph Research *Consumer*

Publishing Co: Michael E. Johnson, 862 Thomas Ave, San Diego, CA 92109-3940; Title Tel # (619) 483-8632
Personnel: Publisher-Michael E. Johnson
Editorial Description: Newsletter for the serious collector of autographs, presenting original research on autograph values, availability and authenticity, including the addresses and autograph signing habits of popular celebrities.
General Info: Yr. Est. 1991, Monthly, Trim Size-8½ x 11, Desktop press, 8 pages, ISSN: 1069-6008
Subscriptions: Indv. $25, Can. $35, For. $35, $3/copy
Advertising: $75.

Bayberry Farm Peddlers *Consumer*

Publishing Co: Bayberry Farm Peddlers, PO Box 447, Perkasie, PA 18944
Editorial Description: Bi-monthly newsletter. Offering reproductions of old cutters and new designs, recipes and decorating ideas for cooks and collectors.
General Info: Monthly
Subscriptions: Indv. $12

Bead and Button
See: HOBBY

Bill Nelson Newsletter *Consumer*

Publishing Co: Nelson Newsletter Publishing Corp., PO Box 41630, Tucson, AZ 85717-1630; Title Tel # (602) 629-0868 Title Fax # (602) 629-0387
Personnel: Publisher, Editor-Bill Nelson, Circ. Mgr.-Julie Nelson
Editorial Description: Covers the exciting world of pin collecting. Articles cover sport, Disney, Olympic, and Coca Cola pins. Also contains advice for beginning pin collectors.
General Info: (Formerly Olympic Collectors Newsletter), Yr. Est. 1985, Monthly, Trim Size-8½ x 11, Offset press, 8 pages, ISSN: 0894-4911, No Color, Matte
Subscriptions: Indv. $20, Can. $30, For. $30, $2/copy
Circulation: Total-90,000, Readership-100,000

Bookplates in the News
See: BOOKS & BOOK TRADE

Bookseller
See: BOOKS & BOOK TRADE

Brandstand
See: HOBBY

Brewster Society News Scope *Consumer, Association*

Publishing Co: Brewster Society, 100 Severn Ave Apt 605, Annapolis, MD 21403-2621; Title Tel # (301) 365-1855
Personnel: Publisher, Editor-Cozy Baker
Editorial Description: For designers and collectors of kaledioscopes.
General Info: Quarterly
Subscriptions: Indv. $35
Printing Co: Hagerstown Bookbinding & Printing, 952 Frederick St, Hagerstown, MD 21740-6821 Tel # (301) 733-2000, Fax # (301) 733-6586

Bridal Collectors News
See: BRIDE

Butterfly Net
See: ANTIQUES & ART GOODS

California Record Collector

Publishing Co: M.AmM.M.A,Co., P.O. Box 92334, Long Beach, CA 90809
Editorial Description: Be it for comic fans, computer hobbyists, motorcycle enthusiasts, or record collectors. This new publication is completely devoted to reporting on record collector convention in California .
General Info: Quarterly, Trim Size-8.5 x 11, 12 pages
Subscriptions: Indv. $2

Candlewick Collector Newsletter, The
See: GLASS, STONE & CLAY

Cane Collector's Chronicle *Consumer, Association*

Publishing Co: Cane Collector's Chronicle, 15 2nd St NE, Washington, DC 20002-7301
Personnel: Publisher-Linda Beeman
Editorial Description: For collectors of walking sticks.
General Info: Quarterly
Subscriptions: Indv. $30
Advertising: Inquire for rates.

Cartomania
See: GEOGRAPHY

Chauffeurs' Badges and Transportation Badges of the World
See: HOBBY

Chicago Playing Card Collectors, Membership Roster
See: HOBBY

Circuit, The
See: PHILATELY & POSTAL AFFAIRS

Coined Freedom Report
See: INVESTMENT

Collectible Newspapers *Consumer, Association*

Publishing Co: Newspaper Collectors Society of America, PO Box 19134, Lansing, MI 48901-9134 Fax # (517) 887-2194; Title Tel # (517) 887-1255
Personnel: Publisher, Editor-Rick Brown
Editorial Description: Contains information for collectors of newspapers as well as organization activities.
General Info: Yr. Est. 1984, Quarterly, Trim Size-8¼ x 10½, Desktop press, 20 pages, ISSN: 1076-4356, 40% ads
Subscriptions: Indv. $18, Inst. $18, Can. $23, For. $28
Advertising: $45.

Diamond Duds
See: BASEBALL

Director
See: HOBBY

ETCetera
See: ANTIQUES & ART GOODS

Edges   *Business*

Publishing Co: Sponsor-American Blade Collectors, Krause Publications, Inc., 700 E. State St., Iola, WI 54990-0001 Fax # (715) 445-4087; Title Tel # (715) 445-2214
Personnel: Publisher-David Kowalski, Editor-Steve Shakleford, Art Ed.-Jim Sasse, Adv. Dir.-John Kronschnabl
Editorial Description: Provides updated knife pricing information while it is hot. Focuses on antique, commemorative, and older factory collectible knives.
General Info: Yr. Est. 1980, Quarterly, Trim Size-8½ x 11, Web press, 24 pages, Newsprint, Saddle-stitched
Subscriptions: Indv. $35, $10/copy
Circulation: Total-5,000, Readership-30,000
List Rental: List Management Co.: Aggressive List Management, 18-2 E Dundee Rd Ste 101, Barrington, IL 60010-5273 Tel # (708) 304-4030, Fax # (708) 304-4032
Printing Co: Target Graphics, PO Box 1272, Chattanooga, TN 37401-1272 Tel # (615) 522-7700

Ertl Blueprinter, The

Publishing Co: Ertl Co., The, PO Box 500, Dyersville, IA 52040-0500; Title Tel # (319) 875-5855 Title Fax # (319) 875-5674
Personnel: Publisher, Editor-Karen Sands
Editorial Description: Informational claering house regarding news and old collectible AMT model kits.
General Info: Yr. Est. 1987, Offset press, 12 pages, 4 Color
Subscriptions: Indv. $8, For. $12, $1/copy
Circulation: Total-20,000
Printing Co: Johnson Graphics, 120 Prentress Lake Road, Box 319, E. Dubuque, IL 61025 Tel # (815) 747-6511

FMCA Newsletter
See: INSURANCE

Fan Club Monitor
See: FAN MAGAZINES-MOVIE, RADIO, TV

Fiesta Collector's Quarterly
See: GLASS, STONE & CLAY

Florence Collector's Club

Publishing Co: Rita Bee, 6960 Abel Stearns Ave., Riverside, CA 92509; Title Tel # (909) 683-1485
Personnel: Editor-Rita Bee
General Info: Bi-monthly
Subscriptions: Indv. $20
Advertising: Inquire for rates.

Front Striker Bulletin   *Consumer, Association*   CPM: $73

Publishing Co: American Matchcover Collecting Club, PO Box 18481, Asheville, NC 28814-0481; Title Tel # (704) 254-4487 Title Fax # (704) 254-1066
Personnel: Circ. Mgr.-Karin Retskin, Publisher, Editor, Circ. Mgr., Promotion Dir.-Bill Retskin
Editorial Description: For matchbook cover collectors.
General Info: Yr. Est. 1986, Quarterly, Sheetfed press, 20 pages, ISSN: 1041-1852, No Color, Newsprint
Subscriptions: Indv. $20, $3/copy
Circulation: Total-750
Advertising: $55. Accepts Inserts.

G.I. Joe Collectors Club   *Consumer, Association*

Publishing Co: G.I. Joe Collectors' Club, 12513 Birchfall Dr., Raleigh, NC 27614 Tel # (919) 847-5263 Fax # (919) 847-5132; Title Tel # (818) 563-1179
Personnel: Publisher-Brian Savage
Editorial Description: Information about collecting popular 60s toy.
General Info: Yr. Est. 1985, Monthly, Mimeo press, 8 pages, No Color
Subscriptions: Indv. $35, Can. $46, For. $80, Free With Membership
Circulation: Total-500
Advertising: Accepts Inserts.

Game Researcher's Notes   *Consumer, Association*

Publishing Co: American Game Collector's Association, 49 Brooks Ave., Lewiston, ME 04240-5901
Personnel: Editor-Lindy Van Fleet
Editorial Description: Newsletter of the American Game Collector's Association.
General Info: Tri-annually, Trim Size-8½ x 11, 24 pages, ISSN: 1050-6608
Subscriptions: Indv. $25
Advertising: $80.

Game Times   *Association*

Publishing Co: American Game Collector's Association, 49 Brooks Ave., Lewiston, ME 04240-5901
Personnel: Editor-Susan Stock
Editorial Description: Contains information about collecting games and history of games.
General Info: Yr. Est. 1985, Tri-annually, Trim Size-8½ x 11, 24 pages, ISSN: 1050-6594
Subscriptions: Indv. $25
Circulation: Total-350
Advertising: Inquire for rates.

George Kamm Paperweights   *Consumer*

Publishing Co: George Kamm Paperweights, 24 Townsend Ct, Lancaster, PA 17603-6797; Title Tel # (717) 872-7858 Title Fax # (717) 397-4294
Editorial Description: Paperweights for sale along with paperweight collecting and conference information.
General Info: Bi-monthly, Trim Size-8½ x 11, 6 pages, 4 Color, Coated
Subscriptions: Indv. $5

Giftbeat
See: DEPARTMENT STORE & RETAIL

Gilligan's Island News
See: CLUBS

GoodNewsletter   *Consumer, Association*

Publishing Co: Enesco Corp. The Memories of Yesterday Collector's Society, PO Box 245, Elk Grove Village, IL 60009-0245 Tel # (708) 640-5200
Editorial Description: Official publication of the Precious Moments Collector's Club.
General Info: Quarterly

Guidon
See: CLUBS

Hall Collector's Club Newsletter
See: GLASS, STONE & CLAY

Hawaiian Shell News
See: NATURAL HISTORY

Illustrator Collector's News, The   *Business*

Publishing Co: Spectrum of Rainbows, 372 Kcahhane Rd., Sequim, WA 98382-1958 Tel # (206) 683-2559 Fax # (206) 683-6559; Title Tel # (360) 683-2559 Title Fax # (360) 683-9708
Personnel: Publisher-Jay Richmond
Editorial Description: For collectors and dealers of old magazine, pin-ups, books, Marilyn Monroe, illustrators 1850's thru 1980's. Free price duides and classifieds.
General Info: Yr. Est. 1983, Bi-monthly, Trim Size-8½ x 11, Offset press, 24 pages
Subscriptions: Indv. $17, $4/copy
Circulation: Total-1,200
Advertising: Accepts Inserts.

Illustrator Magazine & Paper Collector's News   *Business, Consumer*

Publishing Co: T.I.C.N., PO Box 1958, Sequim, WA 98382-1958 Tel # (360) 683-2559 Fax # (360) 683-2559
Personnel: Editor-Denis Charces Jackson, Editorial Page Ed.-Denis C. Jackson, Circ. Mgr.-Marcia Jackson, Mktg. Dir.-Blaine Myhre
Editorial Description: For collectors of old prints, paper collectibles, magazines, etc.
General Info: (Formerly Illustrator Collector's News), Yr. Est. 1983, Bi-monthly, Trim Size-8½ x 11, Desktop press, 24 pages, 25% ads, 2 Color, Saddle-stitched
Subscriptions: Indv. $17, Inst. $12, Can. $18, For. $32, $3/copy
Circulation: Readership-5,000
Advertising: $64. Accepts Inserts.
Printing Co: Richmond Press, 120 W. Bell, Sequim, WA 98382 Tel # (360) 683-0148

Illustratotor's Swap incl JW Anglund Collectors News
See: CHILDREN

In the Groove   *Association*   CPM: $38

Publishing Co: Michigan Antique Phonograph Society, 2609 Devonshire Ave., Lansing, MI 48910-3671; Title Tel # (517) 482-7996
Personnel: Editor-John Whitacre
Editorial Description: Monthly 20 page newsletter with news for the members, classified ads, display ads, letters to Editor, book reviews, how-to-do-it articles, Chapter news, Australia Calling, etc.
General Info: Yr. Est. 1976, Monthly, Trim Size-8½ x 11, Web press, 20 pages, 50% ads, Color-cover, Newsprint
Subscriptions: Indv. $22, Inst. $20, Can. $24, For. $35, $22/copy
Acquistions: Publication Bought
Circulation: Total-920
Advertising: $35. Accepts Inserts.

Joan Walsh Anglund Collector's News
See: CHILDREN

LANSA
See: NUMISMATICS

MFE Collectors' Bookline
See: BOOKS & BOOK TRADE

MIAA Industry News
See: HOBBY

MOOsletter, The
See: DAIRY

Marble Mart Newsletter   *Association*

Publishing Co: Marble Collectors Unlimited, Box 206, Northboro, MA 01532-0206; Title Tel # (508) 393-2923
Personnel: Editor-Beverly Brule
Editorial Description: Information on marble meets, auctions and other activities, notices of new marble books. contains want ads section.
General Info: Yr. Est. 1978, Quarterly, 8 pages, 7% ads, No Color
Subscriptions: Indv. $10
Circulation: Total-800
Advertising: Inquire for rates.
List Rental: Rents Lists

Metro Scene   *Consumer*   **CPM:** $31

Publishing Co: Metro Scene, PO Box 911, Westwood, NJ 07675-0911; Title Tel # (201) 225-0452 Title Fax # (201) 225-0452
Personnel: Publisher-Frank Amico
Editorial Description: Lists autograph signing events in NY, CT, NJ and PA. As well as stores that will ship signed books all over the country. Free promotions for events.
General Info: Monthly, Trim Size-8½ x 11, 8 pages, No Color, Matte
Subscriptions: Indv. $30, $4/copy
Circulation: Total-2,200
Advertising: $70.
Printing Co: Staples, 217/225 M 46 West, Saddlebrook, NJ 07662 Tel # (201) 909-0575

Miller's Market Report
See: GIFTS, GAMES, TOYS

Mini License Plate & Key Chain Tag Newsletter
See: GOLF

Mobilia
See: AUTOMOTIVE

Mystic Light of the Aladdin Knights
See: HOBBY

Nailer News   *Association*

Publishing Co: Texas Date Nail Collectors Assn., 501 W. Horton, Brenham, TX 77833; Title Tel # (409) 830-1495
Editorial Description: Information for collectors of nails used to on railroad ties to identify the date they were laid and the location.
General Info: Yr. Est. 1970, Bi-monthly
Subscriptions: Indv. $14
Circulation: Total-250
List Rental: Rents Lists

New Lovecraft Collector
See: MYSTERY & HORROR

Northern Lights (Minneapolis)
See: ANTIQUES & ART GOODS

Old Abe's News   *Consumer, Association*

Publishing Co: JI Case Collector's Association, 4004 Coal Valley Rd, Vinton, OH 45686-9109
Personnel: Editor-Dave Erb
Editorial Description: For collectors of machinery bearing the JI Case trademark.
General Info: Quarterly, Trim Size-8½ x 11, 54 pages, ISSN: 0896-4955, 2 Color, Matte, Saddle-stitched
Subscriptions: Indv. $20, $5/copy
Advertising: $100.

Opaque News
See: ANTIQUES & ART GOODS

Oz Collector, The
See: HOBBY

PATINAGRAM
See: ANTIQUES & ART GOODS

Pacific Currents
See: BOOKS & BOOK TRADE

Peanut Papers   *Association*

Publishing Co: Peanut Pals, PO Box 4465, Huntsville, AL 35815-4465 Tel # (205) 871-9798; Title Tel # (205) 881-9198
Editorial Description: Contains info about the study of collection of Planters Peanuts memorabilia & info about club activities.
General Info: Yr. Est. 1978, Bi-monthly, 16 pages, Color-cover
Subscriptions: Indv. $20, $2/copy
Circulation: Total-450, Readership-750
Advertising: Inquire for rates.

Postcard Classics   *Association*   **CPM:** $58

Publishing Co: Deltiologists of America, PO Box 8, Norwood, PA 19074-0008; Title Tel # (610) 485-8572
Personnel: Publisher-James Lowe, Editor-Dr. James Lowe, Circ. Mgr.-V.J. Lowe
Editorial Description: Buying, selling, collecting antique (pre-1930) picture postcards.
General Info: (Formerly Deltiology), Yr. Est. 1960, Bi-monthly, Trim Size-8½ x 11, Sheetfed press, 16 pages, ISSN: 0897-4020, 4% ads, No Color, Matte, Saddle-stitched
Subscriptions: Indv. $15, Inst. $15, Can. $18, For. $18, $3/copy
Acquistions: Publication Bought
Circulation: Total-1,100
Advertising: $64. Accepts Inserts.

Prehistoric Times, The   *Consumer*

Publishing Co: Mike Fredericks, 145 Bayline Circle, Folsom, CA 95630
Editorial Description: The first collector newsletter about Dinosaur Toys and models
General Info: Trim Size-8.5 x 11, 30 pages
Subscriptions: Indv. $4

Presidents' Journal
See: HISTORY

Rail Splitter, The   *Consumer*

Publishing Co: Rail Splitter, The, PO Box 275, New York, NY 10044
Editorial Description: A publication for the Abraham Lincoln historical collector.
General Info: Irregular

Rathkamp Matchcover Society-Bulletin
See: HOBBY

Report to Members
See: PHILATELY & POSTAL AFFAIRS

Rusty Iron Monthly
See: ANTIQUES & ART GOODS

St. Patrick Notes   *Consumer*

Publishing Co: Chuck Thompson and Associates, P.O. Box 11652, Houston, TX 77293; Title Tel # (713) 442-7200
Personnel: Publisher-Chuck L. Thompson, Editor-Chuck Thompson
Editorial Description: A 'Club Type' publication for fans who wish to help promote the memory of St. Patrick; contains legends, myths, stories, facts, and other notes about St. Patrick and the Irish. Subscribers include genealogists and others interested in Irish family history.
General Info: (Formerly St. Patrick Card Collectors), Yr. Est. 1995, Trim Size-500 x 8½, Desktop press, 6 pages, No Color
Subscriptions: Free
Circulation: Total-500

Space Autograph News
See: AERONAUTICS/ASTRONAUTICS

Stained Finger, The   *Consumer, Association*

Publishing Co: Society of Inkwell Collectors, 5136 Thomas Ave S, Minneapolis, MN 55410-2241 Fax # (612) 920-7835; Title Tel # (612) 922-2792
Personnel: Publisher-Vincent McGraw, Editor-Michele McGraw, Art Dir.-Kimberly Varnell
Editorial Description: History, identification, and market prices of inkwells, pens & accessories. Also covers repair & cleaning techniques.
General Info: Yr. Est. 1980, Quarterly, 12 pages, 9% ads, No Color
Subscriptions: Indv. $25
Circulation: Total-700
Advertising: Inquire for rates.

Stamp Pals International Newsletter
See: PHILATELY & POSTAL AFFAIRS

Stove Parts Needed
See: ANTIQUES & ART GOODS

Table Top Train News
See: HOBBY

Thimbletter   *Association*

Publishing Co: Thimbletter, 93 Walnut Hill Rd, Newton, MA 02161-1836; Title Tel # (617) 969-9358
Personnel: Publisher, Editor-Lorraine M. Crosby
Editorial Description: A newsletter for thimble collectors, providing information relative to thimbles and thimble collecting.
General Info: Yr. Est. 1973, Bi-monthly, Trim Size-8½ x 11, Offset press, 14 pages, No Color, Recycled, Other
Subscriptions: Indv. $12, Inst. $12, Can. $12, For. $15, $2/copy
Circulation: Total-600
Printing Co: Roberts Printing, 153 California St, Newton, MA 02158-1023 Tel # (617) 382-0650

Toothpick Bulletin
See: HOBBY

Trade Fax
See: SPORTS & SPORTING GOODS

Tuff Stuff's Baseball Bulletin
See: BASEBALL

Viking Import House, Inc. *Consumer*

Publishing Co: Viking Import House, Inc., 690 NE 13th St, Fort Lauderdale, FL 33304-1110; Title Tel # (305) 763-3388
Editorial Description: Limited edition collector's plates, cottages and figurines.
General Info: Monthly, Trim Size-8½ x 11, 6 pages, 2 Color, Matte, Saddle-stitched
Circulation: Total-60,000

Weekly Collectors' Gazette

Publishing Co: Rosie Wells Enterprises, Rr 1 Box 255, Canton, IL 61520-9730 Tel # (309) 668-2211 Fax # (309) 668-2795
Personnel: Publisher, Editor-Rosie Wells, Circ. Mgr.-Bernice Cattron, Production Mgr.-Denise Bankes, Adv. Dir.-Nikki Hadsell, Art Dir.-Michelle Ford, Mktg. Dir.-Mary Maynard
General Info: Weekly, 4 pages
Subscriptions: Indv. $84, $2/copy
List Rental: List Management Co.: Manager: Faye Mathis; Direct Marketing Resources, 301 Duck Rd., Grandview, MO 64030-1664 Tel # (816) 767-9700, Fax # (816) 767-0770

West Coast Lock Collectors *Association*

Publishing Co: West Coast Lock Collectors, C/O Ace Lock & Key, 1427 Lincoln Blvd., Santa Monica, CA 90401-2732; Title Tel # (310) 454-7295
Personnel: Editor-Don Jackson
Editorial Description: Articles on new finds, antique padlocks, keys, and other lock related items.
General Info: Yr. Est. 1978, Quarterly, Trim Size-8½ x 11, Mimeo press, 4 pages, No Color
Subscriptions: Indv. $10
Circulation: Total-175
Advertising: Inquire for rates.

Worldwide Treasure Bureau Newsletter
See: NUMISMATICS

COLLEGE ALUMNI

Birmingham, Alabama

Miles Review, The *Consumer*

Publishing Co: Miles College, Box 3800, Birmingham, AL 35208
Editorial Description: Covers news and activities for and about alumni.
General Info: Yr. Est. 1988, Quarterly, Trim Size-8½ x 11, 12 pages, 4 Color, Coated, Saddle-stitched
Subscriptions: Free To Qualified Recipient
Circulation: Total-8,000

Marion, Alabama

Alumni Bulletin *Consumer*

Publishing Co: Marion Military Institute, Alumni Office, Marion, AL 36756
Personnel: Editor-Edward Bradford
General Info: Quarterly, Trim Size-8½ x 11, 24 pages, No Color, Matte, Saddle-stitched

Mobile, Alabama

Vanguard , The   CPM: $90

Publishing Co: Univ. of South Alabama, The Vanguard Box U-25100, P.O. Drawer U-25100, Mobile, AL 36688-0001; Title Tel # (334) 460-6442 Title Fax # (334) 380-2850
Personnel: Editor-John Livingston Pettie, Editorial Page Ed.-Joy Langston, Circ. Mgr.-Owen Freeland, Adv. Dir.-Amy Oliver
General Info: (Formerly Looking South), Yr. Est. 1965, Weekly, Trim Size-13 x 21, 11 pages, 4 Color, Newsprint
Subscriptions: Indv. $30, Free In Designated Area
Circulation: Total-7,000
Advertising: $630. Accepts Inserts.
Printing Co: Gulf Coast Newspapers, Highway 59 South, Robertsdale, AL 36567 Tel # (334) 947-7712, Fax # (334) 947-7652

Tuscaloosa, Alabama

Stillman Bulletin

Publishing Co: Stillman College, PO Box 1430, Tuscaloosa, AL 35403-1430 Tel # (205) 349-4240; Title Tel # (205) 349-5613 Title Fax # (205) 349-3624
Personnel: Editor-Cresandra W. Smothers
Editorial Description: College news including student assignments, faculty/staff news, updates on alumni, grants & etc.
General Info: Quarterly, Trim Size-8.5 x 11, 16 pages, Color
Subscriptions: Free To Qualified Recipient
Circulation: Total-13,000
Printing Co: The Print Shop, 915 16th Avenue East, Tuscaloosa, AL 35404 Tel # (205) 553-3300, Fax # (205) 553-9401

Fairbanks, Alaska

UAF Alumni Assn. Newsletter *Association*

Publishing Co: University of Alaska Alumni Association, Publications Dept., Fairbanks, AK 99775-0001; Title Tel # (907) 474-7081
General Info: Yr. Est. 1986, Quarterly, 4 pages
Subscriptions: Indv. $25, Free
Circulation: Total-15,500, Readership-31,000

Little Rock, Arkansas

UALR Alumnus *Association*

Publishing Co: Univ. of Arkansas at Little Rock, 2801 S University Ave, Little Rock, AR 72204; Title Tel # (501) 569-3194
Editorial Description: Newsa and information for alumni.
General Info: (Formerly UALR Star), Yr. Est. 1985, Quarterly, 12 pages
Circulation: Total-500

Magnolia, Arkansas

SAU Stater *Association*

Publishing Co: Southern Arkansas Univ., SAU Box 1400, Magnolia, AR 71753 Tel # (501) 235-4000; Title Tel # (501) 235-4990
Personnel: Editor-R. Hoback
Editorial Description: Campus & alumni news.
General Info: Yr. Est. 1962, Quarterly, Trim Size-8½ x 11, Offset press, 16 pages, No Color
Circulation: (100% controlled), Total-10,000

Claremont, California

ASCMC Newsletter

Publishing Co: Claremont McKenna College, 400 E. 9th, Claremont, CA 91711 Tel # (714) 621-8111; Title Tel # (714) 621-8000
General Info: Monthly
Circulation: Total-800

Perspective *Association*

Publishing Co: School of Theology at Claremont, 1325 North College Ave., Public Relations Office, Claremont, CA 91711-3199; Title Tel # (714) 626-3521
Personnel: Editor-Stephanie Graham
Editorial Description: News of interest to supporters, alumni of the school, & those interested in thelogical education.
General Info: Yr. Est. 1957, Quarterly, Trim Size-11½ x 17½, Offset press, 6 pages, 2 Color, Matte, Saddle-stitched
Circulation: Total-12,000

Fullerton, California

Alum News *Association*

Publishing Co: Pacific Christian College, 2500 E Nutwood Ave, Fullerton, CA 92631-3199; Title Tel # (714) 879-3901
Personnel: Editor-Marjorie Weichal
Editorial Description: Alumni news with literary & editorial content.
General Info: Yr. Est. 1984, Quarterly, Offset press, 8 pages, 2 Color, Saddle-stitched
Circulation: (100% controlled), Total-2,000
Printing Co: Robinson/Mayer Lithographers, 1040 Segovia Cir, Placentia, CA 92670-7100 Tel # (714) 630-4244

Irvine, California

Issues, Irvine Valley College *Business*

Publishing Co: Irvine Valley College, 5500 Irvine Center Dr, Irvine, CA 92720-4399 Tel # (714) 559-9300; Title Tel # (714) 559-3277 Title Fax # (714) 559-3270
Personnel: Editor-George Mchory
Editorial Description: Highlights events, activities, & programs at Irvine Valley College.
General Info: Yr. Est. 1988, Quarterly, Trim Size-8½ x 11, Offset press, 2 Color, Coated, Saddle-stitched

National City, California

Pneumo Pneus
See: COLLEGE STUDENT

Oakland, California

Alumni Oak Leaf

Publishing Co: Patten College, 2433 Coolidge Ave, Oakland, CA 94601-2699; Title Tel # (415) 533-8300
Personnel: Editor-Dr. Rebecca Patten
General Info: Every two years, Trim Size-8 x 10, 9 pages
Circulation: Total-500

San Rafael, California

Columbia Pacific University
Alumni Newsletter   *Association*

Publishing Co: Columbia Pacific Univ., 1415 3rd St, San Rafael, CA 94901-2860
Fax # (415) 459-5856; Title Tel # (415) 459-1650
Editorial Description: Articles on C.P.U. student, alumni and university activities.
General Info: Yr. Est. 1980, Semi-annually, Trim Size-8½ x 11, Sheetfed press, 4 pages, No Color
Circulation: Total-10,000

Stockton, California

Humphreys College
Quarterly News Bulletin   *Consumer*

Publishing Co: Humphreys College, 6650 Inglewood Ave, Stockton, CA 95207-3896;
Title Tel # (209) 478-0800 Title Fax # (209) 478-8721
Personnel: Co-Editor-Pamela Knapp, Co-Editor-John Seabreeze
Editorial Description: Newsletter for alumni and students of Humphreys College.
General Info: Quarterly, Trim Size-8½ x 11, Letrpr. press, 4 pages, 2 Color, Matte, Saddle-stitched
Subscriptions: Free
Circulation: Total-20,000
Printing Co: Desktop Publishing and Print, 1704 W Hammer Ln, Stockton, CA 95209-2922
Tel # (209) 477-9209, Fax # (209) 473-4575

Whittier, California

News and Alumni Report   *Association*

Publishing Co: Los Angeles College of Chiropractic, 16200 Amber Valley Dr # B1166, Whittier, CA 90604-4051; Title Tel # (310) 947-8755
Personnel: Editor-Laura Arthur
Editorial Description: College news, chiropractic principles, graduate school opportunities.
General Info: Yr. Est. 1942, Tri-annually, Trim Size-8½ x 11, Desktop press, 12 pages, 2 Color, Coated, Saddle-stitched
Subscriptions: Free With Membership
Circulation: Total-5,000
Printing Co: North Hollywood Printing, 3915 W Burbank Blvd # 6037, Burbank, CA 91505-2118
Tel # (213) 849-6281

Denver, Colorado

Brown & Gold
See: COLLEGE STUDENT

Pueblo, Colorado

USC Alumni Newsletter   *Association*

Publishing Co: Univ. of Southern Colorado, 2200 Bonforte Blvd, Pueblo, CO 81001-4901
Tel # (719) 549-2100; Title Tel # (719) 549-2114 Title Fax # (719) 549-2938
General Info: Trim Size-8½ x 11, 24 pages, Color-cover
Circulation: Total-8,000
Advertising: Inquire for rates.

Fairfield, Connecticut

Night Hawk
See: COLLEGE STUDENT

Waterbury, Connecticut

Postcripts Newsletter   *Consumer*

Publishing Co: Teikyo Post University, 800 Country Club Rd, Waterbury, CT 06708-3200;
Title Tel # (203) 596-4606
Editorial Description: Events and issues at Teikyo Post of concern for alumni and parents.
General Info: Semi-annually, Trim Size-11¼ x 17½, 16 pages, 2 Color, Newsprint, Saddle-stitched

West Haven, Connecticut

Insight   *Association, Scholarly*

Publishing Co: University of New Haven Public Relations Office, 300 Orange Ave, West Haven, CT 06516-1916 Tel # (203) 932-7000; Title Tel # (203) 932-7246 Title Fax # (203) 937-0759
Personnel: Publisher-Cindy Avery, Editor-Mimi Houston
Editorial Description: News & feature stories about members of the Univ. of New Haven community, plus relevant photos.
General Info: Yr. Est. 1978, Quarterly, Trim Size-8½ x 11, Web press, 16 pages, 2 Color, Other, Saddle-stitched
Subscriptions: Free To Qualified Recipient
Circulation: Total-25,000
Printing Co: E.H. Roberts, 510 Washington Ave, North Haven, CT 06473-1313 Tel # (203) 239-0717

Washington, District of Columbia

Alumni Forum   *Association*

Publishing Co: Catholic Univ. of America, Marist Hill, Washington, DC 20064-0001
Tel # (202) 319-5600 Fax # (202) 319-4440; Title Tel # (202) 319-5085
Personnel: Editor-Dr. Elizabeth Stone
General Info: Yr. Est. 1968, Quarterly, Trim Size-8½ x 11, Offset press, 8 pages, No Color
Circulation: Total-2,500

Gallaudet Alumni
Newsletter   *Association*

Publishing Co: Gallaudet University Outreach Services, 800 Florida Ave., NE - KS#6, Washington, DC 20002-3695 Tel # (202) 651-5340 Fax # (202) 651-5708; Title Tel # (202) 651-5060
Personnel: Editor-Mike Kaika
Editorial Description: News of Gallaudet College and its alumni items of interest to the field of deafness.
General Info: Yr. Est. 1965, Monthly, Trim Size-8½ x 11, Sheetfed press, 4 pages, No Color, Newsprint
Circulation: Total-20,000
Printing Co: Baker-Webster Printing, 1121 5th St NW, Washington, DC 20001-3690
Tel # (202) 628-8061

Gainesville, Florida

Graduate School Review

Publishing Co: Campus Communications, Inc., PO Box 115500, Gainesville, FL 32611-5500
Tel # (904) 392-3261; Title Tel # (904) 392-4646
Personnel: Editor-Helen Martin, Circ. Mgr., Production Mgr.-Julie Shih
Editorial Description: Statistical information of graduate students & other information of the Graduate school.
General Info: Yr. Est. 1962, Semi-annually, 4 pages
Circulation: Total-2,500

Jacksonville, Florida

Lamplighter   *Consumer, Association*

Publishing Co: Jacksonville Univ., 2800 University Blvd N, P.O. Box 281-014, Jacksonville, FL 32211-2294 Tel # (904) 745-7526 Fax # (904) 745-7528; Title Tel # (904) 744-3950
Title Fax # (904) 744-0101
Personnel: Publisher-Don Ames, Circ. Mgr.-Janice Moore, Production Mgr.-Dave Pratt, Editor, Art Dir.-Scott Boucher
Editorial Description: A publication of the JU Alumni/Parent Center designed to keep JU grads, parents & friends informed of alumni/parent activities & campus news.
General Info: Yr. Est. 1979, Semi-annually, Web press, 9 pages, Color-cover, Newsprint, Saddle-stitched
Subscriptions: Free To Qualified Recipient
Circulation: Total-13,000
Printing Co: Florida Sun Printing, PO Box 627, Church & Crowey Road, Callahan, FL 32011-0627
Tel # (904) 879-2101, Fax # (904) 879-5029

Lakeland, Florida

Southernnews

Publishing Co: Florida Southern College, 111 Lake Hollingsworth Dr, Lakeland, FL 33801-5607
Tel # (813) 680-4111; Title Tel # (813) 680-4116
General Info: Quarterly, 24 pages
Circulation: Total-17,500

Tallahassee, Florida

Alumni Newsletter, School
of Library & Info Studies   *Association*

Publishing Co: Florida State Univ. Library School, School/Library & Info Studies, Tallahassee, FL 32306-2048; Title Tel # (904) 644-5775 Title Fax # (904) 644-9763
Personnel: Editor-Mary Alice Hunt
Editorial Description: News and pictures about S.L.I.S. alumni and the school.
General Info: Yr. Est. 1949, Quarterly, Trim Size-8½ x 11, Offset press, 6 pages, No Color
Circulation: (100% controlled), Total-2,800

Atlanta, Georgia

Atlanta U-Alumni Update

Publishing Co: Atlanta Univ., 223 James P Brawley Dr SW, Atlanta, GA 30314-4358;
Title Tel # (404) 653-8400

Columbus, Georgia

Columbus College Focus   *Association*

Publishing Co: Columbus College, 101 Richard Hall, Columbus, GA 31907-5645;
Title Tel # (706) 568-2030 Title Fax # (706) 568-2123
Personnel: Editor-Cheryl Gaston
General Info: (Formerly Alumni Update), Quarterly, 16 pages
Subscriptions: Free
Circulation: Total-15,000

Lithonia, Georgia

Pioneer
See: COLLEGE STUDENT

Milledgeville, Georgia

Cadence, The

Publishing Co: Georgia Military College, 201 E. Green St., Milledgeville, GA 31061-3398
Tel # (912) 454-2668 Fax # (912) 454-2867; Title Tel # (912) 454-2700 Title Fax # (912) 454-2688
Personnel: Editor-A. Alling Jones
Editorial Description: A college alumni newsletter.
General Info: (Formerly Alumni Newsletter/GMC Cadence), Bi-monthly, Trim Size-8½ x 11, Web press, 12 pages, Coated, Saddle-stitched
Circulation: Total-6,000

Savannah, Georgia

Alumni Granule

Publishing Co: Savannah State College, PO Box 20482, Savannah, GA 31404-9716
Tel # (912) 356-2187; Title Tel # (912) 356-2240
Personnel: Editor-Edna Jackson
General Info: (Formerly Savannah State Bulletin), Yr. Est. 1947, Quarterly, Offset press, 7 pages, 2 Color
Subscriptions: Indv. $3
Circulation: Total-5,000
Printing Co: Savannah Printing Co., 103 W Park Ave, Savannah, GA 31401-6419
Tel # (912) 233-6240

Waleska, Georgia

Reinhardt Report   *Association*

Publishing Co: Reinhardt College, 7300 Reinhardt College Pkwy., Waleska, GA 30183-0128
Tel # (770) 720-5600; Title Tel # (770) 720-5513 Title Fax # (770) 720-5602
Personnel: Editor-Robby Murray, Sr. Ed.-Marsha Snow
Editorial Description: Reinhardt College alumni and donors' newsletter.
General Info: Tri-annually, Trim Size-8½ x 11, Web press, 8 pages, 2 Color, Coated, Saddle-stitched
Subscriptions: Free To Qualified Recipient
Circulation: (81% controlled), Total-8,000

Honolulu, Hawaii

Alumni News & Notes

Publishing Co: Chaminade University of Honolulu, 3140 Waialae Ave, Honolulu, HI 96816-1510;
Title Tel # (808) 735-4762
Personnel: Editor-Kathy Millwood
General Info: Trim Size-8½ x 11, 8 pages
Circulation: Total-6,200

Champaign, Illinois

University of Illinois, School of Art and Design, Alumni Newsletter
See: ART & SCULPTURE

Charleston, Illinois

Old Main Line

Publishing Co: Eastern Illinois University, Publications, Charleston, IL 61920 Tel # (217) 581-5000;
Title Tel # (217) 581-5981
Personnel: Publisher-D.E. Thornburgh, Art Dir.-Bill Edwards
Editorial Description: Quarterly news paper for EIU alumni.
General Info: (Formerly Eastern Alumnus), Quarterly, Trim Size-11 x 17, Web press, 8 pages
Circulation: (100% controlled), Total-40,000

Chicago, Illinois

Lithuanian-American Bulletin
See: ETHNIC

Bloomington, Indiana

Vibrations
See: LIBRARY

Notre Dame, Indiana

Alumni, the Newsletter for
Notre Dame Alumni   *Association*

Publishing Co: Notre Dame Alumni Assoc., 201 Main Bldg., Notre Dame, IN 46556
Editorial Description: News on alumni and school events.

Saint Meinrad, Indiana

St. Meinrad Newsletter

Publishing Co: Saint Meinrad College, Publications, Saint Meinrad, IN 47577;
Title Tel # (812) 357-6501
General Info: Yr. Est. 1967, Quarterly, 4 pages
Circulation: Total-6,000
Printing Co: Abbey Press, Hill Dr., St. Meinrad, IN 47577 Tel # (817) 357-8011

Upland, Indiana

Profile   *Consumer, Association*

Publishing Co: Taylor Univ., 500 W. Read AVe., Upland, IN 46989 Tel # (317) 998-5797;
Title Tel # (317) 998-5197
General Info: Yr. Est. 1963, Quarterly, 8 pages
Circulation: Total-19,000

Vincennes, Indiana

Views from VU

Publishing Co: Vincennes Univ., 1002 N 1st St, Vincennes, IN 47591-1504 Tel # (812) 882-3350;
Title Tel # (812) 885-4354
General Info: Yr. Est. 1937, Quarterly, 8 pages
Circulation: Total-22,000

Clinton, Iowa

Clarian
See: COLLEGE STUDENT

Davenport, Iowa

Brotherhood, The

Publishing Co: Delta Sigma Chi, Palmer College of Chiropractic, 1000 Brady St., Davenport, IA 52803-5214 Tel # (319) 323-3358
Editorial Description: Newsletter of the Delta Sigma Chi alumni.
General Info: (Formerly Delta Sigma Chi Smut), Bi-monthly

Dubuque, Iowa

Global Issues   *Business, Scholarly*

Publishing Co: Univ. of Dubuque, 2000 University Ave, Dubuque, IA 52001-5050
Tel # (319) 589-3000; Title Tel # (319) 589-3163 Title Fax # (319) 589-5162
Personnel: Editor-Richard Kemmer, Circ. Mgr.-Beth Flemming, Art Dir.-Gregory Noble
Editorial Description: Authoritative insights into business, political, ethical and environmental issues of world wide significance.
General Info: (Formerly From UB to You), Yr. Est. 1993, Irregular, Trim Size-11 x 17, Offset press, 12 pages, 2 Color, Matte
Subscriptions: Indv. $35
Circulation: Total-1,500
Printing Co: Union-Hoermann Press, 2175 Kerper Blvd, Dubuque, IA 52001-2217
Tel # (319) 582-3631

Iowa City, Iowa

Law Alumni Report   *Association*

Publishing Co: University of Iowa College of Law, 290 Boyd Law Building, Iowa City, IA 52242-1113
Tel # (319) 335-9084 Fax # (319) 335-9019; Title Tel # (515) 271-2988
Personnel: Editor-Kitty Cooney Hoye
General Info: Monthly, Trim Size-8½ x 11, Offset press, 4 pages, No Color
Circulation: (100% controlled), Total-2,500

West Des Moines, Iowa

Live Wire

Publishing Co: Natl. Education Ctr., 1119 5th St, West Des Moines, IA 50265-2608;
Title Tel # (515) 223-1486
Personnel: Publisher-Leanne Parsons
General Info: Quarterly, Mimeo press, Newsprint
Circulation: Total-700
Advertising: Inquire for rates.

Emporia, Kansas

S.L.I.M. In-Focus

Publishing Co: Emporia State Univ., School of Library & Info. Management, 1200 Commerical St., Emporia, KS 66801-5087; Title Tel # (316) 343-5203
Personnel: Editor-Rosemary Dukelow
Editorial Description: Designed to keep alumni & area librarians informed of activities at the school of library & information management.
General Info: Semi-annually, Mimeo press, 2 Color
Circulation: (100% controlled), Total-1,500

Haviland, Kansas

Progress
    See: EDUCATION

Kansas City, Kansas

Digest

Publishing Co: Donnelly College, 608 N 18th St, Kansas City, KS 66102-4298;
    Title Tel # (913) 621-6070 Title Fax # (913) 621-0354
Personnel: Editor-Frank Gardner
Editorial Description: Directed to alumni, business & other friends of the college.
General Info: (Formerly Focus), Yr. Est. 1984, Bi-monthly, Sheetfed press, 4 pages, 2 Color
Circulation: Total-4,500
Printing Co: Richman Printing, 827 Minnesota Ave, Kansas City, KS 66101-2683
    Tel # (913) 321-6300

Barbourville, Kentucky

Union College Alumnus   *Association*

Publishing Co: Union College, Box 841, College St., Barbourville, KY 40906;
    Title Tel # (606) 546-4151
Personnel: Editor-Ron Vanover
Editorial Description: Information for alumni & friends of Union College.
General Info: Yr. Est. 1951, Quarterly
Circulation: Total-8,000

London, Kentucky

Alumni Newsletter

Publishing Co: Sue Bennett College, West Fifth, London, KY 40741-1915; Title Tel # (606) 878-9681
General Info: Yr. Est. 1984, Quarterly
Circulation: Total-4,000

Morehead, Kentucky

Morehead Statement   *Association*

Publishing Co: Morehead State University, Alumni Center, Morehead, KY 40351
    Fax # (606) 783-2585; Title Tel # (606) 783-2080 Title Fax # (606) 783-2678
Editorial Description: Contains personal updates on Morehead alumni, feature articles, and general campus information.
General Info: Quarterly, 10 pages
Subscriptions: Free To Qualified Recipient
Circulation: Total-38,000
Printing Co: Account Manager: Jeff Fandin; Park Newspapers, W. First St., Morehead, KY 40351

Pikeville, Kentucky

Echo
    See: COLLEGE STUDENT

New Orleans, Louisiana

White Cap   *Association*

Publishing Co: Charity-Delgado School of Nursing Alumni Assn., 450 S Claiborne Ave, New Orleans, LA 70112-1310; Title Tel # (504) 568-2311
Personnel: Circ. Mgr.-Ruth Wallace, Editor, Art Dir.-Jane Parrish
Editorial Description: Alumni & school news.
General Info: Yr. Est. 1970, Annually, Trim Size-8½ x 11, 12 pages, 2 Color, Saddle-stitched
Circulation: (100% controlled), Total-3,500

Bangor, Maine

Open Door   *Association*

Publishing Co: Bangor Theological Seminary, 300 Union St, Bangor, ME 04401-4642;
    Title Tel # (207) 942-6781
Personnel: Editor-Sharon Bell-Dingman, Circ. Mgr.-Margaret Harvey
Editorial Description: Seminary and alumni/ae news and articles of interest to religious community.
General Info: (Formerly Alumni Bulletin), Yr. Est. 1979, Quarterly, Trim Size-11¼ x 17½, Sheetfed press, 8 pages, 2 Color, Coated, Saddle-stitched
Circulation: Total-7,000
Printing Co: Bacon Printing Co., 1070 Hammond St, Bangor, ME 04401-5704 Tel # (207) 942-5593

Unity, Maine

Unity College Today   *Association*

Publishing Co: Unity College, Quaker Hill Rd., HC 78, Box 1, Unity, ME 04988-9502;
    Title Tel # (207) 948-3131 Title Fax # (207) 948-5626
Personnel: Editor-Molly Hamel
Editorial Description: Class news & articles of interest to alumni.
General Info: Tri-annually, Trim Size-8½ x 11, Sheetfed press, 12 pages, No Color, Coated
Circulation: Total-2,200
Printing Co: Atkins Printing, 155 Main St, PO Box 1169, Waterville, ME 04901-6623
    Tel # (207) 872-5565, Fax # (207) 872-0792

Baltimore, Maryland

Archway

Publishing Co: Catonsville Community College, 800 S Rolling Rd, Baltimore, MD 21228-5384
    Tel # (301) 455-6050; Title Tel # (301) 455-4400
Personnel: Editor-Mary Hilton
General Info: Yr. Est. 1976, 14 pages
Circulation: Total-3,000

St. Mary's Seminary and University Bulletin
    See: RELIGIOUS & THEOLOGICAL

Bowie, Maryland

Alumni Newsletter   *Consumer*

Publishing Co: Bowie State University, 14000 Jericho Park Rd., Bowie, MD 20715;
    Title Tel # (301) 464-3000
General Info: Quarterly, 14 pages
Circulation: Total-6,500

Ann Arbor, Michigan

Dentalum

Publishing Co: Univ. of Michigan, School of Dentistry, Univ. of Michigan, Ann Arbor, MI 48109-1078;
    Title Tel # (313) 763-3376
Personnel: Editor-Judith Dunaway
Editorial Description: Informs alumni of events at the School of Dentistry (e. g. retirements, graduation, honors, student activities, homecoming, etc.); also to inform them of alumni activities & honors.
General Info: (Formerly Alumni News), Yr. Est. 1937, Semi-annually, Trim Size-8½ x 11, Offset press, 24 pages, Color-cover, Newsprint, Saddle-stitched
Circulation: Total-8,000
Printing Co: Ann Arbor Printing & Mailing, 771 Airport Blvd # 4, Ann Arbor, MI 48108-1639
    Tel # (313) 994-0900

Grand Rapids, Michigan

Kendall College of Art and Design
    See: COLLEGE STUDENT

Kalamazoo, Michigan

Westerner, The   *Consumer*

Publishing Co: Western Michigan University Alumni Relations, 1201 Oliver St, Kalamazoo, MI 49008-3804
General Info: Quarterly, Trim Size-11½ x 17½, 8 pages, ISSN: 0279-3628, 4 Color, Coated

Lansing, Michigan

KEY Newsletter
    See: RELIGIOUS & THEOLOGICAL

Brooklyn Park, Minnesota

Alumni News   *Consumer*

Publishing Co: North Hennepin Community College, 7411 85th Ave N, Brooklyn Park, MN 55445-2231; Title Tel # (612) 424-0916
Editorial Description: Newsletter for NHCC Alumni.
General Info: Quarterly

Duluth, Minnesota

Inside Times   *Association*

Publishing Co: College of St. Scholastica, 1200 Kenwood Ave, Duluth, MN 55811-4199
    Tel # (218) 723-6000; Title Tel # (218) 723-6074 Title Fax # (218) 723-6290
Personnel: Editor-Cheryl Reitan, Production Mgr.-Margaret Jensen
Editorial Description: News & features about or by College of St. Scholastica personnel.
General Info: (Formerly Times), Yr. Est. 1971, Quarterly, Trim Size-9 x 12, Sheetfed press, 12 pages, 2 Color, Newsprint, Saddle-stitched
Circulation: Total-12,000
Printing Co: Pro Print, 326 E Central Entrance, Duluth, MN 55811-5514 Tel # (218) 722-9805

Blue Mountain, Mississippi

Bulletin — *Consumer, Association*
Publishing Co: Blue Mountain College, PO Box 160, Blue Mountain, MS 38610-0160; Title Tel # (601) 685-4771 Title Fax # (601) 685-4776
General Info: Quarterly, 6 pages
Subscriptions: Free
Circulation: Total-4,500

Hattiesburg, Mississippi

Southern News and Views — *Association* — CPM: $20
Publishing Co: Univ. of Southern Mississippi, USM Box 5013, Hattiesburg, MS 39406-5013 Tel # (601) 266-4111; Title Tel # (601) 266-5013
Personnel: Editor-Raymond Reeves
Editorial Description: Campus events, alumni activities, keep former students in touch.
General Info: Yr. Est. 1961, Quarterly, Trim Size-11½ x 13¾, Offset press, 8 pages, No Color, Newsprint
Subscriptions: Free With Membership
Circulation: (72% controlled), Total-62,000
Advertising: $1,240.
Printing Co: University of Southern Mississippi Printing Center, SS Box 5085, Hattiesburg, MS 39406 Tel # (601) 266-5397

Meridian, Mississippi

MCC Today
Publishing Co: Meridian Community College, 910 Highway 19 N, Meridian, MS 39307-5890; Title Tel # (601) 483-8241
Personnel: Editor, Art Dir.-Anne Dowdle
Editorial Description: Monthly 4 page newsletter of the Assn. of Alumni & Friends of Meridian Community College.
General Info: Monthly, Offset press, 168 pages
Circulation: Total-6,500

Senatobia, Mississippi

Northwest Now — *Consumer*
Publishing Co: Northwest Mississippi Community College, Publications, Senatobia, MS 38668; Title Tel # (601) 562-3200
General Info: Quarterly, 4 pages
Circulation: Total-4,000

Fulton, Missouri

Echoes from the Woods
Publishing Co: William Woods College, 200 W 12th St, Fulton, MO 65251-1004; Title Tel # (314) 642-2251
Personnel: Editor-Amy Bradshaw
General Info: 6 pages
Circulation: Total-11,500

Kansas City, Missouri

Alumni Hotline — *Consumer*
Publishing Co: Kansas City Art Institute, 4415 Warwick Blvd, Kansas City, MO 64111-1820; Title Tel # (816) 561-4852 Title Fax # (816) 561-3405
Personnel: Editor-Sharon Opdycke
General Info: Monthly, Trim Size-8½ x 11, 10 pages
Subscriptions: Indv. $15, Inst. $20

Alumni News
Publishing Co: Cleveland Chiropractic College, 6401 Rockhill Rd, Kansas City, MO 64131-1181; Title Tel # (816) 333-8230
Personnel: Publisher-Dorothy Marra, Editor-Alan Morgan
General Info: Yr. Est. 1976, Quarterly, 16 pages
Subscriptions: Indv. $20
Circulation: Total-5,000

Blair, Nebraska

Dana Review — *Association*
Publishing Co: Dana College, 2848 College Dr, Blair, NE 68008 Tel # (402) 426-9000; Title Tel # (402) 426-7235 Title Fax # (402) 426-7368
Personnel: Editor-Anna H. George
Editorial Description: College news.
General Info: Yr. Est. 1945, Quarterly, Trim Size-8½ x 11, Offset press, 20 pages, 2 Color, Saddle-stitched
Subscriptions: Free To Qualified Recipient
Circulation: Total-12,000
Printing Co: Interstate Printing Co., 2002 N 16th St # 22, Omaha, NE 68110-2411 Tel # (402) 341-8028, Fax # (402) 341-6168

Omaha, Nebraska

Alumni News — *Consumer*
Publishing Co: Univ. of Nebraska College of Medicine, 600 S. 42nd St., PO Box 985200, Omaha, NE 68198-5200; Title Tel # (402) 559-4354
General Info: Yr. Est. 1960, Semi-annually, 13 pages
Circulation: Total-5,700

Durham, New Hampshire

Alumni Companion — *Business*
Publishing Co: University of New Hampshire, Elliott Alumni Center, 9 Edgewood Road, Durham, NH 03824; Title Tel # (603) 862-2040
General Info: Tri-annually

Hanover, New Hampshire

Dartmouth College Bulletin
Publishing Co: Dartmouth College, 38 North Main Street, Hanover, NH 03755-3762 Tel # (603) 646-2256 Fax # (603) 646-1209

Bloomfield, New Jersey

On-The-Green
  See: COLLEGE STUDENT

New Brunswick, New Jersey

Douglass Alumnae Bulletin — *Association*
Publishing Co: Douglass College, 80 Clifton Ave, New Brunswick, NJ 08901-1568; Title Tel # (201) 247-0700
Personnel: Editor-Eleanor Wyckoff
Editorial Description: Contains news of alumnae, of the college and of higher education in general, in the form of features and class notes.
General Info: Yr. Est. 1926, Quarterly, Trim Size-8½ x 11, Web press, 28 pages, 2 Color
Subscriptions: Indv. $5
Circulation: Total-8,000

Princeton, New Jersey

E-Quad News — *Consumer, Association*
Publishing Co: Princeton Univ., School of Engineering & Applied Science, C-218, E-Quad, Princeton, NJ 08544-0001; Title Tel # (609) 258-3617 Title Fax # (609) 258-6744
Editorial Description: Published for the alumni, faculty, students, corporate affiliates, staff, and friends of Princeton's School of Engineering & Applied Science.
General Info: Yr. Est. 1988, Quarterly, Trim Size-8½ x 11, Offset press, 12 pages, 2 Color, Recycled, Saddle-stitched
Subscriptions: Free To Qualified Recipient
Circulation: (100% controlled), Total-12,500
Printing Co: Princeton University Printing Services, Princeton University, Princeton, NJ 08544-0001

Teaneck, New Jersey

FDU Alumni News
Publishing Co: Fairleigh Dickinson University, 1000 River Rd, Teaneck, NJ 07666-1996 Tel # (201) 692-2000; Title Tel # (201) 692-2436
General Info: Yr. Est. 1960, Quarterly, Web press, 8 pages, 2 Color, Newsprint
Circulation: Total-70,000

Trenton, New Jersey

Invention
  See: COLLEGE STUDENT

Roswell, New Mexico

Eastern Clips — *Association*
Publishing Co: Eastern New Mexico University-Roswell Campus, PO Box 6000, Roswell, NM 88202-6000; Title Tel # (505) 624-7404 Title Fax # (505) 624-7119
Personnel: Publisher, Editor, Mktg. Dir.-Donna Gutierrez
Editorial Description: Campus news sent to friends/employees of college.
General Info: Yr. Est. 1991, Bi-monthly, Trim Size-8½ x 11, Desktop press, 4 pages, 2 Color, Matte
Subscriptions: Free
Circulation: Total-850
Printing Co: Alpha Omega Printing, 211 West Third, Roswe; , NM 88201 Tel # (505) 624-2700, Fax # (505) 624-2733

East Aurora, New York

Christ the King Seminary News

Publishing Co: Christ the King Seminary, 711 Knox Rd., P.O. Box 607, East Aurora, NY 14052-9444; Title Tel # (716) 652-8900
Personnel: Editor-Donald J. Barnett
Editorial Description: Alumni magazine for graduates of CKS. Contains news and information of theological matters for priests, religious, and lay graduates.
General Info: Yr. Est. 1937, Trim Size-8½ x 11, Sheetfed press, 14 pages, 2 Color, Coated, Saddle-stitched
Subscriptions: Free
Circulation: Total-12,000
Printing Co: S&G Press, Knox Rd., E. Aurora, NY 14052 Tel # (716) 652-1250

New Rochelle, New York

Quarterly

Publishing Co: College of New Rochelle, 29 Castle Pl, New Rochelle, NY 10805-2339; Title Tel # (914) 654-5235
Personnel: Editor-Lenore Boytim, Editorial Asst.-Ruth Keeshan, Asst. Ed.-Pat McLoughlin, S.C.
Editorial Description: Articles and news of interest to College of New Rochelle alumni.
General Info: (Formerly Alumnae News), Yr. Est. 1904, Quarterly, Trim Size-11 x 17, 2 Color
Subscriptions: Indv. $4
Circulation: Total-22,000
Printing Co: John D. Lucas Printing Co., 1820 Portal St, Baltimore, MD 21224-6596 Tel # (410) 633-1222, Fax # (410) 633-1202

New York, New York

Columbia Law Alumni Observer   *Association*

Publishing Co: Columbia University -School of Law, 435 W. 116th St. #D25, New York, NY 10027-7201 Tel # (212) 663-8709; Title Tel # (212) 280-2156
Personnel: Editor-Catherina Davidson, Art Dir.-C.S. Ward
Editorial Description: News and features about Columbia Law School and its alumni.
General Info: (Formerly Bulletin), Yr. Est. 1971, Bi-monthly, Trim Size-11½ x 17, Web press, 20 pages, No Color
Subscriptions: Free
Circulation: (100% controlled)

Epilog

Publishing Co: New York Univ. Graduate School of Arts and Science, 25 W 4th St Fl 5, New York, NY 10012-1119; Title Tel # (212) 998-8040
General Info: (Formerly Lions)

Gallatin Today   *Consumer, Association*

Publishing Co: New York Univ. Alumni Dept., 25 W 4th St, New York, NY 10012-1119
Personnel: Editor-Patricia Reardon
Editorial Description: Official newsletter of the Gallatin Division of New York University.
General Info: 10x/yr.
Subscriptions: Free To Qualified Recipient

Metropolitan, The   *Consumer, Association*

Publishing Co: Duke University Metropolitan Area Alumni Association, PO Box 6740, FDR Station, New York, NY 10150 Tel # (212) 439-7280
Editorial Description: The Duke University Metropolitan Area Alumni Association Newsletter.
General Info: Quarterly, Trim Size-8½ x 11, 4 pages, No Color

New York University Education Quarterly
See: EDUCATION

Seminary News
See: RELIGIOUS & THEOLOGICAL

Stern Alumni News & Notes

Publishing Co: New York Univ. Stern School of Business Graduate Div., Public Relations, 40 W. 4th St., Rm. 537, New York, NY 10012-7501 Tel # (212) 998-0600; Title Tel # (212) 998-0670
General Info: (Formerly Sternotes)

Newburgh, New York

MSMC Happenings   *Business, Association*

Publishing Co: Mount St. Mary College, Director of Public Information, Newburgh, NY 12550 Tel # (914) 569-3222 Fax # (914) 562-6762; Title Tel # (914) 561-0800
Personnel: Editor-Brendan Coyne
Editorial Description: Alumni/friend report on College news.
General Info: (Formerly Aquinas News), Yr. Est. 1978, Quarterly, Trim Size-8½ x 11, 16 pages, No Color, Newsprint, Saddle-stitched
Circulation: Total-10,750

Poughkeepsie, New York

What's Happening at Vassar

Publishing Co: Vassar College, Publications, Poughkeepsie, NY 12601 Tel # (914) 437-7000; Title Tel # (914) 437-7400
Personnel: Publisher, Editor-Dixie Sheridan
General Info: Yr. Est. 1984, Sheetfed press, 4 Color, Coated
Circulation: Total-20,000

Rochester, New York

Bulletin from the Hill

Publishing Co: Colgate Rochester Divinity School, 1100 Goodman St S, Rochester, NY 14620-2530; Title Tel # (716) 271-1320
Personnel: Editor-Sally Dodgson
Editorial Description: News of the seminaries and their graduates for alumni/ae and contributors.
General Info: Yr. Est. 1937, Tri-annually, Trim Size-11 x 17, Offset press, 8 pages, ISSN: 8755-450X, No Color
Circulation: (100% controlled), Total-11,600
Printing Co: Canfield & Tack, 925 Exchange St, Rochester, NY 14608-2802 Tel # (716) 235-7710

Staten Island, New York

Alumnotes

Publishing Co: CUNY-College of Staten Island, 130 Stuyvesant Pl, Staten Island, NY 10301-1907; Title Tel # (718) 390-7885
Personnel: Editor, Circ. Mgr.-Francine Raggi, Art Dir.-Mike Metz
Editorial Description: Alumni calendar of events-alumni news-business directory-general information programs & benefits.
General Info: Bi-monthly, Trim Size-8½ x 11, Sheetfed press, 8 pages, 25% ads, No Color
Circulation: Total-23,000
Advertising: Inquire for rates. Accepts Inserts.

Asheville, North Carolina

UNCA Today   *Business, Consumer*

Publishing Co: Univ. of North Carolina at Asheville, Public Information Office, University Heights, Asheville, NC 28804-3251 Tel # (704) 251-6600 Fax # (704) 251-6142; Title Tel # (704) 251-6527
Editorial Description: News and information for faculty and staff.
General Info: (Formerly Inside UNCA), Yr. Est. 1987, Monthly, 2 pages
Circulation: Total-3,000

Durham, North Carolina

Alumni Newsletter - Alpha Alpha Chapter   *Consumer*

Publishing Co: Alpha Alpha Chapter, PO Box 99308, Duke University, Durham, NC 27708-9308
Editorial Description: For Duke University's Alpha Alpha Chapter.
General Info: Yr. Est. 1993, Semi-annually

DukeSource News   *Consumer, Association*

Publishing Co: Duke University Career Development Center, PO Box 90950, Durham, NC 27708-0950; Title Tel # (919) 660-1050
Editorial Description: News on alumni career planning.
General Info: Annually, Trim Size-8½ x 11, 4 pages, No Color

Network

Publishing Co: Duke Univ. History Dept., 614 Chapel Dr, Durham, NC 27706-2500 Tel # (919) 684-5439 Fax # (919) 286-1589; Title Tel # (919) 684-6601

Raleigh, North Carolina

Shaw University Bulletin

Publishing Co: Shaw Univ., 118 E South St, Raleigh, NC 27601-2341; Title Tel # (919) 755-4800

Statelog   *Association*

Publishing Co: North Carolina State Univ., Box 7318, Raleigh, NC 27695-0001; Title Tel # (919) 737-3470
Personnel: Publisher-Lucy Coulbourn, Editor-Alexa Williams
Editorial Description: Updates alumni and others on university accomplishments and contributions.
General Info: Quarterly, Trim Size-9 x 12, Sheetfed press, 8 pages, Color, Newsprint
Circulation: Total-90,000

Berea, Ohio

Pursuit

Publishing Co: Baldwin Wallace College, 120 E Grand St, Berea, OH 44017-2012;
Title Tel # (216) 826-2104
Personnel: Editor-George Richard, Production Mgr.-Jean McKeon, Promotion Dir.-Helen Rathburn
Editorial Description: Alumni news & institutional features relating to Baldwin-Wallace College.
General Info: 5x/yr., Trim Size-11 x 14½, Sheetfed press, 12 pages
Circulation: Total-27,000

Columbus, Ohio

Te Deum
See: RELIGIOUS & THEOLOGICAL

Bartlesville, Oklahoma

Tower

Publishing Co: Bartlesville Wesleyan College, 2201 Silverlake Rd, Bartlesville, OK 74006-6299;
Title Tel # (918) 333-6151
Personnel: Publisher, Editor-Melba Crain
Editorial Description: News of college program & alumni of Bartlesville Wesleyan College.
General Info: Quarterly, Trim Size-8½ x 11, Desktop press, 12 pages, 2 Color, Matte, Saddle-stitched
Circulation: Total-13,000
Printing Co: Printco, 4015 Nowata Rd, Bartlesville, OK 74006-5118 Tel # (918) 333-4303

Edmond, Oklahoma

Alumni Newsletter

Publishing Co: University of Central Oklahoma, 100 N University, Edmond, OK 73034-5209;
Title Tel # (405) 341-2980
Personnel: Editor-Linda Jones, Production Mgr., Art Dir.-Roy Cordell
Editorial Description: News & features about U.C.O. programs & alumni.
General Info: Quarterly, Sheetfed press, 24 pages, Color-cover, Coated
Circulation: Total-7,000

Tulsa, Oklahoma

New Breed   *Association*

Publishing Co: New Breed, PO Box 50126, Tulsa, OK 74150-0126; Title Tel # (918) 258-1588
General Info: Yr. Est. 1976, Quarterly
Circulation: (100% controlled), Total-500

Altoona, Pennsylvania

Ivy Leaf   *Consumer, Association*

Publishing Co: Pennsylvania State Univ., Altoona Campus, 3000 Ivyside Park, Altoona, PA 16601-3760 Tel # (814) 949-5000; Title Tel # (814) 949-5105 Title Fax # (814) 949-5011
Editorial Description: Informs alumni of news, events, and activities on campus.
General Info: Yr. Est. 1966, Semi-annually, Trim Size-8½ x 11, 8 pages, 2 Color, Coated, Saddle-stitched
Circulation: Total-19,000

Bryn Mawr, Pennsylvania

Bryn Mawr Alumnae
Bulletin   *Consumer, Association*

Publishing Co: Bryn Mawr College, Public Information Office, Bryn Mawr, PA 19010-2899;
Title Tel # (215) 526-5000
General Info: Yr. Est. 1907, Quarterly
Circulation: Total-9,500

Lincoln, Pennsylvania

Lion   *Association*

Publishing Co: Lincoln Univ., Office of PR & Publications, Lincoln, PA 19352;
Title Tel # (610) 932-8300 Title Fax # (610) 932-0195
Personnel: Editor-Funso Oluyitan
Editorial Description: Articles generated in-house for & about Alumni.
General Info: Semi-annually, Trim Size-11 x 14, 12 pages, 2 Color
Subscriptions: Free To Qualified Recipient
Circulation: Total-8,000

Philadelphia, Pennsylvania

Apothecary, The   *Association*

Publishing Co: Temple University School of Pharmacy, 3307 N Broad St, Philadelphia, PA 19140-5193 Tel # (215) 221-4946; Title Tel # (215) 707-4946 Title Fax # (215) 707-3678
Personnel: Editor-Joy B. Reighard, Editorial Asst.-Barbara Grissani
Editorial Description: News of alumni and school activities.
General Info: Yr. Est. 1951, 3x/yr., Trim Size-8½ x 11, Desktop press, 6 pages, Color
Subscriptions: Free
Circulation: Total-3,500

Forever Moore   *Scholarly*

Publishing Co: Moore College of Art & Design, College Relations, The Parkway at 20th Street, Philadelphia, PA 19103 Fax # (215) 568-8017; Title Tel # (215) 568-4515
General Info: Quarterly

Moore News
See: COLLEGE STUDENT

Today   *Association*

Publishing Co: Peirce Junior College, Communications Dept., 1420 Pine Street, Philadelphia, PA 19102-4699; Title Tel # (215) 545-6400 Title Fax # (215) 546-5996
Personnel: Editor-Cindy Schlaybach
General Info: Quarterly, Trim Size-8½ x 11, Offset press, 8 pages, No Color, Newsprint
Circulation: Total-23,000
Printing Co: Maxwell Graphic Arts, Inc., 1 Linden Ave # 9, Gibbsboro, NJ 08026-1315

Pittsburgh, Pennsylvania

Panorama
See: RELIGIOUS & THEOLOGICAL

Wayne, Pennsylvania

Forge, The
See: MILITARY & NAVAL

Charleston, South Carolina

Through the Sally Port

Publishing Co: Citadel Military College of SC, The, Association of Citadel Men, 97 Hagood Avenue, Charleston, SC 29409-0001; Title Tel # (803) 953-5006 Title Fax # (803) 792-7084
Personnel: Editor-Samuel Evans, III
Editorial Description: Vehicle for informing college alumni of major campus events.
General Info: Yr. Est. 1983, Quarterly, 8 pages, No Color, Saddle-stitched
Circulation: Total-16,500

Orangeburg, South Carolina

SCSC Review

Publishing Co: South Carolina State College, Publications, Orangeburg, SC 29112 Tel # (803) 536-7000; Title Tel # (803) 536-7061
General Info: Quarterly, 14 pages
Circulation: Total-12,000

Rock Hill, South Carolina

Winthrop Update   *Association*

Publishing Co: Winthrop College, 200 Tillman, Rock Hill, SC 29733 Tel # (803) 323-2211;
Title Tel # (803) 323-2236
Personnel: Editor, Circ. Mgr., Art Dir.-Leigh Handal
Editorial Description: Alumni newsletter/magazine. Purpose to keep alumni (38,000) abreast of Winthrop College.
General Info: (Formerly Winthrop News), Quarterly, Trim Size-8½ x 11, Web press, 24 pages, 2 Color, Newsprint
Circulation: (100% controlled), Total-38,000

Spartanburg, South Carolina

Straight from Sherman
See: HEALTH

Aberdeen, South Dakota

Outline
Association

Publishing Co: Presentation College, 1500 N Main St, Aberdeen, SD 57401-1280
Tel # (605) 225-0420; Title Tel # (605) 229-8454
Personnel: Circ. Mgr.-Kathie Jamieson, Editor, Production Mgr.-James Morgan
Editorial Description: Constituent relations.
General Info: Yr. Est. 1973, Semi-annually, Trim Size-8½ x 11, Offset press, 24 pages, 2 Color, Saddle-stitched
Subscriptions: Free
Acquistions: Publication Bought
Circulation: Total-9,000
Printing Co: Midstates Printing Co., 1216 S Main St, Aberdeen, SD 57401-7051
Tel # (605) 225-5287, Fax # (605) 225-8578

Mitchell, South Dakota

DWU World

Publishing Co: Dakota Wesleyan Univ., 1200 W University Ave, Mitchell, SD 57301-4398
Tel # (605) 995-2814; Title Tel # (605) 995-2615 Title Fax # (605) 995-2699
Personnel: Publisher-Evalyn Claggett
General Info: Quarterly, 12 pages, No Color, Newsprint, Saddle-stitched
Circulation: Total-8,300

Sioux Falls, South Dakota

Sem Times

Publishing Co: North American Baptist Seminary, 1321 W 22nd St, Sioux Falls, SD 57105-1502;
Title Tel # (605) 336-6588
General Info: Weekly, Trim Size-8½ x 11½, 4 pages
Circulation: Total-700

Knoxville, Tennessee

Inside Knoxville College

Publishing Co: Sponsor-Knoxville College Alumni, Knoxville College, 901 College St, Knoxville, TN 37921-4799; Title Tel # (615) 524-6616
Personnel: Publisher-Wilhemina Grey, Editor-Cheryl Ponder
General Info: (Formerly Aurora), Yr. Est. 1979, Quarterly, Offset press, 16 pages, 2 Color, Newsprint
Circulation: (100% controlled), Total-6,000
Printing Co: Campbell Assocs., 405 S Gay St, Knoxville, TN 37902-1104 Tel # (615) 521-6494

Memphis, Tennessee

Allied Health Update

Publishing Co: Univ. of Tennessee for Health Sciences, 800 Madison Ave, Memphis, TN 38103-3400; Title Tel # (901) 528-5516
Personnel: Publisher-Wm. Hinkle, Editor-Anne Frassinelli
Editorial Description: For Univ. of TN graduates of the College of Allied Health Sciences.
General Info: Semi-annually, Trim Size-8½ x 11, 8 pages, 2 Color, Newsprint
Circulation: Total-3,500

Visions Newsletter
Consumer, Association

Publishing Co: Southern College of Optometry, 1245 Madison Ave, Memphis, TN 38104-2222
Fax # (901) 722-3279; Title Tel # (901) 722-3216
Personnel: Editor-Elizabeth Norris
General Info: (Formerly SCO Newsletter), Yr. Est. 1985, Quarterly, Trim Size-8½ x 11, Offset press, 12 pages, Coated, Saddle-stitched
Subscriptions: Free
Circulation: Total-7,000
Printing Co: Sawtelle Printing Co., 3100 Summer Ave., Memphis, TN 38112 Tel # (901) 327-7377

Nashville, Tennessee

Treveccan
Association

Publishing Co: Trevecca Nazarene College, 333 Murfreesboro Rd, Nashville, TN 37210-2834;
Title Tel # (615) 248-1200
Personnel: Editor-Michael T. Johnson
Editorial Description: News bulletin for those interested in college and related topics.
General Info: (Formerly Trevecca Messenger), Yr. Est. 1933, Quarterly, Trim Size-8 x 12, Web press, 16 pages, 4 Color, Matte, Saddle-stitched
Circulation: Total-25,000
Printing Co: Vaughan Printing Co., 411 Cowan St, Nashville, TN 37207-5686 Tel # (615) 256-2244, Fax # (615) 259-4676

Austin, Texas

Texas Alcalde
Association

Publishing Co: Univ. of Texas Ex-Students Association, PO Box 7278, Austin, TX 78713-7278
Tel # (512) 471-8839; Title Tel # (512) 471-3799 Title Fax # (512) 471-8088
Personnel: Editor-Avrel Seale
Editorial Description: Covers the activities of the School, its alumni and foundation.
General Info: (Formerly Alumni Newsletter Insider), Yr. Est. 1951, Bi-monthly
Subscriptions: Indv. $40

Fort Worth, Texas

Alumni Newsletter

Publishing Co: Texas College of Osteopathic Medicine, PO Box 9526, Fort Worth, TX 76147-2526
Tel # (817) 735-2555; Title Tel # (817) 735-2559 Title Fax # (817) 735-2486
Personnel: Editor-Verlie Edwards
Editorial Description: Updates on college activities, alumni association & individual graduates. Includes photographs.
General Info: Yr. Est. 1974, Quarterly, Sheetfed press, 4 pages, 2 Color, Matte
Acquistions: Publication Bought
Circulation: Total-1,400

Southwestern News
Association

Publishing Co: Southwestern Baptist Theological Seminary, Box 22000-3e, Fort Worth, TX 76122-0001; Title Tel # (817) 923-1921
Personnel: Publisher-Russell Dilday, Jr., Editor-John Seelig, Circ. Mgr.-Helen Urrey, Production Mgr.-Mark Wingfield
Editorial Description: Covers Seminary news and a variety of religious issues.
General Info: Yr. Est. 1942, Monthly, Trim Size-8½ x 11, Offset press, 12 pages, ISSN: 0038-4917, Ind/Abs/Online: South.Bap.Per.Ind., Color, Coated, Saddle-stitched
Circulation: Total-50,000
Printing Co: Motheral Printing Co., 510 S Main St # 629, Fort Worth, TX 76104-2408
Tel # (817) 335-1481, Fax # (817) 332-4672

Texas Wesleyan Today

Publishing Co: Texas Wesleyan University, PO Box 50010, Fort Worth, TX 76105-0010;
Title Tel # (817) 531-4400 Title Fax # (817) 531-4262
Editorial Description: Newsletter for alumni and friends of the university.
General Info: Yr. Est. 1993, Quarterly
Circulation: Total-15,000

San Antonio, Texas

Newsletter (Oblate School of Theology) OST News
Consumer, Association

Publishing Co: Sponsor-Oblate Fathers, Oblate School of Theology, 285 Oblate Dr, San Antonio, TX 78216-6631 Tel # (210) 341-1366 Fax # (210) 341-4579; Title Tel # (512) 341-1366
Personnel: Editor-Scott Woodward
Editorial Description: Alumni development newsletter
General Info: (Formerly Informe), Yr. Est. 1947, Semi-annually, Trim Size-8.5 x 11, Roto. press, 8 pages, 2 Color, Matte
Subscriptions: $75/copy
Acquistions: Publication Bought
Circulation: (90% controlled), Total-3,000, Readership-3,000
Printing Co: Impressive Printers, 8060 Vantage Drive, San Antonio, TX Tel # (210) 349-8477

Sherman, Texas

Acknowledge
Association

Publishing Co: Austin College, 900 N Grand Ave # 6h, Sherman, TX 75090-4440
Fax # (903) 813-2415; Title Tel # (903) 813-2386
Personnel: Publisher-J. D. Fuller, Editor-J.D. Fuller
Editorial Description: Campus and alumni news, news of Austin College, higher education.
General Info: (Formerly Austin College Newsletter), Yr. Est. 1909, Quarterly, Trim Size-9 x 12, Web press, 40 pages, 4 Color, Coated, Saddle-stitched
Circulation: (100% controlled), Total-16,000
Printing Co: Hart Graphics, 8000 Shoal Creek Blvd., P.O. Box 968, Austin, TX 78767
Tel # (512) 454-4761

Bennington, Vermont

Quadrille
Association

Publishing Co: Bennington College, Bennington College Campus, Bennington, VT 05201;
Title Tel # (802) 442-5401
Personnel: Editor-Andrea Diehl, Feature Ed.-Rebecca Godwin, Mktg. Dir.-Leslie Noyes
Editorial Description: News and features of interest to friends and alumni.
General Info: (Formerly Bennington College Alumnae Quarterly), Yr. Est. 1966, Quarterly, Trim Size-8½ x 11, Sheetfed press, 16 pages, 2 Color, Newsprint
Circulation: (100% controlled), Total-11,000
Printing Co: A & B Graphics, 29 Lower John St., Hoosick Falls, NY 12089 Tel # (518) 686-5709

Colchester, Vermont

Founders Hall
Association

Publishing Co: St. Michael's College, Winooski Pk., Colchester, VT 05439-0001;
Title Tel # (802) 654-2000 Title Fax # (802) 654-2592
Personnel: Editor-Buff Lindau
Editorial Description: News, analysis, philosophy and plans about St. Michael's College for our alumni and parents. Designed to keep our various readers aware of and interested in the college.
General Info: Yr. Est. 1979, 7x/yr., Trim Size-22 x 25, Sheetfed press, 16 pages, 2 Color, Newsprint
Circulation: Total-18,000
Printing Co: George Little Press, 750 Pine St, Burlington, VT 05401-4944 Tel # (802) 658-3300

Ashland, Virginia

Bulletin of Randolph-Macon
College   *Association*

Publishing Co: Randolph-Macon College, Publications, Ashland, VA 23005;
Title Tel # (804) 752-7317
Personnel: Editor-Linda Evans
Editorial Description: Designed to keep alumnai informed about the educational program and growth of the institution and to give them news of classmates.
General Info: Yr. Est. 1930, Quarterly, Trim Size-8½ x 11, Sheetfed press, 40 pages, Coated, Saddle-stitched
Subscriptions: $1/copy
Circulation: Total-13,500
Printing Co: Carter Printing Co., 2007 N Hamilton St, Richmond, VA 23230-4121
Tel # (804) 359-9206

Bluefield, Virginia

Bluefield College News   *Consumer, Association*

Publishing Co: Bluefield College, 3000 College Dr., Bluefield, VA 24605-1799 Tel # (703) 326-3682 Fax # (703) 326-4288; Title Tel # (540) 326-4212 Title Fax # (540) 326-4288
Personnel: Editor-Dennis Yena
General Info: (Formerly Alumnews), Yr. Est. 1922, Quarterly, Trim Size-8½ x 11, 12 pages
Circulation: Total-8,000
Printing Co: Reliable Printing, P.O. Box 1344, Crab Orchard, WV 25827

Issaquah, Washington

Advance

Publishing Co: Lutheran Bible Institute, Providence Heights, 4221 228 Ave S.E., Issaquah, WA 98027-9988; Title Tel # (206) 392-0400
Personnel: Editor-Corey Bjertness, Production Mgr., Adv. Dir., Art Dir.-Rolf Goetzinger
General Info: Trim Size-11½ x 17¼, Sheetfed press, 8 pages, 2 Color, Newsprint
Circulation: Total-16,000
Printing Co: Continental Printing, 13751 Lake City Way N.E., Seattle, WA 98125
Tel # (206) 362-6903

Bradley, West Virginia

Introspect

Publishing Co: Sponsor-Alumni Assn., Appalachian Bible College, Student Services, PO Box ABC, Bradley, WV 25818; Title Tel # (304) 877-6428 Title Fax # (304) 877-5082
General Info: Quarterly, 8 pages
Circulation: Total-20,000

Madison, Wisconsin

Edgewood College Today

Publishing Co: Edgewood College, 855 Woodrow St, Madison, WI 53711-1997;
Title Tel # (608) 257-4861
Personnel: Editor-Jim Ottney
Editorial Description: Alumni/donor communications.
General Info: (Formerly Edgeword), Yr. Est. 1965, Web press, 8 pages, Coated, Saddle-stitched
Circulation: Total-5,500
Printing Co: Park Printing House, 550 East Verona Ave, Verona, WI 53593-1307
Tel # (608) 265-6515

WIRRA News

Publishing Co: Univ. of Wisconsin, Industrial Relations Research Inst., 1180 Observatory Dr, Madison, WI 53706-1320; Title Tel # (608) 262-5482
Personnel: Editor-Elaine Moran
Editorial Description: Alumni news, faculty news, staff news, placement news, features on subjects of importance to Industrial Relations. Also letters from the Director of IRRI and the presidents of alumni and student organizations.
General Info: 14 pages
Subscriptions: Indv. $10
Circulation: Total-800

Milwaukee, Wisconsin

Ideas, Information & People   *Consumer*

Publishing Co: Milwaukee Institute of Art & Design, 273 E Erie St, Milwaukee, WI 53202-6003;
Title Tel # (414) 276-7889
Editorial Description: Student activities and events.
General Info: Quarterly, Trim Size-10¾ x 10¾, 12 pages, No Color, Coated, Saddle-stitched

CANADA

Wolfville, Nova Scotia

Acadia Divinity College
News   *Consumer*

Publishing Co: Sponsor-Atlantic United Baptist Convention, Acadia Divinity College, Publications, Wolfville, NS B0P 1X0 Canada; Title Tel # (902) 542-2285
Personnel: Editor-Ronald Baxter
Editorial Description: The college is a graduate school of theology, with responsibility to train mistakes, missionaries and other religion workers of the Christian faith.
General Info: Yr. Est. 1968, Quarterly, Trim Size-8½ x 11, Letrpr. press, 2 Color, Newsprint
Circulation: Total-5,100

Guelph, Ontario

Crest
See: VETERINARY

Ontario Agricultural College
Alumni News   *Association*

Publishing Co: University of Guelph School of Engineering, Publications, Guelph, ON N1G 2W1 Canada; Title Tel # (519) 824-4120
Personnel: Publisher-JoAnne Walters, Editor-Richard Buck
Editorial Description: To update alumni on Assn. activities, alumni news & research, development & education in the OAC.
General Info: Yr. Est. 1967, Quarterly, Trim Size-8½ x 11, Offset press, 8 pages, Color, Newsprint
Circulation: (100% controlled), Total-7,000
Printing Co: Wallace Printing Inc., 70 Lewis Rd., Guelph, ON N1H 1G1 Canada
Tel # (519) 822-0371

Ottawa, Ontario

Challenge Fund Journal

Publishing Co: Carleton University Research Services, Dunton Tower, Rm. 1501, 1125 Colonel By Dr., Ottawa, ON K1S 5B6 Canada Tel # (613) 788-7400; Title Tel # (613) 788-3636
Personnel: Editor-Richard Austen
Editorial Description: News & information about the Carleton Univ. Challenge Fund campaign.
General Info: Quarterly, Trim Size-8½ x 11, Desktop press, 2 Color, Newsprint
Circulation: (100% controlled), Total-5,000

Toronto, Ontario

A & S News   *Association, Scholarly*

Publishing Co: Faculty of Arts and Science /Public Relations Dept., University of Toronto, 100 St. George Street, Toronto, ON M5S 1A1 Canada; Title Tel # (416) 978-7253
Title Fax # (416) 971-2374
General Info: Yr. Est. 1995, Semi-annually

A & S Report   *Scholarly, Association*

Publishing Co: Faculty of Arts and Science /Public Relations Dept., University of Toronto, 100 St. George Street, Toronto, ON M5S 1A1 Canada; Title Tel # (416) 978-7253
Title Fax # (416) 971-2374
General Info: Yr. Est. 1995, Annually

Forestry Alumni Newsletter

Publishing Co: Varsity Publications, University of Toronto, 44 St. George St., Toronto, ON M5S 2E4 Canada; Title Tel # (416) 978-2367
Personnel: Publisher-Glenna Sims, Production Mgr.-Helmut Streit, Editor, Art Dir.-Peter Morley
Editorial Description: A newsletter containing information about the Univ. of Toronto faculty of Forestry & its alumni.
General Info: Semi-annually, 14 pages
Circulation: (100% controlled), Total-1,700

COLLEGE STUDENT

Auburn, Alabama

Plainsman

Publishing Co: Auburn University Alumni Assoc., 317 S. College St., Auburn, AL 36849-5150 Fax # (334) 844-5365; Title Tel # (334) 844-4254
Personnel: Editor-Seth Blomely, Production Dir.-George Gouignan
Editorial Description: Student newspaper.
General Info: Yr. Est. 1879, Weekly, Trim Size-13 x 21, Web press, 32 pages, 4 Color
Subscriptions: Indv. $15
Circulation: Total-19,500
Advertising: Inquire for rates. Accepts Inserts.
Printing Co: Columbus Ledger-Enquirer, 17 W 12th St, Columbus, GA 31901-2413
Tel # (706) 576-6243

Birmingham, Alabama

Dr. Free's Radio Remedies

Publishing Co: University of Alabama, Univ. Ctr., 1400 University Blvd., Ste. 135, Birmingham, AL 35294-1150 Tel # (205) 934-4011; Title Tel # (205) 975-6147 Title Fax # (205) 934-3884
Personnel: Publisher, Editor-Tim Herring
Editorial Description: Dr. Tim Herring had left the university in '92-'93.
General Info: Yr. Est. 1987, Quarterly, Trim Size-8½ x 11, 10 pages, 3% ads, Newsprint
Subscriptions: Indv. $5
Circulation: Total-3,500
Advertising: Inquire for rates.
Printing Co: Pete's Printing Co., 2025 2nd Ave., N., Birmingham, AL

Entre Nous

Publishing Co: Samford University, 800 Lakeshore Dr. ROBH 305D, Birmingham, AL 35229-0001 Tel # (205) 870-2959; Title Tel # (205) 870-2011 Title Fax # (205) 870-2654
Editorial Description: A college newsletter for Samford University students.
General Info: Yr. Est. 1909, Annually
Circulation: Total-2,400
Advertising: Inquire for rates.

Grapevine

Publishing Co: Southern Junior College of Business, 115 Office Park Dr, Birmingham, AL 35223-2401; Title Tel # (205) 879-5100 Title Fax # (205) 871-4881

Jefferson State News

Publishing Co: Jefferson State Junior College, 2601 Carson Rd, Birmingham, AL 35215-3007; Title Tel # (205) 853-1200 Title Fax # (205) 893-0340
Editorial Description: A college newsletter.
General Info: Monthly, Offset press, No Color
Circulation: Total-2,300
Advertising: Inquire for rates.

Miles College News   *Consumer*

Publishing Co: Miles College, Box 3800, Birmingham, AL 35208; Title Tel # (205) 923-2771 Title Fax # (205) 923-9292
General Info: Weekly, Trim Size-8½ x 11, 2 pages, No Color

Pioneer

Publishing Co: Jefferson State Junior College, 2601 Carson Rd, Birmingham, AL 35215-3007; Title Tel # (205) 853-1200 Title Fax # (205) 226-4931
Editorial Description: A college newsletter.
General Info: 200 pages
Circulation: Total-2,000

Brewton, Alabama

Beauvoir

Publishing Co: Jefferson Davis State Junior College, Brewton, AL 36426; Title Tel # (334) 867-4832 Title Fax # (334) 867-7399
Editorial Description: A college newsletter.
General Info: 144 pages
Circulation: Total-500

Tarter

Publishing Co: Jefferson Davis State Junior College, Brewton, AL 36426; Title Tel # (334) 867-7399 Title Fax # (334) 867-7399
Editorial Description: A college newsletter.
General Info: Offset press, 4 pages
Circulation: Total-500

Decatur, Alabama

Graffiti

Publishing Co: John C. Calhoun State Community College, PO Box 2216, Decatur, AL 35602-2216; Title Tel # (205) 353-3102
General Info: Letrpr. press, 6 pages
Circulation: Total-1,000

Talon

Publishing Co: John C. Calhoun State Community College, PO Box 2216, Decatur, AL 35602-2216; Title Tel # (205) 353-3102
General Info: 272 pages
Circulation: Total-950

Gadsden, Alabama

Coosada

Publishing Co: Gadsden State Junior College, PO Box 227, Gadsden, AL 35902-0227; Title Tel # (205) 546-0484
General Info: Yr. Est. 1966, Annually
Subscriptions: Indv. $3
Circulation: Total-500
Advertising: Inquire for rates.

Jasper, Alabama

Arcana

Publishing Co: Walker College, Publications, Jasper, AL 35501; Title Tel # (205) 387-0511
General Info: Yr. Est. 1965
Circulation: Total-500

Mobile, Alabama

Newsline

Publishing Co: S.D. Bishop State Junior College, 351 N Broad St, Mobile, AL 36603-5833; Title Tel # (205) 690-6412
Personnel: Editor-Deborah Anthony

Vanguard , The
See: COLLEGE ALUMNI

Monroeville, Alabama

Orator

Publishing Co: Patrick Henry Junior College, PO Box 2000, Monroeville, AL 36461-2000 Tel # (334) 575-2468; Title Tel # (334) 575-3156
General Info: Yr. Est. 1965, Monthly
Circulation: Total-300

Montgomery, Alabama

Bells

Publishing Co: Huntingdon College, Student Life Office, 1500 E. Fairview Ave., Montgomery, AL 36106-2148; Title Tel # (334) 833-4401 Title Fax # (334) 833-4486

Troy State Montgomery Newsletter

Publishing Co: Troy State Univ. in Montgomery, PO Box 4419, Montgomery, AL 36103-4419 Tel # (205) 834-1400
Personnel: Publisher-Sandi Gouge
General Info: Quarterly, Offset press, 4 pages
Circulation: Total-2,000

Normal, Alabama

SGA Newsletter   *Consumer*

Publishing Co: Alabama A & M Univ., Publications, Normal, AL 35762; Title Tel # (205) 851-5000
General Info: Weekly

Tuskegee, Alabama

News of Tuskegee Institute

Publishing Co: Tuskegee Institute, Public Relations Office, Tuskegee, AL 36083 Tel # (334) 727-8349 Fax # (334) 724-4413; Title Tel # (334) 727-8011

Wadley, Alabama

SUC News

Publishing Co: Southern Union State Junior College, Publications, Wadley, AL 36276; Title Tel # (205) 395-2211
General Info: Monthly
Circulation: Total-400

Flagstaff, Arizona

Cardinal Key Bulletin

Publishing Co: Northern Arizona Univ., News & Publications Box 6000, Flagstaff, AZ 86011-0001 Tel # (520) 523-2570 Fax # (520) 523-9313; Title Tel # (602) 523-2232
General Info: Annually

La Cuesta

Publishing Co: Northern Arizona Univ., News & Publications Box 6000, Flagstaff, AZ 86011-0001
Tel # (520) 523-2570 Fax # (520) 523-9313; Title Tel # (602) 523-2232
General Info: Annually
Circulation: Total-1,000

Pine, The

Publishing Co: Northern Arizona Univ., News & Publications Box 6000, Flagstaff, AZ 86011-0001
Tel # (520) 523-2570 Fax # (520) 523-9313; Title Tel # (602) 523-2232
Personnel: Editor-Cheryll Couture
General Info: (Formerly Pine Knots)
Circulation: Total-350

Phoenix, Arizona

Pinstripes   *Consumer*

Publishing Co: Western International University, 9215 N Black Canyon Hwy, Phoenix, AZ 85021-2718; Title Tel # (602) 943-2311 Title Fax # (602) 371-8637
General Info: Bi-monthly, Trim Size-8½ x 11, 8 pages, 2 Color, Matte, Saddle-stitched

Prescott, Arizona

Transitions

Publishing Co: Prescott College, 220 Grove Ave, Prescott, AZ 86301-2990;
Title Tel # (602) 778-2090
General Info: Yr. Est. 1977, Trim Size-8½ x 11, 12 pages, No Color
Circulation: Total-2,500

Tempe, Arizona

Focus

Publishing Co: Arizona State University, Research Publications, P.O Box 878206, Tempe, AZ 85287-8206 Tel # (602) 965-1266 Fax # (602) 965-9684; Title Tel # (602) 965-5229
Personnel: Publisher, Editor-Herbert Kaufman
Editorial Description: Reports on policy-related research on financial markets & institutions.
General Info: Yr. Est. 1988, Semi-annually, Trim Size-8½ x 11, Sheetfed press, 8 pages, 2 Color
Circulation: Total-2,000

Pine Bluff, Arkansas

UAPB Campus Weekly

Publishing Co: Donrey Media Group (Pine Bluff Commercial), 300 S Beech St, Pine Bluff, AR 71601-4039; Title Tel # (501) 541-6564 Title Fax # (501) 535-6227
Personnel: Editor-Patricia Baldwin, Production Mgr.-Kirk Clayborn
Editorial Description: This publication focuses on the administration, teachers and students on the University of Arkansas at the Pine Bluff campus. Articles are written by staff members in the campus' Office of Marketing & News Information Bureau
General Info: (Formerly Wednesday), Yr. Est. 1974, Bi-weekly, Trim Size-11 x 14, Sheetfed press, 4 pages, No Color, Newsprint
Acquistions: Publication Bought
Circulation: Total-4,000
Printing Co: Pine Bluff Commercial, 300 S Beech St, Pine Bluff, AR 71601-4097

Berkeley, California

Cross Currents   *Consumer*

Publishing Co: Dominican School of Philosophy & Theology, Graduate Theological Union, 2401 Ridge Road, Berkeley, CA 94709; Title Tel # (510) 849-2030
General Info: Quarterly, Trim Size-8½ x 11, 4 pages, No Color, Matte

Graduate Theological Union
Currents   *Consumer*

Publishing Co: Graduate Theological Union, 2400 Ridge Rd, Berkeley, CA 94709-1212
Tel # (415) 649-2490; Title Tel # (510) 649-2400
Editorial Description: News about GTU events.
General Info: Quarterly, Trim Size-8½ x 11, 8 pages, 2 Color, Matte, Saddle-stitched
Circulation: Total-400

Public Relations Officer   *Association*

Publishing Co: Vista Community College, 2020 Milvia St., Berkeley, CA 94704-1183
Tel # (501) 841-8431 Parent Co.-Peralta Community Colleges Dist. Office, Oakland;
Title Tel # (510) 841-8431 Title Fax # (510) 841-7333
Personnel: Editor-Shirley Fogarino
Editorial Description: A newsletter for Vista Faculty, staff & students.
General Info: Yr. Est. 1989, Monthly, Desktop press, 4 pages, No Color, Newsprint
Circulation: Total-1,000

Blythe, California

Pirate Log

Publishing Co: Palo Verde College, 811 W. Chanslorway, Blythe, CA 92225-1118
Tel # (619) 922-6168; Title Tel # (714) 922-6168
General Info: Yr. Est. 1945, Annually
Circulation: Total-200
Advertising: Inquire for rates.

Burbank, California

Hotline   *Consumer*

Publishing Co: Woodbury University, PO Box 7846, Burbank, CA 91510-7846;
Title Tel # (818) 767-0888 Title Fax # (818) 504-9320
Personnel: Publisher-Mary Dolan, Production Mgr.-Phlor Torrejos
Editorial Description: The Hotline is published by the Student Services Office to keep the campus community informed of events, policies, & other happenings. We do not accept paid advertising but we sometimes print announcements by off-campus organizations & firms that might interest our students.
General Info: Bi-weekly, Trim Size-8½ x 11, Mimeo press, No Color, Newsprint
Circulation: Total-400

Claremont, California

Theolog
See: RELIGIOUS & THEOLOGICAL

Cupertino, California

Grapevine

Publishing Co: De Anza College, 21250 Stevens Creek Blvd, Cupertino, CA 95014-5797;
Title Tel # (408) 864-5678
General Info: Yr. Est. 1967, Semi-weekly, Trim Size-8½ x 11, Offset press, No Color

Cypress, California

Charge

Publishing Co: Cypress College, 9200 Valley View St, Cypress, CA 90630-5897;
Title Tel # (714) 826-2220
Personnel: Editor-T. Neeman
General Info: Yr. Est. 1966, Weekly, Trim Size-8½ x 11, Offset press, 2 pages, No Color
Circulation: Total-750

Desert Hot Springs, California

Living Music
See: MUSIC & MUSIC TRADES

Inglewood, California

Brief, The   *Consumer*

Publishing Co: University of West Los Angeles, 1155 W Arbor Vitae St, Inglewood, CA 90301-2902
General Info: Monthly, Trim Size-8½ x 11, 8 pages, No Color, Matte, Saddle-stitched
Advertising: Inquire for rates.

Modesto, California

Buccaneer

Publishing Co: Modesto Junior College, College Ave., Modesto, CA 95350 Tel # (209) 575-6498;
Title Tel # (209) 526-2000
General Info: Annually

National City, California

Pneumo Pneus   *Consumer*

Publishing Co: California College for Health Sciences, 222 W 24th St, National City, CA 91950-6605;
Title Tel # (619) 477-4800 Title Fax # (619) 477-4360
Personnel: Publisher-Kenneth Scheiderman, Editor-Cheryl Latif, Circ. Mgr., Production Mgr., Mktg. Dir.-Vanessa Allen
Editorial Description: School newspaper on events and students. Also sells books via mail for courses and student reference.
General Info: Yr. Est. 1979, Quarterly, Trim Size-11 x 14, Sheetfed press, 8 pages, 2 Color, Matte
Subscriptions: Free To Qualified Recipient
Circulation: Total-20,075
Advertising: Accepts Inserts.
Printing Co: Press Plus, 2605 Hoover Ave Ste A, National City, CA 91950-6667
Tel # (619) 474-0666, Fax # (619) 474-9325

North Hollywood, California

Cal Fam
See: PSYCHOLOGY

Palm Springs, California

MUSENET **Business**

Publishing Co: JFO Enterprises, PO Box 818, Palm Springs, CA 92263-0818 Tel # (619) 416-9417; Title Tel # (619) 327-8794
Personnel: Editor, Circ. Mgr.-John Oster
Editorial Description: A newsletter of employment opportunities for the college teaching professional in the music field. Resume writing, formating, storage & referral free with subscription. Free copies to college institution subscribers & advertisers.
General Info: Yr. Est. 1990, Semi-monthly, Trim Size-8½ x 11, 6 pages
Subscriptions: Indv. $120, Inst. $80
Advertising: $450.
Printing Co: Minuteman Press, 67555 Palm Canyon Dr., Cathedral City, CA 92234

San Diego, California

National University Weekly **Association**

Publishing Co: National University, 4141 Camino Del Rio S, San Diego, CA 92108-4193 Tel # (619) 563-7100; Title Tel # (714) 563-7100
General Info: Yr. Est. 1971, Weekly, Letrpr. press
Subscriptions: Free

San Francisco, California

Forum **Consumer**

Publishing Co: Saybrook Institute, 450 Pacific Avenue #300, San Francisco, CA 94133-4640; Title Tel # (415) 441-5034 Title Fax # (415) 441-7556
Personnel: Editor-Melissa Joulwan
General Info: Monthly, Trim Size-8½ x 11, 10 pages, No Color, Matte

San Jose, California

Broadcaster **Association**

Publishing Co: San Jose Bible College, PO Box 1090, San Jose, CA 95108-1090; Title Tel # (408) 293-9058
Personnel: Editor-Ginger McGinty
General Info: Yr. Est. 1968, Bi-monthly, 4 pages
Circulation: (100% controlled), Total-8,000

San Pablo, California

Advocate

Publishing Co: Contra Costa College, 2600 Mission Bell Dr, San Pablo, CA 94806-3195; Title Tel # (415) 235-7800
Personnel: Editor-Claire Anselmo
Editorial Description: Student newspaper of Contra Costa College.
General Info: Yr. Est. 1950, Weekly, Trim Size-13 x 21, Offset press, 6 pages
Subscriptions: Free
Circulation: Total-2,000
Advertising: Inquire for rates.
Printing Co: Gibson Printing & Publishing, 544 Curtola Pky, Vallejo, CA 94590-6925 Tel # (707) 643-2552

San Rafael, California

Columbia Pacific University Alumni Newsletter
  See: COLLEGE ALUMNI

Santa Barbara, California

Fielding Networker, The **Consumer**

Publishing Co: The Fielding Institute, 2112 Santa Barbara St, Santa Barbara, CA 93105-3538; Title Tel # (805) 687-1099
Personnel: Editor-Hilde Keldermans
Editorial Description: Information on this psychology school.
General Info: Semi-annually, Trim Size-11 x 17, 16 pages, No Color, Matte

Santa Paula, California

Thomas Aquinas College
Newsletter **Consumer**

Publishing Co: Thomas Aquinas College, 10000 Ojai Rd, Santa Paula, CA 93060-9622; Title Tel # (719) 549-3218
Personnel: Mktg. Dir.-Gary Franchi
General Info: Quarterly, Trim Size-10¾ x 17, 4 pages, 2 Color, Matte

Stockton, California

Humphreys College Quarterly News Bulletin
  See: COLLEGE ALUMNI

Naranjado

Publishing Co: Univ. of the Pacific, Publishing Bd., 3601 Pacific Ave. Hand Hall, 3rd Fl., Stockton, CA 95211-0001 Tel # (209) 946-2011; Title Tel # (209) 946-2114
General Info: Yr. Est. 1890, Annually
Circulation: Total-2,300
Advertising: Inquire for rates.

West Covina, California

Youth Mission for the Immaculata National Newsletter
  See: RELIGIOUS & THEOLOGICAL

Denver, Colorado

Brown & Gold

Publishing Co: Barnum, Inc., W. 50th & Lowell Blvd., Denver, CO 80221; Title Tel # (303) 458-4152
Personnel: Editor-Elizabeth Stone, Co-Editor-Liz Howard, Circ. Mgr.-Nick Jackson, Adv. Dir.-M.J. Acke
General Info: Yr. Est. 1919, Bi-weekly
Subscriptions: Indv. $12
Circulation: Total-1,200

Iliff Reporter

Publishing Co: Iliff School of Theology, 2201 S University Blvd, Denver, CO 80210-4798; Title Tel # (303) 744-1287
Personnel: Editor-Suzanne Calvin
General Info: Quarterly, Trim Size-8½ x 11, Offset press, 6 pages, 2 Color
Circulation: Total-9,000

La Junta, Colorado

Rattler News **Consumer, Association**

Publishing Co: Otero Junior College, Publications, La Junta, CO 81050 Tel # (303) 384-8721; Title Tel # (719) 384-6821
Personnel: Editor-Bonnie Milenski
General Info: Yr. Est. 1993, Monthly
Circulation: Total-1,000

Danielson, Connecticut

Crazy River Press

Publishing Co: Quinebaug Valley Community-Technical College, 742 Upper Maple St., Danielson, CT 06239-1440; Title Tel # (860) 774-1130 Title Fax # (860) 774-7768
General Info: Yr. Est. 1973, Weekly, Trim Size-8 x 14, Offset press, 6 pages, No Color
Circulation: Total-900

Fairfield, Connecticut

Night Hawk

Publishing Co: Bridgeport Engineering Institute, 785 Unquowa Rd., Fairfield, CT 06430-5002; Title Tel # (203) 259-5717 Title Fax # (203) 259-9372
Editorial Description: General interest.
General Info: Yr. Est. 1924, Semi-annually, Offset press, 4 pages
Circulation: Total-1,500

Groton, Connecticut

Student News

Publishing Co: Univ. of Connecticut-Groton, Publications, Groton, CT 06340; Title Tel # (203) 446-1020
General Info: Weekly, 1 pages

Hartford, Connecticut

Newsletter **Association**

Publishing Co: Hartford Graduate Center, 275 Windsor St, Hartford, CT 06120-2910; Title Tel # (203) 548-2400 Title Fax # (860) 548-7887
Personnel: Editor-Barbara Richards
General Info: Yr. Est. 1970, Tri-annually, Web press, 6 pages, No Color, Coated
Circulation: (100% controlled), Total-9,500
Printing Co: Finlay Brothers, 44 Tobey Rd. #7330, Bloomfield, CT 06002-3538 Tel # (203) 242-2800

New Britain, Connecticut

Central Courier **Consumer**

Publishing Co: Central Connecticut State University, 1615 Stanley St # 101, New Britain, CT 06053-2439
General Info: 8x/yr., Trim Size-8½ x 11, 10 pages, 2 Color, Matte, Saddle-stitched

North Haven, Connecticut

SAC

Publishing Co: Greater New Haven State Technical College, 88 Bassett Rd, North Haven, CT 06473-1901; Title Tel # (203) 234-3304
Personnel: Publisher-Judy Owsiany
General Info: Weekly, Trim Size-8½ x 11, Mimeo press, No Color
Circulation: Total-850

Waterbury, Connecticut

Hillside Highlights

Publishing Co: Univ. of Connecticut, 32 Hillside Ave, Waterbury, CT 06710-2217
Tel # (203) 757-1231
General Info: Bi-weekly, Trim Size-8½ x 11, Desktop press, No Color
Circulation: Total-300
Advertising: Inquire for rates.

West Haven, Connecticut

University of New Haven
Insight   *Consumer*

Publishing Co: University of New Haven, 300 Orange Ave, West Haven, CT 06516-1916;
Title Tel # (203) 932-7000
Editorial Description: Newsletter on events of university.
General Info: Quarterly, Trim Size-8½ x 11, 16 pages, 2 Color, Matte, Saddle-stitched
Circulation: Total-22,000

Winsted, Connecticut

Jabberwocky   *Consumer*

Publishing Co: Northwestern Connecticut Community-Technical College, Rm. 110, Green Woods Hall, Student Activities Office, Winsted, CT 06098; Title Tel # (203) 738-6343
General Info: Weekly, Trim Size-8½ x 11, 4 pages, No Color, Matte

Woodstock, Connecticut

Canto

Publishing Co: Annhurst College, Publishing, Woodstock, CT 06281; Title Tel # (203) 928-7773
General Info: Yr. Est. 1968, Annually, Trim Size-6 x 9, 28 pages
Circulation: Total-300

Wilmington, Delaware

Delaware Law Forum

Publishing Co: Widener Univ. -Delaware Law School, PO Box 7474, Wilmington, DE 19803-0474
Tel # (302) 478-5280; Title Tel # (302) 477-2147
Personnel: Publisher-Tom Manga, Editor-Andrew Hlodio
Editorial Description: Legal periodical - for attorneys, judges, students, family & alumni.
General Info: Yr. Est. 1974, Monthly, Trim Size-11½ x 15, Web press, 20 pages, No Color, Newsprint
Subscriptions: Free
Circulation: Total-7,000
Advertising: Inquire for rates.

Washington, District of Columbia

About Women on Campus

Publishing Co: National Association for Women in Education, 1325 18th St. NW, Ste. 210, Washington, DC 20036-6511; Title Tel # (202) 659-9330 Title Fax # (202) 457-0946
Editorial Description: Up-to-the-minute information about campus climate, the academic workpalce, women in the curriculum, student life, sexual harassment and sexual assault, international issues and conerns, women in nontraditional programs, women of color, women's athletics,gender issues, women's colleges, womens's leadership and many other key issues for women of campus.
General Info: Yr. Est. 1992, Quarterly, ISSN: 1061-768X
Subscriptions: Indv. $20, Inst. $28, Can. $35, For. $35, $5/copy

Adolescent Medicine
See: MEDICINE

Key Reporter
See: CLUBS

Clearwater, Florida

Report   *Consumer*

Publishing Co: Clearwater Christian College, 3400 Gulf To Bay Blvd, Clearwater, FL 34619-4514; Title Tel # (813) 726-1153 Title Fax # (813) 726-8597
General Info: Quarterly, Trim Size-8½ x 11, 6 pages, 2 Color, Matte

Fort Lauderdale, Florida

Buzz

Publishing Co: Art Institute of Ft. Lauderdale, 1799 SE 17th St, Fort Lauderdale, FL 33316-3013
Tel # (305) 527-1799; Title Tel # (305) 463-3000
Personnel: Editor-Robyn Coddington, Mktg. Dir.-Sallie Merit Green
General Info: Monthly

Graceville, Florida

Echoes   *Association, Consumer*

Publishing Co: Florida Baptist Theological College, 5400 College Dr., P.O. Box 1306, Graceville, FL 32440-3306
Personnel: Publisher-Thomas Kinchen, Editor-Marcell Aikens, Mng. Editor-David Knight
Editorial Description: Events and info of college.
General Info: Quarterly, Trim Size-8½ x 11, 16 pages, No Color, Coated, Saddle-stitched

Key West, Florida

Voices

Publishing Co: Florida Keys Community College, 5901 W. Jr. College Rd., Key West, FL 33040-4397; Title Tel # (305) 296-9081
General Info: (Formerly Wrecker's Debris/Log), Yr. Est. 1969, Weekly, 4 pages, Color

Kissimmee, Florida

Sonlife   *Consumer, Association*

Publishing Co: Florida Christian College, 1011 Bill Beck Blvd, Kissimmee, FL 34744-5301;
Title Tel # (407) 847-8966
Editorial Description: Information about college and its programs.
General Info: Monthly, Trim Size-8½ x 11, 4 pages, 2 Color, Coated

Miami, Florida

Antidote

Publishing Co: Miami-Dade Community College-Medical Ctr. Campus, 950 NW 20th St, Miami, FL 33127-4622; Title Tel # (305) 347-4208
Personnel: Editor-Marty Medine
General Info: Monthly, Trim Size-8½ x 11, Desktop press, 4 pages

Mulberry, Florida

Rhema

Publishing Co: Spurgeon Baptist Bible College, 4440 Spurgeon Dr, Mulberry, FL 33860-9531
Personnel: Publisher-Wallace Lont
Editorial Description: In-house student pages of college & related news.
General Info: Yr. Est. 1980, Weekly, No Color

N. Miami Beach, Florida

Sentinel   *Consumer*

Publishing Co: Southeastern University of the Health Sciences, Sentinel, 1750 N.E. 167th Street, N. Miami Beach, FL 33152-3017; Title Tel # (305) 949-4000
General Info: Quarterly, Trim Size-11 x 14, 6 pages, 2 Color, Coated

St. Petersburg, Florida

Eckerd College
Thimblerig

Publishing Co: Eckerd College, Letters Collegium, 4200 54th Avenue South, St. Petersburg, FL 33711 Tel # (813) 864-8238; Title Tel # (813) 867-1166
General Info: Yr. Est. 1961, Bi-weekly, Trim Size-8½ x 11, Offset press, 24 pages, No Color
Circulation: Total-1,100
Advertising: Inquire for rates.

Tampa, Florida

Information X IV   *Consumer*

Publishing Co: Tampa Technical Institute, 2410 E Busch Blvd, Tampa, FL 33612-8410
Fax # (813) 835-7415; Title Tel # (813) 935-5700 Title Fax # (813) 935-7415
Personnel: Publisher, Editor, Adv. Dir.-Wiley Koon, Jr.
Editorial Description: Newsletter for the school campus with emphasis on student success, job placement, news, contests, & happenings.
General Info: (Formerly Information X III), Yr. Est. 1990, Quarterly, Trim Size-8½ x 11, Sheetfed press, 6 pages, 2 Color, Coated, Perfect bound
Circulation: Total-2,000
Advertising: Inquire for rates.
Printing Co: Rinaldi Printing Co., 4514 Adamo Dr, Tampa, FL 33605-5967 Tel # (813) 247-3921, Fax # (813) 242-6705

Atlanta, Georgia

Atlanta University Bulletin   *Consumer*

Publishing Co: Atlanta Univ., 223 James P Brawley Dr SW, Atlanta, GA 30314-4358;
Title Tel # (404) 653-8400
General Info: Semi-annually
Circulation: Total-8,500

Morehouse Update   *Consumer, Association*

Publishing Co: Morehouse College, 317 Gloster Hall, 830 Westview Dr., SW, Atlanta, GA 30314
Tel # (404) 681-2800; Title Tel # (404) 215-2661
Personnel: Publications Director-Robert Bolton
Editorial Description: Events and news of the college.
General Info: Irregular, Trim Size-8½ x 11, 8 pages, 2 Color, Coated, Saddle-stitched
Subscriptions: Free To Qualified Recipient

Lithonia, Georgia

Pioneer   *Association*

Publishing Co: Luther Rice Seminary, 3038 Evans Mill Rd, Lithonia, GA 30038-2454
Tel # (404) 484-1204 Fax # (404) 484-1155; Title Tel # (770) 484-1204 Title Fax # (770) 484-1155
Personnel: Editor-Vanessa Nealey
General Info: Quarterly, Desktop press, 8 pages, 2 Color, Matte
Subscriptions: Free
Circulation: Total-8,000

Waleska, Georgia

On Campus   *Association*

Publishing Co: Reinhardt College, 7300 Reinhardt College Pkwy., Waleska, GA 30183-0128
Tel # (770) 720-5600; Title Tel # (770) 720-5513 Title Fax # (770) 720-5602
Personnel: Publisher-Marsha White, Editor-Kdy Bishop
Editorial Description: Weekly publication for faculty, staff, and students.
General Info: (Formerly This Week/On Campus), Weekly
Circulation: (83% controlled), Total-600
Advertising: Inquire for rates.

Kaneohe, Hawaii

INA

Publishing Co: Hawaii Loa College, 45-045 Kamehameha Hwy, Kaneohe, HI 96744-5297;
Title Tel # (808) 235-3641
Editorial Description: General interest.

Mongoose

Publishing Co: Hawaii Loa College, 45-045 Kamehameha Hwy, Kaneohe, HI 96744-5297;
Title Tel # (808) 235-3641
General Info: Yr. Est. 1991, Bi-weekly
Subscriptions: Free
Advertising: Inquire for rates.

Boise, Idaho

Outreach

Publishing Co: Boise Bible College, 8695 Marigold St, Boise, ID 83714-1220 Tel # (208) 376-7731
Fax # (208) 376-7743
Personnel: Editor-Marian Lawson, Adv. Dir.-Carol Small
Editorial Description: Informational newsletter circulated to donors, interested parties, & prospective students. Material is strictly in-house news of the college.
General Info: Tri-annually, Offset press, 6 pages, 2 Color
Subscriptions: Free
Circulation: Total-15,000
Advertising: Inquire for rates.
Printing Co: Northwest Printing, Inc., 3430 Americana Ter # 8224, Boise, ID 83706-2504
Tel # (208) 345-4545

Lewiston, Idaho

Blue Arrow

Publishing Co: Lewis-Clark State College, 8th Ave. & 6th St., Lewiston, ID 83501
Tel # (208) 799-5272; Title Tel # (208) 746-2341
General Info: Yr. Est. 1955, Annually
Circulation: Total-600
Advertising: Inquire for rates.

Moscow, Idaho

Spur

Publishing Co: Univ. of Idaho, Pubications, Moscow, ID 83843 Tel # (208) 885-6111;
Title Tel # (208) 885-7016
General Info: Quarterly
Advertising: Inquire for rates.

Chicago, Illinois

Campus Watch
See: POLITICS

De Paul Newsline

Publishing Co: De Paul Univ., 1 E Jackson Blvd, Chicago, IL 60604-2201; Title Tel # (312) 362-8690
Title Fax # (312) 362-6639
Personnel: Editor-Al Kipp
Editorial Description: Employees newsletter for faculty & staff.
General Info: Yr. Est. 1968, Monthly, Trim Size-8½ x 11, Web press, 8 pages
Acquistions: Publication Bought
Circulation: Total-2,200

Evanston, Illinois

President's Report   *Business*

Publishing Co: National College of Education, 2840 Sheridan Rd, Evanston, IL 60201-1730
Tel # (708) 475-1100; Title Tel # (708) 256-5150
Personnel: Editor-Janet Messenger
Editorial Description: Informs coroporate and foundation executives of college activities and achievements,recognizes donors to college.
General Info: Semi-annually, Trim Size-8½ x 11, 4 pages, No Color
Circulation: (100% controlled), Total-400

Olney, Illinois

Knightline   *Consumer, Association*

Publishing Co: Olney Central College, 305 N West St, Olney, IL 62450-1043;
Title Tel # (618) 395-4351
General Info: (Formerly Lamplighter), Yr. Est. 1963, Weekly, Trim Size-11 x 14, Desktop press, 4 pages, No Color
Circulation: Total-200
Advertising: Inquire for rates.

Schaumburg, Illinois

Future Actuary, The   *Association*

Publishing Co: Society of Actuaries/Casualty Acturial Society, 475 N. Martingale Rd., Suite 800, Schaumburg, IL 60173-2226; Title Tel # (708) 706-3500 Title Fax # (708) 706-3599
Personnel: Editor-Charles Emma, Editor-Linda Heacox
Editorial Description: Information for students taking actuarial examinations.
General Info: Yr. Est. 1992, 3x/yr., Trim Size-11 x 17, 4 pages, 2 Color
Subscriptions: Indv. $10, Free To Qualified Recipient
Circulation: Total-17,000
Advertising: Inquire for rates.
Printing Co: ABS Graphics, 901 S. Route 53, Addison, IL 60101 Tel # (708) 495-2400, Fax # (708) 495-2400

Urbana, Illinois

Engineering Outlook At the University of Illinois At Urbana-Champaign
See: ENGINEERING

University of Illinois At Urbana-Champaign, College of Agriculture, Current Affairs   *Association*

Publishing Co: Univ. of Illinois at Urbana Champaign, 227 Illini Union, 1401 W. Green Street, Urbana, IL 61801 Tel # (217) 333-1477 Fax # (217) 333-7803; Title Tel # (217) 333-0460
Personnel: Editor, Circ. Mgr.-T. Knecht
Editorial Description: News of current activities to the faculty, staff, alumni, and friends of the College of Agriculture.
General Info: Quarterly, Trim Size-8½ x 11, Letrpr. press, 6 pages, 2 Color
Circulation: (100% controlled), Total-4,100

Elkhart, Indiana

AMBS Bulletin   *Association*

Publishing Co: Goshen Biblical Seminary, 3003 Benham Ave, Elkhart, IN 46517-1999;
Title Tel # (219) 295-3726 Title Fax # (219) 295-0092
Personnel: Publisher-Henry Poettcker, Editor-John Bender, Circ. Mgr.-Jim Metzler
Editorial Description: News of the seminaries, short articles, covering events, theological discourses.
General Info: Yr. Est. 1986, Quarterly, Trim Size-8½ x 11, Offset press, 16 pages, No Color
Circulation: Total-4,000

Hanover, Indiana

Hill Thoughts

Publishing Co: Hanover College, Office of Public Relations, P.O. Box #108, Hanover, IN 47243 Tel # (812) 866-7008
General Info: Yr. Est. 1941, Annually
Circulation: Total-1,000

Ames, Iowa

Adult Students Newsletter   *Association*

Publishing Co: Iowa State Scientist, Inc., 16c Hamilton Hall, Ames, IA 50011-0001 Tel # (515) 294-2180 Fax # (515) 294-5108; Title Tel # (515) 294-5056
Editorial Description: A newsletter for older students at Iowa State Univ. containing info. on important univ. events and special programs for older students.
General Info: 5x/yr., Offset press, 6 pages, No Color
Circulation: (100% controlled), Total-3,700
Printing Co: Iowa State University, Dept. Of English Ross Hall, Ames, IA 50011-0001 Tel # (515) 292-0140

Bettendorf, Iowa

Weekly Update

Publishing Co: Scott Community College, 500 Belmont Rd, Bettendorf, IA 52722-6804; Title Tel # (319) 359-7531
Personnel: Editor-Lisa Brown
General Info: Weekly

Clinton, Iowa

Clarian

Publishing Co: Mount St. Clare College, 400 N Bluff Blvd, Clinton, IA 52732-3910; Title Tel # (319) 242-4023
Personnel: Editor-JoNett Butler
Editorial Description: Published for friends & alumni of Mount St. Clare College, Clinton, IA.
General Info: Quarterly, Offset press, 8 pages, 2 Color, Newsprint
Circulation: Total-8,200

Dubuque, Iowa

Campus Compass

Publishing Co: Univ. of Dubuque, 2000 University Ave, Dubuque, IA 52001-5050 Tel # (319) 589-3000; Title Tel # (319) 589-3164
Personnel: Editor-Frank Duchow, Art Dir.-Barbara Lucke
Editorial Description: This is an internal employee newsletter, but students at the college & seminary read it.
General Info: Yr. Est. 1974, Weekly, Trim Size-8½ x 14, Mimeo press, 2 pages, No Color, Newsprint
Acquistions: Publication Bought
Circulation: (100% controlled), Total-1,000
Printing Co: Univ. of Dubuque, 2000 University Ave, Dubuque, IA 52001-5050 Tel # (319) 589-3164

Fairfield, Iowa

MIU Review   **CPM: $80**

Publishing Co: Maharishi Intl. Univ., 301 S Court St, Fairfield, IA 52556-3452; Title Tel # (515) 472-5031
Personnel: Publisher-Craig Pearson, Editor-Jim Karpen
Editorial Description: Campus newsletter of announcements and achievements.
General Info: (Formerly Ideal Times), Yr. Est. 1985, Bi-weekly, Trim Size-8½ x 11, Letrpr. press, 8 pages, No Color, Newsprint, Saddle-stitched
Subscriptions: Free
Circulation: (100% controlled), Total-2,500
Advertising: $200. Accepts Inserts.
Printing Co: MIU Press, Box 1114, Fairfield, IA 52557-0001 Tel # (515) 472-5031

Grinnell, Iowa

Newsletter

Publishing Co: Grinnell College, PO Box 805, Grinnell, IA 50112-0813 Tel # (515) 269-4000; Title Tel # (515) 269-4901
Personnel: Editor-Bobbie Loucks
Editorial Description: Computer service & telephone service information basically for Grinnell College users.
General Info: (Formerly Input Output), Yr. Est. 1984, Quarterly, Trim Size-8½ x 11, Mimeo press, 20 pages, Color, Newsprint
Subscriptions: Free
Circulation: Total-1,000

Crestview Hills, Kentucky

Utopian   **CPM: $140**

Publishing Co: Thomas More College, 333 Thomas More Pkway., Crestview Hills, KY 41017-3428; Title Tel # (606) 344-3605
Personnel: Editor-Victoria Hoening, Adv. Dir.-Paul Menke, Art Dir.-Jay Costa, Art Dir.-Jason Stelter, Promotion Dir.-Chris Bryson
Editorial Description: General up-to-date college happenings editorials.
General Info: (Formerly Spokesman), Yr. Est. 1968, Monthly, Trim Size-11½ x 15, 12 pages, 13% ads, No Color
Subscriptions: Free
Circulation: Total-1,000
Advertising: $140.
Printing Co: Feike, Web, Cincinnati, OH 45231

Danville, Kentucky

Centrepiece   *Consumer, Association*

Publishing Co: Centre College of Kentucky, 600 W Walnut St, Danville, KY 40422-1309; Title Tel # (606) 236-5211
Personnel: Editor-Diane Fisher Johnson
Editorial Description: Newsletter for Alumni and friends of Centre College of Kentucky.
General Info: Yr. Est. 1924, 5x/yr., Trim Size-11⅜ x 15, Web press, 16 pages, No Color
Circulation: (100% controlled), Total-13,200

Louisville, Kentucky

Student Bulletin

Publishing Co: Jefferson Community College, 109 E Broadway St, Louisville, KY 40202-2000; Title Tel # (502) 584-0181
General Info: Yr. Est. 1970, Weekly, Offset press, 2 pages
Circulation: Total-2,000

Owensboro, Kentucky

Panogram

Publishing Co: Kentucky Wesleyan College, 3000 Frederica St, Owensboro, KY 42301-6055; Title Tel # (502) 926-3111
General Info: Semi-monthly
Circulation: Total-1,200
Advertising: Inquire for rates.

Pikeville, Kentucky

Echo   *Association*

Publishing Co: Pikeville College, Sycamore St., Pikeville, KY 41501 Tel # (606) 432-9200; Tel # (606) 432-9227 Title Fax # (606) 432-9328
Personnel: Editor-Suzanne Rasnick
Editorial Description: News of campus & alumni activities.
General Info: Yr. Est. 1978, Quarterly, Trim Size-11½ x 14, Web press, 16 pages, Color-cover, Newsprint
Subscriptions: Free
Circulation: Total-9,000
Printing Co: Appalachian News Express, PO Box 802, Pikeville, KY 41502-0802 Fax # (606) 437-4246

Baton Rouge, Louisiana

LSU Engineering News   *Association*

Publishing Co: Louisiana State Univ., College of Engineering, 3216 Ceba Bldg., Baton Rouge, LA 70803-0001; Title Tel # (504) 388-6003 Title Fax # (504) 388-5990
Personnel: Publisher-Edward McLaughlin, Editor-Staci Downey, Art Dir.-Son Nguyen
Editorial Description: General update of College of Engineering aimed at alumni.
General Info: Annually, Trim Size-8½ x 11, Desktop press, 30 pages, 2 Color, Newsprint
Circulation: Total-14,000

New Orleans, Louisiana

Communique

Publishing Co: Delgado Community College, 615 City Park Ave, New Orleans, LA 70119-4326

Tulane Tax Institute
See: TAXES

Auburn, Maine

Weekly News Bulletin

Publishing Co: Central Maine Vocational Technical Institute, 1250 Turner St, Auburn, ME 04210-6436; Title Tel # (207) 784-2385
General Info: Yr. Est. 1977, Weekly, Trim Size-8½ x 14, Mimeo press, 2 pages, No Color

Biddeford, Maine

News Flash
Publishing Co: Univ. of New England, 11 Hills Beach Rd, Biddeford, ME 04005-9526
Tel # (207) 283-0171
General Info: Bi-weekly, No Color
Circulation: Total-1,000

Orono, Maine

Uribus
Publishing Co: Univ. of Maine, 265 Stevens Hall, Orono, ME 04469-0001 Tel # (207) 581-1110;
Title Tel # (207) 581-7698
General Info: Yr. Est. 1963
Circulation: Total-500

Presque Isle, Maine

Toward Excellence   *Consumer*
Publishing Co: Northern Maine Technical College, 33 Edgemont Dr, Presque Isle, ME 04769-2016;
Title Tel # (207) 769-2461 Title Fax # (207) 764-8465
General Info: Weekly, Trim Size-8½ x 11, 2 pages, No Color

Unity, Maine

Notable News   *Association*
Publishing Co: Unity College, Quaker Hill Rd., HC 78, Box 1, Unity, ME 04988-9502
Tel # (207) 948-3131 Fax # (207) 948-5626
Personnel: Publisher-Marcia Nance, Editor-Kristy DeRoche
Editorial Description: This is a weekly newsletter representing the student body & faculty/staff, with weekly calendar & contributions from students & staff.
General Info: Weekly, Trim Size-8½ x 11, Mimeo press, Newsprint
Circulation: Total-380

Unity College Today
See: COLLEGE ALUMNI

Baltimore, Maryland

Coppin-Hopkins Newsletter
Publishing Co: Coppin State College, 2500 W North Ave, Baltimore, MD 21216-3698
Tel # (301) 383-4500; Title Tel # (301) 333-7841
Personnel: Editor-John Furlong
General Info: Yr. Est. 1987, Bi-monthly, 6 pages, No Color, Newsprint
Circulation: Total-500

Imagine   *Consumer*
Publishing Co: Sponsor-Study of Exceptional Talent, Johns Hopkins University Press, 2715 N Charles St, Baltimore, MD 21218-4363 Tel # (410) 516-6964; Title Fax # (410) 516-6968
Personnel: Editor-Susan B. Hellerman, Mktg. Dir.-Barbara Berlin Caplan
Editorial Description: News and reviews for academically talented students looking for challenging educational options.
General Info: Yr. Est. 1993, 5x/yr., Trim Size-8½ x 11, 24 pages, 2 Color, Matte
Subscriptions: Indv. $30, Inst. $30, Can. $34, For. $36, $6/copy
List Rental: Rents Lists

Ubique
Publishing Co: Ubique, 1420 N Charles St, Baltimore, MD 21201-5720
Personnel: Editor-John Klender, Production Dir., Art Dir.-Renee Bucharewicz, Adv. Rep., Promotion Mgr.-Carla J. Cunningham
General Info: Yr. Est. 1977, Bi-weekly, Letrpr. press, 20 pages, 35% ads, No Color, Newsprint
Circulation: (100% controlled), Total-2,000
Advertising: Inquire for rates.
List Rental: Rents Lists
Printing Co: Centaur Press, 201 Railroad Ave, Westminster, MD 21157-4823

College Park, Maryland

Commuter, The
See: EDUCATION

Laurel, Maryland

Short Circuit
Publishing Co: Capitol College, 11301 Springfield Rd, Laurel, MD 20708-9759;
Title Tel # (301) 953-0060
Personnel: Editor-Nora Gassek
General Info: Bi-weekly, Trim Size-8½ x 11, Mimeo press, No Color
Advertising: Inquire for rates.

Beverly, Massachusetts

Endicotter   *Association*
Publishing Co: Endicott College, 376 Hale St, Beverly, MA 01915-2098 Tel # (508) 927-0585
Personnel: Editor-Scott Peterson
General Info: Offset press, 16 pages, No Color

Boston, Massachusetts

Spectrum
See: DENTAL

Brookline, Massachusetts

Directions
Publishing Co: Hellenic College, 50 Goddard Ave, Brookline, MA 02146-7496;
Title Tel # (617) 731-3500
Personnel: Editor-George Orfanakos
General Info: Yr. Est. 1978, Weekly, Trim Size-8 x 11, Offset press, 4 pages, No Color
Circulation: Total-250

Cambridge, Massachusetts

Lesley News   *Business*
Publishing Co: Lesley College, 29 Everett St, Cambridge, MA 02138-2790;
Title Tel # (617) 868-9600
Personnel: Editor-Sandra Lish
Editorial Description: Events at and news about the Lesley community.
General Info: (Formerly Lesley Newsletter-Lesley Weekly), Yr. Est. 1970, Monthly, Trim Size-8½ x 11, Offset press, 5 pages, 2 Color, Newsprint
Circulation: Total-1,000

Lowell, Massachusetts

Delta Kappa Phi Bulletin
Publishing Co: Lowell Technological Inst., Publications, Lowell, MA 01854

Dearborn, Michigan

Falcon
Publishing Co: Detroit College of Business, 4801 Oakman Blvd, Dearborn, MI 48126-3799;
Title Tel # (313) 581-4400
Personnel: Editor-Patricia Phillips

Flint, Michigan

This Week at Baker
Publishing Co: Baker College, G-1050 W. Bristol Rd., Flint, MI 48507 Tel # (313) 767-7600;
Title Tel # (313) 766-4100
Personnel: Publisher-Beverly Ferrell, Editor-Janice Siplin
Editorial Description: Calendar information & items of current interest to students, faculty, & staff.
General Info: Weekly, Trim Size-8½ x 11, Mimeo press, No Color, Newsprint
Circulation: Total-750

Grand Rapids, Michigan

Kendall College of Art and Design   *Consumer*
Publishing Co: Kendall College of Art & Design, 111 N Division Ave, Grand Rapids, MI 49503-3102;
Title Tel # (616) 451-2787 Title Fax # (616) 451-9867
Personnel: Editor-Nancy L. Douglas, Production Mgr., Art Dir.-Diane McKnight
General Info: Semi-annually, Trim Size-10¾ x 17, Web press, 12 pages, No Color, Newsprint
Subscriptions: Free
Circulation: Total-60,000

Livonia, Michigan

Madonna Now   *Association*
Publishing Co: Madonna University, 36600 Schoolcraft Rd, Livonia, MI 48150-1176
Tel # (313) 432-5300 Fax # (313) 432-5393; Title Tel # (313) 432-5737
Personnel: Editor-Andrea Nodge
Editorial Description: Development pub. for Madonna University.
General Info: Yr. Est. 1977, Trim Size-11 x 13½, Offset press, 20 pages
Circulation: Total-17,500

Olivet, Michigan

Olivet College Bulletin

Publishing Co: Olivet College, S. Main, Olivet, MI 49076; Title Tel # (616) 749-7000
General Info: Yr. Est. 1900, Monthly
Circulation: Total-5,300
Advertising: Inquire for rates.

Troy, Michigan

Campus Insight

Publishing Co: Walsh College of Accountancy and Business Administration, PO Box 7006, Troy, MI 48007-7006; Title Tel # (313) 689-8282
Personnel: Editor-Marge Winn
General Info: Yr. Est. 1973, Semi-monthly, Trim Size-8½ x 11, Desktop press, 4 pages, No Color
Circulation: (100% controlled)

Brooklyn Park, Minnesota

Retrospect   *Consumer*

Publishing Co: North Hennepin Community College, 7411 85th Ave N, Brooklyn Park, MN 55445-2231; Title Tel # (612) 424-0811
Editorial Description: Annual newsletter describing events of the year.
General Info: Annually, Trim Size-8½ x 11, 6 pages, 2 Color, Matte

Crookston, Minnesota

Trojan Shorts

Publishing Co: Univ. of Minnesota Technical College-Crookston, Crookston, MN 56716-5001; Title Tel # (218) 281-6510
General Info: Yr. Est. 1966, Weekly, Trim Size-8½ x 11, Offset press
Circulation: Total-600

Minnetonka, Minnesota

Razz Ma Tazz   *Consumer*

Publishing Co: Rasmussen Business College, 12450 Wayzata Blvd., Minnetonka, MN 55343
Editorial Description: Events and articles for Rasmussen Business College.
General Info: Quarterly, Trim Size-8½ x 11, 16 pages, No Color, Matte

Moorhead, Minnesota

Bulletin

Publishing Co: Moorhead State Univ., Publications, Moorhead, MN 56563-0001 Tel # (218) 236-2204; Title Tel # (218) 236-2551
Personnel: Editor-Ron Matthies
Editorial Description: Recruitment, retention of students.
General Info: Monthly, 18 pages, Color
Circulation: Total-6,000
Advertising: Inquire for rates.

Rochester, Minnesota

On The Move   *Association*

Publishing Co: Minnesota Bible College, 920 Mayowood Rd SW, Rochester, MN 55902-2382; Title Tel # (507) 288-4563 Title Fax # (507) 288-9046
Personnel: Editor-Nancy Wheeler
General Info: (Formerly MBC Today), Yr. Est. 1935, Quarterly, Web press, 4 pages, 2 Color, Newsprint
Subscriptions: Free
Circulation: Total-12,000

Winona, Minnesota

Campus Notes   *Scholarly*

Publishing Co: Saint Mary's University of Minnesota, 700 Terrace Heights, Campus Box 36, Winona, MN 55987-1399 Fax # (507) 457-6980; Title Tel # (507) 457-1496
General Info: Weekly, Trim Size-8½ x 11, 4 pages, 2 Color

Tougaloo, Mississippi

Tougaloo News

Publishing Co: Tougaloo College, Publications, Tougaloo, MS 39174-9999; Title Tel # (601) 956-4941
Personnel: Editor-Pamela Nall
Editorial Description: College and alumni news.
General Info: (Formerly The Chronicle), Yr. Est. 1965, Monthly, Trim Size-8½ x 11, Offset press, 8 pages
Circulation: Total-9,000
Advertising: Inquire for rates.

Boonville, Missouri

Adjutant

Publishing Co: Kemper Military School & College, 701 3rd St, Boonville, MO 65233-1670; Title Tel # (816) 882-5623
Editorial Description: School & college yearbook.
General Info: Yr. Est. 1844, Annually, Offset press, Color
Circulation: Total-550

Columbia, Missouri

Maneater, The   *Consumer, Association*

Publishing Co: Board of Curators of the Univ of Missouri, University Hall Missouri, University, Columbia, MO 65211-0001; Title Tel # (314) 882-5500 Title Fax # (314) 882-5550
Personnel: Editor-Patrick Strawbridge, Adv. Dir.-Andrew O' Dell
Editorial Description: The Maneater covers campus, city and state news to inform and represent the Univ. of Missouri-Columbia student.
General Info: (Formerly The Missouri Student), Yr. Est. 1955, Semi-weekly, Trim Size-11½ x 16, Web press, 25 pages, 56% ads, 4 Color, Newsprint
Subscriptions: Indv. $35, Free
Circulation: Total-13,000, Readership-24,000
Advertising: Inquire for rates. Accepts Inserts.
Printing Co: Tribune Publishing Co., 100 N. 4th St., Columbia, MO 65202 Tel # (314) 449-3811, Fax # (314) 634-8205

Independence, Missouri

International University Newsletter   *Consumer, Association*

Publishing Co: International University, The, 1301 S Noland Rd, Independence, MO 64055-1390; Title Tel # (816) 461-3633
Personnel: Publisher-Joel Tintori, Editor-John Johnston, Production Mgr.-Josef Walker, Adv. Dir.-Israel Abundis, Circ. Mgr., Art Dir.-Isaac Abundis, Promotion Dir.-Cecil Johnston
Editorial Description: Events of significance involving the collegiate network of the International University.
General Info: Yr. Est. 1973, Quarterly, Trim Size-8½ x 11, Sheetfed press, 12 pages, ISSN: 0748-9684, No Color, Newsprint
Subscriptions: Indv. $300, Inst. $300, For. $300, $75/copy
Circulation: Total-1,500

Jefferson City, Missouri

Alumni Line   *Association*

Publishing Co: Lincoln Univ., Young Hall, 802 Chestnut St., Rm.303, Jefferson City, MO 65102; Title Tel # (314) 681-5103
Personnel: Editor-Mary Simmons
Editorial Description: Presents association news as well as features on campus activities.
General Info: (Formerly Harambee), Yr. Est. 1971, 5x/yr., Trim Size-8½ x 11, Offset press, 16 pages, 2 Color
Circulation: (100% controlled), Total-5,000

Kansas City, Missouri

Music Notes

Publishing Co: Univ. of Missouri Conservatory of Music, 4949 Cherry, Ctr. for the Performing Arts, Kansas City, MO 64110-2229; Title Tel # (816) 276-2949
Personnel: Publisher-Marion Abare, Editor-Catherine Groves
Editorial Description: A forum for dialogue between Christians & New Agers.
General Info: (Formerly Clarion), Yr. Est. 1986, Semi-annually, Trim Size-7 x 8½, Offset press, 8 pages, ISSN: 0899-7292, No Color, Matte
Subscriptions: Indv. $13, Can. $13, For. $19, $4/copy
Circulation: Total-200
Advertising: Inquire for rates.

Kirksville, Missouri

Tenaculum

Publishing Co: Kirksville College of Osteopathic Medicine, 800 W Jefferson St, Kirksville, MO 63501-1497 Tel # (816) 626-2354; Title Tel # (816) 626-2121

Moberly, Missouri

Sentinel, The   *Consumer*

Publishing Co: Central Christian College of the Bible, The Sentinel, 911 Urbandale Drive East, Moberly, MO 65270
General Info: Monthly, Trim Size-8½ x 11, 8 pages, 2 Color, Matte

St. Louis, Missouri

Student Planner

Publishing Co: St. Louis Community College at Florissant Valley, 3400 Pershall Rd, St. Louis, MO 63135-1408 Tel # (314) 595-4465; Title Tel # (314) 595-4200
General Info: Yr. Est. 1973, Semi-annually, Offset press, 64 pages
Circulation: Total-4,000

Student Staff Newsletter

Publishing Co: Rannken Technical Institute, 4431 Finney Ave, Saint Louis, MO 63113-2811
Tel # (314) 371-0233
General Info: Monthly

Trenton, Missouri

Newsletter

Publishing Co: North Central Missouri College, 1301 Main St, Trenton, MO 64683-1824;
Title Tel # (816) 359-3948
General Info: Daily, Mimeo press, No Color
Circulation: Total-250

Hastings, Nebraska

Hastings College Today   *Consumer, Association*

Publishing Co: Hastings College, PO Box 269, Hastings, NE 68902-0269 Tel # (402) 463-7399
Fax # (402) 461-7480; Title Tel # (402) 463-2402 Title Fax # (402) 463-3002
Personnel: Editor-Joyce Ore
Editorial Description: Covers campus personalities & activities.
General Info: (Formerly Hastings College Bulletin), Yr. Est. 1920, Semi-annually, Sheetfed press, 20 pages, Color-cover, Coated, Saddle-stitched
Subscriptions: Free
Circulation: Total-35,000
Printing Co: Account Manager: Rich Portwood; Cornhusker Press, 451 W 2nd St, Hastings, NE 68901-7535 Tel # (402) 463-6702

Omaha, Nebraska

Clarkson College
Connection   *Consumer*

Publishing Co: Clarkson College, 101 S 42nd St, Omaha, NE 68131-2739
General Info: Trim Size-8½ x 11, 8 pages, No Color, Coated, Saddle-stitched

Bloomfield, New Jersey

On-The-Green   *Association*

Publishing Co: Bloomfield College, Publications, Bloomfield, NJ 07003; Title Tel # (201) 748-9000
Title Fax # (201) 743-3998
Personnel: Editor-Bruce Bobbins
General Info: Quarterly, 2 Color
Circulation: Total-7,500

Caldwell, New Jersey

Consort   *Association*

Publishing Co: Caldwell College, 9 Ryerson Ave, Caldwell, NJ 07006-6195;
Title Tel # (201) 228-4424
General Info: Yr. Est. 1980, Monthly, Mimeo press, 4 pages
Circulation: Total-500

Trenton, New Jersey

Invention   *Consumer, Association*

Publishing Co: Thomas Edison State College, 101 W. State St., Trenton, NJ 08608-1176
Tel # (609) 984-1100; Title Tel # (609) 984-4839 Title Fax # (609) 292-9000
Personnel: Editor-Linda Holt
Editorial Description: News about Thomas Edison's college degree programs for adult learners; features on adult students from all 50 states & 70 other nations; news of corporate gifts & grants; alumni updates; stories of interest to adults who wish to complete college degrees.
General Info: (Formerly Invention), Yr. Est. 1973, Quarterly, Trim Size-8½ x 11, Desktop press, 8 pages, 2 Color, Matte
Subscriptions: Free To Qualified Recipient
Circulation: Total-30,000, Readership-30,000

Albuquerque, New Mexico

Dialogue

Publishing Co: University of Albuquerque, St. Joseph's Pl., NW, Albuquerque, NM 87140-0001;
Title Tel # (505) 831-1111
General Info: Monthly, No Color
Circulation: Total-2,500
Advertising: Inquire for rates.

Gallup, New Mexico

Newsletter

Publishing Co: University of New Mexico-Gallup, 200 College Rd, Gallup, NM 87301-5603
Tel # (505) 722-7221
General Info: Yr. Est. 1968
Advertising: Inquire for rates.

Roswell, New Mexico

Eastern Clips
See: COLLEGE ALUMNI

University Park, New Mexico

Swastika

Publishing Co: New Mexico State Univ., Box CC, University Park, NM 88003;
Title Tel # (505) 646-2035
General Info: Annually
Circulation: Total-2,600

Bronx, New York

Maritime College at Fort
Schuyler

Publishing Co: SUNY Maritime College, Ft. Schuyler, Bronx, NY 10465 Tel # (212) 409-7200
Personnel: Editor-Robert Hogg
Editorial Description: Describes current activities of foundation, past contributions.
General Info: Yr. Est. 1976, Quarterly, Trim Size-8½ x 11, Offset press, 4 pages, 2 Color
Circulation: (100% controlled), Total-5,000

Brooklyn, New York

Final Frontier, The
See: SCIENCE FICTION & FANTASY

Footprints

Publishing Co: St. Joseph's College, 245 Clinton Ave, Brooklyn, NY 11205-3688
Tel # (718) 636-6800; Title Tel # (212) 622-4696
General Info: Annually

Odyssey   *Consumer, Association*

Publishing Co: CUNY-Kingsborough Community College, 2001 Oriental Blvd, Brooklyn, NY 11235-2336; Title Tel # (718) 368-5000
General Info: Yr. Est. 1964, Trim Size-9 x 12
Circulation: Total-900

Cazenovia, New York

Cazenovia College Bulletin

Publishing Co: Cazenovia College, c/o Robin Reagan, Cazenovia, NY 13035 Tel # (315) 655-8283;
Title Tel # (315) 655-3466
Personnel: Editor-Vernon W. Smith
General Info: Yr. Est. 1963, Bi-monthly
Circulation: Total-6,000

Highland, New York

Twice Tolled Tales
See: ENTERTAINMENT

Ithaca, New York

Arts & Sciences Newsletter

Publishing Co: College of Arts & Sciences, Cornell University, Gold Smith Hall, Ithaca, NY 14850-3201; Title Tel # (607) 255-7061
Personnel: Editor-L. Abel, Art Dir.-Sally Dutko
Editorial Description: Articles about research & teaching in the College of Arts & Sciences at Cornell Univ.
General Info: Yr. Est. 1979, Semi-annually, Trim Size-11½ x 14, 8 pages, 2 Color, Matte
Circulation: Total-50,200

Dialogue on Campus · *Association*

Publishing Co: Assn for the Coordination of Univ. Religious Affairs, c/o R.L. Johnson, Cornell Univ, Anabel Taylor Hall, Ithaca, NY 14882; Title Tel # (607) 255-6004 Title Fax # (607) 255-9412
Personnel: Editor-Bob Johnson
Editorial Description: Relationship of religion and higher education. Current issues in campus ministry.
General Info: Yr. Est. 1960, Quarterly, Trim Size-8½ x 11, Offset press, 8 pages, ISSN: 0012-2289, Color
Subscriptions: Indv. $5, Free
Circulation: (100% controlled), Total-400
Advertising: Inquire for rates. Accepts Inserts.

Jamaica, New York

Pandora's Box · *Consumer*

Publishing Co: York College, 9420 Guy R Brewer Blvd, Jamaica, NY 11433-1101; Title Tel # (718) 262-2000
Editorial Description: The newspaper of York College and C.U.N.Y. Covers news and features of interest to the college and to the Jamaica community.
General Info: Yr. Est. 1968, Weekly, Trim Size-11½ x 15, Offset press, 14 pages
Circulation: Total-5,000
Advertising: Inquire for rates.

Jamestown, New York

Communicator · *Association*

Publishing Co: Jamestown Community College, 525 Falconer St, Jamestown, NY 14701-1920; Title Tel # (716) 665-5220
Personnel: Editor-Bridget B. Johnson
General Info: Yr. Est. 1950, Weekly, Trim Size-8½ x 11, Letrpr. press, 4 pages, No Color, Newsprint
Circulation: Total-2,000

New York, New York

Changing Scenes · *Business, Consumer*

Publishing Co: New York University Public Affairs Office, 7 E 12th St Fl 11, New York, NY 10003-4475; Title Tel # (212) 998-7070 Title Fax # (212) 995-3656
Personnel: Editor-Craig Gunter
Editorial Description: Information on programs and staff members of NYU's School of Continuing Education.
General Info: Yr. Est. 1991, Quarterly, Trim Size-9¾ x 13½, 6 pages, 4 Color, Matte
Circulation: Total-35,000

CircumSpice
See: LIBRARY

Hunter Arrow

Publishing Co: CUNY-Hunter College, 695 Park Ave., Library, New York, NY 10021-5085 Tel # (212) 772-4000; Title Tel # (212) 570-5566
General Info: Yr. Est. 1914, Semi-weekly
Subscriptions: Indv. $3
Advertising: Inquire for rates.

NY School of Interior Design · *Consumer*

Publishing Co: New York School of Interior Design, 170 E. 70th St., New York, NY 10021-5110 Tel # (212) 472-1500 Fax # (212) 472-1867; Title Tel # (212) 753-5365 Title Fax # (212) 753-2034
Personnel: Editor-Nancy Fox
Editorial Description: College newsletter of the New York School of Interior Design.
General Info: (Formerly Inside), Yr. Est. 1916, Annually, Trim Size-8½ x 11, Offset press, 8 pages
Subscriptions: Free
Circulation: Total-1,500

Newshunter

Publishing Co: CUNY-Hunter College, 695 Park Ave., Library, New York, NY 10021-5085 Tel # (212) 772-4000

Nigerian Students Union in the Americas Newsletter

Publishing Co: Nigerian Consulate General, 828 2nd Ave, New York, NY 10017-4301; Title Tel # (212) 752-1670
General Info: Monthly
Circulation: Total-5,000

Student Aid Newsletter
See: EDUCATION

Newburgh, New York

Happenings · *Consumer, Association*

Publishing Co: Mount St. Mary College, Director of Public Information, Newburgh, NY 12550 Tel # (914) 569-3222 Fax # (914) 562-6762; Title Tel # (914) 561-0800
Editorial Description: News and activities of the college.
General Info: (Formerly Current), Yr. Est. 1978, Quarterly, Offset press, No Color
Circulation: Total-600
Advertising: Inquire for rates.

Poughkeepsie, New York

Vassar Views · *Association*

Publishing Co: Vassar College, Publications, Poughkeepsie, NY 12601 Tel # (914) 437-7000; Title Tel # (914) 437-7400
Personnel: Editor-Dixie Sheridan
Editorial Description: Official college newsletter.
General Info: Yr. Est. 1971, Bi-monthly, Sheetfed press, 8 pages, 4 Color, Coated
Circulation: Total-33,000

Riverdale, New York

Campus Record

Publishing Co: College of Mt. St. Vincent, 6301 Riverdale Ave., Riverdale, NY 10471; Title Tel # (212) 549-8000
General Info: Yr. Est. 1922, Bi-weekly
Subscriptions: Indv. $3
Circulation: Total-1,300
Advertising: Inquire for rates.

Schenectady, New York

Van Curler Newsletter

Publishing Co: Schenectady County Community College, 78 Washington Ave, Schenectady, NY 12305-2215
General Info: Yr. Est. 1970, Semi-monthly, Mimeo press, 4 pages
Circulation: Total-400

Ahoskie, North Carolina

Student Activity Newsletter

Publishing Co: Roanoke-Chowan Technical Institute, Rr 2 Box 46a, Ahoskie, NC 27910-9522; Title Tel # (919) 332-5921
General Info: Yr. Est. 1979, Bi-weekly, Mimeo press, 5 pages
Circulation: Total-519

Durham, North Carolina

Devilirium

Publishing Co: Duke Univ. History Dept., 614 Chapel Dr, Durham, NC 27706-2500 Tel # (919) 684-5439 Fax # (919) 286-1589; Title Tel # (919) 684-2633
Personnel: Editor-John Roth
Editorial Description: Features and news stories covering Duke University Athletics.
General Info: Yr. Est. 1978, 10x/yr., Trim Size-8½ x 11, 8 pages, 2 Color, Newsprint
Subscriptions: Indv. $10
Circulation: Total-5,000
Advertising: Inquire for rates.
Printing Co: Taylor Printing, 115 Clayton Ave, Roxboro, NC 27573-4611 Tel # (919) 599-2146

Grand Forks, North Dakota

Black Student Union Newsletter · *Association*

Publishing Co: Univ. of North Dakota, Box 9040, Univ. Sta., Grand Forks, ND 58202-8237
Personnel: Editor-Kent Burbank

Honors Newsletter

Publishing Co: Univ. of North Dakota, Box 9040, Univ. Sta., Grand Forks, ND 58202-8237

Omniciye · *Association*

Publishing Co: Univ. of North Dakota, PO Box 8274, Grand Forks, ND 58202-8274
Editorial Description: Native american news.
General Info: Semi-annually

Cincinnati, Ohio

University of Cincinnati Evening College
Newsletter *Association*

Publishing Co: Univ. of Cincinnati Evening College, 102 Hanna-Mcmicken Hall, Ml19, Cincinnati, OH 45221-0001; Title Tel # (513) 556-4431
Personnel: Editor-Thomas Beach
Editorial Description: Information and entertainment for students, faculty, and staff of the University of Cincinnati Evening College.
General Info: Yr. Est. 1955, Quarterly, Trim Size-8½ x 14, Offset press, 2 pages, No Color

Cleveland, Ohio

Newsletter

Publishing Co: Cleveland Institute of Art, 11141 East Blvd, Cleveland, OH 44106-1700; Title Tel # (216) 421-4322
Personnel: Editor-Elizabeth Brown
General Info: Monthly

Notes *Association*

Publishing Co: Cleveland Institute of Music, 11021 East Blvd, Cleveland, OH 44106-1705; Title Tel # (216) 791-5000 Title Fax # (216) 791-3063
Personnel: Editor-Rory Sanders, Mktg. Dir.-Susan Schwartz
Editorial Description: Inform the public of activities and programs of the Institute.
General Info: 5x/yr., Trim Size-11 x 17, Sheetfed press, 8 pages, 2 Color, Matte
Circulation: Total-12,000

Columbus, Ohio

Sextant
See: INSURANCE

Delaware, Ohio

Transcript *Association*

Publishing Co: Ohio Wesleyan Univ., English Dept., Slocum Hall, Delaware, OH 43015; Title Tel # (614) 368-3006 Title Fax # (614) 368-3314
Personnel: Editor-Bob West, Circ. Mgr.-Chris Masters
Editorial Description: Independent student newspaper of Ohio Wesleyan University.
General Info: Yr. Est. 1867, Weekly, Trim Size-11½ x 14½, Offset press, 12 pages, 6% ads, No Color, Newsprint
Subscriptions: Indv. $15, Free In Designated Area
Circulation: (74% controlled), Total-1,600
Advertising: Inquire for rates. Accepts Inserts.
Printing Co: Delaware Gazette, 18 E William St, Delaware, OH 43015-4313 Tel # (614) 363-1161

Oberlin, Ohio

Oberlin Other
See: LITERARY REVIEWS

Parma, Ohio

Spectrum

Publishing Co: Cuyahoga Community College-Western Campus, 11000 W. Pleasant Valley Rd, Parma, OH 44130; Title Tel # (216) 987-5000
Personnel: Editor-Aaron-Michael Kaback
General Info: Yr. Est. 1966, Bi-weekly, Trim Size-11½ x 13½, Offset press, 12 pages, No Color
Circulation: Total-3,000
Advertising: Inquire for rates.

Moore, Oklahoma

Insight *Consumer*

Publishing Co: Hillsdale Free Will Baptist College, PO Box 7208, Moore, OK 73153-1208 Fax # (405) 794-6663; Title Tel # (405) 794-6661
General Info: Quarterly

Portland, Oregon

Campus Gram *Consumer*

Publishing Co: Oregon Health Sciences University, 3181 SW Sam Jackson Park Rd, Portland, OR 97201-3011
Editorial Description: Campus news and events.
General Info: Weekly, Trim Size-8½ x 11, 6 pages, 2 Color, Coated

Erie, Pennsylvania

Judean Sand

Publishing Co: Mercyhurst College, 501 E 38th St, Erie, PA 16546-0001 Tel # (814) 825-0200; Title Tel # (814) 864-0681

Gettysburg, Pennsylvania

Gettysburg Seminary Bulletin *Association*

Publishing Co: Lutheran Theological Seminary, 61 N.W. Conferderate Ave., Gettysburg, PA 17325-8421; Title Tel # (717) 334-6286
Personnel: Publisher, Editor-Richard Nelson, Circ. Mgr., Art Dir.-Ruth Fair
General Info: Yr. Est. 1921, Quarterly, 55 pages, ISSN: 0362-0581, Color
Circulation: Total-3,500

Lewisburg, Pennsylvania

What's Happening

Publishing Co: Bucknell University, Lewisburg, PA 17837; Title Tel # (717) 523-1271
Personnel: Publisher-Ruth Burnham
General Info: Yr. Est. 1978, Semi-weekly
Circulation: Total-3,500

Lincoln, Pennsylvania

Lincoln University Newsletter *Business, Association*

Publishing Co: Lincoln Univ., Office of PR & Publications, Lincoln, PA 19352; Title Tel # (610) 932-8300 Title Fax # (610) 932-0195
Personnel: Editor-Funso Oluyitan
Editorial Description: Articles originated in-house about activities of students, faculty & administration.
General Info: Quarterly, Trim Size-11 x 14, 10 pages, 2 Color
Circulation: Total-10,000

Philadelphia, Pennsylvania

Moore News *Scholarly*

Publishing Co: Moore College of Art & Design, College Relations, The Parkway at 20th Street, Philadelphia, PA 19103 Fax # (215) 568-8017; Title Tel # (215) 568-4515 Title Fax # (212) 568-8017
Personnel: Editor-Marigloria Sierra
Editorial Description: A newsletter containing information of interest to alumnae, friends, board members of Moore College of Art and Design.
General Info: Yr. Est. 1990, Monthly, Trim Size-11 x 17, 16 pages, 2 Color, Matte
Subscriptions: Free To Qualified Recipient
Circulation: Total-6,000

Slippery Rock, Pennsylvania

Greensheet

Publishing Co: Slippery Rock Univ., 201 Old Main, Slippery Rock, PA 16057; Title Tel # (412) 738-2091 Title Fax # (412) 738-2098
Editorial Description: Campus news.
General Info: Weekly

Swarthmore, Pennsylvania

Common Speaking

Publishing Co: Swarthmore College, Publications, Swarthmore, PA 19081; Title Tel # (215) 328-8000
Editorial Description: Women's center news.

Wayne, Pennsylvania

Forge, The
See: MILITARY & NAVAL

Williamsport, Pennsylvania

Lycourier, The *Association*

Publishing Co: Lycoming College, Publications, Williamsport, PA 17701; Title Tel # (717) 326-4340
General Info: (Formerly Spectator), Yr. Est. 1990, Semi-monthly, Offset press, 16 pages
Subscriptions: Indv. $20, Free In Designated Area
Circulation: Total-2,000
Advertising: Inquire for rates. Accepts Inserts.

Huron, South Dakota

Smoke Signals

Publishing Co: Huron College, Publications, Huron, SD 57350; Title Tel # (605) 352-8721
General Info: Weekly, Offset press

Sioux Falls, South Dakota

Impact on Ministry   *Consumer*

Publishing Co: North American Baptist Seminary, 1321 W 22nd St, Sioux Falls, SD 57105-1502
General Info: Quarterly, Trim Size-8½ x 11, 8 pages, 2 Color, Matte, Saddle-stitched

Kilian Community College   *Consumer, Association*

Publishing Co: Kilian Community College, 224 N Phillips Ave, Sioux Falls, SD 57102-0316; Title Tel # (605) 336-1711
Personnel: Mktg. Dir.-Becky Hainje
Editorial Description: The mission of Kilian Community College is to provide affordable education to adult students and to meet the training needs of Sioux Falls employers.
General Info: Quarterly, Trim Size-8½ x 11, 15 pages, No Color, Matte, Saddle-stitched

Memphis, Tennessee

HGSR News   *Consumer*

Publishing Co: Harding Graduate School of Religion, 1000 Cherry Rd, Memphis, TN 38117-5424 Tel # (901) 761-1352; Title Tel # (901) 761-1353 Title Fax # (901) 761-1358
Personnel: Editor-Rick Wood
General Info: Yr. Est. 1978, Weekly
Circulation: Total-300

Nashville, Tennessee

Bulletin

Publishing Co: Free Will Baptist Bible College, 3606 W End Ave, Nashville, TN 37205-2498 Tel # (615) 383-1340; Title Tel # (615) 297-4676
General Info: Bi-monthly, Trim Size-8½ x 11, Sheetfed press, 2 Color, Coated

Lamplighter   *Consumer, Scholarly*

Publishing Co: American Baptist Theological Seminary, 1800 Baptist World Ctr. Dr., Nashville, TN 37207 Tel # (615) 262-3433 Fax # (615) 226-7855; Title Tel # (615) 262-1369
General Info: Monthly, Trim Size-8½ x 11, Letrpr. press, 3 pages, No Color
Circulation: Total-150

Alvin, Texas

Intouch   *Association*

Publishing Co: Alvin Community College, 3110 Mustang Rd, Alvin, TX 77511-4895; Title Tel # (713) 331-6111
Personnel: Editor-Bruce Twenhafel
Editorial Description: College newspaper/newsletter.
General Info: (Formerly This Week At ACC), Yr. Est. 1977, Bi-weekly, Trim Size-8½ x 11, Offset press, 10 pages, No Color
Circulation: Total-2,000

Amarillo, Texas

Technoscope   *Association*

Publishing Co: Texas State Technical College-Amarillo, PO Box 11197, Amarillo, TX 79111-0197; Title Tel # (806) 335-2316
Personnel: Publisher-Bob Pearce, Editor-Joann Stern, Graphic Designer-Chrystyal Kott
General Info: (Formerly Texas Traditions, Times of TSTI Amarillo), Yr. Est. 1980, Monthly, Trim Size-8½ x 11, 8 pages, 2 Color
Circulation: Total-1,500

Austin, Texas

Texas Alcalde
See: COLLEGE ALUMNI

El Paso, Texas

Newsletter

Publishing Co: University of Texas at El Paso, 1101 N. Campbell St. News And, Publication Office, El Paso, TX 79968-0001 Tel # (915) 747-5000; Title Tel # (915) 747-5880
Personnel: Editor-Lynne Witch
General Info: Yr. Est. 1979, Semi-annually, 4 pages, No Color, Newsprint
Circulation: Total-200
List Rental: Rents Lists
Printing Co: Texas Western Press, Univ. of Texas at El Paso, El Paso, TX 79901

Houston, Texas

Baylor Medicine   *Association*

Publishing Co: Baylor College of Medicine, 1 Baylor Plz Rm 176b, Houston, TX 77030-3411; Title Tel # (713) 798-4951
General Info: Monthly

News from Fondren
See: LIBRARY

Killeen, Texas

Memogram   *Consumer*

Publishing Co: Central Texas College, PO Box 1800, Killeen, TX 76540-1800 Tel # (817) 526-1150; Title Tel # (817) 526-7161
Editorial Description: Information for students, faculty and staff.
General Info: Yr. Est. 1972, Weekly
Circulation: Total-614

Mesquite, Texas

Eastfield Era

Publishing Co: Eastfield College, 3737 Motley Dr, Mesquite, TX 75150-2099 Tel # (214) 324-7100; Title Tel # (214) 746-3200
General Info: Weekly, Offset press, 8 pages, No Color
Circulation: Total-10,000
Advertising: Inquire for rates.

Pasadena, Texas

Back Page

Publishing Co: Texas Chiropractic College, 5912 Spencer Hwy, Pasadena, TX 77505-1699 Fax # (713) 487-2009; Title Tel # (713) 487-1170
Editorial Description: Weekly campus newsletter to distribute information to students, faculty & staff.
General Info: Weekly, Trim Size-7 x 8½, Mimeo press, 8 pages, No Color, Newsprint
Circulation: Total-365

San Antonio, Texas

News, The   *Consumer*

Publishing Co: University of Texas-Health Science Center at San Antonio, 7703 Floyd Curl Dr, San Antonio, TX 78284-6200; Title Tel # (210) 567-7000 Title Fax # (210) 567-6811
Personnel: Editor-Will Sansom
General Info: Weekly

Waco, Texas

Venture Review   **CPM$1000**

Publishing Co: Baylor Univ., P.O. Box 98011, Waco, TX 76798; Title Tel # (817) 755-2265 Title Fax # (817) 755-2271
Personnel: Editor-Robert Jones, Circ. Dir.-Fadene Shirley
General Info: (Formerly News Venture), Yr. Est. 1990, Quarterly, Trim Size-8½ x 11, 12 pages, No Color
Circulation: Total-1,000
Advertising: $1,000.

Logan, Utah

USU Staff News

Publishing Co: Utah State Univ., Publications, Logan, UT 84322-0001 Tel # (801) 750-1000; Title Tel # (801) 750-1743
Editorial Description: News for and about faculty and staff of Utah State University.
General Info: Yr. Est. 1967, Weekly, Trim Size-8½ x 11, Offset press, 3 pages
Circulation: Total-2,300

Rutland, Vermont

Links

Publishing Co: College of St. Joseph, Clement Rd., Rutland, VT 05701; Title Tel # (802) 773-5900
Personnel: Editor-Charlotte Tate
Editorial Description: Distributed throughout the College Community including students, parents, faculty, alumni, donors, & friends. Its purpose is to keep the College Community apprised of all College events & news.
General Info: Yr. Est. 1979, Quarterly, 8 pages, 2 Color
Printing Co: Quick Print of Rutland, 191 West St, Rutland, VT 05701-2848 Tel # (802) 775-1029

Arlington, Virginia

Strayer College Military
Outreach   *Consumer*

Publishing Co: Strayer College, 3045 Columbia Pike, Arlington, VA 22204-4300;
Title Tel # (703) 769-2676
General Info: Quarterly, Trim Size-8½ x 11, 6 pages, 2 Color, Coated

Big Stone Gap, Virginia

News Briefs

Publishing Co: Mountain Empire Community College, PO Box 700, Big Stone Gap, VA 24219-0700;
Title Tel # (703) 523-2400
General Info: Yr. Est. 1974, Weekly, Trim Size-8½ x 11, 1 pages, Color
Circulation: Total-300

Blacksburg, Virginia

Techgram

Publishing Co: Virginia Polytechnic Institute & State Univ., 101 Deitrick Hall, Blacksburg, VA 24061
Tel # (703) 961-6000; Title Tel # (703) 552-2711
Personnel: Editor-Mary Ann Healy
General Info: Yr. Est. 1930, Bi-weekly
Circulation: Total-31,500

Lawrenceville, Virginia

Saint Paulite   *Association*

Publishing Co: St. Paul's College, 406 Windsor Ave, Lawrenceville, VA 23868-1299;
Title Tel # (804) 848-3111 Title Fax # (804) 848-0403
Personnel: Editor-Jim Nolting
Editorial Description: Original stories promoting students, faculty/staff-administration, alumni &
friends of the college.
General Info: Yr. Est. 1888, Quarterly, Trim Size-8½ x 11, Offset press, 20 pages, 1% ads, Color-
cover
Subscriptions: Free With Membership
Circulation: Total-13,500
Advertising: Inquire for rates.

Norfolk, Virginia

Class Newsletter

Publishing Co: Eastern Virginia Medical School, PO Box 1980, Norfolk, VA 23501-1980
Tel # (804) 446-5600; Title Tel # (804) 446-3600

Richmond, Virginia

Source/Resource   *Consumer*

Publishing Co: Presbyterian School of Christian Education, 1205 Palmyra Ave, Richmond, VA
23227-4417; Title Tel # (804) 254-8049 Title Fax # (804) 254-8061
Personnel: Editor-Nancy Fischer
Editorial Description: Newsletter on issues of the college.
General Info: Trim Size-8½ x 11, 6 pages, 2 Color, Matte, Saddle-stitched
Circulation: Total-150

Auburn, Washington

Knonahi

Publishing Co: Green River Community College Students, 12401 SE 320th St, Auburn, WA
98092-3622; Title Tel # (206) 833-9111
General Info: Yr. Est. 1965, Annually
Circulation: Total-800

Centralia, Washington

Banner, The   *Consumer*

Publishing Co: Centralia College, 600 W Locust St, Centralia, WA 98531-4035 Tel # (360) 736-9391
Editorial Description: Newsletter on student events at Centralia College.
General Info: Weekly, Trim Size-8½ x 11, 4 pages, No Color, Matte

Everett, Washington

Trojan

Publishing Co: Everett Community College, 801 Wetmore Ave, Everett, WA 98201-1390;
Title Tel # (206) 259-7151
General Info: Yr. Est. 1946, Annually
Circulation: Total-850

Issaquah, Washington

Advance
See: COLLEGE ALUMNI

Kirkland, Washington

Northwest   *Association*

Publishing Co: Northwest College, PO Box 579, Kirkland, WA 98083-0579;
Title Tel # (206) 822-8266
General Info: Quarterly, 4 pages
Circulation: Total-5,000

Student Bulletin

Publishing Co: Northwest College, PO Box 579, Kirkland, WA 98083-0579;
Title Tel # (206) 822-8266
General Info: Weekly, 2 pages
Circulation: Total-700

Port Angeles, Washington

Treasure Chest

Publishing Co: Peninsula College, Publications, Port Angeles, WA 98362; Title Tel # (206) 452-9277
General Info: Annually
Circulation: Total-250

Seattle, Washington

Fragments

Publishing Co: Seattle Univ., 12th & E. Columbia, Seattle, WA 98122 Tel # (206) 296-6000;
Title Tel # (206) 626-6200
General Info: Yr. Est. 1958, Quarterly
Circulation: Total-1,000

Yakima, Washington

Hubcaps

Publishing Co: Yakima Valley Community College, PO Box 1647, Yakima, WA 98907-1647;
Title Tel # (509) 575-2350
Personnel: Publisher-Donna West
General Info: Yr. Est. 1928, Weekly, Desktop press, No Color
Circulation: Total-1,000
Advertising: Inquire for rates.

Huntington, West Virginia

Parthenon   *Consumer, Association*

Publishing Co: Marshall Univ., Publications, Huntington, WV 25705; Title Tel # (304) 696-6696
Title Fax # (304) 696-3333
Personnel: Editor-Kevin Melrose, Production Mgr.-Michael Friel, Adv. Dir.-Douglas Jones
Editorial Description: Student newspaper for Marshall University.
General Info: Yr. Est. 1896, Daily, 4 Color, Newsprint
Subscriptions: Indv. $40
Advertising: $293. Accepts Inserts.

Cascade, Wisconsin

NCCCC Newsletter
See: CHILDREN

Hayward, Wisconsin

Lac Courte Oreilles Ojibwa
Community College
News   *Consumer*

Publishing Co: Lac Courte Oreilles Ojibwa Community College, Rr 2 Box 2357, Hayward, WI
54843-9419
Editorial Description: Events of Lac Courte.
General Info: Trim Size-8½ x 11, 4 pages, No Color

Madison, Wisconsin

Orbit, The   *Consumer*

Publishing Co: Wisconsin School of Electronics, 1227 N Sherman Ave, Madison, WI 53704-4257;
Title Tel # (608) 249-6611
Editorial Description: Latest happenings of WSE.
General Info: Yr. Est. 1948, Trim Size-8½ x 11, 4 pages, Matte

Milwaukee, Wisconsin

News & Views   *Association*

Publishing Co: Marquette Univ., 1212 W. Wisconsin Ave., Rm 315, PO Box 1881, Milwaukee, WI 53201-1881 Tel # (414) 228-7553; Title Tel # (414) 288-7553 Title Fax # (414) 288-6519
Personnel: Editor-Christine Orberg
Editorial Description: An internal faculty/staff publication reporting academic and University (i.e. Marquette) news and accomplishments.
General Info: Yr. Est. 1974, Bi-weekly, Trim Size-8½ x 11, Web press, 8 pages, No Color, Newsprint
Subscriptions: Free
Circulation: (100% controlled), Total-2,750
Printing Co: Lake Country Publications, Cardnal Lane, Hartland, WI 53029 Tel # (414) 367-3272, Fax # (414) 367-7414

Saint Francis, Wisconsin

Salt of the Earth   *Consumer*

Publishing Co: Saint Francis Seminary, 3257 S Lake Dr, Saint Francis, WI 53235-3795; Title Tel # (414) 769-3529
Editorial Description: Newsletter of the saint Francis Seminary.
General Info: Monthly, Trim Size-8½ x 11, 8 pages, 2 Color, Matte, Saddle-stitched

Watertown, Wisconsin

Messenger, The   *Consumer*

Publishing Co: Maranatha Baptist Bible College, 745 W Main St, Watertown, WI 53094-7638; Title Tel # (414) 261-9300
Editorial Description: Events and info for Maranatha Baptist Bible College.
General Info: Quarterly, Trim Size-8½ x 11, 4 pages, 2 Color, Matte

Sheridan, Wyoming

Associate, The   *Association*

Publishing Co: Sheridan College, PO Box 1500, Sheridan, WY 82801-1500; Title Tel # (307) 674-6446
Editorial Description: For alumni & friends of Sheridan College.
General Info: Quarterly, 4 pages
Circulation: Total-1,000

CANADA

Vancouver, British Columbia

UBC Gazette

Publishing Co: Univ. of British Columbia, 6251 Cecil Green Park Rd., Vancouver, BC V6K 1W5 Canada; Title Tel # (604) 228-2130
Editorial Description: Decisions of the UBC Board of Governors.
General Info: 10x/yr., Sheetfed press, 4 pages, No Color
Circulation: (100% controlled), Total-2,900

Winnipeg, Manitoba

Mandala

Publishing Co: Univ. of Winnipeg, 230 Lockhart Hall, Winnipeg, MB R3B 2E9 Canada; Title Tel # (204) 786-7537
Personnel: Editor-Laurie Tegelberg
Editorial Description: Collection of poetry, prose, graphics, & photographs submitted by writers & artists at the University of Winnipeg.
General Info: Trim Size-6 x 9, Web press, 58 pages
Subscriptions: $2/copy
Circulation: Total-600

Projector

Publishing Co: Red River Community College, 2055 Notre Dame Ave., Rm. D102, Winnipeg, MB R3H 0J9 Canada Tel # (402) 632-2311; Title Tel # (204) 632-2311

St. John, New Brunswick

Baron, The

Publishing Co: University of New Brunswick, Students Representative, PO Box 5050, St. John, NB E2L 4L5 Canada; Title Tel # (506) 648-5676 Title Fax # (506) 648-5541
Editorial Description: Newspaper of the University of New Brunswick at St. John
General Info: (Formerly Tucker Park Press; St. John Viewpoint), Bi-weekly

Halifax, Nova Scotia

Technical University of Nova Scotia

Publishing Co: Technical Univ. of Nova Scotia, 1360 Barrington St., Halifax, NS B3L 4J1 Canada; Title Tel # (902) 429-8300
Editorial Description: Internal news items related to staff publications, activities, meetings held.
General Info: (Formerly Nova Scotia Technical College), Yr. Est. 1967, Bi-monthly, Trim Size-8½ x 11, Mimeo press, 20 pages, ISSN: 0712-9939, No Color
Circulation: Total-500

Gloucester, Ontario

CIRA Bulletin
   See: EDUCATION

Guelph, Ontario

University of Guelph News Bulletin

Publishing Co: University of Guelph, Dept. of Univ. Communications, Guelph, ON N1G 2W1 Canada Fax # (519) 824-7962; Title Tel # (519) 824-4120
Personnel: Publisher-Douglas Waterston, Editor-Sandra Webster, Art Dir.-Eric Barth
Editorial Description: University of Guelph News.
General Info: Yr. Est. 1969, Weekly, 8 pages, ISSN: 0229-2378
Circulation: Total-8,000

North York, Ontario

York Gazette   *Association*

Publishing Co: Excalibur Publications, 420 Student Center, York Univ., North York, ON M3J 1P3 Canada; Title Tel # (416) 736-5010
Personnel: Editor-Lydia Lobos
Editorial Description: Newsletter for members of faculty and staff of York University.
General Info: Yr. Est. 1970, Bi-weekly, Trim Size-8½ x 11, Offset press, 8 pages
Circulation: Total-5,100

Sudbury, Ontario

Laurentian Gazette

Publishing Co: Laurentian Univ., Ramsey Lake Rd., Sudbury, ON P3E 2C6 Canada; Title Tel # (705) 675-1151
Personnel: Publisher-Jean Baxter, Editor, Production Mgr.-Janet Salian
Editorial Description: University community newsletter, English and French text.
General Info: Yr. Est. 1974, Bi-weekly, Trim Size-8½ x 11, Sheetfed press, 8 pages, ISSN: 0226-7934, No Color
Circulation: (100% controlled), Total-1,250
Printing Co: Laurentian Univ., 935 Remsey, Sudbury, ON P3E 2C6 Canada Tel # (705) 675-1151

Thunder Bay, Ontario

Agora
   See: EDUCATION

Toronto, Ontario

A & S News
   See: COLLEGE ALUMNI

A & S Report
   See: COLLEGE ALUMNI

Waterloo, Ontario

Grebel Now   *Association*

Publishing Co: Conrad Grebel College, Publications, Waterloo, ON N2L 3G6 Canada
Editorial Description: Quarterly alumni newsletter.
General Info: (Formerly Alumni News), Yr. Est. 1983, Quarterly, Roto. press, No Color, Recycled, Saddle-stitched
Printing Co: St. Jacobs Printery, 215 King St. South, St. Jacobs, ON N0B 2N0 Canada

Montreal, Quebec

Quartier Libre   *Association*

Publishing Co: Cegep de Rosemont, 6400 16th Ave., Montreal, PQ H1X 2S9 Canada; Title Tel # (514) 725-7898
Personnel: Editor-Annie Bennet
Editorial Description: Information, discussions, documents related to students at all levels.
General Info: Yr. Est. 1974, Bi-monthly, Trim Size-8½ x 11, Offset press, 16 pages, No Color
Subscriptions: Free
Circulation: Total-1,500

Trois Rivieres, Quebec

La Depeche

Publishing Co: CEGEP de Trois Rivieres, 3500, rue de Courval, Trois Rivieres, PQ G9A 5E6 Canada; Title Tel # (819) 376-1721
Personnel: Editor-Gilels Bourassa, Art Dir.-Danielle Boudreau
General Info: Yr. Est. 1974, Weekly, Trim Size-8½ x 11, Sheetfed press, 12 pages, ISSN: 0317-0632, Color-cover, Saddle-stitched
Circulation: Total-3,000

COLLEGE STUDENT LIFESTYLE

Dothan, Alabama

Logos   *Consumer, Scholarly*

Publishing Co: Troy State Univ. Dothan, 500 University Dr., Box 8368, Dothan, AL 36304; Title Tel # (334) 983-6556 Title Fax # (334) 983-6322
Personnel: Editor-Tony Whetstone
Editorial Description: In-house publication for faculty and staff of Troy State University.
General Info: (Formerly TSUD Today), Monthly, Trim Size-8½ x 11, 8 pages, No Color, Matte, Saddle-stitched
Circulation: Total-250
Printing Co: Houston Printing Co ,Inc, P.O Box 5549, Dothan, AL 36302 Tel # (334) 792-6651

Mobile, Alabama

Vanguard , The
    See: COLLEGE ALUMNI

Berkeley, California

Vegan News, The
    See: ENVIRONMENT & ECOLOGY

Denver, Colorado

Brown & Gold
    See: COLLEGE STUDENT

Hartford, Connecticut

Alert   *Association*

Publishing Co: Assn. of Collegiate Licensing Administrators, 638 Prospect Ave., Hartford, CT 06105-4298; Title Tel # (860) 586-7524 Title Fax # (860) 586-7550
Personnel: Editor-Sue Silvano
Editorial Description: A forum for communication between collegiate licensing professionals, featuring articles by ACLA members that address the current issues of the collegiate licensing industry.
General Info: Yr. Est. 1987, Quarterly, Sheetfed press, 8 pages, No Color, Coated
Circulation: Total-350
List Rental: Actives: 200, $75/M

Washington, District of Columbia

CIC Independent, The   *Business, Association*

Publishing Co: Council of Independent Colleges, 1 Dupont Cir. NW, Ste. 320, Washington, DC 20036-1110; Title Tel # (202) 466-7230 Title Fax # (202) 466-7238
Personnel: Publisher-Stephen Pelletier, Editor-S. Pelletier
Editorial Description: News of CIC projects & programs.
General Info: (Formerly Council for the Advancement of Small Colleges), Yr. Est. 1956, Quarterly, Trim Size-8½ x 11, 16 pages, 2 Color, Coated, Saddle-stitched
Subscriptions: Free To Qualified Recipient
Circulation: Total-6,500

College Republican   *Association*

Publishing Co: College Republican Natl. Committee, The, 440 1st St SE, Suite #303, Washington, DC 20001; Title Tel # (202) 662-1330
Personnel: Publisher-Jack Abramoff, Editor-Kevin Latek
Editorial Description: National, mostly political, directed at college students, general campus news, humor, campaign techniques and news.
General Info: (Formerly CR Report, The), Yr. Est. 1969, Monthly, Offset press, 4 pages
Subscriptions: Indv. $7
Circulation: Total-35,000

Americus, Georgia

Mortarboard   *Association*

Publishing Co: Habitat for Humanity Int'l., Inc., 121 Habitat St., Americus, GA 31709-3423 Fax # (912) 924-6541; Title Tel # (912) 924-6935 Title Fax # (912) 920-4157
Personnel: Publisher-Doug Bright, Editor-Sonja Lewis, Production Mgr.-Joy Highnote, Art Dir.-Jerry Counselman
Editorial Description: News of college students involvement with campus chapters of Habitat for Humanity, a house building Christian ministry.
General Info: Yr. Est. 1990, Quarterly, Trim Size-8½ x 11, 12 pages, 2 Color
Subscriptions: Free
Circulation: Total-12,000
Printing Co: Boyd Brothers, 425 E 15th St, Panama City, FL 32405-5498 Tel # (904) 763-1471, Fax # (904) 769-6526

Indianapolis, Indiana

Perspectives   *Association*

Publishing Co: Assn. of Fraternity Advisors , inc, 3901 W 86th St Ste 390, Indianapolis, IN 46268-1702 Tel # (317) 876-4691
Editorial Description: A publication providing regular news and information to members including feature articles , current research, topical highlights and association updates.
General Info: (Formerly Fraternity Newsletter), Yr. Est. 1973, 8x/yr., 16 pages, Matte, Saddle-stitched
Subscriptions: Free With Membership
List Rental: Rents Lists

College Park, Maryland

Commuter, The
    See: EDUCATION

Hyanas, Massachusetts

Young Adult/Teen Market Report
    See: ADVERTISING & MARKETING

Ridgewood, New Jersey

Collegiate Trends
    See: ADVERTISING & MARKETING

Brooklyn, New York

Hillel Highlights   *Association*

Publishing Co: Brooklyn College Hillel Society, 2900 Bedford Ave, Brooklyn, NY 11210-2814 Tel # (718) 951-5000; Title Tel # (718) 859-1151
Editorial Description: Newsletter for the Brooklyn College Hillel Community.
General Info: Yr. Est. 1993, Bi-monthly, Trim Size-8½ x 11, 4 pages, No Color, Matte

Cary, North Carolina

Cut & Paste   *Business, Consumer*

Publishing Co: DS Design, 2440 SW Cary P'way, #210, Cary, NC 27513-5318; Title Tel # (914) 268-8394 Title Fax # (914) 268-9577
Personnel: Publisher-Jane Scarano
General Info: Yr. Est. 1991, Bi-monthly, Trim Size-8½ x 11, Offset press, 8 pages, 2 Color, Coated, Saddle-stitched
Subscriptions: Indv. $19
Circulation: Total-500

Columbia, South Carolina

Freshman Year Experience
Newsletter   *Consumer, Association*

Publishing Co: University of South Carolina, 1728 College St, Columbia, SC 29201-3918; Title Tel # (803) 777-6029 Title Fax # (803) 777-4699
Personnel: Editor-Dr. Dorothy Fidler, Art Dir.-Eric Graff
Editorial Description: Reports campus programs to enhance success & retention of first-year students.
General Info: Yr. Est. 1988, Quarterly, Trim Size-8½ x 11, Desktop press, 12 pages, ISSN: 1053-2048, Perfect bound
Subscriptions: Indv. $60, $15/copy

Ranger, Texas

School Law Newsletter   *Business, Consumer*

Publishing Co: School Law Newsletter, PO Box 199, Ranger, TX 76470-0199; Title Tel # (817) 647-3300
Personnel: Editor-Joe Mills
Editorial Description: An education law newsletter. Primary distribution to college presidents, deans, attorneys, and school superintendents.
General Info: Yr. Est. 1970, 3x/yr., 8 pages, ISSN: 0891-5474
Subscriptions: Indv. $36, Inst. $36, $6/copy
Circulation: Total-3,500

Madison, Wisconsin

National On-Campus
Report *Consumer*

Publishing Co: Magna Publications, Inc., 611 N Sherman Ave, Madison, WI 53704-4410; Title Tel # (608) 246-3580 Title Fax # (608) 246-3597
Personnel: Publisher-Richard Perkins, Editorial Dir.-Mary Lou Santovec, Editor-Peter Vogt, Circ. Mgr.-Tom Crawford, Adv. Dir.-Tami Cook, Art Dir.-Jim Congdon, Mktg. Dir.-Lisa Collins, Promotion Dir.-Karen Oshman
Editorial Description: Reports on the current activities of college students - student government innovations, publications, recruiting & marketing trends, etc.
General Info: Yr. Est. 1972, Semi-monthly, Trim Size-8½ x 11, Offset press, 6 pages, 2 Color
Subscriptions: Indv. $93, $4/copy
Circulation: Total-2,000
Advertising: Inquire for rates. Accepts Inserts.
List Rental: Rents Lists
Printing Co: Quicksilver Press Inc., 2138 Pennsylvania Ave., Madison, WI 53704-4748 Tel # (608) 244-5040

Recruitment & Retention in Higher Education
See: EDUCATION

Student Leader *Consumer, Association*

Publishing Co: Magna Publications, Inc., 611 N Sherman Ave, Madison, WI 53704-4410 Tel # (608) 246-3580 Fax # (608) 246-3597
Personnel: Editorial Dir.-Doris Green, Editor-Peter Vogt
Editorial Description: Explore and develop student leadership on campuses.
General Info: Monthly, Trim Size-8½ x 11, 6 pages, ISSN: 1057-8722, 2 Color, Recycled
Subscriptions: Indv. $57

CANADA

Toronto, Ontario

A & S News
See: COLLEGE ALUMNI

A & S Report
See: COLLEGE ALUMNI

COMICS

Cartoons by Bulbul

Publishing Co: Arachne Publishing, PO Box 4100, Mountain View, CA 94040-0100; Title Tel # (415) 961-5709
General Info: Yr. Est. 1976, Monthly

Comic Art Studies: A Newsletter from the Russell B. Nye Popular Culture Collection

Publishing Co: Michigan State University Libraries, Publications, E. Lansing, MI 48824-1048
Editorial Description: Has a large collection devoted to the art of comics, containing over 70,000 items. This newsletter documents the work they do & other activities going on around the country.
General Info: Irregular, 8 pages

Dark Horse Insider *Consumer*

Publishing Co: Dark Horse Comics, Inc., 10956 SE Main St, Milwaukie, OR 97222-7644; Title Tel # (503) 652-8815 Title Fax # (503) 654-9440
Personnel: Editor-Kris Young
Editorial Description: Informational magazine on what new comics, collections, and other comic related merchandise is coming out each month from Dark Horse Comics.
General Info: Yr. Est. 1991, Monthly, Trim Size-6⅝ x 10¼, Offset press, 32 pages, Color-cover, Newsprint, Saddle-stitched
Subscriptions: Free

Father Flood Lectionary Series
See: RELIGIOUS & THEOLOGICAL

GAG Recap
See: HUMOR & SATIRE

Illustrator Collector's News, The
See: COLLECTIBLES

Illustrator Magazine & Paper Collector's News
See: COLLECTIBLES

It's Only A Movie
See: ENTERTAINMENT

Kitchen Sink Pipeline *Business*

Publishing Co: Kitchen Sink Press, 320 Riverside, Northampton, MA 01060-2717 Tel # (413) 586-9525 Fax # (413) 586-7040; Title Tel # (414) 295-6922
Personnel: Publisher-Joe Coleman
Editorial Description: Monthly newsletter for comics retailers.
General Info: Monthly, Trim Size-8½ x 11, 16 pages, No Color, Matte, Saddle-stitched

Marvel Requirer *Consumer*

Publishing Co: Marvel Entertainment Group, 387 Park Ave. South, New York, NY 10016-8810; Title Tel # (212) 696-0808
Editorial Description: A monthly guide of what is coming out from Marvel Comics.
General Info: Monthly

Penstuff *Consumer*

Publishing Co: Cartoonist Northwest, PO Box 31122, Seattle, WA 98103
Editorial Description: Primarily for members of the Seattle-area network of cartoonists & illustrators. Packed full of cartoon examples & plenty of news for cartoonists both in Seattle & around the country.
General Info: Irregular
Subscriptions: Indv. $15

Pizazz Comics Unlimited: Newsletter of Pizazz Comics *Consumer*

Publishing Co: Pizazz Comics Unlimited, 1840 Garden Ridge, Apt. #3, Toledo, OH 43614
Editorial Description: The members of Pizazz believe in producing comics which are done in good taste and of high quality. A Pizazz title is one that basically contains no nudity, excessive violence, or vulgar language.
General Info: Irregular
Subscriptions: $1/copy

SSCC Newsletter *Consumer*

Publishing Co: SSCC, PO Box 821143, Dallas, TX 75382-1143
Editorial Description: This is the newsletter for the Southwest Society of Comic Creators, a regional U.S. publication covering comix. Covers a wide variety of comix publishers, writers, & artists. Each issue has lots of art, profiles, & interviews with regional talent.
General Info: Irregular, 8 pages

Tetragammaton Fragments: Official Newsletter of the United Fanzine Organization
See: FAN MAGAZINES-MOVIE, RADIO, TV

Trade Journal Recap
See: HUMOR & SATIRE

Westfield Newsletter *Consumer*

Publishing Co: Westfield Comics, 8608 University Green, Box 620470, Middleton, WI 53562-2510; Title Tel # (608) 836-1945 Title Fax # (608) 836-6950
Personnel: Editor-Joyce Greenholdt
Editorial Description: Newsletter published for mailorder of comic books and comic book collectibles. Features statements of what will be coming out in the comic book industry three months in advance.
General Info: Yr. Est. 1981, Monthly, Trim Size-8½ x 11, 42 pages, Newsprint, Saddle-stitched
Subscriptions: Free To Qualified Recipient

COMPUTERS & AUTOMATION

123 for Windows Report, The *Business, Consumer*

Publishing Co: IDG Newsletter Corporation, 77 Franklin St., Boston, MA 02110 Tel # (617) 482-8785 Fax # (617) 338-0164; Title Tel # (617) 482-8470 Title Fax # (617) 422-8189
Personnel: Publisher-Craig G. Pierce, Editor-Richard Cranford, Circ. Mgr.-Meredith Seller Doesschate, Production Mgr.-John Forgetta
Editorial Description: Dedicated to providing timely, hands-on tips and techniques that enable Lotus 1-2-3 users to become more productive in their jobs.
General Info: (Formerly 123 Windows Report), Monthly
Subscriptions: Indv. $69, For. $99
Circulation: Total-30,000
List Rental: List Management Co.: Mail Marketing, Inc., 171 Terrace St., Haworth, NJ 07641-1899 Tel # (201) 387-1023, Fax # (201) 387-2976, Actives: $120/M

A-E-C Automation Newsletter *Business*

Publishing Co: Technology Publications, Inc., 5920 Roswell Rd., B107336, Atlanta, GA 30328-4922; Title Tel # (770) 565-3282 Title Fax # (770) 565-3286
Personnel: Publisher, Editor in Chief-Carleton R. Howk
Editorial Description: Reports & analyzes automation news for architects, engineers, builders. Also GIS database creation.
General Info: Yr. Est. 1977, Monthly, Trim Size-8½ x 11, Offset press, 16 pages, ISSN: 0277-1659, No Color, Newsprint, Saddle-stitched
Subscriptions: Indv. $225, For. $285, $20/copy
Circulation: Total-3,300, Readership-20,000

A2-Central
Business, Association

Publishing Co: Resource Central, 6339 W. 110th St. #11250, Overland Park, KS 66211-1509; Title Tel # (913) 469-6502 Title Fax # (913) 469-6507

Personnel: Publisher-Tom Weishaar, Editor-Dean Esmay, Editor-Ellen Rosenberg, Circ. Mgr.-Denise Shaffer Cameron

Editorial Description: An international clearinghouse of information for users of all types of Apple II computers.

General Info: (Formerly Open-Apple), Yr. Est. 1985, Monthly, Trim Size-8 x 11, Web press, 8 pages, ISSN: 1066-730X, Ind/Abs/Online: GENIE, No Color, Newsprint

Subscriptions: Indv. $60, Can. $34, For. $34, $3/copy

Acquistions: Publication Bought

Circulation: Total-7,000

List Rental: List Management Co.: Manager: Tom Weishaar; SpeciaLISTS, 1200 Harbor Blvd Ste 9, Weehawken, NJ 07087-6728 Tel # (201) 865-5800, Fax # (201) 867-2450, Actives: $75/M, Expires: $50/M

Printing Co: B&C, Inc., 2820u Roe Ln, Kansas City, KS 66103-1543 Tel # (913) 236-9600

AAMSI News
See: MEDICINE

ACM Systems Documentation Newsletter
Association

Publishing Co: Association for Computing Machinery, 1515 Broadway, 17th Fl., New York, NY 10036-5701 Tel # (212) 869-7440 Fax # (212) 302-5826

Subscriptions: Indv. $125

ADAIC News
Business, Association

Publishing Co: Sponsor-Ada Joint Program Office, Ada Information Clearinghouse, PO Box 1866, Falls Church, VA 22041 Tel # (703) 688-2466 Fax # (703) 681-2869

Personnel: Publications Director-Susan Carlson, Editor-John Walker

Editorial Description: Information on Ada--an internationally standardized, general-purpose computer language used in a variety of applications. Includes news of the Ada community's conferences, events, etc.

General Info: (Formerly Ada Information Clearinghouse Newsletter), Yr. Est. 1982, Quarterly, Trim Size-8½ x 11, 16 pages, ISSN: 1064-1505, Ind/Abs/Online: Internet

Subscriptions: Free

Circulation: Total-20,000

ADRIS Newsletter
Business, Association

Publishing Co: Sponsor-Association for the Development of Religious Information Sys, Association for the Development of Religious Information Syt, P.O Box 210735, Nashville, TN 37221-0735; Title Tel # (615) 662-5189 Title Fax # (615) 662-5251

Personnel: Publisher, Editor-Edward Dodds

General Info: Yr. Est. 1970, Quarterly, Trim Size-7 x 10, 32 pages, Ind/Abs/Online: e-mail:adris@telalink.net

Subscriptions: Indv. $20, Inst. $30, For. $30, $5/copy

Advertising: Accepts Inserts.

AD/Solutions Report
Business

Publishing Co: DataTrends Pubs., Inc., 895 B Harrison Street SE, PO Box 4460, Leesburg, VA 22075 Tel # (703) 779-0574 Fax # (703) 760-9365

Personnel: Editor-Rutrell Yasin

Editorial Description: Information on IBM's SAA-based Ad/Cycle framework.

General Info: Yr. Est. 1991, Bi-weekly

AI Interactions

Publishing Co: Texas Instruments, PO Box 149149, Austin, TX 78714-9149; Title Tel # (512) 250-6580

Editorial Description: Highlights artificial intelligence hardware & software products manufactures by Texas Instruments.

General Info: Yr. Est. 1985, Monthly

Circulation: Total-16,000

AI Trends Newsletter
Business

Publishing Co: Intelligence, PO Box 20008, New York, NY 10025-1510 Tel # (212) 222-1123

Personnel: Publisher-H. Newquist, Editor-Harvey Newquist, Circ. Mgr.-G. Manikin, Circ. Mgr.-C. Rich

Editorial Description: Covers business aspects of artificial intelligence industry & intelligent systems business.

General Info: Yr. Est. 1984, Monthly, Trim Size-8½ x 11, Letrpr. press, 16 pages, ISSN: 0736-5071, 2 Color, Matte, Saddle-stitched

Subscriptions: Indv. $295, Can. $345, For. $345

List Rental: List Management Co.: Manager: C. Rich; WMI/Worldata, 5200 Town Center Circle, Boca Raton, FL 33486 Tel # (407) 393-8200, Fax # (407) 368-8345, Actives: 14,000

AMI Pro Report, The
Business

Publishing Co: IDG Newsletter Corporation, 77 Franklin St., Boston, MA 02110 Tel # (617) 482-8785 Fax # (617) 338-0164; Title Tel # (617) 482-8634 Title Fax # (617) 422-8189

Personnel: Publisher-Craig G. Pierce, Editor-Mark Scappichio, Circ. Mgr.-Meredith Seller Doesschate, Production Mgr.-John forgetta

Editorial Description: Dedicated to providing timely, hands-on tips and techniques that enable Ami Pro users to become more productive in their jobs. The Ami Pro Report offers advice on word processsing and a common sense approach to comnputing.

General Info: Monthly

Subscriptions: Indv. $69, For. $99

Circulation: Total-30,250

List Rental: List Management Co.: Mail Marketing, Inc., 171 Terrace St., Haworth, NJ 07641-1899 Tel # (201) 387-1023, Fax # (201) 387-2976, Actives: 30,240, $135/M

APC Currents
See: ELECTRIC & ELECTRONIC EQUIPMENT

AS/400 Advisory Service

Publishing Co: Computer Economics, Inc., 5841 Edison Pl., Carlsbad, CA 92008-6519; Title Tel # (619) 438-8100 Title Fax # (619) 431-1126

Personnel: Publisher-Bruno Bassi, Editor-Terrin Lovett, Circ. Mgr.-Denise Tondream

Editorial Description: Provides data to optimize your AS/400 hardware investment, budget planning and justification, platform migration strategies, acquisition analyses, and systems planning.

General Info: 6x/yr., Looseleaf

Subscriptions: Indv. $615

List Rental: List Management Co.: Direct Effect, 1049 Camino Del Mar Ste 4b, Del Mar, CA 92014-2651 Tel # (619) 792-9259, Actives: $150/M

ASR News
Business

Publishing Co: Voice Information Association, Inc., 14 Glen Road South ., Box 625, Lexington, MA 02173-5322; Title Tel # (617) 861-6680 Title Fax # (617) 863-8790

Personnel: Publisher-John A. Oberteuffer, Editor-Katherine Carr

Editorial Description: Covers developments in products, marketing, applications, technology, and investments in the automatic speech recognition and synthetic speech industry.

General Info: Yr. Est. 1990, Monthly, Trim Size-8½ x 11, Sheetfed press, 8 pages, ISSN: 1051-4163, 2 Color, Matte

Subscriptions: Indv. $295, Inst. $385, Can. $325, For. $365, $35/copy

List Rental: Rents Lists

ATUNC Newsletter

Publishing Co: ATUNC, PO Box 16427, San Francisco, CA 94116-0427; Title Tel # (415) 731-0829

Personnel: Publisher, Editor-Li Kung Shaw, Promotion Dir.-Ed Suttles

Editorial Description: Technical and general articles on the Apple III computer, its uses, and Apple Three Users of Northern California (ATUNC).

General Info: Yr. Est. 1984, Monthly, Coated, Saddle-stitched

Subscriptions: $2/copy

Circulation: Total-200

Access

Publishing Co: Computer Services Training Centre, City Hall, 453 12th Ave., Vancouver, BC V5Y 1V4 Canada; Title Tel # (604) 873-7981

Personnel: Editor-David Kaufman

General Info: Yr. Est. 1987, Monthly

Acronyms

Publishing Co: Michigan State Univ. Computer Laboratory, 404f Computer Ctr, East Lansing, MI 48824-1042; Title Tel # (517) 353-1802 Title Fax # (517) 353-9847

Personnel: Circ. Mgr.-Diana Gover, Editor, Art Dir.-Linda Dunn

Editorial Description: Procedures, policies, hardware, software notes, education, items interesting computing community.

General Info: Yr. Est. 1971, Quarterly, Trim Size-8½ x 11½, Web press, 40 pages, ISSN: 0163-6774, 2 Color, Saddle-stitched

Circulation: (100% controlled), Total-3,000

Ada Strategies
Business

Publishing Co: Software Strategies & Tactics Inc., Rr 2 Box 713, Harpers Ferry, WV 25425-9416; Title Tel # (304) 725-6542 Title Fax # (304) 725-6543

Personnel: Publisher, Editor-Ralph E. Crafts, Circ. Mgr.-Roseann Crafts

Editorial Description: Presents current trends & issues in the Ada software language industry in both commercial and government applications

General Info: Yr. Est. 1987, Monthly, Trim Size-8½ x 11, 16 pages, ISSN: 0893-0570, No Color

Subscriptions: Indv. $337, Inst. $100, Can. $337, For. $407, $35/copy

Acquistions: Publication Sold

Circulation: Total-500

Advertising: Inquire for rates. Accepts Inserts.

Advanced Intelligent Network News
Business

Publishing Co: Phillips Business Information, Inc., 1201 Seven Locks Rd., Ste 300, Potomac, MD 20854-2958 Tel # (301) 340-1520 Fax # (301) 424-4297; Title Tel # (301) 424-3338 Title Fax # (301) 309-3847

Personnel: Editor-Candice Sams

Editorial Description: Development and deployment of Advanced Integrated Networks.

General Info: (Formerly AIN Report), Yr. Est. 1992, Bi-weekly, ISSN: 1072-0030

Subscriptions: Indv. $597, For. $630

List Rental: Rents Lists

Advanced Office Technologies Report
Business

Publishing Co: Telecommunications Reports, 1333 H St. NW, 2nd Fl., West Tower, Washington, DC 20005 Tel # (202) 842-3022

Editorial Description: Covers electronic mail, electronic data interchage and office automation in fortune 5000 computing environments. Provides market research, new product news and land technical analysis.

General Info: Yr. Est. 1990, Bi-weekly, Trim Size-8½ x 11, Sheetfed press, 8 pages, ISSN: 1054-1462, Ind/Abs/Online: Newsnet, Predicasts

Subscriptions: Indv. $495

Advanced Technology for
Developers   *Business*

Publishing Co: High-Tech Communications, 103 Buckskin Ct, Sewickley, PA 15143-9508;
Title Tel # (412) 741-7699 Title Fax # (412) 741-6094
Personnel: Editor-Jane Kilmasauskas
Editorial Description: For developers working with neural nets, expert systems, genetic algorithms, fuzzy logic, etc.
General Info: Monthly
Subscriptions: Indv. $198

Advanced Wireless Communications
See: TELECOMMUNICATIONS

Agency Law Quarterly Real Estate Intelligence Report
See: REAL ESTATE

Air Quality Data Management Software Report
See: ENVIRONMENT & ECOLOGY

Alldata News   *Business, Consumer*

Publishing Co: Alldata, 9412 Big Horn Blvd., Elk Grove, CA 95758
Editorial Description: Information about the Alldata electronic automotive repair database.
General Info: Yr. Est. 1994, Monthly, Trim Size-8½ x 11, 4 pages, 2 Color, Coated

Ambit International

Publishing Co: Ambit International, Inc., 665 3rd St Ste 508, San Francisco, CA 94107-1923
Tel # (415) 957-9433 Fax # (415) 957-0504

Amiga Culture

Publishing Co: Boston Computer Society, Inc., 101 A First Ave. Suite #2, Waltham, MA 02154
Tel # (617) 290-5700 Fax # (617) 290-5744
General Info: Bi-monthly

Amy Wohl's Trendsletter   *Business*

Publishing Co: Wohl Assocs., 915 Montgomery Ave., Ste. 309, Marberth, PA 19072;
Title Tel # (610) 667-4842 Title Fax # (610) 667-3081
Personnel: Editor-Amy Wohl
General Info: (Formerly Wohl Report on End User Computing), Yr. Est. 1985, Monthly, 12 pages, 2 Color
Subscriptions: Indv. $495, Can. $530, For. $530, $35/copy
Circulation: Total-500
List Rental: Rents Lists

Anderson Report   *Business*

Publishing Co: Altus Inc, PO Box 17869, Milwaukee, WI 53217-0869
Personnel: Publisher-Kenneth Anderson, Editor-Marcia Brooks, Circ. Mgr.-Leona Hollar
Editorial Description: Newsletter on CAD/CAM, CAE.
General Info: (Formerly Anderson Report on Computer Graphics), Yr. Est. 1978, Monthly, Trim Size-8½ x 11, Offset press, 12 pages, ISSN: 0197-7040, No Color, Newsprint
Subscriptions: Indv. $345, Can. $345, For. $395, $20/copy
List Rental: Actives: $170/M

Andrew Seybold's
Outlook on
Communications and
Computing   *Business, Consumer*

Publishing Co: Pinecrest Press Inc., PO Box 917, Brookdale, CA 95007-0917;
Title Tel # (408) 338-7701 Title Fax # (408) 338-7806
Personnel: Publisher, Editor-Andrew Seybold, Circ. Mgr.-Linda Seybold
Editorial Description: Present evaluation of hardware, software, technology from end-user's perspective.
General Info: (Formerly Andrew Seybold's Outlook...Professional...Mobile Computing), Yr. Est. 1982, Monthly, Trim Size-8½ x 11, Sheetfed press, 36 pages, ISSN: 1080-4056, Color-cover, Saddle-stitched
Subscriptions: Indv. $395, Can. $410, For. $425, $30/copy
Acquistions: Publication Bought, Publication Sold
Advertising: Accepts Inserts.

Apple II Software Review

Publishing Co: Delphi and GVC, 1030 Massachusetts Ave., Cambridge, MA 02138-5302;
Title Tel # (617) 491-3393
Editorial Description: Describes the different software packages available through Delphi, the Corps. online service.

Apple Library Users Group
Newsletter   *Business, Consumer*

Publishing Co: Apple Computer, Inc., 4 Infinite Loop, Cupertino, CA 95014-2083;
Title Tel # (408) 974-2552 Title Fax # (408) 725-8502
Personnel: Editor-Monica Ertel, Art Dir.-Bill Vaccaro
Editorial Description: For Apple users in libraries and information centers.
General Info: Quarterly, Trim Size-8½ x 11, 24 pages, ISSN: 0887-2716, 2 Color, Coated, Saddle-stitched

AplePress

Publishing Co: Boston Computer Society, Inc., 101 A First Ave. Suite #2, Waltham, MA 02154
Tel # (617) 290-5700 Fax # (617) 290-5744
General Info: Bi-monthly

Application Development
Strategies   *Business*

Publishing Co: Cutter Information Corp., 37 Broadway, Ste. 1, Arlington, MA 02174-5552
Tel # (617) 648-8700; Title Tel # (617) 648-8702; Title Fax # (617) 648-1950
Personnel: Publisher-Karen Coburn, Editor-Ed Yourdon, Assoc. Ed.-Curt Hall, Circ. Mgr.-Beth O'Neill, Mktg. Dir.-Paul Bergeron, Promotion Mgr.-Laura St. Clair
Editorial Description: For individuals who design, develop or implement software systems. Strategy and practical information on computer aided software engineering.
General Info: (Formerly CASE Strategies), Yr. Est. 1989, Monthly, ISSN: 1045-1986, Ind/Abs/Online: NewsNet, Saddle-stitched
Subscriptions: Indv. $427, Can. $427, For. $487, $30/copy
Advertising: Inquire for rates.
List Rental: Rents Lists

Applications Software
Reports   *Business*

Publishing Co: Faulkner Technical Reports, Inc., 7905 Browning Road, 114 Cooper Center, Pennsauken, NJ 08109; Title Tel # (609) 662-2070 Title Fax # (609) 662-3380
Personnel: Editor-Ellen Walsh, Mng. Editor-JAnice Wright, Circ. Mgr.-Bill Gaul, Production Mgr.-Bill Schmidt, Adv. Dir., Promotion Dir.-Barbara Forkel
Editorial Description: One volume reference service covers human resources, integrated accounting inventory control, manufacturing, general business management and word processing for all computing service.
General Info: Yr. Est. 1970, Monthly, 80 pages, Ind/Abs/Online: Bibl.Charts, No Color, Looseleaf
Subscriptions: Indv. $695

Artificial Intelligence Letter

Publishing Co: Texas Instruments, PO Box 149149, Austin, TX 78714-9149;
Title Tel # (512) 250-6314
Personnel: Editor-Cindy Smith
General Info: Yr. Est. 1984, Monthly

Atex Times
See: HOUSE ORGANS

Audiotex Update   *Business*

Publishing Co: Worldwide Videotex Co., PO Box 3273, Boynton Beach, FL 33424-3273
Fax # (407) 738-2276; Title Tel # (407) 738-2276 Title Fax # (407) 738-2275
Personnel: Editor-Mark Wright
Editorial Description: Provides the latest news & information about the audiotex industry. Voice processing & information products, services, companies & marketing strategies.
General Info: Yr. Est. 1989, Monthly, ISSN: 1045-5795, Ind/Abs/Online: NewsNet, Predicasts
Subscriptions: Indv. $150, Can. $150, For. $165

Authorized OA Dealer Report
See: OFFICE METHODS & EQUIPMENT

AutoGraph   *Business, Association*

Publishing Co: Automated Graphic Systems, 4590 Graphics Dr., White Plains, MD 20695;
Title Tel # (301) 843-1800 Title Fax # (301) 843-6339
Personnel: Editor, Mktg. Mgr.-Eileen Bok
Editorial Description: Desktop publishing tips for Mac and PC users.
General Info: Monthly, Trim Size-8½ x 11, Sheetfed press, 6 pages, 4 Color, Matte, Other
Subscriptions: Free To Qualified Recipient
Circulation: Total-3,400
Printing Co: Automated Graphic Systems, 6810 Cochran Rd., Solon, OH 44139-3908
Tel # (216) 248-7700, Fax # (216) 349-4771

Automation Equipment
Marketing Report

Publishing Co: Cota & Assocs., Inc., PO Box 14070, Sarasota, FL 34278-4070;
Title Tel # (203) 255-0569
Personnel: Publisher, Editor-Ronald Cota
General Info: Yr. Est. 1985, Monthly

BCS 99er

Publishing Co: Boston Computer Society, Inc., 101 A First Ave. Suite #2, Waltham, MA 02154
Tel # (617) 290-5700 Fax # (617) 290-5744
General Info: Bi-monthly

BCS Artificial Intelligence
Newsletter

Publishing Co: Boston Computer Society, Inc., 101 A First Ave. Suite #2, Waltham, MA 02154
Tel # (617) 290-5700 Fax # (617) 290-5744
General Info: Monthly

BCS Construction
Newsletter

Publishing Co: Boston Computer Society, Inc., 101 A First Ave. Suite #2, Waltham, MA 02154
Tel # (617) 290-5700 Fax # (617) 290-5744
General Info: Bi-monthly

BCS Database Newsletter

Publishing Co: Boston Computer Society, Inc., 101 A First Ave. Suite #2, Waltham, MA 02154
Tel # (617) 290-5700 Fax # (617) 290-5744
General Info: Quarterly

BCS Networking Newsletter

Publishing Co: Boston Computer Society, Inc., 101 A First Ave. Suite #2, Waltham, MA 02154
Tel # (617) 290-5700 Fax # (617) 290-5744
General Info: Quarterly

BCS Programming Newsletter

Publishing Co: Boston Computer Society, Inc., 101 A First Ave. Suite #2, Waltham, MA 02154
Tel # (617) 290-5700 Fax # (617) 290-5744
General Info: Quarterly

BCS Robotics Newsletter

Publishing Co: Boston Computer Society, Inc., 101 A First Ave. Suite #2, Waltham, MA 02154
Tel # (617) 290-5700 Fax # (617) 290-5744
General Info: Quarterly

BCS Science & Engineering

Publishing Co: Boston Computer Society, Inc., 101 A First Ave. Suite #2, Waltham, MA 02154
Tel # (617) 290-5700 Fax # (617) 290-5744
General Info: Bi-monthly

BCS T&D

Publishing Co: Boston Computer Society, Inc., 101 A First Ave. Suite #2, Waltham, MA 02154
Tel # (617) 290-5700 Fax # (617) 290-5744
General Info: Bi-monthly

Bank Automation News   *Business*

Publishing Co: Phillips Business Information, Inc., 1201 Seven Locks Rd., Ste 300, Potomac, MD 20854-2958 Tel # (301) 340-1520 Fax # (301) 424-4297; Title Tel # (301) 340-2100 Title Fax # (301) 309-3847
Personnel: Publisher-Chris Scotton, Editor-Kathy Hawk, Production Mgr.-Teresa Fleisher, Adv. Dir.-Kim Hudak, Mktg. Dir.-Kelly Ebbs
Editorial Description: An executive report on bank automation, Marketing and intergration strategies.
General Info: (Formerly Branch Automation News; Bank Automation Contract Watch), Yr. Est. 1989, Bi-weekly, 8 pages, ISSN: 1044-145X, Ind/Abs/Online: NewsNet, DIALOG, Predicasts, Bloomberg, 2 Color
Subscriptions: Indv. $595, For. $630
List Rental: Rents Lists

Bank Network News (Newsletter)
See: BANKING & FINANCE

Bank Operations Bulletin
See: BANKING & FINANCE

Bank Securities Report
See: BANKING & FINANCE

Banking Automation

Publishing Co: Datapro Research Corp., 600 Delran Pky, Delran, NJ 08075-1255
Tel # (609) 764-0100 Fax # (609) 764-2815

Benchmarks

Publishing Co: University of North Texas Computing Center, NT Box 13495, Denton, TX 76203; Title Tel # (817) 565-2324 Title Fax # (817) 565-4060
Personnel: Editor-Claudia Lynch
Editorial Description: Benchmarks provides timely information about topics of interest to the academic computing community and the university.
General Info: Yr. Est. 1980, 9x/yr., Trim Size-8½ x 11, Offset press, 30 pages, ISSN: 1066-0380, No Color, Saddle-stitched
Subscriptions: Free To Qualified Recipient
Circulation: (100% controlled)

Big Byte, The

Publishing Co: University of Calgary, Computer Services, 2500 University Dr., NW, Calgary, AB T2N 1N4 Canada; Title Tel # (403) 220-6616 Title Fax # (403) 282-9199
Personnel: Editor-Jackie Bell
Editorial Description: To inform users of Academic Computing Services about hardware, software (system applications) changes, enchancements to job processing procedures; mainly campus circulation only.
General Info: Yr. Est. 1968, Tri-annually, Trim Size-8½ x 11, Offset press, 50 pages, ISSN: 0045-1991, 2 Color, Matte, Saddle-stitched
Subscriptions: Indv. $15, Can. $20, Free To Qualified Recipient
Circulation: Total-1,300

Bits & Bytes Review

Publishing Co: Bits & Bytes Computer Resources, 623 Iowa Ave, Whitefish, MT 59937-2336; Title Tel # (406) 862-7280 Title Fax # (406) 862-1124
Personnel: Publisher, Editor-John Hughes, Circ. Mgr., Production Mgr., Adv. Dir.-Claire Hughes, Art Dir.-Gail Heinrich
Editorial Description: Detailed reviews of products & resources for academic computing.
General Info: Yr. Est. 1986, Quarterly, Trim Size-8½ x 11, Sheetfed press, 40 pages, ISSN: 0891-2955, Ind/Abs/Online: ISA, SRF, INSPEC, Bus Software Database, 2 Color, Newsprint
Subscriptions: Indv. $55, Inst. $70, Can. $80, For. $85, $6/copy
Circulation: Total-2,500
Printing Co: Towne Printer, 237 Baker Ave, Whitefish, MT 59937-2431 Tel # (406) 862-5770

Boston Area Rainbow News

Publishing Co: Boston Computer Society, Inc., 101 A First Ave. Suite #2, Waltham, MA 02154
Tel # (617) 290-5700 Fax # (617) 290-5744
General Info: Quarterly

Boston Computer Exchange Index   *Consumer*

Publishing Co: Boston Computer Exchange, 55 Temple Pl., Boston, MA 02111-1305; Title Tel # (617) 542-4414 Title Fax # (617) 542-8849
Personnel: Publisher-Alex Randall, Editor-Gary Guhman
Editorial Description: Lists prices for used computers.
General Info: Weekly, 4 pages
Subscriptions: Indv. $250, $10/copy

Boston Kugel

Publishing Co: Boston Computer Society, Inc., 101 A First Ave. Suite #2, Waltham, MA 02154
Tel # (617) 290-5700 Fax # (617) 290-5744
General Info: Quarterly

Bowman's Accounting Report
See: ACCOUNTING

Business Computer Report   *Business, Consumer*

Publishing Co: Guidera Publishing Corp., 3 Myrtle Bank Rd, Hilton Head Island, SC 29926-1809; Title Tel # (803) 681-3399
Personnel: Editor-Lawrence Oakley, Circ. Mgr.-Min Cunningham, Art Dir.-R.C. Chapo, Publisher, Production Mgr., Promotion Dir.-Rosanne Oakley
Editorial Description: Tests & reviews of business related software & hardware. Book reviews, IBM & compatibles exclusively.
General Info: Yr. Est. 1988, Monthly, Trim Size-8½ x 11, Offset press, 8 pages, 2 Color, Matte
Subscriptions: Indv. $50, For. $70, $10/copy
Acquistions: Publication Bought
List Rental: Actives: $85/M
Printing Co: Guidera Fine Printing, 11 Palmetto Pky, Hilton Head Island, SC 29926-3759 Tel # (803) 681-3399

Business Reply

Publishing Co: Boston Computer Society, Inc., 101 A First Ave. Suite #2, Waltham, MA 02154
Tel # (617) 290-5700 Fax # (617) 290-5744
General Info: Bi-monthly

C++ Report   *Business*

Publishing Co: SIGS Publications Group, 71 W. 23rd Street, 3rd Floor, New York, NY 10010-4102
Tel # (212) 246-7447 Fax # (212) 242-7574; Title Tel # (212) 972-7055
Personnel: Publisher-Richard Friedman, Editor-Robert Murray
Editorial Description: Covers the lates developments, applications, trends and new products in the C++ language.
General Info: Yr. Est. 1989, 10x/yr., ISSN: 1040-6042
Subscriptions: Indv. $49, Inst. $79
List Rental: List Management Co.: Statlistics Management, 123 Elm St. Suite 700, Old Saybrook, CT 06475-0936 Tel # (203) 388-4669, Fax # (203) 388-6854, Actives: 6,200, $140/M

CA Business Partners

Publishing Co: Espirit de Corps, 11 Hanover Square, New York, NY 10005; Title Tel # (212) 425-7033
Editorial Description: Computer Associates.
General Info: Yr. Est. 1993, Irregular
Subscriptions: Free

CAD/CAM Update   *Business*

Publishing Co: Worldwide Videotex Co., PO Box 3273, Boynton Beach, FL 33424-3273
Tel # (407) 738-2276 Fax # (407) 738-2276
Editorial Description: Latest news about the CAD/CAM industry.
General Info: Yr. Est. 1989, Monthly, Ind/Abs/Online: NewsNet; DIALOG
Subscriptions: Indv. $150, Inst. $150, Can. $150, For. $165

CAM-I News Alert   *Consumer*

Publishing Co: Computer Aided Manufacturing Intl., 1250 E Copeland Rd Ste 500, Arlington, TX 76011-4913; Title Tel # (817) 265-5328
Editorial Description: Computer assisted manufacturing and the general field of robotics.
General Info: Yr. Est. 1972, Bi-monthly, 6 pages, Color

CCAR Pool
See: LAW

CD Computing News   *Business*

Publishing Co: Worldwide Videotex Co., PO Box 3273, Boynton Beach, FL 33424-3273
Fax # (407) 738-2276; Title Tel # (407) 738-2276 Title Fax # (407) 738-2275
Personnel: Publisher, Editor-Mark Wright, Circ. Mgr.-S. Goldberg
Editorial Description: Provides information & news on CD-ROM projects & products worldwide.
General Info: Yr. Est. 1981, Monthly, Trim Size-11 x 17, Offset press, 8 pages, ISSN: 0893-4843, Ind/Abs/Online: NewsNet, DIALOG, No Color
Subscriptions: Indv. $150, Can. $150, For. $165, $13/copy
Circulation: Total-800

CD-ROM Databases   *Business*

Publishing Co: Worldwide Videotex Co., PO Box 3273, Boynton Beach, FL 33424-3273
Fax # (407) 738-2276; Title Tel # (407) 738-2276 Title Fax # (407) 738-2275
Personnel: Editor-Mark Wright
Editorial Description: Lists latest CD-ROMs being marketed along with prices, vendors, categories.
General Info: Yr. Est. 1988, Monthly, ISSN: 0897-3296, Ind/Abs/Online: NewsNet, DIALOG, Predicasts
Subscriptions: Indv. $150, Can. $150, For. $190

CD-ROM News Extra   *Business, Consumer*

Publishing Co: Online, Inc., 462 Danbury Rd., Wilton, CT 06897-2125 Tel # (203) 761-1466; Title Fax # (203) 761-1444
Editorial Description: Published in alternating months with CD-ROM Professional Magazine.
General Info: Yr. Est. 1993, Bi-monthly
Advertising: Inquire for rates.

CDLA Printout   *Business, Association*

Publishing Co: Computer Leasing & Remarketing Association, 1200 19th St. NW, Ste. 300, Washington, DC 20036-2412; Title Tel # (202) 333-0102 Title Fax # (202) 333-0180
Personnel: Publisher-Kenneth Bouldin, Editor-Douglas McAllister, Production Mgr.-Heather Hogue
Editorial Description: Information on issues of interest to companies engaged in the buying, selling & leasing of new & used computers.
General Info: (Formerly Computer Dealers), Yr. Est. 1976, Quarterly, Trim Size-8½ x 11, Sheetfed press, 16 pages, 2 Color, Coated, Saddle-stitched
Subscriptions: Indv. $24, $6/copy
Circulation: Total-1,500
Printing Co: Affiliated Graphics, 3342 Bladensburg Rd, Brentwood, MD 20722-1898 Tel # (301) 927-3800

CEPA Newsletter   *Association*

Publishing Co: CEPA, Inc., 6408 Bells Mill Rd, Bethesda, MD 20817-1634; Title Tel # (301) 454-8133
Personnel: Publisher, Editor, Circ. Mgr., Art Dir.-Patricia Johnson
Editorial Description: Technical-computers in engineering, architecture, planning. Membership news. New products (computer hardware/software). Upcoming events computer conferences.
General Info: Yr. Est. 1965, Quarterly, Trim Size-8½ x 11, Sheetfed press, 20 pages, ISSN: 8756-0550, 1% ads, Coated, Saddle-stitched
Subscriptions: Indv. $45, For. $60, $15/copy
Circulation: Total-1,000
Advertising: Inquire for rates.
List Rental: Rents Lists

CIRT Newsletter

Publishing Co: Univ. of New Mexico, 2701 Campus Blvd. , N. E., Albuquerque, NM 87131-0001; Title Tel # (505) 277-8147
Personnel: Editor-Barbara Rigg-Healy
Editorial Description: About computing at the U of New Mexico.
General Info: Yr. Est. 1967, 7x/yr., Trim Size-8½ x 11, Sheetfed press, 24 pages, Color-cover, Newsprint
Acquistions: Publication Bought, Publication Sold
Circulation: (100% controlled)
Printing Co: University of New Mexico Printing Plant, Univ. Of New Mexico, Albuquerque, NM 87131-0001 Tel # (505) 277-4055

CKC Report, The Hotel Technology Newsletter
See: HOTEL INDUSTRY

CMC News (Computers in the Media Center)   *Business, Scholarly*   **CPM: $70**

Publishing Co: Computers and the Media Center, 515 Oak St. N., Cannon Falls, MN 55009-1630; Title Tel # (507) 263-3711
Personnel: Publisher, Editor-Jim Deacon, Circ. Mgr.-Barbara Deacon
Editorial Description: Provides information on the application of microcomputers in library/media centers.
General Info: Yr. Est. 1979, Quarterly, Trim Size-8½ x 11, Offset press, 24 pages, ISSN: 0738-8845, Ind/Abs/Online: ERIC, 20% ads, No Color, Newsprint
Subscriptions: Indv. $14, Can. $15, For. $21, $4/copy
Circulation: Total-1,700
Advertising: $120.

CMRR Report

Publishing Co: Center for Magnetic Recording Research, Univ. of California-San Diego, La Jolla, CA 92093-0002; Title Tel # (619) 534-6213 Title Fax # (619) 534-2720
Personnel: Editor-Dawn Talbot
General Info: Yr. Est. 1985, Quarterly, Trim Size-8½ x 11, 4 pages, ISSN: 0888-7381, No Color
Circulation: Total-1,500

COM-AND, Computer Audit News & Developments   *Business*

Publishing Co: Management Advisory Services & Publications, 57 Greylock Rd # 81151, Wellesley Hills, MA 02181-1301 Fax # (617) 235-5446; Title Tel # (617) 235-2895
Personnel: Publisher-J. Kuong, Editor-J.F. Kuong, Production Mgr.-P.A. Kuong, Promotion Dir.-N. Lagos
Editorial Description: Computer audit news & developments. New standards & practices. Tutorials on the impact of EDP on audit & control matters. Practical coverage of technical EDP developments for auditors, & internal controls specialists.
General Info: Yr. Est. 1983, Bi-monthly, Trim Size-8½ x 11, Sheetfed press, 8 pages, ISSN: 0738-4270, No Color, Newsprint
Subscriptions: Indv. $56, Can. $56, For. $62, $10/copy
Advertising: Inquire for rates. Accepts Inserts.

CPA Technology Advisor   *Business*

Publishing Co: Harcourt Brace Professional Publishing, 6277 Sea Harbor Dr, Orlando, FL 32887-0001 Tel # (407) 345-2000 Fax # (800) 874-6418; Title Fax # (800) 336-7377
Personnel: Publisher-Jerry Huss, Editor-Frank Peterson, Circ. Mgr.-Mary Hartzell, Promotion Dir.-Shelley Brannan
Editorial Description: Concise unbiased recommendations on hardware & software for CPAs.
General Info: (Formerly CPA Micro Report), Yr. Est. 1982, Monthly, Offset press, 10 pages, Newsprint
Subscriptions: Indv. $197, $19/copy
Acquistions: Publication Bought
Advertising: Accepts Inserts.
List Rental: Actives: $125/M

Campus Computing and Communications   *Consumer*

Publishing Co: Univ. of British Columbia, Univ. Computing Svces., 6356 Agricultural Rd., Vancouver, BC V6T 1W5 Canada; Title Tel # (604) 822-4783
Personnel: Editor-Wendy Alexander
Editorial Description: In-house newsletter that reports on the various facilities, services and activities of UBC's. Computing and Communications department.
General Info: (Formerly Campus Computing), Yr. Est. 1969, Monthly, Trim Size-8½ x 11, Offset press, 32 pages, 2 Color, Matte, Saddle-stitched
Subscriptions: Indv. $10, Can. $10
Circulation: (100% controlled), Total-6,000

Canadian Index of Computer Literature

Publishing Co: Evans Research Corp. of Canada, 1 Eva Rd. #309, Etobicoke, ON M9C 4Z5 Canada; Title Tel # (416) 621-8814
General Info: Monthly
Subscriptions: Indv. $695

Capacity Management Review   *Business, Association*   **CPM: $856**

Publishing Co: Applied Computer Research, PO Box 82266, Phoenix, AZ 85071-2266 Tel # (602) 995-5929; Title Tel # (602) 997-7374 Title Fax # (602) 861-2587
Personnel: Publisher-Phillip Howard, Editor-Philip Howard, Production Dir.-Dianne Howard, Promotion Dir.-Suzanne Howard
Editorial Description: Reports on computer performance, capacity management, publications, education, software, and membership.
General Info: (Formerly EDP Performance Review), Yr. Est. 1973, Monthly, Trim Size-8½ x 11, Desktop press, 12 pages, ISSN: 0091-7206, Ind/Abs/Online: CmLI, 3% ads, 2 Color, Matte, Saddle-stitched
Subscriptions: Indv. $195, For. $200, $22/copy
Circulation: Total-642
Advertising: $550. Accepts Inserts.
List Rental: Actives: $125/M

Cards & Slots: PCMCIA Market Letter   *Association, Business*

Publishing Co: Dream It, Inc., 1255 Cedar Ridge Ln, Colorado Springs, CO 80919-1403; Title Tel # (719) 598-9000
Editorial Description: For companies who build and resell computer memory cards.
General Info: Yr. Est. 1994, Monthly
Subscriptions: Indv. $495, Can. $495, For. $595

Career Exchange Clearinghouse   *Business, Association*

Publishing Co: Sponsor-Associated Information Managers, Association for Information Management, 1700 Diagonal Rd Ste 300, Alexandria, VA 22314-2866 Parent Co.-Aslib Information House, London, Canada; Title Tel # (703) 836-0250
Personnel: Editor-E. Norman Sims
Editorial Description: Announcement of positions open and wanted for information management professionals.
General Info: Yr. Est. 1978, Monthly, 2 pages
Circulation: (100% controlled), Total-400

CashFlow   *Business*

Publishing Co: Nebs Computer Forms Div., 500 Main St., Groton, MA 01471-0001; Title Fax # (800) 234-4324
Editorial Description: NEBS'newsletter for small business growth.
General Info: Quarterly, Trim Size-10½ x 16, 12 pages, 4 Color, Coated, Saddle-stitched

Catalyst, The — *Business*

Publishing Co: Western Center for Microcomputers, 1259 El Camino Real # 275, Menlo Park, CA 94025-4227; Title Tel # (415) 855-8064
Personnel: Editor-Sue Swezey
Editorial Description: Covers dissemination of information regarding applications of technology in special education and rehabilitation.
General Info: Yr. Est. 1981, Quarterly, Trim Size-8½ x 11, Desktop press, 20 pages, ISSN: 0987-3318
Subscriptions: Indv. $10, Inst. $15, Can. $20, For. $20, $4/copy
Circulation: Total-12,000
Printing Co: PIP Printing, 441 Emerson St, Palo Alto, CA 94301-1605 Tel # (415) 323-8388

Census & You — *Business, Association*

Publishing Co: Bureau of the Census, Data User Services Div., Washington Plaza, Wp-1-317, Washington, DC 20233-0001; Title Tel # (301) 457-1221
Personnel: Editor-Neil Tillman
Editorial Description: Publicizes Census Bureau data products, services, program plans, local information sources.
General Info: (Formerly Data User News), Yr. Est. 1966, Monthly, Trim Size-8½ x 11, Offset press, 12 pages, 2 Color, Recycled
Subscriptions: Indv. $21
Circulation: Total-8,000

Channel
See: LIBRARY

Channelmarker Letter — *Business*

Publishing Co: Merrin Information Services, 2275 E Bayshore Rd, Ste 101, Palo Alto, CA 94303-3220; Title Tel # (415) 493-5050 Title Fax # (415) 493-5480
Personnel: Publisher-Seymour Merrin
Editorial Description: Contains unique perspective and advice regarding the merchandising, distribution, and marketing of personal computers, workstations, and related products, in the U.S. and Europe. Most notably overall trends and vendor & dealer specific issues are identified, clarified, and analyzed.
General Info: Yr. Est. 1988, Monthly, 8 pages, ISSN: 1045-2990, 2 Color, Other, Saddle-stitched
Subscriptions: Indv. $499, Can. $499, For. $599, $45/copy

Church & Synagogue
Computer

Publishing Co: Boston Computer Society, Inc., 101 A First Ave. Suite #2, Waltham, MA 02154 Tel # (617) 290-5700 Fax # (617) 290-5744
General Info: Quarterly

Classic Computer News — *Business*

Publishing Co: Classic Newspaper, 3664 Greenfield Rd, Berkley, MI 48072-3133 Tel # (313) 474-1510; Title Tel # (810) 474-1510
Personnel: Editor-Salvatore Mancuso
Editorial Description: Geared toward users of Windows 3.1, including desktop publishing, highend graphics and multimedia.
General Info: 10x/yr.
Circulation: Total-50,000

Client Server Advisor
Service — *Business*

Publishing Co: Computer Economics, Inc., 5841 Edison Pl., Carlsbad, CA 92008-6519; Title Tel # (619) 438-8100 Title Fax # (619) 431-1126
Personnel: Publisher-Bruno Bassi, Editor-Terrin Lovett, Circ. Mgr.-Denise Tondream
Editorial Description: Provides the hard numbers, resources, and information-intensive analyses you need to take control of yours companies migration to client server technology.
General Info: Yr. Est. 1995, 6x/yr., Looseleaf
Subscriptions: Indv. $895
List Rental: List Management Co.: Direct Effect, 1049 Camino Del Mar Ste 4b, Del Mar, CA 92014-2651 Tel # (619) 792-9259, Actives: $150/M

Client Server News — *Business*

Publishing Co: G2 Computer Intelligence, 3 Maple Place, P.O. Box 7, Glen Head, NJ 11545-9864; Title Tel # (516) 759-7075 Title Fax # (516) 759-7028
Personnel: Publisher-Maureen O'Gara, Editor-Stuart Zipper, Circ. Mgr.-Michael Tablusky
Editorial Description: Information on Microsoft, Windows NY and other products.
General Info: Yr. Est. 1993, Weekly
Subscriptions: Indv. $595
Advertising: Inquire for rates.
List Rental: Rents Lists

Client/Server Economics
Letter — *Business*

Publishing Co: Computer Economics, Inc., 5841 Edison Pl., Carlsbad, CA 92008-6519 Tel # (619) 438-8100 Fax # (619) 431-1126
Personnel: Publisher-Bruno Bassi, Editor-Mark McManus, Circ. Mgr.-Michelle Burrier
Editorial Description: Takes an economic look at the client/server revolution. Covers costs and risks of using client/server computing.
General Info: Yr. Est. 1994, Monthly, Trim Size-8½ x 11, 8 pages, ISSN: 1074-3138, 2 Color, Matte, Saddle-stitched
Subscriptions: Indv. $395, $40/copy
List Rental: List Management Co.: Manager: Denise Tondream; Direct Effect, 1049 Camino Del Mar Ste 4b, Del Mar, CA 92014-2651 Tel # (619) 792-9259, Actives: $150/M

Cole Papers, The
See: NEWSPAPER INDUSTRY

Collected Algorithms from
ACM — *Consumer*

Publishing Co: Association for Computing Machinery, 1515 Broadway, 17th Fl., New York, NY 10036-5701 Fax # (212) 302-5826; Title Tel # (212) 869-7440 Title Fax # (212) 869-0481
Personnel: Publisher-Mark Mandelbaum, Editor-Robert Renka, Circ. Mgr.-Roxanne Carcaterra, Production Mgr.-Lynn O'Addesio, Adv. Dir.-Walter Andrzejewski, Art Dir.-Dennis Ahlgrim, Promotion Dir.-Mike Seiden
General Info: Quarterly, Looseleaf
Subscriptions: Indv. $65, $26/copy
Printing Co: Sheridan Press, 450 Fame Ave, Hanover, PA 17331-9581 Tel # (717) 632-3535, Fax # (717) 633-8900

Color Businesss Report — *Business*

Publishing Co: Blackstone Research Assoc., PO Box 345, Uxbridge, MA 01569-0345; Title Tel # (508) 278-3449 Title Fax # (808) 278-7975
Personnel: Publisher, Editor-Michael Zeis
Editorial Description: Covers color computer and copier products for vendor community.
General Info: (Formerly Color Research Report), Yr. Est. 1991, Monthly, 14 pages, ISSN: 1055-3339, 2 Color, Matte
Subscriptions: Indv. $375, For. $495, $60/copy

Coming to Order — *Business*

Publishing Co: Coming to Order, 660 Fairmont Ave, Westfield, NJ 07090-1361 Fax # (908) 789-7583; Title Tel # (908) 232-4674
General Info: Yr. Est. 1989, Bi-monthly
Subscriptions: Indv. $69

Commercial User's Guide
to the Internet — *Business, Consumer*

Publishing Co: Thompson Publishing Group, 1725 K Street, NW, Washington, DC 20006 Tel # (202) 872-4000
Editorial Description: Monthly updated information on commercial use of the Internet.
General Info: Yr. Est. 1994, Monthly, Looseleaf
Subscriptions: Indv. $395

Communications InfoDisk
See: TELECOMMUNICATIONS

Communications Product
Reports — *Business*

Publishing Co: Phillips Decision Point Resources, 1111 Marlkress Road., P.O. Box 5062, Cherry Hill, NJ 08063-5062 Parent Co.-Phillips Business Information, Inc., Potomac; Title Tel # (609) 424-1100 Title Fax # (609) 424-1999
Personnel: Publisher-Lawrence Feidelman, Editor-Don Stuart, Circ. Mgr.-Carol Bell
Editorial Description: Evaluates voice and data communication products. Includes technical & market overview & evaluation of major products.
General Info: Yr. Est. 1984, Monthly, Offset press, 28 pages, ISSN: 0743-0671, 2 Color, Newsprint, Looseleaf
Subscriptions: Indv. $821, Can. $951, For. $957, $75/copy

Community Memory
Network

Publishing Co: Community Memory Project, 1442a Walnut St # 411, Berkeley, CA 94709-1405; Title Tel # (510) 841-1114
Personnel: Editor-Yavette Holts
Editorial Description: News of a public access computer networking project.
General Info: (Formerly Community Memory News), Yr. Est. 1983, Quarterly, Trim Size-8½ x 11, 8 pages, No Color
Subscriptions: Indv. $10, Inst. $20, $1/copy
Circulation: Total-3,000

Compu-Venture

Publishing Co: Microcomputers Softwares & Consulting, 28 S 12th Ave # 1039, Mount Vernon, NY 10550-2913; Title Tel # (914) 699-2131
Personnel: Editor-Bob James
General Info: Yr. Est. 1988, Bi-monthly, 4 pages
Subscriptions: Indv. $12
Circulation: Total-2,100

Computer &
Communications Library — *Business*

Publishing Co: Faulkner Technical Reports, Inc., 7905 Browning Road, 114 Cooper Center, Pennsauken, NJ 08109; Title Tel # (609) 662-2070 Title Fax # (609) 662-3380
Personnel: Editor-Ellen Walsh, Mng. Editor-Janice Wright, Circ. Mgr.-Bill Gaul, Production Mgr.-Bill Schmidt, Adv. Dir., Promotion Dir.-Barbara Forkel
Editorial Description: Seventeen volume looseleaf reference service covers hardware & software products for mainframes, minis & microcomputers, also voice & data communications.
General Info: Yr. Est. 1963, Monthly, 400 pages, Looseleaf
Subscriptions: Indv. $7,515

Computer Aided Design Report
See: MANUFACTURING

Computer Architecture
Technical Committee
Newsletter

Publishing Co: Computer Society Press, 1730 Massachusetts Ave NW, Washington, DC 20036-1903; Title Tel # (202) 371-0101
Personnel: Editor-Roger Anderson
General Info: Quarterly, 120 pages
Circulation: Total-1,425

Computer Audit Update

Publishing Co: Elsevier Science Inc., 655 Avenue of the Americas, New York, NY 10010-5107 Tel # (212) 633-3916 Fax # (212) 633-3913 Parent Co.-Reed Elsevier, New York
Personnel: Publisher-Andrew Fletcher, Editor-John Meyer, Production Mgr.-J. Whittingham
Editorial Description: Managerial aspects of auditing electronic data processing systems.
General Info: Yr. Est. 1992, Monthly, ISSN: 0960-2593
Subscriptions: Indv. $396

Computer Business   *Business, Association*

Publishing Co: Round Table Assocs. /SAB Inc., PO Box 90776, Los Angeles, CA 90009-0776; Title Tel # (310) 649-2846
Personnel: Publisher, Mag. Ed.-A. Hassan, Asst. Ed.-E. BradFord, Circ. Mgr.-J. Hassan
Editorial Description: Best computer/communications articles of previous month, briefly abstracted.
General Info: Yr. Est. 1978, Monthly, Trim Size-8½ x 11, Letrpr. press, 8 pages, ISSN: 0732-8346, No Color
Subscriptions: Indv. $145, Can. $145, For. $175, $20/copy

Computer Committee Newsletter
See: BOOKS & BOOK TRADE

Computer Communication
Review   *Business, Consumer*

Publishing Co: Bolt Beranek & Newman, 1000 Park Forty Plaza, Suite 300, Durham, NC 27713; Title Tel # (919) 544-9878
Editorial Description: Examines computer performance and uses.
General Info: Monthly

Computer and
Communications Buyer   *Business*

Publishing Co: Technology News of America Co., 110 Greene St Apt 1101, New York, NY 10012-3824; Title Tel # (212) 334-9750
Personnel: Publisher, Editor-H. Wiener
Editorial Description: Annotated statistical reports on capital equipment spending for computer gear.
General Info: Yr. Est. 1980, Monthly, Trim Size-8½ x 11, Sheetfed press, 8 pages, ISSN: 0272-4553, No Color
Subscriptions: Indv. $485, For. $515

Computer Contracts
See: LAW

Computer Counsel   *Business*

Publishing Co: Computer Counsel, Inc., 641 W Lake St # 403, Chicago, IL 60661-1012; Title Tel # (312) 207-6900 Title Fax # (312) 207-1045
Personnel: Publisher, Editor-Richard Robbins, Circ. Mgr.-Tracy Strazzella, Production Mgr.-Troy Griffin, Adv. Dir.-Ed Klass
Editorial Description: Legal software advice for lawyers & law firms.
General Info: Yr. Est. 1988, Monthly, 28 pages, Matte
Subscriptions: Indv. $130, For. $200, $13/copy
Acquistions: Publication Bought
Circulation: Total-1,500
List Rental: Rents Lists
Printing Co: United Letter, Inc., 619 S. LaSalle St., Chicago, IL 60605 Tel # (312) 427-3537

Computer Economic
Report International   *Business*

Publishing Co: Computer Economics, Inc., 5841 Edison Pl., Carlsbad, CA 92008-6519; Title Tel # (619) 438-8100 Title Fax # (619) 431-1126
Personnel: Publisher/President/Advisor-Bruno Bassi, Editor in Chief-Denise Tondream, Editor-Teresa Elms, Circ. Mgr.-Michelle Burrler
Editorial Description: Computer Economics Report- International Edition: 'The Financial Advisor of Data Processing Users'. Written from an end-user perspective, Computer Economics Report provides cost comparisons, price/performance analyses, new product forecasts, and evaluations of acquisition techniques for medium and large computer systems. Computer Economics Report is used by prominent MIS directors at 82% of all For
General Info: Monthly, 8 pages
Subscriptions: Indv. $595, $50/copy
List Rental: List Management Co.: Manager: Luanne Hinkle; Direct Effect, 1049 Camino Del Mar Ste 4b, Del Mar, CA 92014-2651 Tel # (619) 792-9259, Actives: $150/M

Computer Economics
Report   *Business*

Publishing Co: Computer Economics, Inc., 5841 Edison Pl., Carlsbad, CA 92008-6519 Fax # (619) 431-1126; Title Tel # (619) 438-8100 Title Fax # (619) 438-8100
Personnel: Publisher-Bruno Bassi, Editor-Marc McManus, Circ. Mgr.-Michelle Burrler
Editorial Description: Computer Economics Report: 'The Financial Advisor of Data Processing Users' Computer Economics Report provides cost comparisons, price/performance analyses, new product forecasts, and evaluation of acquisition techniques for medium and large computer systems.
General Info: Yr. Est. 1979, Monthly, Trim Size-8½ x 11, Sheetfed press, 8 pages, ISSN: 0739-9874, 2 Color, Saddle-stitched
Subscriptions: Indv. $595, $50/copy
List Rental: List Management Co.: Manager: Denise Tondream; Direct Effect, 1049 Camino Del Mar Ste 4b, Del Mar, CA 92014-2651 Tel # (619) 792-9259, Actives: $150/M

Computer Economics
Sourcebook   *Business*

Publishing Co: Computer Economics, Inc., 5841 Edison Pl., Carlsbad, CA 92008-6519; Title Tel # (619) 438-8100 Title Fax # (619) 431-1126
Personnel: Publisher-Bruno Bassi, Editor-Terrin Lovett, Circ. Mgr.-Denise Tondream
Editorial Description: Computer Economics Sourcebook 'The up-to-date financial guide to DP equipment acquisition and control of DP expenses.' Three volumes with over 1,500 pages of charts, graphs and analyses, it covers list and used equipment prices, residual value forecasts,leasing rates, operating costs, acquisition and disposition strategies, and all the required support resources. An essential management tool for the d
General Info: Yr. Est. 1986, Monthly, Looseleaf
Subscriptions: Indv. $1,895
List Rental: List Management Co.: Manager: Denise Tondream; Direct Effect, 1049 Camino Del Mar Ste 4b, Del Mar, CA 92014-2651 Tel # (619) 792-9259, Actives: $150/M

Computer Entertainer   *Consumer*

Publishing Co: Computer Entertainer, 12115 Magnolia Blvd # 189, North Hollywood, CA 91601
Personnel: Publisher-Marylou Badeaux, Editor-Celeste Dolan
Editorial Description: Reviews & previews, entertainment software for computers/gaming systems.
General Info: (Formerly Video Game Update & Computer Entertainer), Yr. Est. 1982, Monthly, Web press, 16 pages, ISSN: 0890-2143, No Color, Newsprint
Subscriptions: Indv. $25, $3/copy
Circulation: Total-10,000
Printing Co: Newstype Service, 1506 Gardena Ave # 1809, Glendale, CA 91204-2712

Computer Graphics   *Business, Association*

Publishing Co: Association for Computing Machinery, 1515 Broadway, 17th Fl., New York, NY 10036-5701 Fax # (212) 302-5826; Title Tel # (212) 869-7440
Editorial Description: For those interested in computer generated graphics.
General Info: (Formerly SIGRAPH Newsletter), Yr. Est. 1991, Quarterly
Circulation: Total-5,000

Computer Industry Litigation Reporter
See: LAW

Computer Industry Report
(The Gray Sheet)   *Business*

Publishing Co: IDG Intl. Publishing Services, 31 Milk St., Ste. 210, Boston, MA 02109-5104; Title Tel # (617) 423-9030 Title Fax # (617) 423-0712
Personnel: Publisher-P.J. McGovern, Editor-Doug B. McLeod, Circ. Mgr., Production Mgr.-Lee Pillsbury
Editorial Description: Market research and analysis of information processing industry. Annual census of computers as well as market projections.
General Info: (Formerly EDP Industry RPT), Yr. Est. 1964, Semi-monthly, Trim Size-8½ x 11, Sheetfed press, 8 pages, ISSN: 0889-082X, No Color, Saddle-stitched
Subscriptions: Indv. $495, For. $535, $35/copy

Computer Industry Update   *Business*

Publishing Co: IMR, INC-Industry Market Reports, 960 N. San Antonio Rd., Suite 130, Los Altos, CA 94022-1322; Title Tel # (415) 941-6679
Personnel: Publisher-K. V. Blackford, Editor-George Weiser, Circ. Mgr.-Virginia Schnalle
Editorial Description: Abstracts of computer industry trade press organized by market segment; Mainframes, Minicomputers, Terminals & Workstations, Personal Computers, Peripherals and Networking.
General Info: Yr. Est. 1979, Monthly, Trim Size-8½ x 11, Sheetfed press, 80 pages, ISSN: 0744-0081, 2 Color, Matte, Saddle-stitched
Subscriptions: Indv. $345, Can. $345, For. $390
Acquistions: Publication Bought, Publication Sold

Computer Law
See: LAW

Computer Law & Tax
Report

Publishing Co: Roditti Reports Corp., 954 Lexington Ave # 253, New York, NY 10021-5013; Title Tel # (212) 758-1464
Personnel: Publisher, Editor-Esther Schachter, Circ. Mgr.-Amy Fontaine
Editorial Description: Developments in computer law (case decisions, new regs., etc.) tax developments.
General Info: Yr. Est. 1974, Monthly, Trim Size-8½ x 11, Letrpr. press, 16 pages, ISSN: 0361-7203, 2 Color, Newsprint
Subscriptions: Indv. $280, For. $380, $20/copy
Circulation: Total-650
List Rental: Actives: $200/M

Computer Law Reporter   *Business*

Publishing Co: Computer Law Reporter, 1519 Connecticut Ave., NW, Suite 200, Washington, DC 20036-1111 Fax # (202) 328-2430; Title Tel # (202) 462-5755
Personnel: Editor-John Noble, Circ. Mgr.-John Herring
Editorial Description: Information on relevent federal and state computer law cases.
General Info: Yr. Est. 1982, Bi-monthly, Trim Size-8½ x 11, 150 pages, No Color, Looseleaf
Subscriptions: Indv. $475

Computer Law Strategist
See: LAW

Computer Letter   *Business*

Publishing Co: Technologic Partners, 120 Wooster Street, New York, NY 10012; Title Tel # (212) 343-1900 Title Fax # (212) 343-1915
Personnel: Publications Director-John Lo, Publisher, Editor-Richard Shaffer, Sr. Ed.-John W. Wilson, Research Editor-Gillian Fassel, Research Editor-Wayne Gagnon, Production Ed.-Claudia O'Neill, Circ. Mgr.-Matthew Klein, Production Mgr.-Thad Batt, Art Dir.-Natalie Tilton, Mktg. Dir.-Denise Canniff
Editorial Description: Follows business issues in technology & technology issues in business.
General Info: Yr. Est. 1984, 40x/yr., Web press, 8 pages
Subscriptions: Indv. $595, Can. $695, For. $695

Computer Monitor Quarterly
See: DIRECT MAIL

Computer Personnel   *Business*

Publishing Co: Association for Computing Machinery, 1515 Broadway, 17th Fl., New York, NY 10036-5701 Fax # (212) 302-5826; Title Tel # (212) 869-7440
Personnel: Editor-Paul Licker
General Info: Quarterly, ISSN: 0160-2497

Computer Price Guide   *Business*

Publishing Co: Computer Merchants, Inc., 200 Brady Ave., Box 1006, Hawthorne, NY 10532-1823; Title Tel # (914) 769-2686 Title Fax # (914) 769-4897
Personnel: Publisher-Svend Hartmann, Editor-Szend Hartmann, Circ. Mgr.-Jackie Fries
Editorial Description: Compendium of prices for used IBM computers. Includes a newsletter with comments about market trends and developments.
General Info: Yr. Est. 1970, Quarterly, Web press, 48 pages, ISSN: 0045-7841, Color-cover, Matte, Saddle-stitched
Subscriptions: Indv. $58, Can. $58, For. $78, $18/copy
Printing Co: Wayne Printing, 10 Ludlow St, Yonkers, NY 10705-1911 Tel # (914) 739-2100

Computer Price Guide   *Business*

Publishing Co: Computer Economics, Inc., 5841 Edison Pl., Carlsbad, CA 92008-6519 Fax # (619) 431-1126; Title Tel # (619) 438-8100 Title Fax # (619) 438-1126
General Info: Quarterly, Looseleaf
List Rental: Rents Lists

Computer Product Update

Publishing Co: Blackwell Publishers, 238 Main St., Cambridge, MA 02142 Tel # (617) 547-7110 Fax # (617) 547-0789
Editorial Description: New computer products and suppliers.
General Info: Yr. Est. 1990, Bi-weekly

Computer Protocols   *Business*

Publishing Co: Worldwide Videotex Co., PO Box 3273, Boynton Beach, FL 33424-3273 Fax # (407) 738-2276; Title Tel # (407) 738-2276 Title Fax # (407) 738-2275
Personnel: Editor-Mark Wright
General Info: Yr. Est. 1988, Monthly, ISSN: 0899-126X, Ind/Abs/Online: NewsNet, DIALOG, Predicasts
Subscriptions: Indv. $150, Can. $150, For. $165

Computer Publishing & Advertising Report
See: PERIODICAL INDUSTRY

Computer Systems & Peripherals Residual Value Forecasats Multivendor   *Business*

Publishing Co: Computer Economics, Inc., 5841 Edison Pl., Carlsbad, CA 92008-6519 Tel # (619) 438-8100 Fax # (619) 431-1126 Title Tel # (619) 431-1126 Title Fax # (619) 438-8100
Personnel: Publisher-Bruno Bassi, Editor-Terrin Lovett, Circ. Mgr.-Denise Tondream
Editorial Description: Know what your IBM, Dec, HP and sun equipment will be worth years from now. Used by the majority of dealers, lessors, and fortune 500 companies, these are the least expensive, most accurate and widely used forecast.
General Info: Yr. Est. 1995, 8x/yr., Looseleaf
Subscriptions: Indv. $3,450
List Rental: List Management Co.: Manager: Denise Tondream; Direct Effect, 1049 Camino Del Mar Ste 4b, Del Mar, CA 92014-2651 Tel # (619) 792-9259

Computer Workstations   *Business*

Publishing Co: Worldwide Videotex Co., PO Box 3273, Boynton Beach, FL 33424-3273 Tel # (407) 738-2276 Fax # (407) 738-2276
Editorial Description: Computer workstations used in network applications.
General Info: Yr. Est. 1988, Monthly, ISSN: 0899-9783, Ind/Abs/Online: NewsNet; DIALOG
Subscriptions: Indv. $150, Inst. $150, Can. $150, For. $165

Computeriter   *Business*

Publishing Co: Creative Business Communications, PO Box 476, Columbia, MD 21045-0476; Title Tel # (410) 596-5591 Title Fax # (410) 997-7946
Personnel: Publisher, Editor-Linda Elengold
Editorial Description: Microcomputer news and views for the writer, editor.
General Info: Yr. Est. 1984, Monthly, Sheetfed press, 12 pages, ISSN: 8756-7911, No Color, Coated
Subscriptions: Indv. $40, $5/copy
Circulation: Total-4,000

Computers & Society

Publishing Co: Association for Computing Machinery, 1515 Broadway, 17th Fl., New York, NY 10036-5701 Tel # (212) 869-7440 Fax # (212) 302-5826
Personnel: Editor-A.A.J. Hoffman
Editorial Description: Brings together computer professionals, specialists in other fields, and the public at large to address concerns and arouse interest about the impact of computers on sociology
General Info: (Formerly SIGAS Newsletter), Yr. Est. 1968, Quarterly
Subscriptions: Indv. $56
Circulation: Total-1,500

Computers, Control, & Information Theory   *Business*

Publishing Co: National Technical Information Service U.S., 5285 Port Royal Rd., Springfield, VA 22161-0001 Fax # (703) 487-4630; Title Tel # (703) 487-4630
Personnel: Editor-Marie Lawall
Editorial Description: Weekly newsletter containing bibliographic citations of S&T research reports in computer hardware & software; control systems & theory; information processing standards; information theory; & pattern recognition & image processing.
General Info: Weekly, 20 pages, ISSN: 0364-796X
Subscriptions: Indv. $160, Can. $160, For. $225

Computers Foodservice & You   *Business*

Publishing Co: Computers Foodservice & You, 1201 S. Second St., PO Box 338, Raton, NM 87740 Tel # (505) 445-8252; Title Tel # (505) 445-9811 Title Fax # (505) 445-8252
Personnel: Publisher-Mike Pappas, Editor-Kay Van Dyke, Circ. Dir.-Joy Walker
Editorial Description: Computer software and hardware for the foodservice industry.
General Info: Yr. Est. 1990, Bi-monthly, Trim Size-8½ x 11, Desktop press, 12 pages, ISSN: 1051-6476, 2 Color, Matte, Saddle-stitched
Subscriptions: Indv. $119, Can. $125, $25/copy
Circulation: Total-400
List Rental: Rents Lists
Printing Co: Smiths Printing, 303 South Third, Raton, NM 87740 Tel # (505) 445-9018

Computers and Security
See: SECURITY & SURVEILLANCE

Computing & Communications: Law & Protection Report   *Business*

Publishing Co: Assets Protection Publishing, PO Box 5323, Madison, WI 53705-0323; Title Tel # (608) 877-1409
Personnel: Publisher, Editor-Paul Shaw
Editorial Description: Focuses on information systems' legal liability risks including: failure to have a disaster recovery program and improper use of vendor software or systems. Also covers computer-related criminal law applied to deterrence, prosecution, and recovery for loss or damage.
General Info: (Formerly Data Processing & Communication Security), Yr. Est. 1975, Monthly, Trim Size-8½ x 11, Offset press, 8 pages, ISSN: 0749-1484, Ind/Abs/Online: CR. JU. PER. IND., 2% ads, 2 Color, Coated
Subscriptions: Indv. $84, Can. $96, For. $116, $10/copy
Circulation: Total-1,200
List Rental: Actives: $75/M

Computing Newsletter   *Association*

Publishing Co: Kansas State University Computing Center, Cardwell Hall, Manhattan, KS 66506; Title Tel # (913) 532-6311
Personnel: Editor-Betsy Edwards, Circ. Mgr.-Jacque Meisner
Editorial Description: Communication between computing center and computer users.
General Info: (Formerly Computing & Telecommunications Activities), Yr. Est. 1972, Monthly, Trim Size-8½ x 11, Sheetfed press, 8 pages, 2 Color
Acquisitons: Publication Bought
Circulation: (100% controlled), Total-800
Printing Co: Kansas State Univ. Printing Services, Kedzie Hall, Manhattan, KS 66506 Tel # (913) 532-6308

Computing Services Newsletter   *Consumer*

Publishing Co: University of California at Berkeley, 215 Evans Hall, Berkeley, CA 94720-0001; Title Tel # (415) 642-5601
Editorial Description: Describes UC Berkeley computing hardware, software, and services.
General Info: Semi-monthly, Sheetfed press, 36 pages, No Color
Circulation: Total-4,000

Connection Ideas

Publishing Co: Advanced Circuit Technology, 118 Northeastern Blvd, Nashua, NH 03062-1919; Title Tel # (603) 880-6000
Personnel: Editor-Jennifer Foden
Editorial Description: Interconnection tips for engineers & designers.
General Info: Yr. Est. 1987, Quarterly, 4 pages, No Color
Circulation: Total-10,000

Construction Computer Applications Newsletter (CCAN)
See: CONSTRUCTION & BUILDING

Consultants' & Contractors' Newsletter
See: BUSINESS & INDUSTRY

Converge-The Multimedia Developer's Resources *Business, Association*

Publishing Co: Multi-Facet Communications, 499 S Sunnyvale Ave, Sunnyvale, CA 94086-6123; Title Tel # (408) 749-0549 Title Fax # (408) 732-1728
Personnel: Editor-Harrison Rose, Law Ed.-Robert Sabath
Editorial Description: Covers business, technical, legal and marketing hands-on, no fluff advice including technical tips from multimedia tool vendors. Bundled with various multimedia development programs including Apple Computer's Apple Multimedia Program option for their developer programs.
General Info: (Formerly Quick Time Forum), Yr. Est. 1992, Bi-monthly, Trim Size-8½ x 11, Web press, 32 pages, ISSN: 1072-9224, 2 Color, Matte, Saddle-stitched
Subscriptions: Indv. $99, Inst. $99, Can. $114, For. $149, $20/copy
Circulation: Total-3,000
Advertising: Accepts Inserts.

Cook Report on Internet-NREN *Business*

Publishing Co: Cook Network Consultants, 431 Greenway Avenue, Ewing, NJ 08618; Title Tel # (609) 882-2572
Editorial Description: Covers internet systems issues and ideas.
General Info: Monthly, Trim Size-8½ x 11, 24 pages, 2 Color, Matte, Saddle-stitched
Subscriptions: Indv. $85

Corporate EFT Report
See: BANKING & FINANCE

Corporate Internet Strategies *Business*

Publishing Co: Cutter Information Corp., 37 Broadway, Ste. 1, Arlington, MA 02174-5552 Fax # (617) 648-1950; Title Tel # (617) 648-8700 Title Fax # (617) 648-8707
Personnel: Publisher-Karen Coburn, Editor-Ed Yourdor, Circ. Mgr.-Beth O'Neill, Mktg. Dir.-Paul Bergeron
Editorial Description: Features information businesses can use to improve their value though the internet and world wide web.
General Info: Yr. Est. 1995, Monthly, Trim Size-8½ x 11, 16 pages, Saddle-stitched
Subscriptions: Indv. $417, Can. $417, For. $477, $33/copy
Advertising: Inquire for rates.
Printing Co: Benjamin Franklin Smith Printers, 320 Stuart St, Boston, MA 02116-5242 Tel # (617) 426-1160

Counterpoint NewsNotes *Business, Scholarly*

Publishing Co: Counterpoint Publishing, 84 Sherman St., Cambridge, MA 02140 Tel # (617) 547-4515 Fax # (617) 547-9064 Parent Co.-Thomson Publishing Co., New York
Personnel: Publisher-Sandy Friedman, Editor-Jonathan Robbins, Graphic Designer-Greg Saucier
Editorial Description: News and information on online and CD access to the Federal Register and other federal reports.
General Info: Irregular, Trim Size-11 x 15, 4 pages, 2 Color, Matte

Cowles Report on Database Marketing
See: ADVERTISING & MARKETING

Culpepper Letter: Software Intelligence for Growth and Profits *Business*

Publishing Co: Culpepper & Assocs., 7000 Peachtree Dunwoody Rd, NE #10, Atlanta, GA 30328-1615; Title Tel # (404) 668-0616 Title Fax # (770) 668-1095
Personnel: Publisher-Warren Culpepper, Editor-Ginger Kernachan, Production Mgr.-Susan Roth
Editorial Description: How-to sales & marketing management for senior software executives. Features survey-based data & case studies.
General Info: Yr. Est. 1979, Monthly, Sheetfed press, 16 pages, ISSN: 8750-3697, 2 Color, Coated, Saddle-stitched
Subscriptions: Indv. $295, $25/copy
Acquistions: Publication Bought
Circulation: Total-3,000
Printing Co: Ripley Communications, 4508 Bibb Blvd Ste B10, Tucker, GA 30084-6232 Tel # (404) 621-9225

CyberEdge Journal *Business, Scholarly* CPM: $241

Publishing Co: Cyberedge Information Services, #1 Gate Six Rd., Ste. G, Sausalito, CA 94965; Title Tel # (415) 331-3343 Title Fax # (415) 331-3643
Personnel: Publisher, Editor-Ben Delaney, Production Mgr.-Rick Freeman
Editorial Description: Newsletter on virtual reality, & 3D interactive environments.
General Info: Yr. Est. 1991, Bi-monthly, Trim Size-8.5 x 11, Desktop press, 32 pages, ISSN: 1061-3099, Ind/Abs/Online: Newsnet, 4 Color, Matte, Saddle-stitched
Subscriptions: Inst. $249, For. $149
Circulation: Total-3,000
Advertising: $725. Accepts Inserts.
List Rental: Actives: 14,000, $200/M
Printing Co: Publications Ink, 1250 45th Street, Suite 200, Emeryville, CA 94608-2924 Tel # (510) 596-9340, Fax # (510) 596-9318

Cybernautics Digest
See: MEDIA & COMMUNICATIONS

Cyberspace PR Newsletter
See: ADVERTISING & MARKETING

DIGIT

Publishing Co: Univ. of Colorado Computing & Network Services, Campus Box 455, Boulder, CO 80309-0001; Title Tel # (303) 492-8176 Title Fax # (303) 492-4198
Personnel: Editor-Suzanne Kincaid, Art Dir.-Treesa Bernstein
Editorial Description: Newsletter of computing and network services at the University of Colorado at Boulder. Features computing and networking news of general and specific interest.
General Info: Yr. Est. 1967, Bi-monthly
Subscriptions: Free To Qualified Recipient
Circulation: Total-3,000

DLA Bulletin
See: LIBRARY

DOS Authority *Business, Consumer*

Publishing Co: Cobb Group, 9420 Bunsen Pky., Ste. 300, Louisville, KY 40220-4206 Tel # (502) 491-1900 Fax # (502) 491-4200 Parent Co.-Ziff-Davis Publishing Co., New York
Editorial Description: For advanced users of MSD-DOS and PC-DOS systems.
General Info: Monthly
List Rental: List Management Co.: Direct Media, Inc., 200 Pemberwick Rd., PO Box 4565, Greenwich, CT 06830 Tel # (203) 532-3713, Fax # (203) 531-1452

DOT. Com

Publishing Co: Business Communications Co., 25 Van Zant St., Ste.13, Norwalk, CT 06855-1781; Title Tel # (203) 853-4266 Title Fax # (203) 853-0348
Personnel: Publisher-Louis Naturman, Editor-C. Toenne, Mktg. Dir.-Robert Butler
Editorial Description: Updates readers on the commercial use of the internet and related platforms.
General Info: Yr. Est. 1994, Monthly, Trim Size-8½ x 11, 14 pages
Subscriptions: Indv. $375, Can. $425, For. $425, $38/copy
List Rental: List Management Co.: W.I. Mail Marketing, 470 Main St. #317, Ridgefield, CT 06877-4516 Tel # (203) 438-6822, Fax # (203) 438-7756, Actives: 120

D/SNUG

Publishing Co: Boston Computer Society, Inc., 101 A First Ave. Suite #2, Waltham, MA 02154 Tel # (617) 290-5700 Fax # (617) 290-5744
General Info: Quarterly

Data *Association*

Publishing Co: Information Technology Association of America, 1616 Fort Myer Dr Ste 1300, Arlington, VA 22209-3103; Title Tel # (703) 522-5055
Personnel: Editor-Shirley Price
Editorial Description: Association newsletter sent to ADAPSO members.
General Info: Bi-monthly, 20 pages, No Color

Data Base Management

Publishing Co: Auerbach Publishers, One Penn Plz., 42nd Floor, New York, NY 10119-0002 Fax # (212) 971-5024 Parent Co.-Warren, Gorham & Lamont, Boston; Title Tel # (212) 971-5000 Title Fax # (212) 971-5025
Personnel: Publisher-Tom Kelly, Editor-Deb Rhoades, Promotion Dir.-Edward Novack
Editorial Description: Provides timely guidance on how to select, install, implement and maintain data base management systems. Subscription includes main volume and 6 bimonthly updates.
General Info: Bi-monthly, Trim Size-6½ x 9, No Color, Newsprint, Looseleaf
Subscriptions: Indv. $395, Can. $395, For. $514
List Rental: Rents Lists

Data Base Newsletter *Business*

Publishing Co: Data Base Research Group, 1 State St., Ste. 1150, Boston, MA 02109-3507; Title Tel # (617) 227-2583 Title Fax # (617) 227-2396
Personnel: Assoc. Publ.-Anne C. Kenney, Publisher, Editor-Ronald Ross, Circ. Mgr.-Gail Sullivan
Editorial Description: Covers a variety of topics in data adminstration.
General Info: Yr. Est. 1974, Bi-monthly, Trim Size-8½ x 11, 20 pages, ISSN: 0735-3677, No Color, Coated
Subscriptions: Indv. $129, For. $156, $24/copy
Circulation: Total-4,581
List Rental: List Management Co.: Taybi Direct East, Inc., 13321 New Hampshire Ave., Ste. 202, Silver Spring, MD 20904-3450 Tel # (301) 680-3633, Fax # (301) 680-3635
Printing Co: Bay State, 2 Watson Pl, Framingham, MA 01701-4109 Tel # (508) 877-0116

Data Base Product Reports   *Business*

Publishing Co: Phillips Decision Point Resources, 1111 Marlkress Road., P.O. Box 5062, Cherry Hill, NJ 08063-5062 Parent Co.-Phillips Business Information, Inc., Potomac; Title Tel # (609) 424-1100 Title Fax # (609) 424-1999
Personnel: Publisher-Lawrence Feidelman, Editor-Michelle Schener, Circ. Mgr.-Carol Bell
Editorial Description: Evaluations & analyses of data base management systems implemented on all types of computer systems.
General Info: Yr. Est. 1984, Monthly, Trim Size-8½ x 11, Desktop press, 24 pages, ISSN: 0740-6800, No Color, Newsprint, Looseleaf
Subscriptions: Indv. $721, Can. $796, For. $796
Acquistions: Publication Bought

Data Center Operations Management

Publishing Co: Auerbach Publishers, One Penn Plz., 42nd Floor, New York, NY 10119-0002 Fax # (212) 971-5024 Parent Co.-Warren, Gorham & Lamont, Boston; Title Tel # (212) 971-5000 Title Fax # (212) 971-5025
Personnel: Publisher-Tom Kelly, Editor-Irene Kim, Promotion Dir.-Edward Novack
Editorial Description: Helps you make sound lost effective decisions in the planning, design, development and administration of data communication systems. Subscription includes one main volume and bi-monthly updates.
General Info: Bi-monthly, Trim Size-6½ x 9, Looseleaf
Subscriptions: Indv. $395, Can. $395, For. $514
List Rental: Rents Lists

Data Channels   *Business*

Publishing Co: Phillips Business Information, Inc., 1201 Seven Locks Rd., Ste 300, Potomac, MD 20854-2958 Tel # (301) 340-1520; Title Tel # (301) 340-2100 Title Fax # (301) 424-4297
Personnel: Publisher-Chris Scotton, Editor-Susan Aluise, Production Mgr.-Sherry Mitchell, Circ. Mgr.-Promotion Dir.-Ruth Zellers
Editorial Description: A bi-weekly executive report covering the data communications industry including standards and developments in OSI, EDI & E-mail.
General Info: (Formerly Applied Networks Report; Telemedia Monitor), Yr. Est. 1972, Bi-weekly, Trim Size-8½ x 11, Sheetfed press, 8 pages, ISSN: 0093-7290, Ind/Abs/Online: NewsNet, DIALOG, Predicasts, No Color
Subscriptions: Indv. $697, Inst. $697, Can. $697, For. $732, $37/copy
Acquistions: Publication Bought, Publication Sold
Advertising: Accepts Inserts.
List Rental: Rents Lists

Data Conversion Update   *Business*

Publishing Co: Data Conversion Laboratory, 18413 Horace Harding Expy, Fresh Meadows, NY 11365-2207 Tel # (718) 357-8700 Fax # (718) 357-8776

Data Entry Awareness Report   *Business*

Publishing Co: Phillips Decision Point Resources, 1111 Marlkress Road., P.O. Box 5062, Cherry Hill, NJ 08063-5062 Parent Co.-Phillips Business Information, Inc., Potomac; Title Tel # (609) 424-1100 Title Fax # (609) 424-1999
Personnel: Publisher-Lawrence Feidelman, Editor-Randi Koenig, Circ. Mgr.-Carol Bell
Editorial Description: Evaluates a data entry system each month, incl. key-to-disc, intelligent terminals, optical character readers, portable data recorders & voice data entry.
General Info: Yr. Est. 1974, Monthly, Offset press, 28 pages, ISSN: 0747-9549, 2 Color, Newsprint, Saddle-stitched, Looseleaf
Subscriptions: Indv. $721, Can. $821, For. $821

Data Processing Digest   *Business*

Publishing Co: Data Processing Digest, Inc., PO Box 1249, Los Angeles, CA 90078-1249; Title Tel # (213) 851-3156 Title Fax # (213) 851-3156
Personnel: Editor-M. Milligan
Editorial Description: Digests of 200 periodicals.
General Info: Yr. Est. 1955, Monthly, Trim Size-8⅜ x 10⅞, Sheetfed press, 32 pages, ISSN: 0011-6858, 2 Color, Newsprint, Saddle-stitched
Subscriptions: Indv. $175, $12/copy
Circulation: Total-4,500

Data Security Letter   *Business, Scholarly*

Publishing Co: Trusted Information Systems, 3060 Route 97, Glenwood, MD 21738 Tel # (301) 854-6889; Title Tel # (301) 854-5338 Title Fax # (301) 854-5363
Personnel: Editor-Sharon Osuna
Editorial Description: The Data Security letter focuses on computer & communications security, with special emphaisis on the lates research & technology news, written by leading computer security specialists from government & industry
General Info: Yr. Est. 1988, Monthly, Trim Size-8.5 x 11, 16 pages, ISSN: 1065-9986
Subscriptions: Indv. $345, Inst. $345, Can. $370, For. $370
Circulation: Readership-300

Data Security Management

Publishing Co: Auerbach Publishers, One Penn Plz., 42nd Floor, New York, NY 10119-0002 Fax # (212) 971-5024 Parent Co.-Warren, Gorham & Lamont, Boston; Title Tel # (212) 971-5000 Title Fax # (212) 971-5025
Personnel: Publisher-Tom Kelly, Editor-Bob Elliott, Production Mgr.-Geoff Braine, Promotion Dir.-Edward Novack
Editorial Description: Technical & management information for the data security administrator. Subscription includes main volume and 6 bimonthly updates.
General Info: Bi-monthly, Trim Size-6½ x 9, ISSN: 0746-7281, Newsprint, Perfect bound, Looseleaf
Subscriptions: Indv. $395, Can. $395, For. $514
Acquistions: Publication Bought
Circulation: Total-3,000
List Rental: Rents Lists

DataComm Report

Publishing Co: Systems Strategies, Inc., 225 W 34th St, New York, NY 10122-0598; Title Tel # (212) 279-8400
Personnel: Editor-Lynn Tusa
Editorial Description: In-depth reports on data communications topics & news analysis on connectivity issues.
General Info: Yr. Est. 1987, Bi-monthly, Desktop press, 20 pages, No Color, Newsprint, Saddle-stitched
Subscriptions: Indv. $450

DataWorld   *Business*

Publishing Co: Faulkner Technical Reports, Inc., 7905 Browning Road, 114 Cooper Center, Pennsauken, NJ 08109; Title Tel # (609) 662-2070 Title Fax # (609) 662-3380
Personnel: Editor-Larry Abbott, Mng. Editor-Janice Wright, Circ. Mgr.-Bill Gaul, Production Mgr.-Bill Schmidt, Adv. Dir., Promotion Dir.-Barbara Forkel
Editorial Description: Four volume looseleaf reference service covers hardware, software and data communications products for mainframes, minicomputers and microcomputers. Also available on CD-ROM with quarterly updates. Keyword and full text retrieval.
General Info: Monthly, Trim Size-8½ x 11, 300 pages, No Color, Newsprint, Looseleaf
Subscriptions: Indv. $1,515

Database Discussion   *Business, Association*

Publishing Co: Institute for Scientific Information, 3501 Market St., Philadelphia, PA 19104-3302 Tel # (215) 386-0100 Fax # (215) 386-2911
Editorial Description: Newsletter for subsacribers to the institute with computer industry information.
General Info: Quarterly

Database Review

Publishing Co: DataBase Associates, PO Box 215, Morgan Hill, CA 95038-0215; Title Tel # (408) 779-0436 Title Fax # (408) 779-3274
Personnel: Publisher-Colin White
Editorial Description: Reviews key developments in the database marketplace. It provides up-to-the-minute information on technology directions & new products across the complete sepctrum of hardware from mainframes to micros.
General Info: Yr. Est. 1989, Bi-monthly, ISSN: 1042-2595
Subscriptions: Indv. $95, Can. $95, For. $115

Datalab Newsletter   *Business*

Publishing Co: Data Conversion Laboratory, 18413 Horace Harding Expy, Fresh Meadows, NY 11365-2207; Title Tel # (718) 357-8700 Title Fax # (718) 357-8776
Personnel: Editor-Doyle Caton
General Info: Yr. Est. 1987, Quarterly
Subscriptions: Indv. $12

Datalus News   *Business, Consumer*

Publishing Co: Datalus News, 4767 Okemos Rd, Okemos, MI 48864-1634; Title Tel # (517) 347-1333 Title Fax # (517) 347-2466
Editorial Description: Datalus' information on the products it carries with a price list included.
General Info: Quarterly, Trim Size-8½ x 11, 4 pages, No Color, Matte, Saddle-stitched

Datapro Report on Main Frame Converters   *Business*

Publishing Co: Datapro Research Corp., 600 Delran Pky, Delran, NJ 08075-1255 Fax # (609) 764-2815; Title Tel # (609) 764-0100
General Info: Monthly
List Rental: List Management Co.: Mal Dunn & Associates, Inc., Hardscrabble Rd., Croton Falls, NY 10519 Tel # (914) 277-5558, Fax # (914) 277-5636

Datapro Reports on Micro Computers   *Business*

Publishing Co: Datapro Research Corp., 600 Delran Pky, Delran, NJ 08075-1255 Tel # (609) 764-0100 Fax # (609) 764-2815
General Info: Monthly
List Rental: List Management Co.: Mal Dunn & Associates, Inc., Hardscrabble Rd., Croton Falls, NY 10519 Tel # (914) 277-5558, Fax # (914) 277-5636

Davis Database

Publishing Co: Herbert W. Davis & Co., One Executive Dr., Ste. 280, Fort Lee, NJ 07024-3311; Title Tel # (201) 944-5580 Title Fax # (201) 944-2044
Personnel: Editor-William Drumm
General Info: Yr. Est. 1974, Monthly, 4 pages
Circulation: Total-20,000

Dealing with Technology
See: BUSINESS & INDUSTRY

Dec Vax/Axp Advisory Service

Publishing Co: Computer Economics, Inc., 5841 Edison Pl., Carlsbad, CA 92008-6519; Title Tel # (619) 438-8100 Title Fax # (619) 431-1126
Personnel: Publisher-Bruno Bassi, Editor-Terrin Lovett, Circ. Mgr.-Denise Tondreau
Editorial Description: Offers manager with Dec Equipment an opportunity to reduce their costs add anticipate the financial impact of new Dec Technologies.
General Info: 6x/yr., Looseleaf
Subscriptions: Indv. $695
List Rental: List Management Co.: Manager: Denise Tondreau; Direct Effect, 1049 Camino Del Mar Ste 4b, Del Mar, CA 92014-2651 Tel # (619) 792-9259, Actives: $150/M

Decisions
  See: PRINTING/GRAPHIC ARTS

Delphi Report, The
  See: MANAGEMENT

Dental Computer Newsletter
  See: DENTAL

Design Automation Technical Committee Newsletter

Publishing Co: Computer Society Press, 1730 Massachusetts Ave NW, Washington, DC 20036-1903; Title Tel # (202) 371-0101
Personnel: Editor-Joanne DeGrsat
General Info: Quarterly
Circulation: Total-794

Design Drafting News
  See: ENGINEERING

Desktop Direct Marketing News
  See: DIRECT MAIL

Desktop Publishing Trader

Publishing Co: Amerasia, 5621 Liberty Creek Dr W, Indianapolis, IN 46254-1037; Title Tel # (317) 291-1706
Personnel: Publisher-Ben Yanto
General Info: Yr. Est. 1987, Bi-monthly, Trim Size-8$\frac{1}{2}$ x 11, Offset press, 16 pages, 3% ads
Subscriptions: Indv. $6, Inst. $10
Acquistions: Publication Bought
Circulation: Total-5,000
Advertising: Inquire for rates.

Digital Directions Report   *Business*

Publishing Co: Computer Economics, Inc., 5841 Edison Pl., Carlsbad, CA 92008-6519; Title Tel # (619) 438-8100 Title Fax # (619) 431-1126
Personnel: Publisher-Bruno Bassi, Editor-Mark McManus, Circ. Mgr.-Michelle Burrler
Editorial Description: Digital Directions Report 'The Financial Advisor to DEC Users' Written from an end-user perspective,Digital Directions Report has always been the first publication anywhere to provide details on the financial ramifications of future DEC products. DigitalDirections Report,gives you the critical information you need to control costs, develop cost-effective strategies, and understand the impact of rapidl
General Info: Yr. Est. 1989, Monthly, Trim Size-8$\frac{1}{2}$ x 11, 8 pages, ISSN: 1047-1693, 2 Color
Subscriptions: Indv. $525, $50/copy
List Rental: List Management Co.: Manager: Denise Tondream; Direct Effect, 1049 Camino Del Mar Ste 4b, Del Mar, CA 92014-2651 Tel # (619) 792-9259, Actives: $150/M

Digital Expo Update   *Business, Scholarly*

Publishing Co: Zero1 Company, 5114 Balcones Woods Dr., #307-389, Austin, TX 78759; Title Tel # (512) 338-1908 Title Fax # (512) 338-1908
Editorial Description: Provide detailed information on computer and technology related conferences, meeting, expos, symposia, and other events worldwide.
General Info: Yr. Est. 1994, Monthly
Subscriptions: Indv. $175, Can. $190, For. $225

Digital Kids Report, The   *Business*

Publishing Co: Jupiter Communications, 627 Broadway, 2nd Fl., New York, NY 10012-2612 Tel # (212) 780-6060 Fax # (212) 780-6075
Personnel: Publisher-Gene DeRose, Editor-Diana Simeon, Mng. Editor-Yvette DeBow, Art Dir.-Ansel Pitcairn
Editorial Description: Covers all aspects of the 'edutainment' industry including the many companies developing child- and family-oriented products and services.
General Info: Monthly, Trim Size-8$\frac{1}{2}$ x 11, 24 pages, 2 Color, Matte, Saddle-stitched
Subscriptions: Indv. $425

Distributed Computing Monitor   *Business*

Publishing Co: Patricia Seybold's Group, 148 State St., 7th Fl., Boston, MA 02109-2506 Tel # (617) 762-5200 Fax # (617) 764-1028; Title Tel # (617) 742-5200 Title Fax # (617) 742-1028
Personnel: Publisher-Patricia Seybold, Editor-Michael Millikin, Circ. Mgr.-Deborah Hay, Production Mgr.-Doug Freeman, Art Dir.-Melissa Hagan, Promotion Dir.-Richard Allsbrook
Editorial Description: Network monitor analysis architectures, systems, platforms, & applications within the distributed network computing environment.
General Info: (Formerly Patricia Seybold's Network Monitor), Yr. Est. 1986, Monthly, Offset press, 30 pages, 2 Color, Recycled, Saddle-stitched
Subscriptions: Indv. $550, Can. $570, For. $585, $50/copy

Distributed Processing Product Reports

Publishing Co: Phillips Decision Point Resources, 1111 Marlkress Road., P.O. Box 5062, Cherry Hill, NJ 08063-5062 Parent Co.-Phillips Business Information, Inc., Potomac; Title Tel # (609) 424-1100 Title Fax # (609) 424-1999
Personnel: Publisher-Lawrence Feidelman, Editor-Michelle Scherir, Circ. Mgr.-Carol Bell
Editorial Description: Evaluate & describe all sorts of hardware, software, peripherals, communications.
General Info: Monthly, Desktop press, 28 pages, ISSN: 0161-7508, 2 Color, Newsprint, Saddle-stitched
Subscriptions: Indv. $721, Can. $796, For. $796

Distributed Processing Technical Committee Newsletter

Publishing Co: Computer Society Press, 1730 Massachusetts Ave NW, Washington, DC 20036-1903; Title Tel # (202) 371-0101
Personnel: Editor-Jane Liu
Editorial Description: Describes recent advances in all aspects of distributed database systems.
General Info: Quarterly
Circulation: Total-1,208

Division of Computing & Information Technology Update

Publishing Co: Clemson University, 104 Holtzendorff Hall, Clemson, SC 29634-0001 Tel # (803) 656-0518; Title Tel # (803) 365-4307
Personnel: Editor-Pam Purcell
General Info: Yr. Est. 1978, Quarterly, Ind/Abs/Online: Charts.Illus.
Circulation: Total-1,000

Do It with Lotus SmartSuite

Publishing Co: IDG Newsletter Corporation, 77 Franklin St., Boston, MA 02110 Tel # (617) 482-8785 Fax # (617) 338-0164; Title Tel # (617) 482-8634 Title Fax # (617) 422-8189
Personnel: Publisher-Craig G. Pierce, Editor-Valerie Murray, Circ. Mgr.-Meredith Seller Doesschante, Production Mgr.-John Forgetta
Editorial Description: Provides tips, advice and hands-on guidance about using Lotus 1-2-3, Ami Pro, Freelance Graphics, Lotus Approach and Lotus Organizer.
General Info: Monthly
Subscriptions: Indv. $59, For. $89

Do It with Macintosh System 7.5

Publishing Co: IDG Newsletter Corporation, 77 Franklin St., Boston, MA 02110; Title Tel # (617) 482-8785 Title Fax # (617) 338-0164
Personnel: Publisher-Craig G. Pierce, Editor-Scott Fields, Circ. Mgr.-Merediyh Seller Doesschate, Production Mgr.-John Forgetta
Editorial Description: Provides tips, advice, and hands-on guidance about using the Mac's system software, networking potential, and applications.
General Info: Monthly
Subscriptions: Indv. $59, For. $89

Do It with Microsoft Office

Publishing Co: IDG Newsletter Corporation, 77 Franklin St., Boston, MA 02110; Title Tel # (617) 482-8785 Title Fax # (617) 338-0164
Personnel: Publisher-Craig G. Pierce, Editor-Jim Pile, Circ. Mgr.-Meredith Seller Doesschate, Production Mgr.-John Forgetta
Editorial Description: Provides tips, advice and hands-on guidance about using Microsoft Word, Microsoft Excel, PowerPoint Microsoft Access, and Microsoft Mail.
General Info: Monthly
Subscriptions: Indv. $59, For. $89

Do It with Microsoft Publisher

Publishing Co: IDG Newsletter Corporation, 77 Franklin St., Boston, MA 02110; Title Tel # (617) 482-8785 Title Fax # (617) 338-0164
Personnel: Publisher-Craig G. Pierce, Editor-Scott Fields, Circ. Mgr.-Meredith Seller Doesschate, Production Mgr.-John Forgetta
Editorial Description: Provides a plethora of design advice, practical tips, and real projects you can create with Microsoft Publisher.
General Info: Monthly
Subscriptions: Indv. $59, For. $89

Document Center Update
  See: LIBRARY

Document Image Automation
  See: MEDIA & COMMUNICATIONS

Document Imaging Report *Business*

Publishing Co: Phillips Publishing, Phillips Business Information, 1201 Seven Locks Rd. Suite 300, Potomac, MD 20854-2958; Title Tel # (301) 340-7788 Title Fax # (301) 340-0419
Personnel: Publisher-Megan St. John, Mag. Ed.-Mary Crowley, Asst. Ed.-Jeannine Fielding, Mktg. Dir.-Karen Rishioki
Editorial Description: Covers electronic imaging issues, including market strategies, case studies, document management and workglow.
General Info: (Formerly Electronic Imaging Report), Bi-weekly, ISSN: 1071-1295
Advertising: Accepts Inserts.
List Rental: Rents Lists

Document Imaging Report
See: ELECTRIC & ELECTRONIC EQUIPMENT

Document Management
Technology *Business*

Publishing Co: Phillips Business Information, Inc., 1201 Seven Locks Rd., Ste 300, Potomac, MD 20854-2958 Tel # (301) 340-1520 Fax # (301) 424-4297
General Info: Monthly
Subscriptions: Indv. $195
Acquistions: Publication Sold

Dun's Dataline *Business, Consumer*

Publishing Co: Dun & Bradstreet Corp., 3 Sylvan Way, Parsippany, NJ 07054-3805 Tel # (201) 455-0900; Title Tel # (201) 605-6438
Personnel: Editor-Pam Shipp
Editorial Description: Informs online users of database contents & applications.
General Info: Yr. Est. 1984, Trim Size-8½ x 11, 4 pages, 2 Color, Matte
Circulation: Total-12,200

EDI Monthly Report *Business*

Publishing Co: Congressional Information Bureau, Inc., 3030 Clarendon Blvd., Ste. 202, Arlington, VA 22201-2845 Tel # (703) 516-4801 Fax # (703) 516-4804; Title Tel # (202) 347-2275 Title Fax # (202) 347-2278
Personnel: Editor-R.P. Cazalas
Editorial Description: Features new developments in electronic data interchange.
General Info: Yr. Est. 1988, Monthly
Subscriptions: Indv. $250
List Rental: List Management Co.: World Innovators, Inc., 72 Park St., New Canaan, CT 06840 Tel # (203) 966-0374, Fax # (208) 966-0926, Actives: 5,750, $135/M

EDI News
See: BUSINESS & INDUSTRY

EDP Auditing *Business*

Publishing Co: Auerbach Publishers, One Penn Plz., 42nd Floor, New York, NY 10119-0002 Fax # (212) 971-5024 Parent Co.-Warren, Gorham & Lamont, Boston; Title Tel # (212) 971-5000 Title Fax # (212) 971-5025
Personnel: Publisher-Tom Kelly, Editor-Eric Birenbaum, Production Mgr.-Geoff Braine, Promotion Dir.-Edward Novack
Editorial Description: Technical & management information for the EDP audit manager. One year subscription includes one main volume containing 80+ articles and six bi-monthly updates with 24 new articles in all.
General Info: Bi-monthly, ISSN: 0746-7265, Newsprint, Saddle-stitched, Looseleaf
Subscriptions: Indv. $395, Can. $395, For. $514
Acquisitions: Publication Bought
List Rental: Rents Lists

EDP In-Depth Report *Business*

Publishing Co: Evans Research Corp. of Canada, 1 Eva Rd. #309, Etobicoke, ON M9C 4Z5 Canada; Title Tel # (416) 621-8814
Personnel: Editor-Robert Payne, Circ. Mgr., Production Mgr.-Debbie Porter
Editorial Description: Reports of primary research into the Canadian information processing industry.
General Info: Yr. Est. 1981, Monthly, Trim Size-8½ x 11, Letrpr. press, 15 pages, Looseleaf
Subscriptions: Indv. $495, $100/copy
Circulation: Total-450

EDP Weekly *Business*

Publishing Co: Computer Age-Millin Publishing Group, 714 Church Street, Alexandria, VA 22314-4202; Title Tel # (703) 739-8500 Title Fax # (703) 739-8505
Personnel: Publisher-S.L. Millin, Sr. Ed.-Charles Bailey, Mng. Editor-Michael Cotter, Contrib. Ed.-Terry Miller, Circ. Mgr.-Ruth Hill, Mktg. Dir.-Thomas Shack, III
Editorial Description: The nation's oldest computer industry pub. delivers the most comprehensive & up-to-date news coverage on the entire industry.
General Info: Yr. Est. 1958, Weekly, Trim Size-8½ x 11, Sheetfed press, 12 pages, ISSN: 0012-7558, Ind/Abs/Online: Info Access Co.
Subscriptions: Indv. $495, Can. $495, For. $542, $35/copy
Circulation: Total-890
List Rental: Rents Lists

EDPACS: The EDP
Auditing, Control &
Security Newsletter *Business*

Publishing Co: Auerbach Publishers, One Penn Plz., 42nd Floor, New York, NY 10119-0002 Fax # (212) 971-5024 Parent Co.-Warren, Gorham & Lamont, Boston; Title Tel # (212) 971-5000 Title Fax # (212) 971-5025
Personnel: Publisher-Kim Horan Kelly, Editor-Belden Menkus, Exec. Ed.-Robert Elliott, Mng. Editor-Deb Rhoades, Adv. Dir.-Blanca Duque, Mktg. Dir.-Sandra Fox, Mktg. Mgr.-Jeanette Burke
Editorial Description: Provides the latest industry news and techniques to thousands of EDP audit, security & IS professionals.
General Info: Yr. Est. 1974, Monthly, Web press, Saddle-stitched
Subscriptions: Indv. $161, Can. $135, For. $176, $135/copy
Acquistions: Publication Bought
Circulation: Total-5,000
Advertising: Inquire for rates.
List Rental: List Management Co.: Manager: Seena Benedek; WG & L List Management, 1 Penn Plz Fl 42, New York, NY 10119-0002 Tel # (212) 971-5000

EECS/ERL News
See: ENGINEERING, ELECTRICAL

EFT Report
See: BANKING & FINANCE

EPS Decisions
See: PRINTING/GRAPHIC ARTS

East European Kranz
Report *Business, Consumer*

Publishing Co: Kranz Research International, 1979 Catrina Ct., San Jose, CA 95124-5500
Personnel: Editor-Marci Kranz
Editorial Description: Report on computer and telecommunication markets in Eastern Europe.
General Info: Yr. Est. 1992, Monthly
Subscriptions: Indv. $225, $30/copy

Education Technology News
See: EDUCATION

Electro Manufacturing
See: MANUFACTURING

Electromagnetic Field Litigation Reporter
See: LAW

Electronic Business Forecast
See: ADVERTISING & MARKETING

Electronic Claims Processing Report
See: INSURANCE

Electronic Education Report
See: EDUCATION

Electronic Information Report
See: MEDIA & COMMUNICATIONS

Electronic Mail & Micro Systems
See: TELECOMMUNICATIONS

Electronic Materials Technology News
See: ELECTRIC & ELECTRONIC EQUIPMENT

Electronic Messaging News
See: TELECOMMUNICATIONS

Electronic Office:
Management &
Technology *Business*

Publishing Co: Faulkner Technical Reports, Inc., 7905 Browning Road, 114 Cooper Center, Pennsauken, NJ 08109; Title Tel # (609) 662-2070 Title Fax # (609) 662-3380
Personnel: Editor-Janet Mann, Mng. Editor-Janice Wright, Circ. Mgr.-Bill Gaul, Production Mgr.-Bill Schmidt, Adv. Dir., Promotion Dir.-Barbara Forkel
Editorial Description: Two volume looseleaf reference service covers planning, purchasing, implementing, & managing automated office technologies.
General Info: Monthly, Trim Size-8½ x 11, 100 pages, No Color, Newsprint, Looseleaf
Subscriptions: Indv. $1,030

Electronic Payment Journal *Business*

Publishing Co: National Payment Corporation, 100 W Kennedy Blvd Ste 260, Tampa, FL 33602-5116; Title Tel # (813) 222-0333 Title Fax # (813) 221-8651
Personnel: Mktg. Mgr.-Michael Boggs
Editorial Description: A publication of the National Payment Corporation.
General Info: Quarterly, Trim Size-8½ x 11, 4 pages, 2 Color, Coated
Subscriptions: Free

Electronic Services Update   *Business*

Publishing Co: IDG Intl. Publishing Services, 31 Milk St., Ste. 210, Boston, MA 02109-5104; Title Tel # (617) 423-9030 Title Fax # (617) 423-0712
Personnel: Publisher-Diane Gamble, Editor-Steven Sieck, Circ. Mgr.-Lee Pillsbury
Editorial Description: For executives concerned with the information industry.
General Info: (Formerly Electronic Info Report), Yr. Est. 1978, Monthly, Trim Size-8½ x 11, Sheetfed press, 15 pages, ISSN: 0738-3843, Ind/Abs/Online: NewsNet, DIALOG, Predicasts, No Color, Saddle-stitched
Subscriptions: Indv. $495, For. $520

Ellipsis   *Business, Consumer*

Publishing Co: Alphabets, Inc., P.O. Box 5448, Evanston, IL 60204 Tel # (708) 328-2733 Fax # (708) 328-1922
Personnel: Editor-Peter Fraterdeus
Editorial Description: Presents new fonts available and short articles.
General Info: Quarterly, Trim Size-11⅜ x 17, 8 pages, 2 Color, Matte
Subscriptions: Indv. $14

Emerging Technology

Publishing Co: American Society of Civil Engineers, 345 E. 47th St., New York, NY 10017-2398 Tel # (212) 705-7996 Fax # (212) 705-7300; Title Tel # (212) 705-7275
General Info: Bi-monthly
Subscriptions: Indv. $110, For. $120, $20/copy
Printing Co: Edwards Bros., Inc., 2500 S. State St., P.O. Box 1007, Ann Arbor, MI 48106 Tel # (313) 769-1000, Fax # (313) 769-4756

Employment Trends
See: EMPLOYMENT

Enterprise Networking   *Business*

Publishing Co: Faulkner Technical Reports, Inc., 7905 Browning Road, 114 Cooper Center, Pennsauken, NJ 08109; Title Tel # (609) 662-2070 Title Fax # (609) 662-3380
Personnel: Editor-Lawrence Abbott, Mng. Editor-Janice Wright, Circ. Mgr.-Bill Gaul, Production Mgr.-Bill Schmidt, Adv. Dir., Promotion Dir.-Barbara Forkel
Editorial Description: Three volume updated reference service, covers product comparisions, product features, current prices, for data communications equipment & service facilities.
General Info: (Formerly Data Communications), Yr. Est. 1993, Monthly, Trim Size-8½ x 11, 100 pages, No Color, Newsprint, Looseleaf
Subscriptions: Indv. $1,450

Environmental Code Book Software Report
See: ENVIRONMENT & ECOLOGY

Environmental Management Information Systems Report
See: ENVIRONMENT & ECOLOGY

Environmental Software Report
See: ENVIRONMENT & ECOLOGY

Executive Computing
Newsletter   *Business*

Publishing Co: Association of Computer Users, 1250 45th St Ste 200, Emeryville, CA 94608-2924; Title Tel # (415) 549-4300 Title Fax # (415) 549-4331
Personnel: Publisher-James Sinkinson, Editor-Jim Sinkinson, Art Dir.-Cynthia Levitas, Promotion Dir.-Steve gordon
Editorial Description: Provides independent reviews of small computer hardware and software.
General Info: Yr. Est. 1974, Monthly, Offset press, 8 pages, ISSN: 0741-0050, No Color, Newsprint
Subscriptions: Indv. $99, $12/copy
Circulation: Total-13,000

FT Systems   *Business*

Publishing Co: ITOM Intl. Co., PO Box 1450, Los Altos, CA 94023-1450; Title Tel # (415) 948-4516 Title Fax # (415) 948-9153
Personnel: Publisher, Editor-Omri Serlin
Editorial Description: Reports & anlayzes business & technical developments in fault-tolerant computers & transaction systems.
General Info: Yr. Est. 1982, Monthly, 16 pages, ISSN: 0740-4980
Subscriptions: Indv. $695, $60/copy

FasTone

Publishing Co: Boston Computer Society, Inc., 101 A First Ave. Suite #2, Waltham, MA 02154 Tel # (617) 290-5700 Fax # (617) 290-5744
General Info: Quarterly

Federal Computer Market
Report   *Business*

Publishing Co: Computer Age-Millin Publishing Group, 714 Church Street, Alexandria, VA 22314-4202; Title Tel # (703) 739-8500 Title Fax # (703) 739-8505
Personnel: Publisher-S.L. Millan, Sr. Ed.-Charles Bailey, Mng. Editor-Michael Cotter, Contrib. Ed.-Terry Miller, Circ. Mgr.-Ruth Hill, Mktg. Dir.-Thomas Shack, III
Editorial Description: Analyzes government procurement regulations, technical evaluation criteria, minority subcontracting, RFP instructions and other issues of interest to vendors and government buyers. Lists of delegations of procurement authority. Industry shorts.
General Info: (Formerly Procurement Systems Digest), Yr. Est. 1958, Bi-weekly, Trim Size-8½ x 11, Offset press, 10 pages, ISSN: 0163-1489
Subscriptions: Indv. $495, For. $519, $35/copy
Circulation: Total-900
List Rental: Rents Lists

Ferris E-Mail Analyzer   *Business*

Publishing Co: Ferris Networks, 353 Sacramento Street, #600, San Francisco, CA 94111
Editorial Description: For information technology professionals that use E-Mail systems.
General Info: Monthly, Trim Size-8½ x 11, 2 Color
Circulation: Total-4,300
List Rental: List Management Co.: List Information Systems, 320 Northern Blvd Ste 11, Great Neck, NY 11021-4807 Tel # (516) 482-2345, Fax # (516) 487-7721, Actives: 4,306, $650/M

Fiber Distributed Data
Interface (FDDI) News   *Business*

Publishing Co: Information Gatekeepers, Inc., 214 Harvard Ave., Boston, MA 02134-4651 Fax # (617) 782-8562; Title Tel # (617) 232-3111 Title Fax # (617) 734-8562
Personnel: Publisher-Paul Polishuk, Circ. Mgr.-Brendan Monroe, Art Dir.-Diana Towers
Editorial Description: Devoted exclusively to developments in FDDI markets, technology, application, standards, and other competitive information.
General Info: Yr. Est. 1990, Monthly, Letrpr. press, ISSN: 1051-1903, 2 Color
Subscriptions: Indv. $575, Can. $575, For. $625, $50/copy
Advertising: Accepts Inserts.
List Rental: Rents Lists
Printing Co: Eagle Graphics, 30 Lancaster St, Boston, MA 02114-1779 Tel # (617) 742-7575

Fiber Optics Sensors &
Systems (FOS2)   *Business*

Publishing Co: Information Gatekeepers, Inc., 214 Harvard Ave., Boston, MA 02134-4651 Fax # (617) 782-8562; Title Tel # (617) 232-3111 Title Fax # (617) 734-8562
Personnel: Editor-Paul Polishuk
Editorial Description: Offer direct access to information on the markets, technology, & applications of the fiber optic sensors industry. Major research & development activities are now providing practical services for automobile, aircraft, medical & process control.
General Info: Monthly, ISSN: 1051-1946
Subscriptions: Indv. $575, Can. $575, For. $525, $50/copy
Advertising: Accepts Inserts.
List Rental: Rents Lists

Filemaker Report, The   *Business, Consumer*

Publishing Co: Elk Horn Publishing, 25420 Via Cincindela, Carmel, CA 93923-8412 Tel # (408) 626-4361 Fax # (408) 626-4362; Title Tel # (408) 726-1232 Title Fax # (408) 726-1233
Personnel: Publisher-Joe Kroeger
Editorial Description: For users of Filemaker software.
General Info: Yr. Est. 1987, Monthly, ISSN: 0896-0313
Subscriptions: Indv. $49, Inst. $49, Can. $53, For. $67
List Rental: List Management Co.: Direct Effect, 1049 Camino Del Mar Ste 4b, Del Mar, CA 92014-2651 Tel # (619) 792-9259, Actives: 29,000, $125/M

Financial Services Report   *Business*

Publishing Co: Phillips Business Information, Inc., 1201 Seven Locks Rd., Ste 300, Potomac, MD 20854-2958 Tel # (301) 340-1520; Title Tel # (301) 340-2100 Title Fax # (301) 424-4297
Personnel: Publisher-Chris Scotton, Editor-Eric Williams, Production Mgr.-Teresa Fleisher, Adv. Dir.-Kim Hudak, Mktg. Dir.-Kelly Ebbs
Editorial Description: Financial service industry & marketing strategies.
General Info: (Formerly Financial Services Week; Securities Marketing News), Yr. Est. 1984, Bi-weekly, Sheetfed press, 8 pages, ISSN: 0894-7260, Ind/Abs/Online: NewsNet, DIALOG, Predicast, Bloomberg., No Color
Subscriptions: Indv. $795, For. $830, $37/copy
Acquistions: Publication Bought, Publication Sold
List Rental: Rents Lists

First Edition

Publishing Co: Lynx Software, PO Box 3510, Los Angeles, CA 90078-3510; Title Tel # (818) 761-5859 Title Fax # (818) 761-7099
Personnel: Editor-Len Latimer
General Info: Monthly
Subscriptions: Indv. $99

Foreign Exchange

Publishing Co: Boston Computer Society, Inc., 101 A First Ave. Suite #2, Waltham, MA 02154 Tel # (617) 290-5700 Fax # (617) 290-5744
General Info: Bi-monthly

Four Hundred, The

Publishing Co: Technology News of America Co., 110 Greene St Apt 1101, New York, NY 10012-3824; Title Tel # (212) 334-9750
Personnel: Publisher-Hesh Wiener, Editor-Timothy Prickett
Editorial Description: Analytical and management articles on the as/400 market.
General Info: Yr. Est. 1990, Monthly, Trim Size-8½ x 11, 12 pages, ISSN: 1049-7757
Subscriptions: Indv. $175, For. $205
Advertising: Inquire for rates.

Foxtalk   *Business*

Publishing Co: Pinnacle Publishing, Inc., PO Box 888, 1800 72nd Ave. Ste. 217, Kent, WA 98035-0888; Title Tel # (206) 251-1900 Title Fax # (206) 251-5057
Personnel: Publisher-David Johnson, Editor-Glenn Hart, Editorial Dir.-Susan Jamison-Harker
General Info: Yr. Est. 1989, Monthly, ISSN: 1042-6302
Subscriptions: Indv. $149, Can. $164, For. $169, $18/copy
Advertising: Accepts Inserts.
List Rental: List Management Co.: Direct Media, Inc., 200 Pemberwick Rd., PO Box 4565, Greenwich, CT 06830 Tel # (203) 532-3713, Fax # (203) 531-1452

Function Key, The   *Consumer*

Publishing Co: WordPerfect Special Interest Group, The, P.O. Box 39742, Tucson, AZ 85751-0742
Tel # (602) 751-0061 Fax # (602) 751-0498
Personnel: Publisher-Donna C. Kamper
General Info: Yr. Est. 1992, Monthly, Trim Size-4½ x 8½, Desktop press, 24 pages, No Color, Saddle-stitched
Subscriptions: Indv. $18, Inst. $18, Can. $23, $2/copy

GCS Users' Group Newsletter   *Association*

Publishing Co: Sandia Labs Computer Applications Div., Livermore, CA 94550

GEM
See: GOVERNMENT

GIS Law
See: GEOGRAPHY

GUI Program News   *Business*

Publishing Co: Worldwide Videotex Co., PO Box 3273, Boynton Beach, FL 33424-3273
Tel # (407) 738-2276 Fax # (407) 738-2276
Editorial Description: Applications for personal computers.
General Info: Yr. Est. 1990, Monthly, Ind/Abs/Online: NewsNet; DIALOG
Subscriptions: Irídv. $150, Inst. $150, Can. $150, For. $165

Gateway Monitor   *Business*

Publishing Co: Gateway 2000, 610 Gateway Dr., Box 2000, North Sioux City, SD 57049-2000;
Title Fax # (605) 232-2023
Personnel: Editor-Andy VanderWiel, Editor-Ann VanderWiel
Editorial Description: Information about Gateway 2000 and the computer industry.
General Info: Irregular, Trim Size-8½ x 11, 8 pages, 2 Color, Recycled, Saddle-stitched
Printing Co: Printed in Canada

Genealogy Bulletin
See: GENEALOGY

Graphics News

Publishing Co: Boston Computer Society, Inc., 101 A First Ave. Suite #2, Waltham, MA 02154
Tel # (617) 290-5700 Fax # (617) 290-5744
General Info: Quarterly

HP Omnigo World

Publishing Co: Thaddeus Computing, Inc., PO Box 869, Fairfield, IA 52556-0869

HP Palmtop Paper   *Business, Consumer*

Publishing Co: Thaddeus Computing, Inc., PO Box 869, Fairfield, IA 52556-0869;
Title Tel # (515) 472-6330 Title Fax # (515) 472-1879
Personnel: Publisher-Hal Goldstein
Editorial Description: For users of this personal computing tool.
General Info: Bi-monthly
Circulation: Total-20,000
Advertising: Inquire for rates.
List Rental: Rents Lists

Handbook of Communications Systems Management   *Business*

Publishing Co: Auerbach Publishers, One Penn Plz., 42nd Floor, New York, NY 10119-0002
Fax # (212) 971-5024 Parent Co.-Warren, Gorham & Lamont, Boston; Title Tel # (212) 971-5000
Title Fax # (212) 971-5025
Personnel: Publisher-Tom Kelly, Editor-Nancy Tyson, Production Mgr.-Geoff Braine, Promotion Dir.-Edward Booth
Editorial Description: Technical and management information for information center managers. Includes evaluating and selecting hardware and software, training end users, and using technology to achieve corporate goals. Subscription includes main volume and 6 bimonthly updates.
General Info: (Formerly End-User Computing Management; Managing the Information Ctr.), Yr. Est. 1985, Bi-monthly, Trim Size-6½ x 7, No Color, Saddle-stitched, Looseleaf
Subscriptions: Indv. $395, Can. $395, For. $514
Acquistions: Publication Bought
List Rental: Rents Lists

Hard Copy Observer   *Business, Consumer*

Publishing Co: Hard Copy Observer, PO Box 304, Newton Highlands, MA 02161-0004;
Title Tel # (617) 332-0708 Title Fax # (617) 332-0342
Personnel: Publisher, Editor-Charles LeCompte
Editorial Description: For users of computer printers and output devicves.
General Info: Monthly
Subscriptions: Indv. $495

Health Systems Leader
See: MANAGEMENT

HealthCare Systems NewsLetter
See: HEALTH

High Performance Computing & Communications Week   *Business*

Publishing Co: King Communications Group, 627 National Press Building, Washington, DC
20045-1601 Tel # (202) 638-4260 Fax # (202) 662-9719
General Info: Yr. Est. 1992, Weekly
Subscriptions: Indv. $697
List Rental: Rents Lists

High Speed Networking Newsletter   *Business*

Publishing Co: Publications Resource Group, P.O. Box 765, N. Adams, MA 01247;
Title Tel # (413) 664-6185 Title Fax # (413) 664-9343
Editorial Description: Covers trends and developments in broad band network technology.
General Info: (Formerly Broad Band Networks & Applications), Yr. Est. 1992, Bi-weekly
Subscriptions: Indv. $545, Can. $495, For. $545

High-Tech Hot Sheet
See: MEDIA & COMMUNICATIONS

High-Tech Hot Wire
See: MEDIA & COMMUNICATIONS

Home Automation News
See: ELECTRIC & ELECTRONIC EQUIPMENT

Home Economist's Computer Newsletter

Publishing Co: E.M. Enterprises, 3 Hickory Rd, Denville, NJ 07834-9315; Title Tel # (201) 627-0502
Personnel: Editor-Elaine Muller
General Info: Yr. Est. 1983, Monthly
Subscriptions: Indv. $12

Horizons
See: ELECTRIC & ELECTRONIC EQUIPMENT

Hot Off the Computer

Publishing Co: Westchester Library System, 8 Westchester Plaza, Elmsford, NY 10523-1604;
Title Tel # (914) 592-8214 Title Fax # (914) 347-3617
Personnel: Editor-Diane Courtney
Editorial Description: Focuses on administrative & public service applications of microcomputers for public libraries.
General Info: Yr. Est. 1983, 5x/yr., Trim Size-8½ x 11, ISSN: 0737-8076
Subscriptions: Indv. $20, Inst. $20, Can. $20, For. $20, $6/copy
Circulation: Total-250

HumanAwareness and Low Vision Perspectives
See: DISABILITY

IBM Residual Value Forecast for IBM Systems & Peripherals   *Business*

Publishing Co: Computer Economics, Inc., 5841 Edison Pl., Carlsbad, CA 92008-6519;
Title Tel # (619) 438-8100 Title Fax # (619) 431-1126
Personnel: Publisher-Bruno Bassi, Editor-Terrin Lovett
Editorial Description: Provides 7-year forecasts for over 200 IBM machines. Also included is leasing rate, relative performance, and top manufacturers and systems information.
General Info: Quarterly, Looseleaf
Subscriptions: Indv. $2,495
List Rental: Rents Lists

IBM Technical Disclosure Bulletin

Publishing Co: IBM Corp., P.O. Box 218, Yorktown Heights, NY 10598-0218 Tel # (914) 945-3831;
Title Tel # (212) 688-3636
Personnel: Editor-J.K. Mosser
Editorial Description: Informs public of development within IBM in its various fields of interest.
General Info: Yr. Est. 1958, Monthly
Circulation: Total-1,400

I.C. Europe
See: INTERNATIONAL TRADE

IC Strategist

Publishing Co: United Communications Group, 11300 Rockville Pike, Ste. 1100, Rockville, MD
20852-3030 Tel # (301) 816-8950 Fax # (301) 816-8945; Title Tel # (301) 961-8700
Personnel: Publisher, Editor-David Douglass, Circ. Mgr.-Sharon Welch
Editorial Description: For managers of end use computing.
General Info: Yr. Est. 1987, Monthly, 16 pages, No Color, Newsprint
Subscriptions: Indv. $335, $28/copy
List Rental: Rents Lists

I.C.C.P. Newsletter — *Business, Association*

Publishing Co: Institute for Certification of Computer Professionals, 2200 E Devon Ave Ste 268, Des Plaines, IL 60018-4501; Title Tel # (708) 299-4270
Personnel: Editor-Carolyn DuShane
Editorial Description: Computer professionals informed on recognition of their certificate by industry.
General Info: Yr. Est. 1977, Monthly
Circulation: Total-14,200

IDC Japan Report — *Business*

Publishing Co: IDG Intl. Publishing Services, 31 Milk St., Ste. 210, Boston, MA 02109-5104; Title Tel # (617) 423-9030 Title Fax # (617) 423-0712
Personnel: Editor-Yuji Ogino, Circ. Mgr.-Lee Pillsbury, Production Mgr.-Cindy Sparrow
Editorial Description: Detailed analysis of Japanese computer market.
General Info: (Formerly EDP Japan Report), Yr. Est. 1973, Monthly, Trim Size-8½ x 11, Sheetfed press, 12 pages, No Color, Saddle-stitched
Subscriptions: Indv. $495, Can. $535, For. $535, $45/copy

IEEE SMC Newsletter — *Association* — CPM: $78

Publishing Co: Institute of Electrical & Electronics Engineers, Inc., 445 Hoes Lane, PO Box 1331, Piscataway, NJ 08855-1331 Tel # (908) 562-3992 Fax # (908) 981-9334 Parent Co.-Institute of Electrical & Electronics Engineers, New York
Personnel: Editor-Madan Singh, Production Ed.-Ann Skrupski, Adv. Mgr., Sales Mgr.-Susan Schneiderman
Editorial Description: Newsletter of the Systems, Man & Cybernetics Society of the IEEE.
General Info: Quarterly, Trim Size-8½ x 11, 12 pages, Coated, Saddle-stitched
Subscriptions: Free With Membership
Circulation: Total-5,082
Advertising: $400.
List Rental: Rents Lists

IMA Bulletin, The

Publishing Co: Intl. MIDI Assn., 5316 W 57th St, Los Angeles, CA 90056-1339; Title Tel # (213) 649-6434 Title Fax # (213) 215-3380
Personnel: Editor-Lachlan Westfall, Circ. Mgr.-S.D. Westfall
Editorial Description: Info on Musical Instrument Digital Interface (MIDI) software, hardware, products & applications. Newsletter free to members. Distribute the MIDI specification & all of its addenda.
General Info: Yr. Est. 1983, Monthly, Web press, 8 pages, No Color, Newsprint
Subscriptions: Indv. $40, Inst. $85, $3/copy
Acquistions: Publication Bought
Circulation: Total-2,500
List Rental: Actives: $100/M
Printing Co: Corp. Impressions, 14720 Keswick St, Van Nuys, CA 91405-1205 Tel # (818) 787-7567

IN SYNC Magazine — CPM: $300

Publishing Co: Agate Publishing, 3314 Arrowhead Rd, Laporte, CO 80535-9321; Title Tel # (303) 484-2626
Personnel: Publisher, Editor-Gregory Zimmerman
Editorial Description: News and how-to for distributed and cooperative applications. Particularly how to link multiple computer systems to gain best advantage from each.
General Info: Yr. Est. 1991, 10x/yr., Sheetfed press, 16 pages, No Color, Matte, Saddle-stitched
Subscriptions: Indv. $50, $8/copy
Circulation: Total-1,000
Advertising: $300.

IQ Quarterly — *Business, Association* — CPM: $191

Publishing Co: IICS Executive Office, 14657 SW Teal Blvd., Ste. 119, Beaverton, OR 97007-6194; Title Tel # (503) 579-4427 Title Fax # (503) 579-6272
Personnel: Editor-Kandy Arnold, Adv. Dir.-Debra Palm, Mktg. Dir.-Eric F. Nathanson
Editorial Description: Conference notes, IICS announcements, and industry information.
General Info: (Formerly ICS Reporter), Yr. Est. 1983, Quarterly, 8 pages, ISSN: 1047-5346, 20% ads
Subscriptions: Free With Membership
Acquistions: Publication Sold
Circulation: Total-6,000
Advertising: $1,150. Accepts Inserts.
List Rental: Actives: 4,400, $300/M, Expires: 5,000, $300/M

I/S Analyzer — *Business*

Publishing Co: United Communications Group, 11300 Rockville Pike, Ste. 1100, Rockville, MD 20852-3030 Tel # (301) 816-8950 Fax # (301) 816-8945; Title Tel # (301) 961-8700 Title Fax # (301) 961-8666
Personnel: Publisher-Doug O'Boyle, Editor-Barbara Mcnurlin
Editorial Description: Professional reports for data processing management, analyzing significant developments.
General Info: (Formerly EDP Analyzer), Yr. Est. 1963, Monthly, Trim Size-8½ x 11, 14 pages, ISSN: 0012-7523, No Color, Newsprint
Subscriptions: Indv. $169, $15/copy
Acquistions: Publication Bought, Publication Sold
List Rental: Rents Lists

IS Budget — *Business*

Publishing Co: Computer Economics, Inc., 5841 Edison Pl., Carlsbad, CA 92008-6519 Tel # (619) 438-8100 Fax # (619) 431-1126
Personnel: Publisher-Bruno Bassi, Editor-Mark McManus, Circ. Mgr.-Michelle Burrier
Editorial Description: News and analysis of IS expenditures and productivity.
General Info: (Formerly DP Budget), Yr. Est. 1982, Monthly, Trim Size-8½ x 11, 8 pages, 2 Color
Subscriptions: Indv. $525, $50/copy
List Rental: List Management Co.: Manager: Denise Tondream; Direct Effect, 1049 Camino Del Mar Ste 4b, Del Mar, CA 92014-2651 Tel # (619) 792-9259, Actives: $150/M

IS Budget International — *Business*

Publishing Co: Computer Economics, Inc., 5841 Edison Pl., Carlsbad, CA 92008-6519; Title Tel # (619) 438-8100 Title Fax # (619) 431-1126
Personnel: Publisher-Bruno Bassi, Editor-Teresa Elms, Production Mgr.-Michelle Burrier
Editorial Description: IS Budget-International Edition 'The Planning Assistant for MIS Executives'. Published monthly, it is the only newletter that tackles today's toughest IS budgeting issues head-on with exhaustively researched line-item cost comparisons by type of industry, installation size, company revenue, and type pf expenditure.
General Info: (Formerly DP Budget International), Yr. Est. 1982, Monthly, Trim Size-8½ x 11, 8 pages, ISSN: 0890-4316, 2 Color
Subscriptions: Indv. $495, $50/copy
List Rental: Actives: $150/M

IS Capacity Management Handbook Series — *Consumer*

Publishing Co: Applied Computer Research, PO Box 82266, Phoenix, AZ 85071-2266; Title Tel # (602) 995-5929
Personnel: Publisher-Philip Howard
Editorial Description: Analytical methods and tools and techniques for performance management/improvement.
General Info: (Formerly EDP Performance Management Handbook), Yr. Est. 1978, Monthly, Ind/Abs/Online: Comp.Lit.Ind., No Color, Matte, Looseleaf
Subscriptions: Indv. $750, Free With Membership
List Rental: Actives: $125/M

ISA Update
See: TELECOMMUNICATIONS

ISCET Update
See: ENGINEERING, ELECTRICAL

ISDN News — *Business*

Publishing Co: Phillips Business Information, Inc., 1201 Seven Locks Rd., Ste 300, Potomac, MD 20854-2958 Tel # (301) 340-1520; Title Tel # (301) 340-2100 Title Fax # (301) 424-4297
Personnel: Publisher-Ellen Hamm, Editor-Susan Aluise, Production Mgr.-Teresa Lowry, Promotion Dir.-Chris Scotton
General Info: Yr. Est. 1988, Bi-weekly, ISSN: 0899-9554, Ind/Abs/Online: NewsNet, DIALOG, Predicasts
Subscriptions: Indv. $597, For. $630
List Rental: Rents Lists

ISR: Intelligent Systems Report — *Business*

Publishing Co: AI Week Inc., 2555 Cumberland Pkwy., #299, Atlanta, GA 30339 Tel # (707) 431-0867 Fax # (770) 432-6969; Title Tel # (770) 431-0867 Title Fax # (770) 432-6909
Personnel: Publisher-John Llewellyn, Editor-David Blanchard
Editorial Description: Covers news and applications of advanced computing technologies, including virtual reality, fuzzy logic, neural networks, expert systems, and speech recognition.
General Info: (Formerly AI Week), Yr. Est. 1984, Monthly, Trim Size-8½ x 11, Sheetfed press, 20 pages, ISSN: 1054-8696, 2% ads, Matte, Saddle-stitched
Subscriptions: Indv. $299, Can. $299, For. $349, $25/copy
Advertising: Accepts Inserts.
List Rental: Rents Lists

ISTE Update
See: EDUCATION

ISWM News
See: EDUCATION

Icon Analyst — *Business, Consumer*

Publishing Co: University of Arizona Computer Science Dept., Gould-Simpson Building, Tucson, AZ 85721-0001; Title Tel # (602) 621-6609 Title Fax # (602) 621-4246
Personnel: Publisher-Ralph Griswold, Editor-Madge Griswold
Editorial Description: In-depth analysis of technical subjects related to the Icon computer programming language.
General Info: Yr. Est. 1989, Semi-monthly, Trim Size-8½ x 11, Sheetfed press, 12 pages, Matte, Saddle-stitched
Subscriptions: Indv. $25, For. $35
Circulation: Total-200
Advertising: Inquire for rates.
Printing Co: University of Arizona Printing & Publishing, W. Stadium, Tucson, AZ 85721-0001 Tel # (602) 621-2571

Icon Newsletter — *Business*

Publishing Co: University of Arizona Computer Science Dept., Gould-Simpson Building, Tucson, AZ 85721-0001; Title Tel # (602) 621-6609 Title Fax # (602) 621-4246
Personnel: Publisher-Ralph Griswold, Editor-Madge Griswold
Editorial Description: Topical information about the computer programming language Icon.
General Info: Yr. Est. 1978, 3x/yr., Trim Size-8½ x 11, Offset press, 12 pages, No Color, Matte
Subscriptions: Free
Circulation: Total-1,600
Printing Co: University of Arizona Printing & Publishing, W. Stadium, Tucson, AZ 85721-0001 Tel # (602) 621-2571

Imaging Service Bureau
News   *Business*   CPM$1280

Publishing Co: Image Publishing, PO Box 3149, Westport, CT 06880-8149;
Title Tel # (203) 222-9310 Title Fax # (203) 222-7871
Personnel: Publisher-Charles Miles, Adv. Dir.-Lois Posher, Art Dir.-Mary Pat Pino, Promotion Dir.-David Miles
General Info: (Formerly Service Bureau Newsletter; Data Conversion Newsletter), Yr. Est. 1986, Semi-monthly, Trim Size-8½ x 11, Offset press, 24 pages, ISSN: 1055-8098, No Color, Saddle-stitched
Subscriptions: Indv. $190, $35/copy
Circulation: Total-750
Advertising: $960.
List Rental: Actives, 30,000, $125/M

Imaging Supplies Monthly   *Business, Consumer*

Publishing Co: BIS Strategic Decisions, 1 Longwater Cir, Norwell, MA 02061-1620;
Title Tel # (617) 982-9500 Title Fax # (617) 878-6650
Personnel: Publisher-Jay Devin, Editor-Bob Leahey, Circ. Mgr.-Michelle LeBrasseur
Editorial Description: Covers consumables for electronic industries, covering consumables for electronic printers, copiers & other imaging equipment to the office, industry & home.
General Info: Yr. Est. 1987, Monthly, 12 pages, ISSN: 1050-6993, 2 Color
Subscriptions: Indv. $325, Can. $375, For. $375, $25/copy
Printing Co: Fotobeam/Brookside, 260 Lexington St, Waltham, MA 02154-4613 Tel # (617) 893-1600

Imaging Systems   *Business*

Publishing Co: Faulkner Technical Reports, Inc., 7905 Browning Road, 114 Cooper Center, Pennsauken, NJ 08109 Tel # (609) 662-2070; Title Tel # (609) 662-7070
Title Fax # (609) 662-3380
Personnel: Editor-Janet Mann, Mng. Editor-Janice Wright, Circ. Mgr.-Nan Gunderson, Production Mgr.-Bill Schmidt, Promotion Dir.-Barbara Forkel
Editorial Description: One volume reference service provides coverage of all products and technologies related to imaging and document management.
General Info: Monthly, Looseleaf
Subscriptions: Indv. $670

Imaging Technology
Report   *Business*

Publishing Co: Microfilm Publishing, Inc., PO Box 950, Larchmont, NY 10538-0950;
Title Tel # (914) 834-3044 Title Fax # (914) 834-3993
Personnel: Publisher, Editor-Mitchell Badler, Circ. Mgr., Production Mgr., Adv. Dir.-Dorothy Miceli
Editorial Description: Covers news of developments, products, cos., applications, & trends related to optical and business imaging technologies.
General Info: Yr. Est. 1988, Monthly, Trim Size-8½ x 11, Offset press, 16 pages, ISSN: 1041-4320, No Color
Subscriptions: Indv. $168, Can. $168, For. $188, $25/copy
Advertising: $660. Accepts Inserts.
Printing Co: Minuteman Press, 1299 North Ave, New Rochelle, NY 10804-2604 Tel # (914) 576-0335

Imaging Update   *Business*

Publishing Co: Worldwide Videotex Co., PO Box 3273, Boynton Beach, FL 33424-3273
Tel # (407) 738-2276 Fax # (407) 738-2276
Editorial Description: Information on the computer graphics industry.
General Info: Yr. Est. 1990, Monthly, Ind/Abs/Online: NewsNet; DIALOG
Subscriptions: Indv. $150, Inst. $150, Can. $150, For. $165

Impact

Publishing Co: Boston Computer Society, Inc., 101 A First Ave. Suite #2, Waltham, MA 02154
Tel # (617) 290-5700 Fax # (617) 290-5744
General Info: Quarterly

In Command
See: OFFICE METHODS & EQUIPMENT

In Sync   *Business*

Publishing Co: Bucknell Computer & Communications Services, Bucknell Univ., Lewisburg, PA 17837 Tel # (717) 524-1801; Title Tel # (717) 524-1789
Personnel: Editor-Marjorie Heine
Editorial Description: Describes changes in the computer system, documents new programs, presents varied uses of the computer, reports activities of the local ACM, announces current procedures for users.
General Info: (Formerly FRCC Newsletter; BCS Newsletter), Yr. Est. 1963, Bi-monthly, Trim Size-8½ x 11, Desktop press, 10 pages, Color-cover
Subscriptions: Free
Circulation: Total-300

In Touch   *Business*

Publishing Co: Informtech Int'l Inc., 10734 Jefferson Blvd. #516, Culver City, CA 90230-4969;
Title Tel # (213) 836-8993 Title Fax # (213) 836-8992
Editorial Description: Newsletter on Informtech's OEM board information and product line.
General Info: Yr. Est. 1992, Quarterly, Trim Size-8½ x 11, 12 pages, No Color, Matte, Saddle-stitched

InCider's AppleWatch   *Business*

Publishing Co: IDG Communications, 86 Elm St., Peterborough, NH 03458-1052
Tel # (603) 924-0100; Title Tel # (603) 924-9471
Personnel: Publisher-Paul Boule, Editor-Peg Brown
Editorial Description: Monitors developments in the Apple II Computer market.
General Info: Yr. Est. 1985, Semi-monthly, Trim Size-8½ x 11, Sheetfed press, 4 pages, 2 Color, Newsprint
Circulation: (100% controlled), Total-1,841
Printing Co: Savron Graphics, 2 Stratton Rd, Jaffrey, NH 03452-1529 Tel # (603) 532-7726

Industrial Automation
Outlook

Publishing Co: Market Intelligence Research Co., 2525 Charleston Rd, Mountain View, CA 94043-1626; Title Tel # (415) 961-9000 Title Fax # (415) 961-5042
Personnel: Publisher-Wyman Bravard, Circ. Mgr.-Jennifer Wiliiams, Editor, Production Mgr.-Sarah Collings, Art Dir.-Russell Haswell
Editorial Description: Marketing and business news for industrial automation covering CAD, CAM, CAE, material handling, and systems integration.
General Info: (Formerly Factory Automation News), Yr. Est. 1987, Monthly, Trim Size-8½ x 11, 16 pages, ISSN: 1051-9440, Ind/Abs/Online: Newsnet, Color-cover, Saddle-stitched
Subscriptions: Indv. $295, $50/copy
Acquistions: Publication Bought
Advertising: Inquire for rates.
List Rental: Rents Lists

Industrial Controls Intelligence
See: ADVERTISING & MARKETING

Infoperspectives   *Business*

Publishing Co: Technology News of America Co., 110 Greene St Apt 1101, New York, NY 10012-3824; Title Tel # (212) 334-9750
Personnel: Publisher-Hesh Weiner, Editor-Sharon Brady
Editorial Description: Annotated statistical reports on commercial use of computers.
General Info: (Formerly Mainstream), Yr. Est. 1980, Monthly, Trim Size-8½ x 11, Sheetfed press, 8 pages, ISSN: 0733-9305, No Color
Subscriptions: Indv. $485, For. $515

Information & Interactive
Services Report   *Association, Business*

Publishing Co: BRP (Washington DC), 1333 H St., NW, Suite 1100, West Tower, Washington, DC 20005-4707; Title Tel # (202) 842-3006 Title Fax # (202) 842-3047
Personnel: Publisher-Andrew Jacobson, Editor-Kevin McGilly, Circ. Mgr.-Nigel Sonariwo, Mktg. Dir.-Adam Goldstein
Editorial Description: News and analysis for the information industry. Covers online, multimedia, electronic shopping and publishing services.
General Info: Bi-weekly, Trim Size-8½ x 11, 14 pages, ISSN: 1059-731X, Ind/Abs/Online: NewsNet, 2 Color, Matte
Subscriptions: Indv. $495, Inst. $495, Can. $495, For. $531
Printing Co: Jim Buckley Offsetting, 1101 Pennsylvania Ave SE, Washington, DC 20003-2229 Tel # (202) 546-0501

Information Broker
See: MEDIA & COMMUNICATIONS

Info to Go   *Business, Consumer*

Publishing Co: Info to Go, P.O. Box 272, Garden Grove, CA 92642-0272
Personnel: Editor-Barbara Garten
Editorial Description: Information on navigating the Internet.
General Info: Monthly, Trim Size-8½ x 11, 12 pages, ISSN: 1074-522X, 2 Color, Matte
Subscriptions: Indv. $48

Information Hotline   *Business, Association*

Publishing Co: Science Associates/International, Inc., 6 Hastings Rd., Marlboro, NJ 07746-1313;
Title Tel # (212) 873-0656 Title Fax # (212) 873-5587
Personnel: Publisher, Editor-Ivan Lyons, Circ. Mgr.-Roxy Bauer, Production Mgr.-Barbara O'Brien
Editorial Description: News on data bases, information networks, innovative information services, and research projects.
General Info: (Formerly Information News, Sources, Profiles), Yr. Est. 1969, Monthly, Trim Size-8½ x 11, Offset press, 16 pages, ISSN: 0360-5817
Subscriptions: Indv. $150, Can. $175, For. $175, $20/copy

Information Industry Bulletin   *Business*

Publishing Co: Digital Information Group, PO Box 110235, Stamford, CT 06911-0235;
Title Tel # (203) 348-2751 Title Fax # (203) 977-8310
Personnel: Editor-Maureen Fleming
Editorial Description: Intelligence service devoted exclusively to the business of information publishing.
General Info: Yr. Est. 1985, Weekly, Trim Size-8½ x 11, Letrpr. press, 6 pages, ISSN: 0885-7660, No Color
Subscriptions: Indv. $395, For. $345, $20/copy

Information Management: Strategy, Systems and Technologies
Business

Publishing Co: Auerbach Publishers, One Penn Plz., 42nd Floor, New York, NY 10119-0002
Fax # (212) 971-5024 Parent Co.-Warren, Gorham & Lamont, Boston; Title Tel # (212) 971-5000
Title Fax # (212) 971-5025
Personnel: Publisher-Tom Kelly, Editor-Mary Ellen MacIsaac, Production Mgr.-Geoff Braine, Promotion Dir.-Edward Novack
Editorial Description: Technical & management information for the MIS manager. One year subscription includes 2 main volumes containing articles and bi-monthly updates providing 30 new articles.
General Info: (Formerly Data Processing Mgmt.), Bi-monthly, ISSN: 0735-9993, No Color, Newsprint, Perfect bound, Looseleaf
Subscriptions: Indv. $495, Can. $495, For. $644
Acquisitions: Publication Bought
Circulation: Total-3,000
List Rental: Rents Lists

Information Privacy
See: SECURITY & SURVEILLANCE

Information Retrieval & Library Automation
Business

Publishing Co: Lomond Pubs., Inc., PO Box 88, Mount Airy, MD 21771-0088;
Title Tel # (301) 829-1496
Personnel: Publisher-Thomas Hattery, Editor-Susan Johnson
Editorial Description: Topical coverage of new technologies, products/equipment, which improve information systems and library services for science, social science, law and medicine.
General Info: Yr. Est. 1964, Monthly, Trim Size-8$\frac{1}{2}$ x 11, Offset press, 12 pages, ISSN: 0020-0220, No Color
Subscriptions: Indv. $66, Can. $66, For. $80, $6/copy
Circulation: Total-1,160
Printing Co: G&H Printing, 203 E Ridgeville Blvd, Mount Airy, MD 21771-5257 Tel # (301) 829-0155

Information Searcher
See: EDUCATION

Infotech Report
See: PUBLIC MANAGEMENT & PLANNING

Ink on Paper
See: PRINTING/GRAPHIC ARTS

Inside CUE
See: EDUCATION

Inside the Internet
Business, Consumer

Publishing Co: Cobb Group, 9420 Bunsen Pky., Ste. 300, Louisville, KY 40220-4206
Tel # (502) 491-1900 Fax # (502) 491-4200 Parent Co.-Ziff-Davis Publishing Co., New York
Editorial Description: Practical advice and instructions for Internet users.
General Info: Yr. Est. 1994, Monthly
Subscriptions: Indv. $59
List Rental: List Management Co.: Direct Media, Inc., 200 Pemberwick Rd., PO Box 4565, Greenwich, CT 06830 Tel # (203) 532-3713, Fax # (203) 531-1452

Inside Market Data
See: BANKING & FINANCE

Inside the New Computer Industry
Business

Publishing Co: Elk Horn Publishing, 25420 Via Cincindela, Carmel, CA 93923-8412
Tel # (408) 626-4361 Fax # (408) 626-4362; Title Tel # (408) 721-1232 Title Fax # (408) 726-1233
Personnel: Publisher-Joe Kroeger, Editor-Andrew Allison
Editorial Description: Computer industry analysis.
General Info: (Formerly RISC Management), Yr. Est. 1988, 11x/yr., 24 pages
Subscriptions: Indv. $675, Can. $675, For. $725
List Rental: List Management Co.: Direct Effect, 1049 Camino Del Mar Ste 4b, Del Mar, CA 92014-2651 Tel # (619) 792-9259, Actives: 4,400, $195/M

Inside PFS: First Publisher
Business

Publishing Co: Cobb Group, 9420 Bunsen Pky., Ste. 300, Louisville, KY 40220-4206 Parent Co.-Ziff-Davis Publishing Co., New York; Title Tel # (502) 491-1900 Title Fax # (502) 491-4200
Personnel: Editor-Mike O'Mara
Editorial Description: Information and news relating to the desktop software.
General Info: Monthly
Subscriptions: Indv. $59

Inside R&D
See: MANUFACTURING

Inside Report on New Media
See: MEDIA & COMMUNICATIONS

Insider
See: HOUSE ORGANS

Inspec Matters
See: ENGINEERING, ELECTRICAL

Integrated Services Digital Network (ISDN)
Business

Publishing Co: Information Gatekeepers, Inc., 214 Harvard Ave., Boston, MA 02134-4651;
Title Tel # (617) 232-3111 Title Fax # (617) 782-8562
Editorial Description: Gives the latest news and analysis on the markets, technology, standards and applications of ISDN. ISDN tariffs and standards are now in place for rapid deployment of ISDN.
General Info: Monthly, ISSN: 0735-1844
Subscriptions: Indv. $575, Can. $575, For. $625, $50/copy

Integrated Voice/Data PBXs
Business

Publishing Co: U.S. Civil Aeronautics Board, Bureau of Operating Rights, 1825 Connecticut Ave NW, Washington, DC 20428-0001; Title Tel # (202) 557-1433
Editorial Description: Explains operation of integrated voice/data PBX's; describes/ evaluates current/future PBX systems.
General Info: Yr. Est. 1983, Annually, Trim Size-8$\frac{1}{2}$ x 11, 175 pages
Subscriptions: $167/copy

Intelligence: The Future of Computing
Business

Publishing Co: Intelligence, PO Box 20008, New York, NY 10025-1510; Title Tel # (212) 222-1123
Title Fax # (212) 222-1123
Personnel: Publisher, Editor-Edward Rosenfeld, Art Dir.-John Wilton
Editorial Description: Covers technologies, like Neural Networks, that will effect future computing.
General Info: Yr. Est. 1984, Monthly, Trim Size-8$\frac{1}{2}$ x 11, Mimeo press, 8 pages, ISSN: 1042-4296, No Color, Newsprint
Subscriptions: Indv. $395, Can. $450, For. $450, $25/copy
Advertising: Accepts Inserts.
List Rental: Rents Lists

Intelligent Manufacturing
See: MANUFACTURING

Intelligent Software Strategies
Business, Consumer

Publishing Co: Cutter Information Corp., 37 Broadway, Ste. 1, Arlington, MA 02174-5552
Fax # (617) 648-1950; Title Tel # (617) 648-8700 Title Fax # (617) 648-8707
Personnel: Publisher-Karen Coburn, Editor, Assoc. Ed.-Curt Hall, Circ. Mgr.-Kara Lovering, Circ. Mgr.-Beth O'Neill, Production Mgr.-Laura St. Clair
Editorial Description: Software/ hardware reviews, trends & forecasts, vendor profiles, application case studies.
General Info: (Formerly Expert Systems Strategies), Yr. Est. 1985, Monthly, 16 pages, ISSN: 1052-7214, Ind/Abs/Online: NewsNet, No Color, Newsprint
Subscriptions: Indv. $447, Can. $447, For. $507, $33/copy
List Rental: Rents Lists
Printing Co: Benjamin Franklin Smith Printers, 320 Stuart St, Boston, MA 02116-5242
Tel # (617) 426-1160

Intelligent Systems Report
Business

Publishing Co: Lionheart Publishing Inc., 2555 Cumberland Pkwy. #299, Atlanta, GA 30339-3908
Tel # (770) 431-0867 Fax # (770) 432-6969
Editorial Description: Features news and applications of such technologies as expert systems neural networks, fuzzy logic, virtual reality, etc.
General Info: (Formerly AI Week), Monthly, ISSN: 1054-8696
Subscriptions: Indv. $299, Can. $299, For. $349

Interactions
See: TELECOMMUNICATIONS

Interactive Content
Business

Publishing Co: Jupiter Communications, 627 Broadway, 2nd Fl., New York, NY 10012-2612
Tel # (212) 780-6060 Fax # (212) 780-6075; Title Tel # (212) 867-6650
Personnel: Circ. Mgr.-Harry R. Larson, Mktg. Mgr.-John Morris
Editorial Description: Covers Internet, online services, CD-ROM and multimedia.
General Info: Yr. Est. 1994, Monthly, Trim Size-8$\frac{1}{2}$ x 11, 24 pages, 2 Color, Matte, Saddle-stitched
Subscriptions: Indv. $495
List Rental: List Management Co.: List Technology Systems Group, Inc., 1001 Ave. of the Americas, New York, NY 10018 Tel # (212) 719-3850, Fax # (212) 719-1878, Actives: 34,000, $150/M

Interactive Marketing Newsletter
See: ADVERTISING & MARKETING

Interactive Public Relations
See: ADVERTISING & MARKETING

Interactive Travel Report
See: TRAVEL

Interactive Video News
See: TELECOMMUNICATIONS

Intercom
See: MEDIA & COMMUNICATIONS

Interface
See: LAW ENFORCEMENT & PENOLOGY

International Calculator Collector
See: HOBBY

International Computer Law
See: LAW

International MIDI Users
Group Newszine   *Business, Association*   CPM: $11

Publishing Co: G-4 Productions, Box 615, Yonkers, NY 10703-0615; Title Tel # (212) 465-3430
Personnel: Feature Ed.-Pat Reale, Circ. Mgr.-Tammy Wu, Adv. Dir.-Paul Hichak, Art Dir.-Warren Gebert
Editorial Description: Published for MIDI users.
General Info: (Formerly MUG), Yr. Est. 1985, Monthly, Trim Size-8$\frac{1}{2}$ x 11, Offset press, 20 pages, 25% ads, No Color, Matte, Saddle-stitched
Subscriptions: Indv. $20, For. $30, $2/copy
Circulation: Total-30,000
Advertising: $350. Accepts Inserts.
List Rental: Actives: 30,000, $50/M

International Software
Report   *Business*

Publishing Co: RM Publishing Corp., 29327 Stonecrest Rd, Rllng Hls Est, CA 90275-5707; Title Tel # (310) 544-5539
Personnel: Editor-Martha Newton
Editorial Description: News, perspectives, and opportunities in the international software marketplace.
General Info: Yr. Est. 1990, Monthly, Trim Size-8$\frac{1}{2}$ x 11, 8 pages, ISSN: 1050-8570
Subscriptions: Indv. $249, For. $299

International Virtual Reality Association
See: ENTERTAINMENT

Internet Business
Advantage   *Business*

Publishing Co: Wentworth Worldwide Media, 1866 Colonial Village Lane, PO Box 10488, Lancaster, PA 17605-0488 Tel # (717) 393-1000; Title Tel # (717) 390-4363 Title Fax # (717) 393-5752
Editorial Description: Dedicated to help readers use the Internet to improve their business.
General Info: Yr. Est. 1994, Monthly
Subscriptions: Indv. $67

Internet Business
Opportunities Report   *Business*

Publishing Co: Thompson Publishing Group, 1725 K Street, NW, Washington, DC 20006 Tel # (202) 872-4000
Personnel: Publisher-Lucy Caldwell-Stair
Editorial Description: Covers new Internet information, software, interfaces etc.
General Info: Yr. Est. 1994, Monthly
Subscriptions: Indv. $380

Internet Business Report
See: BUSINESS & INDUSTRY

Internet Content Report, The
See: TELEVISION & VIDEO

Internet Marketing &
Technology Report   *Business*

Publishing Co: Computer Economics, Inc., 5841 Edison Pl., Carlsbad, CA 92008-6519; Title Tel # (619) 438-8100 Title Fax # (619) 431-1126
Personnel: Publisher-Bruno Bassi, Circ. Mgr.-Michelle Burrier, Adv. Dir.-Anne Zalatan
Editorial Description: Internet offers your business advice from America's top business marketers and technical experts.
General Info: Monthly, Trim Size-8$\frac{1}{2}$ x 11, 8 pages, 2 Color
Subscriptions: Indv. $287
List Rental: List Management Co.: Direct Effect, 1049 Camino Del Mar Ste 4b, Del Mar, CA 92014-2651 Tel # (619) 792-9259, Actives: $150/M

Internet Medicine
See: MEDICINE

Internet Newsroom, The
See: JOURNALISM

Internet Strategies for Education
See: EDUCATION

Internet Voyager   *Business, Consumer*

Publishing Co: Blue Dolphin Communications, 83 Boston Post Rd, Sudbury, MA 01776-2438; Title Tel # (508) 443-6363 Title Fax # (508) 443-9728
Personnel: Publisher-Donald L. Nicholas, Publications Director-Donna Kelly, Editor-Dick Rubinstein, Mng. Editor-Laura Logan
Editorial Description: 'A guide to mastering the Internet.'
General Info: Yr. Est. 1994, Monthly, Trim Size-8$\frac{1}{2}$ x 11, 8 pages, ISSN: 1078-540X, 2 Color
Subscriptions: Indv. $78, Can. $88, For. $98, $10/copy
Circulation: Total-5,000
List Rental: List Management Co.: Direct Media, Inc., 200 Pemberwick Rd., PO Box 4565, Greenwich, CT 06830 Tel # (203) 532-3713, Fax # (203) 531-1452
Printing Co: Newsletter Services, Inc., 9700 Philadelphia Court, Lanham, MD 20706 Tel # (301) 731-5200, Fax # (301) 731-5201

Internet Week   *Business*

Publishing Co: Phillips Business Information, Inc., 1201 Seven Locks Rd., Ste 300, Potomac, MD 20854-2958 Tel # (301) 340-1520 Fax # (301) 424-4297
General Info: Yr. Est. 1995, Weekly, ISSN: 1081-2474
Subscriptions: Indv. $596

Interrupt

Publishing Co: Computer People for Peace, 291 Sterling Pl, Brooklyn, NY 11238-4403
General Info: Yr. Est. 1973, Quarterly

Investment Newsletter

Publishing Co: Boston Computer Society, Inc., 101 A First Ave. Suite #2, Waltham, MA 02154 Tel # (617) 290-5700 Fax # (617) 290-5744
General Info: Bi-monthly

Japan Robotics   *Consumer*

Publishing Co: Hataye, 43 Deerwood, Aliso Viejo, CA 92656-2105
Personnel: Publisher, Editor-John Hataye
Editorial Description: Newsletter on what Japanese papers report on latest robotics development.
General Info: Yr. Est. 1983, Monthly, 8 pages, Color, Newsprint
Subscriptions: Indv. $175, $20/copy
Circulation: Total-1,000

Job Express
See: BUSINESS & INDUSTRY

Kentucky Appellate
Reporter   *Business*

Publishing Co: Appellate Review, Inc., 500 Country Lane, Louisville, KY 40207 Tel # (502) 897-5079 Fax # (502) 899-7791
Personnel: Publisher-Patricia Owen
Editorial Description: Digests of Kentucky appellate decisions.
General Info: Yr. Est. 1994, Semi-monthly, ISSN: 1075-7791
Subscriptions: Indv. $177

Kermit News   *Business*

Publishing Co: Kermit Development & Distribution, Columbia Academic Info Systems, 612 W. 115th St., New York, NY 10025; Title Tel # (212) 854-3703 Title Fax # (212) 663-8202
Personnel: Editor-Christine M. Gianone
Editorial Description: Information on Kermit communicatons software programs and uses.
General Info: Irregular, Trim Size-8$\frac{1}{2}$ x 11, 32 pages, ISSN: 0899-9309, 2 Color, Matte, Saddle-stitched
Subscriptions: Free To Qualified Recipient

Keywords   *Consumer*

Publishing Co: SPSS Inc., 444 N Michigan Ave, Chicago, IL 60611-3962; Title Tel # (312) 329-2400
Personnel: Editor-Elisabeth Adams
Editorial Description: For users of SPSS Inc. software products.
General Info: (Formerly SPSS Inc. Newsletter), Yr. Est. 1974, Quarterly, Trim Size-8$\frac{1}{2}$ x 11, Sheetfed press, 20 pages, ISSN: 0917-7342, Color, Coated, Saddle-stitched
Circulation: Total-20,000

KidTECH News
See: EDUCATION

LAMALUG: The Apple
COREspondent   *Consumer, Association*

Publishing Co: Lansing Area Mac & Lisa Users Group, PO Box 27372, Lansing, MI 48909-7372
Editorial Description: Info about Apple products and services and events for Lansing Area Mac and Lisa Group Users Group.
General Info: Monthly

LAN Product News   *Business*

Publishing Co: Worldwide Videotex Co., PO Box 3273, Boynton Beach, FL 33424-3273 Tel # (407) 738-2276 Fax # (407) 738-2276
Editorial Description: Information on the computer Local Area Network industry.
General Info: Yr. Est. 1990, Monthly, Ind/Abs/Online: NewsNet; DIALOG
Subscriptions: Indv. $150, Inst. $150, Can. $150, For. $165

LIPService   *Business, Association*

Publishing Co: Long Island Pick Society, c/o ComprehensiveComputerSvces, 555 Broadhollow Rd., Ste. 302, Melville, NY 11747
Personnel: Editor-Walter Bergman
Editorial Description: News and information for PICK programmers.
General Info: Monthly, Trim Size-8$\frac{1}{2}$ x 11, 4 pages, Matte
Subscriptions: Free With Membership

Laboratory Computer Letter
See: SCIENCE

Lap Gazette

Publishing Co: Boston Computer Society, Inc., 101 A First Ave. Suite #2, Waltham, MA 02154 Tel # (617) 290-5700 Fax # (617) 290-5744
General Info: Bi-monthly

Laptopics   *Business*

Publishing Co: FirstGroup, 2013 Crompond Rd, Yorktown Heights, NY 10598-4230;
Title Tel # (914) 245-0701 Title Fax # (914) 245-0655
Personnel: Editor-Morton Sinkoff
General Info: Yr. Est. 1991, Monthly
Subscriptions: Indv. $245

Laser Focus World
Bulletin   *Business*

Publishing Co: PennWell Publishing Company, Ten Tara Blvd., 5th Floor, Nashua, NH 03062-2801
Tel # (603) 891-9174 Fax # (603) 891-0574 Parent Co.-PennWell Publishing Co., Tulsa
Editorial Description: Electro-optic 1/6 page product advertisements that produce high-volume, high-quality sales leads.
General Info: Tri-annually, 100% ads
Circulation: Total-50,000
Advertising: Inquire for rates.

Law Office Automation and Technology
See: LAW

Law Office Technology Review
See: LAW

Lawyers' Micro Users
Group Newsletter   *Business*

Publishing Co: Lawyers' Micro Users Group Newsletter, 333 E Ontario St Apt 2102b, Chicago, IL 60611-3033; Title Tel # (312) 951-8451
Personnel: Publisher-Dolores Finez, Editor-Paul Bernstein
Editorial Description: Law office automation concepts; systems; product reviews. Online resources, data bases & conferencing.
General Info: Yr. Est. 1983, Monthly, Ind/Abs/Online: Newsnet
Subscriptions: Indv. $75
Printing Co: News Type Service, PO Box 1806, Glendale, CA 91209-1806

Lawyer's PC
See: LAW

Leader's Legal Tech
Newsletter

Publishing Co: Leader Publications, Inc., 345 Park Avenue South, New York, NY 10010 Parent Co.-New York Law Publishing Co., New York; Title Tel # (212) 545-6170 Title Fax # (212) 696-1848
Personnel: Publisher-Stuart Wise, Editor in Chief, Editor-Stephen Lief, Circ. Mgr.-Kerry Kyle, Mktg. Dir.-Rose-Ann Morangelei
Editorial Description: Reports on products & trends in law office technology.
General Info: Yr. Est. 1983, Monthly, Trim Size-8½ x 11, Offset press, 8 pages, ISSN: 0738-0186, 2 Color, Newsprint, Saddle-stitched
Subscriptions: Indv. $195, $16/copy
Acquistions: Publication Sold
Printing Co: Columbus Bookbinding, 1343 Belfast Ave, Columbus, OH 31904 Tel # (206) 323-9313, Fax # (206) 323-2987

Leahy Newsletter   *Business*

Publishing Co: Leahy Newsletter, PO Box 467, Tustin, CA 92681-0467; Title Tel # (714) 835-3394
Title Fax # (714) 835-3396
General Info: Yr. Est. 1978, Monthly, Offset press, 4 pages
Subscriptions: Indv. $350, Inst. $350, Can. $350, For. $365
List Rental: List Management Co.: Twin Peaks Press, PO Box 129, Vancouver, WA 98666-0129
Tel # (206) 694-2462, Fax # (206) 696-3210

Legal Publisher, The
See: LAW

Local Area Networks
Newsletter (LAN)   *Business*

Publishing Co: Information Gatekeepers, Inc., 214 Harvard Ave., Boston, MA 02134-4651
Fax # (617) 782-8562; Title Tel # (617) 232-3111 Title Fax # (617) 734-8562
Personnel: Publisher, Editor-Paul Polishuk, Circ. Mgr.-Brendan Monroe, Art Dir.-Diana Towers
Editorial Description: Allows you to remain up-to-date on the markets, technology, standards and applications in the local area network industry. New developments in 100 Mbps twisted wire pairs for FDDI and ATM are also covered.
General Info: Yr. Est. 1983, Monthly, Trim Size-8½ x 11, ISSN: 1051-1962
Subscriptions: Indv. $575, Can. $575, For. $625, $50/copy
Advertising: Accepts Inserts.
List Rental: Rents Lists
Printing Co: Eagle Graphics, 30 Lancaster St, Boston, MA 02114-1779 Tel # (617) 742-7575

LocalNetter Newsletter   *Business, Consumer*

Publishing Co: Architecture Technology Corp., PO Box 24344, Minneapolis, MN 55424-0344
Fax # (612) 829-5871; Title Tel # (612) 935-2035
Personnel: Editor in Chief-Kenneth J. Thurber, Editor-Gordon A. Palzer
Editorial Description: Devoted to all aspects of (computer) local area networking.
General Info: Yr. Est. 1981, Monthly, Trim Size-8½ x 11, Offset press, 36 pages, ISSN: 0886-2397, 2 Color, Matte, Case bound
Subscriptions: Indv. $300, For. $350, $35/copy

MCIC Publication

Publishing Co: Minnesota Computer Industry Coalition, 365 Summit Ave, Saint Paul, MN 55102-2120; Title Tel # (612) 290-2846
Personnel: Editor-Earl Joseph
Editorial Description: Articles related to Minnesota's computer industry. Includes hardware, software, application, services, educational & other areas.
General Info: Yr. Est. 1989, Semi-monthly, 16 pages
Subscriptions: Indv. $16
Circulation: Total-2,000

MIC/INFO   *Business*

Publishing Co: MIC, 1111 Marlkress Rd., P.O. Box 5062, Cherry Hill, NJ 08013;
Title Tel # (609) 424-1100 Title Fax # (609) 484-1999
Personnel: Publisher-L. Feidelman, Editor-J. Fidler, Circ. Mgr.-Carol Bell
Editorial Description: News releases captured electronically, on over 6000 vendors. Contains complete news releases.
General Info: Yr. Est. 1967, Weekly
Subscriptions: Indv. $2,195, Can. $2,270

MLA News
See: LIBRARY

MPC Advantage   *Business, Consumer*

Publishing Co: Microcomputer Publishing Center, Inc., 4 W 20th St, New York, NY 10011-4203
Editorial Description: Information on Apple products.
General Info: Quarterly, Trim Size-8½ x 11, 6 pages, No Color, Coated, Saddle-stitched

MSDS Software Report
See: ENVIRONMENT & ECOLOGY

Macintosh Multimedia &
Product Registry   *Business, Consumer*   CPM: $45

Publishing Co: Redgate Communications Corp., 660 Beachland Blvd., Vero Beach, FL 32963;
Title Tel # (407) 231-6904 Title Fax # (407) 231-7872
Personnel: Editor-Paulette Lee, Circ. Mgr.-Julie Van Goasbeck, Production Mgr.-Joan Hanke, Publisher, Adv. Dir.-Kevin Fallon, Art Dir.-Mark Ballard
Editorial Description: Contains feature articles, case studies & product reviews, plus an extensive directory of more than 8000 Macintosh software, hardware & peripherals, including the Newton message pad and CD-Rom titles.
General Info: Yr. Est. 1984, 10x/yr., Trim Size-8½ x 11, 12 pages, Ind/Abs/Online: America Online, AppleLink, eWorld, 2 Color, Matte, Saddle-stitched
Subscriptions: Indv. $40, Inst. $40, Can. $60, For. $100, $15/copy
Circulation: (BPA), Total-55,000
Advertising: $2,500.
List Rental: List Management Co.: Worldata, 5200 Town Center Circle, Boca Raton, FL 33486
Tel # (407) 368-8200, Fax # (407) 368-8345, Actives: 27,000, $200/M

Macintosh Tips & Tricks   *Business, Consumer*   CPM: $15

Publishing Co: Giles Road Press, PO Box 212, Harrington Park, NJ 07640-0212;
Title Tel # (201) 767-7001 Title Fax # (201) 767-7457
Personnel: Publisher, Editor-Maria Langer
Editorial Description: A news and productivity publication for Apple Macintosh computer users.
General Info: Yr. Est. 1992, Monthly, Trim Size-8½ x 11, Offset press, 8 pages, ISSN: 1070-6720, 2 Color, Other
Subscriptions: Indv. $15, Can. $20, For. $25, $3/copy
Circulation: Total-10,000
Advertising: $150. Accepts Inserts.

Macintosh Update   *Business*

Publishing Co: Datalex Corp., 402 Amherst St Ste 303, Nashua, NH 03063-4228
Personnel: Publisher, Editor-Keith Thompson
General Info: Yr. Est. 1989, Bi-monthly
Subscriptions: Indv. $99, $8/copy
Acquistions: Publication Bought

Mainframe Communications
Report   *Business*

Publishing Co: DataTrends Pubs., Inc., 895 B Harrison Street SE, PO Box 4460, Leesburg, VA 22075 Tel # (703) 779-0574; Title Tel # (703) 641-0444 Title Fax # (703) 760-9365
Personnel: Publisher-Paul Ochs, Editor-Tim Wilson, Circ. Mgr.-Barbara Davis, Promotion Dir.-Steve Ochs
Editorial Description: Covers products that numerous vendors are creating for SNA environment, as well as IBM's improvements & strategies for SNA.
General Info: (Formerly SNA Communications Report), Yr. Est. 1986, Bi-weekly, Trim Size-8½ x 11, Sheetfed press, 10 pages, ISSN: 1040-1393, Ind/Abs/Online: NewsNet, DIALOG, Predicasts, Newsprint
Subscriptions: Indv. $475
Acquistions: Publication Bought, Publication Sold

Mainframe Computing   *Business*

Publishing Co: Worldwide Videotex Co., PO Box 3273, Boynton Beach, FL 33424-3273
Tel # (407) 738-2276 Fax # (407) 738-2276
Editorial Description: Covers computer mainframes.
General Info: Yr. Est. 1990, Monthly, Ind/Abs/Online: NewsNet; DIALOG
Subscriptions: Indv. $150, Inst. $150, Can. $150, For. $165

Managing & User Computing

Publishing Co: Bankers Research Inc., 34 Imperial Ave # 431, Westport, CT 06880-4304; Title Tel # (212) 971-5000
Personnel: Editor-Nancy Tyson
General Info: Yr. Est. 1987, Monthly
Subscriptions: Indv. $96

Managing Open Systems   *Business*

Publishing Co: Faulkner Technical Reports, Inc., 7905 Browning Road, 114 Cooper Center, Pennsauken, NJ 08109; Title Tel # (609) 662-2070 Title Fax # (609) 662-3380
Personnel: Editor-Vic Melis, Mng. Editor-Janice Wright, Circ. Mgr.-Nan Gunderson, Production Mgr.-Bill Schmidt, Promotion Dir.-Barbara Forkel
Editorial Description: Two volume reference set provides 'How To' management articles on open systems migration, along with coverage of vendors and products that support open environments.
General Info: Monthly, 80 pages, Looseleaf
Subscriptions: Indv. $1,075

Managing System Development   *Business*

Publishing Co: Applied Computer Research, PO Box 82266, Phoenix, AZ 85071-2266; Title Tel # (602) 995-5929 Title Fax # (602) 995-0905
Personnel: Publisher-Phillip Howard, Editor-Janet Butler
Editorial Description: Newsletter providing productivity improvement ideas & techniques for software development.
General Info: (Formerly System Development), Yr. Est. 1981, Monthly, Trim Size-8$\frac{1}{2}$ x 11, Web press, 16 pages, ISSN: 0275-6617, Ind/Abs/Online: Comput.Lit.Ind., 3% ads, 2 Color, Newsprint
Subscriptions: Indv. $199, $25/copy
Circulation: Total-600

Manufacturing Applications   *Business*

Publishing Co: Auerbach Publishers, One Penn Plz., 42nd Floor, New York, NY 10119-0002 Fax # (212) 971-5024 Parent Co.-Warren, Gorham & Lamont, Boston; Title Tel # (212) 971-5000
General Info: Yr. Est. 1986, Monthly
Subscriptions: Indv. $68

Manufacturing Market Insider
See: MANUFACTURING

Manufacturing News
See: MANUFACTURING

Manufacturing Technology
See: MANUFACTURING

Maple Tech   *Business, Consumer*

Publishing Co: Sponsor-Waterloo Maple Software, Birkhauser Boston, Inc., 675 Massachusetts Ave., Cambridge, MA 02139 Tel # (617) 876-2333 Fax # (617) 876-1272 Parent Co.-Springer-Verlag Inc., New York
Personnel: Editor-Tony Scott
Editorial Description: Forum for communication between creators and users of Maple software.
General Info: (Formerly Maple Technical Newsletter), Yr. Est. 1987, Semi-annually, ISSN: 1061-5733
Subscriptions: Indv. $36, Inst. $46, $30/copy
Advertising: Accepts Inserts.

Marketing Pulse
See: MEDIA & COMMUNICATIONS

Marketing Technology
See: ADVERTISING & MARKETING

McGraw-Hill's Tech Transfer Report
See: U.S. (& CANADIAN) FED. GOV'T.

McTrans
See: TRAFFIC & TRANSPORTATION

Medical Software Reviews
See: MEDICINE

Medicine on the Net
See: HOSPITALS & NURSING HOMES

Meridian Data, Inc.

Publishing Co: Meridan Data, Inc., 5615 Scotts Valley Dr # 200, Scotts Valley, CA 95066-3424; Title Tel # (408) 476-5858
General Info: Yr. Est. 1988, Quarterly, 6 pages

Metropolitan Area Networks (MAN)   *Business*

Publishing Co: Information Gatekeepers, Inc., 214 Harvard Ave., Boston, MA 02134-4651 Fax # (617) 782-8562; Title Tel # (617) 232-3111 Title Fax # (617) 734-8562
Personnel: Publisher-Paul Polishuk, Circ. Mgr.-Brendan Monroe
Editorial Description: Provides worldwide coverage of the lastest developments in technology, standards & applications of MANs. New techologies such as SONET, ATM and SMDS are providing users & carries with a wide range of new access possibilities.
General Info: Yr. Est. 1990, Monthly, Letrpr. press, ISSN: 1057-5383, 2 Color
Subscriptions: Indv. $575, Can. $575, For. $625, $50/copy
Advertising: Accepts Inserts.
List Rental: Rents Lists
Printing Co: Eagle Graphics, 30 Lancaster St, Boston, MA 02114-1779 Tel # (617) 742-7575

Micro Alert: The Canadian Microcomputer Reference Guide   *Business*

Publishing Co: Roslin Publishing, Inc., 24 Follis Avenue, Toronto, ON M6G 1S3 Canada; Title Tel # (416) 536-1897 Title Fax # (416) 536-5032
Personnel: Publisher, Editor-Doug Sinclair
Editorial Description: Provides product specifications and configuration information on the top 21 microcomputer manufacturers.
General Info: Yr. Est. 1990, Monthly
Subscriptions: Can. $750

Micro Computers & Software   *Business*

Publishing Co: Faulkner Technical Reports, Inc., 7905 Browning Road, 114 Cooper Center, Pennsauken, NJ 08109; Title Tel # (609) 662-2070 Title Fax # (609) 662-3380
Personnel: Editor-Jerry Caron, Mng. Editor-Janice Wright, Circ. Mgr.-Bill Gaul, Production Mgr.-Bill Schmidt, Adv. Dir.-Barbara Forkel
Editorial Description: Two volume looseleaf reference service provides complete coverage of microcomputers, peropherals and PC-based software.
General Info: (Formerly Microworld), Semi-monthly, Trim Size-8$\frac{1}{2}$ x 11, 100 pages, No Color, Newsprint, Looseleaf
Subscriptions: Indv. $1,005

Micro Software Marketing   *Business*

Publishing Co: Micro Software Marketing, PO Box 380, Congers, NY 10920-0380; Title Tel # (914) 268-5925
Personnel: Publisher, Editor-Scott Witt
Editorial Description: Industry newsletter for software publishers & marketers.
General Info: Yr. Est. 1982, Monthly, Offset press, 8 pages, ISSN: 0738-6354, No Color
Subscriptions: Indv. $87, Can. $87, For. $97
List Rental: List Management Co.: WMI/Worldata, 5200 Town Center Circle, Boca Raton, FL 33486 Tel # (407) 393-8200, Fax # (407) 368-8345, Actives: 8,100

MicroView   *Business, Association*

Publishing Co: Canadian Institute of Chartered Accountants, 277 Wellington Street West, Toronto, ON M5V 3H2 Canada Tel # (416) 977-3222 Fax # (414) 204-3416; Title Tel # (416) 962-1242 Title Fax # (416) 962-3375
Personnel: Publisher-R. Cuthbertson, Editor-Hugh Hardie, Editor-Blair Whelan
General Info: Yr. Est. 1986, 10x/yr., Trim Size-8$\frac{1}{2}$ x 11, 200 pages, 2 Color, Matte, Saddle-stitched
Subscriptions: Indv. $205, Can. $195

Microbanker's High-Tech Banking Strategies
See: BANKING & FINANCE

Microcomputer Communications   *Business*

Publishing Co: Faulkner Technical Reports, Inc., 7905 Browning Road, 114 Cooper Center, Pennsauken, NJ 08109; Title Tel # (609) 662-2070 Title Fax # (609) 662-3380
Personnel: Editor-Jerry Caron, Mng. Editor-Janice Wright, Circ. Mgr.-Bill Gaul, Production Mgr.-Bill Schmidt, Adv. Dir., Promotion Dir.-Barbara Forkel
Editorial Description: Management and product reports on PC communications equipment, facilities and software, including E-mail and micro-host links.
General Info: Yr. Est. 1987, Monthly, 100 pages, No Color, Looseleaf
Subscriptions: Indv. $870

Microcomputer Industry Update   *Business*

Publishing Co: IMR, INC-Industry Market Reports, 960 N. San Antonio Rd., Suite 130, Los Altos, CA 94022-1322; Title Tel # (415) 941-6679
Personnel: Publisher-K. V. Blackford, Editor-George Weiser, Circ. Mgr.-Virginia Schnalle
Editorial Description: Abstracts of microcomputer trade press organized by market segment, Personal Computers, High-End Systems, Software, Peripherals, Local Area Networks, & Distribution.
General Info: Yr. Est. 1983, Monthly, Trim Size-8$\frac{1}{2}$ x 11, Sheetfed press, 90 pages, ISSN: 0741-6016, 2 Color, Newsprint, Saddle-stitched
Subscriptions: Indv. $295, Can. $295, For. $340
Acquistions: Publication Bought, Publication Sold

Microcomputer Trainer   *Business*

Publishing Co: Systems Literacy, Inc., 696 9th St, Secaucus, NJ 07094-3029;
Title Tel # (201) 330-8923 Title Fax # (201) 330-0163
Personnel: Publisher, Editor-Loretta Weiss-Morris, Circ. Mgr.-Barbara Schinkle, Production Mgr.-
Susan Lapczynski, Promotion Dir.-Don Hauptman
Editorial Description: The microcomputer trainer provides practical soutions and strategies for the
professional responsible for building end-user skills.
General Info: Yr. Est. 1991, Monthly, 12 pages, ISSN: 1055-3258, 2 Color, Matte
Subscriptions: Indv. $265, Can. $280, For. $290, $25/copy
Circulation: Total-10,000
Printing Co: Admiral Photo, 47 West St., New York, NY 10006

Micrographics Newsletter
See: OFFICE METHODS & EQUIPMENT

Microlink

Publishing Co: Mankato State Univ., PO Box 109, Mankato, MN 56002-0109;
Title Tel # (507) 389-5953
Personnel: Editor-Kenneth Pengelly
General Info: Yr. Est. 1986, Quarterly, 6 pages
Circulation: (100% controlled), Total-350

Microprocessor Report   *Business*

Publishing Co: MicroDesign Resources Inc., 874 Gravenstein Hwy. S., #14, Sebastopol, CA 95472;
Title Tel # (707) 824-4004 Title Fax # (707) 823-0504
Personnel: Publisher-Michael Slater, Editor-Linley Gwennap, Circ. Mgr.-Elaine Stubblefield,
Production Mgr.-Suzanne Gifford, Mktg. Dir.-Joseph McIntyre
Editorial Description: Devoted to covering developments in microprocessors, system design and
chips by providing technical analysis and insight.
General Info: Yr. Est. 1987, 17x/yr., Trim Size-$8\frac{1}{2}$ x 11, 30 pages, ISSN: 0899-9341, 2 Color
Subscriptions: Indv. $495, For. $595
Circulation: Total-2,700

Microsoft Developer
Network News   *Business*

Publishing Co: Microsoft Press, One Microsoft Way, Redmond, WA 98052-6399;
Title Tel # (206) 882-8080 Title Fax # (206) 936-7329
Personnel: Editor-Pat Bellamah, Sales & Mktg. Dir.-Jim McCarthy
Editorial Description: Newsletter for subscribers to Microsoft's Developer Network program.
General Info: Bi-monthly, Trim Size-$11\frac{1}{2}$ x $17\frac{1}{2}$, 16 pages, 2 Color, Newsprint

Microsoft Directions   *Business*

Publishing Co: Redmond Communications, 2661 Bel-Red Road Ste201, Bellevue, WA 98008-5544
Tel # (206) 882-3396 Fax # (206) 885-0848
Personnel: Publisher-Jeff Parker, Editor-Rob Horwitz, Circ. Mgr.-Mary Huber, Production Mgr.-Kelly
Jones, Promotion Dir.-Andy Dellon
Editorial Description: In-depth intelligence about Microsoft's current and emerging technology,
written by Microsoft veterans with privileged access to inside informaiton. Includes monthly news
briefs to keep readers informed on what's happening and what's shipping.
General Info: Yr. Est. 1992, 10x/yr.
Subscriptions: Indv. $595, Inst. $595, Can. $595, For. $648

Microsoft Press Window

Publishing Co: Microsoft Press, One Microsoft Way, Redmond, WA 98052-6399
Tel # (206) 882-8080; Title Tel # (206) 828-7794
Personnel: Editor-Karen Meredith
Editorial Description: Designed to help booksellers understand software & hardware markets so that
informed purchases can be made.
General Info: Yr. Est. 1984, Bi-monthly, 4 pages
Circulation: Total-5,000

Microsoft Quarterly   *Consumer*

Publishing Co: Microsoft Corp., One Microsoft Way, Redmond, CA 98052-6399
Tel # (206) 882-8080 Fax # (800) 546-7516; Title Tel # (212) 245-2100
Personnel: Editor in Chief-Sharon McKenna, Mng. Editor-Jon F. Ganio
Editorial Description: News from Microsoft on events, new hardware and software.
General Info: Quarterly

Microsoft Works in
Education   *Association*

Publishing Co: International Society for Technology in Education, 1787 Agate St, Eugene, OR
97403-1923; Title Tel # (503) 346-4414 Title Fax # (503) 346-5890
Personnel: Publisher-Dave Moursund, Editor-Seymour Hantling, Circ. Mgr.-Patti Van Orstrand,
Production Mgr.-Kerry Lutz, Adv. Dir.-Lynda Ferguson, Art Dir.-Percy Franklin, Promotion Dir.-
Martin Boyesn
Editorial Description: For educators using Microsoft works in the classroom. For pre-college and
college level curriculum. Use with IBM PC's, Apple Macintosh computers.
General Info: Yr. Est. 1989, Quarterly, Trim Size-$8\frac{1}{2}$ x 11, Sheetfed press, 25 pages, ISSN: 1046-
1981, 12% ads, 4 Color, Matte, Saddle-stitched
Subscriptions: Indv. $23, Can. $35, For. $33, $6/copy
Advertising: $370. Accepts Inserts.
List Rental: Hotline: 12,000, $75/M
Printing Co: Univ. of Oregon Press, Univ. of Oregon/Allen Hall, Eugene, OR 97403
Tel # (503) 346-3794, Fax # (503) 346-0935

Midrange Systems
Advisory Service

Publishing Co: Computer Economics, Inc., 5841 Edison Pl., Carlsbad, CA 92008-6519;
Title Tel # (619) 438-8100 Title Fax # (619) 431-1126
Personnel: Publisher-Bruno Bassi, Editor-Terrin Lovett, Circ. Mgr.-Denise Tondream
Editorial Description: Provides objective price/performance comparisons of midrange systems and
products, and analyzes the strengths, weaknesses, and performance of competing midrange
systems from IBM, DEC and HP.
General Info: Yr. Est. 1993, 6x/yr., Looseleaf
Subscriptions: Indv. $995
List Rental: List Management Co.: Manager: Denise Tondream; Direct Effect, 1049 Camino Del Mar
Ste 4b, Del Mar, CA 92014-2651 Tel # (619) 792-9259

Military Robotics
See: MILITARY & NAVAL

Mini' App'les   CPM: $120

Publishing Co: Minnesota Apple Computer Users' Group, Inc., PO Box 796, Hopkins, MN
55343-0796; Title Tel # (612) 229-6952
Personnel: Editor-Michelle Johnson, Circ. Mgr.-Rand Sibet, Production Mgr.-Dave Undlin, Adv. Dir.-
Sharon Gondek
Editorial Description: Features articles on new products & Techniques for Apple Computer users.
General Info: Yr. Est. 1978, Monthly, Trim Size-$8\frac{1}{2}$ x 11, 32 pages, 2% ads, Saddle-stitched
Subscriptions: Indv. $20, $3/copy
Acquistions: Publication Bought
Circulation: Total-1,000
Advertising: $120.
List Rental: Actives: $80/M
Printing Co: Account Manager: Joseph Commers; Commers Printing, Inc., 7130 University Ave NE,
Fridley, MN 55432-3100

Minicomputer Reports   *Business*

Publishing Co: Faulkner Technical Reports, Inc., 7905 Browning Road, 114 Cooper Center,
Pennsauken, NJ 08109; Title Tel # (609) 662-2070 Title Fax # (609) 662-3380
Personnel: Editor-Larry Abbot, Mng. Editor-Janice Wright, Production Mgr.-Bill Schmidt, Adv. Dir.,
Promotion Dir.-Barbara Forkel
Editorial Description: Two volume looseleaf reference guide to mid-range computing issues &
products, covering mid-range hardware & peripherals.
General Info: Yr. Est. 1970, Monthly, 50 pages, Looseleaf
Subscriptions: Indv. $1,190

Minicomputer/LAN
Applications Analyzer   *Business*

Publishing Co: International Management Services, 363 East Central St., Franklin, MA 02038-1300
Fax # (508) 520-1558; Title Tel # (508) 520-1555 Title Fax # (508) 420-3338
Personnel: Publisher-Raymond Wenig, Editor-Terry Pardoe, Circ. Mgr.-Naomi Wehring
Editorial Description: Guidance on use of LAN's personal computers andclient/server systems.
General Info: Yr. Est. 1982, Bi-monthly, Trim Size-$8\frac{1}{2}$ x 11, Desktop press, 12 pages, Saddle-
stitched
Subscriptions: Indv. $95
List Rental: Rents Lists

Mobile Data Report   *Business*

Publishing Co: Telecom Publishing Group, 1101 King St Ste 444, Alexandria, VA 22314-2944 Parent
Co.-Capitol Publications, Inc., Alexandria; Title Tel # (703) 683-4100 Title Fax # (703) 739-6490
Personnel: Publisher-Chris Vestal, Editor-Alan Reiter, Circ. Mgr.-Liz Soper, Production Mgr.-James
Willis, Adv. Dir.-Joe Viviani, Mktg. Dir.-Betsy Martens
Editorial Description: Covers wireless information technology, including mobile electronic
messaging, pages, satellites, & private data networks.
General Info: Yr. Est. 1989, Bi-weekly, Trim Size-$8\frac{1}{2}$ x 11, 12 pages, ISSN: 1040-7022, Ind/Abs/
Online: Newsnet, Predicasts, No Color, Newsprint
Subscriptions: Indv. $495, For. $645
Acquistions: Publication Sold
List Rental: Actives: $185/M
Printing Co: Carr Printing, PO Box 7, Endicott, NY 13761-0007 Tel # (607) 748-0481

Mobile Letter

Publishing Co: IDG Newsletter Corporation, 77 Franklin St., Boston, MA 02110;
Title Tel # (617) 482-8785 Title Fax # (617) 338-0164
Personnel: Publisher-Craig G. Pierce, Editor-J. Gerry Purdy, Circ. Mgr.-Meredith Seller Doesschate,
Production Mgr.-John Forgetta
Editorial Description: Insider's guide to mobile computing and data communications.
General Info: Monthly
Subscriptions: Indv. $595, For. $695

Modem User News   *Business*

Publishing Co: Worldwide Videotex Co., PO Box 3273, Boynton Beach, FL 33424-3273
Tel # (407) 738-2276 Fax # (407) 738-2276
Editorial Description: Information and product news on modems.
General Info: Yr. Est. 1989, Monthly, Ind/Abs/Online: NewsNet; DIALOG
Subscriptions: Indv. $150, Inst. $150, Can. $150, For. $165

Monitor
See: MEDIA & COMMUNICATIONS

Multimedia & Technology   *Business*

Publishing Co: Warren, Gorham & Lamont, 31 Saint James Ave., Boston, MA 02116-4112 Parent Co.-Thomson Professional Publications, Stamford; Title Tel # (617) 423-2020 Title Fax # (617) 423-1914
Personnel: Publisher-Larry Selby, Mktg. Dir.-Sandra Fox
General Info: Yr. Est. 1994, Monthly
Subscriptions: Indv. $195
List Rental: List Management Co.: Manager: Seena Benedek; WG & L List Management, 1 Penn Plz Fl 42, New York, NY 10119-0002 Tel # (212) 971-5000

Multimedia Business Report   *Business, Association*

Publishing Co: Simba Information, Inc., 213 Danbury Rd. PO Box 7430, Wilton, CT 06897-7430 Fax # (203) 834-1771 Parent Co.-Cowles Business Media, New York; Title Tel # (203) 834-0033 Title Fax # (203) 834-0729
Personnel: Publisher-Chris Elwell, Editor-Elizabeth Estroff, Circ. Mgr.-Cara Paul, Mktg. Dir.-Michael Genaro
Editorial Description: The only publication consistently monitoring the strategies companies use to publish, market & sell multimedia titles. Provides a focus on the intellectual property side of new media. Give multimedia's likely impact on important publishing markets.
General Info: (Formerly Multimedia Computing & Presentations), Yr. Est. 1992, Weekly, Trim Size-8½ x 11, Desktop press, 8 pages, ISSN: 1051-953X, 2 Color
Subscriptions: Indv. $496, For. $546
List Rental: Rents Lists
Printing Co: Success Printing, 10 Pearl Street, Norwalk, CT 06850 Tel # (203) 847-1112, Fax # (203) 846-2770

Multimedia Daily   *Business*

Publishing Co: BRP (Washington DC), 1333 H St., NW, Suite 1100, West Tower, Washington, DC 20005-4707 Tel # (202) 842-3006 Fax # (202) 842-3047; Title Tel # (202) 842-0520 Title Fax # (212) 475-1790
Personnel: Publisher-Adam Goldstein, Editor in Chief-Rod Kuckro, Editor-Sharon McLoone
Editorial Description: Focuses on the alliances that are shaping the information marketplace.
General Info: Yr. Est. 1994, Daily, Trim Size-8½ x 11, 4 pages, ISSN: 1079-4212, No Color
Subscriptions: Indv. $595

Multimedia Monitor   *Business*

Publishing Co: Future Systems Incorporated, PO Box 26, Falls Church, VA 22040-0026; Title Tel # (703) 241-1799 Title Fax # (703) 532-0529
Personnel: Publisher, Editor-Rockley Miller, Production Mgr.-Vicki Reeve, Circ. Mgr., Art Dir.-Kiturahn Neppl
Editorial Description: Features applications, technology and industry news for multimedia, interactive video, videodisc, CD-ROM and related fields.
General Info: (Formerly Videodisc Monitor/Multimedia & Videodisc Monitor), Yr. Est. 1983, Monthly, Trim Size-8½ x 11, Letrpr. press, 32 pages, ISSN: 0739-7089, Ind/Abs/Online: Newsnet,Predicasts, No Color, Coated, Saddle-stitched
Subscriptions: Indv. $395, Inst. $150, Can. $425, For. $425, $25/copy
Circulation: Total-1,500
Advertising: Accepts Inserts.
List Rental: List Management Co.: Manager: Vicki Reeve; Performance Marketing, P.O Box 32699, Laughlin, NV 89028 Tel # (702) 299-0011, Fax # (702) 299-0224, Actives: 28,198, $125/M
Printing Co: Corporate Press, 403 Brightseat Rd., Landover, MD 20785-4706 Tel # (301) 499-9200, Fax # (301) 499-5435

Multimedia Networking Newsletter   *Business*

Publishing Co: Publications Resource Group, P.O. Box 765, N. Adams, MA 01247; Title Tel # (413) 664-6185 Title Fax # (413) 664-9343
Editorial Description: Covers multimedia networking systems.
General Info: Yr. Est. 1993, Monthly
Subscriptions: Indv. $545, Can. $495, For. $545

Multimedia Telecommunication News
See: TELECOMMUNICATIONS

NAQP Quick Bytes

Publishing Co: Natl. Assn. of Quick Printers, 401 N. Michigan Ave., Chicago, IL 60611-4267; Title Tel # (312) 644-6610
Personnel: Editor-John Giles, Circ. Mgr., Production Mgr.-Chris Martin, Promotion Dir.-Brian Pugliese
Editorial Description: Briefing on computer hardware & software available to quick printers.
General Info: (Formerly CUG News), Yr. Est. 1982
Circulation: Total-580

NCCBMI Newsletter

Publishing Co: Natl. Consortium for Computer-Based Music Instruction, School of Music, Univ. of Illinois, Urbana, IL 61801; Title Tel # (217) 333-0675
Personnel: Editor-Michael Arenson
General Info: Yr. Est. 1980, Bi-monthly
Subscriptions: Indv. $5
Circulation: Total-300

NFAIS Newsletter
See: LIBRARY

NSRA News   *Business, Association*

Publishing Co: National Service Robot Assn., 900 Victors Way Ste 220, Ann Arbor, MI 48108-1779; Title Tel # (313) 994-6088 Title Fax # (313) 994-3338
Personnel: Editor-Jeffrey Burnstein
Editorial Description: Examines the latest developments in robotics for applications in health care, security, space, home use and related non-manufacturing areas.
General Info: Yr. Est. 1988, Quarterly
Circulation: Total-2,500
List Rental: Rents Lists

NYLA Bulletin
See: LIBRARY

NYSERNet User   *Consumer, Association*

Publishing Co: NYSERNet, Inc., 200 Elwood Davis Rd, Liverpool, NY 13088-6147 Tel # (315) 453-2912 Fax # (315) 453-3052; Title Tel # (315) 443-4120 Title Fax # (315) 425-7518
General Info: (Formerly NYSERNET News), Yr. Est. 1990, Quarterly
Subscriptions: Free To Qualified Recipient

National Information Infrastructure News   *Business*

Publishing Co: Thompson Publishing Group, 1725 K Street, NW, Washington, DC 20006 Tel # (202) 872-4000
Editorial Description: Covers 'inside' Washington news about new standards, latest funding, equipment and more.
General Info: 22x/yr.

National Keyword Forum

Publishing Co: Communication Architects, PO Box 300, Lynnwood, WA 98046-0300; Title Tel # (206) 774-4461
Personnel: Editor-J.G. Lowder
General Info: (Formerly Natl. 2/12/16 Forum), Yr. Est. 1984, Monthly, Letrpr. press, 4 pages
Subscriptions: Indv. $25
Circulation: Total-900

National Report on Computers & Health
See: HEALTH

Natural Resources Computer Newsletter
See: ENVIRONMENT & ECOLOGY

NetWare/Internet Exchange, The

Publishing Co: IDG Newsletter Corporation, 77 Franklin St., Boston, MA 02110; Title Tel # (617) 482-8785 Title Fax # (617) 338-0164
Personnel: Publisher-Craig G. Pierce, Editor-Peter Loshim, Circ. Mgr.-Meredith S. Doesschate, Production Mgr.-John Forgetta
Editorial Description: Technical tips & Techniques and advice for NetWare administrators who need to connect to the Internet.
General Info: Monthly
Subscriptions: Indv. $159, For. $189

Netline   *Business*

Publishing Co: Telecommunications Reports, 1333 H St. NW, 2nd Fl., West Tower, Washington, DC 20005; Title Tel # (202) 842-3022
Editorial Description: The inside report on computer networks. Analysis, discussion of network vendors' products & strategies; solutions for users.
General Info: (Formerly PC Netline), Yr. Est. 1984, Monthly, Trim Size-8½ x 11, Sheetfed press, 16 pages, ISSN: 0892-9467, Ind/Abs/Online: NewsNet, DIALOG, Predicasts, 2 Color, Newsprint, Saddle-stitched
Subscriptions: Indv. $497, $45/copy
Acquistions: Publication Bought, Publication Sold

Network
See: MANAGEMENT

Network Economics Letter   *Business*

Publishing Co: Computer Economics, Inc., 5841 Edison Pl., Carlsbad, CA 92008-6519 Tel # (619) 438-8100 Fax # (619) 431-1126
Personnel: Publisher-Bruno Bussi, Editor-Mark McManus, Circ. Mgr.-Michelle Burrier
Editorial Description: Overview for MIS and network professionals involved in network strategies.
General Info: Yr. Est. 1993, Monthly, Trim Size-8½ x 11, 8 pages, ISSN: 1069-126X, 2 Color
Subscriptions: Indv. $395, $40/copy
List Rental: List Management Co.: Manager: Denise Tondream; Direct Effect, 1049 Camino Del Mar Ste 4b, Del Mar, CA 92014-2651 Tel # (619) 792-9259, Actives: $150/M

Network Management Perspective

Publishing Co: CSI03COM, 3165 Kifer Rd # Csi03com, Santa Clara, CA 95051-0804; Title Tel # (408) 562-6646 Title Fax # (408) 748-1273
Personnel: Publisher-Marianne Cohn, Editor-Suzanne Dowling, Circ. Mgr.-Cynthia Chambers
Editorial Description: Single source objective news letter covering multivendor network management technology.
General Info: Yr. Est. 1988, Monthly
Subscriptions: Indv. $350, For. $385, $29/copy
Circulation: Total-1,000

Network Management Systems & Strategies   *Business, Consumer*

Publishing Co: DataTrends Pubs., Inc., 895 B Harrison Street SE, PO Box 4460, Leesburg, VA 22075 Tel # (703) 779-0574; Title Tel # (703) 760-0660 Title Fax # (703) 760-9365
Personnel: Publisher-Paul Ochs, Editor-Patricia Everett, Circ. Mgr.-Gennifer Chenault, Production Mgr.-Myra Nicholas
Editorial Description: Analysis of new technologies,markets, and network vendor strategies.
General Info: Yr. Est. 1989, Bi-weekly, Desktop press, 10 pages, ISSN: 1043-1217, Ind/Abs/Online: NewsNet,Predicasts, DIALOG, No Color, Other
Subscriptions: Indv. $445, Can. $445, For. $493
Advertising: Accepts Inserts.

Network Security Observations

Publishing Co: DataNet Security Holding Inc., 1825 I Street N.W., Suite #400, Washington, DC 20006 Fax # (202) 429-9574; Title Tel # (202) 775-4947
Personnel: Editor in Chief-F. Bertil Fortrie
General Info: Yr. Est. 2027, Bi-monthly, 1,500 pages, ISSN: 1079-1302, Looseleaf
Subscriptions: Indv. $225
Circulation: Total-2,200

Networks Update   *Business*

Publishing Co: Worldwide Videotex Co., PO Box 3273, Boynton Beach, FL 33424-3273 Tel # (407) 738-2276 Fax # (407) 738-2276
Editorial Description: Information on private, business, and military computer networks.
General Info: Yr. Est. 1989, Monthly, Ind/Abs/Online: NewsNet; DIALOG
Subscriptions: Inst. $150, Can. $150, For. $165

New Media News   *Business, Association*

Publishing Co: Boston Computer Society, Inc., 101 A First Ave. Suite #2, Waltham, MA 02154 Tel # (617) 290-5700 Fax # (617) 290-5744; Title Tel # (617) 252-0600 Title Fax # (617) 577-9365
Personnel: Editor-David Guenette
Editorial Description: Cover computer reliant communications.
General Info: Yr. Est. 1986, Quarterly
Circulation: Total-2,500

New Technology Week
See: SCIENCE

News from the Center

Publishing Co: American Music Center, 30 W. 26th St., #1001, New York, NY 10010-2011; Title Tel # (212) 366-5260
General Info: Yr. Est. 1995, Quarterly

Newsday Connections
See: NEWSPAPER INDUSTRY

Newsletter of Engineering Analysis Software
See: ENGINEERING

NexTech Users Group Newsletter   *Business, Association*

Publishing Co: NexTech Systems Corp., 3671 Old Yorktown Rd., Shrub Oak, NY 10588; Title Tel # (914) 962-6000 Title Fax # (914) 962-1338
Editorial Description: For users of the Interactive Fulfillment System.
General Info: Yr. Est. 1992, Bi-monthly

Next Wave Stocks   *Business*

Publishing Co: Core Communications, 98 Cuttermill Rd., Great Neck, NY 11021 Tel # (516) 487-8322 Fax # (516) 487-8141
Editorial Description: Reports on emerging growth stocks, particularly in new technologies.
General Info: Yr. Est. 1995, Monthly, Trim Size-8½ x 11, 4 pages, 2 Color, Matte

Notes Report, The   *Business*

Publishing Co: IDG Newsletter Corporation, 77 Franklin St., Boston, MA 02110 Tel # (617) 482-8785 Fax # (617) 338-0164; Title Tel # (617) 482-8634 Title Fax # (617) 422-8189
Personnel: Publisher-Craig G. Pierce, Editor-Jim O'Donnell, Circ. Mgr.-Meredith Seller Doesschate, Production Mgr.-John Forgetta
Editorial Description: The Notes Report provides its readers with the latest product information, the hottest tips, and the most knowledgeable forum in the fast-paced Notes marketplace.
General Info: Monthly
Subscriptions: Indv. $295, For. $335
Advertising: Inquire for rates.

Nursing Educators MicroWorld
See: NURSING

OPS: The Data Center Newsletter   *Business*

Publishing Co: Auerbach Publishers, One Penn Plz., 42nd Floor, New York, NY 10119-0002 Fax # (212) 971-5024 Parent Co.-Warren, Gorham & Lamont, Boston; Title Tel # (212) 971-5000
Personnel: Editor-Judy Jones
General Info: Yr. Est. 1986, Monthly
Subscriptions: Indv. $98

OS/2 Connect   *Business*

Publishing Co: M. Bryce & Associates, 777 Alderman Rd, Palm Harbor, FL 34683-2604; Title Tel # (813) 786-4567 Title Fax # (813) 786-4765
Personnel: Publisher-Milt Bryce, Editor, Circ. Mgr.-Tim Bryce
Editorial Description: News and information on IBM's OS/2 operating system.
General Info: (Formerly Management Visions; Antics), Yr. Est. 1995, Monthly, Other press, 100 pages, ISSN: 1081-4892, 5% ads, Color, Saddle-stitched
Subscriptions: Free To Qualified Recipient
Circulation: Total-3,000
Advertising: Inquire for rates.

OSI Product and Equipment News   *Business*

Publishing Co: DataTrends Pubs., Inc., 895 B Harrison Street SE, PO Box 4460, Leesburg, VA 22075 Tel # (703) 779-0574; Title Tel # (703) 760-0660 Title Fax # (703) 760-9365
Personnel: Editor-Michael Cooney
General Info: Yr. Est. 1988, Monthly
Subscriptions: Indv. $465

OSINetter Newsletter   *Business*

Publishing Co: Architecture Technology Corp., PO Box 24344, Minneapolis, MN 55424-0344; Title Tel # (612) 935-2035 Title Fax # (612) 829-5871
Personnel: Editor in Chief-Kenneth Thurber, Editor-Gordon A. Palzer
Editorial Description: Covers products and company activity in the area of open systems interconnection.
General Info: Yr. Est. 1985, Monthly, Trim Size-8½ x 11, Offset press, 30 pages, ISSN: 0888-6997, 2 Color, Matte, Other
Subscriptions: Indv. $372, Can. $432, For. $432, $50/copy
List Rental: Rents Lists

OSRA Newsletter   *Association*

Publishing Co: Office Systems Research Assn., S.W. Missouri State Univ., 901 South National Ave., Springfield, MO 65804-0089; Title Tel # (417) 836-5616 Title Fax # (417) 836-6337
General Info: Yr. Est. 1981, Quarterly, Trim Size-8½ x 11, Desktop press, 8 pages, No Color, Other
Subscriptions: Free With Membership
Circulation: Total-300
Advertising: Inquire for rates.

Object-Oriented Strategies   *Business*

Publishing Co: Cutter Information Corp., 37 Broadway, Ste. 1, Arlington, MA 02174-5552 Tel # (617) 648-8700; Title Tel # (617) 648-8702 Title Fax # (617) 648-1950
Personnel: Publisher-Karen Coburn, Editor-Paul Harmon, Assoc. Ed.-Curt Hall, Circ. Mgr.-Kara Lovering, Circ. Mgr.-Beth O'Neill, Production Mgr.-Ellen McHale, Promotion Dir.-Paul Bergeron
Editorial Description: Features software/hardware reviews, trends, forecasts, analysis, vendor profiles, application studies, etc.
General Info: Yr. Est. 1991, Monthly, Trim Size-8½ x 11, 16 pages, ISSN: 1059-4108, Ind/Abs/ Online: NewsNet, Saddle-stitched
Subscriptions: Indv. $497, Can. $497, For. $567, $33/copy
List Rental: Rents Lists
Printing Co: Benjamin Franklin Smith Printers, 320 Stuart St, Boston, MA 02116-5242 Tel # (617) 426-1160

Off-Line   *Consumer*

Publishing Co: Univ. of Illinois at Urbana Champaign-Computing Svcs. Office, 150 Digital Computer Lab., 1304 W. Springfield, Urbana, IL 61801; Title Tel # (217) 333-6236
Personnel: Editor-Lynn Bilger
General Info: Yr. Est. 1969, Bi-monthly, Trim Size-8½ x 11, Web press, 35 pages, No Color, Newsprint
Circulation: Total-3,500

Office Developer   *Business*

Publishing Co: Pinnacle Publishing, Inc., PO Box 888, 1800 72nd Ave. Ste. 217, Kent, WA 98035-0888 Fax # (206) 251-5057; Title Tel # (206) 251-1900 Title Fax # (360) 257-5057
Personnel: Publisher-Mickey Finedman, Editor-Rob Krumm
Editorial Description: Published for Microsoft users and customizers.
General Info: Yr. Est. 1995, Monthly, ISSN: 1081-9371
Subscriptions: Indv. $149, Can. $164, For. $169, $18/copy
Circulation: Total-2,000
Advertising: Accepts Inserts.

Officemation Product Reports   *Business*

Publishing Co: Phillips Decision Point Resources, 1111 Marlkress Road., P.O. Box 5062, Cherry Hill, NJ 08063-5062 Parent Co.-Phillips Business Information, Inc., Potomac; Title Tel # (609) 424-1100 Title Fax # (609) 424-1999
Personnel: Publisher-Lawrence Feidelman, Editor-Mark Kistre, Circ. Mgr.-Carol Bell
Editorial Description: Objectively evaluates office automation systems, with expert analysis of systems advantages & disadvantages.
General Info: (Formerly Officemation Reports), Yr. Est. 1977, Monthly, Offset press, 28 pages, ISSN: 0161-8768, 2 Color, Newsprint, Saddle-stitched, Looseleaf
Subscriptions: Indv. $721, Can. $821, For. $821

On-Line
Consumer

Publishing Co: Univ. of New Hampshire Computer Service Dept., Kinsbridge Hall, Durham, NH 03824; Title Tel # (603) 862-2323
Editorial Description: Newsletter for computer services to communicate with user community.
General Info: Yr. Est. 1975, Bi-monthly, Trim Size-7 x 11, Offset press, 16 pages, ISSN: 0731-8367, No Color, Newsprint, Saddle-stitched
Circulation: Total-1,650

One to Many

Publishing Co: Boston Computer Society, Inc., 101 A First Ave. Suite #2, Waltham, MA 02154 Tel # (617) 290-5700 Fax # (617) 290-5744
General Info: Bi-monthly

Online Connection

Publishing Co: Boston Computer Society, Inc., 101 A First Ave. Suite #2, Waltham, MA 02154 Tel # (617) 290-5700 Fax # (617) 290-5744
General Info: Bi-monthly

Online Hotline News Service on CD-ROM
See: TELECOMMUNICATIONS

Online Libraries & Microcomputers
See: LIBRARY

Online Marketplace
Business, Consumer

Publishing Co: Jupiter Communications, 627 Broadway, 2nd Fl., New York, NY 10012-2612; Title Tel # (212) 780-6060 Title Fax # (212) 780-6075
Personnel: Publisher-Gene DeRose, Editor-Adam Schoenfield, Mng. Editor-Yvette DeBow, Art Dir.-Ayesha Hakki
Editorial Description: Covers news of electronic commerce in the home including home shopping, electronic banking, travel services, and more.
General Info: Yr. Est. 1995, Monthly, Trim Size-8½ x 11, 24 pages, 2 Color, Matte, Saddle-stitched
Subscriptions: Indv. $545, For. $595

Online News
Business, Association

Publishing Co: Information Access Co., 362 Lakeside Dr, Foster City, CA 94404-1146 Fax # (415) 358-4759 Parent Co.-Thomson Corp., Stamford; Title Tel # (415) 358-4643
Personnel: Publisher-Cindy Larson, Editor-Michael Kure, Mng. Editor-Eric Swartz, Co-Editor-Peter Vigil
Editorial Description: Supports users of Information Access Company and Predicasts online databases.
General Info: (Formerly IAC News), Yr. Est. 1982, Quarterly, Trim Size-8½ x 11, 4 pages, 2 Color, Recycled

Online Newsletter
See: TELECOMMUNICATIONS

Online Tactics
Business

Publishing Co: Simba Information, Inc., 213 Danbury Rd. PO Box 7430, Wilton, CT 06897-7430 Fax # (203) 834-1771 Parent Co.-Cowles Business Media, New York; Title Tel # (203) 834-0033 Title Fax # (203) 834-5068
Personnel: Editor-Elizabeth Estroff, Editorial Dir.-Lorraine Sileo, Mng. Editor-Karen Burka, Circ. Dir.-Joyce Brigish, Mktg. Dir.-Kendra Kalben
Editorial Description: Ideas and marketing strategies for increasing revenue from your online service or web site.
General Info: 12x/yr., ISSN: 1058-5068
Subscriptions: Indv. $345, For. $395, $25/copy

Open Channel
Business, Consumer

Publishing Co: Information Technology, Information Services, University Of Houston, Houston, TX 77204-0001; Title Tel # (713) 743-1500 Title Fax # (713) 743-1512
Editorial Description: Computer and information information for the university.
General Info: Monthly

Open Information Systems
Business

Publishing Co: Patricia Seybold's Group, 148 State St., 7th Fl., Boston, MA 02109-2506 Tel # (617) 762-5200 Fax # (617) 764-1028; Title Tel # (617) 742-5200 Title Fax # (617) 742-1028
Personnel: Publisher-Patricia Seybold, Editor-Judith Hurwitz, Circ. Mgr.-Deborah Hay, Production Mgr.-Doug Freeman, Art Dir.-Melissa Hagan, Promotion Dir.-Richard Allsbrook
Editorial Description: Open Info Systems contains in-depth analysis of commercial Unix trends & applications, and open systems.
General Info: (Formerly Patricia Seybold's Unix in the Office), Yr. Est. 1986, Monthly
Subscriptions: Indv. $550, Can. $570, For. $585, $50/copy

Open: The International Newsletter of Multivendor Networking
Business

Publishing Co: DataTrends Pubs., Inc., 895 B Harrison Street SE, PO Box 4460, Leesburg, VA 22075 Tel # (703) 779-0574; Title Tel # (703) 760-0660 Title Fax # (703) 760-9365
Personnel: Publisher-Paul Ochs, Editor-Patricia Everett, Circ. Mgr.-Gennifer Chenault
Editorial Description: Covers computers, communication products, & equipment in the OPEN Networking arena.
General Info: (Formerly Open: OSI Product & Equipment News), Yr. Est. 1988, Bi-weekly, Trim Size-8½ x 11, Sheetfed press, 8 pages, ISSN: 0898-0489, Ind/Abs/Online: NewsNet, Predicasts, 2 Color, Newsprint
Subscriptions: Indv. $525, Inst. $525, Can. $525, For. $573

Open Systems Economics Letter
Business

Publishing Co: Computer Economics, Inc., 5841 Edison Pl., Carlsbad, CA 92008-6519 Fax # (619) 431-1126; Title Tel # (619) 438-8100
Personnel: Publisher-Bruno Busso, Editor-Mark McManus, Circ. Mgr.-Michelle Burrier
Editorial Description: Addresses economic issues associated with worldwide transformation to open systems.
General Info: Yr. Est. 1994, Monthly, Trim Size-8½ x 11, 8 pages, ISSN: 1071-6394, 2 Color
Subscriptions: Indv. $395, $40/copy
List Rental: List Management Co.: Manager: Denise Tondream; Direct Effect, 1049 Camino Del Mar Ste 4b, Del Mar, CA 92014-2651 Tel # (619) 792-9259, Actives: $150/M

Operating Systems Review

Publishing Co: Association for Computing Machinery, 1515 Broadway, 17th Fl., New York, NY 10036-5701 Fax # (212) 302-5826; Title Tel # (212) 869-7440
Personnel: Editor-William Waite, Production Mgr.-Paul Rivera
Editorial Description: Operating systems.
General Info: Yr. Est. 1972, Quarterly
Subscriptions: Indv. $20
Circulation: Total-6,500

PC Business Products
Business

Publishing Co: Worldwide Videotex Co., PO Box 3273, Boynton Beach, FL 33424-3273 Tel # (407) 738-2276 Fax # (407) 738-2276
Editorial Description: News on hardware and software for those who use PC's for business applications.
General Info: Yr. Est. 1989, Monthly, Ind/Abs/Online: NewsNet; DIALOG
Subscriptions: Indv. $150, Inst. $150, Can. $150, For. $165

PC Digest
Business, Consumer

Publishing Co: National Software Testing Laboratories, PO Box 1000, Plymouth Meeting, PA 19462-0800; Title Tel # (610) 941-9600 Title Fax # (610) 941-9950
Personnel: Publisher-Lawrenc Goldstein
Editorial Description: Independent ratings for selecting PC hardware & peripherals. Ratings are comparative, methodical & reliable.
General Info: Yr. Est. 1986, Monthly, ISSN: 1042-3575
Subscriptions: Indv. $450, $45/copy
List Rental: List Management Co.: WMI/Worldata, 5200 Town Center Circle, Boca Raton, FL 33486 Tel # (407) 393-8200, Fax # (407) 368-8345, Actives: 10,675, $110/M

P.C. Letter
Business

Publishing Co: Industry Publishing Company, 155 Bovet Rd., Ste. 800, San Mateo, CA 94402 Tel # (415) 572-7341; Title Tel # (415) 592-8880 Title Fax # (415) 592-9192
General Info: Yr. Est. 1985, 17x/yr.
Subscriptions: Indv. $395

PC Software & Hardware Evaluation Newsletter
Business, Consumer

Publishing Co: Q-M Consulting Group, Inc., 141 5th Ave 12th Fl, New York, NY 10010-7105 Fax # (212) 481-7045; Title Tel # (212) 779-0710
Personnel: Publisher-Elizabeth Quinn, Editor-Elizabeth Lambert
Editorial Description: Reviews computer software, hardware & related products.
General Info: Yr. Est. 1984, 10x/yr., Desktop press, 16 pages, Other, Saddle-stitched
Subscriptions: Indv. $75, $10/copy
Circulation: Total-10,000

PC World
Business, Consumer

Publishing Co: PC World Communication, Inc., 501 Second Street, San Francisco, CA 94107; Title Tel # (415) 546-7722 Title Fax # (415) 442-1891
Personnel: Publisher-Richard J. Marino, VP Circ., VP Mktng.-Heather Martin Maier
Editorial Description: Covers computer information for users of the PowerPC microchip.
General Info: (Formerly Power PC World), Yr. Est. 1983, 12x/yr.
Subscriptions: Indv. $49
Circulation: (BPA), Total-951,849

PCMCIA Forecast
Business, Association

Publishing Co: Dream It, Inc., 1255 Cedar Ridge Ln, Colorado Springs, CO 80919-1403; Title Tel # (719) 598-9000
Editorial Description: Published for the Personal Computer Memory Card International Association, with industry and membership information.
General Info: Annually, Looseleaf
Subscriptions: Indv. $1,500, Can. $1,500, For. $1,600

PCMCIA Mass Storage Benchmarks
Business, Association

Publishing Co: Dream It, Inc., 1255 Cedar Ridge Ln, Colorado Springs, CO 80919-1403; Title Tel # (719) 598-9000
Editorial Description: Covers memory card storage information for Association members and industry professionals.
General Info: Annually, Looseleaf
Subscriptions: Indv. $3,000, Can. $3,000, For. $3,100

PCNetter Newsletter   *Business*

Publishing Co: Architecture Technology Corp., PO Box 24344, Minneapolis, MN 55424-0344; Title Tel # (612) 935-2035 Title Fax # (612) 829-5871
Personnel: Editor in Chief-Kenneth J. Thurber, Editor-Gordon A. Palzer
Editorial Description: Covers important developments in the field of personal computers and workstations.
General Info: Yr. Est. 1985, Monthly, Trim Size-8½ x 11, Offset press, 44 pages, ISSN: 0893-8075, 2 Color, Matte, Other
Subscriptions: Indv. $275, $35/copy
List Rental: Rents Lists

PC's Mean Business
See: BUSINESS & INDUSTRY

PLC Insider's Newsletter   *Business*

Publishing Co: Sponsor-Instrument Society of America, Carefree Communications, PO Box 5268, Carefree, AZ 85377-5268 Fax # (602) 488-5376; Title Tel # (602) 488-1462
Personnel: Publisher, Editor-Jack Grenard
Editorial Description: News of the programmable logic controllers' market & its people.
General Info: (Formerly PC Insiders Newsletter), Yr. Est. 1981, Monthly, Trim Size-8½ x 11, Sheetfed press, 7 pages, ISSN: 1040-9718, No Color, Newsprint
Subscriptions: Indv. $70, $10/copy
Acquistions: Publication Sold
Advertising: Accepts Inserts.
Printing Co: Eldon Publishing, 6221 E. Cave Creek, Cave Creek, AZ 85331 Tel # (602) 488-2487

PLUS EXTENSIONS   *Consumer*

Publishing Co: Bowker Reed Reference Electronic Publishing, 121 Chanlon Road, New Providence, NJ 07974 Tel # (908) 665-3529; Title Tel # (908) 665-3259 Title Fax # (908) 665-3528
Editorial Description: Electronic bulletin board opens up similar lines of communications with customers enabling them to download software updates, utilities, shareware and customized configurations of CD-ROM products.
General Info: Bi-monthly, ISSN: B-0951
Subscriptions: Indv. $99
Advertising: Inquire for rates.

Packaged Software Reports   *Business*

Publishing Co: Phillips Decision Point Resources, 1111 Marlkress Road., P.O. Box 5062, Cherry Hill, NJ 08063-5062 Parent Co.-Phillips Business Information, Inc., Potomac; Title Tel # (609) 424-1100 Title Fax # (609) 424-1999
Personnel: Publisher-Lawrence Feidelman, Editor-Mark Kistre, Circ. Mgr.-Carol Bell
Editorial Description: Evaluations of business application packages that run on micro and minicomputers.
General Info: Yr. Est. 1975, Monthly, Offset press, 25 pages, ISSN: 0747-9573, 2 Color, Newsprint, Saddle-stitched
Subscriptions: Indv. $721, Can. $821, For. $821

Pen, The   *Consumer*

Publishing Co: Pioneer Electronics, 4800 E 131st St, Cleveland, OH 44105-7132; Title Tel # (216) 587-3600
Editorial Description: Pioneer's newsletter of computer products and software.
General Info: (Formerly Pioneer Report), Quarterly

Perfect Lawyer
See: LAW

PerfectOffice Newsletter   *Business, Consumer*

Publishing Co: IVY Intl. Communications, 270 W. Center St., Orem, UT 84057-4637 Parent Co.-Novell Inc., Provo; Title Tel # (801) 226-5555 Title Fax # (801) 227-3479
General Info: Monthly
Subscriptions: Indv. $69, $8/copy
Circulation: Total-5,740

Pioneers- A Computer Genealogy Newslettter
See: GENEALOGY

Polyspiral

Publishing Co: Boston Computer Society, Inc., 101 A First Ave. Suite #2, Waltham, MA 02154 Tel # (617) 290-5700 Fax # (617) 290-5744
General Info: Quarterly

Poppin' Zits!
See: SOCIOLOGY

Prevention and Prosecution of Computer and High Technology Crime
See: LAW

Printer Impressions   *Business*

Publishing Co: Buyer's Laboratory, Inc., 20 Railroad Ave, Hackensack, NJ 07601-3309; Title Tel # (201) 488-0404 Title Fax # (201) 488-0461
Personnel: Editor-Daria Hoffman, Circ. Mgr.-Marion Davidowicz, Publisher, Promotion Dir.-Burt Meerow
Editorial Description: Track & evaluates new computer printers and typewriters.
General Info: (Formerly Typeline), Yr. Est. 1980, Monthly, Offset press, 4 pages, No Color
Subscriptions: Indv. $365
Circulation: Total-1,600
List Rental: Rents Lists

Printout   *Business*

Publishing Co: BIS Strategic Decisions, 1 Longwater Cir, Norwell, MA 02061-1620 Tel # (617) 982-9500 Fax # (617) 878-6650; Title Tel # (617) 893-9130 Title Fax # (617) 894-5093
Personnel: Publisher-Jay Devin, Editor-Adina Levin, Circ. Mgr.-Michelle LeBrasseur
Editorial Description: Comprehensive coverage of printer industry, analysis of new prodcuts, industry developments, market research.
General Info: Yr. Est. 1977, Monthly, Trim Size-8½ x 11, Sheetfed press, 14 pages, ISSN: 0738-6613, 2 Color, Newsprint
Subscriptions: Indv. $367, Can. $417, For. $417, $25/copy
Printing Co: Fotobeam/Brookside, 260 Lexington St, Waltham, MA 02154-4613 Tel # (617) 893-1600

Prodigy Star

Publishing Co: Prodigy Services Co., 445 Hamilton Ave, White Plains, NY 10601-1807
Editorial Description: For members of the Prodigy interactive personal service.
General Info: Yr. Est. 1988, 8 pages

Productivity Software   *Business*

Publishing Co: Worldwide Videotex Co., PO Box 3273, Boynton Beach, FL 33424-3273 Tel # (407) 738-2276 Fax # (407) 738-2276
Editorial Description: Latest business software products for improving productivity.
General Info: Yr. Est. 1988, Monthly, ISSN: 1040+1482, Ind/Abs/Online: NewsNet; DIALOG
Subscriptions: Indv. $150, Inst. $150, Can. $150, For. $165

Profit Strategies   *Business*

Publishing Co: Microland Electronics Corp., 1883 Ringwood Ave, San Jose, CA 95131-1721; Title Tel # (408) 441-1688 Title Fax # (408) 441-1766
Editorial Description: Forum of ideas for Microland resellers of computer hardware products.
General Info: Monthly, Trim Size-8½ x 11, 4 pages, No Color, Matte, Saddle-stitched

Promptlines

Publishing Co: Allen Communication, Inc., 5 Triad Ctr., 5th Fl., Salt Lake City, UT 84180-1102; Title Tel # (801) 537-7800 Title Fax # (801) 537-7805
Personnel: Publisher-Steven Allen, Editor-Steve Cantwell, Art Dir.-Leo Hall
Editorial Description: For users of publisher's Quest Authoring System software, which trains executives & educators.
General Info: Yr. Est. 1985, Quarterly, Sheetfed press, 14 pages, No Color, Coated, Saddle-stitched
Circulation: Total-5,000
Advertising: Inquire for rates.
Printing Co: Printers Ink, 2185 S 900 E, Salt Lake City, UT 84106-2335

PsycINFO
See: PSYCHOLOGY

Quantum PC Report for CPAs   *Business*

Publishing Co: Quantum Professional Publishing, 700 Larkspur Landing, Suite 199, Larkspur, CA 94939 Tel # (415) 789-8800
Personnel: Editor-Tom McKenna
Editorial Description: Improving productivity with PCs in CPA firms.
General Info: Yr. Est. 1986, Monthly
Subscriptions: Indv. $235

Query
See: SCHOOL ADMINISTRATION

Quick Notes

Publishing Co: Quicksoft, 219 1st Ave. N., #224, Seattle, WA 98109
Editorial Description: Newsletter about PC-Write word processor and other Quicksoft products.
General Info: Quarterly

Quickfill Application Notes   *Business*

Publishing Co: CWC Software, Inc., 150 Grossman Dr Ste 201, Braintree, MA 02184-4902; Title Tel # (617) 843-2010 Title Fax # (617) 843-8365
Personnel: Sales & Mktg. Dir.-Andrew Conti

Quote Quad

Publishing Co: Association for Computing Machinery, 1515 Broadway, 17th Fl., New York, NY 10036-5701 Fax # (212) 302-5826; Title Tel # (212) 869-7440 Title Fax # (212) 944-1318
General Info: Quarterly
Circulation: Total-1,500

RLE Currents
See: ENGINEERING, ELECTRICAL

RUCS Newsletter   *Association*

Publishing Co: Rutgers Univ. Computing Svces., User Services, Box 879-Newsletter, Piscataway, NJ 08855-0879 Tel # (908) 932-2425 Fax # (908) 932-2021; Title Tel # (201) 932-2413
Personnel: Editor-Susan R. Hagan, Editor-Beverly Madron
Editorial Description: To provide information for the Rutgers Univ. mainframe & microcomputer users.
General Info: (Formerly CCIS Newsletter), Yr. Est. 1970, Bi-monthly, Trim Size-8½ x 11, Desktop press, 20 pages, ISSN: 0160-8711, No Color, Matte, Other
Subscriptions: Indv. $10
Circulation: Total-7,500
Printing Co: Rutgers Reprographics, Livingston Campus, Piscataway, NJ 08854

Rapid Prototyping Report   *Business*

Publishing Co: CAD/CAM Publishing, Inc., 1010 Turquoise St., Ste. 320, San Diego, CA 92109-1159; Title Tel # (619) 488-0533 Title Fax # (619) 488-6052
Editorial Description: Newsletter of the desktop manufacturing industry.
General Info: Monthly, Trim Size-8½ x 11, 8 pages, 2 Color, Coated, Saddle-stitched
Subscriptions: Indv. $295, Can. $295, For. $345
List Rental: Rents Lists

Real Estate

Publishing Co: Boston Computer Society, Inc., 101 A First Ave. Suite #2, Waltham, MA 02154 Tel # (617) 290-5700 Fax # (617) 290-5744
General Info: Quarterly

Real Estate Computer Review
See: REAL ESTATE

Real World Software & Computer Newsletter

Publishing Co: Professional Solutions, Inc., 660 Village Trce Ste 203, Marietta, GA 30067-4081; Title Tel # (404) 953-8123
Personnel: Editor-Kenneth Leebow

Really, a Free Newsletter
See: BOOKS & BOOK TRADE

Reengineering Economics Letter
See: ECONOMICS

Rehabilitation Technology Newsletter
See: SOCIAL SERVICES & WELFARE

Release 1.0 Esther Dysons Monthly Report   *Business*

Publishing Co: EDventure Holdings, Inc., 104 Fifth Ave., 20th Floor, New York, NY 10011-6987; Title Tel # (212) 924-8800 Title Fax # (212) 924-0240
Personnel: Publisher-Daphne Kis, Editor-Esther Dyson, Mng. Editor-Jerry Michalski, Circ. Mgr.-Robyn Storm
Editorial Description: Covers emerging technology in the software and telecom industry.
General Info: Yr. Est. 1983, Monthly
Subscriptions: Indv. $595, For. $650

Report on Healthcare Information Management
See: HOSPITALS & NURSING HOMES

Report on IBM   *Business*

Publishing Co: DataTrends Pubs., Inc., 895 B Harrison Street SE, PO Box 4460, Leesburg, VA 22075 Tel # (703) 779-0574; Title Tel # (703) 641-0444 Title Fax # (703) 760-9365
Personnel: Publisher-Paul Ochs, Editor-Rutrell Yasin, Circ. Mgr.-Gennifer Chenault
Editorial Description: Weekly news & analysis on strategies, activities, products of IBM Corp.
General Info: Yr. Est. 1984, Weekly, Trim Size-8½ x 11, Sheetfed press, 12 pages, ISSN: 0742-5341, Ind/Abs/Online: NewsNet, DIALOG, Predicasts, 2 Color, Newsprint
Subscriptions: Indv. $745, Can. $745, For. $795
Acquistions: Publication Bought, Publication Sold

Reports on Information Security

Publishing Co: Datapro Research Corp., 600 Delran Pky, Delran, NJ 08075-1255 Tel # (609) 764-0100 Fax # (609) 764-2815

Reports on PC Communications

Publishing Co: Datapro Research Corp., 600 Delran Pky, Delran, NJ 08075-1255 Tel # (609) 764-0100 Fax # (609) 764-2815

Residual Value Forecasts For DEC Systems and Peripherals   *Business*

Publishing Co: Computer Economics, Inc., 5841 Edison Pl., Carlsbad, CA 92008-6519; Title Tel # (619) 438-8100 Title Fax # (619) 431-1126
Personnel: Publisher-Bruno Bassi, Editor-Terrin Lovett, Circ. Mgr.-Denise Tondream
Editorial Description: Covers 7- year residual value forecasts for over 135 DEC machines, current used price information supported by used price graphs for each piece of forecasted equipment, relative performanceratings, current third-party leasing rates from actual lease transactions, updated listings of the top 50 leading systems and 250 top manufacturers.
General Info: Yr. Est. 1990, Quarterly, Looseleaf
Subscriptions: Indv. $1,495
List Rental: List Management Co.: Manager: Denise Tondream; Direct Effect, 1049 Camino Del Mar Ste 4b, Del Mar, CA 92014-2651 Tel # (619) 792-9259, Actives: $150/M

Residual Value Forecasts For IBM Systems & Peripherals   *Business*

Publishing Co: Computer Economics, Inc., 5841 Edison Pl., Carlsbad, CA 92008-6519; Title Tel # (619) 438-8100 Title Fax # (619) 431-1126
Personnel: Publisher-Bruno Bassi, Editor-Terrin Lovett, Circ. Mgr.-Denise Tondream
Editorial Description: 7-Year Residual Value Forecasts For IBM Systems and Peripherals. Covers 7-year residual value forecasts for over 265 IBM machines, current used price information supported by used price graphs for each piece of forecasted equipment, relative performance ratings, current third-party leasing rates, update listings of the 50 leading systems and 250 top manufacturers with data on revenues, income, and numb
General Info: Yr. Est. 1989, Quarterly, Looseleaf
Subscriptions: Indv. $2,495
List Rental: List Management Co.: Manager: Denise Tondream; Direct Effect, 1049 Camino Del Mar Ste 4b, Del Mar, CA 92014-2651 Tel # (619) 792-9259, Actives: $150/M

Retirement & Tax Planning with 1-2-3
See: ACCOUNTING

Robot Explorer   *Business, Consumer*

Publishing Co: Appropriate Solutions, Inc., 145 Grove St., P.O. Box 458, Peterborough, NH 03458-0458; Title Tel # (603) 924-6079 Title Fax # (603) 525-4923
Personnel: Publisher-Andrew Taylor, Editor-Raymond Cote, Mktg. Dir.-Elizabeth Alpaugh-Cote
Editorial Description: Focus is on innovative research and applications related to robotics. Explores university projects, nonindustrial applications, educational uses and practical designs.
General Info: Yr. Est. 1992, 8x/yr., Trim Size-8½ x 11, Other press, 7 pages, ISSN: 1060-4375, No Color, Other
Subscriptions: Indv. $15, Inst. $15, Can. $15, For. $30, $5/copy
Circulation: Total-500
Advertising: Accepts Inserts.
List Rental: Expires: $100/M
Printing Co: Docunet, 52 Labombard Rd. N., Lebanon, NH 03766

Robot Times

Publishing Co: Robotic Industries Assn., 900 Victors Way, P.O. Box 3724, Ann Arbor, MI 48106; Title Tel # (313) 994-6088 Title Fax # (313) 994-3338
Personnel: Editor-Jeffrey Burnstein
General Info: (Formerly Robotics Quarterly), Yr. Est. 1983, Quarterly, 4 pages
Circulation: Total-5,000

Robotics Technical Committee Newsletter

Publishing Co: Computer Society Press, 1730 Massachusetts Ave NW, Washington, DC 20036-1903; Title Tel # (202) 371-0101
Personnel: Editor-Ramesh Jain
General Info: Quarterly
Circulation: Total-919

Robotronics Age Newsletter   *Business*

Publishing Co: 21st Century Media Communications, 548 Cardero St., Vancouver, BC V6G 2W6 Canada; Title Tel # (604) 261-5712
Personnel: Editor-Frank Ogden
General Info: Ind/Abs/Online: NewsNet

S-Eighty

Publishing Co: Computer Information Exchange, PO Box 159, San Luis Rey, CA 92068-0159
General Info: Monthly

SANYO PC Hacker's Newsletter   *Business, Consumer*

Publishing Co: Victor Frank Publishing, 12450 Skyline Blvd., Woodside, CA 94062-4541; Title Tel # (415) 851-7031
Personnel: Publisher, Editor-Victor Frank
General Info: Yr. Est. 1984, Monthly, Trim Size-8½ x 11, 8 pages, ISSN: 1054-4232, No Color
Subscriptions: Indv. $20, Can. $25, For. $30
Circulation: Total-125

SIA Circuit
See: MANUFACTURING

SIGACT News

Publishing Co: Association for Computing Machinery, 1515 Broadway, 17th Fl., New York, NY 10036-5701 Fax # (212) 302-5826; Title Tel # (212) 869-7440
Personnel: Editor-Michael Langston, Circ. Mgr.-Donna Baglio
Editorial Description: Automata and computability theory.
General Info: Yr. Est. 1969, Quarterly
Subscriptions: Indv. $40, $10/copy
Circulation: Total-2,800

SIGARCH Computer Architecture News
Business, Association

Publishing Co: Association for Computing Machinery, 1515 Broadway, 17th Fl., New York, NY 10036-5701; Title Tel # (212) 869-7440 Title Fax # (212) 302-5826
Personnel: Editor-Doug DeGroot
Editorial Description: SIGARCH serves a unique community of professionals working at the forefront of computer design in both industry and academia.
General Info: Bi-monthly
Subscriptions: Indv. $45, $11/copy

SIGART Newsletter
Association

Publishing Co: Association for Computing Machinery, 1515 Broadway, 17th Fl., New York, NY 10036-5701 Fax # (212) 302-5826; Title Tel # (212) 869-7440
Personnel: Editor-Lewis Johnson
Editorial Description: Artificial intelligence, news, reports, abstracts, educational material, etc. Covers study of the intelligence and its realization in computer systems.
General Info: Quarterly, Trim Size-8½ x 11, Offset press, 32 pages, No Color
Subscriptions: Indv. $25, $8/copy
Circulation: (100% controlled), Total-11,000

SIGBIO Newsletter
See: MEDICINE

SIGCOMM Computer Communications Review
Business, Association

Publishing Co: Association for Computing Machinery, 1515 Broadway, 17th Fl., New York, NY 10036-5701 Fax # (212) 302-5826; Title Tel # (212) 869-7440
Personnel: Editor-Craig Partridge
General Info: Quarterly, ISSN: 0146-4833
Subscriptions: Indv. $37, $10/copy
Circulation: Total-5,500

SIGCPR Newsletter
Business

Publishing Co: Association for Computing Machinery, 1515 Broadway, 17th Fl., New York, NY 10036-5701 Fax # (212) 302-5826; Title Tel # (212) 869-7440
Personnel: Editor-Elias Awad
Editorial Description: Information on computer personnel research.
General Info: Quarterly, 20 pages, ISSN: 0160-2497
Subscriptions: Indv. $26, $10/copy
Circulation: Total-900

SIGCSE Bulletin
Business, Association

Publishing Co: Association for Computing Machinery, 1515 Broadway, 17th Fl., New York, NY 10036-5701 Fax # (212) 302-5826; Title Tel # (212) 869-7440
Editorial Description: Computer science education.
General Info: Quarterly
Subscriptions: Indv. $30, $8/copy
Circulation: Total-3,500

SIGCUE Outlook
Association

Publishing Co: Association for Computing Machinery, 1515 Broadway, 17th Fl., New York, NY 10036-5701 Fax # (212) 302-5826; Title Tel # (212) 869-7440
Editorial Description: For people interested in computer uses in education.
General Info: Yr. Est. 1967, Quarterly, 32 pages, No Color
Subscriptions: Indv. $36, $8/copy
Circulation: Total-2,000
Advertising: Inquire for rates.

SIGDA Newsletter
Association

Publishing Co: Association for Computing Machinery, 1515 Broadway, 17th Fl., New York, NY 10036-5701 Fax # (212) 302-5826; Title Tel # (212) 869-7440
Personnel: Editor-Steven Levitan
Editorial Description: Design automation.
General Info: Quarterly, ISSN: 0163-5743
Subscriptions: Indv. $5, $1/copy

SIGDOC Newsletter
Business, Association

Publishing Co: Association for Computing Machinery, 1515 Broadway, 17th Fl., New York, NY 10036-5701 Fax # (212) 302-5826; Title Tel # (212) 869-7440
Personnel: Editor-Russell Borland
Editorial Description: Reviews & examines the process of producing documentation for the computer industry the process of producing documentation using computers & the end results of the documentation development.
General Info: Quarterly, 32 pages, ISSN: 0163-5956
Subscriptions: Indv. $25, $10/copy
Circulation: Total-2,000

SIGFORTH
Business

Publishing Co: Association for Computing Machinery, 1515 Broadway, 17th Fl., New York, NY 10036-5701 Title Tel # (212) 869-7440 Fax # (212) 302-5826
Personnel: Editor-Charles Curly, Production Mgr.-Pat McCarren
Editorial Description: Dedicated to the advancement of the Forth computer language.
General Info: Quarterly
Subscriptions: Indv. $33
Circulation: Total-1,000

SIGICE Bulletin
Association

Publishing Co: Association for Computing Machinery, 1515 Broadway, 17th Fl., New York, NY 10036-5701 Fax # (212) 302-5826; Title Tel # (212) 869-7440
Personnel: Editor-Ka-Wing Wong
Editorial Description: Fosters the exchange of ideas and information regarding applications and advances in the use of workstations to support the effective use of individual and small group work environments.
General Info: (Formerly SIGSMALL/PC), Quarterly
Subscriptions: Indv. $25

SIGIR Forum
Business, Association

Publishing Co: Association for Computing Machinery, 1515 Broadway, 17th Fl., New York, NY 10036-5701 Fax # (212) 302-5826; Title Tel # (212) 869-7440
Personnel: Editor-Christopher Fox
Editorial Description: Information retrieval.
General Info: Quarterly, ISSN: 0163-5840
Subscriptions: Indv. $32, $10/copy
Circulation: Total-2,400

SIGLINK Review
Association

Publishing Co: Association for Computing Machinery, 1515 Broadway, 17th Fl., New York, NY 10036-5701 Fax # (212) 302-5826; Title Tel # (212) 869-7440
Editorial Description: Covers Hypertext/Hypermedia.
General Info: Yr. Est. 1992, Quarterly, Ind/Abs/Online: acm online products and services publications catalog
Subscriptions: Indv. $12

SIGMETRICS Performance Evaluation Review
Association

Publishing Co: Association for Computing Machinery, 1515 Broadway, 17th Fl., New York, NY 10036-5701 Fax # (212) 302-5826; Title Tel # (212) 869-7440
Personnel: Editor-Blaine Gaither, Production Mgr.-Paul Rivera
Editorial Description: Measurement and evaluation of SIGMETRICS.
General Info: Quarterly
Subscriptions: Indv. $25, $8/copy
Circulation: Total-3,000

SIGMICRO Newsletter
Association

Publishing Co: Association for Computing Machinery, 1515 Broadway, 17th Fl., New York, NY 10036-5701 Fax # (212) 302-5826; Title Tel # (212) 869-7440
Editorial Description: SIGMICRO specializes in computer architecture.
General Info: Quarterly, ISSN: 0163-5751
Subscriptions: Indv. $35, $9/copy

SIGMIS Database
Business, Association

Publishing Co: Association for Computing Machinery, 1515 Broadway, 17th Fl., New York, NY 10036-5701 Fax # (212) 302-5826; Title Tel # (212) 869-7440
Personnel: Editor-Ephraim McLain
Editorial Description: SIGMIS is the Special Interest Group on Management Information Systems.
General Info: (Formerly SIGBDP Database; SIGBIT Database), Quarterly, ISSN: 009-0033
Subscriptions: Indv. $25, $4/copy

SIGMOD Record
Association

Publishing Co: Association for Computing Machinery, 1515 Broadway, 17th Fl., New York, NY 10036-5701 Fax # (212) 302-5826; Title Tel # (212) 869-7440
Personnel: Editor-Jennifer Widom, Production Mgr.-Paul Rivera
Editorial Description: Investigate the development & application of database technology on a full range of computer organizations. A valuable resource for state-of-the-art information & includes the annual conference proceedings.
General Info: Quarterly
Subscriptions: Indv. $27, $8/copy
Circulation: Total-5,000

SIGNUM Newsletter

Publishing Co: Association for Computing Machinery, 1515 Broadway, 17th Fl., New York, NY 10036-5701 Fax # (212) 302-5826; Title Tel # (212) 869-7440
Personnel: Editor-P.W. Gaffney, Circ. Mgr.-Julie Goertz
Editorial Description: Numerical mathematics.
General Info: Yr. Est. 1965, Quarterly
Subscriptions: Indv. $23
Circulation: Total-2,000

SIGOA Newsletter
Association

Publishing Co: Association for Computing Machinery, 1515 Broadway, 17th Fl., New York, NY 10036-5701 Fax # (212) 302-5826; Title Tel # (212) 869-7440
Personnel: Editor-Simon Gibbs
Editorial Description: Office automation.
General Info: Bi-monthly
Subscriptions: Indv. $30, $4/copy

SIGOIS Newsletter
Business, Association

Publishing Co: Association for Computing Machinery, 1515 Broadway, 17th Fl., New York, NY 10036-5701 Tel # (212) 869-7440 Fax # (212) 302-5826; Title Tel # (212) 869-7400
Editorial Description: Office Information Systems.
General Info: Quarterly
Subscriptions: Indv. $30

SIGOPS Operating
Systems Review — *Business, Association*

Publishing Co: Association for Computing Machinery, 1515 Broadway, 17th Fl., New York, NY 10036-5701 Fax # (212) 302-5826; Title Tel # (212) 869-7440
General Info: Quarterly
Subscriptions: Indv. $20, $8/copy
Circulation: Total-6,500

SIGPLAN FORTRAN
Forum — *Association, Consumer*

Publishing Co: Association for Computing Machinery, 1515 Broadway, 17th Fl., New York, NY 10036-5701 Fax # (212) 302-5826; Title Tel # (212) 869-7440 Title Fax # (212) 944-1318
Personnel: Editor-Loren Meissner, Circ. Mgr.-Donna Baglio, Adv. Dir.-Walter Andrzejewski
Editorial Description: Encompasses the Fortran language, its usage, portability, standardization and further evolution as well as the implementation of Fortran processors.
General Info: (Formerly SIGPLANFortec Newsletter), Quarterly
Subscriptions: Indv. $20, $10/copy
Circulation: Total-700
List Rental: List Management Co.: Rubin Response, 1111 Plaza Dr., Schaumburg, IL 60173 Tel # (708) 619-9800, Fax # (708) 619-0150
Printing Co: Cadmus Journal Services, 500 Cadmus Lane, Easton, MD 21601-3857 Tel # (410) 822-2870, Fax # (410) 822-0438

SIGPLAN Notices — *Association*

Publishing Co: Association for Computing Machinery, 1515 Broadway, 17th Fl., New York, NY 10036-5701 Fax # (212) 302-5826; Title Tel # (212) 869-7440 Title Fax # (212) 944-1318
Personnel: Editor-Richard Wexelblat, Circ. Mgr.-Donna Baglio, Adv. Dir.-Walter Andrzejewski
Editorial Description: Programming language development.
General Info: Yr. Est. 1965, Monthly, Offset press, 80 pages, No Color
Subscriptions: Indv. $57, $10/copy
Circulation: Total-8,000
List Rental: List Management Co.: Rubin Response, 1111 Plaza Dr., Schaumburg, IL 60173 Tel # (708) 619-9800, Fax # (708) 619-0150
Printing Co: Cadmus Journal Services, 500 Cadmus Lane, Easton, MD 21601-3857 Tel # (410) 822-2870, Fax # (410) 822-0438

SIGSAC Newsletter — *Business, Association*

Publishing Co: Association for Computing Machinery, 1515 Broadway, 17th Fl., New York, NY 10036-5701 Fax # (212) 302-5826; Title Tel # (212) 869-7440
Personnel: Editor-Catherine Meadows
Editorial Description: Security and Audit Control.
General Info: Quarterly, 32 pages
Subscriptions: Indv. $30, $10/copy
Circulation: Total-2,000

SIGSAM Bulletin — *Association*

Publishing Co: Association for Computing Machinery, 1515 Broadway, 17th Fl., New York, NY 10036-5701 Fax # (212) 302-5826; Title Tel # (212) 869-7440
Personnel: Editor-Franz Winkler, Circ. Mgr.-Julie Goetz
Editorial Description: Symbolic and algebraic manipulation.
General Info: Quarterly
Subscriptions: Indv. $25, $10/copy
Circulation: Total-1,700

SIGSMALL PC Notes — *Association*

Publishing Co: Association for Computing Machinery, 1515 Broadway, 17th Fl., New York, NY 10036-5701 Fax # (212) 302-5826; Title Tel # (212) 869-7440
Editorial Description: Small computing systems applications.
General Info: Quarterly
Subscriptions: Indv. $25, $6/copy

SIGSOFT Software
Engineering Notes — *Business, Association*

Publishing Co: Association for Computing Machinery, 1515 Broadway, 17th Fl., New York, NY 10036-5701 Fax # (212) 302-5826; Title Tel # (212) 869-7440
Personnel: Editor-Peter Neumann
Editorial Description: Newsletter on research and development advances in software engineering.
General Info: Yr. Est. 1977, Quarterly, Offset press, 40 pages, ISSN: 0163-5948, No Color
Subscriptions: Indv. $33, $8/copy
Circulation: (76% controlled), Total-10,500

SIGUCCS Newsletter — *Association*

Publishing Co: Association for Computing Machinery, 1515 Broadway, 17th Fl., New York, NY 10036-5701; Title Tel # (212) 869-7440 Title Fax # (212) 302-5826
Personnel: Editor-Rita Saltz
Editorial Description: Articles and features of interest to professional staff & management of computer installations in higher education & to user-oriented computer professionals in other fields.
General Info: Quarterly, 24 pages, Ind/Abs/Online: ACM online products and services publications catalog, No Color
Subscriptions: Indv. $15, $4/copy

SMUG Notes — *Association*

Publishing Co: Spokane Microcomputer Users Group, Box 10562, Spokane, WA 99209-0562
Personnel: Editor-Sven Pretorious
Editorial Description: Report on SMUG and general microcomputer information.
General Info: Quarterly
Subscriptions: Indv. $15

SNA Perspective

Publishing Co: CSI03COM, 3165 Kifer Rd # Csi03com, Santa Clara, CA 95051-0804; Title Tel # (408) 562-6646 Title Fax # (408) 748-1273
Personnel: Publisher-Marianne Cohn, Editor-Louise Wells, Circ. Mgr.-Cynthia Chambers
Editorial Description: Single source objective newsletter covering IBM's System Network Architecture (SNA).
General Info: Yr. Est. 1980, Monthly, 8 pages, ISSN: 0270-7284
Subscriptions: Indv. $350, For. $385, $29/copy
Acquistions: Publication Sold
Circulation: Total-2,000

SOURCEfile
See: ADVERTISING & MARKETING

SPEX: Small Publishers Exchange
See: BOOKS & BOOK TRADE

SQL Server — *Business*

Publishing Co: Pinnacle Publishing, Inc., PO Box 888, 1800 72nd Ave. Ste. 217, Kent, WA 98035-0888; Title Tel # (206) 251-1900 Title Fax # (206) 251-5057
Personnel: Publisher-Mickey Finedman, Editor-Karon Watterson, Circ. Mgr.-Sharon Whiting
Editorial Description: Information and tips for Microsoft SQL Server users.
General Info: Yr. Est. 1995, Monthly, ISSN: 1081-9355
Subscriptions: Indv. $199, Can. $204, For. $209, $30/copy
Circulation: Total-1,800
Advertising: Accepts Inserts.

SSignals — *Business*

Publishing Co: Silicon Systems, Inc., 14351 Myford Rd, Tustin, CA 92680-7039; Title Tel # (714) 573-6000 Title Fax # (714) 573-6914
Personnel: Editor-Lana Perry
Editorial Description: Newsletter giving info on Silicon System's line of embedded modems.
General Info: Quarterly, Trim Size-$8\frac{1}{2}$ x 11, 8 pages, 2 Color, Coated, Saddle-stitched

Saber Point — *Business*

Publishing Co: Saber Software Corp., PO Box 9088, Dallas, TX 75209-9088
Editorial Description: A complete guide to the Saber LAN workstation.
General Info: Yr. Est. 1991, Quarterly, Trim Size-$8\frac{1}{2}$ x 11, 12 pages, 2 Color, Coated, Saddle-stitched

Sales Automation Success
See: SALESMANSHIP & SELLING

Sarah Stambler's Marketing with Technology News
See: ADVERTISING & MARKETING

Scan Newsletter — *Business*

Publishing Co: Scan Newsletter, 11 Middle Neck Rd., Great Neck, NY 11021-2301; Title Tel # (516) 487-6375 Title Fax # (516) 487-6393
Personnel: Publisher, Editor-George Goldberg, Circ. Mgr.-Teddy Allen
Editorial Description: Bar code scanning & related automatic identification technology.
General Info: Yr. Est. 1977, Monthly, ISSN: 0273-3080
Subscriptions: Indv. $175, Can. $175, For. $195, $15/copy

School Microcomputing
Bulletin

Publishing Co: Learning Publications, Inc., Safe School Coalition, P.O.Box 1338, Holmes Bch., FL 34218; Title Tel # (813) 778-6651
Personnel: Editor-Alan Mcevoy, Circ. Mgr., Production Mgr.-Danna Downing
Editorial Description: Easy-to-read publication for those using micros in educational settings, many field reports.
General Info: Yr. Est. 1982, Monthly, Sheetfed press, 12 pages, ISSN: 0735-9969, No Color
Subscriptions: Indv. $28, $3/copy
Circulation: Total-1,500
Printing Co: Grand Rapids Mailing Service, 1300 Front Ave NW, Grand Rapids, MI 49504-3218 Tel # (616) 451-0657

Script-Central — *Business, Consumer*

Publishing Co: Resource Central, 6339 W. 110th St. #11250, Overland Park, KS 66211-1509; Title Tel # (913) 469-6502 Title Fax # (913) 469-6507
Personnel: Publisher-Tom Weishaar, Editor-Bruce Caplin, Circ. Mgr.-Denise Cameron
Editorial Description: Devoted to Hypercard IIgs & HyperTalk scripting.
General Info: Yr. Est. 1991, Bi-monthly, ISSN: 1066-7318
Subscriptions: Indv. $50, Can. $48, For. $48
Circulation: Total-300
List Rental: Rents Lists

Semiconductor Currents
See: ELECTRIC & ELECTRONIC EQUIPMENT

Seniornet Online Newsletter
See: SENIOR CITIZENS

Sensor Business News — *Business*

Publishing Co: Phillips Business Information, Inc., 1201 Seven Locks Rd., Ste 300, Potomac, MD 20854-2958 Tel # (301) 340-1520 Fax # (301) 424-4297
General Info: Bi-weekly, ISSN: 1079-1132
Subscriptions: Indv. $397, For. $430

Serlin Report on Parallel Processing *Business*

Publishing Co: ITOM Intl. Co., PO Box 1450, Los Altos, CA 94023-1450; Title Tel # (415) 948-4516 Title Fax # (415) 948-9153
Personnel: Publisher, Editor-Omri Serlin
Editorial Description: Business & technical developments in supercomputers and massively-parellel systems.
General Info: Yr. Est. 1987, Monthly, 16 pages, ISSN: 0894-2226
Subscriptions: Indv. $695, $60/copy

Shannon Knows DEC *Business, Consumer*

Publishing Co: Shannon Knows DEC, 135 Leland Farm Road, Ashland, MA 01721; Title Tel # (508) 881-5563
Personnel: Publisher, Editor-Terry Shannon
Editorial Description: Digital Marketplace
General Info: Yr. Est. 1993, Bi-monthly, ISSN: 1079-4379
Subscriptions: Indv. $350, For. $395

Sim-U-Letter
See: GIFTS, GAMES, TOYS

SimAntics
See: GIFTS, GAMES, TOYS

SimPosium
See: EDUCATION

Simulation Digest *Business, Association*

Publishing Co: Association for Computing Machinery, 1515 Broadway, 17th Fl., New York, NY 10036-5701 Fax # (212) 302-5826; Title Tel # (212) 869-7440
Personnel: Editor-Dana L. Wyatt
Editorial Description: SIGSIM seeks the advancement of the state-of-the-art in simulation and modeling.
General Info: (Formerly SIGSIM Simuletter), Quarterly
Subscriptions: Indv. $10, $3/copy

Sinclair-Timex Newsletter

Publishing Co: Boston Computer Society, Inc., 101 A First Ave. Suite #2, Waltham, MA 02154 Tel # (617) 290-5700 Fax # (617) 290-5744
General Info: Quarterly

Singer Report on Managed Care Systems and Technology, The *Business*

Publishing Co: Charles Singer & Co., 401 Edgewater Pl Ste 580, Wakefield, MA 01880-6210 Fax # (617) 246-7737; Title Tel # (617) 246-7585
Personnel: Publisher-Charles J. Singer, Editor-Rich Luhr
Editorial Description: Covers information systems in the managed health care field.
General Info: Yr. Est. 1991, 9x/yr., Trim Size-8½ x 11, Offset press, 8 pages, ISSN: 1071-1910, 2 Color, Matte, Saddle-stitched
Subscriptions: Indv. $395, $40/copy
Circulation: Total-2,000
List Rental: Actives: 400, Expires: 400

Small Business Computer News *Business*

Publishing Co: Phillips Decision Point Resources, 1111 Marlkress Road., P.O. Box 5062, Cherry Hill, NJ 08063-5062 Parent Co.-Phillips Business Information, Inc., Potomac; Title Tel # (609) 424-1100 Title Fax # (609) 424-1999
Personnel: Publisher-Lawrence Feidelman, Editor-Al Powell, Circ. Mgr.-Carol Bell
General Info: Semi-monthly, Desktop press, Newsprint
Subscriptions: Indv. $721, Can. $821, For. $821

Small Business Computing *Business*

Publishing Co: Charles Moore Associates, Inc., PO Box 6, Southampton, PA 18966-0006; Title Tel # (215) 355-6084 Title Fax # (215) 364-2212
Personnel: Editor-Charles Moore, Circ. Mgr.-Nancy Hannigan
Editorial Description: Report to small business executives.
General Info: Yr. Est. 1978, Monthly, Sheetfed press, 16 pages, No Color
Subscriptions: Indv. $49

Small Business Systems *Business*

Publishing Co: Charles Moore Associates, Inc., PO Box 6, Southampton, PA 18966-0006 Tel # (215) 355-6084; Title Tel # (215) 364-2212 Title Fax # (215) 364-2212
Personnel: Editor-Charles Moore, Circ. Mgr.-Nancy Hannigan
Editorial Description: Case histories applying computers to solve small business problems.
General Info: Yr. Est. 1979, Monthly, 4 pages
Subscriptions: Indv. $60
List Rental: List Management Co.: Charles Moore Assocs., PO Box 6, Southampton, PA 18966-0006 Tel # (215) 355-6084, Fax # (215) 364-2212, Actives: 106,250, $80/M

SmallTalk Report *Business* CPM: $280

Publishing Co: SIGS Publications Group, 71 W. 23rd Street, 3rd Floor, New York, NY 10010-4102 Tel # (212) 246-7447 Fax # (212) 242-7574
Personnel: Publisher-Richard Friedman
Editorial Description: For users and programmers of the SmallTalk language.
General Info: 9x/yr.
Circulation: Total-4,000
Advertising: $1,120.

Smart Access

Publishing Co: Pinnacle Publishing, Inc., PO Box 888, 1800 72nd Ave. Ste. 217, Kent, WA 98035-0888 Fax # (206) 251-5057; Title Tel # (206) 251-1900 Title Fax # (360) 257-5057
General Info: Yr. Est. 1993, ISSN: 1066-7911
Subscriptions: Indv. $139, Can. $154, For. $159, $15/copy
Advertising: Accepts Inserts.
List Rental: List Management Co.: Direct Media, Inc., 200 Pemberwick Rd., PO Box 4565, Greenwich, CT 06830 Tel # (203) 532-3713, Fax # (203) 531-1452

Smart Network Services *Business*

Publishing Co: Intel Corp., PO Box 10266, Portland, OR 97210-0266
Editorial Description: Articles and descriptions of Intel LAN products.
General Info: Trim Size-8⅞ x 11, 12 pages, 4 Color, Coated, Saddle-stitched

Soft Letter *Business*

Publishing Co: Soft Letter, 17 Main St, Watertown, MA 02172-4491; Title Tel # (617) 924-3944
Personnel: Publisher, Editor-Jeffrey Tarter, Circ. Mgr.-Allison Shapiro, Production Mgr.-Jane Farber
Editorial Description: Newsletter for microcomputer software developers.
General Info: Yr. Est. 1983, Bi-weekly, Trim Size-8½ x 11, Desktop press, 6 pages, ISSN: 0882-3499, No Color
Subscriptions: Indv. $345, $25/copy
Circulation: Total-1,500
List Rental: List Management Co.: WMI/Worldata, 5200 Town Center Circle, Boca Raton, FL 33486 Tel # (407) 393-8200, Fax # (407) 368-8345, Actives: 10,858, $250/M

Softletter *Business*

Publishing Co: Mercury Group Inc., 17 Main St, Watertown, MA 02172-4491; Title Tel # (617) 924-3944 Title Fax # (617) 924-7288
Personnel: Publisher, Editor-Jeffrey Tarter, Circ. Mgr.-Allison Shapiro
Editorial Description: Trends & strategies in microcomputer software publishing.
General Info: Yr. Est. 1983, Semi-monthly, Trim Size-8½ x 11, Web press, 6 pages, ISSN: 0882-3499, No Color, Newsprint
Subscriptions: Indv. $345, Can. $345, For. $380
Acquistions: Publication Bought
List Rental: Actives: $125/M, Expires: $125/M
Printing Co: Cambridge Offset, 56 Creighton St, Cambridge, MA 02140-2032 Tel # (617) 547-5700

Software Digest *Business, Consumer*

Publishing Co: National Software Testing Laboratories, PO Box 1000, Plymouth Meeting, PA 19462-0800; Title Tel # (610) 941-9600 Title Fax # (610) 941-9950
Personnel: Publisher-Lowrenie Goldstein, Publications Director-Linda Di Biasio, Mag. Ed.-Andrew Froning
Editorial Description: Independent & comparative ratings on IBM PC software. All categories tested free of bias. No adv. is accepted.
General Info: Yr. Est. 1983, Monthly, ISSN: 0896-6486
Subscriptions: Indv. $450
List Rental: List Management Co.: WMI/Worldata, 5200 Town Center Circle, Boca Raton, FL 33486 Tel # (407) 393-8200, Fax # (407) 368-8345, Actives: 45,789, $110/M, Hotline: 7,631, $120/M

Software Economics Letter *Business*

Publishing Co: Computer Economics, Inc., 5841 Edison Pl., Carlsbad, CA 92008-6519; Title Tel # (619) 438-8100 Title Fax # (619) 431-1126
Personnel: Publisher/President/Advisor-Bruno Bassi, Editor-Mark McManus, Circ. Mgr.-Michelle Burrler
Editorial Description: Software Economics Letter ' Maximizing Your Return on Corporate Software'. Software Economics letter, exclusively to the management and cost control of your software investments. This provides the corporate user and IS communities with a concise analysisof software issues. You will use it to stay informed of the latest trends in software and software licensing. It also includes insidghtful analyses of
General Info: Yr. Est. 1992, Monthly, Trim Size-8½ x 11, 8 pages, ISSN: 1065-6146, 2 Color
Subscriptions: Indv. $395, $40/copy
List Rental: List Management Co.: Manager: Denise Tondream; Direct Effect, 1049 Camino Del Mar Ste 4b, Del Mar, CA 92014-2651 Tel # (619) 792-9259, Actives: $150/M

Software Industry Bulletin *Business*

Publishing Co: Digital Information Group, PO Box 110235, Stamford, CT 06911-0235; Title Tel # (203) 348-2751 Title Fax # (203) 977-8310
Personnel: Publisher-Jeff Silverstein
Editorial Description: Weekly news & analysis for micro software publishers.
General Info: Yr. Est. 1985, Weekly, Offset press, 6 pages, ISSN: 0883-5772, No Color, Newsprint
Subscriptions: Indv. $415, $15/copy
List Rental: List Management Co.: Worldata, 5200 Town Center Circle, Boca Raton, FL 33486 Tel # (407) 368-8200, Fax # (407) 368-8345, Actives: 12,956, $125/M

Software Industry Report   *Business*

Publishing Co: Computer Age-Millin Publishing Group, 714 Church Street, Alexandria, VA 22314-4202; Title Tel # (703) 739-8500 Title Fax # (703) 739-8505
Personnel: Publisher-S.L. Millin, Sr. Ed.-Charles Bailey, Mng. Editor-Michael Cotter, Contrib. Ed.-Terry Miller, Circ. Mgr.-Ruth Hill, Mktg. Dir.-Thomas Shack, III
Editorial Description: Tracks worldwide industry and government software activities and opportunities with an emphasis on innovative strategies for MIS executives, market research and new developments in systems technologies.
General Info: (Formerly Software Digest), Yr. Est. 1968, Semi-monthly, Trim Size-8½ x 11, Sheetfed press, 12 pages, ISSN: 0038-0636, Ind/Abs/Online: Info Access Co.
Subscriptions: Indv. $495, Can. $495, For. $519, $35/copy
Circulation: Total-800
List Rental: Rents Lists

Software Law Bulletin
See: LAW

Software Legal Book
See: FISH & FISHERIES

Software and Networks for Learning
See: EDUCATION

Software Reports: Guide to Evaluated Educational Software

Publishing Co: Trade Service Publications, Inc., 10996 Torreyana Rd, San Diego, CA 92121-1105; Title Tel # (619) 457-5920
Personnel: Editor-Bonnie Dudley, Circ. Mgr.-Harry Weber, Adv. Dir.-Charles Penn, Promotion Dir.-Dan Hennahan
Editorial Description: Reviews of software.
General Info: Yr. Est. 1983, Semi-weekly, Trim Size-5½ x 8½, 75 pages, Color-cover
Subscriptions: Indv. $150

Software Reviews on File   *Business, Consumer*

Publishing Co: Facts on File, Inc., 11 Penn Plaza, New York, NY 10001-2006 Tel # (212) 967-8800 Parent Co.-Infobase Holdings Inc., New York; Title Tel # (212) 683-2244 Title Fax # (212) 683-3633
Personnel: Publisher-Remmel Nunn, Editor-James Johnson, Circ. Mgr.-Steve Orlofsky, Production Dir.-Olivia McKean
Editorial Description: Reviews of microcomputer software excerpted from 300 computers journals.
General Info: Yr. Est. 1985, Monthly, Trim Size-8½ x 11, Sheetfed press, 64 pages, ISSN: 8755-7169, No Color, Saddle-stitched, Looseleaf
Subscriptions: Indv. $239, Inst. $239
Acquistions: Publication Bought
List Rental: Rents Lists
Printing Co: Wickersham Printers, 2959 Old Tree Dr, Lancaster, PA 17603-4080 Tel # (717) 299-5731, Fax # (717) 393-7469

Software Success   *Business, Consumer*

Publishing Co: Software Success, 175 Highland Ave., Needham, MA 02194-3034; Title Tel # (408) 446-2504 Title Fax # (408) 255-1098
Personnel: Publisher-David Bowen, Editor-Mark Gordon
General Info: Yr. Est. 1987, Monthly, 16 pages, No Color, Coated, Saddle-stitched
Subscriptions: Indv. $197
Circulation: Total-375
List Rental: List Management Co.: Name-Finders Lists, Inc., 3180 18th St Fl 2, San Francisco, CA 94110-2028 Tel # (510) 533-4177, Fax # (510) 553-8677, Actives: 32,855, $125/M

Software Taxation Letter
See: LAW

Software Technology Transfer
See: ENGINEERING

Software Times

Publishing Co: Sterling Software Marketing, 11050 White Rock Rd # 100, Rancho Cordova, CA 95670-6001; Title Tel # (916) 635-5535
Personnel: Editor-James Hanchett, Circ. Mgr.-Cynthia Wilson, Art Dir.-Tony Kasovich
Editorial Description: Newsletter for IBM/PC mainframe users about Sterling Software products.
General Info: Yr. Est. 1978, Quarterly, Trim Size-8½ x 11, Web press, 12 pages, 2 Color, Coated
Circulation: (80% controlled), Total-20,000, Subscriptions-1,000

The Software User Newsletter   *Business, Consumer*

Publishing Co: Software User, The, 8 Vine Crescent, Barrie, ON L4N 2B3 Canada; Title Tel # (705) 739-7155 Title Fax # (705) 739-7157
Personnel: Publisher, Editor-Jeremy Pollard
Editorial Description: For software users that interface with Allen Bradley programmable controllers.
General Info: Yr. Est. 1993, 6x/yr., Trim Size-8½ x 11, Letrpr. press, 12 pages, ISSN: 1195-8065, No Color, Matte
Subscriptions: Indv. $48, Can. $48, For. $64
Advertising: Accepts Inserts.

Softwatch   *Business*

Publishing Co: Applied Computer Research, PO Box 82266, Phoenix, AZ 85071-2266 Tel # (602) 995-5929; Title Fax # (602) 665-0905
Personnel: Editor-Alan Howard
Editorial Description: Articles from over 200 computer industry related publications.
General Info: Yr. Est. 1992, Quarterly, ISSN: 1064-8860
Subscriptions: Indv. $95, For. $110

Soundwaves

Publishing Co: Boston Computer Society, Inc., 101 A First Ave. Suite #2, Waltham, MA 02154 Tel # (617) 290-5700 Fax # (617) 290-5744
General Info: Bi-monthly

Spang Robinson Report on Artificial Intelligence   *Business*

Publishing Co: John Wiley & Sons, Inc., 605 Third Avenue, New York, NY 10158-0012 Tel # (212) 850-6000 Fax # (212) 850-6088
Personnel: Publisher-Margaret Irwin, Editor-Sara Hedberg, Promotion Dir.-Lonny Stein
Editorial Description: Tracking artificial intelligence applications.
General Info: (Formerly Artificial Intelligence Report), Yr. Est. 1983, Monthly, Trim Size-8½ x 11, 16 pages, ISSN: 0885-9957, Ind/Abs/Online: NewsNet, Newsprint, Saddle-stitched
Subscriptions: Inst. $330, Can. $330, For. $380, $25/copy
List Rental: List Management Co.: American List Counsel, 88 Orchard Cir # Cn-5219, Princeton, NJ 08540-3026 Tel # (908) 874-4300, Fax # (908) 874-4433

Spang Robinson Report on Supercomputing & Parallel Processing   *Business*

Publishing Co: John Wiley & Sons, Inc., 605 Third Avenue, New York, NY 10158-0012 Tel # (212) 850-6000 Fax # (212) 850-6088
Personnel: Publisher-Margaret Irwin, Editor-Richard Hill, Promotion Dir.-Lonny Stein
Editorial Description: Follows business trends in the new field of supercomputing & parallel processing.
General Info: Yr. Est. 1987, Monthly, Trim Size-8½ x 11, 16 pages, Newsprint
Subscriptions: Inst. $305, For. $355, $25/copy
List Rental: List Management Co.: American List Counsel, 88 Orchard Cir # Cn-5219, Princeton, NJ 08540-3026 Tel # (908) 874-4300, Fax # (908) 874-4433

Sprite-The Commodore Newsletter

Publishing Co: Boston Computer Society, Inc., 101 A First Ave. Suite #2, Waltham, MA 02154 Tel # (617) 290-5700 Fax # (617) 290-5744
General Info: Bi-monthly

Step-By-Step Electronic Design   *Business*

Publishing Co: Dynamic Graphics, Inc., 6000 N Forest Park Dr, Peoria, IL 61614-3556 Tel # (309) 688-2300 Fax # (309) 688-3075; Title Tel # (309) 698-0001 Title Fax # (309) 698-0831
Personnel: Editor-Nancy Aldrich-Ruenzel, Production Mgr., Art Dir.-Michael Hammer, Mktg. Dir.-Peter Force
Editorial Description: For electronic designers, illustrators & prepress professionals; how-to articles with step-by-step techniques.
General Info: Yr. Est. 1989, Monthly, Trim Size-8¼ x 10½, Sheetfed press, 16 pages, 4 Color, Matte, Saddle-stitched
Subscriptions: Indv. $48
Circulation: Total-10,000, Readership-13,800
Advertising: Inquire for rates.
List Rental: Actives: $90/M
Printing Co: Performance Press, 1001 3rd Avenue SW, Carmel, IN 46032 Tel # (317) 575-0727, Fax # (517) 496-3700

The Street Irregular
See: POETRY & CREATIVE WRITING

Studio City for the IIGS   *Consumer*

Publishing Co: Resource Central, 6339 W. 110th St. #11250, Overland Park, KS 66211-1509; Title Tel # (913) 469-6502 Title Fax # (913) 469-6507
Personnel: Publisher-Tom Weishaar, Editor-Dean Esmay, Circ. Dir.-Denise Cameron
Editorial Description: Disc-based newsletter for Hyper Studio users. Tips for authors & sample stacks.
General Info: (Formerly Stack-Central), Yr. Est. 1990, Bi-monthly, Desktop press, ISSN: 1066-7334
Subscriptions: Indv. $48, Can. $48, For. $48
Circulation: Total-1,000
List Rental: Rents Lists

Systems Development Management
Business

Publishing Co: Auerbach Publishers, One Penn Plz., 42nd Floor, New York, NY 10119-0002 Fax # (212) 971-5024 Parent Co.-Warren, Gorham & Lamont, Boston; Title Tel # (212) 971-5000 Title Fax # (212) 971-5025
Personnel: Publisher-Tom Kelly, Editor-Mary Ellen Macisaac, Production Mgr.-Geoff Braine, Promotion Dir.-Edward Novack
Editorial Description: Contains more than 80 how-to articles for systems managers, analysts and designers. Provides a wealth of practical solutions to systems development problems in both tradional and client-server environments. Subscription includes main volume and 6 bimonthly updates.
General Info: Bi-monthly, ISSN: 0735-9985, No Color, Newsprint, Saddle-stitched, Looseleaf
Subscriptions: Indv. $395
Acquistions: Publication Bought
Circulation: Total-3,000
List Rental: Rents Lists

Systems Reengineering Economics Letter
Business

Publishing Co: Computer Economics, Inc., 5841 Edison Pl., Carlsbad, CA 92008-6519 Tel # (619) 438-8100 Fax # (619) 431-1126
Personnel: Publisher-Bruno Bassi, Editor-Mark McManus, Circ. Mgr.-Michelle Burrier
Editorial Description: Information on methods, costs and risks of information and business systems process reengineering.
General Info: Yr. Est. 1994, Monthly, Trim Size-8½ x 11, 8 pages, ISSN: 1074-732X, 2 Color
Subscriptions: Indv. $395, $40/copy
List Rental: List Management Co.: Manager: Denise Tondream; Direct Effect, 1049 Camino Del Mar Ste 4b, Del Mar, CA 92014-2651 Tel # (619) 792-9259, Actives: $150/M

Systems Thinker, The
Business

Publishing Co: Pegasus Communications, Inc., P.O. Box 120, Kendall Square, Cambridge, MA 02142 Tel # (617) 576-1231 Fax # (617) 576-3114
Personnel: Mng. Editor-Colleen Lannon-Kim
Editorial Description: Covers systems thinking and organizational learning.
General Info: Yr. Est. 1990, 10x/yr.
Subscriptions: Indv. $117

THEOS Times
Business

Publishing Co: THEOS Software Corporation, 1777 Botelho Drive, Walnut Creek, CA 94596-5022; Title Tel # (510) 935-1118 Title Fax # (510) 935-1177
Personnel: Editor-Callie Webb
Editorial Description: THEOS, published for clients and potential clients, discusses company's activities and products.
General Info: Quarterly, Trim Size-8½ x 11, 32 pages, 4 Color, Coated, Saddle-stitched
Printing Co: Sequoia Litho, 1815 Ygnacio Valley Road, Walnut Creek, CA 94598

TI PPC Notes
Business

Publishing Co: Hanson, 2149 14th Ave SW, Largo, FL 34640-4750
Personnel: Editor-Palmer Hanson
Editorial Description: Supports hand-held computers and programmable calculators manufactured by Texas Instruments such as the CC-40, TI-74, TI-81 and TI95.
General Info: (Formerly 52 Notes), Yr. Est. 1976, Quarterly, Trim Size-8½ x 11, 26 pages, No Color
Subscriptions: Indv. $17, For. $21
Circulation: Total-130

TImes, The
Consumer, Association

Publishing Co: Santa Clara Valley TIPC Users Group, 55 Temescal Ter, San Francisco, CA 94118-4324
Personnel: Editor-Thor Firing
Editorial Description: For Texas Instruments computer users in Santa Clara Valley.
General Info: Monthly

TODDNews
Business

Publishing Co: TODD Enterprises, 31 Water Mill Lane, Great Neck, NY 11021 Tel # (516) 487-3976 Fax # (718) 343-9180
Personnel: Editor-Carol Iglesias
Editorial Description: Information and news for software buyers.
General Info: Quarterly

Tag's Channel Compass
Business

Publishing Co: Ambit International, Inc., 665 3rd St Ste 508, San Francisco, CA 94107-1923; Title Tel # (415) 957-9433 Title Fax # (415) 957-0504
Personnel: Publisher, Editor-Linda Kazares, Production Mgr.-Robin Fenzi, Art Dir.-Marc Richard, Adv. Dir., Promotion Dir.-Linda Gillette
Editorial Description: The report on channel marketing, sales, and development in the computer and multimedia industry.
General Info: Yr. Est. 1991, Monthly, ISSN: 1073-6662
Subscriptions: Indv. $450, Inst. $450, Can. $450, For. $525, $54/copy
Printing Co: Oscar Printing, 2565 3rd St Apt 234, San Francisco, CA 94107-3140 Tel # (415) 641-7763, Fax # (415) 641-8051

TechAgra News
See: AGRICULTURE

Technical Update
Consumer, Scholarly

Publishing Co: Univ. of Cincinnati Computing Info. Tech. Svces., 45 Beecher Hall, Mail Loc. 88, Cincinnati, OH 45221 Tel # (513) 556-9003 Fax # (513) 556-1208; Title Tel # (513) 475-5681
Personnel: Editor-Mary Clark
Editorial Description: Informs users of procedural changes, new programs, etc.
General Info: (Formerly UCCC Technical Update), Yr. Est. 1973, Quarterly, Trim Size-8½ x 11, Sheetfed press, 16 pages, 2 Color, Newsprint
Circulation: Total-2,100

Technologies Tomorrow
Business

Publishing Co: Technologies Tomorrow, 85 W. Stirrup Trail, Monument, CO 80132-8730
Personnel: Editor-F.A. Bick, Circulation-D.L. Bick
Editorial Description: Dedicated to the technologies of and for tomorrow. Each issue is devoted to a specific emerging technology.
General Info: Yr. Est. 1993, 8x/yr.
Subscriptions: Indv. $450
Circulation: Total-500

Technology for Communicators
See: MEDIA & COMMUNICATIONS

Technology Forecasts & Technology Surveys
See: SCIENCE

Technology Industry Growth Forecaster
See: EMPLOYMENT

Technology New York Report
See: BUSINESS & INDUSTRY

Technology Pathfinder for Administrators
Association

Publishing Co: Master Teacher, Inc., Leadership La., Box 1207, Manhattan, KS 66502; Title Tel # (913) 539-0555 Title Fax # (913) 539-7739
Personnel: Publisher-Robert DeBruyn, Editor-Chris Ostrum, Circ. Mgr.-Lori Hanson, Production Mgr.-Sherri Spence, Art Dir.-Barry Anderson
Editorial Description: Monthly source for information , ideas, and solutions to technology issues.
General Info: Yr. Est. 1995, Monthly, Trim Size-8½ x 11, Sheetfed press, 8 pages, 2 Color, Other, Saddle-stitched
Subscriptions: Indv. $40, Can. $40, For. $40
Circulation: Total-1,200

Technology Trends
Business

Publishing Co: Enterprise Technology Corp., 305 Madison Ave., New York, NY 10165-0006; Title Tel # (212) 972-1860 Title Fax # (212) 687-6126
Personnel: Publisher-Christian B. Silge, Editor-Kevin J. Merz
Editorial Description: Discusses current topics in computer software technology, with commentary on their perceived value to the business community. Primarily aimed at chief information officers and information systems managers.
General Info: Yr. Est. 1991, Quarterly, ISSN: 1065-5271
Subscriptions: Free To Qualified Recipient

Technology Watch

Publishing Co: Evans Research Corp. of Canada, 1 Eva Rd. #309, Etobicoke, ON M9C 4Z5 Canada; Title Tel # (416) 498-6664 Title Fax # (416) 498-7275
Editorial Description: Contains a compilation of Evans Research findings & announcements. Technology Watch helps to supplement other reports, & provides on on-going cross-secton of industry-specific information.
General Info: Monthly
Subscriptions: Indv. $475

TelePuting Hotline and Field Computing Source Letter
See: TELECOMMUNICATIONS

Telecom Calendar
See: TELECOMMUNICATIONS

Telecom Newsflash, The
See: TELECOMMUNICATIONS

Telecommuting Review
See: INDUSTRIAL RELATIONS/PERSONNEL

Terry Shannon on DEC   *Business*

Publishing Co: DataTrends Pubs., Inc., 895 B Harrison Street SE, PO Box 4460, Leesburg, VA 22075 Tel # (703) 779-0574; Title Tel # (703) 760-0660 Title Fax # (703) 760-9365
Personnel: Publisher-Paul Ochs, Editor-Dan Carney, Exec. Ed.-Terry Shannon, Circ. Mgr.-Gennifer Chenault
Editorial Description: News and analysis of Digital Equipment Corp.
General Info: (Formerly Monosson Report on DEC and IBM; DataTrends Report on DEC), Yr. Est. 1981, Monthly, Ind/Abs/Online: Predicasts
Subscriptions: Indv. $595, Can. $595, For. $643

Test Technology Newsletter

Publishing Co: Computer Society Press, 1730 Massachusetts Ave NW, Washington, DC 20036-1903; Title Tel # (202) 371-0101
Personnel: Editor-Daniel Graham
General Info: Quarterly, 16 pages
Circulation: Total-1,048

Texas, Natural Resources Information System, Newsletter
See: ENVIRONMENT & ECOLOGY

Tick, Tick, Tick...   *Business, Consumer*

Publishing Co: 2000AD, Inc., 2 Grace Ct., Apt 2U, Brooklyn, NY 11201-4156; Title Tel # (718) 858-6890
Personnel: Editor-Bill Goodwin
Editorial Description: Computer people concerned about the year 2000.
General Info: Yr. Est. 1993, Quarterly, Trim Size-8½ x 11, 8 pages, No Color, Matte

TidBITS   *Business, Consumer*   CPM: $4

Publishing Co: TidBITS, 27541 SE 154th Pl., Issaquah, WA 98027-7340; Title Tel # (206) 392-0553
Personnel: Publisher-Adam Engst, News Ed.-Mark H. Anbinder, Editor, Bk. Rev. Ed., Mktg. Dir.-Tonya Engst
Editorial Description: Electronic newsletter that reports on interesting products and events in the computer industry with an emphasis on the Macintosh and the Internet.
General Info: Yr. Est. 1990, Weekly, Ind/Abs/Online: Internet, America Online, Ziffnet/Mac, CompuServe, GEnie, Delphi, BIX
Subscriptions: Free
Circulation: Total-150,000
Advertising: $700. Accepts Inserts.

TimeOut-Central   *Business, Consumer*

Publishing Co: Resource Central, 6339 W. 110th St. #11250, Overland Park, KS 66211-1509; Title Tel # (913) 469-6502 Title Fax # (913) 469-6507
Personnel: Publisher-Tom Weishaar, Editor-Randy Brandt, Circ. Mgr.-Denise Cameron
Editorial Description: Technical information and complete computer files devoted to Appleworks and the TimeOut series.
General Info: Yr. Est. 1990, Bi-monthly, ISSN: 1066-7326, No Color
Subscriptions: Indv. $50, Can. $48, For. $48
Circulation: Total-500
List Rental: Rents Lists

Times   *Association*   CPM: $720

Publishing Co: National Time Equipment Association, PO Box 13848, Milwaukee, WI 53213-0848; Title Tel # (314) 426-7727 Title Fax # (314) 426-1776
Personnel: Publisher, Editor-Ronald Nowacki
General Info: Yr. Est. 1978, Bi-monthly, Trim Size-7½ x 10, Sheetfed press, 20 pages, 20% ads, 2 Color, Coated
Acquisitions: Publication Bought
Circulation: Total-250
Advertising: $180.

To the Point

Publishing Co: To the Point, RD #1, Box 199, Chester Springs, PA 19425-9801
Editorial Description: Information & ideas for executives marketing technology related products & services.

Token Perspectives Newsletter   *Business*

Publishing Co: Architecture Technology Corp., PO Box 24344, Minneapolis, MN 55424-0344; Title Tel # (612) 935-2035 Title Fax # (612) 829-5871
Personnel: Editor in Chief-Kenneth Thurber, Editor-Gordon A. Palzer
Editorial Description: Covers all developments relating to IBM's Token Ring LAN, and FDDI products and technology
General Info: Yr. Est. 1983, Monthly, Trim Size-8½ x 11, Offset press, 20 pages, ISSN: 0886-2362, 2 Color, Matte, Other
Subscriptions: Indv. $312, For. $372, $40/copy
List Rental: Rents Lists

Trading Systems Technology
See: BANKING & FINANCE

Typendium   *Business*

Publishing Co: Xerox Typographic Marketing, 101 Continental Blvd., El Segundo, CA 90245-4530
Personnel: Editor-Earlene Kerns
General Info: Yr. Est. 1983, Bi-monthly
Circulation: Total-15,000

UCS Dispatch

Publishing Co: Univ. of Alberta General Services, 352 General Svcs. Bldg., Edmonton, AB T6G 2H1 Canada; Title Tel # (403) 492-2462
Personnel: Editor-Vaughn Bowler, Art Dir.-Nada Zeljkovic
Editorial Description: General interest articles on computing & services of Univ. of Alberta, Univ. Computing Systems.
General Info: (Formerly Computing Services Bulletin), Yr. Est. 1966, 10x/yr., Sheetfed press, 16 pages, ISSN: 0840-6235, 2 Color, Newsprint, Saddle-stitched
Subscriptions: Free
Acquistions: Publication Bought
Circulation: Total-3,500
Advertising: Inquire for rates.
Printing Co: Univ. of Alberta Printing Svcs., Genl. Services Bldg., Edmonton, AB T6G 2H1 Canada Tel # (403) 492-4246

UNIX & Software Systems

Publishing Co: Datapro Research Corp., 600 Delran Pky, Delran, NJ 08075-1255 Tel # (609) 764-0100 Fax # (609) 764-2815

UNIX Update   *Business*

Publishing Co: Worldwide Videotex Co., PO Box 3273, Boynton Beach, FL 33424-3273 Tel # (407) 738-2276 Fax # (407) 738-2276
Editorial Description: News and information on UNIX computer systems.
General Info: Yr. Est. 1990, Monthly, Ind/Abs/Online: NewsNet; DIALOG
Subscriptions: Indv. $150, Inst. $150, Can. $150, For. $165

URISA Marketplace
See: LIBRARY

URISA News
See: LIBRARY

Uncle Hank's Shareware Review Newsletter

Publishing Co: Uncle Hank's Shareware, 8 Hendrick St, Easthampton, MA 01027-2525
Editorial Description: Focuses on shareware available for varied applications.
General Info: Bi-monthly
Subscriptions: Indv. $12

Unigram X   *Business*

Publishing Co: G-2 Computer Intelligence, 3 Maple Place, P.O. Box 7, Glen Head, NY 11545-9864; Title Tel # (516) 759-7025 Title Fax # (516) 759-7028
Personnel: Publisher-Maureen O' Gara, Editor-William Fellows, Circ. Mgr.-Michael Tablusky
General Info: Yr. Est. 1984, Weekly
Subscriptions: Indv. $495
Advertising: Inquire for rates.
List Rental: Rents Lists

University Computer Centre Newsletter   *Business*

Publishing Co: Dalhousie University, Computer Centre, Publications, Halifax, NS B3H 4H8 Canada; Title Tel # (902) 494-3472
Personnel: Editor-E. Rowntree
Editorial Description: Computer general information.
General Info: Monthly

University of Hawaii, Computing Center Newsletter   *Association*

Publishing Co: Univ. of Hawaii, Computing Center, 2565 The Mall, Keller Hall, Honolulu, HI 96822-2233; Title Tel # (808) 956-7351
Personnel: Editor-Naomi Okinaga, Production Mgr.-Lee Ann Sakihara
Editorial Description: Center's activities and happenings, services and facilities available, and techniques and problems of using the computer.
General Info: Yr. Est. 1965, Quarterly, Trim Size-8½ x 11, Offset press, 20 pages, 2 Color, Coated, Saddle-stitched
Circulation: Total-1,500

University of New Mexico, Computing Center Newsletter

Publishing Co: University of New Mexico Student Publications, Marron Hall, Rm. 131, Albuquerque, NM 87131-0001; Title Tel # (505) 277-8147
General Info: Yr. Est. 1967, Monthly, Trim Size-8½ x 11, 20 pages, Ind/Abs/Online: Charts.Illus.Cum.Ind.
Circulation: Total-1,400

Update   *Association*

Publishing Co: N.E. Regional Data Ctr. of the State Univ. System of Florida, 112 SSRB-Univ. of Florida, Box 112050, Gainesville, FL 32611-2050; Title Tel # (904) 392-2061
Title Fax # (904) 392-9440
Personnel: Editor-John Ashcraft
Editorial Description: Provides information on system, program, policy, procedural, and accounting changes to users of the Northeast Regional Data Center.
General Info: Yr. Est. 1973, Monthly, Trim Size-8½ x 11, Offset press, 20 pages, No Color, Saddle-stitched
Subscriptions: Free
Circulation: (55% controlled), Total-1,800, Subscriptions-800

Urban & Regional Technology & Development
See: PUBLIC MANAGEMENT & PLANNING

VI Bug Newsletter

Publishing Co: Boston Computer Society, Inc., 101 A First Ave. Suite #2, Waltham, MA 02154
Tel # (617) 290-5700 Fax # (617) 290-5744
General Info: Quarterly

VMEnews

Publishing Co: VME, Inc., 2618 S Shannon Dr, Tempe, AZ 85282-2936; Title Tel # (602) 488-1462
Personnel: Publisher, Editor-Jack Grenard
Editorial Description: Marketing & technical news of & for the VMEnews computer industry.
General Info: Yr. Est. 1987, Monthly, ISSN: 1040-970X
Subscriptions: Indv. $99, Can. $99, For. $99, $21/copy
Advertising: Accepts Inserts.

VTLS EXPRESS A
Publication of VTLS Inc.   *Consumer*

Publishing Co: VTLS inc., 100 Kraft Drive, Blacksburg, VI 24060; Title Tel # (703) 231-3605
Title Fax # (703) 231-3648
Personnel: Editor-Gail Gulbenkin, Asst. Ed.-Barbara Scheid
Editorial Description: The VTLS Z39.50 Server supports all VTLS authority searhes-author, title, subject and Z/subject heading-in addition to full keyword and Boolen searches on any word in any indexed field.
General Info: Yr. Est. 1995, Trim Size-8.5 x 11, 16 pages, ISSN: 0894-4814, 4 Color

Virtual Inc.

Publishing Co: Virtual Fusion, 5160 Calla Bonita, Sierra Vista, AZ 85635
Editorial Description: A newsletter for the online business community
General Info: Trim Size-8.5 x 11, 4 pages
Subscriptions: Indv. $2

Virtual Reality Report   *Business*

Publishing Co: Cobb Group, 9420 Bunsen Pky., Ste. 300, Louisville, KY 40220-4206
Tel # (502) 491-1900 Fax # (502) 491-4200 Parent Co.-Ziff-Davis Publishing Co., New York
Personnel: Publisher-Alan Meckler, Editor-Sandra Meckler, Circ. Mgr.-Mike Hicks
Editorial Description: Keeps companies up-to-date date on the virtual reality industry.
General Info: Monthly, ISSN: 1052-6242
Subscriptions: Indv. $147
Circulation: Total-600

Virus Bulletin   *Business*

Publishing Co: Virus Bulletin, 590 Danbury Rd., Ridgefield, CT 06877-2722;
Title Tel # (203) 431-8720 Title Fax # (203) 431-8165
Personnel: Editor-Richard Ford, Production Mgr.-Victoria Lammer
Editorial Description: An international journal addressing computer viruses, Trojan horses, & other malicious programs. Emphasis is placed on providing technical & procedural countermeasures for businesses using computers.
General Info: Yr. Est. 1989, Monthly, Trim Size-8⅜ x 10¾, Web press, 24 pages, ISSN: 0956-9979, Color-cover, Matte, Saddle-stitched
Subscriptions: Indv. $395, $35/copy

Visual Literacy Review & Newsletter
See: EDUCATION

VoiceNews
See: TELECOMMUNICATIONS

Weigand Report   *Business, Consumer*

Publishing Co: Weigand, 356 Salem Tpke, Bozrah, CT 06334-1518
Personnel: Publisher, Editor-C.J. Weigand
Editorial Description: Working newsletter for Macintosh professionals. Information for communicators, desktop publishers, & small business users. Content is devoted entirely to hard-hitting, decision-making information, including penetrating industry insights, tightly focused product reviews, and time-saving tips & techniques.
General Info: Yr. Est. 1989, 20x/yr., ISSN: 1045-019X
Subscriptions: Indv. $128, Can. $128, For. $148

What's Next?

Publishing Co: Boston Computer Society, Inc., 101 A First Ave. Suite #2, Waltham, MA 02154
Tel # (617) 290-5700 Fax # (617) 290-5744
General Info: Quarterly

Windows 95 Journal,The

Publishing Co: IDG Newsletter Corporation, 77 Franklin St., Boston, MA 02110;
Title Tel # (617) 482-8785 Title Fax # (617) 338-0164
Personnel: Publisher-Craig G. Pierce, Editor-Jim Pile, Circ. Mgr.-Meredith Seller Doesschate, Production Mgr.-John Foegetta
Editorial Description: Provides a wealth of tips, bug reports, networking advice, and road maps to the new Windows interface.
Subscriptions: Indv. $79, For. $109

Windows Letter   *Business*

Publishing Co: Mendham Technology Group, 144 Talmadge Rd., Mendham, NJ 07945;
Title Tel # (201) 543-2273 Title Fax # (201) 543-6033
Personnel: Publisher-D.G. Mennie, Editor-Carole Patton
Editorial Description: Cover Windows ionformation as well as Windows applications.
General Info: (Formerly ACKowledge, the Windows Letter), Yr. Est. 1988, Monthly, ISSN: 1043-0768
Subscriptions: Indv. $245
List Rental: Actives: 10,000

Windows Watcher   *Business*

Publishing Co: Computhink Inc., 15127NE 24th St. #344, Redmond, WA 98052-5547;
Title Tel # (206) 881-7354 Title Fax # (206) 883-1452
Personnel: Publisher, Editor-Jesse Berst, Mng. Editor-Robbin Young, Technology Ed.-Jon Dekeles, Circ. Mgr.-Lori White
Editorial Description: News and info for supervisors and managers of the Windows marketplace.
General Info: Yr. Est. 1990, Monthly
Subscriptions: Indv. $395, Can. $395, For. $445
List Rental: List Management Co.: Statlistics Management, 123 Elm St. Suite 700, Old Saybrook, CT 06475-0936 Tel # (203) 388-4669, Fax # (203) 388-6854, Actives: 19,300, $140/M

Wireless Telecommunications
See: TELECOMMUNICATIONS

Wireless Week
See: TELECOMMUNICATIONS

Workgroup Computing
Report   *Business*

Publishing Co: Patricia Seybold's Group, 148 State St., 7th Fl., Boston, MA 02109-2506
Tel # (617) 762-5200 Fax # (617) 764-1028; Title Tel # (617) 742-5200 Title Fax # (617) 742-1028
Personnel: Publisher-Patricia Seybold, Editor-Ronni Marshak, Circ. Mgr.-Deborah Hay, Production Mgr.-Doug Freeman, Art Dir.-Melissa Hagan
Editorial Description: Contains in-depth product evaluations, vendor profiles, & trend analysis on issues relating to enterprise & workgroup computing, & group area.
General Info: (Formerly Patricia Seybold's Office Computing Report), Yr. Est. 1978, Monthly, Offset press, 25 pages, Ind/Abs/Online: NewsNet, 2 Color, Newsprint, Saddle-stitched
Subscriptions: Indv. $440, Can. $460, For. $475, $50/copy

Workstation Advisory
Service   *Business*

Publishing Co: Computer Economics, Inc., 5841 Edison Pl., Carlsbad, CA 92008-6519;
Title Tel # (619) 438-8100 Title Fax # (619) 431-1126
Personnel: Publisher-Bruno Bassi, Editor-Terrin Lovett, Circ. Mgr.-Denise Tondream
Editorial Description: Indentifies and evaluates the key factors in workstation technology and prices.
General Info: Yr. Est. 1993, 6x/yr., Looseleaf
Subscriptions: Indv. $895
List Rental: List Management Co.: Manager: Denise Tondream; Direct Effect, 1049 Camino Del Mar Ste 4b, Del Mar, CA 92014-2651 Tel # (619) 792-9259, Actives: $150/M

Worldwide Databases
See: PERIODICAL INDUSTRY

Worldwide Videotex Update   *Business*

Publishing Co: Worldwide Videotex Co., PO Box 3273, Boynton Beach, FL 33424-3273
Fax # (407) 738-2276; Title Tel # (407) 738-2276 Title Fax # (407) 738-2275
Editorial Description: Covers television and online related technologies.
General Info: Yr. Est. 1988, Monthly, ISSN: 0731-7891
Subscriptions: Indv. $150, Inst. $150, Can. $150, For. $165

Yardstick   *Business*

Publishing Co: Gartner Group, 56 Top Gallant Rd, Stamford, CT 06902-7700;
Title Tel # (203) 964-0096
Personnel: Editor-Randy Brophy
General Info: (Formerly Top 100), Yr. Est. 1979, Quarterly, Trim Size-9 x 12, 1,000 pages, Looseleaf
Subscriptions: Indv. $2,195, Inst. $2,195, For. $2,195

Yellowstone Desktop
Publishing Letter   *Business*

Publishing Co: Yellowstone Information Services, RR 2 Box 42A, Bloomingdale, OH 43910-9802
Fax # (304) 965-7785; Title Tel # (304) 965-5548 Title Fax # (304) 965-5548
Personnel: Publisher, Editor-Roger Thibault
Editorial Description: Articles on desktop publishing hardware and software, product news, new applications and more. Information covering IBM, Macintosh and other computer types.
General Info: Yr. Est. 1988, Bi-monthly, 10% ads
Subscriptions: Indv. $50, Inst. $50, Can. $60, For. $70
Advertising: $275.
List Rental: List Management Co.: Worldata, 5200 Town Center Circle, Boca Raton, FL 33486 Tel # (407) 368-8200, Fax # (407) 368-8345, Actives: 14,000, $110/M

Yellowstone Multimedia
Letter, The   *Business, Consumer*

Publishing Co: Yellowstone Information Services, RR 2 Box 42A, Bloomingdale, OH 43910-9802;
Title Tel # (304) 965-5548 Title Fax # (304) 965-7785
Personnel: Publisher-Roger Thibault
Editorial Description: Covering world- wide news events, and applizations in cd-rom and multi-media technology.
General Info: Yr. Est. 1993, Monthly, 15% ads
Subscriptions: Inst. $50, Can. $60, For. $70, $10/copy
Advertising: $275. Accepts Inserts.
List Rental: List Management Co.: Worldata, 5200 Town Center Circle, Boca Raton, FL 33486
Tel # (407) 368-8200, Fax # (407) 368-8345, Actives: 25,000, $100/M

Yellowstone Portable
Computing Letter   *Business, Consumer*   CPM: $39

Publishing Co: Yellowstone Information Services, RR 2 Box 42A, Bloomingdale, OH 43910-9802;
Title Tel # (304) 965-5548 Title Fax # (304) 965-7785
Personnel: Editor-Roger Thibault
Editorial Description: For users and those with interests in the area of portable PC computing. Includes articles on hardware, software, news, books, etc.
General Info: Yr. Est. 1991, Bi-monthly
Subscriptions: Indv. $50, Inst. $50, Can. $60, For. $70, $10/copy
Circulation: Total-7,000
Advertising: $275.
List Rental: List Management Co.: Worldata, 5200 Town Center Circle, Boca Raton, FL 33486
Tel # (407) 368-8200, Fax # (407) 368-8345

Yellowstone Windows
Letter   *Business, Consumer*   CPM: $137

Publishing Co: Yellowstone Information Services, RR 2 Box 42A, Bloomingdale, OH 43910-9802
Fax # (304) 965-7785; Title Tel # (304) 965-5548 Title Fax # (304) 965-7485
Personnel: Editor-Roger Thibault
Editorial Description: Centers on computer applications running under Microsoft Windows. Coverage includes reviews, calendar, tips, books, etc.
General Info: Yr. Est. 1991, Bi-monthly, 8 pages, 2 Color, Coated, Saddle-stitched
Subscriptions: Indv. $50, Inst. $50, Can. $60, For. $70, $10/copy
Circulation: Total-2,000
Advertising: $275.
List Rental: List Management Co.: Direct Media, Inc., 200 Pemberwick Rd., PO Box 4565, Greenwich, CT 06830 Tel # (203) 532-3713, Fax # (203) 531-1452, Actives: 16,850, $85/M

ZiffNet Threads   *Business, Consumer*

Publishing Co: ZiffNet Information Service, 25 1st St, Cambridge, MA 02141-1810
Tel # (617) 252-5000 Fax # (617) 252-5551
Editorial Description: Tips and techniques for using ZiffNet's online services.
General Info: Monthly
Subscriptions: Free

CONFECTIONERY

Chocolate News   *Business*

Publishing Co: Hampton Intl. Comm, Inc., 4520 E. Grant Rd., Tucson, AZ 85712-2617;
Title Tel # (212) 682-7320
Personnel: Publisher-Lee Oser, Jr., Editor-Dorothy Pliner
Editorial Description: News relating to the chocolate manufacturing industry.
General Info: Yr. Est. 1979, Bi-monthly
Subscriptions: Indv. $16

Direct Line   *Business, Association*

Publishing Co: Intl. Jelly & Preserve Assn., 5775 Peachtree Dunwoody Rd NE, Ste G500, Atlanta, GA 30342-1507 Tel # (404) 252-3663 Fax # (404) 252-0774
Editorial Description: News and information for producers of jelly and preserves.
General Info: Quarterly

National Confectioners
Assn. of the U.S. News
Bulletin

Publishing Co: Natl. Confectioners Assn., 7900 Westpark Dr Ste A320, Mc Lean, VA 22102-4203;
Title Tel # (703) 790-5750 Title Fax # (703) 790-5752
General Info: Weekly

National Honey Market News
See: AGRICULTURE

Quick Topics   *Association*

Publishing Co: American Wholesale Marketers Assn., 1128 16th St. NW, Washington, DC 20036-4808 Tel # (202) 463-2124 Fax # (202) 467-0559
Personnel: Editor-Shelley Estersohn
Editorial Description: News in abbreviated form; Federal regulations, industry appointments, general industry news. Convention news.
General Info: Bi-weekly, Trim Size-8½ x 11, Offset press, 4 pages, No Color
Circulation: Total-3,200

Sugar Art Sharing
Confectionary Ideas

Publishing Co: Sugar Art Partners, 1301 N Highway 99w # 298, Mcminnville, OR 97128-2722;
Title Tel # (503) 434-5473
Personnel: Circ. Mgr.-John Johnson, Publisher, Editor, Production Mgr., Adv. Dir., Art Dir., Promotion Dir.-Mary Johnson
Editorial Description: Magazine on calcedecorating, candy & all sugar medium arts.
General Info: Yr. Est. 1986, Monthly, Trim Size-8½ x 11, Web press, 88 pages, 4 Color, Coated
Subscriptions: Indv. $30, $3/copy
Circulation: Total-3,000

CONSTRUCTION & BUILDING

A.E. Legal Newsletter
See: LAW

A/E Marketing Journal   *Business, Association*

Publishing Co: Practice Management Associates Ltd., 10 Midland Ave., Newton, MA 02158-1021;
Title Tel # (617) 965-0055 Title Fax # (617) 965-5152
Personnel: Editor-Carolyn Kenney
General Info: Yr. Est. 1973, Monthly, Trim Size-8½ x 11, 8 pages, 2 Color
Subscriptions: Indv. $189, Can. $189, For. $240
List Rental: Rents Lists

AGC National Newsletter   *Business, Association*

Publishing Co: AGC Natl. Newsletter, 1957 East St., N.W., Washington, DC 20006
Fax # (202) 347-4004; Title Tel # (202) 393-2040
Personnel: Publisher-Hubert Beatty, Editor-Damian Hill
Editorial Description: Reports on activities of association and on events, principally actions of the Federal government, likely to affect the construction industry.
General Info: Yr. Est. 1919, Bi-weekly, Trim Size-8½ x 11, Offset press, 4 pages, 2 Color, Newsprint, Other
Subscriptions: Indv. $100
Circulation: Total-15,000

AVA Advisor

Publishing Co: Asbestos Victims of America (AVA), PO Box 559, Capitola, CA 95010-0559;
Title Tel # (408) 476-3646
Personnel: Editor-Heather Maurer
Editorial Description: Informational bulletin on asbestos toxicity. Includes membership news.
General Info: Yr. Est. 1981, Quarterly
Acquistions: Publication Bought
Circulation: Total-18,000

Advanced Construction
Information Service

Publishing Co: Brown's Letters, Inc., 1167 Mcbride Ave, West Paterson, NJ 07424-2539;
Title Tel # (518) 482-6230
General Info: Daily
Subscriptions: Indv. $840

Aluminum Situation
See: METALS & METALWORKING

American Concrete
Pavement Assn.
Newsletter   *Business, Association*

Publishing Co: American Concrete Pavement Assn., 3800 N Wilke Rd Ste 490, Arlington Heights, IL 60004-1268; Title Tel # (708) 394-5577
Personnel: Editor-Sarah Stevens
General Info: Yr. Est. 1964, Monthly

American Institute of
Constructors
Newsletter   *Business, Association*

Publishing Co: American Institute of Constructors, 466 94th Ave. N., Saint Petersburg, FL 33702-2522; Title Tel # (813) 578-0317 Title Fax # (813) 578-9982
Personnel: Editor-Cheryl Harris
General Info: Yr. Est. 1971, Bi-monthly, Trim Size-8½ x 11, Offset press, 16 pages, No Color
Subscriptions: Free With Membership
Circulation: Total-2,000
Advertising: Inquire for rates.
List Rental: Actives: $75/M
Printing Co: Gallaher's, 712 16th St N, Saint Petersburg, FL 33705-1335

American Society for
Concrete Construction
Membership Bulletin   *Association*

Publishing Co: Amer. Soc. for Concrete Construction/E. Burr Bennett, Ltd., 2849 Dundee Rd. #138, Northbrook, IL 60062-2501; Title Tel # (708) 291-0270
Editorial Description: Information in business & technical matters related to concrete construction.
General Info: Yr. Est. 1957, Bi-monthly, Offset press, 4 pages
Circulation: (100% controlled), Total-1,000

Anti-Corrosion Times

Publishing Co: Concrete Reinforcing Steel Inst, 933 N Plum Grove Rd, Schaumburg, IL 60173-4758; Title Tel # (708) 517-1200
Personnel: Editor-Theodore Neff
Editorial Description: Technical information & applications of epoxy-coated reinforcement used as a corrosion protection system in concrete.
General Info: Yr. Est. 1983, Semi-annually
Circulation: Total-25,000

Asbestos Monitor   *Business*

Publishing Co: Monitor Communication Group, 15995 N Barkers Landing Rd Ste, 320, Houston, TX 77079-2461; Title Tel # (713) 496-1734 Title Fax # (713) 531-7229
General Info: Yr. Est. 1989, Monthly
Subscriptions: Indv. $247

Asbestos Removal   *Business*

Publishing Co: Duane Publishing, 319 West St, Braintree, MA 02185; Title Tel # (617) 848-6150 Title Fax # (617) 848-6160
General Info: Yr. Est. 1967, Weekly
Subscriptions: Indv. $630

Asphalt Roofing Manufacturers Assn. - Newsletter

Publishing Co: Asphalt Roofing Manufacturers Assn., 6000 Executive Blvd Ste 201, Rockville, MD 20852-3803; Title Tel # (301) 231-9050
Editorial Description: Membership activities newsletter.
General Info: Bi-monthly

Atlantic Building Supply News   *Association*

Publishing Co: Atlantic Bldg. Supply Dealers Assn., 95 Foundry St., #203, Moncton, NB E1C 5H7 Canada; Title Tel # (506) 858-0700 Title Fax # (506) 859-0064
Personnel: Editor-John Ward
General Info: (Formerly Lumbern Round), Quarterly, Trim Size-8½ x 11, 20 pages, 6% ads
Subscriptions: Free With Membership
Circulation: Total-500
Advertising: Inquire for rates. Accepts Inserts.

BRB Research Briefs

Publishing Co: Building Research Board, Natl. Research Council, 2101 Constitution Ave NW, Washington, DC 20037-2955; Title Tel # (202) 334-3376
Personnel: Editor-Andrew Lerner
General Info: (Formerly ABBE Research Briefs), Bi-monthly, 4 pages
Circulation: Total-2,000

Bechtel Briefs
See: ENGINEERING

Better Building Report

Publishing Co: Pennsylvania State Univ, College of Engineering, 227 Hammond Bldg, University Park, PA 16802-1401; Title Tel # (814) 865-3451
General Info: Yr. Est. 1959

Blue Reports   *Business*

Publishing Co: Blue Reports Inc., 7325 Steele Mill Dr, Springfield, VA 22150-3608; Title Tel # (703) 644-5884 Title Fax # (703) 644-1929
General Info: Yr. Est. 1926, Daily
Subscriptions: Indv. $1,119

Bridge & Building News

Publishing Co: American Railway Bridge & Building Assn., 18154 Harwood Ave., Homewood, IL 60430-2128; Title Tel # (708) 799-4650
Personnel: Editor-Patricia Wisemann
Editorial Description: Covers bridge & building industry.

Brownstoner   *Business, Association*

Publishing Co: Brownstone Revival Committee, PO Box 577, New York, NY 10113-0577; Title Tel # (212) 675-0560
Personnel: Editor-Dorothy Zweighaft
General Info: Yr. Est. 1969, Quarterly, Trim Size-7½ x 11, 10 pages, 8% ads, No Color
Subscriptions: Indv. $25
Circulation: Total-1,500
Advertising: Inquire for rates.

Building & Construction Market Forecast   *Business*

Publishing Co: Delta Communications, Inc., 455 N. Cityfront Plaza Dr., Chicago, IL 60611-5593 Tel # (312) 222-2000 Fax # (312) 222-2026 Parent Co.-Elsevier Business Press, Morris Plains; Title Tel # (617) 964-3030 Title Fax # (617) 630-2100
Personnel: Publisher-Jim Haughey, Editor-Kermit Baker, Circ. Mgr.-Michelle Desmone, Production Mgr.-Chris Blotcher, Mktg. Dir.-Wendy Chambers
Editorial Description: Contains forecasts & analysis of construction activity, (residential, commercial, industrial, institutional, remodeling, public), materials price forecasts, analysis of interest rate trends.
General Info: Yr. Est. 1983, Monthly, Desktop press, 6 pages, Color, Newsprint
Subscriptions: Indv. $187, Can. $187, For. $207, $15/copy
Printing Co: Ben Franklin Smith, 320 Stuart St, Boston, MA 02116-5290 Tel # (617) 426-1160

Building Environment Report   *Business*

Publishing Co: IAQ Publications Inc, 2 Wisconsin Cir., Ste. 430, Chevy Chase, MD 20815-7003; Title Tel # (301) 913-0115 Title Fax # (301) 913-0119
Personnel: Publisher-David Rasmussen, Editor-Jennifer Silverman, Circ. Dir.-Gena McNamara, Mktg. Dir.-Robert Morrow
Editorial Description: Management issues for air quality control.
General Info: Yr. Est. 1993, Monthly, Trim Size-8½ x 11, 16 pages, ISSN: 1063-1615, 2 Color
Subscriptions: Indv. $325, $35/copy
Circulation: Total-800
List Rental: Actives: 100, $200/M

Building Industry Technology   *Business*

Publishing Co: National Technical Information Service U.S., 5285 Port Royal Rd., Springfield, VA 22161-0001 Tel # (703) 487-4630 Fax # (703) 487-4630; Title Tel # (703) 487-4650
Editorial Description: Covers architectural design, environmental design, construction, structural analysis, standards, management, materials, & equipment.
General Info: Weekly, Trim Size-8½ x 11, Offset press, 8 pages, ISSN: 0163-1500
Subscriptions: Indv. $135, Can. $135, For. $195

Building Inspectors' Assn. of British Columbia, News & Report

Publishing Co: Bldg. Inspectors' Assn. of British Columbia, 1158 21st St., W. Vancouver, BC V7V 4B1 Canada
Personnel: Editor-B. Yeomans
General Info: Yr. Est. 1965, Quarterly
Circulation: Total-450

Building Officials and Code Administrators International Bulletin   *Association*

Publishing Co: Building Officials & Code Administrators International, Inc., 4051 Flossmoor Rd, Country Club Hills, IL 60478-5771 Tel # (708) 799-2399; Title Tel # (708) 799-2300 Title Fax # (708) 799-4981
Personnel: Editor-William Even, Mktg. Coord.-Sladjana Drmanic
Editorial Description: Formulates building, zoning, and housing regulations.
General Info: Bi-monthly, Trim Size-8½ x 11, 10 pages
Circulation: (100% controlled), Total-11,500

Building Permits Law Bulletin   *Business*

Publishing Co: Quinlan Publishing, 23 Drydock Ave, Boston, MA 02210-2387 Fax # (617) 345-9646; Title Tel # (617) 542-0048
Personnel: Editor-Kevin Jones
Editorial Description: Info on how municipal building officials overcome legal challenges from developers, contractors, and lawyers.
General Info: Monthly, Trim Size-8½ x 11, 8 pages, ISSN: 1055-193X
Subscriptions: Indv. $63
List Rental: List Management Co.: Stevens-Knox List Management, 304 Park Ave S., New York, NY 10010-5312 Tel # (212) 388-8800, Fax # (212) 388-8890

Bulletin, The
See: GOVERNMENT

Bulletin Board   *Business*

Publishing Co: New Jersey Shore Builders Assn., 190 Oberlin Ave N, Lakewood, NJ 08701-4524; Title Tel # (908) 840-2020
Personnel: Editor-Joanne Capoano
General Info: Monthly
Circulation: Total-1,200

CD-Housing Register
See: REAL ESTATE

CHF Newsbriefs
See: INTERNATIONAL AFFAIRS

CRSI Transportation News

Publishing Co: Concrete Reinforcing Steel Inst, 933 N Plum Grove Rd, Schaumburg, IL 60173-4758; Title Tel # (708) 517-1200
Personnel: Editor-Theodore Neff
Editorial Description: Technical tips & case studies of reinforced concrete used in transportation applications.
General Info: 8 pages

CTDA Tile News & Views

Publishing Co: Ceramic Tile Distributors Assn., 800 Roosevelt Rd Ste C20, Glen Ellyn, IL 60137-5849; Title Tel # (708) 655-3270
General Info: (Formerly Ceramic Tile Distributors Assn. -News & Views), 12 pages, Color-cover, Coated, Saddle-stitched
Advertising: Accepts Inserts.

California Construction Law Reporter
See: LAW

Ceco Scope   *Business*

Publishing Co: Ceco Industries, Inc., 750 Old Hicory Blvd., #150, Brentwood, TN 37027-4502; Title Tel # (312) 242-2000
Personnel: Editor-Joseph F. Jezek
Editorial Description: 4-6 page corporate newsletter to employees, retirees and suppliers.
General Info: Yr. Est. 1920, Quarterly, Trim Size-$8\frac{1}{2}$ x 11, Sheetfed press, 6 pages, 2 Color
Circulation: (100% controlled), Total-10,000
Printing Co: United Letter, Inc., 619 S. LaSalle St., Chicago, IL 60605 Tel # (312) 427-3537

Chalkline   *Association*

Publishing Co: International Union of Bricklayers, 815 Fifteenth St., N.W., Washington, DC 20005-2201; Title Tel # (202) 783-3788
General Info: Yr. Est. 1865

Change Notice, The   *Business*

Publishing Co: R.S. Means Co., Inc., 100 Construction Plaza, Kingston, MA 02364-0100; Title Tel # (617) 585-7880 Title Fax # (617) 585-7466
Personnel: Editor-Howard Chandler
Editorial Description: Trends that affect construction and building costs, performance, etc.
General Info: Yr. Est. 1993, Bi-monthly, Trim Size-$8\frac{1}{2}$ x 11, 20 pages, 4 Color
Subscriptions: Indv. $75
Circulation: Total-30,000

Citator
See: LAW

CoHousing Newsletter
See: ENVIRONMENT & ECOLOGY

Cockshaw's Construction Labor News + Opinion
See: LABOR

Code Authority, The
See: SAFETY

Codes and Standards   *Business*

Publishing Co: Kelly P. Reynolds & Assoc., 833 W Chicago Ave Ste 200, Chicago, IL 60622-5406; Title Tel # (312) 829-6000 Title Fax # (312) 829-8855
Personnel: Publisher-Kelly P. Reynolds, Editor-Kelly Reynolds
Editorial Description: Monthly digest of code related news.
General Info: Yr. Est. 1980, Monthly, Trim Size-$8\frac{1}{2}$ x 11, Web press, 4 pages, Color, Newsprint
Subscriptions: Indv. $75
Circulation: (100% controlled), Total-1,000

Community Living of Florida   *Association*   CPM: $349

Publishing Co: Community Associations Institute, 1630 Duke Street, Alexandria, VA 22314 Tel # (703) 548-8600; Title Tel # (703) 836-6903 Title Fax # (703) 836-6907
Personnel: Editor-Mj Carscallen, Adv. Dir.-Jeff Sandersen
Editorial Description: Serves the information needed of CAI members in the state of Florida. Members include condo and homeowner associations.
General Info: Yr. Est. 1987, Bi-monthly, Trim Size-8.5 x 11, Web press, 8 pages, 25% ads, 2 Color, Coated, Case bound
Subscriptions: Indv. $32
Circulation: Total-2,549
Advertising: $890.

Composites News: Infrastructure
See: PLASTICS

Concrete Openings Newsletter   *Business, Association*   CPM: $166

Publishing Co: Concrete Sawing and Drilling Association, 4900 Blazer Pky, Dublin, OH 43017-3357; Title Tel # (614) 766-3656 Title Fax # (614) 766-3605
Personnel: Editor-Patrick O'Brien
Editorial Description: Published for contractors of concrete sawing & drilling and producers of diamond sawblades & core drills.
General Info: Yr. Est. 1972, Quarterly, Trim Size-$8\frac{1}{2}$ x 11, 20 pages, 2 Color, Coated, Saddle-stitched
Subscriptions: Free To Qualified Recipient
Circulation: Total-6,000
Advertising: $1,000. Accepts Inserts.

Connecticut Builder

Publishing Co: Home Builders Association of Hartford County, Connecticut Home Show, 1310 Silas Deane Highway, Weathersfield, CT 06109-4303; Title Tel # (203) 233-4495
Editorial Description: Legislation for builders.
General Info: 9x/yr.
Circulation: Total-850

Construction & Modernization Report

Publishing Co: American Hotel & Motel Association, 1201 New York Ave NW Ste 600, Washington, DC 20005-3917 Tel # (202) 289-3157 Fax # (202) 289-3110; Title Tel # (202) 289-3100 Title Fax # (202) 289-3158
Personnel: Editor-JB Kaplan
General Info: Monthly, 2 pages, 2 Color
Subscriptions: Free With Membership
Circulation: Total-1,700

Construction Briefings
See: LAW

Construction Claims Monthly   *Business*

Publishing Co: Business Publishers, Inc., 951 Pershing Dr., Silver Spring, MD 20910-4464 Tel # (301) 589-5103 Fax # (301) 589-8493; Title Tel # (301) 587-6300 Title Fax # (301) 587-1081
Personnel: Publisher-Leonard A. Eiserer, Editor-Bruce Jervis, Circ. Mgr.-Brenda Davenport, Production Mgr.-Kathleen Jacob
Editorial Description: Monthly in-depth analysis of court decisions arising from construction-related lawsuits.
General Info: Yr. Est. 1979, Monthly, Trim Size-$8\frac{1}{2}$ x 11, Desktop press, 8 pages, ISSN: 0272-4561, Ind/Abs/Online: Newsnet and Predicasts, No Color, Recycled
Subscriptions: Indv. $233, Can. $233, For. $239
Advertising: Accepts Inserts.
List Rental: List Management Co.: BPI Direct, 951 Pershing Dr., Silver Spring, MD 20910-4464 Tel # (301) 585-5976, Fax # (301) 587-4530

Construction Computer Applications Newsletter (CCAN)   *Business*

Publishing Co: CIP Communications, 6585 Commerce Blvd., Suite 292, Rohnert Park, CA 94928-2407 Fax # (707) 823-1007; Title Tel # (707) 792-2223
Personnel: Publisher, Editor-Royal Maul, Adv. Dir.-Edward Kaplan
Editorial Description: Contains software reviews. Covers construction uses of computers for everyone in the industry. Also includes new product announcements & updates.
General Info: Yr. Est. 1987, Bi-weekly, Trim Size-$8\frac{1}{2}$ x 11, Sheetfed press, 6 pages, Newsprint
Subscriptions: Indv. $89, Inst. $89, For. $109
Acquistions: Publication Bought, Publication Sold
List Rental: Rents Lists
Printing Co: Darrells Graphics & Print, 566 E Cotati Ave, Cotati, CA 94931-4094 Tel # (707) 664-0217

Construction Contractor, The
See: LAW

Construction and Design Law
See: LAW

Construction Equipment Monthly Update   CPM: $124

Publishing Co: Heartland Communications Group, 1003 Central Ave., PO Box 1115, Fort Dodge, IA 50501 Fax # (800) 247-2000; Title Tel # (515) 955-1600
Personnel: Publisher-Joseph Peed, Mktg. Dir.-Denise McLellan
Editorial Description: Listings by category, equipment & parts of sale; auction calendar (dates, product types, sales companies); new product information & changes.
General Info: Yr. Est. 1988, Monthly, Trim Size-$7\frac{5}{8}$ x $10\frac{3}{4}$, Sheetfed press, 4 Color, Saddle-stitched
Subscriptions: Indv. $80
Circulation: Total-4,002
Advertising: $500.
List Rental: Actives: 197,000, $75/M
Printing Co: Allen Printing Co., 215 S Main St, Clarion, IA 50525-1417 Tel # (515) 532-2105

Construction Executive Report   *Association*

Publishing Co: International Builders Exchange Executives, PO Box 2274, Rapid City, SD 57709 Tel # (605) 341-3380
General Info: Quarterly, Offset press, 4 pages

Construction Injury Liability Monthly *Business*

Publishing Co: Business Publishers, Inc., 951 Pershing Dr., Silver Spring, MD 20910-4464
Tel # (301) 589-5103 Fax # (301) 589-8493; Title Tel # (301) 587-6300 Title Fax # (301) 587-1081
Personnel: Publisher-Leonard A. Eiserer, Editor-Tom Ramstack, Circ. Mgr.-Brenda Davenport, Promotion Dir.-Eric Easton
Editorial Description: Case-based advice on how to minimize impact of injury lawsuits in construction. Emphasis on OSHA regulations.
General Info: Yr. Est. 1989, Monthly, Trim Size-8½ x 11, Desktop press, 8 pages, Ind/Abs/Online: Newsnet & Predicasts, No Color, Recycled
Subscriptions: Indv. $173, Can. $173, For. $179
Advertising: Accepts Inserts.
List Rental: List Management Co.: BPI Direct, 951 Pershing Dr., Silver Spring, MD 20910-4464
Tel # (301) 585-5976, Fax # (301) 587-4530

Construction Litigation Reporter
See: LAW

Construction Management World

Publishing Co: Ferrell, 13800 Biola Ave Ste 1488, La Mirada, CA 90639-0002
Personnel: Publisher-W. Marvin Ferrell
General Info: Yr. Est. 1975, Monthly
Subscriptions: Indv. $40

Construction Market Data

Publishing Co: Construction Market Data, 2625 Manhattan Beach Blvd., #110, Redondo Beach, CA 90278-1604; Title Tel # (213) 322-2437
Personnel: Editor-Ted Boone
Editorial Description: Updates for Southern California area builders.

Construction Market Intelligence: Russia *Business*

Publishing Co: R.S. Means Co., Inc., 100 Construction Plaza, Kingston, MA 02364-0100
Tel # (617) 585-7880 Fax # (617) 585-7466
Personnel: Sr. Ed., Engineering Ed.-Phil Waier
Editorial Description: Construction news and developments in Russia.
General Info: Bi-monthly

Construction Marketing Research *Association*

Publishing Co: Construction Assn. of Michigan, 500 Stevenson Highway, Ste. 400, Troy, MI 48083
Tel # (810) 585-1000 Fax # (810) 585-9785; Title Tel # (313) 567-5500 Title Fax # (313) 567-1372
Personnel: Publisher-John Boll, Editor-Anne Fobear, Production Mgr.-Kevin Koehler, Adv. Dir.-James Kostrava, Art Dir.-Denise Metivier
Editorial Description: Weekly reports of Michigan projects in the pre-design & design state. CME informs subscribers on exactly how & when projects will be bid. Over 12 billion in preliminary projects reported each year.
General Info: Yr. Est. 1983, Weekly, 4 pages, No Color
Subscriptions: Indv. $253

Construction News Bulletin

Publishing Co: Construction Assn. of Prince Edward Island, Box 728, Charlottetown, PE C1A 7L3 Canada; Title Tel # (902) 368-3303
Personnel: Editor-Darleen Redy
General Info: Bi-weekly, 6 pages

Contractor Advisory *Business*

Publishing Co: WPI Communications, Inc., 55 Morris Ave, Springfield, NJ 07081-1496;
Title Tel # (201) 467-8700
General Info: Monthly
List Rental: Rents Lists

Crane Safety Report, The
See: SAFETY

DCA News *Business, Association*

Publishing Co: Distribution Contractors Assn., 101 W Renner Rd Ste 250, Richardson, TX 75082-2002; Title Tel # (214) 680-0261 Title Fax # (214) 680-0461
Personnel: Editor-Dennis Kennedy
Editorial Description: Underground pipeline construction.
General Info: (Formerly Distribution Contractors Assn. Newsletter), Yr. Est. 1961, Monthly, Trim Size-8½ x 11, 4 pages, No Color

Daily Construction Report

Publishing Co: Contractor Publishing Co., Inc., 1629 W. Lafayette Blvd., Detroit, MI 48216-1972
Fax # (313) 962-4560; Title Tel # (313) 962-3337
Personnel: Editor-Ken Whiting
Editorial Description: Daily newsletter for the building industry in the Michigan area.
General Info: Daily

Dealmakers *Business* CPM: $258

Publishing Co: TKO Real Estate Group, 100 Youngs Rd., Mercerville, NJ 08619;
Title Tel # (609) 587-6200 Title Fax # (609) 587-3511
Personnel: Publisher-Ted Kraus, Editor-Ann O'Neal
Editorial Description: Published for retailers and shopping center developers.
General Info: Yr. Est. 1981, Weekly, Trim Size-8½ x 11, 4 Color, Coated, Saddle-stitched
Subscriptions: Indv. $197, For. $225, $10/copy
Circulation: (43% controlled), Total-6,200, Subscriptions-3,500
Advertising: $1,600. Accepts Inserts.
List Rental: List Management Co.: Marketry, Inc., 2020 116th NE Ste 100, Bellevue, WA 98004-3017
Tel # (800) 346-2013, Fax # (206) 451-1941, Actives: 6,200, $100/M, Expires: 25,000

Distributor Management Digest
See: MANAGEMENT

Dodge Bulletins

Publishing Co: McGraw-Hill, 1221 Ave. of the Americas, 36th Fl., New York, NY 10020-1095
Tel # (212) 512-2000 Fax # (212) 512-6590
General Info: (Formerly Dodge Reports), Daily, Trim Size-3 x 5, Newsprint

Dome Home Mortgage White Paper *Association*

Publishing Co: Natl. Dome Council, 15th & Main Sts. NW, Washington, DC 20005;
Title Tel # (202) 822-0576
Personnel: Publisher-Arthur Engle, Circ. Mgr.-Kay Warskow, Editor, Adv. Dir.-Donald McClurg
Editorial Description: For mfgrs., builders, designers & dealers of geodesic domes.
General Info: Yr. Est. 1979, Quarterly, Trim Size-8½ x 11, Letrpr. press, 8 pages, 2 Color
Subscriptions: Indv. $6, $2/copy
Circulation: Total-3,000
Advertising: Inquire for rates.

Dredging Contract News
See: ENGINEERING

Drop Cloth, The *Business, Association* CPM: $500

Publishing Co: Texas Council of Painting & Decorating Contractors of Americ, 1601 Rio Grande St Ste 440, Austin, TX 78701-1149; Title Tel # (512) 479-0425
Personnel: Publisher, Editor-Lisa Fry
Editorial Description: Official publication of the Texas Council- Painting and Decorating Contractors of America
General Info: 10x/yr., Trim Size-8½ x 11, Offset press, 12 pages, 15% ads, No Color, Matte
Subscriptions: Free With Membership
Circulation: Total-250
Advertising: $125. Accepts Inserts.

Energy Conservation Digest *Business, Association*

Publishing Co: Editorial Resources, Inc., PO Box 20754, Seattle, WA 98102 Tel # (206) 322-8387
Fax # (206) 329-4149; Title Tel # (202) 783-2929
Personnel: Editor-David Howell
Editorial Description: Focuses oon economic implications of current commercial, presidential, and industrial energy conservation issues. Also monitors legislative and policy development, including least energy conservation programs, news of research and new products, interviews, calendar of events, and notices of publications and other resources.
General Info: (Formerly Facilities Management), Yr. Est. 1977, Semi-monthly
Subscriptions: Indv. $198, Can. $238, For. $263, $17/copy

Energy Exchange
See: PETROLEUM & NATURAL GAS

European Construction - Focus 92 *Business*

Publishing Co: McGraw-Hill, 1221 Ave. of the Americas, 36th Fl., New York, NY 10020-1095
Tel # (212) 512-2000 Fax # (212) 512-6590; Title Tel # (212) 512-2111
Personnel: Editor-C.J. Platt
General Info: Yr. Est. 1989, Monthly
Subscriptions: Indv. $377

Expanded Shale Clay & Slate Institute-Information Sheets
See: GLASS, STONE & CLAY

Facility Manager's Alert *Business*

Publishing Co: Progressive Business Publications, 370 Technology Dr., #3019, Malverne, PA 19355-9863 Parent Co.-American Future Systems, Inc., Bryn Mawr; Title Tel # (610) 695-8600 Title Fax # (610) 647-8089
Personnel: Publisher-Edward M. Satell, Editorial Dir.-Stephen Meyer, Editor-Pieter VanBennekom
Editorial Description: Offers cost-saving strategies to help managers operate more efficient facillities. Updates safety and environmental regulations affecting facillity managers.
General Info: Yr. Est. 1995, Bi-weekly, 8 pages
Subscriptions: Indv. $253

Flexible Conduit, The *Business, Association*

Publishing Co: Electricians, Inspectors, Engineers & Interested Others, 3419 41st Ave., Colmar Manor, MD 20722-1904; Title Tel # (301) 699-8833 Title Fax # (301) 699-8830
Personnel: Mng. Editor-David Shapiro, Contrib. Ed.-Charles Eldridge
Editorial Description: For intellectuals in the electrical industry.
General Info: Yr. Est. 1985, Monthly, Trim Size-8½ x 11, 8 pages, ISSN: 1065-2353
Subscriptions: Free With Membership

Flooring Fax News
See: FURNITURE & HOME FURNISHINGS

Fulcrum   *Association*

Publishing Co: Deep Foundations Institute, 120 Charlotte Pl., Englewood Cliffs, NJ 07632-2607; Title Tel # (201) 567-4232 Title Fax # (201) 729-0732
Personnel: Publisher, Editor-G.R. Compton
Editorial Description: News of the institute and the deep foundations construction industry.
General Info: (Formerly Deep Foundations News), Yr. Est. 1977, Quarterly, Trim Size-8½ x 11, Offset press, 8 pages, No Color, Matte
Circulation: Total-1,000
Advertising: Inquire for rates.
Printing Co: Printing Center Inc., The, Rr 1 Box 831, Lafayette, NJ 07848-9409

General Contractors Association, Bulletin of The
See: ENGINEERING, CIVIL

Hart's Pipeline Digest Update Newsletter
See: PETROLEUM & NATURAL GAS

Hazmat News
See: ENVIRONMENT & ECOLOGY

Home Builders Assn. of Greater New Orleans- Newsletter

Publishing Co: Home Builders Association of Greater New Orleans, 2424 N Arnoult Rd, Metairie, LA 70001-1813; Title Tel # (504) 837-2700
General Info: Weekly

Home Ventilating Guide
See: HEATING, PLUMBING, A/C, REFRIG.

Housing & Development Reporter   *Business*

Publishing Co: Warren, Gorham & Lamont, 31 Saint James Ave., Boston, MA 02116-4112 Parent Co.-Thomson Professional Publications, Stamford; Title Tel # (617) 423-2020 Title Fax # (617) 423-1914
Personnel: Publisher-Larry Selby, Mktg. Dir.-Sandra Fox
Editorial Description: Covers current legislation and judicial opinions affecting housing, community development, real estate, finance, and taxation. Comprised of two components: Current Developments and REference File appearing on alternating weeks.
General Info: Yr. Est. 1973, 50x/yr.
Subscriptions: Indv. $855
List Rental: List Management Co.: Manager: Seena Benedek; WG & L List Management, 1 Penn Plz Fl 42, New York, NY 10119-0002 Tel # (212) 971-5000

Housing Affairs Letter
See: REAL ESTATE

Housing Highlights

Publishing Co: Town of Hempstead Office of Communication & Public Affairs, 1 Washington St, Hempstead, NY 11550-4921; Title Tel # (516) 489-5000
Personnel: Editor-Alexandra Trias
Editorial Description: Housing news within the Town of Hempstead, particularly low income & senior housing. Problem line to answer questions. Just started in autumn.
General Info: Semi-annually
Circulation: Total-10,000

Housing Market Report   *Business*

Publishing Co: CD Publications, 8204 Fenton St., Silver Spring, MD 20910-4571; Title Tel # (301) 588-6380 Title Fax # (301) 588-6385
Personnel: Publisher-Mike Gerecht, Editor-Phil Porado, Circ. Mgr.-Kurt Eisentraut, Mktg. Dir.-Joyce Meals
Editorial Description: U.S. housing markets, news & analyses.
General Info: (Formerly Building & Remodeling Industry Update), Yr. Est. 1976, Semi-monthly, Trim Size-8½ x 11, Sheetfed press, 8 pages, ISSN: 0363-4744, No Color, Matte, Other
Subscriptions: Indv. $327, Can. $337, For. $367, $15/copy
List Rental: List Management Co.: Manager: Amy Seyler; Washington Advertising Service, 8204 Fenton St., Silver Spring, MD 20910 Tel # (301) 588-7920, Fax # (301) 588-6385, Actives: 3,876, $150/M, Expires: $150/M

ICAA News

Publishing Co: Insulation Contractors Assn. of America, PO Box 26237, Alexandria, VA 22313-6237; Title Tel # (301) 590-0030
Personnel: Editor-Lee Edes
General Info: Yr. Est. 1980, Monthly, 8 pages

ICW's Africa Construction Business Report   *Business*

Publishing Co: McGraw-Hill, 1221 Ave. of the Americas, 36th Fl., New York, NY 10020-1095 Tel # (212) 512-2000 Fax # (212) 512-6590; Title Tel # (212) 512-2111
Personnel: Editor-C.J. Platt
Editorial Description: Covers the construction industry in Africa.
General Info: Yr. Est. 1980, Monthly
Subscriptions: Indv. $400

ICW's Asia Construction Business Report   *Business*

Publishing Co: McGraw-Hill, 1221 Ave. of the Americas, 36th Fl., New York, NY 10020-1095 Tel # (212) 512-2000 Fax # (212) 512-6590; Title Tel # (212) 512-2112
Personnel: Publisher-David McGrath, Editor-Christopher Platt, Circ. Mgr.-Paul Herrmannsfeldt
Editorial Description: News of major Asia construction, planning, finance, & design opportunities.
General Info: Yr. Est. 1979, Monthly
Subscriptions: Indv. $400

ICW's Latin American Construction Business Report   *Business*

Publishing Co: McGraw-Hill, 1221 Ave. of the Americas, 36th Fl., New York, NY 10020-1095 Tel # (212) 512-2000 Fax # (212) 512-6590; Title Tel # (212) 512-2112
Personnel: Publisher-David McGrath, Editor-Christopher Platt, Circ. Mgr.-Paul Herrmannsfeldt
Editorial Description: News of major Latin American construction, planning, finance & design opportunities.
General Info: Yr. Est. 1979, Monthly
Subscriptions: Indv. $375

ICW's Mideast Construction Business Report   *Business*

Publishing Co: McGraw-Hill, 1221 Ave. of the Americas, 36th Fl., New York, NY 10020-1095 Tel # (212) 512-2000 Fax # (212) 512-6590; Title Tel # (212) 512-2112
Personnel: Publisher-David McGrath, Editor-Christopher Platt, Circ. Mgr.-Paul Herrmannsfeldt
Editorial Description: News of major Mideast construction, planning, finance & design opportunities.
General Info: Yr. Est. 1979, Monthly
Subscriptions: Indv. $495

IDA: Center City Report

Publishing Co: Intl. Downtown Assn., 915 15th St NW Ste 900, Washington, DC 20005-2375; Title Tel # (202) 783-4963
Personnel: Editor-Evon Chaillet
General Info: (Formerly IDEA: Center City Report), Yr. Est. 1973, Bi-monthly
Circulation: Total-1,000

IFMA News   *Association*

Publishing Co: International Facility Management Association, 1 E Greenway Plz Ste 1100, Houston, TX 77046-0104 Fax # (713) 623-6124; Title Tel # (713) 623-4362 Title Fax # (713) 626-6124
Personnel: Editor-Heather McLean Wiederhoeft
Editorial Description: For facility professionals, filled with information on research, codes and regulation, book reviews, and up-to-date infromation on IFMA news.
General Info: (Formerly Facility Management News), Yr. Est. 1980, Monthly, 8 pages, 2 Color, Newsprint
Subscriptions: Free With Membership
Circulation: (100% controlled), Total-13,000

Indoor Air Bulletin
See: ENVIRONMENT & ECOLOGY

Information-Construction   *Business*

Publishing Co: Assn. Provinciale des Constructeurs d'Habitations du Quebec, 5800 Boul. L.H. Lafontaine, Anjou, PQ H1M 1S7 Canada; Title Tel # (514) 353-9960
Editorial Description: Published in French.
General Info: Yr. Est. 1962, Monthly, Trim Size-8½ x 10⅞, Offset press, 12 pages
Circulation: (100% controlled), Total-6,000
Advertising: Inquire for rates.

John T. Reed's Real Estate Investor's Monthly
See: REAL ESTATE

Journal, The   *Association*

Publishing Co: North American Building Material Distribution Association, 401 N Michigan Ave Ste 2200, Chicago, IL 60611-4206; Title Tel # (312) 321-6845 Title Fax # (312) 644-0310
Personnel: Publisher-Al Leitschuh, Editor-Colleen Hughes
Editorial Description: Dedicated to promotion & advancement of building material distribution. In-depth articles on industry and management issues, legislative actions, sales and marketing, and association events.
General Info: (Formerly NBMDA News & Views), Yr. Est. 1952, Monthly, Trim Size-8½ x 11, 8 pages, 2 Color
Circulation: Total-1,500
Advertising: Inquire for rates.

KC News   *Business*

Publishing Co: Kellogg Corp., 1801 Broadway #1000, Denver, CO 80202-3828; Title Tel # (303) 794-1818
Personnel: Editor-Richard Long
Editorial Description: Newsletter focuses on construction contract disputes, with emphasis on entitlements, damages, schedule analysis & project management.
General Info: Yr. Est. 1984, Quarterly, 8 pages
Circulation: Total-2,200

L'Entrepreneurship *Association*

Publishing Co: Assn. de la Construction du Quebec-Region de Montreal, 470 Place Savoie, 3rd Fl., Montreal, PQ H4P 1Z6 Canada; Title Tel # (514) 739-2381 Title Fax # (514) 341-1216
Personnel: Publisher-Lise Chabot
Editorial Description: News concerning the Quebec construction industry.
General Info: (Formerly Bulletin of Construction--Nouvelles), Yr. Est. 1975, Monthly, Sheetfed press, 4 pages, ISSN: 0833-8396
Circulation: (100% controlled), Total-4,000

Log Cabin News
See: HISTORY

MINFAX *Business*

Publishing Co: Marketing Information Network, 15000 Gulf Blvd Apt 307, Saint Petersburg, FL 33708-2030; Title Tel # (212) 679-0711
Personnel: Editor-Edward C. Birkner, Circ. Mgr.-Elizabeth Birkner
Editorial Description: Monthly newsletter which covers the latest happenings in housing.
General Info: Yr. Est. 1965, Monthly, Trim Size-8½ x 11, Offset press, 12 pages, No Color
Subscriptions: Indv. $125, $20/copy
Circulation: Total-800
List Rental: Rents Lists
Printing Co: Legal Systems, 345 Hudson St, New York, NY 10014-4583 Tel # (212) 691-2460

Manufactured Housing Newsletter *Business*

Publishing Co: Manufactured Housing Newsletter, 598 Shorely Dr., Barrington, IL 60010-3340; Title Tel # (206) 746-6272 Title Fax # (206) 747-1021
Personnel: Editor-Shep Robinson
General Info: Yr. Est. 1969, Semi-monthly, 4 pages, ISSN: 0197-1816, No Color, Newsprint
Subscriptions: Indv. $96
List Rental: Actives: $75/M

Masonry Society-Journal *Business, Association*

Publishing Co: Masonry Society, The, 3970 Broadway, Suite 201D, Boulder, CO 80302-3808 Fax # (303) 444-3239; Title Tel # (303) 939-9700 Title Fax # (303) 541-9215
Personnel: Publisher-William Palmer, Editor-Rochelle Jaffe
Editorial Description: Results of current masonry research.
General Info: Yr. Est. 1978, Semi-annually, Offset press, 106 pages, No Color, Coated, Perfect bound
Subscriptions: Indv. $55, Can. $55, For. $60, $25/copy
Circulation: Total-2,000
List Rental: Rents Lists
Printing Co: Johnson Publishing Co., 1880 S. 57th Ct, Boulder, CO 80301-2827 Tel # (303) 443-1576

Mechanical Contractor

Publishing Co: Mechanical Contractors Assn. of B.C., 3210 Lake City Way, Burnaby, BC V5A 3A4 Canada; Title Tel # (604) 420-9714
Personnel: Editor-J. Traynor
General Info: Yr. Est. 1962, Quarterly
Circulation: Total-5,300

Metric Today
See: CONSUMER INTERESTS

Modern Construction and Development Forms *Business*

Publishing Co: Warren, Gorham & Lamont, 31 Saint James Ave., Boston, MA 02116-4112 Fax # (617) 423-1914 Parent Co.-Thomson Professional Publications, Stamford; Title Tel # (617) 423-2020 Title Fax # (617) 423-2025
Personnel: Publisher-Larry Selby, Mktg. Dir.-Sandra Fox
Editorial Description: Provides proven practical examples of forms.
General Info: Yr. Est. 1975, 2x/yr., Looseleaf
Subscriptions: Indv. $125
List Rental: List Management Co.: Manager: Seena Benedek; WG & L List Management, 1 Penn Plz Fl 42, New York, NY 10119-0002 Tel # (212) 971-5000

NADO News

Publishing Co: Natl. Assn. of Development Organizations, 444 N Capitol St NW Ste 630, Washington, DC 20001-1512; Title Tel # (202) 624-7806 Title Fax # (202) 624-8813
Personnel: Editor-Aliceann Wohlbruck
Editorial Description: Focuses on rural, business, community, economic development policy, & legislation.
General Info: Yr. Est. 1979, Weekly, Mimeo press, 4 pages, No Color, Matte
Subscriptions: Indv. $300, Inst. $1,000
Circulation: Total-500

NAHB Remodelor, The *Association*

Publishing Co: National Association of Home Builders, 1201 15th St NW, Washington, DC 20005-2842; Title Tel # (202) 822-0216
Personnel: Editor-Christopher P. Nicholson
Editorial Description: Newsletter containing information on the remodeling & renovation industry.
General Info: (Formerly Remodelors Council Exchange, The), Bi-monthly, Trim Size-8½ x 11, Desktop press, 12 pages, 2 Color, Newsprint, Saddle-stitched
Subscriptions: Indv. $15
Circulation: Total-6,000
Printing Co: Metro Graphics, Inc., 1211 Conn. Ave., NW, Suite 100, Washington, DC 20036 Tel # (202) 296-4424

NAHWW Newsletter
See: HOME & HOME ENTERTAINMENT

NASFM NEWs
See: MANUFACTURING

NCSBCS News *Association*

Publishing Co: Natl. Conference of States on Building Codes & Standards, 505 Huntmar Park Dr Ste 210, Herndon, VA 22070-5100 Tel # (703) 481-2026; Title Tel # (703) 437-0100 Title Fax # (703) 481-3596
Personnel: Editor-Deborah Brettner
Editorial Description: News for building code officials & the construction industry.
General Info: (Formerly NCSBCS Newsletter), Yr. Est. 1977, Bi-monthly, Trim Size-8½ x 11, Sheetfed press, 12 pages, 2 Color, Matte, Saddle-stitched
Subscriptions: Indv. $35, Free With Membership
Acquistions: Publication Bought
Circulation: Total-500

Nari Focus *Association*

Publishing Co: Natl. Assn. of the Remodeling Industry, 4301 North Fairfax Dr Ste 310, Arlington, VA 22203-1627; Title Tel # (703) 276-7600 Title Fax # (703) 243-3465
Personnel: Editor, Feature Ed.-Susan Maney
Editorial Description: Trade association newsletter for the professional remodeling industry.
General Info: Yr. Est. 1983, Monthly, Trim Size-8½ x 11, Web press, 24 pages, 4 Color, Coated, Saddle-stitched
Circulation: Total-7,500
Printing Co: Publishers Press, Lexington, KY

National Housing Rehabilitation Association Newsletter *Association*

Publishing Co: National Housing Rehabilitation Association, 1726 18th St NW, Washington, DC 20009-2525; Title Tel # (202) 328-9171
Editorial Description: Covers Association news and issues relating to housing rehabilitation.
General Info: Monthly

National Precaster

Publishing Co: National Precast Concrete Association, 10333 N Meridian St Ste 272, Indianapolis, IN 46290-1081; Title Tel # (317) 253-0486 Title Fax # (317) 259-7230
Personnel: Publisher-James Tilford, Editor, Production Mgr., Adv. Dir.-Lucinda Vorhies
Editorial Description: News about association activities & industry information.
General Info: Yr. Est. 1965, Monthly, Trim Size-8½ x 11, Sheetfed press, 24 pages, 3% ads, Color-cover, Matte
Circulation: Total-650
Advertising: Inquire for rates. Accepts Inserts.
Printing Co: Morris Printing, 1502 N College Ave, Indianapolis, IN 46202-2799

National Sash and Door Jobbers Association Newsletter *Association*

Publishing Co: Natl. Sash & Door Jobbers Assn., 2400 E. Devan Ave., Des Plaines, IL 60018; Title Tel # (708) 299-3400
Personnel: Editor-Robert O'Keefe
General Info: Monthly, Offset press, 10 pages
Circulation: Total-1,300

Networld Netlink *Business*

Publishing Co: Blenheim, Ft. Lee Executive Park, One Executive Dr., Ft. Lee, NJ 07024; Title Tel # (201) 346-1400 Title Fax # (201) 346-1602
Editorial Description: Newsletter for the PC Expo Convention.
General Info: Semi-annually, Trim Size-8½ x 11, 6 pages, 2 Color, Matte

New Plant Report *Business*

Publishing Co: Conway Data Inc., 40 Technology Park, Norcross, GA 30092-9990 Fax # (404) 263-8825; Title Tel # (404) 446-6996 Title Fax # (770) 263-8825
Personnel: Editor-Doris Rosser
Editorial Description: Monthly rating of new and expanded facilities for manufacturing, office, distribution, R&D.
General Info: Monthly
Subscriptions: Indv. $600

New York City Building Code
See: LAW

Niagara Construction Association Newsletter *Association*

Publishing Co: Niagara Construction Assn., 34 Scott St., St. Catharines, ON L2R 1C9 Canada; Title Tel # (905) 682-6661
Personnel: Editor-Mrs. C. Tribble
Editorial Description: Construction information on wage rates and collective agreements, cost data, government legislation, plans and specifications for projects out for bid in the Niagara Peninsula.
General Info: Yr. Est. 1966, Weekly
Circulation: Total-250

Occupational Health & Safety News   *Business*

Publishing Co: Stevens Publishing Corp., 3630 J.H. Kultgen Frwy., Waco, TX 76706
Tel # (817) 662-1134 Fax # (817) 662-7075; Title Tel # (817) 776-9000 Title Fax # (817) 776-9018
Personnel: Assoc. Publ.-Dennis Bednarski, Washington Bureau Chief-Mary Crowley, News Ed.-Greg Densmore, Adv. Dir.-Ruth Heard Warren, Art Dir.-Mylynda Callahan, Mktg. Dir.-Terry Duran, Promotion Dir.-Mark Rathe
Editorial Description: Delivers the latest federal legislation and OSHA regulation. Covers current industry news and legislative updates including topics such as ergonomics, drug testing, corporate liability, worker right-to-know and OSHA compliance. Written for the professional responsible for monitoring worker safety and health.
General Info: Yr. Est. 1985, Bi-weekly, Trim Size-81 x 11, Sheetfed press, 16 pages, Saddle-stitched
Subscriptions: Indv. $269, Can. $303, For. $303
Acquistions: Publication Bought
List Rental: Rents Lists

Ontario General Contractors Association - The Generals

Publishing Co: Ontario General Contractors Association, 6303 Airport Rd., Suite 308, Mississauga, ON L4V 1R8 Canada
General Info: (Formerly Ontario General Contractors Association Newsletter), Yr. Est. 1980, Quarterly, 30 pages

PBC Housing Briefs   *Business, Consumer*

Publishing Co: Publishing & Business Consultants, 101 W. 64th St. Unit #3, Inglewood, CA 90302-1255 Tel # (213) 732-3477 Fax # (213) 732-3477
Personnel: Publisher, Editor-Andeson Atia
General Info: Quarterly, ISSN: 1059-2016
Advertising: Inquire for rates.

PENlines

Publishing Co: Natl. Assn. of Student Financial Aid Administrators, 1920 L St. NW, #200, #100, Washington, DC 20036-5020 Fax # (202) 785-1487; Title Tel # (202) 785-0453
Personnel: Editor, Art Dir.-Jeffrey Sheppard
Editorial Description: Users help & computer info for on-line postsecondary news network.
General Info: Yr. Est. 1987, Monthly, Web press, 4 pages, 2 Color, Newsprint
Circulation: Total-600
Printing Co: French-Bray Printing Co., 6731 Baymeadow Dr # 698, Glen Burnie, MD 21060-6410 Tel # (301) 768-6000, Fax # (301) 768-9028

People & Profits   *Business*

Publishing Co: Lee Resources, PO Box 16711, Greenville, SC 29606-7711; Title Fax # (803) 234-6961
General Info: Yr. Est. 1988, Monthly
Subscriptions: Indv. $147

Perspectives on the Construction Industry   *Business*

Publishing Co: Newkirk Products, Inc., 15 Corporate Cir, Albany, NY 12203-5154 Tel # (518) 452-1000
Editorial Description: Custom publication designed for distribution to clients by professionals who advise the construction industry.
General Info: Quarterly, Trim Size-81/2 x 11, 4 pages, 2 Color

Plans on Display Bulletin   *Association*

Publishing Co: Niagara Construction Assn., 34 Scott St., St. Catharines, ON L2R 1C9 Canada Tel # (905) 682-6661; Title Tel # (416) 682-6661
General Info: Weekly, 2 pages

Plastics in Building Construction
See: PLASTICS

Post-Tensioning Institute-Newsletter   *Business*

Publishing Co: Post-Tensioning Institute, 1717 W Northern Ave Ste 114, Phoenix, AZ 85021-5470; Title Tel # (602) 870-7540 Title Fax # (612) 870-7541
Personnel: Editor-Gerard McGuire
General Info: Yr. Est. 1976, Quarterly, 4 pages
Circulation: Total-1,000

Prestressed Concrete Institute, Bridge Bulletin   *Business*

Publishing Co: Prestressed Concrete Institute, 175 W Jackson Blvd Ste 1859, Chicago, IL 60604-2801; Title Tel # (312) 786-0300 Title Fax # (312) 786-0353
Personnel: Editor-Sarah Morris
Editorial Description: Illustrates the use of precast, prestressed concrete in various bridge types.
General Info: 4 pages, 2 Color
Subscriptions: $1/copy

Professional Services Management Journal
See: MANAGEMENT

Project Management   *Business*

Publishing Co: Practice Management Associates Ltd., 10 Midland Ave., Newton, MA 02158-1021; Title Tel # (617) 965-0055 Title Fax # (617) 965-5152
Personnel: Editor-David Stone
General Info: (Formerly Details/Plus), Yr. Est. 1992, Monthly, Trim Size-81/2 x 11, 8 pages, 2 Color
Subscriptions: Indv. $184, Can. $184, For. $234
List Rental: Rents Lists

Punch List

Publishing Co: American Arbitration Assn., 140 W. 51 St., New York, NY 10020-1203 Tel # (212) 484-4000 Fax # (212) 541-4841; Title Tel # (212) 484-4010 Title Fax # (212) 765-4874
Personnel: Editor-Jonathan Rose, Promotion Dir.-Douglas French
Editorial Description: The quarterly newsletter covers the use by the construction & allied industries of alternative dispute resolution, the legal services of the American Arbitration Assn.
General Info: Yr. Est. 1978, Quarterly, Trim Size-81/2 x 11, 8 pages, 2 Color, Matte
Circulation: Total-13,500
Printing Co: Sheridan Printing, 1425 3rd Ave, Alpha, NJ 08865-4695 Tel # (908) 454-0700, Fax # (908) 454-2554

Quebec Construction   *Business*   CPM: $133

Publishing Co: Groupe Constructo, 1500 Bd. Jules Poitras, St. Laurent, PQ H4N 1X7 Canada Fax # (514) 339-2267 Parent Co.-Kerrwil Pubs. Ltd., Mississauga, Canada; Title Tel # (514) 745-5720
Personnel: Publisher-Guy Choiniere, Editor in Chief-Johanne Rouleau, Circ. Mgr.-Francois Blondin, Adv. Dir.-Veronique Tremblay, Adv. Rep.-John Bleuler, Adv. Rep.-Denis Lazure, Art Dir.-Sylvain Renaud
Editorial Description: Mainly read by administrators and decision makers. Features novelties and innovations that solve problems faced by contractors, architects and others that are related to the construction industry in Quebec.
General Info: Yr. Est. 1984, Monthly, Trim Size-83/8 x 111/8, Web press, ISSN: 0829-5263, 50% ads, 4 Color, Perfect bound, Looseleaf
Subscriptions: Indv. $35, Free To Qualified Recipient
Circulation: (CCAB, 100% controlled), Total-23,636, Readership-49,600, Source-I
Advertising: $3,150. Accepts Inserts.

RIEI Information Letter

Publishing Co: Roofing Industry Educational Institute, 14 Inverness Dr., E., Bldg. H, #110, Englewood, CO 80112-5625; Title Tel # (303) 790-7200
Personnel: Editor-Susan Mathews
General Info: Quarterly, 14 pages
Subscriptions: Indv. $12

Real Estate   *Business, Consumer*

Publishing Co: National Research Bureau, 150 N. Wacher Drive, Chicago, IL 60601 Tel # (312) 541-0100 Fax # (312) 541-1492 Parent Co.-Reed Reference Publishing, New Providence; Title Tel # (319) 752-5415 Title Fax # (319) 752-3421
Personnel: Publisher-Michael Darnall, Editor-Barbara Boeding
Editorial Description: Building and remodeling innovations, statistics, designs, regulations, and new products, real estate trends, sales and promotionals.
General Info: Yr. Est. 1933, Monthly, 4 pages
Advertising: Inquire for rates.

Real Estate Investors Classified   *Business*   CPM$1379

Publishing Co: The Dealmakers, 100 Youngs Road, Mercerville, NY 08629; Title Tel # (609) 587-6200 Title Fax # (609) 587-3571
Personnel: Publisher-Ted Kraus, Editor-Ann O'Neal
Editorial Description: Provides commercial property for sale nationwide acquisition requirements of buyers financing sources
General Info: Yr. Est. 1993, Semi-weekly, Trim Size-81/2 x 11
Subscriptions: Indv. $297
Circulation: Total-725, Readership-725
Advertising: $1,000. Accepts Inserts.
List Rental: Actives: 72, $100/M, Expires: 1,500, $100/M

Redwood News
See: ARCHITECTURE

Rocky Mountain CoHousing Quarterly, The
See: ENVIRONMENT & ECOLOGY

SGD Newsletter

Publishing Co: Society of Glass Decorators, 207 Grant St, Port Jefferson, NY 11777-1230; Title Tel # (516) 473-0232
Personnel: Editor-Frank Child
General Info: Yr. Est. 1963, Monthly
Circulation: Total-500

SIGMA Newsletter   *Business, Association*

Publishing Co: Sealed Insulating Glass Manufacturers Assn., 401 N. Michigan Ave., Chicago, IL 60611-4212; Title Tel # (312) 644-6610 Title Fax # (312) 321-6869
Personnel: Editor-Alison Powers
General Info: Yr. Est. 1979, Quarterly, 2 Color
Circulation: Total-800
List Rental: Actives: 4,500

SPEC-DATA Program   *Business, Association*

Publishing Co: Construction Specifications Institute, 601 Madison St., Alexandria, VA 22314-1741; Title Tel # (703) 684-0300 Title Fax # (703) 684-0465
Personnel: Editor-Carol E. Duke
Editorial Description: Standardized presentation of technical construction product info for architectural specifications.
General Info: Yr. Est. 1966, Quarterly, Trim Size-8½ x 11, Web press, Ind/Abs/Online: Spec-Data/Manu-Spec, 4 Color, Newsprint, Looseleaf
Subscriptions: Indv. $80, Free With Membership
Circulation: Total-11,000
Advertising: Inquire for rates. Accepts Inserts.
List Rental: Rents Lists

Sales Leads
See: SALESMANSHIP & SELLING

Scaffold Industry
Association Newsletter   *Association*   **CPM: $560**

Publishing Co: Scaffold Industry Association, 14039 Sherman Way Ste 100, Van Nuys, CA 91405-2599; Title Tel # (818) 782-2012 Title Fax # (818) 786-3027
Personnel: Publisher, Editor-Victor Saleeby, Adv. Dir.-Gary W. Larson
Editorial Description: Articles on construction, safety, development, legislation on safety codes specifically with scaffolding, court decisions.
General Info: Yr. Est. 1972, Monthly, Trim Size-8½ x 11, Sheetfed press, 24 pages, 30% ads, 2 Color, Matte, Saddle-stitched
Acquisitions: Publication Bought
Circulation: Total-1,500
Advertising: $840.

Shavings

Publishing Co: Early American Industries Association, P.O. Box 143, Delmar, NY 12054; Title Tel # (518) 439-2215
General Info: Bi-monthly
Subscriptions: Indv. $30, Inst. $30, Can. $39, For. $39

Shopping Center News   *Business*

Publishing Co: Maclean Hunter Publishing Ltd., Maclean Hunter Building, 777 Bay St., Toronto, ON M5W 1A7 Canada Tel # (416) 596-5000 Fax # (416) 596-5526; Title Tel # (416) 596-5939 Title Fax # (416) 596-5553
Personnel: Publisher-G. Gallagher, Editor-Don Douloff, Circ. Mgr.-Cheryl Treliving
Editorial Description: Information on proposed shopping centres, expansions, space availabilty, etc.
General Info: Monthly, 6 pages
Subscriptions: Indv. $395, Can. $395

Small Contractor   *Business*

Publishing Co: CIP Communications, 6585 Commerce Blvd., Suite 292, Rohnert Park, CA 94928-2407 Fax # (707) 823-1007; Title Tel # (415) 499-7674
Personnel: Publisher-Roderick Crandall
Editorial Description: Information on marketing, management, and computers for the small contractor.
General Info: Yr. Est. 1987, Monthly, Trim Size-8½ x 11, 4 pages, Newsprint
Subscriptions: Indv. $45

Solar Collector
See: ENERGY

Southam Building
Reports   *Business*

Publishing Co: Southam Business Communications, Inc., 1450 Don Mills Rd., Don Mills, ON M3B 2X7 Canada Fax # (416) 442-2200; Title Tel # (416) 445-6641
Personnel: Publisher-Glenn Wagner, Promotion Dir.-Jill Bender
Editorial Description: Advance info on engineering and building projects, statistics and forecasts on construction activity.
General Info: Yr. Est. 1911, Daily, Trim Size-3 x 5, Web press, 200 pages, No Color, Looseleaf
Circulation: (100% controlled), Total-4,300
List Rental: List Management Co.: Cornerstone List Mgrs., 2300 Yonge St., Ste. 2005, Box 2465, Toronto, ON M4P 1E4 Canada Tel # (416) 932-9555, Fax # (416) 932-9566

Sponsorship Report, The   *Business*

Publishing Co: Sponsorship Report, The, 555 Richmond street West, Suite 504, Toronto, ON M5V 3B1 Canada; Title Tel # (416) 360-3894 Title Fax # (416) 360-0204
General Info: Yr. Est. 1988, Monthly
Subscriptions: Indv. $200, Can. $22, For. $200

Staff Leader
See: MANAGEMENT

Super Projects
See: INTERNATIONAL AFFAIRS

TAREI Times
See: REAL ESTATE

TC-HW Reporter   *Association*

Publishing Co: PTN Publishing Co., 445 Broad Hollow Rd., Ste. 21, Melville, NY 11747-3601 Tel # (516) 845-2700 Fax # (516) 845-2736; Title Tel # (617) 848-6150 Title Fax # (617) 848-6160
Personnel: Editor-Dawn James, Circ. Dir.-Jacqueline Serra
Editorial Description: Asbestos & hazardous waste. Bids for removal, consulting, news & awards.
General Info: (Formerly AHW Reporter), Yr. Est. 1967, Weekly, Trim Size-8½ x 11, Mimeo press, 30 pages, 1% ads, Newsprint
Subscriptions: Indv. $630
Acquistions: Publication Bought
Circulation: Total-150
Advertising: Inquire for rates. Accepts Inserts.

Trade Trax
See: WOMEN'S

Tremco News

Publishing Co: Tremco News, 10701 Shaker Blvd, Cleveland, OH 44104-3752
Personnel: Editor-Sherri Kightlinger
Editorial Description: Highlights customer case histories.
General Info: Quarterly
Acquistions: Publication Bought, Publication Sold

USCOLD Newsletter
See: WATER SUPPLY, POWER & WASTE

Utah Construction Report   *Business*

Publishing Co: Univ. of Utah Bureau of Economic & Business Research, 401 Kendall D. Garff Bldg., Salt Lake City, UT 84112 Fax # (801) 581-3354; Title Tel # (801) 581-6333
Personnel: Editor-Austin Sargent, Art Dir.-James Peters
Editorial Description: Monthly and year-to-date statistics on permit-authorized residential and non-residential construction for more than 180 localities throughout the state.
General Info: Yr. Est. 1954, Quarterly, Trim Size-8½ x 11, Offset press, 20 pages, 2 Color
Circulation: (100% controlled), Total-2,000

Vital Link, The   *Business, Association*

Publishing Co: Woodworking Machinery Distributors Association, Adams Bldg., No. 109, 251 DeKalb Pike, King of Prussia, PA 19406 Tel # (215) 265-6668 Fax # (215) 265-3419; Title Tel # (215) 265-6658 Title Fax # (610) 265-3419
Personnel: Editor-R. Franklin Brown, Jr.
Editorial Description: News on this woodworking machinery association.
General Info: (Formerly WMDA News/Bits' N Chips), Yr. Est. 1960, Monthly, Trim Size-8½ x 11, Mimeo press, 6 pages, 1% ads
Subscriptions: Indv. $25, Can. $25, For. $35, Free With Membership
Circulation: Total-120

Western Building &
Remodeling   *Business*

Publishing Co: Sunset Publishing Corp., 80 Willow Rd, Menlo Park, CA 94025-3661 Fax # (415) 328-6215 Parent Co.-Time Inc. Ventures, New York; Title Tel # (415) 321-3600 Title Fax # (415) 321-0551
Personnel: Editor-Mark Hickling
Editorial Description: Distributed to the building & hardware industry in 13 western states.
General Info: (Formerly Western Building & Home Improvement), Bi-monthly
Subscriptions: Free To Qualified Recipient
Circulation: (100% controlled), Total-4,200

Wire Talk
See: SAFETY

Zoning Bulletin   *Business*

Publishing Co: Quinlan Publishing, 23 Drydock Ave, Boston, MA 02210-2387; Title Tel # (617) 542-0048 Title Fax # (617) 345-9646
Editorial Description: Case summaries explaining how zoning decisions may challenged successfully.
General Info: Yr. Est. 1952, Bi-weekly, 8 pages, ISSN: 0514-7905
Subscriptions: Indv. $83
List Rental: List Management Co.: Stevens-Knox List Management, 304 Park Ave S., New York, NY 10010-5312 Tel # (212) 388-8800, Fax # (212) 388-8890

CONSUMER INTERESTS

401(k) Legislative News
See: BANKING & FINANCE

AAFT Quarterly   *Business, Association*

Publishing Co: National Consumers League, 1701 K St. NW, Ste. 1200, Washington, DC 20006; Title Tel # (202) 835-3323 Title Fax # (202) 835-0747
Editorial Description: Educates consumers regarding fraud in telemarketing and how to prevent it.
General Info: Yr. Est. 1899, Quarterly, Trim Size-8½ x 11, Offset press, 4 pages, ISSN: 1055-4491, 2 Color, Newsprint
Subscriptions: Indv. $5, Free With Membership

Abapa Freer
See: LIFESTYLE

Action News

Publishing Co: Action for Corporate Accountability, 910 17th St. NW, Ste. 413, Washington, DC 20006-2601; Title Tel # (202) 882-7711
Personnel: Editor-Carol Linnea-Salmon
General Info: Yr. Est. 1987, Quarterly, Sheetfed press, 4 pages, ISSN: 0895-0636, 2 Color, Newsprint
Subscriptions: Indv. $15, Inst. $60
Circulation: Total-1,000

Advocacy Update

Publishing Co: Public Voice for Food & Health Policy, 1001 Connecticut Ave NW Ste, 522, Washington, DC 20036-5504; Title Tel # (202) 659-5930
General Info: Monthly

Affordable Caribbean, The
See: TRAVEL

Aging America Resources
See: SENIOR CITIZENS

American Law of Products Liability Newsletter
See: LAW

Ample Shopper   *Consumer*

Publishing Co: Ample Shopper, 1150 E Market St, Charlottesville, VA 22902-5351
Editorial Description: Information and buying tips for the large person.
General Info: Quarterly
Subscriptions: Indv. $10

Appalachian Alternatives   *Consumer*

Publishing Co: Appalachia-Science in the Public Interest, PO Box 298, Livingston, KY 40445-0298 Fax # (606) 453-3115; Title Tel # (606) 453-2105
Personnel: Publisher-Al Fritsch, Editor-Mark Spencer
Editorial Description: Making science and technology responsive to the needs of low-income people in central appalachia.
General Info: Quarterly, Desktop press, 8 pages
Subscriptions: Free
Circulation: Total-3,500, Readership-7,000

Association, The   *Consumer*

Publishing Co: Association, 12121 Jasper Ave., Ste. 605, Edmonton, AB T5N 3X8 Canada; Title Tel # (403) 488-2170
Personnel: Publisher, Adv. Dir.-James Patterson, Editor, Art Dir.-Edward Watson
Editorial Description: Covers wide range of subjects of interest to consumers.
General Info: Yr. Est. 1992, Semi-monthly, Trim Size-8½ x 11, Letrpr. press, 4 pages, No Color, Matte
Subscriptions: Indv. $39
Circulation: Total-1,000
Printing Co: Duplicopy Publishing, 10345 124th St., Edmonton, AB T5N 3X8 Canada

At Home with Consumers   *Business, Consumer*

Publishing Co: Direct Selling Education Foundation, 1666 K St., NW, Ste. 1010, Washington, DC 20006-2387; Title Tel # (202) 293-5760 Title Fax # (202) 463-4569
Editorial Description: Contains pro-con debates on timely consumer and civic issues.
General Info: Yr. Est. 1974, 3x/yr., Trim Size-8½ x 11, 12 pages, 2 Color, Matte, Saddle-stitched
Subscriptions: Free
Circulation: Total-23,000

Auto Mi$er
See: AUTOMOTIVE

BBB Member Exchange   *Business, Consumer*

Publishing Co: Better Business Bureau of Eastern Massachusetts, Inc., 20 Park Plz Ste 820, Boston, MA 02116-4303
General Info: (Formerly BBB Tribune), Yr. Est. 1989, Quarterly, Trim Size-8½ x 11, Offset press, 10 pages, 2 Color, Matte, Saddle-stitched

Beauty Spot: News You Can Use
See: MEDIA & COMMUNICATIONS

Best for Less, The   *Consumer*

Publishing Co: Best for Less, The, 14 Washington Place, New York, NY 10003-6609; Title Tel # (212) 673-6297
Personnel: Publisher, Editor-Lydia Cherniakova
Editorial Description: Consumer newsletter that helps upscale consumers live better and spend less.
General Info: Yr. Est. 1982, Monthly, Trim Size-8½ x 11, Desktop press, 4 pages, Matte
Subscriptions: Indv. $33, $5/copy

Bottom Line/Personal   *Consumer*

Publishing Co: Boardroom Publishing, PO Box 2614, 55 Railroad Ave., Greenwich, CT 06836-6378; Title Tel # (203) 625-5216 Title Fax # (203) 861-7442
Personnel: Publisher-Martin Edelston, Editor-Lee Rath, Circ. Mgr.-Laurie Mellon, Production Mgr.-Angela Taormina, Art Dir.-Ray Holland, Promotion Dir.-Brian Kurtz
Editorial Description: Management of personal affairs from investments to personal goods. To help those who are very busy with their careers handle their personal lives more effectively. To bring them the best information from the most knowledgeable sources.
General Info: Yr. Est. 1980, Semi-monthly, ISSN: 0274-4805
Subscriptions: Indv. $49, For. $45, $4/copy
Circulation: Total-2,500,000
List Rental: Actives: $85/M, Hotline: $95/M, Expires: $60/M

Bottom Line/Tomorrow   *Consumer*

Publishing Co: Boardroom Publishing, PO Box 2614, 55 Railroad Ave., Greenwich, CT 06836-6378; Title Tel # (203) 625-5216 Title Fax # (203) 861-7442
Personnel: Publisher-Martin Edelston
Editorial Description: News and information for people in or near retirement.
General Info: Yr. Est. 1994, Monthly, Trim Size-8½ x 11, Matte
Subscriptions: Indv. $30

Boycott Action News   *Consumer*

Publishing Co: Co-Op America, 1612 K St NW Ste 600, Washington, DC 20006 Tel # (202) 872-5307
Editorial Description: Announces boycotts in progress, those which have succeeded and provides information on starting boycotts.
General Info: Quarterly

Bread Pudding Update
See: FOOD

CALPIRG News   *Consumer*

Publishing Co: California Public Interest Research Group, 15 Shattuck Sq., Ste 210, Berkeley, CA 94704 Fax # (510) 644-3460; Title Tel # (510) 644-3454
Personnel: Editor-Faye Park
General Info: Quarterly, 8 pages

CFAnews   *Consumer, Association*

Publishing Co: Consumer Fed. of America, 1424 16th St NW Ste 604, Washington, DC 20036-2211; Title Tel # (202) 387-6121
Personnel: Editor-Barbara Roper
Editorial Description: A public interest newsletter covering consumer federation of America's advocacy efforts on federal consumer issues.
General Info: Yr. Est. 1968, 8x/yr., Sheetfed press, 4 pages, ISSN: 0732-8281, 2 Color
Subscriptions: Indv. $25
Circulation: Total-1,500

COCO Intercom   *Business, Association*

Publishing Co: Conference of Consumer Organizations, Box 158, Newton Centre, MA 02159-0001; Title Tel # (617) 552-8184
Personnel: Editor-Robert McEwen
Editorial Description: News, analysis, opinion on consumer policy.
General Info: (Formerly Intercom), Yr. Est. 1973, Monthly, Trim Size-8½ x 11, Desktop press, 4 pages, Color
Subscriptions: Indv. $10, Inst. $30
Circulation: Total-325

COPIRG Outlook
See: ENVIRONMENT & ECOLOGY

CSA and the Consumer   *Consumer*

Publishing Co: Canadian Standards Association, 178 Rexdale Boulevard, Rexdale, ON M9W 1R3 Canada Tel # (416) 747-4000; Title Tel # (416) 747-4129
Personnel: Editor-Rosemarie MacVicar
Editorial Description: News briefs re: consumer safety, CSA standards and certification programs.
General Info: Yr. Est. 1970, Quarterly, 8 pages
Circulation: Total-880,000

California Products Liability
Actions   *Business*

Publishing Co: Matthew Bender & Co., 11 Penn Plaza, New York, NY 10001-2006 Fax # (212) 244-3188; Title Tel # (212) 967-7707
Personnel: Editor-M. Fenger
Editorial Description: Every aspect of California products liability law for both plaintiff & defendant: investigation, role of experts, pleadings, discovery, proof, defenses, damages, & trials.
General Info: Yr. Est. 1970, Irregular, Looseleaf
Subscriptions: $110/copy

Canadian Commercial Law Guide
See: LAW

Cantu's Newsletter
See: MEDIA & COMMUNICATIONS

Cardtrak
See: CREDIT AND CREDIT UNIONS

Child Labor Monitor · *Business, Association*

Publishing Co: National Consumers League, 1701 K St. NW, Ste. 1200, Washington, DC 20006; Title Tel # (202) 835-3323 Title Fax # (202) 835-0747
Personnel: Editor, Production Mgr.-Darlene Adkins
Editorial Description: Investigates, educates and advocates consumer and worker rights.
General Info: Yr. Est. 1991, Trim Size-8½ x 11, Offset press, 8 pages, ISSN: 1060-6661, 2 Color, Newsprint
Subscriptions: Indv. $12, Inst. $15, Free With Membership
Circulation: Total-1,500, Readership-1,500
Advertising: Accepts Inserts.

Classic Chevrolet Memories
See: AUTOMOTIVE

Closer to the Customer · *Business, Consumer*

Publishing Co: AT&T Closer to the Customer Newsletter, PO Box 1060, Piscataway, NJ 08855-1060
Personnel: Editor-Bill Clausen
Editorial Description: A business newsletter updating AT&T customer services.
General Info: Quarterly, Trim Size-8½ x 11, 8 pages, 4 Color, Coated, Saddle-stitched

Clothing for Less Newsletter

Publishing Co: Prosperity & Profits Unlimited, PO Box 416, Denver, CO 80201-0416; Title Tel # (303) 575-5676
Personnel: Publisher, Editor-A.C. Doyle
Editorial Description: Ideas on getting clothing for less.
General Info: Yr. Est. 1990, Every two years, ISSN: 1053-6507, No Color
Subscriptions: Indv. $4, Inst. $5, Can. $6, For. $8, $4/copy
Circulation: Total-5,000

CoHousing Newsletter
See: ENVIRONMENT & ECOLOGY

College By Mail Etc.- Newsletter
See: EDUCATION

Community First
See: BANKING & FINANCE

Conscious Consumer · *Consumer*

Publishing Co: New Consumer Institute, Inc., PO Box 51, Wauconda, IL 60084; Title Tel # (708) 526-0522
Personnel: Editor-John Wasich
Editorial Description: Critically evaluates socially responsible and environmentally sound products, services/investments, summarizes related articles.
General Info: Yr. Est. 1989, Bi-monthly
Subscriptions: Indv. $30, Can. $35, $3/copy

Conscious Consumer Corporate Edition · *Business*

Publishing Co: New Consumer Institute, Inc., PO Box 51, Wauconda, IL 60084; Title Tel # (708) 526-0522
Personnel: Publisher, Editor-John Wasik
Editorial Description: Evaluate environmentally sound and socially responsible products, services and marketing. Summarizes related articles, research and trade show information.
General Info: Yr. Est. 1990
Subscriptions: Inst. $150, $39/copy

Consumer ActioNews · *Business, Consumer*

Publishing Co: Sponsor-Consumer Action, Consumer Action, 116 New Montgomery St., San Francisco, CA 94105-3607; Title Tel # (415) 777-9648 Title Fax # (415) 777-5267
Personnel: Editor-Michael Heffer
Editorial Description: Banking & phone pricing survey results.
General Info: Yr. Est. 1971, Bi-monthly, Web press, 6 pages, No Color
Subscriptions: Indv. $25, Inst. $25
Circulation: Total-5,000

Consumer Affairs Letter, The · *Business*

Publishing Co: Consumer Affairs Letter, PO Box 65313, Washington, DC 20035-5313 Tel # (202) 362-7279 Fax # (202) 362-4279; Title Tel # (202) 362-4279
Personnel: Publisher, Editor-George Idelson
Editorial Description: Monthly report to management on activities, strategies, personalities, issues of consumer movement.
General Info: Yr. Est. 1979, Monthly, Trim Size-8½ x 11, Sheetfed press, 8 pages, ISSN: 0270-0999, 2 Color, Matte
Subscriptions: Indv. $247, Inst. $125, For. $267, $15/copy
Advertising: Accepts Inserts.
List Rental: Rents Lists

Consumer Alert Comments · *Business, Association*

Publishing Co: Consumer Alert, 1735 I St. NW, Ste. 603, Washington, DC 20006-2402; Title Tel # (209) 524-1738 Title Fax # (209) 524-2316
Personnel: Editor-Scott Pattison
Editorial Description: Keeps members, news media & others informed about our activities & developments of interest to consumers- expression & debate on public policy issues.
General Info: Yr. Est. 1977, Bi-monthly, 5 pages, ISSN: 0740-4964, Color
Subscriptions: Indv. $35, Inst. $75
Circulation: Total-6,600

Consumer Bankruptcy Issues
See: BANKING & FINANCE

Consumer Forum · *Consumer*

Publishing Co: Concerned Consumers League, 436 West Wisconsin Avenue, Milwaukee, WI 53203-2105; Title Tel # (414) 645-1808
Personnel: Editor-Cheryl Gurlik
Editorial Description: News, self-help information, and opinion on consumer issues.
General Info: (Formerly Caveat Vendor), Yr. Est. 1969, Bi-monthly, 4 pages, No Color, Newsprint
Subscriptions: Indv. $10, Inst. $15
Circulation: Total-375

Consumer News and Reviews · *Association*

Publishing Co: American Council on Consumer Interests, 240 Stanley Hall University Of, Missouri, Columbia, MO 65211-0001; Title Tel # (314) 882-3817 Title Fax # (314) 884-6571
Personnel: Editor-Les Dlabay
General Info: (Formerly ACCI Newsletter), Bi-monthly, Trim Size-8½ x 11, Letrpr. press, 6 pages, ISSN: 0010-9975, Color-cover
Subscriptions: Indv. $70, Inst. $135, Can. $147, For. $153, $5/copy
Circulation: Total-1,500
Printing Co: GAP, Columbia, MO

Consumer Product Safety Guide · *Business*

Publishing Co: CCH, Inc., 2700 Lake Cook Rd., Riverwoods, IL 60015 Parent Co.-Kluwer Law & Taxation Publishers, Cambridge; Title Tel # (847) 267-7000 Title Fax # (800) 224-8299
Editorial Description: Reports consumer product safety standards and rules, including automobiles and accessories, tires, electronic radiation emitting devices.
General Info: Yr. Est. 1972, Weekly, Trim Size-6 x 9, Web press, 125 pages, No Color, Looseleaf
Subscriptions: Indv. $972

Consumer Protection Report · *Association*

Publishing Co: National Association of Attorneys General, 444 N Capitol St NW Ste 339, Washington, DC 20001-1512 Tel # (202) 434-8034; Title Tel # (202) 628-0435
Personnel: Editor-Elena Boisvert
Editorial Description: Litigation and proposed legislation in consumer protection, regulation of charitable organizations.
General Info: Yr. Est. 1974, Monthly, Mimeo press, 23 pages
Subscriptions: Indv. $145
Circulation: Total-375

Consumers for World Trade Newsletter
See: INTERNATIONAL TRADE

Con$umer Wi$e · *Consumer*

Publishing Co: Minnesota Ink, Inc., P.O. Box 25376, St. Paul, MN 55125-0376 Tel # (612) 486-7818
Personnel: Publisher-Valerie Hockert, Assoc. Ed.-Glenda Olsen
Editorial Description: How to live better on less.
General Info: Yr. Est. 1994, Monthly
Subscriptions: Indv. $13

Cooking Contest Chronicle
See: FOOD

Cooperative Housing Bulletin
See: REAL ESTATE

Cost Cutter, The · *Business, Association*

Publishing Co: American Purchasing Society, 11910 Oak Trail Way, Port Richey, FL 34668-1037 Fax # (813) 862-8199; Title Tel # (813) 862-7998
Personnel: Publisher, Editor-Harry Hough
General Info: Yr. Est. 1992, Quarterly, Trim Size-8½ x 11, Letrpr. press, 4 pages, 2 Color
Subscriptions: Indv. $59
Circulation: Total-2,500
Advertising: Inquire for rates.
List Rental: Actives: 45,000, $95/M

Debt-Free & Prosperous Living
Business, Consumer

Publishing Co: FINL-Financial Independent Network Ltd., Inc., 310 Second St., Boscobel, WI 53805-1164; Title Tel # (815) 356-8800 Title Fax # (815) 356-8804
Personnel: Women's Editor-Lois Cummuta, Editor, Real Est. Ed.-Mike DiFrisco, Publisher, Finl. Ed., Bk. Rev. Ed.-John Cummuta, Circ. Mgr.-Mike Mikrut, Art Dir.-Michael DiFrisco, Mktg. Dir.-Joh Cummuta
Editorial Description: Strategies and techniques for getting completely debt-free, operating 100% on cash, and building retirement wealth through mutual funds.
General Info: (Formerly Personal Financial Success), Yr. Est. 1993, Monthly, Trim Size-8$\frac{1}{2}$ x 11, Offset press, 12 pages, ISSN: 1076-9676, 2 Color, Matte, Saddle-stitched
Subscriptions: Indv. $120, $6/copy
Circulation: Total-2,500, Readership-7,500
List Rental: List Management Co.: Manager: Michael Mikrut; Conrad Direct, Inc., 300 Knickerbocker Road, Creskill, NJ 07626 Tel # (201) 567-3200, Fax # (201) 567-4959, Actives: 6,000, $75/M, Expires: 5,000, $55/M
Printing Co: PTI Industries, 4813 Kingston Avenue, Lisle, IL 60532 Tel # (708) 241-9800, Fax # (708) 241-9805

Discount & Wholesale Printing Newsletter
See: PRINTING/GRAPHIC ARTS

Dr. Atkins Health Revelations
See: HEALTH

Economic Education Bulletin
See: ECONOMICS

ElderCare Forum
See: WOMEN'S

Energy Design Update
Business, Association

Publishing Co: Cutter Information Corp., 37 Broadway, Ste. 1, Arlington, MA 02174-5552 Tel # (617) 648-8700; Title Tel # (617) 641-5118 Title Fax # (617) 648-1950
Personnel: Publisher-Karen Fine Coburn, Editor-J.D. Ned Nisson, Circ. Mgr.-Carolyn Licata, Production Mgr.-Ellen McHale, Promotion Dir.-Paul Bergeron
Editorial Description: News & analysis on the latest energy efficient building techniques.
General Info: Yr. Est. 1982, Monthly, Trim Size-8$\frac{1}{2}$ x 11, Offset press, 16 pages, ISSN: 0741-3629, Ind/Abs/Online: NewsNet, No Color, Newsprint
Subscriptions: Indv. $337, Can. $337, For. $397, $15/copy
List Rental: Rents Lists
Printing Co: Benjamin Franklin Smith Printers, 320 Stuart St, Boston, MA 02116-5242 Tel # (617) 426-1160

Essential Living
Consumer

Publishing Co: Essential Living, Rr 1 Box 1310, Moretown, VT 05660-9413; Title Tel # (802) 244-1309
Personnel: Editor-Paul Conrad
Editorial Description: Tips on frugal living.
General Info: Bi-monthly

FSC Monthly Bulletin
Association

Publishing Co: Federation of Southern Cooperatives, PO Box 95, Epes, AL 35460-0095 Fax # (205) 652-9678; Title Tel # (205) 652-9676
General Info: Monthly, 8 pages
Subscriptions: Indv. $10
Circulation: Total-3,000
List Rental: Rents Lists

Factory Outlet Newsletter
Consumer

Publishing Co: Factory Outlet Newsletter, 11 Tory Lane Rt. 3, Newtown, CT 06470-1531; Title Tel # (203) 384-2500
Personnel: Editor-Jean Bird
Editorial Description: Directions and information new factory outlet stores.
General Info: Yr. Est. 1972, 8x/yr., Trim Size-8$\frac{1}{2}$ x 11, Offset press, 4 pages, No Color
Subscriptions: Indv. $5, $1/copy
Circulation: Total-3,000

Food Free or Cheap Newsletter
See: HOME ECONOMICS

Frugal Bugle, The
See: BANKING & FINANCE

Frugal Consumers Dollar Stretching Possibility Newsletter
Consumer

Publishing Co: Prosperity & Profits Unlimited, PO Box 416, Denver, CO 80201-0416; Title Tel # (303) 575-5676
Personnel: Publisher-A. Doyle
Editorial Description: Money saving tips for consumers.
General Info: Yr. Est. 1991, Annually, Trim Size-8$\frac{1}{2}$ x 11, ISSN: 0736-3990
Subscriptions: Indv. $5, Inst. $5, Can. $6, For. $7, $5/copy
Circulation: Total-1,500

Frugal Finances
Consumer

Publishing Co: Frugal Finances, PO Box 243, Grayslake, IL 60030-0243
Personnel: Editor-Kristin Fruhwirth, Editor-Richard Fruhwirth, Graphic Designer-Ember Trifonov
Editorial Description: Advocating awareness of excessive and imprudent spending.
General Info: Yr. Est. 1994, Monthly, Trim Size-8$\frac{1}{2}$ x 11, 8 pages, 2 Color, Matte
Subscriptions: Indv. $12

GA-SK Newsletter
See: DEAF

Giving USA Update
See: PHILANTHROPY

Grassroots Economic Organizing (GEO)
Business, Consumer

Publishing Co: Edina, PO Box 5065, New haven, CT 06525 Fax # (203) 486-0387; Title Tel # (203) 389-6194
Editorial Description: GEO reports on constructive gassroots initiative to create new democratic workplaces, environmentally sound enterprises, and community based financial institutions.
General Info: Yr. Est. 1991, Bi-monthly, Trim Size-8$\frac{1}{2}$ x 11, 16 pages
Subscriptions: Indv. $15, Inst. $30, Can. $30, For. $30, $3/copy
Circulation: Total-1,500
Advertising: Inquire for rates. Accepts Inserts.
List Rental: Rents Lists
Printing Co: CommonWealth Printing, 47 East St., Hadley, MA 01035 Tel # (413) 584-2536

Guild News
Association

Publishing Co: Canadian Merchant Service Guild, 1150 Morrison Dr., Ottawa, ON K2H 8S9 Canada Tel # (613) 829-9531
Personnel: Editor-Maury Sjoquist
General Info: Yr. Est. 1979
Subscriptions: $2/copy
Circulation: Total-6,000

Harvest Times
See: ENVIRONMENT & ECOLOGY

Health Facts
See: HEALTH

Healthy & Natural Journal, Part 1 - Health & Natural News
See: HEALTH

How to Manage Your Money

Publishing Co: Christian Financial Concepts, 601 Broad St E, Gainesville, GA 30501-3729; Title Tel # (770) 534-1000
Editorial Description: Money management.
General Info: Monthly

I-Beam
See: LABOR UNION

Impact: A Journal of Safety Litigation and News
See: AUTOMOTIVE

Income Advisor
See: INVESTMENT

Independent Power Report
See: LAW

Indoor Air Quality Update
See: ENVIRONMENT & ECOLOGY

LNG Express Product & Services Directory

Publishing Co: Zeus Development Corporation, P.O. Box 272505, Houston, TX 77277-2505; Title Tel # (713) 952-9500 Title Fax # (713) 782-9594
Editorial Description: Complete references to companies that offer products and services to the LNG subscription vehicle.
General Info: Yr. Est. 1993

Labor/Maintence Update
See: LABOR

Land Use Law Report
See: LAW

Leisure Industry Report
See: BUSINESS & INDUSTRY

Lemon Times
See: AUTOMOTIVE

Living Cheap News   *Consumer*

Publishing Co: ROPUBCO, PO Box 700058, San Jose, CA 95170-0058 Tel # (406) 257-1680;
Title Tel # (408) 257-1680 Title Fax # (408) 446-4257
Personnel: Publisher, Editor-Larry Roth
Editorial Description: Promotes 'practical parsimony' for urban consumers.
General Info: Yr. Est. 1992, 10x/yr.
Subscriptions: Indv. $12, For. $17, $1/copy
Circulation: Total-2,000

Living Healthy
See: HEALTH

Manhattan's User's Guide   *Consumer*

Publishing Co: Manhattan User's Guide, P.O. Box 772, Ansonia Station, New York, NY 10023
Tel # (212) 724-4692
Personnel: Publisher-Charles Suisman
Editorial Description: Consumer information about stores, businesses, restaurants, services, and more in the New York metropolitan area.
General Info: Yr. Est. 1992, Monthly, Trim Size-8½ x 11, 8 pages, No Color, Matte, Looseleaf
Subscriptions: Indv. $39

Mass. Transit
See: TRAFFIC & TRANSPORTATION

Metric Today   *Business, Association*

Publishing Co: Sponsor-U.S. Metric Assn., U.S. Metric Association, Inc., 10245 Andasol Ave, Northridge, CA 91325-1504; Title Tel # (818) 363-5606 Title Fax # (818) 368-7443
Personnel: Circ. Mgr.-Lorelle Young, Publisher, Editor, Production Mgr.-Valerie Antoine
Editorial Description: News of metric conversion activities in U.S. areas & sectors, plus details on U.S. government's progress in its congress-mandated conversion to conduct business in metric units.
General Info: (Formerly USMA Newsletter), Yr. Est. 1966, Bi-monthly, Trim Size-8½ x 11, Letrpr. press, 8 pages, ISSN: 1050-5628, No Color
Subscriptions: Indv. $30, Inst. $150, Can. $35, For. $35, $5/copy
Circulation: (96% controlled), Total-1,500
Printing Co: Reprographics, 8427 Canoga Ave, Canoga Park, CA 91304-2607

Moneytalk

Publishing Co: Moneytalk, Inc., 334 Highlark Dr., Box 1677, Larksville, PA 18704-1699;
Title Tel # (717) 287-6498
Personnel: Publisher, Editor-Jean Kwiatkowski
Editorial Description: Coupon & refund offers made by manufacturers on food & other household items.
General Info: Yr. Est. 1977, Monthly, 76 pages, 3% ads, 2 Color
Subscriptions: Indv. $19, $3/copy
Circulation: Total-30,000
Printing Co: P.A. Hutchison, Scranton, PA 18504

Motorcycle Consumer News
See: CYCLING-BICYCLE & MOTOR

NASCO Newsbriefs   *Association*

Publishing Co: North American Students of Cooperation, 530 S State St # 7715, Ann Arbor, MI 48109-1349; Title Tel # (313) 663-0889
Personnel: Editor-Margaret Martin
Editorial Description: News of NASCO & co-op activities around the US & Canada.
General Info: Monthly, Trim Size-8½ x 11, 2 pages
Subscriptions: Indv. $15
Circulation: Total-800

NCFE Motivator   *Business, Consumer*

Publishing Co: National Center for Financial Education, PO Box 34070, San Diego, CA 92163-4070;
Title Tel # (619) 232-8811
Personnel: Publisher-Loren Dunton, Editor-Paul Richard, Circ. Mgr.-Kim Goco, Circ. Mgr.-Jeff Talmadge
Editorial Description: Provides consumer information & education on spending, saving, investing, insuring & planning. Regular columns: 'Spend Yourself Rich', 'Questions & Answers'.
General Info: Yr. Est. 1982, Quarterly, Trim Size-8½ x 11, Offset press, 8 pages, 2 Color, Newsprint, Saddle-stitched
Subscriptions: Indv. $12, $2/copy
Circulation: (100% controlled), Total-15,000, Readership-25,000
Advertising: Accepts Inserts.

NEISS Data Highlights
See: SAFETY

NYPIRG Agenda   *Consumer, Association*

Publishing Co: New York Public Interest Research Group, Inc., 9 Murray St., New York, NY 10007-2223; Title Tel # (212) 349-6460
Personnel: Publisher, Editor-Matthew Bregman, Art Dir.-Jennine Uerr
Editorial Description: Newsletter of consumer & environmental advocacy organization.
General Info: (Formerly Agenda for Citizen Involvement), Yr. Est. 1980, Quarterly, Trim Size-8¼ x 10⅞, Web press, 16 pages, ISSN: 1044-3134, 2 Color, Newsprint
Subscriptions: Indv. $25
Circulation: Total-60,000
Printing Co: Vanguard Offset Printers, 470 Mundet Place, Hillside, NJ 07205-1115
Tel # (908) 851-2222

National Association of Attorneys General Consumer Protection Newsletter   *Association*

Publishing Co: National Association of Attorneys General, 444 N Capitol St NW Ste 339, Washington, DC 20001-1512 Tel # (202) 434-8034; Title Tel # (202) 628-0435
Personnel: Editor-Elena Boisvert
Editorial Description: Exchanges information between the states' offices.
General Info: Yr. Est. 1980, Monthly, Trim Size-8½ x 11, 20 pages
Circulation: Total-200

National Consumers League Bulletin   *Business, Association*

Publishing Co: National Consumers League, 1701 K St. NW, Ste. 1200, Washington, DC 20006; Title Tel # (202) 835-3323 Title Fax # (202) 835-0747
Personnel: Editor-Cleo Manual, Production Mgr.-Cleo Manuel
Editorial Description: Investigates, educates & advocates consumer & worker rights.
General Info: Yr. Est. 1899, Bi-monthly, Trim Size-8½ x 11, Offset press, 8 pages, ISSN: 1055-923X, 2 Color, Newsprint
Subscriptions: Indv. $20, Inst. $25, Free With Membership
Circulation: Total-4,500

News from ACAP
See: AERONAUTICS/ASTRONAUTICS

Obtaining Low Cost Credit Cards   *Business, Consumer*

Publishing Co: VisionWrite, PO Box 588, San Luis Rey, CA 92068; Title Tel # (619) 753-0794
Personnel: Publisher-Bruce Foley
Editorial Description: Reports on how to seek out and obtain the lowest cost credit cards and best bargains in cards avaliable nationwide. Reveals common credit mistakes made by consumers.
General Info: Yr. Est. 1990, Quarterly, ISSN: 5523-5272
Subscriptions: Indv. $15, $4/copy
Advertising: Inquire for rates.
List Rental: Rents Lists

Officers Call
See: MILITARY & NAVAL

On-Line
See: ADVERTISING & MARKETING

Overflights Newsletter   *Consumer*

Publishing Co: Ulsterites Fight Overflight Noise, PO Box 681, Stone Ridge, NY 12484-0681
General Info: Monthly

PBC Credit Briefs
See: CREDIT AND CREDIT UNIONS

PIRGIM Citizen Connection
See: ENVIRONMENT & ECOLOGY

Photo Marketing Newsline
See: PHOTOGRAPHY

Pocket Change Investor, The   *Consumer*

Publishing Co: Good Advice Press, PO Box 78, Elizaville, NY 12523-0078;
Title Tel # (914) 758-1400 Title Fax # (914) 758-1475
Personnel: Publisher-Nancy Castleman, Editor-Marc Eisenson
Editorial Description: The pocket change investor helps consumers save money on their mortgages, credit cards, and other debts. Also offers techniques to save on expenses like taxes, insurance, vacations, and groceries.
General Info: (Formerly Banker's Secret Bulletin), Yr. Est. 1990, Quarterly, Trim Size-8½ x 11, Web press, 8 pages, ISSN: 1054-8920, No Color, Recycled
Subscriptions: Indv. $13, $6/copy
Printing Co: Johnny's Ideal Printing, 352 Warren St, Hudson, NY 12534-2419 Tel # (518) 826-6666

Practically Green   *Consumer*

Publishing Co: Veridian Press, 4326 S.E. Woodstock Blvd., Suite #500, Portland, OR 97206-6270;
Title Tel # (503) 775-5547
Personnel: Publisher-Michal Angus
Editorial Description: Practical suggestions for reducing, reusind, and recycling.
General Info: Yr. Est. 1994, Monthly, Trim Size-8½ x 11, 4 pages, No Color, Matte
Subscriptions: Indv. $18, For. $24, $2/copy

Privacy & American Business
See: BUSINESS & INDUSTRY

Privacy Newsletter — *Consumer*

Publishing Co: Privacy Newsletter, Dept. OXO1, PO Box 8206, Philadelphia, PA 19101-8206; Title Tel # (215) 533-7373 Title Fax # (215) 533-7373
Personnel: Publisher, Editor-John Featherman
Editorial Description: Shows consumers how to get privacy and keep it. Shares key privacy stories, abuses, and public attitudes. Provides hope, encouragement and inspiration to individuals who seek freedom from Big Brother.
General Info: Yr. Est. 1994, Monthly, Trim Size-8½ x 11, 8 pages
Subscriptions: Indv. $99, For. $149

Product Safety and Liability Reporter — *Business*

Publishing Co: Bureau of National Affairs, Inc., 1231 25th St. NW, Bldg. N-200, Washington, DC 20037-1157; Title Tel # (202) 452-4200 Title Fax # (202) 822-8092
Personnel: Publisher-William A. Beltz, Editor-William Frank, Mng. Editor-Gary A. Weinstein, Circ. Mgr.-Gary C. Seltzer
Editorial Description: A weekly notification & reference service providing comprehensive coverage of current administrative, legislative, judicial, & industry developments relating to product safety & product liability.
General Info: Yr. Est. 1973, Weekly, Trim Size-8½ x 11, Web press, ISSN: 0092-7732, Looseleaf
Subscriptions: Indv. $1,031

Products Liability — *Business*

Publishing Co: Matthew Bender & Co., 11 Penn Plaza, New York, NY 10001-2006 Fax # (212) 244-3188; Title Tel # (212) 967-7707
Personnel: Editor-R. Kaye
Editorial Description: The most frequently cited, respected authority in the field. Covers every facet of the law, including: parties liable, theories of liability, statue of limitations, evidence & newly emerging topics. Discusses over 700 different products & product categories.
General Info: Yr. Est. 1960, Irregular, Looseleaf
Subscriptions: $1,125/copy

Products Liability Reporter — *Business*

Publishing Co: CCH, Inc., 2700 Lake Cook Rd., Riverwoods, IL 60015 Parent Co.-Kluwer Law & Taxation Publishers, Cambridge; Title Tel # (847) 267-7000 Title Fax # (800) 224-8299
Editorial Description: Publishes annotated explanation of liability rules, new court decisions on product-caused injuries; guidelines for manufacturer & retailer avoidance of product liability, full text coverage of current federal & state appellate decisions.
General Info: Yr. Est. 1963, Bi-weekly, Trim Size-6 x 9, Web press, 160 pages, Color, Looseleaf
Subscriptions: Indv. $745

Public Eye
See: LAW

Recipe Greetings Update
See: POETRY & CREATIVE WRITING

Refunding Update - Introduction to Refunding

Publishing Co: Prosperity & Profits Unlimited, PO Box 416, Denver, CO 80201-0416; Title Tel # (303) 575-5676
Personnel: Publisher, Editor-A. Doyle
Editorial Description: An introduction to refunding.
General Info: Yr. Est. 1983, Irregular, Trim Size-8.5 x 11, 4 pages, ISSN: 0736-1688
Subscriptions: Indv. $3, Inst. $3, Can. $4, For. $6, $3/copy
Circulation: Total-2,000

Refundle Bundle — *Consumer*

Publishing Co: Refundle Bundle, Box 141, Centuck Sta., Yonkers, NY 10710-0141; Title Tel # (914) 472-2227 Title Fax # (914) 725-1597
Personnel: Publisher, Editor-Susan Samtur, Circ. Mgr.-Stephen Samtur, Adv. Dir.-Steve Samtur, Art Dir.-Rose Dubin
Editorial Description: A listing of current manufacturer (food & drug) refunds and rebate offers.
General Info: (Formerly Refundle Bundle), Yr. Est. 1973, Bi-monthly, Trim Size-6½ x 10, Web press, 48 pages, ISSN: 0194-0139, 2 Color
Subscriptions: Indv. $10, $2/copy
Circulation: Total-170,000
List Rental: Actives: $50/M
Printing Co: United Printing, 1100 Boston Ave., Bridgeport, CT 06610 Tel # (203) 579-1899

Regulatory Watchdog Service — *Business*

Publishing Co: Washington Business Information, Inc., 1117 19th St N Ste 200, Arlington, VA 22209-1708; Title Tel # (703) 247-3432 Title Fax # (703) 247-3421
Personnel: Publisher-David Swit, Editor-Dave Kramer, Circ. Mgr.-Chris Rogers, Production Mgr.-Jennea Myrick, Mktg. Dir.-Deb Plaskow
Editorial Description: Provides quick access to important documents from the Consumer Product Safety Commission, Food & Drug Administration and other agencies as well as from Capitol Hill and the White House.
General Info: (Formerly Product Safety Watchdog Service), Yr. Est. 1975, Weekly, Trim Size-8½ x 11, Sheetfed press, 5 pages, ISSN: 0275-0902, No Color, Recycled
Subscriptions: Indv. $1,118, Inst. $1,118, Can. $1,118, For. $1,203
Acquistions: Publication Bought
List Rental: Actives: $110/M

Renter's Rag
See: LEASING & RENTING

Retail Operations News Bulletin

Publishing Co: National Retail Federation Enterprises, Inc., 325 7th St. NW, Ste. 1000, Washington, DC 20004-2802 Tel # (202) 783-7971 Fax # (202) 737-2849
General Info: Yr. Est. 1970, Quarterly
Subscriptions: Indv. $30

Rocky Mountain CoHousing Quarterly, The
See: ENVIRONMENT & ECOLOGY

Roman Reports
See: DIRECT MAIL

SF Newsletter
See: LUMBER & WOOD

Safe Food News
See: FOOD

Seafood Soundings

Publishing Co: Boehmer & Boehmer, Box 365, Monhegan Island, ME 04852-0365; Title Tel # (207) 596-0227
Personnel: Publisher-Peter Boehmer, Editor-Raquel Boehmer
Editorial Description: Seafood industry news and developments.
General Info: Yr. Est. 1986, Bi-monthly, Trim Size-8½ x 11, Sheetfed press, 6 pages, ISSN: 0691-4982, No Color
Subscriptions: Indv. $16, Can. $20, $3/copy
Acquistions: Publication Sold
Printing Co: Lakeside Printing, PO Box 654, Rockland, ME 04841-0654 Tel # (207) 594-5216

Shoestring Traveler, The
See: TRAVEL

Shopper Report — *Business, Association*

Publishing Co: Doyle Research Group, PO Box 42753, Philadelphia, PA 19101-2753 Tel # (215) 561-2921; Title Tel # (215) 386-5890 Title Fax # (215) 557-7692
Editorial Description: Consumers news and related information.
General Info: Yr. Est. 1979, 11x/yr., Letrpr. press, 4 pages, 2 Color, Matte
Subscriptions: Indv. $185, $25/copy

Simple Living News — *Consumer*

Publishing Co: Simple Living News, PO Box 1884, Jonesboro, GA 30237 Fax # (404) 471-9048; Title Tel # (404) 471-9048 Title Fax # (770) 471-9048
Personnel: Publisher, Editor-Edith Flowers Kilgo, Circ. Mgr.-Randal Kilgo, Mktg. Dir.-Karen Kilgo
Editorial Description: Geared to baby boomer generation members who want to downscale, destress and deemphasize materialism. Emphasis is on self-help, saving money, learning a more satisfying lifestyle.
General Info: Yr. Est. 1995, 10x/yr., Trim Size-8½ x 11½, 8 pages, ISSN: 1079-6150, Saddle-stitched
Subscriptions: Indv. $16, Can. $20, For. $25, $2/copy
Advertising: Inquire for rates. Accepts Inserts.
List Rental: Rents Lists

Smorgasboard-Plenty to Eat Update
See: FOOD

Soups Cheap or Almost Free
See: FOOD

TidBITS
See: COMPUTERS & AUTOMATION

Tightwad Gazette — *Consumer*

Publishing Co: Tightwad Gazette, RR 1 Box 3570, Leeds, ME 04263-9710 Fax # (207) 524-7962; Title Tel # (207) 524-7962
Personnel: Publisher, Editor-Amy Dacyczyn, Circ. Mgr., Production Mgr.-Jim Dacyczyn
Editorial Description: Promotes thrift as a viable alternative lifestyle.
General Info: Yr. Est. 1990, Monthly, Trim Size-8½ x 11, Letrpr. press, 8 pages, ISSN: 1065-366X, Recycled
Subscriptions: Indv. $12, Inst. $12, Can. $15, For. $21, $1/copy
Circulation: Total-45,000, Readership-150,000
Printing Co: Evergreen Custom Printing, Third St., Auburn, ME Tel # (207) 782-0525

Travel Scoop Consumer Newsletter
See: TRAVEL

Trend/Wire
See: FOOD

Valley Voice
See: GENERAL INTEREST

Wagons of Steel
See: AUTOMOTIVE

COSMETICS & PERFUMES

ANJO Insight
Business

Publishing Co: ANJO Enterprises, 5602 Glenlivet Pl, Greenville, TX 75402-4205;
Title Tel # (214) 321-9113
Personnel: Publisher-Ann Bloskas, Editor-J. D. Bloskas
Editorial Description: Sales items & motivational tips to sales people who sell through ANJO Enterprises.
General Info: Yr. Est. 1976, Monthly, Trim Size-8½ x 11, Offset press, 6 pages, Color

Category Report: HBA
Consumer

Publishing Co: Marketing Intelligence Service, Ltd., 6473D Route 64, Naples, NY 14512;
Title Tel # (716) 374-6326 Title Fax # (716) 374-5217
Personnel: Publisher-Richard Lawrence, Production Mgr.-Patricia Peck
Editorial Description: Combines domestic & foreign new product reviews. Each review typically includes detailed product & packaging descriptions, with illustrations, important manufacturing & marketing innovations, emerging trends, & other background information.
General Info: Yr. Est. 1984, Monthly, Trim Size-8½ x 11, Mimeo press, No Color, Newsprint
Subscriptions: Indv. $1,000

Cosmetic World
Business

Publishing Co: Cosmetic World, Inc., 530 5th Ave. 4th Fl., New York, NY 10036-5101;
Title Tel # (212) 687-6190
Personnel: Publisher-John Ledes, Editor-B. Ledes, Production Mgr.-Joseph Garces, Adv. Dir.-George Ledes
General Info: Yr. Est. 1967, Weekly, Trim Size-8½ x 11, Web press, 6 pages, 4 Color
Subscriptions: Indv. $175, $4/copy
Circulation: Total-4,138
Advertising: Inquire for rates. Accepts Inserts.

Craft Related Newsletters, Periodicals & Publications
See: HOBBY

DCAT Digest
See: DRUGS & PHARMACEUTICALS

Grayson Report
See: ADVERTISING & MARKETING

Healthy & Natural Journal, Part 1 - Health & Natural News
See: HEALTH

NAACS Washington Update
Association

Publishing Co: Natl. Assn. of Acred. Cosmetology Schls., 901 N Washington St Ste 206, Alexandria, VA 22314-1535; Title Tel # (703) 845-1333 Title Fax # (703) 845-1336
Personnel: Publisher, Editor-Ronald Smith
Editorial Description: News & info concerning cosmetology schools legislation & federal agency rules regarding their operation plus news about the industry.
General Info: Yr. Est. 1986, Monthly, Trim Size-8½ x 11, Letrpr. press, 6 pages, 2 Color, Coated
Circulation: (100% controlled), Total-1,400
Printing Co: Balmar Printing Inc., 1528 Tyco Rd., #G, MacLean, VA 22182-2211
Tel # (703) 883-9700

New Product News
See: GROCERY

Potpourri Simple & Easy Update
See: GIFTS, GAMES, TOYS

Rose Sheet, The: Toiletries, Fragrances, and Skin Care
Business

Publishing Co: F-D-C Reports, Inc., 5550 Friendship Blvd, Chevy Chase, MD 20815-7278
Fax # (301) 986-6467; Title Tel # (301) 657-9830 Title Fax # (301) 657-3094
Personnel: Publisher-Wallace Werble, Jr., Editor-Cole Werble, Circ. Mgr.-Edward Picken, Adv. Dir.-Richard Messmer, Mktg. Dir.-Leila Simaika
Editorial Description: Reports on toiletries, fragrance and skin care industry, govt. regulation, industry news including financial review.
General Info: Yr. Est. 1980, Weekly, Trim Size-8½ x 11, Letrpr. press, 25 pages, ISSN: 0297-1110, Ind/Abs/Online: Mead Data, Data-Star, DIALOG, BRS, PNI, No Color
Subscriptions: Indv. $500, For. $575, $18/copy

Scenterpiece Update
See: GIFTS, GAMES, TOYS

Scentouri News
Business, Consumer

Publishing Co: Prosperity & Profits Unlimited, PO Box 416, Denver, CO 80201-0416;
Title Tel # (303) 575-5676
Personnel: Editor-A. Doyle
Editorial Description: Recipes for making potpourri from dried flowers. Listings of sources of fragrant plants.
General Info: Yr. Est. 1983, Irregular, Trim Size-8½ x 11, 17 pages, ISSN: 0741-0816, No Color
Subscriptions: Indv. $4, Inst. $4, Can. $7, For. $8, $4/copy

CRAFTS

ACCI Newsletter
See: HOBBY

AGSA Newsletter
See: GLASS, STONE & CLAY

Black Sheep Newsletter
See: LIVESTOCK

Craftrends Today
Business

Publishing Co: PJS Publications, Inc., 2 News Plaza, PO Box 1790, Peoria, IL 61656
Tel # (309) 682-6626 Parent Co.-K-III Communications, New York
Editorial Description: News and information for craft related industry.

Draft & Design
Consumer

Publishing Co: Robin & Russ Handweavers, 533 N Adams St, McMinnville, OR 97128-5513
Tel # (503) 472-5760
Editorial Description: Techniques for hand looming and weaving.
General Info: Monthly

Project Salvador Crafts
Business, Association

Publishing Co: Project Salvador Crafts, P.O. Box 300105, Denver, CO 80218;
Title Tel # (303) 964-8606 Title Fax # (303) 839-5105
Editorial Description: Project Salvador Crafts are hand-made Salvadorian crafts from new awakening artisan coordination in El Salvador.
General Info: Annually, Looseleaf
Advertising: Inquire for rates.

Scroll Saw News
Consumer

Publishing Co: Nelson Designs, PO Box 422, Dublin, NH 03444-0422 Tel # (603) 563-8306
Editorial Description: For those interested in crafting wood.
General Info: Irregular, Trim Size-8.5 x 11, 11 pages, Color-cover, Newsprint
Subscriptions: Free To Qualified Recipient

Scrollsaw Chatter
Consumer

Publishing Co: Art Factory, The, 1025 West Seminary, Richland Center, WI 53581
Editorial Description: Contains tips and techniques, product news and supply sources for the scrollsaw user.
General Info: Yr. Est. 1995, 8x/yr.
Subscriptions: Indv. $19, Can. $24

Sewing & Crafts Hotline
Consumer

Publishing Co: Sewing & Crafts Wholesale Hotline, PO Box 402091, Miami Beach, FL 33140
Personnel: Publisher, Editor-Mark Weiss
Editorial Description: Lists reader recommended companies, discounts, free samples available and more.
General Info: Yr. Est. 1970, Quarterly, Trim Size-8½ x 14, No Color
Subscriptions: Indv. $10, $3/copy

Size of Craft/Hobby Industry Survey
Business, Association

Publishing Co: Hobby Industry Association, 319 E. 54th St., Elmwood Park, NJ 07407-2712;
Title Tel # (201) 794-1133 Title Fax # (201) 797-0657
Personnel: Publisher-Susan Brandt, Editor-Hope Crawley
Editorial Description: Dollar volume data incorporating retailers, manufacturers & consumers of craft/hobby products.
General Info: Yr. Est. 1990, Every two years, Offset press, 150 pages, No Color, Looseleaf
Subscriptions: $500/copy
Circulation: Total-2,000

Warp & Weft
Consumer

Publishing Co: Robin & Russ Handweavers, 533 N Adams St, McMinnville, OR 97128-5513
Tel # (503) 472-5760
Editorial Description: Weaving information and news for hand weavers.
General Info: Monthly

CREDIT AND CREDIT UNIONS

AICPA Financial Statement Prepartion Manual
See: ACCOUNTING

Alternative Currents
See: BANKING & FINANCE

Bankcard Consumer News

Publishing Co: Bankcard Holders of America, 524 Branch Dr., Salem, VA 24153-4119; Title Tel # (703) 481-1110
Personnel: Editor-Elgie Holstein
Editorial Description: Consumer information on credit & personal finance.
General Info: Bi-monthly, Trim Size-8½ x 11, Web press, 6 pages
Subscriptions: Indv. $18, $2/copy
Circulation: Total-100,000
List Rental: Rents Lists

Bankcard Update   *Business*

Publishing Co: RAM Research Corporation, Box 1700, College Estates, Frederick, MD 21702-0700 Fax # (301) 695-0160; Title Tel # (301) 695-4660 Title Fax # (800) 821-4627
Personnel: Publisher, Editor-Robert McKinley
Editorial Description: Coverage of the bank credit card industry, including legal, marketing, legislative, acquisitions & earnings news. Surveys & ranks cards by interest rate, annual fee & issuer's size.
General Info: Yr. Est. 1986, Monthly, Sheetfed press, 48 pages, ISSN: 0894-2390
Subscriptions: Indv. $695, Inst. $335, Can. $350, For. $435, $35/copy

Card News   *Business*

Publishing Co: Phillips Business Information, Inc., 1201 Seven Locks Rd., Ste 300, Potomac, MD 20854-2958 Tel # (301) 340-1520; Title Tel # (301) 340-2100 Title Fax # (301) 424-4297
Personnel: Publisher-Chris Scotton, Editor-Claire Taylor, Production Mgr.-Teresa Fleisher, Adv. Dir.-Kim Hudak, Mktg. Dir.-Kelly Ebbs
Editorial Description: An Executive report covering the transaction card marketplace, including credit & debit cards, smart cards, proprietary cards, Etc.
General Info: (Formerly Credit Card Insider), Yr. Est. 1986, Bi-weekly, 8 pages, ISSN: 0894-0797, Ind/Abs/Online: NewsNet, DIALOG, Predicasts, Bloomberg, 2 Color
Subscriptions: Indv. $595, For. $630, $37/copy

Cardtrak   *Consumer*

Publishing Co: RAM Research Corporation, Box 1700, College Estates, Frederick, MD 21702-0700 Fax # (301) 695-0160; Title Tel # (301) 695-4660 Title Fax # (800) 821-4627
Personnel: Publisher, Editor-Robert McKinley
Editorial Description: Only report tracking bank credit cards directed towards consumers. Reviews the latest offers and trends. Surveys more than 500 issuers annually. A brief listing of co-branded and affinity cards is also included.
General Info: Yr. Est. 1991, Monthly, 16 pages
Subscriptions: Indv. $60, Inst. $60, Can. $75, For. $100, $5/copy

Collection Agency Report
See: BANKING & FINANCE

Consumer Trends
See: BANKING & FINANCE

Cred-Alert
See: BANKING & FINANCE

Credit Card Collector   *Consumer*

Publishing Co: Credit Card Collector, PO Box 460247, Houston, TX 77056-8247 Tel # (713) 691-1387; Title Tel # (713) 526-2775
Editorial Description: News on the credit card business and the hobby; contains feature articles and editorials.
General Info: Yr. Est. 1986, Bi-monthly
Subscriptions: Indv. $20, Inst. $20, $4/copy
Advertising: Inquire for rates.

Credit Card News   *Business*

Publishing Co: Faulkner & Gray, Inc., 11 Penn Plz., 17th Floor, New York, NY 10001-2006 Tel # (212) 967-7000 Fax # (212) 695-8172 Parent Co.-Thomson Corp., Stamford; Title Tel # (312) 648-0261 Title Fax # (312) 648-9569
Editorial Description: Focuses on credit card related topics.
General Info: Yr. Est. 1988, 26x/yr.
Subscriptions: Indv. $375
List Rental: List Management Co.: Aggressive List Management, 18-2 E Dundee Rd Ste 101, Barrington, IL 60010-5273 Tel # (708) 304-4030, Fax # (708) 304-4032, Actives: 93,839, $95/M, Hotline: 28,151, $105/M

Credit Line

Publishing Co: Stamford Teachers Federal Credit Union, PO Box 2269, Stamford, CT 06906-0269; Title Tel # (203) 324-2144 Title Fax # (203) 327-7202
Editorial Description: Service & financial news provided to member of the Teachers Credit Union.
General Info: Quarterly

Credit Line, The   *Business*

Publishing Co: North Shore Agency, 117 Cutter Mill Rd., Great Neck, NY 11021; Title Tel # (516) 466-9300 Title Fax # (516) 466-9391
Personnel: VP Sales & Mktg.-Doug Harpham
Editorial Description: Information for marketing, credit and collection professionals.
General Info: Quarterly, Trim Size-8½ x 11, No Color
Subscriptions: Indv. $125, $50/copy
Circulation: Total-1,670

Credit Risk Management Report   *Business*

Publishing Co: Phillips Business Information, Inc., 1201 Seven Locks Rd., Ste 300, Potomac, MD 20854-2958 Tel # (301) 340-1520 Fax # (301) 424-4297; Title Tel # (301) 340-2100 Title Fax # (301) 340-0419
Personnel: Publisher-Chris Scotton, Editor-Eric Williams, Production Mgr.-Teresa Fleisher, Adv. Dir.-Kim Hudak, Mktg. Dir.-Kelly Ebbs
Editorial Description: Devoted to the effective management of consumer credit risk. Provides information of risk management, trends, forecasts and legislation in the consumer credit industry.
General Info: Yr. Est. 1990, Bi-weekly, Web press, 64 pages, ISSN: 1054-5069, Ind/Abs/Online: NewsNet, DIALOG, Predicasts, Bloomberg, 2 Color, Coated, Saddle-stitched
Subscriptions: Indv. $595, For. $630, $37/copy
Circulation: Total-2,500
Advertising: Inquire for rates.
List Rental: Rents Lists

Credit Union Digest   *Association*

Publishing Co: California Credit Union League, 2322 S Garey Ave, Pomona, CA 91766-5805; Title Tel # (714) 628-6044
Personnel: Publisher-Laura Kubota, Editor-Carol Payne
Editorial Description: News of & for California credit unions.
General Info: Yr. Est. 1975, Semi-monthly, Offset press, 6 pages
Subscriptions: Indv. $250
Circulation: (100% controlled)

Credit Union Financial Profiles   *Business*

Publishing Co: United Communications Group, 11300 Rockville Pike, Ste. 1100, Rockville, MD 20852-3030 Tel # (301) 816-8950 Fax # (301) 816-8945; Title Tel # (301) 961-8700 Title Fax # (301) 961-8666
Personnel: Publisher-Dan Brown, Circ. Mgr.-Sharon Welch
Editorial Description: An analysis of credit union financial profiles.
General Info: Yr. Est. 1986, Semi-annually
Subscriptions: Indv. $199, $100/copy
List Rental: Rents Lists

Credit Union Information Service   *Association*

Publishing Co: United Communications Group, 11300 Rockville Pike, Ste. 1100, Rockville, MD 20852-3030 Fax # (301) 816-8945; Title Tel # (301) 816-8950 Title Fax # (301) 961-8666
Personnel: Publisher-Martin Zook, Editor-Michael Peck, Circ. Mgr.-Monica Brown
Editorial Description: Contains information for managers of credit unions.
General Info: Yr. Est. 1973, Bi-weekly, Web press, 4 pages, No Color
Subscriptions: Indv. $287, $9/copy
Acquistions: Publication Bought, Publication Sold
List Rental: Rents Lists

Credit Union Manager Newsletter   *Business, Association*

Publishing Co: Credit Union National Association, Inc., 5710 Mineral Point, Madison, WI 53705 Tel # (608) 231-4860 Fax # (608) 231-4858; Title Tel # (608) 231-4080
Personnel: Publisher-Nancy Huepenbecker, Editor-James Hanson, Circ. Mgr.-Mark Condon, Circ. Mgr.-Philip Heckman, Adv. Dir.-Phyllis Peterson
Editorial Description: Trends, perspectives, practical advice on credit union management.
General Info: Yr. Est. 1975, Bi-weekly, Trim Size-8½ x 11, Sheetfed press, 4 pages, No Color
Subscriptions: Indv. $120, $10/copy
Circulation: Total-3,012

CreditWeek   *Association*

Publishing Co: American Financial Services Assn., 919 18th Street, N.W., Washington, DC 20006-5503; Title Tel # (202) 296-5544 Title Fax # (202) 223-0321
Personnel: Publisher-Frances Smith, Editor-Glenn Kaup, Production Mgr., Art Dir.-Lee Westell
Editorial Description: Regulatory, marketplace & congressional events in financial services.
General Info: Yr. Est. 1976, Weekly, Trim Size-8½ x 11, 4 pages, 2 Color, Matte
Subscriptions: Indv. $100, $2/copy
Circulation: Total-1,400

Health Care Collector
See: HEALTH

Managing International Credit & Collections
See: ACCOUNTING

Merchant Connections   *Business*

Publishing Co: Ariad Custom Publishing, 119 Spadina Ave., #1005, Toronto, ON M5V 2L1 Canada Tel # (416) 971-9294
Editorial Description: Information for VISA merchants who deal with the Canadian Imperial Bank of Commerce.
General Info: (Formerly CIBC Connections), Yr. Est. 1992, Quarterly

Nilson Report
See: BANKING & FINANCE

Obtaining Low Cost Credit Cards
See: CONSUMER INTERESTS

Online Marketplace
See: COMPUTERS & AUTOMATION

PBC Credit Briefs   *Business, Consumer*

Publishing Co: Publishing & Business Consultants, 101 W. 64th St. Unit #3, Inglewood, CA 90302-1255 Tel # (213) 732-3477 Fax # (213) 732-3477
Personnel: Publisher, Editor-Andeson Atia
General Info: Quarterly, ISSN: 1059-2059
Subscriptions: Indv. $180
Advertising: Inquire for rates.

Pocket Change Investor, The
See: CONSUMER INTERESTS

Privacy Journal
See: PHILANTHROPY

Senior Membership
Horizons   *Consumer*

Publishing Co: American Express Publishing Corp., 1120 Ave. of the Americas, 9th Floor, New York, NY 10036-6770 Tel # (212) 382-5600 Fax # (212) 382-5879
Personnel: Editor-Denise Shoukas, Art Dir.-Susan Kramer
Editorial Description: Travel, shopping, business and other information for senior American Express card holders.
General Info: Bi-monthly, Trim Size-8½ x 11, 8 pages, 4 Color, Coated, Saddle-stitched

Szabo Collective Wisdom   *Business*

Publishing Co: Szabo Assocs., Inc., 3355 Lenox Rd NE Ste 945, Atlanta, GA 30326-1332; Title Tel # (404) 266-2464 Title Fax # (404) 266-2165
Personnel: Editor-Claudia Dallion
Editorial Description: For collection agents.
General Info: Quarterly
Subscriptions: Free To Qualified Recipient
Circulation: Total-9,000

Today's Collector   *Business*

Publishing Co: Zimmerman & Associates, Inc., 5307 South 92nd St., Hales Corners, WI 53130-1677 Parent Co.-Aspen Publishers, Inc., Gaithersburg; Title Tel # (414) 425-2189
Personnel: Publisher-David Zimmerman, Editor-Bruce Nelson
Editorial Description: Published for professionals in the bill collection field.
General Info: Yr. Est. 1992, Monthly, Sheetfed press, 6 pages, 2 Color, Matte
Subscriptions: Indv. $149, Inst. $149, $13/copy
Circulation: Total-500
Printing Co: TJ Printing, 14150 W National Ave # 406, New Berlin, WI 53151-4529

CROSS-WORD PUZZLES

Fillers for Publications
See: JOURNALISM

Goodenow's Ghosts
See: GENEALOGY

Reporter--Your Editorial Assistant
See: JOURNALISM

Stories that Rhyme, Every Time Kids Pages
See: CHILDREN

Story Rhyme Word
Mapping   *Consumer*

Publishing Co: Story Time Stories that Rhyme, PO Box 416, Denver, CO 80201-0416 Tel # (303) 575-5676; Title Tel # (713) 867-3438
Personnel: Publisher-A. Doyle
Editorial Description: Word mapping puzzles with clues from stories that rhyme.
General Info: Yr. Est. 1992, Annually, Trim Size-8½ x 11, No Color
Subscriptions: Inst. $4, Can. $6, For. $8, $4/copy
Circulation: Total-5,000

Tough Cryptics   *Consumer*

Publishing Co: American Crossword Federation, PO Box 69, Massapequa Park, NY 11762-0069; Title Tel # (516) 795-8823 Title Fax # (516) 795-6788
General Info: (Formerly Crossworder's Own Newsletter), Yr. Est. 1983, Bi-monthly
Subscriptions: Indv. $25

Tough Puzzles   *Consumer*

Publishing Co: American Crossword Federation, PO Box 69, Massapequa Park, NY 11762-0069; Title Tel # (516) 795-8823
Personnel: Publisher-Stanley Newman
Editorial Description: America's most challenging crossword puzzles.
General Info: (Formerly Crossworder's Own Newsletter), Yr. Est. 1983, Bi-monthly, Trim Size-8½ x 11, Offset press, 20 pages, No Color, Newsprint
Subscriptions: Indv. $25, Can. $30, For. $30, $5/copy
Circulation: Total-6,000
List Rental: Actives: $100/M

CULTURE & HUMANITIES

ACE News

Publishing Co: Assn. of Cultural Executives, 133 Barton Ave., Toronto, ON M6G 1R1 Canada; Title Fax # (416) 633-2340
Personnel: Editor-Anthony Schatzky
Editorial Description: Information and articles of interest to cultural managers and professional arts administrators.
General Info: Yr. Est. 1983, Quarterly, Trim Size-8½ x 11, Mimeo press, 9 pages, 1% ads, No Color
Subscriptions: Can. $85
Circulation: Total-225
Advertising: Inquire for rates. Accepts Inserts.

ACLS Newsletter   *Scholarly, Association*

Publishing Co: American Council of Learned Societies, 228 E. 45th St., New York, NY 10017-3398; Title Fax # (212) 697-1505 Title Fax # (212) 949-8058
Personnel: Production Mgr.-Candace Frede
General Info: Quarterly
Circulation: Total-10,000
Printing Co: Citation Graphics, 1249 Glen Ave, Moorestown, NJ 08057 Fax # (609) 231-4696

AHA! Hispanic Arts News
See: ART & SCULPTURE

AIC Newsletter
See: ART & SCULPTURE

Agenda
See: CIVIL RIGHTS

Aging and the Human Spirit Newsletter
See: SENIOR CITIZENS

American Association of Teachers of German Newsletter
See: LITERATURE & LINGUISTICS

American Dreams
See: GENERAL INTEREST

American Studies Assn.
Newsletter   *Association*   CPM: $80

Publishing Co: American Studies Assn., 1120 19th Street NW, Suite 301, Washington, DC 20036; Title Tel # (202) 467-4783 Title Fax # (202) 467-4786
Personnel: Editor-John Stephens
Editorial Description: Its aim is to promote a broader awareness of the complex institutional, economic, & political challenges now facing the American Studies community. ASAN Newsletter also serves as a clearinghouse for news of ASA chapters & committees, conferences & meetin s, fellowships & grants, employment opportunities, publications, & other programs of interest to ASA members.
General Info: (Formerly ASA Newsletter), Yr. Est. 1977, Quarterly, 16 pages, ISSN: 0742-9290, No Color, Perfect bound
Subscriptions: Indv. $50, Free With Membership
Circulation: Total-5,000, Readership-6,000
Advertising: $400. Accepts Inserts.
List Rental: List Management Co.: John Hopkins University Press,Journals Division, 2715 North Charles Street, Baltimore, MD 21218-4319 Tel # (410) 516-6964, Actives: 5,500

Applied Orgonometry   *Consumer*

Publishing Co: RRP Publishers, PO Box 8, Easton, PA 18044-0008; Title Tel # (215) 252-1199
Personnel: Publisher, Editor-Jacob Meyerowitz
Editorial Description: Reich's thought technique. Follows logic of functions. Interdisciplinary. Radical consequences.
General Info: Yr. Est. 1986, Trim Size-8½ x 11, 32 pages, ISSN: 0882-4347, Looseleaf
Subscriptions: Indv. $26, Inst. $32, $9/copy

Arab Voice   *Consumer*

Publishing Co: Arab Voice, 956 Main St., Paterson, NJ 07503; Title Tel # (201) 345-0999 Title Fax # (201) 523-7815
Personnel: Editor in Chief-Walid Rabah, Editor-Alia Shaheen
Editorial Description: The largest Arabic newspaper in the Middle East and the largest bilingual Arabic paper in the US. Contains political analysis, community news, sports, entertainment and advertisment.
General Info: Bi-weekly, Trim Size-11½ x 16¼, 20 pages, No Color, Newsprint, Other
Circulation: Total-20,000
Advertising: Inquire for rates.

Archaeology on Kaua'i
See: ARCHAEOLOGY

Archivists Society of Alberta Newsletter *Association* CPM: $545

Publishing Co: Archives Society of Alberta, P.O. Box 21080, Dominion Postal Outlet, Lelgary, AB T2P 4H5 Canada; Title Tel # (403) 228-0827
Personnel: Editor-Jim Bowman, Production Mgr.-Maigo Loing, Adv. Dir.-Koren Buckley
Editorial Description: Society news and developments in archival science.
General Info: (Formerly Newsletter: Alberta Society of Archivists), Yr. Est. 1981, Quarterly, Trim Size-8½ x 11, Offset press, 20 pages, ISSN: 1199-5122, 2 Color, Matte, Saddle-stitched
Subscriptions: Can. $60, Free With Membership
Circulation: Total-275, Readership-500
Advertising: $150. Accepts Inserts.

Arkansas Country Dancer
See: DANCE

Arts Management *Business*

Publishing Co: Sponsor-Professional Arts Mgt. Inst., Radius, Group, Inc., 408 West 57th Street, New York, NY 10019-3053; Title Tel # (212) 245-3850
Personnel: Publisher, Editor-Alvin Reiss
Editorial Description: Edited for those who finance, manage and communicate cultural activities.
General Info: Yr. Est. 1962, 5x/yr., Trim Size-8½ x 11, Offset press, 4 pages, No Color, Newsprint
Subscriptions: Indv. $18, Can. $19, For. $22, $4/copy
Circulation: Total-6,000

ArtsUSA UpDate *Scholarly*

Publishing Co: American Council for the Arts, 1 E. 53rd St., New York, NY 10022-4294 Fax # (212) 223-4415; Title Tel # (212) 223-2787
Personnel: Publisher-Robert Porter, Editor-Doug Rose
Editorial Description: Monthly news bulletin focusing on arts advocacy, support & recent developments--national legislative actions that affect the arts.
General Info: (Formerly ACA UpDate; Word from Washington), Yr. Est. 1970, Monthly, Trim Size-8½ x 11, Sheetfed press, 8 pages, ISSN: 1054-3570, No Color, Matte, Saddle-stitched
Subscriptions: Indv. $50, Free With Membership
Circulation: Total-1,000
List Rental: Actives: $75/M
Printing Co: Account Manager: Tamar Sokol; Radiant Graphics, 155 Avenue Of The Americas Fl, 4, New York, NY 10013-1507 Tel # (212) 638-8800, Fax # (212) 966-4009

Artsearch
See: EMPLOYMENT

Asia Foundation News

Publishing Co: Asia Foundation, Box 3223, San Francisco, CA 94119
Personnel: Editor-Andrea Hamilton
General Info: Yr. Est. 1976, 2 Color
Circulation: Total-2,000

Asian Studies Newsletter *Association*

Publishing Co: Association for Asian Studies Inc., 1 Lane Hall, Univ. of Michigan, Ann Arbor, MI 48109; Title Tel # (313) 665-2490 Title Fax # (313) 665-3801
General Info: (Formerly Assn. for Asian Studies Newsletter), Yr. Est. 1973, 5x/yr.
Subscriptions: Indv. $15
Circulation: Total-6,300

BCA News
See: ART & SCULPTURE

Bits & Bytes Review
See: COMPUTERS & AUTOMATION

Boletin Informativo Newsletter
See: BOOKS & BOOK TRADE

Bookviews
See: BOOKS & BOOK TRADE

Bradford Compact Newsletter
See: GENEALOGY

Bridges
See: EDUCATION

Bulletin of the American Academy of Arts and Sciences *Association*

Publishing Co: American Academy of the Arts and Sciences, Norton Woods, 136 Irving St., Cambridge, MA 02138; Title Tel # (617) 492-8800
Editorial Description: Reports on the various study groups sponsored by the academy.
General Info: Yr. Est. 1947, 8x/yr., 45 pages, ISSN: 0002-712X, No Color
Subscriptions: $1/copy
Circulation: Total-3,400

CLAG Communication
See: GEOGRAPHY

California Arts Advocate *Association*

Publishing Co: California Confederation of the Arts, 704 O St Fl 2, Sacramento, CA 95814-5506; Title Tel # (916) 447-7811 Title Fax # (916) 447-7891
General Info: (Formerly RADIUS Resources for Local Arts), Yr. Est. 1979, Quarterly
Subscriptions: Indv. $30
Circulation: Total-2,000

California Tomorrow
See: EDUCATION

Carrying Capacity Network Network Clearinghouse Bulletin
See: ENVIRONMENT & ECOLOGY

Celebration News
See: PHILOSOPHY

Children's Video Review Newsletter
See: CHILDREN

China Institute in America Bulletin *Association*

Publishing Co: China Institute in America, 125 E 65th St, New York, NY 10021-7088; Title Tel # (212) 744-8181 Title Fax # (212) 628-4159
Personnel: Editor-Michael Bless
Editorial Description: Highlights the activities of the Institute which focus on Chinese culture & bicultural exchange. Articles & brief notices about lectures, symposia, major exhibitions of Chinese art & cultural objects, & publications are included.
General Info: Quarterly, Trim Size-8½ x 11, Sheetfed press, 8 pages, 2 Color, Matte
Circulation: Total-1,500

Classic Chevrolet Memories
See: AUTOMOTIVE

Come-All-Ye
See: FOLKLORE

Communicator

Publishing Co: Camden County Historical Society, Park Blvd. & Euclid Ave., Camden, NJ 08103; Title Tel # (609) 964-3333
Personnel: Editor-John Dean, Production Mgr.-Margaret Weatherly
Editorial Description: This pub. includes info of interest to our members & genl. public. It includes articles on Camden County listing, program announcements, lists of recent donations, etc.
General Info: Yr. Est. 1970, Quarterly, Color
Subscriptions: Indv. $15
Circulation: Total-800

Communique *Consumer, Association*

Publishing Co: Foundation for Community Encouragement, 109 Danbury Rd Ste 8, Ridgefield, CT 06877-4109; Title Tel # (203) 431-9484 Title Fax # (203) 431-9349
Personnel: Editor-Richard Davies
Editorial Description: Teaches the principles of community and society for today's fragmented world.
General Info: Quarterly
Subscriptions: Free With Membership

Context: Southeast Asians in California

Publishing Co: Southeast Asia Community Resource Center, Folsom Cordova Unified Schools, 2460 Cordova Lane, Rancho Cordova, CA 95670
Editorial Description: Features articles of interest to Asian Americans residing in California.
General Info: (Formerly Refugee Update), 8x/yr.

Cormosea Bulletin *Association*

Publishing Co: Association for Asian Studies Inc., 1 Lane Hall, Univ. of Michigan, Ann Arbor, MI 48109; Title Tel # (313) 665-2490
Personnel: Editor-Carol Mitchell
General Info: Semi-annually
Subscriptions: Indv. $10

Country Dance & Song Society News *Association*

Publishing Co: Country Dance & Song Society, 17 New South St., Northampton, MA 01060-1921 Fax # (413) 585-8726; Title Tel # (413) 584-9913 Title Fax # (413) 585-8728
General Info: Yr. Est. 1966, Bi-monthly, Trim Size-8½ x 11, Offset press, 20 pages, No Color, Recycled, Saddle-stitched
Subscriptions: Indv. $30, Can. $40, For. $40
Circulation: Total-3,500

Crafts News
See: ART & SCULPTURE

Crossings
See: HISTORY

Culture & Psychology

Publishing Co: SAGE Publication, Inc., 2455 Teller Rd., Thousand Oaks, CA 91320-2218
Tel # (805) 499-0721 Fax # (805) 499-0871
General Info: Quarterly, ISSN: 1354-067X
Subscriptions: Indv. $48, Inst. $144

Culturgrams   *Business, Consumer*

Publishing Co: Kennedy Center Publications, Brigham Young University, PO Box 24538, Provo, UT 84602-4538; Title Tel # (801) 378-6528 Title Fax # (801) 378-7075
Personnel: Publisher-Grant Skabelund, Editor-Lisa Ralph, Editor-Susan Sims, Circ. Mgr.-Ferrill Bancroft, Circ. Mgr.-Kristy Gardner, Adv. Dir.-David Deem
Editorial Description: Series of 117 newsletters containing information about individual countries and their customs.
General Info: Yr. Est. 1977, Annually, Trim Size-8½ x 11, 4 pages
Subscriptions: Indv. $75, $3/copy
Circulation: Total-950,000
List Rental: Rents Lists

Deadly Serious
See: MYSTERY & HORROR

Dispatch

Publishing Co: Columbia Univ. American Culture Center, 603 Lewisohn Hall, New York, NY 10027; Title Tel # (212) 854-3774
Personnel: Editor-Jack Salzman

Dispatch/ News
See: HISTORY

Diversity 2000
See: EDUCATION

Documentary Heritage Program Newsletter
See: HISTORY

Dunrobin Piper
See: GENEALOGY

EHE News
See: PARAPSYCHOLOGY

El Puertorriguerto

Publishing Co: Academy of the Street of Puerto Rican Congress, 2315 W North Ave, Chicago, IL 60647-5314; Title Tel # (312) 772-4223
Editorial Description: Promotes mutual aid & understanding in the humanities among Latin Americans.
General Info: Monthly
Circulation: Total-800

Elder Voices
See: SENIOR CITIZENS

FOAFtale News

Publishing Co: Intl. Society for Contemporary Legend Research, Penn State Univ., Hazleton, PA 18201; Title Tel # (717) 450-3026 Title Fax # (717) 450-3182
Editorial Description: Society news and activities.
General Info: Yr. Est. 1988, Quarterly
Subscriptions: Indv. $18

Focus on Festivals
See: MUSIC & MUSIC TRADES

Folk Art Finder
See: ART & SCULPTURE

Food History News
See: FOOD

Ford Foundation Report   *Business, Consumer*

Publishing Co: Ford Foundation, Office of Communications, 320 E. 43rd St., New York, NY 10017-4890; Title Tel # (212) 573-5000
Personnel: Editor-Tom Quinn, Art Dir.-Marylyn Reichstein
Editorial Description: News of grants and program actions.
General Info: (Formerly Ford Foundation Letter), Yr. Est. 1970, Quarterly, Trim Size-8½ x 11, Sheetfed press, 32 pages, ISSN: 0015-699X, 2 Color, Recycled, Saddle-stitched
Subscriptions: Free
Circulation: Total-30,000
Printing Co: Finlay Brothers, 44 Tobey Rd. #7330, Bloomfield, CT 06002-3538 Tel # (203) 242-2800

Gentlestrength Times

Publishing Co: Gentlestrength, 234 W University Dr, Tempe, AZ 85281-3689; Title Tel # (602) 968-4831
Personnel: Editor-Lare Clark
General Info: 8 pages
Advertising: Inquire for rates.

Goodenow's Ghosts
See: GENEALOGY

Guatemala Bulletin

Publishing Co: Guatemala Human Rights Commission, 3321 12th St NE, Washington, DC 20017; Title Tel # (202) 529-6599 Title Fax # (202) 526-4611
Editorial Description: Statistics and analysis.
General Info: Yr. Est. 1996, Bi-monthly, ISSN: 1068-0187
Subscriptions: Indv. $10
Circulation: Total-1,500

Hard Row to Hoe

Publishing Co: Misty Hill Press, PO Box 541i, Healdsburg, CA 95448-0540; Title Tel # (707) 433-9786
Personnel: Editor-Joe Armstrong
Editorial Description: A book review newsletter featuring books of rural America from small presses, a short story and poetry.
General Info: Yr. Est. 1982, 12 pages, No Color
Subscriptions: Indv. $7

Heritage
See: HISTORY

Historic House News
See: HISTORY

ICASALS Newletter
See: AGRICULTURE

IHRC News
See: ETHNIC

Impact!
See: THEATRE

Indian Awareness Center Newsletter
See: HISTORY

Inside the Academy   *Association*

Publishing Co: Wisconsin Academy of Sciences, Arts & Letters, 1922 University Ave, Madison, WI 53705-4013; Title Tel # (608) 263-1692
Personnel: Editor-Andrea Pottos
Editorial Description: Newsletter to members of Wisconsin Academy.
General Info: (Formerly Academy Triforium), Yr. Est. 1973, Bi-monthly
Acquistions: Publication Bought

Insta Mod

Publishing Co: Insta Mod, P.O. Box 4626, Gaithersburg, MD 20885
Editorial Description: a silly zine that has a lot to say about pop culture and the state of phony punks.
General Info: Trim Size-8.5 x 11, 10 pages
Subscriptions: Indv. $1

Institute of Modern Russian Culture Newsletter
See: ETHNIC

International Christian Studies Association Newsletter (ICSA Newsletter)
See: RELIGIOUS & THEOLOGICAL

International Visitor
See: TRAVEL

Iowa Woman
See: WOMEN'S

Japan Society Newsletter   *Association*

Publishing Co: Japan Society, Inc., 333 E 47th St, New York, NY 10017-2399; Title Tel # (212) 832-1155 Title Fax # (212) 755-6752
Personnel: Publisher, Editor-Sandra Faux
Editorial Description: Cultural and educational publication to promote understanding between the U.S. and Japan.
General Info: (Formerly Japan House Newsletter), Yr. Est. 1970, 11x/yr., Trim Size-8½ x 11, Sheetfed press, 10 pages, 2 Color, Matte
Subscriptions: Indv. $40
Circulation: Total-8,000
Printing Co: J & R Litho, 480 Canal St., New York, NY 10017 Tel # (212) 219-1200

Judaica Society International
See: INTERNATIONAL AFFAIRS

Julliard Journal
See: MUSIC & MUSIC TRADES

Keeping the Trust
See: SOCIAL SERVICES & WELFARE

LHAT Bulletin
See: THEATRE

Labor Network News
Business, Association

Publishing Co: National Rainbow Coalition Labor Network, PO Box 27385, Washington, DC 20038-7385 Tel # (202) 728-1180
Editorial Description: Covers the National Rainbow Coalition's Labor Network.
General Info: Semi-annually, Trim Size-8½ x 11, No Color

Las Palabras

Publishing Co: Millicent Rogers Museum, PO Box A, Taos, NM 87571-0546; Title Tel # (505) 758-2462 Title Fax # (505) 758-5751
Personnel: Editor-Patrick Houlihan, Circ. Mgr.-Ione Caley, Production Mgr.-Anita McDaniel
Editorial Description: Supports the museum's purpose--the collection & interpretation of the art, history, & culture of the Native American, Hispanic, & Anglo peoples of the Southwest, focusing on Taos, & northern New Mexico. In-depth information about exhibits & collections, useum news, & a calendar of events.
General Info: Yr. Est. 1980, Quarterly, Trim Size-8½ x 11

Linington Lineup
See: LITERARY REVIEWS

Macedonia, Curiosum
Mundi
Consumer   **CPM: $16**

Publishing Co: Macedonian Arts Council, PO Box 905, New York, NY 10023-0905 Fax # (212) 799-0009; Title Tel # (212) 799-0009
Personnel: Mag. Ed.-Palina Proevsna
Editorial Description: Covers art, history and language.
General Info: Yr. Est. 1992, Quarterly, Trim Size-8 x 11, 6 pages, 4 Color
Subscriptions: Indv. $25, Inst. $2,500, Can. $30, For. $30
Circulation: Total-1,500, Readership-1,500
Advertising: $25.

Memberletter
See: ASTROLOGY

Millennial Prophecy Report
See: RELIGIOUS & THEOLOGICAL

Mind Quest
See: HYPNOSIS

Mirror
See: MUSEUM PUBLICATIONS

Misc.

Publishing Co: Clark Humphrey, 2510 Western Box, Seattle, WA 98121
Editorial Description: A report on Popular Culture in Seattle and Beyond
General Info: Trim Size-8.5 x 11, 4 pages
Subscriptions: Indv. $1

Mongolia Survey
Consumer, Association   **CPM: $111**

Publishing Co: Mongolia Society, 322 Goodbody Hall, Indiana University, Bloomington, IN 47405-2401; Title Tel # (812) 855-4078 Title Fax # (812) 855-7500
Personnel: Editor-John R. Krueger, Jr., Editor-Ruth Meserve
Editorial Description: Contains material on a wide range of topics related to Mongolia, including travel accounts, information on activities of members and programs. This newsletter type of publication embraces cross-Asian and multidisciplinary approaches to Mongolia, past andpresent.
General Info: (Formerly Mongolia Society Newsletter), Yr. Est. 1985, Semi-annually, ISSN: 0895-6523
Subscriptions: Indv. $30, Inst. $30, Can. $30, For. $35, $7/copy
Circulation: Total-450
Advertising: $50. Accepts Inserts.
List Rental: Actives: 450, $250/M

NAD Broadcaster
See: HEARING & SPEECH

NCFLC Quarterly

Publishing Co: North Carolina Foreign Language Ctr., Cumberland County Pub. Lib., 300 Maiden La., Fayetteville, NC 28301-5000; Title Tel # (910) 483-5022 Title Fax # (910) 483-8644
Personnel: Editor-Bin Lin
Editorial Description: Reports on NCFLC activities & on multilingual concerns.
General Info: (Formerly NCFLC Newsletter), Yr. Est. 1977, Quarterly, Trim Size-8½ x 11, Mimeo press, 4 pages, 2 Color
Acquistions: Publication Bought
Circulation: Total-2,326

NH Arts
Consumer

Publishing Co: N.H. State Council on the Arts, 40 N Main St, Concord, NH 03301-4912; Title Tel # (603) 271-2789
Personnel: Editor-Rebecca Lawrence, Circ. Mgr.-Shirley MacAllister, Art Dir.-Sheldon Cassady
Editorial Description: Lists art events taking place in New Hampshire.
General Info: Quarterly
Circulation: Total-600

NIC Exchange
Association

Publishing Co: National Institute for the Conservation of Cultural Property, NIC Exchange, 3299 K Street NW, Washington, DC 20007 Tel # (202) 625-1495
Editorial Description: Promotes public awareness, supports conservation, and coordinates conservation and preservation activities.

National Humanities Center
Newsletter

Publishing Co: National Humanities Ctr. Newsletter, PO Box 12256, Rtp, NC 27709-2256; Title Tel # (919) 549-0661
Personnel: Editor-Jean Leuchtenburg
General Info: Yr. Est. 1979, Semi-annually, Trim Size-6 x 9, 40 pages, ISSN: 0196-1721
Circulation: Total-3,500

New Jersey Humanities
Association

Publishing Co: New Jersey Committee for the Humanities, 28 W State St Ste 6, Trenton, NJ 08608-1602; Title Tel # (201) 932-7726
Personnel: Editor-Susan Loew
Editorial Description: Lists programs funded by the NJCH to apply for funding.
General Info: (Formerly Humanitas), Yr. Est. 1974, Semi-annually, Desktop press, 5 pages, No Color, Newsprint, Saddle-stitched
Circulation: (100% controlled), Total-10,000

News-Can. Musical Heritage Soc./Nouvelles de la Soc. pour le Patrimoine Musical Can.
See: MUSIC & MUSIC TRADES

News Circular

Publishing Co: American Society for Eighteenth-Century Studies, Utah State Univ. USU CC108, Logan, UT 84322-3730; Title Tel # (801) 797-4065 Title Fax # (801) 797-4065
Personnel: Publisher-Jeffrey Smitten, Editor-Jeffrey Smitton, Circ. Mgr.-Deborah Gessamau, Production Mgr.-Hailey Brady
Editorial Description: News of interest to ASECS members.
General Info: Yr. Est. 1969, Quarterly, Trim Size-8½ x 11, Offset press, 4 pages, Newsprint
Subscriptions: Indv. $19
Circulation: (86% controlled), Total-3,000, International-400
List Rental: List Management Co.: John Hopkins University Press,Journals Division, 2715 North Charles Street, Baltimore, MD 21218-4319 Tel # (410) 516-6964, Actives: $10/M
Printing Co: Press Publishing, 1601 W 820 N, Provo, UT 84601-1341 Tel # (801) 373-6996, Fax # (801) 375-2147

Newsletter of the American Handel Society
See: MUSIC & MUSIC TRADES

Nook News Market Bulletin
See: POETRY & CREATIVE WRITING

OHS Bulletin
See: HISTORY

PCAN: Popular Culture
Assn. Newsletter
Association

Publishing Co: Popular Press, Bowling Green State Univ., Bowling Green, OH 43403-0001; Title Tel # (419) 372-7865 Title Fax # (419) 372-8095
Personnel: Editor-M. Marston & C. Jackson
General Info: Yr. Est. 1970
Circulation: Total-2,300
Advertising: Inquire for rates.

PIASA Bulletin, The
See: INTERNATIONAL AFFAIRS

PS: Intelligent Guide to Jewish Affairs
See: POLITICS

Patterns
Consumer

Publishing Co: West Virginia State Dept. of Ed. & The Arts, Cultural Ctr., 1900 Kanawha Blvd. E., Charleston, WV 25305-0300 Fax # (304) 558-2779; Title Tel # (304) 558-0220 Title Fax # (301) 558-2779
Personnel: Editor-Deborah Rainey, Circ. Mgr.-Martha McKee, Production Mgr.-Terri Marion, Art Dir.-Terry Lively
Editorial Description: News & features reflecting the arts & history in W. Virginia.
General Info: (Formerly Culture & History Magazine), Yr. Est. 1977, Semi-annually, Trim Size-10¾ x 6⅛, Sheetfed press, 20 pages, Newsprint, Saddle-stitched
Subscriptions: Free
Circulation: Total-18,000, Readership-18,000
Printing Co: PrinTech Corporation, 2288 Westbrooke Dr, Columbus, OH 43228-9416 Tel # (614) 771-9976, Fax # (614) 771-3899

Percussion News
See: MUSIC & MUSIC TRADES

Perspectives on Contemporary Ukraine
See: INTERNATIONAL AFFAIRS

Plotz

Publishing Co: J. Girl, P.O. Box 819, Peter Stuyvesant St, NY 10019
Editorial Description: The zine for the vaclempt (mostly about Jewish girls)
General Info: Trim Size-5 x 7, 8 pages

Preservation Perspective
See: ARCHITECTURE

RNS Daily News Reports
See: RELIGIOUS & THEOLOGICAL

Race Relations Newsletter
See: ETHNIC

Right of Aesthetic Realism to Be Known, The
See: GENERAL INTEREST

Routes
See: ENTERTAINMENT

SAA Muse
See: LIBRARY

S.I.I.A.S. News
See: MUSEUM PUBLICATIONS

Seattle Arts Newsletter

Publishing Co: Seattle Arts Commission, 312 1st Ave. N, 2nd Floor, Seattle, WA 98109-4501; Title Tel # (206) 684-7171 Title Fax # (206) 684-7172
Personnel: Editor-Doug Lauen
Editorial Description: News of Seattle Arts Commission business, projects, sponsored events, etc. and news of artists, and arts-related events and efforts in the Puget Sound area, regionally, nationally and internationally.
General Info: Yr. Est. 1977, Irregular, Trim Size-8½ x 11, Desktop press, 16 pages, 2 Color, Newsprint
Subscriptions: Free In Designated Area
Circulation: Total-12,000
Printing Co: Pacific Publishing, 2314 Third Ave., Seattle, WA 98121 Tel # (206) 461-1300

Shemp

Publishing Co: Larry Yoshida, 1919 Evergreen Park Dr. SW, Apt 79, Olympia, WA 98502
Editorial Description: The lowlife culture magazine with quick reviews covering a variety of trash culture topics
General Info: Trim Size-8.5 x 11, 8 pages

Sherlockin Tidbits
See: LITERATURE & LINGUISTICS

Six Nations, One Soul
See: INTERNATIONAL AFFAIRS

Sophia Circle

Publishing Co: Sophia Circle, 8319 Fulham Ct, Richmond, VA 23227-1712; Title Tel # (804) 266-7400
Personnel: Editor-D. Gorman
Editorial Description: Analysis of culture and politics.
General Info: Yr. Est. 1987, Trim Size-8½ x 11, Letrpr. press, 4 pages, No Color

Southern Register   *Association*   **CPM: $10**

Publishing Co: Center for the Study of Southern Culture, University of Mississippi, University, MS 38677 Fax # (601) 232-5814; Title Tel # (601) 232-5993 Title Fax # (601) 232-7842
Personnel: Editor-Ann Abadie, Editor-Sue Hart, Circ. Mgr., Production Mgr.-Jennifer Langston, Art Dir.-Susan Lee
Editorial Description: Newsletter for Center for the Study of Southern Culture.
General Info: Yr. Est. 1981, Quarterly, Trim Size-8½ x 11, Sheetfed press, 20 pages, 10% ads, No Color, Matte, Saddle-stitched
Subscriptions: Free
Circulation: (92% controlled), Total-28,000, International-2,000
Advertising: $300.
List Rental: Actives: 25,000
Printing Co: Star-Toot Printing, 670 S Cooper St, Memphis, TN 38104-5353 Tel # (901) 274-3632

Straightalk
See: RELIGIOUS & THEOLOGICAL

Sunspots

Publishing Co: Symphony for United Nations (SUN), 205 West End Ave Apt 21c, New York, NY 10023-4813; Title Tel # (212) 873-2872 Title Fax # (212) 787-7672
Personnel: Publisher-Joseph Eger, Editor-Leonard Rubin
Editorial Description: Seeks to improve understanding among peoples of all nations via the arts.
General Info: 4 pages
Circulation: Total-5,000

Tennessee Arts Report   *Consumer*

Publishing Co: Tennessee Arts Commission, 404 James Robertson Parkway, Suite 160, Nashville, TN 37243-0780; Title Tel # (615) 741-1701 Title Fax # (615) 741-8559
Personnel: Editor-Stephanie Faris
Editorial Description: Information about the arts in Tennessee.
General Info: (Formerly Tennessee Arts Bulletin), Yr. Est. 1974, Quarterly, Trim Size-11 x 17, Offset press, 8 pages, 2 Color, Coated, Saddle-stitched
Subscriptions: Free
Circulation: Total-4,500

Theology & Culture Newsletter
See: RELIGIOUS & THEOLOGICAL

US/ICOMOS Newsletter

Publishing Co: US/ICOMOS, 1600 H St NW, Washington, DC 20006-4907; Title Tel # (202) 842-1866
Personnel: Editor-Terry Morton, Publisher, Circ. Mgr., Adv. Dir., Art Dir.-Ellen Delage
Editorial Description: Covers Intl. activities in historic preservation & cultural resources.
General Info: Yr. Est. 1979, Monthly, Trim Size-8½ x 11, Sheetfed press, 4 pages, No Color, Newsprint
Subscriptions: Indv. $35, Inst. $150
Circulation: Total-700

University Circle Bulletin   *Consumer, Scholarly*

Publishing Co: Univ. Circle Inc., 10831 Magnolia Dr, Cleveland, OH 44106-1807
Personnel: Editor-Whitney Bohan
Editorial Description: News and information about the museums, universities, and other cultural sites located near each other in the Cleveland area.
General Info: Quarterly, Trim Size-8½ x 114, 2 pages, Color, Matte

Utah Ties   *Consumer, Association*

Publishing Co: Utah Endowment for Humanities, 350 S 400 E Ste 110, Salt Lake City, UT 84111-2946; Title Tel # (801) 531-7868
Editorial Description: Discusses grants for humanities public programming.
General Info: (Formerly Utah Humanities News), Quarterly, Looseleaf
Circulation: Total-4,000

Utopus Discovered
See: POLITICS

Voice in the Wilderness   *Consumer, Scholarly*

Publishing Co: JFO Enterprises, PO Box 818, Palm Springs, CA 92263-0818; Title Tel # (619) 416-9417 Title Fax # (619) 416-1036
Personnel: Publisher-John Oster
Editorial Description: For those entertained by excercising mind and wit.
General Info: Yr. Est. 1992, Quarterly, Trim Size-8⅕ x 11, Desktop press, 6 pages, No Color
Subscriptions: Indv. $5, Inst. $10, Can. $8, For. $8, $1/copy
Advertising: Inquire for rates.
Printing Co: Jetcopy & Blueprint, 555 S. Sunrise Way, Palm Springs, CA 92264 Tel # (619) 323-4097

W.P.A.S. Museletter   *Association*

Publishing Co: Washington Performing Arts Society, 2000 L St NW Ste 810, Washington, DC 20036-4907; Title Tel # (202) 393-3600
Personnel: Editor-Linda Suma
Editorial Description: WPAS community & educational programs, advance ticket sales, membership benefits.
General Info: Yr. Est. 1970, Bi-monthly, 12 pages
Subscriptions: Indv. $25
Circulation: (100% controlled), Total-6,500

Women in the Arts Bulletin   *Business, Consumer*

Publishing Co: Women in the Arts Foundation, Inc., 1175 York Ave Apt 2g, New York, NY 10021-7170; Title Tel # (212) 751-1915
Personnel: Editor-Erin Butler
Editorial Description: Forum for women in the visual arts, includes gallery information, articles, reviews, etc.
General Info: (Formerly WIA Newsletter), Yr. Est. 1973, Quarterly, Trim Size-8½ x 11, Desktop press, 8 pages, No Color, Newsprint
Subscriptions: Indv. $9, Inst. $15, Can. $19, For. $19, $1/copy
Acquistions: Publication Bought
Circulation: Total-500
Advertising: Accepts Inserts.
Printing Co: Magic Circle, 13 E. 17th St., New York, NY 10003

Woods Hole Folk Music Society Newsletter
See: MUSIC & MUSIC TRADES

World Heritage Newsletter

Publishing Co: US/ICOMOS, 1600 H St NW, Washington, DC 20006-4907; Title Tel # (202) 842-1866
Personnel: Editor-Terry Morton, Adv. Dir., Art Dir.-Ellen Delage
Editorial Description: News relating to the Intl. Convention for the Protection of the World Cultural & Natural Heritage. The U.S. is one of more than 100 nations that have ratified this Intl. Treaty.
General Info: Yr. Est. 1984, Semi-annually, Trim Size-8½ x 11, Sheetfed press, 4 pages, No Color
Circulation: Total-700

Yiddish of Greater Washington Newsletter
See: LITERATURE & LINGUISTICS

CYCLING-BICYCLE & MOTOR

Alberta Bicycle Assn., Newsletter

Publishing Co: Alberta Bicycle Assn., 11759 Broat, Edmonton, AB T5M 3K6 Canada; Title Tel # (403) 453-8518
General Info: Monthly

Better Bicycling *Consumer*

Publishing Co: Citizens for Safe Cycling (Ottawa-Carleton), PO Box 248, Station B, Ottawa, ON K1P 6C4 Canada; Title Tel # (613) 722-4454 Title Fax # (613) 729-2207
Personnel: Editor-Brett Delmage
Editorial Description: Public information distributed through regional bike stores on safe cycling.
General Info: Bi-monthly, Trim Size-8½ x 11, 4 pages, ISSN: 1195-2091
Circulation: Total-10,000

Bicycle Nova Scotia Newsletter
See: SPORTS & SPORTING GOODS

Bicycle Wholesale Distributors Assn. Newsletter *Association*

Publishing Co: Bicycle Wholesale Distributors Assn., 1900 Arch St, Philadelphia, PA 19103-1498; Title Tel # (215) 564-3484 Title Fax # (215) 564-2175
Personnel: Editor-Dale Zeigier
Editorial Description: For Assn. members.
General Info: Yr. Est. 1978, Quarterly, Trim Size-8½ x 11, Sheetfed press, 8 pages, 2 Color, Newsprint, Case bound
Circulation: (100% controlled), Total-200

Bicycling: BC *Association*

Publishing Co: Bicycling Assn. of British Columbia, 1367 W. Broadway, #332, Vancouver, BC V6H 4A9 Canada; Title Tel # (604) 737-3034 Title Fax # (604) 738-7175
Personnel: Circ. Mgr.-Gerry Parija, Editor, Production Mgr., Adv. Dir.-Danelle Laidlaw
Editorial Description: Book reviews, video reviews. Calendar updates. Announcements. Program updates.
General Info: Yr. Est. 1974, Monthly, Trim Size-8½ x 11, Sheetfed press, 10 pages, 5% ads, No Color, Saddle-stitched
Subscriptions: Indv. $17, Inst. $35
Advertising: Inquire for rates. Accepts Inserts.
List Rental: Actives $250/M
Printing Co: Sport BC Print Shop, 1367 W. Broadway, Vancouver, BC V6H 4A9 Canada Tel # (604) 737-3022

Boston Cyclist *Association*

Publishing Co: Boston Area Bicycle Coalition, Box 1015, Kendall Sq. Branch, Cambridge, MA 02142-0008; Title Tel # (617) 491-7433
Personnel: Editor-Mark Spain
Editorial Description: News about activities of the coalition; opinion & commentary; book reviews, product reviews, humor & other features including regular updates of bicycle advocacy beyond Boston.
General Info: (Formerly Spoke'n Word), Yr. Est. 1979, Bi-monthly, Trim Size-8½ x 11, Sheetfed press, 8 pages, No Color, Newsprint
Subscriptions: Indv. $15
List Rental: Rents Lists
Printing Co: Kwik Kopy Printing, 222 Broadway, Cambridge, MA 02139-1904 Tel # (617) 547-5228

Cheval de Fer *Association*

Publishing Co: Ariel Owners Motorcycle Club, PO Box 1256, Topanga, CA 90290; Title Tel # (310) 455-1476
Personnel: Editor-Ted Faber
General Info: Irregular
Circulation: Total-130

Cheval d'Alliage *Consumer, Association*

Publishing Co: Ariel Owners Motorcycle Club, PO Box 1256, Topanga, CA 90290 Tel # (310) 455-1476
Personnel: Editor-Jack Charney
General Info: Bi-monthly
Circulation: Total-135

Citizens for Safe Cycling Newsletter *Consumer*

Publishing Co: Citizens for Safe Cycling (Ottawa-Carleton), Box 248, Station B, Ottawa, ON K1P 6C4 Canada Tel # (613) 722-4454 Fax # (613) 729-2207
Personnel: Editor-Brett Delmage

Cycle Ontario *Association* CPM: $100

Publishing Co: Ontario Cycling Assn., 1185 Eglington Ave. E. #408, North York, ON M3C 3C6 Canada Tel # (416) 426-7241 Fax # (416) 495-4038; Title Tel # (416) 426-7242 Title Fax # (416) 426-7349
Editorial Description: Provides up-to-date information on the news, issues and activities of cycling across the province from road, track and mountain bike racing to education, advocacy and touring.
General Info: (Formerly Quick Release), Monthly, Trim Size-8½ x 11, 20 pages, Matte, Saddle-stitched
Subscriptions: Indv. $20, Can. $25
Circulation: Total-2,500
Advertising: $250. Accepts Inserts.
List Rental: Actives: 4,000

Fishtail West

Publishing Co: Velocette Owners Club of North America, C/O Phil Swartz, 10623 Darby Ave., Northridge, CA 91326
General Info: Bi-monthly
Circulation: Total-300

Harley Hummer *Association*

Publishing Co: Harley Hummer Club, 4527 Chase Ave., Bethesda, MD 20814; Title Tel # (301) 652-1569
Personnel: Editor-David Hennessey
Editorial Description: For those interested in the preservation & restoration of Harley-Davidson 2 Stroke Motorcycles.
General Info: (Formerly Hummernews), Yr. Est. 1981, Bi-monthly, Trim Size-8½ x 11, Sheetfed press, 6 pages, ISSN: 1077-0062, No Color, Newsprint
Subscriptions: Free With Membership
Circulation: Total-200
Advertising: Inquire for rates.
Printing Co: Business Computer Services, 1559 Rockville Pike, Rockville, MD 20852-1601 Tel # (301) 984-0255

International Bicycle Touring Society Newsletter
See: TRAVEL

Motorcycle Business Newsletter

Publishing Co: Parkhurst Publ. Co., 1812 Alaska Ave, Costa Mesa, CA 92626-2009; Title Tel # (714) 549-2092 Title Fax # (714) 549-4032
General Info: Yr. Est. 1979, 26x/yr.
Subscriptions: Indv. $96

Motorcycle Consumer News *Consumer*

Publishing Co: Fancy Publications, Inc., P.O. Box 6050, Irvine, CA 92718; Title Tel # (714) 855-8822 Title Fax # (714) 855-3045
Editorial Description: Provides product information, evaluation, and analysis on after-market equipment for hobbyists, technicians, and suppliers.
General Info: Monthly
Subscriptions: Indv. $22, $4/copy
Circulation: Total-56,013
Advertising: Inquire for rates.
List Rental: List Management Co.: Manager: Sharon Radt; MacFan Lists, PO Box 6040, Mission Viejo, CA 92690-6040 Tel # (714) 855-8822, Fax # (714) 855-3045, Actives: 56,457, $80/M, Expires: 14,282, $40/M

On One Wheel *Consumer*

Publishing Co: Unicycling Society of America, Inc., PO Box 40534, Redford, MI 48240-0534; Title Tel # (810) 661-0334
Personnel: Editor-Constance Cotter
Editorial Description: Information on unicycles & unicyclists- building, tricks, events, history.
General Info: (Formerly Unicycling Society of America-Newsletter), Yr. Est. 1974, Quarterly, Trim Size-8½ x 11, 20 pages, No Color, Other
Subscriptions: Indv. $15, Can. $20, For. $25, $3/copy
Circulation: Total-870
Advertising: Inquire for rates.
Printing Co: Miller Printing, 19309 Beech Daly Rd, Redford, MI 48240-1420

Outspokin' *Business, Association*

Publishing Co: Natl. Bicycle Dealers Assn., 2240 University Dr # 100, Newport Beach, CA 92660-3319; Title Tel # (714) 722-6909
Personnel: Editor-Fred Clements
Editorial Description: Monthly members newsletter featuring information on retail management and industry news.
General Info: Monthly, 6 pages, No Color, Newsprint
Circulation: (100% controlled), Total-1,200

Pro Bike News *Association*

Publishing Co: Bicycle Institute of America, 1506 21st St NW # 200, Washington, DC 20036-1006; Title Tel # (202) 332-6986 Title Fax # (202) 332-6989
Personnel: Publisher-Bill Wilkinson, Editor-Jim Fremont
Editorial Description: Contains information pertaining to the bicycling and pedestrian community. all issues mailed first class.
General Info: Yr. Est. 1981, Monthly, Sheetfed press, 4 pages, 2 Color
Subscriptions: Indv. $30, Can. $32, For. $35, $2/copy
Circulation: Total-700

Ride On *Association* CPM: $100

Publishing Co: Washington Area Bicyclist Assn., 1819 H St NW Ste 640, Washington, DC 20006-3603; Title Tel # (202) 872-9830 Title Fax # (202) 862-9762
Personnel: Editor-Todd Wallace
Editorial Description: Bicycle advocacy, membership association publication.
General Info: Yr. Est. 1972, Monthly, Trim Size-8½ x 11, Offset press, 4 pages, No Color
Subscriptions: Indv. $20, Inst. $30, Can. $25, For. $27, $1/copy
Circulation: Total-1,000
Advertising: $100.
Printing Co: Serif Press, Inc., 1331 H St. NW, #110LL, Washington, DC 20005 Tel # (202) 737-4650

Twitter

Publishing Co: Gold Star Owners Club, C/O Ron Pallinger, 32450 Walker Rd., Avon Lake, OH 44012; Title Tel # (216) 933-2959
Editorial Description: Promotes the preservation & maintenance & enjoyment of the BSA Gold Star Motorcycle.
General Info: Bi-monthly
Circulation: Total-480

DAIRY

Ag Executive
See: AGRICULTURE

Agri-Mark Monthly   *Association*

Publishing Co: Agri-Mark, Inc., Box 5800, Lawrence, MA 01842-2813; Title Tel # (508) 689-4442
Personnel: Publisher, Editor-Douglas DiMento
Editorial Description: Lists changes in milk prices, legislation, & affects on dairy cooperative milk marketing.
General Info: Monthly, 4 pages
Subscriptions: Indv. $15, $2/copy
Circulation: Total-5,500

B.C.A.I. Newsletter   *Consumer, Association*

Publishing Co: British Columbia Artificial Insemination Centre, Box 40, Milner, BC V0X 1T0 Canada; Title Tel # (604) 530-1141
Personnel: Editor, Art Dir.-Gloria Lawson
Editorial Description: Dairy information- Holstein Friesian.
General Info: Offset press, 4 pages, Color, Newsprint
Subscriptions: Free
Circulation: Total-4,500

Browse
See: AGRICULTURE

Cheese Importers Association of America Bulletin

Publishing Co: Cheese Importers Assn., 460 Park Ave., New York, NY 10022-1906; Title Tel # (212) 753-7500

Cream Separator and Dairy Newsletter   *Association*

Publishing Co: Dr. Paul Dettloff, Rt #3, Arcadia, WI 54612-9803; Title Tel # (608) 323-7470
Personnel: Publisher, Editor-Paul Dettloff
General Info: Yr. Est. 1986, Bi-weekly, Trim Size-8½ x 11, 16 pages, 2 Color
Subscriptions: Indv. $15, Can. $15, $3/copy
Circulation: Total-170, Readership-170
Advertising: Inquire for rates.

DFISA Regulatory Update

Publishing Co: Dairy & Food Industries Supply Assn., Inc., 1451 Dolley Madison Blvd., McLean, VA 22101-3811; Title Tel # (301) 984-1444 Title Fax # (301) 881-7832
Personnel: Editor-S. Shaw
Editorial Description: Summarizes regulatory changes affecting the dairy & food industries.
General Info: Yr. Est. 1985, Bi-monthly, Trim Size-8½ x 11, Letrpr. press, 6 pages, 2 Color, Newsprint
Circulation: Total-1,000

DFISA Technical Bulletin

Publishing Co: Dairy & Food Industries Supply Assn., Inc., 1451 Dolley Madison Blvd., McLean, VA 22101-3811; Title Tel # (301) 984-1444 Title Fax # (301) 881-7832
Personnel: Editor-S. Shaw
General Info: Yr. Est. 1950, Quarterly, Trim Size-8½ x 11, Offset press, 4 pages, 2 Color, Coated
Circulation: Total-975

DSI Bulletin   *Business, Association*

Publishing Co: Dairy Society International, 7185 Ruritan Dr, Chambersburg, PA 17201-9242; Title Tel # (717) 375-4392
Editorial Description: Focuses on Society news and developments in the dairy products industry.
General Info: 3x/yr.

Dairy Center Pipeline

Publishing Co: United Dairy Industry Assn., 6300 River Rd., Rosemont, IL 60018-4289; Title Tel # (708) 696-1860
Personnel: Editor-Jeanne Wegner
General Info: Yr. Est. 1982, Monthly
Circulation: Total-2,300

Dairy and Field Crops Digest

Publishing Co: Cooperative Extension Assn. of Tioga County, 56 Main Street, Owego, NY 13827-1588; Title Tel # (607) 687-4020
Personnel: Publisher-Roger Reinhert, Editor-Richard Eschler
Editorial Description: Contains technical information and research results for commercial dairy farms. Also farm business management information, taxes, estate planning, business organization and labor regulations.
General Info: Yr. Est. 1972, Monthly, Trim Size-8½ x 11, Offset press, 8 pages
Circulation: Total-1,300

Dairy Food Newsletter   *Business*

Publishing Co: Delta Communications, Inc., 455 N. Cityfront Plaza Dr., Chicago, IL 60611-5593 Tel # (312) 222-2000 Fax # (312) 222-2026 Parent Co.-Elsevier Business Press, Morris Plains
Personnel: Publisher-Carolyn Dress, Editor-Ellen Dexheimer, Circ. Mgr., Promotion Dir.-Diane McBride
Editorial Description: Covers government regulation, sales trends, business news, current events in dairy industry.
General Info: Yr. Est. 1978, Weekly, Trim Size-8½ x 11, Sheetfed press, 4 pages, ISSN: 0011-5657, No Color, Newsprint
Subscriptions: Indv. $259, Can. $301, For. $301, $3/copy
Acquisitions: Publication Bought
Circulation: Total-812
List Rental: Actives: $150/M

Dairy Industry Statistics   *Business*

Publishing Co: U.S. Department of Agriculture, California Ag. Stat. Service, PO Box 1258, Sacramento, CA 95812
Editorial Description: Historic & detailed data on above-mentioned categories.
General Info: Annually
Subscriptions: Indv. $10, For. $10

Dairy Information Bulletin   *Business*

Publishing Co: U.S. Department of Agriculture, California Ag. Stat. Service, PO Box 1258, Sacramento, CA 95812
Editorial Description: Production, utilization, & prices of milk & dairy products.
General Info: Monthly
Subscriptions: Indv. $15, For. $20

Dairy Producer News   *Business*

Publishing Co: Kent Feeds, Inc., 1600 Oregon St, Muscatine, IA 52761-1404 Tel # (319) 264-4211; Title Tel # (319) 264-4525
Personnel: Editor-Steve Merriam
Editorial Description: For producers who use Kent feeds and animal care products.
General Info: Bi-monthly

Dairy Products Newsletter   *Business*

Publishing Co: Intl. Data Services, Inc., Box 222, Endwell, NY 13760-0222; Title Tel # (607) 754-8594
Personnel: Publisher, Editor-R.G. Christie
Editorial Description: Organized summary of U. S. , UK & Canadian dairy products pubs.
General Info: Yr. Est. 1985, Monthly, Trim Size-8½ x 11, Letrpr. press, 4 pages, ISSN: 0896-0372, No Color, Newsprint
Subscriptions: Indv. $76
Circulation: (100% controlled), Total-1,000

Feed Facts
See: LIVESTOCK

Food and Drink Weekly
See: FOOD

Food Industry Futures-A Strategy Service
See: FOOD

MOOsletter, The   *Consumer*   CPM: $44

Publishing Co: Cowtree Collector, 240 Wahl Ave, Evans City, PA 16033-1053; Title Tel # (412) 538-5038
Personnel: Editor, Adv. Dir., Art Dir.-Carol J. Peiffer
Editorial Description: 'All the MOOs that's fit to print', newsletter for cow lovers and COWllectors, farmers, bovimaniacs; information on cows, collectibles and cow related merchandise. Official publication of Cow Observers Worldwide (COW.)
General Info: Yr. Est. 1989, Quarterly, Trim Size-5½ x 8½, Desktop press, 32 pages, No Color, Saddle-stitched
Subscriptions: Indv. $7, Can. $9, For. $14, $2/copy
Circulation: Total-450
Advertising: $20. Accepts Inserts.

Milk Market Bulletin

Publishing Co: U.S. Dept. of Agriculture, Milk Market Administrator, 2684 11 Mile Rd, Berkley, MI 48072-3050
Personnel: Editor-Miss Joyce M. Sutherland
General Info: Monthly
Circulation: Total-4,000

National Dairy Council of Canada Direction   *Business, Association*

Publishing Co: Natl. Dairy Council of Canada, 221 Laurier Ave., E., Ottawa, ON K1N 6P1 Canada; Title Tel # (613) 238-4116
Personnel: Editor-Michel Moisan, Editor-Pierre Nadeau
Editorial Description: Text in English & French.
General Info: (Formerly National Dairy Council of Canada Resume), Yr. Est. 1973, Monthly, Trim Size-17 x 22, 4 pages, 2 Color, Coated
Subscriptions: Indv. $15
Circulation: Total-1,300

National Ice Cream & Yogurt Retailers Association Newsletter *Association*

Publishing Co: Natl. Ice Cream & Yogurt Retailers Assn., 1429 King Ave # 210, Columbus, OH 43212-2108; Title Tel # (614) 486-1444 Title Fax # (614) 486-4711
Personnel: Editor-Don Buckley
Editorial Description: Membership and industry news; production tips.
General Info: (Formerly National Ice Cream Retailers Association Newsletter), Yr. Est. 1941, Monthly, 4 pages, 2 Color, Newsprint
Subscriptions: Free With Membership
Circulation: Total-750
Advertising: Inquire for rates.

News for Dairy Co-Ops

Publishing Co: Natl. Milk Producers Fed., 1840 Wilson Blvd., Arlington, VA 22201-3086; Title Tel # (703) 243-6111 Title Fax # (703) 841-9328
General Info: Weekly
Circulation: Total-2,500

Ontario Dairy Council, News & Views *Association*

Publishing Co: Ontario Dairy Council, 6533 Mississauga Rd., #D, Mississauga, ON L5N 1A6 Canada; Title Tel # (905) 542-3620 Title Fax # (905) 542-3624
Personnel: Editor-T.D. Kane
Editorial Description: Newsletter for association members.
General Info: Yr. Est. 1971, Monthly, Trim Size-8$\frac{1}{2}$ x 11, Mimeo press, 8 pages, No Color
Subscriptions: Free
Circulation: Total-400

Tech News Quarterly *Business, Association*

Publishing Co: American Dairy Products Institute, 130 N Franklin St, Chicago, IL 60606-1823; Title Tel # (312) 782-4888 Title Fax # (312) 782-5299
General Info: Yr. Est. 1969, Quarterly, Trim Size-8$\frac{1}{2}$ x 11, Mimeo press, 3 pages, No Color
Circulation: (100% controlled), Total-500

Urner Barry's Price-Current See: POULTRY & POULTRY PRODUCTS

Virginia Hay Clearing House See: AGRICULTURE

Weekly Insiders Dairy & Egg Letter *Business*

Publishing Co: Urner Barry Publications, Inc., PO Box 389, Toms River, NJ 08754-0389; Title Tel # (908) 240-5330 Title Fax # (908) 341-0891
Personnel: Editor-Richard Brown, Production Mgr.-Bill Curro, Adv. Dir.-Lisa Sharkus, Promotion Dir.-Sheila Deane
Editorial Description: Statistical report on eggs and dairy products used as a basis for understanding market conditions of supply, demand, and price.
General Info: Yr. Est. 1858, Weekly, Trim Size-8$\frac{1}{2}$ x 11, Sheetfed press, 4 pages, ISSN: 0270-4153, No Color, Newsprint
Subscriptions: Indv. $164, Can. $174, For. $198, $15/copy

DANCE

American Dance

Publishing Co: American Dance Guild, Inc., 31 W. 21st St. 3 Fl., New York, NY 10010-6806; Title Tel # (212) 627-3790
Personnel: Editor-Susan Glazer
Editorial Description: Informs on dance activities, arts legislation and funding, professional developments; provides reviews of concerts & books; examines current issues affecting the dance professional.
General Info: Yr. Est. 1956, Bi-monthly, Trim Size-8$\frac{1}{2}$ x 11, Offset press, 14 pages, No Color
Circulation: Total-800
Advertising: Inquire for rates.
List Rental: Actives: $37/M

Arkansas Country Dancer *Association*

Publishing Co: Arkansas Country Dance Society, 52 Ridge Dr, Greenbrier, AR 72058-9646; Title Tel # (501) 679-2935 Title Fax # (501) 378-3591
Editorial Description: Society news and features on traditional Arkansas, American and English music and dance.
General Info: Yr. Est. 1980, Bi-monthly
Circulation: Total-143,000
Advertising: Inquire for rates.

Ballroom Review, The *Consumer, Association*

Publishing Co: TBR Communications, Ltd., 60 Gramercy Park North, New York, NY 10010
Personnel: Editor-Nicholas Ullo
Editorial Description: Contains news, articles, announcements, and reviews of ballroom dancing events in the New York, New Jersey, and Connecticut area.
General Info: Yr. Est. 1990, 10x/yr.
Subscriptions: Indv. $25

Boston Swing Dance Society Newsletter *Consumer, Association*

Publishing Co: Boston Swing Dance Society, PO Box 1260, Boston, MA 02134-0008
Personnel: Circ. Mgr.-Laura Sohual, Publisher, Production Mgr.-Benson Wong, Editor, Art Dir.-Roberta Tovey, Mktg. Dir.-Dave Weissburg
Editorial Description: Contains news and articles on the Boston swing dance scene.
General Info: Yr. Est. 1992, Bi-monthly, Trim Size-8$\frac{1}{2}$ x 11, 8 pages
Subscriptions: Indv. $12, Free With Membership
Circulation: (75% controlled), Total-800, Subscriptions-200

CAHPERD Journal/Times See: HEALTH

Cincinnati Folk Life *Consumer, Association*

Publishing Co: Cincinnati Folk Life Organization, PO Box 9008, Cincinnati, OH 45209-9998; Title Tel # (513) 533-4822
Editorial Description: Calendar primarily of folk information (ncluding dancing) but also includes Vintage, Argentine Tango, Swing, and Ballroom dancing. Irish dancing and Cajun dancing.
General Info: Monthly
Subscriptions: Indv. $20, Free With Membership

Company Handbook *Association*

Publishing Co: Natl. Assn. for Regional Ballet, 140 W 79th St Apt 11d, New York, NY 10024-6424; Title Tel # (212) 645-0042
Personnel: Editor-Doris Hering
Editorial Description: Looseleaf managerial and organizational manual for dance companies.
General Info: (Formerly Board Member Handbook), Yr. Est. 1975, Quarterly, Offset press, 2 pages, No Color, Looseleaf
Subscriptions: Indv. $25
Circulation: Total-1,000

Country Dance & Song Society News See: CULTURE & HUMANITIES

DCA News *Association*

Publishing Co: Dance Critics Assn., Box 1882 Chelsea Stn., New York, NY 10011
Personnel: Editor-Rita Felciano, Art Dir.-Sandra Kurtz
General Info: Yr. Est. 1978, Quarterly, 8 pages
Subscriptions: Indv. $40, Inst. $51, Can. $41, For. $41
Circulation: Total-400

Dance on Camera News *Association*

Publishing Co: Dance Films Assn., 31 West 21st Street, 3rd Fl., New York, NY 10010-6806; Title Tel # (212) 727-0764
Personnel: Editor-Deirdre Towers, Publisher, Promotion Dir.-Susan Braun
Editorial Description: News of members & the dance film & video profession.
General Info: Yr. Est. 1967, Bi-monthly, Sheetfed press, 4 pages, Newsprint
Circulation: Total-250
List Rental: Rents Lists

Dance Gypsy *Consumer, Association*

Publishing Co: Dance Gypsy, 57 Sleepy Hollow Rd, Essex Junction, VT 05452-2721
Personnel: Co-Editor-Tom Medve, Co-Editor-Vai Medve
Editorial Description: Covers contra, square, folk, swing and ballroom dancing in western Massachusetts, eastern New York, VErmont, New Hampshire, and Maine.
General Info: Monthly, 6 pages
Subscriptions: Indv. $10

Dance Masters of America-Bulletin

Publishing Co: Dance Masters of America, Inc., PO Box 610533, Bayside, NY 11361-0533
Personnel: Editor-Sharon Fitch Sockalosky
Editorial Description: Information for dance teachers active in the U.S.
General Info: Bi-monthly, 16 pages
Circulation: Total-3,000

Dance Medicine-Health Newsletter *Association*

Publishing Co: International Center for Dance Ortho., 7922 Oceanus Dr., Hollywood, CA 90046-2045; Title Tel # (213) 261-0326
Personnel: Editor-Ernest Washington, M. D.
Editorial Description: Summary of current information on dance medicine & health.
General Info: Yr. Est. 1982, Quarterly, 16 pages
Subscriptions: $8/copy
Circulation: Total-200

Dance Week *Consumer, Association*

Publishing Co: Dance Week, PO Box 55, Mc Lean, VA 22101-0055
Personnel: Editor-Richard Mason
Editorial Description: Contains weekly dance news, up-to-the-minute information on events, people competition results, world-wide.
General Info: Weekly, 6 pages
Subscriptions: Indv. $30

Dance/America *Association*

Publishing Co: Natl. Assn. for Regional Ballet, 140 W 79th St Apt 11d, New York, NY 10024-6424; Title Tel # (212) 645-0042

Editorial Description: A community-oriented newsletter reflecting serious quality dance throughout the U.S.

General Info: (Formerly NARB News), Yr. Est. 1956, Quarterly, Trim Size-8½ x 11, Offset press, 8 pages, Color

Circulation: Total-5,000

Dancers' Dateline *Consumer, Association*

Publishing Co: Dancers' Dateline, PO Box 346, Random Lake, WI 53075-0346; Title Tel # (414) 994-9244 Title Fax # (414) 994-4817

Personnel: Editor-Rod Hagan, Assoc. Ed.-Gary Feider

Editorial Description: A ballroom and social dance calendar for southeastern Wisconsin. Covers events of interest to dancers of all ability levels. Contains information about dance showcases and competitions in the area. Includes dates of open houses and parties at professional dance studios.

General Info: Monthly, Trim Size-8½ x 11, 4 pages, 2 Color, Matte

Subscriptions: Indv. $12

Circulation: Total-750

Dancing USA *Consumer*

Publishing Co: Sponsor-Minnesota Ballroom Operators Assn., DOT Publications, Inc., 10600 University Ave. NW, Minneapolis, MN 55448-6166; Title Tel # (612) 757-4414 Title Fax # (612) 757-6605

Editorial Description: Contains news, articles, announcements, and reviews on ballroom, polka, country, and 50s dancing in the Midwest.

General Info: (Formerly Music Dance News), Yr. Est. 1972, Bi-monthly

Subscriptions: Indv. $22, $4/copy

Circulation: Total-20,000

Advertising: Inquire for rates.

List Rental: Rents Lists

Highland News
See: ETHNIC

In Dance *Consumer, Association* CPM: $440

Publishing Co: Dance Bay Area, 2403 16th St, San Francisco, CA 94103-4210; Title Tel # (415) 252-6240

Editorial Description: Dance news, trends, events, issues, calendar, opportunities. Dance Bay Area membership communication.

General Info: (Formerly West Coast Dance Calendar), Yr. Est. 1973, Bi-monthly, Trim Size-17 x 11, Sheetfed press, 2 pages, ISSN: 0883-9956, Color-cover, Matte

Subscriptions: Indv. $20, Can. $25

Circulation: Total-3,500

Advertising: $1,542. Accepts Inserts.

List Rental: Actives: $80/M

Printing Co: Alonzo Printing Co., Investment Blvd., Hayward, CA 94080 Tel # (510) 293-0522

Information Quarterly
See: MUSIC & MUSIC TRADES

Julliard Journal
See: MUSIC & MUSIC TRADES

Leonard Moss

Publishing Co: Stardust Dance Productions, Church St., Box 157, Woodburne, NY 12788 Tel # (914) 434-6871; Title Tel # (800) 537-2797 Title Fax # (914) 434-3532

Personnel: Publisher, Editor-Leonard Moss, Adv. Dir.-Ann Prince, Art Dir.-Tom Sutton

Editorial Description: Ballroom Dance Programs, Ballroom Dance Resort Weekends, Ballroom Dance Travel Programs, cruises.

General Info: Yr. Est. 1988, Quarterly, Sheetfed press, No Color, Newsprint

Subscriptions: Free

Circulation: Total-15,000

Advertising: Accepts Inserts.

Manisquare

Publishing Co: Square Dance Federation of Manitoba, 195 Enfield, Winnipeg, MB R2H 1B2 Canada Tel # (204) 233-2159

General Info: (Formerly Manitoba Square Dancer), Yr. Est. 1970, 9x/yr.

Manitoba Intl. Folk Dance Assn., Newsletter

Publishing Co: Manitoba Intl. Folk Dance Assn., Box 292, Winnipeg, MB R3M 3S7 Canada; Title Tel # (204) 475-2620

Personnel: Editor-Bill Newman

General Info: Quarterly

Advertising: Inquire for rates.

Next Generation Newsletter *Association*

Publishing Co: Next Generation Swing Dance Club, 236 W Portal Ave Ste 329, San Francisco, CA 94127-1423 Tel # (415) 979-4456

Editorial Description: Information for those interested in swing dancing.

General Info: Yr. Est. 1988, Quarterly

Subscriptions: Free With Membership

Party Platter *Consumer, Association*

Publishing Co: Party Platter, 229 Coolidge Ave. #304, Watertown, MA 02172-1554; Title Tel # (617) 923-8211

Personnel: Publisher, Editor, Circ. Mgr., Production Mgr., Adv. Dir., Art Dir., Mktg. Dir., Promotion Dir.-Anne Atheling

Editorial Description: Covers everything related to dance occurring within 60 miles of Boston. Everything you ever wanted to know about ballroom dancing in New England.

General Info: Quarterly, Trim Size-8½ x 11, Desktop press, 40 pages

Subscriptions: Free To Qualified Recipient

List Rental: Actives: 5,000

Performer

Publishing Co: Natl. Ballet of Canada, 157 King Street East, Toronto, Ont., ON M5C 1G9 Canada; Title Tel # (416) 362-1041 Title Fax # (416) 368-7443

Personnel: Production Mgr.-Haron Vanoerlinde, Editor, Promotion Dir.-Julia Drake

Editorial Description: Contains news and information on the National Ballet of Canada and general articles on dance in Canada.

General Info: (Formerly Balletopics/Front Page News), Yr. Est. 1958, Quarterly, 16 pages, 2 Color, Coated

Acquistions: Publication Bought

Circulation: (100% controlled), Total-15,000

List Rental: Rents Lists

Records of Early English Drama Newsletter
See: LITERATURE & LINGUISTICS

S.W.O.S.D.A. Bugle *Association* CPM: $160

Publishing Co: Southwestern Ontario Square & Round Dance Assn., C/O John & Irene Bullock, 690 Santa Monica Rd., London, ON N6H 3W1 Canada; Title Tel # (519) 472-8050

Personnel: Editor-Irene Bullock, Editor-John Bullock

Editorial Description: Area club news, upcoming events, articles concerning square and round dancing.

General Info: Yr. Est. 1966, 8x/yr., Trim Size-8½ x 11, Mimeo press, 20 pages, No Color

Subscriptions: Indv. $12, $1/copy

Circulation: Total-300, Readership-2,000

Advertising: $48.

Spotlight on Dance
See: EDUCATION

SwingLetter, The *Consumer, Association*

Publishing Co: SwingLetter, The, 306 N Irving St, Arlington, VA 22201-1242 Tel # (703) 527-2052

Editorial Description: Announces swing dances and lessons in the Washington, DC area. Contains articles about swing dancing written by local dancers.

General Info: Irregular

Subscriptions: Indv. $20, Can. $25, For. $30

Textile Museum Bulletin
See: MUSEUM PUBLICATIONS

Update
See: EDUCATION

DEAF

Canadian Cultural Society of the Deaf, CCSD Newsletter

Publishing Co: Canadian Cultural Society of the Deaf, Inc., 11337 61st Ave., House 144, Edmonton, AB T6H 1M3 Canada; Title Tel # (403) 436-2599

Personnel: Editor-Shelly Carver, Circ. Mgr.-Sandra Reid

Editorial Description: Contains information on Canadian cultural activiites & updates. Occasionally includes volunteer & related professional articles.

General Info: Yr. Est. 1972, Trim Size-8½ x 11, Mimeo press, 18 pages, Color-cover

Subscriptions: Indv. $10

Advertising: Inquire for rates. Accepts Inserts.

List Rental: Rents Lists

Printing Co: College Copy Shop, 9906 109th St., Edmonton, AB T5K 1H5 Canada Tel # (403) 423-1458

Coordinating Council on Deafness of Nova Scotia News *Consumer, Association*

Publishing Co: Coordinating Council on Deafness of Nova Scotia, 1660 Hollis, Ste. 803, Halifax, NS B3J 1V7 Canada; Title Tel # (902) 425-0240

Editorial Description: Covers council news and developments of interest to those dealing with the deaf and hearing impaired in Nova Scotia province.

General Info: Yr. Est. 1979, Quarterly

Cubprints
See: HEARING & SPEECH

Deaf Episcopalian, The
See: RELIGIOUS & THEOLOGICAL

Deaf Lutheran
See: RELIGIOUS & THEOLOGICAL

Deafpride Advocate Quarterly

Publishing Co: Deafpride, 1350 Potomac Ave SE, Washington, DC 20003-4412; Title Tel # (202) 675-6700 Title Fax # (202) 547-0547
Editorial Description: Issues relating to deafness and advocacy
General Info: Yr. Est. 1980, Quarterly
Circulation: Total-250
Advertising: Accepts Inserts.

Disability Funding News
See: PHILANTHROPY

GA-SK Newsletter
Business, Association   **CPM: $65**

Publishing Co: Telecommunications for the Deaf, 8719 Colesville Rd Ste 300, Silver Spring, MD 20910-3919; Title Tel # (301) 589-3786 Title Fax # (301) 589-3797
Personnel: Publisher-Alfred Sonnenstrahl, Editor-Kenneth Samson, Editor-Kenneth G Samson, Circ. Dir.-Eleanor McCowan, Production Mgr.-Paula Holbrook, Adv. Dir.-Anne Edwards, Art Dir.-Kate Morgan
Editorial Description: Promotes full visual access to information and telecommunications.
General Info: Yr. Est. 1968, Quarterly, Sheetfed press, 32 pages, 40% ads, 2 Color, Matte, Saddle-stitched
Subscriptions: Indv. $15, Inst. $500, Can. $35, For. $35, Free With Membership
Acquistions: Publication Bought, Publication Sold
Circulation: Total-10,000, Readership-40,000
Advertising: $650. Accepts Inserts.
List Rental: Actives: 50,000, $250/M

NAPH National Newsletter
See: DISABILITY

NFADB Newsletter
Consumer, Association

Publishing Co: Sponsor-National Family Assn. for the Deaf-Blind, Helen Keller Technical Assistance Center, 111 Middle Neck Rd, Sands Point, NY 11050-1298 Fax # (516) 944-7302; Title Tel # (516) 944-8900
Editorial Description: Presents articles on medical info, legislation, resources, and support services for persons who are deaf-blind and their families.
General Info: Yr. Est. 1994, Tri-annually
Subscriptions: Free To Qualified Recipient
Circulation: Total-3,000
Advertising: Accepts Inserts.

National Congress of Jewish Deaf Quarterly
Association

Publishing Co: Natl. Congress of Jewish Deaf, 13580 Osborne St, Arleta, CA 91331-5524
Personnel: Editor-Joshua Mendelsohn
Editorial Description: Activities of NCJD. Articles on Judaism. Officers reports publicity on convention.
General Info: Yr. Est. 1958, Quarterly, Trim Size-8½ x 14, Offset press, 15 pages, 3% ads, Color
Subscriptions: Indv. $15, $1/copy
Circulation: Total-500
Advertising: Inquire for rates. Accepts Inserts.

News n' Notes
See: EDUCATION

Ontario Assn. of the Deaf Newsletter

Publishing Co: Ontario Assn. of the Deaf, 2395 Bayview Ave., North York, ON M2L 1A2 Canada; Title Tel # (416) 925-5258
Personnel: Editor-Lowrie Barry
General Info: Yr. Est. 1986

Our Way - NCSY
CPM: $150

Publishing Co: Orthodox Union, 333 7th Ave, New York, NY 10001-5072; Title Tel # (212) 563-4000 Title Fax # (212) 564-9058
Personnel: Editor-Rabbi Lederfeind
Editorial Description: Magazine for Jewish deaf & hearing impaired.
General Info: Yr. Est. 1973, 20 pages, 2 Color
Subscriptions: Indv. $6
Circulation: Total-2,000
Advertising: $300.
Printing Co: A & D Photo Prints, 11 Stone St., New York, NY 10011 Tel # (212) 269-6896

Radar
Association

Publishing Co: Natl. Catholic Office for the Deaf, 814 Thayer Ave., Silver Spring, MD 20910-4500; Title Tel # (301) 577-1684 Title Fax # (301) 577-1690
Personnel: Editor-Nora Letourneau
General Info: Yr. Est. 1970, Tri-annually
Subscriptions: Free With Membership
Circulation: Total-400

School for the Deaf, Report

Publishing Co: School for the Deaf, 393 50 Gallaudet Dr., Fremont, CA 94538; Title Tel # (415) 794-3666
General Info: Every two years

Speech & Deafness Newsletter
Association

Publishing Co: Hearing, Speech, 1620 18th Ave, Seattle, WA 98122-2739; Title Tel # (206) 323-5770
Personnel: Editor-Patty Tumberg
Editorial Description: Agency newsletter for membership and community.
General Info: Yr. Est. 1935, Quarterly, Trim Size-8½ x 11, Offset press, 8 pages, No Color
Circulation: Total-1,000

TAC Newsletter
See: BLIND

DENTAL

AAP News
Association

Publishing Co: American Academy of Periodontology, 737 N Michigan Ave Ste 800, Chicago, IL 60611-2615; Title Tel # (312) 787-5518
Personnel: Editor-Katie Goss
General Info: (Formerly American Academy of Periodontology Newsletter), Bi-monthly, Trim Size-8½ x 11, 12 pages, 2% ads, No Color, Recycled
Subscriptions: Indv. $30, $3/copy
Circulation: Total-6,200
Advertising: Inquire for rates.
Printing Co: Kelmscott Press, 1665 Mallette Rd, Aurora, IL 60505-1354 Tel # (708) 898-0800

ACFD/AFDC's Forum
Association

Publishing Co: Assn. of Canadian Faculties of Dentistry, 1815 Alta Vista Dr., #109, Ottawa, ON K1G 3Y6 Canada; Title Tel # (604) 822-2413
Personnel: Publisher, Editor, Production Mgr.-R.M. Shah
Editorial Description: Dental education and research in Canada. Text mainly in English, occasionally in French.
General Info: (Formerly ACFD/AFDC Newsletter), Yr. Est. 1968, Trim Size-8½ x 11, Sheetfed press, 40 pages, ISSN: 0820-5949, 2 Color, Newsprint
Subscriptions: Indv. $15, $4/copy
Circulation: (100% controlled), Total-750
Advertising: Inquire for rates.

ADA Compliance Complete Planning & Practice Guide
Business

Publishing Co: Business & Legal Reports, Inc., 39 Academy St., PO Box 1513, Madison, CT 06443-2646 Tel # (860) 245-7448 Fax # (860) 245-2559; Title Tel # (203) 245-7448 Title Fax # (203) 245-2559
Editorial Description: Covers ADA regulations and issues.
General Info: Yr. Est. 1993, Quarterly, Looseleaf

AES Newsletter
Association

Publishing Co: American Endodontic Society, 1440 N Harbor Blvd Ste 719, Fullerton, CA 92635-4120; Title Tel # (714) 870-5590
Editorial Description: Dentists specializing in root canal work.
General Info: Yr. Est. 1969, Quarterly

APPA Digest
See: MEDICINE

ASDC Newsletter
Association

Publishing Co: American Society of Dentistry for Children, 875 N Michigan Ave Ste 4040, Chicago, IL 60611-1901; Title Tel # (312) 943-1244 Title Fax # (312) 943-5341
Personnel: Editor, Promotion Dir.-Dr. George Teuscher
Editorial Description: News items about ASDC activities and items about health matters, legislation, costs, care, drug etc.
General Info: Yr. Est. 1981, Bi-monthly, Trim Size-8½ x 11, Sheetfed press, 8 pages, 2 Color
Circulation: (100% controlled), Total-10,000

Adolescent Medicine
See: MEDICINE

American Academy of Dental Group Practice Newsletter
Association

Publishing Co: American Academy of Dental Group Practice, 5110 N 40th St Ste 250, Phoenix, AZ 85018-2151 Tel # (602) 381-1185; Title Tel # (612) 474-9285
Personnel: Circ. Mgr.-Sue Orlowski
Editorial Description: Dental group practice management information.
General Info: Yr. Est. 1973, Quarterly, Sheetfed press, 4 pages, No Color, Newsprint
Circulation: Total-3,000

American Academy of Esthetic Dentistry Newsletter

Publishing Co: American Academy of Esthetic Dentistry, 500 N. Michigan Ave., Ste 1920, Chicago, IL 60611-3703; Title Tel # (312) 464-2722
Editorial Description: Dentists and other health professionals concerned with aesthetics in dentistry, medicine and psychology.
General Info: Yr. Est. 1975, Semi-annually

American Association of Orthodontists Bulletin

Publishing Co: American Assn. of Orthodontists, 401 N Lindbergh Blvd, Saint Louis, MO 63141-7816; Title Tel # (314) 993-1700
Personnel: Editor-Mike Dillon
Editorial Description: Newsletter discusses Association activities in various areas, including marketing.
General Info: Yr. Est. 1900, 5x/yr., Trim Size-11 x 17, Sheetfed press, 12 pages, 3% ads, 2 Color, Coated, Saddle-stitched
Acquistions: Publication Bought
Circulation: Total-12,000
Advertising: Inquire for rates. Accepts Inserts.
Printing Co: James Mulligan, 1808 Washington Avenue, St. Louis, MO 63103 Tel # (314) 621-0874

American Association of Women Dentists Chronicle   *Association*

Publishing Co: American Assn. of Women Dentists, 401 N. Michigan Ave., Chicago, IL 60611-4212; Title Tel # (312) 644-6610
Editorial Description: Women in dentistry, all aspects of careers.
General Info: (Formerly American Association of Women Dentists Journal), Yr. Est. 1980, Bi-monthly, Trim Size-8½ x 11, Offset press, 6 pages, No Color
Subscriptions: $4/copy
Circulation: Total-2,000
Advertising: Inquire for rates.

American Dental Trade Association Update   *Association*

Publishing Co: American Dental Trade Assn., 4222 King St, Alexandria, VA 22302-1597; Title Tel # (703) 379-7755
Personnel: Editor-Nik Petrovic
General Info: Bi-monthly

Annotations

Publishing Co: Intl. Dental Health Foundation, 11484 Washington Plz., W., Reston, VA 22090-4312; Title Tel # (703) 471-8349
Personnel: Editor-Dr. Dan Watt
General Info: Bi-monthly
Circulation: Total-350

Articulator   *Association*

Publishing Co: North Central Ohio Dental Soc., 2355 W State Route 18, Tiffin, OH 44883-8826; Title Tel # (419) 497-0253
Personnel: Editor, Adv. Dir.-Robert Dornauer
Editorial Description: News, announcements & editorials for NCODS members.
General Info: Trim Size-8½ x 11, Mimeo press, 6 pages, No Color
Advertising: Inquire for rates.

BCDS-Newsletter   *Association*   **CPM: $557**

Publishing Co: Bergen County Dental Society, 1060 Main St, River Edge, NJ 07661-2013; Title Tel # (201) 487-1073
Personnel: Editor-Thomas DiLauro, DDS, Circ. Dir.-Stanley Markman, DDS
Editorial Description: General dental subjects, activities & achievements of members.
General Info: (Formerly Journal of B.C.D.S.), Yr. Est. 1934, Monthly, Trim Size-8½ x 11, Offset press, 6 pages, ISSN: 0092-9832, Ind/Abs/Online: Dent.In., 2 Color
Subscriptions: Indv. $12, For. $10, $2/copy
Circulation: Total-700
Advertising: $390.
Printing Co: James Farnum, 1018 Bergen Boulevard, Fort Lee, NJ 07024 Tel # (201) 886-2481, Fax # (201) 886-8890

Baltimore County Dental Assn. Newsletter   *Association*

Publishing Co: Baltimore County Dental Assn., 201 Pandonia Rd. W., #101, Timomiun, MD 20193; Title Tel # (301) 560-0064
Personnel: Editor-Paul Chyzus

Bridge

Publishing Co: Northwestern University, Dental School, 311 E Chicago Ave # 10-305, Chicago, IL 60611-3008; Title Tel # (312) 503-8335 Title Fax # (312) 503-3831
Personnel: Editor-Carolynn McNally, Circ. Mgr.-Dwight Edwards, Art Dir.-Lynda Karr
Editorial Description: Northwestern Univ. Dental School alumni newsletter.
General Info: Quarterly, 20 pages, 4 Color, Coated
Circulation: Total-7,000
Advertising: Inquire for rates.

Bridging the Gap   *Association*

Publishing Co: San Fernando Valley Dental Assistants Society, 10626 Gothic Ave, Granada Hills, CA 91344-6826; Title Tel # (818) 360-7281
Personnel: Publisher, Editor-Kristy Broquez, RDA, CDA
Editorial Description: Current events in dental assisting.
General Info: Yr. Est. 1976, Bi-monthly, Mimeo press, 4 pages, 2 Color
Subscriptions: Free With Membership
Circulation: Total-200
Advertising: Inquire for rates.

Bulletin of the American Association of Dental Examiners

Publishing Co: American Assn. of Dental Examiners, 211 E Chicago Ave Ste 844, Chicago, IL 60611-2616; Title Tel # (312) 440-7464
Personnel: Editor-Dr. Kathleen Kelly, Promotion Dir.-Molly Nadler
Editorial Description: Reports on events of the Association and Dental Licensure Issues.
General Info: (Formerly Bulletin), Quarterly, Trim Size-8½ x 11, 8 pages, No Color
Circulation: Total-1,000

CDA Update   *Association*   **CPM: $103**

Publishing Co: California Dental Association, 1201 K St. Mall, Sacramento, CA 95814-3906; Title Tel # (916) 443-0505 Title Fax # (916) 443-2943
Personnel: Mng. Editor-Douglas Curley, Circ. Mgr.-Jeannie Bergeron, Adv. Dir.-Ingrid Landis
Editorial Description: Provides up-to-date reports on legal, legislative and association activities affecting the dental profession.
General Info: Yr. Est. 1989, Monthly, Sheetfed press, 8 pages, ISSN: 1048-3594, 5% ads, 4 Color, Matte
Subscriptions: Indv. $24, For. $30, $4/copy
Circulation: Total-18,000
Advertising: $1,865. Accepts Inserts.
Printing Co: W.W. Hobbs, Ltd., 500 20th St, Sacramento, CA 95814-1112 Tel # (916) 448-8950

Canadian Academy of Endodontics Newsletter   *Association*

Publishing Co: Canadian Academy of Endodontics, 103-235 St. Clair Ave., W., Toronto, ON M4V 1R4 Canada Fax # (416) 962-7040; Title Tel # (416) 922-5115 Title Fax # (416) 962-7041
Personnel: Editor-Dr. Barry Chapnick
Editorial Description: Provides information about endodontics to N. American dentists.
General Info: Yr. Est. 1965, Tri-annually, Desktop press, 20 pages, Coated, Perfect bound
Subscriptions: Free With Membership
Circulation: Total-250
Advertising: Inquire for rates.

Central Incisor   *Association*

Publishing Co: Central District Dental Hygiene Society, 1842 Wind Drift Rd, Orlando, FL 32809-6842; Title Tel # (305) 859-1074
Personnel: Editor-Donna Mylrea
General Info: Yr. Est. 1979, Semi-annually, Mimeo press
Circulation: Total-300

College of Dental Surgeons of Saskatchewan, Newsletters   *Association*

Publishing Co: College of Dental Surgeons of Saskatchewan, 202-728 Spadina Crescent E., Saskatoon, SK S7K 4H7 Canada; Title Tel # (306) 244-5072 Title Fax # (306) 244-2476
Personnel: Editor-Dr. Peacock
Editorial Description: Aspects of dentistry.
General Info: Yr. Est. 1940, Bi-monthly, 16 pages, No Color
Circulation: (100% controlled), Total-750

Communicator   *Association*   **CPM: $256**

Publishing Co: Connecticut Dental Assn., 62 Russ St, Hartford, CT 06106-1522; Title Tel # (203) 278-5550
Personnel: Editor-Howard Mark
Editorial Description: Current data on the association.
General Info: Monthly, Trim Size-8½ x 11, Offset press, 12 pages, 2 Color, Saddle-stitched
Subscriptions: Indv. $50, $5/copy
Circulation: Total-2,920
Advertising: $750.
Printing Co: Briarwood Press, 301 Farmington Ave., Rte. 10, Plainville, CT 06062-1319 Tel # (203) 522-9736

Communicator   *Association*

Publishing Co: American Academy of Dental Practice Admin., 1063 S Whippoorwill Ln, Palatine, IL 60067-7064; Title Tel # (708) 934-4404
Personnel: Editor-Walter Hrin
General Info: Bi-monthly, 30 pages

Communicator-Dental   *Association*

Publishing Co: Dental Group Management Assn., 2425 Ashdale Dr Apt 35, Austin, TX 78757-8152; Title Tel # (512) 452-5395
Personnel: Editor-Joann Junkins
Editorial Description: Information on management of dental groups.
General Info: Yr. Est. 1971, Bi-monthly, 8 pages
Circulation: Total-400

Communique   *Association*

Publishing Co: American Association of Public Health Dentistry, 10619 Jousting Ln, Richmond, VA 23235-3838; Title Tel # (319) 335-7204 Title Fax # (319) 335-7155
Personnel: Publisher-Joseph Doherty, Editor-Marsha Cunningham, Circ. Mgr.-Helen Doherty
Editorial Description: Keeps AAPHD members up-to-date on current activities in public health dentistry.
General Info: Yr. Est. 1980, Quarterly, Trim Size-8½ x 11, Mimeo press, 8 pages, 1% ads, No Color
Subscriptions: Indv. $10, $3/copy
Circulation: (100% controlled), Total-625
Advertising: Inquire for rates.

Consultant's Newsletter
See: MANAGEMENT

D.L.A.N.Y. Newsletter   *Association*   **CPM: $425**

Publishing Co: Dental Lab. Assn. of the State of New York, Inc., 1 Barstow Rd., Ste. P20, Great Neck, NY 11021-3501; Title Tel # (516) 829-1144 Title Fax # (516) 829-1988
Personnel: Editor-Teresa M. Sager, Publisher, Circ. Mgr.-Mark Polevoy, Adv. Dir.-Mark Polevy
Editorial Description: News pertaining to the dental lab industry in New York State. Contains technical and management articles.
General Info: Yr. Est. 1989, 11x/yr., Trim Size-8$\frac{1}{2}$ x 10$\frac{7}{8}$, Web press, 12 pages, 3% ads, 4 Color, Saddle-stitched
Subscriptions: Indv. $12, Can. $20, For. $30, $3/copy
Circulation: Total-1,000, Readership-1,000
Advertising: $425.

Dallas Dental News   *Association*

Publishing Co: Dallas County Dental Assistants Assn., 2217 E. Biscayne, Irving, TX 75060-7214; Title Tel # (214) 986-6855
Personnel: Publisher, Editor-Ronda Lane
Editorial Description: Informs local dental assistants of the activities of the DCDAS.
General Info: Yr. Est. 1937, Monthly, Trim Size-8$\frac{1}{2}$ x 11, Mimeo press, 4 pages, No Color
Subscriptions: Indv. $10
Acquistions: Publication Bought
Circulation: (100% controlled), Total-115
Advertising: Inquire for rates.

Dateline: Delta   *Association*

Publishing Co: Delta Dental Plans Assn., 1515 W. 22nd St. #1200, Oak Brook, IL 60521-2007; Title Tel # (312) 337-4707
Personnel: Editor-Kim Volk
Editorial Description: Seeking to expand the provision of dental care in a pre-paid basis.
General Info: (Formerly Natl. Assn. of Dental Service Plans), Yr. Est. 1965, Bi-monthly, Mimeo press, 7 pages
Circulation: Total-1,000

Delta Dictum

Publishing Co: Delta Dental Plans Assn., 1515 W. 22nd St. #1200, Oak Brook, IL 60521-2007; Title Tel # (312) 337-4707
Personnel: Editor-Kim Volk
General Info: Quarterly

Dental Computer Newsletter

Publishing Co: Andent, Inc., 1000 North Ave, Waukegan, IL 60085-2938; Title Tel # (708) 223-5077 Title Fax # (708) 223-5077
Personnel: Publisher, Editor-Ellis Neiburger, Production Mgr.-S. Neiburger, Adv. Dir., Art Dir.-K. Elsbury, Promotion Dir.-B. Alexander
Editorial Description: For dentists & physicians using office computers. Software reviews, industry news, tips, feature stories, book reviews, media news, legislation, new products.
General Info: Yr. Est. 1978, Bi-monthly, 10 pages, ISSN: 0738-9744, 1% ads, Saddle-stitched
Subscriptions: Indv. $20, Can. $30, For. $30, $5/copy
Circulation: Total-3,500
Advertising: Inquire for rates. Accepts Inserts.
List Rental: Rents Lists

Dental Patient Newsletter

Publishing Co: Wentworth Worldwide Media, 1866 Colonial Village Lane, PO Box 10488, Lancaster, PA 17605-0488; Title Tel # (717) 393-1000 Title Fax # (717) 393-5752
Editorial Description: Customized patient education newsletter for dentists.
General Info: Yr. Est. 1983, Monthly
Subscriptions: Indv. $98

Dental Record

Publishing Co: Tufts Univ., Communications & Publ. Rel., 419 Boston Ave., Medford, MA 02155; Title Tel # (617) 956-5705
Editorial Description: Research & school news from Tufts Dental School.
General Info: Yr. Est. 1987, Semi-annually, Trim Size-8$\frac{1}{2}$ x 11, Web press, 8 pages, Newsprint
Circulation: Total-10,000

Dentaletter, The   *Business*

Publishing Co: MPL Communications, Inc., 133 Richmond St. W., Ste. 700, Toronto, ON M5H 3M8 Canada; Title Tel # (416) 869-1177 Title Fax # (416) 869-0456
Personnel: Publisher-Barrie Martland, Publisher-Steven Pepper, Editor-Brian Waters, Circ. Mgr.-David Berger
Editorial Description: A professional source letter for dentists. Subscription also includes special dental reports.
General Info: Yr. Est. 1983, Monthly
Subscriptions: Indv. $119
Advertising: Inquire for rates.
List Rental: Rents Lists

Dentists Medical Digest

Publishing Co: DMD, Inc., 603 Bayville Rd # 402, Locust Valley, NY 11560-1207; Title Tel # (516) 671-7121
Personnel: Publisher, Editor-Dr. R. F. Zambito
Editorial Description: Current medical information plus its impact on dental care.
General Info: Yr. Est. 1979, Monthly, Sheetfed press, 8 pages, ISSN: 0196-2701, No Color, Newsprint
Subscriptions: Indv. $69, Inst. $75, $7/copy
Circulation: (100% controlled)
Printing Co: Northern Type Printing, 10 Morris Ave, Glen Cove, NY 11542-2816

Dentist's Patient Newsletter   *Consumer*

Publishing Co: Doctor's Press, The, 1866 Colonial Village Lane, Lancaster, PA 17605-0488 Tel # (717) 393-1000 Fax # (717) 393-5752; Title Tel # (717) 393-1010
Personnel: Publisher-Cynthia Young, Editor-Kim Conlin, Adv. Dir.-Rem Jackson, Art Dir.-Daniel Hill
Editorial Description: A newsletter for dentists to use to market their practice by providing dental health information that encourages good oral hygiene and regular use of the services offered by the practice.
General Info: Yr. Est. 1983, Quarterly, Trim Size-8$\frac{1}{2}$ x 11, Web press, 4 pages, 2 Color, Matte

Drug Facts and Comparisons Loose Leaf Edition
See: DRUGS & PHARMACEUTICALS

Eastern Dental Society Bulletin   *Association*

Publishing Co: Tim Wong, D.D.S., 85 4th Ave., New York, NY 10003-5205; Title Tel # (212) 581-1090
Personnel: Editor-Tim Wong, D.D.S.
Editorial Description: Announcement, articles relative to the Dental Society.
General Info: Monthly
Circulation: Total-500

Esthetics

Publishing Co: American Academy of Esthetic Dentistry, 500 N. Michigan Ave., Ste 1920, Chicago, IL 60611-3703; Title Tel # (312) 464-2722
Personnel: Editor-Tracy Rados
General Info: Yr. Est. 1980
Circulation: Total-200

Explorer   *Association*

Publishing Co: National Association of Dental Assistants, 900 S Washington St Ste G13, Falls Church, VA 22046-4041; Title Tel # (703) 237-8616
Personnel: Editor-S. Young
Editorial Description: Dentristy news for dental assistants as well as information for personal development.
General Info: Yr. Est. 1974, Monthly, Trim Size-8$\frac{1}{2}$ x 11, Web press, 4 pages, 2 Color
Subscriptions: Indv. $15, Can. $20, For. $20, Free With Membership
Circulation: Total-3,000
List Rental: Actives: 3,000, $90/M, Expires: 2,000

Federation of Prosthodontic Organizations, Newsletter   *Association*

Publishing Co: Federation of Prosthodontic Org., 211 E Chicago Ave Ste 948, Chicago, IL 60611-2616; Title Tel # (312) 642-7538
Personnel: Editor-Dr. Robert Schweitzer
Editorial Description: Association newsletter for the federation of 20 national/regional organizations.
General Info: Yr. Est. 1965, Quarterly, 6 pages
Circulation: (100% controlled), Total-4,500

Forum of Esthetic Dentistry

Publishing Co: Cosmedent Inc., 5419 N. Sheridan Rd, Chicago, IL 60640-1917; Title Tel # (312) 989-6844 Title Fax # (312) 989-1826
Personnel: Editor-Dr. K. Mopper
General Info: Yr. Est. 1983, Bi-monthly
Subscriptions: Indv. $75

Globe   *Association*

Publishing Co: International College of Dentists, 51 Monroe St Ste 1501, Rockville, MD 20850-2408 Tel # (301) 251-8861 Fax # (301) 738-9143
Personnel: Editor-William Hawkins
General Info: Yr. Est. 1975, Annually
Subscriptions: Free With Membership
Printing Co: Hagerstown Bookbinding & Printing, 952 Frederick St, Hagerstown, MD 21740-6821 Tel # (301) 733-2000, Fax # (301) 733-6586

Greater Milwaukee Dental Bulletin   *Association*

Publishing Co: Fox Co., The, 1100 W. Beecher., W. Allis, WI 53227; Title Tel # (414) 461-0230
Personnel: Editor-Dr. Randall Johnson, Adv. Dir.-Edward Keever
Editorial Description: Information for members.
General Info: (Formerly The Bulletin of the Greater Milwaukee Dental Association), Yr. Est. 1935, Monthly, Offset press, 28 pages, Color
Subscriptions: Indv. $20, $2/copy
Circulation: Total-1,200
Advertising: Inquire for rates.
Printing Co: Fox Co., 11000 W. Becher St., W. Allis, WI 53227 Tel # (414) 321-4700

Hartford Dental Society
Newsletter — *Association*

Publishing Co: Hartford Dental Society, 230 Scarborough St, Hartford, CT 06105-1100; Title Tel # (860) 523-8657 Title Fax # (860) 523-8657
Personnel: Editor-Judd R. Fink
Editorial Description: Items of local interest to membership, meeting announcements, new members, necrology local issues.
General Info: Bi-monthly, Trim Size-8½ x 11, 4 pages
Subscriptions: Free With Membership

IAO Straight Talk — *Association*

Publishing Co: Sponsor-International Association for Orthodontics, International Association for Orthodontics, 1100 Lake St Ste 240, Oak Park, IL 60301-1035; Title Tel # (708) 445-0320 Title Fax # (708) 445-0321
Personnel: Publisher, Editor-Joanna Carey
Editorial Description: News of dentistry/orthodontics for members.
General Info: (Formerly Bandelette), Yr. Est. 1969, Monthly, Trim Size-8½ x 11, Web press, 4 pages, Ind/Abs/Online: Ind.Dent.Lit., No Color, Newsprint
Subscriptions: Indv. $15, For. $25, $2/copy
Circulation: Total-2,100

IDDS Newsletter — *Association* — CPM: $294

Publishing Co: Indianapolis District Dental Society, 3901 N Meridian St Ste 10, Indianapolis, IN 46208-4026; Title Tel # (317) 923-8421
Personnel: Editor-Desiree Dimond
General Info: Yr. Est. 1978, Quarterly, Trim Size-8½ x 11, 12 pages
Subscriptions: Indv. $35
Circulation: Total-850
Advertising: $250.
List Rental: Actives: $25/M

ISDA Newsletter — *Association*

Publishing Co: Idaho State Dental Assn., 1220 W. Hays St., Boise, ID 83702-5315; Title Tel # (208) 343-7543

Illinois Dental Hygienists' Association, Bulletin

Publishing Co: Illinois Dental Hygienists Assn., 8051 S Wabash Ave, Chicago, IL 60619-3516
Personnel: Editor-Viola V. Johnson
Subscriptions: Indv. $3
Advertising: Inquire for rates.

Implant Update — *Association*

Publishing Co: Academy for Implants and Transplants, PO Box 223, Springfield, VA 22150-0223; Title Tel # (703) 451-0001
General Info: Yr. Est. 1972, Quarterly

Impressions

Publishing Co: Orange County Dental Society, 295 S Flower St, Orange, CA 92668-3466; Title Tel # (714) 542-8808
Personnel: Publisher-Jim Frickie, Editor-Chris McLean, Adv. Dir.-Debbie Houle, Promotion Dir.-Lucy Barrier
Editorial Description: Dental bulletin for our membership.
General Info: Yr. Est. 1962, 8x/yr., Trim Size-4¹³⁄₁₆ x 7⅜, Sheetfed press, 35 pages, No Color
Subscriptions: Indv. $15
Circulation: Total-1,100

International Academy of Oral Pathology, Bulletin

Publishing Co: International Academy of Oral Pathology, 3900 Reservoir Rd NW, Washington, DC 20007-2187
General Info: Yr. Est. 1962

International Psoriasis Bulletin

Publishing Co: Stanford University, School of Medicine, Dept. of Dermatology, Stanford, CA 94305; Title Tel # (415) 723-2300
General Info: Quarterly
Circulation: Total-10,000

Iowa Dental Bulletin

Publishing Co: Univ. of Iowa College of Dentistry, Publications, Iowa City, IA 52240
Personnel: Editor-Jess Hayden, Jr.
General Info: Yr. Est. 1967, Semi-annually
Subscriptions: Indv. $3
Circulation: Total-3,000
Advertising: Inquire for rates.

Kern County Dental Society
Newsletter — *Business, Consumer*

Publishing Co: Kern County Dental Society, 1701 Westwind Drive, Bakersfield, CA 93301; Title Tel # (805) 327-2666 Title Fax # (805) 327-1229
General Info: Monthly

Keynotes — *Business, Association*

Publishing Co: International College of Dentists, 51 Monroe St Ste 1501, Rockville, MD 20850-2408 Tel # (301) 251-8861 Fax # (301) 738-9143
Personnel: Editor-R.G. Shaffer
General Info: Yr. Est. 1989, Semi-annually
Subscriptions: Free With Membership

Los Angeles Dental Society, Bulletin

Publishing Co: Los Angeles Dental Society, 3660 Wilshire Blvd Ste 1152, Los Angeles, CA 90010-2717; Title Tel # (213) 380-7669
General Info: Bi-monthly

Maryland State Dental Assn. Newsletter — *Association*

Publishing Co: Maryland State Dental Assn., Columbia Business Ctr., 6470 Dobbin Rd., Columbia, MD 21045; Title Tel # (301) 964-2880

Mouthpiece — *Association*

Publishing Co: American Dental Assn., 211 E. Chicago Ave., Chicago, IL 60611-2678 Tel # (312) 440-7649; Title Tel # (312) 440-2639 Title Fax # (312) 440-3542
Personnel: Editor-Robert Faigh
General Info: Yr. Est. 1983, Quarterly, 4 pages
Subscriptions: Indv. $39
Circulation: Total-1,500

NARI Stethoscope
See: MEDICINE

Nebraska Dental Assn. Newsletter — *Association*

Publishing Co: Nebraska Dental Assn., 3120 O St., Ste. A, Lincoln, NE 68510-1533; Title Tel # (402) 476-1704 Title Fax # (402) 476-2641
Personnel: Editor-Tom Bassett, Feature Ed.-Julie Berger, Adv. Dir.-Cindy Boon
General Info: Monthly, Trim Size-8½ x 11, Letrpr. press, 16 pages, 2% ads, No Color
Subscriptions: Indv. $15, Free With Membership
Circulation: Total-1,200, Readership-1,200
Advertising: Inquire for rates. Accepts Inserts.
Printing Co: Alpha Graphics Printshop, 201 N. 14th Street, Lincoln, NE 68508 Tel # (402) 475-0000, Fax # (402) 475-0125

New Hampshire Dental Society Newsletter — *Association*

Publishing Co: New Hampshire Dental Society, Box 2229, 2 S. State St., Concord, NH 03302-2229; Title Tel # (603) 225-5961
Personnel: Editor-James Cassidy
Editorial Description: News and feature material for N.H. dentists and others.
General Info: (Formerly NHDS Newsletter), Yr. Est. 1959, Bi-monthly, Trim Size-8½ x 11, Web press, 6 pages, No Color
Circulation: (100% controlled), Total-650

Newsletter — *Association* — CPM: $750

Publishing Co: Butte-Sierra District Dental Society, 951 Live Oak Blvd Ste 30, Yuba City, CA 95991-3447 Fax # (916) 671-2460; Title Tel # (916) 671-9312
Personnel: Editor-Patricia Fochs
General Info: Bi-monthly
Subscriptions: Indv. $70
Circulation: Total-200
Advertising: $150. Accepts Inserts.

Newsletter of the American Academy of Oral Medicine

Publishing Co: Sponsor-Amer. Academy of Oral Medicine, Gunter Schmidt, 7777 Bonhomme Ave Ste 1400, Saint Louis, MO 63105-1911
Personnel: Circ. Mgr.-Joyce Caplan, Editor, Promotion Dir.-Carl Smith
Editorial Description: Basic organizational activities & notices of important allied meetings/courses.
General Info: Yr. Est. 1946, 8 pages, No Color
Circulation: (100% controlled), Total-900
Printing Co: Montrose Publishing, 10 S Main St # 20, Montrose, PA 18801-1314

North Dakota Dental Association Newsletter — *Association*

Publishing Co: North Dakota Dental Assn., 419 Dakota Ave, Wahpeton, ND 58075-4413; Title Tel # (701) 642-1881
Personnel: Editor-Jack Pfister
General Info: Bi-monthly, 6 pages, No Color
Circulation: Total-350
Printing Co: River Valley Printing, 412 Dakota Ave, Wahpeton, ND 58075-4429 Tel # (701) 642-4006

Northern California Academy of General Dentistry Newsletter *Association*

Publishing Co: Northern California Academy of General Dentistry, 5396 Briar Ridge Dr, Castro Valley, CA 94552-1710; Title Tel # (415) 786-6653
Editorial Description: Controversey in the profession.
General Info: (Formerly Northern California Academy of General Dentistry News), Yr. Est. 1940, 12 pages, No Color
Circulation: Total-700

Northwest Indiana Dental Society Newsletter *Association*

Publishing Co: Northwest Indiana Dental Society, 1205 W Lincoln Hwy Ste 7a, Merrillville, IN 46410-5336; Title Tel # (219) 838-3148
Personnel: Editor-Robert Moon

ODA News *Association* CPM: $150

Publishing Co: Ontario Dental Association, 4 New Street, Toronto, ON M5R 1P6 Canada; Title Tel # (416) 922-3900 Title Fax # (416) 922-9005
Personnel: Publisher-Peter James, Assoc. Publ.-Maureen Lynch, Editor-Nadine Hubert, Circ. Mgr.-Nina Buttice, Art Dir.-Elizabeth Tranter
Editorial Description: Offical Newsletter of the Ontario Dental Association, providing members with timely, accurate information on issues regarding association news, government information, current issues and human interest.
General Info: Yr. Est. 1987, 10x/yr., 8 pages, 50% ads, 2 Color, Recycled, Saddle-stitched
Subscriptions: Free With Membership
Circulation: Total-6,000
Advertising: $900.
Printing Co: Account Manager: Mike Schofield; General Printers, 1001 Ritson Rd., S., Oshawa, ON L1H 4G5 Canada Tel # (416) 490-6000, Fax # (905) 436-0813

Omicron Kappa Upsilon Bulletin

Publishing Co: OKU Dental Honorary Society, 40th & Holdrege, Lincoln, NE 68583-0001; Title Tel # (402) 472-1375
Personnel: Editor-Dr. Stephen Leeper
General Info: Annually, Trim Size-8$\frac{1}{2}$ x 11, 8 pages
Circulation: Total-10,000

Oracle *Association*

Publishing Co: Southern Maryland Dental Society, 4920 Niagara Rd Ste 306, College Park, MD 20740-1110; Title Tel # (301) 589-6062
General Info: Yr. Est. 1964, Monthly, Offset press, 4 pages, No Color
Circulation: Total-730

Pankey-Gram *Association*

Publishing Co: L.D. Pankey Institute, 240 Crandon Blvd., Ste. 302, Dupont Pl. Ctr., Key Biscayne, FL 33149-1543; Title Tel # (305) 361-5433
Personnel: Publisher-Christian Sager, Editor-Reba Foster
Editorial Description: L. D. Pankey Institute activities & educational offerings.
General Info: Yr. Est. 1971, Quarterly, Trim Size-8$\frac{1}{2}$ x 11, 4 pages, 2 Color
Subscriptions: Indv. $25, Inst. $15
Circulation: Total-8,000

Passaic County, Dental Society, Bulletin *Association* CPM$1166

Publishing Co: Passaic County Dental Society, 999 Mcbride Ave. #2, W. Paterson, NJ 07424-2534; Title Tel # (201) 812-1101 Title Fax # (201) 890-2460
General Info: 7x/yr.
Circulation: Total-300, Readership-300
Advertising: $350.

Professional Placement Newsnotes
See: HOSPITALS & NURSING HOMES

Professional Practice Today
See: MANAGEMENT

Royal College of Dentists of Canada

Publishing Co: Royal College of Dentists of Canada, 67 Berkeley St., Toronto, ON M5A 2W5 Canada; Title Tel # (416) 367-5373
Personnel: Editor-Kay Montgomery
General Info: Yr. Est. 1983, Semi-annually, 8 pages
Circulation: Total-800

SDA Dentist

Publishing Co: La Fierra University, 4700 Pierce St., Riverside, CA 92515-8247 Tel # (909) 785-2181 Fax # (909) 785-2199
Personnel: Editor-Hugh C. Love, D.D.S.
General Info: Yr. Est. 1962, Quarterly
Subscriptions: Indv. $3
Circulation: Total-1,450
Advertising: Inquire for rates.

San Diego County Dental Society, Facets *Association*

Publishing Co: San Diego County Dental Society, 1275 W Morena Blvd # B, San Diego, CA 92110-3837; Title Tel # (619) 275-7188
Personnel: Publisher-Dorothy Greaves, Editor-Joseph Mayer, Circ. Mgr., Production Mgr., Adv. Dir.-Patricia Beach
Editorial Description: In-house information to members of the San Diego County Dental Society.
General Info: (Formerly San Diego County Dental Society, Bulletin), Yr. Est. 1930, Monthly, Trim Size-4$\frac{3}{4}$ x 4$\frac{3}{4}$, Letrpr. press, 8 pages, ISSN: 0036-4010, No Color
Subscriptions: Indv. $20
Circulation: Total-1,300
Advertising: Inquire for rates.
Printing Co: Arts & Crafts, 3590 Kettner Blvd, San Diego, CA 92101-1139 Tel # (619) 297-0261

San Gabriel Valley Dental Society, Bulletin

Publishing Co: San Gabriel Valley Dental Society, 312 E Las Tunas Dr, San Gabriel, CA 91776-1502
Personnel: Editor-Dr. Esler Johnson
General Info: Yr. Est. 1937, Monthly
Subscriptions: Indv. $6

Sixth District Dental Assn. Newsletter *Business, Association*

Publishing Co: Sixth District Dental Assn., 6721 Government St., Baton Rouge, LA 70806-6239
Personnel: Editor-Timothy St. Romain

South Carolina Dental Bulletin

Publishing Co: South Carolina Dental Bulletin, 120 Stonemark Ln, Columbia, SC 29210-3841; Title Tel # (803) 799-3649
Personnel: Editor-Dr. Charles Hanna
General Info: Yr. Est. 1982, Monthly
Circulation: Total-1,100

South Dakota Dental Assn. Newsletter *Association* CPM$1000

Publishing Co: South Dakota Dental Assn., PO Box 1194, Pierre, SD 57501-1194; Title Tel # (605) 224-9133 Title Fax # (605) 224 9168
Personnel: Editor-Trudy Feigum
Editorial Description: Information for dentists in South Dakota.
General Info: Yr. Est. 1970, Monthly, Trim Size-8$\frac{1}{2}$ x 11, Sheetfed press, 3 pages, Ind/Abs/Online: ADAL, 3% ads, No Color, Matte
Subscriptions: Indv. $20, $2/copy
Circulation: Total-500
Advertising: $500. Accepts Inserts.
Printing Co: State Publishing Co., 303 E Sioux Ave, Pierre, SD 57501-3138 Tel # (605) 224-9999

Southern California Dental Laboratory Association, Bulletin *Business, Association*

Publishing Co: Southern California Dental Laboratory Association, 3333 Glendale Blvd Ste 4, Los Angeles, CA 90039-1840
Personnel: Editor-Richard Falge
General Info: Yr. Est. 1944, Monthly
Subscriptions: Indv. $3
Circulation: Total-2,000
Advertising: Inquire for rates.

Spectrum *Association*

Publishing Co: Boston University Goldman School of Graduate Dentistry, 100 East Newton St, Boston, MA 02118-2392; Title Tel # (617) 638-4700
Personnel: Editor-Shirley Levine
Editorial Description: Feature stories, events, research, etc. at the BU Goldman School of Graduate Dentistry.
General Info: (Formerly News), Yr. Est. 1982, Quarterly, Offset press, 6 pages
Circulation: Total-2,300

TMJ Update (Temporomandibular Joint Update)

Publishing Co: Anadem, Inc., 3620 N High St Ste 310, Columbus, OH 43214-3643; Title Tel # (614) 262-2539
Personnel: Publisher-Will Kuhlmann, Editor-Donald Bowers, Circ. Mgr.-Cindy Taylor, Adv. Dir.-L. Joe Gaietto, Promotion Dir.-Karla Gayle
Editorial Description: Digests medical & dental journal articles about TMJ disorders & craniofacial pain.
General Info: Yr. Est. 1983, Bi-monthly, Trim Size-8$\frac{1}{2}$ x 11, ISSN: 0885-9191
Subscriptions: Indv. $69, Inst. $69, Can. $79, For. $84, $8/copy

Tennessee Dental Association News   *Association*

Publishing Co: Tennessee Dental Assn., 2104 Sunset Place, PO Box 120188, Nashville, TN 37212; Title Tel # (615) 383-8962
Personnel: Editor-David Horvat
Editorial Description: Current news about dentistry in TN.
General Info: Yr. Est. 1958, Monthly, 4 pages
Circulation: Total-2,100

Tenth Times   *Association*

Publishing Co: Austin Tenth District Dental Society, 3303 Northland Dr Ste 313, Austin, TX 78731-4956
Personnel: Editor-Dr. William Dabilek
General Info: (Formerly Austin Dental News), Yr. Est. 1962, Monthly
Subscriptions: Indv. $15
Circulation: Total-450
Advertising: Inquire for rates.

Tri-County Dental Society, Bulletin

Publishing Co: Tri-County Dental Society, 110 Madison Ave, Morristown, NJ 07960-6013; Title Tel # (201) 538-2177
Personnel: Publisher, Editor-Harvey Nisselson
Editorial Description: Dental-related news of local interest.
General Info: Yr. Est. 1920, 5x/yr., Trim Size-8½ x 11
Circulation: Total-400
Advertising: Inquire for rates.

Univ. of Nebraska College of Dentistry Alumni Bulletin   *Association*

Publishing Co: University of Nebraska College of Dentistry Alumni Assn., 1520 R St, Lincoln, NE 68508-1651; Title Tel # (402) 472-2811
Editorial Description: News bulletin for college alumni.
General Info: Yr. Est. 1937, Semi-annually, Trim Size-5½ x 8, Sheetfed press, 24 pages, 2 Color, Newsprint, Saddle-stitched
Circulation: Total-2,000

Update

Publishing Co: Univ. of Florida College Dentistry, Public Relations-Alumni Dept., Box J-40, Gainesville, FL 32602
General Info: Semi-annually
Circulation: Total-3,200

Utah Dental Assn. Newsletter   *Association*

Publishing Co: Utah Dental Assn., 1151 E. 3900 SB-160, Salt Lake City, UT 84124-1216; Title Tel # (801) 261-5315
Personnel: Editor-Monte Thompson

WSDA News   *Association*   **CPM: $158**

Publishing Co: Washington State Dental Assn, 2033 6th Ave Ste 333, Seattle, WA 98121-2514; Title Tel # (206) 448-1914 Title Fax # (206) 443-9266
Personnel: Editor-Richard Mielke, Adv. Dir.-Kerry Alexander
Editorial Description: Association news and other items of interest to members.
General Info: Yr. Est. 1960, Monthly, Trim Size-8½ x 11, Offset press, 32 pages, ISSN: 0083-7431, 2 Color, Coated, Saddle-stitched
Subscriptions: Indv. $40, Can. $50, For. $50, $5/copy
Circulation: (100% controlled), Total-3,160
Advertising: $500.
Printing Co: Springs Printing, 425 3rd Ave W, Seattle, WA 98119-4001

WSDHA Newsletter   *Association*

Publishing Co: Washington State Dental Hygienists' Assn., PO Box 389, Lynnwood, WA 98046-0389; Title Tel # (206) 771-3201
Personnel: Editor-Cathy Dire
General Info: Bi-monthly, Trim Size-8½ x 11, Offset press, 12 pages, No Color
Circulation: Total-1,000
Advertising: Inquire for rates.

West Coast Dental Assn. Newsletter   *Association*

Publishing Co: West Coast Dental Assn., 9720 N Armenia Ave # F, Tampa, FL 33612-7539; Title Tel # (813) 968-7505
Personnel: Editor-Dr. Niles Kinnunen

Westviews   *Association*

Publishing Co: Western Dental Society, 6242 Westchester Pky Ste 220, Los Angeles, CA 90045-4820; Title Tel # (213) 641-5561 Title Fax # (213) 641-3258
Personnel: Publisher-Margaret O'Brien, Editor-Victor Pineschi
General Info: Yr. Est. 1972, Monthly, Trim Size-11 x 17, Offset press, 10 pages, 2 Color, Saddle-stitched
Subscriptions: Indv. $10
Acquistions: Publication Bought
Circulation: Total-925
Advertising: Inquire for rates. Accepts Inserts.
Printing Co: JAM Graphics, 22817 Lockness Ave, Torrance, CA 90501-5103 Tel # (213) 325-8062

Wireline   *Association*

Publishing Co: American Communications Exchange, 312 E Wisconsin Ave Ste 601, Milwaukee, WI 53202-4305; Title Tel # (214) 343-0805 Title Fax # (214) 343-1628
Personnel: Editor-Bret Cullers, Mktg. Dir.-Gennifer Golden
Editorial Description: News on seminars & membership activities.
General Info: (Formerly American Orthodontic Society Newsletter), Yr. Est. 1975, Quarterly, 8 pages, No Color
Circulation: Total-12,000
List Rental: Rents Lists

Wyoming Dental Association Newsletter   *Association*

Publishing Co: Wyoming Dental Association, 330 S Center St Ste 322, Casper, WY 82601-2875; Title Tel # (307) 234-0777
Personnel: Editor-Ben Chesebro

DEPARTMENT STORE & RETAIL

Barnard's Retail Marketing Report   *Business*

Publishing Co: Barnard Enterprises, Inc., 515 Mountain Avenue, #100, Berkeley, NJ 07922-2500
Personnel: Publisher, Editor-Kurt Barnard
Editorial Description: Marketing trends, developments, problems, opportunities affecting retailers, their suppliers & bankers, & shopping center developers. We analyze & forecast retailing trends.
General Info: Yr. Est. 1984, Monthly, 4 pages, ISSN: 0882-6218
Subscriptions: Indv. $175, Can. $185, For. $195

Card News
See: CREDIT AND CREDIT UNIONS

Cred-Alert
See: BANKING & FINANCE

Credit Risk Management Report
See: CREDIT AND CREDIT UNIONS

Employment Trends
See: EMPLOYMENT

Fashion International   *Business*

Publishing Co: FI Publishing, Inc., 153 E. 87th St., New York, NY 10128; Title Tel # (212) 289-0420
Personnel: Publisher, Editor-Ruth Finley
Editorial Description: Fashion news, market digest, trends, & forecasts, boutique info.
General Info: Yr. Est. 1972, Monthly
Subscriptions: Indv. $85, $20/copy
Circulation: Total-1,500

Giftbeat   *Business*

Publishing Co: Giftbeat, 145 Woodland Ave., Westwood, NJ 07675-3217; Title Tel # (201) 358-6868 Title Fax # (201) 664-6464
Personnel: Publisher, Editor-Joyce Washnik
Editorial Description: Tracks sales and overviews market of gift retailers.
General Info: Yr. Est. 1992, Monthly, Trim Size-10 x 14½, 8 pages, 2 Color, Coated, Saddle-stitched
Subscriptions: Indv. $129, Can. $139, For. $159

Inside Retailing   *Business*

Publishing Co: Lebhar-Friedman Inc., 425 Park Ave., New York, NY 10022-3556 Tel # (212) 756-5000; Title Tel # (212) 371-9400
Personnel: Publisher-J.R. Friedman, Editor-David Mahler
Editorial Description: Insights into chain store behavior & the strategies behind it all.
General Info: Yr. Est. 1975, Bi-weekly, Trim Size-8½ x 11, Web press, 4 pages, No Color, Newsprint
Subscriptions: Indv. $137, $5/copy

JonesReport
See: ADVERTISING & MARKETING

Monday Report on Retailers   *Business*

Publishing Co: Maclean Hunter Publishing Ltd., Maclean Hunter Building, 777 Bay St., Toronto, ON M5W 1A7 Canada Tel # (416) 596-5000 Fax # (416) 596-5526; Title Tel # (416) 596-5939 Title Fax # (416) 596-5553
Personnel: Publisher-Gloria Gallagher, Editor-Don Douloff, Circ. Mgr.-Cheryl Treliving
Editorial Description: Information on Canada's chain retailers: chain expansion plans, financial information, merchandising policy changes, new retail chains opening.
General Info: Yr. Est. 1973, Weekly, 6 pages
Subscriptions: Indv. $395, Can. $395
List Rental: Rents Lists

NAMSB News
See: APPAREL & ACCESSORIES

NASFM NEWs
See: MANUFACTURING

Online Marketplace
See: COMPUTERS & AUTOMATION

Peter Berlin Report on Shrinkage Control - Executive Edition   *Business*

Publishing Co: Peter Berlin Retail Consulting Group, Inc., 380 N Broadway Ste 206, Jericho, NY 11753-2109; Title Tel # (516) 932-0450 Title Fax # (516) 932-9393
Personnel: Publisher-Peter Berlin
General Info: Yr. Est. 1981, 7x/yr., 8 pages
Subscriptions: Indv. $135, For. $149

Peter Berlin Report on Shrinkage Control - Store Manager's Edition   *Business*

Publishing Co: Peter Berlin Retail Consulting Group, Inc., 380 N Broadway Ste 206, Jericho, NY 11753-2109; Title Tel # (516) 932-0450 Title Fax # (516) 932-9393
General Info: Yr. Est. 1985, 10x/yr., 4 pages
Subscriptions: Indv. $120

RTW Review
See: APPAREL & ACCESSORIES

Retail Performance Monitor   *Business*

Publishing Co: CSM Communications Co., Inc., 195 Smithtown Blvd., Nesconset, NY 11767-1869; Title Tel # (516) 265-3900 Title Fax # (516) 265-3281
Personnel: Publisher, Editor-Ralph Sullivan, Circ. Mgr.-Peter Chamberlin, Production Mgr.-John Walsh
Editorial Description: Monitors retail performance including strategy, financial condition, operations, sales & earnings personnel, expansion activity, stock, labor, inventory, management, holdings, insider trading, demographic & market trends, bankruptcies, mergers & acquisitions, interest rates, consumer credit, spending, & the economy.
General Info: Yr. Est. 1990, Bi-weekly, Trim Size-8½ x 11, Sheetfed press, 8 pages, ISSN: 1050-1789, No Color, Matte, Saddle-stitched
Subscriptions: Indv. $358, Can. $390, For. $399, $20/copy
Acquistions: Publication Bought
Printing Co: Print Shack, 430 Oser Ave, Hauppauge, NY 11788-3611 Tel # (516) 231-5588

Retail Roundup   *Business, Association*

Publishing Co: Comex Rista Co., 22 Juniper Rd, Port Washington, NY 11050-1435; Title Tel # (516) 767-9331 Title Fax # (516) 767-3710
Personnel: Publisher, Editor-John Santelli
Editorial Description: Tracks retail strategy shifts in sales & marketing, print media advertising, trends, sales promotion developments, expansions & diversifications.
General Info: Yr. Est. 1986, Monthly, 10 pages
Subscriptions: Indv. $195
Advertising: Inquire for rates.
List Rental: Rents Lists

Retail Systems Alert   *Business*

Publishing Co: Retail Systems Alert, P.O. Box 332, 77 Oak Street, Newton Upper Falls, MA 02164-9806; Title Tel # (617) 527-4626 Title Fax # (617) 527-8102
Personnel: Publisher, Editor-Thomas Freidman, Editorial Coord.-Eric Olson, Mktg. Dir.-Patrice Fallon
Editorial Description: Reports on implementation of technology and strategies of top retailers
General Info: Yr. Est. 1988, Monthly, Trim Size-11 x 8½, Offset press, 8 pages, ISSN: 0898-8439, 2 Color, Matte, Other
Subscriptions: Indv. $295
Acquisitions: Publication Bought
Circulation: Total-800
List Rental: List Management Co.: WMI/Worldata, 5200 Town Center Circle, Boca Raton, FL 33486 Tel # (407) 393-8200, Fax # (407) 368-8345, Actives: 14,603, $150/M

Retailing Today   *Business*

Publishing Co: Robert Kahn & Associates, PO Box 249, Lafayette, CA 94549-0249; Title Tel # (510) 254-4434 Title Fax # (510) 284-5612
Personnel: Publisher, Editor-Robert Kahn, Circ. Mgr.-Annabelle Farrell
Editorial Description: Written for CEO and other senior retail executives. Provides analysis of current activities, innovative research studies and emphasis on ethical conduct.
General Info: Yr. Est. 1965, Monthly, Trim Size-8½ x 11, Offset press, 6 pages, ISSN: 0360-606X, No Color
Subscriptions: Indv. $60, Can. $54, For. $72, $6/copy
Circulation: Total-1,000

SSAP Newsletter
See: ENVIRONMENT & ECOLOGY

SalesCoach   *Business*

Publishing Co: Report Communications, 9595 Whitley Dr Ste 100, Indianapolis, IN 46240-1308 Tel # (317) 844-9024 Fax # (317) 848-6953
Personnel: Editor-Maureen Gilmer, Circ. Mgr.-Patty Williams, Production Mgr.-Bridget Gurtowsky, Publisher, VP Mktng.-Phil Stillerman
Editorial Description: Tips and information for successful retail selling.
General Info: Yr. Est. 1992, Monthly, Trim Size-8½ x 11, Offset press, 4 pages, Matte
Subscriptions: Indv. $30, Can. $50
Circulation: Total-5,000
Printing Co: Corporate Printing, 5220 W 79th St, Indianapolis, IN 46268-1604 Tel # (317) 872-8480, Fax # (317) 875-5939

Shopping Center Ad Trends   *Business*

Publishing Co: National Research Bureau, 150 N. Wacher Drive, Chicago, IL 60601 Tel # (312) 541-0100 Fax # (312) 541-1492 Parent Co.-Reed Reference Publishing, New Providence; Title Tel # (319) 752-5415 Title Fax # (319) 752-3421
Personnel: Publisher-Michael Darnall, Editor-Teresa Levinson
Editorial Description: A monthly review of advertising and promotions from shopping centers across the country and other nations.
General Info: Monthly, Trim Size-8½ x 11, Offset press, 25 pages, Color-cover, Matte, Looseleaf
Subscriptions: $34/copy

Shopping Center Digest   *Business*

Publishing Co: Jomurpa Publishing Inc., 7 S Myrtle Ave # 1708, Spring Valley, NY 10977-5543; Title Tel # (914) 426-0040 Title Fax # (914) 426-0802
Personnel: Publisher, Editor-Murray Shor, Mng. Editor-Stephanie Strapka, Circ. Mgr.-Diana Hill, Adv. Dir.-Joyce Shor-Johnson
Editorial Description: Information on new and expanding shopping center in the U.S. and Canada and expansion plans of retail chains. Names, addresses and telephone numbers of those responsible for leasing and development.
General Info: Yr. Est. 1973, Semi-monthly, Trim Size-8¼ x 11, Offset press, 12 pages, ISSN: 0885-209X, 20% ads, 4 Color, Coated, Saddle-stitched
Subscriptions: Indv. $209, Can. $224, For. $224, $15/copy
Advertising: $2,350. Accepts Inserts.
List Rental: Rents Lists

Shopping Center Newsletter   *Business*

Publishing Co: National Research Bureau, 150 N. Wacher Drive, Chicago, IL 60601 Tel # (312) 541-0100 Fax # (312) 541-1492 Parent Co.-Reed Reference Publishing, New Providence; Title Tel # (319) 752-5415 Title Fax # (319) 752-3421
Personnel: Publisher-Michael Darnall, Editor-Teresa Levinson
Editorial Description: Highlights promotions and events conducted by shopping centers across the country.
General Info: Yr. Est. 1955, Monthly, Trim Size-8½ x 11, Sheetfed press, 4 pages, 2 Color, Newsprint
Subscriptions: Indv. $57

Store Planning Service

Publishing Co: Retail Reporting Corp., 302 5th Ave Fl 11, New York, NY 10001-3604 Fax # (212) 279-7014; Title Tel # (212) 279-7000
Editorial Description: Color photographs showing interiors, departments, fixtures, etc., of newly opened American stores.
General Info: Yr. Est. 1941, Monthly, ISSN: 0039-'859
Subscriptions: Indv. $35

Wholesale Trade   *Business, Association*

Publishing Co: Statistics Canada, Holland Ave/RH Coats, Holland Ave/Tunney's Pasture, Ottawa, ON K1A O26 Canada Tel # (613) 951-8116 Fax # (613) 951-0581; Title Tel # (613) 951-1581 Title Fax # (613) 951-1584
Editorial Description: Estimated dollar sales and inventories of wholesale merchants for 26 business groups. 63-008.
General Info: Yr. Est. 1935, Monthly, 24 pages, ISSN: 0380-7894
Subscriptions: Indv. $17, Can. $14, For. $20
List Rental: Actives: 38,000

DIRECT MAIL

AAFT Quarterly
See: CONSUMER INTERESTS

Alliance Report   *Business, Association*

Publishing Co: Alliance of Nonprofit Mailers, 2001 S St NW Ste 301, Washington, DC 20009-1125 Tel # (202) 462-5132
Editorial Description: Keeps mailers of non-profit pieces informaed of developements in Congress, USPS and the Postal rate Commssion.
General Info: Bi-monthly

Art of Self Promotion, The
See: ADVERTISING & MARKETING

Book Marketing Update
See: BOOKS & BOOK TRADE

Bruce Report, The   *Business*
Publishing Co: Bruce, Dean & Company, 116 New Montgomery St., Suite 914, San Francisco, CA 94105-3607; Title Tel # (415) 512-7305 Title Fax # (415) 512-7308
Personnel: Publisher-William Dean, Assoc. Publ.-Kathleen Shlutz, Editor-Hannah Bruce, Editor-Scott Fitzgerrell, Circ. Mgr.-Phred Huben
Editorial Description: Provides strategic and financial information on the catalog industry.
General Info: Yr. Est. 1990, Monthly, ISSN: 1055-3525
Subscriptions: Indv. $295

Business Marketing Notepad
See: ADVERTISING & MARKETING

Change   *Business, Consumer*
Publishing Co: Lifestyle Change Communications, 5885 Glenridge Dr., Atlanta, GA 30328 Fax # (404) 250-4295; Title Tel # (404) 252-0554 Title Fax # (404) 252-4295
Personnel: Publisher-Robert Perlstein, Mng. Editor-Catherine Hagin, Production Dir., Mktg. Dir.-Kimberly Merritt
Editorial Description: Covers innovations, technical developments, and controversies in direct marketing, alternative media, and data programs.
General Info: Yr. Est. 1992, Quarterly, Trim Size-8½ x 11, Desktop press, 8 pages, 2 Color, Coated, Saddle-stitched
Subscriptions: Free
Circulation: Total-2,500

Circulation Council Newsletter   *Association, Business*
Publishing Co: Direct Marketing Association, PMDS Book Distribution Co., PO Box 391, Annapolis Junction, MD 20701-0391 Tel # (301) 604-0187 Fax # (301) 206-9789; Title Tel # (212) 768-7277
Editorial Description: Direct Marketing Association Circulation Council info on marketing.
General Info: Quarterly, Trim Size-8½ x 11, 16 pages, 2 Color, Matte, Saddle-stitched
Advertising: $325.

Computer Monitor Quarterly   *Business*
Publishing Co: Direct Media, 200 Pemberwick Rd, P.O. Box 4565, Greenwich, CT 06830-4273 Fax # (203) 531-1452; Title Tel # (203) 532-1000
Editorial Description: Tips and ideas on list rentals and direct marketing.
General Info: Yr. Est. 1992, Quarterly
Subscriptions: Free To Qualified Recipient
List Rental: Rents Lists

Connections to Mail Order/World Trade and Homebased Business Info.
See: ADVERTISING & MARKETING

DB Publisher
See: PRINTING/GRAPHIC ARTS

Day Break   *Business*
Publishing Co: Direct Marketing Day in New York, Inc., 65 Commerce Rd., Stamford, CT 06902-4549
Personnel: Publisher-Loren Granville, Art Dir.-Dennis Sirrine
Editorial Description: Information for direct marketers and about the Direct Marketing Day program.

Desktop Direct Marketing News   *Business*
Publishing Co: Jet Products, 5656 Buffalo Ave, Van Nuys, CA 91401-4505; Title Fax # (818) 785-3914
Editorial Description: Covers hardware and software and events for direct marketers using PC's.
General Info: Monthly
Subscriptions: Free To Qualified Recipient

Development Director's Letter
See: PHILANTHROPY

Direct Line   *Association*
Publishing Co: Direct Marketing Association, PMDS Book Distribution Co., PO Box 391, Annapolis Junction, MD 20701-0391 Tel # (301) 604-0187 Fax # (301) 206-9789; Title Tel # (212) 768-7277
Personnel: Editor-Sanna Levine
Editorial Description: Newsletter serving the direct mail industry.
General Info: Monthly

Direct Marketing Optimization Letter   *Business*
Publishing Co: Lee Marc Stein Ltd., 41 Executive Dr, Hauppauge, NY 11788-2112; Title Tel # (516) 724-3765 Title Fax # (516) 724-6202
Editorial Description: Information and how-to's on direct marketing.
General Info: Monthly, Trim Size-8½ x 11, 4 pages, No Color, Matte
Subscriptions: Indv. $192

Direct Marketing Savings Report   *Business*
Publishing Co: Sayers Publishing Co., P.O. Box 3323, Marietta, GA 30061 Fax # (404) 928-8411; Title Tel # (404) 928-7423 Title Fax # (770) 928-8411
Personnel: Publisher-Charlie Sayers
Editorial Description: Suggestions and information about efficient list rentals.
General Info: Yr. Est. 1994, Monthly
Subscriptions: Indv. $198

Direct Marketing Success Letter   *Business*
Publishing Co: Nicholas Direct, PO Box 877, Indian Rocks Beach, FL 34635-0877; Title Tel # (813) 596-4966 Title Fax # (813) 596-6900
Personnel: Publisher-Ted Nicholas
Editorial Description: Marketing ideas and strategies.
General Info: (Formerly Ted Nicholas Letter), 10x/yr., Trim Size-8½ x 11, 8 pages, No Color, Matte
Subscriptions: Indv. $177

Direct Marketing Tips and Targets   *Business*
Publishing Co: West, Adams, Christopher & Associates, 1000 W. McNab Rd., Suite 158, Pompano, FL 33069-9871 Tel # (305) 384-8500 Fax # (305) 578-4200
Editorial Description: Covers latest in database management, direct mail, telemarketing and list marketing.
General Info: Weekly

Direct Response   *Business*
Publishing Co: Creative Direct Marketing, 1815 W 213th St Ste 210, Torrance, CA 90501-2839; Title Tel # (310) 212-5727 Title Fax # (310) 212-5773
Personnel: Publisher-Craig Huey, Editor-Kent Komae, Circ. Mgr., Production Mgr.-Rhonda Held, Art Dir.-Eric Oxenberg
Editorial Description: Summarizes new and profitable direct marketing info.
General Info: (Formerly Direct Marketing News Digest), Yr. Est. 1977, Monthly, Trim Size-8½ x 11, Sheetfed press, 12 pages, No Color, Other
Subscriptions: Indv. $79, For. $88
Circulation: Total-700

Direct Response Specialist   *Business*
Publishing Co: Stilson & Stilson, PO Box 1075, Tarpon Springs, FL 34688-1075; Title Tel # (813) 786-1411
Personnel: Publisher, Editor-Galen Stilson, Assoc. Ed.-Jean Stillson, Circ. Mgr.-Jean Bunner
Editorial Description: Effective response/profit techniques for professional mail marketers.
General Info: (Formerly Mail Order Connection), Yr. Est. 1982, Monthly, 8 pages, Newsprint
Subscriptions: Indv. $77, Can. $77, For. $92

Direct Success Ideas   *Business*
Publishing Co: Teague Publishing Group, PO Box 14689, Dayton, OH 45413-0689
Personnel: Publisher-Bob Teague, Editor-Rob Eugene
Editorial Description: Insider direct response marketing plus hard-to-get sources. Covers copywriting, advertising, direct mail classifieds, etc.
General Info: (Formerly Mail Order Resource; Direct Response Report), Yr. Est. 1985, 6x/yr., Trim Size-8½ x 11, Offset press, 8 pages, No Color
Subscriptions: Indv. $49, Inst. $60, Can. $55, For. $75, $6/copy
Circulation: Total-11,000

Direction   *Business*
Publishing Co: Direct Marketing Consultants, Inc., 705 Franklin Tpke, Allendale, NJ 07401-1637; Title Tel # (201) 327-9213 Title Fax # (201) 327-9213
Personnel: Publisher, Editor-Hugh Curley
Editorial Description: Gives valuable hints re direct mail & sales promotion.
General Info: Yr. Est. 1979, Bi-monthly, Desktop press, 4 pages, 2 Color
Subscriptions: Indv. $40, For. $60, $10/copy
Circulation: (82% controlled), Total-4,126
Advertising: Accepts Inserts.

Directions
See: HOUSE ORGANS

Drop Shipping News
See: ADVERTISING & MARKETING

FRM Weekly
See: PHILANTHROPY

Group 1 Report   *Business*
Publishing Co: Group 1 Software, 4200 Parliament Place, Suite 600, Lanham, MD 20706; Title Tel # (301) 731-2300 Title Fax # (301) 731-0360
Personnel: Editor-Suzanne Porter-Kuchay
Editorial Description: Direct marketing information from Group 1 Software.
General Info: Yr. Est. 1984, Semi-annually, Trim Size-8½ x 11, Offset press, 6 pages, 2 Color, Matte
Subscriptions: Free
Circulation: Total-23,000

Home Income Quarterly
See: ADVERTISING & MARKETING

I'm Too Busy To Read Marketing Report Service
See: ADVERTISING & MARKETING

Inside Mail Order (Mellinger Mail Order Profit Letter)

Publishing Co: Mellinger Co., 6100 Variel Ave, Woodland Hills, CA 91367-3721; Title Tel # (818) 884-4400 Title Fax # (818) 594-5804
Personnel: Editor-B.L. Mellinger, III
General Info: Yr. Est. 1977, Monthly, Trim Size-11 x 17, Sheetfed press, 6 pages, 2 Color, Newsprint
Subscriptions: Indv. $49
Acquistions: Publication Sold
Printing Co: Mellinger Co., 6100 Variel Ave, Woodland Hills, CA 91367-3721

Interactive Marketing News
Business

Publishing Co: Phillips Business Information, Inc., 1201 Seven Locks Rd., Ste 300, Potomac, MD 20854-2958 Tel # (301) 340-1520 Fax # (301) 424-4297; Title Tel # (202) 546-5005 Title Fax # (202) 546-8759
Personnel: Publisher-Donald R. Libey
Editorial Description: Covers the strategic future of direct marketing in North America. Incudes information on magazine publishing trends.
General Info: (Formerly Pub.Trends&Trendsetters; InteractiveFacts; InteractiveMktpl.), Yr. Est. 1989, Monthly, ISSN: 1078-6821
Subscriptions: Indv. $495, For. $530
Advertising: Accepts Inserts.

Just Classified Catalog
Business

Publishing Co: Eastern Digital Resources, 438 Malone Avenue North, Augusta, SC 29841 Tel # (803) 593-0870
Editorial Description: Catalog/newsletter catering to responders and users of direct response advertising.
General Info: Bi-monthly, Trim Size-8½ x 11, 2 Color, Matte, Saddle-stitched
List Rental: List Management Co.: J.F. Glaser, Inc., 999 N Main St Ste 103, Glen Ellyn, IL 60137-3504 Tel # (708) 469-2075, Fax # (708) 790-5244, Actives: 5,007, $95/M

List News
Business

Publishing Co: Names in the News - California, 1 Bush St., Ste. 300, San Francisco, CA 94104-4425; Title Tel # (415) 989-3350 Title Fax # (415) 433-7796
General Info: Weekly
List Rental: Rents Lists

List Update
Business

Publishing Co: Ed Burnett/Database America, 100 Paragon Dr, Montvale, NJ 07645-1718 Fax # (201) 476-2405; Title Tel # (201) 476-2300 Title Fax # (201) 476-2416
Editorial Description: Ed Burnett's list info for clients and potential customers.
General Info: Bi-monthly, Trim Size-8½ x 11, 2 pages, No Color, Coated

Mail Order Digest
Business, Association

Publishing Co: National Mail Order Association, 2807 Polk St. NE., Minneapolis, MN 55418-2954; Title Tel # (612) 788-1673 Title Fax # (612) 788-1147
Personnel: Editor-Paul Muchnick, Publisher, Editor-John Schulte
Editorial Description: Reports successful direct marketing techniques, new products, books, government regulations and other pertinent information concerning mail order.
General Info: Yr. Est. 1972, Monthly, Trim Size-8½ x 11, Sheetfed press, 8 pages, Newsprint
Subscriptions: Indv. $75, Can. $90, For. $150

MailShot
Business

Publishing Co: IBIS International Direct, 249 W. 17th St. 10th Fl., New York, NY 10011-5300; Title Tel # (212) 779-1344 Title Fax # (212) 779-1349
Editorial Description: List rental information from IBIS to potential and current customers.
General Info: Quarterly, Trim Size-8½ x 11, 4 pages, 2 Color, Matte

MarketWave
Consumer

Publishing Co: MarketWave, PO Box 27587, Fresno, CA 93729-7587; Title Tel # (209) 434-4946
Personnel: Publisher-Leonard Clements
Editorial Description: Analyzes and reviews the multi-level marketing industry.
General Info: Yr. Est. 1991, Bi-monthly, Trim Size-8½ x 11, 12 pages
Subscriptions: Indv. $39

Mature Market Report
See: SENIOR CITIZENS

Newsletter Editor's Resource
See: PERIODICAL INDUSTRY

Numbers News
See: ADVERTISING & MARKETING

Online Marketplace
See: COMPUTERS & AUTOMATION

Passport
See: PHILATELY & POSTAL AFFAIRS

Publicity & Marketing Ideas
See: ADVERTISING & MARKETING

Publisher's Multinational Direct
See: ADVERTISING & MARKETING

Roman Reports
Business, Consumer

Publishing Co: Roman Reports Pub., 12600 Rockside Rd Ste 107, Garfield Heights, OH 44125-4525; Title Tel # (216) 662-4593
Personnel: Publisher, Editor-D.L. Roman
Editorial Description: Reviews mail order business, opportunity & get rich ads.
General Info: Yr. Est. 1973, Bi-monthly, Trim Size-8.5 x 11, 8 pages, No Color
Subscriptions: Indv. $39, $5/copy
Circulation: Total-5,000
List Rental: Actives: 6,000, $45/M

Royal Mail, The
Business

Publishing Co: Royal Mail, 152 Madison Ave., Ste. 304, New York, NY 10157-1973; Title Tel # (212) 725-5460
Personnel: Editor-Geoff Brown
Editorial Description: News and information for direct mail marketers who market overseas.
General Info: Quarterly, Trim Size-11¾ x 16½, 4 pages, 2 Color, Coated

SORT'ing News
See: OFFICE METHODS & EQUIPMENT

Selling to Seniors
See: ADVERTISING & MARKETING

Sharing Memories
See: HOBBY

Small Business Builder
See: BUSINESS & INDUSTRY

Success Ads
See: ADVERTISING & MARKETING

Who's Mailing What!
Business   **CPM: $555**

Publishing Co: North American Publishing Co., 401 N. Broad St., Philadelphia, PA 19108 Tel # (215) 238-5300 Fax # (215) 238-5270; Title Tel # (215) 235-5300
Personnel: Editor-Denison Hatch, Circ. Mgr.-Paul Goldberg, Production Mgr.-Margaret Cook
Editorial Description: A newsletter reviewing the mailing efforts of the direct mail industry.
General Info: Yr. Est. 1984, 10x/yr., Trim Size-8½ x 11, Sheetfed press, 16 pages, ISSN: 8755-2671, 2 Color, Matte
Subscriptions: Indv. $195, For. $198, $12/copy
Circulation: Total-1,800
Advertising: $1,000.
List Rental: List Management Co.: D-J Associates, 77 Danbury Rd., Box 2048, Ridgefield, CT 06877 Tel # (203) 431-8777, Fax # (203) 431-3302, Actives: 30,322, $100/M
Printing Co: Star Press, P.O. Box 748, Holyoke, MA 01040-4994 Tel # (413) 532-7091

Worldata Direct Mail List Letter
Business

Publishing Co: Worldata, 5200 Town Center Circle, Boca Raton, FL 33486; Title Tel # (407) 393-8200 Title Fax # (407) 368-8345
Personnel: VP Mktng.-Geoffrey Hodes
Editorial Description: For list marketers with tips and Worldata list info.
General Info: Quarterly, Trim Size-8½ x 11, 8 pages, 2 Color, Matte
Subscriptions: Free

DISABILITY

AACPDM News
See: HEALTH

ABDC Newsletter
See: HEALTH

ADA Compliance Guide
See: LAW

ADA Update
Business, Association

Publishing Co: NYPER Publications, PO Box 662, Latham, NY 12110-0662 Fax # (518) 458-8582; Title Tel # (518) 786-1654 Title Fax # (518) 452-8582
Personnel: Editor-Harvey Randall
General Info: Yr. Est. 1991, Monthly, ISSN: 1071-7382
Subscriptions: Indv. $95, Inst. $95
Advertising: Accepts Inserts.

ASR News
See: COMPUTERS & AUTOMATION

A.T. Quarterly
See: BUSINESS & INDUSTRY

Accessible Journeys *Consumer*

Publishing Co: Accessible Journeys, 35 W Sellers Ave, Ridley Park, PA 19078-2113
Tel # (610) 521-0339 Fax # (610) 521-0339; Title Tel # (610) 747-0171 Title Fax # (610) 521-6959
Personnel: Publisher-Howard J. McCoy, RN, Editor-Deborah A. Hoover, RN
General Info: Yr. Est. 1985, Quarterly
Subscriptions: Indv. $15, Can. $20
Circulation: Total-5,000, Readership-5,000, Source-IS
Advertising: Inquire for rates.

Accommodating Disabilities: Business Management Guide *Business*

Publishing Co: CCH, Inc., 2700 Lake Cook Rd., Riverwoods, IL 60015 Fax # (800) 224-8299 Parent
Co.-Kluwer Law & Taxation Publishers, Cambridge; Title Tel # (847) 267-7000
Title Fax # (800) 554-8299
Editorial Description: Explains the federal requirements for accommodating individuals with
disabilities with respect to employment, access to public accommodations and commercial facilities,
and access to transportation vehicles and services.
General Info: Yr. Est. 1992, Monthly, 8 pages
Subscriptions: Indv. $420

Accommodating Disability Decisions
See: LAW

Administration & Management Special Interest Section Newsletter
See: HEARING & SPEECH

Adventures in Movement
See: SOCIAL SERVICES & WELFARE

Affirmative Action/EEO Update
See: CIVIL RIGHTS

Alert, National Service Dog Center Newsletter
See: DOGS

Americans with Disabilites Cases *Business*

Publishing Co: Bureau of National Affairs, Inc., 1231 25th St. NW, Bldg. N-200, Washington, DC
20037-1157; Title Tel # (202) 452-4200 Title Fax # (202) 822-8092
Personnel: Publisher-William A. Beltz, Mng. Editor-Nancy J. Sedmak, Circ. Mgr.-Gary C. Seltzer
Editorial Description: A one-binder, biweekly service, reporting in full text significant decisions under
federal & state disabilities laws.
General Info: Yr. Est. 1993, Bi-weekly, Trim Size-6 x 9, Offset press, Ind/Abs/Online: Westlaw,
Looseleaf
Subscriptions: Indv. $551

Americans with Disabilities Newsletter *Business, Association*

Publishing Co: Positive Workforce for America, Inc., PO Box 365, Hillsdale, NY 12529-0365
Tel # (518) 325-5260
Personnel: Publisher-Thomas P. Carty, Editor-Howard Van Lenten
Editorial Description: Focuses on the implications of the passage of The Americans with Disabilities
Act for both employers and people with disabilities.
General Info: Yr. Est. 1993, Monthly, Trim Size-8½ x 11, Sheetfed press, 20 pages, ISSN: 1077-
2987, 2 Color, Coated, Saddle-stitched
Subscriptions: Indv. $75, Inst. $150, Free To Qualified Recipient
Circulation: (52% controlled), Subscriptions-1,200
Advertising: Accepts Inserts.
Printing Co: Quality Printing, 3 Federico Dr, Pittsfield, MA 01201-3842 Tel # (413) 442-4166

BNA's Americans with Disabilities Act Manual *Business, Association*

Publishing Co: Bureau of National Affairs, Inc., 1231 25th St. NW, Bldg. N-200, Washington, DC
20037-1157; Title Tel # (202) 452-4200 Title Fax # (202) 822-8092
Personnel: Publisher-William A. Beltz, Mng. Editor-Jeff Day, Circ. Mgr.-Gary Seltzer
Editorial Description: A reference service, update monthly, providing practical guidance on the
provisions of the Americans with Disabilities Act which concern employers most: employment &
public accomodations. Also includes a monthly newsletter covering new developments & trends, &
legal decisions.
General Info: Yr. Est. 1992, Monthly, Trim Size-8½ x 11, Offset press, 6 pages, Looseleaf
Subscriptions: Indv. $737

BNA's Americans with Disabilities Act Manual Newsletter *Business*

Publishing Co: Bureau of National Affairs, Inc., 1231 25th St. NW, Bldg. N-200, Washington, DC
20037-1157; Title Tel # (202) 452-4200 Title Fax # (202) 822-8092
Personnel: Publisher-William A. Beltz, Mng. Editor-Jeff Day, Circ. Mgr.-Gary C. Seltzer
Editorial Description: A monthly newsletter that provides prompt notification of developments &
trends concerning all provisions of the Americans with Disabilities Act.
General Info: Yr. Est. 1992, Monthly, Trim Size-8½ x 11, Offset press, ISSN: 1063-3111
Subscriptions: Indv. $165

Bell, The
See: PSYCHOLOGY

Breaking New Ground *Business*

Publishing Co: Purdue University Agriculture Dept., Dept. Agricultural Engineering, 1146 Ag.
Engineering Bldg., West Lafayette, IN 47907 Fax # (317) 496-1115; Title Tel # (317) 494-5088
Title Fax # (317) 496-1356
Personnel: Editor-Bill Field
Editorial Description: News and information of interest to farmers with physical disabilities.
General Info: Yr. Est. 1982, Quarterly
Circulation: Total-7,500

CANCH-Gram

Publishing Co: California Assn. for Newly Handicapped Children, 17583 Daves Ave, Monte Sereno,
CA 95030-3214
General Info: Yr. Est. 1960, 5x/yr.
Subscriptions: Indv. $25

CAPTALK *Business*

Publishing Co: CAPTEK Custom Applied Technology, PO Box 888, Southeastern, PA 19399-0888
Tel # (261) 096-2114; Title Tel # (610) 296-2114 Title Fax # (610) 296-0488
Personnel: Publisher, Editor-Lee Benham, Editor-Mary Ann Case, Food Editor, Research Editor-John
Blankenbaker
Editorial Description: CAPTEK's newsletter to the rehab, education, and eyecare professionals it
serves. Americans with Disabilities Acts (ADA) accommodation.
General Info: Yr. Est. 1993, Quarterly, Trim Size-8½ x 11, Sheetfed press, 4 pages, 2 Color, Coated,
Saddle-stitched
Subscriptions: Free

C.H.A.D.D.ER Box *Association*

Publishing Co: Children & Adults With Attention Deficit Disorders, 499 Northwest 70th Ave., Suite
308, Plantation, FL 33317; Title Tel # (305) 587-3700 Title Fax # (305) 587-4599
Editorial Description: Events and news for those who have, or have children who have, attention
deficit disorders.
General Info: Monthly, Trim Size-8½ x 11, 12 pages, 2 Color, Coated, Saddle-stitched

Can-Do *Consumer*

Publishing Co: Can-Do, 6737 Morella Ave, North Hollywood, CA 91606-1618;
Title Tel # (214) 631-7438
Personnel: Editor-Bill Baugh
Editorial Description: Information on devices & methods to reduce physical limitations.
General Info: Yr. Est. 1987, Bi-monthly, 6 pages
Subscriptions: Indv. $9
Circulation: Total-600

Capitol Capsule

Publishing Co: National Assn. of State Mental Retardation Prgm Directors, 113 Oronoco St,
Alexandria, VA 22314-2015; Title Tel # (703) 683-4202
General Info: Yr. Est. 1971, Monthly
Subscriptions: Indv. $30

Caring Community
See: RELIGIOUS & THEOLOGICAL

Christian Horizons Newsletter *Consumer*

Publishing Co: Christian Horizons Newsletter, 384 Arthur St., S., Elmira, ON N3B 2P4 Canada;
Title Tel # (519) 669-1571
Personnel: Editor-Joyce Wagler
Editorial Description: Updates on trends, legislation, & programs for mentally retarded persons.
General Info: Yr. Est. 1983, Bi-monthly, Trim Size-8½ x 14, Letrpr. press, 8 pages, No Color
Subscriptions: Indv. $1
Circulation: Total-7,500

Communique *Consumer, Association*

Publishing Co: Society for Manitobans with Disabilities, 825 Sherbrook St., Winnipeg, MB R3A 1M5
Canada Tel # (204) 786-5601 Fax # (204) 783-2919
Personnel: Editor-Terry Wiebe
Editorial Description: Covers current issues relevant to people with physical disabilities.
General Info: (Formerly Society Focus), Yr. Est. 1985, Semi-annually, Trim Size-8½ x 11, 4 pages,
No Color, Matte
Subscriptions: Free To Qualified Recipient
Circulation: Total-23,000, Readership-100,000
Advertising: Inquire for rates.

Contact
See: PHYSIOLOGY

Cubprints
See: HEARING & SPEECH

Daily Word in Large Type
See: RELIGIOUS & THEOLOGICAL

Diabetic Traveler
See: TRAVEL

Disabilities Issues

Publishing Co: Info Ctr. for Individuals with Disabilities, 29 Stanhope St., Boston, MA 02116-5111; Title Tel # (617) 727-5540
Personnel: Editor-Linda Hillyer
Editorial Description: Newsletter for people with disabilities & relatives & friends in MA on all subjects related to living with disabilities - trends, issues, events, etc.
General Info: Yr. Est. 1980, Monthly, Trim Size-8½ x 11, Mimeo press, 8 pages, 2% ads, No Color, Matte
Subscriptions: Inst. $25, Can. $30, For. $35, Free To Qualified Recipient
Circulation: Total-4,500
Advertising: Inquire for rates.
List Rental: Actives: $80/M

Disabilities in the Workplace Alert
See: LAW

Disability Advocates Bulletin

Publishing Co: Boston University School of Law, 765 Commonwealth Ave., Boston, MA 02215-1401; Title Tel # (617) 353-2904 Title Fax # (617) 353-5995
Personnel: Publisher, Editor-Henry Beyer, Production Mgr.-Cynthia Dunn
Editorial Description: Summarizes recent judicial opinions, statutes, regulations, articles, & other materials of importance to people with disabilities & their advocates. An associated advocacy clearinghouse provides complete texts of many of these materials.
General Info: (Formerly P&A Newsletter), Yr. Est. 1977, Bi-monthly, Trim Size-8½ x 11, Sheetfed press, 40 pages, No Color, Newsprint, Other
Subscriptions: Indv. $60, Inst. $120, $10/copy
Circulation: Total-650, Readership-700
Advertising: Accepts Inserts.

Disability Compliance for Higher Education *Business, Scholarly*

Publishing Co: LRP Publications, 747 Dresher Rd., P.O. Box 980, Horsham, PA 19044-0980 Tel # (215) 784-0910 Fax # (215) 784-0317
Editorial Description: Covers disability compliance issues for coleges, universities, and higher learning institutes.
General Info: Monthly

Disability Funding News
See: PHILANTHROPY

Disability Law Compliance Report *Business*

Publishing Co: Warren, Gorham & Lamont, 31 Saint James Ave., Boston, MA 02116-4112 Parent Co.-Thomson Professional Publications, Stamford; Title Tel # (617) 423-2020 Title Fax # (617) 423-1914
Personnel: Publisher-Larry Selby, Mktg. Dir.-Sandra Fox
General Info: Yr. Est. 1992, Monthly
Subscriptions: Indv. $135
List Rental: List Management Co.: Manager: Seena Benedek; WG & L List Management, 1 Penn Plz Fl 42, New York, NY 10119-0002 Tel # (212) 971-5000

Disability Resources Monthly *Consumer*

Publishing Co: Sponsor-Disability Resources, Disability Resources, Inc., 4 Glatter Ln, Centereach, NY 11720-1032; Title Tel # (516) 585-0290
Personnel: Publisher-Avery Klauber, Editor-Julie Klauber
Editorial Description: Features short topical articles and news items about books, periodicals, software, organizations and other resources for and about people with disabilities. Geared for libraries, disability organizations, health, social service and education professionals, and interested consumers.
General Info: Yr. Est. 1993, Monthly, ISSN: 1070-7220
Subscriptions: Indv. $25, Can. $30, For. $35, $3/copy

Division on Visual Handicaps Quarterly
See: BLIND

Dykes, Disability & Stuff *Consumer* CPM: $266

Publishing Co: Dykes, Disability & Stuff, PO Box 8773, Madison, WI 53708-8773
General Info: Yr. Est. 1988, Quarterly
Subscriptions: Indv. $25
Circulation: Total-750
Advertising: $200.

ElderCare Forum
See: WOMEN'S

Employment Health Law & Benefits
See: INDUSTRIAL RELATIONS/PERSONNEL

Gathered View, The *Association*

Publishing Co: Prader Willi Syndrome Assn., 2510 S Brentwood Blvd Ste 220, Saint Louis, MO 63144-2326
Personnel: Publisher-Don Goranson, Editor-Linda Kedar, Circ. Mgr.-Russ Myler
Editorial Description: Newsletter of the national organization which serves as a center for communication for interested/concerned persons, dedicated to the sharing of experiences & development of facilities.
General Info: Yr. Est. 1975, Bi-monthly, Trim Size-17 x 11, Desktop press, 6 pages, No Color, Coated
Subscriptions: Indv. $30, Inst. $40, Can. $40, For. $40
Circulation: Total-1,700

Golden Gateway
See: TRAVEL

Goodwill News *Association*

Publishing Co: Goodwill Industries of Houston Inc., PO Box 21185, Houston, TX 77226-1185; Title Tel # (713) 692-6221 Title Fax # (713) 692-0923
Personnel: Editor-Sherri Lowe
Editorial Description: A composite of information pertaining to the activities & opportunities disabled people & disadvantaged people through Goodwill Ind. of volunteers & special events are also highlighted.
General Info: Yr. Est. 1945, Trim Size-8½ x 11, Letrpr. press, 5 pages, 2 Color, Coated
Acquistions: Publication Bought
Circulation: Total-7,100

HAI News
See: SOCIAL SERVICES & WELFARE

Handicap News

Publishing Co: Handicap News, 3060 E Bridge St Lot 342, Brighton, CO 80601-2724; Title Tel # (303) 659-4463
Personnel: Editor-Phyllis Burns
Editorial Description: Feature articles, fiction, poetry & news of interest to the disabled & those who work with them.
General Info: Yr. Est. 1984, Monthly
Subscriptions: Indv. $13, Can. $23, For. $35

HumanAwareness and Low Vision Perspectives *Business, Consumer*

Publishing Co: HumanWare, Inc., 6245 King Rd., Loomis, CA 95650-8801; Title Tel # (916) 652-7253 Title Fax # (916) 652-7296
Personnel: Publisher-Jim Halliday
Editorial Description: Newsletter about HumanWare, Inc.'s line of computer products geared for education and helping the disabled. Newsletter for retinal specialist who help patients with low vision.
General Info: Quarterly, Trim Size-8½ x 11, 8 pages, 2 Color, Coated, Saddle-stitched

In Action
See: HEALTH

Inclusion Times *Consumer*

Publishing Co: Natl. Professional Resources, 25 South Regent Street, P.O. Box 1479, Pt. Chester, NY 10573 Tel # (914) 937-8879 Fax # (914) 937-9327
Personnel: Editor-Daniel Sage
Editorial Description: Written to ensure that children with disabilities are included in regular school and community environments.
General Info: Quarterly, ISSN: 1072-3811
Subscriptions: Indv. $30, Inst. $30, Can. $30, For. $40

Inclusive Education Programs
See: EDUCATION

Individuals with Disabilities Education Law Reporter *Business*

Publishing Co: LRP Publications, 747 Dresher Rd., P.O. Box 980, Horsham, PA 19044-0980 Tel # (215) 784-0910 Fax # (215) 784-0317
Personnel: Publisher-Ken Kahn, Editor-Melinda Maloney, Promotion Dir.-Marcy Witt
Editorial Description: Full text case reporter including special education judicial decisions, SEA decisions, and OCR & OSEP rulings.
General Info: (Formerly Education for the Handicapped Law Report), Yr. Est. 1978, 24x/yr., ISSN: 1055-520X, Ind/Abs/Online: LRPnet
Subscriptions: Indv. $855
List Rental: List Management Co.: Manager: Anne Magowen; Axon Lists, 747 Dresher Rd. Ste. 500, Box 980, Horsham, PA 19044 Tel # (215) 784-0860, Fax # (215) 784-0870, Actives: 13,924, $125/M

Infocus
See: ELECTRIC & ELECTRONIC EQUIPMENT

It's Okay
See: SEX

Job Training and Placement Report
Business   **CPM: $202**

Publishing Co: Jones Publishing Inc., N7450 Aanstad Rd., PO Box 5000, Iola, WI 54945-5000; Title Tel # (715) 445-5000 Title Fax # (715) 445-4053
Personnel: Publisher-Scott Kolpien, Asst. Pub.-Gregory Bayer, Editor-Diane Harrington, Circ. Mgr.-Barb Beyersdorf, Product Mgr.-Dave Mills, Art Dir.-Julie King
Editorial Description: Source of up-to-date information for administrators and professionals who train and place mentally and physically handicapped persons in quality jobs.
General Info: Yr. Est. 1976, Monthly, Trim Size-8½ x 11, Sheetfed press, 13 pages, ISSN: 1041-1488, 2 Color, Matte
Subscriptions: Indv. $117, Can. $128, For. $127
Circulation: Total-1,200
Advertising: $243.
List Rental: Actives: 1,130, $150/M, Expires: 9,477, $125/M

LDA Newsbriefs
Association

Publishing Co: Learning Disabilities Association of America, 4156 Library Rd., Pittsburgh, PA 15234-1349; Title Tel # (412) 341-1515 Title Fax # (412) 344-0224
Editorial Description: Parents of children with learing disabilities; interested professionals.
General Info: Bi-monthly, ISSN: 0739-909X
Subscriptions: Indv. $14, Can. $30, For. $30, $3/copy

LaBods Journal
Consumer

Publishing Co: The Orton Dyslexia Society, 823 Cresswell Ln, Opelousas, LA 70570-5881
Editorial Description: Information for dyslexics.
General Info: Quarterly, Trim Size-8½ x 11, 6 pages, No Color, Matte, Saddle-stitched

Learning Disabilities Assn. of California
See: SOCIAL SERVICES & WELFARE

Meeting Ground
Consumer

Publishing Co: AHA Stroke Connections, 7272 Greenville Ave, Dallas, TX 75231-5129 Tel # (214) 706-1556 Fax # (214) 696-5211; Title Tel # (612) 520-0438
Editorial Description: Written by and for families and professionals in the rehabilitation/medical/education community to foster communication and the sharing of information, interests, and experiences.
General Info: Yr. Est. 1972, Quarterly, Trim Size-8½ x 11, Sheetfed press, 8 pages, ISSN: 1047-4993, 2 Color, Matte, Other
Subscriptions: Free To Qualified Recipient

NAFC Quarterly Newsletter
See: HEALTH

NAPH National Newsletter
Association   **CPM: $100**

Publishing Co: Natl. Assn. of the Physically Handicapped. Inc., 244 W. Sturbridge Dr., Medina, OH 44256-3887; Title Tel # (513) 961-8040
Personnel: Publisher, Editor-Joann Edwards, Circ. Mgr.-Helen Roudebush, Adv. Dir.-Gerald Snyder
Editorial Description: Advance economic, social and physical welfare of all physically handicapped persons.
General Info: Yr. Est. 1958, Quarterly, Trim Size-8½ x 11, Desktop press, 24 pages, ISSN: 0741-1405, 1% ads, No Color, Other, Saddle-stitched
Subscriptions: Indv. $12, $3/copy
Circulation: (100% controlled), Total-1,000
Advertising: $100.

NARHA News
See: SPORTS & SPORTING GOODS

National
See: EDUCATION

National Disability Law Reporter
See: LAW

National Reye's Syndrome Foundation-In the News
See: HEALTH

New Directions

Publishing Co: National Assn. of State Mental Retardation Prgm Directors, 113 Oronoco St, Alexandria, VA 22314-2015; Title Tel # (703) 683-4202
Personnel: Editor-Sally Carson
General Info: Yr. Est. 1970, Monthly
Subscriptions: Indv. $35

New Horizons
See: SOCIAL SERVICES & WELFARE

News Digest
Association

Publishing Co: National Information Center for Children with Disabilities, PO Box 1492, Washington, DC 20013-1492; Title Tel # (202) 884-8200 Title Fax # (202) 884-8441
Personnel: Editor-Lisa Kupper
Editorial Description: Compilation of articles on current research & relevant program information in the disabilities field.
General Info: Yr. Est. 1970, Quarterly, Trim Size-8½ x 11, 15 pages, Ind/Abs/Online: ERIC, 2 Color, Matte, Saddle-stitched
Subscriptions: Free To Qualified Recipient
Circulation: Total-63,000

Newswheel
See: SPORTS & SPORTING GOODS

North Texas Amputee Support Group News

Publishing Co: North Texas Amputee Support Group, 3714 Lisa Ln, Mesquite, TX 75150-2659; Title Tel # (214) 631-7438
Editorial Description: Support group news and activities, related topics.
General Info: Yr. Est. 1988, 11x/yr.
Subscriptions: Indv. $12

Nova Scotia Special Olympics Newsletter
See: SPORTS & SPORTING GOODS

One Step Ahead
Consumer

Publishing Co: EKA Publications, Inc., 1050 Connecticut Avenue, NW, Suite 1250, Washington, DC 20036; Title Tel # (202) 296-1488 Title Fax # (202) 861-1645
Personnel: Publisher-Evan J. Kemp, Jr., Editor in Chief-Robert J. Funk, Editor-Leye Chrzanowski, Mktg. Dir.-Marsha Sussman
Editorial Description: A newsletter by people with disabilities for people with disabilities, their familiees and their friends.
General Info: Yr. Est. 1994, Bi-weekly
Subscriptions: Indv. $30

Over the Rainbow
See: TRAVEL

PIP College 'HELPS'
See: EDUCATION

Paragraphic
Association

Publishing Co: Canadian Paraplegic Assn, British Columbia Div., 780 SW Marine Dr., Vancouver, BC V6P 5Y7 Canada; Title Tel # (604) 324-3611
Personnel: Editor-Wayne Stevens
Editorial Description: Newsletter circulated to members describing activities of the association.
General Info: Yr. Est. 1957, Quarterly, 12 pages, No Color
Subscriptions: Indv. $5
Circulation: Total-2,500

Parent Care News Brief
See: BABY

Peoplenet
See: LIFESTYLE

Projects with Industry Forum

Publishing Co: Multi Resource Centers, Inc., 1900 Chicago Ave, Minneapolis, MN 55404-1903; Title Tel # (612) 879-5429 Title Fax # (612) 879-5400
Personnel: Editor-Jim Roth
Editorial Description: News and information regarding employment of people with disabilities.
General Info: (Formerly PWI Pioneer), Yr. Est. 1984, Bi-monthly, 4 pages
Subscriptions: Free To Qualified Recipient
Circulation: Total-2,000

Quality of Care
Consumer, Scholarly

Publishing Co: Quality of Care for Mentally Disabled, 99 Washington Ave Ste 1002, Albany, NY 12210-2801; Title Tel # (518) 473-6304 Title Fax # (518) 473-6296
Personnel: Editor-Marcus Gigliotti
Editorial Description: Advocacy and monitoring issues including legal related to the quality of care for people with mental disabilities.
General Info: Yr. Est. 1980, Bi-monthly, Trim Size-11 x 14, 12 pages
Subscriptions: Free
Circulation: Total-13,000
Printing Co: Dodge Graphics Press, 1501 Broad St, Utica, NY 13501-1098 Tel # (315) 735-9266

RESNA News
See: HEALTH

RFB News

Publishing Co: Recording for the Blind, 20 Roszel Rd, Princeton, NJ 08540-6294; Title Tel # (609) 452-0606
Personnel: Editor-Elizabeth Callahan
Editorial Description: Issues affecting people with print disabilities and non-profit, voluntary organizations; activities and programs of RFB.
General Info: (Formerly Recording for the Blind News), Yr. Est. 1951, Quarterly, Trim Size-8½ x 11, Web press, 6 pages, 2 Color, Coated
Subscriptions: Free
Circulation: (100% controlled), Total-30,000
Printing Co: Contempo Press, 8 Industry Ct, Trenton, NJ 08638-2716 Tel # (609) 530-0800, Fax # (609) 530-0880

Rampart

Publishing Co: The Canadian Paraplegic Assn.-Newfoundland & Labrador Inc., The Roberts Bldg. Ste. 202, 95 LeMarchant Rd., St. Johns, NF A1C 2H1 Canada Fax # (709) 753-4224; Title Tel # (709) 753-5901
General Info: Quarterly

Reaching Out *Consumer, Association*

Publishing Co: Cornelia de Lange Syndrome Foundation, 60 Dyer Ave, Collinsville, CT 06022-1201; Title Tel # (203) 697-0159 Title Fax # (203) 693-6819
Editorial Description: Features medical information about Cornelia de Lange Syndrome.
General Info: Yr. Est. 1977, Bi-monthly, 12 pages, 2 Color, Saddle-stitched
Subscriptions: Indv. $15, Inst. $25, Free With Membership
Circulation: Total-3,500

Rehab Tab *Association*

Publishing Co: Rehabilitation Society of Calgary, #7, 11 St. SE, Calgary, AB T2E 4Z2 Canada Fax # (403) 269-2735; Title Tel # (403) 263-8341
Editorial Description: Articles relating to self-help and advocacy for handicapped people, reports on organizational issues and activities.
General Info: Yr. Est. 1960, Irregular, Trim Size-8½ x 11, Mimeo press, 20 pages, No Color
Subscriptions: Indv. $2, $1/copy
Acquistions: Publication Bought
Circulation: (100% controlled), Total-300
Advertising: Inquire for rates.

Rehab Update
See: MEDICINE

Rehabilitation Technology Newsletter
See: SOCIAL SERVICES & WELFARE

Report on Disability Programs *Business*

Publishing Co: Business Publishers, Inc., 951 Pershing Dr., Silver Spring, MD 20910-4464 Tel # (301) 589-5103 Fax # (301) 589-8493; Title Tel # (301) 587-6300 Title Fax # (301) 587-1081
Personnel: Publisher-Eric Easton, Editor-Lisa Rabasca, Circ. Mgr.-Kathleen Harrow, Promotion Dir.-Connie Arnold
Editorial Description: The only national newsletter covering disability issues from a policy perspective, with full coverage of the implementation of the Americans with Disabilities Act, and the Rehabilitation Act, as well as other civil rights issues affecting Americans with disabilities.
General Info: (Formerly Handicapped Rights & Regulations; Handicapped Americans Rept), Yr. Est. 1978, Bi-weekly, Trim Size-8½ x 11, Desktop press, 8 pages, ISSN: 0191-6734, Ind/Abs/Online: Newsnet and Predicasts, No Color, Recycled
Subscriptions: Indv. $286, Can. $286, For. $299
Advertising: Accepts Inserts.
List Rental: List Management Co.: Manager: Don Peterson; BPI Direct, 951 Pershing Dr., Silver Spring, MD 20910-4464 Tel # (301) 585-5976, Fax # (301) 587-4530

Report on Education of the Disadvantaged
See: EDUCATION

Saskatchewan Society for Autistic Children Newsletter
See: PSYCHOLOGY

Saskatchewan Special Olympics Society Newsletter
See: SPORTS & SPORTING GOODS

Section 504 Compliance Guide
See: LAW

Special Education Leadership
See: EDUCATION

Special Educator, The
See: EDUCATION

Successful Job Accomodation Strategies *Business*

Publishing Co: LRP Publications, 747 Dresher Rd., P.O. Box 980, Horsham, PA 19044-0980 Tel # (215) 784-0910 Fax # (215) 784-0317
Editorial Description: Provides practical tips and solutions for your job accomodation questions.
General Info: Monthly

TASH Newsletter *Association*

Publishing Co: TASH: The Assn. for Persons with Severe Handicaps, 29 W. Susquehanna Ave., Ste. 210, Baltimore, MD 21204-5201 Tel # (410) 828-8274 Fax # (410) 828-6706; Title Tel # (206) 361-8870 Title Fax # (206) 361-9208
Personnel: Editor-Sheryl Ball, Adv. Dir.-Mary Hensley, Mktg. Dir.-Kimberly Doyle
Editorial Description: Covers articles on integration, supported employment, community living, results of significant court costs, upcoming conferences, workshops, training inservice programs, resources and new publications..
General Info: Yr. Est. 1975, Monthly, 12 pages, No Color, Newsprint
Subscriptions: Indv. $15, Can. $15, Free With Membership
Circulation: Total-9,000
Advertising: Inquire for rates.
List Rental: Actives: 8,000, $95/M

TD Access & Safety Report
See: TRAFFIC & TRANSPORTATION

Torch Bearer
See: EDUCATION

Transition Summary *Consumer*

Publishing Co: Sponsor-U.S. Office of Special Education Programs, National Information Center for Children with Disabilities, PO Box 1492, Washington, DC 20013-1492; Title Tel # (202) 884-8200 Title Fax # (202) 884-8441
Personnel: Editor-Lisa Kupper
Editorial Description: Compilations of articles dealing with issues of transition of individuals with disabilities form youth to adulthood.
General Info: Yr. Est. 1985, Annually, Trim Size-8½ x 11, Offset press, 10 pages, No Color, Saddle-stitched
Subscriptions: Free
Circulation: Total-10,000

Travelin' Talk
See: TRAVEL

Update on Quality
See: SOCIAL SERVICES & WELFARE

DOGS

Alaskan Malamute Club of America Newsletter *Association*

Publishing Co: Alaskan Malamute Club of America, 8565 Hill Rd S, Pickerington, OH 43147-8536; Title Tel # (614) 837-7702
General Info: Monthly

Alert, National Service Dog Center Newsletter *Consumer, Association*

Publishing Co: Sponsor-Pedigree Food for Dogs, Delta Society, 289 Perimeter Rd. E., Renton, WA 98055-1329; Title Tel # (206) 226-7357 Title Fax # (206) 235-1076
Personnel: Editor-Maureen Fredrickson, Production Mgr.-Andrea Leigh Ptak
Editorial Description: Covers issues related to training, handling, and partnership with service dogs for people with disablties.
General Info: (Formerly Alert), Yr. Est. 1993, Quarterly, 4 pages, ISSN: 1069-0743, 2 Color, Matte
Subscriptions: Indv. $6, Inst. $6, Can. $9, For. $9, Free To Qualified Recipient
Circulation: (80% controlled), Total-2,500

Animal Sheltering Magazine
See: ANIMALS

Beastly News *Consumer, Association*

Publishing Co: Beastly News, 718 Earp St, Philadelphia, PA 19147-5723; Title Tel # (215) 755-4030
Personnel: Publisher-Jane Brydon, Art Dir.-Deborah Woolwine
Editorial Description: Informs Delaware Valley dog lovers of dog related activities, sports, club events, medical information, etc.
General Info: Yr. Est. 1990, Quarterly, Trim Size-17 x 11, Offset press, 10 pages
Advertising: $80. Accepts Inserts.

Canine Courier
See: LAW ENFORCEMENT & PENOLOGY

Canine Listener *Consumer, Association*

Publishing Co: Dogs for the Deaf, Inc., 10175 Wheeler Rd., Central Point, OR 97502-9360; Title Tel # (541) 826-9220 Title Fax # (541) 826-6696
Personnel: Editor-Robin Dickson
Editorial Description: Information about the Dogs for the Deaf program which rescues stray dogs and trains them to help deaf and hard of hearing people.
General Info: Yr. Est. 1977, Quarterly
Circulation: Total-35,000

Chi-Chatter Newsletter *Consumer, Association*

Publishing Co: Chihuahua Club of America, 11530 Second Branch Rd., Chesterville, VA 23832; Title Tel # (804) 790-1618
Personnel: Co-Editor-Cindy Seibert, Co-Editor-Sandra Whittle
Editorial Description: Reports all aspects of caring for & breeding chihuahua dogs.
General Info: Bi-monthly

Curly Commentator

Publishing Co: Curly-Coated Retriever Club of America, C/O Mary Alice Hembree, 951 Brown Rd., Bridgewater, NJ 08807; Title Tel # (908) 722-1409
Personnel: Publisher-Michele Flickinger, Editor-Mary Alice Hembree
Editorial Description: Carries items on all aspects of curly-coated Retriever ownership.
General Info: Yr. Est. 1979, Bi-monthly, Mimeo press, 36 pages, 1% ads, No Color
Subscriptions: Indv. $12
Circulation: (100% controlled), Total-125

Dog Industry Newsletter *Business*

Publishing Co: Good Communications, Inc., PO Box 10069, Austin, TX 78766; Title Tel # (512) 454-6090 Title Fax # (512) 454-3420
Personnel: Publisher, Editor-Ross Becker, Mng. Editor-Judi Sklar, Adv. Dir.-Karen Laufer
Editorial Description: Monthly newsletter for Senior Executives in the dog products industry. Provides sensitive information on new products due out in the next year, strategies, industry data, new consumer promotions, dog food business.
General Info: Yr. Est. 1989, Monthly, Trim Size-8½ x 11, 9 pages, ISSN: 1074-777x, No Color
Subscriptions: Indv. $295

DogGone
See: TRAVEL

French Bulldog Club of America Newsletter
Publishing Co: French Bulldog Club of America, 86 Gold Rd, Wappingers Falls, NY 12590-3534; Title Tel # (201) 334-2682
Personnel: Editor-Richard Hoover

Golden Retriever Club of America News
Publishing Co: Golden Retriever Club of America, 3 Station Plaza, Ramsey, NJ 07446-1805; Title Tel # (201) 327-5555
General Info: 8x/yr.

Harness & Greyhound Racing Handicapping
See: GAMBLING

Humane News
See: ANIMALS

Info   *Association*
Publishing Co: International Sled Dog Racing Association, C/o Team & Trail Printers, RR#4, Box 381, Tyrone, PA 16686; Title Tel # (814) 684-3594
Personnel: Editor-Nancy Molburg, Production Mgr.-Donna Hawlly
Editorial Description: Technical info. on all facets of sled dog racing.
General Info: Yr. Est. 1961, Monthly, Trim Size-8½ x 11, Sheetfed press, 24 pages, 2% ads, No Color
Subscriptions: Indv. $20, $2/copy
Circulation: (100% controlled)
Advertising: Inquire for rates.
List Rental: Rents Lists
Printing Co: Team & Trail Printers, PO Box 128, Center Harbor, NH 03226-0128

International Pet Industry News
See: ANIMALS

Irish Setter Club of American, Memo to Members
Publishing Co: Irish Setter Club of American, 12318 Hwy. 62, Charlestown, IN 47111-1634 Tel # (812) 256-3649
General Info: Monthly

K-9 Courier   *Consumer*   **CPM: $45**
Publishing Co: Mellowbriar Enterprises, Box 49, Jerico Springs, MD 64756; Title Tel # (417) 398-2876 Title Fax # (417) 398-2830
Personnel: Publisher, Editor-Allene Reynolds
Editorial Description: Newsletter for people who raise dogs. Short articles, free advertising, breeder's directory.
General Info: Yr. Est. 1983, Monthly, Mimeo press, 10 pages, 40% ads, No Color
Subscriptions: Indv. $14, $2/copy
Circulation: Total-550
Advertising: $25.

MASKC Komondor News
Publishing Co: Middle Atlantic States Komondor Club, Inc., 102 Russell Rd, Princeton, NJ 08540-6773; Title Tel # (609) 924-0199
Personnel: Editor-Joy Levy
Editorial Description: News & views about the Komondor as show dog, houseguard, & livestock guard dog. History, records, translation from foreign material.
General Info: Yr. Est. 1974, Bi-monthly, Trim Size-8½ x 11, Sheetfed press, 40 pages, ISSN: 0146-9436, No Color
Subscriptions: Indv. $20, For. $25, $4/copy
Circulation: Total-350
Advertising: Inquire for rates.
Printing Co: Press Room, 10 S Tulane St, Princeton, NJ 08542-6913 Tel # (609) 924-5240

Mastiff Newsletter
Publishing Co: Mastiff Club of America, 355 Jasontown Rd, Westminster, MD 21158-3523; Title Tel # (301) 848-3281
General Info: Quarterly

Norwich and Norfolk Terrier News   *Association*
Publishing Co: Old Dominion Press, Inc., 310 Tarrytown Dr, Richmond, VA 23229-7323; Title Tel # (804) 740-8139
Editorial Description: Informative breed digest on Norwich and Norfolk Terriers.
General Info: (Formerly Norwich Terrier News), Yr. Est. 1962, Semi-annually, Trim Size-6 x 9, Offset press, 32 pages, No Color, Saddle-stitched
Subscriptions: $3/copy
Circulation: Total-500

PETA News
See: ENVIRONMENT & ECOLOGY

Pekingese Club of America, Bulletin   *Association*
Publishing Co: Pekingese Club of America, 3 Carolyn Terrace, Southboro, MA 01772
General Info: Quarterly
Circulation: Total-225

Political Watchdog
Publishing Co: Activists for Protective Animal Legislation, PO Box 11743, Costa Mesa, CA 92627-0743
General Info: Quarterly
Circulation: Total-500

Silky Terrier Club of America Newsletter   *Association*
Publishing Co: Silky Terrier Club of America, PO Box 1132, Alameda, CA 94501-0116
Personnel: Editor-Shelby Rust
General Info: Yr. Est. 1955, Monthly, Sheetfed press, No Color
Advertising: Inquire for rates.

Skye Terrier Club of America-Bulletin
Publishing Co: Skye Terrier Club of America, Dale, 180 Marsh Creek Road, Gettysburg, MD 17325-7121; Title Tel # (301) 840-9556
General Info: Yr. Est. 1938, Monthly, 6 pages
Circulation: Total-200
Advertising: Inquire for rates.

Tatoo-A-Pet News
See: ANIMALS

Veterinary Industry Newsletter
See: VETERINARY

Warning Letter Bulletin
See: LAW

Welsh Wag
Publishing Co: Welsh Terrier Club of America, 139 Hood School Rd, Indiana, PA 15701-9208; Title Tel # (708) 831-0313
Personnel: Editor-Virginia Winters
Editorial Description: Contains articles & info of interest to owners, breeders & exhibitors of Welsh terrier dogs.
General Info: Yr. Est. 1981, Bi-monthly, 6 pages
Circulation: Total-300

Wolf Park News
See: ANIMALS

Yorkie Express   *Association*
Publishing Co: Yorkie Express, 1058 Citrus Ave NE, Palm Bay, FL 32905-4847; Title Tel # (407) 725-8821
Editorial Description: About Yorkshire Terriers; health, stories, articles, records, statistics, etc.
General Info: Yr. Est. 1951, Bi-monthly, 10 pages
Circulation: Total-400

Your Dog   *Consumer*
Publishing Co: Tufts University School of Veterinary Medicine, 200 Westboro Rd., North Grafton, MA 01536
Personnel: Editor-Gloria Parkinson
Editorial Description: Covers dog behavior, health and other issues for pet owners.
General Info: Yr. Est. 1995, Monthly, Trim Size-8½ x 11, Offset press, 4 pages, 2 Color, Newsprint, Other

DRUGS & PHARMACEUTICALS

AACP News   *Association*
Publishing Co: American Assn. of Colleges of Pharmacy, 1426 Prince St, Alexandria, VA 22314-2815; Title Tel # (703) 739-2330
Personnel: Editor-Mary Bassler
Editorial Description: Activities and issues of interest to pharmacy education.
General Info: Yr. Est. 1972, Monthly, Trim Size-8½ x 11, Letrpr. press, 8 pages, Color
Subscriptions: Indv. $35
Circulation: Total-2,200
Advertising: Inquire for rates.

AIDS Clinical Care Newsletter
See: MEDICINE

AIDS Treatment News
See: MEDICINE

AIHP Notes
See: HISTORY

ASHP Newsletter *Association*

Publishing Co: American Society of Health System Pharmacists, 7272 Wisconsin Ave., Bethesda, MD 20814-3410 Fax # (301) 657-1641; Title Tel # (301) 657-3000 Title Fax # (301) 657-1615
Personnel: Editor-Rebecca Wilfinger, Sr. Ed.-Renee Brehio, Mktg. Dir.-Kevin P. Whorton
Editorial Description: Covers current developments in pharmacy and health care for institutional patients and activities of the American Society of Hospital Pharmacists.
General Info: Yr. Est. 1968, Monthly, 8 pages, ISSN: 0001-2483, 2 Color, Newsprint
Circulation: Total-30,000
List Rental: List Management Co.: Manager: Mylene San Gabriel; Business Mailers, Inc., 2000 York Rd., Oak Brook, IL 60521 Fax # (708) 574-6121, Actives: 25,000, $125/M
Printing Co: Bladen Lithographics, 8235 Beechcraft Drive, Gaithersburg, MD 20879-5507 Tel # (301) 948-9600

Academy Reporter
See: MEDICINE

Addiction Letter, The
See: HEALTH

Alcoholism & Drug Abuse Weekly
See: HEALTH

Alcoholism Briefs
See: HEALTH

Allegheny County Pharmacist *Association*

Publishing Co: Allegheny County Pharmaceutical Assn., 2 Parkway Ctr Ste 111, Pittsburgh, PA 15220-3501; Title Tel # (412) 922-2440
Personnel: Editor-Carole Ladik
Editorial Description: Drug info.-organization business-meetings.
General Info: Yr. Est. 1947, Monthly, 8 pages, No Color
Subscriptions: Indv. $50
Circulation: Total-800
Advertising: Inquire for rates.

American Society of Pharmacognosy Newsletter *Association*

Publishing Co: Temple University School of Pharmacy, 3307 N Broad St, Philadelphia, PA 19140-5193 Tel # (215) 221-4946; Title Tel # (215) 770-7946 Title Fax # (215) 707-3678
Personnel: Editor-Joy Reighard, Editorial Asst.-Barbara Grissani
Editorial Description: News of the American Society of Pharmacognosy.
General Info: Yr. Est. 1959, Quarterly, Desktop press
Circulation: Total-1,200

Animal Pharm World Animal Health & Nutrition News
See: VETERINARY

Approved Bioequivalency Codes *Business*

Publishing Co: Facts & Comparisons, Inc., 111 West Port Plaza, Suite 300, St. Louis, MO 63146-3098 Tel # (314) 878-2515; Title Tel # (314) 787-2515 Title Fax # (314) 878-5563
Editorial Description: A user friendly publication containing the FDA's current data on bioequivalency evaluations. Data includes: prescription drug information, OTC drug lists, patient exclusivity information, and a drug manufacturers index updated monthly.
General Info: Yr. Est. 1992, Monthly, Looseleaf
Subscriptions: Indv. $79

Arizona Poison Control System Newsletter *Business, Consumer*

Publishing Co: Univ. of Arizona, College of Pharmacy, Publications, Tucson, AZ 85721-0001; Title Tel # (602) 626-4063
Personnel: Editor-Lory Fischler
Editorial Description: Inform physicians and pharmacists of new techniques and management in poisoning and overdose.
General Info: Yr. Est. 1959, Quarterly, Trim Size-8½ x 11, 4 pages, No Color
Circulation: Total-3,000

Association des Pharmaciens des Etablissements de Sante du Quebec. Bulletin d'information. *Association*

Publishing Co: APES, 50 Cremazie O, Montreal, PQ H2P 2T2 Canada; Title Tel # (514) 381-7904
General Info: Yr. Est. 1968, Bi-monthly, Web press, 12 pages, 1% ads, 2 Color
Circulation: Total-850

BBI Newsletter, The
See: HOSPITALS & NURSING HOMES

Biotechnology News
See: SCIENCE

Blue Sheet: Health Policy & Biomedical Research, The *Business*

Publishing Co: F-D-C Reports, Inc., 5550 Friendship Blvd, Chevy Chase, MD 20815-7278; Title Tel # (301) 657-9830 Title Fax # (301) 986-6467
Personnel: Publisher-Wallace Werble, Jr., Editor-Cole Werble, Circ. Mgr.-Edward Picken, Mktg. Dir.-Leila Simaika
Editorial Description: Review of government policy in health care and biomedical research.
General Info: (Formerly Drug Research Reports), Yr. Est. 1957, Weekly, Trim Size-8½ x 11, Offset press, 30 pages, ISSN: 0162-3605, Ind/Abs/Online: Mead Data, No Color
Subscriptions: Indv. $390, Can. $390, For. $465, $18/copy

Bulletin

Publishing Co: Ohio Society of Hospital Pharmacists, 53 Haddam Pl W, Westerville, OH 43081-1266; Title Tel # (614) 891-6176
Personnel: Editor, Adv. Dir.-Amy Bennett
Editorial Description: Covers assn. news, events, pharmacy, & continuing education.
General Info: Yr. Est. 1979, Bi-monthly, Trim Size-8½ x 11, Offset press, 8 pages, 2% ads, 2 Color, Newsprint, Saddle-stitched
Subscriptions: Indv. $10
Circulation: Total-700
Printing Co: Spencer Walker Press, 107 W Main St, Newark, OH 43055-5007 Tel # (614) 345-3465

Bulletin of the Bureau of Pharmaceutical Services *Association*

Publishing Co: Univ. of Mississippi Pharmacy School, School of Pharmacy, University, MS 38677; Title Tel # (601) 232-7080
Personnel: Editor-Mickey C. Smith
Editorial Description: Continuing education topics for pharmacists.
General Info: Yr. Est. 1963, Monthly, Trim Size-8½ x 11, Offset press, 4 pages, 2 Color
Circulation: Total-3,000

Cahners Pharmaceuticals Economic Review *Business*

Publishing Co: Cahners Publishing Co., 275 Washington St., Newton, MA 02158-1630 Tel # (617) 964-3030 Fax # (617) 558-4470 Parent Co.-Reed Elsevier, New York; Title Tel # (617) 630-2117 Title Fax # (617) 630-2100
General Info: Yr. Est. 1987, Quarterly
Subscriptions: Indv. $129

Canadian Biotech News *Business*

Publishing Co: Canadian Biotechnology News Svce., 20 Stone Park Lane, Nepean, ON K2H 9P4 Canada; Title Tel # (613) 726-0115 Title Fax # (613) 726-7344
Personnel: Publisher, Editor-Peter Winter, Technology Ed.-Ainsley Allan, Medical Ed.-Hans Giese, Science Ed.-Fred Haynes, News Ed.-Paul Hollis, Health Editor-Alan Ledger
Editorial Description: Analysis of the business activities of biotechnology companies, organizations & government. New product announcements, reports & surveys, personality profiles also included.
General Info: (Formerly New Biotech Business), Yr. Est. 1988, Weekly, 24 pages, Ind/Abs/Online: bioweb, 2% ads, 2 Color, Coated, Saddle-stitched
Subscriptions: Indv. $180, Inst. $400, Can. $180, For. $450, $10/copy
Acquistions: Publication Bought
Circulation: Total-3,000
Advertising: Accepts Inserts.
List Rental: Actives: 10,317, $150/M

Canadian Wholesale Drug Assn., Bulletin

Publishing Co: Canadian Wholesale Drug Assn., 1110 Sherbrooke St. W., #2206, Montreal, PQ H3A 1G8 Canada; Title Tel # (514) 842-8627 Title Fax # (514) 842-3061
Personnel: Editor-Desmond Lartigue
General Info: Quarterly, 16 pages
Acquistions: Publication Bought
Circulation: Total-450

Chi Miera

Publishing Co: Chi Chapter, Phi Delta Chi Frat, School of Pharmacy, Auburn University, Auburn, AL 36849 Tel # (334) 844-4000 Fax # (334) 844-8331

Chimera *Association*

Publishing Co: Chi Chapter, Phi Delta Chi Frat, School of Pharmacy, Auburn University, Auburn, AL 36849 Tel # (334) 844-4000 Fax # (334) 844-8331; Title Tel # (205) 844-4000
Personnel: Editor-William R. Ravis
Editorial Description: Informs national and regional fraternity chapters of Chi's activities.
General Info: Yr. Est. 1959, Semi-annually, Trim Size-8½ x 11, 14 pages, No Color
Circulation: (100% controlled), Total-500

Civil Abolitionist
See: HEALTH

Clin-Alert *Business*

Publishing Co: Information Today, Inc., 143 Old Marlton Pike, Medford, NJ 08055-8758; Title Tel # (609) 654-6266 Title Fax # (609) 654-4309
Personnel: Publisher-Thomas Hogan, Editor-Ramona Scheible-Jacobs, Circ. Mgr.-Joan Gianvito
Editorial Description: Adverse drug reactions, interactions, and related therapeutic hazards, as reported in hundreds of journals.
General Info: Yr. Est. 1962, Semi-monthly, ISSN: 0069-4770
Subscriptions: Indv. $100, For. $110

Clinical Abstracts/Current Therapeutic Findings   *Scholarly*

Publishing Co: Harvey Whitney Books Co., PO Box 42696, Cincinnati, OH 45242-0696; Title Tel # (513) 793-3555 Title Fax # (513) 793-3600
Personnel: Publisher, Editor-Harvey Whitney, Circ. Mgr.-Brenda Bailey, Production Mgr.-Donna Thordsen
Editorial Description: Abstracts of articles on drug therapy, drug action, reactions & interactions.
General Info: (Formerly Clinical Abstracts), Yr. Est. 1982, Monthly, Trim Size-8½ x 11, Sheetfed press, 8 pages, ISSN: 1043-3031, 2 Color, Newsprint, Saddle-stitched
Subscriptions: Indv. $44, Inst. $68, Can. $83, For. $83, $5/copy
Circulation: Total-1,000
Advertising: Accepts Inserts.
List Rental: Rents Lists

Clinical Consult

Publishing Co: American Society of Consultant Pharmacists, 1321 Duke St., 4 Floor, Alexandria, VA 22204-2320 Tel # (703) 739-1300 Fax # (703) 739-1321; Title Tel # (703) 920-8492 Title Fax # (703) 486-2997
Personnel: Publisher-R. Tim Webster, Editor-James Cooper, Production Mgr.-Catherine Burdette
Editorial Description: Editorial focuses on geriatric drug therapy &/or chronic illness & offers guidance to readers on drug therapy monitoring criteria.
General Info: Trim Size-8½ x 11
Circulation: Total-4,400
Printing Co: Corporate Press II, 8900 Lee Hwy, Fairfax, VA 22031-1423 Tel # (703) 641-0900

Clinical Investigator News   *Business*

Publishing Co: CTB International Publishing, Inc., P.O. Box 218, Maplewood, NJ 07040-0218; Title Tel # (201) 379-7749 Title Fax # (201) 379-1158
Personnel: Publisher-Oyukue Brogna, Editor in Chief-Christopher Brogna, Editor-Mark Via, Circ. Mgr.-William Robinson, Mktg. Dir.-Ann Light
Editorial Description: Helps investigators identify new drug study opportunities. Timely and concise reports on companies targeting what compounds for what indications, where they stand in their research, and when they plan to begin trials.
General Info: Yr. Est. 1992, Monthly, Trim Size-8½ x 11, Offset press, 32 pages, ISSN: 1068-1191, Saddle-stitched
Subscriptions: Indv. $548, Inst. $548, Can. $548, For. $578, $69/copy

Clinical Trials Monitor   *Business*

Publishing Co: CTB International Publishing, Inc., P.O. Box 218, Maplewood, NJ 07040-0218 Fax # (201) 379-1158; Title Tel # (201) 379-7749 Title Fax # (202) 379-1158
Personnel: Publisher-Oyukue Brogna, Editor in Chief-Christopher Brogna, Circ. Mgr.-William Robinson, Promotion Dir.-Oykue Brogma
Editorial Description: Monthly monitoring of clinical trials of human pharmaceuticals. Tracks clinical trials of drugs in vivo, imaging agents, and extra corporal therapies from beginning to end.
General Info: (Formerly Clinical Trials), Yr. Est. 1992, Monthly, Trim Size-8½ x 11, Offset press, 78 pages, ISSN: 1061-608X, No Color, Saddle-stitched
Subscriptions: Indv. $1,137, Inst. $1,137, Can. $1,137, For. $1,199, $142/copy

College of Pharmacists of British Columbia, the Bulletin   *Association*

Publishing Co: College of Pharmacists of British Columbia, 1765 W. 8th Ave., #200, Vancouver, BC V6J 1V8 Canada
Personnel: Editor-Sharon Kerr-Eng
General Info: Yr. Est. 1977, 10x/yr.
Subscriptions: Indv. $17, Inst. $10, Can. $10, For. $10
Circulation: Total-3,300

Communicator

Publishing Co: Phi Delta Chi, PO Box 6565, Athens, GA 30604; Title Tel # (706) 613-0100 Title Fax # (706) 613-0200
Editorial Description: Editorials, chapter reports, regional conferences, grand councils, achievement awards and scholarship presentations.
General Info: Yr. Est. 1883, Quarterly, 20 pages, Color

Consumer Reports on Health
See: HEALTH

DATA - The Brown University Digest of Addiction Theory and Application
See: MEDICINE

DCAT Digest   *Business, Association*

Publishing Co: Drug, Chemical and Allied Trades Assn., 2 Roosevelt Ave., Syosset, NY 11791-3012; Title Tel # (516) 496-3317
Editorial Description: Assn. activities, meetings, Washington Digest, regulatory affairs, legislation, etc.
General Info: Yr. Est. 1890, Monthly, Offset press, 4 pages
Circulation: Total-1,500

DES Litigation Reporter
See: LAW

Dia Newsletter   *Association*

Publishing Co: Drug Information Assn., Inc., PO Box 3113, Maple Glen, PA 19002-8113; Title Tel # (215) 628-2288
Personnel: Editor-Thomas Teal
General Info: Quarterly, Trim Size-8½ x 11, Web press, 20 pages, No Color, Coated
Subscriptions: Indv. $40
Circulation: Total-5,000
List Rental: Actives: $50/M

Diagnostics Intelligence   *Business*

Publishing Co: CTB International Publishing, Inc., P.O. Box 218, Maplewood, NJ 07040-0218; Title Tel # (201) 379-7749 Title Fax # (201) 379-1158
Personnel: Publisher-OyKue Brogna, Editor in Chief-Christopher Brogna, Circ. Mgr.-William Robinson, Promotion Mgr.-Ann Light
Editorial Description: Monthly intelligence for the medical diagnostic industry. Designed specifically for and devoted to the in-vitro diagnostic business.
General Info: Yr. Est. 1989, Monthly, Trim Size-8½ x 11, Offset press, 18 pages, ISSN: 1054-9609, No Color
Subscriptions: Indv. $414, Inst. $414, Can. $414, For. $434, $52/copy
List Rental: Rents Lists

Dickinson's FDA Review   *Business, Consumer*

Publishing Co: Ferdic, Inc., PO Box 367, Las Cruces, NM 88004-0367 Tel # (505) 527-8634 Fax # (505) 527-8858
Editorial Description: FDA regulatory information.
General Info: (Formerly Dickinson's FDA; Dickinson's FDA Inspection), Yr. Est. 1984, Monthly
Subscriptions: Indv. $685, Can. $685, For. $745

Dickinson's FDA Update by Fax   *Business*

Publishing Co: Ferdic, Inc., PO Box 367, Las Cruces, NM 88004-0367 Tel # (505) 527-8634; Title Fax # (505) 527-8858
Editorial Description: FDA regulations.
General Info: Yr. Est. 1995, Weekly
Subscriptions: Indv. $395, Inst. $395, Can. $395, For. $395

Dickinson's Pharmacy   *Business*

Publishing Co: Ferdic, Inc., PO Box 367, Las Cruces, NM 88004-0367 Fax # (505) 527-8858; Title Tel # (505) 527-8634
Personnel: Editor-James Dickinson
General Info: Yr. Est. 1986, Monthly
Subscriptions: Indv. $175

Drackett Diamonds
See: HOUSE ORGANS

Drug & Alcohol Abuse Education
See: HEALTH

Drug & Device Recall Bulletin

Publishing Co: RX-Data-Pac Service, PO Box 42020, Cincinnati, OH 45242-0020; Title Tel # (513) 489-0943
Personnel: Editor-I.H. Goodman
Editorial Description: Monthly info about drug & device recalls, Compiled from
General Info: Yr. Est. 1985, Monthly, 4 pages, ISSN: 8456-5935, No Color
Subscriptions: Indv. $50, $5/copy

Drug & Market Development   *Business*

Publishing Co: Drug & Market Development, 2124 Broadway Ste 1200, New York, NY 10023-1722; Title Tel # (212) 873-8140 Title Fax # (212) 580-3975
Personnel: Publisher, Editor-Timothy Tankosic, MD, Circ. Dir.-Mimi Meyer Falcone
Editorial Description: Provides pharmaceutical, biotechnology, and other health care industry professionals with comprehensive analyses of developments in human therapeutics.
General Info: Yr. Est. 1990, Monthly, 20 pages, ISSN: 1053-1564
Subscriptions: Indv. $695, Can. $745, For. $745

Drug Abuse Newsletter

Publishing Co: Committees of Correspondence, Inc., 57 Conant, #113, Danvers, MA 01923-2952; Title Tel # (617) 774-2641
General Info: Yr. Est. 1980, Quarterly
Circulation: Total-1,000

Drug Facts and Comparisons Loose Leaf Edition   *Business*

Publishing Co: Facts & Comparisons, Inc., 111 West Port Plaza, Suite 300, St. Louis, MO 63146-3098; Title Tel # (314) 878-2515 Title Fax # (314) 878-5563
Editorial Description: The definitive source of objecstive drug information groups more than 16,000 drug products, including over 6,000 OTC items, by therapeutic class for ease of camparison. Contains over 600 unique charts and tables not found in any other publication.
General Info: Yr. Est. 1946, Monthly, Looseleaf
Subscriptions: Indv. $220

Drug GMP Report *Business*

Publishing Co: Washington Business Information, Inc., 1117 19th St N Ste 200, Arlington, VA 22209-1708; Title Tel # (703) 247-3425 Title Fax # (703) 247-3421
Personnel: Publisher-David Swit, Editor-Dennis Melamed, Circ. Dir.-Chris Rogers, Production Dir.-Jennea Myrick
Editorial Description: Covers FDA regulation of Good Manufacturing Practices of prescription, and OTC drugs.
General Info: Yr. Est. 1992, Monthly, Trim Size-8½ x 11, Sheetfed press, 8 pages, ISSN: 1061-2335, Ind/Abs/Online: BRS, Data-Star, DIALOG, Diogenes, No Color
Subscriptions: Indv. $457, Inst. $457, Can. $457, For. $492

Drug Interaction Facts Package *Business*

Publishing Co: Facts & Comparisons, Inc., 111 West Port Plaza, Suite 300, St. Louis, MO 63146-3098 Fax # (314) 878-5563; Title Tel # (314) 878-2515 Title Fax # (314) 878-2515
Personnel: Editor-Bernie Olin, Mktg. Dir.-Barb Wright, Mktg. Mgr.-Regina Trull
Editorial Description: This comprehensive reference includes information all drug/food interatctions of clinical significance, as well as interactions which are suspected but unsubstanciatied. Significant rateing codes establish the clinical relevance of the onset, severity and documentation of the interaction.
General Info: Quarterly, Looseleaf
Subscriptions: Indv. $95

Drug Law Report *Business*

Publishing Co: Clark Boardman Callaghan, 375 Hudson St, New York, NY 10014-3685 Fax # (212) 807-6209; Title Tel # (212) 929-7500 Title Fax # (212) 924-0460
Personnel: Publisher-David Doughty, Promotion Dir.-Robert Arkin
Editorial Description: Authoritative articles plus recent cases & developments in drug law. Prepared under the auspices of NORML.
General Info: Yr. Est. 1983, Bi-monthly, Sheetfed press, 12 pages, ISSN: 0734-6166
Subscriptions: Indv. $175, $15/copy
List Rental: Rents Lists
Printing Co: Port City Press, 1323 Greenwood Rd, Pikesville, MD 21208-3611 Tel # (410) 486-3000, Fax # (410) 486-0706

Drug Metabolism Newsletter

Publishing Co: American Society for Pharmacology, 9650 Rockville Pike, Bethesda, MD 20814-3998; Title Tel # (301) 530-7060
General Info: Yr. Est. 1908, Quarterly

Drug Newsletter *Business*

Publishing Co: Facts & Comparisons, Inc., 111 West Port Plaza, Suite 300, St. Louis, MO 63146-3098 Fax # (314) 878-5563; Title Tel # (314) 878-2515 Title Fax # (314) 878-5523
Personnel: Publisher-Sue Sewester, Editor-Bernie Olin, Production Mgr.-Toni Kasparek, Mktg. Dir.-Barbara Wright
Editorial Description: Helping the professional stay abreast of the ever changing world of pharmacy. Includes a review of current topics of interest in drug therapy, drug of choice, and recent reports, actions and reactions, new drugs, drug interactions and over the counter products.
General Info: Yr. Est. 1982, Monthly, Trim Size-8½ x 11, 8 pages, ISSN: 0731-5163
Subscriptions: Indv. $60, $5/copy

Drug Policy Letter *Consumer, Association*

Publishing Co: Drug Policy Foundation, 4455 Connecticut Ave. NW, Ste. B-500, Washington, DC 20008-2328 Tel # (202) 537-5005 Fax # (202) 537-3007
Personnel: Editor in Chief-Arnold Trebach
Editorial Description: Discusses drug policy reform and legalization. Also is a catalog of books and gifts with drug reform themes.
General Info: Bi-monthly, Trim Size-8½ x 11, 16 pages, No Color, Matte
Subscriptions: Indv. $25

Drug Product Liability
See: LAW

Drug Utilization Review

Publishing Co: American Health Consultants, Inc., 3525 Piedmont Rd., Building #6, Ste. 400, Atlanta, GA 30305-0056 Tel # (404) 262-7436 Fax # (404) 284-3291; Title Tel # (404) 351-4523 Title Fax # (404) 352-1971
Personnel: Publisher-Lauren Oden, Editor-Monica Browns, Circ. Mgr.-Laura HAyes, Production Mgr.-Mike Witter, Mktg. Mgr.-Michelle Titus
Editorial Description: Guides hospitals in drug use, evaluation, monitoring & cost containment.
General Info: Yr. Est. 1985, Monthly, 12 pages, ISSN: 0884-8998
Subscriptions: Indv. $177, $14/copy
Circulation: Total-1,125
List Rental: Actives: $145/M

Drugs and Drug Abuse Education

Publishing Co: Editorial Resources, Inc., PO Box 20754, Seattle, WA 98102; Title Tel # (206) 322-8387 Title Fax # (206) 329-4149
Personnel: Publisher, Editor-David Howell, Circ. Mgr.-D. Hancock
Editorial Description: Covers all aspects of the drug scene, including pharmacological effects, psychological and sociological aspects, legislation, enforcement issues, etc.
General Info: Yr. Est. 1969, Monthly, Trim Size-8½ x 11, Offset press, 10 pages, ISSN: 0744-2823
Subscriptions: Indv. $98, Inst. $98, Can. $113, For. $138
Acquistions: Publication Bought

Drugs in the Workplace *Business*

Publishing Co: Research Institute of America, 1340 Braddock Pl., Ste. 400, Alexandria, VA 22314-1651 Tel # (703) 706-8260 Fax # (703) 683-4824; Title Tel # (202) 842-0520 Title Fax # (212) 475-1790
Personnel: Publisher-John Roche, Editor-Rhodes Henderer, Editor-Alison Knopf, Circ. Mgr.-Loretta Netzer, Production Mgr.-Amy Ryan
Editorial Description: Covers business strategies for lawful prevention, detection & treatment of drug abuse in the work force.
General Info: Yr. Est. 1986, Monthly, Sheetfed press, 8 pages
Subscriptions: Indv. $275
List Rental: List Management Co.: Taybi Direct East, Inc., 13321 New Hampshire Ave., Ste. 202, Silver Spring, MD 20904-3450 Tel # (301) 680-3633, Fax # (301) 680-3635
Printing Co: Jim Buckley Offsetting, 1101 Pennsylvania Ave SE, Washington, DC 20003-2229 Tel # (202) 546-0501

Emerging Pharmaceuticals *Business*

Publishing Co: CTB International Publishing, Inc., P.O. Box 218, Maplewood, NJ 07040-0218; Title Tel # (201) 379-7749 Title Fax # (201) 379-1158
Personnel: Publisher-Oykue Brogna, Editor in Chief-Christopher Brogna, Circ. Mgr.-William Robinson, Promotion Dir.-Ann Light
Editorial Description: Covers preclinical drug development, from discovery, through preclinical trials and research on small molecule drugs.
General Info: Yr. Est. 1992, Monthly, Trim Size-8½ x 11, Offset press, 14 pages, ISSN: 1061-6098, No Color
Subscriptions: Indv. $457, Inst. $457, Can. $457, For. $477, $57/copy
List Rental: Rents Lists

Environmental Compliance Litigation & Strategy
See: LAW

Europe Drug & Device Report *Business*

Publishing Co: Washington Business Information, Inc., 1117 19th St N Ste 200, Arlington, VA 22209-1708; Title Tel # (703) 247-3425 Title Fax # (703) 247-3421
Personnel: Publisher-David Swit, Editor-Sara Lewis, Circ. Dir.-Chris Rogers, Production Dir.-Jennea Myrick, Mktg. Dir.-Deb Plaskow
Editorial Description: Covers the drug and medical device regulation in Europe.
General Info: Yr. Est. 1991, Bi-weekly, Trim Size-8½ x 11, Sheetfed press, 8 pages, ISSN: 1056-179X, Ind/Abs/Online: BRS, Data-Star, DIALOG, Diogenes, No Color, Recycled
Subscriptions: Indv. $797, Inst. $797, Can. $797, For. $862

F-D-C Report -- 'The Tan Sheet'

Publishing Co: F-D-C Reports, Inc., 5550 Friendship Blvd, Chevy Chase, MD 20815-7278; Title Tel # (301) 657-9830 Title Fax # (301) 986-6467
Personnel: Publisher-Wallace Werble, Jr., Editor-Cole Palmer Werble, Circ. Mgr.-Edward Picken, Adv. Dir.-Richard Messmer, Mktg. Dir.-Leila Simaika
Editorial Description: Reports to Industry on Non-Prescription Pharmaceuticals and Nutritionals.
General Info: Yr. Est. 1993, Weekly, ISSN: 1068-5316
Subscriptions: Indv. $650, For. $725, $18/copy

FDA Advertising and Promotion Manual
See: LAW

FDA Enforcement Manual
See: LAW

FDA Outline
See: GOVERNMENT

The Father, The Son

Publishing Co: The Father, The Son, P.O. Box 561, Milwaukee, WI 53007
Editorial Description: A strange grab bag with ideas about religion mixed with drug nostalgia.
General Info: Trim Size-8.5 x 11, 16 pages
Subscriptions: Indv. $2

Fax-Stat on Drugs *Business*

Publishing Co: Facts & Comparisons, Inc., 111 West Port Plaza, Suite 300, St. Louis, MO 63146-3098; Title Tel # (314) 878-2515 Title Fax # (314) 878-5563
Personnel: Publisher-Sue Sewester, Mktg. Dir.-Barbara Wright
Editorial Description: Weekly faxed transmissions of the latest drug news. Including, new drugs, dosage forms, indications, approvables and recalls. Also includes news scans from journals and newspapers.
General Info: Yr. Est. 1992, Weekly, ISSN: 1064-5055
Subscriptions: Indv. $95

Food & Drink Daily
See: FOOD

Food & Drug Letter, The   *Business*

Publishing Co: Washington Business Information, Inc., 1117 19th St N Ste 200, Arlington, VA 22209-1708; Title Tel # (703) 247-3424 Title Fax # (703) 247-3421
Personnel: Publisher-David Swit, Editor-Mike Dolan, Circ. Mgr.-Chris Rogers, Production Mgr.-Jennea Myrick, Mktg. Dir.-Deb Plaskow
Editorial Description: Interprets key issues in Federal control of drugs and cosmetics.
General Info: Yr. Est. 1976, Bi-weekly, Trim Size-8½ x 11, Sheetfed press, 8 pages, ISSN: 0362-6466, Ind/Abs/Online: BRS, Data-Star, DIALOG, Diogenes, No Color, Newsprint
Subscriptions: Indv. $945, Inst. $945, Can. $945, For. $1,011
Acquistions: Publication Bought
List Rental: Actives: $110/M

Food Drug Cosmetic Law
Reports   *Business, Association*

Publishing Co: CCH, Inc., 2700 Lake Cook Rd., Riverwoods, IL 60015 Parent Co.-Kluwer Law & Taxation Publishers, Cambridge; Title Tel # (847) 267-7000 Title Fax # (800) 224-8299
Editorial Description: Covers regulation of adulteration, packaging & labeling of foods, drugs & cosmetics, including food additives, color additives, & animal drugs. Includes full text of laws, regulations, court decisions.
General Info: Yr. Est. 1938, Weekly, ISSN: 0162-1122, Looseleaf
Subscriptions: Indv. $2,250

Forensic Drug Abuse
Advisor   *Business, Consumer*

Publishing Co: Forensic Drug Abuse Advisor, PO Box 5139, Berkeley, CA 94705-0139; Title Tel # (510) 849-0923 Title Fax # (510) 849-0958
Editorial Description: Medical research on drug abuse.
General Info: Yr. Est. 1989, Monthly, ISSN: 1048-8731
Subscriptions: Indv. $187, Inst. $187, Can. $187, For. $197, $20/copy
Circulation: Total-1,100

GMP Letter, The
See: HEALTH

Gene Therapy Newsletter
See: GENETICS

Generic Line   *Business*

Publishing Co: Scitec Services, Inc., 5324 Sinclair Rd, Columbus, OH 43229-5002; Title Tel # (614) 433-0648 Title Fax # (614) 433-0432
Personnel: Publisher-Frank McKim, Editor-Ronald M. Schwartz, Assoc. Ed.-David Carlson, Asst. Ed.-Brenda Baily, Circ. Mgr.-Nancy Hahn
Editorial Description: Generic line provides coverage of the generic drug industry.
General Info: (Formerly Health Commerce Line), Yr. Est. 1984, Bi-monthly, Trim Size-8½ x 11, Desktop press, 16 pages, ISSN: 1076-884X, Matte
Subscriptions: Indv. $295, Can. $305, For. $345
Acquistions: Publication Bought

Genetic Technology News
See: GENETICS

Gold Sheet: Quality Control
Reports   *Business*

Publishing Co: F-D-C Reports, Inc., 5550 Friendship Blvd, Chevy Chase, MD 20815-7278; Title Tel # (301) 657-9830 Title Fax # (301) 986-6467
Personnel: Publisher-Wallace Werble, Jr., Editor-Cole Palmer Werble, Circ. Mgr.-Edward Picken
Editorial Description: Reviews government guidelines for good manufacturing practices, especially as they refer to the medical and pharmaceutical industries.
General Info: Yr. Est. 1967, Monthly, Trim Size-11 x 17, Offset press, 4 pages, ISSN: 0163-2418, Ind/Abs/Online: Newsnet, No Color
Subscriptions: Indv. $250, For. $260, $25/copy

Green Sheet: Weekly
Pharmacy Reports   *Business*

Publishing Co: F-D-C Reports, Inc., 5550 Friendship Blvd, Chevy Chase, MD 20815-7278; Title Tel # (301) 657-9830 Title Fax # (301) 986-6467
Personnel: Publisher-Wallace Werble, Editor-Cole Palmer Werble, Circ. Mgr.-Edward Picken, Mktg. Dir.-Leila Simaika
Editorial Description: New pharmaceuticals, govt. regulatory activity, legislation, etc. For Retail & Wholesale pharmacy.
General Info: Yr. Est. 1951, Weekly, Trim Size-8½ x 11, Letrpr. press, 4 pages, ISSN: 0043-1893, Ind/Abs/Online: PNI, Mead Data, No Color
Subscriptions: Indv. $60, Can. $60, For. $70

Guide to Good Clinical Practice
See: MANAGEMENT

HCPA Pharmacist   *Association*

Publishing Co: Hamilton County Pharmaceutical Association, PO Box 19923, Cincinnati, OH 45219-0923; Title Tel # (513) 961-8665
Personnel: Editor-Doug Moehring
Editorial Description: For practicing pharmacists retail, hospital & commercial.
General Info: Yr. Est. 1960, Monthly, Offset press, 12 pages, 5% ads, No Color
Circulation: (100% controlled), Total-460

Health Victory Bulletin
See: HEALTH

HealthLetter   *Consumer*

Publishing Co: AARP Pharmacy Service, PO Box 883, Libertyville, IL 60048-0883
Editorial Description: Health information for customers.
General Info: Bi-monthly

Histamine Club Bulletin   *Association*

Publishing Co: Cornell Univ. Medical College, 1300 York Ave # 61, New York, NY 10021-4805 Tel # (212) 472-5300; Title Tel # (212) 472-5971
Editorial Description: Includes directory.
General Info: Annually

Hospital Pharmacy
Director's Monthly
Management Series

Publishing Co: RX-Data-Pac Service, PO Box 42020, Cincinnati, OH 45242-0020; Title Tel # (513) 489-0943
Personnel: Editor-I.H. Goodman
Editorial Description: Confidential, practical monthly guide to successful hospital pharmacy management. Concise, fast-reading, provides ideas & strategies. Daily guide to easier, more effective, satisfying managing. Improves decision making, curbs absenteeism, etc.
General Info: Yr. Est. 1979, Monthly, 4 pages, ISSN: 0739-957X, No Color
Subscriptions: Indv. $50, $5/copy

ImmunoFacts   *Business*

Publishing Co: Facts & Comparisons, Inc., 111 West Port Plaza, Suite 300, St. Louis, MO 63146-3098 Tel # (314) 878-2515; Title Tel # (314) 878-5563
Editorial Description: The first comprehensive updatable reference on vaccines and immunologic drugs. Designed for the professionals who prescribe, administer and dispense vaccines. Over 100 detailed monographs cover vaccines, toxoids, immune globulins, immunologic mediators and hypersensitivity agents. Contains both adult and pediatrics dosages. Semi-annual newsletter included.
General Info: Semi-annually
Subscriptions: Indv. $89

Infection Control Weekly   *Business, Association*

Publishing Co: C.W. Henderson Publisher, Medical Center II, P.O. Box 5528, Atlanta, GA 31107-0528 Tel # (404) 507-7777 Fax # (404) 507-7788; Title Tel # (404) 377-8895 Title Fax # (404) 378-5411
Personnel: Publisher-C.W. Henderson, Editor-WM. Edgar Boggan, Bk. Rev. Ed.-Alan D. Henderson, Calendar Ed.-Ken Kimsey
Editorial Description: Conrol of infection in hospital setting; drug resistant strains. Coverag of journals and periodicals worldwide, news, meetings and conferences.
General Info: Yr. Est. 1994, Weekly, ISSN: 1074-2905
Subscriptions: Indv. $995, Can. $995, For. $1,195

InfoPack   *Consumer*

Publishing Co: Community Prescription Service, 349 W. 12th St., P.O. Box 1937, New York, NY 10014 Fax # (212) 229-9102; Title Tel # (212) 229-9102 Title Fax # (212) 229-9108
Personnel: Publisher-Stephen Gendin, Editor-Adam Turner
Editorial Description: Pharmaceutical treatment information from this mail order pharmaceutical service for people with AIDS/HIV.
General Info: Yr. Est. 1991, Quarterly, Trim Size-8½ x 11, 20 pages, ISSN: 1085-3014, 2 Color, Matte, Saddle-stitched
Subscriptions: Free
Circulation: Total-25,000
Advertising: Accepts Inserts.
List Rental: List Management Co.: Strubco Media Group, Inc., Old Chelsea Station, P.O. Box 1274, New York, NY 10113-0920 Tel # (212) 242-1900, Fax # (212) 242-1963, Actives: $125/M

Instant Up-Date

Publishing Co: RX-Data-Pac Service, PO Box 42020, Cincinnati, OH 45242-0020; Title Tel # (513) 489-0943
Personnel: Editor-I.H. Goodman
Editorial Description: Concise, monthly newsletter keeps hospital pharmacy staff informed at-a-glance. Staff quizzes with repro rights. Assists in documenting JCAHO educational program compliance. New products, product changes, recalls, FDA, Washington neews. Fast reading easy to retain information.
General Info: Yr. Est. 1978, Monthly, Trim Size-8½ x 11, 4 pages, ISSN: 0739-9561
Subscriptions: Indv. $70, $6/copy

Intelli-Scope   *Consumer*

Publishing Co: Smart Products, Inc., 870 Market St Ste 1262, San Francisco, CA 94102-2907
Editorial Description: Information on vitamins and 'Smart drugs'.
General Info: Monthly, Trim Size-8½ x 11, 8 pages, 2 Color, Matte

InterPharmacy Forum   *Business*

Publishing Co: Facts & Comparisons, Inc., 111 West Port Plaza, Suite 300, St. Louis, MO 63146-3098; Title Tel # (314) 878-2515 Title Fax # (314) 878-5563
Personnel: Publisher-Sue Sewester, Editor-Bernie Olin, Production Mgr.-Michele Ryan, Mktg. Dir.-Barbara Wright
Editorial Description: An easy to read newsletter of questions and answers on pharmacy related issues. Covers a wide range of timely, practical topics for practicing healthcare professionals.
General Info: Yr. Est. 1993, Monthly, Trim Size-8½ x 11, 4 pages, ISSN: 1065-9412
Subscriptions: Indv. $40

International Medical Device Regulatory Monitor
Business

Publishing Co: Newsletter Services, Inc., 9700 Philadelphia Ct., Lanham, MD 20706-4405; Title Tel # (301) 731-5202 Title Fax # (301) 731-5203
Personnel: Publisher-Lisa A. Anthony, Editor-Joanne Eglovitch, Circ. Mgr.-Priscilla Arenas, Mktg. Mgr.-Susan Pangman, Promotion Dir.-Dennis Cunningham
Editorial Description: Provides official, English-language texts of regulations regarding approval and marketing of medical devices. Covers international standardization efforts, as well as regulations from individual countries.
General Info: (Formerly International Drug & Device Regulatory Monitor), Yr. Est. 1974, Monthly, Trim Size-8½ x 11, Web press, 30 pages, ISSN: 0888-6393, 2 Color
Subscriptions: Indv. $495, Can. $495, For. $537
Acquistions: Publication Bought, Publication Sold
List Rental: List Management Co.: Manager: Joanne Eglovitch; Taybi Direct East, Inc., 13321 New Hampshire Ave., Ste. 202, Silver Spring, MD 20904-3450 Tel # (301) 680-3633, Fax # (301) 680-3635, Actives: $150/M, Expires: $75/M
Printing Co: Newsletter Services, Inc., 9700 Philadelphia Court, Lanham, MD 20706 Tel # (301) 731-5200, Fax # (301) 731-5201

International Pharmaceutical Regulatory Monitor
Business

Publishing Co: Newsletter Services, Inc., 9700 Philadelphia Ct., Lanham, MD 20706-4405; Title Tel # (301) 731-5202 Title Fax # (301) 731-5203
Personnel: Publisher-Lisa A. Anthony, Publisher-Joanne Egbvitch, Exec. VP/Group Publisher-Jerry Boin, Exec. VP/Group Publisher-Michael Nagan, Circ. Mgr.-Priscilla Arenas, Mktg. Dir.-Susan Pangman, Mktg. Mgr.-Ruth P. Davis
Editorial Description: Provides official, English-language texts of regulations regarding approval and marketing of drugs. Covers international standardization efforts, as well as regulations from individual countries.
General Info: (Formerly International Drug & Device Regulatory Monitor), Yr. Est. 1974, Monthly, ISSN: 0888-6393
Subscriptions: Indv. $495, Can. $495, For. $549
List Rental: List Management Co.: Taybi Direct East, Inc., 13321 New Hampshire Ave., Ste. 202, Silver Spring, MD 20904-3450 Tel # (301) 680-3633, Fax # (301) 680-3635

Japan Medical Review
See: MEDICINE

Language Matters
See: LITERATURE & LINGUISTICS

Lawrence Review of Natural Products
Business

Publishing Co: Facts & Comparisons, Inc., 111 West Port Plaza, Suite 300, St. Louis, MO 63146-3098; Title Tel # (314) 878-2515 Title Fax # (314) 878-5563
Personnel: Publisher-Sue Sewester, Editor-Bernie Olin, Production Mgr.-Michele Ryan, Mktg. Dir.-Barbara Wright
Editorial Description: Monthly monographs provide detailed information on natural products including their biology, history, chemistry, pharmacology, medical uses, abuses and toxicology.
General Info: Yr. Est. 1980, Monthly, Trim Size-8½ x 11, Offset press, 2 pages, ISSN: 0734-4961, Looseleaf
Subscriptions: Indv. $60, For. $63, $5/copy

Legal-eyes
Association

Publishing Co: Legalize? SIG, PO Box 3240, Charlottesville, VA 22903-0240; Title Tel # (804) 296-9692
Personnel: Editor-Ellis Godard
Editorial Description: Articles relating to the debate of drug legalization, especially of marijuana.
General Info: Yr. Est. 1989, Bi-monthly, Desktop press, 18 pages
Subscriptions: Indv. $15, Free With Membership
Advertising: $20. Accepts Inserts.

Life Sciences & Biotechnology Update
See: BIOLOGY

LifelineLetter
See: NUTRITION

Managed Pharmaceutical Report
Business

Publishing Co: Capitol Publications, Inc., 1101 King St., Ste. 444, Alexandria, VA 22314-2968; Title Tel # (703) 683-4100 Title Fax # (703) 739-6501
Personnel: Publisher-Cynthia Carter, Editor-Jim Gutman, Circ. Mgr.-Peggy Dwyer, Production Mgr.-Billy Adams, Art Dir.-Linda McDonald, Mktg. Dir.-Mary Lou Probka, Promotion Dir.-Kelly Baptiste
Editorial Description: This independent briefing service on managed pharmaceuticals helps subscribers identify new business opportunities and keep costs down.
General Info: Yr. Est. 1994, Monthly, Trim Size-8½ x 11, 12 pages
Subscriptions: Indv. $287, Inst. $287
List Rental: Actives: $150/M
Printing Co: Capitol Publications, Inc., 1101 King St., Ste. 444, Alexandria, VA 22314-2968 Tel # (703) 683-4100, Fax # (703) 739-6501

Manitoba Pharmaceutical Assn., News Bulletin

Publishing Co: Manitoba Pharmaceutical Assn., 187 St Mary's Rd., Winnipeg, MB R2H 1J2 Canada
Personnel: Editor-S. Wilcox
General Info: Bi-monthly, 4 pages
Circulation: Total-1,000

Massachusetts College of Pharmacy, Bulletin

Publishing Co: Massachusetts College of Pharmacy, 179 Longwood Ave, Boston, MA 02115-5896; Title Tel # (617) 732-2800
General Info: Yr. Est. 1966, 4x/yr., ISSN: 0025-4789
Circulation: Total-8,000

Mealey's Litigation Report: Drugs & Medical Devices
See: LAW

Medical Bulletin
Consumer, Scholarly

Publishing Co: Sponsor-Department of Health and Human Services, U.S. Food & Drug Administration, 5600 Fishers Ln., Rm. 15A-07, Rockville, MD 20852; Title Tel # (301) 443-5470
Personnel: Editor-T. Arrowsmith-Long
Editorial Description: Technical information about drugs, biologics, foods, radiological & medical devices.
General Info: (Formerly FDA Drug Bulletin), Yr. Est. 1970, Offset press, 8 pages, Ind/Abs/Online: BRS, DIALOG, No Color
Subscriptions: Free
Circulation: (100% controlled), Total-100,000

Medical Devices Reporter
Association, Business

Publishing Co: CCH, Inc., 2700 Lake Cook Rd., Riverwoods, IL 60015 Parent Co.-Kluwer Law & Taxation Publishers, Cambridge; Title Tel # (847) 267-7000 Title Fax # (800) 224-8299
Editorial Description: Reports the Food & Drug Administration's rules controlling the manufacture & marketing of medical & dental devices-classification, standards, inspection, etc. Includes full text regulations & court decisions.
General Info: Yr. Est. 1976, Monthly, Trim Size-6 x 9, Web press, 40 pages, No Color, Looseleaf
Subscriptions: Indv. $671

Medical Letter on Drugs and Therapeutics
Business, Scholarly

Publishing Co: Medical Letter, Inc., 1000 Main St, New Rochelle, NY 10801-7500; Title Tel # (914) 235-0500
Personnel: Editor-M. Abramowicz
Editorial Description: Appraisals for physicians, etc. of drugs in terms of their effectiveness, toxicity and side effects.
General Info: Yr. Est. 1959, Bi-weekly, Trim Size-8½ x 11, Offset press, 4 pages, Ind/Abs/Online: Medline, BRS, DIALOG, No Color, Matte
Subscriptions: Indv. $43, $1/copy
Circulation: Total-160,000
List Rental: Rents Lists

Medical Materials Update
See: MEDICINE

Mercy Hospital Pharmacy Newsletter
Association

Publishing Co: Mercy Hospital, 1000 N. Village Ave., Rockville, NY 11570; Title Tel # (516) 255-2407 Title Fax # (516) 678-8666
Personnel: Editor-Zachary Hannon
General Info: (Formerly Drug Information Network), Monthly
Subscriptions: Indv. $5

Misuse of Medications
See: SENIOR CITIZENS

NABP Newsletter
Association

Publishing Co: Natl. Assn. of Boards of Pharmacy, 700 Busse Hwy, Park Ridge, IL 60068-2402; Title Tel # (708) 698-6227
Editorial Description: Legislative, regulatory & licensure affairs of state pharmacy boards. Association activities, pharmacy professional affairs.
General Info: (Formerly NABP Bulletin, NABP Quarterly), Yr. Est. 1904, Monthly, Trim Size-8½ x 11, Offset press, 8 pages, 2 Color
Subscriptions: Indv. $25
Circulation: Total-1,100
List Rental: Actives: $55/M

NACDS Executive Newsletter
Business, Association

Publishing Co: Natl. Assn. of Chain Drug Stores, Box 1417-D49, Alexandria, VA 22313 Fax # (703) 836-4869; Title Tel # (703) 549-3001
Personnel: Editor-John Covert, Production Mgr.-Kathleen Collins
Editorial Description: Association activities, government and executive changes within the industry.
General Info: (Formerly NACDS Legislative Newsletter), Bi-weekly, 4 pages
Subscriptions: Indv. $100
Circulation: Total-2,500

NAPM News Bulletin
Business, Association

Publishing Co: Natl. Assn. of Pharmaceutical Manufacturers, 320 Old Country Road, Suite #205, Garden City, NY 11530-1743 Tel # (516) 741-3699 Fax # (516) 741-3696; Title Tel # (212) 838-3720
Personnel: Editor-Robert Milanese
General Info: Monthly, 8 pages
Subscriptions: Indv. $100
Circulation: (100% controlled), Total-1,300

NFP News

Publishing Co: Natl. Fed. of Parents for Drug Free Youth, 11159b S Towne Sq, Saint Louis, MO 63123-7814; Title Tel # (314) 845-1933
General Info: Yr. Est. 1980, Quarterly, 2 pages
Circulation: Total-5,000

NWDA Executive
Newsletter *Business, Association*

Publishing Co: Natl. Wholesale Druggists' Assn., 1821 Michael Faraday Dr., Ste. 400, Reston, VA 22090-5348; Title Tel # (703) 787-0000
Personnel: Editor-Lauren Asplen
Editorial Description: News and announcements on association programs and services, the membership and the industry.
General Info: Bi-weekly, Offset press, 4 pages, 2 Color
Circulation: Total-2,500

Narcotics Law Bulletin
See: LAW

National Association of
Boards of Pharmacy
Survey of Pharmacy Law *Business*

Publishing Co: Natl. Assn. of Boards of Pharmacy, 700 Busse Hwy, Park Ridge, IL 60068-2402; Title Tel # (708) 698-6227
Personnel: Editor-Carmen Catizone
Editorial Description: State pharmacy law, licensing laws, etc.
General Info: Yr. Est. 1953, Annually, Trim Size-$8\frac{1}{2}$ x 11, Offset press, 25 pages, 2 Color
Subscriptions: Indv. $25, $20/copy
Circulation: Total-1,000

National Association of
Pharmaceutical
Manufacturers News
Bulletin *Association*

Publishing Co: Natl. Assn. of Pharmaceutical Manufacturers, 320 Old Country Road, Suite #205, Garden City, NY 11530-1743 Tel # (516) 741-3699 Fax # (516) 741-3696; Title Tel # (212) 838-3720 Title Fax # (212) 753-6832
Personnel: Editor-Robert Milanese
Editorial Description: Information, regulatory, legal, technical.
General Info: Yr. Est. 1955, Monthly, Trim Size-$8\frac{1}{2}$ x 11, Offset press, 8 pages, No Color, Newsprint
Circulation: (100% controlled), Total-1,300
Printing Co: Walton Press, 2555 Boston Rd, Bronx, NY 10467-9099 Tel # (212) 547-4300

National Consumers League Bulletin
See: CONSUMER INTERESTS

National Report on
Substance Abuse *Business, Consumer*

Publishing Co: LRP Publications, 747 Dresher Rd., P.O. Box 980, Horsham, PA 19044-0980 Tel # (215) 784-0910 Fax # (215) 784-0317
Personnel: Publisher-Ken Kahn, Editor-Marilyn Schaefer, Production Mgr.-Kathleen Neely, Mktg. Dir.-Jana Shellington
Editorial Description: Review of federal, state, and local laws and regulations involving alchohol and drug abuse.
General Info: Yr. Est. 1986, Bi-weekly, Trim Size-$8\frac{1}{2}$ x 11, Sheetfed press, 8 pages, ISSN: 0891-5709, Ind/Abs/Online: HRIN, 2 Color, Newsprint
Subscriptions: Indv. $377, For. $399, $16/copy
Acquistions: Publication Bought, Publication Sold

New Developments in Medicine & Drug Therapy
See: MEDICINE

New Epidemiology Monitor, The
See: HEALTH

New Hampshire Pharmacy
News *Association*

Publishing Co: New Hampshire Pharmacy Assn., 2 Eagle Sq. 3400, Concord, NH 03001 Tel # (603) 229-0292
Editorial Description: Association news, events, and information.

Nurses' Drug Alert *Business*

Publishing Co: M.J. Powers, 374 Millburn Ave, Millburn, NJ 07041-1361 Fax # (201) 912-8883; Title Tel # (201) 467-4556
Personnel: Publisher-Michael Powers, Editor-Sally Wicklund
General Info: Yr. Est. 1976, Monthly
Subscriptions: Indv. $24, Can. $30

Ontario Pharmacist *Association*

Publishing Co: Ontario Pharmacist, 23 Les Mill Rd., Ste. 301, Don Mill, ON M3B 3P6 Canada; Title Tel # (416) 441-0788
Personnel: Editor-R. Franceschini
General Info: (Formerly O.R.D.A. Bulletin), Yr. Est. 1962, Monthly
Circulation: Total-1,700

Oregon Pharmacist *Association*

Publishing Co: Oregon State Pharmacists Assn., 1460 State St, Salem, OR 97301-4247; Title Tel # (503) 585-4887 Title Fax # (503) 378-9067
Personnel: Editor-Chuck Gress
General Info: Monthly, 28 pages, 2% ads
Subscriptions: Indv. $40, Free
Circulation: Total-1,300
Advertising: Inquire for rates.

Orphan Disease Update

Publishing Co: Orphan Disease Update, PO Box 8923, New Fairfield, CT 06812-8923; Title Tel # (203) 746-6518
Personnel: Editor-Abbey Meyers
General Info: Yr. Est. 1983, Trim Size-$8\frac{1}{2}$ x 11, Desktop press, 12 pages, Ind/Abs/Online: CompuServe, No Color, Coated
Circulation: (100% controlled), Total-17,000
Printing Co: EMG Printing, 43 Beaver Brook Rd, Danbury, CT 06810-6210 Tel # (203) 744-2071

PDA Letter *Association* CPM: $158

Publishing Co: Parenteral Drug Association, Inc., 7500 Old Georgetown Rd., Suite 620, Bethesda, MD 20814 Tel # (310) 986-0293 Fax # (310) 986-0296; Title Tel # (301) 986-0293
Personnel: VP & Exec. Ed.-E.M. Fry, Mktg. Mgr.-Margaret Wanca
Editorial Description: Newsletter covering association activities.
General Info: Yr. Est. 1964, Monthly, Trim Size-$8\frac{1}{2}$ x 11, Sheetfed press, 8 pages, 2 Color, Matte
Subscriptions: Free With Membership
Circulation: (100% controlled), Total-4,700
Advertising: $745.

Patient Drug Facts Package *Business, Consumer*

Publishing Co: Facts & Comparisons, Inc., 111 West Port Plaza, Suite 300, St. Louis, MO 63146-3098; Title Tel # (314) 878-2515 Title Fax # (314) 878-5563
Personnel: Editor in Chief-Bernie Olin, Mktg. Dir.-Barbara Wright, Mktg. Mgr.-Regina Trull
Editorial Description: Contains drug monographs that are written in 'patient-friendly' language and are designed to be copied for use as patient handouts. Contains more than 450 monographs on the most commonly prescribed drugs. Includes book and 3 quarterly updates.
General Info: Yr. Est. 1989, Quarterly, Looseleaf
Subscriptions: Indv. $75

Pharma Japan *Business*

Publishing Co: F-D-C Reports, Inc., 5550 Friendship Blvd, Chevy Chase, MD 20815-7278; Title Tel # (301) 657-9830 Title Fax # (301) 986-6467
Editorial Description: News report on the Japanese pharmaceutical industry.
General Info: Weekly

Pharmaceutical Litigation Reporter
See: LAW

Pharmaceutical
Manufacturers Assn. of
Canada Newsletter *Business, Association*

Publishing Co: Pharmaceutical Manufacturers Assn. of Canada, 1111 Prince of Wales Dr., #302, Ottawa, ON K2C 3T2 Canada Tel # (613) 727-1380 Fax # (613) 727-1407
Personnel: Publications Director-Rob Andrews
General Info: Monthly
Subscriptions: Free With Membership
Circulation: Total-10,000

Pharmaceutical
Manufacturers
Association, Trademark
Bulletin

Publishing Co: Pharmaceutical Manufacturers Assn., 1100 15th St NW Ste 900, Washington, DC 20005-1707; Title Tel # (202) 296-2440
General Info: Weekly

Pharmaceutical
Manufacturers
Association. Yearbook

Publishing Co: Pharmaceutical Manufacturers Assn., 1100 15th St NW Ste 900, Washington, DC 20005-1707; Title Tel # (212) 296-2440
General Info: Yr. Est. 1959, Annually

Pharmaceutical Outcomes
News

Publishing Co: Zitter Group, The, 90 New Montgomery St., Suite #820, San Francisco, CA 94105; Title Tel # (415) 495-2450 Title Fax # (415) 495-2453
Personnel: Publisher-Mark Zitter, Publications Director-Susan Keller, Mag. Ed.-Karl Thiel
Editorial Description: Outcomes-related information related to pharmaceutical prouducts.
General Info: Yr. Est. 1992, Monthly

Pharmaceutical Production Tech Source
Business

Publishing Co: Medical Manufacturing Tech Source, 40 N Huron St, Ypsilanti, MI 48197-2608; Title Tel # (313) 487-5989
Editorial Description: For supplier managers to drug and pharmaceutical manufacturers.
General Info: Monthly
Subscriptions: Indv. $100
List Rental: Actives: 17,905, $80/M

Pharmaceutical Ventures
Business

Publishing Co: Scitec Services, Inc., 5324 Sinclair Rd, Columbus, OH 43229-5002; Title Tel # (614) 433-0648 Title Fax # (614) 433-0432
Personnel: Publisher-Frank McKim, Editor-David Carlson, Assoc. Ed.-Brenda Bailey, Circ. Mgr.-Nancy Hahn
Editorial Description: Provides insight and information on small-growth firms and development-phase companies in pharmaceutical industry.
General Info: Yr. Est. 1991, Weekly, Trim Size-8½ x 11, Desktop press, 12 pages, ISSN 1076-9382
Subscriptions: Indv. $360, Can. $380, For. $410

Pharmacy & Therapeutics Forum

Publishing Co: Univ. of California At San Francisco, Box 0622, 3rd Ave. & Parnassus, San Francisco, CA 94143-0001; Title Tel # (415) 476-4240
Personnel: Editor-Linda Hart, Production Mgr.-Susan Heath
Editorial Description: Contains articles on drug information and rational drug therapy as well as changes in the hospital formulary.
General Info: Yr. Est. 1981, Bi-monthly, Trim Size-8½ x 11, Offset press, 4 pages, 2 Color
Circulation: Total-5,000
Printing Co: V.I.P. Litho, 1 Newhall St, San Francisco, CA 94124-1420 Tel # (415) 695-8888

Pharmacy Cost Control News
Business

Publishing Co: Aspen Publishers, Inc., 200 Orchard Ridge Dr., Ste 200, Gaithersburg, MD 20878-5440 Fax # (301) 417-7655 Parent Co.-Wolters Kluwer US Corporation, New York; Title Tel # (301) 417-7500 Title Fax # (301) 417-7550
Personnel: Editor-Curtis Johnson, Editor-Stephen Zimmerman, Mktg. Dir.-Trudi Graham
Editorial Description: Reports on current, effective, program-proven methods to maintain a cost-efficient pharmacy.
General Info: Yr. Est. 1995, Monthly, 8 pages, ISSN: 1081-2407
Subscriptions: Indv. $189, For. $227, $20/copy

Pharmacy Health-Line

Publishing Co: RX-Data-Pac Service, PO Box 42020, Cincinnati, OH 45242-0020; Title Tel # (513) 489-0943
Personnel: Editor-I.H. Goodman
Editorial Description: Personalized, professional pharmacy hospital-employee & patient monthly wellness-bulletin. Improves pharmacist's image, expands clinical activities. Low cost, effective, public relations aid. New drugs, news briefs,
General Info: Yr. Est. 1982, Monthly, 2 pages, No Color
Subscriptions: Indv. $50, $5/copy

Pharmacy Law Digest
Business

Publishing Co: Facts & Comparisons, Inc., 111 West Port Plaza, Suite 300, St. Louis, MO 63146-3098; Title Tel # (314) 878-2515 Title Fax # (314) 878-5563
Personnel: Editor in Chief-Bernie Olin, Mktg. Dir.-Barbara Wright
Editorial Description: A compilation of up-to-date legal information, addresses federal laws regulating controlled substances, constitutional consideration indealing with governmental inspections, drug control law civil liability, business law, and criminal cases involving practice of pharmacy. Includes book and one update.
General Info: Yr. Est. 1965, Semi-annually, Web press, 250 pages, No Color, Newsprint, Looseleaf
Subscriptions: Indv. $75
Printing Co: Corley, 3777 S Rider Trl, Earth City, MO 63045-1114 Tel # (314) 739-3777

Pharmacy News
Association   **CPM:** $36

Publishing Co: National Psoriasis Foundation/USA, 6600 SW 92nd Ave. #300, Portland, OR 97223-7195; Title Tel # (503) 244-7404 Title Fax # (503) 245-0626
Personnel: Editor-Sheri Decker, Adv. Dir.-Susan Terry, Art Dir.-Robyn Baumbach
Editorial Description: Provides consumer information for people who have psoriasis.
General Info: Yr. Est. 1989, 3x/yr., Trim Size-8½ x 11, Web press, 24 pages, 2 Color, Matte, Saddle-stitched
Subscriptions: Free With Membership
Circulation: Total-50,000, Readership-50,000
Advertising: $1,800.
Printing Co: Times-Litho, 1829 Pacific Ave., PO Box 7, Forest Grove, OR 97116-2333 Tel # (503) 359-0300, Fax # (503) 357-3754

Pharmacy News and Review
Association, Business

Publishing Co: Pennsylvania Pharmacists Assn, 508 N 3rd St, Harrisburg, PA 17101-1112; Title Tel # (717) 234-6151 Title Fax # (717) 236-1618
Editorial Description: Professional and business aspects of publishing.
General Info: Monthly
Subscriptions: Indv. $75, Inst. $75, $3/copy
Circulation: Total-2,900

Pharmacy Student
Consumer

Publishing Co: Student American Pharmaceutical Assn., 2215 Constitution Ave NW, Washington, DC 20037-2975; Title Tel # (202) 628-4410
Personnel: Editor-Vicki Meade
Editorial Description: Practical information to help pharmacy students grow professionally is the love of this quarterly publication of the Academy of Students of Pharmacy (ASP).
General Info: Yr. Est. 1978, Quarterly, ISSN: 0279-5272
Subscriptions: Indv. $25
Circulation: Total-12,000
List Rental: Rents Lists

Pharmacy USC

Publishing Co: Univ. of Southern California, School of Pharmacy, Univ. Park, Los Angeles, CA 90007; Title Tel # (213) 226-2501

Pharmacy Week
See: EMPLOYMENT

Pharmascope
Business

Publishing Co: Transpharma, Inc., 13072 Camino Del Valle, Poway, CA 92064-1917
Personnel: Publisher-William J. Richardson, Editor-Elvera R. Richardson
Editorial Description: Investigational drugs & new products.
General Info: Yr. Est. 1961, Monthly, Trim Size-8½ x 11, Offset press, 14 pages, ISSN: 0048-3648
Subscriptions: Indv. $525, $45/copy
Advertising: Inquire for rates.

Physiology Canada
See: PHYSIOLOGY

Pink Sheet: Prescription and OTC pharmaceuticals
Business

Publishing Co: F-D-C Reports, Inc., 5550 Friendship Blvd, Chevy Chase, MD 20815-7278; Title Tel # (301) 657-9830 Title Fax # (301) 986-6467
Personnel: Publisher-Wallace Werble, Jr., Editor-Cole Werble, Circ. Mgr.-Edward Picken, Adv. Dir.-Richard Messmer, Mktg. Dir.-Leila Simaika
Editorial Description: Specialized newsletter for executives in the pharmacentical industry, marketing, financial, regulatory, research news.
General Info: Yr. Est. 1939, Weekly, Trim Size-8½ x 11, Offset press, 35 pages, ISSN: 0734-6514, Ind/Abs/Online: Mead Data, Data-Star, DIALOG, BRS, PNI, Color
Subscriptions: Indv. $750, For. $825, $18/copy
Advertising: Inquire for rates.

Prescriber's Letter
Business

Publishing Co: Therapeutic Research Center, PO Box 8190, Stockton, CA 95208-0190; Title Tel # (209) 472-2240 Title Fax # (209) 472-2249
Personnel: Editor-Jeff Jellin, Circ. Mgr.-Lisa Shawhan
Editorial Description: Advice on drug therapy for pharmacists, and physicians.
General Info: (Formerly Pharmacist's Letter), Yr. Est. 1994, Monthly, ISSN: 1073-7219
Subscriptions: Indv. $85

Primary Care Medicine Drug Alerts
Business

Publishing Co: M.J. Powers, 374 Millburn Ave, Millburn, NJ 07041-1361 Fax # (201) 912-8883; Title Tel # (201) 467-4556
Personnel: Publisher-John Roche
General Info: (Formerly Physicians' Drug Alert), Yr. Est. 1978, Monthly, ISSN: 0277-4194, 2 Color
Subscriptions: Indv. $59
Circulation: Total-5,000

Psychiatry Drug Alerts
Business

Publishing Co: M.J. Powers, 374 Millburn Ave, Millburn, NJ 07041-1361 Fax # (201) 912-8883; Title Tel # (201) 467-4556
Personnel: Publisher-Michael Powers, Editor-Dory Greene
General Info: Yr. Est. 1986, Monthly
Subscriptions: Indv. $59

Public Policy Quarterly

Publishing Co: National Association of State Alcohol & Drug Abuse Directors, 444 N Capitol St NW Ste 642, Washington, DC 20001-1512; Title Tel # (202) 783-6868 Title Fax # (202) 783-2704
Personnel: Editor-Diane Canova
General Info: (Formerly Alcohol &I Drug Abuse Report), Yr. Est. 1978, Semi-monthly, 12 pages
Subscriptions: Indv. $80
Circulation: Total-350

Public Safety and Justice Policies/State Capitals
See: LAW ENFORCEMENT & PENOLOGY

R & D Focus Drug News
Business

Publishing Co: IMS America, 660 W. Germantown Pike #905, Plymouth Meeting, PA 19462-1048 Tel # (610) 834-5000; Title Tel # (215) 834-5330 Title Fax # (610) 834-5018
Personnel: Editor-Tim Reynolds, Mktg. Mgr.-Will Hau
Editorial Description: Weekly newsletter on new drugs entering the pharmaceutical market.
General Info: Weekly, Trim Size-8½ x 11, 12 pages, No Color, Matte, Saddle-stitched

R & D Innovator
See: TELECOMMUNICATIONS

Recall/Regulatory Analysis

Publishing Co: McVicker Assocs., Inc., PO Box 6353, Silver Spring, MD 20916-6353;
Title Tel # (301) 460-8821
Personnel: Editor-William McVicker
General Info: Yr. Est. 1986, Monthly, Trim Size-8½ x 11, 16 pages, ISSN: 0890-8451
Subscriptions: Indv. $225

Reference Guide to Managing Addiction Programs
See: HEALTH

Regulatory Watchdog Service
See: CONSUMER INTERESTS

Russia Market News:
Drugs & Medical Devices   *Business*

Publishing Co: Thompson Publishing Group, 1725 K Street, NW, Washington, DC 20006
Tel # (202) 872-4000
Editorial Description: News on regulatory developments and marketing opportunities in Russia.
General Info: Monthly

Rutgers Pharmacy
Newsletter   *Association*

Publishing Co: Rutgers University, College of Pharmacy, Publications, New Brunswick, NJ 08903;
Title Tel # (908) 932-2675
Personnel: Editor, Circ. Mgr.-Roy Bowers, Art Dir.-Ann Kurtzenberger
Editorial Description: Feature stories on pharmacy, news, personals.
General Info: Yr. Est. 1978, Semi-annually, Trim Size-8 x 11, Letrpr. press, 8 pages
Circulation: (100% controlled), Total-10,000

SB News   *Association*

Publishing Co: SmithKline Beecham, One Franklin Plaza, PO Box 7929, Philadelphia, PA
19101-7929; Title Tel # (215) 751-4000
Personnel: Editor-Mary Ellen Seitz
Editorial Description: Info on the company's drugs and phramaceuticals research.
General Info: Bi-monthly

Saskatchewan
Pharmaceutical Assn.
Newsletter

Publishing Co: Saskatchewan Pharmaceutical Assn., 2631 28th Ave., Ste. 301, Regina, SK S4S 6X3
Canada; Title Tel # (306) 584-2292
Personnel: Editor-Nancy McBean
General Info: Yr. Est. 1981, Bi-monthly, 6 pages
Circulation: Total-1,400

Scrip World
Pharmaceutical News   *Business, Association*

Publishing Co: Pharmabooks, 1775 Broadway Ste 511, New York, NY 10019-1903;
Title Tel # (212) 262-8230 Title Fax # (212) 262-8234
Personnel: Publisher-Philip Brown, Editor-Moira Dower, Adv. Dir.-Peter Coltart
General Info: Yr. Est. 1972, Semi-weekly, Trim Size-209mm x 294mm, Offset press, 28 pages, 2
Color, Newsprint, Saddle-stitched
Subscriptions: Indv. $1,050
Circulation: (PSS), Total-10,000
Advertising: Inquire for rates.

Sneeze the Day
See: HEALTH

Strategic Advantage
See: HOSPITALS & NURSING HOMES

Street Pharmacologist
See: HEALTH

Substance Abuse Letter

Publishing Co: Pace Publications, 443 Park Ave. South, New York, NY 10016 Tel # (212) 685-5450
Fax # (212) 679-4701; Title Tel # (202) 835-1770
Personnel: Publisher-Sid Goldstein, Editor-Molly R. Parrish
General Info: Bi-monthly, ISSN: 1076-979X
Subscriptions: Indv. $195

Substance Abuse Report
See: HEALTH

Tablet, The   *Association*

Publishing Co: British Columbia Pharmacy Assn., 3751 Shell Rd., Ste. 150, Richmond, BC V6X 2W2
Canada Tel # (604) 279-2053 Fax # (604) 279-2065
Personnel: Editor-Judy Schlachter
Editorial Description: Information of specific importance to the practice of pharmacy in B.C.,
employment relations, member benefits, legislative changes, etc.
General Info: (Formerly In Pharmation), Yr. Est. 1971, Monthly, Trim Size-11¼ x 15, Web press, 8
pages, 2 Color, Newsprint
Circulation: Total-1,600
Advertising: Inquire for rates.
Printing Co: College Printers, 865 Terminal Avenue, Vancouver, BC V6A 2N3 Canada
Tel # (604) 685-6322, Fax # (604) 685-0743

Tactical Technology
See: MILITARY & NAVAL

Technology Access Report
See: SCIENCE

Therapeutic Drug
Monitoring & Toxicology   *Consumer, Association*

Publishing Co: American Assn. for Clinical Chemistry, Inc., 2101 L St., NW, Ste. 202, Washington,
DC 20037-1526 Fax # (202) 887-5093; Title Tel # (202) 857-0717
Editorial Description: Educational and professional development services to its members to improve
level at which chemistry is practiced in chemical labs.
General Info: Yr. Est. 1979, Monthly, Mimeo press, 20 pages, ISSN: 0740-7726, 2 Color, Looseleaf
Subscriptions: Indv. $295, Inst. $295, Can. $295, For. $295, $25/copy

U.S. Regulatory Reporter   *Business*

Publishing Co: Parexel Intl. Corp., 195 West St., Waltham, MA 02154-1116;
Title Tel # (617) 487-9900 Title Fax # (617) 487-0525
Personnel: Editor-Mark Mathieu, Circ. Mgr.-Kris Clouthier, Mktg. Dir.-Carolyn Newman
Editorial Description: U.S FDA regulation of drugs & biologics.
General Info: Yr. Est. 1984, Monthly, ISSN: 0749-5005
Subscriptions: Indv. $395, For. $445

Unlisted Drugs

Publishing Co: Pharmaeo-Medical Documentation, Inc., 205 Main St, Chatham, NJ 07928-2408;
Title Tel # (201) 822-9200 Title Fax # (201) 765-0722
Personnel: Editor-B. R. Anzlowar
Editorial Description: Reports worldwide investigational drugs and news pharmaceutical products:
experimental codes, trademarks, composition, producer, activity, bibliography.
General Info: Yr. Est. 1949, Monthly
Subscriptions: Indv. $390, $13/copy
Circulation: Total-1,100
Advertising: Inquire for rates.

Veterinary Industry Newsletter
See: VETERINARY

Vital Signs Pharmacy-
Nursing Newsletter

Publishing Co: RX-Data-Pac Service, PO Box 42020, Cincinnati, OH 45242-0020;
Title Tel # (513) 489-0943
Personnel: Editor-I.H. Goodman
Editorial Description: Concise, inexpensive, monthly hospital pharmacy-nursing newsletter for
communicating with staff. Aids in complying with JCAHO regulations. Includes master copy with
repro rights. New products, news briefs, quizzes, terminology, etc. Easy to personalize for
institution.
General Info: Yr. Est. 1978, Monthly, 4 pages, ISSN: 0739-9588, No Color
Subscriptions: Indv. $75, $7/copy

Voice of the Pharmacist

Publishing Co: American College of Apothecaries, 205 Daingerfield Rd, Alexandria, VA 22314-2833;
Title Tel # (703) 684-8603
Personnel: Editor-D.C. Huffman
Editorial Description: Pharmaceutical news both local and national.
General Info: Yr. Est. 1948, Quarterly, Offset press, 4 pages, 2 Color
Subscriptions: Indv. $35
Circulation: Total-1,200

Washington Drug Letter   *Business*

Publishing Co: Washington Business Information, Inc., 1117 19th St N Ste 200, Arlington, VA
22209-1708; Title Tel # (703) 247-3426 Title Fax # (703) 247-3421
Personnel: Publisher-David Swit, Editor-John Briley, III, Circ. Mgr.-Chris Rogers, Production Mgr.-
Jennea Myrick
Editorial Description: Coverage of the Food & Drug Administration.
General Info: (Formerly Washington Drug), Yr. Est. 1969, Weekly, Trim Size-8½ x 11, Sheetfed
press, 6 pages, ISSN: 0194-1291, Ind/Abs/Online: BRS, Data-Star, DIALOG, Diogenes, No Color,
Recycled
Subscriptions: Indv. $737, Inst. $737, Can. $737, For. $822
Acquistions: Publication Bought
List Rental: Actives: $110/M

Wellspring Services
Business, Consumer

Publishing Co: ICI Pharmaceuticals, PO Box 751, Wilmington, DE 19897-0001; Title Tel # (302) 886-3000
Editorial Description: Diet and medication taking information for ICI's customers.
General Info: Bi-weekly
Subscriptions: Free To Qualified Recipient
Circulation: Total-475,000

White Sheet

Publishing Co: Roxane Laboratories, Inc., PO Box 16532, Columbus, OH 43216-6532; Title Tel # (614) 276-4000
Personnel: Editor-Richard E. Surface
Editorial Description: Drug information, management tips, and timely items for pharmacists practicing in hospital and institutional settings.
General Info: (Formerly Hospital Pharmacy,), Yr. Est. 1967, Monthly, Trim Size-8½ x 11, Sheetfed press, 4 pages, No Color, Coated
Circulation: Total-38,000

Wisconsin Pharmacy Extension Bulletin

Publishing Co: Univ. of Wisconsin, Extension Services in Pharmacy, Pharmacy Bldg. Rm. 2308, Madison, WI 53706; Title Tel # (608) 262-3130
Personnel: Editor-Melvin H. Weinswig
Editorial Description: Maintain professional competency & update pharmacists knowledge.
General Info: Yr. Est. 1967, Monthly, 6 pages
Circulation: Total-1,500

ECONOMICS

A Monetary Time Bomb is Ticking, Ticking, Ticking
Business, Consumer

Publishing Co: Seraphim Press, 4805 Courageous Ln, Carlsbad, CA 92008-3783 Tel # (619) 720-0107 Fax # (619) 720-4208
Editorial Description: Discusses US monetary problems.
General Info: Irregular
Subscriptions: $29/copy

AOI Business Viewpoint
See: BUSINESS & INDUSTRY

APEE Newsletter
See: BUSINESS & INDUSTRY

AS/400 Advisory Service
See: COMPUTERS & AUTOMATION

Abstract of American Economic Trend Analysis
Business, Association

Publishing Co: Maxiplan Financial Club, Box 5255 Stn. C, 12687 52nd Ave., Montreal, PQ H1E 2H6 Canada; Title Tel # (514) 648-2953
Editorial Description: Covers economic activity outlook; development strategy; US financial market timing; investment strength; productivity growth.
General Info: Yr. Est. 1980, Quarterly
Subscriptions: Indv. $60, $25/copy

Abstract of International Economic Trend Analysis
Business, Association

Publishing Co: Maxiplan Financial Club, Box 5255 Stn. C, 12687 52nd Ave., Montreal, PQ H1E 2H6 Canada; Title Tel # (514) 648-2953
Personnel: Editor-Marcel Wistaff
Editorial Description: Discusses international economic activity outlook; international trade in perspective; multinational investment strength; multicountry productivity growth.
General Info: Yr. Est. 1990, Quarterly, Trim Size-8½ x 11, Offset press, 4 pages, No Color
Subscriptions: Indv. $60, $25/copy

Agenda Newsletter, The
See: REGIONAL INTEREST

Agora, Inc.
See: BANKING & FINANCE

American Economic Foundation Newsletter

Publishing Co: American Economic Foundation, 1215 Terminal Tower, Cleveland, OH 44113; Title Tel # (216) 781-1212 Title Fax # (216) 575-0911
Personnel: Editor-Homer Giles
Editorial Description: Economic reform and capitalism.
General Info: Monthly
Acquistions: Publication Bought
Circulation: Total-11,500
Advertising: Accepts Inserts.

America's Future
See: POLITICS

Arizona Blue Chip Economic Forecast
Business

Publishing Co: Arizona State University, Economic Outlook Center, PO Box 874406, Tempe, AZ 85287-4406; Title Tel # (602) 965-5543 Title Fax # (602) 965-5458
Personnel: Editor-Tracy Clark, Editor-Lee McPheters, Circ. Mgr.-Michelle Moss, Production Mgr.-Nan Beams
Editorial Description: Contains consensus economic forecasts by month for Arizona. Includes 4 quaterly issues of Metro Phoenix Blue Chip Journal.
General Info: Yr. Est. 1984, Monthly, Trim Size-8½ x 11, Desktop press, 4 pages, ISSN: 1042-6787, 2 Color, Coated, Saddle-stitched
Subscriptions: Indv. $99, $5/copy
Acquisitions: Publication Bought
Circulation: (78% controlled), Total-836, Subscriptions-176
Printing Co: Vista Press, 411 Semini Drive, Tempe, AZ 85283 Tel # (602) 820-0910

Arizona Economic Indicators Chartbook
Business

Publishing Co: Univ. of Arizona, College of Business & Public Admin., Mcclelland Hall 204a, Tucson, AZ 85721-0001; Title Tel # (602) 621-2155
Personnel: Publications Director-Diana Hunter, Production Dir.-Constantine Georgelos
Editorial Description: Chartbook containing demographic, economic information in tables & graphs.
General Info: Yr. Est. 1984, Semi-annually, Trim Size-8½ x 11, Offset press, 52 pages, Color-cover, Other, Saddle-stitched
Subscriptions: Indv. $14, Inst. $14, Can. $20, For. $20, $7/copy
Circulation: Total-400

Asset Sales Report
See: BANKING & FINANCE

Atlantic Provinces Economic Council, Newsletter
Business, Consumer

Publishing Co: Atlantic Provinces Economic Council, 5121 Sackville St., #500, Halifax, NS B3J 1K1 Canada; Title Tel # (902) 422-6516 Title Fax # (902) 429-6803
Personnel: Editor-Maurice Mandale
Editorial Description: General topics of interest to private sector--government policies, economic reports, etc.
General Info: Yr. Est. 1957, 8x/yr., Trim Size-8½ x 11, Sheetfed press, 8 pages, ISSN: 0044-989X, Ind/Abs/Online: CBI, CMI, No Color, Matte
Subscriptions: Can. $63
Circulation: Total-1,600

Aura Wealth Newsletter
See: INVESTMENT

Austrian Economics Newsletter
Business, Association

Publishing Co: Mises Institute, Auburn Univ., Auburn, AL 36849 Fax # (205) 844-2583; Title Tel # (205) 844-2500
Personnel: Publisher-L. H. Rockwell, Jr., Editor-Peter G. Klein, Production Mgr.-Judy Thommesen, Promotion Dir.-Pat Heckman
Editorial Description: Articles on modern, free-market economics of Mises, Hayek, etc.
General Info: Yr. Est. 1977, Semi-annually, Trim Size-8.5 x 11, Desktop press, 16 pages, 2 Color, Coated, Saddle-stitched
Circulation: Total-5,000

Barter Update - Barter Basics Edition
See: BUSINESS & INDUSTRY

Billington's Stock Focus II
See: INVESTMENT

Blue Chip Economic Indicators
See: BUSINESS & INDUSTRY

Blue Chip Job Growth Update: Ranking the States and MSAs
Business

Publishing Co: Arizona State University, Economic Outlook Center, PO Box 874406, Tempe, AZ 85287-4406; Title Tel # (602) 965-5543 Title Fax # (602) 965-5458
Personnel: Editor-Yolanda Strozier
Editorial Description: Statistical listing of latest available figures on job growth in the US by state and city.
General Info: Yr. Est. 1990, Irregular
Subscriptions: Indv. $79, $5/copy
Circulation: Total-112
Printing Co: Alpha Graphics, One Renaissance Square, 2 N. Central, Phoenix, AZ 85004 Tel # (602) 271-9525

Blue Chip Stocks
See: INVESTMENT

Boot Cove Economic Forecast   *Business*

Publishing Co: Voight Industries, Inc., PO Box 200, Lubec, ME 04652-0200; Title Tel # (207) 733-5593
Personnel: Editor-R. Voight
Editorial Description: Evaluates the major national political and economic events, forecasts specific parameters.
General Info: Yr. Est. 1970, Monthly, 6 pages, Ind/Abs/Online: NewsNet
Subscriptions: Indv. $380

Browning Newsletter
See: INVESTMENT

CBASSE Newsletter
See: SOCIOLOGY

CEP Research Report   *Business, Consumer*

Publishing Co: Sponsor-Council on Economic Priorities, Council on Economic Priorities, 30 Irving Pl., New York, NY 10003-2303; Title Tel # (212) 420-1133 Title Fax # (212) 420-0988
Personnel: Publisher-Alice Marlin, Editor-Patrick Vance, Circ. Mgr.-Lindae Feinberg, Production Mgr., Art Dir.-Eugene Chollick, Promotion Dir.-Leslie Gottlieb
Editorial Description: Newsletters on status and findings of CEP's studies.
General Info: Yr. Est. 1969, Monthly, Trim Size-8½ x 11, Sheetfed press, 6 pages, ISSN: 0193-4066, 2 Color, Newsprint
Subscriptions: Indv. $25, For. $350, $4/copy
Circulation: (100% controlled), Total-7,500
List Rental: Rents Lists
Printing Co: Faculty Press, 75 Varick St Frnt 5, New York, NY 10013-1917 Tel # (212) 941-0702, Fax # (212) 941-0708

CJCEE Newsletter
See: EDUCATION

CRA Review   *Business*

Publishing Co: Charles River Associates, Inc., 200 Clarendon St., T-33, Boston, MA 02116-5092; Title Tel # (617) 425-3000 Title Fax # (617) 425-3132
Personnel: Editor-Harriet Ullman, Circ. Mgr.-Cindy Thompson, Art Dir.-Patsy Cushing
Editorial Description: Highlights CRA's work in enconomics, finance, transportation, energy, metals, regulations, environment, engineering, automotive pharmaceuticals, telecommunications, transfer pricing, chemicals.
General Info: (Formerly CRA Research Review.), Yr. Est. 1972, Quarterly, Trim Size-8½ x 11, Letrpr. press, 4 pages, 2 Color, Coated
Subscriptions: Free
Circulation: (57% controlled), Total-35,000, Single Copy/Newsstand-15,000
Printing Co: Ben Franklin Smith, 320 Stuart St, Boston, MA 02116-5290 Tel # (617) 426-1160

Caribbean Update
See: INTERNATIONAL TRADE

Center Focus
See: EDUCATION

Center for Rural Affairs Newsletter
See: AGRICULTURE

Center for Self Sufficiency Update
See: PHILANTHROPY

Charting the Economy   *Business*

Publishing Co: Charting the Economy, PO Box 829, New Haven, CT 06504-0829; Title Tel # (203) 269-3225
Personnel: Publisher, Editor-Robert Williams
Editorial Description: Concise view/forecast of the economy, profusely illustrated with charts.
General Info: Yr. Est. 1982, Monthly, Trim Size-8½ x 11, Offset press, 4 pages, Coated
Subscriptions: Indv. $95
Printing Co: Picturesque Photo Graphics, 25 Business Park Dr., Branford, CT 06405 Tel # (203) 488-6966

Chief Economist (Straight Talk)

Publishing Co: Conference Board, Inc., 845 3rd Ave., New York, NY 10022-6679 Tel # (212) 759-0900
Personnel: Editor-Gail Fossler
Editorial Description: Newsletter for professional economists.

Chile Economic Report
See: INTERNATIONAL TRADE

Client Server Advisor Service
See: COMPUTERS & AUTOMATION

Comecon Reports   *Business*

Publishing Co: World Reports Ltd., 280 Madison Ave Rm 1209, New York, NY 10016-0801; Title Tel # (212) 689-7442 Title Fax # (212) 481-0915
Personnel: Publisher, Editor-Christopher Story
General Info: Quarterly
Subscriptions: Indv. $500
Acquistions: Publication Bought

Commodex (R) System, The
See: INVESTMENT

Commodity Futures Forecast (R) Service
See: INVESTMENT

CommonWealth Letters
See: INVESTMENT

Community Development Services, Inc.
See: PUBLIC MANAGEMENT & PLANNING

Community Economics

Publishing Co: Institute for Community Economics, 57 School St, Springfield, MA 01105-1331; Title Tel # (413) 746-8660 Title Fax # (413) 746-8862
Personnel: Publisher, Editor-Kirby White, Circ. Mgr.-Mike Kusek, Art Dir.-Lisa Berger
Editorial Description: News on community land trusts, community loan funds, affordable housing policy, and community economic development iniatives.
General Info: Yr. Est. 1982, Quarterly, Roto. press, 20 pages, ISSN: 1045-4322, No Color, Matte
Subscriptions: Indv. $15, Inst. $25, Can. $20, For. $20
Circulation: (71% controlled), Total-7,000, Subscriptions-2,000, International-300
List Rental: Actives: $65/M
Printing Co: CommonWealth Printing, 47 East St., Hadley, MA 01035 Tel # (413) 584-2536

Computer Economic Report International
See: COMPUTERS & AUTOMATION

Computer Economics Report
See: COMPUTERS & AUTOMATION

Computer Economics Sourcebook
See: COMPUTERS & AUTOMATION

Computer Systems & Peripherals Residual Value Forecasats Multivendor
See: COMPUTERS & AUTOMATION

Conservative Speculator
See: INVESTMENT

Consumer Price Index   *Business*

Publishing Co: Bureau of Labor Statistics, 230 S. Dearborn, Chicago, IL 60604-1505; Title Tel # (312) 353-1880
Personnel: Editor-Ronald Guzicki
Editorial Description: Includes CPI figures for Chicago, Detroit, Cincinnati, Cleveland, Minneapolis, St. Paul and Milwaukee. As well as the US city average.
General Info: Monthly, Trim Size-8½ x 11, Offset press, 4 pages, No Color
Circulation: Total-18,000

Credit Review

Publishing Co: Standard & Poor's Corp., 25 Broadway, New York, NY 10004 Tel # (212) 208-8000 Parent Co.-McGraw-Hill, New York
Personnel: Publisher-Byron Klapper, Editor-Paul Stanwick, Production Mgr.-Georgine Fitzsimons
General Info: ISSN: 0731-1974

Current Economic Bulletin   *Business, Association*

Publishing Co: American Trucking Assn., Inc., Statistics Dept., 2200 Mill Rd., Alexandria, VA 22314-4686; Title Tel # (703) 838-1799 Title Fax # (703) 683-9751
Editorial Description: Compilation of economic trend data: output, interest rates, consumer & producer prices, fuel rates, housing costs, etc.
General Info: Yr. Est. 1989, Weekly, 4 pages
Subscriptions: Indv. $120
Circulation: Total-104

Daily Report for Executives   *Business*

Publishing Co: Bureau of National Affairs, Inc., 1231 25th St. NW, Bldg. N-200, Washington, DC 20037-1157; Title Tel # (202) 452-4200 Title Fax # (202) 822-8092
Personnel: Publisher-William A. Beltz, Mng. Editor-Toby McIntosh, Circ. Mgr.-Gary C. Seltzer
Editorial Description: A daily notification service covering legislative, regulatory, legal, tax, & economic developments which affect both natl. & intl. businesses.
General Info: Yr. Est. 1943, Daily, Trim Size-8½ x 11, Web press, 65 pages, ISSN: 0148-8155, Ind/Abs/Online: Lexis, Nexis, HRIN, Dialcom, Westlaw
Subscriptions: Indv. $5,811

Dec Vax/Axp Advisory Service
See: COMPUTERS & AUTOMATION

Digital Directions Report
See: COMPUTERS & AUTOMATION

Dimensions of the Independent Sector

Publishing Co: Independent Sector, 1828 L St NW, Washington, DC 20036-5107; Title Tel # (202) 223-8100
Personnel: Editor-Virginia Ann Hodgkinson

ETDD Newsletter
See: PUBLIC MANAGEMENT & PLANNING

Early Warning Forecast
See: BUSINESS & INDUSTRY

Economic & Business Outlook
See: BANKING & FINANCE

Economic Developments   *Association*

Publishing Co: National Council for Urban Economic Development, 1730 K St NW Ste 915, Washington, DC 20006-3868; Title Tel # (202) 223-4735
Personnel: Editor-Wayne Welch
Editorial Description: Covers public-private projects & relevant local-state-federal programs & regulations.
General Info: (Formerly Urban Economic Developments), Semi-monthly, Trim Size-8½ x 11, Offset press, 6 pages, 2 Color, Newsprint
Subscriptions: Indv. $250, Inst. $550
Circulation: (100% controlled), Total-1,200
Advertising: Inquire for rates.

Economic Education Bulletin   *Consumer, Association*

Publishing Co: American Institute for Economic Research, PO Box 1000, Great Barrington, MA 01230-1000; Title Tel # (413) 528-1216 Title Fax # (413) 528-0103
Personnel: Editor-Robert Gilmour, Bk. Rev. Ed.-Lawrence Pratt
Editorial Description: Analyses of economic developments based on statistical data; personal finance.
General Info: Yr. Est. 1933, Monthly, Trim Size-8½ x 11, Offset press, 24 pages, ISSN: 0424-2769, No Color
Subscriptions: Indv. $25
Circulation: Total-10,000

Economic Indicators   *Business*

Publishing Co: Norwest Corp. -Economics Dept., Sixth & Marquette, Minneapolis, MN 55479-0001; Title Tel # (612) 667-1234
Personnel: Publisher-Dr. Sung Won Sohn, Editor-Larry Wips, Circ. Mgr.-Nancy Fakhreddine
Editorial Description: Summary of economic & financial prospects & regional & agricultural conditions.
General Info: Bi-monthly, 4 pages
Circulation: Total-10,000

Economic Issues   *Scholarly*

Publishing Co: Economic Issues, 179 East Franklin Street, Post Office Box 989, Chapel Hill, NC 27514-0989; Title Tel # (919) 549-6431 Title Fax # (919) 489-3024
Personnel: Editor-Lawrence J. McQuillan
Editorial Description: Economic issues is a newsletter which reviews economic journal articles that are relevant to current public policy topics. The reviews, on such topics as monetary and fiscal policy and government regulation, provoke thought and enrich understanding of critical national issues.
General Info: Yr. Est. 1995, 8x/yr., Trim Size-17 x 11, Offset press, 4 pages, ISSN: 1074-9241, 2 Color, Matte
Subscriptions: Inst. $95, Can. $45, For. $45

Economic and Legal Information from Poland
See: INTERNATIONAL TRADE

Economic Logic
See: INVESTMENT

Economic Notes
See: LABOR

Economic Outlook   *Business*

Publishing Co: Economic Outlook, 1187 Laurel Loop NE, Albuquerque, NM 87122-1108; Title Tel # (505) 293-5268
General Info: Monthly

Economic Reform   *Business*

Publishing Co: Committee on Monetary and Economic Reform, 3284 Yonge St., Ste. 500, Toronto, ON M4N 3M7 Canada; Title Tel # (416) 486-4686 Title Fax # (416) 486-4674
General Info: (Formerly COMER Comment), Monthly
Subscriptions: Indv. $18, Free With Membership

Economic Trends   *Business*

Publishing Co: Federal Reserve Bank of Cleveland, E. 6th & Superior, Cleveland, OH 44114 Fax # (216) 579-3050; Title Tel # (216) 579-2157 Title Fax # (216) 579-2477
Personnel: Editor-Tess Ferg, Production Mgr.-Robin Ratliff, Art Dir.-Michael Galka
Editorial Description: Booklet of charts & explanations of what is happening in particular economic series.
General Info: (Formerly Economic Presentation), Yr. Est. 1912, Monthly, Trim Size-8½ x 11, Sheetfed press, 20 pages, ISSN: 0748-2922, 2 Color, Newsprint, Saddle-stitched
Subscriptions: Free
Circulation: Total-15,000
Printing Co: Watt Printing Co., 1278 W 9th St., Ste. 600, Cleveland, OH 44113-1046 Tel # (216) 696-5000

Economic Update
See: GOVERNMENT

Economic Week   *Business*

Publishing Co: Citibank/GFNA, 55 Water St., 43rd Floor, New York, NY 10043-0001
General Info: Yr. Est. 1973, Weekly, Ind/Abs/Online: Mead Data Central

Economy At A Glance

Publishing Co: Argus Research Corp., 17 Battery Pl., New York, NY 10004-1101; Title Tel # (212) 425-7500 Title Fax # (212) 509-5408
Personnel: Editor-John Eade
Editorial Description: Report summarizing economic trends & offering forecasts.
General Info: Yr. Est. 1989, Semi-monthly
Subscriptions: Indv. $160
Printing Co: Argus Printing & Mailing, 226 New York Ave, Huntington, NY 11743-2748 Tel # (516) 423-7710

Econoscope, The Royal Bank of Canada

Publishing Co: Royal Bank of Canada, 9th fl., South Tower, Royal Bank Plaza, Toronto, ON M5J 2J5 Canada
Editorial Description: Information on the current state of the Canadian economy.
General Info: Yr. Est. 1989, Monthly

Ecosources

Publishing Co: Sunset Hill School, 400 W 51st St, Kansas City, MO 64112-2316
Personnel: Editor-Janet Woerner
General Info: Yr. Est. 1972, Monthly
Circulation: Total-250

Empire State Development
See: BUSINESS & INDUSTRY

Employment & Training Reporter
See: EMPLOYMENT

Employment Opportunities
See: EMPLOYMENT

Emprise Investment Newsletter
See: INVESTMENT

Euronomics Review
See: BANKING & FINANCE

FRBSF Weekly Letter
See: BANKING & FINANCE

Family Incomes   *Business, Association*

Publishing Co: Statistics Canada, Holland Ave/RH Coats, Holland Ave/Tunney's Pasture, Ottawa, ON K1A O26 Canada Tel # (613) 951-8116 Fax # (613) 951-0581; Title Tel # (613) 990-8116
Editorial Description: Distributions by size of income, major source, region, age, sex, etc. 13-208.
General Info: Yr. Est. 1971, Annually, 30 pages, ISSN: 0703-7368
Subscriptions: Indv. $23, Can. $19, For. $27

Fed Letter
See: BANKING & FINANCE

Fed Tracker, The   *Business*

Publishing Co: Seraphim Press, 4805 Courageous Ln, Carlsbad, CA 92008-3783 Fax # (619) 720-4208; Title Tel # (619) 720-0107
Personnel: Publisher-Kenneth Coleman, Editor, Adv. Dir.-C.C. Chambers, Promotion Dir.-S.R. Rinaudo
Editorial Description: The reality of our nation's economy and body politic.
General Info: (Formerly Fed Tracker Reality Theory; Fed Tracker Special Report), Yr. Est. 1982, Monthly, 6 pages, ISSN: 0739-3563, No Color
Subscriptions: Indv. $96, Can. $52, For. $55
Circulation: Total-2,300

Fernand Braudel Center-Newsletter
See: SOCIOLOGY

Financial Planning Update

Publishing Co: Securities Sources, Box 85600, Univ. Station, Seattle, WA 98145-1600; Title Tel # (206) 285-1730 Title Fax # (206) 284-5249
Personnel: Publisher, Editor-Robert Fry
Editorial Description: Financial planning matters of interest to members of public.
General Info: Yr. Est. 1979, Bi-monthly, Trim Size-8½ x 11, Letrpr. press, 6 pages, ISSN: 0739-8697, No Color
Subscriptions: Indv. $75, $10/copy
Circulation: Total-2,500

First Hawaiian Bank
Economic Indicators   *Business*

Publishing Co: First Hawaiian Bank, PO Box 3200, Honolulu, HI 96847-0001; Title Tel # (808) 525-6151
Personnel: Editor-Leroy Laney
Editorial Description: Economic and business conditions in Hawaii; current statistics.
General Info: Yr. Est. 1961, Bi-monthly, Trim Size-8 1/2 x 11, Sheetfed press, 8 pages, 4 Color, Coated, Other
Subscriptions: Free
Circulation: Total-2,800
Printing Co: Edward Enterprises, PO Box 30468, 641 Waiakamilo Rd., Honolulu, HI 96820-0468 Tel # (808) 841-4231

Florida Population Studies   *Business*

Publishing Co: Bureau of Economic & Business Research, University of Florida, 221 Matherly Hall, Box 117145, Gainesville, FL 32611-7145 Tel # (352) 392-0171 Fax # (352) 392-4739; Title Tel # (904) 392-0171 Title Fax # (904) 392-4739
Personnel: Editor-Stanley K. Smith, Circ. Mgr.-Pam Middleton, Publications Director, Production Mgr.-Ann Pierce
Editorial Description: Reports changes in Florida population for a variety of geographic and demographic categories.
General Info: (Formerly Population Studies), Yr. Est. 1967, Tri-annually, Trim Size-8 1/2 x 11, Offset press, 8 pages, ISSN: 0071-6030, Ind/Abs/Online: AUBER Bibliography, 2 Color, Matte, Saddle-stitched
Subscriptions: Indv. $30, $8/copy
Circulation: Total-800

Focus

Publishing Co: Institute for Research on Poverty, 1800 Observatory Dr., 3412 Soc. Sci., Madison, WI 53706; Title Tel # (608) 262-6358 Title Fax # (608) 265-3119
Personnel: Editor-Elizabeth Hur
Editorial Description: Shows the work of the Institute for Research on Poverty, by means of short essays on selected pieces of research.
General Info: Yr. Est. 1976, 3x/yr., Trim Size-8 1/2 x 11, Letrpr. press, 24 pages, ISSN: 0195-5705, 2 Color, Newsprint
Circulation: Total-7,000

Focus
See: EDUCATION

Forecaster Moneyletter,
The   *Business, Consumer*

Publishing Co: Forecaster Publishing Co., 19623 Ventura Blvd., Tarzana, CA 91356-2918 Tel # (818) 340-5014; Title Tel # (818) 345-4421 Title Fax # (818) 345-0468
Personnel: Publisher, Editor-John Kamin, Circ. Mgr.-Audrey Nedry
Editorial Description: A weekly moneyletter containing forecasts, predictions, strategies for fields outside securities and commodity futures; covering rare coins, gold/silver coins, old cars, distressed property, wholesale auctions, proprietary businesses; how to make money in other unusual speculations. Assesses/forecasts trends that affect work/money/lifestyle.
General Info: (Formerly Forecaster), Yr. Est. 1962, 40x/yr., Offset press, 8 pages, ISSN: 0095-294X, No Color, Other, Other
Subscriptions: Indv. $150, Can. $170, For. $180, $8/copy
Acquisitions: Publication Bought
List Rental: Expires: 18,200, $130/M

Foreign Markets Advisory
See: INVESTMENT

Fraser Forum   *Business*

Publishing Co: National Media Archive, 626 Bute St., Vancouver, BC V6E 3M1 Canada Parent Co.-Fraser Institute, Vancouver, Canada; Title Tel # (604) 688-0221 Title Fax # (604) 688-8539
Personnel: Publisher-Mike Walker, Editor-Sally Pipes, Promotion Dir.-Lorna Hoye
Editorial Description: Collection of commentaries, articles & other materials produced by the institutes authors.
General Info: Yr. Est. 1974, Monthly, Offset press, 20 pages, No Color
Subscriptions: Indv. $48, $4/copy
Circulation: (100% controlled), Total-5,000
Printing Co: College Printers, 865 Terminal Avenue, Vancouver, BC V6A 2N3 Canada Tel # (604) 685-6322, Fax # (604) 685-0743

Fraser Opinion Letter   *Business*

Publishing Co: Fraser Management Associates, PO Box 494, Burlington, VT 05402-0494; Title Tel # (802) 658-0322 Title Fax # (802) 658-0260
Personnel: Publisher, Editor-James Fraser
Editorial Description: Philosophical survey of current economic events and trends in business, finance and public thinking.
General Info: Yr. Est. 1964, Bi-weekly, Trim Size-8 1/2 x 11, Letrpr. press, 2 pages, ISSN: 0740-0276
Subscriptions: Indv. $100, Can. $112, For. $116
Circulation: Total-675

Free Market

Publishing Co: Auburn University, Ludwig von Mises Institute, Auburn, AL 36849; Title Tel # (205) 844-2500
Personnel: Editor-L. Rockwell, Jr.
Editorial Description: Features articles delving into aspects of free market economics.
General Info: Yr. Est. 1983

FutureScan
See: ADVERTISING & MARKETING

Futures and Options Factors
See: INVESTMENT

Gallup Poll, The
See: POLITICS

Good News
See: INVESTMENT

Government Business Worldwide Reports
See: GOVERNMENT

Grassroots Economic Organizing (GEO)
See: CONSUMER INTERESTS

Great Lakes Newsletter
See: ENVIRONMENT & ECOLOGY

Green Party News
See: ENVIRONMENT & ECOLOGY

Guatemala Bulletin
See: CULTURE & HUMANITIES

Henry George News   *Consumer, Association*

Publishing Co: Henry George School of Social Science, 121 E 30th St, New York, NY 10016-7302; Title Tel # (212) 889-8020
Personnel: Editor-Alice Elizabeth Davis
Editorial Description: News of land economics and commentary as well as accounts of school activities.
General Info: Yr. Est. 1943, Monthly, Trim Size-8 1/2 x 11, Offset press, 4 pages
Subscriptions: Indv. $15
Circulation: Total-1,000

History of Economics
Soc. Bulletin, The   *Business, Association*

Publishing Co: Univ. of Richmond History of Economics Society, Economics Dept., Richmond, VA 23173; Title Tel # (804) 289-8566
Personnel: Editor-J. Patrick Raines
Editorial Description: Publishes research notes on history of economics.
General Info: Yr. Est. 1972, Web press
Subscriptions: Indv. $6, $4/copy
Circulation: Total-600
Advertising: Inquire for rates.

Holistic Resource Management Quarterly
See: ENVIRONMENT & ECOLOGY

Horizons
See: AGRICULTURE

Human Economy
Newsletter   *Scholarly*

Publishing Co: Mankato State University Human Economy Center, Box 14, Economics Dept., Mankato, MN 56002-0014; Title Tel # (507) 389-2963 Title Fax # (507) 389-5497
Personnel: Editor-Gerald Smith
General Info: Quarterly, 16 pages
Subscriptions: Indv. $15

IAEE Newsletter
See: ENERGY

I/B/E/S Monthly Comments
See: BANKING & FINANCE

IE News: Engineering
Economy   *Association*   CPM: $256

Publishing Co: Institute of Industrial Engineers, 25 Technology Park/Atlanta, Norcross, GA 30092-2988 Tel # (770) 449-0461; Title Tel # (404) 449-0460 Title Fax # (770) 263-8532
Personnel: Production Mgr.-Dona Brown
Editorial Description: Newsletter for IIE Engineering Economy Division.
General Info: Quarterly, Trim Size-8 1/2 x 11, Sheetfed press, 4 pages, 2 Color, Matte, Saddle-stitched
Circulation: (100% controlled), Total-1,850
Advertising: $475. Accepts Inserts.
List Rental: Rents Lists

IMF Survey   *Business*

Publishing Co: International Monetary Fund, 700 19th St NW Ste 10-540, Washington, DC 20431-0001; Title Tel # (202) 623-7430 Title Fax # (202) 623-7201
Personnel: Editor-David Cheney, Promotion Dir.-Lori Newsom
Editorial Description: Topical report of Fund activities & expert coverage & analysis of major economic news & financial events. Reports on intl. financial developments in the broader context of the world economy.
General Info: Semi-weekly, Trim Size-8 1/2 x 11, ISSN: 0047-083X, 2 Color
Subscriptions: Indv. $79
Circulation: Total-30,000

IRA-Individual Retirement Account Stocks
See: INVESTMENT

IS Budget International
See: COMPUTERS & AUTOMATION

ISLA
See: INTERNATIONAL AFFAIRS

Ideas & Action
See: LABOR

Income Stocks
See: INVESTMENT

Indicators of Industrial Activity

Publishing Co: Organization for Economic Cooperation & Development, 2001 L St NW Ste 650, Washington, DC 20036-4910; Title Tel # (202) 785-6323 Title Fax # (202) 785-0350
Editorial Description: Trends in major industries with detailed charts and graphs.
General Info: Yr. Est. 1979, Quarterly, Trim Size-7$\frac{7}{8}$ x 10$\frac{5}{8}$, Offset press, 120 pages, 2 Color
Subscriptions: Indv. $80

Industry Forecast *Business*

Publishing Co: Industry Forecast Inc., 223 N Greeley Ave # 26, Chappaqua, NY 10514-3411 Fax # (914) 238-7940; Title Tel # (914) 238-3665 Title Fax # (914) 238-4599
Personnel: Publisher-Jay Levy, Editor-David Levy, Circ. Mgr.-Walter Mills
Editorial Description: Forecasts business conditions twelve months ahead.
General Info: Yr. Est. 1949, Monthly, Trim Size-8$\frac{1}{2}$ x 11, Sheetfed press, 4 pages, 2 Color
Subscriptions: Indv. $295
Circulation: Total-4,000
List Rental: Actives: 16,000, $125/M

Info Franchise Newsletter
See: BUSINESS & INDUSTRY

International Association of Agriculture Economists-Proceedings of Conferences
See: AGRICULTURE

International Currency Report
See: BANKING & FINANCE

International Economic Scoreboard *Business*

Publishing Co: Conference Board, Inc., 845 3rd Ave., New York, NY 10022-6679; Title Tel # (212) 759-0900
Personnel: Editor-Edward Siedler
Editorial Description: Report on leading economic indicators in seven major industrial countries.
General Info: Yr. Est. 1979, Monthly, Trim Size-8$\frac{1}{2}$ x 11, Sheetfed press, 4 pages, No Color
Subscriptions: Indv. $495

International Marketing Intelligence News
See: INTERNATIONAL TRADE

Internet Marketing & Technology Report
See: COMPUTERS & AUTOMATION

InvesTech Mutual Fund Advisor
See: INVESTMENT

JEI Report
See: INTERNATIONAL TRADE

Japan Economic Survey
See: INTERNATIONAL AFFAIRS

Japan-U.S. Business Report
See: INTERNATIONAL TRADE

John Naisbitt's Trend Letter *Business*

Publishing Co: Global Network, Inc., 1101 30th Street, NW, Suite 130, Washington, DC 20007; Title Tel # (202) 337-5960 Title Fax # (202) 333-5198
Personnel: Publisher-Daniel Levinas, Editor-Jerry Kline
Editorial Description: Predicts trends that will affect business.
General Info: Yr. Est. 1982, Bi-weekly, Trim Size-8$\frac{1}{2}$ x 11, 8 pages, No Color, Matte, Saddle-stitched
Subscriptions: Indv. $195
Circulation: Total-12,000
List Rental: List Management Co.: Walter Karl Business Lists, One American Lane, Greenwich, CT 06831 Tel # (203) 552-6700, Fax # (203) 552-6799, Actives: 5,299, $125/M
Printing Co: Newsletter Services, Inc., 9700 Philadelphia Court, Lanham, MD 20706 Tel # (301) 731-5200, Fax # (301) 731-5201

LAMA's Watch on Washington
See: BUSINESS & INDUSTRY

Left Business Observer
See: BUSINESS & INDUSTRY

Listen Real Loud: News of Women's Liberation Worldwide
See: WOMEN'S

Low Priced Stocks
See: INVESTMENT

MH-Edie Economics *Business*

Publishing Co: Manufacturers Hanover Trust, 270 Park Ave., New York, NY 10017-2040; Title Tel # (212) 957-1244
Personnel: Editor-Irwin L. Kellner
General Info: Monthly

Mankato Area Business & Economic Indicators *Business, Association*

Publishing Co: Mankato State Univ. Economics Dept., MSU 14, P.O. Box 8400, Mankato, MN 56002-8400 Tel # (507) 389-6767; Title Tel # (507) 389-1623
Editorial Description: A monthly listing of area economic indicators.
General Info: Yr. Est. 1973, Monthly, 4 pages, No Color
Circulation: Total-275

Market: Europe
See: INTERNATIONAL TRADE

Market: Latin America
See: INTERNATIONAL TRADE

Marketips *Business, Association*

Publishing Co: General Services Admin., 18th and F Streets, Washington, DC 20406-0001; Title Tel # (703) 557-5480
Personnel: Editor-Ruth Lyons, Art Dir.-B. Kravinsky
Editorial Description: For Federal agencies with information on travel and transportation procurement, and Gov't services & people.
General Info: Quarterly, Web press, Newsprint, Saddle-stitched

Meat Sheet
See: MEAT & MEAT PROVISIONS

Metropolitan Washington D.C. Area Labor Summary
See: LABOR

Mexico Business Monthly
See: INTERNATIONAL TRADE

Midrange Systems Advisory Service
See: COMPUTERS & AUTOMATION

Missouri Enterprise *Business, Association*

Publishing Co: Missouri State Dept. of Economic Development, PO Box 1157, Jefferson City, MO 65102-1157; Title Tel # (314) 526-6796
Personnel: Editor-Mildred Robertson
Editorial Description: Narrative and statistical description relative to Missouri's economy, by selected areas.
General Info: Yr. Est. 1962, Bi-monthly, Offset press, 6 pages, ISSN: 0279-3261, 2 Color
Subscriptions: Indv. $2,800, Free
Circulation: Total-2,500

Monthly Business Failure *Business*

Publishing Co: Dun & Bradstreet, PO Box 870, Wilton, CT 06897 Tel # (212) 593-6800; Title Tel # (212) 285-7417
Personnel: Editor-Rowena Wyant
Editorial Description: Number and liabilities in 39 lines of business; in 5 liability size groups; in regions, states, large cities, and Federal Reserve districts; comment and interpretations.
General Info: Yr. Est. 1900, Monthly
Subscriptions: Indv. $30
Circulation: Total-1,565

Mortgage Marketplace
See: BANKING & FINANCE

Multiple Linear Regression Viewpoints
See: PSYCHOLOGY

NABE News *Business, Association* CPM: $138

Publishing Co: National Association of Business Economists, 1233 20th St., NW, Suite 505, Washington, DC 20036-2304; Title Tel # (202) 463-6223 Title Fax # (202) 463-6239
Personnel: Editor-Ann Picker, Production Mgr., Adv. Dir.-Susan Doolittle
Editorial Description: NABE News is published bimonthly & contains timely feature articles, news of local chapters & Roundtables, reviews of seminars & meetings, personal notes & advertisements of interest to the business economist.
General Info: Bi-monthly, Trim Size-8$\frac{1}{2}$ x 11, Offset press, 24 pages, Color-cover, Matte, Saddle-stitched
Subscriptions: Indv. $55, Can. $55, For. $75
Circulation: Total-3,600
Advertising: $500.
List Rental: Actives: $150/M

NABE Outlook, Industry Survey & Policy Survey *Business*

Publishing Co: National Association of Business Economists, 1233 20th St., NW, Suite 505, Washington, DC 20036-2304 Tel # (202) 463-6223
Personnel: Production Mgr., Adv. Dir.-Susan Doolittle
Editorial Description: The NABE conducts a quarterly survey of a special panel of its members on the outlook for selected macro economic variables including GNP, CPI, auto sales, housing starts, unemployment, & others. Another panel is queried quarterly on business conditions within their company/industry. Questions are asked on changes in demand, employment, inventories, & capital spending, etc.
General Info: Quarterly, Sheetfed press, 8 pages, Saddle-stitched
Subscriptions: Indv. $55, Inst. $300, For. $75
Circulation: Total-3,700
List Rental: Actives: $150/M
Printing Co: Watt Printing Co., 1278 W 9th St., Ste. 600, Cleveland, OH 44113-1046 Tel # (216) 696-5000

NBER Digest

Publishing Co: National Bureau of Economic Research, 1050 Massachusetts Ave., Cambridge, MA 02138 Fax # (617) 868-2742; Title Tel # (617) 868-3900
Personnel: Editor-Donna Zerwitz
General Info: Yr. Est. 1978, Monthly
Acquistions: Publication Bought
Circulation: Total-13,000

NC State Economist *Association, Business*

Publishing Co: North Carolina Cooperative Extension Service, Box 8119, Ncsu, Raleigh, NC 27695-0001; Title Tel # (919) 515-2607 Title Fax # (919) 515-6268
Personnel: Editor-W.D. Eickhoff
General Info: (Formerly Tar Heel Economist), Yr. Est. 1952, Monthly
Circulation: (100% controlled), Total-5,000

NCBA Reports
See: LAW

NQB Pink Sheets for Equities
See: INVESTMENT

NQB Yellow Sheets for Taxable Bonds
See: INVESTMENT

NYSE-Weekly Stock Buys
See: INVESTMENT

Nebraska County Profiles
See: BUSINESS & INDUSTRY

Nebraska Development News *Business*

Publishing Co: Nebraska State Dept. of Economic Development, PO Box 94666, Lincoln, NE 68509-4666 Fax # (402) 471-3778; Title Tel # (402) 471-3111
Personnel: Editor-Information Officer
Editorial Description: To update readers on state economic development activities.
General Info: (Formerly Nebraska Economic Developments), Yr. Est. 1986, Monthly, Trim Size-8½ x 11, Offset press, 12 pages, 2 Color, Saddle-stitched
Subscriptions: Free
Circulation: Total-5,600

Network *Business*

Publishing Co: North Dakota Dept. of Economic Development and Finance, 1833 E Bismarck Expy, Bismarck, ND 58504-6708 Tel # (701) 328-2374; Title Tel # (701) 224-2810 Title Fax # (701) 223-3081
Personnel: Publisher-Fred Haeffner, Editor-Kim Stenchgem
Editorial Description: Business/industrial development news of interest to community.
General Info: (Formerly EDC Newsletter), Yr. Est. 1957, Bi-monthly, Trim Size-10 x 15, Sheetfed press, 8 pages, ISSN: 0029-2729, 2 Color, Newsprint
Circulation: Total-4,200
Printing Co: New Salem Journal, New Salem, ND 58501

New England Economic Review *Business, Consumer*

Publishing Co: Fedl. Reserve Bank of Boston, PO Box 2076, Boston, MA 02106-2076; Title Tel # (617) 973-3397
Personnel: Research Editor-Anita Denault
Editorial Description: Articles on topics relating to the national economy.
General Info: Yr. Est. 1920, Bi-monthly, Trim Size-8½ x 11, Web press, 50 pages, ISSN: 0028-4726, No Color, Matte, Saddle-stitched
Subscriptions: Free To Qualified Recipient
Circulation: Total-12,000

New Hampshire Journal of Economic Development
See: REGIONAL INTEREST

New z Letter

Publishing Co: Freedom Lawyers of the USA, PO Box 309, South Haven, MI 49090-0309; Title Tel # (616) 637-6557 Title Fax # (616) 637-2422
Personnel: Publisher-Sheldon Waxman, Circ. Mgr., Art Dir.-Shelly Waxman
Editorial Description: Lively politics/economic commentary.
General Info: Yr. Est. 1978, Mimeo press, 91 pages, No Color
Subscriptions: Indv. $15, $5/copy
Advertising: Inquire for rates.

New York Mercantile Exchange, Daily Futures Report

Publishing Co: New York Mercantile Exchange, 4 World Trade Center, New York, NY 10048-0137 Tel # (212) 748-3000; Title Tel # (212) 966-2600
Personnel: Editor-Rose Gerbasio
Editorial Description: Daily trading statistics-prices, trading volume and open interest.
General Info: Yr. Est. 1951, Daily, Trim Size-8½ x 14, Offset press, 2 pages, Color
Subscriptions: Indv. $50
Circulation: Total-500

News From ICS
See: POLITICS

North Star Compass
See: INTERNATIONAL AFFAIRS

Northeast-Midwest Economic Review

Publishing Co: Northeast-Midwest Institute, 218 D St., SE, Washington, DC 20003-1900; Title Tel # (202) 544-5200
Personnel: Publisher-Dick Munson, Editor-John Dineen
Editorial Description: Natl. & regional economic policy articles, congressional & regional economic news, regional demographics, aimed primarily at Members fo Congress, state & regional government, business, labor & academic leaders.
General Info: Yr. Est. 1988, Bi-weekly, Sheetfed press, 16 pages, 2 Color
Subscriptions: Indv. $195
Printing Co: D.L. Printing, PO Box 70209, Washington, DC 20024-0209 Tel # (202) 543-2082

Notes from FEE

Publishing Co: Foundation for Economic Education, Inc., 30 S Broadway, Irvington, NY 10533-1861; Title Tel # (914) 591-7230
Personnel: Publisher-Bruce Evans, Editor-Beth Hoffman
General Info: Yr. Est. 1956, Trim Size-8½ x 11, Sheetfed press, 4 pages, 2 Color, Newsprint
Circulation: Total-30,000

Our Washington Newsletter

Publishing Co: Industrial Newsletters, 1545 New York Ave NE, Washington, DC 20002-1765; Title Tel # (202) 529-5700 Title Fax # (202) 636-3992
Personnel: Editor-Peter S. Nagan
Editorial Description: Business outlook and prospects for prices, wages, interest rates, and government regulation.
General Info: Monthly

Parametric World *Association* CPM: $571

Publishing Co: International Society of Parametic Analysts, PO Box 6402, Chesterfield, MO 63006-6402
Personnel: Editor-Nina Tahir
Editorial Description: Members are cost analysts working principally in the field of defense and weapons systems.
General Info: (Formerly Whisper), Yr. Est. 1980, Bi-monthly, Desktop press, 8 pages, 4 Color, Saddle-stitched
Subscriptions: Indv. $45
Circulation: Total-700
Advertising: $400. Accepts Inserts.

Partners *Business, Association*

Publishing Co: Junior Achievement, Inc., National Headquarters, One Education Way, Colorado Springs, CO 80906-4477 Fax # (719) 540-8000; Title Tel # (719) 540-8000 Title Fax # (719) 540-6299
Personnel: Publisher-Everlyn Taylor, Editor-Julia Maitino, Circ. Mgr.-Susan Michael, Art Dir.-Kathy Lippencott, Production Mgr., Promotion Dir.-Laura Banks
Editorial Description: The natl. newsletter of Junior Achievement. Discusses issues of importance to business & economic education. Features interviews with leading figures in the economics, business & education world.
General Info: Yr. Est. 1986, Quarterly, Sheetfed press, 12 pages, 4 Color, Coated
Subscriptions: $1/copy
Circulation: Total-30,000
Printing Co: Fittje Bros., 2830 Delta Dr, Colorado Springs, CO 80910-1011 Tel # (719) 392-4286

Patriot Cannon
See: POLITICS

Pennsylvania's Labor Force...A Monthly Statistical Analysis
See: EMPLOYMENT

Perryman Report

Publishing Co: Texas Economic Publishers, Inc., 510 N. Valley Mills Dr., Ste. 300, Waco, TX 76710-6076 Tel # (817) 755-8811; Title Tel # (800) 789-8705 Title Fax # (817) 755-0381
Personnel: Publisher-Ray Perryman, Editor-Nancy Cunningham, Adv. Dir.-Leigh Martinez, Promotion Dir.-Brooke Bulow
Editorial Description: Newsletter fousing on state, national, and international economic events the affect business exclutives.
General Info: Monthly, Offset press, 8 pages, ISSN: 1047-8280, 2 Color, Matte, Saddle-stitched
Subscriptions: Indv. $135
Circulation: Total-2,500, Readership-10,000

Perryman Texas Letter, The   *Business*

Publishing Co: Texas Economic Publishers, Inc., 510 N. Valley Mills Dr., Ste. 300, Waco, TX 76710-6076 Tel # (817) 755-8811; Title Tel # (817) 755-8705 Title Fax # (817) 755-0381
Personnel: Publisher-Ray Perryman, Editor-Bill Bancroft, Editor-Kevin Gleghorn, Asst. Ed.-Nancy Cunningham, Circ. Mgr.-Eliska Beaty
General Info: Yr. Est. 1990, Monthly, Offset press, 4 pages, ISSN: 1052-5254, 2 Color, Matte
Subscriptions: Indv. $135
Circulation: Total-2,500, Readership-10,000

Perspectives on Contemporary Ukraine
See: INTERNATIONAL AFFAIRS

Policy Currents
See: PUBLIC MANAGEMENT & PLANNING

Positive Economist Bulletin   *Business, Consumer*

Publishing Co: Code of the West Publishing, 1633 Best Ln, Eugene, OR 97401-5030; Title Tel # (503) 345-9379
Personnel: Publisher, Editor-E.G. Ross, Circ. Dir.-Susan Peterson
Editorial Description: Positive economic developments in the free market.
General Info: Yr. Est. 1991, Bi-monthly, Trim Size-8½ x 11, Desktop press, 8 pages, No Color, Matte
Subscriptions: Indv. $30, Can. $30, For. $30, $5/copy
Circulation: Total-3,000

Prairie Progress Newsletter
See: BUSINESS & INDUSTRY

Printing Sales Index

Publishing Co: National Association of Printers & Lithographers, 780 Palisade Ave., Teaneck, NJ 07666-3129; Title Tel # (201) 342-0707 Title Fax # (201) 692-0286
Personnel: Editor-Andrew Papacozzi, Art Dir.-Catherine Vitale
Editorial Description: Tracks sales growth of commercial printers in the U.S. & Canada. Over 450 participating firms. Includes commentary on economic trends affecting the commercial printing industry.
General Info: Yr. Est. 1989, Bi-monthly, Sheetfed press, 2 pages, 2 Color, Coated
Circulation: (19% controlled), Total-5,000, Subscriptions-4,050

Pro$perity Alert   *Business, Consumer*

Publishing Co: Pro$perity Network, PO Box 1406, Hoboken, NJ 07030-1301; Title Tel # (201) 714-4953 Title Fax # (201) 714-4693
Personnel: Editor-Paul Mladjenovic
Editorial Description: Covers issues affecting American economic situations. Also provides practical information on personal finance, tax , investing and entrapeneur matters.
General Info: Quarterly, Trim Size-8½ x 11, 4 pages, No Color
Subscriptions: Indv. $29, Free With Membership
Circulation: Readership-2,000
Advertising: Accepts Inserts.
List Rental: Actives: 2,000, $50/M

Provincial - Industry Economic Services

Publishing Co: Royal Bank of Canada, 9th fl., South Tower, Royal Bank Plaza, Toronto, ON M5J 2J5 Canada
Editorial Description: Economic reports of each Canadian province - one for each province.
General Info: Yr. Est. 1990, Semi-annually

Quarterly Domestic & Global Forecasts of Key Economic Indicators
See: BUSINESS & INDUSTRY

Quarterly Labour Force Statistics   *Business, Association*

Publishing Co: Organization for Economic Cooperation & Development, 2001 L St NW Ste 650, Washington, DC 20036-4910; Title Tel # (202) 785-6323 Title Fax # (202) 785-0350
Editorial Description: Presents statistics on total labor force, unemployment, and employment by sector for 13 OECD countries.
General Info: Quarterly, Trim Size-7⅞ x 10⅝, Offset press, 90 pages, ISSN: 0255-3627, No Color, Newsprint
Subscriptions: Indv. $60, $15/copy

Reading Labor Market News Release
See: GOVERNMENT

Recession-Recovery Watch   *Business*

Publishing Co: Center for Intl. Business Cycles Research, Columbia Univ., Business School, Uris Hall, New York, NY 10027-2399; Title Tel # (212) 280-2916
Personnel: Editor-Dr. Geoffrey Moore
General Info: Yr. Est. 1979, Quarterly
Subscriptions: Indv. $950, Inst. $950, Can. $950
Circulation: Total-455

Reengineering Economics Letter   *Business*

Publishing Co: Computer Economics, Inc., 5841 Edison Pl., Carlsbad, CA 92008-6519; Title Tel # (619) 438-8100 Title Fax # (619) 431-1126
General Info: Monthly, Trim Size-8½ x 11, 8 pages, 2 Color
Subscriptions: $395/copy
List Rental: Rents Lists

Reference Guide to Addiction Counseling
See: HEALTH

Regional Economies & Markets   *Business*

Publishing Co: Conference Board, Inc., 845 3rd Ave., New York, NY 10022-6679; Title Tel # (212) 759-0900
Personnel: Editor-Fabian Linden
Editorial Description: Examines economic trends & prospects in the nine major U.S. regions.
General Info: Yr. Est. 1986, Quarterly, Trim Size-8½ x 11, 8 pages, ISSN: 0896-2537
Subscriptions: Indv. $295
Circulation: Total-8,400

Research Reports   *Business*

Publishing Co: American Institute for Economic Research, PO Box 1000, Great Barrington, MA 01230-1000; Title Tel # (413) 528-1216 Title Fax # (413) 528-0103
Personnel: Editor-Larry Pratt
Editorial Description: Scientific analysis of economic & monetary issues.
General Info: Yr. Est. 1933, Semi-monthly, Trim Size-8½ x 11, Offset press, 4 pages, ISSN: 0034-5407, No Color
Subscriptions: Indv. $59, $2/copy
Circulation: Total-8,500

Residual Value Forecasts For DEC Systems and Peripherals
See: COMPUTERS & AUTOMATION

Residual Value Forecasts For IBM Systems & Peripherals
See: COMPUTERS & AUTOMATION

Rezo
See: SOCIOLOGY

Ron Paul Survival Report
See: INVESTMENT

Runzheimer on Cars & Living Costs   *Business*

Publishing Co: Runzheimer Intl., Runzheimer Park, Rochester, WI 53167 Fax # (414) 767-2254; Title Tel # (414) 767-2200
Personnel: Publisher-Bradford Burris, Editor-Peter Packer
General Info: Yr. Est. 1963, Quarterly, Trim Size-5½ x 8½, Sheetfed press, 4 pages, No Color, Coated
Acquistions: Publication Bought, Publication Sold

Russian Business News Update
See: INTERNATIONAL TRADE

SF Newsletter
See: LUMBER & WOOD

Salary Characteristics   *Business, Association*

Publishing Co: National Association of Business Economists, 1233 20th St., NW, Suite 505, Washington, DC 20036-2304 Tel # (202) 463-6223
Personnel: Publisher-Susan Doolittle, Editor-Bruce Kratofil, Production Mgr.-susan Doolittle
Editorial Description: The only authoritative source on salaries of business economists and business analysts. Included are median salary data by industry, geographic area, area of responsibility, size of firm, number supervised, attained education and years of experience.
General Info: (Formerly Salary Survey), Yr. Est. 1964, Every two years, Trim Size-8½ x 11, Sheetfed press, 8 pages, Saddle-stitched, Looseleaf
Subscriptions: For. $31, $26/copy
Circulation: Total-3,600
List Rental: Actives: $150/M

Saskatchewan Monthly Statistical Review

Publishing Co: Bureau of Statistics, 2350 Albert St., 5th fl., Regina, SK S4P 4A6 Canada; Title Tel # (306) 787-6327 Title Fax # (306) 787-6311
General Info: Yr. Est. 1975, Monthly, 13 pages, No Color
Circulation: Total-500

Senior Economist
Consumer

Publishing Co: Economics America - Natl. Council on Economic Education, 1140 Avenue of Americas, New York, NY 10036-5803; Title Tel # (212) 730-7007
Personnel: Publisher-Joan Baranski
Editorial Description: Economic concepts described with accompanying teaching activities.
General Info: Yr. Est. 1986, Quarterly, Trim Size-8½ x 11, 16 pages, 2 Color, Looseleaf
Subscriptions: Indv. $17, $5/copy
Circulation: Total-1,000

Small Business-USA
See: BUSINESS & INDUSTRY

Software Economics Letter
See: COMPUTERS & AUTOMATION

South Asia Forum Quarterly
See: ETHNIC

Straight Shooter
Consumer

Publishing Co: Straight Shooter, PO Box 1584, Ridgewood, NJ 07451-1584; Title Tel # (201) 444-6517
Personnel: Publisher-Walter Williams, Exec. Ed.-Doug Gillespie
Editorial Description: Covers the economic, political and financial environment of the USA. Also available in weekly faxed format.
General Info: Monthly
Subscriptions: Indv. $55

Straight Talk
Business

Publishing Co: Conference Board, Inc., 845 3rd Ave., New York, NY 10022-6679; Title Tel # (212) 759-0900
Personnel: Editor-Gail Foster
General Info: Yr. Est. 1990, 10x/yr.
Subscriptions: Indv. $495

System of National Accounts, Financial Flow Accounts
Business, Association

Publishing Co: Statistics Canada, Holland Ave/RH Coats, Holland Ave/Tunney's Pasture, Ottawa, ON K1A O26 Canada Tel # (613) 951-8116 Fax # (613) 951-0581; Title Tel # (613) 990-8116
Editorial Description: Contains matrices, economic sector & financial category tables. Catalog #13-002.
General Info: Yr. Est. 1968, Quarterly, 161 pages, ISSN: 0380-092X
Subscriptions: Indv. $15, Can. $13, For. $18

System of National Accounts-Financial Flow Accounts: Preliminary Data
Business, Association

Publishing Co: Statistics Canada, Holland Ave/RH Coats, Holland Ave/Tunney's Pasture, Ottawa, ON K1A O26 Canada Tel # (613) 951-8116 Fax # (613) 951-0581; Title Tel # (613) 990-8116
Editorial Description: Advance data for 13-002, cat. #13-002P.
General Info: Yr. Est. 1938, Quarterly, 10 pages, ISSN: 0380-0938
Subscriptions: Indv. $15, Can. $13, For. $18

System of National Accounts, National Income and Expenditure Accounts
Business, Association

Publishing Co: Statistics Canada, Holland Ave/RH Coats, Holland Ave/Tunney's Pasture, Ottawa, ON K1A O26 Canada Tel # (613) 951-8116 Fax # (613) 951-0581; Title Tel # (613) 990-8116
Editorial Description: GNP and its principal components. 13-001.
General Info: Yr. Est. 1953, Quarterly, 60 pages, ISSN: 0318-708X
Subscriptions: Indv. $24, Can. $20, For. $28, $24/copy

Transition: The Newsletter About Reforming Economies
See: INTERNATIONAL AFFAIRS

Trends & Projections
Business

Publishing Co: Standard & Poor's Corp., 25 Broadway, New York, NY 10004 Parent Co.-McGraw-Hill, New York; Title Tel # (212) 208-8000
Personnel: Publisher-Stephen Sanborn, Editor-David Biitzer
Editorial Description: Monthly overview of the economy and leading industries.
General Info: Monthly
Subscriptions: Indv. $80

UNITE!
See: INTERNATIONAL AFFAIRS

URPE Newsletter
Association CPM: $100

Publishing Co: Union for Radical Political Economics, Univ. of CA Dept. of Economics, Riverside, CA 92521-0001 Tel # (909) 787-1580 Fax # (909) 787-5685; Title Tel # (714) 787-3538
Personnel: Editor-Robert Pollin
Editorial Description: Provides organizational updates, analysis of current events within the framework of radical political economy. Advertises conference, workshops, job openings, publications. Written for professionals and laypersons with an interest in radical economic thought.
General Info: Yr. Est. 1968, Quarterly, Trim Size-11 x 17, Offset press, 20 pages, Matte, Saddle-stitched
Subscriptions: Indv. $10, Inst. $10, Can. $10, For. $10
Circulation: Total-3,000
Advertising: $300. Accepts Inserts.
List Rental: Actives: $75/M, Expires: $75/M

Understanding Defense
See: MILITARY & NAVAL

Vermont Labor Market
See: LABOR

View, The
See: CHAMBER OF COMMERCE

Virginia Agriculture Commodity Newsletter
See: AGRICULTURE

Voluntaryist, The
See: POLITICS

Washington Watch
See: BABY

Week in Germany, The
See: INTERNATIONAL AFFAIRS

Weekly Business Failures

Publishing Co: Dun & Bradstreet, PO Box 870, Wilton, CT 06897 Tel # (212) 593-6800; Title Tel # (212) 285-7417
Personnel: Editor-Rowena Wyant
Editorial Description: Numbers in week ended previous Thursday; comment and analysis by liability size, industry, geographic regions.
General Info: Yr. Est. 1900, Weekly
Subscriptions: Indv. $45
Circulation: Total-1,400

West Virginia Economic Summary
Business

Publishing Co: West Virginia Bureau of Employment Programs, 112 California Ave., Charleston, WV 25305-0112; Title Tel # (304) 558-2660 Title Fax # (304) 558-0301
Personnel: Publisher-David Calvert
Editorial Description: State & area narratives with 16 tables relating to employment, unemployment, wages.
General Info: (Formerly Employment Trends; West Virginia Labor Market Trends), Yr. Est. 1950, Monthly, Trim Size-8½ x 11, Letrpr. press, 14 pages, No Color
Subscriptions: Free
Circulation: Total-3,000

Westchester Business Partnership

Publishing Co: Westchester Business Partnership, 427 Bedford Rd., Pleasantville, NY 10570; Title Tel # (914) 769-3591
Editorial Description: A non-profit joint venture of the public and private sectors to foster a positive business climate in Westchester County.
General Info: Quarterly, Trim Size-8.5 x 11, 4 pages, 4 Color

Western Blue Chip Economic Forecast

Publishing Co: Arizona State University, Economic Outlook Center, PO Box 874406, Tempe, AZ 85287-4406; Title Tel # (602) 965-5543 Title Fax # (602) 965-5458
Personnel: Editor-Tracy Clark, Editor-Lee McPheters, Circ. Mgr.-Michelle Moss, Production Mgr.-Nan Beams
Editorial Description: Consensus forecasts on economic conditions & performance for 10 Western states: Arizona, California, Colorado, Idaho, Nevada, New Mexico, Texas, Oregon, Utah, & Washington.
General Info: Yr. Est. 1987, 10x/yr., Trim Size-8½ x 11, Desktop press, 12 pages, ISSN: 1042-6795, 2 Color, Coated, Saddle-stitched
Subscriptions: Indv. $99
Circulation: (52% controlled), Total-563, Subscriptions-270
Printing Co: Vista Press, 411 Semini Drive, Tempe, AZ 85283 Tel # (602) 820-0910

What Is to Be Read
See: BOOKS & BOOK TRADE

Wolfe's Version — *Business*

Publishing Co: Wolfe's Version, PO Box 99, Blue Springs, MO 64013-0099;
Title Tel # (314) 635-3154
Personnel: Editor-James Wolfe
Editorial Description: Missouri and natl. politics; hard money economics.
General Info: Yr. Est. 1975, Monthly, Sheetfed press, 4 pages, No Color
Subscriptions: Indv. $24

Workstation Advisory Service
See: COMPUTERS & AUTOMATION

World Bank Publications Update
See: INTERNATIONAL AFFAIRS

Yardstick
See: COMPUTERS & AUTOMATION

EDUCATION

3 R's: Research, Reports & Reviews — *Association*

Publishing Co: Master Teacher, Inc., Leadership La., Box 1207, Manhattan, KS 66502
Tel # (913) 539-0555 Fax # (913) 539-7739
Personnel: Publisher, Editor-Robert DeBruyn, Circ. Mgr.-Lori Hansom, Production Mgr.-Brad Roberts, Art Dir.-Barry Anderson
Editorial Description: A research quarterly which synthesizes the most recent research in the field of education.
General Info: Yr. Est. 1989, Quarterly, Sheetfed press, 4 pages, Other
Subscriptions: Indv. $25, Inst. $22, Can. $25, For. $25
Printing Co: Educational Publishers, 3201 Marlatt Ave, Manhattan, KS 66502-8143
Tel # (913) 539-2469

A2-Central
See: COMPUTERS & AUTOMATION

AACE Bonus Briefs — *Business, Association*

Publishing Co: American Assn. for Career Education, 2900 Amby Pl, Hermosa Beach, CA 90254-2216; Title Tel # (310) 376-7378 Title Fax # (310) 374-1360
Personnel: Editor-Pat Nellor Wickwire
Editorial Description: Current information on careers, education and work.
General Info: Yr. Est. 1991, Quarterly, Desktop press, Looseleaf
Subscriptions: Free With Membership

AACE Careers Update — *Business, Association*

Publishing Co: American Assn. for Career Education, 2900 Amby Pl, Hermosa Beach, CA 90254-2216; Title Tel # (310) 376-7378 Title Fax # (310) 374-1360
Personnel: Editor-Pat Nellor Wickwire
Editorial Description: Current career education information.
General Info: (Formerly AACE Update), Quarterly, Trim Size-8½ x 11, Offset press, 6 pages, ISSN: 1074-9551, Other
Subscriptions: Indv. $13, Free With Membership

AACRAO Data Dispenser — *Association*

Publishing Co: American Assn. of Collegiate Registrars & Admissions Officer, 1 Dupont Cir NW Ste 330, Washington, DC 20036-1171; Title Tel # (202) 293-9161 Title Fax # (202) 872-8857
Personnel: Editor-Eileen Kennedy, Mktg. Dir.-Jennifer Harrison
Editorial Description: Association newsletter for U.S. & foreign postsecondary educational institution professionals involved in admissions, records & registration, data management, financial aid, institutional research & international education.
General Info: Yr. Est. 1981, 10x/yr., Trim Size-8½ x 11, Offset press, 12 pages, ISSN: 1040-8924, 2 Color, Matte, Saddle-stitched
Subscriptions: Indv. $30, $3/copy
Acquistions: Publication Bought, Publication Sold
Circulation: Total-8,800
Printing Co: CLB Publishers & Lithographers, 10580 Metropolitan Ave, Kensington, MD 20895-2606
Tel # (301) 933-5220, Fax # (301) 933-2498

AACS Newsletter — *Association*

Publishing Co: American Assn. of Christian Schools, 4500 Selsa Rd., Blue Springs, MD 64015-2221; Title Tel # (703) 818-7150 Title Fax # (703) 818-7281
Personnel: Editor-Dr. Carl Herbster
General Info: (Formerly AACS Annunciator), Monthly, Offset press, 4 pages, Color, Newsprint
Circulation: Total-1,500

AACSB Newsline — *Business, Association* — CPM: $120

Publishing Co: American Assembly of Collegiate Schools of Business, 600 Emerson Rd Ste 300, Saint Louis, MO 63141-6762; Title Tel # (314) 872-8481 Title Fax # (314) 872-8495
Personnel: Editor-Sharon Barber
Editorial Description: Covers AACSB activities as well as administration/management and accounting education programs at the baccalaureate and master's degree levels. includes analyses of trends and data reports.
General Info: Yr. Est. 1916, Quarterly, Trim Size-8½ x 11, Web press, 32 pages, ISSN: 0360-697X, 2 Color, Coated, Saddle-stitched
Subscriptions: Indv. $15, Inst. $15, Can. $20, For. $20
Circulation: Total-7,000
Advertising: $840.

AACTE Briefs — *Association* — CPM: $53

Publishing Co: American Assn. of Colleges for Teacher Education, 1 Dupont Cir NW Ste 610, Washington, DC 20036-1110 Fax # (202) 457-8095; Title Tel # (202) 293-2450
Personnel: Editor-Elizabeth Foxwell
Editorial Description: Contains general education & assn. news.
General Info: Yr. Est. 1980, Bi-weekly, Trim Size-8½ x 11, Sheetfed press, 8 pages, 2 Color, Saddle-stitched
Subscriptions: Indv. $30, For. $40
Circulation: (100% controlled), Total-6,000
Advertising: $320.
List Rental: Actives: 6,400
Printing Co: Weadon Printing, 6430 General Green Way, Alexandria, VA 22312-2413
Tel # (703) 750-0800, Fax # (703) 750-0807

AAHE Bulletin — *Association*

Publishing Co: American Association for Higher Education, 1 Dupont Cir NW Ste 360, Washington, DC 20036-1110; Title Tel # (202) 293-6440
Personnel: Mng. Editor-Bry Pollack
Editorial Description: Articles on higher education academic affairs, innovative programs, professional development.
General Info: (Formerly College and University Bulletin), Yr. Est. 1947, Monthly, Trim Size-8 x 12, Sheetfed press, 16 pages, ISSN: 0162-7910, 2 Color, Newsprint, Saddle-stitched
Subscriptions: Indv. $35, $4/copy
Circulation: Total-8,000
List Rental: Rents Lists

AATE Newsletter
See: THEATRE

AATF National Bulletin — *Association*

Publishing Co: American Association of Teachers of French, 57 E Armory Ave, Champaign, IL 61820-6601; Title Tel # (217) 333-2842 Title Fax # (217) 333-2842
Personnel: Editor-Jane Black Goepper, Circ. Mgr.-Fred Jenkins
Editorial Description: Announcements and short articles on French language and cultural activities in the U.S.
General Info: Yr. Est. 1975, Quarterly, Trim Size-8½ x 11, Offset press, 24 pages, No Color, Newsprint, Other
Subscriptions: Inst. $35, Can. $38, For. $38, Free With Membership
Circulation: Total-11,000
List Rental: Rents Lists
Printing Co: Printec Press Inc., 2602 N Mattis Ave, Champaign, IL 61821-1053 Tel # (217) 359-2219

ABCDE Focus — *Association*

Publishing Co: Sponsor-Association of B.C. Drama Educators, British Columbia Teachers' Federation, 100-550 West 6th Avenue, Vancouver, BC V5Z 4P2 Canada;
Title Tel # (604) 871-2283 Title Fax # (604) 871-2289
General Info: Irregular
Circulation: Total-300

ACAT News
See: HEALTH

ACJS Today — *Association* — CPM: $66

Publishing Co: Academy of Criminal Justice Sciences, Northern Kentucky University, Nunn Hall 402, Nunn Drive, Highland Hts, KY 41099-5998; Title Tel # (606) 572-5634 Title Fax # (606) 572-6665
Personnel: Editor-Jeff Walker, Adv. Dir., Promotion Dir.-Pat DeLancey
Editorial Description: Professors and institutions who teach courses in criminology, law enforcement and corrections.
General Info: Yr. Est. 1963, 4x/yr., Trim Size-8½ x 11, Offset press, 28 pages, Newsprint, Saddle-stitched
Subscriptions: Indv. $45, Inst. $100, Free With Membership
Circulation: (100% controlled), Total-3,000
Advertising: $200.
List Rental: Actives: 3,000, $200/M

ACJU Higher Education Report

Publishing Co: Association of Jesuit Colleges and Universities, 1 Dupont Cir NW Ste 405, Washington, DC 20036-1110; Title Tel # (202) 667-3889
Personnel: Editor-Fa. James Sauve, Circ. Mgr.-Sr. Paulette, Circ. Mgr.-James Sauve
Editorial Description: Net-working; informatory trend-setting.
General Info: Yr. Est. 1977, Monthly, Trim Size-8½ x 11, Offset press, 8 pages, 2 Color
Subscriptions: Indv. $128, $2/copy
Circulation: Total-1,000
List Rental: Rents Lists
Printing Co: Webb/Mason, Inc., 6600 York Rd Ste 209, Baltimore, MD 21212-2024
Tel # (410) 532-8500

ACS Bulletin AEC — *Scholarly, Association* — CPM: $400

Publishing Co: Association for Canadian Studies, Box 8888, Station Centre-Ville, Montreal, PQ H3C 3P8 Canada; Title Tel # (514) 987-7784 Title Fax # (514) 987-8210
Personnel: Editor-Danielle Comeau
Editorial Description: News and articles on the various aspects of the study of Canada.
General Info: (Formerly ACS Newsletter/Bulletin de l'AEC), Yr. Est. 1979, Quarterly, Trim Size-8½ x 11, 48 pages, ISSN: 1196-8036, 1% ads, No Color
Subscriptions: Indv. $40, Inst. $75, Can. $40, For. $45, $4/copy
Circulation: Total-1,000
Advertising: $400. Accepts Inserts.
List Rental: Actives: $120/M
Printing Co: Imprimerie Gagne, 80 Ave. Saint Martin, Louiseville, PQ J5V 1B4 Canada
Tel # (819) 228-2766, Fax # (819) 228-8390

ADCIS Newsletter
Association   **CPM: $857**

Publishing Co: Association for Dev. of Computer-Based Instructional Systems, 1601 W 5th Ave, Columbus, OH 43212-2367; Title Tel # (614) 487-1528 Title Fax # (614) 487-1528
Personnel: Publisher-Carol Norris
Editorial Description: Information from special interest groups such as computer based training and instructional systems.
General Info: 5x/yr., 10% ads
Subscriptions: Free With Membership
Circulation: Total-700
Advertising: $600. Accepts Inserts.
List Rental: Actives: 1,300

ADHD Report
See: PSYCHOLOGY

AFSA News
See: SCHOOL ADMINISTRATION

AFT Action
Association

Publishing Co: American Federation of Teachers, 555 New Jersey Ave., NW, Washington, DC 20001-2079 Tel # (202) 879-4430 Fax # (202) 783-2014
Personnel: Editor-Trish Gorman, Art Dir.-Charles Glendinning
Editorial Description: Information for leadership of the AFT.
General Info: Yr. Est. 1970, Bi-monthly, Trim Size-11 x 17, Offset press, 4 pages, No Color, Newsprint, Other
Subscriptions: Indv. $1
Circulation: (84% controlled), Total-13,000

AGHE Exchange
See: SENIOR CITIZENS

AGS Quarterly: Bulletin of the Association for Gravestone Studies
See: HISTORY

ANR Educator
Business

Publishing Co: Michigan State Univ., Dept. of Ag. & Ext. Ed., 409 Ag. Hall, East Lansing, MI 48824-1039; Title Tel # (517) 355-6580 Title Fax # (517) 353-4981
Personnel: Editor-Jake Wamhoff, Production Mgr.-Diane Davis
Editorial Description: Newsletter sent to Michigan's agriscience & natural resource teachers & others interested in agricultural education.
General Info: Yr. Est. 1974, Bi-monthly, Trim Size-8½ x 11, Desktop press, 16 pages, No Color, Recycled, Saddle-stitched
Subscriptions: Free In Designated Area
Acquistions: Publication Bought
Circulation: (100% controlled), Total-300
Advertising: Accepts Inserts.

AOI Business Viewpoint
See: BUSINESS & INDUSTRY

AOSA Foresight
Business   **CPM: $100**

Publishing Co: American Optometric Assn. (AOA), 243 N. Lindbergh Blvd., St. Louis, MO 63141-7881; Title Tel # (314) 991-4100 Title Fax # (314) 991-4101
Personnel: Production Mgr.-Carol Freihaut
General Info: (Formerly AOSA Review), Quarterly, Trim Size-8½ x 11, Desktop press, 20 pages, 3% ads, 4 Color, Saddle-stitched
Subscriptions: Indv. $20, Free With Membership
Circulation: Total-6,000
Advertising: $600.

APEE Newsletter
See: BUSINESS & INDUSTRY

ASCA Counselor
Association

Publishing Co: American Counseling Assn., 5999 Stevenson Ave., Alexandria, VA 22304-3300 Fax # (703) 823-0252; Title Tel # (703) 823-9800
Personnel: Editor-Dolores Ehrlich
General Info: Yr. Est. 1962, Bi-monthly, Trim Size-8½ x 11, Sheetfed press, 16 pages, 1% ads, No Color, Newsprint
Circulation: (100% controlled)
List Rental: Actives: $65/M
Printing Co: American Graphics, PO Box 364, Gastonia, NC 28053-0364 Tel # (704) 864-5745

ASCD Update
Publishing Co: Association for Supervision & Curriculum Development, 1250 N Pitt St, Alexandria, VA 22314-1457; Title Tel # (703) 549-9110
Personnel: Publisher-Ronald Brandt, Editor-Scott Willis
Editorial Description: News on contemporary education issues & information on ASCD programs.
General Info: (Formerly News Exchange)
Circulation: Total-180,000
List Rental: List Management Co.: MGI-Marketing General Inc., 105 Oronoco St., Alexandria, VA 22314-2015 Tel # (703) 739-1000

ASSC Newsletter
Business, Association

Publishing Co: Arkansas School Study Council, 234 Graduate Education Bldg., Univ. of Arkansas, Fayetteville, AR 72701; Title Tel # (501) 575-4207 Title Fax # (501) 575-4681
Personnel: Editor-Martin Schoppmeyer, Circ. Mgr.-Sonja Bennett
Editorial Description: Research & developments of interest to Arkansas education professionals. Specificlly, school finance and equity.
General Info: Yr. Est. 1976, Monthly
Subscriptions: Free With Membership
Circulation: Total-650
Advertising: Accepts Inserts.

ASTC Newsletter
See: SCIENCE

ATENS News
Association

Publishing Co: Nova Scotia Teachers Union, 3106 Dutch Village Rd., Halifax, NS B3L 4L7 Canada Fax # (902) 477-3818; Title Tel # (902) 477-5621 Title Fax # (902) 477-3517
Personnel: Editor-Paul McCormick
Editorial Description: Items of interest to teachers of English Language Arts K-12.
General Info: (Formerly ATENS Newsletter), Yr. Est. 1970, Bi-monthly, 4 pages, No Color
Subscriptions: Indv. $10, Can. $10
Circulation: Total-400

AVA Update
Publishing Co: Association for Volunteer Administration, PO Box 4584, Boulder, CO 80306-4584; Title Tel # (303) 541-0238 Title Fax # (303) 541-0277
Personnel: Editor-Martha Martin
Editorial Description: Info of value to administrators of volunteer services.
General Info: (Formerly AAVS Newsletter), Yr. Est. 1961, Bi-monthly, 4 pages
Printing Co: Mathis Printing, INc., 3801 Old Pearl, Boulder, CO 80301

AWAIR News
See: ETHNIC

Academic Leader: The Newsletter for Academic Deans and Department Chairs
Consumer, Association

Publishing Co: Magna Publications, Inc., 611 N Sherman Ave, Madison, WI 53704-4410; Title Tel # (608) 246-3580 Title Fax # (608) 246-3597
Personnel: Publisher-Richard C. Perkins, Editor-Doris Green, Editorial Dir.-Mary Lou Santovec, Circ. Mgr.-Tom Crawford, Art Dir.-Tami Cook, Mktg. Dir.-Lisa Collins
Editorial Description: Provides information useful to Academic Deans and Department Chairs
General Info: Yr. Est. 1991, Monthly, Trim Size-8½ x 11, Offset press, 8 pages, ISSN: 8750-7730, 2 Color, Recycled
Subscriptions: Indv. $83
Circulation: Total-2,100
Advertising: Inquire for rates. Accepts Inserts.
List Rental: Actives: 2,300, $90/M
Printing Co: Sprint Print, 2610 Damon Rd, Madison, WI 53713-2388 Tel # (608) 251-3110

Accelerator Newsletter
Association

Publishing Co: Saskatchewan Science Teachers' Society, Box 1108, 2317 Arlington Ave., Saskatoon, SK S7K 3N3 Canada Parent Co.-Saskatchewan Teachers' Federation, Saskatoon, Canada
Personnel: Editor-Sharon Bender
General Info: Yr. Est. 1966, Irregular, Trim Size-5½ x 8½, Offset press, 20 pages, ISSN: 0316-2893, No Color
Subscriptions: Can. $20
Circulation: Total-300
Advertising: Inquire for rates.

Access
Business, Consumer   **CPM: $333**

Publishing Co: American Forum for Global Education, 120 Wall St Ste 2600, New York, NY 10005-4001; Title Tel # (212) 732-8606 Title Fax # (212) 791-4132
Personnel: Editor-Elizabeth Mahony, Circ. Mgr.-Don Miller, Promotion Dir.-Jaimie Cloud
Editorial Description: Presents current and important information on events, resources, and news on global/international educational concerns.
General Info: Yr. Est. 1979, 8x/yr., Web press, 20 pages, 2 Color
Subscriptions: Indv. $25
Circulation: Total-600
Advertising: $200.
List Rental: Rents Lists

Access
Scholarly

Publishing Co: Stamats Communications, Inc., 427 6th Ave. SE, Cedar Rapids, IA 52401-1931 Fax # (319) 364-4278; Title Tel # (319) 364-6167 Title Fax # (319) 365-5421
Editorial Description: Newsletter for educational proffesionals to improve recruiting & retaining students of color.
General Info: Yr. Est. 1993, 8x/yr.
Subscriptions: Indv. $99, Inst. $99, Can. $109
Circulation: Total-632, Readership-1,100

Accrediting Association of Bible Colleges Newsletter   *Consumer, Association*

Publishing Co: Accrediting Assn. of Bible Colleges, PO Box 1523, Fayetteville, AR 72702-1523; Title Tel # (501) 521-8164 Title Fax # (501) 521-9202
Personnel: Editor-Randall Bell, Circ. Mgr.-Joniva Monragon, Publisher, Production Mgr., Art Dir.-Joniva Mondragon
Editorial Description: Information,resources/seminars,employment opportunities revelant to Christian higher education.
General Info: Yr. Est. 1948, Tri-annually, Trim Size-8½ x 11, 20 pages, ISSN: 0094-260x, Matte, Saddle-stitched
Subscriptions: Indv. $6, $2/copy
Circulation: (83% controlled), Total-1,200, Subscriptions-200, Readership-1,200
Printing Co: Just-Us Printers, 555 N Old Missouri Rd, Springdale, AR 72764-3637 Tel # (501) 751-0385

Accrediting Association of Bible Colleges Newsletter
See: RELIGIOUS & THEOLOGICAL

Action Agenda
See: MEDIA & COMMUNICATIONS

Activity   *Business*

Publishing Co: American College Testing, 2201 N. Dodge St., Iowa City, IA 52243-0168; Title Tel # (319) 337-1410 Title Fax # (319) 339-3020
Personnel: Editor-Dan Lechay, Art Dir.-Henry Twanicki
Editorial Description: For counselors, administrators, advisors, and educators generally.
General Info: Yr. Est. 1961, Quarterly, 12 pages, 2 Color
Subscriptions: Free
Circulation: Total-100,000

Administrative Focus
See: SCHOOL ADMINISTRATION

Administrative Information Report

Publishing Co: National Association of Secondary School Principals, 1904 Association Dr., Reston, VA 22091-1537; Title Tel # (703) 860-0200 Title Fax # (703) 476-5432
Personnel: Editor-Thomas Koerner
General Info: Yr. Est. 1975, Monthly, Trim Size-8½ x 11, Sheetfed press, 4 pages, 2 Color, Matte
Subscriptions: $2/copy
Circulation: Total-40,000

Administrator: The Source for Practical Ideas and Key Issues in Higher Education
See: SCHOOL ADMINISTRATION

Adult & Continuing Education Today   *Business, Association*

Publishing Co: Learning Resources Network, 1550 Hayes Dr, Manhattan, KS 66502-5068; Title Tel # (913) 539-5376 Title Fax # (913) 539-7766
Personnel: Production Mgr.-Ed Dobmeyer, Publisher, Editor, Art Dir.-William Draves
Editorial Description: Natl. news letter for continuing educators.
General Info: (Formerly Learning Connection), Yr. Est. 1970, Bi-weekly, Trim Size-8½ x 11, Sheetfed press, 8 pages, ISSN: 0001-8473, 2 Color, Newsprint, Saddle-stitched
Subscriptions: Indv. $95
Acquistions: Publication Bought, Publication Sold
Circulation: (100% controlled), Total-3,200
Advertising: Inquire for rates.
List Rental: Actives: $85/M
Printing Co: Hawley Printing, 1660 Hayes Dr, Manhattan, KS 66502-5070 Tel # (913) 776-6731

Adventures in Movement
See: SOCIAL SERVICES & WELFARE

Advisor   *Association*

Publishing Co: Assn. of Community College Trustees, 1740 N Street, N.W., Washington, DC 20036-2907; Title Tel # (202) 775-4667
Personnel: Publisher-Ray Taylor, Editor-Sally Hutchins
Editorial Description: Covers association news, community college news, & trustee education information.
General Info: Yr. Est. 1972, Bi-monthly, Trim Size-8½ x 11, Sheetfed press, 12 pages, ISSN: 1044-8152, 2 Color, Coated, Saddle-stitched
Subscriptions: Indv. $35, $6/copy
Circulation: (93% controlled), Total-8,000
Printing Co: Hundley Lithograph, Inc., 6503 Chillum Pl NW, Washington, DC 20012-2189 Tel # (202) 829-7800

Advocate, The   *Association*   CPM: $65

Publishing Co: NEA New York, 217 Lark St, Albany, NY 12210-1101; Title Tel # (518) 462-6451
Personnel: Publisher-Greory Nash, Editor-Mollie Marchione
Editorial Description: Membership publication of the New York state branch of the National Education Assn.
General Info: Yr. Est. 1976, 9x/yr., Trim Size-11⅜ x 12, 16 pages, ISSN: 0161-7982, 2 Color, Newsprint
Subscriptions: Indv. $10, Free With Membership
Circulation: Total-38,000
Advertising: $2,500.

Aero-Gramme   *Consumer*

Publishing Co: Alternative Education Resource Organization, 417 Roslyn Rd, Roslyn Heights, NY 11577-2620 Fax # (516) 625-3257; Title Tel # (516) 621-2195 Title Fax # (516) 625-3057
Editorial Description: Features information of interest to homeschoolers and alternative educators.
General Info: (Formerly Atro-Gramme), Yr. Est. 1990, Quarterly, ISSN: 1067-9219
Subscriptions: Indv. $15
Circulation: Total-5,000

African Studies Center Newsletter   *Consumer, Association*

Publishing Co: African Studies Center, Michigan State University, 100 International Center, E. Lansing, MI 48824-1035; Title Tel # (517) 353-1700 Title Fax # (517) 432-1209
Personnel: Editor-David Wiley
Editorial Description: Contains information about Africa and related events at Michigan State Univ.
General Info: (Formerly Michigan Info on Africa Newsletter), Yr. Est. 1976, Semi-annually, Trim Size-17 x 11, Desktop press, 17 pages, No Color, Saddle-stitched
Subscriptions: Free
Acquistions: Publication Bought
Circulation: Total-990

Aging Research & Training News
See: SENIOR CITIZENS

Agora   *Association*

Publishing Co: Lakehead University, Oliver Rd., Thunder Bay, ON P7B 5E1 Canada; Title Tel # (807) 343-8300
Personnel: Editor-Katherine Shedden, Art Dir.-Ben Kaminski
Editorial Description: Lakehead Univ.'s staff and faculty newspaper publishes news and information on campus events.
General Info: (Formerly LU Week 2), Yr. Est. 1969, Monthly, Trim Size-11¼ x 17, Sheetfed press, 12 pages, No Color, Matte, Saddle-stitched
Circulation: (80% controlled), Total-2,000
Printing Co: Rainbow Printing, 380 Mooney St., Thunder Bay, ON P7B 5R4 Canada Tel # (807) 345-2364

Aid for Education Report   *Business*

Publishing Co: CD Publications, 8204 Fenton St., Silver Spring, MD 20910-4571; Title Tel # (301) 588-6380 Title Fax # (301) 588-6385
Personnel: Publisher-Mike Gerecht, Editor-Dave Zuckerman, Circ. Mgr.-Kurt Eisentraut, Mktg. Dir.-Joyce Meals
Editorial Description: Public and private funding opportunities for all levels of education, plus updates on application deadlines, eligibility requirements, funding levels and budget trends.
General Info: Yr. Est. 1991, Semi-monthly, Trim Size-8½ x 11, Sheetfed press, 16 pages, ISSN: 1058-1324, No Color, Matte, Other
Subscriptions: Indv. $259, Can. $269, For. $299, $15/copy
List Rental: List Management Co.: Manager: Amy Seyler; Washington Advertising Service, 8204 Fenton St., Silver Spring, MD 20910 Tel # (301) 588-7920, Fax # (301) 588-6385, Actives: 19,720, $150/M, Expires: 2,210, $150/M

Alberta Counselletter

Publishing Co: Alberta Teachers' Association, 11010-142 St., Edmonton, AB T5N 2R1 Canada Tel # (403) 453-2411
Personnel: Editor-Carole Solberg
Editorial Description: News of events, ideas, etc. For Guidance Counselors.
General Info: Trim Size-11 x 17, Mimeo press, 12 pages, ISSN: 0381-5951, No Color, Newsprint, Saddle-stitched
Subscriptions: Indv. $20, $2/copy
Circulation: (100% controlled), Total-500

Alberta Teachers' Association-Learning Resources Council-Newsletter

Publishing Co: Alberta Teachers' Association, 11010-142 St., Edmonton, AB T5N 2R1 Canada Tel # (403) 453-2411
Personnel: Editor-Teddy Moline
Editorial Description: Librarian newsletter- news, updates, resources.
General Info: Quarterly, Trim Size-8½ x 11, Mimeo press, 12 pages, ISSN: 0380-8491, No Color, Newsprint
Subscriptions: Indv. $30
Circulation: (100% controlled), Total-600

Alternative Models Newsletter
See: RELIGIOUS & THEOLOGICAL

Alumni Newsletter

Publishing Co: Jewish Labor Committee, 25 E. 21st St., 2nd Fl., New York, NY 10010-6297; Title Tel # (212) 477-0707 Title Fax # (212) 477-1918
Personnel: Editor-Arieh Lebowitz
Editorial Description: Newsletter of American public secondary school teachers who teach about the Holocaust and Jewish Resistance to the Nazis during World War II.
General Info: Yr. Est. 1983, Semi-annually, Trim Size-8½ x 11, Sheetfed press, 8 pages, No Color, Matte, Saddle-stitched
Circulation: Total-6,000

American Association of Teachers of German Newsletter
See: LITERATURE & LINGUISTICS

American Association of Teachers of Italian
See: LITERATURE & LINGUISTICS

American Association of Teachers of Slavic & Eastern European Languages News
See: LITERATURE & LINGUISTICS

American Nudist Research Library
See: LIFESTYLE

American Trade Schools
Directory

Publishing Co: Croner Publications, Inc., 34 Jericho Tpke, Jericho, NY 11753-1042; Title Tel # (516) 333-9085 Title Fax # (516) 338-4986
Personnel: Publisher-Ron Guggenheimer, Editor-Carol Sixt, Circ. Mgr.-Regina Friel
Editorial Description: Lists approximately 8,000 trade, technical & vocational schools in the US. Institutions are alphabetically classified by trades taught & listed by state & city. Includes name, address & telephone number as well as subjects taught, accrediting & approvingagencies.
General Info: Yr. Est. 1953, Monthly, Trim Size-7 x 9, Offset press, Looseleaf
Subscriptions: Indv. $100

America's Future
See: POLITICS

Arbitration in the Schools
See: LABOR

Arbitration in the Schools
See: LAW

Arkansas Vocational Visitor

Publishing Co: State Board of Education, Vocational Div., Education Building West-303D, Little Rock, AR 72201; Title Tel # (501) 682-2363
Personnel: Circ. Mgr.-Lucille McCall, Editor, Circ. Mgr.-Diane Murrell
Editorial Description: Significant instruction/activities in home economics education.
General Info: Trim Size-11 x 17, Letrpr. press, 4 pages, No Color
Subscriptions: Free
Circulation: (100% controlled), Total-650

Artistic Opportunities   *Consumer*

Publishing Co: Greene County Council on the Arts, 398 Main Street, Catskill, NY 12414 Tel # (518) 943-3400
Editorial Description: Information on workshops, grants, internships, and more for artists.
General Info: Irregular

Asian Studies Newsletter
See: CULTURE & HUMANITIES

Assessment Update
See: SCHOOL ADMINISTRATION

Association of American Law Schools, Newsletter
See: LAW

Assn. of Professors & Researchers in Religious Education Newsletter
See: RELIGIOUS & THEOLOGICAL

Assn. Provinciale des Enseignantes et Enseignants des Ecoles Fransaskoises Newsletter   *Association*

Publishing Co: Saskatchewan Teachers' Federation, Box 1108, Saskatoon, SK S7K 3N3 Canada
Editorial Description: News and information for French-speaking teachers in Saskatchewan. Text in French.
General Info: Yr. Est. 1994, Irregular
Subscriptions: Indv. $15

Association for Social Anthropology in Oceania Newsletter   *Association*

Publishing Co: Association for Social Anthropology in Oceania, Department Of Anthropology, University Of Washingto, Seattle, WA 98195-0001; Title Tel # (206) 543-1414
Personnel: Editor-Barbara Burns McGrath
General Info: Quarterly
Subscriptions: Indv. $20

Association of Teachers of Exceptional Children   *Association*

Publishing Co: Nova Scotia Teachers Union, 3106 Dutch Village Rd., Halifax, NS B3L 4L7 Canada Fax # (902) 477-3818; Title Tel # (902) 477-5621
Personnel: Editor-Fred Atkinson
General Info: Irregular
Subscriptions: Indv. $5

Athletic Director   *Association*

Publishing Co: National Association for Sport & Physical Education, 1900 Association Dr., Reston, VA 22091 Fax # (703) 496-9527; Title Tel # (703) 476-3410 Title Fax # (703) 476-9527
Editorial Description: Interest to athletic directors & coaches.
General Info: Yr. Est. 1969, Semi-annually, 4 pages, ISSN: 0004-6647, 2 Color
Subscriptions: Free With Membership
Circulation: Total-1,500
List Rental: Rents Lists

Awareness
See: RELIGIOUS & THEOLOGICAL

B.C. Alternate Education Association Newsletter   *Association*

Publishing Co: Sponsor-B.C. Alternate Education Association Newsletter, British Columbia Teachers' Federation, 100-550 West 6th Avenue, Vancouver, BC V5Z 4P2 Canada; Title Tel # (604) 871-2283 Title Fax # (604) 871-2289
General Info: Irregular
Circulation: Total-250

B.C. School Counsellors Newsletter   *Association*

Publishing Co: Sponsor-B.C. School Counsellor's Association, British Columbia Teachers' Federation, 100-550 West 6th Avenue, Vancouver, BC V5Z 4P2 Canada; Title Tel # (604) 871-2283 Title Fax # (604) 871-2289
General Info: Irregular, ISSN: 0382-8190
Circulation: Total-600

B.C. Science Teacher   *Association*

Publishing Co: British Columbia Teachers' Federation, 100-550 West 6th Avenue, Vancouver, BC V5Z 4P2 Canada Title Tel # (604) 871-2283 Fax # (604) 871-2289
Personnel: Editor-Gordon Gore
General Info: Yr. Est. 1972, Bi-monthly, 30 pages, Ind/Abs/Online: Can.Ed.In.
Subscriptions: Indv. $5
Circulation: Total-700

BCAMT Newsletter   *Association*

Publishing Co: Sponsor-B.C. Association of Mathematics Teachers, British Columbia Teachers' Federation, 100-550 West 6th Avenue, Vancouver, BC V5Z 4P2 Canada; Title Tel # (604) 871-2283 Title Fax # (604) 871-2289
General Info: Irregular

BCMEA Newsletter   *Association*

Publishing Co: British Columbia Teachers' Federation, 100-550 West 6th Avenue, Vancouver, BC V5Z 4P2 Canada; Title Tel # (604) 871-2283 Title Fax # (604) 871-2289
General Info: Irregular
Circulation: Total-800

Baltic Studies Newsletter   *Scholarly, Association*   **CPM: $33**

Publishing Co: Assn. for the Advancement of Baltic Studies,Inc, 111 Knob Hill Rd, Hackettstown, NJ 07840-4222; Title Tel # (908) 852-5258 Title Fax # (908) 852-3233
Personnel: Publisher-Janis Gaigulis, Editor-Sandra Milevska
Editorial Description: Provides information about the activities of the AABS, Baltic scholarly conferences, academic exchanges with the Baltic republics, & recent publications on Baltic history & current developments.
General Info: (Formerly AABS Newsletter), Yr. Est. 1976, Quarterly, Trim Size-8½ x 11, Offset press, 28 pages, ISSN: 1077-405x, 5% ads
Subscriptions: Indv. $25, Inst. $25, Can. $25, For. $25, $7/copy
Circulation: Total-3,000
Advertising: $100.
Printing Co: Augstums Printing Service, 1621 S 17th St, Lincoln, NE 68502-2602 Tel # (402) 474-1591

Bargaining Bulletin   *Association*

Publishing Co: British Columbia Teachers' Federation, 100-550 West 6th Avenue, Vancouver, BC V5Z 4P2 Canada Fax # (604) 871-2289; Title Tel # (604) 871-2283
Personnel: Editor-George North
Editorial Description: Provides data, information, articles, advice on bargaining matters.
General Info: Yr. Est. 1981, Irregular, Trim Size-8½ x 11, Offset press, 4 pages, 2 Color, Coated, Looseleaf
Circulation: (100% controlled), Total-950

Barter Update - Barter Basics Edition
See: BUSINESS & INDUSTRY

Baseball Coach
See: BASEBALL

Beacon
See: RELIGIOUS & THEOLOGICAL

Beta Parents
Consumer, Association

Publishing Co: National Beta Club, 151 West Lee Street, Spartanburg, SC 29306-3012
Tel # (803) 583-4553 Fax # (803) 542-9300; Title Tel # (864) 583-4553 Title Fax # (864) 542-9300
Personnel: Editor-Marggi Roldan
Editorial Description: Articles of interest to parents preparing to send a child to college. Topics include financial aid, choosing a college/career, and the admission process.
General Info: Yr. Est. 1990, Annually, Web press, 16 pages, 2 Color, Matte, Saddle-stitched
Subscriptions: $1/copy
Circulation: Total-70,000
Printing Co: Beacon Press, Inc., 4731 Eubank Rd., P.O. Box 26905, Richmond, VA 23261
Tel # (804) 226-2120

Better Teaching: Tips & Techniques to Improve Student Learning

Publishing Co: National School Public Relations Assn., 1501 Lee Hwy Ste 201, Arlington, VA 22209-1109 Fax # (703) 528-7017; Title Tel # (703) 528-5840
Personnel: Publisher-Joseph Scherer, Editor-Rodney Davis, Promotion Dir.-Keenan Bradshaw
General Info: Yr. Est. 1987, Semi-monthly, 4 pages, 2 Color, Newsprint
Subscriptions: Indv. $69
Circulation: Total-6,000

Between Classes/ Elderhostel Catalog
Consumer, Association

Publishing Co: Elderhostel, Inc., 75 Federal St., Boston, MA 02110-1904; Title Tel # (617) 426-7788 Title Fax # (617) 426-8351
Personnel: Editor-Michael Zoob
Editorial Description: Seasonal listings of elderhostel- sponsored educational programs offered by most colleges, universities and other educational cultural institutions in the U.S., Canada and 47 countries overseas.
General Info: 10x/yr., Web press, 120 pages, 2 Color, Newsprint, Saddle-stitched
Subscriptions: Free In Designated Area
Circulation: Total-600,000
Printing Co: Noll Printing Company, Inc., 100 Noll Plz, Huntington, IN 46750-1696
Tel # (800) 348-2886

Beyond Words

Publishing Co: Beyond Words, 1534 Wells Dr NE, Albuquerque, NM 87112-6383; Title Tel # (505) 275-2558
General Info: 10x/yr.
Subscriptions: Indv. $10

Blumenfeld Education Newsletter

Publishing Co: Blumenfeld Education Newsletter, PO Box 45161, Boise, ID 83711-5161; Title Tel # (208) 343-3790
Personnel: Editor-Samuel Blumenfeld
Editorial Description: Education in commentary & home schooling.
General Info: Monthly
Subscriptions: Indv. $36

Boletin

Publishing Co: Center for the Teaching of the Americas, Immaculata College, c/o Sister, Immaculata, PA 19345-9999; Title Tel # (215) 647-4400
Personnel: Editor-Sr. Mary Consuela
Editorial Description: School teaching of the Americas.
General Info: (Formerly Focus on the Americas), Yr. Est. 1968, Quarterly
Subscriptions: Indv. $1

Books to Build a New Society
See: BOOKS & BOOK TRADE

Border Connections
Association

Publishing Co: Los Ninos, 9765 Marconi Dr Ste 105, San Ysidro, CA 92173-3264; Title Tel # (619) 661-6912 Title Fax # (619) 661-1363
Personnel: Editor-Tammy Fishback
Editorial Description: Describes non-profits programs in Mexicali and Tijuana, Mexico.
General Info: (Formerly Los Ninos Notas), 3x/yr., 8 pages
Subscriptions: Free

Borod & Huggins Educational Services- Newsletter
Business

Publishing Co: Borod & Huggins Educational Services, Inc., 245 Wagner Pl Ste 200, Memphis, TN 38103-3815; Title Tel # (901) 526-7000
General Info: Monthly

Bridges
Association

Publishing Co: AFS Intercultural Programs, 220 East 42nd Street, Third Floor, New York, NY 10017-5806; Title Tel # (212) 949-4242 Title Fax # (212) 949-9379
Personnel: Editor-Nancy Stuve, Art Dir.-Mary Whiting
Editorial Description: Newsletter for AFS's U.S. volunteers.
General Info: (Formerly Directions), Yr. Est. 1988, Monthly, Trim Size-8½ x 11, 6 pages, ISSN: 1063-0910, No Color
Subscriptions: Free In Designated Area
Circulation: Total-10,000

Bridging The Gap
See: PHILOSOPHY

Briefings
See: LIBRARY

Briefs

Publishing Co: Packaging Education Foundation, 481 Carlisle Dr., Herndon, VA 22070-4819
Tel # (703) 318-8975; Title Tel # (703) 620-2155
Personnel: Editor-Cynthia Pslaum
General Info: Yr. Est. 1980, Quarterly
Circulation: Total-2,000

Brighton Times

Publishing Co: Brighton Academy, Foundation of Human Understanding, 1121 NE 7th St, Grants Pass, OR 97526-1421 Tel # (541) 474-6865
Personnel: Editor-Cynthia Cournoyer
Editorial Description: Home schooling.
General Info: Monthly
Subscriptions: Indv. $18

Bueno
See: LITERATURE & LINGUISTICS

Bulletin

Publishing Co: New Brunswick School Trustees' Assn., Box 501, Fredericton, NB E3B 4Z9 Canada; Title Tel # (506) 450-4066
Personnel: Editor-Marven Betts
General Info: Bi-monthly, 4 pages, ISSN: 0832-8358
Circulation: Total-5,000

Bulletin
Association

Publishing Co: Canadian Commission for UNESCO, 99 Metcalfe, Box 1047, Ottawa, ON K1P 5V8 Canada; Title Tel # (613) 598-4325 Title Fax # (613) 598-4405
Personnel: Publisher, Editor-Brigitte Morissette
Editorial Description: Activities of the Canadian Commission for Unesco & Unesco news of particular interest to Canadians.
General Info: Yr. Est. 1959, Quarterly, 12 pages, ISSN: 0008-4557
Circulation: Total-5,000

Bulletin Nouvelles
Association

Publishing Co: Sponsor-Assn. Provinciale des Professeurs de l'Immersion et du, British Columbia Teachers' Federation, 100-550 West 6th Avenue, Vancouver, BC V5Z 4P2 Canada Fax # (604) 871-2289; Title Tel # (604) 871-2283 Title Fax # (604) 633-2938
General Info: Irregular

Bulletin de Service
Association

Publishing Co: Saskatchewan Association of Teachers of French, Box 1108, 2317 Arlington Ave., Saskatoon, SK S7K 3N3 Canada Parent Co.-Saskatchewan Teachers' Federation, Saskatoon, Canada; Title Tel # (306) 373-1660
Personnel: Publisher-J. Henderson, Editor-Katherine Pugh, Circ. Mgr.-B. Shih
Editorial Description: Information for French language teachers in Saskatchewan. Text in French.
General Info: (Formerly SATF Newsletter), Yr. Est. 1964, 3x/yr., Trim Size-8½ x 11, Offset press, 6 pages, No Color
Subscriptions: Indv. $15
Circulation: (100% controlled), Total-375

Business Currents
See: LABOR

Business/Education Insider

Publishing Co: Heritage Foundation, 214 Massachusetts Ave NE, Washington, DC 20002-4999; Title Tel # (202) 546-4400 Title Fax # (202) 544-2260
Personnel: Editor-Jeanne Allen
General Info: Yr. Est. 1990, Monthly
Subscriptions: Indv. $8

CAEL News
Association **CPM: $244**

Publishing Co: Council for Adult & Experiential Learning, 243 S Wabash Ave # 800, Chicago, IL 60604-2302 Tel # (312) 922-5909; Title Tel # (312) 922-5907 Title Fax # (312) 922-1769
Personnel: Editor-Lynn Schroeder
Editorial Description: Expanding lifelong learning opportunities for adults.
General Info: Yr. Est. 1974, Tri-annually
Subscriptions: Indv. $15, For. $20
Circulation: Total-2,450
Advertising: $600.

CAFA Report
Association

Publishing Co: Confederation of Alberta Faculty Assn., 11043 90th Ave., Univ. of Alberta, Edmonton, AB T6G 2E1 Canada Fax # (403) 492-6145
General Info: Yr. Est. 1982, Quarterly
Circulation: Total-4,000

CAHPERD Journal/Times
See: HEALTH

CAL/NX211 Collectors Society Newsletter
See: HISTORY

CANS Newsletter

Publishing Co: Nova Scotia Teachers Union, 3106 Dutch Village Rd., Halifax, NS B3L 4L7 Canada
Fax # (902) 477-3818; Title Tel # (902) 477-5621 Title Fax # (902) 477-3517
Personnel: Editor-Ann Blackwood
General Info: Yr. Est. 1989, Irregular, 4 pages, No Color
Subscriptions: Indv. $15, Can. $15, $5/copy
Circulation: Total-200
Printing Co: Nova Scotia Teachers Union, Box 1060, Halifax, NJ B3L 4L7 Canada

CAPE Outlook   *Association*

Publishing Co: Council for American Private Educ., 1726 M St NW Ste 1102, Washington, DC
20036-4502; Title Tel # (202) 659-0016 Title Fax # (202) 659-0018
Personnel: Mktg. Dir.-Suzanne Cambria
General Info: Yr. Est. 1971, 10x/yr., Trim Size-8½ x 11, 4 pages, ISSN: 0271-1451, Color-cover,
Matte
Subscriptions: Indv. $15, $1/copy
Acquistions: Publication Bought
Circulation: (71% controlled), Total-2,800, Subscriptions-800
List Rental: Rents Lists
Printing Co: Serif Press, Inc., 1331 H St. NW, #110LL, Washington, DC 20005 Tel # (202) 737-4650

CAPS Capsule

Publishing Co: ERIC Counseling & Personnel Services Clearinghouse, 2108 School of Education,
Univ. of Michigan, Ann Arbor, MI 48109-1259; Title Tel # (313) 764-9492
Editorial Description: Covers news about ERIC & the counselling clearinghouse & developments in
the fields of education & counseling.
General Info: Quarterly, Trim Size-8½ x 11, Offset press, 4 pages, Color
Circulation: Total-7,500

CASE Newsletter   *Association*

Publishing Co: Council of Administrators of Special Education, 615 16th St., NW, Albuquerque, NM
87104; Title Tel # (505) 243-7622 Title Fax # (505) 247-4822
Editorial Description: Info to CASE members on issues pertinent to education of youth with special
needs.
General Info: Yr. Est. 1960, Quarterly, 8 pages, No Color
Subscriptions: Free With Membership
Circulation: Total-4,000

CAUSN Newsletter/
   Bulletin d'Information   *Association*

Publishing Co: Canadian Assn. of Univ. Schools of Nursing, 350 Albert Street, Suite 325, Ottawa,
ON K1R 1B1 Canada; Title Tel # (613) 563-1236
Personnel: Publisher, Editor-J. Bouchard
Editorial Description: News & activities of interest to nurse educators in university programs across
Canada. Bilingual publication.
General Info: Yr. Est. 1970, Quarterly, 4 pages, ISSN: 0835-9660, 4% ads, No Color
Acquistions: Publication Sold
Circulation: (100% controlled), Total-750
Advertising: Inquire for rates.
List Rental: Rents Lists
Printing Co: Kwik Kopy, 300 Slater St., Ottawa, ON K1P 6A6 Canada Tel # (613) 234-8826

CB Report

Publishing Co: Texas Higher Education Coordinating Board, PO Box 12788, Austin, TX 78711-2788;
Title Tel # (512) 483-6111
Personnel: Editor-Teri E. Flack
Editorial Description: Articles relating to higher education in Texas.
General Info: Yr. Est. 1966, Quarterly, Trim Size-8½ x 11, Sheetfed press, 8 pages, No Color,
Saddle-stitched
Subscriptions: Free To Qualified Recipient
Acquistions: Publication Bought
Circulation: Total-1,000

CBASSE Newsletter
See: SOCIOLOGY

CBE Report

Publishing Co: Sponsor-Assn. for Community Based Education, Assn. for Community Based
Education, 1806 Vernon St NW, Washington, DC 20009-1217; Title Tel # (202) 462-6333
Editorial Description: For educ. institutions covering news, fundraising, workshops, resources.
General Info: (Formerly Raps), Yr. Est. 1977, Monthly, Trim Size-8½ x 11, Sheetfed press, 12 pages,
2 Color
Subscriptions: Indv. $30, Can. $30, For. $50
Circulation: Total-2,000

CCAS Newsletter   *Association*

Publishing Co: Council of Colleges of Arts & Sciences, 186 University Hall, 230 N. Oval Mall,
Columbus, OH 43210-1319; Title Tel # (614) 292-1882 Title Fax # (614) 292-8666
Personnel: Editor-R.J. Hopkins, Feature Ed.-Melinda Nelson
Editorial Description: Membership newsletter to inform deans about arts and sciences issues.
General Info: Yr. Est. 1968, Bi-monthly, Trim Size-8½ x 11, Desktop press, 6 pages, No Color
Subscriptions: Free With Membership
Circulation: (100% controlled), Total-1,400
Printing Co: PS Printing Service, 1768 Hightower Dr, Columbus, OH 43235-1928

CCLI Newsletter
See: LIBRARY

CEA Forum   *Scholarly, Association*   CPM: $166

Publishing Co: College English Assn., Inc., English Dept., Youngstown State Univ., Youngstown, OH
44555-0001; Title Tel # (216) 742-3414
Personnel: Editor-Bege Bowers, Editor-Patricia Kelvin, Mng. Editor-Laaren Whitcombe
Editorial Description: Provides information for teachers of college English.
General Info: Yr. Est. 1970, Semi-annually, Trim Size-11 x 14, Sheetfed press, 15 pages, ISSN:
0007-8034, 1% ads, No Color, Coated
Subscriptions: Indv. $25, Inst. $30, Free With Membership
Circulation: Total-1,200
Advertising: $200.
Printing Co: Customer Printing, 1640 Mahoning Ave., Youngstown, OH 44509 Tel # (216) 793-2046

CEA News & Notes   *Association*

Publishing Co: Correctional Education Assn. Region VII, L.A. County Office of Ed., 9300 E. Imperial
Hwy., Downey, CA 90242; Title Tel # (310) 803-8546
Personnel: Co-Editor-Ted Price, Co-Editor-Silvia Ruiz
Editorial Description: International Correctional Education Association Newsletter.
General Info: Quarterly, Trim Size-8½ x 11, 12 pages, 2 Color, Matte, Saddle-stitched
Circulation: Total-3,500

CEA Newsletter   *Association*

Publishing Co: Canadian Education Association, 252 Bloor St. W., Ste. 8-200, Toronto, ON M5S
1V5 Canada; Title Tel # (416) 924-7721 Title Fax # (416) 924-3188
Personnel: Editor-Harriett Goldsborough
Editorial Description: News about school boards & departments of education for Canadian school
administrators. Text in English.
General Info: Yr. Est. 1946, 9x/yr., Trim Size-8½ x 11½, Desktop press, 6 pages, ISSN: 0008-3445,
Ind/Abs/Online: CEI,EI, Color, Matte
Subscriptions: Indv. $15, $2/copy
Circulation: Total-9,000

CEMA Update

Publishing Co: Connecticut Educational Media Assoc., 25 Elmwood Ave, Trumbull, CT 06611-3503;
Title Tel # (203) 774-7755
Personnel: Editor-Jim Weigel
General Info: Yr. Est. 1981, 10x/yr.
Subscriptions: Indv. $18

CFLE Network
See: SOCIAL SERVICES & WELFARE

CHE Letter

Publishing Co: Middle States Assn. of Colleges & Schools, 3624 Market St., Philadelphia, PA
19104-2614; Title Tel # (215) 662-5600 Title Fax # (215) 662-5950
General Info: (Formerly Higher Commission Letter), Quarterly
Circulation: Total-2,700

CIRA Bulletin   *Association*

Publishing Co: Canadian Intramural Recreation Association, 1600 James Naismith Drive, Suite 601,
Gloucester, ON K1B 5N4 Canada; Title Tel # (613) 748-5639 Title Fax # (613) 748-5706
Personnel: Editor-Suzanne Bray
Editorial Description: Association newsletter of practical ideas, feature articles, association
updates & conference highlights- in the area of intramurals.
General Info: Yr. Est. 1985, Bi-monthly, Trim Size-8½ x 11, Desktop press, 20 pages, ISSN: 1187-
0818, Ind/Abs/Online: SIRC, 2 Color, Recycled, Saddle-stitched
Subscriptions: Can. $40, Free With Membership
Circulation: Total-1,500

CJCEE Newsletter

Publishing Co: Connecticut Joint Council on Economic Education, Univ. of Connecticut, U-55, One
Bishop Circle, Storrs, CT 06269-4055; Title Tel # (203) 486-2327
Personnel: Editor-Emmett Cutter
Editorial Description: A semi-annual bulletin of upcoming programs and seminars for Council
memberrs and teachers (k-12) in Connecticut.
General Info: Yr. Est. 1974, Semi-annually, 4 pages
Circulation: Total-3,200

CLAG Communication
See: GEOGRAPHY

COPRED Peace Chronicle
See: POLITICS

COSSA Washington Update
See: POLITICS

CPC Salary Survey
See: EMPLOYMENT

CPF National News — *Association*

Publishing Co: Canadian Parents for French, 309 Cooper St., Suite 210, Ottawa, ON K2P 0G5 Canada; Title Tel # (613) 235-1481 Title Fax # (613) 230-5940
Personnel: Editor-Cynthia Steers
Editorial Description: For those interested in French language learning opportunities for young Canadians.
General Info: (Formerly CPF News; CPF National Newsletter), Yr. Est. 1977, Trim Size-8½ x 11, Offset press, 8 pages, ISSN: 0715-8904, 2 Color
Subscriptions: Indv. $25, Inst. $125, Free With Membership
Circulation: (100% controlled), Total-12,000

C/S Newsletter

Publishing Co: Center for Instructional Services, Purdue Univ., W. Lafayette, IN 47907; Title Tel # (317) 494-9454
Personnel: Editor-Vickie Lojek, Production Mgr.-Donna Miller
Editorial Description: Contains descriptions of CIS services & articles about instructional techniques.
General Info: Yr. Est. 1982, 7x/yr., Trim Size-8½ x 11, Sheetfed press, 4 pages, No Color
Circulation: Total-7,000

CSFA News

Publishing Co: Citizens' Scholarship Foundation of America, 1505 Riverview Rd, Saint Peter, MN 56082-1556; Title Tel # (507) 931-1682
Personnel: Editor-Liz Weiss, Circ. Mgr.-Joe Peterson
Editorial Description: Focuses on student aid programs in the private sector used to address recruitment of employees, high dropout rates, & creating & sustaining community scholarship foundation.
General Info: Monthly, Trim Size-8½ x 11, Web press, 6 pages, 2 Color, Matte
Circulation: (80% controlled), Total-4,500
List Rental: Rents Lists
Printing Co: Nelsen Printing, 838 N Minnesota Ave, Saint Peter, MN 56082-2425 Tel # (507) 931-1207

C.S.T. Connection
See: BUSINESS & INDUSTRY

CTF Link

Publishing Co: Canadian Teachers' Fed., 110 Argyle Ave., Ottawa, ON K2P 1B4 Canada; Title Tel # (613) 232-1505
Personnel: Editor-Maurice Bourque
General Info: Quarterly, 16 pages
Circulation: Total-5,200

CUSO Forum — *Scholarly, Association*

Publishing Co: CUSO, 2255 Carling Ave, Ste 400, Ottawa, ON K2B 1A6 Canada Tel # (613) 829-7445 Fax # (613) 829-7996; Title Tel # (613) 563-1242 Title Fax # (613) 563-8068
Personnel: Publisher-Christine Sotteau, Editor-Barbara Green, Production Mgr.-Brenda Hollett, Art Dir.-Suzanne Hall
Editorial Description: Describes CUSO work in Canada & the Third World.
General Info: (Formerly CUSO Journal), Yr. Est. 1969, Tri-annually, Trim Size-8½ x 11, Offset press, 8 pages, ISSN: 0823-5740, 2 Color, Newsprint, Saddle-stitched
Subscriptions: Free
Circulation: (100% controlled), Total-10,000

CWC Communicator
See: WOMEN'S

Cal Fam
See: PSYCHOLOGY

California School Law Digest — *Business, Consumer*

Publishing Co: LRP Publications, 747 Dresher Rd., P.O. Box 980, Horsham, PA 19044-0980 Tel # (215) 784-0910 Fax # (215) 784-0317; Title Tel # (908) 889-6336 Title Fax # (908) 889-6339
Personnel: Editor-Fred Rossi, Circ. Mgr.-Sandra Smith, Publisher, Promotion Dir.-Joel Whitaker
Editorial Description: News & administrative/court decision & pertaining to the law, the courts & California schools.
General Info: Yr. Est. 1973, Monthly, Trim Size-8½ x 11, Desktop press, 6 pages, ISSN: 0094-2057, No Color, Other
Subscriptions: Indv. $131, $15/copy
List Rental: List Management Co.: The Lake Group, 411 Theodore Freund Ave., Rye, NY 10580-1497 Tel # (914) 925-2400, Fax # (914) 925-2499, Actives: 29,196, $70/M

California Tomorrow — *Consumer, Association*

Publishing Co: California Tomorrow, Ft. Mason Ctr. Bldg. B, #345, San Francisco, CA 94123-1380; Title Tel # (415) 441-7631 Title Fax # (415) 775-4529
Personnel: Editor-Carol Dewell, Editor-Katherine Kam, Art Dir.-John Prestianni, Art Dir.-Alison Wood, Mktg. Dir.-May Li
Editorial Description: Illustrates need for system of comprehensive state/regional planning, responsive to public interest in California.
General Info: (Formerly Cry California), Yr. Est. 1965, Irregular, Trim Size-7 x 10, Offset press, 24 pages, ISSN: 0011-2224, No Color
Circulation: Total-2,618
Advertising: Accepts Inserts.

Campus Perspective — *Business, Association*

Publishing Co: Elizabeth City State Univ., Box 841, Elizabeth City, NC 27909; Title Tel # (919) 335-3246 Title Fax # (919) 335-3731
Personnel: Publisher, Editor-Shelia Johnson
Editorial Description: Provides news, activities of interest tofaculty and staff, etc.
General Info: Yr. Est. 1990, Monthly, Desktop press

Campus Watch
See: POLITICS

Canadian AIDS News
See: HEALTH

Canadian Association for University Continuing Education Bulletin — *Association*

Publishing Co: K. Clements Executive Dir. Assn. of Universities, 350 Albert St., Ottawa, ON K1R 1B1 Canada Fax # (613) 563-7739; Title Tel # (613) 563-1236
Personnel: Editor-Richard Levens, Circ. Mgr., Art Dir.-K. Clements
Editorial Description: Eng/Fr text.
General Info: Yr. Est. 1967, Trim Size-8½ x 11, Offset press, 14 pages, No Color
Subscriptions: Can. $80
Circulation: (100% controlled), Total-450

Canadian Association of University Research Administrators Research Bulletin

Publishing Co: Canadian Assn. of Univ. Research Administrators, c/o Office Research Admin., York Univ., 4700 Keele St., North York, ON MSJ 1P3 Canada; Title Tel # (416) 736-5055 Title Fax # (416) 736-5512
General Info: Bi-monthly

Canadian Assn. of Univ. Teachers of German, Newsletter — *Consumer, Association*

Publishing Co: Canadian Assn. of Univ. Teachers of German, Univ. of Victoria, PO Box 3045, Dept. of Germanic Studies, Victoria, BC V8W 3P4 Canada; Title Tel # (604) 721-6329 Title Fax # (604) 721-7319
Editorial Description: News of the assn. and German language teaching.
General Info: Semi-annually

Canadian Home & School — *Consumer, Association*

Publishing Co: Canadian Home & School Parent Teacher Federation, 858 Bank St., Ste. 109B, Ottawa, ON K1S 3W3 Canada Fax # (613) 234-3913
General Info: Annually

Canadian Institute of Ukrainian Studies, Newsletter

Publishing Co: Sponsor-Univ. of Alberta, Canadian Institute of Ukrainian Studies, 352 Athabasca Hall, Univ. of Alberta, Edmonton, AB T6G 2E8 Canada; Title Tel # (403) 492-2972 Title Fax # (403) 492-4967
Personnel: Editor-Bahdan Klid, Circ. Mgr., Promotion Dir.-Khrystyna Jendyk
Editorial Description: A bilingual (English & Ukrainian) pub. issued once a year detailing the activities of the Canadian Institute of Ukrainian Studies & its staff.
General Info: Yr. Est. 1976, Annually, Trim Size-8½ x 11, 80 pages, ISSN: 0702-8474, No Color, Newsprint
Subscriptions: Free
Circulation: Total-4,500
Advertising: Accepts Inserts.

Canadian Quill — *Association*

Publishing Co: New Brunswick Teachers' Assn., Box 752, Fredericton, NB E3B 5R6 Canada; Title Tel # (506) 455-8921
Personnel: Editor-Woody Hayes, Art Dir.-Dawn Parousiadis
Editorial Description: Teachers of English in New Brunswick.
General Info: (Formerly Chautauqua), Yr. Est. 1964, Trim Size-8½ x 11, Offset press, 16 pages, ISSN: 0710-7757, 2 Color
Circulation: (100% controlled), Total-490

Canadian Studies Update

Publishing Co: Association for Canadian Studies in the U.S., 1 Dupont Cir. NW, Ste. 620, Washington, DC 20036-1182; Title Tel # (202) 887-6375 Title Fax # (202) 296-8379
Personnel: Editor-Joan Guberman
Editorial Description: Canadian Studies Update is a part of membership in the Association for Canadian Studies in the U.S. - lists conferences, seminars, etc.
General Info: (Formerly ACSUS Newsletter), Yr. Est. 1971, Quarterly, Trim Size-8½ x 11, Web press, 10 pages, ISSN: 0734-4546, 2 Color, Coated, Saddle-stitched
Subscriptions: Indv. $60, Inst. $105, Free With Membership
Circulation: Total-1,500
List Rental: Actives: $275/M
Printing Co: To Change

Cardinal Principles — *Association*

Publishing Co: University of Louisville Alumni Assn., 2001 S. Brook St., Louisville, KY 40292-0001; Title Tel # (502) 852-6186
Personnel: Editor-Anne Domeck
Editorial Description: Information about programs and research activities of the school of education.
General Info: Semi-annually, 15 pages, 2 Color
Subscriptions: Free

Career Connections *Association*

Publishing Co: International Career Association Network, 2900 Amby Pl, Hermosa Beach, CA 90254-2216; Title Tel # (310) 376-7378
Personnel: Editor-Pat Nellor Wickwire
Editorial Description: Networking publication for associations and individuals interested in career education, career guidance, and career development.
General Info: Yr. Est. 1985, Trim Size-8½ x 11, 8 pages
Circulation: Total-2,500
Advertising: Accepts Inserts.

Career Planning & Adult Development Network Newsletter
See: LABOR

Careers Bridge Newsletter

Publishing Co: St. Louis Public Schools, 901 Locust St, St. Louis, MO 63101-1401; Title Tel # (314) 231-3720
Personnel: Editor-Susan Katzman, Circ. Mgr.-Pam Collier, Production Mgr.-Richard Hey, Adv. Dir.-Carol Duncan, Art Dir.-Betty Tobler, Promotion Dir.-Ken Roberts
Editorial Description: Newsletter available to educators & business/community persons on collaborative activities & promotion of career, & self-awareness education in pre-school to grade 12.
General Info: Yr. Est. 1980, Bi-monthly
Circulation: Total-11,000

Carnegie Quarterly *Association*

Publishing Co: Carnegie Corp. of New York, 437 Madison Avenue, New York, NY 10022-7001; Title Tel # (212) 371-3200
Personnel: Editor-Avery Russell
Editorial Description: Describes projects supported by Carnegie Corp. a philanthropic foundation.
General Info: Yr. Est. 1953, Quarterly, Trim Size-8½ x 11, Sheetfed press, 16 pages, 4 Color, Coated
Subscriptions: Free
Circulation: Total-38,500

Carolina Justice Policy Center News
See: LAW ENFORCEMENT & PENOLOGY

Catalyst, The
See: COMPUTERS & AUTOMATION

Catalyst *Association*

Publishing Co: Sponsor-B.C. Science Teacher's Association, British Columbia Teachers' Federation, 100-550 West 6th Avenue, Vancouver, BC V5Z 4P2 Canada; Title Tel # (604) 871-2283 Title Fax # (604) 871-2289
General Info: Irregular
Circulation: Total-500

Catalyst: Voices of Chicago School Reform

Publishing Co: Community Renewal Society, 332 S. Michigan Ave., Siute #500, Chicago, IL 60604-9863 Tel # (312) 427-4830 Fax # (312) 427-6130
Personnel: Publisher-Linda Lenz, Circ. Mgr.-Marvlun Reed
Editorial Description: An independent publication that documents, analyzes and supports school improvement efforts in chicago's public schools.
General Info: Yr. Est. 1990, 9x/yr., ISSN: 0528-2616
Subscriptions: Indv. $20, Inst. $25, For. $46, $2/copy
Circulation: (85% controlled), Subscriptions-1,200

Celo Education Notes

Publishing Co: Arthur Morgan School, 1901 Hannah Branch Rd, Burnsville, NC 28714-7582; Title Tel # (704) 675-4262
Personnel: Editor-Jeff Goodman, Circ. Mgr., Production Mgr.-Ernest Morgan
Editorial Description: Articles about the Arthur Morgan School & alternative education.
General Info: Yr. Est. 1962, Annually, Sheetfed press, 8 pages, No Color
Circulation: Total-1,500

Center for Creative Leadership
See: MANAGEMENT

Center Focus

Publishing Co: Sponsor-Center of Concern, Center of Concern, 3700 13th St NE, Washington, DC 20017-2592; Title Tel # (202) 635-2757 Title Fax # (202) 832-9494
Personnel: Publisher-Peter HEnriot, Editor-John Prendergast, Production Mgr.-Lance Hinds, Promotion Dir.-Lucien Chauvin
General Info: Yr. Est. 1971, Bi-monthly, 6 pages, 2 Color
Circulation: Total-12,000

Center for Health Services Newsletter
See: HEALTH

Center for Parent Education Newsletter

Publishing Co: Center for Parent Education, 81 Wyman St., Wapham, MA 02160; Title Tel # (617) 964-2442
Personnel: Editor-Burton White
General Info: Yr. Est. 1978, Bi-monthly
Subscriptions: Indv. $25

Center Update, The *Association*

Publishing Co: American Council on Education, 1 Dupont Cir NW, Ste 800, Washington, DC 20036-1193 Tel # (202) 939-9300 Fax # (202) 833-4762; Title Tel # (202) 939-9731 Title Fax # (202) 939-9793
Personnel: Editor-Stephen Sattler, Assoc. Ed.-Judith Cangialosi, Assign. Ed.-Laura Mullane
General Info: (Formerly Office on Educational Credit & Credentials News), Yr. Est. 1942, Semi-annually, Trim Size-11 x 17, Offset press, 16 pages, 2 Color, Saddle-stitched
Subscriptions: Free To Qualified Recipient
Circulation: Total-25,000
List Rental: Rents Lists

Centergram

Publishing Co: Center on Education & Training for Employment, 1900 Kenny Rd, Columbus, OH 43210-1016; Title Fax # (614) 290-1260
Personnel: Editor-Judy Balogh
General Info: Yr. Est. 1965, Bi-monthly
Subscriptions: Free To Qualified Recipient
Circulation: Total-14,139

Central Missouri State University News *Association*

Publishing Co: Central Missouri State University Public Relations, Administration 302, Warrensburg, MO 64093; Title Tel # (816) 543-4640 Title Fax # (816) 543-4911
Personnel: Publisher/President/Advisor-John Inglish, Editor-Tammy Dugan
Editorial Description: Faculty and staff weekly newsletter.
General Info: Yr. Est. 1980, Weekly, Sheetfed press, 4 pages, No Color, Matte
Subscriptions: Free
Printing Co: Account Manager: John Sarantakos; Central Missouri State University, Printing Services, Warrensburg, MO 64093

Chalk Talk *Association*

Publishing Co: Fresno Teachers Assn, 5334 N Fresno St # A, Fresno, CA 93710-6828; Title Tel # (209) 224-8430
Personnel: Editor-Pat Imperatrice, Circ. Mgr., Adv. Dir., Art Dir.-Cherry Henmi
Editorial Description: Improvement of public education and of the states of public school teachers and of their working conditions.
General Info: Yr. Est. 1958, Quarterly, 6 pages, 2 Color
Subscriptions: Indv. $2, $1/copy
Circulation: (100% controlled), Total-2,300

Challenging Times *Consumer*

Publishing Co: Natl. Professional Resources, 25 South Regent Street, P.O. Box 1479, Pt. Chester, NY 10573; Title Tel # (914) 937-8879 Title Fax # (914) 937-9327
Personnel: Editor-Donald J. Coe, Ed.D.
Editorial Description: Addresses the needs of service providers for children and youth at-risk. Information about issues related to curriculum, demonstration projects, grants, policy and procedures, networking and more.
General Info: (Formerly SubstanceAbuse inSchools&AIDS Update; Educating Youth atRisk), Bi-monthly
Subscriptions: Indv. $50, Inst. $50, Can. $50, For. $60

Chicago South Asia Newsletter *Association*

Publishing Co: Sponsor-Outreach Educational Project, South Asia Language & Area Center, 5848 S. University Ave., Chicago, IL 60637-1515; Title Tel # (312) 702-8635 Title Fax # (312) 702-9673
Personnel: Editor-Greg Grieve, Editor-Sandra Mulholland, Circ. Mgr.-Sameera Iyengar, Adv. Dir.-Sputnik Padmi Hum
Editorial Description: Reports on projects & activities of the Outreach Educational Project of the Center. Recurring features include a calendar of events, news of research & publications, & educational opportunities.
General Info: Yr. Est. 1977, 3x/yr., Mimeo press, 12 pages, No Color, Coated, Saddle-stitched
Subscriptions: Free
Acquistions: Publication Bought
Circulation: Total-2,000, Readership-6,000
Advertising: Accepts Inserts.
Printing Co: University of Chicago Printing Services, 5020 S Cornell Ave, Chicago, IL 60615-3016 Tel # (312) 702-1999, Fax # (312) 753-2977

Chicago Union Teacher
See: LABOR UNION

Chiefline
See: SCHOOL ADMINISTRATION

Child and Adolescent Psychopharmacology News
See: PSYCHOLOGY

Child Assessment News
See: PSYCHOLOGY

Children's Video Review Newsletter
See: CHILDREN

Christian Anti-Communism Crusade Newsletter
See: RELIGIOUS & THEOLOGICAL

Christian Civic League Record
See: RELIGIOUS & THEOLOGICAL

Christian Literacy Outreach

Publishing Co: Christian Literacy Assocs., 541 Perry Hwy, Pittsburgh, PA 15229-1851;
Title Tel # (412) 364-3777
Personnel: Editor-Joseph Mosca
General Info: Yr. Est. 1978, Quarterly, Mimeo press, 4 pages, No Color, Newsprint
Circulation: Total-3,500

Christian School Comment
See: RELIGIOUS & THEOLOGICAL

Chuchoteries

Publishing Co: Le Conseil Francais/Alberta Teachers Assn., 11010-142nd St., Edmonton, AB T5N 2R1 Canada
General Info: Semi-monthly, Mimeo press, Ind/Abs/Online: Can Educ Ind.
Circulation: Total-630

Circumference   *Association*

Publishing Co: Phi Epsilon Phi, 1290 Bayshore Highway, Suite 2, Burlingame, CA 94010-1821;
Title Tel # (415) 347-1765
Personnel: Editor-Cheryl Coulter
Editorial Description: To acquaint all members with what is going on in our sorority.
General Info: Quarterly, Trim Size-7 x 8½, Offset press, 10 pages, No Color
Circulation: Total-700

Citizens Business
See: PUBLIC MANAGEMENT & PLANNING

Classroom Connect   *Business*

Publishing Co: Wentworth Worldwide Media, 1866 Colonial Village Lane, PO Box 10488, Lancaster, PA 17605-0488; Title Tel # (717) 393-1000 Title Fax # (717) 393-5752
Personnel: Mng. Editor-Eileen Mauskapf
Editorial Description: Information on educational resources via the Internet for K-12 teachers.
General Info: Yr. Est. 1994, Monthly
Subscriptions: Indv. $39

Clothing for Less Newsletter
See: CONSUMER INTERESTS

College By Mail Etc.-
Newsletter   *Consumer*

Publishing Co: Prosperity & Profits Unlimited, PO Box 416, Denver, CO 80201-0416;
Title Tel # (303) 575-5676
Personnel: Publisher-A.C. Doyle
Editorial Description: Sources for college degrees that can be obtained by mail.
General Info: Yr. Est. 1991, Annually, Letrpr. press, 4 pages, ISSN: 0740-395X
Subscriptions: Indv. $7, Inst. $7, Can. $11, For. $11, $7/copy
Circulation: Total-10,000

College Placement Council-Spotlight
See: EMPLOYMENT

Colloquy on Teaching
World Affairs   *Business*

Publishing Co: World Affairs Council of North Califfornia, 312 Sutter St Ste 200, San Francisco, CA 94108-4311; Title Tel # (415) 982-3263 Title Fax # (415) 982-5028
Personnel: Editor-Cassie Todd
General Info: Yr. Est. 1971, 3x/yr.
Circulation: Total-3,500

Common Sense on Energy & Our Envirnoment
See: ENVIRONMENT & ECOLOGY

Communicate   *Association*

Publishing Co: Northwest Territories Teachers Assn., Box 2340, Yellowknife, NT X1A 2P7 Canada;
Title Tel # (403) 873-8501 Title Fax # (403) 873-2366
Personnel: Editor-J.T. Maurke
General Info: 8x/yr., 12 pages
Subscriptions: Indv. $10
Circulation: Total-1,400
Advertising: Accepts Inserts.

Communicator
See: SCHOOL ADMINISTRATION

Communicator

Publishing Co: Ontario Alliance of Christian Schools, 777 Hwy 53 East, Ancaster, ON L9K 1J4 Canada; Title Tel # (416) 648-2100
General Info: Yr. Est. 1979, Bi-monthly
Subscriptions: Free To Qualified Recipient
Circulation: Total-2,500

Commuter, The

Publishing Co: Natl. Clearinghouse for Commuter Programs, 1195 Stamp Student Union Univ., University of Maryland, College Park, MD 20742-0001; Title Tel # (301) 314-5274
Title Fax # (301) 314-9874
Personnel: Editor-Barbara Jacoby
Editorial Description: Services, programs, advocacy and research for commuter students in higher education.
General Info: Yr. Est. 1974, Quarterly, Desktop press, 12 pages, Other
Subscriptions: Indv. $30
Circulation: Total-400

Co-Operatively Speaking   *Consumer, Association*

Publishing Co: U.S. Office, PO Box 90410, Indianapolis, IN 46290-0410; Title Tel # (519) 673-4070
Personnel: Editor-Carol Mitchell
Editorial Description: A forum for parent participation preschools to promote parent involvement along with qualified early childhood educators.
General Info: Yr. Est. 1984, Quarterly, 8 pages, ISSN: 0048-2978
Subscriptions: Indv. $25, Can. $25, Free With Membership
Circulation: Total-3,000

Composition Studies/
Freshman English
News

Publishing Co: Sponsor-Dept. of English, Texas Christian Univ., Box 32929, Fort Worth, TX 76129;
Title Tel # (817) 921-7240 Title Fax # (817) 921-7333
Personnel: Editor-Christina Murphy, Circ. Mgr.-Toni Howell
Editorial Description: Theoretical and practical articles on rhetorical theory.
General Info: (Formerly Freshman English News), Yr. Est. 1972, Semi-annually, 44 pages, 3% ads, No Color, Newsprint
Subscriptions: Indv. $8, Inst. $20, $5/copy
Circulation: Total-900
Advertising: Inquire for rates. Accepts Inserts.

Concerns   *Consumer, Association*

Publishing Co: Alcohol & Drug Concerns, 4500 Sheppard Ave., E., Ste. 112H, Scarborough, ON M1F 3R6 Canada; Title Tel # (416) 293-3400 Title Fax # (416) 293-1142
Personnel: Editor-K.N. Burden
Editorial Description: Preventive education in the field of alcohol and drug abuse.
General Info: (Formerly The Advocate), Yr. Est. 1902, Quarterly, ISSN: 0045-779X, 2 Color
Subscriptions: Indv. $12
Circulation: Total-15,000

Connect   *Business*

Publishing Co: Teachers' Laboratory Inc., 28 Birge St., PO Box 6480, Brattleboro, VT 05302-6480;
Title Tel # (802) 254-3457 Title Fax # (802) 254-5233
Personnel: Editor-Casey Murrow
Editorial Description: New developments in science & math instruction for the K-8 teacher.
General Info: Yr. Est. 1987, 5x/yr., Trim Size-8½ x 11, Letrpr. press, 20 pages, ISSN: 1041-682X, 2 Color, Other, Saddle-stitched
Subscriptions: Indv. $18, Can. $22, For. $30, $6/copy
Acquistions: Publication Bought
Circulation: (25% controlled), Total-2,000, Subscriptions-1,500

Connecticut Libraries
See: LIBRARY

Connection   *Association*

Publishing Co: National Association of State Boards of Education, Inc., 1012 Cameron St, Alexandria, VA 22314-2427; Title Tel # (703) 684-4000
Editorial Description: An informal newsletter for state board of education members.
General Info: (Formerly Focus), Yr. Est. 1981, Monthly, Offset press, 10 pages, 2 Color, Newsprint
Circulation: Total-750

Connections
See: MEDICINE

Contact-British Columbia
Hospital/Homebound
Teachers Association   *Association*

Publishing Co: Sponsor-Hospital/Homebound Provincial Specialist Assoication, British Columbia Teachers' Federation, 100-550 West 6th Avenue, Vancouver, BC V5Z 4P2 Canada;
Title Tel # (604) 871-2283 Title Fax # (604) 871-2289
General Info: Irregular, ISSN: 0226-1456

Continuation Education

Publishing Co: California Continuation Education Assn., 6501 Balboa Blvd., Van Nuys, CA 91406-5526
Personnel: Editor-A.C. Laudon
Subscriptions: Indv. $5

Core Teacher   *Association*

Publishing Co: Natl. Assn. for Core Curriculum, 1100 E Summit St Ste 5, Kent, OH 44240-4094; Title Tel # (216) 677-5008 Title Fax # (216) 677-5008
Personnel: Editor-Gordon Vars
Editorial Description: News of the national association and the core movement in general.
General Info: Yr. Est. 1951, Quarterly, Trim Size-8½ x 11, Offset press, 8 pages, ISSN: 0045-8538, No Color
Subscriptions: Indv. $10, Can. $12, For. $15, $3/copy
Circulation: Total-300

Cormosea Bulletin
See: CULTURE & HUMANITIES

Cornerstone

Publishing Co: Center for Education of Women, University of Michigan, Ann Arbor, MI 48109-1189; Title Tel # (313) 998-7080
Editorial Description: Research, advocacy, and service to women in terms of education and professional advancement.
General Info: (Formerly Center for Continuing Education of Women Newsletter), Yr. Est. 1964, Offset press, 4 pages, No Color
Subscriptions: Free To Qualified Recipient
Circulation: Total-12,500

Council Actions   *Consumer, Association*

Publishing Co: Kentucky Council on Higher Education, 1050 US 127 S., Suite #101, Frankfort, KY 40601-4333; Title Tel # (502) 564-3553
Editorial Description: News of Kentucky Council on Higher Education's activities and of higher education in the state.
General Info: (Formerly Council Report), Yr. Est. 1977, Quarterly, Sheetfed press, 2 pages, Matte
Circulation: Total-1,200
Printing Co: Kentucky Dept. Of Finance, Div. of Printing, 300 Myrtle Ave, Frankfort, KY 40601-3070 Tel # (502) 564-2670

Council on School Administration Newsletter

Publishing Co: Alberta Teachers' Association, 11010-142 St., Edmonton, AB T5N 2R1 Canada Tel # (403) 453-2411
Personnel: Editor-Lorelei Rogers
General Info: (Formerly Visions), Trim Size-8½ x 11, Sheetfed press, 4 pages, Saddle-stitched
Subscriptions: Indv. $15
Circulation: Total-1,200

Counterforce

Publishing Co: Society for the Advancement of Good English, 4501 Riverside Ave # 30, Anderson, CA 96007-2759; Title Tel # (916) 365-8026
General Info: Quarterly
Circulation: Total-1,000

Coupon Treasure Hunt Newsletter
See: HOME ECONOMICS

Courier
See: INTERNATIONAL AFFAIRS

Courier Alberta Teachers' Association, Modern and Classical Languages Council, Newsletter   *Association*

Publishing Co: Alberta Teachers' Association, 11010-142 St., Edmonton, AB T5N 2R1 Canada Tel # (403) 453-2411
Personnel: Editor-Carolyn King
Editorial Description: Articles on classroom practices and subjects of interest to teachers of French, German and Ukrainian.
General Info: Yr. Est. 1963, Monthly, Trim Size-8½ x 11, Offset press, 10 pages, ISSN: 0318-0220, No Color, Newsprint
Subscriptions: Indv. $20
Circulation: (79% controlled), Total-600

Course Trends in Adult Learning   *Business, Association*

Publishing Co: Learning Resources Network, 1550 Hayes Dr, Manhattan, KS 66502-5068; Title Tel # (913) 539-5376 Title Fax # (913) 537-2834
Personnel: Publisher-William Draves, Editor, Production Mgr., Art Dir.-Julie Coates
Editorial Description: Trends in noncredit classes for adults.
General Info: (Formerly Program Trends in Business & Industry), Yr. Est. 1970, Monthly, Trim Size-8½ x 11, Sheetfed press, 16 pages, Color-cover, Newsprint, Saddle-stitched
Subscriptions: Indv. $95, $7/copy
Acquistions: Publication Bought, Publication Sold
Circulation: (100% controlled), Total-1,500
Advertising: Inquire for rates. Accepts Inserts.
List Rental: List Management Co.: Infocore, 5605 Avenida Del Parque, Rancho Santa Fe, CA 92067 Tel # (619) 634-5064, Actives: $85/M
Printing Co: Hawley Printing, 1660 Hayes Dr, Manhattan, KS 66502-5070 Tel # (913) 776-6731

Cranial Letter
See: HEALTH

Creation/Evolution
See: SCIENCE

Cross & Quill, the Christian Writers Newsletter   *Consumer, Association*

Publishing Co: Christian Writers Fellowship International, Rr 3 Box 1635, Clinton, SC 29325-9542 Tel # (803) 697-6035; Title Tel # (615) 522-3026 Title Fax # (803) 697-6035
Personnel: Publisher, Editor-Sandy Brooks
Editorial Description: Contains marketing information & concise how-to on writing. CWFI offers a critique service; market consultation; networking with other Christian writers and organizations, online access.
General Info: Yr. Est. 1976, Bi-monthly, Trim Size-8½ x 11, Desktop press, 8 pages, Ind/Abs/Online: America Online , Compuserve, No Color, Other
Subscriptions: Indv. $18, Can. $21, For. $25, Free With Membership
Circulation: Readership-1,000
Advertising: Inquire for rates. Accepts Inserts.
List Rental: List Management Co.: Twin Peaks Press, PO Box 129, Vancouver, WA 98666-0129 Tel # (206) 694-2462, Fax # (206) 696-3210

Cubprints
See: HEARING & SPEECH

Current News on File
See: GOVERNMENT

DCS News

Publishing Co: Division of Continuing Studies, University of Nebraska-Lincoln, Lincoln, NE 68583-0001; Title Tel # (402) 472-2175
Personnel: Editor-Brad Gifford

DEC Communicator

Publishing Co: Division for Early Childhood, Ctr. For Persons W/Disability, Utah State Univ., Logan, UT 84322-0001
Personnel: Editor-Sarah Rule
General Info: Yr. Est. 1978, Quarterly, 6 pages
Circulation: Total-7,000

D.H.E. Data Briefs   *Association*

Publishing Co: New Jersey State Dept. of Education, Public Information Office, 225 W. State St., CN 500, Trenton, NJ 08625-0500; Title Tel # (609) 984-1666
General Info: Yr. Est. 1974, Bi-monthly

DICD New Times   *Association*

Publishing Co: Council for Exceptional Children, 1920 Association Dr., Reston, VA 22091-1589; Title Tel # (703) 620-3660 Title Fax # (703) 264-9494
Personnel: Editor-Christine DeSouza
Editorial Description: Information concerning education & welfare of children & youth with communication disorders.
General Info: (Formerly Division for Children w/Communication Disorders Newsletter), Yr. Est. 1980, Semi-annually, Trim Size-8½ x 11, Offset press, 12 pages, No Color, Saddle-stitched
Subscriptions: Free With Membership
Circulation: Total-2,500
List Rental: Actives: $60/M
Printing Co: Naecker Printing

DLD Times   *Association*

Publishing Co: Council for Exceptional Children, 1920 Association Dr., Reston, VA 22091-1589; Title Tel # (703) 620-3660 Title Fax # (703) 264-9494
Personnel: Editor-Katherine Garnett
Editorial Description: Information concerning education & welfare of children & youth with learning disabilities.
General Info: Yr. Est. 1983, Trim Size-8½ x 11, Offset press, 8 pages, No Color, Saddle-stitched
Circulation: Total-14,100
List Rental: Actives: $60/M
Printing Co: Beyer Offset, R.D. #2, Central Square, NY 13036 Tel # (315) 668-2880

Dallas Institute Newsletter, The
See: PUBLIC MANAGEMENT & PLANNING

Dallas Memorial Center for Holocaust Studies Newsletter
See: HISTORY

Day Care Guide
See: CHILDREN

Dearborn School News   *Consumer, Association*

Publishing Co: Dearborn Public Schools, PO Box 2812, Dearborn, MI 48123-2812; Title Tel # (313) 582-3010
General Info: Quarterly

Decision Line   *Association*

Publishing Co: Decision Sciences Institute, University Plaza, Atlanta, GA 30303
Tel # (404) 651-4073 Fax # (404) 651-2804; Title Tel # (404) 651-4000
Personnel: Editor-K. Roscoe Davis, Production Mgr.-Harold Jacobs, Adv. Dir.-Carol Latta
Editorial Description: Contains articles on education, business, and decision sciences as well as available positions and textbook advertising.
General Info: Yr. Est. 1973, 5x/yr., Trim Size-8½ x 11, Web press, 32 pages, No Color, Coated
Subscriptions: Indv. $6
Circulation: Total-5,000
Advertising: Inquire for rates.
List Rental: Actives: $50/M
Printing Co: Vision Web, 5305 Webb Pky NW, Lilburn, GA 30247-5944 Tel # (404) 279-2209

Delta Kappa Gamma News
See: CLUBS

Department Chair
See: SCHOOL ADMINISTRATION

Department of Education
Newsletter   *Association*

Publishing Co: Government of Newfoundland, Box 8700, St. John's, NF A1B 4J6 Canada;
Title Tel # (709) 576-2991
Personnel: Editor-Robert Forsey
Editorial Description: News from the Department of Education as it relates to the Province's teachers. Notices from all divisions, curriculum, administration, special, school services, etc.
General Info: Yr. Est. 1950, Quarterly, Trim Size-8½ x 11, Offset press, 12 pages, No Color, Saddle-stitched
Circulation: (100% controlled), Total-8,000
Printing Co: Hawk Publications, Normans Ave., Mt. Pearl, NF A1C 3R9 Canada
Tel # (709) 368-3235

Dept. of Education Reports

Publishing Co: Feistritzer Pubs., 4401a Connecticut Ave NW # 212, Washington, DC 20008-2325;
Title Tel # (202) 362-3444 Title Fax # (202) 362-3493
Personnel: Editor-David Chester
General Info: (Formerly Education Reports), Yr. Est. 1979, Weekly, 8 pages
Subscriptions: Indv. $347, Can. $360, For. $385

Design & Technology
Education Bulletin   *Business, Association*

Publishing Co: Design & Tech. Teachers Assn. of ON, 38 Patina Dr., c/o Keith McLaren, Willowdale, ON M2H 1R1 Canada
Personnel: Publisher-Denis Etienne, Editor-Brian Carswell, Adv. Dir.-Peter Morris, Art Dir.-Jim O'Shea
Editorial Description: Industrial arts education in the schools of Ontario.
General Info: (Formerly Ontario Industrial Arts Bulletin), Yr. Est. 1942, Semi-annually, Trim Size-8½ x 11, Mimeo press, 45 pages, Ind/Abs/Online: Can.Ed.In., No Color
Subscriptions: Indv. $30
Acquisitions: Publication Bought, Publication Sold
Circulation: (100% controlled), Total-1,000
Advertising: Inquire for rates.

DeskTop Presentations &
Publishing   *Business*

Publishing Co: Doron & Associates, 1213 Ridgecrest Cir, Denton, TX 76205-5421;
Title Tel # (817) 566-1366
Personnel: Publisher, Editor-Tom Doron, Circ. Mgr.-Susan Byrd, Product Mgr.-Mac Page
Editorial Description: Computer generated publications, presentations & visual aids for education & business.
General Info: Yr. Est. 1991, Bi-monthly, Trim Size-8½ x 11, Web press, 16 pages, 2 Color, Matte, Saddle-stitched
Subscriptions: Indv. $60, $5/copy
Circulation: Total-60,000

Developer, The

Publishing Co: Natl. Staff Development Council, PO Box 240, Oxford, OH 45056-0240;
Title Tel # (513) 523-6029 Title Fax # (513) 523-0638
Personnel: Editor-Dennis Sparks, Circ. Mgr.-Shirley Havens
Editorial Description: Devoted to staff development for educational personnel.
General Info: Yr. Est. 1980, 10x/yr., 8 pages
Circulation: Total-7,000
Advertising: Inquire for rates.
List Rental: Actives: 4,986, $95/M
Printing Co: American Printing, 528 S 7th St, Hamilton, OH 45011-3619 Tel # (513) 867-0602

Digital Kids Report, The
See: COMPUTERS & AUTOMATION

Disability Compliance for Higher Education
See: DISABILITY

Distant Drums
See: PHILOSOPHY

Diversity 2000   *Business, Consumer*

Publishing Co: Holocaust Resource Center, Kean College - Dr. J. Preil, 1000 Morris Avenue, Union, NJ 07083-7131
Personnel: Editor-J. Preil
Editorial Description: Offers ideas and issues on multicultural school education programs.
General Info: Yr. Est. 1993, Bi-monthly

Division on Visual Handicaps Quarterly
See: BLIND

Documentary Heritage Program Newsletter
See: HISTORY

Drug & Alcohol Abuse Education
See: HEALTH

EDUCOM Update

Publishing Co: EDUCOM, 1112 16th St NW Ste 600, Washington, DC 20036-4823;
Title Tel # (202) 872-4200 Title Fax # (202) 872-4200
Editorial Description: News and information pertaining to information technology in higher education.
General Info: Yr. Est. 1992, Bi-monthly
Subscriptions: Free With Membership

ERIC/CRESS Bulletin   *Consumer*

Publishing Co: Sponsor-US Dept. of Edu., Off. of Edu. Research & Improvement, ERIC Clearinghouse on Rural Education, PO Box 1348, Charleston, WV 25325-1348 Parent Co.-Appalachia Educational Laboratory, Inc., Charleston; Title Tel # (304) 347-0400
Title Fax # (304) 347-0487
Personnel: Editor-Patricia Cahape Hammer
Editorial Description: Covers all aspects of education pertaining to American Indians, Mexican Americans, migrants, outdoor education, rural education and small schools.
General Info: (Formerly CRESS Notes), Yr. Est. 1988, 3x/yr., Trim Size-8½ x 11, Web press, 4 pages, No Color, Matte, Saddle-stitched
Subscriptions: Free
Circulation: (100% controlled), Total-3,500
Printing Co: Red Clay Press, Route 16, Mt. Zion, WV 26147 Tel # (304) 354-6159

ERIC/EECE Newsletter   *Consumer, Scholarly*

Publishing Co: ERIC EECE, Univ. of Illinois, 805 W. PA Ave., Urbana, IL 61801;
Title Tel # (217) 333-1386 Title Fax # (217) 333-3767
Personnel: Editor-Bernard Cesarone, Circ. Mgr.-James Ennis
Editorial Description: Elementary and early childhood education, day care, parental behavior, and child development from the prenatal period through early adolescence.
General Info: Yr. Est. 1968, Semi-annually, Trim Size-8½ x 11, Offset press, 4 pages, ISSN: 0740-1132, 2 Color, Matte
Subscriptions: Free
Circulation: Total-8,000

ERIC/IR Update   *Business, Consumer*

Publishing Co: Syracuse University, 4-194 Cst, Syracuse, NY 13244-0001;
Title Tel # (315) 443-3640 Title Fax # (315) 443-5448
Personnel: Editor-Jane Janis
Editorial Description: Information on the widening of access to educational information.
General Info: Yr. Est. 1977, Semi-annually, Trim Size-8½ x 11, Offset press, 6 pages, Newsprint
Circulation: Total-4,600
Printing Co: Syracuse Univ. Printing Services, 820 Comstock Ave., Syracuse, NY 13244-0001

ETS Developments

Publishing Co: Educational Testing Service, Rosedale Rd., Princeton, NJ 08541-0001;
Title Tel # (609) 734-1129
Personnel: Editor-Wendy Nardi
Editorial Description: Quarterly newsletter in developments in educational testing, research, and services at ETS.
General Info: Yr. Est. 1951, Quarterly, 12 pages, ISSN: 0046-1547, 2 Color, Coated, Saddle-stitched
Acquistions: Publication Bought
Circulation: Total-75,000

ETV Newsletter
See: TELEVISION & VIDEO

Early Childhood Reporter   *Consumer, Association*

Publishing Co: LRP Publications, 747 Dresher Rd., P.O. Box 980, Horsham, PA 19044-0980
Tel # (215) 784-0910 Fax # (215) 784-0317
Personnel: Publisher-Kenneth Kahn, Editor-Caroline Ryan, Mktg. Dir.-Marcy Witt
Editorial Description: Educational newsletter for parents & professionals, at the local state & federal levels, responsible for the design & implementation of early childhood programs. Operates from a policy perspective & the impact of state & federal activity on such programs.
General Info: Yr. Est. 1990, Monthly, ISSN: 1058-6482, Ind/Abs/Online: LRPnet, 2 Color
Subscriptions: Indv. $145
List Rental: List Management Co.: Manager: Anne McGowen; Axon Lists, 747 Dresher Rd. Ste. 500, Box 980, Horsham, PA 19044 Tel # (215) 784-0860, Fax # (215) 784-0870, Actives: $125/M
Printing Co: Axon-Chancellor, 1660 DeKalb Ave., King of Prussia, PA 19405 Tel # (215) 265-1007

Eastern Clips
See: COLLEGE ALUMNI

Ecolacy   *Association*

Publishing Co: Sponsor-Environmental Educators' Provincial Specialist Association, British Columbia Teachers' Federation, 100-550 West 6th Avenue, Vancouver, BC V5Z 4P2 Canada; Title Tel # (604) 871-2283 Title Fax # (604) 871-2289
General Info: Irregular
Circulation: Total-200

Economic Education Bulletin
See: ECONOMICS

Economic Opportunity Report
See: SOCIAL SERVICES & WELFARE

EdPress News   *Business, Association*

Publishing Co: Educational Press Association of America, Rowan College of New Jersey, 201 Mullica Hill Rd., Glassboro, NJ 08028-1701; Title Tel # (609) 256-4610 Title Fax # (609) 256-4926
Personnel: Mng. Editor-Lloyd W. Kline, Exec. Ed.-Donald R. Stoll, Circ. Mgr.-Deborah A. Culotta, Editor, Design Ed.-, Art Dir.-Julia M. Mercier
Editorial Description: Newsletter of issues, skills, events, and trends relevent to education publishing.
General Info: Yr. Est. 1939, Monthly, Trim Size-8½ x 11, Letrpr. press, 8 pages, 2 Color, Matte
Subscriptions: Indv. $50, Inst. $130, Free With Membership
Circulation: Total-1,000
List Rental: Actives: $135/M
Printing Co: Glassboro Printing Inc., 30 Academy St N, Glassboro, NJ 08028-1911 Tel # (609) 881-2600, Fax # (609) 881-0257

Ed.WORD   *Association*

Publishing Co: Arizona Dept. of Education, 1535 W Jefferson St, Phoenix, AZ 85007-3280; Title Tel # (602) 542-4700
Personnel: Editor-Jim Whitelaw
Editorial Description: Educational news in Arizona and the nation, and events in the Department of Education.
General Info: (Formerly Alert), Yr. Est. 1976, Weekly, Trim Size-8½ x 14, Offset press, 2 pages, No Color
Circulation: (100% controlled), Total-2,000

Edgewise

Publishing Co: Edgewood College, 855 Woodrow St, Madison, WI 53711-1997; Title Tel # (608) 257-4861
Personnel: Editor-Jim Otttney
General Info: Yr. Est. 1986, Bi-weekly, Trim Size-11 x 17, Offset press, 4 pages
Circulation: Total-450
Printing Co: Econo Print, 1402 Greenway Cross, Madison, WI 53713-3111 Tel # (608) 274-4400

EduQuest Connections
See: BUSINESS & INDUSTRY

Educated Traveler, The
See: TRAVEL

Educating for Employment
See: EMPLOYMENT

Education Beat   *Business, Association*

Publishing Co: Political Pulse, 926 J St., Ste. 1218, Sacramento, CA 95814-2708; Title Tel # (916) 446-2048 Title Fax # (916) 446-5302
Personnel: Editor-Larry Lynch
Editorial Description: News of California education--kindergarten through university level.
General Info: Yr. Est. 1990, Semi-monthly
Subscriptions: Indv. $110
Circulation: Total-380
List Rental: Rents Lists

Education Daily   *Business*

Publishing Co: Capitol Publications, Inc., 1101 King St., Ste. 444, Alexandria, VA 22314-2968; Title Tel # (703) 683-4100 Title Fax # (703) 739-6501
Personnel: Publisher-Cynthia Carter, Editor-Annette Licitra, Exec. Ed.-Joe McGavin, Circ. Mgr.-Peggy Dwyer, Production Mgr.-Billy Adams, Art Dir.-Linda McDonald, Mktg. Dir.-Mary Lou Probka, Promotion Dir.-Susan Pangman
Editorial Description: Timely reports on federal policy funding & research affecting schools, school districts, college's and universities and state education agencies.
General Info: Yr. Est. 1967, Daily, Trim Size-8½ x 11, 6 pages, ISSN: 0013-1261, Ind/Abs/Online: NewsNet
Subscriptions: Indv. $581, Inst. $581, $5/copy
List Rental: Actives: $150/M
Printing Co: Capitol Publications, Inc., 1101 King St., Ste. 444, Alexandria, VA 22314-2968 Tel # (703) 683-4100, Fax # (703) 739-6501

Education in Focus   *Consumer*

Publishing Co: Books for All Times, Inc., PO Box 2, Alexandria, VA 22313-0002; Title Tel # (703) 548-0457 Title Fax # (703) 548-0457
Personnel: Editor-Joe David
Editorial Description: A look at education from a rational and humane viewpoint in order to enlighten readers about specific concerns.
General Info: Yr. Est. 1990, Semi-annually, Trim Size-8½ x 11, 6 pages, ISSN: 1049-7250
Subscriptions: Indv. $18, Inst. $18, Can. $18, For. $28, $3/copy
Circulation: Total-1,000
Advertising: Inquire for rates. Accepts Inserts.

Education Forward   *Association*

Publishing Co: Education Forward, PO Box 7841, Madison, WI 53707-7841; Title Tel # (608) 266-4499
Personnel: Editor-Mark Ibach
Editorial Description: Sent to Wisconsin school administrators, libraries, and teachers.
General Info: Yr. Est. 1947, 10x/yr., Trim Size-11 x 15, Web press, 24 pages, 2 Color, Newsprint
Circulation: Total-14,000
List Rental: Rents Lists

Education Funding News   *Business*

Publishing Co: Education Funding Research Council, 4301 Fairfax Dr Ste 875, Arlington, VA 22203-1627; Title Tel # (703) 528-1082 Title Fax # (703) 528-6060
Personnel: Publisher-James Marshall, Editor-Lisa Sierra, Circ. Mgr.-Thomas Wright, Promotion Dir.-Richard Erb
Editorial Description: Newsletter on federal funding for elementary and secondary education.
General Info: Yr. Est. 1971, Weekly, 10 pages, ISSN: 0273-4443, No Color
Subscriptions: Indv. $297
Acquistions: Publication Bought, Publication Sold
Printing Co: Newsletter Press, 76 Valley St, East Providence, RI 02914-4424 Tel # (401) 438-5352

Education Grants Alert
See: PHILANTHROPY

Education Jobs

Publishing Co: National Education Service Center, PO Box 1279, Riverton, WY 82501-1279; Title Tel # (307) 856-0170
Personnel: Editor-Lucretia Ficht
General Info: Yr. Est. 1981, Weekly

Education Law
See: LAW

Education Leader

Publishing Co: B.C. School Trustees Assn., 1155 W. 8th Ave., Vancouver, BC V6H 1C5 Canada
Personnel: Editor-Jeremy Cato, Adv. Dir.-Marjam Kimia
Editorial Description: Canada's most comprehensive & timely education pub. Stories explore current issues & trends in education while also providing in-depth news coverage.
General Info: Yr. Est. 1904, Bi-weekly, Web press, 6 pages
Subscriptions: Indv. $59
Circulation: Total-7,000
Advertising: Inquire for rates.

Education Newsletter
See: RELIGIOUS & THEOLOGICAL

Education Newsline

Publishing Co: Natl. Assn. of Christan Educators, PO Box 3200, Costa Mesa, CA 92628-3200; Title Tel # (714) 251-9333 Title Fax # (714) 251-9466
Personnel: Publisher-Robert Simonds, Editor-Kathi Hudson
Editorial Description: Articles pertinent to public education for teachers & parents, current trends & solutions, the work of Citizens for Excellence In Education.
General Info: Yr. Est. 1985, Bi-monthly, Desktop press, 8 pages, Color, Newsprint
Subscriptions: Indv. $20
Acquistions: Publication Bought
Circulation: (11% controlled), Total-18,000, Single Copy/Newsstand-1,000, Subscriptions-15,000

Education Personnel
Notes   *Business, Association*

Publishing Co: NYPER Publications, PO Box 662, Latham, NY 12110-0662 Fax # (518) 458-8582; Title Tel # (518) 786-1654
Personnel: Editor-Harvey Randall
Editorial Description: Summarizes important court and administrative discussions of interest to educators
General Info: Yr. Est. 1986, Monthly, ISSN: 1071-7420
Subscriptions: Indv. $95, Inst. $95, Can. $95, For. $115
Advertising: Accepts Inserts.

Education Perspectives   *Consumer, Association*

Publishing Co: Education Students' Assn., Univ. of British Columbia, Vancouver, BC Canada Tel # (604) 822-5632
General Info: Yr. Est. 1975, Annually
Advertising: Inquire for rates.

Education Quarterly   *Consumer, Association*

Publishing Co: New Jersey State Dept. of Education, Public Information Office, 225 W. State St., CN 500, Trenton, NJ 08625-0500; Title Tel # (609) 292-4040
Personnel: Editor-Richard Vespucci
General Info: (Formerly NJ Education Bulletin), Yr. Est. 1982, Monthly, Trim Size-8½ x 11, Web press, 6 pages, No Color, Coated
Circulation: Total-10,000
Printing Co: Trenton Printing Co., 1200 Southard St, Trenton, NJ 08638-5006

Education Reporter
See: JOURNALISM

Education Technology
News
Business

Publishing Co: Business Publishers, Inc., 951 Pershing Dr., Silver Spring, MD 20910-4464
Tel # (301) 589-5103 Fax # (301) 589-8493; Title Tel # (301) 587-6300 Title Fax # (301) 587-1081
Personnel: Publisher-Leonard A. Eiserer, Editor-Howard Fields, Circ. Mgr.-Brenda Davenport, Mktg. Mgr.-Mark Fullem
Editorial Description: Programs and funding available to assist secondary and elementary schools in teaching computer literacy.
General Info: Yr. Est. 1984, Monthly, Trim Size-8½ x 11, Desktop press, 8 pages, Ind/Abs/Online: Newsnet, Information Access Company, No Color, Recycled
Subscriptions: Indv. $297, Inst. $297, Can. $297, For. $310
Advertising: Accepts Inserts.
List Rental: List Management Co.: BPI Direct, 951 Pershing Dr., Silver Spring, MD 20910-4464
Tel # (301) 585-5976, Fax # (301) 587-4530

Education U.S.A.
Business

Publishing Co: Capitol Publications, Inc., 1101 King St., Ste. 444, Alexandria, VA 22314-2968;
Title Tel # (703) 683-4100 Title Fax # (703) 739-6501
Personnel: Publisher-Cynthia Carter, Publisher-Helen Hoart, Exec. Ed.-Joe McGavin, Circ. Mgr.-Peggy Dwyer, Production Mgr.-Billy Adams, Art Dir.-Linda McDonald, Mktg. Dir.-Mary Lou Probka, Promotion Dir.-Susan Pangman
Editorial Description: Comprehensive overview of the national education scene. Includes reports on special ed, billigual ed, chapter 1 programs and more.
General Info: Yr. Est. 1958, Bi-weekly, Trim Size-8½ x 11, Offset press, 8 pages, ISSN: 0013-1571, No Color
Subscriptions: Indv. $128, Inst. $128
List Rental: Actives $150/M
Printing Co: Capitol Publications, Inc., 1101 King St., Ste. 444, Alexandria, VA 22314-2968
Tel # (703) 683-4100, Fax # (703) 739-6501

Education Update
Association

Publishing Co: AFL-CIO Department of Education, 815 16th St. NW, Ste. 407, Washington, DC 20006-4104 Fax # (202) 637-5058; Title Tel # (202) 637-5152
Personnel: Editor-David Cohen
Editorial Description: Labor education conferences, resources, issues, new publications, films, & videos.
General Info: Yr. Est. 1978, Bi-monthly, Trim Size-8½ x 11, 8 pages, 2 Color
Subscriptions: Free
Circulation: Total-6,800

Educational Marketer
See: ADVERTISING & MARKETING

Educator
See: SCHOOL ADMINISTRATION

Educators Against Racism and Apartheid
See: CIVIL RIGHTS

Educator's Guide to Controlling Sexual Harassment
See: LAW

Educatus
Scholarly, Association

Publishing Co: Education Students' Assn., Univ. of British Columbia, Vancouver, BC Canada;
Title Tel # (604) 822-5632
General Info: Yr. Est. 1974, Bi-weekly

Effective Classrooms:
Research Based
Solutions to Improve
Learning

Publishing Co: Effective Classrooms, 14110 S Park Blvd, Cleveland, OH 44120-1326;
Title Tel # (216) 397-1030 Title Fax # (216) 397-1030
Personnel: Publisher, Editor-Ruth Kendel
General Info: (Formerly Effective Classrooms: The In-Service Newsletter), Yr. Est. 1989, 6x/yr., Trim Size-8½ x 11, 4 pages, 2 Color
Subscriptions: Indv. $175, Inst. $185
Circulation: Total-150
Printing Co: Bisco Printers, 2904 W Clay St, Richmond, VA 23230-4807 Tel # (804) 353-7292, Fax # (804) 353-0390

Electronic Education
Report
Business

Publishing Co: Simba Information, Inc., 213 Danbury Rd. PO Box 7430, Wilton, CT 06897-7430
Tel # (203) 834-0033 Fax # (203) 834-1771 Parent Co.-Cowles Business Media, New York
Personnel: Publisher-Chris Elwell, Editor-Michael P. Hayes, Editorial Dir.-Claire Schoen, Assoc. Ed.-Victor Rubell, Circ. Mgr.-Joyce Brigish, Mktg. Dir.-Michael Genaro
Editorial Description: Electronic Education Report provides industry decision-makers with the prudent business decisions in a rapidly evolving market.
General Info: Yr. Est. 1994, Bi-weekly
Subscriptions: Indv. $349, Can. $349, For. $399
List Rental: Rents Lists

Employee Ownership Report
See: BUSINESS & INDUSTRY

Employment & Training Reporter
See: EMPLOYMENT

Employment Opportunities

Publishing Co: National Guild of Community Schools of the Arts, Box 8018, 40 N. Van Brunt St., Englewood, NJ 07631 Fax # (201) 871-7639; Title Tel # (201) 871-3337
Editorial Description: Features annoucements of job opportunities in the field of community arts education.
General Info: Monthly, Ind/Abs/Online: NewsNet
Subscriptions: Indv. $60

English Leadership
Quarterly
Association

Publishing Co: Sponsor-NCTE, Natl. Coun. of Teachers of English, 1111 W Kenyon Rd, Urbana, IL 61801-1096; Title Tel # (217) 328-3870 Title Fax # (217) 328-0977
Personnel: Editor-Henry Kiernan, Production Mgr.-Michelle Sander Johlas
Editorial Description: Teaching of English for secondary school English Department chairpersons.
General Info: (Formerly CSSEDC Newsletter), Yr. Est. 1982, Quarterly, Trim Size-8½ x 11, Web press, 12 pages, ISSN: 1054-1578, 2 Color, Newsprint, Saddle-stitched
Subscriptions: Indv. $15, $3/copy
Circulation: Total-2,200
List Rental: Rents Lists

English Resource, The
See: LITERATURE & LINGUISTICS

Equal Education Alert

Publishing Co: NOWLDEF/Peer, 1333 H St. NW, 14th Fl., Washington, DC 20005-4707;
Title Tel # (202) 682-0940
Personnel: Editor-Theresa Cusick
Editorial Description: Reports on current educational policy affecting women & girls.
General Info: (Formerly Peer Perspectives), Yr. Est. 1980, Monthly, 8 pages, No Color
Subscriptions: Indv. $50
Circulation: Total-500

Equity for the Education of Women & Girls
See: WOMEN'S

Esperanto U.S.A.
See: LITERATURE & LINGUISTICS

Everglades Reporter
See: ENVIRONMENT & ECOLOGY

Exclaimer
See: AGRICULTURE

Extensions - Newsletter of
the High/Scope
Curriculum
Consumer, Association

Publishing Co: High Scope Educational Resource Foundation, 600 N River St, Ypsilanti, MI 48198-2821 Tel # (313) 485-2000 Fax # (800) 442-4329
Personnel: Editor-Lynn Taylor, Circ. Mgr.-Jana Federer, Mktg. Dir.-Rita Toderan
Editorial Description: Teacher guide for users of the High/Scope curriculum.
General Info: Yr. Est. 1970, Bi-monthly, Trim Size-8 x 11, Offset press, 8 pages, 2 Color, Matte
Subscriptions: Indv. $30, For. $33

FACTA Newsletter
Association

Publishing Co: Alberta Teachers' Association, 11010-142 St., Edmonton, AB T5N 2R1 Canada
Tel # (403) 453-2411
Personnel: Editor-Kay Anderson
Editorial Description: Fine arts newsletter.
General Info: Yr. Est. 1966, Trim Size-8½ x 11, Mimeo press, 12 pages, ISSN: 0014-5556, No Color, Newsprint
Subscriptions: Indv. $20
Circulation: (100% controlled), Total-620

FFA Update
See: AGRICULTURE

FIERF Newsletter

Publishing Co: Forging Industry Educational & Research Foundation, LTV Bldg. 300/25 Prospect Ave., Cleveland, OH 44115; Title Tel # (216) 781-5040 Title Fax # (216) 781-5065
Personnel: Editor-Ila Pearl
General Info: Yr. Est. 1968, Semi-annually
Subscriptions: Free With Membership
Circulation: Total-3,000

Facing History & Ourselves
News

Publishing Co: Facing History and Ourselves National Foundation, Inc., 16 Hurd Rd, Brookline, MA 02146-6919; Title Tel # (617) 232-1595
Personnel: Editor-Margot Strom
General Info: Yr. Est. 1983, Quarterly
Circulation: Total-10,000

Faculty Affairs *Association*

Publishing Co: Langara Faculty Association, Langara College, 100 W. 49th Ave., Vancouver, BC V5Y 2Z6 Canada Fax # (604) 327-3234; Title Tel # (604) 324-5343
Personnel: Editor-John Howard-Gibbon, Promotion Dir.-David Mitton
Editorial Description: College activities, post-secondary education, occasional light essays.
General Info: Yr. Est. 1967, Quarterly, Trim Size-8½ x 11, Mimeo press, 16 pages, No Color
Circulation: Total-450

Fast Break
See: SPORTS & SPORTING GOODS

Federal Auditing Information Service for Higher Education
See: ACCOUNTING

Federal Grants & Contracts Weekly
See: PHILANTHROPY

Federal Research Report *Business*

Publishing Co: Business Publishers, Inc., 951 Pershing Dr., Silver Spring, MD 20910-4464 Tel # (301) 589-5103 Fax # (301) 589-8493; Title Tel # (301) 587-6300 Title Fax # (301) 587-1081
Personnel: Publisher-Leonard A. Eiserer, Editor-Leonard Eiserer, Circ. Mgr.-Brenda Davenport
Editorial Description: Federal grants & contracts for colleges in areas including health, education, social sciences.
General Info: Yr. Est. 1965, Weekly, Trim Size-8½ x 11, Offset press, 8 pages, ISSN: 0148-4109, Ind/Abs/Online: Newsnet, No Color
Subscriptions: Indv. $270, Can. $270, For. $295
List Rental: Rents Lists

Federation of C.P.T.A.s of Ontario Newsletter *Association*

Publishing Co: Federation of Cath. Parent/Teacher Assn. of Ontario, 80 Sheppard Ave., Toronto, ON M2N 6E8 Canada; Title Tel # (416) 229-5333
Personnel: Publisher-Glorya Nanne, Editor-Jack MacKinnon, Production Mgr.-Norman Prieur
General Info: Yr. Est. 1974, Quarterly, ISSN: 0700-9070, Ind/Abs/Online: to the ministry of education & to other education assns. in Ontario.'
Circulation: Total-42,000

Federation Update

Publishing Co: Ontario Secondary School Teachers' Federation, 60 Mobile Dr., Toronto, ON M4A 2P3 Canada Fax # (416) 751-3394; Title Tel # (416) 751-8300
Personnel: Editor-Jack Hutton
Editorial Description: Material of interest to secondary school teachers, primarily in Ontario.
General Info: (Formerly Intercom), Yr. Est. 1974, 40x/yr., 4 pages
Circulation: Total-40,000

Ferguson-Florissant Schools *Consumer*

Publishing Co: Ferguson-Florissant School District R-2, 1005 Waterford Dr, Florissant, MO 63033-3649; Title Tel # (314) 831-4411
Editorial Description: Provides residents of the school district with information about public schools.
General Info: Yr. Est. 1958, Quarterly, Trim Size-11 x 17, Offset press, 4 pages, 2 Color
Circulation: Total-32,000

Five Minutes with ACHE *Association*

Publishing Co: Association for Continuing Higher Education, P.O Box 118067, CE-P, Charleston, SC 29423-8067; Title Tel # (803) 722-5546 Title Fax # (803) 722-5520
Personnel: Editor-Wayne Whelan
Editorial Description: Membership news.
General Info: (Formerly Assn. for Continuing Higher Educ.), Yr. Est. 1977, Monthly, 4 pages
Subscriptions: Indv. $25, Inst. $20, Can. $25, For. $35
Circulation: Total-1,500
List Rental: Actives: 1,600, $200/M

Florida School Herald
See: HEARING & SPEECH

Focus

Publishing Co: Florida Education Association, 118 N Monroe St, Tallahassee, FL 32301-1531; Title Tel # (904) 224-1161 Title Fax # (904) 681-2905
Personnel: Publisher-Pat Tornillo, Editor-Frank Ciarlo, Editorial Asst.-Elisia Dames, Art Dir.-Danny Capps
Editorial Description: Emphasizes such issues as education, unionism and politics.
General Info: (Formerly Solidarity's Focus), Yr. Est. 1989, Quarterly, Trim Size-8½ x 11, Offset press, 8 pages, Matte, Other
Advertising: Accepts Inserts.

Focus *Business, Association*

Publishing Co: Freedoms Foundation At Valley Forge, PO Box 706, Valley Forge, PA 19482-0706; Title Tel # (610) 933-8825
Personnel: Publisher-Ron Leymeister, Editor-George Blake, Circ. Mgr.-Henshaw Chappie, Production Mgr.-Abdul Faber, Art Dir.-Iggy Wilson, Promotion Dir.-Michael Albert Moyer
Editorial Description: Strives to teach Americans about America and promote responsible citizenship through educatiuonal programs anjd awards designed to recognize outstanding Americans.
General Info: (Formerly Report from Valley Forge), Yr. Est. 1949, Quarterly, Trim Size-8 x 11, Sheetfed press, 6 pages, 2 Color, Matte, Saddle-stitched
Circulation: Total-30,000

Focus on Festivals
See: MUSIC & MUSIC TRADES

Focus on Seattle Public Schools

Publishing Co: Seattle Public Schools, 815 4th Ave. N., Seattle, WA 98109-3902; Title Tel # (206) 298-7000 Title Fax # (206) 298-7101
Personnel: Editor-Edna Kellman
Editorial Description: Highlights news & achievements of students & staff in SPS.
General Info: Yr. Est. 1983, Bi-monthly, 8 pages, 2 Color
Circulation: (100% controlled), Total-45,000

Food Free or Cheap Newsletter
See: HOME ECONOMICS

Forefront
See: AGRICULTURE

Foreign Student Service Council Newsletter *Consumer*

Publishing Co: Foreign Student Service Council, 2337 18th St NW, Washington, DC 20009-1814; Title Tel # (202) 232-4979
Editorial Description: Non-profit organization dedicated to promote understanding between international students and Americans.
General Info: Yr. Est. 1956, Semi-annually, Trim Size-8½ x 14, Letrpr. press, Color
Subscriptions: Free
Circulation: Total-1,500

Forest Forum
See: FORESTRY

Forum
See: INTERNATIONAL AFFAIRS

Forum *Association*

Publishing Co: Educators for Social Responsibility, 23 Garden St, Cambridge, MA 02138-3623; Title Tel # (617) 492-1764 Title Fax # (617) 864-5164
Personnel: Editor-Laura Parker Roerden
Editorial Description: Educators concerned with children's ethical and social development, focusing especially on conflict resolution, violence prevention, and prejudice reduction.
General Info: Yr. Est. 1981, Quarterly, Trim Size-8½ x 11, 16 pages, No Color
Subscriptions: Indv. $35
Circulation: Total-12,000

Foundations Monthly Newsletter

Publishing Co: Foundations of Education, College of Education, Univ. of Florida, Gainsville, FL 32611; Title Tel # (904) 392-0724
Personnel: Editor-Dr. Robert Primack
Editorial Description: Discusses influence of education on society, society on education.
General Info: Yr. Est. 1983, Monthly
Subscriptions: Indv. $10, Inst. $20, $1/copy

Free Materials for Schools & Libraries *Business*

Publishing Co: Connaught Education Services, Box 34069, Dept. 349, Seattle, WA 98124; Title Tel # (604) 876-3377 Title Fax # (604) 876-3377
Personnel: Editor-Jim Clark, Circ. Mgr.-Sylvia Lim, Production Mgr.-Hardy Fischer, Art Dir.-Pat Lavac
Editorial Description: Provides schools & libraries with a reliable list of recommended free materials & services. Subject headings included.
General Info: (Formerly Free Newsletter), Yr. Est. 1979, 5x/yr., Trim Size-7¼ x 11, Offset press, 16 pages, ISSN: 0836-0073, 1% ads, Color, Other
Subscriptions: Indv. $20, Inst. $20, Can. $21, For. $22
Circulation: Total-2,500
Advertising: Inquire for rates.
Printing Co: New Leaf, 12357 82A Ave., Surrey, BC V3W 0L5 Canada

Freedom & Enterprise

Publishing Co: Natl. Schools Committee for Economic Education, Inc., PO Box 295, Cos Cob, CT 06807-0295; Title Tel # (203) 869-1706
Personnel: Editor-John Murphy
General Info: (Formerly American Way '76)
Circulation: Total-4,000

Freshman Year Experience Newsletter
See: COLLEGE STUDENT LIFESTYLE

Fulbright News

Publishing Co: Metro-Intl. Program Services of N.Y., 285 W. Roadway, #450, New York, NY 10013; Title Tel # (212) 431-1195
Personnel: Editor-Andrea Nemetz
General Info: Bi-monthly
Circulation: Total-245

Fulbrighters' Newsletter   *Association*

Publishing Co: Fulbright Alumni Assn., 1130 17th St NW Ste 310, Washington, DC 20036-4604
Fax # (202) 331-1979; Title Tel # (202) 331-1590 Title Fax # (203) 331-1979
Personnel: Editor-Jane L. Anderson
Editorial Description: Intl. educational & cultural exchange, alumni news.
General Info: (Formerly Fulbright Alumni Assn.), Yr. Est. 1977, Tri-annually, Offset press, 16 pages, 3% ads, 2 Color, Newsprint
Subscriptions: Free With Membership
Circulation: (100% controlled), Total-10,000
Advertising: Inquire for rates.
Printing Co: Delancey Printing, 444 Swann Ave, Alexandria, VA 22301-1085 Tel # (703) 836-4628, Fax # (703) 836-4628

GED Items   *Consumer, Association*   CPM: $41

Publishing Co: American Council on Education, 1 Dupont Cir NW, Ste 800, Washington, DC 20036-1193 Tel # (202) 939-9300 Fax # (202) 833-4762; Title Tel # (202) 939-9490 Title Fax # (202) 775-8578
Personnel: Circ. Mgr.-Debra Louallen, Editor, Adv. Dir.-Lisa Richards
Editorial Description: Newsletter of the GED Testing Service. Articles focus on adult education programs, teaching tips, GED graduate success stories, administration of the GED Testing Program.
General Info: Yr. Est. 1984, 5x/yr., Trim Size-8$\frac{1}{2}$ x 11, Offset press, 12 pages, 2 Color
Subscriptions: Free
Circulation: (91% controlled), Total-24,000
Advertising: $1,000.
List Rental: Rents Lists
Printing Co: Reproductions, Inc., Rockville, MD

GLCA Faculty Newsletter   *Association*

Publishing Co: Great Lakes Colleges Assn., 2929 Plymouth Rd., Ann Arbor, MI 48105-3206; Title Tel # (313) 761-4833
Personnel: Editor-Jeanine Elliott
Editorial Description: Highlights programs sponsored by a consortium. The consortium membership is twelve independent, liberal arts colleges in Indiana, Michigan, & Ohio.
General Info: Yr. Est. 1969, 5x/yr., Letrpr. press, 6 pages, No Color
Circulation: Total-3,500
Printing Co: First Impression, 4109 Jackson Ave, Ann Arbor, MI 48103-1890 Tel # (313) 662-6541

Geography Education Program UPDATE
See: GEOGRAPHY

German-American World   *Consumer*   CPM: $12

Publishing Co: Gak-Law Communications Media, Inc., 529A Central Ave, Jersey City, NJ 07307-2538; Title Tel # (201) 420-0159 Title Fax # (201) 420-0469
Personnel: Publisher-Elizabeth Larson, Editor-John Lawrora
Editorial Description: Educational pub. centered on history, culture, music & the arts. Fosters the teaching of the German language & promotes festivals & excursions. Also involved in computer training programs for WordPerfect, Word, Lotus, etc.
General Info: Yr. Est. 1968, Monthly, Trim Size-8$\frac{1}{2}$ x 11, Mimeo press, 16 pages, 3% ads, No Color, Saddle-stitched
Subscriptions: Free
Circulation: Total-6,000
Advertising: $75. Accepts Inserts.
List Rental: Rents Lists
Printing Co: Gak-Law Communications Media, Inc., 529-A Central Ave., P.O. Drawer 7 A-L, Jersey City, NJ 07307 Tel # (201) 420-0159

Getting and Spending   *Business*

Publishing Co: Magna Publications, Inc., 611 N Sherman Ave, Madison, WI 53704-4410; Title Tel # (608) 246-3580 Title Fax # (608) 246-3597
Personnel: Publisher-Richard C. Perkins, Editor-Doris Green, Editorial Dir.-Mary Lou Santovec, Circ. Mgr.-Tom Crawford, Art Dir.-Tami Cook, Mktg. Dir.-Lisa Collins, Promotion Mgr.-Karen Oshman
Editorial Description: Finding and allocating funds in higher education.
General Info: Yr. Est. 1996, Monthly, Trim Size-8$\frac{1}{2}$ x 11, 8 pages, 2 Color
Subscriptions: Indv. $197
Advertising: Accepts Inserts.
List Rental: Rents Lists

Global Talk!
See: INTERNATIONAL AFFAIRS

Golden Taffy   *Association*

Publishing Co: Saskatchewan English Teachers' Assn., Box 1108, Saskatoon, SK S7K 3N3 Canada
Parent Co.-Saskatchewan Teachers' Federation, Saskatoon, Canada; Title Tel # (306) 373-1660
Personnel: Editor-Paulette Hubbs
General Info: Yr. Est. 1964, Irregular, Trim Size-8$\frac{1}{2}$ x 11, Offset press, No Color
Subscriptions: Indv. $20, Can. $20
Circulation: (100% controlled), Total-500

Government Union Critique
See: LABOR UNION

Graduate School of Library and Information Science Newsletter
See: LIBRARY

Grant Advisor   *Association*

Publishing Co: The Grant Advisor, PO Box 520, Linden, VA 22642-0520; Title Tel # (703) 636-1529 Title Fax # (703) 636-7313
Personnel: Publisher-Robert Toft, Editor-Chris Watkins
Editorial Description: Lists more than 1400 federal & private foundation grant programs per year. Also available in computer form (IBM & compatible) with search capabilites ($358/yr.).
General Info: Yr. Est. 1983, Monthly, Trim Size-8$\frac{1}{2}$ x 11, Mimeo press, 20 pages, ISSN: 0740-5383, No Color, Recycled
Subscriptions: Indv. $152
Circulation: Total-450
Printing Co: Demand Tech, 10201 Lee Highway, Fairfax, VA 22030 Tel # (703) 591-2800, Fax # (703) 352-2405

Grants for School Districts Monthly Hotline   *Business*

Publishing Co: Quinlan Publishing, 23 Drydock Ave, Boston, MA 02210-2387 Fax # (617) 345-9646; Title Tel # (617) 542-0048
Editorial Description: Listing of grants available for schools across the country.
General Info: Monthly
Subscriptions: Indv. $83
List Rental: List Management Co.: Stevens-Knox List Management, 304 Park Ave S., New York, NY 10010-5312 Tel # (212) 388-8800, Fax # (212) 388-8890

Grapevine, The (Genesee Valley)
See: ETHNIC

Great Lakes Basin Report
See: FISH & FISHERIES

HANDI Information Center Update
See: HEALTH

HANDI Quarterly
See: HEALTH

HE-XTRA
See: HEALTH

HEA Advocate

Publishing Co: Houston Education Assn., 1415 Southmore Blvd, Houston, TX 77004-5845; Title Tel # (713) 528-1968
Personnel: Editor-Deborah Abbott
General Info: Yr. Est. 1971, Monthly, Trim Size-8$\frac{1}{2}$ x 11, Sheetfed press, 5 pages, No Color, Matte
Acquistions: Publication Bought
Circulation: Total-8,500
Advertising: Inquire for rates.

Hands On!

Publishing Co: Technical Education Research Centers, 2067 Massachusetts Ave., Cambridge, MA 02140; Title Tel # (617) 547-0430
Personnel: Editor-Peggy Kapisovsky
General Info: Irregular
Subscriptions: Indv. $10

Harvard Education Letter   *Consumer*

Publishing Co: Harvard Educational Review, 35 Longfellow Hall / Gutman, 6 Appian Way, Ste. 349, Cambridge, MA 02138; Title Tel # (617) 496-9984
Personnel: Editor-Adria Steinberg, Circ. Mgr.-Karen Maloney, Mktg. Dir.-Joanne Durham
General Info: Yr. Est. 1985, Bi-monthly, Trim Size-8$\frac{1}{2}$ x 11, 8 pages, Color, Matte
Subscriptions: Indv. $26
Circulation: Total-14,000
List Rental: List Management Co.: MGI-Marketing General Inc., 105 Oronoco St., Alexandria, VA 22314-2015 Tel # (703) 739-1000, Actives: 11,799, $100/M

Health Education Reports
See: HEALTH

Health Grants & Contracts Weekly
See: PHILANTHROPY

Health Professions Report   *Business*

Publishing Co: Manisses Communications Group, Inc., PO Box 3357, Providence, RI 02906-0757 Tel # (401) 831-6020 Fax # (401) 861-6370; Title Tel # (908) 889-6336 Title Fax # (908) 889-6339
Personnel: Editor-Anne Bittner, Circ. Mgr.-Sandra Smith, Publisher, Promotion Dir.-Joel Whitaker
Editorial Description: News on health professions education.
General Info: Bi-weekly, Trim Size-8$\frac{1}{2}$ x 11, Desktop press, 8 pages, ISSN: 0736-9077, Ind/Abs/Online: Newsnet, No Color, Other
Subscriptions: Indv. $271, Inst. $271, Can. $321, For. $321, $15/copy
List Rental: List Management Co.: The Lake Group, 411 Theodore Freund Ave., Rye, NY 10580-1497 Tel # (914) 925-2400, Fax # (914) 925-2499, Actives: 29,196, $70/M

Higher Education & National Affairs   *Scholarly, Association*

Publishing Co: American Council on Education, 1 Dupont Cir NW, Ste 800, Washington, DC 20036-1193 Tel # (202) 939-9300; Title Tel # (202) 939-9365 Title Fax # (202) 833-4762
Personnel: Editor-Janetta Hammock, Mag. Ed.-Laura Wilcox
Editorial Description: Current events dealing with higher education.
General Info: Yr. Est. 1952, Bi-weekly, 8 pages, No Color
Subscriptions: Indv. $60, Can. $75, For. $75, Free With Membership
Circulation: Total-25,000

Highland Highlights
See: HOBBY

Historical Time Capsules of Monroe County
See: HISTORY

Holistic Resource Management Quarterly
See: ENVIRONMENT & ECOLOGY

Home & School Connection   *Consumer*

Publishing Co: Resources For Educators, 1717 Commonwealth Drive, Front Royal, VA 22630 Tel # (703) 635-9911
Editorial Description: Educational information and news.
General Info: Yr. Est. 1990, Monthly
Subscriptions: Indv. $185

Home & School News   *Consumer, Association*

Publishing Co: Home & School Parent Teacher Fed. of Manitoba, 1 Sir John Franklin Rd., Winnipeg, MB R3N 1Z9 Canada; Title Tel # (204) 489-7741
Personnel: Editor-Jackie DeRuyck, Adv. Dir.-A. DeRuyck
Editorial Description: Articles of interest to parents dealing with educational issues, parent involvement in education, parenting, health & safety issues re: children & provincial & local organization activities.
General Info: Yr. Est. 1980, Bi-monthly, Trim Size-8½ x 11, Offset press, 5% ads, Newsprint, Saddle-stitched
Circulation: Total-12,000
Advertising: Accepts Inserts.
Printing Co: Kildonan Printing, 215 Oakland Avenue, Winnepeg, MB R2G 0A7 Canada Tel # (204) 338-0329, Fax # (204) 334-4873

Home Business Idea Possibility Newsletter
See: BUSINESS & INDUSTRY

Home Ec News
See: HOME ECONOMICS

Hot Topics   *Association*

Publishing Co: Assn for Media & Technology in Education in Canada, 3-1750 the Queensway, Ste. 1318, Etobicoke, ON M9C 5H5 Canada
Personnel: Editor-Wayne Blair
Editorial Description: Each issue provides an in-depth look at a topical subject in educational technology.
General Info: Irregular

How to Be Your Own Publisher Update
See: BOOKS & BOOK TRADE

HumanAwareness and Low Vision Perspectives
See: DISABILITY

Humphreys College Quarterly News Bulletin
See: COLLEGE ALUMNI

IACET Reporter   *Business, Association*

Publishing Co: International Association for Continuing Education, 1200 19th St NW Ste 300, Washington, DC 20036-2412; Title Tel # (202) 857-1122 Title Fax # (202) 223-4579
Personnel: Editor-Judy Kohl
Editorial Description: Association news and developments.
General Info: (Formerly CCEU Reporter), Yr. Est. 1977, Quarterly, 8 pages
Subscriptions: Free With Membership
Circulation: Total-750, Readership-750
Advertising: Inquire for rates.
List Rental: Actives: 550
Printing Co: Tuxedo Press, 3501 Windom Rd, Brentwood, MD 20722-1095 Tel # (301) 864-6400

IASL Newsletter
See: LIBRARY

ICAE News

Publishing Co: International Council for Adult Education, 720 Bathurst St., #500, Toronto, ON M5S 2R4 Canada; Title Tel # (416) 588-1211 Title Fax # (416) 588-5725
Personnel: Editor-Erma Stultz
General Info: (Formerly News from the Secretariat), Yr. Est. 1983, Quarterly, Desktop press, 16 pages, ISSN: 0834-9789, 2 Color
Subscriptions: Can. $35
Acquistions: Publication Bought
Circulation: Total-2,000
Printing Co: Is Five, 400 Mount Pleasant, Toronto, ON Canada

ICYE-US Newsletter
See: RELIGIOUS & THEOLOGICAL

IDRA Newsletter

Publishing Co: Intercultural Development Research Assn., 5835 Callaghan Rd Ste 350, San Antonio, TX 78228-1125; Title Tel # (210) 684-8180 Title Fax # (210) 684-5389
Personnel: Editor-Jose Cardenas, Exec. Ed.-Dr. Maria R. Montecel, Production Mgr.-Christie Goodman
Editorial Description: The IDRA newsletter provides information for educators, administrators, parents, and the general public regarding current issues in public education.
General Info: (Formerly Tee Newsletter), Yr. Est. 1973, Monthly, ISSN: 1069-5672
Acquistions: Publication Bought
Circulation: Total-7,000
Advertising: Inquire for rates.

IEEE Education Society Newsletter   *Association*   **CPM: $133**

Publishing Co: Institute of Electrical & Electronics Engineers, Inc., 445 Hoes Lane, PO Box 1331, Piscataway, NJ 08855-1331 Tel # (908) 562-3992 Fax # (908) 981-9334 Parent Co.-Institute of Electrical & Electronics Engineers, New York
Personnel: Editor-Donald Kirk, Production Ed.-Ann Skrupski, Adv. Mgr., Sales Mgr.-Susan Schneiderman
Editorial Description: Joint newsletter of the the IEEE Education Society and the ASEE Electrical Engineering Division. Published for those involved and interested in Electrical Engineering education.
General Info: Tri-annually, Trim Size-8½ x 11, 12 pages, Matte, Saddle-stitched
Subscriptions: Free With Membership
Circulation: Total-2,996
Advertising: $400.
List Rental: Rents Lists

IHE Newsletter

Publishing Co: Institute of Higher Education, Univ. of Georgia, Candler Hall, Athens, GA 30602; Title Tel # (404) 542-3464
Personnel: Editor-Cameron Fincher
General Info: Yr. Est. 1971, Trim Size-8½ x 11, Letrpr. press, 6 pages, No Color, Matte
Circulation: Total-1,000

ILSA Newsletter
See: LAW

ISTE Update   *Business, Association*

Publishing Co: International Society for Technology in Education, 1787 Agate St, Eugene, OR 97403-1923 Tel # (503) 346-4414 Fax # (503) 346-5890
Editorial Description: Provides articles on current issues and membership activities.
General Info: 7x/yr.
Subscriptions: Indv. $20, Can. $32, For. $30

ISWM News   *Association*   **CPM: $500**

Publishing Co: International Society of Weighing & Measurement, 2299 Brockett Rd, Tucker, GA 30084-4400 Tel # (404) 939-2200 Fax # (404) 939-7924
Personnel: Publisher-Mimi Harlan
General Info: Tri-annually, Trim Size-8½ x 11, 232 pages, 2 Color, Coated, Saddle-stitched
Subscriptions: Free With Membership
Circulation: Total-1,400
Advertising: $700.

Iggeret
See: LITERATURE & LINGUISTICS

Illinois TESOL/BE Newsletter
See: LITERATURE & LINGUISTICS

Imagine
See: COLLEGE STUDENT

Impact: A Journal of Safety Litigation and News
See: AUTOMOTIVE

In Touch   *Association*

Publishing Co: Prince Edward Island School Trustees Assn., 3 Queen St., Box 2000, Charlottetown, PE C1A 7N8 Canada; Title Tel # (902) 368-5027 Title Fax # (902) 368-5055
Personnel: Editor-Elaine Noonan
General Info: (Formerly On Board), Quarterly, Trim Size-8½ x 11, 6 pages, No Color
Acquistions: Publication Bought
Circulation: Total-350
Advertising: Inquire for rates. Accepts Inserts.

In Touch Newsletter   *Association*

Publishing Co: Canadian Assn. for Health, Physical Edu. Recreation & Dance, 1600 James Naismith Dr., Gloucester, ON K1B 5N4 Canada; Title Tel # (613) 748-5622 Title Fax # (613) 748-5737
Personnel: Editor-Debbie Vanderburgh
Editorial Description: News items for CAHPERD members, position on issues pertaining to physical activity in Canada.
General Info: (Formerly CAHPER News), Yr. Est. 1974, 3x/yr., Trim Size-8½ x 11, Offset press, 20 pages, ISSN: 0848-1733, 2 Color, Matte, Saddle-stitched
Subscriptions: Free With Membership
Circulation: Total-1,000, Readership-1,000
Advertising: Accepts Inserts.
Printing Co: Performance Printing, 65 Lorne Ave., Box 158, Smith's Falls, ON K7A 4T1 Canada Tel # (613) 283-5650, Fax # (613) 283-7480

In Touch-Newsletter of PITA of B.C.   *Association*

Publishing Co: Sponsor-Provincial Intermediate Teachers' Association, British Columbia Teachers' Federation, 100-550 West 6th Avenue, Vancouver, BC V5Z 4P2 Canada; Title Tel # (604) 871-2283 Title Fax # (604) 871-2289
General Info: Irregular
Circulation: Total-900

Inclusive Education Programs   *Business, Consumer*

Publishing Co: LRP Publications, 747 Dresher Rd., P.O. Box 980, Horsham, PA 19044-0980 Tel # (215) 784-0910 Fax # (215) 784-0317
Personnel: Publisher-Ken Kahn, Editor-Karen Diamond, Mktg. Dir.-Marcy Witt
Editorial Description: Gives practical advice on educating students with disabilities in regular settings.
General Info: Monthly, Ind/Abs/Online: LRPnet
Subscriptions: Indv. $115

Independent Scholar   *Association*

Publishing Co: Sponsor-National Coalition of Independent Scholars, Independent Scholar, 8202 Kenfield Court, Bethesda, MD 20817-3147; Title Tel # (301) 469-9489
Personnel: Editor-Harold Orlans
Editorial Description: Publishes articles by independent scholars & information on groups, programs, issues & events of interest to them.
General Info: Yr. Est. 1987, Quarterly, Trim Size-8½ x 11, Offset press, 20 pages, ISSN: 1066-5633
Subscriptions: Indv. $12, Can. $14, For. $14, $4/copy
Circulation: Total-380
Advertising: Inquire for rates.

Independent Thinking Review   *Consumer*

Publishing Co: Resources for Independent Thinking, 4067 Hardwick St # 129, Lakewood, CA 90712-2350; Title Tel # (310) 630-3678 Title Fax # (310) 630-7389
Personnel: Editor-Sharon Presley, Production Mgr.-Julie Filatoff
Editorial Description: Books that help people think for themselves. Gives reviews and descriptions of books, buttons, bumper stickers, organizations.
General Info: (Formerly Resources for Independent Thinking Review), Yr. Est. 1994, Quarterly, Trim Size-8½ x 11, 12 pages, No Color, Matte
Subscriptions: Indv. $18, $5/copy
Printing Co: Printmaster, 6116 Orange Avenue, Long Beach, CA 90805 Tel # (310) 428-5391

Indian Affairs
See: ETHNIC

Indiana History Bulletin
See: HISTORY

Individuals with Disabilities Education Law Reporter
See: DISABILITY

Infochange

Publishing Co: Assn. for Humanistic Education & Development, 404 W Warren St, Shelby, NC 28150-5330; Title Tel # (317) 284-7511
Personnel: Publisher, Editor, Production Mgr.-Steve Leatherwood
Editorial Description: Promotes education & development for human benefit.
General Info: Yr. Est. 1951, Quarterly, Trim Size-8½ x 11, Sheetfed press, 16 pages, 2 Color, Newsprint
Subscriptions: Indv. $2
Acquistions: Publication Bought
Circulation: Total-3,500
Advertising: Inquire for rates.

Infolines
See: HEALTH

Info

Publishing Co: Univ. Minnesota Dept. of Extension Classes, 180 Westbrook Hall, 77 Pleasant St., SE, Minneapolis, MN 55455 Tel # (312) 624-3854 Fax # (312) 624-8238; Title Tel # (612) 624-3300
Personnel: Editor-Charles Cheeserough
Editorial Description: A newsletter for adult & part time college students at the Univ. of MN.
General Info: Yr. Est. 1972, 9x/yr., Trim Size-8½ x 11, Sheetfed press, 6 pages, No Color, Newsprint
Circulation: Total-70,000

Information North
See: SCIENCE

Information Searcher   *Business, Scholarly*

Publishing Co: Datasearch Group, 14 Hadden Rd, Scarsdale, NY 10583-3328; Title Tel # (914) 723-1995 Title Fax # (914) 723-1995
Personnel: Publisher, Editor-Pam Berger
General Info: (Formerly Online Searcher), Yr. Est. 1988, 5x/yr., ISSN: 1055-3916
Subscriptions: Indv. $34, Inst. $34, Can. $39, $6/copy
Advertising: $530.

Innovator

Publishing Co: Univ. of Michigan Assoc. in the Social Found. of Educ., 4001 School of Educ. Bldg., Ann Arbor, MI 48104; Title Tel # (313) 763-4880
Personnel: Editor-Eric Warden
Editorial Description: For professional educators and alumni of University of Michigan's School of Education.
General Info: Yr. Est. 1969, Quarterly, Trim Size-8½ x 11, Web press, 20 pages, No Color, Newsprint, Saddle-stitched
Subscriptions: Free
Printing Co: Swenk-Tuttle Press, 320 Springbrook Ave # 745, Adrian, MI 49221-2055 Tel # (517) 263-4615, Fax # (517) 263-0819

Inside AESES

Publishing Co: Assn. of Employees Supporting Education Services, 405 - 275 Broadway, Winnipeg, MB R3C 4M6 Canada; Title Tel # (204) 949-5200
General Info: Yr. Est. 1974, Monthly
Circulation: (100% controlled), Total-2,000

Inside CUE   *Association*

Publishing Co: Sponsor-Computer-Using Educators of B.C., British Columbia Teachers' Federation, 100-550 West 6th Avenue, Vancouver, BC V5Z 4P2 Canada; Title Tel # (604) 871-2283 Title Fax # (604) 871-2289
General Info: Irregular
Circulation: Total-600

Inside GMAC

Publishing Co: Graduate Management Admission Council, 2400 Broadway St Ste 230, Santa Monica, CA 90404-3064; Title Tel # (213) 478-1433 Title Fax # (213) 473-2388
Personnel: Editor-Deborah Perrin
Editorial Description: Contains information for member schools.
General Info: (Formerly GMAC Newsletter), Quarterly
Circulation: Total-300

Insiders Report
See: LABOR UNION

Insights
See: BLIND

Insights Into Open Education

Publishing Co: Univ. of North Dakota, PO Box 7189, Grand Forks, ND 58202-7189; Title Tel # (701) 777-4421 Title Fax # (701) 777-4365
Personnel: Editor-Sara Hanhan
General Info: Yr. Est. 1968, 8x/yr., Trim Size-8½ x 11, 10 pages
Subscriptions: Indv. $7
Circulation: Total-500
Printing Co: Univ. Of North Dakota, Univ. Printing Services, Box 8006, University Station, Grand Forks, ND 58202 Tel # (701) 777-2544

Interaction (Ontario Teachers Federation)   *Association*

Publishing Co: Ontario Teachers Federation, 1260 Bay St., Suite 700, Toronto, ON M5R 2B5 Canada Fax # (416) 966-5450; Title Tel # (416) 966-3424
Personnel: Editor-Rosemarie Stasios
Editorial Description: Education news, Federation activities.
General Info: Yr. Est. 1974, Quarterly, Trim Size-8½ x 11, Web press, 8 pages, ISSN: 0316-3903, Color
Circulation: (100% controlled), Total-190,900
Printing Co: Del Charters Litho., Inc., 10 Henderson Ave., Brampton, ON L6Y 2A4 Canada Tel # (905) 451-0830

Interface
See: MEDIA & COMMUNICATIONS

Interfraternity Bulletin   *Association*

Publishing Co: Natl. Interfraternity Foundation, 3901 W 86th St Ste 380, Indianapolis, IN 46268-1799; Title Tel # (317) 872-3304
Personnel: Editor-Kris Riske, Circ. Mgr.-Mary Barbee
Editorial Description: Developments in higher education, research in areas affecting colleges and news of interest to fraternities and sororities.
General Info: (Formerly IRAC Bulletin), Yr. Est. 1946, Monthly, Trim Size-8½ x 11, Desktop press, 4 pages, No Color
Subscriptions: Indv. $6, $1/copy
Circulation: Total-3,000

International Association of Educators for World Peace, Circulation Newsletter
See: POLITICS

International Christian Studies Association Newsletter (ICSA Newsletter)
See: RELIGIOUS & THEOLOGICAL

International Dateline
Publishing Co: Univ. of Minnesota, Office of Intl. Education, Univ. Of Minnesota, 216 Pillsbury Drive, S.E., Minneapolis, MN 55455; Title Tel # (612) 624-5580 Title Fax # (612) 626-1730
Personnel: Editor-Gayla Marty
Editorial Description: Intl. campus update for students, faculty, staff, community.
General Info: (Formerly QUIN: Quarterly Univ. Intl. News), Yr. Est. 1982, Trim Size-8½ x 11, Desktop press, Color
Subscriptions: Free
Circulation: Total-10,200
Printing Co: Univ. of Minnesota, Printing Services, 2818 Como Ave., SE, Minneapolis, MN 55414 Tel # (612) 625-9500

International Notes   *Scholarly*
Publishing Co: Capstone Intl. Program Center, Univ. of Alabama, Box 870254, Tuscaloosa, AL 35487; Title Tel # (205) 348-5256 Title Fax # (205) 348-5298
Personnel: Editor-Marilyn Emplaincourt
Editorial Description: Provides news about international activities at the Univ. of Alabama, in Alabama, & in the Southeast.
General Info: Yr. Est. 1970, Monthly, 4 pages
Circulation: Total-1,500

International Update
Publishing Co: American Council on International Intercultural Education, c/o AACTC, 1 Dupont Circle #410, Washington, DC 20036-1110; Title Tel # (202) 728-0200
Personnel: Editor-Yukie Tokuyama
Editorial Description: American & foreign colleges & other entities interested in intl. education. Information on curricula, exchanges, etc.
General Info: Yr. Est. 1972, Monthly, Trim Size-8 x 11, 6 pages
Subscriptions: Indv. $50
Circulation: Total-2,000
Printing Co: Newsletter Services, Inc., 9700 Philadelphia Court, Lanham, MD 20706 Tel # (301) 731-5200, Fax # (301) 731-5201

Internet Strategies for Education   *Business*
Publishing Co: Nelson B. Heller & Associates, 1910 1st St Ste 303, Highland Park, IL 60035-3146; Title Tel # (708) 831-6604 Title Fax # (708) 926-0202
Personnel: Publisher-Nelson Heller, Editor-Roberta Salvador
Editorial Description: Covers marketing of technology and telecommunications to educators at all levels.
General Info: (Formerly Heller Report on Educational Technology & Telecommunications), Yr. Est. 1989, Monthly, Trim Size-8½ x 11, 12 pages, ISSN: 1047-5230, Matte
Subscriptions: Indv. $395, Can. $395, For. $415, $40/copy
Acquistions: Publication Bought
Circulation: Total-800
Advertising: Accepts Inserts.

Invention
See: COLLEGE STUDENT

Iowa PTA Bulletin   *Association*
Publishing Co: Iowa Congress of Parents, 610 Merle Hay Towers, Des Moines, IA 50310-1327; Title Tel # (515) 244-6246
Personnel: Editor-Marguerite Boss
Editorial Description: In-house information plus updates on legislation, media and cultural arts.
General Info: 8x/yr., 8 pages, No Color
Subscriptions: Indv. $3, $1/copy
Circulation: Total-1,000
Printing Co: Carter Printing, 1739 E Grand Ave, Des Moines, IA 50316-3611 Tel # (515) 265-6139

Issues in Higher Education
Publishing Co: Southern Regional Education Bd, 592 10th St NW, Atlanta, GA 30318-5776; Title Tel # (404) 875-9211 Title Fax # (404) 872-1477
Personnel: Editor-Margaret Sullivan
Editorial Description: Deals with current issues affecting higher education in 15 SREB-member states.
General Info: Yr. Est. 1971, Trim Size-8½ x 11, Sheetfed press, 9 pages, Newsprint
Subscriptions: $1/copy
Circulation: (100% controlled), Total-7,800

It Starts on the Front Line   *Association*
Publishing Co: National School Public Relations Assn., 1501 Lee Hwy Ste 201, Arlington, VA 22209-1109; Title Tel # (703) 528-5840 Title Fax # (703) 528-7017
Personnel: Publisher-Joseph Scherer, Editor-Judi Cowan, Circ. Mgr.-Laura Bono, Circ. Mgr.-Keenan Bradshaw
Editorial Description: Devoted to classroom and teacher public relations techniques and ideas.
General Info: (Formerly It Starts in the Classroom), Yr. Est. 1935, Monthly, Trim Size-8½ x 11, Offset press, 8 pages, 2 Color, Newsprint
Subscriptions: Indv. $65
Circulation: Total-2,500

Italic Newsletter   *Consumer*
Publishing Co: Portland State Univ., Continuing Education Pr., Box 1491, Portland, OR 97207 Fax # (503) 725-4840; Title Tel # (503) 725-4846 Title Fax # (502) 725-4840
Personnel: Editor-Tena Spears
Editorial Description: A newsletter for people who care about legibility
General Info: Yr. Est. 1987, Semi-annually, Desktop press, 2 pages, Color
Subscriptions: Free
Circulation: Total-15,000

JACS Volunteer
See: EMPLOYMENT

Jefferson Research Letter   *Association*
Publishing Co: Thomas Jefferson Research Center, 2700 E. Foothill Blvd., #302, Pasadena, CA 91107-3443; Title Tel # (818) 792-8130
Personnel: Editor-Frank Goble
General Info: (Formerly Jefferson Research), Yr. Est. 1966, Bi-monthly, Letrpr. press, 4 pages
Subscriptions: Indv. $5, $1/copy
Circulation: Total-3,000

Jersey Journeys   *Association*
Publishing Co: New Jersey Historical Society, 230 Broadway, Newark, NJ 07104-3926 Fax # (201) 483-1988; Title Tel # (201) 483-3939
Personnel: Editor-Kathryn Grover
Editorial Description: Magazine for elementary students on topics in NJ history.
General Info: Yr. Est. 1980, Monthly, Trim Size-11 x 17, Offset press, 4 pages, Ind/Abs/Online: NJ His., Color, Newsprint
Subscriptions: Indv. $10, Inst. $65
Circulation: Total-25,000
Printing Co: Johnston Letter, 267 Mount Pleasant Ave, Newark, NJ 07104-3796 Tel # (201) 482-7535

Jewish Educators Assembly Yearbook
See: RELIGIOUS & THEOLOGICAL

Jobs in Higher Education   *Business, Association*
Publishing Co: Jobs in Higher Education, PO Box 10100, Colorado Springs, CO 80932-1100; Title Tel # (719) 475-9797 Title Fax # (719) 475-9693
Editorial Description: Job listings in higher education levels.
General Info: Monthly, ISSN: 1074-5475, 4 Color, Matte, Saddle-stitched
Subscriptions: Indv. $48
Circulation: Total-2,000
Advertising: Inquire for rates.

KEY Newsletter
See: RELIGIOUS & THEOLOGICAL

KRC Letter
Publishing Co: KRC Letter, 4 Gelber St., Larchmont, NY 10536 Fax # (914) 834-2587; Title Tel # (914) 834-7825
General Info: Yr. Est. 1970, 10x/yr.
Subscriptions: Indv. $35

Kaleidoscope
Publishing Co: Evansville-Vanderburgh School Corp., 1 SE 9th St, Evansville, IN 47708-1821; Title Tel # (812) 426-5041
Personnel: Editor-Patti S. Coleman
Editorial Description: A staff publication-for and about employees of the Evansville-Vanderburgh School Corporation.
General Info: Yr. Est. 1975, Monthly, Trim Size-8½ x 11, Offset press, 8 pages, Color
Circulation: Total-3,000

Kaufman Letter, The
See: SAFETY

Keeping the Trust
See: SOCIAL SERVICES & WELFARE

Keeping Up
Publishing Co: ERIC Clearinghouse for Social Studies/Social Science Educati, Univ. of Indiana, Bloomington, 2805 E. 10th St., Suite 120, Bloomington, IN 47408; Title Tel # (812) 855-3838
Personnel: Editor-Vickie Schlene
General Info: Yr. Est. 1970, Quarterly

Ken Keyes College Newsletter
Publishing Co: Ken Keyes College, 1620 Thompson Rd., Coos Bay, OR 97420-2150; Title Tel # (503) 267-6412
Personnel: Publisher-Ken Keyes, Editor-Walter Hill, Production Mgr.-Andrea Keeler, Art Dir.-Claudia Lowman
Editorial Description: Articles on the science of happiness & a schedule of workshops taught on that subject at the college & on the road.
General Info: Quarterly, Trim Size-8½ x 11, Web press, 12 pages, 4 Color, Newsprint
Subscriptions: Free
Circulation: Total-60,000
Printing Co: Courier Printing, PO Box 268, Reedsport, OR 97467-0268 Tel # (503) 271-3633

Kentucky Commission on Human Rights, Reports and Newsletter
See: CIVIL RIGHTS

Keying In
See: BUSINESS & INDUSTRY

KidTECH News   *Consumer*

Publishing Co: KidTECH/BG Associates, PO Box 200, New York, NY 10044-0204
Fax # (212) 935-7873; Title Tel # (212) 935-7873
Personnel: Editor-Barbara Gollon
Editorial Description: Reviews the connection and ideas concerning children and their use of technology in the learning process. Resources for skills development software sources are reviewed.
General Info: Yr. Est. 1994, Bi-monthly, Trim Size-8½ x 11, 12 pages, No Color, Matte
Subscriptions: Indv. $25, Inst. $50, Can. $60, $5/copy
Advertising: Inquire for rates.

Kindergarten Connection   *Consumer*

Publishing Co: Resources For Educators, 1717 Commonwealth Drive, Front Royal, VA 22630
Tel # (703) 635-9911
Editorial Description: Practical ideas for busy parents to improve their child's school success.
General Info: Yr. Est. 1994, Monthly
Subscriptions: Indv. $47

Kobrin Letter, The
See: CHILDREN

Kol Bana'Yikh   *Association*

Publishing Co: United Synagogue of Conservative Judaism, 155 5th Ave, New York, NY 10010-6811
Tel # (212) 533-7800 Fax # (212) 353-9439; Title Tel # (212) 260-8450
Personnel: Editor, Production Mgr.-Edya Arzt
Editorial Description: For Jewish educators.
General Info: Yr. Est. 1979, Quarterly, 4 pages
Subscriptions: Indv. $5
Circulation: Total-1,000

LAI Notes
See: INTERNATIONAL AFFAIRS

LAMA Manager
See: MANAGEMENT

LATA Newsletter   *Association*

Publishing Co: Sponsor-Learning Assistance Teacher's Association, British Columbia Teachers' Federation, 100-550 West 6th Avenue, Vancouver, BC V5Z 4P2 Canada;
Title Tel # (604) 871-2283 Title Fax # (604) 871-2289
General Info: Irregular
Circulation: Total-400

L.D. Forum

Publishing Co: Council for Learning Disabilities, PO Box 40303, Overland Park, KS 66204-4303
Fax # (913) 492-2546; Title Tel # (913) 492-8755
Personnel: Editor-Brian Bryant
Editorial Description: Provides up-to-date information about activities of the Council for Learning Disabilities, plus numerous articles of interest to teachers of students with learning disabilities.
General Info: (Formerly CLD Newsletter), Yr. Est. 1978, Quarterly, 32 pages, No Color, Coated, Saddle-stitched
Circulation: Total-3,200
List Rental: Rents Lists

LEA News

Publishing Co: Lutherans Education Assn., 7400 Augusta St, River Forest, IL 60305-1402;
Title Tel # (708) 771-8300
Personnel: Editor-Mary Lou Krause
Editorial Description: Membership activities, pubs., conferences.
General Info: Quarterly, 5 pages
Circulation: Total-3,500

LRE Report   *Consumer, Association*

Publishing Co: American Bar Association, 750 N. Lake Shore Dr., Chicago, IL 60611-4497
Tel # (312) 988-6115 Fax # (312) 988-6030; Title Tel # (312) 988-5522 Title Fax # (312) 988-5528
Personnel: Editor-Paula Nessel
Editorial Description: Publishes news and articles of interest on topics related to law and citizenship education.
General Info: Yr. Est. 1980, Tri-annually, Trim Size-8½ x 11, Sheetfed press, 16 pages, ISSN: 0731-9711, 2 Color, Coated, Saddle-stitched
Subscriptions: Free
Circulation: Total-5,000
List Rental: Rents Lists

LSBA Quarter Notes

Publishing Co: Louisiana School Boards Assn., 7912 Summa Ave, Baton Rouge, LA 70809-3416
Personnel: Editor-Victor Hodgkins, Circ. Mgr.-Art Greene
Editorial Description: News articles relative to the association, feature stories on research.
General Info: Yr. Est. 1987, Bi-monthly, Sheetfed press, 6 pages, No Color, Coated
Circulation: Total-2,900
Printing Co: Printing, Inc., 3019 Plank Rd, Baton Rouge, LA 70805-6599 Tel # (504) 357-5961

LUNO   *Business, Consumer*

Publishing Co: Learning Information Network of Oregon, 31960 SE Chin St, Boring, OR 97009-9708
Personnel: Publisher-Gene Lehman
Editorial Description: Newsletter of the Learning Information Network of Oregon.
General Info: Monthly

Labor Arbitration in Government
See: LABOR UNION

Labor Studies Forum
See: LABOR

Latin America/Chicago

Publishing Co: Center for Latin American Studies, Univ of Chicago, 5848 S.University Ave., Chicago, IL 60611-1798; Title Tel # (312) 702-8420 Title Fax # (312) 702-1755
Personnel: Editor-Michael Rosenfeld
Editorial Description: Listing of Latin America-related events in Greater Chicago.
General Info: Yr. Est. 1977, Monthly, Mimeo press, 4 pages
Subscriptions: Free
Circulation: Total-1,000

Latino
See: ETHNIC

Le Bulletin de l'ACE   *Business, Association*

Publishing Co: Association Canadienne d'Education, 252 Bloor St. W, #8-200, Toronto, ON M5S 1V5 Canada; Title Tel # (416) 924-7721 Title Fax # (416) 924-3188
Personnel: Editor-Daniel Fitzgerald
Editorial Description: News of interest to officials of educational school boards. Text in French
General Info: Yr. Est. 1965, 9x/yr., Trim Size-8½ x 11, Desktop press, 8 pages, ISSN: 0004-5306, 2 Color
Subscriptions: Indv. $15, Free With Membership
Circulation: Total-1,400
Advertising: Inquire for rates.

Leader
See: FAMILY

Leadership Times   *Association*

Publishing Co: Natl. Professional Resources, 25 South Regent Street, P.O. Box 1479, Pt. Chester, NY 10573; Title Tel # (914) 937-8879 Title Fax # (914) 937-9327
Editorial Description: Information about the resources available to special education personnel.
General Info: (Formerly Effective Special Services Management), Bi-monthly
Subscriptions: Indv. $50, Inst. $50, Can. $50, For. $60
List Rental: Rents Lists

Leaflet

Publishing Co: New England Assn. of Teachers of English, PO Box 291, Chelmsford, MA 01824-0291; Title Tel # (617) 646-2575
Personnel: Editor-Barbara Von Villas
Editorial Description: Articles about teaching of English each issue focuses on a specific theme. Recent research on teaching English is of special interest.
General Info: Yr. Est. 1901
Subscriptions: Indv. $20, Inst. $25
Circulation: Total-1,000

Learning Disabilities Assn. of California
See: SOCIAL SERVICES & WELFARE

Learning Edge   *Association*

Publishing Co: Sponsor-Clonlara Home Based Education Program, Clonlara, Inc., 1289 Jewett St, Ann Arbor, MI 48104-6201; Title Tel # (313) 769-4515
Personnel: Publisher-Pat Montgomery, Editor, Circ. Mgr.-Jo Hinsdale
Editorial Description: Newsletter serving home educators, teachers, students & interested individuals.
General Info: Yr. Est. 1978, Bi-monthly, Trim Size-8½ x 11, Web press, 32 pages, ISSN: 0896-8756, No Color, Newsprint
Subscriptions: Indv. $15, For. $20, $3/copy
Printing Co: IMP, 24555 Industrial, Ann Arbor, MI 48104 Tel # (313) 474-6464

Learning Exchange News

Publishing Co: Learning Exchange News, 2940 N Lincoln Ave, Chicago, IL 60657-4109
Personnel: Editor-Diane Kinishi
General Info: Yr. Est. 1974, Quarterly
Subscriptions: Indv. $15
Circulation: Total-8,000

Learning Together News   *Consumer*

Publishing Co: Prima Publishing, Box 1260 HS, Rocklin, CA 95677-1260 Tel # (916) 632-4400
Fax # (916) 632-4405
Personnel: Publisher-Ben Dominitz, Editor-Sally Palow
Editorial Description: Learning Together News features latest technology, education news, and hints from homeschooling families.
General Info: 13x/yr., Trim Size-8½ x 11, 4 pages, Matte
Subscriptions: Indv. $30
List Rental: Rents Lists

Learning Unlimited Network
of Oregon   *Consumer, Association*

Publishing Co: Learning Unlimited Network of Oregon, 31960 SE Chin St, Boring, OR 97009-9708; Title Tel # (503) 663-5153 Title Fax # (503) 492-3716
Personnel: Editor-Gene Lehman
Editorial Description: LUNO is a networking newsletter that reaches out to all interested in alternatives to traditional (un)thinking about education, schools & government and offers positive alternatives. Copying & sharing of pages, including Phonetic Fun pages challenging basic language skills on all levels, is encouraged.
General Info: Yr. Est. 1985, 10 pages
Subscriptions: Indv. $10, $2/copy
Acquistions: Publication Bought

Legal Notes for Education

Publishing Co: Data Research, Inc., 4635 Nicols Rd Ste 100, Eagan, MN 55122-3337; Title Tel # (612) 452-8267 Title Fax # (612) 452-8694
Editorial Description: Summaries of court decisions dealing with education law.
General Info: Yr. Est. 1973, Monthly, Trim Size-8½ x 11, Sheetfed press, 8 pages, ISSN: 0093-397X, No Color
Subscriptions: Indv. $108
Circulation: Total-6,000
Printing Co: Helgeson Press, 7600 14th Ave S, Richfield, MN 55423-4530 Tel # (612) 869-6828

Legislative Update

Publishing Co: United States Students Assn., 1612 K St. NW, Ste. 510, Washington, DC 20006; Title Tel # (202) 347-8772 Title Fax # (202) 393-5886
General Info: Bi-weekly

Lemon Times
See: AUTOMOTIVE

Lex Collegii
See: LAW

Liaison Bulletin

Publishing Co: National Association of State Directors of Special Education, 1800 Diagonal Rd Ste 320, Alexandria, VA 22314-2840; Title Tel # (202) 296-1800
Personnel: Editor-Dr. William Schipper
General Info: Yr. Est. 1975, Bi-weekly
Subscriptions: Indv. $40
Circulation: Total-1,500

Library Notes
See: LIBRARY

Lifeline
See: RELIGIOUS & THEOLOGICAL

Liftoff   *Consumer, Association*

Publishing Co: World University Roundtable, PO Box 2470, Benson, AZ 85602-2470; Title Tel # (520) 586-2985
Personnel: Publisher-H.J. Zitko, Editor-Howard Zitko
Editorial Description: International newsletter reporting current happenings within the World University community.
General Info: (Formerly International Newsletter), Yr. Est. 1947, Bi-monthly, Trim Size-8½ x 11, Letrpr. press, 4 pages, ISSN: 0730-9066, No Color, Matte
Subscriptions: Indv. $35, Inst. $35, $1/copy
Circulation: Total-1,000

l'Infoscolaire   *Association*

Publishing Co: Assn. Francaise des Conseils Scolaires de l'Ontario, 435 Blvd Saint Laurent, Ottawa, ON K1K 2Z8 Canada; Title Tel # (613) 745-3195
Personnel: Publisher, Editor-Anne-Josee Delcorde
Editorial Description: Internal publication reporting activities and developments Re: association interests.
General Info: Yr. Est. 1972, Monthly, 8 pages, No Color
Circulation: (100% controlled), Total-800

Link   *Business, Association*

Publishing Co: Appalachia Educational Laboratory, Inc., PO Box 1348, Charleston, WV 25325-1348; Title Tel # (304) 347-0400
Personnel: Editor-Carolyn Luzader
Editorial Description: A newsletter for educators providing research summaries, education news, and news of AEL products, services and events.
General Info: Yr. Est. 1982, Quarterly, Trim Size-8½ x 11, Offset press, 12 pages, 2 Color, Other, Saddle-stitched
Subscriptions: Free In Designated Area
Circulation: Total-8,000

Lisle Interaction   *Consumer, Association*

Publishing Co: Lisle Fellowship, 433 W Sterns Rd, Temperance, MI 48182-9568; Title Tel # (313) 847-7126 Title Fax # (419) 530-1245
Personnel: Publisher-Mark Kinney, Editor-Orion Six
Editorial Description: Describes Lisle programs, experiences in intercultural human relations, & updates Lisle alumni to activities of the organization & its alumni.
General Info: Yr. Est. 1944, Quarterly, Trim Size-8¼ x 10¾, 12 pages, 2 Color, Matte
Subscriptions: Free To Qualified Recipient
Circulation: Total-1,700
List Rental: Rents Lists

Living Music
See: MUSIC & MUSIC TRADES

Lovejoy's Guidance Digest   *Consumer*

Publishing Co: Lovejoy's College Guide, Inc., Drawer Q, Red Bank, NJ 07701-8039; Title Tel # (908) 741-5640 Title Fax # (908) 671-5322
Personnel: Publisher, Circ. Mgr.-Barbarasue Straughn, Editor, Adv. Dir.-Charles T. Straughn
Editorial Description: Covers college, vocational school, prep school and graduate school. Lists curricula, admissions, scholarships, tuition, summer programs, etc.
General Info: Yr. Est. 1947, 10x/yr., Trim Size-8½ x 11, Offset press, 6 pages, ISSN: 0024-7022, Color, Other
Subscriptions: Indv. $60, Can. $67, For. $75, $6/copy
Circulation: Total-3,000
Printing Co: J.V. Graphics, Linden Pl., Red Bank, NJ 07701 Tel # (908) 842-5617

MAGnet: Newsletter in
Mixed-Age Grouping   *Consumer, Scholarly*

Publishing Co: ERIC EECE, Univ. of Illinois, 805 W. PA Ave., Urbana, IL 61801 Tel # (217) 333-1386 Fax # (217) 333-3767
Personnel: Editor-Diane E. McClellan, Circ. Dir.-James Ennis
Editorial Description: Provides information on topics related tot the use of mixed-age groups in elementary classrooms
General Info: Yr. Est. 1992, Semi-annually, ISSN: 1065-6782
Subscriptions: Indv. $6
Circulation: Total-1,000

MASC Bulletin
See: SCHOOL ADMINISTRATION

MASRC Newsletter
See: ETHNIC

MATSOL Newsletter

Publishing Co: Massachusetts Assn. of Teachers of English to Speakers of Ot, 730 Commonwealth Ave., Boston Univ., Boston, MA 02159-1133; Title Tel # (617) 353-4233
Personnel: Editor-Ruth Spack
Editorial Description: Articles on teaching techniques & applied linguistics for instructors of ESL. Includes Assn. news, book reviews, conference notes, news of research, references, etc.
General Info: Yr. Est. 1972
Circulation: Total-575
Advertising: Inquire for rates.

MBA Newsletter

Publishing Co: Kwartler Communications Inc., 79 Verbena Ave., Floral Park, NY 11001-3014; Title Tel # (516) 488-2010 Title Fax # (516) 488-2025
Personnel: Editor-Dick Kwartler
Editorial Description: Global coverage of graduate management education.
General Info: Yr. Est. 1991, Monthly, Trim Size-8½ x 11, 12 pages, 2 Color, Saddle-stitched
Subscriptions: Indv. $267, Inst. $267, Can. $282, For. $292, $28/copy
Advertising: Inquire for rates. Accepts Inserts.

M.E.A. Today   *Association*

Publishing Co: Montana Education Assn., 1232 E 6th Ave, Helena, MT 59601-3995; Title Tel # (406) 442-4250 Title Fax # (406) 443-5081
Personnel: Publisher-Eric Feaver, Editor-Nancy Starrett
Editorial Description: National and state association news, legislative political action, classroom features.
General Info: Yr. Est. 1882, Monthly, Trim Size-8½ x 11, Sheetfed press, 20 pages, 51% ads, 2 Color, Other
Subscriptions: Free With Membership
Circulation: Total-11,000
Advertising: Inquire for rates.

MIU Review
See: COLLEGE STUDENT

MLA Newsletter
See: LITERATURE & LINGUISTICS

MN Educational Resource
Guide   *Business*

Publishing Co: MN Licensing Data Services, Market Communications, PO Box 16568, St. Paul, MN 55116; Title Tel # (612) 222-7393 Title Fax # (612) 222-4208
Editorial Description: Lists names and addresses of all school districts; public and private schools in alpha and zip code order.
General Info: Annually
Subscriptions: Indv. $40
List Rental: Rents Lists

MPAEA Newsletter   *Association*

Publishing Co: Mountain Plains Adult Education Association, Box 3374, University of Wyoming, Laramie, WY 82071 Tel # (307) 766-3042; Title Tel # (307) 766-5198
Personnel: Editor-Marjorie Slotten
Editorial Description: Keeps members up to date on activities in 8 states, focuses on all aspects of adult education.
General Info: Yr. Est. 1954, Semi-annually, Offset press, 8 pages, No Color
Subscriptions: Indv. $20, Inst. $45
Circulation: Total-600

MSBA Update
Association

Publishing Co: Maine School Boards Assn., 49 Community Dr, Augusta, ME 04330-9405;
Title Tel # (207) 622-4971
Personnel: Editor-Paul Brunelle
Editorial Description: Information to assist members; labor relation, school law, school board oriented material.
General Info: Monthly, 4 pages, No Color
Circulation: Total-2,700

MSLAVA Journal/MSLAVA Newsletter
See: LIBRARY

Malvern Examiner
See: INSURANCE

Manitoba Association of School Trustees Newsletter
Association

Publishing Co: Manitoba Assn. of School Trustees, 191 Provencher Blvd., Winnipeg, MB R2H 0G4 Canada; Title Tel # (204) 233-1595
Personnel: Editor-Heather Shepherd
General Info: Yr. Est. 1965, Monthly, Trim Size-8½ x 11, Mimeo press, 7 pages, No Color
Circulation: (100% controlled), Total-1,200

Manitoba Assn. for Schooling At Home, Newsletter

Publishing Co: Manitoba Assn. for Schooling At Home, 98 Baltimore Rd., Winnipeg, MB R3L 1H1 Canada; Title Tel # (204) 334-4763
Personnel: Editor-Charles Small, Circ. Mgr.-Kristy Peterson
General Info: Yr. Est. 1983, Bi-monthly, Mimeo press, 8 pages, No Color
Subscriptions: Indv. $10
Circulation: Total-130
Advertising: Inquire for rates.

Manitoba Science Teacher
See: SCIENCE

Marine Education

Publishing Co: Sea Grant College Program, PO Box 1675, Galveston, TX 77553-1675;
Title Tel # (409) 762-9800
Personnel: Editor-Amy Broussard
General Info: Yr. Est. 1981, Quarterly, ISSN: 0744-0162
Circulation: Total-5,000

Marketing Health Classes
Business

Publishing Co: Learning Resources Network, 1550 Hayes Dr, Manhattan, KS 66502-5068;
Title Tel # (913) 539-5376 Title Fax # (913) 539-7766
Personnel: Publisher-William Draves, Editor, Production Mgr.-Julie Coates
Editorial Description: Adult education targeted to health professionals.
General Info: (Formerly Marketing Classes), Yr. Est. 1989, Quarterly, Sheetfed press, Matte
Subscriptions: Indv. $95, $7/copy
Circulation: Total-350
List Rental: List Management Co.: Infocore, 5605 Avenida Del Parque, Rancho Santa Fe, CA 92067 Tel # (619) 634-5064
Printing Co: Hawley Printing, 1660 Hayes Dr, Manhattan, KS 66502-5070 Tel # (913) 776-6731

Marketing Higher Education
Scholarly

Publishing Co: Topor & Assocs., 655 Castro Street, Suite 8, Mountain View, CA 94041;
Title Tel # (415) 961-6121 Title Fax # (415) 962-1155
Personnel: Publisher-Robert Topor, Editor-Peg McKenna
Editorial Description: For the science, art, and craft of marketing schools.
General Info: Yr. Est. 1986, Monthly, Trim Size-8½ x 11, 8 pages, ISSN: 0896-7156, 2 Color, Coated, Saddle-stitched
Subscriptions: Indv. $95, Can. $95
Circulation: Total-2,000
Advertising: Inquire for rates.
Printing Co: Pace Printing, 5695 Dugan Ave, La Mesa, CA 91942-2331

Marketing Recreation Classes
Business, Association

Publishing Co: Learning Resources Network, 1550 Hayes Dr, Manhattan, KS 66502-5068;
Title Tel # (913) 539-5376 Title Fax # (913) 537-2834
Personnel: Publisher, Editor-William Draves, Production Mgr.-Julie Coates
Editorial Description: Successful new class ideas & promotion techniques for recreators.
General Info: (Formerly Resources), Yr. Est. 1980, Quarterly, Trim Size-8½ x 11, Sheetfed press, 8 pages, Newsprint, Saddle-stitched
Subscriptions: Indv. $95, $7/copy
Acquistions: Publication Bought, Publication Sold
Circulation: (62% controlled), Total-800
List Rental: Actives: $85/M
Printing Co: Hawley Printing, 1660 Hayes Dr, Manhattan, KS 66502-5070 Tel # (913) 776-6731

Martimer
See: HEARING & SPEECH

Maryland PTA Bulletin
Association

Publishing Co: Maryland Congress of Parents, 3121 Saint Paul Street, Suite 25, Baltimore, MD 21218-3857; Title Tel # (301) 685-0865
Personnel: Editor-Norm Otis
Editorial Description: Educational and legislative information for PTA leaders concerning children, schools.
General Info: 9x/yr., Trim Size-11½ x 15, Offset press, 6 pages, No Color, Newsprint
Subscriptions: Indv. $3, $1/copy
Circulation: Total-2,000
Advertising: Inquire for rates.

Massachusetts Home Learning Assn. Newsletter
Consumer, Association

Publishing Co: Massachusetts Home Learning Assn., 23 Mountain St, Sharon, MA 02067-2234;
Title Tel # (617) 784-8006
Personnel: Editor-Sharon Terry
Editorial Description: Home schooling.
General Info: Yr. Est. 1988, Quarterly, Trim Size-14 x 8½, Desktop press, 24 pages
Subscriptions: Indv. $10
Circulation: Total-200

Master Teacher
Association

Publishing Co: Master Teacher, Inc., Leadership La., Box 1207, Manhattan, KS 66502;
Title Tel # (913) 539-0555 Title Fax # (913) 539-7739
Personnel: Publisher-Robert L. DeBruyn, Editor-Robert DeBruyn, Circ. Mgr.-Lori Hanson, Production Mgr.-Brad Roberts, Art Dir.-Barry Anderson
Editorial Description: Inservice program for teachers dealing with the human side of teaching.
General Info: Yr. Est. 1970, Weekly, Trim Size-3½ x 8½, Sheetfed press, 1 pages, ISSN: 0889-6259, Color, Other
Subscriptions: Indv. $17
Circulation: (100% controlled), Total-226,000
Printing Co: Educational Publishers, 3201 Marlatt Ave, Manhattan, KS 66502-8143 Tel # (913) 539-2469

Matrix Newsletter

Publishing Co: Sponsor-Dept. of CCTE, Teachers College Dept. Communications in Education, Columbia University, Box 8, New York, NY 10027-0008; Title Tel # (212) 678-3344
Personnel: Publisher, Editor-Marie Sayer
Editorial Description: Newsletter describing activities and interests of Dept. of Communication, Computing and Technology.
General Info: Yr. Est. 1983, Semi-annually, Trim Size-7 x 11, Offset press, 14 pages, No Color, Newsprint
Circulation: Total-1,500

Med Ed News

Publishing Co: University of Toronto Faculty of Medicine, Medical Sciences Building, 1 King's College Circ Rm 2388A, Toronto, ON M5S 1A8 Canada; Title Tel # (416) 978-2717
Personnel: Editor-Ken McCraig
General Info: Yr. Est. 1984, Quarterly, 4 pages
Circulation: Total-4,000

Media News
Association

Publishing Co: Assn for Media & Technology in Education in Canada, 3-1750 the Queensway, Ste. 1318, Etobicoke, ON M9C 5H5 Canada
Personnel: Editor-Julie Bowerman
Editorial Description: Covers news media education, conferences, and comments on current activities of the association.
General Info: Quarterly

Mel Gabler's Newsletter
Consumer

Publishing Co: Educational Research Analysts, PO Box 7518, Longview, TX 75607-7518;
Title Tel # (903) 753-5993 Title Fax # (903) 753-7788
Personnel: Publisher-Mel Gabler, Editor-Chad Rosenberger
Editorial Description: Educational information pertaining to curricula used in schools.
General Info: Yr. Est. 1961, Semi-annually, Trim Size-8½ x 11, Offset press, 8 pages, 2 Color, Newsprint
Circulation: Total-12,000

Melton Center for Jewish Studies-Newsletter

Publishing Co: Melton Center for Jewish Studies, 399 Dulles Hall, 230 W. 17th Ave., Columbus, OH 43210; Title Tel # (614) 292-0967
Personnel: Editor-Melton Center
General Info: Yr. Est. 1979, 6 pages
Circulation: Total-5,000
Printing Co: Ohio State University Printing Services, 2500 Kenny Rd, Columbus, OH 43210-1017 Tel # (614) 292-3450

Memo to the President
Association

Publishing Co: American Assn. of State Colleges & Universities, One Dupont Circle, Washington, DC 20036-1192; Title Tel # (202) 293-7070 Title Fax # (202) 296-5819
Personnel: Editor-Gay Clyburn, Circ. Mgr., Production Mgr.-Trudy James
Editorial Description: Contains general information on higher education as well as activities of the Association and of the member institutions.
General Info: Yr. Est. 1966, Weekly, Trim Size-8½ x 11½, Offset press, 20 pages, ISSN: 0047-6692, No Color
Subscriptions: Indv. $65
Circulation: Total-1,450

Mentor
See: GENERAL INTEREST

Microsoft Works in Education
See: COMPUTERS & AUTOMATION

Mid Life Woman
See: WOMEN'S

Middle School Companion, The *Scholarly*
Publishing Co: Totally for Teachers, 55 Larchwood Drive, Pittsford, NY 14534-2458 Tel # (716) 387-9438; Title Tel # (716) 385-2849
Personnel: Publisher, Editor-Carla S. Clark
Editorial Description: A newsletter filled with practical tips and activities for the classroom. Teachers from 6, 7 & grades and all subjects submit straight-to-the-point ideas that others can easily adapt to their own needs.
General Info: (Formerly Teacher to Teacher; Totally for Teachers), Yr. Est. 1994, Bi-monthly, Trim Size-8½ x 11, Offset press, 8 pages, No Color, Other, Other
Subscriptions: Inst. $42
Circulation: Total-400
Printing Co: Webster Printing, 2010 Empire Blvd, Webster, NY 14580-1915 Tel # (716) 671-1533

Mind Garden Newsletter, The
See: FAMILY

Mind Science Foundation News
See: PSYCHOLOGY

Mini' App'les
See: COMPUTERS & AUTOMATION

Minnesota Education Update *Association*
Publishing Co: Office of Library Development & Services, 440 Capital Square Bldg., 550 Cedar St., St. Paul, MN 55101 Tel # (612) 296-2821; Title Tel # (612) 296-6418
Personnel: Editor-James Lee
Editorial Description: Policies of & activities in elementary & secondary education in the state.
General Info: Yr. Est. 1966, Monthly, Trim Size-11 x 17, Web press, 8 pages, No Color, Newsprint
Circulation: (100% controlled), Total-60,000

Minnesota English Newsletter
Publishing Co: Minnesota Council of Teachers of English, c/o Terrance Flaherty, Mankato State University, Mankato, MN 56001; Title Tel # (507) 389-1821
General Info: Bi-monthly, ISSN: 0544-3520

Minnesota International Center
See: INTERNATIONAL AFFAIRS

Minnesota Landscape Arboretum News
See: GARDENING & HORTICULTURE

Missouri Parent-Teacher
Publishing Co: Missouri Congress of Parents, 324 S 11th St, Bowling Green, MO 63334-1914
General Info: Yr. Est. 1920, Monthly
Subscriptions: Indv. $1

Missouri Schools
Publishing Co: Missouri Dept. of Education, PO Box 480, Jefferson City, MO 65102-0480; Title Tel # (314) 751-3469
Personnel: Editor-James L. Morris, Production Mgr.-Concerned With Educ
Editorial Description: Concerned with successful educational programs & state education policy.
General Info: Yr. Est. 1935, Bi-monthly, Trim Size-8½ x 11, Offset press, 28 pages, ISSN: 0745-1237, 2 Color
Circulation: Total-8,000

Mixed Media
See: ART & SCULPTURE

Mixin'
See: BEVERAGES - BREWING

Modern Languages Newsletter *Association*
Publishing Co: Sponsor-B.C. Association of Teachers of Modern Languages, British Columbia Teachers' Federation, 100-550 West 6th Avenue, Vancouver, BC V5Z 4P2 Canada; Title Tel # (604) 871-2283 Title Fax # (604) 871-2289
General Info: Irregular
Circulation: Total-600

Monday Memo *Association*
Publishing Co: Jefferson County Public Schools, PO Box 34020, Louisville, KY 40232-4020; Title Tel # (502) 473-3343
Personnel: Publisher-Stephanie M Bateman, Editor-Becky Greenlee, Art Dir.-Kim Katzman
Editorial Description: Weekly report to all employees.
General Info: Yr. Est. 1975, Weekly, Trim Size-8½ x 14, Sheetfed press, 2 pages, No Color, Newsprint
Circulation: (100% controlled), Total-10,500

Montana Parent-Teacher
Publishing Co: Montana Congress of Parents, Cascade, MT 59421
General Info: Yr. Est. 1950, 8x/yr.
Subscriptions: Indv. $1

Montana Schools *Consumer*
Publishing Co: Montana Office of Public Instruction, State Capitol, Helena, MT 59620-0001 Tel # (406) 444-3095; Title Tel # (406) 444-3160
Personnel: Editor-Ellen Meloy
Editorial Description: Information about people, programs and activities in Montana education.
General Info: Yr. Est. 1950, 5x/yr., Trim Size-11⅜ x 17, Web press, 12 pages, Color
Subscriptions: Free
Circulation: Total-11,000

Montessori Observer *Consumer, Association*
Publishing Co: International Montessori Society, 912 Thayer Ave Ste 207, Silver Spring, MD 20910-4570; Title Tel # (301) 589-1127
Personnel: Editor-Lee Havis
Editorial Description: Programs, services & resources in Montessori education.
General Info: Yr. Est. 1980, Quarterly, Trim Size-8½ x 11, 4 pages, ISSN: 0889-5643, No Color, Coated
Subscriptions: Indv. $20, Inst. $25, $2/copy
Circulation: (40% controlled), Total-1,000, Subscriptions-600
Advertising: Inquire for rates.

Morim Bulletin
Publishing Co: Jewish Teachers Assn., 45 E. 33rd St., New York, NY 10016-5336; Title Tel # (212) 684-0556
General Info: 5x/yr.

Mortarboard
Publishing Co: Sponsor-Alumni Assn., College of St. Elizabeth, Publications, Convent Station, NJ 07961 Tel # (201) 292-6300
Editorial Description: Newsletter for faculty, students & staff of College of St. Elizabeth.
General Info: Yr. Est. 1977, Bi-weekly, 8 pages
Circulation: Total-1,650

Multicultural Messenger
See: REGIONAL INTEREST

Multimedia Business Report
See: COMPUTERS & AUTOMATION

Multiple Linear Regression Viewpoints
See: PSYCHOLOGY

Municipal News
See: REGIONAL INTEREST

Murder is Academic *Association*
Publishing Co: Hunter College English Dept., English Dept., 695 Park Ave., New York, NY 10021 Tel # (212) 772-5180 Fax # (212) 772-5005
Personnel: Publisher, Editor-B.J. Rahn
Editorial Description: 'The teaching and criticism of Crime Fiction on campus.'
General Info: Yr. Est. 1992, 3x/yr.
Subscriptions: Indv. $20
Circulation: Total-600

NAACLS News *Association*
Publishing Co: Natl. Accrediting Agency for Clinical Lab. Sciences, 8410 W. Bryn Mawr Ave., Ste. 670, Chicago, IL 60631-3402; Title Tel # (312) 714-8880 Title Fax # (312) 714-8886
Personnel: Circ. Mgr.-Mildred Adamson, Editor, Adv. Dir.-Megan Hennessy-Eggert
Editorial Description: Distributed to agency program officials. News related to allied health education.
General Info: Yr. Est. 1976, Tri-annually, Trim Size-8½ x 11, Desktop press, 12 pages, 2 Color, Matte, Saddle-stitched
Subscriptions: Indv. $15, $2/copy
Acquistions: Publication Bought, Publication Sold
Circulation: Total-1,600
Advertising: Inquire for rates.
List Rental: Rents Lists
Printing Co: Mid American Printing Systems, 517 S. Jefferson St. #800, Chicago, IL 60607 Tel # (312) 663-4720

NABE News
Association   CPM: $366

Publishing Co: Natl. Assn. for Bilingual Education, 1220 L St NW Ste 605, Washington, DC 20005-4018; Title Tel # (202) 898-1829 Title Fax # (202) 289-1829
Personnel: Editor-Nancy Zelasko
Editorial Description: Articles/news on the education of linguistic minority populations and bilingualism.
General Info: Yr. Est. 1978, Monthly, Trim Size-8$\frac{1}{2}$ x 11, Offset press, 24 pages, 20% ads, No Color
Subscriptions: Indv. $35
Circulation: (100% controlled), Total-3,000
Advertising: $1,100.
List Rental: Actives: $250/M, Expires: $250/M
Printing Co: Discount Newsletter Printing, 1487 Persisterce Dr., PO Box 1487, Woodbridge, VA 22193-0487 Tel # (703) 690-1788, Fax # (703) 491-2563

NACAC Bulletin
Association

Publishing Co: National Association of College Admission Counselors, 1631 Prince St., Alexandria, VA 22314-2818; Title Tel # (703) 836-2222 Title Fax # (703) 836-8015
General Info: Monthly
Circulation: Total-4,000

NACCAS Review
Business, Association   CPM: $285

Publishing Co: Natl. Accrediting Commission of Cosmetology Arts & Sciences, 901 N Stuart St., Ste 900, Arlington, VA 22203-1854 Fax # (403) 527-8811; Title Tel # (703) 527-7600 Title Fax # (703) 527-8811
Personnel: Editor-Mary E. Bird, Esq., Circ. Mgr., Production Mgr., Adv. Dir.-Amy Speiser
Editorial Description: Information on accreditation, cosmetology schools and any federal regulations affecting accreditation and post secondary education.
General Info: (Formerly Washington Dateline), 3x/yr., 28 pages, 15% ads
Subscriptions: Indv. $45, Free To Qualified Recipient
Circulation: (100% controlled), Total-3,500
Advertising: $1,000.
Printing Co: Corporate Press, 403 Brightseat Rd., Landover, MD 20785-4706 Tel # (301) 499-9200, Fax # (301) 499-5435

NAEA News
CPM: $46

Publishing Co: Natl. Art Education Assn., 1916 Association Dr., Reston, VA 22091-1590; Title Tel # (703) 860-8000 Title Fax # (703) 860-2960
Personnel: Editor-Stacie Lequar
Editorial Description: Natl., state, & local news affecting visual art education.
General Info: Yr. Est. 1960, Bi-monthly, Trim Size-11$\frac{1}{4}$ x 15, 24 pages, ISSN: 0160-6395, 1% ads, No Color, Newsprint
Subscriptions: $4/copy
Circulation: (94% controlled), Total-16,700
Advertising: $780.
List Rental: List Management Co.: MGI-Marketing General Inc., 105 Oronoco St., Alexandria, VA 22314-2015 Tel # (703) 739-1000, Actives: 19,163, $85/M
Printing Co: Freeport Press Inc., 121 Main St., Freeport, OH 43973 Tel # (614) 658-3315

NAEIR Advantage
Business, Association

Publishing Co: National Assn. for the Exchange of Industrial Resources, 560 McClure St, Galesburg, IL 61401-4286; Title Tel # (309) 343-0704 Title Fax # (309) 343-0862
Personnel: Publisher-Gary Smith, Editor-Jack Zavada
Editorial Description: Tells how businesses, schools, and nonprofits benefit when businesses donate excess inventory to NAEIR. Donors get above cost tax deduction; recipients get new supplies at minimal cost. Contains features, instructional articles and photos.
General Info: Yr. Est. 1977, Bi-monthly, Trim Size-8$\frac{1}{2}$ x 11, Offset press, 8 pages, 2 Color, Coated, Saddle-stitched
Subscriptions: Free To Qualified Recipient
Circulation: Total-40,000
Printing Co: Logan Printing, 200 NE Perry Ave, Peoria, IL 61603-3626

NAEN Bulletin
See: SCHOOL ADMINISTRATION

NAFC Quarterly Newsletter
See: HEALTH

NAFSA Newsletter
Consumer, Association   CPM: $85

Publishing Co: NAFSA Association of International Educators, 1875 Connecticut Ave., NW, Washington, DC 20009-5728; Title Tel # (202) 462-4811 Title Fax # (202) 667-3419
Personnel: Editor-Steven Kennedy
Editorial Description: Publishes news and information related to international educational exchange.
General Info: Yr. Est. 1949, 8x/yr., Trim Size-8$\frac{1}{2}$ x 11, Sheetfed press, 32 pages, ISSN: 0027-5824, 40% ads, 2 Color, Recycled, Saddle-stitched
Subscriptions: Free With Membership
Acquistions: Publication Bought
Circulation: (88% controlled), Total-8,100, Subscriptions-600, International-500
Advertising: $690.
List Rental: Actives: 7,200, $85/M
Printing Co: AGS, 188 DeMarr Rd., White Plains, MD 20695 Tel # (301) 843-1800, Fax # (301) 843-6339

NAIEC Newsletter
Association

Publishing Co: National Association for Industry - Education Cooperation, 235 Hendricks Blvd, Buffalo, NY 14226-3304 Fax # (716) 834-7047; Title Tel # (716) 834-7047
Personnel: Editor-Dr. Vito Pace, Promotion Dir.-Donald M. Clark
Editorial Description: Highlights programs, issues and major developments in industry-education cooperation, school improvement,career development, human resource and economic development.
General Info: Yr. Est. 1964, Bi-monthly, Trim Size-8$\frac{1}{2}$ x 11, Offset press, 4 pages, 2 Color
Subscriptions: Indv. $25, $5/copy
Circulation: (100% controlled), Total-1,200
Advertising: Inquire for rates. Accepts Inserts.
List Rental: Actives: $135/M
Printing Co: Aherst Quick Printing, 2076 Eggert Rd, Amherst, NY 14226 Tel # (716) 835-4831, Fax # (716) 835-5017

NAPNSC Newsletter: Current Events & Comments
Business, Association

Publishing Co: National Assn. of Private Non-Traditional Schools and Colleg, 182 Thompson Rd., Grand Junction, CO 81503-2246; Title Tel # (970) 243-5441 Title Fax # (970) 242-4392
Personnel: Editor-H. Earl Heusser
Editorial Description: Informs constituents of current events and the accreditation progress member and applying institutions.
General Info: (Formerly Notes & Comments), Yr. Est. 1974, Irregular, Trim Size-8$\frac{1}{2}$ x 11, 5 pages
Subscriptions: Indv. $30, Free With Membership
Printing Co: NAPNSC. Notes & Comments, 182 Thompson Rd, Grand Junction, CO 81503-2246 Tel # (303) 243-5441

NAPSEC News
Consumer, Association

Publishing Co: Natl. Assn. of Private Schools for Exceptional Children, 1522 K St NW Ste 1032, Washington, DC 20005; Title Tel # (202) 408-3338 Title Fax # (202) 408-3340
General Info: Quarterly
Acquistions: Publication Sold
Circulation: Total-320
List Rental: List Management Co.: Mail Advertising, Inc., 300 N Stonestreet Ave, Rockville, MD 20850-1655, Actives: 2,600

NASFAA Newsletter
Association

Publishing Co: Natl. Assn. of Student Financial Aid Administrators, 1920 L St. NW, #200, #100, Washington, DC 20036-5020 Fax # (202) 785-1487; Title Tel # (202) 785-0453 Title Fax # (212) 785-1487
Personnel: Editor-Madeleine McLean, Adv. Dir.-Mindy Kaplan
Editorial Description: News covering student financial aid legislation & regulations.
General Info: Yr. Est. 1970, Semi-monthly, Trim Size-8$\frac{1}{2}$ x 11, Desktop press, 24 pages, ISSN: 0882-4630, 10% ads, 2 Color, Saddle-stitched
Advertising: Inquire for rates.
List Rental: Rents Lists
Printing Co: Charter Printing Co., 4202 Wheeler Ave, Alexandria, VA 22304-6413 Tel # (703) 370-1010, Fax # (703) 370-2009

NASJE News
See: LAW

NASPA Forum
Association   CPM: $58

Publishing Co: National Association of Student Personnel Administration, 1875 Connecticut Ave NW Ste, 418, Washington, DC 20009-5728; Title Tel # (202) 265-7500 Title Fax # (202) 797-1157
Personnel: Editor-Sybil Walker
Editorial Description: Communication organ for the association and the student affairs profession.
General Info: Yr. Est. 1980, Monthly, Trim Size-8$\frac{1}{2}$ x 11, Web press, 8 pages, ISSN: 0271-1672, 2 Color, Matte, Perfect bound
Subscriptions: Free With Membership
Circulation: Total-6,800
Advertising: $400.
List Rental: Rents Lists
Printing Co: Hagerstown Bookbinding & Printing, 952 Frederick St, Hagerstown, MD 21740-6821 Tel # (301) 733-2000, Fax # (301) 733-6586

NASPE News

Publishing Co: National Association for Sport & Physical Education, 1900 Association Dr., Reston, VA 22091 Fax # (703) 496-9527; Title Tel # (703) 476-3410
Personnel: Editor-Bob Kraft
General Info: 8 pages, 2 Color, Newsprint
Subscriptions: Free With Membership
Circulation: Total-23,000

NASSP Curriculum Report
See: SCHOOL ADMINISTRATION

NASSP Legal Memorandum
See: SCHOOL ADMINISTRATION

NASTAT News
Association

Publishing Co: N. American Society of Teachers of the Alexander Technique, 826 S. Dakes Street, Tacoma, WA 98405-2726; Title Tel # (217) 359-3529
Personnel: Editor-Jerry Sontag
Editorial Description: NASTAT News is a pub. of the N. American Society of Teachers of the Alexander Technique, a psycho-physical educational approach, for its members.
General Info: Yr. Est. 1987, Quarterly, Trim Size-8$\frac{1}{2}$ x 11, Sheetfed press, 8 pages, No Color
Subscriptions: Indv. $20, For. $35, $5/copy
Circulation: Total-500
Advertising: Accepts Inserts.

NATE News
See: RELIGIOUS & THEOLOGICAL

NATIE News Notes   *Association*

Publishing Co: Natl. Assn. for Trade & Industrial Education, PO Box 1665, Leesburg, VA 22075-1665; Title Tel # (703) 777-1740
General Info: Yr. Est. 1973, Quarterly, 4 pages
Circulation: Total-1,500

NBTA News
See: HOUSE ORGANS

NCAE News Bulletin

Publishing Co: North Carolina Assn. of Educators, PO Box 27347, Raleigh, NC 27611-7347; Title Tel # (919) 832-3000 Title Fax # (919) 829-1626
Personnel: Editor-Jacqueline Vaughn
Editorial Description: News for educators on state of education in North Carolina.
General Info: Yr. Est. 1970, Bi-monthly, 2% ads, 2 Color
Subscriptions: Indv. $1
Circulation: Total-55,000

NCBA Reports
See: LAW

NCCCC Newsletter
See: CHILDREN

NCEA Notes
See: RELIGIOUS & THEOLOGICAL

NCRTL Special Report

Publishing Co: Sponsor-Natl. Ctr. for Research on Teacher Education, Institute for Research on Teaching, Michigan State Univ., College of Education, East Lansing, MI 48824-0001; Title Tel # (517) 353-0658 Title Fax # (517) 353-6393
Personnel: Editor-Sandra Gross
General Info: (Formerly NCRTE Colloquy), Yr. Est. 1987, Semi-annually, Trim Size-8$\frac{1}{2}$ x 11, Sheetfed press, 24 pages, ISSN: 0896-3932, 2 Color, Newsprint, Saddle-stitched
Circulation: Total-6,000

NCSE Reports   *Consumer, Association*

Publishing Co: National Center for Science Education, 925 Kearney St., El Cerrito, CA 94530-2810 Fax # (510) 526-1675; Title Tel # (510) 526-1674 Title Fax # (510) 843-2237
Personnel: Publisher-Eugenie Scott, Editor-Andrew J. Petto, Circ. Mgr.-Erik Wheston
Editorial Description: Covers discussion and commentary on evolution education and the creation/evolution debate.
General Info: (Formerly Creation/Evolution Newsletter), Yr. Est. 1981, Quarterly, Offset press, 24 pages, No Color, Matte, Saddle-stitched
Subscriptions: Inst. $25, Can. $32, For. $32, $3/copy
Circulation: Total-3,200
List Rental: Actives: 3,000, $125/M
Printing Co: New Earth Press, 1921 Ashby Ave., Berkeley, CA 94703 Tel # (510) 549-0176, Fax # (510) 549-1514

NCSIE Inservice

Publishing Co: Natl. Council of States on Inservice Education, Syracuse Univ. 402 Huntington, Hall, Syracuse, NY 13244-0001; Title Tel # (315) 443-4167 Title Fax # (315) 443-5732
Personnel: Editor-James Collins
Editorial Description: Professional development, staff development, inservice education.
General Info: Yr. Est. 1976, Quarterly, Trim Size-8$\frac{1}{2}$ x 11, Web press, 20 pages, No Color, Newsprint
Subscriptions: Indv. $15, Inst. $15, Can. $20, For. $20, $4/copy
Acquistions: Publication Bought
Circulation: Total-3,000
Advertising: Inquire for rates.
List Rental: Actives: $10/M
Printing Co: Trident Printing, 2201 Teall Ave, Syracuse, NY 13206-1544 Tel # (315) 437-2834

ND Council on Vocational Education-Biennial Evaluation Report

Publishing Co: Council on Vocational Education; ND, PO Box 1373, Bismarck, ND 58502-1373
Personnel: Editor-Larry Barnhardt
General Info: Every two years, ISSN: 0094-8306
Circulation: Total-2,000

NEA Higher Education Advocate   *Association*

Publishing Co: National Education Association, 1201 16th St., NW, Washington, DC 20036; Title Tel # (202) 822-7214 Title Fax # (202) 822-7206
Personnel: Publisher-Alicia Sandoual, Editor-Rebecca Robbins, Production Mgr.-Penny Grayson, Adv. Dir.-Susan Wade
Editorial Description: Newsletter reporting NEA & general higher education news.
General Info: Yr. Est. 1983, 13x/yr., Trim Size-7 x 10, Offset press, 4 pages
Subscriptions: Indv. $30
Circulation: (100% controlled), Total-80,000
Printing Co: Mt. Vernon Printing, 3229 Hubbard Rd, Landover, MD 20785-2008 Tel # (301) 341-5600, Fax # (301) 341-1359

NEA Now

Publishing Co: National Education Association, 1201 16th St., NW, Washington, DC 20036 Tel # (202) 822-7214 Fax # (202) 822-7206
Personnel: Art Dir.-Marion Clayton

NEATE Newsletter   *Association*

Publishing Co: New England Assn. of Teachers of English, PO Box 291, Chelmsford, MA 01824-0291; Title Tel # (617) 646-2575
Personnel: Editor-Irene Harris
Editorial Description: Articles about teaching of Enlgish. Recent research, both formal & informal, on teaching English is of special interest. Book reviews also included.
General Info: Yr. Est. 1901, Quarterly, Trim Size-8$\frac{1}{2}$ x 11, Letrpr. press, 20 pages, No Color, Matte
Subscriptions: Indv. $15, Inst. $18
Circulation: Total-950
Advertising: Inquire for rates. Accepts Inserts.

NEHC Update
See: HOME ECONOMICS

NETC News
See: THEATRE

NEWSCOPE

Publishing Co: Institute for Massachusetts Studies, Box 237, Westfield, MA 01086 Tel # (413) 572-5431 Fax # (413) 572-5477; Title Tel # (413) 568-3311
Personnel: Editor, Art Dir.-Jeanne Julian
Editorial Description: Newsletter about campus activities, accomplishments of students & faculty.
General Info: (Formerly Westfield 150), Yr. Est. 1988, Sheetfed press, 2 pages, Matte

NFME News

Publishing Co: National Fund for Medical Education, 8905 Kingston Pike, #12-483, Knoxville, TN 37923-5011
Personnel: Editor-Marla Driscoll
General Info: (Formerly News About Medical Education), Yr. Est. 1967, Annually
Circulation: Total-1,500

NHSC Report

Publishing Co: National Home Study Council, 1601-18th St., N.W., Washington, DC 20009; Title Tel # (202) 234-5100
Personnel: Editor-Sally Welch
General Info: Yr. Est. 1975, Semi-annually
Circulation: Total-2,000

N.J.S.D.C. Research Bulletin

Publishing Co: Rutgers University, Graduate School of Education, Publications, New Brunswick, NJ 08903
Personnel: Editor-Dr. Lawrence Kaplan
General Info: Yr. Est. 1956, Quarterly
Subscriptions: Indv. $2
Circulation: Total-2,500

NLTA Bulletin   *Association*   **CPM: $45**

Publishing Co: Newfoundland Labrador Teachers Association, 3 Kenmount Rd., St. John's, NF A1B 1W1 Canada; Title Tel # (709) 726-3223 Title Fax # (709) 726-4302
Personnel: Editor-Jacqio Tam
Editorial Description: Text in English.
General Info: (Formerly NTA Bulletin), Yr. Est. 1958, 8x/yr., Trim Size-8$\frac{1}{2}$ x 11, 28 pages, ISSN: 1189-9662
Subscriptions: Indv. $10, Inst. $10, Can. $7
Circulation: Total-10,000
Advertising: $450.

NMHA Prevention Update
See: PSYCHOLOGY

NOLPE Notes   *Association*

Publishing Co: Natl. Organization on Legal Problems of Education, 3601 SW 29th St., Ste. 223, Topeka, KS 66614-2047; Title Tel # (913) 273-3550 Title Fax # (913) 273-2001
Personnel: Publisher-Robert Wagner, Editor-Terry Leas
Editorial Description: Presents information on NOLPE activities, commentary on significant legal developments, and case notes on important education law decisions.
General Info: Yr. Est. 1969, Monthly, Trim Size-8$\frac{1}{2}$ x 11, 16 pages, Looseleaf
Subscriptions: Indv. $95, Can. $105, For. $115
Circulation: Total-2,000
List Rental: Rents Lists

NOLPE School Law Reporter
See: LAW

NOTES Plus
Association

Publishing Co: Natl. Coun. of Teachers of English, 1111 W Kenyon Rd, Urbana, IL 61801-1096 Tel # (217) 328-3870
Personnel: Editor-Felice Kaufmann
Editorial Description: A quarterly of pratical teaching ideas contributed by teachers across the country
General Info: Quarterly, Trim Size-8.5 x 11, 16 pages, ISSN: 0738-8624, 2 Color
Subscriptions: Indv. $55
Circulation: Total-27,300
List Rental: Rents Lists

NREA News
Association

Publishing Co: National Rural Education Assoc., Education Bldg., Rm. 230, Colorado State University, Fort Collins, CO 80523-1588 Tel # (970) 491-7022 Fax # (970) 491-1317; Title Tel # (303) 491-7022 Title Fax # (303) 491-1317
Personnel: Publisher, Editor, Circ. Mgr., Adv. Dir., Art Dir., Promotion Dir.-Joseph Newlin
Editorial Description: Newsletter for rural and small school administrators, staff.
General Info: (Formerly Rural, Regional Education Assoc.Newsletter), Yr. Est. 1908, Trim Size-8½ x 11, Sheetfed press, 24 pages, 2 Color, Coated
Subscriptions: Indv. $75, Inst. $85
Circulation: Total-1,080, Readership-1,080
Advertising: Inquire for rates. Accepts Inserts.
List Rental: Actives $50/M
Printing Co: Citizen Printing Co., Inc., 1309 Webster Ave, Fort Collins, CO 80524-2776 Tel # (303) 482-2537

NSSBA Newsletter
See: SCHOOL ADMINISTRATION

NUCEA News
Consumer, Association   **CPM: $175**

Publishing Co: Natl. University Continuing Education Assn., 1 Dupont Cir NW Ste 615, Washington, DC 20036-1110 Tel # (202) 659-3031 Fax # (202) 785-0374; Title Tel # (202) 659-3130
Personnel: Publications Director, Editor-Susan Goewey
Editorial Description: The NUCEA newsletter reports on NUCEA activities; federal legislation and government agencies; innovative programming at institutions across the country; member institutions; trends in continuing and part time education; resources; professional development opportunities within the field; and changes in member personnel.
General Info: Monthly, Trim Size-8½ x 11, Desktop press, 14 pages, 2 Color, Matte, Saddle-stitched
Subscriptions: Indv. $45, For. $55
Circulation: Total-2,000
Advertising: $350.
List Rental: Rents Lists

National
Consumer, Association

Publishing Co: Learning Disabilities Assn. of Canada, Kildare House, 323 Chapel, Ottawa, ON K1N 7Z2 Canada; Title Tel # (613) 238-5721 Title Fax # (613) 235-5391
Personnel: Production Dir.-Claudette Gudranson, Adv. Dir.-Bonnie Copping
Editorial Description: Various perspectives of learning disabilities. Articles, book reviews, resource listings (videos, etc.) to help adults and parents of children with learning disabilities as well as professionals in the field. Editions in English and French.
General Info: (Formerly Post, The), Yr. Est. 1964, Quarterly, Trim Size-8½ x 11, Desktop press, 16 pages, ISSN: 0709-1370, Color-cover, Matte, Saddle-stitched
Subscriptions: Indv. $15, Inst. $15, Can. $15
Circulation: Total-10,000
Advertising: Inquire for rates.
Printing Co: Love Printing Services Ltd., 5972 Hazeldean Rd., Stittsville, ON K2S 1B9 Canada Tel # (613) 831-5683

National Association for the Advancement of Black Americans in Vocational Education-Newsle

Publishing Co: Natl. Assn. for Advancement of Black Americans in Vocation, Southern Ill. Univ., Edwardsville, IL 62026-0001; Title Tel # (618) 692-2131
Personnel: Editor-Dr. Wilbur Campbell
General Info: Yr. Est. 1980, Quarterly
Subscriptions: Indv. $10
Circulation: Total-600

National Association of Language Laboratory Directors Newsletter

Publishing Co: International Association for Learning Laboratories, 304C Moore College Bldg., UGA Language Labs, Athens, GA 30602; Title Tel # (713) 749-2716
General Info: Quarterly

National Association for Vietnamese & American Education-Newsletter

Publishing Co: Natl. Assn. for Vietnamese & American Education, 3206 Wynford Dr, Fairfax, VA 22031-2831; Title Tel # (703) 971-1018
Personnel: Editor-Nguyen Ngoc Bich
General Info: Quarterly
Subscriptions: Indv. $10
Circulation: Total-500

National Braille Association Bulletin
Consumer, Association

Publishing Co: National Braille Association, Inc., 3 Townline Cir, Rochester, NY 14623-2513 Tel # (716) 427-8260 Fax # (716) 427-0263
Editorial Description: Designed to educate and inform braille transcribers, narrators and teachers of the visualy impaired.
General Info: (Formerly National Braille Club Bulletin), Yr. Est. 1945, Quarterly, Trim Size-8½ x 11, Offset press, 32 pages, ISSN: 0550-5666, Saddle-stitched
Subscriptions: Inst. $30, Can. $40, For. $40, Free With Membership
Circulation: Total-2,000
Printing Co: Advanced QuickPrint, Jefferson Rd., Rochester, NY 14623

National Coalition News
Association

Publishing Co: National Coalition of Alternative Community Schools, PO Box 15036, Santa Fe, NM 87506-5036
Personnel: Editor-Mary Ellen Bowen
Editorial Description: Newsletter serving alternative schools & home schools, teachers, students, & interested individuals.
General Info: Yr. Est. 1976, Quarterly, Trim Size-8½ x 11, Offset press, 20 pages, ISSN: 1062-0869, No Color, Recycled
Subscriptions: Indv. $20, Inst. $30
Circulation: (100% controlled), Total-1,500
Advertising: Inquire for rates.

National Faculty Forum
Scholarly, Association

Publishing Co: Natl. Faculty of the Humanities, Arts & Sciences, 57 Forsythe St., Ste. 600, Atlanta, GA 30303; Title Tel # (404) 525-0525

National Faculty Placement Bureau Bulletin

Publishing Co: O'Brien, 4985 Meadowbrook Rd, Williamsville, NY 14221-4215
Personnel: Editor-D. O'Brien
General Info: Yr. Est. 1972, Quarterly
Subscriptions: Indv. $25
Circulation: Total-3,300

National Homeschool Assn. Newsletter
Association

Publishing Co: Natl. Homeschool Assn., PO Box 157290, Cincinnati, OH 45215-7290
Editorial Description: Information on what's happening within NHA and the homeschool community across the nation. Network for individuals and support groups.
General Info: Quarterly, Trim Size-5½ x 8½, 28 pages
Subscriptions: Indv. $15, $2/copy
Circulation: Total-1,550

National Monitor of Education
Consumer

Publishing Co: California Monitor of Education, PO Box 402, Alamo, CA 94507-0402; Title Tel # (510) 945-6745
Personnel: Publisher, Editor-Betty Arras, Circ. Mgr.-Kenneth Arras
Editorial Description: Supports traditional moral & academic values in education. Summarizes current litigation in education. Covers grades K-12. Discusses implications of psychological & social programs in the schools.
General Info: Yr. Est. 1977, 10x/yr., Trim Size-11 x 17, Sheetfed press, 10 pages, No Color
Subscriptions: Indv. $20, Inst. $30, $2/copy
Acquistions: Publication Bought
Circulation: Total-3,000
List Rental: Actives: $90/M

National On-Campus Report
See: COLLEGE STUDENT LIFESTYLE

National Psoriasis Foundation-Bulletin
See: MEDICINE

National Teaching & Learning Forum
Business

Publishing Co: James Rhem & Associates, Inc., 213 Potter Street, Madison, WI 53715 Fax # (608) 258-9955 Parent Co.-Oryx Press, The, Phoenix; Title Tel # (608) 258-8747
Personnel: Exec. Ed.-James Rhem, Circ. Mgr.-Karen Heuman Parry, Mktg. Dir.-Barbara Flaxman
Editorial Description: Provides opportunity for higher education faculty to share thoughts and experiences to motivate students to reach higher levels of learning.
General Info: Yr. Est. 1991, Bi-monthly, Trim Size-8½ x 11, 12 pages, ISSN: 1057-2880, 2 Color, Matte, Saddle-stitched
Subscriptions: Indv. $39, For. $45
Circulation: Total-3,000, Readership-3,000

Needle Tips & the Hepatitis B Coalition News
See: HEALTH

Net News
See: SPORTS & SPORTING GOODS

Nevada Families
See: GOVERNMENT

New Hampshire Educator   *Association*

Publishing Co: Natl. Education Assn. -New Hampshire, 103 N State St, Concord, NH 03301-4334; Title Tel # (603) 224-7751
Personnel: Editor, Adv. Dir.-Martha Allen
Editorial Description: The advancement of education in the state and nation and promotion of the welfare of educators.
General Info: Yr. Est. 1920, Monthly, Web press, 10 pages, ISSN: 0279-3539, 3% ads, Color
Subscriptions: Indv. $4
Circulation: (100% controlled), Total-9,000
Advertising: Inquire for rates.

New Horizons
See: RELIGIOUS & THEOLOGICAL

New Horizons   *Consumer*

Publishing Co: Natl. Registration Center for Study Abroad, PO Box 1393, Milwaukee, WI 53201-1393; Title Tel # (414) 278-0631 Title Fax # (414) 271-8884
Personnel: Publisher-Barbara Wittig, Circ. Mgr.-Ethel Dzik, Editor, Adv. Dir.-Mike Wittig, Art Dir.-Reuel Zielke
Editorial Description: Learning vacations & study abroad programs in 17 countries. With focus on programs offered by the 88 schools. Over 3,000 programs available annually ranging from one week to several months.
General Info: (Formerly Whole Enchilada), Yr. Est. 1980, Semi-annually, Trim Size-11 x 17, Web press, 12 pages, 2 Color, Matte
Subscriptions: Indv. $10
Circulation: Total-7,500
Advertising: Accepts Inserts.
List Rental: Actives $86/M

New Images

Publishing Co: METCO, Inc., 55 Dimock St, Boston, MA 02119-1029; Title Tel # (617) 427-1545
Personnel: Publisher, Editor-J.M. Mitchell, Sr., Production Mgr.-Jeannette Sanders
Editorial Description: Newsletter mailed to METCO parents and educational institutions local and national. METCI has contact with over 2200 families in the Boston area.
General Info: Quarterly, Sheetfed press, 4 pages, No Color
Subscriptions: Free
Circulation: Total-3,000
Printing Co: Sir Speedy Printing Co., 437 Boylston St., Boston, MA 02116 Tel # (617) 267-9711

New Jersey Education Association, Research Bulletin

Publishing Co: New Jersey Education Assn., 180 W State St, P.O. Box 1211, Trenton, NJ 08608-1104; Title Tel # (609) 599-4561

New Jersey Education Law Report   *Business*

Publishing Co: Whitaker Newsletters, 313 South Ave., Box 340, Fanwood, NJ 07023-1350 Tel # (908) 889-6336; Title Tel # (908) 322-7797 Title Fax # (908) 889-6339
Personnel: Publisher-Joel Whitaker, Editor-Ervine Evers, Circ. Mgr.-Sandra Smith
Editorial Description: Court decisions & rulings on employment in New Jersey schools.
General Info: Yr. Est. 1981, Monthly, Trim Size-8½ x 11, Desktop press, 8 pages, ISSN: 0279-8557, No Color, Newsprint
Subscriptions: Indv. $193, Inst. $193, $15/copy
Acquisitions: Publication Bought, Publication Sold
List Rental: List Management Co.: The Lake Group, 411 Theodore Freund Ave., Rye, NY 10580-1497 Tel # (914) 925-2400, Fax # (914) 925-2499, Actives: 29,196, $70/M

New Sense Bulletin
See: SOCIOLOGY

New York African Studies Association Newsletter   *Association*

Publishing Co: New York African Studies Association, STL-G14 Suny, New Paltz, NY 12561; Title Tel # (914) 257-3680 Title Fax # (914) 257-3670
Personnel: Editor-Thomas Nyquist
Editorial Description: The NYASA Newsletter includes articles, news items, conference highlights, book & film reviews, useful lists, etc. of interest to Africanists teaching at all levels.
General Info: (Formerly NYASA Newsletter), Yr. Est. 1974, 3x/yr., Trim Size-8½ x 11, Sheetfed press, 8 pages, ISSN: 0148-7264, Color-cover, Matte, Saddle-stitched
Subscriptions: Indv. $10, Can. $10, For. $10
Acquisitions: Publication Bought
Circulation: Total-300
Printing Co: Franklin Printing, 15 Mulberry St, New Paltz, NY 12561-1418 Tel # (914) 255-1158

New York Education Law Report   *Business, Consumer*

Publishing Co: LRP Publications, 747 Dresher Rd., P.O. Box 980, Horsham, PA 19044-0980 Tel # (215) 784-0910 Fax # (215) 784-0317; Title Tel # (908) 889-6336 Title Fax # (908) 889-6339
Personnel: Publisher-Joel Whitaker, Editor-Fred Rossi, Circ. Mgr.-Sandra Smith
General Info: Yr. Est. 1987, Monthly, Trim Size-8½ x 11, Desktop press, 8 pages, ISSN: 0896-4122, No Color
Subscriptions: Indv. $131, Inst. $131, $15/copy
Acquisitions: Publication Bought, Publication Sold
List Rental: List Management Co.: The Lake Group, 411 Theodore Freund Ave., Rye, NY 10580-1497 Tel # (914) 925-2400, Fax # (914) 925-2499, Actives: 29,196, $70/M

New York Parent-Teacher Quarterly

Publishing Co: New York Parent-Teacher Quarterly, 10 Plymouth St, New Hyde Park, NY 11040-3143
Personnel: Editor-Mrs. Robert White
General Info: Yr. Est. 1969, Quarterly
Subscriptions: Indv. $1

New York University Education Quarterly   *Consumer, Scholarly*

Publishing Co: New York University, 537 East Bldg., 239 Greene St., New York, NY 10003; Title Tel # (212) 598-2031
Personnel: Editor-Lila Rosenblum
Editorial Description: Articles cover issues and research in education, health, nursing and the arts professions.
General Info: Yr. Est. 1969, Quarterly, Trim Size-8½ x 11, Offset press, 32 pages, Ind/Abs/Online: Ed.In.
Circulation: Total-53,000

News, The   *Scholarly, Association*

Publishing Co: Christian College Coalition, 329 8th St., NE, Washington, DC 20002-6158; Title Tel # (202) 293-6177
Personnel: Editor-Sandy Swartzentruber
Editorial Description: National development of & cooperation among Christian liberal arts colleges, & universities, including faculty development, student programs, public relations & legal affairs.
General Info: (Formerly Christian College News), Yr. Est. 1976, Monthly, Trim Size-8½ x 11, Offset press, 4 pages, 2 Color, Matte
Subscriptions: Free
Circulation: Total-4,000

News & Notes

Publishing Co: Alberta Teachers' Association, 11010-142 St., Edmonton, AB T5N 2R1 Canada; Title Tel # (403) 453-2411
Personnel: Editor-Norman Mathew
Editorial Description: News affecting industrial arts and vocational education, project ideas, direction of industrial education.
General Info: Yr. Est. 1968, Annually, Trim Size-7 x 10, Offset press, 30 pages, No Color, Saddle-stitched
Circulation: Total-542

News & Notes
See: INDUSTRIAL RELATIONS/PERSONNEL

News & Views   *Association*

Publishing Co: National Association of Biology Teachers, 11250 Roger Bacon Dr Ste 19, Reston, VA 22090-5202; Title Tel # (703) 471-1134
Personnel: Publisher-Patricia McWethy, Editor, Promotion Dir.-Cheryl Merrill
Editorial Description: Contains news of the organization, its members, research notes & development opportunities for teachers.
General Info: Yr. Est. 1956, Quarterly, Trim Size-8½ x 11, Web press, 16 pages, 2 Color, Newsprint, Saddle-stitched
Circulation: (100% controlled), Total-7,000
List Rental: Actives: $45/M

News & Views

Publishing Co: Michigan Reading Assn., PO Box 7509, Grand Rapids, MI 49510-7509; Title Tel # (616) 361-2232
Personnel: Editor-Marilyn Rose, Circ. Mgr.-Diana Muller
Editorial Description: Articles on reading in grades K-12.
General Info: Yr. Est. 1967, Quarterly, 10 pages, 2 Color
Subscriptions: Indv. $20, $4/copy
Circulation: (100% controlled), Total-5,000
Advertising: Inquire for rates.

News Digest
See: DISABILITY

News from Fondren
See: LIBRARY

News, Notes and Quotes
See: CLUBS

News n' Notes   CPM: $291

Publishing Co: NTID at Rochester Inst. of Technology, LBJ 2264, Box 9887, Rochester, NY 14623-0887; Title Tel # (716) 475-6201 Title Fax # (716) 475-6500
Personnel: Publisher, Editor-Judy Egelston-Dodd
Editorial Description: Newsletter of the Convention of the American Instructors of the Deaf: convention news; membership information; education legislation advocacy; personal contributions; scholarly articles; professional events.
General Info: Yr. Est. 1987, Quarterly, 12 pages, No Color, Matte
Circulation: Total-1,200
Advertising: $350.
List Rental: Rents Lists
Printing Co: Advanced QuickPrint, Jefferson Rd., Rochester, NY 14623

NewsLinks
Scholarly, Association   CPM: $75

Publishing Co: International Schools Services, 15 Roszel Rd., P.O. Box 5910, Princeton, NJ 08543-5910 Parent Co.-Peterson's Guides, Princeton; Title Tel # (609) 452-0990 Title Fax # (609) 452-2690
Personnel: Editor-Gina Parziale, Circ. Mgr.-Anne Schlesinger
Editorial Description: Articles and information relevant to international and American teachers around the world. Directed to the 500 American and international schools around the world.
General Info: Yr. Est. 1961, 5x/yr., Trim Size-11 x 17, Web press, 32 pages, ISSN: 1043-3724, 3% ads, Color-cover, Newsprint
Subscriptions: Free
Circulation: Total-12,000
Advertising: $910.

NewsNotes: Teaching Women's Studies from An Intl. Perspective

Publishing Co: Sponsor-Southwest Institute for Research on Women, Univ. of Arizona, Douglass Bldg., #102, Tucson, AZ 85721-0001; Title Tel # (602) 621-7338
Personnel: Editor-Janice Monk
General Info: Yr. Est. 1985, 10 pages, No Color
Circulation: Total-183

Newsletter and Ideas Collection--British Columbia Primary Teachers' Association
Association

Publishing Co: Sponsor-B.C. Primary Teachers' Association, British Columbia Teachers' Federation, 100-550 West 6th Avenue, Vancouver, BC V5Z 4P2 Canada; Title Tel # (604) 871-2283 Title Fax # (604) 871-2289
General Info: Irregular, ISSN: 0382-5671
Circulation: Total-2,450

Newsletter on Intellectual Freedom
Consumer, Association

Publishing Co: American Library Association, 50 E Huron St, Chicago, IL 60611-2795 Tel # (312) 944-6780; Title Tel # (312) 280-4223 Title Fax # (312) 440-9374
Personnel: Editor-Judith F. Krug
Editorial Description: A bi-monthly newsletter reporting on censorship incidents & court decisions, with book reviews & articles on censorship & intellectual freedom.
General Info: Yr. Est. 1951, Bi-monthly, Trim Size-8½ x 11, Offset press, 36 pages, ISSN: 0028-9485, Ind/Abs/Online: Lib.Lit., No Color
Subscriptions: Indv. $40, For. $45, $8/copy
Circulation: Total-3,200

Newsletter for the National Center for Collective Bargaining
See: LABOR

Newsletter-Special Education Association
Association

Publishing Co: Sponsor-Special Education Association, British Columbia Teachers' Federation, 100-550 West 6th Avenue, Vancouver, BC V5Z 4P2 Canada; Title Tel # (604) 871-2283 Title Fax # (604) 871-2289
General Info: Irregular, ISSN: 0381-8144
Circulation: Total-600

Newsletter of The Teaching Company (Update)

Publishing Co: Teaching Co., The, 7405 Alban Court, Ste. A107, Springfield, VA 22150; Title Fax # (703) 912-7756
Editorial Description: Versatile literature, audio cassette & videos on increasing the coverage of philosophy in the 20th century.
General Info: Bi-monthly, Trim Size-8.5 x 11, 8 pages, 4 Color
Subscriptions: Indv. $549

Newswire

Publishing Co: Journalism Education Association, Kansas State University, 103 Kedzie Hall, Manhattan, KS 66506-1505; Title Tel # (913) 532-5532 Title Fax # (913) 532-7309
Personnel: Circ. Mgr.-Connie Fulkerson, Production Mgr.-Nancy Hall, Editor, Adv. Dir., Promotion Dir.-H.L. Hall
Editorial Description: Provides members with up-to-date information on activities and members of the organization.
General Info: 12 pages, 2% ads, 2 Color, Matte, Saddle-stitched
Subscriptions: Indv. $35, Inst. $40, Can. $41, For. $42
Advertising: Inquire for rates.
List Rental: Actives: $90/M

Non-Credit Learning News
Business

Publishing Co: Learning for All Seasons, Inc., 6 Saddle Club Rd # 579x, Lexington, MA 02173-2115; Title Tel # (617) 861-0379 Title Fax # (617) 860-0237
Personnel: Publisher, Editor-Susan Capon
Editorial Description: Marketing information for directors & marketers of non-credit programs.
General Info: Yr. Est. 1986, 10x/yr., Trim Size-8½ x 11, Sheetfed press, 8 pages, ISSN: 0886-0165, 2 Color, Newsprint
Subscriptions: Indv. $74, $7/copy
Circulation: Total-1,300

North Carolina Public School Bulletin

Publishing Co: North Carolina State Dept. of Public Instruction, Raleigh, NC 27602; Title Tel # (919) 733-3813
Personnel: Editor-A. C. Brooks
Editorial Description: Educational news of particular interest to N.C. public school superintendents, principals, supervisors, and boards of education.
General Info: Yr. Est. 1936, 9x/yr.
Circulation: Total-11,000

Northeast Conference Newsletter
CPM: $19

Publishing Co: Northeast Conference on the Teaching of Foreign Languages, 29 Ethan Allen Ave # 4, Colchester, VT 05446-3339; Title Tel # (603) 862-3124
Personnel: Editor-Barbara Wing
Editorial Description: News of recent happenings in foreign language teaching and reviews of films and computer software.
General Info: Yr. Est. 1977, Semi-annually, Trim Size-8½ x 11, Web press, 48 pages, 5% ads, Newsprint, Saddle-stitched
Circulation: Total-42,000
Advertising: $825.

Northwest Association of Schools & Colleges-Newsletter
Association

Publishing Co: Northwest Association of Schools & Colleges, 1910 University Dr, Boise, ID 83725-0001; Title Tel # (208) 334-3226 Title Fax # (202) 334-3228
Personnel: Editor-David Steadman
Editorial Description: Report of the Association' activities.
General Info: Semi-annually, Trim Size-8½ x 11, Letrpr. press, 8 pages, No Color, Coated
Circulation: Total-1,500
Printing Co: Northwest Printing, Inc., 3430 Americana Ter # 8224, Boise, ID 83706-2504 Tel # (208) 345-4545

Northwest Report

Publishing Co: Northwest Regional Educational Laboratory, 101 SW Main, #500, Portland, OR 97204-3213; Title Tel # (503) 275-9500
Personnel: Editor-Lee Caudell
Editorial Description: Provides information on research & development activities of the N.W. Regional Educational Laboratory, an independent nonprofit institution that assists schools & other agencies in improving their programs. Contains abstracts & ordering information for r search reports, training manuals & other NWREL documents & products.
General Info: Yr. Est. 1967, Monthly, 12 pages, 2 Color, Newsprint
Circulation: Total-10,000

Notes

Publishing Co: Univ. of Michigan Assoc. in the Social Found. of Educ., 4001 School of Educ. Bldg., Ann Arbor, MI 48104; Title Tel # (313) 668-7196
Personnel: Editor-Prof. C. A. Eggertsen
Editorial Description: Reports in the area of social foundations of education.
General Info: Yr. Est. 1963, Trim Size-5½ x 8, Offset press, 14 pages, No Color, Newsprint, Saddle-stitched
Circulation: Total-300
Printing Co: University of Michigan Printing Services, 1919 Green Rd, Ann Arbor, MI 48105-2554 Tel # (313) 764-4392, Fax # (313) 763-5147

Notes for ESL
Association

Publishing Co: Sponsor-English as a Second Language Provincial Specialist Assn., British Columbia Teachers' Federation, 100-550 West 6th Avenue, Vancouver, BC V5Z 4P2 Canada; Title Tel # (604) 871-2283 Title Fax # (604) 871-2289
General Info: Irregular
Circulation: Total-500

Notes Plus
Association

Publishing Co: Natl. Council of Teachers of English, 1111 W Kenyon Rd, Urbana, IL 61801-1010 Fax # (217) 328-9645; Title Tel # (217) 328-3870
Personnel: Editor-Felice Kaufmann, Promotion Dir.-Kent Williamson
Editorial Description: Secondary periodical featuring usable teaching ideas for teachers by teachers.
General Info: Yr. Est. 1983, Quarterly, Trim Size-8½ x 11, 16 pages, ISSN: 0738-8524
Circulation: Total-22,000
List Rental: List Management Co.: MGI-Marketing General Inc., 105 Oronoco St., Alexandria, VA 22314-2015 Tel # (703) 739-1000
Printing Co: Kowa Press, 510 N. Hickory, Champagne, IL 61820 Tel # (217) 359-6700

Nouvelles
Association

Publishing Co: AEFNB, CP 712, Fredericton, NB E3B 5B4 Canada Tel # (506) 452-1743; Title Tel # (506) 452-8921 Title Fax # (506) 453-9795
Personnel: Editor-Nicole Dupere
Editorial Description: Published in French for members of the AEFNB and interested persons in the field of education in New Brunswick.
General Info: Yr. Est. 1970, Monthly, Trim Size-8½ x 11, Web press, 20 pages, ISSN: 0229-7558, 2 Color, Saddle-stitched
Circulation: Total-4,150
Printing Co: FENB, CP 1535, Fredericton, NB E3B 5Q2 Canada Tel # (506) 452-8921, Fax # (506) 453-9795

Nouvelles Universitaires *Association*

Publishing Co: Fed. des Associations de Professeurs des Universites du Queb, 2715 Ch. de la Cote Ste-Cath., Montreal, PQ H3T 1B6 Canada; Title Tel # (514) 735-3654
Personnel: Publisher-Michel Croteau.
Editorial Description: News of University activities and experiences. Text in French.
General Info: Yr. Est. 1979, 17x/yr., Trim Size-11 x 17, Sheetfed press, 4 pages, ISSN: 0709-8006, No Color
Circulation: Total-5,500

Nursing Educators MicroWorld
See: NURSING

Nutrition Funding Report, The
See: HEALTH

Nutrition News
See: NUTRITION

OSCA Reports *Association*

Publishing Co: Naylor Communications, 920 Yonge St 6th flr, Toronto, ON M4W 3C7 Canada Tel # (416) 961-1028 Fax # (416) 924-4408; Title Tel # (416) 449-9321 Title Fax # (416) 449-9321
Personnel: Editor-Lori Knowles
General Info: (Formerly OSCAR), Yr. Est. 1966, 3x/yr., 30 pages
Subscriptions: Free With Membership
Circulation: Readership-1,000

Official Journal - American College of Medical Quality
See: MEDICINE

Oklahoma English Bulletin

Publishing Co: Phillips Univ., Pillipian Dept., 100 South University Road, Enid, OK 73701 Tel # (405) 237-4433
Personnel: Editor-Glenn Doyle
General Info: Yr. Est. 1973, Semi-annually
Subscriptions: Indv. $2

On Campus with Women

Publishing Co: Association of American Colleges and Univ., 1818 R St NW, Washington, DC 20009-1604 Tel # (202) 387-3760 Fax # (202) 265-9532; Title Tel # (202) 357-3760
General Info: Yr. Est. 1971, Quarterly
Subscriptions: Indv. $20

On the Level
See: HEALTH

On Location
See: PSYCHOLOGY

Ontario Vacation Farms
See: TRAVEL

Options in Learning *Consumer, Association*

Publishing Co: Alliance for Parental Involvement in Education, Inc., PO Box 59, East Chatham, NY 12060-0059; Title Tel # (518) 392-6900
Personnel: Editor-Katharine Houk, Editor-Seth Rockmuller
Editorial Description: Offers parents articles on educational alternatives (public, private and homeschooling), educational reform, and information about being involved in their children's education. It includes educational resources for families, book and product reviews, andinformation about ALLPIE's upcoming conferences and workshops.
General Info: Yr. Est. 1989, Quarterly, Trim Size-8½ x 11, Offset press, 20 pages, ISSN: 1066-2855, No Color, Saddle-stitched
Subscriptions: Indv. $20, Can. $20, For. $32, $6/copy
Circulation: Total-2,000, Readership-3,000

Opus
See: MUSIC & MUSIC TRADES

Oregon PTA Bulletin *Association*

Publishing Co: Oregon PTA Publ., 531 SE 14th Ave, Portland, OR 97214-2427; Title Tel # (503) 234-3928
Personnel: Editor-Pat Fuhrer, Circ. Mgr.-Aleen Klingforth
General Info: Yr. Est. 1922, 7x/yr., Offset press, 4 pages, No Color
Subscriptions: Indv. $2
Circulation: (100% controlled), Total-2,000
Advertising: Inquire for rates.

Otoscope
See: HEARING & SPEECH

PCTE Bulletin

Publishing Co: Pennsylvania Council of Teachers of English, Williamsport Area Community Co, Williamsport, PA 17701
Personnel: Editor-Robert Ulrich
General Info: Semi-annually

PEB Exchange *Association*

Publishing Co: Organization for Economic Cooperation & Development, 2001 L St NW Ste 650, Washington, DC 20036-4910; Title Tel # (202) 785-6323 Title Fax # (202) 785-0350
Editorial Description: Published by the Program on Educational Building division of the OECD. Describes issues and policies that plan, design and manage school and college facilities.
General Info: Tri-annually, Trim Size-8¼ x 11⅝, Offset press, 16 pages, ISSN: 1018-9327, Color
Subscriptions: Indv. $34

PENlines
See: CONSTRUCTION & BUILDING

PEPSA Newsletter *Association*

Publishing Co: British Columbia Teachers' Federation, 100-550 West 6th Avenue, Vancouver, BC V5Z 4P2 Canada; Title Tel # (604) 871-2283 Title Fax # (604) 871-2289
General Info: Irregular
Circulation: Total-850

PIP College 'HELPS' *Association, Consumer*

Publishing Co: Partners in Publishing, PO Box 50347, Tulsa, OK 74150-0347; Title Tel # (918) 835-8258 Title Fax # (918) 835-8258
Personnel: Publisher, Editor-P.M. Fielding, Circ. Mgr.-Hazel Moss
Editorial Description: For learning disabled college students and teachers/counselors & parents of learning disabled youth.
General Info: Yr. Est. 1976, 13x/yr., Trim Size-8½ x 11, 6 pages, ISSN: 0732-5256, No Color
Subscriptions: Indv. $33, Inst. $33, Can. $35, For. $40, $3/copy
Circulation: Total-1,000
List Rental: Rents Lists
Printing Co: Kinkos Copies, 2603 E 11th St, Tulsa, OK 74104-3911 Tel # (918) 584-2774

PSI Newsletter

Publishing Co: Georgetown University, Center for Personalized Instruction, Loyola Hall, Georgetown Univer, Washington, DC 20057-0001; Title Tel # (202) 687-5055
Subscriptions: Indv. $4

PTA National Bulletin

Publishing Co: National Association of Hebrew Day School PTA's, 160 Broadway, New York, NY 10038-4201; Title Tel # (212) 674-6700
Editorial Description: Educational events in day school field relating to PTA movement. News of national and regional groups.
General Info: Yr. Est. 1960, Quarterly

PTA in Pennsylvania Bulletin *Association*

Publishing Co: Pennsylvania PTA, PO Box 4384, Harrisburg, PA 17111-0384; Title Tel # (717) 564-8985
General Info: (Formerly Pennsylvania Parent Teacher Bulletin), Monthly
Subscriptions: Indv. $1

Painted Monkey
See: ART & SCULPTURE

Parent & Preschooler *Business, Association*

Publishing Co: Preschool Pubs., Inc., PO Box 1167, Cutchogue, NY 11935-0888; Title Tel # (516) 765-5450 Title Fax # (516) 835-4927
Personnel: Publisher, Editor-Betty Farber, Food Editor-Amy Houts, Art Dir.-Farrar Thurber
Editorial Description: An international resource for parents and professionals. Explores child development ideas, activities, recipes, & books for children & parents in a concise professional style. Also available in bilingual English-Spanish edition.
General Info: Yr. Est. 1986, Monthly, Trim Size-8½ x 11, 4 pages, ISSN: 0887-0365
Subscriptions: Indv. $28, Can. $28, For. $40
Circulation: Total-4,500
Printing Co: Merit Printing, 100 Jericho Tpke, Floral Park, NY 11001-2003

Parents Make the Difference! *Consumer*

Publishing Co: Parent Institute, The, PO Box 7474, Fairfax Station, VA 22039-7474; Title Tel # (703) 323-9170 Title Fax # (703) 323-9173
Personnel: Publisher-John Wherry, Production Mgr.-R. Hasty Norrell, Mktg. Dir.-Laura D. Bono
Editorial Description: Practical ideas for parents to help their children. Ways to get involved in your child's education from K-6 grades.
General Info: Yr. Est. 1989, 9x/yr., Trim Size-8½ x 11, Web press, 4 pages, ISSN: 1046-0446, 2 Color, Matte
Subscriptions: Indv. $79
Printing Co: Newsletter Services, Inc., 9700 Philadelphia Court, Lanham, MD 20706 Tel # (301) 731-5200, Fax # (301) 731-5201

Parents Still Make the Difference! *Consumer*

Publishing Co: Parent Institute, The, PO Box 7474, Fairfax Station, VA 22039-7474; Title Tel # (703) 323-9170 Title Fax # (703) 323-9173
Personnel: Publisher, Editor-John H. Wherry, Production Mgr.-R. Hasty Norrell, Mktg. Dir.-Laura D. Bono
Editorial Description: Practical ideas for parents to help their children ways to get involved in childs education from grades 7-12.
General Info: Yr. Est. 1993, 9x/yr., Trim Size-8½ x 11, Web press, 4 pages, 2 Color, Matte
Subscriptions: Indv. $79
Printing Co: Newsletter Services, Inc., 9700 Philadelphia Court, Lanham, MD 20706 Tel # (301) 731-5200, Fax # (301) 731-5201

Parish Coordinator/Director of Religious Education
See: RELIGIOUS & THEOLOGICAL

Parish Teacher
See: RELIGIOUS & THEOLOGICAL

Participatory Formation
Association

Publishing Co: Northern Illinois University Education Dept., Office of Public Affairs NIU, DeKalb, IL 60115 Tel # (815) 753-1681 Fax # (815) 753-3299; Title Tel # (815) 753-1430 Title Fax # (815) 753-2100
Personnel: Editor-Phyllis Cunningham
Editorial Description: Critical review and discussion of issues surrounding international training of popular educators.
General Info: Yr. Est. 1987
Subscriptions: $5/copy

Partners in Education
Association

Publishing Co: Natl. Assn. of Partners in Education, 601 Wythe St Ste 200, Alexandria, VA 22314-1937; Title Tel # (703) 836-4880
Personnel: Editor-Ted McConnell
Editorial Description: Current information on educational partnerships.
General Info: (Formerly Volunteer in Education), Yr. Est. 1976, 10x/yr., 6 pages, 2 Color, Newsprint
Subscriptions: Indv. $35
Circulation: Total-8,000

Passing Marks
Consumer, Association

Publishing Co: San Bernardino City Unified School District, 777 N F St, San Bernardino, CA 92410-3017; Title Tel # (909) 381-1250
Personnel: Editor-Jan Bell
Editorial Description: Educational resume of school activities, covering instruction, personnel, administration, board of education, etc.
General Info: Yr. Est. 1945, Monthly, Trim Size-8½ x 11, Sheetfed press, 12 pages, 2 Color, Newsprint, Saddle-stitched
Circulation: (100% controlled), Total-4,500

Passport To Legal Understading

Publishing Co: American Bar Association, 750 N. Lake Shore Dr., Chicago, IL 60611-4497 Tel # (312) 988-6115 Fax # (312) 988-6030; Title Tel # (312) 988-5522 Title Fax # (312) 988-5528
Personnel: Editor-Cynthia Canary
Editorial Description: Coverage of programs and publications which promote public understandin g about the law. Includes book reviews, news analysis and commentary.
General Info: Yr. Est. 1983, Quarterly, Trim Size-8½ x 11, 12 pages
Circulation: Total-10,000
List Rental: Rents Lists

Pathways
Consumer

Publishing Co: Bank Street College of Education, 610 W 112th St, New York, NY 10025-1898 Tel # (212) 875-4400; Title Tel # (212) 875-4528 Title Fax # (212) 875-4753
Personnel: Editor-Phoebe Speck, Design Ed.-Joan Auclair, Asst. Ed.-Cathleen Harvey
Editorial Description: Provides information on the Pathways to Teaching Careers Program, a national project funded by the DeWitt Wallace-Readers' Digest Fund to foster improvement of education and develope careers opportunities.
General Info: Yr. Est. 1995, Semi-annually, Trim Size-8½ x 11, 8 pages, 2 Color, Matte, Saddle-stitched

Peace Chronical
CPM: $125

Publishing Co: COPRED, George Mason University, 4400 University Drive, Fairfax, VA 22030; Title Tel # (703) 323-2806 Title Fax # (703) 764-6515
Personnel: Editor-Maire Dugan
General Info: Yr. Est. 1975, Bi-monthly, 24 pages, 5% ads, No Color
Subscriptions: Indv. $20, Inst. $125, $4/copy
Circulation: Total-800
Advertising: $100.
List Rental: Actives: 800, $50/M, Expires: $50/M
Printing Co: Association Printers, 1250 Connecticut Avenue NW, Washington, DC 20005

Peace Press
See: POLITICS

Pen and Ink
Association

Publishing Co: Sponsor-B.C. Art Teachers' Association, British Columbia Teachers' Federation, 100-550 West 6th Avenue, Vancouver, BC V5Z 4P2 Canada; Title Tel # (604) 871-2283 Title Fax # (604) 871-2289
General Info: Irregular
Circulation: Total-750

Pennsylvania Crafts
See: HOBBY

Pennsylvania Dutch News and Views
See: FOLKLORE

Pennsylvania Education
Consumer, Association

Publishing Co: Pennsylvania Department of Education, 333 Market St Fl 10, Harrisburg, PA 17126-0333 Fax # (717) 783-4517; Title Tel # (717) 783-9802
Personnel: Editor-Beth Boyer
Editorial Description: Informs Pennsylvania educators on state department programs, legislation, court decisions and federal programs.
General Info: Yr. Est. 1968, 8x/yr., Trim Size-8 x 10½, Web press, 8 pages, No Color
Subscriptions: Free
Circulation: Total-190,000

Pennsylvania Home Schoolers Newsletter

Publishing Co: Pennsylvania Home Schoolers Newsletter, Rr 2 Box 117, Kittanning, PA 16201-9311; Title Tel # (412) 783-6512
Personnel: Publisher-Susan Richman
Editorial Description: Pennsylvania state homeschooling newsletter. Full of personal stories by homeschooling parents & children, reviews of homeschooling materials & news about homeschooling in Pennsylvania.
General Info: (Formerly Western Pa Homeschoolers), Yr. Est. 1982, Quarterly, Trim Size-8½ x 11, Sheetfed press, 32 pages, 1% ads, No Color, Saddle-stitched
Subscriptions: Indv. $10, Can. $15, $3/copy
Circulation: Total-1,400
Advertising: Inquire for rates.
Printing Co: Matthews Printing, Penn Ave., Pittsburgh, PA

Pennsylvania School Boards Association, Information Legislative Service
See: SCHOOL ADMINISTRATION

Percussion News
See: MUSIC & MUSIC TRADES

Personal Career Directions
Business, Association

Publishing Co: SRC Software Research Corp., PO Box 6519, Depot 1, Victoria, BC V8P 5M4 Canada; Title Tel # (604) 721-1214 Title Fax # (604) 721-1785
Personnel: Publisher-A.E. Wright, Editor-Dr. Walker, Production Mgr.-D. Anderson
Editorial Description: Computerized career counselling & related issues.
General Info: Yr. Est. 1982, Quarterly, Trim Size-8½ x 11, Desktop press, 6 pages, No Color
Subscriptions: Free In Designated Area
Circulation: Total-5,000
List Rental: Actives: $24/M

Perspective
Association   **CPM: $80**

Publishing Co: Assn. of Teachers of Latin American Studies, PO Box 620754, Flushing, NY 11362-0754; Title Tel # (718) 428-1237
Personnel: Editor-Daniel Mugan
Editorial Description: Promotes the teaching of Latin America in US schools and colleges.
General Info: Yr. Est. 1970, Bi-monthly, Web press, 10 pages, No Color, Coated
Subscriptions: Indv. $12, Inst. $12, $4/copy
Circulation: Total-750
Advertising: $60. Accepts Inserts.

Perspective
See: LAW

Perspective
Association

Publishing Co: Institute for Christian Studies, 229 College St., Toronto, ON M5T 1R4 Canada Tel # (416) 979-2331
Personnel: Editor-Robert E. VanderVennen, Art Dir.-Willem Hart
Editorial Description: Informs people of the work of the Institute, a graduate school for teaching and research with a Christian philosophy.
General Info: Yr. Est. 1967, Quarterly, Trim Size-8½ x 11, 8 pages, ISSN: 0847-0324, 2 Color
Subscriptions: Indv. $15, Can. $15
Circulation: Total-4,500
Printing Co: Guardian Press, 609 Trinity Rd., Box 7257, Ancaster, ON L9G 3N6 Canada Tel # (416) 648-8720

Perspective
See: SCHOOL ADMINISTRATION

Perspectives
See: COLLEGE STUDENT LIFESTYLE

Perspectives on Contemporary Ukraine
See: INTERNATIONAL AFFAIRS

Perspectives on Dyslexia
Business, Association

Publishing Co: Orton Dyslexia Society, 8600 LaSalle Rd., Chester Bldg., Suite 382, Baltimore, MD 21286-2044 Tel # (301) 296-0232 Fax # (410) 321-5069; Title Tel # (410) 296-0232
Personnel: Editor-Rosemary Bowler
Editorial Description: Articles on dyslexia research & treatment. Meeting announcements/reports; brief reviews of current literature & publications etc.
General Info: Yr. Est. 1975, Quarterly, Trim Size-8.5 x 11, 32 pages, Color-cover
Subscriptions: Free With Membership
Circulation: Total-11,000
Printing Co: Printing Corp. of America, 15 W. Aylesbury Rd., Timonium, MD 21093 Tel # (301) 561-5533

Perspectives for
Policymakers *Association*

Publishing Co: New Jersey School Boards Assn., 413 W State St # 909, Trenton, NJ 08618-5617
Tel # (609) 695-7600 Fax # (609) 695-0413
Personnel: Editor-Missy Martin
Editorial Description: Each issue focuses on a specific topic in education providing background, activities, and resources.
General Info: Yr. Est. 1990, Semi-annually, Trim Size-8½ x 11, 8 pages, 2 Color, Matte
Subscriptions: Indv. $30, $15/copy
Circulation: Total-1,800
Printing Co: American Press, Neptune, NJ 07753

Pharmacy News
See: DRUGS & PHARMACEUTICALS

Phi Chi Chronicles
See: MEDICINE

Philanthropic Digest
See: PHILANTHROPY

Pinnacle

Publishing Co: Jefferson County Public Schools, PO Box 34020, Louisville, KY 40232-4020;
Title Tel # (502) 473-3622
Personnel: Publisher-Stephanie M. Bateman, Editor-Tammy Jones, Production Mgr.-Ralph Guess, Art Dir.-Kim Katzman
Editorial Description: Annual report.
General Info: Yr. Est. 1984, Annually, Sheetfed press, 18 pages, 2 Color, Coated, Saddle-stitched
Circulation: Total-6,000

Placement Bulletin
See: EMPLOYMENT

Plowshares Update

Publishing Co: Disarm Education Fund, 36 E. 12th St., 6th Fl., New York, NY 10003-4604;
Title Tel # (212) 475-3232
General Info: Semi-annually
List Rental: Actives: $65/M, Expires: 9,630, $55/M

Practitioner
See: SCHOOL ADMINISTRATION

Prehistoric Times
See: ARCHAEOLOGY

President's Newsletter *Association*

Publishing Co: Saskatchewan Middle Years Association, Box 1108, Saskatoon, SK S7K 3N3 Canada Parent Co.-Saskatchewan Teachers' Federation, Saskatoon, Canada
Personnel: Editor-Mark Eggleston
General Info: 3x/yr., ISSN: 0823-695X
Subscriptions: Indv. $15
Advertising: Inquire for rates.

Priority

Publishing Co: Cheryl Pryor, 5304 Kingswood Dr., Orlando, FL 32810; Title Tel # (407) 293-4915
Personnel: Editor-Cherly Pryor
General Info: Bi-monthly, Trim Size-8½ x 11, 12 pages
Subscriptions: Indv. $15, $3/copy

Private Education Law
Report

Publishing Co: Data Research, Inc., 4635 Nicols Rd Ste 100, Eagan, MN 55122-3337;
Title Tel # (612) 452-8267 Title Fax # (612) 452-8694
General Info: Yr. Est. 1986, Monthly, Trim Size-8½ x 11, Sheetfed press, 6 pages, ISSN: 0890-121X, No Color
Subscriptions: Indv. $97
Circulation: Total-1,500
Printing Co: Helgeson Press, 7600 14th Ave S, Richfield, MN 55423-4530 Tel # (612) 869-6828

Private Higher Education

Publishing Co: American Assn. of Presidents of Independent Colleges and Uni, Rick College, Rexburg, ID 83460-0001; Title Tel # (208) 356-1113
General Info: Yr. Est. 1968, Annually

Proceedings *Association*

Publishing Co: Southern Assn. of Colleges, 1866 Southern Ln, Decatur, GA 30033-4033;
Title Tel # (404) 679-4500 Title Fax # (404) 679-4556
Personnel: Editor-Teresa Green
Editorial Description: Association news, book reviews, education commentary.
General Info: Yr. Est. 1947, Bi-monthly, Trim Size-8½ x 11, Sheetfed press, 16 pages, ISSN: 0038-3813, 2 Color, Coated, Saddle-stitched
Subscriptions: Indv. $10
Circulation: Total-18,000
Printing Co: Standard Press, 1210 Menlo Dr NW, Atlanta, GA 30318-4173 Tel # (404) 351-6780

Professional Development Tips
See: INSURANCE

Program Plans/Nursing
Basic *Business*

Publishing Co: EPSCO-Educational Planning Services Corp., PO Box 930, East Sandwich, MA 02537-0930; Title Tel # (508) 888-3257
Personnel: Publisher-Robert Terrill, Editor-Jessica Terrill
Editorial Description: Instructor's program and employee summary for training nonprofessional nursing staff.
General Info: Yr. Est. 1979, Monthly, Trim Size-8½ x 11, Desktop press, 6 pages, ISSN: 0734-1431, Matte, Looseleaf
Subscriptions: Indv. $76
Circulation: Total-2,000
List Rental: List Management Co.: Mailing Clearing House, 601 E. Marshall St., Sweet Springs, MO 65351 Tel # (816) 335-6373
Printing Co: Sandwich Print Shop, 150 Rte. 6A, Sandwich, MA 02563 Tel # (508) 888-1540

Progress *Association*

Publishing Co: Barclay College, Box 288, 607 N. Kingman, Haviland, KS 67059-0288;
Title Tel # (316) 862-5252 Title Fax # (316) 862-5403
Personnel: Publisher, Editor, Circ. Mgr., Production Mgr., Adv. Dir., Art Dir., Promotion Dir.-Jeff Blackburn
Editorial Description: Campus and alumni news.
General Info: (Formerly Bulletin) Yr. Est. 1932, Quarterly, Offset press, 12 pages, 2 Color, Matte
Subscriptions: Free
Circulation: Total-5,500
Printing Co: Taylor Printing, 402 S Main St, Pratt, KS 67124-2625

Progressive Teacher, The *Business*

Publishing Co: Progressive Publishing Co., 2678 Henry St, Augusta, GA 30904-4656;
Title Tel # (404) 868-1691
Personnel: Editor-M.S. Adcock
General Info: Quarterly, Trim Size-9 x 12, ISSN: 0033-0825
Subscriptions: Indv. $7
Circulation: Total-10,450
Advertising: Inquire for rates.

Promptlines
See: COMPUTERS & AUTOMATION

Protestant Teachers Association Newsletter
See: RELIGIOUS & THEOLOGICAL

Public Education Alert *Consumer*

Publishing Co: Public Education Association, 39 W. 32nd, New York, NY 10001-3803;
Title Tel # (212) 868-1640 Title Fax # (212) 268-7344
Personnel: Publisher-Ray Domanico, Editor-Judith Baum
Editorial Description: Provides information & consumer-oriented analysis of key policy issues & current developments in New York City public education; reflects the advocacy agenda of the non-partisan, non-profit Public Education Association.
General Info: (Formerly PEA Reports), Yr. Est. 1974, Bi-monthly, Sheetfed press, 6 pages, No Color, Matte
Subscriptions: Indv. $25
Circulation: Total-4,000

Pulse
See: HEALTH

Pure Facts
See: HEALTH

Quality Teaching *Association*

Publishing Co: National Council for Accreditation of Teacher Education, 2010 Massachusetts Ave NW, Ste #500, Washington, DC 20036-1023; Title Tel # (202) 466-7496 Title Fax # (202) 296-6620
Personnel: Editor-Jane Leibbrand
Editorial Description: Membership activities newsletter for education leaders.
General Info: (Formerly NCATE Update), Yr. Est. 1991, Tri-annually, Trim Size-8½ x 11, 8 pages, 2 Color, Matte
Subscriptions: Indv. $6
Circulation: Total-15,500
List Rental: Rents Lists

Quarterly Review of
Doublespeak *Consumer, Association*

Publishing Co: Natl. Council of Teachers of English, 1111 W Kenyon Rd, Urbana, IL 61801-1010;
Title Tel # (217) 328-3870 Title Fax # (217) 328-9645
Personnel: Editor-William Lutz, Promotion Dir.-Kent Williamson
Editorial Description: Provides information on the misuse and abuse of language.
General Info: (Formerly Public Doublespeak Newsletter), Yr. Est. 1971, Quarterly, Sheetfed press, 8 pages, ISSN: 0735-5920, No Color, Newsprint, Saddle-stitched
Subscriptions: Indv. $10, $3/copy
Circulation: Total-6,000
List Rental: List Management Co.: MGI-Marketing General Inc., 105 Oronoco St., Alexandria, VA 22314-2015 Tel # (703) 739-1000, Actives: 1,814, $95/M

Quebec Homeschooling Advisory Newsletter

Publishing Co: Quebec Homeschooling Advisory, 4650 Acadia, Lachine, PQ H8T 1N5 Canada
Personnel: Publisher, Editor-Jocelyn Maskerman
General Info: Yr. Est. 1983, Trim Size-8½ x 11, Mimeo press, 4 pages, 1% ads, No Color, Looseleaf
Subscriptions: Indv. $5, $2/copy
Advertising: Inquire for rates. Accepts Inserts.

Query
See: SCHOOL ADMINISTRATION

REACH
See: RELIGIOUS & THEOLOGICAL

REEAction
See: REAL ESTATE

RFB News
See: DISABILITY

RIF Newsletter   *Consumer, Association*

Publishing Co: Reading is Fundemental, Inc., 600 Maryland Avenue SW Room, Suite #600, Washington, DC 20024-2569; Title Tel # (202) 287-3220 Title Fax # (202) 287-3196
Personnel: Editor-Gail Oerke
Editorial Description: Describes RIF's nationwide reading motivation program. The Newsletter reaches the general public, RIF volunteers, public officials, & other interested individuals & groups.
General Info: Yr. Est. 1972, Quarterly, Trim Size-11 x 15, Sheetfed press, 8 pages, ISSN: 0364-8389, No Color, Matte, Other
Circulation: Total-12,000

RUCS Newsletter
See: COMPUTERS & AUTOMATION

Rampant Lion
See: ETHNIC

Re: Quest   *Scholarly*

Publishing Co: Stamats Communications, Inc., 427 6th Ave. SE, Cedar Rapids, IA 52401-1931 Fax # (319) 364-4278; Title Tel # (319) 364-6167 Title Fax # (319) 365-5421
Editorial Description: Newsletter for educational professionals to improve recruiting & retention of nontraditional students.
General Info: Yr. Est. 1995, Irregular
Subscriptions: Indv. $99, Inst. $99, Can. $109
Circulation: Total-532, Readership-532

Read, America!   *Scholarly, Association*   CPM: $99

Publishing Co: Place in the Woods, The, 3900 Glenwood Ave., Golden Valley, MN 55422-5302; Title Tel # (612) 374-2120 Title Fax # (612) 593-5593
Personnel: Publisher, Editor-Roger Hammer
Editorial Description: News, book reviews, ideas for librarians, & reading program leaders. Distributed to reading-programs and literacy leaders at schools and community centers across the country.
General Info: (Formerly Supply Side), Yr. Est. 1981, Quarterly, Trim Size-8½ x 11, Sheetfed press, 8 pages, ISSN: 0891-4214, 20% ads, 2 Color, Newsprint
Subscriptions: Indv. $20, Inst. $20, $8/copy
Circulation: (100% controlled), Total-10,000, Readership-40,000
Advertising: $995. Accepts Inserts.
List Rental: Rents Lists

Reading Programs with Stories that Educate, Inform, Entertain and Rhyme
See: CHILDREN

Recreation News

Publishing Co: Innovative Marketing, Inc., PO Box 912, Meredith, NH 03253-0912; Title Tel # (603) 968-7349
Personnel: Publisher, Editor-Jayne Cohen, Circ. Dir.-Beth Kondos
Editorial Description: Features on varied types of recreation facilities and activities.
General Info: Bi-monthly
Subscriptions: Indv. $30, $5/copy
Advertising: Inquire for rates.

Recruitment & Retention in Higher Education   *Scholarly*

Publishing Co: Magna Publications, Inc., 611 N Sherman Ave, Madison, WI 53704-4410; Title Tel # (608) 246-3580 Title Fax # (608) 246-3597
Personnel: Publisher-Richard C. Perkins, Editorial Dir., Editor-Mary Lou Santovec, Circ. Mgr.-Tom Crawford, Art Dir.-Tami Cook, Mktg. Dir.-Lisa Collins
Editorial Description: News and trends related to recruiting and retaining students at colleges and universities.
General Info: Yr. Est. 1987, Monthly, Trim Size-8½ x 11, ISSN: 0891-012X, 2 Color
Subscriptions: Indv. $189
Circulation: Total-1,400
Advertising: Inquire for rates. Accepts Inserts.
List Rental: Actives: 1,250, $90/M

Refunding Update - Introduction to Refunding
See: CONSUMER INTERESTS

Regional Spotlight

Publishing Co: Southern Regional Education Bd, 592 10th St NW, Atlanta, GA 30318-5776; Title Tel # (404) 875-9211 Title Fax # (404) 872-1477
Personnel: Editor-Margaret Sullivan
Editorial Description: News of educational interest directed to 15 SREB-member states.
General Info: Yr. Est. 1968, Trim Size-8½ x 11, 9 pages, 2 Color
Subscriptions: $1/copy
Circulation: (100% controlled), Total-7,500

Religious Education Newsletter
See: RELIGIOUS & THEOLOGICAL

Renaissance Educator

Publishing Co: Renaissance Educational Assocs., 4817 N. County Rd., #29, Loveland, CO 80538-9515; Title Tel # (303) 679-4300
Personnel: Publisher, Editor-Kristy Clark, Circ. Mgr., Adv. Dir., Art Dir., Promotion Dir.-Betsy Koenig
Editorial Description: This quarterly pub. highlights educators around the world who are revealing the effectiveness of integrity in education.
General Info: Yr. Est. 1985, Quarterly, 8 pages, 2 Color, Coated
Subscriptions: Indv. $15
Printing Co: Kendall Printing Co., 2015 2nd Ave Ste N, Greeley, CO 80631-7256 Tel # (303) 353-8895

Report to the Board   *Consumer, Association*

Publishing Co: Vermont State Department of Education, 120 State St, Montpelier, VT 05602-2703; Title Tel # (802) 828-3135
Editorial Description: Commissioner of Education's monthly report to the State Board of Education.
General Info: Monthly
Circulation: Total-1,300

Report on Education of the Disadvantaged   *Business*

Publishing Co: Business Publishers, Inc., 951 Pershing Dr., Silver Spring, MD 20910-4464 Tel # (301) 589-5103 Fax # (301) 589-8493; Title Tel # (301) 587-6300 Title Fax # (301) 587-1081
Personnel: Publisher-Eric Easton, Editor-Rosemary Lally, Circ. Mgr.-Kathleen Harrow, Promotion Dir.-Sherri Filllingham
Editorial Description: Tracks federal aid to education and other programs helping disadvantaged children in elementary and secondary schools, including Chapter 1 & Chapter 2 programs, migrant education, and dropout prevention
General Info: Yr. Est. 1967, Bi-weekly, Trim Size-8½ x 11, Desktop press, ISSN: 0034-4680, Ind/Abs/Online: Newsnet and Predicasts, No Color, Recycled
Subscriptions: Indv. $273, Can. $273, For. $286
Advertising: Accepts Inserts.
List Rental: List Management Co.: Manager: Donald Peterson; BPI Direct, 951 Pershing Dr., Silver Spring, MD 20910-4464 Tel # (301) 585-5976, Fax # (301) 587-4530

Report on Education Research   *Business*

Publishing Co: Capitol Publications, Inc., 1101 King St., Ste. 444, Alexandria, VA 22314-2968; Title Tel # (703) 683-4100 Title Fax # (703) 739-6501
Personnel: Publisher-Cynthia Carter, Exec. Ed.-Joe McGavin, Circ. Mgr.-Peggy Dwyer, Production Mgr.-Billy Adams, Art Dir.-Linda McDonald, Mktg. Dir.-Mary Lou Probka, Promotion Dir.-Susan Pangman
Editorial Description: Timely updates on the best research on learning, testing and classroom practice. New research on such issues as school improvement, assessment, setting & meeting student & achievement standards & more.
General Info: Yr. Est. 1969, Bi-weekly, Trim Size-8½ x 11, Sheetfed press, 10 pages, ISSN: 0034-4699, 2 Color
Subscriptions: Indv. $247, Inst. $247
List Rental: Actives: $150/M
Printing Co: Capitol Publications, Inc., 1101 King St., Ste. 444, Alexandria, VA 22314-2968 Tel # (703) 683-4100, Fax # (703) 739-6501

Report on Literacy Programs
Business

Publishing Co: Business Publishers, Inc., 951 Pershing Dr., Silver Spring, MD 20910-4464
Tel # (301) 589-5103 Fax # (301) 589-8493; Title Tel # (301) 587-1081 Title Fax # (301) 587-1081
Personnel: Publisher-Eric Easton, Editor-David Speights, Circ. Mgr.-Kathleen Harrow, Mktg. Dir.-Pat Nussman
Editorial Description: Covers the efforts of business and government to provide literacy training for adults focusing on the effects of illiteracy in the workplace.
General Info: Yr. Est. 1989, Bi-weekly, Trim Size-8½ x 11, Desktop press, 8 pages, Ind/Abs/Online: Newsnet and Predicasts, No Color, Recycled
Subscriptions: Indv. $260, Can. $260, For. $273
Advertising: Accepts Inserts.
List Rental: List Management Co.: Manager: Donald Peterson; BPI Direct, 951 Pershing Dr., Silver Spring, MD 20910-4464 Tel # (301) 585-5976, Fax # (301) 587-4530

Report on Preschool Programs

Publishing Co: Business Publishers, Inc., 951 Pershing Dr., Silver Spring, MD 20910-4464
Tel # (301) 589-5103 Fax # (301) 589-8493; Title Tel # (301) 587-6300 Title Fax # (301) 587-1081
Personnel: Publisher-Eric Easton, Circ. Mgr.-Kathleen Harrow, Promotion Dir.-Sherri Fillingham
Editorial Description: Covers new Headstart regulations, federal funding policies, state trends in pre-kindergardens, and other news and research as it develops.
General Info: (Formerly PreSchool Perspectives), Yr. Est. 1968, Semi-monthly, Trim Size-8½ x 11, Desktop press, 8 pages, Ind/Abs/Online: Newsnet, Predicasts, No Color, Recycled
Subscriptions: Indv. $286, Can. $286, For. $299
Advertising: Accepts Inserts.
List Rental: List Management Co.: Manager: Donald Peterson; BPI Direct, 951 Pershing Dr., Silver Spring, MD 20910-4464 Tel # (301) 585-5976, Fax # (301) 587-4530

Reporting Classroom Research
Association, Scholarly

Publishing Co: Canadian Education Association, 252 Bloor St. W., Ste. 8-200, Toronto, ON M5S 1V5 Canada Tel # (416) 924-7721 Fax # (416) 924-3188; Title Tel # (416) 428-6622
Editorial Description: Deals mainly with research related to teaching, learning and school problems.
General Info: Yr. Est. 1972, Quarterly, Trim Size-8½ x 11, Offset press, 8 pages, ISSN: 0315-369X
Subscriptions: Indv. $12, For. $17
Circulation: (100% controlled), Total-7,000

Reprint Mailing

Publishing Co: Laucks Foundation, PO Box 5012, Santa Barbara, CA 93150-5012
Personnel: Publisher, Editor-Eulah Laucks
Editorial Description: The Reprint Mailing is a publication of Laucks Foundation, Inc., a small private nonprofit organization interested in furthering efforts toward world peace, equity among peoples & environmental responsibility.
General Info: Yr. Est. 1969, Bi-monthly, Trim Size-8½ x 11, 10 pages, No Color
Subscriptions: Free
Circulation: Total-450

Research News
See: SCIENCE

Resume

Publishing Co: ACCIS - The Graduate Workforce Professionals, 1209 King St. W., #205, Toronto, ON M6K 1G2 Canada; Title Tel # (416) 535-8126 Title Fax # (416) 532-0934
Personnel: Editor-Nancy Graham
General Info: (Formerly UCPA Newsletter), Yr. Est. 1978, 8x/yr., ISSN: 0849-1518
Circulation: (83% controlled), Total-600, International-10
Advertising: Inquire for rates.

Retired Teacher
Association

Publishing Co: Nova Scotia Retired Teachers Assn., 3106 Dutch Village Road, Halifax, NS B3L 4L7 Canada; Title Tel # (902) 477-5621 Title Fax # (902) 477-3517
Personnel: Editor-Leonie M. Poirier
General Info: Yr. Est. 1965, 3x/yr., Trim Size-11 x 17, Offset press, 4 pages, ISSN: 0382-408X, 2 Color, Newsprint
Subscriptions: Free To Qualified Recipient
Circulation: Total-2,000
Printing Co: Dartmouth Printing, 69 Lyme Rd., Hanover, NH 03755-1293 Tel # (603) 643-2220, Fax # (603) 643-5479

Retirement Facility Guide
See: SENIOR CITIZENS

Right of Aesthetic Realism to Be Known, The
See: GENERAL INTEREST

SASS News & Notes
See: ETHNIC

SCWEA Newsletter
Association

Publishing Co: Saskatchewan Teachers' Federation, Box 1108, Saskatoon, SK S7K 3N3 Canada
Personnel: Editor-Anna Marie Donovan
Editorial Description: Information for and about the Saskatchewan Career/Work Education Assn.
General Info: 3x/yr.
Subscriptions: Indv. $20, Can. $20

SDA Newsletter
See: THEATRE

SHETA Newsletter
Association

Publishing Co: Saskatchewan Home Economics Teachers' Association, Box 1108, Saskatchewan, SK S7K 3N3 Canada Parent Co.-Saskatchewan Teachers' Federation, Saskatoon, Canada
Personnel: Editor-Sharon Baker
Editorial Description: News and information for and about the Association
General Info: Semi-annually

SIGCUE Outlook
See: COMPUTERS & AUTOMATION

SIROW Newsletter
See: WOMEN'S

SJTA News
Association

Publishing Co: San Jose Teachers Assn., 2476-A Almaden expwy., San Jose, CA 95125-2901
Tel # (408) 267-0411

SKOLE: The Journal of Alternative Education
Consumer   **CPM: $183**

Publishing Co: Down-To-Earth Books, 72 Philip St, Albany, NY 12202-1729 Fax # (518) 462-6836; Title Tel # (518) 432-1578 Title Fax # (518) 432-8934
Personnel: Editor-Mary Leue
Editorial Description: Publishes articles, poems, and research by people engaged in alternative education. Also contains reprints of relative material from a wide variety of sources.
General Info: Yr. Est. 1985, Quarterly, Trim Size-5½ x 8, Desktop press, 200 pages, ISSN: 9100-1139, No Color, Perfect bound
Subscriptions: Indv. $15, Inst. $20, Can. $21, For. $25, $8/copy
Circulation: Total-300
Advertising: $55. Accepts Inserts.
Printing Co: Account Manager: Ed Hamilton; Celecom, Inc., 357 Shaker Rd # 588, East Longmeadow, MA 01028-3125 Tel # (413) 525-4771

SLATE Newsletter
Association

Publishing Co: Natl. Coun. of Teachers of English, 1111 W Kenyon Rd, Urbana, IL 61801-1096
Tel # (217) 328-3870
Personnel: Editor-Charles Suhor
Editorial Description: Short articles on concerns such as censorshi, trends, issues and testing. Slate Support for the learning and teaching of english, serves the political action arm of NCTE.
General Info: Trim Size-8.5 x 11, 8 pages, No Color
Subscriptions: Indv. $15
Advertising: Inquire for rates.

SMEA Newsletter
Association

Publishing Co: Saskatchewan Music Educators Association, Box 519, Cudworth, SK S0K 1B0 Canada Tel # (306) 256-3372 Fax # (306) 256-3489 Parent Co.-Saskatchewan Teachers' Federation, Saskatoon, Canada; Title Tel # (306) 373-9673 Title Fax # (306) 244-4545
Personnel: Editor-Doug McCosh
General Info: 6x/yr., Trim Size-6½ x 8½, Desktop press, 30 pages, Color-cover, Recycled
Subscriptions: Indv. $30, $30/copy
Advertising: Inquire for rates.
Printing Co: Mr. Print, Saskatoon, SK Canada

SNEA Impact: The Student Voice of the United Teaching Profession

Publishing Co: Student National Education Association, 1201 16th St., N.W., Washington, DC 20036-3207; Title Tel # (202) 822-7910
General Info: 7x/yr.
Subscriptions: Indv. $5
Circulation: Total-90,000

SPEA Newsletter
See: SPORTS & SPORTING GOODS

SSC Booknews
See: BOOKS & BOOK TRADE

S.S.E.A. Newsletter
Association

Publishing Co: Saskatchewan Society for Education Through Art, Box 1108, 2317 Arlington Ave., Saskatoon, SK S7K 3N3 Canada Parent Co.-Saskatchewan Teachers' Federation, Saskatoon, Canada; Title Tel # (306) 373-1660
Personnel: Editor-Norm Yakel, Circ. Mgr.-D. Andres
Editorial Description: Stresses importance of art and art education.
General Info: Yr. Est. 1970, Irregular, Trim Size-8½ x 11
Circulation: (100% controlled), Total-200

SSTS Newsletter
Association

Publishing Co: Saskatchewan Science Teachers' Society, Box 1108, 2317 Arlington Ave., Saskatoon, SK S7K 3N3 Canada Parent Co.-Saskatchewan Teachers' Federation, Saskatoon, Canada; Title Tel # (306) 373-1660
General Info: Yr. Est. 1966, Trim Size-5½ x 8½, Offset press, 4 pages, No Color
Circulation: Total-530
Advertising: Inquire for rates.

STA News

Publishing Co: Seattle Teachers Assn., 720 Nob Hill Ave N, Seattle, WA 98109-4195
Personnel: Editor-Bernard Pearce
General Info: Yr. Est. 1970, Semi-monthly
Subscriptions: Indv. $1
Circulation: Total-5,000

STEADY
See: HEARING & SPEECH

STFM Messenger
See: MEDICINE

SWOAM News
See: FORESTRY

Safety Is Elementary
See: SAFETY

San Bernardino County Museum Association Newsletter
See: MUSEUM PUBLICATIONS

Saskatchewan Assn. of Teachers of French Bulletin   *Association*

Publishing Co: Saskatchewan Association of Teachers of French, Box 1108, 2317 Arlington Ave., Saskatoon, SK S7K 3N3 Canada Parent Co.-Saskatchewan Teachers' Federation, Saskatoon, Canada; Title Tel # (306) 373-1660
Personnel: Publisher-Denis Ferre, Editor-Daniel Gerle, Circ. Mgr.-D. Andres
Editorial Description: Eng./Fr. text.
General Info: Yr. Est. 1974, Irregular, Trim Size-8½ x 11, Offset press, 5 pages, No Color
Subscriptions: Indv. $5
Circulation: (100% controlled), Total-375

Saskatchewan Safety Council Link
See: SAFETY

School Bulletin

Publishing Co: Independent School District No. 709, Communications, Lake Ave. & Second St., Duluth, MN 55802; Title Tel # (218) 723-4155
Personnel: Publisher-Charles Anderson, Editor-Glenn Sandvik, Circ. Mgr.-Mary Greene
Editorial Description: Reports to school district staff and the community on issues concerning education in Duluth and throughout the state of Minnesota.
General Info: (Formerly School Record), Yr. Est. 1970, Bi-weekly, Trim Size-8½ x 11, Sheetfed press, 8 pages, No Color, Newsprint
Circulation: Total-3,500

School Emergencies
See: SCHOOL ADMINISTRATION

School Health Alert
See: HEALTH

School Law Bulletin   *Business*

Publishing Co: Quinlan Publishing, 23 Drydock Ave, Boston, MA 02210-2387 Fax # (617) 345-9646; Title Tel # (617) 542-0048
Editorial Description: Covers cases and laws pertaining to schools.
General Info: Monthly, 8 pages
Subscriptions: Indv. $60
List Rental: List Management Co.: Stevens-Knox List Management, 304 Park Ave S., New York, NY 10010-5312 Tel # (212) 388-8800, Fax # (212) 388-8890

School Law News   *Business*

Publishing Co: Capitol Publications, Inc., 1101 King St., Ste. 444, Alexandria, VA 22314-2968; Title Tel # (703) 683-4100 Title Fax # (703) 739-6501
Personnel: Publisher-Cynthia Carter, Editor-Annette Licitra, Exec. Ed.-Joe McGavin, Circ. Mgr.-Peggy Dwyer, Production Mgr.-Billy Adams, Art Dir.-Linda McDonald, Mktg. Dir.-Mary Lou Probka, Promotion Dir.-Susan Pangman
Editorial Description: The lastest legal decisions, pending court cases & critical legal issues that affect schools, colleges & universities.
General Info: Bi-weekly, Trim Size-8½ x 11, 10 pages, ISSN: 0194-2271
Subscriptions: Indv. $267, Inst. $267
List Rental: Actives: $150/M
Printing Co: Capitol Publications, Inc., 1101 King St., Ste. 444, Alexandria, VA 22314-2968 Tel # (703) 683-4100, Fax # (703) 739-6501

School Law Newsletter
See: COLLEGE STUDENT LIFESTYLE

School Librarian's Workshop
See: LIBRARY

School Marketing Newsletter
See: ADVERTISING & MARKETING

School Microcomputing Bulletin
See: COMPUTERS & AUTOMATION

School Musician

Publishing Co: American School Band Directors Assn., PO Box 146, Otsego, MI 49078-0146 Tel # (616) 694-2092; Title Tel # (209) 835-2037
General Info: Yr. Est. 1953, Monthly

School Scene

Publishing Co: American Industrial Arts Students Assn., 1908 Association Dr., Reston, VA 22091; Title Tel # (703) 860-9000
Editorial Description: Information of interest to industrial arts students.
General Info: Yr. Est. 1978
Subscriptions: Indv. $4

School Science and Mathematics   *Association*

Publishing Co: School Science & Mathematics Association, Inc., 400 East 2nd Street, Bloomsburg University, Bloomsburg, PA 17815-1301; Title Tel # (717) 389-4915 Title Fax # (717) 389-3894
Personnel: Editor-Robert Underhill, Circ. Mgr.-Donald Pratt
Editorial Description: Topics in science and mathematics education at the K - 16 grade level.
General Info: Yr. Est. 1901, 8x/yr., Trim Size-8½ x 11, Offset press, 54 pages, Ind/Abs/Online: Chem.Abs.,Ed.In., No Color
Subscriptions: Indv. $30, Inst. $38, Can. $46, For. $46, $6/copy
Circulation: Total-7,500
Advertising: Inquire for rates.
List Rental: Rents Lists

School Violence Alert: Maintaining Safe Schools   *Business*

Publishing Co: LRP Publications, 747 Dresher Rd., P.O. Box 980, Horsham, PA 19044-0980 Tel # (215) 784-0910 Fax # (215) 784-0317
Editorial Description: Focuses on the legal and practical issues involved in preventing and responding to violent acts in schools.
General Info: Monthly, Ind/Abs/Online: LRPnet

School to Work   *Business*

Publishing Co: MII Publications, Inc., 1211 Conn. Ave. NW, #705, Washington, DC 20036-2701; Title Tel # (202) 293-1740 Title Fax # (202) 293-0377
Personnel: Publisher-Cecilio Morales, Editor-Chris McKenna, Mng. Editor-Richard Sayre
Editorial Description: Covers education reform, tech-prep, vocational education, and programs designed to enhance education for employment.
General Info: Yr. Est. 1994, Bi-weekly, Trim Size-8½ x 11, 8 pages, 2 Color
Subscriptions: Indv. $298, $12/copy
List Rental: Rents Lists
Printing Co: Plymouth Printing, 1200 Cushing Pl SE, Washington, DC 20003-3599 Tel # (202) 488-7777, Fax # (202) 863-1078

School-to-Work Report

Publishing Co: Business Publishers, Inc., 951 Pershing Dr., Silver Spring, MD 20910-4464 Tel # (301) 589-5103 Fax # (301) 589-8493
General Info: 12x/yr., Trim Size-8½ x 11, Desktop press, 8 pages, No Color

School Zone

Publishing Co: West Aurora Public Schools, District 129, 80 S. River Street, PO Box 14, Aurora, IL 60507-0014; Title Tel # (708) 844-4400
Personnel: Editor, Adv. Dir.-Laurel Chivari
Editorial Description: Inform the community of what is happening in their schools, with their students, with their tax dollars, etc.
General Info: (Formerly Waubonsee), Yr. Est. 1974, 5x/yr., 4 pages
Circulation: Total-13,600

Science Education Newsletter

Publishing Co: Univ. of Hawaii at Manoa Education Dept., College of Education, 1776 Univ. Ave., Hall 132, Honolulu, HI 96822; Title Tel # (808) 956-7863 Title Fax # (808) 956-9486
Personnel: Editor-Donald Young
General Info: Yr. Est. 1982, Quarterly, Trim Size-8½ x 11, Sheetfed press, 12 pages, No Color, Matte, Saddle-stitched
Subscriptions: Free To Qualified Recipient
Circulation: Total-13,500

Science for the Handicapped Good Newsletter

Publishing Co: Science for the Handicapped Assn., C/O Ben Thompson, SHA/UWEC Brewer 271, Eau Claire, WI 54701 Tel # (715) 834-9388; Title Tel # (715) 832-5357
Personnel: Editor-Dr. Ben Thompson
General Info: Yr. Est. 1973, Sheetfed press, 8 pages
Subscriptions: Indv. $5
Circulation: Total-900

Scleroderma Spectrum
See: MEDICINE

Scrabble News
See: GIFTS, GAMES, TOYS

Script-Central
See: COMPUTERS & AUTOMATION

Scroll & Stylus

Publishing Co: Kappa Delta Pi, PO Box A, West Lafayette, IN 47906-0576;
Title Tel # (317) 743-1705
Personnel: Editor-Ken Mele
Editorial Description: Info on the honor society's activities in education & on research projects.
General Info: Quarterly
Circulation: Total-55,000

Scrutiny   *Consumer, Association*

Publishing Co: Scrutiny, Box 1, Sub Post Off. 6, Saskatoon, SK S7N 0W0 Canada;
Title Tel # (306) 966-7521 Title Fax # (306) 966-8719
Personnel: Editor-Donald Cochrane
Editorial Description: Covers issues relating to education in Saskatchewan province.
General Info: Yr. Est. 1987, Monthly, ISSN: 0838-4525
Subscriptions: Indv. $8, Inst. $16
Circulation: Total-400

Self Employment Update - Business Idea Letters Edition
See: BUSINESS & INDUSTRY

Self Publishing Update - How to Basics Edition
See: BOOKS & BOOK TRADE

Senior Economist
See: ECONOMICS

Sextant
See: INSURANCE

Sharing Space   *Consumer, Association*

Publishing Co: Sponsor-Creative Urethanes, Children's Creative Response to Conflict, 521 N.
Broadway, P.O. Box 271, Nyack, NY 10960-0271; Title Tel # (914) 353-1796
Title Fax # (914) 358-4924
Editorial Description: Trains all those working with children to communicate positivity and
cooperation.
General Info: Yr. Est. 1972, Tri-annually, Trim Size-8½ x 11, Web press, 12 pages, No Color
Subscriptions: Indv. $15, $5/copy
Circulation: (33% controlled), Total-3,000
Advertising: Inquire for rates.

Signature   *Association*

Publishing Co: Sponsor-B.C. Business Education Association, British Columbia Teachers'
Federation, 100-550 West 6th Avenue, Vancouver, BC V5Z 4P2 Canada Fax # (604) 871-2289;
Title Tel # (604) 871-2283
Personnel: Editor, Adv. Dir.-Ken Horne
Editorial Description: Business education/Computers, methods of teaching, equipment,
supplimentary materials, events.
General Info: Yr. Est. 1960, Irregular, Trim Size-8½ x 11, 15 pages, No Color
Subscriptions: Indv. $15
Circulation: Total-350
Advertising: Inquire for rates.

SimPosium   *Business*

Publishing Co: Maxis, 2 Theatre Sq Ste 230, Orinda, CA 94563-3346 Tel # (510) 254-9700
Editorial Description: For teachers using Maxis software in the classroom.
General Info: Quarterly, Trim Size-8½ x 11, 6 pages, 4 Color, Coated
Subscriptions: Free To Qualified Recipient

Six Months to Six Years   *Business*

Publishing Co: Crescent Park Press, PO Box 448, Eureka Springs, AR 72632-0448
Fax # (501) 253-7196; Title Tel # (501) 253-8686
Personnel: Publisher-Ross Sackett, Editor-R. Sackett
Editorial Description: For those serving pre-school, early childhood, & kindergarden education.
General Info: Yr. Est. 1981, Bi-monthly, Trim Size-8½ x 11, Sheetfed press, 12 pages, 2 Color,
Newsprint
Subscriptions: Indv. $58, $15/copy
Circulation: Total-400
Advertising: Inquire for rates.

Sky Calendar   *Consumer*

Publishing Co: Abrams Planetarium, Michigan State University, Publications, East Lansing, MI
48824; Title Tel # (517) 355-4676
Personnel: Editor-Robert Victor, Circ. Mgr.-Teresa Griffiths
Editorial Description: Illustrated guide to planets, sky events; evening starmap on reverse.
General Info: Yr. Est. 1968, Monthly, Trim Size-8½ x 11, Web press, 2 pages, ISSN: 0733-6314, Ind/
Abs/Online: Sci. & Child., No Color, Looseleaf
Subscriptions: Indv. $8, Can. $14, For. $14
Circulation: Total-12,000

Skylark   *Association*

Publishing Co: Saskatchewan English Teachers' Assn., Box 1108, Saskatoon, SK S7K 3N3 Canada
Parent Co.-Saskatchewan Teachers' Federation, Saskatoon, Canada; Title Tel # (306) 373-1660
Personnel: Editor-Mable Fleming
General Info: Yr. Est. 1964, Irregular, Trim Size-8½ x 11, Offset press, 50 pages, ISSN: 0226-353X,
No Color
Subscriptions: Indv. $20, Can. $20
Circulation: (100% controlled), Total-500

Slate Newsletter

Publishing Co: Natl. Council of Teachers of English, 1111 W Kenyon Rd, Urbana, IL 61801-1010
Fax # (217) 328-9645; Title Tel # (217) 328-3870
Editorial Description: Short articles on concerns such as censorship, trends and issues, and testing.
SLATE serves as the political action arm of NCTE.
General Info: Yr. Est. 1976
Subscriptions: Indv. $10, For. $12
Circulation: Total-2,600
List Rental: List Management Co.: MGI-Marketing General Inc., 105 Oronoco St., Alexandria, VA
22314-2015 Tel # (703) 739-1000

Slovak Studies Assn. Newsletter
See: ETHNIC

Society for Values in Higher Education-Newsletter   *Business, Association*

Publishing Co: Society for Values in Higher Education, Georgetown Univ., PO Box 571205,
Washington, DC 20057-0001 Fax # (202) 687-5094; Title Tel # (202) 687-3653
Title Fax # (202) 687-7084
Personnel: Editor, Circ. Mgr., Production Mgr., Adv. Dir., Art Dir., Mktg. Dir., Promotion Dir.-M.
Kathleen McGrory
Editorial Description: Info on education and membership issues.
General Info: Quarterly, 10 pages
Subscriptions: Free To Qualified Recipient
Circulation: Total-2,000
List Rental: Rents Lists

Software and Networks for Learning   *Scholarly*   CPM: $812

Publishing Co: Shrewbury Publishing, PO Box 3894, Santa Barbara, CA 93130-3894
Fax # (805) 687-0904; Title Tel # (516) 765-2378 Title Fax # (516) 765-2544
Editorial Description: The world's best newsletter on educational software and networks, with inside
info on the Net and hundreds of descriptions, and specs of educational computer programs.
General Info: (Formerly EPIEgram), Yr. Est. 1974, Irregular, ISSN: 1046-1493
Subscriptions: Indv. $65, Can. $75, For. $80, $7/copy
Circulation: Total-550
Advertising: $447. Accepts Inserts.
List Rental: Actives: $150/M

Software Reports: Guide to Evaluated Educational Software
See: COMPUTERS & AUTOMATION

Solutions: an idea exchange for CPCU and IIA course leaders
See: INSURANCE

Sound Off   *Consumer, Association*

Publishing Co: Utah Congress of Parents & Teachers, 1037 E South Temple, Salt Lake City, UT
84102-1506; Title Tel # (801) 359-3875
Personnel: Editor-Rowan C. Stutz
General Info: (Formerly Utah PTA Bulletin), 10x/yr.
Subscriptions: Indv. $6
Circulation: Total-3,500

Sounds of Reading   *Association*

Publishing Co: Reading Reform Foundation, PO Box 98785, Tacoma, WA 98498-0785;
Title Tel # (206) 588-3436
Editorial Description: Restoration of intensive phonics to beginning reading instruction.
General Info: Yr. Est. 1961, 5x/yr., Offset press, 8 pages, No Color
Subscriptions: Indv. $25
Circulation: Total-17,000

Southeastern Historical Keyboard Society Newsletter
See: MUSIC & MUSIC TRADES

Southwest Marine Educators Assn. Newsletter

Publishing Co: Southwest Marine Education Assn., Monterey Bay Aquarium, 886 Cannery Row,
Monterey, CA 93940-1085; Title Tel # (619) 943-0205
Personnel: Editor-Nanette Sterman
Editorial Description: SWMEA Newsletter is for marine educatiors throughout California, Arizona &
Nevada. SWMEA's major purpose is to provide a medium for exchange of ideas, information &
teaching materials among marien educators.
General Info: Yr. Est. 1981, Quarterly, Desktop press, 9 pages, No Color, Newsprint
Subscriptions: Indv. $27
Circulation: Total-300
Advertising: Inquire for rates.
List Rental: Rents Lists
Printing Co: University of California Printing, 2120 Oxford St. Univ. Of, California, Berkeley, CA
94720-7340

Southwestern Archivist
See: LIBRARY

Speaking of Safety
See: SAFETY

SpeciaList
See: LIBRARY

Special Education Law
Update
Publishing Co: Data Research, Inc., 4635 Nicols Rd Ste 100, Eagan, MN 55122-3337; Title Tel # (612) 452-8267 Title Fax # (612) 452-8694
General Info: (Formerly Special Education & the Handicapped), Yr. Est. 1983, Monthly, Trim Size-8$\frac{1}{2}$ x 11, Sheetfed press, 6 pages, ISSN: 8756-3746, No Color, Newsprint
Subscriptions: Indv. $117
Circulation: Total-5,000
Printing Co: Helgeson Press, 7600 14th Ave S, Richfield, MN 55423-4530 Tel # (612) 869-6828

Special Education
Leadership   *Consumer*
Publishing Co: Sunday School Board Southern Baptist Convention, 127 9th Avenue, North, Nashville, TN 37234-0001 Tel # (615) 251-3649 Fax # (615) 251-2795; Title Tel # (615) 251-3916 Title Fax # (615) 251-3866
Personnel: Design Ed.-Ellen Cambell, Asst. Ed.-Carol Yarnell, Artist-Pam Goodwin
Editorial Description: Covers special education issues relating to religious education.
General Info: Yr. Est. 1988, Quarterly, Trim Size-8$\frac{1}{4}$ x 10$\frac{3}{4}$, 52 pages, ISSN: 0896-7784, Color-cover, Newsprint, Saddle-stitched
Subscriptions: Indv. $9

Special Education Report   *Business*
Publishing Co: Capitol Publications, Inc., 1101 King St., Ste. 444, Alexandria, VA 22314-2968; Title Tel # (703) 683-4100 Title Fax # (703) 739-6501
Personnel: Publisher-Cynthia Carter, Editor-Annette Licitra, Exec. Ed.-Joe McGavin, Circ. Mgr.-Peggy Dwyer, Production Mgr.-Billy Adams, Art Dir.-Linda McDonald, Mktg. Dir.-Mary Lou Probka, Promotion Dir.-Susan Pangman
Editorial Description: Source of news on federal legislation, regulation, policies & funding of special education programs. Helps subs stay on top of federal & state litigation on IDEA & other laws.
General Info: (Formerly Education of the Handicapped), Yr. Est. 1974, Bi-weekly, Trim Size-8$\frac{1}{2}$ x 11, 10 pages, ISSN: 0194-2255, Ind/Abs/Online: NewsNet
Subscriptions: Indv. $266, Inst. $266
List Rental: Actives: $150/M
Printing Co: Capitol Publications, Inc., 1101 King St., Ste. 444, Alexandria, VA 22314-2968 Tel # (703) 683-4100, Fax # (703) 739-6501

Special Education Support
Newsletter   *Consumer*
Publishing Co: SpEds, PO Box 68578, Virginia Beach, VA 23455
Editorial Description: For parents of special education children with tips and information.
General Info: Monthly

Special Educator, The   *Consumer, Association*
Publishing Co: LRP Publications, 747 Dresher Rd., P.O. Box 980, Horsham, PA 19044-0980 Tel # (215) 784-0910 Fax # (215) 784-0317; Title Tel # (215) 784-0860 Title Fax # (215) 784-9645
Personnel: Publisher-Kenneth Kahn, Editor-Melinda Maloney, Promotion Dir.-Marcy Witt
Editorial Description: Covers important issues in the field of special education, including such topics as law & administrative policy.
General Info: Yr. Est. 1978, Bi-weekly, Sheetfed press, 22 pages, ISSN: 1047-1618, Ind/Abs/Online: LRPnet, 2 Color
Subscriptions: Indv. $215
List Rental: List Management Co.: Manager: Anne Magowen; Axon Lists, 747 Dresher Rd. Ste. 500, Box 980, Horsham, PA 19044 Tel # (215) 784-0860, Fax # (215) 784-0870, Actives: $125/M

Special Teacher   *Business, Association*
Publishing Co: New York State Assn. of Teachers of Mentally Retarded, 1721 E 54th St, Brooklyn, NY 11234-3921; Title Tel # (718) 949-1155
Personnel: Editor-Stanley Scher
General Info: Yr. Est. 1973, Semi-annually
Subscriptions: Indv. $10
Circulation: Total-3,000
Advertising: Inquire for rates.

Spectrum
See: SCHOOL ADMINISTRATION

Sport Scene
See: SPORTS & SPORTING GOODS

Spotlight   *Association*
Publishing Co: College Placement Council, Inc., 62 Highland Ave., Bethlehem, PA 18017-9481; Title Tel # (215) 868-1421 Title Fax # (610) 868-0208
Editorial Description: College career planning, placement, and recruitment field.
General Info: Yr. Est. 1940, Bi-weekly, ISSN: 0162-1068
Subscriptions: Indv. $72, Inst. $72, Can. $72, For. $92, $2/copy
Circulation: Total-4,200

Spotlight on Dance
Publishing Co: American Alliance for Health, Physical Education, Recreation, 1900 Association Dr, Reston, VA 22091-1599 Tel # (703) 476-3400; Title Tel # (703) 476-3436 Title Fax # (703) 476-9527
Editorial Description: News of National Dance Assn. activities; national events in dance education; limited articles on dance education on special topics.
General Info: Yr. Est. 1966, Quarterly, 12 pages
Circulation: Total-3,000
List Rental: Rents Lists

Spotlight on Youth Sports   *Consumer, Association*
Publishing Co: Sponsor-Youth Sports Institute, Inst. for the Study of Youth Sports, Michigan State Univ., 212 I.M. Sports Circle, E. Lansing, MI 48824; Title Tel # (517) 353-6689 Title Fax # (517) 353-6393
Personnel: Editor in Chief-Robert Malina, Editor-Vern Seefeldt, Art Dir.-Nancy Seefeldt
Editorial Description: Published for parents, coaches, and youth sports administrators.
General Info: Yr. Est. 1979, Quarterly, Trim Size-8$\frac{1}{2}$ x 11, Web press, 6 pages, ISSN: 0740-0802, 2 Color
Subscriptions: Indv. $3, Can. $4, For. $4, Free In Designated Area
Printing Co: Stone Printing Co., 136 E Main St, Lansing, MI 48933-2421 Tel # (517) 482-2231

Springfield Public Schools,
News and Views   *Association*
Publishing Co: Springfield Public Schools, 940 N Jefferson Ave, Springfield, MO 65802-3718; Title Tel # (417) 864-3734
Editorial Description: Items of interest to staff of school district about the district and education in general.
General Info: Yr. Est. 1952, 10x/yr., Trim Size-8$\frac{3}{4}$ x 11$\frac{1}{4}$, Offset press, 8 pages, Color
Circulation: Total-3,000

Statwise; Statistical and
Research Newsletter
Publishing Co: State Board of Ed., Planning, Research & Evaluation Div., PO Box 1402, Dover, DE 19903-1402; Title Tel # (302) 736-4583
Editorial Description: Statistical data relating to Delaware Public Schools.
General Info: Mimeo press, 2 pages, 2 Color
Circulation: Total-350

Stories that Rhyme, Every Time Kids Pages
See: CHILDREN

Story Bag: A National
Storytelling Newsletter   *Consumer, Association*
Publishing Co: Harlynne Geisler, 5361 Javier St, San Diego, CA 92117-3215; Title Tel # (619) 569-9399
Personnel: Publisher, Editor-Harlynne Geiser
General Info: (Formerly Story Bag Newsletter), Yr. Est. 1981, Bi-monthly, Trim Size-8$\frac{1}{2}$ x 11, 8 pages, No Color, Newsprint
Subscriptions: Indv. $20, Inst. $20, Can. $20, For. $25, $4/copy
Circulation: Total-300
Advertising: Accepts Inserts.
List Rental: Rents Lists

Story Rhyme Reproducible
Newsletter   *Consumer, Association*
Publishing Co: Story Time Stories that Rhyme, PO Box 416, Denver, CO 80201-0416; Title Tel # (303) 575-5676
Personnel: Publisher-A. Doyle
Editorial Description: Stories that educate entertain, inform & rhyme in newsletter format.
General Info: Yr. Est. 1994, 6x/yr., Trim Size-8$\frac{1}{2}$ x 11, Looseleaf
Subscriptions: Inst. $3, Can. $4, For. $6, $3/copy
Circulation: Total-5,000

Story Rhyme Word Mapping
See: CROSS-WORD PUZZLES

Story Time Stories That Rhyme
See: CHILDREN

Straight from Sherman
See: HEALTH

Street Scenes   *Business*
Publishing Co: Bank Street College of Education, 610 W 112th St, New York, NY 10025-1898; Title Tel # (212) 875-4400 Title Fax # (212) 875-4761
Personnel: Editor-Antonella Severo
Editorial Description: New ideas in education.
General Info: (Formerly Bank Street Reporting), Yr. Est. 1975, Semi-annually, Trim Size-11 x 11$\frac{3}{8}$, Web press, 8 pages, 2 Color, Newsprint
Circulation: Total-2,000

Street Voice
Publishing Co: Street Voice Outreach, 101 W. Read St. #421, Baltimore, MD 21201
Editorial Description: An outreach tool for education and survival, a short newsletter devoted to the homeless/IV drug community in Baltimore.
General Info: Trim Size-8.5 x 11, 2 pages

Stroudsburg Area
Teachers Association
News
Publishing Co: Stroudsburg Area Teachers Assn., 11 S 8th St, Stroudsburg, PA 18360-1612
Personnel: Editor-Harry G. Anton
General Info: Bi-monthly
Circulation: Total-250
Advertising: Inquire for rates.

Student Aid News   *Business*

Publishing Co: Capitol Publications, Inc., 1101 King St., Ste. 444, Alexandria, VA 22314-2968;
Title Tel # (703) 683-4100 Title Fax # (703) 739-6501
Personnel: Publisher-Cynthia Carter, Editor-Annette Licitra, Exec. Ed.-Joe McGavin, Circ. Mgr.-Peggy
Dwyer, Production Mgr.-Billy Adams, Art Dir.-Linda McDonald, Mktg. Dir.-Mary Lou Probka,
Promotion Dir.-Susan Pangman
Editorial Description: News on developments of the DSL program and all other federal student aid
programs. Reports on new program initiatives, eligibility requirements, new regulations and more.
General Info: Yr. Est. 1973, Weekly, Trim Size-8½ x 11, Sheetfed press, 10 pages, ISSN: 0194-
2212, Ind/Abs/Online: NewsNet, 2 Color, Newsprint
Subscriptions: Indv. $298, Inst. $298
Acquistions: Publication Bought
List Rental: Actives: $150/M
Printing Co: Capitol Publications, Inc., 1101 King St., Ste. 444, Alexandria, VA 22314-2968
Tel # (703) 683-4100, Fax # (703) 739-6501

Student Aid Newsletter   *Consumer*

Publishing Co: Scovill, Paterson Inc., 141 Fifth Avenue, New York, NY 10010 Tel # (212) 673-6090
Fax # (212) 673-6603
Editorial Description: Timely information and advice on college and graduate scholarships, grants,
loans and awards.
General Info: Yr. Est. 1955, Quarterly, ISSN: 1060-2275
Subscriptions: Indv. $49

Study of Play

Publishing Co: Assn. for the Study of Play, Box 6375, Southwestern Univ., Georgetown, TX 78626
Editorial Description: Focuses on research into aspects of play.
General Info: Yr. Est. 1974
Subscriptions: Indv. $15

Study War No More   *Consumer, Association*   **CPM: $211**

Publishing Co: University Conversion Project, PO Box 748, Cambridge, MA 02142-0006;
Title Tel # (617) 354-9363 Title Fax # (617) 354-9363
Personnel: Editor-Rich Cowan
Editorial Description: A publication which provides tools for activists, academics, and journalists who
wish to examine the influence of the military in our society. It provides bibliographies, articles, lists
of relevant organizations, statistics, and research ideas.
General Info: (Formerly War Research Info Service), Yr. Est. 1991, Quarterly, ISSN: 1073-2349
Subscriptions: Indv. $25, Inst. $35, Can. $40, For. $40, $3/copy
Circulation: Total-900
Advertising: $190.

Success Orientation
See: MANAGEMENT

Suffolk University Report   *Association*

Publishing Co: Suffolk Univ., 8 Ashburton Pl, Boston, MA 02108-2701 Tel # (617) 573-8447
Editorial Description: Information about the university for alumni, students, faculty and others.

Suffolk University Sun   *Association*

Publishing Co: Suffolk Univ., 8 Ashburton Pl, Boston, MA 02108-2701; Title Tel # (617) 573-8447
Personnel: Editor-Louis Connelly
Editorial Description: A publication for faculty and staff.
General Info: Yr. Est. 1971, Monthly, Offset press, 12 pages
Circulation: Total-1,000

Superintendents Only
See: SCHOOL ADMINISTRATION

Supported Employment InfoLines
See: EMPLOYMENT

Synagogue School
See: RELIGIOUS & THEOLOGICAL

Synthesis/Synthese

Publishing Co: Canadian Bureau for Intl. Education, 85 Albert St., #1400, Ottawa, ON K1P 6A4
Canada; Title Tel # (613) 237-4820 Title Fax # (613) 237-1300
Personnel: Circ. Mgr.-Margot Geruld, Editor, Production Mgr., Adv. Dir.-Jennifer Humphries
Editorial Description: International education, news and issues; available in English and French.
General Info: Yr. Est. 1990, Quarterly, 16 pages, Color-cover, Matte, Saddle-stitched
Subscriptions: Indv. $20, For. $30, $4/copy
Circulation: Total-2,500
Advertising: Inquire for rates.

TAC Newsletter
See: BLIND

TAM Newsletter   *Association*

Publishing Co: Council for Exceptional Children, 1920 Association Dr., Reston, VA 22091-1589;
Title Tel # (703) 620-3660 Title Fax # (703) 264-9494
Personnel: Editor, Production Mgr., Adv. Dir.-David Edyburn
Editorial Description: Information concerning use of technology & media for handicapped & gifted
children & youth.
General Info: Yr. Est. 1985, Bi-monthly, Trim Size-8½ x 11, Offset press, 8 pages, No Color, Saddle-
stitched
Circulation: Total-1,800
Advertising: Inquire for rates.
List Rental: Actives: $60/M

TASH Newsletter
See: DISABILITY

TEA Newsletter

Publishing Co: Tucson Education Assn., 4625 E 2nd St, Tucson, AZ 85711-1198;
Title Tel # (602) 795-8870
Personnel: Editor-Gene M. Brooks
General Info: Yr. Est. 1957, Weekly
Circulation: Total-2,500

THESA Newsletter   *Association*

Publishing Co: Sponsor-Teachers of Home Economics Specialist Association, British Columbia
Teachers' Federation, 100-550 West 6th Avenue, Vancouver, BC V5Z 4P2 Canada;
Title Tel # (604) 871-2283 Title Fax # (604) 871-2289
General Info: Irregular, ISSN: 0702-7133
Circulation: Total-500

TRACE Newsletter
See: RELIGIOUS & THEOLOGICAL

Tag Update   *Association*

Publishing Co: Assn. for the Gifted-Council for Exceptional Children, Kent State U, 401 White Hall,
729 21st St., Kent, OH 44242-0001; Title Tel # (216) 672-2477
Personnel: Publisher-Jan Yoder, Editor-James Demaio
Editorial Description: Information regarding events, legislation, conferences related to gifted
education.
General Info: (Formerly Talents & Gifts), Yr. Est. 1977, Quarterly, Sheetfed press, 8 pages, Color,
Newsprint
Circulation: (100% controlled), Total-2,500

Take a Breather...
See: HEALTH

Te Deum
See: RELIGIOUS & THEOLOGICAL

Teacher Education Reports   *Consumer, Association*

Publishing Co: Feistritzer Pubs., 4401a Connecticut Ave NW # 212, Washington, DC 20008-2325;
Title Tel # (202) 362-3444 Title Fax # (202) 362-3493
Personnel: Editor-David Chester
General Info: Yr. Est. 1979, Bi-weekly, Trim Size-8½ x 11, 8 pages
Subscriptions: Indv. $247, Can. $260, For. $270
Printing Co: Frank's Duplicating, 529 14th St., N.W., Washington, DC 20045 Tel # (202) 628-7883

Teacher's Guide to Classroom Management   *Business*

Publishing Co: Economics Press, Inc., 12 Daniel Rd., Fairfield, NJ 07004-2565;
Title Tel # (201) 227-1224 Title Fax # (201) 227-9742
Personnel: Editor-Robert Guder
Editorial Description: Bulletins showing teachers how to solve problems and avoid problematic
situations.
General Info: Bi-weekly
Subscriptions: Indv. $25
Circulation: Total-1,200
List Rental: List Management Co.: Manager: Michael Korman; Names in the News, 411 Theodore
Fremd Ave., Rye, NY 10580 Tel # (914) 925-2400, Actives: $85/M
Printing Co: Beckley Press, 2 Sperry Rd, Fairfield, NJ 07004-2056 Tel # (201) 227-6350

Teachers In Touch   *Consumer*

Publishing Co: ISM Independent School Management, Inc., 1316 N. Union St., Wilmington, DE
19806-2534; Title Tel # (302) 656-4944 Title Fax # (302) 656-0647
Personnel: Adv. Dir.-Christin Dworsky
Editorial Description: Newsletter for professional sharing among teachers on topics of teaching
excellence and teacher renewal. Focus or professional development and self renewal.
General Info: Yr. Est. 1993, 5x/yr.
Subscriptions: Indv. $23, Inst. $5
Circulation: Total-2,500

Teacher's PET Term Paper   *Business*

Publishing Co: Zero Population Growth Inc., 1400 16th St NW Ste 320, Washington, DC
20036-2290; Title Tel # (202) 332-2200 Title Fax # (202) 332-2302
Personnel: Editor-Pamela Wasserman, Production Mgr.-Susan Bryant
Editorial Description: Offers population education classroom activities for grades K-12, reviews of
population education resources, news of training opportunities, ideas contributed by teachers,
answers to frequently asked questions about population trends.
General Info: Yr. Est. 1985, Quarterly, Offset press, 4 pages, 2 Color, Newsprint
Subscriptions: Indv. $3
Circulation: Total-4,500
List Rental: List Management Co.: Names in the News-California, 1 Bush St Bsmt 3, San Francisco,
CA 94104-4425 Tel # (415) 989-3350, Fax # (415) 433-7796, Actives: 41,177, $70/M, Expires:
29,829, $35/M
Printing Co: Eco-Print, 9335 Fraser Ave, Silver Spring, MD 20910-1228 Tel # (301) 585-7077

Teaching Forum

Publishing Co: University of Guelph Educational Practice, Publications, Guelph, ON N1G 2W1 Canada; Title Tel # (519) 824-4120
Editorial Description: Informs faculty and graduate students of current ideas in the area of teaching and learning.
General Info: Yr. Est. 1970, Trim Size-8½ x 11, Offset press, 4 pages, No Color
Subscriptions: Free
Circulation: Total-2,000

Teaching Georgia Government Newsletter　　*Consumer*

Publishing Co: Carl Vinson Institute of Georgia, Univ. of Georgia, 201 N. Milledge Ave., Athens, GA 30602; Title Tel # (706) 542-2736 Title Fax # (706) 542-9301
Personnel: Editor-Inge Whittle
Editorial Description: Provides teaching ideas for instruction in Georgia government, history,geography, law-related education; news of events in Georgia government; news of relevant publications, programs for teachers.
General Info: Tri-annually
Subscriptions: Free
Circulation: Total-1,000

Teaching Notes

Publishing Co: University of Guelph Educational Practice, Publications, Guelph, ON N1G 2W1 Canada; Title Tel # (519) 824-4120
Editorial Description: Informs faculty & graduate students of practical or new items in the area of teaching & learning.
General Info: Yr. Est. 1987, Monthly, Desktop press, 4 pages, No Color, Newsprint
Circulation: Total-1,100

Teaching Opportunities Overseas Bulletin　　*Consumer*

Publishing Co: Overseas Academic Opportunities, P.O. Box 768, Merrick, NY 11566-0368 Tel # (908) 774-1040; Title Tel # (908) 774-1004 Title Fax # (908) 774-1040
Personnel: Publisher-Thomas Towey, Editor, Circ. Mgr.-Susan Towey
Editorial Description: Employment information on elementary, secondary & college teaching positions overseas.
General Info: Yr. Est. 1973, Monthly, Trim Size-8½ x 11, Web press, 6 pages, ISSN: 0889-8839, No Color
Subscriptions: Indv. $38, Inst. $38, Can. $40, For. $43, $4/copy
Circulation: Total-2,500
Advertising: Accepts Inserts.
List Rental: Rents Lists
Printing Co: Banner Associates, 1109 Banner Ave, Brooklyn, NY 11235-5214 Tel # (718) 934-7857

Teaching Professor　　*Consumer, Association*　　CPM: $62

Publishing Co: Magna Publications, Inc., 611 N Sherman Ave, Madison, WI 53704-4410; Title Tel # (608) 246-3580 Title Fax # (608) 246-3597
Personnel: Publisher-Richard C. Perkins, Editorial Dir.-Mary Lou Santovec, Editor-Maryellen Weimer, Asst. Ed.-Bob Magnan, Circ. Mgr.-Tom Crawford, Art Dir.-Tami Cook, Promotion Dir.-Lisa Collins
Editorial Description: A resource for college faculty whose primary responsibility is teaching.
General Info: Yr. Est. 1987, Monthly, Trim Size-8½ x 11, 6 pages, ISSN: 0892-2209, 2 Color
Subscriptions: Indv. $41, $3/copy
Circulation: Total-16,000
Advertising: $1,000. Accepts Inserts.
List Rental: Actives: 6,000, $90/M, Hotline: 1,000, $100/M, Expires: 10,000, $80/M

Technology Applications Quarterly　　*Business*

Publishing Co: University of the State of New York - State Education Dept., Office Of Middle/ Secondary Ed., Room 967 EBA, Albany, NY 12234-0001; Title Tel # (518) 474-1280 Title Fax # (518) 486-5295
Personnel: Editor-Ann Ardell
Editorial Description: Covers developments and uses in technology for edcucation.
General Info: Yr. Est. 1989, Quarterly, 40 pages, 2 Color
Subscriptions: Free To Qualified Recipient
Circulation: Readership-185,000

Technology Pathfinder for Administrators
See: COMPUTERS & AUTOMATION

Telluride Newsletter　　*Association*

Publishing Co: Telluride Newsletter, 217 West Ave, Ithaca, NY 14850-3911; Title Tel # (607) 273-5011
Personnel: Editor-Eric Lerner
Editorial Description: News of interest to alumni of Telluride Association sponsored programs.
General Info: Yr. Est. 1913, Trim Size-8½ x 11, Letrpr. press, 8 pages, No Color
Circulation: Total-3,000

Tennessee Arts Education

Publishing Co: Tennessee Arts Commission, 404 James Robertson Parkway, Suite 160, Nashville, TN 37243-0780 Fax # (615) 741-8559; Title Tel # (615) 741-1701
General Info: Yr. Est. 1989, Quarterly, 4 pages

Tennessee Observer
See: HEARING & SPEECH

Tennessee Parent-Teacher Bulletin　　*Consumer, Association*

Publishing Co: Tennessee Congress of Parents, 1905 Acklen Ave., Nashville, TN 37212-3713; Title Tel # (615) 383-9740
Personnel: Editor-Diane Dozier
Editorial Description: Provides local PTA's with State and National news relative to PTA work.
General Info: Yr. Est. 1924, 10x/yr., Trim Size-8½ x 11, Offset press, 6 pages, No Color
Subscriptions: Indv. $4
Acquistions: Publication Bought
Circulation: Total-1,400
Advertising: Inquire for rates.

Tennessee School Board Bulletin　　*Association*

Publishing Co: Tennessee School Boards Assn., 500 13th Ave. , N., Nashville, TN 37203-2808; Title Tel # (615) 251-1518
Personnel: Publisher-Daniel Tollett, Editor-Holly Hewitt
Editorial Description: Articles of interest to boards of education; announcements.
General Info: Yr. Est. 1950, 8x/yr., Trim Size-8½ x 11, Offset press, 6 pages, ISSN: 0049-3406, No Color, Coated
Subscriptions: Indv. $20
Circulation: (100% controlled), Total-2,000
Printing Co: Pollock Printing, 928 6th Ave S, Nashville, TN 37203-4679 Tel # (615) 255-0526

Texas Alcalde
See: COLLEGE ALUMNI

Texas Standard

Publishing Co: Texas State Teachers Assn., 316 W 12th St, Austin, TX 78701-1892 Tel # (512) 476-5355
General Info: Yr. Est. 1874, 5x/yr.
Subscriptions: Indv. $2
Circulation: Total-9,800
Advertising: Inquire for rates.

Thanks to Scandinavia Newsletter

Publishing Co: Thanks to Scandinavia, 745 5th Ave., New York, NY 10151-0002; Title Tel # (212) 486-8600
Editorial Description: Educational opportunities for Scandinavians at American univs. & medical centers.

Tidbits　　*Association*

Publishing Co: Natl. Association for Legal Support of Alternative Schools, PO Box 2823, Santa Fe, NM 87504-2823; Title Tel # (505) 471-6928
Personnel: Editor-Ed Nagel
Editorial Description: Information and legal advice to those involved in non-public educational facilities.
General Info: Yr. Est. 1976, Quarterly, Trim Size-8½ x 11, Web press, 12 pages, No Color
Circulation: Total-4,000

TimeOut-Central
See: COMPUTERS & AUTOMATION

Tips for Principals
See: SCHOOL ADMINISTRATION

Tipsheet　　*Consumer*

Publishing Co: Minnesota Arthritis Foundation, Arthritis Fndn. MN Chapter, 1730 Clifton Pl. #A1, Minneapolis, MN 55403-3242 Fax # (612) 874-9332; Title Tel # (612) 874-1201
Personnel: Editor-Judy Peters
Editorial Description: Describes chapter activities & limited information on arthritis.
General Info: (Formerly Connection), Quarterly, 8 pages
Circulation: Total-40,000

Today's Science on File
See: SCIENCE

Together We Can　　*Association*

Publishing Co: Valley UniServ, 620 Hawkins St, Harrisonburg, VA 22801-4312 Tel # (703) 434-5564; Title Tel # (703) 943-4511
Personnel: Publisher-Ron Emery, Editor-Harriet Aylor
Editorial Description: Internal communication organ of Waynesboro Education Association.
General Info: Yr. Est. 1963, Monthly, Trim Size-8½ x 11, Letrpr. press, 2 pages
Circulation: Total-200

Torah Aura Newsletter
See: RELIGIOUS & THEOLOGICAL

Torch Bearer　　*Consumer*

Publishing Co: New York Special Olympics, 504 Balltown Rd., Schenectady, NY 12304-2201; Title Tel # (518) 388-0793 Title Fax # (518) 388-0795
Personnel: Editor-Deborah Sturm
General Info: Yr. Est. 1970, Semi-annually, 4 pages
Subscriptions: Indv. $15, Free With Membership
Circulation: Total-90,000

Torch; U.S.

Publishing Co: Junior Classical League, Miami Univ., Oxford, OH 45056; Title Tel # (513) 529-7741
Personnel: Editor-Dennis Bartlow

Totline Newsletter

Publishing Co: Warren Publishing House, Inc., PO Box 2250, Everett, WA 98203-0250; Title Tel # (206) 353-3100 Title Fax # (206) 355-7007
Personnel: Publisher-Jean Warren, Editor-Gayle Bittinger, Circ. Mgr.-Melody Olney, Production Mgr.-JoAnn Brock, Art Dir.-Jill Lustig, Mktg. Dir.-David Warren
Editorial Description: Creative activities for working with toddlers and preschool children.
General Info: (Formerly Totline), Yr. Est. 1979, Bi-monthly, Trim Size-8½ x 11, Web press, 32 pages, ISSN: 0734-4473, 2 Color, Newsprint, Saddle-stitched
Subscriptions: Indv. $24, $4/copy
Circulation: Total-10,000
List Rental: Actives $70/M
Printing Co: Renton Printery, 315 S 3rd St, Renton, WA 98055-2092 Tel # (206) 235-1776, Fax # (206) 271-9148

Towers
See: BLIND

Trager Newsletter
See: HEALTH

Training Trends
See: INDUSTRIAL RELATIONS/PERSONNEL

Trans-Parent-Focus

Publishing Co: Commission des Ecoles Catholiques de Montreal, 3737 Sherbrooke St., E., Montreal, PQ Canada
General Info: Quarterly
Circulation: Total-40,000

Trends
See: RELIGIOUS & THEOLOGICAL

Tutor Newsletter

Publishing Co: Christian Literacy Assocs., 541 Perry Hwy, Pittsburgh, PA 15229-1851; Title Tel # (412) 364-3777
Personnel: Editor-Joe Mosca
General Info: Yr. Est. 1977, Quarterly, Mimeo press, 4 pages
Circulation: Total-2,300

Twin Services Reporter
See: BABY

UAA Communication
See: PUBLIC MANAGEMENT & PLANNING

UAA Newsletter

Publishing Co: University Aviation Association, 3410 Skyway Dr, Opelika, AL 36801-7123; Title Tel # (205) 844-2434 Title Fax # (334) 844-2432
Personnel: Editor-Gary Kiteley, Production Mgr.-Carolyn Williamson
Editorial Description: The newsletter is a comprehensive report of the activities & projects of the association, as well as a summary of events & items of interest in the aviation industry that relate to collegiate aviation education.
General Info: Yr. Est. 1977, Bi-monthly, Desktop press, 15 pages, 1% ads, No Color
Subscriptions: Indv. $15, $3/copy
Circulation: Total-450
Advertising: Accepts Inserts.

UME Letter
See: RELIGIOUS & THEOLOGICAL

Ultimate Early Childhood Music Resource

Publishing Co: Miss Jackie Music Co., 10001 El Monte, Overland Park, KS 66207-3631; Title Tel # (913) 381-3672
Personnel: Publisher-Jackie Weissman, Editor-Emily Smith
Editorial Description: Designed to assist parents, teachers to those engaged in early childhood.
General Info: (Formerly Early Childhood Music), Yr. Est. 1984, Quarterly, Trim Size-8½ x 11, Offset press, 16 pages, ISSN: 0747-5446, 1% ads
Subscriptions: Indv. $20, $4/copy
Circulation: Total-2,000
Advertising: Inquire for rates.
Printing Co: PIP Printing, 4567 Indian Creek Pkwy., Overland Pk., KS 66207 Tel # (913) 649-8727

Union Wire   *Association*

Publishing Co: Association of College Unions-International, 400 E. 7th St., Bloomington, IN 47405-3085 Tel # (812) 855-8455; Title Tel # (812) 855-8550 Title Fax # (812) 855-0162
Personnel: Editor-Ann Vest
Editorial Description: Assn. announcements & news of union & activities profession.
General Info: Yr. Est. 1968, Bi-monthly, Trim Size-8½ x 11, Offset press, 6 pages, 2 Color, Other
Subscriptions: Free With Membership
Circulation: (100% controlled), Total-1,800
Advertising: Inquire for rates. Accepts Inserts.
List Rental: Rents Lists

United Student Aid Funds Newsletter   *Business*

Publishing Co: United Student Aid Funds, Inc., PO Box 6180, Indianapolis, IN 46206-6180; Title Tel # (317) 578-6094
Personnel: Publisher-Nelson Scharadin, Editor-Dena Weisbard
Editorial Description: USA Funds Education Loan products & services information.
General Info: (Formerly College on Credit), Yr. Est. 1961, Bi-monthly, Sheetfed press, 8 pages, 2 Color, Newspaper, Saddle-stitched
Subscriptions: Free
Circulation: Total-7,500
Printing Co: Metropolitan Printing Services,Inc, 720 S Morton St, Bloomington, IN 47403-2462

Universe in the Classroom   *Consumer*

Publishing Co: Astronomical Society of the Pacific, 390 Ashton Ave, San Francisco, CA 94112-1722; Title Tel # (415) 337-1100 Title Fax # (415) 337-5205
Personnel: Editor-George Musser, Circ. Mgr.-Lucile Taber, Production Mgr.-Joseph O'sullivan
Editorial Description: On teaching astronomy in grades 3 - 12. Includes astronomical news, teaching resources & classroom activities. Available free to teachers who request it on school stationary.
General Info: Yr. Est. 1984, Quarterly, Trim Size-8½ x 11, Sheetfed press, 6 pages, ISSN: 0890-6866, No Color, Other
Subscriptions: Free To Qualified Recipient
Circulation: Total-11,000

University of Michigan, Bureau of School Services, Letter to Schools   *Business*

Publishing Co: Univ. of Michigan Assoc. in the Social Found. of Educ., 4001 School of Educ. Bldg., Ann Arbor, MI 48104; Title Tel # (313) 764-8241
Editorial Description: University resources and high interest subjects in the field of education (teaching and administration).
General Info: Yr. Est. 1948, Quarterly, Trim Size-8½ x 11, Offset press, 4 pages, No Color, Newsprint
Subscriptions: Free
Circulation: Total-4,500
Printing Co: University of Michigan Printing Services, 420 Maynard St, Ann Arbor, MI 48109-1314 Tel # (313) 764-0550

Univ. of New Mexico, Office of Research, Research Notes   *Business, Consumer*

Publishing Co: Univ. of New Mexico, Office of Research, 102 Scholes Hall, Albuquerque, NM 87131-0001; Title Tel # (505) 277-2256
Personnel: Editor-Denise Waller
Editorial Description: Sponsored award opportunities.
General Info: Yr. Est. 1971, Semi-monthly
Subscriptions: Indv. $15
Circulation: Total-1,500

University of South Carolina Education Report   *Business*

Publishing Co: Univ. of South Carolina, College of Education, Publications, Wardlaw 301, Columbia, SC 29208-0001 Tel # (803) 777-6301 Fax # (803) 777-3090; Title Tel # (803) 777-5901
Personnel: Editor-Susan Alexander
Editorial Description: Contains articles summarizing educational research and news of the College.
General Info: Yr. Est. 1957, Semi-annually, Trim Size-8½ x 11, Desktop press, 4 pages, Color
Subscriptions: Free
Circulation: Total-3,000

Unschoolers Network

Publishing Co: Unschoolers Network, 2 Smith St, Farmingdale, NJ 07727-1006; Title Tel # (908) 938-2473
Personnel: Publisher, Editor-Nancy Plent
Editorial Description: Information and support for families teaching their children at home.
General Info: Yr. Est. 1978, Tri-annually, Trim Size-8½ x 11, Mimeo press, 14 pages, No Color
Subscriptions: Indv. $15, $2/copy
Circulation: Total-200
Advertising: Inquire for rates.

Up with People News   *Business*

Publishing Co: Up with People, 1 International Ct, Broomfield, CO 80021-3482; Title Tel # (602) 327-7351
Editorial Description: News of the multifaceted activities and educational experiences involved in the Up With People program and its outreach into communities around the world.
General Info: Yr. Est. 1971, Quarterly, Trim Size-12⅜ x 19, Web press, 6 pages, 2 Color, Newsprint
Circulation: Total-90,000

Update   *Association*

Publishing Co: Association of Catholic Colleges/Universities, 1 Dupont Cir NW Ste 650, Washington, DC 20036-1110; Title Tel # (202) 457-0650
Personnel: Publisher, Editor-Alice Gallin
Editorial Description: Update in all areas of Catholic higher education.
General Info: (Formerly College Newsletter), Yr. Est. 1899, Bi-monthly, Trim Size-8½ x 11, Offset press, 8 pages, No Color
Subscriptions: Indv. $65
Circulation: Total-1,950

Update
Association   **CPM: $41**

Publishing Co: American Alliance for Health, Physical Education, Recreation, 1900 Association Dr, Reston, VA 22091-1599 Tel # (703) 476-3400 Fax # (703) 476-9527; Title Tel # (703) 476-3484
Personnel: Editor-Linda Topper, Adv. Dir.-Tim Burton
Editorial Description: Newsletter of American Alliance Health, P.E., Recreation, & Dance.
General Info: Yr. Est. 1970, Bi-monthly, Trim Size-11 x 16, Web press, 16 pages, ISSN: 0199-932X, 2 Color, Newsprint
Subscriptions: Indv. $45, Free With Membership
Circulation: Total-29,000
Advertising: $1,200.
List Rental: Actives: $60/M
Printing Co: Newspaper Printers, Inc., 28a Industrial Park Dr, Waldorf, MD 20602-2707 Tel # (301) 843-9400, Fax # (301) 870-7361

Updating School Board
Policies

Publishing Co: National School Boards Assn., 1680 Duke St., Alexandria, VA 22314-3493; Title Tel # (703) 838-6722
Personnel: Editor-Brenda Greene
General Info: 11x/yr.
Circulation: Total-18,000

Upwellings
See: ENVIRONMENT & ECOLOGY

Uqaqta
Association   **CPM: $83**

Publishing Co: Nunavut Teachers Association, 40 Box 761, Iqaluit, NT X0A-0H0 Canada; Title Tel # (819) 979-1226 Title Fax # (819) 979-5994
Personnel: Publisher, Editor-J.T. Maurice
Editorial Description: Newsletter of the Nunavut teachers association.
General Info: Yr. Est. 1995, Semi-annually, Trim Size-8$\frac{1}{2}$ x 11, 8 pages, 33% ads, No Color
Subscriptions: Free
Circulation: Total-600, Readership-700
Advertising: $50. Accepts Inserts.
List Rental: Actives: 700, $25/M

VEWAA Newsletter
Association

Publishing Co: Vocational Evaluation & Work Adj. Assn., 1234 Haley Ctr, Auburn University, AL 36849 Fax # (205) 844-2080; Title Tel # (205) 844-5943 Title Fax # (334) 844-2080
Personnel: Publisher-Ronald Fry, Editor-Clarence D. Brown
Editorial Description: News & info about the practice of vocational evaluation & work adjustment.
General Info: Yr. Est. 1976, Quarterly, 8 pages
Subscriptions: Free With Membership
Circulation: Total-1,700

VICA Professional: VP
Newsletter
Association

Publishing Co: Vocational Industrial Clubs of America, PO Box 3000, Leesburg, VA 22075-0300 Fax # (703) 777-8999; Title Tel # (703) 777-8810
Personnel: Publisher-Stephen Denby, Circ. Mgr.-Judy Garrison, Editor, Production Mgr.-Heidi Ambrose
Editorial Description: Trends in vocational education, assn. news & new ideas.
General Info: (Formerly Professional News), Quarterly, 4 pages
Subscriptions: Indv. $10
Circulation: Total-19,300

V.I.P., Views, Insights &
Practice

Publishing Co: Master Teacher, Inc., Leadership La., Box 1207, Manhattan, KS 66502; Title Tel # (913) 539-0555 Title Fax # (913) 539-7739
Personnel: Publisher, Editor-Robert Debruyn, Circ. Mgr.-Lori Hanson, Production Mgr.-Brad Roberts, Art Dir.-Barry Anderson
General Info: (Formerly V.I.P , Views , Insights and Perspective), Yr. Est. 1969, Bi-monthly, Trim Size-8$\frac{1}{2}$ x 11, Sheetfed press, 16 pages, 4 Color, Matte, Saddle-stitched
Subscriptions: Indv. $20, Inst. $16, Can. $20, For. $20
Circulation: (100% controlled), Total-5,000
Printing Co: Educational Publishers, 3201 Marlatt Ave, Manhattan, KS 66502-8143 Tel # (913) 539-2469

VSBA Newsletter

Publishing Co: Vermont School Boards Assn., 2 Prospect St, Montpelier, VT 05602-3555; Title Tel # (802) 223-3580
Personnel: Editor-Donald Jamieson
Editorial Description: General information.
General Info: Yr. Est. 1961, Monthly, Mimeo press, 16 pages, No Color
Subscriptions: Indv. $10, Inst. $50
Circulation: Total-2,000

Vexillum
Association

Publishing Co: British Columbia Assn. of Teachers of Classics, 2235 Burrard St., Vancouver, BC V6J 3H9 Canada; Title Tel # (604) 731-8121
Personnel: Editor-Fred Cadman
Editorial Description: Ideas and information for teachers of Latin and Greek.
General Info: Yr. Est. 1960, Offset press, 20 pages, No Color
Circulation: Total-125

Viands In Verse
See: FOOD

View
Association

Publishing Co: Sponsor-B.C. Technology Education Association, British Columbia Teachers' Federation, 100-550 West 6th Avenue, Vancouver, BC V5Z 4P2 Canada; Title Tel # (604) 871-2283 Title Fax # (604) 871-2289
General Info: Irregular, ISSN: 0700-5407
Circulation: Total-450

Viewpoints
See: ART & SCULPTURE

Views & News
Association

Publishing Co: Assn. of Episcopal Colleges, 815 Second Ave., New York, NY 10017-4559; Title Tel # (212) 986-0989 Title Fax # (212) 949-6781
Personnel: Editor-John C. Powers, Art Dir.-Kate Chisholm
Editorial Description: Program, personnel, & church relationships of the twelve Episcopal Colleges.
General Info: (Formerly AEC News), Yr. Est. 1962, Semi-annually, Trim Size-8$\frac{1}{2}$ x 11, Desktop press, 8 pages, 2 Color
Subscriptions: Free
Circulation: Total-12,000
Printing Co: Lithoprint, 328 State St, North Haven, CT 06473-3179 Tel # (203) 248-0422, Fax # (203) 248-5072

Views and Visions
Association

Publishing Co: Wisconsin Vocational Association, 44 E Mifflin St Ste 104, Madison, WI 53703-2800 Tel # (608) 283-2595; Title Tel # (608) 833-5858
Personnel: Editor-Linda Stemper
Editorial Description: News for teachers of vocational & adult education.
General Info: Bi-monthly, Sheetfed press, 12 pages, Color-cover, Newsprint
Circulation: Total-2,500
Advertising: Inquire for rates. Accepts Inserts.
List Rental: Actives: $50/M

Visual Literacy Review &
Newsletter
Association

Publishing Co: International Visual Literacy Association, Inc., Virginia Tech., Old Security Bldg., #LRC, Blacksburg, VA 24061-0232; Title Tel # (703) 231-8992
Personnel: Editor-Richard Couch
Editorial Description: Forum for sharing research & practice within an educational context in the area of visual communication.
General Info: (Formerly Visual Literacy Newsletter), Bi-monthly, Trim Size-8$\frac{1}{2}$ x 11, Desktop press, 8 pages, No Color, Newsprint
Subscriptions: Indv. $40, For. $45, Free With Membership
Circulation: Total-250

Vocational Training News
Business

Publishing Co: Capitol Publications, Inc., 1101 King St., Ste. 444, Alexandria, VA 22314-2968; Title Tel # (703) 683-4100 Title Fax # (703) 739-6501
Personnel: Publisher-Cynthia Carter, Editor-Dave Harrison, Exec. Ed.-Joe McGavin, Circ. Mgr.-Peggy Dwyer, Production Mgr.-Billy Adams, Art Dir.-Linda McDonald, Mktg. Dir.-Mary Lou Probka, Promotion Dir.-Susan Pangman
Editorial Description: Comprehensive updates on major developments affecting federal vocational ed & job training program's. Follows new program initiatives, new funding possibilities, new regulations & more.
General Info: Yr. Est. 1971, Weekly, Trim Size-8$\frac{1}{2}$ x 11, Sheetfed press, 10 pages, ISSN: 0047-5785, 2 Color, Newsprint
Subscriptions: Indv. $298, Inst. $298
List Rental: Actives: $150/M
Printing Co: Capitol Publications, Inc., 1101 King St., Ste. 444, Alexandria, VA 22314-2968 Tel # (703) 683-4100, Fax # (703) 739-6501

Voices
Association

Publishing Co: Sponsor-English Language Arts Council, Alberta Teachers' Association, 11010-142 St., Edmonton, AB T5N 2R1 Canada Tel # (403) 453-2411
Personnel: Editor-Moira Juliebo
Editorial Description: Curriculum ideas and news for English teachers.
General Info: Yr. Est. 1968, Quarterly, Trim Size-8$\frac{1}{2}$ x 11, Sheetfed press, 8 pages, ISSN: 0832-8315, Ind/Abs/Online: Can.Educ.Ind., No Color
Subscriptions: Indv. $15
Circulation: (100% controlled), Total-1,100

Voices in Black Studies

Publishing Co: Natl. Council for Black Studies, Memorial Hall West 105, Indiana Univ., Bloomington, IN 47405; Title Tel # (812) 855-6581
General Info: Bi-monthly
Circulation: Total-1,000
List Rental: Rents Lists

WCER Highlights
Scholarly

Publishing Co: Wisconsin Center for Education Research, 1025 W. Johnston St. #785, Madison, WI 53706-1706; Title Tel # (608) 263-8814 Title Fax # (608) 263-6448
Personnel: Editor-Paul Baker, Art Dir.-Laura Moberly
Editorial Description: Reports results of current education research conducted at the Wisconsin Center for Education Research.
General Info: (Formerly Wisconsin Center for Education Research News), Quarterly, Trim Size-8$\frac{1}{2}$ x 11, Sheetfed press, 8 pages, ISSN: 1073-1822, 2 Color, Matte, Saddle-stitched
Subscriptions: Free
Circulation: Total-8,000

WEA Action

Publishing Co: Washington Education Association, 33434 8th Ave S, Auburn, WA 98003-6323;
Title Tel # (206) 941-6700
Personnel: Editor-Jeanne Giardina
General Info: Yr. Est. 1962, Monthly
Subscriptions: Indv. $10, $1/copy
Circulation: (100% controlled), Total-41,000

WYO Network   *Association*

Publishing Co: Wyoming Congress of Parents & Teachers, 5030 E 17th St, Casper, WY
82609-3726; Title Tel # (307) 265-2494 Title Fax # (307) 234-4646
Personnel: Editor-Mary Hein
Editorial Description: Schools, legislation, family life, health & children.
General Info: (Formerly Wyoming PTA News), Yr. Est. 1929, Quarterly, Trim Size-8½ x 11, Offset
press, 8 pages, No Color
Subscriptions: Indv. $3, $1/copy
Circulation: (100% controlled), Total-500

Washington Counseletter   *Business*

Publishing Co: Chronicle Guidance Publications, Inc., PO Box 1190, Moravia, NY 13118-1190
Fax # (315) 497-3359; Title Tel # (315) 497-0330
Personnel: Publisher-Gary Fickeisen, Editor-Dr. Samuel Kavruck
Editorial Description: News of interest to educators, counselors, behavioral scientists.
General Info: Yr. Est. 1963, Monthly, Trim Size-8½ x 11, Offset press, 8 pages, 4 Color, Coated
Subscriptions: Indv. $33
Circulation: Total-3,926

Water Current
See: SCIENCE

West Coast Environmental Law Research Foundation Newsletter
See: ENVIRONMENT & ECOLOGY

West Coast Lifeliner
See: HEALTH

What's Happening in
Washington   *Association*

Publishing Co: Office of Governmental Relations-Natl. PTA, 2000 L St NW Ste 600, Washington, DC
20036-4907; Title Tel # (202) 331-1380
Personnel: Editor-Susan Kushner
Editorial Description: Reports on legislation, regulations and court cases affecting children and
youth.
General Info: Semi-monthly, Trim Size-8½ x 11, Web press, 4 pages, ISSN: 0732-8362, 2 Color
Subscriptions: Indv. $6
Circulation: Total-5,500

What's Working in Parent
Involvement

Publishing Co: Parent Institute, The, PO Box 7474, Fairfax Station, VA 22039-7474;
Title Tel # (703) 323-9170 Title Fax # (703) 323-9173
Personnel: Publisher, Editor-John Wherry, Production Mgr.-R. Hasty Norrell, Mktg. Dir.-Laura P.
Beno
Editorial Description: Focuses on parent involvement in children's education. Ideas schools can use
to promote parent involvement.
General Info: Yr. Est. 1990, 10x/yr., Trim Size-8½ x 11, Web press, 6 pages, ISSN: 1053-2609, 2
Color, Matte
Subscriptions: Indv. $89
Printing Co: Newsletter Services, Inc., 9700 Philadelphia Court, Lanham, MD 20706
Tel # (301) 731-5200, Fax # (301) 731-5201

Whole Idea, The   *Consumer*

Publishing Co: Wright Group, The, 19201 120th Ave NE, Bothell, WA 98011-9507;
Title Tel # (206) 486-8011
Personnel: Publisher-Thomas Wright, Editor-Michael Ford, Production Dir.-Karen Hynemann, Art Dir.-
Steven Hauge
Editorial Description: An 'ideas' newsletter for innovative and holistic elementary school educators.
General Info: Yr. Est. 1989, Quarterly, Trim Size-8½ x 11, Web press, 16 pages, ISSN: 1069-3866, 4
Color, Newsprint, Saddle-stitched
Subscriptions: Indv. $16, $4/copy
Circulation: Total-20,000

Willa Cather Pioneer
Memorial Newsletter   *Consumer, Association*

Publishing Co: Willa Cather Pioneer Memorial, 326 N Webster St, Red Cloud, NE 68970-2550;
Title Tel # (402) 746-2653 Title Fax # (402) 746-2652
Personnel: Editor-John J. Murphy, Circ. Mgr.-Patricia K. Phillips
Editorial Description: Promotes interest in Willa Cather. Makes readers aware of Cather events &
new scholarship on the life & art of Willa Cather. Invites pub. of Cather related papers.
General Info: Yr. Est. 1955, Quarterly, No Color
Subscriptions: Indv. $15, For. $21
Circulation: Total-1,700
Printing Co: Vaughans Printers, Inc., 222 Eastside Blvd., P.O. Box 128, Hastings, NE 68902-0128
Tel # (402) 463-7721

Wisconsin Parent Teacher   *Association*

Publishing Co: Wisconsin PTA, 4797 Hayes Rd. #2, Madison, WI 53704-7333;
Title Tel # (608) 244-1455
Personnel: Editor-Jane Shibilski
Editorial Description: Deals with issues affecting the health, education or welfare of children or
youth, as well as communicating PTA organizational information.
General Info: (Formerly Wisconsin Parent Teacher Bulletin), 9x/yr., Trim Size-8½ x 11, Offset press,
4 pages, Color
Subscriptions: Indv. $5
Circulation: Total-2,000

Women's History Network
News   *Association*

Publishing Co: Natl. Women's History Project, 7738 Bell Rd, Windsor, CA 95492-8518
Fax # (707) 838-1478; Title Tel # (707) 838-6000 Title Fax # (707) 838-0478
Personnel: Editor-Mary Ruthsdotter
Editorial Description: U.S. women's history news.
General Info: Yr. Est. 1983, Quarterly, Trim Size-8½ x 11, Desktop press, 8 pages, No Color,
Newsprint
Subscriptions: Indv. $25, Inst. $50
Circulation: Total-1,000

Word of Mouth

Publishing Co: School Health Alert, PO Box 13716, San Antonio, TX 78213-0716;
Title Tel # (512) 433-7327
Personnel: Publisher-Rose Karin Newton
Editorial Description: News and information of interest to educators.
General Info: Bi-monthly
Subscriptions: Indv. $20

World Gifted

Publishing Co: World Council for Gifted & Talented Children, Purdue University, 1446 S. Campus
Courts, Bldg. G, West Lafayette, IN 47907
Circulation: Total-600

World Goodwill Commentary
See: INTERNATIONAL AFFAIRS

Worldlit   *Business, Association*

Publishing Co: World Literary of Canada, 59 Front St. E., Toronto, ON M5E 1B3 Canada;
Title Tel # (416) 863-6262 Title Fax # (416) 601-6984
Personnel: Editor-Mamta Mishra
Editorial Description: Updates on WLC overseas projects, Canadian literacy update, conferences, &
workshop news.
General Info: Yr. Est. 1967, Semi-annually, Desktop press, 4 pages, ISSN: 0820-6686, Recycled
Subscriptions: Indv. $25, Can. $25, Free With Membership
Acquistions: Publication Bought
Circulation: Total-3,000
Printing Co: Dolphin Printers, 7 Labatt Ave., Toronto, ON M5A 1Z1 Canada Tel # (416) 365-7446

Writing Lab Newsletter   *Consumer, Association*

Publishing Co: Purdue University, Dept. of English, 1356 Heavilon, W. Lafayette, IN 47907-1356;
Title Tel # (317) 494-7268 Title Fax # (317) 494-3780
Personnel: Editor-Muriel Harris, Asst. Ed., Circ. Mgr.-Mary Jo Turley
Editorial Description: Covers activities of writing labs and writing tutorials.
General Info: Yr. Est. 1977, Monthly, Trim Size-8½ x 11, Desktop press, 16 pages, ISSN: 1040-3779
Subscriptions: Indv. $15, Inst. $15, Can. $20, For. $40, $3/copy
Circulation: Total-900
List Rental: Actives: 900, $75/M, Expires: 900, $75/M

Written Word

Publishing Co: CEGA Services, PO Box 81826, Lincoln, NE 68501-1826; Title Tel # (402) 464-0602
Title Fax # (402) 464-5931
Personnel: Editor-Lisa Olivigni Maddox
Editorial Description: Communicate to those working in the field of functional illiteracy.
General Info: Yr. Est. 1978, Monthly, 8 pages, 2 Color, Newsprint
Subscriptions: Indv. $18, Can. $23, For. $30
Circulation: Total-1,000
Printing Co: CEGA Publishing Services, PO Box 81826, Lincoln, NE 68501-1826
Tel # (402) 464-0602

York University Institute for Social Research Newsletter
See: SOCIOLOGY

Young Audiences
Newsletter   *Consumer*

Publishing Co: Young Audiences, Inc., 115 E 92nd St, New York, NY 10128-1688;
Title Tel # (212) 831-8110 Title Fax # (212) 289-1202
Personnel: Editor-Jane Bak
Editorial Description: Published by the national office of Young Audiences, Inc., a national non-profit
organization sponsoring performing arts education programs in schools & communities.
General Info: Yr. Est. 1969, Annually
Circulation: Total-3,000

ZPG Reporter, The
See: ENVIRONMENT & ECOLOGY

ELECTRIC & ELECTRONIC EQUIPMENT

APC Currents
Business

Publishing Co: American Power Conversion, 132 Fairgrounds Rd., P.O. Box 278, West Kingston, RI 02892-9920 Tel # (401) 789-5735 Fax # (401) 789-3180
Editorial Description: News about power protection and information about power protection products from American Power Conversion.
General Info: Semi-annually, Trim Size-8½ x 11, 18 pages, 4 Color, Coated, Saddle-stitched

ASR News
See: COMPUTERS & AUTOMATION

Advanced Battery
Technology
Business   **CPM: $529**

Publishing Co: Seven Mountains Scientific, Inc., Box 650, Boalsburg, PA 16804-0651 Tel # (814) 466-6559 Fax # (814) 466-6559; Title Tel # (607) 547-5314 Title Fax # (607) 547-5314
Personnel: Publisher, Editor-E. Thomas Chesworth, Circ. Mgr.-Sally Horn
Editorial Description: A key source for important aspects of the battery industry; research, engineering, manufacturing, and sales.
General Info: Yr. Est. 1965, Monthly, Trim Size-8½ x 11, Offset press, 16 pages, ISSN: 0001-8627, 30% ads, No Color, Matte, Saddle-stitched
Subscriptions: Indv. $135, Inst. $135, Can. $135, For. $165, $12/copy
Circulation: Total-850
Advertising: $450. Accepts Inserts.
Printing Co: Colonial Press, 124 Chambers Alley, Broalsburg, PA 16827 Tel # (814) 238-8445

Airborne Electronics Forecast
See: AERONAUTICS/ASTRONAUTICS

Audio Week
Business

Publishing Co: Warren Publishing, Inc., 2115 Ward Ct. NW, Washington, DC 20037-1213; Title Tel # (202) 872-9200 Title Fax # (202) 293-3435
Personnel: Publisher-Albert Warren, Editor-Paul Gluckman, Circ. Mgr.-Betty Alvine, Mktg. Dir.-Gary Madderom
Editorial Description: Exclusive weekly, coverage of consumer audio.
General Info: Yr. Est. 1989, Weekly, Trim Size-8 x 11, 8 pages, ISSN: 1044-7601, Ind/Abs/Online: Newsnet, Predicasts
Subscriptions: Indv. $579, For. $625

Battery & EV Technology
See: ENGINEERING, ELECTRICAL

CBM News
Association

Publishing Co: Certified Ballast Manufacturers Association, 1422 Euclid Ave Ste 402, Cleveland, OH 44115-1901; Title Tel # (216) 241-0711 Title Fax # (216) 241-0713
Personnel: Editor-Clark Davies
Editorial Description: Information on ballasts for fluorescent lighting.
General Info: Yr. Est. 1956, Semi-annually, 2 Color
Subscriptions: Free
Circulation: Total-11,000

Circuit Breaker

Publishing Co: Municipal Electric Assn., 20 Eglinton Ave. W., #500, Box 2004, Toronto, ON M4R 1K8 Canada; Title Tel # (416) 483-7739 Title Fax # (416) 483-9039
Personnel: Editor-Sheree Bond
General Info: (Formerly OMEA Newsletter), Monthly, Web press, 8 pages, 2 Color, Matte, Saddle-stitched
Circulation: Total-2,000

Co-Op Currents
Consumer

Publishing Co: Washington Electric Co-Op, Box 8, Rte. 14, E. Montpelier, VT 05651-0008; Title Tel # (802) 223-5245
Personnel: Publisher-Joseph Bongiovanni, Editor-Douglas Wilhelm
Editorial Description: Items of general interest to consumer-members.
General Info: Yr. Est. 1939, Monthly, Trim Size-10 x 13½, Desktop press, 8 pages, ISSN: 0746-8784, 2 Color, Newsprint
Circulation: Total-6,500
Printing Co: The Herald, 30 Pleasant St, Randolph, VT 05060-1156 Tel # (802) 728-3232

Connections
Association

Publishing Co: Canadian Electrical Assn., 1 Westmount Sq., Montreal, PQ H3Z 2P9 Canada; Title Tel # (514) 937-6181
Personnel: Editor-D. Roberts
Editorial Description: Association newsletter - articles relevant to Canadian electrical utilities.
General Info: (Formerly Lea Bulletin), 10x/yr., Trim Size-5½ x 11, Web press, 6 pages, Color
Circulation: Total-4,800

Consumer Electronics Edge
Business, Consumer

Publishing Co: Twin Creeks Entertainment, PO Box 410867, San Francisco, CA 94141-0867; Title Tel # (415) 777-1964 Title Fax # (415) 777-0187
Personnel: Publisher-Hamilton Bryan, Editor-Rebecca Day, Art Dir.-Ming Lau
Editorial Description: Features consumer electronic goods.
General Info: Yr. Est. 1992, Monthly, ISSN: 1065-7223
Subscriptions: Indv. $40, Inst. $90, Can. $50

Consumer Information - Appliances
See: TELECOMMUNICATIONS

Contact
Business

Publishing Co: Furnas Electric Co, 1000 Mckee St, Batavia, IL 60510-1682; Title Tel # (708) 879-6000
Personnel: Editor-Steve Wilcox
Editorial Description: Application of electric motor controls to electrically operated machinery and equipment.
General Info: Yr. Est. 1946, Quarterly, Trim Size-8½ x 11, Offset press, 12 pages, 2 Color
Subscriptions: Free
Circulation: (100% controlled), Total-4,000

Current
See: BOATS & BOATING

Cybernautics Digest
See: MEDIA & COMMUNICATIONS

Data Security Letter
See: COMPUTERS & AUTOMATION

Design & Technology Education Bulletin
See: EDUCATION

Dialogue

Publishing Co: Ontario Electrical League, 2 Lansing Square, Suite 1000, North York, ON M2J 4P8 Canada; Title Tel # (416) 495-0052 Title Fax # (416) 495-1804
Personnel: Publisher-R.S. McCarten, Circ. Mgr.-P. Norwood, Sales Mgr.-Leslie Krok, Adv. Dir.-, Mktg. Dir.-Wm Masson
Editorial Description: Serves the electric industry in the province of Ontario. Includes industry news, developments, editorial comments, chapter and contractor news.
General Info: (Formerly DIALOGUE), Yr. Est. 1979, 6x/yr., Trim Size-8⅛ x 10¾, Web press, 24 pages, 40% ads, Color, Coated, Saddle-stitched
Subscriptions: Free With Membership
Circulation: (100% controlled), Total-10,000
Advertising: Inquire for rates. Accepts Inserts.
List Rental: Rents Lists
Printing Co: General Printers, 1001 Ritson Rd., S., Oshawa, ON L1H 4G5 Canada Tel # (416) 490-6000, Fax # (905) 436-0813

Display Technology News
Business

Publishing Co: Business Communications Co., 25 Van Zant St., Ste.13, Norwalk, CT 06855-1781; Title Tel # (203) 853-4266 Title Fax # (203) 853-0348
Personnel: Publisher-Louis Naturman, Editor-Robert Moran, Mktg. Dir.-Robert Butler
Editorial Description: Market reports technology updated on these topics newsmaterials, news applications, products, patents, technology transfer, processing and equipmente.
General Info: Yr. Est. 1995, Monthly
Subscriptions: Indv. $325, Can. $375, For. $375, $31/copy
Advertising: Inquire for rates.
List Rental: List Management Co.: W.I. Mail Marketing, 470 Main St. #317, Ridgefield, CT 06877-4516 Tel # (203) 438-6822, Fax # (203) 438-7756

Document Imaging Report
Business

Publishing Co: Phillips Business Information, Inc., 1201 Seven Locks Rd., Ste 300, Potomac, MD 20854-2958 Tel # (301) 340-1520 Fax # (301) 424-4297; Title Tel # (301) 340-1200 Title Fax # (301) 309-3847
Personnel: Publisher-Christopher Scotton, Grp. Pub.-Megan St. John, Editor-Sheila Sweeney, Mng. Editor-Mary Crowley, Production Mgr.-Sherry Mitchell, Circ. Mgr., Mktg. Dir.-Ruth Zellers
Editorial Description: Presents the most timely and actionable information on electronic imaging applications, products, and user implementation.
General Info: (Formerly Electronic Imaging Report; Imaging Business Report), Yr. Est. 1989, Bi-weekly, ISSN: 1071-1295
Subscriptions: Indv. $597, For. $630
Advertising: Inquire for rates.
List Rental: Rents Lists

Dunn Report
See: PRINTING/GRAPHIC ARTS

EASA Currents

Publishing Co: Electrical Apparatus Service Assn., Inc., 1331 Baur Blvd, Saint Louis, MO 63132-1903; Title Tel # (314) 993-2220
General Info: Monthly
Circulation: Total-3,300

EDI Monthly Report
See: COMPUTERS & AUTOMATION

EDP Weekly
See: COMPUTERS & AUTOMATION

Early Warning Report
Business

Publishing Co: Warren Publishing, Inc., 2115 Ward Ct. NW, Washington, DC 20037-1213; Title Tel # (202) 872-9200 Title Fax # (202) 293-3435
Personnel: Publisher-Albert Warren, Editor-David Lachenbruch, Circ. Mgr.-Betty Alvine, Mktg. Dir.-Gary Madderom
Editorial Description: Recap of national sales and inventory of television sets, VCRS, projection T.V.'s and stereo units.
General Info: Yr. Est. 1977, Monthly, Trim Size-8½ x 11, 2 pages, ISSN: 0193-3655, Ind/Abs/Online: Newsnet, 2 Color, Newsprint
Subscriptions: Indv. $1,118, For. $1,131
Acquistions: Publication Bought

Electric Leaguer
See: HOUSE ORGANS

Electrical Marketing
Newsletter   *Business*

Publishing Co: Intertec Publishing Corporation, 9800 Metcalf Ave., PO Box 12901, Overland Park, KS 66212-2215 Tel # (913) 341-1300 Fax # (913) 967-1898 Parent Co.-K-III Communications, New York
Personnel: Publisher-Rich Hathaway, Mng. Editor-Dale Funk, Mng. Editor-Timothy Kasen, Circ. Mgr.-Michelle Bartlett
Editorial Description: News and analysis of developments in the marketing of electrical products, especially construction products.
General Info: Yr. Est. 1975, Bi-monthly, Trim Size-8½ x 11, Offset press, 12 pages, Ind/Abs/Online: LEXIS, No Color, Looseleaf
Subscriptions: Indv. $495, Can. $495, For. $600, $30/copy
Acquistions: Publication Bought

Electrical Product News   *Business*

Publishing Co: Business Marketing & Publishing, Inc., PO Box 7457, Wilton, CT 06897-7457; Title Tel # (203) 834-9959
Personnel: Publisher, Editor-George Young
Editorial Description: Electrical product news on manufacturers, computer companies, equipment, etc.
General Info: Quarterly, 5% ads
Subscriptions: Indv. $20, $5/copy
Advertising: $825. Accepts Inserts.
List Rental: Rents Lists

Electrical Safety Bulletin

Publishing Co: Min. of Municipal Affairs, Recreation & Culture, c/o Crown Publications, 546 Yates St., Victoria, BC V8W 1K8 Canada; Title Tel # (604) 386-4636
Editorial Description: Focuses on electrical safety issues.
General Info: Monthly

Electromagnetic Field Litigation Reporter
See: LAW

Electronic Materials
Technology News   *Business*

Publishing Co: Business Communications Co., 25 Van Zant St., Ste.13, Norwalk, CT 06855-1781; Title Tel # (203) 853-4266 Title Fax # (203) 853-0348
Personnel: Publisher-Louis Naturman, Editor-Marc Favrean, Mktg. Dir.-Robert Butler
Editorial Description: Reports on electronic materials and processes, patents, companies involved, trends and business opportunities.
General Info: Yr. Est. 1986, Monthly, Trim Size-8½ x 11, ISSN: 1045-0955, Ind/Abs/Online: DIALOG, No Color, Matte
Subscriptions: Indv. $350, Can. $400, For. $400, $35/copy
List Rental: List Management Co.: W.I. Mail Marketing, 470 Main St. #317, Ridgefield, CT 06877-4516 Tel # (203) 438-6822, Fax # (203) 438-7756, Actives: 120

Electronic Warfare Forecast
See: MILITARY & NAVAL

Electronics
Communicator, The   *Business*

Publishing Co: Evert Communications Ltd., 1296 Carling Ave., Ottawa, ON K1Z 7K8 Canada; Title Tel # (613) 728-4621 Title Fax # (613) 728-0385
Personnel: Publisher, Editor-Gordon Hutchison, Assoc. Ed.-Mark Henderson, Assoc. Ed.-Trevor Marshall, Circ. Mgr.-Carole Jeffrey
Editorial Description: Developments that affect the manufacturing and distribution of electronic goods in Canada.
General Info: Yr. Est. 1969, 40x/yr., Trim Size-8½ x 11, Sheetfed press, 6 pages, ISSN: 0446-1733, No Color, Matte
Subscriptions: Inst. $575, Can. $575, For. $575
List Rental: Actives: $850/M
Printing Co: Bradda Printing Services, 130 Slater Street, Ottawa, ON K1P 6E2 Canada Tel # (613) 238-5433

Electrotechnology
See: ENGINEERING, ELECTRICAL

Executive Update   *Business*

Publishing Co: Natl. Electrical Manufacturers Assn., 1300 N. 17th St., Ste. 1847, Arlington, VA 22209-3801 Tel # (703) 841-3200 Fax # (703) 841-3300; Title Tel # (202) 457-8455 Title Fax # (202) 457-8411
Personnel: Editor-J.M. Gabel
Editorial Description: News of interest to electrical manufacturers.
General Info: (Formerly Management Information Bulletin), Monthly, No Color

Factory Sales of Electric
Storage Batteries   *Business, Association*

Publishing Co: Statistics Canada, Holland Ave/RH Coats, Holland Ave/Tunney's Pasture, Ottawa, ON K1A O26 Canada Tel # (613) 951-8116 Fax # (613) 951-0581; Title Tel # (613) 951-1581 Title Fax # (613) 951-1584
Editorial Description: Sales by type, number, and value. Cat #43-005.
General Info: Yr. Est. 1935, Monthly, 4 pages, ISSN: 0380-7061
Subscriptions: Indv. $6, Can. $5, For. $7, $6/copy

Federal Computer Market Report
See: COMPUTERS & AUTOMATION

Flexible Conduit, The
See: CONSTRUCTION & BUILDING

Global Electronics

Publishing Co: Pacific Studies Center, 222b View St, Mountain View, CA 94041-1344; Title Tel # (415) 969-1545 Title Fax # (415) 968-1126
Personnel: Editor-Leonard Siegel
Editorial Description: News items detailing the industry throughout the world, & the social, environmental & military implications of production & application.
General Info: (Formerly Global Electronics Information Newsletter), Yr. Est. 1980, Monthly, Trim Size-8½ x 11, 4 pages, ISSN: 0739-0416
Subscriptions: Indv. $12, Can. $14, For. $18, $1/copy
Circulation: Total-400

HDTV Report
See: TELEVISION & VIDEO

Henderson Electronic
Market Forecast   *Business*

Publishing Co: Henderson Ventures, 101 1st St Ste 444, Los Altos, CA 94022-2706 Tel # (915) 961-2900 Fax # (415) 961-2900; Title Tel # (415) 961-2900 Title Fax # (415) 961-3090
Personnel: Publisher-R. E. HEnderson
Editorial Description: Electronic industry forecasts & analysis, including equipemnt, components & competitors.
General Info: Yr. Est. 1983, 11x/yr., Trim Size-8½ x 11, 24 pages, No Color, Newsprint, Saddle-stitched
Subscriptions: Indv. $750, Can. $750, For. $795, $100/copy

Home Automation News   *Business, Association*   CPM: $666

Publishing Co: Home Automation Association, 808 17th St NW Ste 200, Washington, DC 20006-3910; Title Tel # (202) 223-9669 Title Fax # (202) 223-9569
Personnel: Editor-Mark Wright, Adv. Dir.-Diane Calvert
Editorial Description: Current issues and developments in home automation.
General Info: Yr. Est. 1988, Monthly, Trim Size-8½ x 11, Offset press, 8 pages, ISSN: 1057-8536, 2 Color, Matte, Saddle-stitched
Subscriptions: Indv. $150, Free With Membership
Circulation: Total-600
Advertising: $400. Accepts Inserts.
List Rental: Actives: 3,500, $170/M

Horizons

Publishing Co: Best Power Technology, PO Box 280, Necedah, WI 54646-0280; Title Tel # (608) 565-7200 Title Fax # (608) 565-2221
Personnel: Editor-Susan Mascott
Editorial Description: Deals with computer-grade power and how it can protect computers, telecommunications equipment and other equipment.
General Info: Yr. Est. 1984, Monthly, Trim Size-8½ x 11, 4 pages, No Color, Coated
Acquisitions: Publication Bought

IEEE Bulletin
See: ENGINEERING, ELECTRICAL

IEEE Publications Bulletin
See: PERIODICAL INDUSTRY

Impact   *Business*   CPM: $163

Publishing Co: American Electronics Assn., 5201 Great America Pkwy., Ste. 520, Santa Clara, CA 95054-1133; Title Tel # (408) 987-4200 Title Fax # (408) 970-8565
Personnel: Editor-April Neilson, Circ. Mgr., Production Mgr.-Virignia McIlmoil, Publisher, Adv. Dir.-Rick Wood, Art Dir.-Libby Dickinson
Editorial Description: News & business information for U.S. electronics industry executives.
General Info: (Formerly Update), Yr. Est. 1979, Monthly, Web press, 16 pages, 4 Color
Subscriptions: Indv. $72, For. $110
Circulation: (PSS), Total-35,000
Advertising: $5,730.
Printing Co: Howard Quinn Co., 298 Alabama St, San Francisco, CA 94103-4218 Tel # (415) 621-3750, Fax # (415) 621-0430

Independent Medical
Distributors Association
Update

Publishing Co: Independent Medical Distributors Assn., 5818 Reeds Rd., Mission, KS 66202-2740; Title Tel # (913) 262-4510
Personnel: Editor-Chris Bale
Editorial Description: High-technology, sophisticated, medical equipment.
General Info: Yr. Est. 1978, Monthly, 4 pages

Infocus   *Consumer*

Publishing Co: TeleSensory Corporation, 455 Bernardo Ave, Mountain View, CA 94043-5237
Editorial Description: Offers the lastest electronic viewing products in aiding visionally impaired students and professionals.
General Info: Quarterly

Inside Defense Electronics
See: MILITARY & NAVAL

Inside R&D
  See: MANUFACTURING

International Contractors, Volume II
  See: MILITARY & NAVAL

Japan Consumer
Electronics Scan

Publishing Co: Kyodo News Intl., 50 Rockefeller Plaza #803, New York, NY 10020-1605; Title Tel # (212) 397-3723 Title Fax # (212) 397-3721
Editorial Description: New electronic product announcements from Japanese manufacturers.
General Info: Yr. Est. 1988, Weekly

Land & Sea-Based Electronics Forcast
  See: MILITARY & NAVAL

Leased Access Report - Audience
  See: TELEVISION & VIDEO

Lightrays   *Association*

Publishing Co: American Home Lighting Inst, 435 N. Michigan Ave., #1770, Chicago, IL 60611-4008; Title Tel # (312) 644-0828
Editorial Description: Aids members in offering representative display of quality home lighting fixtures, services of trained staff lighting consultants, promotion of decorative, efficient lighting.
General Info: Yr. Est. 1972, Bi-monthly, Trim Size-8½ x 11, Offset press, 8 pages, Color

MACS ACTION!
  See: AUTOMOTIVE

MACS Service Reports
  See: AUTOMOTIVE

Mainly Marketing
  See: ADVERTISING & MARKETING

Manufacturing Market Insider
  See: MANUFACTURING

Measurement Chain, The
  See: INSTRUMENTS

Microwave News
  See: HEALTH

Microwaves and Food
Newsletter   *Business*

Publishing Co: Food & Nutrition Press Inc., 2 Corporate Drive, Box 374, Trumbull, CT 06611-1338; Title Tel # (203) 261-8587 Title Fax # (203) 261-9724
Personnel: Editor-Robert V. Decareau
Editorial Description: Covers new food products, production, packaging, quality assurance, microbiology, shelf-life, and microwave equipment.
General Info: Monthly
Subscriptions: Indv. $55
List Rental: Rents Lists

N E M A News

Publishing Co: Natl. Electrical Manufacturers Assn., 1300 N. 17th St., Ste. 1847, Arlington, VA 22209-3801; Title Tel # (703) 841-3200 Title Fax # (703) 841-3300
Personnel: Editor in Chief-Margaret Newton, Sr. Ed.-Jacqui Showers
Editorial Description: Official publications of the National Electrical Manufacturers Association. Reports on industry developments of interest to association members, and includes features on member activities and association events.
General Info: Monthly
Circulation: Total-81,000

NESDA Update   *Business, Association*

Publishing Co: Natl. Electronics Service Dealers Assn., 2708 W. Berry St., Ft. Worth, TX 76109-2397; Title Tel # (817) 921-9061 Title Fax # (817) 921-3741
Personnel: Publisher-Clyde Nabors, Editor-Wallace Harrison, Adv. Dir.-Barbara Bubin
Editorial Description: Official newsletter of the National Electronics Service Dealers Association.
General Info: Yr. Est. 1979, Quarterly, Trim Size-8½ x 11, 4 pages, No Color, Matte
Subscriptions: Free With Membership
Circulation: Total-1,000
List Rental: Rents Lists

National Electrical
Contractors Association,
Newsletter   *Association*

Publishing Co: National Electrical Contractors Assn., Inc., 3 Bethesda Metro Ctr., Suite 1100, Bethesda, MD 20814-5372 Fax # (301) 415-4500; Title Tel # (301) 657-3110
Personnel: Editor-Bonnie Duncan
Editorial Description: Construction developments, marketing trends, government affairs, and small business issues.
General Info: Weekly, Trim Size-8½ x 11, Sheetfed press, 4 pages, No Color
Circulation: (100% controlled), Total-6,900

PV News
  See: ENERGY

Perspectives   *Business, Association*

Publishing Co: International Sign Association, 801 N Fairfax St Ste 205, Alexandria, VA 22314-1757; Title Tel # (703) 836-4012 Title Fax # (703) 836-8353
Personnel: Editor, Editor-Suzy Beamer
Editorial Description: Newsletter for legislative issues
General Info: Yr. Est. 1990, Quarterly, Trim Size-8½ x 11, Sheetfed press, 12 pages, 2 Color, Other
Subscriptions: Free With Membership
Circulation: Total-1,200

Powerline   *Association*   CPM: $464

Publishing Co: Electrical Generating Systems Association, 10251 W Sample Rd # Sv-B, Coral Springs, FL 33065-3939; Title Tel # (305) 755-2677 Title Fax # (305) 755-2679
Personnel: Editor-Gordon Johnson
Editorial Description: For manufacturers and distributors of electrical energy not directly supplied by the public utility companies.
General Info: (Formerly EGSA Marketer), Yr. Est. 1964, Bi-monthly, Trim Size-8½ x 11, Sheetfed press, 32 pages, No Color
Subscriptions: Indv. $10
Circulation: (100% controlled), Total-2,500
Advertising: $1,160.
Printing Co: Nationwide Business Forms, 10895 N.W. 50th St., Sunrise, FL 33351 Tel # (305) 572-0888, Fax # (305) 572-0994

Radar Forecast
  See: AERONAUTICS/ASTRONAUTICS

Representor   *Association*

Publishing Co: Electronic Representatives Assn., 20 E Huron St, Chicago, IL 60611-2706; Title Tel # (312) 649-1333
Editorial Description: Topics of the electronics industry, legislation, to member firms of ERA.
General Info: Yr. Est. 1953, Monthly, Trim Size-8½ x 11, Web press, 12 pages, No Color, Coated
Subscriptions: Indv. $72, $6/copy
Circulation: Total-4,500
Advertising: Inquire for rates.
Printing Co: Fremont-Grafics, 619 S. Lasalle, Chicago, IL 60605 Tel # (312) 435-6780

SANYO PC Hacker's Newsletter
  See: COMPUTERS & AUTOMATION

SIA Circuit
  See: MANUFACTURING

SIBS Newsletter   *Business*

Publishing Co: HTE Research, Inc., 400 Oyster Pt. Blvd., Ste. 220, S. San Francisco, CA 94080-1918; Title Tel # (415) 871-4377 Title Fax # (415) 871-0513
Personnel: Publisher-Steve Szrom, Editor-Paul Plansky, Asst. Ed.-Amy Whaley
Editorial Description: Semiconductor industry, product and financial news.
General Info: Yr. Est. 1979, 15x/yr., Mimeo press, 24 pages, 2 Color, Matte, Saddle-stitched
Subscriptions: Indv. $595, For. $745
Advertising: Inquire for rates.

SSignals
  See: COMPUTERS & AUTOMATION

Semiconductor Currents   *Business*

Publishing Co: Semiconductor Currents, 930 Brookgrove Ln, Cupertino, CA 95014-4668; Title Tel # (408) 996-9764 Title Fax # (408) 446-3714
Personnel: Publisher, Editor-Sten Dymling
Editorial Description: News and developments pertaining to the semiconductor industry.
General Info: Yr. Est. 1988, Monthly
Subscriptions: Indv. $410

Semiconductor Reliability
News   *Business*

Publishing Co: DM Data, Inc., 10170 E Jenan Dr, Scottsdale, AZ 85260-5921; Title Tel # (602) 451-7449
Personnel: Editor-Howard Dicken
Editorial Description: Focuses on semiconductor reliability and related topics.
General Info: Yr. Est. 1989, Monthly
Subscriptions: Indv. $195, For. $275

Sensor Technology
  See: ENGINEERING, ELECTRICAL

Shannon Knows DEC
  See: COMPUTERS & AUTOMATION

Signals
Business, Association

Publishing Co: International Sign Association, 801 N Fairfax St Ste 205, Alexandria, VA 22314-1757; Title Tel # (703) 836-4012 Title Fax # (703) 836-8353
Personnel: Editor-Suzy Beamer
Editorial Description: Information on current business trends, safety information, and trade show updates.
General Info: (Formerly NESA News), Yr. Est. 1970, Bi-monthly, Trim Size-8½ x 11, Sheetfed press, 12 pages, 2 Color, Other
Subscriptions: Free With Membership
Circulation: (83% controlled), Total-1,200, International-200, Readership-1,200

Southwest Technology Report
See: ENGINEERING, ELECTRICAL

Switch Mode Power Conversion SMP/FAX Report
See: POWER & POWER PLANTS

Table Top Train News
See: HOBBY

Television Digest with Consumer Electronics
See: TELEVISION & VIDEO

This Week
Business, Association

Publishing Co: Electro Federation, 10 Carlson Court, #210, Rexdale, ON M9W 6L7 Canada Tel # (416) 674-7410 Fax # (416) 674-7412
Personnel: Editor-Lise de la Busantaye
Editorial Description: News and information updates for electrical manufacturers.
General Info: Weekly

TidBITS
See: COMPUTERS & AUTOMATION

Two Way Transmissions
See: LUMBER & WOOD

Up to the Minute
Business

Publishing Co: North American Publishing Co., 401 N. Broad St., Philadelphia, PA 19108 Tel # (215) 238-5300 Fax # (215) 238-5270
Editorial Description: Fax newsletter that covers the consumer electronics market.
General Info: Yr. Est. 1994, Weekly

Video Services News
See: TELEVISION & VIDEO

Video Technology Newsletter
See: TELEVISION & VIDEO

WaferNews Confidential
Business

Publishing Co: PennWell Publishing Company, Ten Tara Blvd., 5th Floor, Nashua, NH 03062-2801 Tel # (603) 891-9174 Fax # (603) 891-0574 Parent Co.-PennWell Publishing Co., Tulsa
Editorial Description: Provides semiconductor equipment industry executives with information on developments, trends, news and market insights. Subscription includes e-mail transmission of newsletter or the annual Solid State Technology Resource Guide.
General Info: Yr. Est. 1996, Semi-monthly
Subscriptions: Indv. $350, Can. $350, For. $375, $15/copy

William Hardash Auction Newsletter
See: ART & SCULPTURE

Wire Talk
See: SAFETY

The Word
Business, Association　　**CPM: $100**

Publishing Co: Electronic Service Dealers Assn. of Illinois, 4927 W Irving Park Rd, Chicago, IL 60641-2620; Title Tel # (312) 282-9400
Personnel: Editor-George Weiss
Editorial Description: Business, technical, and editorial items of interest to electronic service dealers. Features book reviews, articles relating to ethical issues, client relations, government & industry and more.
General Info: (Formerly Illinois Word), Yr. Est. 1951, Monthly, Trim Size-8⅞ x 10⅞, Sheetfed press, 8 pages, 3% ads, No Color, Newsprint
Subscriptions: Indv. $12, $2/copy
Circulation: Total-3,000
Advertising: $300. Accepts Inserts.
List Rental: Actives: $50/M
Printing Co: Progress Press, 2328 W Touhy Ave, Chicago, IL 60645-3493 Tel # (312) 465-5601

World Aerospace & Defense Intelligence
See: AERONAUTICS/ASTRONAUTICS

Yardstick
See: COMPUTERS & AUTOMATION

Yellowstone Portable Computing Letter
See: COMPUTERS & AUTOMATION

Yellowstone Windows Letter
See: COMPUTERS & AUTOMATION

EMPLOYMENT

AACE Bonus Briefs
See: EDUCATION

AACE Careers Update
See: EDUCATION

ADA Update
See: DISABILITY

ASAE Career Opportunities
Business

Publishing Co: CEO Job Opportunities Update - ARA, 325 7th St. NW, Ste. 1000, Washington, DC 20004-2801 Tel # (202) 331-3828; Title Tel # (202) 408-7900
Personnel: Editor-Don DeBolt
Editorial Description: Lists executive jobs in the $30,000 to $50,000 range.
General Info: Monthly

Accommodating Disability Decisions
See: LAW

Administrative Assistant's Update
Business

Publishing Co: MPL Communications, Inc., 133 Richmond St. W., Ste. 700, Toronto, ON M5H 3M8 Canada; Title Tel # (416) 869-1177 Title Fax # (416) 869-0456
Personnel: Publisher-Barrie Martland, Publisher-Steven Pepper, Editor-Audrey Greer, Circ. Mgr.-David Berger
Editorial Description: A professional newsletter combining Secretary's Update, Receptionist's Update and The Memo. A source for office administration staff.
General Info: (Formerly Secretary's Update, Receptionist's Update, The Memo), Yr. Est. 1989, Monthly, 8 pages
Subscriptions: Indv. $139
List Rental: Rents Lists

Affirmative Action/EEO Update
See: CIVIL RIGHTS

After the Fact

Publishing Co: After the Fact, 4100 N 58th Ave Apt 210, Hollywood, FL 33021-1532; Title Tel # (305) 961-3431
Personnel: Publisher-Cindy Spritzer, Editor-Jane Mayer
General Info: Yr. Est. 1988, Bi-monthly
Subscriptions: Indv. $12

Alabama Employment Law Letter
See: LAW

Americans with Disabilities Newsletter
See: DISABILITY

Arizona Economic Trends
Business

Publishing Co: Arizona Dept. of Economic Security, Research Administration, Box 6123, SC-733A, Phoenix, AZ 85005-6123; Title Tel # (602) 542-3871 Title Fax # (602) 542-6474
Personnel: Editor-Brent Fine, Mng. Editor-Ron Simon, Research Mgr.-Dan Anderson
Editorial Description: Employment opportunities & economy are analyzed.
General Info: (Formerly Arizona Labor Market Information Newsletter), Yr. Est. 1976, Monthly, Trim Size-8½ x 11, Sheetfed press, 24 pages, ISSN: 0743-5657, 2 Color, Coated, Saddle-stitched
Acquistions: Publication Bought
Circulation: Total-5,000
Printing Co: Arizona Dept. Of Economic Security, Phoenix, AZ 85040

Arkansas Employment Law Letter
See: LAW

Artsearch
Business

Publishing Co: Theatre Communications Group, Inc., 355 Lexington Ave., New York, NY 10017-6695; Title Tel # (212) 697-5230 Title Fax # (212) 983-4842
Personnel: Editor-Laura Romanowski
Editorial Description: The national employment service bulletin for the performing arts.
General Info: Yr. Est. 1981, Bi-weekly, ISSN: 0730-9023, No Color, Newsprint
Subscriptions: Indv. $54, Inst. $75, For. $100
Circulation: Total-6,400
Advertising: Inquire for rates.
Printing Co: Intercounty Lithograph, 13 Edison St, Amityville, NY 11701-2813 Tel # (516) 842-1950

BNA's Americans with Disabilities Act Manual
See: DISABILITY

BNA's Americans with Disabilities Act Manual Newsletter
See: DISABILITY

BNA's Workers' Compensation Report
Business

Publishing Co: Bureau of National Affairs, Inc., 1231 25th St. NW, Bldg. N-200, Washington, DC 20037-1157; Title Tel # (202) 452-4200 Title Fax # (202) 822-8092
Personnel: Publisher-William A. Beltz, Mng. Editor-Jeff Day, Circ. Dir.-Gary C. Seltzer
Editorial Description: Provides comprehensive coverage of national & state workers' compensation developments. Provides information on important legal, legislative & industry developments, actions & trends related to workers' compensation.
General Info: Yr. Est. 1990, Bi-weekly, Trim Size-8½ x 11, Offset press, 16 pages, ISSN: 1051-4775, Ind/Abs/Online: Hrin, Looseleaf
Subscriptions: Indv. $476

BOMI Newsletter
Association   **CPM: $453**

Publishing Co: Box Office Management International, 250 W. 37th Street, Suite 722, New York, NY 10107; Title Tel # (212) 581-0600 Title Fax # (212) 581-0885
Personnel: Editor-Patricia Spira
Editorial Description: Articles about systems, technological advances, employment practics.
General Info: Yr. Est. 1982, 8x/yr., Sheetfed press, 12 pages, 3% ads, Color, Newsprint
Subscriptions: Free With Membership
Circulation: Total-1,400
Advertising: $635. Accepts Inserts.
List Rental: Actives: $90/M
Printing Co: Emery Printing, 1545 1st Ave, New York, NY 10028-3903 Tel # (212) 628-7700

Bank Personnel News
See: BANKING & FINANCE

Bank Wage-Hour & Personnel Report
Business

Publishing Co: A.S. Pratt & Sons, 1911 Fort Myer Dr., Ste 308, Arlington, VA 22209-1603 Tel # (703) 528-1045; Title Tel # (703) 528-0145
Personnel: Publisher-Alan Rice, Editor-T. W. Buschman
Editorial Description: The Federal employment laws for financial institutions, wage-hours, equal employment requirements, Disability Act, FMLA, and general personnel matters.
General Info: Semi-monthly, Trim Size-6 x 9, ISSN: 0744-8767, Looseleaf
Subscriptions: Indv. $225
Advertising: Inquire for rates.

Blue Chip Job Growth Update: Ranking the States and MSAs
See: ECONOMICS

Business Currents
See: LABOR

CPA Network, The
Consumer

Publishing Co: MBA Track, Inc., 10 Bay St Ste 104, Westport, CT 06880-4324 Tel # (203) 227-9155 Fax # (203) 227-9210
Editorial Description: Lists employment opportunities for CPAs.
General Info: Yr. Est. 1992, Monthly
Subscriptions: Indv. $70, Inst. $70, Can. $82, For. $88, $10/copy
List Rental: Rents Lists

CPA Personnel Report
Business

Publishing Co: Strafford Pubs., Inc., 590 Dutch Valley Rd., N.E., Postal Drawer 13729, Atlanta, GA 30324-0729; Title Tel # (404) 881-1141 Title Fax # (404) 881-0074
Personnel: Publisher-Richard M. Ossoff, Editor-Suzanne Verity, Production Ed.-C. Malone Tumlin, Circ. Mgr.-Marianne Mueller, Mktg. Coord.-Emily Callahan
Editorial Description: Helps CPA firms excel in recruiting and retaining professional and non-professional staff, in competing with other firms to attract the best talent, in making informed hiring and firing decisions, and staying abreast of evaluation, compensation and benefits strategies and management & motivational techniques.
General Info: Yr. Est. 1982, 12x/yr., Trim Size-8½ x 11, Sheetfed press, 16 pages, ISSN: 0745-0877, 1% ads, No Color, Other
Subscriptions: Indv. $227, Can. $257, For. $282, $18/copy
Acquistions: Publication Bought, Publication Sold
List Rental: Expires: $105/M

CPC Salary Survey

Publishing Co: College Placement Council, Inc., 62 Highland Ave., Bethlehem, PA 18017-9481; Title Tel # (215) 868-1421 Title Fax # (610) 868-0208
Personnel: Publisher-Alan Yost, Editor-Dawn Oberman, Circ. Mgr.-Kathy Katchur
Editorial Description: Reports average beginning salary offers for graduating college students.
General Info: Yr. Est. 1960, Quarterly, Trim Size-8½ x 11, Offset press, 36 pages, ISSN: 0196-1004, 2 Color, Saddle-stitched, Looseleaf
Subscriptions: Indv. $220, Can. $220, For. $235
Circulation: (100% controlled), Total-4,000

CWC Communicator
See: WOMEN'S

California Compensation Cases
Business

Publishing Co: Matthew Bender & Co., 11 Penn Plaza, New York, NY 10001-2006 Fax # (212) 244-3188; Title Tel # (212) 967-7707
Personnel: Mng. Editor-W.H. Ryan
Editorial Description: All en banc & selected panel decisions of Workers' Compensation Appeals Board: digests of significant Appeals Board decisions denied judicial review; published & unpublished California Appellate Court & Supreme Court opinions in workers' compensation cases; published state court opinions in related areas.
General Info: Yr. Est. 1960, Monthly, Looseleaf
Subscriptions: Indv. $175

California Employer
Association

Publishing Co: California State Employment Development Dept., 800 Capitol Mall, Sacramento, CA 95814-4807; Title Tel # (916) 445-1952
Personnel: Editor-Lois McNally
Editorial Description: Advice to employers of California workers on payroll tax and insurance tax changes and regulations and on mandatory employment regulations and other employee legislation.
General Info: Yr. Est. 1947, Quarterly, Trim Size-8½ x 11, Offset press, 4 pages, No Color
Circulation: Total-585,000

California Employer Advisor
Business

Publishing Co: California Employer Alert, Inc., 98 Main Street, Suite 700, Tiburon, CA 94920; Title Tel # (415) 435-9360
Personnel: Editor-Larry J. Shapiro
Editorial Description: Guide to California employment law and employment relations.
General Info: Yr. Est. 1991, Monthly, Trim Size-8½ x 11, Sheetfed press, 8 pages, ISSN: 1058-4293, No Color, Matte
Subscriptions: Indv. $167, $20/copy
Advertising: Accepts Inserts.

California Employment Law Monitor
See: LAW

California Law of Employee Injuries and Workmen's Compensation
Business

Publishing Co: Matthew Bender & Co., 11 Penn Plaza, New York, NY 10001-2006 Fax # (212) 244-3188; Title Tel # (212) 967-7707
Personnel: Editor-Carolyn D. Jones, Editor-William H. Ryan, Editor-Ryan James L. Weinberger
Editorial Description: Standard work on California substantive and procedural law of employee injuries and workman's compensation.
General Info: Irregular, Looseleaf
Subscriptions: $350/copy

Canadian Employer, The
Business

Publishing Co: Carswell, 2075 Kennedy Road, One Corporate Plaza, Scarborough, ON M1T 3V4 Canada Fax # (416) 298-5094; Title Tel # (416) 609-8000 Title Fax # (416) 298-5063
Personnel: Publisher-Barry Garnet, Editor-Ellen Mole, Circ. Mgr.-Mike Moore, Adv. Dir.-Melanie Causton
Editorial Description: A monthly newsletter for the Human Resource/Personnel Manager, Business Executive & Professional Adviser. Written in an easily understood journalistic style the author deals with the critical issues affecting hiring, discrimination, employment standards, health & safety, discipline & firing.
General Info: Monthly, Trim Size-8½ x 11, 8 pages, ISSN: 0840-626X
Subscriptions: Indv. $150

Canadian Employment Law
See: LAW

Canadian Employment Law Today
Business

Publishing Co: MPL Communications, Inc., 133 Richmond St. W., Ste. 700, Toronto, ON M5H 3M8 Canada; Title Tel # (416) 869-1177 Title Fax # (416) 869-0456
Personnel: Publisher-Barrie Martland, Publisher-Steven Pepper, Editor-Stephanie Stoyan, Circ. Mgr.-David Berger
Editorial Description: Information to help employers avoid hassles in employment process.
General Info: Yr. Est. 1987, Bi-weekly, Sheetfed press, 8 pages, No Color, Newsprint
Subscriptions: Indv. $278
List Rental: Rents Lists

Canadian HR Reporter
Business

Publishing Co: MPL Communications, Inc., 133 Richmond St. W., Ste. 700, Toronto, ON M5H 3M8 Canada; Title Tel # (416) 869-1177 Title Fax # (416) 869-0456
Personnel: Publisher-Barrie Martland, Publisher-Steve Pepper, Editor-George Pearson, Circ. Mgr.-David Berger, Adv. Dir.-Shelly Legault
Editorial Description: The primary source of information for the human resources industry.
General Info: Bi-weekly, 16 pages
Subscriptions: Indv. $98
Advertising: Inquire for rates. Accepts Inserts.
List Rental: Rents Lists

Career Connections
See: EDUCATION

Career Opportunities News   *Business*

Publishing Co: Garrett Park Press, PO Box 190, Garrett Park, MD 20896-0190; Title Tel # (301) 946-2553
Personnel: Publisher, Editor-Robert Calvert, Jr., Assoc. Ed.-Mary French
Editorial Description: Presents information on career trends, jobs of the future and resources in this area.
General Info: Yr. Est. 1983, Bi-monthly, Trim Size-8½ x 11, 12 pages, ISSN: 0739-5043, No Color
Subscriptions: Indv. $30, Inst. $20, $4/copy
Circulation: Total-3,000

Career Outplacement
See: INDUSTRIAL RELATIONS/PERSONNEL

Career Planning & Adult Development Network Newsletter
See: LABOR

Caretaker Gazette, The   *Consumer*

Publishing Co: Caretaker Gazette, The, 1845 NW Dean Stay, Pullman, WA 99163-3509; Title Tel # (509) 332-0806 Title Fax # (509) 332-0806
Personnel: Publisher-Gary Dunn, Editor-Thea Dunn
Editorial Description: Lists domestic and international caretaking, agricultural and environmental positions.
General Info: Yr. Est. 1983, Bi-monthly, Trim Size-8½ x 11, Offset press, 8 pages, ISSN: 1074-3642, No Color, Matte, Perfect bound
Subscriptions: Indv. $24, Inst. $24, Can. $24, For. $30, $5/copy
Acquistions: Publication Sold
Circulation: Total-3,000, Readership-6,000
Advertising: Inquire for rates. Accepts Inserts.
List Rental: Actives: 3,000, $75/M, Expires: 3,000, $75/M
Printing Co: Western Printing, 409 S. Jackson, Moscow, ID 83843 Tel # (208) 882-6700, Fax # (208) 883-8205

Chief Economist (Straight Talk)
See: ECONOMICS

College Placement Council-Spotlight   *Business*

Publishing Co: College Placement Council, Inc., 62 Highland Ave., Bethlehem, PA 18017-9481; Title Tel # (215) 868-1421
Personnel: Editor-Patricia Sinnott, Circ. Mgr.-Sarita Hunter
Editorial Description: For college career planning, placement & recruitment field.
General Info: Yr. Est. 1978, 21x/yr., Trim Size-8½ x 11, Sheetfed press, 4 pages, ISSN: 0162-1068, No Color, Newsprint
Subscriptions: Indv. $60
Circulation: (100% controlled), Total-3,500
List Rental: Rents Lists

Communicator, The

Publishing Co: New York State Public Employees Federation, AFL-CIO, 1168 Troy Schenectady Rd # 70, Latham, NY 12110-1006; Title Tel # (518) 785-1900
Personnel: Editor-Sherry Halbrook, Exec. Ed.-Ronald Kermani, Adv. Dir.-John Townsend
General Info: ISSN: 0745-6514

Connecticut Employment Law Letter
See: LAW

Connecticut Labor Situation   *Business, Association*

Publishing Co: Connecticut Labor Dept., Business Management, 200 Folly Brook Blvd., Wethersfield, CT 06109-1114; Title Tel # (203) 566-4374
Personnel: Publisher-Richard Vannuccini, Editor-C. Richard Ficks
Editorial Description: Prepared in cooperation with U.S. Bureau of Labor Statistics.
General Info: (Formerly Employment Wages, Hours in Connecticut), Monthly, 8 pages, No Color
Circulation: Total-2,000

Connections
See: SHIPS & SHIPPING

Consultants' & Contractors' Newsletter
See: BUSINESS & INDUSTRY

The Contingency Crier

Publishing Co: The Contingency Crier, P.O. Box 16875, Phoenix, AZ 85011
Editorial Description: This is a short newsletter covering legislation and legal issues for today's growing temporary workforce.
General Info: Trim Size-8.5 x 11, 2 pages
Subscriptions: Indv. $7

Cornerstone
See: EDUCATION

Corporate Jobs Outlook!   *Business*

Publishing Co: Corporate Jobs Outlook!, PO Box 670466, Dallas, TX 75367-0466; Title Tel # (214) 692-1085 Title Fax # (214) 692-0105
Personnel: Publisher-Jack Plunkett
Editorial Description: In-depth reports on rapidly growing corporate, employers. Includes rating on each employer's financial, salaries, benefits, training and growth.
General Info: Yr. Est. 1986, Bi-monthly, Trim Size-8½ x 11, Sheetfed press, 40 pages, ISSN: 0892-5232, Ind/Abs/Online: Newsnet, HRIN, Matte
Subscriptions: Indv. $170
Circulation: Total-1,000

Council on Postsecondary Accreditation-Presidents Bulletin
See: SCHOOL ADMINISTRATION

Drugs in the Workplace
See: DRUGS & PHARMACEUTICALS

EMA Reporter   *Business, Association*

Publishing Co: Employment Management Association, 4101 Lake Boone Trl Ste 201, Raleigh, NC 27607-7506; Title Tel # (919) 787-6010 Title Fax # (919) 787-5302
Personnel: Editor-Susan Rexer
Editorial Description: Employment Management Association member newsletter.
General Info: Yr. Est. 1969, Bi-monthly, Sheetfed press, 8 pages, Ind/Abs/Online: Emanet, 2 Color, Coated
Circulation: Total-1,800
Advertising: Inquire for rates.
List Rental: Actives: $350/M

Economic Opportunity Report
See: SOCIAL SERVICES & WELFARE

Educating for Employment   *Business*

Publishing Co: LRP Publications, 747 Dresher Rd., P.O. Box 980, Horsham, PA 19044-0980 Tel # (215) 784-0910 Fax # (215) 784-0317
Editorial Description: Discusses how to prepare students for work, obtain funding and establish effective transition programs.
General Info: Monthly, Ind/Abs/Online: LRPnet

Education Jobs
See: EDUCATION

Education Update
See: EDUCATION

Employee Benefits for Non-Profits   *Business*

Publishing Co: NP Publishing, Inc., 7936 Bressingham Dr., Fairfax Station, VA 22039-3157; Title Tel # (703) 922-4225 Title Fax # (703) 922-4226
Personnel: Publisher, Editor-Kevin G. Moore
Editorial Description: Covers latest court decisions and agency rulings and legislative initiative on all aspects of employee benefits as they relate to non-profit organizations.
General Info: Yr. Est. 1984, Monthly
Subscriptions: Indv. $150
Circulation: Total-650

Employee Relations in Action
See: LABOR UNION

Employee Testing & the Law   *Business*

Publishing Co: Vanguard Information Pubs., PO Box 667, Chapel Hill, NC 27514-0667; Title Tel # (919) 967-2420
Personnel: Publisher-Merle Thorpe, Editor-Ted Shults
Editorial Description: Reports legal, technical & business developments affecting employee testing.
General Info: Yr. Est. 1986, Monthly, Offset press, 10 pages, ISSN: 0889-5422, No Color, Newsprint, Saddle-stitched
Subscriptions: Indv. $295

Employers' Immigration Compliance Guide
See: LAW

Employment & the Economy: Atlantic Coastal Region   *Business*

Publishing Co: New Jersey Department of Labor, Office of Research & Planning, CN 056, Trenton, NJ 08625-0056; Title Tel # (609) 292-7567
Personnel: Editor, Circ. Mgr.-Mary Ann Unger
Editorial Description: Describes employment and current economic trends in Atlantic Coastal Region.
General Info: Yr. Est. 1940, Quarterly, Trim Size-8½ x 11, Offset press, 8 pages, No Color

Employment & the Economy: Northern Region
Business

Publishing Co: New Jersey Department of Labor, Office of Research & Planning, CN 056, Trenton, NJ 08625-0056; Title Tel # (609) 292-7567
Personnel: Editor, Circ. Mgr.-Mary Ann Unger
Editorial Description: Describes employment and current economic trends in Northern New Jersey Region.
General Info: (Formerly New Jersey Area Trends in Employment, Jersey City), Yr. Est. 1940, Quarterly, Trim Size-8½ x 11, Offset press, 11 pages, No Color

Employment & the Economy: Southern Region
Business

Publishing Co: New Jersey Department of Labor, Office of Research & Planning, CN 056, Trenton, NJ 08625-0056; Title Tel # (609) 292-7567
Personnel: Editor, Circ. Mgr.-Mary Ann Unger
Editorial Description: Employment, unemployment and current economic trends in Southern New Jersey Region.
General Info: (Formerly New Jersey Area Trends in Employment Camden Labor Area), Yr. Est. 1940, Quarterly, Trim Size-8½ x 11, Offset press, 9 pages, No Color

Employment & Training Reporter
Business

Publishing Co: MII Publications, Inc., 1211 Conn. Ave. NW, #705, Washington, DC 20036-2701; Title Tel # (202) 293-1740 Title Fax # (202) 293-0377
Personnel: Publisher-Cecilio Morales, Editor-Tracy Fine, Mag. Ed.-Midred C. Greene, Production-Linda A. Morgan
Editorial Description: Covers job training, work-welfare, vocational education programs, retraining and layoffs.
General Info: (Formerly Manpower Information Service), Yr. Est. 1969, Weekly, Trim Size-8½ x 11, Web press, 28 pages, ISSN: 0146-9673
Subscriptions: Indv. $698, Can. $731, $14/copy
Acquistions: Publication Bought
Circulation: Total-1,010
List Rental: Rents Lists
Printing Co: McArdle Printing Co., 800 Commerce Dr, Upper Marlboro, MD 20772-8792 Tel # (301) 390-8500

Employment Alert
Business

Publishing Co: Research Institute of America, 117 E Stevens Ave, Valhalla, NY 10595-1264; Title Tel # (212) 645-4800 Title Fax # (212) 337-4380
Personnel: Editor-George Burke
Editorial Description: Latest developments governing the private employment relationship.
General Info: Yr. Est. 1984, 26x/yr., Trim Size-8½ x 11, Offset press, 8 pages
Subscriptions: Indv. $104, $7/copy
List Rental: List Management Co.: WG & L List Management, 1 Penn Plz Fl 42, New York, NY 10119-0002 Tel # (212) 971-5000, Actives: $95/M

Employment Equity Update
Business, Consumer

Publishing Co: Employment Equity Update, 44 Laird Drive, Ste. 300, Toronto, ON M4G 3T2 Canada Tel # (416) 696-9199 Fax # (416) 696-8409
Personnel: Publisher-Susan Baka
Editorial Description: Covers Canadaian employment equity news.
General Info: Yr. Est. 1994, Monthly
Subscriptions: Indv. $297

Employment Guide
Business

Publishing Co: Bureau of National Affairs, Inc., 1231 25th St. NW, Bldg. N-200, Washington, DC 20037-1157; Title Tel # (202) 452-4200 Title Fax # (202) 822-8092
Personnel: Publisher-William A. Beltz, Mng. Editor-Bill L. Manville, Circ. Mgr.-Gary C. Seltzer
Editorial Description: An easy-to-read, practical reference guide to a broad range of employment topics, designed for the small to medium sized organization.
General Info: Yr. Est. 1986, Bi-weekly, Trim Size-8½ x 11, Web press, 6 pages, ISSN: 0896-3452, Ind/Abs/Online: HRIN
Subscriptions: Indv. $470

Employment and Labor Lawcast
See: LAW

Employment Law Deskbook
See: INDUSTRIAL RELATIONS/PERSONNEL

Employment Law News
See: LAW

Employment Law Report, The

Publishing Co: Concord Publishing Ltd., 14 Prince Arthur Avenue, Toronto, ON M5R 1A9 Canada Tel # (612) 225-9550 Fax # (612) 298-0291; Title Tel # (416) 964-2758 Title Fax # (416) 964-0659

Employment Law Report
See: LAW

Employment Law Strategist
See: LAW

Employment in New York State
Association

Publishing Co: New York State Dept. of Labor, State Campus, Pubs. Unit Bldg., 12 Room 511, Albany, NY 12240-0001; Title Tel # (518) 457-1130
Personnel: Editor-Vincent DeSantis
Editorial Description: Highlights current New York State employment and unemployment developments; includes statistical tables.
General Info: Yr. Est. 1960, Monthly, Trim Size-8½ x 11, Offset press, 2 pages, 2 Color, Newsprint
Circulation: Total-2,000
Printing Co: Labor Dept., 55 W. 125th St., New York, NY 10027 Tel # (212) 870-8102

Employment Opportunities
Association

Publishing Co: National Association of Business Economists, 1233 20th St., NW, Suite 505, Washington, DC 20036-2304 Tel # (202) 463-6223
Personnel: Editor, Circ. Mgr., Promotion Dir.-Susan Doolittle
Editorial Description: Employment Opportunities, a quarterly listing of job openings, is published in March, June, September & December. It is also available continually on the Association's electronic bulletin board. new listings are posted to the bulletin board as received.
General Info: Quarterly, Trim Size-8½ x 11, Offset press, 6 pages
Subscriptions: Indv. $55, For. $75
Circulation: Total-3,600
List Rental: Actives: $150/M

Employment Practices Decisions

Publishing Co: CCH, Inc., 2700 Lake Cook Rd., Riverwoods, IL 60015 Parent Co.-Kluwer Law & Taxation Publishers, Cambridge; Title Tel # (847) 267-7000 Title Fax # (800) 224-8299
Editorial Description: Bound volumes of federal and state court cases involving issues of employment discrimination on account of race, color, sex, religion, national origin, age, handicap/disability, and of veterans' job rights.
General Info: Looseleaf
Subscriptions: Indv. $50

Employment Practices Guide
Business

Publishing Co: CCH, Inc., 2700 Lake Cook Rd., Riverwoods, IL 60015 Fax # (800) 224-8299 Parent Co.-Kluwer Law & Taxation Publishers, Cambridge; Title Tel # (847) 267-7000
Editorial Description: Spans actions of the EEOC, OFCCP and state FEP agencies - laws, court and administrative decisions, plus Equal Pay rules.
General Info: Yr. Est. 1965, Weekly, Trim Size-6 x 9, Web press, 50 pages, No Color, Looseleaf
Subscriptions: Indv. $934

Employment Report for Maryland

Publishing Co: Maryland Dept. of Employment, 1100 N Eutaw St, Baltimore, MD 21201-2206; Title Tel # (301) 383-5644
Personnel: Editor-Osborne P. Beall
General Info: (Formerly Manpower Trends), Yr. Est. 1970, Monthly
Circulation: Total-5,000

Employment Safety and Health Guide
See: SAFETY

Employment Screening
Business

Publishing Co: Matthew Bender & Co., 11 Penn Plaza, New York, NY 10001-2006 Tel # (212) 967-7707 Fax # (212) 244-3188
Editorial Description: This important guide details each of the major employment screening devices currently in use, analyzing the legal & constitutional considerations, statutory restrictions & legal acceptance of each.
General Info: Yr. Est. 1988, Irregular, Looseleaf

Employment Security Activities

Publishing Co: Georgia State Dept. of Labor, 148 International Blvd NE, Atlanta, GA 30303-1751; Title Tel # (404) 656-3032
General Info: Monthly

Employment and Total Wages Paid by Employers Subject to the Louisiana Employment Security
See: LAW

Employment Trends
Business, Scholarly

Publishing Co: Rawski & Associates, PO Box 815, Minocqua, WI 54568
Personnel: Publisher-T. Rawski, Circ. Mgr.-A. Rawski
Editorial Description: Provides information about companies that are expanding--creating jobs or those that are downsizing--eliminating jobs.
General Info: Yr. Est. 1991, Bi-monthly, Trim Size-8½ x 11, Desktop press, 4 pages, 2 Color, Coated
Circulation: Total-568

Environmental Opportunities
Business, Consumer

Publishing Co: Sponsor-Antioch New England Env. Studies Dept., Environmental Opportunities, PO Box 547158, Surfside, FL 33154; Title Tel # (305) 866-0084
Personnel: Publisher, Editor, Adv. Dir.-Sanford Berry
Editorial Description: Lists comprehensive environmental job openings throughout the U.S.
General Info: Yr. Est. 1982, Monthly, Trim Size-8$\frac{1}{2}$ x 11, Sheetfed press, 12 pages, ISSN: 0736-9603, Ind/Abs/Online: Dialog, No Color, Recycled
Subscriptions: Indv. $47, Can. $50, For. $60, $5/copy
Circulation: Total-3,800, Readership-11,000
Printing Co: Braden Printing, Inc., 19 Ralston St # 571, Keene, NH 03431-3643 Tel # (603) 357-1513, Fax # (603) 352-3262

Equal Employer, The
Business, Consumer

Publishing Co: Y.S. Publications, Inc., 4736 Lee Highway, Ste. 202, Arlington, VA 22207; Title Tel # (703) 525-0465
Personnel: Publisher-E. Targin
Editorial Description: Contains accurate & complete digests of the latest critical decisions of all courts & U.S. Government agencies bearing on employment discrimination; expert editorial comment & equal employment developments.
General Info: Yr. Est. 1977, Bi-weekly, 8 pages
Subscriptions: Indv. $245
Circulation: Total-200

Equal Employment Compliance Update
See: CIVIL RIGHTS

Ethics in Government Reporter
See: GOVERNMENT

Exec-U-Tary
See: OFFICE METHODS & EQUIPMENT

Exec-u-Net
Business

Publishing Co: Exec-u-Net, 25 Van Zant St., Ste. 15-3, Norwalk, CT 06855; Title Tel # (203) 851-5180 Title Fax # (203) 851-5177
Editorial Description: Career opportunity listings.
General Info: Yr. Est. 1988, Bi-weekly
Subscriptions: Indv. $260

Executive Search Review

Publishing Co: Hunt-Scanlon Publishing Co., Inc., Two Pickwick Plaza, Greenwich, CT 06830; Title Tel # (203) 629-3629 Title Fax # (203) 629-3701
Personnel: Editor-Scott Scanlon, Circ. Mgr., Promotion Dir.-Jeffrey Cobain
General Info: Yr. Est. 1989, Monthly, 12 pages, ISSN: 1050-9003, 3% ads, 2 Color, Saddle-stitched
Subscriptions: Indv. $210, For. $240, $20/copy
Acquistions: Publication Bought
Advertising: Inquire for rates. Accepts Inserts.

Fair Employment Practices
See: LAW

Fair Employment Practices Guidelines
Business

Publishing Co: Bureau of Business Practice, 24 Rope Ferry Rd, Waterford, CT 06386-0001 Tel # (806) 442-4365 Fax # (860) 434-3341 Parent Co.-Prentice Hall, Waterford; Title Tel # (860) 442-4365
Personnel: Publisher-Martin E. Kenney, Jr., Editor-Russ Case, Art Dir.-Deni Fedeli
Editorial Description: Covers equal employment opportunity legislation, regulations and court developments. Primarily directed at Human resource professionals.
General Info: Yr. Est. 1977, Semi-monthly, ISSN: 1069-921X
Subscriptions: Indv. $150

Fair Employment Practices Summary of Latest Developments
See: LAW

Fair Employment Report
Business

Publishing Co: Business Publishers, Inc., 951 Pershing Dr., Silver Spring, MD 20910-4464 Tel # (301) 589-5103 Fax # (301) 589-8493; Title Tel # (301) 587-6300 Title Fax # (301) 587-1081
Personnel: Publisher-Leonard A. Eiserer, Editor-Chuck Knebl, Circ. Mgr.-Brenda Davenport, Production Mgr.-Kathleen Jacob
Editorial Description: Covers legislation, regulations & litigation that affect personnel officers.
General Info: Yr. Est. 1963, Bi-weekly, Trim Size-8$\frac{1}{2}$ x 11, Desktop press, 8 pages, ISSN: 0014-6919, Ind/Abs/Online: Newsnet and Predicasts, No Color, Recycled
Subscriptions: Indv. $299, Can. $299, For. $312
Advertising: Accepts Inserts.
List Rental: List Management Co.: BPI Direct, 951 Pershing Dr., Silver Spring, MD 20910-4464 Tel # (301) 585-5976, Fax # (301) 587-4530

Federal Career Opportunities
Business, Association

Publishing Co: Federal Research Service, Inc., 243 Church Street, N.W., Vienna, VA 22180-4434; Title Tel # (703) 281-0200 Title Fax # (703) 281-7639
Personnel: Publisher-J.A. McArdle, Editor-Katherine Dausch, Circ. Mgr.-Sharon Patterson
Editorial Description: Contains over 4,000 Federal jobs, all professions, nationwide & overseas, where & how to apply.
General Info: (Formerly Federal Research Service Report), Yr. Est. 1974, Bi-weekly, Trim Size-8 x 11, Web press, 64 pages, ISSN: 0279-2230, Newsprint, Saddle-stitched
Subscriptions: Indv. $175, Inst. $175, Can. $253, $8/copy
Circulation: Total-10,000
List Rental: Actives: 10,000, $100/M, Expires: 35,000, $100/M
Printing Co: McArdle Printing Co., 800 Commerce Dr, Upper Marlboro, MD 20772-8792 Tel # (301) 390-8500

Federal Ethics Report
See: GOVERNMENT

Florida Employment Law Letter
See: LAW

Fordyce Letter
Business

Publishing Co: Kimberly Organization, PO Box 31011, Saint Louis, MO 63131-0011; Title Tel # (314) 965-3883 Title Fax # (314) 965-8177
Personnel: Publisher, Editor-Paul Hawkinson, Circ. Mgr.-John Cranston, Production Mgr.-Kim Hellyar
Editorial Description: Personnel & search info. for executive recruiters & professional placement professionals.
General Info: Yr. Est. 1966, Monthly, Trim Size-8$\frac{1}{2}$ x 11, Sheetfed press, 12 pages, ISSN: 0733-0324, No Color, Newsprint, Saddle-stitched
Subscriptions: Indv. $96, Can. $96, For. $136, $7/copy
Acquistions: Publication Bought
Circulation: Total-9,000

Forty Plus Newsletter

Publishing Co: Forty Plus of New York, 15 Park Row, New York, NY 10038-2334; Title Tel # (212) 233-6086
Personnel: Editor-Bertram Newman
Editorial Description: Executives over 40 years/age and currently unemployed and seeking employment.
General Info: Yr. Est. 1939, Quarterly, Trim Size-8$\frac{1}{2}$ x 11, Mimeo press, 4 pages
Circulation: Total-1,800

Georgia Employment Law Letter
See: LAW

Goodwill Dimensions
See: SOCIAL SERVICES & WELFARE

Grain and Feed Merchants, The
See: FEED, GRAIN & MILLING

Grassroots Economic Organizing (GEO)
See: CONSUMER INTERESTS

HR Reporter
See: INDUSTRIAL RELATIONS/PERSONNEL

Hiring & Firing Newsletter
Business

Publishing Co: Carswell, 2075 Kennedy Road, One Corporate Plaza, Scarborough, ON M1T 3V4 Canada Tel # (416) 609-8000; Title Tel # (416) 609-3800 Title Fax # (416) 298-5094
Personnel: Publisher-Bob McElman
General Info: Yr. Est. 1985, Monthly, 8 pages, ISSN: 0829-5700, Ind/Abs/Online: Indexed, Color
Subscriptions: Indv. $160
Acquistions: Publication Bought, Publication Sold
Circulation: Total-3,200

How to Succeed in Rotten Times
Business, Consumer   CPM: $333

Publishing Co: Business Scribe Inc., 105 Randolphs Grn, Williamsburg, VA 23185-6554
Personnel: Publisher, Editor-Hal Gieseking, Publisher, Production Mgr.-Bob Atkinson
Editorial Description: Tips for job-hunters and new business start-ups. Success stories of individuals succeeding in spite of difficult economic times.
General Info: Monthly, 10% ads
Subscriptions: Indv. $13, $2/copy
Circulation: Total-300
Advertising: $100.
List Rental: Actives: $45/M

Human Resources Briefing

Publishing Co: Conference Board, Inc., 845 3rd Ave., New York, NY 10022-6679; Title Tel # (212) 759-0900
Personnel: Editor-Theresa Brothers
General Info: 10x/yr., ISSN: 0896-257X
Subscriptions: Indv. $85

Human Resources Equal Employment Opportunity

Publishing Co: CCH, Inc., 2700 Lake Cook Rd., Riverwoods, IL 60015 Parent Co.-Kluwer Law & Taxation Publishers, Cambridge; Title Tel # (847) 267-7000 Title Fax # (800) 224-8299
Editorial Description: Shows what companies and government contractors can do, can't do, and should do to comply with federal and state fair employment, affirmative action and equal pay rules.
General Info: Monthly, Looseleaf
Subscriptions: Indv. $417

Human Resources Management OSHA Compliance
See: MANAGEMENT

IBIS Briefing Service
See: BUSINESS & INDUSTRY

Idaho Employment   *Business, Association*

Publishing Co: Idaho State Dept. of Employment, 317 Main St., Boise, ID 83735-0001; Title Tel # (208) 334-6100
Editorial Description: Cojntains information and statistics about employment and job trends in Idaho.
General Info: Monthly, Trim Size-8½ x 11, Offset press, 16 pages, 2 Color, Newsprint
Circulation: Total-1,700
Printing Co: State of Idaho Print Shop, 550 W. State, Boise, ID 83720-0001 Tel # (208) 334-2124

Illinois Employment Law Letter
See: LAW

Indiana Employment Law Letter
See: LAW

Individual Employment Rights
See: LAW

Inside Labor Relations
See: LABOR UNION

Inside NAPS   *Business, Association*

Publishing Co: National Association of Personnel Services, 3133 Mount Vernon Ave, Alexandria, VA 22305-2640; Title Tel # (703) 684-0180 Title Fax # (703) 684-0071
Editorial Description: News and information for personnel service professionals.
General Info: Bi-monthly, Trim Size-8½ x 11, 12 pages, No Color

InternAmerica   *Consumer, Association*

Publishing Co: InternAmerica, 105 Chestnut St., #34, Needham, MA 02192
Personnel: Publisher-Bernard Ford, Adv. Dir.-Ellen Miller
Editorial Description: Information for college career guidance officials about available internships. Contains reviews of relevant videos and software.
General Info: Yr. Est. 1992, Bi-monthly, Trim Size-8½ x 11, 8 pages, ISSN: 1061-7337, No Color, Matte
Subscriptions: Indv. $50
Advertising: Inquire for rates.

International Employment Hotline   *Business*

Publishing Co: Cantrell Corp., PO Box 3030, Oakton, VA 22124-9030; Title Tel # (703) 620-1972
Personnel: Publisher, Editor-Will Cantrell
Editorial Description: Monitors international job market. Features current job openings & helpful advice.
General Info: Yr. Est. 1980, Monthly, 8 pages, ISSN: 0748-8890, No Color, Matte
Subscriptions: Indv. $39, For. $51
Circulation: Total-6,000
List Rental: List Management Co.: Direct Communications Corp., 24 Wales St. Box 6628, Rutland, VT 05702-6628 Tel # (802) 747-3322, Fax # (802) 747-3376, Actives: 6,000, $85/M

JACS Volunteer   *Association*

Publishing Co: Joint Action in Community Service, 5225 Wisconsin Ave NW Ste 404, Washington, DC 20015-2014; Title Tel # (202) 537-0996 Title Fax # (202) 363-0239
Personnel: Editor-Ana Gomez
Editorial Description: Activities of volunteers serving Job Corps youth.
General Info: Yr. Est. 1968, Quarterly, Trim Size-8½ x 11, Desktop press, 8 pages, 2 Color, Matte, Saddle-stitched
Subscriptions: Free
Circulation: Total-5,000
Printing Co: Homart Press & Envelope Co., PO Box 346, Bladensburg, MD 20710-0346 Tel # (301) 277-8836

JWB Personnel Reporter   *Association*

Publishing Co: Jewish Community Centers Assn. of North America, 15 E. 26 St., New York, NY 10010-1579; Title Tel # (212) 532-4949
Personnel: Editor-Mrs. Bessie Pine
Editorial Description: Listing of professional employment opportunities in JWB affiliated Jewish Community Centers.
General Info: Yr. Est. 1968, Quarterly, Offset press, 28 pages, No Color, Coated
Circulation: Total-6,000
Printing Co: Astoria Press, Inc., 435 Hudson St., New York, NY 10014 Tel # (212) 627-2122

Job Announcements

Publishing Co: National Center for State Courts, 300 Newport Ave, Williamsburg, VA 23185-4147; Title Tel # (804) 253-2000 Title Fax # (804) 220-0449
Personnel: Editor-Kim Swanson
Editorial Description: Lists court-related job openings.
General Info: Yr. Est. 1984, Semi-monthly, Trim Size-8½ x 11, 10 pages, No Color, Saddle-stitched
Subscriptions: Indv. $30, $4/copy
Circulation: Total-750

Job Bank, The   *Association*

Publishing Co: Water Environment Federation, 601 Wythe St, Alexandria, VA 22314-1994; Title Tel # (703) 684-2400 Title Fax # (703) 684-2492
Personnel: Editor-Macarena de la Piedra, Production Mgr.-Jennifer Darnell, Publisher, Mktg. Dir.-Matthew Rowan, Promotion Dir.-Joan Martin
Editorial Description: List job openings in international wastewater treatment field.
General Info: Bi-monthly, Trim Size-8½ x 11, Mimeo press, 8 pages, 100% ads, Matte
Subscriptions: Indv. $72, For. $84
Circulation: Total-750
Advertising: Inquire for rates.
List Rental: Actives: $135/M

Job Express
See: BUSINESS & INDUSTRY

Job Finder   *Association*

Publishing Co: Western Governmental Research Assn., 1250 Bellflower Blvd., Long Beach, CA 90840-0001; Title Tel # (310) 985-5419 Title Fax # (310) 985-1624
Personnel: Editor-Mel Powell, Circ. Mgr., Adv. Dir.-Linda Berger
Editorial Description: Listing of job openings in public administration & government research in the Western states.
General Info: Yr. Est. 1954, Monthly, Trim Size-8½ x 14, Offset press, 8 pages, No Color
Subscriptions: Indv. $20, Inst. $30
Circulation: Total-2,000

Job Training and Placement Report
See: DISABILITY

Jobmart   *Business, Association*

Publishing Co: American Planning Association, 1313 E 60th St, Chicago, IL 60637-2891; Title Tel # (312) 955-9100 Title Fax # (312) 955-8312
Personnel: Editor-Jeri Parish
Editorial Description: Publication consists entirely of classified help wanted ads placed by employers seeking professional city planners.
General Info: (Formerly Jobs in Planning), Yr. Est. 1952, Semi-monthly, Trim Size-8½ x 11, Web press, 12 pages, No Color, Matte
Subscriptions: Indv. $30
Circulation: Total-4,800
Advertising: Inquire for rates.
List Rental: Actives: 27,000, $60/M
Printing Co: Sheffield Press, 2040 164th Pl, Hammond, IN 46320-2803 Tel # (219) 844-2520

Jobs in Higher Education
See: EDUCATION

Jobs Impact Bulletin

Publishing Co: National Commission for Full Employment, 815 16th St NW Ste 301, Washington, DC 20006-4104; Title Tel # (202) 842-7816
Personnel: Editor-J. Scott
General Info: Yr. Est. 1981, 10x/yr.
Subscriptions: Indv. $20

Kansas Monthly Employment Review

Publishing Co: Kansas Dept. of Human Resources, 401 SW Topeka Blvd, Topeka, KS 66603-3151; Title Tel # (913) 296-5058
Personnel: Publisher-William Layes
Editorial Description: Employment newsletter inlcudes statistics for state and metropolitan areas of Kansas.
General Info: Yr. Est. 1950, Monthly
Circulation: Total-300

Kennedy's Career Strategist   *Business, Consumer*

Publishing Co: Career Strategies, 1150 Wilmette Ave., Wilmette, IL 60091-2603; Title Tel # (708) 251-1661 Title Fax # (708) 251-5191
Personnel: Publisher, Editor-Marilyn Moats Kennedy, Circ. Mgr.-Linda Mitchell
Editorial Description: A monthly guide to career planning success & job satisfaction.
General Info: Yr. Est. 1986, Monthly, Web press, 16 pages, ISSN: 0891-2572, Color-cover, Newsprint, Saddle-stitched
Subscriptions: Indv. $59, Can. $69, For. $69, $5/copy
Circulation: Total-2,500

Kentucky Employment Law Letter
See: LAW

Labor and Employment Arbitration
See: LABOR

Labor and Employment Law Newsletter
See: LAW

Labor Lines

Publishing Co: Nebraska Dept. of Labor, 550 S 16th St, Lincoln, NE 68508-2601;
Title Tel # (402) 471-4189
Personnel: Editor-Don Atwater
Editorial Description: Topics about Dept. of Labor programs & activities.
General Info: (Formerly Administrative News), Yr. Est. 1960, Monthly, Trim Size-8½ x 11, Sheetfed press, 8 pages, No Color, Newsprint
Circulation: Total-1,000

Labor Trends, Albany Local
Office   *Business, Association*

Publishing Co: Oregon Employment Division, PO Box 751, Salem, OR 97308-0751;
Title Tel # (503) 378-2324
Personnel: Editor-Earl Fairbanks
Editorial Description: Labor trends and general economic news for Linn and Benton County; monthly estimates of employment and unemployment.
General Info: Monthly, Trim Size-8½ x 11, 10 pages, Color
Circulation: (100% controlled), Total-500

Labor Trends, Salem
Metropolitan Area

Publishing Co: Oregon Employment Division, PO Box 751, Salem, OR 97308-0751;
Title Tel # (503) 378-2324
Personnel: Editor-Earl Fairbanks
Editorial Description: Employment trends & general economic news, employment & unemployment estimates.
General Info: Monthly, 10 pages, Color
Circulation: (100% controlled), Total-700

Law School Placement Bulletin
See: LAW

Lawyers Job Bulletin
Board   *Association*

Publishing Co: Federal Bar Association, 1815 H St. NW, Ste. 408, Washington, DC 20006-3697;
Title Tel # (202) 638-0252 Title Fax # (202) 775-0295
Personnel: Editor-Margaret Simon
Editorial Description: Legal position vacancies in public. private, & goverment/military sectors.
General Info: (Formerly Placement Newsletter), Yr. Est. 1920, Monthly, Trim Size-8½ x 11, 10 pages, No Color, Matte
Subscriptions: Indv. $30, Inst. $30
Circulation: (100% controlled), Total-350
Advertising: Inquire for rates.

Legislative Network for Nursing
See: NURSING

L'Employeur Canadien

Publishing Co: Carswell, 2075 Kennedy Road, One Corporate Plaza, Scarborough, ON M1T 3V4 Canada Tel # (416) 609-8000 Fax # (416) 298-5094; Title Tel # (416) 445-4940 Title Fax # (416) 445-5352
Personnel: Publisher-Barry Garnet, Editor-Ellen Mole, Circ. Mgr.-Mike Moore, Adv. Dir.-Melanie Causton
General Info: Yr. Est. 1988, Monthly, ISSN: 0840-8149
Subscriptions: Indv. $160

MBA Track   *Consumer*

Publishing Co: MBA Track, Inc., 10 Bay St Ste 104, Westport, CT 06880-4324;
Title Tel # (203) 227-9155 Title Fax # (203) 227-9210
Editorial Description: Lists employment opportunities for MBAs entry to executive level.
General Info: (Formerly The MBA Network), Yr. Est. 1991, Monthly
Subscriptions: Indv. $72, Inst. $72, Can. $84, For. $90, $11/copy
List Rental: Rents Lists

MESC Messenger

Publishing Co: Michigan Employment Security Commission, 7310 Woodward Ave, Detroit, MI 48202-3152; Title Tel # (313) 876-5488
Personnel: Editor-Ann Costa, Art Dir.-Ronald Kangas
Editorial Description: Contains news items, features and columns on Commission offices, branches, activities, policies.
General Info: (Formerly Michigan Employment Security Commission Report), Yr. Est. 1951, Monthly, Trim Size-8½ x 11, Offset press, 8 pages, Color
Circulation: (100% controlled), Total-6,500

Managed Dental Care

Publishing Co: Business Information Services, 12811 N Point Ln, Laurel, MD 20708-2341;
Title Tel # (301) 604-4001 Title Fax # (301) 604-5126
Personnel: Publisher-James Gutman, Editor-Sheila Moldover, Circ. Mgr.-Kathleen Gutman, Mktg. Dir.-Seth Sprecher
Editorial Description: Independent news and analysis source covering major events and trends affeeting the managed dental care industry.
General Info: Yr. Est. 1995, Monthly, Trim Size-8½ x 11, Offset press, 12 pages, ISSN: 1083-3641, 2 Color, Other, Other
Subscriptions: Indv. $267, $25/copy
Advertising: Accepts Inserts.
List Rental: Rents Lists
Printing Co: Newsletter Services, Inc., 9700 Philadelphia Court, Lanham, MD 20706 Tel # (301) 731-5200, Fax # (301) 731-5201

Managing Laboratory Personnel
See: MANAGEMENT

Maryland Employment Law Letter
See: LAW

Massachusetts Employment Law Letter
See: LAW

Medical Industry Employment Opportunities
See: MEDICINE

Mertens Current Tax
Highlights

Publishing Co: Clark Boardman Callaghan & Co., 155 Pfingsten Rd., Deerfield, IL 60015;
Title Tel # (708) 948-7000 Title Fax # (708) 948-8955
General Info: Monthly
Subscriptions: Indv. $295

Michigan Department of
Civil Service, Newsletter

Publishing Co: Michigan Dept. of Civil Service, 320 S Walnut St # 30002, Lansing, MI 48933-2014;
Title Tel # (517) 373-3030

Michigan Employment Law Letter
See: LAW

Minnesota Employment Law Letter
See: LAW

Minnesota Labor Market Review
See: LABOR

Missouri Employment Law Letter
See: LAW

NABE News
See: ECONOMICS

NADAP News/Report   *Consumer, Association*

Publishing Co: Natl. Assn. on Drug Abuse Problems, Inc., 355 Lexington Ave., New York, NY 10017-6603; Title Tel # (212) 986-1170 Title Fax # (212) 697-2939
Personnel: Editor-Patricia Stickney
Editorial Description: Dedicated to fighting drug and alcohal abuse in the family,the community and the workplace.
General Info: Yr. Est. 1972, Irregular, 12 pages
Circulation: Total-6,500

NALP Bulletin   *Business, Association*   CPM: $424

Publishing Co: National Association for Law Placement, 1666 Connecticut Ave NW Ste, 325, Washington, DC 20009-1039; Title Tel # (202) 667-1666 Title Fax # (202) 265-6735
Personnel: Publications Director-Janet Smith
General Info: Monthly, Trim Size-8½ x 11, Offset press, 12 pages, 25% ads, No Color, Matte
Subscriptions: Indv. $75
Circulation: Total-1,060
Advertising: $450.
List Rental: Rents Lists

NJCAA Proof Sheet   *Association*

Publishing Co: National Job Corps Alumni Association, 607 14th St. NW, Ste. 610, Washington, DC 20005-2000 Tel # (202) 638-3810 Fax # (202) 638-3807
Personnel: Editor-Hope Hall
Editorial Description: Newsletter for former job corps students who are now members of national Job Corps Alumni Assn. (NJCAA).
General Info: (Formerly NJCAA-Alumni News), Yr. Est. 1981, Quarterly, Trim Size-8½ x 11, Desktop press, 6 pages, 2 Color, Matte, Saddle-stitched
Subscriptions: Free To Qualified Recipient
Circulation: Total-15,000, Readership-15,000
Advertising: Inquire for rates.
Printing Co: Doyle Printing & Offset, 6911 Old Landover Rd, Landover, MD 20785-1503 Tel # (301) 322-4800, Fax # (301) 372-2860

National Employment Law Project Library Bulletin
See: LAW

National Public Employment Reporter
See: LAW

New Account Selling
See: SALESMANSHIP & SELLING

New Jersey Employment Law Letter
See: LAW

New Jersey Labor and Employment Law Quarterly
See: LABOR

New York Civil Service
Update
Business, Association

Publishing Co: NYPER Publications, PO Box 662, Latham, NY 12110-0662 Fax # (518) 458-8582;
Title Tel # (518) 786-1654
Personnel: Editor-Harvey Randall
Editorial Description: Information of interest to civil service professionals.
General Info: (Formerly Civil Service Personnel Notes), Yr. Est. 1985, Monthly, ISSN: 1071-7435
Subscriptions: Indv. $95, Inst. $95
Advertising: Accepts Inserts.

New York Employment
Law Letter
Business

Publishing Co: M. Lee Smith Publishers & Printers ,LCC, P.O. Box 198867, 162 Fourth Avenue North, Nashville, TN 37219-8867 Tel # (615) 242-7395 Fax # (615) 256-6601
Personnel: Publisher-M Lee Smith, Editor-Mike Curley, Circ. Mgr.-Cathy Bradford
Editorial Description: New York employment law information.
General Info: Yr. Est. 1994, Monthly, Trim Size-8½ x 11, 8 pages, ISSN: 1072-9178, 2 Color
Subscriptions: Indv. $97
List Rental: Rents Lists
Printing Co: M. Lee Smith Publishers & Printers ,LLC, PO Box 198867, 162 Fourth Avenue, Nashville, TN 37219-8867 Tel # (615) 242-7395, Fax # (615) 256-6601

News & Views

Publishing Co: West Virginia Bureau of Employment Programs, 112 California Ave E Rm 101, Charleston, WV 25305-0004; Title Tel # (304) 348-3305
Personnel: Editor-Bob Rosier
Editorial Description: All aspects of employment security news-local, state and national.
General Info: Yr. Est. 1943, Monthly, Trim Size-5½ x 8½, Offset press, 24 pages, No Color, Saddle-stitched
Circulation: (55% controlled), Total-1,900

North Carolina Employment Law Letter
See: LAW

Nutshell
Business

Publishing Co: Country Press, Inc., PO Box 5880, Snowmass Village, CO 81615-5880; Title Tel # (303) 923-3210
Personnel: Editor-Nanette Mosiman
Editorial Description: A digest of employee benefit publications.
General Info: Yr. Est. 1974, Monthly
Subscriptions: Indv. $156

O-Hayo Sensei

Publishing Co: O-Hayo Sensei, 1032 Irving St. Ste# 508, San Francisco, CA 94122
Editorial Description: The newsletter of teaching jobs in japan.
General Info: Trim Size-8.5 x 11, 6 pages
Subscriptions: Indv. $5

O'Dwyer PR Marketplace
Business

Publishing Co: J.R. O'Dwyer Company, Inc., 271 Madison Ave Ste 600, New York, NY 10016-1001 Tel # (212) 679-2471
General Info: Yr. Est. 1988, Bi-weekly, 4 pages
Subscriptions: Indv. $24
Circulation: Total-5,000
Advertising: Inquire for rates.

OFCCP Federal Contract
Compliance Manual

Publishing Co: CCH, Inc., 2700 Lake Cook Rd., Riverwoods, IL 60015 Parent Co.-Kluwer Law & Taxation Publishers, Cambridge; Title Tel # (847) 267-7000 Title Fax # (800) 224-8299
Editorial Description: Reflects OFCCP policies & procedures, tell how its staff investigates & enforces contractor adherence to pledges made to comply with affirmative action rules to increase job opportunities for women, racial minorities, handicapped persons, disabled & Vietnam veterans.
General Info: Monthly, Looseleaf
Subscriptions: Indv. $318

Officers Call
See: MILITARY & NAVAL

Ohio Employment Law Letter
See: LAW

Oklahoma Employment Law Letter
See: LAW

Options Unlimited

Publishing Co: Davcol Group, 1660 Oak Tree Rd # 155, Edison, NJ 08820-2805; Title Tel # (201) 668-8164
Personnel: Publisher, Editor-Sheri Davis-Collins
General Info: Yr. Est. 1985, Bi-monthly, 8 pages
Circulation: Total-300

Oregon Employment Law Letter
See: LAW

Organize Your Luck!
Business

Publishing Co: Behavioral Images, Inc., 302 Leland, Bloomington, IL 61701-5646; Title Tel # (309) 829-3931 Title Fax # (309) 829-9677
Personnel: Publisher-Stephen Johnson, Art Dir.-Sharon Johnson
Editorial Description: Finding, getting, and keeping a job through self-marketing skills.
General Info: Yr. Est. 1976, Trim Size-8½ x 11, Sheetfed press, 4 pages, ISSN: 0734-1776, 2 Color, Newsprint
Subscriptions: Indv. $75
Circulation: (100% controlled), Total-3,000
List Rental: Actives: $36/M

PBC Employment Briefs
Business, Consumer

Publishing Co: Publishing & Business Consultants, 101 W. 64th St. Unit #3, Inglewood, CA 90302-1255 Tel # (213) 732-3477 Fax # (213) 732-3477
Personnel: Publisher, Editor-Andeson Atia
General Info: Quarterly, ISSN: 1095-2040
Subscriptions: Indv. $180
Advertising: Inquire for rates.

PR Marcom Jobs East
Business, Scholarly   CPM: **$33**

Publishing Co: Rachel P.R. Services, 1650 S. Pacific Coast Hwy., Suite #200-C, Redondo Beach, CA 90277 Tel # (310) 792-1313 Fax # (310) 792-1309
Personnel: Publisher, Editor-Janis Brett-Elspas
Editorial Description: Most comprehensive listing of advertising, public relations, journalism, marketing communications & writing jobs on the East Coast. Covers New York, Boston, Washington, DC & surrounding states.
General Info: Yr. Est. 1991, Semi-monthly, Trim Size-17 x 11, Desktop press, 8 pages, 2 Color, Recycled, Saddle-stitched
Subscriptions: Indv. $99, $15/copy
Circulation: Total-6,000
Advertising: $200. Accepts Inserts.
List Rental: Actives: 3,000, $100/M, Hotline: 3,000, $100/M, Expires: 3,000, $100/M
Printing Co: Printmasters, 20807 Higgins Ct, Torrance, CA 90501-1830 Tel # (310) 320-5310, Fax # (310) 782-2460

PR Marcom Jobs Mid-
America
Business, Scholarly   CPM: **$66**

Publishing Co: Rachel P.R. Services, 1650 S. Pacific Coast Hwy., Suite #200-C, Redondo Beach, CA 90277 Tel # (310) 792-1313 Fax # (310) 792-1309
Personnel: Publisher, Editor-Janis Brett-Elspas
Editorial Description: Most comprehensive listing of jobs in advertising, public relations, journalism, marketing communications & writing. Covers Midwest, South, SE, SW, & Rocky Mountain states.
General Info: Yr. Est. 1993, Bi-weekly, Trim Size-17 x 11, Desktop press, 8 pages, 2 Color, Recycled, Saddle-stitched
Subscriptions: Indv. $99, $15/copy
Circulation: Total-3,000, Readership-3,000
Advertising: $200. Accepts Inserts.
List Rental: Rents Lists

PR Marcom Jobs West-
No. Calif./Pacific
Nothwest
Business, Scholarly   CPM: **$10**

Publishing Co: Rachel P.R. Services, 1650 S. Pacific Coast Hwy., Suite #200-C, Redondo Beach, CA 90277 Tel # (310) 792-1313 Fax # (310) 792-1309
Personnel: Publisher, Editor-Janis Brett-Elspas
Editorial Description: Most comprehensive listing of advertising, public relations, journalism, marketing communications & writing jobs in Northern California & the Pacific Northwest.
General Info: Yr. Est. 1989, Semi-monthly, Trim Size-17 x 11, Sheetfed press, 8 pages, 2 Color, Recycled, Saddle-stitched
Subscriptions: Indv. $99, $15/copy
Circulation: Total-20,000, Readership-20,000
Advertising: $200. Accepts Inserts.
List Rental: Rents Lists

PR Marcom Jobs West-
So. Calif.
Business, Scholarly   CPM: **$10**

Publishing Co: Rachel P.R. Services, 1650 S. Pacific Coast Hwy., Suite #200-C, Redondo Beach, CA 90277 Tel # (310) 792-1313 Fax # (310) 792-1309
Personnel: Publisher, Editor-Janis Brett-Elspas
Editorial Description: Most comprehensive listing of advertising, public relations, journalism, marketing communications & writing jobs in Southern California.
General Info: Yr. Est. 1988, Semi-monthly, Trim Size-8½ x 11, Desktop press, 8 pages, 2 Color, Recycled, Saddle-stitched
Subscriptions: Indv. $99, $15/copy
Circulation: Total-20,000, Readership-20,000
Advertising: $200. Accepts Inserts.
List Rental: Actives: 3,000, $100/M, Hotline: 3,000, $100/M, Expires: 3,000, $100/M
Printing Co: Printmasters, 20807 Higgins Ct, Torrance, CA 90501-1830 Tel # (310) 320-5310, Fax # (310) 782-2460

Pa Unemployment
Compensation State
Business

Publishing Co: Bureau of Research and Statistics, 300 Capitol Associates Bld., Harrisburg, PA 17120-0034; Title Tel # (717) 787-6466 Title Fax # (717) 772-2168
Editorial Description: Statwide report provides monthly employment, quarterly total & taxable wages & annual averages at 3-digit SIC level. County report provides annual average employment & total wages by county at 2 digit industry level with comparisons to previous year.
General Info: (Formerly Employment and W. of Workers Covered by the PA Unemp), Yr. Est. 1950, Annually
Subscriptions: Free

Pathways
See: EDUCATION

Payroll Practitioner's Compliance Handbook
See: MANAGEMENT

Pennsylvania Employment Law Letter
See: LAW

Pennsylvania's Labor Force...A Monthly Statistical Analysis   *Business*
Publishing Co: Bureau of Research and Statistics, 300 Capitol Associates Bld., Harrisburg, PA 17120-0034; Title Tel # (717) 787-6466 Title Fax # (717) 772-2168
Personnel: Editor-Donald Laughery
Editorial Description: Provides labor force, employment & unemployment in PA including detail by county & major labor market area, nonagricultural wage & salary jobs by industrial detail (statewide only), current statistics on average hours worked & average earnings for production workers in manufacturing & selected nonmanufacturing industries & a brief discussion of recent unemployment compensation.
General Info: (Formerly Pennsyania Employment & Earnings), Yr. Est. 1989, Monthly
Subscriptions: Free

People and Jobs
Publishing Co: Louisiana Dept. of Labor, Box 94094, Baton Rouge, LA 70804-9094 Tel # (504) 342-3111

People Trends
See: INDUSTRIAL RELATIONS/PERSONNEL

Personnel Insights   *Association*
Publishing Co: MEMA-Motor & Equipment Manufacturers Assn., PO Box 13966, Rtp, NC 27709-3966 Tel # (919) 549-4800 Fax # (919) 549-4824
Personnel: Publisher-J. J. Conner, Editor-H.L. Coor
Editorial Description: Lists situations and personnel available in automotive industry.
General Info: Monthly, Trim Size-8½ x 11, Sheetfed press, Color

Personnel Practice Ideas
See: MANAGEMENT

Perspectives
See: HISTORY

Pharmacy Week   *Business, Association*   CPM: $327
Publishing Co: Pharmacy Week, PO Box 552, Madison, WI 53701 Tel # (608) 245-1112; Title Tel # (608) 251-1112 Title Fax # (608) 251-1155
Personnel: Publisher-Paul Barnes, Mktg. Dir.-Gail Scherer
Editorial Description: A national newsletter for pharmacists actively seeking advancement opportunities in hospitals and home infusion pharmacies, editorial consists of management, drug information and employment articles.
General Info: Yr. Est. 1992, Weekly, Trim Size-8⅜ x 10⅞, Web press, 16 pages, 75% ads, 2 Color, Coated, Saddle-stitched
Subscriptions: Free To Qualified Recipient
Circulation: (BPA, 100% controlled), Total-7,628
Advertising: $2,500. Accepts Inserts.
List Rental: Actives: 10,968, $95/M

Placement Bulletin   *Association*
Publishing Co: Association of American Law Schools, 1201 Conn. Ave. NW, #800, Washington, DC 20036-2605; Title Tel # (202) 296-8851 Title Fax # (202) 296-8869
Personnel: Editor, Circ. Mgr.-Janet Kulick
General Info: Yr. Est. 1976, Bi-monthly, Trim Size-8½ x 11, Sheetfed press, 12 pages, 2 Color, Matte, Saddle-stitched
Subscriptions: Indv. $59, Inst. $59, Can. $59, For. $59, $14/copy
Advertising: Inquire for rates.
Printing Co: Good Printers, 213 Dry River Rd, Bridgewater, VA 22812-1242 Tel # (703) 828-4663

Portable Practitioner: Opportunities in the Healing Arts
See: HEALTH

Prevention at Work
See: LAW

Principles of Payroll Administration
See: MANAGEMENT

Profiles in PDM
See: MANAGEMENT

Project Equality-Update
See: CIVIL RIGHTS

Public Employment Law Notes
See: LAW

Public Employment Reports
See: GOVERNMENT

Public Safety Personnel Updance
See: LAW ENFORCEMENT & PENOLOGY

Public Sector Job Bulletin   *Consumer*
Publishing Co: Public Sector Job Bulletin, PO Box 1222, Newton, IA 50208-1222; Title Tel # (515) 791-9019 Title Fax # (515) 791-1005
Personnel: Publisher, Editor-Gerald Pecinovsky
Editorial Description: Bi-weekly listing of job opportunities in local and state government. (National listing).
General Info: Yr. Est. 1985, Bi-weekly, Trim Size-8½ x 11, Sheetfed press, 8 pages, ISSN: 1072-3773, Color-cover
Subscriptions: Indv. $22, Can. $29
Circulation: (4% controlled), Total-3,500, Subscriptions-3,200
Advertising: Inquire for rates.

Quality 1st.
See: INDUSTRIAL RELATIONS/PERSONNEL

RAP Session   *Business*
Publishing Co: Training Consultants, Inc., PO Box 31052, Saint Louis, MO 63131-0052; Title Tel # (314) 965-0291 Title Fax # (314) 965-8177
Personnel: Publisher-Paul Hawkinson, Editor-Phyllis Fleck
Editorial Description: Training material for employment & recruiting professionals.
General Info: Yr. Est. 1981, Weekly, Trim Size-8½ x 11, Sheetfed press, 2 pages, 2 Color, Newsprint
Subscriptions: Indv. $130, $3/copy
Circulation: Total-1,600

ReCareering Newsletter   *Business, Consumer*
Publishing Co: Publications Plus, 655 Rockland Road, Suite 7, Lake Bluff, IL 60044-1700 Tel # (708) 735-1980 Fax # (708) 735-0046
Personnel: Publisher, Editor-Sharon Schuster
Editorial Description: Ideas, resources, and news for downsized managers and others in career transition.
General Info: Yr. Est. 1992, Monthly, Trim Size-8½ x 11, ISSN: 1068-199X, 2 Color
Subscriptions: Indv. $59, Inst. $590, Can. $59, For. $75, $7/copy
Advertising: Inquire for rates. Accepts Inserts.
List Rental: Rents Lists

Ready Or Not
Publishing Co: Manpower Education Inst., 715 ladd Rd., New York, NY 10471; Title Tel # (212) 548-4200
Personnel: Editor-Ed Townsend
General Info: Yr. Est. 1977, Monthly
Subscriptions: Indv. $20

Recruiting & Search Report   *Business*
Publishing Co: PRI Group, PO Box 9433, Panama City Beach, FL 32417-9433; Title Tel # (904) 235-3733
Personnel: Editor-Kenneth Cole
Editorial Description: Technique, research & commentary for executive search community. Special emphasis on resources to perform work efficiently, & improve proficiency.
General Info: Yr. Est. 1981, Quarterly, Trim Size-8½ x 11, Sheetfed press, 10 pages, No Color, Newsprint, Saddle-stitched
Acquistions: Publication Bought
Circulation: Total-7,500
List Rental: Actives: $175/M
Printing Co: Curry Printing, 23 Harrison Ave, Panama City, FL 32401-2723 Tel # (904) 769-2679

Recruiting Trends   *Business*
Publishing Co: Remy Publishing Co., 350 W Hubbard St # 440, Chicago, IL 60610-4011; Title Tel # (312) 464-0300 Title Fax # (312) 464-0166
Personnel: Publisher-Robert Root, Editor-Elizabeth Hintch, Circ. Mgr.-Trish Bissell
Editorial Description: Covers trends and practices, the latest news, legal developments, and issues in the recruiting field.
General Info: Yr. Est. 1962, Monthly, Trim Size-8½ x 11, 4 pages, No Color
Subscriptions: Indv. $155, Inst. $155, Can. $155, For. $185, $155/copy

Report on Disability Programs
See: DISABILITY

Report on Literacy Programs
See: EDUCATION

Resume
See: EDUCATION

Rhode Island Department of Employment Security, Employment Bulletin
Publishing Co: Rhode Island Dept. of Employment Security, 101 Friendship St, Providence, RI 02903-3716; Title Tel # (401) 277-3600
General Info: Yr. Est. 1954, Monthly
Circulation: Total-2,000

Rocky Mountain
Employment Newsletter   *Consumer*

Publishing Co: Intermountain Referral Service, 311 14th St, Glenwood Springs, CO 81601-3949; Title Tel # (303) 945-8991 Title Fax # (303) 945-5140
Personnel: Publisher, Editor-Heath Harrison
Editorial Description: Lists current job openings in CO, WY, AZ, NM, ID, MT, WA, OR.
General Info: Yr. Est. 1977, Semi-monthly, Trim Size-8½ x 14, Sheetfed press, 4 pages, 3% ads, No Color, Other
Subscriptions: Indv. $116, $15/copy
Acquisitions: Publication Bought, Publication Sold
Circulation: (100% controlled), Total-3,000
Advertising: Inquire for rates. Accepts Inserts.
List Rental: Actives: $65/M, Expires: $50/M
Printing Co: Discount Printer, Glenwood Springs, CO 81601

SBANE Enterprise
See: BUSINESS & INDUSTRY

Salary Characteristics
See: ECONOMICS

Salesmanship
See: SALESMANSHIP & SELLING

Small Business-USA
See: BUSINESS & INDUSTRY

Social Service Jobs
See: SOCIAL SERVICES & WELFARE

South Carolina Employment Law Letter
See: LAW

Specialty Lab Update
See: PHOTOGRAPHY

Staffing Industry Report   *Business*

Publishing Co: Staffing Industry Analysts, 2235 Grant Rd # 3, Los Altos, CA 94024-6954; Title Tel # (415) 903-9494 Title Fax # (415) 903-9811
Personnel: Publisher, Editor-Peter Yessne, Production Ed.-Laura Lebherz, Fulflmnt. Mgr.-Jennifer Julian, Circ. Mgr.-Michele Reed, Adv. Dir.-Grant Landis, Assoc. Ed., Asst. Ed., Mktg. Dir.-Theresa Daly
Editorial Description: News and resources for the temporary help and employment services industries. Includes company news, industry trends, hiring surveys, association news, industry calendar, includes Annual Yearbook and more.
General Info: Yr. Est. 1990, Semi-monthly, Trim Size-8⅜ x 11, Letrpr. press, 16 pages, ISSN: 1051-3051, Color-cover, Matte, Saddle-stitched
Subscriptions: Indv. $285, Can. $285, For. $347, $18/copy
Circulation: (19% controlled), Subscriptions-2,000
Advertising: Inquire for rates. Accepts Inserts.
Printing Co: Account Manager: Ramsey Nijmeh; Diamond Printing, 10070 N Blaney Ave, Cupertino, CA 95014-2328

Successful Closing Techniques
See: SALESMANSHIP & SELLING

Supported Employment
InfoLines   *Business*

Publishing Co: Training Resource Network, PO Box 439, Saint Augustine, FL 32085-0439; Title Tel # (904) 823-9800 Title Fax # (904) 829-2001
Personnel: Publisher-Dale DiLeo, Editor-Dawn Langton
Editorial Description: Practical information related to employment & job development strategies for people who support persons with a range of physical, mental or psychiatric disabilities. Topics include training techniques, natural supports, job analysis, employer negotiation & behavior practices. Examples of various job placements are analyzed.
General Info: Yr. Est. 1990, Monthly, Trim Size-17 x 11, Offset press, 8 pages, ISSN: 1047-952X, 4% ads, Color, Matte
Subscriptions: Indv. $89, Can. $89, For. $129, $10/copy
Circulation: Total-4,000
Advertising: Inquire for rates.
Printing Co: Acme Printing, 1300 S. Dixie Highway, St. Augustine, FL 32084 Tel # (904) 824-9235

TSM Reports
See: INDUSTRIAL RELATIONS/PERSONNEL

Teaching Opportunities Overseas Bulletin
See: EDUCATION

Technology Industry
Growth Forecaster   *Business*

Publishing Co: CorpTech, 12 Alfred St., Ste. 200, Woburn, MA 01801-1915; Title Tel # (617) 932-3939 Title Fax # (617) 932-6335
Personnel: Publisher-Andrew Campbell, Editor-Deborah Nielsen
Editorial Description: Details future employment growth in the technology industry.
General Info: Monthly, Trim Size-8½ x 11, 4 pages, Matte
Subscriptions: Indv. $120, Can. $150, For. $150, Free To Qualified Recipient
Circulation: Readership-8,000
List Rental: Rents Lists

Telecommuting Review
See: INDUSTRIAL RELATIONS/PERSONNEL

Tennessee Employment Law Update
See: LAW

Texas Chapter NSLA
Newsletter

Publishing Co: Texas Automotive Dismantlers & Recyclers Assn., 823 Congress Ave. #1300, Austin, TX 78701-2429; Title Tel # (512) 479-0425
Personnel: Publisher, Editor-Lisa Peek
Editorial Description: Official publication of the Texas Chapter National Staff Leasing Association.
General Info: Quarterly, Mimeo press, 4 pages, No Color, Matte
Printing Co: Austex Printing Co., 501 W 3rd St, Austin, TX 78701-3807 Tel # (512) 476-7581

Texas Employment Law Letter
See: LAW

TrainMaster
See: INDUSTRIAL RELATIONS/PERSONNEL

Trained Men

Publishing Co: Intl. Correspondence Schools, Oak & Pawnee St., Scranton, PA 18515-0001; Title Tel # (717) 342-7701
Personnel: Editor-George Carpenter
Editorial Description: Articles dealing with training, new management methods, interesting topics for industrial management readers.
General Info: Yr. Est. 1920, Quarterly
Circulation: Total-16,000

Transition Summary
See: DISABILITY

Unemployment Insurance
Reports   *Consumer*

Publishing Co: CCH, Inc., 2700 Lake Cook Rd., Riverwoods, IL 60015 Parent Co.-Kluwer Law & Taxation Publishers, Cambridge; Title Tel # (847) 267-7000 Title Fax # (800) 224-8299
Editorial Description: Social security taxes, old age survivors and disability benefits, supplemental security income, into to medicine, unemployment insurance, explanations, tables, laws, and court cases.
General Info: Yr. Est. 1935, 30x/yr., ISSN: 0572-9920, Looseleaf
Subscriptions: Indv. $2,470

United Nations Jobs
Newsletter   *Consumer*

Publishing Co: Thomas F. Burola & Assoc., 6477 Telephone Rd Ste 7r, Ventura, CA 93003-4459
Editorial Description: Covers employment conditions within the United Nations system. Includes vacancy notices for organizations such as the World Bank, USAID, International Red Cross, and related private sector consulting companies.
General Info: Monthly
Subscriptions: Indv. $110
Circulation: Total-17,500

Utah Labor Market Report

Publishing Co: Utah State Dept. of Employment Security, 174 Social Hall Ave # 11249, Salt Lake City, UT 84111-1504; Title Tel # (801) 536-7800 Title Fax # (801) 536-7869
Personnel: Publisher-William Horner, Editor-Lelia Langston
Editorial Description: Analysis & statistics about labor market conditions & trends in the state of Utah.
General Info: (Formerly Utah Employment Review), Monthly, Trim Size-8½ x 11, Desktop press, 16 pages, 2 Color, Saddle-stitched
Circulation: Total-4,200

Vermont Labor Market
See: LABOR

View, The
See: CHAMBER OF COMMERCE

Virginia Employment Law Letter
See: LAW

WG&L Human Resources Forms with Commentary
See: INDUSTRIAL RELATIONS/PERSONNEL

Washington Employment
Law Letter   *Business*

Publishing Co: M. Lee Smith Publishers & Printers ,LCC, P.O. Box 198867, 162 Fourth Avenue North, Nashville, TN 37219-8867 Tel # (615) 242-7395 Fax # (615) 256-6601
Personnel: Publisher-M. Lee Smith, Editor-Michael Reynvaan, Circ. Mgr.-Cathy Bradford, Mktg. Dir.-Dave Yates
Editorial Description: Employment law information.
General Info: Yr. Est. 1994, Monthly, Trim Size-8½ x 11, 8 pages, ISSN: 1072-0588, 2 Color
Subscriptions: Indv. $97
Printing Co: M. Lee Smith Publishers & Printers ,LLC, PO Box 198867, 162 Fourth Avenue, Nashville, TN 37219-8867 Tel # (615) 242-7395, Fax # (615) 256-6601

Weekly Outlook

Publishing Co: Univ. of Illinois at Urbana Champaign, 227 Illini Union, 1401 W. Green Street, Urbana, IL 61801 Tel # (217) 333-1477 Fax # (217) 333-7803; Title Tel # (217) 333-2666 Title Fax # (217) 333-1952
Personnel: Publisher-Darrel Good
Editorial Description: Anticipates reports & interprets current Market information, supply, demand & price outlook for Agricultural products.
General Info: Weekly
Subscriptions: Indv. $30

Welfare to Work   *Business*

Publishing Co: MII Publications, Inc., 1211 Conn. Ave. NW, #705, Washington, DC 20036-2701; Title Tel # (202) 293-1740 Title Fax # (202) 293-0377
Personnel: Publisher-Cecilio Morales, Editor-Lucas Graves, Mag. Ed.-Richard Sayre
Editorial Description: Covers welfare reform, job training for public assistance recipiants, powerty and employment issues.
General Info: Yr. Est. 1992, Bi-weekly, Trim Size-8½ x 11, 8 pages, ISSN: 1060-5622, 2 Color
Subscriptions: Indv. $267, $11/copy
List Rental: Rents Lists
Printing Co: Plymouth Printing, 1200 Cushing Pl SE, Washington, DC 20003-3599 Tel # (202) 488-7777, Fax # (202) 863-1078

West Virginia Economic Summary
See: ECONOMICS

Wisconsin Employment Law Letters
See: LAW

Workamper News
See: TRAVEL

Workcamp News

Publishing Co: Service Civil Intl. USA, Rr 2 Box 506, Crozet, VA 22932-9510; Title Tel # (804) 823-1826 Title Fax # (804) 823-5027
Personnel: Editor-Anne Smucker
General Info: Yr. Est. 1981, Semi-annually, Offset press, 4 pages, No Color
Subscriptions: Indv. $25
Circulation: Total-1,500

Workers Compensation Guide
See: INDUSTRIAL RELATIONS/PERSONNEL

Worker's Compensation Law Bulletin
See: LAW

Workforce Strategies   *Association*

Publishing Co: Bureau of National Affairs, Inc., 1231 25th St. NW, Bldg. N-200, Washington, DC 20037-1157; Title Tel # (202) 452-4200 Title Fax # (202) 822-8092
Personnel: Publisher-William A. Beltz, Mng. Editor-Jeff Day, Circ. Mgr.-Gary C. Seltzer
Editorial Description: A monthly newsletter providing analysis & case studies of developments in training, recruiting, & employee development.
General Info: Yr. Est. 1990, Monthly, Trim Size-8½ x 11, Offset press, 6 pages, ISSN: 1062-8991
Subscriptions: Indv. $148

Working Age
See: SENIOR CITIZENS

Working Options

Publishing Co: Assn. of Part-Time Professionals, 7700 Leesburg Pike Ste 216, Falls Church, VA 22043-2615; Title Tel # (703) 734-7975
Personnel: Editor-Maureen Kenney
Editorial Description: Part time employment: trends, profiles, employer use.
General Info: (Formerly Part-Time Professional Newsletter), Yr. Est. 1981, Monthly, 6 pages, ISSN: 0739-2931
Subscriptions: Indv. $45, Inst. $75
Circulation: Total-1,500

Working Together
See: INDUSTRIAL RELATIONS/PERSONNEL

Working at Home   *Consumer*

Publishing Co: Mrs. H.C. McGarity, PO Box 200504, Cartersville, GA 30120-9009; Title Tel # (404) 386-1257
Personnel: Publisher, Editor-H.C. McGarity
General Info: Yr. Est. 1985, Tri-annually, Trim Size-8½ x 11, Sheetfed press, 6 pages
Subscriptions: Indv. $12, For. $17, $3/copy
Circulation: Total-375
Advertising: Inquire for rates. Accepts Inserts.
Printing Co: Tallent Printers, 735 Joe Frank Harris Pky SE, Cartersville, GA 30120-2469 Tel # (404) 386-0086

Workmen's Compensation   *Business*

Publishing Co: Matthew Bender & Co., 11 Penn Plaza, New York, NY 10001-2006 Fax # (212) 244-3188; Title Tel # (212) 967-7707
Personnel: Editor-S. Weisenfeld
Editorial Description: Includes legal principles, working rules, procedures and forms.
General Info: (Formerly Law of Workmen's Compensation), Yr. Est. 1952, Looseleaf
Subscriptions: $1,095/copy

Workplace in the
Community

Publishing Co: Volunteer - The National Center, 736 Jackson Pl NW, Washington, DC 20503-0007; Title Tel # (703) 276-0542
Personnel: Editor-Brenda Hanlon
Editorial Description: Corporate employee volunteer programs; public/private partnerships.
General Info: Yr. Est. 1984, 8 pages, Color, Newsprint
Acquistions: Publication Bought
Circulation: Total-3,700

ENERGY

21st Century Fuels   *Business*

Publishing Co: Hart Publications, 7811 Montrose Rd., Potomac, MD 20854 Tel # (301) 340-2100 Parent Co.-Phillips Business Information, Inc., Potomac
Personnel: Publisher-Frederick Potter, Asst. Pub.-Brian Crotty, Editor-Kevin Adler, Circulation, Mktg. Dir.-Paul Caplan
Editorial Description: Trends & monthly statistics and analysis on supply and demand for clean gasolines and diesel fuels as well as alternative fuels.
General Info: (Formerly Oxygenate Outlook), Yr. Est. 1983, Monthly, Ind/Abs/Online: Newsnet and Predicasts
Subscriptions: Indv. $445, Can. $495, For. $495

AWEA Wind Energy
Weekly   *Business*

Publishing Co: American Wind Energy Assn., 122 C St. NW, Washington, DC 20001 Tel # (202) 383-2500; Title Tel # (202) 383-2508
Personnel: Editor-Randall Swishe
Editorial Description: Legistlative, regulatory, business, technical news (national and international).
General Info: (Formerly AWEA Update), Yr. Est. 1982, Weekly, 8 pages, ISSN: 0747-5500, No Color, Newsprint
Subscriptions: Indv. $175
Circulation: Total-460

Access to Energy   *Consumer*

Publishing Co: Access to Energy, PO Box 1250, Cave Junction, OR 97523; Title Tel # (541) 592-4142
Personnel: Publisher, Editor-Arthur Robinson
Editorial Description: Pro-science pro-technology, pro-free enterprise.
General Info: Yr. Est. 1973, Monthly, Trim Size-8½ x 11, Sheetfed press, 4 pages, Ind/Abs/Online: Cumulative Index, No Color, Newsprint
Subscriptions: Indv. $35, Inst. $60, Can. $37, For. $40, $3/copy
Circulation: Total-4,000

Alcohol Week
See: PETROLEUM & NATURAL GAS

Alert
See: PUBLIC UTILITIES

Alternative Energy
Trends & Forecasts   *Business*

Publishing Co: Technology Forecasts, 205 S Beverly Dr Ste 208, Beverly Hills, CA 90212-3873; Title Tel # (310) 273-3486 Title Fax # (310) 858-8272
Personnel: Publisher-Irwin Stambler, Circ. Mgr.-S. Nemiroff
Editorial Description: Reports on trends; major advances and future prospects for key alternative energy sectors including solar; wind; biomass electric vehicles, geothermal; synfuels and fusion.
General Info: Yr. Est. 1979, Monthly
Subscriptions: Indv. $95, Can. $99, For. $109

American Association for
Fuel Cells Newsletter   *Association*

Publishing Co: American Association for Fuel Cells, 50 San Miguel Ave, Daly City, CA 94015-3950; Title Tel # (413) 774-6051
Editorial Description: Association newsletter promoting use of fuel cells in automotives.
General Info: Quarterly, Trim Size-8½ x 11, 8 pages

Bechtel Briefs
See: ENGINEERING

CRA Review
See: ECONOMICS

California Energy Markets   *Business*

Publishing Co: NewsData Corp., P.O. Box 900928, Seattle, WA 98119-9228 Tel # (206) 285-4848 Fax # (206) 281-8035; Title Tel # (415) 824-3222 Title Fax # (415) 824-3223
Personnel: Publisher-Cyrus Noe, Editor-Arthur O'Donnell, Production Mgr.-Karen Hatch, Mktg. Dir.-Daniel Sackett
Editorial Description: Covers public utility & energy policy, market developments and energy litigation in california, nevada, arizona and new mexico.
General Info: Yr. Est. 1989, Weekly, Trim Size-8½ x 11, Offset press, 20 pages, ISSN: 1044-2022, Ind/Abs/Online: Semi-Annual Index, No Color, Recycled, Other
Subscriptions: Indv. $989
List Rental: Rents Lists
Printing Co: A & A Printing, 320 Queen Anne Ave N, Seattle, WA 98109-4512 Tel # (206) 285-1700

Canada Petroleum Industry
See: PETROLEUM & NATURAL GAS

Canadian Energy News   *Business*

Publishing Co: CCH Canadian Ltd., 6 Garamond Ct., North York, ON M3C 1Z5 Canada
Fax # (416) 444-8011 Parent Co.-CCH, Inc., Riverwoods; Title Tel # (416) 441-2992
Title Fax # (416) 444-9011
Personnel: Editor-Brad Morrison
Editorial Description: Current reporting on Canada's energy problems. Legislative and administrative activities, as well as economic and technological developments.
General Info: Yr. Est. 1980, Bi-monthly, Trim Size-8½ x 11, Offset press, 8 pages, ISSN: 0319-3403, No Color
Subscriptions: Can. $390

Canadian Energy Program
Reporter   *Business*

Publishing Co: CCH Canadian Ltd., 6 Garamond Ct., North York, ON M3C 1Z5 Canada
Fax # (416) 444-8011 Parent Co.-CCH, Inc., Riverwoods; Title Tel # (416) 441-2992
Title Fax # (416) 444-9011
Editorial Description: Reports on Canada's national energy program.
General Info: Monthly, Trim Size-6 x 9, Web press, No Color, Looseleaf
Subscriptions: Can. $265

Chronicle

Publishing Co: U.S. Government Energy Regulatory Commission, 826 N Capitol St NE, Washington, DC 20002-4233; Title Tel # (202) 208-0680
Personnel: Editor-Robert Cecil
Editorial Description: Government publication regarding energy policy.
General Info: Yr. Est. 1990, Monthly, Sheetfed press, 8 pages, Color-cover, Matte
Subscriptions: Indv. $12, Inst. $12, $1/copy
Advertising: Inquire for rates.

Clearing Up   *Business*

Publishing Co: NewsData Corp., P.O. Box 900928, Seattle, WA 98119-9228; Title Tel # (206) 285-4848 Title Fax # (206) 281-8035
Personnel: Publisher-Cyrus Noe, Editor-Ben Tansey, Production Mgr.-Karen Hatch, Circ. Mgr., Mktg. Dir., Promotion Dir.-Daniel Sackett
Editorial Description: Clearing up covers public utility & energy litigation, energy policy, resource development & utility capital financing in the Pacific Northwest & Western Canada.
General Info: Yr. Est. 1982, Weekly, Trim Size-8½ x 11, Offset press, 20 pages, ISSN: 0738-2332, Ind/Abs/Online: Subject-oriented index included semi-annually., No Color, Matte
Circulation: Total-800
List Rental: Rents Lists
Printing Co: A & A Printing, 320 Queen Anne Ave N, Seattle, WA 98109-4512 Tel # (206) 285-1700

Coal & Synfuels
Technology   *Business*

Publishing Co: Pasha Publications, Inc, 1616 N. Fort Myer Dr., #1000, Arlington, VA 22209-3103; Title Tel # (703) 528-1244 Title Fax # (703) 528-4926
Personnel: Publisher-Tod Sedgwick, Editor-Audrey Haar, Mng. Editor-Jeff Schomisch, Assoc. Ed.-Lataunja Beale, Circ. Mgr.-Kathy Thorne, Production-Rob Traister, Mktg. Coord.-Mary Anvari, Mktg. Coord.-Julie Johnson
Editorial Description: Complete coverage of clean coal technology funding, project financing, oil shale, scrubbers, R & D, coal fuels, power plant projects.
General Info: (Formerly Synfuels Week; Coal Technology Report), Yr. Est. 1979, Weekly, Trim Size-8½ x 11, Web press, 8 pages, ISSN: 0883-9735, Ind/Abs/Online: DIALOG, Predicasts, Matte
Subscriptions: Indv. $790, For. $820, $16/copy
Circulation: Total-425
List Rental: Actives: $95/M

Coal Focus   *Business, Association*   CPM: $71

Publishing Co: Coal Assn. of Canada, 205 9th Ave. SE, #502, Calgary, AB T2G 0R3 Canada; Title Tel # (403) 262-1544
Personnel: Editor-Jim Wood
Editorial Description: Canadian coal industry newsletter.
General Info: Yr. Est. 1977, Monthly, 4 pages, ISSN: 0821-7068, Recycled
Subscriptions: Free In Designated Area
Circulation: Total-700
Advertising: $50.

Coal Outlook
See: MINING & MINERALS

Coal Tech International

Publishing Co: McGraw-Hill, 1221 Ave. of the Americas, 36th Fl., New York, NY 10020-1095 Tel # (212) 512-2000 Fax # (212) 512-6590; Title Tel # (212) 512-6410
Personnel: Publisher-John Slater, Editor-Kevin Hamilton
General Info: (Formerly Clean-Coal/Synfuels Letter), Weekly, Ind/Abs/Online: DIALOG, Dow Jones, NewsNet, Nexis
Subscriptions: Indv. $825

Coal Transportation Report   *Business*

Publishing Co: Fieldston Co., 1920 N Street, N.W., Ste. 210, Washington, DC 20036; Title Tel # (202) 775-0240 Title Fax # (202) 872-8045
Personnel: Publisher-James Heller, Editor-John Gallagher, Sr. Ed.-Sue Follett, Asst. Ed.-Mike Harms, Circ. Mgr.-Martha Lotry, Mktg. Dir.-Laura Dowe
Editorial Description: News and information relating to coal transportation.
General Info: Yr. Est. 1982, 24x/yr., Trim Size-8½ x 11, 12 pages
Subscriptions: Indv. $595
Printing Co: Plymouth Printing, 1200 Cushing Pl SE, Washington, DC 20003-3599 Tel # (202) 488-7777, Fax # (202) 863-1078

Coal Week
See: MINING & MINERALS

Coal Week International
See: MINING & MINERALS

Coaldat Marketing Report   *Business*

Publishing Co: Pasha Publications, Inc, 1616 N. Fort Myer Dr., #1000, Arlington, VA 22209-3103 Fax # (703) 528-4926; Title Tel # (703) 528-1244
Personnel: Publisher-Tod Sedgwick, Editor-Ron McMahon, Circ. Mgr.-Kathy Thorne, Promotion Dir.-Wade Martin
Editorial Description: Lists coal prices paid by utilities & specs.
General Info: (Formerly Coaldat Monthly), Yr. Est. 1979, Monthly, Trim Size-8½ x 11, Mimeo press, 55 pages
Subscriptions: Indv. $595, For. $635, $100/copy
Acquistions: Publication Bought, Publication Sold
List Rental: Rents Lists

Coaldat Quarterly   *Business*

Publishing Co: Pasha Publications, Inc, 1616 N. Fort Myer Dr., #1000, Arlington, VA 22209-3103 Fax # (703) 528-4926; Title Tel # (703) 528-1244
Personnel: Publisher-Harry Baisden, Editor-Ron McMahon, Circ. Mgr.-Kathy Thorne, Promotion Dir.-Wade Martin
General Info: Yr. Est. 1986, Quarterly, 60 pages
Subscriptions: Indv. $695, For. $775, $200/copy

Cogeneration Letter

Publishing Co: Energy Engineering, 700 Indian Trail Rd NW, Lilburn, GA 30247-3724; Title Tel # (404) 925-9388 Title Fax # (770) 381-9865
Personnel: Editor-Anna Faye Williams, Circ. Mgr.-Lisa O'Sullivan
Editorial Description: A newsletter detailing what you should know about the fast-growing field of cogeneration. Providing insight into issues such as market directions, new cogeneration technologies, investments, competitive products, & project developments. Covering all segm nts of the market, small & large projects, commercials, institution & industrial, small pre-packaged & large custom-designed plants.
General Info: Yr. Est. 1985, Monthly, 8 pages, ISSN: 0749-5617
Subscriptions: Indv. $195, For. $210
Circulation: Total-250

Comfortline
See: HEATING, PLUMBING, A/C, REFRIG.

Common Sense on Energy & Our Envirnoment
See: ENVIRONMENT & ECOLOGY

Critical Mass Energy
Bulletin

Publishing Co: Public Citizen's Critical Mass Energy Project, 215 Pennsylvania Ave., SE, Washington, DC 20003-1155; Title Tel # (202) 546-4996 Title Fax # (202) 547-7392
Personnel: Publisher, Editor-Ken Bossong
Editorial Description: Pressing to decrease reliance on nuclear and fossil fuels.
General Info: Yr. Est. 1983, Quarterly, Trim Size-8½ x 11, Web press, 10 pages, No Color
Subscriptions: Indv. $12, Inst. $36, For. $30, $3/copy
Circulation: (90% controlled), Total-1,200, Subscriptions-120
List Rental: Rents Lists

Cureletter
See: MANUFACTURING

Current Marketing

Publishing Co: Natl. Food & Energy Council, Inc., 409 Vandiver W., Ste. 202, Bldg. 4, Columbia, MO 65202-1587
Personnel: Editor-Richard Hiatt
Editorial Description: Promotes electrical energy use/management for agricultural enterprises.
General Info: Yr. Est. 1985, Bi-monthly, Trim Size-8½ x 11, Letrpr. press, 4 pages, 2 Color, Coated
Subscriptions: Indv. $35
Circulation: Total-270

Daily Oil Bulletin
See: PETROLEUM & NATURAL GAS

Dakota Counsel *Association*

Publishing Co: Dakota Resource Council, PO Box 1095, Dickinson, ND 58602-1095; Title Tel # (701) 227-1851 Title Fax # (701) 225-8315
Personnel: Editor-Mark Trechok, Production Mgr.-Aleta Hendricks
Editorial Description: Grassroots group organizing aournd energy & rural survival issues produce research materials on topics such as ground water protection, farm bill, economic development, air quality, energy development energy taxation.
General Info: Yr. Est. 1978, Quarterly, Trim Size-8½ x 11, 8 pages, No Color
Subscriptions: Indv. $20
Acquistions: Publication Bought
Circulation: Total-723
Advertising: Accepts Inserts.

Dialogue
See: ELECTRIC & ELECTRONIC EQUIPMENT

Dialogue
See: PRODUCE

Drilling & Land Report

Publishing Co: Petroleum Resources Div., Ministry of Energy Mines & Petrole, Parliament Bldg., Victoria, BC V8V 1X4 Canada
General Info: Monthly
Subscriptions: Indv. $30

Drilling & Well Servicing Worldwide
See: PETROLEUM & NATURAL GAS

ECPA Newsline *Association*

Publishing Co: Energy Consumers and Producers Assn., PO Box 1288, Muskogee, OK 74402-1288; Title Tel # (405) 382-5363
Personnel: Editor-Patti Gipson
Editorial Description: Update on federal oil & gas legislation & regulations affecting independent producers.
General Info: Yr. Est. 1977, Monthly, Trim Size-8½ x 11, 4 pages, No Color
Circulation: Total-400

EMF Update

Publishing Co: Energy Modeling Forum, Stanford Univ., Terman Engineering Ctr., Stanford, CA 94305-1901; Title Tel # (415) 723-0645
Personnel: Editor-Dorothy Sheffield
General Info: Yr. Est. 1980, Semi-annually
Circulation: Total-3,000

ENERCOM *Consumer*

Publishing Co: New York State Energy Office, Two Rockefeller Plaza, Albany, NY 12223-0001; Title Tel # (518) 474-2161
Personnel: Editor-Gary Sheffer
Editorial Description: Quarterly news communique of the New York state energy office.
General Info: Yr. Est. 1983, Quarterly, Offset press, 10 pages, 2 Color, Newsprint, Saddle-stitched
Subscriptions: Free
Circulation: Total-5,200

Electric Leaguer
See: HOUSE ORGANS

Electric Power
See: WATER SUPPLY, POWER & WASTE

Electric Power Alert *Business*

Publishing Co: Inside Washington Publishers, P.O. Box 7167, Ben Franklin Station, Washington, DC 20044 Tel # (703) 512-1800; Title Tel # (703) 892-8516 Title Fax # (703) 685-2606
Personnel: Mng. Editor-Lia Parisien
Editorial Description: Provides comprehensive coverage of the electric power industry. Contains information on power supply, producers, regulators and related topics.
General Info: Bi-weekly

Electric Utilities Industry - U.S. and Canada
See: PUBLIC UTILITIES

Electric Utility Week
See: PUBLIC UTILITIES

Electric Utility Week's Demand-Side Report
See: PUBLIC UTILITIES

Electric Vehicle News
See: TRAFFIC & TRANSPORTATION

Electric Vehicle Progress
See: AUTOMOTIVE

Energizer, The *Consumer, Association*

Publishing Co: Solar Energy Assn. of Oregon, 418 SW Washington Street, Suite 306, Portland, OR 97204-2209; Title Tel # (503) 224-7867 Title Fax # (503) 241-4260
General Info: (Formerly Oregon Energizer), Yr. Est. 1987, Quarterly, Trim Size-8½ x 11, 6 pages, 4 Color
Subscriptions: $50/copy
Circulation: Total-1,000

Energy *Business*

Publishing Co: National Technical Information Service U.S., 5285 Port Royal Rd., Springfield, VA 22161-0001 Fax # (703) 487-4630; Title Tel # (703) 487-4630
Editorial Description: Covers energy sources, energy use, supply & demand, power & heat generation, energy conversion & storage, energy transmission, & fuel conversion processes.
General Info: Weekly, Trim Size-8½ x 11, Offset press, 40 pages, ISSN: 0148-446X, No Color
Subscriptions: Indv. $160, Can. $160, For. $225
Circulation: Total-100,000

Energy & Environmental News

Publishing Co: Naval Energy & Environmental Support Activities, 1001 Lyons St Ste 1, Port Hueneme, CA 93043-4339; Title Tel # (805) 982-3512
Personnel: Editor-Jean Grant
General Info: (Formerly Clean Slate), Yr. Est. 1973, Quarterly, 8 pages
Circulation: Total-4,500

Energy Analects

Publishing Co: Southam Information & Technology Group, 999 8th St. SW, #300, Calgary, AB T2R 1N7 Canada; Title Tel # (403) 244-6111 Title Fax # (403) 245-8666
Personnel: Circ. Mgr.-Kay Isaac, Editor, Promotion Dir.-Dale Lunan
Editorial Description: News & developments in the energy marketing field in Canada.
General Info: Yr. Est. 1972, Weekly, Trim Size-8½ x 11, Offset press, 8 pages, ISSN: 0315-1654, No Color
Subscriptions: Indv. $537

Energy Conservation Digest

Publishing Co: Editorial Resources, Inc., PO Box 21129, Washington, DC 20009-0629; Title Tel # (202) 783-2929
Personnel: Publisher, Editor-David Howell, Circ. Mgr.-D. Hancock
Editorial Description: Covers commercial, residential, industrial, energy & conservation issues. Includes coverage of legislative/policy developments, least-cost planning, state & local programs, new products, callendar & resources.
General Info: Bi-weekly, Trim Size-8½ x 11, Sheetfed press, 10 pages, ISSN: 0270-823X
Subscriptions: Indv. $167

Energy Conservation News *Business*

Publishing Co: Business Communications Co., 25 Van Zant St., Ste.13, Norwalk, CT 06855-1781; Title Tel # (203) 853-4266 Title Fax # (203) 853-0348
Personnel: Publisher-Louis Naturman, Editor-Kevin Gainer, Mktg. Dir.-Robert Butler
Editorial Description: Reports on energy conservation in industry.
General Info: Yr. Est. 1978, Monthly, Trim Size-8½ x 11, Offset press, 12 pages, ISSN: 0660-1083, Ind/Abs/Online: DIALOG, No Color, Matte
Subscriptions: Indv. $325, Can. $375, For. $375, $31/copy
List Rental: List Management Co.: W.I. Mail Marketing, 470 Main St. #317, Ridgefield, CT 06877-4516 Tel # (203) 438-6822, Fax # (203) 438-7756

Energy Daily, The *Business, Association*

Publishing Co: King Communications Group, 627 National Press Building, Washington, DC 20045-1601 Tel # (202) 638-4260; Title Tel # (202) 662-9724 Title Fax # (202) 662-9719
Personnel: Publisher-Llewellyn King, Editor-Dennis Wamstead, Circ. Mgr.-Dawn Miles, Production Mgr.-Tony Russell, Art Dir.-Tony Campana
General Info: Yr. Est. 1973, Daily, Trim Size-8.5 x 11, Sheetfed press, 6 pages, ISSN: 0364-5274, Ind/Abs/Online: Newsnet, DIALOG, 2 Color, Newsprint, Perfect bound
Subscriptions: Indv. $1,495, $11/copy
Acquistions: Publication Bought
List Rental: Rents Lists

Energy Design Update
See: CONSUMER INTERESTS

Energy Detente *Business*

Publishing Co: Tele-Drop Inc., PO Box 3996, North Hollywood, CA 91609-0996; Title Tel # (818) 768-5111 Title Fax # (818) 768-0537
Personnel: Publisher, Editor-Trilby Lundberg
Editorial Description: Covers international energy policy, resource development, fuel prices, & refining.
General Info: Yr. Est. 1980, Semi-monthly, Trim Size-8½ x 11, Sheetfed press, 20 pages, No Color
Subscriptions: Indv. $500, Inst. $250, Can. $500, For. $500, $50/copy

Energy Efficiency News & Views
Business, Association

Publishing Co: IRT Environment, Inc./Results Center, The, PO Box 2239, Basalt, CO 81612; Title Tel # (970) 927-3155 Title Fax # (970) 927-9428
Personnel: Publisher, Editor-Ted Flanigan, Circ. Mgr., Production Mgr.-Bill Flanigan
Editorial Description: Provides coverage of new events, issues and programs in the energy industry and includes an industry forum for an exchange of view points on current issues.
General Info: Yr. Est. 1995, Monthly, Desktop press, 8 pages, ISSN: 1080-5133, No Color, Matte
Subscriptions: Indv. $200, Inst. $500
Circulation: Total-500
Printing Co: Basalt Printing, Basalt, CO 81612-3039 Tel # (970) 927-4705

Energy Futures
Business, Consumer

Publishing Co: Energy Probe, 225 Brunswick Ave., Toronto, ON M5S 2M6 Canada; Title Tel # (416) 964-9223
Editorial Description: Hardnosed economic analysis; grassroots knowledge of forces shaping public opinion.
General Info: Yr. Est. 1984, Bi-monthly, Sheetfed press, 8 pages, 4 Color
Subscriptions: $30/copy
Circulation: Total-250

Energy Information Administration New Releases

Publishing Co: Natl. Energy Information Center, Forrestal Bldg., Washington, DC 20585-0001; Title Tel # (202) 586-8800
Editorial Description: Lists new reports.
General Info: Bi-monthly
Subscriptions: Free

Energy Law and Transactions
Business

Publishing Co: Matthew Bender & Co., 11 Penn Plaza, New York, NY 10001-2006 Tel # (212) 967-7707 Fax # (212) 244-3188
Personnel: Editor-William A. Mogel, Editor-David J. Muchow
Editorial Description: Covers all major sources of energy--from gas, oil, coal & electric, to nuclear, hydroelectric power, cogeneration, solar & biomass. Discussions of each energy source explain production transmission & distribution, as well as the typical transactions encountered.
General Info: Yr. Est. 1990, Irregular, Looseleaf

Energy Management and Federal Energy Guidelines
Business

Publishing Co: CCH, Inc., 2700 Lake Cook Rd., Riverwoods, IL 60015 Parent Co.-Kluwer Law & Taxation Publishers, Cambridge; Title Tel # (847) 267-7000 Title Fax # (800) 224-8299
Editorial Description: Weekly reporting on federal petroleum allocation rules, local conservation efforts, the cost of fuel, data on new energy technology, plus laws, regulations, government releases.
General Info: (Formerly Energy Management), Yr. Est. 1973, Bi-weekly, Trim Size-6 x 9, Web press, 300 pages, No Color, Looseleaf
Subscriptions: Indv. $1,534

Energy News Exchange
See: APPLIANCES

Energy Newsbrief
Business, Association

Publishing Co: IRT Environment, Inc./Results Center, The, PO Box 2239, Basalt, CO 81612; Title Tel # (970) 927-3155 Title Fax # (970) 927-9428
Personnel: Publisher, Editor-Ted Flanigan, Circ. Mgr., Production Mgr., Promotion Dir.-Bill Flanigan
Editorial Description: Covers means of developing a global sustainable environment.
General Info: (Formerly IRT: Issues, Review, & Tracking), Yr. Est. 1986, Bi-weekly, Desktop press, 8 pages, ISSN: 1059-289X, No Color, Matte
Subscriptions: Indv. $195, Inst. $295, Can. $295, For. $295, $10/copy
Circulation: Total-500

Energy Outlook

Publishing Co: Virginia Polytechnic Inst. Virginia Cntr. for Coal & Energy, 617 N Main St, Blacksburg, VA 24060-3348; Title Tel # (703) 231-5038
Editorial Description: Reporting on events, issues, research on coal & energy in Virginia & SE U.S. region.
General Info: Yr. Est. 1981, Bi-monthly, Trim Size-8½ x 11, 6 pages, ISSN: 0279-6635, No Color, Recycled
Acquistions: Publication Bought
Circulation: Total-3,500
List Rental: Rents Lists
Printing Co: VA Tech Print Shop, Virginia Polytechnic Institute, Blacksburg, VA 24061 Tel # (703) 231-6701

Energy Prices & Taxes
Business, Association

Publishing Co: Organization for Economic Cooperation & Development, 2001 L St NW Ste 650, Washington, DC 20036-4910; Title Tel # (202) 785-6323 Title Fax # (202) 785-0350
Editorial Description: International compilation of energy prices at all market levels for the main petroleum products, coal, and electricity.
General Info: Quarterly, Trim Size-7⅞ x 10⅝, Offset press, 350 pages, ISSN: 0256-2332, No Color
Subscriptions: Indv. $230, $59/copy

Energy Pricing News
Business

Publishing Co: Southam Business Communications, Inc., 1450 Don Mills Rd., Don Mills, ON M3B 2X7 Canada Fax # (416) 442-2200; Title Tel # (416) 445-6641
Personnel: Publisher, Editor, Circ. Mgr., Promotion Dir.-Paul Harris
Editorial Description: Actual selling prices for all major energy commodities in Canada.
General Info: Yr. Est. 1981, Monthly, 12 pages, ISSN: 0836-7744, 4 Color
Subscriptions: Indv. $467
List Rental: List Management Co.: Cornerstone List Mgrs., 2300 Yonge St., Ste. 2005, Box 2465, Toronto, ON M4P 1E4 Canada Tel # (416) 932-9555, Fax # (416) 932-9566

Energy Report, The
Business

Publishing Co: Pasha Publications, Inc, 1616 N. Fort Myer Dr., #1000, Arlington, VA 22209-3103 Fax # (703) 528-4926; Title Tel # (703) 528-1244
Personnel: Publisher-Tod Sedgwick, Editor-Bryan Lee, Mng. Editor-Jeff Schomisch, Assoc. Ed.-Tom Yancy, Circ. Mgr.-Kathy Thorne, Production-Rob Traister, Mktg. Coord.-Mary Anvari, Mktg. Coord.-Julie Johnson
Editorial Description: Coverage includes comprehensive federal and state policies and issues affecting oil, natural gas, electricity, cogeneration, power markets, nuclear energy, taxation, global warming and other topics.
General Info: Yr. Est. 1986, Weekly, 20 pages, ISSN: 0888-8183, Ind/Abs/Online: Mead Data Central, DIALOG, Predicasts
Subscriptions: Indv. $695, For. $769, $14/copy
List Rental: Rents Lists

Energy Savers
Business

Publishing Co: Alberta Dept. of Energy, 9945 108th St., 7th Floor, Edmonton, AB T5K 2G6 Canada; Title Tel # (403) 427-5200 Title Fax # (403) 422-0494
Editorial Description: A series of fact sneets about energy effiency measures in Alberta. Each issue highlights a different technology and its successful use in the province.
General Info: Yr. Est. 1990, Irregular
Subscriptions: Free
Circulation: Total-2,500

Energy Summary

Publishing Co: Oliphant Washington News Service, PO Box 9808, Washington, DC 20016-8808 Tel # (202) 298-7226; Title Tel # (202) 296-0924
Personnel: Editor-John Oliphant
Editorial Description: Covers Energy Dept. FERC & related agencies.
General Info: Yr. Est. 1972, Weekly, Trim Size-8½ x 11, Sheetfed press, 8 pages, ISSN: 0733-0219
Subscriptions: Indv. $300

Energy Today

Publishing Co: Trends Publishing, Inc., 1079 Natl. Press Bldg., Washington, DC 20045-0001; Title Tel # (202) 393-0031 Title Fax # (202) 393-1732
Personnel: Publisher, Editor-A. Kranish
General Info: Yr. Est. 1972, Monthly, Trim Size-8½ x 11, Offset press, 8 pages, ISSN: 0093-806X, No Color
Subscriptions: Indv. $795

Enhanced Energy Recovery News
Business

Publishing Co: Business Communications Co., 25 Van Zant St., Ste.13, Norwalk, CT 06855-1781; Title Tel # (203) 853-4266 Title Fax # (203) 853-0348
Personnel: Publisher-Louis Naturman, Editor-Anna Crull, Editor-Diana Mulloy, Mktg. Dir.-Robert Butler
Editorial Description: Highlights R&D materials developments, commercial applications & government activity in energy recov
General Info: Yr. Est. 1980, Monthly, Trim Size-8½ x 11, 10 pages, ISSN: 0271-7085, Ind/Abs/Online: Predicasts, No Color, Matte
Subscriptions: Indv. $350, Can. $400, For. $400, $35/copy
List Rental: List Management Co.: W.I. Mail Marketing, 470 Main St. #317, Ridgefield, CT 06877-4516 Tel # (203) 438-6822, Fax # (203) 438-7756, Actives: 120

Environmental Success Index
Consumer

Publishing Co: Renew America, 1400 16th St NW Ste 710, Washington, DC 20036-2217; Title Tel # (202) 232-2252 Title Fax # (202) 232-2617
Personnel: Publisher-Tina Hobson, Circ. Mgr.-Ric Barrick
Editorial Description: Promotes succeful environmental programs of all types across the nation.
General Info: (Formerly Renew America Report; Sun Times), Yr. Est. 1978, Quarterly, Trim Size-8½ x 11, Desktop press, 16 pages, ISSN: 0278-582X, 2 Color, Newsprint
Subscriptions: $2/copy
Acquistions: Publication Bought
Circulation: Total-15,000
Advertising: Inquire for rates.
List Rental: Actives: 7,500
Printing Co: Discount Newsletter Printing, 1487 Persisterce Dr., PO Box 1487, Woodbridge, VA 22193-0487 Tel # (703) 690-1788, Fax # (703) 491-2563

Exploratory Research Letter
See: POWER & POWER PLANTS

FERC Daily Release Service
Business

Publishing Co: CCH Washington Service Bureau, Inc., 655 15th St NW Ste 275, Washington, DC 20005-5701 Tel # (202) 508-0600 Fax # (202) 508-0694
Personnel: Editor-Michelle George, Circ. Mgr.-Trent Seibert
Editorial Description: Daily release service of the opinions, notices, and agendas issued by the Federal Energy Regulatory Commission.
General Info: Yr. Est. 1981, Daily, Looseleaf

FERC Practice & Procedure
Manual
Business

Publishing Co: Thompson Publishing Group, 1725 K Street, NW, Washington, DC 20006; Title Tel # (202) 872-4000
Personnel: Publisher-Richard Thompson, Editor-William Mogel, Circ. Mgr.-Dale Miller, Production Mgr.-Martha Dahlman, Promotion Dir.-Lucy Caldwell-Stair
Editorial Description: Designed for natural gas lawyers, energy consultants, and others who practice before the Commission. Subscription includes monthly replacement pages.
General Info: Annually, Sheetfed press, Newsprint, Looseleaf
Subscriptions: Indv. $947

Federal Energy Regulatory
Commission Reports
Business

Publishing Co: CCH, Inc., 2700 Lake Cook Rd., Riverwoods, IL 60015 Parent Co.-Kluwer Law & Taxation Publishers, Cambridge; Title Tel # (847) 267-7000 Title Fax # (800) 224-8299
Editorial Description: Spans law, proposed and final regulations and preambles, delegation orders and notices and orders and decisions of the Commission.
General Info: Yr. Est. 1979, Irregular, Trim Size-6 x 9, Web press, 50 pages, Color, Looseleaf
Subscriptions: Indv. $1,247

Field Reports
See: BUSINESS & INDUSTRY

Foster Natural Gas Report
See: PETROLEUM & NATURAL GAS

Fusion Power Report
Business

Publishing Co: Business Publishers, Inc., 951 Pershing Dr., Silver Spring, MD 20910-4464 Tel # (301) 589-5103 Fax # (301) 589-8493; Title Tel # (301) 587-6300 Title Fax # (301) 587-1081
Personnel: Publisher-Leonard A. Eiserer, Editor-Thecla Fabian, Circ. Mgr.-Brenda Davenport, Mktg. Mgr.-Keith Payne
Editorial Description: New technology and funding for fusion power research and applications worldwide.
General Info: Yr. Est. 1980, Monthly, Trim Size-8½ x 11, Desktop press, 8 pages, ISSN: 0276-2919, Ind/Abs/Online: Information Access Company, No Color, Recycled
Subscriptions: Indv. $749, Can. $749, For. $755
Advertising: Accepts Inserts.
List Rental: List Management Co.: BPI Direct, 951 Pershing Dr., Silver Spring, MD 20910-4464 Tel # (301) 585-5976, Fax # (301) 587-4530

GRID

Publishing Co: Gas Research Institute, 8600 W. Bryn Mawr, Chicago, IL 60631-3562; Title Tel # (312) 399-8100
Personnel: Editor-C. Drugan, Circ. Mgr.-C. Holmes, Art Dir.-G. Allen
Editorial Description: Reports on gas energy research & development sponsored by the Institute.
General Info: (Formerly Gas Research Institute Digest), Yr. Est. 1978, Quarterly, Trim Size-8½ x 11, Sheetfed press, 48 pages, 4 Color, Coated
Acquistions: Publication Bought
Circulation: (100% controlled), Total-14,000

Gas Daily
Business

Publishing Co: Pasha Publications, Inc, 1616 N. Fort Myer Dr., #1000, Arlington, VA 22209-3103 Fax # (703) 528-4926; Title Tel # (703) 528-1244 Title Fax # (703) 528-1253
Personnel: Publisher-Tom Sedgwick, Grp. Pub.-Joan Henderson, Editor-Robert Barton, Circ. Mgr.-Kathy Thorne, Production-Eva Absher, Mktg. Coord.-Delores Baisden
Editorial Description: Daily news and prices in the natural gas industry.
General Info: Yr. Est. 1985, Daily, 6 pages, ISSN: 0885-5935
Subscriptions: Indv. $1,095, For. $1,183, $21/copy

Gas Energy Review
Business, Association

Publishing Co: American Gas Association, 1515 Wilson Blvd., Arlington, VA 22209-2469 Tel # (703) 841-8400 Fax # (703) 841-8406; Title Tel # (703) 841-8496
Personnel: Editor-Bryan White
Editorial Description: Analyzes issues of importance to the natural gas industry.
General Info: (Formerly Gas Supply Review), Yr. Est. 1972, Monthly, Desktop press, 20 pages, No Color
Subscriptions: Indv. $60, For. $100
Circulation: Total-1,000

Gas Markets Week
See: PETROLEUM & NATURAL GAS

Gas Transactions Report
See: PETROLEUM & NATURAL GAS

Gas Transportation Report
See: PETROLEUM & NATURAL GAS

Gas Turbine forecast
Business

Publishing Co: Forecast International/DMS, Inc., 22 Commerce Rd., Newtown, CT 06470-1643 Fax # (203) 426-1964; Title Tel # (203) 426-0800 Title Fax # (203) 426-4262
General Info: Monthly, Looseleaf
Subscriptions: Indv. $1,395

Gas Utilities Industry - Worldwide
See: PUBLIC UTILITIES

Geyser Geothermal
Energy Newsletter

Publishing Co: Geyser, Inc., The, PO Box 1738, Santa Monica, CA 90406-1738; Title Tel # (213) 395-1856
Personnel: Editor-Steve Moore, Circ. Mgr.-Jackson Amason, Publisher, Adv. Dir.-James Miner, Art Dir.-Dennis Gerondale
Editorial Description: International geothermal and energy information -- Federal land lease announcements.
General Info: Yr. Est. 1974, 18x/yr., Trim Size-8½ x 11, Offset press, 4 pages, Color
Subscriptions: Indv. $195, $11/copy
Advertising: Inquire for rates.

Gulf of Mexico Newsletter
Business

Publishing Co: Offshore Data Services, Inc., PO Box 19909, Houston, TX 77224-1909; Title Tel # (713) 781-2713 Title Fax # (713) 781-9594
Personnel: Publisher-Loran Sheffer, Editor-Blake Wright, Circ. Mgr.-Linda Parreno, Production Mgr.-Charles Meadows, Promotion Dir.-Marie Sheffer
Editorial Description: Covers oil & gas exploration and field development in the Gulf of Mexico.
General Info: Yr. Est. 1986, Weekly, Trim Size-8½ x 11, Offset press, 6 pages, ISSN: 1058-5885, No Color, Matte
Subscriptions: Indv. $115, Can. $115, For. $115, $5/copy
Acquistions: Publication Bought
Advertising: Accepts Inserts.
List Rental: Actives: $75/M
Printing Co: Offshore Data Services, Inc., PO Box 19909, Houston, TX 77224-1909 Tel # (713) 781-7213, Fax # (713) 781-9594

Hanford News

Publishing Co: U.S. Energy Research, Rockwell Intl., Atomics Intl., Richland, WA 99352 Tel # (509) 376-7411

Hanford Update Newsletter
See: WATER SUPPLY, POWER & WASTE

Hart's Pipeline Digest Update Newsletter
See: PETROLEUM & NATURAL GAS

Hawaii Health Planning
News
Association

Publishing Co: Hawaii State Health Planning, 335 Merchant St Ste 214e, Honolulu, HI 96813-2921; Title Tel # (808) 548-4050
Personnel: Editor-Kinau Boyd Kamalii
General Info: Yr. Est. 1975, Bi-monthly, Mimeo press, 2 pages, 2 Color
Circulation: Total-600

Houston Petroleum Industry
See: PETROLEUM & NATURAL GAS

Huttlinger's Energy
Reports

Publishing Co: Huttlinger's Energy Reports, PO Box 409, Poolesville, MD 20837-0409; Title Tel # (301) 972-8100
Personnel: Publisher, Editor-Stan Janet
Editorial Description: Covers energy industry with U.S. & Worldwide plus energy technology & markets.
General Info: (Formerly Intl. Energy Markets), Yr. Est. 1980, Weekly, Trim Size-8½ x 11, Mimeo press, 8 pages, 2 Color
Subscriptions: Indv. $298
Acquistions: Publication Bought
List Rental: Rents Lists

Huttlinger's Natural Gas
Bulletin

Publishing Co: Huttlinger's Energy Reports, PO Box 409, Poolesville, MD 20837-0409; Title Tel # (301) 972-8100
Personnel: Publisher, Editor-Stan Janet
Editorial Description: Covers U.S. natural gas & oil industries.
General Info: Yr. Est. 1980, Weekly, Mimeo press, 8 pages, 2 Color
Subscriptions: Indv. $360
Acquistions: Publication Bought
List Rental: Rents Lists

Huttlinger's Pipeline
Report

Publishing Co: Huttlinger's Energy Reports, PO Box 409, Poolesville, MD 20837-0409; Title Tel # (301) 972-8100
Personnel: Publisher, Editor-Stan Janet
Editorial Description: Covers U.S. natural gas and oil pipeline construction industries.
General Info: Yr. Est. 1960, Weekly, Desktop press, 8 pages
Subscriptions: Indv. $360
Acquistions: Publication Bought
List Rental: Rents Lists

Hydrowire
See: POWER & POWER PLANTS

IAEE Newsletter
Association   CPM: $220

Publishing Co: International Association for Energy Economics, 28790 Chagrin Blvd., Ste. 210, Cleveland, OH 44122-4630 Fax # (216) 464-5365; Title Tel # (216) 464-5365 Title Fax # (216) 464-2737
Personnel: Editor, Production Mgr., Adv. Dir.-David Williams
Editorial Description: For those professionally interested in energy economics.
General Info: Yr. Est. 1977, Quarterly, Trim Size-8½ x 11, Offset press, 24 pages, 2 Color, Coated, Saddle-stitched
Subscriptions: Indv. $60, Inst. $1,250, $10/copy
Circulation: (26% controlled), Total-3,400
Advertising: $750.
List Rental: Actives: 3,400
Printing Co: IAEE, 28790 Chagrin Blvd Ste 210, Cleveland, OH 44122-4630 Tel # (216) 464-5365, Fax # (216) 464-2737

IE News: Energy, Environment & Plant Engineering
Association   CPM: $475

Publishing Co: Institute of Industrial Engineers, 25 Technology Park/Atlanta, Norcross, GA 30092-2988 Tel # (770) 449-0461; Title Tel # (404) 449-0460 Title Fax # (770) 263-8532
Personnel: Production Mgr.-Dona Brown
Editorial Description: Newsletter for IIE Energy, Environment & Plant Engineering Division.
General Info: (Formerly IE News: Energy Management), Quarterly, Trim Size-8½ x 11, Sheetfed press, 6 pages, 2 Color, Matte, Saddle-stitched
Circulation: (100% controlled), Total-1,000
Advertising: $475. Accepts Inserts.
List Rental: Rents Lists

I&M Inventories Database License
Business

Publishing Co: Forecast International/DMS, Inc., 22 Commerce Rd., Newtown, CT 06470-1643 Fax # (203) 426-1964; Title Tel # (203) 426-0800 Title Fax # (203) 426-4262
General Info: Quarterly, Looseleaf
Subscriptions: Indv. $4,790

Illinois Energy Newsletter
Consumer

Publishing Co: Energy Resources Center, Univ. of Ill. at Chicago, 1919 W. Taylor Street, Chicago, IL 60612-7246; Title Tel # (312) 248-0912
Personnel: Editor-James Wiet
Editorial Description: Focuses on energy news, programs & research in Illinois.
General Info: Yr. Est. 1974, Bi-monthly
Circulation: Total-5,500

Improved Recovery Week
Business

Publishing Co: Pasha Publications, Inc, 1616 N. Fort Myer Dr., #1000, Arlington, VA 22209-3103 Tel # (703) 528-1244 Fax # (703) 528-4926; Title Tel # (703) 680-0914
Personnel: Publisher-Tod Sedgwick, Editor-F. Jay Schempf, Circ. Mgr.-Kathy Thorne, Mktg. Dir.-Jeff Grizzel
Editorial Description: Enhanced oil recover projects and methods being used. Also includes Advanced Recovery methods such as horizontal drilling.
General Info: (Formerly ERW, Advanced Recovery Week), Yr. Est. 1980, Weekly, Trim Size-8½ x 11, Offset press, 6 pages, ISSN: 1050-1347, Ind/Abs/Online: DIALOG, Mead Data Central, Predicasts, No Color
Subscriptions: Indv. $495, For. $525, $10/copy
Acquistions: Publication Bought, Publication Sold
List Rental: Rents Lists

Independent Liquid Terminals Assn. -Newsletter
See: CHEMISTRY & CHEMICALS

Independent Power Markets Quarterly
Business

Publishing Co: McGraw-Hill, 1221 Ave. of the Americas, 36th Fl., New York, NY 10020-1095 Tel # (212) 512-2000 Fax # (212) 512-6590
Personnel: Editor in Chief-Richard Schwartz
Editorial Description: Updates project development activities, solicitations, regulations, and utility avoided-cost rates in all 50 states in the US and 10 provinces in Canada.
General Info: Quarterly
Subscriptions: Indv. $675

Independent Power Report
See: LAW

Industrial Energy Bulletin
Business

Publishing Co: McGraw-Hill, 1221 Ave. of the Americas, 36th Fl., New York, NY 10020-1095 Tel # (212) 512-2000 Fax # (212) 512-6590; Title Tel # (212) 512-2036
Editorial Description: News and developments in industrial energy.
General Info: Ind/Abs/Online: Dow Jones, DIALOG, NewsNet, Nexis
Subscriptions: Indv. $485

Inside CAODC
See: PETROLEUM & NATURAL GAS

Inside Energy/with Federal Lands
Business, Association

Publishing Co: McGraw-Hill, 1221 Ave. of the Americas, 36th Fl., New York, NY 10020-1095 Tel # (212) 512-2000 Fax # (212) 512-6590; Title Tel # (212) 512-6410
Personnel: Publisher-John Slater, Editor in Chief-William Loveless, Circ. Mgr.-Georgia Safos, Promotion Dir.-Suzanne Godman
Editorial Description: Focuses on those areas of federal government where energy policy is made.
General Info: (Formerly Inside DOE), Yr. Est. 1978, Weekly, ISSN: 0278-2227, Ind/Abs/Online: Dow Jones, DIALOG, NewsNet, Nexis
Subscriptions: Indv. $965, Can. $965, For. $990

Inside F.E.R.C.
Consumer

Publishing Co: McGraw-Hill, 1221 Ave. of the Americas, 36th Fl., New York, NY 10020-1095 Tel # (212) 512-2000 Fax # (212) 512-6590; Title Tel # (202) 463-1600
Personnel: Publisher-John Slater, Editor in Chief-Larry Foster, Editor-Christine Vestal, Mng. Editor-Christopher Newkurnet, Circ. Mgr.-Peggy Collins
Editorial Description: In-depth coverage of the Federal Energy Regulatory Commission's activities.
General Info: Yr. Est. 1979, Weekly, Ind/Abs/Online: DIALOG, Dow Jones, NewsNet, Nexis

Inside FERC's Gas Market Report
Consumer

Publishing Co: McGraw-Hill, 1221 Ave. of the Americas, 36th Fl., New York, NY 10020-1095 Tel # (212) 512-2000 Fax # (212) 512-6590
Personnel: Publisher-John Slater, Editor in Chief-Larry Foster, Editor-Stephen Munro, Circ. Mgr.-Peggy Collins, Production Mgr.-Marion Marino
General Info: Yr. Est. 1985, Bi-weekly, Ind/Abs/Online: DIALOG, Dow Jones, NewsNet, Nexis

Integrated Waste Management
Business

Publishing Co: McGraw-Hill, 1221 Ave. of the Americas, 36th Fl., New York, NY 10020-1095 Tel # (212) 512-2000 Fax # (212) 512-6590; Title Tel # (212) 512-6410
Personnel: Editor in Chief-Kevin Hamilton, Sr. Ed.-Steven Lang, Mng. Editor-Alexandra Rudenko
General Info: (Formerly Waste-To-Energy Report), Yr. Est. 1985, Bi-weekly, Trim Size-8½ x 11, 4 pages, Ind/Abs/Online: DIALOG, Dow Jones, NewsNet, Nexis, No Color
Subscriptions: Indv. $745, Can. $745, For. $770

International Energy Business

Publishing Co: Huttlinger's Energy Reports, PO Box 409, Poolesville, MD 20837-0409; Title Tel # (301) 972-8100
Personnel: Publisher, Editor-Stan Janet
Editorial Description: Covers international energy business news.
General Info: Weekly
Subscriptions: Indv. $360
List Rental: Rents Lists

International Fluidized Bed Review
Business, Consumer

Publishing Co: International Fluidized Bed Institute, 4440 Mountain View Ave, Oakland, CA 94605-1210; Title Tel # (515) 472-2561
Personnel: Publisher, Editor-David Turner
Editorial Description: Focuses on fluid bed related topics.
General Info: (Formerly Fluid Bed Review), Yr. Est. 1987, Monthly, Trim Size-8½ x 11, 4 pages, ISSN: 0896-8144
Subscriptions: Indv. $300
Circulation: Readership-60
Advertising: $500. Accepts Inserts.

International Gas Technology Highlights
See: PETROLEUM & NATURAL GAS

International Petroleum Industry
See: PETROLEUM & NATURAL GAS

International Private Power Quarterly
Business

Publishing Co: McGraw-Hill, 1221 Ave. of the Americas, 36th Fl., New York, NY 10020-1095 Tel # (212) 512-2000 Fax # (212) 512-6590
Personnel: Editor in Chief-Richard Schwartz
Editorial Description: A country-by-country review of emerging private power markets in Asia, the Pacific Rim, Latin America, Western & Eastern Europe, and key republics of the former Soviet Union.
General Info: Yr. Est. 1993, Quarterly
Subscriptions: Indv. $845

International Solar Energy Intelligence Report
Business

Publishing Co: Business Publishers, Inc., 951 Pershing Dr., Silver Spring, MD 20910-4464 Tel # (301) 589-5103 Fax # (301) 589-8493; Title Tel # (301) 587-6300 Title Fax # (301) 585-9075
Personnel: Publisher-Leonard A. Eiserer, Editor-Bob Shepard, Mktg. Dir.-Fay S. Gold
Editorial Description: Worldwide news on governmental support & new technology in solar, wind power, hydroelectic, photovoltaic & all other forms of renewable energy.
General Info: Yr. Est. 1975, Bi-weekly, Trim Size-8½ x 11, Desktop press, 10 pages, ISSN: 0148-4095, Ind/Abs/Online: NewsNet, DIALOG, No Color, Recycled
Subscriptions: Indv. $416, Can. $416, For. $429
Advertising: Accepts Inserts.
List Rental: List Management Co.: Manager: Jim Hauschild; BPI Direct, 951 Pershing Dr., Silver Spring, MD 20910-4464 Tel # (301) 585-5976, Fax # (301) 587-4530

Inventors News
See: SCIENCE

Israeli Investor Network   *Business, Association*

Publishing Co: Energy Investment Research, Inc., Box 73, Glenville Sta., Greenwich, CT 06831-0773; Title Tel # (914) 937-6939
Personnel: Editor-M. Enowitz
Editorial Description: Devoted to Israeli Business.
General Info: (Formerly Envest), Yr. Est. 1994, 12x/yr.
Subscriptions: Indv. $118

Japan Energy Scan

Publishing Co: Kyodo News Intl., 50 Rockefeller Plaza #803, New York, NY 10020-1605; Title Tel # (212) 397-3723 Title Fax # (212) 397-3721
Editorial Description: Discussing Japan's energy scene.
General Info: Yr. Est. 1988, Weekly

Land Rig Newsletter, The
See: PETROLEUM & NATURAL GAS

Laser Report   *Business*

Publishing Co: PennWell Publishing Company, Ten Tara Blvd., 5th Floor, Nashua, NH 03062-2801 Tel # (603) 891-9174 Fax # (603) 891-0574 Parent Co.-PennWell Publishing Co., Tulsa
Personnel: Publisher-Dr. Morris Levitt, Editor-David Kales, Circ. Mgr.-Judith Simers
Editorial Description: A marketing newsletter covering economic and market outlook, companies and personnel change, laser applications, energy production, government contacts. Subscription includes Annual Economic Review and Outlook.
General Info: Yr. Est. 1966, Semi-monthly, Trim Size-8½ x 11, Offset press, 8 pages
Subscriptions: Indv. $360, Can. $360, For. $370, $10/copy
Circulation: Total-400

Lewis Letter on Energy
Communication   *Business*

Publishing Co: Lewis Assocs., Inc., PO Box 567, Housatonic, MA 01236-0567; Title Tel # (413) 274-6100 Title Fax # (413) 528-1753
Personnel: Publisher-John Mooney, Editor, Circ. Mgr.-Eileen Willner
Editorial Description: Advice on communication techniques for professional public utility communicators.
General Info: Yr. Est. 1980, Bi-weekly, Sheetfed press, 4 pages, 2 Color, Newsprint
Subscriptions: Indv. $135, $6/copy
Acquistions: Publication Bought

Lundberg Letter   *Business*

Publishing Co: Tele-Drop Inc., PO Box 3996, North Hollywood, CA 91609-0996; Title Tel # (818) 768-5111 Title Fax # (818) 768-0537
Personnel: Publisher, Editor-Trilby Lundberg
Editorial Description: Vital statistics and analyses of U.S. oil marketing, primary data.
General Info: Yr. Est. 1974, Semi-monthly, Trim Size-8½ x 11, Sheetfed press, 12 pages, No Color
Subscriptions: Indv. $798, Can. $798, For. $798, $50/copy

Mid-Continent States Petroleum Industry
See: PETROLEUM & NATURAL GAS

Midwest Energy Newsletter

Publishing Co: Midwest Universities Energy Consortium, PO Box 5478, Chicago, IL 60680-5478; Title Tel # (312) 996-4490
Personnel: Editor-James Hartnett
General Info: Yr. Est. 1980, Quarterly
Circulation: Total-4,000

NFEC News & Notes

Publishing Co: Natl. Food & Energy Council, Inc., 409 Vandiver W., Ste. 202, Bldg. 4, Columbia, MO 65202-1587; Title Tel # (314) 875-7155
Personnel: Editor-Kenneth McFate
General Info: (Formerly Farm Electrification Council Letter), Yr. Est. 1962, Bi-monthly
Circulation: Total-700

NFPA Reporter

Publishing Co: Natl. Fluid Power Assn., 3333 N Mayfair Rd Ste 311, Milwaukee, WI 53222-3219 Tel # (414) 778-3347; Title Tel # (414) 778-3344 Title Fax # (414) 778-3361
Personnel: Editor-Carrie Tatman Schwartz
Editorial Description: Association news, fluid power industry news.
Subscriptions: Indv. $50

NGI's Daily Gas Price Index
See: PETROLEUM & NATURAL GAS

NGI's Gas Price Index
See: PETROLEUM & NATURAL GAS

NPGA Reports

Publishing Co: Natl. Propane Gas Assn., 1600 Eisenhower Ln, Lisle, IL 60532-2167; Title Tel # (708) 515-0600 Title Fax # (708) 515-8774
Personnel: Editor-James Burnham
Editorial Description: Conveys news about-& of interest to-the LP-Gas Industry.
General Info: (Formerly NLPGA Management News), Yr. Est. 1982, Bi-weekly, Trim Size-8½ x 11, Letrpr. press, 4 pages, No Color, Newsprint
Subscriptions: Indv. $25
Circulation: Total-9,000
Printing Co: Associated Equipment Distributors, 615 W 22nd St, Oak Brook, IL 60521-8807 Tel # (708) 574-0650

NRMA Newsletter

Publishing Co: Nuclear Records Management Assn., 210 5th Ave., New York, NY 10010-2102; Title Tel # (215) 683-9221
Personnel: Editor-Rodd Excelbert
General Info: Yr. Est. 1979, Quarterly
Circulation: Total-375

National Coal Leader   *Business, Association*

Publishing Co: Altizer, Fisher, & Assoc., PO Box 250, Richlands, VA 24641-0250; Title Tel # (703) 963-2779
Personnel: Publisher-Barbara Altizer, Circ. Mgr.-Anne West, Adv. Dir.-Emily Fisher
General Info: Yr. Est. 1966, Monthly, ISSN: 0192-7239, Color
Subscriptions: Indv. $12
Circulation: Total-8,500
Advertising: Inquire for rates.
Printing Co: Richlands News press, PO Box 818, Richlands, VA 24641-0818 Tel # (703) 963-1081

Natural Gas Contracts   *Business*

Publishing Co: Thompson Publishing Group, 1725 K Street, NW, Washington, DC 20006 Tel # (202) 872-4000; Title Tel # (202) 872-1766 Title Fax # (410) 543-2921
Personnel: Publisher-Richard Thompson, Editor-Gary Anderson, Circ. Mgr.-Dale Miller, Production Mgr.-Lisa Anderson, Promotion Dir.-Conrad Heibel
Editorial Description: Sample clauses for various types of natural gas contracts.
General Info: Yr. Est. 1984, Quarterly, Sheetfed press, 115 pages, No Color, Newsprint, Looseleaf
Subscriptions: Indv. $657
Circulation: Total-800

Natural Gas Intelligence
See: PETROLEUM & NATURAL GAS

New Fuels Report

Publishing Co: Inside Washington Publishers, P.O. Box 7167, Ben Franklin Station, Washington, DC 20044 Tel # (703) 512-1800; Title Tel # (703) 892-8500
Editorial Description: Covers the fuel alcohol, alternative fuel and related industries. Features on industry news and trends, new legislation, government policy, conferences, etc.
General Info: Weekly
Subscriptions: Indv. $550
List Rental: Actives: 22,192, $105/M

News from ECNP

Publishing Co: Environmental Coalition on Nuclear Power, 433 Orlando Ave, State College, PA 16803-3477; Title Tel # (814) 237-3900
Personnel: Editor-J.H. Johnsrud
Editorial Description: Current information on nuclear energy, radioactive waste, radiation health effects.
General Info: Yr. Est. 1970
Subscriptions: Indv. $10, Inst. $25

Northeast Power Report   *Business*

Publishing Co: McGraw-Hill, 1221 Ave. of the Americas, 36th Fl., New York, NY 10020-1095 Tel # (212) 512-2000 Fax # (212) 512-6590; Title Tel # (212) 512-2306
Personnel: Publisher-John Slater, Editor in Chief-Daniel Tanz, Mng. Editor-Ray Pospisil
General Info: Bi-weekly, Ind/Abs/Online: Dialog, Dow Jones, NewsNet

Northeast States Petroleum Industry
See: PETROLEUM & NATURAL GAS

Northwest Energy News

Publishing Co: Northwest Power Planning Council, 851 SW 6th Ave Ste 1100, Portland, OR 97204-1348; Title Tel # (503) 222-5161
Personnel: Editor-Carlotta Collette, Art Dir.-Stephen Sasser
General Info: Yr. Est. 1982, Bi-monthly, Trim Size-8½ x 11, 32 pages, 2 Color, Recycled

Nuclear Fuel
See: NUCLEAR ENERGY

Nuclear Remediation Week
See: NUCLEAR ENERGY

Octane Week
See: PETROLEUM & NATURAL GAS

Offshore Field Development International
Business

Publishing Co: Offshore Data Services, Inc., PO Box 19909, Houston, TX 77224-1909; Title Tel # (713) 781-2713 Title Fax # (713) 781-9594
Personnel: Publisher-Loran Sheffer, Editor-Anthony Guegel, Circ. Mgr.-Linda Parreno, Promotion Dir.-Marie Sheffer
Editorial Description: Worldwide listing of each platform, pipeline, subsea completion, and mooring terminal under construction and planned with specifications and contract information.
General Info: (Formerly Ocean Construction Locator), Yr. Est. 1979, Monthly, Trim Size-8½ x 11, Offset press, 250 pages, ISSN: 1058-5869, No Color, Matte, Saddle-stitched, Looseleaf
Subscriptions: Indv. $795, Can. $795, For. $870, $200/copy
Acquistions: Publication Bought
Circulation: Total-700
Advertising: Accepts Inserts.
List Rental: Actives: $75/M
Printing Co: Offshore Data Services, Inc., PO Box 19909, Houston, TX 77224-1909 Tel # (713) 781-7213, Fax # (713) 781-9594

Offshore International Newsletter
See: PETROLEUM & NATURAL GAS

Offshore Rig Locator International
Business   **CPM: $474**

Publishing Co: Offshore Data Services, Inc., PO Box 19909, Houston, TX 77224-1909; Title Tel # (713) 781-2713 Title Fax # (713) 781-9594
Personnel: Publisher-Loran Sheffer, Editor-Terry Childs, Circ. Mgr.-Linda Parreno, Promotion Dir.-Marie Sheffer
Editorial Description: World wide report listing all offshore rigs working and under construction, the tupe of well they are drilling, where, for whom and future contract status of rig.
General Info: Yr. Est. 1974, Monthly, Trim Size-8½ x 11, Offset press, 150 pages, ISSN: 0733-0928, No Color, Matte, Saddle-stitched, Looseleaf
Subscriptions: Indv. $545, Can. $545, For. $585, $60/copy
Acquistions: Publication Bought
Circulation: Total-980
Advertising: $465. Accepts Inserts.
List Rental: Actives: $75/M
Printing Co: Offshore Data Services, Inc., PO Box 19909, Houston, TX 77224-1909 Tel # (713) 781-7213, Fax # (713) 781-9594

Offshore Rig Newsletter
Business

Publishing Co: Offshore Data Services, Inc., PO Box 19909, Houston, TX 77224-1909; Title Tel # (713) 781-2713 Title Fax # (713) 781-9594
Personnel: Publisher-Loran Sheffer, Editor-Tom Marsh, Circ. Mgr.-Linda Parreno, Promotion Dir.-Marie Sheffer
Editorial Description: Rig utilization, day rates, new rig construction, cost trends, industry growth, labor problems, accidents, new drilling contracts, drilling trends, financing trends.
General Info: Yr. Est. 1974, Monthly, Trim Size-8½ x 11, Offset press, 12 pages, ISSN: 0147-1481, No Color, Matte
Subscriptions: Indv. $220, Can. $220, For. $235, $25/copy
Acquistions: Publication Bought, Publication Sold
Circulation: Total-750
Advertising: Accepts Inserts.
List Rental: Actives: $75/M
Printing Co: Offshore Data Services, Inc., PO Box 19909, Houston, TX 77224-1909 Tel # (713) 781-7213, Fax # (713) 781-9594

Oil Spill Intelligence Report
See: ENVIRONMENT & ECOLOGY

Oil/Energy Statistics Bulletin
See: PETROLEUM & NATURAL GAS

Oliphant Washington Svc.
See: PETROLEUM & NATURAL GAS

On the Watch
Association

Publishing Co: New England Coalition on Nuclear Pollution, Inc., 67 Main St. , Box 545, Brattleboro, VT 05302; Title Tel # (802) 257-0336
Personnel: Editor-David Pyles, Circ. Mgr., Adv. Dir.-Annette Larson
Editorial Description: NECNP's activities, nuclear power, alternative energy resources, radioactive waste pollution.
General Info: (Formerly NECNP Newsletter), Yr. Est. 1971, Irregular, Trim Size-8½ x 11, Desktop press, 16 pages, ISSN: 0738-9477, No Color, Saddle-stitched
Subscriptions: Indv. $25, Free With Membership
Circulation: Total-1,200
Advertising: Inquire for rates.

Oxy-Fuel News
See: PETROLEUM & NATURAL GAS

PV News
Business, Association

Publishing Co: PV Energy Systems, Inc., PO Box 290, Casanova, VA 22017-0290; Title Tel # (703) 788-9626 Title Fax # (703) 788-9626
Personnel: Publisher, Editor-Paul Maycock
Editorial Description: Covers international photovoltaic technology, products, people, markets, meetings, reports, economics & analysis.
General Info: Yr. Est. 1981, Monthly, Trim Size-8½ x 11, Sheetfed press, 8 pages, ISSN: 0739-4829, No Color, Newsprint
Subscriptions: Indv. $100, Can. $100, For. $120, $5/copy
Circulation: Total-1,000
Printing Co: Betty's Printing & Stationary, 7805 Schelhorn Rd, Alexandria, VA 22306-2825 Tel # (703) 765-7276

Permian Basin Petroleum Industry
See: PETROLEUM & NATURAL GAS

Petrochemical Industry - Worldwide
See: PETROLEUM & NATURAL GAS

Pipeline - Worldwide
See: PETROLEUM & NATURAL GAS

Platt's Energy Litigation Report
Business

Publishing Co: McGraw-Hill, 1221 Ave. of the Americas, 36th Fl., New York, NY 10020-1095 Tel # (212) 512-2000 Fax # (212) 512-6590; Title Tel # (202) 463-1676
Personnel: Editor-Joseph Link
General Info: Semi-weekly, 4 pages, ISSN: 0278-226X

Platt's Oil Export/Import Report
See: PETROLEUM & NATURAL GAS

Power Source, The
See: POWER & POWER PLANTS

Prospect Review
Business

Publishing Co: Hart Publications, 7811 Montrose Rd., Potomac, MD 20854 Tel # (301) 340-2100 Parent Co.-Phillips Business Information, Inc., Potomac
Editorial Description: Covers drilling opportunities worldwide.
General Info: Yr. Est. 1993, Bi-weekly
Subscriptions: Indv. $395

Quad Report, The
Business, Consumer

Publishing Co: Consumer Energy Council of America Research Foundation, 2000 L St., NW, Ste. 802, Washington, DC 20036-4907; Title Tel # (202) 659-0404 Title Fax # (202) 659-0407
Personnel: Publisher-Ellen Berman, Assoc. Publ.-Agatha Aurbach, Assoc. Publ.-John McCaughey, Exec. Ed.-Kennedy Maize, Circ. Mgr.-Joan Von Drehle
Editorial Description: Covers issues and events on the general topic of energy efficiency and the relationship of energy efficiency to the environment. Also covers energy policy and demand-side management.
General Info: Yr. Est. 1992, Monthly, Trim Size-8½ x 11, Web press, 8 pages, ISSN: 1072-3179, 2 Color, Matte
Subscriptions: Indv. $495, Inst. $495, Can. $495, For. $495, $45/copy
Circulation: Total-20,000
List Rental: Rents Lists
Printing Co: District Lithograph Co., Inc., 4000 Penn Belt Pl, Forestville, MD 20747-4736 Tel # (301) 736-4444

Quad Special Reports, The
Consumer

Publishing Co: Consumer Energy Council of America Research Foundation, 2000 L St., NW, Ste. 802, Washington, DC 20036-4907; Title Tel # (202) 659-0404 Title Fax # (202) 659-0407
Personnel: Publisher-Ellen Berman, Assoc. Publ.-Agatha Aurbach, Assoc. Publ.-John McCaughey, Editor-Kennedy Maize, Circ. Mgr.-Joan Von Drehle
Editorial Description: Unique studies on specific energy related topics, such as demand-side management, energy efficiency programs, etc.
General Info: Yr. Est. 1992, Quarterly, Trim Size-8½ x 11, 12 pages, ISSN: 1072-3137, 2 Color, Matte
Subscriptions: Indv. $195, Inst. $195, Can. $195, For. $195
Circulation: Total-20,000
List Rental: Rents Lists
Printing Co: District Lithograph Co., Inc., 4000 Penn Belt Pl, Forestville, MD 20747-4736 Tel # (301) 736-4444

RE News Digest
Business, Consumer

Publishing Co: Sun Words, 332 Furman St., Schenectady, NY 12304-1118; Title Tel # (518) 372-1799
Personnel: Publisher, Editor-Sandra Oddo
Editorial Description: Renewable energy news summarized, intended for renewable energy professionals & people with a strong interest in the area.
General Info: Yr. Est. 1986, Monthly, Sheetfed press, 8 pages, ISSN: 0895-5700, Newsprint
Subscriptions: Indv. $60, Can. $70, For. $80, $5/copy

Radiological Inspection Reports
See: NUCLEAR ENERGY

Refining & Gas Processing Worldwide
See: PETROLEUM & NATURAL GAS

The Regulatory Times   *Business*

Publishing Co: Southam Information & Technology Group, 999 8th St. SW, #300, Calgary, AB T2R 1N7 Canada; Title Tel # (403) 244-6111 Title Fax # (403) 245-8666
Personnel: Publisher-Rick Charland, Editor-Darlene West, Sales-Dan Cole
Editorial Description: Covers energy regulation in Canada wwith a focus on oil and gas pipeline developments, rate hearings, gas 7 electric utility regulation, Canadian regulatory policy. Also covers the National Energy Board and provincial public utility board hearings.
General Info: (Formerly Nickle's Regulatory Times), Yr. Est. 1992, Bi-weekly
Subscriptions: Can. $547

Saving Energy   *Business*

Publishing Co: Saving Energy, 5411 117th Ave SE, Bellevue, WA 98006-3324; Title Tel # (206) 643-4248
Personnel: Publisher, Editor-Larry Liebman, Circ. Mgr.-Melissa Kranor, Adv. Dir., Mktg. Dir., Promotion Dir.-Jean Liebman
Editorial Description: Energy conservation ideas for business & industry.
General Info: Yr. Est. 1977, Monthly, Web press, 8 pages, ISSN: 0279-2338, No Color
Subscriptions: Indv. $75, $5/copy
Acquistions: Publication Bought
Advertising: Accepts Inserts.
List Rental: Actives: 4,000

Science for Democratic Action
See: POLITICS

Solar Collector

Publishing Co: Florida Solar Energy Ctr., 1679 Clearlake Rd., Cocoa, FL 32922-5703; Title Tel # (407) 783-0300 Title Fax # (407) 783-2571
Personnel: Art Dir.-Terri Grossman
Editorial Description: For distribution to persons with a special interest in solar energy utilization.
General Info: 4 pages, 2 Color
Circulation: Total-10,000

Southeast Power Report   *Business*

Publishing Co: McGraw-Hill, 1221 Ave. of the Americas, 36th Fl., New York, NY 10020-1095 Tel # (212) 512-2000 Fax # (212) 512-6590; Title Tel # (212) 512-6410 Title Fax # (212) 512-2723
Personnel: Editor in Chief-Richard Schwartz
Editorial Description: Covers new independent and utility power projects, demand-side management, facility siting, fuel supply issues, and more.
General Info: Yr. Est. 1992, Bi-weekly, Ind/Abs/Online: Dialog, Dow Jones, NewsNet
Subscriptions: Indv. $695, Can. $695, For. $745

Southeast States Petroleum Industry
See: PETROLEUM & NATURAL GAS

Statistical Handbook for
Canada's   *Business, Association*

Publishing Co: Canadian Assn. of Petroleum Producers, 2100-350 Seventh Ave., SW, Calgary, AB T2P 3N9 Canada Tel # (403) 267-1100; Title Fax # (403) 261-4622
Editorial Description: Annual oil & gas statistics.
General Info: (Formerly CPA Statistical Handbook), Yr. Est. 1955, Annually, ISSN: 0068-9432, Looseleaf
Subscriptions: Can. $100, $70/copy
Circulation: Total-900

Switch Mode Power Conversion SMP/FAX Report
See: POWER & POWER PLANTS

Technologies for Energy Management
See: POWER & POWER PLANTS

Texas Energy

Publishing Co: Texas A&M Univ., Ctr. for Energy & Mineral Resources, College Station, TX 77843-1243 Tel # (409) 845-8025
Personnel: Editor-MaryAnn Williams
Editorial Description: Provides news of energy issues in Texas tips on energy conservation & information on energy resources.
General Info: (Formerly Texas Energy & Mineral Resources), Yr. Est. 1974, Bi-monthly, Trim Size-8½ x 11, Web press, 8 pages, 2 Color, Coated, Saddle-stitched
Circulation: Total-7,800

Texas Energy Reporter

Publishing Co: Texas Energy Research Assoc., 5926 Balcones Dr Ste 220, Austin, TX 78731-4263; Title Tel # (512) 452-9872 Title Fax # (512) 452-9007
Personnel: Publisher, Editor-Edward Selig, Circ. Mgr.-Janice Bennett, Art Dir.-David Timmons
Editorial Description: Quarterly review of Texas energy arena.
General Info: Yr. Est. 1983, Quarterly, Sheetfed press, 8 pages, ISSN: 0739-8050, Ind/Abs/Online: ENG. ABS. /POL. ANAL, 2 Color, Saddle-stitched
Subscriptions: Indv. $85, $7/copy
Acquistions: Publication Bought
Printing Co: Am. Printers Exchange, 515 W 15th St Ste 103, Austin, TX 78701-1511 Tel # (512) 452-5058

Texas Petroleum Industry
See: PETROLEUM & NATURAL GAS

Tiger on Spreads
See: INVESTMENT

U.S. Lease Price Report

Publishing Co: Lierle Public Relations, PO Box 440745, Aurora, CO 80044-0745; Title Tel # (303) 792-0507
Personnel: Publisher, Editor, Circ. Mgr.-Doug Lierle, Production Mgr.-Andy Anderson
Editorial Description: Covers oil & gas leases, prices, rental & royalty ranges in Continental U.S.
General Info: Yr. Est. 1980, Monthly, Letrpr. press, 30 pages, No Color, Newsprint
Subscriptions: Indv. $250, $25/copy
Circulation: Total-600
Printing Co: Tudor House Press, 2505 W 2nd Ave, Denver, CO 80219-1600 Tel # (303) 937-9030

Utility Reporter-Fuels,
Energy & Power   *Business*

Publishing Co: Infoteam, Inc., PO Box 15640, Plantation, FL 33318-5640 Fax # (954) 472-0544; Title Tel # (954) 473-9560 Title Fax # (954) 473-0544
Personnel: Publisher, Editor-Merton Allen
Editorial Description: Covers energy, utilities, systems, products, R&D, power plants, engines, devices, regulatory, nuclear, coal, oil, gas, solar, wind, etc.
General Info: Yr. Est. 1984, Monthly, Trim Size-8½ x 11, Sheetfed press, 18 pages, ISSN: 0890-2984, Ind/Abs/Online: Data-star, DIALOG, NewsNet, Predicasts, No Color, Newsprint
Subscriptions: Indv. $269, Can. $309, For. $379, $25/copy

WSEO Dispatch   *Association*

Publishing Co: Washington State Energy Office, 809 Legion Way, SE, Olympia, WA 98504-0001; Title Tel # (206) 956-2039
Personnel: Editor-Jim Erickson
Editorial Description: Energy-related issues, programs & technologies that are of interest primarily to Washington State & Northwest region.
General Info: 5x/yr., 12 pages, No Color
Subscriptions: Free
Circulation: Total-5,300

Waste Recovery Report
See: ENVIRONMENT & ECOLOGY

Weekly Propane Newsletter   *Business*

Publishing Co: Butane-Propane News, Inc., 338 E Foothill Blvd # 660698, Arcadia, CA 91006-2542; Title Tel # (818) 357-2168 Title Fax # (818) 303-2854
Personnel: Publisher-Natalie Peal, Editor-Lon Richardson, Circ. Mgr.-Charlene Lyman
General Info: Yr. Est. 1971, Weekly
Subscriptions: Indv. $150

Western States Petroleum Industry
See: PETROLEUM & NATURAL GAS

Whisper in the Woods
See: ENVIRONMENT & ECOLOGY

Wind Energy Weekly

Publishing Co: American Wind Energy Assn., 122 C St. NW, Washington, DC 20001 Tel # (202) 383-2500; Title Tel # (202) 408-8988 Title Fax # (202) 408-8536
Personnel: Editor-Tom Gray
Editorial Description: News and developments in the wind energy field.
General Info: 48x/yr.
Subscriptions: Indv. $225

Windletter   *Association*

Publishing Co: American Wind Energy Assn., 122 C St. NW, Washington, DC 20001 Tel # (202) 383-2500; Title Tel # (703) 276-8334
Personnel: Editor-Thomas Gray
Editorial Description: To further the art and science of using the wind's energy for human purposes.
General Info: Yr. Est. 1974, 8x/yr., Offset press, 4 pages, ISSN: 0270-3394, Color, Newsprint
Subscriptions: Indv. $35
Circulation: Total-800

Windmillers' Gazette
See: AGRICULTURE

Wisconsin Energy News   *Business, Association*

Publishing Co: Wisconsin Energy Bureau, PO Box 7868, Madison, WI 53707-7868; Title Tel # (608) 266-8871 Title Fax # (608) 267-6931
Personnel: Editor-Barbara Samuel
Editorial Description: The newsletter is designed to inform readers about programs, policies, and research in energy conservation, renewable energy technology and other resources in Wisconsin and the upper Midwest.
General Info: (Formerly Energy Program News), Yr. Est. 1977, Bi-monthly, Trim Size-8½ x 11, Offset press, 8 pages, Color, Recycled
Subscriptions: Free
Circulation: Total-6,500

Wisconsin Environmental Law and Regulation Report
See: ENVIRONMENT & ECOLOGY

World Diesel & Off-Highway News
See: TRAFFIC & TRANSPORTATION

Wyoming Geological Association Oil & Gas Fields Guide Book/ Symposium
Business, Association

Publishing Co: Wyoming Geological Association, PO Box 545, Casper, WY 82602-0545; Title Tel # (307) 237-0027
Editorial Description: Contains technical reports describing oil & gas fields in selected areas of Wyoming.
General Info: Yr. Est. 1943, Annually, Letrpr. press, Coated, Looseleaf
Circulation: Total-1,000
Advertising: Inquire for rates.
Printing Co: Mountain States Litho, 133 S Mckinley St, Casper, WY 82602 Tel # (307) 234-9325

ENGINEERING

A-E-C Automation Newsletter
See: COMPUTERS & AUTOMATION

AABC Newsletter
Business, Association

Publishing Co: Associated Air Balance Council, 1518 K St NW Ste 503, Washington, DC 20005-1203; Title Tel # (202) 737-0202
Editorial Description: To provide council news, technical information & news affecting test & balance engineers.
General Info: Yr. Est. 1964, Monthly, Trim Size-8½ x 11, Mimeo press, 4 pages, 2 Color

AACC Newsletter
Association

Publishing Co: AACC Secretariat, Northwestern Univ., Dept. EES, 2145 Sheridan Rd., Evanston, IL 60208-0001; Title Tel # (708) 491-3641 Title Fax # (708) 491-4455
Personnel: Editor-Bonnie Heck
Editorial Description: News on meetings of American Automatic Control Council.
General Info: Yr. Est. 1982, Semi-annually, Trim Size-8½ x 11, Letrpr. press, 4 pages, No Color, Matte
Circulation: Total-2,500
List Rental: Actives: $200/M

A.E. Legal Newsletter
See: LAW

AIPE Newsline
See: MANUFACTURING

AISES Newsletter
See: SCIENCE

ALERTA
See: INTERNATIONAL TRADE

ANSI Reporter/Standards Action
Association

Publishing Co: American Natl. Standards Inst, 11 W 42nd Sreet, 13th Fl., New York, NY 10036-8002; Title Tel # (212) 642-4900 Title Fax # (212) 302-1286
Editorial Description: Reports to members on activities of the American National Standards Institute, the national clearinghouse and coordinating agency for voluntary standardization in the United States.
General Info: Yr. Est. 1918, Monthly, Trim Size-8½ x 11, Sheetfed press, 20 pages, ISSN: 0038-9633, No Color, Newsprint
Subscriptions: Indv. $200
Circulation: Total-7,500

Alternative Energy Trends & Forecasts
See: ENERGY

American Engineering Model Society Newsletter
Business, Association

Publishing Co: American Engineering Model Soc., 1 Walnut St., Boston, MA 02108-3616; Title Tel # (617) 227-5551
Personnel: Editor-Walter Clothier
General Info: Yr. Est. 1968, Bi-monthly
Circulation: Total-1,000

Application Development Strategies
See: COMPUTERS & AUTOMATION

Association of Polish Engineers in Canada, Bulletin
Association

Publishing Co: Association of Polish Engineers in Canada, 206 Beverley, Toronto, ON Canada; Title Tel # (416) 977-7723
Personnel: Editor-G. Sobocki
General Info: Yr. Est. 1978, Quarterly

BMES Bulletin
Association

Publishing Co: Biomedical Engineering Soc., PO Box 2399, Culver City, CA 90231-2399; Title Tel # (310) 618-9322
Personnel: Editor-Jerry Collins, Production Mgr.-Rita Schaffer
Editorial Description: Contains bioengineering science articles, public affairs announcements, employment opportunities, calendar of events, conference announcements, editorials & letters.
General Info: Yr. Est. 1968, Quarterly, Offset press, 16 pages, No Color, Saddle-stitched
Subscriptions: Indv. $25, Free With Membership
Circulation: Total-2,000
List Rental: Actives: $175/M

Backsights

Publishing Co: Surveyors Historical Society, 31457 Hugh Way, Hayward, CA 94544-7741; Title Tel # (415) 471-3905
General Info: Semi-annually, Web press
Circulation: Total-2,000

Bechtel Briefs
Business

Publishing Co: Bechtel Corp., 50 Beale St, San Francisco, CA 94105-1895; Title Tel # (415) 768-7904
Personnel: Editor-Jeff Berger, Circ. Mgr.-Barbara Pohan
General Info: Quarterly, Trim Size-8¼ x 11, Offset press, 32 pages, 4 Color, Coated, Saddle-stitched

Biomaterials Forum
See: MEDICINE

Bulletin of Tau Beta Pi
Association

Publishing Co: Tau Beta Pi Assn., Inc., Box 8840, Univ. Station, Knoxville, TN 37996-0001 Fax # (615) 546-4579; Title Tel # (615) 546-4578
Personnel: Editor-James Froula
Editorial Description: Articles on chapter management, annual convention, and membership election procedures.
General Info: Yr. Est. 1925, Trim Size-8½ x 11, Offset press, 8 pages, ISSN: 8755-5670, 2 Color, Newsprint, Saddle-stitched
Subscriptions: Free
Circulation: (100% controlled), Total-12,000

CESSE Quill

Publishing Co: Sponsor-Cesse, Council of Engineering, C/o AGU, 2000 Florida Ave., NW, Washington, DC 20009; Title Tel # (202) 462-6903
Personnel: Editor-W. Cullison
Editorial Description: For staff professionals of engineering and scientific societies.
General Info: Yr. Est. 1949, Trim Size-8½ x 11, Web press, 8 pages, No Color, Coated
Circulation: (100% controlled), Total-700

Central Hudson Newsletter
See: HOUSE ORGANS

Cercular
See: ENVIRONMENT & ECOLOGY

Cleveland Engineering
Association

Publishing Co: Cleveland Engineering Society, 3100 Chester Ave, Cleveland, OH 44114-4683; Title Tel # (216) 361-3100
Personnel: Editor-Elaine Ryback, Circ. Mgr.-Alva Wood, Circ. Mgr., Adv. Dir., Art Dir.-Elaine Rybak
Editorial Description: Society events and news of interest to members.
General Info: Yr. Est. 1916, Monthly, Trim Size-8½ x 11, Sheetfed press, 8 pages, ISSN: 0009-8809, 2 Color, Newsprint
Subscriptions: Indv. $24, $2/copy
Acquistions: Publication Bought
Circulation: (100% controlled)
Advertising: Inquire for rates.

Clinical Lab Letter
See: MEDICINE

Coal & Synfuels Technology
See: ENERGY

Commentary
Business, Association

Publishing Co: Consulting Engineers of British Columbia, #514, 409 Granville St., Vancouver, BC V6C 1T2 Canada; Title Tel # (604) 687-2811 Title Fax # (604) 688-7110
Personnel: Editor-John Wilkins
Editorial Description: External marketing tool of CEBC to inform about issues pertaining to consulting engineering.
General Info: (Formerly Consulting Engineers of British Columbia Newsletter), Yr. Est. 1975, Quarterly, Offset press, 4 pages, 2 Color, Coated
Subscriptions: Free With Membership
Circulation: Total-2,000
List Rental: Rents Lists

Communique
Association

Publishing Co: Assn. of Consulting Engineers of Canada, 130 Albert Street, Suite 616, Ottawa, ON K1P 5G4 Canada Fax # (613) 236-6193; Title Tel # (613) 236-0569
Personnel: Publisher-Anthony Burges, Editor-J. Daniel Matko
General Info: (Formerly ACEC Information), Yr. Est. 1976, Quarterly, Trim Size-8½ x 11, Offset press, 6 pages, 2 Color
Circulation: Total-1,700
List Rental: Actives: 1,700, $250/M

Composites & Adhesives Newsletter   *Business*

Publishing Co: T/C Press, PO Box 36006, Los Angeles, CA 90036-0006; Title Tel # (213) 938-6923 Title Fax # (213) 938-6923
Personnel: Publisher, Editor-George Epstein, Circ. Mgr.-Irene Stone, Mktg. Dir.-Jerry Hartman
Editorial Description: Composite/adhesives news highlights--materials, processes, NDT, applications, industry; ALERTS. Design/processing hints, special section entitled 'Hot Out of the Autoclave.' Also: Flash reports of special news, sent via fax to participants as part of subscriptions
General Info: Yr. Est. 1984, Quarterly, Trim Size-8½ x 11, Sheetfed press, 20 pages, ISSN: 0888-1227, Ind/Abs/Online: Predicasts, Newsnet, 2 Color, Newsprint, Saddle-stitched
Subscriptions: Indv. $150, Inst. $150, Can. $150, For. $170, $40/copy
Circulation: Total-250, Readership-2,000
Advertising: Accepts Inserts.
Printing Co: MetroPress A-1 Printing (Los Angeles, CA 90036), Los Angeles, CA 90036

Connecticut Engineers   *Association*   CPM: $137

Publishing Co: Connecticut Joint Federation, 2600 Dixwell Ave., Hamden, CT 06514-1833; Title Tel # (203) 281-4322 Title Fax # (203) 248-8932
Personnel: Editor-Paul Brady
Editorial Description: News and legislation concerning professional engineers.
General Info: (Formerly Connecticut Professional Engineer), Monthly, Trim Size-8½ x 11, Sheetfed press, 12 pages, 50% ads, No Color, Coated, Saddle-stitched
Subscriptions: Free With Membership
Circulation: Total-1,200
Advertising: $165.
Printing Co: Ace Printing, 41 Walnut St, Hartford, CT 06120-2842 Tel # (203) 522-2155

Construction Marketing Research
See: CONSTRUCTION & BUILDING

Consultant   *Association*

Publishing Co: Consulting Engineers Council of NJ, 66 Morris Ave., Springfield, NJ 07081-1409; Title Tel # (201) 379-1100 Title Fax # (201) 379-6507
Personnel: Editor-Debra Hart, Circ. Mgr.-Peter Allen
Editorial Description: Association activities and news.
General Info: (Formerly Blueprints), Bi-monthly, Trim Size-8½ x 11, 4 pages
Circulation: (100% controlled), Total-500

Department of Civil and Environmental Engineering Newsletter
See: ENGINEERING, CIVIL

Derivatives Engineering & Technology

Publishing Co: Waters Information Services, PO Box 2248, Binghamton, NY 13902-2248 Tel # (607) 770-4075; Title Tel # (607) 770-8535 Title Fax # (607) 770-9435
General Info: Yr. Est. 1992, Bi-weekly
Subscriptions: Indv. $595

Design Drafting News   *Association*   CPM: $160

Publishing Co: American Design Drafting Association, PO Box 799, Rockville, MD 20848-0799; Title Tel # (301) 460-6875 Title Fax # (301) 460-8591
Personnel: Editor-Rachel Howard
Editorial Description: Membership newsletter of the American Design Drafting Assn.
General Info: Yr. Est. 1959, Monthly, Trim Size-8½ x 11, 8 pages, Newsprint
Subscriptions: Free With Membership
Circulation: Total-2,500
Advertising: $400.

Diamond Industry Week
See: SCIENCE

Dredging Contract News

Publishing Co: Dredging Contract News, PO Box 1487, Fort Collins, CO 80522-1487; Title Tel # (303) 484-9562 Title Fax # (303) 484-5778
Personnel: Publisher-Judith Powers, Editor-Mara Cykoski
Editorial Description: Lists open dredging contracts & bid results. Listing is free for all contract owners.
General Info: Yr. Est. 1984, Bi-weekly, Mimeo press, 6 pages, No Color, Newsprint
Subscriptions: Indv. $125, $5/copy

E-Quad News
See: COLLEGE ALUMNI

ECCOMAS Newsletter
See: SCIENCE

ESE Notes
See: ENVIRONMENT & ECOLOGY

Editor & M & E Appraiser

Publishing Co: American Society of Appraisers, Detroit, 2450 Burns St, Detroit, MI 48214-1802
Personnel: Publisher-Leslie Miles, Jr., Editor-Ralph Alberti, Production Mgr.-Sylvia Olson
Editorial Description: Technical publication devoted to appraisal of machinery & equipment.
General Info: Yr. Est. 1984, Quarterly, Trim Size-8½ x 11, Letrpr. press, 8 pages, 1% ads, Color-cover, Matte, Saddle-stitched
Subscriptions: $15/copy
Circulation: Total-650
Advertising: Inquire for rates.

Electrostatic Precipitator   *Business*

Publishing Co: McIlvaine Co., The, 2970 Maria Ave., Northbrook, IL 60062-2024; Title Tel # (847) 272-0010 Title Fax # (847) 272-9673
Personnel: Publisher-R.W. McIlvaine, Editor-Juanita Brand
Editorial Description: High and low voltage precipitators for all applications. A Knowledge Network that is a complete information system with Manual, Newsletter, Catalog, Fact Finder, and 300 service units.
General Info: Yr. Est. 1976, Monthly
Subscriptions: Indv. $690, Can. $750, For. $750
List Rental: Rents Lists

Engineering Automation Report   *Business*

Publishing Co: Technology Automation Services, PO Box 3593, Englewood, CO 80155-3593; Title Tel # (303) 770-1728 Title Fax # (303) 770-3660
Personnel: Publisher, Editor-David E. Weisberg, Circ. Mgr.-Kim Draper
Editorial Description: In the context of the use of computers in engineering design, reviews the latest advances in computer systems, graphics, & communication technology; provides concise analyses of these developments; keeps track of the key primary vendors in this market; &provides information on how users are implementing new engineering design tools.
General Info: Yr. Est. 1992, Monthly, Trim Size-8½ x 11, Sheetfed press, 16 pages, ISSN: 1065-6952, 2 Color, Coated, Saddle-stitched
Subscriptions: Indv. $235, Inst. $235, Can. $235, For. $285, $20/copy
List Rental: Rents Lists
Printing Co: Business Word, 5350 S. Roslyn Street, Englewood, CO 80111-2125 Tel # (303) 290-8500, Fax # (303) 290-9025

Engineering Forum

Publishing Co: Univ. of Toronto, Faculty of Applied Science, 35 St. George St., Toronto, ON M5S 1A4 Canada
Circulation: Total-22,000

Engineering Information Inc.   *Consumer*

Publishing Co: Engineering Information, Inc., 1 Castle Point Terr, Hoboken, NJ 07030-5996 Tel # (201) 216-8500; Title Tel # (201) 216-8514 Title Fax # (201) 216-8532
Editorial Description: For the scientific information provider, meeting the needs of engineers, scientists and information specialists in diverse settings.
General Info: Quarterly

Engineering Outlook At the University of Illinois At Urbana-Champaign   *Business, Association*

Publishing Co: Univ. of Illinois at Urbana-Champaign, Engineering Pubs. Off, 1308 W. Green St., Urbana, IL 61801-2936; Title Tel # (217) 333-1510 Title Fax # (217) 244-7705
Personnel: Editor-Maureen Tan, Art Dir.-Richard Maul
Editorial Description: Popular coverage of research in the UIUC College of Engineering.
General Info: Yr. Est. 1960, Quarterly, Trim Size-8⅜ x 10⅞, Sheetfed press, 12 pages, ISSN: 0013-8088, 4 Color, Coated
Circulation: Total-25,500
Printing Co: Univ. of Illinois at Urbana-Champaign Printing Division, 542 E. Gregory Dr., Champaign, IL 61820 Tel # (217) 333-0428, Fax # (217) 244-7277

Engineers   *Business*

Publishing Co: American Assn. of Engineering Societies, 1111 19th St. NW, Ste. 608, Washington, DC 20036-3603; Title Tel # (202) 296-2237 Title Fax # (202) 296-1151
Personnel: Editor-Richard Ellis, Circ. Mgr., Adv. Dir.-Gordon Davis
Editorial Description: Reports on selected developments in engineering and technical manpower, for manpower managers in industry, government and education.
General Info: (Formerly Engineers Joint Council/Engineering Manpower Bulletin), Yr. Est. 1965, Trim Size-8½ x 11, Letrpr. press, 5 pages, ISSN: 0013-8037, 2 Color
Subscriptions: Indv. $110, $14/copy
Circulation: Total-800

Engineers-Quarterly bulletin   *Business, Association*

Publishing Co: American Assn. of Engineering Societies, 1111 19th St. NW, Ste. 608, Washington, DC 20036-3603; Title Tel # (202) 296-2237 Title Fax # (202) 296-1151
Personnel: Editor-Richard Ellis, Promotion Dir.-Claire LeBuffe
Editorial Description: A quarterly bulletin on the engineering profession. Detailed, timely articles and data on engineering employment, salaries,enrollment,degrees, women and minorities in engineering, and many other topics.
General Info: (Formerly Enginering Workforce Bulletin), Yr. Est. 1995, Quarterly, Trim Size-8½ x 11, 16 pages, ISSN: 1079-7211, 2 Color
Subscriptions: Indv. $25, For. $35, $5/copy

Exchange

Publishing Co: Consulting Engineers Council of Metropolitan Washington, 8811 Colesville Rd Apt G106, Silver Spring, MD 20910-4343; Title Tel # (301) 588-6616
Personnel: Publisher-Tom Cohn, Editor-John Bachner, Circ. Mgr.-Annie Vasquez, Production Mgr.-J. Lewis, Adv. Dir.-Mary Lou Schenkel
Editorial Description: News of the Council; Information concerning events & developments in the industry.
General Info: Monthly
Subscriptions: Indv. $100
Circulation: Total-300

Export Action   *Business, Association*

Publishing Co: Assn. of Consulting Engineers of Canada, 130 Albert Street, Suite 616, Ottawa, ON K1P 5G4 Canada; Title Tel # (613) 236-0569 Title Fax # (613) 236-6193
Personnel: Publisher-Anthony Burges, Editor-J. Daniel Matko
Editorial Description: Consulting engineering exporters' newsletter.
General Info: Yr. Est. 1990, Quarterly, Trim Size-5½ x 11, Offset press, 6 pages, 2 Color, Saddle-stitched
Subscriptions: Free With Membership
Circulation: Total-700

Facilities Forum
    See: MANUFACTURING

Finishing Line
    See: PAINT

Flying Engineers Newsletter
    See: AERONAUTICS/ASTRONAUTICS

Groundwater Newsletter, The
    See: WATER SUPPLY, POWER & WASTE

Gulf of Mexico Newsletter
    See: ENERGY

H.E.S. Bulletin   *Association*

Publishing Co: Society of Harvard Engineers, Harvard Univ., Rm. G12B, Pierc, Cambridge, MA 02138-3800

Human Factors & Ergonomics Society Bulletin
    See: ENVIRONMENT & ECOLOGY

IACM Bulletin
    See: SCIENCE

IE News: Aerospace & Defense
    See: AERONAUTICS/ASTRONAUTICS

IE News: Energy, Environment & Plant Engineering
    See: ENERGY

IE News: Engineering Economy
    See: ECONOMICS

IE News: Ergonomics   *Association*   CPM: $306

Publishing Co: Institute of Industrial Engineers, 25 Technology Park/Atlanta, Norcross, GA 30092-2988 Tel # (770) 449-0461; Title Tel # (404) 449-0460 Title Fax # (770) 263-8532
Personnel: Production Mgr.-Dona Brown
Editorial Description: Newsletter for IIE Ergonomics Division.
General Info: Quarterly, Trim Size-8½ x 11, Sheetfed press, 4 pages, 2 Color, Matte, Saddle-stitched
Circulation: (100% controlled), Total-1,550
Advertising: $475. Accepts Inserts.
List Rental: Rents Lists

IE News: Facilities Planning & Design
    See: MANUFACTURING

IE News: Financial Services
    See: BANKING & FINANCE

IE News: Industrial & Labor Relations
    See: INDUSTRIAL RELATIONS/PERSONNEL

IE News: Operations
Research   *Association*   CPM: $237

Publishing Co: Institute of Industrial Engineers, 25 Technology Park/Atlanta, Norcross, GA 30092-2988 Tel # (770) 449-0461; Title Tel # (404) 449-0460 Title Fax # (770) 263-8532
Personnel: Production Mgr.-Dona Brown
Editorial Description: Newsletter for IIE Operations Research Division.
General Info: Quarterly, Trim Size-8½ x 11, Sheetfed press, 8 pages, 2 Color, Matte, Saddle-stitched
Circulation: (100% controlled), Total-2,000
Advertising: $475. Accepts Inserts.
List Rental: Rents Lists

IE News: Quality Control and Reliability Engineering
    See: MANUFACTURING

IE News: Utilities
    See: PUBLIC UTILITIES

IE News: Work Measurement & Methods Engineering
    See: MANUFACTURING

IEEE Vehicular Technology Society
News   *Association*   CPM: $84

Publishing Co: Institute of Electrical & Electronics Engineers, Inc., 445 Hoes Lane, PO Box 1331, Piscataway, NJ 08855-1331 Tel # (908) 562-3992 Fax # (908) 981-9334 Parent Co.-Institute of Electrical & Electronics Engineers, New York
Personnel: Editor-Robert McKnight, Production Ed.-Ann Scrupski, Production Mgr.-Robert Smrek, Adv. Mgr.-Susan Schneidermen
Editorial Description: Information on technology in development and use of vehicles of all kinds.
General Info: Yr. Est. 1953, Quarterly, Trim Size-8½ x 11, 36 pages, ISSN: 1068-5731, Color, Saddle-stitched
Subscriptions: Free With Membership
Circulation: Total-4,733
Advertising: $400.
List Rental: Rents Lists

Indicator   *Association*

Publishing Co: Canadian Council of Professional Engineers, 116 Albert Street, Suite 401, Ottawa, ON K1P 5G3 Canada; Title Tel # (613) 232-2474
Personnel: Editor-Alison Baiguee
Editorial Description: Fr & Eng text. Reports on the supply and demand for engineering manpower, including post-secondary enrolements, immigration, etc.
General Info: Yr. Est. 1974, Quarterly, Trim Size-8¼ x 10½, 4 pages, ISSN: 0828-7198, No Color
Subscriptions: Indv. $60, $15/copy
Circulation: Total-800

Indoor Air Bulletin
    See: ENVIRONMENT & ECOLOGY

Info
    See: BIBLIOGRAPHY

Innovator's Digest
    See: MANAGEMENT

Interactions   *Association*

Publishing Co: Society of American Value Engineers, 60 Revere Dr., Northbrook, IL 60062-1563; Title Tel # (708) 480-1730 Title Fax # (708) 480-9282
Personnel: Editor-Jill Hronek, Production Mgr.-Mary Dulabaum
Editorial Description: Monthly newsletter about society.
General Info: Yr. Est. 1959, Monthly, Trim Size-8½ x 11, 8 pages, ISSN: 0195-0193, 4% ads, Newsprint, Saddle-stitched
Circulation: (100% controlled), Total-1,500
Advertising: Inquire for rates.
List Rental: Rents Lists
Printing Co: Bloomington Offset, U.S. 150 and Veterans Parkway, Bloomington, IL 61702

International Contractors, Volume I
    See: AERONAUTICS/ASTRONAUTICS

JETS Report   *Association*

Publishing Co: Junior Engineering Technical Society, 1420 King St Ste 405, Alexandria, VA 22314-2750; Title Tel # (703) 548-5387 Title Fax # (703) 836-4875
Personnel: Editor, Production Mgr.-Cathy McGowan
Editorial Description: Newsletter for high school students. Engineering, career news, activities, guidance information.
General Info: Yr. Est. 1952, Semi-annually, Trim Size-8½ x 11, 12 pages, 2 Color, Coated, Saddle-stitched
Subscriptions: Indv. $4
Circulation: Total-35,000

Jet News
    See: WATER SUPPLY, POWER & WASTE

LSU Engineering News
    See: COLLEGE STUDENT

Last Word   *Business*

Publishing Co: American Consulting Engineers Council, 1015 15th Street NW, Washington, DC 20005-2670; Title Tel # (202) 347-7474
Personnel: Editor-Jean Quick
Editorial Description: Independent, private practice engineering companies.
General Info: Yr. Est. 1973, Weekly, Trim Size-8½ x 14, 2 pages, No Color
Circulation: Total-9,400
List Rental: Rents Lists

Light Aircraft Manufacturers Assn. -Newsletter
    See: AERONAUTICS/ASTRONAUTICS

MHI News   *Association*

Publishing Co: Material Handling Industry of America, 8720 Red Oak Blvd Ste 201, Charlotte, NC 28217-3990; Title Tel # (704) 522-8644 Title Fax # (704) 522-7826
Personnel: Editor-Lisa Woodie
General Info: Yr. Est. 1955, Quarterly, Trim Size-8½ x 11, Sheetfed press, 8 pages, 2 Color, Matte, Saddle-stitched
Circulation: Total-1,000

MIT Sea Grant Quarterly Report
See: OCEANOGRAPHY

Manhattan College
Engineer   *Business*

Publishing Co: Manhattan College, School of Engineering, Manhattan College Parkway, Bronx, NY 10471-4097; Title Tel # (212) 548-1400
Personnel: Editor-Tracey Gorman
Editorial Description: Developments & projects performed in the fields of science, engineering, mathematics & computer technology.
General Info: Yr. Est. 1940, Quarterly, Trim Size-8½ x 10, Offset press, 30 pages, Color
Subscriptions: Indv. $5, $3/copy
Circulation: Total-2,000
Advertising: Inquire for rates.

Manufacturing News
See: MANUFACTURING

Maple Tech
See: COMPUTERS & AUTOMATION

Materials Sciences   *Business*

Publishing Co: National Technical Information Service U.S., 5285 Port Royal Rd., Springfield, VA 22161-0001 Tel # (703) 487-4630 Fax # (703) 487-4630; Title Tel # (703) 487-4650
Editorial Description: Covers ablation, adhesives, sealants, carbon, graphite, ceramics, refractors, glass, coatings, colorants, finishes, corrosion, & elastomers.
General Info: Weekly, Trim Size-8½ x 11, Offset press, ISSN: 0364-4928, No Color
Subscriptions: Indv. $145, Can. $145, For. $205

McGraw-Hill's Tech Transfer Report
See: U.S. (& CANADIAN) FED. GOV'T.

Millipore Process News

Publishing Co: Millipore Corp., PO Box 255, Bedford, MA 01730-0255; Title Tel # (617) 275-9200
General Info: 4 pages

Milwaukee Engineering   *Consumer*

Publishing Co: Engineers & Scientists of Milwaukee, Inc., PO Box 644, Milwaukee, WI 53201-0644; Title Tel # (414) 288-5490 Title Fax # (414) 277-7470
Personnel: Editor-Sabrina Radke
Editorial Description: Milwaukee and Wisconsin news of interest to engineers and executives.
General Info: Yr. Est. 1904, 9x/yr., Sheetfed press, 8 pages, 3% ads, 2 Color, Newsprint
Subscriptions: Indv. $9, $1/copy
Circulation: (90% controlled), Total-500
Advertising: Inquire for rates.
Printing Co: Econo Print, 1402 Greenway Cross, Madison, WI 53713-3111 Tel # (608) 274-4400

Municipal Engineers Assn.
Newsletter

Publishing Co: Municipal Engineers Assn., 530 Otto Road, Unit #2, Mississauga, ON L5T 2L5 Canada Tel # (905) 795-2555 Fax # (905) 795-2660; Title Tel # (519) 524-7412
Personnel: Editor-P. Jeffery Secton
General Info: Quarterly
Subscriptions: Indv. $25

NASA STI Bulletin
See: AERONAUTICS/ASTRONAUTICS

NCAC Newsletter   *Business, Association*

Publishing Co: National Council of Accoustical Consultants, 66 Morris Ave., Suite 1A, Springfield, NJ 07081-1409; Title Tel # (201) 564-5859 Title Fax # (201) 564-7480
Personnel: Circ. Mgr., Adv. Dir.-Virginia Maquire
General Info: Yr. Est. 1962, Quarterly, Trim Size-8½ x 11, 5% ads, No Color
Subscriptions: Free With Membership
Acquistions: Publication Sold
Circulation: Total-500
Advertising: Accepts Inserts.
Printing Co: Mayor Printing, Union, NY Tel # (908) 686-7296

NCEES Registration
Bulletin   *Association*

Publishing Co: Natl. Council of Examiners for Engineering & Surveying, PO Box 1686, Clemson, SC 29633-1686; Title Tel # (803) 654-6824 Title Fax # (803) 654-6033
Personnel: Publisher, Editor-Laura Griffis
Editorial Description: Engineering and land surveying registration; state board news.
General Info: Quarterly, Trim Size-8½ x 11, Web press, 8 pages, ISSN: 0199-8994, Color, Coated, Saddle-stitched
Circulation: (100% controlled), Total-6,500
Printing Co: Electric City, PO Box 1920, Anderson, SC 29622-1920 Tel # (803) 224-3339

NCSPA News

Publishing Co: Natl. Corrugated Steep Pipe Assn., 1255 23rd St NW Ste 850, Washington, DC 20037-1125; Title Tel # (202) 223-2217
Personnel: Editor-Venlo Wolfson
General Info: Yr. Est. 1973, 11x/yr., 8 pages
Circulation: Total-1,700

NICET Newsletter

Publishing Co: National Inst. for Certification in Engineering Technology, 1420 King St., Alexandria, VA 22314-2794 Tel # (703) 684-2834; Title Tel # (703) 684-2835
Personnel: Editor-John Antrim
Editorial Description: Available only to persons passing NICET certification requirements via examination.
General Info: (Formerly ICET Newsletter), Yr. Est. 1962, Quarterly, Trim Size-8½ x 11, 4 pages, 2 Color, Newsprint
Circulation: (100% controlled), Total-40,000

NTIAC Newsletter

Publishing Co: Nondestructive Testing Info Analysis Center, 415 Crystal Creek Dr, Austin, TX 78746-4725 Tel # (512) 263-2106; Title Tel # (512) 563-2106 Title Fax # (512) 263-3530
Personnel: Editor-Gary Carriverv, Circ. Mgr.-M.C. Carriverv
Editorial Description: News & technical information on current nondestructive testing technology.
General Info: Yr. Est. 1974, Bi-monthly, 8 pages, No Color, Newsprint
Subscriptions: Free
Circulation: Total-3,200

NanoNews
See: SCIENCE

Nanotechnology &
Microengineering
Progress   *Association*

Publishing Co: STICS Inc., 9714 S Rice Ave, Houston, TX 77096-4138; Title Tel # (713) 723-3949
Personnel: Publisher-Anna Crull, Editor-Donald Saxman
Editorial Description: Interdisciplinary approach to micron-scale technology, molecular engineering, micro sensors & nanotechnology.
General Info: Yr. Est. 1988, Quarterly, Desktop press, 40 pages, ISSN: 1041-5831, No Color
Subscriptions: Indv. $200, $50/copy
List Rental: Rents Lists

National Council of
Acoustical Consultants-
Directory   *Business*

Publishing Co: National Council of Accoustical Consultants, 66 Morris Ave., Suite 1A, Springfield, NJ 07081-1409 Tel # (201) 564-5859 Fax # (201) 564-7480
Personnel: Editor-Virginia Maquire
General Info: Yr. Est. 1962, Annually, Trim Size-8½ x 11, 40 pages, 2 Color
Subscriptions: $15/copy
Circulation: Total-650
List Rental: Rents Lists

New Technology Week
See: SCIENCE

Newsletter of Engineering
Analysis Software   *Business, Association*

Publishing Co: Frank Maga & Assocs., Box 6805, Pine Mountain Club, CA 93222 Tel # (805) 242-6952; Title Tel # (805) 424-6952 Title Fax # (805) 242-6953
Personnel: Publisher, Editor-Frank Maga, Circ. Mgr.-Earla Quakenbush
Editorial Description: Computer program and application abstracts in structures, structural mechanics, dynamics. CAE news,conferences, calls for papers, and more.
General Info: Yr. Est. 1978, Monthly, Trim Size-8½ x 11, Sheetfed press, 20 pages, ISSN: 0739-697X, No Color, Matte
Subscriptions: Indv. $205, Inst. $205, Can. $215, For. $215

Night Hawk
See: COLLEGE STUDENT

Northland   *Consumer*

Publishing Co: Inst. of Northern Engineering, Univ. of Alaska, Fairbanks, AK 99775-0001; Title Tel # (907) 474-6113 Title Fax # (907) 474-6087
Personnel: Editor-S. Faussett
Editorial Description: Reviews Alaskan research on artic & northern engineering.
General Info: Yr. Est. 1984, Semi-annually, Sheetfed press, 4 pages, Color-cover, Matte
Subscriptions: Free
Circulation: Total-2,200

Object-Oriented Strategies
See: COMPUTERS & AUTOMATION

Offshore Field Development International
See: ENERGY

Optical Materials and Engineering News
See: OPTICAL

PEG Times

Publishing Co: Black Rose Communications, PO Box 464, Dublin, OH 43017-0464; Title Tel # (703) 684-2833
Personnel: Editor-Marji Bayers, Production Mgr.-Steve Storts
Editorial Description: The newsletter for engineers employed by federal, state, & local govt.
General Info: Yr. Est. 1983, Bi-monthly, 8 pages
Subscriptions: Indv. $5
Circulation: Total-8,500

Parametric World
See: ECONOMICS

Perspectives in Engineering
Business, Association   **CPM: $56**

Publishing Co: New Jersey Society of Prof. Engineers, 150 W. State St., Trenton, NJ 08608; Title Tel # (609) 393-0099 Title Fax # (609) 396-5361
Personnel: Publisher, Editor-John Patterson
General Info: (Formerly New Jersey Professional Engineer), Yr. Est. 1939, Quarterly, Trim Size-8$\frac{1}{2}$ x 11, Offset press, 8 pages, 40% ads, 2 Color, Matte, Saddle-stitched
Subscriptions: Indv. $25, Inst. $25, $7/copy
Circulation: Total-12,000
Advertising: $675. Accepts Inserts.
Printing Co: Hermitage Press Inc., 1595 Fifth Ave., Ewing, NJ 08638 Tel # (609) 882-3600, Fax # (609) 882-1137

Pipeline

Publishing Co: Natl. Corrugated Steep Pipe Assn., 1255 23rd St NW Ste 850, Washington, DC 20037-1125; Title Tel # (202) 223-2217

President's Forum

Publishing Co: Milwaukee School of Engineering, 1025 N Milwaukee St # 644, Milwaukee, WI 53202-3118; Title Tel # (414) 277-7140
General Info: Semi-annually

Professional Edge, The
Association

Publishing Co: Assn. of Professional Engineers of Saskatchewan, 2255 13th Ave., Regina, SK S4P 0V6 Canada; Title Tel # (306) 525-9547 Title Fax # (306) 525-0851
Editorial Description: Advises membership of legislation changes, new products, engineering advancements, news of council, etc.
General Info: Yr. Est. 1968, Bi-monthly, Trim Size-216mm-8.5 x 280mm-11, 16 pages, 2 Color, Coated, Other
Subscriptions: Inst. $10, For. $17
Advertising: Inquire for rates.

Professional Ethics Report
See: SCIENCE

RAC Journal
Business   **CPM: $77**

Publishing Co: Reliability Analysis Center, 201 Mill St # 4700, Rome, NY 13440-6916; Title Tel # (315) 339-7075 Title Fax # (315) 337-9932
Personnel: Publisher-Nan Pfrimmer, Editor-Anthony Coppola, Production Mgr.-Jeanne Crowell
Editorial Description: News of interest to Reliability Engineering Community.
General Info: (Formerly RAC Newsletter), Yr. Est. 1969, Quarterly, Trim Size-8$\frac{1}{2}$ x 11, Desktop press, 16 pages, 2 Color
Subscriptions: Free
Circulation: Total-20,000
Advertising: $1,550.

Radiology & Imaging Letter
See: MEDICINE

Report on Performance Materials
Business

Publishing Co: McGraw-Hill, 221 Main Street, 8th Floor, San Francisco, CA 94105; Title Tel # (415) 954-9733 Title Fax # (415) 954-9786
Personnel: Publisher-Thomas Woodall, Editor-Richard Piellisch, Circ. Mgr.-James Amerson, Promotion Dir.-Patricia Maffei
Editorial Description: Covers markets for high-tech materials in aerospace, defense, & automotive fields.
General Info: Yr. Est. 1986, 25x/yr.
Subscriptions: Indv. $447, $9/copy
Acquisitions: Publication Bought, Publication Sold
List Rental: List Management Co.: Performance Marketing, P.O Box 32699, Laughlin, NV 89028 Tel # (702) 299-0011, Fax # (702) 299-0224, Actives: $150/M

Research Horizons

Publishing Co: Georgia Institute of Technology, Student Services Building, Atlanta, GA 30332-0290; Title Tel # (404) 894-6987
Personnel: Editor-Mark Hodges
General Info: Quarterly, 16 pages

Robot Explorer
See: COMPUTERS & AUTOMATION

Rochester Engineer
Association

Publishing Co: Rochester Engineering Society, 1806 Lyell Ave, Rochester, NY 14606-2396; Title Tel # (716) 254-2350 Title Fax # (716) 254-2237
Personnel: Publisher, Editor, Circ. Mgr., Adv. Dir.-Joseph Campbell
Editorial Description: News of local engineering organizations and members.
General Info: Yr. Est. 1922, Monthly, Trim Size-8$\frac{1}{2}$ x 11, Sheetfed press, 40 pages, ISSN: 0035-7405, 2% ads, 2 Color, Newsprint, Saddle-stitched
Subscriptions: Indv. $14, $2/copy
Circulation: (100% controlled), Total-6,100
Advertising: Inquire for rates.

SME News
Association

Publishing Co: Society of Manufacturing Engineers, One SME Dr., Box 930, Dearborn, MI 48121; Title Tel # (313) 271-1500 Title Fax # (313) 271-2861
Personnel: Editor-Tom Akas, Production Mgr.-Dale Michelson, Publisher, Adv. Dir.-Tom Drozda, Art Dir.-Kathy Lake
Editorial Description: Society activities and news. Education, professional engineering, chapter news, professional certification covered.
General Info: Yr. Est. 1965, Quarterly, Trim Size-8$\frac{1}{4}$ x 11$\frac{1}{4}$, Web press, 16 pages, No Color, Newsprint
Acquistions: Publication Bought
Circulation: (100% controlled), Total-81,000
Printing Co: Wisconsin Color Press, Inc., 5400 W Good Hope Rd, Milwaukee, WI 53223-4732 Tel # (414) 353-5400, Fax # (414) 353-0829

SPEC-DATA Program
See: CONSTRUCTION & BUILDING

SPEEA Spotlite
See: LABOR UNION

Society for Health Systems News
See: HEALTH

Society for Industrial Archeology Newsletter
See: ARCHAEOLOGY

Software Technology Transfer

Publishing Co: COSMIC/University of Georgia, 382 E Broad St, Athens, GA 30601-2819; Title Tel # (706) 542-3265 Title Fax # (706) 542-4807
Editorial Description: Brief descriptions of new computer systems from the U.S. National Aeronautical and Space Administration (NASA).
General Info: (Formerly COSMIC Update), Yr. Est. 1988, Monthly
Subscriptions: Free
Circulation: Total-10,000

Soletter
Association

Publishing Co: Society of Logistics Engineers, 8100 Professional Pl Ste 211, Hyattsville, MD 20785-2225 Tel # (301) 459-8446
General Info: Yr. Est. 1966, 11x/yr.
Subscriptions: Indv. $15

Staveley NDTech News
See: MANUFACTURING

Superconductivity News
See: SCIENCE

Systems
Association   **CPM: $86**

Publishing Co: Institute of Industrial Engineers, 25 Technology Park/Atlanta, Norcross, GA 30092-2988 Tel # (770) 449-0461; Title Tel # (404) 449-0460 Title Fax # (770) 263-8532
Personnel: Production Mgr.-Dona Brown
Editorial Description: Newsletter for IIE's Society for Engineering & management Systems.
General Info: (Formerly IE News: Management), Quarterly, Trim Size-8$\frac{1}{2}$ x 11, Sheetfed press, 4 pages, No Color, Matte, Saddle-stitched
Circulation: (100% controlled), Total-5,500
Advertising: $475. Accepts Inserts.
List Rental: Rents Lists

TI PPC Notes
See: COMPUTERS & AUTOMATION

Technimet Topics

Publishing Co: Technimet Corp., 2345 S 170th St, New Berlin, WI 53151-2701; Title Tel # (414) 782-6344
Personnel: Editor-Robert Hutchinson
General Info: Yr. Est. 1982, Quarterly
Circulation: Total-1,800

Technology Alert
See: MANAGEMENT

Technology Forecasts & Technology Surveys
See: SCIENCE

Technology New York Report
See: BUSINESS & INDUSTRY

Technology Notebook — *Business*

Publishing Co: Technical Univ. of Nova Scotia, 1360 Barrington St., Halifax, NS B3L 4J1 Canada; Title Tel # (902) 429-8300
Editorial Description: Technology Newsletter.
General Info: Yr. Est. 1981, Weekly, Mimeo press, 4 pages, ISSN: 0824-0353
Circulation: Total-1,000

Total Productive Maintenance
See: BUSINESS & INDUSTRY

Update — *Business*

Publishing Co: R.W. Beck, 2101 4th Ave Ste 600, Seattle, WA 98121-2375; Title Tel # (206) 441-7500 Title Fax # (206) 441-4962
Personnel: Publisher, Editor, Production Mgr.-John Forman, Art Dir.-Geri Rudolph
Editorial Description: Innovations in techniques/technology & experience regarding multiple engineering disciplines from firm that leads the fields of electrical engineering, solid waste management/recycling, water/wastewater management, management consulting, environmental engineering and construction management.
General Info: Yr. Est. 1965, Quarterly, Trim Size-$8\frac{1}{2}$ x 11, Sheetfed press, 8 pages, 4 Color, Recycled, Saddle-stitched
Subscriptions: Free To Qualified Recipient
Acquistions: Publication Bought
Circulation: Total-8,500
Printing Co: Account Manager: Don Dvorak; United Graphics, 1401 Broadway # 24287, Seattle, WA 98122-3808 Tel # (206) 325-4400

Utility Reporter-Fuels, Energy & Power
See: ENERGY

Value Engineering & Management Digest — *Business*

Publishing Co: Tufty Communications, Inc., 2107 National Press Building, Washington, DC 20045; Title Tel # (202) 347-8998 Title Fax # (202) 543-6776
Personnel: Publisher, Editor-Harold Tufty
Editorial Description: Cost control by value engineered or value managed alternates.
General Info: Yr. Est. 1960, Monthly, Trim Size-$8\frac{1}{2}$ x 11, Offset press, 12 pages, ISSN: 0275-4371, 2 Color, Other, Other
Subscriptions: Indv. $180, For. $195, $15/copy
Circulation: Total-5,000

Vision
See: MANUFACTURING

Voice Coil Newsletter
See: SOUND ENGINEERING

WOTS/Water Operations Technical Support
See: ENVIRONMENT & ECOLOGY

Water Newsletter/Research and Development News
See: ENVIRONMENT & ECOLOGY

Wood Design Focus — *Business* — CPM: $400

Publishing Co: Forest Products Society, 2801 Marshall Ct., Madison, WI 53705-2257; Title Tel # (608) 231-1361 Title Fax # (608) 231-2152
Personnel: Publisher-Arthur B. Brauner, Editor-Robert Leichti, Production Mgr.-Theresa Gray, Promotion Dir.-Jennifer McBlaine
Editorial Description: Contemporary engineering information pertaining to design, specification, construction and maintenance of structural systems and components where wood is a principal material.
General Info: Yr. Est. 1990, Quarterly, Trim Size-$8\frac{1}{2}$ x 11, 24 pages, ISSN: 1066-5757, 5% ads, 2 Color, Matte, Saddle-stitched
Subscriptions: Indv. $48, Inst. $125, Can. $48, For. $58, $15/copy
Circulation: (10% controlled), Total-1,000, Subscriptions-900
Advertising: $400.

Yellowstone Portable Computing Letter
See: COMPUTERS & AUTOMATION

Yellowstone Windows Letter
See: COMPUTERS & AUTOMATION

ENGINEERING, CHEMICAL

CPIA Bulletin
See: AERONAUTICS/ASTRONAUTICS

Composites & Adhesives Newsletter
See: ENGINEERING

ConnTAP Quarterly
See: ENVIRONMENT & ECOLOGY

CryoGas International
See: CHEMISTRY & CHEMICALS

High-Tech Materials Alert
See: MANUFACTURING

International Fluidized Bed Review
See: ENERGY

Membrane Technology — *Business*

Publishing Co: Elsevier Science Inc., 655 Avenue of the Americas, New York, NY 10010-5107 Tel # (212) 633-3916 Fax # (212) 633-3913 Parent Co.-Reed Elsevier, New York
Personnel: Publisher-G. Kitteringham, Editor-David Sleeman, Mktg. Dir.-Cerdine Champney
General Info: Monthly, ISSN: 0958-2118
Subscriptions: Indv. $449
List Rental: Rents Lists

ORSANCO Quality Monitor
See: WATER SUPPLY, POWER & WASTE

Octane Week
See: PETROLEUM & NATURAL GAS

Oxy-Fuel News
See: PETROLEUM & NATURAL GAS

Thermoanalysis News
See: CHEMISTRY & CHEMICALS

ENGINEERING, CIVIL

A-E-C Automation Newsletter
See: COMPUTERS & AUTOMATION

ALS News — *Association*

Publishing Co: Alberta Land Surveyors Assn., 14403 115th Ave., Edmonton, AB T5M 3B8 Canada; Title Tel # (403) 452-7662 Title Fax # (403) 453-1824
Personnel: Editor-G.K. Allred, Circ. Mgr., Adv. Dir., Art Dir.-S. Stecyk
Editorial Description: Association activities, historical, biographical, legal and technical articles related to land surveying.
General Info: Yr. Est. 1961, Bi-monthly, Sheetfed press, 40 pages, ISSN: 0703-4228, 3% ads, No Color, Matte, Saddle-stitched
Circulation: (100% controlled)
Advertising: Inquire for rates. Accepts Inserts.
Printing Co: Peerless Printing, 407 Gilbert Ave, Cincinnati, OH 45202-2287

American Shore & Beach Preservation Assn. -Newsletter
See: ENVIRONMENT & ECOLOGY

American Society of Sanitary Engineering Newsletter — *Association*

Publishing Co: American Society for Sanitary Engineering, PO Box 40326, Bay Village, OH 44140-0326; Title Tel # (216) 835-3040
General Info: Yr. Est. 1906, Annually

Center for Dredging Studies Newsletter — *Business, Scholarly*

Publishing Co: Center for Dredging Studies, Texas A & M Univ., Civil Engineering Dept., College Station, TX 77843-3136; Title Tel # (409) 845-4516 Title Fax # (404) 862-1542
Personnel: Editor-R.E. Randall
General Info: Yr. Est. 1968, Semi-annually, 4 pages
Subscriptions: Free
Circulation: Total-3,300

Civil Engineering — *Business*

Publishing Co: National Technical Information Service U.S., 5285 Port Royal Rd., Springfield, VA 22161-0001 Fax # (703) 487-4630; Title Tel # (703) 487-4630
Editorial Description: Covers civil engineering, highway engineering, flood control, materials, supplies, soil & rock mechanics, and construction equipment.
General Info: Weekly, Trim Size-$8\frac{1}{2}$ x 11, Offset press, 8 pages, ISSN: 0163-1454, No Color
Subscriptions: Indv. $135, Can. $135, For. $195

Composites News: Infrastructure
See: PLASTICS

Crane Safety Report, The
See: SAFETY

DIGGER Reporter — *Business*

Publishing Co: Underground Contractors Assn., 7041 Koll Center Pky Bldg 130, Pleasanton, CA 94566-3128; Title Tel # (415) 829-7800
Personnel: Publisher-Mark Breslin, Editor-Michael Rocco
Editorial Description: Underground & heavy highway engineering.
General Info: Monthly, 1 pages, 5% ads
Circulation: Total-1,500
Advertising: Inquire for rates. Accepts Inserts.

Department of Civil and Environmental Engineering Newsletter *Business*

Publishing Co: Duke University Civil Eng. Dept., Dept. Civil/Environmental Eng., Box 90287, Durham, NC 27708-0287
Editorial Description: Newsletter of events and seminars from Duke's Department of Civil and Environmental Engineering.
General Info: Quarterly

Dredging Contract News
See: ENGINEERING

EERC News *Association*

Publishing Co: University of California at Berkeley Earthquake Engineering, Research Center, 1301 South 46th Street, Richmond, CA 94804-4698 Tel # (510) 231-9468 Fax # (510) 231-9461; Title Tel # (510) 231-9413
Personnel: Editor-Ruth Wrentmore, Circ. Mgr.-Shirley Edwards
Editorial Description: Highlights research and public service activities conducted at the Earthquake Engineering Research Center. Recurring features include listings of new library acquisitions & EERC reports, announcements of new computer applications software, notices of publications available, & news of other activities at the Center.
General Info: (Formerly NISEE/EERC News), Yr. Est. 1977, Quarterly, Trim Size-8⅜ x 10¾, Offset press, 6 pages, ISSN: 0739-7704, No Color, Saddle-stitched
Circulation: (100% controlled), Total-5,300

General Contractors Association, Bulletin of The

Publishing Co: General Contractors Assn., 60 E 42nd St, New York, NY 10165-3510; Title Tel # (212) 687-3131 Title Fax # (212) 808-5267
Editorial Description: Heavy engineering construction.
General Info: Yr. Est. 1909, Monthly, 6 pages
Circulation: Total-5,700

Guidelines for Improving Practice: Architects and Engineers Professional Liability
See: ARCHITECTURE

Gulf Business Report
See: INTERNATIONAL TRADE

Liability Update
See: LAW

Newsletter of Engineering Analysis Software
See: ENGINEERING

Newslog *Association* CPM: $460

Publishing Co: ASFE-Assn. of Professional Firms Practicing the Geosciences, 8811 Colesville Rd Apt G106, Silver Spring, MD 20910-4343 Fax # (301) 589-2017; Title Tel # (301) 565-2733
Personnel: Publisher-John Bachner, Editor-Chris Meier, Adv. Dir.-Stacy Johnson
Editorial Description: News of the Assn., profession, legal developments.
General Info: Yr. Est. 1969, Semi-monthly, Trim Size-8½ x 11, Offset press, 22 pages, Other
Subscriptions: Indv. $100
Circulation: (100% controlled), Total-1,400
Advertising: $645.
List Rental: Actives: $250/M
Printing Co: Image Graphics, 1200 Indian Creek Ct., Beltsville, MD 20705 Tel # (301) 470-2700, Fax # (301) 470-2701

Quarterly CERCular Information Bulletin
See: OCEANOGRAPHY

TransitPulse
See: TRAFFIC & TRANSPORTATION

USCOLD Newsletter
See: WATER SUPPLY, POWER & WASTE

Wisconsin Environmental Law and Regulation Report
See: ENVIRONMENT & ECOLOGY

Wood Design Focus
See: ENGINEERING

ENGINEERING, ELECTRICAL

BACUS News CPM: $254

Publishing Co: SPIE International Society for Optical Engineering, 1000 20th St., Bellingham, WA 98225-6705 Fax # (360) 647-1445; Title Tel # (360) 676-3290
Editorial Description: Contains monthly meeting presentations, excerpts of related papers and news items relevant to the development of photomask process.
General Info: Yr. Est. 1985, Monthly, 30% ads
Circulation: Total-3,500
Advertising: $890.

Battery & EV Technology *Business*

Publishing Co: Business Communications Co., 25 Van Zant St., Ste.13, Norwalk, CT 06855-1781 Fax # (203) 853-0348; Title Tel # (203) 853-4266 Title Fax # (203) 353-0348
Personnel: Publisher-Louis Naturman, Co-Editor-Anna Crull, Co-Editor-Dick Hilton, Co-Editor-Donald Saxman, Mktg. Dir.-Robert Butler
Editorial Description: Advanced technology & product development in batteries & electric vehicles.
General Info: Yr. Est. 1981, Monthly, Trim Size-8½ x 11, Offset press, 12 pages, ISSN: 0271-7093, Ind/Abs/Online: DIALOG, Predicasts, No Color, Matte
Subscriptions: Indv. $395, Can. $445, For. $445, $38/copy
Circulation: (100% controlled), Total-200
List Rental: List Management Co.: W.I. Mail Marketing, 470 Main St. #317, Ridgefield, CT 06877-4516 Tel # (203) 438-6822, Fax # (203) 438-7756, Actives: $120/M

C-CORE News
See: OCEANOGRAPHY

C3I News
See: MILITARY & NAVAL

Circuit Breaker
See: ELECTRIC & ELECTRONIC EQUIPMENT

EECS/ERL News *Consumer*

Publishing Co: Univ. of California at Berkeley, Dept. of Electrical Eng., 203 Cory Hall, Berkeley, CA 94720-1770; Title Tel # (510) 643-6685 Title Fax # (510) 643-6694
Personnel: Editor-Janie Ellison
Editorial Description: Research, faculty, student, & administrative news about EECS Dept. at Berkeley for corporate, government, & private sponsors.
General Info: (Formerly U.C. Electronics Newsletter), Semi-annually, Offset press, 16 pages, 2 Color, Newsprint, Saddle-stitched
Circulation: Total-1,800
Printing Co: University of California Printing, 2120 Oxford St. Univ. Of, California, Berkeley, CA 94720-7340

EP&P Nepcon East Show Daily *Business, Association*

Publishing Co: Cahner's Publishing Co., 1350 E. Touhy Ave., Des Plaines, IL 60018-3358 Tel # (708) 390-2363 Fax # (708) 635-6856; Title Tel # (708) 635-8800
General Info: Yr. Est. 1991
Advertising: $1,995.

Electronic Display World *Business*

Publishing Co: Sanford Resources, Inc., PO Box 20324, San Jose, CA 95160-0324 Fax # (448) 448-4445; Title Tel # (408) 448-4440 Title Fax # (408) 448-4445
Personnel: Publisher-Joseph Castellano, Editor-Brian Barretto, Circ. Mgr.-Rose Castellano, Production Mgr.-Darren Itow
Editorial Description: News, events, markets, & technology relating to electronic displays & systems.
General Info: Yr. Est. 1980, Monthly, Trim Size-8½ x 11, Desktop press, 30 pages, ISSN: 0742-1532, No Color, Coated
Subscriptions: Indv. $495, Inst. $495, Can. $495, For. $495, $35/copy
Circulation: Total-400

Electronic Imaging CPM: $250

Publishing Co: SPIE International Society for Optical Engineering, 1000 20th St., Bellingham, WA 98225-6705 Fax # (360) 647-1445; Title Tel # (360) 676-3290
Editorial Description: Contains short technical and opinion articles on the title subject.
General Info: Yr. Est. 1991, Quarterly, 30% ads
Circulation: (71% controlled), Total-3,500, Single Copy/Newsstand-500, Subscriptions-500
Advertising: $876.

Electronics *Business* CPM: $41

Publishing Co: Penton Publishing, 2025 Gateway Pl Ste 354, San Jose, CA 95110-1006; Title Tel # (408) 441-7336 Title Fax # (408) 441-6052
Personnel: Publisher-Jonah NcLeod, Editor-Jonah McLeod
Editorial Description: News, trends, and analyses for global electronic leaders.
General Info: Yr. Est. 1930, Monthly, Trim Size-8½ x 11, 16 pages, Ind/Abs/Online: DIALOG, 4 Color
Subscriptions: Indv. $98
Circulation: Total-149,000
Advertising: $6,188.
List Rental: List Management Co.: Penton Lists, 1100 Superior Ave, Cleveland, OH 44114-2534 Tel # (216) 696-7000, Fax # (216) 696-6662, Actives: 8,119, $90/M

Electrotechnology *Business*

Publishing Co: National Technical Information Service U.S., 5285 Port Royal Rd., Springfield, VA 22161-0001 Fax # (703) 487-4630; Title Tel # (703) 487-4630
Editorial Description: Covers antennas, circuits, electromechanical devices, electron tubes, optoelectronic devices & systems, power & signal transmission devices, and semiconductors.
General Info: Weekly, Trim Size-8½ x 11, Offset press, ISSN: 0163-1462, No Color
Subscriptions: Indv. $135, Can. $135, For. $195

Facility Manager's Alert
See: CONSTRUCTION & BUILDING

Flexible Conduit, The
See: CONSTRUCTION & BUILDING

Fotec Fiber Optic Testing
News *Business*

Publishing Co: Fotec, Inc., 529 Main St., Box 246, Boston, MA 02129-1101 Tel # (617) 241-7810; Title Tel # (617) 396-6155
Personnel: Editor-James Hayes
Editorial Description: Technical information on testing Fiber Optic Communication Systems & Components. Also introduction of cos. FO testing products.
General Info: Yr. Est. 1983, Quarterly, Trim Size-8½ x 11, 6 pages, No Color
Subscriptions: Free To Qualified Recipient
Circulation: Total-15,000

Guidelines for Improving Practice: Architects and Engineers Professional Liability
See: ARCHITECTURE

Holography   CPM: $250

Publishing Co: SPIE International Society for Optical Engineering, 1000 20th St., Bellingham, WA 98225-6705 Fax # (360) 647-1445; Title Tel # (360) 676-3290
Editorial Description: Contains short technical and opinion articles on the title subject.
General Info: Yr. Est. 1991, Quarterly, 30% ads
Subscriptions: Free With Membership
Circulation: (71% controlled), Total-3,500, Single Copy/Newsstand-500, Subscriptions-500
Advertising: $876.

ICECAP Report   *Business, Association*

Publishing Co: Integrated Circuit Engineering Corp., 15022 N 75th St, Scottsdale, AZ 85260-2425; Title Tel # (602) 998-9780 Title Fax # (602) 948-1935
Personnel: Editor-William McClean, Adv. Dir.-Pat Frascello
Editorial Description: Semiconductor industry coverage, particularly technology & business trends.
General Info: Yr. Est. 1981, Monthly, 16 pages
Subscriptions: Indv. $445, Can. $465, For. $465, $50/copy
Circulation: Total-250

IEEE Bulletin   *Association*   CPM: $86

Publishing Co: Institute of Electrical & Electronics Engineers, Inc., 1515 West 190th Street, Suite 530, Gardena, CA 90248-4323; Title Tel # (310) 715-6796 Title Fax # (310) 715-6798
Personnel: Editor-Erin Lipsitz
General Info: 10x/yr., Trim Size-8¼ x 10⅞, Web press, 12 pages, ISSN: 0162-3842, 5% ads, Color
Subscriptions: Indv. $8
Circulation: Total-14,500
Advertising: $1,260.

IEEE Education Society Newsletter
See: EDUCATION

IEEE Instrumentation & Measurement Society Newsletter
See: INSTRUMENTS

IEEE SMC Newsletter
See: COMPUTERS & AUTOMATION

IEEE Standards Bearer

Publishing Co: Institute of Electrical & Electronics Engineers, Inc., 445 Hoes Lane, PO Box 1331, Piscataway, NJ 08855-1331 Tel # (908) 562-3992 Fax # (908) 981-9334 Parent Co.-Institute of Electrical & Electronics Engineers, New York; Title Tel # (908) 562-3830 Title Fax # (908) 562-1571
Personnel: Publisher-Judith Gorman, Editor-Rochelle Stern, Art Dir.-Esaleta Corbin, Circ. Mgr., Production Mgr., Promotion Dir.-Karen McCabe
Editorial Description: Provides information on latest developments in electrical & electronics standards.
General Info: Yr. Est. 1987, Quarterly, Trim Size-10½ x 14, Sheetfed press, 8 pages, ISSN: 0896-1425, 2 Color, Newsprint
Acquistions: Publication Bought, Publication Sold
Circulation: Total-50,000

ISCET Update   *Association*

Publishing Co: International Society of Certified Electronics Technicians, 2708 W. Berry, Ft. Worth, TX 76109-2356 Fax # (817) 921-9101; Title Tel # (817) 921-9101 Title Fax # (817) 921-3741
Personnel: Publisher-Clyde Nabors, Bk. Rev. Ed.-Barbara Rubin, Editor, Production Mgr.-Wallace Harrison
Editorial Description: Technical information pertinent to the electronics industry
General Info: Yr. Est. 1970, Quarterly, Sheetfed press, 4 pages, No Color, Newsprint
Subscriptions: Indv. $35, Free With Membership
Circulation: (100% controlled), Total-2,100
Advertising: Accepts Inserts.
List Rental: Actives: $60/M

Inspec Matters   *Business, Association*

Publishing Co: INSPEC, 445 Hoes Ln., PO Box 1331, Piscataway, NJ 08855-1331 Parent Co.-Institute of Electrical & Electronics Engineers, New York; Title Tel # (908) 562-5549 Title Fax # (908) 562-8737
Editorial Description: Describes what's new on the INSPEC Database.
General Info: Quarterly, Trim Size-8½ x 11, 8 pages, ISSN: 0266-1616, 2 Color, Matte, Saddle-stitched
Subscriptions: Free
Circulation: Total-16,000

Integrated Circuits
International   *Business*

Publishing Co: Elsevier Science Inc., 655 Avenue of the Americas, New York, NY 10010-5107 Tel # (212) 633-3916 Fax # (212) 633-3913 Parent Co.-Reed Elsevier, New York
Personnel: Publisher-Andrew Flectcher, Editor-Roy Sweda, Circ. Mgr.-R. Sheppard
Editorial Description: Monthly newsletter for suppliers and users of integrated circuits.
General Info: (Formerly Microcomputer News International), Yr. Est. 1977, Monthly, 16 pages, ISSN: 0263-6522, Ind/Abs/Online: DIALOG, Predicasts
Subscriptions: Indv. $541

International Society for Hybrid Microelectronics
Newsletter   *Consumer, Association*

Publishing Co: International Society for Hybrid Microelectronics, 1850 Centennial Park Drive, #105, Reston, VA 22091 Tel # (703) 758-1060; Title Tel # (703) 471-0066
Personnel: Editor-Robert Lagow
General Info: Yr. Est. 1967, Bi-monthly
List Rental: Rents Lists

Japan Semiconductor
Weekly   *Business*

Publishing Co: Kyodo News Intl., 50 Rockefeller Plaza #803, New York, NY 10020-1605; Title Tel # (212) 397-3723 Title Fax # (212) 397-3721
Personnel: Publisher, Editor-M. Suito, Circ. Mgr.-Toshiaki Mitsudome
Editorial Description: General survey of the Japanese semiconductor industry with R&D developments.
General Info: Yr. Est. 1984, Weekly, 4 pages, Ind/Abs/Online: Newsnet

Liability Update
See: LAW

Mainly Marketing
See: ADVERTISING & MARKETING

Microelectronics
Technology Alert   *Business*

Publishing Co: Technical Insights, Inc., PO Box 1304, Fort Lee, NJ 07024-9967; Title Tel # (201) 568-4744 Title Fax # (201) 568-8247
Personnel: Publisher-Kenneth A. Kovaly, Circ. Mgr.-Barbara Chaffee, Mktg. Dir.-Lyn A. Schmidt
Editorial Description: Tracks significant developments in electronics, optoelectronics, data storage & transfer, focusing on the manufacture of devices using techniques such as vapor deposition & ultralithography. Major changes in industry & novel designs for electronic components & systems are covered.
General Info: Yr. Est. 1995, Weekly, 7 pages, ISSN: 1084-4546
Subscriptions: Indv. $890, For. $990
List Rental: Actives: $185/M

Mighty Mopars
See: AUTOMOTIVE

Open Systems Communications
See: TELECOMMUNICATIONS

Optical Computing   CPM: $250

Publishing Co: SPIE International Society for Optical Engineering, 1000 20th St., Bellingham, WA 98225-6705 Fax # (360) 647-1445; Title Tel # (360) 676-3290
Editorial Description: Contains short technical and opinion articles on the title subject.
General Info: Yr. Est. 1991, Quarterly, 30% ads
Subscriptions: Free With Membership
Circulation: (71% controlled), Total-3,500, Single Copy/Newsstand-500, Subscriptions-500
Advertising: $876.

Optical Signal & Image
Processing   CPM: $250

Publishing Co: SPIE International Society for Optical Engineering, 1000 20th St., Bellingham, WA 98225-6705 Fax # (360) 647-1445; Title Tel # (360) 676-3290
Editorial Description: Contains short technical and opinion articles on the title subject.
General Info: Yr. Est. 1991, Quarterly, 30% ads
Subscriptions: Free With Membership
Circulation: (71% controlled), Total-3,500, Single Copy/Newsstand-500, Subscriptions-500
Advertising: $876.

PV News
See: ENERGY

RLE Currents   *Business*

Publishing Co: MIT-Research Laboratory of Electronics, MIT Rm. 36-412, Cambridge, MA 02139-4307; Title Tel # (617) 253-2566 Title Fax # (617) 258-7864
Personnel: Editor-Dorothy Fleischer, Photo Ed.-John F. Cook, Production Mgr.-Barbara Passero
Editorial Description: A newsletter that describes the intellectual concerns & activities of RLE investigators. Each issue focuses on a specific area of research & includes historical photographs & list new RLE pubs.
General Info: Yr. Est. 1987, Semi-annually, Trim Size-8½ x 11, 24 pages, ISSN: 1040-2012, 2 Color, Coated, Saddle-stitched
Subscriptions: Free
Circulation: Total-5,400

Radio and Electrical Engineering Division, Bulletin

Publishing Co: National Research Council of Canada, Research Journals, 1200 Montreal Rd., Bldg. M-55, Ottawa, ON K1A 0R6 Canada Tel # (613) 993-9084 Fax # (613) 952-7656
General Info: Yr. Est. 1951, Quarterly

Robotics
CPM: $250

Publishing Co: SPIE International Society for Optical Engineering, 1000 20th St., Bellingham, WA 98225-6705 Tel # (360) 676-3290 Fax # (360) 647-1445
Editorial Description: Contains short technical and opinion articles on the title subject.
General Info: Yr. Est. 1991, Quarterly, 30% ads
Subscriptions: Free With Membership
Circulation: (71% controlled), Total-3,500, Single Copy/Newsstand-500, Subscriptions-500
Advertising: $876.

SANYO PC Hacker's Newsletter
See: COMPUTERS & AUTOMATION

Sensor Technology
Business

Publishing Co: Technical Insights, Inc., PO Box 1304, Fort Lee, NJ 07024-9967; Title Tel # (201) 568-4744 Title Fax # (201) 568-8247
Personnel: Publisher-Kenneth A. Kovaly, Editor-Angelo DePalma, Circ. Mgr.-Barbara Chaffee
Editorial Description: Monitors and analyzes breakthroughs in all areas of sensing - including micromachining, biosensors, instrumentation, corrosion detection, optoelectronics, image processing, and more.
General Info: Yr. Est. 1985, Monthly, Trim Size-8½ x 11, Sheetfed press, 10 pages, ISSN: 8756-4017, 2 Color, Matte, Other
Subscriptions: Indv. $610, For. $670
List Rental: Actives: $180/M, Expires: $235/M
Printing Co: Allied Lettercraft, 307 W. 36th St., New York, NY 10018 Tel # (212) 279-4800

Southwest Technology Report
Business

Publishing Co: C/S Communications, Inc., PO Box 23899, Tempe, AZ 85285-3899; Title Tel # (602) 345-1118 Title Fax # (602) 345-1119
Personnel: Publisher, Editor-Walter Schuch
Editorial Description: High Technology news & events in Southwestern U. S.
General Info: Yr. Est. 1986, Semi-monthly, Trim Size-8½ x 11, Sheetfed press, 6 pages, ISSN: 1041-2379
Subscriptions: Indv. $69, $5/copy
Circulation: Total-500
Printing Co: Drum Printing, 1618 E Mcdowell Rd, Phoenix, AZ 85006-3098 Tel # (602) 252-3947

Technical Brief
See: THEATRE

ENGINEERING, MECHANICAL

Aura Wealth Newsletter
See: INVESTMENT

C-CORE News
See: OCEANOGRAPHY

CryoGas International
See: CHEMISTRY & CHEMICALS

Division of Mechanical Engineering, Newsletter
Consumer

Publishing Co: National Research Council of Canada, Research Journals, 1200 Montreal Rd., Bldg. M-55, Ottawa, ON K1A 0R6 Canada Tel # (613) 993-9084 Fax # (613) 952-7656
Editorial Description: Text in English, French/describing current R&D work.
General Info: Offset press, 6 pages
Circulation: (100% controlled), Total-15,193

Equipment & Materials Update
See: MANAGEMENT

Facility Manager's Alert
See: CONSTRUCTION & BUILDING

Guidelines for Improving Practice: Architects and Engineers Professional Liability
See: ARCHITECTURE

Heat Transfer/Fluid Flow Data Books
Consumer

Publishing Co: Genium Publishing Corp., 1 Genium Plz, Schenectady, NY 12304-4607; Title Tel # (518) 377-8854 Title Fax # (518) 377-1891
Personnel: Editor-Frank Kreith, Publisher, Circ. Mgr., Production Mgr.-Robert Roy, Promotion Dir.-Paul Hans
Editorial Description: Practical engineering design data & worked out problems.
General Info: (Formerly Heat Transfer), Yr. Est. 1943, Trim Size-11 x 81, Sheetfed press, 30 pages, Newsprint, Looseleaf
Subscriptions: Indv. $116, Can. $116, For. $174
Circulation: Total-1,500
List Rental: Actives: $85/M

International Fluidized Bed Review
See: ENERGY

Liability Update
See: LAW

Mighty Mopars
See: AUTOMOTIVE

Modern Drafting Practices & Standards Manual & Updating Service
Consumer

Publishing Co: Genium Publishing Corp., 1 Genium Plz, Schenectady, NY 12304-4607; Title Tel # (518) 377-8854 Title Fax # (518) 377-1891
Personnel: Publisher, Editor, Circ. Mgr., Production Mgr.-Robert Roy, Promotion Dir.-Paul Hans
Editorial Description: Guide to mechanical/electrical drafting practices.
General Info: Yr. Est. 1901, Trim Size-8½ x 11, Sheetfed press, 30 pages, No Color, Newsprint, Looseleaf
Subscriptions: Indv. $91, Can. $91, For. $116
Circulation: Total-2,400
List Rental: Actives: $85/M

National Fluid Power Association Reporter
Association

Publishing Co: Natl. Fluid Power Assn., 3333 N Mayfair Rd Ste 311, Milwaukee, WI 53222-3219 Tel # (414) 778-3347 Fax # (414) 778-3361; Title Tel # (414) 778-3344
Personnel: Publisher-Linda Western, Editor-Carrie Tatman Schwartz, Production Mgr., Art Dir.-Janet Long
Editorial Description: News on hydraulic and pneumatic product standards, marketing & management seminars in fluid power, and the NFPA spring & fall conferences.
General Info: Yr. Est. 1953, Bi-monthly, Trim Size-8½ x 11, Sheetfed press, 16 pages, ISSN: 0271-782X, 2 Color
Subscriptions: Indv. $50, $9/copy
Circulation: Total-2,000
Printing Co: Zimmerman Printing Co., 3418 Washington Ave # 931, Sheboygan, WI 53081-6405 Tel # (414) 457-5021

Newsletter of Engineering Analysis Software
See: ENGINEERING

Technical Brief
See: THEATRE

Thermodynamics At Texas A&M
Business

Publishing Co: Thermodynamics Rsrch. Ctr., Texas Engineering Exprmt Station, Texas A&m University, College Station, TX 77843-0001; Title Tel # (409) 845-4940 Title Fax # (409) 847-8590
Editorial Description: Brief technical articles and announcements of meetings etc. of interest to thermodynamicists and engineers.
General Info: (Formerly TRC Current Data News), Yr. Est. 1973, Semi-annually, Sheetfed press, 4 pages, 2 Color
Acquistions: Publication Sold
Circulation: Total-4,500
Printing Co: Texas A&M Graphics Arts Center, Texas A&m University, College Station, TX 77843-0001

ENTERTAINMENT

1H3PA Newsletter & Poker Tips
Consumer

Publishing Co: Scotty Barclay Poker Products, 220 East Flamingo Road, Suite 127, Las Vegas, NV 89109; Title Tel # (702) 893-9851
Personnel: Publisher, Editor-Tony Wuehle
Editorial Description: Published for home & private club poker players who are seriously interested in the game & who especially like tournaments.
General Info: (Formerly Scotty Barclay's Poker Chips), Yr. Est. 1984, Bi-monthly, Mimeo press, 4 pages, Newsprint
Subscriptions: Indv. $7, Can. $10, For. $12, $1/copy
Circulation: Total-250, Readership-300

AGVA News
Association

Publishing Co: American Guild of Variety Artists, 184 5th Ave, New York, NY 10010-5995; Title Tel # (212) 675-1003
General Info: Yr. Est. 1950, Bi-monthly
Circulation: Total-16,000
Advertising: Inquire for rates.

AMOA Location
Association

Publishing Co: Amusement & Music Operators Assn., 401 N. Michigan Ave., Chicago, IL 60611-4267; Title Tel # (312) 245-1021 Title Fax # (312) 321-6869
Personnel: Editor-Fred Newton
General Info: Bi-monthly, 8 pages, 2 Color, Saddle-stitched
Circulation: Total-2,000

ARSC Newsletter
See: SOUND ENGINEERING

Anglofile
Consumer

Publishing Co: Goody Press, PO Box 33515, Decatur, GA 30033-0515; Title Tel # (404) 633-5587 Title Fax # (404) 321-3109
Personnel: Editor-E.L. King, Circ. Mgr.-Scott Mowry, Production Mgr.-Justia Stonehouse, Publisher, Adv. Dir.-William King, Art Dir.-Mitch Darling, Promotion Dir.-Jane Skelton
Editorial Description: News, reviews & articles concerning British entertainment & pop culture.
General Info: Yr. Est. 1988, Monthly, Trim Size-8⅝ x 11, Desktop press, 2 pages, 3% ads, No Color, Coated
Subscriptions: Indv. $12, Can. $13, For. $15, $1/copy
Circulation: Total-3,000, Readership-9,000
Advertising: Inquire for rates. Accepts Inserts.
Printing Co: Walton Press, Inc., 402 Mayfield Dr., P.O. Box 1047, Monroe, GA 30655-1706 Tel # (404) 267-2596

Arts Vancouver
Consumer

Publishing Co: Community Arts Council of Vancouver, 837 Davey St., Vancouver, BC V6Z 1B7 Canada Tel # (604) 683-4358
Editorial Description: Listing of cultural events and articles of local interest about the visual and performing arts.
General Info: (Formerly Community Arts Council News), Yr. Est. 1947, Quarterly
Circulation: Total-1,000

Asian Travel & Nigthlife
See: TRAVEL

Atterbury Letter
See: TRAVEL

Autograph Research
See: COLLECTIBLES

Beyond Gaming

Publishing Co: Randy H. Smith, 89 Arundel Place, St. Louis, MO 63105
Editorial Description: Many interesting discussions and commentary on Neo-Geo, Genesis & Super Nintendo. The many book reviews make up the bulk of the issue.
General Info: Trim Size-8.5 x 11, 14 pages

Bullet, The
See: TELEVISION & VIDEO

Calliage

Publishing Co: Clowns of America, 210 Glen Haven Rd., New Haven, CT 06513-1145; Title Tel # (301) 282-8141
General Info: Yr. Est. 1968, Monthly
Circulation: Total-11,000

Capitol Comedy
See: HUMOR & SATIRE

Cartoon Tips
Consumer

Publishing Co: Hartman Publishing Co., Box 30567, Lincoln, NE 68503-0367; Title Tel # (402) 435-3191
Personnel: Publisher, Editor-George Hartman
Editorial Description: Markets for amateur and professional cartoonists plus articles, news, etc. Cartoon lessons, tips, business cartoon plans, articles on cartooning and gagwriting.
General Info: (Formerly Information Guide), Yr. Est. 1935, Monthly, Offset press, 28 pages, No Color, Coated
Subscriptions: Indv. $50, Can. $55, $5/copy
Circulation: Total-175
Advertising: Inquire for rates. Accepts Inserts.

Casino Chronicle
Business

Publishing Co: Casino Chronicle Inc., 10880 Crescendo Circle, Boca Raton, FL 33498; Title Tel # (407) 477-3082 Title Fax # (407) 477-3082
Personnel: Editor-Ben Borowsky
Editorial Description: Covers the casino gaming industry.
General Info: Yr. Est. 1983, Weekly, ISSN: 0889-9797
Subscriptions: Indv. $175, Can. $185, For. $225
Circulation: Total-1,500

Casino News & Entertainment Review
Business, Consumer

Publishing Co: Casino Tourism Assn. Review, 225 Ferris Rd., Toronto, ON M4B 1H2 Canada; Title Tel # (416) 759-2121
Personnel: Publisher-William Rondeau
General Info: Yr. Est. 1980, Quarterly, Sheetfed press, 8 pages, No Color, Coated
Acquistions: Publication Bought
Circulation: (100% controlled), Total-100,000
Printing Co: GRI Tony Masood, 487 Bryant St, San Francisco, CA 94107-1316 Tel # (415) 227-0698, Fax # (415) 442-0208

Celebration News
See: PHILOSOPHY

Cheap Leisure Thrills
See: FAMILY

Circus Report
Business   CPM: $60

Publishing Co: Circus Report, 525 Oak St, El Cerrito, CA 94530-3699; Title Tel # (510) 525-3332
Personnel: Editor-Don Marcks
Editorial Description: Circus news, stories, reports, plus magic news.
General Info: Yr. Est. 1972, Weekly, Trim Size-7 x 8½, Offset press, 40 pages, ISSN: 0889-5996, 5% ads, No Color, Recycled, Saddle-stitched
Subscriptions: Indv. $40, Can. $50, For. $55, $1/copy
Circulation: Total-2,000
Advertising: $120.

Circus Week

Publishing Co: Circus Week, PO Box 3952, San Bernardino, CA 92413-3952; Title Tel # (714) 381-1025
Personnel: Editor-Tony Major
Editorial Description: Covers news, events, & personalities in the circus industry.
General Info: Yr. Est. 1987, Weekly, Trim Size-8½ x 11, Letrpr. press, 8 pages, No Color, Newsprint
Subscriptions: Indv. $20
Advertising: Accepts Inserts.
Printing Co: Major Pubs., PO Box 3952, San Bernardino, CA 92413-3952

Dark Shadows Announcement
See: FAN MAGAZINES-MOVIE, RADIO, TV

Day Care Guide
See: CHILDREN

Entertainment Industry Contracts
See: LAW

Entertainment Marketing Letter

Publishing Co: EPM Communications, Inc., 160 Mercer St., 3rd Floor, New York, NY 10012-3212; Title Tel # (212) 941-0099 Title Fax # (212) 941-1622
Personnel: Publisher-Ira Mayer, Editor-Michael Schau, VP Mktng.-Michele Jensen
Editorial Description: Entertainment Marketing Letter helps marketers at entertainment companies build promotional alliances by linking them to decision-makers at packaged goods, food , beverage, pharmaceutical, fast food and other firms, as well as at film studiois; record companies; TV,cable, and radio networks; home video labels; sales/promotion agencies and more. Plus, every issue of EML brings readers the names, compan
General Info: Yr. Est. 1988, Monthly, Trim Size-8½ x 11, Offset press, 12 pages, 2 Color
Subscriptions: Indv. $319, Can. $319, For. $349, $35/copy
List Rental: Actives: $250/M, Expires: $250/M

Entertainment and Travel Mode
Business, Consumer

Publishing Co: Lion Publishing Company, Box 150-559 Van Brunt Station, Brooklyn, NY 11215-0559; Title Tel # (718) 266-5117
Personnel: Publisher, Editor-Lawrence Heller
Editorial Description: Commentary on entertainment and travel experiences.
General Info: Semi-weekly, Trim Size-8½ x 11, Sheetfed press, 100 pages, Saddle-stitched
Subscriptions: Indv. $250
Advertising: $1,000.

Fairs & Expositions

Publishing Co: International Association of Fairs & Expositions, 3043 E Cairo St # 985, Springfield, MO 65802-6204; Title Tel # (417) 862-5771
Personnel: Editor-Max Willis
General Info: Yr. Est. 1946, 10x/yr., 3% ads
Subscriptions: Indv. $20
Circulation: Total-2,750
Advertising: Inquire for rates.

Fan Club Monitor
See: FAN MAGAZINES-MOVIE, RADIO, TV

Festivities · *Consumer*

Publishing Co: Festive Occasions, 1205 Cliffwood Ln, La Crosse, WI 54601-6084;
Title Tel # (608) 788-5742
Editorial Description: Party ideas, themes, invitations, menus, activities for all age groups.
General Info: Yr. Est. 1986, 5x/yr., 8 pages
Subscriptions: $7/copy
Advertising: Inquire for rates.

Film Analyst, The
See: FILM

Forum
See: THEATRE

Friends of Doctor Who Newsletter
See: SCIENCE FICTION & FANTASY

Frump Update

Publishing Co: In House Personal Publishing, PO Box 1047, Winter Park, FL 32790-1047;
Title Tel # (407) 644-3431
General Info: Yr. Est. 1984, Monthly
Subscriptions: Indv. $10

Fun Seekers

Publishing Co: Fun Seekers, 3455 Euclid Ave, Concord, CA 94519-2320; Title Tel # (415) 798-3866
Title Fax # (415) 825-6492
Personnel: Editor-Paige Goddard
General Info: Yr. Est. 1980, Monthly
Subscriptions: Indv. $25

GAG Recap
See: HUMOR & SATIRE

Gene Lees Jazzletter
See: MUSIC & MUSIC TRADES

Girl Groups ('60's Rock N' Roll) Gazette
See: FAN MAGAZINES-MOVIE, RADIO, TV

Gold Coast News
See: REGIONAL INTEREST

HAI News
See: SOCIAL SERVICES & WELFARE

Humor Digest and Conversation Piece - Chuckles & Grins
See: HUMOR & SATIRE

Inside Moves · *Association*

Publishing Co: Association of Asian/Pacific American Artists, 10153 1/2 Riverside Dr # 199, Toluca
Lake, CA 91602-2533; Title Fax # (213) 874-4755
Personnel: Editor-Robert Lee
General Info: Quarterly
Circulation: Total-700

International Virtual Reality Association · *Association* · CPM: $533

Publishing Co: International Virtual Reality Assn., 2765 N. Scottsdale Rd., Ste. 104-D, Scottsdale,
AZ 85257; Title Tel # (602) 949-7848 Title Fax # (602) 990-1958
Personnel: Publisher, Editor, Adv. Dir.-Thomas R. Cutler, Production Mgr., Art Dir.-Daniel Flynn
Editorial Description: Focus are owners of virtual reality entertainment centers and trends in the
marketing of the Virtual Reality industry.
General Info: Yr. Est. 1995, Quarterly, Trim Size-8½ x 11, Web press, 16 pages, Color-cover
Subscriptions: Indv. $400, Inst. $400, Can. $500, For. $500, Free With Membership
Circulation: (33% controlled), Total-1,500, Subscriptions-1,000, International-250
Advertising: $800.

Irish Music & Dance Assn. - Newsletter · *Consumer*

Publishing Co: Irish Music & Dance Assn., PO Box 65187, Saint Paul, MN 55165-0187;
Title Tel # (612) 227-5090
Personnel: Editor-Patty Bronson
Editorial Description: For the Irish community in Minnesota.
General Info: Yr. Est. 1983, Monthly
Subscriptions: Indv. $12
Circulation: Total-275

It's Only A Movie · *Consumer, Scholarly*

Publishing Co: Psychotronic Film Society, PO Box 14683, Chicago, IL 60614-0683;
Title Tel # (312) 509-4958
Personnel: Publisher, Editor-Michael Flores, Art Dir.-Pat Schenning
Editorial Description: Review of drive in films, interviews with reviews of TV and popular culture.
General Info: Yr. Est. 1988, Monthly, Trim Size-8½ x 11, Sheetfed press, 24 pages, Ind/Abs/Online:
rock music, 2% ads, No Color, Newsprint
Subscriptions: Indv. $12, $1/copy
Circulation: Total-600
Advertising: Inquire for rates.
Printing Co: Copy Shop, 920 W Diversey Pky, Chicago, IL 60614-1416 Tel # (312) 549-0740

Jack Benny Times
See: FAN MAGAZINES-MOVIE, RADIO, TV

Key

Publishing Co: Falcon Pubs., 8432 Steller Dr, Culver City, CA 90232-2425 Tel # (310) 204-5922
General Info: Weekly
Subscriptions: Indv. $22

Laugh It Up
See: HUMOR & SATIRE

Leak News Service and Room 101 Revisited

Publishing Co: Juxtapedia Press, PO Box 25771, Albuquerque, NM 87125-0771;
Title Tel # (505) 898-5390
General Info: Yr. Est. 1968

Leisure Industry Report
See: BUSINESS & INDUSTRY

Multimedia Business Report
See: COMPUTERS & AUTOMATION

Munsters & the Addams Family Reunion
See: FAN MAGAZINES-MOVIE, RADIO, TV

NATAS News
See: TELEVISION & VIDEO

NETC News
See: THEATRE

National Amusement Park Historical News · *Business, Association*

Publishing Co: Natl. Amusement Park Historical Assn., PO Box 83, Mount Prospect, IL 60056-0083
Personnel: Publisher-Thomas Kohout, Editor-James Abbate, Promotion Dir.-Tom Keefe
Editorial Description: Contains information & photos concerning amusement, parks, past & present.
General Info: Yr. Est. 1978, Semi-monthly, Trim Size-8½ x 11, 44 pages, No Color, Newsprint,
Saddle-stitched
Subscriptions: Indv. $30, Inst. $25, Can. $30, For. $40
Circulation: Total-500

New York Opera Newsletter · *Consumer*

Publishing Co: New York Opera Newsletter, PO Box 278, Maplewood, NJ 07040-0278;
Title Tel # (201) 378-9549 Title Fax # (201) 378-2372
Personnel: Publisher-David Wood, Editor in Chief-Barry Lenson, Production Mgr.-Mary Ann Foster,
Adv. Dir.-Jeanne Whiting
Editorial Description: Information for NY opera lovers and professional singers.
General Info: 11x/yr., Trim Size-8½ x 11, Offset press, 32 pages, ISSN: 1043-2361, 2 Color, Matte
Subscriptions: Indv. $48
Circulation: Total-3,000
Advertising: Inquire for rates.
List Rental: Actives: 1,900, $150/M

OABA News
See: PARKS & RECREATION AREAS

Oakland Artscape
See: REGIONAL INTEREST

Party Design Quarterly · *Business*

Publishing Co: Celebration Decor, 410 Plateau Ave, Santa Cruz, CA 95060-6353;
Title Tel # (408) 423-3557
Editorial Description: Published for special event professionals. Contains 'How-To' articles, design,
and product information.
General Info: Yr. Est. 1992, Quarterly, Trim Size-8½ x 11, Desktop press, 40 pages, Other
Advertising: Inquire for rates. Accepts Inserts.

Passing Show
See: THEATRE

Past Times

Publishing Co: Moonstone Press, 7308 Fillmore Dr, Buena Park, CA 90620-3882
Personnel: Editor-Randy Skretvedt, Circ. Dir.-Dorothy Steiman
Editorial Description: The nostalgia entertainment newsletter.
General Info: Yr. Est. 1992, Quarterly, Trim Size-8½ x 11, 20 pages, ISSN: 1050-5504
Subscriptions: Indv. $11

Pay TV Newsletter
See: TELEVISION & VIDEO

Performance

Publishing Co: St. Clair Group, The, 30 St Clair Ave W #805, Toronto, ON M4V 3A1 Canada
   Fax # (416) 926-1858; Title Tel # (416) 926-7595 Title Fax # (416) 926-0407
Personnel: Editor-Laurie Payne
General Info: Quarterly, Trim Size-8¼ x 10⅞, Web press
Subscriptions: Indv. $9, $2/copy
Advertising: $10,645.

Practical Gourmet
See: TRAVEL

Public Domain Report
See: ART & SCULPTURE

Pun American Newsletter
See: HUMOR & SATIRE

Pundit, The
See: HUMOR & SATIRE

Reading Programs with Stories that Educate, Inform, Entertain and Rhyme
See: CHILDREN

Recreation News
See: EDUCATION

Recycling Stories that Rhyme Newsletter
See: ENVIRONMENT & ECOLOGY

Retirement Facility Guide
See: SENIOR CITIZENS

Romantic Notions
See: ROMANCE

Routes
Consumer

Publishing Co: OCR, 521 W. 23rd St., New York, NY 10011; Title Tel # (212) 627-5241
Personnel: Publisher, Editor in Chief-Ronald Bunn, Acting Ed.-Barbara Lewis, Staff Writer-Perri Gafney, Staff Writer-Estelle Whiting
Editorial Description: Guide to African-American cultural events in New York City.
General Info: Yr. Est. 1992, 48x/yr.
Subscriptions: Indv. $36
Advertising: Inquire for rates.

Showboat Centennials
See: HISTORY

Showmen's League News Flashes

Publishing Co: Showmen's League of America, 300 W Randolph St, Chicago, IL 60606-1705; Title Tel # (312) 332-6236
General Info: Monthly

Sorcerer's Scroll

Publishing Co: Don Chaddock, Chaddock Productions, 216 Brimmer Road, 216 brimmer Road, CA 95340
Editorial Description: This used to be Magus News, but now has a new tabloid format. Pretty much the same stuff, like rope playing games, & comix fantasy.
General Info: Trim Size-8.5 x 11, 8 pages
Subscriptions: Indv. $1

Stories that Rhyme, Every Time Kids Pages
See: CHILDREN

Story Rhyme Reproducible Newsletter
See: EDUCATION

Syndication News
See: TELEVISION & VIDEO

Trade Journal Recap
See: HUMOR & SATIRE

Trebas Track
See: SOUND ENGINEERING

Twice Tolled Tales

Publishing Co: AGEHR, Inc. The, 99 Sunnybrook Cir, Highland, NY 12528-1324

U.S. Outdoor Drama
See: THEATRE

Vanguard , The
See: COLLEGE ALUMNI

Video Industry Statistical Report
See: TELEVISION & VIDEO

Winning!
Consumer   CPM: $23

Publishing Co: NatCom, Inc., 5300 City Plex Tower, 2448 E. 31st St., Tulsa, OK 74137-4207
   Tel # (918) 491-6190 Fax # (918) 491-9410; Title Tel # (918) 366-4441 Title Fax # (918) 366-4439
Personnel: Publisher-Gerald Pope, Editor-Simon McCaffery, Circ. Mgr.-Bob Pope, Circ. Mgr.-Ed Schondorf, Assoc. Publ., VP Adv.-Ellie Shimer
Editorial Description: Winning! has editorial which is designed to help its readers increase their odds for winning the big money prize of their dreams. Subjects covered are contests, sweepstakes, lotteries, TV game shows, Vegas-style gaming & methods of earning extra income.
General Info: (Formerly National Reporter), Yr. Est. 1976, Monthly, Trim Size-8 x 10⅞, Web press, 16 pages, 25% ads, 2 Color, Matte, Saddle-stitched
Subscriptions: Indv. $24, $2/copy
Circulation: (PSS), Total-150,000, Readership-840,000
Advertising: $3,500.
List Rental: Actives: 139,909, $60/M, Hotline: 47,000, $65/M, Expires: 154,824, $35/M
Printing Co: Ringier America, 4708 Krueger Dr, Jonesboro, AR 72401-6714 Tel # (501) 935-7000

Young Audiences Newsletter
See: EDUCATION

ENTOMOLOGY

AMCA Newsletter

Publishing Co: American Mosquito Control Assn., Inc., 707 E Prien Lake Rd # 5416, Lake Charles, LA 70601-8613 Fax # (318) 478-9434; Title Tel # (318) 474-2723 Title Fax # (810) 478-9434
Personnel: Editor-Dr. Jimmie Long, Production Mgr., Adv. Dir., Promotion Dir.-Sharon Colvin
Editorial Description: Reports new products & developments in the mosquito control industry.
General Info: Yr. Est. 1975, Quarterly, 16 pages, ISSN: 0195-4180, No Color
Subscriptions: Indv. $5
Circulation: Total-2,000
List Rental: Rents Lists

Beekeeping Notes
See: GARDENING & HORTICULTURE

Bunker Banner
See: GENEALOGY

Civil Abolitionist
See: HEALTH

ESA Newsletter
Consumer, Association

Publishing Co: Entomological Society of America, 9301 Annapolis Rd., Lanham, MD 20706-3125; Title Tel # (301) 731-4535 Title Fax # (301) 731-4538
Personnel: Editor-Elizabeth Blinn, Production Mgr.-Raymond L. Everngam, Jr., Adv. Dir.-Denise McCall
Editorial Description: News and member information relating to entomology.
General Info: Yr. Est. 1953, Monthly, Trim Size-8½ x 11, Sheetfed press, ISSN: 0273-7353, 2 Color, Newsprint, Perfect bound
Subscriptions: Indv. $7, $1/copy
Circulation: (100% controlled), Total-9,000
List Rental: Rents Lists

Entomological Society of Canada, Bulletin
Association   CPM: $71

Publishing Co: Entomological Society of Canada, 393 Winston Ave., Ottawa, ON K2A 1Y8 Canada; Title Tel # (613) 725-2619 Title Fax # (613) 725-9349
Personnel: Editor-H. Barclay
General Info: Yr. Est. 1969, Quarterly, 50 pages, 2% ads
Subscriptions: Free With Membership
Circulation: Total-1,400
Advertising: $100.

Entomological Society of Manitoba, Newsletter

Publishing Co: Entomological Society of Manitoba, c/o Agriculture Canada, 195 Dafoe Rd., Winnipeg, MB R3T 2M9 Canada Tel # (204) 983-5533; Title Tel # (204) 983-1631 Title Fax # (204) 983-4604
Personnel: Editor-B. Galka
General Info: Yr. Est. 1973, Quarterly, Trim Size-8½ x 11, 6 pages, ISSN: 0826-306X
Subscriptions: Indv. $15
Circulation: Total-160

Lepidopterists' Society
News   *Association*

Publishing Co: Lepidopterists Society, 1900 John St., Manhattan Beach, CA 90266-2608
Tel # (310) 545-9415
Personnel: Publisher-Allen Press, Editor-Marc & Maria Minno
Editorial Description: Material of timely interest to amateur & professional scientists who study butterflies and moths.
General Info: Yr. Est. 1947, Quarterly, 12 pages, No Color
Subscriptions: Indv. $35, Inst. $50, Can. $50, For. $50
Circulation: Total-170
List Rental: Actives: 1,500, $80/M

Minnesota Pest Report
See: AGRICULTURE

Pest Bulletin   *Business, Consumer*

Publishing Co: Moore Consulting, PO Box 9527, Berkeley, CA 94709-0527;
Title Tel # (510) 524-1163
Personnel: Publisher-Wayne Moore, Assoc. Ed.-Nancy Hamalian
Editorial Description: Covers household pest control. Customized for pest control companies to mail to their clients.
General Info: (Formerly Pest Patrol News), Yr. Est. 1989, Bi-monthly
Circulation: Total-100,000

Pest Control Letter
See: SANITATION

Tribolium Information
Bulletin   *Consumer*

Publishing Co: California State Univ. Biology Dept., School of Natural Sciences, Biology Dept., San Bernardino, CA 92407; Title Tel # (909) 880-5305 Title Fax # (909) 880-7005
Personnel: Editor-Alexander Sokoloff
Editorial Description: Includes research, technical & teaching notes on Tribolium & current bibliography as well as personal & geographic directory of investigators using flour & other beetles in their research, & lists where mutant/stocks are available.
General Info: Yr. Est. 1958, Annually, Offset press, 165 pages, ISSN: 0082-6391, No Color
Subscriptions: Indv. $24, Inst. $26
Circulation: Total-110
List Rental: Rents Lists

Wood Duck
See: NATURAL HISTORY

ENVIRONMENT & ECOLOGY

AALS Newsletter
See: AGRICULTURE

ABDC Newsletter
See: HEALTH

ASFI Bulletin

Publishing Co: American Sport Fishing Institute, 1033 N. Fairfax St., Ste. 200, Alexandria, VA 22314-1540; Title Tel # (703) 519-9691
Personnel: Editor-G.E. Radonski, Production Mgr.-Stephen Phillips
Editorial Description: Presents findings from fishing research, developments in resource management and associated matters judged significant to sport fish conservation.
General Info: (Formerly SFI Bulletin), Yr. Est. 1951, 10x/yr., Trim Size-8½ x 11, Offset press, 8 pages
Subscriptions: Indv. $10, $1/copy
Circulation: Total-15,000

AWPI Newsletter
See: LUMBER & WOOD

Aboveground Storage Tank
Guide   *Business*

Publishing Co: Thompson Publishing Group, 1725 K Street, NW, Washington, DC 20006; Title Tel # (202) 872-4000 Title Fax # (202) 296-1091
Personnel: Editor in Chief-Jeffrey L. Leiter
Editorial Description: Manual dealing with state regulations, tire codes and SPCC plans for aboveground storage tanks. Subscription monthly newsletters covering latest developments in AST regulations.
General Info: Yr. Est. 1991, Monthly, Looseleaf
Subscriptions: Indv. $397

Abundant Life Seed Foundation Newsletter
See: GARDENING & HORTICULTURE

Advocate
See: POLITICS

Agrarian Advocate   *Association*

Publishing Co: Community Alliance with Family Farmers, PO Box 464, Davis, CA 95617-0464
Fax # (916) 756-7587; Title Tel # (916) 756-8518 Title Fax # (916) 756-7857
Personnel: Co-Editor-Erin Barnett, Co-Editor-Tom Haller
Editorial Description: Issues of concern to rural CA residents: groundwater pollution, pesticides, sustainable agriculture.
General Info: (Formerly CAAP Newsletter), Yr. Est. 1977, Bi-monthly, Trim Size-8½ x 11, Offset press, 8 pages, 2% ads, No Color, Newsprint
Subscriptions: Indv. $25, Inst. $25

Air & Water Pollution
Control   *Business*

Publishing Co: Bureau of National Affairs, Inc., 1231 25th St. NW, Bldg. N-200, Washington, DC 20037-1157; Title Tel # (202) 452-4200 Title Fax # (202) 822-8092
Personnel: Publisher-William A. Beltz, Mng. Editor-Karan Walker, Circ. Mgr.-Gary C. Seltzer
Editorial Description: A review of developments in polution laws, regulations, & trends in government & industry.
General Info: Yr. Est. 1979, Bi-weekly, Trim Size-8½ x 11, Offset press, 8 pages, ISSN: 0890-0396
Subscriptions: Indv. $331

Air Currents   *Business, Association*

Publishing Co: Bay Area Air Quality Management District, 939 Ellis St, San Francisco, CA 94109-7714; Title Tel # (415) 749-4900 Title Fax # (415) 928-8560
Personnel: Publisher-Edward McHugh, Editor, Production Mgr.-Lucia Libretti
Editorial Description: Describes regulation changes and other information of interest to the air pollution control community.
General Info: Yr. Est. 1959, Monthly, Web press, 4 pages, ISSN: 0400-8510, No Color, Coated
Subscriptions: Free
Circulation: (100% controlled), Total-5,000
Printing Co: Union Offset, 120 8th St, San Francisco, CA 94103-2716 Tel # (415) 861-4706

Air Pollution Control   *Business*

Publishing Co: Bureau of National Affairs, Inc., 1231 25th St. NW, Bldg. N-200, Washington, DC 20037-1157; Title Tel # (202) 452-4200 Title Fax # (202) 822-8092
Personnel: Publisher-William A. Beltz, Editor-Eileen Joseph, Mng. Editor-Karen Walker, Circ. Mgr.-Gary C. Seltzer
Editorial Description: A reference and advisory service on the control of air pollution, designed to meet the information needs of individuals responsible for complying with EPA and state air pollution control regulations.
General Info: Yr. Est. 1980, Bi-weekly, Trim Size-8½ x 11, Offset press, 8 pages
Subscriptions: Indv. $772

Air Pollution Monitoring &
Sampling   *Business*

Publishing Co: McIlvaine Co., The, 2970 Maria Ave., Northbrook, IL 60062-2024; Title Tel # (847) 272-0010 Title Fax # (847) 272-9673
Personnel: Publisher-R.W. McIlvaine, Editor-Christine Hennig
Editorial Description: Ambient and Stack testing, continuous emission monitors. A complete information system with Manual, Newsletter, Catalog, Fact Finder, and 300 service units for reprints, advice, audio and video tapes, and on line fax answers.
General Info: Yr. Est. 1980, Monthly, 8 pages
Subscriptions: Indv. $690, Can. $750, For. $750, Free With Membership
List Rental: Rents Lists

Air Quality Data
Management Software
Report   *Business, Consumer*

Publishing Co: Donley Technology, PO Box 152, 220 Garfield Avenue, Colonial Beach, VA 22443-0152; Title Tel # (804) 224-9427 Title Fax # (804) 224-7958
Personnel: Publisher-Elizabeth Donley, Editor-Veronica Deschambault, Asst. Ed.-Karen Roberts
Editorial Description: Describes more than 45 systems which manage air quality data, including modeling/monitoring , reporting, emissions inventory and regulatory compliance features.
General Info: Yr. Est. 1995, Irregular, ISSN: 1084-9394
Subscriptions: $195/copy

Air Quality Week   *Business*

Publishing Co: Air Daily Ltd., 4418 MacArthur Blvd. NW, Ste. 202, Washington, DC 20007-2563; Title Tel # (202) 298-8201 Title Fax # (202) 298-8210
Personnel: Publisher, Editor-George Spencer
Editorial Description: Clean air issues specializing on the Clean Air Act.
General Info: Weekly

AirDaily   *Association*

Publishing Co: Air Daily Ltd., 4418 MacArthur Blvd. NW, Ste. 202, Washington, DC 20007-2563; Title Tel # (202) 298-8201 Title Fax # (202) 298-8210
Personnel: Publisher, Editor-George Spencer
Editorial Description: For quality air managers with focus on air pollution credit allowance buying and selling.
General Info: Yr. Est. 1993, Daily
Subscriptions: Indv. $367
List Rental: Rents Lists

AirTECH News
Business

Publishing Co: HazTECH Publications, Inc., 14120 Huckleberry Ln, Silver Spring, MD 20906-2012
Fax # (301) 460-5869; Title Tel # (301) 871-3289 Title Fax # (301) 460-5859
Personnel: Editor-Cathy Dombrowski
Editorial Description: Technologies for controlling air pollution, business developments in the industry.
General Info: Yr. Est. 1991, Monthly, ISSN: 1066-193X
Subscriptions: Indv. $345, Can. $345, For. $360

Air/Water Pollution Report's Environment Week
Business

Publishing Co: Business Publishers, Inc., 951 Pershing Dr., Silver Spring, MD 20910-4464
Tel # (301) 589-5103 Fax # (301) 589-8493; Title Tel # (301) 587-6300 Title Fax # (301) 587-1081
Personnel: Publisher-Leonard A. Eiserer, Editor-David Goeller, Mktg. Dir.-Fay S. Gold
Editorial Description: Independent newsletter covering legislation, regulations & litigation, as well as technical developments of all aspects of environmental issues.
General Info: Yr. Est. 1963, Weekly, Trim Size-8½ x 11, Desktop press, 8 pages, Ind/Abs/Online: NewsNet, Predicasts, DIALOG, No Color, Recycled
Subscriptions: Indv. $595, Inst. $595, Can. $595, For. $620
Advertising: Accepts Inserts.
List Rental: List Management Co.: Manager: Donald Peterson; BPI Direct, 951 Pershing Dr., Silver Spring, MD 20910-4464 Tel # (301) 585-5976, Fax # (301) 587-4530

Al-Anon in Institutions
See: SOCIAL SERVICES & WELFARE

Alabama Environmental Compliance Update
See: LAW

Alberta Agrologist
See: AGRICULTURE

Amanaka'a
Consumer, Association

Publishing Co: Amazon Network, 339 Lafayette St # 8, New York, NY 10012-2725;
Title Tel # (212) 674-4646 Title Fax # (212) 674-9139
Editorial Description: Dedicated to preserving the Amazon culture and environment.
General Info: Quarterly, Trim Size-8½ x 11, 8 pages

American Rivers
Association

Publishing Co: American Rivers, 801 Pennsylvania Ave., SE, #400, Washington, DC 20003-2167;
Title Tel # (202) 547-6900 Title Fax # (202) 543-6142
Personnel: Editor-Randy Showstack
Editorial Description: Reports on the activities of American Rivers, the nation's leaders river-saving organization.
General Info: Yr. Est. 1973, Quarterly, Sheetfed press, 12 pages, Color-cover, Coated, Saddle-stitched
Subscriptions: Free With Membership
Circulation: Total-20,000
List Rental: List Management Co.: Manager: Mary E. Kukbride; RMI Direct Marketing, Inc., 4 Skyline Dr, Hawthorne, NY 10532-2133 Tel # (914) 345-4615, Fax # (914) 347-2954
Printing Co: Eco-Print, 9335 Fraser Ave, Silver Spring, MD 20910-1228 Tel # (301) 585-7077

American Shore & Beach Preservation Assn. - Newsletter
Association

Publishing Co: American Shore & Beach Preservation Assn., 1724 Indian Way, Oakland, CA 94611-1221 Tel # (510) 339-2818 Fax # (510) 339-6710; Title Tel # (510) 642-2666 Title Fax # (510) 642-9143
Personnel: Editor-Gerald Giefer
Editorial Description: Contains information on books, reports, and government action on beaches and other coastal areas for geologists, geographers, engineers, coastal zone managers, etc.
General Info: Yr. Est. 1954, Quarterly, Trim Size-8½ x 11, Desktop press, 4 pages, ISSN: 0517-4856
Subscriptions: Indv. $40, Inst. $40, Can. $40, For. $59, Free With Membership
Circulation: Total-900

American Wildlands
Business, Association

Publishing Co: American Wildlands, 40 E. Main St., Ste. 2, Bozeman, MT 59715
Tel # (403) 586-8175; Title Tel # (406) 586-8175 Title Fax # (406) 586-8242
Personnel: Publisher, Editor-Sally Ranney
Editorial Description: Promotes ecologically sustainable uses of public wildland resources including forests, wilderness, wildlife, fisheries, and rivers.
General Info: (Formerly American Wilderness Alliance), Yr. Est. 1977, Quarterly, 4 Color, Coated
Subscriptions: Indv. $25
Acquistions: Publication Bought
Circulation: Total-3,000
List Rental: Actives: $75/M

America's At Our Doorstep
See: HUMOR & SATIRE

Animal Welfare Institute Quarterly

Publishing Co: Animal Welfare Institute, PO Box 3650, Washington, DC 20007-0150;
Title Tel # (202) 337-2333 Title Fax # (202) 338-9478
Personnel: Publisher-Christine Stevens, Editor-Henry Herbermann
Editorial Description: Promote the reduction of total pain and fear inflicted on animals by man.
General Info: (Formerly Animal Welfare Institute Information Report), Yr. Est. 1951, Quarterly, Trim Size-8½ x 11, Web press, 20 pages, 2 Color, Newsprint, Saddle-stitched
Subscriptions: Indv. $15, Free
Circulation: Total-20,000
Printing Co: Sauls Lithograph, 2424 Evarts St NE, Washington, DC 20018-2120
Tel # (202) 529-9100

Antarctica Project Newsletter, The
Consumer, Association

Publishing Co: Antarctica & Southern Ocean Coalition, 424 C St NE, Washington, DC 20002-5818
Tel # (202) 544-0236
Personnel: Editor-J. Barnes, Editor-B. Marks, Science Ed.-Beth Marks, Circ. Mgr., Production Mgr.-Tania Blagrove
General Info: Yr. Est. 1992, Quarterly, Desktop press, 4 pages, No Color, Recycled
Subscriptions: Free With Membership
Circulation: Total-1,000
Advertising: Inquire for rates.

Appalachian Alternatives
See: CONSUMER INTERESTS

Appledore Times
See: OCEANOGRAPHY

Applied Demography
See: PUBLIC MANAGEMENT & PLANNING

Aquaphyte
See: SCIENCE

Aquatic Plant Control Research Program Newsletter

Publishing Co: U.S. Army Engineer Waterways Experiment Station, 3909 Halls Ferry Rd, Vicksburg, MS 39180-6133; Title Tel # (601) 634-3616
Personnel: Editor-Bobby Baylot
General Info: (Formerly Aquatic Plant Control Research Program Info Bulletin), Quarterly
Circulation: Total-1,000

Arbor Day
See: FORESTRY

Archives Sharing Bulletin
See: HEALTH

Arizona Environment
Business, Association

Publishing Co: Arizona Dept. of Environmental Quality, OCSEA Section, 3033 N. Central Ave, Phoenix, AZ 85012 Tel # (602) 207-2300; Title Tel # (602) 207-4333 Title Fax # (602) 207-4872
Personnel: Publisher-Marian Slavin, Editor-Ray Jackson, Circ. Mgr.-Marlene Roden
Editorial Description: Describes current activities of Arizona Dept. of Environmental Quality in areas of air quality, water quality & waste programs.
General Info: (Formerly Environmental Scene), Yr. Est. 1988, Quarterly, Trim Size-8½ x 11, Web press, 8 pages
Subscriptions: Free
Acquistions: Publication Bought
Circulation: Total-3,000, Readership-3,000
Printing Co: K & M Printing, 75 Baseline Road, Suite D-27, Gilbert, AZ 85233 Tel # (602) 926-0123, Fax # (602) 926-3097

Arizona Environmental Law Update
See: LAW

Arroyo
See: WATER SUPPLY, POWER & WASTE

Asbestos & Lead Abatement Report

Publishing Co: Business Publishers, Inc., 951 Pershing Dr., Silver Spring, MD 20910-4464
Tel # (301) 589-5103 Fax # (301) 589-8493; Title Tel # (301) 587-6300 Title Fax # (301) 587-1081
Personnel: Publisher-John Wills, Editor-Corby Anderson, Circ. Mgr.-Elizabeth Early, Promotion Dir.-Loretta Keller
Editorial Description: Cover national and state policies and regulations governing the asbestos and lead abatement industry. Features business, litigation, and technology news on asbestos and lead detection and abatement.
General Info: (Formerly Asbestos Abatement Report; Asbestos Control Report), Yr. Est. 1987, Bi-weekly, Trim Size-8½ x 11, Offset press, 8 pages, ISSN: 1068-2643, Ind/Abs/Online: HRIN, 2 Color, Newsprint
Subscriptions: Indv. $497, Can. $497, For. $510
Acquistions: Publication Bought, Publication Sold
List Rental: List Management Co.: BPI Direct, 951 Pershing Dr., Silver Spring, MD 20910-4464 Tel # (301) 585-5976, Fax # (301) 587-4530
Printing Co: Plymouth Printing, 1200 Cushing Pl SE, Washington, DC 20003-3599 Tel # (202) 488-7777, Fax # (202) 863-1078

Asbestos Monitor
See: CONSTRUCTION & BUILDING

Asbestos Removal
See: CONSTRUCTION & BUILDING

Audubon Society of Rhode Island Report *Association*

Publishing Co: Audubon Society of Rhode Island, 12 Sanderson Rd, Smithfield, RI 02917-2606; Title Tel # (401) 231-6444
Personnel: Publisher-Alfred Hawkes, Editor, Circ. Mgr., Adv. Dir., Art Dir.-Eugenia Marks
Editorial Description: Current & historical natural history & ecology topics, RI focused.
General Info: (Formerly Audubon Society of RI), Yr. Est. 1966, Bi-monthly, Web press, 8 pages, ISSN: 0274-502X, No Color
Subscriptions: Indv. $5, $1/copy
Circulation: Total-4,500
Advertising: Inquire for rates.
Printing Co: Beacon Press, 132 Meadow St, Warwick, RI 02886-6909 Tel # (401) 737-1601

Aullwood

Publishing Co: Aullwood Audubon Ctr. & Farm, 1000 Aullwood Rd, Dayton, OH 45414-1129; Title Tel # (513) 890-7360
Personnel: Publisher, Editor-John Ritzenthaler
Editorial Description: Program information, articles of interest to members, friends of Aullwood.
General Info: (Formerly Aullwood Notes), Yr. Est. 1957, Bi-monthly, Trim Size-8½ x 11, Offset press, 12 pages, No Color
Subscriptions: Indv. $35, Free With Membership
Circulation: (100% controlled), Total-1,400
Advertising: Inquire for rates.
Printing Co: C.L. Graphics, 642 W National Rd, Vandalia, OH 45377-1032

B.C. Naturalist
See: NATURAL HISTORY

BNA's Environmental Compliance Bulletin *Association, Business*

Publishing Co: Bureau of National Affairs, Inc., 1231 25th St. NW, Bldg. N-200, Washington, DC 20037-1157; Title Tel # (202) 452-4200 Title Fax # (202) 822-8092
Personnel: Publisher-William A. Beltz, Mng. Editor-Karen S. Walker, Circ. Mgr.-Gary C. Seltzer
Editorial Description: Provides practical, hands-on, how-to help & information on environmental compliance obligations. Covers topics such as: compliance deadlines & procedures, changing laws & regulations, pollution prevention methods, inspections & enforcement, training opportunities, new technologies, & industry stategies.
General Info: Yr. Est. 1993, Bi-weekly, Trim Size-8½ x 11, Offset press, 8 pages, ISSN: 1073-5798
Subscriptions: Indv. $498

BNA's Environmental Due Diligence Guide *Business*

Publishing Co: Bureau of National Affairs, Inc., 1231 25th St. NW, Bldg. N-200, Washington, DC 20037-1157; Title Tel # (202) 452-4200 Title Fax # (202) 822-8092
Personnel: Publisher-William A. Beltz, Mng. Editor-Anne M. Lange, Circ. Mgr.-Gary C. Seltzer
Editorial Description: A reference manual which describes how environmental law affects real estate transactions & how 'due diligence' can provide protection against Superfund (CERCLA) & RCRA cleanup liabilities.
General Info: Yr. Est. 1992, Monthly, Trim Size-8½ x 11, Offset press, 50 pages, Looseleaf
Subscriptions: Indv. $674

BNA's Health Care Facilities Guide
See: HEALTH

BNA's State Environment & Safety Regulatory Monitoring *Business*

Publishing Co: Bureau of National Affairs, Inc., 1231 25th St. NW, Bldg. N-200, Washington, DC 20037-1157; Title Tel # (202) 452-4200 Title Fax # (202) 822-8092
Personnel: Publisher-William A. Beltzer, Mng. Editor-Kevin Fetherston, Circ. Mgr.-Gary C. Seltzer
Editorial Description: A biweekly report that covers regulatory developments for all 50 states & the District of Columbia. It is organized by state & then by topic within each state. Each summary includes a brief description of the regulatory action, administrative code citation, effective telephone number, & comment deadlines.
General Info: Yr. Est. 1993, Bi-weekly, Trim Size-8½ x 11, Offset press, ISSN: 1065-8076
Subscriptions: Indv. $931

Backyard Wildlife
See: NATURAL HISTORY

Barrier Islands Newsletter

Publishing Co: National Wildlife Federation, 8925 Leesburg Pike, Vienna, VA 22184-0001 Tel # (703) 790-4000 Fax # (703) 442-7332; Title Tel # (202) 797-6839
Personnel: Editor-Kathie Dixon
Editorial Description: Newsletter for activists interested in the protection of America's four coasts, specifically in the expansion of the Coasta Barrier Resources system & improvement of the Natl. Flood Insurance Program.
General Info: Yr. Est. 1980, Quarterly, Sheetfed press, 8 pages
Circulation: Total-6,200

Beaver Defenders

Publishing Co: Unexpected Wildlife Refuge, PO Box 765, Newfield, NJ 08344-0765; Title Tel # (609) 697-3541
Personnel: Editor-Hope Sawyer Buyukmihci
Editorial Description: About the unexpected wildlife refuge & about issues concerning beavers everywhere.
General Info: Yr. Est. 1971, Quarterly, 8 pages
Subscriptions: Indv. $10
Circulation: Total-200

Bibliography of Plant Protection
See: BOTANY

BioWorld Today *Business*

Publishing Co: American Health Consultants, Inc., 3525 Piedmont Rd., Building #6, Ste. 400, Atlanta, GA 30305-0056 Tel # (404) 262-7436 Fax # (404) 284-3291
Personnel: Publisher-Don Johnston
General Info: Monthly
Subscriptions: Indv. $784
Acquistions: Publication Sold
List Rental: Actives: $145/M

Bioremediation Report, The *Business, Consumer*

Publishing Co: King Communications Group, 627 National Press Building, Washington, DC 20045-1601 Tel # (202) 638-4260 Fax # (202) 662-9719
Editorial Description: Provides information on technology and applications of environmental clean-up.
General Info: Yr. Est. 1993, Monthly
Subscriptions: Indv. $395
List Rental: Rents Lists

Bioworld Financial *Business*

Publishing Co: American Health Consultants, Inc., 3525 Piedmont Rd., Building #6, Ste. 400, Atlanta, GA 30305-0056 Tel # (404) 262-7436 Fax # (404) 284-3291
Personnel: Publisher-Don Johnston
General Info: Monthly
Acquistions: Publication Sold
List Rental: Actives: $145/M

Bioworld Week *Business*

Publishing Co: American Health Consultants, Inc., 3525 Piedmont Rd., Building #6, Ste. 400, Atlanta, GA 30305-0056 Tel # (404) 262-7436 Fax # (404) 284-3291
Personnel: Publisher-Don Johnston
General Info: Weekly
Acquistions: Publication Sold
List Rental: Actives: $145/M

Blue Goose Flyer *Association*

Publishing Co: Sponsor-Natl. Wildlife Refuge Assn., Natl. Wildlife Refuge Assn., PO Box 60318, Potomac, MD 20859-0318 Fax # (301) 986-9498; Title Tel # (301) 983-9498 Title Fax # (301) 983-9498
Personnel: Exec. VP/Group Publisher-Ginger Merchant, Editor-Russel Clapper
Editorial Description: Wildlife Refuge System stewardship.
General Info: Yr. Est. 1975, Quarterly, Trim Size-8½ x 11, 10 pages, 2 Color
Subscriptions: Indv. $20
Circulation: Total-1,250
Printing Co: Copy Shoppe, 1351 N Main St, Liberty, TX 77575-3707 Tel # (409) 336-5761

Books to Build a New Society
See: BOOKS & BOOK TRADE

Border Connections
See: EDUCATION

Bottle/Can Recycling Update *Business, Association*

Publishing Co: Resource Recycling, Inc., PO Box 10540, Portland, OR 97210-0540 Fax # (503) 229-6135; Title Tel # (503) 227-1319 Title Fax # (503) 227-6135
Personnel: Publisher-Judy Roumpf, Editor-Jerry Powell, Circ. Mgr.-Carol Hendrickson, Art Dir.-Suzette DuCharme
Editorial Description: Covers all aspects of recycling glass & plastic bottles, and steel & aluminum cans. Includes market trends, economics, collection processes, equipment news, industry actors, governmental activities & information sources.
General Info: Yr. Est. 1990, Monthly, Trim Size-8½ x 11, 16 pages, ISSN: 1052-4916
Subscriptions: Indv. $75, Can. $75, For. $75
Circulation: Total-1,000
List Rental: Actives: $75/M

Building Systems Review *Business*

Publishing Co: National Association of Home Builders, 1201 15th St NW, Washington, DC 20005-2842 Tel # (202) 822-0216; Title Tel # (202) 822-0576
Personnel: Publisher-James R. Birdsong, Editor-Kelly M. Romigh
Editorial Description: News information summary for the sutems built housing industry & their product service suppliers.
General Info: (Formerly Housing America), Yr. Est. 1987, Monthly
Subscriptions: Free With Membership
Circulation: Total-750

Business Associate *Business, Association*

Publishing Co: Western Pennsylvania Conservancy, 316 4th Ave., Pittsburgh, PA 15222-2075; Title Tel # (412) 288-2777
Personnel: Editor-William Randour
Editorial Description: Reports on land conservation projects of the Western Pennsylvania Conservancy (land acquisition, land studies, & feature articles on conservation of natural resources) to business members of the organization.
General Info: Yr. Est. 1984, Semi-annually
Subscriptions: Free With Membership
Circulation: Total-1,000

Business and the Environment
See: BUSINESS & INDUSTRY

CBE Environmental Review

Publishing Co: Citizens for A Better Environment, 407 S Dearborn St Ste 1775, Chicago, IL 60605-1198; Title Tel # (612) 824-8637
Personnel: Editor-Sarah Johanneson
Editorial Description: Evironmental matters specific to Illiois Minnesota & Wisconsin.
General Info: Yr. Est. 1975, Quarterly, Trim Size-8.5 x 11, Offset press, 4 pages, 2 Color, Newsprint, Other
Subscriptions: Indv. $30, Inst. $30
Circulation: Total-22,000

CENYC Environmental Bulletin *Consumer*

Publishing Co: Council on the Environment of NYC, 51 Chambers St Ste 228, New York, NY 10007-1208; Title Tel # (212) 788-7900
Personnel: Editor-Veronica Green
Editorial Description: Environmental briefs of interest to New York City area residents and other individuals and organizations.
General Info: Yr. Est. 1970, Bi-monthly, Trim Size-8½ x 11, 2 pages, No Color
Circulation: Total-150

CLAG Communication
See: GEOGRAPHY

COPIRG Outlook *Association*

Publishing Co: Colorado Public Interest Research Group, 1530 Blake St., #220, Denver, CO 80202-1336; Title Tel # (303) 573-7474
Personnel: Editor-Richard McClintock, Circ. Mgr.-Sam Goldberg
Editorial Description: Consumer rights,environmental protection & citizen action organization.
General Info: (Formerly Colorado Outlook), Quarterly, Trim Size-8½ x 11, Web press, 8 pages, No Color, Newsprint, Saddle-stitched
Subscriptions: Indv. $20
Circulation: Total-25,000

COSSMHO Reporter, The
See: HEALTH

California Environmental Compliance Monitor *Business*

Publishing Co: M. Lee Smith Publishers & Printers ,LCC, P.O. Box 198867, 162 Fourth Avenue North, Nashville, TN 37219-8867; Title Tel # (615) 242-7395 Title Fax # (615) 256-6601
Personnel: Publisher-M Lee Smith, Editor-Dan McGovern, Circ. Dir.-Cathy Bradford, Mktg. Dir.-David Yates
Editorial Description: Covers environmental issues and developments in California.
General Info: (Formerly BNA California Environment Reporter), Yr. Est. 1990, 26x/yr., ISSN: 1052-813X
Subscriptions: Indv. $417
Printing Co: M. Lee Smith Publishers & Printers ,LLC, PO Box 198867, 162 Fourth Avenue, Nashville, TN 37219-8867 Tel # (615) 242-7395, Fax # (615) 256-6601

California Environmental Insider *Business*

Publishing Co: California Environmental Insider, PO Box 10106, San Rafael, CA 94912-0106; Title Tel # (415) 456-8411 Title Fax # (415) 456-1314
Personnel: Publisher-Jerry Cadagan, Editor-Roger Pearson
Editorial Description: Covers environmental developments and issues in California.
General Info: Yr. Est. 1987, Semi-monthly, ISSN: 0985-2299
Subscriptions: Indv. $355
Advertising: Inquire for rates.
List Rental: Hotline: 9,750, $125/M

California Environmental Law and Land Use Practice
See: LAW

California Today *Association*

Publishing Co: Planning and Conservation League, 926 J St Ste 612, Sacramento, CA 95814-2707; Title Tel # (916) 444-8726 Title Fax # (916) 448-1789
Personnel: Publisher, Editor-Dr. Gerald Meral
Editorial Description: Review of California environmental legislation and activities of PCL.
General Info: Yr. Est. 1965, Bi-monthly, Trim Size-8½ x 11, Offset press, 8 pages, ISSN: 0739-8042, 2 Color, Recycled, Saddle-stitched
Subscriptions: Indv. $33, Free With Membership
Circulation: Total-12,000
Printing Co: Fruitridge Printing & Litho, 3258 Stockton Blvd., Sacramento, CA 95820-1418 Tel # (916) 452-9213

Canadian Conservation Institute Technical Bulletin *Association*

Publishing Co: Canadian Conservation Institute, 1030 Innes Rd., Ottawa, ON K1A 0M5 Canada; Title Tel # (613) 998-3721 Title Fax # (613) 998-4721
Personnel: Circ. Mgr.-A. Dorning
Editorial Description: Variety of subjects on conservation of collections.
General Info: Yr. Est. 1972, Semi-annually, Trim Size-8½ x 11, ISSN: 0706-4152, Ind/Abs/Online: AATA, No Color
Subscriptions: Free
Circulation: Total-3,500

Canadian Environmental Control Newsletter *Business*

Publishing Co: CCH Canadian Ltd., 6 Garamond Ct., North York, ON M3C 1Z5 Canada Fax # (416) 444-8011 Parent Co.-CCH, Inc., Riverwoods; Title Tel # (416) 441-2992 Title Fax # (416) 444-9011
Editorial Description: Covers the general topic of pollution and the environmental control measures designed to fight it.
General Info: Yr. Est. 1945, Semi-monthly, Trim Size-6 x 9, Web press, ISSN: 0318-0794, No Color
Subscriptions: Can. $365

Canadian Plains Bulletin *Association*

Publishing Co: Canadian Plains Research Center, University of Regina, Regina, SK S4S 0A2 Canada; Title Tel # (306) 585-4758 Title Fax # (306) 585-4699
Personnel: Editor-Brian Mlazgar
Editorial Description: Informs individuals of current developments in the prairie region & the center. Multi-disciplinary research.
General Info: (Formerly Canadian Plains Area Studies Bulletin), Yr. Est. 1970, 2x/yr., Trim Size-8½ x 11, Offset press, 8 pages, ISSN: 0316-0343, No Color, Newsprint, Saddle-stitched
Circulation: Total-1,800

Canadian Society of Environmental Biologists Newsletter *Scholarly, Association* CPM: $388

Publishing Co: Canadian Society of Environmental Biologists, Box 962, Station F, Toronto, ON M4Y 2N9 Canada
Personnel: Editor-Patrick Stewart, Publisher, Adv. Dir.-Gary Ash
General Info: Yr. Est. 1962, Quarterly, Trim Size-8.5 x 11, Offset press, 36 pages, ISSN: 0318-5133, Color-cover, Matte, Saddle-stitched
Subscriptions: Indv. $25, For. $35, $10/copy
Circulation: Total-450
Advertising: $175. Accepts Inserts.

Canopy

Publishing Co: Rainforest Alliance, 65 Bleeker Street, New York, NY 10012-2187; Title Tel # (212) 677-1900 Title Fax # (212) 677-2187
General Info: Yr. Est. 1988, Quarterly

Caretaker Gazette, The
See: EMPLOYMENT

Carrying Capacity Network Network Clearinghouse Bulletin *Business, Consumer*

Publishing Co: Carrying Capacity Network, 2000 P St. NW, Ste.240, Washington, DC 20036-5915; Title Tel # (202) 296-4548 Title Fax # (202) 296-4609
Personnel: Editor-Monique Miller, Circ. Mgr.-Jennifer Correa
Editorial Description: Conducts Advocacy oriented initiatives focusing on solutions , such as immigration limitation , population stabilization and resource conservation to preserve our heritage and quality of life.
General Info: (Formerly Carrying Capacity Network Clearinghouse Bulletin), Yr. Est. 1991, Monthly, Trim Size-8½ x 11, 8 pages, ISSN: 1066-5404, 2 Color, Matte
Subscriptions: Indv. $25, Inst. $85, $2/copy
Acquistions: Publication Sold
Advertising: Accepts Inserts.
Printing Co: Ecoprint, 9335 Fraser Ave, Silver Spring, MD 20910 Tel # (301) 585-7077, Fax # (301) 585-4899

Center for Health Services Newsletter
See: HEALTH

Center for Rural Affairs Newsletter
See: AGRICULTURE

Center for Self Sufficiency Update
See: PHILANTHROPY

Central Alberta Naturalist *Association*

Publishing Co: Red Deer River Naturalists Society, Box 785, Red Deer, AB T4N 5H2 Canada Tel # (403) 347-8200
Personnel: Editor-Anna Robertson
General Info: (Formerly Red Deer River Naturalist), Monthly, 12 pages
Subscriptions: Indv. $15
Circulation: Total-3,200
Advertising: Inquire for rates.

Central Park Good Times
See: REGIONAL INTEREST

Cercular
Publishing Co: U.S. Army Engineer Waterways Experiment Station, 3909 Halls Ferry Rd, Vicksburg, MS 39180-6133; Title Tel # (601) 634-2016
Personnel: Editor-Andre Szuwalski
General Info: (Formerly Cercular Information Bulletin), Yr. Est. 1976, Quarterly
Circulation: Total-2,500

Changemakers
See: SOCIAL SERVICES & WELFARE

ChemEcology
See: CHEMISTRY & CHEMICALS

Chemical Process Safety *Business*
Publishing Co: Thompson Publishing Group, 1725 K Street, NW, Washington, DC 20006; Title Tel # (202) 872-4000 Title Fax # (202) 296-1091
Editorial Description: Features all federal and state regulations regarding chemical process safety. Subscription includes monthly newsletter and updates tracking new regulation and other related issues.
General Info: Yr. Est. 1990, Monthly, Looseleaf
Subscriptions: Indv. $349

Chesapeake Bay Foundation News
Publishing Co: Chesapeake Bay Foundation, 162 Prince George St, Annapolis, MD 21401-1758; Title Tel # (410) 268-8816 Title Fax # (410) 268-6687
Personnel: Editor-Flannery Davis
Editorial Description: Activities of CBF and problems concerning the Chesapeake Bay.
General Info: (Formerly Chesapeake Report), Yr. Est. 1969, Quarterly, Trim Size-8½ x 11, Sheetfed press, 8 pages, 2 Color, Matte, Saddle-stitched
Subscriptions: Free With Membership
Circulation: Total-75,000

Chihuahuan Desert Newsbriefs *Consumer*
Publishing Co: Chihuahuan Desert Research Institute, PO Box 1334, Alpine, TX 79831-1334
General Info: Yr. Est. 1983, Semi-annually, 4 pages, No Color, Newsprint
Circulation: Total-5,000

Children's Environments Quarterly
Publishing Co: Center for Human Environments, 33 W 42nd St, New York, NY 10036-8003; Title Tel # (212) 790-4550
General Info: (Formerly Childhood City Quarterly), Yr. Est. 1974, Quarterly
Subscriptions: Inst. $40

Citizen Alert Newsletter *Association*
Publishing Co: Citizen Alert, PO Box 5339, Reno, NV 89513-5339; Title Tel # (702) 827-4200
Personnel: Publisher-Bill Vincent, Editor-F. McGhe
Editorial Description: Raise awareness about nuclear, military and environmental issues facing Nevada.
General Info: (Formerly Great Basin Mx Alliance Newsletter), Yr. Est. 1975, Quarterly, Desktop press, 16 pages, No Color
Subscriptions: Indv. $10
Advertising: Inquire for rates.

Citizen Forester, The; Western Forest Report
See: FORESTRY

City Sierran
Publishing Co: Sierra Club-NYC Group, 625 Broadway Fl 2, New York, NY 10012-2611; Title Tel # (212) 473-7841
Personnel: Editor-Don Young, Adv. Dir.-Andrew Andriuk
General Info: Yr. Est. 1984, Quarterly, Trim Size-8½ x 11, Offset press, 16 pages, No Color, Newsprint
Circulation: Total-16,000
Printing Co: Vanguard Offset Printers, 470 Mundet Place, Hillside, NJ 07205-1115 Tel # (908) 851-2222

City Trees
See: PUBLIC MANAGEMENT & PLANNING

Clean Air News *Business*
Publishing Co: Progressive Business Publications, 370 Technology Dr., #3019, Malverne, PA 19355-9863 Parent Co.-American Future Systems, Inc., Bryn Mawr; Title Tel # (610) 695-8600 Title Fax # (610) 647-8089
Personnel: Publisher-Edward M. Satell, Editor-Matthew Harrington, Editorial Dir.-Steve Meyer, Mktg. Dir.-Ed Moore
Editorial Description: Business-to-business newslrtter to keep companies abreast of changing environmental regulations and new compliance strategies.
General Info: Yr. Est. 1992, Bi-weekly, 8 pages
Subscriptions: Indv. $299
Circulation: Total-15,000
List Rental: List Management Co.: Mail Marketing, Inc., 171 Terrace St., Haworth, NJ 07641-1899 Tel # (201) 387-1023, Fax # (201) 387-2976

Clean Air Permits *Business*
Publishing Co: Thompson Publishing Group, 1725 K Street, NW, Washington, DC 20006; Title Tel # (202) 872-4000 Title Fax # (202) 296-1091
Editorial Description: Manual dealing with state and federal clean air programs. Subscription includes monthly newsletter and updates.
General Info: Yr. Est. 1992, Monthly, Looseleaf
Subscriptions: Indv. $298

Clean Air Report
Publishing Co: Inside Washington Publishers, P.O. Box 7167, Ben Franklin Station, Washington, DC 20044 Tel # (703) 512-1800; Title Tel # (703) 416-8500
Personnel: Publisher-Alan Sosenko, Editor-Rick Weber
Editorial Description: Focuses on air pollution and related environmental issues.
General Info: Yr. Est. 1990, 26x/yr.
Subscriptions: Indv. $425

Clean Air Technology News *Business, Association*
Publishing Co: Inst. of Clean Air Companies, 1707 L St NW Ste 570, Washington, DC 20036-4201 Tel # (202) 331-1388; Title Tel # (202) 457-0911
Personnel: Editor-Jeffrey Smith
Editorial Description: Industrial air pollution control.
General Info: (Formerly Clean Air News), Yr. Est. 1960, Semi-annually

Clean Water Report *Business*
Publishing Co: Business Publishers, Inc., 951 Pershing Dr., Silver Spring, MD 20910-4464 Tel # (301) 589-5103 Fax # (301) 589-8493; Title Tel # (301) 587-6300 Title Fax # (301) 587-1081
Personnel: Publisher-Leonard A. Eiserer, Editor-Elaine Eiserer
Editorial Description: Safe drinking water act, water resources projects, water quality & effluent standards.
General Info: (Formerly Water Reporter), Yr. Est. 1964, Bi-weekly, Offset press, 8 pages, ISSN: 0009-8620, Ind/Abs/Online: Newsnet
Subscriptions: Indv. $268, Can. $268, For. $285
List Rental: List Management Co.: BPI Direct, 951 Pershing Dr., Silver Spring, MD 20910-4464 Tel # (301) 585-5976, Fax # (301) 587-4530

Clearwater Navigator *Consumer*
Publishing Co: Clearwater Navigator, 112 Market St, Poughkeepsie, NY 12601-4031; Title Tel # (914) 454-7673
Personnel: Editor-Mona Burkhart
Editorial Description: Covers Clearwater Revival programs and environmental issues.
General Info: Bi-monthly, Trim Size-7 x 11, 8 pages
Subscriptions: Free With Membership

Clippings
See: GARDENING & HORTICULTURE

CoHousing Newsletter *Consumer*
Publishing Co: CoHousing Newsletter, 2169 E. San Francisco Blvd., Ste. E, San Rafael, CA 94901 Tel # (510) 528-2212
Editorial Description: New and information Residential communities with shared facilities.
Subscriptions: Indv. $20

Coastal Reporter *Association*
Publishing Co: American Littoral Society, Sandy Hook, Highlands, NJ 07732; Title Tel # (908) 291-0055 Title Fax # (908) 872-8041
General Info: Semi-annually
Subscriptions: Inst. $30, For. $35, Free With Membership
Circulation: Total-8,000

Coastal Society Bulletin, The *Association*
Publishing Co: The Coastal Society, PO Box 25408, Alexandria, VA 22313-5408; Title Tel # (703) 768-1599
Personnel: Editor-Robert Boyles, Editor-Darlene Finch
Editorial Description: Covers multi-disciplinary issues (management, law, science, etc.) related to the world's coasts.
General Info: Yr. Est. 1975, Quarterly
Subscriptions: Indv. $35, Inst. $250, Can. $40, For. $40, $3/copy
Circulation: (83% controlled), Total-300, International-50

Colorado Environmental Compliance Update
See: LAW

Common Sense on Energy & Our Envirnoment *Consumer*
Publishing Co: Common Sense on Energy & Our Environment, PO Box 215, Morrisville, PA 19067-0215 Tel # (215) 736-1153; Title Tel # (215) 321-6479 Title Fax # (215) 321-6479
Editorial Description: Reports on environmental issues and provides information about protecting resources. Focuses on educational programs.
General Info: Yr. Est. 1990, Bi-monthly, ISSN: 1052-6331
Subscriptions: Indv. $49, Inst. $79
Circulation: Total-150, Readership-150

Community & Worker Right to Know News *Business*

Publishing Co: Thompson Publishing Group, 1725 K Street, NW, Washington, DC 20006; Title Tel # (202) 872-4000 Title Fax # (202) 296-1091
Personnel: Publisher-Richard Thompson, Editor-Mary Belferman
Editorial Description: Covers a variety of environmental issues.
General Info: Yr. Est. 1986, 22x/yr., Trim Size-8½ x 11, 10 pages
Subscriptions: Indv. $379

Community Right to Know Manual *Business*

Publishing Co: Thompson Publishing Group, 1725 K Street, NW, Washington, DC 20006
Tel # (202) 872-4000; Title Tel # (202) 872-1766
Personnel: Publisher-Richard Thompson, Editor-June Bolstridge
Editorial Description: Covers a variety of SARA Title III issues. Subscription includes monthly updates and bulletins covering current federal and state developments.
General Info: Yr. Est. 1986, 22x/yr., Looseleaf
Subscriptions: Indv. $324

Compassionate Shopper *Association*

Publishing Co: Beauty Without Cruelty, 175 W 12th St Apt 16g, New York, NY 10011-8220; Title Tel # (212) 989-8073
Personnel: Publisher, Editor-Ethel Thurston
Editorial Description: Apparel & cosmetics manufactured & tested without harm to animals.
General Info: Yr. Est. 1973, 4 pages
Subscriptions: Indv. $15, $1/copy
Circulation: Total-4,000

Compendium Newsletter 'Your Guide to the Worlds Environmental Crises' *Business, Consumer*

Publishing Co: Educational Communications, Environmental Res. Library, Box 351419, Los Angeles, CA 90035-9119; Title Tel # (310) 559-9160
Personnel: Editor-Nancy Pearlman
Editorial Description: Comprehensive summary of environmental issues & activities. Natl. emphasis; lists radio & TV shows produced by Educational Communications. Book reviews, resources available, special reports, calendar.
General Info: Yr. Est. 1972, Bi-monthly, Mimeo press, 20 pages, ISSN: 0198-9103, No Color
Subscriptions: Indv. $20
Acquistions: Publication Bought
Circulation: Total-900

Compliance Strategies Review *Business*

Publishing Co: Fieldston Co., 1920 N Street, N.W., Ste. 210, Washington, DC 20036; Title Tel # (202) 775-0240 Title Fax # (202) 872-8045
Personnel: Publisher-James Heller, Publications Director-Jay Kumar, Editor-Sue Follett, Asst. Ed.-John Gallagher, Asst. Ed.-Mike Harms, Mktg. Dir.-Laura Dowe
Editorial Description: Briefing on the Clean Air Act of 1990.
General Info: 24x/yr., Trim Size-8½ x 11, 12 pages
Subscriptions: Indv. $625
Printing Co: Newsletter Services, Inc., 9700 Philadelphia Court, Lanham, MD 20706 Tel # (301) 731-5200, Fax # (301) 731-5201

Composting News *Business, Association*

Publishing Co: McEntee Media Corp., 13727 Holland Rd., Cleveland, OH 44142-3920; Title Tel # (216) 362-7979 Title Fax # (216) 362-6553
Personnel: Publisher, Editor-Ken McEntee, Adv. Rep.-Kevin Freas, Adv. Rep.-Carol Garbo, Adv. Dir., Mktg. Dir.-Rick Downing
Editorial Description: Monthly news about municipal, backyard, industrial, and agricultural composting.
General Info: Yr. Est. 1992, Monthly, Trim Size-8½ x 11, Sheetfed press, 16 pages, ISSN: 1064-1440, 33% ads, 2 Color, Recycled, Saddle-stitched
Subscriptions: Indv. $89, Can. $90, For. $105, $10/copy
Advertising: Inquire for rates.

ConnTAP Quarterly *Business*

Publishing Co: Connecticut Technical Assistance Program, 50 Columbus Blvd Ste 4, Hartford, CT 06106-1910 Tel # (203) 241-0777 Fax # (203) 244-2017
Personnel: Publisher-Rita Lomasney, Editor, Production Mgr., Art Dir.-Lauren Daus Shea
Editorial Description: Practical case-studies and advice about a range of pollution prevention issues. Designed to assist small- to medium-sized businesses relaize the cost savings inherent in pollution prevention.
General Info: Yr. Est. 1988, Quarterly, Trim Size-8½ x 11, Desktop press, 8 pages, 2 Color, Matte
Circulation: (100% controlled)
Printing Co: Lebon Press, 73 Homestead Ave, Hartford, CT 06112-2333 Tel # (203) 278-6355, Fax # (203) 527-3786

Connecticut Environmental Compliance Update
See: LAW

Conscious Consumer
See: CONSUMER INTERESTS

Conscious Consumer Corporate Edition
See: CONSUMER INTERESTS

Conservation *Association*

Publishing Co: National Wildlife Federation, 8925 Leesburg Pike, Vienna, VA 22184-0001 Tel # (703) 790-4000 Fax # (703) 442-7332; Title Tel # (202) 797-6800
Personnel: Editor-Dena Leibman, Editor-Caroline Taylor, Editorial Asst.-Fannie Mae Keller
Editorial Description: Digest of national conservation legislation, published when Congress is in session, available to members only!.
General Info: Yr. Est. 1939, Bi-weekly, 24 pages, ISSN: 1074-1283
Circulation: Total-27,000

Conservation Commission News *Consumer, Association*

Publishing Co: New Hampshire Assn. of Conservation Commissions, 54 Portsmouth St, Concord, NH 03301-5486; Title Tel # (603) 224-7867
Personnel: Editor-Marjory Swope
Editorial Description: National, state, local information and issues dealing with natural resources and the environment.
General Info: Yr. Est. 1967, Quarterly, Trim Size-8½ x 11, Offset press, 8 pages, ISSN: 0027-6537, 1% ads, No Color
Subscriptions: Indv. $5
Circulation: Total-1,700
Advertising: Inquire for rates.
Printing Co: Town Line Printing, 102 Main St, Suncook, NH 03275-1236 Tel # (603) 485-8850

Conservation Voter *Association*

Publishing Co: California League of Conservation Voters, 10951 W Pico Blvd Ste 201, Los Angeles, CA 90064-2126; Title Tel # (310) 441-4162 Title Fax # (310) 441-1685
Personnel: Editor-Christine Quirk
Editorial Description: Environmental politic affairs/analysis.
General Info: Yr. Est. 1981, Trim Size-11⅜ x 17½, Web press, 4 pages, 2 Color, Newsprint
Subscriptions: Indv. $30
Circulation: Total-35,000
Printing Co: Rogers & McDonald Graphics, 1141 Sandhill Ave, Carson, CA 90746-1314 Tel # (310) 604-1012, Fax # (310) 537-0250

Conserve *Association*

Publishing Co: Western Pennsylvania Conservancy, 316 4th Ave., Pittsburgh, PA 15222-2075; Title Tel # (412) 288-2777
Personnel: Editor-William Randour
Editorial Description: Reports on land conservation projects of the Western Pennsylvania Conservancy (land acquisition, land studies, and feature articles on conservation of natural resources).
General Info: Yr. Est. 1971, Semi-annually, Trim Size-9½ x 13½, Offset press, 6 pages, 2 Color
Subscriptions: Free With Membership
Circulation: Total-20,000

Courier
See: INTERNATIONAL AFFAIRS

Cultivar: Newsletter of the UCSC Center for Agroecology & Sustainable Food Systems
See: AGRICULTURE

Current
See: BOATS & BOATING

Cycle/the Waste Paper

Publishing Co: Environmental Action Coalition, 625 Broadway Fl 2, New York, NY 10012-2611; Title Tel # (212) 677-1601
Personnel: Editor-Jenny Tichenor
Editorial Description: Environmental issues, opinions, and reporting. Special sections on recycling and education.
General Info: Yr. Est. 1970, Quarterly, 8 pages
Circulation: Total-2,500

D&A Hazardous Waste Hotline
See: CHEMISTRY & CHEMICALS

DGS Greenthumb

Publishing Co: Dept. of General Services, Manhattan Municipal Bldg., 1 Centre St., 17th Fl. S., New York, NY 10007; Title Tel # (212) 669-7140 Title Fax # (212) 669-8992
Editorial Description: Focuses on Operation Greenthumb personnel, community garden projects, awards, etc.
General Info: Yr. Est. 1981, Quarterly
Circulation: Total-3,000

Dakota Counsel
See: ENERGY

Deep Spring Newsletter
See: RELIGIOUS & THEOLOGICAL

Digest of Environmental Law
See: LAW

Digit Fund

Publishing Co: Digit Fund, 45 Inverness Dr., E., Englewood, CO 80112-5411; Title Tel # (303) 790-2345
Personnel: Editor-Claude Ramsey
General Info: 8x/yr.

Disaster Research

Publishing Co: Natural Hazards Information Center, Box 482, Univ. of Colorado, Boulder, CO 80309-0001 Fax # (303) 492-2151; Title Tel # (303) 492-6819 Title Fax # (810) 492-2151
Personnel: Editor-David Butler
Editorial Description: Disaster Research is an electronic newsletter, distributed by computer network, for creators and users of hazards and disasters information. It deals with all aspects of human adaption to natural hazards - floods, earthquakes, volcanoes, hurricanes, tornadoes, etc.
General Info: Yr. Est. 1987, Semi-monthly
Subscriptions: Free
Circulation: Total-1,400
List Rental: Rents Lists

Divining Rod   *Business, Consumer*

Publishing Co: New Mexico Water Resources Research Institute, Box 30001, Dept. 3167, Las Cruces, NM 88003-0001; Title Tel # (505) 646-1813 Title Fax # (505) 646-6418
Personnel: Editor-Catherine O. Klett
Editorial Description: Reports on water issues & water research in New Mexico.
General Info: Yr. Est. 1977, Quarterly, Trim Size-8½ x 11, Offset press, 12 pages, 2 Color, Matte, Saddle-stitched
Subscriptions: Free
Circulation: Total-3,000

Doctors for Disaster Preparedness
See: HEALTH

E & P Environment   *Business*

Publishing Co: Pasha Publications, Inc, 1616 N. Fort Myer Dr., #1000, Arlington, VA 22209-3103 Fax # (703) 528-4926; Title Tel # (703) 528-1244 Title Fax # (703) 528-1253
Personnel: Publisher-Tod Sedgwick, Editor-Jerry Grisham, Mng. Editor-Jeff Schomisch, Circ. Mgr.-Kathy Thorne, Production-Rob Traister, Mktg. Coord.-Mary Anvari, Mktg. Coord.-Julie Johnson
Editorial Description: Reports on environmental regulations, advances in technology, and litigation involving the exploration and production segments of the oil and gas industry.
General Info: Bi-weekly, ISSN: 1054-6464
Subscriptions: Indv. $395, For. $430, $17/copy

ECOAlert   *Association*

Publishing Co: CCNB, 180 St. John St., Fredericton, NB E3B 4A9 Canada; Title Tel # (506) 458-8747 Title Fax # (506) 458-1047
Personnel: Editor-Merrideth Brewer
Editorial Description: Environmental issues.
General Info: (Formerly Conservation), Yr. Est. 1978, Bi-monthly, Trim Size-8½ x 11, Web press, 12 pages, ISSN: 0833-448X, Ind/Abs/Online: CPI, No Color, Newsprint
Subscriptions: Indv. $18, Can. $18
Circulation: Total-600
Advertising: Inquire for rates.

ECOL News   *Business, Association*

Publishing Co: Environmental Conservation Library, 300 Nicollet Mall, Minneapolis, MN 55401-1925; Title Tel # (612) 372-6570
Personnel: Editor-William Johnston
Editorial Description: Environmental information; update on resources available in the Environmental Conservation Library (ECOL); bibliographies on specific topics.
General Info: Yr. Est. 1972, Semi-annually, Trim Size-8½ x 11, 4 pages, Color-cover
Circulation: Total-4,000

EDF Letter   *Business, Association*

Publishing Co: Environmental Defense Fund, 257 Park Ave S Fl 16, New York, NY 10010-7386; Title Tel # (212) 505-2100 Title Fax # (212) 505-2375
Personnel: Editor-Norma Watson, Photo Ed., Staff Writer-Tim Conner, Circ. Mgr.-Rosemary Ostergen
Editorial Description: Reports EDF efforts to protect environmental quality, & public health.
General Info: Yr. Est. 1970, Bi-monthly, Trim Size-8½ x 11, Web press, 8 pages, ISSN: 0163-2566, No Color, Newsprint, Saddle-stitched
Subscriptions: Indv. $20, Free With Membership
Circulation: Total-285,000
List Rental: List Management Co.: Names in the News-California, 1 Bush St Bsmt 3, San Francisco, CA 94104-4425 Tel # (415) 989-3350, Fax # (415) 433-7796, Actives: 187,174, $70/M, Expires: 82,559, $50/M
Printing Co: Instant Web, 7951 Powers Blvd, Chanhassen, MN 55317-9502 Tel # (612) 474-0961

EER Environmental Events
Record   *Business, Association*

Publishing Co: United Nations Publications, Two UN Plaza, Room DC2-853, New York, NY 10017 Tel # (212) 963-8302 Fax # (212) 963-3489
Editorial Description: Maintains a record of recent environmental occurences.
General Info: Yr. Est. 1990, Monthly

ENFO

Publishing Co: Environmental Info Ctr., 1251b Miller Ave, Winter Park, FL 32789-4827; Title Tel # (407) 644-5377
Personnel: Editor-Marcia Ramsdell
Editorial Description: Describe environmental matters important to Florida such as water resources, parks, wildlife, air quality, growth management, government & private actions.
General Info: Yr. Est. 1971, Bi-monthly, 12 pages, ISSN: 0276-9956
Subscriptions: Indv. $20, Inst. $25
Circulation: Total-1,100

EPA Bulletin

Publishing Co: U.S. Environmental Protection Agency, 401 M St., S.w., A-107, Washington, DC 20460-0001; Title Tel # (202) 755-0890
General Info: Yr. Est. 1972, Monthly

EPA Enforcement Manual   *Business*

Publishing Co: Thompson Publishing Group, 747 Third Ave., New York, NY 10017 Tel # (212) 888-7220 Fax # (212) 486-3400
Personnel: Editor-Barry M. Hartman, Editor-Cheryl Lieber, Mktg. Dir.-Kevin Mahon
Editorial Description: All matters (state and federal) of environmental enforcement. Deals with regulations, cases and agency decisions.
General Info: Yr. Est. 1993, Annually, 8 pages, 2 Color, Looseleaf
Subscriptions: Indv. $449, $449/copy

EPA Policy Alert

Publishing Co: Inside Washington Publishers, P.O. Box 7167, Ben Franklin Station, Washington, DC 20044 Tel # (703) 512-1800; Title Tel # (703) 892-8500
Personnel: Publisher-Alan Sosenko, Editor-Rick Weber
General Info: Yr. Est. 1984, Bi-weekly, Trim Size-8½ x 11, Sheetfed press, 14 pages
Subscriptions: Indv. $295

EPA Reusable News   *Business, Consumer*

Publishing Co: US EPA, Office Of Solid Waste 401 M, Street SW, Washington, DC 20460-0001
Editorial Description: Newsletter on recycling and the environment.

ESE Notes   *Association*

Publishing Co: UNC Dept. Envir. Sci. & Eng., Sch. Of Public Health Cb#7400, Chapel Hill, NC 27599-0001; Title Tel # (919) 966-1171
Editorial Description: Reports research and training activities of the Department.
General Info: Yr. Est. 1964, Quarterly, Trim Size-8½ x 11½, Offset press, 8 pages, ISSN: 0546-4552, 2 Color
Circulation: Total-2,200

Earth Impact   *Consumer*

Publishing Co: Seventh Generation, Colchester, VT 05446-1672; Title Fax # (800) 456-1139
Editorial Description: Environmental information .
General Info: Bi-monthly
Subscriptions: Free With Membership
List Rental: Rents Lists

Earth Patrol   *Consumer*

Publishing Co: Earth Matters, 6 Patriot Ln, Newington, CT 06111-4421
Editorial Description: Environmental issues reported simply, with activities, books, and more for kids 4-12.
General Info: Quarterly

Earth System Monitor
See: OCEANOGRAPHY

EarthQuest

Publishing Co: Univ. Corp. for Atmospheric Research, Box 3000, Boulder, CO 80307-3000; Title Tel # (303) 497-1682 Title Fax # (303) 497-1679
Personnel: Editor-Carol Ramussen, Circ. Mgr.-Diane Ehret
Editorial Description: Covers natl. & intl. programs addressing global environmental change.
General Info: Yr. Est. 1987, Quarterly, Trim Size-8 x 11, Sheetfed press, 16 pages, 2 Color, Matte, Saddle-stitched
Circulation: Total-12,000

Earthkeeping Ontario
See: AGRICULTURE

Earthstewards Network
News

Publishing Co: Holyearth Foundation, Box 10697, Winslow, WA 98110-0697; Title Tel # (206) 842-7986
Personnel: Editor-Irv Thomas
Editorial Description: Voice for earthstewards-caretakers of the planet & each other. Sustainable, harmonious living. Global friendships.
General Info: (Formerly Holyearth Network News), Yr. Est. 1980, Bi-monthly, Trim Size-8½ x 11, Offset press, 24 pages, No Color
Subscriptions: Indv. $18
Circulation: Total-2,000

Earthwatch Oregon   *Association*

Publishing Co: Oregon Environmental Council, 520 SW 6th Avenue, #940, Portland, OR 97204-1535; Title Tel # (503) 222-1963
Personnel: Editor-Martha Prinz
Editorial Description: Environmental issues of current importance in Oregon.
General Info: Yr. Est. 1969, Quarterly, Trim Size-8½ x 11, Web press, 8 pages, ISSN: 0890-1201, 3% ads, No Color, Newsprint
Subscriptions: Indv. $25
Circulation: (100% controlled), Total-2,000
Advertising: Inquire for rates.
List Rental: Actives: 2,000, $70/M

Eco-Humane Letter *Association*

Publishing Co: Intl. Ecology Society, 1471 Barclay St, Saint Paul, MN 55106-1405; Title Tel # (612) 774-4971
Personnel: Publisher-R.J.F. Kramer, Editor-Stephanie O'Brien
Editorial Description: Brings to light issues concerning animals, wildlife and the environment.
General Info: Yr. Est. 1976, Irregular, Trim Size-8½ x 11, Offset press, 10 pages, Color, Recycled, Other
Subscriptions: Indv. $10
Acquistions: Publication Bought, Publication Sold
Circulation: (100% controlled), Total-6,000
Advertising: Inquire for rates.
List Rental: Rents Lists
Printing Co: Sunrise Publishing, Box 6767, Seeger Sq. Stn., St. Paul, MN 55106-0767 Tel # (612) 774-4971

Eco Newsletter *Association*

Publishing Co: Sponsor-Antarctic & Southern Ocean Coalition, Antarctica & Southern Ocean Coalition, 424 C St NE, Washington, DC 20002-5818 Tel # (202) 544-0236; Title Tel # (202) 544-2600 Title Fax # (202) 544-8483
Personnel: Editor-J. Barnes, Science Ed.-B. Marks
General Info: Quarterly
Subscriptions: Free To Qualified Recipient
Circulation: Total-500

Eco-Politics

Publishing Co: California League of Conservation Voters, 10951 W Pico Blvd Ste 201, Los Angeles, CA 90064-2126 Tel # (310) 441-4162; Title Tel # (415) 397-7780
Personnel: Editor-Sven Serrano
General Info: Quarterly, 4 pages
Subscriptions: Indv. $25

Eco-Profiteer, The
See: INVESTMENT

Eco/Log Canadian Pollution Legislation
See: LAW

Eco/Log Week *Business*

Publishing Co: Southam Business Communications, Inc., 1450 Don Mills Rd., Don Mills, ON M3B 2X7 Canada Fax # (416) 442-2200; Title Tel # (416) 445-6641
Personnel: Publisher-Mary Mancini, Editor-Deborah Orchard, Circ. Mgr.-Saundra Dobroski
Editorial Description: Legislation & regulations, techniques & equipment re: effluent treatment, emission controls, waste disposal, & recycling.
General Info: Yr. Est. 1973, Weekly, Trim Size-8½ x 11, Desktop press, 6 pages, ISSN: 0315-0380, Ind/Abs/Online: North. Tit., No Color, Recycled
Subscriptions: Indv. $470, Can. $519
List Rental: List Management Co.: Cornerstone List Mgrs., 2300 Yonge St., Ste. 2005, Box 2465, Toronto, ON M4P 1E4 Canada Tel # (416) 932-9555, Fax # (416) 932-9566, Actives: $80/M

EcoPsychology Newsletter
See: PSYCHOLOGY

Ecological Illness Law Reports
See: LAW

Ecology Notes
See: PRINTING/GRAPHIC ARTS

Ecology Reports

Publishing Co: Ecology Center of Ann Arbor, 417 Detroit St, Ann Arbor, MI 48104-1117; Title Tel # (313) 761-3186
Editorial Description: Promote environmental awareness through local & state research & education.
General Info: Yr. Est. 1970, 5x/yr., Offset press, 8 pages, No Color, Newsprint
Subscriptions: Indv. $30, $2/copy
Circulation: Total-2,000
Advertising: Inquire for rates.

Ecology USA

Publishing Co: Business Publishers, Inc., 951 Pershing Dr., Silver Spring, MD 20910-4464 Tel # (301) 589-5103 Fax # (301) 589-8493; Title Tel # (301) 587-6300
Personnel: Publisher-Leonard A. Eiserer, Editor-Elaine Eiserer
Editorial Description: Newsletter covering the protection of aquatic and terrestrial ecosystems.
General Info: Yr. Est. 1976, Bi-weekly, Trim Size-8½ x 11, Offset press, 8 pages, ISSN: 0098-6615, No Color
Subscriptions: Indv. $121, Can. $121, For. $137

Ecolution: The Eco-Home Newsletter *Consumer*

Publishing Co: Eco-Home Network, 4344 Russell Ave, Los Angeles, CA 90027-4508; Title Tel # (213) 662-5207
Personnel: Editor-Julia Russell
Editorial Description: Enhance quality of life through education.
General Info: Yr. Est. 1985, Quarterly, 12 pages, No Color
Subscriptions: Indv. $25
Circulation: Total-1,200

Economic News Notes

Publishing Co: National Association of Home Builders, 1201 15th St NW, Washington, DC 20005-2842 Tel # (202) 822-0216; Title Tel # (202) 822-0434
General Info: Yr. Est. 1954, Monthly
Circulation: Total-6,000

Ecosphere Magazine/ Newsletter

Publishing Co: Intl. Ecosystems Univ., 310 Oak Vue Rd, Pleasant Hill, CA 94523-3618; Title Tel # (415) 671-2900 Title Fax # (415) 946-1500
Personnel: Publisher-Claus Hetzer, Editor-Dr. Nicolas Hetzer, Circ. Mgr.-Franco Battaglia, Adv. Dir.-J. McCormack, Art Dir.-Jeannie Graves
Editorial Description: Environment, Culture, & Humans form the Ecosystem we live in. We want to enlighten & educate through good reporting, analysis scientific & popular articles & through outh
General Info: (Formerly International Ecosystems University -Bulletin), Yr. Est. 1965, Quarterly
Subscriptions: Indv. $12
Circulation: Total-25,000
Advertising: Accepts Inserts.
List Rental: Actives: $80/M

Electric Vehicle Progress
See: AUTOMOTIVE

Electrical Sensitivity News

Publishing Co: Weldon Publishing, 202 Cactus Dr., #20, PO Box 4146, Prescott, AZ 86302
Personnel: Editor-Lucinda Grant
Editorial Description: Electrical Sensitivity News is an international newsletter about the latest environmental illness-electrical sensitivity from electromagnetic fields.
General Info: Yr. Est. 1996, Bi-monthly, ISSN: 1086-2897
Subscriptions: Indv. $20, For. $35, $4/copy

Elm Research Institute Newsletter

Publishing Co: Elm Research Institute, J.P. Hansel, Harrisville, NH 03450; Title Tel # (603) 827-3048
Personnel: Editor-J.P. Hansel
General Info: Quarterly, 6 pages

Endangerspeak

Publishing Co: R.K. Jones, POB 3502, Camarillo, CA 93011
Editorial Description: To inform the public of their threat to wildlife and to promote a more balanced and creative ecology through fiction, essays, artwork and photos.
General Info: Yr. Est. 1995, Semi-annually, ISSN: 1076-576X
Subscriptions: Indv. $4, Inst. $4, Can. $6, For. $6, $2/copy
Advertising: Inquire for rates.

Energy & Environment Alert *Association*

Publishing Co: National Council for Environmental Balance, Inc., 4169 Westport Rd., Box 7732, Louisville, KY 40257-0732; Title Tel # (502) 896-8731 Title Fax # (502) 339-1745
Personnel: Editor-Irwin Tucker, Ph.D.
Editorial Description: Technical information on energy environment, agriculture, chemistry, entomology, & mineral resources in Layman's language.
General Info: Yr. Est. 1977, Quarterly, Trim Size-8½ x 11, Mimeo press, 4 pages, Color
Subscriptions: Indv. $20, Inst. $25
Circulation: Total-1,000
Printing Co: General Printing Co., 1700 S 5th St, Louisville, KY 40208-1795 Tel # (502) 637-6277

Energy & Environmental News
See: ENERGY

Energy Conservation News
See: ENERGY

Energy Design Update
See: CONSUMER INTERESTS

Energy Savers
See: ENERGY

Entomological Society of Canada, Bulletin
See: ENTOMOLOGY

Enviro Update *Business*

Publishing Co: Flint Ink Corp., 33105 Schoolcraft Rd, Livonia, MI 48150-1625
Editorial Description: Provides information on environmental issues relevant to the printing industry.
General Info: Quarterly, Trim Size-8½ x 11, 2 pages, 2 Color, Matte
Subscriptions: Free To Qualified Recipient

Environment & Development *Association*

Publishing Co: American Planning Association, 1313 E 60th St, Chicago, IL 60637-2891; Title Tel # (312) 955-9100 Title Fax # (312) 955-8312
Personnel: Editor-Jim Schwab, Art Dir.-Lisa Barton, Mktg. Dir.-Kenneth East
Editorial Description: Publication is geared to the needs ot urban planners, developers, consultants and other efficials dealing with environmental planning problems.
General Info: Yr. Est. 1992, Monthly, Trim Size-8½ x 11, Desktop press, 4 pages, 2 Color
Subscriptions: Indv. $50, Inst. $50, Can. $60, For. $60, $5/copy
Acquistions: Publication Sold
Circulation: Total-2,195, Readership-2,200
List Rental: Actives: 2,250, $300/M

Environment Health & Safety Management *Business*

Publishing Co: Environment Group, Inc., The, PO Box 1269, Wainscott, NY 11975-1269; Title Tel # (516) 324-3508 Title Fax # (516) 329-1209
Personnel: Publisher, Editor-J. Gary Taylor, PhD, Circ. Dir.-Lynn Lutjen, Production Dir.-Patricia Scharlin
Editorial Description: Policy information and news for health and safety managers.
General Info: Yr. Est. 1990, Bi-weekly, Trim Size-8½ x 11, Sheetfed press, 8 pages, Color-cover, Matte
Subscriptions: Indv. $397
Circulation: Total-1,000
List Rental: Actives: 5,000, $60/M, Expires: 300, $60/M

Environment Ohio *Association*

Publishing Co: Ohio Environmental Protection Agency, PO Box 163669, Columbus, OH 43216-3669; Title Tel # (614) 644-2160
Personnel: Publisher-Patricia Madigan, Editor-Carol Porter, Art Dir.-Yvonne Foster-Smith
Editorial Description: Covers the activities of the Ohio EPA regarding air, water & land pollution plus public water supply; including pollution problems in Ohio & their control. New policies, regulations, significant Agency actions are covered as well.
General Info: Yr. Est. 1975, Bi-monthly, Trim Size-8½ x 11, Offset press, 8 pages, 2 Color, Newsprint
Circulation: Total-4,500

Environment Reporter *Business*

Publishing Co: Bureau of National Affairs, Inc., 1231 25th St. NW, Bldg. N-200, Washington, DC 20037-1157; Title Tel # (202) 452-4200 Title Fax # (202) 822-8092
Personnel: Publisher-William A. Beltz, Editor-Wallis E. McClain, Jr., Mng. Editor-Patricia Spencer, Circ. Mgr.-Gary C. Seltzer
Editorial Description: Covers legislative, administrative, judicial, industrial, & technical developments in pollution control & environment protection.
General Info: Yr. Est. 1970, Weekly, Trim Size-8½ x 11, Web press, 30 pages, ISSN: 0013-9211, Ind/Abs/Online: Lexis, Westlaw, HRIN, Mead Data Central, Nexis
Subscriptions: Indv. $2,310

Environment Watch: Latin America *Business*

Publishing Co: Cutter Information Corp., 37 Broadway, Ste. 1, Arlington, MA 02174-5552 Fax # (617) 648-1950; Title Tel # (617) 648-8700 Title Fax # (617) 648-8707
Personnel: Publisher-Karen Coburn, Editor-Jeffrey Stoub, Circ. Mgr.-Dennis Crowley, Production Mgr.-Ellen McHale, Mktg. Dir.-Paul Bergeron
Editorial Description: News and analysis for business and policy professionals.
General Info: Yr. Est. 1991, Monthly, Trim Size-8½ x 11, 16 pages, ISSN: 1060-1414
Subscriptions: Indv. $537, Can. $537, For. $597, $20/copy
List Rental: Rents Lists
Printing Co: Benjamin Franklin Smith Printers, 320 Stuart St, Boston, MA 02116-5242 Tel # (617) 426-1160

Environment Watch: Western Europe *Business*

Publishing Co: Cutter Information Corp., 37 Broadway, Ste. 1, Arlington, MA 02174-5552 Tel # (617) 648-8700 Fax # (617) 648-1950
Personnel: Publisher-Karen Coburn, Editor-Tony Carritt, Editor-Stephanie Gehlen, Circ. Mgr.-Dennis Crowley, Production Mgr.-Ellen McHale, Mktg. Dir.-Paul Bergeron
Editorial Description: News and analysis for business and policy professionals.
General Info: Yr. Est. 1992, Semi-monthly, Trim Size-8½ x 11, 8 pages, ISSN: 1066-6001, No Color
Subscriptions: Indv. $657, Can. $657, For. $757, $23/copy
List Rental: Rents Lists

Environmental Advisor
See: PRINTING/GRAPHIC ARTS

Environmental Bulletin

Publishing Co: N.J. Conservation Foundation, 300 Mendham Rd., Morristown, NJ 07960-4806; Title Tel # (201) 539-7540
Personnel: Editor-Pat Baxter
Editorial Description: State environmental legislative bulletin.
General Info: Yr. Est. 1971, Monthly, Mimeo press, 4 pages, No Color, Newsprint, Saddle-stitched
Subscriptions: Indv. $30
Circulation: Total-500

Environmental Bulletin *Association*

Publishing Co: American Assn. of State Highway Transportation Officials, 444 N Capitol St NW Ste 249, Washington, DC 20001-1512; Title Tel # (202) 624-5800
Personnel: Editor-David Clawson, Mktg. Dir.-Patty Kelley
Editorial Description: Environmental information for highway and transportation planners.
General Info: Yr. Est. 1992, Irregular, Trim Size-8½ x 11, Mimeo press, 12 pages
Subscriptions: Inst. $100, Can. $100, For. $125

Environmental Business Journal *Business*

Publishing Co: Environmental Business International, Inc., PO Box 371769, San Diego, CA 92137-1769; Title Tel # (619) 295-7685 Title Fax # (619) 295-5743
Personnel: Editor-Grant Ferrier, Circ. Mgr.-Jeff Turner
Editorial Description: Strategic business analysis for environmental industry executives.
General Info: Yr. Est. 1988, Monthly, 16 pages, ISSN: 1045-8611, No Color, Matte
Subscriptions: Indv. $395, Inst. $395, Can. $395, For. $445

Environmental Code Book Software Report *Business, Consumer*

Publishing Co: Donley Technology, PO Box 152, 220 Garfield Avenue, Colonial Beach, VA 22443-0152; Title Tel # (804) 224-9427 Title Fax # (804) 224-7958
Personnel: Publisher-Elizabeth Donley, Editor-Veronica Deschambault
Editorial Description: Profiles 25 systems with federal, State, and international environmental laws and regulations on CD-Rom, diskettes or on line.
General Info: Yr. Est. 1994, Irregular, 60 pages, ISSN: 1074-7591
Subscriptions: $89/copy

Environmental Compliance Alert *Business*

Publishing Co: Progressive Business Publications, 370 Technology Dr., #3019, Malverne, PA 19355-9863 Parent Co.-American Future Systems, Inc., Bryn Mawr; Title Tel # (610) 695-8600 Title Fax # (610) 647-8089
Personnel: Publisher-Edward M. Satell, Editor-Tom Guay, Editorial Dir.-Steve Meyer, Mktg. Dir.-Ed Moore
Editorial Description: Business-to-business newsletter to keep companies abreast of changing environmental regulations and new compliance stategies. Geared towards air, water, and waste issues.
General Info: Yr. Est. 1993, Bi-weekly, 8 pages
Subscriptions: Indv. $299
Circulation: Total-36,000
List Rental: List Management Co.: Mail Marketing, Inc., 171 Terrace St., Haworth, NJ 07641-1899 Tel # (201) 387-1023, Fax # (201) 387-2976

Environmental Compliance Litigation & Strategy
See: LAW

Environmental Compliance Report, The *Business*

Publishing Co: Southam Business Communications, Inc., 1450 Don Mills Rd., Don Mills, ON M3B 2X7 Canada Tel # (416) 445-6641; Title Tel # (416) 446-6641 Title Fax # (416) 442-2200
Personnel: Publisher-Mary Mancini, Sr. Ed.-Mark Sabourin, Circulation-Aileen Manganaro, Mktg. Dir.-Ian Rhind
Editorial Description: Legislative, regulatory, and judicial developments relative to the Canadian environment.
General Info: (Formerly Eco/Log Canadian Pollution Legislation Monthly Report), Yr. Est. 1983, Monthly, Trim Size-8½ x 11, Sheetfed press, 8 pages, ISSN: 1187-0125, Ind/Abs/Online: Predicasts, No Color
Subscriptions: Can. $815
List Rental: List Management Co.: Cornerstone List Mgrs., 2300 Yonge St., Ste. 2005, Box 2465, Toronto, ON M4P 1E4 Canada Tel # (416) 932-9555, Fax # (416) 932-9566

Environmental Compliance Tool Kit *Business*

Publishing Co: Thompson Publishing Group, 1725 K Street, NW, Washington, DC 20006 Tel # (202) 872-4000
Personnel: Editor-David J. Mason
Editorial Description: Simplifies paperwork and helps in the collection of data for an ongoing environmental compliance program. Subscription includes updates and a monthly newsletter.
General Info: Annually, Looseleaf
Subscriptions: Indv. $395

Environmental Compliance in (Your State) *Business*

Publishing Co: Business & Legal Reports, Inc., 39 Academy St., PO Box 1513, Madison, CT 06443-2646; Title Tel # (860) 245-7448 Title Fax # (860) 245-2559
Personnel: Publisher-Robert Brady, Editor-Faith Kuhn, Adv. Dir.-John Brady, Art Dir.-John Kallio, Mktg. Dir.-Kathy Long, Promotion Dir.-Jay Schleifer
Editorial Description: Provides accurate & timely 'how to' information on compliance for environmental regulations at both the state & federal level.
General Info: Yr. Est. 1990, Monthly, Trim Size-8½ x 11, 2 Color, Matte, Saddle-stitched, Looseleaf
Subscriptions: Indv. $595
Circulation: Total-2,500
List Rental: List Management Co.: Manager: Denise Shurkus; Marketing List Professionals, 39 Academy St # 1513, Madison, CT 06443-2646 Tel # (860) 245-2076, Fax # (860) 245-2559

Environmental Contract Opportunity Report

Publishing Co: United Communications Group, 11300 Rockville Pike, Ste. 1100, Rockville, MD 20852-3030; Title Tel # (301) 816-8950 Title Fax # (301) 816-8945
Personnel: Publisher-Nancy Becker, Editor-Neil Griffin
Editorial Description: Reports on environmental contracts, related topics.
General Info: Yr. Est. 1991, Weekly
Subscriptions: Indv. $527
List Rental: Rents Lists

Environmental Control News for Southern Industry   *Business*

Publishing Co: E.F. Williams, 751 E Brookhaven Cir, Memphis, TN 38117-4501; Title Tel # (901) 685-2077 Title Fax # (901) 685-2261
Personnel: Publisher-E.F. Williams, Asst. Ed.-Alex Williams, Circ. Mgr.-Etta Crisp, Adv. Dir.-Sue Reid
Editorial Description: Update on developments in pollution control for Southern industry, e.g., regulation, legislation, environment, technical.
General Info: Yr. Est. 1971, Monthly, Trim Size-8½ x 11, Offset press, 12 pages, ISSN: 0013-9238, No Color
Subscriptions: Indv. $30, $3/copy
Circulation: (100% controlled), Total-300
Advertising: Inquire for rates.

Environmental Counselor, The
See: LAW

Environmental Digest   *Business, Consumer*

Publishing Co: Sydenham Publishing, 344 23rd Street West, Owen Sound, ON N4K 4G7 Canada Tel # (519) 371-6289 Fax # (519) 371-3676
Personnel: Publisher-Jeffrey Elie, Editor-Stella Coultas
Editorial Description: Environmental news review for Canada.
General Info: Yr. Est. 1990, Bi-weekly, ISSN: 1183-8795
Subscriptions: Indv. $235

Environmental Engineering News   *Consumer*

Publishing Co: Purdue University Civil Engineering Dept., Civil Engineering Bldg., W. Lafayette, IN 47907 Tel # (317) 494-2164; Title Tel # (317) 494-2194
Personnel: Editor-John Bell
Editorial Description: Concerns environmental engineering.
General Info: Yr. Est. 1944, Monthly, 2 pages, No Color
Acquistions: Publication Bought
Circulation: Total-6,000

Environmental File, The   *Business*

Publishing Co: Environmental Healthcare, Inc., PO Box 2286, Delray Beach, FL 33447-2286; Title Tel # (407) 279-9901 Title Fax # (407) 265-0035
Editorial Description: Provides records management information to the environmental industry.
General Info: Yr. Est. 1992, Quarterly
Subscriptions: Indv. $195

Environmental Health & Safety CFR Update   *Business*

Publishing Co: Government Institutes, Inc., 4 Research Pl Ste 200, Rockville, MD 20850-3226; Title Tel # (301) 921-2355
General Info: Monthly
Subscriptions: Indv. $225

Environmental Health Letter   *Business*

Publishing Co: Business Publishers, Inc., 951 Pershing Dr., Silver Spring, MD 20910-4464 Tel # (301) 589-5103 Fax # (301) 589-8493; Title Tel # (301) 587-6300 Title Fax # (301) 587-1081
Personnel: Publisher-Leonard A. Eiserer, Editor-Pat Phibbs, Mktg. Dir.-Fay S. Gold
Editorial Description: Concise information on scientific research, legislation and issues that shape environmental health policy.
General Info: Yr. Est. 1962, Bi-weekly, Trim Size-8½ x 11, Offset press, 8 pages, ISSN: 0196-0598, Ind/Abs/Online: Newsnet
Subscriptions: Indv. $312, Can. $325, For. $325
List Rental: List Management Co.: Manager: Jim Hauschild; BPI Direct, 951 Pershing Dr., Silver Spring, MD 20910-4464 Tel # (301) 585-5976, Fax # (301) 587-4530

Environmental Health News   *Business*

Publishing Co: Univ. of Washington, School of Public Health, Dept. Of Environmental Health, Seattle, WA 98195-0001; Title Tel # (206) 543-3222
Personnel: Editor-David Kalman, Circ. Mgr.-Lynn Salter, Production Mgr.-Jerry Ongerth
Editorial Description: Concerns occupational health, air pollution and safety.
General Info: Yr. Est. 1951, Quarterly, 15 pages, No Color
Subscriptions: Free
Circulation: Total-2,500

Environmental Impact in New York   *Business*

Publishing Co: Matthew Bender & Co., 11 Penn Plaza, New York, NY 10001-2006 Tel # (212) 967-7707 Fax # (212) 244-3188
Editorial Description: This unique publication takes project applicants, opponents, & regulators through every stage of the exacting compliance requirements & procedures of SEQRA & New York City's Environmental Quality Review. It dicusses how to mesh them with local laws & regulations & analyzes the court & administrative decisions
General Info: Yr. Est. 1990, Irregular, Looseleaf

Environmental Invester's Green Market Report
See: INVESTMENT

Environmental Investor's Newsletter
See: INVESTMENT

Environmental LAWCAST
See: LAW

Environmental Laboratory Washington Report
See: LAW

Environmental Law
See: LAW

Environmental Law Journal
See: LAW

Environmental Liability Enforcement & Penalties Report
See: LAW

Environmental Life Newsletter   *Consumer*

Publishing Co: Parsons Holder Lifestyle Institute, PO Box 10979, Daytona Beach, FL 32120-1979 Tel # (904) 767-0670
Editorial Description: Shares ideas for living 'the environmental life' and lists environmental products.
Subscriptions: Free

Environmental Management Information Systems Report   *Business, Consumer*

Publishing Co: Donley Technology, PO Box 152, 220 Garfield Avenue, Colonial Beach, VA 22443-0152; Title Tel # (804) 224-9427 Title Fax # (804) 224-7958
Personnel: Publisher-Elizabeth Donley, Editor-Veronica Deschambault
Editorial Description: Describes 22 comprehensive environmental management information systems which allow environmental health and safety professionals to use one system to help comply with regulations under several different programs.
General Info: Yr. Est. 1995, Irregular, 80 pages, ISSN: 1081-2989
Subscriptions: $195/copy

Environmental Manager   *Business*

Publishing Co: John Wiley & Sons, Inc., 605 Third Avenue, New York, NY 10158-0012 Tel # (212) 850-6000 Fax # (212) 850-6088; Title Tel # (212) 645-7880 Title Fax # (212) 645-1160
Personnel: Editor-Sarah Magee
Editorial Description: Current environmental news & practical information, featuring case studies of solutions to problems such as toxic waste cleanups, waste minimization, underground storage tank leaks, clean air standards; coverage of regulation & legislation, & new cleanup technology & methods.
General Info: Yr. Est. 1989, Monthly, Trim Size-8½ x 11, Sheetfed press, 16 pages, ISSN: 1043-786X, Ind/Abs/Online: Data courier, 2 Color, Recycled, Saddle-stitched
Subscriptions: Indv. $135, Can. $135, For. $185
Advertising: Inquire for rates.
List Rental: Rents Lists
Printing Co: Williams Printing Co., 811 Cowan St, Nashville, TN 37207-5694 Tel # (615) 256-7125

Environmental Manager's Compliance Advisor   *Business*

Publishing Co: Business & Legal Reports, Inc., 39 Academy St., PO Box 1513, Madison, CT 06443-2646 Fax # (860) 245-2559; Title Tel # (860) 245-7448 Title Fax # (860) 245-1513
Personnel: Editor-Alan Borner, Art Dir.-John Kallio, Mktg. Dir.-Kathy Long, Publisher, Adv. Dir., Promotion Dir.-John Brady
Editorial Description: Practical advice on compliance with the lastest environmental and hazardous waste regulation, including state national & Federal Register news.
General Info: Yr. Est. 1984, Semi-monthly, Sheetfed press, 16 pages, Newsprint
Subscriptions: Indv. $270, $9/copy
Circulation: Total-5,000
List Rental: List Management Co.: Manager: Denise Sharkus; Marketing List Professionals, 39 Academy St # 1513, Madison, CT 06443-2646 Tel # (860) 245-2076, Fax # (860) 245-2559, Actives: $90/M, Hotline: $95/M

Environmental News

Publishing Co: N.J. Dept. of Environmental Protection, 401 E. State St., CN 402, Trenton, NJ 08608-1501; Title Tel # (609) 984-6773
Personnel: Editor-Edith Joseph
Editorial Description: Informs public about N.J. programs to address environmental concerns-- cleaner air, water, land management, conservation & preservation of natural resources-- flora, fauna, & historic heritage. Also, solid waste management and hazardous waste management.
General Info: (Formerly NJ Environmental Times), Yr. Est. 1968, Bi-monthly, Sheetfed press, 8 pages, 2 Color
Circulation: (100% controlled), Total-20,000

Environmental Newsletter, The *Consumer*

Publishing Co: Town of Rochester Environmental Commission, PO Box 65, Accord, NY 12404-0065
General Info: Quarterly, Trim Size-8½ x 11, 4 pages, No Color, Matte

Environmental Notice Bulletin *Business*

Publishing Co: New York State Department of Environmental Conservation, Division of Water, 50 Wolf Rd., Albany, NY 12233 Tel # (518) 457-3014; Title Tel # (518) 457-2344 Title Fax # (518) 485-7786
Personnel: Editor-Betty-Jo Daly
Editorial Description: Legal notice vehicle for state environmental quality review actions.
General Info: Weekly, Sheetfed press, 35 pages, No Color, Newsprint
Subscriptions: Indv. $12
Circulation: (100% controlled), Total-15,000
Printing Co: Eagle Press & Graphics, 20 S Ferry St, Albany, NY 12202-2058 Tel # (518) 462-2640

Environmental Opportunities See: EMPLOYMENT

Environmental Outlook

Publishing Co: Univ. of Washington, Engineering Annex, Fm-12, Seattle, WA 98195-0001; Title Tel # (206) 543-1812 Title Fax # (206) 543-2025
Personnel: Editor-Polly Dyer
Editorial Description: Regional & local environmental education.
General Info: Yr. Est. 1973, 10x/yr., Trim Size-8½ x 11, Sheetfed press, 4 pages, No Color
Circulation: Total-2,000
Printing Co: University of Washington Duplicating, Printing Deptartment, Seattle, WA 98195-0001 Tel # (206) 685-0305

Environmental Packaging: U.S. Guide to Green Labeling, Packaging and Recycling See: PACKAGING

Environmental Policy Alert

Publishing Co: Inside Washington Publishers, P.O. Box 7167, Ben Franklin Station, Washington, DC 20044 Tel # (703) 512-1800; Title Tel # (703) 892-8500 Title Fax # (703) 685-2606
Personnel: Publisher-Alan Sosenko, Editor-Rick Weber
Editorial Description: Developments in environmental policy.
General Info: Yr. Est. 1976, 26x/yr.
Subscriptions: Indv. $425

Environmental Pollution & Control *Business*

Publishing Co: National Technical Information Service U.S., 5285 Port Royal Rd., Springfield, VA 22161-0001 Fax # (703) 487-4630; Title Tel # (703) 487-4630
Editorial Description: Covers air, noise, solid waste, water pollution, radiation, environmental health & safety, and pesticide pollution & control.
General Info: Weekly, Trim Size-8½ x 11, Offset press, 34 pages, ISSN: 0364-4936, No Color
Subscriptions: Indv. $160, Can. $160, For. $225

Environmental Problems & Remediation *Business*

Publishing Co: Infoteam, Inc., PO Box 15640, Plantation, FL 33318-5640 Tel # (954) 473-9560 Fax # (954) 472-0544; Title Tel # (954) 473-7560 Title Fax # (954) 473-0544
Personnel: Publisher, Editor-Merton Allen
Editorial Description: Covers topics relating to environmental problems and solutions.
General Info: Yr. Est. 1994, Monthly, Trim Size-8½ x 11, Sheetfed press, 16 pages, ISSN: 1077-1395, Ind/Abs/Online: NewsNet, DIALOG, Predicasts, No Color, Newsprint
Subscriptions: Indv. $269, Can. $309, For. $379

Environmental Protection News *Business*

Publishing Co: Stevens Publishing Corp., 3630 J.H. Kultgen Frwy., Waco, TX 76706 Tel # (817) 662-1134 Fax # (817) 662-7075; Title Tel # (817) 776-9000 Title Fax # (817) 776-9018
Personnel: Publisher-L. Alan Stevens, Editor-Jim Pinkham, Mng. Editor-William C. Wallack, Editorial Asst.-Brian Feagans, Assoc. Ed.-Ellen S. Carey, Assoc. Ed.-Lisa Caruso, Assoc. Ed.-Stephen Davies, Circ. Mgr.-Tammy Meredith, Production Mgr.-Eliska Beaty, Adv. Dir.-Ruth Heard Warren, Art Dir.-Mylynda Callahan, Mktg. Mgr.-Mark Rathe, Promotion Dir.-Sherman George
Editorial Description: Reports on waste legal issues, technological advances and trends developing in the environmental arena. covers all media - air, water & land at all levels of government. Target audience: managers who want to know how to comply with EPA regulations.
General Info: Yr. Est. 1985, Semi-monthly, Trim Size-8½ x 11, Sheetfed press, 16 pages, ISSN: 1057-171X, Saddle-stitched
Subscriptions: Indv. $332, Can. $348, For. $366
Acquistions: Publication Bought
List Rental: Actives: 30,854, $75/M

Environmental Regulation/ State Capitals *Business, Consumer*

Publishing Co: Wakeman/Walworth, 300 N. Washington St., Alexandria, VA 22314-2530; Title Fax # (703) 549-8606 Title Fax # (703) 549-1372
Personnel: Publisher-Keyes Walworth
Editorial Description: Reviews state laws and programs affecting air & water pollution, solid waste, hazardous waste, ground water protection, insurance protection, etc.
General Info: (Formerly From the State Capitals Waste Disposal & Pollution Control), Weekly, ISSN: 1061-9682
Subscriptions: Indv. $265, Inst. $216, Can. $235, For. $255

Environmental Remediation Technology *Business*

Publishing Co: Business Publishers, Inc., 951 Pershing Dr., Silver Spring, MD 20910-4464 Tel # (301) 589-5103 Fax # (301) 589-8493; Title Tel # (301) 587-6300 Title Fax # (301) 585-9075
Personnel: Publisher-Leonard A. Eiserer, Editor-Andrew Ronak, Mktg. Dir.-Fay S. Gold
General Info: Bi-weekly, No Color, Other
Subscriptions: Indv. $437, Inst. $437, Can. $437, For. $450
List Rental: List Management Co.: Manager: Jim Hauschild; BPI Direct, 951 Pershing Dr., Silver Spring, MD 20910-4464 Tel # (301) 585-5976, Fax # (301) 587-4530

Environmental Resources Research Institute, Newsletter *Consumer*

Publishing Co: Environmental Resources Research Institute, Pennsylvania State Univ., University Park, PA 16802; Title Tel # (814) 863-0291 Title Fax # (814) 865-3378
Personnel: Editor-Joy Drohan
Editorial Description: Features on research projects on land, water, air & mining, institute news; announcements of new publications/reports.
General Info: Yr. Est. 1970, Quarterly, Trim Size-8½ x 11, Offset press, 6 pages, ISSN: 1041-701X, Ind/Abs/Online: Pencycle bulletin board (610.3533.5295)abstracted by Cambridge Scientific, 2 Color, Coated, Saddle-stitched
Subscriptions: Free To Qualified Recipient
Circulation: Total-2,500, Readership-2,500
Printing Co: University Printing Services (Penn State), 101 Business Services Bldg, University Park, PA 16802

Environmental Software Report *Business, Consumer*

Publishing Co: Donley Technology, PO Box 152, 220 Garfield Avenue, Colonial Beach, VA 22443-0152; Title Tel # (804) 224-9427 Title Fax # (804) 224-7958
Personnel: Publisher-Elizabeth Donley, Editor-Veronica M. Deschambault, Asst. Ed.-Karen Roberts
Editorial Description: The Environmental Software Report delivers information on new software packages, online systems, and databases. It describes both commercial and government systems relating to hazardous substance management, environmental assessments, regulatory compliance, ground water contamination studies, chemical profiles, air pollution modeling, risk management, and environmental impact assessments.
General Info: Yr. Est. 1988, 8x/yr., Trim Size-8½ x 11, Offset press, 24 pages, ISSN: 1043-2884, 2 Color, Matte, Saddle-stitched
Subscriptions: Indv. $125, Inst. $125, Can. $145, For. $145
Printing Co: Riverside Printing, PO Box 1267, Oak Grove, VA 22443-1067

Environmental Times, The *Association*

Publishing Co: Environmental Assessment Association, 8383 E. Evans Rd., Scottsdale, AZ 85260-3614; Title Tel # (602) 483-8100 Title Fax # (602) 998-8022
Editorial Description: News and information concerning issues of the environment.
General Info: (Formerly Environmental Inspector, The), Quarterly
Subscriptions: Indv. $30

Environs *Association*

Publishing Co: Environmental Law Society, U.C. Davis School of Law, Davis, CA 95616; Title Tel # (916) 752-6703
Personnel: Publisher-Darro Frommer, Circ. Mgr.-Dawn Andrews, Production Mgr.-Karen Hamilton, Editor, Promotion Dir.-Leslie Frank
Editorial Description: Non-partisan environmental law & natural resources newsletter on current issues affecting the West.
General Info: Yr. Est. 1977, Quarterly, Web press, 16 pages, No Color
Subscriptions: Indv. $13, Inst. $50
Acquistions: Publication Bought
Circulation: Total-1,000
Printing Co: Reprographics, Univ. of California, Davis, CA 95616 Tel # (916) 752-1011

Environs

Publishing Co: Dept. of Environmental Protection, 59-17 Junction Blvd., #3FL, Flushing, NY 11373-5107; Title Tel # (212) 669-8200
Personnel: Editor-Jinna Holmes
General Info: Yr. Est. 1986

Everglades Reporter *Association*

Publishing Co: Friends of the Everglades, 101 Westward Dr Ste 2, Miami Springs, FL 33166-5211; Title Tel # (305) 888-1230
Personnel: Editor-Joe Podgor
Editorial Description: Newsletter of Friends of the Everglades.
General Info: Yr. Est. 1969, Annually, Trim Size-8½ x 11, 4 pages
Circulation: Total-3,000

Everyone's Backyard

Publishing Co: Citizen's Clearinghouse for Hazardous Wastes, PO Box 6806, Falls Church, VA 22040-6806; Title Tel # (703) 237-2249
Personnel: Editor-Jeri Hawkins
Editorial Description: Covers environmental and waste disposal topics.
General Info: Yr. Est. 1982, Bi-monthly, Trim Size-8½ x 11, Letrpr. press, 32 pages, ISSN: 0749-3940, Color-cover, Saddle-stitched
Subscriptions: Indv. $25, Inst. $150
Acquistions: Publication Bought
Circulation: (72% controlled), Total-18,000, Subscriptions-5,000, International-300
Advertising: Inquire for rates. Accepts Inserts.

FGD & DeNOx   *Business*

Publishing Co: McIlvaine Co., The, 2970 Maria Ave., Northbrook, IL 60062-2024; Title Tel # (847) 272-0010 Title Fax # (847) 272-9673
Personnel: Publisher-Robert McIlvaine, Editor-Jeanene Dueber
Editorial Description: Desulfurization and Denitrification for coal fired boilers. A knowledge network that is a complete information system with manual, newsletter, catalog, fact finder, and 300 service units for reprints, advice, audio and video tapes, and online fax answers.
General Info: Yr. Est. 1976, Monthly
Subscriptions: Indv. $635, Can. $680, For. $680
List Rental: Rents Lists

Fabric Filter   *Business*

Publishing Co: McIlvaine Co., The, 2970 Maria Ave., Northbrook, IL 60062-2024 Tel # (847) 272-0010 Fax # (847) 272-9673; Title Tel # (708) 272-0010 Title Fax # (708) 272-9673
Personnel: Publisher-R.W. McIlvaine, Editor-Mary Carpenter
Editorial Description: A Knowledge Network, that is a complete information system with manual, newsletter, catalog, fact finder, and 300 service units for reprints, advice, audio and video tapes, and online fax answers.
General Info: Yr. Est. 1976, Monthly
Subscriptions: Indv. $635, Can. $680, For. $680
List Rental: Rents Lists

Facets of Freshwater

Publishing Co: Freshwater Foundation, 2500 Shadywood Road, Navarre, MN 55331 Tel # (612) 471-9773 Fax # (612) 471-7605; Title Fax # (612) 471-8142
General Info: Quarterly, Trim Size-8½ x 11, 12 pages, 2 Color
Subscriptions: Indv. $25, Inst. $50

Fathom
See: OCEANOGRAPHY

Feather in the Wind

Publishing Co: Last Chance Forever, 506 Avenue A, San Antonio, TX 78215-1221; Title Tel # (512) 655-6049
Personnel: Editor-John Carter
Editorial Description: Helps educate the public concerning birds of prey & their relation to the environment.
General Info: Semi-annually

Federation Highlights   *Business, Association*

Publishing Co: Water Environment Federation, 601 Wythe St, Alexandria, VA 22314-1994 Fax # (703) 684-2492; Title Tel # (703) 684-2400 Title Fax # (702) 684-2492
Personnel: Publisher-Quincalee Brown, Editor-Nancy Blatt, Production Mgr.-Jennifer Darnell, Mktg. Dir.-Matthew Rowann, Promotion Dir.-Jean Martin
Editorial Description: Newsletter of Water Pollution Control Fed. Covers Federation activities and items of concern to the water pollution control industry in general.
General Info: Yr. Est. 1964, Monthly, Trim Size-11 x 15, Offset press, 8 pages, ISSN: 0049-6987, 2 Color, Matte
Subscriptions: Indv. $19, Can. $29, For. $29, $2/copy
Circulation: Total-38,000
List Rental: Actives: 38,000, $135/M, Expires: 8,000
Printing Co: Reproductions, Inc., 7621 Rickenbacker Dr, Gaithersburg, MD 20879 Tel # (301) 840-5400, Fax # (301) 590-1065

Fibre Market News
See: PAPER

Fish & Wildlife Reference Service Newsletter

Publishing Co: Fish & Wildlife Reference Service Newsletter, 5430 Grosvenor Ln Ste 110, Bethesda, MD 20814-2142; Title Tel # (800) 582-3421 Title Fax # (301) 564-4059
Personnel: Editor-Geoffrey Yeadon
Editorial Description: Lists the reports of the Federal Aid in Fish & Wildlife Program.
General Info: Yr. Est. 1967, Quarterly, Trim Size-8½ x 11, 6 pages, ISSN: 0098-8170, 2 Color
Subscriptions: Free
Circulation: Total-12,000
Advertising: Inquire for rates.

Flashpoint   *Association*

Publishing Co: Natl. Assn. of Chemical Recyclers, 1200 G St NW Ste 800, Washington, DC 20005-3814; Title Tel # (202) 986-8150 Title Fax # (202) 986-8102
Personnel: Editor-Kimberly Levy
Editorial Description: Overview of legislative & regulatory issues affecting chemical recycling, hazardous waste fuel blending & related industries.
General Info: Monthly, 8 pages, Recycled
Subscriptions: Indv. $75, Can. $75, For. $75
Circulation: Total-145

Florida Environmental Compliance Update
See: LAW

Florida Fish & Wildlife News   *Association*

Publishing Co: Florida Wildlife Federation, PO Box 6870, Tallahassee, FL 32314-6870; Title Tel # (904) 656-7113 Title Fax # (904) 942-4431
Personnel: Publisher-Manley Fuller, Editor-Richard Farren
Editorial Description: Environmental news, conservation news concerning Florida's fish & wildlife.
General Info: Yr. Est. 1987, Monthly, Trim Size-11 x 14, Web press, 16 pages, 3% ads, 2 Color, Newsprint
Subscriptions: Indv. $25
Circulation: Total-12,000
Advertising: Accepts Inserts.
Printing Co: Camilla Enterprise, PO Box 365, Camilla, GA 31730-0365 Tel # (912) 336-5265

Florida PIRG Citizen Agenda   *Consumer, Association*

Publishing Co: Florida Public Interest Research Group, 420 E. Call St., Tallahassee, FL 32301-7612; Title Tel # (904) 224-5304
Personnel: Publisher-Ann Whitfield, Editor-Susan Infantine
Editorial Description: FPIRG is a consumer/environmental advocacy org. for FL.
General Info: (Formerly Florida Citizen Agenda), Yr. Est. 1983, Quarterly, Offset press, 4 pages, 2 Color, Recycled
Subscriptions: Indv. $20
Circulation: Total-20,000
Printing Co: Fund for Public Interest Research, 29 Temple Pl., Boston, MA 02111 Tel # (617) 292-4805

Flyway, The

Publishing Co: Detroit Audubon Society, 1320 N Campbell Rd, Royal Oak, MI 48067-1573; Title Tel # (313) 545-2929
Personnel: Editor-Grant Ruttinger
Editorial Description: Discusses issues affecting environmental & wildlife protection in Great Lakes Region.
General Info: 10x/yr., Trim Size-8½ x 11, Desktop press, 4 pages, No Color, Newsprint
Subscriptions: Indv. $30, $1/copy
Circulation: Total-7,500
Advertising: Inquire for rates.

Focus on International Joint Commission Activities   *Business, Association*

Publishing Co: Intl. Joint Commission, Great Lakes Regional Office, Box 32869, Detroit, MI 48232-2869; Title Tel # (313) 226-2170 Title Fax # (519) 257-6700
Personnel: Editor-Sally Cole-Misch, Art Dir.-Bruce Jamieson
Editorial Description: Provides latest information on Great Lakes water quality & quantity issues.
General Info: (Formerly Focus on Great Lakes Water Quality), Yr. Est. 1974, 3x/yr., Trim Size-8½ x 11, Sheetfed press, 24 pages, ISSN: 0832-6673, 2 Color, Recycled, Saddle-stitched
Subscriptions: Free
Circulation: Total-14,000
Printing Co: Preney Print & Litho, 2714 Dougall Ave., Windsor, ON N9E 1R9 Canada Tel # (519) 966-3412

Food First Books
See: FOOD

Food First News & Views
See: SOCIAL SERVICES & WELFARE

Footprints

Publishing Co: N.J. Conservation Foundation, 300 Mendham Rd., Morristown, NJ 07960-4806; Title Tel # (201) 539-7540
Personnel: Editor-Patricia Baxter
Editorial Description: Newsletter to members about activities, related issues.
General Info: Yr. Est. 1973, Bi-monthly, Sheetfed press, 6 pages, 2 Color, Newsprint
Subscriptions: Indv. $25
Circulation: Total-4,500

Forest Forum
See: FORESTRY

GEM Notes
See: WATER SUPPLY, POWER & WASTE

Game Manager
See: HUNTING & FISHING

Georgia Environmental Law Letter
See: LAW

Gildea Resource Newsletter

Publishing Co: Community Environmental Council, 930 Miramonte Dr, Santa Barbara, CA 93109-1384; Title Tel # (805) 962-2210
Personnel: Editor-Michael Colin
Editorial Description: Newsletter sent to members of our community based environmental organization.
General Info: Semi-annually
Circulation: Total-750

Global Environmental Change Report — *Business*

Publishing Co: Cutter Information Corp., 37 Broadway, Ste. 1, Arlington, MA 02174-5552 Tel # (617) 648-8700; Title Tel # (617) 641-5118 Title Fax # (617) 648-1950
Personnel: Publisher-Karen Fine Coburn, Editor-Lelani Arris, Circ. Mgr.-Carolyn Licata, Mktg. Dir.-Paul Bergeron
Editorial Description: Features developments in the environment worldwide, including ozone depletion, acid rain and CFC policy.
General Info: Yr. Est. 1989, Semi-monthly, ISSN: 1049-9083, Ind/Abs/Online: NewsNet
Subscriptions: Indv. $457, Inst. $257, Can. $457, For. $557, $16/copy
List Rental: Rents Lists
Printing Co: Benjamin Franklin Smith Printers, 320 Stuart St, Boston, MA 02116-5242 Tel # (617) 426-1160

Golob's Oil Pollution Bulletin — *Consumer*

Publishing Co: World Information Systems, Box 535, Harvard Square Station, Cambridge, MA 02238 Tel # (617) 492-3310; Title Tel # (617) 491-5100 Title Fax # (617) 492-3312
Personnel: Publisher, Editor in Chief-Richard S. Golob, Editor-Eric Brus, Circ. Mgr.-Lisa Jasak
Editorial Description: An international newsletter on oil pollution prevention, control, and cleanup.
General Info: Weekly, Trim Size-$\frac{1}{2}$ x 11, 8 pages, ISSN: 1051-6255, 2 Color, Matte, Other
Subscriptions: Indv. $335, Can. $335, For. $375

Great Lakes Basin Report
See: FISH & FISHERIES

Great Lakes Newsletter — *Consumer*

Publishing Co: Great Lakes Commission, Argus II Bldg., 400 4th St., Ann Arbor, MI 48103; Title Tel # (313) 665-9135 Title Fax # (313) 665-4370
Personnel: Editor-Carol Ratza
Editorial Description: Concerns current developments relating to activities of the Great Lakes Commission & its eight member states; including environment, economy & Great Lakes related issues. Regional focus on binational Great Lakes region states & provinces.
General Info: Yr. Est. 1956, Bi-monthly, Trim Size-8$\frac{1}{2}$ x 11, Offset press, 12 pages, Ind/Abs/Online: Indexed by Center for Environmental Info (Rochester, N.Y.), 2 Color, Matte
Subscriptions: Free
Circulation: (60% controlled), Total-2,500
Printing Co: Partners Press, Washington St., Ann Arbor, MI 48103

Green Business Letter, The
See: BUSINESS & INDUSTRY

Green Guide, The — *Consumer*

Publishing Co: Mothers & Others for a Livable Planet, 40 W. 20 St., New York, NY 10011-4211 Tel # (212) 242-0010; Title Tel # (212) 424-0010 Title Fax # (212) 242-0545
Personnel: Editor-Mindy Pennybacker, Production Mgr.-Kristin Ebbert, Adv. Dir.-Renae Vorgert, Art Dir.-Iris Karp, Mktg. Dir.-Elaine Lipson
Editorial Description: The Green Guide, a publication of Mothers & others for a livable planet, presents hands-on, solutions-oriented information about green alternatives for health and the environment in an easy-to-access format.
General Info: Yr. Est. 1994, 15x/yr., Trim Size-8$\frac{1}{2}$ x 11, Offset press, 6 pages, 2 Color, Matte
Subscriptions: Indv. $15, Can. $20, For. $25, $2/copy
Circulation: (26% controlled), Total-15,000
Advertising: Inquire for rates.

Green Horizon — *Consumer*

Publishing Co: Green Politics Network, Rr 2 Box 3292, Bowdoinham, ME 04008-9606
Editorial Description: For U.S. green activists.
General Info: Yr. Est. 1994, Quarterly
Subscriptions: Indv. $25

Green Party News — **CPM: $80**

Publishing Co: Green Party of British Columbia, 505-620 View Street, Vancouver, BC V8W 1J6 Canada; Title Tel # (604) 254-8165 Title Fax # (604) 254-8166
Personnel: Publisher-Rosalinde Compton
General Info: (Formerly BC Green Party News), Yr. Est. 1983, Tri-annually, Trim Size-8$\frac{1}{2}$ x 11, Web press, 12 pages, ISSN: 0843-0322, Ind/Abs/Online: & international news of the Green movement from British Columbia'.', 2 Color
Subscriptions: Indv. $10, Inst. $25, Can. $10, For. $25
Circulation: Total-5,000
Advertising: $400.

GreenMoney Journal
See: INVESTMENT

GreenViews — *Consumer*

Publishing Co: Greenhome, 3705 N Spaulding Ave, Chicago, IL 60618-4411; Title Tel # (312) 267-1480
Editorial Description: Newsletter which features environmental tips and information on ecologically sound products.
General Info: Quarterly, Trim Size-8$\frac{1}{2}$ x 11, 4 pages, No Color, Matte

Greenpeace — *Consumer*

Publishing Co: Greenpeace, 1436 U St. NW, Washington, DC 20009-3994 Tel # (202) 462-1177; Title Tel # (202) 319-2444 Title Fax # (202) 462-4507
Personnel: Editor-Andre Carothers, Sr. Ed.-Robert Schaeffer, Assoc. Ed.-Judy Christrup
Editorial Description: Articles on Greenpeace activities worldwide as well as about social, political & environmental issues of interest to Greenpeace members.
General Info: (Formerly Greenpeace Examiner), Yr. Est. 1980, Bi-monthly, Trim Size-11 x 17, Web press, 4 pages, 4 Color, Coated, Saddle-stitched
Subscriptions: Indv. $30
Circulation: Total-1,200,000
List Rental: Actives: 786,000, $75/M

Ground Water Monitor — *Business*

Publishing Co: Business Publishers, Inc., 951 Pershing Dr., Silver Spring, MD 20910-4464; Title Tel # (301) 589-5103 Title Fax # (301) 589-8493
Personnel: Publisher-Leonard A. Eiserer, Editor-John Leonard, Circ. Mgr.-Brendae Davenport, Mktg. Mgr.-Keith Payne, Promotion Dir.-Adam Goldstein
Editorial Description: Covers national and local policies and regulations concerning the disposal and beneficial use of biosolids. All reports on legal, technological, and business aspects of the biosolids industry.
General Info: Yr. Est. 1985, Bi-weekly, Offset press, ISSN: 0882-6188, Ind/Abs/Online: Information Access Company
Subscriptions: Indv. $497, Inst. $497, Can. $497, For. $510
List Rental: List Management Co.: BPI Direct, 951 Pershing Dr., Silver Spring, MD 20910-4464 Tel # (301) 585-5976, Fax # (301) 587-4530

Groundwater Newsletter, The
See: WATER SUPPLY, POWER & WASTE

Growing for Market
See: AGRICULTURE

Growing Native Newsletter
See: GARDENING & HORTICULTURE

Gulf Business Report
See: INTERNATIONAL TRADE

HR Update — *Business*

Publishing Co: Bureau of Natl. Affairs, Inc. -Executive Telecom System, 1200 Quince Orchard Blvd, Gaithersburg, MD 20878-4103
Personnel: Publisher-John Hawkins, Editor-Becky Van Winkle, Circ. Mgr.-Pete Blainey, Circ. Mgr.-John Gill, Adv. Dir., Promotion Dir.-Leslie Burns
Editorial Description: A free monthly newsletter for users of the Human Resources Information Network (HRIN) on online information retrieved & communication service designed by & specifically for HR professionals.
General Info: Yr. Est. 1984, Monthly, Trim Size-8$\frac{1}{2}$ x 11, Web press, 4 pages, 2 Color
Circulation: Total-7,000

Hanford Update Newsletter
See: WATER SUPPLY, POWER & WASTE

Harvest Times — *Consumer*

Publishing Co: Harvest Times, PO Box 27, Mount Tremper, NY 12457-0027 Tel # (914) 688-5030
Editorial Description: Reports on and provides useful tips on starting a Community Supported Agriculture program.
General Info: Quarterly
Subscriptions: Indv. $10

HazMat Transport News
See: TRUCKING

Hazardous Materials Intelligence Report — *Consumer*

Publishing Co: World Information Systems, Box 535, Harvard Square Station, Cambridge, MA 02238 Tel # (617) 492-3310; Title Tel # (617) 491-5100 Title Fax # (617) 492-3312
Personnel: Publisher, Editor in Chief-Richard S. Golob, Editor-George Stubbs, Circ. Mgr.-Lisa Jasak
Editorial Description: An international weekly newsletter on hazardous materials and hazardous wastes.
General Info: Yr. Est. 1980, Weekly, Trim Size-8$\frac{1}{2}$ x 11, Web press, 8 pages, ISSN: 0272-9628, 2 Color, Coated
Subscriptions: Indv. $375, Can. $445, For. $445
Circulation: Total-1,000
Advertising: Inquire for rates.

Hazardous Materials Transportation
See: TRAFFIC & TRANSPORTATION

Hazardous Materials Transportation — *Business*

Publishing Co: Washington Business Information, Inc., 1117 19th St N Ste 200, Arlington, VA 22209-1708; Title Tel # (703) 247-3424 Title Fax # (703) 247-3421
Personnel: Publisher-David Swit, Editor-Bob Billings, Circ. Mgr.-Chris Rogers, Production Mgr.-Jennea Myrick
Editorial Description: Monitors harzardous materials transportation regulations on state and federal levels.
General Info: Yr. Est. 1978, Bi-weekly, Trim Size-8$\frac{1}{2}$ x 11, Sheetfed press, 8 pages, ISSN: 0197-3177, No Color, Recycled
Subscriptions: Indv. $657, Inst. $657, Can. $657, For. $722

Hazardous Regulation Guide
See: CHEMISTRY & CHEMICALS

Hazardous Substances & Public Health
See: WATER SUPPLY, POWER & WASTE

Hazardous Waste Guide
See: CHEMISTRY & CHEMICALS

Hazardous Waste News   *Business*

Publishing Co: Business Publishers, Inc., 951 Pershing Dr., Silver Spring, MD 20910-4464 Tel # (301) 589-5103 Fax # (301) 589-8493; Title Tel # (301) 587-6300 Title Fax # (301) 587-1081
Personnel: Publisher-Leonard A. Eiserer, Editor-Jerry Ashworth, Circ. Mgr.-Brenda Davenport, Mktg. Mgr.-Keith Payne
Editorial Description: Covers RICRA, CERCLA & all issues related to hazardous waste disposal nationwide, including legislation, regulation, court cases and business opportunities in hazardous waste redemption.
General Info: (Formerly Hazardous Waste Report), Yr. Est. 1979, Weekly, Trim Size-8½ x 11, Desktop press, 10 pages, ISSN: 0275-374X, Ind/Abs/Online: NewsNet, Information Access Company, No Color, Recycled
Subscriptions: Indv. $570, Can. $570, For. $595
Advertising: Accepts Inserts.
List Rental: List Management Co.: Manager: Donald Peterson; BPI Direct, 951 Pershing Dr., Silver Spring, MD 20910-4464 Tel # (301) 585-5976, Fax # (301) 587-4530

Hazardous Waste Regulatory Guide
See: CHEMISTRY & CHEMICALS

Hazmat News   *Business, Consumer*

Publishing Co: Stevens Publishing Corp., 3630 J.H. Kultgen Frwy., Waco, TX 76706 Tel # (817) 662-1134; Title Tel # (817) 662-7100 Title Fax # (817) 662-7075
Personnel: Publisher-Wallace Bennett, Editor-Kurt Mahler, Circ. Mgr.-Tammy Meredith, Production Mgr.-Terry Kelly, Adv. Dir.-Ruth Heard Warren, Art Dir.-Mylynda Callahan, Promotion Dir.-Mark Rathe
Editorial Description: Covers a variety of environmental topics.
General Info: Yr. Est. 1990, Bi-weekly, Trim Size-8½ x 11, Sheetfed press, 16 pages, Saddle-stitched
Subscriptions: Indv. $290, Can. $417, For. $446
Acquistions: Publication Bought
List Rental: Rents Lists

Haztech News   *Business*

Publishing Co: HazTECH Publications, Inc., 14120 Huckleberry Ln, Silver Spring, MD 20906-2012 Fax # (301) 460-5869; Title Tel # (301) 871-3289 Title Fax # (301) 460-5859
Personnel: Publisher, Editor-Cathy Dombrowski
Editorial Description: Covers technologies for treating hazardous wastes and cleaning up contaminated sites. Business developments in the waste management industry.
General Info: Yr. Est. 1986, Bi-weekly, ISSN: 1051-3221
Subscriptions: Indv. $360, Can. $360, For. $375

Headwaters   *Association*

Publishing Co: Friends of the River, Bldg. C, Ft. Mason Ctr., San Francisco, CA 94123-1380; Title Tel # (415) 771-0400
Personnel: Editor-Andrew Hidas, Circ. Mgr., Production Mgr., Adv. Dir.-Ted Cuzzillo
Editorial Description: News of river conservation, recreation, water policy in the West.
General Info: Yr. Est. 1975, Bi-monthly, Trim Size-11 x 15, Web press, 20 pages, 4% ads, 4 Color, Newsprint
Subscriptions: Indv. $25
Advertising: Inquire for rates. Accepts Inserts.
List Rental: Rents Lists
Printing Co: Paradise Post, 5399 Clark Rd, Paradise, CA 95969-6325 Fax # (916) 877-5213

Health & Environment
Digest   *Business, Association*

Publishing Co: Freshwater Foundation, 2500 Shadywood Road, Navarre, MN 55331 Tel # (612) 471-9773 Fax # (612) 471-7605; Title Tel # (612) 471-9292
Personnel: Editor-Jeanne Mettner
Editorial Description: Contains credible, medically accurate information on the public health effects of environmental containants of water, air, & soil. Peer reviewed journal discussing the human health effects of environmental containments.
General Info: Yr. Est. 1987, Monthly, Trim Size-8½ x 1011, 8 pages, 2 Color, Newsprint
Subscriptions: Indv. $90, Inst. $110, Can. $125, $10/copy
Circulation: Total-1,200, Readership-1,300
List Rental: Actives: $120/M, Expires: $150/M

Holistic Resource
Management Quarterly   *Business, Association*

Publishing Co: Center for Holistic Resource Management, PO Box 7128, Albuquerque, NM 87194-7128; Title Tel # (505) 842-5252 Title Fax # (505) 843-7900
Personnel: Editor-Jody Butterfield, Assoc. Ed.-Sandra Halpin
Editorial Description: Contains articles, questions & answers, and editorials on range, livestock, wildlife, forest & human resource management.
General Info: (Formerly Savory Letter; Ctr. for Holistic Resource Newsletter), Yr. Est. 1982, Quarterly, Trim Size-8½ x 11, Web press, 24 pages, ISSN: 1069-2789, No Color, Matte, Saddle-stitched
Subscriptions: Indv. $25, Inst. $25, Can. $30, For. $30, $3/copy
Circulation: Total-2,000
Advertising: Inquire for rates.
Printing Co: Web Southwest, 7201 Washington St NE, Albuquerque, NM 87109-4518 Tel # (505) 345-7824

Hotline

Publishing Co: Ohio Environmental Council, OEC 400 Dublin Ave, Suite #120, Columbus, OH 43215; Title Tel # (614) 224-4900
Personnel: Editor-Stephen Sedam
General Info: 10x/yr., 4 pages
Subscriptions: Indv. $20

Housing Pipeline   *Association*

Publishing Co: Natl. Fed. of Housing Counselors, PO Box 5607, Savannah, GA 31414-5607
Personnel: Publisher-Jimmy Bennett
Editorial Description: Information & resource network working for safe & affordable housing for low & moderate income persons. Monitors impact of govt. action as well as lending institutions. Feature updates on funding sources, legislative & regulatory reports.
Circulation: Total-500

Human Factors &
Ergonomics Society
Bulletin   *Association*   **CPM: $207**

Publishing Co: Human Factors and Ergonomics Society, PO Box 1369, Santa Monica, CA 90406-1369; Title Tel # (310) 394-1811 Title Fax # (310) 394-2410
Personnel: Production Mgr.-Lois Smith
Editorial Description: News of human factors, profession, and people, calendar of meetings and conferences, announcements of new publications, listings of employment opportunities.
General Info: Yr. Est. 1957, Monthly, Trim Size-8½ x 11, Offset press, 8 pages, ISSN: 0438-1629, Color-cover, Matte, Saddle-stitched
Subscriptions: Indv. $36
Circulation: Total-5,300
Advertising: $1,100.
List Rental: Rents Lists
Printing Co: Sheridan Press, 450 Fame Avenue, Hanover, PA 17331-9581 Tel # (717) 632-3535, Fax # (717) 633-8900

Huntsman Marine Science News
See: FISH & FISHERIES

IAEE Newsletter
See: ENERGY

I.A.F.W.A. Newsletter   *Association*

Publishing Co: International Association of Fish and Wildlife Agencies, 444 N. Capitol St. NW, Suite 544, Washington, DC 20001-1512 Fax # (202) 624-7891; Title Tel # (202) 624-7890 Title Fax # (202) 624-7890
Personnel: Editor-Mark Reeff, Art Dir.-Hwlwn Turner
Editorial Description: Current legislative brief and current bills involved with fish & wildlife conservation, fishing, wildlife management budgets.
General Info: Yr. Est. 1902, Bi-monthly, Trim Size-8½ x 11, Letrpr. press, 8 pages, Color-cover
Subscriptions: Indv. $25
Circulation: Total-450
Printing Co: Serif Press, Inc., 1331 H St. NW, #110LL, Washington, DC 20005 Tel # (202) 737-4650

ICASALS Newletter
See: AGRICULTURE

INGAA Washington Report
See: PETROLEUM & NATURAL GAS

INTECOL Newsletter   *Association*

Publishing Co: International Association for Ecology, Savannah River Ecology Lab., Drawer E, Aiken, SC 29802; Title Tel # (404) 725-2472 Title Fax # (770) 725-3309
Personnel: Editor-Rebecca Sharitz
Editorial Description: Reports news of ecology, & environmental science.
General Info: Yr. Est. 1971, Bi-monthly, Trim Size-8 x 11, Sheetfed press, 6 pages, No Color, Newsprint
Subscriptions: Indv. $25, Inst. $40
Circulation: (66% controlled), Total-1,500, Single Copy/Newsstand-500
List Rental: Rents Lists

The ISC Newsletter
See: ZOOLOGY

ISRI Report
See: METALS & METALWORKING

IWRA Update

Publishing Co: International Water Resources Association, Economics Building, UNM, Albuquerque, NM 87131; Title Tel # (505) 277-9400 Title Fax # (505) 277-9405
Personnel: Editor-Glenn Stout
Editorial Description: Covers developments in all areas related to water resources.
General Info: Yr. Est. 1973, Quarterly, Trim Size-8½ x 11, Desktop press, 8 pages, No Color, Newsprint
Subscriptions: Free In Designated Area
Circulation: Total-700
List Rental: Actives: $150/M
Printing Co: Univ. of Illinois at Urbana-Champaign Printing Division, 542 E. Gregory Dr., Champaign, IL 61820 Tel # (217) 333-0428, Fax # (217) 244-7277

Illinois Department of Conservation, Outdoor Highlights
Consumer

Publishing Co: Illinois Dept. of Conservation, 524 S. Second, Springfield, IL 62701
Tel # (217) 785-8552; Title Tel # (217) 782-7454 Title Fax # (217) 785-9236
Personnel: Editor-Gary Thomas, Circ. Mgr.-Vera Smith, Art Dir.-Dave Ambrose
Editorial Description: News and events on Illinois' natural resources, in conservation, environment and outdoor recreation.
General Info: Yr. Est. 1973, Bi-weekly, Trim Size-8½ x 11, Offset press, 24 pages, ISSN: 0279-8700, 2 Color
Subscriptions: Indv. $8
Circulation: (100% controlled), Total-40,000

Illinois Division of Game Management, Technical Bulletin

Publishing Co: Illinois Dept. of Conservation, 524 S. Second, Springfield, IL 62701
Tel # (217) 785-8552
General Info: Yr. Est. 1958

Illinois Environmental Law Letter
See: LAW

In Brief
Association

Publishing Co: Sierra Club Legal Defense Fund, 180 Montgomery St., Ste. 1400, San Francisco, CA 94104-4209; Title Tel # (415) 627-6700 Title Fax # (415) 627-6740
Personnel: Circ. Mgr.-Carol Redman, Publisher, Editor, Production Mgr., Art Dir.-Tom Turner
Editorial Description: News of legal actions by SCLDF to protect the environment.
General Info: Yr. Est. 1982, Quarterly, Trim Size-8½ x 11, Web press, 12 pages, 2 Color, Recycled, Saddle-stitched
Circulation: Total-140,000

In Good Tilth
See: AGRICULTURE

Indiana Environmental Compliance Update
See: LAW

Indoor Air Bulletin
Business, Consumer

Publishing Co: Indoor Air Information Service, PO Box 8446, Santa Cruz, CA 95061-8446; Title Tel # (408) 426-6624 Title Fax # (408) 426-6522
Personnel: Publisher, Editor-Hal Levin, Circ. Dir.-Gina Bendy
Editorial Description: Technological and governmental developments in indoor air quality.
General Info: Yr. Est. 1991, Monthly, Trim Size-8½ x 11, 16 pages, ISSN: 1055-5242, 2 Color
Subscriptions: Indv. $195, Inst. $195, Can. $235, For. $235, $16/copy
Circulation: Total-560, Readership-560
Advertising: Accepts Inserts.
Printing Co: Pilot Printing, 1725 Seabright Ave, Santa Cruz, CA 95062-2118 Tel # (408) 429-1109

Indoor Air Quality Update
Business, Consumer

Publishing Co: Cutter Information Corp., 37 Broadway, Ste. 1, Arlington, MA 02174-5552
Tel # (617) 648-8700; Title Tel # (617) 641-5118 Title Fax # (617) 648-1950
Personnel: Publisher-Charles Gibbs, Editor-Carlton Vogt, Circ. Mgr.-Carolyn Licata, Production Mgr.-Lorell Lambert, Promotion Dir.-Paul Bergeron
Editorial Description: A guide to the practical control of indoor air problems.
General Info: Yr. Est. 1988, Monthly, Trim Size-8½ x 11, 16 pages, ISSN: 1040-0533, 2 Color, Newsprint
Subscriptions: Indv. $317, Can. $317, For. $377, $25/copy
List Rental: Rents Lists
Printing Co: Benjamin Franklin Smith Printers, 320 Stuart St, Boston, MA 02116-5242
Tel # (617) 426-1160

Indoor Health
Consumer

Publishing Co: Ecodex, 584 Marrett Rd # 16-18, Lexington, MA 02173-7606 Tel # (617) 862-3440
Editorial Description: Information on keeping indoor environments safe.
General Info: Quarterly

Indoor Pollution News
See: CHEMISTRY & CHEMICALS

Industrial Bioprocessing
See: BIOCHEMISTRY

Industrial Environment
Business

Publishing Co: Worldwide Videotex Co., PO Box 3273, Boynton Beach, FL 33424-3273
Tel # (407) 738-2276 Fax # (407) 738-2276
Editorial Description: Products and procedures in business that help improve environment.
General Info: Yr. Est. 1991, Monthly, Ind/Abs/Online: NewsNet; DIALOG
Subscriptions: Inst. $150, Can. $150, For. $165

Inform Reports
Business, Association

Publishing Co: Inform., Inc., 120 Wall Street, New York, NY 10005-3904; Title Tel # (212) 689-4040
Title Fax # (212) 447-0689
Personnel: Publisher-Joanna Underwood, Editor-Joseph Mohbat, Circ. Mgr.-Katherine Valyi, Production Mgr.-Elisa Last
Editorial Description: Inform is a nonprofit environmental research & education organization that identifies & reports on practical actions for the preservation & conservation of natural resources & public health. Its current research focuses on such critical environmental issues as hazardous waste reduction, garbage management and urban air pollution.
General Info: Yr. Est. 1981, Quarterly, Trim Size-8½ x 11, Desktop press, 6 pages, ISSN: 0275-522X, 2 Color, Matte
Subscriptions: Indv. $25
Circulation: Total-2,500
Printing Co: Bilmar Printing, 169a New Hwy, Amityville, NY 11701-1132 Tel # (516) 789-3010

Info

Publishing Co: Bryan Memorial Hospital, 1600 S 48th St, Lincoln, NE 68506-1299;
Title Tel # (402) 483-3675
Personnel: Editor-Paul Hadley
Editorial Description: Employee news for health care workers.
General Info: Weekly, 2 pages
Circulation: (100% controlled), Total-500

Inside EPA's Clean Air Report

Publishing Co: Clean Air Report, Box 7167, Ben Franklin Station, Washington, DC 20044-7167
Tel # (800) 424-9068; Title Tel # (703) 892-8500
General Info: Bi-weekly

Inside EPA's Environmental Policy Alert

Publishing Co: Inside Washington Publishers, P.O. Box 7167, Ben Franklin Station, Washington, DC 20044 Tel # (703) 512-1800; Title Tel # (202) 452-4200 Title Fax # (202) 822-8092
Editorial Description: Covers environmental policy issues.
General Info: Yr. Est. 1984, 26x/yr.
Subscriptions: Indv. $350

Inside EPA's Superfund Report

Publishing Co: Inside Washington Publishers, P.O. Box 7167, Ben Franklin Station, Washington, DC 20044; Title Tel # (703) 512-1800 Title Fax # (703) 685-2606
Personnel: Editor-Robert Harrelson
General Info: Yr. Est. 1987, Bi-weekly
Subscriptions: Indv. $295

Inside EPA's Weekly Report

Publishing Co: Inside Washington Publishers, P.O. Box 7167, Ben Franklin Station, Washington, DC 20044 Tel # (703) 512-1800; Title Tel # (703) 892-8500
Personnel: Publisher-Alan Sosenko, Editor-Jane Moody
Editorial Description: News and developments in the Environmental Protection Agency.
General Info: Yr. Est. 1979, Weekly, Trim Size-8½ x 11, Sheetfed press, 14 pages
Subscriptions: Indv. $760
List Rental: Actives: 30,808, $85/M

Institute for Social Ecology Newsletter
Business, Association

Publishing Co: Institute for Social Ecology, PO Box 89, Plainfield, VT 05667-0089;
Title Tel # (802) 454-8493
General Info: Yr. Est. 1989, Semi-annually, 10 pages
Subscriptions: Indv. $10
Circulation: Total-4,000

Integrated Waste Management
See: ENERGY

Interaction
Business, Association

Publishing Co: Global Tomorrow Coalition, 1325 G St NW Ste 1010, Washington, DC 20005-3104;
Title Tel # (202) 628-4016 Title Fax # (202) 628-4018
Personnel: Editor-Donald Lesh
Editorial Description: GTC and member organization news, book notes, calendar, commentary and features on sustainable development.
General Info: Yr. Est. 1981, Quarterly, Trim Size-10 x 14, Web press, 8 pages, ISSN: 8756-6281, Color, Newsprint, Other
Subscriptions: Indv. $25, Free With Membership
Circulation: Total-370
Printing Co: Newspaper Printers, Inc., 28a Industrial Park Dr, Waldorf, MD 20602-2707
Tel # (301) 843-9400, Fax # (301) 870-7361

Interior Concerns
Newsletter *Business, Consumer*
Publishing Co: Interior Concerns Publications, PO Box 2386, Mill Valley, CA 94942-2386
Tel # (415) 389-8049 Fax # (415) 488-8322
Editorial Description: Published for environmentally concerned interior designers, architects, and other professionals.
General Info: Yr. Est. 1991, Bi-monthly, Trim Size-8½ x 11, 16 pages, 2 Color, Matte
Subscriptions: Indv. $30
Advertising: Inquire for rates.

International Bear News
See: ZOOLOGY

International Environment
Reporter *Business*
Publishing Co: Bureau of National Affairs, Inc., 1231 25th St. NW, Bldg. N-200, Washington, DC 20037-1157; Title Tel # (202) 452-4200 Title Fax # (202) 822-8092
Personnel: Publisher-William A. Beltz, Mng. Editor-Marlon B. Allen, Circ. Mgr.-Gary C. Seltzer
Editorial Description: A four-binder information & reference service covering intl. environmental law & developing policy in the major industrial nations.
General Info: Yr. Est. 1978, Monthly, Trim Size-8½ x 11, Web press, 65 pages, ISSN: 0149-8738, Ind/Abs/Online: Nexis, Lexis, Looseleaf
Subscriptions: Indv. $1,695

International Fluidized Bed Review
See: ENERGY

International Protection of the Environment
See: LAW

International Society for
Animal Rights Report *Consumer, Association*
Publishing Co: International Society for Animal Rights, Inc., 421 S. State St., Clarks Summit, PA 18411-1540; Title Tel # (717) 586-2200 Title Fax # (717) 586-9580
Personnel: Editor-Lynn Manheim
Editorial Description: News of ISAR, Inc. & animal rights field.
General Info: Yr. Est. 1959, Quarterly, Trim Size-8½ x 11, Offset press, 8 pages, 2 Color
Subscriptions: Free With Membership
Circulation: Total-49,000

International Society of Islands
See: INTERNATIONAL AFFAIRS

International Solar Energy Intelligence Report
See: ENERGY

Inventors News
See: SCIENCE

Jersey Sierran *Consumer, Association*
Publishing Co: Sierra Club, New Jersey Chapter, 57 Mountain Ave, Princeton, NJ 08540-2611; Title Tel # (609) 924-3141
Personnel: Editor-Mary Penney
Editorial Description: Focuses on conservation issues statewide and nationwide. Also features news on club meetings, hikes and other events.
General Info: Bi-monthly
Subscriptions: Indv. $8
Circulation: Total-15,000
Advertising: Inquire for rates.

Jewish Vegetarians Newsletter
See: RELIGIOUS & THEOLOGICAL

Kansas/Iowa Environmental Compliance Update
See: LAW

Keep Tahoe Blue *Association*
Publishing Co: League to Save Lake Tahoe, 989 Tahoe Keys Blvd Ste 6, South Lake Tahoe, CA 96150-7133; Title Tel # (916) 541-5388 Title Fax # (916) 541-5454
Editorial Description: Dedicated to preserving the environmental balance, scenic beauty and recreational opportunities of the Tahoe Basin.
General Info: Yr. Est. 1956, Quarterly, Trim Size-8½ x 11, 8 pages, 2 Color
Circulation: (100% controlled), Total-6,000

LRIS Newsletter *Business, Association*
Publishing Co: Alberta Environmental Protection, Resource Planning Branch, 9820 106th St., 9th Fl., Edmonton, AB T5K 2J5 Canada Tel # (403) 427-3608 Fax # (403) 422-9684; Title Tel # (403) 422-1413 Title Fax # (403) 427-0360
Editorial Description: The Land-Related Information Systems Coordination Project newsletter reports on developments and activities in the field.
General Info: Yr. Est. 1979, Bi-monthly, ISSN: 0709-4590

Land Letter
Publishing Co: W.J. Chandler Assocs., 7410 Recard Ln, Alexandria, VA 22307-1846; Title Tel # (202) 783-7762
Personnel: Editor-William Chandler
Editorial Description: Covers natl. land use & conservation policy.
General Info: Yr. Est. 1982, Bi-weekly, 8 pages
Subscriptions: Indv. $165

Land Use Law Report
See: LAW

Law of Hazardous Waste: Management, Cleanup, Liability and Litigation, The
See: LAW

Lead Poisoning Report *Business*
Publishing Co: IAQ Publications Inc, 2 Wisconsin Cir., Ste. 430, Chevy Chase, MD 20815-7003 Tel # (301) 913-0115 Fax # (301) 913-0119
Editorial Description: Covers news and issues of the lead poisoning industry.
General Info: Monthly, ISSN: 1059-4930
Subscriptions: Indv. $325

League Leader
Publishing Co: Izaak Walton League of America, 1401 Wilson Blvd., Level B, Arlington, VA 22209-2318; Title Tel # (703) 528-1818 Title Fax # (703) 528-1836
Personnel: Publisher-Jack Lorenz, Editor-Laury Forbes
Editorial Description: Works to educate the public to conserve, maintain, protect & restore the sail, forest water & other natural resources of the U.S.
General Info: Yr. Est. 1922, Bi-monthly, Web press, 4 pages, No Color, Matte
Circulation: Total-2,200
Printing Co: Discount Newsletter Printing, 1487 Persisterce Dr., PO Box 1487, Woodbridge, VA 22193-0487 Tel # (703) 690-1788, Fax # (703) 491-2563

Legislative Agenda
Publishing Co: Sierra Club, 923 12th St Ste 200, Sacramento, CA 95814-2923; Title Tel # (916) 557-1100
Personnel: Editor-Teresa Schilling
Editorial Description: An up-to-the minute summary of environmental news in the California Legislature, focusing on key legislation.
General Info: Yr. Est. 1980, Semi-monthly, Trim Size-11 x 17, Offset press, 8 pages, No Color
Subscriptions: Indv. $15, Inst. $25
Acquistions: Publication Bought, Publication Sold
Circulation: Total-1,000

Letters from Abraham Lincoln
See: ART & SCULPTURE

Lightning Flash *Consumer*
Publishing Co: Lightning Technologies, Inc., 10 Downing Pkwy., Pittsfield, MA 01201-3839; Title Tel # (413) 499-2135 Title Fax # (413) 499-2503
Personnel: Circ. Mgr., Adv. Dir.-Connie McKenzie, Editor, Art Dir.-J.A. Plumer
Editorial Description: Abstracts of technical papers, reports, conferences standards & other items or events of interest to those concerned with lightning & protection.
General Info: Yr. Est. 1977, Bi-monthly, 12 pages, ISSN: 0164-0011
Subscriptions: Indv. $75, Can. $75, For. $85
Acquistions: Publication Bought, Publication Sold
Circulation: Total-200

Lines to Leaders
See: FISH & FISHERIES

Liquid Filtration *Business*
Publishing Co: McIlvaine Co., The, 2970 Maria Ave., Northbrook, IL 60062-2024; Title Tel # (847) 272-0010 Title Fax # (847) 272-9673
Personnel: Publisher-R.W. McIlvaine, Editor-Ross Ardell
Editorial Description: Dewatering and separation using presses, drums, leaf and belt filters. A complete information system with Manual, Newsletter, Catalog, Fact Finder, and 300 service units for reprints, advice, tapes, and online fax answers.
General Info: Yr. Est. 1976, Monthly, 8 pages
Subscriptions: Indv. $635, Can. $680, For. $680
List Rental: Rents Lists

Littoral Drift *Association*
Publishing Co: Univ. of Wisconsin Sea Grant Institute, 1800 University Ave, Madison, WI 53705-4090 Tel # (608) 262-0905; Title Tel # (608) 263-3259 Title Fax # (608) 263-2063
Personnel: Editor-Stephen Wittman, Production Mgr.-Christine Kohler
Editorial Description: News of Wisconsin Sea Grant research, outreach activities, staff, publications & conferences. Focuses on the national Sea Grant and current Great Lakes issues.
General Info: (Formerly The Chocolate Door Knob), Yr. Est. 1975, 10x/yr., Trim Size-8½ x 11, 2 pages, Recycled
Subscriptions: Free
Circulation: Total-720
Printing Co: University of Wisconsin-Extension Printing, 30 N Murray St, Madison, WI 53715-1227 Tel # (608) 263-6555

Long Trail News, The
See: OUTDOORS

Louisiana Coastal Law
See: LAW

Louisiana Environmental Compliance Update
See: LAW

MSDS Software Report   *Business, Consumer*

Publishing Co: Donley Technology, PO Box 152, 220 Garfield Avenue, Colonial Beach, VA 22443-0152; Title Tel # (804) 224-9427 Title Fax # (804) 224-7958
Personnel: Publisher-Elizabeth Donley, Editor-Veronica Deschambault
Editorial Description: Profiles 61 material safety data sheets (MSDS) software systems.
General Info: Yr. Est. 1995, Irregular, 186 pages, ISSN: 1074-1984
Subscriptions: $189/copy

MSRC Bulletin Series

Publishing Co: Marine Sciences Research Center, State Univ. Of Ny, Stony Brook, NY 11794-0001; Title Tel # (516) 632-8700 Title Fax # (516) 632-8820
Personnel: Editor-T. Bell, Art Dir.-L. Palmer
Editorial Description: Covers issues of regional and global interest, eg. 'The Brown Tide,' 'Sea Level Rise,' and Long Island's Fish and Fisheries.
General Info: Yr. Est. 1990, Irregular, Trim Size-8½ x 11, 6 pages, 2 Color, Newsprint, Looseleaf
Subscriptions: Indv. $12, Free To Qualified Recipient
Circulation: (54% controlled), Total-1,000, International-240
Printing Co: Shannon & Sons, 1 Comac Loop, Ronkonkoma, NY 11799 Tel # (516) 981-1616

MSW Solutionsr
See: SANITATION

Mackinac   *Consumer, Association*   **CPM: $16**

Publishing Co: Sierra Club, Mackinac Chapter, 300 Washington Sq. N., Ste. 411, Lansing, MI 48933-1223; Title Tel # (517) 484-2372
Personnel: Editor-Kathy Mitchell
Editorial Description: Publication of state-wide chapter of Sierra Club in Michigan.
General Info: Quarterly
Subscriptions: Indv. $4
Circulation: Total-12,000
Advertising: $200.

Maine Environment   *Association*

Publishing Co: Natural Resources Council of Maine, 271 State St, Augusta, ME 04330-6912; Title Tel # (207) 622-3101 Title Fax # (207) 622-4343
Personnel: Editor-Judy Berk
Editorial Description: News bulletin of environmental activities & issues in Maine.
General Info: Yr. Est. 1961, Bi-monthly, Trim Size-8½ x 11, Offset press, 8 pages, No Color, Recycled, Saddle-stitched
Subscriptions: Indv. $28
Circulation: Total-8,000
Printing Co: Letter Systems Inc., PO Box 48, Hallowell, ME 04347-0048 Tel # (207) 622-7126

Maine Environment
See: ENVIRONMENT & ECOLOGY

Maine Legacy   *Association*

Publishing Co: Nature Conservancy, Maine Chapter, 14 Maine St., Ste. 401, Brunswick, ME 04011 Parent Co.-Nature Conservancy, Arlington; Title Tel # (207) 729-5181
Editorial Description: Emphasis on Nature Conservancy projects in Maine.
General Info: (Formerly Maine Chapter News), Yr. Est. 1956, Quarterly, Trim Size-8½ x 11, Offset press, 8 pages, Matte, Saddle-stitched
Subscriptions: Free With Membership
Circulation: Total-13,000

Manitoba Naturalists Society, Bulletin   *Consumer, Association*

Publishing Co: Manitoba Naturalists Society, 63 Albert St. Rm. 401, Winnipeg, MB R3B 1G4 Canada; Title Tel # (204) 943-9029
Personnel: Editor-Kevin Hill
Editorial Description: Articles on natural history & environmental topics as well as program information for members.
General Info: Yr. Est. 1977, 11x/yr., Trim Size-8½ x 11, Desktop press, 16 pages, ISSN: 0823-2911, 3% ads, No Color, Saddle-stitched
Subscriptions: Indv. $30
Circulation: Total-1,400
Advertising: Inquire for rates. Accepts Inserts.
Printing Co: Liveware, Inc., 546 Edison Ave., Winnipeg, MB R2G 0M4 Canada Tel # (204) 663-6747

Marine Bulletin   *Business, Association*

Publishing Co: National Coalition for Marine Conservation, 3 W. Market St., #100, Leesburg, VA 22075-2901
Personnel: Editor-Ken Hinman
Editorial Description: Covers issues relative to ocean fish, conservation, and environmental protection.
General Info: (Formerly Right Rigger!), Yr. Est. 1985, Monthly, Trim Size-8½ x 11, 6 pages, 2 Color
Subscriptions: Indv. $25
Circulation: Total-1,500

Marine Conservation News   *Association*

Publishing Co: Center for Marine Conservation, 1725 Desales St NW Ste 500, Washington, DC 20036-4408; Title Tel # (202) 429-5609
Personnel: Editor-Rose Bierce
Editorial Description: Updates marine conservation issues; whales, seals, sea turtles, and habitat.
General Info: (Formerly CEE Report), Yr. Est. 1989, Quarterly, Trim Size-8½ x 11, Web press, 24 pages, 2 Color, Recycled, Saddle-stitched
List Rental: Actives: $55/M

Marine Ecology Research Highlights   *Business, Association*

Publishing Co: U.S. Environmental Protection Agency, South Ferry Rd., Narragansett, RI 02882
General Info: Yr. Est. 1973, Semi-annually

Marine Safety Report
See: SAFETY

Maryland Environmental Law Letter
See: LAW

Maryland Tomorrow   *Business, Consumer*

Publishing Co: Maryland Dept. of State Planning, 301 W Preston St Ste 1101, Baltimore, MD 21201-2305; Title Tel # (301) 225-4500
Personnel: Editor-Ann Wilmer
General Info: (Formerly Maryland Dept. of State Planning-Newsletter), Yr. Est. 1985, Quarterly, 8 pages
Circulation: Total-3,000

Massachusetts Environmental Compliance Update
See: LAW

Massachusetts Environmental Law Handbook
See: LAW

Mawewi
See: GENERAL INTEREST

Mealey's Litigation Report: Lead
See: LAW

Mealey's Litigation Report: Superfund
See: LAW

Media Update Environment
See: MEDIA & COMMUNICATIONS

Medical Waste News   *Business*

Publishing Co: Business Publishers, Inc., 951 Pershing Dr., Silver Spring, MD 20910-4464; Title Tel # (301) 589-5103 Title Fax # (301) 589-8493
Personnel: Publisher-Leonard A. Eiserer, Editor-Joan Murphy, Circ. Mgr.-Brenda Davenport, Mktg. Mgr.-Keith Payne
Editorial Description: Legislative, regulatory, legal, and technological information on the identification, handling, transportation, treatment, and disposal of medical waste.
General Info: Yr. Est. 1989, Bi-weekly, Trim Size-8½ x 11, Desktop press, 8 pages, Ind/Abs/Online: Newsnet, Information Access Company, No Color, Recycled
Subscriptions: Indv. $390, Can. $390, For. $403
Advertising: Accepts Inserts.
List Rental: List Management Co.: BPI Direct, 951 Pershing Dr., Silver Spring, MD 20910-4464 Tel # (301) 585-5976, Fax # (301) 587-4530

Michigan Environmental Compliance Update
See: LAW

Mind-Expander
See: PHILOSOPHY

Minnesota Division of Game and Fish, Technical Bulletin

Publishing Co: Minnesota Dept. of Conservation, 90 Plato Blvd W, Saint Paul, MN 55107-2004
General Info: Yr. Est. 1944

Minnesota Landscape Arboretum News
See: GARDENING & HORTICULTURE

Missouri Environmental Compliance Update
See: LAW

Mohonk Preserve Newsletter   *Association*

Publishing Co: Mohonk Preserve, Inc., Mohonk Lake, New Paltz, NY 12561; Title Tel # (914) 255-0919
General Info: Quarterly, Trim Size-8½ x 11, Offset press, 8 pages, No Color
Circulation: (100% controlled), Total-3,500
Printing Co: Walden Printing Co., 63 Orange Ave, Walden, NY 12586-1816 Tel # (914) 778-3575

Mono Lake Newsletter
See: WATER SUPPLY, POWER & WASTE

Morris Arboretum Newsletter
See: BOTANY

NAA Reporter
See: FORESTRY

NCAMP's Technical Report
Publishing Co: National Coalition Against the Misuse of Pesticides, 701 E St. S.E., Ste. 200, Washington, DC 20003-2841 Tel # (292) 543-5450; Title Tel # (202) 543-5450 Title Fax # (202) 543-4791
Personnel: Publisher-Jay Feldman, Editor-Sandra Schubert, Circ. Mgr.-Sarah Sullivan
General Info: Yr. Est. 1986, Monthly, Desktop press, 4 pages, ISSN: 1084-2136, No Color, Looseleaf
Subscriptions: Indv. $45, Inst. $50, $4/copy
Circulation: Total-350

NCWA Letter   *Consumer, Association*
Publishing Co: National Center for Wilderness Activities, PO Box 655, Pomona, NY 10970-0655 Tel # (914) 354-3717
Editorial Description: Promotes participation in nature-based activities,
General Info: Bi-monthly
Subscriptions: Free With Membership

NETA Newsletter   *Association*   **CPM: $325**
Publishing Co: National Environmental Training Assn., 2930 E Camelback Rd Ste 185, Phoenix, AZ 85016-4412; Title Tel # (602) 956-6099 Title Fax # (602) 956-6399
Personnel: Editor-C.L. Richardson
Editorial Description: Membership newsletter for instructional technology & technical subject matter specialists in the environmental field.
General Info: Yr. Est. 1977, Semi-monthly, Trim Size-8½ x 11, Desktop press, 12 pages, 2% ads, Color, Recycled, Saddle-stitched
Subscriptions: Indv. $25
Circulation: Total-2,000
Advertising: $650.
List Rental: Actives: 1,400, $100/M

NJPIRG   *Association*
Publishing Co: New Jersey Public Interest Research Group, 11 N Willow St, Trenton, NJ 08608-1203; Title Tel # (908) 247-4606
Personnel: Publisher-Deborah Ennis, Editor-Ken Ward
Editorial Description: Report of NJPIRG, a consumer & environmental advocacy organization for New Jersey.
General Info: Semi-annually, 8 pages
Subscriptions: Indv. $15
Circulation: Total-19,000

NOACA News
See: PUBLIC MANAGEMENT & PLANNING

NRDC Newsline   *Association*
Publishing Co: Natural Resources Defense Council, 40 W 20th St Fl 11, New York, NY 10011-4211; Title Tel # (212) 727-2700 Title Fax # (212) 727-1773
Personnel: Editor-Susan Henriksen
Editorial Description: A newsletter chronicling NRDC's activities, including lawsuits, testimony & pubs.
General Info: Yr. Est. 1983, Bi-monthly, 4 pages, 2 Color, Newsprint
Subscriptions: Indv. $10
Circulation: Total-150,000
List Rental: Actives: $65/M, Expires: 14,000, $55/M

N.S. Conservation
Publishing Co: NS Department of Natural Resources, Box 68, Truro, NS B2N 5B8 Canada; Title Tel # (902) 893-5647 Title Fax # (902) 893-6102
Personnel: Editor-Bob Bancroft
Editorial Description: Wildlife & conservation topics pertinent to Nova Scotia.
General Info: Yr. Est. 1977, Quarterly, Trim Size-6 x 9, Sheetfed press, 16 pages, ISSN: 0702-732X, Color, Coated
Circulation: Total-19,600

NTIS Newsline   *Business*
Publishing Co: National Technical Information Service U.S., 5285 Port Royal Rd., Springfield, VA 22161-0001 Tel # (703) 487-4630 Fax # (703) 487-4630; Title Tel # (703) 487-4650
Personnel: Editor-Dorothy Aukofer
Editorial Description: Current info about the National technical Information Service and its products that report on the health care/medicine and environmental businesses.
General Info: Quarterly, Trim Size-8½ x 11, 16 pages, ISSN: 1045-3350, 2 Color, Matte, Saddle-stitched
Subscriptions: Free To Qualified Recipient

NYPIRG Agenda
See: CONSUMER INTERESTS

NYS Environment   *Association*
Publishing Co: New York State Department of Environmental Conservation, Division of Water, 50 Wolf Rd., Albany, NY 12233 Tel # (518) 457-3014 Fax # (518) 485-7786; Title Tel # (518) 457-2344
Personnel: Editor-Bob DeVillenueve
Editorial Description: Controversial environmental issues in NY. Environmental legislation regulations affecting NYS Environment.
General Info: Yr. Est. 1971, Bi-weekly, Trim Size-8½ x 11, Sheetfed press, 20 pages, ISSN: 0048-0053, No Color
Circulation: (100% controlled), Total-38,000

Naddum News
Publishing Co: Natl. Assn. of Dumpster Driver & Urban Miners, PO Box 8040, Bigfork, MT 59911-8040; Title Tel # (406) 837-5548
Personnel: Publisher, Editor-Edmund Fitzgerald
Editorial Description: Covers Association news, environmental issues, etc.
General Info: Yr. Est. 1990, Bi-monthly
Subscriptions: Indv. $20

National Coalition News
See: EDUCATION

National Environmental
Enforcement Journal   *Association*
Publishing Co: National Association of Attorneys General, 444 N Capitol St NW Ste 339, Washington, DC 20001-1512 Tel # (202) 434-8034
Personnel: Editor-C.H. Evans
Editorial Description: Litigation & inventive settlements in cases of waste dumping, pollution.
General Info: (Formerly Environmental Protection Report), Monthly, 35 pages
Subscriptions: Indv. $195, Inst. $95

National Weather Assn. Newsletter
See: METEOROLOGY

National Wetlands Newsletter
See: WATER SUPPLY, POWER & WASTE

Natural Hazards Observer
Publishing Co: Natural Hazards Information Center, Box 482, Univ. of Colorado, Boulder, CO 80309-0001 Tel # (303) 492-6819; Title Tel # (303) 492-6818 Title Fax # (303) 492-2151
Personnel: Editor-David Butler, Circ. Mgr.-Janet Clark
Editorial Description: Reports on hazards and programs; legislation and programs; applications of research at federal, state & local levels, recent events, new publications and other information sources.
General Info: Yr. Est. 1976, Bi-monthly, Trim Size-8½ x 11, Offset press, 24 pages, Ind/Abs/Online: Ind., Color, Matte, Saddle-stitched
Subscriptions: $2/copy
Circulation: Total-13,000
List Rental: Rents Lists

Natural Resources & Earth
Sciences   *Business*
Publishing Co: National Technical Information Service U.S., 5285 Port Royal Rd., Springfield, VA 22161-0001 Fax # (703) 487-4630; Title Tel # (703) 487-4630
Editorial Description: Covers the mineral indsutry, natural resources management, hydrology, limnology, soil conservation, watershed management, forestry, soil sciences, & geology.
General Info: (Formerly Weekly Government Abstracts, Natural Resources), Weekly, Trim Size-8½ x 11, Offset press, 12 pages, ISSN: 0163-1438, No Color
Subscriptions: Indv. $115, Can. $115, For. $155

Natural Resources
Computer Newsletter   *Business, Association*
Publishing Co: Michaelsen's Micro Magic, Inc., PO Box 7332, Fredericksburg, VA 22404-7332; Title Tel # (703) 775-3059
Personnel: Publisher, Editor, Production Mgr.-Nancy L. Michaelsen, Circ. Mgr., Adv. Dir., Promotion Dir.-Hope McCullough
Editorial Description: Provides timely, in depth articles about computer hardware and software applications in all natural resource disciplines -- forestry, fisheries, wildlife, environmental, ecology, etc.
General Info: Yr. Est. 1986, 9x/yr., Letrpr. press, 12 pages, ISSN: 0890-5673, 2% ads, No Color, Newsprint
Subscriptions: Indv. $98, Can. $104, For. $114, $10/copy
Circulation: Readership-1,000
Advertising: $95. Accepts Inserts.
List Rental: Actives: $100/M
Printing Co: Printing Ideas Inc., 9925 Main St, Fairfax, VA 22031-3904 Tel # (703) 591-1708

Nebraska Pest Control Association Newsletter
See: AGRICULTURAL SUPPLIES

Nebraska Resources
Publishing Co: Sponsor-State of Nebraska, Nebraska Natural Resources Comm., 301 Centennial Mall S # 94876, Lincoln, NE 68508-2529; Title Tel # (402) 471-2081
Personnel: Editor, Art Dir.-Terry Cartwright
General Info: Yr. Est. 1978, Quarterly, Trim Size-11 x 25, Offset press, 6 pages, ISSN: 0047-9217, 2 Color, Newsprint
Circulation: Total-1,700

New Abolitionist — *Association*

Publishing Co: Nuclear Free America, 325 E. 25th St., Baltimore, MA 21218-5303; Title Tel # (301) 235-3575 Title Fax # (301) 235-5457
Personnel: Publisher, Editor-Chuck Johnson
Editorial Description: Newsletter of nuclear free america and the nuclear free zone and socially responsible investment movement.
General Info: Yr. Est. 1983, Quarterly, Web press, 12 pages, 2% ads, No Color, Newsprint
Subscriptions: Indv. $15, Inst. $17, For. $17, $4/copy
Circulation: Total-5,000
Advertising: Accepts Inserts.

New England Sierran — *Consumer, Association*

Publishing Co: Sierra Club, New England Chapter, 3 Joy St., Boston, MA 02108; Title Tel # (617) 227-5339
Personnel: Editor-Susan Evans
Editorial Description: Focuses on conservation issues in the New England region and nationwide. Also features news on club meetings, hikes and other events.
General Info: 10x/yr.
Subscriptions: Indv. $10

New Environment Bulletin — *Association*

Publishing Co: New Environment Association, 270 Fenway Dr, Syracuse, NY 13224-1537; Title Tel # (315) 446-8009
Personnel: Editor-Harry Schwarzlander, Circ. Mgr.-Hank Manwell
Editorial Description: New patterns of living which will ease the basic social and environmental problems of humankind.
General Info: Yr. Est. 1974, Monthly, Trim Size-8$\frac{1}{2}$ x 11, Desktop press, 6 pages, No Color, Matte
Subscriptions: Indv. $10, Can. $10, For. $14
Circulation: Total-150

New Hampshire Audubon
See: ORNITHOLOGY

New York/New Jersey Environmental Law Letter
See: LAW

News Abstracts — *Association*

Publishing Co: American Fund for Alternatives to Animal Research (AFAAR), 175 W 12th St Apt 16g, New York, NY 10011-8220; Title Tel # (212) 989-8073 Title Fax # (212) 989-8073
Personnel: Publisher-Ethel Thurston, Ph. D., Editor-Dr. Ethel Thurston
Editorial Description: Provides financial support to develope substitutes for animals in research.
General Info: Yr. Est. 1978, 6 pages
Subscriptions: Indv. $20, For. $25
Circulation: Total-4,000

News from Mote
See: SCIENCE

Newsletter
See: WATER SUPPLY, POWER & WASTE

Ngoma: The Talking Drum
See: SOCIAL SERVICES & WELFARE

North American Association for Environmental Education — *Association*

Publishing Co: North American Assn. for Environmental Education, PO Box 400, Troy, OH 45373-0400; Title Tel # (513) 339-6835 Title Fax # (513) 335-5823
General Info: Bi-monthly, 24 pages, No Color, Recycled
Subscriptions: Indv. $35, Inst. $150, Free With Membership

North Carolina Environmental Bulletin — *Association*

Publishing Co: North Carolina Office of Intergovernmental Relations, 116 W Jones St, Raleigh, NC 27603-1300
General Info: Quarterly

North Carolina Environmental Law Letter — *Business*

Publishing Co: M. Lee Smith Publishers & Printers ,LCC, P.O. Box 198867, 162 Fourth Avenue North, Nashville, TN 37219-8867; Title Tel # (615) 242-7395 Title Fax # (615) 256-6601
Personnel: Publisher-M. Lee Smith, Editor-R.H. Grubbs, Circ. Mgr.-Cathy Bradford, Mktg. Dir.-Dave Yates
Editorial Description: Review of environmental law developments that affect North Carolina companies.
General Info: Yr. Est. 1991, Monthly, Trim Size-8$\frac{1}{2}$ x 11, 8 pages, ISSN: 1047-4633, 2 Color
Subscriptions: Indv. $117
List Rental: Rents Lists
Printing Co: M. Lee Smith Publishers & Printers ,LLC, PO Box 198867, 162 Fourth Avenue, Nashville, TN 37219-8867 Tel # (615) 242-7395, Fax # (615) 256-6601

North Star — CPM: $116

Publishing Co: North Country Trail Assn., 3777 Sparks Drive, Suite 105, Grand Rapids, MI 49546; Title Tel # (616) 975-0831
Personnel: Editor-Wes Boyd
Editorial Description: Biking, trail buiding, outdoor newsletter
General Info: (Formerly North Country Trail Assn. Newsletter), Yr. Est. 1988, 5x/yr., Trim Size-8$\frac{1}{4}$ x 10 $\frac{5}{16}$, Offset press, 24 pages, 17% ads, No Color, Matte, Other
Subscriptions: Indv. $7, Free With Membership
Circulation: Total-600, Readership-1,000
Advertising: $70.

Northbound
See: FORESTRY

Northern Perspectives

Publishing Co: Canadian Arctic Resources Committee, 1 Nicholas St., Ste. 412, Ottawa, ON K1N 7B7 Canada; Title Tel # (613) 236-7379
Personnel: Editor-Alan Saunders, Art Dir.-Anne Kneif
Editorial Description: To clarify central issues concerning Canada's North (environmental, social, and resource-related).
General Info: Yr. Est. 1973, Quarterly, Trim Size-8$\frac{1}{2}$ x 11, Offset press, 12 pages, ISSN: 0380-5522, Ind/Abs/Online: CPI, 2 Color, Newsprint, Saddle-stitched
Subscriptions: Indv. $25, Inst. $25, Can. $25, $1/copy
Circulation: Total-14,000

Northwest Indian Fisheries Commission News
See: FISH & FISHERIES

Notes from Illinois South

Publishing Co: Illinois South Project, Inc., PO Box 648, Rochester, IL 62563-0648; Title Tel # (618) 942-6613
General Info: Yr. Est. 1975, Quarterly, 8 pages, ISSN: 0270-4439
Circulation: Total-3,100

Nuclear Remediation Week
See: NUCLEAR ENERGY

Nuclear Waste News
See: NUCLEAR ENERGY

ORSANCO Quality Monitor
See: WATER SUPPLY, POWER & WASTE

OTS Liana — *Consumer, Association*

Publishing Co: Organization for Tropical Studies, PO Box 90632, Durham, NC 27708-0632; Title Tel # (919) 684-5774 Title Fax # (919) 684-5661
Personnel: Editor-Jonathan Giles, Mng. Editor-Carol Mozell
Editorial Description: Info on the wise and eductaed use of the Tropic's natural resoources.
General Info: Tri-annually, Desktop press, 24 pages, No Color, Other, Saddle-stitched
Subscriptions: Indv. $30, Free With Membership
Circulation: Total-3,500

Occupational Health & Safety News
See: CONSTRUCTION & BUILDING

Ohio Environmental Law Letter
See: LAW

Ohio Environmental Report

Publishing Co: Ohio Environmental Council, OEC 400 Dublin Ave, Suite #120, Columbus, OH 43215; Title Tel # (614) 224-4900
Personnel: Editor-Stephen Sedam
Editorial Description: Current news on environmental issues, research, and projects in Ohio.
General Info: Yr. Est. 1969, Monthly, Trim Size-8$\frac{1}{2}$ x 11, Offset press, 4 pages, No Color
Subscriptions: Indv. $20, Inst. $50
Circulation: (50% controlled), Total-2,000

Ohio Naturalist Newsletter, The — *Consumer, Association*

Publishing Co: Ohio Naturalist Newsletter, The, PO Box 429142, Cincinnati, OH 45242-9142
Personnel: Publisher-Jane Van Coney
Editorial Description: Contains news about wildlife and environmental issues in Ohio, featuring articles from relevant organizations.Doesn't include hunting or fishing.
General Info: Yr. Est. 1993, Bi-monthly, Trim Size-8$\frac{1}{2}$ x 11, 12 pages
Subscriptions: Indv. $12
Advertising: $80.

Oil Spill Intelligence
Report
Business

Publishing Co: Cutter Information Corp., 37 Broadway, Ste. 1, Arlington, MA 02174-5552
Tel # (617) 648-8700; Title Tel # (617) 641-5125 Title Fax # (617) 648-1950
Personnel: Publisher-Edward Coburn, Editor-Faith Yando, Circ. Mgr.-Dennis Crowley, Production Mgr.-Heather Black, Adv. Dir.-Tom Coggeshall, Promotion Dir.-Paul Bergeron
Editorial Description: Provides timely, exclusive coverage of oil spills and spill-related events as they occur worldwide.
General Info: Yr. Est. 1978, Weekly, Trim Size-8½ x 11, Offset press, 6 pages, ISSN: 0195-3524, Ind/Abs/Online: NewsNet, Predicasts, No Color, Newsprint
Subscriptions: Indv. $617, Can. $617, For. $717, $11/copy
Acquistions: Publication Sold
Advertising: Accepts Inserts.
List Rental: Rents Lists
Printing Co: Benjamin Franklin Smith Printers, 320 Stuart St, Boston, MA 02116-5242
Tel # (617) 426-1160

Oil Spill Law Information
Service
Business

Publishing Co: Thompson Publishing Group, 747 Third Ave., New York, NY 10017
Tel # (212) 888-7220; Title Tel # (212) 888-1242 Title Fax # (212) 486-3400
Personnel: Editor-Cheryl Lieber, Production Mgr.-R. D. Whitney, Mktg. Dir.-Kevin Mahon
Editorial Description: Deales with requirements of OPA's monthly newsletter/monthly update 2 volume.
General Info: Yr. Est. 1990, Monthly, 8 pages, Looseleaf
Subscriptions: Indv. $678, For. $819
Circulation: Total-300

Oil Spill Planning Manual,
The
Business

Publishing Co: Thompson Publishing Group, 1725 K Street, NW, Washington, DC 20006
Tel # (202) 872-4000
Personnel: Publisher-Richard Thompson, Editor-Bryan Lee, Circ. Mgr.-Dale Miller, Production Mgr.-Lisa Granderson, Mktg. Dir.-Conrad Heibel
Editorial Description: Provides information pertaining to Federal oil spill contingency planning. Subscription includes monthly updates and monthly newsletter.
General Info: Yr. Est. 1992, Monthly, Looseleaf
Subscriptions: Indv. $548
Circulation: Total-580

Oil Spill U.S. Law Report
See: LAW

On the Edge
Association

Publishing Co: Wildlife Preservation Trust International, 3400 W Girard Ave, Philadelphia, PA 19104-1139; Title Tel # (215) 222-3636 Title Fax # (215) 222-2191
Editorial Description: Animal conservation, endangered species, captive breeding, fieldwork, research, education.
General Info: Yr. Est. 1974, Trim Size-8½ x 11, Offset press, 16 pages, 2 Color, Saddle-stitched
Subscriptions: Free With Membership
Circulation: Total-4,000
Printing Co: Consolidated Business Forms, 143-147 E. Main St. #2C, Lock Haven, PA 17745
Tel # (717) 748-5540, Fax # (717) 748-7592

On the Watch
See: ENERGY

Ontario Conservation News
Business, Association

Publishing Co: Conservation Council of Ontario, 489 College St., #506, Toronto, ON M6G 1A5 Canada; Title Tel # (416) 969-9637 Title Fax # (416) 960-8053
Personnel: Publisher, Editor-Chris Winter
Editorial Description: Informs people of Council activities, positions, events, and highlights issues on conservation and preservation in Ontario.
General Info: (Formerly Conservation News), Yr. Est. 1973, Bi-monthly, Trim Size-8½ x 11, Sheetfed press, 8 pages, ISSN: 0383-6479, 2 Color
Subscriptions: Indv. $25, Inst. $50, Free With Membership
Circulation: Total-1,000
Printing Co: Dolphin Printing, 936 Eastern Ave., Toronto, ON M4L 1A4 Canada
Tel # (416) 465-1885, Fax # (416) 465-1757

Ontario Recycling Update
Business, Association **CPM: $400**

Publishing Co: Recycling Council of Ontario, 489 College St., #504, Toronto, ON M6G 1A5 Canada
Tel # (416) 960-1025 Fax # (416) 960-8053
Personnel: Editor-Pat McFarlane
General Info: Yr. Est. 1981, Quarterly, 24 pages, ISSN: 0823-6143, 2 Color
Subscriptions: Indv. $30, Inst. $100
Circulation: Total-1,500
Advertising: $600. Accepts Inserts.

Oscar Report
See: PETROLEUM & NATURAL GAS

Our Green Emerald
See: GENERAL INTEREST

Outdoor News Bulletin
Association

Publishing Co: Wildlife Management Institute, 1101 14th St NW Ste 801, Washington, DC 20005-5601; Title Tel # (202) 371-1808 Title Fax # (202) 408-5059
Personnel: Editor-Lonnie Williamson
Editorial Description: Conservation and wildlife topics of immediate interest, (conservation).
General Info: Yr. Est. 1947, Bi-weekly, Trim Size-8½ x 11, Sheetfed press, 4 pages, No Color, Newsprint
Subscriptions: Free With Membership
Circulation: Total-4,000

Oxy-Fuel News
See: PETROLEUM & NATURAL GAS

Ozone Depleter
Compliance Guide
Business

Publishing Co: Thompson Publishing Group, 1725 K Street, NW, Washington, DC 20006
Tel # (202) 872-4000
Editorial Description: Provides guidance on how federally mandated CFC replacement affects everything from air conditioning to the viability of entire product lines. Subscription includes monthly newsletter and updates.
General Info: Annually, Looseleaf
Subscriptions: Indv. $398

PAS

Publishing Co: American Planning Association, 1313 E 60th St, Chicago, IL 60637-2891
Fax # (312) 955-8312; Title Tel # (312) 955-9100
Personnel: Publisher-Israel Stollman, Editor-Marya Morris, Promotion Dir.-Ken East
Editorial Description: Short pieces on all aspects of planning, including housing and economic development.
General Info: Yr. Est. 1970, Monthly, Trim Size-8½ x 11, Web press, 4 pages, No Color
Circulation: (100% controlled), Total-1,700

PETA News
Association

Publishing Co: Sponsor-PETA, People for the Ethical Treatment of Animals, PO Box 42516, Washington, DC 20015-0516; Title Tel # (301) 770-7382 Title Fax # (301) 770-8907
Personnel: Editor-Ingrid E. Newkirk, Production Mgr.-Robin Perry, Art Dir.-Anthony Lawrence
Editorial Description: Anti-vivisection activist newsletter.
General Info: Yr. Est. 1980, Quarterly, Trim Size-6 x 10⅞, Web press, 32 pages, ISSN: 0899-9708, 4 Color, Coated, Saddle-stitched
Subscriptions: Free With Membership
Circulation: (10% controlled), Total-250,000, Subscriptions-225,000
List Rental: Actives: $60/M
Printing Co: Account Manager: Dan Peterka; Nahan Printing, 6380 Saukview Dr, Saint Cloud, MN 56303-0943 Tel # (612) 259-1378

PIRGIM Citizen Connection
Association

Publishing Co: Public Interest Research Group on Michigan, 338 1/2 S State St, Ann Arbor, MI 48104-2412; Title Tel # (313) 662-6597
Personnel: Publisher-Elise Jacques, Editor-Susan Hurley, Circ. Mgr.-Sam Godlberg, Production Mgr.-Rich Hannigan
Editorial Description: To promote research, public education & advocacy for environmental & consumer protection.
General Info: Quarterly, Trim Size-8½ x 11, Sheetfed press, 8 pages, No Color, Newsprint, Saddle-stitched
Subscriptions: Indv. $15
Circulation: Total-40,000

PSR Reports
Association

Publishing Co: Physicians for Social Responsibility, 1101 14th St NW Ste 700, Washington, DC 20005-5601; Title Tel # (202) 898-0150
Personnel: Editor-Meg Duskin
Editorial Description: Articles & events about nuclear war prevention & health and environmental programs by physicians' groups.
General Info: (Formerly PSR Newsletter), Yr. Est. 1971, Quarterly, Trim Size-1 x 15, Web press, 8 pages, No Color
Subscriptions: Indv. $15
Circulation: Total-20,000
Printing Co: Record Printing & Publishing, 7676 Fenton St, Silver Spring, MD 20910-4903
Tel # (301) 589-6400

Pacific Science Association Information Bulletin
See: SCIENCE

Pacific Seabird Group Bulletin
See: ORNITHOLOGY

Pack & Paddle

Publishing Co: Ozark Society, PO Box 2914, Little Rock, AR 72203-2914; Title Tel # (501) 225-1795
Personnel: Publisher, Editor, Production Mgr.-John Heuston
Editorial Description: Official news journal of the Ozark Society, Inc. ; a regional (Arkansas, Missouri, Oklahoma & Louisiana) conservation organization.
General Info: Yr. Est. 1962, Quarterly
Subscriptions: Indv. $10
Circulation: Total-1,600

Paper Recycler
See: PAPER

Paper Stock Report:News and Trends of the Paper recycling Markets
Business   CPM: $25

Publishing Co: McEntee Media Corp., 13727 Holland Rd., Cleveland, OH 44142-3920; Title Tel # (216) 362-7979 Title Fax # (216) 362-6553
Personnel: Publisher, Editor, Production Mgr.-Ken McEntee, Adv. Dir.-Rick Downing
Editorial Description: Covers paper recycling markets. Reports industry news & tracks prices of various grades of waste paper.
General Info: Yr. Est. 1990, Bi-weekly, Trim Size-8½ x 11, Sheetfed press, 12 pages, ISSN: 1064-1432, 50% ads, 2 Color, Recycled, Saddle-stitched
Subscriptions: Indv. $108, Inst. $108, Can. $135, For. $235, $15/copy
Circulation: Total-28,000
Advertising: $700.

Peace Letter
See: POLITICS

Peace Press
See: POLITICS

Pesticide & Toxic Chemical News
See: CHEMISTRY & CHEMICALS

Planet, The
Consumer, Association

Publishing Co: Sierra Club, 85 Second St., San Francisco, CA 94105-3441 Tel # (415) 923-5653 Fax # (415) 776-0850; Title Tel # (415) 776-2211 Title Fax # (415) 776-0350
Personnel: Editor-Kurt Rosenthal, Production Mgr.-Paul Larmer
Editorial Description: Summary of news on national environmental issues and legislation.
General Info: (Formerly Sierra Club National News Report), Yr. Est. 1968, Bi-weekly, Trim Size-8½ x 11, Sheetfed press, 8 pages, ISSN: 0049-044X, No Color
Subscriptions: Indv. $18
Circulation: Total-5,100

Planning in Progress
Business, Association

Publishing Co: Alberta Environmental Protection, Resource Planning Branch, 9820 106th St., 9th Fl., Edmonton, AB T5K 2J5 Canada Tel # (403) 427-3608 Fax # (403) 422-9684
Editorial Description: Describes the integrated resource and planning program being conducted for Alberta's public lands and natural resources.
General Info: (Formerly Planning Newsletter), Yr. Est. 1983, Irregular, ISSN: 0824-1880
Subscriptions: Free
Circulation: Total-2,500

Plant Conservation Newsletter

Publishing Co: Center for Plant Conservation, Box 299, Saint Louis, MD 83100-0200; Title Tel # (617) 524-6988
Personnel: Publisher-Donald Falk, Editor-Peggy Olwell
Editorial Description: News on conservation efforts and rare and endangered U.S. plants.
Advertising: Inquire for rates.

Plastics Recycling Update
Business, Association

Publishing Co: Resource Recycling, Inc., PO Box 10540, Portland, OR 97210-0540 Fax # (503) 229-6135; Title Tel # (503) 227-1319 Title Fax # (503) 227-6135
Personnel: Publisher-Judy Roumpf, Editor-Jerry Powell, Circ. Mgr., Circ. Mgr.-Mary Decius, Art Dir.-Suzette DuCharme
Editorial Description: Covers all aspects of post-consumer plastics waste recycling -- market developments, legislation, economics, events, equipment, industry actors, export date, and packaging trends. Includes annual directory of U.S. & Canadian Scrap Plastics Processors & Buyers.
General Info: Yr. Est. 1988, Monthly, 16 pages, ISSN: 1052-4908
Subscriptions: Indv. $49, Can. $49, For. $49
Advertising: $525.
List Rental: Actives: $75/M

Plastron Papers
See: ZOOLOGY

Policy Currents
See: PUBLIC MANAGEMENT & PLANNING

Pollution Law

Publishing Co: Business Law Reporting Service, Box 1762, Kingston, ON K7L 5J6 Canada
Editorial Description: Compiled Information & laws, regulations with updates & newsletter, 2 binder service.
General Info: Yr. Est. 1977, Monthly, Trim Size-8½ x 11
Subscriptions: Can. $290

Popline

Publishing Co: Population Institute, 110 Maryland Ave. NE, Washington, DC 20002-5626; Title Tel # (202) 544-3300
Editorial Description: News and feature articles and editorials on international population issues.
General Info: Yr. Est. 1979, Bi-monthly, Web press, 4 pages, No Color
Subscriptions: Indv. $25, Inst. $25
Circulation: Total-60,181

Potomac Basin Reporter
Business, Association

Publishing Co: Interstate Commission on the Potomac River Basin, 6110 Executive Blvd Ste 300, Rockville, MD 20852-3903; Title Tel # (301) 984-1908 Title Fax # (301) 984-5841
Personnel: Editor-Curtis Dalpra
Editorial Description: Highlights water quality and resource issues for Potomac River basin.
General Info: Yr. Est. 1940, Bi-monthly, Trim Size-6 x 11, Sheetfed press, 8 pages, No Color, Recycled
Subscriptions: Free
Circulation: Total-17,500, Readership-20,000
Printing Co: Envelopes Unlimited, 649 N Horners Ln, Rockville, MD 20850-1299 Tel # (301) 424-3300

Practically Green
See: CONSUMER INTERESTS

Prairie Center Newsletter

Publishing Co: Grassland Heritage Foundation, PO Box 394, Shawnee Mission, KS 66201-0394; Title Tel # (913) 677-3326
General Info: Quarterly
Circulation: Total-1,500

Prehistoric Times
See: ARCHAEOLOGY

Preservation New York
See: HISTORY

Preserving Family Lands

Publishing Co: American List Counsel, 88 Orchard Cir # CN-5219, Princeton, NJ 08543; Title Tel # (617) 728-9616
Editorial Description: Articles on the preservation of family lands and related products.
Subscriptions: Indv. $35

ProTECt
Association

Publishing Co: Tennessee Environmental Council, 1700 Hayes St Ste 101, Nashville, TN 37203-3014; Title Tel # (615) 321-5075 Title Fax # (615) 321-5082
Editorial Description: Quarterly update on environmental happenings across the state.
General Info: Yr. Est. 1976, Quarterly, Trim Size-8½ x 11, Other press, 8 pages, 2 Color, Recycled, Other
Subscriptions: Free With Membership
List Rental: Actives: $50/M

Prop 65 Litigation Reporter
See: LAW

Prop 65 News
Business, Consumer

Publishing Co: American Environmental Institute, 45 Belden St., 3rd Fl., San Francisco, CA 94104-2808 Tel # (415) 544-0111 Fax # (415) 544-0112; Title Tel # (415) 544-3111 Title Fax # (415) 548-0112
Personnel: Publisher-Alejandro Levins, Editor-Lana Beckett, Product Mgr.-Drew Corpeneter
Editorial Description: Information on California's Proposition 65--chemical 'right-to-know' law.
General Info: Yr. Est. 1987, Monthly
Subscriptions: Indv. $325

Public Lands Council-Washington Highlight Report

Publishing Co: Public Lands Council, 1301 Penn Ave. NW, #300, Washington, DC 20004; Title Tel # (202) 347-5355
Personnel: Editor-James Smits
General Info: Yr. Est. 1976, Quarterly
Circulation: Total-2,000

Quad Report, The
See: ENERGY

Quad Special Reports, The
See: ENERGY

Quinnehtukqut
CPM: $36

Publishing Co: Sierra Club, Connecticut Chapter, 118 Oak St, Hartford, CT 06106-1514; Title Tel # (203) 529-3984
Personnel: Editor-Richard Hathaway, Production Mgr.-Kate Tilton, Adv. Dir.-Joan Drucker
Editorial Description: Focuses on conservation issues statewide and nationwide. Also features news on club meetings, hikes and other events.
General Info: Bi-monthly, Trim Size-10 x 14½, 8 pages, 18% ads, No Color, Newsprint
Circulation: Total-9,000, Readership-10,500
Advertising: $325.
Printing Co: Naugatuk Daily News, 71 Weid Dr, Naugatuck, CT 06770-4764 Tel # (203) 729-2228

RCRA Corrective Action

Publishing Co: Thompson Publishing Group, 747 Third Ave., New York, NY 10017 Tel # (212) 888-7220 Fax # (212) 486-3400
Personnel: Editor-Cheryl Lieber, Production Mgr.-R.D. Whitney, Mktg. Dir.-Kevin Mohon
Editorial Description: RCRA corrective actier issues explains EPA's requirements for implementing a corrective action plan. Contains fiederal laws, reps, and court cases.
General Info: Monthly, 8 pages, 2 Color
Subscriptions: Indv. $387

RCRA Corrective Action
Manual
Business

Publishing Co: Thompson Publishing Group, 1725 K Street, NW, Washington, DC 20006
Tel # (202) 872-4000
Editorial Description: Guide to EPA's RCRA corrective action program.
General Info: Monthly
Subscriptions: Indv. $387

RE News Digest
See: ENERGY

Rachel's Environment &
Health Weekly

Publishing Co: Environmental Research Foundation, PO Box 5036, Annapolis, MD 21403-7036
Fax # (410) 263-8944; Title Tel # (410) 263-1584
Personnel: Editor-Peter Montague, Assoc. Ed.-Maria B. Pellerano, Asst. Ed.-Annette Eubank
Editorial Description: A weekly bulletin providing news & resources to the Movement for Environmental Justice. The newsletter covers technical issues but is written in plain language that anyone can understand.
General Info: (Formerly Rachel's Hazardous Waste News), Yr. Est. 1980, Weekly, ISSN: 1078-103X
Subscriptions: Indv. $40, Inst. $45, Can. $51, For. $56

Radiological Inspection Reports
See: NUCLEAR ENERGY

Radon News Digest
Business

Publishing Co: Hoosier Environmental Pubs., 801 Congressional Blvd # 200, Carmel, IN 46032-5650; Title Tel # (317) 843-0788 Title Fax # (317) 573-9964
Personnel: Publisher-Richard Jordan, Editor-Scott Abel
Editorial Description: A quarterly update on Radon news in the area of testing, mitigation, legislation, law, medicine & market trends.
General Info: Yr. Est. 1987, Quarterly, Trim Size-8½ x 11, Sheetfed press, 12 pages, ISSN: 0896-7180, Ind/Abs/Online: NewsNet, 2 Color, Matte, Saddle-stitched
Subscriptions: Indv. $250, Inst. $250, Can. $300, For. $300
List Rental: Actives: $100/M

Ram's Horn
See: AGRICULTURE

Real Estate/Environmental Liability News
See: LAW

Recnotes

Publishing Co: U.S. Army Engineer Waterways Experiment Station, 3909 Halls Ferry Rd, Vicksburg, MS 39180-6133; Title Tel # (601) 634-3616
Personnel: Editor-Bobby Baylot
General Info: Yr. Est. 1978, Quarterly, 8 pages
Circulation: Total-1,250

Recycled Paper News
Business, Consumer

Publishing Co: Center for Earth Resource Management Applications, 5528 Hempstead Way, Springfield, VA 22151-4009; Title Tel # (703) 750-1158 Title Fax # (703) 642-1258
Personnel: Publisher-Edward Pechan, Editor-Alicia Pitzer
Editorial Description: Explores key issues relating to recycled paper including: definitions, labels, standards, legislation, etc.
General Info: Yr. Est. 1991, 10x/yr.
Subscriptions: Indv. $195

Recycling Advocate, The

Publishing Co: Sponsor-California Against Waste, Californians Against Waste, PO Box 289, Sacramento, CA 95812-0289; Title Tel # (916) 443-5422
Editorial Description: Natural resource conservation, recycling, anti-litter issues in California.
General Info: (Formerly CAW Waste Watch), Yr. Est. 1978, Quarterly, Trim Size-8½ x 11, Web press, 6 pages, 3% ads, 2 Color, Newsprint
Subscriptions: $5/copy
Circulation: Total-24,000

Recycling Canada
Business, Consumer

Publishing Co: Sydenham Publishing, 344 23rd Street West, Owen Sound, ON N4K 4G7 Canada; Title Tel # (519) 371-6289 Title Fax # (519) 371-3676
Personnel: Publisher-Jeffrey Elie, Editor-Stella Coultas
Editorial Description: A insiders' report on waste management for resource recovery.
General Info: (Formerly Environmental Digest), Yr. Est. 1990, Monthly, ISSN: 1183-8809
Subscriptions: Indv. $110

Recycling Related
Newsletters, Publications,
Etc; A Reference
Business, Consumer

Publishing Co: Prosperity & Profits Unlimited, PO Box 416, Denver, CO 80201-0416; Title Tel # (303) 575-5676
Personnel: Publisher, Editor-A.C. Doyle
Editorial Description: Covers recycling periodicals, publications: newsletters, pamphlets & more.
General Info: Yr. Est. 1990, Irregular, Trim Size-8½ x 11, 10 pages, ISSN: 1053-0525, Looseleaf
Subscriptions: Indv. $9, Inst. $9, Can. $11, For. $11, $9/copy

Recycling Stories that
Rhyme Newsletter
Consumer

Publishing Co: Prosperity & Profits Unlimited, PO Box 416, Denver, CO 80201-0416; Title Tel # (303) 575-5676
Personnel: Publisher-A. Doyle
Editorial Description: Rhyming stories on recycling for children.
General Info: Yr. Est. 1991, Annually, Trim Size-8½ x 11
Subscriptions: Indv. $5, Inst. $5, Can. $7, For. $9, $5/copy
Circulation: Total-1,500

Recycling Update
Business, Consumer

Publishing Co: Prosperity & Profits Unlimited, PO Box 416, Denver, CO 80201-0416; Title Tel # (303) 575-5676
Personnel: Publisher, Editor-A.C. Doyle
Editorial Description: A newsletter that lists upcoming conferences, publications, products and covers other topics related to recycling.
General Info: Yr. Est. 1983, Semi-annually, Trim Size-8.5 x 11, 4 pages, ISSN: 0736-1890, No Color
Subscriptions: Indv. $3, Inst. $3, Can. $4, For. $6, $3/copy
Circulation: Total-1,000

Recycling World
Business, Association

Publishing Co: Environmental Defense Fund, 257 Park Ave S Fl 16, New York, NY 10010-7386; Title Tel # (212) 505-2100
Personnel: Editor-Tim Connor, Circ. Mgr.-Rosemary Ostergren
Editorial Description: Reports on practical action to protect the environment.
General Info: Yr. Est. 1990, Quarterly, Sheetfed press, 6 pages, ISSN: 0163-2566, Matte
Subscriptions: Indv. $20, Free
Circulation: Total-300,000
List Rental: List Management Co.: Names in the News-California, 1 Bush St Bsmt 3, San Francisco, CA 94104-4425 Tel # (415) 989-3350, Fax # (415) 433-7796, Actives: 187,174, $70/M, Expires: 82,559, $50/M
Printing Co: Times Printing, 1209 Main St, Swoyersville, PA 18704-1338 Tel # (717) 288-7603, Fax # (717) 283-3145

Regulatory Update
See: PLASTICS

Remediation Review
Business

Publishing Co: New York State Department of Environmental Conservation, Division of Water, 50 Wolf Rd., Albany, NY 12233 Tel # (518) 457-3014 Fax # (518) 485-7786
Personnel: Editor-Dianne Ritter
Editorial Description: Hazardous waste site cleanup & remediation issues in NY.
General Info: Yr. Est. 1988, Quarterly, Trim Size-8½ x 11, Web press, 8 pages, 2 Color, Saddle-stitched
Subscriptions: Free
Circulation: Total-13,000

Report from the Hill
See: SOCIAL SERVICES & WELFARE

Resolve
Consumer, Association

Publishing Co: Conservation Foundation, 2828 Pennsylvania Ave., NW, Ste.402, Washington, DC 20007 Parent Co.-World Wildlife Fund-U.S., Washington; Title Tel # (202) 944-2300
Personnel: Editor-Paul DeLong
Editorial Description: Articles, case studies, announcements about environmental dispute resolution alternatives.
General Info: (Formerly Environmental Consensus), Yr. Est. 1978, Quarterly, 20 pages
Subscriptions: Free
Circulation: Total-6,500

Resource Hotline
See: FORESTRY

Resource Recovery
Report
Business

Publishing Co: Resource Recovery Report, 5313 38th St NW, Washington, DC 20015-1831; Title Tel # (202) 362-6034 Title Fax # (202) 362-6632
Personnel: Publisher, Editor-Frank McManus, Circ. Mgr.-Virginia Casey, Production Mgr.-Ursula Hauff, Adv. Dir.-Richard Will
Editorial Description: Energy & materials recovery & recycling from solid waste.
General Info: Yr. Est. 1976, Monthly, Trim Size-8½ x 11, Letrpr. press, 12 pages, ISSN: 0735-3081, 4 Color, Recycled
Subscriptions: Indv. $227, Inst. $227, For. $245
Advertising: Accepts Inserts.
List Rental: Rents Lists
Printing Co: City Duplicating Center, 1617 Eye St., NW, Washington, DC 20006 Tel # (202) 296-0700

Resource Review
Association

Publishing Co: Iowa State Dept. of Soil Conservation, Wallace State Office Bldg., Des Moines, IA 50319-0001; Title Tel # (515) 281-5851
Personnel: Editor-Judy Lawson
Editorial Description: Reports of activities of individuals and organizations participating in the field of soil and water conservation, and surface mining.
General Info: Yr. Est. 1985, Monthly, Trim Size-8½ x 11, Offset press, 4 pages, 2 Color
Circulation: Total-850

Resources
Association

Publishing Co: Resources for the Future, Inc., 1616 P St NW, Washington, DC 20036-1400; Title Tel # (202) 328-5113
Personnel: Editor-Samuel Allen, Circ. Mgr.-Anne Shapiro, Production Mgr.-Brigitte Coulton
Editorial Description: Contains news of research & policy analysis regarding natural resources & the environment.
General Info: Yr. Est. 1959, Quarterly, Trim Size-8½ x 11, Offset press, 20 pages, ISSN: 0048-7376, Ind/Abs/Online: UMI, Color, Newsprint
Subscriptions: Free
Circulation: Total-20,000
Printing Co: Sowers Printing Co., N. 10th & Scull St., Box 479, Lebanon, PA 17042-0479 Tel # (717) 272-6667, Fax # (717) 276-2928

Reuse/Recycle

Publishing Co: Technomic Publishing Co., Inc., 851 New Holland Ave. #3535, Lancaster, PA 17601-5644; Title Tel # (717) 291-5609 Title Fax # (717) 295-4538
Personnel: Editor-Jack Milgrom, Production Mgr.-Tony Deraco
Editorial Description: New processes, machinery, & uses for both industrial & municipal recycling.
General Info: Yr. Est. 1970, Monthly, Trim Size-8½ x 11, Offset press, 11 pages, ISSN: 0048-7457
Subscriptions: Indv. $195, $17/copy
Circulation: Total-180
List Rental: Rents Lists

Rhodes Real Estate Review
See: LAW

Risk Management Program Handbook
See: MANUFACTURING

Robin
Association

Publishing Co: Yankee Permaculture, PO Box 672, Dahlonega, GA 30533-0672
Personnel: Publisher, Editor-Dan Hemenway
Editorial Description: For Forest Ecosystem Rescue Network & Solutions Network. Covers sustainability, esp. for forest rescue.
General Info: Yr. Est. 1984, Irregular, Trim Size-8½ x 11, 25 pages, ISSN: 1041-5955, No Color, Matte
Subscriptions: Indv. $17, Inst. $17, Can. $18, For. $18, Free With Membership
Circulation: Total-200
Advertising: Accepts Inserts.

Rocky Mountain CoHousing Quarterly, The
Consumer

Publishing Co: Rocky Mountain CoHousing, 1705 14th St # 317, Boulder, CO 80302-6321 Tel # (303) 442-3280
Editorial Description: Regional newsletter on resident defined shared facility communities.
General Info: Quarterly

Rural Network Advocate
See: LIFESTYLE

Rural Property Investor
See: REAL ESTATE

Rutgers University, Bureau of Conservation and Environmental Science, News

Publishing Co: Rutgers Univ., Publications, New Brunswick, NJ 08903 Tel # (201) 932-1766

SF Newsletter
See: LUMBER & WOOD

SSAP Newsletter
Association

Publishing Co: Suitainable Society Action Project, Inc, 525 Midvale road, Upper Darby, PA 19082-3607; Title Tel # (610) 352-2689
Personnel: Publisher, Editor-Ernest Cohen
General Info: 4x/yr., 6 pages, Other
Subscriptions: Free With Membership
Circulation: Total-350

SWOAM News
See: FORESTRY

Safe Food News
See: FOOD

Safety & Health Bulletin
See: WATER SUPPLY, POWER & WASTE

Safety Management
See: SAFETY

St. John-Aroostock-RC&D Newsletter
Association

Publishing Co: St. John-Aroostock-RC&D, PO Box 745, Presque Isle, ME 04769-0745; Title Tel # (207) 764-4126 Title Fax # (207) 764-4126
General Info: Yr. Est. 1966, Bi-monthly, Mimeo press, 3 pages, Color-cover
Circulation: Total-2,500
List Rental: Rents Lists

Salar Newsletter
See: FISH & FISHERIES

Save-The-Redwoods League Bulletin

Publishing Co: Save-The-Redwoods League, 114 Sansome St Ste 605, San Francisco, CA 94104-3814; Title Tel # (415) 362-2352
Editorial Description: Report to our members on the program and progress of the Save-the-Redwoods League.
General Info: Yr. Est. 1918, Semi-annually, Trim Size-8½ x 11, Sheetfed press, 4 pages, 4 Color

Scales and Tales
See: ZOOLOGY

Scenic Hudson News
Business, Consumer

Publishing Co: Scenic Hudson, 9 Vassar St, Poughkeepsie, NY 12601-3091 Fax # (914) 473-2648; Title Tel # (914) 473-4440
Personnel: Editor-Carol Sondheimer
General Info: Semi-annually, 4 pages
Subscriptions: Indv. $15
Circulation: Total-7,500

Science for Democratic Action
See: POLITICS

Scrubber/Adsorber
Business

Publishing Co: McIlvaine Co., The, 2970 Maria Ave., Northbrook, IL 60062-2024; Title Tel # (847) 272-0010 Title Fax # (847) 272-9673
Personnel: Publisher-R.W. McIlvaine, Editor-Virginia Grimse
Editorial Description: Adsorption, absorption and dust scrubbing except coal-fired boilers. A complete information system with Manual, Newsletter, Catalog, Fact Finder, and 300 service units for reprints, advice audio and video tapes, and online fax answers.
General Info: Yr. Est. 1975, Monthly, 8 pages
Subscriptions: Indv. $690, Can. $750, For. $750
Circulation: Total-150
List Rental: Rents Lists

Seafare
Business, Consumer

Publishing Co: University of New Hampshire Sea Grant Program, Kingman Farm, Durham, NH 03824; Title Tel # (603) 749-1565 Title Fax # (603) 743-3997
Personnel: Editor-Steve Adams, Editor-Kathleen Lignell, Art Dir.-MaJo Keleshian
Editorial Description: Seafare seeks to increase awareness of the freshwater, estuarine, coastal & marine environments in northern New England & beyond and to encourage the wise use of these resources.
General Info: (Formerly Windward), Yr. Est. 1978, Semi-annually, Trim Size-11 x 17, Offset press, 6 pages, 2 Color, Coated
Subscriptions: Free
Circulation: Total-5,000

Seafood Soundings
See: CONSUMER INTERESTS

Sedimentation & Centrifugation
Business

Publishing Co: McIlvaine Co., The, 2970 Maria Ave., Northbrook, IL 60062-2024; Title Tel # (847) 272-0010 Title Fax # (847) 272-9673
Personnel: Publisher-R.W. McIlvaine, Editor-Ellen Smith
Editorial Description: A Knowledge Network, a complete information system with Manual, Newsletter, Catalog, Fact Finder and 300 service units.
General Info: Yr. Est. 1980, Monthly, 8 pages
Subscriptions: Indv. $690, Can. $750, For. $750
List Rental: Rents Lists

Seed Savers Exchange
See: GARDENING & HORTICULTURE

Seedling News
Association

Publishing Co: Treepeople, 12601 Mulholland Dr, Beverly Hills, CA 90210-1364; Title Tel # (818) 753-4600 Title Fax # (818) 753-4625
Personnel: Editor-Kate Hahn
Editorial Description: Newsletter of TreePeople, an environmentally-oriented, non-profit organization.
General Info: Yr. Est. 1978, Bi-monthly, Trim Size-8½ x 11, Sheetfed press, 4 pages, No Color
Subscriptions: Indv. $25, Free With Membership
Circulation: Total-25,000

Seiche, The
Business, Association

Publishing Co: Sea Grant, Univ. of Minnesota, 2305 East 5th Street, Duluth, MN 55812; Title Tel # (218) 726-8106
Personnel: Editor-Marie Sales
Editorial Description: Covers research & extension articles of MN Sea Grant: Great Lakes fisheries, water policy, biotechnology, economic development and exotic species.
General Info: Yr. Est. 1976, Quarterly, Sheetfed press, 12 pages, Ind/Abs/Online: gopher:seagrnt.d.umn.edu
Subscriptions: Free
Acquistions: Publication Bought
Circulation: Total-3,500

Sheepherder, The
Association

Publishing Co: Society for the Conservation of Bighorn Sheep, 2106 Mesita Ave, West Covina, CA 91791-2720; Title Tel # (818) 794-0027
Personnel: Editor-George Taylorson
Editorial Description: Promotes the conservation, propagation & preservation of the wild sheep of North America.
General Info: Yr. Est. 1964, Quarterly, 20 pages

Sierra Atlantic
Association   **CPM: $22**

Publishing Co: Sierra Club, Atlantic Chapter, 353 Hamilton St, Albany, NY 12210-1709; Title Tel # (914) 361-1322
Personnel: Publisher-Don Young, Editor-Ann Botshon, Production Mgr., Adv. Dir.-Richard Botshon
Editorial Description: Environmental news of interest to Sierra Club members in New York State.
General Info: Yr. Est. 1974, Quarterly, Trim Size-8$\frac{1}{4}$ x 10$\frac{7}{8}$, Web press, 32 pages, ISSN: 0164-825X, 3% ads, 2 Color, Newsprint, Perfect bound
Subscriptions: Indv. $8, Inst. $8, Can. $8, For. $10, $2/copy
Circulation: Total-35,000
Advertising: $800.
Printing Co: Walden Printing Co., 63 Orange Ave, Walden, NY 12586-1816 Tel # (914) 778-3575

Sludge Newsletter
Business

Publishing Co: Business Publishers, Inc., 951 Pershing Dr., Silver Spring, MD 20910-4464; Title Tel # (301) 589-5103 Title Fax # (301) 589-8493
Personnel: Publisher-Leonard A. Eiserer, Editor-John Leonard, Circ. Mgr.-Brenda Davenport, Mktg. Mgr.-Keith Payne
Editorial Description: Covers national and local policies and regulations concering the disposal and beneficial use of biosolids. All reports on legal, technological, and business aspects of the biosolids industry.
General Info: Yr. Est. 1976, Bi-weekly, Trim Size-8$\frac{1}{2}$ x 11, Desktop press, 8 pages, ISSN: 0148-4125, Ind/Abs/Online: Information Access Company, No Color, Recycled
Subscriptions: Indv. $351, Can. $351, For. $364
Advertising: Accepts Inserts.
List Rental: List Management Co.: BPI Direct, 951 Pershing Dr., Silver Spring, MD 20910-4464 Tel # (301) 585-5976, Fax # (301) 587-4530

Solid Waste Report
Business

Publishing Co: Business Publishers, Inc., 951 Pershing Dr., Silver Spring, MD 20910-4464 Tel # (301) 589-5103 Fax # (301) 589-8493; Title Tel # (301) 587-6300 Title Fax # (301) 587-1081
Personnel: Publisher-Leonard A. Eiserer, Circ. Mgr.-Kathleen Harrow, Mktg. Dir.-Fay Gold
Editorial Description: Federal & local regulation of solid waste management including landfills, incineration & waste to energy recyling, composting & disposal.
General Info: Yr. Est. 1970, Weekly, Trim Size-8$\frac{1}{2}$ x 11, Desktop press, 10 pages, ISSN: 0038-1128, Ind/Abs/Online: NewsNet, Predicasts, DIALOG, No Color, Recycled
Subscriptions: Indv. $547, Inst. $547, Can. $547, For. $550
Advertising: Accepts Inserts.
List Rental: List Management Co.: Manager: Jim Hauschild; BPI Direct, 951 Pershing Dr., Silver Spring, MD 20910-4464 Tel # (301) 585-5976, Fax # (301) 587-4530

South Carolina Environmental Compliance Update
See: LAW

Spill Briefs
Business

Publishing Co: Spill Control Association of America, 400 Renaissance Ctr, Detroit, MI 48243; Title Tel # (313) 567-0500 Title Fax # (313) 849-2685
Personnel: Editor-Marc Shaye
Editorial Description: Discusses activities, trends, laws & regulations affecting the oil/hazardous material spill cleanup & control industry.
General Info: Yr. Est. 1973, Monthly
Circulation: Total-250

Spirit!
See: HOUSE ORGANS

Spyhopper
Association

Publishing Co: American Cetacean Society, PO Box 1391, San Pedro, CA 90733-1391; Title Tel # (310) 548-6279 Title Fax # (310) 548-6950
Personnel: Editor-Sue Mayter
Editorial Description: Marine Mammal concerns.
General Info: (Formerly Whale News), Yr. Est. 1980, Quarterly, Trim Size-8$\frac{1}{2}$ x 11, 12 pages, No Color
Subscriptions: Indv. $35, For. $35, Free With Membership
Circulation: Total-3,000
Printing Co: Instant Print King, 454 W 6th St, San Pedro, CA 90731-2632 Tel # (213) 548-6666

State Solid Waste Report
Association

Publishing Co: American Forest Foundation, 1111 19th Street NW, Washington, DC 20036-3603; Title Tel # (202) 463-2420
Personnel: Editor-Ann Mattheis
General Info: (Formerly Solid Waste Issues), Yr. Est. 1978, Monthly, 4 pages
Circulation: Total-600

Steward, The
Business, Association

Publishing Co: Alberta Environmental Protection, Resource Planning Branch, 9820 106th St., 9th Fl., Edmonton, AB T5K 2J5 Canada Tel # (403) 427-3608 Fax # (403) 422-9684
Editorial Description: Reflects the expanding roles of the Natural & Protected Areas Program and the Stewards in conserving all of Alberta's Natural regions.
General Info: (Formerly Natural Areas Newsletter), Yr. Est. 1988, Quarterly

Stormwater Permit Manual
Business

Publishing Co: Thompson Publishing Group, 1725 K Street, NW, Washington, DC 20006; Title Tel # (202) 872-4000 Title Fax # (202) 296-1091
Editorial Description: Manual dealing with federal and state stormwater programs. Subscription includes monthly updates and newsletters highlighting new developments and compliance strategies.
General Info: Yr. Est. 1991, Monthly, Looseleaf
Subscriptions: Indv. $398

Student Conservation Association Newsletter
Association

Publishing Co: SCA Student Conservation Assn., PO Box 550, Charlestown, NH 03603-0550; Title Tel # (603) 826-4301 Title Fax # (603) 826-7755
Personnel: Editor-Janet Warren
Editorial Description: Recent developments in the S.C.A nationwidehigh school and adult volunteer management program.Activities of 17000 alumni highlighted.
General Info: Yr. Est. 1957, Semi-annually, Trim Size-8$\frac{1}{2}$ x 11, Offset press, 6 pages, 2 Color, Coated
Subscriptions: Indv. $10
Circulation: Total-30,000
Advertising: Accepts Inserts.
List Rental: Actives: $70/M

Sunnyside Gardener

Publishing Co: Sunnyside Foundation, 4518 Skillman Ave, Sunnyside, NY 11104-2117; Title Tel # (718) 392-9139
Personnel: Production Mgr.-Nina Rappaport
Editorial Description: Community preservation newsletter for Natl. Register Historic District. Community planning & preservation issues.
General Info: Yr. Est. 1983, Quarterly, 12 pages
Circulation: Total-3,000

Survival Update
See: FISH & FISHERIES

Sylvanian
Consumer, Association

Publishing Co: Sierra Club, Pennsylvania Chapter, 305 Christopher Street, Export, PA 15632; Title Tel # (412) 785-7861
Personnel: Editor-Philip Coleman
Editorial Description: Focuses on conservation issues statewide and nationwide. Also features news on club meetings, hikes and other events.
General Info: Yr. Est. 1983, Bi-monthly
Subscriptions: Indv. $10
Circulation: Total-19,000

TRAFFIC U S A
Business, Association

Publishing Co: World Wildlife Fund-U.S., 1250 24th St NW Ste 400, Washington, DC 20037-1175; Title Tel # (202) 293-4800 Title Fax # (202) 775-8287
Personnel: Editor-Andrea Gaski
Editorial Description: Studies international trade in wild plants & animals, with emphasis on endangered & threatened species.
General Info: Yr. Est. 1979, Quarterly, 12 pages, ISSN: 0740-199X, Saddle-stitched
Subscriptions: Free
Circulation: Total-3,000

Talking Leaves Newsletter
See: OUTDOORS

Teacher's PET Term Paper
See: EDUCATION

Technologies for Energy Management
See: POWER & POWER PLANTS

Technology Industry Growth Forecaster
See: EMPLOYMENT

Tennessee Environmental Law Letter
See: LAW

Texas Environmental Law Letter
See: LAW

Texas, Natural Resources Information System, Newsletter   *Business*

Publishing Co: Natural Resources Information System, PO Box 13231, Austin, TX 78711-3231
Fax # (512) 463-7274; Title Tel # (512) 463-8337 Title Fax # (513) 463-7274
Personnel: Publisher, Editor-Charles Palmer, Circ. Mgr.-Lisa Ernst
Editorial Description: Describes TNRIS services for users of Natural Resources, socioeconomic and related data, new data files, new capabilities, linkages to other data systems, educational offerings.
General Info: Yr. Est. 1976, Quarterly, Trim Size-8½ x 11, Offset press, 2 pages, No Color
Subscriptions: Free
Circulation: (60% controlled), Total-500

Texas Pollution Report

Publishing Co: Report Publications, Inc., PO Box 12368, Austin, TX 78711-2368;
Title Tel # (512) 478-5663
Personnel: Editor-Bill Kidd, Circ. Mgr.-Shirl Scott
Editorial Description: Air, water, solid and hazardous wastes, nuclear waste pollution; regulatory developments, court action, etc. affecting Texas industries.
General Info: Yr. Est. 1937, Weekly, Trim Size-7 x 9, 4 pages, No Color
Subscriptions: Indv. $76, $2/copy
Circulation: Total-400

Tortoise Burrow Bulletin

Publishing Co: Gopher Tortoise Council, Florida Museum of Natural Hist, ory, Univ. of Florida, Gainesville, FL 32611; Title Tel # (904) 392-1721
Personnel: Editor-Patricia Ashton
Editorial Description: Articles on efforts to preserve populations of the gopher tortoise.
General Info: (Formerly Gopher Tortoise Council)
Advertising: Inquire for rates.

Totem

Publishing Co: State of Washington, 1111 Washington St. South E, P.O. Box 47001, Olympia, WA 98504-0001; Title Tel # (206) 902-1022
Personnel: Editor-Catherine Rucker
Editorial Description: Natural resource management.
General Info: Yr. Est. 1973, Bi-monthly, Trim Size-8½ x 11, 8 pages
Circulation: Total-16,000

Toxics Law Reporter
See: LAW

Tranet
See: POLITICS

Treatise on Environmental Law
See: LAW

Treeworker
See: FORESTRY

Tropicus

Publishing Co: Conservation Intl., 1015 18th St. NW, #1002, Washington, DC 20036-5203;
Title Tel # (202) 429-5660 Title Fax # (202) 887-5188
Editorial Description: Membership newsletter of Conservation International Foundation.
General Info: Quarterly
Circulation: Total-30,000
List Rental: Actives: $65/M

Trumpeter Swan Society Newsletter
See: ORNITHOLOGY

Tuesday Letter

Publishing Co: National Association of Conservation Districts, 509 Capitol Ct NE, Washington, DC 20002-4937; Title Tel # (202) 547-6223 Title Fax # (202) 547-6450
Personnel: Editor-R. Neil Sampson
Editorial Description: Articles and news pertaining to land and water conservation, environmental affairs, resource conservation, resource education.
General Info: Yr. Est. 1952, Weekly, Trim Size-8½ x 11, 4 pages
Subscriptions: Indv. $50
Circulation: Total-40,000

Turning the Tide   *Business, Association*

Publishing Co: Maine State Planning Office, Station 38, State House, Augusta, ME 04333-0001;
Title Tel # (207) 289-3261 Title Fax # (207) 289-5756
Editorial Description: Information about the Gulf of Maine & International policy initiatives for managing its resources.
General Info: (Formerly Maine's Coastal Program Newsletter), Yr. Est. 1990, Quarterly
Circulation: Total-2,000

USCID Newsletter   *Association*

Publishing Co: U.S. Committee on Irrigation & Drainage, 1616 17th St Ste 483, Denver, CO 80202-1277; Title Tel # (303) 628-5430 Title Fax # (303) 628-5431
Personnel: Editor-Larry Stephens
Editorial Description: Brief news items regarding natl. & intl. developments on water resources development, especially irrigation, drainage & flood control.
General Info: (Formerly ICID Newsletter), Yr. Est. 1958, Quarterly, Trim Size-8½ x 11, Desktop press, 24 pages, No Color, Newsprint, Saddle-stitched
Subscriptions: Indv. $50, Inst. $250, Free With Membership
Circulation: Total-700

USCOLD Newsletter
See: WATER SUPPLY, POWER & WASTE

Underground Storage Tank Guide   *Business*

Publishing Co: Thompson Publishing Group, 1725 K Street, NW, Washington, DC 20006
Tel # (202) 872-4000
Personnel: Editor in Chief-Jeffrey Leiter
Editorial Description: Comprehensive guide to underground storage tank regulations with information on planning and compliance. Subscription includes monthly newsletter and updates.
General Info: Irregular, Looseleaf
Subscriptions: Indv. $279

Underground Storage Tank News
See: PETROLEUM & NATURAL GAS

U.S. MAB Bulletin   *Association*

Publishing Co: U.S. MAB Secretariat, OES/ETC/MAB, Department of State, Washington, DC 20522-4401; Title Tel # (202) 776-8318 Title Fax # (202) 776-8367
Personnel: Editor-Antoinette Condo
Editorial Description: News on the United States Man and the Biosphere Program which is an interagency organization with mission to explore, demonstrate, promote, and encourage harmonious relationships between people and their environments building on the MAB network of Biosphere Reserves and interdisciplinary research.
General Info: Yr. Est. 1976, Quarterly, Trim Size-8½ x 11, Desktop press, 8 pages, ISSN: 1078-6295, 2 Color, Recycled
Subscriptions: Free
Circulation: Total-11,000

U.S. PIRG Citizen Agenda   *Association*

Publishing Co: U.S. Public Interest Research Group, MA PIRG, 29 Temple Pl, Boston, MA 02111
Parent Co.-U.S. Public Interest Research Group, Washington; Title Tel # (617) 292-4800
Title Fax # (617) 292-8057
Personnel: Editor-Richard Hannigan
Editorial Description: Report of U.S. PIRG, a national consumer & environmental org.
General Info: (Formerly U.S. Citizen Agenda), Yr. Est. 1983, Quarterly, 8 pages
Subscriptions: Indv. $25
Circulation: Total-14,000

Update
See: ENGINEERING

Upwellings   *Business, Association*

Publishing Co: Michigan Sea Grant College Program, 2200 Bonisteel Blvd., Ann Arbor, MI 48109-2099; Title Tel # (313) 764-1138 Title Fax # (313) 747-0768
Personnel: Editor-Carol Allaire, Circ. Mgr.-Barbara Latham, Art Dir.-Mildred Flory
Editorial Description: Upwellings is a quarterly newsletter that reports on Michigan Sea Grant research extension, education & other Great Lakes issues and activities.
General Info: Yr. Est. 1976, Quarterly, Trim Size-8½ x 11, Offset press, 6 pages, ISSN: 0886-2664, Ind/Abs/Online: Great Lake Information Network (GLIN) through Great Lakes Commission., 2 Color, Recycled, Saddle-stitched
Subscriptions: Free
Circulation: (100% controlled), Readership-9,000
Printing Co: University of Michigan Printing Services, 1919 Green Rd, Ann Arbor, MI 48105-2554
Tel # (313) 764-4392, Fax # (313) 763-5147

Urban Audubon

Publishing Co: New York City Audubon Society, 71 W 23rd St Ste 1430, New York, NY 10010-4102;
Title Tel # (212) 691-7483
Personnel: Editor-Danielle Ponsolle
Editorial Description: Environmental issues concerning mainly NYC.
General Info: Yr. Est. 1979, 9x/yr., 6 pages
Subscriptions: Indv. $5
Circulation: Total-10,000

Urban Wildlife Manager's Notebook   *Association, Consumer*

Publishing Co: Natl. Institute for Urban Wildlife, P.O. Box 3015, Shepherdstown, WV 25443-3015
Personnel: Publisher-Gomer Jones, Editor-Louise Dove
Editorial Description: Methods for enhancing and enjoying desirable species of urban wildlife.
General Info: Yr. Est. 1983, Quarterly, Trim Size-8½ x 11, 5 pages, ISSN: 0882-584X, Ind/Abs/Online: Wildlife Review, No Color, Looseleaf
Subscriptions: Indv. $25, Inst. $50, $1/copy
Circulation: Total-1,000

Urban Wildlife News

Publishing Co: Natl. Institute for Urban Wildlife, P.O. Box 3015, Shepherdstown, WV 25443-3015; Title Tel # (301) 596-3311
Personnel: Publisher-Gomer E. Jones, Editor-Louise Dove
Editorial Description: Current information on research & management techniques for urban wildlife.
General Info: Yr. Est. 1977, Quarterly, Trim Size-8½ x 11, Offset press, 6 pages, ISSN: 0882-5858, Color-cover, Coated
Subscriptions: Indv. $25, Inst. $50, $1/copy
Circulation: Total-1,000

Utah Environmental News

Publishing Co: Utah State Div. of Health, Environmental Health Branch, 44 N Medical Dr, Salt Lake City, UT 84113-1105; Title Tel # (801) 533-6121
Personnel: Editor-Mary C. Sewall
Editorial Description: Informs Utah citizens of state environmental programs, with an emphasis of prognosis and treatment.
General Info: Monthly, Trim Size-8½ x 11, Offset press, 4 pages
Circulation: Total-1,500

Utility Environment Report
See: POWER & POWER PLANTS

Valley Voice
See: GENERAL INTEREST

Vegan News, The   *Consumer, Association*

Publishing Co: Vegan Action, P.O. Box 4353, Berkeley, CA 94704; Title Tel # (510) 654-6297
Personnel: Publisher-Leor Jacobi, Adv. Dir.-Mark Schlosberg, Promotion Dir.-Ori Brafman
Editorial Description: Contains information on health, environmental, and animal issues.
General Info: (Formerly East Bay Vegan News, The), Yr. Est. 1993, Trim Size-8½ x 11, Offset press, 8 pages, Coated, Saddle-stitched
Subscriptions: Indv. $10, Can. $13, For. $15, Free In Designated Area
Circulation: Total-10,000, Readership-10,000
Advertising: Inquire for rates.

Viands In Verse
See: FOOD

Views from the Rim

Publishing Co: Fossil Rim Wildlife Ctr., Rr 1 Box 210, Glen Rose, TX 76043-9729; Title Tel # (817) 897-2960
Personnel: Editor-Gail Rankin
Editorial Description: News relating to the preservation of endangered and rare species.
General Info: (Formerly Fossil Rim News), Quarterly, Trim Size-8½ x 11, 8 pages, No Color, Recycled, Saddle-stitched
Subscriptions: Indv. $10, Free With Membership
Advertising: Inquire for rates.

Virginia Environmental Compliance Update
See: LAW

Visibility
See: SPORTS & SPORTING GOODS

Voices
See: WOMEN'S

WOTS/Water Operations Technical Support

Publishing Co: U.S. Army Engineer Waterways Experiment Station, 3909 Halls Ferry Rd, Vicksburg, MS 39180-6133; Title Tel # (601) 634-3616
Personnel: Editor-Bobby Baylot
General Info: (Formerly EWQOS: Environmental & Water Quality Operational Studies), Yr. Est. 1978, Quarterly, 8 pages
Circulation: Total-3,000

Wary Canary   *Consumer, Association*

Publishing Co: Wary Canary Press, PO Box 2204, Ft. Collins, CO 80522-2204 Tel # (970) 493-8089; Title Tel # (303) 224-0083
Personnel: Production Mgr.-Karma Randegger, Publisher, Editor, Art Dir.-Suzanne Randegger, Co-Editor, Promotion Dir.-Ed Randegger
Editorial Description: For and about victims of environmental illnes. An educational tool for doctors, legislators, relatives, & employers, and others to promote understanding of environmental illness or multiple chemical sensitivities.
General Info: Quarterly, Trim Size-8½ x 11, Sheetfed press, ISSN: 0899-1405, Saddle-stitched
Subscriptions: Indv. $20, Can. $24, For. $27, $6/copy
Circulation: (50% controlled), Total-1,000, Subscriptions-500

Washington Environmental Compliance Update   *Business*

Publishing Co: M. Lee Smith Publishers & Printers ,LCC, P.O. Box 198867, 162 Fourth Avenue North, Nashville, TN 37219-8867 Tel # (615) 242-7395 Fax # (615) 256-6601
Personnel: Publisher-M Lee Smith, Editor-Doug Little, Circ. Mgr.-Cathy Bradford, Mktg. Dir.-Dave Yates
Editorial Description: State environmental laws and issues.
General Info: Yr. Est. 1994, Monthly, Trim Size-8½ x 11, 8 pages, ISSN: 1072-0596, 2 Color
Subscriptions: Indv. $117
Printing Co: M. Lee Smith Publishers & Printers ,LLC, PO Box 198867, 162 Fourth Avenue, Nashville, TN 37219-8867 Tel # (615) 242-7395, Fax # (615) 256-6601

Washington Environmental Protection Report   *Business*

Publishing Co: Callahan Pubs., PO Box 1173, McLean, VA 22101-1173; Title Tel # (703) 356-1925 Title Fax # (703) 356-9614
Personnel: Publisher, Editor-Vincent F. Callahan, Jr.
Editorial Description: Legislation, research & development and contracting opportunities in federal environment field.
General Info: (Formerly Federal Programs Report), Yr. Est. 1964, Semi-monthly, Trim Size-8½ x 11, Offset press, 8 pages, ISSN: 0014-9136, No Color
Subscriptions: Indv. $190, For. $200

Washington Update   *Business, Association*

Publishing Co: Assn. of Local Air Pollution Control Officials, 444 N Capitol St NW Ste 306, Washington, DC 20001-1512; Title Tel # (202) 624-7864
Personnel: Editor-Tod Friedman
Editorial Description: Shares headquarters & staff with the state & territorial air pollution program administrators.
General Info: Yr. Est. 1971, Monthly, Mimeo press
Circulation: Total-270

Waste Minimization & Recycling Report   *Business*

Publishing Co: Government Institutes, Inc., 4 Research Pl Ste 200, Rockville, MD 20850-3226 Tel # (301) 921-2355; Title Tel # (301) 251-9250 Title Fax # (301) 251-0638
Editorial Description: Devoted to recycling and waste minimization developments and information.
General Info: Yr. Est. 1986, Monthly
Subscriptions: Indv. $198, Can. $198, For. $225

Waste Recovery Report   *Business*

Publishing Co: ICON Information Concepts, Inc., 211 S. 45th St., Philadelphia, PA 19104-2995 Fax # (216) 349-6500; Title Tel # (215) 349-6500 Title Fax # (215) 349-6502
Personnel: Publisher, Editor-Alan Krigman
Editorial Description: Reports on the recovery of material and energy from municipal, commercial, and industrial waste. Topics include reuse, recycling, waste-to-energy, composting, soil remediation, heat & solvent recovery, and landfill reclamation. Format allows quick skimming with contact names and addresses on all items.
General Info: (Formerly Recovery Engineering News), Yr. Est. 1976, Monthly, Trim Size-8½ x 11, Sheetfed press, 6 pages, ISSN: 0889-0072, No Color, Recycled
Subscriptions: Indv. $50, Can. $50, For. $75, $5/copy
Circulation: Total-500
Printing Co: Jade Press, 4420 Walnut St, Philadelphia, PA 19104-2947 Tel # (215) 556-0691, Fax # (215) 385-9495

Waste Watch   *Business, Association*

Publishing Co: California Against Waste, PO Box 289, Sacramento, CA 95812-0289; Title Tel # (916) 443-5422
Personnel: Editor-Bill Shireman
General Info: Quarterly, 8 pages, Recycled
Subscriptions: Indv. $20

Wastewater Works News
See: WATER SUPPLY, POWER & WASTE

Water Connection   *Business*

Publishing Co: NEIWPCC, 255 Ballardvale St, Wilmington, MA 01887-1013; Title Tel # (617) 367-8522
Personnel: Editor-Ellen Frye
Editorial Description: Water polution control legislation and activities.
General Info: Yr. Est. 1970, Quarterly, Trim Size-11 x 14, 6 pages, Color
Circulation: Total-2,000

Water Current
See: SCIENCE

Water Desalination Report
See: WATER SUPPLY, POWER & WASTE

Water Environment Lab Solutions
See: WATER SUPPLY, POWER & WASTE

Water Highlights   *Business*

Publishing Co: DC Water Resources Research Ctr., Univ. of Dist. of Columbia, 4200 Connecticut Ave., Washington, DC 20008; Title Tel # (202) 274-6690 Title Fax # (202) 274-6687
Personnel: Editor-Hame Watt, Asst. Ed.-Kathryn E. Friedman
General Info: Yr. Est. 1982, Quarterly, Trim Size-8½ x 11, Sheetfed press, 6 pages, 2 Color
Subscriptions: Free
Circulation: Total-1,000

Water Newsletter/Research and Development News
Business, Consumer

Publishing Co: Water Information Center, Inc., 1099 18th St., Ste 2150, Denver, CO 80202-1921 Parent Co.-Geraghty & Miller, Inc., Danver; Title Tel # (303) 391-8799 Title Fax # (303) 294-1239
Personnel: Publisher-Fred Troise, Editor-Karen Kliegle, Mng. Editor-Fred L. Troise, Bk. Rev. Ed.-Dee Farrell, Circ. Mgr.-Michelle Hankins
Editorial Description: Provides the latest news in supply, pollution control, conservation, water legislation, and government activities. Subscription includes a section, announcing upcomming meetings & new publications, and the monthly supplement . International Water Report
General Info: Yr. Est. 1959, Monthly, Trim Size-8 x 10, Offset press, 6 pages, ISSN: 0043-1273, 2 Color
Subscriptions: Indv. $127, Can. $127, For. $157, $11/copy

Water Pollution Control
Business

Publishing Co: Bureau of National Affairs, Inc., 1231 25th St. NW, Bldg. N-200, Washington, DC 20037-1157; Title Tel # (202) 452-4200 Title Fax # (202) 822-8092
Personnel: Publisher-William A. Beltz, Mng. Editor-Karen Walker, Circ. Mgr.-Gary C. Seltzer
Editorial Description: A reference & advisory service on the control of water pollution, designed to meet the information needs of individuals responsible for complying with EPA & state water pollution control regulations.
General Info: Yr. Est. 1979, Bi-weekly, Trim Size-8½ x 11, Offset press, 8 pages
Subscriptions: Indv. $667

Water Quality Newsletter
See: WATER SUPPLY, POWER & WASTE

Water Regulation Watch
See: WATER SUPPLY, POWER & WASTE

Water Resources Center News

Publishing Co: Univ. of Delaware Water Resource Ctr., 133 Townsend Hall, Newark, DE 19717-1303; Title Tel # (302) 831-2191
Personnel: Editor-Deanna Benson
General Info: Yr. Est. 1971, Semi-annually, 4 pages
Circulation: Total-800

Water Resources Research Institute News

Publishing Co: Univ. of North Carolina, Campus Box 7912, Raleigh, NC 27695-0001
Personnel: Editor-Jeri Gray
Editorial Description: Distributed to 2,500 federal & state agencies, university personnel, multi-county planning regions, city & local officials, & engineers. Regularly covers water-related topics, current federal & state activities, & new research findings.
General Info: Yr. Est. 1964, Bi-monthly, 16 pages
Circulation: Total-2,500

Water Review
See: WATER SUPPLY, POWER & WASTE

Watergardening News
See: GARDENING & HORTICULTURE

Weather & Climate Report

Publishing Co: Nautilus Press, Inc., 1054 National Press Building, Washington, DC 20045-2001; Title Tel # (202) 347-6643 Title Fax # (202) 484-0087
Personnel: Publisher-John Botzum, Editor-Diane Garner, Circ. Mgr.-Priscilla Capra
Editorial Description: Federal actions impacting weather & climate research & Global Climate change.
General Info: Yr. Est. 1978, Monthly
Subscriptions: Indv. $95

Well Log, The
Association

Publishing Co: National Ground Water Association, 2600 Ground Water, Columbus, OH 43219; Title Tel # (614) 337-1949 Title Fax # (614) 337-8445
Personnel: Editor-Susan McKinley
Editorial Description: For contractors, manufacturers, and suppliers of the ground water industry.
General Info: (Formerly NGWA Newsletter), Yr. Est. 1968, Monthly, Trim Size-8½ x 11, 6 pages, ISSN: 0271-230X, Coated
Circulation: Total-6,000

Wellness Newsletter, The
See: HEALTH

West Coast Environmental Law Research Foundation Newsletter
Association

Publishing Co: West Coast Environmental Law Research Foundation, 207 W. Hastings St., Ste. 1001, Vancouver, BC V6B 1H7 Canada; Title Tel # (604) 684-7378 Title Fax # (604) 684-1512
Personnel: Editor-W.J. Andrews, Production Mgr.-Catherine Ludgate
General Info: Yr. Est. 1980, Monthly, Trim Size-8.5 x 11, Offset press, 4 pages, ISSN: 0715-4275, 2 Color, Recycled, Other
Subscriptions: Indv. $20, Inst. $20
Printing Co: Press Gang Printers, 603 Powell Street, Vancouver, BC V6A 1H2 Canada Tel # (604) 253-1224

Western States Water
Business, Association

Publishing Co: Western States Water Council, 942 E. 7145 S., #A201, Midvale, UT 84047-1763; Title Tel # (801) 561-5300 Title Fax # (801) 255-9642
Personnel: Editor-Tony Willardson
Editorial Description: Covers Western Water Law, policy & federal/state management issues.
General Info: Yr. Est. 1974, Weekly, Desktop press, 2 pages, No Color
Subscriptions: Indv. $100
Circulation: Total-400

Whalewatch
Consumer, Association

Publishing Co: International Wildlife Coalition, 70 E Falmouth Hwy, East Falmouth, MA 02536-5900; Title Tel # (508) 548-8328 Title Fax # (508) 548-8542
Editorial Description: Information on work done to protect the remaining humpback whales and other marine animals.
General Info: Quarterly, Trim Size-8½ x 11, 8 pages, 2 Color, Recycled
List Rental: Actives: 116,309, $65/M

Whisper in the Woods

Publishing Co: Gaia Group, 2108 Reynolds St., Regina, SK S4N 3N1 Canada; Title Tel # (306) 352-4804
Personnel: Editor, Circ. Mgr., Production Mgr.-Jim Elliott
Editorial Description: A review of environmental, peace, disarmament, & issues related to society. Mainly Canadian issues, but includes some international issues that impact on Canada. Investigate Gaia Hypothesis & methods of modifying lifestyle.
General Info: Yr. Est. 1988, Bi-monthly, 8 pages, No Color
Subscriptions: Inst. $25, Can. $25, For. $30, $3/copy
Acquistions: Publication Bought, Publication Sold
Advertising: Inquire for rates.

Wildlife Resource Notes
Consumer

Publishing Co: U.S. Army Engineer Waterways Experiment Station, 3909 Halls Ferry Rd, Vicksburg, MS 39180-6133; Title Tel # (601) 634-3958
Personnel: Editor-Chester Martin
General Info: Yr. Est. 1983, Irregular, Mimeo press, 8 pages
Circulation: Total-2,000

Wildlifer, The
Consumer, Association

Publishing Co: Wildlife Society, 5410 Grosvenor Ln, Bethesda, MD 20814-2197; Title Tel # (301) 897-9770 Title Fax # (301) 530-2471
Personnel: Editor-Harry Hodgdon, Production Mgr.-Yanin Walker
Editorial Description: Official publication for The Wildlife Society.
General Info: Yr. Est. 1937, Bi-monthly, Trim Size-8½ x 11, Offset press, 16 pages, ISSN: 0163-6359, 2 Color
Subscriptions: Indv. $38
Circulation: Total-9,500
Printing Co: Bladen Lithographics, 8235 Beechcraft Drive, Gaithersburg, MD 20879-5507 Tel # (301) 948-9600

WindStar Wildlife Institute Journal
See: OUTDOORS

Windstar Newsletter/ Products Catalog

Publishing Co: Windstar Foundation, 2317 Snowmass Creek Rd, Snowmass, CO 81654-9198; Title Tel # (303) 927-4777
Personnel: Editor-Steve Blomeke
General Info: 8 pages

Winging It
See: ORNITHOLOGY

Wisconsin Environmental Compliance Update
Business

Publishing Co: M. Lee Smith Publishers & Printers ,LCC, P.O. Box 198867, 162 Fourth Avenue North, Nashville, TN 37219-8867 Tel # (615) 242-7395 Fax # (615) 256-6601
Personnel: Publisher-M Lee Smith, Editor-Paul Kent, Circ. Mgr.-Cathy Bradford, Mktg. Dir.-Dave Yates
Editorial Description: State environmental law information.
General Info: Yr. Est. 1994, Monthly, ISSN: 1072-9151
Subscriptions: Indv. $117
Printing Co: M. Lee Smith Publishers & Printers ,LLC, PO Box 198867, 162 Fourth Avenue, Nashville, TN 37219-8867 Tel # (615) 242-7395, Fax # (615) 256-6601

Wisconsin Environmental Law and Regulation Report
Business

Publishing Co: Environmental Information Services, Ltd., PO Box 391, Brookfield, WI 53008-0391; Title Tel # (414) 778-0093 Title Fax # (414) 778-1181
Personnel: Exec. Ed.-Chesley P. Erwin, Circ. Mgr.-C. M. Kimball, Mktg. Mgr.-Allen Busse
Editorial Description: A comprehensive report on the ever changing environmental laws and regulations in Wisconsin.
General Info: Yr. Est. 1990, Semi-monthly, Trim Size-8.5 x 11, Desktop press, 26 pages, No Color, Newsprint, Other
Subscriptions: Indv. $450, Inst. $445, $30/copy

Wolf Park News
See: ANIMALS

Wood Duck
See: NATURAL HISTORY

Woodland Report
See: FORESTRY

World Automotive Alternative Energy & Fuels Bulletin
See: AUTOMOTIVE

World Automotive Environment & Safety Bulletin
Business

Publishing Co: Forecast International/DMS, Inc., 22 Commerce Rd., Newtown, CT 06470-1643 Fax # (203) 426-1964; Title Tel # (203) 426-0800 Title Fax # (203) 426-4262
General Info: Monthly
Subscriptions: Indv. $475

World Environment Report

Publishing Co: Business Publishers, Inc., 951 Pershing Dr., Silver Spring, MD 20910-4464 Tel # (301) 589-5103 Fax # (301) 589-8493; Title Tel # (301) 587-6300 Title Fax # (301) 587-1081
Personnel: Publisher-Leonard A. Eiserer, Editor-David Bottorff, Circ. Mgr.-Brenda Devenport, Mktg. Mgr.-Keith Payne
Editorial Description: Covers energy, resource management, pollution, economic development, and environmental business opportunities around the world.
General Info: (Formerly Multinational Environmental Outlook), Yr. Est. 1975, Bi-weekly, Trim Size-8½ x 11, Offset press, 8 pages, ISSN: 0098-8235, Ind/Abs/Online: Information Access Company, 2 Color
Subscriptions: Indv. $494, Can. $494, For. $507
List Rental: List Management Co.: Manager: Kim Brown; BPI Direct, 951 Pershing Dr., Silver Spring, MD 20910-4464 Tel # (301) 585-5976, Fax # (301) 587-4530

World Goodwill Commentary
See: INTERNATIONAL AFFAIRS

World Rainforest Report
Business, Association

Publishing Co: Rainforest Action Network, 450 Sansome St., Ste. 700, San Francisco, CA 94111-3315; Title Tel # (415) 398-4404 Title Fax # (415) 398-2732
General Info: Yr. Est. 1985, Quarterly
Subscriptions: Indv. $25, Inst. $25, Can. $25, For. $25, $1/copy
Circulation: (1% controlled), Total-35,000, Single Copy/Newsstand-500, Subscriptions-34,000, International-750
List Rental: List Management Co.: Names in the News-California, 1 Bush St Bsmt 3, San Francisco, CA 94104-4425 Tel # (415) 989-3350, Fax # (415) 433-7796, Actives: 21,011, $65/M

World Rivers Review

Publishing Co: International Rivers Network, 1847 Berkeley Way, Berkeley, CA 94703-1576; Title Tel # (510) 848-1155 Title Fax # (510) 848-1008
Personnel: Editor-Lori Pottinger
Editorial Description: Articles relating to rivers and conservation.
General Info: Yr. Est. 1986, Quarterly, Trim Size-8.5 x 11, 16 pages, 2 Color
Subscriptions: Indv. $35, Inst. $100, Free With Membership
Printing Co: Westcoast Print Center, 2618 8th St, Berkeley, CA 94710-2514

World Wildlife Fund-U.S.- Focus
Association

Publishing Co: World Wildlife Fund-U.S., 1250 24th St NW Ste 400, Washington, DC 20037-1175; Title Tel # (202) 293-4800
Personnel: Editor-David Slater
Editorial Description: WWF projects, news, current events on international wildlife conservation.
General Info: Bi-monthly, Trim Size-11 x 16½, Web press, 8 pages, 2 Color, Newsprint
Subscriptions: Indv. $15
Circulation: (100% controlled), Total-800,000, Readership-800,000
List Rental: Actives: $65/M, Hotline: $75/M
Printing Co: Press Star Printing Corp., 12201 Old Columbia Pike, Silver Spring, MD 20904-1968 Tel # (301) 622-5000, Fax # (301) 622-5403

Wyoming Sierran

Publishing Co: Sierra Club, Northern Plains Region, 1427 Desmet Dr., Sheridan, WY 82801; Title Tel # (307) 672-0425
Personnel: Editor-Patricia Colberg
Editorial Description: Focuses on conservation issues in the Northern Plains region and nationwide. Also features news on club meetings, hikes and other events.
General Info: Quarterly
Circulation: Total-800

ZPG Reporter, The
Consumer, Association

Publishing Co: Zero Population Growth Inc., 1400 16th St NW Ste 320, Washington, DC 20036-2290; Title Tel # (202) 332-2200 Title Fax # (202) 332-2302
Personnel: Editor-Sharon Pickett, Production Mgr.-Nadia Steinzor, Art Dir.-Bill Raue
Editorial Description: Informs ZPG members and the press of current population/environmental issues legislation, local initiatives, programs & suggested solutions. Educates readers on population impact and a variety of issues related to popluation growth.
General Info: Yr. Est. 1984, Bi-monthly, Trim Size-11½ x 15, Web press, 8 pages, ISSN: 0199-0071, Color, Newsprint
Subscriptions: Indv. $20, Inst. $10, Can. $14, For. $18, Free With Membership
Circulation: Total-60,000
List Rental: List Management Co.: Names in the News-California, 1 Bush St Bsmt 3, San Francisco, CA 94104-4425 Tel # (415) 989-3350, Fax # (415) 433-7796, Actives: 41,177, $70/M, Expires: 29,829, $35/M
Printing Co: Comprint, 9030 Comprint Ct, Gaithersburg, MD 20877-1313 Tel # (301) 921-2822, Fax # (301) 948-1967

ETHNIC

General Ethnic Periodicals-
(For specific ethnicities, look under the name of the specific ethnic group)

ASA News
See: INTERNATIONAL AFFAIRS

Canadian Ethnic Studies Association Bulletin

Publishing Co: University of Saskatchewan - Ethnic Studies Assoc., Publications, Saskatoon, SK S7N 0W0 Canada; Title Tel # (306) 966-6774
Editorial Description: Regional Canadian ethnic studies in English and French.
General Info: Yr. Est. 1974, ISSN: 0315-8705
Acquistions: Publication Bought
Advertising: Inquire for rates.

Center for Migration Studies Newsletter
See: SOCIOLOGY

Civil Rights/State Capitals
See: CIVIL RIGHTS

Ethnic Reporter

Publishing Co: Natl. Assn. for Ethnic Studies, Dept. of English, Arizona State U. Box 870302, Tempe, AZ 85287-0302; Title Tel # (602) 965-3391 Title Fax # (602) 965-1093
Personnel: Publisher-Catherine Udall, Editor-Gretchen Bataille, Circ. Mgr.-Miguel Carranza
Editorial Description: Reports on the activities of NAES, provides news & includes short articles.
General Info: (Formerly NAES Newsletter), Yr. Est. 1975, Semi-annually, Trim Size-8½ x 11, Desktop press, 45 pages, Ind/Abs/Online: UMI, No Color, Newsprint
Subscriptions: Indv. $35, Inst. $45, Can. $40, For. $45, $5/copy
Circulation: Total-300
Advertising: Inquire for rates.
List Rental: Actives: $25/M

Genealogical Society of Flemish Americans Newsletter
Consumer, Association

Publishing Co: Genealogical Society of Flemish Americans, 18740 Thirteen Mile Rd., Roseville, MI 48066
Personnel: Editor-Margaret Roets
General Info: Semi-annually, Trim Size-8½ x 11, 4 pages, Matte
Subscriptions: Free With Membership

IHRC News
Association

Publishing Co: Univ. of Minnesota Immigration History Research Center, Immigration History Res. Ctr., 826 Berry St., St. Paul, MN 55114-1076; Title Tel # (612) 627-4208 Title Fax # (612) 627-4190
Personnel: Editor-Judith Rosenblatt
Editorial Description: Brief reports on staff, new acquisitions, research & visitors at the Immigration History Research Ctr.
General Info: Yr. Est. 1980, Tri-annually, Trim Size-8½ x 11, Desktop press, 10 pages, No Color, Saddle-stitched
Subscriptions: Free
Circulation: Total-2,100

Immigration Newsletter
See: LAW

Interracial Club of Buffalo Newsletter
Consumer, Association

Publishing Co: Interracial Club of Buffalo, 7 Harwood Dr. #400, Buffalo, NY 14226-4610; Title Tel # (716) 875-6958 Title Fax # (716) 839-5079
Personnel: Publisher, Editor-Mary Murchison Edwords
Editorial Description: Addresses the needs and interests of interracial couples, families, biracial individuals, and those who have adopted across racial lines.
General Info: Yr. Est. 1988, Monthly, Trim Size-8½ x 11, 10 pages
Subscriptions: Indv. $19, Inst. $19, Can. $25, For. $35, $2/copy
Circulation: Total-150, Readership-500

Magnes News
    See: MUSEUM PUBLICATIONS

Minorities in Business Insider
    See: BUSINESS & INDUSTRY

Monday: a weekly newsletter on refugee and immigration issues   *Consumer, Association*

Publishing Co: Church World Service, 475 Riverside Dr Ste 656, New York, NY 10115-0122; Title Tel # (212) 870-3153 Title Fax # (212) 870-2132
Personnel: Editor-Jane Lowicki
Editorial Description: Covers refugee and immigration issues from an ecumenical perspective.
General Info: Yr. Est. 1982, Weekly, Trim Size-8½ x 11, Offset press, 4 pages, Matte
Subscriptions: Free To Qualified Recipient
Circulation: Total-2,700

National Farm Workers Minority Newsletter
    See: AGRICULTURE

Pennsylvania Ethnic Heritage Newsletter

Publishing Co: Pennsylvania Ethnic Heritage Studies Center, 405 Bellfield Hall, 315 Bell-f, ield Ave. Univ. of Pittsburgh, Pittsburgh, PA 15260; Title Tel # (412) 648-7420
Personnel: Editor-Joseph Markarweicz
Editorial Description: Articles & news items concerned with the immigrant & ethnic heritage of Pennsylvania.
General Info: Yr. Est. 1975, 8 pages
Subscriptions: Indv. $2

Project Equality of Wisconsin-Newsletter & Buyers' Guide
    See: LABOR

Race Relations Newsletter   *Consumer*

Publishing Co: CH II Publishing, 200 W. 57th St., 15th Floor, New York, NY 10019 Tel # (212) 399-1084 Fax # (212) 245-1973 Parent Co.-Hanover Publishers, New York
Personnel: Publisher-Theodore Cross
Editorial Description: Covers race relations in the USA.
General Info: Yr. Est. 1993, Monthly

Routes
    See: ENTERTAINMENT

Saenger-Zeitung
    See: MUSIC & MUSIC TRADES

USET Gaming
    See: GAMBLING

Valley Women's Voice
    See: WOMEN'S

Virginia/West Virginia Queries
    See: GENEALOGY

African

Africa Fund
    See: CIVIL RIGHTS

JULUKA Newsletter   *Business, Association*   CPM: $173

Publishing Co: JULUKA Corporation, The, PO Box 34095, Bethesda, MD 20827-0095; Title Tel # (301) 652-5754 Title Fax # (301) 652-5756
Personnel: Publisher, Editor-Cliff Matheson
Editorial Description: A newsletter for those intereted in South Africa. Opinion and commentary on news affecting South and Southern Africa. Coverage politics, sports, business, travel, arts, opinion and culture.
General Info: Yr. Est. 1991, Bi-monthly, Trim Size-8½ x 11, Web press, 12 pages, 30% ads, No Color, Matte, Saddle-stitched
Subscriptions: Indv. $20, Inst. $20, Can. $22, For. $30, $4/copy
Circulation: Total-5,200, Readership-15,000
Advertising: $900. Accepts Inserts.
List Rental: List Management Co.: Pinnacle List Company, 2800 Shirlington Rd Ste 405b, Arlington, VA 22206-3601 Tel # (703) 379-4394, Fax # (703) 379-5312, Actives: 5,000, $100/M
Printing Co: Account Manager: Brandon Hymen; Newsletter Services, Inc., 9700 Philadelphia Court, Lanham, MD 20706 Tel # (301) 731-5200, Fax # (301) 731-5201

Mamaroots
    See: WOMEN'S

Nigerian Students Union in the Americas Newsletter
    See: COLLEGE STUDENT

African-American

African-American Family History Assn. Newsletter
    See: GENEALOGY

Black Congressional Monitor
    See: GOVERNMENT

Black History News & Notes
    See: HISTORY

CBMR Digest
    See: MUSIC & MUSIC TRADES

Education Program Calendar
    See: MUSEUM PUBLICATIONS

NOMMO; Power of the Word

Publishing Co: Afro-American Studies Center, Purdue Univ., 110 Matthews Hall, W. Lafayette, IN 47907; Title Tel # (317) 494-5680
Personnel: Editor-Ceola Ross Baber
General Info: Yr. Est. 1976
Circulation: Total-1,500

Nubian Exchange News
    See: AFRICAN-AMERICAN INTEREST

People's Guide

Publishing Co: People's Guide, 5927 Dr. M.L. King Dr., St. Louis, MO 63112
Personnel: Editor-J. Vaughn Chapman

Voices in Black Studies
    See: EDUCATION

Albanian

Drita E Vertete/True Light

Publishing Co: Albanian Orthodox Archdiocese in America, 523 E Broadway, South Boston, MA 02127-4415; Title Tel # (617) 268-7808
Personnel: Editor-Rev. Bishop Mar Lippa
Editorial Description: Text in Albanian and English.
General Info: Yr. Est. 1958, Monthly
Subscriptions: Indv. $10
Circulation: Total-1,500

Arabic

ADC Times   CPM: $80

Publishing Co: ADC Research Institute, 4201 Connecticut Ave NW Ste, 500, Washington, DC 20008-1158; Title Tel # (202) 244-2990 Title Fax # (202) 244-3196
Personnel: Editor-Ghauda Khouri
Editorial Description: Concerned with fighting against discrimination and promoting a positive image of the Arab-American community. Explores contemporary issues.
General Info: (Formerly ADC Reports), Yr. Est. 1980, Monthly, ISSN: 0749-2642
Subscriptions: Indv. $35, Inst. $50, Can. $40, For. $60
Circulation: Total-10,000
Advertising: $800. Accepts Inserts.

AWAIR News   *Consumer, Association*

Publishing Co: AWAIR (Arab World Islamic Resources & School Services), 1865 Euclid Ave Apt 4, Berkeley, CA 94709-1301; Title Tel # (510) 704-0517
Editorial Description: Increase knowledge of Muslim religion and culture to Americans through implementing programs in education systems.
General Info: Yr. Est. 1992, Quarterly

Iraq Views & News
    See: INTERNATIONAL AFFAIRS

Armenian

ACOM Newsletter

Publishing Co: Armenian Cultural Organization of Minnesota, 18275 Hummingbird Rd., Deephaven, MN 55391-3226; Title Tel # (612) 473-4936
Personnel: Editor-Peggy Merjanian
Editorial Description: News of particular interest to members of the Armenian Cultural Organization of Minnesota. Covers Armenian culture and heritage.
General Info: Yr. Est. 1980, Quarterly
Acquistions: Publication Bought

Armenian Welfare Association of New York News

Publishing Co: Armenian Welfare Assn. of New York Inc., 137 45th Ave., Flushing, NY 11355
Personnel: Editor-Nazaret Cherkezian
General Info: Yr. Est. 1970, 5x/yr.

NAASR Newsletter

Publishing Co: Sponsor-Natl. Assn for Armenian Studies & Research, Natl. Assn. for Armenian Studies & Research, Inc., 395 Concord Ave, Belmont, MA 02178-3036; Title Tel # (617) 489-1610
Personnel: Editor-Barbara Merguerian, Circ. Mgr., Adv. Dir., Promotion Dir.-Sandra Jurigian
General Info: Yr. Est. 1984, Quarterly, Trim Size-8½ x 11, Sheetfed press, 8 pages, ISSN: 0890-3794, 1% ads, 2 Color, Newsprint
Subscriptions: Indv. $8, For. $10, $2/copy
Circulation: Total-1,200
Printing Co: Arvest Press, 31 Coolidge Hill Rd, Watertown, MA 02172-2816 Tel # (617) 924-1101

Yettem   *Association*

Publishing Co: St. Mary Armenian Apostolic Church, PO Box 367, Yettem, CA 93670-0367; Title Tel # (209) 528-6892
Personnel: Editor-Vartan Kasparian, Circ. Mgr.-Carolyn Mikaelian
Editorial Description: Church-oriented publication on Armenian community life & education.
General Info: Yr. Est. 1971, Monthly, Trim Size-8½ x 11, 8 pages
Circulation: Total-315

Asian

CWAS Newsletter
See: WOMEN'S

Contact
See: INTERNATIONAL AFFAIRS

Context: Southeast Asians in California
See: CULTURE & HUMANITIES

CrossCurrents   *Consumer*

Publishing Co: Asian American Studies Center, 405 Hilgard Ave., University of California, Los Angeles, CA 90095-1546 Tel # (310) 825-2968 Fax # (310) 206-9844; Title Tel # (213) 825-3415
Personnel: Circ. Mgr.-Jean Yip, Publisher, Editor, Art Dir.-Glenn Omatsu
Editorial Description: Covers issues relating to Asian Pacific Americans on campuses and in communities.
General Info: Yr. Est. 1977, Semi-annually, Trim Size-8½ x 11, Letrpr. press, 14 pages, No Color, Coated, Saddle-stitched
Subscriptions: Free To Qualified Recipient
Circulation: Total-3,000
Printing Co: UCLA Publication Svcs., 405 Hilgard Ave, Los Angeles, CA 90024-1561 Tel # (213) 825-7040

In America

Publishing Co: Refugee Service Center, Center for Applied Linguistics, 1118 22nd St. NW, Washington, DC 20037
Editorial Description: Contains essays on Indochinese and Amerasian refugees and their adaption to the United States.
General Info: Bi-monthly

South Asia Forum
Quarterly   *Consumer, Association*   CPM$3336

Publishing Co: South Asia Forum, 4615 Morgan Dr, Chevy Chase, MD 20815-5314
Personnel: Publisher, Editor-Mohsin Siddique, Circ. Mgr., Promotion Dir.-Sachi Dastidar
Editorial Description: Deals with cultural, social, economic, political and other issues relating to the South Asian countries of the Indian subcontinent.
General Info: (Formerly South Asia Forum Newsletter), Yr. Est. 1988, Quarterly, Offset press, 10 pages, ISSN: 1047-7691, No Color, Coated
Subscriptions: Indv. $10, Inst. $20, Can. $15, For. $25, $3/copy
Circulation: Total-300
Advertising: $1,001. Accepts Inserts.

Basque

Basque Studies Program-
Newsletter

Publishing Co: Basque Studies Program 322, Univ. Of Nevada Library, Reno, NV 89557-0001; Title Tel # (702) 784-4854 Title Fax # (702) 784-1355
Personnel: Editor-Linda White, Production Ed.-Jill Berner
General Info: Yr. Est. 1968, Semi-annually, Trim Size-6½ x 8½, 12 pages, ISSN: 1047-2932, No Color, Saddle-stitched
Subscriptions: Free
Circulation: Total-8,700

Brazilian

GloboFax   *Business, Consumer*

Publishing Co: O Globo/Multimedia Inc., 7061 Grand National Dr., Ste. 127, Orlando, FL 32819-8377; Title Tel # (407) 363-1555 Title Fax # (407) 363-9809
Personnel: Publisher-Robert O. Marinho, Editor-Merval Pereira, Circ. Mgr.-Fernando Mariano, Production Mgr.-Henrique Caban, Mktg. Mgr.-Luis Eduardo Vasconcelos
Editorial Description: Covers political, economic, cultural and sports news of Brazil. Portuguese and English editions.
General Info: Yr. Est. 1993, Daily, Trim Size-8½ x 11, Desktop press, 2 pages, No Color, Other
Subscriptions: Indv. $432, $5/copy
Circulation: Total-600

British

Tam Kernewek

Publishing Co: Cornish American Heritage Society, Chy An Eglos, 2405 N. Brookfield Rd., Brookfield, WI 53045; Title Tel # (908) 776-5909
Personnel: Editor-Nanct Heydt
Editorial Description: Covers articles about Cornwall and the Cornish North American Community, book reviews, what's happening, society announcements, genealogy articles and queries, folklore, language etc.
General Info: Yr. Est. 1983, Quarterly, Trim Size-11 x 17, Desktop press, 10 pages, ISSN: 1085-1267, No Color, Newsprint, Other
Subscriptions: Indv. $10
Circulation: Total-450

Caribbean

Caribbean Newsletter
See: INTERNATIONAL AFFAIRS

Montserrat Progressive
Society of New York
Newsletter   *Association*

Publishing Co: Montserrat Progressive Society of N.Y., 584 Broadway, New York, NY 10012; Title Tel # (212) 941-8899
General Info: Quarterly
Circulation: Total-250

Chinese

CAA Newsletter
See: CIVIL RIGHTS

China Focus
See: INTERNATIONAL AFFAIRS

China/Judaic Connection   *Consumer, Association*

Publishing Co: China Judaic Studies Association, Oakton Community College, 1600 Goff Rd., Des Plaines, IL 60016 Tel # (847) 635-1848 Fax # (847) 635-1987; Title Tel # (708) 635-1848 Title Fax # (708) 635-1987
Personnel: Editor-Beverly Friend, Ph.D
Editorial Description: Newsletter of the China Judaic Studies Association.
General Info: Yr. Est. 1991, Semi-annually, Trim Size-8½ x 11, No Color
Subscriptions: Indv. $20, Inst. $20, Free With Membership
Circulation: Total-600

Chinese American Medical Society Newsletter
See: MEDICINE

Chinese Historical Society of America Bulletin
See: HISTORY

Music From China
See: MUSIC & MUSIC TRADES

OCA Image   *Association*   CPM: $300

Publishing Co: Organization of Chinese Americans, Inc., 1001 Connecticut Ave NW Ste, 707, Washington, DC 20036-5504; Title Tel # (202) 223-5500 Title Fax # (202) 296-0540
Personnel: Editor-Cindy Tong
Editorial Description: Surveys issues concerning Chinese Americans & Asian Americans-current events, cultural history.
General Info: Yr. Est. 1974, Quarterly, Trim Size-8½ x 11, Offset press, 28 pages, 2 Color, Coated, Saddle-stitched
Subscriptions: Indv. $25, Free With Membership
Circulation: Total-5,000
Advertising: $1,500. Accepts Inserts.
Printing Co: Duke Printing, 773 E Gude Dr, Rockville, MD 20850-1329 Tel # (301) 424-5599, Fax # (301) 424-5801

Czech

American Bulletin, The

Publishing Co: Czechoslovak Nat'l Council of America, 2137 S Lombard Ave Rm 202, Cicero, IL 60650-2037; Title Tel # (708) 656-1117
Editorial Description: News and assorted features of interest to the Czech community.
General Info: Monthly, ISSN: 0517-032X
Subscriptions: Indv. $5

Czechoslovak History
Newsletter   *Association*

Publishing Co: Valdosta State College Dept. Political Science, Publications, Valdosta, GA 31698-0001; Title Tel # (912) 333-5771
Personnel: Publisher, Editor-James Peterson
Editorial Description: Newsletter of the Czechoslovak History Conference.
General Info: (Formerly Czech Marks), Yr. Est. 1977, Semi-annually, Desktop press, 23 pages, 1% ads, No Color, Newsprint
Subscriptions: Indv. $8, Inst. $10, Can. $8, For. $8, $2/copy
Circulation: Total-150
Advertising: Inquire for rates. Accepts Inserts.

Nase Ceske Dedictvi   *Scholarly, Association*

Publishing Co: Czech Heritage Foundation, Inc., PO Box 761, Cedar Rapids, IA 52406-0761; Title Tel # (319) 857-4462
Personnel: Editor-Adeline Voleskey, Editorial Page Ed.-Adeline Volesky
Editorial Description: Czechoslovak history & culture, genealogy, traditions, & family histories. Local, natl. & intl. involvement.
General Info: (Formerly Our Czech Heritage), Yr. Est. 1973, Quarterly, Trim Size-8½ x 11, 16 pages, Color-cover, Saddle-stitched
Subscriptions: Indv. $3, Free With Membership
Circulation: Total-1,300
Printing Co: Lilly Printing, 301 3rd Ave SW, Cedar Rapids, IA 52404

Vestnik

Publishing Co: Czechoslovak Nat'l Council of America, 2137 S Lombard Ave Rm 202, Cicero, IL 60650-2037; Title Tel # (708) 656-1117
Editorial Description: News and features of interest to people of Czech descent.
General Info: Yr. Est. 1958, Monthly

Vestnik

Publishing Co: Czechoslovak Assn. of Canada, 740 Spadina Ave., Toronto, ON M5S 2J2 Canada; Title Tel # (416) 925-2241
Personnel: Editor-Karla Hartl
General Info: Yr. Est. 1948, Bi-monthly, 12 pages, No Color

Danish

Danish Odd Fellow Bulletin
See: CLUBS

Harbor Highlights
See: CLUBS

Dutch

De Nieuwe
Amsterdammer   *Business, Consumer*   CPM: $150

Publishing Co: De Nieuwe Amsterdammer, 54 W 39th St Fl 11, New York, NY 10018-3808; Title Tel # (212) 764-2284 Title Fax # (212) 764-2284
Editorial Description: Covers news and information for the Dutch speaking community in the U.S.
General Info: Yr. Est. 1991, Monthly, Offset press, No Color
Subscriptions: Indv. $30, For. $35, $3/copy
Circulation: Total-2,000
Advertising: $300.

East European

BATUN News   *Association*

Publishing Co: United Baltic Appeal, 115 W 183rd St, Bronx, NY 10453-1103; Title Tel # (212) 367-8802
Personnel: Editor-Paul Luedig
Editorial Description: To present informatioon on Baltic issues to the Baltic community and to those who are interested.
General Info: Yr. Est. 1980, Quarterly, Trim Size-8½ x 11, Sheetfed press, 16 pages, No Color, Newsprint
Subscriptions: $2/copy
Acquistions: Publication Bought
Circulation: Total-1,200

Bialystoker Stimme   *Association*

Publishing Co: Bialystoker Center, 228 E Broadway, New York, NY 10002-5699; Title Tel # (212) 475-7755
Personnel: Editor-Izaak Rybal
Editorial Description: Dedicated to the preservation of hometown memories and traditions; contains memoirs, a literary section, organizational reports, illustrations and news of Bialystoker Home for the Aged.
General Info: (Formerly Bialystoker Nursing Home), Yr. Est. 1920, Semi-annually, 80 pages, Color
Subscriptions: Indv. $35, $3/copy
Circulation: Total-6,000
Advertising: Inquire for rates.
Printing Co: Empire Press, 550 Empire Blvd, Brooklyn, NY 11225-3131 Tel # (718) 756-1473

Newsletter of the Society
Farsarotul   *Association*

Publishing Co: Society Farsarotul, PO Box 753, Trumbull, CT 06611-0753; Title Tel # (203) 375-0600 Title Fax # (203) 375-5003
Personnel: Publisher, Editor-Nicholas Balamaci
Editorial Description: Articles (mainly in English) concerning the history & culture of the Arumanians (also known as Vlachs) & Arumanian communities in Europe & America.
General Info: Yr. Est. 1986, Semi-annually, Trim Size-7 x 10, 24 pages, ISSN: 1042-3230, No Color
Circulation: (44% controlled), Total-450, Subscriptions-250

Russia and Her Neighbors, Facts & Views on Daily Life
See: INTERNATIONAL AFFAIRS

Estonian

Free Estonian Word

Publishing Co: World Association of Estonians, 243 E 34th St, New York, NY 10016-4852; Title Tel # (212) 684-0336
Personnel: Editor-Harold Raudsepp
General Info: Yr. Est. 1949, Weekly
Circulation: Total-3,900

Finnish

FACS Newsletter
See: CLUBS

Finnam Newsletter   *Consumer, Association*

Publishing Co: Finnish-American Historical Society of the West, PO Box 5522, Portland, OR 97228-5522; Title Tel # (503) 654-0448
Personnel: Editor-Gene Knapp
Editorial Description: Advocate & publicize Finnish-American Historical Preservation (Especially Western.).
General Info: Yr. Est. 1962, Quarterly, Trim Size-8½ x 11, Letrpr. press, 6 pages, Newsprint
Subscriptions: Indv. $8, Free With Membership
Circulation: Total-400
Advertising: Inquire for rates.
Printing Co: Laser Quick Print, 3001 SW Cedar Hills Blvd, Beaverton, OR 97005-1341 Tel # (503) 644-9196

Finnish-American Heritage

Publishing Co: Finnish-American Heritage Society, Inc., 1027 Rhode Island Ave N, Minneapolis, MN 55427-4522; Title Tel # (612) 786-1076
Editorial Description: News and features covering topics of interest to those of Finnish ancestry.
General Info: (Formerly Finnish American Soc. Inc., News & Views), Yr. Est. 1972, Monthly

Finnish-American Soc. of
Santa Clara Cnty.
Newsletter

Publishing Co: Finnish-American Soc. of Santa Clara Cnty., 878 Hummingbird Dr, San Jose, CA 95125-2918; Title Tel # (408) 266-0777
Editorial Description: News of interest to those of Finnish ancestry. Covers variety of society functions and events.
General Info: Yr. Est. 1985, Monthly

French

Informaction   *Association*

Publishing Co: Action for Franco-Americans, PO Box 504, Manchester, NH 03105-0504; Title Tel # (603) 622-2883
Personnel: Publisher-Real Gilbert, Editor-Tom Luce, Production Mgr.-Josee Vachon
General Info: Yr. Est. 1982, Bi-monthly, Trim Size-8½ x 11, Sheetfed press, 6 pages, No Color, Newsprint
Subscriptions: Indv. $5
Acquistions: Publication Bought
Circulation: Total-3,000
List Rental: Actives: $40/M

French Canadian

Chuchoteries
See: EDUCATION

German

German American Business Council
See: INTERNATIONAL TRADE

German-American World
See: EDUCATION

Grawunder and Graffunder Connection, The
See: GENEALOGY

Immigrant Genealogical Society Newsletter
See: GENEALOGY

LBI News
Association

Publishing Co: Leo Baeck Institute, Inc., 129 E. 73rd Street, New York, NY 10021
Tel # (212) 744-6400; Title Tel # (212) 333-5222 Title Fax # (212) 315-1716
Personnel: Editor-Gabrielle Bamberger
Editorial Description: Reportage on the work and activities of the Leo Baeck Institute and of material available in the Institute's archives and library relating to the history of German Jewry.
General Info: Yr. Est. 1960, Semi-annually, Trim Size-8½ x 11, Offset press, 12 pages
Circulation: Total-2,500

Nachrichten der Donauschwaben in Chicago
Association   **CPM: $250**

Publishing Co: Society of the Danube Swabians, Chicago, 625 Seegers Rd, Des Plaines, IL 60016-3041
Personnel: Editor-Annerose George
Editorial Description: Text: Ger.
General Info: (Formerly Nachrichten der Donauschwaben in Amerika), Yr. Est. 1955, Monthly, Trim Size-8½ x 11, 8 pages
Circulation: Total-600, Readership-3,000
Advertising: $150.
Printing Co: Weber Printing, 5746 N Western Ave, Chicago, IL 60659-5114

Ninth Manhattan Masonic News
See: CLUBS

Pennsylvania Dutch News and Views
See: FOLKLORE

Schale (Westfalen) Newsletter
See: GENEALOGY

Vorwarts, Forward
See: CLUBS

Yorker Palatine Newsletter
See: GENEALOGY

Greek

Campana
Consumer

Publishing Co: Campana Printing Co., 3096 42nd St, Astoria, NY 11103-3031;
Title Tel # (718) 278-3014 Title Fax # (718) 278-3023
Personnel: Publisher, Editor-Costas Athanasiades, Circ. Mgr.-Costas Athanasiandes, Adv. Dir.-E. Stan
Editorial Description: Text in Greek. Materials on Greeks in U.S.
General Info: Yr. Est. 1917, Semi-monthly, Offset press, 20 pages
Subscriptions: Indv. $20, For. $25
Circulation: Total-8,200

Greek Canadian Reportage
Consumer

Publishing Co: Greek Canadian Reportage, 7438 Durocher St., Montreal, PQ H3N 2A3 Canada
Tel # (514) 279-7772; Title Tel # (514) 279-2610
Personnel: Publisher, Editor-Anthony Bartzakos, Adv. Dir.-D. Peths
Editorial Description: Greek and English text.
General Info: Yr. Est. 1974, Weekly, Trim Size-11 x 17, Offset press
Subscriptions: Indv. $50
Advertising: Inquire for rates.

Modern Greek Studies Association Bulletin
See: HISTORY

Neo-Hellenika

Publishing Co: Center for Neo-Hellenic Studies, 1010 W 22nd St, Austin, TX 78705-5306;
Title Tel # (512) 477-5526
General Info: Annually

Pan Hellenic Society Inventors of Greece in U.S.A. Newsletter
See: PATENTS/COPYRIGHTS/TRADE MARKS

Velouchi Bulletin
Association

Publishing Co: Evry Tanian Assn. of America, 121 Greenwich Rd., Charlotte, NC 28211-2343;
Title Tel # (704) 366-6571
Personnel: Publisher, Editor-Serafim Nikopoulos
General Info: Yr. Est. 1946, Quarterly, Letrpr. press, 11 pages, No Color
Subscriptions: $1/copy
Circulation: Total-2,000
Advertising: Inquire for rates.

Hispanic

Agenda
See: CIVIL RIGHTS

Boletin de Divulgacion Martiana
Consumer

Publishing Co: DPA International, PO Box 440817, Houston, TX 77244-0817;
Title Tel # (713) 558-3052
Personnel: Editor-Andres Puello
General Info: Quarterly, ISSN: 1064-9824

COSSMHO Reporter, The
See: HEALTH

Enlace
Consumer

Publishing Co: Washington Office on Latin America, 110 Maryland Avenue, NE, Suite 404, Washington, DC 20002; Title Tel # (202) 544-8045 Title Fax # (202) 546-5288
Editorial Description: Political and cultural issues facing Latin Americans.
General Info: Yr. Est. 1992, Quarterly, Trim Size-8½ x 11, 10 pages, ISSN: 1059-6402
Subscriptions: Indv. $20

Grand Lodge
See: CLUBS

Hispanic Link Weekly Report
See: MEDIA & COMMUNICATIONS

Hispanic Newsletter
See: LAW

Journal Update
See: POLITICS

LULAC News
Consumer, Association

Publishing Co: League of United Latin American Citizens, 2100 M St. NW, Ste. 602, Washington, DC 20037-1207; Title Tel # (202) 628-0717
General Info: Monthly
Circulation: Total-1,200,000

Latino
Association

Publishing Co: Latino Institute, 228 S. Wabash, Ste. 600, Chicago, IL 60604-2314;
Title Tel # (312) 663-3603 Title Fax # (312) 663-4023
Personnel: Editor-Mayra Martinez
Editorial Description: Reports and secondary documentation on Chicago's latino community.
General Info: (Formerly Lider), Yr. Est. 1983, Quarterly, Trim Size-8½ x 11, Offset press, 8 pages, No Color
Subscriptions: Indv. $5, $2/copy
Acquistions: Publication Bought, Publication Sold
Circulation: Total-3,500

Latinogram

Publishing Co: Moraga & Associates, 1915 E Glencove St, Mesa, AZ 85203-4520;
Title Tel # (213) 397-6057
Personnel: Editor-Peter Moraga
Editorial Description: Covers events in the Latino community of Southern California. Examines problems in health, education & housing.
General Info: Yr. Est. 1978, Semi-monthly
Subscriptions: Indv. $30

Leading Hispanics
See: CIVIL RIGHTS

Malcriado/Voice of the Farm Worker
See: LABOR UNION

National Hispanic Reporter

Publishing Co: Hispanic Foundation, 1377 K St NW Ste 611, Washington, DC 20005-3303;
Title Tel # (202) 293-6245
General Info: Quarterly

Noticias de Aztlan
See: POETRY & CREATIVE WRITING

Plus Ultra

Publishing Co: Spanish Benevolent Society, 239 W 14th St, New York, NY 10011-7144
General Info: Annually

Southwest Alliance for Latin America Bulletin

Publishing Co: Southwest Alliance for Latin America, 1700 Asp Ave., Norman, OK 73037-0001;
Title Tel # (405) 325-1941
General Info: Bi-monthly

Hungarian

American Hungarian Educator

Publishing Co: American Hungarian Educators Assn., PO Box 4103, Silver Spring, MD 20914-4103;
Title Tel # (301) 384-4657
Personnel: Editor-Eniko Basa
Editorial Description: News of the AHEA & Hungarian studies, scholarly exchanges, professional activities.
General Info: Yr. Est. 1978, Trim Size-8½ x 11, 6 pages, ISSN: 0163-0040
Subscriptions: Indv. $15, $5/copy
Circulation: Total-250

American Hungarian Foundation Report
See: LITERATURE & LINGUISTICS

Hungarian Studies Newsletter

Publishing Co: American Hungarian Foundation, P.O. Box 1084, New Brunswick, NJ 08901-2248;
Title Tel # (908) 846-5777 Title Fax # (908) 249-7033
Personnel: Editor-August J. Molnar
General Info: Yr. Est. 1973, Quarterly, Trim Size-8½ x 11, Sheetfed press, 8 pages, ISSN: 0194-164X, No Color
Subscriptions: Indv. $10, Inst. $10, Can. $10, For. $12, $6/copy
Circulation: Total-1,500
Advertising: Inquire for rates.

Magyar Cserke'sz
See: CLUBS

Indian

Committee on South Asian Women Bulletin   *Consumer, Association*

Publishing Co: Committee on South Asian Women, Texas A & M Univ., Pschology Dept., College Station, TX 77843-0001 Tel # (409) 845-2576
Personnel: Editor-J. Vaid
Editorial Description: Publishes original essays, reports, interviews, reviews and creative works by and about South Asian women on various aspects of women's struggle and achievements in South Asia.
General Info: (Formerly Newsletter Committee on South Asian Women), Yr. Est. 1984, Semi-annually, ISSN: 0885-4319
Subscriptions: Indv. $18, Inst. $30, For. $15, $7/copy

Irish

Ducas   *Association*

Publishing Co: Irish American Culture Institute, 2115 Summit Ave # 5026, Saint Paul, MN 55105-1048 Tel # (612) 962-6040; Title Tel # (612) 662-6040 Title Fax # (612) 962-6043
Personnel: Editor-James Bohen
Editorial Description: Irish & Irish American historical items, reports of institute activities & accomplishments, & news of events in Ireland.
General Info: Yr. Est. 1971, Bi-monthly, Sheetfed press, 8 pages, 2 Color, Newsprint, Saddle-stitched
Circulation: Total-8,000
Advertising: Inquire for rates.
Printing Co: Sexton Printing, 250 E. Lothenbach Ave, W. St. Paul, MN 55118-3535 Tel # (612) 457-9255, Fax # (612) 457-7040

Gander, The

Publishing Co: Wild Geese, The, 6 N Water St, Greenwich, CT 06830-5817;
Title Tel # (203) 531-7755
Personnel: Publisher-Roger Lourie, Editor-Niall Healy, Production Mgr.-Dave Wheeler
Editorial Description: Concerned with the activities & special events of the Wild Geese, a group of Irish Americans interested in Irish culture.
General Info: Yr. Est. 1982, Monthly, Trim Size-8½ x 11, Sheetfed press, 16 pages, 2 Color, Newsprint
Acquisitions: Publication Bought, Publication Sold
Circulation: (100% controlled), Total-2,500

The Septs
See: GENEALOGY

Israel

Israel MarketFax
See: INVESTMENT

United Israel Bulletin   *Association*

Publishing Co: United Israel World Union, 1123 Broadway, New York, NY 10010-2007;
Title Tel # (212) 675-4863

Italian

ACIM News   *Association*

Publishing Co: American Committee on Italian Migration, 352 W 44th St, New York, NY 10036-5419;
Title Tel # (212) 247-7373
Personnel: Editor-Fr. Mariano Cisco
Editorial Description: Immigration policies.
General Info: (Formerly ACIM Dispatch), Yr. Est. 1953, Annually, Trim Size-8.5 x 11, Offset press, 8 pages, No Color, Newsprint, Other
Circulation: Total-10,000

America Italy Society Newsletter

Publishing Co: America Italy Society, 3 E 48th St Fl 6, New York, NY 10017-1027;
Title Tel # (212) 838-1560
Personnel: Editor-L. Caputo
Editorial Description: Information on cultural events of an Italian nature, (calendar of events of the Society), events in the Italian community (Manhattan).
General Info: Yr. Est. 1949, Mimeo press, 6 pages, 2% ads, No Color, Newsprint
Circulation: Total-3,000
Advertising: Inquire for rates. Accepts Inserts.
List Rental: Rents Lists
Printing Co: Dart Printing

American Italian Heritage Association Newsletter

Publishing Co: American Italian Heritage Association, PO Box 419, Morrisville, NY 13408-0419;
Title Tel # (315) 684-9502
Personnel: Editor-Prof. Philip J. DiNovo
Editorial Description: Our goals are to record and preserve the Italian heritage & culture. The newsletter includes traditions, customs, news about Italy and Italian Americans, culture, heritage, recipes, etc. Membership dues: $14/couple, $12/person, $18/couples and $8 for religious, clergy and students under 22. All inquiries answered by mail.
General Info: Yr. Est. 1979, Bi-monthly, Letrpr. press, 16 pages, No Color
Subscriptions: Indv. $12, Inst. $16, Can. $18, $3/copy
Circulation: Total-1,485
Advertising: Inquire for rates.
Printing Co: Acme Printing, 423 Broad St, Utica, NY 13501-1204 Tel # (316) 724-9734

American Italian Historical Association Newsletter   *Association*

Publishing Co: University of Illinois Alumni Assn., c/o Univ. Mail Service, 1919 W. Taylor St., Rm. B59, Chicago, IL 60612-7247 Tel # (312) 996-2885; Title Tel # (312) 996-3144
Personnel: Editor-Dominic Candeloro
Editorial Description: New publications, members and chapter activities, grant projects.
General Info: Yr. Est. 1967, Trim Size-8½ x 11, 20 pages, No Color
Subscriptions: Indv. $17, $1/copy
Circulation: Total-700

Bulletin

Publishing Co: Middletown Bulletin, Inc., PO Box 906, Middletown, CT 06457-0906;
Title Tel # (203) 346-8183
Personnel: Editor-B. Max Corvo
Editorial Description: In Italian.
General Info: Weekly

Italian-American Cultural Society Newsletter   *Consumer, Association*

Publishing Co: Italian American Cultural Society, 28111 Imperial Dr, Warren, MI 48093-4281;
Title Tel # (810) 751-2855
Editorial Description: Seeks to preserve Italian culture and recognize Italian contributions to the U.S.
General Info: Monthly
Subscriptions: Free With Membership
Circulation: Total-10,000
Advertising: Inquire for rates.

Italian Charities of America Bulletin
See: PHILANTHROPY

Messaggero/Messenger   *Consumer*

Publishing Co: Messenger Publishing Co., PO Box 30300, Kansas City, MO 64112-3300
Personnel: Editor-Dr. J. Bisceglia
Editorial Description: Text in English & Italian.
General Info: Yr. Est. 1921, Monthly, Trim Size-11 x 17
Subscriptions: Indv. $1
Circulation: Total-1,000
Advertising: Inquire for rates.

NIAF News, The   *Association*

Publishing Co: Natl. Italian American Foundation, 1860 19th St. NW, Washington, DC 20009-5501;
Title Tel # (202) 387-0600 Title Fax # (202) 387-0800
Personnel: Editor-Dona DeSanctis
Editorial Description: Articles of interest to the Italian-American community.
General Info: (Formerly washington Newsletter), Yr. Est. 1976, 5x/yr., Web press, 16 pages, No Color, Matte, Saddle-stitched
Subscriptions: $3/copy
Circulation: Total-25,000, Readership-25,000

Sicilia Parra   *Association*

Publishing Co: Sponsor-Arba Sicula, Arba Sicula, PO Box 040328, Brooklyn, NY 11204-0328; Title Tel # (718) 331-0613
Personnel: Production Mgr.-Henry Barbera, Editor, Circ. Mgr., Art Dir.-Gaetano Cipolla
Editorial Description: Bilingual English/Sicilian.
General Info: Yr. Est. 1989, Semi-annually, Trim Size-8½ x 11, Web press, 32 pages, 2% ads, 2 Color, Newsprint, Perfect bound
Subscriptions: Indv. $20, Inst. $25, $4/copy
Circulation: Total-2,000
Advertising: Inquire for rates.
Printing Co: Mill River Press, 176 Johnston St., Brooklyn, NY 11201 Tel # (718) 875-5832

Japanese

Canada Letter
See: BUSINESS & INDUSTRY

Japan-America Society
Bulletin   *Association*

Publishing Co: Japan-America Society of Washington, Inc., 1020 19th Street NW, #LL, Washington, DC 20036-6101; Title Tel # (202) 289-8290
Personnel: Editor-Patricia Kearns
Editorial Description: Keeps members informed of coming events in fields of cultural and educational activities. Carries articles on U.S. - Japan relations.
General Info: Yr. Est. 1957, Monthly, Trim Size-8½ x 11, Offset press, 7 pages, Color
Circulation: (37% controlled), Total-2,000
Advertising: Inquire for rates.

Japan Folio
See: SOCIOLOGY

Nippon Club Dayori
See: CLUBS

Jewish

Canadian Zionist
See: POLITICS

Highlights
See: CLUBS

Kosher Kettle   *Consumer*

Publishing Co: Five Star Publications, 4696 West Tyson St., Chandler, AZ 85226-2903; Title Tel # (602) 940-8182 Title Fax # (602) 940-8787
Personnel: Publisher, Editor-Linda F. Radke
Editorial Description: Devoted to Jewish life and interests. Includes Kosher recipes from around the globe and Jewish gift guide.
General Info: 3x/yr., ISSN: 1079-0829
Subscriptions: Indv. $19

Latin American Jewish
Studies   *Association*

Publishing Co: Latin American Jewish Studies Assn., 2104 Georgetown Blvd., Ann Arbor, MI 48105-1535; Title Tel # (313) 996-2880
Personnel: Publisher-Judith Laikin Elkin, Editor-Judith Laikin Elkin
Editorial Description: News of professional developments, research, conferences, pubs. in field, book reviews.
General Info: Yr. Est. 1980, Semi-annually, Trim Size-8½ x 11, Sheetfed press, 8 pages, ISSN: 0738-1379
Subscriptions: Indv. $25, Inst. $35
Circulation: Total-500, Readership-750
Advertising: Inquire for rates. Accepts Inserts.
List Rental: Rents Lists
Printing Co: Partners Press, 410 W Washington St, Ann Arbor, MI 48103-4230 Tel # (313) 662-8681

Yesha Report, The

Publishing Co: Pro Israel/Yesha Heartland Campaign, 17 East 45th Street, Suite 603, New York, NY 10017
Editorial Description: News and opinions from the yesa council of Jewish communities in Judea, Samaria & Gaza.

Latvian

Jauna Gaita

Publishing Co: Jauna Gaita, 636 Iroquuois Ave., Ancaster, ON L9G 3B4 Canada
Editorial Description: Community interest articles and news geared towards those of Latvian descent.
General Info: Yr. Est. 1955, 5x/yr.
Subscriptions: Indv. $29, Inst. $23, Can. $29, For. $29, $7/copy

Kristus Draudzes Vestis

Publishing Co: Kristus Draudzes Vestis, 4025 Chowen Ave S, Minneapolis, MN 55410-1013
Editorial Description: Ethnic, religious and general news of special significance to the Latvian-American population.
General Info: Yr. Est. 1972

Latvian Dimensions   *Association*   **CPM: $25**

Publishing Co: American Latvian Association in the U.S., PO Box 4578, Rockville, MD 20849-4578 Tel # (301) 340-1914 Fax # (301) 762-5438; Title Tel # (301) 340-8174 Title Fax # (301) 340-8732
Personnel: Editor-Martin Zvaners
Editorial Description: Reviews current affairs in Latvia and the Latvian community in the United States. Text in English.
General Info: (Formerly Latvian News Digest), Yr. Est. 1976, Quarterly, Trim Size-8½ x 11, Letrpr. press, 16 pages, ISSN: 1062-9505, Color, Saddle-stitched
Subscriptions: Indv. $25, Free With Membership
Circulation: Total-5,000
Advertising: $125.
Printing Co: Pinnacle Printing, 625 A Lofstrand Lane, Rockville, MD 20850 Tel # (301) 762-6300

Latvian House, Inc. Bulletin

Publishing Co: Latvian House, Inc., PO Box 18491, Minneapolis, MN 55418-0491; Title Tel # (612) 789-1575
General Info: Annually

Oregonietis

Publishing Co: Oregon Latvian Society, 1245 Hallinan St, Lake Oswego, OR 97034-4935
Editorial Description: Features news and special interest items devoted to the Latvian-American community.
General Info: Yr. Est. 1958, Monthly

Toronto Centra

Publishing Co: Latvian Canadian Cultural Centre, 4 Credit Union Dr., Toronto, ON M4A 2N8 Canada; Title Tel # (416) 759-4900
Editorial Description: News and cultural articles dealing with the ethnic Latvian community in Canada.
General Info: Yr. Est. 1978

Vinipegas Latviesu
Biedribas Izdevums
Informators

Publishing Co: Winnipeg Latvian Society, C/o O. Radovskias, 97 Lennox Ave., Winnipeg, MB R2M 1B1 Canada
Editorial Description: News and information relating to ethnic Latvians in Canada.
General Info: Yr. Est. 1983, Monthly

Lithuanian

Genealogija
See: GENEALOGY

Lithuanian-American
Bulletin   *Association*

Publishing Co: Lithuanian American Council, Inc., 6500 S Pulaski Rd, Chicago, IL 60629-5136; Title Tel # (312) 778-6900
Personnel: Publisher, Editor-Rev. Prunskis
Editorial Description: Current events concerning work of Lith. -Ameri. council & Lith. -Amer. activities; current events in Lithuania.
General Info: Yr. Est. 1972, Bi-weekly, Trim Size-8½ x 11, 3 pages, No Color, Matte
Circulation: Total-1,000

Lithuanian Museum Review
See: MUSEUM PUBLICATIONS

Musu Zinios   *Association*

Publishing Co: Jesuit Fathers of Della Strada, 5620 S Claremont Ave, Chicago, IL 60636-1039; Title Tel # (312) 767-8400
Personnel: Editor-Antanas Saulaitis, Circ. Mgr., Adv. Dir.-Petras Kleinotas, Art Dir.-Petras Aleksa
Editorial Description: Illustrated accounts of cultural & ethnics activities of Lithuanian Youth Center & Lithuanian Jesuit Fathers.
General Info: Yr. Est. 1972, Monthly, Trim Size-9 x 11¼, Offset press, 20 pages, No Color
Subscriptions: Indv. $5
Circulation: Total-700
Advertising: Inquire for rates.
Printing Co: Morkunas Printing Co., 3001 W 59th St, Chicago, IL 60629-2501 Tel # (312) 737-8230

Tiesa
See: CLUBS

Maltese

Maltese-American Social
Club of San Francisco
Newsletter   *Association*

Publishing Co: Maltese-American Social Club of San Francisco, 1789 Oakdale Ave, San Francisco, CA 94124-2326; Title Tel # (415) 647-9766
General Info: Semi-monthly

Mexican

Carta Abierta   *Association*

Publishing Co: Texas Lutheran College, 1000 W Court St, Seguin, TX 78155-5999
Tel # (210) 372-8028; Title Tel # (210) 372-6059 Title Fax # (210) 372-8096
Personnel: Publisher, Editor-Juan Rodriguez, Circ. Mgr.-Casimiro Rojo, Adv. Dir.-Arturo Garatusa
Editorial Description: Reviews, letters, news of Chicano literary world.
General Info: Yr. Est. 1975, Quarterly, Trim Size-8 x 11½, Sheetfed press, 12 pages, ISSN: 0198-1021, No Color
Subscriptions: Indv. $10, Inst. $20, $2/copy
Circulation: Total-1,000
Advertising: Inquire for rates.

El Machete Mecha
See: POETRY & CREATIVE WRITING

MALDEF Newsletter
See: CIVIL RIGHTS

MASRC Newsletter

Publishing Co: Mexican American Studies & Research Center, University Of Arizona Douglas, Bldg., Rm. 315, Tucson, AZ 85721-0001; Title Tel # (602) 621-7551
Personnel: Editor-Thomas Gelsinon
Editorial Description: For all the friends & supporters, including professors, staff & students of universities throughout the country.
General Info: (Formerly Mexican American Studies & Research Center-Newsletter), Yr. Est. 1981, Web press, 8 pages, 2 Color, Coated, Saddle-stitched
Circulation: (100% controlled), Total-1,000
List Rental: Actives: $40/M

TQS News
See: LITERATURE & LINGUISTICS

Mongolian

Mongolia Survey
See: CULTURE & HUMANITIES

Native American

AFN Newsletter   *Association*

Publishing Co: Alaska Federation of Natives, 1577 C St. #201, Anchorage, AK 99501-5138; Title Tel # (907) 274-3611 Title Fax # (907) 276-7989
Personnel: Editor-Jeffry Silverman
General Info: Trim Size-8½ x 11, 16 pages

Achimowin   *Association*

Publishing Co: Sagitawa Friendship Centre, Box 5083, Peace River, AB T8S 1R7 Canada; Title Tel # (403) 624-2443 Title Fax # (403) 624-2728
General Info: Semi-annually
Subscriptions: Indv. $6
Circulation: Total-200

American Indian Libraries Newsletter
See: LIBRARY

American Indian Society Newsletter   *Association*

Publishing Co: American Indian Society, 22226 Cool Water Dr, Ruther Glen, VA 22546-3309; Title Tel # (804) 448-3707
Personnel: Editor-Mitchell Bush, Art Dir.-Stephen Gonyea, Promotion Dir.-Verde Halley
General Info: Yr. Est. 1966, Monthly, Trim Size-8½ x 11, Offset press, 10 pages, No Color
Subscriptions: Indv. $8, Free With Membership
Circulation: Total-500, Readership-550
Advertising: Inquire for rates.
Printing Co: Serif Press, Inc., 1331 H St. NW, #110LL, Washington, DC 20005 Tel # (202) 737-4650

American Native Press
See: PERIODICAL INDUSTRY

Americans Before Columbus   *Consumer, Association*   CPM: $43

Publishing Co: National Indian Youth Council, 318 Elm St SE, Albuquerque, NM 87102-3614
Fax # (505) 247-4251; Title Tel # (505) 247-2251
Personnel: Editor-Sherry Robinson
Editorial Description: Indian issues--land, water, and fishing rights; education; history.
General Info: Bi-monthly, Web press, 8 pages, Newsprint
Subscriptions: Free With Membership
Circulation: Total-8,000
Advertising: $350.
List Rental: Actives: $60/M

Char-Koosta

Publishing Co: Confederated Salish, PO Box 278, Pablo, MT 59855-0278; Title Tel # (406) 675-4800
Personnel: Editor-Ron Bick, Circ. Mgr.-Francis McDonald, Production Mgr.-Paul Homuth, Adv. Dir.-Patti Sessions Blomquist, Art Dir.-Robert Billie
Editorial Description: News, art, and poetry and photography about native Americans, specifically Flathead/Kootenais.
General Info: (Formerly Charlo), Yr. Est. 1957, Bi-weekly, Trim Size-8½ x 11, Sheetfed press, 28 pages, ISSN: 0528-8592, Color
Subscriptions: Indv. $22, $1/copy
Circulation: (100% controlled)
Advertising: Inquire for rates.

Cherokee Boys Club- Newsletter & Cherokee Voice

Publishing Co: Cherokee Boys Club, PO Box 507, Cherokee, NC 28719-0507 Tel # (704) 497-9101 Fax # (704) 497-3140; Title Tel # (704) 497-5001 Title Fax # (704) 497-5818
Personnel: Editor-Joy Evans Widenhouse
Editorial Description: News and information about the activities of the cherokee boys club in cherokee, North Carolina. The cherokee Voice contains news and information regarding the activities of the cherokee center for family services the human services department of the boys club.
General Info: Yr. Est. 1965, Quarterly, Trim Size-8½ x 11, 12 pages, ISSN: 0890-5193, Other
Circulation: Total-5,500, Readership-5,500

DNA Newsletter
See: LAW

Domestic Abuse Is Not An Indian Tradition
See: SOCIAL SERVICES & WELFARE

Grapevine, The (Genesee Valley)   *Consumer, Association*

Publishing Co: Genesee Valley Indian Association Ctr., 609 W Court St, Flint, MI 48503-5019; Title Tel # (810) 239-6621
Editorial Description: News and information for and about the Native American community.
General Info: Yr. Est. 1975, Quarterly, Trim Size-8½ x 11, 8 pages, No Color, Matte
Subscriptions: Free
Acquistions: Publication Bought
Circulation: Total-2,500
Advertising: Inquire for rates.
List Rental: Rents Lists

Indian Affairs   *Association*

Publishing Co: Association on American Indian Affairs, PO Box 268, Sisseton, SD 57262; Title Tel # (605) 698-3998
Personnel: Editor-Arlene Hirschfelder, Circ. Mgr.-Pauline Pierro
Editorial Description: American Indian, Alaska Native rights, legislation, economic development, health, education.
General Info: Yr. Est. 1949, Trim Size-8½ x 11, Sheetfed press, 8 pages, 2 Color, Newsprint
Subscriptions: Indv. $10, $4/copy
Acquistions: Publication Bought
Circulation: Total-45,000

Indian Awareness Center Newsletter
See: HISTORY

Indian Report
See: U.S. (& CANADIAN) FED. GOV'T.

Indian Voice

Publishing Co: Canadian Indian Voice Society, 429 E. 6th St., N. Vancouver, BC V7L 1P8 Canada
Personnel: Editor-Donna Doss, Circ. Mgr.-Viola Starcevich
Editorial Description: Discusses topics affecting the native Indian, to serve as a communications vehicle.
General Info: Yr. Est. 1969, Quarterly, Trim Size-10 x 15, Offset press, 16 pages, ISSN: 0073-6732, No Color
Subscriptions: Indv. $7, $1/copy
Circulation: (CCAB), Total-2,800
Advertising: Inquire for rates.

Itza Voice   *Association*   CPM: $8

Publishing Co: Kaweah Indian Nation, PO Box 3121, Hutchinson, KS 67504-3121; Title Tel # (316) 665-3614
Personnel: Editor-Thunderbird Webber
Editorial Description: Tribal paper of Kaweah Indian Nation (Native Americans).
General Info: Yr. Est. 1980, Quarterly, Sheetfed press, 8 pages
Subscriptions: Indv. $6, Can. $7, For. $8, $1/copy
Circulation: (60% controlled), Total-5,000, Subscriptions-2,000
Advertising: $40.

Journal of American Indian Research Monthly Newsletter
See: GENEALOGY

Linkages
See: FAMILY

Meeting Ground

Publishing Co: D'Arcy McNickle Center for History of American Indian, the N, 60 W Walton St, Chicago, IL 60610-3305; Title Tel # (312) 943-9090
Personnel: Editor-Brenda Mannelito
Editorial Description: Activities & events of McNickle Center & alumni.
General Info: Yr. Est. 1972, Semi-annually, 8 pages
Subscriptions: Free
Circulation: Total-4,000

NAPBC Newsletter
See: BROADCASTING

NARF Legal Review
See: LAW

Nakodabi, The Assiniboine
People   *Consumer*

Publishing Co: Friends of the Assiniboines Foundation, 623 Knapp St, Wolf Point, MT 59201-1806; Title Tel # (406) 653-1804
Personnel: Editor-Bob Saindon
Editorial Description: Official publication of the Friends of the Assiniboines Foundation.
General Info: Quarterly
Subscriptions: Indv. $25

National Indian Council on Aging News
See: SENIOR CITIZENS

Native American
Connection   *Consumer*

Publishing Co: Native American Connections, PO Box 414, Coos Bay, OR 97420-0043
Editorial Description: Cultural events, editorials and information about Native American lifestyles.
General Info: Monthly, Trim Size-11 x 15, 8 pages

Native American Policy Network
See: SOCIOLOGY

Native Arts Update
See: ART & SCULPTURE

Native Child Advocate
See: CHILDREN

Native Sun

Publishing Co: Detroit American Indian Ctr., 22720 Plymouth Rd., 360 John Rd., Detroit, MI 48239-1327; Title Tel # (313) 535-2966
Personnel: Editor-Andrew Butterfly
Editorial Description: Contains local & natl. news pertaining to Native Americans.
General Info: Yr. Est. 1975, Monthly, Trim Size-8½ x 11, Mimeo press, 10 pages, No Color
Subscriptions: Indv. $8, $1/copy
Circulation: Total-200

Navajo Area Newsletter

Publishing Co: U.S. Bur. of Indian Affairs, PO Box 1060, Gallup, NM 87305-1060; Title Tel # (602) 871-5156
Personnel: Editor-Frank Hardwick
General Info: (Formerly Navajo Educ. Newsletter), Yr. Est. 1977, Monthly
Circulation: Total-4,000

Newsletter

Publishing Co: Foundation for Indian Leadership, Hal Schultz, PO Box 5340, Santa Fe, NM 87505; Title Tel # (505) 989-6300

North American Indian
See: POLITICS

North River Trading Post   *Consumer*

Publishing Co: N.R. Trading Co., HCR 77 Box 382, Cosmopolis, WA 98537-9600; Title Tel # (206) 538-1240
Personnel: Publisher-Charles Peterson, Art Dir.-Jade Peterson
Editorial Description: Articles and recipes of interest to Native Americans.
General Info: Yr. Est. 1990, Quarterly, Trim Size-4¼ x 8, Desktop press, 8 pages, 50% ads, No Color, Matte
Subscriptions: Indv. $8, $2/copy
Advertising: Inquire for rates.

Oh Hi Yoh Noh

Publishing Co: Seneca Nation of Indians, Box 231, Plummer Bldg., Salamanca, NY 14779-0231
Personnel: Editor-Eldena Halftown
Editorial Description: News and special interest pieces devoted to the Seneca Nation of Indians.
General Info: Yr. Est. 1970, Monthly
Circulation: Total-500

Omniciye
See: COLLEGE STUDENT

Red Cloud Country

Publishing Co: Red Cloud Indian School, Inc., Holy Rosary Mission, Pine Ridge, SD 57770; Title Tel # (605) 867-5491
Personnel: Editor-Fr. Roger
Editorial Description: American Indian interests.
General Info: Yr. Est. 1960, Quarterly, Letrpr. press, 4 pages, Color, Coated
Subscriptions: Indv. $10, $10/copy
Circulation: (81% controlled), Total-160,000

Shenandoah Newsletter

Publishing Co: Shenadoah Newsletter Co., 736 W Oklahoma St, Appleton, WI 54914-3733; Title Tel # (414) 832-9525
Personnel: Publisher, Editor, Circ. Mgr.-Paul Skenandore
Editorial Description: Native American treaty rights & history.
General Info: Yr. Est. 1973, Monthly, Trim Size-8½ x 11, Mimeo press, 21 pages, Newsprint
Subscriptions: Indv. $15, Inst. $20, $2/copy
Circulation: Total-1,000

Tekakwitha Conference
Newsletter

Publishing Co: Tekakwitha Conference Natl. Ctr., PO Box 6768, Great Falls, MT 59406-6768; Title Tel # (406) 727-0147
Personnel: Editor-Gilbert Hemauer
General Info: Yr. Est. 1979, Quarterly, 28 pages, 2 Color, Newsprint
Circulation: Total-15,000
List Rental: Actives: $50/M

Treaty Council News
See: GOVERNMENT

Tribal Spokesman

Publishing Co: Inter-Tribal Council of California, 2755 Cottage Way, Ste. 14, Sacramento, CA 95825-1221 Tel # (916) 973-9581
Personnel: Editor-Darlene Brown
Editorial Description: American Indian interests.
General Info: Yr. Est. 1969, Monthly
Subscriptions: Indv. $5
Circulation: Total-6,500

Unity

Publishing Co: Assn. of Iroquois and Allied Indians, R.R. 2, Southwold, ON N0L 2G0 Canada
Personnel: Editor-Shelly Bressette
Editorial Description: Covers news and issues of importance to the Indian peoples.
General Info: (Formerly Strength in Unity), Quarterly

Web, The   *Consumer, Association*

Publishing Co: Akwe-Kon Press/Cornell University, 300 Caldwell Hall, Cornel University, Ithaca, NY 14853-8605 Tel # (607) 255-4308; Title Tel # (607) 255-4300 Title Fax # (607) 255-0185
Personnel: Editor-Jose Barreiro, Circ. Dir.-Jennifer Bedell, Production Mgr.-Susan Dixon
Editorial Description: Staff and student written pieces.
General Info: (Formerly Cornell Web), Yr. Est. 1984, Tri-annually
Circulation: (44% controlled), Total-5,000, International-200

Wicozanni Wowapi Good Health Newsletter
See: HEALTH

Norwegian

News of Norway
See: INTERNATIONAL AFFAIRS

Northwood Ermissaeren
See: HOSPITALS & NURSING HOMES

Norwegian-American
Historical Association
Newsletter   *Association*

Publishing Co: Norwegian-American Historical Assn., St. Olaf College, 1510 St. Olaf Ave., Northfield, MN 55057-1097; Title Tel # (507) 646-3221 Title Fax # (507) 646-3734
Personnel: Editor-Lloyd Hustvedt
General Info: Semi-annually, Trim Size-6 x 9
Subscriptions: Free With Membership
Circulation: (83% controlled), Total-1,800
List Rental: Rents Lists

Norwegian-American Museum Newsletter
See: MUSEUM PUBLICATIONS

Norwegian Tracks
See: GENEALOGY

Sanger-Hilsen/Singers Greetings
Association

Publishing Co: Norwegian Singers Assn. of America, Rr 2 Box 137, Kenyon, MN 55946-9340; Title Tel # (812) 925-4658
Personnel: Editor-Donald L. Berg
Editorial Description: Printed in Norwegian and English.
General Info: Yr. Est. 1892, Bi-monthly, Web press, 16 pages
Subscriptions: Indv. $5
Circulation: Total-1,000
Printing Co: Shakopee Valley Printing, 5101 Valley Industrial Blvd S, Shakopee, MN 55379-1821 Tel # (612) 445-8260, Fax # (612) 496-0007

Polish

Association of Polish Engineers in Canada, Bulletin
See: ENGINEERING

Canadian Polish Congress. Information Bulletin

Publishing Co: Canadian Polish Congress, 288 Roncesvalles Ave., Toronto, ON M6R 2M4 Canada; Title Tel # (416) 532-2876
Personnel: Editor-Marie Brodeki
General Info: Yr. Est. 1967, Quarterly, 32 pages
Subscriptions: Indv. $4, $1/copy

Dom Polski

Publishing Co: Polish Festivals, Inc., 7128 W Rawson Ave, Franklin, WI 53132-9280; Title Tel # (414) 529-2140
Personnel: Editor-Ray Trzesniewski, Jr.
General Info: (Formerly Polski Dom), Yr. Est. 1985, Quarterly, Trim Size-8½ x 11, 4 pages, 2 Color, Coated
Circulation: Total-5,000
Printing Co: Metropolitan Graphics, 7512 W. Oklahoma Ave., West Allis, WI 53219

Hamersky & Allied Families Newsletter
See: GENEALOGY

Hejna

Publishing Co: Polish-American Cultural Soc. /St. Louis, 12205 Kollingsford Dr., Florissant, MO 63033; Title Tel # (314) 741-2763
Personnel: Editor-Delphine Kaminski
Editorial Description: Ethnic news, both local and national. Educational features.
General Info: Yr. Est. 1979, Quarterly, ISSN: 0748-7568
Subscriptions: Indv. $6
Circulation: Total-1,800

Kombatant W Ameryce
See: CLUBS

Kosciuszko Foundation Newsletter
Association

Publishing Co: Kosciuszko Foundation, 15 E 65th St, New York, NY 10021-6595; Title Tel # (212) 734-2130
Personnel: Editor-Monica Olszer-Jasinska
Editorial Description: Informs members of the Foundation activity.
General Info: Yr. Est. 1947, Semi-monthly, Trim Size-8½ x 11, Letrpr. press, 16 pages, No Color, Newsprint
Subscriptions: Indv. $35
Circulation: Total-4,000
Printing Co: Polstar, 134 Greenpoint Ave., Brooklyn, NY 11222 Tel # (718) 383-9587

Liga
Consumer, Association

Publishing Co: Catholic League for Religious Assistance to Poland, 1200 N. Ashland Ave., Chicago, IL 60622-2259; Title Tel # (312) 276-2334
Editorial Description: News of religious assistance to Poland.
General Info: Yr. Est. 1943, Quarterly
Circulation: Total-2,500

PAHA Newsletter
Consumer, Association   **CPM: $133**

Publishing Co: Polish American Historical Assn., Jersey City State College, Jersey City, NJ 07305
Personnel: Editor-James S. Pula
Editorial Description: Reports on association and members; activities in the area of Polish American studies.
General Info: Yr. Est. 1942, Quarterly, Trim Size-8½ x 11, Desktop press, 8 pages, ISSN: 0739-9766, No Color, Matte
Subscriptions: Indv. $20, Inst. $35, $10/copy
Circulation: Total-750
Advertising: $100.
List Rental: Actives: $75/M

PIASA Bulletin, The
See: INTERNATIONAL AFFAIRS

Polish Arts Club Bulletin

Publishing Co: Polish Arts Club of Chicago, 5378 N Lynch Ave, Chicago, IL 60630-1443
Personnel: Editor-Lillian Zukowski
Editorial Description: News and feature articles revolving around the Polish Arts Club and its functions, activities.
General Info: Yr. Est. 1946, Quarterly

Polish Assistance Bulletin

Publishing Co: Polish Assistance, Inc., 15 E. 65th St., New York, NY 10021-6501; Title Tel # (212) 245-2087
General Info: Semi-annually

Polonian
CPM: $25

Publishing Co: Polish Community Service Center, 165 11th St, San Francisco, CA 94103-2534; Title Tel # (415) 864-6100 Title Fax # (415) 431-6450
Personnel: Editor-Dalegor Suchecki
Editorial Description: Publication of editorial comment directed to the ethnic Polish community. Lists Polish cultural events, religious services, radio broadcasts, etc.
General Info: (Formerly Daleger Wladyslaw Suchecki Newsletter), Yr. Est. 1962, Monthly, Trim Size-8½ x 11, Sheetfed press, 2 pages, 2% ads, 2 Color, Matte
Subscriptions: Indv. $10, Can. $20, For. $40, $5/copy
Circulation: (50% controlled), Total-4,000, Single Copy/Newsstand-1,000, Subscriptions-1,000, International-127
Advertising: $100.
Printing Co: Tempo Press, 9118 Dice Rd., Santa Fe, CA 90670 Tel # (213) 946-5803

Portuguese

Erensia Sefardi
Association, Consumer

Publishing Co: Turkish Sephardi Federation, 46 Benson Pl., Fairfield, CT 06430-6904; Title Tel # (203) 255-4432 Title Fax # (203) 256-8819
Personnel: Editor-Albert de Vidas
Editorial Description: Information about and for the descendants of Spanish and Portuguese Jews - from 1492 to present.
General Info: Yr. Est. 1993, Quarterly, Trim Size-8½ x 11, 6 pages, No Color, Matte
Subscriptions: Indv. $25, Inst. $50
Circulation: Total-2,000

First Portugese Canadian News (Noticias)

Publishing Co: First Portuguese Canadian Club, Inc., 722 College St., Toronto, ON M6G 1C4 Canada
General Info: Monthly

Puerto Rican

Ecos Nacionales

Publishing Co: Natl. Conference of Puerto Rican Women, 5 Thomas Cir., NW, Washington, DC 20005-4153; Title Tel # (202) 387-4716
Editorial Description: Info of interest to the Hispanic community, especially women.
General Info: Yr. Est. 1972

El Puertorriguerto
See: CULTURE & HUMANITIES

Nacion Taina
Consumer, Association

Publishing Co: Nacion Taina, PO Box 883, New York, NY 10025-0883; Title Tel # (212) 866-4573
Editorial Description: For the restoration of the Taino people in Puerto Rico.
General Info: Yr. Est. 1993, Monthly

Romanian

Information Bulletin

Publishing Co: Romanian American Heritage Ctr., 2540 Grey Tower Rd, Jackson, MI 49201-9120; Title Tel # (517) 522-8260
Personnel: Editor-Valerian Trifa
Editorial Description: Information and news of interest to those of Romanian extraction. Explores Romanian culture and heritage.
General Info: Yr. Est. 1983, Quarterly

Romanian American Heritage Center Information Bulletin

Publishing Co: Romanian American Heritage Ctr., 2540 Grey Tower Rd, Jackson, MI 49201-9120; Title Tel # (517) 522-8260
Editorial Description: Covers the evolution of the Romanian-American community.
General Info: Yr. Est. 1983, Bi-monthly
Subscriptions: Indv. $10

Union

Publishing Co: Union, 1367 W 65th St, Cleveland, OH 44102-2109
Personnel: Publisher-Rev. Mircea M. Toderich
Editorial Description: In Romanian and English.
General Info: Monthly
Circulation: Total-2,200

Russian

Institute of Modern Russian Culture Newsletter

Publishing Co: Sponsor-Institute of Modern Russian Culture, Institute of Modern Culture, Univ. Of Southern California, Mc 4353, Los Angeles, CA 90089-0001; Title Tel # (213) 743-8162
Personnel: Editor, Circ. Mgr.-John Bowlt, Publisher, Art Dir.-Ivan Verbliud
Editorial Description: Newsletter reports on cultural activities of the Institute.
General Info: Yr. Est. 1979, Semi-annually, Trim Size-8½ x 11, Mimeo press, 15 pages, ISSN: 0738-7105, 2 Color, Newsprint
Subscriptions: Indv. $25
Circulation: Total-1,200
Printing Co: Printing Palace, 513 Wilshire Blvd, Santa Monica, CA 90401-1444

Pervopokhodnik

Publishing Co: Obedinenie Pervopokhodnikov, 1315 Chelten Way, South Pasadena, CA 91030-3911
Editorial Description: Text: Russ.
General Info: Yr. Est. 1971, Bi-monthly
Subscriptions: Indv. $6

Scandinavian

SASS News & Notes   *Association*

Publishing Co: Society for the Advancement of Scandinavian Study, 3003 JKHB, Brigham Young Univ., Provo, UT 84602 Tel # (801) 378-5598 Fax # (801) 378-4649; Title Tel # (206) 543-0645
Personnel: Editor-Terje Leiren
Editorial Description: Newsletter of the Society for the Advancement of Scandinavian Study.
General Info: Yr. Est. 1974, Quarterly, Trim Size-8½ x 11, 12 pages, ISSN: 0891-7477, No Color
Circulation: Total-575

Scan   *Association*

Publishing Co: American-Scandinavian Foundation, The, 725 Park Ave, New York, NY 10021-5025; Title Tel # (212) 879-9779 Title Fax # (212) 249-3444
Personnel: Publisher-Patricia McFate
Editorial Description: Covers events sponsored by and related to the foundation's educational and cultural mission.
General Info: Quarterly
Circulation: (100% controlled), Total-3,500

Thanks to Scandinavia Newsletter
See: EDUCATION

Scottish

An Drochaid   *Association*

Publishing Co: Clans & Scottish Societies of Canada, St. Andrew's Church, 73 Simcoe St., Toronto, ON M5J 1W9 Canada; Title Tel # (416) 593-0518
Personnel: Publisher-W.N. Fraser, Editor-Marie Fraser, Exec. Ed.-Ian McGregor
Editorial Description: Contains information from & about Scottish groups & events.
General Info: Yr. Est. 1976, 5x/yr., Trim Size-8½ x 11, Desktop press, 8 pages, ISSN: 0703-1491
Subscriptions: Indv. $8, Can. $10
Circulation: Total-300

Calling All Scots   *Association*

Publishing Co: American Scottish Foundation, Box 537, Lenox Hill Sta., New York, NY 10021-0033; Title Tel # (212) 249-5556
Editorial Description: Activities & information of interest to American-Scottish Foundation.
General Info: Quarterly
Circulation: Total-4,000

Clan Fraser Society of N. America, Canadian Region Newsletter

Publishing Co: Clan Fraser Society of N.A., Canadian Region, 71 Charles St. E., #1101, Toronto, ON M4Y 2T3 Canada; Title Tel # (416) 920-6851
Personnel: Editor-W. Neil Fraser
General Info: (Formerly Clan Fraser Society of N. America, Ontario Chapter Newslette), Yr. Est. 1982, 5x/yr., Trim Size-8½ x 11, Desktop press, 6 pages, ISSN: 1184-1141
Circulation: Total-200

Dobie Connection
See: GENEALOGY

Dunrobin Piper
See: GENEALOGY

Fesse Cheguy

Publishing Co: Clan Stewart Society in America, Inc., 28 Harwich Rd, Morristown, NJ 07960-2640; Title Tel # (201) 267-1675
Personnel: Editor-Donald Livingston
Editorial Description: Scottish heritage articles; current Scottish/American events affecting our society.
General Info: Yr. Est. 1975, Quarterly, Trim Size-8½ x 11, Offset press, 8 pages, No Color, Newsprint
Subscriptions: Indv. $15
List Rental: Actives: $50/M

Highland News

Publishing Co: U.S. Highland Dancing Association, 5135 Kneale Dr, Lyndhurst, OH 44124-1226
General Info: Bi-monthly

Kennedy Gazette
See: GENEALOGY

Pibroch   *Association*

Publishing Co: St. Andrew Society of the State of N.Y., 71 W. 23rd St., New York, NY 10010 Fax # (212) 807-1730; Title Tel # (212) 807-1730 Title Fax # (212) 807-1877
Personnel: Editor-Robert Campbell, Jr.
Editorial Description: Scottish and society business also Scottish events.
General Info: Yr. Est. 1946, Semi-annually, 16 pages, No Color
Circulation: (100% controlled), Total-2,000

Rampant Lion   *Consumer, Association*

Publishing Co: Scottish Historic & Research Society of Delaware Valley, 102 Saint Pauls Rd, Ardmore, PA 19003-2811; Title Tel # (610) 649-4144
Personnel: Editor-Blair Stonier, Adv. Dir.-P. J. Stonier
Editorial Description: Articles on all phases of Scottish culture, travel, history, etc.
General Info: Yr. Est. 1964, Monthly, Trim Size-8½ x 11, Offset press, 8 pages, 1% ads, No Color, Newsprint
Subscriptions: Indv. $15
Acquistions: Publication Bought
Circulation: (100% controlled), Total-600
Advertising: Inquire for rates. Accepts Inserts.

Serbian

Kanadski Srbobran   *Association*

Publishing Co: Serbian League of Canada, 335 Britannia Avenue, Hamilton, ON L3H 1Y4 Canada; Title Tel # (416) 549-4079
Personnel: Circ. Mgr.-Gvozden Bajic
General Info: Yr. Est. 1951, Weekly, Trim Size-6 x 15, Offset press, 8 pages, No Color
Subscriptions: Indv. $25
Circulation: Total-1,750
Advertising: Inquire for rates.

Serbia

Publishing Co: Serbian Chetniks War Vets Assn., Box 70, Fruitland, ON L0R 1L0 Canada Tel # (905) 643-9212
Personnel: Editor-M. Devrnja
General Info: Monthly
Subscriptions: Indv. $10
Circulation: Total-4,000
Advertising: Inquire for rates.

Slavic

AAASS Newsletter   *Consumer, Association*

Publishing Co: American Assn. for Advancement of Slavic Studies, 8 Story St., Cambridge, MA 02138 Tel # (617) 495-0677; Title Tel # (415) 723-9668 Title Fax # (415) 725-7737
Personnel: Publisher-Dorothy Atkinson, Production Mgr., Adv. Dir.-Paqui Nelson
Editorial Description: Carries news of the association and its members, institutional announcements, grants, and fellowships offered and awarded and a calendar of conferences.
General Info: Yr. Est. 1960, 5x/yr., Trim Size-8½ x 11, Offset press, 40 pages, ISSN: 0883-9549, Ind/Abs/Online: ABSEES, 1% ads, No Color, Matte
Subscriptions: Indv. $20, $5/copy
Circulation: Total-4,000
Advertising: Inquire for rates.
List Rental: Actives: $80/M

American Association of Teachers of Slavic & Eastern European Languages News
See: LITERATURE & LINGUISTICS

CAS Newsletter — *Association* — CPM: $135

Publishing Co: Canadian Association of Slavists, Dept. Comparative Literature, 347 Arts Bldg.-Univ.of Alberta, Edmonton, AB T6G 2E6 Canada; Title Tel # (403) 492-2566 Title Fax # (403) 492-2715
Personnel: Editor-G. Olson
Editorial Description: News of profession (CAS is interdisciplinary, academic organization devoted to Soviet & E. Europe).
General Info: Yr. Est. 1961, Semi-annually, Trim Size-8½ x 11, Offset press, 16 pages, ISSN: 0381-6133, 1% ads, No Color
Subscriptions: Indv. $6, Can. $6, $3/copy
Circulation: Total-370
Advertising: $50. Accepts Inserts.
List Rental: Actives: $100/M

Slovak

Floridsky Slovak

Publishing Co: Slovak Garden, Inc., 3110 Howell Branch Rd., Ste. 5075, Winter Park, FL 32792-6006; Title Tel # (407) 677-6894 Title Fax # (407) 677-8442
Editorial Description: General interest articles and ethnic pieces of interest to Slovak-Americans.
General Info: Yr. Est. 1967, Quarterly

SAYN

Publishing Co: Summit Impressions, Inc., Hwy. 36, Airport Plz., Hazlet, NJ 07730
General Info: Monthly
Subscriptions: Indv. $12

Slovak Heritage Live — *Consumer, Association* — CPM: $22

Publishing Co: Slovak Heritage and Cultural Society of British Columbia, 3804 Yale Street, Burnaby, BC V5C 1P6 Canada; Title Tel # (604) 291-8065 Title Fax # (604) 291-1966
Personnel: Publisher-Vladimir Linder
Editorial Description: For the Slovak community of British Columbia & the world.
General Info: Yr. Est. 1993, Quarterly, Trim Size-8½ x 11, 16 pages, ISSN: 1198-6077
Subscriptions: Indv. $15, Inst. $50, Can. $15, For. $15, $5/copy
Circulation: Total-8,800
Advertising: $200.
Printing Co: Laser Graphics, 250 East Broadway, Vancouver, BC V5T 1W3 Canada Tel # (604) 812-3231, Fax # (604) 812-2640

Slovak Press Digest — *Association*

Publishing Co: Slovak-American Cultural Center, 20219 36th Ave, Bayside, NY 11361-1157; Title Tel # (914) 428-0703
Personnel: Editor-Jozef Ihnat
Editorial Description: Digesting news from Slovak life and achievements of Slovaks.
General Info: Yr. Est. 1969, Quarterly, Trim Size-8½ x 11, 10 pages, No Color
Circulation: Total-500
Advertising: Inquire for rates.

Slovak Studies Assn. Newsletter — *Association*

Publishing Co: Slavic Dept., Indiana Univ., Bloomington, IN 47405
Personnel: Publisher, Editor-Louise Hammer
General Info: Yr. Est. 1977, Semi-annually, Trim Size-8½ x 11, Sheetfed press, 20 pages, No Color, Newsprint
Subscriptions: Indv. $5, Inst. $10
Circulation: (100% controlled)

Spanish

Yeshiva University Sephardic Bulletin — *Association*

Publishing Co: Yeshiva University, 500 W 185th St, New York, NY 10033-3299; Title Tel # (212) 960-5398
Personnel: Editor-Rabbi Mitchell Serels
Editorial Description: Purpose of the bulletin is to disseminate information about Sephardic studies and community activities programs.
General Info: Yr. Est. 1973, Annually, Trim Size-8½ x 11, Offset press, 9 pages, No Color
Subscriptions: Free
Circulation: Total-14,000

Sri Lankan

Sri Lankan — *Association*

Publishing Co: Sri Lanka Association of New York, Inc., 19 Lake Ave, New Rochelle, NY 10801-2311; Title Tel # (914) 235-1744
Personnel: Publisher, Editor, Adv. Dir.-Dallas De Soyza
Editorial Description: Issues relating to the Sri Lanka Association of New York, Inc. and its members residing in the Greater New York area, the contiguous states, and the New England States.
General Info: Quarterly, Trim Size-8½ x 11, Offset press, 4 pages, No Color
Circulation: (100% controlled), Total-150

Swedish

ASI Posten — *Consumer, Association*

Publishing Co: American Swedish Institute, 2600 Park Ave, Minneapolis, MN 55407-1090; Title Tel # (612) 871-4907 Title Fax # (612) 871-8682
Personnel: Editor-Jan McElfish
General Info: (Formerly Happenings), Yr. Est. 1969, 11x/yr., Trim Size-8½ x 11, Offset press, 12 pages, 2 Color, Saddle-stitched
Subscriptions: Indv. $33
Circulation: Total-5,500
Printing Co: Carlson Printing, 2001 Chicago Ave, Minneapolis, MN 55404

American Swedish Historical Foundation and Museum Newsletter — *Consumer, Association*

Publishing Co: American Swedish Historical Foundation, 1900 Pattison Ave, Philadelphia, PA 19145-5901; Title Tel # (215) 389-1776 Title Fax # (215) 389-7701
Personnel: Editor-Ann Brown
Editorial Description: Covers cultural exhibition & activities events of interest to Museum membership.
General Info: Yr. Est. 1976, Quarterly, Letrpr. press, 4 pages, 2 Color
Circulation: Total-1,000
Advertising: Inquire for rates. Accepts Inserts.
Printing Co: Bailey Printing, Baltimore Pl., Springfield, PA 19078 Tel # (215) 544-6700

Svithiod Journal
See: CLUBS

Swenson Center News — *Association*

Publishing Co: Swenson Swedish Immigration Research Ctr., Augustana College, 639 38th Street, Rock Island, IL 61201-2273; Title Tel # (309) 794-7204 Title Fax # (309) 794-7443
Personnel: Editor-Dag Blanck
Editorial Description: Covers Swedish immigration to N. America, as related to collections, programs & services of the Swenson Ctr.
General Info: Yr. Est. 1986, Annually, Trim Size-8½ x 11, Sheetfed press, 8 pages, ISSN: 0895-7126, No Color, Coated
Subscriptions: Free
Circulation: Total-4,800
Advertising: Inquire for rates.

Swiss

Orangeburgh German-Swiss Newsletter
See: GENEALOGY

Swiss-American Historical Society Review
See: HISTORY

Swiss Canadian News
See: CLUBS

Swiss Connection, The
See: GENEALOGY

Yoder Newsletter
See: GENEALOGY

Turkish

Macedonia, Curiosum Mundi
See: CULTURE & HUMANITIES

News from Turkey

Publishing Co: Turkish-American Assn. for Cultural Exchange, 1600 Broadway, New York, NY 10019-7413 Tel # (212) 956-1560; Title Tel # (212) 354-0737
Personnel: Editor-M. Peker
Editorial Description: Text: Turkish.
General Info: Yr. Est. 1965, Semi-annually

Quintcentennial Quarterly, The

Publishing Co: Quintcentennial Foundation of Istanbul, c/o GCI Group, 777 Third Avenue, 23rd Fl, New York, NY 10017; Title Tel # (212) 546-1548 Title Fax # (212) 546-2381
Editorial Description: Celebrates 500 years of peaceful living in Turkish lands by Jews expelled from Spain in 1492.
General Info: Yr. Est. 1989, Quarterly

Turkish-American Associations Newsletter — *Consumer, Association*

Publishing Co: Turkish-American Assn. for Cultural Exchange, 1600 Broadway, New York, NY 10019-7413; Title Tel # (212) 956-1560 Title Fax # (212) 956-1562
Personnel: Editor-I. Fenik
General Info: Bi-monthly, Trim Size-8½ x 11, 6 pages
Circulation: Total-10,000

Ukrainian

Federation of Ukrainian Student Organizations of America Newsletter
Consumer, Association

Publishing Co: Fed. of Ukrainian Student Organizations of America, 2 E 79th St, New York, NY 10021-0106; Title Tel # (212) 288-8660

Kredytova Kooperatyva Pivnichnoho Vinnipegu Biuleten North Winnipeg Credit Union Ltd. Bull
Association

Publishing Co: North Winnipeg Credit Union Ltd., 544 Selkirk Ave., Winnipeg, MB R2W 2M9 Canada; Title Tel # (204) 586-8469
Personnel: Editor-Maurice Bugera
Editorial Description: Self-help and credit organization for people of Ukrainian descent.
General Info: Yr. Est. 1959, Quarterly, 8 pages, Color

Maloda Ukraina
Consumer, Association

Publishing Co: Ukrainian Youth Assn., 133 Fairview Ave., Toronto, ON M6P 3A6 Canada
General Info: Monthly

Novyny z Akademii (UVAN)

Publishing Co: Ukrainian Academy of Arts, 206 W 100th St, New York, NY 10025-5018; Title Tel # (212) 222-1866
Personnel: Circ. Mgr.-Oksana Radysh
Editorial Description: Text: Ukrainian. Articles on activity of the Ukrainian Academy, biographical artices etc.
General Info: (Formerly Novyny & UVAN), Yr. Est. 1970, Annually, Letrpr. press, 8 pages
Subscriptions: $2/copy
Circulation: Total-1,000
Printing Co: Svoboda Press, Ukrainian Natl., 30 Montgomery St., Jersey City, NJ 07302

Ukrainian Canadian Committee Bulletin
Association

Publishing Co: Ukrainian Canadian Congress, 456 Main St., Winnipeg, MB R3B 1B6 Canada Tel # (204) 942-4627 Fax # (204) 947-3882; Title Tel # (204) 943-1927
Personnel: Editor-W. Werbeniuk, Circ. Mgr.-Jennie May
Editorial Description: Activity of the Ukranian Canadian Committee and its 30 branch offices operating in 9 provinces of Canada.
General Info: Yr. Est. 1953, Semi-annually, Trim Size-8½ x 11, 40 pages, ISSN: 0503-1036, No Color
Subscriptions: Indv. $10, $3/copy
Circulation: (52% controlled), Total-19,000, Subscriptions-9,000

Ukrainian Cultural Inst. Newsletter

Publishing Co: Ukrainian Cultural Institute, DSU Box 6, Dickinson, ND 58601
Editorial Description: Expores Ukrainian cultural heritage, reports on Institute activities.
General Info: Yr. Est. 1980, Quarterly

Ukrainian Professional & Business Club Bulletin
See: CLUBS

Ukrainian Times

Publishing Co: Ukrainian Culture Center, 4315 Melrose Ave, Los Angeles, CA 90029-3510 Tel # (213) 665-3703
Personnel: Editor-Orysia Bulczak

Vietnamese

Vietnamese Association's Newsletter
Association

Publishing Co: Vietnamese Assn., Toronto, 1364 Dundas St., W., Toronto, ON M6J 1Y2 Canada; Title Tel # (416) 536-3611 Title Fax # (416) 536-8364
General Info: Yr. Est. 1979, Monthly, Trim Size-8½ x 11, Mimeo press, 8 pages, ISSN: 0712-1288, No Color
Subscriptions: Indv. $12
Circulation: (100% controlled), Total-600

Yiddish

Book Peddler/der Pakn-Treger
See: BOOKS & BOOK TRADE

Yugoslavian

Yugoslav-American Society Newsletter

Publishing Co: Yugoslav-American Society, PO Box 23336, Minneapolis, MN 55423-0336
Editorial Description: Illuminates ethnic heritage of Yugoslovian-Americans, reports on Society activities.
General Info: Yr. Est. 1987, Bi-monthly

FAMILY

Abstract of Marital Relationship Analysis
See: PSYCHOLOGY

Academy of Family Films & Family Television Newsletter

Publishing Co: Academy of Family Films & Family Television, 334 W 54th St, Los Angeles, CA 90037-3806; Title Tel # (213) 752-5811
Personnel: Editor-Dr. Donald Reed
General Info: Yr. Est. 1980, Quarterly
Circulation: Total-1,000

Academy Newsletter
See: MUSEUM PUBLICATIONS

Adams Family Chronicle
See: GENEALOGY

Adoption Law and Practice
See: LAW

Adoption Today Newsletter
Association

Publishing Co: Concerned Persons for Adoption, PO Box 179, Whippany, NJ 07981-0179; Title Tel # (908) 273-5694
Personnel: Editor-Barbara James, Circ. Mgr.-Ann Pontown
Editorial Description: Contains committee reports, current adoption in formation, social news & editorial features. We publish monthly for our members.
General Info: Yr. Est. 1972, Monthly, 14 pages, 2 Color
Subscriptions: Indv. $20, Inst. $10, For. $25
Acquistions: Publication Bought
Circulation: Total-425
Printing Co: Triangle Offset Printing, 177 Main St, East Brunswick, NJ 08816-4448

Adoption Update
Consumer, Association

Publishing Co: Natl. Adoption Center, 1500 Walnut St Ste 701, Philadelphia, PA 19102-3507; Title Tel # (215) 735-9988 Title Fax # (215) 735-9410
Personnel: Editor-Gloria Hochman
General Info: (Formerly National Adoption Center News), Yr. Est. 1983, Semi-annually, 8 pages, No Color, Coated
Acquistions: Publication Bought
Circulation: Total-12,000

Alateen Talk
See: SOCIAL SERVICES & WELFARE

Alimony, Child Support and Counsel Fees--Award, Modification and Enforcement
See: LAW

American Mother

Publishing Co: Sponsor-American Mothers, Inc., Greene Recorder, 701 Park St, Greene, IA 50636-9439; Title Tel # (212) 755-2539 Title Fax # (212) 755-2539
Personnel: Editor-Sylvia Hawker
Editorial Description: Quarterly pub. news & communicatiosn of American Mothers, Inc. Lessons on all aspects of Motherhood helps in teaching children moral values & promoting family happiness.
General Info: Quarterly, Trim Size-8½ x 11, 20 pages, 2 Color
Subscriptions: Indv. $10, $3/copy
Circulation: Total-5,000
Advertising: Inquire for rates.

American Nudist Research Library
See: LIFESTYLE

Army Families
See: MILITARY & NAVAL

Barney Family News
See: GENEALOGY

Benedict Family News, The
See: GENEALOGY

Beta Parents
See: EDUCATION

Bulletin of the NPA
See: BABY

Burnett Family Newsletter
See: GENEALOGY

CF Child Care Bulletin   *Association*

Publishing Co: Children's Foundation, 725 15th St NW Ste 505, Washington, DC 20005-2109;
  Title Tel # (202) 347-3300 Title Fax # (202) 347-3382
Personnel: Editor-Sandra Gellert, Publisher, Circ. Mgr.-Kay Hollestelle
Editorial Description: A national information resource for family day care homes.
General Info: (Formerly Family Day Care Bulletin), Yr. Est. 1977, Bi-monthly, Trim Size-8½ x 11,
  Sheetfed press, 8 pages, No Color
Subscriptions: Indv. $18, Inst. $25, $4/copy
Circulation: Total-3,000
Printing Co: District Service, 5004 Jackson St, Hyattsville, MD 20781-1009 Tel # (301) 779-3040

CFLE Network
See: SOCIAL SERVICES & WELFARE

CUB Communicator   *Consumer, Association*

Publishing Co: Concerned United Birthparents, 2000 Walker St., Des Moines, IA 50317-5201;
  Title Tel # (515) 263-9558
Personnel: Editor-Marylee MacDonald
Editorial Description: CUB is a nonprofit organization for families separated by adoption.
General Info: Yr. Est. 1976, Monthly, Trim Size-8 x 11, 20 pages, No Color
Subscriptions: Indv. $50, Inst. $50, Can. $65, For. $65, $3/copy
Circulation: Total-1,500

CWC Communicator
See: WOMEN'S

California Family Law Monthly
See: LAW

California Family Law-Practice and Procedure
See: LAW

California Family Tax Planning
See: TAXES

California Tomorrow
See: EDUCATION

Camps Canada
See: PARKS & RECREATION AREAS

Canadian Family Law
Guide   *Business*

Publishing Co: CCH Canadian Ltd., 6 Garamond Ct., North York, ON M3C 1Z5 Canada
  Fax # (416) 444-8011 Parent Co.-CCH, Inc., Riverwoods; Title Tel # (416) 441-2992
  Title Fax # (416) 444-9011
Editorial Description: Federal, provincial, territorial statutes re family law in Canada. Court decisions
  concerning custody and maintenance of children, maintenance of deserted wives and parents, etc.
General Info: Monthly, Trim Size-6 x 9, Web press, No Color, Looseleaf
Subscriptions: Can. $500

Center for Plain Living Newsletter
See: LIFESTYLE

Cheap Leisure Thrills   *Consumer*

Publishing Co: HUB Publishing, PO Box 45025, Seattle, WA 98145-0025
Editorial Description: Advice for families trying to find inexpensive entertainment ideas.
General Info: Bi-monthly
Subscriptions: Indv. $12

Cheapskate Monthly
See: BANKING & FINANCE

Child Care Employee News   *Consumer*

Publishing Co: National Center for Early Childhood Workforce, 733 15th St NW Ste 800,
  Washington, DC 20005-2112; Title Tel # (202) 737-7700 Title Fax # (202) 737-0370
Personnel: Editor-Marcy Whitebrook
General Info: Yr. Est. 1980, Quarterly, 12 pages
Subscriptions: Indv. $25, Inst. $35, Can. $25
Circulation: Total-3,500

Child Custody and Visitation Law and Practice
See: LAW

Child Welfare Report (CWR)
See: SOCIAL SERVICES & WELFARE

Children's Video Review Newsletter
See: CHILDREN

Children's Writer
See: BOOKS & BOOK TRADE

Choosing Home   *Consumer*

Publishing Co: Choosing Home, PO Box 15868, Fort Wayne, IN 46885-5868;
  Title Tel # (219) 486-0287
Personnel: Publisher-Valerie Sanders
Editorial Description: Covers issues for parenting.
General Info: Monthly

Collier Family Law and the Bankruptcy Code
See: LAW

Communications in Family
Planning

Publishing Co: Planned Parenthood Assn. of Halifax & Dartmouth, 3115 Veith St., 3rd Fl., Halifax,
  NS B3K 3G9 Canada; Title Tel # (902) 492-0444
General Info: 10 pages
Subscriptions: Indv. $10
Circulation: Total-500

Community Service Newsletter
See: SOCIOLOGY

Compassionate Friends
Newsletter   *Association, Consumer*

Publishing Co: Compassionate Friends, Inc., Box 3696, Oak Brook, IL 60522-3696;
  Title Tel # (708) 990-0010
Personnel: Publisher-Susan Salisbury Richards, Editor-Judy Kaplan
Editorial Description: Information and inspiration for parents whose children have died.
General Info: Yr. Est. 1972, Quarterly, Trim Size-8½ x 11, Offset press, 8 pages, No Color
Subscriptions: Indv. $15, Can. $18, For. $20
Circulation: Total-5,000

Connecticut Hospice
Newsletter

Publishing Co: Connecticut Hospice, Inc., 61 Burban Dr, Branford, CT 06405-4003;
  Title Tel # (203) 481-6231
Personnel: Editor-John Abbott
General Info: Semi-annually, 16 pages
Subscriptions: Indv. $3

Contact
See: HEARING & SPEECH

Contraceptive Technology
Update   *Consumer*

Publishing Co: American Health Consultants, Inc., 3525 Piedmont Rd., Building #6, Ste. 400,
  Atlanta, GA 30305-0056 Tel # (404) 262-7436 Fax # (404) 284-3291
Personnel: Publisher-Connie Austin, Editor-Joy Daughtery, Editor-Terry Murphy, Circ. Mgr.-Linda
  Slayton, Production Mgr.-Mike Witter, Mktg. Mgr.-Rebecca S. Torres, Promotion Dir.-Kathryn
  Russell
Editorial Description: Latest news in contraceptive research, family planning issues.
General Info: Yr. Est. 1980, Monthly, Trim Size-8½ x 11, Offset press, 16 pages, ISSN: 0274-726X,
  Ind/Abs/Online: Mead Data Central, 2 Color
Subscriptions: Indv. $259, $25/copy
Circulation: Total-1,500
List Rental: Actives: $125/M

Coryell Newsletter
See: GENEALOGY

Cottage Connections
See: REGIONAL INTEREST

Desert Voice
See: RELIGIOUS & THEOLOGICAL

Digital Kids Report, The
See: COMPUTERS & AUTOMATION

Disputed Paternity
Proceedings   *Business*

Publishing Co: Matthew Bender & Co., 11 Penn Plaza, New York, NY 10001-2006
  Fax # (212) 244-3188; Title Tel # (212) 967-7707
Personnel: Editor-J. Borvick
Editorial Description: Defense strategy and tactics, reports on new biochemical blood tests that
  determine paternity.
General Info: Yr. Est. 1944, Irregular, Looseleaf
Subscriptions: $210/copy

Double Feature

Publishing Co: Parents of Multiple Births Assn. of Canada, Inc., 4981 Hwy. #7 E., Unit 12A #161, Markham, ON L3R 1N1 Canada; Title Tel # (416) 513-7506
Personnel: Editor-Barbara Cooper, Production Mgr.-Sheryl McInnes
Editorial Description: Canada's newsletter for parents of twins & other multiple births.
General Info: Yr. Est. 1977, Quarterly, Trim Size-8½ x 11, Offset press, 16 pages, ISSN: 0824-278X, Saddle-stitched
Subscriptions: Indv. $12, $3/copy
Circulation: Total-1,800
Advertising: Inquire for rates.

Double Talk

Publishing Co: Karen Kerkhoff Gromada, Box 412, Dept. NP, Amelia, OH 45102-0412; Title Tel # (513) 231-8946
Personnel: Editor-Karen Dromoda
General Info: Yr. Est. 1981, Quarterly, 16 pages
Subscriptions: Indv. $6
Circulation: Total-1,600

Dovetail: A Newsletter By and For Jewish-Christian Families
See: RELIGIOUS & THEOLOGICAL

ERIC/EECE Newsletter
See: EDUCATION

ElderCare Forum
See: WOMEN'S

Families in Crisis Funding Report *Business*

Publishing Co: CD Publications, 8204 Fenton St., Silver Spring, MD 20910-4571; Title Tel # (301) 588-6380 Title Fax # (301) 588-6385
Personnel: Publisher-Mike Gerecht, Editor-Richard Walker, Circ. Mgr.-Kurt Eisentraut, Mktg. Dir.-Joyce Meals
Editorial Description: Helps organizations working with families to identify and gain access to financial support.
General Info: Yr. Est. 1994, Semi-monthly, Trim Size-8½ x 11, Sheetfed press, 16 pages, ISSN: 1075-3184, No Color, Matte, Other
Subscriptions: Indv. $259, Can. $269, For. $299, $15/copy
List Rental: List Management Co.: Manager: Amy Seyler; Washington Advertising Service, 8204 Fenton St., Silver Spring, MD 20910 Tel # (301) 588-7920, Fax # (301) 588-6385, Actives: 7,009, $150/M, Expires: $150/M

Family in America *Consumer*

Publishing Co: Rockford Institute, 934 N Main St, Rockford, IL 61103-7061; Title Tel # (815) 964-5053 Title Fax # (815) 965-1826
Personnel: Publisher-Allan Carlson, Publications Director-Guy Reffett, Editor-Bryce Christiansen, Art Dir.-Amanda Lundgren
Editorial Description: Features a major essay and reports on events, trends, and literature relating to family life.
General Info: (Formerly Persuasion At Work), Yr. Est. 1978, Monthly, Trim Size-8¼ x 11, Sheetfed press, 12 pages, ISSN: 0892-2691, 2 Color, Newsprint
Subscriptions: Indv. $24, Can. $27, For. $27, $2/copy
Circulation: (PSS, 25% controlled), Total-3,756, Subscriptions-2,796
List Rental: List Management Co.: Manager: Rochelle Frank; Main Street Agency, 934 N Main St, Rockford, IL 61103-7061 Tel # (815) 964-5811, Actives: 1,870, $110/M

Family Law Handbook

Publishing Co: Gould Publications, Inc, 1333 N US Highway 17-92, Longwood, FL 32750-3724 Tel # (407) 695-9500 Fax # (407) 695-2906; Title Tel # (607) 724-3000
Editorial Description: Book. Supplemented annually at additional cost. Includes social service laws and domestic relation law.
General Info: Annually, Trim Size-5½ x 8½, Sheetfed press, 250 pages, No Color, Looseleaf
Subscriptions: Indv. $13, $22/copy

Family Law Reporter *Business*

Publishing Co: Bureau of National Affairs, Inc., 1231 25th St. NW, Bldg. N-200, Washington, DC 20037-1157; Title Tel # (202) 452-4200 Title Fax # (202) 822-8092
Personnel: Publisher-William A. Beltz, Editor-Randy Auerbach, Mng. Editor-David B. Jackson, Circ. Mgr.-Gary C. Seltzer
Editorial Description: A weekly notification & reference service dealing with all significant state & federal developments in the field of family law. (Marriage, divorce, child custody, adoption, family relations).
General Info: Yr. Est. 1974, Weekly, Trim Size-8½ x 11, Web press, 16 pages, ISSN: 0148-7922, Looseleaf
Subscriptions: Indv. $595

Family Law: Texas Practice and Procedure
See: LAW

Family Policy

Publishing Co: Family Research Council, 700 13th St NW Ste 500, Washington, DC 20005-3960; Title Tel # (202) 393-2100 Title Fax # (203) 393-2134
Personnel: Publisher-Gary Baver, Editor-William Mattox
Editorial Description: Reviews current research and policy developments on family issues.
General Info: Yr. Est. 1988, Bi-monthly, Sheetfed press, 8 pages, 2 Color, Newsprint, Saddle-stitched
Subscriptions: Indv. $15
Circulation: Total-28,000
Printing Co: Corporate Press, 403 Brightseat Rd., Landover, MD 20785-4706 Tel # (301) 499-9200, Fax # (301) 499-5435

Family Relations/State Capitals
See: LAW

Family Research Report *Consumer*

Publishing Co: Family Research Institute, Inc., PO Box 62640, Colorado Springs, CO 80962; Title Tel # (703) 690-8536
Personnel: Publisher, Editor-Paul Cameron, Circ. Mgr.-Virginia Cameron, Production Mgr.-Kirk Cameron, Art Dir.-Karyn Knapp, Promotion Dir.-Kelly Cameron
Editorial Description: Focuses on the impact of sexuality, particularly homosexuality, on society. Promotes incentives instead of punishment.
General Info: (Formerly Family Research Newsletter), Yr. Est. 1982, Bi-monthly, Trim Size-8½ x 11, Desktop press, 8 pages, 2 Color, Saddle-stitched
Subscriptions: Indv. $20, Inst. $20, Can. $30, For. $30
Circulation: Total-6,500

Family Resource Coalition Report *Association*

Publishing Co: Family Resource Coalition, 200 S Michigan Ave Ste 1520, Chicago, IL 60604-2404; Title Tel # (312) 341-0900 Title Fax # (312) 341-9361
Personnel: Editor, Production Mgr.-Joan Silvern
Editorial Description: Information for professional and staff workers working with families.
General Info: Yr. Est. 1982, Quarterly, Trim Size-8½ x 11, Web press, 24 pages, ISSN: 1041-8660, Ind/Abs/Online: ERIC, 2 Color
Subscriptions: Indv. $35, Inst. $75, $4/copy
Acquisitions: Publication Bought
Circulation: Total-7,500
List Rental: Actives: $50/M
Printing Co: Booklet Publishing Co., 1902 Elmhurst Rd, Elk Grove Village, IL 60007-5913 Tel # (708) 364-1544

Famlee Talk

Publishing Co: Famlee Talk, 136 S 10th St, Quakertown, PA 18951-1504; Title Tel # (215) 538-4530
General Info: Quarterly
Subscriptions: Indv. $10

Federated News
See: WOMEN'S

Florida Family Law
See: LAW

Florida Family Law Reporter
See: LAW

Frugal Finances
See: CONSUMER INTERESTS

Genealogy Bulletin
See: GENEALOGY

Get Organized! News, The
See: GENERAL INTEREST

Gloria Pitzer's Secret Recipes Publications
See: FOOD

Goodenow's Ghosts
See: GENEALOGY

Grad Family Newsletter
See: GENEALOGY

Green Guide, The
See: ENVIRONMENT & ECOLOGY

Guide
See: WOMEN'S

Homeworking Mothers

Publishing Co: Mother's Home Business Network, PO Box 423, East Meadow, NY 11554-0423; Title Tel # (516) 997-7394
Personnel: Editor-Georganne Fiumara
General Info: Yr. Est. 1984, Quarterly

ICEA Journal *Consumer*

Publishing Co: International Childbirth Education Assn., PO Box 20048, Minneapolis, MN 55420-0048; Title Tel # (612) 854-8660
Personnel: Editor-Mary O'Brien
Editorial Description: Information on group organization, administration, needs.
General Info: Yr. Est. 1978, Trim Size-8½ x 11, Sheetfed press, 8 pages, Color, Newsprint, Saddle-stitched
Subscriptions: $2/copy
Circulation: Total-2,500

IDRA Newsletter
See: EDUCATION

Inside Al-Anon
See: HEALTH

Intensive Caring Unlimited
Association

Publishing Co: Intensive Caring Unlimited, 910 Bent Ln., Philadelphia, PA 19118-1008; Title Tel # (215) 233-6994 Title Fax # (215) 233-5795
Personnel: Editor-Lenette Moses, Adv. Dir.-Phyllis DiFilice, Art Dir.-Judy Haas
Editorial Description: Children premature, needing special care, newsletter. Grieving, high-risk pregnancy. Developmental delays.
General Info: Yr. Est. 1983, Bi-monthly, Trim Size-8$\frac{1}{2}$ x 11, Web press, 16 pages, 2% ads, No Color, Coated
Subscriptions: Indv. $10, Inst. $12, Can. $10, For. $10, $1/copy
Circulation: Total-3,000
Advertising: Inquire for rates.

Interracial Club of Buffalo Newsletter
See: ETHNIC

Johnson/Johansson Family News
See: GENEALOGY

Juvenile Law Reports
See: LAW

Kaleidoscope

Publishing Co: Univ. of Connecticut, 1776 Ellington Rd, South Windsor, CT 06074-2708 Tel # (203) 282-7050; Title Tel # (203) 344-7500 Title Fax # (334) 344-7595
Personnel: Editor, Production Mgr.-Lisa Glidden
General Info: Yr. Est. 1987, Quarterly, Trim Size-8$\frac{1}{2}$ x 11, Desktop press, 10 pages, 2 Color
Subscriptions: Indv. $7, Inst. $15
Circulation: Total-1,500

Kennedy Gazette
See: GENEALOGY

Kershner Kinfolk
See: GENEALOGY

Kid News
See: APPAREL & ACCESSORIES

Kinder Family
See: GENEALOGY

LAAF Quarterly
CPM: $114

Publishing Co: Latin American Adoptive Families, 23 Evangeline Rd, Falmouth, MA 02540-2201; Title Tel # (617) 934-6756
Personnel: Publisher, Editor-Marilyn Rowland
Editorial Description: Information on adoption child care & development & Latin American countries for persons interested in Latin American adoption.
General Info: Yr. Est. 1987, Quarterly, Trim Size-8$\frac{1}{2}$ x 11, 36 pages, 1% ads, Saddle-stitched
Subscriptions: Indv. $24, Inst. $48, Can. $24, $4/copy
Circulation: Total-700
Advertising: $80.

Leader
Consumer

Publishing Co: Active Parenting Publishers, 810 Franklin Ct Ste B, Marietta, GA 30067-8943; Title Tel # (770) 429-0565 Title Fax # (770) 429-0334
Personnel: Publisher-Michael Popkin
Editorial Description: Highlights leaders in parent education, loss education, self-esteem education and teacher training.
General Info: (Formerly AP Leader), Yr. Est. 1985, Bi-monthly, 20 pages, Coated, Saddle-stitched
Subscriptions: Free To Qualified Recipient
Circulation: Total-45,000

Let's Talk Families

Publishing Co: Family Service Canada, 220 Laurier Ave. W., Ste. 600, Ottawa, ON K1P 5Z9 Canada Tel # (613) 230-9960; Title Fax # (613) 230-5884
General Info: Yr. Est. 1983, Quarterly, 8 pages
Circulation: Total-2,500

Lindey on Separation Agreements and Antenuptial Contracts
See: LAW

Linkages

Publishing Co: TCI, Inc., 2126 Connecticut Ave NW # 52, Washington, DC 20008-1729; Title Tel # (202) 333-6350 Title Fax # (202) 965-0246
Personnel: Publisher-Thomas Clary, Editor-Nancy Gale, Circ. Mgr., Production Mgr., Promotion Dir.-Corinne Levy
Editorial Description: American Indian child welfare; Indian family law; Indians against alcohol & drug abuse.
General Info: Yr. Est. 1984, Bi-monthly, Letrpr. press, 16 pages, ISSN: 0889-6423, 2 Color, Saddle-stitched
Subscriptions: Indv. $48, $10/copy
Circulation: (100% controlled), Total-4,500
List Rental: Rents Lists
Printing Co: Global Printing, Inc., 4116 Wheeler Ave, Alexandria, VA 22304-6411 Tel # (703) 751-3611

Little Times, The
Consumer

Publishing Co: Little/Silver Times, The, 100 6th Ave., 7th Fl., New York, NY 10013-1605 Tel # (212) 765-3301; Title Tel # (212) 397-3924 Title Fax # (212) 765-3630
Personnel: Editor in Chief-Lori Bernstein, Adv. Dir.-Tim Delanty
Editorial Description: News and views for busy parents.
General Info: Yr. Est. 1992, Monthly, Trim Size-8$\frac{1}{2}$ x 11, 20 pages, No Color, Matte, Saddle-stitched
Subscriptions: Indv. $39
Circulation: Total-25,000
Advertising: Inquire for rates.
Printing Co: Sanford Graphics, 250 Hudson St., New York, NY 10013 Tel # (212) 242-5444

Living Healthy
See: HEALTH

Locke Sickle & Sword
See: GENEALOGY

Manitoba Assn. for Schooling At Home, Newsletter
See: EDUCATION

Men & Wife Newsletter

Publishing Co: P.G. Springer, 206 N Woods St, Urbana, IL 61801-2620
Editorial Description: Discusses issues pertaining to gay men & their wives.
General Info: 5x/yr.
Subscriptions: Indv. $9
Circulation: Total-200

Menninger Letter, The
See: PSYCHOLOGY

Mind Garden Newsletter, The
Consumer

Publishing Co: Children's Resource Center, P.O Box 8697, Scootsdale, AZ 85257; Title Tel # (602) 483-9130
Personnel: Publisher, Editor-Janet Tubbs
Editorial Description: Articles by experts in the fields of parenting, health, education, humor and child development.
General Info: Yr. Est. 1994, Quarterly, 8 pages, No Color
Subscriptions: Indv. $15
Circulation: Total-1,000
Printing Co: Children's Resource Center, P.O Box 8697, Scottsdale, AZ 85252

Modern Divorce
See: LIFESTYLE

Mom to Mom
See: WOMEN'S

Mom's Apple Pie
See: GAY & LESBIAN INTEREST

Mother-To-Mother

Publishing Co: Mothers Without Custody, PO Box 27418, Houston, TX 77227-7418; Title Tel # (713) 840-1622
Personnel: Editor-Jennifer Isham
Editorial Description: Provides support to women living apart from one or more of their minor children for any reason, including court decisions, exchange of custody with an ex-spouse or intervention by a state agency.
General Info: Yr. Est. 1980, Bi-monthly, Trim Size-8$\frac{1}{2}$ x 11, 12 pages, No Color
Subscriptions: Indv. $20, Inst. $30, $3/copy
Acquistions: Publication Bought
Circulation: (100% controlled), Total-550
Advertising: Inquire for rates.

NAPSAC News
Consumer

Publishing Co: Sponsor-NAPSAC Intl., Natl. Assn. of Parents, RR 1 Box 646, Marble Hill, MO 63764-9725; Title Tel # (314) 238-2010 Title Fax # (314) 238-2010
Personnel: Editor, Circ. Mgr.-Lee Stewart
Editorial Description: Pregnancy, childbirth, newborn care, pediatrics, obstetrics, midwifery, home birth, breast feeding.
General Info: Yr. Est. 1976, Quarterly, Trim Size-5$\frac{1}{2}$ x 8$\frac{1}{2}$, Desktop press, 28 pages, ISSN: 0192-1223, 8% ads, Color-cover, Saddle-stitched
Subscriptions: Indv. $20, Inst. $50, Can. $22, For. $22, $3/copy
Circulation: (100% controlled)
Advertising: $200.
List Rental: Rents Lists
Printing Co: Napsac Reproductions, Rr 1 Box 646, Marble Hill, MO 63764-9725

NARAL News
See: HEALTH

NCFR Report
Association **CPM: $107**

Publishing Co: Natl. Council on Family Relations, 3989 Central Ave. NE, Ste. 550, Minneapolis, MN 55421-3972; Title Tel # (612) 781-9331 Title Fax # (612) 781-9348
Personnel: Editor-Kathy Collins Royce
Editorial Description: Up to date information for members on national, international, and Council affairs as well as broad family field news and current issues.
General Info: Quarterly, Trim Size-11½ x 16, Web press, 20 pages, 2 Color, Newsprint
Subscriptions: Indv. $12
Circulation: Total-4,000
Advertising: $430.
List Rental: Actives: $75/M
Printing Co: Sunshine Graphics, 1021 East First Street, Cambridge, MN 55008 Tel # (612) 689-5499

NFADB Newsletter
See: DEAF

NPA Bulletin
See: BABY

National Adoption Reports
Consumer, Association

Publishing Co: Natl. Council for Adoption, Inc., 1930 17th St NW, Washington, DC 20009-6235; Title Tel # (202) 328-1200 Title Fax # (202) 332-0935
Editorial Description: Adoption issues, legislation (Current).
General Info: Yr. Est. 1980, Quarterly, 8 pages
Subscriptions: Indv. $36

National Advocate

Publishing Co: Natl. Foster Parent Assn., 4874 Bloom Ave, White Bear Lake, MN 55110-2734; Title Tel # (612) 429-7855
Personnel: Editor-Dorothy Bodlovick
Editorial Description: Enlightening foster parents & social workers about natl. foster care.
General Info: Yr. Est. 1975, Bi-monthly, 20 pages, No Color
Circulation: Total-3,500

National Association for Family Day Care-Natl. Perspective

Publishing Co: Natl. Assn. for Family Day Care, 5558 Walden Wood Dr, Salt Lake City, UT 84123-5458; Title Tel # (215) 622-0663
General Info: Yr. Est. 1982, Quarterly
Subscriptions: $3/copy
Circulation: Total-1,600
Advertising: Accepts Inserts.

National Council for Adoption-Memo

Publishing Co: Natl. Council for Adoption, Inc., 1930 17th St NW, Washington, DC 20009-6235; Title Tel # (202) 328-1200 Title Fax # (202) 332-0935
Editorial Description: Current adoption legislation, media watch on adoption; Federal developments in adoption.
General Info: Bi-weekly

National Homeschool Assn. Newsletter
See: EDUCATION

National Pulse

Publishing Co: National Life Center, Inc., 686 N Broad St, Woodbury, NJ 08096-1672; Title Tel # (609) 848-1819 Title Fax # (609) 848-2380
Editorial Description: Dissemanates information to chapters regarding organization's progress and other social issues which impact on the organization's services.
General Info: (Formerly Life Guardian), Yr. Est. 1992, Bi-monthly, Trim Size-8½ x 11, Offset press, 4 pages, Color-cover, Matte
Subscriptions: Free To Qualified Recipient
Circulation: Total-1,000

National Report on Work
Consumer

Publishing Co: Business Publishers, Inc., 951 Pershing Dr., Silver Spring, MD 20910-4464 Tel # (301) 589-5103 Fax # (301) 589-8493; Title Tel # (301) 587-6300 Title Fax # (301) 587-1081
Personnel: Publisher-John Wills, Editor-Richard Hagan, Circ. Mgr.-Elizabeth Early, Promotion Dir.-Loretta Keller
General Info: (Formerly National Report on Work & Family), Yr. Est. 1987, Bi-weekly, Trim Size-8½ x 11, Sheetfed press, 8 pages, ISSN: 0896-3002, Ind/Abs/Online: HRIN, 2 Color, Newsprint
Subscriptions: Indv. $528, Can. $528, For. $540, $18/copy
Acquistions: Publication Bought, Publication Sold
List Rental: List Management Co.: BPI Direct, 951 Pershing Dr., Silver Spring, MD 20910-4464 Tel # (301) 585-5976, Fax # (301) 587-4530
Printing Co: Plymouth Printing, 1200 Cushing Pl SE, Washington, DC 20003-3599 Tel # (202) 488-7777, Fax # (202) 863-1078

National Reye's Syndrome Foundation-In the News
See: HEALTH

Nature Views
See: NATURAL HISTORY

Network
Consumer, Association

Publishing Co: Family Health International, PO Box 13950, Rtp, NC 27709-3950 Fax # (919) 544-7261; Title Tel # (919) 544-7040
Personnel: Mng. Editor-Bill Finger, Circ. Mgr.-Debbie Crumpler, Production Mgr.-Marguerite Rogers
Editorial Description: Research on reproductive health, contraceptives, family planning.
General Info: Yr. Est. 1979, Quarterly, Trim Size-8½ x 12, 28 pages, ISSN: 0270-3637, 2 Color, Saddle-stitched
Subscriptions: Free To Qualified Recipient
Circulation: Total-20,000

Network-French Edition
See: HEALTH

Network-Spanish Edition
See: HEALTH

Nevada Families
See: GOVERNMENT

New Beginnings
See: BABY

New Jersey Family Lawyer

Publishing Co: New Jersey State Bar Association, New Jersey Law Center, 1 Constitution Sq., New Brunswick, NJ 08901-1520 Tel # (908) 249-5000 Fax # (908) 828-0034; Title Tel # (201) 249-5000 Title Fax # (201) 249-2815
Personnel: Editor-L.M. Hymerling, Publisher, Production Mgr., Promotion Dir.-Glenn Hintze
Editorial Description: New Jersey Family Lawyer offers substantive articles, (4-6 each issue), along with regular editorial columns & book reviews. We now have a national focus, where by two articles in each issue are on topics of national interest.
General Info: (Formerly Family Law Newsletter), Yr. Est. 1981, 8x/yr., Letrpr. press, 24 pages, No Color, Newsprint
Circulation: Total-1,800
Printing Co: B & R Photo Offset Printers, 211 Stokes Ave, Trenton, NJ 08638-3729 Tel # (609) 882-9270, Fax # (609) 882-9660

New Moon Network
Consumer

Publishing Co: New Moon Publishing, PO Box 3620, Duluth, MN 55803-3620; Title Tel # (218) 728-5507
Personnel: Publisher-Nancy Gruver, Editor-Joe Kelly, Adv. Dir.-Angie Miller
Editorial Description: For adults who care about raising girls ages 8-14.
General Info: (Formerly New Moon Parenting), Yr. Est. 1993, Bi-monthly, Trim Size-8½ x 11, Sheetfed press, 16 pages, ISSN: 1083-5970, No Color, Matte, Saddle-stitched
Subscriptions: Indv. $25, Can. $35, For. $37, $7/copy
Circulation: Total-3,500, Readership-7,000
Advertising: Inquire for rates. Accepts Inserts.
List Rental: Actives: 3,300, $100/M, Expires: 3,000, $100/M
Printing Co: Davidson Printing Co., 4631 Mike Colalillo Dr, PO Box 16990, Duluth, MN 55807-2733 Tel # (218) 628-1016

New York Practice Guide: Domestic Relations
See: LAW

Newswire
Association

Publishing Co: Sponsor-Family Service America, Families International, 11700 W Lake Park Dr, Milwaukee, WI 53224-3044; Title Tel # (414) 359-2111
Personnel: Editor-Eva Augustin Rumpf
Editorial Description: Information on family issues, problems, programs to strengthen family life, & on Family Service America, natl. headquarters of the family service movement.
General Info: (Formerly Highlights), Yr. Est. 1940, Quarterly, Trim Size-8½ x 11, Offset press, 6 pages, 2 Color
Circulation: (100% controlled), Total-8,000

Nurturing News
Consumer

Publishing Co: Nurturing Press, 975 York Street, JW Mahan, San Francisco, CA 94110-2812; Title Tel # (415) 861-0847
Personnel: Publisher, Editor-David Giveans
Editorial Description: Quarterly forum for today's changing male roles.
General Info: Yr. Est. 1979, Quarterly, Trim Size-8½ x 11, Offset press, 24 pages, ISSN: 0379-7615, 1% ads, 2 Color
Subscriptions: Indv. $16, $4/copy
Circulation: (100% controlled), Total-3,000
Advertising: Inquire for rates.
Printing Co: Northwind Productions, 3232 Balboa St, San Francisco, CA 94121-2732

Open Adoption Birthparent
Consumer

Publishing Co: R-Squared Press, 2113 Arborview Blvd., Ann Arbor, MI 48103-3513; Title Tel # (810) 543-0997
Personnel: Publisher-Daniel Romanchik, Editor-Brenda Romanchik
Editorial Description: Provides practical information to birthparents in open adoptions.
General Info: Yr. Est. 1994, Quarterly, ISSN: 1078-0831
Subscriptions: Indv. $12, $3/copy
Circulation: Total-200

Operation Wildlife News
Consumer, Association

Publishing Co: Nat'l. Wildlife Federation Corporate Conservation Council, 1400 16th Street NW, Washington, DC 20036-2266
Personnel: Editor-Susan De Treville
General Info: Bi-monthly, 16 pages
Subscriptions: Indv. $10
Advertising: Inquire for rates.

Options in Learning
See: EDUCATION

Over 30 Parenting   *Consumer*
Publishing Co: Over 30 Parenting, PO Box 57046, Sherman Oaks, CA 91413-2046; Title Tel # (818) 988-0854
Editorial Description: Parenting issues for older parents.
General Info: Monthly

Parent & Preschooler
See: EDUCATION

Parent Care Advisor
See: SENIOR CITIZENS

Parent Finders-Edmonton   *Association*
Publishing Co: Parent Finders, Box 12031, Edmonton, AB T5J 3L2 Canada; Title Tel # (403) 466-3335
Personnel: Editor-Angela Clark, Circ. Mgr.-John Schmidt
General Info: Yr. Est. 1976, Monthly, Trim Size-8½ x 11, 8 pages
Subscriptions: Indv. $15, Can. $15, Free With Membership
Circulation: Total-700

Parent Hotline
Publishing Co: Child Growth & Development Corp., 599 Broadway Fl 9, New York, NY 10012-3235; Title Tel # (212) 226-4518
Personnel: Editor-Maggie Agoglia
General Info: Yr. Est. 1988, Monthly

Parent SIG
Publishing Co: Parent SIG, PO Box 2377, New York, NY 10185-2377; Title Tel # (714) 371-2080
Personnel: Publisher-M.D. Schuyten, Editor-Lawrence Stanley
General Info: (Formerly Parent SIG), Yr. Est. 1980, Trim Size-8½ x 11, 4 pages
Subscriptions: Indv. $15

ParentAge   *Consumer*
Publishing Co: ParentAge, 27 W 20th St Ste 305, New York, NY 10011-3707
Editorial Description: Dedicated to the interests of new parents over the age of 35.
General Info: Monthly
Subscriptions: Indv. $30

Parental Discretion   *Consumer*
Publishing Co: Parental Discretion, PO Box 758, Colleyville, TX 76034-0758; Title Tel # (817) 428-2001
Editorial Description: Movie reviews for families with young children.
General Info: Monthly

Parenting Center Newsletter
Publishing Co: Parenting Center Newsletter, 92nd St. Y, 1395 Lexington, New York, NY 10128; Title Tel # (212) 427-6000
Editorial Description: Help for parents of infants and toddlers.
General Info: Monthly, 8 pages
Subscriptions: Indv. $5

Parenting for Peace & Justice Network-Newsletter
Publishing Co: Institute for Peace & Justice, 4144 Lindell Blvd Ste 122, Saint Louis, MO 63108-2931; Title Tel # (314) 533-4445
Personnel: Editor-Jim Ford
Editorial Description: Focus on peace & justice issues in family life.
General Info: (Formerly Natl. Parenting for Peace & Justice Network-Newsletter), Yr. Est. 1981, Bi-monthly, Desktop press, 8 pages, No Color
Subscriptions: Indv. $15, Inst. $50, $1/copy

Pediatrics for Parents   *Consumer*
Publishing Co: Pediatrics for Parents, Inc., PO Box 1069, Bangor, ME 04402-1069; Title Tel # (207) 942-6212 Title Fax # (207) 947-3134
Personnel: Editor-Richard Sagall, M. D., Editorial Asst.-Rachel Poole, Art Dir.-Rosella Park-Sagall
Editorial Description: Informative, and relevant information on children's health.
General Info: Yr. Est. 1981, Monthly, Trim Size-8½ x 11, Offset press, 12 pages, Ind/Abs/Online: DIALOG, 2 Color, Newsprint, Saddle-stitched
Subscriptions: Indv. $18, Inst. $18, Can. $23, For. $33, $2/copy
Circulation: Total-1,500
List Rental: Actives: $100/M, Hotline: $75/M, Expires: $75/M

Pennsylvania Divorce & Domestic Relations Reporter
See: LAW

Penny Pincher   *Business, Consumer*
Publishing Co: Penny Pincher, PO Box 809, Kings Park, NY 11754-0809; Title Tel # (516) 724-1868
Personnel: Editor-Jackie Iglehart, Circ. Mgr.-John Ventura
Editorial Description: Money-saving tips for households.
General Info: Yr. Est. 1992, Monthly, Trim Size-8½ x 11, Desktop press, 8 pages, Color, Matte, Saddle-stitched
Subscriptions: Indv. $15, Can. $17, For. $19, $1/copy
Circulation: Total-4,000
List Rental: List Management Co.: Lone Star Direct, 12180 N Mo Pac Expy Ste D, Austin, TX 78758-2909 Tel # (512) 836-9573, Fax # (512) 836-9579, Actives: 4,000, Expires: 800
Printing Co: Printery, 2193 Jericho Tpke, Commack, NY 11725-2904 Tel # (516) 499-4455, Fax # (516) 499-4549

Pied Piper, The   *Consumer, Association*
Publishing Co: Organization for the Enforcement of Child Support, 1712 Deer Park Rd, Finksburg, MD 21048-2032; Title Tel # (301) 833-2458
Personnel: Editor-Elaine Fromm, Editor-William Fromm
Editorial Description: Makes people aware of their rights under the child support laws and provides information on resources and referrals.
General Info: Yr. Est. 1979, Quarterly, Mimeo press
Subscriptions: Indv. $10
Acquistions: Publication Sold

Pipings, The
See: GENEALOGY

Planned Parenthood of Seattle-King County
Publishing Co: Planned Parenthood of Seattle-King County, 2211 E Madison St, Seattle, WA 98112-5336
Personnel: Editor-Marilyn Knight
General Info: Quarterly, Trim Size-8½ x 11, 4 pages, No Color

Practically Green
See: CONSUMER INTERESTS

Priority Parenting   *Consumer*
Publishing Co: Priority Parenting Pubs., 830 S Union St, Warsaw, IN 46580-4701 Tel # (219) 268-1415; Title Tel # (219) 453-3864
Personnel: Publisher, Editor-Tamra Orr
Editorial Description: A newsletter designed to support & encourage natural parents to follow their hearts & instincts not society's dictates.
General Info: Yr. Est. 1987, Monthly, Trim Size-5 x 8, Sheetfed press, 20 pages, 10% ads, No Color, Newsprint, Other
Subscriptions: Indv. $14, Can. $16, $2/copy
Acquistions: Publication Bought
Circulation: Total-250
Advertising: Inquire for rates. Accepts Inserts.
Printing Co: Instant Copy, Warsaw, IN 46580

Raising Your Child's Self-Esteem
See: CHILDREN

Refunding Makes Cents
See: BANKING & FINANCE

Representing the Child Client
See: LAW

Resolve National Newsletter   *Consumer, Association*
Publishing Co: Resolve, Inc., 1310 Broadway, Somerville, MA 02144-1779; Title Tel # (617) 623-1156 Title Fax # (617) 623-0252
Personnel: Editor-Lynette Aznavourian
Editorial Description: Current information on medical and emotional aspects of infertility, including coverage of related issues such as adoption and living child-free.
General Info: Yr. Est. 1975, Quarterly, Trim Size-8½ x 11, Offset press, 16 pages, ISSN: 1042-0290, 2 Color, Matte, Saddle-stitched
Subscriptions: Indv. $45, For. $60, $4/copy
Circulation: Total-15,000
Printing Co: Fidelity Press, 2401 Revere Beach Pky, Everett, MA 02149-5999 Tel # (617) 389-6220

San Bernardino County Museum Association Newsletter
See: MUSEUM PUBLICATIONS

Scouter's Digest
See: YOUTH

Shema Newsletter
See: RELIGIOUS & THEOLOGICAL

Shop Talk (Lubbock)
Publishing Co: Shop Talk Inc., 5737 64th St, Lubbock, TX 79424-1261
Personnel: Publisher, Editor-Thomas Morris
General Info: Yr. Est. 1987, Monthly, Sheetfed press, 8 pages, 2 Color, Newsprint, Saddle-stitched
Subscriptions: Indv. $24, $4/copy
Circulation: (100% controlled), Total-500

Sibling Information Network Newsletter

Publishing Co: Univ. of Connecticut, 1776 Ellington Rd, South Windsor, CT 06074-2708
Tel # (203) 282-7050; Title Tel # (203) 344-7500 Title Fax # (203) 344-7595
Personnel: Publisher-A.J. Pappanikou, Editor-Lisa Glidden
General Info: Yr. Est. 1981, Quarterly, Desktop press, 10 pages, 2 Color
Subscriptions: Indv. $9, Inst. $15
Circulation: Total-2,000

SingleMOTHER   *Consumer, Association*

Publishing Co: National Organization of Single Mothers, PO Box 68, Midland, NC 28107-0068
Tel # (704) 888-2337; Title Tel # (704) 888-5437 Title Fax # (704) 888-1752
Editorial Description: Information and support for single mothers.
General Info: Yr. Est. 1991, Bi-monthly, Trim Size-8½ x 11, ISSN: 1074-0775, Recycled
Subscriptions: Indv. $13, Can. $19, $3/copy
Circulation: Total-15,000
Advertising: Inquire for rates.
Printing Co: Leesburg Printing Co., 1100 North Blvd E, Leesburg, FL 34748-5350
Tel # (904) 787-3348, Fax # (904) 787-2210

Sisterhood Newsletter
See: WOMEN'S

Smart Dads   *Consumer*

Publishing Co: Family University, PO Box 270616, San Diego, CA 92198-2616;
Title Tel # (619) 487-7099 Title Fax # (619) 487-7356
Personnel: Publisher, Editor-Paul Lewis, Adv. Dir.-Michael Martin
Editorial Description: News and creative ideas resource forbusy dads and healthy family living.
General Info: (Formerly Dads Only), Yr. Est. 1978, Bi-monthly, Offset press, 12 pages, ISSN: 0199-655X, 3% ads, 2 Color, Newsprint
Subscriptions: Indv. $19
List Rental: List Management Co.: Bernice Bush Co./Springdale Lists, 15052 Springdale St., Huntington Beach, CA 92649-1178 Tel # (714) 891-3344, Fax # (714) 897-0650, Actives: 12,100, $80/M
Printing Co: Sidekick Printers, 100 W. 35 St., National City, CA 92050 Tel # (619) 420-3831

Speak Out for Children   **CPM: $46**

Publishing Co: Natl. Council for Children's Rights, 220 Eye Street N.W., Ste. 230, Washington, DC 20002-4307; Title Tel # (202) 547-6227 Title Fax # (202) 546-6589
Personnel: Editor-David Levy, Adv. Dir.-Jan Fletcher
Editorial Description: To strengthen families & to assist children of separation & divorce.
General Info: Yr. Est. 1985, Quarterly, Desktop press, 20 pages, ISSN: 1042-3559, 1% ads
Subscriptions: Indv. $35
Circulation: Total-4,000
Advertising: $185.
List Rental: Actives: $75/M, Expires: $40/M

Sport Scene
See: SPORTS & SPORTING GOODS

Stepfamilies   *Association*

Publishing Co: Nextstep Publications, 475 Simpson Rd., Greensburg, KY 42743-9460;
Title Tel # (503) 325-8828 Title Fax # (503) 325-1454
Personnel: Publisher, Editor-Jan Fletcher
Editorial Description: Articles and information, by, for and about stepfamily life.
General Info: Yr. Est. 1981, Quarterly, Trim Size-8½ x 11, 16 pages, ISSN: 0195-5969, No Color, Newsprint
Subscriptions: Indv. $14, Inst. $22, For. $16, $5/copy
Acquistions: Publication Bought
Circulation: Total-2,500
Advertising: Inquire for rates.
List Rental: Rents Lists

Stepfamilies & Beyond   *Consumer*

Publishing Co: Listening Inc., 8716 Pine Ave, Gary, IN 46403-1441; Title Tel # (219) 938-6962
Personnel: Publisher-Richard Bennett, Editor-Patricia W. Bennett
Editorial Description: America's first independent newsletter about remarriage.
General Info: (Formerly Stepparent News), Yr. Est. 1980, Monthly, Trim Size-8½ x 11, Desktop press, 6 pages, ISSN: 0271-3225, Color, Newsprint
Subscriptions: Indv. $12, Inst. $15, Can. $20, For. $22, $1/copy

Stires Family Newsletter
See: GENEALOGY

Stockwell Family Association Newsletter   *Association*

Publishing Co: Stockwell Family Association, Donald F. Stockwell, 10 Fruit St., Mansfield, MA 02048

Story Time Stories That Rhyme
See: CHILDREN

Straight Talk on Your Money
See: BANKING & FINANCE

Texas Family Law Reporter
See: LAW

Texas Family Law Trial Guide
See: LAW

Today's Dads   *Association, Consumer*   **CPM: $125**

Publishing Co: Wisconsin Fathers for Equal Justice, Inc., 4406 Evergreen Rd, Wausau, WI 54403-9447; Title Tel # (608) 255-3237
Personnel: Editor-Bill Fetzner
Editorial Description: Advocacy: children need their fathers; fathers have right to parent; equal responsibility for mothers; positive image of families & fatherhood.
General Info: Yr. Est. 1988, Monthly, Trim-8½ x 11, Sheetfed press, 6 pages, No Color, Matte
Subscriptions: Indv. $20, Inst. $30, $2/copy
Circulation: Total-800
Advertising: $100. Accepts Inserts.
Printing Co: Community News, Monona Ave., Monona, WI 53703

Toiyable Indian Health Project, Inc.

Publishing Co: Family Services Program, PO Box 1296, Bishop, CA 93515-1296;
Title Tel # (619) 873-6394
Editorial Description: Articles concerning medical, dental, optical, counseling, & outreach medical care service.
General Info: (Formerly Family Service Newsletter), Yr. Est. 1978, Quarterly, Mimeo press, 8 pages, No Color
Circulation: (100% controlled), Total-1,200

Twin Services Reporter
See: BABY

Twins Letter
See: SCIENCE

Unmarried Parents Today   *Association, Consumer*

Publishing Co: Natl. Council for Adoption, Inc., 1930 17th St NW, Washington, DC 20009-6235; Title Tel # (202) 328-1200
Editorial Description: Maternity & pregnancy issues; teenage mothers; AIDS; teenage sex & marriage.
General Info: Quarterly

VHL Family Forum
See: MEDICINE

WYO Network
See: EDUCATION

Washington Watch
See: BABY

William Petschek Natl. Jewish Family Center- Newsletter

Publishing Co: William Petschek Natl. Jewish Family Ctr.-American Jewish C, 165 E 56th St, New York, NY 10022-2709; Title Tel # (212) 751-4000
Personnel: Editor-Sherry Rosen
General Info: Yr. Est. 1981, Semi-annually, 6 pages
Circulation: Total-5,000

Young People and Cults
See: RELIGIOUS & THEOLOGICAL

FAN MAGAZINES-MOVIE, RADIO, TV

Autograph Research
See: COLLECTIBLES

Bullet   *Business, Consumer*

Publishing Co: EQ/EW Intl. U.S.A., 1021 Gregory St, Normal, IL 61761-4236 Tel # (510) 754-6692;
Title Tel # (309) 888-4715
Personnel: Col. Ed.-Lenore Hutton
Editorial Description: Narrow-Focus International Newsletter, going to fans & media around the world, specializing in Edward Woodward (Callan, Breaker Morant, The Equalizer, Over My Dead Body), his career, past, present, & future, & the major players in his life.
General Info: Yr. Est. 1989, Irregular, Trim Size-8½ x 11, Letrpr. press, 10 pages, No Color, Matte
Subscriptions: Indv. $12, Can. $18, $3/copy
Circulation: Total-500
Advertising: Inquire for rates. Accepts Inserts.

Celebrity Service Intl. Social Calendar

Publishing Co: Celebrity Service Intl., 1780 Broadway Ste 300, New York, NY 10019-1414;
Title Tel # (212) 757-7979
Personnel: Editor-Sara Weiner, Production Mgr.-Vicki Bagley
General Info: Weekly
Subscriptions: Indv. $150

Dark Shadows
Announcement
Consumer, Association CPM: $20

Publishing Co: Fan Club Publishing Co. / Louis Wendruck, Box 69A04-Dept. OX, West Hollywood, CA 90069-0066; Title Tel # (213) 650-5112
Personnel: Publisher, Editor-Louis Wendruck
Editorial Description: Covers Dark Shadow television show, the 1960s gothic soap opera, with videos, pictures etc.
General Info: Yr. Est. 1986, Quarterly, Trim Size-8½ x 11, Offset press, 24 pages
Subscriptions: Indv. $20, Can. $30, For. $30, $6/copy
Acquistions: Publication Sold
Circulation: Total-10,000, Readership-25,000
Advertising: $200. Accepts Inserts.
List Rental: Rents Lists

Deanna Gram
See: TELEVISION & VIDEO

Elvis Now Fan Club
Newsletter
Association

Publishing Co: Elvis Now Fan Club, PO Box 6581, San Jose, CA 95150-6581; Title Tel # (408) 923-0978
Personnel: Publisher, Editor-Sue McCasland
Editorial Description: Articles and news relating to Elvis Presley.
General Info: Yr. Est. 1973, Quarterly, Trim Size-5½ x 8½, Offset press, 14 pages, No Color, Other
Subscriptions: Indv. $11, Inst. $15
Circulation: (100% controlled), Total-307

Elvis Worldwide Fan Club
CPM: $80

Publishing Co: Elvis Worldwide Fan Club, 3081 Sunrise St, Memphis, TN 38127-1437; Title Tel # (901) 357-9910
Personnel: Co-Editor-Will McDaniel, Co-Editor-Don Wilson
Editorial Description: About Elvis and different events going on in Memphis during Elvis Weeks in January & August. Write-up from some of his friends and stories told by them. All the good things about Elvis.
General Info: (Formerly President), Yr. Est. 1989, Quarterly
Subscriptions: $3/copy
Circulation: Total-250
Advertising: $20.

Fan Club Monitor
Association CPM: $100

Publishing Co: National Association of Fan Clubs, PO Box 7487, Burbank, CA 91510-7487; Title Tel # (818) 763-3280 Title Fax # (818) 752-4848
Editorial Description: The fan club industry's only trade newsletter.
General Info: Yr. Est. 1977, Quarterly, Trim Size-8½ x 11, Offset press, 24 pages, ISSN: 1081-5538, Ind/Abs/Online: E-Mail: LKNAFC@aol.com, No Color, Other, Saddle-stitched
Subscriptions: Indv. $10, $2/copy
Circulation: Total-500
Advertising: $50.

Fluff

Publishing Co: Lori Key, 11-34 44th Dr. #7, Long Island City, NY 11101
Editorial Description: A messy but fun-filled collection of stuff.
General Info: Trim Size-5 x 7, 14 pages
Subscriptions: Indv. $2

Friends of Doctor Who Newsletter
See: SCIENCE FICTION & FANTASY

Gilligan's Island News
See: CLUBS

Girl Groups ('60's Rock N' Roll) Gazette
Consumer, Association CPM: $10

Publishing Co: Fan Club Publishing Co. / Louis Wendruck, Box 69A04-Dept. OX, West Hollywood, CA 90069-0066; Title Tel # (213) 650-5112
Personnel: Publisher, Editor, Production Mgr., Adv. Dir.-Louis Wendruck
Editorial Description: Fan magazine covering news and developments relating to girl Rock 'n Roll groups of the 60s, & 70s.
General Info: (Formerly Girl Groups Gazette), Yr. Est. 1987, Quarterly, Trim Size-8½ x 11, Offset press, 24 pages, 10% ads
Subscriptions: Indv. $20, Inst. $20, Can. $30, For. $30, $6/copy
Acquistions: Publication Sold
Circulation: Total-20,000
Advertising: $200. Accepts Inserts.
List Rental: Rents Lists

Grateful Dead Almanac
Consumer, Association

Publishing Co: Grateful Dead Mercantile Co., PO Box X, Novato, CA 94948-1210; Title Tel # (415) 892-3421 Title Fax # (415) 898-9695
Editorial Description: Official newsletter of the Grateful Dead band.
General Info: Trim Size-11½ x 17, 12 pages, 4 Color, Matte

Hello Again
CPM: $125

Publishing Co: Jay Hickerson, PO Box 4321, Hamden, CT 06514-0321; Title Tel # (203) 248-2887 Title Fax # (203) 281-1322
Personnel: Editor-Jay Hickerson
Editorial Description: For fans and collectors of old-time radio shows.
General Info: Yr. Est. 1970, Bi-monthly, Trim Size-8½ x 11, Letrpr. press, 6 pages, No Color
Subscriptions: Indv. $12, $2/copy
Circulation: Total-400
Advertising: $50.

Hoppy Talk
Consumer, Association

Publishing Co: Friends of Hopalong Cassidy, 6310 Friendship Dr, New Concord, OH 43762-9708; Title Tel # (614) 826-4850
Personnel: Editor-Laura Bates
General Info: Yr. Est. 1991, Quarterly, Trim Size-8½ x 11, Offset press, 4 pages, Matte, Other
Subscriptions: Indv. $15, Can. $20, $3/copy
Circulation: Total-500
Advertising: Accepts Inserts.

It's Only A Movie
See: ENTERTAINMENT

Jack Benny Times
Association

Publishing Co: International Jack Benny Fan Club, 3190 Oak Rd., Apt. 303, Walnut Creek, CA 94596-7736; Title Tel # (510) 933-3879
Personnel: Publisher, Editor-Laura Lee
Editorial Description: Collection of articles and information pertaining to Jack Benny and his associates.
General Info: Yr. Est. 1980, 3x/yr., Trim Size-8½ x 11, Offset press, 16 pages, No Color, Recycled, Other
Subscriptions: Indv. $6
Acquistions: Publication Bought, Publication Sold
Circulation: Total-200, Readership-300
Advertising: Accepts Inserts.

Linington Lineup
See: LITERARY REVIEWS

Metro Scene
See: COLLECTIBLES

Millennium Pop
See: MUSIC & MUSIC TRADES

Munsters & the Addams
Family Reunion
Consumer, Association CPM: $10

Publishing Co: Fan Club Publishing Co. / Louis Wendruck, Box 69A04-Dept. OX, West Hollywood, CA 90069-0066; Title Tel # (213) 650-5112
Personnel: Publisher, Editor, Adv. Dir., Art Dir.-Louis Wendruck
Editorial Description: Magazine for fans of the 1960's TV comedy shows, and movies the Munsters and The Addams Family.
General Info: Yr. Est. 1987, Quarterly, Trim Size-8½ x 11, Offset press, 24 pages, 10% ads
Subscriptions: Indv. $20, Can. $30, For. $30, $6/copy
Acquistions: Publication Sold
Circulation: Total-20,000
Advertising: $200. Accepts Inserts.
List Rental: Rents Lists

Oz Observer
Consumer, Association

Publishing Co: International Wizard of Oz Club, 220 N 11th St, Escanaba, MI 49829-3523
Personnel: Editor-Fred Meyer
Editorial Description: For members of the International Wizard of Oz Club.
General Info: Yr. Est. 1993, Quarterly

The Realm of Out-There

Publishing Co: Haratio, P.O. Box 5092, Wilmington, DE 19808
Editorial Description: The unabridge newsletter of all things horatio, a short collection of comments and general weirdness from a struggle musician and fan of high weirdness by mail.
General Info: Trim Size-8.5 x 11, 8 pages

TV Game Show: Newsletter
for Game Show Fans
Consumer

Publishing Co: TV Game Show, PO Box 157, Agoura Hills, CA 91376-0157; Title Tel # (818) 865-1999
Personnel: Publisher-Stacy Harris, Editor-David Wagner
Editorial Description: Articles and information on TV game shows.
General Info: Yr. Est. 1993, Quarterly
Subscriptions: Indv. $10
Circulation: Total-8,000

Tetragammaton Fragments: Official Newsletter of the United Fanzine Organization   *Consumer*

Publishing Co: United Fanzine Organization, 7534 Kingsgate Way, West Chester, OH 05069
Editorial Description: The United Fanzine Organization is a group of small-press publishers who believe in publishing zines, mostly comix zines.
General Info: Irregular
Subscriptions: $2/copy

Who: The Relay, The
See: MUSIC & MUSIC TRADES

Working Class Hero Beatles Club, The   *Consumer, Association*

Publishing Co: Working Class Hero Beatles Club, The, 3311 Niagara St, Pittsburgh, PA 15213-4223
Personnel: Editor-Barbara Whatmough, Co-Editor-Sue Link, Circ. Mgr.-Susan Link, Production Mgr.-Alan Ratliff, Adv. Dir.-Cynthia Knighton, Art Dir.-Maxwell Cameron, Mktg. Dir.-Vickie Smallwood, Promotion Dir.-Pamela Henkel
Editorial Description: A Non-profit newsletter for and by Beatle fans.
General Info: (Formerly Beatle Peace Followers), Yr. Est. 1968, 3x/yr., Trim Size-8 x 10, 20 pages
Subscriptions: Indv. $10, For. $15
Advertising: $50. Accepts Inserts.

FEED, GRAIN & MILLING

AFIA Safetygram
See: AGRICULTURE

Agrow World Crop Protection News
See: AGRICULTURE

Bluebook Update Newsletter
See: AGRICULTURE

Broadwater Market Letter
See: AGRICULTURE

Calfornia Grain & Feeders Report   *Business*

Publishing Co: Federal State Market News, 1220 N St. #216, Box 942871, Sacramento, CA 94271-0001 Tel # (209) 654-0298; Title Tel # (916) 654-0298 Title Fax # (916) 654-1046
Personnel: Editor-Jim Carroll
Editorial Description: Values paid by feed manufacturers & other users & suppliers, delivered plant or receiving station. Grower prices F.O.B. Ranch.
General Info: (Formerly Grain Market News), Yr. Est. 1954, Weekly, Trim Size-8½ x 11, Mimeo press, 6 pages
Subscriptions: Indv. $66
Circulation: Total-400

California Grain and Feeders Report   *Business*

Publishing Co: California Dept. of Food & Agriculture, Communications Dept., 1220 N St. Rm. 100, Sacramento, CA 95814 Tel # (916) 654-0466; Title Tel # (916) 654-0298 Title Fax # (916) 654-1046
Editorial Description: Covers grain, feedstuffs, hay, livestock, poultry and egg prices. Reports on grain market situation, Futures, and exports.
General Info: Weekly, Trim Size-8½ x 11, 4 pages, No Color
Subscriptions: Indv. $99, Can. $99, For. $144, $6/copy
Circulation: Total-400

Canola Digest   *Business*

Publishing Co: Canola Council of Canada, 400-167 Lombard Ave., Winnipeg, MB R3B OT6 Canada; Title Tel # (204) 982-2100
Personnel: Editor-Dawn Harris, Publisher, Circ. Mgr., Production Mgr.-Wendy Miller
Editorial Description: Features Council news and industry developments.
General Info: (Formerly Rapeseed Digest), Yr. Est. 1967, 8x/yr., Letrpr. press, 12 pages, 7% ads, 2 Color, Newsprint
Subscriptions: Indv. $25
Circulation: Total-1,100
Advertising: Inquire for rates.
Printing Co: Mid Canada Press, 21 Burnett, Winnipeg, MB Canada

Feed Additive Compendium   **CPM: $646**

Publishing Co: Miller Publishing Co., 12400 Whitewater Dr., Ste. 160, Minnetonka, MN 55343-9466; Title Tel # (612) 931-0211 Title Fax # (612) 938-1832
Personnel: Publisher-Michael Ford, Editor-Sarah Muirhead, Circ. Mgr.-Steve Joss, Adv. Dir.-Gary Ashbacher
Editorial Description: Feed additive regulations, labeling, drug use levels and claims information.
General Info: Yr. Est. 1963, Annually, Trim Size-8¼ x 11½, Offset press, 500 pages, 4 Color, Looseleaf
Subscriptions: Indv. $199, Inst. $170, Can. $235, For. $235
Circulation: Total-3,000, Readership-3,000
Advertising: $1,940.

Feed Bulletin

Publishing Co: Jacobsen Publishing Co., 300 W Adams St Ste 835, Chicago, IL 60606-5109; Title Tel # (312) 726-6600

Feedgram
See: AGRICULTURE

Forage Notes   *Consumer*

Publishing Co: Canada Dept. of Agriculture, 930 Carling Ave., Ottawa, ON K1A 0C7 Canada
Personnel: Editor-M.A. Faris
General Info: Yr. Est. 1955, Semi-annually
Circulation: Total-500

Grain and Feed Merchants, The   *Association*

Publishing Co: Nebraska Grain and Feed Association, 1233 Lincoln Mall, Lincoln, NE 68508-2847; Title Tel # (402) 476-6174 Title Fax # (402) 476-3401
Personnel: Publisher, Editor-Richard Sanne, Circ. Mgr., Adv. Dir.-Mary Effle
Editorial Description: Inform dealers of elevator and grain information.
General Info: Yr. Est. 1962, Monthly, Trim Size-8½ x 11, Offset press, 24 pages, 3% ads
Subscriptions: $4/copy
Circulation: (100% controlled), Total-1,000
Advertising: Inquire for rates.

Grain and Livestock Market News
See: LIVESTOCK

Grain Matters   *Business*

Publishing Co: Canadian Wheat Board, PO Box 816, Station Main, Winnipeg, MB R3C 2P5 Canada; Title Tel # (204) 983-3421
Personnel: Editor-Brian Stacey
Editorial Description: Newsletter on Canadian grain industry.
General Info: Yr. Est. 1976, Bi-monthly, Trim Size-8½ x 11, Sheetfed press, 8 pages, 2 Color, Newsprint
Circulation: Total-135,000
Printing Co: Kromar Printing, 725 Portage Ave., Winnipeg, MB R3G 0M8 Canada Tel # (204) 775-8721, Fax # (204) 783-8985

Gulf Grain Guide

Publishing Co: King Publishing Corp., 6914 Office Park Cir # 52210, Knoxville, TN 37909-1161 Tel # (619) 584-6214; Title Tel # (615) 584-6294 Title Fax # (615) 558-6101
Editorial Description: Detailed grain marketing & export information.
General Info: Weekly, Trim Size-8½ x 11, 12 pages, ISSN: 0885-5811, No Color, Matte
Subscriptions: Indv. $547, For. $572

Livestock
See: LIVESTOCK

Livestock Grain Market News Report

Publishing Co: Louisiana Dept. of Agriculture, Office of Marketing, Box 3334, Baton Rouge, LA 70821; Title Tel # (504) 922-1328
Personnel: Editor-Dave Foster
General Info: Weekly, 2 pages
Circulation: Total-15,811

Milwaukee Grain Exchange, Market Report

Publishing Co: Milwaukee Grain Exchange, 1900 S Harbor Dr, Milwaukee, WI 53207-1027; Title Tel # (414) 271-0585
General Info: Daily

Molasses Market News
See: SUGAR

North American Bull Buyers Guide
See: LIVESTOCK

Pacific Northwest Grain and Feed Association Newsletter   *Association*

Publishing Co: Pacific Northwest Grain, 200 SW Market St Ste 1730, Portland, OR 97201-5718; Title Tel # (503) 227-0234
Personnel: Editor-Jonathan Schlueter
General Info: Bi-weekly

RBA Insight
See: FOOD

St. Louis Market Record   *Association*

Publishing Co: Merchants' Exchange of Saint Louis, 5100 Oakland Avenue, St. Louis, MO 63110-1441; Title Tel # (314) 535-2400
Editorial Description: Commodity quotes.
General Info: Daily
Subscriptions: Indv. $150

Tiger on Spreads
See: INVESTMENT

Trading Trends
See: INVESTMENT

U.S. Wheatletter *Business*

Publishing Co: U.S. Wheat Assocs., 1620 Eye St., NW, #801, Washington, DC 20006;
Title Tel # (202) 463-0999
Personnel: Editor-Susan Zillinger
Editorial Description: Current events affecting the supply, production & trade of U.S. wheat, with information on intl. markets & competing nations.
General Info: Bi-weekly, Trim Size-8½ x 11, Sheetfed press, 4 pages, No Color, Newsprint
Circulation: Total-2,575
Printing Co: City Duplicating Center, 1617 Eye St., NW, Washington, DC 20006
Tel # (202) 296-0700

Virginia Agriculture Commodity Newsletter
See: AGRICULTURE

Washington Feedline
See: LIVESTOCK

FICTION

Children's Writer
See: BOOKS & BOOK TRADE

Deadly Serious
See: MYSTERY & HORROR

Fiction Digest
See: BOOKS & BOOK TRADE

Reading Woman *Consumer*

Publishing Co: Bering Communications, PO Box 19116, Minneapolis, MN 55419;
Title Tel # (612) 822-1271 Title Fax # (612) 822-1271
Personnel: Publisher-Chris Wiencke, Editor-David Wiencke
General Info: Yr. Est. 1993, Quarterly, Trim Size-8½ x 11
Subscriptions: Indv. $15, Inst. $15, Can. $19, $4/copy
Circulation: Total-855
Printing Co: Northwest Printing Company, 3010 N 2nd St, Minneapolis, MN 55411-1608
Tel # (612) 588-7506, Fax # (612) 588-2265

FILM

AFVA Bulletin *Association*

Publishing Co: American Film & Video Assn., 760 Plantation Rd, Merritt Island, FL 32952-4039;
Title Tel # (708) 698-6440
Personnel: Publisher-Don Sager, Editorial Dir.-Dennis Husking
Editorial Description: Updates in nontheatrical film/video distribution & programming.
General Info: Yr. Est. 1977, Quarterly, Trim Size-8½ x 11, Sheetfed press, 8 pages, 2 Color, Matte
Subscriptions: Indv. $175
Circulation: Total-1,200

AMIA Newsletter (Assn. of Moving Image Archivists)
See: LIBRARY

Association of Film Commissioners Newsletter *Association*

Publishing Co: AFC c/o Wyoming Film Office, 1-25 At College Dr., Cheyenne, WY 82002-0001;
Title Tel # (800) 458-6657
Personnel: Editor-Bill Lindstrom
Editorial Description: Members are local government representatives responsible for bringing movie & TV industry to their areas.
General Info: Yr. Est. 1985, Quarterly, Sheetfed press, 4 pages, No Color, Matte, Saddle-stitched
Circulation: (100% controlled), Total-225

Black Camera *Business, Association*

Publishing Co: Indiana University Department of Afro-American Studies, Memorial Hall #32, Bloomington, IN 47405; Title Tel # (812) 855-6041 Title Fax # (812) 855-3874
Personnel: Editor-Gloria J. Gibson-Hudson
Editorial Description: Covers news of the Black Film Center & its archives, related events dealing with black cinema.
General Info: Yr. Est. 1985, Semi-annually, Trim Size-8½ x 11, 6 pages, Matte

Bullet, The
See: TELEVISION & VIDEO

Common Ground News
See: THEATRE

Digest of the Univ. Film & Video Assn. *Association*

Publishing Co: Univ. Film & Video Assn., Univ. of N. Texas, Dept of RTVF, Box 13108, Denton, TX 76203-3108; Title Tel # (817) 565-2537 Title Fax # (817) 565-2518
Personnel: Editor-Steve Fore, Editor-Gerry Veeler
General Info: 5x/yr., Desktop press
Subscriptions: Free With Membership
Circulation: Total-850

Express Exchange *Association*

Publishing Co: Sponsor-Philadelphia Independent Film/Video Assn., Philadelphia Independent Film/Video Assn., 3701 Chestnut St., Philadelphia, PA 19104-3104; Title Tel # (215) 895-6594 Title Fax # (215) 895-6562
Personnel: Editor-David Haas, Asst. Ed.-Jerry White
Editorial Description: Newsletter of Philadelphia Independent Film/Video Association, a service organization for film, video and audio artists and producers working on independent, non-commercial projects in the greater Philadephia area.
General Info: (Formerly Mid-Atlantic Arts Exchange), Yr. Est. 1979, Monthly, Trim Size-8½ x 11, Desktop press, 10 pages, No Color, Matte
Subscriptions: Indv. $25, Inst. $50, Free With Membership
Circulation: Total-530, Readership-550
List Rental: Actives: 438

Fast Foreward *Association*

Publishing Co: Association of Audio-Visual Technicians, PO Box 603, Farmingdale, NY 11735-0603;
Title Tel # (303) 698-1820
Editorial Description: U.S. and foreign audio-visual technicians in schools, industry and service shops.
General Info: Yr. Est. 1975, Monthly, Trim Size-8½ x 11, Offset press, 12 pages, 1% ads, Newsprint, Saddle-stitched
Subscriptions: Inst. $65, $3/copy
Circulation: Total-1,200
Advertising: Inquire for rates.

Film Analyst, The *Consumer*

Publishing Co: Film Analyst, 2404 Narbonne Way, Costa Mesa, CA 92627-1424;
Title Tel # (714) 645-3825
Personnel: Publisher-Arthur Taussig
Editorial Description: Intelligent reviews of movies from a cultural perspective - not too simple or academically complicated.
General Info: Monthly, Trim Size-8½ x 11, 12 pages, No Color, Matte, Saddle-stitched
Subscriptions: Indv. $15, $2/copy
Circulation: Total-1,000

Film Councilor

Publishing Co: Council of Film Organizations, 334 W 54th St, Los Angeles, CA 90037-3806;
Title Tel # (213) 752-5811 Title Fax # (213) 752-5811
Personnel: Editor-Dr. Donald Reed
General Info: Yr. Est. 1980, Quarterly
Circulation: Total-1,000
Advertising: Inquire for rates.

Film Technology News *Business, Association*

Publishing Co: Film Technology Co., 726 Cole Ave, Los Angeles, CA 90038-3606;
Title Tel # (213) 464-3456 Title Fax # (213) 464-7439
Editorial Description: Film technology developments.
General Info: Quarterly
Subscriptions: Free

Genealogy Bulletin
See: GENEALOGY

Hollywood Stuntmen's Hall of Fame News *Business, Association* CPM$1500

Publishing Co: Hollywood Stuntmen's Hall of Fame, Inc., 8305 Lewis River Rd., Ariel, WA 98603-9736; Title Tel # (801) 259-6100
Personnel: Editor-John Hagner, Adv. Dir.-Doricca Brewer
General Info: Yr. Est. 1987, Monthly, Trim Size-17 x 11, 4 pages
Subscriptions: Indv. $25, Can. $35, For. $45
Circulation: Total-500
Advertising: $750. Accepts Inserts.

Independent Eye

Publishing Co: Canadian Filmmakers Distribution Centre, 67A Portland St., Toronto, ON M5V 2M9 Canada; Title Tel # (416) 593-1808 Title Fax # (416) 593-8661
Personnel: Editor-Paul Couillard
Editorial Description: A periodical devoted to news, interviews, reviews & articles concerning independent & avant-garde film.
General Info: Yr. Est. 1971, Trim Size-8½ x 11, Offset press, 68 pages, ISSN: 0225-9192, No Color
Subscriptions: Indv. $15, Inst. $20, Can. $10, For. $20, $5/copy
Circulation: (16% controlled), Single Copy/Newsstand-500, Subscriptions-500
Advertising: Inquire for rates. Accepts Inserts.

Infocus   *Association*

Publishing Co: Academy of Canadian Cinema and Television, 158 Pearl St., Toronto, ON M5H 1L3 Canada Fax # (416) 591-2157; Title Tel # (416) 591-2040
Personnel: Editor-Jody Scotchmer
Editorial Description: Newsletter that helps stimulate, recognize and celebrate exceptional, creative achievement in the Canadian film and television industry.
General Info: Yr. Est. 1979, Quarterly, Trim Size-8½ x 11, Offset press, 20 pages, Coated, Saddle-stitched
Subscriptions: Free With Membership
Circulation: Total-2,000
Advertising: Inquire for rates.

It's Only A Movie
See: ENTERTAINMENT

Laser Disc Newsletter, The
See: HOME & HOME ENTERTAINMENT

Leased Access Report - Audience
See: TELEVISION & VIDEO

Lyon Lamb Newsletter

Publishing Co: Lyon Lamb, 4531 W Empire Ave, Burbank, CA 91505-1143; Title Tel # (818) 843-4831
Personnel: Editor-David Goggin
General Info: Bi-monthly

Millennium Pop
See: MUSIC & MUSIC TRADES

Motion Picture Investor   *Business*

Publishing Co: Paul Kagan Associates Inc., 126 Clock Tower Pl., Carmel, CA 93923-8746; Title Tel # (408) 624-1536 Title Fax # (408) 625-3225
Personnel: Publisher-Paul Kagan, Circ. Mgr.-Judy Pinney, Adv. Dir.-Johanne Hardy
Editorial Description: Analysis of private & public values of movies & movie stock.
General Info: Yr. Est. 1984, Monthly, Trim Size-7¼ x 10, Other press, 15 pages, ISSN: 0742-8839, No Color, Other, Saddle-stitched
Subscriptions: Indv. $675
Advertising: $1,560.

News Reel

Publishing Co: Federation of Motion Picture Council, 142 N Tucker St, Memphis, TN 38104-2656; Title Tel # (901) 725-4987
General Info: Monthly

Old Time Western Film Club-Newsletter   *Consumer*

Publishing Co: Old Time Western Film Club, PO Box 142, Siler City, NC 27344-0142
Personnel: Publisher, Editor-Milo Holt
Editorial Description: The showing & preserving of old western movies.
General Info: Yr. Est. 1970, Bi-monthly, Mimeo press, 2 pages
Circulation: Total-400
List Rental: Rents Lists

Pantheist Vision
See: PHILOSOPHY

Subway Entertainment Guide
See: MUSIC & MUSIC TRADES

TEA News

Publishing Co: Theatre Equipment Assn., 244 W 49th St Ste 305, New York, NY 10019-7411; Title Tel # (212) 246-6460

TVM Report

Publishing Co: Tom V. Murphy Enter., PO Box 740875, Dallas, TX 75374-0875; Title Tel # (214) 234-2986
Personnel: Publisher, Editor-Tom Murphy
Editorial Description: Texas film,video & other entertainment industries insiders newsletter.
General Info: Yr. Est. 1984, Semi-monthly, Offset press, 4 pages, No Color
Subscriptions: $3/copy
Circulation: Total-200

Ten Thousand Words
See: MEDIA & COMMUNICATIONS

Trebas Track
See: SOUND ENGINEERING

Variety Deal Memo   *Business*

Publishing Co: Baskerville Communications, 2455 Teller Rd, Newbury Park, CA 91320-2218 Parent Co.-SAGE Publication, Inc., Thousand Oaks; Title Tel # (805) 499-0721 Title Fax # (805) 499-0871
Personnel: Publisher-Tim Baskerville, Group Editor-Meredith Amdur, Mktg. Dir.-Allen Kriegshauser
Editorial Description: Covers global theatrical and post-theatrical rights and markets.
General Info: Yr. Est. 1994, Bi-weekly
Advertising: Inquire for rates.
List Rental: Rents Lists

WRITE!   *Business*

Publishing Co: Hank Roll Co., 2419 Greensburg Pike, Pittsburgh, PA 15221-3665
Personnel: Editor-Hank Roll
Editorial Description: Features topics of interest to screenwriters.
General Info: Yr. Est. 1991, Monthly, Trim Size-5½ x 8½, 20 pages, Color-cover
Subscriptions: Indv. $7, Inst. $10, Can. $10, For. $10, $1/copy
Advertising: $50.

FIRE PROTECTION

Arson Prevention Idea File

Publishing Co: Fire-Medic Services, 19 Joslin St., Providence, RI 02909-2599; Title Tel # (401) 751-6217
Personnel: Publisher, Editor-Thomas Lopatosky
Editorial Description: News and features relating to arson, its effects and causes. Special emphasis on practical ideas for government agencies, citizen organizations, and private individuals to use in preventing arson.
General Info: Yr. Est. 1990, Bi-monthly, Trim Size-8½ x 11, Sheetfed press, 8 pages, No Color, Matte
Subscriptions: Indv. $11, Can. $11, For. $11, $2/copy

CSAA Dispatch
See: SECURITY & SURVEILLANCE

Canadian Assn. of Fire Chiefs, Dialogue

Publishing Co: Canadian Assn. of Fire Chiefs, Inc., 2425-1 Don Reid Dr., Ottawa, ON K1H 1A4 Canada; Title Tel # (613) 736-0576 Title Fax # (613) 736-0684
Personnel: Editor-Ferris Clark
General Info: Bi-monthly, ISSN: 0706-1382
Circulation: Total-2,000

Canadian Association of Fire Chiefs, Inc.

Publishing Co: Canadian Assn. of Fire Chiefs, Inc., 2425-1 Don Reid Dr., Ottawa, ON K1H 1A4 Canada; Title Tel # (613) 736-0576 Title Fax # (613) 736-0684
General Info: Yr. Est. 1979, Bi-monthly

Chief Officer's Aide

Publishing Co: Fire-Medic Services, 19 Joslin St., Providence, RI 02909-2599; Title Tel # (401) 751-6217
Editorial Description: Information to assist Fire Service chief Officers more effectively manage personnel and operations.
General Info: Yr. Est. 1990, Bi-weekly, Looseleaf
Subscriptions: Indv. $35, $2/copy

Commish   *Business*

Publishing Co: Quinlan Publishing, 23 Drydock Ave, Boston, MA 02210-2387 Fax # (617) 345-9646; Title Tel # (617) 542-0048
Personnel: Editor-Leo Stapleton
Editorial Description: For the firefighting community with tips and information.
General Info: Monthly
Subscriptions: Indv. $68

Dispatcher

Publishing Co: Fire-Medic Services, 19 Joslin St., Providence, RI 02909-2599; Title Tel # (401) 751-6217
Personnel: Publisher, Editor-Thomas Lopatosky
Editorial Description: News, ideas and information for fire department and other emergency service agency dispatchers.
General Info: Yr. Est. 1991, Bi-monthly, Sheetfed press, 8 pages, No Color, Matte
Subscriptions: Indv. $9

E.M.S. Officer's Notebook
See: MEDICINE

Emergency Management Today
See: GOVERNMENT

Emergency Preparedness News
See: SAFETY

Emergency Services Chaplain
See: RELIGIOUS & THEOLOGICAL

Fire & Emergency World   *Business*

Publishing Co: Fire-Medic Services, 19 Joslin St., Providence, RI 02909-2599; Title Tel # (401) 751-6217
Personnel: Publisher, Editor-Thomas Lopatosky
Editorial Description: Newsletter (with magazine supplement) for fire, rescue, & emergency medical services. Available in New England, US and International editions.
General Info: Yr. Est. 1983, Semi-monthly, Trim Size-8½ x 11, Web press, 10 pages, ISSN: 0738-3940, 4% ads, No Color
Subscriptions: Indv. $34, Can. $34, For. $34, $1/copy
Circulation: Total-14,000
Advertising: Inquire for rates. Accepts Inserts.

Fire & Flammability Bulletin   *Business*

Publishing Co: Elsevier Science Inc., 655 Avenue of the Americas, New York, NY 10010-5107
   Tel # (212) 633-3916 Fax # (212) 633-3913 Parent Co.-Reed Elsevier, New York;
   Title Tel # (212) 867-9040
Personnel: Publisher-Christopher Lloyd, Editor-Stephen Grayson, Circ. Mgr.-Karen Richardson
Editorial Description: A monitor of the international fire scene.
General Info: (Formerly Rubber & Plastics, Fire & Flammability Bulletin), Yr. Est. 1979, Monthly,
   ISSN: 0142-9353
Subscriptions: Indv. $390

Fire Bell Club News Notes   *Association*

Publishing Co: Fire Bell Club of New York, Inc., 150 E. 23rd St., New York, NY 10010-4501;
   Title Tel # (212) 505-2681
Personnel: Publisher, Editor-Jack Lerch, Circ. Dir.-Ira Hoffman, Production Mgr.-Steven Scher, Adv.
   Dir.-Martin Schwartzberg, Promotion Dir.-Barry Gintel
General Info: Yr. Est. 1968, Monthly, Trim Size-8½ x 11, Offset press, 4 pages, Newsprint
Subscriptions: Free With Membership
Circulation: Total-1,000

Fire Control Digest   *Business*

Publishing Co: Washington Capital News Reports, 3918 Prosperity Ave Ste 318, Fairfax, VA
   22031-3333; Title Tel # (703) 573-1600 Title Fax # (703) 573-1604
Personnel: Publisher, Editor-R.J. O'Connell, Circ. Dir.-Nancy Van Wyen
General Info: Yr. Est. 1975, Monthly, Trim Size-8½ x 11, 10 pages, ISSN: 0889-5740
Subscriptions: Indv. $145, Can. $147, For. $156
Circulation: Total-1,000

Fire Findings   *Business*

Publishing Co: Fire Findings, 820 Lions Park Drive, PO Box 493, St. Joseph, MI 49085-0493;
   Title Tel # (616) 983-2113 Title Fax # (616) 983-7805
Personnel: Publisher-Mary Cahill, Editor-Jack Sanderson
Editorial Description: Fire investigation's newsletter for building successful origin & cause cases.
General Info: Yr. Est. 1993, Quarterly, Trim Size-8½ x 11, Sheetfed press, 16 pages, ISSN: 1073-
   6972, 2 Color, Matte, Saddle-stitched
Subscriptions: Indv. $36, Can. $42, For. $61, $10/copy
Circulation: Total-1,825
Advertising: Accepts Inserts.
Printing Co: Howard Printing Co., 7419 Sprinkle Rd, Kalamazoo, MI 49001-9791
   Tel # (616) 329-0022, Fax # (616) 329-1966

Fire Lines

Publishing Co: Uniformed Fire Fighters Assn. of Greater NY, 225 Broadway, New York, NY
   10007-3092
Personnel: Editor-Robert Di Virgilio
General Info: Yr. Est. 1973, Monthly
Advertising: Inquire for rates.

Fire News

Publishing Co: Canadian Assn. of Fire Chiefs, Inc., 2425-1 Don Reid Dr., Ottawa, ON K1H 1A4
   Canada Tel # (613) 736-0576 Fax # (613) 736-0684
Personnel: Editor-Ferris Clark
General Info: Yr. Est. 1979, Bi-monthly, 2 pages
Circulation: Total-2,000

Fire News   *Association*

Publishing Co: Natl. Fire Protection Assn., 1 Batterymarch Park, Quincy, MA 02169
   Tel # (617) 770-3000 Fax # (617) 984-7090; Title Tel # (617) 984-7268
Personnel: Editor-Michael Hazell
Editorial Description: NFPA news, and developments in fire prevention, protection, suppression.
General Info: Yr. Est. 1916, Bi-monthly, Trim Size-11 x 14, Web press, 8 pages, 2 Color, Matte
Subscriptions: Indv. $95, Free With Membership
Circulation: (86% controlled), Total-61,000
Printing Co: MacDonald & Evans, 1 Rex Dr, Braintree, MA 02184-5290 Tel # (617) 848-9090

Fire Officer's Notebook

Publishing Co: Fire-Medic Services, 19 Joslin St., Providence, RI 02909-2599;
   Title Tel # (401) 751-6217
Personnel: Publisher-Thoams Lopatosky, Editor-Thomas Lopatosky
Editorial Description: Ideas and information to assist officers of fire companies with their supervisory
   and related duties.
General Info: Yr. Est. 1990, Bi-weekly, Sheetfed press, 8 pages, No Color, Matte, Looseleaf
Subscriptions: Indv. $35, $2/copy

Fire Police

Publishing Co: Fire-Medic Services, 19 Joslin St., Providence, RI 02909-2599;
   Title Tel # (401) 751-6217
Personnel: Publisher, Editor-Thomas Lopatosky
Editorial Description: News, features and ideas for fire police units (usually associated with fire
   companies).
General Info: Yr. Est. 1991, Sheetfed press, No Color, Matte
Subscriptions: Indv. $9, $2/copy

Fire and Police Personnel Reporter
   See: LABOR

Fire Service Information

Publishing Co: Fire Service Ext., Iowa State Univ., Ames, IA 50011-0001; Title Tel # (515) 294-6817
Personnel: Editor-Keith Royer
Editorial Description: Fire service information.
General Info: Yr. Est. 1947, Bi-monthly, Trim Size-8½ x 11½, Offset press, 8 pages, Color
Circulation: Total-8,000

Fire Service Labor Monthly

Publishing Co: Justex Systems, PO Box 6224, Huntsville, TX 77342-6224 Fax # (409) 294-0984;
   Title Tel # (409) 291-7981
Personnel: Editor-Jerry Dowling
General Info: Yr. Est. 1987, Monthly, 10 pages, ISSN: 0890-8494
Subscriptions: Indv. $89

Firehouse Lawyer Monthly
   See: LAW

Flame Retardancy News   *Business*

Publishing Co: Business Communications Co., 25 Van Zant St., Ste.13, Norwalk, CT 06855-1781;
   Title Tel # (203) 853-4266 Title Fax # (203) 853-0348
Personnel: Publisher-Louis Naturman, Editor-Anna Crull, Editor-Dick Hilton, Mktg. Dir.-Robert Butler
Editorial Description: New advances in flame retardent materials, patents, corporate activity, trends
   and business opportunities.
General Info: Monthly, Trim Size-8½ x 11, 14 pages, Ind/Abs/Online: Dialog Newsnet, Information
   Access, No Color, Matte
Subscriptions: Indv. $365, Can. $415, For. $415, $35/copy
List Rental: List Management Co.: W.I. Mail Marketing, 470 Main St. #317, Ridgefield, CT
   06877-4516 Tel # (203) 438-6822, Fax # (203) 438-7756, Actives: 120

Gated Wye

Publishing Co: Oregon State Fire Marshal, 4760 Portland Rd NE # 534, Salem, OR 97305-1760;
   Title Tel # (503) 373-1540 Title Fax # (503) 373-1825
Personnel: Circ. Mgr.-Norma Howe, Editor, Circ. Mgr., Production Mgr.-Colleen Olson
Editorial Description: Covers general fire protection and related items (prevention, investigation,
   suppression.).
General Info: (Formerly Fire Service Bulletin), Yr. Est. 1983, Monthly, Trim Size-8½ x 11, Offset
   press, 8 pages, 1% ads, No Color
Subscriptions: Indv. $25, Can. $41, For. $41
Circulation: Total-1,400
Advertising: Inquire for rates.
Printing Co: Printing Division, 550 Airport Rd SE, Salem, OR 97310-1202

Hot Flashes   *Consumer, Association*

Publishing Co: State of CT Commission on Fire Prevention, PO Box 3383, Windsor Locks, CT
   06096-3383; Title Tel # (203) 627-6363
Personnel: Editor-Cynthia Colton-Reichler
Editorial Description: News, information concerning fire fighting, fire prevention, public fire safety
   education.
General Info: (Formerly Connecticut Fire Bulletin), Yr. Est. 1976, Semi-annually, Trim Size-8½ x 11,
   Desktop press, 4 pages, 2 Color, Matte
Subscriptions: Free To Qualified Recipient
Circulation: Total-6,000

IAFC On Scene   CPM: $232

Publishing Co: International Association of Fire Chiefs, Inc., 4025 Fair Ridge Drive, Fairfax, VA
   22033-2868; Title Tel # (202) 833-3420 Title Fax # (202) 452-0684
Personnel: Editor-Timothy Elliott, Adv. Dir.-Scott Bolton
Editorial Description: Provides very up-to-date information for fire service and EMS leaders.
   Information includes latest in state and Federal fire service and building codes regulations, as well
   as features and announcements.
General Info: Yr. Est. 1987, Bi-weekly, Trim Size-11 x 14, Sheetfed press, 8 pages, ISSN: 0893-
   3936, Ind/Abs/Online: IChiefs Network, 15% ads, 2 Color, Matte
Subscriptions: Indv. $60
Circulation: Total-8,600
Advertising: $2,000.
List Rental: Rents Lists
Printing Co: CLB Publishers & Lithographers, 10580 Metropolitan Ave, Kensington, MD 20895-2606
   Tel # (301) 933-5220, Fax # (301) 933-2498

Indiana Public Safety Letter
   See: PUBLIC MANAGEMENT & PLANNING

NAFI Newsletter   *Association*

Publishing Co: National Association of Fire Investigators, PO Box 957257, Hoffman Estates, IL
   60195-7257; Title Tel # (312) 939-6050
General Info: Yr. Est. 1962, Quarterly, Offset press, 8 pages, 2 Color
Subscriptions: $3/copy
Circulation: Total-3,500

National Newsline
   See: SECURITY & SURVEILLANCE

New England Harbormaster
   See: GOVERNMENT

Northeastern Forest Fire Protection Commission Compact News

Publishing Co: Northeastern Forest Fire Protection Commission, 66 Buckley Hwy, Stafford Springs, CT 06076-4406
General Info: Quarterly

Prometheus Report: Journal of Firesafety   *Business*

Publishing Co: Clark Publishing, 904 Merridale Blvd, Mount Airy, MD 21771-5266
General Info: Yr. Est. 1982, Monthly
Subscriptions: Indv. $24

Public Safety Management   *Business*

Publishing Co: Fire-Medic Services, 19 Joslin St., Providence, RI 02909-2599;
   Title Tel # (401) 751-6217
Personnel: Publisher, Editor-Thomas Lopatosky
Editorial Description: Covers current police, fire, EMS issues for local government management.
General Info: Yr. Est. 1984, Weekly, Trim Size-8½ x 11, Sheetfed press, 8 pages, ISSN: 0748-9927, No Color, Newsprint
Subscriptions: Indv. $130, $3/copy

Recruiting & Retention Idea File

Publishing Co: Fire-Medic Services, 19 Joslin St., Providence, RI 02909-2599;
   Title Tel # (401) 751-6217
Personnel: Publisher, Editor-Thomas Lopatosky
Editorial Description: Information on recruiting and retaining firefighters, rescue workers, EMS personnel and support staff in volunteer agencies.
General Info: Yr. Est. 1990, Bi-monthly, Looseleaf
Subscriptions: Indv. $7, $2/copy

Rescue Officer's Notebook

Publishing Co: Fire-Medic Services, 19 Joslin St., Providence, RI 02909-2599;
   Title Tel # (401) 751-6217
Personnel: Publisher, Editor-Thomas Lopatosky
Editorial Description: Ideas and information to assist officers of rescue companies and agencies (including search & rescue) with their supervisory and related duties.
General Info: Yr. Est. 1990, Bi-weekly, Looseleaf
Subscriptions: Indv. $35, $2/copy

SFM

Publishing Co: California State Fire Marshal, 7171 Bowling Dr Ste 600, Sacramento, CA 95823-2034; Title Tel # (916) 427-4175
Personnel: Editor-Joan Jennings
Editorial Description: Fire prevention.
General Info: (Formerly State Fire Marshal Newsletter), Yr. Est. 1960, Bi-monthly, Trim Size-8½ x 11, Web press, 16 pages, 2 Color
Circulation: (100% controlled), Total-8,000

School Emergencies
See: SCHOOL ADMINISTRATION

Selected Articles for Arson Investigators   *Business, Association*

Publishing Co: International Association of Arson Investigators, 300 S Broadway # 100, Saint Louis, MO 63102-2800; Title Tel # (502) 239-7228 Title Fax # (502) 239-7324
Personnel: Publisher-Alex Ahart, Editor-David Icove
Editorial Description: General and education reference information on fire and arson investigation.
General Info: Yr. Est. 1970, Annually, Web press, 1,200 pages, Looseleaf
Subscriptions: Indv. $72
Printing Co: V.G. Reed & Co., 1500 Arlington Ave, Louisville, KY 40206-3109 Tel # (502) 589-3770

Speaking of Fire   *Association*

Publishing Co: Fire Protection Pubs., Ok State Univ., Stillwater, OK 74078-0001;
   Title Tel # (405) 744-5723 Title Fax # (405) 744-8204
Personnel: Publisher-Doug Forsman, Editor-Cynthia Brakhage, Art Dir.-Don Davis, Adv. Dir., Promotion Dir.-Kay Getz
Editorial Description: Manuals & informational texts, newsletter & other training material for the Fire Service. Speaking of Fire contains articles on Fire Fighting, HazMat, Prevention, Computers, book reviews & educational announcements.
General Info: (Formerly International Fire Service Training Association Newsletter), Yr. Est. 1934, Quarterly, Trim Size-8½ x 11, Offset press, 8 pages, 2 Color
Subscriptions: Free
Circulation: (100% controlled), Total-117,000

United Fire Equipment Service Association Information Bulletin

Publishing Co: International Fire Equipment, 22155 W. Hwy. 22, Box 141, Lake Zurich, IL 60047;
   Title Tel # (847) 438-2343 Title Fax # (847) 438-1869
General Info: Quarterly

U.S. Fire Sprinkler Reporter   *Business*

Publishing Co: Wakeman/Walworth, 300 N. Washington St., Alexandria, VA 22314-2530;
   Title Tel # (703) 549-8606 Title Fax # (703) 549-1372
Personnel: Publisher-Keyes Walworth, Editor-Mark Farrell, Production Mgr.-Thang Vu
Editorial Description: Written for those on the front lines of development and installation of fire sprinklers.
General Info: Yr. Est. 1980, Monthly, Trim Size-8½ x 11, Offset press, 10 pages, 5% ads, 4 Color, Saddle-stitched
Subscriptions: Indv. $60, Can. $65, For. $90
Advertising: $630. Accepts Inserts.

Vulcan Newsletter

Publishing Co: Vulcan Society, Vulcan Hall, 739 Eastern Pky, Brooklyn, NY 11213-3410;
   Title Tel # (718) 778-7978
Personnel: Editor-Edward Thomas
General Info: Monthly
Circulation: (100% controlled), Total-600

Wyoming Fire News   *Business*

Publishing Co: Wyoming State Department of Fire Prevention, Herschler Bldg., 1 West, Cheyenne, WY 82002; Title Tel # (307) 777-7288 Title Fax # (307) 777-7119
Personnel: Editor-Donna Depew
Editorial Description: Information pertinent to fire chiefs and electricians.
General Info: (Formerly Fire Marshall Bulletin), Yr. Est. 1985, Quarterly, Trim Size-8½ x 11, Mimeo press, 6 pages, Color
Subscriptions: Free
Circulation: Total-1,000

FISH & FISHERIES

Alternative Aquaculture Network   *Consumer, Association*

Publishing Co: Alternative Aquaculture Association, PO Box 109, Breinigsville, PA 18031-0109;
   Title Tel # (215) 395-5854 Title Fax # (610) 683-9280
Personnel: Publisher, Editor-Steven Van Gorder
Editorial Description: Provides basic information on state-of-the-art alternative methods of aquaculture. Includes small-scale, backyard methods.
General Info: (Formerly Rodale's Network), Yr. Est. 1981, Quarterly, Trim Size-8½ x 11, Web press, 8 pages, ISSN: 8755-7894, No Color
Subscriptions: Indv. $14, $3/copy
Circulation: Total-1,000
Printing Co: Rhoads Press, 6265 Hamilton Blvd, Allentown, PA 18106-9698 Tel # (215) 395-8000

American Fish Decoy Association
See: HOBBY

American Wildlands
See: ENVIRONMENT & ECOLOGY

Aquaculture Newsletter International   *Business*

Publishing Co: Aquaculture Newsletter International, 3 Pinefield, Weston, CT 06883
   Tel # (203) 221-8494 Fax # (203) 221-8269
Personnel: Publisher-Sandra Martin
Editorial Description: Covers the trends and activities in the aquaculture industry worldwide.
General Info: Yr. Est. 1994, Monthly, Trim Size-8½ x 11, 8 pages, ISSN: 1080-0298, No Color, Matte, Saddle-stitched
Subscriptions: Indv. $89

BOAT/U.S. Reports
See: BOATS & BOATING

Delta Pride News

Publishing Co: Delta Catfish Processors, Inc., Industrial Park, Box 850, Indianola, MS 38751;
   Title Tel # (601) 887-5401
Personnel: Editor-Carolyn Ann Sledge
General Info: Yr. Est. 1984, Quarterly, 6 pages

Fish & Wildlife Reference Service Newsletter
See: ENVIRONMENT & ECOLOGY

Fish Lines   *Consumer*

Publishing Co: Natl. Aquarium Society, Dept. Of Commerce Bldg. Rm., B-037, Washington, DC 20230-0001; Title Tel # (202) 482-2825 Title Fax # (202) 482-4946
Personnel: Editor-Sarah Rosenbaum
Editorial Description: Explores current marine research, legislation and related events. Devoted to the general public. Publicizes nat. aquarium events and happenings to members.
General Info: Yr. Est. 1982, Quarterly
Circulation: Total-600

Fish News

Publishing Co: New England Fisheries Development Foundation, Inc., 309 World Trade Center, Boston, MA 02210-2001; Title Tel # (617) 542-8890
Personnel: Editor-Ken Coon
General Info: Yr. Est. 1982, Bi-weekly
Subscriptions: Indv. $25
Circulation: Total-279

Fisheries Market News
Report   *Business*

Publishing Co: Urner Barry Publications, Inc., PO Box 389, Toms River, NJ 08754-0389; Title Tel # (908) 240-5330 Title Fax # (908) 341-0891
Personnel: Editor-Joseph T. Soja, Production Mgr.-Bill Curro
General Info: (Formerly Weekly Statistical Fishery Report/NMFS Fisheries Market News), Yr. Est. 1981, Semi-weekly, Trim Size-11 x 17, Sheetfed press, 10 pages, Ind/Abs/Online: COMTELL Fish, No Color, Newsprint
Subscriptions: Indv. $282, Can. $302, For. $423, $15/copy
Circulation: Total-700

Fishery Bulletin

Publishing Co: Illinois Dept. of Conservation, 524 S. Second, Springfield, IL 62701 Tel # (217) 785-8552; Title Tel # (217) 782-6424

Fishery Market News
Reports (New Orleans-
Goldenrod Sheet)   *Business*

Publishing Co: Natl. Marine Fisheries Service, 1 Canal Place, Ste. 2340, 365 Canal St., New Orleans, LA 70130; Title Tel # (800) 932-0617
Personnel: Editor-Joe Soja
Editorial Description: Gulf shrimp landings, spiny lobster, crab, oyster, finfish; wholesale prices; NY, Alaska prices; imp
General Info: Semi-weekly
Subscriptions: Indv. $50

Fishery Market News
Reports (New York
Green Sheet)   *Business*

Publishing Co: U.S. Dept. of Commerce, 201 Varick St Rm 951, New York, NY 10014-4811; Title Tel # (212) 620-3405
Editorial Description: Current market information on wholesale prices & receipts at N.Y. City's Fulton Fish Market.
General Info: Yr. Est. 1937, Semi-weekly, Trim Size-8½ x 14, Mimeo press, 5 pages
Subscriptions: Indv. $50, $20/copy

Foreign Fishery Information
Release   *Association*

Publishing Co: National Marine Fisheries Service, 501 W Ocean Blvd Ste 4200, Long Beach, CA 90802-4221; Title Tel # (213) 514-6679
Personnel: Editor, Circ. Mgr., Art Dir.-Dr. Sunee Sonu
Editorial Description: Information translated from foreign journals and periodicals which have major impact on U.S. fisheries and seafood markets.
General Info: Yr. Est. 1961, Bi-weekly, Trim Size-8½ x 14, Mimeo press, 4 pages, Color
Circulation: Total-500

Great Lakes Basin Report   *Business, Association*

Publishing Co: Great Lakes Sport Fishing Council, PO Box 297, Elmhurst, IL 60126-0297; Title Tel # (708) 941-1351
Personnel: Publisher, Editor-Dan Thomas, Production Mgr.-J.L. Thomas
Editorial Description: Seeks to protect and enhance the Great Lakes sport fishery and its ecology, and to educate and inform council members and the general public.
General Info: Yr. Est. 1972, Monthly, Trim Size-8 x 10, Offset press, 10 pages, 2 Color, Recycled, Other
Subscriptions: Can. $12, For. $25, $1/copy
Advertising: Accepts Inserts.

Huntsman Marine Science
News   *Business, Association*

Publishing Co: Huntsman Marine Science Centre, Brandy Cove Rd., St. Andrews, NB E0G 2X0 Canada; Title Tel # (506) 529-1200 Title Fax # (506) 529-1212
Editorial Description: Covers education & research issues & developments in the marine sciences.
General Info: (Formerly Marine Science News), Yr. Est. 1988, Semi-annually, ISSN: 0843-5340
Subscriptions: Free
Circulation: Total-2,000

I.A.F.W.A. Newsletter
See: ENVIRONMENT & ECOLOGY

Lines to Leaders   *Association*

Publishing Co: Trout Unlimited, 1500 Wilson Blvd., Arlington, VA 22209-2404 Tel # (703) 281-1100 Fax # (703) 281-1825; Title Tel # (703) 522-0200
Personnel: Editor-Alison Rice
Editorial Description: Information for T.U. chapter presidents and council chairmen and other T U volunteer leaders.
General Info: Monthly
Subscriptions: Free To Qualified Recipient
Circulation: Total-900

Littoral Drift
See: ENVIRONMENT & ECOLOGY

MSRC Bulletin Series
See: ENVIRONMENT & ECOLOGY

Marine Fish Management

Publishing Co: Nautilus Press, Inc., 1054 National Press Building, Washington, DC 20045-2001; Title Tel # (202) 347-6643
Personnel: Publisher, Editor-John Botzum
Editorial Description: Coverage of the field of fisheries management within the new U.S. 200-mile zone, plus world fish management news.
General Info: Yr. Est. 1975, Monthly, Trim Size-8½ x 11, Offset press, 8 pages
Subscriptions: Indv. $88, $4/copy

NFLCC Gazette
See: CLUBS

National Wetlands Newsletter
See: WATER SUPPLY, POWER & WASTE

Natural Resources Computer Newsletter
See: ENVIRONMENT & ECOLOGY

News from Mote
See: SCIENCE

Northwest Energy News
See: ENERGY

Northwest Indian Fisheries
Commission News

Publishing Co: Northwest Indian Fisheries Commission, 6730, Dept. DB, Martin Way E., Olympia, WA 98506
Editorial Description: The Indian perspective & the facts about the health of the fish in the Northwest Coast.

Nutmeg Notes

Publishing Co: Nutmeg Chapter, Trout Unlimited, PO Box 1594, Fairfield, CT 06430-1594
Editorial Description: News and information for memebers of the Nutmeg Chapter of Trout Unlimited.

Pacific States Marine
Fisheries Commission
Newsletter   *Business, Association*

Publishing Co: Pacific States Marine Fisheries Commission, 45 82nd Street Drive, #100, Gladstone, OR 97027-2522 Tel # (503) 326-7025
Personnel: Editor-Guy Thornburgh
Editorial Description: Notice of major events, review of recent meetings of Commission, action on regulations, news of people and places.
General Info: Yr. Est. 1962, Quarterly, Offset press, 10 pages, No Color
Circulation: Total-1,100

Pacific Trollers Association
Newsletter   *Association*

Publishing Co: Pacific Trollers' Assn., 5960 #6 Rd. #625, Richmond, BC V6V 1Z1 Canada Tel # (604) 273-4213

Salar Newsletter   *Consumer, Association*

Publishing Co: Atlantic Salmon Federation, PO Box 807, Calais, ME 04619-0807; Title Tel # (506) 529-4581 Title Fax # (506) 529-4985
Editorial Description: Articles on the conservation and propagation of Atlantic salmon.
General Info: Quarterly, Trim Size-8½ x 11
Circulation: Total-12,000

Sea Grant Extension
Programs Newsletter   *Business*

Publishing Co: Univ. California-Davis Dept. Wildlife and Fisheries Biology, Univ. of California-Davis, Davis, CA 95616-8751; Title Tel # (916) 752-1497
Personnel: Editor-Christopher Dewees
Editorial Description: Topics for commercial & recreational fishing industries & seafood processors.
General Info: (Formerly Marine Advisory Programs Newsletter), Yr. Est. 1973, Bi-monthly, Trim Size-8½ x 11, 4 pages, No Color
Subscriptions: Free
Circulation: Total-4,200

Seafood Price-Current *Business*

Publishing Co: Urner Barry Publications, Inc., PO Box 389, Toms River, NJ 08754-0389; Title Tel # (908) 240-5330 Title Fax # (908) 341-0891
Personnel: Editor-Paul Brown, Jr., Editor-Joseph T. Soja, Circ. Mgr.-Karen Mick, Production Mgr.-Bill Curro, Adv. Dir.-Lisa Sharkus, Promotion Dir.-Sheila Deane
Editorial Description: Market price and news report for the fin fish and shellfish industry.
General Info: Yr. Est. 1972, Semi-weekly, Trim Size-8½ x 11, Sheetfed press, 8 pages, ISSN: 0270-417X, Ind/Abs/Online: COMTELL-FISH, Color, Newsprint
Subscriptions: Indv. $295, Can. $315, For. $363, $15/copy
Circulation: Total-1,200
Advertising: Inquire for rates.

Seafood Soundings
See: CONSUMER INTERESTS

Seiche, The
See: ENVIRONMENT & ECOLOGY

Shellfish Soundings *Association*

Publishing Co: Shellfish Institute of North America, 1525 Wilson Blvd Ste 500, Arlington, VA 22209-2411; Title Tel # (202) 296-5090
Personnel: Editor-Mr. Everett A. Tolley
Editorial Description: A digest of the shellfish industry for assistance and benefit of our members.
General Info: Yr. Est. 1908, Monthly, Trim Size-8½ x 11, Mimeo press, 6 pages
Subscriptions: Indv. $5
Circulation: Total-600

Shrimp Notes *Business*

Publishing Co: Shrimp World, Inc., 417 Eliza St, New Orleans, LA 70114-2335; Title Tel # (504) 368-1571 Title Fax # (504) 368-1573
Personnel: Publisher-William Chauvin, Editor, Promotion Dir.-Pamela Menesses
Editorial Description: Market news analysis of the U.S. shrimp industry.
General Info: Yr. Est. 1979, Monthly, 4 pages
Subscriptions: Indv. $225, For. $240

Software Legal Book *Business*

Publishing Co: Shafer Books, Inc., PO Box 40, Croton On Hudson, NY 10520-0040; Title Tel # (914) 271-6919 Title Fax # (914) 271-5193
Personnel: Publisher-Paul Hoffman
Editorial Description: Computer software proprietary rights and contracting.
General Info: Yr. Est. 1981, Annually, Looseleaf
Subscriptions: $235/copy

Spoof Newsletter
See: OCEANOGRAPHY

Survival Coalition

Publishing Co: B.C. Fisheries Survival Coalition, Box 147-401 West Georgia St., Vancouver, BC V6B -5A1 Canada; Title Tel # (604) 684-8903 Title Fax # (604) 687-0462
Editorial Description: Provides the fishing industry on the west coast of B.C.
General Info: Yr. Est. 1992, 3x/yr.
Circulation: Total-12,000

Survival Update *Association* CPM: $25

Publishing Co: Survivor Update, Sutie 380, 401 W Georgia St., Box 147, Vancouver, BC V4N4J6 Canada; Title Tel # (604) 684-8903 Title Fax # (604) 684-8903
Personnel: Editor, Production Mgr.-Phil Eidsuik, Circ. Mgr., Production Mgr., Adv. Dir.-Sandy Smith
Editorial Description: Fishing industry news update to our membership.
General Info: Trim Size-11 x 8½, 12 pages, 2 Color, Coated
Circulation: Total-12,000
Advertising: $300.

Upwellings
See: ENVIRONMENT & ECOLOGY

Urchin, Abalone, Kelp News *Business, Association*

Publishing Co: Univ. California-Davis Dept. Wildlife and Fisheries Biology, Univ. of California-Davis, Davis, CA 95616-8751; Title Tel # (916) 752-1497
Personnel: Editor-Leon Davies
Editorial Description: Topics of interest to researchers, agency staff, and fishing industry personnel.
General Info: Yr. Est. 1992, Semi-annually
Subscriptions: Free
Circulation: Total-300, Readership-320

Vancouver Aquascene Aquarium Newsletter
See: NATURAL HISTORY

Watergardening News
See: GARDENING & HORTICULTURE

FLORIST

ABC Dialogue
See: BRIDE

Bridal Collectors News
See: BRIDE

California Ornamental Crops Report *Business, Association*

Publishing Co: USDA-AMS-F&V. Div., 630 Sansome St Ste 727, San Francisco, CA 94111-2215; Title Tel # (415) 705-1300 Title Fax # (415) 705-1301
Personnel: Editor-Frederick Teensma
Editorial Description: Provides FOB shipping point price information on selected ornamentals. Included is information from major California areas. Competing U.S. shipping point areas, import prices through Miami, selected wholesale markets around the U.S. and the San Diego Flower Auction.
General Info: Semi-weekly, Trim Size-8½ x 14, 4 pages, No Color, Matte
Subscriptions: Indv. $180, Can. $180, For. $360

Connecticut Greenhouse Newsletter *Business, Association*

Publishing Co: University of Connecticut, U-67, 1376 Storrs Rd., Storrs, CT 06269-4067; Title Tel # (203) 486-3435
Personnel: Editor-Richard McAvoy
Editorial Description: Original research papers, timely cultural articles, and comments on greenhouse operation.
General Info: Yr. Est. 1964, Bi-monthly, Trim Size-5½ x 8¼, Offset press, 20 pages, No Color, Newsprint, Saddle-stitched
Subscriptions: Indv. $6, $1/copy
Circulation: (100% controlled), Total-2,000

Holland Flower *Association*

Publishing Co: Flower Council of Holland, PO Box 749, Glenwood, NY 11547-0749
Editorial Description: Info on fresh cut flowers.
General Info: Yr. Est. 1981, Quarterly
Subscriptions: Indv. $10, Can. $13
Circulation: Total-19,000

Letters from Abraham Lincoln
See: ART & SCULPTURE

Minnesota State Florists' Bulletin *Business*

Publishing Co: Minnesota Extension Service, 231 ClassRm. Office Bldg., 1994 Buford Avenue., St. Paul, MN 55108-6040; Title Tel # (612) 624-9703
Personnel: Editor-John Erwin
Editorial Description: Horticulture commercial flower production, cultural practices.
General Info: Yr. Est. 1951, Semi-monthly, 25 pages
Subscriptions: Indv. $30
Circulation: Total-300

Ohio Florists' Association Bulletin *Association*

Publishing Co: Ohio Florists' Assn., 2130 Stella Ct., #200, Columbus, OH 43215-1033; Title Tel # (614) 422-8200
Editorial Description: Information on production handling and marketing of floral crops: laws and regulations: business aids.
General Info: Yr. Est. 1930, Monthly, Trim Size-8½ x 11, Letrpr. press, 10 pages, 2 Color
Subscriptions: $2/copy
Circulation: Total-3,300

Ornamental Crops National Market Trends *Business, Association*

Publishing Co: USDA-AMS-F&V. Div., 630 Sansome St Ste 727, San Francisco, CA 94111-2215; Title Tel # (415) 705-1300 Title Fax # (415) 705-1301
Personnel: Editor-Frederick Teensma
Editorial Description: This report contains price trends for ornamental at shopping points in California, Massachusetts, and Florida, and information through Miami. It includes volume information on imports and interstate shipments for major cut flowers from California. Also includes a section on prices at various wholesale markets in the U.S.
General Info: Weekly, Trim Size-8½ x 14, Offset press, 3 pages, No Color, Matte
Subscriptions: Indv. $120, Can. $120, For. $240
Circulation: Total-150

San Francisco Wholesale Ornamental Crops Report
See: GARDENING & HORTICULTURE

FOLKLORE

AGS Quarterly: Bulletin of the Association for Gravestone Studies
See: HISTORY

Archaeoastronomy & Ethnoastronomy News
See: ASTRONOMY

Archaeology on Kaua'i
See: ARCHAEOLOGY

Beech Grove
See: GENEALOGY

Celebration News
  See: PHILOSOPHY

Come-All-Ye   *Consumer*   CPM: $50

Publishing Co: Legacy Books, PO Box 494, Hatboro, PA 19040-0494; Title Tel # (215) 675-6762
  Title Fax # (215) 674-2826
Personnel: Editor-Richard Burns, Publisher, Assoc. Ed.-Lillian Krelove
Editorial Description: Contains reviews of monographs in American Studies, ethnic & cultural studies, folktales, & legends. Also covers folkdance, international folk songs, & instrumental tunes from sources all over the world.
General Info: Yr. Est. 1977, Quarterly, Trim Size-8½ x 10⅞, Sheetfed press, 16 pages, ISSN: 0736-6132, Ind/Abs/Online: BK. REV. IN., No Color, Matte
Subscriptions: Indv. $6, Can. $7, For. $8, $2/copy
Circulation: Total-2,000
Advertising: $100.
Printing Co: Hirsch Printing Co., 457 Easton Rd, Horsham, PA 19044-2508 Tel # (215) 674-3830

Country Dance & Song Society News
  See: CULTURE & HUMANITIES

Dispatch/ News
  See: HISTORY

Dobie Connection
  See: GENEALOGY

Flax Craft
  See: TEXTILES

Florida Folklore Society
Newsletter   *Association*

Publishing Co: Florida Folklore Society, 4011 State Rd., 52, Dade City, FL 33525-8240;
  Title Tel # (904) 397-2192
Personnel: Publisher, Editor-Pat Robar, Circ. Mgr.-Eric Larsen, Art Dir.-Peggy Clark
Editorial Description: Folklore events publications, job openings and media notes. News of the Florida folklife program.
General Info: (Formerly Florida Folklife News), Yr. Est. 1983, Trim Size-8½ x 11, Desktop press, 7 pages, No Color
Subscriptions: Indv. $10
Circulation: (100% controlled), Total-225

Folklore Society of
Greater Washington
Newsletter

Publishing Co: Folklore Society of Greater Washington, P.O. Box 5693, Washington, DC 20016-5693; Title Tel # (202) 546-2228
Personnel: Circ. Mgr.-Cecily Pilzer
Editorial Description: Used to publicize events of Folklore Society to its member s& promote other traditional art events in the Washington, DC area.
General Info: Yr. Est. 1964, Monthly, Trim Size-8½ x 11, Sheetfed press, 20 pages, No Color, Newsprint
Subscriptions: Indv. $18, $3/copy
Advertising: Inquire for rates.

Gypsy Lore Society Newsletter
  See: ANTHROPOLOGY

Herbal Healer Academy Newsletter
  See: HEALTH

The ISC Newsletter
  See: ZOOLOGY

Jewish Storytelling
Newsletter   *Association*

Publishing Co: 92nd St.-YM-YWHA, 1395 Lexington Ave, New York, NY 10128-1647; Title Tel # (212) 415-5542 Title Fax # (212) 415-5575
Personnel: Editor-Peninnah Schram, Production Mgr.-Steven Siegel
General Info: Yr. Est. 1985, ISSN: 0896-8152
Subscriptions: Indv. $10
Circulation: Total-350

Kennedy Gazette
  See: GENEALOGY

Lead Belly Letter
  See: MUSIC & MUSIC TRADES

Nase Ceske Dedictvi
  See: ETHNIC

Newsletter of the North
Carolina Folklore Soc.

Publishing Co: North Carolina Folklore Society, Appalachian State Univ. Dept., Of English, Boone, NC 28608-0001; Title Tel # (704) 262-2323
Personnel: Editor-Thomas McGowan
Editorial Description: News on folklife activites, calender, directory, teacher's corner, & film notes.
General Info: Yr. Est. 1978, Quarterly, Web press, 16 pages, ISSN: 0888-6121, No Color
Subscriptions: Indv. $6, Inst. $8, For. $10, $1/copy
Circulation: Total-1,000
List Rental: Actives: $25/M
Printing Co: Shelby Printing, 1450 E Dixon Blvd, Shelby, NC 28152-6846 Tel # (704) 482-1454

Ohio Folklore

Publishing Co: Bowling Green State Univ., Bowling Green State Campus, Bowling Green, OH 43403-0001
Personnel: Editor-Donalk M. Winkelman
General Info: Yr. Est. 1967
Subscriptions: $1/copy

Pennsylvania Dutch News
and Views   *Consumer, Association*

Publishing Co: Pennsylvania Dutch Folk Culture Society, Inc., Lenhartsville, PA 19534; Title Tel # (215) 562-4803
Personnel: Publisher-Milton Blatt, Editor-Florence Baver
Editorial Description: Preservation of the folklore and history of the ancestry of the Pa. German people.
General Info: Yr. Est. 1965, Semi-annually, Sheetfed press, 20 pages, 2 Color
Subscriptions: $1/copy
Circulation: Total-400
Printing Co: Shoemakersville Press, 620 Franklin St, Shoemakersville, PA 19555-1617 Tel # (215) 567-8551

Pipings, The
  See: GENEALOGY

S.F.S. Flyer

Publishing Co: Seattle Folklore Society, PO Box 30141, Seattle, WA 98103-0141; Title Tel # (206) 782-0505
Personnel: Circ. Mgr.-Lucy Bodilly, Adv. Dir.-Dion Rossi, Editor, Art Dir.-John Watt
Editorial Description: Current folk,ethnic events in N.W.
General Info: Yr. Est. 1973, Monthly, Trim Size-8½ x 11, Sheetfed press, 6 pages, 2% ads, Newsprint
Subscriptions: Indv. $15
Circulation: (100% controlled), Total-2,500
Advertising: Inquire for rates.

Sherlockin Tidbits
  See: LITERATURE & LINGUISTICS

Smithsonian Talk Story   *Consumer*

Publishing Co: Smithsonian Institution-Folklife Programs & Cultural Studies, 955 L'Enfant Plaza, SW, Ste. 2600, MRC 914, Washington, DC 20560 Tel # (202) 287-3210; Title Tel # (202) 287-3424 Title Fax # (202) 287-3699
Personnel: Editor-Carla Borden
Editorial Description: A publication of the Center for Folklife Programs and Cultural Studies.
General Info: Quarterly

Spirit!
  See: HOUSE ORGANS

Story Bag: A National Storytelling Newsletter
  See: EDUCATION

Superstition Mountain Historical Society-Newsletter
  See: HISTORY

Violent Kin
  See: HISTORY

Welland Historical Museum Newsletter
  See: MUSEUM PUBLICATIONS

Wilson Museum Bulletin
  See: MUSEUM PUBLICATIONS

Yiddish of Greater Washington Newsletter
  See: LITERATURE & LINGUISTICS

FOOD

A La Carte   *Consumer*

Publishing Co: La Cuisine Kitchenware, 323 Cameron St, Alexandria, VA 22314-3219; Title Tel # (703) 836-4435
Personnel: Publisher-Nancy Purves Pollard
Editorial Description: Culinary newsletter published by La Cuisine Kitchenwware.
General Info: Semi-annually

AFFI Letter — *Association*

Publishing Co: American Frozen Food Inst, 2000 Corporate Ridge, Mc Lean, VA 22102-4399; Title Tel # (703) 821-0770 Title Fax # (703) 821-1350
Personnel: Circ. Mgr.-Jenifer Voskiul, Publisher, Editor, Production Mgr.-Traci Carneal
Editorial Description: News of interest to top management in the frozen food industry, covering primarily legislative, regulatory, technical and marketing developments.
General Info: (Formerly Weekly Report), Yr. Est. 1942, Semi-monthly, Trim Size-8½ x 11, Sheetfed press, 4 pages, 2 Color, Matte
Subscriptions: Free With Membership
Circulation: Total-1,400
Printing Co: Newsletter Services, Inc., 9700 Philadelphia Court, Lanham, MD 20706 Tel # (301) 731-5200, Fax # (301) 731-5201

AFI Newsletter — *Association*

Publishing Co: Assn. of Food Industries, 5 Ravine Dr, Matawan, NJ 07747-3106; Title Tel # (908) 583-8188
Personnel: Editor-Richard Solomon
General Info: Yr. Est. 1906, Bi-monthly

Advertising Via Telemarketing Script Presentations Newsletter
See: BUSINESS & INDUSTRY

Alberta Agrologist
See: AGRICULTURE

American Deli-Bakery News
See: BAKING

American Harvest — *Consumer*

Publishing Co: Cornucopia Press, 3 Golf Ctr Ste 221, Hoffman Estates, IL 60195-3710; Title Tel # (708) 934-7655
Personnel: Publisher-Tamara Sellman
Editorial Description: Covers low-fat cooking with ideas and information for growing own produce.
General Info: Yr. Est. 1993, Quarterly, Trim Size-8½ x 11, 20 pages, No Color
Subscriptions: Indv. $15
Advertising: Inquire for rates.

American Institute for Cancer Research Newsletter
See: HEALTH

American Meat Institute, Newsletter — *Association*

Publishing Co: American Meat Institute, 1700 N Moore St Ste 1600, Arlington, VA 22209-1903; Title Tel # (703) 841-2400
Editorial Description: Reports on issues affecting meat and poultry packing and processing industry.
General Info: Yr. Est. 1966, Weekly, Trim Size-8½ x 11, 4 pages, 4 Color
Subscriptions: Free With Membership
Circulation: Total-2,700
Printing Co: Newsletter Services, Inc., 9700 Philadelphia Court, Lanham, MD 20706 Tel # (301) 731-5200, Fax # (301) 731-5201

American Wine & Food

Publishing Co: American Institute of Wine & Food, 1550 Bryant St., San Francisco, CA 94103-4832; Title Tel # (415) 255-3000
Personnel: Editor-Robert Clark
Editorial Description: Covers institute & restaurant industry news.
General Info: Semi-monthly, ISSN: 0892-7642
Subscriptions: Indv. $20
Circulation: Total-5,000

America's Future Foods Report — *Business*

Publishing Co: TRA Information Svcs., Division of Technomic, Inc., 300 S Riverside Plz Ste 1940, Chicago, IL 60606-6613; Title Tel # (312) 876-0004 Title Fax # (312) 876-1158
Personnel: Publisher, Editor-John Hofer
Editorial Description: Identifies hot food trends and restaurant concepts, with discussion and analysis.
General Info: (Formerly Ron Paul's Future Foods Report), Yr. Est. 1989, Bi-monthly
Subscriptions: Indv. $195

Andre Gayot's Tastes
See: TRAVEL

Art of Eating — *Consumer*

Publishing Co: Art of Eating, The, P.O. Box 242, Peacham, VT 05862
Personnel: Publisher-Edward Behr
Editorial Description: Detailed articles and book reviews with photos and illustrations.
General Info: Quarterly

Asian Foodbookery — *Consumer*

Publishing Co: Asian Foodbookery, PO Box 15947, Seattle, WA 98115-0947
Personnel: Publisher, Editor-R.W. Lucky
Editorial Description: Explores the foods and foodways of Asia. Includes reviews and recipes as well as travel notes.
General Info: Yr. Est. 1996, Quarterly, Trim Size-8½ x 11, 8 pages, No Color, Matte
Subscriptions: Indv. $14, Can. $14, For. $18, $4/copy

Atlanta Wholesale Fruit
See: PRODUCE

BFC Flyer — *Business, Association*

Publishing Co: Boston Food Cooperative, 449 Cambridge St, Allston, MA 02134-2010; Title Tel # (617) 787-1416
Editorial Description: For the Boston Food Co-Operative grocery stores.
General Info: Monthly, 6 pages
Subscriptions: Indv. $5
Circulation: Total-2,000
Advertising: Inquire for rates.

Beem
See: LIFESTYLE

Bistro Bistro Bits — *Consumer*

Publishing Co: Bistro Bistro Bits, 4021 28th St S, Arlington, VA 22206-2201; Title Tel # (703) 379-0300
Personnel: Publisher-Kathy Edwards
Editorial Description: Baking and cooking tips.
General Info: Yr. Est. 1993, Quarterly

Blooming Foods

Publishing Co: Bloomington Cooperative Services, PO Box 821, Bloomington, IN 47402-0821; Title Tel # (812) 336-5300
Personnel: Editor-Nanette Esseck
General Info: 10x/yr., Trim Size-8 x 11, 8 pages

Bread Pudding Update — *Consumer*

Publishing Co: Prosperity & Profits Unlimited, PO Box 416, Denver, CO 80201-0416; Title Tel # (303) 575-5676
Personnel: Publisher, Editor-A.C. Doyle
Editorial Description: A newsletter that gives new ideas to making bread pudding.
General Info: Yr. Est. 1989, Annually, Trim Size-8½ x 11, Letrpr. press, 4 pages, ISSN: 1042-7139, No Color
Subscriptions: Indv. $5, Inst. $5, Can. $8, For. $9, $5/copy
Circulation: Total-2,000

COFIC Newsletter
See: LAW

Cachepot
See: GARDENING & HORTICULTURE

California Prune News — *Business, Association*

Publishing Co: California Prune Board, 5990 Stoneridge Dr Ste 101, Pleasanton, CA 94588-3234; Title Tel # (510) 734-0150 Title Fax # (510) 734-0525
General Info: Quarterly
Subscriptions: Free To Qualified Recipient
Circulation: Total-1,500

Calorie Control Commentary
See: HEALTH

Canadian College & Univ. Food Service Assn., Newsletter — *Business, Association*

Publishing Co: Canadian College & Univ. Food Service Assn., Food Service Dept., McMaster University, Hamilton, ON L85 4K1 Canada; Title Tel # (905) 525-9140 Title Fax # (905) 527-7274
Personnel: Editor-Julie Gigante
General Info: Yr. Est. 1984, Quarterly
Advertising: Inquire for rates.

Cat Industry Newsletter
See: CATS

Category Report: Foods — *Consumer*

Publishing Co: Marketing Intelligence Service, Ltd., 6473D Route 64, Naples, NY 14512; Title Tel # (716) 374-6326 Title Fax # (716) 374-5217
Personnel: Publisher-Richard Lawrence, Production Mgr.-Patricia Peck
Editorial Description: Combines domestic & foreign new product reviews. Each review typically includes detailed product & packaging descriptions, with illustrations, important manufacturing & marketing innovations, emerging trends, & other background information.
General Info: Monthly, Trim Size-8½ x 11, Mimeo press, No Color
Subscriptions: Indv. $1,000

Catering Service Idea Newsletter
See: BUSINESS & INDUSTRY

Center for Self Sufficiency Update
See: PHILANTHROPY

Cereal Industry Newsletter

Publishing Co: American Phytopathological Society, 3340 Pilot Knob Rd, St. Paul, MN 55121-2055
Fax # (612) 454-0766; Title Tel # (612) 454-7250
Personnel: Publisher-Steven Nelson, Editor-Jody Grider
Editorial Description: Newsletter appears as 1-2 screen pages within each monthly issue of the feature & news journal Cereal Foods World, published by American Assn. of Cereal Chemists, Inc.
General Info: Monthly, ISSN: 0146-6283
Circulation: Total-4,800

Changing Markets   *Business, Consumer*

Publishing Co: National Research Bureau, 150 N. Wacher Drive, Chicago, IL 60601
Tel # (312) 541-0100 Fax # (312) 541-1492 Parent Co.-Reed Reference Publishing, New Providence; Title Tel # (319) 752-5415 Title Fax # (319) 752-3421
Personnel: Publisher-Michael Darnall
Editorial Description: Food trends, promotionals, restaurant, beverage chiefly directed to retail. Marketing trends in all industries.
General Info: (Formerly Food Facts), Yr. Est. 1933, Monthly, Trim Size-8½ x 11, Sheetfed press, 4 pages, 2 Color

Concessionaire, The   *Association*

Publishing Co: Natl. Assn. of Concessionaires, 35 E. Wacker Dr., Ste. 1545, Chicago, IL 60601-2202; Title Tel # (312) 236-3858 Title Fax # (312) 236-7809
Personnel: Editor-Susan Cross
Editorial Description: Monthly newsletter describing new products, industry news for leisure time food service.
General Info: Yr. Est. 1959, Quarterly, Trim Size-8½ x 11, Offset press, 12 pages, 2 Color, Coated
Circulation: Total-1,200
Printing Co: Reinhardt-LaShore Press, 1104 S. Wabash Ave., Chicago, IL 60605
Tel # (312) 427-7377, Fax # (312) 427-0970

Convivium   *Consumer*

Publishing Co: Convivium, PO Box 835, East Liverpool, OH 43920-5835
Personnel: Publisher-Catherine Vodrey
Editorial Description: Cooking tips and recipes as well as cookbook and catalog reviews.
General Info: Bi-monthly, Trim Size-8½ x 11, 8 pages
Subscriptions: Indv. $22

Cook & Tell   *Consumer*

Publishing Co: Cook & Tell, Love's Cove, W. Southport, ME 04576; Title Tel # (207) 633-3928
Personnel: Publisher-Karyl Bannister
Editorial Description: Thoughts about food and cooking.
General Info: Yr. Est. 1982, 10x/yr., Trim Size-7 x 8.5, Offset press, 12 pages, Matte, Saddle-stitched
Subscriptions: Indv. $16, Can. $18, For. $23, $2/copy
Circulation: Total-2,000
Printing Co: Lincoln County Publishing Co., Box 36 Damariscotta, Newcastle, ME 04553
Tel # (207) 563-3171

Cook Speak   *Business, Consumer*

Publishing Co: Food Ink, PO Box 155, Wallingford, VT 05773-0155 Tel # (802) 446-7381
Fax # (802) 775-6085; Title Tel # (802) 446-2381
Personnel: Publisher, Editor, Circ. Mgr., Production Mgr., Adv. Dir., Art Dir., Mktg. Dir., Promotion Dir.-Sharon Nimtz
Editorial Description: A seasonal narrative with recipes
General Info: (Formerly Food Ink), Yr. Est. 1994, Bi-monthly, Trim Size-8½ x 11, Offset press, 10 pages, Matte
Subscriptions: Indv. $18, $4/copy
Printing Co: Prime Offset, 56 West St, Rutland, VT 05701 Tel # (802) 773-7211, Fax # (802) 747-7754

Cookbook Gossip Newsletter   *Consumer*   **CPM: $400**

Publishing Co: Cookbook Collectors Club of America, PO Box 56, Saint James, MO 65559-0056; Title Tel # (314) 265-8296
Editorial Description: Monthly newsletter of the Cookbook Collectors Club of America.
General Info: Yr. Est. 1990, Monthly, Trim Size-8½ x 11, Offset press, 11 pages, Other
Subscriptions: Indv. $20, $2/copy
Circulation: Total-250
Advertising: $100.
List Rental: Rents Lists
Printing Co: Triad Printing Co., 630 S Bishop Ave, Rolla, MO 65401-4349

Cookbook Review, The
See: BOOKS & BOOK TRADE

Cookies
See: BAKING

Cooking Connection, The   *Consumer*

Publishing Co: Recipes Unlimited, 12125 16th Ave S # 1271, Burnsville, MN 55337-2982; Title Tel # (612) 890-6655
Personnel: Editor-Janet L. Sadlack
Editorial Description: Up-to-date microwave cooking information, including recipes, methods, new features and answers to questions.
General Info: (Formerly Microwave Times), Yr. Est. 1975, Bi-monthly, 16 pages, No Color, Newsprint, Saddle-stitched
Subscriptions: Indv. $12, Can. $13
List Rental: List Management Co.: Aggressive List Management, 18-2 E Dundee Rd Ste 101, Barrington, IL 60010-5273 Tel # (708) 304-4030, Fax # (708) 304-4032, Actives: 20,000, $75/M

Cooking Contest Chronicle   *Business, Consumer*

Publishing Co: Cooking Contest Chronicle, Box 10792, Merrillville, IN 46411-0792; Title Tel # (219) 736-1168
Personnel: Publisher, Editor-Karen Martis
Editorial Description: Cooking contests, prize-winning recipes, contest hints, tips, food trends, book reviews, free recipe booklets, entry blanks and subscriber news.
General Info: Yr. Est. 1985, Monthly, Trim Size-8½ x 11, Letrpr. press, 8 pages, 2 Color
Subscriptions: Indv. $20, Can. $23, $3/copy
Acquistions: Publication Bought, Publication Sold
Circulation: Total-2,500

Cooking Contest Newsletter   *Consumer*

Publishing Co: Cooking Contest Newsletter, PO Box 339, Summerville, SC 29484-0339; Title Tel # (803) 871-1570
Personnel: Publisher-Joyce Campagna
Editorial Description: Contests, winning recipes, and industry news as well as cookbook reviews and cooking tips.
General Info: Yr. Est. 1991, Monthly, Trim Size-8½ x 11, 6 pages, ISSN: 1061-4729, 2 Color, Coated
Subscriptions: Indv. $20

Cooking on the Edge   *Consumer*

Publishing Co: Cooking on the Edge, 175 Fifth Avenue, Suite 2117, New York, NY 10010
Personnel: Publisher-Julie Cornfield, Graphic Designer-Julie Schuman
Editorial Description: The only food newsletter with al chocolate cake recipe in every issue. Covers what's worth making from the back of the box, personal views on cooking and eating in unusual circumstances, recipes you never got around to clipping, reader request cheerfully answered, famous recipes reconsidered, and reader's fave recipes.
General Info: Bi-monthly
Subscriptions: Indv. $18

Cooks Corner, The   *Consumer*

Publishing Co: Cooks Corner, PO Box 50116, Irvine, CA 92619-0116; Title Tel # (310) 641-9105
Title Fax # (310) 641-9105
Personnel: Publisher-William Bracken, Editor-Michelle Bracken, Production Mgr.-Frank DeLuna
Editorial Description: Cooking tips, recipes, and ideas for those who love to cook.
General Info: Yr. Est. 1993, Bi-monthly, Trim Size-8½ x 11, Desktop press, 8 pages, 2 Color, Saddle-stitched
Subscriptions: Indv. $22, Inst. $18, Can. $22, $4/copy
Circulation: Total-375, Readership-400
Advertising: Accepts Inserts.
List Rental: Rents Lists

Cook's Notebook

Publishing Co: Gingerbread House Pubs., 11216 N 500 E, Ossian, IN 46777-9728; Title Tel # (219) 622-4868
Personnel: Publisher, Editor-Avis Hulvey
Editorial Description: Recipe sharing newsletter, test-kitchen memberships, sponsors recipe round robins.
General Info: Yr. Est. 1983, Bi-monthly, Trim Size-5½ x 8½, Offset press, 16 pages, No Color
Subscriptions: Indv. $8, $2/copy

Corporate Consumer Forum Trendletter
See: HOME ECONOMICS

Cranberry Station Newsletter

Publishing Co: Cranberry Experiment Station, Glen Charlie Rd., Box 569, E. Wareham, MA 02538; Title Tel # (617) 295-2212 Title Fax # (508) 285-6387
Personnel: Editor-Anne Averill
General Info: 10x/yr., 2 pages
Printing Co: Printman, 13253 Brunswick Rd, Grass Valley, CA 95945-9388 Tel # (416) 273-7354

Curmudgeon's Home Companion, The   *Consumer*

Publishing Co: The Curmudgeon's Home Companion, PO Box 3312, Yountville, CA 94599-3312
Personnel: Publisher, Editor-Dan Goldberg
Editorial Description: A rabid little newsletter about food and the dark side of modern manners, with recipes.
General Info: Yr. Est. 1993, Monthly, Trim Size-8½ x 11, Sheetfed press, 4 pages, ISSN: 1069-3564, No Color, Matte
Subscriptions: Indv. $18, Inst. $18, Can. $22, For. $28, $3/copy
Circulation: Total-750

D'Agostino Consumer Newsletter   *Consumer*

Publishing Co: D'Agostino Supermarkets, 1385 Boston Post Rd, Larchmont, NY 10538-3904
Personnel: Editor-Mary Stoner Moore
Editorial Description: Food, diet, and product info from D'Agostino's.
General Info: Quarterly, Trim Size-8½ x 11, 6 pages, 4 Color, Coated

DFISA Technical Bulletin
See: DAIRY

Dog Industry Newsletter
See: DOGS

Down the Hatch

Publishing Co: Mofungo Foundation, 92 Perry St Apt 9, New York, NY 10014-5513
Personnel: Editor-Robert Sietsema
General Info: Bi-monthly

Dreaded Broccoli   *Consumer*

Publishing Co: Dreaded Broccoli, 121 W. 92nd St., New York, NY 10025; Title Tel # (212) 662-5451
Title Fax # (212) 663-2407
Editorial Description: Covers low-fat foods and cooking.
General Info: Yr. Est. 1992, Quarterly
Subscriptions: Indv. $14

Environment News Digest (END)

Publishing Co: Foodservice & Packaging Institute Inc., 1901 N Moore St Ste 1111, Arlington, VA 22209-1706; Title Tel # (202) 822-6420
Personnel: Editor-Charles Felix
General Info: Quarterly, 24 pages, 2 Color, Newsprint
Subscriptions: Indv. $5
Circulation: Total-5,000
Printing Co: Potomac Press, 405 Glenn Dr Ste 5, Sterling, VA 20164-4432 Tel # (703) 450-7827

Epicurean Revue   *Consumer*

Publishing Co: Epicurean Revue, PO Box 35128, Sarasota, FL 34242-5128; Title Tel # (813) 346-2008 Title Fax # (813) 349-4370
Personnel: Publisher-J. Prade, Adv. Dir.-G. Brown
Editorial Description: Features information on fine food and cuisine.
General Info: Yr. Est. 1983, Monthly, Trim Size-8½ x 11, 8 pages
Subscriptions: Indv. $89
Circulation: Total-10,000

FDA Outline
See: GOVERNMENT

FISA Distributor News   *Business, Association*

Publishing Co: Food Industries Suppliers Assn., 401 Brokenwood Lane, Farifield Glade, TN 38558; Title Tel # (615) 456-2205
Personnel: Editor-Thomas Watkins
Editorial Description: Distributors who sell equipment & supplies to the food processing industry.
General Info: Yr. Est. 1968, Quarterly, Trim Size-11 x 14
Circulation: Total-475

FPM & SA Focus   *Business, Association*

Publishing Co: Food Processing Machinery & Supplies Assn., 200 Daingerfield Rd., Alexandria, VA 22314-2884; Title Tel # (703) 684-1080 Title Fax # (703) 548-6563
Personnel: Publisher-George Melnykovich, Editor-Wesley Trochlil
General Info: (Formerly Executive Update), Yr. Est. 1977, Bi-monthly, Sheetfed press, 16 pages, 2 Color, Coated
Circulation: Total-3,000

Fare Share-The Food Letter *Consumer*

Publishing Co: Fare Share Co., 4709 Weyhill Dr, Arlington, TX 76013-5450; Title Tel # (817) 457-2273
Personnel: Editor-Gail Curnutt
Editorial Description: Recipe exchange publication and cookbook news.
General Info: Yr. Est. 1983, Bi-monthly, 12 pages, ISSN: 1052-3898, Matte
Subscriptions: Indv. $16, Can. $17, For. $19, $3/copy

Feasting Fancies

Publishing Co: Fanciful Feasting Caterers, 486 Union Ave, Brooklyn, NY 11211-3435; Title Tel # (718) 782-6875
Editorial Description: Tips on party & menu planning, recipes & full menus for groups of various sizes.
General Info: Yr. Est. 1985, Quarterly, Mimeo press, 4 pages
Subscriptions: $3/copy

Festivities
See: ENTERTAINMENT

Food & Beverage Newsletter
See: SAFETY

Food & Drink Daily   *Association, Business*

Publishing Co: King Communications Group, 627 National Press Building, Washington, DC 20045-1601 Fax # (202) 662-9719; Title Tel # (202) 638-4260 Title Fax # (202) 662-9744
Personnel: Publisher-Llewellyn King, Editor-Linda Gasparello, Circ. Mgr.-Dawn Miles, Production Mgr.-Tony Russell, Art Dir.-Tony Campana
Editorial Description: News on the food & beverage industry world-wide. Food and drink daily also covers newly emerging nutracenticals and functional foods.
General Info: (Formerly World Food & Drink Report), Yr. Est. 1985, Daily, Trim Size-8½ x 11, Sheetfed press, 10 pages, ISSN: 0885-7946, Ind/Abs/Online: NewsNet, DIALOG, Predicasts, 2 Color, Newsprint, Saddle-stitched
Subscriptions: Indv. $925, $7/copy
Acquistions: Publication Bought

Food & Nutrition

Publishing Co: U.S. Dept. of Agriculture, Food & Nutrition Service, Alexandria, VA 22302 Tel # (202) 447-8046
Personnel: Editor-Jan Kern
Editorial Description: Info on nutrition and family service programs.
General Info: Yr. Est. 1971, Quarterly
Subscriptions: Indv. $5
Circulation: Total-5,000

Food & Nutrition Bulletin

Publishing Co: U.N. Univ., Cambridge Programme Office, MIT, Cambridge, MA 02139-3594
General Info: Yr. Est. 1978, Quarterly
Subscriptions: Indv. $30
Circulation: Total-5,500

Food & Nutrition Newsletter
See: NUTRITION

Food Chemical News   *Business*

Publishing Co: CRC Press Inc., 1101 Pennsylvania Ave SE, Washington, DC 20003-2229; Title Tel # (202) 544-1980 Title Fax # (202) 546-3890
Personnel: Publisher-Majorie Weiner, Editor-Natalie Pargas, Circ. Dir.-Iris Shamaskin, Mktg. Dir.-Jill Casasola
Editorial Description: Covers regulation of food & color additives, pesticides & allied products.
General Info: Yr. Est. 1959, Weekly, Trim Size-8½ x 11, Sheetfed press, 70 pages, ISSN: 0015-6337, Ind/Abs/Online: Predicasts,NewsNet, Dialog, 2 Color
Subscriptions: Indv. $1,097

Food Conspiracy Newsletter

Publishing Co: Food Conspiracy, Inc., 412 N 4th Ave, Tucson, AZ 85705-8443; Title Tel # (602) 624-4821
Personnel: Publisher, Editor-Sue James, Adv. Dir.-John Mulle
Editorial Description: Discussions of cooperative businesses, natural food, health.
General Info: (Formerly Coyote), Yr. Est. 1972, Monthly, Trim Size-11⅜ x 17, Web press, 8 pages, No Color, Newsprint
Subscriptions: Indv. $5, Free
Circulation: (100% controlled)
Advertising: Inquire for rates. Accepts Inserts.

Food Distribution Research Society Newsletter   *Association*

Publishing Co: Food Distributor Research Society, PO Box 441110, Fort Washington, MD 20749-1110; Title Tel # (301) 292-1970 Title Fax # (301) 292-1787
Personnel: Editor-Dale Anderson
General Info: Yr. Est. 1972, Quarterly, Sheetfed press, 16 pages, Newsprint
Subscriptions: Indv. $50, Inst. $25
Circulation: Total-400
Printing Co: Silesia Companies, Inc., 619 Broad Creek Dr, Fort Washington, MD 20744-5806 Tel # (301) 292-2600

Food and Drink Weekly   *Business*

Publishing Co: Sparks Companies Inc., 6708 Whittier Ave, Mc Lean, VA 22101-4529 Tel # (703) 734-8787 Fax # (703) 893-1065
Editorial Description: A weekly up to date information on the food and beverage industry
General Info: (Formerly Food and Drink Daily), Yr. Est. 1985, Weekly, ISSN: 1044-1433
Subscriptions: Indv. $925

Food Drug Cosmetic Law Reports
See: DRUGS & PHARMACEUTICALS

Food First Books   *Association*

Publishing Co: Institute for Food & Development, 398 60th St, Oakland, CA 94618-1212; Title Tel # (510) 654-4400 Title Fax # (510) 654-4551
Personnel: Publisher-Denise Newman
Editorial Description: Membership newsletter, lists relevant books.
General Info: Yr. Est. 1975, Quarterly, Trim Size-8½ x 11, 4 pages, Matte, Saddle-stitched
Subscriptions: Indv. $30, Free To Qualified Recipient
Circulation: Total-15,000
List Rental: Rents Lists

Food History News   *Business, Consumer*

Publishing Co: Food History News, HCR 81, Box 354A, Islesboro, ME 04848; Title Tel # (207) 734-8140
Personnel: Publisher, Editor-Sandra L. Oliver
Editorial Description: Covers domestic and military foodways in the US from the earliest settlements to the 20th century. Includes food history events, exhibits, symposia and practical information on recreating past foodways. Serves museum cooks, reenactors, culinary historians, food professionals and others interested in food history.
General Info: Yr. Est. 1989, Quarterly, 10 pages, ISSN: 1067-1951, Matte
Subscriptions: Indv. $12, Inst. $15, Can. $12, For. $18, $2/copy
Circulation: Total-600
Printing Co: County Copy, Main St., Belfast, ME 04915

Food Industry Futures-A Strategy Service *Business*

Publishing Co: C.R.S., Inc., PO Box 430, Fayetteville, NY 13066-0430; Title Tel # (315) 682-7455
Title Fax # (315) 682-7455
Personnel: Publisher, Editor-Ian Cuthill
Editorial Description: Makes industry leaders aware of new developments concerning management or marketing practices, mergers & aquisitions, products, processes, packages, technology, economics, government regulations, trade policies, etc. It covers the industry from farm to r tail stores, mostly in the U.S. but also internationally.
General Info: Yr. Est. 1971, Semi-monthly, Trim Size-8½ x 11, Letrpr. press, 4 pages, ISSN: 0046-4414, No Color
Subscriptions: Indv. $150, For. $180, $10/copy
Acquistions: Publication Bought
List Rental: Rents Lists

Food Industry Newsletter *Business*

Publishing Co: Newsletters, Inc., P.O. Box 342730, Bethesda, MD 20827-2730;
Title Tel # (301) 469-8507 Title Fax # (301) 469-7271
Personnel: Publisher-Ellis Meredith, Editor-Ray Marsili, Circ. Mgr.-Alice Corcoran
Editorial Description: Concise, objective report for busy food excutives, covering major industry deverlopments, including mergers and acouisitions, new trends & products, corporate & marketing strategies, FTC.
General Info: (Formerly Food Marketing Briefs), Yr. Est. 1972, 30x/yr., Trim Size-8½ x 11, Web press, 6 pages, ISSN: 0890-720X, Matte
Subscriptions: Indv. $245, Inst. $245, Can. $270, For. $290, $15/copy
Acquistions: Publication Bought
Printing Co: Plymouth Printing, 1200 Cushing Pl SE, Washington, DC 20003-3599
Tel # (202) 488-7777, Fax # (202) 863-1078

Food Industry Report *Business*

Publishing Co: Food & Nutrition Press Inc., 2 Corporate Drive, Box 374, Trumbull, CT 06611-1338
Tel # (203) 261-8587 Fax # (203) 261-9724
Personnel: Editor-Gerald C. Melson
Editorial Description: Significant news of the food and related industries including: new products, food laws & regulations, price trends of ingredients, food career opportunities, and more.
General Info: Monthly
Subscriptions: Indv. $55

Food Institute Report *Business*

Publishing Co: The Food Institute, 28-12 Broadway, Fair Lawn, NJ 07410-3913
Fax # (201) 791-5222; Title Tel # (201) 791-5570 Title Fax # (201) 794-4568
Personnel: Editor-Brian Todd
Editorial Description: Weekly posting on developments affecting distribution of food products.
General Info: Yr. Est. 1928, Weekly, 24 pages, ISSN: 0745-4503
Subscriptions: Indv. $550, For. $535
Circulation: Total-6,500

Food Labeling & Nutrition News

Publishing Co: CRC Press Inc., 1101 Pennsylvania Ave SE, Washington, DC 20003-2229
Tel # (202) 544-1980 Fax # (202) 546-3890
Personnel: Publisher-Mariorie Weiner, Editor-Brenon McDunell, Circ. Dir.-Iris Shasmakin, Mktg. Dir.-Jill Casasola
Editorial Description: A comprehensive information source on legislation and regulation of food and beverage labeling, advertising, and packaging.
General Info: (Formerly Food Labeling News), Yr. Est. 1992, Weekly, Letrpr. press, 30 pages, Saddle-stitched
Subscriptions: Indv. $797

Food Labeling: A user's Manual *Business, Association*

Publishing Co: National Food Processors Assn., 1401 New York Ave. NW, Washington, DC 20005-2154 Tel # (202) 639-5934 Fax # (202) 637-8068; Title Tel # (202) 393-0890
Editorial Description: A comprehensive, loose-leaf guide to food labeling regulations, for in-plant use, including nutrition labeling, serving sizes rules, ingredient declarations, and nutrient content claims.
General Info: Looseleaf
Subscriptions: Indv. $750, Can. $750, For. $850

Food Marketing Briefs
See: ADVERTISING & MARKETING

Food News for Consumers *Consumer*

Publishing Co: U.S. Dept. of Ag-FSIS, Rm. 1165, S. Bldg. 12th &, Independence, Washington, DC 20250-0001; Title Tel # (202) 447-9351 Title Fax # (202) 475-5460
Personnel: Editor-Mary Parmley, Art Dir.-Loren Gifford
Editorial Description: An update on USDA stands on food safety & nutrition research.
General Info: Yr. Est. 1980, Quarterly, Trim Size-8½ x 11, 16 pages, 2 Color, Coated
Subscriptions: Indv. $5
Acquistions: Publication Bought
Circulation: Total-13,000

Food, the Newsletter! *Consumer*

Publishing Co: QEC & S, 4057 North Drake, Chicago, IL 60618-2219 Tel # (312) 267-5269
Editorial Description: Recipes, tips, information on free recipe booklets, food news.
General Info: Yr. Est. 1995, Bi-monthly
Subscriptions: $2/copy

Food Packaging and Labeling Newsletter *Business*

Publishing Co: Food & Nutrition Press Inc., 2 Corporate Drive, Box 374, Trumbull, CT 06611-1338
Tel # (203) 261-8587; Title Tel # (203) 227-6596 Title Fax # (203) 261-9724
Personnel: Publisher-John O'Neil, Editor-Stanley Sacharow
Editorial Description: Contains information on the latest trends, emerging markets, and legislation in food packaging and labeling.
General Info: Yr. Est. 1977, Monthly, Trim Size-8½ x 11
Subscriptions: Indv. $74, Inst. $71, Can. $71, For. $90, $6/copy

Food Processing Machinery News

Publishing Co: Werner Lehara, Inc., 301 East Erie Street, Chicago, IL 60611-3037;
Title Tel # (616) 784-3111
Personnel: Editor-Roy G. Hlavacek
General Info: (Formerly F.P.M. News), Yr. Est. 1984, Quarterly, 6 pages
Circulation: Total-4,000

Food Protection Report

Publishing Co: Charles Felix Assocs., PO Box 1581, Leesburg, VA 22075-1581;
Title Tel # (703) 777-7448 Title Fax # (703) 777-4453
Personnel: Publisher, Editor-Charles Felix, Circ. Mgr.-Kathleen Felix
Editorial Description: Covers food protection issues of interest to Federal, State & Local Health Officials & food industry executives responsible for quality, safety, or training.
General Info: Yr. Est. 1985, Monthly, Offset press, 12 pages, ISSN: 0884-0806, 2 Color, Newsprint
Subscriptions: Indv. $135, $10/copy
Circulation: Total-3,000
Printing Co: Potomac Press, 405 Glenn Dr Ste 5, Sterling, VA 20164-4432 Tel # (703) 450-7827

Food Safety Notebook

Publishing Co: LYDA Assocs., Inc., PO Box 700, Palisades, NY 10964-0700;
Title Tel # (914) 359-8282 Title Fax # (914) 359-1229
Personnel: Publisher, Editor-Lillian Langseth, PH.D., Mng. Editor-Jennifer Shapiro, Circ. Mgr.-Karen Isaksen
Editorial Description: Covers food safety issues.
General Info: Yr. Est. 1990, 10x/yr., Trim Size-8½ x 11, Offset press, 10 pages, ISSN: 1050-1843, Ind/Abs/Online: DIALOG, EBSCO, UMI, Information Access, Color-cover, Matte
Subscriptions: Indv. $75, Inst. $55, Can. $55, For. $65, $6/copy
Circulation: Total-600
Printing Co: Minuteman Press, 260 Livington St., Northvale, NJ 07647 Tel # (201) 767-5604, Fax # (201) 767-6471

Food Service Management Briefing *Business*

Publishing Co: Qualified Solutions Consulting Group, 23629 Suncrest Avenue, Moreno Valley, CA 92553 Tel # (909) 653-8778
Editorial Description: Information on improving restaurant profitability.
General Info: Yr. Est. 1994, Monthly
Subscriptions: Indv. $240

Foods Adlibra *Consumer*

Publishing Co: Komp Information Services, Inc., 811 Fountain Ave, Louisville, KY 40222-6729;
Title Tel # (502) 426-7754
Personnel: Publisher, Editor-Joel Komp
Editorial Description: Current awareness newsletter with citations.
General Info: Yr. Est. 1974, Semi-monthly, Trim Size-8½ x 11, Sheetfed press, 60 pages, ISSN: 0146-9304, Ind/Abs/Online: DIALOG, No Color
Subscriptions: Indv. $75, For. $275, $10/copy

Foodservice Newsletter *Business*

Publishing Co: United Fresh Fruit & Vegetable Assn., 727 N Washington St, Alexandria, VA 22314-1924; Title Tel # (703) 836-3410
Personnel: Editor-Elaine McLaughlin
General Info: Yr. Est. 1979, Monthly, ISSN: 0194-763X
Subscriptions: Indv. $20
Circulation: Total-4,800

Foodservice Planning
See: RESTAURANTS & CATERING

Foodtalk *Business, Consumer*

Publishing Co: Foodtalk, Box 6543, San Francisco, CA 94101-0120; Title Tel # (415) 386-3067
Personnel: Publisher, Editor-Elaine Douglas Cahn, Art Dir.-Tara Cahn
Editorial Description: Deals with the background of food: history, ceremony, folklore, ritual, habit, etc. It also features interviews with people professionally involved with food & book reviews.
General Info: Yr. Est. 1978, Quarterly, Trim Size-8½ x 11, Offset press, 8 pages, ISSN: 1065-0067, No Color
Subscriptions: Indv. $15, Inst. $18, Can. $19, For. $19, $4/copy
Circulation: Total-5,000

Fried Rice Times
See: RESTAURANTS & CATERING

Frugal Consumers Dollar Stretching Possibility Newsletter
See: CONSUMER INTERESTS

Garlic Times
See: NUTRITION

Gift Basket Idea Newsletter
See: GIFTS, GAMES, TOYS

Gloria Pitzer's Secret
Recipes Publications   *Business, Consumer*

Publishing Co: Gloria Pitzer's Secret Recipes Publications, PO Box 237, Marysville, MI 48040-0237; Title Tel # (810) 329-7696 Title Fax # (810) 329-0811
Personnel: Editor-Gloria Pitzer, Circ. Mgr., Adv. Dir.-Paul Pitzer
Editorial Description: Contains 80 recipes per issue, restaurant reviews, cookbook reviews, household hints, radio broadcast food reviews and recipe presentations, humorous & thoughtful articles.
General Info: Yr. Est. 1973, Quarterly, Trim Size-8½ x 11, Web press, 20 pages, No Color, Saddle-stitched
Subscriptions: Indv. $16, $5/copy
Acquistions: Publication Bought
Circulation: Total-5,000

Gluten Free Pantry   *Consumer*

Publishing Co: Gluten Free Pantry, PO Box 881, Glastonbury, CT 06033-0881; Title Tel # (203) 633-3826
Personnel: Publisher-Beth Hilson
Editorial Description: Fat-free, healthy recipes, tips and information for your favorite foods.
General Info: Bi-monthly

Gold Coast News
See: REGIONAL INTEREST

Grace Kirschenbaum's
World of Cookbooks   *Consumer*

Publishing Co: World of Cookbooks, 1645 S. Vineyard Ave, Los Angeles, CA 90019-5735; Title Tel # (213) 933-1645 Title Fax # (213) 933-1645
Personnel: Publisher, Editor-Grace Kirschenbaum
Editorial Description: Reviews of cookbooks. Each issue authoritatively reviews 70+ cookbooks & other food-related books, American & foreign, primarily new & some antiquarian & past published. Also contains inside news of forthcoming books, authors, new trends, editorial matte s regarding cookbooks, etc.
General Info: (Formerly World of Cookbooks), Yr. Est. 1987, Quarterly
Subscriptions: Indv. $40, Inst. $65, Can. $50, For. $50

Grilled News   *Consumer*

Publishing Co: Austin Grill, 2404 Wisconsin Ave NW, Washington, DC 20007-1845; Title Tel # (202) 337-8080
Editorial Description: Tex-mex cooking tips and recipes.
General Info: Quarterly

Guide to U.S. Food Labeling Law
See: ADVERTISING & MARKETING

Guide to U.S. Food Safety
Law   *Business*

Publishing Co: Thompson Publishing Group, 747 Third Ave., New York, NY 10017 Tel # (212) 888-7220 Fax # (212) 486-3400; Title Fax # (800) 999-2320
Personnel: Publisher-Ken Gesser, Editor-James Martin, Production Mgr.-R.D. Whitney, Mktg. Dir.-Kevin Mahon
Editorial Description: Analyses all FDA, USDA, and EPA food safety regulations, including HACCP requirements and new standards on microbiological tests, irradiation, and more. Subscription includes monthly updates and bulletins plus special reports on latest changes.
General Info: Yr. Est. 1994, Monthly, Looseleaf
Subscriptions: Indv. $547

Healthy Eating   *Business, Association*

Publishing Co: Paul Gillette Enterprises, 3284 Barham Blvd Apt 201, Los Angeles, CA 90068-1454; Title Tel # (213) 876-7590 Title Fax # (213) 876-4090
Personnel: Publisher-Paul Gillette, Editor-Norvelle A. Harris, M.D., Adv. Dir.-Marc Wright
Editorial Description: Articles by physicians on the pleasures of the table, consistent with good health. Includes recipes, book reviews, and interviews.
General Info: Yr. Est. 1992, Irregular, ISSN: 1071-4449
Subscriptions: Indv. $48, Inst. $96, Can. $100, For. $120, $5/copy
Advertising: Accepts Inserts.
List Rental: Actives: 14,000

Healthy Exchanges   *Consumer*

Publishing Co: Healthy Exchanges, PO Box 124, Des Moines, IA 50301-0124
Editorial Description: Low fat healthy food recipes and ideas.
General Info: Monthly

Hivelights   *Business, Association*

Publishing Co: Fran Kay & Associates, RR#2, Chase, BC Canada Tel # (604) 679-5362 Fax # (604) 679-5362; Title Tel # (306) 862-3844 Title Fax # (306) 862-5122
Personnel: Editor-Linda Gane
General Info: (Formerly Canadian Honey Council News), Quarterly, 10 pages
Subscriptions: Indv. $30
Circulation: Total-800
Advertising: Inquire for rates.
List Rental: Rents Lists

IFMA World   *Association*

Publishing Co: Intl. Foodservice Mfrs. Assn., 180 N Stetson Ave Fl 4400, Chicago, IL 60601-6710; Title Tel # (312) 644-8989
Personnel: Publisher-Michael Licata, Editor-Jane Rustigan
General Info: Yr. Est. 1981, Bi-monthly, 8 pages, 2 Color, Newsprint
Circulation: (100% controlled), Total-1,800

IFPRI Report
See: INTERNATIONAL AFFAIRS

Ice Cream Reporter   *Business*

Publishing Co: FIND/SVP, the Information Clearinghouse, Inc., 625 Avenue of Americas, New York, NY 10011-2095; Title Tel # (212) 645-4500 Title Fax # (212) 645-7681
Personnel: Editor-Howard Waxman
Editorial Description: News on ice cream products and the industry.
General Info: Yr. Est. 1987, Monthly, 8 pages, ISSN: 0897-3261, Ind/Abs/Online: Newsnet
Subscriptions: Indv. $395
List Rental: Rents Lists
Printing Co: Mathias & Carr, 75 Varick St., New York, NY 10013 Tel # (212) 226-6000, Fax # (212) 966-0712

Il Cuoco   *Consumer*

Publishing Co: Galileo, 1110 21st St NW, Washington, DC 20036-3303; Title Tel # (202) 331-0997
Personnel: Publisher-Roberto Donna
Editorial Description: Discusses travels and cooking ideas from Chef Roberto Donna.
General Info: Bi-monthly

In the Kitchen   *Consumer*

Publishing Co: Meredith Corp., 1716 Locust St, Des Moines, IA 50309-3023 Tel # (515) 284-3000 Fax # (515) 284-3343
Personnel: Editor-Jan Turner Hazard
Editorial Description: Reports on restaurant, cooking, market and nutrition news.
General Info: Yr. Est. 1994, Monthly, Trim Size-8½ x 11, 8 pages

International Cooking
Contest Newsletter

Publishing Co: Lorensen International Communications, PO Box 380022, San Antonio, TX 78280-0022
Personnel: Publisher-Mary Otero Lorensen
Editorial Description: News on a wide range of cooking contests.
General Info: Yr. Est. 1987, Bi-monthly
Subscriptions: Indv. $18

International Food
Regulatory Monitor   *Business*

Publishing Co: Newsletter Services, Inc., 9700 Philadelphia Ct., Lanham, MD 20706-4405; Title Tel # (301) 731-5202 Title Fax # (301) 731-5203
Personnel: Publisher-Lisa A. Anthony, Editor-Jerome Boin, Circ. Mgr.-Priscilla Arenas, Mktg. Dir.-Susan Pangman
Editorial Description: Provides official, English language texts of regulations regarding food safety, labeling, transportation & storage. Covers intl. standardizatiion efforts as well as regulations from individual countries.
General Info: Yr. Est. 1995, Monthly
Subscriptions: Indv. $495, For. $545

Jewish Vegetarians Newsletter
See: RELIGIOUS & THEOLOGICAL

Just Good Food   *Consumer*

Publishing Co: Just Good Food, 1955 W Cornelia Ave, Chicago, IL 60657-1021; Title Tel # (312) 549-9139
Personnel: Publisher, Editor-John Ryan
Editorial Description: For busy people who love to cook good foods.
General Info: Monthly
Subscriptions: Indv. $24

Kamora Culinary Trends   *Association, Consumer*

Publishing Co: Kamora Culinary Club, PO Box 11172, Chicago, IL 60611-0172
Editorial Description: Facts about Mayan/Mexican culture interspersed with recipes for food and drinks from this liqueur maker.
General Info: Quarterly

Kashrus Faxletter   *Business, Consumer*

Publishing Co: Yeshiva Birkas Reuven, PO Box 204, Brooklyn, NY 11204-0204; Title Tel # (718) 336-8544
Personnel: Publisher-Yosef Wikler, Editor-Yosef Winkler, Circ. Mgr., Mktg. Dir.-Faigie Weingarten
Editorial Description: Faxed monthly product update for kosher consumers and the kosher food trade.
General Info: Yr. Est. 1991, Monthly
Subscriptions: Indv. $30
Circulation: Total-125, Readership-125

Katherine's of Broadway Market
Business, Consumer

Publishing Co: Ken Weisbrod Productions, PO Box 5359, Chatsworth, CA 91313-5359; Title Tel # (818) 718-0644
Personnel: Publisher-Dolores Weisbrod, Editor-Emily Adamczyk, Circ. Mgr.-Kary Weisbrod, Production Dir.-Ken Weisbrod, Art Dir.-Louis Weisbrod
Editorial Description: Food industry and product news, etc.
General Info: Yr. Est. 1987, Trim Size-8½ x 11, Sheetfed press, 8 pages, 4 Color, Coated
Advertising: $500.

Keeping Pace
Consumer

Publishing Co: Pace Foods, Ltd., PO Box 12636, San Antonio, TX 78212-0636
Editorial Description: For aficionados of Pace's picante sauce.
General Info: Quarterly, Trim Size-8½ x 11, 8 pages, 4 Color, Coated, Saddle-stitched

Kitchen Times

Publishing Co: Howard Wilson & Co., 185 Marlborough St., Boston, MA 02116-1827; Title Tel # (617) 266-2453 Title Fax # (617) 437-9983
Personnel: Publisher, Editor-Howard Wilson, Adv. Dir.-Patrice Pisano, Art Dir.-Tracey Lethbridge, Circ. Mgr., Production Mgr., Promotion Dir.-Patricia Connolly
Editorial Description: Readable, witty, newsletter on food & cooking.
General Info: Yr. Est. 1975, Monthly, Mimeo press, 8 pages, 2 Color, Newsprint
Subscriptions: Indv. $27, $3/copy
Circulation: Total-500
List Rental: Rents Lists

Kosher Kettle
See: ETHNIC

Life Enthusiast Newsletter

Publishing Co: Life Enthusiast Co-Op, PO Box 4415, Federal Way, WA 98063-4415; Title Tel # (206) 952-4264
Personnel: Publisher-Larry Meier
General Info: Yr. Est. 1989, Monthly, 4 pages
Subscriptions: $2/copy

Link, The
Business, Association   CPM: $208

Publishing Co: R&D Associates, 16607 Blanco Rd Ste 501, San Antonio, TX 78232-1940; Title Tel # (210) 493-8024 Title Fax # (210) 493-8036
Personnel: Publisher-James Fagan, Editor-Maryeene Fagan
Editorial Description: News of interest to R&D associates. Latest foodservice, equipment, and food news in Armed Forces.
General Info: Yr. Est. 1946, Quarterly, Trim Size-8½ x 11, Offset press, 16 pages, Color
Subscriptions: Indv. $40, Inst. $25, Can. $40, $20/copy
Circulation: (100% controlled), Total-1,200, Readership-11,000
Advertising: $250. Accepts Inserts.
List Rental: Actives: 9,000, $100/M

Low Fat for Life
Consumer   CPM: $23

Publishing Co: Coffee Pot Press, PO Box 3906, Greenville, SC 29608-3906; Title Tel # (803) 294-9807 Title Fax # (803) 246-7340
Personnel: Publisher-William Mason, Editor-Elizabeth Mason
Editorial Description: Lowfat recipes, product information, motivational material recipe analysis.
General Info: (Formerly Recipe Friends), Yr. Est. 1993, Monthly, Trim Size-8½ x 11, 6 pages, Other
Subscriptions: Indv. $15
Circulation: Total-300
Advertising: $7. Accepts Inserts.

Magic Bread Letter
See: BAKING

Mail Order Spice House
Consumer

Publishing Co: Mail Order Spice House, PO Box 1633, Milwaukee, WI 53201-1633
Editorial Description: Variety of spices along with recipes and cooking ideas.
General Info: Annually

Make it Tasty with No/Low Salt--How To & Receipe Blends Edition
Business, Consumer

Publishing Co: Prosperity & Profits Unlimited, PO Box 416, Denver, CO 80201-0416; Tel # (303) 575-5676
Personnel: Editor-A. Doyle
Editorial Description: Spice blends & recipes with no or low salt.
General Info: Yr. Est. 1989, Irregular, Trim Size-8½ x 11
Subscriptions: Indv. $7, Inst. $7, Can. $9, For. $12, $7/copy

Make it Tasty Spice Co. Blends Food Business Newsletter
Business

Publishing Co: Prosperity & Profits Unlimited, PO Box 416, Denver, CO 80201-0416; Title Tel # (303) 575-5676
Personnel: Publisher-A. Doyle
Editorial Description: Recipes for food businesses using various no-salt spice blends.
General Info: (Formerly Food Business Letter), Yr. Est. 1993, Annually, Trim Size-8½ x 11
Subscriptions: Indv. $25, Inst. $25, Can. $29, For. $32, $25/copy
Circulation: Total-3,000

Market Strategy Forecast
Business

Publishing Co: Cahners Publishing Co., 275 Washington St., Newton, MA 02158-1630 Fax # (617) 558-4470 Parent Co.-Reed Elsevier, New York; Title Tel # (617) 964-3030
Personnel: Publisher-Barry Reese, Editor-Lori Brassaw, Circ. Mgr.-Michelle Desimone, Production Mgr.-Chris Blotcher
Editorial Description: Economic outlook & analysis for the foodservice industry & its major suppliers. Written for professionals on the foodservice industry to help them plan & market better.
General Info: Monthly, Desktop press, 6 pages, Color, Matte
Subscriptions: Indv. $159, For. $179, $15/copy

Marvelous Market
Consumer

Publishing Co: Marvelous Market, 5016 Connecticut Ave NW, Washington, DC 20008-2023
Editorial Description: Contains information on breads, pastry, and other foods.
General Info: Quarterly
Subscriptions: Free To Qualified Recipient

Microwaves and Food Newsletter
See: ELECTRIC & ELECTRONIC EQUIPMENT

Mimi Sheraton's Taste
See: RESTAURANTS & CATERING

Monthly Price Review
Business

Publishing Co: Urner Barry Publications, Inc., PO Box 389, Toms River, NJ 08754-0389; Title Tel # (908) 240-5330 Title Fax # (908) 341-0891
Personnel: Editor-Paul Brown, Production Mgr.-Bill Curro, Adv. Dir.-Lisa Sharkus, Promotion Dir.-Sheila Deane
Editorial Description: Lists monthly prices & averages for poultry, eggs, & egg products.
General Info: Yr. Est. 1858, Monthly, Trim Size-11 x 17, Sheetfed press, 4 pages, ISSN: 0566-3628, No Color, Newsprint
Subscriptions: Indv. $125, Can. $128, For. $134, $15/copy
Circulation: Total-307

NACUFS News Wave

Publishing Co: Natl. Assn. of College Univ. Food Services, 1405 S. Harrison, Manly Miles Bldg., Ste 304, E. Lansing, MI 48824; Title Tel # (517) 332-2494 Title Fax # (517) 332-8144
Personnel: Editor-Mary Jo Custer
Editorial Description: Covers news of interest to Food Service industry personnel in academic institutions.
General Info: (Formerly NACUFS Newsletter Digest), Yr. Est. 1968, Quarterly, Sheetfed press, 32 pages, Color, Newsprint
Circulation: Total-2,600

NPFFA News
Association

Publishing Co: National Prepared Frozen Food Assn., 1415 Queene Ann Rd #201, Teaneck, NJ 07666-3521; Title Tel # (201) 837-8200 Title Fax # (201) 837-9770
Personnel: Editor-Vee Soto
Editorial Description: Newsletter that tells what is going on in the association & important topics, areas of concern or news inthe industry.
General Info: (Formerly Executive Bulletin), Quarterly, Trim Size-8½ x 11, Offset press, 4 pages, 2 Color, Newsprint
Circulation: Total-300
Printing Co: Graphic House, PO Box 1017, Passaic, NJ 07055-1017 Tel # (201) 472-2800, Fax # (201) 472-0773

N.Y. Food Letter
Consumer

Publishing Co: N.Y. Food Letter, 50 W 67th St # 6c, New York, NY 10023-6227; Title Tel # (212) 873-9068
Personnel: Publisher-William Gillen
Editorial Description: Shopping and cooking advice.
General Info: Monthly, Trim Size-8½ x 11, 6 pages, ISSN: 1065-7967
Subscriptions: Indv. $20, $2/copy

National Food Processors Association - Information Letter
Association   CPM: $205

Publishing Co: National Food Processors Assn., 1401 New York Ave. NW, Washington, DC 20005-2154 Fax # (202) 637-8068; Title Tel # (202) 639-5934 Title Fax # (202) 637-8018
Personnel: Editor-Michelle Spring, Adv. Dir.-Jenet K. Hawkins, Art Dir.-John Klinovsky
Editorial Description: A bi-weekly update on food industry activities, including new regulations new legislation, consumer issues, scientific & technical developments & more.
General Info: (Formerly Information Letter), Yr. Est. 1923, Bi-weekly, Trim Size-8½ x 11, Offset press, 8 pages, 2 Color, Matte
Subscriptions: Indv. $100, Inst. $50, For. $110, $4/copy
Circulation: Total-2,800
Advertising: $575.
List Rental: Actives: 2,800, $200/M

National Packing News
Business   CPM: $80

Publishing Co: National Packing News, 403 Main St # 1349, Murphys, CA 95247-9628; Title Tel # (209) 728-1455 Title Fax # (209) 728-3277
Personnel: Publisher, Editor-Jack W. Soward, Adv. Dir.-Beryl E. Day
Editorial Description: A newsletter for & about the food processing industry. Directed toward production & marketing management personnel. Contians information about plants, products, trends, and people.
General Info: Yr. Est. 1937, Monthly, Trim Size-8½ x 11, Offset press, 8 pages, 40% ads, Color
Subscriptions: Indv. $25, Can. $35, For. $48
Circulation: Total-2,500
Advertising: $200.

Natural Selections
Consumer

Publishing Co: Isla Vista Food Co-Op, 6575 Seville Rd, Isla Vista, CA 93117-5073; Title Tel # (805) 968-1411
Personnel: Editor-Robert Terry
Editorial Description: Isla Vista Food Coop Newsletter about nutrition, health, ecology, consumer news and cooperated news.
General Info: Monthly, Trim Size-8½ x 11, Letrpr. press, 8 pages, Recycled
Subscriptions: Indv. $20, Inst. $20, Can. $20, For. $30, $2/copy
Circulation: Total-500
Advertising: Inquire for rates.
Printing Co: Alternative Graphics, 5780 Hollister Ave, Goleta, CA 93117-3418 Tel # (805) 964-8875

New Product News
See: GROCERY

News from CAST
See: AGRICULTURE

Newsletter for People with Lactose Intolerance and Milk Allergy
See: HEALTH

North River Trading Post
See: ETHNIC

Nutrition Funding Report, The
See: HEALTH

Nutrition Legislation News
See: NUTRITION

Ontario Dairy Council, News & Views
See: DAIRY

Organic Food Business News
Business   **CPM: $400**

Publishing Co: Hotline Publishing, PO Box 161132, Altamonte Springs, FL 32716-1132 Tel # (407) 628-1377 Fax # (407) 628-9355; Title Tel # (701) 774-8757 Title Fax # (701) 774-0419
Personnel: Publisher, Editor-Dennis Blank
Editorial Description: For buyers, sellers, growers, manufacturers, etc. in the organic food industry.
General Info: Yr. Est. 1989, Monthly, 12 pages
Subscriptions: Indv. $84, Can. $84, For. $84
Circulation: Total-1,000
Advertising: $400.
List Rental: Actives: 2,000, $85/M

P-Nutty News & Notes
Consumer

Publishing Co: Virginia Carolina Peanut Promotions, PO Box 8, Nashville, NC 27856-0008 Tel # (919) 459-9977 Fax # (918) 459-7396; Title Tel # (919) 446-3097
Personnel: Editor-Betsy Owens
Editorial Description: Promotes increased use & consumption of peanuts via receipes & photos.
General Info: Yr. Est. 1957, Quarterly, 1 pages, No Color
Circulation: (100% controlled), Total-17,000
Printing Co: Herald Printing Co., 116 N. McGlohon, Ahoskie, NC 27910 Tel # (919) 332-2123

Peanut Butter & Nut Processors Assn. - Bulletin

Publishing Co: Peanut Butter & Nut Processors Assn., 9005 Congressional Ct, Potomac, MD 20854-4608; Title Tel # (301) 365-4080
Personnel: Editor-James Mack
General Info: Yr. Est. 1939
Circulation: Total-240

Perdue Newsletter
Consumer

Publishing Co: Perdue Farms, P.O. Box 2417 NCL, Salisbury, MD 21802
Editorial Description: Contains recipes, health advice and news.
General Info: Yr. Est. 1994, Quarterly, Trim Size-8½ x 11, 4 pages, 4 Color, Coated

Positively Pasta!
Business, Consumer

Publishing Co: National Pasta Association, 2101 Wilson Blvd., Ste. 920, Arlington, VA 22201-3055; Title Tel # (703) 841-0818 Title Fax # (703) 528-6507
Personnel: Editor-Donna Chowning Reid
Editorial Description: Consumer newsletter with tips and facts on pasta, loaded withrecipes, and nutritional information.
General Info: (Formerly Pastahhh), Yr. Est. 1985, 3x/yr., Trim Size-8½ x 11, Sheetfed press, 8 pages, 4 Color, Coated
Subscriptions: Indv. $4
Circulation: Total-10,000
List Rental: Rents Lists

Practical Gourmet
See: TRAVEL

Pure Facts
See: HEALTH

Quick, Easy, Cheap and Simple..the Newsletter
See: HOME ECONOMICS

RBA Insight
Business, Association

Publishing Co: Retail Bakers of America, 14239 Park Center Dr, Laurel, MD 20707-5261; Title Tel # (301) 725-2149 Title Fax # (301) 725-2187
Editorial Description: Fast facts, tips and ideas for the bakery business mind. Covers trends and developments in the baking industry. Caters to all bakery variations including independent, in store, single or multi-unit specialty bakeries.
General Info: Yr. Est. 1995, Monthly, Trim Size-8.5 x 13, Sheetfed press, 16 pages, 4 Color, Coated, Saddle-stitched
Subscriptions: Free With Membership
Circulation: Readership-4,000

Raisin Consciousness

Publishing Co: Southern California Cooperating Warehouse, 3547 White House Pl, Los Angeles, CA 90004-5944; Title Tel # (213) 233-2667
Personnel: Editor-Mike Cluster
General Info: Quarterly, 20 pages
Subscriptions: Indv. $8

Report on Institutional Foodservice
Business

Publishing Co: Information Central, PO Box 3900, Prescott, AZ 86302-3900 Fax # (602) 445-6407; Title Tel # (602) 778-1513
Personnel: Publisher-A.W. Woodman, Editor-Julie Woodman
Editorial Description: Trends in foodservice for schools, colleges, healthcare, employee foodservices, with major emphasis on the large operation. Prime audience: food & equipment, marketing executives.
General Info: Yr. Est. 1987, Monthly, Sheetfed press, 8 pages
Subscriptions: Indv. $210, Inst. $190, Can. $200, For. $225

Research Notes

Publishing Co: Peat, Marwick, Main & Co., Thanksgiving Tower, 200 Crescent Court St. #300, Dallas, TX 75201-1885; Title Tel # (214) 754-2330
Personnel: Editor-Margaret McClure
General Info: Bi-monthly

Safe Food News
Business, Consumer

Publishing Co: Food & Water, Inc., Rr 1 Box 30, Marshfield, VT 05658-9701; Title Tel # (802) 426-3700 Title Fax # (802) 426-3711
Personnel: Editor-Michael Colby, Mng. Editor-Marion Chartoff
Editorial Description: Provides information about hazards in food and water.
General Info: (Formerly Radiation Reports), Yr. Est. 1991, Quarterly, 6 pages
Subscriptions: Indv. $25, Inst. $100
Circulation: Total-20,000

Savory Thymes
Business

Publishing Co: Savory Times (The), P.O. Box 9115, Stockton, CA 95212 Tel # (209) 931-0434
Editorial Description: Local business in the food, wine and culinary fields.
General Info: Yr. Est. 1994, Monthly
Subscriptions: Indv. $18

Seafood Trend Newsletter
Business

Publishing Co: Seafood Trend Assoc., 8227 Ashworth Ave N, Seattle, WA 98103-4434; Title Tel # (206) 523-2280 Title Fax # (206) 526-8719
Personnel: Publisher, Editor-Ken Talley
Editorial Description: Covers the seafood market.
General Info: Yr. Est. 1984, Bi-weekly, 4 pages
Subscriptions: Indv. $220
Circulation: Total-1,000

Seed Savers Exchange
See: GARDENING & HORTICULTURE

Shiitake News

Publishing Co: Southeastern Minnesota Forest Resource Ctr., Rr 2 Box 156a, Lanesboro, MN 55949-9648; Title Tel # (507) 467-2437
Personnel: Editor-Joe Deden, Art Dir.-Mancie McCormish
General Info: Yr. Est. 1984, 16 pages
Subscriptions: Indv. $25
Circulation: Total-1,000

Shrimp Notes
See: FISH & FISHERIES

Simple Cooking
Consumer

Publishing Co: Simple Cooking, PO Box 88, Steuben, ME 08680-0008
Personnel: Editor-John Thorne, Editor-Matt Lewis Thorne
Editorial Description: Essays on food & cooking, cookbook & product reviews.
General Info: Yr. Est. 1980, Bi-monthly, Trim Size-8½ x 11, Web press, 12 pages, ISSN: 0749-176X, No Color, Matte
Subscriptions: Indv. $24, Can. $27, For. $30, $24/copy
Circulation: Total-2,000
List Rental: Actives: $100/M
Printing Co: L.H. Thompson, 20 S Main St, Brewer, ME 04412-2112 Tel # (207) 989-3280

Smorgasboard-Plenty to Eat Update
Consumer

Publishing Co: Prosperity & Profits Unlimited, PO Box 416, Denver, CO 80201-0416; Title Tel # (303) 575-5676
Personnel: Publisher-A. Doyle
Editorial Description: Possibilites for getting food cheap or almost free.
General Info: (Formerly Smorgasboard U.S.A. Update), Yr. Est. 1983, Irregular, Trim Size-8½ x 11, 20 pages, ISSN: 0738-7458, No Color
Subscriptions: Indv. $3, Inst. $3, Can. $5, For. $6, $3/copy

Soups Cheap or Almost Free
Consumer

Publishing Co: Prosperity & Profits Unlimited, PO Box 416, Denver, CO 80201-0416; Title Tel # (303) 575-5676
Personnel: Publisher, Editor-A. Doyle
General Info: Yr. Est. 1990, Every two years
Subscriptions: Indv. $4, Inst. $4, Can. $5, For. $7, $4/copy

Sproutletter
See: NUTRITION

Stocks for Tomorrow

Publishing Co: N.U. Pizza, 15414 Cabrito Ave., Suite A, Van Nuys, CA 91406
Personnel: Editor-Mark Schultz
Editorial Description: N.U. Pizza holding cororation trades on the O.T.C. bulletin board and operates a chain of restaurants under the name Numero Uno, specializing in pizza and Italian foods.
General Info: Yr. Est. 1973, Trim Size-8½ x 11, 4 pages, 2 Color, Coated, Other

Sugar Notes and News
See: SUGAR

Super Snack News
See: NEWSPAPER INDUSTRY

Supermarket Savvy Information Resource Service
Business

Publishing Co: Leni Reed Associates, Inc., PO Box 666, Herndon, VA 22070-0666; Title Tel # (703) 742-3364 Title Fax # (703) 742-3316
Personnel: Publisher, Editor-Leni Reed
Editorial Description: Up-to-date information about new healthier food products.
General Info: (Formerly Supermarket Scoop), Yr. Est. 1988, Bi-monthly, Trim Size-8½ x 11, 8 pages, ISSN: 1065-3260, 2 Color, Matte, Saddle-stitched
Subscriptions: Indv. $89, Inst. $89, Can. $89, For. $109, $20/copy
Circulation: Total-1,500, Readership-3,000
Advertising: Inquire for rates. Accepts Inserts.
List Rental: Rents Lists
Printing Co: Middleburg Printers, 6 East Federal Street, Middleburg, VA 22117

Supermarket Strategic Alert
See: GROCERY

Survival Food Storage Newsletter

Publishing Co: Survival Food Storage Newsletter, PO Box 362, Calico Rock, AR 72519-0362
General Info: Bi-monthly, 12 pages
Subscriptions: Indv. $4

Taste of Elegance

Publishing Co: Robert Ciraulo, Taste of Elegance, 141 Algonquin Rd, Hampton, VA 23661
Editorial Description: Sensual Foods, Choice Wines, Exciting Travel
General Info: Trim Size-8.5 x 11, 8 pages
Subscriptions: Indv. $2

Tea Times
See: BEVERAGES - BREWING

Technomic Foodservice Digest
Business

Publishing Co: TRA Information Svcs., Division of Technomic, Inc., 300 S Riverside Plz Ste 1940, Chicago, IL 60606-6613; Title Tel # (312) 876-0004 Title Fax # (312) 876-1158
Personnel: Publisher-Ronald Paul, Publications Director-Jan Sneesby, Editor-Mary Sue Mohnke
Editorial Description: Abstracts from 100 publications covering food and the foodservice industry.
General Info: (Formerly TRA Foodservice Digest), Yr. Est. 1971, Monthly
Subscriptions: Indv. $195

Telemarketing Update-Catering Service Business Script Presentations
See: ADVERTISING & MARKETING

Telemarketing Update-Copier Service Business Script Presentations
See: ADVERTISING & MARKETING

Tomato Club, The
See: GARDENING & HORTICULTURE

Transmedia News

Publishing Co: Transmedia, P.O. Box 619400, North Miami, FL 33261; Title Tel # (305) 892-3300 Title Fax # (305) 892-3317
Editorial Description: A Benefit Directory in addition to restaurant listings, many opportunities to use savings on both lodging and dining at the same hotel. Benefits directory to Lodging, Sports & Leisure and more.
General Info: Bi-monthly

Travel Food & Wine
See: TRAVEL

Trend/Wire
Business, Association

Publishing Co: Credenza Company, The, 6620 W. 93 rd Street, Overland Park, KS 66212 Fax # (913) 648-7492; Title Tel # (913) 648-7492
Personnel: Publisher-Art Siemering, Circ. Mgr.-Carol J. Siemering
Editorial Description: A weekly advisory letter on consumer trends that affect the food industey.
General Info: Yr. Est. 1944, Weekly, Trim Size-8½ x 11, Offset press, 2 pages, Matte
Subscriptions: Indv. $175, Can. $245, For. $245, $5/copy
Circulation: Total-500, Readership-1,500

Uncommon Cook

Publishing Co: Golden Apple Pubs., 15208 Carnell St, Whittier, CA 90603-2205; Title Tel # (213) 698-4607
Personnel: Publisher-Carl Nelson, Editor-Esther Nelson
Editorial Description: Culinary articles and information.
General Info: Yr. Est. 1982, Monthly

Urner Barry's Price-Current (West Coast Edition)
Business

Publishing Co: Urner Barry Publications, Inc., PO Box 389, Toms River, NJ 08754-0389; Title Tel # (908) 240-5330 Title Fax # (908) 341-0891
Personnel: Editor-Paul Brown, Sr., Production Mgr.-Bill Curro, Adv. Dir.-Lisa Sharkus, Promotion Dir.-Sheila Deane
Editorial Description: Price quotes for poultry, dairy & egg products on the West Coast.
General Info: Yr. Est. 1978, Semi-weekly, Trim Size-8½ x 11, Sheetfed press, 4 pages, ISSN: 0273-5016, Ind/Abs/Online: COMTELL, Newsprint
Subscriptions: Indv. $140, Can. $160, For. $208, $15/copy
Circulation: Total-150

VFDA Update
Business

Publishing Co: Virginia Food Dealers Assn., Inc., 517 W. Grace St., Richmond, VA 23220-4928; Title Tel # (804) 644-0731 Title Fax # (804) 644-1423
Personnel: Editor-Nadine Kadlubowski
Editorial Description: General information of interest to food retailers & convenience stores.
General Info: Bi-monthly, Trim Size-8½ x 11, Mimeo press, 4 pages, No Color
Circulation: (100% controlled), Total-1,000

VSDC News

Publishing Co: Vegetarian Society of the District of Columbia, PO Box 4921, Washington, DC 20008-0121; Title Tel # (301) 589-0722
Personnel: Editor-Carol South
Editorial Description: Events & articles of interest to vegetarians in the DC area.
General Info: Bi-monthly, Trim Size-8½ x 11, Offset press, 8 pages, 1% ads, No Color, Newsprint
Subscriptions: Indv. $15
Circulation: Total-1,000
Advertising: Inquire for rates. Accepts Inserts.
List Rental: Rents Lists

Vegan News, The
See: ENVIRONMENT & ECOLOGY

Vegetarian Journal's Foodservice Update
Consumer

Publishing Co: Vegetarian Resource Group, PO Box 1463, Baltimore, MD 21203-8804 Tel # (410) 366-8343
Editorial Description: Newsletter for foodservice personnel and others working for healthier food in schools, restaurants, hospitals and other institutions.
General Info: Yr. Est. 1994, Quarterly, ISSN: 1072-0820
Subscriptions: Indv. $20
Circulation: Total-2,000
List Rental: List Management Co.: Names in the News-California, 1 Bush St Bsmt 3, San Francisco, CA 94104-4425 Tel # (415) 989-3350, Fax # (415) 433-7796, Actives: $200/M

Vermont Foodnews Paper
Business, Consumer

Publishing Co: Food Ink, PO Box 155, Wallingford, VT 05773-0155 Tel # (802) 446-7381 Fax # (802) 775-6085
Editorial Description: Chat about food, recipes, news, and trends with the primary focus on Vermont food.
General Info: Yr. Est. 1993, Monthly

Viands In Verse
Business, Association

Publishing Co: Original Traveling Chef, 31 Ridge St, Pittston, PA 18640-9526
Personnel: Editor-Robert Bernoskie, Production Mgr.-K. Vanderoux, Promotion Dir.-B. Delesio
Editorial Description: Covers society news which includes culinary arts, literature, world hunger, environment, health, global brotherhood.
General Info: Yr. Est. 1991, Monthly, 2% ads
Subscriptions: Indv. $22, $4/copy
Advertising: Inquire for rates. Accepts Inserts.

Vinegar Views
Association

Publishing Co: Vinegar Institute, 5775 Peachtree Dunwoody Rd NE, Ste G500, Atlanta, GA 30342-1507; Title Tel # (404) 252-3663 Title Fax # (404) 252-0774
General Info: (Formerly Vinegar Institute News), Quarterly

Virginia Wine Line
Consumer

Publishing Co: Sharline, 586 Truslow Road, Fredericksburg, VA 22406 Tel # (703) 373-1371
Editorial Description: Provides a connection supplying wine lovers with information to enhance their enjoyment of wine, and especially Virginia wine.
General Info: Yr. Est. 1994, Monthly
Subscriptions: Indv. $24

WGA Update
Business, Association

Publishing Co: Wisconsin Grocers Association, 2601 Crossroads Dr Ste 185, Madison, WI 53704-7923; Title Tel # (608) 244-7150
Editorial Description: News and info about the Wisconsin grocers industry.
General Info: Yr. Est. 1992, 5x/yr., Trim Size-8½ x 11, No Color, Matte, Saddle-stitched
Circulation: Total-1,500
Advertising: Inquire for rates.

Weekly Insiders Dairy & Egg Letter
See: DAIRY

Western Growers Assn. - Update

Publishing Co: Western Growers Assn., PO Box 2130, Newport Beach, CA 92658-8944; Title Tel # (714) 863-1000
Personnel: Editor-Gregg Payne
General Info: Yr. Est. 1972, Bi-weekly
Circulation: Total-2,700

Working Wine Guide, The
See: BEVERAGES - BREWING

World Chemical News
Business

Publishing Co: Food Chemical News, 1101 Pennsylvania Ave SE, Washington, DC 20003-2229 Parent Co.-CRC Press, Inc., Boca Raton; Title Tel # (202) 544-1980 Title Fax # (202) 546-3890
Personnel: Publisher-Marjorie Weiner, Editor-Declan Conray, Mktg. Dir.-Jill Casasola
Editorial Description: Covers international development in food and beverage regulation.
General Info: Yr. Est. 1994, Bi-weekly, ISSN: 1073-2357, Ind/Abs/Online: newsnet, dialog
Subscriptions: Indv. $787

World of Cookbooks
Consumer

Publishing Co: World of Cookbooks, 1645 S. Vineyard Ave, Los Angeles, CA 90019-5735; Title Tel # (213) 933-1645
Personnel: Editor-Grace Kirschenbaum
Editorial Description: Extensive information on cookbooks, culinary news, etc.
General Info: Yr. Est. 1986, Quarterly
Subscriptions: Indv. $40

The Zealot

Publishing Co: Jeff McFadden, R.E. Foods, 820 Struthers, Grand Junction, CO 81501
Editorial Description: The Zealot is a tongue-in-cheek behind-the-scenes look at R.E. foods and the people that work there.
General Info: Trim Size-8.5 x 11, 2 pages

FOOTBALL

5th Down
Association

Publishing Co: Football Writers Association of America, PO Box 1022, Edmond, OK 73083-1022; Title Tel # (405) 341-4731
Personnel: Editor-Volney Meece
Editorial Description: Established to improve working conditions in college press boxes.
General Info: Yr. Est. 1964, 7x/yr.
Subscriptions: Free With Membership
Circulation: Total-825
Printing Co: Edmond Printing, Edmond, OK 73083

Draft Insiders' Digest
Consumer

Publishing Co: Draft Insiders' Digest, PO Box 702, Red Bank, NJ 07701-0702 Tel # (908) 842-4749
Editorial Description: Covers National Football League season and draft picks. Rates top 600 college players and top 30 teams.
General Info: 6x/yr., Trim Size-8½ x 11, 10 pages
Subscriptions: Indv. $20

G&W Recruiting Service
Business

Publishing Co: G&W Recruiting Service, PO Box 2021, Sanatoga, PA 19464-0902; Title Tel # (610) 327-2553
Personnel: Publisher-Phil Grosz
Editorial Description: Covers the high school football player recruiting done by colleges.
General Info: 7x/yr.
Subscriptions: Indv. $35

Gold Sheet

Publishing Co: Nation Wide Sports Publications, 2316 216th Pl NE, Redmond, WA 98053-6324; Title Tel # (206) 868-2907
Personnel: Editor, Adv. Dir.-Ronald Ward
Editorial Description: Football & baseball game analysis, predictions, logs & statistical studies.
General Info: Yr. Est. 1956, Weekly, 20 pages, Ind/Abs/Online: Newsnet, Coated
Subscriptions: Indv. $150, $5/copy

Insider, The
Consumer

Publishing Co: Inside Publishing, 2351 W. Northwest Hwy., Ste. 2115, Dallas, TX 75220-4434 Tel # (214) 233-7547
Personnel: Publisher-David Vaughn
Editorial Description: Dallas football plus other Texas sports team information faxed three times a week.
General Info: Yr. Est. 1990, Semi-weekly, Trim Size-8½ x 11, 2 pages
Subscriptions: Indv. $149
Advertising: Inquire for rates.

People to People Sports Newsletter
See: SPORTS & SPORTING GOODS

South Bend Football Recruiting News
Consumer

Publishing Co: South Bend Football Recruiting News, 281 Bruce Ct., Westerville, OH 43081
Editorial Description: Complete coverage of Notre Dame (IN) recruiting.
General Info: 5x/yr.
Subscriptions: Indv. $18

Sports Weekly Newsletter-Football
Consumer

Publishing Co: R.W. Livingston, Publishing, PO Box 60008, North Charleston, SC 29419-0008; Title Tel # (803) 797-6173
Personnel: Editor-R. W. Livingston
General Info: Weekly, Trim Size-11 x 17, Offset press, 4 pages
Subscriptions: Indv. $40
Circulation: Total-500

Woof!
Consumer, Association

Publishing Co: Western New York Browns Backers, 106 Woodgate Terrace, Rochester, NY 14625 Fax # (716) 288-3122; Title Tel # (716) 482-3641 Title Fax # (714) 288-3122
Editorial Description: Monthly newsletter for fans of the Cleveland Browns.
General Info: Yr. Est. 1992, Monthly
Subscriptions: Indv. $10, Can. $20, For. $30
Circulation: Total-400, Readership-600

FORESTRY

Alaska Branching Out

Publishing Co: University of Alaska, Cooperative Extension, 193 Arctic Health Bldg., Fairbanks, AK 99775-6180; Title Tel # (907) 474-6356 Title Fax # (907) 474-7439
Personnel: Editor-Tony Gasbarro
Editorial Description: Focuses on forestry in Alaska.
General Info: Yr. Est. 1983, Quarterly, 6 pages
Subscriptions: Free
Circulation: Total-835

Alaska Forest Products Newsletter
Business

Publishing Co: University of Alaska, Cooperative Extension, 193 Arctic Health Bldg., Fairbanks, AK 99775-6180; Title Tel # (907) 474-6356 Title Fax # (907) 474-7439
Personnel: Editor-Tony Gasbarro
Editorial Description: Developments of interest to forest products industry in Alaska.
General Info: Yr. Est. 1966, Quarterly, Trim Size-8½ x 11, Offset press, 10 pages, 1% ads, No Color, Newsprint
Subscriptions: Free
Circulation: Total-660
Advertising: Inquire for rates.
List Rental: Rents Lists

American Bamboo Society-Newsletter
See: GARDENING & HORTICULTURE

American Wildlands
See: ENVIRONMENT & ECOLOGY

Arbor Day

Publishing Co: National Arbor Day Foundation, 100 Arbor Ave, Nebraska City, NE 68410-1099; Title Tel # (402) 474-5655
Personnel: Editor-John Rosenow
Editorial Description: Promotes trees & the tree-related activities of the Foundation & other groups.
General Info: (Formerly Arbor Day Foundation News), Yr. Est. 1978, Bi-monthly, Trim Size-8½ x 11, Web press, 8 pages, 4 Color, Coated
Subscriptions: Free With Membership
Circulation: Total-1,000,000
List Rental: List Management Co.: List Services Corp., 6 Trowbridge Dr., PO Box 516, Bethel, CT 06801-2858 Tel # (203) 743-2600, Fax # (203) 743-0589, Actives: 1,025,000, $75/M, Hotline: 100,000, $85/M

Arizona Forestry Notes *Consumer*

Publishing Co: Northern Arizona University, School of Forestry, Publications, Flagstaff, AZ 86011-0001; Title Tel # (602) 523-3031
Personnel: Editor-L.D. Garrett
General Info: Yr. Est. 1966, 20 pages
Circulation: Total-500

Association of BC Professional Foresters Newsletter *Business, Association*

Publishing Co: Assn. of British Columbia Foresters, 1130 W. Pendes Street, Ste 1201, Vancouver, BC V6E 4A4 Canada; Title Tel # (604) 687-8027 Title Fax # (604) 687-3264
Personnel: Publisher, Editor-A. Furniss
Editorial Description: Action taken on all assoc. business by elected members of council at monthly meetings.
General Info: Yr. Est. 1947, Bi-monthly, Trim Size-8½ x 11, Mimeo press, 10 pages, No Color
Subscriptions: Indv. $35, Can. $43, Free With Membership
Circulation: Total-3,000

Association of British Columbia Professional Foresters, Highlights

Publishing Co: Assn. of British Columbia Foresters, 1130 W. Pendes Street, Ste 1201, Vancouver, BC V6E 4A4 Canada Fax # (604) 687-3264; Title Tel # (604) 687-8027
General Info: Monthly

Chips
See: CLUBS

Citizen Forester, The; Western Forest Report *Consumer, Association*

Publishing Co: Public Forestry Foundation, PO Box 371, Eugene, OR 97440-0371; Title Tel # (503) 687-1993
Editorial Description: Promotes socially responsible forestry thorugh citizen involvement and education.
General Info: (Formerly Publica Forester, The), Quarterly
Subscriptions: Indv. $25, Inst. $50, Free With Membership

City Trees
See: PUBLIC MANAGEMENT & PLANNING

Entomological Society of Canada, Bulletin
See: ENTOMOLOGY

FPRS Member Newsletter *Consumer, Association*

Publishing Co: Forest Products Society, 2801 Marshall Ct., Madison, WI 53705-2257 Fax # (608) 231-2152; Title Tel # (608) 231-1361
Personnel: Editor-Arthur Brauner
Editorial Description: FPRS and its members' activities.
General Info: Yr. Est. 1968, Semi-annually, Trim Size-8½ x 11, Offset press, 4 pages, No Color
Circulation: Total-4,500

FPRS Technical Newsletter Series: Timber Harvesting and Merchandising
See: LUMBER & WOOD

Fish & Wildlife Reference Service Newsletter
See: ENVIRONMENT & ECOLOGY

Forest Forum *Consumer, Association*

Publishing Co: Canadian Forestry Assn., 185 Somerset St. W., #203, Ottawa, ON K2P 0J2 Canada; Title Tel # (613) 232-1815 Title Fax # (613) 232-4210
Personnel: Editor-Glen Blouin
General Info: (Formerly Forestry on the Hill), Yr. Est. 1983, Semi-annually, 80 pages, ISSN: 0828-6299, No Color, Saddle-stitched
Subscriptions: Indv. $25, Can. $25
Circulation: Total-2,000
Advertising: Inquire for rates.
Printing Co: Mutual Hadwen Imaging Technologies, 2211 Thurston Dr., Ottawa, ON K1B 3R1 Canada Tel # (613) 736-1380, Fax # (613) 736-1143

Forest Industry Affairs

Publishing Co: Ahlfeld & Assocs., PO Box 19187, Washington, DC 20036-9187; Title Tel # (301) 320-3416
Personnel: Editor-Bill Ahlfeld
Editorial Description: Covers public policy issues of concern to both wood and paper companies.
General Info: Yr. Est. 1966, Semi-monthly, Trim Size-8½ x 11, 4 pages
Subscriptions: Indv. $175, Can. $195

Forest Land Owner *Association*

Publishing Co: Forest Landowners of California, 3807 Pasadena Ave Ste 100, Sacramento, CA 95821-2863; Title Tel # (916) 972-0273
Personnel: Publisher, Editor-Thomas Kerr, Circ. Mgr.-Janice Kabel
Editorial Description: Newsletter reporting on legislation, regulation, & related issues of concern to small woodland owners in California & the West.
General Info: Bi-monthly, Trim Size-8½ x 11, Letrpr. press, 6 pages, ISSN: 0735-8199, No Color
Subscriptions: Indv. $75, $7/copy
Circulation: Total-200
Advertising: Inquire for rates.

Forest Log *Association*

Publishing Co: Oregon Dept. of Forestry, 2600 State St., Salem, OR 97310-1336; Title Tel # (503) 945-7422 Title Fax # (503) 945-7212
Personnel: Publisher-Doug Decker, Editor-Brian Ballou
Editorial Description: For Oregon forest landowners, educators and news media; reports on department services, statewide forestry issues, etc.
General Info: Yr. Est. 1930, Bi-monthly, Trim Size-8½ x 11, Offset press, 8 pages, No Color
Subscriptions: Free
Circulation: (100% controlled), Total-3,000

Forest People *Association* CPM: $156

Publishing Co: Ontario Forestry Association, 150 Consumers Rd., Suite 502, Willowdale, ON M2J 1P9 Canada; Title Tel # (416) 493-4565 Title Fax # (416) 493-4608
Personnel: Editor-J.D. Coats
Editorial Description: Promotes full utlization and protection of Onatrio's natural resources.
General Info: (Formerly Ontario Forestry Association Newsletter), Yr. Est. 1968, Quarterly, Trim Size-8½ x 11, Sheetfed press, 16 pages, ISSN: 0834-2008, 2 Color, Newsprint, Saddle-stitched
Subscriptions: Indv. $35
Circulation: (75% controlled), Total-800
Advertising: $125. Accepts Inserts.

Forestry Alumni Newsletter
See: COLLEGE ALUMNI

Forestry, Conservation Communications Association News and Views

Publishing Co: Forestry, Conservation Communications Assn. News, 3821 Roosevelt Road, West Little Rock, AR 72204-6369 Tel # (501) 664-2531
Editorial Description: Technical journal designed to inform Canadian forestry personnel of developments in the fields of forest management, wild life management, economics, soils and other phases of forestry.
General Info: Quarterly
Subscriptions: Indv. $8, $3/copy
Circulation: Total-2,500
Advertising: Inquire for rates.

Forestry Update *Consumer*

Publishing Co: Oregon State University, School of Forestry, Publications, Corvallis, OR 97331; Title Tel # (503) 737-3700
Personnel: Editor-Dave Cleaves
Editorial Description: Describes research and new forestry techniques of interest to land managers in Pacific Northwest.
General Info: Yr. Est. 1975, Quarterly, Trim Size-8½ x 11, 8 pages, No Color
Circulation: Total-3,000

Health and Safety Resource *Business, Association*

Publishing Co: Ontario Natural Resources Safety Assn., PO Box 2050, Stn. Main, 690 McKeownn Ave., North Bay, ON P1B 9P1 Canada Tel # (705) 474-7233; Title Tel # (705) 472-7233 Title Fax # (705) 472-5800
Personnel: Editor-G. V. Lightfoot
Editorial Description: Resource carries news & feature stories about current issues in health & safety for the mining, forestry & pulp & paper industries in Ontario.
General Info: (Formerly Tallyboard; Safety News; Paper Maker, The), Yr. Est. 1954, Bi-monthly, Trim Size-8½ x 11, 8 pages, ISSN: 0712-3094, 2 Color
Circulation: (100% controlled), Total-2,500

ISTF News
Business, Association   CPM: $245

Publishing Co: International Society of Tropical Foresters, 5400 Grosvenor Ln, Bethesda, MD 20814-2161; Title Tel # (301) 897-8720 Title Fax # (301) 897-3690
Personnel: Publisher-Warren T. Doolittle, Editor-Frank Wadsworth, Production Mgr.-James Clark, Adv. Dir.-Rodney Young
Editorial Description: Information on tropical forestry.
General Info: Yr. Est. 1980, Quarterly, Trim Size-8½ x 11, Web press, 12 pages, ISSN: 0276-2056, No Color, Matte
Subscriptions: Indv. $25, Inst. $40, Can. $25
Circulation: (45% controlled), Total-2,200, International-1,200
Advertising: $540.
Printing Co: Printing Impressions ,Inc., 671A South Lawn Lane, Rockville, MD 20850 Tel # (301) 217-0400, Fax # (301) 217-0404

Illinois Forest Management Newsletter

Publishing Co: Univ. of Illinois at Urbana Champaign, 227 Illini Union, 1401 W. Green Street, Urbana, IL 61801 Tel # (217) 333-1477 Fax # (217) 333-7803; Title Tel # (217) 333-2666 Title Fax # (217) 333-1952
Personnel: Publisher-Michael Bolin
Editorial Description: Management information & tips for woodland owners on silviculture, planting, wildlife management, forest investments & taxes, marketing, harvesting; insect & disease problems residential tree care & care of wood products.
General Info: Semi-annually
Subscriptions: Indv. $6

Information Forestry

Publishing Co: Sponsor-Canadian Forestry Service, Forestry Canada Pacific & Yukon, 506 W. Burnside Road, Victoria, BC V8Z 1M5 Canada Tel # (604) 363-0610; Title Tel # (604) 388-0600
Personnel: Publisher, Editor-Elaine Teske
General Info: Yr. Est. 1972, Trim Size-8½ x 11, Offset press, 8 pages, Saddle-stitched
Subscriptions: Free
Circulation: Total-3,250

Kentucky's Growing Gold   *Business, Consumer*

Publishing Co: Kentucky Div. of Forestry, Forest Products Utilization Secti, 627 Commanche Trl, Frankfort, KY 40601-1753; Title Tel # (502) 564-4496 Title Fax # (502) 564-6553
Personnel: Publisher, Editor-Larry Lowe
Editorial Description: Advertisements & items of interest to the lumbering and wood industry with private timber stumpage for sale.
General Info: Yr. Est. 1960, Quarterly, Trim Size-8½ x 11, Sheetfed press, 10 pages, No Color, Recycled, Saddle-stitched
Subscriptions: Free
Circulation: (100% controlled), Total-600
Advertising: Inquire for rates. Accepts Inserts.

Madison's Canadian Lumber Reporter
See: LUMBER & WOOD

Morris Arboretum Newsletter
See: BOTANY

NAA Reporter

Publishing Co: Natl. Arborist Assn. (NAA), Meeting Place Mall, PO Box 1094 Rt. 101, Amherst, NH 03031-1094 Tel # (603) 673-8952 Fax # (603) 672-2613; Title Tel # (603) 673-3311
Personnel: Editor-Robert Felix
Editorial Description: Assn. newsletter for member firms.
General Info: Monthly, No Color
Subscriptions: Free With Membership
Circulation: Total-1,000

Natural Resources Computer Newsletter
See: ENVIRONMENT & ECOLOGY

Northbound   *Association*

Publishing Co: Trees for Tomorrow Inc., 611 Sheridan St., Eagle River, WI 54521; Title Tel # (715) 479-6456 Title Fax # (715) 479-2318
Personnel: Editor-Nicholas Petterssen
Editorial Description: An educational pub. focusing on natural resource issues for members, teachers & students in Wisconsin, Upper Peninsula of Michigan, & Northern Illinois schools.
General Info: (Formerly Tree Tips), Yr. Est. 1944, Quarterly, Trim Size-11¼ x 13½, Offset press, 12 pages, 2 Color, Newsprint
Subscriptions: Indv. $15, Free With Membership
Circulation: Total-3,000
Printing Co: Vilas County News Review, 330 W. Division, Eagle River, WI 54521 Tel # (715) 479-4421

Nut Kernel, The
See: PRODUCE

Nutshell The
See: AGRICULTURE

Out of the Woods

Publishing Co: Western Forest Industries Assn., 1500 SW Taylor St, Portland, OR 97205-1894; Title Tel # (503) 224-5455
Personnel: Editor-Ralph Saperstein
General Info: Yr. Est. 1946, Weekly
Circulation: Total-200

Resource Hotline

Publishing Co: American Forests, 1516 P St NW, Washington, DC 20005-1932; Title Tel # (202) 667-3300 Title Fax # (202) 667-7751
Personnel: Publisher-Richard Thompson, Editor-Gerald Gray, Production Dir.-Pamela Keogh
Editorial Description: Hotline covers late-breaking national forestry and natural resource policy news.
General Info: Yr. Est. 1985, Bi-weekly, Sheetfed press, 32 pages, 2 Color, Newsprint
Subscriptions: Indv. $45, $2/copy
Circulation: (100% controlled), Total-2,000
Printing Co: Reprint Co., 4019 5th Rd N, Arlington, VA 22203-2102 Tel # (703) 524-8600

Robin
See: ENVIRONMENT & ECOLOGY

SF Newsletter
See: LUMBER & WOOD

SWOAM News   *Business, Association*   CPM: $58

Publishing Co: Small Woodland Owners Association of Maine (SWOAM), PO Box 926, Augusta, ME 04332-0926; Title Tel # (207) 626-0005
Personnel: Editor-Abbott Ladd, Production Mgr.-Debra Ladd
Editorial Description: SWOAM extends knowledge about ownership and management to Maine's 180,000 small woodland owners. SWOAM stresses the value of holding woodlands for the long periods of time that good management practices require.
General Info: Yr. Est. 1975, Monthly, 12 pages, 4% ads, 2 Color, Matte, Saddle-stitched
Subscriptions: Indv. $20, Inst. $25, Can. $25
Circulation: (5% controlled), Total-1,700, Subscriptions-1,600
Advertising: $100.

Save-The-Redwoods League Bulletin
See: ENVIRONMENT & ECOLOGY

Seedling News
See: ENVIRONMENT & ECOLOGY

Treeworker

Publishing Co: Natl. Arborist Assn. (NAA), Meeting Place Mall, PO Box 1094 Rt. 101, Amherst, NH 03031-1094 Tel # (603) 673-8952; Title Tel # (603) 673-3311 Title Fax # (603) 672-2613
Personnel: Editor-Brian Barnard
Editorial Description: Newsletter containing articles on aboriculture.
General Info: Yr. Est. 1982, Monthly, Trim Size-8½ x 11, Offset press, 6 pages, No Color, Matte
Subscriptions: Indv. $15
Circulation: Total-1,500
Printing Co: Min-a-Print, Lincoln Street, Manchester, NH Tel # (603) 669-5221

Two Way Transmissions
See: LUMBER & WOOD

UBC Forester

Publishing Co: Univ. of British Columbia Forest Club, McMillan Bldg., Vancouver, BC Canada; Title Tel # (604) 228-6740
Personnel: Editor-Todd Bell, Adv. Dir.-Pierre LeCourt, Art Dir.-Ken Leader
Editorial Description: A short glimpse at the forestry undergraduate program at the University of British Columbia.
General Info: Yr. Est. 1948, Annually, 78 pages, Color-cover, Coated, Perfect bound
Subscriptions: Indv. $25, Can. $25
Circulation: Total-220
Advertising: Inquire for rates.

Woodland Report   *Association*

Publishing Co: National Woodland Owners Association, 374 Maple Ave E., Ste 210, Vienna, VA 22180-4718 Tel # (703) 255-2700; Title Tel # (703) 255-2300
Personnel: Publisher-Keith Argow, Editor-Eric Johnson
Editorial Description: Late breaking news from Washington DC & state capitals of interest to woodland owners. Includes reports from 32 state affiliates.
General Info: Yr. Est. 1983, 8x/yr., Trim Size-8½ x 14, Offset press, 2 pages, Newsprint
Subscriptions: Indv. $25, Can. $28
Circulation: Total-2,200

Woody Points   *Association*

Publishing Co: NRCAN - Canadian Forest Service, PO Box 6028, St. John's, NF A1C 5X8 Canada; Title Tel # (709) 772-4117 Title Fax # (709) 772-2576
Personnel: Editor-Doug Rex
Editorial Description: An annotated mediagraphy on career and family issues.
General Info: Yr. Est. 1968, Quarterly, Trim Size-8½ x 11, Offset press, 16 pages, ISSN: 0825-6411, 2 Color, Newsprint, Saddle-stitched
Subscriptions: Free
Circulation: (81% controlled), Total-1,200

Yankee Woodlot   *Business*

Publishing Co: Univ. of Maine Cooperative Ext. Serv., 103 Nutting Hall, Orono, ME 04469-0001; Title Tel # (207) 581-2892
Personnel: Editor-Bud Blumenstock
General Info: Yr. Est. 1942
Circulation: Total-4,500

FUNERAL SERVICE

CFSA Newsletter   *Association*

Publishing Co: Casket & Funeral Supply Assn. of America, 708 Church St., Evanston, IL 60201-3867; Title Tel # (708) 866-8383
Personnel: Editor-George Lemke
Editorial Description: News of interest to firms in the funeral supply industry.
General Info: (Formerly CMA Newsletter), Monthly, Trim Size-8½ x 11, Offset press, 4 pages, No Color
Subscriptions: Indv. $75
Circulation: (100% controlled), Total-400

Calgary Co-Operative Memorial Society Ltd. Newsletter   *Consumer*

Publishing Co: Calgary Co-Operative Memorial Society Ltd., 28 Norseman Pl., N.W., Calgary, AB T2K 5M6 Canada; Title Tel # (403) 274-5120
Personnel: Editor-Rick Green
Editorial Description: Information re. funeral preplanning costs, customs and legal requirements.
General Info: Yr. Est. 1957, Annually, Trim Size-9 x 14, 2 pages, No Color

Canadian Estate Planning & Administration Reporter
See: LAW

Funeral Monitor   *Business*

Publishing Co: Abbott & Hast Publications, Inc., 761 Lighthouse Ave., Ste. A, Monterey, CA 93940-1033; Title Tel # (408) 622-9032
Personnel: Publisher-Ronald Hast, Editor-Jean DeSapio, Fashion Ed.-Yytas Banionis, Circ. Mgr.-Gregory Abbott, Production Mgr.-Michael Abbott
Editorial Description: For funeral directors and others related to the funeral industry, including manufacturers, suppliers and dealers of funeral merchandise and equipment, embalmers, cemeteries and students.
General Info: Yr. Est. 1992, Weekly, Trim Size-8½ x 11, 8 pages
Subscriptions: Indv. $199, Can. $218, For. $218, $5/copy
Circulation: Total-1,150

Funeral Service Insider   *Business*

Publishing Co: United Communications Group, 11300 Rockville Pike, Ste. 1100, Rockville, MD 20852-3030 Tel # (301) 816-8950 Fax # (301) 816-8945; Title Tel # (212) 873-3760 Title Fax # (212) 799-1728
Personnel: Publisher-Beverley Walker, Editor-Jean De Sapio, Circ. Mgr.-Pamela Ortiz, Production Mgr.-Eladia Orellana, Art Dir.-Rise Cappadonna, Promotion Dir.-Anne Cheevers
Editorial Description: Newsletter for owners and managers of funeral homes and related services.
General Info: (Formerly Director's Insider, The), Yr. Est. 1963, Weekly, Trim Size-8½ x 11, Sheetfed press, 8 pages, ISSN: 0148-6705, No Color, Newsprint
Subscriptions: Indv. $249, Can. $230, For. $265, $10/copy
Acquistions: Publication Bought, Publication Sold
Circulation: Total-1,500
List Rental: List Management Co.: George Mann & Associates, 569 Abbington Dr., PO Box 930, Hightstown, NJ 08520-9990 Tel # (609) 443-1330, Fax # (609) 443-0397, Actives: $85/M, Hotline: $85/M, Expires: $75/M

Mortuary Science Monitor   *Business*

Publishing Co: Abbott & Hast Publications, Inc., 761 Lighthouse Ave., Ste. A, Monterey, CA 93940-1033 Tel # (408) 622-9032; Title Tel # (213) 665-0101 Title Fax # (213) 665-3068
Personnel: Publisher-Ronald Hast, Editor-Jean DeSapio, Circ. Mgr.-Gregory Abbott, Production Mgr.-Michael Abbott, Promotion Mgr.-Vytas Banionis
Editorial Description: Concerned with the care and preparation of deceased persons for burial. Directed towards licensed embalmers, cornoers, students, mortuary schools, tissue banks, and related professions.
General Info: Yr. Est. 1993, Monthly, Trim Size-8½ x 11, 8 pages
Subscriptions: Indv. $72, Can. $82, For. $82, $7/copy
Circulation: Total-120

NFFS News   *Business, Association*

Publishing Co: Foundation of Funeral Services, 2250 E Devon Ave Ste 250, Des Plaines, IL 60018-4509 Fax # (708) 827-6342; Title Tel # (708) 827-6337
Personnel: Editor-Howard Rather
General Info: (Formerly Facts from the Foundation), Quarterly
Subscriptions: Indv. $20, Free To Qualified Recipient
Circulation: Total-20,000, Readership-20,000
Advertising: Accepts Inserts.

National Selected Morticians Bulletin

Publishing Co: National Selected Morticians, 5 Revere Dr., Ste. 340, Northbrook, IL 60062-8009; Title Tel # (847) 559-9569 Title Fax # (847) 559-9571
General Info: Monthly

State Officers Bulletin   *Association*

Publishing Co: NFDA Publications Inc., 11121 W Oklahoma Ave, P.O. Box 27641, Milwaukee, WI 53227-0641; Title Tel # (414) 541-2500 Title Fax # (414) 541-1909
Personnel: Editor-Robert Harden
Editorial Description: Information pertinent to NFDA state association volunteer leadership regarding the funeral service profession.
General Info: (Formerly NFDA Bulletin to State Officers), Yr. Est. 1948, Bi-weekly, Trim Size-8½ x 11, Mimeo press, 10 pages, Color-cover, Matte, Looseleaf
Subscriptions: Indv. $100, Free To Qualified Recipient
Circulation: Total-550

Woodlawn Cemetery News   *Consumer*

Publishing Co: Woodlawn Cemetery, Webster Ave. & 233rd St., New York, NY 10470 Tel # (718) 920-0556
Personnel: Editor-Jeanne Capodilupo
Editorial Description: Information about Woodlawn Cemetery and activities taking place there.
General Info: Quarterly, Trim Size-8½ x 11, 4 pages, Coated
Subscriptions: Free To Qualified Recipient

FUR

Appraiser, The
See: ANTIQUES & ART GOODS

Fashion Reports   *Business*

Publishing Co: American Fur Industry (AFI), 101 W 30th St # 512, New York, NY 10001-4001; Title Tel # (212) 564-5133
General Info: Yr. Est. 1958, Monthly

Fur Production   *Business, Association*

Publishing Co: Statistics Canada, Holland Ave/RH Coats, Holland Ave/Tunney's Pasture, Ottawa, ON K1A O26 Canada Tel # (613) 951-8116 Fax # (613) 951-0581; Title Tel # (613) 990-8116
Editorial Description: Production of pelts by provinces with source, wildlife or ranch-raised. (#23-207)
General Info: Yr. Est. 1919, Annually, 16 pages, ISSN: 0318-787X
Subscriptions: Indv. $41, Can. $34, For. $48, $41/copy

N.S. Trappers Newsletter   *Business, Association*

Publishing Co: NS Department of Natural Resources, Box 68, Truro, NS B2N 5B8 Canada; Title Tel # (902) 893-5647 Title Fax # (902) 893-6102
Personnel: Editor-Bob Bancroft
Editorial Description: Trapping and furbearer management in Nova Scotia.
General Info: Yr. Est. 1965, Annually, Trim Size-6 x 9, Offset press, 20 pages, ISSN: 0705-4831, 2 Color, Recycled, Saddle-stitched
Circulation: Total-5,100

PETA News
See: ENVIRONMENT & ECOLOGY

Sandy Parker Reports: Weekly Intl. Fur News   *Business*

Publishing Co: Sandford Advertising, Inc., 363 7th Ave, New York, NY 10001-3904; Title Tel # (212) 947-1144 Title Fax # (516) 791-4751
Personnel: Publisher, Editor-Sandy Parker
Editorial Description: Summary & analysis of trade developments.
General Info: Yr. Est. 1977, Weekly, Trim Size-8½ x 11, Sheetfed press, 4 pages, No Color
Subscriptions: Indv. $135, Can. $135, For. $160, $3/copy
Circulation: Total-800
List Rental: Actives: $150/M
Printing Co: Mailchute, 360a W Merrick Rd, Valley Stream, NY 11580-5344

FURNITURE & HOME FURNISHINGS

Commercial Carpet Digest   *Business*

Publishing Co: G. Wentworth Smith, PO Box 71, Columbus, WI 53925-0071; Title Tel # (414) 623-5183 Title Fax # (414) 623-2810
Personnel: Publisher, Editor-G. Wentworth Smith
Editorial Description: Commentary & practical use of carpet terms & industry analysis.
General Info: Yr. Est. 1979, 10x/yr., Sheetfed press, 4 pages, ISSN: 0890-0027
Subscriptions: Indv. $49, Can. $49, For. $60
Circulation: (100% controlled), Total-2,000

Flooring Fax News   *Business*

Publishing Co: Douglas Publications, 9609 Gayton Rd., Ste. 100, Richmond, VA 23233-4904 Tel # (804) 741-6704 Fax # (804) 750-2399
Personnel: Editor-Dave Foster
General Info: Semi-weekly
Circulation: Total-300

Forum   *Business*

Publishing Co: COSEC Intl., Inc., 8141 E 44th St, Tulsa, OK 74145-4846; Title Tel # (918) 622-3903
Personnel: Editor-Robin Larsen
General Info: Yr. Est. 1974, Bi-monthly

Forum Canada

Publishing Co: Tyjak, Inc., 4731 El Camino Ave, Carmichael, CA 95608-4938; Title Tel # (916) 485-8993
Personnel: Publisher-Jack Brandwein
Editorial Description: Canadian furniture news.
General Info: Monthly
Subscriptions: Indv. $110
List Rental: Rents Lists

Forum Furniture FAX

Publishing Co: Tyjak, Inc., 4731 El Camino Ave, Carmichael, CA 95608-4938; Title Tel # (916) 485-8993
Personnel: Publisher-Jack Brandwein
Editorial Description: Furniture news.
General Info: Weekly
Subscriptions: Indv. $99

Forum International

Publishing Co: Forum Intl. Group, Inc., PO Box 6415, High Point, NC 27262-6415; Title Tel # (919) 884-5732
General Info: Yr. Est. 1984, Monthly
Subscriptions: Indv. $200

Furniture Forum

Publishing Co: Forum Intl. Group, Inc., PO Box 6415, High Point, NC 27262-6415; Title Tel # (919) 884-5732
Personnel: Publisher-Jack Brandewein, Editor-Bob Keningham
General Info: Yr. Est. 1973, Monthly

Furniture Transporter

Publishing Co: Bohman Industrial Traffic Consultants, Inc., 335 Broadway, Box 889, Gardner, MA 01440; Title Tel # (508) 632-1913 Title Fax # (508) 945-4815
Personnel: Editor-Ray Bohman, Jr.
Editorial Description: News digest of important developments in packaging, shipping, and transporting that affect the furniture and allied products industries.
General Info: Yr. Est. 1966, Semi-monthly, Trim Size-8½ x 11½, Offset press, 20 pages
Subscriptions: Indv. $49, $2/copy
Circulation: Total-1,000

Haverty's Half Hour   *Business*

Publishing Co: Haverty Furniture Cos. Inc., 866 West Peachtree St NW, Atlanta, GA 30308-1123; Title Tel # (404) 881-1911
Personnel: Editor-Bonnie Webb
General Info: Yr. Est. 1929, Quarterly, Trim Size-8½ x 11, Offset press, 12 pages, 2 Color
Circulation: Total-1,650

IFMA News
See: CONSTRUCTION & BUILDING

ISA Newsletter   *Association*

Publishing Co: International Society of Appraisers, 16040 Christensen Rd., Suite #320, Seattle, WA 98188-2929; Title Tel # (206) 241-0359 Title Fax # (206) 241-0436
Editorial Description: Articles on the practice of personal property appraising upcoming events, and news of the Society.
General Info: (Formerly Appraiser Information Exchange), Yr. Est. 1980, Bi-monthly, Trim Size-11 x 8½, Desktop press, 20 pages, No Color, Matte, Saddle-stitched
Subscriptions: Indv. $12, Inst. $10, $2/copy
Circulation: Total-2,000, Readership-2,000
Advertising: Inquire for rates. Accepts Inserts.
List Rental: Actives: $100/M

Interior Fashion News   *Business*

Publishing Co: Publishing Dynamics, Inc., 15 Bank St., Ste. 101, Stamford, CT 06901-3008; Title Tel # (203) 357-0028 Title Fax # (203) 357-0075
Personnel: Publisher-Martin Johnson, Editor-Anne McConney
Editorial Description: Covers all facets of wallcoverings industry.
General Info: (Formerly Wallcoverings Letter), Yr. Est. 1970, Monthly, 5 pages, No Color, Newsprint
Subscriptions: Indv. $75, For. $80
Circulation: (ABC), Total-7,169

Living in Style

Publishing Co: Citicorp Diners Club-Carte Blanche, 183 Inverness Dr W, Englewood, CO 80112-5203
General Info: Quarterly, Trim Size-8⅛ x 10⅝, 36 pages, 4 Color, Coated, Saddle-stitched
List Rental: Actives: 422,559, $85/M, Hotline: 47,217, $100/M, Expires: 123,525, $90/M

Monday Morning Message

Publishing Co: Forum Intl. Group, Inc., PO Box 6415, High Point, NC 27262-6415; Title Tel # (919) 884-5732
Personnel: Publisher-Jack Brandwein, Editor-John Tobin
General Info: Yr. Est. 1963, Weekly
Subscriptions: Indv. $88

NHMA Reports   *Business, Association*

Publishing Co: National Housewares Manufacturers Assn., 6400 Shafer Ct Ste 650, Rosemont, IL 60018-4929; Title Tel # (708) 292-4200 Title Fax # (708) 292-4211
Personnel: Editor-Deborah Teschke, Production Mgr.-Thomas Goodman
Editorial Description: Promotional news of association activities for association members.
General Info: (Formerly NHMA News), Bi-monthly, Desktop press, 8 pages, 2 Color, Recycled, Saddle-stitched
Subscriptions: Free With Membership
Circulation: Total-5,500
Printing Co: Monarch Printing, 1938 Raymond Dr, Northbrook, IL 60062-6715 Tel # (708) 438-0680, Fax # (708) 498-0688

Perspectives

Publishing Co: Natl. Kitchen & Bath Assn., 687 Willow Grove St., Hackettstown, NJ 07840; Title Tel # (908) 852-0033
Personnel: Editor-Joyce Laurie
Editorial Description: Designers, dealers, distrib, of kitchen cabinets.
General Info: (Formerly National Kitchen; American Institute of Kitchen Dealers), Yr. Est. 1964, Monthly, Desktop press, 12 pages, Color, Newsprint
Circulation: Total-5,000
List Rental: Rents Lists

Tips for Salesmen

Publishing Co: Natl. Wholesale Furniture Assn., 164 S. Main St., #404, Box 2482, High Point, NC 27261-2482; Title Tel # (312) 644-6610
General Info: Monthly

UFAC Volunteer

Publishing Co: Upholstered Furniture Action Council, PO Box 2436, High Point, NC 27261-2436; Title Tel # (919) 885-5065
Personnel: Publisher-E.L. Briggs
General Info: Yr. Est. 1978, Semi-annually, Trim Size-8½ x 11, Letrpr. press, 4 pages, No Color, Newsprint
Circulation: Total-3,000
Printing Co: Crown Printing, Edgeworth St., High Point, NC 27261 Tel # (919) 884-1133

GAMBLING

1H3PA Newsletter & Poker Tips
See: ENTERTAINMENT

Atlantic City Action
See: HOTEL INDUSTRY

Casino Journal's National Gaming Summary   *Business*

Publishing Co: Nevada Casino Journal, 3100 W Sahara Ave Ste 205, Las Vegas, NV 89102-6008 Tel # (702) 253-6230; Title Fax # (702) 253-6804
Personnel: Publisher-Glenn Fine, Editor-Adam Fine
Editorial Description: Information on the national gaming industry including stock update.
General Info: Weekly
Subscriptions: Indv. $198
List Rental: Rents Lists

Contest News Wire   *Consumer*

Publishing Co: S.A. Toney & Assoc., 3750 W Union Ave, Denver, CO 80236-3631; Title Tel # (303) 795-6954
Personnel: Editor-S.A. Toney
Editorial Description: Easy how-to information on the most current sweepstakes and contests. Winning tips. Proven rating system shows best sweepstakes and contests to enter.
General Info: Monthly, Trim Size-8½ x 11, 8 pages, No Color
Subscriptions: Indv. $22, $3/copy
Advertising: Accepts Inserts.

Contest/Sweepstakes Bulletin   *Consumer*

Publishing Co: Eggleston Enterprize, PO Box 27, Milford, NY 13807-0027; Title Tel # (607) 286-3371
Personnel: Editor-Dolores Kilts
Editorial Description: Complete information and rules for entering Sweepstake Contests. Also services.
General Info: Yr. Est. 1937, Bi-weekly
Subscriptions: Indv. $21
Circulation: Total-2,000

Current Blackjack News   *Consumer*

Publishing Co: Pi Yee Press, 7910 Ivanhoe Ave # 34, La Jolla, CA 92037-4511 Tel # (617) 456-4080 Fax # (619) 456-8076
Personnel: Publisher, Editor-Stanford Wong
Editorial Description: Casino by casino update of rules & playing conditions for blackjack.
General Info: Yr. Est. 1979, Monthly, Trim Size-8½ x 11, Desktop press, 8 pages, ISSN: 1081-2363, No Color, Matte, Looseleaf
Subscriptions: Indv. $79, Inst. $79, Can. $79, For. $79, $10/copy
Circulation: Total-750

Experts Blackjack Newsletter   *Consumer*

Publishing Co: Gambling Times, Inc., 16140 Valerio St. #B, Van Nuys, CA 91406-2916; Title Tel # (818) 781-9355 Title Fax # (818) 781-3125
Personnel: Publisher-Stanley Sludikoff, Editor-Cecil Suzuki
Editorial Description: Blackjack (gambling) inside information.
General Info: Yr. Est. 1982, Bi-monthly, Trim Size-8½ x 11, Sheetfed press, 24 pages, 2 Color, Matte, Saddle-stitched
Subscriptions: Indv. $30, $6/copy
Circulation: Total-1,000
List Rental: Actives: $65/M, Expires: $150/M

Gaming Confidential

Publishing Co: Geno Munari, 3426 Biela Ave, Las Vegas, NV 89120-2208;
Title Tel # (702) 456-0621
Personnel: Editor-Geno Munari
General Info: Yr. Est. 1984
Subscriptions: Indv. $24
Circulation: Total-1,000

Handicapping Monthly

Publishing Co: CHRN, PO Box 539, Medinah, IL 60157-0539
Personnel: Publisher-Roger Bruce
Editorial Description: Shows the reader the many ways to handicap horse races. Lists whole races & handicaps two race tracks in each issue.
General Info: Yr. Est. 1982, Semi-monthly, 8 pages, 1% ads
Subscriptions: Indv. $40, Can. $44, $10/copy
Acquisitions: Publication Bought, Publication Sold
Circulation: Total-10,000
Advertising: Inquire for rates.
List Rental: Rents Lists

Harness & Greyhound Racing Handicapping

Publishing Co: CHRN, PO Box 539, Medinah, IL 60157-0539; Title Tel # (708) 307-1333
General Info: Yr. Est. 1990, Bi-monthly
Subscriptions: Indv. $40

Indiana Gaming Insight   *Consumer*

Publishing Co: Insight Group, PO Box 383, Noblesville, IN 46060-0383; Title Tel # (317) 773-8715 Title Fax # (317) 773-9998
Editorial Description: Info on riverboats, horse racing, lottery, bingo, and Indiana raffles.
General Info: Yr. Est. 1993, Weekly, ISSN: 1076-867X
Subscriptions: Indv. $325
Circulation: Total-175
Advertising: Accepts Inserts.
List Rental: Rents Lists

International Gamblers' Club Newsletter   *Consumer*

Publishing Co: Intl. Gaming, Inc., Box 73, Thornhill, ON L3T 3N1 Canada; Title Tel # (905) 731-5457
Personnel: Publisher, Editor-Lance Humble, Ph.D.
Editorial Description: Quarterly, dedicated to the professional gambler, covers all gambling games.
General Info: Yr. Est. 1974, Quarterly, Trim Size-8$\frac{1}{2}$ x 11, Web press, 24 pages, 5% ads, No Color
Subscriptions: Indv. $24, $6/copy
Circulation: Total-1,900
Advertising: Inquire for rates.

Jackpotunities   *Consumer*

Publishing Co: Jackpotunities, Inc., Box 393, Centuck Station, Yonkers, NY 10710-0393 Parent Co.-Direct American Marketers, Inc., Irvine; Title Tel # (914) 664-5242
Personnel: Editor-Shirley Liss, Adv. Dir.-Harriet Levy
Editorial Description: Sweepstakes newsletter.
General Info: Yr. Est. 1978, Bi-monthly, Trim Size-6 x 10$\frac{1}{2}$, Web press, 28 pages, 2 Color
Subscriptions: Indv. $20, $2/copy
Circulation: Total-100,000

Las Vegas Advisor
See: TRAVEL

Las Vegas Insider
See: TRAVEL

Leisure Industry Report
See: BUSINESS & INDUSTRY

Lottery, Paramutual & Casino Regulations/State Capitals   *Business*

Publishing Co: Wakeman/Walworth, 300 N. Washington St., Alexandria, VA 22314-2530;
Title Tel # (703) 549-8606 Title Fax # (703) 549-1372
Personnel: Publisher-Keyes Walworth
Editorial Description: Regulation & development of state lottery programs, prize structures, ticket marketing policies, taxation of casinos and other wagering operations.
General Info: (Formerly Lottery, Parimuteul & Casino Regulations from the State Capi), Yr. Est. 1990, Weekly, Trim Size-8$\frac{1}{2}$ x 11, 6 pages, ISSN: 1047-8493
Subscriptions: Indv. $365, Inst. $293, Can. $325, For. $345

Lottery Retailer

Publishing Co: Washington State Lottery, Box 43000, Olympia, WA 98504-0001;
Title Tel # (206) 753-1412
Personnel: Editor-Janine Patry

Overlay, The   *Consumer*

Publishing Co: Gambler's Book Club, 630 S 11th St, Las Vegas, NV 89101-7106;
Title Tel # (702) 382-7555 Title Fax # (702) 382-7594
Personnel: Editor, Mktg. Dir.-Howard Schwartz
Editorial Description: Books, videotapes, and computer software for gamblers, researchers.
General Info: Yr. Est. 1976, Quarterly, Trim Size-8 x 11, 20 pages
Subscriptions: Free
Circulation: Total-40,000

Privacy Newsletter
See: CONSUMER INTERESTS

So You Wanna Be a Gambler   *Consumer*

Publishing Co: John Patrick Productions, P.O. Box 289, Short Hills, NJ 07078-0289
Tel # (201) 467-4665
Editorial Description: Information on where to find the best casino game conditions as well as instruction from gaming experts.
General Info: Monthly, Trim Size-8$\frac{1}{2}$ x 11, 8 pages, 2 Color
Subscriptions: Indv. $28

USET Gaming   *Business, Association*

Publishing Co: United South & Eastern Tribes, Inc., 711 Stewarts Ferry Pike # 100, Nashville, TN 37214-2634
Editorial Description: Provides news and information of the United South and Eastern Tribes Gaming Assn.
General Info: Yr. Est. 1993, Quarterly

Winning Ways   *Consumer*

Publishing Co: ICON Information Concepts, Inc., 211 S. 45th St., Philadelphia, PA 19104-2995 Fax # (216) 349-6500; Title Tel # (215) 349-6500 Title Fax # (215) 349-6502
Personnel: Publisher, Editor-Alan Krigman
Editorial Description: Each issue contains four separate feature articles discussing various aspects of casino gambling--ranging from specifics about machines and table games to generalizations about gambling philosophy, theories and probabilities underlying games of chance and how players can make the most of the casino experience.
General Info: Yr. Est. 1996, Monthly
Subscriptions: Indv. $25, Can. $25, For. $40, $4/copy
Advertising: Inquire for rates. Accepts Inserts.

GARDENING & HORTICULTURE

AABGA Newsletter   *Association*

Publishing Co: American Association of Botanical Gardens and Arboreta, 786 Church Rd, Wayne, PA 19087-4713 Fax # (215) 293-0149; Title Tel # (215) 688-1120 Title Fax # (610) 293-0149
Personnel: Publisher-Sharon Lee, Editor-Cindy Loman
Editorial Description: Promotes the botanical, horticultural and educational advancement of botanical gardens and arboreta.
General Info: Yr. Est. 1940, Monthly, Trim Size-8$\frac{1}{2}$ x 11, Offset press, 8 pages, ISSN: 0569-2423, Newsprint
Subscriptions: Indv. $50, Free With Membership
Circulation: (100% controlled), Total-1,800
List Rental: Actives: 350, $50/M, Expires: 2,000, $150/M

Abundant Life Seed Foundation Newsletter   *Consumer*

Publishing Co: Abundant Life Seed Foundation, Box 772, Pt. Townsend, WA 98368-0772;
Title Tel # (206) 385-5660 Title Fax # (360) 385-7455
Personnel: Editor-Forest Shomer
Editorial Description: Announcements of calendar events: seminars, meetings, etc., update of annual catalog of seeds, books.
General Info: Yr. Est. 1975, Irregular, Trim Size-8$\frac{1}{2}$ x 14, Offset press, 2 pages, No Color
Subscriptions: Indv. $8, Can. $10, For. $15
Circulation: Total-20,000

Alberta Horticulturist   *Association*

Publishing Co: Alberta Horticultural Assn, A.H.A. Secretary, c/o Adamson, Box 1 of 3, Lacombe, AB T0C 1S0 Canada; Title Tel # (403) 973-3351
Editorial Description: Minutes of meetings; horticultural society reports; show reports; horticulture articles; related pictures; articles on gardening.
General Info: Yr. Est. 1958, Quarterly, Trim Size-8$\frac{1}{2}$ x 11$\frac{1}{2}$, 4 pages, No Color
Circulation: Total-800

American Bamboo Society-Newsletter

Publishing Co: American Bamboo Society, 750 Krumkill Road, Albany, NY 12203-5976;
Title Tel # (518) 458-7618 Title Fax # (518) 458-7625
Personnel: Editor-Michael Bartholomen
General Info: Yr. Est. 1979, Bi-monthly, Trim Size-8$\frac{1}{2}$ x 11, Offset press, 24 pages, No Color
Subscriptions: Indv. $30, Can. $30, For. $30
Circulation: Total-1,100

American Harvest
See: FOOD

American Herb Association -Quarterly Newsletter
Consumer, Association **CPM: $245**

Publishing Co: American Herb Association, PO Box 1673, Nevada City, CA 95959-1673; Title Tel # (916) 265-9552
Personnel: Publisher-Bob Brucia, Editor-Kathi Keville, Assoc. Ed.-Amanda McQuade- Crawford, Production Mgr.-Marian Wycoff, Art Dir.-David Hoffman
Editorial Description: Reports on scientific studies, legal aspects of medicinal herbs, and environmental concerns. Includes movie, video, and book reviews.
General Info: Yr. Est. 1981, Quarterly, Trim Size-7 x 10, Offset press, 20 pages, No Color, Matte, Saddle-stitched
Subscriptions: Indv. $20, Can. $25, For. $28, $5/copy
Circulation: Total-1,000, Readership-2,000
Advertising: $245.

American Horticultural Society Newsletter
Consumer, Association

Publishing Co: American Horticultural Society, 7931 E Boulevard Dr, Alexandria, VA 22308-1300 Tel # (703) 768-5700
Personnel: Editor-Kathleen Fisher, Bk. Rev. Ed.-David Ellis, Production Mgr.-Terri Huck, Adv. Dir.- Bonnie Fowler
Editorial Description: Provides practical advice and information for gardeners.
General Info: Bi-monthly
Subscriptions: $2/copy
List Rental: Rents Lists
Printing Co: Cadmus Journal Services, 2901 Byrdhill Rd., Richmond, VA 23228-5867 Tel # (804) 264-2711, Fax # (804) 266-0832

American Peony Society Bulletin
Association

Publishing Co: American Peony Society, 250 Interlachen Rd, Hopkins, MN 55343-8526; Title Tel # (612) 938-4706
Personnel: Editor, Circ. Mgr., Adv. Dir., Art Dir.-Greta Kessenich
Editorial Description: Increasing the general interest in and use of the peony. Registration of new varieties. Research, hybridizing and diseases.
General Info: Yr. Est. 1903, Quarterly, Trim Size-6 x 9, Letrpr. press, 48 pages, No Color
Subscriptions: Indv. $8, $2/copy
Circulation: Total-850
Advertising: Inquire for rates.

Amerigold Newsletter

Publishing Co: Marigold Society of America, National Headquarters, P.O. Box 5112, New Britain, PA 18901
Personnel: Editor-William R. Morris
Editorial Description: To spread information about the beauty, versatility & use of marigolds; to promote the marigold for the international friendship flower; to promote the marigold for U.S. postage stamp.
General Info: Yr. Est. 1979, Quarterly, 8 pages
Subscriptions: Indv. $12

Appalachian Alternatives
See: CONSUMER INTERESTS

Avant Gardener
Consumer

Publishing Co: Horticultural Data Processors, PO Box 489, New York, NY 10028-0005
Personnel: Publisher, Editor-Thomas Powell
Editorial Description: Covers news of new plants, products and techniques, plus articles on all aspects of indoor and outdoor gardening.
General Info: Yr. Est. 1968, Monthly, Trim Size-8½ x 11, Web press, 8 pages, ISSN: 0005-1926, No Color
Subscriptions: Indv. $20, Can. $24, For. $24, $2/copy
Circulation: Total-6,000

Backyard Wildlife
See: NATURAL HISTORY

Baer's Garden Newsletter

Publishing Co: John Baer's Sons, PO Box 328, Lancaster, PA 17608-0328; Title Tel # (717) 392-0733
Personnel: Editor-Gerald Lestz
Editorial Description: For new & experienced gardeners; data on news products & services, history, & folklore.
General Info: Yr. Est. 1979, Quarterly, Trim Size-8½ x 11, 4 pages
Subscriptions: Indv. $4

Beekeeping Notes

Publishing Co: Plant Industry Branch, Horticultural Crops, N.S. Dept. of Agriculture, Box 550, Truro, NS B2N 5E3 Canada; Title Tel # (902) 895-1571 Title Fax # (902) 893-0244
Personnel: Editor-Dick Rogers
Circulation: Total-825
Advertising: Inquire for rates.

Bonsai Bark
Consumer

Publishing Co: Bonsai by the Bay, PO Box 1246, Trinidad, CA 95570-1246 Tel # (707) 677-4100 Fax # (707) 677-4102
Editorial Description: Information on how to care for bonsai trees.
General Info: Quarterly

Bonsai Business
Business

Publishing Co: Lowenthal & Miller, 25601 SW 137th Ave, Princeton, FL 33032-6726; Title Tel # (305) 258-5520 Title Fax # (305) 258-6929
Personnel: Editor in Chief-Mary Miller
Editorial Description: Information for bonsai purists, retailers and wholesalers.
General Info: Yr. Est. 1994, Bi-monthly, Trim Size-8½ x 11, 6 pages, ISSN: 1076-3538, No Color, Matte
Subscriptions: Indv. $24
Advertising: Inquire for rates.

Bulletin
See: BOTANY

Cachepot
Consumer

Publishing Co: Cornucopia Press, 3 Golf Ctr Ste 221, Hoffman Estates, IL 60195-3710; Title Tel # (708) 934-7655
Personnel: Publisher-Tamara Saliman
Editorial Description: Practical information on edible plants growing.
General Info: Yr. Est. 1994, 9x/yr., 2 pages
Subscriptions: Indv. $15

California Ornamental Crops Report
See: FLORIST

Clippings
Consumer, Association

Publishing Co: Atlanta Botanical Garden, PO Box 77246, Atlanta, GA 30357-1246 Fax # (404) 876-7472; Title Tel # (404) 876-5859
Personnel: Editor in Chief-Julie Herron, Mng. Editor-Laura Anne Middlesteadt
Editorial Description: Newsletter for our 10,000 members, our donors, sponsors and over 1,000 people in the media. Garden news, events, feature articles and horticultural how-to's.
General Info: Yr. Est. 1981, Quarterly, Trim Size-8½ x 11, Sheetfed press, 20 pages, 5% ads, 2 Color, Matte, Saddle-stitched
Subscriptions: Indv. $35, Free With Membership
Circulation: Total-14,000, Readership-14,000
Advertising: Inquire for rates.
Printing Co: Ripley Communications, 4508 Bibb Blvd Ste B10, Tucker, GA 30084-6232 Tel # (404) 621-9225

Composting News
See: ENVIRONMENT & ECOLOGY

Cucurbits
Association

Publishing Co: World Pumpkin Confederation, 14050 Rt. 62, Collins, NY 14034-9704 Fax # (716) 632-5690; Title Tel # (716) 532-5995 Title Fax # (716) 532-5690
Personnel: Asst. Pub.-Darleen Stry, Publisher, Editor-Ray Waterman, Circ. Dir.-Karen Fisher
Editorial Description: World Pumpkin Confederation news-letter. Club membership in 30 countries.
General Info: (Formerly Espirit De Corps), Yr. Est. 1983, Quarterly, 24 pages
Subscriptions: Indv. $15, Can. $20, For. $25
Circulation: Total-2,500
Advertising: Inquire for rates.

Cycad Newsletter
See: BIOLOGY

Dawes Arboretum Newsletter

Publishing Co: Dawes Arboretum, 7770 Jacksontown Rd SE, Newark, OH 43056-9358; Title Tel # (614) 323-2355
Personnel: Editor-Alan Cook
General Info: Yr. Est. 1968, Monthly, Trim Size-8½ x 11, 8 pages
Circulation: Total-1,800

Epiphyllum Society of America Bulletin
Association

Publishing Co: Epiphyllum Society of America, PO Box 1395, Monrovia, CA 91017-1395 Tel # (818) 447-9688
Editorial Description: Strictly limited to the care, growing and hybridizing of Epiphyllums and related epiphytes.
General Info: Yr. Est. 1940, Bi-monthly, 10 pages
Subscriptions: Indv. $10, For. $16
Circulation: Total-500
Advertising: Inquire for rates.

Euro-Turf
Business

Publishing Co: Argus Agronomics, PO Box 1420, 14920 Highway 61N, Clarksdale, MS 38614 Tel # (601) 624-8503 Fax # (601) 627-1977 Parent Co.-Argus Business, Atlanta
Editorial Description: Information for professional turf managers in Europe.
General Info: Bi-monthly

Expanded Shale Clay & Slate Institute-Information Sheets
See: GLASS, STONE & CLAY

Fiddlehead Forum   *Association*

Publishing Co: American Fern Society, 326 West St., NW, Vienna, VA 221814151 a;
    Title Tel # (202) 357-2568
Personnel: Editor-Cindy Johnson-Groh, Circ. Coord.-David B. Lellinger
Editorial Description: Notes, news, information about ferns for lay persons.
General Info: (Formerly News and Views), Yr. Est. 1974, Bi-monthly, Trim Size-8½ x 11, Offset press, 6 pages, No Color
Subscriptions: Can. $8, For. $11, Free With Membership
Circulation: (100% controlled), Total-1,600
Printing Co: Omega Lithographers, 126 Mount Vernon Ave, Mount Vernon, NY 10550-2425
    Tel # (914) 664-1214

Flax Craft
See: TEXTILES

Garden Club of America
Newsletter   *Association*

Publishing Co: Garden Club of America, 598 Madison Ave, New York, NY 10022-1693;
    Title Tel # (212) 753-8287
Personnel: Editor-Marion White Kahn, Circ. Mgr.-Millie Roman, Adv. Dir.-Joanne Riddick
Editorial Description: Includes feature articles, personality profiles, organizational news, & legislative news on issues of specific interest.
General Info: Yr. Est. 1922, Semi-monthly, Trim Size-8½ x 11, 8 pages, 1% ads, 2 Color, Newsprint
Subscriptions: Indv. $8
Circulation: Total-16,000
Advertising: Inquire for rates.
Printing Co: Parkin Printing, Asher Ave., Little Rock, AR

Garden Newsletter   *Association*   CPM: $400

Publishing Co: Friends of the State Botanical Garden of Georgia, Inc., University of Georgia, 2450 S. Milledge, Athens, GA 30605-1624; Title Tel # (706) 542-1244 Title Fax # (706) 542-3091
Personnel: Editor-Mollie Henry, Circ. Mgr.-Beverly Moore
Editorial Description: Ongoing events and accomplishments at the State Botanical Garden; Stories of horticulture interest.
General Info: (Formerly Friends of the Univ. of Georgia Botanical Garden-Newsletter), Yr. Est. 1972, Quarterly, Sheetfed press, 12 pages, 2 Color, Newsprint
Subscriptions: Indv. $25, Free With Membership
Acquistions: Publication Bought
Circulation: Total-1,500
Advertising: $600. Accepts Inserts.

Garden Sampler   *Consumer*

Publishing Co: Blue Moon Publishing, PO Box 7, Peru, VT 05152-0007; Title Tel # (802) 824-5890
Personnel: Publisher-Stewart Read, Editor-Dorothy Read
Editorial Description: For New England gardeners.
General Info: Bi-monthly, Trim Size-8½ x 11, 16 pages, 2 Color, Matte, Saddle-stitched
Subscriptions: Indv. $20

Gardenesque

Publishing Co: Gardenesque, 14 Gertrude Place, Toronto, ON M4J 1R3 Canada;
    Title Tel # (416) 463-5334
Personnel: Publisher, Editor, Art Dir.-Juliet Mannock
General Info: Yr. Est. 1985, 8x/yr., Trim Size-8½ x 11, Mimeo press, 4 pages, No Color
Subscriptions: $2/copy
Circulation: Total-300

Germinations   *Consumer*

Publishing Co: Butterbrooke Farm, 78 Barry Rd, Oxford, CT 06478-1529; Title Tel # (203) 888-2000
Personnel: Publisher, Editor-Thomas Butterworth
Editorial Description: Articles on organic gardening/sustainable agriculture by & for growers.
General Info: Yr. Est. 1979, Quarterly, Trim Size-8½ x 11, Mimeo press, 6 pages, No Color
Subscriptions: Indv. $8, $2/copy
Circulation: (100% controlled), Total-300

Gourd   *Association*

Publishing Co: American Gourd Society, PO Box 274, Mount Gilead, OH 43338-0274;
    Title Tel # (419) 362-6446 Title Fax # (419) 362-6446
Personnel: Publisher-Jean McClentock, Editor-Ted Modrowski, Mktg. Dir., Promotion Dir.-Jean McClintock
Editorial Description: Information on gourds, culture & craft, members experiences.
General Info: (Formerly Gourd Seed), Yr. Est. 1970, Quarterly, Trim Size-8½ x 11, Letrpr. press, 24 pages, ISSN: 0888-5672, No Color, Matte, Saddle-stitched
Subscriptions: Indv. $5, Can. $8, For. $8, $1/copy
Printing Co: Account Manager: Marilyn Supple; Hartman Printing Co., 4240 Cord, 115, Mt. Gilead, OH 43338 Tel # (419) 946-2854

Green World News   *Scholarly, Association*

Publishing Co: Bonsai & Orchid Association, 26 Pine St., Dover, DE 19901-4452;
    Title Tel # (302) 736-6781 Title Fax # (302) 736-6763
Personnel: Editor-Leroy Rench
General Info: Yr. Est. 1984, Monthly
Subscriptions: Indv. $20, Free With Membership
Circulation: Total-2,300
Advertising: Inquire for rates.

Grow Letter   *Business*

Publishing Co: Vegetable Factory, Inc., 495 Post Road East, WestPort, CT 06880-4400
    Tel # (203) 454-0040 Fax # (203) 454-0020; Title Tel # (203) 324-0010
Personnel: Publisher, Editor-Fred Small, Art Dir.-S.O. Schwartz
Editorial Description: Newsletter for owners of Vegetable Factory solar greenhouses.
General Info: Yr. Est. 1970, Quarterly, Trim Size-8½ x 11, Offset press, 12 pages, No Color, Matte, Saddle-stitched
List Rental: List Management Co.: ZED Marketing, 3100 Cactus Dr., Edmond, OK 73013-7934
    Tel # (405) 348-8145, Fax # (405) 348-5541, Actives: $55/M, Expires: $60/M

Growing for Market
See: AGRICULTURE

Growing Native Newsletter   *Consumer*

Publishing Co: Growing Native Research Institute, PO Box 489, Berkeley, CA 94701-0489;
    Title Tel # (510) 232-9865
Personnel: Publisher, Editor-Louise Lacey
Editorial Description: For gardeners, landscapers, and revegetation specialists; thorough and engaging information about California native plants.
General Info: Yr. Est. 1989, Bi-monthly, Trim Size-8.5 x 11, Web press, 16 pages, No Color, Matte
Subscriptions: Indv. $30, Free

Heather Notes
See: BOTANY

Herbarium Pacificum News

Publishing Co: Bishop Museum, 1525 Bernice St # 19000-A, Honolulu, HI 96817-2704;
    Title Tel # (808) 847-3511
General Info: Semi-annually

Historical Gardener, The   *Consumer*

Publishing Co: Historical Gardener, 1910 N 35th Pl, Mount Vernon, WA 98273-8981;
    Title Tel # (206) 424-3154
Personnel: Publisher, Editor-Kathleen McClelland
Editorial Description: Covers all regions and eras of North American garden history for professional museum gardeners, seed savers, and home gardeners.
General Info: Yr. Est. 1994, Quarterly, Trim Size-8½ x 11, 12 pages, Ind/Abs/Online: Garden Literature Index, Boston MA, No Color
Subscriptions: Indv. $12, Can. $14, For. $20

Home Gardener's
Newsletter   *Business, Consumer*

Publishing Co: Moore Consulting, PO Box 9527, Berkeley, CA 94709-0527;
    Title Tel # (510) 524-1163
Personnel: Publisher, Editor-Wayne Moore, Assoc. Ed.-Nancy Hamalian
Editorial Description: What to do in the garden each month. Customized for garden centers to mail to their customers.
General Info: Yr. Est. 1983, Monthly, Trim Size-8½ x 11, Letrpr. press, 1 pages, No Color
Circulation: Total-100,000
Printing Co: Super Print, 10176 San Pablo Ave., El Cerrito 94530

Hort-News

Publishing Co: Horticulture Awareness Assn., C/O Christopher Van Oosterhout, 14575 Mercury Dr., Grand Haven, MI 49417; Title Tel # (616) 846-3864
General Info: Bi-monthly

HortIdeas   *Business, Consumer*

Publishing Co: Hort Ideas, 460 Black Lick Rd, Gravel Switch, KY 40328-9306;
    Title Tel # (606) 332-7606
Personnel: Publisher-Pat Williams, Editor-Gregory Williams
Editorial Description: Covers a wide range of horticultural and gardening topics.
General Info: Yr. Est. 1984, Monthly, Trim Size-8½ x 11, Sheetfed press, 12 pages, ISSN: 0742-8219
Subscriptions: Indv. $22, Inst. $20, Can. $26, For. $35, $2/copy
Circulation: Total-1,500
Printing Co: Diamond Graphics, 914 National Ave, Lexington, KY 40502-1436 Tel # (502) 252-6578

K.T.F. Newsletter

Publishing Co: Kansas Turfgrass Foundation Dept. of Horticulture, Waters Hall, Kansas State University, Manhattan, KS 66506-4000; Title Tel # (913) 532-6170
Personnel: Editor-Larry Luthold
General Info: (Formerly C.P.T.F. Newsletter), Bi-monthly, 6 pages
Circulation: (100% controlled), Total-150

Kansas Crop Improvement
Assn. -News Letter

Publishing Co: Kansas Crop Improvement Assn., 2000 Kimball Ave, Manhattan, KS 66502-3354;
    Title Tel # (913) 532-6118
Personnel: Editor-Daryl Strouts
General Info: Monthly
Circulation: Total-5,000

Medianite   *Association*

Publishing Co: Median Iris Society, 1440 N Fountain Blvd, Springfield, OH 45504-1425;
Title Tel # (513) 399-2308
Personnel: Editor, Adv. Dir.-Alice Kelly
Editorial Description: Culture, hybridizing and promotion of middle-sized (Median) bearded irises,
10-28 inches in height.
General Info: Yr. Est. 1960, Quarterly, Trim Size-8½ x 11, Offset press, 20 pages, No Color
Subscriptions: Indv. $3, $1/copy
Circulation: Total-500

Michigan Organic News

Publishing Co: Federated Organic Clubs of Michigan, 4401 Maple Lane Rd, Rives Junction, MI
49277-9647; Title Tel # (517) 569-3905
Personnel: Publisher, Circ. Mgr.-Russ Severance, Editor, Adv. Dir.-Marcia Severance, Art Dir.-Kisti
Beckwith
Editorial Description: Holistic health and organic gardening and farming, regional.
General Info: (Formerly Federated Organic News), Yr. Est. 1981, Quarterly, Trim Size-5½ x 8½,
Offset press, 56 pages, 1% ads, No Color, Newsprint
Subscriptions: Indv. $5, $1/copy
Circulation: Total-1,300
Advertising: Inquire for rates.
Printing Co: Quick Print, 226 East Capitol St., Jackson, MI 39201 Tel # (601) 355-8195

Minnesota Landscape
Arboretum News   *Business, Association*

Publishing Co: Minnesota Landscape Arboretum Foundation, 3675 Arboretum Blvd # 39,
Chanhassen, MN 55317-9338; Title Tel # (612) 443-2460
Personnel: Editor-Maria Klein
Editorial Description: Information for members and readers about Arboretum news and events plus
horticultural and environmental articles, with emphasis on what the Arb is doing.
General Info: Yr. Est. 1981, Bi-monthly, Trim Size-8½ x 11, Offset press, 16 pages, 2 Color, Coated,
Saddle-stitched
Subscriptions: Free With Membership
Circulation: (92% controlled), Total-13,000
Printing Co: Gopher State Litho, 3232 E 40th St, Minneapolis, MN 55406-3236 Tel # (612) 724-3600

Minnesota Pest Report
See: AGRICULTURE

Morris Arboretum Newsletter
See: BOTANY

NAA Reporter
See: FORESTRY

N.C. Botanical Garden
Newsletter

Publishing Co: Botanical Garden Foundation, NC Botanical Garden UNC, CB, 3375 Totten Center,
Chapel Hill, NC 27599-3375; Title Tel # (919) 962-0522 Title Fax # (919) 962-3531
Personnel: Editor-Sandra Brooks
Editorial Description: The North Carolina Botanical Garden, a teaching, research, & public service
facility of the University of North Carolina at Chapel Hill, is a center for the study, display,
interpretation, & conservation of plants & of the natural areas of which these plants are a part.
General Info: Yr. Est. 1971, Bi-monthly, Trim Size-11 x 17, Desktop press, 12 pages, Saddle-stitched
Subscriptions: Indv. $20, Inst. $35
Circulation: Total-2,500
Printing Co: University of North Carolina Printing, CB 1110 Bennett Bldg., Chapel Hll, NC 27514
Tel # (919) 962-5566

NCAMP's Technical Report
See: ENVIRONMENT & ECOLOGY

NLA Landscape News   *Association*

Publishing Co: Natl. Landscape Assn., 1250 Eye St. NW, #500, Washington, DC 20004-1901;
Title Tel # (202) 789-2900
Personnel: Publisher-David Peiffer, Editor-Angela Hutcherson
Editorial Description: Mgt. info. for landscape nursery businesses.
General Info: Bi-monthly, Trim Size-8½ x 11, Sheetfed press, 8 pages, Color, Coated
Circulation: Total-1,000

Nebraska Pest Control Association Newsletter
See: AGRICULTURAL SUPPLIES

Norfolk Botanical Garden
Society Bulletin   *Association*

Publishing Co: Norfolk Botanical Garden Society, Azalea Garden Rd., Norfolk, VA 23518;
Title Tel # (804) 425-5344
Personnel: Circ. Mgr.-Marie Wright, Adv. Dir.-Winnie Ciucci, Editor, Art Dir.-William Genz, Promotion
Dir.-Brian O'Neill
Editorial Description: Disseminates plant and gardening information to members as well as a
calendar of events, Society news, etc.
General Info: Yr. Est. 1940, Monthly, Trim Size-8½ x 11, Offset press, 6 pages, 3% ads, Color,
Newsprint
Subscriptions: Indv. $15
Circulation: (100% controlled)
Printing Co: Sir Speedy, 3008 Virginia Beach Blvd, Virginia Beach, VA 23452-6904
Tel # (804) 463-5300

Nutshell The
See: AGRICULTURE

OALA News
See: ARCHITECTURE

On the Garden Line   *Business, Consumer*

Publishing Co: On the Garden Line, PO Box 6047, Wexon, MI 48393; Title Tel # (313) 960-1600
Personnel: Publisher-Kim Gasior
Editorial Description: Gardening tips and information.
General Info: Monthly
Circulation: Total-58,000
List Rental: List Management Co.: Rubin Response, 1111 Plaza Dr., Schaumburg, IL 60173
Tel # (708) 619-9800, Fax # (708) 619-0150

Orchid Hunter   *Consumer*   **CPM: $200**

Publishing Co: Ferraro & Associates, Rr 1 Box 62a, Adamsville, PA 16110-8706
Tel # (412) 932-3449; Title Tel # (412) 824-5066
Personnel: Publisher, Editor-Terry Ferraro, Circ. Mgr., Adv. Dir.-Sam Ferraro, Production Mgr., Art
Dir.-Ted Smiley
Editorial Description: News and information for orchid growers (hobby and commercial.)
General Info: Yr. Est. 1988, Monthly, Trim Size-8½ x 11, Offset press, 10 pages, ISSN: 0005-9760, 2
Color, Matte
Subscriptions: Indv. $17, Can. $17, For. $23, $2/copy
Circulation: Total-1,000
Advertising: $200. Accepts Inserts.
List Rental: Actives: 1,000

Ornamentals Northwest   *Consumer*

Publishing Co: Jim Green, Horticulture Department, OSU, Corvallis, OR 97331;
Title Tel # (503) 737-5452 Title Fax # (503) 737-3479
Personnel: Editor, Circ. Mgr.-James Green, Art Dir.-Tom Weeks
Editorial Description: Commercial production and use of landscape plants.
General Info: (Formerly Ornamental & Nursery Digest), Yr. Est. 1975, Bi-monthly, Trim Size-8 x 10,
Sheetfed press, 28 pages, ISSN: 0030-4778, Ind/Abs/Online: BAg, 2 Color, Coated, Saddle-stitched
Subscriptions: Indv. $10, For. $15, $2/copy
Circulation: (100% controlled), Total-5,000
Printing Co: Oregon State Univ. Department of Printing, Oregon State University, Industrial Bldg.
124, Corvallis, OR 97331-4203 Tel # (503) 737-0123

Pest Control Progress   *Business, Association*

Publishing Co: Interstate Professional Applicators Assn., PO Box 1420, Milton, WA 98354;
Title Tel # (206) 922-9437
Editorial Description: Info. for chemical applicators-- chemicals, legislation, infestations.
General Info: Yr. Est. 1963, Quarterly, Trim Size-8½ x 11, Letrpr. press, 8 pages, 1% ads, No Color,
Newsprint
Subscriptions: Free With Membership
Circulation: Total-450
Advertising: Inquire for rates.
Printing Co: Lakewood Printing, 6111 Steilacoom Blvd SW, Tacoma, WA 98499-2698
Tel # (206) 582-6670

PlantWise   *Business, Consumer*

Publishing Co: Botanical Dimensions, PO Box 807, Occidental, CA 95465-0807
Personnel: Editor-Kathleen Harrison
Editorial Description: The use of plants for medicinal purposes.
General Info: Bi-monthly
Subscriptions: Indv. $20

Plants & Gardens News   *Association*

Publishing Co: Brooklyn Botanic Garden, 1000 Washington Ave, Brooklyn, NY 11225-1008;
Title Tel # (718) 622-4433 Title Fax # (718) 857-2430
Personnel: Publisher-Judy Zuk, Editor-Betsy Kissam, Art Dir.-Anne Garland
Editorial Description: Covers latest horticultural/gardening how-tos, trends & technology.
General Info: (Formerly Brooklyn Botanic Garden Newsletter), Yr. Est. 1985, Quarterly, Trim Size-8½
x 11, Sheetfed press, 16 pages, 2 Color, Newsprint, Saddle-stitched
Subscriptions: Indv. $35, Free With Membership
Circulation: Total-180,000

Potpourri from Herbal Acres
See: HOBBY

Potpourri Simple & Easy Update
See: GIFTS, GAMES, TOYS

Potting Shed

Publishing Co: Charles Moore Associates, Inc., PO Box 6, Southampton, PA 18966-0006;
Title Tel # (215) 355-6084 Title Fax # (215) 364-2212
Personnel: Editor-Charles Moore, Circ. Mgr.-Nancy Hannigan
General Info: Yr. Est. 1977, Monthly, 8 pages
Subscriptions: Indv. $24
Circulation: Total-1,500

Queens Botanical Garden
News   *Association*

Publishing Co: Queens Botanical Garden Society Inc., 4350 Main St, Flushing, NY 11355-4742; Title Tel # (718) 886-3800 Title Fax # (718) 463-0263
Personnel: Editor-Joyce Leiz
Editorial Description: Newsletter covering items important to visitors and members, plus program schedules, descriptions.
General Info: Yr. Est. 1980, Quarterly, Trim Size-8½ x 11, Desktop press, 4 pages, No Color
Subscriptions: Free
Circulation: Total-3,000
Printing Co: Jo Capa Inc., 191 Victory Blvd, Staten Island, NY 10301-2918 Tel # (718) 875-3333

Robin
See: ENVIRONMENT & ECOLOGY

Rosarian   *Association*

Publishing Co: Canadian Rose Society, 10 Fairfax Cres., Scarborough, ON M1L 1Z8 Canada; Title Tel # (416) 757-8809 Title Fax # (416) 757-4796
Personnel: Editor-Ron Capon
Editorial Description: Rose culture.
General Info: (Formerly Rose Bulletin, The), Yr. Est. 1913, 35 pages, No Color
Subscriptions: Inst. $23, Can. $21
Circulation: Total-1,000
Advertising: Inquire for rates.

Rose Letter

Publishing Co: Heritage Roses Group, Box 228, RD 1, Clinton Corners, NY 12514-0228; Title Tel # (914) 266-3562
General Info: Quarterly
Circulation: Total-2,700

San Francisco Wholesale
Ornamental Crops Report   *Business, Association*

Publishing Co: USDA-AMS-F&V. Div., 630 Sansome St Ste 727, San Francisco, CA 94111-2215; Title Tel # (415) 705-1300 Title Fax # (415) 705-1301
Personnel: Editor-Frederick Teensma
Editorial Description: Provides prices of cut flowers, cut foliage, and flowering potted plants on the San Francisco wholesale flower market, by variety, color or sizes. Prices are for over the counter sales by wholesalers to local retailers.
General Info: Weekly, Trim Size-8½ x 14, 4 pages, Matte
Subscriptions: Indv. $120, Can. $120, For. $240

Scentouri News
See: COSMETICS & PERFUMES

Seed Savers Exchange   *Consumer*

Publishing Co: Kent Whealy, 3076 N Winn Rd, Decorah, IA 52101-7776; Title Tel # (319) 382-5990 Title Fax # (319) 382-5872
Personnel: Editor-Kent Whealy
Editorial Description: A grassroots genetic preservation project whose members work together to save our vanishing vegetable heritage.
General Info: (Formerly True Seed Exchange), Yr. Est. 1975, Tri-annually, Trim Size-7½ x 10½, Web press, 200 pages, No Color, Newsprint
Subscriptions: Indv. $25, Can. $30, For. $40
Circulation: Total-7,000

Seedling News
See: ENVIRONMENT & ECOLOGY

Sego Lily   *Consumer, Association*

Publishing Co: Utah Native Plant Society, PO Box 520081, Salt Lake City, UT 84152-0081 Tel # (801) 581-3744; Title Tel # (801) 581-5322
Personnel: Editor-Kathy Mutz
General Info: Yr. Est. 1977, 6x/yr., Trim Size-8½ x 11, Other press, 8 pages, Matte, Saddle-stitched
Subscriptions: $10/copy
Circulation: Total-200
Advertising: Inquire for rates.
Printing Co: Kinko's, VT

Shade Tree   *Association*

Publishing Co: Sponsor-NJ Shade Tree Foundation, New Jersey Shade Tree Federation, Box 231, Blake Hall, Cook College, New Brunswick, NJ 08903-0231; Title Tel # (908) 246-3210
Personnel: Editor-Donald Lacey, Production Mgr.-William Porter
General Info: Yr. Est. 1928, Bi-monthly, Trim Size-5½ x 8½, Sheetfed press, 16 pages, No Color, Recycled, Saddle-stitched
Subscriptions: Indv. $65, Free With Membership
Advertising: Inquire for rates.
Printing Co: Mariano Press, 13 N Talmadge St, New Brunswick, NJ 08901-3198 Tel # (908) 247-6828

Society for Louisiana
Irises Newsletter   *Association*   CPM: $106

Publishing Co: Society for Louisiana Irises, Box 40175, USL, Lafayette, LA 70504-0175; Title Tel # (318) 235-8700
Personnel: Editor-Marie Caillet
General Info: Quarterly, Trim Size-8½ x 11, Offset press, 14 pages, No Color
Circulation: Total-375
Advertising: $40.

Talking Leaves Newsletter
See: OUTDOORS

Tomato Club, The   *Consumer*

Publishing Co: Tomato Club, The, 114 E. Main St., Bogota, NJ 07603; Title Tel # (201) 488-2231 Title Fax # (201) 489-4609
Personnel: Circ. Mgr.-Dorothy Oyen, Production Mgr., Art Dir.-Penelope Foran, Publisher, Editor, Mktg. Dir.-Robert D. Ambrose
Editorial Description: The Tomato Club newsletter is primarily a gardening publication which concentrates on tomatoes. Varieties information is an important second objective since the number & diversity of tomatoes is immense, history, recipes, poetry & other tomato related subjects & included.
General Info: Yr. Est. 1993, Bi-monthly, Trim Size-8½ x 11, Web press, 8 pages, 2 Color, Matte, Saddle-stitched
Subscriptions: Indv. $16, Can. $19, For. $21
Circulation: Total-1,600
Printing Co: Chernay Printing, 7483 S. Main St., PO Box 199, Coopersburg, PA 18036 Tel # (215) 282-3774, Fax # (610) 282-2982

Treeworker
See: FORESTRY

TurfGrass Trends   *Business*

Publishing Co: Turf Grass Trends, 1775 T Street NW, Washington, DC 20009; Title Tel # (202) 483-8873 Title Fax # (202) 483-5797
Personnel: Publisher-Juesgen Haber, Editor-Todd Natkin
General Info: Yr. Est. 1992, Monthly, Trim Size-8½ x 11, Web press, 16 pages, ISSN: 1076-7207, 2 Color, Matte, Saddle-stitched
Subscriptions: Indv. $120, Inst. $120, Can. $120, For. $120, $10/copy
Circulation: Total-500
Printing Co: Newsletter Services, Inc., 9700 Philadelphia Court, Lanham, MD 20706 Tel # (301) 731-5200, Fax # (301) 731-5201

Update   *Association*

Publishing Co: American Assn. of Nurserymen, 1250 I St NW Ste 500, Washington, DC 20005-3922; Title Tel # (202) 789-2900
General Info: Bi-weekly, 2 pages

Vesterheim Rosemaling
Letter

Publishing Co: Norwegian American Museum Corp., 502 W Water St, Decorah, IA 52101-1782; Title Tel # (319) 382-9682 Title Fax # (319) 382-8828
Personnel: Editor-Enid Grindland
General Info: Yr. Est. 1967, Quarterly, 22 pages, Newsprint
Subscriptions: Indv. $23
Circulation: (100% controlled), Total-1,800

Watergardening News   CPM: $19

Publishing Co: Vivicon Productions Inc., 1000 Whitetail Court, Duncansville, PA 16635 Tel # (814) 695-4325; Title Tel # (814) 695-4375 Title Fax # (814) 695-1722
Personnel: Publisher-Roseanne D. Conrad, Circ. Mgr.-Roxanne Barr
Editorial Description: For entry-Level to veteran pond enthusiasts.
General Info: Yr. Est. 1995, Bi-monthly, Trim Size-8½ x 11, Desktop press, 16 pages, No Color, Matte, Saddle-stitched
Subscriptions: Indv. $20, Can. $30, For. $40
Circulation: Total-12,000
Advertising: $230.

GAY & LESBIAN INTEREST

AMALGM Newsletter

Publishing Co: Alliance of Massachusetts Asian Lesbians & Gay Men, Box 543, Boston, MA 02199
Editorial Description: Newsletter for Asian lesbians and gay men in Massachusetts.
General Info: (Formerly BAGMAL Newsletter), Yr. Est. 1988, Quarterly

Amazon Times   *Consumer*

Publishing Co: Amazon Times, Box 135, Owing Mills, MD 21170-0135
Personnel: Editor-Charlotte Zinser
Editorial Description: For working class lesbians.
Subscriptions: Indv. $20, Inst. $25

American Gay & Lesbian
Atheist   *Consumer, Association*

Publishing Co: American Gay Atheists, Inc., PO Box 66711, Houston, TX 77266-6711 Fax # (713) 862-3283; Title Tel # (713) 862-3283
Personnel: Editor-Don Sanders, Production Mgr.-Mark Franceschini
Editorial Description: Newsletter reporting on issues of state/church separation, First Amendment issues, civil & human rights issues, Gay/Lesbian concerns, commentary, poetry, movie & book reviews all from an Atheist perspective.
General Info: (Formerly American Gay Atheist), Yr. Est. 1983, Bi-monthly, Trim Size-8½ x 11, Web press, 12 pages, No Color
Subscriptions: Indv. $24, Can. $36, For. $50, $3/copy
Circulation: (5% controlled), Single Copy/Newsstand-1,800, Subscriptions-1,000, Readership-4,500, Source-I
Advertising: Inquire for rates.
Printing Co: American Atheist Press, 7215 Cameron Rd, Austin, TX 78752-2973 Tel # (512) 458-1244, Fax # (512) 467-9525

Amethyst
Consumer   CPM: $32

Publishing Co: SYOL, Box 728 Westview Stn., Binghamton, NY 13905-0728;
Title Tel # (607) 729-1921
Editorial Description: To educate and organize the gay and lesbian communities of NY'S Southern tier.
General Info: Yr. Est. 1988, Bi-monthly, Trim Size-8 x 10, Web press, 24 pages, 25% ads, Newsprint, Other
Subscriptions: Indv. $10
Circulation: Total-2,000
Advertising: $65. Accepts Inserts.

Association of New Gay & Lesbian Entrepreneurs
Association   CPM: $533

Publishing Co: Association of New Gay & Lesbian Entrepreneurs (A.N.G.L.E.), 2765 N. Scottsdale Rd., Ste. 104-D, Scottsdale, AZ 85257; Title Tel # (602) 949-7848 Title Fax # (602) 990-1958
Personnel: Publisher, Editor, Adv. Dir.-Thomas R. Cutler, Production Mgr., Art Dir.-Daniel Flynn
Editorial Description: Contains informative and educational information for Gay & Lesbian Entrepreneurs on how to maximized marketing and sales opportunities with the community.
General Info: Yr. Est. 1995, Quarterly, Trim Size-8$\frac{1}{2}$ x 11, Web press, 16 pages, No Color
Subscriptions: Indv. $400, Inst. $400, Can. $500, For. $500, Free With Membership
Circulation: (33% controlled), Total-1,500, Subscriptions-1,000, International-250
Advertising: $800.

Atalanta: Newsletter of the Atlanta Lesbian Feminist Alliance
See: WOMEN'S

Bi Women Newsletter
Consumer   CPM: $187

Publishing Co: Boston Bisexual Women' Network, C/O Bisexual Resource Center, PO Box 639, Cambridge, MA 02140; Title Tel # (617) 424-9595
Personnel: Editor-Linda Blair, Editor-Debbie Block-Schwenk
Editorial Description: News, articles, book reviews, poetry, artwork of interest to bisexual women & their friends.
General Info: Yr. Est. 1983, Bi-monthly, Trim Size-11 x 17, Offset press, 800 pages, Matte
Subscriptions: Indv. $25
Circulation: Total-800
Advertising: $150.

BiFocus
Consumer

Publishing Co: BiFocus, PO Box 30372, Philadelphia, PA 19103-8372; Title Tel # (215) 729-8750
Editorial Description: For Philadelphia's bisexual community.
General Info: Quarterly, Trim Size-8$\frac{1}{2}$ x 11, 16 pages, No Color
Advertising: $130.

Bondings
See: RELIGIOUS & THEOLOGICAL

CLAGS
Consumer, Association

Publishing Co: Center for Lesbian and Gay Studies, CUNY Graduate Center, 33 W. 42nd St., Rm.404N, New York, NY 10036-8099
Subscriptions: Free With Membership
Circulation: Readership-8,500

CLGRO Newsletter
Association

Publishing Co: Coalition for Lesbian & Gay Rights in Ontario, Box 822, Station A, Toronto, ON M5W 1G3 Canada; Title Tel # (416) 533-6824
Editorial Description: Committed to the fight for liberation for lesbians, gay men, and bisexuals.
General Info: (Formerly CGRO Newsletter), Yr. Est. 1975, Quarterly, 8 pages, Color-cover
Subscriptions: Indv. $25

Celebrate the Self
See: SEX

Center Voice

Publishing Co: Gay & Lesbian Community Center, 208 W 13th St, New York, NY 10011-7702; Title Tel # (212) 620-7310
Personnel: Publisher-Richard Burns, Editor-Benjamin Stilp, Adv. Dir.-Paul Hepworth
Editorial Description: News of New York's gay & lesbian community.
General Info: Yr. Est. 1985, Monthly, Trim Size-8$\frac{1}{2}$ x 11, Sheetfed press, 8 pages, ISSN: 0894-8984, No Color, Matte
Subscriptions: Indv. $25
Circulation: Total-23,000

Centre/Fold
Scholarly, Association

Publishing Co: Toronto Centre for Gay and Lesbian Studies, 2 Bloor Street West, Suite 100-129, Toronto, ON M4W 3E2 Canada; Title Tel # (416) 925-9872
Editorial Description: CENTRE/FOLD is the newsletter of the Toronto Centre for Lesbian and Gay Studies. We advance a critical understanding of the lives, histories and cultures of all lesbians and gay men in the context of sexuality, race, gneder and class. By building a financially sound, community-based, lively organization, we stimulate, support and promote lesbian and gay exploration.
General Info: Yr. Est. 1990, Semi-annually, ISSN: 1180-8101
Subscriptions: Indv. $25, $3/copy

Dinah
Consumer

Publishing Co: Lesbian Activist Bureau, Inc., PO Box 1485, Cincinnati, OH 45201-1485
Editorial Description: Local: lesbian news, interviews, humor, poetry, opinions, letters, graphics, short articles, short fiction. National: book reviews, major news.
General Info: (Formerly Dinah Soar News), Yr. Est. 1974, Bi-monthly, 16 pages, 10% ads, No Color
Subscriptions: Indv. $10, $2/copy
Advertising: $75.

Dykes, Disability & Stuff
See: DISABILITY

FLGC Newsletter

Publishing Co: Friends for Lesbian & Gay Concerns, 143 Campbell Avenue, Ithaca, NY 14850-0222 Tel # (215) 234-8424; Title Tel # (607) 272-1024 Title Fax # (607) 272-0801
Personnel: Editor-Janis Kelly
Editorial Description: For gay & lesbian Quakers.
General Info: Yr. Est. 1972, Quarterly, 8 pages, Newsprint
Subscriptions: Indv. $10
Circulation: Total-770

Franchise Wise (Quarterly newsletter of the intl gay & lesbian franchise assoc.)
Association

Publishing Co: T R C Publishing, 2765 N. Scottsdale Rd, Suite 104-D, Scottsdale, AZ 85257 Fax # (602) 992-1958; Title Tel # (602) 949-7848 Title Fax # (602) 990-1958
Personnel: Publisher, Editor, Adv. Dir.-Thomas R. Cutler, Product Mgr., Art Dir.-Daniel Flynn
Editorial Description: It is published for gay and lesbian franchises and potential franchises wishing to know which franchisors are receptive to the community. Also a forum for franchisors proactively seeking to market to the gay and lesbian community.
General Info: (Formerly Gay & Lesbian Franchise News, The), Yr. Est. 1995, Quarterly, Trim Size-17 x 11, Web press, 50 pages, No Color, Newsprint, Other
Subscriptions: Inst. $400, Can. $500, For. $300, Free
Circulation: (20% controlled), Total-2,500, Subscriptions-1,000, International-250
Advertising: Inquire for rates.

GLAAD Newsletter

Publishing Co: The Gay & Lesbian Alliance Against Defamation, Inc., 150 W 26th St Rm 503, New York, NY 10001-6813; Title Tel # (212) 966-1700
Personnel: Editor-Craig Davidson, Editor-Karin Schwartz

GLTF Newsletter
Association

Publishing Co: Gay, Lesbian and Bisexual Task Force, American Library Assn., 50 E. Huron St., Chicago, IL 60611-2795 Title Tel # (312) 280-4204 Fax # (312) 440-9374
Personnel: Editor-Kathy Anderson
Editorial Description: Published to assist librarians in providing improved services to the gay and lesbian community.
General Info: Yr. Est. 1987, Quarterly, Trim Size-8$\frac{1}{2}$ x 11, Desktop press, 8 pages, ISSN: 1045-2893
Subscriptions: Indv. $5, Inst. $5, Can. $7, For. $10
Circulation: Total-300
Advertising: Inquire for rates.

GOAL Gazette
Association

Publishing Co: Gay Officers Action League, Box 2038, Canal St. Stn., New York, NY
Editorial Description: Newsletter of the Gay Officers Action League.
General Info: Monthly

Gay Airline & Travel Club Newsletter, The
See: TRAVEL

Gay Center Voice

Publishing Co: Lesbian & Gay Community Svcs. Ctr., Inc., 208 W 13th St, New York, NY 10011-7702; Title Tel # (212) 620-7310
Personnel: Publisher-Richard Burns, Editor-Robert Woodworth, Adv. Dir.-Paul Hepworth
Editorial Description: Covers news & events in New York's gay community.
General Info: Yr. Est. 1983, Monthly, Sheetfed press, 16 pages, ISSN: 0894-8984, 2 Color, Coated
Subscriptions: Indv. $25
Circulation: Total-22,000

G'vanim
See: RELIGIOUS & THEOLOGICAL

HIC Newsletter
Association

Publishing Co: Homosexual Information Center, 115 Monroe St, Bossier City, LA 71111-4539; Title Tel # (318) 742-4709
Personnel: Editor-Don Slater
Editorial Description: Newsletter on issues facing homosexuals today.
General Info: (Formerly Tangents), Yr. Est. 1965, Bi-monthly, Mimeo press, 6 pages
Circulation: Total-1,000

InfoPack
See: DRUGS & PHARMACEUTICALS

Jewish Gaily Forward, The
See: RELIGIOUS & THEOLOGICAL

Lambda Update
See: CIVIL RIGHTS

Lesbian and Gay Archivist

Publishing Co: Canadian Lesbian & Gay Archives, P.O Box 639, Station A, Toronto, ON M5W 1G2 Canada Fax # (416) 251-8285; Title Tel # (416) 777-2755 Title Fax # (905) 257-8285
Editorial Description: Lesbian and gay issues especially concerning archives, libraries and history.
General Info: (Formerly Gay Archivist), Yr. Est. 1979, Trim Size-8½ x 11, Desktop press, 8 pages, ISSN: 0714-3605, Matte
Subscriptions: Free
Advertising: Accepts Inserts.

Lesbian Herstory Archives
News
Business, Consumer

Publishing Co: Lesbian Herstory Educational Foundation, Inc., PO Box 1258, New York, NY 10116-1258; Title Tel # (718) 768-3953
Personnel: Publisher, Editor-Deborah Edel
Editorial Description: A newsletter about the work of the Lesbian Herstory Educational Foundation, Inc. Includes reference materials, bibliographies and cultural items on all aspects of Lesbian history and culture. The collection serves as a source of infomation as well as anArchival collection on Lesbian history.
General Info: Yr. Est. 1975, Irregular, Offset press, 24 pages, No Color, Other, Saddle-stitched
Subscriptions: Inst. $10
Circulation: Total-8,000

Lesbian/Gay Law Notes
Scholarly, Association

Publishing Co: Lesbian & Gay Law Association of Greater New York, 799 Broadway #340, New York, NY 10003-6811; Title Tel # (212) 353-9118 Title Fax # (212) 353-2970
Personnel: Editor-Arthur S. Leonard, Circ. Mgr.-Daniel R. Schaffer
Editorial Description: Concise summary of legal developments affecting lesbians & gay and community.
General Info: (Formerly Law Group Notes), Yr. Est. 1979, Monthly, ISSN: 8755-9021
Subscriptions: Indv. $25, Can. $50, For. $57

Lesbianline
Business, Consumer **CPM: $27**

Publishing Co: Clothespin Fever Press, 10393 Spur Ct, La Mesa, CA 91941; Title Tel # (619) 234-2656
Personnel: Editor-Jenny Wrenn
Editorial Description: News items of note to gay/lesbian writers, publishers, & interested readers.
General Info: Yr. Est. 1987, Irregular, Trim Size-11 x 17, Web press, 8 pages, 10% ads, Newsprint
Subscriptions: Indv. $2, Can. $3, For. $4, $1/copy
Circulation: (80% controlled), Total-5,000
Advertising: $138. Accepts Inserts.
List Rental: Hotline: $291/M
Printing Co: San Dieguito Publishing, 1910 Diamond St, San Marcos, CA 92069-5120 Tel # (619) 744-0910

Loving Brotherhood
Newsletter
Consumer, Association

Publishing Co: Loving Brotherhood, PO Box 556, Sussex, NJ 07461-0556; Title Tel # (201) 875-4710
Personnel: Publisher, Editor-Ralph Walker
Editorial Description: Transformational journal from gay men to all loving people everywhere.
General Info: Yr. Est. 1977, Monthly, Trim Size-8½ x 11, Web press, 13 pages, 4 Color, Newsprint
Subscriptions: Indv. $18, Inst. $35, For. $20, $2/copy
Circulation: (100% controlled), Total-200
List Rental: Rents Lists
Printing Co: Lightning Press, Route 23, Pompton Plains, NJ 07444 Tel # (201) 839-1470

Mastering Life
See: SEX

Media Reporter
Business, Association

Publishing Co: Gay & Lesbian Press Assn., PO Box 8185, Universal City, CA 91608-0185; Title Tel # (818) 902-1476
Personnel: Editor-R.J. Curry
Editorial Description: Newsletter information about gay/lesbian publishing, broadcasts, writing, & assn. news.
General Info: Yr. Est. 1980, Bi-monthly, Trim Size-8½ x 11, 16 pages, 4% ads, No Color, Newsprint
Subscriptions: Indv. $40, Inst. $150
Circulation: (100% controlled), Total-1,000
Advertising: Inquire for rates.
List Rental: Actives: $50/M

Military & Police Uniform Association Newsletter
See: CLUBS

Momentum
Association

Publishing Co: Human Rights Compaign Fund, PO Box 1396, Washington, DC 20013; Title Tel # (202) 628-4160 Title Fax # (202) 347-5323
Personnel: Editor-Gregory J. King, Asst. Ed., Asst. Ed.-Beth Allen
Editorial Description: Newsletter for members of the Human Rights Campign fund.
General Info: Quarterly, Trim Size-8½ x 11, 12 pages, 2 Color, Matte, Other

Mom's Apple Pie
Association **CPM: $300**

Publishing Co: Lesbian Mothers Natl. Defense Fund, PO Box 21567, Seattle, WA 98111-3567; Title Tel # (206) 325-2643
Personnel: Editor-Jenny Sayward, Promotion Dir.-Misha Williams
Editorial Description: Covers news, updates on lesbian & gay custody cases, and offers information and support on donor insemination, adoption, and lesbian & gay parenting.
General Info: Yr. Est. 1974, Quarterly, Trim Size-8½ x 11, Offset press, 16 pages, No Color
Subscriptions: Indv. $15, Inst. $15, Can. $20, For. $20, $2/copy
Acquistions: Publication Bought
Circulation: Total-500
Advertising: $150. Accepts Inserts.

More Light Update
Association

Publishing Co: Presbyterians for Lesbian & Gay Concerns, c/o James D. Anderson, Box 38, New Brunswick, NJ 08903-0038; Title Tel # (908) 249-1016 Title Fax # (908) 932-6916
Personnel: Publisher, Editor-James Anderson
Editorial Description: Lesbian & gay concerns within the Presbyterian Church (U.S.A.).
General Info: Yr. Est. 1980, Monthly, Trim Size-5½ x 8½, Sheetfed press, 20 pages, ISSN: 0889-3985, Ind/Abs/Online: PresbyNet, 10% ads, No Color, Other
Subscriptions: Indv. $10, $1/copy
Advertising: $200. Accepts Inserts.
Printing Co: Brunswick Typographic, Inc., 230 Brunswick Ave, Spotswood, NJ 08884-1050 Tel # (908) 251-8220

Newsbreaks
Association **CPM: $100**

Publishing Co: New York Advertising & Communications Network, Inc., Box 149, 332 Bleecker St., New York, NY 10014-2980; Title Tel # (212) 517-0380
Personnel: Editor-Jack Schlegel, Production Mgr., Adv. Dir.-Kent C. Dillon, Art Dir.-Lanny Richman
Editorial Description: With more than 900 lesbian and gay members, NYACN is the biggest and busiest of the metropolitan-area professional groups.
General Info: Monthly, Trim Size-8½ x 11, 16 pages, 2 Color, Matte
Subscriptions: Indv. $45, $5/copy
Circulation: Total-2,500
Advertising: $250.

One-IGLA Bulletin

Publishing Co: One Institute, PO Box 69679, West Hollywood, CA 90069 Tel # (310) 854-0271
Personnel: Editor-Ernie Potvin
Editorial Description: Newsletter of ONE Institute/International Gay and Lesbian Archives.
General Info: (Formerly One Institute/International Gay and Lesbian Archives), Yr. Est. 1995, Irregular
Subscriptions: Indv. $10, Inst. $10, Can. $10, For. $10

OurStories

Publishing Co: Gay & Lesbian Historical Soc. of Northern California, 2940 16th Street, San Francisco, CA 94103; Title Tel # (415) 626-0980
Personnel: Editor-Les Wright
General Info: (Formerly Newsletter of the Gay and Lesbian Historical Society.), Quarterly, ISSN: 0896-162X

Out and About
See: TRAVEL

Out in the Mountains
Consumer

Publishing Co: Out in the Mountains, PO Box 177, Burlington, VT 05402-0177
Personnel: Editor-Deborah Lashman, Circ. Mgr.-Terry Wolf, Production Mgr.-Bruce Howden, Adv. Dir.-Ellen Hetherington
Editorial Description: Serves as a voice for lesbians, gay men and bisexuals and their supporters in Vermont. Includes news, features, advertising.
General Info: Yr. Est. 1986, Monthly, Trim Size-8½ x 11, Offset press, 24 pages, 2 Color
Subscriptions: Indv. $20, $2/copy
Printing Co: BMH Graphics, 32 N Champlain St, Burlington, VT 05401-4320 Tel # (802) 864-7198

Ozark Feminist Review
See: WOMEN'S

Pride of Lions

Publishing Co: Columbia Gay & Lesbian Alliance, Columbia Univ., 304 Earl Hall, New York, NY 10027-2399; Title Tel # (212) 280-5113
General Info: Monthly

Privacy Newsletter
See: CONSUMER INTERESTS

Program and Legislative Action
See: POLITICS

SAGE Bulletin

Publishing Co: Senior Action in A Gay Environment, 208 W 13th St, New York, NY 10011-7702; Title Tel # (212) 741-2247
Personnel: Editor-Cynthia Kessler
Editorial Description: Monthly update of current events & activities of oldest & largest organization serving gay & lesbian seniors.
General Info: Yr. Est. 1983, Monthly, 4 pages
Circulation: Total-3,500
Advertising: Accepts Inserts.
List Rental: Rents Lists
Printing Co: Buda Graphics, Ltd., 210 11th Ave., New York, NY 10001 Tel # (212) 627-2000

SAGE News

Publishing Co: Senior Action in A Gay Environment, 208 W 13th St, New York, NY 10011-7702; Title Tel # (212) 741-2247
Editorial Description: Organizational news of oldest, largest gay seniors' group in U.S.
General Info: (Formerly SAGE Voices), Yr. Est. 1981, Semi-annually, 12 pages, Newsprint
Circulation: Total-12,000

Shamakami   *Consumer*

Publishing Co: Shamakami, PO Box 460456, San Francisco, CA 94146-0456
Editorial Description: For South Asian lesbians and bi-sexuals.
General Info: Quarterly
Subscriptions: Indv. $10

Task Force Report

Publishing Co: Natl. Gay & Lesbian Task Force, 1734 14th St NW, Washington, DC 20009-4309; Title Tel # (202) 332-6483
Personnel: Editor-Robert Bray
Editorial Description: News on gay & lesbian political issues nationwide & review of National Gay & Lesbian Task Force programs.
General Info: Yr. Est. 1973, Quarterly, Trim Size-11½ x 17, Offset press, 8 pages
Circulation: Total-17,000
Advertising: Inquire for rates.
List Rental: Rents Lists

Tripod, The   *Association*

Publishing Co: Triangle Foundation, 19641 W 7 Mile Rd, Detroit, MI 48219-2721; Title Tel # (313) 537-3323 Title Fax # (810) 539-3379
Personnel: Editor-John Monahan, Circ. Mgr.-Henry Messer, Art Dir.-Eric Hansen
Editorial Description: Gay/Lesbian news and features relating to current issues in human rights.
General Info: (Formerly MOHR News & Notes), Yr. Est. 1978, Trim Size-8½ x 11, 8 pages, No Color, Matte
Subscriptions: Free To Qualified Recipient
Circulation: Total-12,500
Advertising: Inquire for rates.

Valley Women's Voice
See: WOMEN'S

Waves   *Consumer, Association*

Publishing Co: United Church Coalition for Lesbian/Gay Concerns, 18 N College St, Athens, OH 45701-2436 Tel # (614) 593-7301 Fax # (614) 592-4846; Title Tel # (203) 683-8943
Personnel: Editor-April Allison
Editorial Description: Publicizes coalition events and churches that have declared themselves 'open'.
General Info: Yr. Est. 1975, Quarterly, Trim Size-8½ x 11, Offset press, 12 pages, No Color, Other
Subscriptions: Free With Membership

GENEALOGY

3-D Data   *Consumer*

Publishing Co: 3-D Data, C/O M.D. Chamberlain, 13650 No. Frontage Rd. #334, Yuma, AZ 85367
Personnel: Editor-Marjorie Chamberlain
Editorial Description: A newsletter of the Dyckman/Dikeman/Dykeman family.
General Info: Quarterly

AFG News   *Association*

Publishing Co: American French Genealogical Society, PO Box 2113, Pawtucket, RI 02861-0113 Tel # (401) 769-8079; Title Tel # (401) 765-6141 Title Fax # (401) 465-6141
Personnel: Editor-Sylvia Bantholomy, Circ. Mgr.-Roger Beauday, Mktg. Dir.-Roger Bearday
Editorial Description: French Canadian history and genealogy
General Info: Yr. Est. 1990, Bi-monthly, Trim Size-8½ x 11, Offset press, 2 pages, 2 Color, Other, Other
Subscriptions: Indv. $20, Inst. $25, Free With Membership
Circulation: Total-1,400

AGS Quarterly: Bulletin of the Association for Gravestone Studies
See: HISTORY

About Alfords

Publishing Co: About Alfords, 1403 Kingsford Dr., Florissant, MD 63061; Title Tel # (314) 831-8648
Personnel: Editor-Gilbert Alford

About Towne

Publishing Co: Towne Family Association, 145 Oriole, Batesville, AR 72501-6500

Acadian Genealogy
Exchange   *Consumer, Scholarly*

Publishing Co: Acadian Genealogy Exchange, 863 Wayman Branch Rd, Covington, KY 41015-2201; Title Tel # (606) 356-9825 Title Fax # (606) 356-9825
Personnel: Publisher, Editor-Janet Jehn
Editorial Description: Restricted to Acadian,Cajun and/or French-Canadian genealogy and history; free queries.
General Info: Yr. Est. 1972, Quarterly, Trim Size-8½ x 11, Desktop press, 30 pages, ISSN: 0199-9591, No Color, Matte, Other
Subscriptions: Indv. $17, Can. $17, For. $17, $5/copy
Circulation: Total-800
Printing Co: J & J Printing, 856 Crocus Lane, Covington, KY 41015

Acorns to Oaks   *Association*

Publishing Co: Oakland Co. Genealogical Soc., PO Box 1094, Birmingham, MI 48012-1094
Personnel: Editor-Pamela Epple, Bk. Rev. Ed.-Marge Kalec
Editorial Description: Publication for members of the Oakland County Genealogical Society and those interested in Oakland County Michigan genealogy research.
General Info: Yr. Est. 1977, Quarterly, Trim Size-8½ x 11, Sheetfed press, 26 pages, ISSN: 1045-537X, No Color, Other, Saddle-stitched
Subscriptions: Indv. $10, Can. $13, For. $15, Free With Membership

Adams County Trumpeter
See: HISTORY

Adams Family Chronicle   *Association*

Publishing Co: Adams Family Assoc., 1294 W Nancy Creek Dr NE, Atlanta, GA 30319-1690; Title Tel # (404) 457-6564
Personnel: Editor-L.H. Adams, Jr.
General Info: (Formerly Adams Family Newsletter), Yr. Est. 1979, Quarterly, Trim Size-8½ x 11, Sheetfed press, 6 pages, ISSN: 8755-5026, No Color, Newsprint
Circulation: (100% controlled), Total-850
Printing Co: Action Printing Center, 3400 Clairmont Rd NE, Atlanta, GA 30319-3720 Tel # (404) 321-7457

Advance Notice

Publishing Co: Advance Notice, PO Box 1223, Princeton, NJ 08542-1223
Personnel: Publisher-James B. Bell, Editor-Thomas Jay Kemp
General Info: Quarterly
Subscriptions: Indv. $24

African-American Family
History Assn. Newsletter

Publishing Co: African/Amer. Family Hist. Assn., PO Box 115268, Atlanta, GA 30310-8268
Personnel: Editor-Herman Mason
Editorial Description: Black family & genealogical pub.
General Info: Quarterly, Trim Size-8½ x 11, Offset press, 8 pages, No Color
Acquistions: Publication Bought

Alabama Genealogical
Society Newsletter   *Association*

Publishing Co: AGS Depository Hdqtrs., Samford Univ. Lib. 800, Lakeshore Dr., Birmingham, AL 35229-0001
Personnel: Editor-Nancy Robinson
General Info: Quarterly

Alberta Genealogical
Society Newsletter

Publishing Co: Alberta Genealogical Society, Box 12015, Edmonton, AB T5J 3L2 Canada Tel # (403) 455-7028

Alexander Agenda   *Association*

Publishing Co: Bette Butcher Topp, 1304 W. Cliffwood Ct., Spokane, WA 99218-2917; Title Tel # (509) 467-2299
Personnel: Publisher, Editor-Bette Butcher Topp
Editorial Description: For those studying the name Alexander.
General Info: Yr. Est. 1983, Irregular, Trim Size-8½ x 11, Sheetfed press, 40 pages, ISSN: 0890-9482, Color-cover
Subscriptions: $5/copy

Allee's All Around

Publishing Co: Allee's All Around, PO Box 347, Friendswood, TX 77546-0347; Title Tel # (713) 482-2839
Personnel: Publisher, Editor-Ginger Allee
Editorial Description: Family information from census, marriage, war, bible, land records. Includes Alley, Ally, Allie, Alyea.
General Info: Yr. Est. 1984, Quarterly, 50 pages, ISSN: 0883-5926
Subscriptions: Indv. $15, $4/copy

Allen Ancestors   *Association*

Publishing Co: Lusa R. Franklin, 4604 Virginia Loop Rd., Apt. 3156-G, Montgomery, AL 36116-4739
Editorial Description: Research source for persons searching for Data on ancestors bearing the Allen Surname.
General Info: Quarterly, Trim Size-8½ x 11, 25 pages
Subscriptions: Indv. $10, Inst. $10, $3/copy
Advertising: $9. Accepts Inserts.

Allen Family Circle
Consumer, Association

Publishing Co: Allen Family Circle, 4906 Ridgeway Ave, Kansas City, MO 64133-2545; Title Tel # (816) 353-4976
Personnel: Editor-Lois Allen
Editorial Description: Genealogical queries & clearinghouse for surname: Allen.
General Info: Annually, Trim Size-8½ x 11, 12 pages, ISSN: 0865-3215, No Color, Matte
Subscriptions: $3/copy

American Conference for Irish Studies Newsletter

Publishing Co: American Conference for Irish Studies, Indiana Univ. Eng. Dept., Ft. Wayne, IN 46805; Title Tel # (215) 328-8000
Personnel: Editor-Jim Donnelly

Among the Coles

Publishing Co: Cole County Genealogical Society, PO Box 225, Charleston, IL 61920-0225
Personnel: Editor-Les Hickenbottom
General Info: Yr. Est. 1975, 11x/yr., Trim Size-8½ x 11, 8 pages, No Color
Circulation: Total-250

Ancestor Hunt

Publishing Co: Ashtabula County Genealogical Society, Geneva Library, 117 West Main Street, Geneva, OH 44041-1227 Tel # (216) 466-4521
Personnel: Editor-Marion Holmes
Editorial Description: Genealogical material relating to Ashtabula County, reviews, queries, instruction, registry.
General Info: Yr. Est. 1973, Quarterly, Trim Size-8½ x 11, Letrpr. press, 34 pages, ISSN: 0736-9115, No Color, Newsprint
Subscriptions: Indv. $10, Inst. $10, $3/copy
Acquistions: Publication Bought, Publication Sold
Circulation: Total-325
Printing Co: Mentor Office Center, 7490 Center St, Mentor, OH 44060-5804

Ancestry Newsletter

Publishing Co: Ancestry, Inc., PO Box 476, Salt Lake City, UT 84110-0476; Title Tel # (801) 531-1790
Personnel: Publisher-John Sittner, Editor-Robb Barr
Editorial Description: Practical, instructional, & informative pieces specifically applicable to the field of genealogy. Articles on research techniques & genealogical collections are sought. No family histories.
General Info: Yr. Est. 1984, Bi-monthly, Trim Size-8½ x 11, Sheetfed press, 16 pages, ISSN: 0749-5927, 2 Color, Newsprint, Saddle-stitched
Subscriptions: Indv. $12, $3/copy
Circulation: Total-8,000

Ancestry Trails

Publishing Co: Trumbull County Chapter, PO Box 309, Warren, OH 44482-0309
Editorial Description: Research information, county records, chapter news, notice of seminars, etc.
General Info: Monthly, Trim Size-8½ x 11, Mimeo press, 8 pages

Appler Family Newsletter

Publishing Co: Charles R. Appler, 10417 New Bedford Ct SE, Lehigh Acres, FL 33936-7253; Title Tel # (941) 368-6373
Personnel: Publisher, Editor-Charles R. Appler
Editorial Description: Provides data on past & current generations of Appler Family.
General Info: Yr. Est. 1982, Quarterly, Trim Size-8½ x 11, Mimeo press, 8 pages, ISSN: 1047-684X, No Color
Subscriptions: Indv. $7, $2/copy
Circulation: Total-150

Archibald Clan Newsletter
Association

Publishing Co: Clan Archibald in America, 302 S Wilson St, Hillsboro, KS 67063-1826; Title Tel # (316) 947-3691
Personnel: Publisher-Elbert Archibald, Editor-Peggy Goertzen
Editorial Description: To provide a network of Archibald family researchers & source data for Archibald research.
General Info: Yr. Est. 1981, Quarterly, Trim Size-8½ x 11, Mimeo press, 22 pages, No Color, Newsprint
Subscriptions: Indv. $10, $3/copy

Arkansas Family Historian
Association

Publishing Co: AR Genealogical Society Inc., PO Box 908, Hot Springs, AR 71902-0908; Title Tel # (501) 262-4513 Title Fax # (501) 262-4513
Personnel: Publisher, Editor-Margaret Hubbard
Editorial Description: Primary & secondary research material, generally concentrated on Arkansas families, counties, etc.
General Info: Yr. Est. 1962, Quarterly, Trim Size-8½ x 11, Offset press, 48 pages, ISSN: 0571-0472, 10% ads, No Color, Saddle-stitched
Subscriptions: Indv. $15
Circulation: Total-1,600

Armiger's News
Consumer, Association

Publishing Co: American College of Heraldry, Inc., PO Box Cg, Tuscaloosa, AL 35486-2870
Personnel: Editor-David Robert Wooten
Editorial Description: Lists coats of arms borne in America and armiger biographies.
General Info: Yr. Est. 1979, Quarterly, Trim Size-8½ x 11, Letrpr. press, 18 pages, No Color
Subscriptions: Indv. $25, Inst. $10
Circulation: Total-1,028

Ashby Newsletter

Publishing Co: Ashby Newsletter, 1013 Illinois St, Bicknell, IN 47512-3000; Title Tel # (812) 735-2530
Personnel: Publisher, Editor-Carol Hulen
Editorial Description: Clearinghouse for all Ashby family records, everywhere. Queries & ads free to subscribers.
General Info: Yr. Est. 1985, Quarterly, Mimeo press, 10 pages, Perfect bound
Subscriptions: Indv. $10, $3/copy
Advertising: Inquire for rates. Accepts Inserts.

Atlantic County Historical Society Newsletter
Association

Publishing Co: Atlantic County Historical Society, 907 Shore Rd # 301, Somers Point, NJ 08244-2335; Title Tel # (609) 927-9776
General Info: Quarterly, 8 pages
Subscriptions: Free With Membership

Augustaeum
Consumer

Publishing Co: Augustan Society, Inc., PO Box P, Torrance, CA 90508-0210 Tel # (310) 320-7766
Editorial Description: Newsletter of the Augustan Society.
General Info: Quarterly
Advertising: Inquire for rates.

Autrey, Autry, Autery Bulletin

Publishing Co: Autrey Family Assn., AFA-199, Rt. I, Box 106-B, Thomasville, AL 36784; Title Tel # (205) 385-2503
Personnel: Editor-Kirk Boutwell, Publisher, Circ. Mgr.-Milton Autry
Editorial Description: This international genealogical & historical quarterly serves those doing research on the many spelling variations of the Autry name including Awtry, Otray, D'Autry, Aughtry & more. 20 to 40 pages.
General Info: Yr. Est. 1986, Quarterly, Sheetfed press, 30 pages, ISSN: 0892-0303, No Color
Subscriptions: Indv. $15, $5/copy
Circulation: Total-319

B.C.G.S. News

Publishing Co: Bond County Genealogical Society, C/o Nelda Anthony, Corr. Sec., 911 Killarney, Greenville, IL 62246

BR(E)ASHE(A)R(S) Family Branches
Consumer

Publishing Co: BR(E)ASHE(A)R(S) Family Branches, 817 Stratford Dr., Bedford, TX 76021-5321; Title Tel # (817) 268-1581
Personnel: Publisher, Editor-Arzella Spear
Editorial Description: A collection of data, relating to the BRASHEAR (many different spellings) families & related lines.
General Info: Yr. Est. 1984, Monthly, Trim Size-8½ x 11, 12 pages, ISSN: 1044-5552, No Color, Matte
Subscriptions: Indv. $20
Advertising: Accepts Inserts.

Baker Family Newsletter International
Business, Association

Publishing Co: Crystal Jensen, 118 Saw Mill Rd, Union, MO 63084-4012
Personnel: Publisher, Editor-Crystal Jensen
General Info: Yr. Est. 1987, Annually, Trim Size-8½ x 11, Desktop press, 80 pages, ISSN: 0893-5831, No Color, Newsprint
Subscriptions: Indv. $15
Circulation: Total-227
Advertising: Inquire for rates. Accepts Inserts.
Printing Co: Ye Olde Homestead, 326 Panhorst St, Staunton, IL 62088-1829 Tel # (618) 635-3259

Baldwin By-Lines
Association

Publishing Co: Bette Butcher Topp, 1304 W. Cliffwood Ct., Spokane, WA 99218-2917; Title Tel # (509) 467-2299
Personnel: Publisher, Editor-Bette Topp
Editorial Description: Research info for the last name of Baldwin.
General Info: Yr. Est. 1985, Irregular, Sheetfed press, ISSN: 0890-9474
Subscriptions: $6/copy
Acquistions: Publication Sold

Band of Botsford Bulletin

Publishing Co: Botsford Family Historical Assn., c/o Mrs. Janet Elton, 80 E. Main St., Plymouth, CT 06782

Barnes Family Digest
Consumer, Association

Publishing Co: PBS-Professional Business Svces., 450 Potter St, Wauseon, OH 43567-1138; Title Tel # (419) 335-6485
Personnel: Editor-Howard Fausey, Asst. Ed.-Shelly Ackley
Editorial Description: The Barnes Family Quarterly is published in Feb. - May, Aug. - Nov. & covers all known Barnes branches in the U.S.
General Info: (Formerly Barnes Family Quarterly), Yr. Est. 1983, Quarterly
Subscriptions: Indv. $12
List Rental: Actives: 1,000

Barney Family News   *Association*

Publishing Co: William Barney, 7361 Silver Pine Dr, Springfield, VA 22153-1819;
Title Tel # (703) 451-3916 Title Fax # (703) 451-2814
Personnel: Publisher-William C. Barney
Editorial Description: Focus on family history and genealogy.
General Info: Yr. Est. 1979, Quarterly, Trim Size-8½ x 11, Offset press, 32 pages, ISSN: 1045-344X,
Ind/Abs/Online: http:softaid.net/anchor/barney/barney.html, Coated, Saddle-stitched
Subscriptions: Indv. $8, Inst. $8, $2/copy
Circulation: Total-400, Readership-1,000

Batchelder Review

Publishing Co: Pioneer Publications, PO Box 1179, Tum Tum, WA 99034-1179;
Title Tel # (509) 276-9841
Personnel: Publisher-Shirley Oakes
Editorial Description: Genealogical data collected on the surname,lineage & Queries accepted free.
General Info: Yr. Est. 1986, Irregular, Trim Size-8½ x 11, Offset press, 25 pages, ISSN: 0897-7429,
No Color
Subscriptions: $6/copy
Acquistions: Publication Bought

Bean Stalk

Publishing Co: Southern Bean Assn., Mary Kirk-McCrary, 209 Kinwood Dr., Murfreesboro, TN
37130; Title Tel # (615) 893-5667

Bear Tracks

Publishing Co: Hunting for Bears, Inc., 3878 W 3200 S, Salt Lake City, UT 84120-2154;
Title Tel # (801) 298-6339
Personnel: Editor-Nicholas Murray, Production Mgr., Adv. Dir., Art Dir.-David Murray, Publisher, Circ.
Mgr., Promotion Dir.-Joyce Murray
Editorial Description: National publication - personal view of genealogy with emphasis on
computers. H.F.B., Inc. has computer databank of marriages from 16 southern & midwestern
states.
General Info: Yr. Est. 1978, Quarterly, Trim Size-8½ x 11, Web press, 16 pages, 1% ads, No Color,
Saddle-stitched
Subscriptions: Indv. $10, $3/copy
Advertising: Inquire for rates.
List Rental: Rents Lists
Printing Co: DABCO

Beaver Briefs

Publishing Co: Willamette Valley Genealogical Society, PO Box 2083, Salem, OR 97308-2083

Beech Grove

Publishing Co: Mark Hagenbuch, 821 W Siddonsburg Rd, Dillsburg, PA 17019-9320
Tel # (717) 432-8911; Title Tel # (717) 743-0303
Personnel: Editor-Mark Hagenbuch, Production Mgr.-Diane Brosius
Editorial Description: Not only includes information on Hagenbuch families and related lines, past
present, and future. Also includes frequent articles on American History, Pennsylvania German
Folklore and life.
General Info: Yr. Est. 1982, Semi-annually, Mimeo press, 25 pages
Subscriptions: Indv. $4, $2/copy
Circulation: Total-115

Belcher Bulletin

Publishing Co: Belcher Bulletin, PO Box 10, Belcher, KY 41513-0010
Personnel: Editor-Fon Belcher, Circ. Mgr.-Jonathan Belcher, Production Mgr.-Camilia Belcher
Editorial Description: Covers the life & times of colonial governor Jonathan Belcher; & history/
biography of the Belcher family in the U.S., Nova Scotia, & Great Britain; & Belcher place names.
General Info: Annually, Trim Size-8½ x 11, Offset press, Ind/Abs/Online: GPAI, BPI, No Color,
Saddle-stitched
Subscriptions: Indv. $20, $2/copy

Belgian Laces
See: HISTORY

Bell Chimes   *Association*   **CPM: $20**

Publishing Co: Sponsor-International Bell Society, Bell Chimes, PO Box 451, Springfield, VT
05156-0451; Title Tel # (802) 885-3151
Personnel: Editor-Irving Bell
Editorial Description: News & genealogies relating to Bells of Scottish & English descent
everywhere.
General Info: Yr. Est. 1980, Bi-monthly, Trim Size-8½ x 11, Web press, 8 pages, No Color
Subscriptions: Indv. $25, $2/copy
Circulation: Total-982
Advertising: $20.

Benedict Family News, The   *Association*

Publishing Co: Benedict Family News, The, 718 S. 35th St., Galesburg, MI 49053;
Title Tel # (616) 665-9697
Personnel: Editor-Mary A. Grindol, Circ. Mgr.-Larry Grindol
Editorial Description: Newsletter devoted to researching a publishing genealogical and newsworthy
information about all families surnamed Benedict.
General Info: Yr. Est. 1993, Quarterly, Trim Size-8½ x 11, Desktop press, 14 pages, Matte, Saddle-
stitched
Subscriptions: Indv. $12, $3/copy
Circulation: Total-150, Readership-150

Berry-By-Lines

Publishing Co: Pioneer Publications, PO Box 1179, Tum Tum, WA 99034-1179;
Title Tel # (509) 276-9841
Personnel: Publisher-Shirley Penna Oakes
Editorial Description: Genealogical data collected on the Surname, lineage and queries accepted
free.
General Info: Yr. Est. 1991, Irregular, Trim Size-8½ x 11, 25 pages
Subscriptions: $6/copy

Berry Newsletter

Publishing Co: Berry Newsletter, 1013 Illinois St, Bicknell, IN 47512-3000; Title Tel # (812) 735-2530
Personnel: Publisher, Editor-Carol Hulen
Editorial Description: Clearinghouse for all Berry/Barry family records, everywhere. Queries & ads
free to subscribers.
General Info: Yr. Est. 1985, Quarterly, Mimeo press, 10 pages
Subscriptions: Indv. $10, $3/copy

Bicknell Heritage

Publishing Co: Sponsor-Bicknell Family Assn., Ashby Newsletter, 1013 Illinois St, Bicknell, IN
47512-3000; Title Tel # (812) 735-2530
Personnel: Editor-Carol Hulen
Editorial Description: Information on descendents at William Bicknell died Amherst County, VA,
1781.
General Info: Yr. Est. 1985, Quarterly, Mimeo press, 6 pages, No Color, Newsprint
Subscriptions: Indv. $4, $2/copy

Black Swamp Heritage

Publishing Co: Black Swamp Heritage, 18620 W Moline Martin Rd, Martin, OH 43445-9720
Personnel: Editor-Grace Luebke

Blaisdell Papers

Publishing Co: Blaisdell Family Nat'l. Assn., PO Box 707, Amarillo, TX 79105-0707

Bonnet-T-E's and Kin   *Consumer*

Publishing Co: Bonnet-T-E's, 314 Glenwood Rd, Lake Forest, IL 60045-3020;
Title Tel # (708) 234-4804
Personnel: Publisher, Editor-Howard Bonnett
Editorial Description: Carries genealogical information for Bonnet-T-E and allied families.
General Info: Yr. Est. 1973, Annually, Trim Size-8½ x 11, Sheetfed press, 10 pages, ISSN: 0743-
0957, No Color, Newsprint
Circulation: Total-400
Printing Co: Vogue Printers Inc., 2421 Green Bay Rd, North Chicago, IL 60064-3010
Tel # (708) 689-4044

Boone County Genealogical
Society Newsletter

Publishing Co: Boone County Genealogical Society, PO Box 453, Boone, IA 50036-0453;
Title Tel # (515) 432-5920

Boone County Historian

Publishing Co: Boone County Historical & Railroad Society, Inc., PO Box 1094, Harrison, AR
72602-1094
Personnel: Editor-Sammie Rose, Production Mgr.-Virginia Phillips
General Info: Yr. Est. 1978, Trim Size-8½ x 11, Offset press, 32 pages, No Color
Subscriptions: Indv. $10, Inst. $25, $3/copy
Circulation: Total-300

Boone Geneaological
Quarterly   *Association*

Publishing Co: Boone County Genealogical Society, PO Box 306, Madison, WV 25130-0306;
Title Tel # (304) 369-2769
Personnel: Editor-Janet Hager, Circ. Mgr.-Lenore Ferrell
General Info: (Formerly Boone Co. Gen. Soc. Newsletter), Yr. Est. 1975, Quarterly, Sheetfed press,
16 pages
Subscriptions: Indv. $6, $2/copy
Circulation: Total-300

Born Young Newsletter

Publishing Co: Born Young, 347 12th Ave. N, St. Paul, MN 55075-1957; Title Tel # (612) 455-3626
Personnel: Editor-Vicki Young Albu
Editorial Description: A newsletter for genealogists researching persons with the surname Young
(Yung, Jung, etc.) Free queries accepted.
General Info: Yr. Est. 1983, Quarterly, Trim Size-8½ x 11, Sheetfed press, 20 pages, ISSN: 0885-
1247, No Color, Newsprint
Subscriptions: Indv. $15, $3/copy
Circulation: Total-200
Advertising: Accepts Inserts.

Bouchard Family Newsletter

Publishing Co: Bouchard Family Newsletter, PO Box 13548, Saint Louis, MO 63138-0548
Personnel: Editor-Maryann Schicker

Bouquet (Buckey) Newsletter *Association*

Publishing Co: Genz Assoc. of America, 5821 Rowland Hill Rd., Cascade, MD 21719-1939; Title Tel # (301) 416-2660
Personnel: Editor-Victor Gebhart
General Info: Annually, Mimeo press, No Color
Subscriptions: Indv. $2

Bowen Newsletter

Publishing Co: Bowen Newsletter, 1013 Illinois St, Bicknell, IN 47512-3000; Title Tel # (812) 735-2530
Personnel: Publisher, Editor-Carol Hulen
Editorial Description: Clearinghouse for all Bowen family records, everywhere. Queries & ads free for subscribers.
General Info: Yr. Est. 1985, Quarterly, Mimeo press, 10 pages
Subscriptions: Indv. $10, $3/copy

Bozarth Beacon *Consumer*

Publishing Co: Bozarth Beacon, 38518 Kickbush Ln, Springfield, OR 97478-8667
Tel # (541) 746-9736; Title Tel # (503) 746-9736
Personnel: Publisher, Editor-Gayle Rose Mark
Editorial Description: A quarterly pub. of genealogical & historical materials on Bozarth.
General Info: Yr. Est. 1987, Quarterly, Mimeo press, 30 pages, ISSN: 1045-862X, Color-cover, Recycled
Subscriptions: Indv. $10, $3/copy
Acquistions: Publication Sold
Circulation: Total-132

Bradford Compact Newsletter *Association*

Publishing Co: Governor William Bradford Compact, 5204 Kenwood Ave, Chevy Chase, MD 20815-6604; Title Tel # (301) 654-7233
Personnel: Medical Ed., Feature Ed., News Ed., Photo Ed., Society Ed., Bk. Rev. Ed., Calendar Ed.-John M. Pogue, MD, Circ. Mgr.-Herbert M. Giffin, MD, Editor, Production Mgr.-John M. Pogue, MD, Publisher, Art Dir.-Mary Ellen Pogue
Editorial Description: A genealogical newsletter serving to keep members informed of meetings, current events, new books, projects, genealogical and other information on members (including obituaries). Contains essays, artwork, photographs, news, and more.
General Info: (Formerly Descendants of Governor William Bradford of Plymouth Colony), Yr. Est. 1946, Annually, Trim Size-8½ x 11, 20 pages, ISSN: 0892-9238, Matte
Subscriptions: $8/copy
List Rental: Rents Lists
Printing Co: Bethesda Business Sevice, Spring Center, 8629 16th St., Silver Spring, MD 20910 Tel # (301) 495-9660

Branches & Acorns

Publishing Co: Southwest Texas Genealogical Society, PO Box 295, Uvalde, TX 78802-0295; Title Tel # (512) 563-2976
Personnel: Editor-Gloria Benacci
Editorial Description: Promotes collection, preservation, exchange of genealogical data in Southwest Texas.
General Info: Yr. Est. 1985, Quarterly, Trim Size-8½ x 11, Sheetfed press, 40 pages, No Color, Newsprint
Subscriptions: Indv. $15, $6/copy
Circulation: Total-300
Printing Co: Accuracy Printing, 126 S Getty St, Uvalde, TX 78801-5500 Tel # (512) 278-6505

Bricker Branches

Publishing Co: Pioneer Publications, PO Box 1179, Tum Tum, WA 99034-1179; Title Tel # (509) 276-9841
Personnel: Publisher-Shirley Oakes
Editorial Description: Genealogical data on the Bricker surname, etc.
General Info: Yr. Est. 1985, Irregular, Trim Size-8½ x 11, Mimeo press, 25 pages, ISSN: 0897-7879
Subscriptions: $6/copy

Brief Case

Publishing Co: Brief Case, PO Box 98234, Tacoma, WA 98498-0234
Personnel: Editor-Glenda Thayer

Brookside Columns: Newsletter of the Saratoga County Museum

Publishing Co: Saratoga County Historical Society, Saratoga County Museum, 6 Charlton Street, Ballston Spa, NY 12020-1707 Tel # (518) 885-4000; Title Tel # (516) 885-4000
Personnel: Editor-Fran Finkbeiner

Broyles Family Newsletter

Publishing Co: Broyles Printing, Rr 3 Box 178, Clinton, TN 37716-9803; Title Tel # (615) 457-5866
Personnel: Editor-John Broyles, Sr.
Editorial Description: Family research, cemetery, marriage, birth, death records, renunions, census records. Newspaper items. Etc.
General Info: Yr. Est. 1982, Bi-monthly, Trim Size-8½ x 11, Sheetfed press, 20 pages, ISSN: 1044-856X, No Color, Matte
Subscriptions: Indv. $12, $2/copy
Acquistions: Publication Bought
Advertising: Inquire for rates. Accepts Inserts.

Bryant County Heritage Quarterly

Publishing Co: Bryan County Heritage Assn., PO Box 153, Calera, OK 74730-0153; Title Tel # (405) 434-5848
Personnel: Publisher-Wanda Shelton, Editor-Margie Buchheister
General Info: Yr. Est. 1982, Quarterly
Subscriptions: Indv. $13, $3/copy
Acquistions: Publication Sold
Circulation: Total-135

Bucks County Genealogical Society Newsletter *Association*

Publishing Co: Bucks County Genealogical Society, PO Box 1092, Doylestown, PA 18901-0020; Title Tel # (215) 230-9410
Personnel: Editor-Donna Humphrey
Editorial Description: Contains a Query Column, news of reunions, & genealogical news, abstracts of Bucks Co. information, articles of general interest, records of activities of members.
General Info: Yr. Est. 1981, Quarterly, ISSN: 1047-2770
Subscriptions: Indv. $15, Can. $15, $3/copy
Acquistions: Publication Sold
Circulation: Total-750

Bunker Banner *Association*

Publishing Co: Bunker Family Assn., Carole Bunker, 9 Sommerset Rd., Turnersville, NJ 08012; Title Tel # (609) 589-6140
Personnel: Publisher-G.W. Bunker, Editor-Carole Bunker
Editorial Description: Genealogical information, articles & stories, events, queries, family reunions & general information about the Bunker name & family.
General Info: Yr. Est. 1970, Quarterly, Trim Size-8½ x 11, Offset press, 16 pages, Matte
Subscriptions: Indv. $15, Can. $17, For. $17, Free With Membership
Circulation: Total-590
Printing Co: R.J. Miller Printing Company, Box 721A, RD #2, Turnersville, NJ 08012 Tel # (609) 228-3213, Fax # (609) 232-8251

Burbank Banner

Publishing Co: John R. Burbank, 31 Congress St, Saint Albans, VT 05478-1610; Title Tel # (802) 524-3529
Personnel: Editor-John Burbank
Editorial Description: A genealogical & historical newsletter of the Burbank-Burbanck family in America, updating the 1928 genealogy.
General Info: (Formerly Burbank Family News), Yr. Est. 1980, Irregular, Trim Size-8½ x 11, Mimeo press, 8 pages, ISSN: 1071-7013, No Color
Subscriptions: $1/copy
Circulation: Total-175

Burnett Family Newsletter *Association*

Publishing Co: Burnett Family Genealogical Assn., 3891 Commander Dr, Chamblee, GA 30341-1854; Title Tel # (770) 455-6445
Personnel: Editor-Thomas Burnett
General Info: Yr. Est. 1981, Quarterly, Trim Size-8½ x 11, Offset press, 22 pages, ISSN: 0730-4978, No Color, Other, Other
Subscriptions: Indv. $15, Can. $20, For. $20, $5/copy
Circulation: (100% controlled), Total-200

Bush Branches *Association*

Publishing Co: Bette Butcher Topp, 1304 W. Cliffwood Ct., Spokane, WA 99218-2917; Title Tel # (509) 467-2299
Personnel: Publisher, Editor-Bette Butcher Topp
Editorial Description: Research information for the last name of Bush.
General Info: Yr. Est. 1983, Irregular, Trim Size-8½ x 11, Sheetfed press, ISSN: 0890-944X
Subscriptions: $6/copy

Bush-Meeting Dutch *Association*

Publishing Co: Illinois College, Dr. David Koss, Prof. of Religion, Jacksonville, IL 62650
Personnel: Editor-David Koss
Editorial Description: Local history & genealogy of the former Evangelical United Bretheren church, its predecessors, and sister churches.
General Info: Yr. Est. 1984, Quarterly, Trim Size-8½ x 11
Subscriptions: Indv. $5

Bushong Bulletin

Publishing Co: Bushong Bulletin, 1504 E. 52nd St., Odessa, TX 79762-4457; Title Tel # (915) 366-6861 Title Fax # (915) 366-2929
Personnel: Editor-Carol W. Bell
General Info: Yr. Est. 1985, Quarterly, 16 pages
Subscriptions: Indv. $10, $3/copy

Butcher Block *Association*

Publishing Co: Bette Butcher Topp, 1304 W. Cliffwood Ct., Spokane, WA 99218-2917; Title Tel # (509) 467-2299
Personnel: Publisher, Editor-Bette Butcher Topp
Editorial Description: Research info for the last name of Butcher.
General Info: Yr. Est. 1984, Irregular, Trim Size-8½ x 11, Sheetfed press, ISSN: 0890-9466
Subscriptions: $6/copy

Byberry Walton Newsletter

Publishing Co: Byberry Walton Newsletter, 6940 Southern Vista Dr, Enon, OH 45323-1544
Personnel: Editor-J.D. Whitehead

C.T.C. Cousin-To-Cousin
Coast to Coast Courier

Publishing Co: Shirley Baughman-O'Leary, PO Box 641, Belle Fourche, SD 57717-0641

California Genealogical
Society Newsletter   *Association*

Publishing Co: California Genealogical Society, PO Box 77105, San Francisco, CA 94107-0105; Title Tel # (415) 777-9936 Title Fax # (415) 777-0932
Personnel: Editor-Marg Kelt, Adv. Dir.-Jan Kusco
Editorial Description: Organizational news, items of genealogical interest, primary source materials, book reviews, queries.
General Info: Yr. Est. 1898, Bi-monthly, Offset press, 7 pages, ISSN: 8756-694X, 1% ads, Matte, Other
Subscriptions: Indv. $30, Inst. $30, $3/copy
Circulation: Total-825
Advertising: Inquire for rates.

Calvert County Genealogy
Newsletter   *Consumer, Association*

Publishing Co: Calvert County Genealogy Society, PO Box 9, Sunderland, MD 20689-0009; Title Tel # (410) 535-0839
Personnel: Editor-Mildred Bowen O'Brien, Publisher, Editor-Jerry O'Brien
Editorial Description: Genealogical data on Calvert County origins from 1640 to date. A clearing house for inquiries, answered promptly. Goal is to accumulate & distribute all Calvert Co. genealogy records data.
General Info: Yr. Est. 1986, Monthly, 10 pages, ISSN: 0895-8939, Matte
Subscriptions: Indv. $15, Can. $15, $2/copy
Acquistions: Publication Bought, Publication Sold
Circulation: Total-160
Advertising: Inquire for rates.

Camden County Historical
Society Bulletin

Publishing Co: Camden County Historical Society, Park Blvd. & Euclid Ave., Camden, NJ 08103; Title Tel # (609) 964-3333
Personnel: Editor-Gail Greenberg
General Info: Yr. Est. 1922, Offset press, 12 pages, Color-cover, Newsprint
Subscriptions: $3/copy
Acquistions: Publication Bought

Campbell Connections   *Business*

Publishing Co: Pioneer Publications, PO Box 1179, Tum Tum, WA 99034-1179; Title Tel # (509) 276-9841
Personnel: Publisher, Editor-Shirley Oakes
Editorial Description: Genealogical data on Surname.
General Info: Yr. Est. 1994, Irregular
Subscriptions: $6/copy

Canada Reports

Publishing Co: Canada Reports, External Info. Svcs. Div., Dept. of External Affairs, Ottawa, ON K1A 0G2 Canada

Cantwell-Conteville
Family Newsletter

Publishing Co: Cantwell-Conteville Family Assn., 3402 Fairlawn Dr, Glenview, IL 60025-4520; Title Tel # (708) 729-0301
Personnel: Publisher-Henry Cantwell, Editor-Donald Cantwell, Circ. Mgr.-Altie Bird
Editorial Description: Genealogical publication covering association information.
General Info: (Formerly Woody Cantwell Newsletter), Yr. Est. 1979, Quarterly, Trim Size-8½ x 11, Mimeo press, 20 pages, Color-cover, Newsprint
Subscriptions: Indv. $10, $3/copy
Advertising: Accepts Inserts.
Printing Co: Printing While You Wait, 1410 Waukegan Rd, Glenview, IL 60025-2182 Tel # (208) 729-6688

Carpenter Chronicles   *Business*

Publishing Co: Bette Butcher Topp, 1304 W. Cliffwood Ct., Spokane, WA 99218-2917; Title Tel # (509) 467-2299
Personnel: Publisher, Editor-Bette Butcher Topp
Editorial Description: Research information for the last name of Carpenter.
General Info: Yr. Est. 1988, Irregular, Trim Size-8½ x 11, Sheetfed press, 40 pages, ISSN: 0899-272X, 2 Color
Subscriptions: $6/copy

Cass County Connections   *Association, Consumer*

Publishing Co: Cass County Genealogical Society, PO Box 880, Atlanta, TX 75551-0880
Personnel: Publisher-John Livingston, Bk. Rev. Ed.-Melba Times
General Info: (Formerly Cass County Genealogical Society), Yr. Est. 1973, Quarterly, Trim Size-8.5 x 11, Other press, 26 pages, ISSN: 1074-5742, Other, Other
Subscriptions: Indv. $10
Circulation: Total-246

Chamberlain Chain

Publishing Co: Weidner Words, 2206 W Borden Rd, Spokane, WA 99204-9668; Title Tel # (509) 448-9263
Personnel: Publisher, Editor-Carolyn Weidner
Editorial Description: Chamberlain Chain: Surname booklet on chamberlain (all spellings.) Indexed by every name & locality.
General Info: Yr. Est. 1985, Irregular, Trim Size-8½ x 11, Desktop press, 35 pages, ISSN: 1041-6579, No Color, Matte
Subscriptions: Can. $8, For. $10, $8/copy
Advertising: Accepts Inserts.

Chamberlain Chain Master
Index

Publishing Co: Weidner Words, 2206 W Borden Rd, Spokane, WA 99204-9668; Title Tel # (509) 448-9263
Personnel: Publisher, Editor-Carolyn Weidner
Editorial Description: Chamberlian Chain Master Index V. 1-17. Index by names and localities.
General Info: Irregular, Trim Size-8½ x 11, Desktop press, 55 pages, No Color, Matte
Subscriptions: Can. $23, For. $25, $20/copy

Charbonneau Connection

Publishing Co: Charbonneau Connection, 9040 Farley Rd, Pinckney, MI 48169-9148; Title Tel # (313) 878-3680
Personnel: Publisher, Editor-Milton Charboneau
Editorial Description: Exchange of information on all derivatives of name of (Harbonneau, Sharronno, Cole, Coleman, etc.).
General Info: Yr. Est. 1984, Quarterly, 8 pages, ISSN: 1046-5901
Subscriptions: Indv. $5, $1/copy

Chautauqua Genealogist

Publishing Co: Chautauqua County Geneological Society, PO Box 404, Fredonia, NY 14063-0404
General Info: Yr. Est. 1978, Quarterly

Chestnut Tree

Publishing Co: Pierre Chastain Family Assn., 1903 Forest Green Dr NE, Atlanta, GA 30329-2604

Chronicles of St. Mary's
See: HISTORY

Circuit Rider
See: HISTORY

Claiborne Parish Trails

Publishing Co: J & W Enterprises, PO Box 17706, Shreveport, LA 71138-0706; Title Tel # (318) 686-5089
Personnel: Editor-Wanda Head
General Info: Yr. Est. 1986, Mimeo press, 404 pages
Subscriptions: Indv. $12, $3/copy
Acquistions: Publication Bought, Publication Sold

Clan Donald Bulletin

Publishing Co: Clan Donald Assn. of Nova Scotia, c/o St. Francis Xavier Univers, P.O. Box 5000, Antigonish, NS B2G 2W5 Canada; Title Tel # (902) 863-3300
General Info: Quarterly

Clan McCullough/McCulloch
Newsletter   *Consumer*

Publishing Co: Betty K. Summers, 2618 Dumire Ct., Port Collins, CO 80526-6208; Title Tel # (303) 634-3031
Personnel: Publisher, Editor-Betty Summers
Editorial Description: Publishing queries, contributions & original research-all states, time periods.
General Info: Yr. Est. 1978, Quarterly, 35 pages, No Color
Circulation: Total-175

Clandigger

Publishing Co: Alberta Genealogical Society, Box 12015, Edmonton, AB T5J 3L2 Canada Tel # (403) 455-7028; Title Tel # (403) 435-2691

Clark Clarion

Publishing Co: Ruth Lanphear, 633 E 13th St, Bowling Green, KY 42101-2531
Personnel: Publisher, Editor-Ruth Lanphear
Editorial Description: Focuses on queries and genealogical data for Clark(e) family researchers.
General Info: Yr. Est. 1977, Quarterly, Letrpr. press, 11 pages, No Color
Subscriptions: Indv. $8, $2/copy
Circulation: Total-115

Cleveland Kol   *Association*

Publishing Co: Jewish Genealogical Soc. of Cleveland, 996 Eastlawn Dr, Highland Heights, OH 44143-3126; Title Tel # (216) 449-2326 Title Fax # (216) 621-7560
Personnel: Editor-Arlene Rich
Editorial Description: Devoted to Jewish genealogy with a local emphasis.
General Info: Yr. Est. 1986, Quarterly, Trim Size-8½ x 11, Desktop press, 120 pages, No Color, Saddle-stitched
Subscriptions: Indv. $25, $7/copy
Circulation: Total-225

Coffey Cousin's Clearinghouse   *Association*

Publishing Co: Bonnie Culley, 1416 Green Berry Rd, Jefferson City, MO 65101-3620; Title Tel # (314) 635-9057
Personnel: Editor-Bonnie Culley
General Info: Yr. Est. 1981, Quarterly, Trim Size-8½ x 11, Offset press, 10 pages, ISSN: 0749-758X, No Color, Recycled, Other
Subscriptions: Indv. $8, For. $10, $2/copy
Circulation: Total-200
Printing Co: Ketch's Printing Company, 925 Madison St, Jefferson City, MO 65101-3455

Coleraine Pageant

Publishing Co: Coleraine Historical Society, 1442 Cedar Ave, Cincinnati, OH 45224-3062; Title Tel # (513) 541-8706
Personnel: Publisher, Editor, Adv. Dir.-Ruth J. Wells
Editorial Description: Meeting information and local history.
General Info: Yr. Est. 1964, Quarterly, 5 pages, ISSN: 0888-6784
Subscriptions: Indv. $3
Circulation: Total-120
Printing Co: Blanks, Hamilton Ave., Cincinnati, OH 45224 Tel # (513) 591-0246

Connecticut Maple Leaf   *Consumer*

Publishing Co: French-Canadian Genealogical Society of Connecticut, Inc., PO Box 45, Tolland, CT 06084-0045
Personnel: Editor-Susan Paquette
General Info: Semi-annually
Subscriptions: Indv. $20

Connector   *Association*

Publishing Co: Hamilton National Genealogical Society, Inc., 215 SW 20th Terrace, Oak Grove, MD 64075-9248; Title Tel # (816) 690-7768
Personnel: Publisher, Editor-L.M. Hamilton
Editorial Description: A family monthly devoted to genealogical data on Hamiltons.
General Info: Yr. Est. 1979, Monthly, Trim Size-17 x 11, Offset press, 20 pages, ISSN: 1051-9300, No Color
Subscriptions: Indv. $20, Free With Membership
Acquistions: Publication Bought
Circulation: Total-450

Cornerstone, The   *Consumer, Association*

Publishing Co: Lemont Area Historical Society, PO Box 126, Lemont, IL 60439-0126; Title Tel # (708) 257-2972
Personnel: Publisher, Editor-Mary Letson
Editorial Description: Publishes news, information, and research from the Lemont Area Historical Society.
General Info: Yr. Est. 1970, Bi-monthly, Desktop press, 6 pages, No Color
Subscriptions: Indv. $10, Inst. $30, Free With Membership
Circulation: Total-300

Cornsilk from DeKalb County, IL

Publishing Co: DeKalb County Historical & Genealogical Society, PO Box 295, Sycamore, IL 60178-0295; Title Tel # (815) 784-2015
Personnel: Editor-Sheila Larson
Editorial Description: Genealogical recorders of DeKalb County, IL. Purpose is to preserve & store county records.
General Info: Quarterly, 30 pages, ISSN: 0730-501X, No Color
Subscriptions: Indv. $10, $2/copy
Circulation: Total-250

Coryell Newsletter

Publishing Co: Coryell Newsletter, PO Box 662, Santa Barbara, CA 93102-0662; Title Tel # (805) 965-3749
Personnel: Editor-N. Burr Coryell
General Info: Yr. Est. 1970, Semi-annually, Trim Size-8½ x 14, Offset press, 4 pages, ISSN: 0883-7600, Color
Circulation: Total-200
Printing Co: Kinkos, 4141 Holister Avenue, Santa Barbara, CA

County Line
See: HISTORY

Courtney Chronicle

Publishing Co: Courtney Chronicle, RR 1 Box 77A, Pawnee, IL 62558-9710
Personnel: Editor-Stanley Courtney

Cousins et Cousines   *Association*

Publishing Co: NWTC & FHC, PO Box 29397, Brooklyn Center, MN 55429-0397
Personnel: Editor-Judith Bougie, Publications Director, Circ. Mgr.-Al Dahlquist
Editorial Description: French-Canadian & Franco-American genealogy, & metis.
General Info: Yr. Est. 1977, Tri-annually, Trim Size-5½ x 8½, Offset press, 12 pages, No Color
Subscriptions: Indv. $4, $1/copy
Circulation: Total-1,300
Advertising: Inquire for rates.

Coweta County Genealogical Society Magazine

Publishing Co: Coweta County Genealogical Society, PO Box 1014, Newnan, GA 30264-1014

Cox Heritage

Publishing Co: Palouse Publications, SE 310 Camino, Pullman, WA 99163-2206; Title Tel # (509) 334-1732
Personnel: Publisher, Editor-Janet Damm
Editorial Description: This is a surname book relating to the Cox name. All spellings accepted. Includes book reviews, queries, every name index, etc.
General Info: Yr. Est. 1987, Irregular, Mimeo press, 35 pages, ISSN: 0895-4062, No Color
Subscriptions: $7/copy

Crane Flock Newsletter   *Association*

Publishing Co: Crane Flock Newsletter, Poinsettia Drive #21, Ft. Myers, FL 33905-4343; Title Tel # (813) 693-2343
Personnel: Publisher, Editor-Edith Breker
Editorial Description: Information & queries on the Crane Family. Also Crain, Crayne, Krayne, etc.
General Info: Yr. Est. 1979, Quarterly, Offset press, 8 pages
Subscriptions: Indv. $8, $2/copy
Circulation: Total-150
Advertising: Accepts Inserts.
Printing Co: Regency Printing, 1001 Lee Blvd, Lehigh Acres, FL 33936-4942 Tel # (813) 368-1453

Crisp Newsletter   *Consumer, Association*

Publishing Co: Phillip Genealogical Heritage House, 605 Benton Ave., Missoula, MT 59801-8633; Title Tel # (406) 543-3495
Personnel: Publisher-Ruth Phillip, Editor-Jennie Crisp, Adv. Mgr.-Arthur Wigfield
Editorial Description: Includes editorial, genealogy information, vital news of today about the Crisp family name.
General Info: Annually
Subscriptions: Indv. $5, Inst. $4, $5/copy
Advertising: Accepts Inserts.
List Rental: Rents Lists
Printing Co: Phillip Heritage Genealogy House., 605 Benton Ave, Missoula, MT 59801-8633 Tel # (406) 543-3495

Cross Collections

Publishing Co: Anne Long, Rr 2 Box 671, Grangeville, ID 83530-9635; Title Tel # (208) 983-0515
Editorial Description: Surname booklet: Research, lineages, queries & book reviews. Everyname & location indexes.
General Info: Yr. Est. 1987
Subscriptions: $6/copy

Crossings
See: HISTORY

Crowl Connections   *Association*

Publishing Co: Crowl Family Association, 9603 Bel Glade St, Fairfax, VA 22031-1105
General Info: Yr. Est. 1985, Quarterly, Trim Size-8½ x 11, Desktop press, 12 pages
Subscriptions: Indv. $12, Inst. $6, $4/copy
Circulation: Readership-80

Da Lee Newsletter   *Consumer*

Publishing Co: Da Lee Newsletter, 1810 Linwood Blvd, Oklahoma City, OK 73106-2626; Title Tel # (405) 232-8843
Personnel: Publisher, Editor-Martha DaLee Haidek
Editorial Description: Devoted research on the families of Da Lee, Daily, Dailey, Daley, Daly, etc.
General Info: Yr. Est. 1985, Quarterly, Trim Size-8½ x 11, 7 pages
Subscriptions: Indv. $10

Dadswell Family Bulletin

Publishing Co: Dadswell Family Bulletin, 1310 Brydges St., London, ON N5W 2C4 Canada; Title Tel # (519) 451-7594
Personnel: Publisher-Barbara Nethercott, Editor-B. Nethercott
Editorial Description: Family history & genealogy.
General Info: Yr. Est. 1982, Semi-annually, Trim Size-8½ x 11, Sheetfed press, 8 pages, ISSN: 0824-7730, No Color, Coated
Subscriptions: Indv. $6, $2/copy
Acquistions: Publication Sold

Dakota Homestead Historical Newsletter   *Consumer, Association*

Publishing Co: Bismarck-Mandan Historical & Genealogical Soc., PO Box 485, Bismarck, ND 58502-0485
Personnel: Editor-Jeff Smith
General Info: Yr. Est. 1971, Quarterly, Trim Size-8½ x 11, Offset press, 24 pages
Subscriptions: Indv. $8, $3/copy
Circulation: Total-240

Dalton Data

Publishing Co: Bell Enterprises, PO Box 10328, Spokane, WA 99209-1328
Personnel: Editor-Mary Ann Bell

Dameron-Damron Family Assn. Newsletter

Publishing Co: Dameron-Damron Family Assn., 203 E Portland St, Springfield, MO 65807-2036

Daniel Cole Society Newsletter *Association*

Publishing Co: Daniel Cole Society, PO Box 367, Mahopac Falls, NY 10542-0367; Title Tel # (914) 628-0912
Personnel: Editor-Mrs. Cole
Editorial Description: Society news and genealogical information.
General Info: Yr. Est. 1986, Quarterly, Mimeo press; 6 pages, No Color
Subscriptions: Indv. $10
Acquistions: Publication Bought

Day Researcher

Publishing Co: Day Researcher, 319 N Houston Lake Blvd, Centerville, GA 31028-1117
Personnel: Editor-Addie Howell

Dean & Creech Newsletter *Association*

Publishing Co: Dean, 6770 US 60 E., Morehead, KY 40351; Title Tel # (606) 784-9145
Personnel: Editor-Lloyd Dean
Editorial Description: Seeks to preserve the history of the Dean and Creech families in America.
General Info: Yr. Est. 1975, Annually, Trim Size-8$\frac{1}{2}$ x 11, Mimeo press, 3 pages, No Color
Circulation: Total-500

Dearborn Historian

Publishing Co: Dearborn Historical Commission, 915 S Brady Rd, Dearborn, MI 48124-2322

Delaware Genealogist *Association*

Publishing Co: Delaware County Chapter OGS, PO Box 1126, Delaware, OH 43015-8126; Title Tel # (614) 369-4969
Editorial Description: A quarterly newsletter dealing with genealogy and history of Delaware County, Ohio.
General Info: Yr. Est. 1984, Quarterly, Trim Size-8$\frac{1}{2}$ x 11, 16 pages
Subscriptions: Indv. $10, Inst. $10, Free With Membership

Descendants of Peter Shaklee (1756-1834)

Publishing Co: William Shaklee, 14901 North Pennsylvania Ave., # 369, Oklahoma City, OK 73134-6072 Tel # (405) 755-8921; Title Tel # (405) 233-3118
Personnel: Editor-William Shaklee
General Info: Yr. Est. 1981, Quarterly, Trim Size-8$\frac{1}{2}$ x 11, Offset press, 14 pages, ISSN: 1044-7873, No Color
Subscriptions: Indv. $7, $2/copy

Disbrow Family Newsletter

Publishing Co: Disbrow Family Newsletter, 435 N Franklin Ave, Sioux Falls, SD 57103-0825; Title Tel # (605) 336-8012
Personnel: Editor-Cash Disbrow
General Info: Yr. Est. 1984, Quarterly
Subscriptions: Indv. $8

Dobie Connection

Publishing Co: Dobie Clan of North America, 20001 Ridge Rd, Cleveland, OH 44133-6270; Title Tel # (216) 237-6657
Personnel: Editor-George Dobie
Editorial Description: Reports of annual family clan gatherings. Medium for exchange of Scottish family connection to establish ancestral lines for individual. Items promoting interest in family heritage.
General Info: Yr. Est. 1977, Semi-annually, Sheetfed press, 4 pages, Looseleaf
Subscriptions: Can. $8, $5/copy

Dorney (Turni) Newsletter *Association*

Publishing Co: Genz Assoc. of America, 5821 Rowland Hill Rd., Cascade, MD 21719-1939; Title Tel # (301) 416-2660
Personnel: Editor-Victor Gebhart
General Info: Annually, Mimeo press, No Color
Subscriptions: $2/copy

Dorot

Publishing Co: Jewish Genealogical Society, Inc., PO Box 6398, New York, NY 10128-0004; Title Tel # (212) 330-8257
Personnel: Editor-Alex Friedlander, Production Mgr.-Steven Siegel
Editorial Description: Jewish genealogical news, announcements of future events, reports on past programs.
General Info: Yr. Est. 1979, Quarterly, Trim Size-8$\frac{1}{2}$ x 11, Offset press, 20 pages, ISSN: 0886-2796, No Color, Saddle-stitched
Subscriptions: Indv. $18, Can. $18, For. $18
Circulation: Total-1,000

Doughty Tree *Association*

Publishing Co: Doughty Family Assn., PO Box 203, Mays Landing, NJ 08330-0203; Title Tel # (609) 625-5459
Personnel: Editor-Clarence Doughty
Editorial Description: History of Doughty, Dowty, Dawdy, Doty, Doughtie families.
General Info: Yr. Est. 1977, Quarterly, Trim Size-8$\frac{1}{2}$ x 11, Sheetfed press, 25 pages, ISSN: 0897-3350, No Color
Subscriptions: Indv. $10, $4/copy
Circulation: Total-250
Printing Co: Chris Martin, 189 Margal Rd., Jericho, NY 11753 Tel # (516) 681-9714

Douglas Trails & Traces *Consumer*

Publishing Co: Douglas County Genealogical Society, PO Box 113, Tuscola, IL 61953-0113
Personnel: Editor-M. Tracy Carpenter, Circ. Mgr.-Kathryn Brandenbur
Editorial Description: Deaths, marriages, newspaper items, wills, county court records, queries, etc.
General Info: Yr. Est. 1977, Quarterly, Mimeo press, 20 pages, ISSN: 0741-6954
Subscriptions: Indv. $8, $2/copy
Circulation: Total-150

Dunahay

Publishing Co: Lowell Dunahay, 4513 Lake Haven Blvd, Sebring, FL 33872-5227; Title Tel # (813) 382-2522
General Info: Yr. Est. 1987

Dunrobin Piper

Publishing Co: Clan Sutherland Society of N. America, Inc., 2922 Primrose Cir, Nashville, TN 37212-6016; Title Tel # (615) 297-1528 Title Fax # (615) 343-6909
Personnel: Publisher, Editor-Mary Nell Snoddy
Editorial Description: Newsletter of Clan Sutherland Society of N. America.
General Info: Yr. Est. 1976, Monthly, Trim Size-8$\frac{1}{2}$ x 11, Mimeo press, 4 pages, ISSN: 0741-5273, No Color
Acquistions: Publication Bought
Circulation: Total-350
Printing Co: Kinkos Copies, 2901 Medical Arts St, Austin, TX 78705-3325 Tel # (512) 476-3242

Durch Die Fensterscheibe (Through the Windowpane) *Consumer*

Publishing Co: BGM Pubs., 28635 W Old Hideway Rd, Cary, IL 60013-9794; Title Tel # (708) 639-2400
Personnel: Publisher, Editor-Betty Massman
Editorial Description: Genealogical information on Scheib/Shipe/Shive surname.
General Info: Yr. Est. 1981, Quarterly, Mimeo press, 25 pages, ISSN: 0882-5874
Subscriptions: Indv. $18, $6/copy
Circulation: Total-675

Durkee Family Newsletter *Association*

Publishing Co: Soc. of Genealogy of Durkee, Bernice Gunderson, 3753 E. 15th St., Long Beach, CA 90804-2943; Title Tel # (310) 494-2836
Personnel: Editor-Bernice Gunderson
Editorial Description: Features one Durkee family group in each issue & explores the background & genealogy of that particular branch. Reprints family records & photos, records VR in Durkee family.
General Info: Yr. Est. 1984, Quarterly, Trim Size-8$\frac{1}{2}$ x 11, 12 pages, ISSN: 0892-208X, Color-cover
Subscriptions: Indv. $8, Can. $9, For. $15, $2/copy
Circulation: Total-400

East Wind

Publishing Co: Jonna Baker, PO Box 217, Omaha, AR 72662-0217

Eastern Genealogical PPQ *Consumer, Association*

Publishing Co: Kross Publications & Research Services, PO Box 9, Franklin Park, NJ 08823-0009
Editorial Description: Cover Eastern genealogical people, places and queries.
General Info: Yr. Est. 1992, Quarterly, Trim Size-8$\frac{1}{2}$ x 11, 24 pages, No Color
Subscriptions: Indv. $18

Edward Howell Family Assn. -Newsletter

Publishing Co: Edward Howell Family Assn., 22723 Rio Gusto Ct, Valencia, CA 91354-2355
Personnel: Editor-Carol Morton
Editorial Description: Directed toward descendants of Edward Howell (founder of Southampton, NY) & other genealogists. Contains reunion news; genealogy notes; & news of members. Illustrated.
General Info: Yr. Est. 1979, Trim Size-8$\frac{1}{2}$ x 11, 8 pages, ISSN: 1045-2605
Circulation: Total-400
List Rental: Rents Lists

Eller Cronicles

Publishing Co: Eller Family Assn., 914 James St, Independence, OR 97351-9404

Ellis Cousins Newsletter

Publishing Co: Ellis Cousins Nationwide, 1201 Maple Ave, Friona, TX 79035-1405;
Title Tel # (806) 247-3053
Personnel: Editor-Bill Ellis, Production Mgr.-Carol Ellis
Editorial Description: A clearinghouse for genealogical data on all Ellis families in US & Canada. Not limited to any one Ellis family group.
General Info: (Formerly Ellis Family Newsletter), Yr. Est. 1973, Quarterly, Trim Size-8½ x 11, Sheetfed press, 20 pages, ISSN: 0740-1477, No Color
Subscriptions: Indv. $15, Can. $19, $3/copy
Acquistions: Publication Bought
Circulation: Total-600

Emerick Family Newsletter

Publishing Co: Ohio Connection, PO Box 14296, Dayton, OH 45413-0296;
Title Tel # (513) 279-0385
Personnel: Editor-Ann Fenley
General Info: Yr. Est. 1984, Quarterly, Trim Size-8½ x 11, ISSN: 0887-5693
Subscriptions: Indv. $16

Estep Family Journal   *Association*

Publishing Co: Estep Family Assn., 12206 Brisbane Ave, Dallas, TX 75234-6528;
Title Tel # (214) 241-2739 Title Fax # (214) 620-1416
Personnel: Editor-Nova Lemons
Editorial Description: A clearinghouse for the surname Eastep/Estep.
General Info: Yr. Est. 1991, Quarterly, Trim Size-8½ x 11, Mimeo press, 10 pages, ISSN: 1076-6138, No Color, Newsprint
Subscriptions: Indv. $10
Circulation: Readership-55

FGS   *Consumer, Association*   CPM: $36

Publishing Co: Fed. of Genealogical Societies, 2003 E 12th St, Davenport, IA 52803-3917
Personnel: Editor-Sandra Luebking
Editorial Description: News and information of interest to genealogists and member societies.
General Info: (Formerly Federation of Genealogical Societies Forum), Yr. Est. 1989, Quarterly, Trim Size-8½ x 11, Offset press, 40 pages, ISSN: 0894-3265, 10% ads, No Color, Saddle-stitched
Subscriptions: Indv. $15
Circulation: Total-5,500
Advertising: $200.

Falconer Facets

Publishing Co: Falconer Facets, 2431 Crestwood Dr SW, Huntsville, AL 35805-3150;
Title Tel # (205) 536-0375
Personnel: Editor-Floyd Falconer
Editorial Description: The official Colin Falconer/Phoebe Cheney Family Assn. newsletter.
General Info: Quarterly, ISSN: 0884-867X
Subscriptions: Indv. $5, Can. $7

Family Connection of the Cothren-Cochrane Surname

Publishing Co: Family Connection, 730 Grand Ave, Pomona, CA 91765-4462
General Info: ISSN: 0896-9302
Subscriptions: Indv. $15

Family Connection of the O'Neil-Neil-O'Neill Surname

Publishing Co: Family Connection, 730 Grand Ave, Pomona, CA 91765-4462
Editorial Description: Established to preserve our heritage whether Scot &/or Irish & for the purpose of providing a clearing hosue for family data.
General Info: Semi-annually
Subscriptions: Indv. $15, $4/copy

Family Treebune

Publishing Co: Thomas Nash Descendants Assn., c/o D. Roberts, 2733 Running B, Dallas, TX 75228
General Info: Quarterly
Subscriptions: Indv. $6

Fanfare   *Consumer*

Publishing Co: Sterling Communications, 1920 Ellesmere Road, Suite 104, Scarborough, ON M1H 2WY Canada Tel # (416) 513-2218; Title Tel # (416) 512-2218 Title Fax # (416) 512-6493
Personnel: Editor-Barbara Fanson
General Info: Yr. Est. 1990, Semi-annually, Trim Size-8½ x 11, 4 pages, Matte

Farr Footnotes

Publishing Co: Pioneer Publications, PO Box 1179, Tum Tum, WA 99034-1179;
Title Tel # (509) 276-9841
Personnel: Publisher, Editor-Shirley Oakes
Editorial Description: Genealogical data on the Farr surname. Lineages, miscellaneous info. Queries free.
General Info: Yr. Est. 1985, Irregular, Trim Size-8½ x 11, Mimeo press, 25 pages, ISSN: 0897-778X
Subscriptions: $6/copy
Acquistions: Publication Bought, Publication Sold

Fellowship of Brethren Genealogists Newsletter

Publishing Co: Fellowship of Brethren Genealogists, 518 Miller Dr, Elgin, IL 60123-7256

Fenstermaker Newsnotes

Publishing Co: Fenstermaker Newsnotes, 4223 Hackett Ave, Lakewood, CA 90713-3207;
Title Tel # (213) 421-6595
Personnel: Publisher, Editor-Roy Fenstermaker
Editorial Description: Genealogy notes & current family news: Fenstermaker-Cyphert Families.
General Info: Yr. Est. 1982, Quarterly, Trim Size-7 x 8½, Mimeo press, 12 pages, No Color, Newsprint
Subscriptions: Indv. $5, $1/copy
Circulation: Total-175

Fields Family Findings

Publishing Co: Fields Family Findings, 4740 Roosevelt Ave., Sacramento, CA 95820-4522;
Title Tel # (916) 451-1076
Personnel: Feature Ed.-S.R. Thomas, Publisher, Editor, Circ. Mgr., Production Mgr., Adv. Dir., Art Dir., Mktg. Dir., Promotion Dir.-Mary A. Thomas
Editorial Description: For Field-Fields genealogy & their related families.
General Info: Yr. Est. 1984, Quarterly, Trim Size-8½ x 11, Desktop press, 25 pages, ISSN: 0883-8585, 1% ads, No Color, Newsprint
Subscriptions: Indv. $22, Inst. $22, $6/copy
Acquistions: Publication Bought
Circulation: Total-350
Advertising: Inquire for rates.

Fisher Families   *Consumer, Association*

Publishing Co: Fisher Families, 3960 German Rd., Kettle Falls, WA 99141-9402;
Title Tel # (509) 738-6731
Personnel: Publisher, Editor-Susan Gallyon Dechant
General Info: Yr. Est. 1986, Irregular, 30 pages, ISSN: 0890-9458
Subscriptions: $7/copy
Acquistions: Publication Sold

Fisk(E) Family Assn. Newsletter

Publishing Co: Fisk(E) Family Assn., 2215 Anderson Ave, Manhattan, KS 66502-3608;
Title Tel # (213) 681-5533
Personnel: Publisher, Editor-Irwin Fisk
Editorial Description: A genealogical newsletter for persons researching Fisk or Fiske history.
General Info: Yr. Est. 1976, Semi-annually, Sheetfed press, 16 pages, No Color, Newsprint
Subscriptions: Indv. $9
Circulation: Total-500
Printing Co: Litho Press, 742 E Alosta Ave, Glendora, CA 91740-3510 Tel # (818) 914-1221

Flipping Flippins   *Association*

Publishing Co: Flippin Family Assn., 12206 Brisbane Ave, Dallas, TX 75234-6528;
Title Tel # (214) 241-2739 Title Fax # (214) 620-1416
Personnel: Editor-Nova Lemons
Editorial Description: A clearinghouse for the surname. Flippin/Flippen/Flipping ancestry.
General Info: Yr. Est. 1987, Quarterly, Trim Size-8½ x 11, Mimeo press, 20 pages, ISSN: 0893-5041, No Color, Newsprint
Subscriptions: Indv. $15
Circulation: Readership-65
Advertising: Inquire for rates. Accepts Inserts.

Florida Parishes Genealogical Newsletter

Publishing Co: Florida Parishes Genealogical Newsletter, 20011 Will Hughes Road, Livingston, LA 70754-2642
Personnel: Publisher, Editor-Donna Adams
Editorial Description: Genealogical and historical data for researchers.
General Info: Yr. Est. 1979, Bi-monthly, Trim Size-8½ x 11, Mimeo press, 8 pages, ISSN: 8756-2316, Ind/Abs/Online: Annual Ind., No Color
Subscriptions: Indv. $8, $2/copy

Footprints in Time

Publishing Co: Gaston/Lincoln Genealogical Society, PO Box 584, Mount Holly, NC 28120-0584;
Title Tel # (704) 827-6437
Personnel: Editor-Annette Williams
General Info: Yr. Est. 1987, Quarterly, 40 pages
Subscriptions: Indv. $10
Circulation: Total-200

Forgotten Pathways

Publishing Co: Genealogical Society of Hancock Co., PO Box 146, Hawesville, KY 42348-0146;
Title Tel # (502) 927-8095
Editorial Description: Quarterly of the Hancock County Kentucky Genealogical Society.

The Fountain

Publishing Co: Links Genealogy Publications, 7677 Abaline Way, Sacramento, CA 95823-4224; Title Tel # (916) 428-2245
Personnel: Editor-Iris Carter Jones
Editorial Description: Newsletter for descendants and researchers tracing the surname WELCH/WELSH/WALSH.
General Info: Yr. Est. 1983, Quarterly, Trim Size-8½ x 11, Desktop press, 20 pages, ISSN: 1060-9261
Subscriptions: Indv. $12, Can. $15, For. $17, $3/copy
Advertising: Inquire for rates.

Franklintonian   *Consumer, Association*

Publishing Co: Franklin County Genealogical Society, Box 3406, Columbus, OH 43216-2406; Title Tel # (614) 469-1300
Editorial Description: Genealogical and historical information of Franklin County and society members.
General Info: Yr. Est. 1979, Bi-monthly, Trim Size-8½ x 11, Mimeo press, 20 pages, 1% ads, No Color, Newsprint
Subscriptions: Indv. $14, $2/copy
Acquistions: Publication Sold
Circulation: Total-550
Printing Co: Tuller Graphics, 5828 Sawmill Rd, Dublin, OH 43017-1589 Tel # (614) 889-5959

Frary Family Newsletter   *Association*

Publishing Co: Frary Family Association, 12 Lohmann Pl., Dumont, NJ 07628-1521; Title Tel # (201) 384-2111
Personnel: Editor-Grace Frary
Editorial Description: News on Frary descendants & news about the association activities.
General Info: Yr. Est. 1970, Semi-annually, Trim Size-8½ x 11, Mimeo press, 8 pages, ISSN: 0887-6312, No Color, Newsprint
Subscriptions: Indv. $6, Can. $6, For. $6, Free With Membership

Freeborn County Tracer   *Association*

Publishing Co: Freeborn County Genealogical Soc., PO Box 403, Albert Lea, MN 56007-0403
Personnel: Publisher-Vickie Storlie, Editor-Cathy Wittmer
Editorial Description: To inform, teach, help members/public; to preserve & promote interest in genealogy.
General Info: Yr. Est. 1980, Bi-monthly, Trim Size-8½ x 11, Letrpr. press, 10 pages, 2 Color
Subscriptions: Free With Membership
Circulation: Total-120

Freeland

Publishing Co: Freeland Family Assn., 220 4th St, Del Mar, CA 92014-3254; Title Tel # (619) 755-1284
Personnel: Publisher-Barney T. Freeland, Editor-Barney Freeland, Production Mgr.-Maxine Wade
Editorial Description: Geneology on all Freeland families with emphasis on English ancestry to the Norman Times and the Allied Families of Calvert County, Maryland, etc.
General Info: (Formerly Freeland Quarterly), Yr. Est. 1971, Trim Size-8½ x 11, Offset press, 20 pages, No Color, Looseleaf
Subscriptions: $4/copy
Circulation: (100% controlled)

Fremont County Nostalgia News

Publishing Co: Fremont County Genealogical Society, Riverton Branch Library, 1330 W. Park, Riverton, WY 82501
Personnel: Editor-Marlys Bias
General Info: Yr. Est. 1981, Quarterly, Trim Size-8½ x 11, Mimeo press, 25 pages, ISSN: 8756-8446, No Color
Subscriptions: Indv. $10, $4/copy
Acquistions: Publication Bought, Publication Sold

Friends of the Springer Homestead

Publishing Co: Friends of the Springer Homestead, 22 Hortense St, Uniontown, PA 15401-3025; Title Tel # (301) 799-5221
Personnel: Editor-Gerald Cunningham, Circ. Mgr.-Paul Cunningham
Editorial Description: To inform current members of restoration progress & acquire new members interested in the Springer Homestead.
General Info: (Formerly Architectural Society for Preservation), Yr. Est. 1984, Letrpr. press, 1 pages
List Rental: Rents Lists

Frost on the Vine   *Association*

Publishing Co: Frost Family Assn., 2665 Orchard St, Soquel, CA 95073-2625
Personnel: Publisher, Editor-Debbie Fulmer
General Info: Yr. Est. 1984, Quarterly, Trim Size-8½ x 11, Mimeo press, 9 pages, ISSN: 0882-2514, No Color
Subscriptions: Indv. $10

Fuller Society Newsletter   *Consumer, Association*

Publishing Co: Fuller Society, Hc 69 Box 675, Friendship, ME 04547-9610; Title Tel # (207) 832-7298
Editorial Description: Geneaolgy information for descendants of Mayflower pirigms Edward and Dr. Samuel Fuller.
General Info: Yr. Est. 1992, Tri-annually
Subscriptions: Indv. $10
Circulation: Total-300

Gage Family Newsletter

Publishing Co: Gage Family Newsletter, 29 Seminole Ct. NE, Winter Haven, FL 33881-9451; Title Tel # (941) 294-2496
Personnel: Editor-John Gage
Editorial Description: All information published & unpublished concerning the Gage Family.
General Info: Yr. Est. 1985, Quarterly, 10 pages
Subscriptions: Indv. $8, $2/copy
List Rental: Rents Lists

Gates Gazette

Publishing Co: Pioneer Publications, PO Box 1179, Tum Tum, WA 99034-1179; Title Tel # (509) 276-9841
Personnel: Publisher, Editor-Shirley Oakes
Editorial Description: Genealogical data; queries and lineages printed free. On surname Gates.
General Info: Yr. Est. 1985, Irregular, Trim Size-8½ x 11, Mimeo press, 25 pages, ISSN: 0897-7798
Subscriptions: $6/copy

Gebhart Society of America Newsletter   *Association*

Publishing Co: Genz Assoc. of America, 5821 Rowland Hill Rd., Cascade, MD 21719-1939; Title Tel # (301) 416-2660
Personnel: Editor-Victor Gebhart
General Info: Quarterly, Trim Size-8½ x 11, Mimeo press, 4 pages, No Color
Subscriptions: Indv. $6, $2/copy

Genealogical Society of Flemish Americans Newsletter
See: ETHNIC

Genealogical Society of Okeechobee Newsletter

Publishing Co: Genealogical Society of Okeechobee, PO Box 371, Okeechobee, FL 34973-0371
Personnel: Editor-Joy Morley
Editorial Description: A genealogical newsletter sent to members of the Society & also donated to some libraries; exchanged with some other genealogical societies.
General Info: Yr. Est. 1982, Quarterly, Mimeo press, 5 pages
Subscriptions: Indv. $10, Free With Membership

Genealogija

Publishing Co: Balzekas Museum of Lithuanian Culture, 6500 S Pulaski Rd, Chicago, IL 60629-5136; Title Tel # (312) 582-6500
General Info: Quarterly

Genealogy Bulletin   *Consumer, Association*

Publishing Co: AGLL, P.O. Box 329, Bountiful, UT 84011; Title Tel # (801) 298-5358 Title Fax # (801) 298-5468
Personnel: Circ. Mgr.-Barbara Moore, Production Mgr.-William Dollardide, Art Dir.-Danielle Hunger, Publisher, Mktg. Dir.-Bradley W. Stewart
Editorial Description: The Genealogy Bulletin features articles on pursuing your genealogical research. Each issue contains 3,000 name-date-place queries and keeps you current on whats happening in the field of genealogy.
General Info: Bi-monthly, Trim Size-8½ x 11, Web press, 56 pages, ISSN: 1049-9571, 2 Color, Matte, Perfect bound
Subscriptions: Indv. $18, Inst. $18, Can. $23, For. $23, $4/copy
Circulation: Total-5,000
Printing Co: AGLL, P.O. Box 329, 560 W. 100 N., Bountiful, UT 84011 Tel # (801) 298-5358, Fax # (801) 298-5468

Genealogy Workshop Bulletin   *Consumer*

Publishing Co: Brooklyn Historical Society, 128 Pierrepont St, Brooklyn, NY 11201-2794 Fax # (718) 875-3869; Title Tel # (718) 624-0890
Personnel: Editor, Circ. Mgr.-Elizabeth Feldhusen
General Info: Yr. Est. 1970, Bi-monthly, Offset press, 4 pages
Subscriptions: Indv. $6, $2/copy
Circulation: Total-150

Generations

Publishing Co: New Brunswick Genealogical Soc., Box 3235, Sta. A, Fredericton, NB E3A 5G9 Canada
Personnel: Editor-C. Williston
General Info: Yr. Est. 1978, Quarterly, Trim Size-8½ x 11, Sheetfed press, 72 pages, ISSN: 0821-5359, 2 Color, Saddle-stitched
Subscriptions: Indv. $20, Inst. $25, $5/copy
Circulation: Total-900
Advertising: Inquire for rates.

Gileland/Gilliland Newsletter

Publishing Co: Gileland/Gilliland Newsletter, 1400 Glenwood Rd Apt 201, Glendale, CA 91201-1919
Personnel: Editor-Lillian Brender

Gillet, Gillette, Gillett Pride 'n' Joy

Publishing Co: B.E. Gillett, 1103 W. 1st St., McCook, NE 69001-2504; Title Tel # (308) 345-5358
Personnel: Publisher, Editor, Production Mgr.-B.E. Gillett
Editorial Description: Covers Gillett Family history. This is for any person researching any spelling of the Gillett name.
General Info: Yr. Est. 1986, Quarterly, Trim Size-8½ x 11, ISSN: 0890-4022
Subscriptions: Indv. $10

Goddard Newsletter

Publishing Co: Goddard Assn. of America, 118 S. Volustia, Wichita, KS 67211-2038; Title Tel # (316) 682-4942
Personnel: Editor-Kathryn Meyer
General Info: Yr. Est. 1977, Quarterly, Trim Size-8½ x 11, Letrpr. press, 12 pages, Newsprint
Acquistions: Publication Bought
Circulation: Total-980

Goodenow's Ghosts *Association*

Publishing Co: Goodenow Family Association, Rt. 2 Box 718, Shepherdstown, WV 25443; Title Tel # (304) 876-2008
Personnel: Publisher-Theodore Banvard, Editor-Miriam Colvin
Editorial Description: Family newsletter containing biographical, historical, & genealogical stories, records, & misc. papers. Coordinates articles and information on Goodenows, Goodnos, Goodnoughs, Goodenoughs and related surnames.
General Info: (Formerly Goodenough's Ghosts), Yr. Est. 1980, Quarterly, Trim Size-8½ x 11, Other press, 26 pages, Color-cover
Subscriptions: Indv. $20
Circulation: Total-200

Goodwin News

Publishing Co: Goodwin Family Organization, 39 Lost Trail Rd, Roswell, NM 88201-9509; Title Tel # (505) 625-0961
Personnel: Publisher, Editor, Circ. Mgr., Production Mgr.-Murray Sharp
Editorial Description: Newsletter of the Goodwin Family Organization, vital records, research, genealogies.
General Info: Yr. Est. 1979, Semi-annually, Trim Size-8½ x 11, Offset press, 24 pages, ISSN: 0892-1423, No Color, Newsprint
Subscriptions: Indv. $10, Inst. $5, Can. $12, For. $12
Circulation: Total-245

Grad Family Newsletter *Association*

Publishing Co: Eli Grad, 22 Haven Rd., Wellesley Hills, CA 02181-2405
Personnel: Publisher, Editor-Eli Grad
Editorial Description: Quarterly newsletter of the Grad family - covering 7 generations of history/genealogy & current affairs of world-wide family.
General Info: Yr. Est. 1986, Quarterly

Grand River Times

Publishing Co: Grand River Historical Society, Grand Rapids Publ. Library, 2016 Eastern Ave SE, Grand Rapids, MI 49507; Title Tel # (616) 245-8737
Personnel: Editor-Gordon Olson

Grapevine: Kniffin-Sniffen Family Newsletter *Consumer, Association*

Publishing Co: Paul Sniffen, PO Box 124, Red Bank, NJ 07701-0124; Title Tel # (908) 530-2065 Title Fax # (908) 530-2065
Personnel: Publisher, Editor-Paul Sniffen, Circ. Mgr.-Joanne Sniffen
Editorial Description: History of the Kniffin-Sniffen lineage along with allied families, reunions, & exchange of family history data.
General Info: Yr. Est. 1983, Semi-annually, Trim Size-8½ x 11½, 2 pages, No Color, Coated
Acquistions: Publication Bought

Grawunder and Graffunder Connection, The *Consumer, Association*

Publishing Co: Grawunder Technical Services, 13108 Penn Ave., Burnsville, MN 55337-2015; Title Tel # (612) 890-3240
Personnel: Co-Editor-Gladys Grovender, Co-Editor-Linnea Grovender, Production Mgr.-John Grovender
Editorial Description: Connect family data into family trees and include all know information ex. health history, occupation, personal description etc.
General Info: (Formerly Grawunder Connection, The), Yr. Est. 1987, Quarterly, Trim Size-11 x 8½, Desktop press, 8 pages
Subscriptions: Indv. $5, $1/copy

Great Migration Newsletter *Consumer, Scholarly*

Publishing Co: New England Historic Genealogical Society, 101 Newbury St., Boston, MA 02116-3007 Tel # (617) 536-5740 Fax # (617) 536-7307
Personnel: Editor-Robert Charles Anderson
Editorial Description: Information on genealogy studying.
General Info: Yr. Est. 1990, Quarterly, Trim Size-8½ x 11, 34 pages, ISSN: 1049-8087
Subscriptions: Indv. $8
Circulation: Total-3,150

Green Country Quarterly *Association, Consumer*

Publishing Co: Broken Arrow Genealogical Society, PO Box 1244, Broken Arrow, OK 74013-1244; Title Tel # (918) 455-8619
Editorial Description: Records of Oklahoma's Green Country (Eastern) area. Genealogy research tips; queries from researchers; review of genealogy publications.
General Info: Yr. Est. 1980, Quarterly, Trim Size-8½ x 11, 12 pages, ISSN: 0743-2828
Subscriptions: Indv. $10, $3/copy

Green Family Quarterly

Publishing Co: Alton Moran, 18435 S Mission Hills Ave, Baton Rouge, LA 70810-7943; Title Tel # (504) 756-2303
Personnel: Publisher, Editor-Alton Moran
Editorial Description: Genealogical information pertaining to Greens of the southern U.S.
General Info: Yr. Est. 1985, Quarterly, 40 pages, Color-cover
Subscriptions: Indv. $15, $4/copy
List Rental: Rents Lists

Guelph Historical Society Newsletter
See: HISTORY

Halfyard Heritage *Association*

Publishing Co: Halfyard Heritage, R. R. Halfyard, St. Catharines, ON L2M 2E1 Canada; Title Tel # (905) 934-3651
Personnel: Publisher, Editor-Robert Halfyard
Editorial Description: Historical/genealogical publication for those interested in the Halfyard name.
General Info: Yr. Est. 1985, Quarterly, Trim Size-8½ x 11, Desktop press, 10 pages, ISSN: 0828-9557, No Color, Other
Subscriptions: Indv. $10, Inst. $10, Can. $10, For. $10
Printing Co: Skyway Reprographics, 288 Lake St., St. Catharines, ON L2N 4H2 Canada Tel # (905) 646-5303

Hamersky & Allied Families Newsletter *Consumer*

Publishing Co: Hamersky & Allied Families Newsletter, PO Box 1334, San Diego, CA 92112-1334
Personnel: Editor-Michael Hamersky
Editorial Description: News relating to the Hamersky and allied families.
General Info: Yr. Est. 1980, Bi-monthly, 10 pages, ISSN: 0882-4150
Subscriptions: Indv. $8, Can. $12, For. $12, $1/copy

Hancock Heritage

Publishing Co: Hancock County Chapter, OGS, PO Box 672, Findlay, OH 45839-0672
General Info: 20 pages

Harbour-Witt Family Association Bulletin

Publishing Co: Harbour-Witt Family Assn., Inc., 7904 Joliet Ave, Lubbock, TX 79423-1720; Title Tel # (806) 795-5136
Personnel: Editor-Bettye Atkins Cartwright
Editorial Description: Ancestors/descendants of Thomas & Sarah Witt Harbour of VA. (all variations of spelling: Harbour/Harbor/Harber and Witt/Whitt/Whit)
General Info: Yr. Est. 1978, Quarterly, Trim Size-7 x 8½, Web press, 32 pages, No Color, Saddle-stitched
Subscriptions: Indv. $12, $4/copy
Acquistions: Publication Bought
Circulation: Total-270

Harden Newsletter

Publishing Co: Harden Newsletter, 7041 Kilbourne Rd, Sunbury, OH 43074-9567; Title Tel # (614) 524-4301
Personnel: Publisher-Clyde Harden, Editor-John Hardin
General Info: Yr. Est. 1983, Quarterly, Offset press, 50 pages
Subscriptions: $4/copy
Circulation: Total-400

Harrington/Herrington Kin

Publishing Co: Harrington/Herrington Kin, 1013 Illinois St, Bicknell, IN 47512-3000; Title Tel # (812) 735-2530
Personnel: Publisher, Editor-Carol Hulen
Editorial Description: Clearinghouse for all Harrington/Herrington family records, everywhere. Queries & ads free to subscribers.
General Info: Yr. Est. 1985, Quarterly, Mimeo press, 10 pages, No Color, Perfect bound
Subscriptions: Indv. $10, $3/copy

Hart Lines Newsletter *Association*

Publishing Co: Hart Lines Newsletter, 15875 Interurban Rd., Platte City, MO 64079-9185; Title Tel # (816) 858-3599 Title Fax # (816) 858-5556
Personnel: Publisher, Editor-Betty N. Soper
Editorial Description: Publishes queries, book reviews, and research information on the Hart surname.
General Info: Yr. Est. 1990, Irregular, Trim Size-8½ x 11, Offset press, 10 pages, ISSN: 1080-5761, No Color
Subscriptions: Indv. $5
Circulation: Total-200
Printing Co: Citizen Printing, PO Box 888, Platte City, MO 64079-0888

Haskins-Haskins Annals

Publishing Co: Haskins-Haskins Annals, 2635 153rd Ave SE, Bellevue, WA 98007-6513
Personnel: Editor-Mary Lou Hackett-Magnuso

Hatton Family Newsletter   *Consumer, Association*

Publishing Co: Hatton Heritage Assn., 1451 Sandy Ln, Clearwater, FL 34615-2044
Editorial Description: Designed to gather and disseminate information on various Hatton lines. Articles and queries are cheerfully accepted.
General Info: Quarterly
Subscriptions: Indv. $7, Can. $8, For. $10
Acquistions: Publication Bought

Hawkins Newsletter   *Association*

Publishing Co: Genz Assoc. of America, 5821 Rowland Hill Rd., Cascade, MD 21719-1939; Title Tel # (301) 416-2660
Personnel: Editor-Victor Gebhart
General Info: Annually, Mimeo press, No Color
Subscriptions: $2/copy

Hear Ye Hear Ye   *Association*

Publishing Co: Rochester Genealogical Society, PO Box 10501, Rochester, NY 14610-0501
Personnel: Publisher, Editor-J. Markham, Editor-J. Paprocki
Editorial Description: Contains articles, research tips, inquiries, & society news of interest to genealogists. Primary emphasis on Rochester, NY & surrounding counties.
General Info: Tri-annually, Trim Size-8½ x 11, Desktop press, 10 pages, No Color
Subscriptions: Indv. $10
Circulation: Total-250

Heard Heritage

Publishing Co: Genealogical Researcher, c/o Lynda S. Eller, Box 249, Lanett, AL 36863; Title Tel # (205) 576-2797
Personnel: Editor-Linda Eller
Editorial Description: History of people of Heard Co. GA.
General Info: Yr. Est. 1976, Semi-annually, ISSN: 0149-5046
Subscriptions: Indv. $8, $8/copy
Circulation: Total-150

Heartlines

Publishing Co: Heart of America Genealogical Society, C/O K.C. Public Lib., 311 E 12th St., Kansas City, MO 64106-2412 Tel # (816) 221-2685; Title Tel # (816) 483-8144
Personnel: Editor-Betty McGettigan
Editorial Description: For members only-society news-library acquistions-genealogical events.
General Info: Yr. Est. 1976, Bi-monthly, Trim Size-8½ x 11, Sheetfed press, 8 pages, No Color, Newsprint
Circulation: Total-300

Heller Helper   *Consumer*

Publishing Co: BGM Pubs., 28635 W Old Hideway Rd, Cary, IL 60013-9794; Title Tel # (708) 639-2400
Personnel: Editor-Betty Massman
General Info: Yr. Est. 1982, Quarterly, Mimeo press, 25 pages, ISSN: 0882-5882
Subscriptions: Indv. $18, $6/copy
Circulation: Total-700

Henderson Highlights

Publishing Co: Bell Enterprises, PO Box 10328, Spokane, WA 99209-1328

Henkel Newsletter   *Association*

Publishing Co: Genz Assoc. of America, 5821 Rowland Hill Rd., Cascade, MD 21719-1939; Title Tel # (301) 416-2660
Personnel: Editor-Victor Gebhart
General Info: (Formerly Genz Newsletter), Annually, Mimeo press, No Color
Subscriptions: $2/copy

Henry County Historicalog   *Association*

Publishing Co: Henry County Historical Soc., 606 S 14th St, New Castle, IN 47362-3339; Title Tel # (317) 529-4028
Personnel: Editor-Richard Ratcliff
Editorial Description: Society activites. Information about the history of Henry County, Indiana and its people, past and present.
General Info: Yr. Est. 1973, Semi-annually, Trim Size-8½ x 11, 8 pages, No Color
Subscriptions: Indv. $6
Circulation: Total-1,100

Heritage

Publishing Co: Heritage, 35145 Balboa Pl SE, Albany, OR 97321-9751; Title Tel # (503) 928-2582
Personnel: Publisher-Dick Milligan, Editor-Pamela Knofler
General Info: Monthly, ISSN: 0898-4824
Subscriptions: Indv. $12

Heritage, The
See: HISTORY

Heritage of Stone   *Association*

Publishing Co: Stone County Historical Society, PO Box 284, Mountain View, AR 72560-0284; Title Tel # (501) 269-3132
Personnel: Editor-Freda Massey
Editorial Description: Articles about Stone County, its people, & history.
General Info: (Formerly Stone County Historical Society Nesletter), Yr. Est. 1972, Semi-annually, Mimeo press, 35 pages, No Color
Subscriptions: Indv. $10, $3/copy

Higdon Family Newsletter

Publishing Co: Higdon Family Assn., Inc., PO Box 26008, Alexandria, VA 22313-6008
General Info: Yr. Est. 1972, Monthly, Trim Size-8½ x 14, Sheetfed press, 4 pages, ISSN: 0739-3199
Circulation: Total-200

Highpoint   *Consumer, Association*

Publishing Co: Ohio Genealogical Society Summit County Chapter, PO Box 2232, Akron, OH 44309-2232
Personnel: Publisher, Editor-Marilyn Kirn Kovatch
Editorial Description: Free queries - Reports on new family histories, chapter news, Summit County Court, cemetery. Vital statistics & any data pertinent to this area.
General Info: Yr. Est. 1971, 10x/yr., Trim Size-11 x 8½, 14 pages, No Color
Subscriptions: Indv. $7, Can. $10, For. $10
Circulation: Total-365

Hinkle (Henkel) Newsletter   *Association*

Publishing Co: Genz Assoc. of America, 5821 Rowland Hill Rd., Cascade, MD 21719-1939; Title Tel # (301) 416-2660
Personnel: Editor-Victor Gebhart
General Info: Annually
Subscriptions: $2/copy

Historical Footnotes
See: RELIGIOUS & THEOLOGICAL

Historical Tidings   *Consumer, Association*

Publishing Co: Franklin County Historical Society, PO Box 130, Winchester, TN 37398-0130; Title Tel # (615) 962-1476
Editorial Description: Listing activities of society, receipts or genealogical information, & requests for genealogical records.
General Info: Yr. Est. 1969, Quarterly, Trim Size-8½ x 11
Subscriptions: Free With Membership

Historical Time Capsules of Monroe County
See: HISTORY

Hoffmann Newsletter   *Association*

Publishing Co: Genz Assoc. of America, 5821 Rowland Hill Rd., Cascade, MD 21719-1939; Title Tel # (301) 416-2660
Personnel: Editor-Victor Gebhart
General Info: Yr. Est. 1990, Annually, Mimeo press, No Color
Subscriptions: Indv. $2

Hollowell Heritage

Publishing Co: Palouse Publications, SE 310 Camino, Pullman, WA 99163-2206; Title Tel # (509) 334-1732
Personnel: Publisher, Editor-Janet Damm
Editorial Description: This is a surname book relating to the Hollowell name. All spellings accepted. Includes book reviews, queries, every name index, etc.
General Info: Yr. Est. 1987, Irregular, Mimeo press, 35 pages, ISSN: 0891-270X, No Color
Subscriptions: $7/copy

Hood County Genealogical Society Newsletter   *Association*

Publishing Co: Hood County Genealogical Society, PO Box 1623, Granbury, TX 76048-8623; Title Tel # (817) 573-2840
Personnel: Editor-Merle McNeese
Editorial Description: Provides information about the pioneer families of Hood County, Texas.
General Info: Yr. Est. 1984, Quarterly, ISSN: 1071-1112
Subscriptions: Indv. $10, Free With Membership
Circulation: Total-200

Houp Houpe Houpt Haupt Family Historian Quarterly

Publishing Co: Houp Houpe Houpt Haupt Family Assn., PO Box 608, Alma, AR 72921-0608; Title Tel # (501) 632-4687
Personnel: Editor-J. Randall Houp
General Info: Yr. Est. 1981, Quarterly, 20 pages
Subscriptions: Indv. $10

Howard Historian, The

Publishing Co: Howard Historian, Inc., 2904 SE 35th Ave., Portland, OR 97202-1802; Title Tel # (503) 231-4349
Personnel: Editor-Barbara Howard, Art Dir.-Jeff Stewart, Publisher, Mktg. Dir.-Kent Haldorson
Editorial Description: Genealogical newsletter of the Howard also Heyward, and Hayward surnames. Contains biological information, queries, lineages & published text reviews.
General Info: Yr. Est. 1986, Quarterly, Trim Size-8½ x 11, Sheetfed press, 56 pages, ISSN: 0886-9103, Matte, Saddle-stitched
Subscriptions: Indv. $18, Can. $18, $6/copy
Advertising: $50. Accepts Inserts.

Howe Research Newsletter *Consumer, Association*

Publishing Co: Yoder Distributors, 1422 Wealthy St SE, Grand Rapids, MI 49506-2717;
Title Tel # (616) 774-0520
Personnel: Editor-Harry Walter Yoder
Editorial Description: Research information & query sharing.
General Info: Yr. Est. 1984, Irregular, Mimeo press, 8 pages, Looseleaf
Subscriptions: $2/copy

Howell Lines

Publishing Co: Bell Enterprises, PO Box 10328, Spokane, WA 99209-1328
Personnel: Editor-Mary Ann Van Za Bell

Hubbell Family Historical Society-Family Notes

Publishing Co: Hubbell Family Historical Society, 106 W. 14th St., 25th Fl., Kansas City, MO 64105-1992
Editorial Description: News of the Society and of members.
General Info: Yr. Est. 1981, Semi-annually, Trim Size-8½ x 11, Letrpr. press
Acquistions: Publication Bought
Circulation: Total-300

Hunterdon Historical Newsletter
See: HISTORY

Immigrant Genealogical Society Newsletter *Association*

Publishing Co: Immigrant Genealogical Society, PO Box 7369, Burbank, CA 91510-7369;
Title Tel # (818) 848-3122
Personnel: Editor-Jean Nepsund
Editorial Description: Items of interest to German genealogy hobbyists.
General Info: Yr. Est. 1982, Monthly, Trim Size-8½ x 11, Mimeo press, 4 pages, No Color
Subscriptions: Indv. $15, For. $25
Acquistions: Publication Bought
Circulation: Total-600

Immigration Digest

Publishing Co: Family History World, PO Box 22045, Salt Lake City, UT 84122-0045;
Title Tel # (801) 250-6717
Personnel: Editor-Arlene Eakle, Circ. Mgr.-JoAnn Jackson
Editorial Description: Contains information for those tracing immigrant heritage. Includes naming patterns, passenger lists, naturalizations, & reviews.
General Info: Yr. Est. 1987, Irregular, Trim Size-8½ x 11, 50 pages, 1% ads, No Color
Subscriptions: $11/copy
Acquistions: Publication Bought
Circulation: Total-1,000
Advertising: Inquire for rates.

Ingalls Inquirer

Publishing Co: Arlene Ingalls Schrader, 5640 W Chadwick Rd, Dewitt, MI 48820-9116;
Title Tel # (517) 669-3219
Personnel: Editor-Arlene Ingalls Schrader
Editorial Description: Family newsletter for all spellings of Ingallss, Ingle, Ingles, Engel, Ingall.
General Info: Yr. Est. 1984, Trim Size-8½ x 11, 18 pages
Subscriptions: $2/copy

International Molyneux Family Association

Publishing Co: Wesley Mullenneix, PO Box 5402, Salton City, CA 92275-5402
Personnel: Editor-Wesley L. Mullenneix
Editorial Description: Quarterly results of research of Molyneux, Mullinix, and more than 200 such spellings of the name.
General Info: Yr. Est. 1986, Quarterly, Trim Size-8½ x 11¼, Mimeo press, 18 pages
Subscriptions: Indv. $8, Can. $10, For. $8, $2/copy
Circulation: Total-288

International Society for British Genealogy and Family History Newsletter *Association*

Publishing Co: Intl. Society for British Genealogy and Family History, PO Box 3115, Salt Lake City, UT 84110-3115
Personnel: Editor-Sherry Irvine
General Info: Yr. Est. 1979, Quarterly, Sheetfed press, 16 pages, ISSN: 0736-8054, No Color
Subscriptions: $3/copy
Circulation: Total-800

Iowa Genealogical Society Newsletter *Association*

Publishing Co: Iowa Genealogical Society, PO Box 7735, Des Moines, IA 50322-7735;
Title Tel # (515) 276-0287
Personnel: Circ. Mgr.-Rhonda Q. Riordan
Editorial Description: Research help, chapter info, new publications.
General Info: Yr. Est. 1978, Bi-monthly, Trim Size-8½ x 11, Desktop press, 12 pages, No Color, Other, Other
Subscriptions: Indv. $20, Inst. $20, For. $20, Free With Membership
Circulation: Total-3,000, Readership-3,000

Iredell County Tracks

Publishing Co: Genealogical Soc. of Iredell Co., PO Box 946, Statesville, NC 28687-0946;
Title Tel # (704) 878-5384

Irish Family Newsletter

Publishing Co: Irish Family Newsletter, PO Box 13548, Saint Louis, MO 63138-0548
Personnel: Editor-Maryann Schicker

Irish Queries

Publishing Co: Pioneer Publications, PO Box 1179, Tum Tum, WA 99034-1179;
Title Tel # (509) 276-9841
Personnel: Editor-Shirley Oakes
Editorial Description: Queries related to Irish ancestors-worldwide.
General Info: Yr. Est. 1986, Irregular, Trim Size-8½ x 11, Mimeo press, 25 pages, ISSN: 1044-6923
Subscriptions: $6/copy
Acquistions: Publication Bought

Iroquois County Historical Society Newsletter

Publishing Co: Iroquois County Historical Society, 103 W Cherry St, Watseka, IL 60970-1524;
Title Tel # (815) 432-2215
Personnel: Editor-Marie Hanford
Editorial Description: Includes local geneology society news and news of the museum.
General Info: Monthly, Trim Size-8½ x 11, 8 pages, No Color, Newsprint
Circulation: Total-1,150
Printing Co: Twin States Publishing Co. Inc., 1492 E Walnut St, Watseka, IL 60970-1806
Tel # (815) 432-5227

Jahnke Newsletter *Association*

Publishing Co: Genz Assoc. of America, 5821 Rowland Hill Rd., Cascade, MD 21719-1939;
Title Tel # (301) 416-2660
Personnel: Editor-Victor Gebhart
Editorial Description: Traces the history of the Jahnke family name.
General Info: Annually, Trim Size-8½ x 11, Mimeo press, 4 pages, No Color, Matte
Subscriptions: $2/copy

Jameson Newsletter

Publishing Co: Jameson Newsletter, 112 Belaire Cir, Windsor Locks, CT 06096-2809;
Title Tel # (203) 623-5790
Personnel: Publisher, Editor-Scott Jameson
Editorial Description: Comprehensive newsletter on Jamesons (includes all surname variations). Contents-50% source records (US), annual surname & subject indexes, directory, articles-historical & personal, research listings, queries, charts, & forums.
General Info: Yr. Est. 1985, Quarterly, Trim Size-8½ x 11, Mimeo press, 28 pages, No Color, Newsprint, Saddle-stitched
Subscriptions: Indv. $12, Can. $9, For. $10, $3/copy
Circulation: Total-150

Janney Journal *Association*

Publishing Co: Susan Wight, PO Box 413, Duchesne, UT 84021-0413; Title Tel # (208) 233-8542
Personnel: Editor-Susan Wight
Editorial Description: The Janney Journal is a genealogical newsletter for the Janney family.
General Info: Yr. Est. 1984, Quarterly, Mimeo press, 12 pages, No Color
Subscriptions: Indv. $6, $2/copy
Circulation: Total-130

Jay News

Publishing Co: Jay Family Assn. West, 4406 Moffett Rd, Ceres, CA 95307-9427;
Title Tel # (209) 538-3855
Personnel: Editor-Loretta Davis
Editorial Description: Jay News & Davis Data exchange are only printed when enough material is obtained. Compiling a book on surname of Duck. Any Duck descendents who wish to be included. Patterson Prints is my printing business. Will give estimates on offset printing, upon request.
General Info: (Formerly Jay-Bird News Update), Yr. Est. 1976
Subscriptions: $7/copy

Johnson/Johansson Family News *Consumer, Association*

Publishing Co: Johnson/Johansson Family News, 171 Clinton Rd, Brookline, MA 02146-5815;
Title Tel # (617) 232-5946 Title Fax # (617) 734-8233
Personnel: Publisher, Editor-Joyce Graff
Editorial Description: Current and historical family information from the Johnson family history project.
General Info: Yr. Est. 1991, Irregular, Trim Size-8½ x 11, Desktop press, 12 pages, ISSN: 1066-6427, 2 Color, Recycled
Subscriptions: Indv. $10, Inst. $40, $3/copy
Circulation: Total-150, Readership-400
Advertising: Inquire for rates. Accepts Inserts.
List Rental: Rents Lists

Johnston County Genealogical Society Journal
Association

Publishing Co: Johnston County Genealogical Society, 305 E Market St, Smithfield, NC 27577-3919; Title Tel # (919) 934-8146
Personnel: Co-Editor-Elizabeth Ross, Co-Editor-Virginia Lee Satterfield
Editorial Description: Johnston County Genealogical info, abstracts, cemeteries, family bibles, news items.
General Info: (Formerly Johnston County Genealogical Society Newsletter), Yr. Est. 1973, Quarterly, Trim Size-8½ x 11, Offset press, 20 pages
Subscriptions: Indv. $10
Circulation: Total-275
Printing Co: D&S Printing Co., Raiford St., Selma, NC 27576 Tel # (919) 965-2465

Joseph Lines
Consumer

Publishing Co: Orland Stanley, RR 2 Box 97, Sullivan, IN 47882-9612; Title Tel # (812) 382-4236
General Info: Yr. Est. 1986, Quarterly

Jots from the Point
Association

Publishing Co: Western Pennsylvania Genealogical Society, 4400 Forbes Ave., Pittsburgh, PA 15213-4080; Title Tel # (412) 681-5533
Personnel: Editor-Helen Harriss
General Info: Monthly, 8 pages
Subscriptions: Indv. $10

Journal of American Indian Research Monthly Newsletter

Publishing Co: Histree, 803 S 5th Ave, Yuma, AZ 85364-3842; Title Tel # (714) 859-1659
Personnel: Editor-Larry Watson, Circ. Mgr.-Louis Simone
Editorial Description: Current events & activities in the Native American community - calendar of events.
General Info: Yr. Est. 1988, Monthly, Mimeo press, 16 pages, ISSN: 1040-6581, No Color, Newsprint
Subscriptions: Indv. $59, Can. $75, $7/copy

Journal of the Predmore/ Pridemore/Pridmore/ Prigmore Assn.
Association

Publishing Co: Pridemore/Pridmore/Prigmore Assn., 545 Jefferson St, Kimberly, ID 83341-1825; Title Tel # (208) 423-4293
Personnel: Publisher-Howard Johnston, Editor-June Welch
General Info: Yr. Est. 1986, Quarterly, Trim Size-8½ x 11, Mimeo press, 65 pages, No Color
Subscriptions: Indv. $20, $5/copy

Judkins Journal
Association, Consumer

Publishing Co: Judkins Family Assn., 1538 NW 60th St, Seattle, WA 98107-2328
Personnel: Publisher, Editor-Kathi Abendroth, Production Mgr.-Kathi Judkins
Editorial Description: Family oriented genealogy.
General Info: Yr. Est. 1985, Quarterly, Trim Size-8½ x 11, Desktop press, 20 pages, Saddle-stitched
Subscriptions: Indv. $14, $4/copy
Circulation: Total-115
Printing Co: American Press and Graphics, 595 15th N.W., Seattle, WA 98107 Tel # (206) 789-6497

Kalamazoo Valley Heritage
Scholarly, Association

Publishing Co: Kalamazoo Valley Genealogical Society, Box 405, Comstock, MT 49041; Title Tel # (616) 665-9697
Personnel: Editor-Mary Alice Benedict, Grindol
Editorial Description: Society news and genealogical news, original records and other items.
General Info: Yr. Est. 1983, Monthly, Trim Size-8½ x 11, Desktop press, 12 pages, ISSN: 1052-7672, No Color
Subscriptions: Free With Membership
Circulation: Total-370, Readership-370
Printing Co: Office Max, Portage, MI 49002

Kane Family News Notes

Publishing Co: Mullac Co., 822 Bonaparte Ave, Baltimore, MD 21218-6219; Title Tel # (301) 235-6697
Personnel: Editor-Agnes Callum
Editorial Description: Black genealogy & history, current family events.
General Info: Yr. Est. 1978, Quarterly
Subscriptions: Indv. $5
Circulation: Total-102

Keeping up with the Jones
Association

Publishing Co: Lusa R. Franklin, 4604 Virginia Loop Rd., Apt. 3156-G, Montgomery, AL 36116-4739
Editorial Description: Resource for persons researching ancestors bearing the jones surname.
General Info: Quarterly, Trim Size-8½ x 11, 25 pages
Subscriptions: Indv. $10, Inst. $10, $3/copy
Advertising: $9. Accepts Inserts.

Kennedy Gazette
Consumer, Association

Publishing Co: Kennedy Society of America, Inc., 520 Harrison Ave., Cambridge, OH 43725-1472; Title Tel # (614) 432-6263
Personnel: Editor-Donald Canaday
General Info: Yr. Est. 1977, Quarterly, Trim Size-8 x 10½, 8 pages
Subscriptions: Indv. $25, $1/copy

Kentucky Kinfolk

Publishing Co: Kentucky Tree-Search, PO Box 22621, Lexington, KY 40522-2621
Personnel: Editor-Gwendolyn Tippie, Circ. Mgr.-Heather Evans, Production Mgr.-Guy Evans, Adv. Dir.-Bruce Layne, Promotion Dir.-William Tippie
General Info: Quarterly
Subscriptions: Indv. $15, $4/copy

Kershner Kinfolk
Association

Publishing Co: Kershner Family Association, 1449 Fox Run Dr, Charlotte, NC 28212-7125
Personnel: Publisher, Editor-W. Kershner
Editorial Description: History and genealogy of descendants of Endres Kirschner (b 1570) of Hesse, Germany.
General Info: Yr. Est. 1982, Quarterly, Trim Size-8½ x 11, Other press, 30 pages, ISSN: 0736-0886, No Color, Other
Subscriptions: Indv. $14, $4/copy
Circulation: Total-300

Kilgore Clan, The

Publishing Co: Charleston Chapter SCGS, PO Box 20266, Charleston, SC 29413-0266; Title Tel # (803) 766-1667
General Info: Bi-monthly, Looseleaf
Subscriptions: Indv. $10
Advertising: $6. Accepts Inserts.

Kinder Family
Consumer

Publishing Co: Kinder Family, PO Box 264, Acworth, GA 30101-0264; Title Tel # (404) 926-8732
Personnel: Publisher, Editor-Gerald Purcell
Editorial Description: Consist of articles, queries, lineages, births, deaths, marriages, census, family group charts & others.
General Info: Yr. Est. 1990, Quarterly, ISSN: 1046-7998
Subscriptions: $3/copy

Kindred Spirits
Association

Publishing Co: Ontario Genealogical Society: Whitby-Oshawa Branch, Box 174, Whitby, ON L1N 5S1 Canada; Title Tel # (905) 668-1362
Personnel: Editor-Deana Shaver
General Info: Yr. Est. 1982, Quarterly, Trim Size-8½ x 11, Offset press, 16 pages, ISSN: 0823-8367, No Color, Other
Subscriptions: Indv. $12, Inst. $14, Can. $12

Kinfolks & Connections
Association

Publishing Co: Alexander County Genealogical Soc. NC, PO Box 241, Hiddenite, NC 28636-0241; Title Tel # (704) 632-3998
Personnel: Editor-Linda Correll
Editorial Description: Genealogical material contains family, local, county and surrounding areas records.
General Info: Yr. Est. 1983, Quarterly, Trim Size-8½ x 11, Mimeo press, 30 pages, No Color
Subscriptions: Indv. $8, $3/copy
Acquisitions: Publication Sold
Circulation: Total-200

Kingston Relations
Association

Publishing Co: Kingston Branch, Ontario Genealogical Soc., Box 1394, Kingston, ON K7L 5C6 Canada
Personnel: Editor-Stephanie Stone
Editorial Description: Genealogical news of Frontenac, & Lennox & Addington Counties, of Ontario, Canada.
General Info: (Formerly Kingston Branch Newsletter), Yr. Est. 1973, Bi-monthly, Trim Size-8½ x 11, Mimeo press, 12 pages, ISSN: 0316-5183, No Color
Subscriptions: Indv. $10
Circulation: Total-600

Kinship Kronicle

Publishing Co: Rockingham Society of Genealogists, PO Box 81, Exeter, NH 03833-0081; Title Tel # (603) 436-5824
Personnel: Publisher, Editor-Carl Brage
Editorial Description: Primary interest on ancestry of persons who resided in Rockingham County of New Hampshire. Secondarily on those who lived adjacent to this county.
General Info: Yr. Est. 1978, Quarterly, Trim Size-8½ x 11, Sheetfed press, 16 pages, ISSN: 0882-9802, 1% ads, Matte
Subscriptions: Indv. $7, Can. $9, For. $13, $2/copy
Circulation: Total-250
Advertising: Inquire for rates. Accepts Inserts.
Printing Co: Jiffy Copy Ctr., 149 Congress St, Portsmouth, NH 03801-4086 Tel # (603) 436-8286

Kinship Tales

Publishing Co: Grand Travese Area Genealogical Society, PO Box 2015, Traverse City, MI 49685-2015
Personnel: Editor-Barbara Martin
Editorial Description: Genealogical information for the local area.
General Info: Yr. Est. 1983, Quarterly, Trim Size-5½ x 8½, Mimeo press, 20 pages, No Color, Newsprint
Subscriptions: Indv. $10, $3/copy
Circulation: Total-132
Printing Co: Speedy Print, 308 E Front St, Traverse City, MI 49684-2528 Tel # (616) 946-2679

Koch Newsletter   *Association*

Publishing Co: Genz Assoc. of America, 5821 Rowland Hill Rd., Cascade, MD 21719-1939;
Title Tel # (301) 416-2660
Personnel: Editor-Victor Gebhart
General Info: Annually, Mimeo press, No Color
Subscriptions: $2/copy

Krefeld Immigrants and Their Descendants

Publishing Co: Links Genealogy Publications, 7677 Abaline Way, Sacramento, CA 95823-4224;
Title Tel # (916) 428-2245
Personnel: Editor-Iris Carter Jones
Editorial Description: Genealogical & historical information on the original Dutch/German pioneers to Germantown, PA & on their allied families & descendants.
General Info: Yr. Est. 1984, Semi-annually, Trim Size-8½ x 11, Desktop press, 40 pages, ISSN: 0883-7961
Subscriptions: Indv. $14, Can. $17, For. $19, $7/copy
Acquistions: Publication Sold
Advertising: Inquire for rates. Accepts Inserts.

L'Ancetre   *Association*

Publishing Co: Societe de Genealogie de Quebec, C.P. 9066, Ste. Foy, PQ G1V 4A8 Canada;
Title Tel # (418) 651-9127
Personnel: Editor-Jacques Saintonge, Circ. Mgr.-Raymond Deraspe
Editorial Description: Genealogical research and ancestors history.
General Info: Yr. Est. 1974, Monthly, Mimeo press, 40 pages, ISSN: 0316-0513, No Color
Subscriptions: Indv. $30, $2/copy
Acquistions: Publication Bought, Publication Sold
Circulation: Total-1,300

Land Newsletter

Publishing Co: Ruth Land Hatten, 86 Saint Andrews Dr, Jackson, MS 39211-2467;
Title Tel # (601) 636-9337
Personnel: Editor-Ruth Land Hatten
General Info: Yr. Est. 1982, Quarterly, Desktop press, 10 pages, No Color
Subscriptions: Indv. $15

Lapeer County Genealogical Society Newsletter   *Association, Consumer*

Publishing Co: Lapeer County Genealogical Society, 921 W Nepessing St, Lapeer, MI 48446-1872
Personnel: Editor-Alice Bohnsack
Editorial Description: Quarterly with local birth, death & marriage records. Cemetery readings, ancestor charts, family histories, queries, & membership list.
General Info: Yr. Est. 1983, Quarterly, 12 pages, ISSN: 8756-7067, Ind/Abs/Online: Indexed, Color-cover
Circulation: Total-250

Latah County Genealogical Society Newsletter

Publishing Co: Latah Co. Genealogical Society, 327 E 2nd St, Moscow, ID 83843-2852;
Title Tel # (208) 882-1004
Personnel: Editor-Dorothy Viets Schell
Editorial Description: Local genealogical records.
General Info: 8x/yr., ISSN: 0747-6663, Ind/Abs/Online: PSI

Leaf of the Branch   *Association*

Publishing Co: S.W. Branch, Manitoba Genealogical Soc., 53 Almond Cres., Brandon, MB R7B 1A2 Canada; Title Tel # (204) 728-2857
Personnel: Publisher-Jim Wall, Editor-Margaret Goodman, Editor-Beth Wall
General Info: Yr. Est. 1984, Quarterly, Trim Size-8 x 11, Other press, 10 pages, Other
Subscriptions: Free With Membership

Leaves of Greene   *Consumer, Association*

Publishing Co: Greene County Chapter, OGS, PO Box 706, Xenia, OH 45385-0706;
Title Tel # (513) 376-4952
Personnel: Editor-Richard Keister
General Info: Yr. Est. 1981, Semi-monthly, ISSN: 1061-8791
Subscriptions: Indv. $8
Circulation: Total-275

Lehmer-Leamer-Lamer Newsletter

Publishing Co: Laurence Leamer, 221 Torrance Ave, Vestal, NY 13850-1328;
Title Tel # (607) 748-6021
Personnel: Editor-Laurence Leamer
General Info: Yr. Est. 1977, Semi-annually, Trim Size-5½ x 8½, Sheetfed press, 24 pages, No Color
Subscriptions: Indv. $3
Circulation: Total-200

Lesher Families in America

Publishing Co: Lesher Families in America, 18310 Florwood Ave., Torrance, CA 90504
Personnel: Editor-Don Lesher
Editorial Description: Newsletter of the Lesher Family.
General Info: Quarterly, ISSN: 0985-0768

Lewis Unlimited

Publishing Co: Pioneer Publications, PO Box 1179, Tum Tum, WA 99034-1179;
Title Tel # (509) 276-9841
Personnel: Publisher, Editor-Shirley Oakes
Editorial Description: Genealogical data on surname. Lineage & Queries accepted for free.
General Info: Yr. Est. 1994, Irregular, Trim Size-8½ x 11, Mimeo press, 25 pages
Subscriptions: $6/copy

Life Times Family History Quarterly

Publishing Co: Rayve Productions, Inc., PO Box 726, Windsor, CA 95492-0726;
Title Tel # (707) 838-6200
Personnel: Editor-Barbara Ray
Editorial Description: Devoted to those interested in their family history.
General Info: Yr. Est. 1990, Quarterly
Subscriptions: Indv. $18

Lifeline   *Consumer, Association*

Publishing Co: New York State Council of Genealogical Organizations, PO Box 2593, Syracuse, NY 13220-2593
Personnel: Editor-Joyce Cook
Editorial Description: For New York State genealogical associations.
General Info: Quarterly

Linder Quarterly

Publishing Co: Linder Family Assn., Hc 73 Box 989, Walker, MN 56484-9531
General Info: Yr. Est. 1967, Quarterly, Trim Size-8½ x 11, Sheetfed press, 10 pages

Lipscomb Newsletter   *Consumer, Association*

Publishing Co: Phillip Genealogical Heritage House, 605 Benton Ave., Missoula, MT 59801-8633;
Title Tel # (406) 543-3495
Personnel: Publisher-Ruth Phillip, Editor-Jennie Crisp, Adv. Dir.-Arthur Wigfield
Editorial Description: Annual Lipscomb Newsletter including editorial, genealogy information, & present day vital statistics.
General Info: Yr. Est. 1981, Annually, Trim Size-8½ x 11, Mimeo press
Subscriptions: Indv. $5, Inst. $4, $5/copy
Acquistions: Publication Sold
Advertising: Accepts Inserts.
List Rental: Rents Lists
Printing Co: Phillip Heritage Genealogy House., 605 Benton Ave, Missoula, MT 59801-8633
Tel # (406) 543-3495

Lively Newsletter

Publishing Co: Nat'l. Assn. of Lively Families, Rte. 1, Box 36904, Butler, AL 36904-9801
Personnel: Editor-Carolyn Lively

Livingston Genealogical Register

Publishing Co: Friends of Clermont, The, One Clermont Avenue, Germantown, NY 12526
Editorial Description: This up-to-date record of the descendants of Robert Livingston (1654-1728), first proprietor of Llvingston manor, and Robert Livingston 'The Nephew' (1663-1725), replaces teh 19891 and 1986 editions of the Livingston Genealogy, which was compiled by James D. Livingston, Clare Brandt and Arthur Kelly and which was produced in loose-leaf binder format. This publication will be limited to 300 compies, an
General Info: Looseleaf
Subscriptions: $75/copy

Locke Sickle & Sword   *Association*

Publishing Co: Locke Family Assn., 102 Crooked Spring Rd., Chelmsford, MA 01863-2307;
Title Tel # (508) 251-4804
Personnel: Editor-Donald Hayes
Editorial Description: Association events and projects; research on John Locke of N.H. family, and William Locke of Woburn, MA family.
General Info: (Formerly Locke Family Association Newsletter), Yr. Est. 1972, Quarterly, Trim Size-11 x 17, Desktop press, 4 pages, No Color, Coated
Subscriptions: Indv. $7, $2/copy
Circulation: Total-400

Long Point Genealogist, The
Association

Publishing Co: Norfolk Historical Society, 109 Norfolk St., S., Simcoe, ON N3Y 2W3 Canada; Title Tel # (519) 426-1583
Editorial Description: Local history and genealogy for Norfolk county, Ontario.
General Info: Yr. Est. 1980, Semi-monthly, Desktop press, 10% ads
Subscriptions: Indv. $20, Inst. $20, Can. $20, For. $20
Circulation: Total-650
Advertising: Inquire for rates.

Lonoke County Historical Society Newsletter
Association

Publishing Co: LCHS, PO Box 14, Lonoke, AR 72086-0014; Title Tel # (501) 676-2467
General Info: Semi-annually

Lookin' for Lockes
Association

Publishing Co: Lookin' for Lockes, 7650 Fairview Rd., Tillamook, OR 97141-9009; Title Tel # (503) 842-6036
Personnel: Editor-Orella Chadwick
Editorial Description: This newsletter covers all Locks/Lockes except New England ones covered by another organization.
General Info: Yr. Est. 1979, Quarterly, Mimeo press, 20 pages, No Color
Subscriptions: Indv. $15, $4/copy

Love Letters

Publishing Co: Love Letters, 1300 Arbolita Dr., La Habra, CA 90631-3206; Title Tel # (213) 690-4306
Personnel: Art Dir.-Pat Stubblefield
Editorial Description: Surname newsletter of all Love records to aid in genealogical research.
General Info: Yr. Est. 1984, Quarterly, Sheetfed press, 15 pages, No Color
Subscriptions: Indv. $10, $3/copy
Acquistions: Publication Bought
Circulation: Total-200

Low Country Courier

Publishing Co: Sponsor-S. Carolina Gen. Soc., Charleston Chapter SCGS, PO Box 20266, Charleston, SC 29413-0266; Title Tel # (803) 766-1667
Personnel: Editor-Doris O'Brien
General Info: Yr. Est. 1976, Monthly, Trim Size-8½ x 11, Sheetfed press, 12 pages, No Color, Looseleaf
Subscriptions: Indv. $12, Inst. $8
Acquistions: Publication Bought
Circulation: Total-320

Lowery Newsletter
Association

Publishing Co: Genz Assoc. of America, 5821 Rowland Hill Rd., Cascade, MD 21719-1939; Title Tel # (301) 416-2660
Personnel: Editor-Victor Gebhart
General Info: Annually, Mimeo press, No Color
Subscriptions: $2/copy

Luptonian

Publishing Co: Luptonian, P.O. Box 43, Bayboro, NC 28515-0443 Tel # (919) 745-3569; Title Tel # (919) 745-7037
Personnel: Editor-David W. Lupton, Circ. Mgr.-Dorothy R. Lupton
Editorial Description: Presents articles & family histories pertaining to the surname Lupton.
General Info: Yr. Est. 1974, Irregular, Trim Size-8½ x 11, Offset press, 20 pages, ISSN: 0099-1791, Ind/Abs/Online: Geneal.Per.Ind., No Color
Subscriptions: Free
Circulation: (100% controlled), Total-300, Readership-300

Luther Family Newsletter
Association

Publishing Co: Luther Family Association, 2531 Lakeview St, Lakeland, FL 33801-2556; Title Tel # (941) 665-5788
Personnel: Editor-George Luther
Editorial Description: Devoted to interests of decendants of Captain John Luther of Massachusetts Bay Colony of 1630-35.
General Info: Yr. Est. 1986, Quarterly, Trim Size-8½ x 11, 10 pages, No Color
Subscriptions: Indv. $10, Inst. $10, Can. $10, For. $10
Acquistions: Publication Bought
Circulation: Total-850

Lybarger Linkages
Association

Publishing Co: Lybarger Memorial Associates, PO Box 7792, West Trenton, NJ 08628-0792; Title Tel # (609) 396-1099
Personnel: Editor-Lee Lybarger
Editorial Description: Report, promote, educate about Lybarger relations, history, & reunion activities.
General Info: Yr. Est. 1985, Semi-annually, 8 pages, ISSN: 0887-9354, Saddle-stitched
Subscriptions: Indv. $10, Free
Acquistions: Publication Bought
Circulation: Total-800

Madden Family Newsletter
Consumer

Publishing Co: Madden Family Newsletter, 1101 Wilmington Ave Apt A, Dayton, OH 45420-1681; Title Tel # (513) 293-0779
Personnel: Editor-Mariam Schaefer
Editorial Description: Genealogy research of name Madden--BAS(By Any Spelling.)
General Info: Yr. Est. 1984, Quarterly, Trim Size-8½ x 11, Mimeo press, 31 pages, ISSN: 0883-556X, Newsprint
Subscriptions: Indv. $15, For. $25, $4/copy
Acquistions: Publication Bought
Circulation: Total-150
Advertising: Inquire for rates.

Magny Families Association Newsletter
Association

Publishing Co: Magny Families Association, PO Box 684, Windsor, CT 06095-0684 Tel # (203) 683-8943; Title Tel # (860) 683-8943
Personnel: Publisher, Editor-Dorothy Many
Editorial Description: Information on genealogical and historical gleanings by family association historian (surnames: Many, Manney, Manny, Maney, Manee, Manna, Magny, Manaugh - mainly French in origin); Census data, journal excerpts, and other research aids; announcements of family publications and reunions; current personals.
General Info: Yr. Est. 1980, Semi-annually, Trim Size-8½ x 11, Sheetfed press, 8 pages, Matte
Subscriptions: Free With Membership
Circulation: Total-600
Printing Co: Spaulding Printers, Wallingford, CT 06492

Main Gazette
Consumer

Publishing Co: Nancy L. Childress Svces., 3709 W Gardenia Ave., Phoenix, AZ 85051-8266; Title Tel # (602) 841-7478
Personnel: Publisher-Nancy L. Childress
Editorial Description: Genealogy for the Mayne/Maine/Main/Mehn surname.
General Info: Yr. Est. 1990, Quarterly, Trim Size-8½ x 11, 24 pages
Subscriptions: Indv. $10, Can. $12, For. $15

Maine Genealogical Society Newsletter
Association

Publishing Co: Maine Genealogical Society, PO Box 221, Farmington, ME 04938-0221
Personnel: Editor-Marlene Grores
General Info: Yr. Est. 1986, Quarterly, Trim Size-8½ x 11, 16 pages, No Color, Newsprint
Subscriptions: Indv. $20
Circulation: Total-1,200
Advertising: Inquire for rates.

Manley Family Newsletter
CPM: $133

Publishing Co: Manley Family Newsletter, 171 Nathan Dr, Bohemia, NY 11716-1319; Title Tel # (516) 567-0386
Personnel: Editor-Trudi Manley
Editorial Description: Documents Manley/Manly family history, genealogy & heritage, both past & present. Includes lineage charts, biographies, & researched historical data, photographs and queries.
General Info: Yr. Est. 1983, Semi-annually, Trim Size-8½ x 11, Desktop press, 56 pages, ISSN: 0883-7805, Ind/Abs/Online: GPAI, No Color, Other
Subscriptions: Indv. $15
Circulation: Total-225
Advertising: $30. Accepts Inserts.
List Rental: Rents Lists

Marion Memories

Publishing Co: Marion Area Genealogical Society, 671 Vernon Heights Blvd, Marion, OH 43302-5377; Title Tel # (614) 382-4179
Personnel: Editor, Production Mgr.-Maxine Marshall
General Info: Quarterly, 11 pages
Subscriptions: Indv. $8
Circulation: Total-240
Advertising: Accepts Inserts.

Marshland to Heartland
Association

Publishing Co: Ohio Genealogical Society, Ottawa County Chapter, Box 193, Port Clinton, OH 43452; Title Tel # (419) 734-7396
Editorial Description: Publication containing data of interest to genealogists interested in Ottawa County, Ohio.
General Info: Yr. Est. 1987, Quarterly, Trim Size-8½ x 11, 30 pages, Ind/Abs/Online: Indexed
Subscriptions: Indv. $8, $2/copy
Printing Co: Dogwood Printing Co., PO Box 716, Ozark, MO 65721-0716 Tel # (417) 485-8585

Martin Newsletter
Consumer, Association

Publishing Co: Phillip Genealogical Heritage House, 605 Benton Ave., Missoula, MT 59801-8633; Title Tel # (406) 543-3495
Personnel: Publisher-Ruth Phillip, Editor-Jennie Crisp, Adv. Dir.-Arthur Wigfield
Editorial Description: Annual newsletter including editorial, genealogy information, present day vital statistics.
General Info: Yr. Est. 1981, Annually, Trim Size-8½ x 11, Mimeo press, 10 pages
Subscriptions: Indv. $5, Inst. $4, $5/copy
Acquistions: Publication Sold
Advertising: Accepts Inserts.
Printing Co: Phillip Heritage Genealogy House., 605 Benton Ave, Missoula, MT 59801-8633 Tel # (406) 543-3495

Maryland & Delaware Genealogy

Publishing Co: Family Line Pubs., 63 E Main St Rear, Westminster, MD 21157-5026; Title Tel # (301) 876-6101
General Info: Semi-annually

Mason Family Newsletter   *Consumer, Association*

Publishing Co: COMPU-CHART, 363 S. Park Victoria Dr., Milpitas, CA 95035-5708; Title Tel # (408) 262-1051
Personnel: Editor-Paula Mortensen
General Info: Yr. Est. 1987, Quarterly, Trim Size-8½ x 11, Mimeo press, 12 pages, ISSN: 0895-4496, No Color
Subscriptions: Indv. $10, For. $15

Mass-Pocha   *Association*

Publishing Co: Jewish Genealogical Society of Greater Boston, Inc., PO Box 366, Newton Highlands, MA 02161-0003; Title Tel # (617) 784-0387
Personnel: Editor-Jim Yarin
Editorial Description: Newsletter of the Jewish Genealogical Society of Greater Boston.
General Info: Yr. Est. 1991, Quarterly, Trim Size-8½ x 11, 12 pages, No Color
Subscriptions: Indv. $12, $3/copy

McCoy Material

Publishing Co: Bell Enterprises, PO Box 10328, Spokane, WA 99209-1328

McCrary

Publishing Co: McCrary, 406 Jefferson Dr, Charlotte, NC 28270-5344; Title Tel # (704) 366-3474
Personnel: Editor-Leslie McCrary, Publisher, Circ. Mgr.-Perry McCrary
Editorial Description: Family Assn. (Family History & Genealogy) Newsletter.
General Info: Yr. Est. 1978, Quarterly, Trim Size-8½ x 11, Sheetfed press, 8 pages, No Color, Newsprint
Subscriptions: Indv. $8
Acquistions: Publication Bought
Circulation: Total-300
Advertising: Accepts Inserts.

Mennonite Historians of Eastern PA   *Association*

Publishing Co: Mennonite Historians of Eastern PA, PO Box 82, Harleysville, PA 19438-0082; Title Tel # (215) 256-3020
Personnel: Editor-Carolyn Nolan
General Info: Yr. Est. 1974, Bi-monthly, Trim Size-8½ x 11, Desktop press, 12 pages, ISSN: 0895-0903, No Color
Subscriptions: Indv. $20, Inst. $30, Can. $26, $1/copy

Mick Family Newsletter

Publishing Co: Mick Family Newsletter, 6555 Manson Dr, Waterford, MI 48329-2736; Title Tel # (313) 623-6062
Personnel: Publisher, Editor-Emma Smith, Promotion Dir.-John Mick, Jr.
Editorial Description: Dedicated to finding first immigrant in America & connecting all family branches.
General Info: Yr. Est. 1979, Quarterly, Trim Size-8½ x 11, Mimeo press, 11 pages, No Color, Newsprint
Subscriptions: Indv. $5, $1/copy
Acquistions: Publication Bought
Advertising: Accepts Inserts.
List Rental: Rents Lists
Printing Co: Impressive Type, 5734 Williams Lake Rd, Waterford, MI 48329-3274 Tel # (313) 673-0511

Mid-Atlantic Queries & Reviews

Publishing Co: Pioneer Publications, PO Box 1179, Tum Tum, WA 99034-1179; Title Tel # (509) 276-9841
Personnel: Publisher, Editor-Shirley Oakes
Editorial Description: Queries pertaining to ancestors in Pennsylvania or those who passed through.
General Info: (Formerly Pennsylvania Queries), Yr. Est. 1986, Irregular, Trim Size-8½ x 11, Mimeo press, 25 pages, ISSN: 1044-6915
Subscriptions: $6/copy
Acquistions: Publication Bought

Mifflin County Historical News See: HISTORY

Minnesota Genealogical Society Newsletter   *Association*

Publishing Co: Minnesota Genealogical Society, PO Box 16069, St. Paul, MN 55116-0069; Title Tel # (612) 645-3671
Personnel: Editor-Mark Abbott
Editorial Description: Society newsletter giving details of upcoming events.
General Info: Yr. Est. 1969, Quarterly, Trim Size-8½ x 11, Letrpr. press, 8 pages, No Color
Subscriptions: Free With Membership
Circulation: Total-1,500
Advertising: Inquire for rates.

Mirror See: MUSEUM PUBLICATIONS

Monroe Juneau Jackson Counties Genealogy Newsletter   *Association*

Publishing Co: Carolyn Habelman, RR 3, Box 253, Black River Falls, WI 54615-9405; Title Tel # (608) 378-4388 Title Fax # (608) 378-3006
Editorial Description: Genealogical information on Monroe, Juneau, & Jackson counties Wisconsin.
General Info: Quarterly
Subscriptions: Indv. $7, Inst. $10, Can. $12, Free With Membership
Circulation: Total-225

Moore Family Register

Publishing Co: Ophelia Wade, Rr 1 Box 26, Bragg City, MO 63827-9705

Morgan Link   *Association*

Publishing Co: Ohio Genealogical Society Morgan County Chapter, Box 418, McConnelsville, OH 43756-0418
General Info: Yr. Est. 1986, Quarterly, Trim Size-8½ x 11, Offset press, 12 pages, Color
Subscriptions: Indv. $8, $2/copy
Circulation: Total-300

Moriarty Clan

Publishing Co: Gerald Moriarty, 8657 Golfview Drive, Orland Park, IL 60462; Title Tel # (708) 460-2193 Title Fax # (708) 423-6991
Personnel: Editor-Dan Moriarty
General Info: Yr. Est. 1978, Semi-annually, 8 pages
Subscriptions: Indv. $6
Circulation: Total-250

Morton Heritage

Publishing Co: Palouse Publications, SE 310 Camino, Pullman, WA 99163-2206; Title Tel # (509) 334-1732
Personnel: Publisher, Editor-Janet Damm
Editorial Description: This is a surname book relating to the Morton name. All spellings accepted. Includes book reviews, queries, index, etc.
General Info: Yr. Est. 1987, Irregular, Mimeo press, 35 pages, ISSN: 0894-3974, No Color
Subscriptions: $7/copy

Moultrie County Heritage See: HISTORY

Mountain Empire Genealogical Quarterly   *Consumer, Association*

Publishing Co: Mountain Empire Genealogical Soc., PO Box 628, Pound, VA 24279-0628; Title Tel # (703) 796-5233
General Info: Quarterly
Subscriptions: Indv. $20
Circulation: Total-800
Advertising: Inquire for rates.

Mylan Messenger

Publishing Co: Home Publisher, PO Box 451, Coeur D Alene, ID 83816-0451; Title Tel # (208) 765-9474
Personnel: Publisher, Editor, Production Mgr., Adv. Dir., Art Dir.-Joisse Knowles
General Info: Quarterly
Subscriptions: Indv. $10, $3/copy

NEHGS Nexus   *Association*   CPM: $22

Publishing Co: New England Historic Genealogical Society, 101 Newbury St., Boston, MA 02116-3007; Title Tel # (617) 536-5740 Title Fax # (617) 536-7307
Personnel: Editor-Robert Shaw Scott C. Steward, Publisher, Contrib. Ed.-Gary Boyd Roberts, Circ. Mgr.-Linda Skinner, Adv. Dir.-Donald Nielsen, Art Dir.-Alice Ledogar
Editorial Description: Genealogical/historical articles & query column. Society events and news.
General Info: (Formerly NEXUS), Yr. Est. 1984, 5x/yr., Trim Size-8½ x 11, 52 pages, ISSN: 0747-9891, 10% ads, No Color, Saddle-stitched
Subscriptions: Indv. $10, Free With Membership
Circulation: Total-16,600
Advertising: $375.
Printing Co: Daamen Printing, West Rutland Industrial Pk., W. Rutland, VT 05777 Tel # (802) 438-5472

NGS Newsletter   *Association*

Publishing Co: National Genealogical Society, 4527 17th St. N, Arlington, VA 22207-2399; Title Tel # (703) 525-0050 Title Fax # (703) 525-0052
Personnel: Publisher-Russell Henderson
General Info: Yr. Est. 1975, Bi-monthly, Trim Size-8½ x 11, Sheetfed press, 28 pages, ISSN: 0887-1353, No Color, Newsprint, Saddle-stitched
Subscriptions: Indv. $40, Inst. $30
Circulation: Total-14,500

NHSG Newsletter

Publishing Co: New Hampshire Society of Genealogists, Inc., PO Box 2316, Concord, NH 03302-2316 Tel # (603) 269-4371 Fax # (603) 269-4524; Title Tel # (603) 436-5824
Personnel: Editor-Jane Bramwell
Editorial Description: New Hampshire genealogy & society news.
General Info: (Formerly 40), Yr. Est. 1981, Quarterly, Trim Size-8½ x 11, Sheetfed press, 14 pages, ISSN: 8755-173X, 1% ads, No Color, Matte
Subscriptions: $1/copy
Advertising: Inquire for rates.
Printing Co: Jiffy Copy Ctr., 149 Congress St, Portsmouth, NH 03801-4086 Tel # (603) 436-8286

NYG&B Newsletter, The   *Consumer, Association*

Publishing Co: New York Genealogical & Biographical Society, 122 E. 58th St., New York, NY 10022-1939; Title Tel # (212) 755-8532
Personnel: Co-Editor-Henry Hoff, Co-Editor-Harry Macy
General Info: Yr. Est. 1990, Quarterly, Trim Size-8½ x 11, Offset press, 8 pages, ISSN: 1049-8826, Matte, Saddle-stitched
Subscriptions: $2/copy
Circulation: Total-2,000

Nash Notations   *Consumer*

Publishing Co: Culver Research Pubs., 840 Mesman Dr, Grants Pass, OR 97527-6018; Title Tel # (818) 333-5917
Personnel: Editor-Lois Culver
Editorial Description: Research of the surname Nash (& its variations) in the U.S. including allied lines. Free queries to subscribers.
General Info: Yr. Est. 1981, Quarterly, Trim Size-8½ x 11, 18 pages, ISSN: 8756-4718
Subscriptions: Indv. $12, Can. $14, $3/copy
Acquistions: Publication Bought

Nebraska Ancestree

Publishing Co: Nebraska State Genealogical Society, 704 Maple St, Kimball, NE 69145-1814

Nelson County Genealogist

Publishing Co: Nelson County Genealogical Round Table, PO Box 409, Bardstown, KY 40004-0409

New Brass Key

Publishing Co: Nebraska State Genealogical Society, 704 Maple St, Kimball, NE 69145-1814

New England Queries & Reviews

Publishing Co: Pioneer Publications, PO Box 1179, Tum Tum, WA 99034-1179; Title Tel # (509) 276-9841
Personnel: Publisher, Editor-Shirley Oakes
Editorial Description: Queries pertaining to ancestors in all New England states or those who passed through.
General Info: (Formerly Massachusetts Queries), Yr. Est. 1986, Irregular, Trim Size-8½ x 11, 25 pages, ISSN: 0897-7739
Subscriptions: $6/copy
Acquistions: Publication Bought

New Notes from Suggett House   *Association*

Publishing Co: Cortland County Historical Society, 25 Homer Ave, Cortland, NY 13045-2018; Title Tel # (607) 756-6071
Personnel: Editor-Rachel Savage
Editorial Description: Cortland County local history & genealogy newsletter.
General Info: Yr. Est. 1983, Bi-monthly, Trim Size-8½ x 11, Sheetfed press, 2 pages, No Color
Subscriptions: Indv. $15, $1/copy
Circulation: (100% controlled), Total-750

New York State Queries

Publishing Co: Weidner Words, 2206 W Borden Rd, Spokane, WA 99204-9668; Title Tel # (509) 448-9263
Personnel: Publisher, Editor-Carolyn Weidner
Editorial Description: New York State queries:25 pages of queries & book reviews plus index of names & localities
General Info: Yr. Est. 1987, Irregular, Trim Size-8½ x 11, Desktop press, 35 pages, ISSN: 1041-6560, No Color, Matte
Subscriptions: Can. $8, For. $10, $8/copy
Advertising: Accepts Inserts.

New York State Queries Master Index

Publishing Co: Weidner Words, 2206 W Borden Rd, Spokane, WA 99204-9668 Tel # (509) 448-9263; Title Tel # (509) 448-9283
Personnel: Publisher, Editor-Carolyn Weidner
Editorial Description: New York State Queries Master Index V. 1-11. Index by names and localities.
General Info: Yr. Est. 1994, Irregular, Trim Size-8½ x 11, Desktop press, 50 pages, No Color, Matte
Subscriptions: Can. $23, For. $25, $20/copy

Newman News

Publishing Co: Newman Family Society c/o Shirley Ann Sheets, 1675 S Steele St, Denver, CO 80210-2939; Title Tel # (303) 733-4935
Personnel: Publisher-R.N. Sheets, Editor-Shirley Ann Sheets
Editorial Description: Contains information on ancestors, descendants, lineal, collateral, of Robert Newman of 1775 Boston lantern fame.
General Info: Yr. Est. 1975, Annually, Trim Size-8½ x 11, Mimeo press, 4 pages, No Color, Newsprint
Subscriptions: Indv. $10
Circulation: Total-130

News from the Congregational Christian Historical Society
See: RELIGIOUS & THEOLOGICAL

Newsletter of the German Genealogical Society of America   *Consumer, Association*

Publishing Co: German Genealogical Society of America, PO Box 291818, Los Angeles, CA 90029-8818; Title Tel # (909) 593-0509
Personnel: Editor-T.M. Schoenky
General Info: 10x/yr., Trim Size-8½ x 11, Sheetfed press, 12 pages, No Color
Subscriptions: Indv. $18, For. $28, $2/copy
Circulation: Total-3,000

Newsletter of the Knarr-Knerr-Knorr Family

Publishing Co: Larry Knarr, 7657 Squirrel Creek Ln, Cincinnati, OH 45247-3614; Title Tel # (513) 385-3422
Personnel: Editor-Larry Knarr
General Info: Bi-monthly, Trim Size-8½ x 11, Mimeo press, 10 pages, No Color, Newsprint
Subscriptions: Indv. $5, $1/copy

Newsletter of the North Suburban Genealogical Society   *Association*

Publishing Co: North Suburban Genealogical Society, C/o Winnetka Public Library, 768 Oak St., Winnetka, IL 60093; Title Tel # (708) 446-7220
Personnel: Editor-Allison Childs, Circ. Mgr.-Bonita Barcus, Circ. Mgr.-Hosmer Morse
Editorial Description: Genealogical news, research and bible records, members' descents; library services.
General Info: Yr. Est. 1975, Bi-monthly, Trim Size-8½ x 11, Offset press, 10 pages, ISSN: 0743-1341, Ind/Abs/Online: PGAI, PERSI, Color
Subscriptions: Indv. $10
Circulation: (100% controlled), Total-200

Newsletter of the Society Farsarotul
See: ETHNIC

Newsletter of South Suburban Genealogical and Historical Society   *Association*

Publishing Co: South Suburban Genealogical & Historical Society, PO Box 96, S. Holland, IL 60473-0096; Title Tel # (708) 333-9474
Personnel: Editor-Janice Helge
Editorial Description: News of data bases, information networks & services, research & legislation affecting the genealogical community.
General Info: (Formerly Southsubkin), Yr. Est. 1972, Monthly, Trim Size-8½ x 11, 4 pages, ISSN: 0896-4408, No Color, Newsprint
Subscriptions: Indv. $15
Circulation: (100% controlled), Total-460

Nicola Valley Archives-Quarterly   *Association*

Publishing Co: Nicola Valley Museum Archives Assn., 2202 Jackson Ave., Box 1262, Merritt, BC V0K 2B0 Canada; Title Tel # (604) 378-4145
Personnel: Editor-Pat Lean
Editorial Description: To record and disseminate the history of the Nicola Valley, British Colombia.
General Info: (Formerly Nicola Valley Archives Association Newsletter), Yr. Est. 1977, Quarterly, Trim Size-8½ x 11, Sheetfed press, 10 pages, ISSN: 0708-8132, No Color
Subscriptions: Indv. $15, Inst. $25, $3/copy
Circulation: Total-500

North/South Carolina Queries

Publishing Co: Pioneer Publications, PO Box 1179, Tum Tum, WA 99034-1179; Title Tel # (509) 276-9841
Personnel: Publisher, Editor-Shirley Oakes
Editorial Description: Queries pertaining to ancestors in North Carolina & South Carolina or those who passed through.
General Info: Yr. Est. 1986, Irregular, Trim Size-8½ x 11, Mimeo press, 25 pages, ISSN: 0897-7755
Subscriptions: $6/copy
Acquistions: Publication Bought

Norwegian-American Historical Association Newsletter
See: ETHNIC

Norwegian Tracks   *Association*

Publishing Co: Norwegian Tracks, 4909 Sherwood Rd, Madison, WI 53711-1343;
Title Tel # (608) 271-8826
Personnel: Publisher, Editor-Gerhard Naeseth
Editorial Description: Information for Norwegian genealogists.
General Info: Yr. Est. 1975, Quarterly, Trim Size-8½ x 11, Offset press, 4 pages
Subscriptions: Indv. $16
Circulation: Total-1,400

Notes
See: GOVERNMENT

Nuggets from Paradise   *Consumer, Association*

Publishing Co: Paradise Genealogical Society, PO Box 460, Paradise, CA 95967-0460
Tel # (916) 877-2330
Personnel: Editor-Bill Arnold
Editorial Description: Promotion of genealogy as a hobby and support of membership with current useful guides and references.
General Info: Yr. Est. 1981, Monthly, Trim Size-8½ x 11, Sheetfed press, 6 pages, ISSN: 1055-8632, No Color, Other, Other
Subscriptions: Free With Membership
Circulation: (100% controlled), Total-280

Nyando Roots   *Association*

Publishing Co: Nyando Roots Genealogical Club, PO Box 175, Massena, NY 13662-0175
Editorial Description: Information of St. Lawrence & Franklin Counties, Northern New York.
General Info: Yr. Est. 1983, Quarterly, Mimeo press, 20 pages, No Color
Subscriptions: Indv. $10
Acquistions: Publication Sold
Circulation: Total-800

OHS Bulletin
See: HISTORY

Oakes Acorn

Publishing Co: Pioneer Publications, PO Box 1179, Tum Tum, WA 99034-1179;
Title Tel # (509) 276-9841
Personnel: Publisher, Editor-Shirley Oakes
Editorial Description: Genealogical information on all spellings of Oakes. Lineages, Oakes information and queries.
General Info: Yr. Est. 1985, Irregular, Trim Size-8½ x 11, Mimeo press, 25 pages, ISSN: 0897-7771
Subscriptions: $6/copy
Acquistions: Publication Bought, Publication Sold

Ogden Newsletter   *Consumer*

Publishing Co: Ogden Newsletter, 1801 Ardath Ave, Wichita Falls, TX 76301-6001;
Title Tel # (817) 767-6658
Personnel: Editor-H. Ogden, Jr.
Editorial Description: Publishes information on all branches of Ogden family. Small space given to Ogan, Ogburn, Oden, & Osborn (& many spelling variations for these names). No longer published on a regular basis but back issues are available only if it will help with individual problems.
General Info: Yr. Est. 1979, Irregular, Letrpr. press, 15 pages, ISSN: 0891-2602, No Color

Ogle County Links Newsletter

Publishing Co: Ogle County Illinois Genealogical Soc., PO Box 251, Oregon, IL 61061-0251

Ohio Archivist
See: HISTORY

Ohio Indiana Iowa Queries and Reviews

Publishing Co: Pioneer Publications, PO Box 1179, Tum Tum, WA 99034-1179;
Title Tel # (509) 276-9841
Personnel: Editor-Shirley Oakes
Editorial Description: Queries pertaining to ancestors in Ohio or those who passed through.
General Info: (Formerly Ohio Queries), Yr. Est. 1986, Irregular, Trim Size-8½ x 11, Mimeo press, 25 pages, ISSN: 0897-7747
Subscriptions: $6/copy
Acquistions: Publication Bought

Ohio's Last Frontier   *Association*

Publishing Co: Williams County Genealogical Society, PO Box 293, Bryan, OH 43506-0293;
Title Tel # (419) 636-3295
Personnel: Editor-Marlene Smith
General Info: Yr. Est. 1981, 11x/yr., Trim Size-8½ x 11, Sheetfed press, 10 pages, No Color, Other
Subscriptions: Free With Membership

Old Fort Log   *Consumer, Association*

Publishing Co: Old Fort Genealogical Society of SE Kansas, 502 S National Ave, Fort Scott, KS 66701-1327 Tel # (316) 223-3300
Personnel: Editor-Margie Williams, Circ. Mgr.-Sara Eshelbrenner
Editorial Description: Cemetery transcriptions, marriages, obituaries, family history, early schools, local history.
General Info: Yr. Est. 1974, Tri-annually, Trim Size-8½ x 11, Offset press, 25 pages, No Color, Looseleaf
Subscriptions: Indv. $14, $2/copy
Circulation: Total-200

Old Fort News

Publishing Co: Allen County, Ft. Wayne Historical Soc., 302 E Berry St, Fort Wayne, IN 46802-2708;
Title Tel # (219) 426-2882 Title Fax # (219) 424-4419
Personnel: Editor-Michael Hawfield
Editorial Description: Magazine of history devoted to the preservation and dissemination of the heritage of Fort Wayne and northeastern Indiana.
General Info: Yr. Est. 1952, Semi-annually
Subscriptions: Indv. $20, Inst. $30, $2/copy

Old Oregon Country News   *Consumer*

Publishing Co: Frontier Genealogy Resources, PO Box 22026, Milwaukie, OR 97269-2026;
Title Tel # (503) 786-0166
Personnel: Editor-Mary Howard
Editorial Description: Genealogical news and queries for Oregon.
General Info: Yr. Est. 1993, Monthly, Trim Size-8½ x 11, 16 pages
Subscriptions: Indv. $18
Advertising: Inquire for rates.

Olde Mecklenburg Genealogical Society Quarterly   *Association*

Publishing Co: OMGS, PO Box 32453, Charlotte, NC 28232-2453; Title Tel # (704) 376-6817
Personnel: Publisher, Editor-Ronald Touchstone, Circ. Mgr.-T. Melvin Cook
General Info: Yr. Est. 1982, Quarterly
Subscriptions: Indv. $15, Inst. $15, Free With Membership

Ontario Genealogy Society Newsleaf   *Association*

Publishing Co: Ontario Genealogical Society, 40 Orchard View Blvd., #251, Toronto, ON M4R 1B9 Canada; Title Tel # (416) 489-0734 Title Fax # (416) 489-9803
Editorial Description: Family history research news and sources of aid to genealogists.
General Info: (Formerly Newsleaf), Yr. Est. 1971, Quarterly, Trim Size-6 x 9, Offset press, 12 pages, ISSN: 0380-1616, No Color
Subscriptions: Free With Membership
Circulation: Total-7,000

Orange Peelings

Publishing Co: Orange County Genealogical Society, PO Box 344, Paoli, IN 47454-0344

Orangeburgh German-Swiss Newsletter

Publishing Co: Orangeburgh German Swiss Genealogical Society, PO Box 974, Orangeburg, SC 29116-0974; Title Tel # (803) 723-2235
Personnel: Editor-Beverly Shuler, Promotion Dir.-Alfred Gramling
Editorial Description: Research reports & queries on families of Orangeburgh, 1735-1800.
General Info: Yr. Est. 1981, Quarterly, Sheetfed press, Looseleaf
Subscriptions: Indv. $15
Circulation: Total-400

Origins   *Association, Consumer*

Publishing Co: Family Ties Genealogy, 3950 60th St Apt 22a, Woodside, NY 11377-3418;
Title Tel # (718) 898-7048
Personnel: Publisher-Jeff Salak, Editor-Jean Trinite
Editorial Description: Accounts and information about genealogical research methods and tools.
General Info: Yr. Est. 1994, Quarterly, Trim Size-8½ x 11, 20 pages, 2 Color

Orrell Family Genealogical Assn. Newsletter

Publishing Co: Orrell Family Genealogical Assn., PO Box 4828, South Daytona, FL 32121-4828;
Title Tel # (904) 788-7083
Personnel: Editor-Robert S. Orrell

Ottawa Branch News   *Association*

Publishing Co: Ontario Genealogical Society, Ottawa Branch, Box 8346, Ottawa, ON K1G 3H8 Canada; Title Tel # (613) 745-0200
Personnel: Editor-Brian O'Regan
Editorial Description: To provide genealogical information to help satisfy the family history needs of all interested persons who have Ottawa & Ottawa Valley ancestors.
General Info: Yr. Est. 1970, Bi-monthly, Trim Size-6 x 9, Mimeo press, 20 pages, ISSN: 0708-5583, 2 Color, Matte
Subscriptions: Indv. $12, $2/copy
Circulation: (15% controlled), Total-1,100, Subscriptions-900
Advertising: Accepts Inserts.
Printing Co: Moonlighy Printing, 1203 Wellington St., Ottawa, ON KIY 2Z8 Canada
Tel # (613) 722-1062, Fax # (613) 722-0873

Our Foster Forefathers   *Consumer, Association*

Publishing Co: Lusa R. Franklin, 4604 Virginia Loop Rd., Apt. 3156-G, Montgomery, AL 36116-4739
Editorial Description: For persons researching ancestors bearing thje Foster surname.
General Info: Yr. Est. 1994, Quarterly, Trim Size-8½ x 11, 25 pages
Subscriptions: Indv. $10, Inst. $10, $3/copy
Advertising: $9. Accepts Inserts.

Owen County History & Genealogy
Consumer, Association

Publishing Co: Owen County Historical & Genealogical Society, 110 E Market St, Spencer, IN 47460-1867
Personnel: Editor-Roger Peterson
Editorial Description: For and by the Owen County Historical and Genealogical Society.
General Info: Yr. Est. 1989, Quarterly, ISSN: 1063-7400
Subscriptions: Indv. $10, Free With Membership

Oxford Tracer
Association

Publishing Co: Ontario Genealogical Society, Oxford County Branch, Box 1092, Woodstock, ON N4S 8P6 Canada
Personnel: Publisher, Editor-Mary Evans
Editorial Description: Informs readers of resources, helpful holdings, queries for members & articles of special interest of Oxford County, Ontario.
General Info: Yr. Est. 1979, Monthly, Mimeo press, 5 pages, No Color
Subscriptions: Can. $8
Circulation: Total-400

Ozar'Kin

Publishing Co: Ozark Genealogical Society, P.O. Box 3945, Springfield, MO 65808-3945
General Info: Yr. Est. 1979, Quarterly, Trim Size-8½ x 11, Offset press, 50 pages
Subscriptions: Indv. $15, Can. $20
Circulation: Total-1,000

Page Pedigree

Publishing Co: Pioneer Publications, PO Box 1179, Tum Tum, WA 99034-1179; Title Tel # (509) 276-9841
Personnel: Publisher, Editor-Shirley Oakes
Editorial Description: Genealogical data on the surname page. Lineages & Queries accepted free.
General Info: Yr. Est. 1985, Irregular, Trim Size-8½ x 11, Mimeo press, 25 pages, ISSN: 0897-7763
Subscriptions: $6/copy
Acquisitions: Publication Bought, Publication Sold

Palatine Patter
Association

Publishing Co: Sponsor-Palatines to America, Palatines to America, Capital Univ., Box 101, Columbus, OH 43209-2394; Title Tel # (614) 236-8281
Personnel: Editor-P. Torrance
Editorial Description: A newsletter containing information on national and regional activities of the society as well as other groups of interest. Free queries published for members.
General Info: Yr. Est. 1975, Quarterly, Trim Size-8½ x 11, Web press, 12 pages, ISSN: 8755-6014
Subscriptions: Indv. $20, Can. $30, For. $40, Free With Membership
Circulation: Total-2,500
Printing Co: C.P.M.M. Services Group, 3785 Indianola Ava, Columbus, OH 43214 Tel # (614) 447-0165

Parke Society Newsletter
Association

Publishing Co: Parke Society, Inc., P O Box 590, Milwaukee, WI 53201 Tel # (414) 332-9984
Personnel: Editor-David Parke
General Info: Yr. Est. 1963, Tri-annually, ISSN: 0148-3994
Subscriptions: Free To Qualified Recipient
Circulation: (27% controlled), Total-930, Subscriptions-645, International-25

Pass Genealogical Reporter

Publishing Co: San Gorgonio Pass Gen. Soc., PO Box 3261, Beaumont, CA 92223-1204
Personnel: Editor-Lila Hubbard
General Info: Yr. Est. 1986, Quarterly

Pate Pioneers

Publishing Co: Clovis Herring, Rr 1 Box 123a, Buffalo, TX 75831-9717; Title Tel # (214) 322-5462
Personnel: Editor-Clovis Herring
General Info: Yr. Est. 1986, ISSN: 0887-1280

Patton Exchange Letter

Publishing Co: Barbara Nivison-Patton, 1912 Powder Horn Rd, Toms River, NJ 08755-1709
Personnel: Editor-Barbara Patton Nivison
Editorial Description: Genealogical information for those researching the surname Patton & various spellings of the name. Queries are free to members.
General Info: Yr. Est. 1976, Quarterly, 12 pages, Color-cover
Subscriptions: Indv. $15, $4/copy
Acquisitions: Publication Bought
Advertising: Accepts Inserts.
Printing Co: Cottrell Printing, 2121 Rt. #9, Toms River, NJ 08755 Tel # (908) 349-7430

Pennsylvania Traveler-Post

Publishing Co: Pennsylvania Traveler-Post, PO Box 776, Newtown, PA 18940-0776
Personnel: Publisher, Editor-Richard Williams
General Info: Yr. Est. 1964, Quarterly
Subscriptions: Indv. $8

Perkins Family Newsletter
Consumer, Association

Publishing Co: COMPU-CHART, 363 S. Park Victoria Dr., Milpitas, CA 95035-5708; Title Tel # (408) 262-1051
Personnel: Editor-Paula Perkins Mortensen
General Info: Yr. Est. 1986, Quarterly, Trim Size-8½ x 11, Mimeo press, 12 pages, ISSN: 0895-4488, No Color
Subscriptions: Indv. $10, For. $15

Phipps Quarterly

Publishing Co: Phipps Quarterly, Mrs. Gaye Phipps Pencin, 1316 Harley Dr, Woodland, CA 95695-4430; Title Tel # (916) 662-7486
General Info: Yr. Est. 1977, Annually
Subscriptions: Indv. $10

Piatt County Historical Society
Association

Publishing Co: Piatt County Historical Society, Box 111, Monticello, IL 61856-0111
Personnel: Editor-Carlene Snell
Editorial Description: Piatt County, IL historical and genealogical articles.
General Info: Yr. Est. 1979, Quarterly, Trim Size-8½ x 11, Offset press, 15 pages, No Color
Subscriptions: Indv. $8, $2/copy
Circulation: Total-250

Pile (Pyle) Family
Association

Publishing Co: Genz Assoc. of America, 5821 Rowland Hill Rd., Cascade, MD 21719-1939 Tel # (301) 416-2660
Personnel: Editor-Victor Gebhart
General Info: Annually, Mimeo press, No Color
Subscriptions: Indv. $2

Pilger News

Publishing Co: Marsha Lockerby-Pilger, 807 Madison Ave, Council Bluffs, IA 51503-6735
Editorial Description: Historical data pertaining to the Pilger Families in America & Europe & their migration patterns & contributions to their communities. Includes associated female branches.

Pioneer, The
Business, Consumer

Publishing Co: Douglas County Genealogical Soc., PO Box 3664, Lawrence, KS 66046-0664
General Info: (Formerly Douglas County Genealogical Society Newsletter), Quarterly
Subscriptions: Indv. $15

Pioneer Branches

Publishing Co: Northeast Washington Genealogical Society, S. 195 Oak, C/O Colville Public Library, Colville, WA 99114; Title Tel # (509) 684-4092
Personnel: Publisher-Susan Dechant, Editor-Wallace Baucom
Editorial Description: Stevens & Ferry counties genealogical information.
General Info: Yr. Est. 1985, Quarterly, Trim Size-8½ x 11, Sheetfed press, 30 pages, No Color
Subscriptions: Indv. $13, $3/copy

Pioneer Echoes
Consumer, Association

Publishing Co: Noble County Historical Society, PO Box 152, Albion, IN 46701-0152
General Info: Irregular
Subscriptions: $5/copy

Pioneers- A Computer Genealogy Newslettter
Consumer

Publishing Co: Marthe Arends, PO Box 1571, Snohomish, WA 98291-1571; Title Tel # (206) 776-7978 Title Fax # (206) 775-7983
Personnel: Publisher, Editor-Marthe Arends
Editorial Description: A newsletter for genealogists who use computers.
General Info: (Formerly Pioneers), Yr. Est. 1994, Bi-monthly, Desktop press, 6 pages, ISSN: 1079-4425, Other, Other
Subscriptions: Indv. $14, Inst. $14, Can. $16, For. $16, $2/copy

Pipings, The
Association

Publishing Co: Clan Gillean U.S.A., PO Box 4061, Alvin, TX 77512-4061
Personnel: Publisher, Editor-David McLane
Editorial Description: A family-oriented newsletter issued for members of Scottish Highland clan.
General Info: (Formerly Pipings of MacLeans), Yr. Est. 1961, Quarterly, Trim Size-8½ x 11, Offset press, 13 pages, Saddle-stitched
Subscriptions: Indv. $15
Circulation: Total-350
Advertising: Inquire for rates.

Pocahontas Trails Quarterly

Publishing Co: Pocahontas Trails Genealogical Soc., 6015 Robin Hill Dr, Lakeport, CA 95453-6007
General Info: Quarterly

Polish Genealogical Society Bulletin
Association

Publishing Co: Polish Genealogical Society, 984 N Milwaukee Ave, Chicago, IL 60622-4101; Title Tel # (312) 586-4242
Personnel: Editor-Edward Peckwas
Editorial Description: Printed in English, deals with doing research on the old Kingdom of Poland, & Polish genealogical research in general.
General Info: Yr. Est. 1979, Semi-annually, Trim Size-8½ x 11, Web press, 20 pages, ISSN: 0735-9349, No Color, Newsprint
Subscriptions: Indv. $15, Inst. $8, $8/copy
Circulation: Total-1,200
Advertising: Inquire for rates.

Portage Path to Genealogy
Portage Co. Chapter

Publishing Co: Ohio Genealogical Soc., 6252 Spring St, Ravenna, OH 44266-1338

Porter Settlements   *Consumer*

Publishing Co: Nancy L. Childress Svces., 3709 W Gardenia Ave., Phoenix, AZ 85051-8266;
   Title Tel # (602) 841-7478
Personnel: Publisher-Nancy L. Childress
Editorial Description: Genealogy of the Porter surname and variations.
General Info: Quarterly, Trim Size-8½ x 11, 32 pages
Subscriptions: Indv. $12, Can. $15, For. $15
Acquistions: Publication Bought

Potthast Newsletter   *Association*

Publishing Co: Genz Assoc. of America, 5821 Rowland Hill Rd., Cascade, MD 21719-1939;
   Title Tel # (301) 416-2660
Personnel: Editor-Victor Gebhart
General Info: Yr. Est. 1990, Annually, Mimeo press, No Color
Subscriptions: $2/copy

Poweshiek County
Historical & Genealogical
Society   *Association*

Publishing Co: Poweshiek County Historical & Genealogical Soc., 206 N. Mill St., Montezuma, IA
   50171; Title Tel # (515) 623-3322
Personnel: Editor-Leta Hollmann, Editor-Ferne Norris
Editorial Description: Genealogy, Poweshiek County, Iowa Meetings also noted.
General Info: Yr. Est. 1978, Quarterly, Trim Size-8½ x 11, Mimeo press, 14 pages, No Color
Subscriptions: Indv. $5, $1/copy
Circulation: Total-175

Prather Bulletin   *Consumer*

Publishing Co: Ellsbury Records, PO Box 206, Chillicothe, MO 64601-0206;
   Title Tel # (816) 646-4409
Personnel: Editor-Elizabeth Ellsberry
General Info: Yr. Est. 1973, Bi-monthly
Subscriptions: Indv. $5

Preston Scoop, The

Publishing Co: Charleston Chapter SCGS, PO Box 20266, Charleston, SC 29413-0266;
   Title Tel # (803) 766-1667
General Info: Bi-monthly, Looseleaf
Subscriptions: Indv. $10
Advertising: $6. Accepts Inserts.

Prince George's County
Genealogical Society
Bulletin   *Association*

Publishing Co: Prince George's County Genealogical Society, PO Box 819, Bowie, MD 20718-0819;
   Title Tel # (301) 490-8441
Personnel: Co-Editor-Robert Clark, Co-Editor-Roberta Pohl
Editorial Description: Family histories & genealogical source material, primarily dealing with Prince
   George's county, MD.
General Info: Yr. Est. 1969, 10x/yr., Trim Size-7 x 8½, Sheetfed press, 20 pages, ISSN: 1052-1380,
   Ind/Abs/Online: General Per.In., No Color, Saddle-stitched
Subscriptions: Indv. $12, $2/copy

Professional Business
Services

Publishing Co: PBS-Professional Business Svces., 450 Potter St, Wauseon, OH 43567-1138;
   Title Tel # (419) 335-6485
List Rental: Rents Lists

Putnam County Heritage
See: HISTORY

Quaker Yeomen   *Consumer*

Publishing Co: Yeomen Genealogy Services, 2330 SE Brookwood Ave Apt 108, Hillsboro, OR
   97123-8168; Title Tel # (503) 640-2217
Personnel: Publisher, Editor-James Bellarts
Editorial Description: Quaker genealogy and history.
General Info: Yr. Est. 1974, Quarterly, Trim Size-8½ x 11, Sheetfed press, 10 pages, ISSN: 0737-
   8246, No Color
Subscriptions: Indv. $17, For. $22, $5/copy
Circulation: (100% controlled), Total-400

Quarterly   *Association*

Publishing Co: Barton County Genealogical Society, PO Box 425, Great Bend, KS 67530-0425;
   Title Tel # (316) 793-7304
Personnel: Editor-Karen Neuforth
Editorial Description: Genealogical, biographical, & historical coverage of Barton County, KS &
   vicinity.
General Info: (Formerly Barton Gen. Soc. Newsletter), Yr. Est. 1980, Quarterly, Trim Size-8½ x 11,
   Mimeo press, 15 pages, 2 Color
Subscriptions: Indv. $13
Acquistions: Publication Bought

Questing Heirs
Genealogical Society   *Consumer, Association*

Publishing Co: Questing Heirs Genealogical Soc., PO Box 15102, Long Beach, CA 90815-0102
General Info: Monthly

Rampant Lion
See: ETHNIC

Ranck Reporter

Publishing Co: Ranck/Rank Clan, 300 Valleybrook Dr, Lancaster, PA 17601-4633
Personnel: Publisher-Harriet Ranck

Ray Newsletter

Publishing Co: Ray's Surname Index File, Box 482, McCook, NE 69001-0482;
   Title Tel # (308) 345-1443
Personnel: Publisher, Editor-Robert Ray
Editorial Description: Material dealing with the Ray surname with various spellings.
General Info: Yr. Est. 1983, Quarterly, Trim Size-8½ x 11, Mimeo press, 12 pages
Subscriptions: Indv. $10, $3/copy
Advertising: Inquire for rates.

Regional Archivist
See: HISTORY

Reid Family Newsletter &
Data

Publishing Co: Reid Family Newsletter & Data, PO Box 488, Due West, SC 29639-0488
Personnel: Publisher-Elizabeth Austin

Research News   *Business*

Publishing Co: Family History World, PO Box 22045, Salt Lake City, UT 84122-0045;
   Title Tel # (801) 250-6717
Personnel: Publisher, Editor-Arlene Eakle, Circ. Mgr.-JoAnn Jackson
Editorial Description: Research tips, reviews, how-to suggestions, new source publication.
General Info: Yr. Est. 1982, Irregular, Trim Size-8½ x 11, Desktop press, 4 pages, Ind/Abs/Online:
   GAPI, No Color
Subscriptions: $4/copy
Acquistions: Publication Bought
Circulation: Total-10,000
Advertising: Inquire for rates.

Researcher

Publishing Co: Researcher, PO Box 206, Chillicothe, MO 64601-0206
Personnel: Publisher-Elizabeth Ellsberry

Researchin' Ouachita-
Calhoun Counties AR

Publishing Co: O-C Genealogical Society, PO Box 2092, Camden, AR 71701-2092
General Info: ISSN: 8756-9817
Subscriptions: Indv. $10, $6/copy

Rhodes Crossroads
Newsletter   *Consumer*

Publishing Co: Craig Rhodes, 133 Montclair Loop, Daphne, AL 36526-8151;
   Title Tel # (205) 626-6573
Personnel: Editor-Debbie Owen
Editorial Description: Bible, census, cemetary records and genealogical articles about the rhodes
   (all spellings) surname and famillies in USA and other countries.
General Info: Yr. Est. 1994, Quarterly, Trim Size-8½ x 11, Mimeo press, 15 pages
Subscriptions: Indv. $12, $3/copy
Circulation: Total-200

Richardson Family
Researcher and
Historical News   *Consumer*

Publishing Co: Richardson Heritage Society, 944 S G St # 123, Broken Bow, NE 68822-2444;
   Title Tel # (308) 872-2167
Personnel: Editor-Harry Richardson
Editorial Description: For researchers of the Richardson and Moore family lines.
General Info: Quarterly, 16 pages, ISSN: 0147-2488
Subscriptions: Indv. $10, $3/copy
Circulation: Total-1,000
Advertising: Inquire for rates.

Ritchie County Historical
Society Newsletter   *Association*

Publishing Co: Ritchie Co. Historical Society, 200 S Church St, Harrisville, WV 26362-1246
Editorial Description: contains queries; society activities, projects and meeting minutes; articles of
   historical interest copied from old newspapers or publications or written by the editor.
General Info: Yr. Est. 1973, Quarterly, Trim Size-8½ x 11, 15 pages
Subscriptions: Indv. $3
Circulation: Total-175

Roadrunner

Publishing Co: Chaparral Genealogical Soc., PO Box 606, Tomball, TX 77377-0606; Title Tel # (713) 255-9081
Personnel: Editor-Janice Duhe

Roaming Roots: A Kent Family History   *Consumer*

Publishing Co: Roaming Roots, 75 Pitt Ave., Scarborough, ON M1L 2R5 Canada; Title Tel # (416) 288-1602
Personnel: Publisher-Michael S. Young
Editorial Description: Articles and photographs of the Young Family of Kent, England and branches. Main branches include Pilcher, Hawkins, Hayward, Silk, Goldup, Luckhurst, and Raines. Includes biographies, family group sheets, pedigree charts and census information. Material ranges form the 1600's to the present.
General Info: Yr. Est. 1990, Quarterly, Trim Size-8½ x 11, Desktop press, 10 pages, ISSN: 1180-5714
Subscriptions: Indv. $10, $2/copy

Robb Relatives   *Association*

Publishing Co: Barbara Robb Kabel, 421 Kemmerer Rd, State College, PA 16801-6408; Title Tel # (814) 237-6447
Personnel: Editor-Barbara Robb Kabel
Editorial Description: Information & history on the family of William Robbe of Peterborough, New Hampshire 1692-1769 also queries from any Rob, Robb, Rabb, Robbe.
General Info: Yr. Est. 1985, Semi-annually, Trim Size-8½ x 11, Desktop press, 7 pages, No Color, Other, Other
Subscriptions: Indv. $5
Advertising: $20.

Robbins Cousins

Publishing Co: Ashby Newsletter, 1013 Illinois St, Bicknell, IN 47512-3000; Title Tel # (812) 735-2530
Personnel: Publisher, Editor-Carol Hulen
Editorial Description: Clearinghouse for all Robbins family records, everywhere. Queries & ads free to subscribers.
General Info: Yr. Est. 1985, Quarterly, Mimeo press
Subscriptions: Indv. $10, $3/copy

Robert McKay Clan Newsletter   *Association*

Publishing Co: Robert McKay Clan Newsletter, 5319 Manning Pl NW, Washington, DC 20016-5311; Title Tel # (202) 363-3663
Personnel: Editor-Dorothy Shipp, Editor-Wallace Shipp
Editorial Description: News of family members, deaths, marriages, donations, changes of address, reunions. Historical articles, genealogy & resources.
General Info: Yr. Est. 1965, Annually, Trim Size-8½ x 11, Offset press, 24 pages, 2 Color, Newsprint, Saddle-stitched
Subscriptions: Indv. $10, Free To Qualified Recipient
Acquistions: Publication Bought, Publication Sold
Circulation: Total-221
Printing Co: Stickley Printing Co., 2293 Lewis Ave, Rockville, MD 20851-2333 Tel # (301) 881-4121

Root Digger Newsletter   *Association*

Publishing Co: Solano County Genealogical Society, Inc., PO Box 2494, Fairfield, CA 94533-0249; Title Tel # (707) 446-6869
Personnel: Editor-Jennie Wright
Editorial Description: Current events of Solano County Genealogical Society. Historical records of Solano county , such as church indexes, newspapers , vital records, etc.
General Info: Yr. Est. 1981, Monthly, Trim Size-8½ x 11, 20 pages, No Color
Subscriptions: Indv. $13
Circulation: Total-260

Roots & Leaves   *Consumer, Association*

Publishing Co: Eastern Nebraska Genealogical Society, 8686 N 204th St, Elkhorn, NE 68022-3900
General Info: Yr. Est. 1973, Quarterly
Subscriptions: Indv. $7
Circulation: Total-300
Advertising: Inquire for rates.

Rose Family Newsletter   *Association*

Publishing Co: Rose Family Assn., 1474 Montelegre Dr., San Jose, CA 95120-4831; Title Tel # (408) 268-2137 Title Fax # (408) 268-2165
General Info: Quarterly, 10 pages
Circulation: Total-700

Royce Quarterly   *Association*

Publishing Co: Royce Family Assn., 4033 Somerdale Ln, Charlotte, NC 28205-4639; Title Tel # (704) 563-2216
Personnel: Publisher, Editor-E. Allen Royce, III
Editorial Description: Dealing with Royce, Rice & Roys families and descendants.
General Info: Yr. Est. 1979, Quarterly, Trim Size-8½ x 11, Offset press
Subscriptions: Indv. $5
Circulation: Total-200
Advertising: Inquire for rates.

Rucker Ruckus   *Association*

Publishing Co: Mary Rucker Snyder, 1516 Elliott Ave, Jeffersonville, IN 47130-4502
Personnel: Editor-Mary Rucker Snyder
Editorial Description: Information on descendants of Peter Rucker, Essex Co., VA.
General Info: Yr. Est. 1983, Quarterly, 10 pages
Subscriptions: Indv. $15, Inst. $10, $4/copy

Rushing Past

Publishing Co: Jack Rushing, PO Box 15, Liberty Corner, NJ 07938-0015
Editorial Description: International family newsletter.
General Info: Yr. Est. 1979, Quarterly, 12 pages
Subscriptions: Indv. $5, $3/copy
Circulation: Total-500

Russell Register

Publishing Co: Frances Nelson, 4041 Pedley Rd Spc 18, Riverside, CA 92509-2822; Title Tel # (714) 685-8936

St. Louis Genealogical Society, News and Notes   *Association*

Publishing Co: St. Louis Genealogical Society, 9011 Manchester Rd Ste 3, St. Louis, MO 63144-2643; Title Tel # (314) 968-2763
Personnel: Editor-Ann Fleming
Editorial Description: Dated genealogical information - society meetings, family reunions, addresses, classes.
General Info: Yr. Est. 1967, Monthly, Trim Size-8½ x 11, Letrpr. press, 4 pages, ISSN: 1065-5255, No Color
Subscriptions: Free With Membership
Circulation: Total-2,300

San Angelo Genealogical & Historical Society Newsletter

Publishing Co: San Angelo Genealogical & Historical Soc., PO Box 3453, San Angelo, TX 76902-3453

San Diego Historical Society Times
See: HISTORY

Sauermann Newsletter   *Association*

Publishing Co: Genz Assoc. of America, 5821 Rowland Hill Rd., Cascade, MD 21719-1939; Title Tel # (301) 416-2660
Personnel: Editor-Victor Gebhart
General Info: Annually, Mimeo press, No Color
Subscriptions: $2/copy

Schale (Westfalen) Newsletter   *Association*

Publishing Co: David Koss, 114 Dundee Ave., Barrington, IL 60010-4202
Personnel: Editor-David Koss
Editorial Description: Genealogy of descendants of families from Schale, Westfalen, Germany.
General Info: Yr. Est. 1984, Quarterly, Trim Size-8½ x 11, Offset press, 8 pages
Subscriptions: Indv. $5

Schneider Connections   *Consumer*

Publishing Co: BGM Pubs., 28635 W Old Hideway Rd, Cary, IL 60013-9794; Title Tel # (708) 639-2400
Personnel: Publisher, Editor-Betty Massman
Editorial Description: Genealogical records & information on the Schneider & variations on the surname.
General Info: Yr. Est. 1984, Quarterly, Trim Size-8½ x 11, Mimeo press, 25 pages, ISSN: 0882-5904, No Color
Subscriptions: Indv. $18, $6/copy
Circulation: Total-1,000

Schutt Newsletter   *Association*

Publishing Co: Genz Assoc. of America, 5821 Rowland Hill Rd., Cascade, MD 21719-1939; Title Tel # (301) 416-2660
Personnel: Editor-Victor Gebhart
General Info: Annually, Mimeo press, No Color
Subscriptions: $2/copy

Scottish Heritage U.S.A. Newsletter

Publishing Co: Scottish Heritage USA, Inc., PO Box 457, Pinehurst, NC 28374-0457; Title Tel # (919) 295-4448
Personnel: Editor-Jacqueline Stewart
General Info: Yr. Est. 1968, Quarterly
Circulation: Total-3,000

Searchlight *Consumer*

Publishing Co: Searchlight, Route #8, Carmel, NY 10512-9808
Personnel: Publisher, Editor-Betty M. Light-Behr
Editorial Description: Carries archival, genealogical, biographical & historical data on Light (& variants) families.
General Info: Yr. Est. 1979, Quarterly, Offset press, 10 pages, ISSN: 1059-9843, No Color
Subscriptions: Indv. $8, For. $9, $2/copy
Circulation: Total-300
Printing Co: Peppertree Press, Seymour Hall,pres., Rt. #376, Hopewell Junct., NY 12533 Tel # (914) 226-6755, Fax # (914) 227-6723

Seneca Searchers *Association*

Publishing Co: Seneca County Genealogical Society, PO Box 157, Tiffin, OH 44883-0157; Title Tel # (419) 457-8082
Personnel: Editor-Don Rogier, Editor, Co-Editor-Joan Dysinger
General Info: Yr. Est. 1981, Bi-monthly, Trim Size-8½ x 11, Offset press, 16 pages, ISSN: 1046-5545, Ind/Abs/Online: PERSI
Subscriptions: Indv. $10, For. $12, Free To Qualified Recipient
Circulation: (98% controlled)
Printing Co: Bookmyer Printing, 68 E Market St, Tiffin, OH 44883-2830 Tel # (419) 447-3883

The Septs *Association* CPM: $58

Publishing Co: Sponsor-Minnesota Genealogical Society, Irish Genealogical Society, Intl., PO Box 16585, St. Paul, MN 55116-0585; Title Tel # (612) 574-1436 Title Fax # (612) 574-0316
Editorial Description: Newsletter of the Irish Genealogical Society.
General Info: Yr. Est. 1978, Quarterly, Trim Size-8½ x 11, 65 pages, No Color
Subscriptions: Indv. $15, Can. $20, For. $20, $5/copy
Circulation: Total-1,700, Readership-1,700
Advertising: $100.

Shelby Exchange

Publishing Co: Carol Peterson, PO Box 536, Freeman, SD 57029-0536; Title Tel # (605) 925-7186
Personnel: Editor-Carol Peterson
Editorial Description: Information about the Shelby family.
General Info: Yr. Est. 1988, Quarterly, Trim Size-8½ x 11, Mimeo press, 20 pages, No Color
Subscriptions: Indv. $13

Shem Tov

Publishing Co: Jewish Genealogical Society of Canada (Toronto), Box 446, Sta. A, Willowdale, ON M2N 5T1 Canada; Title Tel # (416) 638-3280
Editorial Description: Dedicated to publishing articles of personal research experiences, informing its members of new & tried research sources acting as part of an international network of experienced family historians & beginning genealogists.
General Info: Yr. Est. 1988, Quarterly, Trim Size-8½ x 11, Desktop press, 12 pages, ISSN: 0843-6924, Saddle-stitched
Subscriptions: Indv. $30, Inst. $30, Can. $30, For. $30, $4/copy
Acquistions: Publication Bought
Advertising: $60. Accepts Inserts.

Sherbondy Beacon *Association*

Publishing Co: Sherbondy Family Assn., 6509 W 102nd St, Overland Park, KS 66212-1723; Title Tel # (913) 341-8641
Personnel: Editor-Jeffrey Sherbondy
Editorial Description: Current & historical information on living & deceased Sherbondy descendants.
General Info: Yr. Est. 1984, Annually, 22 pages, ISSN: 8755-0547, No Color, Newsprint
Subscriptions: Indv. $4

Shumate Newsletter *Association*

Publishing Co: Genz Assoc. of America, 5821 Rowland Hill Rd., Cascade, MD 21719-1939; Title Tel # (301) 416-2660
Personnel: Editor-Victor Gebhart
General Info: Annually, Mimeo press, No Color
Subscriptions: $2/copy

Sims Seeker *Consumer*

Publishing Co: BGM Pubs., 28635 W Old Hideway Rd, Cary, IL 60013-9794; Title Tel # (708) 639-2400
Editorial Description: Genealogical research & information on the SIMS, SIMMS, SIMMES (et var) surname.
General Info: Yr. Est. 1989, Quarterly, Trim Size-8½ x 11, Mimeo press, 25 pages, ISSN: 1045-9987
Subscriptions: Indv. $18, $6/copy
Circulation: Total-350

Sleeper News
See: REGIONAL INTEREST

Small Siblings

Publishing Co: Pioneer Publications, PO Box 1179, Tum Tum, WA 99034-1179; Title Tel # (509) 276-9841
Personnel: Publisher, Editor-Shirley Oakes
Editorial Description: Genealogical data; queries and lineages printed free.
General Info: Irregular, Trim Size-8½ x 11, Mimeo press, 25 pages, ISSN: 0897-7860
Subscriptions: $6/copy
Acquistions: Publication Bought, Publication Sold

South Bend Area Genealogical Society *Consumer*

Publishing Co: South Bend Genealogical Society, PO Box 1222, South Bend, IN 46624-1222
Personnel: Editor-Arlene Martin
General Info: Quarterly
Subscriptions: Indv. $12

Southern Echoes *Association*

Publishing Co: Augusta Genealogical Soc., Inc., PO Box 3743, Augusta, GA 30914-3743; Title Tel # (706) 738-2241
Personnel: Editor-Carrie Adamson, Bk. Rev. Ed.-Marguerite Fogleman, Art Dir.-H. Evans
Editorial Description: Genealogical educational items; queries, historical essays, surname files.
General Info: Yr. Est. 1979, Monthly, Trim Size-8½ x 11, Sheetfed press, 10 pages, ISSN: 0735-6870, No Color
Subscriptions: Indv. $25, $1/copy
Circulation: (100% controlled), Total-1,300

Southern Indiana Genealogical Society Quarterly

Publishing Co: Southern Indiana Genealogical Soc., PO Box 665, New Albany, IN 47151-0665
General Info: Quarterly
Subscriptions: $3/copy

Southwestern Archivist
See: LIBRARY

Stackhouse Newsletter *Association*

Publishing Co: Genz Assoc. of America, 5821 Rowland Hill Rd., Cascade, MD 21719-1939; Title Tel # (301) 416-2660
Personnel: Editor-Victor Gebhart
General Info: Annually, Mimeo press, No Color
Subscriptions: $2/copy

Stalkin-Kin

Publishing Co: San Angelo Genealogical & Historical Soc., PO Box 3453, San Angelo, TX 76902-3453

Stand Sure

Publishing Co: Clan Anderson Society Ltd., 1947 Kensington High St SW, Lilburn, GA 30247-2523
Personnel: Editor-Laurie Anderson
General Info: Yr. Est. 1977, Quarterly, Mimeo press, Newsprint
Subscriptions: Indv. $10

Steger Family Newsletter

Publishing Co: Steger Family Newsletter, 12717 Gores Mill Rd, Reisterstown, MD 21136-5100; Title Tel # (410) 833-5416
Editorial Description: Promotes research of Steger families in the United states.
General Info: Yr. Est. 1989, 2x/yr., Trim Size-8½ x 11, 36 pages
Subscriptions: Indv. $4, $2/copy
Circulation: Total-200

Stires Family Newsletter *Association*

Publishing Co: Stires Family Newsletter, Rr 2 Box 3249, Livermore Falls, ME 04254-9549; Title Tel # (207) 897-4222
Personnel: Editor-W. Dennis Stires
Editorial Description: Genealogy & family history articles about present & past Stires families.
General Info: Yr. Est. 1977, Monthly, Mimeo press, 3 pages
Subscriptions: Indv. $10, $1/copy

Strange Branches & Twigs

Publishing Co: Clover Ann Hankins, 5373 Sunset Ave, Indianapolis, IN 46208-2538; Title Tel # (317) 255-6210
Personnel: Publisher-Gay Menefee, Editor, Circ. Mgr., Adv. Dir.-Clover Ann Hankins, Art Dir.-Melanie Menefee
General Info: (Formerly Strange Family Tree), Yr. Est. 1968, Quarterly, 7 pages
Subscriptions: Indv. $10, $3/copy
Acquistions: Publication Bought, Publication Sold
Advertising: Inquire for rates.

Studebaker Family

Publishing Co: Studebaker Family Natl. Assn., 6555 S State Route 202, Tipp City, OH 45371-9468; Title Tel # (513) 667-4451 Title Fax # (513) 667-9322
Personnel: Editor-Ruth Studebaker
Editorial Description: Family news & family history, past & present.
General Info: Yr. Est. 1966, Quarterly, Sheetfed press, 12 pages, Color-cover
Subscriptions: Indv. $10
Acquistions: Publication Bought
Circulation: Total-1,700
Printing Co: Graphic Printing, 310 N Clay St, New Carlisle, OH 45344-1705 Tel # (513) 845-3757

Sullivan County Historical Society Newsletter

Publishing Co: Sullivan County Historical Society, PO Box 326, Sullivan, IN 47882-0326; Title Tel # (812) 268-6253

Swenson Center News
See: ETHNIC

Swiss Connection, The

Publishing Co: Swiss Connection, The, 2845 N 72nd St, Milwaukee, WI 53210-1106; Title Tel # (404) 778-1224 Title Fax # (414) 778-2109
Personnel: Editor-Maralyn Wellauer
Editorial Description: A genealogical and cultural newsletter for the Swiss.
General Info: Yr. Est. 1993, Quarterly, Trim Size-8½ x 11, 12 pages, ISSN: 1067-1080
Subscriptions: Indv. $8, For. $15
Advertising: Inquire for rates.

Talley, Tally Researcher

Publishing Co: Midwestern Enterprises, 5412 Raytown Rd, Kansas City, MO 64133-2744; Title Tel # (816) 356-5100
Personnel: Publisher, Editor-Hugh Burton
Editorial Description: Provide a central point to collect, index & publish data that is not, as well as data that is, a matter of public record for these & similar families.
General Info: Yr. Est. 1979, Quarterly, Trim Size-8½ x 11, Mimeo press, 8 pages, No Color, Newsprint
Subscriptions: Indv. $8
Advertising: Accepts Inserts.

Terrebonne Life Lines

Publishing Co: Terrebone Genealogical Society, Sta. #2, Box 295, Houma, LA 70360
Personnel: Editor-Audrey Westerman
General Info: Yr. Est. 1981, Quarterly, Trim Size-8½ x 11, Offset press, 80 pages, ISSN: 0735-2794, No Color, Newsprint
Subscriptions: Indv. $20, Inst. $18, $6/copy
Circulation: Total-600

Terrell Trails

Publishing Co: Terrell Society of American, Inc., Rr 5 Box 211, Bassett, VA 24055-8964; Title Tel # (703) 647-9574
Personnel: Publisher, Editor-Dan Brinson
Editorial Description: Covers Terrell family history.
General Info: Yr. Est. 1985, Quarterly, Trim Size-8½ x 11, Sheetfed press, 20 pages, ISSN: 0884-2108, No Color
Subscriptions: Indv. $12, Inst. $10, Can. $15, For. $15, $5/copy
Circulation: Total-400

Texarkana U.S.A. Quarterly   *Consumer, Association*

Publishing Co: Texarkana Genealogical Soc., 2404a Briar Rose Dr, Texarkana, AR 75502-3304; Title Tel # (501) 772-3955
Editorial Description: Information on most Texas counties.
General Info: (Formerly Texarkana Quarterly), Yr. Est. 1974, Quarterly, ISSN: 0741-6105
Subscriptions: Indv. $10
Circulation: Total-300

Texas Gulf Historical & Biographical Records

Publishing Co: Texas Gulf Historical Soc., PO Box 1621, Beaumont, TX 77704-1621

Think On

Publishing Co: Clan McClellan in America, Inc., 8636 Don Carol Dr, El Cerrito, CA 94530-2733; Title Tel # (510) 527-6867
Personnel: Editor-Aubrey McClellan
Editorial Description: Contains material on Clan MacLellan activities genealogical queries & stories, reports on Scottish games, book reports & items on Scotland: All related to MacLellans (any spelling).
General Info: Yr. Est. 1982, Quarterly, Trim Size-8½ x 11, 12 pages, ISSN: 1066-601X, No Color
Subscriptions: Free With Membership
Circulation: Total-500

Tiller Trails

Publishing Co: Tiller Trails, PO Box 787, Winston, OR 97496-0787; Title Tel # (503) 679-9648
Personnel: Editor-Lavonnie Brimhall
Editorial Description: Tiller Trails Vol. 2 available. 206+ pages. A joint effort with other Tiller researchers.
General Info: Yr. Est. 1986, Mimeo press

Timber Trails   *Association, Business*

Publishing Co: Yamhill County- Genealogical Society, PO Box 568, Mcminnville, OR 97128-0568
Personnel: Editor-Ruth Stoller, Circ. Mgr.-Miriam Blair, Adv. Dir., Art Dir.-Peg Morgan
Editorial Description: Materials of genealogical interest including free queries.
General Info: Yr. Est. 1980, Quarterly, Trim Size-8½ x 11, Mimeo press, 28 pages, Color, Other
Subscriptions: Indv. $10, $3/copy
Circulation: Total-250
Advertising: Inquire for rates.

Timmons Family Newsletter   *Consumer*

Publishing Co: Bunnie Timmons-Runman, PO Box 262, Montrose, MN 55363-0262; Title Tel # (612) 675-3457
General Info: Yr. Est. 1981, Quarterly, Trim Size-8½ x 11, Offset press, 6 pages, ISSN: 1062-7820
Subscriptions: $1/copy
Advertising: Accepts Inserts.
Printing Co: Mr. Print, 5330 Cedar Lake Rd., St. Louis Park, MN 55416 Tel # (612) 544-4576

Traces   *Association*

Publishing Co: South Central Kentucky Historical & Genealogical Society, In, PO Box 157, Glasgow, KY 42142-0157
Personnel: Editor-Martha Reneau
Editorial Description: Historical & geneological information of S. Central KY.
General Info: Yr. Est. 1973, Quarterly, Trim Size-8½ x 11, 36 pages
Subscriptions: Indv. $10, Free With Membership
Circulation: Total-450

Tracking in Crawford County   *Association*

Publishing Co: Ohio Genealogical Society, Crawford County Chapter, PO Box 92, Galion, OH 44833-0092
Personnel: Editor-Frances Reiter
General Info: 8x/yr., Trim Size-8½ x 11, Offset press, 10 pages, No Color
Subscriptions: Indv. $6, Free With Membership
Printing Co: A-1 Printing Company, 825 S Sandusky Ave, Bucyrus, OH 44820-2633 Tel # (419) 562-3111

Tracks & Traces   *Consumer*

Publishing Co: Union County Genealogical Society C/O Barton Library, 200 E 5th St, El Dorado, AR 71730-3824
Personnel: Editor-Dorathy Boulden
General Info: Semi-annually, Mimeo press, 70 pages, No Color
Subscriptions: Indv. $10, $5/copy
Circulation: Total-150

Treasure State Lines   *Association*

Publishing Co: Great Falls Genealogy Society, 1400 1st Ave N, Great Falls, MT 59401-3205; Title Tel # (406) 727-3922
Personnel: Editor-Alice Heisel
Editorial Description: Genealogical and historical information and records; also news about the association.
General Info: Yr. Est. 1975, Quarterly, Trim Size-8½ x 11, Sheetfed press, 20 pages, ISSN: 1060-0337, No Color
Subscriptions: Indv. $20, $3/copy
Advertising: $50.
Printing Co: Easter Seal Society, 4400 Central Ave, Great Falls, MT 59405-1695 Tel # (406) 761-3680

Trees & Trails

Publishing Co: Flathead Valley Genealogical Soc., PO Box 584, Kalispell, MT 59903-0584; Title Tel # (406) 752-5446

Tri-County Genealogy   *Association*

Publishing Co: Tri-County Genealogical Society, PO Box 580, Marvell, AR 72366-0580; Title Tel # (501) 829-2772
Personnel: Editor-Jo Claire English
Editorial Description: Covers genealogy in Monroe, Lee & Phillips counties, AR.
General Info: Yr. Est. 1985, Trim Size-8½ x 11, 40 pages, ISSN: 0896-419x
Subscriptions: Indv. $15, $5/copy
Circulation: Total-434

Tri-County Researcher   *Business*

Publishing Co: Tri-County Researcher, PO Box 196, Proctor, WV 26055-0196; Title Tel # (304) 455-3203
Personnel: Publisher, Editor-Linda Goddard Stout
Editorial Description: Courthouse records, cemetery records, federal census, family histories, queries, covering Marshall, Wetzel, & Tyler Counties, WV.
General Info: Yr. Est. 1976, Quarterly, Mimeo press, 35 pages, No Color
Subscriptions: Indv. $16, $4/copy
Circulation: Total-350

Tucker Times

Publishing Co: Pioneer Publications, PO Box 1179, Tum Tum, WA 99034-1179; Title Tel # (509) 276-9841
Personnel: Publisher, Editor-Shirley Oakes
Editorial Description: Genealogical data on Surname. Lineage & Queries accepted for free.
General Info: Yr. Est. Irregular, Trim Size-8½ x 11, Mimeo press, 25 pages
Subscriptions: $6/copy

Tufts Kinsmen   *Association*

Publishing Co: Tufts Kinsmen Assn., PO Box 571, Dedham, MA 02027-0571;
Title Tel # (617) 296-0997
Personnel: Editor-Herbert Adams
Editorial Description: Official bulletin of the Tufts Kinsmen Association, a non-profit organization dedicated to Tufts Heritage.
General Info: Yr. Est. 1975, Quarterly, Trim Size-8½ x 11, Offset press, 10 pages
Subscriptions: $2/copy
Circulation: Total-1,000

Upper South Carolina Genealogy & History

Publishing Co: Piedmont Historical Soc., PO Box 8096, Spartanburg, SC 29305-8096

Utah Genealogical Assn. Newsletter   *Association*   **CPM:** $85

Publishing Co: Utah Genealogical Association, PO Box 1144, Salt Lake City, UT 84110-1144;
Title Tel # (801) 240-2091
Personnel: Editor-Rosemarie Finter, Editor-Rea Whitker
General Info: Yr. Est. 1971, Quarterly, ISSN: 0146-2229
Circulation: Total-700
Advertising: $60.

Van Zandt Ancestors

Publishing Co: Bell Enterprises, PO Box 10328, Spokane, WA 99209-1328

Vance Family Assn. Newsletter

Publishing Co: William R. Huss, 10 Carter Dr, Chelmsford, MA 01824-2808;
Title Tel # (508) 256-9647
Personnel: Editor-Vance Voss Smith
Editorial Description: Researching & publishing Vance history, lists members, individual lines.
General Info: Yr. Est. 1985, Quarterly, Trim Size-8½ x 11, Desktop press, 26 pages, No Color, Newsprint
Subscriptions: Indv. $15, Inst. $8, For. $10, $2/copy
Acquisitions: Publication Sold
Circulation: Total-200
Advertising: Accepts Inserts.

Vandal Newsletter

Publishing Co: Wayne Vandal Masterson, PO Box 193, Bull Shoals, AR 72619-0193
Editorial Description: Communication link between descendants of Abraham & Mary Vandal.

Veitch Chronicle

Publishing Co: Veitch Historical Society, 6060 SW Coyote Ave, Redmond, OR 97756-9536;
Title Tel # (503) 548-4113
Personnel: Publisher-Wanda Clark, Editor-Barbara Veach
Editorial Description: Study & information on the Veitch family.
General Info: Yr. Est. 1978, 48 pages
Subscriptions: Indv. $15, $3/copy
Circulation: Total-500

Viking Kinfolk

Publishing Co: Floyd Oydegard, 114 Trenethan Ave., Box 2201, Santa Cruz, CA 95062-1312
Personnel: Editor-Floyd D.P. Oydegaard
Editorial Description: Information gathering source with historical content - reprints of genealogical charts.
General Info: Yr. Est. 1979, Monthly, Trim Size-8½ x 11, Mimeo press, 3 pages, Color
Subscriptions: Indv. $5
Circulation: Total-150

Violent Kin
See: HISTORY

Virginia Genealogical Society Newsletter   *Consumer, Association*

Publishing Co: Virginia Genealogical Society, 5001 W Broad St Ste 115, Richmond, VA 23230-3023;
Title Tel # (804) 285-8954
Personnel: Editor-Joanne Nance, Editor-Barbara Vines Little
Editorial Description: Articles, news, book reviews, and queries of interest to Virginia genealogical research.
General Info: Yr. Est. 1974, Semi-monthly, Trim Size-8½ x 11, Desktop press, 18 pages, ISSN: 1084-5852, No Color, Matte, Saddle-stitched
Subscriptions: Indv. $23, Inst. $23
Circulation: Total-2,900
List Rental: Actives: $100/M
Printing Co: Copy Van, Dickens Rd., Richmond, VA 23261

Virginia/West Virginia Queries

Publishing Co: Bette Butcher Topp, 1304 W. Cliffwood Ct., Spokane, WA 99218-2917;
Title Tel # (509) 467-2299
Personnel: Publisher-Bette B. Topp, Editor-Betty B. Topp
General Info: Yr. Est. 1987, Irregular, Trim Size-8½ x 11, ISSN: 0890-9423
Subscriptions: $6/copy

WI Genealogical Council Newsletter   *Association*

Publishing Co: Carolyn Habelman, RR 3, Box 253, Black River Falls, WI 54615-9405;
Title Tel # (608) 378-4388 Title Fax # (608) 378-3006
Personnel: Editor-Pat Kell
Editorial Description: Genealogical information of interest to state clubs.
General Info: Yr. Est. 1987, Quarterly, Trim Size-8½ x 11, Desktop press, 8 pages, No Color, Matte
Subscriptions: Indv. $5, Inst. $10
Circulation: Total-220

Wake County Genealogical Society Newsletter   *Association*

Publishing Co: Wake County Genealogical Society, 5253 Vann St, Raleigh, NC 27606-1579;
Title Tel # (919) 851-2593
Personnel: Publisher-Mary Louise James
Editorial Description: Genealogy.
General Info: Yr. Est. 1982, Monthly, Mimeo press, 10 pages, No Color
Circulation: Total-149

Watauga Ancestry   *Consumer, Association*

Publishing Co: Genealogical Society of Watauga Co., NC, 530 Forrest Hill Dr, Boone, NC 28607-4428; Title Tel # (704) 264-7813
Personnel: Circ. Mgr.-Joyce Ryals, Editor, Production Mgr.-Sanna Gaffney
Editorial Description: Contains local history, news extracts from 100 year old Watauga Democrat, tombstone inscripture, court records, queries plus other genealogical data.
General Info: Yr. Est. 1987, Quarterly, Trim Size-8½ x 11, Offset press, 20 pages, No Color, Newsprint, Looseleaf
Subscriptions: Indv. $10, $2/copy
Circulation: Total-200

Weather - Watch

Publishing Co: Robert Weatherford, 531 Majestic Ave, Bellmawr, NJ 08031-1461
Personnel: Publisher, Editor-R.E. Weatherford
Editorial Description: A publication for all Weatherford descendants of Weatherford ancestry.
General Info: Yr. Est. 1979, Quarterly, Trim Size-5½ x 8½, Sheetfed press, 24 pages, 2 Color, Newsprint
Subscriptions: Indv. $8, $2/copy
Circulation: Total-125
Printing Co: Art Press Printing, 124 E. Clemens Bridge Rd., Barrington, NJ 08007
Tel # (609) 547-8953

West Central Kentucky Family Research Assoc. Bulletin   *Association*

Publishing Co: West Central Kentucky Family Research Assoc., PO Box 1932, Owensboro, KY 42302-1932; Title Tel # (502) 684-4150
Personnel: Editor-Margaret Alford
Editorial Description: Kentucky genealogical articles.
General Info: Yr. Est. 1968, Quarterly, Trim Size-8½ x 11, Offset press, 20 pages, No Color
Subscriptions: Indv. $15, $2/copy
Circulation: Total-800

Western Reserve Historical Society Genealogical Committee Bulletin   *Association*

Publishing Co: Western Reserve Historical Society, 10825 East Blvd., Cleveland, OH 44106-1703;
Title Tel # (216) 721-5722
Personnel: Editor, Circ. Mgr.-Gina Hamister
Editorial Description: Designed to further the study of genealogy. By publishing articles on research methods and source material in the WRHS library, & identify other important repositories & their resources.
General Info: Yr. Est. 1982, Quarterly, Trim Size-8½ x 11, Sheetfed press, 8 pages, ISSN: 0883-9069, No Color, Newsprint
Subscriptions: Indv. $4, $1/copy
Circulation: Total-500

Weymouth Surname Newsletter

Publishing Co: Albert Weymouth, Jr., RR 1, Box 120, Belfast, ME 04915-9704;
Title Tel # (207) 942-8775
Personnel: Publisher, Editor, Circ. Mgr., Production Mgr., Art Dir., Promotion Dir.-Al Weymouth
Editorial Description: Past & present informative articles about persons and places with Weymouth surname.
General Info: Yr. Est. 1985, Trim Size-8½ x 11, Offset press, 6 pages, 2 Color, Newsprint
Subscriptions: Indv. $5, $1/copy

White Press   *Business, Association*

Publishing Co: Bette Butcher Topp, 1304 W. Cliffwood Ct., Spokane, WA 99218-2917;
Title Tel # (509) 467-2299
Editorial Description: Research information for the last name of White.
General Info: Yr. Est. 1994, Irregular, Trim Size-8½ x 11, 45 pages
Subscriptions: Indv. $6, $6/copy

Wigfield (Wingfield)
Newsletter   *Consumer, Association*

Publishing Co: Phillip Genealogical Heritage House, 605 Benton Ave., Missoula, MT 59801-8633; Title Tel # (406) 543-3495
Personnel: Publisher-Ruth Phillip, Editor-Jennie Crisp, Adv. Dir.-Arthur Wigfield
Editorial Description: 20 years of research of the Wigfield-Wingfield line. Yearly editorial, genealogy present day vital statistics.
General Info: Yr. Est. 1971, Annually, Trim Size-8½ x 11, Mimeo press, 20 pages, No Color
Subscriptions: Indv. $5, Inst. $4, $5/copy
Acquistions: Publication Sold
Advertising: Accepts Inserts.
List Rental: Rents Lists
Printing Co: Phillip Heritage Genealogy House., 605 Benton Ave, Missoula, MT 59801-8633 Tel # (406) 543-3495

Wilcox Excerpts

Publishing Co: Bell Enterprises, PO Box 10328, Spokane, WA 99209-1328

Williams' Family Bulletin

Publishing Co: John Williams, PO Box 970, Taylors, SC 29687-0970
Editorial Description: Published for the numerous Williams' descendants.
General Info: Yr. Est. 1966, Quarterly
Subscriptions: Indv. $12
Advertising: Inquire for rates.

Williams Wandering

Publishing Co: Pioneer Publications, PO Box 1179, Tum Tum, WA 99034-1179; Title Tel # (509) 276-9841
Personnel: Publisher-Shirley Penna Oakes
Editorial Description: Genealogical data collected on the durname, lineage and queries accepted free.
General Info: Yr. Est. 1996, Irregular, Trim Size-8½ x 11, 25 pages
Subscriptions: $6/copy

Wine Press Newsletter   *Consumer, Association*

Publishing Co: Napa Valley Genealogical and Biographical Society, PO Box 385, Napa, CA 94559-0385; Title Tel # (707) 252-2252
Personnel: Editor-Danda Winford
Editorial Description: Society & genealogical news.
General Info: Yr. Est. 1976, Monthly, Trim Size-8½ x 11, Web press, 4 pages, No Color
Subscriptions: Indv. $25
Acquistions: Publication Bought
Circulation: Total-260

Wood County Chapter Ohio Genealogical Society
Newsletter   *Association*

Publishing Co: Wood County Chapter Ohio Genealogical Society, PO Box 722, Bowling Green, OH 43402-0722
General Info: Yr. Est. 1977, Bi-monthly, Trim Size-8½ x 11, Offset press, 12 pages, ISSN: 0893-1593
Subscriptions: Indv. $8, $2/copy

Woolford Newsletter

Publishing Co: Genz Assoc. of America, 5821 Rowland Hill Rd., Cascade, MD 21719-1939; Title Tel # (301) 416-2660
Personnel: Editor-Victor Gebhart
General Info: Annually, Mimeo press, No Color
Subscriptions: $2/copy

Wordens Past

Publishing Co: Pat Worden, 1201 Glendale St, Midland, MI 48642-5105

Worthington Descendants

Publishing Co: Bette Brengle-Poole, 2203 Aquila's Delight, Faliston, MA 21047-1035
Personnel: Publisher, Editor-Bette Brengle Poole
Editorial Description: Coverign all branches of the Worthington lineage. It is published quarterly at a cost of 15.00 yearly. Has unlimited fill queries.
General Info: Quarterly, ISSN: 8756-0445

WyMonDak Messenger   *Consumer, Association*

Publishing Co: Tri-State Genealogical Society, 905 5th Ave, Belle Fourche, SD 57717-1702; Title Tel # (605) 892-4407
Personnel: Editor-Pat Engebretson, Circ. Mgr.-Vicki Ross
Editorial Description: Genealogy covering the counties of Carter, MT; Crook, WY; Butte, & Harding, SD.
General Info: Yr. Est. 1980, Quarterly, Desktop press, 8 pages, No Color
Subscriptions: Indv. $5, $1/copy
Advertising: Inquire for rates.

Wyandot Tracers

Publishing Co: Ohio Genealogical Society, PO Box 414, Upper Sandusky, OH 43351-0414
Editorial Description: Each newsletter contains announcements, queries and relevant genealogical items.
General Info: Yr. Est. 1983, Trim Size-8½ x 11, 14 pages

Yoder Newsletter   *Consumer*

Publishing Co: Yoder Newsletter, PO Box 594, Goshen, IN 46527-0594; Title Tel # (219) 825-9318
Personnel: Editor-Christopher Yoder, Circ. Dir.-John Yoder, Circ. Mgr.-Ben Yoder
Editorial Description: Information to readers, special interest memos, family history & news.
General Info: Yr. Est. 1983, Semi-annually, Trim Size-8½ x 11, Sheetfed press, 8 pages, No Color, Coated
Subscriptions: Indv. $3, $2/copy
Circulation: Total-770
Printing Co: News Printing Co, 114 S Main St, Goshen, IN 46526-3702

Yorker Palatine Newsletter   *Association*

Publishing Co: Palatines to America, Elpis Rd., RD #1, Box 128, Camden, NY 13316; Title Tel # (315) 245-0990
Personnel: Editor-Eila Schiffer
Editorial Description: Early German arrivals to U.S. (1850's). Palatines society holds meetings, writes articles, has speakers, offers research techniques, tours, surname exchange lists, answers queries.
General Info: Yr. Est. 1981, Quarterly, 8 pages
Subscriptions: Indv. $19, Can. $30, For. $40
Circulation: Total-500

Yucaipa Valley Family
Finders   *Consumer*

Publishing Co: Y.V.G.S., PO Box 32, Yucaipa, CA 92399-0032
Personnel: Editor-Helen Alexander
General Info: Yr. Est. 1982, Monthly, Mimeo press, 3 pages
Subscriptions: Indv. $8, $4/copy
Acquistions: Publication Bought, Publication Sold

Yurek Herald

Publishing Co: Kevin J. Tankersley, 524 E Luray Ave, Alexandria, VA 22301-1606
Personnel: Publisher, Editor-Kevin Tankersley
Editorial Description: A genealogical & family history newsletter for Yurek & Associated Families of Baltimore, MD.
General Info: Yr. Est. 1983, Trim Size-8½ x 11, Mimeo press, 3 pages, No Color

GENERAL INTEREST

American Dreams   *Consumer*

Publishing Co: American Dreams, 11875 Dublin Blvd., #D-272, Dublin, CA 94568; Title Tel # (510) 803-1100 Title Fax # (510) 803-1088
Personnel: Publisher-James Bickford
Editorial Description: Positive success stories for inspiration and motivation.
General Info: Yr. Est. 1993, Quarterly
Subscriptions: Indv. $40

American Information
Newsletter

Publishing Co: American Information Newsletter, 2308 N Cole Rd Ste G, Boise, ID 83704-7361; Title Tel # (208) 385-9655
Editorial Description: Digest of over 300 publications.
General Info: Monthly
Subscriptions: Indv. $48

At Your Command

Publishing Co: USAA Federal Savings Bank, Marketing Programs Usaa, Building, San Antonio, TX 78288-0001; Title Tel # (210) 498-7859
Editorial Description: A Newsletter for USAA Credit Card Holders
General Info: Quarterly

Backboard

Publishing Co: Backspace Ink, 1131 Galvez Dr, Pacifica, CA 94044-4210
Personnel: Editor-Joanne Shwed
Editorial Description: Features poetry, music, art, current news & other topics of interest. Includes interviews.
General Info: Yr. Est. 1986, Irregular, Trim Size-8½ x 11

Belle Ringer   *Consumer, Association*

Publishing Co: Bennett College, 900 E Washington St, Greensboro, NC 27401-3298; Title Tel # (919) 370-8629 Title Fax # (910) 378-0511
Personnel: Publisher, Circ. Mgr.-Ellease Colston
General Info: Quarterly, 12 pages, Color-cover, Coated, Saddle-stitched
Circulation: Total-6,700
Printing Co: Deal Printing Co., 616 S Elm St, Greensboro, NC 27406-1328 Tel # (919) 273-3152

Blue Chip Stocks
See: INVESTMENT

Chautauqua

Publishing Co: Luciano Curuchet, 532 W. Olive ST #8, Inglewood, CA 90301
Editorial Description: Tiny four-point type of reviews and other stuff, like recipes, interviews and rants about TV.
General Info: Trim Size-8.5 x 11, 10 pages
Subscriptions: Indv. $1

College By Mail Etc.- Newsletter
See: EDUCATION

Cruise & Freighter Travel Letter
See: TRAVEL

DOE
See: SCIENCE FICTION & FANTASY

Digest of Attorney General Opinions
See: LAW

Donald R. Morris Newsletter
See: NEWSPAPER INDUSTRY

Eagle-Eye Communicator   *Consumer*
Publishing Co: Stellar-7 Communications, 532 Lakeview Ave # 2, Jamestown, NY 14701-3352; Title Tel # (716) 484-2208
Personnel: Editor-Douglas Arters
General Info: Yr. Est. 1989, Monthly
Subscriptions: Indv. $21

Editorials on File
See: NEWSPAPER INDUSTRY

Facts on File World News Digest
See: INTERNATIONAL AFFAIRS

The Feat Sheet
Publishing Co: Derrick & Ida, P.O. Box 981, Columbia, MO 65205
Editorial Description: Newsletter for foot bag enthusiasts
General Info: Trim Size-8.5 x 11, 7 pages

Fernand Braudel Center-Newsletter
See: SOCIOLOGY

Festivities
See: ENTERTAINMENT

Friendship Letter, The   *Consumer*
Publishing Co: Friendship Letter, The, PO Box 278, Friendship, ME 04547-0278
Personnel: Publisher-Michael Cooney
Editorial Description: Folksy information about this and that.
General Info: Monthly

Frugal Bugle, The
See: BANKING & FINANCE

Future Trends
Publishing Co: Minnesota Futurists, 365 Summit Ave., Saint Paul, MN 55102-2120; Title Tel # (612) 290-2846 Title Fax # (612) 290-2847
Personnel: Editor-Earl Joseph
Editorial Description: Editorials & wide ranging topical articles on alternative futures, peace futures, futures bibliographic, key quotes on futures, & meeting announcements.
General Info: Yr. Est. 1967, 9x/yr., Desktop press, 14 pages
Subscriptions: Indv. $10
Circulation: Total-1,000

Get Organized! News, The   *Business, Consumer*
Publishing Co: SEP Publishing, PO Box 144, Gotha, FL 34734; Title Tel # (407) 292-0225 Title Fax # (407) 292-0225
Editorial Description: Information designed to introduce the reader to new ways to save time, save money, organize many different areas of their personal and business lives.
General Info: Yr. Est. 1993, Monthly, Trim Size-8.5 x 11, Desktop press, 8 pages, No Color
Subscriptions: Indv. $20, Can. $26, $2/copy

Grapevine, The (Genesee Valley)
See: ETHNIC

Guatemala Human Rights
See: CIVIL RIGHTS

IFTF Perspectives   *Business*
Publishing Co: Institute for the Future, 2740 Sand Hill Rd, Menlo Park, CA 94025-7020; Title Tel # (415) 854-6322 Title Fax # (415) 854-7850
Personnel: Editor-Joe Donzelli, Art Dir.-Janet Chambers
Editorial Description: Covers topics of general interest to anyone involved in long-term planning as well as those in the futures field. It includes a calendar of futures-oriented events.
General Info: (Formerly Institute for the Future Newsletter), Yr. Est. 1984, Quarterly, 8 pages, Matte
Circulation: Total-1,400

IRA-Individual Retirement Account Stocks
See: INVESTMENT

Income Stocks
See: INVESTMENT

Inside Out   *Consumer*
Publishing Co: Select Publishing Society, 6756 Towne Lane Road, PO Box 1231A, McLean, VA 22101-1231; Title Tel # (703) 356-1092 Title Fax # (703) 821-3077
Personnel: Editor-Paulena Meyer
Editorial Description: Thought provoking articles by educators, consultants, and practitioners to encourage awareness and positive empowerment.
General Info: Yr. Est. 1993, Monthly, Trim Size-8½ x 11, 8 pages, ISSN: 1066-9833
Subscriptions: Indv. $18

Lefty's Letter   *Consumer*
Publishing Co: Richard W. Unger Publications, 610 4th St. E., Box 212, Spiritwood, SK S0J 2M0 Canada Tel # (306) 445-5172; Title Tel # (306) 883-2462
Personnel: Publisher, Editor-Richard Unger
Editorial Description: Articles aimed to inform and encourage left-handers.
General Info: Yr. Est. 1992, 10x/yr., Trim Size-8½ x 11, Mimeo press, 6 pages, ISSN: 1192-2915, Ind/Abs/Online: Annual Index, Color, Matte
Subscriptions: Indv. $17, Inst. $17, Can. $17, For. $27, $2/copy
Printing Co: Valley Web, 1299 Stowe Avenue, Medford, OR 97504 Tel # (503) 772-7039

Lesko's Info-Power Newsletter
See: BUSINESS & INDUSTRY

Low Priced Stocks
See: INVESTMENT

Mawewi   *Consumer*
Publishing Co: Adastra West, Inc., PO Box 874, Mahwah, NJ 07430-0874; Title Tel # (201) 529-1144 Title Fax # (201) 529-1404
Personnel: Editor-Maja Britton, Editor-Alex Rainer
Editorial Description: An eclectic blend of compact articles on a wide range of topics, including current events, astronomy, ecology, history, etymology and more.
General Info: Yr. Est. 1988, Bi-monthly, Trim Size-8½ x 11, Sheetfed press, 6 pages, ISSN: 1053-4423, No Color, Matte
Subscriptions: Indv. $10, Can. $15, For. $15, $2/copy
Circulation: (20% controlled), Total-2,500, Subscriptions-2,000
Printing Co: Ramsey Press, 2 E Main St, Ramsey, NJ 07446-1923

Medical Abstracts Newsletter
See: HEALTH

Mentor   *Business, Association*
Publishing Co: A Great Mother company, PO Box 4382, Overland Park, KS 66204-0382; Title Tel # (913) 362-7889
Personnel: Publisher, Editor-Maureen Waters
Editorial Description: Recreating community through the art and practice of mentoring.
General Info: Yr. Est. 1989, Quarterly, Trim Size-8½ x 11, Letrpr. press, 12 pages, ISSN: 1045-4985, 2 Color, Matte, Saddle-stitched
Subscriptions: Indv. $24, Can. $30, For. $40, $6/copy
Acquistions: Publication Sold
Circulation: Total-500
Advertising: Inquire for rates.

Metric Today
See: CONSUMER INTERESTS

Middletown Bulletin
Publishing Co: Middletown Bulletin, Inc., 380 Main St, Cromwell, CT 06416-2309; Title Tel # (203) 346-8183
Personnel: Editor-Max B. Corvo
Editorial Description: General news.
General Info: Yr. Est. 1948, Weekly
Circulation: Total-1,335

Mitzymitzy Ennui
Publishing Co: Narcissus Press, P.O. Box 2430, Chandler, AZ 85244-2430
Editorial Description: A zine that takes brief looks at various movements, along with a bit of Erisian/ Discordian stuff and a few other things thrown in.
General Info: Trim Size-8.5 x 11, 7 pages

Monitor, We the People & Our Two Cents Worth
Publishing Co: ETS Research, 80 Narcissa Dr # 700-32, Rancho Palos Verdes, CA 90275-5910; Title Tel # (213) 377-7608
Personnel: Publisher-Enrica Tonello-Stuart, Editor-Erica Tonello-Stuart, Circ. Mgr., Production Mgr.-Erica Stuart, Adv. Dir.-Charles Stuart
Editorial Description: Contains letters & articles on public issues.
General Info: (Formerly We the People & Our Two Cents Worth), Yr. Est. 1988, Quarterly, Trim Size-11 x 17, Web press, 8 pages, No Color
Subscriptions: Indv. $5
Circulation: (100% controlled), Total-5,000
Advertising: Inquire for rates. Accepts Inserts.
Printing Co: Glendale Rotary Offset Printing, 112 S Maryland Ave # 696, Glendale, CA 91205-1027 Tel # (213) 245-1825

NYSE-Weekly Stock Buys
See: INVESTMENT

Network for Citizen Enlightenment

Publishing Co: DeClare Publishing, PO Box 1475, Clackamas, OR 97015-1475
Personnel: Publisher, Editor-Will DeClare
General Info: Yr. Est. 1986, Monthly, Trim Size-8$\frac{1}{2}$ x 11, 16 pages, Color
Subscriptions: Indv. $20, $2/copy
Advertising: Inquire for rates.

News Notice

Publishing Co: News Notice, 4758 Ridge Rd # 2633, Cleveland, OH 44144-3327
Personnel: Publisher, Editor-Gary Skeens
General Info: Yr. Est. 1980, Quarterly
Subscriptions: Indv. $10

Ninety Three Point Five

Publishing Co: Maestro Takatak, The Sonic Buffalo, P.O. Box 734, Mt Angel, OR 97362
Editorial Description: The maestro prints media commentary, fiction, rants, and other miscellaneous ramblings.
General Info: Monthly
Subscriptions: Indv. $2

The Omnipotent Nectarine

Publishing Co: The Omnipotent Nectarine, 286 Croidin Place, #2E, Brooklyn, NY 11235
Editorial Description: A mostly hand-written effort with messy drawings, rants, and a funny piece where people write in to 'Ask the Incredible Rabbi,' who dispenses advice about love, piercings, and other such things
General Info: Trim Size-8.5 x 11, 14 pages
Subscriptions: Indv. $1

Operation Mind Fuck

Publishing Co: A.C.A.A., Box 25, 197 Hunter St W, Peterborough, ON K9H 2L1 Canada
Editorial Description: A really cool zine from someone who has a a knack for finding obscure conspiracy-oriented clips to reprint, a very interesting article revealing secrets of the Gulf War.
General Info: Trim Size-8.5 x 11, 10 pages
Subscriptions: Indv. $2

Our Green Emerald

Publishing Co: Aquarian Print, Box 1657, Edmonton, AB T5J 2N9 Canada;
   Title Tel # (403) 463-7311
Editorial Description: Available to members of interested non-profit groups. Currently: New Age International; 21st Century Science & Technology Foundation.
General Info: Yr. Est. 1990, Quarterly, Sheetfed press, Color-cover
Subscriptions: Indv. $50, Can. $50, For. $50
Acquistions: Publication Bought

Outreach
   See: COLLEGE STUDENT

Patriot Review

Publishing Co: CPA Publishing, PO Box 905, Sandy, OR 97055-0905; Title Tel # (503) 668-4941
   Title Fax # (503) 657-4631
Personnel: Editor-Richard Flowers
General Info: Yr. Est. 1984, Monthly, Web press, 16 pages
Subscriptions: Indv. $20, $2/copy
Circulation: Total-8,500
Advertising: Inquire for rates.

Pen Pals Northwest

Publishing Co: Nuxoll Newsletters, E. 1419 Marietta Ave., Spokane, WA 99207;
   Title Tel # (509) 487-3383
General Info: 24x/yr.
Subscriptions: Indv. $6

Popline
   See: ENVIRONMENT & ECOLOGY

PopularLife

Publishing Co: LAMAR, 96 Hillside Avenue, Rochester, NY 14610
Editorial Description: A wonderful collection of funny newsclips, xerox/fax memes, vintage ads, detoured comics, and text/image collages.
General Info: Trim Size-5 x 7, 18 pages
Subscriptions: Indv. $2

The Quill Pen Pal

Publishing Co: Quill Corp., 100 Schelter Rd, Lincolnshire, IL 60069-3621 Tel # (708) 634-4800;
   Title Fax # (708) 634-6723
Editorial Description: A friendly newsletter to you from quill
General Info: Monthly

Radio Resistors Bulletin

Publishing Co: Frank Haulgren, P.O. Box 3038, Bellingham, WA 98227
Editorial Description: This bulletin provides an open discussions of alternative and community radio and reports on stimulating new broadcasts and projects.
General Info: Trim Size-8.5 x 11, 10 pages
Subscriptions: Indv. $1

Rational Enquirer

Publishing Co: Eric Robison, 33 Gaymor Lane, Commack, NY 11725
Editorial Description: This a very entertaining zine devoted exclusively to thought-provoking questions and intelligent answers.
General Info: Trim Size-5 x 7, 16 pages
Subscriptions: Indv. $2

Recycling Related Newsletters, Publications, Etc; A Reference
   See: ENVIRONMENT & ECOLOGY

Recycling Update
   See: ENVIRONMENT & ECOLOGY

Release
   See: HEALTH

Right of Aesthetic Realism to Be Known, The   *Consumer, Scholarly*

Publishing Co: Aesthetic Realism Foundation, 141 Greene St., New York, NY 10012
   Tel # (212) 777-4490; Title Fax # (212) 777-4426
Personnel: Editor-Ellen Reiss
Editorial Description: Contains works by Eli Siegel, founder of Aesthetic Realism; commentary by Ellen Reiss, Class Chairman; articles by Aesthetic Realism consultants. Explains world events and questions of self, showing that personally and internationally 'Contempt is the great failure of man' and 'man's deepest desire...is to like the world.
General Info: Yr. Est. 1973, Weekly, ISSN: 0882-3731
Subscriptions: Indv. $18, Can. $28, For. $40

Rural Network Advocate
   See: LIFESTYLE

SORT'ing News
   See: OFFICE METHODS & EQUIPMENT

Saskatchewan Safety Council Link
   See: SAFETY

Self-Reliant Living
   See: SURVIVAL, WEAPONS

Senior Writers Network News

Publishing Co: Nuxoll Newsletters, E. 1419 Marietta Ave., Spokane, WA 99207;
   Title Tel # (509) 747-4468
General Info: Yr. Est. 1984, Quarterly
Subscriptions: Indv. $8

Sinkfull Of Dishes

Publishing Co: Sink Full of Dirty Dishes, P.O. Box 160122, St. Louis, MO 63116
Editorial Description: An almost haphazard collection of stories, comics, poems, dream transcripts, and celebrity fan club addresses.
General Info: Trim Size-8.5 x 11, 20 pages
Subscriptions: Indv. $2

Skinflint News   *Consumer*

Publishing Co: Skinflint News, 1460 Noell Blvd, Palm Harbor, FL 34683-5637;
   Title Tel # (813) 785-7759
Personnel: Editor-Melodie Moore
Editorial Description: Information for consumers on how to save money.
General Info: Monthly, Trim Size-8$\frac{1}{2}$ x 11, 12 pages
Subscriptions: Indv. $10
Circulation: Total-40,000

Slacker   *Association, Consumer*

Publishing Co: Third Millenium, 817 Broadway Fl 6, New York, NY 10003-4709 Tel # (212) 979-2001
Editorial Description: Newsletter for generation x'ers.
General Info: Yr. Est. 1994, Quarterly
Subscriptions: $2/copy
Circulation: Total-3,000

Solitary Pleasures

Publishing Co: Alva Svoboda, P.O. Box 10604, Oaland, CA 94610 ; '''
Editorial Description: A short occasional pamphlet on various subjects, this one is simply four pages of Alva's personal history with religion and beliefs about abortion.
General Info: Trim Size-8.5 x 11, 4 pages
Subscriptions: Indv. $1

Song's for Peace

Publishing Co: Sharleen Leahey, P.O. Box 090-312, Brooklyn, NY 11209-0006
Editorial Description: A unique publication explores the power of song to transform life and create peace on Earth.
General Info: Trim Size-8.5 x 11, 23 pages
Subscriptions: Indv. $6

Spectrum Tidbits   *Consumer*

Publishing Co: Spectrum Concepts, 2117 Foothill blvd., Ste. 138, La Verne, CA 91750
Editorial Description: Condensed news items on a variety of subjects directed to readers over 50.
General Info: Bi-monthly
Subscriptions: Indv. $15

Streetlife

Publishing Co: Massachusetts Coalition for the Homeless, 288 A St, Boston, MA 02210-1600;
Title Tel # (617) 451-0707
General Info: Bi-monthly, 6 pages
Subscriptions: Indv. $15

Tabloid Tattler   *Consumer*

Publishing Co: Tabloid Tattler, P.O. Box 93944, Hollywood, CA 90093 Tel # (213) 665-7157
Fax # (213) 913-9791
Personnel: Publisher-Sondra Lowell
Editorial Description: A publication for people who want to know what's happening in the tabloids but shun the publicity of buying or reading the publications at the checkout stand.
General Info: Yr. Est. 1993, 50x/yr., 2 pages
Subscriptions: Indv. $25

Teaching Thinking and
Problem Solving   *Business, Consumer*

Publishing Co: Lawrence Erlbaum Associates, Inc., 10 Industrial Ave., Mahwah, NJ 07430-2205
Tel # (201) 236-9500 Fax # (201) 236-0072 Parent Co.-Taylor & Francis, Bristol;
Title Tel # (201) 666-4110
Personnel: Editor-Francine Beyer
Editorial Description: Issues on thinking and problem solving.
General Info: Bi-monthly, ISSN: 0887-0217
Subscriptions: Indv. $28, Inst. $54, For. $48

Transitions
See: MEN'S

Valley Voice   *Consumer, Association*   CPM: $350

Publishing Co: Concerned Citizens of the Delaware Valley, PO Box 47, Bryn Mawr, PA 19010-0047;
Title Tel # (610) 525-1129
Personnel: Editor-Harry Hyde, Jr.
Editorial Description: A newsletter for the Delaware Valley citizen-activist/public-interest network.
General Info: (Formerly Delaware Valley/South Jersey Transportation), Yr. Est. 1966, Quarterly, Trim Size-7¹/₂ x 12.5, Other press, 10 pages, ISSN: 1082-0027, Other
Subscriptions: Indv. $3, $1/copy
Acquistions: Publication Bought, Publication Sold
Circulation: Total-200
Advertising: $70. Accepts Inserts.

Vermont Academy of Arts &
Sciences

Publishing Co: Vermont Academy of Arts, 2 Buxton Ave, Middletown Springs, VT 05757-4231;
Title Tel # (802) 235-2302
Personnel: Editor-Frances Krouse
Editorial Description: Newsletter of president's message & pertinent news of the Academy.
General Info: Semi-annually, Trim Size-17 x 22, Sheetfed press, 8 pages, 2 Color, Newsprint
Acquistions: Publication Bought
Circulation: Total-1,000

Weekly World Digest   *Business, Consumer*

Publishing Co: Facts on File, Inc., 11 Penn Plaza, New York, NY 10001-2006 Tel # (212) 967-8800
Parent Co.-Infobase Holdings Inc., New York
Personnel: Editor-Thomas Hitchings
Editorial Description: Condensed world news reports.
General Info: Weekly, Trim Size-8¹/₂ x 11, 20 pages
Subscriptions: Indv. $640

Westerner, The

Publishing Co: Old West Shop Publishing, Box 5232-19, Vienna, WV 26105;
Title Tel # (304) 295-3143
Personnel: Publisher, Editor-Roger Crowley
Editorial Description: Articles, stories, and information for wild west enthusiasts.
General Info: Yr. Est. 1986, Monthly
Subscriptions: Indv. $20
Advertising: Inquire for rates.

World of A.S.P.
See: LIFESTYLE

GENETICS

ABDC Newsletter
See: HEALTH

Applied Genetics News   *Consumer*

Publishing Co: Business Communications Co., 25 Van Zant St., Ste.13, Norwalk, CT 06855-1781;
Title Tel # (203) 853-4266 Title Fax # (203) 853-0348
Personnel: Publisher-Louis Naturman, Editor-Jack Miskell, Mktg. Dir.-Robert Butler
Editorial Description: Reports on development in all aspects of biotechnology.
General Info: Yr. Est. 1980, Monthly, Trim Size-8¹/₂ x 11, Offset press, 12 pages, ISSN: 0271-7107,
Ind/Abs/Online: Predicasts, No Color, Matte
Subscriptions: Indv. $375, Can. $425, For. $425, $38/copy
Circulation: (100% controlled), Total-250
List Rental: List Management Co.: W.I. Mail Marketing, 470 Main St. #317, Ridgefield, CT
06877-4516 Tel # (203) 438-6822, Fax # (203) 438-7756, Actives: $120/M

Biotech Business   *Business*

Publishing Co: Worldwide Videotex Co., PO Box 3273, Boynton Beach, FL 33424-3273
Fax # (407) 738-2276; Title Tel # (407) 738-2276 Title Fax # (407) 738-2275
Personnel: Editor-Mark Wright
Editorial Description: Provides the latest detailed information & news on biotechnology companies & products. It reports on the financial & business standings & prospects of biotech companies.
General Info: Yr. Est. 1987, Monthly, ISSN: 0899-5702, Ind/Abs/Online: NewsNet, DIALOG, Predicasts
Subscriptions: Indv. $150, Can. $150, For. $165, $13/copy
List Rental: Actives: 30,024, $235/M

Biotechnology News
See: SCIENCE

Biotechnology Newswatch   *Business*

Publishing Co: McGraw-Hill, 1221 Ave. of the Americas, 36th Fl., New York, NY 10020-1095
Fax # (212) 512-6590; Title Tel # (212) 512-2000
Personnel: Publisher-John Slater
Editorial Description: Newsletter focusing on the business of biotechnology.
General Info: Yr. Est. 1980, Bi-weekly, Ind/Abs/Online: DIALOG, NEXIS, Dow Jones, NewsNet
Subscriptions: Indv. $775, $50/copy

Biotechnology Patent
Watch   *Business*

Publishing Co: McGraw-Hill, 1221 Ave. of the Americas, 36th Fl., New York, NY 10020-1095
Tel # (212) 512-2000 Fax # (212) 512-6590; Title Tel # (212) 512-6090
Personnel: Publisher-John Slater
General Info: Yr. Est. 1986

Clinical Trials Monitor
See: DRUGS & PHARMACEUTICALS

Connective Issues
See: MEDICINE

Diagnostics Intelligence
See: DRUGS & PHARMACEUTICALS

Down Syndrome News   *Consumer*

Publishing Co: National Down Syndrome Congress, 1605 Chantilly Dr. NE, #250, Atlanta, GA
30324-3269 Fax # (404) 232-2817; Title Fax # (770) 232-2817
Personnel: Editor-Margaret Lewis
Editorial Description: Newsletter carrying up-to-date information on a variety of aspects of Down Syndrome aimed at parents.
General Info: (Formerly Down's Syndrome News), Yr. Est. 1975, 10x/yr., Trim Size-8¹/₂ x 11, Offset press, 16 pages, ISSN: 0161-0716, No Color, Newsprint
Subscriptions: Indv. $15, Inst. $25
Acquistions: Publication Bought
Circulation: Total-200,000
Printing Co: Peace Institute Printing, 4436 Olive St, Saint Louis, MO 63108-1808

Drosophila
See: SCIENCE

DuPont Biotech Update
See: BIOCHEMISTRY

Emerging Pharmaceuticals
See: DRUGS & PHARMACEUTICALS

Fungal Genetics Newsletter
See: BIOLOGY

Gathered View, The
See: DISABILITY

Gene Therapy Newsletter

Publishing Co: Derwent Information Ltd, 1420 Spring Hill Road, Suite 525, Maclean, VA 22102
Tel # (703) 790-0400 Fax # (703) 790-1426
Personnel: Mng. Editor-Rumana Huq, Production Mgr.-Karen Munasinghe, Art Dir.-Christy Campbell, Mktg. Dir.-Fiona Racher
Editorial Description: Information included scanned from 1,00 biomedical journals and patents from 40 patent issuing authorities. Provides scientists & Sr. Managers in biotech & pharmaceutical industries with monthly R & D updates in gene therapy area.
General Info: Monthly, 25 pages, ISSN: 1354-8662, Color-cover, Matte, Saddle-stitched
Subscriptions: Indv. $500

GeneWATCH   *Association*

Publishing Co: Council for Responsible Genetics, 5 Upland Rd # 3, Cambridge, MA 02140-2717; Title Tel # (617) 868-0870 Title Fax # (617) 491-5344
Personnel: Mng. Editor-Judith Glaubman
Editorial Description: Analyzes the political, ethical, and social impact of new biotechnologies and genetic engineering both in the U.S. and abroad. Feature articles, news notes, and reviews cover bioweapons, genetic discrimination, novel organisms in the environment, and more.
General Info: Yr. Est. 1984, Bi-monthly, Sheetfed press, 16 pages, ISSN: 0740-9737, Ind/Abs/Online: ALT. API., No Color, Saddle-stitched
Subscriptions: Indv. $24, Inst. $30, Can. $27, For. $30
Circulation: Total-1,100
List Rental: Rents Lists

Genetic Engineering Letter   *Consumer*

Publishing Co: Environews, Inc., 408 Neale Ct, Silver Spring, MD 20901-4436
Personnel: Editor-Gershon Fishbein
Editorial Description: News and analysis of recombinant DNA, etc., emphasis on public policy aspects.
General Info: Yr. Est. 1981, Semi-monthly, Trim Size-8½ x 11, Offset press, 4 pages, ISSN: 0276-1882, No Color, Newsprint
Subscriptions: Indv. $295, Can. $295, For. $295

Genetic Technology News   *Business*

Publishing Co: Technical Insights, Inc., PO Box 1304, Fort Lee, NJ 07024-9967; Title Tel # (201) 568-4744 Title Fax # (201) 568-8247
Personnel: Publisher-Kenneth A. Kovaly, Editor-Albert S. Hester, Circ. Mgr.-Barbara Chaffee, Mktg. Dir.-Lyn Schmidt
Editorial Description: Details all significant technical & business developments in every area of genetic engineering & related technologies, analyzing their applications in the chemical, pharmaceutical, food, processing, & energy industries as well as in agriculture, animal breeding & medicine. Three special supplements: GTN Patent Update, GTN Strategic Partners Report, & Strategic Forecast.
General Info: Yr. Est. 1986, Monthly, Trim Size-8½ x 11, Sheetfed press, 18 pages, ISSN: 0272-9032, 2 Color, Matte, Other
Subscriptions: Indv. $650, For. $710
List Rental: Actives: $180/M, Expires: $235/M
Printing Co: Allied Lettercraft, 307 W. 36th St., New York, NY 10018 Tel # (212) 279-4800

Genetically Speaking

Publishing Co: Natl. Foundation for Jewish Genetic Diseases, Inc., 250 Park Ave Ste 1000, New York, NY 10177-1099; Title Tel # (212) 682-5550
Personnel: Editor-Joan Samsen
Editorial Description: Info on the 7 known Jewish diseases.
General Info: Yr. Est. 1975, Semi-annually
Circulation: Total-15,000

Genetics in Practice

Publishing Co: March of Dimes Birth Defects Foundation, 1275 Mamaroneck Ave., Professional Svcs. Dept., White Plains, NY 10605-5298; Title Tel # (914) 997-4527
Personnel: Publisher-Beverly Raff, Editor-Dr. Kenneth Garver, Production Mgr.-Suzanne Golia
Editorial Description: Provides the clinical practitioner & social worker with concise abstracts of the newest developments in clinical genetics including advances in prenatal testing & updated findings on syndromes.
General Info: Yr. Est. 1983, Quarterly, Trim Size-8½ x 11, Offset press, 7 pages, 2 Color, Newsprint
Subscriptions: Indv. $5
List Rental: Rents Lists
Printing Co: Science Press, 300 W Chestnut St, Ephrata, PA 17522-2002 Tel # (717) 738-9300, Fax # (717) 738-9413

Genetics Society of Canada
Bulletin   *Consumer*

Publishing Co: National Research Council of Canada, Research Journals, 1200 Montreal Rd., Bldg. M-55, Ottawa, ON K1A 0R6 Canada Tel # (613) 993-9084 Fax # (613) 952-7656; Title Tel # (613) 232-9459
Personnel: Editor-E. Nestmann
Editorial Description: Genetics research, news for Genetics Society of Canada.
General Info: Yr. Est. 1959, Quarterly, Trim Size-6½ x 10, ISSN: 0316-4357, No Color
Subscriptions: $3/copy
Circulation: Total-700

HANDI Information Center Update
See: HEALTH

HANDI Quarterly
See: HEALTH

Lotus Newsletter   *Consumer*

Publishing Co: Univ. of Missouri, P. R. Beuselinck, 207 Waters, Columbia, MO 65211-0001; Title Tel # (314) 882-2405
Editorial Description: Research on the forage legume Birdsfoot Trefoil and relatives.
General Info: Yr. Est. 1970, Annually, Trim Size-8½ x 11, Mimeo press, 40 pages, ISSN: 0316-0106, Ind/Abs/Online: Plant.Breed.Abstr., No Color
Circulation: Total-175

Maize Genetics
Cooperation News Letter

Publishing Co: Univ. of Missouri, Curtis Hall, Columbia, MO 65211-0001; Title Tel # (314) 882-2768
Personnel: Editor-Edward H. Coe, Jr.
Editorial Description: Reports research on corn maize genetics from cooperators throughout the world.
General Info: Yr. Est. 1932, Annually, Trim Size-8½ x 11, Offset press, 180 pages, No Color
Subscriptions: Indv. $10
Circulation: Total-800

R & D Innovator
See: TELECOMMUNICATIONS

Seiche, The
See: ENVIRONMENT & ECOLOGY

VHL Family Forum
See: MEDICINE

VHL News   *Association*

Publishing Co: VHL Foundation, PO Box 733, Toms River, NJ 08754-0733; Title Tel # (908) 244-7635
Editorial Description: Newsletter of the Van Hippel-Lindau Syndrome Foundation. Provides information on current research on the disease, as well as resoure information for affected families
General Info: 3x/yr.

GEOGRAPHY

AAG Newsletter   *Association*   CPM: $109

Publishing Co: Association of American Geographers, 1710 16th St NW, Washington, DC 20009-3104; Title Tel # (202) 234-1450 Title Fax # (202) 234-2744
Personnel: Editor-Linda Bradshaw
Editorial Description: Announcements, meetings, minutes of association council, short articles, publications available, important items of association business.
General Info: Yr. Est. 1967, Monthly, Trim Size-8½ x 11, Offset press, 24 pages, ISSN: 0275-3995, 2 Color, Saddle-stitched
Subscriptions: Indv. $12, Free With Membership
Circulation: Total-7,310
Advertising: $800.
List Rental: Actives: $100/M
Printing Co: Automated Graphic Systems, 4590 Graphics Drive, White Plains, MD 20695 Tel # (301) 843-1800, Fax # (301) 843-6339

AALS Newsletter
See: AGRICULTURE

ALS News
See: ENGINEERING, CIVIL

Association of Canadian Map Libraries & Archives Bulletin
See: LIBRARY

CLAG Communication   *Association*

Publishing Co: Conference of Latin Americanist Geographers, P.O. Box 7819, Univ. of Texas Press, Austin, TX 78713; Title Tel # (512) 471-5116
Personnel: Editor-Gregory Knapp
Editorial Description: Reports on conference programs & activities, study programs in Latin America, grants available, & other Latin American assns., conferences & workshops.
General Info: Yr. Est. 1971, Quarterly, Sheetfed press, 16 pages, 2 Color, Newsprint, Saddle-stitched
Subscriptions: Indv. $25, Inst. $25
Acquistions: Publication Sold
Circulation: (17% controlled), Total-560, Subscriptions-400, International-60

Cartomania   *Association*   CPM: $300

Publishing Co: Assn. of Map Memorabilia, c/o Siegfried Feller, 8 Amherst Rd., Pelham, MA 01002-9746; Title Tel # (413) 253-3115
Personnel: Publisher, Editor-Siegfried Feller
Editorial Description: Information on map collecting & map memorabilia.
General Info: Yr. Est. 1986, Semi-annually, Trim Size-8½ x 11, 24 pages, ISSN: 0894-2595
Subscriptions: Indv. $14, Inst. $14, Can. $14, For. $18, $8/copy
Circulation: Total-200
Advertising: $60. Accepts Inserts.

Disaster Research
See: ENVIRONMENT & ECOLOGY

Expedition News
See: OUTDOORS

G-Map, the Geographic Information, Mapping & Publishing Newsletter   *Business*

Publishing Co: Phillips Business Information, Inc., 1201 Seven Locks Rd., Ste 300, Potomac, MD 20854-2958 Tel # (301) 340-1520 Fax # (301) 424-4297; Title Tel # (301) 340-2100
Editorial Description: Covers technology, market, product & user trends in electronic navigation, digital positioning, digital mapping, geographic information systems & spatial databases. Looks at market size & growth, new developments in vehicle positioning & location systems software & databases for GIS.
General Info: Yr. Est. 1989, Monthly, Sheetfed press, 2 Color, Matte
Subscriptions: Indv. $425, Can. $425, For. $465, $35/copy
List Rental: Rents Lists

GIS Law   *Association*

Publishing Co: GIS Law and Policy Institute, 370-R Neff Ave., Harrisonburg, VA 22801 Tel # (540) 434-3307 Fax # (540) 434-3143
Personnel: Co-Editor-H. Bishop Dansby, Co-Editor-Louis Milrad, Co-Editor-Harlan Onsrud
Editorial Description: Examines legal and public policy issues surrounding the use of geographic information systems.
General Info: Yr. Est. 1993, Quarterly, ISSN: 1064-2027
Subscriptions: Indv. $98

Geography Education Program UPDATE

Publishing Co: National Geographic Society, 1145 17th St NW, Washington, DC 20036-4701; Title Tel # (202) 857-7000
Personnel: Editor-Roger Hirschland, Editorial Asst.-Emmy Scammahorn, Production Mgr.-George Zeller, Art Dir.-Cynthia Scudder
Editorial Description: Keeps educators and decision-makers informed about the Geography Education Program's activities and accomplishments. Each issue also contains geography lesson plans for classroom use.
General Info: Yr. Est. 1985, 3x/yr., Trim Size-$8\frac{1}{2}$ x $10\frac{7}{8}$, Sheetfed press, 20 pages, 2 Color, Matte, Saddle-stitched
Circulation: Total-80,000

Historical Geography

Publishing Co: California State Univ. Dept. of Geography, Publications, Northridge, CA 91330-0001; Title Tel # (818) 885-3532
Personnel: Editor-Robert Newcomb
General Info: Yr. Est. 1971, Letrpr. press, 40 pages, No Color, Saddle-stitched
Subscriptions: Indv. $5, Inst. $8, Can. $5, For. $8

History of Geography Newsletter   *Consumer, Association*

Publishing Co: Sponsor-Southern Connecticut State Univ., Association of American Geographers, 1710 16th St NW, Washington, DC 20009-3104 Tel # (202) 234-1450 Fax # (202) 234-2744; Title Tel # (203) 397-4355
Personnel: Editor, Circ. Mgr.-Geoffrey Martin
Editorial Description: Specialist literature on the history & philosophy of geography. . . emphasis on North America.
General Info: Yr. Est. 1981, Annually
Subscriptions: Indv. $5
Circulation: Total-200
Advertising: Inquire for rates.

Information North
See: SCIENCE

Mapline   *Association*

Publishing Co: Newberry Library, Renaissance Center, 60 W. Walton St., Chicago, IL 60610-3380 Tel # (312) 255-3514; Title Tel # (312) 943-9090
Personnel: Editor-James Akerman
Editorial Description: News of cartographic developments; focus on history of cartography.
General Info: Yr. Est. 1976, Quarterly, Trim Size-$8\frac{1}{2}$ x 11, Sheetfed press, 12 pages, ISSN: 0196-0881, No Color
Subscriptions: Indv. $8, Can. $8, For. $10, $2/copy
Circulation: Total-700
List Rental: Actives: $30/M

Maps on File   *Consumer*

Publishing Co: Facts on File, Inc., 11 Penn Plaza, New York, NY 10001-2006 Tel # (212) 967-8800 Parent Co.-Infobase Holdings Inc., New York; Title Tel # (212) 683-2244 Title Fax # (800) 678-3633
Editorial Description: About 400 maps, indexed, designed for photocopying.
General Info: Annually, Looseleaf
Subscriptions: Indv. $175, Inst. $175

Natural Hazards Observer
See: ENVIRONMENT & ECOLOGY

Northbound
See: FORESTRY

Sand Paper, The
See: HOBBY

Texas, Natural Resources Information System, Newsletter
See: ENVIRONMENT & ECOLOGY

GEOLOGY

AEG News   *Association*

Publishing Co: Association of Engineering Geologists, 323 Boston Post Road, Suite 2D, Sudbury, MA 01776-3022 Tel # (409) 845-9682 Fax # (508) 443-2948; Title Tel # (508) 443-4639
Personnel: Editor-Edwin Blackey
Editorial Description: Contains reports by president & committees, association, technical & section news.
General Info: Yr. Est. 1957, Quarterly, 40 pages, ISSN: 0514-9142, 1% ads, Color
Circulation: Total-3,800
Advertising: Inquire for rates.
List Rental: Rents Lists

AIH Bulletin   *Business, Association*

Publishing Co: American Institute of Hydrology, 2499 Race St. Ste. 135, St. Paul, MN 55113 Tel # (612) 484-8169 Fax # (612) 484-8357; Title Tel # (612) 379-1030 Title Fax # (612) 379-0169
Personnel: Publisher, Circ. Mgr., Promotion Dir.-Helen Klose
Editorial Description: Registers & certifies hydrologists & hydrogeologists. Provides educational & continuing education services.
General Info: Yr. Est. 1981, Quarterly, Trim Size-11 x 17, Sheetfed press, 6 pages, 1% ads, 2 Color, Coated
Subscriptions: Indv. $16, Inst. $20, Can. $20, For. $24, $5/copy
Acquistions: Publication Bought, Publication Sold
Circulation: Total-1,100
Advertising: Inquire for rates. Accepts Inserts.
List Rental: Actives: 1,100, $120/M

American Assn. of Stratigraphic Palynologists-Newsletter   *Association*

Publishing Co: American Assn. of Stratigraphic Palynologists, Arco Alaska Inc., 700 G St., Anchorage, AK 99501 Tel # (907) 265-1135 Fax # (907) 265-1515; Title Fax # (416) 978-3938
Personnel: Editor-Martin Head, Mng. Editor-David Goodman
Editorial Description: Contains national & international news of interest to micropaleontologists & paleobotonists.
General Info: Yr. Est. 1967, Quarterly, Trim Size-$8\frac{1}{2}$ x 11, Sheetfed press, 20 pages, ISSN: 0732-6041, No Color, Newsprint
Subscriptions: Indv. $20, Inst. $30
Circulation: Total-1,100

American Paleontologist   *Association*   CPM: $191

Publishing Co: Paleontological Research Institution, 1259 Trumansburg Rd, Ithaca, NY 14850-1313; Title Tel # (607) 273-6623
Personnel: Editor-Warren Allmon
Editorial Description: News and features about earth history, geology, life on earth.
General Info: (Formerly Paleontological Research Institution-Newsletter; PS-PSI News), Yr. Est. 1979, Quarterly, Trim Size-$8\frac{1}{2}$ x 11, 12 pages, ISSN: 1066-8772, 8% ads
Subscriptions: Indv. $20, Inst. $20, $4/copy
Circulation: Total-1,150
Advertising: $220.
List Rental: Actives: 1,150
Printing Co: Fine Line Printing, 409 1/2 W State St, Ithaca, NY 14850-5219 Tel # (607) 272-1177

American Shore & Beach Preservation Assn. -Newsletter
See: ENVIRONMENT & ECOLOGY

Arizona Geology   *Consumer, Scholarly*

Publishing Co: Arizona Geological Survey, 416 W Congress St., #100, Tucson, AZ 85701-1315; Title Tel # (520) 770-3500
Editorial Description: Summaries of survey research, announcements of meetings, and descriptions of new publications.
General Info: (Formerly Fieldnotes), Yr. Est. 1971, Quarterly, Trim Size-$8\frac{1}{2}$ x 11, Offset press, 4 pages, ISSN: 1045-4802, Color, Coated
Subscriptions: Free In Designated Area
Printing Co: Alpha Graphics, 812 N Tyndall Ave, Tucson, AZ 85719-4829 Tel # (602) 882-0410

Bulletin of the Global Volcanism Network
See: GEOPHYSICS

C-CORE News
See: OCEANOGRAPHY

CSPG Reservoir   *Consumer*

Publishing Co: Canada Society of Petroleum Geologists, 505, 206-7 Ave. SW, Calgary, AB T2P 0W7 Canada; Title Tel # (403) 264-5610
Personnel: Publisher-Hans Speelman, Editor-Lisa Henri Kirkland, Circ. Mgr.-Sheila Dylke, Adv. Dir.-Peter Harrington
General Info: Yr. Est. 1972, Monthly, 20 pages, 2% ads, No Color
Circulation: Total-4,400
Advertising: Inquire for rates.

Coastal Research
See: SCIENCE

Contact, The
Association **CPM: $133**

Publishing Co: Wyoming Geological Association, PO Box 545, Casper, WY 82602-0545; Title Tel # (307) 237-0027
Editorial Description: Contains abstracts of weekly luncheon talks, calendar of events, regional geology news, job notices, scholarship news.
General Info: Monthly, Trim Size-8½ x 11, Offset press, 14 pages, No Color
Subscriptions: Indv. $18, Free With Membership
Circulation: Total-750
Advertising: $100.
Printing Co: Best Impressions, 128 S Center St, Casper, WY 82601-2522 Tel # (307) 235-8823

Empire State Geogram-
Research Issue
Business

Publishing Co: New York State Museum, Cultural Education Center Rm., 3136, Albany, NY 12230-0001; Title Tel # (518) 486-2020
Personnel: Editor-William Rogers
Editorial Description: Canvas of current research -- NY Geology; articles of regional scope; theoretical and applied geology; mineral industry information.
General Info: (Formerly Empire State Geogram), Yr. Est. 1962, Semi-annually, Trim Size-8½ x 11, Offset press, 32 pages, ISSN: 0013-676X, No Color
Subscriptions: Free
Circulation: Total-2,500

GIS Newsletter
Association

Publishing Co: Geoscience Information Society, 4220 King St, Alexandria, VA 22302-1507; Title Tel # (812) 855-7170 Title Fax # (812) 855-6614
General Info: Bi-monthly, ISSN: 0046-5801
Subscriptions: Indv. $40, Inst. $40, Can. $40, For. $45, $10/copy
Circulation: Total-300

Gaea
Association **CPM: $237**

Publishing Co: Sponsor-Assoc. for Women Geoscientist, Association for Women Geoscientists, 4779 126th St. N., St. Paul, MN 55110-5910; Title Tel # (612) 426-3316 Title Fax # (612) 426-5449
Personnel: Editor-Sarah Stoll, Adv. Dir.-Virginia Sand
Editorial Description: Covers issues affecting women in the geosciences.
General Info: Yr. Est. 1981, Bi-monthly, Trim Size-8½ x 11, Offset press, 16 pages, 1% ads, 2 Color, Recycled, Saddle-stitched
Subscriptions: Indv. $50, Inst. $100, Can. $55, For. $60, $7/copy
Circulation: Total-1,347
Advertising: $320. Accepts Inserts.
List Rental: Actives: 1,000, Expires: 400

Geo-Monitor
Business, Scholarly

Publishing Co: Geo-Monitor, 65 Washington St # 400, Santa Clara, CA 95050-6138; Title Tel # (408) 749-6770
Personnel: Publisher, Editor-Vincent T. Migliore
Editorial Description: Dedicated to earthquake prediction, amateur geophysical monitoring and earth mysteries.
General Info: Yr. Est. 1991, Monthly, Trim Size-8½ x 11, 10 pages, ISSN: 1057-4492, No Color, Matte
Subscriptions: Indv. $15, Inst. $15, Can. $15, For. $30, $2/copy
Circulation: Total-400
Advertising: Accepts Inserts.

Geolog
Association **CPM: $24**

Publishing Co: Sponsor-Geological Assn. of Canada, Geological Assn. of Canada, Dept. of Earth Sciences, Dept.of Earth Sciences, Memorial University of NF, St. John's, NF A1B 3X5 Canada; Title Tel # (709) 737-7660 Title Fax # (709) 737-2532
Personnel: Editor, Adv. Dir.-Paul Metcalfe
General Info: Yr. Est. 1970, Quarterly, Trim Size-5½ x 8⅜, Offset press, 48 pages, ISSN: 0227-3713, 5% ads, Color-cover, Matte, Saddle-stitched
Subscriptions: Indv. $15, Inst. $150, Can. $15, For. $15, $3/copy
Circulation: Total-3,500
Advertising: $85. Accepts Inserts.
Printing Co: Love Printing Services Ltd., 5972 Hazeldean Rd., Stittsville, ON K2S 1B9 Canada Tel # (613) 831-5683

Geological Newsletter
Association

Publishing Co: Geological Society of Oregon Country, PO Box 907, Portland, OR 97207-0907; Title Tel # (503) 221-0757
Personnel: Editor-Donald Barr, Circ. Mgr.-Rosemary Kenney
Editorial Description: Articles on earth sciences, reports of lectures, meeting notices, notices of field trips, and news of members.
General Info: Yr. Est. 1935, Monthly, Trim Size-8½ x 11, Offset press, 6 pages, ISSN: 0270-5451, No Color, Other
Subscriptions: Indv. $10, Inst. $13, Can. $13, For. $13, $1/copy

Gulf of Mexico Newsletter
See: ENERGY

ISEM Newsletter

Publishing Co: Institute for the Study of Earth & Moon, Southern Methodist Univ. Box, 274, Dallas, TX 75275-0001; Title Tel # (214) 692-2425
Personnel: Editor-Jane Albritton
General Info: Yr. Est. 1972, Semi-annually, 6 pages
Circulation: Total-1,200

International Oil News
See: PETROLEUM & NATURAL GAS

LRIS Newsletter
See: ENVIRONMENT & ECOLOGY

Market: Africa/Mid-East
Business

Publishing Co: W-Two Publications, 202 The Commons, #401, Ithaca, NY 14850-5578; Title Tel # (607) 277-0934 Title Fax # (607) 277-0935
Editorial Description: Explores demographics and lifestyles of consumers in africa and the mid-east and the opportunities they create for business.
General Info: Yr. Est. 1995, Monthly, ISSN: 1083-5512
Subscriptions: Inst. $279, $32/copy
Advertising: Accepts Inserts.

Meteor News
See: SCIENCE

NCA Cave Talk
Association

Publishing Co: National Caves Association, 4138 Dark Hollow Road, McMinnville, TN 37110-8629 Fax # (615) 668-3988; Title Tel # (615) 668-3925 Title Fax # (615) 668-8629
Personnel: Editor-Barbara Munson
Editorial Description: Newsletter to keep membership informed about current trends & activities.
General Info: Yr. Est. 1973, Bi-monthly, Trim Size-8½ x 11, Desktop press, 4 pages, No Color, Other
Subscriptions: Free With Membership
Circulation: Total-125

NDGS Newsletter

Publishing Co: Geological Survey, Univ. Station, Grand Forks, ND 58202; Title Tel # (701) 777-2231
Personnel: Editor-Robert Biek
Editorial Description: Articles of general interest on North Dakota geology.
General Info: Yr. Est. 1974, Semi-annually, Offset press, 25 pages, ISSN: 0889-3594, No Color, Newsprint
Circulation: Total-2,500
Printing Co: Quality Printing, 2306 E Broadway Ave, Bismarck, ND 58501-4932 Tel # (701) 255-3900

Newsletter
Association

Publishing Co: National Cartographic Information Ctr., USGS, 509 National Ctr., Reston, VA 22092-0001; Title Tel # (703) 648-5906
Personnel: Editor-Doris Eazarsky, Circ. Mgr.-MaryJane Chirichella
Editorial Description: Natl. Cartographic Information Center newsletter, Natl. Mapping Div. , U. S. Geological Survey.
General Info: Yr. Est. 1975, Semi-annually, Offset press, 8 pages, ISSN: 0364-7064, No Color
Circulation: Total-3,000

Northbound
See: FORESTRY

Offshore International Newsletter
See: PETROLEUM & NATURAL GAS

Preliminary Determination
of Epicenters
Business, Scholarly

Publishing Co: U.S. Gov't Printing Office, 2100 2nd St. S.W., Washington, DC 20593-0001
General Info: Monthly, 32 pages
Subscriptions: Indv. $14, For. $18

Sand Paper, The
See: HOBBY

Seismograph Report
Association

Publishing Co: West Virginia Univ. School of Journalism, Box 6010, Morgantown, WV 26506-6010 Tel # (304) 293-3505 Fax # (304) 293-3072; Title Tel # (304) 293-5603
Personnel: Editor-R.W. Laird
Editorial Description: Earthquake times, phases, location and depth.
General Info: Yr. Est. 1950, Semi-annually, 25 pages, No Color

Society of Independent
Professional Earth
Scientists, Newsletter
Consumer, Association

Publishing Co: Society of Independent Professional Earth Scientists, 4925 Greenville Ave Ste 170, Dallas, TX 75206-4008; Title Tel # (214) 363-1780
Personnel: Editor, Adv. Dir.-John Silvernail
Editorial Description: News of members, local chapters (11) and Society committee reports.
General Info: Yr. Est. 1964, Quarterly, Trim Size-8½ x 11, 20 pages, No Color, Coated
Circulation: Total-1,100

Subsurface
Business

Publishing Co: Budinger & Assoc., 3820 E Broadway Ave, Spokane, WA 99202-4525; Title Tel # (509) 535-8841 Title Fax # (509) 535-9589
Personnel: Publisher, Editor, Promotion Dir.-Jo Ann Bender
General Info: Yr. Est. 1985, Quarterly, Trim Size-8½ x 11, Desktop press, 3 pages, 2 Color, Newsprint
Subscriptions: Indv. $10
Circulation: (100% controlled)

Surview   *Consumer*

Publishing Co: Wisconsin Geological & National History Survey, 3817 Mineral Point Rd, Madison, WI 53705-5121; Title Tel # (608) 262-1705 Title Fax # (608) 262-8086
Personnel: Circ. Mgr.-Leona Rane, Editor, Production Mgr.-Mindy James, Art Dir.-Susan Hunt
Editorial Description: Provides brief coverage of Wisconsin Geological Survey activities & programs.
General Info: Yr. Est. 1980, Semi-annually, Trim Size-8½ x 11, Sheetfed press, 8 pages, ISSN: 0733-8813, No Color, Coated
Subscriptions: Free
Circulation: Total-3,500

Underground Storage Tank News
See: PETROLEUM & NATURAL GAS

Wilson Museum Bulletin
See: MUSEUM PUBLICATIONS

Wyoming Geological Association Oil & Gas Fields Guide Book/Symposium
See: ENERGY

GEOPHYSICS

Asynchronous Transfer Mode (ATM) Newsletter   *Business*

Publishing Co: Information Gatekeepers, Inc., 214 Harvard Ave., Boston, MA 02134-4651 Fax # (617) 782-8562; Title Tel # (617) 232-3111 Title Fax # (617) 734-0562
Editorial Description: Provides comprehensive coverage of Asynchronous Transfer Mode (ATM) technology, markets and applications worldwide. One of the most exciting new technologies for local, metropolitan and long distance networks.
General Info: Monthly, ISSN: 1067-5221
Subscriptions: Indv. $575, Can. $575, For. $625, $50/copy
Advertising: Accepts Inserts.
List Rental: Rents Lists

Bulletin of the Global Volcanism Network   *Association*

Publishing Co: Global Volcanism Network, Natl. Museum Of Nat. History, Mail Stop 129, Washington, DC 20560-0001; Title Tel # (202) 357-1511 Title Fax # (202) 357-2476
Editorial Description: Covers current volcanic activity and major earthquakes.
General Info: (Formerly Scientific Events Alert Network Bulletin), Yr. Est. 1975, Monthly, ISSN: 1050-4818
Subscriptions: Indv. $18, For. $28

Bulletin of the Seismographic Stations   *Consumer*

Publishing Co: Univ. of California Earth Sciences Dept., Rm. 475, Earth Sci Bldg., Berkeley, CA 94720-0001; Title Tel # (415) 642-3977
Personnel: Editor-Robert Uhrhammer
Editorial Description: Northern California earthquake listing plus phase readings for worldwide earthquakes.
General Info: Yr. Est. 1910, Annually, Mimeo press, 80 pages, ISSN: 0041-946X, No Color, Newsprint
Subscriptions: $10/copy
Circulation: Total-435
Printing Co: University of California Printing, 2120 Oxford St. Univ. Of, California, Berkeley, CA 94720-7340

C-CORE News
See: OCEANOGRAPHY

Consortium for Continental Reflection Profiling-Newsletter   *Business*

Publishing Co: Consortium for Continental Reflection Profiling, Cornell Univ., Dept. of Geological Studies, Ithaca, NY 14850-3995; Title Tel # (607) 255-3474 Title Fax # (607) 254-4780
Personnel: Editor-Larry Brown
General Info: Yr. Est. 1976, 6 pages
Circulation: Total-350

Empire State Geogram-Research Issue
See: GEOLOGY

Gaea
See: GEOLOGY

Geo-Monitor
See: GEOLOGY

NASA STI Bulletin
See: AERONAUTICS/ASTRONAUTICS

Recorder   *Association*

Publishing Co: Canadian Society of Exploration Geophysicists, 206 7th Ave. S.W., Rm. 406, Calgary, AB T2P 0W7 Canada Fax # (403) 262-7383; Title Tel # (403) 262-0015
Personnel: Editor-Barbara Young, Adv. Dir.-Dave Siegfried
Editorial Description: Publication that promotes the science of geophysics, especially as it applies to exploration, and to promote fellowship and co-operation among those persons interested in geophysical prospecting.
General Info: 10x/yr.
Subscriptions: Free With Membership
Advertising: Inquire for rates.

World Geophysical News   *Business*

Publishing Co: Petroleum Information Corp., PO Box 2612, Denver, CO 80201-2612 Tel # (303) 740-7100
Editorial Description: Comprehensive geophysical activity report offering detailed crew location, statistical summaries, and industry news.
General Info: Semi-monthly
Subscriptions: Indv. $252, For. $342

GIFTS, GAMES, TOYS

Consumer Electronics Edge
See: ELECTRIC & ELECTRONIC EQUIPMENT

Craft Related Newsletters, Periodicals & Publications
See: HOBBY

Director
See: HOBBY

Dollmasters, The
See: ANTIQUES & ART GOODS

G.I. Joe Collectors Club
See: COLLECTIBLES

Game Researcher's Notes
See: COLLECTIBLES

Game Times
See: COLLECTIBLES

Gift Basket Idea Newsletter   *Consumer*

Publishing Co: Prosperity & Profits Unlimited, PO Box 416, Denver, CO 80201-0416; Title Tel # (303) 575-5676
Personnel: Editor-A.C. Doyle
Editorial Description: Features ideas for unique gift baskets.
General Info: Yr. Est. 1991, Every two years, Trim Size-8½ x 11, 6 pages, No Color
Subscriptions: Indv. $5, Inst. $5, Can. $12, For. $15, $5/copy
Circulation: Total-2,400

Giftbeat
See: DEPARTMENT STORE & RETAIL

GoodNewsletter
See: COLLECTIBLES

Illustratotor's Swap incl JW Anglund Collectors News
See: CHILDREN

International Gamblers' Club Newsletter
See: GAMBLING

International Virtual Reality Association
See: ENTERTAINMENT

Kosher Kettle
See: ETHNIC

Living in Style
See: FURNITURE & HOME FURNISHINGS

Manhattan Chess Club News
See: SPORTS & SPORTING GOODS

Marble Mart Newsletter
See: COLLECTIBLES

Miller's Market Report

Publishing Co: Miller's, P.O. Box 8722, Spokane, WA 99203-0722; Title Fax # (509) 455-6115
Personnel: Publisher, Editor-Barbara Miller, Mag. Ed.-Dan Miller, Photo Ed.-Alan Bisson, Art Dir.-Mauri Pullinen
Editorial Description: Dedicated to bringing dealers and collectors the news and information they need to buy and sell Barie dolls profitably.
General Info: Monthly, Trim Size-11½ x 16, 8 pages, 4 Color, Newsprint
Subscriptions: Indv. $25, Can. $28, For. $35

The Neo-Geo Gamer

Publishing Co: Andrew Duba, 6307 Alexander Drive, St. Louis, MO 63105
Editorial Description: The hottest gaming system today. Full of extensive reviews and tips for the games and even includes some photos taken off the screens.
General Info: Trim Size-8.5 x 11, 17 pages
Subscriptions: Indv. $2

Oz Collector, The
See: HOBBY

Party Design Quarterly
See: ENTERTAINMENT

Potpourri Simple & Easy Update

Publishing Co: Prosperity & Profits Unlimited, PO Box 416, Denver, CO 80201-0416; Title Tel # (303) 575-5676
Personnel: Publisher-A. Doyle
Editorial Description: Potpourri recipes that are unusual and easy to make.
General Info: Yr. Est. 1990, Every two years, Trim Size-8½ x 11
Subscriptions: Indv. $5, Inst. $5, Can. $7, For. $9, $5/copy
Circulation: Total-1,500

Practical Gift Planner, The *Business*

Publishing Co: Charitable Gift Planning News, 41 Sutter St Ste 1129, San Francisco, CA 94104-4903; Title Tel # (214) 978-3326 Title Fax # (214) 978-3395
General Info: Yr. Est. 1992, Bi-monthly
Subscriptions: Indv. $72

Scenterpiece Update *Consumer*

Publishing Co: Prosperity & Profits Unlimited, PO Box 416, Denver, CO 80201-0416; Title Tel # (303) 575-5676
Personnel: Editor-A.C. Doyle
Editorial Description: Features recipes for potpourri.
General Info: Yr. Est. 1990, Annually, Trim Size-8½ x 11, 4 pages, No Color
Subscriptions: Indv. $5, Inst. $5, Can. $9, For. $9, $5/copy
Circulation: Total-2,500

Scrabble News *Consumer, Association*

Publishing Co: National Scrabble Association, PO Box 700, Greenport, NY 11944-0700; Title Tel # (516) 477-0033 Title Fax # (516) 477-0294
Personnel: Publisher-John Williams, Editor-Joe Edley, Adv. Dir.-Jane Willams
Editorial Description: Information and news for Scrabble players.
General Info: 8x/yr.
Subscriptions: Indv. $18, Can. $20, For. $25, Free With Membership
Circulation: Total-9,000
Advertising: Inquire for rates.

Sharing Memories
See: HOBBY

Sim-U-Letter *Consumer*

Publishing Co: Maxis, 2 Theatre Sq Ste 230, Orinda, CA 94563-3346 Tel # (510) 254-9700
Personnel: Editor in Chief-Sally Vandershaf, Production Dir.-Vera Jaye
Editorial Description: Newsletter on Maxis' line of electronic software games.
General Info: Quarterly, Trim Size-8½ x 11, 6 pages, 4 Color, Coated
Subscriptions: Free To Qualified Recipient

SimAntics *Consumer*

Publishing Co: Maxis, 2 Theatre Sq Ste 230, Orinda, CA 94563-3346 Tel # (510) 254-9700
Editorial Description: Newsletter for kids who play Maxis software games.
General Info: Yr. Est. 1994, Quarterly, Trim Size-8½ x 11, 6 pages, 4 Color, Coated

Snow Biz
See: ANTIQUES & ART GOODS

Story Rhyme Word Mapping
See: CROSS-WORD PUZZLES

Strategist *Association, Consumer*

Publishing Co: Strategy Gaming Society, 87 Park Ave Apt 6, Worcester, MA 01605-3929; Title Tel # (508) 831-5339
Personnel: Editor-Jack Ellis
Editorial Description: For those who are interested in board and role playing games.
General Info: Yr. Est. 1973, Monthly, Trim Size-8½ x 11, Offset press, 10 pages, No Color
Subscriptions: Indv. $12, Inst. $12, Can. $12, $1/copy
Circulation: Total-150

Table Top Train News
See: HOBBY

Today's Hospital Gift
Shop Business *Business* **CPM: $93**

Publishing Co: Nason & Associates, PO Box 8204, Asheville, NC 28814-8204 Tel # (704) 258-1323; Title Tel # (704) 258-1341 Title Fax # (704) 253-3726
Personnel: Publisher-Marilyn Nason, Production Dir.-Michelle Ramsey, Mktg. Dir.-Jack Mossman
Editorial Description: Monthly newsletter bringing together hospital gift shop managers to help them maximize their shop operations and profits.
General Info: Yr. Est. 1974, Bi-monthly, Trim Size-8½ x 11, Offset press, ISSN: 1084-6352
Subscriptions: Indv. $25, Can. $40, For. $50, $2/copy
Circulation: Total-8,000, Readership-20,000
Advertising: $750. Accepts Inserts.
List Rental: Actives: 7,500, $90/M

Traders' Horn *Consumer*

Publishing Co: Traders' Horn, 1903 Schoettler Valley Dr., Chesterfield, MO 63017-5203; Title Tel # (314) 532-3871
Personnel: Circ. Mgr.-Renee Atkinson, Production Mgr.-Erin Atkinson, Adv. Dir.-J. F. Atkinson, Publisher, Editor, Promotion Dir.-J.F. Atkinson
Editorial Description: Buy, sell and swap lists for collectors of die cast, promotional and plastic kit automotive models.
General Info: Yr. Est. 1971, Bi-monthly, Trim Size-8½ x 14, Offset press, 12 pages, 91% ads, No Color, Matte, Saddle-stitched
Subscriptions: Indv. $12, Inst. $12, Can. $13, For. $18, $2/copy
Circulation: Total-1,000, Readership-1,000
Advertising: Inquire for rates.

Viking Import House, Inc.
See: COLLECTIBLES

Working Wine Guide, The
See: BEVERAGES - BREWING

Yo-Yo Times *Consumer* **CPM: $750**

Publishing Co: Creative Communications, Inc., Box 1519-OX, Herndon, VA 22070-1524; Title Tel # (703) 742-9696
Personnel: Publisher, Editor-Stuart Crump, Jr., Circ. Mgr.-Margaret Crump
Editorial Description: News from the world of yo-yoing, including new tricks, interviews, new products, and yo-yoing tips.
General Info: Yr. Est. 1988, Quarterly, Trim Size-8½ x 11, Roto. press, 8 pages, ISSN: 0897-7704, 25% ads, No Color, Matte
Subscriptions: Indv. $12, $3/copy
Circulation: Total-500
Advertising: $375. Accepts Inserts.
List Rental: Actives: 500, Expires: 3,000

GLASS, STONE & CLAY

AGSA Newsletter *Association*

Publishing Co: Art Glass Supplies Association Intl., 1100 Brandywine Blvd. #H, PO Box 2188, Zanesville, OH 43701-2188 Tel # (614) 451-4541; Title Tel # (614) 452-4541 Title Fax # (614) 452-2552
Personnel: Circ. Mgr.-Tricia Ritchey, Publisher, Editor, Editorial Page Ed., Feature Ed., Bk. Rev. Ed., Production Mgr., Adv. Dir., Art Dir., Mktg. Dir., Promotion Dir.-Paula Morris
Editorial Description: Information about legislative issues, about members & those involved in the art glass industry. Articles about how to use national art glass promotions, features on running a small business, design & marketing articles. It also features information about the International Art Glass Supplies Trade Show held each June in a different major city in the U.S.A.
General Info: Yr. Est. 1986, Quarterly, Trim Size-8½ x 11, Web press, 16 pages, 2 Color, Matte, Other
Subscriptions: Indv. $12, $2/copy
Circulation: (100% controlled), Total-4,800, Readership-4,800
Advertising: Inquire for rates.

Akro Agate Gem

Publishing Co: Akro Agate Art Assn., PO Box 1524, Salem, NH 03079-1141; Title Tel # (603) 898-4547
General Info: Quarterly

American Carnival Glass News

Publishing Co: American Carnival Glass Assn., Inc., 153 Douglas Dr, Rittman, OH 44270-1329; Title Tel # (216) 927-2496
Personnel: Editor-Joan Anderson
General Info: Yr. Est. 1966, Quarterly
Circulation: Total-1,000

CMP Newsletter
See: METALS & METALWORKING

Cambridge Crystal Ball

Publishing Co: Natl. Cambridge Collectors, Inc., PO Box 416, Cambridge, OH 43725-0416; Title Tel # (614) 432-7823
Personnel: Editor-Phyllis Smith
General Info: Yr. Est. 1973, Monthly, 16 pages
Circulation: Total-1,500

Candlewick Collector Newsletter, The

Publishing Co: Sponsor-National Candlewick Collector's Club, Candlewick Publications, 6534 South Ave., Holland, OH 43528 Tel # (419) 866-6350; Title Tel # (706) 866-6350
Personnel: Feature Ed.-Cliff McCaslin, Circ. Mgr.-Connie Doll, Publisher, Production Mgr.-Ron Doll, Editor, Adv. Dir.-Virginia R. Scott
Editorial Description: Disseminates specific information about Imperial Glass Corp.'s Candlewick pattern, giving information about pieces, prices, look-likes, colors, decorations, sizes, dates, answers collectors' questions & tells about finds. Discusses reproductions.
General Info: Yr. Est. 1976, Quarterly, Trim Size-8½ x 11, Web press, 10 pages, No Color, Coated
Subscriptions: Indv. $7, Can. $8, $1/copy
Circulation: Total-670
Advertising: Inquire for rates.
Printing Co: BQ Printing, 1007 McCord Ave., Holland, OH 43528

Craft News
Business, Association　　CPM: $216

Publishing Co: Ontario Crafts Council, 35 McCaul St., Toronto, ON M5T 1V7 Canada; Title Tel # (416) 977-3551 Title Fax # (416) 977-3552
Personnel: Publisher-Sarah Lupmanis, Editor-Anne McPherson, Mng. Editor-Wendy Jacob, Circ. Mgr.-Emily Otterman, Adv. Dir.-Susan Browne
Editorial Description: Contains a calendar of craft events, business and marketing articles, and features; covers craft marketing, competitions, and award recipients.
General Info: Yr. Est. 1976, Quarterly, Trim Size-11⅜ x 17, Web press, 16 pages, ISSN: 0139-7832, Ind/Abs/Online: Micromedia, 5% ads, No Color, Newsprint
Subscriptions: $2/copy
Circulation: Total-4,600
Advertising: $995.
List Rental: Rents Lists
Printing Co: Weller Publishing Co., 78 Advance Rd., Etobicoke, ON M8Z 2T7 Canada Tel # (416) 233-2123

Diamond Industry Week
See: SCIENCE

Egg Cup Collectors Corner
See: HOBBY

Expanded Shale Clay & Slate Institute- Information Sheets
Business

Publishing Co: Expanded Shale Clay & Slate Institute, 2225 E. Murray Holladay Rd., Suite #102, Salt Lake City, UT 84117-5382; Title Tel # (801) 272-7070 Title Fax # (801) 272-3377
Personnel: Publisher-John Ries, Circ. Mgr.-Claris Powers
Editorial Description: Technical information report on the uses of lightweight expanded shale, clay & slate aggregates in concrete masonry, structural, geotechnical, horticultural and road projects.
General Info: Yr. Est. 1952, Looseleaf
Acquistions: Publication Bought
Circulation: Total-150
Advertising: Accepts Inserts.

Facets of Fostoria

Publishing Co: Fostoria Glass Society of America, PO Box 826, Moundsville, WV 26041-0826; Title Tel # (304) 845-1050
Personnel: Editor-Cliff Bucy
General Info: Bi-monthly
Circulation: Total-800

Fiesta Collector's Quarterly

Publishing Co: Fiesta Collector's Quarterly, PO Box 471, Valley City, OH 44280-0471
Editorial Description: Newsletter all about FIESTA, America's favorite collectible dinnerware since 1936.
General Info: Quarterly
Subscriptions: $2/copy

Glass Reflections
Association

Publishing Co: Flat Glass Marketing Assn., 3310 S.W. Harrison St., Topeka, KS 66611-2252; Title Tel # (913) 266-7013 Title Fax # (913) 266-0272
General Info: Yr. Est. 1949, Monthly

Glass Shards Newsletter

Publishing Co: Natl. Early American Glass Club, PO Box 57, Fishers Hill, VA 22626-0057; Title Tel # (703) 465-8580
Personnel: Editor-Sylvia Applebee Lyon
Editorial Description: Glass seminar(s) News; Official National EArly American glass club newsletter; chapter news; glass calendar lists antique glass shows, museum seminars for collectors, etc.
General Info: Yr. Est. 1985, Semi-annually, Trim Size-8½ x 11, Sheetfed press, 4 pages, Matte
Subscriptions: Indv. $15, Inst. $25
Circulation: Total-1,200

Hall Collector's Club Newsletter

Publishing Co: Hall Collector's Club Newsletter, PO Box 360488, Cleveland, OH 44136
Editorial Description: Contians club news and information on collecting Hall China Teapots & kitchenware, Autumn Leaf, Poppy, Tavern & Crocus patterns.

Heartbeat
Business, Consumer

Publishing Co: Degenhart Paperweight & Glass Museum, 65323 Highland Hills Rd # 186, Cambridge, OH 43725-9657; Title Tel # (614) 432-2626
Editorial Description: Contains articles and information on glassware, especially Degenhart Crystal Art glass, and a schedule of Degenhart Museum events.
General Info: Yr. Est. 1981, Quarterly
Subscriptions: Free With Membership
Circulation: Total-400
Advertising: Inquire for rates.

International Porcelain Artists/Teachers News
See: ART & SCULPTURE

Neon News
See: LIGHTING

Newsletter
Association

Publishing Co: Potters Guild of British Columbia, 1359 Cartwright St., Vancouver, BC V6H 3R7 Canada; Title Tel # (604) 683-9623
Personnel: Editor-Janet Kidnie
Editorial Description: A pub. with function of keeping guild members, informed & in touch throughout British Columbia.
General Info: Yr. Est. 1965, Monthly, Offset press, 8 pages, ISSN: 6319-812X, 12% ads, No Color
Subscriptions: Indv. $20, Inst. $30
Circulation: (71% controlled), Total-350
Advertising: Inquire for rates.

Opaque News
See: ANTIQUES & ART GOODS

Refractory News
Business

Publishing Co: Refractories Institute, The, 500 Wood St Ste 326, Pittsburgh, PA 15222-2414; Title Tel # (412) 281-6787 Title Fax # (412) 281-6881
General Info: Yr. Est. 1980, Monthly
Subscriptions: Indv. $24, $2/copy
Circulation: Total-1,000

SIGMA Newsletter
See: CONSTRUCTION & BUILDING

Slag Runner
Association

Publishing Co: Natl. Slag Assn., 900 Spring St, Silver Spring, MD 20910-4015
Personnel: Publisher-William E. Mattison
Editorial Description: Contains a description of the three types of steel industry blast furnace slag, i.e. air cooled, expanded, and granulated.
General Info: (Formerly Slag Technical Bulletin), Yr. Est. 1978, Bi-monthly, 16 pages, Color

TGA Newsletter
Association　　CPM: $71

Publishing Co: Texas Automotive Dismantlers & Recyclers Assn., 823 Congress Ave. #1300, Austin, TX 78701-2429; Title Tel # (512) 479-0425 Title Fax # (512) 495-4031
Editorial Description: Official publication of the Texas Glass Association.
General Info: Quarterly, Trim Size-8½ x 11, Offset press, 12 pages, 40% ads, No Color, Matte, Saddle-stitched
Circulation: Total-1,400
Advertising: $100.
Printing Co: Austex Printing Co., 501 W 3rd St, Austin, TX 78701-3807 Tel # (512) 476-7581

Thistle
Association

Publishing Co: Pairpoint Cup Plate Collectors of America, Box A2058, New Bedford, MA 02741-2058; Title Tel # (617) 997-1813
Editorial Description: Deals with cup plates, information on background, production and availability.
General Info: Yr. Est. 1976, Quarterly, 8 pages
Subscriptions: Inst. $7
Circulation: (100% controlled), Total-1,500

Tiffin Glassmasters
Consumer, Association

Publishing Co: Tiffin Glass Collectors Club, PO Box 554, Tiffin, OH 44883-0554
Editorial Description: Information about club, old glass factory & workers, and on identification of glass.
General Info: Yr. Est. 1985, Quarterly

Toothpick Bulletin
See: HOBBY

Town Pump
See: HOBBY

GOLF

ACM Monthly
See: PLASTICS

Briefing
Business, Association

Publishing Co: Golf Course Superintendents Assn. of America, 1421 Research Park Dr, Lawrence, KS 66049-3858 Fax # (913) 832-4455; Title Tel # (913) 841-2240 Title Fax # (913) 832-4433
Personnel: Editor-Brad Short, Mng. Editor-Terry Ostmeyer
Editorial Description: Covers Association news & golf course management issues as they relate to regulatory and legislative matters.
General Info: Yr. Est. 1989, Monthly
Circulation: Total-15,000

Canadian Professional Golfers' Assn., Bulletin
Business, Association

Publishing Co: Canadian Professional Golfers' Assn., 13450 Dublin Line, RR #1, Acton, ON L7S 2W7 Canada; Title Tel # (416) 744-2212 Title Fax # (416) 744-2215
Personnel: Publisher, Editor-Dave Colling
General Info: Quarterly, Trim Size-8½ x 11, 12 pages, No Color
Circulation: Total-2,000
Advertising: Inquire for rates.

El Moligan
Business

Publishing Co: Father & Son Publishing, 1959 Loiza St., #912, Santurce, PR 00911-1850; Title Tel # (809) 796-4392 Title Fax # (809) 796-4392
Personnel: Publisher-Pedro Rodriquez
General Info: Yr. Est. 1995, Weekly, Desktop press, 2 Color, Saddle-stitched
Subscriptions: Indv. $25
Circulation: Total-2,000
Advertising: Inquire for rates. Accepts Inserts.

Gary Galyean's Golf Letter
Consumer

Publishing Co: Gary Galyean's Golf Letter, PO Box 3899, Vero Beach, FL 32964; Title Tel # (407) 778-2288
Personnel: Publisher-Gary Galyean
Editorial Description: Covers and reviews international golf resorts.
General Info: Monthly
Subscriptions: Indv. $78

Golf Clubmaker
Business, Association

Publishing Co: Professional Golf Club Repairmen's Assn., 2295 Dan Hogan Dr., Dunedin, FL 34698-2612; Title Tel # (813) 787-6890
Editorial Description: Covers repair and maintenance of golf clubs. Features industry and Association news and developments.
General Info: Quarterly
Circulation: Total-1,000

Golf Collectors Society Bulletin
Consumer, Association

Publishing Co: Golf Collectors Society, 600 E Cathedral Rd Apt G307, Philadelphia, PA 19128-1929; Title Tel # (215) 828-4492
General Info: Yr. Est. 1970, Bi-monthly

Golf Travel: The Guide for Discriminating Golfers

Publishing Co: Travel Guide Inc., PO Box 3485, Charlottesville, VA 22903-0485; Title Tel # (804) 295-1200 Title Fax # (804) 296-0948
Personnel: Publisher-Terence Sieg, Editor-Daniel Friedman, Assoc. Ed.-W. Carter Hoerr, Art Dir.-Barbara Sieg
Editorial Description: Upscale travel/golf opportunities.
General Info: Yr. Est. 1992, Monthly
Subscriptions: Indv. $67

Golf Update Newsletter

Publishing Co: Golf Update Newsletter, 821 Lone Pine Rd., Bloomfield Hills, MI 48302; Title Tel # (810) 647-4669
Personnel: Publisher, Editor-Bob McHenry
Editorial Description: Golf marketing activities.
General Info: Yr. Est. 1994, Trim Size-8½ x 14, 4 pages
Subscriptions: Indv. $24, Free To Qualified Recipient
Circulation: Total-3,000

Golf Writers Association of America Newsletter
See: JOURNALISM

International Golfer
Consumer

Publishing Co: Owenoak International, 3 Parklands Dr., Darien, CT 06830 Fax # (203) 656-1651
Editorial Description: Tours and events centering around golf.
General Info: Trim Size-8½ x 11, 6 pages, 4 Color, Coated

Mini License Plate & Key Chain Tag Newsletter

Publishing Co: Dr. Edward H. Miles, 888 8th Ave., New York, NY 10019-5704; Title Tel # (212) 765-2660
Personnel: Editor-Dr. Edward Miles
Editorial Description: Mini license plate collectors newsletter. Features chauffeurs badges, automobile windshield stickers, paper drivers licenses and registrations, disabled veterans key chains and others auto related items.
General Info: Yr. Est. 1984, Bi-monthly, 30 pages, No Color
Subscriptions: Indv. $10, $2/copy
Circulation: Total-109
Advertising: Inquire for rates. Accepts Inserts.

Newsline
Business, Association

Publishing Co: Golf Course Superintendents Assn. of America, 1421 Research Park Dr, Lawrence, KS 66049-3858 Fax # (913) 832-4455; Title Tel # (913) 841-2240
Personnel: Editor-Carol Hayes
General Info: Monthly, Trim Size-8½ x 11, 4 pages, No Color
Circulation: Total-15,000

On Course
Business

Publishing Co: O.M. Scott & Sons Co., 14111 Scottslawn Rd., Marysville, OH 43041-0001; Title Tel # (513) 644-0011 Title Fax # (513) 644-7679
Editorial Description: Published for professional turf managers at golf courses.
General Info: Semi-annually, Trim Size-8½ x 11, 4 pages, 2 Color, Coated

PGA Tour News
Business, Association

Publishing Co: PGA Tour, 112 TPC Blvd., Ponte Vedra Beach, FL 32082; Title Tel # (904) 285-3700
Personnel: Editor-Dave Lancer
General Info: Yr. Est. 1975, Quarterly, 4 pages
Circulation: Total-4,000

Senior Golf

Publishing Co: Senior Golf of America, 3013 Church St, Myrtle Beach, SC 29577-5820 Tel # (803) 448-1569; Title Tel # (803) 448-1560
General Info: Yr. Est. 1981, Bi-monthly

Southpaw Activities

Publishing Co: Natl. Assn. of Left-Handed Golfers, PO Box 801223, Houston, TX 77280-1223; Title Tel # (713) 464-8683
Personnel: Publisher, Editor-Ken Ahrens
Editorial Description: Lists tournament schedules; Secretary's /Treasurer's results of those tournaments; items for sale, or trade; necrology; letters of appreciation; etc.
General Info: Yr. Est. 1936, 9x/yr., Trim Size-8½ x 11, 8 pages, 2% ads, Color-cover, Newsprint
Subscriptions: $60/copy
Advertising: Inquire for rates. Accepts Inserts.
Printing Co: Cosmo Printing, 10226 Hammerly Blvd, Houston, TX 77043-2196 Tel # (713) 932-7503

GOVERNMENT

14-Point Program to Reform and Restructure the U.N. System
Business, Consumer

Publishing Co: Campaign for U.N. Reform, 713 D St SE, Washington, DC 20003-2153; Title Tel # (202) 546-3956
Personnel: Editor-Eric Cox
General Info: Yr. Est. 1975, Annually, 16 pages, Saddle-stitched
Subscriptions: Free

AACE Bonus Briefs
See: EDUCATION

AACE Careers Update
See: EDUCATION

ADA Update
See: DISABILITY

AFFI Letter
See: FOOD

AIDS/STD News Report
See: PHILANTHROPY

AKCENS
Business, Consumer

Publishing Co: Alaska State Data Center, Alaska Dept. of Labor, Box 25504, Juneau, AK 99802-5504; Title Tel # (907) 465-4500 Title Fax # (907) 465-2101
Personnel: Editor-Kathryn Lizik
General Info: Yr. Est. 1983, Quarterly, Desktop press, 8 pages, 2 Color, Newsprint
Subscriptions: Free
Circulation: Total-700

Accountants SEC Practice Manual
See: ACCOUNTING

Across the Table · *Association*

Publishing Co: New York Conference of Mayors, 119 Washington Ave, Albany, NY 12210-2291; Title Tel # (518) 463-1185
Editorial Description: Public sector labor relations.
General Info: Yr. Est. 1974, Monthly, Trim Size-8½ x 11, Offset press, 12 pages, ISSN: 0362-8493, No Color
Subscriptions: Inst. $15, $5/copy
Circulation: Total-1,200

Agenda Newsletter, The
See: REGIONAL INTEREST

Aging News Alert
See: SENIOR CITIZENS

Air/Water Pollution Report's Environment Week
See: ENVIRONMENT & ECOLOGY

Alcoholic Beverage Control/State Capitals
See: BEVERAGES - BREWING

Alternatives
See: PUBLIC MANAGEMENT & PLANNING

American Shore & Beach Preservation Assn. -Newsletter
See: ENVIRONMENT & ECOLOGY

America's Future
See: POLITICS

Antitrust and Trade Regulation Report
See: LAW

Applying Government Accounting Principles
See: ACCOUNTING

Applying Government Auditing Standards
See: ACCOUNTING

Archivists Society of Alberta Newsletter
See: CULTURE & HUMANITIES

Arkansas Report

Publishing Co: Wallace Assn., PO Box 1836, Little Rock, AR 72203-1836; Title Tel # (501) 372-6512
Personnel: Publisher, Editor-Douglas Wallace
Editorial Description: Reporting & analyzing Arkansas political, legislative & state government news.
General Info: Yr. Est. 1983, Monthly, ISSN: 0273-2742
Subscriptions: Indv. $70
Circulation: Total-500

BNA's Health Care Policy Report
See: HEALTH

Beacon Hill Roll Call · *Business, Association*

Publishing Co: Bay State News Service, 8 Whittier Place, (Suite 7A), Boston, MA 02114-1437; Title Tel # (617) 720-1562
Personnel: Publisher, Editor-Bob Katzen
Editorial Description: A weekly report covering the Massachusetts Legislature. Includes the voting records of all elected state senators & representatives.
General Info: Yr. Est. 1976, Weekly, Offset press, 5 pages

Best's Intelligencer
See: INSURANCE

Bill Shipp's Georgia · *Business, Consumer*

Publishing Co: Word Merchants, Inc., PO Box 440755, Kennesaw, GA 30144-9513 Tel # (772) 577-9194 Fax # (770) 422-0227; Title Tel # (404) 422-2543 Title Fax # (404) 522-3715
Personnel: Publisher, Editor-Bill Shipp, Circ. Mgr., Production Mgr.-Joyce Manson
General Info: Yr. Est. 1987, Weekly, Desktop press, 6 pages, ISSN: 0894-9697, 2 Color, Matte
Subscriptions: Indv. $195, $4/copy
Circulation: (100% controlled), Total-2,000
List Rental: List Management Co.: Political Resources, Inc., List Managment Division, Box 3177, Burlington, VT 05401 Tel # (802) 660-2869, Fax # (802) 864-9502, Actives: 1,150

Black Congressional Monitor · *Business, Association*

Publishing Co: Len Mor Pubs., PO Box 75035, Washington, DC 20013-0035; Title Tel # (202) 488-8879 Title Fax # (202) 554-3116
Personnel: Publisher, Editor-Lenora Moragne, Ph.D, Circ. Mgr., Production Mgr.-Nora Champion, Ph.D
Editorial Description: Twice Month report of legislative and executive branch Federal Government initiatives pertaining to African Americans. Also reports activities of Congressional Black Caucus members.
General Info: Yr. Est. 1987, Semi-monthly, Trim Size-8½ x 11, Sheetfed press, 8 pages, ISSN: 0895-1780, 2 Color, Coated
Subscriptions: Indv. $39, Inst. $39, Can. $50, For. $50
Acquistions: Publication Bought
List Rental: Actives: $65/M

Board of Contract Appeals Bid Protest Decisions

Publishing Co: Federal Pubs., Inc., 1120 20th St., NW, Fifth Floor, South Building, Washington, DC 20036-3484 Tel # (202) 337-7000 Fax # (202) 659-2233
Subscriptions: Indv. $608

Boycott Law Bulletin
See: INTERNATIONAL TRADE

Briefing · *Consumer*

Publishing Co: Jacksonville Community Council, 21 W. Church Street, Jacksonville, FL 32202-3155; Title Tel # (904) 396-3052
Editorial Description: Newsletter of public affairs local organization.
General Info: Yr. Est. 1975, Bi-monthly, 4 pages
Circulation: Total-700

Briefing Papers
See: LAW

Bronx Report, The
See: PUBLIC MANAGEMENT & PLANNING

Brooklyn Newsletter · *Business, Consumer*

Publishing Co: Office of the Borough President, 209 Joralemon St., Rm 320, Brooklyn, NY 11201 Tel # (718) 802-3700; Title Fax # (718) 802-3778
Personnel: Editor-Diane Moogan
Editorial Description: Social and political activities in Brooklyn.
General Info: Semi-annually, Trim Size-7 x 11, 4 pages, No Color

Bruce Bortz's Maryland Report

Publishing Co: Bancroft Information Group, Inc., PO Box 65360, Baltimore, MD 21209-0560; Title Tel # (410) 358-0658 Title Fax # (410) 764-1967
Personnel: Publisher, Editor-Bruce Bortz
Editorial Description: Bi-weekly newsletter on Maryland government, politics, & business.
General Info: Yr. Est. 1988, Bi-weekly, Trim Size-8½ x 11, 8 pages, ISSN: 1042-1564, No Color, Newsprint
Subscriptions: Indv. $200
Circulation: Total-350
Advertising: Accepts Inserts.
List Rental: List Management Co.: Political Resources, Inc., List Managment Division, Box 3177, Burlington, VT 05401 Tel # (802) 660-2869, Fax # (802) 864-9502, Actives: 350
Printing Co: Speed-D-Print, 9121 Reisterstown Rd., Baltimore, MD 21117 Tel # (301) 363-2116

Budget Message of the Governor of New Jersey

Publishing Co: Budget Message of the Governor of New Jersey, Office of the Governor, Trenton, NJ 08625
General Info: Annually

Bulletin, The · *Association* · **CPM: $250**

Publishing Co: Building Officials Assn. of Texas, 1601 Rio Grande St Ste 440, Austin, TX 78701-1149; Title Tel # (512) 479-0425
Personnel: Editor-Lisa Fry
Editorial Description: Official publication of the Building Officials Association of Texas. B.O.A.T. is an association of professionals who are interested in improving the quality of construction, code enforcement, and state and local laws of code officials in Texas.
General Info: Quarterly, Trim Size-8½ x 11, Offset press, 12 pages, 25% ads, No Color, Matte
Subscriptions: Free With Membership
Circulation: Total-400
Advertising: $100.
Printing Co: Austex Printing Co., 501 W 3rd St, Austin, TX 78701-3807 Tel # (512) 476-7581

Bulletin-N.D.

Publishing Co: North Dakota League of Cities, PO Box 2235, Bismarck, ND 58502-2235; Title Tel # (701) 223-3518 Title Fax # (701) 223-5174
Personnel: Editor-Robert Johnson
Editorial Description: For city officials.
General Info: Yr. Est. 1950, 10x/yr., Trim Size-7¾ x 11, Web press, 16 pages, ISSN: 0040-800X, 2 Color
Subscriptions: Indv. $10, $1/copy
Circulation: Total-2,900
Advertising: Inquire for rates.
Printing Co: Quality Printing, 2306 E Broadway Ave, Bismarck, ND 58501-4932 Tel # (701) 255-3900

CBASSE Newsletter
See: SOCIOLOGY

CD-Housing Register
See: REAL ESTATE

COGEL Guardian   *Association*

Publishing Co: The Council of State Governments, Iron Works Pike, P.O Box 11910, Lexington, KY 40578-1910 Tel # (606) 244-8000 Fax # (606) 244-8001; Title Tel # (606) 231-1920 Title Fax # (606) 231-1858
Personnel: Editor-Joyce Bullock
Editorial Description: A periodical which covers government campaign finance, ethics, & lobby law developments at the state, federal & provincial levels.
General Info: Yr. Est. 1984, Quarterly, 24 pages, ISSN: 1059-6224, No Color, Newsprint
Subscriptions: Indv. $54
Circulation: (100% controlled), Total-300

COHA's Washington Report on the Hemisphere
See: INTERNATIONAL AFFAIRS

CRA/HMDA Update
See: BANKING & FINANCE

CSBS Examiner
See: BANKING & FINANCE

Cal-OSHA Reporter
See: SAFETY

California Employer Newsletter
See: TAXES

California Public Finance
See: BANKING & FINANCE

California Statesman

Publishing Co: William Shearer, 8158 Palm St, Lemon Grove, CA 91945-3028; Title Tel # (619) 460-4484
Personnel: Publisher, Editor-William Shearer
Editorial Description: Political subjects: historical information memorable political leaders.
General Info: Yr. Est. 1962, Monthly, 8 pages
Subscriptions: Indv. $15
Circulation: Total-1,700

Canadian Employment Benefits and Pension Guide
See: INDUSTRIAL RELATIONS/PERSONNEL

Canadian Goods & Services Tax Reporter
See: TAXES

Canadian Tax Forms
See: TAXES

Capital Journal
See: BUSINESS & INDUSTRY

Capitol Connection
See: HEALTH

Capitol Government Reports Weekly

Publishing Co: Capitol Government Reports Weekly, P.O. Box 602, Santa Fe, NM 87504; Title Tel # (505) 988-9835 Title Fax # (505) 988-9835
Personnel: Asst. Pub.-Rene Parker, Editor-Jack Flynn
Editorial Description: Features timely government news.
General Info: Weekly
Subscriptions: Indv. $245

Capitol Update   *Business, Association*

Publishing Co: Texas State Directory Press, 1800 Nueces St, Austin, TX 78701-1120; Title Tel # (512) 477-5698 Title Fax # (512) 473-2447
Personnel: Publisher-Scott Sayers, Editor-Nancy Barnes
Editorial Description: Features government news and related developments.
General Info: Yr. Est. 1982, Bi-weekly
Subscriptions: Indv. $50

Career Connections
See: EDUCATION

Carolina Justice Policy Center News
See: LAW ENFORCEMENT & PENOLOGY

Carolina Report   *Business, Association*

Publishing Co: Broach, Mijeski & Assoc., PO Box 12074, Rock Hill, SC 29731-2074; Title Tel # (803) 323-2200
Editorial Description: South Carolina government news, etc.
General Info: Yr. Est. 1986, Monthly
Subscriptions: Indv. $64

Caveat Emptor
See: PURCHASING

Child Protection Report
See: CHILDREN

Citizens Union Reports

Publishing Co: Citizens Union of the City of New York, 198 Broadway, New York, NY 10038-2515; Title Tel # (212) 227-0342 Title Fax # (212) 227-0345
Personnel: Publisher, Editor-Jeannette Kahlenberg
Editorial Description: Commentary on New York City civic affairs & Citizens Union activities; includes special candidate evaluation edition.
General Info: (Formerly Across from City Hall), Yr. Est. 1897, Quarterly, Trim Size-8½ x 11, Offset press, 6 pages, 2 Color, Other
Subscriptions: Indv. $20, Free With Membership
Circulation: Total-3,000

City Beat

Publishing Co: City of San Antonio, Texas, PO Box 839966, San Antonio, TX 78283-3966; Title Tel # (512) 299-7235
Personnel: Editor-Carmen Vazques-Gonzale
Editorial Description: Employee newsletter for the City of San Antonio.
General Info: (Formerly City Hall & Elsewhere), Yr. Est. 1972, Monthly, Trim Size-8½ x 11, Offset press, 8 pages, Color-cover, Newsprint
Circulation: Total-9,000

City Leaders Institute Briefings

Publishing Co: City Leaders Institute, Inc., 3045 Thayen Pl, Boise, ID 83709-3953; Title Tel # (208) 362-4332 Title Fax # (208) 362-4332
Personnel: Publisher-Karen Forrey, Editor, Production Mgr.-Wayne Forrey
Editorial Description: Provides management and technical information exclusively for Mayors and elected city officials in small to medium size cities within all regions of the USA. This information is provided for members of the Institute only.
General Info: Yr. Est. 1989, Monthly, Web press, 4 pages, ISSN: 1044-6222, 2 Color, Matte
Subscriptions: $10/copy
Acquistions: Publication Bought
Circulation: Total-400
Printing Co: Mike Printing Co., 270 S Cole Rd, Boise, ID 83709-0934

Civil Rights/State Capitals
See: CIVIL RIGHTS

Clear News
See: LAW

Code Authority, The
See: SAFETY

Code of Maryland Regulations   *Business, Association*

Publishing Co: Maryland Division of State Documents, PO Box 2249, Annapolis, MD 21404-2249; Title Tel # (410) 974-2486 Title Fax # (410) 974-2546
Personnel: Publisher-Robert J. Colborn, Circ. Mgr.-Marcia Diamond
Editorial Description: All Maryland state agency regulations, governor's executive orders & Ethics Commission opinions.
General Info: Yr. Est. 1974, Annually, Trim Size-6 x 9, Offset press, 22,000 pages, No Color, Looseleaf
Subscriptions: $850/copy
Circulation: Total-6,000
Printing Co: Fry Communications, Inc., 800 W Church Rd, Mechanicsburg, PA 17055-3198 Tel # (717) 766-0211, Fax # (717) 691-0341

Cold War International History Project Bulletin
See: POLITICS

Commerce Contact   *Business*

Publishing Co: Minnesota Department of Commerce, 133 7th St E, Saint Paul, MN 55101-2333; Title Tel # (612) 296-6984
General Info: Semi-annually, 6 pages
Subscriptions: Free
Circulation: Total-80,000

Committee

Publishing Co: Association of the Bar of the City of New York, 42 W 44th St, New York, NY 10036-6686; Title Tel # (212) 382-6655
General Info: Yr. Est. 1919, Bi-monthly, Mimeo press
Circulation: Total-500

Commodity Futures Law Reports
See: INVESTMENT

Communicator-Government   *Business, Association*

Publishing Co: Clark Boardman Callaghan, 50 Broad St. E., Rochester, NY 14694-0001 Tel # (716) 546-1490; Title Tel # (703) 823-4821
Personnel: Editor-Dan Hall
General Info: Monthly

Community Change
Association

Publishing Co: Center for Community Change, 1000 Wisconsin Ave NW, Washington, DC 20007-3651; Title Tel # (202) 342-0594
Personnel: Editor-Timothy Saasta, Circ. Mgr.-Virgie Tilghman
Editorial Description: Articles about low-income housing, community & economic development, funding for community-based organizations.
General Info: (Formerly Monitor), Quarterly, Sheetfed press, 12 pages, No Color, Newsprint
Subscriptions: Indv. $20
Circulation: Total-2,000

Community Development Services, Inc.
See: PUBLIC MANAGEMENT & PLANNING

Community Health Funding Report
See: PHILANTHROPY

Comptroller General
Procurement Decisions
Business

Publishing Co: Federal Pubs., Inc., 1120 20th St., NW, Fifth Floor, South Building, Washington, DC 20036-3484 Fax # (202) 659-2233; Title Tel # (202) 337-7000 Title Fax # (800) 292-4330
General Info: Yr. Est. 1974, Monthly
Subscriptions: Indv. $1,216

Congressional Research
Report
Business

Publishing Co: Penny Hill Press, 6440 Wiscasset Rd, Bethesda, MD 20816-2115 Parent Co.-Thunderstruck, Ltd., Bethesda; Title Tel # (301) 229-8229 Title Fax # (301) 229-6988
Editorial Description: Abstracts of congressional research service reports and studies.
General Info: Yr. Est. 1983, Monthly, Trim Size-8$\frac{1}{2}$ x 11, 16 pages
Subscriptions: Indv. $140, Inst. $140, For. $170, $15/copy

Connecticut Law Journal
See: LAW

Conserve Neighborhoods
Consumer, Association

Publishing Co: National Trust for Historic Preservation, 1785 Massachusetts Ave., NW, Washington, DC 20036-2117 Tel # (202) 673-4035; Title Tel # (202) 673-4047
Personnel: Publisher, Editor-Susan Hyatt, Circ. Mgr.-Lisa Calhoun, Production Mgr., Art Dir.-Janet Walker
Editorial Description: Tips on improving quality of life in local communities and neighborhoods.
General Info: Yr. Est. 1978, Monthly, Trim Size-8$\frac{1}{2}$ x 11, Web press, Color
Subscriptions: $2/copy
Circulation: Total-7,000

Constitution

Publishing Co: National Center for Constitutional Studies, PO Box 841, West Jordan, UT 84084-0841 Tel # (801) 565-1787; Title Tel # (801) 280-1787
Personnel: Publisher, Editor-Andrew Allison, Circ. Mgr.-Bryan Neville, Production Mgr.-Bob Johnson, Adv. Dir.-Jay Perry, Art Dir.-Susan Hurd, Promotion Dir.-Zeldon Nelson
Editorial Description: Constitutional history, current attitudes and practical solutions to constitutional problems.
General Info: (Formerly Families for America Update), Yr. Est. 1971, Monthly, Trim Size-8$\frac{1}{4}$ x 10$\frac{3}{4}$, Sheetfed press, 32 pages, ISSN: 0882-5955, 2 Color, Coated, Perfect bound
Subscriptions: Indv. $30, Inst. $28, $3/copy
Circulation: Total-10,000

Council Spotlight
Association

Publishing Co: World Affairs Council of North Califfornia, 312 Sutter St Ste 200, San Francisco, CA 94108-4311; Title Tel # (415) 982-2541 Title Fax # (415) 982-5028
Personnel: Editor-K. Weichel
General Info: Yr. Est. 1947, Monthly, 8 pages
Circulation: Total-11,000

County News
Consumer   **CPM:** $83

Publishing Co: Nat'l Assn. of Counties, 440 1st St NW, 8th Fl., Washington, DC 20001-2080; Title Tel # (202) 393-6226 Title Fax # (202) 393-2630
Personnel: Publisher-Larry Naake, Editor-Beverly Schlotterbeck, Circ. Mgr.-Anne Powell
General Info: Yr. Est. 1970, Bi-weekly, Trim Size-11$\frac{1}{2}$ x 14, Web press, 24 pages, ISSN: 0744-9798, 4 Color
Subscriptions: Indv. $75
Circulation: (90% controlled), Total-30,000
Advertising: $2,495.

Credit Union Accountant
See: BANKING & FINANCE

Crime & Drug Report
See: LAW ENFORCEMENT & PENOLOGY

Crime Prevention News
See: LAW ENFORCEMENT & PENOLOGY

Current News on File
Consumer

Publishing Co: Facts on File, Inc., 11 Penn Plaza, New York, NY 10001-2006 Tel # (212) 967-8800 Parent Co.-Infobase Holdings Inc., New York; Title Tel # (212) 683-2244 Title Fax # (212) 683-3633
Personnel: Publisher-Remmel Nunn, Editor-Fran Claro, Circ. Dir.-Steve Orlofsky, Production Dir.-Olivia McKean
Editorial Description: Indexed summary of US and international news for students.
General Info: (Formerly Current Events on File), Yr. Est. 1990, 24x/yr., Trim Size-8$\frac{1}{2}$ x 11, Sheetfed press, 16 pages, ISSN: 1058-8124, No Color, Matte
Subscriptions: Indv. $244, Inst. $244
Circulation: Total-1,900
List Rental: Rents Lists
Printing Co: Science Press, 300 W Chestnut St, Ephrata, PA 17522-2002 Tel # (717) 738-9300, Fax # (717) 738-9413

DGS Digest
Association

Publishing Co: Dept. of General Services, Manhattan Municipal Bldg., 1 Centre St., 17th Fl. S., New York, NY 10007; Title Tel # (212) 669-7140 Title Fax # (212) 669-8992
Personnel: Editor-Daniel Levine, Editor-Andrea Patterson
Editorial Description: Covers the department's personnel activities, projects, achievements & awards presentations.
General Info: Yr. Est. 1989
Circulation: Total-3,500

DGS Powerlines

Publishing Co: Dept. of General Services, Manhattan Municipal Bldg., 1 Centre St., 17th Fl. S., New York, NY 10007; Title Tel # (212) 669-7140 Title Fax # (212) 669-8992
Personnel: Editor-Daniel Levine, Editor-Andrea Patterson
Editorial Description: Focuses on OEC personnel, conservation projects, etc.
General Info: (Formerly DGS Energy Manager), Yr. Est. 1989, Semi-annually

Daily Report for Executives
See: ECONOMICS

Daily Treasury Statement
See: BANKING & FINANCE

Data Security Letter
See: COMPUTERS & AUTOMATION

Defense Contract Awards
Business, Association

Publishing Co: Murray Felsher, 1057-B Natl. Press Bldg., Washington, DC 20045; Title Tel # (202) 393-3640 Title Fax # (202) 393-3640
Personnel: Publisher, Editor-Murray Felsher
Editorial Description: Focuses on defense contracts and contractors.
General Info: Yr. Est. 1993, Semi-monthly, Offset press, 8 pages, ISSN: 1061-0613, 2 Color, Newsprint
Subscriptions: Indv. $510, Can. $510, For. $800

Defense Week
See: MILITARY & NAVAL

Deficit Letter, The
See: U.S. (& CANADIAN) FED. GOV'T.

Dept. of Education Reports
See: EDUCATION

Dickinson's FDA Review
See: DRUGS & PHARMACEUTICALS

Dickinson's FDA Update by Fax
See: DRUGS & PHARMACEUTICALS

Dickinson's Pharmacy
See: DRUGS & PHARMACEUTICALS

Digest of Attorney General Opinions
See: LAW

Disabilities in the Workplace Alert
See: LAW

Donald R. Morris Newsletter
See: NEWSPAPER INDUSTRY

Drug Policy Report
See: LAW ENFORCEMENT & PENOLOGY

ETDD Newsletter
See: PUBLIC MANAGEMENT & PLANNING

Economic Development/State Capitals
See: BUSINESS & INDUSTRY

Economic Issues
See: ECONOMICS

Economic Opportunity Report
See: SOCIAL SERVICES & WELFARE

Economic Update   *Consumer, Association*

Publishing Co: Economics Group, Ways & Means Committee State, Capitol, Room 412, Albany, NY 12248-0001; Title Tel # (518) 455-4006
Editorial Description: Economic report from the NYS Assembly Ways and Means Committee.
General Info: Yr. Est. 1993

Edison Entrepreneur   *Business*

Publishing Co: Thomas Edison Program, Ohio Dept. Of Development Box, 1001, Columbus, OH 43266-0001; Title Tel # (614) 466-3887
General Info: Yr. Est. 1984, Quarterly, 4 pages, No Color, Coated
Circulation: Total-22,000

Editorials on File
See: NEWSPAPER INDUSTRY

Election Connection

Publishing Co: New York City Board of Elections, 200 Varick St Fl 10, New York, NY 10014-4810
General Info: Quarterly

Electronic Public Information Newsletter
See: PUBLIC MANAGEMENT & PLANNING

Emergency Management
Today   *Business, Consumer*

Publishing Co: Emergency Management Group, 1508 E 86th St., Ste 315, Indianapolis, IN 46240-1986 Tel # (317) 475-9572; Title Tel # (317) 466-4339 Title Fax # (317) 475-9403
Personnel: Publisher, Editor in Chief-Douglas L. Crichlow, Mng. Editor-C.M. Heller, Art Ed.-Jenny Crichlow, Assoc. Ed.-S.A. Katt, Circ. Mgr.-A.J. Strong
Editorial Description: Report of trends in the management of disasters and major emergencies. Details developments and lessons learned in recent emergencies. Focuses on incidents caused by natural, technological and human behavioral hazards.
General Info: Yr. Est. 1983, Bi-weekly, Trim Size-8½ x 11, Offset press, 8 pages, Ind/Abs/Online: AOL, 2 Color, Matte, Saddle-stitched
Subscriptions: Indv. $90, Inst. $185, Can. $212
Circulation: Total-1,819
Advertising: Accepts Inserts.
Printing Co: Valley Web, 1299 Stowe Avenue, Medford, OR 97504 Tel # (503) 772-7039

Empire State Development
See: BUSINESS & INDUSTRY

Employment & Training Reporter
See: EMPLOYMENT

Employment Tax Forms
See: TAXES

Environment Watch: Western Europe
See: ENVIRONMENT & ECOLOGY

Environmental Regulation/State Capitals
See: ENVIRONMENT & ECOLOGY

Ernie Mills' Legislative
Report   *Business, Association*

Publishing Co: Mills Capitol Observer, PO Box 5141, Santa Fe, NM 87502-5141; Title Tel # (505) 421-4452
Personnel: Publisher-Ernie Mills, Editor-Lorene Carpenter
Editorial Description: Covers legislative developments and news.
General Info: Yr. Est. 1972, Weekly
Subscriptions: Indv. $225

Ethics in Government
Reporter   *Business, Association*

Publishing Co: CCH Washington Service Bureau, Inc., 655 15th St NW Ste 275, Washington, DC 20005-5701 Tel # (202) 508-0600 Fax # (202) 508-0694; Title Tel # (202) 833-9200 Title Fax # (202) 659-3655
Personnel: Editor-Matthew Merrick, Circ. Dir.-Michelle McCaulley
Editorial Description: Full text of statutes, executive orders, federal agency regulations, case rulings and office of Government Ethics advisory opinions that define federal ethics law for contractors and federal employees. Includes free subsription to the current awareness newsletter - 'Federal Ethics Reports'.
General Info: Yr. Est. 1980, Monthly, ISSN: 0279-2869, Looseleaf
Subscriptions: Indv. $650

FCL Newsletter
See: CIVIL RIGHTS

FDA Outline   *Business*

Publishing Co: Hotline Publishing, PO Box 161132, Altamonte Springs, FL 32716-1132 Tel # (407) 628-1377 Fax # (407) 628-9355
General Info: Bi-monthly
Subscriptions: Indv. $257
List Rental: Actives: 20,000, $85/M

F.E.A.R. Chronicles
See: CIVIL RIGHTS

Facts on File World News Digest
See: INTERNATIONAL AFFAIRS

Fair Labor Standards
Handbook   *Business*

Publishing Co: Thompson Publishing Group, 1725 K Street, NW, Washington, DC 20006 Tel # (202) 872-4000; Title Tel # (202) 872-1766
Personnel: Publisher-Richard Thompson, Editor-Kathleen Dunten, Circ. Mgr.-Judy Ellingsworth, Art Dir.-Kathy Stein, Promotion Dir.-Carol Bray
Editorial Description: Assists state and local government managers as well as school administrators in complying with the Fair Labor Standards Act. Subscription includes monthly updates and newsletters covering major developments in the field.
General Info: Yr. Est. 1985, Monthly, Trim Size-8½ x 11, Offset press, 25 pages, No Color, Newsprint, Looseleaf
Subscriptions: Indv. $254

Families in Crisis Funding Report
See: FAMILY

Family, Law and
Democracy Report

Publishing Co: Political Report, 717 2nd St., N.E., Washington, DC 20002; Title Tel # (202) 546-3000 Title Fax # (202) 546-7689
General Info: Monthly
Subscriptions: Indv. $50

Family Relations/State Capitals
See: LAW

Fed/Direct
See: ADVERTISING & MARKETING

Federal Action Affecting the States/State Capitals
See: U.S. (& CANADIAN) FED. GOV'T.

Federal Assistance Monitor
See: PHILANTHROPY

Federal Budget Report   *Business, Consumer*

Publishing Co: Price Waterhouse, 1251 Ave. of Americas, New York, NY 10020; Title Tel # (212) 596-7000
Personnel: Editor-Stanley Collender
Editorial Description: Analyzes the federal budget and actions of the administration and congress.
General Info: Bi-weekly
Subscriptions: Indv. $295
Acquistions: Publication Bought, Publication Sold

Federal Computer Market Report
See: COMPUTERS & AUTOMATION

Federal Court Procurement
Decisions   *Business*

Publishing Co: Federal Pubs., Inc., 1120 20th St., NW, Fifth Floor, South Building, Washington, DC 20036-3484 Tel # (202) 337-7000 Fax # (202) 659-2233
General Info: Monthly
Subscriptions: Indv. $820

Federal Ethics Report

Publishing Co: CCH Washington Service Bureau, Inc., 655 15th St NW Ste 275, Washington, DC 20005-5701 Tel # (202) 508-0600 Fax # (202) 508-0694
Personnel: Editor-Susan Kavanagh, Circ. Mgr.-Michelle McCaulley
Editorial Description: In-depth coverage of current policy developments and coverage of all legislative and regulatory initiatives. Valuable source for both government agency ethics officials and for government contractors.
General Info: Yr. Est. 1994, Monthly
Subscriptions: Indv. $195

Federal Physicians, The
See: MEDICINE

Federal Procurement
Update

Publishing Co: United Communications Group, 11300 Rockville Pike, Ste. 1100, Rockville, MD 20852-3030; Title Tel # (301) 816-8950 Title Fax # (301) 816-8945
General Info: Monthly
Subscriptions: Indv. $197
List Rental: Rents Lists

Federal Quality News   *Business, Association*

Publishing Co: U.S. Office of Personnel Management, Office Of Workforce Info., 1900 E. St. NW #7494, Washington, DC 20415-0001 Tel # (202) 606-2684 Fax # (202) 606-1719; Title Tel # (202) 376-3753
Editorial Description: Covers issues of quality in government.
General Info: Yr. Est. 1991, Quarterly, Trim Size-8½ x 11, 12 pages, No Color

Federal Securities Law Reports
See: LAW

Federal Technology Report   *Business*

Publishing Co: McGraw-Hill, 1200 G St NW Ste 1100, Washington, DC 20005-3814
Tel # (202) 383-3700 Parent Co.-McGraw-Hill, New York; Title Tel # (202) 383-2240
Personnel: Editor in Chief-Bill Loveless
Editorial Description: News on government technology policies.
General Info: (Formerly Tech Transfer Report), Yr. Est. 1988, Bi-weekly, Trim Size-8½ x 11, 14
pages, Ind/Abs/Online: Dialog, Dow Jones, NewsNet, Nexis, 2 Color, Matte
Subscriptions: Indv. $495

Federal Update

Publishing Co: Natl. Conference of State Legislatures, 1560 Broadway, Ste. 700, Denver, CO
80202-5140; Title Tel # (303) 830-2200 Title Fax # (303) 863-8003
Editorial Description: Covers Conference news, related legislative issues.
General Info: 15x/yr.
Subscriptions: Indv. $35

Field Reports
See: BUSINESS & INDUSTRY

Fire & Emergency World
See: FIRE PROTECTION

Fiscal Letter   *Business, Association*

Publishing Co: Natl. Conference of State Legislatures, 1560 Broadway, Ste. 700, Denver, CO
80202-5140; Title Tel # (303) 830-2200 Title Fax # (303) 863-8003
Personnel: Editor-Judy Zelio, Circ. Mgr.-Gail Loos
Editorial Description: Source of fiscal news provided to legislators and legislative staff.
General Info: Yr. Est. 1978, Bi-monthly, Trim Size-8½ x 11, Offset press, 12 pages, ISSN: 0197-
288X, No Color, Saddle-stitched
Subscriptions: Indv. $35, Can. $38, $7/copy
Circulation: Total-2,100

Florida Administrative Law Reports
See: LAW

Florida Insight   *Business, Association*

Publishing Co: Florida Communications Network, Inc., PO Box 2099, Gainesville, FL 32602-2099;
Title Tel # (904) 378-4154
Personnel: Publisher-Jon Mills, Editor-John Hotaling
Editorial Description: Reports on Florida government and politics at the local, state, and federal
level.
General Info: Yr. Est. 1989, 20x/yr., Trim Size-8½ x 11, Offset press, 8 pages
Subscriptions: Indv. $95, Inst. $95, $8/copy
Circulation: Total-220

Florida Workers' Compensation Law Bulletin
See: LAW

Focus on Canadian Municipal Assessment & Taxation
See: REAL ESTATE

Food Chemical News
See: FOOD

Food Drug Cosmetic Law Reports
See: DRUGS & PHARMACEUTICALS

Freedom Forum   *Consumer, Association*

Publishing Co: Mountain States Legal Foundation, 1660 Lincoln St Ste 2300, Denver, CO
80264-2301; Title Tel # (303) 861-0244
General Info: (Formerly Litigator), Quarterly, 4 pages
Circulation: Total-20,000

Frontiers of Freedom

Publishing Co: Frank Parsons, 10235 SE 13th Pl, Bellevue, WA 98004-6728;
Title Tel # (206) 454-2420
Personnel: Publisher, Editor-Frank Parsons
Editorial Description: Material pertinent to the freedom of all Americans.
General Info: Yr. Est. 1983, Monthly, Mimeo press, 8 pages
Subscriptions: Indv. $20

GEM

Publishing Co: Government Management Information Sciences, PO Box 926, Wichita Falls, TX
76307-0926; Title Tel # (817) 692-3707
Personnel: Editor-Charles Collier
Editorial Description: State and local government agencies involved in data processing.
General Info: Yr. Est. 1969, Bi-monthly, Trim Size-8½ x 11, 15 pages, 1% ads, No Color, Newsprint
Circulation: Total-800
Printing Co: Wichita Printing, 2914 Kemp Blvd, Wichita Falls, TX 76308-1017 Tel # (817) 723-7214

GFOA Newsletter
See: PUBLIC MANAGEMENT & PLANNING

Gallup Poll, The
See: POLITICS

Georgia Courts Journal
See: LAW

Gerald R. Ford Foundation
Newsletter

Publishing Co: Gerald R. Ford Foundation, 1000 Beal Ave., Ann Arbor, MI 48109-2114;
Title Tel # (313) 668-2218
Personnel: Editor-Karen Holzhausen
Editorial Description: Foundation news and events.
General Info: Yr. Est. 1982, 6 pages, 2 Color, Coated
Circulation: Total-3,000

Global Statesmanship
Ratings of the U.S.
House   *Consumer*

Publishing Co: Campaign for U.N. Reform, 713 D St SE, Washington, DC 20003-2153;
Title Tel # (202) 546-3956
General Info: Annually, Trim Size-8½ x 11
Subscriptions: Free

Government Accounting and Auditing Update
See: ACCOUNTING

Government Business
Worldwide Reports   *Business*

Publishing Co: Government Bus. Worldwide Rpts., PO Box 5997, Washington, DC 20016-1597;
Title Tel # (202) 244-7050 Title Fax # (202) 244-5410
Personnel: Publisher, Editor-J. Wagner
Editorial Description: Monthly information on international, governments and economic affairs.
General Info: (Formerly Defensed & Economy World Repor), Yr. Est. 1969, Monthly, Trim Size-8½ x
11, Offset press, 15 pages, ISSN: 0017-2588, Looseleaf
Subscriptions: Indv. $400, For. $400

Government Contract
Compliance Guide   *Business*

Publishing Co: Thompson Publishing Group, 1725 K Street, NW, Washington, DC 20006
Tel # (202) 872-4000
Editorial Description: Comprehensive guide to complying with federal contracting rules.
General Info: Monthly
Subscriptions: Indv. $447

Government Contract Costs Pricing & Accounting Report
See: LAW

Government Contractor
See: LAW

Government Contracts
Citator

Publishing Co: Federal Pubs., Inc., 1120 20th St., NW, Fifth Floor, South Building, Washington, DC
20036-3484; Title Tel # (202) 337-7000 Title Fax # (202) 659-2233
General Info: Quarterly
Subscriptions: Indv. $828

Government Employee
Relations Report   *Business*

Publishing Co: Bureau of National Affairs, Inc., 1231 25th St. NW, Bldg. N-200, Washington, DC
20037-1157 Fax # (202) 822-8092; Title Tel # (202) 452-4200 Title Fax # (202) 452-4603
Personnel: Publisher-William A. Beltz, Editor-Anthony Harris, Mng. Editor-James F. Fitzpatrick, Circ.
Mgr.-Gary C. Seltzer, Product Mgr.-Robert Fuchs
Editorial Description: A notification service that covers federal, state & municipal government
employee relations.
General Info: Yr. Est. 1963, Weekly, Trim Size-8½ x 11, Web press, 32 pages, ISSN: 0017-260X,
Ind/Abs/Online: HRIN, Lexis, Westlaw, Nexis, Personnel Literture Index (OPM)
Subscriptions: Indv. $873

Government
Microcomputer Letter
(GML)   *Business, Association*   CPM: $57

Publishing Co: The Innovation Groups, PO Box 16645, Tampa, FL 33687-6645
Fax # (813) 664-0051; Title Tel # (813) 622-8484 Title Fax # (813) 622-8484
Personnel: Publisher-Robert Havlick, Editor-Alicia Murray, Feature Ed., Bk. Rev. Ed.-Liz Diaz
Editorial Description: Informs on what town, cities, counties, agencies are doing in microcomputer
applications. Features: Hardware and Software liser profiles, new products, review of software,
books, computer training.
General Info: Yr. Est. 1983, Quarterly, Trim Size-8½ x 11, Sheetfed press, 8 pages, ISSN: 0882-
6587, 25% ads, No Color, Coated
Subscriptions: Indv. $19, Can. $24, For. $24, Free With Membership
Acquistions: Publication Bought
Circulation: Total-4,000, Readership-5,000
Advertising: $230.
List Rental: Rents Lists

Government Pubs. News   *Business*

Publishing Co: Bernan, 4611f Assembly Dr, Lanham, MD 20706-4370; Title Tel # (301) 459-7666 Title Fax # (301) 459-0056
Personnel: Publisher-Donald Hagen, Editor-Rebecca Dempsey, Promotion Dir.-Aine O'Dwyer
Editorial Description: Free pub. for customers with an established account. Covers government information issues; lists newly-released & forthcoming government pubs.
General Info: Yr. Est. 1988, Monthly, Trim Size-8½ x 11, Sheetfed press, 12 pages, ISSN: 0897-5728, Ind/Abs/Online: Internet, 2 Color, Newsprint
Circulation: Total-4,500
Printing Co: Todd-Allan Printing Co., Inc., 6011 Blair Rd NW, Washington, DC 20011-1463

Government Relations   *Association*

Publishing Co: American Society of Association Executives, 1575 'I' St., N.W., 11th Fl., Washington, DC 20005-1168 Tel # (202) 626-2711 Fax # (202) 408-9633; Title Tel # (202) 626-2739
Personnel: Editor-Jospeh Cavarretta
Editorial Description: For governmental relations professionals of non-profit organizations.
General Info: Monthly, 11 pages
Subscriptions: Free With Membership
Circulation: Total-1,800, Readership-3,000
List Rental: Actives: 1,664, $175/M

Government Training News

Publishing Co: Business Publishers, Inc., 951 Pershing Dr., Silver Spring, MD 20910-4464 Fax # (301) 589-8493; Title Tel # (301) 589-5103 Title Fax # (301) 587-1081
Personnel: Publisher-Henry E. Kleiner, Editor-Leonard A. Eiserer
Editorial Description: Training news and related information.
General Info: Yr. Est. 1976, Monthly
Subscriptions: Indv. $175, Inst. $175, Can. $175, For. $189
List Rental: Rents Lists

Government Union Critique
   See: LABOR UNION

Government WasteWatch   *Consumer*

Publishing Co: Citizens Against Goverment Waste, Suite 400, 1301 Conneticut Ave., NW, Washington, DC 20036
Personnel: Editor-Mark Rhoads
Editorial Description: Info about goverment spending and wasteful legislation.
General Info: Quarterly

Governmental Affairs Newsletter

Publishing Co: Governmental Affairs Newsletter, 206 Professional Bldg. Univ., Of Missouri-Columbia, Columbia, MO 65211-0001; Title Tel # (314) 882-6401
Editorial Description: Explores governmental affairs and related areas.
General Info: Yr. Est. 1966, 11x/yr.
Subscriptions: Indv. $15

Governors' Bulletin   *Association*

Publishing Co: Natl. Governors' Assn., 444 N Capitol St NW Ste 267, Washington, DC 20001-1512; Title Tel # (202) 624-5330 Title Fax # (202) 624-8832
Personnel: Editor-Alan Janesch
Editorial Description: Issues of interest to states, including state & federal programs, legislation, & regulations.
General Info: (Formerly Governor's Weekly Bulletin), Bi-weekly, Trim Size-8½ x 11, 4 pages, ISSN: 0888-8647, 2 Color, Newsprint
Subscriptions: Indv. $50
Circulation: Total-4,000
Printing Co: State Services Organization, 444 N. Capitol St., Washington, DC 20001 Tel # (202) 624-5490

Grant Advisor
   See: EDUCATION

Guide to Government Contracting

Publishing Co: CCH, Inc., 2700 Lake Cook Rd., Riverwoods, IL 60015 Parent Co.-Kluwer Law & Taxation Publishers, Cambridge; Title Tel # (847) 267-7000 Title Fax # (800) 224-8299
Editorial Description: Provides an all explanation, basic understanding of the government contracting field. Over 1,500 pages cite the significant cases, and contain the relevant statutes and applicable sections of FAR necessary to do business with the federal government.
General Info: Monthly, Looseleaf
Subscriptions: Indv. $416

Guide to Medical Device Regulation
   See: MEDICINE

Guide to Transfer Pricing
   Compliance   *Business*

Publishing Co: Thompson Publishing Group, 1725 K Street, NW, Washington, DC 20006 Tel # (202) 872-4000
Editorial Description: Compliance guide covering transfer pricing regulation.
General Info: Monthly

Guide to U.S. Food Safety Law
   See: FOOD

Guide to Used Oil Regulations
   See: OILS & FATS

HLB Newsletter
   See: MEDICINE

HR Sample Policies and
   Government Forms   *Business*

Publishing Co: Bureau of National Affairs, Inc., 1231 25th St. NW, Bldg. N-200, Washington, DC 20037-1157; Title Tel # (202) 452-4200 Title Fax # (202) 822-8092
Personnel: Publisher-William A. Beltz, Mng. Editor-Bill Manville, Circ. Mgr.-Gary C. Seltzer
Editorial Description: A four-volume set: 2 volumes 'Sample Policies & Forms: & 2 volumes 'Government Forms, Notices, & Posters.' Part of the BNA Policy & Practice Series.
General Info: Yr. Est. 1993, Irregular, Trim Size-8½ x 11, Offset press, Looseleaf
Subscriptions: Indv. $376

Hay Market News
   See: AGRICULTURE

Hazardous Materials Transportation
   See: ENVIRONMENT & ECOLOGY

Hazardous Waste News
   See: ENVIRONMENT & ECOLOGY

Hidden Child, The   *Consumer, Association*

Publishing Co: Hidden Child Foundation/ADL, 823 United Nations Plaza, New York, NY 10017
Editorial Description: For those who were children hidden during WWII.
General Info: Yr. Est. 1991, Quarterly

Highway Financing & Construction/State Capitals
   See: ROADS & STREETS

Hill Report, The
   See: POLITICS

Honolulu Employee Journal   *Consumer, Association*

Publishing Co: Honolulu Office of Information, City Hall, Honolulu, HI 96813; Title Tel # (808) 523-4385
Personnel: Editor-Francis Marzen
Editorial Description: Areas of interest for employees in their work, including safety, training, towards programs, collective bargaining, health fund, retirement, classification and pay, labor relations.
General Info: Yr. Est. 1971, Bi-monthly, Trim Size-8½ x 11, Web press, 8 pages, No Color
Circulation: (100% controlled), Total-9,500

Housing Affairs Letter
   See: REAL ESTATE

Housing Law Bulletin
   See: PUBLIC MANAGEMENT & PLANNING

IPS, Local Government
   Newsletter

Publishing Co: Institute of Public Service, Univ. of Conn., Box U14, Storrs, CT 06268; Title Tel # (203) 486-2829
Personnel: Editor-John Azzaretto
General Info: Quarterly, 4 pages
Circulation: Total-3,000

IRRC Mediator   *Business, Consumer*

Publishing Co: Independent Regulatory Review Commission, 333 Market St Fl 14, Harrisburg, PA 17101-2210; Title Tel # (717) 783-5417
Editorial Description: For those intersted in the regulatory review process of Pennsylvania.
General Info: Yr. Est. 1993, Monthly

Idaho Cities   *Association*

Publishing Co: Assn. of Idaho Cities, 3314 Grace St, Boise, ID 83703-5836; Title Tel # (208) 344-8594 Title Fax # (208) 344-8677
Personnel: Editor-William Jarocki, Adv. Dir.-Marc Eesley
Editorial Description: Idaho city government and various state/federal activities impacting cities.
General Info: Yr. Est. 1974, Monthly, Trim Size-8½ x 11, Offset press, 12 pages, 3% ads, 2 Color, Newsprint
Subscriptions: Indv. $18
Circulation: Total-2,200
Advertising: Inquire for rates.

Illinois Voter
   See: POLITICS

Illinois Workers' Compensation Law Bulletin
   See: LAW

Immigration 2000

Publishing Co: Federation for American Immigration Reform, 1666 Connecticut Ave NW, Ste. 400, Washington, DC 20009-1039; Title Tel # (202) 328-7004
Editorial Description: For anyone who is thinking of writing or determining government economic policies on immigration.
Subscriptions: Indv. $8

Immigration Report   *Association*

Publishing Co: FAIR, 1666 Conneticut Ave., N.W., Suite 400, Washington, DC 20009; Title Tel # (202) 328-7004 Title Fax # (202) 387-3447
Personnel: Editor-Louisa Parker
Editorial Description: News on legal and illegal immigration into the United States.
General Info: Yr. Est. 1979, Monthly, Trim Size-8$\frac{1}{2}$ x 11, 6 pages, ISSN: 1067-3337, 2 Color, Matte, Saddle-stitched
Subscriptions: Indv. $25
Circulation: Total-32,694
List Rental: List Management Co.: MPG List Company, 115 South Union Street, Suite 308, Alexandria, VA 22314 Tel # (703) 683-3635, Actives: $125/M
Printing Co: Balmar Graphics, 1021 15th St NW, Washington, DC 20005-2601 Tel # (202) 659-3610

Import and Customs Compliance Guide   *Business*

Publishing Co: Thompson Publishing Group, 1725 K Street, NW, Washington, DC 20006 Tel # (202) 872-4000
Editorial Description: Comprehensive guide to complying with U.S. Customs regulations.
General Info: Monthly
Subscriptions: Indv. $547

Indian Affairs
See: ETHNIC

Indiana Issues

Publishing Co: David Lantz, Government Affairs Consultant, 7802 Cannonade Dr, Indianapolis, IN 46217-4302; Title Tel # (317) 887-0970
Editorial Description: Focuses on government affairs in Indiana.
General Info: 26x/yr.
Subscriptions: Indv. $80

Indiana Law Reporter
See: LAW

Indiana Legislative Insight *Business*

Publishing Co: Insight Group, PO Box 383, Noblesville, IN 46060-0383; Title Tel # (317) 773-8715 Title Fax # (317) 773-9998
Personnel: Publisher, Editor-Edward D. Feigenbaum
Editorial Description: Focuses on Indiana legislative activity.
General Info: Yr. Est. 1989, 44x/yr., Trim Size-8$\frac{1}{2}$ x 11, Desktop press, 8 pages, ISSN: 1076-8661
Subscriptions: Indv. $295
Circulation: Total-350
Advertising: Accepts Inserts.
List Rental: List Management Co.: Political Resources, Inc., List Managment Division, Box 3177, Burlington, VT 05401 Tel # (802) 660-2869, Fax # (802) 864-9502, Actives: 300

Indiana Public Safety Letter
See: PUBLIC MANAGEMENT & PLANNING

Indochina Newsletter
See: INTERNATIONAL AFFAIRS

Industries in Transition
See: BUSINESS & INDUSTRY

Inside the Administration

Publishing Co: Inside Washington Publishers, P.O. Box 7167, Ben Franklin Station, Washington, DC 20044 Tel # (703) 512-1800; Title Tel # (703) 892-8800 Title Fax # (703) 685-2606
Editorial Description: Government news and developments.
General Info: Yr. Est. 1982, Weekly
Subscriptions: Indv. $490

Inside EPA's Superfund Report
See: ENVIRONMENT & ECOLOGY

Inside the Pentagon
See: MILITARY & NAVAL

Inside the Pentagon's Electronic Combat Report
See: MILITARY & NAVAL

Inside U.S. Trade
See: INTERNATIONAL TRADE

Insider

Publishing Co: City of Cincinnati, City Hall, 801 Plum St., #106, Cincinnati, OH 45202; Title Tel # (513) 352-3216
Personnel: Editor-Mike Gorman
Editorial Description: News & information for city of Cincinnati employees.
General Info: (Formerly Cincy News), Yr. Est. 1982, Monthly, Trim Size-8$\frac{1}{2}$ x 11, Offset press, 4 pages, No Color
Subscriptions: $1/copy
Circulation: (100% controlled), Total-5,600

Insurance Department Directory   *Business*

Publishing Co: National Association of Insurance Commissioners, 120 W. 12th St., Ste. 1100, Kansas City, MO 64105-1925; Title Tel # (816) 842-3600 Title Fax # (816) 471-7004
Personnel: Editor-Karen Montalto, Production Mgr.-Michael Adams, Art Dir.-Therese Manweiler
Editorial Description: Contact information for state insurance departments.
General Info: Yr. Est. 1991, Quarterly, Trim Size-8$\frac{1}{2}$ x 11, 190 pages, No Color, Matte, Other
Subscriptions: Indv. $25
Circulation: Total-1,200

Insurance Regulation/State Capitals
See: INSURANCE

Insurance Regulator
See: INSURANCE

Interaction
See: CHAMBER OF COMMERCE

Interaction
See: ENVIRONMENT & ECOLOGY

Internal Revenue Manual-Audit and Administration
See: TAXES

International Institute of Municipal Clerks Directory   *Association*   **CPM: $52**

Publishing Co: Intl. Institute of Municipal Clerks, 1206 N San Dimas Canyon Rd., San Dimas, CA 91773-1223; Title Tel # (909) 592-4462 Title Fax # (909) 592-1555
Personnel: Publisher-John Devine, Editor-Erin Gathard
General Info: Yr. Est. 1947, Monthly, Trim Size-8$\frac{1}{2}$ x 11, 24 pages, 2 Color, Matte, Saddle-stitched
Subscriptions: Indv. $90, Free With Membership
Circulation: Total-10,000
Advertising: $525. Accepts Inserts.
List Rental: Rents Lists

Iowa Legislative News Service Bulletin   *Association*

Publishing Co: Iowa Legislative News Service, Inc., PO Box 8370, Des Moines, IA 50301-8370; Title Tel # (515) 288-4676
Editorial Description: Legislative news of Iowa.
General Info: Yr. Est. 1954, Daily
Subscriptions: Indv. $260, $4/copy
Circulation: Total-300

Issue Bulletin

Publishing Co: Heritage Foundation, 214 Massachusetts Ave NE, Washington, DC 20002-4999; Title Tel # (202) 546-4400
Editorial Description: Examination of bills currently before congress.
General Info: Letrpr. press, 12 pages
Subscriptions: Indv. $125, $3/copy

John Pugsley's Journal
See: BANKING & FINANCE

Journal Update
See: POLITICS

Judaica Society International
See: INTERNATIONAL AFFAIRS

Kentucky Attorney General Opinions
See: LAW

Kentucky Horizons

Publishing Co: Kentucky Legislative Research Commission, Capitol #300, Frankfort, KY 40601; Title Tel # (502) 564-8100 Title Fax # (502) 223-5094
Editorial Description: Covers legislative issues, etc.
General Info: Yr. Est. 1988, Monthly
Subscriptions: Indv. $10

LIC International
Business

Publishing Co: LIC International, Inc, PO Box 10265, Arlington, VA 22210-1265
Tel # (703) 516-9919 Fax # (703) 243-1197
General Info: Yr. Est. 1993, Monthly
Subscriptions: Indv. $50, Inst. $80, Can. $90, For. $96, $6/copy
Circulation: Total-500

Labor Arbitration in Government
See: LAW

Law Enforcement-New England
See: LAW ENFORCEMENT & PENOLOGY

Left Out
See: POLITICS

Legal-Legislative Reporter
See: LAW

Legi-Slate Letter

Publishing Co: Legi-Slate, Inc., Washington Post Co., 777 N Capitol St NE Ste 900, Washington, DC 20002-4239; Title Tel # (202) 898-2300
Personnel: Editor-Nancy Hartwell
General Info: 4 pages

Legiscon Statehouse Report

Publishing Co: Legiscon Statehouse Report, 703 N 7th St, Baton Rouge, LA 70802-5327; Title Tel # (504) 343-9829 Title Fax # (504) 338-5243
Personnel: Editor-Jim Lee
Editorial Description: Statehouse news and legislative issues.
General Info: Yr. Est. 1975, Weekly
Subscriptions: Indv. $300

Lender Liability Law Report
See: LAW

Lesbian/Gay Law Notes
See: GAY & LESBIAN INTEREST

Liaison
Business, Association   **CPM: $250**

Publishing Co: Intergovernmental Committee on Urban & Regional Research, 150 Eglinton Ave. E., #301, Toronto, ON M4P 1E8 Canada; Title Tel # (416) 973-5644 Title Fax # (416) 973-1375
Personnel: Editor-Wayne Berry
Editorial Description: Provides a forum for the exchange of information on urban, rural and regional research in Canada.
General Info: Yr. Est. 1989, Bi-monthly, Trim Size-8½ x 11, 32 pages, ISSN: 0843-5278, Color-cover, Matte, Saddle-stitched
Subscriptions: Indv. $60, $10/copy
Circulation: Total-1,500
Advertising: $375.
List Rental: Rents Lists

Lobby Law Update

Publishing Co: Bonsib Agencies Inc., PO Box 6152, Bloomington, IN 47407-6152
Circulation: Total-275

Local Government Newsnet
See: TELEVISION & VIDEO

Local Health Officers News
Business, Association   **CPM: $555**

Publishing Co: U.S. Conference of Local Health Officers, 1620 Eye St. , N. W., Washington, DC 20006; Title Tel # (202) 293-7330 Title Fax # (202) 293-2352
Personnel: Publisher-J. Thomas Cochran, Editor-Alan E. Gambrell, Production Ed.-Stephen K. Horn
Editorial Description: Local health dept. information, federal & state policy updates.
General Info: (Formerly City Health Officers News), Yr. Est. 1960, Bi-monthly, Trim Size-8½ x 11, Desktop press, 6 pages, 2 Color, Recycled, Saddle-stitched
Subscriptions: Indv. $35, $5/copy
Circulation: Total-900
Advertising: $500.
List Rental: Actives: 2,000, $250/M

Local/State Funding Report

Publishing Co: Government Information Services, Inc., 4301 Fairfax Dr., Ste. 875, Arlington, VA 22203-1627 Tel # (703) 528-1000; Title Tel # (703) 528-1082 Title Fax # (703) 528-6060
Personnel: Publisher-James J. Marshall, Editor-Jeanne M. Williams, Circ. Mgr.-Joyce Gulizia, Mktg. Dir.-Richard Erb
Editorial Description: Details private & federal sources of financial aid & technical assistance for state, city, county govts. & community & non-profit groups. Includes weekly Grant Alerts with new programs, funding opportunities, and Federal Register announcements.
General Info: (Formerly Local Government Funding Report), Yr. Est. 1973, Weekly, 18 pages, ISSN: 0741-3173
Subscriptions: Indv. $239
List Rental: Rents Lists
Printing Co: Newsletter Press, 76 Valley St, East Providence, RI 02914-4424 Tel # (401) 438-5352

Lottery, Paramutual & Casino Regulations/State Capitals
See: GAMBLING

MIRS Legislative Report & Capitol Capsule

Publishing Co: Michigan Information & Research Service, Inc., 421 W Ionia St, Lansing, MI 48933-1103; Title Tel # (517) 482-2125 Title Fax # (517) 482-1307
Personnel: Editor-Todd Carter
Editorial Description: Features legislative news and related items.
General Info: Yr. Est. 1961, Daily
Subscriptions: Indv. $1,200

MSW Solutionsr
See: SANITATION

Manhattan Borough Watch
See: REGIONAL INTEREST

Manhattan Forum
See: REGIONAL INTEREST

Manitoba Decisions, Civil and Criminal Cases
See: LAW

Maryland State Data Center Newsletter

Publishing Co: Maryland Office of Planning, State Office Bldg., 301 W. Preston, Baltimore, MD 21201 Tel # (410) 225-4500
General Info: Yr. Est. 1980, Quarterly

Medical Devices Reporter
See: DRUGS & PHARMACEUTICALS

Medical Office Report

Publishing Co: Washington G-2 Reports, 1111 14th St NW Ste 711, Washington, DC 20005-5603; Title Tel # (202) 789-1034
Personnel: Editor-Jim Curren

Mental Health Law Reporter
See: PSYCHOLOGY

Michigan Workers' Compensation Law Reporter
See: LAW

Midwest Political Consultant
See: POLITICS

Minnesota Government Report

Publishing Co: Minnesota Government Report, PO Box 441, Willernie, MN 55090-0441; Title Tel # (612) 429-0423
Personnel: Publisher-Jean Dawson
Editorial Description: Covers the state government.
General Info: Yr. Est. 1978
Subscriptions: Indv. $240

Monday: a weekly newsletter on refugee and immigration issues
See: ETHNIC

Montana League of Cities
See: PUBLIC MANAGEMENT & PLANNING

Monthly Product Announcement
See: BUSINESS & INDUSTRY

Mortgage Marketplace
See: BANKING & FINANCE

Motor Vehicle Regulation/State Capitals
See: AUTOMOTIVE

Municipal Litigation Reporter
See: LAW

Municipal News
See: REGIONAL INTEREST

Municipal Open Line   *Association*

Publishing Co: Union of Nova Scotia Municipalities, Suite 1106, 1809 Barrington Street, Halifax, NS B3J 3K8 Canada; Title Tel # (902) 423-8331
Personnel: Editor-Sherman Zwicker
Editorial Description: Information of interest or concern to municipal governments.
General Info: Yr. Est. 1973, Monthly, Mimeo press, 10 pages
Subscriptions: Indv. $10
Circulation: Total-870

NAIC News, The
See: INSURANCE

NC State Data Center Newsletter

Publishing Co: Office of State Budge & Mgmt., 116 W Jones St, Raleigh, NC 27603-8005

NCLG Newsletter

Publishing Co: Natl. Conference of Lieutenant Governors, C/O Council of State Govts., Box 11910, Lexington, KY 40578-1910; Title Tel # (606) 231-1813 Title Fax # (606) 231-1970
General Info: Quarterly

NIGP Technical Bulletin
See: PURCHASING

NIMLO Congressional News

Publishing Co: Natl. Institute of Municipal Law Officers, 1000 Connecticut Ave NW Ste, 902, Washington, DC 20036-5302; Title Tel # (202) 466-5424 Title Fax # (202) 785-0152
Personnel: Editor-Benjamin Brown
Editorial Description: Municipal law developments in Congress.
General Info: Yr. Est. 1986, Bi-monthly

NOTES

Publishing Co: NYC Dept. of Records & Information Services, 31 Chambers St Rm 305, New York, NY 10007-1210; Title Tel # (212) 566-0598 Title Fax # (212) 385-4253
Editorial Description: Information from a variety of municipal departments.
General Info: Yr. Est. 1913, Quarterly
Subscriptions: Indv. $10

NSI Advisory
See: SECURITY & SURVEILLANCE

Nash & Cibinic Report, The
See: LAW

National Association for State Information Newsletter-Exchange

Publishing Co: National Association for State Information Systems, Inc., Box 11910 Iron Works Pike, Lexington, KY 40578-1910; Title Tel # (606) 231-1870 Title Fax # (606) 231-1870
Personnel: Editor-Louise Spieler
General Info: Yr. Est. 1970, Semi-annually
Circulation: Total-900

National Bulletin   *Association*

Publishing Co: Jewish Civil Service Employees, Inc., Box 688, G.P.O., New York, NY 10121-0035
Personnel: Editor-Elias Levin
General Info: Semi-annually
Circulation: Total-10,000
Advertising: Inquire for rates.

National Public Employment Reporter
See: LAW

Nevada Families

Publishing Co: Nevada Families Eagle Forum, PO Box 656, Sparks, NV 89432-0656; Title Tel # (702) 358-5313
Personnel: Publisher, Editor-Janine Hansen
Editorial Description: Issues concerning family, natl. defense, tax reduction-constitutional government, pro life.
General Info: (Formerly ProFamily Coalition), Yr. Est. 1975, Monthly, Letrpr. press, 6 pages
Subscriptions: Indv. $10
Circulation: Total-2,500

New American View   *Business, Association*

Publishing Co: New American View, PO Box 999, Herndon, VA 22070-0999; Title Tel # (703) 478-0592 Title Fax # (703) 478-0142
Personnel: Publisher, Editor-Victor Marchetti, Circ. Dir., Production Mgr.-Donna McGrath, Promotion Dir.-W.G. Sweet
Editorial Description: Seeks to counter the excessive infuence in the American government and Congress of the single-issue, pro-Israeli lobby and promote a balanced U.S. policy towards the Middle East.
General Info: Yr. Est. 1987, Semi-monthly
Subscriptions: Indv. $100, $5/copy

New England City & Town
See: PUBLIC MANAGEMENT & PLANNING

New England Harbormaster

Publishing Co: Thomas Lopatosky, 19 Joslin Street, Providence, RI 02909-2599; Title Tel # (401) 751-6217
Personnel: Publisher, Editor-Thomas J. Lopatosky
Editorial Description: News and ideas for harbormasters.
General Info: Yr. Est. 1995, 10x/yr., Trim Size-8½ x 11, 10 pages, Matte
Subscriptions: Indv. $20, Inst. $20, $3/copy

New Forces

Publishing Co: New Force Publishing, 6505 E Central Ave # 176, Wichita, KS 67206-1924
Personnel: Publisher, Editor-Timothy Mayer
Editorial Description: New Forces is a nationalist publication that covers issues in culture, politics, foreign affairs, literature, & the national interest.
General Info: Yr. Est. 1989, Monthly, 4 pages
Subscriptions: Indv. $5, Can. $6, For. $8

New Technology Week
See: SCIENCE

New Urban Voice   CPM: $152

Publishing Co: Saskatchewan Urban Municipalities Assn., 200-1819 Cornwall St., Regina, SK S4P 2K4 Canada; Title Tel # (306) 525-3727 Title Fax # (306) 565-3550
Personnel: Editor-Janice Sierawitch, Adv. Dir.-J. Doris Lerner
General Info: (Formerly Urban Voice), Bi-monthly, Trim Size-8½ x 11, Web press, 20 pages, 3% ads, No Color, Saddle-stitched
Circulation: Total-3,000
Advertising: $456. Accepts Inserts.
Printing Co: Commercial Printers, 1935 Albert St., Regina, SK S4P 2T6 Canada Tel # (306) 352-8671

New York Civil Service Update
See: EMPLOYMENT

New York Legislative Service City Report   *Business*

Publishing Co: New York Legislative Service, 299 Broadway, New York, NY 10007-1978; Title Tel # (212) 962-2826 Title Fax # (212) 962-1420
Personnel: Editor-Laird Ehlert
Editorial Description: New York city council and state legislation information.
General Info: Yr. Est. 1980, Weekly, Desktop press, 15 pages, Looseleaf
Subscriptions: Indv. $800, Inst. $800

New York Legislative Service State Report   *Business*

Publishing Co: New York Legislative Service, 299 Broadway, New York, NY 10007-1978; Title Tel # (212) 962-2826 Title Fax # (212) 962-1420
Personnel: Editor-Laird Ehlert
Editorial Description: Categorized reports of all legislation introduced in New York State & of all laws passed & vetoed.
General Info: Yr. Est. 1946, Weekly, Desktop press, 30 pages, Recycled, Looseleaf
Subscriptions: Indv. $1,200, Inst. $1,200

New York State Contract Reporter

Publishing Co: NYS Contract Reporter, PO Box 4452, Utica, NY 13504-4452; Title Tel # (518) 283-0393 Title Fax # (518) 282-0920
General Info: Yr. Est. 1989, Weekly
Subscriptions: Indv. $150

New York State Law Digest
See: LAW

News Digest   *Association*   CPM: $51

Publishing Co: Intl. Institute of Municipal Clerks, 1206 N San Dimas Canyon Rd., San Dimas, CA 91773-1223; Title Tel # (909) 592-4462 Title Fax # (909) 592-1555
Personnel: Publisher-John Devine, Editor-Erin Gothard
Editorial Description: Published for municipal clerks worldwide.
General Info: (Formerly News for Officers of the State Clerks Assn.), Monthly, Trim Size-8½ x 11, Desktop press, 24 pages, 50% ads, No Color, Matte, Saddle-stitched
Subscriptions: Free With Membership
Circulation: Total-10,200
Advertising: $525.

North Star Compass
See: INTERNATIONAL AFFAIRS

Northwest Territories Assn. of Municipalities Newsletter

Publishing Co: Northwest Territories Assn. of Municipalities, Box 1529, Yellowknife, NT X1A 2P2 Canada; Title Tel # (403) 873-8359 Title Fax # (403) 873-5801
Editorial Description: Association news and events.
General Info: Monthly
Circulation: Total-200

Notes

Publishing Co: New York City Dept. of Records & Info Services, 31 Chambers St Rm 305, New York, NY 10007-1210; Title Tel # (212) 566-0598 Title Fax # (212) 385-4253
Personnel: Editor-Jeanette Martinez
Editorial Description: NOTES informs potential reference service users, such as genealogists, historians, researchers, students, subscribers, journalists, city officials and legislative aides about our vast collection of archival, legislative and other reference materials. It also describes the records management techniques and benefits we provide all NYC mayoral agencies.
General Info: Yr. Est. 1914, Quarterly, Trim Size-5½ x 8½, Web press, 16 pages, ISSN: 0731-2385, No Color, Saddle-stitched
Subscriptions: Indv. $10, For. $15, $3/copy
Acquistions: Publication Bought
Circulation: Total-5,000
Advertising: Accepts Inserts.

Nova Scotia Government Employees Union Newsletter
See: LABOR

Nutrition Legislation News
See: NUTRITION

OBD News

Publishing Co: New York City Office of Business Development, 17 John St., New York, NY 10038-4010; Title Tel # (212) 513-6448
Personnel: Editor-Mark Kaufman
Editorial Description: Includes information on city business assistance programs, legislation that affects businesses & taxation issues.
General Info: Quarterly

OGLC Exchange

Publishing Co: Ontario Government Libraries Council, C/o Legislative Library, Toronto, ON M7A 1A2 Canada
Personnel: Editor-Bob Gardner
General Info: Yr. Est. 1984, Bi-monthly, 10 pages, ISSN: 0826-7871

OKI Topics Newsletter
See: PUBLIC MANAGEMENT & PLANNING

OMB Watcher

Publishing Co: OMB Watch/Focus Project, 1731 Connecticut Ave., N.W., Washington, DC 20009-1146; Title Tel # (202) 234-8494 Title Fax # (202) 234-8584
General Info: Yr. Est. 1983, Bi-monthly
Subscriptions: Indv. $35

OMSSA Newsletter

Publishing Co: Ontario Municipal Social Services Assn., 5780 Timberlea Blvd., #108, Mississauga, ON L4W 4W8 Canada; Title Tel # (416) 629-3115
Personnel: Editor-John Anderson
General Info: (Formerly Frontliner), Bi-monthly, 20 pages
Circulation: (100% controlled), Total-800

ORSANCO Quality Monitor
See: WATER SUPPLY, POWER & WASTE

Off the Shelf
See: PURCHASING

Ohio Attorney General Opinions
See: LAW

Ohio Monthly Record
See: LAW

Oil Spill Law Information Service
See: ENVIRONMENT & ECOLOGY

Oil Spill U.S. Law Report
See: LAW

Older Americans Report
See: SENIOR CITIZENS

On Principle

Publishing Co: Apriori Assoc., 278 Gorwin Dr, Holliston, MA 01746-1535
General Info: Yr. Est. 1982, 26x/yr.
Subscriptions: Indv. $52

Ontario Assn. of Committees of Adjustment Newsletter

Publishing Co: Ontario Assn. of Committees of Adjustment, 4 Egan Circle, 1 Huron St., Stratford, ON N4Z 1C7 Canada
Personnel: Editor-Gary Cook
General Info: Quarterly, 6 pages
Circulation: Total-700

Ontario Corporations Law Guide
See: LAW

Ontario Statute Citator

Publishing Co: Canada Law Book Co., Inc., 240 Edward St., Aurora, ON L4G 3S9 Canada Fax # (416) 841-5085; Title Tel # (416) 841-6472
Personnel: Editor-L. R. MacTavish
General Info: Quarterly, Looseleaf
Subscriptions: Indv. $170, Can. $170, For. $170

Operation Big Vote Newsletter

Publishing Co: National Coalition on Black Voter Participation, 1629 K St NW Ste 801, Washington, DC 20006-1602; Title Tel # (202) 898-2220 Title Fax # (202) 659-5025
General Info: Yr. Est. 1976, Quarterly
Subscriptions: Free

Oregon Governmental Notes *Association*

Publishing Co: Bureau of Governmental Research and Service, U. of Oregon, PO Box 3177, Eugene, OR 97403-0177; Title Tel # (503) 686-5232
Personnel: Circ. Mgr., Production Mgr.-Joyce Ray
General Info: Yr. Est. 1977, Quarterly, Trim Size-8½ x 11, Offset press, 8 pages, 2 Color
Circulation: Total-2,000

Ottawa Letter
See: LAW

Our Washington Newsletter
See: ECONOMICS

Outlook/State Capitals, The *Business, Consumer*

Publishing Co: Wakeman/Walworth, 300 N. Washington St., Alexandria, VA 22314-2530; Title Tel # (703) 549-8606 Title Fax # (703) 549-1372
Personnel: Publisher-Keyes Walworth
Editorial Description: Covers all areas of state government and important changes in public policy. Each week is devoted to a different topic.
General Info: (Formerly Outlook from the State Capitals), Yr. Est. 1946, Weekly, Trim Size-8½ x 11, Offset press, ISSN: 1061-9690, No Color
Subscriptions: Indv. $265, Inst. $212, Can. $235, For. $255

PAR Analysis *Association*

Publishing Co: Public Affairs Research Council of Louisiana, Inc., 4664 Jamestown Ave, #300, Baton Rouge, LA 70808; Title Tel # (504) 926-8414 Title Fax # (504) 926-8417
Personnel: Publisher, Editor-Jan Carlock
Editorial Description: Research report on subjects related to state and local government in Louisiana.
General Info: (Formerly PAR News Analysis), Yr. Est. 1951, Trim Size-5½ x 8½, Web press, 6 pages, ISSN: 0030-7807, 2 Color, Coated
Subscriptions: $3/copy
Acquistions: Publication Bought
Circulation: Total-6,000
Printing Co: Franklin Press, 1391 Highland Rd, Baton Rouge, LA 70802-7500 Tel # (504) 387-0504

PAR Legislative Bulletin *Association*

Publishing Co: Public Affairs Research Council of Louisiana, Inc., 4664 Jamestown Ave, #300, Baton Rouge, LA 70808; Title Tel # (504) 926-8414 Title Fax # (504) 926-8417
Personnel: Publisher, Editor-Jan Brashear Carlock
Editorial Description: Analysis of current major bills and resolutions before the Legislature.
General Info: Yr. Est. 1952, Weekly, Trim Size-5½ x 8½, Web press, 8 pages, 2 Color, Newsprint
Subscriptions: $1/copy
Circulation: (100% controlled), Total-6,000
Printing Co: Franklin Press, 1391 Highland Rd, Baton Rouge, LA 70802-7500 Tel # (504) 387-0504

PBC Government Programs Newsletter *Business, Consumer*

Publishing Co: Publishing & Business Consultants, 101 W. 64th St. Unit #3, Inglewood, CA 90302-1255 Tel # (213) 732-3477 Fax # (213) 732-3477
Personnel: Publisher, Editor-Andeson Atia
General Info: Quarterly, 60 pages, ISSN: 1059-2069
Subscriptions: Indv. $180
Advertising: Inquire for rates.

PCS Market Sourcebook *Business*

Publishing Co: BRP (Washington DC), 1333 H St., NW, Suite 1100, West Tower, Washington, DC 20005-4707 Tel # (202) 842-3006 Fax # (202) 842-3047
Editorial Description: Directory of data on FCC auctions for PCS licenses.
General Info: Monthly

PTI Prism *Consumer, Association*

Publishing Co: Public Technology, Inc., 1301 Pennsylvania Ave NW, Washington, DC 20004-1793; Title Tel # (202) 626-2400 Title Fax # (202) 626-2698
Personnel: Editor-Shaden Tageldin
Editorial Description: Management & technological applications for local government to improve productivity & quality of services.
General Info: (Formerly Public Technology News /Public Technology), Yr. Est. 1994, Quarterly, Trim Size-8½ x 11, Offset press, 16 pages, ISSN: 0882-1445, 2 Color
Subscriptions: Free
Circulation: Total-10,000

Patriot Cannon
See: POLITICS

Peace Gazette
See: POLITICS

Pennsylvania Civil Service Commission Observations

Publishing Co: Pennsylvania Civil Service Commission, PO Box 569, Harrisburg, PA 17108-0569; Title Tel # (717) 783-2926
Personnel: Publisher, Editor-George Young, Jr.
Editorial Description: Information on merit system (civil service) activities in Pennsylvania.
General Info: Yr. Est. 1957, Bi-monthly, Trim Size-8½ x 11, 3 pages, Color
Circulation: (100% controlled), Total-2,600

Pennsylvania Discovery & Evidence Reporter
See: LAW

Pennsylvania Divorce & Domestic Relations Reporter
See: LAW

Pennsylvania Injuries & Damages Reporter
See: LAW

Pennsylvania Workers' Compensation Law Reporter
See: LAW

Personnelly Speaking

Publishing Co: City of Wichita, 455 N Main St, Wichita, KS 67202-1603; Title Tel # (316) 268-4351 Title Fax # (316) 268-4519
Editorial Description: News items of importance to city employees.
General Info: (Formerly City Highlight), Yr. Est. 1960, Monthly, Trim Size-8½ x 11, Offset press, 4 pages, No Color, Newsprint
Subscriptions: Free In Designated Area
Circulation: Total-4,200

Pesticide & Toxic Chemical News
See: CHEMISTRY & CHEMICALS

Phyllis Schafly Report *Association*

Publishing Co: Eagle Forum, PO Box 618, Alton, IL 62002-0618 Fax # (618) 462-8909; Title Tel # (618) 462-5415
Personnel: Publisher-Phyllis Schlafly
Editorial Description: Reports legislative activities concerning family, education, defense, economics.
General Info: (Formerly Eagle Forum Newsletter), Yr. Est. 1975, Monthly, Trim Size-8½ x 11, 4 pages, Matte
Subscriptions: Indv. $20
Circulation: Total-60,000
List Rental: Rents Lists

Policy Currents
See: PUBLIC MANAGEMENT & PLANNING

Political Finance & Lobby Reporter
See: POLITICS

Polling Report
See: POLITICS

Positive Economist Bulletin
See: ECONOMICS

Post Industrial Issues

Publishing Co: Center for Technology and Democracy, PO Box 460516, San Francisco, CA 94146-0516; Title Tel # (415) 648-5742
General Info: Yr. Est. 1988, 10x/yr.
Subscriptions: Indv. $28

Presidents' Journal
See: HISTORY

Privacy Journal
See: PHILANTHROPY

Privatization Watch *Business, Consumer*

Publishing Co: Reason Foundation, 3415 S Sepulveda Blvd Ste 400, Los Angeles, CA 90034-6060; Title Tel # (310) 391-2245 Title Fax # (310) 391-4395
Personnel: Publisher-Robert Poole, Jr., Editor-John O'Leary, Adv. Dir.-Raymond Ng
Editorial Description: Reports latest developments in privatization especially ventures in which private companies are awarded exclusive contracts for the provision of a wide array of public services.
General Info: (Formerly Fiscal Watchdog), Yr. Est. 1976, Monthly, Trim Size-8½ x 11, Offset press, 6 pages, Color, Coated
Subscriptions: Indv. $135, Inst. $75, $5/copy
Advertising: Accepts Inserts.
List Rental: Actives: $50/M
Printing Co: Westcoast Printing, 1608 Santa Monica Blvd, Santa Monica, CA 90404-1808 Tel # (310) 828-8708

Problem Solving Information for State & Local Governments
See: BIBLIOGRAPHY

Procedures Review
See: NUCLEAR ENERGY

Prop 65 News
See: ENVIRONMENT & ECOLOGY

Proposed Consolidated Plan

Publishing Co: Department of City Planning, 22 Reade Street 4N, New York, NY 10007

Provincial Legislative Record *Business*

Publishing Co: CCH Canadian Ltd., 6 Garamond Ct., North York, ON M3C 1Z5 Canada Fax # (416) 444-8011 Parent Co.-CCH, Inc., Riverwoods; Title Tel # (416) 441-2992 Title Fax # (416) 444-9011
Personnel: Editor-Joe Wiesberg
Editorial Description: Contains status information of provincial bills, Cumulative record.
General Info: Monthly
Subscriptions: Can. $145

Public Affairs

Publishing Co: Governmental Research Bureau, Univ. of S.D., Vermillion, SD 57069; Title Tel # (605) 677-5702
Personnel: Editor-Steve Feimer
Editorial Description: Extended scholarly treatment of matters of relevance in political science and public administration, usually with application to South Dakota.
General Info: Yr. Est. 1960, Trim Size-8½ x 11, Offset press, 12 pages, Ind/Abs/Online: PAIS, Color
Subscriptions: Free
Circulation: Total-2,000

Public Assistance & Welfare Trends/State Capitals
See: SOCIAL SERVICES & WELFARE

Public Employment Law Notes
See: LAW

Public Employment Reports

Publishing Co: NYPER Publications, PO Box 662, Latham, NY 12110-0662 Tel # (518) 786-1654 Fax # (518) 458-8582; Title Tel # (518) 786-1656 Title Fax # (518) 456-8582
Personnel: Editor-Harvely Randall
General Info: Yr. Est. 1980, Monthly, ISSN: 0889-9789
Subscriptions: Indv. $95, Inst. $95
Advertising: Accepts Inserts.
List Rental: Rents Lists

Public Safety and Justice Policies/State Capitals
See: LAW ENFORCEMENT & PENOLOGY

Public Safety Management
See: FIRE PROTECTION

Public Safety Personnel Updance
See: LAW ENFORCEMENT & PENOLOGY

Public Sector Job Bulletin
See: EMPLOYMENT

Quality of Care
See: DISABILITY

Quorum Report

Publishing Co: Texas Analyst, PO Box 8, Austin, TX 78767-0008; Title Tel # (512) 444-4574
Title Fax # (512) 326-2126
Personnel: Editor-Harvey Kronberg
General Info: Yr. Est. 1982, 22x/yr.
Subscriptions: Indv. $125

RCRA Corrective Action
See: ENVIRONMENT & ECOLOGY

Reading Labor Market
News Release   *Business, Association*

Publishing Co: Penn. Dept. of Labor & Industry/Bureau of Research & Statist, 625 Cherry St, Reading, PA 19602-1152; Title Tel # (215) 378-4314
Editorial Description: Labor market info, industrial employment, unemployment, unemployment rate for Berks County. Factory wage & hour data.
General Info: (Formerly Reading Labor Market Letter), Bi-monthly, Trim Size-8½ x 11½, Mimeo press, 6 pages, No Color
Circulation: Total-1,300

Regional View
See: REGIONAL INTEREST

Regulatory Compliance Watch
See: BANKING & FINANCE

Remediation Review
See: ENVIRONMENT & ECOLOGY

Republican Woman

Publishing Co: National Federation of Republican Women, 310 1st St SE, Washington, DC 20003-1801; Title Tel # (202) 547-9341
Personnel: Publisher-Judy Hughes, Circ. Mgr.-Nina Henson, Editor, Production Mgr., Art Dir.-Karen Johnson
General Info: (Formerly Challenge '88), Yr. Est. 1979, Bi-monthly, Web press, 16 pages, 2 Color, Coated
Subscriptions: Indv. $15
Circulation: Total-140,000

Republican Women of
Capitol Hill Truckline   *Business, Association*

Publishing Co: National Federation of Republican Women, 310 1st St SE, Washington, DC 20003-1801; Title Tel # (202) 547-9341
Personnel: Editor-Lori Stillman
General Info: Yr. Est. 1963, Monthly
Circulation: Total-300

Research Perspectives

Publishing Co: City of Boulder Div. of Research, PO Box 791, Boulder, CO 80306-0791; Title Tel # (303) 441-3270
Personnel: Editor-Thomas Miller, Art Dir.-Susan Ross
Editorial Description: Synopsis of local and national research for Boulder policymakers.
General Info: Yr. Est. 1981, Semi-annually, Trim Size-8½ x 11, Sheetfed press, 4 pages, 2 Color
Circulation: Total-600

Richardson Today   *Consumer*

Publishing Co: City of Richardson Texas, 411 West Arataho, Richardson, TX 75080; Title Tel # (214) 238-4100
Personnel: Editor-Rick McGarry
Editorial Description: Report to keep residents informed about municipal government in its many facets.
General Info: Yr. Est. 1961, Monthly, Trim Size-11 x 17, Web press, 20 pages, No Color, Matte
Acquistions: Publication Bought
Circulation: (83% controlled), Total-30,000

Risky Business

Publishing Co: Risk Manaement Unit, 100 Church Street, 20th Floor, New York, NY 10007
Tel # (212) 788-1430
Editorial Description: Newsletter of the risk management unit.

Rockefeller Institute Bulletin   *Consumer*

Publishing Co: Nelson A. Rockefeller Institute of Govt., 411 State St, Albany, NY 12203-1003
Tel # (518) 443-5258; Title Tel # (518) 443-5522 Title Fax # (518) 443-5788
Personnel: Editor-Michael Malbin, Production Mgr.-Michael Cooper
General Info: Yr. Est. 1991, Annually, Trim Size-8½ x 11, Web press, 88 pages, 2 Color, Coated, Saddle-stitched
Subscriptions: Free To Qualified Recipient

SDACC County Comment   *Association*

Publishing Co: South Dakota Assn. of County Commissioners, 207 E. Capitol, #203, Pierre, SD 57501-3161; Title Tel # (605) 224-4554 Title Fax # (605) 224-4833
Personnel: Production Mgr.-Dennis Hanson, Editor, Circ. Mgr., Art Dir.-Susan Comer
Editorial Description: Covers county government: taxation, welfare, planning, elections. Also views of county officials; calendar of events.
General Info: Yr. Est. 1948, Monthly, Trim Size-8½ x 11, Offset press, 8 pages, ISSN: 1049-7838, 2 Color, Saddle-stitched
Subscriptions: Indv. $12, $1/copy
Circulation: (100% controlled), Total-1,025
Advertising: Inquire for rates.
Printing Co: State Publishing Co., 303 E Sioux Ave, Pierre, SD 57501-3138 Tel # (605) 224-9999

SEC Accounting Rules
See: ACCOUNTING

SEC Case Monitor   *Business*

Publishing Co: Worldwide Videotex Co., PO Box 3273, Boynton Beach, FL 33424-3273; Title Tel # (407) 738-2276 Title Fax # (407) 738-2276
Editorial Description: Decisions on U.S. Securities and Exchange Commission.
General Info: Yr. Est. 1991, Monthly

SEC Docket
See: INVESTMENT

SERB Official Reporter
See: LAW

SNL Weekly ComplianceFax
See: BANKING & FINANCE

Saskatchewan Decisions Civil and Criminal Cases
See: LAW

Searchlight on the City
Council   *Business, Consumer*

Publishing Co: Citizens Union of the City of New York, 198 Broadway, New York, NY 10038-2515; Title Tel # (212) 227-0342 Title Fax # (212) 227-0345
Personnel: Publisher-Jeannette Kahlenberg, Editor-Lenore Chester
Editorial Description: Periodic reporting on & evaluation of the actions of the New York City Council.
General Info: Yr. Est. 1990, Bi-monthly, Trim Size-8½ x 11, 8 pages, 2 Color, Saddle-stitched
Subscriptions: Free To Qualified Recipient
Circulation: Total-12,000

Seattle Arts Newsletter
See: CULTURE & HUMANITIES

Secrecy & Goverment
Bulletin   *Consumer*

Publishing Co: Fed. of American Scientists, 307 Massachusetts Ave NE, Washington, DC 20002-5793; Title Tel # (202) 675-1012
Personnel: Editor-Steven Aftergood
Editorial Description: Challenges excessive government secrecy and promotes free exchange of info to public.
General Info: Monthly, ISSN: 1061-0340

Shenandoah Newsletter
See: ETHNIC

South Dakota Data
Supplement   *Business*

Publishing Co: Business Research Bureau, 414 E. Clark, U of SD, Vermillion, SD 57069; Title Tel # (605) 677-5287
Personnel: Publisher, Editor-Donald Lewis
Editorial Description: Current sales tax comparisons for South Dakota counties & cities.
General Info: Yr. Est. 1984, Bi-monthly, 8 pages, Looseleaf
Subscriptions: Indv. $6
Circulation: Total-200

South Dakota Sales & Use
Tax Report   *Business*

Publishing Co: Business Research Bureau, 414 E. Clark, U of SD, Vermillion, SD 57069; Title Tel # (605) 677-5287
Personnel: Editor, Circ. Mgr.-Donald Lewis
Editorial Description: State,county and city sales tax data.
General Info: Yr. Est. 1983, Bi-monthly, Trim Size-8½ x 11, 175 pages, 2 Color, Looseleaf
Subscriptions: Indv. $60, $10/copy

Spacewatch
See: AERONAUTICS/ASTRONAUTICS

Spectrum Regulation
Handbook
Business

Publishing Co: BRP (Washington DC), 1333 H St., NW, Suite 1100, West Tower, Washington, DC 20005-4707 Tel # (202) 842-3006 Fax # (202) 842-3047
Editorial Description: Rules and procedures for bidding on FCC licenses for wireless communications.
General Info: Monthly

Springfield Scene, The
See: BUSINESS & INDUSTRY

State Budget & Tax News

Publishing Co: State Policy Research, Inc., 182 W. Royal Forest Blvd., Columbus, OH 43214-2029; Title Tel # (614) 447-9443 Title Fax # (614) 447-2077
Personnel: Editor-Harold Hovey, Production Mgr.-Denise Hovey
Editorial Description: State government tax & budget issues, including legislative actions.
General Info: Yr. Est. 1982, Semi-monthly, Trim Size-8½ x 11, Letrpr. press, 12 pages, ISSN: 0742-0498, No Color
Subscriptions: Indv. $220
List Rental: Rents Lists

State CDBG Update

Publishing Co: State CDBG Update, 444 N Capitol St NW Ste 224, Washington, DC 20001-1512 Fax # (202) 393-6435; Title Tel # (202) 393-6435
Editorial Description: Covers developments in the state CDBS programs.
General Info: Bi-monthly, Desktop press, 12 pages, No Color, Newsprint
Subscriptions: Indv. $60
Circulation: Total-200

State Government Alert

Publishing Co: American Institute of Architects, 1735 New York Ave., NW, Washington, DC 20006-5209 Tel # (202) 626-7300; Title Tel # (202) 626-7459
Personnel: Publisher-Sally Wise
Editorial Description: Covers government affairs.
General Info: Quarterly

State Health Notes
See: HEALTH

State Legislative Report
Association

Publishing Co: Natl. Conference of State Legislatures, 1560 Broadway, Ste. 700, Denver, CO 80202-5140 Tel # (303) 830-2200 Fax # (303) 863-8003; Title Tel # (303) 623-7800
Personnel: Circ. Mgr.-Gail Loos
Editorial Description: Brief discussions of current state legislative issues.
General Info: Yr. Est. 1975, Irregular, Looseleaf
Circulation: Total-500

State Policy Reports

Publishing Co: State Policy Research, Inc., 182 W. Royal Forest Blvd., Columbus, OH 43214-2029; Title Tel # (614) 447-9443 Title Fax # (614) 447-2077
Personnel: Publisher, Editor-harold Hovey, Production Mgr.-Denise Hovey
Editorial Description: State revenue & spending policies of significance in all 50 states.
General Info: Yr. Est. 1983, Semi-monthly, Trim Size-8½ x 11, 36 pages, ISSN: 8750-6637, No Color
Subscriptions: Indv. $405, For. $420
List Rental: Rents Lists

State of the Region

Publishing Co: Coastal Bend Council of Governments, Box 9909, Corpus Christi, TX 78469-9909; Title Tel # (512) 883-5743
Personnel: Editor-Juliet Winger
Editorial Description: Issues of regional interest to local governments.
General Info: Yr. Est. 1969, Quarterly, Offset press, 8 pages, No Color, Coated
Circulation: Total-1,100

Substance Abuse Funding News
See: PHILANTHROPY

Taxation and Revenue Policies/State Capitals
See: TAXES

Taxes-Property/State Capitals
See: TAXES

Tennessee Tax Quarterly
See: TAXES

Texas Administration Code

Publishing Co: Hart Information Systems, 8030 Shoal Creek Blvd, Austin, TX 78757-8039; Title Tel # (512) 454-3786
Personnel: Publisher-Chris Hart, Editor-Nita Yeck
Editorial Description: All state agency regulations separated into 15 titles, 22 volumes.
General Info: Yr. Est. 1985, Quarterly, Offset press, 1,500 pages, No Color, Looseleaf
Circulation: Total-1,200
Printing Co: Hart Graphics, 8000 Shoal Creek Blvd., P.O. Box 968, Austin, TX 78767 Tel # (512) 454-4761

This Week in Washington
See: SOCIAL SERVICES & WELFARE

Town Crier
Business　　　　CPM$1035

Publishing Co: Sponsor-Natl. Association of Towns & Townships, Natl. Center for Small Communities, 1522 K St NW Ste 600, Washington, DC 20005-1202; Title Tel # (202) 737-5200 Title Fax # (202) 289-7996
Personnel: Editor-Ronnie Kweller
Editorial Description: News about the National Center for Small Communities, the research and training program of the National Association of Towns and Townships. The Center offers small-town officials training materials on rural job creation, recycling, hazardous materials response and innovative financing.
General Info: Yr. Est. 1984, 3x/yr., Offset press, 4 pages, ISSN: 0748-5883, 2 Color, Newsprint
Circulation: Total-1,000
Advertising: $1,035.
List Rental: Rents Lists

Trailblazer

Publishing Co: Rails to Trails Conservancy, 1400 16th St., NW, Ste. 300, Washington, DC 20036-2217; Title Tel # (202) 797-5400 Title Fax # (202) 797-5411
Personnel: Publisher-David Burwell, Promotion Dir.-David Hintz
General Info: Trim Size-8½ x 11
List Rental: Actives: $65/M

Train It
See: RAILROADS

Treaty Council News

Publishing Co: Intl. Indian Treaty Council Info. Office, 54 Mint St., Ste. 400, San Francisco, CA 94103-1823
Personnel: Editor-Andrea Carmen
Subscriptions: Indv. $15, Inst. $25, For. $35, $4/copy
Printing Co: GRAPH-X, 740 H St, Fresno, CA 93721-2820

Underground Storage Tank News
See: PETROLEUM & NATURAL GAS

Understanding Defense
See: MILITARY & NAVAL

U.S. Cuba Bulletin

Publishing Co: Cuban-American Committee, Inc., 1601 Connecticut Ave NW Ste, 500, Washington, DC 20009-1035; Title Tel # (202) 667-6367
General Info: Quarterly

U.S. ITC Update
Business

Publishing Co: Worldwide Videotex Co., PO Box 3273, Boynton Beach, FL 33424-3273; Title Tel # (407) 738-2276 Title Fax # (407) 738-2276
Editorial Description: Reports on the International Trade Commission's decisions.
General Info: Yr. Est. 1991, Monthly

U.S. Regulatory Reporter
See: DRUGS & PHARMACEUTICALS

United We Stand America
See: POLITICS

University of Alaska.
Cooperative Extension
Service. Local
Government Hi-Lites
Business, Association

Publishing Co: University of Alaska, Cooperative Extension, 193 Arctic Health Bldg., Fairbanks, AK 99775-6180 Tel # (907) 474-6356; Title Tel # (907) 278-3141
Personnel: Publisher, Editor-Anthony Nakazawa, Circ. Mgr., Adv. Dir., Art Dir.-Eva Alexie
Editorial Description: Selected topics in Alaska local government financial and management operations.
General Info: Yr. Est. 1976, Bi-monthly, Trim Size-8½ x 11, Sheetfed press, 6 pages, Color
Circulation: Total-1,000

University of Virginia News
Letter

Publishing Co: Center for Public Service, UVA, 918 Emmet Street N., #300, Charlottesville, VA 22903-4832; Title Tel # (804) 924-3396 Title Fax # (804) 924-4538
Personnel: Editor-Sandra Wiley
Editorial Description: Each monthly article focuses on a pressing public policy concern & its impact on Virginia State and/or local government.
General Info: Yr. Est. 1925, 10x/yr., Trim Size-8½ x 11, Letrpr. press, 8 pages, ISSN: 0042-0271, 2 Color, Matte
Subscriptions: $4/copy
Circulation: Total-4,300
Printing Co: Univ. Printing Office, Univ. of Virginia, Ivy Rd., Charlottesville, VA 22903 Tel # (804) 924-7186

Urban, State & Local Law
News
Association

Publishing Co: American Bar Association, 750 N. Lake Shore Dr., Chicago, IL 60611-4497 Tel # (312) 988-6115 Fax # (312) 988-6030; Title Tel # (312) 988-5522 Title Fax # (312) 988-5528
General Info: Yr. Est. 1978, ISSN: 0195-7686, 2 Color, Newsprint, Saddle-stitched
Circulation: Total-6,000
List Rental: Rents Lists

Utah Foundation Research
Report · *Association, Business*
Publishing Co: Utah Foundation, 10 W 100 S Ste 323, Salt Lake City, UT 84101-1544;
Title Tel # (801) 364-1837
Editorial Description: Studies of State and Local Government in Utah.
General Info: Yr. Est. 1945, Monthly, Trim Size-8½ x 11, Offset press, 4 pages, No Color
Subscriptions: Indv. $30, $1/copy

Vietnam Insight
Publishing Co: Nat'l United Front for the Liberation of Vietnam, PO Box 7826, San Jose, CA 95150;
Title Tel # (408) 363-6892
Editorial Description: A forum sponsored by the National United Front for the Liberation of Vietnam.
Subscriptions: Indv. $12, Can. $24, For. $24

Virginia Municipal Review
Publishing Co: Review Publishing Co., Inc., 2601 W Cary St, Richmond, VA 23220-5118;
Title Tel # (804) 782-1043
Personnel: Publisher-Richard Walker
General Info: Trim Size-7 x 10
Subscriptions: Indv. $6
Circulation: Total-2,000

Washington Bakery Report
See: BAKING

Washington Federal Science Newsletter
See: SCIENCE

Washington Newsletter · *Association*
Publishing Co: Natl. Council of Jewish Women, 53 W. 23rd St., New York, NY 10010-4299
Tel # (212) 645-4040; Title Tel # (212) 532-1740
Personnel: Editor-Joan Suall
Editorial Description: Legislative news.
General Info: Quarterly

Washington Watch
See: BABY

Water Current
See: SCIENCE

Ways & Means · *Association*
Publishing Co: Center for Policy Alternatives, 1875 Connecticut Ave NW Ste, 710, Washington, DC
20009-5728 Fax # (202) 986-2539; Title Tel # (202) 387-6030
Personnel: Publisher-Linda Tarr-Whelan, Editor-Farley Peters, Production Mgr.-Scott Johnson, Circ.
Mgr., Promotion Dir.-Judy Goldsmith
Editorial Description: Alternative legislation for solutions to state and local government problems.
General Info: Yr. Est. 1975, Quarterly, Trim Size-8½ x 11, Sheetfed press, 8 pages, ISSN: 0193-
4716, Ind/Abs/Online: UBB. AFF. ABS., 2 Color
Subscriptions: Indv. $30, $2/copy
Circulation: Total-3,300

Webster Agricultural Letter
See: AGRICULTURE

West Virginia Economic Summary
See: ECONOMICS

What's Happening · *Business, Association*
Publishing Co: Metropolitan Area Planning Agency, 2222 Cuming St, Omaha, NE 68102-4328
Fax # (404) 342-0949; Title Tel # (402) 444-6866
Personnel: Publisher-Lou Violi, Production Mgr.-John Bair, Editor, Promotion Dir.-Pat Jesse
Editorial Description: Features MAPA programs & data products, up-coming meetings & special
events, federal & state programs & requirements, and regional news items.
General Info: (Formerly MAPA Capsule), Yr. Est. 1967, Monthly, Trim Size-8½ x 11, Letrpr. press, 4
pages, No Color, Matte
Subscriptions: Free
Circulation: (100% controlled), Total-950

White House Weekly
Publishing Co: Feistritzer Pubs., 4401a Connecticut Ave NW # 212, Washington, DC 20008-2325;
Title Tel # (301) 386-3444 Title Fax # (301) 322-4350
Personnel: Publisher-C. Emily Feistritzer, Editor-Warren Rogers, Circ. Mgr.-Betty Moran
General Info: Yr. Est. 1981, 50x/yr.
Subscriptions: Indv. $295

Wisconsin Law Reporter
See: LAW

Wisconsin Taxpayer
See: TAXES

World Aeroospace & Defense Intelligence
See: AERONAUTICS/ASTRONAUTICS

World Chemical News
See: FOOD

World Federalist News
See: INTERNATIONAL AFFAIRS

Yes on 23/Liberty
Amendment News · *Consumer*
Publishing Co: Liberty Amendment Committee of the USA, PO Box 2386, El Cajon, CA 92021-0386;
Title Tel # (619) 579-8500
Personnel: Editor-Armin Moths
General Info: Irregular, Trim Size-11¼ x 17, 4 pages, No Color, Newsprint

Your Wisconsin
Government · *Association*
Publishing Co: Wisconsin Taxpayers Alliance, 335 W Wilson St, Madison, WI 53703-3612;
Title Tel # (608) 255-4581
Personnel: Editor-James Morgan
Editorial Description: Legislative activity, state & local government & taxation.
General Info: Yr. Est. 1961, Bi-weekly, Offset press, 2 pages, No Color
Subscriptions: Indv. $44
Circulation: Total-2,400

Youth Record
See: YOUTH

GROCERY

Cat Industry Newsletter
See: CATS

Cleveland Food Dealer · *Business* · CPM: $203
Publishing Co: Cleveland Food Dealers Association, Inc., 5800 Grant Ave, Cleveland, OH 44105;
Title Tel # (216) 641-2444 Title Fax # (216) 641-2446
Personnel: Editor, Adv. Dir.-Alvin Palack
Editorial Description: News of the retail food industry.
General Info: (Formerly Cleveland Grocer, The), Yr. Est. 1914, Monthly, Trim Size-9 x 12, Offset
press, 18 pages, No Color
Subscriptions: Indv. $12, $1/copy
Circulation: Total-760
Advertising: $155.
Printing Co: Elkon Graphics, 4529 Detroit Ave, Cleveland, OH 44102-2213 Tel # (216) 651-9777,
Fax # (216) 651-9779

Communicator · *Association*
Publishing Co: Certified Grocers of Calif., Ltd., 2601 S Eastern Ave, Los Angeles, CA 90040-1401;
Title Tel # (213) 723-7476
Personnel: Editor-Shelley Machock
Editorial Description: For retail members of certified Grocers of California, Ltd.
General Info: Monthly, Trim Size-11 x 17, Sheetfed press, 4 pages, No Color, Newsprint
Circulation: Total-1,500

Creative Marketing Newsletter
See: ADVERTISING & MARKETING

Dog Industry Newsletter
See: DOGS

HBE Buyer
Publishing Co: Bantam Doubleday Dell Publishing Group, 1540 Broadway, New York, NY
10036-4039; Title Tel # (212) 354-6500
Personnel: Editor-Sara Sheldon, Adv. Dir.-Barney O'Hara
Editorial Description: Newsletter for supermarket buyers and rack jobbers of health and beauty aids.
Sales, marketing, and merchandising information, new product news.
General Info: Monthly, Trim Size-8½ x 11, 6 pages
Subscriptions: Indv. $15
Circulation: Total-2,500
Advertising: Inquire for rates.

Healthy Eating
See: FOOD

Independent Grocer · *Association*
Publishing Co: Canadian Fed. of Independent Grocers, 2235 Sheppard Ave. E., Ste. 902,
Willowdale, ON M2J 5B5 Canada; Title Tel # (416) 492-2311
Personnel: Editor-A. Wilshaw
Editorial Description: Canada's leading news bulletin for the independent grocer.
General Info: (Formerly Headlines), Yr. Est. 1961, Monthly, Trim Size-8½ x 11, Offset press, 8
pages, No Color
Circulation: (100% controlled), Total-5,300

Issues Bulletin *Business, Association*

Publishing Co: Food Marketing Institute, 800 Connecticut Ave., N.W., Washington, DC 20006-2701; Title Tel # (202) 452-8444
Personnel: Editor-Elizabeth Wise
Editorial Description: Issues & ideas important to food distribution industry.
General Info: Yr. Est. 1977, Monthly, Trim Size-8½ x 11, Sheetfed press, 8 pages, ISSN: 0275-8059, 2 Color, Newsprint, Saddle-stitched
Subscriptions: Indv. $35, Inst. $35, Free With Membership
Circulation: Total-4,100
Printing Co: Allen-Wayne, Ltd., 5404a Port Royal Rd, Springfield, VA 22151-2301
Tel # (703) 321-7414, Fax # (703) 321-8179

Louisiana Market Bulletin *Business, Association*

Publishing Co: Louisiana Dept. of Agriculture, Office of Marketing, Box 3334, Baton Rouge, LA 70821; Title Tel # (504) 922-1328
Personnel: Editor-Renee Tulle
Editorial Description: Covers selling, buying, and exchanging surplus agricultural items in Louisiana and other states.
General Info: Yr. Est. 1916, Weekly, Trim Size-17 x 22, Offset press, 4 pages, No Color
Circulation: Total-32,500
Advertising: Inquire for rates.

New Product News *Business*

Publishing Co: BPI Communications, The Merchandise Mart, Suite 936, Chicago, IL 60654; Title Tel # (312) 464-8501 Title Fax # (312) 464-8550
Personnel: Publisher-Lynn Dornblaser, Editor-Martin Friedman
Editorial Description: Covers new product introductions in supermarkets, gourmet shops, and health food stores. Provides statistics and analysis.
General Info: (Formerly Gorman's New Product News), Yr. Est. 1964, Monthly, Trim Size-8½ x 11, Sheetfed press, 60 pages, ISSN: 1048-020X, 2 Color, Newsprint
Subscriptions: Indv. $359, Inst. $359, Can. $432, For. $432, $40/copy
Acquistions: Publication Sold
Circulation: Total-1,100
Advertising: Inquire for rates. Accepts Inserts.
List Rental: Actives: 1,100
Printing Co: Arlington Press, 1187 Tower Road, Schaumburg, IL 60173 Tel # (708) 884-8414, Fax # (708) 882-1863

RBA Insight
See: FOOD

Retail Food Store Design *Association*

Publishing Co: CRMA Commercial Refrigerator Manufacturers Assn., 1101 Connecticut Ave NW Ste, 700, Washington, DC 20036-4303; Title Tel # (202) 857-1145
General Info: 30 pages
Subscriptions: $1/copy

Retail Food Store Energy Conservation *Association*

Publishing Co: CRMA Commercial Refrigerator Manufacturers Assn., 1101 Connecticut Ave NW Ste, 700, Washington, DC 20036-4303; Title Tel # (202) 857-1145
General Info: 30 pages
Subscriptions: $1/copy

Supermarket Strategic Alert *Business*

Publishing Co: Pollack Associates, 140 E. 81st St., Apt 5E, New York, NY 10028-1875; Title Tel # (212) 734-0753 Title Fax # (212) 988-9394
Personnel: Publisher, Editor, Adv. Dir., Promotion Dir.-Mary Pollack
Editorial Description: Supermarket Strategic Alert summarizes news and information about the supermarket industry from more than 70 daily, weekly and monthly general business and trade publications.
General Info: Yr. Est. 1990, Monthly, Trim Size-8½ x 11, ISSN: 1053-3648
Subscriptions: Indv. $795, Can. $795, For. $795, $80/copy
Circulation: Total-1,000
List Rental: List Management Co.: JAMI Marketing, 2 Blue Hill Plz, Pearl River, NY 10965-3101 Tel # (914) 620-0700, Fax # (914) 620-1885, Actives: 17,000, $100/M

Trend/Wire
See: FOOD

Western Grocery News *Business*

Publishing Co: Sunset Publishing Corp., 80 Willow Rd, Menlo Park, CA 94025-3661 Tel # (415) 321-3600 Fax # (415) 328-6215 Parent Co.-Time Inc. Ventures, New York; Title Tel # (310) 312-8981 Title Fax # (310) 312-8918
Personnel: Editor-Janis Hashe
Editorial Description: Distributed to key members of grocery industry in 13 western states.
General Info: Bi-monthly
Subscriptions: Free To Qualified Recipient
Circulation: (100% controlled), Total-8,400

GUNS & FIREARMS

American Gunsmith *Business*

Publishing Co: A.G Media, P.O Box 2626, Almeda, CA 06836; Title Tel # (203) 661-6111
Editorial Description: Gun repair,customizing and maintenance
General Info: Yr. Est. 1992
Subscriptions: Free With Membership

Crime & Drug Report
See: LAW ENFORCEMENT & PENOLOGY

Drug Policy Report
See: LAW ENFORCEMENT & PENOLOGY

North-South Skirmish Association Newsletter *Association*

Publishing Co: North-South Skirmish Assn. Inc., 9700 Royerton Dr, Richmond, VA 23228-1218; Title Tel # (804) 266-0898
Editorial Description: Contains articles, news, letters & discussions of muzzle loading guns as they pertain to North-South.
General Info: Yr. Est. 1952, Bi-monthly, Letrpr. press
Subscriptions: $1/copy
Circulation: Total-3,500
Advertising: Inquire for rates.

Ontario Rifle Assn. Newsletter

Publishing Co: Ontario Rifle Assn., 31 Marchington Cir., 1207 Albion Rd., Scarborough, ON M1R 3M6 Canada
Personnel: Editor-C. Bullock
General Info: Quarterly, 10 pages
Circulation: Total-650

Shooting the Breeze
See: HOBBY

U.S. Handgunner *Association*

Publishing Co: Sponsor-United States Revolver Association, U.S. Revolver Assn., 40 Larchmont Ave, Taunton, MA 02780-1397; Title Tel # (617) 881-2617
Personnel: Publisher, Editor-Brian Barer
Editorial Description: Reports of matches, new guns, book reviews, legislation pertinent to the sport, articles of general interest to handgun shooters.
General Info: Yr. Est. 1900, Bi-monthly, Trim Size-8½ x 11, 8 pages, ISSN: 0746-6625, 3% ads, No Color
Subscriptions: Indv. $10
Circulation: Total-1,420
Advertising: Inquire for rates.
Printing Co: Trade Press, 230 Cold Spring Ave, West Springfield, MA 01089-3494

Violent Kin
See: HISTORY

HARDWARE

ACDQ Journaliste *Association*

Publishing Co: Assn. Canadienne des Detaillants en Quincaillerie, 6800 Campobello Rd., Mississagua, ON L5N 2L8 Canada; Title Tel # (416) 821-3470
Editorial Description: French edition of CRHA Reporter. For the hardware retail industry.
General Info: Yr. Est. 1966, Monthly, Letrpr. press, 8 pages, No Color
Circulation: Total-500

American Hardware Manufacturers Assn. Newsletter *Business, Association*

Publishing Co: American Hardware Mfgs. Assn., 801 N. Plaza Dr., Schaumburg, IL 60173-4977; Title Tel # (708) 605-1025
Personnel: Publisher-William Farrell, Editor-Jake Kelleher
General Info: Yr. Est. 1983, Bi-monthly, 24 pages, 2 Color
Circulation: Total-1,500

American Lock Collectors Association Newsletter
See: COLLECTIBLES

Armstrong Saw Engineer *Association*

Publishing Co: Armstrong Mfg. Co., PO Box 3008, Portland, OR 97208-3008; Title Tel # (503) 228-8381 Title Fax # (503) 228-8384
Personnel: Editor-Tracy Thompson
General Info: Yr. Est. 1931, Semi-annually, Trim Size-6 x 9, Letrpr. press, 16 pages, 2 Color
Circulation: Total-4,000

Builders' Hardware Manufacturers Association, Bulletin *Business*

Publishing Co: Builders' Hardware Manufacturers Assn., Inc., 355 Lexington Ave Fl 17, New York, NY 10017-6603; Title Tel # (212) 661-4261
Personnel: Editor-J. Waldner, CAE
General Info: Monthly, 2 pages, No Color

CRHA Reporter
Association

Publishing Co: Canadian Retail Hardware Assn., 6800 Campobello Rd., Mississauga, ON L5N 2L8 Canada; Title Tel # (905) 821-3470 Title Fax # (905) 821-8946
Personnel: Circ. Dir.-Linda Nolet
Editorial Description: For hardware/home centre retailers, articles pertaining to business of operating retail outlet. English edition of ACDQ Journaliste.
General Info: Yr. Est. 1966, Monthly, Trim Size-8½ x 11, Offset press, 8 pages, No Color
Subscriptions: Free With Membership
Circulation: (100% controlled), Total-2,200

Doorknob Collector, The
See: HOBBY

HACV

Publishing Co: Hardware Assn. of the Carolinas & Virginia, 5822 W. 74th St., Indianapolis, IN 46278-1756; Title Tel # (704) 332-3141
Personnel: Editor-Paul Gelsleichter
Editorial Description: Lists of association member stores.
General Info: Annually

Journal, The
See: CONSTRUCTION & BUILDING

NAHWW Newsletter
See: HOME & HOME ENTERTAINMENT

West Coast Lock Collectors
See: COLLECTIBLES

HEALTH

A Friend Indeed
See: WOMEN'S

A Guide to Rehabilitation
Business

Publishing Co: Matthew Bender & Co., 11 Penn Plaza, New York, NY 10001-2006 Tel # (212) 967-7707 Fax # (212) 244-3188
Editorial Description: An invaluable handbook for the rehabilitation professional.
General Info: Yr. Est. 1985, Irregular, Looseleaf

AAB Bulletin
See: SCIENCE

AACPDM News
Association

Publishing Co: American Academy for Cerebral Palsy & Developmental Medicine, 6300 N River Rd Ste 727, Rosemont, IL 60018-4238; Title Tel # (708) 698-1635
General Info: 12 pages
Circulation: Total-1,300

AARN Newsletter
See: NURSING

ABDC Newsletter
Consumer, Association

Publishing Co: Assn. of Birth Defect Children, 827 Irma Ave, Orlando, FL 32803-3806; Title Tel # (407) 245-7035
Personnel: Editor-Betty Mekdici
Editorial Description: Reports on environmental causes and other information on birth defects.
General Info: Yr. Est. 1982, Quarterly, Trim Size-8½ x 11, 8 pages, 2 Color, Newsprint
Subscriptions: Free With Membership
Circulation: Total-8,000

ACAT News
Consumer, Association

Publishing Co: American Center for the Alexander Technique, Inc., 129 W 67th St, New York, NY 10023-5917; Title Tel # (212) 799-0468
Personnel: Editor-Sheldon Berkowitz
Editorial Description: Membership news for the American Ctr. For The Alexander Technique (A method of postural education).
General Info: Tri-annually, 6 pages
Subscriptions: Indv. $12
Circulation: Total-150
Printing Co: Support Services Alliance, Scharie, NY 12157

ACHA Action
Association

Publishing Co: American College Health Assn., PO Box 28937, Baltimore, MD 21240-8937; Title Tel # (301) 963-1100
Personnel: Editor-Cynthia Launchbaugh
Editorial Description: Reports items of interest to those at work in the college/university health field. Includes legislative items, news of affiliates, & news of ACHA activities.
General Info: Yr. Est. 1970, Quarterly, Trim Size-8½ x 11, Offset press, 16 pages, ISSN: 0002-7952, 2 Color, Newsprint, Saddle-stitched
Circulation: Total-2,500
List Rental: Rents Lists

ACLS Alert
See: MEDICINE

ACPA/CPF Newsletter
See: MEDICINE

ADHD Report
See: PSYCHOLOGY

AHCA Notes
Association

Publishing Co: American Health Care Assn., 1201 L St NW, Washington, DC 20005-4046 Tel # (202) 842-4444; Title Tel # (202) 898-2854 Title Fax # (202) 842-3860
Personnel: Editor-Marla Gold
Editorial Description: Covers major policy issues affecting the nursing home industry.
General Info: (Formerly AHCA Weekly Notes), Yr. Est. 1972, Bi-weekly, 4 pages
Subscriptions: Indv. $150
Circulation: Total-9,000

AHP Connect
See: HOSPITALS & NURSING HOMES

AIDS Alert

Publishing Co: American Health Consultants, Inc., 3525 Piedmont Rd., Building #6, Ste. 400, Atlanta, GA 30305-0056 Tel # (404) 262-7436 Fax # (404) 284-3291; Title Tel # (404) 351-4523
Personnel: Publisher-Lauren Oden, Editor-Richard Jarvis, Circ. Mgr.-Monica Brown, Production Mgr.- Mike Witter, Mktg. Dir.-David Price
Editorial Description: Covers risks, hazards, cost, research, prevention, etc. of AIDS & related conditions.
General Info: Yr. Est. 1986, Monthly, Trim Size-8½ x 11
Subscriptions: Indv. $219
Circulation: Total-3,200
List Rental: Actives: $145/M

AIDS Clinical Care Newsletter
See: MEDICINE

AIDS Information Exchange

Publishing Co: U.S. Conference of Mayors, 1620 I St NW, Washington, DC 20006-4073
Personnel: Editor-Paul Jones
General Info: Quarterly
Subscriptions: Indv. $25, Free To Qualified Recipient
Circulation: Total-5,000, Readership-5,000

AIDS Literature & Law Review
See: LAW

AIDS Litigation Reporter
See: LAW

AIDS Report, The
See: MEDICINE

AIDS Treatment News
See: MEDICINE

AIDS World Newsletter
See: MEDICINE

AIDS/STD News Report
See: PHILANTHROPY

AMFAR Report

Publishing Co: American Foundation for AIDS Research, 733 3rd Ave Fl 12, New York, NY 10017-3204; Title Tel # (212) 682-7440 Title Fax # (212) 682-9812
Personnel: Editor-David Kirby
Editorial Description: Quarterly newsletter which describes current activities of the American Foundation for AIDS Research (AMFAR).
General Info: Quarterly, Trim Size-8 x 11, 4 pages, 2 Color
Circulation: Total-60,000

AMPRA Review
See: MEDICINE

APLA Update

Publishing Co: AIDS Project Los Angeles, 6721 Romaine St, Los Angeles, CA 90038-2417; Title Tel # (213) 993-1600 Title Fax # (213) 962-3475
Personnel: Editor-Paul Serchia
Editorial Description: APLA Update, produced by the Communications Dept. of AIDS Project Los Angeles & volunteer contributors, presents news about AIDS & programs of AIDS Project Los Angeles to people affected by the disease.
General Info: Yr. Est. 1988, 8x/yr., Web press, 20 pages, 2 Color, Newsprint, Saddle-stitched
Circulation: Total-10,000
Printing Co: Rodgers & McDonald Graphics, 1141 Sandhill Ave # 6270, Carson, CA 90746-1314 Tel # (310) 604-1012

APLIC International Communicator
See: LIBRARY

APS Bulletin
Association   CPM: $287

Publishing Co: American Pain Society, 5700 Old Orchard Rd., 1st fl., Skokie, IL 60077-1057
Fax # (708) 966-9418; Title Tel # (708) 966-5595
Personnel: Editor-Peter Vicente, Circ. Dir.-Kay Warskow, Adv. Dir.-Kathy Checea
Editorial Description: Features articles, organization news and a calendar of events.
General Info: Yr. Est. 1991, Bi-monthly, Trim Size-8½ x 11, Desktop press, 18 pages, 2 Color, Coated, Saddle-stitched
Subscriptions: Free With Membership
Circulation: Total-2,000
Advertising: $575.
List Rental: Actives: 2,000
Printing Co: Sundance Press, 817 E 18th St, Tucson, AZ 85719-6614 Tel # (602) 622-5233, Fax # (602) 620-1593

ARN News
Association

Publishing Co: Association of Rehabilitation Nurses, 5700 Old Orchard Rd., 1st fl., Skokie, IL 60077-1057; Title Tel # (708) 966-3433 Title Fax # (708) 966-9418
Personnel: Mng. Editor-Joann Abkemeier, Circ. Dir.-Kay Warskow, Adv. Dir.-Kathy Checea, Production Mgr., Art Dir.-Dot Vartan, Natl. Sales Mgr.-Kerry Lawton, Promotion Dir.-Kathleen Klaeser
Editorial Description: ARN News is written for the members of the Association of Rehabilitation Nurses. It focuses on association news, upcoming educational events, committee functions, news items of interest to all in the field of nursing and the specialty of rehabilitation nursing.
General Info: Yr. Est. 1984, 10x/yr., Trim Size-8½ x 11, Sheetfed press, 20 pages, ISSN: 1075-5764, 12% ads, 2 Color, Matte, Saddle-stitched
Subscriptions: Free With Membership
Advertising: $1,410.
List Rental: Actives: 8,200, $120/M
Printing Co: Sundance Press, 817 E 18th St, Tucson, AZ 85719-6614 Tel # (602) 622-5233, Fax # (602) 620-1593

ASCA Quarterly
Business, Association   CPM: $61

Publishing Co: American Subacute Care Association, 1440 Kennedy Crossway, Suite 421, North Bay Village, FL 33141 Fax # (305) 868-0905; Title Tel # (305) 864-0396
Personnel: Editor-Michael Kesti, Circ. Mgr.-Stephanie K. Fredman, Production Mgr.-Jeff Borg, Publisher, Adv. Dir.-Mike Freedman
Editorial Description: Covers news and developments regarding the subacute care industry, including personnel, products, trends, and meetings. Our readers include subacute care providers, professionals, and vendors.
General Info: Yr. Est. 1993, Quarterly, Trim Size-8½ x 11, Sheetfed press, 16 pages, ISSN: 1073-9475, 4 Color, Coated, Saddle-stitched
Subscriptions: Free With Membership
Circulation: Total-9,000, Readership-10,000
Advertising: $550. Accepts Inserts.

ASH Smoking & Health Review

Publishing Co: Action on Smoking and Health, 2013 H St. NW, Washington, DC 20006-4207; Title Tel # (202) 659-4310
Editorial Description: Update on legal action on behalf of non-smokers.
General Info: (Formerly ASH Newsletter), Yr. Est. 1967, Bi-monthly, Trim Size-8½ x 11, Web press, 16 pages, 2 Color
Subscriptions: Indv. $15, Inst. $15, $2/copy
Circulation: Total-35,000
List Rental: Actives: $75/M, Expires: $50/M

ASHP Newsletter
See: DRUGS & PHARMACEUTICALS

AVSC News
Business, Association

Publishing Co: AVSC International, 79 Madison Ave., New York, NY 10016-7802
Fax # (212) 729-9439; Title Tel # (212) 561-8000 Title Fax # (212) 779-9439
Personnel: Editor-Joanne Tzanis, Art Dir.-Renee Santhouse
Editorial Description: Information on voluntary sterilization, norplant implants, IUDs and other contraceptive methods; reproductive health issues in the U.S and abroad.
General Info: Yr. Est. 1963, 4x/yr., Trim Size-8½ x 11, Offset press, 8 pages, ISSN: 0001-2904, 2 Color, Other
Subscriptions: Indv. $25
Circulation: Total-7,000
Printing Co: Official Offset Corp., 8600 New Horizons Blvd, Amityville, NY 11701-1154 Tel # (516) 957-8500

Abortion Research Notes
See: PSYCHOLOGY

Abstract

Publishing Co: Natl. Tumors Registrars Assn., Inc., 505 E. Hawley St., Mundelein, IL 60060-2458; Title Tel # (301) 984-1748
Personnel: Production Mgr.-Carol Johnson, Editor, Adv. Dir.-Connie Creitz
Editorial Description: Articles on theory, practice, & current issues relating to tumor registries & cancer program management.
General Info: Bi-monthly, Trim Size-7½ x 10, Sheetfed press, 24 pages, 2 Color, Newsprint
Subscriptions: Indv. $10
Circulation: Total-1,800
Advertising: Accepts Inserts.
List Rental: Rents Lists
Printing Co: Old Dominion Printing Co., 444 Swann Ave, Alexandria, VA 22301-1047

Access

Publishing Co: Canadian Rehabilitation Council for the Disabled, 45 Sheppard Ave. E., #801, Toronto, ON M2N 5W9 Canada; Title Tel # (416) 250-7490 Title Fax # (416) 229-1371
Personnel: Editor-Heather Ney
Editorial Description: General news on rehabilitation in Canada and CRCD activities.
General Info: Yr. Est. 1978, Bi-monthly, Trim Size-8½ x 11, Desktop press, 4 pages, ISSN: 0226-2657, No Color, Recycled, Saddle-stitched
Subscriptions: Free
Circulation: Total-1,000
List Rental: Rents Lists

Accident Facts Up-to-Date
See: SAFETY

Action News
See: CONSUMER INTERESTS

Acupressure Workshop

Publishing Co: Acu Press, 1533 Shattuck Ave, Berkeley, CA 94709-1516; Title Tel # (415) 845-1059
Personnel: Publisher, Editor-Michael Gach
Editorial Description: Vocational training program catalog outlining required courses for certification.
General Info: Every two years, Offset press, 16 pages, No Color, Newsprint, Saddle-stitched
Subscriptions: $1/copy
Circulation: Total-25,000

Addiction Letter, The
Business

Publishing Co: Manisses Communications Group, Inc., PO Box 3357, Providence, RI 02906-0757; Title Tel # (401) 831-6020 Title Fax # (401) 861-6370
Personnel: Publisher-Fraser Lang, Editor-Marcia Lawton, Ph. D., Circ. Mgr.-Deb Zajas, Promotion Dir.-Betty Lang
Editorial Description: Aimed at professionals in alcohol & drug addiction treatment and prevention.
General Info: Yr. Est. 1985, Monthly, Offset press, 8 pages, ISSN: 8756-405X, Ind/Abs/Online: DIALOG
Subscriptions: Indv. $97, Inst. $129, Can. $107, For. $117, $6/copy
Acquistions: Publication Bought, Publication Sold
Circulation: Total-2,500
List Rental: List Management Co.: Manager: Betty Lang; Conrad Direct, Inc., 300 Knickerbocker Road, Creskill, NJ 07626 Tel # (201) 567-3200, Fax # (201) 567-4959, Actives: 4,000, Expires: 4,000
Printing Co: Newsletter Press, 76 Valley St, East Providence, RI 02914-4424 Tel # (401) 438-5352

Adult Day Care Letter
See: HOSPITALS & NURSING HOMES

Adventures in Movement
See: SOCIAL SERVICES & WELFARE

African Alternatives
Business, Consumer

Publishing Co: Africa Operations Research & Technical Assistance Project, Population Council, One Dag Hammarskjold Plaza, New York, NY 10017-2291 Tel # (212) 339-0500
Editorial Description: Contains articles on the activities of the project, including such subjects as education for family planning jointly undertaken by the Africa OR/TA Project and other cooperating agencies and the success in distributing contraceptives and information on HIV/AIDS at factories in Dar es Salaam.
General Info: Semi-annually, 12 pages
Subscriptions: Free To Qualified Recipient

Akwa Letter
Association   CPM: $143

Publishing Co: Aquatic Exercise Assoc., PO Box 1609, Nokomis, FL 34274; Title Tel # (813) 486-8600
Personnel: Publisher-Ruth Sova, Editor-Gina Taucher, Adv. Dir.-Lynn Van Epern, Art Dir.-Cheryl Gorton
Editorial Description: Contains timely articles on aquatic fitness and therapy as well as information on research, mail order books and videos to keep aquatic professionals informed on the latest trends in the industry.
General Info: Yr. Est. 1987, Bi-monthly, Trim Size-8½ x 11, Letrpr. press, 20 pages, 3% ads, 2 Color, Matte, Saddle-stitched
Subscriptions: Indv. $35, Inst. $95, Can. $50, For. $60, $2/copy
Circulation: (10% controlled), Total-5,000, Single Copy/Newsstand-500, Subscriptions-4,000, International-100
Advertising: $715.
List Rental: Rents Lists
Printing Co: Heritage Publishing Co., Port Washington, WI 53074

Al-Anon in Institutions
See: SOCIAL SERVICES & WELFARE

Alcoholism & Drug Abuse Weekly
Business

Publishing Co: Manisses Communications Group, Inc., PO Box 3357, Providence, RI 02906-0757; Title Tel # (401) 831-6020 Title Fax # (401) 861-6370
Personnel: Publisher-Fraser Lang, Editor-Gary Enos, Circ. Mgr.-Deb Zajas, Promotion Dir.-Betty Lang
Editorial Description: Provides practical, in-depth reports on the alcohol and drug abuse field. Public policy and economic issues for those in public, private, and non-profit sectors.
General Info: (Formerly Drug Abuse Report), Yr. Est. 1989, Weekly, Offset press, ISSN: 1042-1394
Subscriptions: Indv. $397, Inst. $437, Can. $437, For. $467
Acquistions: Publication Bought, Publication Sold
Circulation: Total-1,500
List Rental: List Management Co.: Conrad Direct, Inc., 300 Knickerbocker Road, Creskill, NJ 07626 Tel # (201) 567-3200, Fax # (201) 567-4959, Actives: 2,500, Expires: 2,500
Printing Co: Newsletter Press, 76 Valley St, East Providence, RI 02914-4424 Tel # (401) 438-5352

Alcoholism Briefs *Consumer*

Publishing Co: Del Mar Publications, 1165 Elmwood Pl., Deerfield, IL 60015-1209; Title Tel # (708) 945-1790
Personnel: Publisher, Editor-Bob Aitchison
Editorial Description: Promotes services, ideas, & issues on correcting alcoholism. Provides a clearing house & exchange for information on alcoholism, drug abuse & related subjects. Reports on policy, treatment & prevention programs & research in the field.
General Info: Yr. Est. 1986, Quarterly, Trim Size-8½ x 11, Roto. press, 4 pages, ISSN: 1076-2507, No Color
Subscriptions: Indv. $9
Circulation: Total-1,300

Alert *Consumer*

Publishing Co: Universal Fellowship of Metropolitan Community Churches, 5300 Santa Monica Blvd Ste 304, Los Angeles, CA 90029-1131; Title Tel # (213) 464-5100 Title Fax # (213) 464-2123
Personnel: Publisher-Ravi Verma, Editor-Rev. Stephen Pieters, Circ. Mgr.-Nancy Fackrell
Editorial Description: Covers news on AIDS legislation, education, research, & treatment.
General Info: Yr. Est. 1987, Quarterly, Trim Size-8½ x 11, Offset press, 4 pages, 2 Color, Newsprint
Subscriptions: Indv. $10, $1/copy
Circulation: (58% controlled), Total-1,600, International-100

Alert, National Service Dog Center Newsletter
See: DOGS

Allergy and Asthma Industry News
See: MEDICINE

Allergy Edge
See: MEDICINE

Allied Health Update
See: COLLEGE ALUMNI

Alternative Health Therapies Newsletter

Publishing Co: Science of Mind Church Counseling & Healing Ctr., PO Box 1439, La Jolla, CA 92038-1439
Personnel: Publisher, Editor-Thomas Clary, Ph.D., Production Mgr.-Corinne Levy
Editorial Description: Healing: spiritual, psychological & physical, metaphysical, hypnosis, imagery, counseling, sex therapy.
General Info: Yr. Est. 1982, Monthly, Letrpr. press, 4 pages, ISSN: 0899-5974, 2 Color
Circulation: Total-3,000
List Rental: List Management Co.: Dependable Lists, 950 25th Ave, Bellwood, IL 60104-2203 Tel # (708) 544-1000, Fax # (708) 544-1094
Printing Co: Global Printing, Inc., 4116 Wheeler Ave, Alexandria, VA 22304-6411 Tel # (703) 751-3611

Alternatives for the Health Conscious Individual *Consumer*

Publishing Co: Mountain Home Publishing, PO Box 829, Ingram, TX 78025-0829; Title Tel # (210) 367-4492 Title Fax # (210) 367-5314
Personnel: Publisher-Brenda Lyman, Editor-David Williams, Circ. Mgr.-Tabetha Ashcraft
Editorial Description: Health news and information.
General Info: Yr. Est. 1985, Monthly
Subscriptions: Indv. $40, Can. $50, For. $55
Circulation: Readership-200,000
List Rental: Actives: 70,000, $95/M

Alzheimer's Association Newsletter *Association*

Publishing Co: Alzheimer's Association, 919 N Michigan Ave Ste 1000, Chicago, IL 60611-1676; Title Tel # (312) 335-8700 Title Fax # (312) 335-1110
Personnel: Editor-Mary Anne Pecora
Editorial Description: Newsletter of interest to Alzheimer families & others interested in Alzheimer's Disease.
General Info: (Formerly ADRDA Newsletter), Yr. Est. 1980, Quarterly, 12 pages, 2 Color, Matte, Saddle-stitched
Circulation: Total-600,000

Ambulance Industry Digest *Association*

Publishing Co: American Ambulance Assn., 3800 Auburn Blvd Ste C, Sacramento, CA 95821-2102; Title Tel # (916) 483-3827
Personnel: Publisher-Charles Clark, Editor-Brenda Staffian, Circ. Mgr.-Susan Saunders
Editorial Description: Private & public ambulance & patient aid suppliers.
General Info: Quarterly, Trim Size-8½ x 11, Sheetfed press, 32 pages, 4% ads, 2 Color, Newsprint, Saddle-stitched
Circulation: Total-2,500
Advertising: Inquire for rates.

American Anorexia/Bulimia Assn. -Newsletter *Consumer, Association*

Publishing Co: American Anorexia/Bulimia Assn., Inc., 293 Central Park W., Suite 12, New York, NY 10024-3009; Title Tel # (212) 501-8351
Personnel: Editor-Phyllis Ehrenfeld
General Info: Yr. Est. 1977, Quarterly, 16 pages, ISSN: 1064-4210, 1% ads, Color, Newsprint
Subscriptions: Indv. $50
Acquistions: Publication Bought, Publication Sold
Circulation: Total-7,000
Printing Co: United Publ. & Prtg. Co., 23 Acosta St # 1232, Stamford, CT 06902-4601 Tel # (203) 348-6455

American Art Therapy Assn. -Newsletter
See: ART & SCULPTURE

American Industrial Hygiene Assn. Newsletter *Association*

Publishing Co: American Industrial Hygiene Association, 2700 Prosperity Ave # 250, Fairfax, VA 22031-4320 Tel # (703) 849-8888 Fax # (703) 207-3561; Title Tel # (216) 762-7294
Editorial Description: Provides news and information of and by association members.
General Info: Bi-monthly

American Institute for Cancer Research Newsletter *Consumer*

Publishing Co: American Institute for Cancer Research, 1759 R St NW, Washington, DC 20009-2583 Fax # (202) 328-7226; Title Tel # (202) 328-7744
Personnel: Publisher-Marilyn Gentry, Editor-Christine Murray, Production Mgr.-Gina Grieb
Editorial Description: Consumer newsletter on diet and cancer. Provides updates on cancer research and information on nutrition and health.
General Info: Yr. Est. 1983, Quarterly, Web press, 12 pages, 2 Color, Matte
Subscriptions: Free
Circulation: Total-1,600,000
List Rental: List Management Co.: RMI Direct Marketing, Inc., 4 Skyline Dr, Hawthorne, NY 10532-2133 Tel # (914) 345-4615, Fax # (914) 347-2954
Printing Co: Account Manager: Mark Rowell; The Fisher Group, 2121 N Towne Ln NE, Cedar Rapids, IA 52402-1913

American Nudist Research Library
See: LIFESTYLE

American Society of Bariatric Physicians Newsletter
See: MEDICINE

Americans with Disabilities Newsletter
See: DISABILITY

Americans for Nonsmokers' Rights Update *Consumer, Association*

Publishing Co: Americans for Nonsmokers' Rights, 2530 San Pablo Ave.,Ste. #J, Berkeley, CA 94702-2000; Title Tel # (415) 841-3032
Personnel: Editor in Chief-Mark Pertschuk, Exec. Ed.-Julia Carol, Art Dir.-Tim Mancusi
Editorial Description: Focuses its attention on removing what researchers call environmental tobacco smoke, or ETS--the stuff that gets in your eyes, lungs, hair, and clothes.
General Info: Quarterly, Trim Size-8½ x 11, Offset press, 6 pages, 2 Color, Recycled
Subscriptions: Indv. $35, Inst. $50, For. $40
Circulation: Total-10,000
List Rental: List Management Co.: Names in the News-California, 1 Bush St Bsmt 3, San Francisco, CA 94104-4425 Tel # (415) 989-3350, Fax # (415) 433-7796

Applied Orgonometry
See: CULTURE & HUMANITIES

Archives Sharing Bulletin *Consumer, Association*

Publishing Co: Al-Anon Family Group Headquarters, Inc., 1600 Corporate Landing Pkwy., Virginia Beach, VA 23456 Tel # (804) 563-1600; Title Tel # (212) 302-7240 Title Fax # (212) 869-3757
Personnel: Editor-Claire Ricewasser
Editorial Description: Archival preservation of Al-Anon material.
General Info: Yr. Est. 1987, Semi-annually, ISSN: 1054-0709
Subscriptions: Free
Circulation: Total-300

Arizona Nurse
See: NURSING

Arthritis News *Consumer*

Publishing Co: ArthritiSource, 2045 Kassner Drive, Green Bay, WI 54304; Title Tel # (414) 592-9922 Title Fax # (414) 592-1306
Personnel: Publisher, Editor, Circ. Mgr., Production Mgr., Adv. Dir.-Marjorie L. Riggio
Editorial Description: Specializes in providing up-to-date and accurate information about arthritis.
General Info: Yr. Est. 1995, Bi-monthly, Trim Size-8½ x 11, 4 pages, 2 Color, Matte
Subscriptions: Indv. $10, Inst. $10, Can. $10, For. $16
Circulation: (50% controlled), Total-2,000, Subscriptions-1,000

Aspen's Advisor for Nurse Executives
See: NURSING

Atlantis, The Imagery Newsletter
See: MEDICINE

Automated Medical Payments News
See: INSURANCE

Aviation Medical Bulletin
See: AERONAUTICS/ASTRONAUTICS

B.A.S.H., Inc.

Publishing Co: B.A.S.H., 12161 Lackland Rd # 101, Saint Louis, MO 63146-4003;
Title Tel # (314) 567-4080
Personnel: Editor-Felix Laroca
General Info: Yr. Est. 1981, Monthly, 12 pages
Subscriptions: Indv. $25
Circulation: Total-15,000

BCHA News   *Association*

Publishing Co: British Columbia Health Assn., 1333 W. Broadway, Suite 600, Vancouver, BC V6H
4C7 Canada; Title Tel # (604) 734-2423 Title Fax # (604) 734-7202
Personnel: Editor-John Braddock
Editorial Description: For trustees, administration of hospitals, long term care & allied organizations
in B.C.
General Info: Yr. Est. 1972, Monthly, Web press, 16 pages, 1% ads, No Color
Circulation: (86% controlled), Total-4,600
Printing Co: Westco Mktg., 2040 W. 12th Ave., Vancouver, BC V6J 2G2 Canada
Tel # (604) 736-6754

B.E.A.M. (Being Energetic About Multiplicity)
See: PSYCHOLOGY

BNA's Health Care
Facilities Guide   *Business*

Publishing Co: Bureau of National Affairs, Inc., 1231 25th St. NW, Bldg. N-200, Washington, DC
20037-1157; Title Tel # (202) 452-4200 Title Fax # (202) 822-8092
Personnel: Publisher-William A. Beltz, Mng. Editor-Randy Kubetin, Circ. Mgr.-Gary C. Seltzer
Editorial Description: Explains environmental & worker safety & health regulations that affect health
care facilities. HCFG is designed for environment & safety & health professionals in health care
facilities & provides plain English explanations of all of these regulations.
General Info: Monthly, Trim Size-8½ x 11, 6 pages
Subscriptions: Indv. $695

BNA's Health Care Policy
Report   *Business*

Publishing Co: Bureau of National Affairs, Inc., 1231 25th St. NW, Bldg. N-200, Washington, DC
20037-1157; Title Tel # (202) 452-4200 Title Fax # (202) 822-8092
Personnel: Publisher-William A. Beltz, Mng. Editor-Paul Albergo, Circ. Mgr.-Gary C. Seltzer
Editorial Description: A weekly notification service providing timely & objective coverage of federal,
state, & private sector efforts to reform & manage the U.S. health care system.
General Info: Yr. Est. 1993, Weekly, Trim Size-8½ x 11, Offset press, 40 pages, ISSN: 1068-1213,
Ind/Abs/Online: Lexis, Nexis
Subscriptions: Indv. $716

BNA's Health Law Reporter   *Business, Association*

Publishing Co: Bureau of National Affairs, Inc., 1231 25th St. NW, Bldg. N-200, Washington, DC
20037-1157; Title Tel # (202) 452-4200 Title Fax # (202) 822-8092
Personnel: Mng. Editor-Susan Webster, Circ. Mgr.-Gary C. Seltzer
Editorial Description: A weekly notification service that provides comprehensive coverage of the
wide range of legal, regulatory, & legislative developments that have impact on health care
attorneys & top-flight health care executives, in such areas as antitrust, tax, professional liability,
insurance, fraud & abuse, reimbursement, medical health law, Medicare, Medicaid, & licensure.
General Info: Yr. Est. 1992, Weekly, Trim Size-8½ x 11, 32 pages, ISSN: 1064-2137, Ind/Abs/Online:
Lexis, Nexis, Other
Subscriptions: Indv. $1,044

BSR on Fitness

Publishing Co: Bay Sports Review, P.O. Box 4520, Berkeley, CA 94704; Title Tel # (510) 633-9096
Title Fax # (510) 635-2981
Personnel: Publisher-Christopher Weills
Editorial Description: BSR on Fitness is mailed to the owners and managers of 500 s.f. Bay area
health and fitness clubs. Contains industry news, releases, interviews reports, schedules and job
listings.
General Info: Yr. Est. 1995, Bi-monthly, Trim Size-8½ x 11, 4 pages
Subscriptions: Free To Qualified Recipient
Circulation: Total-800
List Rental: Actives: 600, $100/M

Back Letter, The
See: MEDICINE

Batting the Breeze   *Association*

Publishing Co: Emphysema Anonymous, Inc., 726 N. Highland Ave., Clearwater, FL 34615-5463;
Title Tel # (813) 391-9977
Personnel: Publisher, Editor-William Jaeckle
Editorial Description: To help those with emphysema toward a more useful life by means of
education, encouragement and mutual assistance.
General Info: Yr. Est. 1965, Bi-monthly, Trim Size-8 x 11, Offset press, 16 pages, ISSN: 0005-6367,
1% ads, No Color
Subscriptions: Indv. $15, Can. $20, $3/copy
Circulation: (3% controlled), Total-3,300, Subscriptions-3,200
Advertising: Inquire for rates.

Beauty Spot: News You Can Use
See: MEDIA & COMMUNICATIONS

Being Well   *Association*

Publishing Co: Center for Professional Well Being, 21 W Colony Pl Ste 150, Durham, NC
27705-5589 Tel # (919) 419-0011; Title Tel # (919) 489-9167 Title Fax # (919) 403-8605
Editorial Description: Improving quality of life of professionals. Preventing burnout. Coaching in
career decisions. Malpractice risk reduction. Family stress resolution. Emphasis on physicians and
other health care professionals.
General Info: (Formerly Bulletin of the Society for Professional Well Being), Yr. Est. 1988, Quarterly,
Web press, 10 pages, Color
Subscriptions: Indv. $55, Free With Membership
Acqusitions: Publication Bought
Circulation: Total-5,000

Bell, The
See: PSYCHOLOGY

Benefits Communicator
See: MANAGEMENT

Best of Health   *Consumer*

Publishing Co: Best of Health, Box 40-1232, Brooklyn, NY 11240-1232; Title Tel # (718) 756-2245
Personnel: Editor-Wista Johnson
General Info: Yr. Est. 1987, Quarterly
Subscriptions: Indv. $14

Better Health   *Consumer*

Publishing Co: Nebraska State Dept. of Health, 301 Centennial Mall S # 95007, Lincoln, NE
68508-2529; Title Tel # (402) 471-4047
Personnel: Editor-Marla Augustine
Editorial Description: Public health issues in Nebraska.
General Info: Yr. Est. 1930, Quarterly, Desktop press, 4 pages, Color
Circulation: (100% controlled), Total-16,000
Printing Co: South Carolina State Printing Co., 1210 Key Rd, Columbia, SC 29201-4739
Tel # (803) 799-9550

Bio/Med Technology Alert
See: MEDICINE

Black Lung Reporter
See: LABOR

Blue Sheet: Health Policy & Biomedical Research, The
See: DRUGS & PHARMACEUTICALS

Body Bulletin

Publishing Co: Rodale Press, 33 East Minor St., Emmaus, PA 18098-0001 Tel # (610) 967-5171
Fax # (610) 967-8963; Title Tel # (215) 967-5171 Title Fax # (610) 967-6263
Personnel: Editor-Chris Hill, Circ. Mgr.-Susan Sidler
Editorial Description: A company-sponsored health and fitness newsletter for employees. Covers
exercise, how-to-do-it health care, stress management, recipes and more.
General Info: Yr. Est. 1981, Monthly, Trim Size-8½ x 11, 4 pages
Subscriptions: $5/copy

Body Renaissance

Publishing Co: Rising Sun, PO Box 627, Milesburg, PA 16853-0627; Title Tel # (814) 355-9850
Personnel: Publisher, Editor-Hope Woodring
Editorial Description: Devoted to a variety of health and fitness related topics.
General Info: Yr. Est. 1991, Semi-annually, Looseleaf
Subscriptions: Indv. $15, $10/copy

Bottom Line/Personal
See: CONSUMER INTERESTS

Breast Implant Litigation Reporter
See: LAW

Bresler Center News
See: MEDICINE

Briefings on Assisted Living *Business*

Publishing Co: Opus Communications, Inc., Box 1168, 100 Hoods Lane, Marblehead, MA 01945; Title Tel # (617) 639-1872 Title Fax # (617) 639-2982
Personnel: Publisher-Jennifer Cofer, Editor-Suzanne Perney
Editorial Description: A guide for administrators of assisted living facilities. Interprets standards & regulations and how best to meet them.
General Info: Yr. Est. 1995, Monthly, Trim Size-8½ x 11, 12 pages, ISSN: 1082-5827, 2 Color, Matte, Saddle-stitched
Subscriptions: Indv. $177
List Rental: Rents Lists

Briefings on Hospital Safety
See: HOSPITALS & NURSING HOMES

Briefings on JCAHO
See: HOSPITALS & NURSING HOMES

Briefings on JCAHO-Home Care
See: HOSPITALS & NURSING HOMES

Briefings on Laboratory Safety and Accreditation
See: HOSPITALS & NURSING HOMES

Briefings on Long-Term Care Regulations
See: HOSPITALS & NURSING HOMES

Briefings on Practice Management
See: MANAGEMENT

Briefings on Subacute Care: Regulations & Reimbursement
See: HOSPITALS & NURSING HOMES

Brown University Child and Adolescent Behavior Letter, The
See: CHILDREN

Brown University Geriatric Research Application Digest, The *Business*

Publishing Co: Manisses Communications Group, Inc., PO Box 3357, Providence, RI 02906-0757; Title Tel # (401) 831-6020 Title Fax # (401) 861-6370
Personnel: Publisher-Fraser Lang, Editor-Anne Christner, Ph.D., Circ. Mgr.-Deb Zajas, Mktg. Dir.-Betty Lang
Editorial Description: An authoritative review of significant research in geriatrics.
General Info: Yr. Est. 1993, Monthly, ISSN: 1067-7372
Subscriptions: Indv. $97, Inst. $127, Can. $137, For. $147
Circulation: Total-1,000
List Rental: List Management Co.: Conrad Direct, Inc., 300 Knickerbocker Road, Creskill, NJ 07626 Tel # (201) 567-3200, Fax # (201) 567-4959, Actives: 1,000, $100/M

Brown University Long Term Care Quality Letter, The *Business*

Publishing Co: Manisses Communications Group, Inc., PO Box 3357, Providence, RI 02906-0757; Title Tel # (401) 831-6020 Title Fax # (401) 861-6370
Personnel: Publisher-Fraser Lang, Editor-Barry Fogel, M.D., Editor-Vincent Mor, Ph.D., Circ. Mgr.-Deb Zajas, Promotion Dir.-Betty Lang
Editorial Description: Contains practical reports for health care professionals working in long term care facilities, and home health agencies.
General Info: (Formerly Brown University Long Term Care Letter), Yr. Est. 1988, Bi-weekly, 8 pages, ISSN: 1042-1386, Ind/Abs/Online: DIALOG
Subscriptions: Indv. $247, Inst. $297, Can. $262, For. $272, $10/copy
Circulation: Total-1,500
List Rental: List Management Co.: Conrad Direct, Inc., 300 Knickerbocker Road, Creskill, NJ 07626 Tel # (201) 567-3200, Fax # (201) 567-4959, Actives: 3,000, $100/M, Expires: 3,000, $100/M
Printing Co: Newsletter Press, 76 Valley St, East Providence, RI 02914-4424 Tel # (401) 438-5352

Bulletin

Publishing Co: Saskatchewan Abilities Council, 2310 Louise Ave., Saskatoon, SK S7J 2C7 Canada; Title Tel # (306) 374-4448 Title Fax # (306) 373-2665
Personnel: Editor-J. Dombroski
General Info: Quarterly, ISSN: 0929-4224
Subscriptions: Indv. $30
Acquistions: Publication Bought
Circulation: Total-9,500

Bulletin of the NPA
See: BABY

Bulletin de l'Assurance
See: INSURANCE

C. Everett Koop Foundation Health Letter *Consumer*

Publishing Co: C. Everett Koop Foundation, P.O. Box 998, Hanover, NH 03755
Editorial Description: Information on loosing and maintaining weight.
General Info: Bi-monthly
Subscriptions: Indv. $25

CAAA Reports *Association*

Publishing Co: California Association of AIDS Agencies, 926 J St Ste 803, Sacramento, CA 95814-2707 Tel # (916) 447-7199 Fax # (916) 447-5302
Editorial Description: Membership and health information for California AIDS agencies.
General Info: Bi-monthly

CAHPERD Journal/Times *Association*

Publishing Co: California Assn. for Health, Phys. Ed., Recreation & Dance, 1501 El Camino Ave Ste 3, Sacramento, CA 95815-2748; Title Tel # (916) 922-3596 Title Fax # (916) 922-0133
Personnel: Publisher, Editor in Chief-Phyllis Blatz
Editorial Description: Research/articles in fields of health, p.e., recreation & dance. Appealing primarily to educators in those disciplines, including sports & athletics.
General Info: (Formerly CAHPER Journal), Yr. Est. 1937, 8x/yr., Trim Size-8½ x 11, Web press, 26 pages, ISSN: 0273-6896, 1% ads, Color-cover, Coated, Saddle-stitched
Subscriptions: Indv. $56, For. $75
Circulation: Total-4,300
Advertising: Inquire for rates.
Printing Co: Griffin Printing, 4141 N Freeway Blvd, Sacramento, CA 95834-1209 Tel # (916) 448-3511, Fax # (916) 448-3597

CCH Monitor: The Newsletter of Managed Care *Business*

Publishing Co: CCH, Inc., 2700 Lake Cook Rd., Riverwoods, IL 60015 Parent Co.-Kluwer Law & Taxation Publishers, Cambridge; Title Tel # (847) 267-7000 Title Fax # (800) 224-8299
Editorial Description: Provides complete coverage of the issues facing today's managed care providers, with practical advice on managed care plans; 'how-to' tips on compliance, coverage, and certification requirements; and analysis of legal developments affecting managed caresystems.
General Info: Yr. Est. 1993, 26x/yr.
Subscriptions: Indv. $360

CCH Pulse: The Resource Guide to Health Care Reform

Publishing Co: CCH, Inc., 2700 Lake Cook Rd., Riverwoods, IL 60015 Parent Co.-Kluwer Law & Taxation Publishers, Cambridge; Title Tel # (847) 267-7000 Title Fax # (800) 224-8299
General Info: Looseleaf
Subscriptions: Indv. $565
List Rental: Rents Lists

CHAC Info/Info ACCS *Association*

Publishing Co: Catholic Health Association of Canada, 1247 Kilborn Pl., Ottawa, ON K1H 6K9 Canada; Title Tel # (613) 731-7148 Title Fax # (613) 731-7797
Personnel: Editor, Production Mgr.-Maryse Blouin
Editorial Description: Newsletter for members.
General Info: Yr. Est. 1983, Quarterly, Trim Size-8½ x 11, Offset press, 2 pages, ISSN: 0822-8426, No Color, Newsprint
Subscriptions: Free With Membership
Circulation: (100% controlled), Total-2,300
Printing Co: Mutual Hadwen Imaging Technologies, 2211 Thurston Dr., Ottawa, ON K1B 3R1 Canada Tel # (613) 736-1380, Fax # (613) 736-1143

CHAS Communique *Consumer, Association*

Publishing Co: Catholic Health Assn. of Saskatchewan, 1702 20th St., W., Saskatoon, SK S7M 0Z9 Canada; Title Tel # (306) 664-5330
Personnel: Editor-Sr. Anne Collins
Editorial Description: Ethical & social justice issues dealing with health care; feature articles on membership, and in-service seminars.
General Info: Yr. Est. 1982, Bi-monthly, Trim Size-8½ x 11, 4 pages, ISSN: 0831-0548, Color-cover
Acquistions: Publication Sold
Circulation: Total-700
Printing Co: Apex Graphics, 1002 Broadway Ave., Saskatoon, SK S7N 1B9 Canada Tel # (306) 652-1967, Fax # (306) 656-9763

CHI (City Health Information) Newsletter

Publishing Co: New York City Department of Health, 125 Worth St., Box 44, New York, NY 10013-4006; Title Tel # (212) 566-7153
Personnel: Editor-Cortnie Lowe
Editorial Description: An epidemiological bulletin that features current & original data, analysis, & news from programs operated by the New York City Dept. of Health.
General Info: Yr. Est. 1952, Monthly, Trim Size-8½ x 11, Sheetfed press, 4 pages, Ind/Abs/Online: Bibl., Color
Circulation: Total-40,000
Printing Co: Astoria Press, Inc., 435 Hudson St., New York, NY 10014 Tel # (212) 627-2122

CIRA Bulletin
See: EDUCATION

COSSMHO Reporter, The   *Consumer, Association*

Publishing Co: National Coalition of Hispanic Health & Human Services Orgs, 1501 16th St NW, Washington, DC 20036-1401; Title Tel # (202) 387-5000
Editorial Description: Dedicated to providing health and human services for Hispanics in the USA.
General Info: Yr. Est. 1972, Quarterly, Trim Size-8 1/2 x 11, Offset press, 24 pages, 2 Color, Coated, Saddle-stitched
Subscriptions: Indv. $40, Free With Membership
Circulation: Total-3,000
Advertising: Inquire for rates.
Printing Co: District Lithograph Co., Inc., 4000 Penn Belt Pl, Forestville, MD 20747-4736
   Tel # (301) 736-4444

CPHA Health Digest/ACSP
Selection Sante   *Association*

Publishing Co: Canadian Public Health Assn., 1565 Carling Ave., #400, Ottawa, ON K1Z 8R1 Canada; Title Tel # (613) 725-3769 Title Fax # (613) 725-9826
Personnel: Assoc. Ed.-Karen Craven, Circ. Mgr.-Ellen McWeeny
Editorial Description: Newsletter on association activities and public health issues.
General Info: Quarterly, Trim Size-8.5 x 11, 16 pages, ISSN: 0703-5426, 2 Color, Coated, Saddle-stitched
Circulation: Total-3,000
Printing Co: MOM Printing, 300 Parkdale, Ottawa, ON K1Y 1G2 Canada Tel # (619) 729-4303

CTD News   *Business*

Publishing Co: Center for Workplace Health, The, 410 Lancaster Ave., Ste. 15, PO Box 239, Haverford, PA 19041-0239; Title Tel # (610) 896-2770 Title Fax # (610) 896-2762
Personnel: Publisher-James Kinsella, Mktg. Dir.-Brad Aronson
Editorial Description: Covers ergonomics, treatment and prevention of cumulative trauma disorders/repetitive stress injuries in the workplace.
General Info: Yr. Est. 1991, Monthly, Trim Size-8 1/2 x 11, 14 pages, ISSN: 1062-6743, No Color, Saddle-stitched
Subscriptions: Indv. $147, Inst. $147, Can. $147, For. $147, $13/copy
Circulation: Total-10,000
Advertising: Inquire for rates. Accepts Inserts.
List Rental: Actives: 10,000, $125/M

Cadre

Publishing Co: Commonwealth Alliance for Drug Rehab & Ed, Off. of Att. Genl., 101 N. 8th, Richmond, VA 23219
Personnel: Editor-Donald Carignan

Cal-OSHA Reporter
See: SAFETY

California Morbidity   *Association*

Publishing Co: State of California Dept. of Health Services, 2151 Berkeley Way, Berkeley, CA 94704-1011; Title Tel # (415) 540-2566
Personnel: Editor-James Chin
Editorial Description: Cases of notifiable diseases by current week; same week last two years; cumulative totals through current week and similar totals for two preceding years.
General Info: Yr. Est. 1913, Weekly, Trim Size-8 1/2 x 11 1/2, Offset press, 2 pages, No Color
Circulation: (100% controlled), Total-4,500

Calorie Control
Commentary   *Consumer*

Publishing Co: Calorie Control Council, 5775 Peachtree Dunwoody Rd NE, Ste G500, Atlanta, GA 30342-1507; Title Tel # (404) 252-3663 Title Fax # (404) 252-0774
Personnel: Publisher-Keith Keeney
Editorial Description: Developments related to low-calorie and low-fat foods & beverages, low calorie ingredients and dieting.
General Info: Yr. Est. 1979, Semi-annually, 6 pages, ISSN: 1049-1791
Subscriptions: Can. $10, For. $10, Free In Designated Area
Circulation: Total-12,000

Can-Do
See: DISABILITY

Canadian AIDS News   *Association, Consumer*

Publishing Co: Canadian Public Health Assn., 1565 Carling Ave., #400, Ottawa, ON K1Z 8R1 Canada; Title Tel # (613) 725-3769 Title Fax # (613) 725-9826
Personnel: Editor-Judy Redpath
Editorial Description: Features articles on AIDS education in Canada in French and English.
General Info: (Formerly New Facts of Life, The), Yr. Est. 1987, Quarterly, Trim Size-8 1/2 x 11, Web press, 55 pages, ISSN: 0841-9396, 2 Color, Saddle-stitched
Subscriptions: Free
Circulation: (8% controlled), Total-11,500, Readership-16,000
Printing Co: MOM Printing, 300 Parkdale, Ottawa, ON K1Y 1G2 Canada Tel # (619) 729-4303

Canadian Childbirth
Educator   *Business*   **CPM: $625**

Publishing Co: Professional Publishing Associates, 269 Richmond St. W., Toronto, ON M5V 1X1 Canada; Title Tel # (416) 596-8680 Title Fax # (416) 596-1991
Personnel: Publisher-Beverly Topping, Editor-Winnifred Hunsberger, Circ. Mgr.-Molly Binney, Production Mgr.-Kathy Bergen, Natl. Sales Mgr.-Cheryl Weaver
Editorial Description: Professional newsletter for childbirth educators/prenatal instructors.
General Info: Yr. Est. 1987, Quarterly, Trim Size-8 1/2 x 11, Sheetfed press, 16 pages, Saddle-stitched
Circulation: (PSS, 100% controlled), Total-5,800
Advertising: $3,630. Accepts Inserts.

Canadian Health Facilities
Law Guide   *Business*

Publishing Co: CCH Canadian Ltd., 6 Garamond Ct., North York, ON M3C 1Z5 Canada
   Fax # (416) 444-8011 Parent Co.-CCH, Inc., Riverwoods; Title Tel # (416) 441-2992
   Title Fax # (416) 444-9011
Personnel: Adv. Dir.-Michael Dyet, Mktg. Dir.-Rick Humphrey
Editorial Description: Statutes and commentary related to health care facilities.
General Info: Yr. Est. 1983, Monthly, Trim Size-6 x 9, Web press, No Color, Looseleaf
Subscriptions: Can. $470

Canadian Nursing Management
See: BUSINESS & INDUSTRY

Canadian Society of Cytology Bulletin
See: HOSPITALS & NURSING HOMES

Cancer Challenge, The
See: MEDICINE

Cancer Letter, The
See: MEDICINE

Candid Facts

Publishing Co: Canadian Cystic Fibrosis Foundation, 2221 Yonge St. #601, Toronto, ON M4S 2B4 Canada
Personnel: Editor-Carol Hill
General Info: Quarterly, Web press, 12 pages, 2 Color, Matte, Saddle-stitched
Printing Co: Scion Communications, 430 Rue McGill, Montreal, PQ H2Y 2G1 Canada
   Tel # (514) 398-0746

Capitation & Medical Practice
See: HOSPITALS & NURSING HOMES

Capitation Management
Report   *Business*

Publishing Co: National Health Information, L.L.C., 4671 E Forest Peak, Marietta, GA 30066-1763 Fax # (404) 977-8603; Title Tel # (404) 977-8113 Title Fax # (770) 977-8603
Personnel: Publisher/President/Advisor-David Schwartz
Editorial Description: Offers practical, sophisticated guidance on the management of group practices and hospitals under at-risk, capitated managed care contracts.
General Info: Yr. Est. 1994, Monthly
Subscriptions: Indv. $259, Inst. $259, Can. $269, For. $279

Capitol Connection   *Association*

Publishing Co: Health Industry Distributors Assn., 225 Reinekers Ln Ste 650, Alexandria, VA 22314-2875; Title Tel # (703) 549-4432 Title Fax # (703) 549-6495
Personnel: Editor-Donna Slingluff
General Info: (Formerly Government Report), Monthly
Circulation: Total-1,075

Capsule
See: SOCIAL SERVICES & WELFARE

Cardiovascular Coding:
The Monthly Advisor on
Coding &
Reimbursment   *Business*

Publishing Co: St. Anthony Consulting Group, 11410 Isaac Newton Sq., N., Ste. 200, Alexandria, VA 22090-5012; Title Tel # (703) 549-0100
Personnel: Publisher-Eugene W. Lorenz, Editor-Marlis McCollum, Circ. Mgr.-Kathi Lawson, Production Mgr.-Lisa Woodward, Art Dir.-Laura Daras, Promotion Dir.-Lori Liggett
General Info: Yr. Est. 1991, Monthly, Trim Size-8 1/2 x 11, 4 pages
Subscriptions: Indv. $119, $10/copy
List Rental: Hotline: $110/M

Catalyst, The
See: COMPUTERS & AUTOMATION

Catherine's Aloe Journal   *Consumer*

Publishing Co: Aloes International Inc., 2421 Curry Ford Rd, Orlando, FL 32806-2503
Personnel: Publisher-Pat Butt
Editorial Description: Information on aloe along with a variety of aloe products including lotions, juices, capsules, gels and skin care products.
General Info: Quarterly, Trim Size-8 1/2 x 11, 16 pages, 4 Color, Coated, Saddle-stitched
Advertising: Inquire for rates.

Celiac News   *Business, Association*

Publishing Co: Canadian Celiac Assn. L'Assn. Canadienne de la Maladie Coel, 6519B Mississauga Rd., Mississauga, ON L5N 1A6 Canada; Title Tel # (416) 567-7195 Title Fax # (905) 567-0710
Personnel: Publisher, Editor, Production Mgr., Promotion Dir.-Rosie Wartecker
Editorial Description: Contains information for individuals with Celiac Disease & Dermatitis Herpetiformis, its diagnosis & treatment.
General Info: Yr. Est. 1981, Quarterly, Trim Size-8½ x 11, Letrpr. press, 12 pages, ISSN: 0833-1464, 3% ads, 2 Color, Recycled, Perfect bound
Subscriptions: Indv. $25, Can. $20, For. $30, $5/copy
Acquistions: Publication Bought
Advertising: Inquire for rates. Accepts Inserts.
List Rental: Rents Lists
Printing Co: Topline Printing & Graphics, 6350 Tomken Rd., #5, Mississauga, ON L5T 1K2 Canada Tel # (416) 564-4600

Center for Health Services Newsletter

Publishing Co: Center for Health Services, Vanderbilt Medical Ctr., #17, Nashville, TN 37232-0001; Title Tel # (615) 322-4773
General Info: Semi-annually, Trim Size-8½ x 11, Sheetfed press, 4 pages, Color, Coated
Circulation: Total-1,000

Center Post   *Association*

Publishing Co: Presbyterian Medical Ctr. of Philadelphia-Univ. of PA, Public Relations, 39th St. & Market, Philadelphia, PA 19104 Tel # (215) 662-9139; Title Tel # (215) 662-9140
Personnel: Editor-Carol Barrale
Editorial Description: Info on health and health related topics from cardiology, ophthalmology to nutrition, stress etc. Purpose is to increase awareness among and educate audience on health subjects.
General Info: Bi-monthly, 8 pages, No Color
Circulation: Total-20,000

Changing Medical Markets
See: MEDICINE

ChemEcology
See: CHEMISTRY & CHEMICALS

Child and Adolescent Psychopharmacology News
See: PSYCHOLOGY

Child Health Talk   *Consumer*

Publishing Co: Black Child Development Inst, 1023 15th Street NW, Suite 600, Washington, DC 20005; Title Tel # (202) 387-1281
Personnel: Editor-Noreen Yazejian
General Info: Yr. Est. 1987, Quarterly, 8 pages, 2 Color, Coated
Subscriptions: Indv. $8
Acquistions: Publication Bought, Publication Sold
Circulation: Total-15,000
Printing Co: Corporate Press, 403 Brightseat Rd., Landover, MD 20785-4706 Tel # (301) 499-9200, Fax # (301) 499-5435

Choices   *Consumer, Association*

Publishing Co: Choice In Dying Inc., 200 Varick Street, New York, NY 10014-4810; Title Tel # (212) 366-5540 Title Fax # (212) 366-5337
Personnel: Editor-Sam Davol, Mag. Ed.-Jackie Coleman, Mktg. Dir.-Maryanne Shanahan
Editorial Description: Coverage of new developments and important legal psychosocial and practical aspects of medical care at the end of life.
General Info: (Formerly Newsletter of Choice In Dying,The), Yr. Est. 1981, Quarterly, Trim Size-11 x 8½, Web press, 8 pages, 2 Color, Matte, Other
Subscriptions: Indv. $25, Inst. $65, $15/copy
Circulation: Total-65,000
List Rental: List Management Co.: Manager: Cathy Boyles; Names in the News-California, 1 Bush St Bsmt 3, San Francisco, CA 94104-4425 Tel # (415) 989-3350, Fax # (415) 433-7796, Actives: 90,000, $75/M, Expires: 31,000, $60/M

Christian Brotherhood Newsletter
See: INSURANCE

Christian Chiropractor & CCA Bulletin
See: RELIGIOUS & THEOLOGICAL

Chronic Pain Letter   *Consumer*

Publishing Co: Robert J. Fabian Foundation, Box 1303, Old Chelsea Stn., New York, NY 10011-1303; Title Tel # (718) 797-0015 Title Fax # (212) 614-9266
Personnel: Editor-Alice DeLury, Publisher, Circ. Mgr.-Dorothy Fabian
Editorial Description: Chronic Pain Letter brings current information on the management of chronic pain to the sufferer & the health professional. Abstracts relevant literature and contains original articles on specific therapies for pain management.
General Info: Yr. Est. 1984, Bi-monthly, Trim Size-8½ x 11, 6 pages, 2 Color, Newsprint, Other
Subscriptions: Indv. $20, Inst. $35, $2/copy
Circulation: (13% controlled), Total-1,500

Citizens for Health   *Consumer*

Publishing Co: Citizens for Health, PO Box 2260, Boulder, CO 80306-2260; Title Tel # (303) 417-0772
General Info: Monthly
Subscriptions: Indv. $20, Free With Membership

Civil Abolitionist   *Consumer*

Publishing Co: Coalition to Protect Animals in Parks & Refuges, PO Box 26, Slain, NY 14884-0026; Title Tel # (607) 545-6213
Personnel: Editor-Bina Robinson
Editorial Description: Highly political animal-rights zine that also deals with general health and environmental concerns. News of adverse effects of animal experimentation on human health.
General Info: Yr. Est. 1983, Quarterly, Trim Size-8½ x 11, Offset press, 8 pages, Matte, Other
Subscriptions: Indv. $15, Can. $5, For. $6
Circulation: Total-2,000
Printing Co: Maple City Printing, Hornell, NY 14843 Tel # (607) 324-7474

Clear News
See: LAW

Clinical Cardiology Alert

Publishing Co: American Health Consultants, Inc., 3525 Piedmont Rd., Building #6, Ste. 400, Atlanta, GA 30305-0056 Tel # (404) 262-7436 Fax # (404) 284-3291; Title Tel # (404) 351-4523 Title Fax # (404) 352-1971
Personnel: Publisher-David Wilson, Editor-Peter Jenkins, Circ. Mgr.-Monica Brown, Production Mgr.-Kent Anderson, Mktg. Dir.-Debbie Zelnio
Editorial Description: Abstracts of clinical studies in medical literature pertaining to cardiology.
General Info: Yr. Est. 1982, Monthly, 4 pages, ISSN: 0741-4218, 2 Color
Subscriptions: Indv. $159
List Rental: Actives: $100/M

Clipboard   *Business, Association*

Publishing Co: Nova Scotia Association of Health Organizations, 2 Dartmouth Rd., Bedford, NS B4A 2K7 Canada Tel # (902) 832-8500; Title Tel # (902) 429-4020 Title Fax # (902) 429-5882
Personnel: Editor-Robert Purcell, Mng. Editor-Helen Patriquin
Editorial Description: Gathers health related news items from print media source.
General Info: Yr. Est. 1991, Bi-weekly, Trim Size-8½ x 14, Desktop press, 2 pages, Color, Recycled
Subscriptions: Indv. $20, Can. $20, For. $24, $4/copy
Circulation: Total-1,800, Readership-4,500
Advertising: Inquire for rates.

Commitment   *Consumer, Association*

Publishing Co: Cystic Fibrosis Foundation, 6931 Arlington Rd, Bethesda, MD 20814-5200; Title Tel # (301) 951-4422 Title Fax # (301) 951-6378
Personnel: Publisher-Robert J. Beall, Ph.D., Publisher-C.R. Mattingly, Editor-Christina Pietrasanta, Medical Ed.-Carolyn Habbersett
Editorial Description: Highlights medical advancements, chapter fundraising successes & information for people with CF.
General Info: Yr. Est. 1955, Semi-annually, Trim Size-8½ x 11, Web press, 8 pages, 2 Color, Matte
Subscriptions: Free
Circulation: Total-60,000
Printing Co: Balmar Printing, 16780 Oakmont Ave, Gaithersburg, MD 20877-4188 Tel # (301) 258-0700

Communique
See: DISABILITY

Community Alert
See: MEDICINE

Community Health Funding Report
See: PHILANTHROPY

Competitive Healthcare Market Reporter   *Business*

Publishing Co: Health Resource Publishing, 3100 Hwy. 138, PO Box 1442, Wall Township, NJ 07719-1442 Tel # (908) 681-1133 Fax # (908) 681-0490
Personnel: Publisher-Robert Jenkins, Editor-Melanie Jenkins
Editorial Description: Keeps track of the changing healthcare market including strategic issues, market facts, mergers and acquisitions, network alliances, and new managed care products.
General Info: Yr. Est. 1993, Semi-monthly, Trim Size-8½ x 11, Letrpr. press, 8 pages, ISSN: 1073-6816, No Color, Newsprint
Subscriptions: Indv. $377, $16/copy
Advertising: Accepts Inserts.
List Rental: Actives: $125/M
Printing Co: ACN Graphics, 1602 Birchwood Ln, Neptune, NJ 07753-6910 Tel # (908) 681-6083

Concerned Friends   *Consumer*

Publishing Co: Concerned Friends of Ontario Citizens in Care Facilities, 170 Merton Street, Toronto, ON M4S 1A1 Canada; Title Tel # (416) 489-0146
Personnel: Editor-Joan Fussell
Editorial Description: Discusses events & issues pertaining to reform of long-term care in Ontario.
General Info: (Formerly Concern), Yr. Est. 1981, Quarterly
Subscriptions: Indv. $15
Circulation: Total-1,000

Connective Issues
See: MEDICINE

Constructive Action
Newsletter *Consumer*

Publishing Co: Act-Action, 417 Churchill Ave., Apt. 2306, Syracuse, NY 13205-2123; Title Tel # (315) 471-4644
Personnel: Publisher, Editor-Shirley Burghard
Editorial Description: Advocates self-help, use of the arts, exercise, rest, vitamins and other therapies for former mental patients. Maintains an anti-psychiatry point of view. Urges readers to participate in yearly alternative therapy conferences.
General Info: Yr. Est. 1960, Monthly, Trim Size-8½ x 14, Mimeo press, 10 pages, ISSN: 0010-6992, No Color
Subscriptions: Indv. $10, $2/copy
Circulation: Total-150
Advertising: Inquire for rates.

Consumer Health
Newsletter

Publishing Co: Consumer Health Organization of Canada, 250 Sheppard Ave. E. #205, Box 248, Willowdale, ON M2N 5S9 Canada; Title Tel # (416) 222-6517 Title Fax # (416) 225-1243
Personnel: Publisher, Editor-Ian Pearce
Editorial Description: Canada's largest consumer health information centre providing info on healing alternatives to convention/medicine. Holds annual conventions in Toronto in April. 1990 will be our 13th. Library of books, audio & video-tapes available to members. Licensed, non-profit organization with taxfree license.
General Info: Yr. Est. 1975, Monthly, 4 pages
Subscriptions: Indv. $30, Can. $30, For. $40
Acquistions: Publication Bought

Consumer Reports on
Health *Consumer*

Publishing Co: Consumer Union, 101 Truman Avenue, Yonkers, NY 10703-1057 Tel # (914) 378-2000; Title Tel # (914) 378-2567 Title Fax # (914) 378-2907
Personnel: Publisher-James Davis, Editor-Michael Leff
Editorial Description: A monthly report on nutrition and fitness; preventive measures and new treatments; medical breakthrough and medical hype; health frauds and other critical issues. A source of frank, objective, reliable reporting on health.
General Info: (Formerly Consumer Reports Health Letter), Yr. Est. 1989, Monthly, Trim Size-8 x 10½, Web press, 16 pages, ISSN: 1044-3139, Ind/Abs/Online: DIALOG, 2 Color
Subscriptions: Indv. $24, Can. $30, For. $30, $3/copy
Printing Co: Offset House Printers, 89 Sand Hill Rd., Essex, VT 05451

Contact
See: PHYSIOLOGY

Contact Lens Update
See: OPTICAL

Contemporary Health
Journal

Publishing Co: C.H. Raine, 1320 Wisconsin Ave, Racine, WI 53403-1978; Title Tel # (414) 636-2718
Personnel: Editor-C.H. Raine, MD
General Info: Yr. Est. 1983, Monthly, ISSN: 0882-4479
Circulation: Total-220

Continuing Care
Connection *Business, Association*

Publishing Co: Healtcare Assn. of N.Y. State, 74 N. Pearl St., Albany, NY 12207-2788; Title Tel # (518) 431-7600 Title Fax # (518) 431-7915
Editorial Description: Association activities and relevant health care issues and updates dealing with continuing care.
General Info: Yr. Est. 1993, Bi-weekly, Trim Size-8½ x 11, Sheetfed press, 6 pages, 2 Color, Matte
Subscriptions: Indv. $150, Free With Membership
Circulation: Total-1,000

Cooperative Connection

Publishing Co: Nurse Healers-Professional Assocs., Inc., 85 Hawthorne Rd, Williamstown, MA 01267-2700; Title Tel # (413) 458-9181
General Info: Yr. Est. 1980, Quarterly
Circulation: Total-1,000
Advertising: Inquire for rates.

Corhealth *Consumer, Association* CPM: $416

Publishing Co: American Correctional Health Services Assn., PO Box 2307, Dayton, OH 45401-2307; Title Tel # (513) 223-9630 Title Fax # (513) 223-6307
Personnel: Editor-H.A. Rosefield
Editorial Description: Information of value to persons involved or interested in correctional health care.
General Info: Yr. Est. 1975, Bi-monthly, Trim Size-8½ x 11, Offset press, 8 pages, 1% ads, 2 Color, Newsprint
Subscriptions: Indv. $45, Free With Membership
Circulation: Total-1,200, Readership-8,000
Advertising: $500. Accepts Inserts.
List Rental: Actives: $100/M

Courage News

Publishing Co: AHA Stroke Connections, 7272 Greenville Ave, Dallas, TX 75231-5129 Tel # (214) 706-1556 Fax # (214) 696-5211; Title Tel # (612) 520-0263
Personnel: Editor-Kay Cady
General Info: (Formerly Minnesota Crippled Children News), Yr. Est. 1952, 8 pages
Circulation: Total-100,000

Cranial Letter *Business, Association* CPM: $150

Publishing Co: Cranial Academy, 3500 Depauw Blvd Ste 1080, Indianapolis, IN 46268-1136; Title Tel # (317) 879-0713 Title Fax # (317) 879-0718
Personnel: Editor-R.C. Clark
Editorial Description: Published for the membership of the Cranial Academy. Contains articles on osteopathy in the cranial field, news of cources & conferences.
General Info: (Formerly Cranial Academy Newsletter), Yr. Est. 1948, Quarterly
Circulation: Total-800
Advertising: $120.

Creative Escapes *Consumer*

Publishing Co: Creative Escapes, PO Box 1257, Piscataway, NJ 08855-1257 Tel # (201) 761-4573 Fax # (908) 436-3794
Editorial Description: Focuses on health and relaxation techniques for African-American women, with information about spa retreats.
General Info: Yr. Est. 1995, Quarterly
Subscriptions: Free
Circulation: Total-5,000
Advertising: Inquire for rates.

Creative Health Newsletter

Publishing Co: Biokinesiology Institute, 5432 Highway 227, Trail, OR 97541-9710; Title Tel # (503) 878-2080
Personnel: Publisher, Editor-John Barton, Circ. Mgr.-Linda Vice, Adv. Dir.-Shiela Shirtcliff, Production Mgr., Art Dir.-Rossetta Resue, Promotion Dir.-Genevra Pope
Editorial Description: Wholistic health research journal.
General Info: Yr. Est. 1978, Bi-monthly, 10 pages
Circulation: Total-400

Cryer, The
See: SOCIAL SERVICES & WELFARE

DATA - The Brown University Digest of Addiction Theory and Application
See: MEDICINE

DES Action Voice *Consumer, Association*

Publishing Co: DES Action USA, 1615 Broadway, Ste. 510, Oakland, CA 94612-2125; Title Tel # (510) 465-4011 Title Fax # (510) 465-4815
Personnel: Editor-Pat Cody
Editorial Description: Medical & legal information for those exposed prenatally to DES.
General Info: Yr. Est. 1979, Quarterly, 8 pages, 2 Color, Matte
Subscriptions: Indv. $30, $3/copy
Circulation: Total-2,800
Printing Co: Inkworks Press, 2727 8th St, Berkeley, CA 94710-2630 Tel # (510) 845-7111

Dairy Council Digest
See: NUTRITION

Damon Runyon-Walter
Winchell Cancer
Research Fund
Newsletter *Association*

Publishing Co: Damon Runyon-Walter Winchell Cancer Research Fund, 131 E 36th St, New York, NY 10016-3404
Personnel: Editor-Rebecca Kry
Editorial Description: Information on organization and cancer research.
General Info: Yr. Est. 1982, Semi-annually, 4 pages, No Color
Circulation: (100% controlled), Total-14,000

Daycare Health *Business*

Publishing Co: Mathanna Publications, PO Box 5351, Bellingham, WA 98227-5351; Title Tel # (206) 671-4350
Personnel: Publisher, Editor-Paula Kobos
General Info: Yr. Est. 1987, 5x/yr., 8 pages, ISSN: 0893-9020
Subscriptions: Indv. $27, Inst. $27, Can. $32, For. $32

Deep Spring Newsletter
See: RELIGIOUS & THEOLOGICAL

Delaware Biweekly
Morbidity Report *Association*

Publishing Co: Bureau of Disease Control, Div. of Public Health, Dover, DE 19901; Title Tel # (302) 678-4745
Editorial Description: Statewide disease statistics; articles and case reports of preventable disease interest.
General Info: Trim Size-8½ x 14, 2 pages, Color
Circulation: Total-1,580

Dennis Barry's Reimbursement Advisor
Business

Publishing Co: Aspen Publishers, Inc., 200 Orchard Ridge Dr., Ste 200, Gaithersburg, MD 20878-5440 Fax # (301) 417-7655 Parent Co.-Wolters Kluwer US Corporation, New York; Title Tel # (301) 417-7500 Title Fax # (301) 417-7550
Personnel: Editor-Dennis Barry, Mktg. Mgr.-Trudi Graham
Editorial Description: Hospital cost reimbursement. Insights and overhauls of the payment system by Congress, HCFAs changing interpretations and budget-cutting initiatives, civil penalties, PRO sanctions, and more.
General Info: Monthly, 8 pages, ISSN: 0084-2795
Subscriptions: Indv. $235, For. $282, $24/copy
List Rental: List Management Co.: Stevens-Knox List Management, 304 Park Ave S., New York, NY 10010-5312 Tel # (212) 388-8800, Fax # (212) 388-8890

Dentist's Patient Newsletter
See: DENTAL

Devices & Diagnostics Letter
Business

Publishing Co: Washington Business Information, Inc., 1117 19th St N Ste 200, Arlington, VA 22209-1708; Title Tel # (703) 247-3427 Title Fax # (703) 247-3421
Personnel: Publisher-David Swit, Editor-Steve Mardon, Circ. Mgr.-Chris Rogers, Production Mgr.-Jennea Myrick, Mktg. Dir.-Deb Plaskow
Editorial Description: Coverage of federal regulation of medical devices.
General Info: Yr. Est. 1974, Weekly, Trim Size-8½ x 11, Sheetfed press, 6 pages, ISSN: 0098-7530, Ind/Abs/Online: BRS, Data-Star, DIALOG, Diogenes, No Color, Matte
Subscriptions: Indv. $667, Inst. $697, Can. $697, For. $782
Acquistions: Publication Bought
List Rental: Actives: $110/M

Diabetes Self-Management
Business

Publishing Co: Phillips Publishing, Inc., 7811 Montrose Rd., Potomac, MD 20854-3394 Parent Co.-Phillips Business Information, Inc., Potomac; Title Tel # (301) 340-2100 Title Fax # (301) 294-1307
Personnel: Publisher-Thomas Phillips
Editorial Description: One of a kind publication addresses the needs of this special group with the latest medical breakthroughs techniques, nutrition, exercise & products geared toward health management.
Subscriptions: Indv. $18, $5/copy
List Rental: List Management Co.: Manager: John Baldwin; Phillips Publishing List Marketing, 7811 Montrose Rd., Potomac, MD 20854-3394 Tel # (301) 340-2100, Fax # (301) 294-1307, Actives: 300,000, $85/M, Expires: $150/M

Diabetes Update
Association

Publishing Co: Greater Boston Diabetes Society, 1330 Beacon St., Brookline, MA 02146-3202; Title Tel # (617) 731-2972
Personnel: Editor-Krista Anderson, Adv. Dir.-Faye Gordon
Editorial Description: Contains current information of interest to all diabetics, particularly recent research in diabetes, methods of self-care, proper diets.
General Info: (Formerly Diabetes Dialogue), Yr. Est. 1945, Quarterly, Trim Size-8½ x 11, Letrpr. press, 4 pages, 1% ads
Subscriptions: Indv. $10
Circulation: (100% controlled)
Advertising: Accepts Inserts.

Diabetic Traveler
See: TRAVEL

Dickinson's FDA Review
See: DRUGS & PHARMACEUTICALS

Dickinson's FDA Update by Fax
See: DRUGS & PHARMACEUTICALS

Dickinson's Pharmacy
See: DRUGS & PHARMACEUTICALS

Diet Business Bulletin
Business, Consumer

Publishing Co: Marketdata Enterprises, Inc., 181 S Franklin Ave Ste 608, Valley Stream, NY 11581-1101; Title Tel # (516) 791-6579 Title Fax # (516) 791-7759
Personnel: Publisher, Editor-John S. LaRosa
Editorial Description: Market research publication covering developments in weight loss programs and services. Feature stories plus eight regular departments.
General Info: Yr. Est. 1992, Quarterly, Trim Size-8½ x 11, 16 pages, ISSN: 1062-9289, Matte
Subscriptions: Indv. $119, Inst. $119, Can. $119, For. $145, $25/copy
Circulation: Total-300
List Rental: Actives: 1,100, $250/M

Different Drummer

Publishing Co: Office of Alcohol & Drug Abuse Prevention, 105 Pleasant St, Concord, NH 03301-3852; Title Tel # (603) 271-4636
Personnel: Production Mgr.-Pamela Rowell, Editor, Circ. Mgr., Art Dir.-Victoria Come
Editorial Description: Notes from director; personality profile; service highlights; current substance abuse articles, trends in New Hampshire, etc.
General Info: (Formerly Drummer), Yr. Est. 1981, Sheetfed press, 8 pages, 2 Color
Circulation: (100% controlled), Total-3,500
Advertising: Accepts Inserts.

Diplomate
See: PSYCHOLOGY

Disabilities Issues
See: DISABILITY

Disease Management News

Publishing Co: Business Information Services, 12811 N Point Ln, Laurel, MD 20708-2341
Personnel: Publisher, Editor-James Gutman, Circ. Mgr.-Kathleen Gutman, Mktg. Dir.-Seth Sprecher
Editorial Description: Independent news and analysis source covering major events and trends affecting the disease management sector of the health care industry.
General Info: Yr. Est. 1995, Semi-monthly, Trim Size-8½ x 11, Offset press, 8 pages, ISSN: 1084-7146, 2 Color, Other
Subscriptions: Indv. $377, $20/copy
Advertising: Accepts Inserts.
List Rental: Rents Lists
Printing Co: Newsletter Services, Inc., 9700 Philadelphia Court, Lanham, MD 20706 Tel # (301) 731-5200, Fax # (301) 731-5201

Doctors for Disaster Preparedness
Consumer, Association

Publishing Co: Doctors for Disaster Preparedness, 2509 N Campbell Ave # 272, Tucson, AZ 85719-3304; Title Tel # (602) 325-2680
Editorial Description: Covers topics related to emergency preparedness, homeland defense, natural disasters, technology accidents, and chemical, biological & nuclear weapons.
General Info: (Formerly Triage), Yr. Est. 1982, Bi-monthly
Subscriptions: Free With Membership

Doctor's Office Lab News
See: MEDICINE

Dr. Alexander Grant's Health Gazette
Consumer

Publishing Co: Alexander Grant Associates, Inc., PO Box 1786, Indianapolis, IN 46206-1786; Title Fax # (317) 253-8582
Personnel: Publisher-James Armstrong, Editor-Alexander Grant, Medical Ed.-Alexander Grant, MD
Editorial Description: Digest of medical facts & news for consumers.
General Info: (Formerly Healthwise), Yr. Est. 1978, 10x/yr., Trim Size-8½ x 11, Letrpr. press, 4 pages, ISSN: 0740-1086, Newsprint
Subscriptions: Indv. $25, Inst. $30, Can. $35, For. $45
Circulation: Total-63,823, Readership-63,823
List Rental: List Management Co.: Stevens-Knox List Management, 304 Park Ave S., New York, NY 10010-5312 Tel # (212) 388-8800, Fax # (212) 388-8890, Actives: 63,823, $75/M

Dr. Atkins Health Revelations
Consumer

Publishing Co: National Information Corp., 1101 King Street, Alexandria, VA 22314; Title Tel # (703) 548-2400
Personnel: Publisher-Marianne Parrish, Editor-Robert Atkins
Editorial Description: Information for consumers interested in alternative health care methods.
General Info: Yr. Est. 1993, Monthly
Subscriptions: Indv. $40
List Rental: List Management Co.: Wellness List Marketing, 1700 Diagonal Rd Ste 430, Alexandria, VA 22314-2866 Tel # (703) 836-8002, Actives: 27,108, $90/M

Dr. Scholl's Foot Health Forum

Publishing Co: Scholl, Inc., 3030 Jackson Ave., 150 E. Huron St., Memphis, TN 38112-2020; Title Tel # (901) 320-4666
General Info: Semi-annually
Circulation: Total-54,000

Dreaded Broccoli
See: FOOD

Drug & Alcohol Abuse Education

Publishing Co: Editorial Resources, Inc., PO Box 21129, Washington, DC 20009-0629; Title Tel # (202) 332-2267
Editorial Description: Focuses on substance abuse education.
General Info: Yr. Est. 1968, Monthly
Subscriptions: Indv. $55

Drug Abuse and Alcoholism Newsletter

Publishing Co: Vista Hill Foundation, 2355 Northside Dr, San Diego, CA 92108-2795; Title Tel # (619) 563-1770
Personnel: Editor-Marc Schukit, Circ. Mgr.-Beckie Van Houten
General Info: Yr. Est. 1971, Bi-monthly, Trim Size-8½ x 11, 4 pages, Ind/Abs/Online: Psychol. Abstr., 2 Color, Newsprint
Subscriptions: Free
Circulation: (100% controlled), Total-11,000
Printing Co: Eye Comm. Inc., 7946 Convoy Ct, San Diego, CA 92111-1212 Tel # (619) 565-6111

Drug Educator *Association*

Publishing Co: American Council for Drug Education, 136 E 64th St, New York, NY 10021-7360
Personnel: Editor-Lee Dogoloff
Editorial Description: Summarizes scientific findings on psychoactive drugs; highlights ACDE's education/prevention efforts. Contains editorials on emergent issues on drug education & prevention.
General Info: (Formerly AMMC News), Yr. Est. 1977, Quarterly, Web press, 6 pages
Subscriptions: Indv. $25
Circulation: Total-15,000
List Rental: Rents Lists

Drug GMP Report
See: DRUGS & PHARMACEUTICALS

Drug Resistance Weekly *Business, Association*

Publishing Co: C.W. Henderson Publisher, Medical Center II, P.O. Box 5528, Atlanta, GA 31107-0528 Tel # (404) 507-7777 Fax # (404) 507-7788; Title Tel # (404) 377-8895 Title Fax # (404) 378-5411
Personnel: Publisher-C.W. Henderson, Science Ed.-Alan D. Henderson, Calendar Ed.-Ken Kimsey, Bk. Rev. Ed.-Michelle Marble
Editorial Description: Timely worldwide coverage of drug resistant strains of infection, including research findings alternative therapies, and public health updates.
General Info: Yr. Est. 1994, ISSN: 1074-2913

Dystonia Medical Research Foundation Newsletter *Consumer*

Publishing Co: Dystonia Medical Research Found., 1 E Wacker Dr Ste 2900, Chicago, IL 60601-2001; Title Tel # (312) 755-0198 Title Fax # (312) 803-0138
Personnel: Editor-Dana Klosner
General Info: Yr. Est. 1977, Quarterly, Trim Size-8$\frac{1}{2}$ x 11, 8 pages, 2 Color, Coated, Saddle-stitched
Acquistions: Publication Bought
Circulation: Total-9,500

ED Management *Business, Consumer*

Publishing Co: American Health Consultants, Inc., 3525 Piedmont Rd., Building #6, Ste. 400, Atlanta, GA 30305-0056 Tel # (404) 262-7436 Fax # (404) 284-3291
Personnel: Publisher-David Wilson
General Info: Monthly
Subscriptions: Indv. $198
List Rental: Actives: $100/M

EPI-Gram

Publishing Co: Maine Dept. of Human Services, Bureau Of Health 157 Capitol, Street, Augusta, ME 04333-0001; Title Tel # (207) 287-5301
Personnel: Publisher-Rollin Ives, Editor-Geoff Beckett
Editorial Description: Current disease control and environment information, ex. hepatitis, V.D., T.B., salmonella, grid of cured diseases.
General Info: Yr. Est. 1981, Monthly, 8 pages
Circulation: Total-2,700

Early Intervention
See: BABY

Ecological Illness Law Reports
See: LAW

Economic Trends
See: HOSPITALS & NURSING HOMES

ElderCare Forum
See: WOMEN'S

Elderly Health Services Letter *Business*

Publishing Co: Health Resource Publishing, 3100 Hwy. 138, PO Box 1442, Wall Township, NJ 07719-1442; Title Tel # (908) 681-1133 Title Fax # (908) 681-0490
Personnel: Publisher-Robert Jenkins, Editor-Edward Miller
Editorial Description: Newsletter on trends and projections for health services which will be provided for the elderly: inpatient care, long term care, outpatient, home care, primary care, ambulatory care, day care, health promotion, disease prevention, support groups, health education, even residential care.
General Info: Yr. Est. 1986, Monthly, Trim Size-8$\frac{1}{2}$ x 11, Offset press, 8 pages, ISSN: 0891-9275, No Color, Newsprint
Subscriptions: Indv. $157, $12/copy
Advertising: Accepts Inserts.
List Rental: Actives: $95/M
Printing Co: ACN Graphics, 1602 Birchwood Ln, Neptune, NJ 07753-6910 Tel # (908) 681-6083

Electrical Sensitivity News
See: ENVIRONMENT & ECOLOGY

Elisabeth Kubler-Ross Center Newsletter

Publishing Co: Elisabeth Kubler-Ross Center, South Rt. 616, Head Waters, VA 24442; Title Tel # (703) 396-3441
Personnel: Editor-Elisabeth Ross
General Info: Yr. Est. 1980, Quarterly, 8 pages
Subscriptions: Indv. $15
Circulation: Total-30,000

Employee Benefit Notes
See: INDUSTRIAL RELATIONS/PERSONNEL

Employee Health and Fitness

Publishing Co: American Health Consultants, Inc., 3525 Piedmont Rd., Building #6, Ste. 400, Atlanta, GA 30305-0056 Fax # (404) 284-3291; Title Tel # (404) 262-7436 Title Fax # (800) 284-3291
Personnel: Publisher-Connie Austin, Editor-Linda Morningstar, Circ. Mgr.-Monica Brown, Production Mgr.-Mike Witter, Mktg. Mgr.-Robin Prows
Editorial Description: The executive update on health improvement programs.
General Info: Yr. Est. 1979, Monthly, Trim Size-8$\frac{1}{2}$ x 11, ISSN: 0199-6304, Ind/Abs/Online: Mead Data Central
Subscriptions: Indv. $219, $22/copy
Circulation: Total-1,100
List Rental: Actives: $100/M

Employer's Health Benefits Bulletin *Business*

Publishing Co: Thompson Publishing Group, 1725 K Street, NW, Washington, DC 20006 Tel # (202) 872-4000; Title Tel # (202) 872-1766
Personnel: Publisher-Richard Thompson, Editor-Richard Quinn, Promotion Dir.-Vicki Black
Editorial Description: Contains news on congressional action and how it will affect benefits programs.
General Info: Yr. Est. 1987, Monthly, Trim Size-8$\frac{1}{2}$ x 11, Offset press, 8 pages, 2 Color
Subscriptions: Indv. $249

Employers' Health Benefits Management Letter
See: INDUSTRIAL RELATIONS/PERSONNEL

Employment Health Law & Benefits
See: INDUSTRIAL RELATIONS/PERSONNEL

Employment Safety and Health Guide
See: SAFETY

Endometriosis Assn. International Newsletter *Association*

Publishing Co: International Endometriosis Assn., 8585 N 76th Pl, Milwaukee, WI 53223-2633; Title Tel # (414) 355-2200 Title Fax # (414) 355-6065
Personnel: Editor-Mary Lou Ballweg
Editorial Description: Presents information related to endometriosis.
General Info: (Formerly Endometriosis Assn. Natl. Newsletter), Yr. Est. 1980, Bi-monthly, Trim Size-8.5 x 11, 8 pages, ISSN: 0897-1870
Subscriptions: Indv. $25, Inst. $30, Can. $35

Environmental Health Letter
See: ENVIRONMENT & ECOLOGY

Epi Notes *Association*

Publishing Co: North Carolina Dept. of Environment, PO Box 27687, Raleigh, NC 27611-7687; Title Tel # (919) 733-3421 Title Fax # (919) 733-0490
Personnel: Editor-J. N. MacCormack, M.D., Circ. Mgr.-Hazel King
Editorial Description: Covers communicable disease control, occupational health, vital statistics, highway safety, & injury control environmental epidemiology & other epidemiology division programs & issues.
General Info: (Formerly Epidemiologic Notes & Comm. Dis. Report), Yr. Est. 1969, Monthly, Trim Size-8$\frac{1}{2}$ x 11, Offset press, Color
Acquistions: Publication Bought
Circulation: (100% controlled), Total-1,200
List Rental: Rents Lists

Epidemiology Bulletin

Publishing Co: Oklahoma State Dept. of Health, 1000 NE 10th St, Oklahoma City, OK 73117-1299; Title Tel # (405) 271-4060
Personnel: Editor-Scott McNabb, Production Mgr.-Shelley Lanser, Art Dir.-Nancy Ballard
Editorial Description: Contains monthly summary of communicable diseases in Okla. with descriptive or editorial comment; latest practices in epidemiology, immunization procedures.
General Info: Yr. Est. 1964, Monthly, Trim Size-8$\frac{1}{2}$ x 11, Offset press, 6 pages, Color
Circulation: Total-3,000

Ethics and Medics
See: MEDICINE

Executive Briefings on Hospital Regulation
See: MEDICINE

Executive Edge
See: MANAGEMENT

Executive Health's Good
Health Report *Business*

Publishing Co: Executive Health Publications, 383 Route 46 West, Fairfield, NJ 07004-2402; Title Tel # (201) 227-9358
Personnel: Editor-Rob Laufer, Circ. Mgr.-Mary E. Setter, Publisher, Adv. Dir.-A.C. Bushnell
Editorial Description: Preventive medicine.
General Info: (Formerly Executive Health Report), Yr. Est. 1963, Monthly, Sheetfed press, 8 pages, ISSN: 0882-2131, Ind/Abs/Online: Information Access Co; University Microfilms; Health & Nutrition Index., 2 Color, Recycled
Subscriptions: Indv. $34, $3/copy
Acquisions: Publication Bought
Circulation: Total-11,000
List Rental: List Management Co.: Compuname, Inc., 411 Theodore Fremd Ave., Rye, NY 10580 Tel # (914) 925-4000, Fax # (914) 925-2499, Actives: $85/M

Executive Report on
Managed Care *Business*

Publishing Co: Health Resource Publishing, 3100 Hwy. 138, PO Box 1442, Wall Township, NJ 07719-1442; Title Tel # (908) 681-1133 Title Fax # (908) 681-0490
Personnel: Publisher-Robert Jenkins, Editor-Melanie Jenkins
Editorial Description: A monthly report giving news of how major employers are implementing managed care programs. Helps companies prepare to evaluate & monitor various managed care proposals in terms of their cost effectiveness, quality & liability to the employer.
General Info: Yr. Est. 1988, Monthly, Trim Size-8½ x 11, Sheetfed press, 8 pages, ISSN: 0898-9753, No Color, Newsprint
Subscriptions: Indv. $222, $15/copy
Advertising: Accepts Inserts.
List Rental: Rents Lists
Printing Co: ACN Graphics, 1602 Birchwood Ln, Neptune, NJ 07753-6910 Tel # (908) 681-6083

Exercise Standards & Malpractice Reporter, The
See: LAW

Facilitator

Publishing Co: Wentworth Worldwide Media, 1866 Colonial Village Lane, PO Box 10488, Lancaster, PA 17605-0488; Title Tel # (717) 393-1000 Title Fax # (717) 393-5752
General Info: Yr. Est. 1992, Monthly

Family Health *Consumer*

Publishing Co: Sacred Heart Hospital, 421 Chew St., Allentown, PA 18102-3490; Title Tel # (215) 776-4500 Title Fax # (610) 776-5149
Personnel: Editor-Thomas Moylan, Production Mgr.-Helreigel-Keena Advertising
Editorial Description: Medical/consumer health information.
General Info: Quarterly, Trim Size-8½ x 11, 4 pages, 2 Color
Circulation: Total-120,000

Farmsafe

Publishing Co: Farm Safety Assn., Inc., 340 Woodlawn Rd. W., #22, Guelph, ON N1H 7K6 Canada
General Info: Yr. Est. 1976, Bi-monthly, 8 pages
Circulation: Total-26,000

Federal Veterinarian
See: VETERINARY

Fed. of Medical Women of Canada, Newsletter
See: MEDICINE

Felix Letter
See: NUTRITION

Fitfax Journal

Publishing Co: Fitness Motivation, Institute of America, 36 Harold Ave, San Jose, CA 95117-1026; Title Tel # (408) 246-9191
Personnel: Editor-Ron Useldiaga
General Info: Bi-monthly, Trim Size-8½ x 11, 6 pages
Subscriptions: Indv. $20

Fitness Bulletin *Consumer*

Publishing Co: Steen Publishing Co., RR #1, Cheltenham, ON L0P 1C0 Canada Tel # (908) 833-0943 Fax # (905) 838-0948; Title Tel # (416) 491-5830
Personnel: Publisher, Editor-David Steen, Circ. Mgr.-Joy Stewart
Editorial Description: Professional advice regarding exercise, nutrition, stress management and associated subjects.
General Info: (Formerly The Fitness Institute Bulletin), Yr. Est. 1978, Monthly, Trim Size-8½ x 11, Sheetfed press, 4 pages, 2 Color, Newsprint
Subscriptions: Indv. $30, Can. $30, For. $44, $5/copy
Acquisions: Publication Sold
Circulation: Total-3,500
Printing Co: C&S Printing, 119 Mill St., Georgetown, ON L7G 2C7 Canada Tel # (416) 877-9423

Fitnews CPM: $45

Publishing Co: American Health & Fitness, PO Box 530489, Livonia, MI 48153-0489; Title Tel # (313) 537-7343
Personnel: Editor-Robert Carzon, Publisher, Adv. Dir.-Kathleen Carzon
Editorial Description: Features a variety of informative articles on different health and fitness topics; interviews; profiles.
General Info: Yr. Est. 1988, Quarterly
Subscriptions: $2/copy
Circulation: (20% controlled), Total-10,000, Subscriptions-8,000
Advertising: $450.

Floating

Publishing Co: Floatation Tank Assn., PO Box 1396, Grass Valley, CA 95945-1396; Title Tel # (916) 432-3794 Title Fax # (916) 432-3794
Personnel: Editor-Lee Perry
General Info: (Formerly Flotation Tank Association Newsletter), Yr. Est. 1987, Trim Size-8½ x 11, 1% ads, No Color, Coated
Subscriptions: $4/copy
Circulation: Total-1,000
Advertising: Inquire for rates.

Florida Healthtrac
See: LAW

Flower Essence Society
Newsletter *Association*

Publishing Co: Flower Essence Society, PO Box 459, Nevada City, CA 95959-0459; Title Tel # (916) 265-0247 Title Fax # (916) 265-6467
Personnel: Editor-Patricia Kaminski
Editorial Description: Holistic health, nature awareness, clinical use of essences, networking.
General Info: Yr. Est. 1979, Semi-annually, Trim Size-8½ x 11, Desktop press, 40 pages, Color, Newsprint, Perfect bound
Subscriptions: Indv. $20, Inst. $50, For. $30, Free With Membership
Acquisions: Publication Sold
Circulation: Total-100,000
Printing Co: North Star Press, Nevada City, CA 95959 Tel # (916) 265-6923

Flying Lizards Newsletter
See: TRACK & FIELD

Focus on Geriatric Care &
Rehabilitation *Business*

Publishing Co: Aspen Publishers, Inc., 200 Orchard Ridge Dr., Ste 200, Gaithersburg, MD 20878-5440 Tel # (301) 417-7500 Parent Co.-Wolters Kluwer US Corporation, New York; Title Tel # (301) 251-7500 Title Fax # (301) 417-7655
Personnel: Publisher-Michael Brown, Publisher-Richard Kravitz, Editor-Joan K. Glickstein, PhD, Production Mgr.-Ruth Mckendry, Adv. Dir.-Frances Ray, Promotion Dir.-Janis Treacy
Editorial Description: Written for nurses, physical therapists, occupational therapists & administrators in geriatric settings.
General Info: Yr. Est. 1987, 10x/yr., Trim Size-11 x 8½, Other press, 8 pages, 2 Color, Recycled, Other
Subscriptions: Indv. $80, For. $96, $11/copy
Circulation: Total-3,400
List Rental: List Management Co.: Stevens-Knox List Management, 304 Park Ave S., New York, NY 10010-5312 Tel # (212) 388-8800, Fax # (212) 388-8890

Focus: Social and
Preventive Medicine *Association*

Publishing Co: Community Health Services Association, 455-2nd Ave., N., Saskatoon, SK S7K 2C2 Canada; Title Tel # (306) 664-4243
Personnel: Editor-Sheila Ragush
Editorial Description: Information bulletin for membership of the co-operative and the general public.
General Info: Yr. Est. 1962, Quarterly, Trim Size-8½ x 11, Letrpr. press, 6 pages, Color
Subscriptions: Indv. $5
Circulation: Total-5,300
Advertising: Inquire for rates.
Printing Co: Print West Communications, Saskatoon, SK Canada

Food & Nutrition Letter

Publishing Co: Rodale Press, 33 East Minor St., Emmaus, PA 18098-0001 Tel # (610) 967-5171 Fax # (610) 967-8963; Title Tel # (215) 567-5171 Title Fax # (610) 967-6263
Personnel: Editor-Martha Capwell
Editorial Description: Promotes the benefits of a healthy diet. Features health news, cooking tips, consumer information and much more.
General Info: Yr. Est. 1990, Monthly
Subscriptions: Indv. $24
List Rental: List Management Co.: Direct Media, Inc., 200 Pemberwick Rd., PO Box 4565, Greenwich, CT 06830 Tel # (203) 532-3713, Fax # (203) 531-1452, Actives: 40,820, $75/M

Food Drug Cosmetic Law Reports
See: DRUGS & PHARMACEUTICALS

Food, Nutrition & Health
See: NUTRITION

Frontiers *Consumer, Association*

Publishing Co: Parents Anonymous, 675 W Foothill Blvd Ste 220, Claremont, CA 91711-3475; Title Tel # (310) 649-5212
Editorial Description: Concerned about child abuse problems & issues.
General Info: Quarterly

Fruitful Yield Nutrition & Health Update   *Consumer*

Publishing Co: Fruitful Yield Inc., 550 Mitchell Rd., Glendale Heights, IL 60139-2581; Title Tel # (708) 893-2037
Personnel: Publisher-Elwood Richard, Editor-Dave Richard
Editorial Description: Subjects ranging from prenatal care to health & nutrition for all age groups.
General Info: Yr. Est. 1972, Semi-annually, 12 pages
Circulation: Total-15,000

Future Skinnies of America

Publishing Co: Future Skinnies of America, Rr 2 Box 423, Claysville, PA 15323-9418
Personnel: Editor-Judy Kerns
Editorial Description: Diet/friendship club by mail. Send for information to Judy Kerns, RD #2, Box 423, Claysville, Pa 15323-9418.
General Info: Monthly, Mimeo press
Subscriptions: Indv. $5, $3/copy
Acquistions: Publication Bought

GFP Notes

Publishing Co: Association of American Medical Colleges, 2450 N Street, N.W., Washington, DC 20037-1167 Tel # (202) 828-0400; Title Tel # (202) 828-0490
Personnel: Editor-Robert D'Antuono
Editorial Description: Articles of interest to administrators of faculty practice plans.
General Info: Yr. Est. 1988, Quarterly, 8 pages
Circulation: Total-400

GHAA Journal   *Association*

Publishing Co: Group Health Assn. of America, Inc., 1129 20th St NW, Ste. 600, Washington, DC 20036-3403 Tel # (202) 778-3200 Fax # (202) 331-7487
Personnel: Publisher, Editor-James Doherty
Editorial Description: Professional journal concentrating on health maintenance organizations.
General Info: (Formerly Group Health Journal), Yr. Est. 1980, Semi-annually, ISSN: 0196-6332
Subscriptions: Indv. $35
Circulation: Total-2,500

GHAA News   *Association*

Publishing Co: Group Health Assn. of America, Inc., 1129 20th St NW, Ste. 600, Washington, DC 20036-3403 Fax # (202) 331-7487; Title Tel # (202) 778-3200
Personnel: Editor-Lisa Lopez
Editorial Description: Bimonthly magazine providing indepth analysis of issues, features for HMOs.
General Info: (Formerly Group Health News), Yr. Est. 1959, Bi-monthly, 32 pages, Color
Subscriptions: Indv. $75
Circulation: Total-5,000

GMP Letter, The   *Business*

Publishing Co: Washington Business Information, Inc., 1117 19th St N Ste 200, Arlington, VA 22209-1708; Title Tel # (703) 247-3424 Title Fax # (703) 247-3421
Personnel: Publisher-David Swit, Editor-Samuel Gilston, Circ. Mgr.-Chris Rogers, Production Mgr.-Jennea Myrick, Mktg. Dir.-Deb Plaskow
Editorial Description: Good manufacturing processes - federal regulations, re: production and quality control in the medical device field.
General Info: Yr. Est. 1980, Monthly, Trim Size-8½ x 11, Sheetfed press, 8 pages, ISSN: 0196-626X, Ind/Abs/Online: Diogenes, BRS, Data-Star, DIALOG, No Color, Matte
Subscriptions: Indv. $377, Inst. $377, Can. $377, For. $412
Acquistions: Publication Bought
List Rental: Actives: $110/M

Gaucher's Disease Registry Newsletter   *Association*

Publishing Co: National Gaucher Foundation, 11140 Rockville Pike, #350, Rockville, MD 20852-3106; Title Tel # (312) 990-8800
Personnel: Editor-Karen Cohen
General Info: Yr. Est. 1981, Bi-monthly, 8 pages, No Color
Circulation: Total-3,000

Generations   *Association*

Publishing Co: Natl. Ataxia Foundation, 15500 Wayzata Blvd Ste 750, Wayzata, MN 55391-1490; Title Tel # (612) 473-7666 Title Fax # (612) 473-9289
Personnel: Editor-Donna Gruetzmacher
Editorial Description: Information for persons interested in hereditary ataxia and related disorders.
General Info: Yr. Est. 1957, Quarterly, Trim Size-8½ x 11, Sheetfed press, 32 pages, No Color, Newsprint, Saddle-stitched
Subscriptions: Indv. $25, Can. $30
Circulation: Total-7,600
Printing Co: Madison Daily Leader, PO Box 348, Madison, SD 57042-0348 Tel # (605) 256-4555

Genesis   *Association*

Publishing Co: American Society for Psychoprophylaxis in Obstetrics, 1200 19th St NW Ste 300, Washington, DC 20036-2412; Title Tel # (202) 857-1128 Title Fax # (202) 223-4579
Personnel: Editor-Roberta Scaer
Editorial Description: Concerned with pregnancy, maternal/child health, family centered maternity care.
General Info: Yr. Est. 1979, Quarterly, Trim Size-8⅛ x 10⅞, Desktop press, 8 pages, ISSN: 657710, 2 Color, Other, Saddle-stitched
Subscriptions: Inst. $30, $5/copy
Circulation: (100% controlled), Total-4,500
Advertising: Accepts Inserts.
List Rental: Actives: 4,000
Printing Co: Hagerstown Bookbinding & Printing, 952 Frederick St, Hagerstown, MD 21740-6821 Tel # (301) 733-2000, Fax # (301) 733-6586

Genetically Speaking
See: GENETICS

Georgia Health Law Update   *Business*

Publishing Co: M. Lee Smith Publishers & Printers ,LCC, P.O. Box 198867, 162 Fourth Avenue North, Nashville, TN 37219-8867 Tel # (615) 242-7395 Fax # (615) 256-6601
Personnel: Publisher-M Lee Smith, Editor-George Hendrix, Circ. Mgr.-Cathy Bradford, Mktg. Dir.-Dave Yates
Editorial Description: Health information for Georgia.
General Info: (Formerly Georgia Health Alert), Yr. Est. 1994, Monthly, Trim Size-8½ x 11, 8 pages, ISSN: 1073-0559, 2 Color
Subscriptions: Indv. $177
Printing Co: M. Lee Smith Publishers & Printers ,LLC, PO Box 198867, 162 Fourth Avenue, Nashville, TN 37219-8867 Tel # (615) 242-7395, Fax # (615) 256-6601

Geriatric Care News

Publishing Co: DRS Geriatric Pub. Co., 4210 95th Ave SE, Mercer Island, WA 98040-4230; Title Tel # (206) 232-9689
Personnel: Publisher-Denise Schramke, Editor-Frances Greer
General Info: Yr. Est. 1972, Monthly, Offset press, 8 pages, ISSN: 0745-5070, 2 Color
Subscriptions: Indv. $59, $6/copy

Gerofiles
See: SENIOR CITIZENS

Gluten Free Pantry
See: FOOD

Gluten Intolerance Group's Newsletter
See: NUTRITION

Good-News-Letter
See: NUTRITION

Grace Kirschenbaum's World of Cookbooks
See: FOOD

Gray Sheet: Medical Devices, Diagnostics & Instrumentation Reports
See: MEDICINE

Green Guide, The
See: ENVIRONMENT & ECOLOGY

Green Sheet: Weekly Pharmacy Reports
See: DRUGS & PHARMACEUTICALS

HANDI Information Center Update   *Consumer, Association*

Publishing Co: Natl. Hemophilia Foundation, 110 Greene St Apt 303, New York, NY 10012-3832 Tel # (212) 219-8180 Fax # (212) 966-9247; Title Tel # (212) 431-8541 Title Fax # (212) 431-0906
Personnel: Editor-Suzanne Tracy, Promotion Dir.-Suzanne Trace
Editorial Description: STET & AIDS/HIV Network for the Dissemination of Information newsletter for members of the bleeding disorders community.
General Info: Yr. Est. 1990, Bi-monthly, Trim Size-8½ x 11, Desktop press, 2 pages, Color-cover, Other
Subscriptions: Free
Circulation: Total-1,800

HANDI Quarterly   *Consumer, Association*

Publishing Co: Natl. Hemophilia Foundation, 110 Greene St Apt 303, New York, NY 10012-3832 Tel # (212) 219-8180 Fax # (212) 966-9247; Title Tel # (212) 431-8541 Title Fax # (212) 431-0906
Personnel: Editor, Promotion Dir.-Suzanne Tracy
Editorial Description: Semi annual newsletter for members of the bleeding disorders community.
General Info: Yr. Est. 1990, Semi-annually, Trim Size-8½ x 11, Offset press, 8 pages, ISSN: 1050-2505, 2 Color, Recycled, Saddle-stitched
Subscriptions: Free
Circulation: Total-3,200, Readership-3,200

HANYS News
Business, Association

Publishing Co: Healtcare Assn. of N.Y. State, 74 N. Pearl St., Albany, NY 12207-2788; Title Tel # (518) 431-7600 Title Fax # (518) 431-7915
Editorial Description: Association activities and relevant health issues and updates.
General Info: (Formerly Healthcare Association of New York State News), Yr. Est. 1969, Weekly, Trim Size-8½ x 11, Sheetfed press, 4 pages, Matte
Subscriptions: Indv. $500, Free With Membership
Circulation: Total-2,000

HE-XTRA
Association   **CPM: $38**

Publishing Co: Assn. for the Advancement of Health Education, 1900 Association Dr, Reston, VA 22091-1502; Title Tel # (703) 476-3437 Title Fax # (703) 476-6638
Personnel: Editor-Linda Moore
Editorial Description: Promotes health education to professionals.
General Info: Yr. Est. 1936, 5x/yr., Trim Size-11½ x 15, Offset press, 8 pages, 2 Color, Newsprint
Subscriptions: Free With Membership
Circulation: Total-8,500
Advertising: $325.
List Rental: Rents Lists
Printing Co: Silver Communications Inc, 102A Executive Drive, Sterling, VA 20166 Tel # (703) 471-7339, Fax # (703) 471-9145

HEF News

Publishing Co: Health Education Foundation, 600 N.H. Ave. NW, #452, Washington, DC 20037; Title Tel # (202) 338-3501
Personnel: Publisher-Marion Chafetz, Editor-Marion Clafetz
Editorial Description: Information, perspectives on behavior, lifestyle, trends relating to health, well-being.
General Info: Yr. Est. 1977, Quarterly, Trim Size-8½ x 11, Sheetfed press, 4 pages, No Color
Subscriptions: Indv. $15
Circulation: Total-1,000

HESCA Feedback
Association

Publishing Co: Health Sciences Communications Association, 6728 Old Mclean Village Dr, Mc Lean, VA 22101-3906 Tel # (703) 556-9324 Fax # (703) 556-8729; Title Tel # (314) 556-9324 Title Fax # (314) 556-8729
Personnel: Editor-Chery Kilday
Editorial Description: Announces news & reviews books/programs in health sciences education, & reports on member activities.
General Info: Yr. Est. 1975, Bi-monthly, Trim Size-8½ x 11, Letrpr. press, 8 pages, No Color, Coated
Subscriptions: Indv. $60, Can. $55, For. $55
Acquistions: Publication Bought
Circulation: (100% controlled), Total-400
List Rental: Actives: 350

HIDA Headlines
Business, Association

Publishing Co: Health Industry Distributors Assn., 225 Reinekers Ln Ste 650, Alexandria, VA 22314-2875; Title Tel # (703) 549-4432 Title Fax # (703) 549-6495
Personnel: Editor-Laura Colnes
Editorial Description: Newsletter for medical products distributors.
General Info: Yr. Est. 1985, Monthly, Trim Size-8½ x 11, 4 pages, 2 Color
Circulation: Total-3,100

HIV Connect
Consumer, Association

Publishing Co: Library for AIDS/HIV Resources, NYC Dept. of Health, 125 Worth Street, Box A/1, New York, NY 10013; Title Fax # (212) 788-4278
Personnel: Editor-Wendy Levine
Editorial Description: Info on prevention and care services and professional opportunities in NYC.
General Info: Yr. Est. 1992, Monthly, Trim Size-8½ x 11, 16 pages, 2 Color, Matte

HLABC Forum
Association

Publishing Co: Sponsor-Univ. of BC, Health Libraries Association of British Columbia, 1383 W. 8th Ave., Vancouver, BC V6H 4C4 Canada Fax # (604) 737-8582; Title Tel # (604) 733-6671
Personnel: Editor-Andrew Stefanelli
General Info: Yr. Est. 1976, Quarterly, Trim Size-8½ x 11, Mimeo press, 20 pages, ISSN: 0826-0135, No Color
Subscriptions: Can. $15

HMO Managers Letter
Business, Association

Publishing Co: Group Health Assn. of America, Inc., 1129 20th St NW, Ste. 600, Washington, DC 20036-3403 Fax # (202) 331-7487; Title Tel # (202) 778-3200
Personnel: Editor-Pam Schwartz
Editorial Description: Breaking news about HMO industry, legislation.
General Info: Yr. Est. 1984, Bi-weekly
Subscriptions: Indv. $125
Circulation: Total-2,000

HPV News
Association

Publishing Co: American Social Health Assn., PO Box 13827, Research Triangle Pk, NC 27709-3827; Title Tel # (919) 361-8400 Title Fax # (919) 361-8425
Personnel: Editor-Charles Ebel
Editorial Description: Research reports and other information on Human Papillomavirus.
General Info: Yr. Est. 1991, Quarterly, Trim Size-7 x 11, Offset press, 12 pages, 2 Color, Matte, Saddle-stitched
Subscriptions: Indv. $25, $5/copy

Harvard AIDS Letter
See: MEDICINE

Harvard Health Letter
Consumer

Publishing Co: Harvard Medical School Health Publications Group, 164 Longwood Ave, Fl. 1, Boston, MA 02115-5818 Tel # (617) 432-1802; Title Tel # (617) 432-1485 Title Fax # (617) 432-1506
Personnel: Editor-Patricia Thomas, Publisher, Circ. Mgr.-Andrea Graham, Production Mgr.-Timothy Evans
Editorial Description: Accurate & timely health information for the layperson.
General Info: (Formerly Harvard Medical School Health Letter), Yr. Est. 1975, Monthly, Trim Size-8½ x 11, Web press, 8 pages, ISSN: 1052-1577, Ind/Abs/Online: CD Plus Technologies, Information Access, EBSCO, 2 Color, Matte, Saddle-stitched
Subscriptions: Indv. $24, Can. $36, For. $39, $4/copy
Circulation: Total-300,000
List Rental: List Management Co.: The Lake Group, 411 Theodore Freund Ave., Rye, NY 10580-1497 Tel # (914) 925-2400, Fax # (914) 925-2499, Actives: 226,381, $85/M, Hotline: 14,526, $90/M

Harvard Heart Letter
Consumer

Publishing Co: Harvard Medical School Health Publications Group, 164 Longwood Ave, Fl. 1, Boston, MA 02115-5818 Tel # (617) 432-1802 Fax # (617) 432-1506
Personnel: Publications Director-Andrea Graham
General Info: Monthly

Harvard Mental Health Letter
See: PSYCHOLOGY

Harvard Women's Health Watch
Consumer

Publishing Co: Harvard Medical School Health Publications Group, 164 Longwood Ave, Fl. 1, Boston, MA 02115-5818 Tel # (617) 432-1802 Fax # (617) 432-1506; Title Tel # (617) 432-1485
Personnel: Publisher-Andrea Graham, Editor in Chief-Celeste Robb-Nicholson, MD, Editor-Beverly Merz, Product Mgr.-Timothy Evans
Editorial Description: Health newsletter addressing issues unique to women, such as mammography and hormone replacement therapy. Covers topics in medicine, psychology, and health science policy that are of particular interest to women.
General Info: Yr. Est. 1993, Monthly, Trim Size-8½ x 11, 8 pages, ISSN: 1070-910X, Ind/Abs/Online: EBSCO, Information Acess, 2 Color, Matte, Saddle-stitched
Subscriptions: Indv. $24, Can. $36, $4/copy
Circulation: Total-250,000

Hawaii Health Messenger
Consumer

Publishing Co: Hawaii State Dept. of Health, Box 3378, Communication Office, Honolulu, HI 96801-3378; Title Tel # (808) 586-4442
Personnel: Editor-Maxine Sandison, Art Dir.-Elizabeth Rider
Editorial Description: Current policies and programs of the hawaii State Health Dept.
General Info: Yr. Est. 1941, Quarterly, 4 pages, 2 Color
Circulation: Total-5,500

Hazardous Substances & Public Health
See: WATER SUPPLY, POWER & WASTE

Hazelden Voice
See: SOCIAL SERVICES & WELFARE

Heal Prints

Publishing Co: HEAL of Louisiana, 8618 GSRI Ave., Baton Rouge, LA 70810-6221; Title Tel # (504) 383-2028
Personnel: Editor, Adv. Dir.-Diane Hamilton
Editorial Description: Promotes good human ecology.
General Info: (Formerly Louisiana HEAL Newsletter), Yr. Est. 1984, Quarterly, Trim Size-8½ x 11, 8 pages
Circulation: Total-500
Advertising: Inquire for rates.

Healing Currents

Publishing Co: Whole Health Institute, 4817 N County Road 29, Loveland, CO 80538-9515; Title Tel # (303) 679-4306
Personnel: Editor, Circ. Mgr., Adv. Dir.-Kathy Bassett, Art Dir.-Victor Summers
Editorial Description: Considers a wide variety of topics in the healing arts, with emphasis on the spiritual integration in everyday living which results in health & practical approach to healing.
General Info: Yr. Est. 1976, Quarterly, 32 pages, Color
Subscriptions: Indv. $20, For. $24, $4/copy
Circulation: Total-1,500

Healing Newsletter
Business, Consumer

Publishing Co: Gerson Institute, PO Box 430, Bonita, CA 91908-0430; Title Tel # (619) 472-7450
Personnel: Editor-Gar Hildenbrand
Editorial Description: The Healing Newsletter is the membership organ of the Gerson Institute, a non-profit education & research institute.
General Info: Quarterly, Offset press, 8 pages, No Color
Subscriptions: Indv. $15
Circulation: Total-3,000
Printing Co: Axis Printing, 1441 C St, San Diego, CA 92101-5717 Tel # (619) 231-0847

Healing Woman, The
See: WOMEN'S

Health & Environment Digest
See: ENVIRONMENT & ECOLOGY

Health & Healing
See: MEDICINE

Health & Longevity   *Consumer*

Publishing Co: Agora, Inc., 105 W. Monoment St., Baltimore, MD 21202-4702 Tel # (410) 783-2647
  Fax # (410) 223-2662
Personnel: Publisher-William Bonner, Editor-Robert D. Willix
Editorial Description: Health information from Dr. Robert D. Willix, Jr.
General Info: (Formerly Health for Life), Monthly
Subscriptions: Indv. $40
Circulation: Total-66,800

Health & Nutrition Update   *Association*   **CPM$1200**

Publishing Co: Canadian Schizophrenia Foundation, 16 Florence Ave., North York, ON M2N 1E9
  Canada; Title Tel # (416) 733-2117 Title Fax # (416) 733-2352
Personnel: Publisher, Editor, Production Mgr., Adv. Dir., Promotion Dir.-Steven Carter
Editorial Description: Health, nutrition, new treatments for schizophrenia, children's learning &
  behavior disorders.
General Info: Yr. Est. 1974, Quarterly, Trim Size-8½ x 11, Web press, 20 pages, ISSN: 0831-8530,
  Ind/Abs/Online: Excerp.Med., 1% ads, No Color, Coated, Saddle-stitched
Subscriptions: Indv. $25, Inst. $25, Can. $25, For. $30, $8/copy
Acquistions: Publication Bought
Circulation: Total-375
Advertising: $450.

Health Advocate
See: LAW

Health Advocate   *Business, Association*   **CPM: $347**

Publishing Co: Nova Scotia Association of Health Organizations, 2 Dartmouth Rd., Bedford, NS B4A
  2K7 Canada; Title Tel # (902) 832-8500 Title Fax # (902) 429-5882
Personnel: Editor-Robert Purcell, Adv. Dir.-Greg Phipps
General Info: (Formerly NSAHO Newsletter), Yr. Est. 1980, Monthly, Trim Size-8½ x 11, Offset
  press, 4 pages, 25% ads, Color, Saddle-stitched
Subscriptions: Indv. $24, Can. $24, For. $24, $5/copy
Circulation: Total-2,000, Readership-5,000
Advertising: $695. Accepts Inserts.
Printing Co: Printer, The, 2411 Agricola St., Halifax, NS B3K 3B5 Canada Tel # (902) 423-2679,
  Fax # (902) 422-3706

Health Alert   *Consumer*

Publishing Co: Health Alert, PO Box 22620, Carmel, CA 93922; Title Tel # (408) 372-2103
  Title Fax # (408) 372-3805
Personnel: Publisher, Editor-Bruce West
Editorial Description: Natural healing, health and fitness information, techniques and remedies.
General Info: (Formerly Natural Fitness Newsletter), Yr. Est. 1984, Monthly, Offset press, 8 pages,
  ISSN: 1083-8325
Subscriptions: Indv. $39, $3/copy
Circulation: Total-25,000, Readership-25,100
List Rental: List Management Co.: Harbor Press, P.O. Box 919, Gig Harbor, WA 98335
  Tel # (206) 857-5190, Fax # (206) 851-5191, Actives: 25,000, $75/M

Health Alliance Alert
See: LAW

Health Care
See: HOSPITALS & NURSING HOMES

Health Care Antitrust
See: LAW

Health Care Biller   *Business*

Publishing Co: Zimmerman & Associates, Inc., 5307 South 92nd St., Hales Corners, WI 53130-1677
  Parent Co.-Aspen Publishers, Inc., Gaithersburg; Title Tel # (414) 424-2189
  Title Fax # (414) 425-4807
Personnel: Publisher-David Zimmerman, Editor-Bruce Nelson
Editorial Description: A communication network for America's health care billers.
General Info: Yr. Est. 1992, Monthly, Trim Size-8½ x 11, Sheetfed press, 6 pages, 2 Color, Matte
Subscriptions: Indv. $177, Inst. $177, $15/copy
Circulation: Total-1,000
Printing Co: TJ Printing, 14150 W National Ave # 406, New Berlin, WI 53151-4529

Health Care Capitation and
Risk Contracting Manual   *Business*

Publishing Co: Thompson Publishing Group, 747 Third Ave., New York, NY 10017
  Tel # (212) 888-7220; Title Tel # (212) 888-7292 Title Fax # (212) 486-3400
Personnel: Publisher-Kenneth R. Gesser, Editor-Guy Masters, Production Mgr.-Mauro Vaisman,
  Mktg. Dir.-Barbara McGee
General Info: Yr. Est. 1994, Monthly, 8 pages, 2 Color, Looseleaf
Subscriptions: Indv. $395

Health Care Collector   *Business*

Publishing Co: Zimmerman & Associates, Inc., 5307 South 92nd St., Hales Corners, WI 53130-1677
  Parent Co.-Aspen Publishers, Inc., Gaithersburg; Title Tel # (414) 425-2189
  Title Fax # (414) 425-4807
Personnel: Publisher-David Zimmerman, Editor-Lori Zindl, Art Dir.-Kathleen Hamm
Editorial Description: Covers how to successfully collect health care account while maintaining good
  patient relations. Provides useful tips on collecting from patients and insurance companies.
General Info: Yr. Est. 1987, Monthly, Sheetfed press, 8 pages, 2 Color, Matte
Subscriptions: Indv. $157, Inst. $157
Circulation: Total-6,376
Printing Co: TJ Printing Inc., 14150 W National Ave # 406, New Berlin, WI 53151-4529

Health Care Labor Manual & Newsletter
See: LABOR

Health Care Law: A Practical Guide
See: LAW

Health Care Law Newsletter
See: LAW

Health Care Newsletter
See: SAFETY

Health Care Reform Week   *Business*

Publishing Co: United Communications Group, 11300 Rockville Pike, Ste. 1100, Rockville, MD
  20852-3030 Fax # (301) 816-8945; Title Tel # (301) 816-8950 Title Fax # (301) 961-8666
Personnel: Publisher-Richard Hadley, Editor-Burt Schorr, Circ. Mgr.-Monica Brown
Editorial Description: Reports on developments of health care reform and regulation.
General Info: (Formerly Health Policy Week), Yr. Est. 1972, Weekly, Trim Size-8½ x 11, Offset
  press, 4 pages, ISSN: 0732-7493, 2 Color, Newsprint
Subscriptions: Indv. $395, $8/copy
Acquistions: Publication Bought
List Rental: Actives: $125/M
Printing Co: Newsletter Services, Inc., 9700 Philadelphia Court, Lanham, MD 20706
  Tel # (301) 731-5200, Fax # (301) 731-5201

Health Care Registrar   *Business*

Publishing Co: Zimmerman & Associates, Inc., 5307 South 92nd St., Hales Corners, WI 53130-1677
  Parent Co.-Aspen Publishers, Inc., Gaithersburg; Title Tel # (414) 425-2189
Personnel: Editor-Bruce Nelson, Publisher, Adv. Dir.-David Zimmerman, Art Dir.-Kathleen I. Hamm
Editorial Description: Published for health care registration professionals.
General Info: Yr. Est. 1991, Monthly, Sheetfed press, 8 pages, 2 Color, Coated
Subscriptions: Indv. $187, Inst. $187, $15/copy
Circulation: Total-1,200
Printing Co: TJ Printing, 14150 W National Ave # 406, New Berlin, WI 53151-4529

Health Comp

Publishing Co: Boston Computer Society, Inc., 101 A First Ave. Suite #2, Waltham, MA 02154
  Tel # (617) 290-5700 Fax # (617) 290-5744
General Info: Quarterly

Health Confidential

Publishing Co: Boardroom Publishing, PO Box 2614, 55 Railroad Ave., Greenwich, CT 06836-6378;
  Title Tel # (203) 625-5216 Title Fax # (203) 861-7442
Editorial Description: Provides affluent consumers with up-to-date information from today's leading
  health authorities.
Subscriptions: Indv. $30
List Rental: Rents Lists

Health Education Reports   *Business, Association*

Publishing Co: Feistritzer Pubs., 4401a Connecticut Ave NW # 212, Washington, DC 20008-2325;
  Title Tel # (202) 362-3444 Title Fax # (202) 362-3493
Personnel: Publisher-David Chester, Editor-Lawrence O'Rourke
General Info: Yr. Est. 1980, Bi-weekly, 8 pages
Subscriptions: Indv. $198, Can. $210, For. $220

Health Exchange   *Business, Consumer*

Publishing Co: Medical Group Management Association, 104 Inverness Terrace E., Englewood, CO
  80112-5306 Fax # (303) 397-1824; Title Tel # (303) 799-1111 Title Fax # (303) 643-4427
Personnel: Editor, Circ. Mgr., Production Mgr., Art Dir.-Marilee Aust, Promotion Dir.-Dennis Barnhardt
Editorial Description: Patient education newsletter. Distributed to clinics in bulk. Health & wellness.
General Info: (Formerly Health Matters), Yr. Est. 1983, Quarterly, Trim Size-8½ x 11, Sheetfed
  press, 4 pages, ISSN: 1040-2314, 2 Color, Recycled, Other
Subscriptions: Free To Qualified Recipient
Circulation: Total-100,000, Readership-100,000
Printing Co: Lange Graphics, 1360 S Lipan St, Denver, CO 80223-3409 Tel # (303) 777-1737

Health Express
See: NUTRITION

Health Facts *Consumer*

Publishing Co: Center for Medical Consumers, 237 Thompson St, New York, NY 10012-1017; Title Tel # (212) 674-7105
Personnel: Publisher-Arthur Levin, Editor-Maryann Napoli
Editorial Description: Medical & health topics based on review of current scientific literature with consumer point of view.
General Info: Yr. Est. 1976, Monthly, Offset press, 6 pages, No Color
Subscriptions: Indv. $21, Can. $24, For. $32, $2/copy
Circulation: Total-14,000

Health Grants & Contracts Weekly
See: PHILANTHROPY

Health Industry Today *Business*   CPM: $687

Publishing Co: Business Word, Inc., 5350 S. Roslyn St., Ste. 400, Englewood, CO 80111-2125; Title Tel # (303) 290-8500 Title Fax # (303) 290-9025
Personnel: Publisher-Donald Johnson, Editor-Damon Braly, Circ. Mgr.-Linda Gamble, Production Mgr.-Barb Wilson, Adv. Dir.-Dave Jeans
Editorial Description: For healthcare distribution executives.
General Info: (Formerly Surgical Business), Yr. Est. 1937, Monthly, Trim Size-8½ x 11, Sheetfed press, 24 pages, ISSN: 0745-4678, 2 Color, Matte, Saddle-stitched
Subscriptions: Indv. $277, Can. $283, For. $295, $25/copy
Circulation: Total-800
Advertising: $550.
List Rental: Actives: $325/M
Printing Co: Lancaster Press, 3575 Hempland Rd., P.O Box 3657, Lancaster, PA 17604-3657 Tel # (717) 285-9095, Fax # (717) 285-7261

Health Labor Relations Reports
See: INDUSTRIAL RELATIONS/PERSONNEL

Health Law Digest
See: LAW

Health Lawyers News Report *Association*

Publishing Co: Natl. Health Lawyers Assn., 1120 Connecticut Ave NW Ste, 950, Washington, DC 20036-3902; Title Tel # (202) 833-1100 Title Fax # (202) 833-1105
Personnel: Editor-Cynthia Barvin
General Info: Yr. Est. 1971, Monthly, Trim Size-8½ x 11, Desktop press, 8 pages, ISSN: 0145-4129, 2 Color
Subscriptions: Indv. $34
Circulation: Total-5,500

Health Legislation & Regulation

Publishing Co: Faulkner & Gray Healthcare Information Center, 1133 15th St NW, Ste. 450, Washington, DC 20005-2710 Parent Co.-Faulkner & Gray, Inc., New York; Title Tel # (202) 828-4148
Personnel: Publisher-L. Koizumi, Editor-Scott Tong, Circ. Mgr.-Mattie Steward
Editorial Description: Covers Congressional activity on legislation related to health care.
General Info: Yr. Est. 1947, Weekly, Trim Size-8½ x 11, Web press, 8 pages, ISSN: 0043-0730, 2 Color, Newsprint
Subscriptions: Indv. $565
Acquistions: Publication Bought, Publication Sold
List Rental: List Management Co.: Aggressive List Management, 18-2 E Dundee Rd Ste 101, Barrington, IL 60010-5273 Tel # (708) 304-4030, Fax # (708) 304-4032, Actives: 2,918

Health Master *Consumer*   CPM: $12

Publishing Co: Conscious Living Foundation, PO Box 9, Drain, OR 97435-0009; Title Tel # (503) 673-2475 Title Fax # (503) 836-2358
Personnel: Editor-Janai Lowenstein, Publisher, Editor-Tim Lowenstein
Editorial Description: Articles and products reviewed for mastering stress and life pressure.
General Info: (Formerly Stress Master), Yr. Est. 1976, Semi-annually, Trim Size-11½ x 17½, Web press, 8 pages, 3% ads, No Color, Newsprint, Saddle-stitched
Subscriptions: $1/copy
Circulation: Total-80,000
Advertising: $975.
List Rental: Actives: $65/M
Printing Co: Eagle Web Press, P.O. Box 12008, Salem, OR 97305-1128 Tel # (503) 635-8811, Fax # (503) 635-8817

Health News *Consumer, Association*

Publishing Co: Hilborn Group Ltd., The, 109 Vanderhoof Ave., Ste. 200, Toronto, ON M4G 2H7 Canada Tel # (416) 696-8146 Fax # (416) 424-3016; Title Tel # (416) 978-5411 Title Fax # (416) 978-1774
Personnel: Publisher-Jim Hilborn, Editor-June Engel, Circ. Mgr.-Xavier Anasartnam
Editorial Description: To provide accurate and up-to-date medical and health information for the lay public.
General Info: Yr. Est. 1983, Bi-monthly, Trim Size-8½ x 11, Offset press, 8 pages, ISSN: 0821-3925, Ind/Abs/Online: Information Access, 2 Color, Matte, Saddle-stitched
Subscriptions: Indv. $25, Inst. $25, Can. $19, For. $25, $3/copy
Circulation: (16% controlled), Total-30,000, Subscriptions-25,000
List Rental: Rents Lists
Printing Co: Delta-Webb, Middlefield Rd., Scarborough, ON Canada Tel # (416) 298-1680

Health News *Consumer*

Publishing Co: Massachusetts Medical Society-Publ. Dir, 1440 Main St., Waltham, MA 02154-1649 Tel # (617) 893-3800 Fax # (617) 893-8103
Personnel: Publisher-Robert Bouenschulte, Editor-Holly Atkinson, M.D, News Ed.-Patrick Skerrett, Production Mgr.-Susan Haering
Editorial Description: Provides information on current issues in medicine.
General Info: Yr. Est. 1995, 19x/yr., Trim Size-8½ x 11, 10 pages, 4 Color, Saddle-stitched
Subscriptions: Indv. $29
Printing Co: Lane Press, 1000 Hinesburg Rd., PO Box 130, Burlington, VT 05403-7612 Tel # (802) 863-5555, Fax # (802) 865-2470

Health News Daily *Business*

Publishing Co: F-D-C Reports, Inc., 5550 Friendship Blvd, Chevy Chase, MD 20815-7278 Fax # (301) 986-6467; Title Tel # (301) 657-9830 Title Fax # (301) 657-3094
Personnel: Publisher-Wallace Werble, Editor-Cole Palmer Werble, Circ. Dir.-Edward Picken, Mktg. Dir.-Leila Simaika
Editorial Description: Provides comprehensive healthcare news via FAX to health industry professionals. Covers a broad range of topics affecting the health fields.
General Info: Yr. Est. 1989, Daily, ISSN: 1042-2781
Subscriptions: Indv. $1,195, Can. $1,195, For. $1,445

Health Physics Society Newsletter *Association*

Publishing Co: Sponsor-Health Physics Society, Health Physics Society, Rte. 1, Box 139H, Elysian, MN 56028; Title Tel # (507) 362-8958
Personnel: Editor in Chief-Genevieve Roessler
General Info: Yr. Est. 1959, Monthly, 16 pages, ISSN: 0073-1498
Circulation: Total-7,000
Advertising: Inquire for rates.
List Rental: Rents Lists

Health Professions Report
See: EDUCATION

Health Revelations

Publishing Co: Agora, Inc., 105 W. Monoment St., Baltimore, MD 21202-4702 Tel # (410) 783-2647 Fax # (410) 223-2662
Personnel: Publisher-William Bonner
Editorial Description: Health information from Dr. Atkin's.
General Info: Monthly
Subscriptions: Indv. $40
List Rental: Actives: 47,700, $95/M

Health and Safety Resource
See: FORESTRY

Health Sentry

Publishing Co: Performance Resource Press, Inc., 1863 Technology Dr, Troy, MI 48083-4244 Tel # (810) 588-7733; Title Tel # (313) 643-9580
Personnel: Publisher-George Watkins, Editor-Brent Chartier
Editorial Description: Newsletter for employee health concerns.
General Info: Quarterly, Trim Size-8½ x 11, 8 pages, ISSN: 1042-699X, No Color, Coated, Saddle-stitched
Subscriptions: Indv. $2, $12/copy

Health Technology Trends *Business*

Publishing Co: ECRI, 5200 Butler Pike, Plymouth Meeting, PA 19462-1298 Tel # (610) 825-6000; Title Tel # (215) 825-6000 Title Fax # (610) 834-1275
Personnel: Editor-Cynthia Wallace, Circ. Mgr.-Diane Schwartztrauber, Promotion Dir.-Michele Carlin
Editorial Description: Technology news for health care executives on existing & emerging technologies, planning & purchasing, litigation, regulations, interviews, & consultants' advice.
General Info: Yr. Est. 1989, Monthly, Trim Size-8½ x 11, Sheetfed press, 12 pages, 2 Color, Coated
Subscriptions: Indv. $295, For. $325, $30/copy
Acquistions: Publication Bought

Health Victory Bulletin *Business, Consumer*

Publishing Co: Arlin J. Brown Information Center Inc., PO Box 251, Fort Belvoir, VA 22060-0251; Title Tel # (540) 752-9511 Title Fax # (540) 752-4324
Personnel: Publisher, Editor, Circ. Mgr.-Arlin Brown
Editorial Description: Contains updates on the latest, important alternative developments on cancer and health.
General Info: (Formerly Cancer Victory Bulletin), Yr. Est. 1975, Monthly, Trim Size-8½ x 11, Offset press, 4 pages, No Color, Newsprint
Subscriptions: Indv. $20, $2/copy
Circulation: Total-210
Printing Co: Sundra Printing, 14508c Lee Rd, Chantilly, VA 22021-1604 Tel # (703) 378-3500

Health Wisdom for Women
See: WOMEN'S

Health Words for Women   *Consumer*

Publishing Co: Dowden Publishing Co., 110 Summit Ave., Montvale, NJ 07645-1712
  Fax # (201) 391-2778; Title Tel # (201) 391-9100
Personnel: Publisher-Alfred J. Lucchesi, Editor-Wulf H. Utan, MD, PhD, Mng. Editor-Lisa Kelly, Assoc. Adv. Mgr.-Marlene Bauer
Editorial Description: Women's health newsletter for ages 45-65.
General Info: Yr. Est. 1992, Quarterly, Trim Size-8½ x 11, Web press, 8 pages, 4 Color, Coated, Saddle-stitched
Subscriptions: Free In Designated Area
Circulation: Total-1,500,000
Advertising: Inquire for rates.
List Rental: Rents Lists

Health in the Workplace   *Business*

Publishing Co: Carswell, 2075 Kennedy Road, One Corporate Plaza, Scarborough, ON M1T 3V4 Canada Tel # (416) 609-8000; Title Tel # (416) 609-3800 Title Fax # (416) 298-5094
Personnel: Publisher-Bob McElman, Editor-Laurie Blake
Editorial Description: This publication is designed to help employers meet new rules & regulations on health & safety standards within their organizations.
General Info: Yr. Est. 1988, Monthly, Trim Size-8½ x 11, 8 pages, 2 Color
Subscriptions: Indv. $184
Acquistions: Publication Bought, Publication Sold
Circulation: Total-200

HealthAction

Publishing Co: Kelly Communications, Rr 13 Box 28, Charlottesville, VA 22901-7927; Title Tel # (804) 296-5676 Title Fax # (804) 296-3972
Personnel: Publisher-Joseph Kelly, Editor-Tom Allen, Production Mgr.-Paxson MacDonald, Art Dir.-Steven Black
Editorial Description: Covers health & related issues to enable readers to take an active role in maintaining their health.
General Info: Yr. Est. 1985, Monthly, Trim Size-8½ x 11, 8 pages, ISSN: 0886-1986, 4 Color, Coated, Saddle-stitched

HealthCare Systems NewsLetter   *Business, Consumer*

Publishing Co: J.E. Sparks & Associates, 1404 N. Floyd Rd., Richardson, TX 75080-4138; Title Tel # (214) 238-8593 Title Fax # (214) 238-0509
Personnel: Publisher-Jim Sparks
Editorial Description: Empowers health care professionals and providers to take advantage of the benefits of Information systems & technology.
General Info: Yr. Est. 1991, Semi-annually, Trim Size-8½ x 11, Offset press, 6 pages, 2 Color, Recycled
Subscriptions: Free
Circulation: Total-1,500

HealthInform

Publishing Co: InfoLink, P.O. Box 306, 31 Albany Post Rd, Montrose, NY 10458 Tel # (914) 736-1565 Fax # (914) 736-3806
Personnel: Publisher-Janet Gotking, Editor-Katherine Mason-Page
Editorial Description: healthinform is atwice monthly fax digest on alternative and complementary medicine specifically to device time, vital 'need to know' information to busy health care professions.
General Info: ISSN: 1082-6734
Subscriptions: Indv. $47, Can. $97

HealthSense

Publishing Co: Kelly Communications, Rr 13 Box 28, Charlottesville, VA 22901-7927; Title Tel # (804) 296-5676 Title Fax # (804) 296-3972
Editorial Description: Features developments in health maintenance, etc.
General Info: Yr. Est. 1987, Bi-monthly

Healthbeat   *Consumer*

Publishing Co: Niagara Falls Memorial Medical Ctr., 621 10th St., Niagara Falls, NY 14301-1890; Title Tel # (716) 278-4528
Personnel: Editor-R. Seymour Smith, Promotion Dir.-Lori Barrette
Editorial Description: Preventive health journal for our community.
General Info: Yr. Est. 1986, Quarterly, Trim Size-11 x 16, 8 pages, 2 Color, Coated
Acquistions: Publication Bought
Circulation: (100% controlled), Total-50,000

Healthcare Advocate
  See: HOSPITALS & NURSING HOMES

Healthcare Business & Legal Strategies
  See: MANAGEMENT

Healthcare Community Relations & Marketing Letter   *Business*

Publishing Co: Health Resource Publishing, 3100 Hwy. 138, PO Box 1442, Wall Township, NJ 07719-1442; Title Tel # (908) 681-1133 Title Fax # (908) 681-0490
Personnel: Publisher, Editor-Robert Jenkins
Editorial Description: Written for the professional manager, HCR&M Letter helps you stay atop of the latest innovations, keep pace with the changes in the healthcare field and puts you in touch with other directors of community relations, public relations practitioners, administrators, marketing and advertising pros who are staying abreast of the field and adopting new techniques and strategies.
General Info: Yr. Est. 1987, Monthly, ISSN: 0894-9980
Subscriptions: Indv. $197, $11/copy
Advertising: Accepts Inserts.
List Rental: Actives: $90/M
Printing Co: ACN Graphics, 1602 Birchwood Ln, Neptune, NJ 07753-6910 Tel # (908) 681-6083

Healthcare Leadership Review
  See: HOSPITALS & NURSING HOMES

Healthcare PR & Marketing News   *Business*

Publishing Co: Phillips Business Information, Inc., 1201 Seven Locks Rd., Ste 300, Potomac, MD 20854-2958 Tel # (301) 340-1520 Fax # (301) 424-4297
Personnel: Publisher-Ellen Stuhlmann, Editor-Kathy Beisler
General Info: (Formerly Healthcare PR News), Yr. Est. 1992, Bi-weekly, ISSN: 1072-3684, Ind/Abs/Online: NEWSNET, Predicasts
Subscriptions: Indv. $397, For. $430, $37/copy
Advertising: Accepts Inserts.
List Rental: Rents Lists

Healthcare Quality Abstracts
  See: HOSPITALS & NURSING HOMES

Healthcare System Reform Alert   *Business*

Publishing Co: Health Resource Publishing, 3100 Hwy. 138, PO Box 1442, Wall Township, NJ 07719-1442; Title Tel # (908) 681-1133 Title Fax # (908) 681-0490
Personnel: Publisher-Robert Jenkins, Editor-Melanie Jenkins
Editorial Description: Hospital administrators, planners, financial officers, and other executives concerned with access to capital & restructuring.
General Info: (Formerly Hospital Capital Formation Management Letter), Yr. Est. 1982, Monthly, Trim Size-8½ x 11, Offset press, 8 pages, ISSN: 0738-6370, No Color, Newsprint
Subscriptions: Indv. $227, $15/copy
Advertising: Inquire for rates. Accepts Inserts.
List Rental: Rents Lists
Printing Co: ACN Graphics, 1602 Birchwood Ln, Neptune, NJ 07753-6910 Tel # (908) 681-6083

Healthcare Trends Report   *Business*

Publishing Co: Health Trends Inc., 4405 East-West Highway, Ste. 406, Bethesda, MD 20814; Title Tel # (301) 652-8937 Title Fax # (301) 907-6790
Editorial Description: This monthly report gives a 3-5 year perspective on major trends related to the health care industry.
General Info: Monthly
List Rental: List Management Co.: Affinity Marketing Group Inc., P.O. Box 2409, Fairfax, VA 22031 Tel # (703) 978-4927, Fax # (703) 425-4537

Healthletters   *Consumer*

Publishing Co: Santa Fe Health Education Project, PO Box 577, Santa Fe, NM 87504-0577; Title Tel # (505) 982-3236
Editorial Description: Health information for women in English and Spanish.
Subscriptions: $1/copy

Healthline   *Consumer*

Publishing Co: Healthline, 830 Menlo Ave., Ste. 100, Menlo Park, CA 90425; Title Tel # (415) 325-6457 Title Fax # (415) 322-2436
Personnel: Editor-Paul Insel
Editorial Description: Health & fitness information for healthcare professionals & the general public alike. Covers weight control, nutrition, exercise, sports medicine, aging, child health & many other topics.
General Info: Yr. Est. 1981, Monthly, ISSN: 0736-7929
Subscriptions: Indv. $24, For. $36
Circulation: Total-11,000
List Rental: List Management Co.: Kleid Company, Inc., 530 5th Ave., 17 Floor, New York, NY 10036-5101 Tel # (212) 819-3406, Fax # (212) 719-9788, Actives: 9,000, $65/M

Healthlines   *Business, Association*

Publishing Co: University of Michigan Fitness Research Center, 401 Washtenaw Ave., Ann Arbor, MI 48109-2214; Title Tel # (313) 763-2462
Personnel: Editor-Marilyn Pearce-Edington, Circ. Dir.-Lin Wei Wang
General Info: Yr. Est. 1982, Monthly, Trim Size-8½ x 11, 4 pages, ISSN: 8756-453X, 2 Color
Subscriptions: Indv. $15
Circulation: Total-4,500

Healthtrac Tallahassee Report on Health Care Issues

Publishing Co: Healthtrac, Inc., PO Box 13552, Tallahassee, FL 32317-3552; Title Tel # (904) 222-8180
Personnel: Editor-Thomas Poulton
Editorial Description: Reports on health care issues and developments.
General Info: Yr. Est. 1985, 30x/yr.
Subscriptions: Indv. $385

Healthy & Natural Journal, Part 1 - Health & Natural News *Consumer*

Publishing Co: Measurements & Data Corporation, 100 Wallace Ave., Ste. 100, Sarasota, FL 34237 Tel # (941) 366-1153 Parent Co.-Measurements & Data, Pittsburgh
Personnel: Assoc. Ed.-Greg Mann, Publisher, Adv. Dir.-Robert S. Aronson, Adv. Mgr.-Jessica A. Higel, Advertising & Sales, Advertising & Sales-Kathleen P. Flynn, Art Dir.-Michael L. Keenan
Editorial Description: Contains product information on natural foods, supplements, herbal products, natural cosmetics, books, and more.
General Info: Bi-monthly, Trim Size-8¼ x 10¾, 50 pages, 4 Color, Coated, Saddle-stitched
Subscriptions: Free To Qualified Recipient
Advertising: Inquire for rates.

Healthy Eating
See: FOOD

Healthy Exchanges
See: FOOD

Healthy Information *Consumer*

Publishing Co: Alcoholism Council of Greater NY, 49 E 21st St Fl 3, New York, NY 10010-6213; Title Tel # (212) 252-7001
Personnel: Editor-Joseph Barbato
General Info: Yr. Est. 1966, Bi-monthly
Subscriptions: Indv. $25

Healthy Talk *Consumer*

Publishing Co: Vitamin Shoppe, 4700 Westside Ave., N. Bergen, NJ 07047-9808
Personnel: Publisher-Helen Howard, Editor-Ann Louise Gittleman
Editorial Description: Nutrition and health information.
General Info: Yr. Est. 1996, Monthly, Trim Size-8½ x 11, 8 pages, 2 Color, Matte, Saddle-stitched
Subscriptions: Indv. $40

Heart Direct *Consumer*

Publishing Co: McMurry Publishing Inc., 8805 N 23rd Ave Ste 11, Phoenix, AZ 85021-4171 Tel # (602) 395-5850; Title Tel # (206) 395-5850
Personnel: Publisher-Preston V. McMurry, Editor-Fred Petrovsky, Art Dir.-Linda Longmire
Editorial Description: Nationally syndicated cardiovascular health newsletter.
General Info: Yr. Est. 1991, Quarterly, Trim Size-8½ x 11, 8 pages, 4 Color
Subscriptions: Free To Qualified Recipient
Circulation: (100% controlled), Total-219,000
List Rental: List Management Co.: Coolidge List Marketing, 25 W. 43rd St., New York, NY 10036-7491 Tel # (212) 274-0630, Fax # (212) 274-0650

Heart to Heart *Association*

Publishing Co: British Columbia Heart Foundation, 1212 West Broadway, Vancouver, BC V6H 3V2 Canada; Title Tel # (604) 736-4404
Personnel: Editor-Linda Muller
Editorial Description: Articles on heart disease, heart research, diagnosis and treatment. House organ for volunteers.
General Info: (Formerly Straight From the Heart), Yr. Est. 1957, Trim Size-8½ x 11, 4 pages, 2 Color, Coated
Subscriptions: Free
Circulation: (100% controlled), Total-2,000

Heart Net *Consumer, Association*

Publishing Co: Mountain State Mended Hearts, PO Box 4665, Star City, WV 26504; Title Tel # (304) 296-5158
Personnel: Publisher-George L. Rosier, Editor-Kay Bailey
General Info: Yr. Est. 1987, Quarterly, Trim Size-8½ x 11, 4 pages
Subscriptions: Free With Membership

Heart Sense *Business, Consumer*

Publishing Co: Phillips Publishing, Inc., 7811 Montrose Rd., Potomac, MD 20854-3394 Fax # (301) 294-1307 Parent Co.-Phillips Business Information, Inc., Potomac; Title Tel # (301) 340-2100 Title Fax # (301) 424-6228
Personnel: Publisher-Thomas L. Phillips, Editor-Stephen Sinatra, Mktg. Dir.-Laurie Hoffman
Editorial Description: Education & prevention of heart disease.
General Info: (Formerly Cardiac Alert), Yr. Est. 1978, Monthly, Trim Size-8½ x 11, 8 pages, ISSN: 0194-2557, 2 Color, Matte
Subscriptions: Indv. $49, $7/copy
Acquistions: Publication Bought, Publication Sold
Advertising: Inquire for rates.
List Rental: List Management Co.: Manager: John Balwin; Phillips Publishing List Marketing, 7811 Montrose Rd., Potomac, MD 20854-3394 Tel # (301) 340-2100, Fax # (301) 294-1307, Actives: 7,377, $125/M, Expires: 9,025, $85/M

Heartline

Publishing Co: Coronary Club, Inc., 9500 Euclid Ave., #EE37, Cleveland, OH 44195-0001 Parent Co.-Penton Publishing, Cleveland; Title Tel # (216) 444-3690 Title Fax # (216) 444-9385
Personnel: Publisher-Fredric J. Pashkow, MD, Editor-Jean Rothman
Editorial Description: All facets of heart care & rehabilitation.
General Info: (Formerly Coronary Club Bulletin), Yr. Est. 1972, Monthly, Trim Size-8½ x 11, 6 pages, ISSN: 8755-5271, 2 Color, Coated
Subscriptions: Indv. $29, $3/copy
Circulation: Total-10,000

Helper *Association*

Publishing Co: American Social Health Assn., PO Box 13827, Research Triangle Pk, NC 27709-3827; Title Tel # (919) 361-8400 Title Fax # (919) 361-8425
Personnel: Editor-Charles Ebel
Editorial Description: Research reports and other information on Herpes Simplex.
General Info: Yr. Est. 1979, Quarterly, Trim Size-8½ x 11, Offset press, 12 pages, 2 Color, Saddle-stitched
Subscriptions: Indv. $25, Can. $25, For. $25, $5/copy
Circulation: Total-10,000

Hemophilia Ontario *Association*

Publishing Co: Canadian Hemophilia Society, Ontario Chapter, 1300 Yonge St., #506, Toronto, ON M4T 1X3 Canada; Title Tel # (416) 972-0641 Title Fax # (416) 972-0307
Personnel: Editor-Joan Kent
General Info: Yr. Est. 1969, Quarterly, Offset press, 6 pages, Color
Subscriptions: Indv. $25
Circulation: Total-2,400

Hepatitis B Coalition News *Association*

Publishing Co: Immunization Action Coalition, 1573 Selby Ave Ste 229, St. Paul, MN 55104-6328 Fax # (612) 647-9131; Title Tel # (612) 647-9009 Title Fax # (612) 647-9137
Personnel: Editor-Deborah L. Wexler, MD
Editorial Description: A publication of the Hepatitis B Coalition which promotes hepatitis B vaccination for all infants & adolescents; HBsAg screening for all pregnant women; testing for high-risk groups; & education & treatment for hepatitis B carriers. The coalition is a program of the Immunization Action Coalition, a non-Profit organization.
General Info: (Formerly Hepatitis B Coalition News), Yr. Est. 1991, 3x/yr., Trim Size-8½ x 11, 16 pages, No Color, Matte, Saddle-stitched
Subscriptions: Free In Designated Area
Circulation: Total-65,000

Herbal Healer Academy Newsletter *Consumer, Association*

Publishing Co: Herbal Healer Academy, HC 32 Box 97B, Mt. View, AR 72560-9106; Title Tel # (501) 269-4177 Title Fax # (501) 269-5424
Personnel: Publisher, Editor-Marijah M.H. McCain
Editorial Description: Herbal remedies, recipes and 'hands-on' healing experiences are discussed. Dedicated to the non-aggressive field of the healing arts.
General Info: Yr. Est. 1988, Quarterly
Subscriptions: Indv. $10, $2/copy

High Performance Optometry
See: MEDICINE

Hippocrates Health Institute-Newsletter

Publishing Co: Hippocrates Health Institute, 1443 Palmdale Ct, West Palm Beach, FL 33411-3388; Title Tel # (617) 267-9525
Editorial Description: Nutrition institute notes, book & equipment lists.
General Info: Yr. Est. 1963, Trim Size-8½ x 11, Sheetfed press, 12 pages, Coated, Saddle-stitched
Circulation: Total-50,000

Holistic

Publishing Co: Holistic Health/Academy, 218 Avenue B, Redondo Beach, CA 90277-4706
General Info: Monthly, Trim Size-8½ x 11, 4 pages
Subscriptions: Indv. $48

Holistic & Preventive Update

Publishing Co: International Academy Holistic Health/Medicine, 218 Avenue B, Redondo Beach, CA 90277-4706; Title Tel # (213) 540-0564
General Info: Monthly, 4 pages
Subscriptions: Indv. $18

Holistic Dental Digest Plus *Consumer*

Publishing Co: Once Daily, Inc., 263 West End Ave Apt 2a, New York, NY 10023-2613; Title Tel # (212) 874-4212 Title Fax # (212) 874-4212
Personnel: Editor-Jerry Mittelman, DDS
Editorial Description: Holistic news for people who want to save their teeth.
General Info: (Formerly Holistic Dental Digest), Yr. Est. 1980, Bi-monthly, Trim Size-8½ x 11, 4 pages, No Color, Newsprint
Subscriptions: Indv. $10
Circulation: Total-3,000
List Rental: Rents Lists

    ©1996, Oxbridge Communications, Inc.

Holistic Living
Consumer

Publishing Co: Holistic Health Assn. of the Princeton Area, 360 Nassau St, Princeton, NJ 08540-4615; Title Tel # (609) 924-8580
Personnel: Editor-Jackie Schilder-McLaug
General Info: Yr. Est. 1978, Bi-monthly, 32 pages, 2 Color, Newsprint
Subscriptions: Indv. $20
Circulation: Total-22,000
Advertising: Inquire for rates.
Printing Co: Allied Printing, 280 Midland Ave, Saddle Brook, NJ 07663-6404 Tel # (201) 794-0400

Home Advantage
See: ADVERTISING & MARKETING

Home Health Agency Gazette
Business

Publishing Co: American Federation of Home Health Agencies, 1320 Fenwick Ln Ste 500, Silver Spring, MD 20910-3514; Title Tel # (301) 588-1454 Title Fax # (301) 588-4732
Personnel: Editor-Joan Guberman
Editorial Description: Focuses on regulatory & legislative issues of interest to the home health care industry.
General Info: Yr. Est. 1981, 1% ads
Circulation: Total-300

Home Health Business Report
Business

Publishing Co: Staffing Industry Analysts, 2235 Grant Rd # 3, Los Altos, CA 94024-6954; Title Tel # (415) 903-9494 Title Fax # (415) 903-9811
Personnel: Publisher, Editor-Peter Yessne
Editorial Description: Business news & resources for home healthcare agencies and companies, covering all sectors of come care - nursing equipment & infusion.
General Info: Yr. Est. 1994, Monthly, Trim Size-8½ x 11, 20 pages
Subscriptions: Indv. $187, Inst. $159, Can. $187, For. $227
Circulation: (25% controlled), Total-2,000, Subscriptions-1,500
Advertising: Accepts Inserts.

Home Health Care Reimbursement Report, The

Publishing Co: Zimmerman & Associates, Inc., 5307 South 92nd St., Hales Corners, WI 53130-1677 Parent Co.-Aspen Publishers, Inc., Gaithersburg; Title Tel # (414) 425-2189 Title Fax # (414) 425-4807
Personnel: Editorial Dir.-Jo Ann Petaschnick
General Info: Yr. Est. 1993, Monthly
Subscriptions: Indv. $157

Home Health Line
Business

Publishing Co: United Communications Group, 11300 Rockville Pike, Ste. 1100, Rockville, MD 20852-3030 Tel # (301) 816-8950 Fax # (301) 816-8945; Title Tel # (301) 586-0100
Personnel: Publisher-Richard Hadley, Editor-Rishard Falknor
Editorial Description: Home care's independent Washington line on service programs, legistation & regulations.
General Info: Yr. Est. 1975, Weekly, 6 pages
Subscriptions: Indv. $399, $5/copy
Acquisitions: Publication Bought, Publication Sold
Circulation: Total-10,000
Advertising: Inquire for rates.

Home Infusion Therapy Management
Business, Consumer

Publishing Co: American Health Consultants, Inc., 3525 Piedmont Rd., Building #6, Ste. 400, Atlanta, GA 30305-0056 Tel # (404) 262-7436 Fax # (404) 284-3291
Personnel: Publisher-Connie Austin, Editor-Cheli Brown, Circ. Mgr.-Monica Brown, Production Mgr.-Mike Witter, Mktg. Mgr.-Rebecca Swancott-Torres
Editorial Description: Covers home therapy industry news.
General Info: Yr. Est. 1993, Monthly
Subscriptions: Indv. $259, $26/copy
List Rental: Actives: $145/M

Homecare Administrative Horizons
Business

Publishing Co: Beacon Health Corp., 1001 W. Glen Oaks Ln., Suite 104, Mequon, WI 53092-3366 Fax # (414) 241-4488; Title Tel # (414) 241-3765 Title Fax # (414) 241-8477
Personnel: Publisher-Richard Omdahl, Editor-Cory Anshus, Circ. Mgr.-Donna Schwierske, Production Mgr.-Don Gawronski
Editorial Description: Focuses on strategic issues and management techniques for homecare administrators and directors.
General Info: Yr. Est. 1994, Monthly
Subscriptions: Indv. $237, $24/copy

Homecare Direction
Business

Publishing Co: Beacon Health Corp., 1001 W. Glen Oaks Ln., Suite 104, Mequon, WI 53092-3366; Title Tel # (414) 241-3765 Title Fax # (414) 241-4488
Personnel: Publisher-Richard Omdahl, Editor in Chief-Diane Omdahl, RN, MS, Editor-Cory Anshus, Circ. Mgr.-Donna Schwierske, Production Mgr.-Don Gawronski
Editorial Description: Focuses on the problems of managers, nurses, therapist, social workers, and others involved with home health care.
General Info: Yr. Est. 1993, Monthly, ISSN: 1069-4560
Subscriptions: Indv. $197, $19/copy

Homeopathy Today
See: MEDICINE

Hope Health Letter

Publishing Co: Sponsor-Hope Heart Institute, International Health Awareness Ctr., 350 E Michigan Ave Ste 301, Kalamazoo, MI 49007-3854; Title Tel # (616) 343-0770 Title Fax # (616) 343-6260
Personnel: Adv. Dir.-Debra Seeley
Editorial Description: Developments and issues in the health field.
General Info: Yr. Est. 1979, Monthly, 8 pages, 2 Color, Newsprint
Subscriptions: Indv. $20, Can. $30

Hope News

Publishing Co: People-To-People Health Foundation/Project Hope, Millwood, VA 22646-9999; Title Tel # (703) 837-2100 Title Fax # (703) 837-1813
Personnel: Editor-Maggie Peterson
Editorial Description: Progress report on worldwide activities of Project HOPE, an international non-profit health foundation.
General Info: Yr. Est. 1963, Quarterly, Trim Size-8½ x 11, Web press, 8 pages, 2 Color, Matte
Acquistions: Publication Bought
Circulation: Total-150,000

Horizon
Association

Publishing Co: Huntington Society of Canada, 13 Water St. N., #3, Box 1269, Cambridge, ON N1R 7G6 Canada; Title Tel # (519) 622-1002 Title Fax # (519) 622-7370
Personnel: Editor-Isla Horvath
Editorial Description: To inform families, health professionals, & interested others about Huntington's Disease.
General Info: Yr. Est. 1974, Quarterly, Trim Size-8½ x 11, Sheetfed press, 14 pages, ISSN: 0827-7605, No Color, Matte
Subscriptions: Free With Membership
Circulation: Total-8,109
Printing Co: Highland Printcraft, 50 Raglin Pl., Cambridge, ON N1R 7J2 Canada Tel # (519) 621-5390

Horse Report, The
See: HORSES

Hospice Forum
CPM: $190

Publishing Co: Hospice Association of America, 519 C St., N.E., Stanton Park, Washington, DC 20002-5809; Title Tel # (202) 547-7424 Title Fax # (202) 547-3540
Personnel: Editor-Janet Neigh, Circ. Mgr.-Stewart Jordan, Adv. Dir.-Christopher Adams
Editorial Description: Keeps the hospice professional up-to-date with issues affecting the industry. Each issue contains legislative and regulatory updates, research news, marketing strategies and general information on the hospice world.
General Info: Yr. Est. 1986, Bi-monthly, Sheetfed press, 4 pages, 10% ads, No Color, Coated
Subscriptions: Indv. $105, Can. $120, For. $120
Circulation: Total-2,100
Advertising: $400.
List Rental: Rents Lists

Hospital Cost Management & Accounting
See: HOSPITALS & NURSING HOMES

Hospital Hazardous Materials Management

Publishing Co: ECRI, 5200 Butler Pike, Plymouth Meeting, PA 19462-1298; Title Tel # (610) 825-6000 Title Fax # (610) 834-1275
Personnel: Editor-Shana Halpern, Circ. Mgr.-Diane Schwarztranger, Promotion Dir.-Michele Carlin
Editorial Description: Legal, regulatory & technical aspects of managing hazardous materials in hospitals.
General Info: Yr. Est. 1987, Monthly, Trim Size-8½ x 11, Sheetfed press, 12 pages, ISSN: 0895-7169, No Color, Coated
Subscriptions: Indv. $225, For. $250
Acquistions: Publication Bought
Circulation: Total-1,000

Hospital Litigation Reporter
See: LAW

How to Get Paid
See: MANAGEMENT

Human Resources Management OSHA Compliance
See: MANAGEMENT

Huna Work
See: RELIGIOUS & THEOLOGICAL

IAHP Newsletter
See: MEDICINE

ICA Today   *Association*

Publishing Co: International Chiropractors Assn., 1110 N. Glebe Rd., Ste. 1000, Arlington, VA 22201-4795; Title Tel # (703) 528-5000 Title Fax # (703) 528-5023
Personnel: Editor-Molly Bangnath, Production Mgr.-Gwen Cofield
Editorial Description: News about chiropractic, general health issues & the association.
General Info: (Formerly ICA Newsletter), Yr. Est. 1978, Quarterly, Trim Size-9½ x 13, Offset press, 4 pages, 2 Color, Newsprint
Circulation: Total-6,500
List Rental: Rents Lists
Printing Co: Presstar Printing, 12201 Old Columbia Pike, Silver Spring, MD 20904-1968 Tel # (301) 622-5000, Fax # (301) 622-5403

ICA Update

Publishing Co: Interstitial Cystitis Assn., Inc., Box 1553, Madison Sq. Sta., New York, NY 10159-1553; Title Tel # (212) 979-6057 Title Fax # (212) 677-6139
Personnel: Editor-Deborah Slade
Editorial Description: News on IC.
General Info: Quarterly
Subscriptions: Indv. $35, For. $60

IDEA Fitness Manager
See: SPORTS & SPORTING GOODS

IFFLP Bulletin

Publishing Co: International Federation for Family Life Promotion, 2009 14th St N Ste 512, Arlington, VA 22201-2514; Title Tel # (202) 783-0137
Personnel: Editor-Dr. William Pruzensky
General Info: (Formerly IFFLP Newsletter), Yr. Est. 1977, Semi-annually, 10 pages, No Color
Subscriptions: Free With Membership
Circulation: Total-1,500

IPHA Newsletter   *Association*

Publishing Co: Sponsor-Iowa Public Health Assn., Iowa Public Health Association, PO Box 4772, Des Moines, IA 50306-4772; Title Tel # (515) 281-4900
Personnel: Publisher-Linda White, Editor-Anne Snell
General Info: Bi-monthly, Desktop press, 20 pages, No Color, Newsprint
Subscriptions: Free
Circulation: Total-450
Printing Co: Carter Printing, 1739 E Grand Ave, Des Moines, IA 50316-3611 Tel # (515) 265-6139

ISSD News
See: PSYCHOLOGY

I.V.U.N. News   *Consumer*

Publishing Co: Gazette International Networking Institute, 4207 Lindell Boulevard, #110, St. Louis, MO 63108; Title Tel # (314) 534-0475 Title Fax # (314) 534-5070
Personnel: Publisher-Joan Headley, Editor-Judith Fischer
Editorial Description: Provides a world wide network for ventilator users & their families.
General Info: Yr. Est. 1987, Semi-annually, Trim Size-8½ x 11, Sheetfed press, 16 pages, ISSN: 1066-534X, No Color, Recycled
Subscriptions: Indv. $8, Inst. $20, Can. $10, For. $12
Circulation: Total-1,200

Icarus File, The
See: HOSPITALS & NURSING HOMES

Imaging & Radiology PCS

Publishing Co: ECRI, 5200 Butler Pike, Plymouth Meeting, PA 19462-1298; Title Tel # (610) 825-6000 Title Fax # (610) 834-1275
Personnel: Editor-Gary Hayner, Circ. Mgr.-Diane Schwarztrauber, Promotion Dir.-Michele Carlin
Editorial Description: Product comparison information in binder system with monthly updates.
General Info: Yr. Est. 1984, Monthly, 12 pages, ISSN: 0892-7340, No Color, Newsprint, Looseleaf
Subscriptions: Indv. $695, For. $745

In Action   *Business, Association*

Publishing Co: Leprosy Mission Canada, 40 Wynford Dr., #216, Don Mills, ON M3C 1J5 Canada; Title Tel # (416) 441-3618
Personnel: Editor-Peter Derrick, Production Mgr.-Nicholas Hunter
General Info: (Formerly Without the Camp), Yr. Est. 1973, Quarterly, Trim Size-5½ x 8½, 16 pages, 2 Color
Subscriptions: Free
Circulation: Total-20,000

In Search

Publishing Co: Juvenile Diabetes Foundation, 49 The Donway West, Suite 320, Don Mills, ON M3C 3M9 Canada; Title Tel # (416) 510-1350 Title Fax # (416) 510-1357
Personnel: Editor-Glenn peterson
General Info: Yr. Est. 1983, Irregular, Trim Size-8½ x 11, 3% ads
Circulation: Total-10,500
Advertising: Inquire for rates.

In Touch for Health   *Association*

Publishing Co: Touch for Health Foundation, 11194 Spruce Ave, Bloomington, CA 92316-3226
Personnel: Publisher-Jon Thie, Circ. Mgr., Production Mgr.-David Koch, Adv. Dir., Art Dir.-Jayne Merritt, Editor, Promotion Dir.-Rob Aboulache
Editorial Description: Methods, applications and teaching health enhancement using kinesiology, accupressure massage.
General Info: Yr. Est. 1974, Bi-monthly, Web press, 16 pages, 1% ads, Newsprint, Saddle-stitched
Subscriptions: Indv. $30, $4/copy
Circulation: (100% controlled), Total-1,500
Advertising: Inquire for rates.

In Touch Newsletter
See: EDUCATION

Indoor Air Quality Update
See: ENVIRONMENT & ECOLOGY

Indoor Health
See: ENVIRONMENT & ECOLOGY

Industrial Health & Hazards Update
See: SAFETY

InfoPack
See: DRUGS & PHARMACEUTICALS

Infolines

Publishing Co: AID Atlanta, Inc., 1430 W. Peachtree St., NW, Ste. 100, Atlanta, GA 30309; Title Tel # (404) 872-0600 Title Fax # (404) 885-6799
Personnel: Editor-Pat Grindel, Production Mgr.-Rebecca Poynor-Burns
Editorial Description: A general interest newletter for persons interested in AIDS health services, support and public education in Atlanta, and in the nation. Special emphasis is placed on the role of AID Atlanta, Inc., a multiservice, community-based, volunteer-supported organization.
General Info: Monthly, Web press, 4 pages, No Color, Newsprint
Acquistions: Publication Bought

Info
See: BIBLIOGRAPHY

Innovations in Head Injury
Rehabilitation   *Business*

Publishing Co: Matthew Bender & Co., 11 Penn Plaza, New York, NY 10001-2006 Tel # (212) 967-7707 Fax # (212) 244-3188
Editorial Description: A hands-on volume for the rehabilitation professional.
General Info: Yr. Est. 1988, Monthly, Looseleaf

Inside Al-Anon   *Consumer, Association*

Publishing Co: Al-Anon Family Group Headquarters, Inc., 1600 Corporate Landing Pkwy., Virginia Beach, VA 23456 Tel # (804) 563-1600; Title Tel # (212) 302-7240 Title Fax # (212) 869-3757
Personnel: Editor-Sandra Forte
Editorial Description: Presents news, policy, & commentary from volunteers, staff & readers sharing experiences of individual & group growth through service, to families and friends of alcoholics.
General Info: Yr. Est. 1979, Bi-monthly, Trim Size-8½ x 11, Web press, 4 pages, ISSN: 1054-1438, 2 Color, Matte
Subscriptions: Indv. $3, Free To Qualified Recipient
Circulation: (93% controlled), Total-32,000
Printing Co: Woodhaven Press, 424 W. 33rd St., New York, NY 10001 Tel # (212) 967-7230

Inside Health Law
See: HOSPITALS & NURSING HOMES

Insiders' Health Letter

Publishing Co: Agora, Inc., 105 W. Monoment St., Baltimore, MD 21202-4702 Tel # (410) 783-2647 Fax # (410) 223-2662
Personnel: Publisher-William Bonner, Editor-Bob Arnot
General Info: Monthly
Subscriptions: Indv. $40

Institute for Positive Weight
Management Newsletter   *Consumer, Association*

Publishing Co: Institute for Positive Weight Management, 301 Mac Ave. #101, East Lansing, MI 48823-4330; Title Tel # (407) 750-7004
Personnel: Publisher, Editor, Production Mgr., Promotion Dir.-Lynn Brown
Editorial Description: Features articles sharing the Institute's philosophy, research findings, answers to weight management questions and many practical tips.
General Info: Yr. Est. 1990, Quarterly, Trim Size-8½ x 11, 8 pages
Subscriptions: Indv. $10

Integrated Health Care
Delivery: Business and
Legal Forms   *Business*

Publishing Co: Thompson Publishing Group, 747 Third Ave., New York, NY 10017; Title Tel # (212) 888-7220 Title Fax # (212) 486-3400
Personnel: Editor-Allan Fine, Production Mgr.-Mauro Vaisman, Mktg. Dir.-Michael Carrano
General Info: Yr. Est. 1993, Quarterly, Looseleaf
Subscriptions: Indv. $295

Intelli-Scope
See: DRUGS & PHARMACEUTICALS

International Guild of Professional Electrologists-Newsletter
See: MEDICINE

International Healthwatch
Report

Publishing Co: Foundation for the Advancement of Compassion & Truth, PO Box 90140, Arlington, TX 76004-3140
Editorial Description: Covers health related issues worldwide.
General Info: Yr. Est. 1987, Monthly
Subscriptions: Indv. $25

Iridis
See: PARAPSYCHOLOGY

Ironic Blood
See: MEDICINE

Issues

Publishing Co: SSM Health Care System, 477 N Lindbergh Blvd, Saint Louis, MO 63141-7832
Tel # (314) 994-7910 Fax # (314) 994-7900; Title Tel # (314) 768-1699 Title Fax # (314) 768-1700
Editorial Description: Issues and developments in the health care field.
General Info: Yr. Est. 1986, Bi-monthly
Subscriptions: Indv. $125

Issues: A Critical Examination of Contemporary Ethical Issues in Health Care

Publishing Co: SSM Health Care System, 477 N Lindbergh Blvd, Saint Louis, MO 63141-7832
Tel # (314) 994-7910 Fax # (314) 994-7900
Personnel: Editor-Dennis Brodeur, Mng. Editor-Carol Bales
General Info: Bi-monthly
Subscriptions: Indv. $125
List Rental: Rents Lists

It's Your Cholesterol — *Consumer*

Publishing Co: George Washington University Medical Center, 2300 I St NW, Washington, DC 20037-2337
Personnel: Editor in Chief-Diane Stoy
Editorial Description: Explains news on cholesterol.
General Info: Monthly
Subscriptions: Indv. $25

Jin Shin Do Acupressure Newsletter — *Consumer, Association*

Publishing Co: Jin Shin Do Foundation Newsletter, P O Box 1097, Felton, CA 95018;
Title Tel # (408) 338-9454
Personnel: Editor-Iona Teeguarden
Editorial Description: Typed acupressure system practitioner newsletter.
General Info: Yr. Est. 1982, Annually, Trim Size-8½ x 11, Offset press, 12 pages, No Color, Matte
Subscriptions: Indv. $3, Free To Qualified Recipient
Circulation: Total-7,500, Readership-15,000
Advertising: Inquire for rates. Accepts Inserts.
List Rental: Actives: 7,000, $70/M
Printing Co: Community Printers, 1827 Soquel Ave, Santa Cruz, CA 95062-1385
Tel # (408) 426-4682

Johns Hopkins Health After 50 — *Consumer*

Publishing Co: Medletter Assocs., Inc., 632 Broadway, New York, NY 10012-2614;
Title Tel # (212) 505-2255 Title Fax # (212) 505-5462
Personnel: Publisher, Editor-Rodney Friedman
Editorial Description: Health newsletter for people over 50.
General Info: Yr. Est. 1989, Monthly, Trim Size-8½ x 11, Web press, 8 pages, ISSN: 1042-1882, No Color
Subscriptions: Indv. $28, Can. $29, For. $30, $3/copy
Acquistions: Publication Sold
Circulation: Total-550,000
List Rental: List Management Co.: List Services Corp., 6 Trowbridge Dr., PO Box 516, Bethel, CT 06801-2858 Tel # (203) 743-2600, Fax # (203) 743-0589, Actives: 425,000, $85/M, Hotline: 80,000, $95/M, Expires: 408,206, $55/M
Printing Co: Tempographics, 455 E North Ave, Carol Stream, IL 60188-2167 Tel # (708) 462-8200, Fax # (708) 462-0350

Journal of Hospital Occupational Health
See: MEDICINE

Journal of the Senses — *Business, Association* — CPM: $30

Publishing Co: Elysium Institute, 814 Robinson Rd, Topanga, CA 90290-3627;
Title Tel # (310) 455-1000 Title Fax # (310) 455-1000
Personnel: Publisher-Ed Lange, Editorial Dir.-Art Kunkin, Circ. Mgr., Adv. Dir.-Chris Moran
Editorial Description: Newsletter of the Elysium Institute, an organization promoting nudism. Focuses on the latest issues concerning fredom of choice, body awareness, body acceptance, and the clothing-optional lifestyle. Bound with Elysium Living.
General Info: Yr. Est. 1961, Quarterly, Trim Size-8 x 10½, 40 pages, ISSN: 0741-8787, 4 Color, Newsprint, Saddle-stitched
Subscriptions: Inst. $2, Can. $3, For. $3, $2/copy
Circulation: Total-10,000
Advertising: $300.

Journal Watch
See: MEDICINE

Kaufman Letter, The
See: SAFETY

Kidfit Newsletter
See: CHILDREN

LPI Newsletter
See: MEDICINE

Lab Hotline — *Business*

Publishing Co: Univ. of Iowa Univ. Hygienic Lab., Oakdale Campus, Iowa City, IA 52242-0001;
Title Tel # (319) 335-4500
Personnel: Editor-Theodore Heald
Editorial Description: Topics of interest in the clinical and environmental laboratory fields.
General Info: Yr. Est. 1965, Monthly, Trim Size-8½ x 11, Offset press, 20 pages, No Color
Circulation: Total-1,000

L'Association Pour la Sante Publique de Quebec Bulletin — *Association* — CPM: $200

Publishing Co: Association pour la Sante Publique de Quebec, 3958 Rue Dandurand, Montreal, PQ H1X 1P7 Canada; Title Tel # (514) 593-9939 Title Fax # (514) 593-4554
Editorial Description: Public health, health promotion.
General Info: Yr. Est. 1943, Quarterly, 4 pages, ISSN: 0826-9203
Subscriptions: Indv. $40, Inst. $250, Can. $125
Circulation: Total-500
Advertising: $100. Accepts Inserts.

Laughter Prescription Newsletter
See: HUMOR & SATIRE

Laughter Works
See: HUMOR & SATIRE

Life Enthusiast Newsletter
See: FOOD

Life Entitlements — *Consumer*

Publishing Co: Life Entitlements, 4 World Trade Ctr., Ste. 5270, New York, NY 10048-0204;
Title Tel # (212) 775-1400 Title Fax # (212) 775-8039
Editorial Description: Advises terminally ill people with decisions of legal, health and quality of life concerns.
General Info: Quarterly, Trim Size-8½ x 11, 4 pages, 2 Color, Matte

Life Extension Society News — *Consumer*

Publishing Co: Life Extension Society, 990 Powhatan St., Arlington, VA 22205 Tel # (703) 534-7277
Editorial Description: Reports on events and activities in the mid-atlantic region related to life extension, nutrition and cryogenic preservation of humans.
General Info: Yr. Est. 1994, Quarterly
Subscriptions: Indv. $10

Life Sciences & Biotechnology Update
See: BIOLOGY

LifeLines — *Business*

Publishing Co: Economics Press, Inc., 12 Daniel Rd., Fairfield, NJ 07004-2565;
Title Tel # (201) 227-1224 Title Fax # (201) 227-9742
Personnel: Editor-Robert Guder, Circ. Mgr.-Ann Lanahan
Editorial Description: Biweekly series of messages that give employees the information they need to help them stay healthy.
General Info: Yr. Est. 1983, Bi-weekly
Subscriptions: Indv. $60
Circulation: Total-18,548
List Rental: List Management Co.: Manager: Michael Korman; Names in the News, 411 Theodore Fremd Ave., Rye, NY 10580 Tel # (914) 925-2400, Actives: $85/M
Printing Co: Beckley Press, 2 Sperry Rd, Fairfield, NJ 07004-2056 Tel # (201) 227-6350

Lifelines
Association

Publishing Co: Oil, Chemical & Atomic Workers, PO Box 281200, Lakewood, CO 80228-8200
Tel # (303) 288-2712; Title Tel # (303) 987-2229
Personnel: Editor-Sylvia Kieding
Editorial Description: Describes work of the health and safety department of the Oil, Chemical, and Atomic Workers Union.
General Info: Bi-monthly, Trim Size-8 x 11, Web press, 4 pages, No Color
Subscriptions: Indv. $5
Circulation: (100% controlled), Total-100,000

Lifetime Health Letter

Publishing Co: University of Texas, 1100 Holcombe Blvd., Houston, TX 77030-3907;
Title Tel # (713) 792-4265
Personnel: Editor-Joe Sigler
General Info: Yr. Est. 1989, Monthly, 8 pages
Subscriptions: Indv. $24
Circulation: Total-35,000

Living Health Bulletin

Publishing Co: GOTACH Center for Health, 7051 Poole Jones Rd # 606, Frederick, MD 21702-2447; Title Tel # (301) 662-6726

Living Healthy
Business, Consumer

Publishing Co: Mitchell & Assoc., 5654 Willow Terrace Dr, Bethel Park, PA 15102-3528;
Title Tel # (412) 831-0891
Personnel: Publisher, Editor-Juliann Mitchell
General Info: Yr. Est. 1992, Quarterly, Desktop press, 4 pages, 2 Color, Matte
Subscriptions: Indv. $11, For. $15
Printing Co: J & G Printing, 4320 Library Rd., Library, PA 15141 Tel # (412) 854-3320

Local Health Officers News
See: GOVERNMENT

Long Term Care Monitor
Business

Publishing Co: MPL Communications, Inc., 133 Richmond St. W., Ste. 700, Toronto, ON M5H 3M8 Canada; Title Tel # (416) 869-1177 Title Fax # (416) 869-0456
Personnel: Publisher-Steve Pepper, Editor-Chris Garbutt, Circ. Mgr.-Diana Yeo, Production Mgr.-Adam Mirowski
Editorial Description: Published for administrators and senior staff of long term care organizations in Canada. Provides news from the field and practical advice for the daily management of long term care.
General Info: Yr. Est. 1990, 10x/yr., Sheetfed press, 8 pages, ISSN: 1180-2189, 2 Color, Matte
Subscriptions: Indv. $107, Can. $107
List Rental: Rents Lists

Longevity Letter
Association

Publishing Co: American Longevity Assn., 1000 W Carson St, Torrance, CA 90502-2004;
Title Tel # (213) 533-2764
Editorial Description: Association news and developments relating to longevity.
General Info: Yr. Est. 1983, Monthly
Subscriptions: Indv. $47

Looking Forward
Business, Association

Publishing Co: International Health Awareness Ctr., 350 E Michigan Ave Ste 301, Kalamazoo, MI 49007-3854; Title Tel # (616) 343-0770
Personnel: Editor-Carol Garzona, Circ. Mgr.-Jeff Rubleski, Production Mgr.-Sandi Harville, Adv. Dir.-Debra Seeley, Art Dir.-Fred Birchman, Promotion Dir.-Shawn Connors
Editorial Description: Senior health pub. that is UPBEAT & POSITIVE with relavent topics.
General Info: Yr. Est. 1988, Quarterly, Web press, 8 pages, ISSN: 0896-7032, 2 Color, Newsprint
Subscriptions: Indv. $20

Lose Weight Naturally Newsletter
See: NUTRITION

Low Fat for Life
See: FOOD

MA Report

Publishing Co: Mothers of Asthmatics, Inc., 3554 Chain Bridge Rd Ste 200, Fairfax, VA 22030-2709;
Title Tel # (703) 385-4403 Title Fax # (703) 352-4354
Editorial Description: News and developments of interest to families with asthma and allergies.
General Info: Yr. Est. 1985, Monthly
Subscriptions: Indv. $25, Can. $25, For. $25
Circulation: Total-15,000

MDR Watch
Business

Publishing Co: Washington Business Information, Inc., 1117 19th St N Ste 200, Arlington, VA 22209-1708; Title Tel # (703) 247-3418 Title Fax # (703) 247-3421
Personnel: Publisher-David Swit, Editor-Sean Oberle, Circ. Mgr.-Chris Rogers, Production Mgr.-Jennea Myrick, Mktg. Dir.-Deb Plaskow
Editorial Description: Medical device reporting. Closely monitors your competitor's (and your own) compliance with FDA's tough Medical Device Reporting (MDR) rules. Provides detailed charts.
General Info: Yr. Est. 1986, Monthly, Trim Size-8½ x 11, Sheetfed press, 19 pages, ISSN: 0890-7587, No Color, Recycled
Subscriptions: Indv. $597, Inst. $597, Can. $597, For. $652
Acquistions: Publication Bought
List Rental: Actives: $110/M

MDS News
Association

Publishing Co: Massachusetts Dental Society, 83 Speen St., Natick, MA 01760-4144;
Title Tel # (508) 651-7511 Title Fax # (508) 653-7115
Personnel: Editor-Peg Pollard
Editorial Description: Timely articles of interest to dentists in Mass.
General Info: Yr. Est. 1964, 7x/yr., Trim Size-8½ x 11, Offset press, 8 pages, ISSN: 0738-4556, No Color, Recycled
Subscriptions: Indv. $20, $3/copy
Circulation: Total-4,259
Advertising: Inquire for rates.

MIBCA Scope

Publishing Co: Sponsor-MIBCA, Minnesota Institute on Black Chemical Abuse, 2616 Nicollet Ave, Minneapolis, MN 55408-1628; Title Tel # (612) 871-7878
Personnel: Editor, Circ. Mgr.-David Grant
Editorial Description: Drug abuse & prevention notes/focus on black community.
General Info: Yr. Est. 1977, Quarterly, Trim Size-8½ x 11, Web press, 4 pages, 2 Color, Newsprint
Circulation: Total-12,000

MLA News
See: LIBRARY

MRO Update
Business, Association

Publishing Co: Sponsor-American College of Occupational and Enviornmental Medicine, American College of Occupational and Environmental Medicine, 55 W. Seegers Rd., Arlington Hts., IL 60005-3922 Tel # (847) 228-6850 Fax # (847) 228-1856
Personnel: Mng. Editor-Mariane Dreger, MA
General Info: Yr. Est. 1995, 10x/yr., Trim Size-8½ x 11, 8 pages, ISSN: 1079-3291, 2 Color, Matte
Subscriptions: Indv. $225
Circulation: Total-650
List Rental: Actives: 650, $100/M
Printing Co: Clyde Printing, 3520 S. Morgan, Chicago, IL 60609

MS Canada
Association

Publishing Co: Multiple Sclerosis Society of Canada, 250 Bloor St. E., #820, Toronto, ON M4W 3P9 Canada; Title Tel # (416) 922-6065 Title Fax # (416) 922-7538
Personnel: Editor-Deanna Groetzinger, Asst. Ed.-Susan Talbot
Editorial Description: Developments in multiple sclerosis research, treatments, management of disease.
General Info: Yr. Est. 1974, Quarterly, Trim Size-8½ x 11, Sheetfed press, 16 pages, ISSN: 0315-1131, 2 Color, Recycled, Saddle-stitched
Subscriptions: Can. $12, Free With Membership
Circulation: (5% controlled), Total-26,000

Maine Events
Association

Publishing Co: Maine Lung Assn., 128 Sewall St, Augusta, ME 04330-6822;
Title Tel # (207) 622-6394
Personnel: Editor-Peter King
Editorial Description: Association news. Lung disease information.
General Info: (Formerly Maine TB), Yr. Est. 1949, Quarterly, Trim Size-5½ x 8½, Offset press, 16 pages, 2 Color
Circulation: Total-3,000

Make it Tasty with No/Low Salt--How To & Receipe Blends Edition
See: FOOD

Make it Tasty Spice Co. Blends Food Business Newsletter
See: FOOD

Managed Care & Health Care Marketing
Business

Publishing Co: Healthcare Publishing, 200 McCleary Ct., Raleigh, NC 27607;
Title Tel # (919) 852-0552 Title Fax # (910) 852-0552
Personnel: Publisher-Don Brandy, Editor-Don Brady, Circ. Mgr.-Sandy Mueller
Editorial Description: Marketing information for healthcare facilities on HMO's, PPO's developing contracts with insurance companies and general marketing quidelines for managed care.
General Info: (Formerly Marketing Rehabilitation), Yr. Est. 1990, Monthly, 10 pages, ISSN: 54-158285, 2 Color
Subscriptions: Indv. $145

Managed Care Outlook
See: HOSPITALS & NURSING HOMES

Managed Care Week
Business

Publishing Co: Atlantic Information Svcs., Inc., 1100 17th St. NW, Ste. 300, Washington, DC 20036-5503; Title Tel # (202) 775-9008 Title Fax # (202) 331-9542
Personnel: Publisher-Richard Biehl, Circ. Mgr.-Gwen Arnold, Production Dir.-Gary Peterson, Mktg. Mgr.-Christine Burdell
Editorial Description: Timely, reliable newsom innovative managed care aramgents & the business affairs and compliance strategies of HMOS, PPOs and POS Plans.
General Info: Yr. Est. 1991, Weekly
Subscriptions: Indv. $439
List Rental: List Management Co.: Tony Murray & Assoc., P.O. Box 2409, Fairfax, VA 22031-3739 Tel # (703) 425-5356, Fax # (703) 425-4537

Managed Dental Care
See: EMPLOYMENT

Managed Pharmaceutical Report
See: DRUGS & PHARMACEUTICALS

Managing Integration and Operations: A Guide to Quality Health Care Systems
See: HOSPITALS & NURSING HOMES

Manitoba League of the Physically Handicapped, Update

Publishing Co: Manitoba League of the Physically Handicapped, Inc., 294 Portage Ave., #200, Winnipeg, MB R3C 0B9 Canada; Title Tel # (204) 943-6099
Personnel: Editor-David Martin
General Info: Monthly, 16 pages
Circulation: Total-575

Massage Therapy Focus on Health Care
Business, Consumer

Publishing Co: Massage Therapy Focus on Health Care, 324 OakDale Avenue, Ottawa, ON Canada; Title Tel # (613) 722-8588
Personnel: Publisher, Editor-Doug Alexander, Circ. Mgr., Mktg. Dir.-Leona Alexander
Editorial Description: Information for massage therapists to present to clients.
General Info: Yr. Est. 1982, Irregular, Trim Size-11 x 17, Desktop press, 4 pages
Subscriptions: Indv. $12, Inst. $12, Can. $12, For. $12, $3/copy
Acquistions: Publication Sold
Circulation: Readership-5,000
Printing Co: Ottawa Laser Copy, 880 Wellington St., Ottawa, ON K1R 6K7 Canada Tel # (613) 563-3210

Materiel Manager
See: HOSPITALS & NURSING HOMES

Mature Market Report
See: SENIOR CITIZENS

Mayo Clinic Health Letter
Consumer

Publishing Co: Mayo Foundation-Mayo Medical School, 200 1st St SW, Rochester, MN 55905-0001 Tel # (507) 284-2511; Title Tel # (507) 284-4660 Title Fax # (507) 284-5410
Personnel: Editor-Charles Kennedy, M.D., Editor-David Swanson, Circ. Mgr.-Jane Biers, Circ. Mgr.-Christie Smith
Editorial Description: Covers issues relating to good health.
General Info: Yr. Est. 1983, Monthly, Trim Size-8½ x 11, Web press, 8 pages, ISSN: 0741-6245, 4 Color, Coated
Subscriptions: Indv. $24, $3/copy
Circulation: Total-380,000
List Rental: List Management Co.: Kleid Company, Inc., 530 5th Ave., 17 Floor, New York, NY 10036-5101 Tel # (212) 819-3406, Fax # (212) 719-9788, Actives: 383,386, $75/M, Hotline: 64,347, $90/M, Expires: 69,003, $65/M
Printing Co: Brown Brinting, 2300 Brown Avenue, US Hwy 14 W., PO Box 1549, Waseca, MN 56093-0517 Tel # (507) 835-2410, Fax # (507) 835-0420

Mealey's Litigation Report: Breast Implants
Business

Publishing Co: Mealey Publications, Inc., PO Box 446, Wayne, PA 19087-0446; Title Tel # (610) 688-6566 Title Fax # (610) 688-7552
Personnel: Publisher-Michael Mealey, Editor-Jennifer Hahn
Editorial Description: Provides detailed coverage of jury verdicts, medical studies, multi-district litigation, discovery coordination, class-action updates, etc.
General Info: Yr. Est. 1993, Semi-monthly, ISSN: 1067-0246
Subscriptions: Indv. $825, For. $945, $50/copy

Mealey's Litigation Report: Norplant
Business

Publishing Co: Mealey Publications, Inc., PO Box 446, Wayne, PA 19087-0446; Title Tel # (610) 688-6566 Title Fax # (610) 688-7552
Personnel: Publisher-Michael Mealey, Editor-Jon Hansen, Mktg. Dir.-Kathy Roach
Editorial Description: Document and editorial coverage of nationwide Norplant Litigation.
General Info: Yr. Est. 1994, Semi-monthly, Trim Size-8½ x 11
Subscriptions: Indv. $650, For. $746, $50/copy

Med News
Business, Consumer

Publishing Co: Cypress Publishing, PO Box 777, Cypress, TX 77429-0777 Fax # (713) 256-1722; Title Tel # (713) 373-9142 Title Fax # (713) 373-4450
Personnel: Editor-Linda Hadfield, Art Dir.-Jeff Morgan
Editorial Description: News, articles, and information on health issues.
General Info: Yr. Est. 1992, Monthly, Trim Size-8½ x 11, Offset press, 3 pages, 2 Color, Coated, Other

Medical Abstracts Newsletter
Consumer

Publishing Co: Georgetown Publishing House, 1101 30th St., NW, Washington, DC 20007 Tel # (202) 337-5980 Fax # (202) 337-1512
Personnel: Publisher-Daniel Lavinas, Editor-Toni Goldfarb, Circ. Mgr.-Debra Schulle, Mktg. Dir.-Carline Anglade-Cole
Editorial Description: Easy-to-understand summaries of latest medical breakthroughs & discoveries, abstracted from over 150 authoritative medical journals.
General Info: Yr. Est. 1981, Monthly, Trim Size-8½ x 11, Letrpr. press, 6 pages, ISSN: 0730-7810, Ind/Abs/Online: CHNI, 2 Color, Other
Subscriptions: Indv. $40, Can. $50, $5/copy
List Rental: List Management Co.: Mail Marketing, Inc., 171 Terrace St., Haworth, NJ 07641-1899 Tel # (201) 387-1023, Fax # (201) 387-2976, Actives: 93,797, $80/M
Printing Co: Country Marketing List Mgr., 155 E. Main St., Brewster, NY 10509 Tel # (914) 278-9744, Fax # (914) 278-9747

Medical Alert
Association, Consumer

Publishing Co: National Association of People with AIDS (NAPWA), 1413 K Street NW, Washington, DC 20005; Title Tel # (202) 898-0414 Title Fax # (202) 898-0435
Editorial Description: For people with AIDS from the NAPWA.
General Info: Bi-monthly
Subscriptions: Free
Circulation: Total-35,000

Medical Benefits
Business

Publishing Co: Aspen Publishers, Inc., 200 Orchard Ridge Dr., Ste 200, Gaithersburg, MD 20878-5440 Fax # (301) 417-7655 Parent Co.-Wolters Kluwer US Corporation, New York; Title Tel # (301) 417-7500 Title Fax # (301) 417-7550
Personnel: Editor-Margaret Mucklo
Editorial Description: For professionals responsible for controlling healthcare costs.
General Info: Yr. Est. 1991, Semi-monthly, ISSN: 0743-8079
Subscriptions: Indv. $196, For. $235
List Rental: List Management Co.: Stevens-Knox List Management, 304 Park Ave S., New York, NY 10010-5312 Tel # (212) 388-8800, Fax # (212) 388-8890

Medical Business Letter, The
Business, Association

Publishing Co: ARSI Group, The, 19W068 Granville Road, Itasca, IL 60143; Title Tel # (708) 773-1395 Title Fax # (708) 773-1396
Personnel: Editor-James Muscler, Circ. Mgr.-Karen Schumacher, Art Dir.-Mike Malone
Editorial Description: Information for the business side of medicine. Business office management and process re-engineering.
General Info: Yr. Est. 1988, Monthly, Trim Size-8½ x 11, Offset press, 8 pages, 2 Color, Coated, Saddle-stitched
Subscriptions: Indv. $227, Inst. $189
Circulation: Total-3,400, Readership-3,400
Advertising: Accepts Inserts.
List Rental: Actives: 3,400

Medical Business Review

Publishing Co: Cast, Hursh & Assoc., 4601 N. Wash. Rd, Ft. Wayne, IN 46804; Title Tel # (219) 432-3036
Personnel: Editor-William Cast
General Info: (Formerly Medical Businessman), Yr. Est. 1981, Monthly, Trim Size-8½ x 11, Sheetfed press, 8 pages, 2 Color, Newsprint
Subscriptions: Indv. $144
Circulation: Total-2,500

Medical Devices Bulletin
Business, Association

Publishing Co: Food & Drug Administration, 5600 Fishers La., Rockville, MD 20852-1750; Title Tel # (301) 443-5360 Title Fax # (301) 227-6834
Personnel: Editor-Susan Gerhold
Editorial Description: Monthly newsletter that goes out to 4,000 medical device manufacturers.
General Info: Yr. Est. 1983, Monthly, Trim Size-8½ x 11, 6 pages, Color
Subscriptions: Free
Circulation: Total-5,000

Medical Devices Reporter
See: DRUGS & PHARMACEUTICALS

Medical Mission Sisters News
Consumer, Association

Publishing Co: Society of Catholic Medical Missionaries, Inc., 8400 Pine Rd, Philadelphia, PA 19111-1312; Title Tel # (215) 742-6100 Title Fax # (215) 342-3948
Personnel: Circ. Mgr.-Fran MacAllister, Editor, Art Dir.-Monica McGinley
Editorial Description: Information about Medical Mission Sisters and their worldwide concerns.
General Info: (Formerly Medical Missionary), Yr. Est. 1927, Quarterly, Trim Size-8½ x 11, Web press, 4 pages, 4 Color, Coated
Subscriptions: Free
Circulation: Total-57,000
List Rental: Rents Lists
Printing Co: Triune Color Corp., 7155 Airport Cir., Pennsauken, NJ 08109 Tel # (609) 663-5155

Medical Network Strategy Report
See: HOSPITALS & NURSING HOMES

Medical Offfice Biller

Publishing Co: Zimmerman & Associates, Inc., 5307 South 92nd St., Hales Corners, WI 53130-1677 Parent Co.-Aspen Publishers, Inc., Gaithersburg; Title Tel # (414) 425-2189 Title Fax # (414) 425-4807
Personnel: Editorial Dir.-Jo Ann Petaschnick
General Info: Yr. Est. 1994, Monthly
Subscriptions: Indv. $197

Medical Records Briefing
See: HOSPITALS & NURSING HOMES

Medical Reform
See: MEDICINE

Medical Staff Briefing
See: HOSPITALS & NURSING HOMES

Medical Update   *Consumer*

Publishing Co: Medical Education & Research Foundation, 1100 Waterway Blvd, Indianapolis, IN 46202-2156; Title Tel # (317) 636-8881
Personnel: Publisher-C.J. Servaas, Editor-Jack Grambling, Circ. Mgr.-Susan Hanley, Promotion Dir.-Greg Joray
Editorial Description: Disseminates health and nutrition information to the general public.
General Info: Yr. Est. 1977, Monthly, Trim Size-8.5 x 11, Sheetfed press, 6 pages, Ind/Abs/Online: DIALOG, 2 Color, Coated
Subscriptions: Indv. $15, Inst. $12, Can. $19, For. $19, $2/copy
Circulation: Total-20,000
List Rental: List Management Co.: Media Marketplace, 140 Terry Drive, P.O. Box 500, Newtown, PA 18940-0500 Tel # (215) 968-5020, Fax # (215) 968-9410, Actives: $65/M

Medical Utilization Management
See: MEDICINE

Medicare Compliance Alert   *Business*

Publishing Co: United Communications Group, 11300 Rockville Pike, Ste. 1100, Rockville, MD 20852-3030 Tel # (301) 816-8950 Fax # (301) 816-8945
Editorial Description: News on healthcare business.
General Info: Bi-weekly

Medicare Report

Publishing Co: Bureau of National Affairs, Inc., 1231 25th St. NW, Bldg. N-200, Washington, DC 20037-1157; Title Tel # (202) 452-4200 Title Fax # (202) 822-8092
Editorial Description: Medicare developments and news.
General Info: Yr. Est. 1990, 26x/yr.
Subscriptions: Indv. $526

Medicine & Health

Publishing Co: Faulkner & Gray Healthcare Information Center, 1133 15th St NW, Ste. 450, Washington, DC 20005-2710 Tel # (202) 828-4148 Parent Co.-Faulkner & Gray, Inc., New York; Title Tel # (202) 828-4150
Personnel: Publisher-Luci Koizumi, Editor-Craig Havighurst
Editorial Description: Federal & Natl. Health Policy.
General Info: Yr. Est. 1947, Weekly, Trim Size-8½ x 11, Web press, 8 pages, ISSN: 0043-0730, Color, Newsprint
Subscriptions: Indv. $450
Acquistions: Publication Bought, Publication Sold
List Rental: Actives: $95/M

Medicine on the Net
See: HOSPITALS & NURSING HOMES

Mended Hearts Newsletter

Publishing Co: Mended Hearts, Inc., 7320 Greenville Ave, Dallas, TX 75231-4502; Title Tel # (214) 750-5442
General Info: Quarterly, 12 pages, Color
Circulation: Total-9,000

Menninger Letter, The
See: PSYCHOLOGY

Men's Confidential
See: MEN'S

Mental Health Law News   *Business, Consumer*

Publishing Co: Interwood Publications, 3 Interwood Pl., Box 20241, Cincinnati, OH 45220-1821; Title Tel # (513) 221-3715
Personnel: Publisher, Editor-Frank Bardack
Editorial Description: Mental health case law summaries.
General Info: Yr. Est. 1985, Monthly, Trim Size-8½ x 11, Sheetfed press, 6 pages, ISSN: 0889-017X, No Color, Newsprint
Subscriptions: Indv. $89, For. $100

Mental Health Weekly   *Business*

Publishing Co: Manisses Communications Group, Inc., PO Box 3357, Providence, RI 02906-0757; Title Tel # (401) 831-6020 Title Fax # (401) 861-6370
Personnel: Publisher-Fraser Lang, Editor-Gary Enos, Circ. Mgr.-Deb Zajas, Mktg. Dir.-Betty Lang
Editorial Description: Provides the most current, complete coverage of mental health issues for field professionals.
General Info: (Formerly Behavior Today), Yr. Est. 1991, Weekly, Offset press, ISSN: 1058-1103
Subscriptions: Indv. $397, Inst. $427, Can. $447, For. $467
Circulation: Total-1,500
List Rental: List Management Co.: Conrad Direct, Inc., 300 Knickerbocker Road, Creskill, NJ 07626 Tel # (201) 567-3200, Fax # (201) 567-4959, Actives: 1,030, $90/M, Expires: 2,266, $90/M
Printing Co: Newsletter Press, 76 Valley St, East Providence, RI 02914-4424 Tel # (401) 438-5352

Messenger, The
See: HOSPITALS & NURSING HOMES

Miami Health Letter   *Consumer*

Publishing Co: Miami Medical Letter, Inc., 9700 SW 67th Ave, Miami, FL 33156-3272; Title Tel # (305) 284-8466 Title Fax # (305) 284-1019
Editorial Description: Features information contributing to the awareness and understanding of current medical knowledge and opinion.
General Info: (Formerly Miami Medical Letter), Yr. Est. 1987, Monthly, ISSN: 1047-2509
Subscriptions: Indv. $36, Inst. $36, Can. $36, For. $48, $3/copy
Circulation: Total-5,000
List Rental: Rents Lists

Miami Health Letter en
Espanol   *Consumer*

Publishing Co: Miami Medical Letter, Inc., 9700 SW 67th Ave, Miami, FL 33156-3272; Title Tel # (305) 284-8466 Title Fax # (305) 284-1019
Editorial Description: Information on current medical knowledge and opinion. Text in Spanish.
General Info: (Formerly Miami Health Letter en Espanol), Monthly
Subscriptions: Indv. $36, Inst. $36, Can. $36, For. $48, $3/copy
Circulation: Total-5,000
List Rental: Rents Lists

Michigan Organic News
See: GARDENING & HORTICULTURE

Microwave News   *Business*   **CPM$1200**

Publishing Co: Microwave News, Box 1799, Grand Central Sta., New York, NY 10163-1799; Title Tel # (212) 517-2800 Title Fax # (212) 734-0316
Personnel: Publisher, Editor-Louis Slesin, Mng. Editor-Robert Dietrich
Editorial Description: Health risks and interference issues related to radiation, exposure to power lines, cellular phones and other electromagnetic field hazards..
General Info: Yr. Est. 1981, Bi-monthly, Trim Size-8½ x 11, Offset press, 16 pages, ISSN: 0275-6595, 2% ads, No Color, Matte, Saddle-stitched
Subscriptions: Indv. $285, Can. $315, For. $315, $50/copy
Circulation: Total-1,000
Advertising: $1,200.

Mid Life Woman
See: WOMEN'S

Mind/Body Medicine
Newsletter, The   *Consumer*

Publishing Co: Institute for the Study of Human Knowledge, Center for Health Sciences, PO Box 176, Los Altos, CA 94023
Personnel: Co-Editor-Robert Ornstein, PhD, Co-Editor-David Sobel, MD
Editorial Description: Focuses on treatments which involve the mind and body jointly.
General Info: Yr. Est. 1995, Quarterly, Trim Size-8½ x 11, 8 pages, 2 Color
Subscriptions: Indv. $10

Mindell Letter, The   *Consumer*

Publishing Co: Phillips Publishing, Inc., 7811 Montrose Rd., Potomac, MD 20854-3394 Parent Co.-Phillips Business Information, Inc., Potomac; Title Tel # (301) 340-2100 Title Fax # (301) 294-1307
Personnel: Publisher-Thomas L. Phillips, Editor-Earl Mindell, Mktg. Dir.-Laurie Hoffman
Editorial Description: Guide to healthier living through proper nutrition.
General Info: (Formerly Earl Mindell's Joy of Health), Yr. Est. 1993, Monthly
Subscriptions: Indv. $40
List Rental: List Management Co.: Manager: John Baldwin; Phillips Publishing List Marketing, 7811 Montrose Rd., Potomac, MD 20854-3394 Tel # (301) 340-2100, Fax # (301) 294-1307, Actives: 48,038, $125/M, Expires: 34,191, $85/M

Minnesota Nursing Accent
See: NURSING

Missouri Monthly Vital
Statistics   *Business, Consumer*

Publishing Co: Department of Health, Center for Health Statistics, PO Box 570, Jefferson City, MO 65102-0570 Tel # (314) 751-6278; Title Tel # (314) 751-6400
Personnel: Editor-Garland Land
Editorial Description: Contains vital statistics, data and short analytical articles concrning public health issues.
General Info: Yr. Est. 1967, Monthly
Subscriptions: Free
Circulation: Total-800

Modern Nutrition News
See: NUTRITION

Monday Morning Report

Publishing Co: Alcohol Research Info Svc., 1106 E Oakland Ave, Lansing, MI 48906-5513; Title Tel # (517) 485-9900 Title Fax # (517) 485-1928
Personnel: Editor-Robert Hammond
Editorial Description: Brief articles & news items on alcohol related issues & problems.
General Info: Yr. Est. 1976, Semi-monthly, 2 pages
Subscriptions: Indv. $30, Can. $40, For. $40
Circulation: (20% controlled), Total-1,000, Subscriptions-800

Monthly Newsletter for Mothers of Asthmatics

Publishing Co: Jennifer Miller, 3554 Chain Bridge Rd Ste 200, Fairfax, VA 22030-2709; Title Tel # (703) 385-4403 Title Fax # (703) 352-4354
Personnel: Publisher-Jennifer Miller
Editorial Description: Patient education/resource information on managing asthma and allergies.
General Info: Yr. Est. 1986, Monthly
Subscriptions: Indv. $25, Can. $35, For. $35
Circulation: Total-5,000

Museletter, The   *Consumer, Association*

Publishing Co: National Association for Poetry Therapy, PO Box 551, Port Washington, NY 11050-0105; Title Tel # (516) 944-9781 Title Fax # (516) 944-5818
Personnel: Editor-Donna Husby
Editorial Description: Provides information on events in the world of poetry therapy and within NAPT.
General Info: (Formerly NAPT Museletter), Yr. Est. 1981, Trim Size-8½ x 11, 8 pages, No Color, Matte, Saddle-stitched
Subscriptions: Indv. $5, Free With Membership
Circulation: Total-1,000
Advertising: Inquire for rates.

NAACLS News
See: EDUCATION

NAAP News
See: HOSPITALS & NURSING HOMES

NACHRI Newsletter
See: HOSPITALS & NURSING HOMES

NAEB Bulletin
See: PURCHASING

NAF Update   *Association*

Publishing Co: National Abortion Federation, 1436 U St NW Ste 103, Washington, DC 20009-3997; Title Tel # (202) 546-9060
Personnel: Editor-Pat Donovan, Art Dir.-Daphne Petty, Promotion Dir.-Barbara Radford
Editorial Description: NAF news and information about all aspects of abortion.
General Info: (Formerly NAF Quarterly), Yr. Est. 1985, Semi-annually, Trim Size-8½ x 11, 10 pages, No Color, Newsprint
Subscriptions: Indv. $50, $1/copy
Circulation: Total-1,000
Advertising: Inquire for rates.

NAFC Quarterly Newsletter   *Consumer, Association*

Publishing Co: National Association for Continence, PO Box 8310, Spartanburg, SC 29305-8310 Tel # (864) 579-7900 Fax # (864) 579-7902; Title Tel # (803) 579-7900
Personnel: Publisher-Terry Lowp, Editor, Adv. Dir.-Lisa Verdell, Mktg. Dir.-Stacey Brewer
Editorial Description: Educational materials for incontinent people. Comprensive resource guide to products and services, audiovisuals, patient education leaflets.
General Info: (Formerly HIP Report), Yr. Est. 1982, Quarterly, Trim Size-8½ x 11, 8 pages
Subscriptions: Indv. $15
Circulation: Total-100,000
Advertising: Inquire for rates. Accepts Inserts.

N.A.H.C. Report

Publishing Co: National Association for Home Care, 519 C St NE, Washington, DC 20002-5809 Fax # (202) 547-3751; Title Tel # (202) 547-7424 Title Fax # (202) 547-3540
Personnel: Publisher-Val Hacamandaris, Editor-Andrea Brummit, Circ. Mgr.-Stewart Jordan, Production Mgr.-D. Richard McDew, Adv. Dir.-Christopher Adams, Art Dir.-Dian Van DeMark
Editorial Description: NAHC Report provides the most up-to-date information on the latest developments in legislative, regulatory, operational and financial issues affecting the home care field.
General Info: Yr. Est. 1983, Weekly, Letrpr. press, 8 pages, Matte
Subscriptions: Indv. $175, $3/copy
Circulation: (75% controlled)
Advertising: Inquire for rates.
Printing Co: National Assn. for Home Care, 519 C St NE, Washington, DC 20002-5809

NAPSAC News
See: FAMILY

NARAL News

Publishing Co: National Abortion Rights Action League, Communications Office, 1156 15th St. NW, Ste. 700, Washington, DC 20005-1704; Title Tel # (202) 828-9300 Title Fax # (202) 973-3099
Personnel: Editor, Production Mgr.-Victoria Jaffe
Editorial Description: Newsletter Provding updates on legislation regarding abortion.
General Info: Quarterly, Letrpr. press, 6 pages, ISSN: 0195-2862, 2 Color, Newsprint
Subscriptions: Indv. $20
Acquistions: Publication Bought
Circulation: Total-124,000
Printing Co: Homart Press & Envelope Co., PO Box 346, Bladensburg, MD 20710-0346 Tel # (301) 277-8836

NARHA News
See: SPORTS & SPORTING GOODS

NCAMP's Technical Report
See: ENVIRONMENT & ECOLOGY

NCI Catalyst   *Consumer*

Publishing Co: North Conway Institute, Inc., 14 Beacon St, Boston, MA 02108-3746; Title Tel # (617) 742-0424
Personnel: Editor-Priscilla Martin
Editorial Description: Alcohol use/abuse, and other forms of drug abuse.
General Info: Yr. Est. 1967, Quarterly, Trim Size-8½ x 11, Offset press, 8 pages, No Color
Subscriptions: Indv. $15
Circulation: (100% controlled), Total-10,000

NCOSH
See: INDUSTRIAL RELATIONS/PERSONNEL

NCRP News
See: SAFETY

NFPRHA News   *Association*

Publishing Co: Natl. Family Planning & Reproductive Health Assn., 122 C St NW Ste 380, Washington, DC 20001-2109; Title Tel # (202) 628-3535
Personnel: Publisher-Scott Swirling, Editor, Circ. Mgr.-Penny Bates
Editorial Description: Newsletter of natl. family planning trade assn.
General Info: Yr. Est. 1981, Bi-monthly, Trim Size-11½ x 15, 12 pages, 1% ads, 2 Color, Newsprint
Subscriptions: Indv. $125, Inst. $375
Circulation: (100% controlled), Total-3,000
List Rental: Actives: $100/M
Printing Co: Suburban Record/Record Printing Co., 7676 Fenton St, Silver Spring, MD 20910-4903

NHF Headlines   *Business, Association*

Publishing Co: Sponsor-National Headache Foundation, Silent Partners, 8727 Shoal Creek Blvd., Austin, TX 78757-6815; Title Tel # (512) 458-1191 Title Fax # (512) 458-1234
Personnel: Publisher-Lori Brix, Editor-Arthur Elkind, MD
Editorial Description: Information in headache causes & treatments; research updates; foundation news; reader question and answer section; book/article review; educational information area form.
General Info: (Formerly NHF Newsletter; National Migraine Foundation), Yr. Est. 1970, Quarterly, Trim Size-8½ x 11, 16 pages, Color, Matte
Subscriptions: Indv. $15, For. $15, Free With Membership
Circulation: Total-45,000, Readership-45,000

NHO Newsline
See: MEDICINE

NIH Record

Publishing Co: National Center for Research Resources Information Ctr., Bldg. 31, Room 2B03, 9000 Rockville Pike, Bethesda, MD 20892; Title Tel # (301) 496-2125
Personnel: Editor-Herschel Cribb
Editorial Description: Scientific developments (biomedical) in law, language, plus general news of NIH.
General Info: Yr. Est. 1949, Bi-weekly, 12 pages, No Color
Circulation: (100% controlled), Total-18,250

NIHB Health Reporter   *Business*

Publishing Co: National Indian Health Board, 1385 S. Colorado Blvd., #A-708, Denver, CO 80222-3304
Personnel: Editor-John O'Connor
General Info: Yr. Est. 1980, Bi-monthly, Trim Size-8½ x 11, 24 pages, 2 Color, Matte, Saddle-stitched

NMHA Prevention Update
See: PSYCHOLOGY

NOCIRC Newsletter   *Consumer*

Publishing Co: Natl. Org. of Circumcision Info. Res. Ctrs., PO Box 2512, San Anselmo, CA 94979-2512; Title Tel # (415) 488-9883 Title Fax # (415) 488-9660
Personnel: Editor-Marilyn Milos, R.N.
Editorial Description: Newsletter of the National Organization ok Circumcision Information Resource Centers.
General Info: Yr. Est. 1986, Semi-annually, 6 pages, ISSN: 1070-3721, No Color, Other
Subscriptions: Free With Membership
Acquistions: Publication Sold
Circulation: Total-18,000

NOHA News
See: NUTRITION

NSCA Bulletin   *Association*

Publishing Co: Natl. Strength & Conditioning Assn., PO Box 38909, Colorado Springs, CO 80937-8909; Title Tel # (719) 632-6722 Title Fax # (719) 636-7976
Personnel: Editor-Lori Warner, Mktg. Dir.-Donna Welsh
Editorial Description: Currant eventsin the strenght and condition ig fuild ws
General Info: Yr. Est. 1978, Bi-monthly, Sheetfed press, 16 pages, No Color, Newsprint
Circulation: Total-11,000
Advertising: Inquire for rates. Accepts Inserts.
List Rental: Actives: $90/M
Printing Co: Nebraska Business Printing, 5612 S 49th St, Lincoln, NE 68516-2501

NTSA Newsletter   *Association*

Publishing Co: Natl. Tuberous Sclerosis Assn., Inc., 8000 Corporate Dr Ste 120, Landover, MD 20785-2239; Title Tel # (301) 459-9888
Editorial Description: Info to parents, professionals about research, treatment of Tuberous Sclerosis.
General Info: Yr. Est. 1974, Quarterly, Trim Size-11 x 17, Offset press, 8 pages, No Color
Subscriptions: Indv. $20, Free
Circulation: (100% controlled), Total-6,000

Narcotics and Drug Abuse
A-Z   *Consumer*

Publishing Co: Croner Publications, Inc., 34 Jericho Tpke, Jericho, NY 11753-1042; Title Tel # (516) 333-9085 Title Fax # (516) 338-4986
Personnel: Publisher-Ron Guggenheimer, Editor-Carol Sixt, Circ. Mgr.-Regina Friel
Editorial Description: A directory, dictionary and guide to information sources on drug abuse.
General Info: Quarterly
Subscriptions: Indv. $80

National, The
See: MEDICINE

National Consumers League Bulletin
See: CONSUMER INTERESTS

National Council Against
Health Fraud Newsletter   *Business, Association*

Publishing Co: National Council Against Health Fraud, PO Box 1276, Loma Linda, CA 92354-1276; Title Tel # (909) 824-4690 Title Fax # (909) 824-4838
Personnel: Editor-William Jarvis, Art Dir.-Ellis Jones
Editorial Description: Information about health fraud, quackery and misinformation.
General Info: (Formerly California Council Against Health Fraud, Inc.), Yr. Est. 1978, Bi-monthly, Trim Size-8½ x 11, Offset press, 4 pages, ISSN: 0890-3417, No Color, Other
Subscriptions: Indv. $15, $3/copy
Acquistions: Publication Bought, Publication Sold
Circulation: (100% controlled), Total-2,600
Printing Co: Loma Linda University Press, 24887 Taylor St Ste 101, Loma Linda, CA 92354-2809 Tel # (714) 796-3741

National Pulse
See: FAMILY

National Report on
Computers & Health   *Business*

Publishing Co: United Communications Group, 11300 Rockville Pike, Ste. 1100, Rockville, MD 20852-3030; Title Tel # (301) 816-8950 Title Fax # (301) 816-8945
Personnel: Publisher-Richard Hadley, Editor-Doug O'Boyle, Circ. Mgr.-Monica Brown
Editorial Description: News on DP, clinical info systems for hospital info system executives.
General Info: Yr. Est. 1980, Bi-weekly, Trim Size-8½ x 11, Offset press, 8 pages, ISSN: 0273-4974, Ind/Abs/Online: Predicast PTS Newsletter Database, DIALOG, NewsNet
Subscriptions: Indv. $387, Inst. $427, $18/copy
List Rental: Actives: $125/M

National Reye's Syndrome
Foundation-In the News   *Association*

Publishing Co: National Reye's Syndrome Foundation, PO BOX 829, Bryan, OH 43506-0829; Title Tel # (419) 636-2679 Title Fax # (419) 636-3366
Personnel: Publisher-Sandi Nelson, Editor-Terri Freudenberger, Circ. Mgr.-Terri Freudenberger
General Info: Yr. Est. 1974, Semi-annually, Trim Size-8½ x 11, Letrpr. press, 12 pages, 4 Color, Coated
Subscriptions: Free With Membership
Circulation: Total-5,000

National Women's Health
Report   *Association, Consumer*

Publishing Co: National Women's Health Resource Center, 2440 M St NW Ste 325, Washington, DC 20037-1404 Tel # (202) 293-6045 Fax # (202) 293-7256
Personnel: Editor-Heidi Rosvold-Brenholtz, Circ. Mgr.-Laura Bayer, Circ. Mgr.-Laura Brown, Production Mgr.-Philip Beauregard, Art Dir.-Caroline Arlen
Editorial Description: Timely health topics and preventive medicine information for women of all ages.
General Info: Yr. Est. 1983, Bi-monthly, Web press, 8 pages, ISSN: 0741-9147, Color, Newsprint
Subscriptions: Indv. $25, Inst. $75, For. $75
Acquistions: Publication Bought
Circulation: Total-30,000
Advertising: Accepts Inserts.
List Rental: Actives $65/M
Printing Co: Newsletter Services, Inc., 9700 Philadelphia Court, Lanham, MD 20706 Tel # (301) 731-5200, Fax # (301) 731-5201

Natural Hygiene Soc. of New Jersey Newsletter
See: NUTRITION

Naturally Well   *Consumer*

Publishing Co: Phillips Publishing, Inc., 7811 Montrose Rd., Potomac, MD 20854-3394 Parent Co.-Phillips Business Information, Inc., Potomac; Title Tel # (301) 340-2100 Title Fax # (301) 294-1307
Personnel: Publisher-Thomas L. Phillips, Editor-Marcus Laux, Mktg. Dir.-Karen Phillips
Editorial Description: Information from the Malibu Health and Rehab clinic on health issues.
General Info: (Formerly Malibu Natural Health Letter), Yr. Est. 1994, Monthly
Subscriptions: Indv. $40
List Rental: List Management Co.: Manager: John Baldwin; Phillips Publishing List Marketing, 7811 Montrose Rd., Potomac, MD 20854-3394 Tel # (301) 340-2100, Fax # (301) 294-1307, Actives: 43,893, $125/M, Expires: 5,814, $85/M

Needle Tips & the Hepatitis
B Coalition News   *Association*

Publishing Co: Immunization Action Coalition, 1573 Selby Ave Ste 229, St. Paul, MN 55104-6328; Title Tel # (612) 647-9009 Title Fax # (612) 647-9131
Personnel: Editor-Deborah L. Wexler, MD
Editorial Description: Published by the Immunization Action Coalition for individuals and organizations concerned about vaccine-preventable diseased children and adults.
General Info: (Formerly Needle Tips), Yr. Est. 1990, Semi-annually, Trim Size-8½ x 11, 28 pages, No Color, Matte, Saddle-stitched
Subscriptions: Free
Circulation: Total-125,000
Printing Co: Winslow Printing, 1225 N. Seventh Street, Minneapolis, MN 55411 Tel # (612) 522-3868, Fax # (612) 522-0025

Network
See: FAMILY

Network

Publishing Co: Parkinson Foundation of Canada, 55 Bloor St. West, Ste. 230, Toronto, ON M4W 1A5 Canada Tel # (416) 964-1155
Personnel: Editor-Grazyna Bergman
General Info: (Formerly Parkinson Foundation of Canada Bulletin Quarterly), Yr. Est. 1978, ISSN: 0824-7315
Subscriptions: Indv. $25
Circulation: Total-5,000

Network-French Edition   *Consumer, Association*

Publishing Co: Family Health International, PO Box 13950, Rtp, NC 27709-3950 Fax # (919) 544-7261
Personnel: Editor-Mary Bean, Circ. Mgr.-Debbie Crumpler, Production Mgr.-Marguerite Rogers
Editorial Description: Research on reproductive health, contraceptives.
General Info: Quarterly, ISSN: 0270-3637
Subscriptions: Free To Qualified Recipient
Circulation: Total-14,000

Network News
See: WOMEN'S

Network-Spanish Edition   *Consumer, Association*

Publishing Co: Family Health International, PO Box 13950, Rtp, NC 27709-3950 Fax # (919) 544-7261
Personnel: Editor-Marina McCune, Circ. Mgr.-Debbie Crumpler, Production Mgr.-Marguerite Rogers
Editorial Description: Research on reproductive health, contraceptives, family planning.
General Info: Quarterly, Trim Size-8.5 x 11, ISSN: 0270-3637
Subscriptions: Free To Qualified Recipient
Circulation: Total-20,000

New Brunswick Health
Records Assn.
Newsbreak   *Association*

Publishing Co: New Brunswick Health Records Assn., 1750 Sunset Drive, Bathurst, NB E2A 4A4 Canada Tel # (506) 548-8961 Fax # (506) 548-9850
Personnel: Editor-Catherine Parry
General Info: Yr. Est. 1966, Semi-annually, 25 pages, 2 Color
Subscriptions: Indv. $5
Circulation: Total-130

New Developments in Medicine & Drug Therapy
See: MEDICINE

New England Private Ambulance Report
See: MEDICINE

New Epidemiology Monitor, The
Business, Association   **CPM: $452**

Publishing Co: Epidemiology Monitor, 2560 Whisper Wind Ct., Roswell, GA 30076-3664
Fax # (404) 594-0997; Title Tel # (404) 594-1613 Title Fax # (770) 594-0997
Personnel: Publisher, Editor-Roger Bernier, MPH, PhD, Circ. Mgr.-Teresa Reinsel, Mng. Editor, Adv. Dir.-Virginia Mason, Mktg. Dir., Promotion Dir.-Ann Liakos
Editorial Description: News and information in epidemiology and public health.
General Info: (Formerly Epidemiology Monitor), Yr. Est. 1980, Monthly, Trim Size-8½ x 11, Offset press, 20 pages, ISSN: 0774-0898, 45% ads, 2 Color, Matte, Saddle-stitched
Subscriptions: Indv. $30, Inst. $45
Circulation: Total-2,200
Advertising: $995.
List Rental: Actives: 5,000, $130/M

New York Health Law Update
Business

Publishing Co: M. Lee Smith Publishers & Printers ,LCC, P.O. Box 198867, 162 Fourth Avenue North, Nashville, TN 37219-8867 Tel # (615) 242-7395 Fax # (615) 256-6601
Personnel: Publisher-M Lee Smith, Editor-John O'Connor, Circ. Mgr.-Cathy Bradford, Mktg. Dir.-David Yates
Editorial Description: New York health information.
General Info: (Formerly New York Health Alert), Yr. Est. 1994, Monthly, ISSN: 1073-0443
Subscriptions: Indv. $177
Printing Co: M. Lee Smith Publishers & Printers ,LLC, PO Box 198867, 162 Fourth Avenue, Nashville, TN 37219-8867 Tel # (615) 242-7395, Fax # (615) 256-6601

News & Views
See: MEDICINE

News Reports

Publishing Co: Natl. Health Lawyers Assn., 1120 Connecticut Ave NW Ste, 950, Washington, DC 20036-3902; Title Tel # (202) 833-1100
General Info: Monthly, 8 pages
Circulation: Total-5,000

Newsletter
Association

Publishing Co: British Columbia Chiropractic Assn., 532 W. Broadway, Vancouver, BC V5Z 1E9 Canada; Title Tel # (604) 873-6827
Personnel: Editor-Chas. Kibble
Editorial Description: Inhouse newsletter for the office.
General Info: Yr. Est. 1973, Quarterly, Trim Size-8½ x 14, 13 pages, No Color
Circulation: Total-400
Advertising: Inquire for rates.

Newsletter
Consumer, Association

Publishing Co: American Industrial Health Council, 2001 Pennsylvania Ave. NW, Suite 760, Washington, DC 20006-1850; Title Tel # (202) 659-0060
Personnel: Editor-Marsha Lawson
Editorial Description: Actions ensuring sound science in chronic health hazard policy development.
General Info: Yr. Est. 1977, Quarterly, Trim Size-8½ x 11, Sheetfed press, 10 pages, 2 Color
Circulation: (100% controlled), Total-1,200

Newsletter, The
Association

Publishing Co: Arthritis Foundation - NJ Chapter, 200 Middlesex Turnpike, Iselin, NJ 08830; Title Tel # (908) 283-4300 Title Fax # (908) 283-4633
Personnel: Editor-Stephen G. Pitts
Editorial Description: Arthritis info and association news.
General Info: 3x/yr., Letrpr. press, 6 pages, 2 Color
Subscriptions: Free To Qualified Recipient
Circulation: Total-40,000

Newsletter from Dick B on The Spiritual Roots of AA
Consumer, Association

Publishing Co: Good Book Publishing Company, 2747 S. Kihei Road, Kihei, HI 96753-9622
Fax # (808) 876-4876; Title Tel # (808) 874-4876 Title Fax # (808) 874-4876
Personnel: Publisher, Editor in Chief-Dick B, Product Mgr.-Ken B
Editorial Description: Covers the biblical and spiritual orgins of A.A. comments, reviews, news of research, directories and locations of historical data.
General Info: (Formerly The Spiritual Roots of Alchoholics Anonymous), Yr. Est. 1992, Bi-monthly, Trim Size-8½ x 11, Desktop press, 2 pages, ISSN: 1068-302X, Color, Other
Subscriptions: Free
Circulation: Total-1,000
Advertising: Inquire for rates. Accepts Inserts.
List Rental: Rents Lists

Newsletter of Medical Rehabilitation Administrators

Publishing Co: Assn. of Medical Rehabilitation Administrators, 1733 Forest Hills Dr, Vienna, WV 26105-3313; Title Tel # (304) 485-5842
Personnel: Editor-Millie Coty
Editorial Description: Items relating to individual members as well as rehabilitation administration, management and rehabilitation trends.
General Info: Yr. Est. 1989, Quarterly, Sheetfed press, 6 pages, No Color, Matte, Saddle-stitched
Circulation: Total-250
Advertising: Inquire for rates.
List Rental: Rents Lists

Newsletter for People with Lactose Intolerance and Milk Allergy
Consumer

Publishing Co: Jane Zukin, PO Box 3129, Ann Arbor, MI 48106-3129; Title Tel # (313) 572-9134
Title Fax # (313) 572-9134
Personnel: Publisher, Editor-Jane Zukin
Editorial Description: Medical tips and information for sufferers of these problems.
General Info: Yr. Est. 1987, Bi-monthly, Trim Size-8½ x 11, 8 pages
Subscriptions: Indv. $15, Inst. $29, Can. $36, For. $36
Circulation: Total-1,000
Advertising: Inquire for rates.
List Rental: Actives: $100/M

Newswatch

Publishing Co: Hospital Council of Southern California, 201 N. Figueroa St., 4th Fl., Los Angeles, CA 90012-2623; Title Tel # (213) 250-5600
Personnel: Editor-Steven Scholl
Editorial Description: Reprint of 10 healthcare news stories each month.
General Info: Yr. Est. 1982, Monthly
Subscriptions: Indv. $60

Noetic Sciences Bulletin
See: PHILOSOPHY

Noise Regulation Report
See: HEARING & SPEECH

North Texas Amputee Support Group News
See: DISABILITY

Not for Children Only

Publishing Co: Time Out to Enjoy, Inc., c/o CDR 208 LaSalle, Suite 1330, Chicagon, IL 60604; Title Tel # (312) 444-9484
Personnel: Editor-Jane Johnston
General Info: Yr. Est. 1977, Quarterly
Subscriptions: Indv. $10
Circulation: Total-600

Notes from the Underground
Consumer

Publishing Co: People With AIDS (PWA) Health Group, 150 W 26th St Rm 201, New York, NY 10001-6813; Title Tel # (212) 255-0520 Title Fax # (212) 255-2080
Personnel: Editor-Theo Smart
Editorial Description: Health info for people with AIDS.
General Info: Bi-monthly
Subscriptions: Indv. $35, Inst. $75

Nutrition & the M.D.
Association

Publishing Co: PM Inc., 1185 Ave of The Americas, New York, NY 10036-2601; Title Tel # (213) 873-4399 Title Fax # (818) 997-1316
Personnel: Publisher-Mervyn Oakner, Editor-Mara Stein, Circ. Mgr.-Carol Nowotarski, Production Mgr.-John Pearce
Editorial Description: A continuing education source for the health care professional involved in the field of clinical nutrition.
General Info: Yr. Est. 1974, Monthly, Letrpr. press, 8 pages, ISSN: 0732-0167
Subscriptions: Indv. $48, Can. $48, For. $73, $5/copy
Acquistions: Publication Bought, Publication Sold
Circulation: Total-8,000
List Rental: Actives: $125/M

Nutrition & the M.D.
See: NUTRITION

Nutrition Forum
See: NUTRITION

Nutrition Funding Report, The
Consumer, Association

Publishing Co: Nutrition Legislation Services, PO Box 75035, Washington, DC 20013-0035; Title Tel # (202) 488-8879 Title Fax # (202) 554-3116
Personnel: Publisher-Lenora Moragne, PH.D, Editor-Lenora Moragne, Ph.D., Circ. Mgr.-Nora Champion, Ph.D., Circ. Mgr., Production Mgr.-Nora Champion
Editorial Description: A monthly guide to locating funds,publications, public policy documents, scholarships and fellowships, information and other resources for nutrition and health research and service initiatives.
General Info: Yr. Est. 1986, Monthly, Trim Size-8½ x 11, Sheetfed press, 8 pages, ISSN: 0892-1474, 2 Color, Other
Subscriptions: Indv. $45, Inst. $45, Can. $50, For. $50, $5/copy
Acquistions: Publication Bought

Nutrition Legislation News
See: NUTRITION

Nutrition News
See: NUTRITION

Nutrition Notes
See: NUTRITION

Nutrition Research Newsletter
See: NUTRITION

Nutrition Week
See: NUTRITION

OASAS Today
Business

Publishing Co: New York State Dept. Div. of Substance Abuse Services, 1450 Western Ave., Albany, NY 12203- 352; Title Tel # (518) 457-6040 Title Fax # (518) 474-3004
Personnel: Editor-Richard Chody, Co-Editor-Leslie Connor, Art Dir.-Terri Novak
Editorial Description: Features current issues on alcoholism & substance abuse in New York State.
General Info: (Formerly Outlook), Yr. Est. 1980, Bi-monthly, Trim Size-8½ x 11, Offset press, 20 pages, 2 Color, Recycled, Saddle-stitched
Subscriptions: Free
Circulation: Total-10,000
Advertising: Inquire for rates.

OR Manager
Business   **CPM: $308**

Publishing Co: OR Manager, PO Box 17487, Boulder, CO 80308-0487; Title Tel # (303) 442-1661 Title Fax # (303) 442-5960
Personnel: Publisher-Elinor Schrader, Editor-Pat Patterson, Adv. Dir.-John R. Schmus
Editorial Description: Provides information for managers of operating rooms. Topics include human resources, finance, health care policy, environmental control, and more.
General Info: Yr. Est. 1985, Monthly, Trim Size-8¼ x 11, Sheetfed press, 28 pages, ISSN: 8756-8047, Ind/Abs/Online: CINAHL, Hosp.Lit.Ind., HP&Adb, 25% ads, 4 Color, Coated, Saddle-stitched
Subscriptions: Indv. $68, Can. $74, For. $78, $10/copy
Circulation: Total-3,400
Advertising: $1,050.
List Rental: Actives: 3,000, $300/M
Printing Co: Account Manager: Doug Groskopf; Alpine Printing, 5620b Kendall Ct, Arvada, CO 80002-2730 Tel # (303) 424-2089, Fax # (303) 424-8491

OSERS News in Print

Publishing Co: Clearinghouse on the Handicapped, 330 C St. SW Switzer Bldg., Rm. 3132, Washington, DC 20202-0001; Title Tel # (202) 732-1241
Personnel: Editor-Jean Nathanson
Editorial Description: Focuses on federal activities affecting people with disabilities & new developments in the information field.
General Info: Yr. Est. 1967, Bi-monthly

OSHA Compliance Encyclopedia & Newsletter
See: SAFETY

OSHA Week
See: INDUSTRIAL RELATIONS/PERSONNEL

OT Week
See: MEDICINE

Occupational Safety & Health Reporter
See: SAFETY

Officers Call
See: MILITARY & NAVAL

Ohio Health Law Update
See: LAW

Ohio Health Letter
Consumer

Publishing Co: Ohio Health Letter, 224 Pleasant St, Yellow Springs, OH 45387-2015; Title Tel # (513) 767-9361
Personnel: Editor-Jeffrey Simons
Editorial Description: Health and fitness information and advice.
General Info: Monthly
Subscriptions: Indv. $24

Oklahoma Health Bulletin

Publishing Co: Oklahoma State Dept. of Health, 1000 NE 10th St, Oklahoma City, OK 73117-1299; Title Tel # (405) 271-5601
Personnel: Editor-Shelli Stidham, Production Mgr.-Nancy Ballard
Editorial Description: Public health related news.
General Info: Quarterly, Trim Size-11 x 17, Offset press, 8 pages, 2 Color
Subscriptions: Free
Circulation: (100% controlled), Total-3,000

Older Americans Report
See: SENIOR CITIZENS

On the Level
Consumer, Association

Publishing Co: Vestibular Disorders Association, PO Box 4467, Portland, OR 97208-4467; Title Tel # (503) 229-7705 Title Fax # (503) 229-8064
Personnel: Editor-Jerry Underwood
Editorial Description: Quarterly newsletter for people with inner-ear balance disorders.
General Info: Yr. Est. 1985, Quarterly, Trim Size-8½ x 11, 10 pages, No Color
Subscriptions: Indv. $15, For. $15
Circulation: Total-6,000

On Your Mark
See: SUGAR

One Spirit
See: PHILOSOPHY

Open Minds, the Behavioral Health Industry Analyst
See: PSYCHOLOGY

Optimist

Publishing Co: AIDS Project Los Angeles, 6721 Romaine St, Los Angeles, CA 90038-2417; Title Tel # (213) 993-1600 Title Fax # (213) 962-3475
Personnel: Editor-Paul Serchia
Editorial Description: Optimist, produced by the Communications Dept. of AIDS Project Los Angeles & volunteer contributors, presents news about AIDS & programs of AIDS Project Los Angeles to the general public.
General Info: Yr. Est. 1989, Quarterly, Web press, 24 pages, 2 Color, Newsprint, Saddle-stitched
Circulation: Total-70,000
Printing Co: Rodgers & McDonald Graphics, 1141 Sandhill Ave # 6270, Carson, CA 90746-1314 Tel # (310) 604-1012

Oregon Health Sciences University News

Publishing Co: Oregon Health Sciences University Foundation, 1121 SW Salmon Street, Portland, OR 97201-3098 Tel # (503) 228-3548 Fax # (503) 228-3548; Title Tel # (503) 225-8231
Personnel: Editor-Marlys Levin Pierson
Editorial Description: News and events of Oregon's only academic health institution.
General Info: Quarterly, Trim Size-11 x 17, 12 pages
Circulation: Total-27,500

Oregon Heartline
Association

Publishing Co: American Heart Assn., Oregon Affiliate, Inc., 1425 NE Irving St Ste 100, Portland, OR 97232-4201 Tel # (503) 233-0100; Title Tel # (503) 226-2575
Personnel: Editor-Kelly Leer
Editorial Description: Assn. activities and programs; issues relating to cardiovascular disease.
General Info: (Formerly Pacesetter), Yr. Est. 1976, Quarterly, Trim Size-8½ x 11, Web press, 16 pages, 2 Color, Newsprint, Saddle-stitched
Circulation: (100% controlled), Total-11,000

Organic Consumer Report

Publishing Co: Eden Ranch, PO Box 370, Topanga, CA 90290-0370; Title Tel # (213) 455-2065
Personnel: Editor-Patricia Moore
General Info: Weekly, 2 pages
Subscriptions: Indv. $5

Ortho Newsletter
Association

Publishing Co: American Orthopsychiatric Assn., 330 7th Ave., 18th Floor, New York, NY 10001-5010 Tel # (212) 564-5930 Fax # (212) 564-6180; Title Tel # (212) 354-5770
Personnel: Editor-Dr. Herbert Sohn, Circ. Mgr.-Terri Thal, Adv. Dir.-Muriel Benjamin
Editorial Description: Trends & issues in mental health.
General Info: Tri-annually, Trim Size-7⅛ x 9¼, Sheetfed press, 40 pages
Circulation: Total-10,500
List Rental: Actives: $45/M
Printing Co: Boyd Printing Co., Inc., 49 Sheridan Ave, Albany, NY 12210-2735 Tel # (518) 436-9686, Fax # (518) 436-7433

Our Voice
Consumer

Publishing Co: Our Voice, 365 W 25th St Apt 13e, New York, NY 10001-5816; Title Tel # (212) 929-4299 Title Fax # (212) 929-4099
Personnel: Mng. Editor-Midge Kovacs
Editorial Description: Published for the Spasmodic Dysphonia patient and the medical professionals who serve them. Covers medical developments concerning this voice disorder and ideas for coping.
General Info: Yr. Est. 1990, Semi-annually, Trim Size-8½ x 11, Sheetfed press, 6 pages, ISSN: 1064-0207, No Color
Subscriptions: Indv. $20, Inst. $20, Can. $22, For. $22

Outcomes Measurement & Management

Publishing Co: Zitter Group, The, 90 New Montgomery St., Suite #820, San Francisco, CA 94105; Title Tel # (415) 495-2450 Title Fax # (415) 495-2453
Personnel: Publisher-Mark Zitter, Publications Director-Susan Keller, Mag. Ed.-Karl Thiel
Editorial Description: Outcomes information dedicated to improvement in health care & health care delivery.
General Info: Yr. Est. 1991, Bi-monthly

Outlook
Business, Consumer

Publishing Co: Piact/Path, 4 Nickerson St., Seattle, WA 98109-1699; Title Tel # (206) 285-3500 Title Fax # (206) 285-6619
Personnel: Editor-Jacqueline Sherris
Editorial Description: Features international drug regulatory decisions, safety issues & other reproductive health related articles.
General Info: Yr. Est. 1983, Quarterly, Trim Size-8 x 10, Offset press, 10 pages, ISSN: 0737-3732, 2 Color, Coated
Subscriptions: Indv. $20, Free To Qualified Recipient
Circulation: Total-16,000
Printing Co: Evergreen Printing, 4246 24th Ave W, Seattle, WA 98199-1216

Over 50 and Fit

Publishing Co: Over 50 and Fit, 1202 E. Pike Street Suite #740, P.O. Box 22050, Seattle, WA 98122; Title Tel # (206) 527-6240 Title Fax # (206) 527-6651
Personnel: Publisher-Alan A. Cooper, Editor-Karin T. Collins
Editorial Description: The newsletter for active adults!
General Info: Yr. Est. 1995, Monthly, Trim Size-8$\frac{1}{2}$ x 11, 8 pages, ISSN: 1078-5035, 2 Color, Matte
Subscriptions: Indv. $49, Can. $58, $6/copy

Ovulation Method Newsletter
Business, Association

Publishing Co: Ovulation Method Teachers Assn., Box 10-1780, Anchorage, AK 99510-1780; Title Tel # (907) 343-4623
Editorial Description: Fertility, natural family planning and related health issues.
General Info: Quarterly, Mimeo press, 12 pages
Subscriptions: Indv. $10, $3/copy
Circulation: Total-500
Advertising: Inquire for rates.

PAA Affairs
Association

Publishing Co: Population Assn. of America, 1722 N. Street, NW, Washington, DC 20036; Title Tel # (202) 429-0891
Personnel: Editor-Felicia Le Clere, Adv. Dir.-Kathy London
Editorial Description: Information about association activities.
General Info: Yr. Est. 1972, Quarterly, Trim Size-8$\frac{1}{2}$ x 11, Sheetfed press, 12 pages, No Color, Newsprint
Subscriptions: Indv. $5, Free With Membership
Circulation: Total-3,000
List Rental: Rents Lists
Printing Co: Boyd Printing Co., Inc., 49 Sheridan Ave, Albany, NY 12210-2735 Tel # (518) 436-9686, Fax # (518) 436-7433

PANdemic
See: RELIGIOUS & THEOLOGICAL

PBC Comprehensive Health Briefs
Business, Consumer

Publishing Co: Publishing & Business Consultants, 101 W. 64th St. Unit #3, Inglewood, CA 90302-1255 Tel # (213) 732-3477 Fax # (213) 732-3477
Personnel: Publisher, Editor-Andeson Atia
General Info: Quarterly, 60 pages, ISSN: 1059-2069
Subscriptions: Indv. $180
Advertising: Inquire for rates.

PSR Reports
See: ENVIRONMENT & ECOLOGY

PWA Coalition Newsline

Publishing Co: People With AIDS Coalition (N.Y.), 245 8th Ave # 316, New York, NY 10011-1607; Title Tel # (212) 532-0290 Title Fax # (212) 447-1508
Personnel: Editor-Bree Scott-Hartland, Editorial Asst.-Susan Shaw, Production Mgr.-Laura Antoniou
Editorial Description: News and information for persons with AIDS and those who are HIV positive.
General Info: Yr. Est. 1985, Monthly, Trim Size-8$\frac{1}{2}$ x 11, Web press, 72 pages, No Color, Newsprint
Subscriptions: Indv. $35, Inst. $35, Free To Qualified Recipient
Circulation: Total-14,000
Advertising: Accepts Inserts.
Printing Co: Kimmel and Milas Advertising, 17-10 River Rd Ste 4d, Fair Lawn, NJ 07410-1250 Tel # (201) 796-5855, Fax # (201) 796-6005

Pacific Report
Association

Publishing Co: Canadian Cancer Society-B.C. Div., 565 W. 10th Ave., Vancouver, BC V5Z 4J4 Canada Fax # (604) 870-4533; Title Tel # (604) 872-4400 Title Fax # (604) 879-4533
Personnel: Editor-Sandra Bishop
Editorial Description: Reports society efforts of education, fundraising, research, patient services & public relations. Focus on cancer prevention.
General Info: (Formerly Provincial News), Yr. Est. 1984, Semi-annually, Trim Size-8$\frac{1}{2}$ x 11, Offset press, 8 pages, 4 Color, Matte, Saddle-stitched
Subscriptions: Free
Acquistions: Publication Bought
Circulation: (100% controlled), Total-7,500
Advertising: Accepts Inserts.
Printing Co: Hazeldine Press Ltd., 55 W. 8th Ave., Vancouver, BC V5Y 1N1 Canada Tel # (604) 872-0611, Fax # (604) 325-1559

Paraelite

Publishing Co: Canadian Paraplegic Assn. -New Brunswick, 65 Brunswick St., Fredericton, NB E3B 1G5 Canada; Title Tel # (506) 458-1189
Personnel: Editor-Linda Stephenson
General Info: Bi-monthly

Parapsychology, Hypnosis, & Alternative Health
See: PARAPSYCHOLOGY

Paratracks

Publishing Co: Canadian Paraplegic Assn., Manitoba, 825 Sherbrook Street, Winnipeg, MB R3A 1M5 Canada; Title Tel # (204) 786-4753 Title Fax # (204) 786-1140
Editorial Description: Discusses activities of Association in rehabilitation of paraplegics and other disabled persons, programs, prosthetic appliances and equipment, and improvements in the welfare field.
General Info: Yr. Est. 1963, Quarterly
Circulation: Total-900

Parkinsonian Speak-Out

Publishing Co: Parkinsonian Speak-Out, 55 Merrick St, Rumford, RI 02916-2520; Title Tel # (401) 521-1025
Personnel: Publisher-Robert Bernen
General Info: Yr. Est. 1987, Monthly
Subscriptions: Indv. $14

Parkinson's Disease Update
See: MEDICINE

Part A News

Publishing Co: United Communications Group, 11300 Rockville Pike, Ste. 1100, Rockville, MD 20852-3030 Tel # (301) 816-8950 Fax # (301) 816-8945; Title Tel # (301) 961-8700 Title Fax # (301) 916-8666
Personnel: Publisher-Richard Hadley, Editor-Judy Haberek, Circ. Mgr.-Sharon Welch
Editorial Description: Washington news, practical strategies for maximizine Medicare Part A, PPS payments.
General Info: (Formerly Prospective Payment Guide), Yr. Est. 1983, Monthly, Trim Size-8$\frac{1}{2}$ x 11, Offset press, 8 pages, ISSN: 8756-3274, 2 Color, Newsprint
Subscriptions: Indv. $379, $30/copy
Acquistions: Publication Bought
List Rental: Actives: $125/M

Part B Answer Book
Business

Publishing Co: United Communications Group, 11300 Rockville Pike, Ste. 1100, Rockville, MD 20852-3030; Title Tel # (301) 816-8950 Title Fax # (301) 816-8945
Personnel: Publisher-Richard Hadley, Editor-Roxanne Bolinger
Editorial Description: Reference formatted medicare billing rules for physicians.
General Info: Yr. Est. 1992, Monthly, Looseleaf
Subscriptions: Indv. $245, Inst. $245
List Rental: Rents Lists

Part B News
Business

Publishing Co: United Communications Group, 11300 Rockville Pike, Ste. 1100, Rockville, MD 20852-3030; Title Tel # (301) 816-8950 Title Fax # (301) 816-8945
Personnel: Publisher-Richard Hadley, Editor-Carol Monaco, Lit. Ed.-Diane Turner, Circ. Mgr.-Monica Brown
Editorial Description: Washington news, practical strategies for maximizing Medicare Part B physician reimbursement.
General Info: Yr. Est. 1987, Bi-weekly, Trim Size-8$\frac{1}{2}$ x 11, 12 pages, ISSN: 0893-8121
Subscriptions: Indv. $446, Inst. $446, $19/copy
List Rental: Rents Lists

Participaper
Consumer, Association

Publishing Co: Ontario Federation for the Cerebral Palsied, 1630 Lawrence Ave. W., #104, Toronto, ON M6L 1C5 Canada
Personnel: Editor-Mark Evans
General Info: (Formerly Proud & Happy Times), Yr. Est. 1978, Quarterly, 12 pages
Subscriptions: Indv. $4

Pathways to Health
Association

Publishing Co: A.R.E. Clinic, 4017 N 40th St, Phoenix, AZ 85018-5204; Title Tel # (602) 955-0551
Personnel: Editor-Scott Brady, Circ. Mgr.-Anna Blackstone
Editorial Description: Holistic health tips, research articles, medical news, Edgar Cayce principles.
General Info: Yr. Est. 1979, Quarterly, Trim Size-8$\frac{1}{2}$ x 11, Sheetfed press, 8 pages, Color, Newsprint
Subscriptions: Indv. $22
Circulation: (100% controlled), Total-32,000

Peak Performance

Publishing Co: United Research, 1020 108th Ave NE Ste 102, Bellevue, WA 98004-4310; Title Tel # (206) 451-8337
Personnel: Editor-Jack Smith
Editorial Description: Health & athletic club marketing.
General Info: Semi-monthly
Subscriptions: Indv. $189

Pediatric Report's Child Health Newsletter
See: MEDICINE

Pennsylvania Nurse
See: NURSING

Periscoop   CPM: $258

Publishing Co: Association pour la Sante Publique de Quebec, 3958 Rue Dandurand, Montreal, PQ H1X 1P7 Canada; Title Tel # (514) 593-9939 Title Fax # (514) 593-4554
General Info: Yr. Est. 1995, Quarterly
Subscriptions: Indv. $25, Inst. $100
Circulation: Total-3,100, Readership-6,000
Advertising: $800. Accepts Inserts.

Perrin & Treggett's
Review   *Consumer*

Publishing Co: Perrin & Treggett Booksellers, 937 Jamestown Rd., Hightstown, NJ 08520-5645; Title Tel # (609) 497-1122
Personnel: Editor-Thomas Perrin
Editorial Description: Commentary on books covering all aspects of all addictions: alcohol, drugs, work, sex, codependency.
General Info: (Formerly COA Review), Yr. Est. 1983, Bi-monthly, Trim Size-8½ x 11, Letrpr. press, 4 pages, ISSN: 0730-1395, No Color
Subscriptions: Indv. $3
Circulation: (100% controlled), Total-15,000
Advertising: Inquire for rates. Accepts Inserts.

Personal Fitness

Publishing Co: Cromwell-Sloan Pub. Co., 63 Vine Rd, Stamford, CT 06905-2012; Title Tel # (203) 323-6839
Personnel: Publisher-Marlene Cromwell, Editor-Paul Sloan
Editorial Description: Nutrition, exercise, stress management, holistic health, tips on fitness motivation.
General Info: Yr. Est. 1983, Monthly, Trim Size-8½ x 11, Offset press, 8 pages, ISSN: 0738-7857, 2 Color
Subscriptions: Indv. $47
Acquistions: Publication Bought

Perspectives on
Addictions Nursing   *Scholarly*   CPM: $268

Publishing Co: Natl. Nurses Society on Addictions, 4101 Lake Boone Trail, Ste. 201, Raleigh, NC 27607; Title Tel # (919) 787-5181
Personnel: Editor-Christine Vourakis, Circ. Dir.-Kay Warskow, Production Dir.-Chris Bennett, Adv. Dir.-Kathryn Checea
Editorial Description: Includes clinical and research content as well as information about the NNSA, the field of nursing, and the specialty of addictions nursing.
General Info: Yr. Est. 1984, Bi-monthly, Trim Size-8½ x 11, 12 pages, ISSN: 1057-1639, 2 Color
Subscriptions: Inst. $20, Free With Membership
Circulation: Total-1,100
Advertising: $295.
List Rental: Actives: 1,000, $200/M

Perspectives in
Respiratory Nursing   *Association*   CPM: $196

Publishing Co: Respiratory Nursing Society, 4700 W. Lake Ave., Glenview, IL 60025; Title Tel # (708) 375-4721 Title Fax # (708) 375-4777
Personnel: Editor-Michele Geiger-Bronsky, Circ. Dir.-Kay Warskow, Production Dir.-Chris Bennett, Adv. Dir.-Kathryn Checea
Editorial Description: Features RNS news and educational topics related to repiratory nursing health care.
General Info: Yr. Est. 1990, Quarterly, Trim Size-8½ x 11, 12 pages
Subscriptions: Indv. $35, Inst. $35, Can. $40, For. $40, Free With Membership
Circulation: Total-1,500
Advertising: $295.
List Rental: Actives: $50/M
Printing Co: Sundance Press, 817 E 18th St, Tucson, AZ 85719-6614 Tel # (602) 622-5233, Fax # (602) 620-1593

Pet Partners Newsletter
See: ANIMALS

Pharmacy News
See: DRUGS & PHARMACEUTICALS

Physician Laboratory
Regulations Manual   *Business*

Publishing Co: Thompson Publishing Group, 747 Third Ave., New York, NY 10017 Tel # (212) 888-7220; Title Tel # (212) 888-9765 Title Fax # (212) 486-3400
Personnel: Publisher-Kenneth Gesser, Editor-Delicia Honen, Production Mgr.-R.D. Whitney, Mktg. Dir.-Kevin Mahon
Editorial Description: Federal regulations for physician office laboratories-from the health care financing adminstration the centers for disease control and prevention, the FDA and other organizations.
General Info: Yr. Est. 1990, Monthly, 8 pages, 2 Color
Subscriptions: Indv. $379

Physician Office Lab
News   *Business*

Publishing Co: United Communications Group, 11300 Rockville Pike, Ste. 1100, Rockville, MD 20852-3030; Title Tel # (301) 816-8950 Title Fax # (301) 816-8945
Personnel: Publisher-Richard Hadley, Editor-Lori Launi
Editorial Description: Covers CLIA, OSHA, Medicare rules affecting physician in office labs.
General Info: Yr. Est. 1992, Monthly
Subscriptions: Indv. $123, Inst. $123
List Rental: Rents Lists

Physicians Managed Care Report
See: MEDICINE

Physician's Patient
Newsletter   *Consumer*

Publishing Co: Doctor's Press, The, 1866 Colonial Village Lane, Lancaster, PA 17605-0488; Title Tel # (717) 393-1000 Title Fax # (717) 393-5752
Personnel: Publisher-Cynthia Young, Editor-Kim Conlin, Adv. Dir.-Rem Jackson, Art Dir.-Daniel Hill
Editorial Description: Newsletter for physicians, particularly Family Practice Specialists and General Practioners, to use to market their practices by providing health information that educates patients and encourages use of the services offered by the practice.
General Info: Yr. Est. 1983, Quarterly, Trim Size-8½ x 11, Web press, 4 pages, 2 Color, Matte

Physiotherapy Today   *Association*   CPM: $250

Publishing Co: Ontario Physiotherapy Assn., 55 Eglinton Avenue East, Suite #210, Toronto, ON M4P 1G8 Canada Tel # (416) 322-6866 Fax # (416) 322-6705; Title Tel # (416) 391-4700 Title Fax # (416) 391-4702
Personnel: Editor-Don Butcher, Production Mgr.-Caroline Snow
Editorial Description: General information on and job and educational opportunities in physiotherapy.
General Info: Bi-monthly, Trim Size-8½ x 11, Offset press, 12 pages, 50% ads, 2 Color, Newsprint
Subscriptions: Indv. $25
Circulation: Total-3,200
Advertising: $800. Accepts Inserts.
Printing Co: Brock Graphics & Printing, 1755 Plummer Street, Unit # 21, Pickering, ON L1W 3S1 Canada

Pink Sheet: Prescription and OTC pharmaceuticals
See: DRUGS & PHARMACEUTICALS

Planetalk   *Association*

Publishing Co: Planetree Health Resource Ctr., 2040 Webster St, San Francisco, CA 94115-2330; Title Tel # (415) 923-3680
Editorial Description: A pub. of Planetree-a consumer health organization.
General Info: Yr. Est. 1981, Semi-annually, Trim Size-8½ x 11, Offset press, 4 pages, 2 Color
Circulation: Total-5,000

PlantWise
See: GARDENING & HORTICULTURE

Plastic Surgery Outlook
See: MEDICINE

Podiatrist's Patient
Newsletter   *Consumer*

Publishing Co: Doctor's Press, The, 1866 Colonial Village Lane, Lancaster, PA 17605-0488 Tel # (717) 393-1000 Fax # (717) 393-5752; Title Tel # (717) 393-1010
Personnel: Publisher-Cynthia Young, Editor-Kim Conlin, Adv. Dir.-Rem Jackson, Art Dir.-Daniel Hill
Editorial Description: Newsletter for podiatrists to use to market the practice by providing foor health information thta educates patients and encourages of use of services offered by the practice.
General Info: Yr. Est. 1983, Quarterly, Trim Size-8½ x 11, Offset press, 4 pages, 2 Color, Matte

Popline
See: ENVIRONMENT & ECOLOGY

Portable Practitioner: Opportunities in the Healing Arts *Business*

Publishing Co: Monica Gruler & Co., PO Box 2095, Petoskey, MI 49770-2095; Title Fax # (616) 347-0409
Personnel: Publisher, Editor-Monica Gruler
Editorial Description: Worldwide resource and networking guide for health and healing arts professionals.
General Info: Yr. Est. 1993, Quarterly, Trim Size-8½ x 11, 12 pages, Matte
Subscriptions: For. $25, Free With Membership
Circulation: Total-2,000
Advertising: Inquire for rates. Accepts Inserts.
List Rental: Rents Lists

Positive Living *Consumer*

Publishing Co: AIDS Project Los Angeles, 6721 Romaine St, Los Angeles, CA 90038-2417 Tel # (213) 993-1600; Title Tel # (213) 993-1470
Editorial Description: Health issues for HIV Positive people.
General Info: Monthly

Practical Gourmet See: TRAVEL

Primum Non Nocere

Publishing Co: U.S. Section-World Fed. of Doctors Who Respect Human Life, PO Box 508, Oak Park, IL 60303-0508; Title Tel # (708) 848-3835
Personnel: Publisher, Editor-Herbert Ratner, Circ. Mgr.-Michael Dovel, Production Mgr.-Andrew Scholberg
Editorial Description: Newsletter in the Hippocratic tradition. Topics include abortion & euthanasia.
General Info: Yr. Est. 1974, Trim Size-8½ x 11, 12 pages
Subscriptions: Indv. $10
Circulation: Total-1,400

Priorities

Publishing Co: American Council on Science and Health, 18th Floor, 1995 Broadway, New York, NY 10023; Title Tel # (212) 362-7044 Title Fax # (212) 362-4919
Personnel: Editor-Elizabeth Whelan
General Info: Yr. Est. 1978, Quarterly
Subscriptions: Indv. $25

Professional Regulation News *Business, Association*

Publishing Co: Natl. Organization for Competency Assurance, 1200 19th St NW Ste 300, Washington, DC 20036-2412; Title Tel # (202) 857-1165 Title Fax # (202) 223-4579
Personnel: Publisher-Michael S. Ham, Editor-Sean Casey, Circ. Mgr.-Susan Davies
Editorial Description: News & trends in professional licensing, certification, and competence.
General Info: Yr. Est. 1991, 10x/yr., Trim Size-17 x 11, Desktop press, 4 pages, ISSN: 0741-4749, No Color, Newsprint
Subscriptions: Indv. $20
Circulation: (100% controlled), Total-1,000
Printing Co: Tuxedo Press, 3501 Windom Rd, Brentwood, MD 20722-1095 Tel # (301) 864-6400

Professional Report *Association*

Publishing Co: National Rehabilitation Counseling Assn., 1910 Association Dr # 206, Reston, VA 22091-1502; Title Tel # (703) 836-7677
Personnel: Editor-Dr. Richard Wolfe
General Info: Bi-monthly

Progress in Public Health

Publishing Co: Ohio Dept. of Health, 246 N. High St., P.O. Box 118, Columbus, OH 43215-2429; Title Tel # (614) 462-8562
Personnel: Editor-Shawn Summers, Art Dir.-Jean Thomas
Editorial Description: Communications vehicle from Ohio Department of Health central office to local health departments and public health personnel throughout the state.
General Info: (Formerly Ohio's Health), Quarterly, Trim Size-8½ x 11, Offset press, 8 pages, No Color
Circulation: Total-5,000

Projection *Association*

Publishing Co: Addiction Research Foundation, 33 Russell St., Toronto, ON M5S 2S1 Canada Fax # (416) 593-4694; Title Tel # (416) 595-6059 Title Fax # (416) 595-5017
Editorial Description: Reviews & assessment of A/V material on drug & alcohol use & abuse.
General Info: Yr. Est. 1972, Bi-monthly, Trim Size-8½ x 11, Letrpr. press, 7 pages, ISSN: 0229-2947, No Color, Looseleaf
Subscriptions: Indv. $18, Can. $18, For. $18, $2/copy
Circulation: Total-600

Prospective Payment Guide

Publishing Co: United Communications Group, 11300 Rockville Pike, Ste. 1100, Rockville, MD 20852-3030 Tel # (301) 816-8950 Fax # (301) 816-8945; Title Tel # (301) 656-6666
Personnel: Publisher-Bruce Levenson, Editor-Ed Peskowitz, Production Mgr.-Frank Joseph
Editorial Description: Guidance for healthcare institutions on PPS.
General Info: Monthly
Subscriptions: Indv. $299
List Rental: Rents Lists

Psychopharmacology Update See: PSYCHOLOGY

Psychotherapy Letter, The See: PSYCHOLOGY

Public Assistance & Welfare Trends/State Capitals See: SOCIAL SERVICES & WELFARE

Public Citizen Health Letter *Consumer, Association*

Publishing Co: Public Citizen, 2000 P St., NW, #610, Washington, DC 20036
Editorial Description: Covers health issues such as public policy, environmental health, safer workplaces, etc.
General Info: Yr. Est. 1971, Monthly, ISSN: 0882-598X
Subscriptions: Indv. $18, Inst. $18, Can. $28, For. $38
Circulation: Total-90,000
List Rental: List Management Co.: AZ Marketing Services, Inc., 31 River Rd, Cos Cob, CT 06807-2745 Tel # (203) 629-8088, Fax # (203) 661-1068

Public Health Letter

Publishing Co: Los Angeles Health Services, 313 N Figueroa St, Los Angeles, CA 90012-2659; Title Tel # (213) 974-7941
Personnel: Editor-Robert Gates
Editorial Description: Public health and AIDS.

Public Health/State Capitals *Consumer*

Publishing Co: Wakeman/Walworth, 300 N. Washington St., Alexandria, VA 22314-2530 Fax # (703) 549-1372; Title Tel # (703) 549-8606
Personnel: Publisher-Keyes Walworth
Editorial Description: Devoted to all state issues affecting public health including Medicaid legislation, AIDS disclosure and testing, drug programs, smoking restrictions, etc.
General Info: (Formerly Public Health from the State Capitals), Yr. Est. 1946, Weekly, Trim Size-8½ x 11, Offset press, 10 pages, ISSN: 0734-1156, No Color
Subscriptions: Indv. $265, Inst. $212, Can. $235, For. $255

Pulse *Association*

Publishing Co: American School Health Association, PO Box 708, 7263 State Rte. 43, Kent, OH 44240-0708
Editorial Description: School health programs concerned with the health and well-being of children and youth.
General Info: Quarterly
List Rental: List Management Co.: MGI-Marketing General Inc., 105 Oronoco St., Alexandria, VA 22314-2015 Tel # (703) 739-1000, Actives: 3,860, $85/M

Pure Facts *Consumer, Association*

Publishing Co: Feingold Association of the U.S., PO Box 6550, Alexandria, VA 22306-0550; Title Tel # (703) 768-3287
Personnel: Editor-Jane Hersey
Editorial Description: Relationship between foods, food additives & behavior/learning problems.
General Info: Yr. Est. 1981, 10x/yr., Trim Size-8½ x 11, 6 pages, No Color, Newsprint
Subscriptions: Indv. $25
Circulation: Total-10,000

Quality Care Advocate *Business, Association*

Publishing Co: National Citizens' Coalition for Nursing Home Reform, 1424 16th St. NW, Ste 202, Washington, DC 20036 Tel # (202) 332-2275 Fax # (202) 332-2949; Title Tel # (202) 393-2018 Title Fax # (202) 393-4122
Personnel: Editor-Nicole Gudzowsky
Editorial Description: To improve quality of care and life for nursing home, board, and home care residents nationwide.
General Info: Yr. Est. 1986, Bi-monthly, Trim Size-8½ x 11, Sheetfed press, 12 pages, No Color, Recycled, Saddle-stitched
Subscriptions: Indv. $45, Inst. $45, Can. $45, For. $45, Free With Membership
Circulation: Readership-30,000
Advertising: Inquire for rates.
Printing Co: Leesburg Printing Co., 1100 North Blvd E, Leesburg, FL 34748-5350 Tel # (904) 787-3348, Fax # (904) 787-2210

Quarterly Community Health Center News *Association*

Publishing Co: Community Health Center, 635 Main St, Middletown, CT 06457-2730
General Info: Yr. Est. 1977, Quarterly
Subscriptions: $3/copy
Circulation: Total-14,000

RBRVS Fee Schedule : A Plain-English Guide *Business*

Publishing Co: United Communications Group, 11300 Rockville Pike, Ste. 1100, Rockville, MD 20852-3030; Title Tel # (301) 816-8950 Title Fax # (301) 816-8945
Personnel: Publisher-Richard D. Hadley, Editor-Roxanne Bolinger
Editorial Description: Helps physicians understand new Medicare RBRVS Fee Schedule and calculate their payments under it.
General Info: Yr. Est. 1991, Monthly, Looseleaf
Subscriptions: Indv. $370, Inst. $370
List Rental: Rents Lists

RESNA News
Association

Publishing Co: RESNA Technical Assistance Project, 1700 N. Moore St., Ste. 1540, Arlington, VA 22209; Title Tel # (703) 524-6686 Title Fax # (202) 223-4579
Personnel: Publisher-Patricia Horner, Editor-Lynn Phillips, Circ. Mgr.-Susan Leone
Editorial Description: Information about assistive technology programs and other issues related to RESNA members.
General Info: Yr. Est. 1982, Bi-monthly, Offset press, 16 pages, ISSN: 0882-2476, 2 Color, Newsprint
Subscriptions: Indv. $25, $2/copy
Circulation: Total-1,500
Advertising: Inquire for rates. Accepts Inserts.
List Rental: Actives $100/M
Printing Co: Dependable Printing Co., 5349 46th Ave, Hyattsville, MD 20781-2309 Tel # (301) 779-9200

Radiance Technique Newsletter, The
Association **CPM: $150**

Publishing Co: Radiance Technique Association International, Inc., PO Box 40570, Saint Petersburg, FL 33743-0570; Title Tel # (813) 392-9278
Personnel: Editor-Marvelle Lightfields, Editor-F.W. Wright
Editorial Description: For members of the Radiance Technique Association International & others interested in the Radiance Technique.
General Info: (Formerly Reiki Journal, The), Yr. Est. 1980, 3x/yr., Trim Size-8½ x 11, Sheetfed press, 20 pages, ISSN: 1040-5836, 4% ads, Color, Coated, Saddle-stitched
Subscriptions: Indv. $10
Circulation: Total-1,000
Advertising: $150.

Radiological Health Bulletin
Business, Association

Publishing Co: Food & Drug Administration, 5600 Fishers La., Rockville, MD 20852-1750; Title Tel # (301) 443-5860 Title Fax # (301) 227-6834
Personnel: Editor-Mickie Kivel
Editorial Description: Information on food & drug administration programs & activities to protect the public health by preventing unneccesary exposure to ionizing & non-ionizing radiation.
General Info: (Formerly BRH Bulletin), Yr. Est. 1967, Monthly, Trim Size-8½ x 11, 4 pages
Subscriptions: Free To Qualified Recipient
Circulation: Total-4,500

Rampart
See: DISABILITY

Real Living with Diabetes

Publishing Co: Cobb Group, 9420 Bunsen Pky., Ste. 300, Louisville, KY 40220-4206 Fax # (502) 491-4200 Parent Co.-Ziff-Davis Publishing Co., New York; Title Tel # (502) 491-1900 Title Fax # (502) 491-5162
Personnel: Publisher-Tom Noland, Editor in Chief-Toni Bowers, Mktg. Dir.-Jim Heffley
Editorial Description: Practical help, sharing and inspiration for people with diabetes.
General Info: Yr. Est. 1994, Bi-monthly
Subscriptions: Indv. $20

Real Living with Multiple Sclerosis
Consumer

Publishing Co: Cobb Group, 9420 Bunsen Pky., Ste. 300, Louisville, KY 40220-4206 Fax # (502) 491-4200 Parent Co.-Ziff-Davis Publishing Co., New York; Title Tel # (502) 491-1900
Personnel: Publisher-Tom Noland, Editor-Toni Bowers
Editorial Description: To inform and energize those with MS.
General Info: Yr. Est. 1993, Monthly
Subscriptions: Indv. $39

Receivables Report
See: ACCOUNTING

Record, The
Association

Publishing Co: Alberta Health Records Association, Box 1752, Edmonton, AB T5J 2P1 Canada
General Info: (Formerly A.H.R.A. Record), Yr. Est. 1980, Bi-monthly, 25 pages
Subscriptions: Indv. $30
Circulation: Total-550

Reference Guide to Addiction Counseling
Business, Consumer

Publishing Co: Manisses Communications Group, Inc., PO Box 3357, Providence, RI 02906-0757 Fax # (401) 861-6370; Title Tel # (401) 831-6020 Title Fax # (401) 561-6370
Personnel: Publisher-Fraser Lang, Editor-Anne M. Christine, PhD, Circ. Mgr.-Deb Zajas, Mktg. Dir.-Betty Lang
Editorial Description: Comprehensive guide designed to help counselors and other mental health professionals stay up-to-date.
General Info: Yr. Est. 1991, Annually, Looseleaf
Subscriptions: Indv. $198, Inst. $198, Can. $208, For. $238
Circulation: Total-1,000
List Rental: Rents Lists

Reference Guide to Counseling Children & Adolescents
See: CHILDREN

Reference Guide to Managing Addiction Programs
Business

Publishing Co: Manisses Communications Group, Inc., PO Box 3357, Providence, RI 02906-0757; Title Tel # (401) 831-6020 Title Fax # (401) 861-6370
Personnel: Publisher-Fraser Lang, Editor-Anne M. Christner, Ph.D., Adv. Dir.-Deb Zajas, Mktg. Dir.-Betty Lang
General Info: Yr. Est. 1992, Annually, 350 pages, Looseleaf
Subscriptions: Indv. $197, Inst. $198, Can. $218, For. $238
Circulation: Total-1,000
Printing Co: Newsletter Press, 76 Valley St, East Providence, RI 02914-4424 Tel # (401) 438-5352

Registry
Association

Publishing Co: National Registry of Emergency Medical Technicians, PO Box 29233, Columbus, OH 43229-0233; Title Tel # (614) 888-4484
Personnel: Editor-Teri Tatman
Editorial Description: Relates latest policies and procedures to all nationally registered EMTs.
General Info: Yr. Est. 1971, Semi-annually, 8 pages, 2 Color
Circulation: Total-92,000

Regulatory Watchdog Service
See: CONSUMER INTERESTS

Rehab Update
See: MEDICINE

Release
Association

Publishing Co: Sedona Institute, 4501 N 22nd St Ste 100, Phoenix, AZ 85016-4625; Title Tel # (602) 264-0123
Personnel: Publisher, Editor-Virginia Lloyd, Circ. Mgr., Production Mgr.-Janet Bechtel
Editorial Description: The newsletter of the Sedona Method, a stress elimination technique.
General Info: Yr. Est. 1978, Monthly, Trim Size-8½ x 11, Offset press, 6 pages, ISSN: 8755-3333, 2 Color
Circulation: Total-7,900

Report on Disability Programs
See: DISABILITY

Report on Medical Guidelines and Outcomes Research
See: HOSPITALS & NURSING HOMES

Resolve National Newsletter
See: FAMILY

Respiratory Care Manager
See: HOSPITALS & NURSING HOMES

Ridge News
Association

Publishing Co: Wheat Ridge Regional Ctr., 10285 Ridge Rd, Wheat Ridge, CO 80033-2399; Title Tel # (303) 424-7791
Personnel: Editor-Marie Muller
General Info: Yr. Est. 1953, Quarterly, Trim Size-8½ x 11, Offset press, 10 pages, No Color
Subscriptions: Indv. $2
Circulation: Total-1,727

Round Table
Consumer, Association

Publishing Co: Cerebral Palsy Association of B.C., 4423 Boundry Rd., Vancouver, BC V5R 2N3 Canada Tel # (604) 431-3833
Personnel: Editor-Beth Lawrence
General Info: Bi-monthly
Subscriptions: Indv. $10
Circulation: Total-1,000

Running & FitNews
Consumer, Association

Publishing Co: American Running & Fitness Association, 4405 East West Hwy Ste 405, Bethesda, MD 20814-4535; Title Tel # (301) 913-9517 Title Fax # (301) 913-9520
Personnel: Publisher-Susan Kalish, Editor-Trevor Smith, Circ. Mgr.-Lorie Allion
Editorial Description: Covers latest developments in sports medicine research, training, nutrition, and health information.
General Info: (Formerly Running & Fitness), Yr. Est. 1968, Monthly, Trim Size-8½ x 11, Web press, 8 pages, ISSN: 0898-5162, Ind/Abs/Online: Indexed, 2 Color
Subscriptions: Indv. $25, Inst. $40, Can. $40, For. $40, $3/copy
Circulation: Total-35,000, Readership-35,000
Advertising: Accepts Inserts.
List Rental: List Management Co.: Manager: Susan Kalish; Infocus Communications, 341 Victory Dr, Herndon, VA 22070-5217 Tel # (703) 834-0100, Fax # (703) 834-0110, Actives: 24,000, $70/M, Hotline: 15,000, $80/M, Expires: 15,000, $55/M
Printing Co: Newsletter Services, Inc., 9700 Philadelphia Court, Lanham, MD 20706 Tel # (301) 731-5200, Fax # (301) 731-5201

Ryan Advisory for Health, Facilities Governing Boards

Publishing Co: Advisory Newsletter Group, Inc., PO Box 90833, Washington, DC 20090-0833; Title Tel # (301) 656-1995
Personnel: Editor-Michael Ryan, Publisher, Circ. Mgr.-John Ryan
Editorial Description: Publication on trends, innovation & news for healthcare boards & executives.
General Info: Yr. Est. 1973, Monthly, Desktop press, 4 pages, 2 Color
Subscriptions: Indv. $59
Printing Co: Metro Graphics, Inc., 1211 Conn. Ave., NW, Suite 100, Washington, DC 20036 Tel # (202) 296-4424

SAHO News   *Association*

Publishing Co: Saskatchewan Assn of Health Organizations, 1445 Park St., Regina, SK S4N 4C5 Canada Tel # (306) 347-5500; Title Tel # (306) 525-2741 Title Fax # (306) 525-1960
Personnel: Editor-Loretta Fritz, Production Mgr., Art Dir.-Andrew Caswell
General Info: (Formerly Continuum of Care, The), Yr. Est. 1950, Quarterly, Trim Size-8½ x 11, Web press, 8 pages, 4 Color, Matte, Saddle-stitched
Subscriptions: Free In Designated Area
Circulation: Total-3,000
List Rental: Rents Lists
Printing Co: Printwest Communications, 1150 8th Ave., Regina, SK Canada Tel # (306) 525-2304

SB Current

Publishing Co: Spina Bifida & Hydrocephalus Assn. of Ontario, 35 McCaul Street, Suite 310, Toronto, ON M5T 1V7 Canada; Title Tel # (416) 979-5514 Title Fax # (416) 364-5437
Personnel: Editor-Marie Lloyd
General Info: Yr. Est. 1986, Quarterly, Trim Size-8½ x 11, Web press, 20 pages, 2 Color, Matte, Saddle-stitched
Subscriptions: Free With Membership
Acquistions: Publication Bought, Publication Sold
Circulation: Total-3,000

SIGBIO Newsletter
See: MEDICINE

SSM Network

Publishing Co: SSM Health Care System, 477 N Lindbergh Blvd, Saint Louis, MO 63141-7832 Tel # (314) 994-7910; Title Tel # (314) 994-7800 Title Fax # (314) 994-7900
Personnel: Editor-Carol Bales
General Info: Yr. Est. 1984, Quarterly
Circulation: Total-9,000

Safety & Health Bulletin
See: WATER SUPPLY, POWER & WASTE

Safety Is Elementary
See: SAFETY

St. Anthony's Coding for OB/GYN Reimbursement Newsletter

Publishing Co: St. Anthony Consulting Group, 11410 Isaac Newton Sq., N., Ste. 200, Alexandria, VA 22090-5012; Title Tel # (703) 549-0100 Title Fax # (703) 706-5700
Personnel: Publisher-Eugene Lorenz, Editor-Marlis McCollum, Circ. Mgr.-Kathi Lawson, Promotion Dir.-Elise Schumacher
Editorial Description: Coding tool for OB/GYN billing personnel.
General Info: Monthly
Subscriptions: Indv. $87
List Rental: Actives, 71,500, $100/M

St. Anthony's Coding for Orthopaedic Reimbursement

Publishing Co: St. Anthony Consulting Group, 11410 Isaac Newton Sq., N., Ste. 200, Alexandria, VA 22090-5012; Title Tel # (703) 549-0100 Title Fax # (703) 706-5700
Personnel: Publisher-Eugene Lorenz, Editor-Marlis McCollum, Circ. Mgr.-Kathi Lawson, Promotion Dir.-Elise Schumacher
Editorial Description: Coding tool for orthopaedic billing personnel.
General Info: Yr. Est. 1990, Monthly, Trim Size-8½ x 11, 4 pages, No Color, Matte
Subscriptions: Indv. $93
List Rental: Actives, 71,500, $100/M

St. Anthony's Coding for Physician Reimbursement Newsletter

Publishing Co: St. Anthony Consulting Group, 11410 Isaac Newton Sq., N., Ste. 200, Alexandria, VA 22090-5012; Title Tel # (703) 549-0100 Title Fax # (703) 706-5700
Personnel: Publisher-Eugene Lorenz, Editor-Marlis McCollum, Circ. Mgr.-Kathi Lawson, Promotion Dir.-Elise Schumacher
Editorial Description: ICDD-9-CM and CPT coding and regulatory information for healthcare professionals.
General Info: Monthly
Subscriptions: Indv. $98
List Rental: Actives, 71,500, $100/M

St. Anthony's Healthcare Resources Alert

Publishing Co: St. Anthony Consulting Group, 11410 Isaac Newton Sq., N., Ste. 200, Alexandria, VA 22090-5012; Title Tel # (703) 549-0100 Title Fax # (703) 706-5700
Personnel: Publisher-Eugene Lorenz, Editor-Kate Holden, Circ. Mgr.-Kathi Lawson, Promotion Dir.-Pat Nussman
Editorial Description: News, resources and services for practicing healthcare professionals.
General Info: Monthly, Trim Size-8½ x 11, 8 pages, 2 Color, Matte
List Rental: Actives, 71,500, $100/M

St. Anthony's Physicians Resources Alert

Publishing Co: St. Anthony Consulting Group, 11410 Isaac Newton Sq., N., Ste. 200, Alexandria, VA 22090-5012; Title Tel # (703) 549-0100 Title Fax # (703) 706-5700
Personnel: Publisher-Eugene Lorenz, Editor-Kate Holden, Circ. Mgr.-Kathi Lawson, Promotion Dir.-Elise Schumacher
Editorial Description: News, resources and services for physicians' offices.
General Info: Monthly, 8 pages, 2 Color, Matte
List Rental: Actives, 71,500, $100/M

St. John Ambulance, Instructor's Digest

Publishing Co: St. John Ambulance, British Columbia Council, 6111 Cambie St., Vancouver, BC V5Z 3B2 Canada; Title Tel # (604) 321-2651 Title Fax # (604) 321-5316
Editorial Description: Digest for St. John Ambulance first aid and CPR instructors. Includes information on upcoming events, updates in first aid procedures and protocols and articles relating to training.
General Info: Yr. Est. 1981, Quarterly, Trim Size-8½ x 11, 12 pages

St. John News

Publishing Co: St. John Ambulance, 312 Laurier Ave. East, Box 388, Station A, Ottawa, ON K1N 8V4 Canada; Title Tel # (613) 236-7461
Personnel: Editor-Julie Fenn
General Info: (Formerly Canadian First Aid), Yr. Est. 1952, Quarterly, Trim Size-8½ x 11, 20 pages, ISSN: 0380-8181, 2 Color, Newsprint
Circulation: Total-6,500

St. Luke's Insight

Publishing Co: Sponsor-St. Luke's Hospital, St. Luke's Hospital, 1227 E Rusholme St, Davenport, IA 52803-2498; Title Tel # (319) 326-6896
Personnel: Editor-Blake Lewis, III, Circ. Mgr.-Regina Howell, Art Dir.-Rick Reed
Editorial Description: General information on community-related health issues.
General Info: Yr. Est. 1983, Bi-monthly, Trim Size-5½ x 8½, 6 pages, 2 Color, Coated
Circulation: Total-2,100

Sanus Healthy Update   *Consumer*

Publishing Co: Sanus Health Plan of Greater New York/New Jersey, 75-20 Astoria Blvd., Jackson Heights, NY 11370; Title Tel # (718) 899-3600
Editorial Description: Health tips and information from Sanus Life Insurance.
General Info: Semi-annually, Trim Size-8½ x 11, 16 pages, 4 Color, Coated, Saddle-stitched

Saskatchewan Dietetic Assn. Newsletter   *Association*

Publishing Co: Saskatchewan Dietetic Assn., BOX 3894, Regina, SK S4P 3R8 Canada; Title Tel # (306) 359-3040 Title Fax # (306) 757-8161
Personnel: Editor-Susan Halland
Editorial Description: Informs members of national and provincial operations, etc.
General Info: Yr. Est. 1958, Bi-monthly, Trim Size-5 x 8, Desktop press, 16 pages, Color-cover
Subscriptions: Can. $20
Circulation: Total-200
Advertising: Inquire for rates. Accepts Inserts.

School Health Alert

Publishing Co: School Health Alert, PO Box 13716, San Antonio, TX 78213-0716; Title Tel # (512) 433-7327
Personnel: Editor-Jerry Newton, Circ. Mgr.-Rose Karin
Editorial Description: Focuses on school health issues.
General Info: Yr. Est. 1985, Trim Size-8½ x 11, Desktop press, 8 pages
Subscriptions: Indv. $25, $3/copy

Science/Health Abstracts   *Consumer*

Publishing Co: Yuchi Pines Institute, PO Box 319, Fort Mitchell, AL 36856-0319;
Title Tel # (404) 288-5495
Personnel: Editor, Promotion Dir.-Phylis Austin
Editorial Description: Health & natural living.
General Info: Yr. Est. 1980, Bi-monthly, Trim Size-8½ x 11, Sheetfed press, 4 pages, No Color, Matte
Subscriptions: Indv. $6, $1/copy
Circulation: Total-1,000

Scientific American Medicine
See: MEDICINE

Scleroderma Spectrum
See: MEDICINE

Scrip World Pharmaceutical News
See: DRUGS & PHARMACEUTICALS

Second Opinion   *Consumer*

Publishing Co: Soundview Publications, 7100 Peachtree Dunwoody Rd., Suite #100, Atlanta, GA 30328-4134; Title Tel # (770) 668-0432 Title Fax # (770) 668-0692
Personnel: Publisher-Wallis W. Wood, Editor in Chief-Wm. Campbell Douglass, Production Mgr.-Penny Lane, Art Dir.-Elizabeth Bame, Mktg. Dir.-Joyce Morris
Editorial Description: Provides a 'skeptics view' of today's 'accepted' health and medicine procedures from a classically trained M.D. telling readers the sometimes unpleasant truth about how the medical, pharmaceutical system really works, what doctors & hospitals really don't know about how to cure, and how readers can make decisions which make them healthier, not their doctors richer.
General Info: (Formerly Cutting Edge, The), Yr. Est. 1987, Monthly
Subscriptions: Indv. $39, $5/copy
List Rental: List Management Co.: Carnegie Marketing Assocs., Koll Executive Plaza, 3878 Carson St., Suite 220, Torrance, CA 90503 Tel # (310) 540-4757, Fax # (310) 540-7407, Actives: 56,687, $110/M

Seeing Clearly   *Consumer*

Publishing Co: National Association for Visually Handicapped, 22 W. 21st St., New York, NY 10010-6904; Title Tel # (212) 889-3141 Title Fax # (212) 727-2931
Personnel: Editor-Lorraine Marchi
Editorial Description: Provides the adult partially-seeing, their families, friends & professionals who serve them with an update on services, technological advances, large print products; also accepts for publication original essays, short fiction, poetry & drawings by & forthe partial seeing.
General Info: Yr. Est. 1975, Annually, Trim Size-9 x 12, 26 pages, Color-cover
Subscriptions: Free
Circulation: Total-19,500

Senior Housing: Assisted Living & Long-term Care Manual
See: SENIOR CITIZENS

Singer Report on Managed Care Systems and Technology, The
See: COMPUTERS & AUTOMATION

Ski for Light Bulletin

Publishing Co: Ski for Light, 1455 W. Lake St., Minneapolis, MN 55408-2648; Title Tel # (612) 827-3232
Personnel: Editor-Barbara Kvigne Rostad
General Info: (Formerly HEALTHsports Bulletin), Yr. Est. 1976, Quarterly, 8 pages
Circulation: Total-3,000

Skin Facts   *Consumer*

Publishing Co: New York Univ. Medical Center, 550 1st Ave, New York, NY 10016-6481
Personnel: Editor-Edward Edelson
Editorial Description: Newsletter on dermatology and skin concerns,.
General Info: Quarterly, Trim Size-8½ x 11, 4 pages, No Color, Matte

Smart's Health and Safety Newsletter

Publishing Co: Kaslow & Associates, 2203 Los Angeles Ave, Berkeley, CA 94707-2619; Title Tel # (415) 632-2200
Editorial Description: Covers health and safety news and developments.
General Info: 10x/yr.
Subscriptions: Indv. $35

Smart's National Comp & Health Bulletin
See: INSURANCE

Smoking and Health Newsletter   *Consumer*

Publishing Co: Natl. Interagency Council on Smoking, 7320 Greenville Ave, Dallas, TX 75231-4502
Personnel: Editor-Robert Wallace
General Info: Yr. Est. 1965, Quarterly
Circulation: Total-10,000

Sneeze the Day   *Consumer*

Publishing Co: Good Communications, Inc., PO Box 10069, Austin, TX 78766; Title Tel # (512) 454-6090 Title Fax # (512) 454-3420
Personnel: Publisher-Ross Becker, Editor-Rebecca Reynolds, Mng. Editor-Judi Sklar, Adv. Dir.-Karen Laufer
Editorial Description: Focuses on allergy relief for people suffering from allergies and asthma. You'll get information on all types of allergic reactions, plus the latest medical research, the real story on medication, shots and products for the allergic. The independent newsletter for people with allergies
General Info: Yr. Est. 1994, Monthly, Trim Size-8½ x 11, 12 pages, ISSN: 1080-143x, 2 Color, Matte, Saddle-stitched
Subscriptions: Indv. $27
Advertising: $550.

Society for Health Systems News   *Association*

Publishing Co: Institute of Industrial Engineers, 25 Technology Park/Atlanta, Norcross, GA 30092-2988 Tel # (770) 449-0461; Title Tel # (404) 449-0460 Title Fax # (770) 263-8532
Personnel: Production Mgr.-Dona Brown
General Info: Yr. Est. 1989, Quarterly, 12 pages, 2 Color, Coated
Subscriptions: Free With Membership
Circulation: (100% controlled)
Advertising: $475. Accepts Inserts.
List Rental: Rents Lists

South Shore Cerebral Palsy News

Publishing Co: Cerebral Palsy of the South Shore Area, Inc., 105 Adams St, Quincy, MA 02169-2004; Title Tel # (617) 479-7443 Title Fax # (617) 479-7577
Personnel: Editor-Arthur Ciampa
Editorial Description: Contains program information on cerebral palsy.
General Info: Yr. Est. 1959, Quarterly, Trim Size-8½ x 11, Mimeo press, 8 pages, No Color
Subscriptions: Free
Acquistions: Publication Bought
Circulation: (100% controlled), Total-2,000

Southern Health Update

Publishing Co: Southern Health Assn., c/o Metro Health Dept., 311 23rd Avenue N, Nashville, TN 37203; Title Tel # (615) 327-9313
Personnel: Editor-Durward Collier
General Info: Yr. Est. 1981, Quarterly, Trim Size-9¹³⁄₁₆ x 12⁷⁄₈, 12 pages
Circulation: Total-1,000

Sower   *Consumer, Association*

Publishing Co: Beatrice State Development Ctr., 3000 Lincoln Blvd, Beatrice, NE 68310-3300; Title Tel # (402) 223-2302
Personnel: Editor-Jerry Crisp
Editorial Description: Information for parents, friends, & persons working in the field of mental retardation. Current programs, goals & objectives, needs & actual happenings at the institution.
General Info: (Formerly Broadcaster), Yr. Est. 1981, Quarterly, Trim Size-8½ x 11½, Sheetfed press, 12 pages, Color-cover
Circulation: Total-5,500

Spa Specs   *Business, Association*

Publishing Co: Spa Specs International, 21548 Hyde Rd, Sonoma, CA 95476-9732; Title Tel # (415) 457-9092 Title Fax # (415) 461-6958
Personnel: Publisher, Editor-Eva M. Jensch, Mktg. Dir.-Monique Phelan
Editorial Description: Trade newsletter targeted toward professionals in the health spa industry. Our publication attempts to explore the most recent findings in the maintenance of good health.
General Info: Yr. Est. 1990, Bi-monthly, Letrpr. press, 12 pages, 2 Color, Matte
Subscriptions: Indv. $59, For. $79, Free To Qualified Recipient
Circulation: (75% controlled), Total-1,000, Subscriptions-250, International-300
Advertising: Inquire for rates. Accepts Inserts.
Printing Co: UltraPrint, 1137 4th St, San Rafael, CA 94901-3006

Speaking of Safety
See: SAFETY

Specialty Capitation Manual: Rate Setting, Evaluation and Implementation

Publishing Co: Thompson Publishing Group, 747 Third Ave., New York, NY 10017 Tel # (212) 888-7220; Title Tel # (212) 888-7295 Title Fax # (212) 486-3400
Personnel: Publisher-Kenneth R. Gesser, Editor-Rosalie L. Donlon, Production Mgr.-R.D. Whitney, Mktg. Dir.-Kevin Mohon
Editorial Description: Comprehensive guidance for negotiating specialty capitation contracts.
General Info: Yr. Est. 1995, Looseleaf
Subscriptions: Indv. $395

Spina Bifida Assn. of British Columbia Newsletter

Publishing Co: Spina Bifida Assn. of British Columbia, 9460 140th St., Surrey, BC V3V 5Z4 Canada; Title Tel # (604) 584-1361
General Info: Quarterly

Sports Medicine in Primary Care
See: MEDICINE

Sports Medicine Standards & Malpractice Reporter, The
See: LAW

Sproutletter
See: NUTRITION

State Health Notes   *Business, Association*

Publishing Co: Intergovernmental Health Policy Project, 2021 K St NW Ste 800, Washington, DC 20006-1003 Fax # (202) 785-0114; Title Tel # (202) 872-1445
Personnel: Publisher-Richard Merritt, Editor-Linda Demkovich, Circ. Mgr.-Lorraine Stief
General Info: Yr. Est. 1979, Bi-weekly, Offset press, 8 pages, 2 Color
Subscriptions: Indv. $277, $10/copy
Circulation: Total-2,000
List Rental: Actives: 2,000, $150/M

State Health Watch   *Business, Scholarly*

Publishing Co: State Health Watch, 704 Stony Hill Road, Ste. 154, Yardley, PA 19067 Fax # (215) 321-3370; Title Tel # (215) 295-2304 Title Fax # (215) 428-3782
Editorial Description: Tracks health policy/trends in all 50 states.
General Info: Yr. Est. 1994, Monthly, Trim Size-8.5 x 11, Offset press, 12 pages, ISSN: 1074-4754, 2 Color, Saddle-stitched
Subscriptions: Indv. $247, $20/copy
List Rental: Rents Lists
Printing Co: Spruce Printing, West trenton, NJ Tel # (609) 538-0011

Statewide Comprehensive Plan for Mental Health Services
See: PSYCHIATRY

Staying Well Newsletter   *Business, Association*

Publishing Co: Foundation for Chiropractic Education and Research, 66 Washington, Des Moines, IA 50314; Title Tel # (515) 282-7118 Title Fax # (515) 282-3347
Personnel: Editor-Thomas Wolfe
Editorial Description: Health & fitness newsletter.
General Info: Yr. Est. 1982, Bi-monthly, 4 pages
Circulation: Total-120,000

Straight from Sherman   *Association*

Publishing Co: Sherman College of Straight Chiropractic, 2020 Springfield Rd., PO Box 1452, Spartanburg, SC 29304; Title Tel # (803) 578-8770 Title Fax # (803) 599-7145
Personnel: Publisher-Thomas Gelardi, D.C., Circ. Mgr.-Valerie Massey, Editor, Production Mgr.- Art Dir.-Teresa Salley
Editorial Description: Seeks to promote advancement of straight chiropractic health care.
General Info: Yr. Est. 1978, Quarterly, Sheetfed press, 16 pages, 2 Color, Matte, Saddle-stitched
Subscriptions: Free To Qualified Recipient
Circulation: (100% controlled), Total-5,500, Readership-5,500

Strategic Advantage
See: HOSPITALS & NURSING HOMES

Strategic Health Care Marketing   *Business*

Publishing Co: Health Care Communications, 11 Heritage Ln, Rye, NY 10580-3713; Title Tel # (914) 967-6741
Personnel: Publisher, Editor-Michele Von Dambrowski
Editorial Description: Marketing strategies for hospitals, medical group practices, home health services, and managed care organizations.
General Info: Yr. Est. 1984, Monthly, Trim Size-8½ x 11, Sheetfed press, 12 pages, ISSN: 0749-5153, 2 Color, Matte, Saddle-stitched
Subscriptions: Indv. $249, Inst. $259, Can. $259, For. $274, $25/copy
List Rental: Rents Lists

Strategies for Healthcare Excellence
See: HOSPITALS & NURSING HOMES

Street Pharmacologist

Publishing Co: Up Front Drug Information, 5701 Biscayne Blvd Apt 602, Miami, FL 33137-2602; Title Tel # (305) 757-2566
Personnel: Editor-James Hall, Circ. Mgr.-Roman Dominguez
Editorial Description: Drug education/information suitable for secondary schools/college libraries/ drug programs.
General Info: Yr. Est. 1973, Bi-monthly, Trim Size-8½ x 11, Desktop press, 8 pages, ISSN: 0735-6544, No Color, Coated
Subscriptions: Indv. $25, $3/copy
Circulation: Total-500
List Rental: Rents Lists

Stroke Connection

Publishing Co: AHA Stroke Connections, 7272 Greenville Ave, Dallas, TX 75231-5129 Tel # (214) 706-1556 Fax # (214) 696-5211
Personnel: Editor-Pat Kasell
Editorial Description: Personal experiences of stroke survivors & caregivers and educational information on strokes.
General Info: Yr. Est. 1980, Bi-monthly, 16 pages, ISSN: 1047-014X, 2 Color
Subscriptions: Indv. $8
Circulation: Total-8,000, Readership-44,000
Advertising: Inquire for rates.

Subacute Care: A Guide to Development, Implementation and Management
See: HOSPITALS & NURSING HOMES

Substance Abuse Funding News
See: PHILANTHROPY

Substance Abuse Report   *Business*

Publishing Co: Research Institute of America, 1340 Braddock Pl., Ste. 400, Alexandria, VA 22314-1651 Tel # (703) 706-8260 Fax # (703) 683-4824; Title Tel # (202) 842-0520 Title Fax # (212) 475-1790
Personnel: Publisher-John Roche, Editor-Alison Knopf, Circ. Mgr.-Ellen Hartman, Production Mgr.- Amy Ryan, Promotion Dir.-Ron Lippock
Editorial Description: Concentrates on regulatory news, trends, & developments in drug & alcohol abuse. Written for employee assistance directors, hospitals, treatment & care providers.
General Info: Yr. Est. 1970, Semi-monthly, Sheetfed press, 8 pages
Subscriptions: Indv. $275
List Rental: List Management Co.: Taybi Direct East, Inc., 13321 New Hampshire Ave., Ste. 202, Silver Spring, MD 20904-3450 Tel # (301) 680-3633, Fax # (301) 680-3635
Printing Co: Jim Buckley Offsetting, 1101 Pennsylvania Ave SE, Washington, DC 20003-2229 Tel # (202) 546-0501

Sudden Infant Death Syndrome Foundation of Washington Newsletter

Publishing Co: Children's Hospital & Medical Center, CG-07, P.O Box 5371, Seattle, WA 98105; Title Tel # (206) 526-2110 Title Fax # (206) 527-5726
Personnel: Editor-Teresa Peterson
Editorial Description: Covers local research, meetings, new research leads, refutes incorrect information, publishes copies of correct SIDS, newspaper articles.Provides emotional support.
General Info: Yr. Est. 1970, Bi-monthly, Trim Size-8½ x 11, 8 pages, No Color
Subscriptions: Free
Circulation: Total-3,400, Readership-3,400

Sun & Skin News   *Consumer, Association*

Publishing Co: Skin Cancer Foundation, 245 Fifth Ave., Ste. 2402, New York, NY 10016; Title Tel # (212) 725-5176
Editorial Description: Quarterly publication written in non-technical language for the prevention and treatment of skin cancer.
General Info: Yr. Est. 1984, Quarterly, Trim Size-8½ x 11, 4 pages, No Color, Newsprint
Subscriptions: Free With Membership
Circulation: Total-60,000

Supermarket Savvy Information Resource Service
See: FOOD

Survivors   *Association, Consumer*

Publishing Co: Parents of Murdered Children, 100 E. 8th St., #B-41, Cincinnati, OH 45202-2129; Title Tel # (513) 721-5683 Title Fax # (513) 345-4489
Personnel: Editor-Nancy Ruhe
General Info: Quarterly, 6 pages
Subscriptions: Indv. $10

Synapse

Publishing Co: Univ. of Nebraska Medical Ctr., 600 So. 42nd St., Omaha, NE 68198-0001
Personnel: Editor-Betty Dyhrberg, Art Dir.-Judy Hogan
Editorial Description: Research projects at the Univ. of Nebraska Medical Center.
General Info: Quarterly, Offset press, Saddle-stitched
Subscriptions: Free To Qualified Recipient
Circulation: Total-4,500

Synergy

Publishing Co: Canadian Society for International Health, 170 Laurier Ave. W, Suite #902, Ottawa, ON K1P 5V5 Canada; Title Tel # (613) 230-2654 Title Fax # (613) 230-8401
Personnel: Editor-Mary Bridgeo
Editorial Description: Canadian intl. health iniatives.
General Info: (Formerly Tropica-Canada), Yr. Est. 1987, Quarterly, Trim Size-8½ x 11, Letrpr. press, 20 pages, ISSN: 0838-0368, Color-cover, Matte, Saddle-stitched
Subscriptions: Indv. $12, Can. $15, Free In Designated Area
Circulation: Total-1,200
Advertising: Inquire for rates. Accepts Inserts.

TJFR Health News Reporter
See: MEDIA & COMMUNICATIONS

TMJ Update (Temporomandibular Joint Update)
See: DENTAL

Take a Breather...   *Consumer*

Publishing Co: Lung Association -Metro Toronto & York Region, 573 King Street East, Suite 201, Toronto, ON M5A 4L3 Canada; Title Tel # (416) 864-1112 Title Fax # (416) 864-9916
Personnel: Publisher-Andre C. Roberts
General Info: Quarterly, Trim Size-8.5 x 11, Offset press, 12 pages, 4 Color, Other, Saddle-stitched
Subscriptions: Free
Printing Co: National Printing Group, 110 Denison Street, Unit 4, Maukham, ON 90543-7584

Teachers In Touch
See: EDUCATION

Tennessee Health Law Update
See: LAW

Texas Health Bulletin

Publishing Co: Texas Dept. of Health, 1100 W 49th St, Austin, TX 78756-3199
Personnel: Editor-Al. Williams
General Info: Monthly, 12 pages
Circulation: Total-3,500

Thanatology Librarian

Publishing Co: Center for Thanatology Research, 391 Atlantic Ave, Brooklyn, NY 11217-1701;
Title Tel # (718) 858-3026
Personnel: Editor-Roberta Halporn
General Info: 4 pages

Thyrobulletin   *Association*

Publishing Co: Thyroid Foundation of Canada, 1040 Gardiners Rd., Kingston, ON K7P 1R7 Canada;
Title Tel # (613) 634-3426 Title Fax # (613) 634-3483
Personnel: Editor-Robert MacTavish
General Info: (Formerly Thyroid Foundation of Canada, Newsletter), Yr. Est. 1980, Quarterly, Trim Size-8½ x 11, Offset press, 16 pages, ISSN: 0832-7076, No Color, Matte
Subscriptions: Indv. $15, Free With Membership
Circulation: Total-4,000

Tipsheet
See: EDUCATION

To Your Health

Publishing Co: International Chiropractors Assn., 1110 N. Glebe Rd., Ste. 1000, Arlington, VA 22201-4795 Fax # (703) 528-5023; Title Tel # (703) 528-5000
Personnel: Publisher-Molly Rangnath, Editor, Production Mgr.-Heidi Freerks, Circ. Mgr., Art Dir.-Ted Glazer
Editorial Description: A one-page, two-sided quarterly subscription newsletter designed as a public editions/marketing tool for distribution by chiropractors to their patients. Filled with interesting articles about chiropractic-related & seasonal subjects.
General Info: Yr. Est. 1985, Quarterly, Offset press, 1 pages, No Color, Coated
Subscriptions: Indv. $69
Printing Co: Minuteman, Washington, DC

Tobacco on Trial
See: TOBACCO

Today's Team

Publishing Co: Wentworth Worldwide Media, 1866 Colonial Village Lane, PO Box 10488, Lancaster, PA 17605-0488; Title Tel # (717) 393-1000 Title Fax # (717) 393-5752
Editorial Description: Team-building and group process skills for team members.
General Info: Yr. Est. 1991, Monthly

TopHealth   *Business*

Publishing Co: Health Source Corporation, The, 443 Western Ave, Boston, MA 02135-1010;
Title Tel # (617) 254-5000 Title Fax # (617) 254-2599
Personnel: Publisher-Arnon Dreyfuss, M.D.
Editorial Description: Sold in bulk for employers to distribute to their employees. Contains health and safety info. Available in English and Spanish.
General Info: Yr. Est. 1987, 10x/yr., Trim Size-8½ x 11, 2 pages
Circulation: Total-750,000

Torch Bearer
See: EDUCATION

Tourette Syndrome
Association Newsletter   *Association*

Publishing Co: Tourette Syndrome Association, 4240 Bell Blvd, Bayside, NY 11361-2820;
Title Tel # (718) 224-2999 Title Fax # (718) 279-9596
Personnel: Editor-David Spiler
Editorial Description: Review of research and advocacy programs.
General Info: Yr. Est. 1972, Quarterly, Trim Size-8 x 11, 8 pages, Color
Circulation: Total-25,000

Trager Newsletter   *Association*

Publishing Co: Trager Institute, 21 Locust Ave., Mill Valley, CA 94941-2806;
Title Tel # (415) 388-2688 Title Fax # (415) 388-2710
General Info: (Formerly Trager Institute Newsletter), Yr. Est. 1980, Tri-annually, Trim Size-8½ x 11, 20 pages, No Color, Other, Saddle-stitched
Subscriptions: Indv. $45, Free With Membership
Circulation: Total-1,800
List Rental: Rents Lists

Traumagram Newsletter   *Association*

Publishing Co: American Trauma Society, 8903 Presidential Pky Ste 512, Upper Marlboro, MD 20772-2656; Title Tel # (301) 420-4189 Title Fax # (301) 420-0617
General Info: Quarterly, 12 pages, 2 Color
Subscriptions: Free With Membership
Circulation: Total-6,000
Advertising: Inquire for rates.
List Rental: Rents Lists

Traveling Healthy Newsletter
See: TRAVEL

Trying Times   *Consumer*

Publishing Co: Trying Times, 18295 Clearbrook Cir, Boca Raton, FL 33498-1946
Personnel: Publisher-Susan Cohen Strange
Editorial Description: For those undergoing infertility treatment.
General Info: Yr. Est. 1993, Bi-monthly
Subscriptions: Indv. $20

Turn Back the Clock   *Consumer*

Publishing Co: Turn Back the Clock, 12020 Sunrise Valley Drive, Reston, VA 22090
Editorial Description: Alternative healing, weight loss, and health ideas and techniques.
General Info: Monthly, Trim Size-8½ x 11, 20 pages, 4 Color, Coated, Saddle-stitched
Subscriptions: Indv. $52
Circulation: Total-14,000
List Rental: List Management Co.: Listworks, 1 Campus Dr., Pleasantville, NY 10570-1602
Tel # (914) 769-7100, Fax # (914) 769-8070, Actives: 14,000

Turner's Syndrome News   *Association*

Publishing Co: Turner's Syndrome Society, 7777 Keele St. Fl. 2, Concord, ON L4K 1Y7 Canada;
Title Tel # (905) 660-7766 Title Fax # (905) 660-7450
General Info: (Formerly T.S.S. News), Yr. Est. 1981, Quarterly, 16 pages
Circulation: Total-400

Twin Services Reporter
See: BABY

UC People, Etc.   *Association*

Publishing Co: United Cerebral Palsy Assn., Inc., 7 Penn Plz Ste 804, New York, NY 10001-3900;
Title Tel # (212) 481-6345
Personnel: Editor-A. Nicolai, Jr.
Editorial Description: Information of use to affiliates and health care professionals.
General Info: (Formerly Crusader), Bi-monthly, Trim Size-11 x 13¾, 8 pages, 2 Color
Circulation: Total-16,000

UPF Newsletter   *Consumer, Association*

Publishing Co: United Parkinson Foundation, 833 W Washington Blvd, Chicago, IL 60607-2316;
Title Tel # (312) 733-1893
Personnel: Editor-Judy Rosner
Editorial Description: Educational.
General Info: Yr. Est. 1963, Quarterly, Trim Size-8½ x 11, Letrpr. press, 16 pages, No Color
Subscriptions: Indv. $25
Circulation: Total-38,000

Understanding and Living
with Glaucoma   *Consumer*

Publishing Co: Glaucoma Research Fondation, 490 Post St Ste 830, San Francisco, CA 94102-1409
Fax # (415) 986-3162; Title Tel # (415) 986-3162 Title Fax # (415) 986-3763
Personnel: Editor-Lisa Clark
General Info: Yr. Est. 1984
Subscriptions: Free
Circulation: Total-100,000

Une Veritable Amie
See: WOMEN'S

Universal Healthcare Almanac
See: HOSPITALS & NURSING HOMES

University of California at
Berkeley, Wellness
Letter   *Association*

Publishing Co: Healthletter Assocs., 632 Broadway, New York, NY 10012-2614;
Title Tel # (212) 505-2255 Title Fax # (212) 505-5462
Personnel: Publisher, Editor-Rodney Friedman
Editorial Description: Deals with nutrition, fitness, & stress management.
General Info: Yr. Est. 1984, Monthly, Trim Size-8½ x 11, Web press, 8 pages, ISSN: 0748-9234, Ind/Abs/Online: DIALOG, 2 Color, Newsprint
Subscriptions: Indv. $24, Can. $29, For. $30, $3/copy
Acquistions: Publication Sold
Circulation: Total-500,000
List Rental: List Management Co.: List Services Corp., 6 Trowbridge Dr., PO Box 516, Bethel, CT 06801-2858 Tel # (203) 743-2600, Fax # (203) 743-0589, Actives: 750,000, $80/M, Hotline: 50,000, $90/M, Expires: 579,217, $50/M
Printing Co: Tempographics, 455 E North Ave, Carol Stream, IL 60188-2167 Tel # (708) 462-8200, Fax # (708) 462-0350

University of Texas
Lifetime Health Letter   *Consumer*

Publishing Co: University of Texas Health Science Center, 7000 Fannin, Houston, TX 77030-3907; Title Tel # (713) 792-4265 Title Fax # (713) 792-4986
Personnel: Editor-Joe Sigler, Circ. Mgr.-Todd Hendrichs
Editorial Description: General consumer health newsletter with useful news about health, fitness, nutrition and mental well-being from a major medical school.
General Info: Yr. Est. 1989, Monthly
Subscriptions: Indv. $24, $3/copy
Circulation: Total-75,000
List Rental: List Management Co.: Kleid Company, Inc., 530 5th Ave., 17 Floor, New York, NY 10036-5101 Tel # (212) 819-3406, Fax # (212) 719-9788, Actives: 46,766, $85/M, Expires: 20,329, $65/M
Printing Co: Newsletter Services, Inc., 9700 Philadelphia Court, Lanham, MD 20706 Tel # (301) 731-5200, Fax # (301) 731-5201

Unlimited Horizons   *Association*

Publishing Co: Metascience Foundation, PO Box 32, Kingston, RI 02881
Personnel: Editor-George Meek
General Info: Quarterly, 12 pages
Subscriptions: Indv. $30

Update
See: EDUCATION

VHL Family Forum
See: MEDICINE

VHL News
See: GENETICS

Vaccine Weekly

Publishing Co: C.W. Henderson Publisher, Medical Center II, P.O. Box 5528, Atlanta, GA 31107-0528 Tel # (404) 507-7777 Fax # (404) 507-7788; Title Tel # (404) 377-8895 Title Fax # (404) 378-5411
Personnel: Publisher-C.W. Henderson, Editor-Daniel J. Denoon, Science Ed.-Alan D. Henderson, Calendar Ed.-Ken Kimsey
Editorial Description: International coverage of vaccine development, gene therapies, clinical trials and immune booster research, developments and outcomes.
General Info: Yr. Est. 1994, ISSN: 1074-2921
Subscriptions: Indv. $995, Can. $995, For. $1,195

Vegan News, The
See: ENVIRONMENT & ECOLOGY

Vegetarian Journal's Foodservice Update
See: FOOD

Virginia's Health   *Association*

Publishing Co: Virginia State Health Dept., 109 Governor St # 515, Richmond, VA 23219-3623; Title Tel # (804) 786-2002
Personnel: Editor, Art Dir.-Henry Brown, Jr.
Editorial Description: Covers health subjects of interest to the people of Virginia. Reports on the activities of the State Health Department and the programs being undertaken for the benefit of the public.
General Info: (Formerly Virginia Health Bulletin), Yr. Est. 1979, Quarterly, Trim Size-11 x 14, Offset press, 8 pages, No Color
Circulation: (100% controlled), Total-10,000

Vita-Mix Health Digest, The   *Consumer*

Publishing Co: Vita-Mix Corp., 8615 Usher Rd, Cleveland, OH 44138-2103; Title Fax # (216) 235-3726
Editorial Description: Newsletter from Vita-Mix describing health issues and Vita-Mix's products that also serves as a catalog for ordering the products.
General Info: Trim Size-8½ x 11, 18 pages, 4 Color, Coated, Saddle-stitched
Subscriptions: Indv. $3, Can. $4

Vitality

Publishing Co: Foundation for Education About Eating Disorders, 5238 Duvall Dr, Bethesda, MD 20816-1876; Title Tel # (301) 371-8880
Personnel: Publisher, Editor-Caroline Adams Miller
Editorial Description: Vitality helps educate people about eating disorders, matches pen pals, & publishes stories by & about recovering eating disorder sufferers.
General Info: Yr. Est. 1988, Bi-monthly, Web press, 6 pages, 2% ads, 2 Color, Newsprint
Subscriptions: Indv. $25, $4/copy
Acquisitions: Publication Bought
Circulation: Total-350
Advertising: Inquire for rates.
Printing Co: Rosedale Printing Co., Inc., 2250 Reisterstown Rd, Baltimore, MD 21217-1928 Tel # (301) 669-4000

WYO Network
See: EDUCATION

Walker's World Newsletter
See: SPORTS & SPORTING GOODS

Wary Canary
See: ENVIRONMENT & ECOLOGY

Washington Drug Letter
See: DRUGS & PHARMACEUTICALS

Washington Health
Record

Publishing Co: Faulkner & Gray Healthcare Information Center, 1133 15th St NW, Ste. 450, Washington, DC 20005-2710 Tel # (202) 828-4148 Parent Co.-Faulkner & Gray, Inc., New York; Title Tel # (202) 828-4150
Personnel: Publisher-Luci Koizumi
Editorial Description: Listings of new health bills, meetings.
General Info: Yr. Est. 1979, 50x/yr., Trim Size-8½ x 11, Web press, 4 pages, ISSN: 0164-1514, Ind/Abs/Online: developments.', 2 Color, Newsprint
Subscriptions: Indv. $175
Acquisitions: Publication Bought, Publication Sold
List Rental: List Management Co.: Aggressive List Management, 18-2 E Dundee Rd Ste 101, Barrington, IL 60010-5273 Tel # (708) 304-4030, Fax # (708) 304-4032

Washington Health Week
See: PUBLIC MANAGEMENT & PLANNING

Washington Memo

Publishing Co: Alan Guttmacher Institute, 120 Wall Street, New York, NY 10005; Title Tel # (212) 248-1111 Title Fax # (212) 248-1952
Personnel: Publisher-Jeannie Rosoff, Editor-Terry Sollom, Circ. Mgr.-Lourdes Lebron
Editorial Description: Natl. & state legislative & policy developments affecting family planning, maternal & child health, abortion & intl. aid.
General Info: Yr. Est. 1966, Bi-weekly, Trim Size-8½ x 11½, Desktop press, 4 pages, ISSN: 0739-4179, 2 Color
Subscriptions: Indv. $35, Inst. $45, For. $55, $5/copy
Circulation: Total-3,000, Readership-3,400
List Rental: Rents Lists
Printing Co: Casillas Press, 1717 K St NW, Washington, DC 20006-1501 Tel # (202) 223-1220

Weekly Epidemiological
Record

Publishing Co: World Health Organization, United Nations, New York, NY 10017-3582
Editorial Description: A unique global update on epidemiology & the control of disease. Text in English and French.
General Info: Yr. Est. 1926, Weekly, 12 pages, ISSN: 0049-8114, Ind/Abs/Online: ExMd, Abs.Hyg., Trop.Dis.Bul.
Subscriptions: Indv. $152

Wellness Newsletter, The   *Consumer*

Publishing Co: The Wellness Newsletter, 3451 Central Ave, Saint Petersburg, FL 33713-8522
Personnel: Publisher, Editor-Carolyn Chambers Clark, Circ. Mgr., Adv. Dir.-Tony Auriemma
Editorial Description: Health promotion, disease prevention focus, including wellness research program summaries, self-care information written by an registered nurse practitioner.
General Info: Yr. Est. 1980, Bi-monthly, 8 pages, ISSN: 0740-8498, Ind/Abs/Online: CHID, Color
Subscriptions: Indv. $30, Can. $35, For. $40, $4/copy
List Rental: List Management Co.: List Services Corp., 6 Trowbridge Dr., PO Box 516, Bethel, CT 06801-2858 Tel # (203) 743-2600, Fax # (203) 743-0589, Actives: 620,000, $85/M, Hotline: $95/M, Expires: 675,093, $55/M

West Coast Lifeliner   *Association*

Publishing Co: Royal Life Saving Society Canada, 1235 W. Pender, Vancouver, BC V6E 2V6 Canada; Title Tel # (604) 684-6368 Title Fax # (604) 685-6802
General Info: Quarterly, Offset press, 8 pages, No Color, Newsprint, Saddle-stitched
Subscriptions: Free With Membership
Advertising: Accepts Inserts.

Whole Person's Health
Letter

Publishing Co: SMB Whole Health, PO Box 263, Little Falls, NJ 07424-0263; Title Tel # (201) 256-4261
Personnel: Editor-S.N. Zahorian
Editorial Description: Covers a wide range of health related topics.
General Info: Yr. Est. 1984, Quarterly
Subscriptions: Indv. $15

Wicozanni Wowapi Good
Health Newsletter

Publishing Co: Wicozanni Wowapi Good Health Newsletter, PO Box 572, Lake Andes, SD 57356-0572; Title Tel # (605) 487-7072 Title Fax # (605) 487-7964
Personnel: Editor-Charon Asetoyer
General Info: Yr. Est. 1987, Quarterly, Trim Size-8½ x 11, Desktop press, 4 pages, Color, Recycled
Subscriptions: Free
List Rental: Rents Lists

Wisconsin State Laboratory
of Hygiene Laboratory
Newsletter   *Association*

Publishing Co: Univ. of Wisconsin, 465 Henry Mall, Madison, WI 53706-1501; Title Tel # (608) 262-1293
Personnel: Editor-Ronald Laessig, Ph.D.
Editorial Description: Activities and current recommendations of the State Public Health laboratory.
General Info: Yr. Est. 1962, Trim Size-8¼ x 11, Offset press, 8 pages, No Color
Circulation: (100% controlled), Total-7,000

Wise Ideas
See: SENIOR CITIZENS

Women's Health Center
Management   *Business*

Publishing Co: American Health Consultants, Inc., 3525 Piedmont Rd., Building #6, Ste. 400, Atlanta, GA 30305-0056 Tel # (404) 262-7436 Fax # (404) 284-3291
Personnel: Publisher-Connnie Austin, Editor-Joy Daughtery, Circ. Mgr.-Monica Brown, Production Mgr.-Mike Whitter, Mktg. Mgr.-Rebecca Swancott-Torres
Editorial Description: For administrators in the women's health industry.
General Info: Yr. Est. 1993, Monthly
Subscriptions: Indv. $279, $27/copy
List Rental: Actives: $145/M

Women's Health Issues
See: WOMEN'S

Women's Health Letter
See: WOMEN'S

Women's Health Matters   *Consumer*

Publishing Co: Women's College Hospital, 76 Grenville Street, Toronto, ON M6S 1B2 Canada; Title Tel # (416) 323-7322 Title Fax # (416) 813-4721
Personnel: Editor-Kristine Culp, Circ. Mgr.-Gary Cowie, Art Dir.-Portia Tam
Editorial Description: WOMEN'S HEALTH MATTERS discusses health issues pertaining to women, such as menopause, pregnancy and reproductive concerns, osteoporosis, women's nutritional needs, heart disease and stress with an emphasis on disease prevention and healthy living. WHM also takes into account the impact of social role on women's health.
General Info: Yr. Est. 1994, 10x/yr., Trim Size-8½ x 11, Sheetfed press, 8 pages, ISSN: 1201-1800, 2 Color, Matte, Saddle-stitched
Subscriptions: Indv. $30, Can. $30, For. $36, $3/copy
Circulation: (1% controlled), Total-6,000
Printing Co: Canada Direct, 743 Renaud Avenue, Montreal, PQ H9P 2N1 Canada Tel # (514) 422-8835, Fax # (514) 422-8525

Working Times
See: HOUSE ORGANS

Working Together   *Association*

Publishing Co: National Association of Anorexia Nervosa & Assoc. Disorder, PO Box 7, Highland Park, IL 60035-0007; Title Tel # (708) 831-3438 Title Fax # (708) 433-4032
Personnel: Editor-Amy Grabowski
General Info: Yr. Est. 1976, Quarterly, Offset press, 4 pages, No Color
Subscriptions: Indv. $25
Circulation: Total-22,000

Worksite Wellness Works   *Business, Association*

Publishing Co: Wellness Councils of America, Community Health Plaza, #311, 7101 Newport Ave., Omaha, NE 68152-2100; Title Tel # (402) 572-3590 Title Fax # (402) 572-3594
Personnel: Editor, Circ. Mgr., Production Mgr.-Sandra Wendel
Editorial Description: Promotes health at the worksite.
General Info: Yr. Est. 1985, Monthly, Sheetfed press, 1 pages, ISSN: 1053-492X, 2 Color, Recycled, Saddle-stitched
Subscriptions: Free With Membership
Circulation: (100% controlled), Total-12,000
List Rental: List Management Co.: Manager: Sandra Wendel; Taybi Direct ,Inc, 10468 San Pablo Ave., El Cerrito, CA 94530 Tel # (510) 525-1500, Fax # (510) 525-7225, Actives: 18,500, $125/M

World Medical Relief-
Newsletter   *Business*

Publishing Co: World Medical Relief, 11745 12th St., Detroit, MI 48206-1270; Title Tel # (313) 866-5333
General Info: Trim Size-8½ x 11, 5 pages, No Color, Newsprint
Printing Co: Robot Printing Co., 25215 Glendale, Redford, MI 48239-2675 Tel # (313) 255-2280

World Right-To-Die
Newsletter   *Association*

Publishing Co: Derek Humphry, 24829 Norris Ln, Junction City, OR 97448-9559; Title Tel # (503) 998-1873 Title Fax # (503) 998-1873
Personnel: Publisher, Editor-Marilynne Seguin
Editorial Description: Provides information on issues associated with the subject of the right to die.
General Info: Yr. Est. 1976, Semi-annually, Trim Size-8½ x 11, 8 pages, ISSN: 0742-535X
Subscriptions: Free With Membership

Yale Children's Health
Letter   *Consumer*

Publishing Co: Yale University, School of Medicine, 333 Cedar St, New Haven, CT 06510-3206
Personnel: Editor-Joseph Warshaw, MD
Editorial Description: Covers health issues about children from infancy to adolescence.
General Info: Yr. Est. 1995, Monthly
Subscriptions: Indv. $45

York University Institute for Social Research Newsletter
See: SOCIOLOGY

Your Child's Wellness
See: BABY

Your Health
See: MEDICINE

Your Health Report   *Consumer*

Publishing Co: Curriculum Innovations Group, 3001 Cindel Dr., Delran, NJ 08370 Tel # (609) 786-1000; Title Tel # (708) 205-3000 Title Fax # (708) 564-8197
Personnel: Publisher-Bernard Berkin, Editor-Nancy Dreher, Production Mgr.-Roy Shlagman, Art Dir.-Ami Koenig, Adv. Dir., Promotion Dir.-Donna Gedwill
Editorial Description: Good health, diet, exercise, and self-motivation articles.
General Info: Yr. Est. 1969, Quarterly, Web press, 6 pages, 4 Color
Circulation: Total-200,000
Printing Co: Chicago Press, 1112 N Homan Ave, Chicago, IL 60651-4007 Tel # (312) 276-1500, Fax # (312) 276-4595

Yours For Health

Publishing Co: Panos Communications Ltd., R.R. 5, Box 867, Big Pine, FL 33043-9404; Title Tel # (301) 986-0908
Personnel: Publisher, Editor-Anne Panos
Editorial Description: Generic practice letter for health care professionals.
General Info: Yr. Est. 1984, Bi-monthly, Trim Size-11 x 17, Sheetfed press, 4 pages, No Color, Newsprint
Subscriptions: Indv. $560
Circulation: Total-5,000

ZPG Reporter, The
See: ENVIRONMENT & ECOLOGY

Zimmerman Letter, The   *Business*

Publishing Co: Zimmerman & Associates, Inc., 5307 South 92nd St., Hales Corners, WI 53130-1677 Parent Co.-Aspen Publishers, Inc., Gaithersburg; Title Tel # (414) 425-2189
Personnel: Publisher, Editor-David Zimmerman, Circ. Mgr.-Bruce A. Necson, Art Dir.-Kathleen I. Hamm
Editorial Description: Presents new concepts; reviews of vendors; and funding ideas for health care facilities.
General Info: Yr. Est. 1991, Monthly, Sheetfed press, 8 pages, 2 Color, Matte
Subscriptions: Indv. $397, Inst. $397
Circulation: Total-3,700
Printing Co: TJ Printing, 14150 W National Ave # 406, New Berlin, WI 53151-4529

HEARING & SPEECH

AIF/NERF News

Publishing Co: American Interprofessional Foundation, 601 Driftwood Ln, Northbrook, IL 60062-5501; Title Tel # (708) 564-4641

ASR News
See: COMPUTERS & AUTOMATION

Administration &
Management Special
Interest Section
Newsletter   *Business*

Publishing Co: American Occupational Therapy Assn., 4720 Montgomery Lane, PO Box 31220, Bethesda, MD 20824-1220 Tel # (301) 652-2682 Fax # (301) 652-7711; Title Tel # (301) 948-9626
Personnel: Editor-Marla Dittman
Editorial Description: 9 sections of health and safety management.
General Info: Quarterly, ISSN: 8756-629X
Subscriptions: Indv. $15

Between Friends   *Consumer*

Publishing Co: Beltone Electronics Corp., 4201 W Victoria St, Chicago, IL 60646-6700; Title Tel # (312) 583-3600
Personnel: Editor-Renee Rockoff, Circ. Mgr.-Kathy Cody, Production Mgr.-Shelly Jacobson, Adv. Dir.-Dennis Roy, Art Dir.-Shelley Jacobson
Editorial Description: For hearing aid wearers: quizzes, jokes, health, recipes and financial items.
General Info: Yr. Est. 1986, Bi-monthly, Trim Size-7½ x 8½, Sheetfed press, 6 pages, 2 Color, Newsprint
Circulation: (100% controlled), Total-200,000
List Rental: List Management Co.: Qualified Lists Corp., 135 Bedford Rd, Armonk, NY 10504-1937 Tel # (914) 273-6606, Actives: $55/M
Printing Co: Darwill Press, 11900 Roosevelt Rd, Hillside, IL 60162-2070 Tel # (708) 449-7770

Clinical Connection

Publishing Co: American Advertising Distributors of Northern VA, 708 Pendleton St, Alexandria, VA 22314-1819; Title Tel # (703) 549-5126
Personnel: Publisher-Georgina Ruley-Parks, Editor-Georgina Ruley Parks
Editorial Description: Covers speech language pathology.
General Info: Quarterly
Subscriptions: Indv. $36

Connections
See: MEDIA & COMMUNICATIONS

Contact
CPM: $92

Publishing Co: Cochlear Implant Club International, PO Box 464, Buffalo, NY 14223-0464; Title Tel # (716) 838-4662 Title Fax # (716) 838-4662
Personnel: Publisher-Camille Jones, Editor-Larry Orloff, Circ. Dir.-Craig Carpenter, Production Mgr.-Jacqueline Carpenter, Adv. Dir.-George Lambert
Editorial Description: News and features of interest to deaf cochlear implant users, their families and to support professionals.
General Info: Yr. Est. 1984, Quarterly, Trim Size-8$\frac{1}{2}$ x 11, 44 pages, ISSN: 1060-2496, 18% ads, 2 Color, Matte
Subscriptions: Indv. $18, Inst. $60, Can. $25, For. $30, Free With Membership
Circulation: Total-1,300
Advertising: $120.
Printing Co: Phillipone Business Services, 802 Kenmore Ave, Buffalo, NY 14216-1506 Tel # (216) 873-2028

Cubprints
Business, Association

Publishing Co: California School for the Deaf, 3044 Horace St, Riverside, CA 92506-4420; Title Tel # (909) 782-6500 Title Fax # (909) 782-6509
Personnel: Publisher-Gena Fischer, Publisher-Bob Greathouse, Editor, Circ. Mgr., Promotion Dir.-Zibby Bayarsky
Editorial Description: News of school serving hearing impaired youths from 3-22 years. Includes community events, programs for the deaf and parent education.
General Info: (Formerly California Palms), Yr. Est. 1953, Monthly, Trim Size-8$\frac{1}{2}$ x 11, Sheetfed press, 12 pages, 2 Color
Subscriptions: Free To Qualified Recipient
Circulation: (PSS, 66% controlled), Total-1,200, Readership-2,000, Source-I
Advertising: Inquire for rates. Accepts Inserts.

Florida School Herald
Association

Publishing Co: Florida School for the Deaf & the Blind, 207 San Marco Ave., St. Augustine, FL 32084-2762; Title Tel # (904) 823-4000 Title Fax # (904) 823-4018
Personnel: Publisher-Robert Dawson, Editor-Mary Jane Dillon
Editorial Description: Stories about students & activities at FSDB. Information for parents.
General Info: Yr. Est. 1891, 6x/yr., Trim Size-8$\frac{1}{2}$ x 11, Sheetfed press, 8 pages, ISSN: 0015-4288, Coated, Saddle-stitched
Subscriptions: Indv. $6
Circulation: (77% controlled), Total-2,200, Subscriptions-500

Gallaudet Alumni Newsletter
See: COLLEGE ALUMNI

Hearing Research Developments
Consumer, Association

Publishing Co: C.H.E.A.R., Inc., 928 Mclean Ave, Yonkers, NY 10704-4103; Title Tel # (914) 237-2676
Personnel: Publisher-Sidney Goldblatt, Editor-Philip Miller
Editorial Description: Events, newest developments in research announcements, available information.
General Info: Yr. Est. 1974, Quarterly, Trim Size-8$\frac{1}{2}$ x 11, 5 pages, Color
Circulation: Total-1,800
Advertising: Inquire for rates.

IASCP Bulletin

Publishing Co: Institute for Advanced Study of the Communication Processes, Dauer Hall 63, ASB-63, Gainesville, FL 32611; Title Tel # (904) 392-2046
Personnel: Editor-Dr. Alice Dyson
Editorial Description: Reports of research in speech, hearing & language, activities, publications, grants, etc. of members of institute.
General Info: Yr. Est. 1974, Semi-annually, Trim Size-8$\frac{1}{2}$ x 11, Mimeo press, 40 pages
Circulation: (100% controlled), Total-500

Junior NAD Newsletter
Association

Publishing Co: Junior Nat'l. Assn. for the Deaf, 814 Thayer Ave., Silver Springs, MD 20910-4500; Title Tel # (301) 587-1788 Title Fax # (301) 587-1791
Personnel: Editor-Fred Weiner
Editorial Description: For deaf youth, subscription rate includes Junior Deaf American Magazine.
General Info: (Formerly Junior NAD American), Yr. Est. 1968, Monthly, Trim Size-8$\frac{1}{2}$ x 11, Desktop press, 12 pages, 2 Color, Coated
Subscriptions: Indv. $8, $1/copy
Circulation: Total-2,000

Kentucky Standard
Association

Publishing Co: School for the Deaf, PO Box 27, S. Second St., Danville, KY 40423-0027; Title Tel # (606) 236-5132 Title Fax # (606) 239-7006
Personnel: Editor-Frank Powell
Editorial Description: School program, alumni news, educational articles on deafness, calendar of coming events, history, student activities.
General Info: Yr. Est. 1823, 8x/yr., Trim Size-8$\frac{1}{2}$ x 11, Offset press, 12 pages, No Color, Newsprint, Saddle-stitched
Subscriptions: Indv. $3
Circulation: Total-1,525

MN Speech-Language-Hearing Assn.

Publishing Co: MN Speech-Language-Hearing Assn., PO Box 26115, St. Louis Park, MN 55426-0115; Title Tel # (612) 920-0787 Title Fax # (612) 920-6098
Personnel: Editor-Maxine Slobof
General Info: Bi-monthly, Trim Size-8$\frac{1}{2}$ x 11, 10 pages, 1% ads, No Color, Newsprint
Subscriptions: Indv. $25, Inst. $25, $5/copy
Circulation: Total-800
List Rental: Actives: $75/M

Martimer
Consumer, Association

Publishing Co: APSEA-RCHI, Box 308, Amherst, NS B4H 3Z6 Canada; Title Tel # (902) 667-3808 Title Fax # (902) 667-0893
Personnel: Editor-Phyllis Cameron
Editorial Description: Periodical describing programs & services provided by the APSEA-Resource Centre for the Hearing Impaired. Audience would be parents, school districts & friends of the school.
General Info: Yr. Est. 1975, Quarterly, Trim Size-8$\frac{1}{2}$ x 11, 8 pages, ISSN: 0704-0652

NAD Broadcaster

Publishing Co: Natl. Assn. of the Deaf, 814 Thayer Ave., Silver Spring, MD 20910-4500; Title Tel # (301) 587-1788 Title Fax # (301) 578-1791
Personnel: Editor, Adv. Dir.-Anita Farb
Editorial Description: Monthly newsletter distributed to members of NAD, containing stories and articles and columns about the deaf community.
Subscriptions: Indv. $10, Inst. $10

NJSHA Newsletter
Association

Publishing Co: NJ Speech-Language-Hearing Assn., 2 Greentree Centre, Suite 225 / Box 955, Marlton, NJ 08053; Title Tel # (609) 985-2878
Personnel: Editor-Lisa Hastings, Adv. Dir.-Beth Krchnavek
Editorial Description: For professional assn. of speech-language pathologists & audiologists.
General Info: Yr. Est. 1955, Bi-monthly, 10 pages
Subscriptions: Indv. $15
Circulation: Total-1,700
Advertising: Inquire for rates.

News n' Notes
See: EDUCATION

Newsletter of American Hearing Research Foundation
Association

Publishing Co: American Hearing Research Found., 55 E Washington St., Ste. 2022, Chicago, IL 60602-2202; Title Tel # (312) 726-9670
Personnel: Editor-William Lederer
Editorial Description: Concerned with hearing research and education.
General Info: Yr. Est. 1970, 3x/yr., Trim Size-8$\frac{1}{2}$ x 11, Offset press, 6 pages, Color, Coated
Subscriptions: Indv. $15
Circulation: Total-13,000

Noise Regulation Report
Business

Publishing Co: Business Publishers, Inc., 951 Pershing Dr., Silver Spring, MD 20910-4464 Tel # (301) 589-5103 Fax # (301) 589-8493; Title Tel # (301) 587-6300 Title Fax # (301) 587-1081
Personnel: Publisher-Leonard A. Eiserer, Editor-Charlotte Gavey, Mktg. Dir.-Fay S. Gold
Editorial Description: Federal, state and local regulation of noise control and vibration issues.
General Info: (Formerly Noise Control Report), Yr. Est. 1974, Bi-weekly, Trim Size-8$\frac{1}{2}$ x 11, Desktop press, 8 pages, Ind/Abs/Online: Newsnet and Predicasts, No Color, Recycled
Subscriptions: Indv. $455, Inst. $455, Can. $455, For. $468
List Rental: List Management Co.: Manager: Jim Hauschild; BPI Direct, 951 Pershing Dr., Silver Spring, MD 20910-4464 Tel # (301) 585-5976, Fax # (301) 587-4530

On the Level
See: HEALTH

Otoscope
Consumer

Publishing Co: EAR Foundation, 2000 Church St # 111, Nashville, TN 37236-0001 Fax # (615) 329-7935; Title Fax # (615) 340-4606
Personnel: Editor-Sonya Walley Tate
Editorial Description: Covers medical developments, patient coping strategies, communication methods and information on general interest to the hearing impaired.
General Info: Yr. Est. 1978, 3x/yr.
Circulation: Total-16,500

Our Voice
See: HEALTH

RLE Currents
See: ENGINEERING, ELECTRICAL

Registry, The
Business, Consumer

Publishing Co: National Temporal Bone, Hearing, & Balance Pathology Registry, Deafness Research Foundation, 15 W. 39th St., New York, NY 10018-3806; Title Tel # (212) 684-6556 Title Fax # (212) 779-2125
Personnel: Editor-Ron Wudarsky
Editorial Description: To help stimulate otopathological research.
General Info: Yr. Est. 1992, Semi-annually, Trim Size-8$\frac{1}{2}$ x 11, 6 pages

Rehabilitation Technology Newsletter
See: SOCIAL SERVICES & WELFARE

Reverberations *Association*

Publishing Co: Speech & Hearing Assn. of Nova Scotia, Box 775 Sta M, 5919 South St., Halifax, NS B3J 2V2 Canada; Title Tel # (902) 423-9331
Personnel: Editor-Robert Ikley
General Info: Trim Size-5½ x 8½, Sheetfed press, 16 pages, 2% ads, No Color, Coated, Saddle-stitched
Circulation: (100% controlled), Total-175
Advertising: Inquire for rates.

SHAA Newsletter *Association*

Publishing Co: Speech & Hearing Assn. of Alberta, 10060 Jafper Ave., Suite 2210, Edmonton, AB T5J 3R8 Canada; Title Tel # (403) 944-1609
Personnel: Editor-C. Dearden, Editor-Joan Sullivan
General Info: Quarterly, 25 pages
Circulation: Total-550
Advertising: Inquire for rates.

STEADY *Consumer*

Publishing Co: EAR Foundation, 2000 Church St # 111, Nashville, TN 37236-0001 Fax # (615) 329-7935; Title Fax # (615) 340-4606
Personnel: Editor-Sonya Walley Tate
Editorial Description: Newsletter of the Meniere's Network, a national network of support groups for those with Meniere's Disease. Provides information about the condition, treatment alternatives, and coping strategies.
General Info: Yr. Est. 1988, Quarterly
Subscriptions: Indv. $25
Circulation: Total-2,000

Spectra *Association*

Publishing Co: Speech Communication Association, 5105 Backlick Rd Bldg E, Annandale, VA 22003-6005; Title Tel # (703) 750-0533 Title Fax # (703) 914-9471
Personnel: Editor-James L. Gaudino, Circ. Mgr.-Norma Geiger
Editorial Description: A membership newsletter with timely reports on federal legislation, curriculum, & research etc.
General Info: Yr. Est. 1964, Monthly, Trim Size-8½ x 11, Letrpr. press, 16 pages, Ind/Abs/Online: BRS, DIALOG, No Color, Newsprint
Subscriptions: Indv. $36
Circulation: (92% controlled), Total-7,600
List Rental: Actives: $50/M
Printing Co: Harpers Graphics, 1 Post Office Rd, Waldorf, MD 20602-2710 Tel # (301) 843-6950

Tennessee Observer

Publishing Co: Tennessee School for the Deaf, 2725 Island Home Blvd., Knoxville, TN 37920-2700; Title Tel # (423) 594-6022
General Info: Bi-monthly
Subscriptions: Indv. $2

Views *Consumer, Association*

Publishing Co: Registry of Interpreters for the Deaf, 8719 Colesville Rd Ste 310, Silver Spring, MD 20910-3919; Title Fax # (301) 608-0508
General Info: (Formerly Interpreter Views), Yr. Est. 1964, Monthly, Offset press, 24 pages, 2% ads, 2 Color, Newsprint, Saddle-stitched
Subscriptions: Indv. $24, $3/copy
Circulation: Total-4,000
Advertising: Inquire for rates.
Printing Co: McArdle Printing Co., 800 Commerce Dr, Upper Marlboro, MD 20772-8792 Tel # (301) 390-8500

WID News *Association*

Publishing Co: Western Institute for the Deaf, 2125 W. 7th Ave., Vancouver, BC V6K 1X9 Canada; Title Tel # (604) 736-7391
Personnel: Publisher-Lynn Siddaway, Editor-Helen Parker
Editorial Description: Information of interest to the membership as well as items of interest within the hearing impaired community.
General Info: Yr. Est. 1970, Quarterly, Trim Size-8½ x 11, Desktop press, 6 pages, 2 Color, Saddle-stitched
Subscriptions: Indv. $10
Circulation: (100% controlled), Total-900
Advertising: Inquire for rates.

HEATING, PLUMBING, A/C, REFRIG.

ACCA News *Association*

Publishing Co: Air Conditioning Contractors of America, 1712 New Hampshire Ave NW, Washington, DC 20009-2502; Title Tel # (202) 483-9370 Title Fax # (202) 234-4721
Personnel: Editor-Elaine Smith
Editorial Description: Informs members of assn. & industry news.
General Info: Yr. Est. 1969, 10x/yr., Trim Size-8½ x 11, 8 pages, 2 Color, Coated
Circulation: (100% controlled), Total-2,500

ARCA Update *Association*

Publishing Co: ARCA/NJ, 66 Morris Ave., Springfield, NJ 07081-1409; Title Tel # (201) 379-1100
Personnel: Editor-Debbie Hart, Circ. Mgr.-Jim Grassi
Editorial Description: Industry trends, association news for air conditioning/refrigeration contractors.
General Info: Yr. Est. 1983, Monthly, Trim Size-8½ x 11, Offset press, 4 pages, 2 Color
Circulation: (100% controlled), Total-175

ARW Supplier News *Association*

Publishing Co: Air-Conditioning & Refrigeration Wholesalers, 10251 W Sample Rd # B, Coral Springs, FL 33065-3939; Title Tel # (305) 771-1000
Personnel: Publisher-David Kellough, Editor-Nicholas Aramino
Editorial Description: Information pertinent to suppliers of products to wholesaler members.
General Info: Yr. Est. 1935, Trim Size-8½ x 11, 6 pages, 2 Color

ASA News *Business, Association*   CPM: $184

Publishing Co: American Supply Association, 222 Merchandise Mart Plz., Ste. 1360, Chicago, IL 60654-1016; Title Tel # (312) 464-0090 Title Fax # (312) 464-0091
Personnel: Publisher-Peter Schwartz, Editor-Paul Zuziak, Circ. Mgr.-Alan Rusinski, Production Mgr.-Tommy Connor, Adv. Dir.-Molly Frank-Stewart
Editorial Description: Covers ASA activities and events in the plumbing, heating, cooling and piping supply industry.
General Info: (Formerly ASA Newsletter), Yr. Est. 1968, Bi-monthly, Trim Size-15 x 11, Web press, 24 pages, 4 Color, Matte, Saddle-stitched
Subscriptions: Inst. $11, Free
Circulation: (BPA, 100% controlled), Total-13,023
Advertising: $2,408.
Printing Co: Thrift-Remsen Printers, 739 20th St, Rockford, IL 61104-3504 Tel # (815) 397-1022, Fax # (815) 397-1029

Comfortline

Publishing Co: Graham Communications, PO Box 222, Georgetown, MA 01833-0322; Title Tel # (800) 696-4526
Personnel: Publisher-Jim Townsend, Editor-John Graham, Art Dir.-Jan Byorkman
Editorial Description: A newsletter from Townsend Oil Co., Inc.
General Info: Yr. Est. 1989, Quarterly, Sheetfed press, 4 pages, 2 Color, Matte, Perfect bound
Circulation: Total-20,000
Printing Co: Ink Spot, The, 40 Oval Rd, Quincy, MA 02170-3813 Tel # (617) 273-7605, Fax # (617) 471-8810

Counterline *Association*

Publishing Co: Air-Conditioning & Refrigeration Wholesalers, 10251 W Sample Rd # B, Coral Springs, FL 33065-3939; Title Tel # (305) 771-1000
Personnel: Publisher-David Kellough, Editor-Charles Willits
General Info: Yr. Est. 1935, Quarterly, Desktop press

Forum Information

Publishing Co: National Trust for Historic Preservation, 1785 Massachusetts Ave., NW, Washington, DC 20036-2117 Tel # (202) 673-4035; Title Tel # (202) 673-4296
Personnel: Publisher-Margaret Heimbold, Editor-CAtharine Gilliam, Circ. Mgr.-Lajeune Farmer, Production Mgr.-Polly Arenberg
Editorial Description: Provides technical information to a natl. network of preservation professionals & organizations.
General Info: Yr. Est. 1987, Bi-monthly, 8 pages, Ind/Abs/Online: Provides technical information to a national network of preservation profes, 2 Color
Subscriptions: Indv. $75, $5/copy
Circulation: Total-4,000
Printing Co: Smith Lithograph Corp., 1029 E Gude Dr, Rockville, MD 20850-1333 Tel # (301) 424-1400

HRAI News *Business, Association*

Publishing Co: Heating, Refrigerating & Air Conditioning Inst. of Canada, 5045 Orbitor Drive, Building 11, Suite 300, Mississauga, ON L4W 4Y4 Canada Tel # (905) 602-4700 Fax # (905) 602-1197; Title Tel # (416) 239-8191
Personnel: Editor-Gerald Smith
General Info: (Formerly Environment), Yr. Est. 1968, Semi-annually, Offset press, 4 pages, 2 Color, Saddle-stitched
Subscriptions: Free With Membership
Circulation: (100% controlled), Total-1,800

Home Ventilating Guide *Business, Association*

Publishing Co: Home Ventilating Institute, Div. of AMCA, 30 W. University Dr., Arlington Heights, IL 60004-1806; Title Tel # (708) 394-0150 Title Fax # (708) 253-0088
Editorial Description: Bulletin covering proper home ventilation.
General Info: Irregular
Subscriptions: Free

Impact Compressors/ Turbines News & Patents *Business*

Publishing Co: Impact Pubs., PO Box 3113, Ketchum, ID 83340-3113; Title Tel # (208) 726-2133 Title Fax # (208) 726-2115
Personnel: Publisher, Editor-Mary Jo Helmeke
Editorial Description: Report describing new compressor/turbine patents & new developments in compressor/turbine field. Includes listings of current articles, seminars, books, industry news, etc.
General Info: (Formerly Impact Compressors), Yr. Est. 1975, 10x/yr., Trim Size-8½ x 11, Mimeo press, 30 pages, ISSN: 0884-2264, Color-cover
Subscriptions: Indv. $60, For. $70, $6/copy
Advertising: Inquire for rates.
List Rental: Rents Lists

Impact Pump News & Patents
Business

Publishing Co: Impact Pubs., PO Box 3113, Ketchum, ID 83340-3113; Title Tel # (208) 726-2133 Title Fax # (208) 726-2115
Personnel: Publisher, Editor-Mary Jo Helmeke
Editorial Description: Describes all types of new pumps as they are introduced. Includes listings of current articles, seminars, books, industry news, and patents from gazette arranged by category.
General Info: Yr. Est. 1973, 10x/yr., Trim Size-8½ x 11, Mimeo press, 45 pages, ISSN: 1056-1536, Color-cover
Subscriptions: Indv. $100, For. $110, $10/copy
Advertising: Inquire for rates.
List Rental: Rents Lists

Impact Valve News & Patents
Business

Publishing Co: Impact Pubs., PO Box 3113, Ketchum, ID 83340-3113; Title Tel # (208) 726-2133 Title Fax # (208) 726-2115
Personnel: Publisher, Editor-Mary Jo Helmeke
Editorial Description: Describes all types of new valves as they are introduced. Includes patents form gazette arranged by category.
General Info: Yr. Est. 1974, 10x/yr., Trim Size-8½ x 11, Mimeo press, 50 pages, ISSN: 1506-1544, Color-cover
Subscriptions: Indv. $150, For. $160, $15/copy
Advertising: Inquire for rates.
List Rental: Rents Lists

Koldfax
Association

Publishing Co: Air-Conditioning & Refrigeration Institute (ARI), 4301 Fairfax Dr Ste 425, Arlington, VA 22203-1627; Title Tel # (703) 524-8800 Title Fax # (703) 528-3816
Personnel: Editor, Circ. Mgr.-Maura Shannon
Editorial Description: Membership newsletter for manufacturers of air-conditioning & refrigeration equipment.
General Info: Monthly, Trim Size-8½ x 11, Letrpr. press, 8 pages, Color
Subscriptions: Free With Membership
Circulation: (100% controlled), Total-2,400
Printing Co: Corporate Press, 403 Brightseat Rd., Landover, MD 20785-4706 Tel # (301) 499-9200, Fax # (301) 499-5435

Maryland News and Views

Publishing Co: Maryland Plumbing Heating Cooling Contractors, Inc., 10176 Baltimore National Pike, Ste 205, Ellicott City, MD 21042-3672; Title Tel # (301) 461-5977 Title Fax # (301) 750-2507
Personnel: Adv. Dir.-Phil Maher, Art Dir.-Diane Kastner
Editorial Description: Covers new products in the plumbing, heating cooling field, legislation, code and license requirements, technical information.
General Info: Monthly, Letrpr. press, 24 pages, 4 Color, Coated
Circulation: Total-2,000
Advertising: Inquire for rates.
Printing Co: Graphic Expressions, 5418 Harford Rd, Baltimore, MD 21214-2215 Tel # (301) 254-4998

Minuteman

Publishing Co: Air-Conditioning & Refrigeration Institute (ARI), 4301 Fairfax Dr Ste 425, Arlington, VA 22203-1627 Fax # (703) 528-3816; Title Tel # (703) 524-8800
Editorial Description: Government affairs policy letter.
General Info: Monthly
Subscriptions: Free To Qualified Recipient

Radiator Reporter
Business

Publishing Co: Runzheimer Intl., Runzheimer Park, Rochester, WI 53167 Tel # (414) 767-2200 Fax # (414) 767-2254; Title Tel # (708) 291-9011 Title Fax # (708) 291-9581
Personnel: Publisher-Bradford Burris, Editor-Ralph McDarmont
General Info: Yr. Est. 1973, Monthly, Trim Size-8½ x 11, Sheetfed press, ISSN: 0739-2060, No Color, Newsprint
Subscriptions: Indv. $125, Can. $160, $15/copy
Acquistions: Publication Bought, Publication Sold
List Rental: Rents Lists

Refrigeration News
Association

Publishing Co: NRCA, 1900 Arch St, Philadelphia, PA 19103-1404; Title Tel # (215) 564-3484 Title Fax # (215) 963-9785
Personnel: Editor-Dale Zeigler
Editorial Description: Assn. newsletter.
General Info: Quarterly, Trim Size-8.5 x 11, Desktop press, 8 pages, No Color, Matte, Other
Subscriptions: Free

Spotlight on Service & Maintenance

Publishing Co: Mechanical Contractors Association of Eastern PA, Inc., 1601 Market St Fl 550, Philadelphia, PA 19103-2337; Title Tel # (215) 563-9498
Personnel: Publisher-Bill Lindsay, Editor-Bill Redstreake, Circ. Mgr.-Jeanette Lindsay, Production Mgr.-Greg Norbert, Art Dir.-Barbara Hebding
Editorial Description: Newsworthy reports about innovations & applications to improve HVAC/R installations.
General Info: Yr. Est. 1979, Quarterly, Sheetfed press, 4 pages, 2 Color, Coated
Circulation: Total-8,500
Printing Co: Winchell Marketing Communications, 1315 Cherry St., Philadelphia, PA 19107 Tel # (215) 568-1770

Stove Parts Needed
See: ANTIQUES & ART GOODS

Trade Association News

Publishing Co: Roofing Metal, 167 W Walnut Pk Dr, Philadelphia, PA 19120-1010; Title Tel # (215) 276-1675
General Info: Yr. Est. 1903, Monthly
Circulation: Total-968

Washington Plumbing and Heating Contractor
Association

Publishing Co: Ballard Printing, 11732 1st Ave NE, Seattle, WA 98125-4714; Title Tel # (206) 363-9647

HISTORY

ABH Bulletin
Association

Publishing Co: Association for the Bibliography of History, Pullen Lib., GSU, Ref. Dept., Atlanta, GA 30303; Title Tel # (404) 651-2422
Personnel: Editor-Carol Jones
Editorial Description: Association news and activities relating to historical bibliography.
General Info: (Formerly Assn. for the Bibliography of History Newletter), Yr. Est. 1978, Semi-annually, ISSN: 0892-4600
Subscriptions: Indv. $10, Inst. $10

ACA Bulletin
Association

Publishing Co: Sponsor-Univ. of Regina, Association of Canadian Archivists, Box 2596, Station D, Ottawa, ON K1P 5W6 Canada; Title Tel # (613) 443-0251 Title Fax # (613) 443-0261
Personnel: Editor-E. Diamond
Editorial Description: This newsletter publishes topical information on archival concerns in Canada & the world.
General Info: (Formerly Archives Bulletin), Yr. Est. 1975, Bi-monthly, 24 pages, ISSN: 0709-4604, Color-cover, Saddle-stitched
Subscriptions: Inst. $80, Can. $86, For. $80
Circulation: Total-750, Readership-750
Advertising: Accepts Inserts.

AGS Quarterly: Bulletin of the Association for Gravestone Studies
Association **CPM: $95**

Publishing Co: Assn. for Gravestone Studies, 30 Elm St, Worcester, MA 01609-2504; Title Tel # (508) 831-7753
Personnel: Editor-Miranda Levin
Editorial Description: Contains feature articles, regional & topical columns, news items, book reviews, member activities, assn. news.
General Info: (Formerly Association for Gravestone Studies Newsletter), Yr. Est. 1977, Quarterly, Trim Size-8½ x 11, Offset press, 28 pages, ISSN: 0146-5783, No Color
Subscriptions: Indv. $25, Inst. $30, $3/copy
Circulation: Total-1,050
Advertising: $100.
List Rental: Rents Lists
Printing Co: Marie's Direct Mail, 105 Fremont St, Worcester, MA 01603-2308 Tel # (508) 755-9853, Fax # (508) 755-7523

AIC Newsletter
See: ART & SCULPTURE

AIHP Notes
Association

Publishing Co: American Institute of the History of Pharmacy, 425 N. Charter Street, Madison, WI 53706; Title Tel # (608) 262-5378
Personnel: Publisher-Gregory J. Higby, Editor-Jonathon Grant, Circ. Mgr.-Carrie Massey, Production Mgr.-Elaine Stroud, Production Mgr.-Rosemary Zurlo-Cuva
Editorial Description: News abbout the institute and the history of pharmacy field, including future programming and seetings collector's column.
General Info: Yr. Est. 1959, Quarterly, Trim Size-8½ x 11, Offset press, 4 pages, Newsprint
Subscriptions: Free With Membership
Circulation: Total-1,250, Readership-2,000
Advertising: Inquire for rates.

AMIA Newsletter (Assn. of Moving Image Archivists)
See: LIBRARY

APVA Newsletter
See: ARCHITECTURE

ARA Journal
See: POLITICS

ASCH Newsletter
Association

Publishing Co: Sponsor-Assn. for the Study of Connecticut History, Emerson College, 100 Beacon St, Boston, MA 02116-1596 Tel # (617) 578-8500; Title Tel # (617) 578-8762
Personnel: Editor-Robert Roetger
Editorial Description: Short articles & bibliographic essays focusing on any aspect of Connecticut history. News of the Organization.
General Info: Semi-annually, Trim Size-5 x 8, Offset press, 16 pages, No Color
Circulation: Total-250

ATHA Newsletter
See: HOBBY

Acadian Genealogy Exchange
See: GENEALOGY

Adams County Trumpeter

Publishing Co: Adams County Historical Society, PO Box 262, Decatur, IN 46733-0262
Editorial Description: Covers Historical Society activities, & Indiana.'
General Info: Yr. Est. 1978, Trim Size-8½ x 11, 6 pages
Subscriptions: Free With Membership
Circulation: Total-400

Advance Notice
See: GENEALOGY

Allen County Historical Society, Newsletter   *Association*

Publishing Co: Allen County Historical Society, 620 W Market St, Lima, OH 45801-4604; Title Tel # (419) 222-9426
Personnel: Editor-Raymond Schuck
General Info: Yr. Est. 1983, Bi-monthly, Trim Size-8½ x 11, 2 pages, Newsprint
Subscriptions: Indv. $10
Circulation: Total-610
Printing Co: News Gazette Printing Co., 324 W Market St, Lima, OH 45801-4714

Alumni Newsletter
See: EDUCATION

American Brahms Society Newsletter
See: MUSIC & MUSIC TRADES

American Friends of Lafayette   *Association*

Publishing Co: Lafayette College Library, Skillman Library, Easton, PA 18042 Tel # (610) 250-5161; Title Tel # (614) 025-0516 Title Fax # (610) 252-0370
Personnel: Editor-Leonard Panaggie
Editorial Description: Covers the organization, Marquis de Lafayette and Franco-American relations.
General Info: Yr. Est. 1932, Annually, Trim Size-8½ x 11, Offset press, 4 pages, No Color
Subscriptions: Indv. $20
Circulation: (100% controlled), Total-150

American Italian Historical Association Newsletter
See: ETHNIC

American Studies Assn. Newsletter
See: CULTURE & HUMANITIES

Americans Before Columbus
See: ETHNIC

Annotation   *Scholarly*

Publishing Co: National Historical Publications and Records Commission, National Archives Bldg., Washington, DC 20408-0001; Title Tel # (202) 501-5600 Title Fax # (202) 501-5601
Personnel: Editor-Laurie Baty, Editor-Daniel Stokes
Editorial Description: Preservation and publication of historical manuscripts and records.
General Info: Yr. Est. 1973, Tri-annually, Trim Size-8½ x 11, Offset press, 12 pages, ISSN: 0160-8460, No Color, Matte, Saddle-stitched
Subscriptions: (Free)
Circulation: (100% controlled)

Archaeoastronomy & Ethnoastronomy News
See: ASTRONOMY

Archaeology on Kaua'i
See: ARCHAEOLOGY

Archival Outlook   *Association*

Publishing Co: Society of American Archivists, 600 S. Federal St., Ste. 504, Chicago, IL 60605-1898; Title Tel # (312) 922-0140 Title Fax # (312) 347-1452
Personnel: Editor, Adv. Dir.-Teresa Brinati
Editorial Description: Articles covering archival theory and practice.
General Info: (Formerly SAA Newsletter), Yr. Est. 1973, Bi-monthly, Trim Size-8½ x 11, 36 pages, ISSN: 0091-5971, 1% ads, No Color, Newsprint
Circulation: (100% controlled), Total-3,900
Advertising: Inquire for rates.
List Rental: Rents Lists

Archives of Labor
See: LABOR

Arkansas Preservation Digest   *Consumer, Association*

Publishing Co: Historic Preservation Alliance of Arkansas, PO Box 305, Little Rock, AR 72203-0305 Tel # (501) 372-4757
Personnel: Publisher-Douglas Wallace, Editor-Ruth Mitchell
Editorial Description: Publication on the historic preservation of Arkansas.
General Info: Quarterly
Subscriptions: $2/copy

Association for the History of Chiropractic-Bulletin
See: MEDICINE

Atlantic County Historical Society Newsletter
See: GENEALOGY

August Derleth Society Newletter

Publishing Co: August Derleth Society, PO Box 481, Sauk City, WI 53583
General Info: 4x/yr., ISSN: 0272-9911

Augustana Historian

Publishing Co: Augustana Historical Society, Augustana College, Rock Island, IL 61201-2296; Title Tel # (309) 794-7228
Personnel: Editor-Dr. Melbert Peterson
General Info: (Formerly Augustana Historical Society-Newsletter), Yr. Est. 1983, Semi-annually
Circulation: Total-300

Bancroftiana   *Association*

Publishing Co: Friends of the Bancroft Library, Inc., The, Univ. Of Calif., Berkeley, CA 94720-6000 Tel # (510) 642-7589; Title Tel # (510) 642-3781
Editorial Description: Informational news for members of the organization that supports the Library of Western Americana, Latin Americana and rare books in general.
General Info: Yr. Est. 1950, Trim Size-6 x 9½, Letrpr. press, 12 pages, No Color, Saddle-stitched
Subscriptions: Free With Membership
Circulation: Total-1,600, Readership-1,600

Baptist Heritage Update
See: RELIGIOUS & THEOLOGICAL

Barney Family News
See: GENEALOGY

Beech Grove
See: GENEALOGY

Belgian Laces   *Association*

Publishing Co: Belgian Researchers, 62073 Fruitdale Ln., La Grande, OR 97850-5312; Title Tel # (541) 963-6697 Title Fax # (541) 962-7604
Personnel: Publisher-Pierre Inghels, Editor-Leen Inghels, Art Dir.-Carmelo Bellavia
General Info: Yr. Est. 1976, Quarterly, Trim Size-8½ x 11, Roto. press, 24 pages, ISSN: 1046-0462, Color-cover, Saddle-stitched
Subscriptions: Indv. $15, Can. $15, For. $18, $4/copy
Circulation: Total-450
List Rental: Rents Lists
Printing Co: La Grande Quick Print, Jefferson Ave., La Grande, OR 97850

Benedict Family News, The
See: GENEALOGY

Berea College Appalachian Center Newsletter   *Association*

Publishing Co: Berea College, Publications, Berea, KY 40404-0001 Tel # (606) 986-9341 Fax # (606) 986-9494
Personnel: Editor-Tom Parrish, Production Mgr.-Loyal Jones
Editorial Description: News of Appalachian region, especially Appalachian studies.
General Info: Yr. Est. 1972, Quarterly, Trim Size-8½ x 11, Offset press, 4 pages
Subscriptions: Indv. $3, Free
Circulation: (100% controlled), Total-1,800

Bethel Courier   *Consumer, Association*

Publishing Co: Bethel Historical Society, Inc., 14 Broad St # 12, Bethel, ME 04217-3802; Title Tel # (207) 824-2908
Personnel: Publisher, Editor-Stanley Howe
Editorial Description: Local & regional history, book reviews, genealogy, & society news.
General Info: Yr. Est. 1976, Quarterly, Trim Size-8½ x 11, Sheetfed press, 8 pages, ISSN: 0749-9108, No Color, Newsprint
Subscriptions: Indv. $10, Inst. $25
Circulation: Total-1,200

Black History News & Notes   *Consumer*

Publishing Co: Indiana Historical Society, 315 W Ohio St, Indianapolis, IN 46202-3210 Tel # (317) 233-3157; Title Tel # (317) 232-1879 Title Fax # (317) 233-3109
Personnel: Editor-Wilma Gibbs
Editorial Description: Quarterly newsletter of the Black History program of the Indiana Historical Society (IHS). Contains information about IHS collections and articles and relevant announcements on Indiana black history.
General Info: Yr. Est. 1979, Quarterly, Sheetfed press, ISSN: 1058-4900, Matte, Saddle-stitched
Subscriptions: Inst. $20, Free With Membership
Circulation: Total-800
Printing Co: Graphics Ltd., Inc., 401 N College Ave, Indianapolis, IN 46202-3605 Tel # (317) 263-3456

Boletin
See: EDUCATION

Book Newsletter & Catalog
See: BOOKS & BOOK TRADE

Book, The: Newsletter of the Program in the History of the Book in American Culture
See: BOOKS & BOOK TRADE

Boombah Herald   *Scholarly*

Publishing Co: Boombah Herald, 15 Park Blvd, Lancaster, NY 14086-2510; Title Tel # (716) 681-9720
Personnel: Publisher, Editor-Loren Geiger
Editorial Description: Band history.
General Info: Yr. Est. 1973, Semi-annually, Trim Size-8½ x 11, Sheetfed press, 12 pages, ISSN: 8755-5832, No Color
Subscriptions: Indv. $10, $5/copy
Printing Co: A.G. Halldin Co., 954 N. Bash Rd., Indiana, PA 15701 Tel # (412) 463-8450

Born Young Newsletter
See: GENEALOGY

Bradford Compact Newsletter
See: GENEALOGY

British Studies Intelligencer

Publishing Co: Sponsor-North American Conference on British Studies, Georgetown Univ. Dept. of History, Georgetown Univ., Washington, DC 20057-0001; Title Tel # (202) 687-5909
Personnel: Editor-Peter Dunkley
General Info: Sheetfed press, 40 pages, No Color
Circulation: Total-850

Brooklyn Historical Society Newsletter, The   *Consumer*

Publishing Co: Brooklyn Historical Society, 128 Pierrepont St, Brooklyn, NY 11201-2794; Title Tel # (718) 624-0890 Title Fax # (718) 875-3869
Personnel: Editor-Jill Levey
Editorial Description: Featuring news at the Brooklyn Historical Society & information on Society's events. Some feature stories about Brooklyn history.
General Info: Yr. Est. 1986, 3x/yr., Trim Size-5½ x 11, Offset press, 4 pages, 2 Color, Newsprint
Subscriptions: Indv. $35
Circulation: Total-5,000

Bulletin

Publishing Co: Cortland County Historical Society, 25 Homer Ave, Cortland, NY 13045-2018; Title Tel # (607) 756-6071
Personnel: Editor-Mary Ann Kane
General Info: Yr. Est. 1947, Trim Size-5½ x 8½, 4 pages, No Color
Circulation: Total-750

Bulletin of the Historical Society of Haddonfield

Publishing Co: Historical Society of Haddonfield, 343 Kings Hwy E, Haddonfield, NJ 08033-1214; Title Tel # (609) 429-7375
Personnel: Editor-Connie Reeves
Editorial Description: Local history of news of coming events.
General Info: Yr. Est. 1958, Quarterly, 4 pages, No Color
Subscriptions: Free With Membership
Circulation: Total-400

Bulletin from Johnny Cake Hill   *Association*

Publishing Co: Old Dartmouth Historical Soc., 18 Johnny Cake Hill, Whaling Museum, New Bedford, MA 02740-6317; Title Tel # (508) 997-0046 Title Fax # (508) 997-0018
Personnel: Editor, Promotion Dir.-Frederic Hood
Editorial Description: Information on new exhibitsm and acquisitions. Devoted to area history, including whaling in the 1800s.
General Info: Yr. Est. 1974, 3x/yr., Trim Size-8½ x 11, Offset press, 6 pages, 2 Color
Subscriptions: Indv. $15, Free With Membership
Circulation: (100% controlled), Total-2,400

Bulletin of the Kentucky Historical Society   *Association*

Publishing Co: Kentucky Historical Society, PO Box H, Frankfort, KY 40602-2108; Title Tel # (502) 564-3016 Title Fax # (502) 564-4701
Personnel: Editor-Gretchen Haney
Editorial Description: Local societies news & historical events, includes some book notes, feature stories.
General Info: Yr. Est. 1974, Quarterly, Trim Size-8½ x 11, Sheetfed press, 8 pages, No Color
Subscriptions: Indv. $25, Inst. $30, $1/copy
Circulation: (100% controlled), Total-6,200
Printing Co: Commonwealth of Kentucky, Frankfort, KY 40601

Bunker Banner
See: GENEALOGY

Bush-Meeting Dutch
See: GENEALOGY

Business History Bulletin
See: BUSINESS & INDUSTRY

CAL/NX211 Collectors Society Newsletter   *Association*

Publishing Co: C.A.L./NX211 Collector's Society, 727 Youn Kin Pky S, Columbus, OH 43207-4788; Title Tel # (614) 497-9517
Editorial Description: Forum for the study and collection of Lindbergh memorabilia and history.
General Info: Yr. Est. 1989, Quarterly
Subscriptions: Indv. $20, Free With Membership

CHI Dispatch   *Consumer*

Publishing Co: Confederate Historical Institute, PO Box 7388, Little Rock, AR 72217-7388; Title Tel # (501) 225-3996 Title Fax # (501) 225-5167
Personnel: Publisher, Editor-Jerry Russell
Editorial Description: News, articles on history of Confederate States of America & the preservation of Civil War sites.
General Info: Yr. Est. 1979, Bi-monthly, Trim Size-8½ x 11, Mimeo press, 20 pages, No Color
Subscriptions: Indv. $20
Circulation: Total-525
Advertising: Inquire for rates.

CN Lines
See: RAILROADS

California Statesman
See: GOVERNMENT

Campaign
See: PHILATELY & POSTAL AFFAIRS

Canadian Historical Association Newsletter/ Bulletin   *Association*

Publishing Co: Canadian Historical Association, 395 Wellington St., Ottawa, ON K1A 0N3 Canada; Title Tel # (613) 233-7885 Title Fax # (613) 567-3110
Personnel: Editor-Donald Wright
Editorial Description: Membership news in English and French.
General Info: Yr. Est. 1975, Tri-annually, 24 pages
Subscriptions: Indv. $60, Inst. $70
Circulation: Total-2,500

Carolina Comments

Publishing Co: North Carolina Division of Archives & History, 109 E Jones St, Raleigh, NC 27601-2806 Fax # (919) 733-1439; Title Tel # (919) 733-7442
Personnel: Editor-Robert Topkins
Editorial Description: News of state and local historical societies; agencies and history-related activities in North Carolina.
General Info: Yr. Est. 1952, Bi-monthly, Trim Size-6¾ x 10, Offset press, 24 pages, No Color
Subscriptions: Indv. $5, $1/copy
Circulation: (100% controlled)

Carroll County History Journal   *Consumer, Association*

Publishing Co: Historical Society of Carroll County, 210 E Main St, Westminster, MD 21157-5225 Tel # (401) 848-6494; Title Tel # (410) 848-6494
Personnel: Editor-Jay Graybeal
Editorial Description: Articles and notices about local history and special events in Carroll County; including information about membership activities.
General Info: Yr. Est. 1952, Quarterly, Trim Size-8½ x 11, Sheetfed press, 6 pages, No Color, Newsprint
Circulation: (100% controlled), Total-1,000

Cass County Connections
See: GENEALOGY

Castle Light   *Association*

Publishing Co: Passaic County Historical Society, Lambert Castle, 3 Valley Rd., Paterson, NJ 07503; Title Tel # (201) 881-2761
Editorial Description: News and information from the Passaic County Historical Society.
General Info: Semi-annually

Cavalry Journal, The
See: MILITARY & NAVAL

Center for Migration Studies Newsletter
See: SOCIOLOGY

Center for Reformation Research, Newsletter

Publishing Co: Center for Reformation Research, 6477 San Bonita Ave, St. Louis, MO 63105-3117; Title Tel # (314) 727-6655
Personnel: Editor-William S. Maltby
Editorial Description: Facilitates communication among those interested in the 16th century.
General Info: (Formerly Foundation for Reformation Research Monthly Newsletter), Yr. Est. 1968, Quarterly, Trim Size-8½ x 11, Offset press, 6 pages
Circulation: Total-3,400
Advertising: Inquire for rates.

Center for Socialist History Interbulletin

Publishing Co: Center for Socialist History, 2633 Etna St, Berkeley, CA 94704-3408; Title Tel # (415) 843-4658
Personnel: Editor-Ernest Haberkern
General Info: Yr. Est. 1981
Subscriptions: Indv. $10, $3/copy

Central Kentucky Researcher *Association*

Publishing Co: Taylor County Historical Society, PO Box 14, Campbellsville, KY 42719-0014; Title Tel # (502) 465-5207
Personnel: Editor-Gwynette Sullivan
Editorial Description: Taylor County history.
General Info: Yr. Est. 1971, Quarterly, Trim Size-8½ x 11, 20 pages, No Color
Subscriptions: Indv. $8, $2/copy
Printing Co: Greensburg Printing Co., 26 Columbia Hwy., Greensburg, KY 42743 Tel # (502) 932-7113

Chadburn

Publishing Co: Great Lakes Historical Society, Inland Seas Maritime Museum, 480 Main St., Vermilion, OH 44089-1015 Fax # (216) 967-1519; Title Tel # (216) 967-3467
Personnel: Editor-Rita Howley
General Info: Yr. Est. 1976, Quarterly

Children's Historical Newsletter *Consumer*

Publishing Co: Jenny Wren Press, 11 E. Main St., P.O. Box 505, Mooresville, IN 46158 Fax # (317) 831-1387; Title Tel # (317) 831-1044
Editorial Description: Historical craft ideas, games, history lessons and party ideas for children.
General Info: Yr. Est. 1994, Bi-monthly
Subscriptions: Indv. $15
Circulation: Total-300, Readership-300

Chinese Historical Society of America Bulletin

Publishing Co: Chinese Historical Society of America, 650 Commercial St, San Francisco, CA 94111-2504; Title Tel # (415) 391-1188
Personnel: Editor-Annie Soo
General Info: Yr. Est. 1963, Monthly, Trim Size-5½ x 8¾, 4 pages, No Color, Newsprint
Circulation: Total-500

Chronica *Association*

Publishing Co: Medieval Assn. of the Pacific, Scripps College, Claremont, CA 91711; Title Tel # (714) 621-8000
Personnel: Editor-Thomas Head
Editorial Description: Current scholarly projects of Medieval Assoc. of Pacific members; meeting announcements.
General Info: Yr. Est. 1967, Annually, Mimeo press, 40 pages, No Color
Subscriptions: Indv. $10
Circulation: Total-375

Chronicles of St. Mary's *Association*

Publishing Co: Sponsor-St. Mary's County Hist. Soc., St. Mary's County Historical Society, PO Box 212, Leonardtown, MD 20650-0212; Title Tel # (301) 475-2467
Personnel: Editor-Regina Combs Hammett
General Info: Yr. Est. 1953, Quarterly, Trim Size-8½ x 11, Offset press, 8 pages, No Color
Subscriptions: Indv. $20, $3/copy
Circulation: Total-800
Printing Co: Kirby Lithographic Co., 2900 S. Eads St., Arlington, VA 22202-4099 Tel # (703) 684-7600, Fax # (703) 683-5918

Circuit Rider *Association* CPM: $80

Publishing Co: Historical Confederation of Kentucky, PO Box 1792, Frankfort, KY 40602-1792; Title Tel # (502) 564-3016 Title Fax # (502) 564-4701
Personnel: Editor-Karla Nicholson, Asst. Ed.-Julia Curry
Editorial Description: Provides information for and about Kentucky's historical organizations.
General Info: Yr. Est. 1978, Quarterly, Trim Size-8½ x 11, 20 pages, ISSN: 0898-0330, 5% ads, Other
Subscriptions: Indv. $10, $3/copy
Circulation: Total-2,500
Advertising: $200. Accepts Inserts.

Civil War Library & Museum *Consumer*

Publishing Co: Civil War Library & Museum, 1805 Pine St, Philadelphia, PA 19103-6601; Title Tel # (215) 735-8196 Title Fax # (215) 735-3812
Personnel: Editor-David W. Letcher
Editorial Description: A library and museum publication covering the Civil War.
General Info: Yr. Est. 1888, Quarterly

Civil War Round Table Digest *Association*

Publishing Co: Civil War Round Table Assoc., PO Box 7388, Little Rock, AR 72217-7388; Title Tel # (501) 225-3996
Personnel: Editor-Jerry Russell, Publisher, Adv. Dir.-J. L. Russell
Editorial Description: News about historic preservation, contemporary interest in Civil War history.
General Info: Yr. Est. 1968, Monthly, Trim Size-8½ x 11, Mimeo press, 20 pages, No Color
Subscriptions: Indv. $13, Free With Membership
Circulation: Total-1,450

Clio's Pscyhe
See: PSYCHOLOGY

Collectible Newspapers
See: COLLECTIBLES

Colorado History News *Association*

Publishing Co: Colorado Historical Society, 1300 Broadway, Denver, CO 80203-2104; Title Tel # (303) 866-3670 Title Fax # (303) 866-5739
Personnel: Assoc. Publ.-christine Genouese, Publisher, Editor-David Wetzel, Art Dir.-Susan Romansky
Editorial Description: Brief historical articles; news about state and local historical and preservation activities.
General Info: (Formerly Colorado Heritage News), Yr. Est. 1964, Monthly, Trim Size-11½ x 15, Sheetfed press, 12 pages, ISSN: 0895-0083, 2 Color, Newsprint
Subscriptions: Indv. $30, Inst. $35
Circulation: Total-17,000
Printing Co: Barnum Publishing Co., 314 Federal Blvd, Denver, CO 80219-1537 Tel # (303) 936-2345

Columns *Association*

Publishing Co: State Historical Society of Wisconsin, 816 State St., Madison, WI 53706-1488 Tel # (608) 264-6400 Fax # (608) 264-6404; Title Tel # (608) 264-6482 Title Fax # (608) 264-6486
Personnel: Editor-Deborah Johnson
Editorial Description: Society newsletter.
General Info: (Formerly Wisconsin Then & Now), Yr. Est. 1980, Bi-monthly, Trim Size-8½ x 11, Sheetfed press, 12 pages, ISSN: 0196-1306, 2 Color, Saddle-stitched
Subscriptions: Free With Membership
Circulation: (100% controlled), Total-6,600
Printing Co: American Printing, 2909 Syene Rd., Madison, WI 53713-3293 Tel # (608) 271-6544, Fax # (608) 271-3475

Columns *Consumer, Association*

Publishing Co: Sponsor-Saratoga County Historical Soc., Saratoga County Historical Society, Saratoga County Museum, 6 Charlton Street, Ballston Spa, NY 12020-1707; Title Tel # (518) 885-4000
Personnel: Editor-Ted R. Beardsley
Editorial Description: Covers Saratoga County history.
General Info: (Formerly Grist Mill), Bi-monthly, 6 pages, No Color, Coated
Subscriptions: Free With Membership
Circulation: Total-700
Printing Co: Shipmates Printmates, Village Plaza, Clifton Park, NY 12065 Tel # (518) 371-0883

Constitution Chronicle
See: MUSEUM PUBLICATIONS

Cormorant News Bulletin
See: AUTOMOTIVE

Cornell Modern Indonesia Project:
See: INTERNATIONAL AFFAIRS

Cornerstone *Association*

Publishing Co: Alberta Historical Resources Foundation, 8820-112 St., Edmonton, AB T6G 2P8 Canada; Title Tel # (403) 297-7320
Personnel: Editor-Mark Rasmussen
Editorial Description: Heritage activities in Alberta, Canada.
General Info: (Formerly News and Views), Yr. Est. 1977, Quarterly, Trim Size-8½ x 11, 20 pages, No Color, Newsprint, Saddle-stitched
Subscriptions: Indv. $10
Circulation: Total-2,000
Printing Co: GTO Printing, 2316 27th Ave. NE, Calgary, AB T2E 7A7 Canada Tel # (403) 250-2779

Cornerstone

Publishing Co: Nebraska State Historical Society, Box 82554, Lincoln, NE 68501-2554 Tel # (402) 471-3270; Title Tel # (402) 471-4767 Title Fax # (402) 471-3100
Personnel: Editor-L. R. Puschendorf, Art Dir.-Steve Ryan
Editorial Description: Newsletter & journal of historic preservation in Nebraska.
General Info: Yr. Est. 1977, Quarterly, Trim Size-8½ x 11, Sheetfed press, 6 pages, ISSN: 0270-5699, No Color, Newsprint
Circulation: (100% controlled), Total-7,000
Printing Co: State of Nebraska, DAS Material Div., Box 94847, Lincoln, NE 68509 Tel # (402) 471-2331

Cornerstone, The
See: GENEALOGY

Cornsilk from DeKalb County, IL
See: GENEALOGY

Corral Dust
Association

Publishing Co: Panhandle-Plains Historical Society, WTAMU Box 967, 2401 Fourth Ave., Canyon, TX 79016-0001; Title Tel # (806) 656-2244 Title Fax # (806) 656-2250
Personnel: Editor, Mktg. Dir.-Linda Moreland
Editorial Description: News & upcoming events of Museum & Historical Society.
General Info: Yr. Est. 1983, Quarterly, Trim Size-8½ x 11, Sheetfed press, 4 pages, 2 Color, Coated
Subscriptions: Indv. $20, Inst. $10
Circulation: Total-1,200

Coryell Newsletter
See: GENEALOGY

County Line

Publishing Co: Taylor Publishing Co., 1550 W Mockingbird Ln, Dallas, TX 75235-5007; Title Tel # (214) 394-6642
Personnel: Publisher-Bob Jonson
Editorial Description: Promote interest in local give an outlet to local historical writing & provide material for local consumption.'
General Info: Yr. Est. 1988, Trim Size-8½ x 11, Sheetfed press, 6 pages, No Color
Subscriptions: Indv. $16, Inst. $12, $4/copy
Acquistions: Publication Bought
Circulation: Total-2,500
Printing Co: Kissel Printing Co., Inc., 7218 Harry Hines Blvd, Dallas, TX 75235-4012 Tel # (214) 357-8396

Courier
Association

Publishing Co: Tennessee Historical Commission, 701 Broadway, Nashville, TN 37243-0442; Title Tel # (615) 742-6716 Title Fax # (615) 742-6594
Personnel: Editor-Herbert Harper
Editorial Description: Reports the Commission's work in the areas of historic preservation, historical publications, and historical markers in Tennessee.
General Info: Yr. Est. 1964, Trim Size-8½ x 11, Offset press, 8 pages, 2 Color
Subscriptions: Free
Circulation: (100% controlled), Total-9,000
Printing Co: College Press, PO Box 400, Collegedale, TN 37315-0400 Tel # (615) 396-2164

Cousins et Cousines
See: GENEALOGY

Crosscurrents
See: MUSIC & MUSIC TRADES

Crossings
Association

Publishing Co: Stearns County Historical Society, C/O David Ebnet, 235 South 33rd Ave. Box 702, St. Cloud, MN 56302-0702; Title Tel # (320) 253-8424 Title Fax # (320) 253-2172
Personnel: Publisher-David Ebnet, Editor-Ann Brown, Assoc. Ed.-John Decker, Production Mgr.-Lorie Fischer
Editorial Description: Publication on & for the history of Stearns County & Minnesota.
General Info: (Formerly Stearns County Historical Society-Newsletter), Yr. Est. 1975, Bi-monthly, Trim Size-8½ x 11, Offset press, 12 pages, Color-cover, Coated, Saddle-stitched
Subscriptions: Indv. $25, Inst. $125, $4/copy
Circulation: Readership-1,250
Printing Co: Nissen Graphics, 520 Sundial Dr., Waite Park, MN 56387-1526 Tel # (320) 251-8000, Fax # (320) 252-0378

Crossroads
Consumer, Association

Publishing Co: Orphan Train Heritage Society of America, 4912 Trout Farm Rd, Springdale, AR 72762-8834; Title Tel # (501) 756-2780 Title Fax # (501) 756-0769
Editorial Description: Gathers, preserves, and desseminates history of Orphan Train Riders who were placed out from NYC and Boston, 1854-1929.
General Info: Quarterly, Trim Size-9 x 10½, Offset press, 26 pages, 2 Color, Coated, Saddle-stitched
Subscriptions: $7/copy
Circulation: Total-800, Readership-1,500
Printing Co: S.o.s., PO Box 1281, Granbury, TX 76048-8281

Czechoslovak History Newsletter
See: ETHNIC

Dallas Memorial Center for Holocaust Studies Newsletter
Consumer, Association

Publishing Co: Dallas Memorial Center for Holocaust Studies, 7900 Northaven Rd, Dallas, TX 75230-3352; Title Tel # (214) 750-4654 Title Fax # (214) 750-4672
Editorial Description: Reduces prejudice by teaching about Holocaust.
General Info: Yr. Est. 1984, Tri-annually, Trim Size-8½ x 11, 14 pages, Matte, Saddle-stitched
Subscriptions: Free With Membership
Circulation: Total-4,700
List Rental: Rents Lists
Printing Co: Business Express Press, 14110 Dallas Parkway, Dallas, TX Tel # (214) 233-4700

Desert Voice
See: RELIGIOUS & THEOLOGICAL

Dispatch, The
Consumer, Association

Publishing Co: Amityville Historical Society, PO Box 764, Amityville, NY 11701-0764; Title Tel # (516) 598-1486
Personnel: Editor-Seth Purdy
Editorial Description: History of local area.
General Info: (Formerly Newsletter), Yr. Est. 1970, Quarterly, Trim Size-7 x 8½, Sheetfed press, 8 pages, ISSN: 0894-94-9, No Color, Newsprint
Circulation: Total-460
Printing Co: Speedomical, 125 Merrick Rd, Amityville, NY 11701-3416 Tel # (516) 598-3370

Dispatch/ News

Publishing Co: Illinois State Historical Society, Old State Capital, Springfield, IL 62701 Fax # (217) 524-8042; Title Tel # (217) 782-2635
Personnel: Editor-Greg Olson
Editorial Description: For members of ISHS on events & items of historical interest in state of Illinois.
General Info: (Formerly Dispatch), Quarterly, 16 pages, 2 Color, Coated, Saddle-stitched
Circulation: Total-3,200
List Rental: Rents Lists
Printing Co: Emerson Press, 103 West Dodds, Divernon, IL 62530 Tel # (217) 628-3441

Distant Drums
See: PHILOSOPHY

Docket
Association

Publishing Co: Berrien County Historical Assn., PO Box 261, Berrien Springs, MI 49103-0261; Title Tel # (616) 471-1202
General Info: Quarterly
Subscriptions: Indv. $15, Inst. $30
Circulation: Total-350

Documentary Heritage Program Newsletter
Association, Consumer

Publishing Co: WNY Documentary Heritage Program, 4455 Genesee Street, PO Box 400, Buffalo, NY 14225-0400; Title Tel # (716) 633-0705 Title Fax # (716) 633-1736
Personnel: Editor-Heidi Bamford
Editorial Description: Technical information & general news of events, training opportunities, organizations in WNY region. Serving museums historical societies, libraries, archives, & other institutions with historical records programs or interest in regional collections.
General Info: (Formerly WNY Documentary Heritage Program), Yr. Est. 1988, Tri-annually, Trim Size-8½ x 11, Desktop press, 10 pages, ISSN: 1076-9544, No Color, Other, Other
Subscriptions: Indv. $15, Inst. $15, Can. $15, For. $15, $5/copy
Acquistions: Publication Bought
Circulation: Readership-1,600
Advertising: Accepts Inserts.
List Rental: Rents Lists

Dr. Samuel A. Mudd Society Newsletter
Consumer, Association

Publishing Co: Dr. Samuel A. Mudd Society, P.O. Box 1043, LaPlata, MD 20646-1043; Title Tel # (301) 934-8464 Title Fax # (202) 783-5966
Personnel: Publisher-John Mooney, Editor-Louise Mudd Arehart, Promotion Dir.-Catherine Whitehurst
Editorial Description: Covers historical facts about the life of Dr. Mudd. Also includes current news concerning the Museum & Society.
General Info: Yr. Est. 1979, Bi-weekly, Trim Size-8½ x 11, Letrpr. press, 4 pages, No Color, Saddle-stitched
Subscriptions: Indv. $12
Circulation: Total-450

Ducas
See: ETHNIC

ETCetera
See: ANTIQUES & ART GOODS

East-Florida Gazette
Association

Publishing Co: St. Augustine Historical Society, 271 Charlotte St, Saint Augustine, FL 32084-5033; Title Tel # (904) 824-2872
Personnel: Editor-Jean Waterbury
Editorial Description: St. Augustine history and personalities.
General Info: Yr. Est. 1977, 3x/yr., Trim Size-8½ x 11, Letrpr. press, 4 pages, No Color, Newsprint
Subscriptions: Indv. $30, Inst. $50, $15/copy
Circulation: Total-500
List Rental: Actives: 650, $100/M, Expires: 1,000
Printing Co: Townet Printing Co., 5 Highland Avenue, Box 932, St. Augustine, FL 32084 Tel # (904) 829-9997

Echoes
Association

Publishing Co: Ohio Historical Society, 1982 Velma Ave, Columbus, OH 43211-2497 Tel # (614) 297-2360 Fax # (614) 297-2367; Title Tel # (614) 297-2310 Title Fax # (614) 297-2411
Personnel: Editor-Corinne Colbert
Editorial Description: Current news of happenings concerned with the Ohio Historical Society.
General Info: (Formerly Museum Echoes), Yr. Est. 1928, Monthly, Trim Size-8½ x 11, Sheetfed press, 4 pages, ISSN: 0012-933X, Color-cover, Matte
Subscriptions: Indv. $5, $1/copy
Circulation: Total-13,500

Editing History · *Association*

Publishing Co: Sixteenth Century Publishers, NMSU LB 115, Kirksville, MO 63501; Title Tel # (816) 785-4665 Title Fax # (816) 785-4181
Personnel: Publisher, Editor-R.V. Schnucker
Editorial Description: For editors of history & humanities pubs.
General Info: Yr. Est. 1984, Semi-annually, Trim Size-8½ x 11, Sheetfed press, 12 pages, ISSN: 0883-3532, 1% ads, No Color, Newsprint
Subscriptions: Indv. $25, $15/copy
Circulation: Total-280
Advertising: Inquire for rates.
List Rental: Rents Lists

Elk Horn · *Association*

Publishing Co: Elk County Historical Society, 109 Center St # 361, Ridgway, PA 15853-1701; Title Tel # (814) 776-1032
Personnel: Editor-Iva Fay, Circ. Mgr.-Sydney Blaskett
Editorial Description: History & pictures of towns, townships, County of Elk; biography of early settlers.
General Info: Yr. Est. 1965, Trim Size-8½ x 13, Offset press, 8 pages, No Color
Subscriptions: $1/copy
Circulation: Total-645
Printing Co: Ridgway Publishing Co., Main St., Ridgway, PA 15853 Tel # (814) 773-3161

Erensia Sefardi
See: ETHNIC

European Studies
Newsletter · *Scholarly*

Publishing Co: Council for European Studies, 808-809 International Aff.Bldg, Columbia Univ., New York, NY 10027-0044; Title Tel # (212) 854-4172 Title Fax # (212) 749-0397
Personnel: Editor-Marion Kaplan
Editorial Description: Notices of research, publications, conferences, fellowships, grants, social sciences: focus on modern Europe.
General Info: Yr. Est. 1971, Bi-monthly, Trim Size-8 x 10, 24 pages, ISSN: 0046-2802, No Color
Subscriptions: Indv. $25, Inst. $30, Can. $35, For. $35, $5/copy
Acquistions: Publication Bought
Circulation: Total-1,500
Advertising: Inquire for rates.
List Rental: Actives: $200/M
Printing Co: Boyd Printing Co., Inc., 49 Sheridan Ave, Albany, NY 12210-2735 Tel # (518) 436-9686, Fax # (518) 436-7433

Ex-P O W Bulletin
See: MILITARY & NAVAL

Fernand Braudel Center-Newsletter
See: SOCIOLOGY

Focus
See: EDUCATION

Food History News
See: FOOD

Forest History Cruiser · *Consumer, Association*

Publishing Co: Forest History Society, Inc., 701 Vickers Ave, Durham, NC 27701-3162; Title Tel # (919) 682-9319
Personnel: Editor-Harold Steen
Editorial Description: Newsletter of the Forest History Society.
General Info: Yr. Est. 1977, Tri-annually, Trim Size-11 x 17, Offset press, 4 pages, No Color
Subscriptions: Indv. $30, Inst. $45, $5/copy
Circulation: Total-1,800

Franklin Pierce Times · *Consumer*

Publishing Co: Franklin Pierce Times, 79 Elm Hill Street, Springfield, VT 05156-2501; Title Tel # (802) 885-3151
Personnel: Editor-Irving Bell
Editorial Description: Articles about the life, letters, and legacy of the 14th US president.
General Info: Yr. Est. 1992, Quarterly, Trim Size-8½ x 11, 4 pages
Subscriptions: Indv. $12, $3/copy
Circulation: Total-200

Front and Center
See: ADVERTISING & MARKETING

G.H.S. Foot-Notes · *Association*

Publishing Co: Georgia Historical Society, 501 Whitaker St, Savannah, GA 31401-4889; Title Tel # (912) 651-2125
Personnel: Editor-Todd Groce, Ph.D
Editorial Description: Informs membership of: new members, recent gifts, current events at the GA Historical Society, upcoming exhibits at Society.
General Info: Yr. Est. 1972, Quarterly, Offset press, 10 pages, No Color
Subscriptions: Indv. $35, Inst. $40, For. $45
Circulation: (100% controlled), Total-2,400

Gate-Keeper · *Association*

Publishing Co: Friends of Historic Meridian, PO Box 155, Okemos, MI 48805-0155; Title Tel # (517) 347-7300
Personnel: Editor-Paula Gangopadhyay
General Info: Yr. Est. 1971, Quarterly, Trim Size-8½ x 11, 6 pages
Subscriptions: Indv. $10
Circulation: Total-120

Generation After

Publishing Co: TGA, Inc., PO Box 290014, Brooklyn, NY 11229-0014; Title Tel # (718) 743-6640
Personnel: Editor-John Ranz
Editorial Description: Pubs. is committed to the lessons of the holocaust, human rights & social justice.
General Info: Yr. Est. 1980, Trim Size-8½ x 11, Web press, 12 pages, Looseleaf
Subscriptions: Indv. $18
Circulation: Total-2,000

George C. Marshall
Foundation Topics

Publishing Co: George C. Marshall Foundation, Box 1600, VMI Parade Grounds, Lexington, VA 24450-1600; Title Tel # (703) 463-7103 Title Fax # (703) 464-5229
Personnel: Publisher-Gordon Beyer, Editor-Joellen Bland, Circ. Mgr.-Lisa Howeth, Art Dir.-Jeanne Pedersen
Editorial Description: Covers foundation activities & Marshalliana.
General Info: Yr. Est. 1962, Quarterly, Sheetfed press, 6 pages, 2 Color, Matte
Acquisitions: Publication Bought
Circulation: Total-11,500
Printing Co: McClung Printing, 550 N Commerce Ave, Waynesboro, VA 22980-2897

Girl Groups ('60's Rock N' Roll) Gazette
See: FAN MAGAZINES-MOVIE, RADIO, TV

Good Earth Times
See: MUSEUM PUBLICATIONS

Great Migration Newsletter
See: GENEALOGY

Green Country Quarterly
See: GENEALOGY

Guelph Historical Society
Newsletter · *Consumer, Association*

Publishing Co: Guelph Historical Society, Box 1502, Guelph, ON N1H 6N9 Canada; Title Tel # (519) 822-1709
Personnel: Editor-Bob Cripps, Circ. Mgr.-S. Mooney
Editorial Description: Information about the City of Guelph, its people, buildings, events & its environs from its founding to the present. Members also receive a copy of that year's volume of Historic Guelph - The Royal City.
General Info: Yr. Est. 1973, Bi-monthly, ISSN: 0709-5562
Subscriptions: Indv. $14, Can. $10, Free With Membership
Circulation: Total-700

Guidon
See: CLUBS

Gypsy Lore Society Newsletter
See: ANTHROPOLOGY

HAC Techline
See: AERONAUTICS/ASTRONAUTICS

Hamersky & Allied Families Newsletter
See: GENEALOGY

Hammerterz Forum

Publishing Co: Hammerterz Verlag, PO Box 13448, Baltimore, MD 21202
Editorial Description: Entirely devoted to the history of swordplay.
General Info: Quarterly
Subscriptions: Indv. $30

Harlow's Wooden Man · *Association*

Publishing Co: Marquette County Historical Society, Inc., 213 N Front St, Marquette, MI 49855-4220; Title Tel # (906) 226-3571
General Info: Yr. Est. 1964, Quarterly, Trim Size-5½ x 8½, 12 pages, No Color
Subscriptions: $2/copy
Circulation: Total-750

Harriet Beecher Stowe
House & Library

Publishing Co: Stowe-Day Foundation, 77 Forest St., Hartford, CT 06105-3243; Title Tel # (860) 522-9258 Title Fax # (860) 522-9259
Personnel: Editor-Earl French
General Info: (Formerly Stowe-Day Foundation), Yr. Est. 1986, Bi-monthly, Trim Size-8½ x 11, Sheetfed press, No Color
Circulation: Total-1,500
Printing Co: Colonial Press, 22 Dunn Hill Rd, Durham, CT 06422-1104 Tel # (203) 349-9865

Hastings Historian   *Association*

Publishing Co: Hastings Historial Society, 41 Washington Ave, Hastings On Hudson, NY 10706-2204; Title Tel # (914) 478-2249
Personnel: Editor-Mary Allison, Editor-David W. McCullough, Circ. Mgr.-Barbara McManus
Editorial Description: Society news & historical research articles.
General Info: Yr. Est. 1971, Quarterly, Trim Size-8½ x 11, Offset press, 16 pages, No Color, Matte, Saddle-stitched
Subscriptions: Indv. $10, Inst. $25, Can. $15, For. $15, $3/copy
Circulation: Total-1,200
Printing Co: Morgan Press, 145 Pailsades Ave., Dobbs Ferry, NY 10522 Tel # (914) 693-0023

Haversack, The
See: MUSEUM PUBLICATIONS

Henry County Historicalog
See: GENEALOGY

Heritage   *Association*   CPM: $250

Publishing Co: American Jewish Historical Society, 2 Thornton Rd, Waltham, MA 02154-7711; Title Tel # (617) 891-8110 Title Fax # (617) 899-9208
Editorial Description: Featuring news of the American Jewish Historical Society and American Jewish history.
General Info: (Formerly AJHS Report), Yr. Est. 1976, 3x/yr., Trim Size-12 x 18, Letrpr. press, 8 pages, ISSN: 0732-0194, 2 Color, Coated
Subscriptions: Indv. $50, Inst. $50, Free With Membership
Circulation: Total-4,000
Advertising: $1,000.
List Rental: List Management Co.: AB Data, 8050 N Port Washington Rd, Milwaukee, WI 53217-2600 Tel # (414) 352-4404, Fax # (414) 352-3994, Actives: 4,100

Heritage, The   *Association*

Publishing Co: Gwinnett Historical Society, Inc., PO Box 261, Lawrenceville, GA 30246-0261; Title Tel # (404) 822-5174
Personnel: Editor-Donna Black, Circ. Mgr.-Bill Dalton
Editorial Description: Material of genealogical or historical interest. Accent on preservation of buildings & sites.
General Info: (Formerly Heritage Quarterly), Yr. Est. 1971, Quarterly, Trim Size-8¼ x 10¾, Offset press, 24 pages, No Color
Subscriptions: Indv. $15, $3/copy
Circulation: Total-750, Readership-750

Heritage and History   *Association*

Publishing Co: Ventura County Historical Society, 100 E Main St, Ventura, CA 93001-2698 Fax # (805) 653-5267; Title Tel # (805) 653-0323
Personnel: Editor-Stan Wisenhunt
Editorial Description: Events and developments concerning the Ventura County Historical Museum.
General Info: Yr. Est. 1977, Monthly, Trim Size-8½ x 11, Offset press, 4 pages, No Color
Subscriptions: Indv. $35
Circulation: Total-1,788

Historian's Digest
See: RELIGIOUS & THEOLOGICAL

Historic House News

Publishing Co: Sponsor-New York City Dept. of Parks & Recreation, Historic House Trust of New York City, 830 5th Ave, Room 203, New York, NY 10021-7001; Title Tel # (212) 360-8282 Title Fax # (212) 360-8201
Personnel: Editor-Valerie Kalas, Acting Ed.-Elizabeth B. Leckie
Editorial Description: Focuses on the activities of the 16 historic house museums owned by the City of New York and the efforts of the Historic House Trust, which helps to preserve and promote these houses.
General Info: Yr. Est. 1989, Quarterly, Trim Size-8½ x 11, 12 pages, No Color
Subscriptions: Free With Membership
Circulation: Total-1,200
List Rental: Rents Lists

Historic Kansas City
Foundation Gazette   *Association*

Publishing Co: Historic Kansas City Found., 712 Broadway St Ste 404, Kansas City, MO 64105-1537; Title Tel # (816) 471-3391
Editorial Description: Subject matter: historic preservation, restoration, architecture, built environment research/education.
General Info: (Formerly Historic Kansas City News), Yr. Est. 1976, Bi-monthly, Offset press, 8 pages, 3% ads, 2 Color, Newsprint
Circulation: (100% controlled), Total-1,600

Historic New Orleans
Collection Quarterly

Publishing Co: Kemper/Leila Williams Foundation Historic New Orleans Collec, 533 Royal St., New Orleans, LA 70130-2113; Title Tel # (504) 523-4662
Personnel: Co-Editor-Patricia Brady, Co-Editor-Louise Hoffman
Editorial Description: Information about activities of the institution & about local history.
General Info: Yr. Est. 1983, Quarterly, Trim Size-8½ x 11, Offset press, 16 pages, ISSN: 0886-2109, 2 Color, Coated, Saddle-stitched
Subscriptions: Free
Circulation: Total-5,800
Printing Co: Harvey Press, 246 Harbor Cir, New Orleans, LA 70126-1104 Tel # (504) 246-8474, Fax # (504) 242-2007

Historic Richmond Town

Publishing Co: Staten Island Historical Society, 441 Clarke Ave, Staten Island, NY 10306-1125 Tel # (718) 351-1611
Editorial Description: Covers restoration of Richmondtown.
General Info: (Formerly Richmond Town Restoration)

Historical Bulletin
See: RELIGIOUS & THEOLOGICAL

Historical Footnotes   *Association*

Publishing Co: Stonington Historical Soc., PO Box 103, Stonington, CT 06378-0103 Tel # (203) 535-1131; Title Tel # (203) 535-0018
Personnel: Publisher-Taliaferro Boatwright, Adv. Dir.-Robert Vested
General Info: Yr. Est. 1962, Quarterly, 12 pages, ISSN: 0886-5272, Coated
Subscriptions: Indv. $10, $2/copy
Circulation: Total-800
Advertising: Inquire for rates.
Printing Co: Mystic Pubs., 10 Masons Island Rd, Mystic, CT 06355-2937

Historical Footnotes
See: RELIGIOUS & THEOLOGICAL

Historical Gardener, The
See: GARDENING & HORTICULTURE

Historical Roller Skating
Overview   *Association*

Publishing Co: Natl. Museum of Roller Skating, 4730 South St, Lincoln, NE 68506-1256; Title Tel # (402) 483-7551 Title Fax # (402) 483-1465
Personnel: Editor-Barbara Sorenson
Editorial Description: Covers roller skating history, sports and industry, 1700 to present.
General Info: Yr. Est. 1982, Quarterly, Trim Size-8½ x 11, Sheetfed press, 8 pages, ISSN: 0896-1379, No Color, Newsprint
Subscriptions: Indv. $15
Circulation: Total-600

Historical Society of
Michigan   *Association*

Publishing Co: Historical Society of Michigan, 2117 Washtenaw Ave., Ann Arbor, MI 48104-4599; Title Tel # (313) 769-1828 Title Fax # (313) 769-4267
Personnel: Publisher-Hugh Gurney, Art Dir.-Laurie Torbet
Editorial Description: Reports on activities sponsored by state & local historical groups.
General Info: Yr. Est. 1978, Quarterly, Trim Size-8½ x 11, Desktop press, 8 pages, No Color, Coated, Saddle-stitched
Subscriptions: Indv. $35, $2/copy
Circulation: Total-2,867
Advertising: Accepts Inserts.
List Rental: Actives: 4,000, $50/M
Printing Co: White Pine, Inc., 5204 Jackson Ave, Ann Arbor, MI 48103-1800 Tel # (313) 761-2670

Historical Time Capsules of
Monroe County   *Association*

Publishing Co: Monroe City Hist. Soc., PO Box 422, Sparta, WI 54656-0422; Title Tel # (608) 269-8680
Personnel: Editor-James Schlosser
Editorial Description: Features early history of Monroe Co., WI.
General Info: (Formerly Portals of Time), Yr. Est. 1975, Quarterly, Trim Size-8½ x 11, Sheetfed press, 16 pages, No Color, Newsprint
Subscriptions: Indv. $5
Circulation: Total-210

Historicalog   *Association*

Publishing Co: Warren County Hist. Society, PO Box 223, Lebanon, OH 45036-0223; Title Tel # (513) 932-1817
Personnel: Editor-Pat George
Editorial Description: Newsletter designed to keep membership and friends informed of activities and business news.
General Info: Yr. Est. 1974, Quarterly, Trim Size-8½ x 11, 4 pages, No Color
Subscriptions: Free With Membership
Circulation: (100% controlled), Total-700
Printing Co: Star Printing, 28 E. Mulberry, Lebanon, OH 45036

History News Dispatch   *Association*

Publishing Co: American Assn. for State & Local History, 530 Church St Ste 600, Nashville, TN 37219-2325; Title Tel # (615) 255-2971 Title Fax # (615) 255-2979
Personnel: Editor, Production Mgr.-Susan Cantrell, Adv. Dir.-David Rector, Art Dir.-Sasan Cantrell
Editorial Description: Current news from the state & local history field.
General Info: Monthly, Trim Size-8½ x 11, Web press, 8 pages, 2 Color, Newsprint
Subscriptions: Indv. $50, Inst. $75
Circulation: (100% controlled), Total-6,000, Readership-8,000
Advertising: Inquire for rates.
List Rental: Actives: $75/M
Printing Co: Pollock Printing, 928 6th Ave S, Nashville, TN 37203-4679 Tel # (615) 255-0526

History of Science
Society-Newsletter   *Association*   CPM: $116

Publishing Co: History of Science Society, Inc., The, Univ. of Washington, 351330, Seattle, WA 98195-1330; Title Tel # (206) 543-9366 Title Fax # (206) 685-9544
Personnel: Editor-Michael Sokal
Editorial Description: News of interest to members of the History of Science Society.
General Info: Yr. Est. 1972, Quarterly, Trim Size-8½ x 11, Offset press, 28 pages, ISSN: 0739/4934, No Color, Saddle-stitched
Subscriptions: Inst. $25
Circulation: Total-3,000
Advertising: $350.
List Rental: Rents Lists
Printing Co: University of Chicago Press, 5720 S Woodlawn Ave, Chicago, IL 60637-1603 Tel # (312) 702-7676, Fax # (312) 702-0172

Hobo Times
See: LIFESTYLE

Holocaust Project/1990

Publishing Co: Through the Flower Corp., PO Box 5280, Santa Fe, NM 87502-5280
Personnel: Editor-Judy Chicago
Editorial Description: Explores significance of Holocaust through art.

Howard Historian, The
See: GENEALOGY

Huguenot Trails
See: RELIGIOUS & THEOLOGICAL

Hungarian Studies Newsletter
See: ETHNIC

Hunterdon Historical
Newsletter   *Association*

Publishing Co: Hunterdon County Historical Society, 114 Main St, Flemington, NJ 08822-1415; Title Tel # (201) 782-1091
Personnel: Editor-Roxanne Carkhuff
Editorial Description: Hunterdon County history & genealogy; society news.
General Info: Yr. Est. 1965, Trim Size-8½ x 11, Offset press, 8 pages, ISSN: 0018-7850, No Color
Subscriptions: Indv. $15, $5/copy
Circulation: Total-525

Huron Historical Notes   *Association*

Publishing Co: Huron County Historical Society, RR1 Box 16, Bayfield, ON N0M 1G0 Canada; Title Tel # (519) 565-5200
Personnel: Editor-Mrs. T. Clark
Editorial Description: History of people, places and events relative to the County of Huron. Subscription includes yearbook.
General Info: Yr. Est. 1965, Semi-annually, Trim Size-8½ x 11, Mimeo press, 34 pages, ISSN: 0822-9503
Subscriptions: $5/copy
Circulation: Total-200

IHRC News
See: ETHNIC

Immigration History
Newsletter

Publishing Co: Immigration History Society, 18 S 7th St, Philadelphia, PA 19106-2314; Title Tel # (215) 925-8090 Title Fax # (215) 925-8195
Personnel: Editor-M. Mark Stolarik
Editorial Description: Published in conjuction with the Journal of American Ethnic History.
General Info: Yr. Est. 1968, Semi-annually, Mimeo press, 24 pages, No Color
Circulation: Total-850

In Focus
See: PHOTOGRAPHY

Indian Awareness Center
Newsletter   *Association*

Publishing Co: Fulton County Historical Society, Inc., 37 E. 375 North, Rochester, IN 46975-8384; Title Tel # (219) 223-4436
Personnel: Editor-Shirley Willard
Editorial Description: History and news about Indiana Indians.
General Info: Yr. Est. 1984, Quarterly, Trim Size-8½ x 11, 10 pages, No Color, Saddle-stitched
Subscriptions: Indv. $5, Inst. $8, $2/copy
Circulation: Total-150
Advertising: Inquire for rates. Accepts Inserts.

Indiana History Bulletin   *Consumer, Association*

Publishing Co: Indiana Historical Bureau, 140 N Senate Ave Rm 408, Indianapolis, IN 46204-2207 Tel # (317) 232-2537 Fax # (317) 232-2296
Editorial Description: Newsletter reparting events from Indiana Historical Organizations.
General Info: Yr. Est. 1920, Quarterly, Trim Size-8½ x 11, Offset press, 16 pages, ISSN: 0019-6649, No Color, Matte, Saddle-stitched
Subscriptions: Indv. $5, $1/copy
Circulation: Total-4,500

Indochina Newsletter
See: INTERNATIONAL AFFAIRS

International Calculator Collector
See: HOBBY

Iowa Genealogical Society Newsletter
See: GENEALOGY

Itza Voice
See: ETHNIC

James Fenimore Cooper Society Newsletter
See: LITERATURE & LINGUISTICS

Johnson/Johansson Family News
See: GENEALOGY

Journal of Muscle Shoals
History

Publishing Co: Tennessee Valley Historical Society, Univ. of N. Alabama, Dept. of History, Florence, AL 35630-0001; Title Tel # (205) 760-4306
Personnel: Editor-Kenneth Johnson
Editorial Description: Scholarly journal on history of Northwest Alabama.
General Info: Yr. Est. 1973, Annually, Trim Size-7 x 8½, Sheetfed press, 150 pages, No Color, Coated
Subscriptions: $10/copy
Circulation: Total-1,000
Printing Co: Morris Publishing, Sheffield, AL 35660

Kansas State Historical
Society Mirror   *Association*

Publishing Co: Center for Historical Research, 6425 SW 6th Street, Topeka, KS 66615-1099 Tel # (913) 272-8681 Fax # (913) 271-3358; Title Tel # (913) 296-4784 Title Fax # (913) 296-1005
Personnel: Editor-Bobbie Pray, Circ. Mgr.-Colene Bailes
Editorial Description: News of the Kansas State Historical Society & its eleven depts., from archeology to pubs.
General Info: Yr. Est. 1955, Bi-monthly, Trim Size-8½ x 11, Offset press, 8 pages, No Color
Subscriptions: Indv. $25, Inst. $25, Free With Membership
Circulation: Total-3,400
Printing Co: Pro-Print, 2028 SW Gage Blvd, Topeka, KS 66604-3340 Tel # (913) 272-0070

Kelso Courier   *Association*

Publishing Co: Brimfield Memorial House Assn., Inc., PO Box 1231, Kent, OH 44240-0024; Title Tel # (216) 673-8987
Personnel: Editor-Edgar McCormick
Editorial Description: Local history, preservation and appreciation.
General Info: Yr. Est. 1965, 8x/yr., Trim Size-8½ x 11, Mimeo press, 4 pages, No Color
Subscriptions: Free
Circulation: Total-325

Kennedy Gazette
See: GENEALOGY

Kentucky Archivist

Publishing Co: Kentucky Council on Archives, Univ. Archives & Records Ctr., Univ. Of Louisville, Louisville, KY 40292-0001
Personnel: Editor-Jeffrey Duff
Editorial Description: Provides information relating to the the Center's archival and manuscript repositories.
General Info: Yr. Est. 1978, Semi-annually
Subscriptions: Indv. $6
Circulation: Total-120

Kindred Spirits   *Consumer*

Publishing Co: Kindred Spirits, PO Box 252, White Plains, NY 10602-0252
Personnel: Publisher-Thomas Illari
Editorial Description: Covers the history of New York's Hudson River Valley.
General Info: Yr. Est. 1994, Quarterly
Subscriptions: Indv. $14

Kings County Historical
Society Newsletter   *Association*

Publishing Co: Sponsor-Kings County Hist. & Archival Soc. Inc., Kings County Historical Society, c/o W. Harvey Dalling, Sec., Hampton, NB E0G 1Z0 Canada; Title Tel # (506) 433-3244
Personnel: Publisher, Adv. Dir.-W. Harvey Dalling
Editorial Description: Covers history of rural districts.
General Info: Yr. Est. 1968, 7x/yr., 7 pages, No Color
Subscriptions: Indv. $10, Can. $15, $1/copy
Acquistions: Publication Bought, Publication Sold
Circulation: Total-303
Advertising: Inquire for rates.

Kingston Relations
See: GENEALOGY

Kittochtinny Newsletter

Publishing Co: Kittochtinny Historical Society, 175 E King St # 733, Chambersburg, PA 17201-1806; Title Tel # (717) 264-1667
Personnel: Editor-H.B. Mattingly
Editorial Description: Includes historical articles, notice of meetings, new acquisitions, calendar, board news & applicable pictures or sketches.
General Info: Yr. Est. 1986, 8x/yr., Trim Size-11 x 17, 4 pages, Matte
Circulation: Total-451

Kurt Weill Newsletter
See: MUSIC & MUSIC TRADES

Lambton County Historical Society, Bulletin

Publishing Co: Lambton County Historical Society, c/o Edward Phelps, 1777 Lakeshore Rd., Sarnia, ON Canada
Personnel: Editor-Edward Phelps
General Info: Yr. Est. 1965, Semi-annually
Subscriptions: Indv. $2

L'Ancetre
See: GENEALOGY

Landmarks Observer *Business, Consumer* CPM: $33

Publishing Co: Greater Portland Landmarks, Inc., 165 State St, Portland, ME 04101-3701; Title Tel # (207) 774-5561
Personnel: Editor-Linda J. Murnik
Editorial Description: Preservation of historical buildings, local architecture and history, preservation techniques and issues.
General Info: Yr. Est. 1967, Semi-annually, Trim Size-11½ x 16½, Offset press, 16 pages, No Color, Newsprint
Subscriptions: Free
Circulation: Total-6,000
Advertising: $200.
Printing Co: Biddeford Journal Tribune, Alfred Rd., Biddeford, ME 04005 Tel # (207) 282-1535

Latin American Jewish Studies
See: ETHNIC

Legacy Newsletter *Association*

Publishing Co: Daughters of Utah Pioneers Museum, 300 N Main St, Salt Lake City, UT 84103-1632; Title Tel # (801) 538-1050
Personnel: Editor-Emma Olsen, Circ. Mgr.-Louise Green, Art Dir.-Eileen Dunyon
Editorial Description: Descriptions & articles of membership activities.
General Info: Yr. Est. 1982, Quarterly, Trim Size-8½ x 11, 2 Color, Coated
Circulation: Total-22,000
Printing Co: Paragon Press, 200 S West Temple, Salt Lake City, UT 84101-1909

Lethbridge Historical Society Newsletter *Association*

Publishing Co: Lethbridge Historical Society, Box 974, Lethbridge, AB T1J 4A2 Canada
Editorial Description: Records local & regional history, & Society activities.
General Info: Bi-monthly, Trim Size-8½ x 11, Sheetfed press, 4 pages, ISSN: 0838-7249
Subscriptions: Indv. $9
Acquistions: Publication Sold
Circulation: Total-210

Lexington Quarterly
See: TRAFFIC & TRANSPORTATION

Lincarnations *Association*

Publishing Co: Association of Lincoln Presenters, 1143 River Rd., Neshanic, NJ 08853; Title Tel # (908) 369-7648
Editorial Description: Dedicated to supporting and encouraging the presenting of the Lincolns in arts, speeches and ceremonies to the American people.
General Info: Yr. Est. 1991, Semi-annually
Subscriptions: Indv. $20, Free With Membership
Circulation: Total-300, Readership-300

Lincoln Ledger *Association*

Publishing Co: Lincoln Fellowship of Wisconsin, 1923 Grange Ave, Racine, WI 53403-2328
Personnel: Editor-Steven Rogstad
Editorial Description: Covers matters concerning Abraham Lincoln and the state of Wisconsin.
General Info: Quarterly
Subscriptions: Indv. $20
Advertising: Inquire for rates.

Log Cabin News *Consumer, Association*

Publishing Co: Flax Craft, 3503 Edwards Rd, Sodus, MI 49126-9707; Title Tel # (616) 944-5719 Title Fax # (616) 944-5719
Personnel: Editor-Virginia Handy
Editorial Description: A quarterly compendium of log cabin lore contributed by members of the Log Cabin Society of Michigan, which sponsors the unique statewide Log Cabin Day tours and festivals every year on the last Sunday of June, with Log Cabin history, news, preservation,books, the 1840 Log Cabin Campaign, and miscellanea.
General Info: Yr. Est. 1989, Quarterly, Trim Size-8½ x 11, 8 pages, ISSN: 1061-5857, No Color, Other
Subscriptions: Indv. $20, Inst. $30, Can. $23, $3/copy
Circulation: (34% controlled), Total-500, Subscriptions-320, International-10, Readership-500
Advertising: Inquire for rates.

Long Point Genealogist, The
See: GENEALOGY

Longyear Museum Quarterly News
See: MUSEUM PUBLICATIONS

Loyal Legion Historical Journal
See: CLUBS

M.H.S. Miscellany *Scholarly, Association*

Publishing Co: Massachusetts Historical Society, 1154 Boylston St, Boston, MA 02215-3695; Title Tel # (617) 536-1608 Title Fax # (617) 859-0074
Personnel: Editor-Conrad Wright
Editorial Description: Calls to the attention of friends & scholars the accessions & activities of the Massachusetts Historical Society.
General Info: Yr. Est. 1955, Tri-annually, Trim Size-8½ x 11, Sheetfed press, 7 pages, No Color, Saddle-stitched
Subscriptions: Free
Circulation: (87% controlled), Total-4,000

Macedonia, Curiosum Mundi
See: CULTURE & HUMANITIES

Magnes News
See: MUSEUM PUBLICATIONS

Magny Families Association Newsletter
See: GENEALOGY

Mail Call *Consumer*

Publishing Co: Mail Call, Dept. S, Box 5031, South Hackensack, NJ 07606 Tel # (201) 296-0419 Parent Co.-Distant Frontier Press, South Hackensack
Editorial Description: Collection of civil war letters and diaries.
General Info: Yr. Est. 1990, Bi-monthly
Subscriptions: Indv. $25, $5/copy

Manitoba Historical Society, Newsletter *Association*

Publishing Co: Manitoba Historical Society, The Grain Exchange, 470-167 Lombard Avenue, Winnipeg, MB R3B 0T6 Canada; Title Tel # (204) 947-0559
Personnel: Editor-Carol Barbee
Editorial Description: Notice of meetings and other society events, news of the societies various projects, museums, competitions, recent books available, and historical events occurring throughout Manitoba.
General Info: Yr. Est. 1969, Bi-monthly, Trim Size-8½ x 11, Desktop press, 8 pages, ISSN: 0226-5036, No Color
Circulation: Total-880

Manitowoc County Historical Society Pinecrest Spirit Newsletter *Consumer, Association*

Publishing Co: Manitowoc County Historical Society, PO Box 574, Manitowoc, WI 54221-0574; Title Tel # (414) 684-4445
Personnel: Editor-Robert Fay
Editorial Description: Local history, society activities, & projects, Pinecrest Historical Village events.
General Info: (Formerly Manitowoc County Historical Society Newsletter), Yr. Est. 1987, Quarterly, Trim Size-8½ x 11, Desktop press, 6 pages
Subscriptions: Indv. $15, Inst. $15, Free With Membership
Circulation: Total-1,200
Printing Co: Econo Print, 2710 Custer St, Manitowoc, WI 54220-5554 Tel # (414) 682-1903

Manley Family Newsletter
See: GENEALOGY

Maryland Historical Society News and Notes
Consumer, Association

Publishing Co: Maryland Historical Society, 201 W Monument St, Baltimore, MD 21201-4674 Tel # (410) 685-3750 Fax # (410) 385-2105; Title Tel # (301) 685-3750
Personnel: Editor-Richard Gorelick, Bk. Rev. Ed.-Ernest Scott
Editorial Description: Maryland Historical Society News.
General Info: (Formerly Maryland History Notes), Yr. Est. 1943, Quarterly, Trim Size-8½ x 11, Offset press, 4 pages, ISSN: 0162-3826, 2 Color
Subscriptions: Indv. $4, Free With Membership
Circulation: Total-6,000
List Rental: Rents Lists

Medallion
Consumer

Publishing Co: Sponsor-Texas Historical Commission, Texas Historical Commission, PO Box 12276, Austin, TX 78711-2276 Tel # (512) 463-6100; Title Tel # (512) 475-4960 Title Fax # (512) 305-9246
Personnel: Editor-Roni Morales, Mng. Editor-Phil Parisi, Assoc. Ed.-Philip Parisi, Circ. Mgr.-Marty Moulthrop, Production Mgr.-Lin Altman
Editorial Description: News of historic preservation activities in Texas.
General Info: Yr. Est. 1963, Bi-monthly, Trim Size-8½ x 11, Sheetfed press, 8 pages, ISSN: 0890-7595, 2 Color, Matte, Saddle-stitched
Subscriptions: Indv. $7
Circulation: Total-2,300
List Rental: Actives 2,200, $50/M
Printing Co: Water Commission Print Shop, 2105 Denton Dr, Austin, TX 78758-4505 Tel # (512) 837-6782

Meeting Ground
See: ETHNIC

Member News, Minnesota Historical Society
Association

Publishing Co: Minnesota Historical Society, 345 Kellogg Blvd W, St. Paul, MN 55102-1906 Tel # (612) 296-2264 Fax # (612) 297-1345; Title Tel # (612) 296-4566
Personnel: Co-Editor-Therese Downey, Co-Editor-Brenda Kramer
Editorial Description: Report of the society to its members.
General Info: (Formerly Minnesota History News), Yr. Est. 1959, Monthly, Trim Size-11 x 17, Sheetfed press, 8 pages, ISSN: 0544-358X, 2 Color, Recycled
Subscriptions: Free With Membership
Circulation: (97% controlled), Total-8,200, International-200

Michigan Gazette
Association

Publishing Co: Bentley Historical Library, 1150 Beal Ave, The University of Michigan, Ann Arbor, MI 48109-2113; Title Tel # (313) 764-3482 Title Fax # (313) 936-1333
Editorial Description: Articles on accessions & activities of Bentley Historical Library, Univ. of Michigan.
General Info: Yr. Est. 1967, Annually, Letrpr. press, 6 pages, No Color, Newsprint
Circulation: (100% controlled), Total-1,500
List Rental: Rents Lists

Mid-Atlantic Archivist
See: LIBRARY

Mifflin County Historical News
Business, Association

Publishing Co: Mifflin County Historical Society, 1 W Market St # 1, Lewistown, PA 17044-2128; Title Tel # (717) 242-1022
General Info: Yr. Est. 1975, Quarterly
Subscriptions: Indv. $10, Inst. $50, $2/copy
Circulation: Total-750

Mirror
See: MUSEUM PUBLICATIONS

Mississippi History Newsletter
Association

Publishing Co: Mississippi State Dept of Archives, PO Box 571, Jackson, MS 39205-0571; Title Tel # (601) 359-6850 Title Fax # (601) 359-6905
Personnel: Publisher-Elbert Hilliard, Editor-Chrissy Wilson
Editorial Description: News of Miss. history events, dept. programs, books.
General Info: Yr. Est. 1959, Monthly, Trim Size-8½ x 11, Offset press, Color
Subscriptions: Free
Circulation: Total-6,500

Missouri Archeological Society Quarterly
See: ARCHAEOLOGY

Mistletoe Leaves
Association

Publishing Co: Oklahoma Historical Society, 2100 N Lincoln Blvd, Oklahoma City, OK 73105-4997; Title Tel # (405) 522-5243 Title Fax # (405) 521-2492
Personnel: Editor-Bob L. Blackburn, Assoc. Ed.-Mary Ann Blochowiak
Editorial Description: Reports on the activities, programs, and events of the Society and notes what is happening in the historical community in the state.
General Info: Yr. Est. 1893, Monthly, Trim Size-11½ x 15, Web press, 8 pages, 2 Color, Matte
Subscriptions: Indv. $20, Inst. $30, Can. $35, For. $35
Circulation: Total-6,600
Printing Co: Shawnee News-Star, 215 N. Bell, Shawnee, OK 74801 Tel # (405) 273-4200

Modern Greek Studies Association Bulletin
Scholarly, Association

Publishing Co: Modern Greek Studies Association, Box 1826, New Haven, CT 06508; Title Tel # (203) 392-5668
Personnel: Editor-John Iatrides
Editorial Description: Articles and announcements of MGSA; index of Modern Greek Studies programs at American & Greek Universities.
General Info: Yr. Est. 1976, Semi-annually, Trim Size-8½ x 11, 75 pages, ISSN: 0047-7702, No Color
Subscriptions: Indv. $25, $5/copy
Circulation: (100% controlled), Total-500

Monroe County Heritage
Association

Publishing Co: Monroe County Historical Society, PO Box 538, Woodsfield, OH 43793-0538
General Info: Quarterly
Subscriptions: Indv. $10, $1/copy

Monroe County of Wisconsin Historical Society Time Capsules
Association, Consumer

Publishing Co: Carolyn Habelman, RR 3, Box 253, Black River Falls, WI 54615-9405; Title Tel # (608) 378-4388 Title Fax # (608) 378-3006
Personnel: Editor-Jim Schlosser
Editorial Description: Historical info on Monroe County, Wisconsin.
General Info: Yr. Est. 1976, Quarterly, Desktop press
Subscriptions: Indv. $5, Free With Membership
Circulation: Total-225

Montana Post
Business, Association

Publishing Co: Montana Historical Society, 225 N. Roberts St., P.O. Box 201201, Helena, MT 59620-1201; Title Tel # (406) 444-4708 Title Fax # (406) 444-2696
Personnel: Editor-Marilyn Grant, Assoc. Ed.-Pam Otto, Circ. Mgr.-Tammy Ryan
Editorial Description: News & pictures relating to present-day activities of the Montana Historical Society & historical features taken from holdings of The Montana Historical Society Library. Also includes events & happenings in the region.
General Info: Yr. Est. 1963, Quarterly, Trim Size-8½ x 11, Offset press, 4 pages, ISSN: 0047-7958, 2 Color, Other, Other
Subscriptions: Free With Membership
Circulation: Total-8,200
List Rental: List Management Co.: Coolidge List Marketing, 25 W. 43rd St., New York, NY 10036-7491 Tel # (212) 274-0630, Fax # (212) 274-0650, Actives: 8,000, $75/M, Expires: 5,000
Printing Co: Artcraft Printers, 1207 E Front St, Butte, MT 59701-2935

Morgan Link
See: GENEALOGY

Moultrie County Heritage

Publishing Co: Moultrie County Historical & Genealogical Society, PO Box 588, Sullivan, IL 61951-0588

Mountain Light

Publishing Co: Idaho State Historical Society, 210 Main St, Boise, ID 83702-7264; Title Tel # (208) 338-3428 Title Fax # (208) 334-3198
Personnel: Editor-Judith Austin
Editorial Description: History of Idaho and pacific northwest: historical society activities.
General Info: (Formerly Idaho State Historical Society), Yr. Est. 1956, Quarterly, Trim Size-8½ x 11, Web press, 12 pages, 2 Color, Coated
Subscriptions: Indv. $15
Circulation: Total-2,500

Museum of the Great Plains Newsletter
See: MUSEUM PUBLICATIONS

Museum of Staten Island News
See: MUSEUM PUBLICATIONS

NAASR Newsletter
See: ETHNIC

NAVA News
Scholarly, Association

Publishing Co: North American Vexillological Association, 1977 N Olden Avenue Ext Ste, 225, Trenton, NJ 08618-2193
Personnel: Circ. Mgr.-Grace R. Cooper, Editor, Production Mgr.-Art Dir.-James A. Croft
Editorial Description: Contains articles on current and historical flags and seals with particular interest paid to North America.
General Info: Yr. Est. 1967, Bi-monthly, Trim Size-8½ x 11, Offset press, 8 pages, ISSN: 1053-3338, Other, Saddle-stitched
Subscriptions: Free With Membership
Circulation: Total-383, Readership-383

NEHGS Nexus
See: GENEALOGY

NYG&B Newsletter, The
See: GENEALOGY

Nase Ceske Dedictvi
See: ETHNIC

Nebraska State Historical Society Historical Newsletter — *Association*

Publishing Co: Nebraska State Historical Society, Box 82554, Lincoln, NE 68501-2554; Title Tel # (402) 471-3270 Title Fax # (402) 471-3100
Personnel: Editor-Bob Selzer, Art Dir.-Alice Filbert
Editorial Description: To inform members of society about current events in the historical field, primarily in Nebraska.
General Info: Yr. Est. 1947, Monthly, Trim Size-8½ x 11, Sheetfed press, 4 pages, ISSN: 0028-1859, No Color, Newsprint
Subscriptions: Indv. $25
Circulation: (100% controlled), Total-4,700

New Hampshire Historical Society Newsletter — *Association*

Publishing Co: New Hampshire Historical Society, 30 Park St, Concord, NH 03301-6316; Title Tel # (603) 225-3381 Title Fax # (603) 224-0463
Personnel: Editor-Lesve Scammon
Editorial Description: New Hamsphire Historical Society news.
General Info: Yr. Est. 1964, Quarterly, Trim Size-8½ x 11, Web press, 8 pages, Color
Acquistions: Publication Bought
Circulation: Total-4,600
Printing Co: Northlight Studio Press, Rte. 14, Box 568, Barre, VT 05641-0568 Tel # (802) 479-0565

New Jersey Historical Commission Newsletter — *Consumer, Scholarly*

Publishing Co: New Jersey Historical Commission, Cn305, Trenton, NJ 08608-0305; Title Tel # (609) 292-6062 Title Fax # (606) 633-8168
Personnel: Editor-Lee R. Parks, Bk. Rev. Ed.-Howard L. Green, Product Mgr.-Nancy H. Dellaire
Editorial Description: New Jersey historical news, including grants-in-aid, symposia, workshops, research projects, publications commemorative programs, oral history programs, book reviews.
General Info: Yr. Est. 1970, 10x/yr., Trim Size-8½ x 11, Web press, 8 pages, ISSN: 0047-9772, No Color, Matte, Saddle-stitched
Subscriptions: Indv. $10, Inst. $10, $1/copy
Circulation: Total-1,000
Printing Co: Heidelberg Press, PO Box 599, 2206 Rte 38 East, Hainesport, NJ 08036 Tel # (609) 265-0454, Fax # (609) 265-0864

New Jersey Historical Society News — *Consumer, Association*

Publishing Co: New Jersey Historical Society, 230 Broadway, Newark, NJ 07104-3926; Title Tel # (201) 483-3939 Title Fax # (201) 483-1988
Personnel: Editor-Robert Burnett
Editorial Description: Relates to activities and news at the New Jersey Historical Society.
General Info: (Formerly New Jersey Messenger), Yr. Est. 1958, 3x/yr., Sheetfed press, 4 pages, ISSN: 0028-582X, No Color, Newsprint
Subscriptions: Indv. $25, Inst. $30
Circulation: Total-2,500
List Rental: Rents Lists
Printing Co: Johnston Letter, 267 Mount Pleasant Ave, Newark, NJ 07104-3796 Tel # (201) 482-7535

New River News

Publishing Co: Historical Society of Fort Lauderdale, PO Box 14043, Fort Lauderdale, FL 33302-4043; Title Tel # (305) 463-4431
Personnel: Editor-Daniel Hobby
Editorial Description: Information regarding activities of Ft. Lauderdale Historical Society & articles relatign to the history of Ft. Lauderdale & Broward County, FL.
General Info: Yr. Est. 1962, Quarterly
Subscriptions: Indv. $10, $1/copy
Circulation: Total-740

Newark Historical Society Newsletter — *Association*

Publishing Co: Sponsor-Newark, DE, Historical Society, Newark Historical Society, PO Box 711, Newark, DE 19715-0711; Title Tel # (302) 451-1972
Personnel: Editor-George Miller
Editorial Description: Articles related to Newark, DE, history.
General Info: Yr. Est. 1982, Annually, Offset press, 4 pages, Newsprint
Subscriptions: Indv. $10, $3/copy
Circulation: Total-500

News — *Association*

Publishing Co: Historical Society of Rockland County, 20 Zukor Rd, New City, NY 10956-4302; Title Tel # (914) 634-9629
Personnel: Editor-Marianne Leese
Editorial Description: Happenings in the historical society-volunteer activity, events, exhibits.
General Info: Yr. Est. 1984, Semi-annually, Trim Size-8½ x 11, Sheetfed press, 8 pages, No Color, Newsprint
Circulation: Total-2,000

News-Can. Musical Heritage Soc./Nouvelles de la Soc. pour le Patrimoine Musical Can.
See: MUSIC & MUSIC TRADES

News from the Congregational Christian Historical Society
See: RELIGIOUS & THEOLOGICAL

News Notes from the Suggett House
See: MUSEUM PUBLICATIONS

Newsletter of the Afro-American Religious History Group
See: RELIGIOUS & THEOLOGICAL

Newsletter from Dick B on The Spiritual Roots of AA
See: HEALTH

Newsletter of the Maryland Archives

Publishing Co: Maryland Hall of Records, 350 Rowe Blvd, Annapolis, MD 21401-1685; Title Tel # (301) 974-3914
Personnel: Editor-Steve Cooper
Editorial Description: News of State Archives; Maryland history and records.
General Info: Yr. Est. 1984, Trim Size-8½ x 11, Offset press, 6 pages, 2 Color
Circulation: (100% controlled), Total-3,000

Newsletter of St. Lawrence City Historical Association — *Association*

Publishing Co: St. Lawrence County Historical Association, 3 E Main St, P.O Box 8, Canton, NY 13617-0008 Fax # (315) 386-8134; Title Tel # (315) 386-8133
Personnel: Editor-Stu Wilson
Editorial Description: Informational newsletter for members and general public.
General Info: Yr. Est. 1980, Bi-monthly, Trim Size-8½ x 11, Desktop press, 4 pages
Subscriptions: Indv. $25, Inst. $35, Free With Membership
Circulation: Total-1,000
Printing Co: Commercial Press, Canton, NY 13617

Newsletter of the Society of Maine Archivists — *Association*

Publishing Co: Society of Maine Archivists, The Edmund S. Muskie Archives, Baker College, 70 Campus Ave., Lewiston, ME 04240-6018; Title Tel # (207) 786-6354 Title Fax # (207) 786-6035
Personnel: Editor-Judy Franke, Production Ed.-Christopher M. Beam
Editorial Description: Newsletter for members.
General Info: Yr. Est. 1990, Quarterly, Mimeo press, 12 pages, No Color
Subscriptions: Free With Membership
Circulation: Total-150, Readership-150
Advertising: Accepts Inserts.

Newsletter (Talladega County Historical Assn.) — *Association*

Publishing Co: Talladega County Historical Assn., 106 Broome St, Talladega, AL 35160-2167; Title Tel # (205) 362-2219
Personnel: Editor-Vern Scott, Art Dir.-Frances Upchurch
Editorial Description: Obituary-eulogies.
General Info: Yr. Est. 1972, Monthly, Trim Size-8½ x 11, Mimeo press, 20 pages, ISSN: 0896-3630, 10% ads, No Color, Newsprint
Subscriptions: Indv. $10
Circulation: Total-485

Newsline — *Consumer, Association*

Publishing Co: East Tennessee Historical Society, 500 W Church Ave, Knoxville, TN 37902-2505; Title Tel # (615) 544-5732
Personnel: Editor-W. Tedd Groce
General Info: Yr. Est. 1985, Quarterly
Subscriptions: Free With Membership
Circulation: Total-2,000

North American Society for Sports History Newsletter
See: SPORTS & SPORTING GOODS

North Country Notes — *Association*

Publishing Co: Clinton County Historical Association, 48 Court St, Plattsburgh, NY 12901-2831; Title Tel # (518) 561-0340
Personnel: Publisher-Helen Allan
General Info: Yr. Est. 1960, Monthly
Subscriptions: Indv. $20, Inst. $30, Can. $30, For. $30, $1/copy
Circulation: Total-650

North-South Skirmish Association Newsletter
See: GUNS & FIREARMS

Norwegian-American Historical Association Newsletter
See: ETHNIC

Nouvelles Nouvelles — *Scholarly*

Publishing Co: Center for Medieval & Renaissance Studies, Ohio State Univ. Rm. 256 Cunz, 1841 Millikin Rd., Columbus, OH 43210; Title Tel # (614) 292-7495
Personnel: Editor-Dawn Metcalf
General Info: Yr. Est. 1972, Quarterly, Trim Size-5½ x 8½, Desktop press, 20 pages, No Color, Saddle-stitched
Subscriptions: Free
Circulation: Total-518

Nuclear Resister
See: POLITICS

OAH Newsletter

Publishing Co: Organization of American Historians, 112 N Bryan Ave, Bloomington, IN 47408-4141; Title Tel # (812) 855-7311
Personnel: Editor-Brad Young, Circ. Mgr.-Ginger Foutz, Production Mgr.-Michael Regoli, Adv. Dir., Promotion Dir.-Debby Davis
Editorial Description: Contains articles & information of interest to American historians.
General Info: Quarterly, Trim Size-10 x 12½, Web press, 24 pages, ISSN: 0197-3341, 1% ads, Color-cover, Newsprint
Subscriptions: Inst. $80
Circulation: Total-12,000
Advertising: Inquire for rates.
List Rental: Actives: $70/M
Printing Co: Herald Times, Inc., 190 S Walnut St # 909, Bloomington, IN 47404-6107 Tel # (812) 332-4401

OHS Bulletin   *Association*   CPM: $337

Publishing Co: Ontario Historical Society, 34 Parkview Ave., Willowdale, ON M2N 3Y2 Canada; Title Tel # (416) 226-9011 Title Fax # (416) 226-2740
Personnel: Circ. Mgr.-Barbara Truax, Editor, Adv. Dir.-Meribeth Clow
Editorial Description: Short articles of topical interest to members plus news on the activities & concerns of local heritage groups in Province.
General Info: (Formerly Newsletter), Yr. Est. 1968, Bi-monthly, Trim Size-11¼ x 17, Web press, 8 pages, ISSN: 0714-6736, 10% ads, 2 Color, Newsprint
Subscriptions: Indv. $20, Inst. $20, $2/copy
Circulation: Total-3,000
Advertising: $1,013.
Printing Co: Versatel Corporate Services Ltd., 1905 Leslie St., Don Mills, ON M3B 2M3 Canada Tel # (416) 449-6805, Fax # (416) 449-2584

OIW Communique   *Association*

Publishing Co: Order of the Indian Wars, PO Box 7401, Little Rock, AR 72217-7401; Title Tel # (501) 225-3996
Personnel: Publisher, Editor-Jerry Russell
Editorial Description: News of contemporary activities relevant to study of Indian Wars history.
General Info: Yr. Est. 1979, Monthly, Mimeo press, 20 pages
Subscriptions: Indv. $20
Circulation: Total-485

Ohio Archivist   *Association*

Publishing Co: Society of Ohio Archivists, 2700 Kenny Road, Columbus, OH 43210-1157; Title Tel # (216) 444-2929 Title Fax # (216) 444-5446
Personnel: Editor-Frederick Lautzenheiser
Editorial Description: Professional activities of persons interested in preservation and use of Ohio source materials.
General Info: Yr. Est. 1970, Semi-annually, Trim Size-9 x 12, Offset press, 20 pages, ISSN: 1047-5400, No Color
Subscriptions: Indv. $10, Inst. $15, $5/copy
Circulation: (100% controlled), Total-200, Readership-200
Advertising: Inquire for rates.

Ohio's Historical Detective

Publishing Co: Dukeman Publications Company, 4111 Yellowood Street, Lima, OH 45806-1121
Editorial Description: This newsleter includes research from the entire state, a yearly index issue, which includes alphabeticla listings of all surnames and another list of surnames by locality, and also historical stories and information from the Ohio area
General Info: Yr. Est. 1994

Oklahoma Anthropological Society, Newsletter
See: ANTHROPOLOGY

Old Fort News
See: GENEALOGY

Olde Mecklenburg Genealogical Society Quarterly
See: GENEALOGY

Oral History Association
Newsletter   *Association*

Publishing Co: Oral History Assn., Baylor Universtiy, Po Box 97234, Waco, TX 76798-7234 Tel # (817) 755-2764 Fax # (817) 755-1571; Title Tel # (703) 379-8164
Personnel: Editor-Mary Kay Quinlan
Editorial Description: Oral History Newsletter announces oral history projects, describes new developments, and provides a forum for exchange of views on practical and intellectual problems.
General Info: Yr. Est. 1967, Quarterly, 12 pages, Color
Subscriptions: $3/copy
Circulation: (100% controlled), Total-1,400

Osler Library Newsletter
See: LIBRARY

Over the Edge   *Consumer, Association*

Publishing Co: Vore Buffalo Jump Foundation, PO Box 369, Sundance, WY 82729-0369; Title Tel # (307) 283-1192
Editorial Description: Covers issues and events on buffalo jumping sites explored by the foundation.
General Info: Quarterly, Trim Size-8½ x 11, No Color

PAHA Newsletter
See: ETHNIC

Passing Show
See: THEATRE

Past-Present Prints   *Association*

Publishing Co: Iron County Historical Museum Society, PO Box 272, Caspian, MI 49915-0272; Title Tel # (906) 265-2617
Personnel: Editor-Marcia Bernhardt
General Info: Yr. Est. 1968, Annually, Trim Size-8½ x 11, 8 pages
Subscriptions: Free To Qualified Recipient
Circulation: Total-1,800

Patterns
See: CULTURE & HUMANITIES

Perspectives   *Association*   CPM: $30

Publishing Co: American Historical Association, 400 A St. SE, Washington, DC 20003-3807; Title Tel # (202) 544-2422 Title Fax # (202) 544-8307
Personnel: Editor-Wendi Maloney, Production Mgr.-Roxanne Myers Spencer, Adv. Dir.-Robert Townsend
Editorial Description: The newsletter of the historical profession, with regular columns on teaching, research, technology, public history, and the presentation of history in the media. Principal source of job listings for history profession.
General Info: (Formerly AHA Newsletter), Yr. Est. 1962, 9x/yr., Trim Size-8½ x 11, Web press, 40 pages, ISSN: 0743-7021, No Color, Matte, Saddle-stitched
Subscriptions: Inst. $85, $3/copy
Circulation: Total-16,500
Advertising: $500.
List Rental: Actives: 16,000, $100/M
Printing Co: Cadmus Journal Services, 2901 Byrdhill Road, Richmond, VA 23261

Pervopokhodnik
See: ETHNIC

Peterborough Historical
Society, Bulletin   *Association*

Publishing Co: Peterborough Historical Society, Hutchison House, 270 Brock St., Peterborough, ON K9H 2P9 Canada; Title Tel # (705) 743-9710
Personnel: Publisher, Editor-Florence Maynes
Editorial Description: Announcements of and reports of meetings, queries column, current happenings, etc.
General Info: Yr. Est. 1968, 8x/yr., Trim Size-7 x 8½, Offset press, 4 pages, ISSN: 0380-6642, No Color
Subscriptions: Indv. $10
Circulation: Total-500
Printing Co: Pronto-Print, 248 Rink St., Peterborough, ON Canada Tel # (705) 748-4141

Pioneer Echoes
See: GENEALOGY

Pioneers- A Computer Genealogy Newslettter
See: GENEALOGY

Pipings, The
See: GENEALOGY

Plains Talk: The Quarterly
Newsletter of the State
Historical Society of
North Dakota   *Association*

Publishing Co: State Historical Soc. of N.D., North Dakota Heritage Ctr., Bismarck, ND 58505-0830; Title Tel # (701) 328-2799 Title Fax # (701) 328-3710
Personnel: Publisher-James Sperry, Editor-Janet Lysengen, History Ed.-Ann Rathke, Mktg. Coord.-Sue Berg
Editorial Description: Activities of the agency's divisions, county and local historical societies in North Dakota, and events and exhibits at North Dakota Heritage Center.
General Info: Yr. Est. 1963, Quarterly, Trim Size-8½ x 11, Offset press, 12 pages, 2 Color, Newsprint
Subscriptions: Indv. $30, Inst. $25, For. $30, Free With Membership
Circulation: Total-1,900

Points East
See: INTERNATIONAL AFFAIRS

Pony Express Mail   *Consumer, Association*

Publishing Co: Sponsor-Patee House Museum, Pony Express Historical Assn., Inc., Box 1022, 12th & Penn, St. Joseph, MO 64502-1022 Tel # (816) 232-8200; Title Tel # (816) 232-8206
Personnel: Editor-Gary Chilcote, Circ. Mgr.-Carolyn Chilcote
Editorial Description: Chronicles the Pony Express-Jesse James involvement with St. Joseph. Official pub. for Patee House Museum & the Jesse James Home Museum. Covers modern activities including the National Pony Express rerun each year.
General Info: Yr. Est. 1972, 10x/yr., Trim Size-8½ x 14, Desktop press, 4 pages, Color, Newsprint
Subscriptions: Indv. $10
Circulation: Total-350

Portage County Historical
Society Newsletter   *Association*

Publishing Co: Portage County Historical Society Newsletter, 6549 N Chestnut St, Ravenna, OH 44266-3907; Title Tel # (216) 296-3523
General Info: Yr. Est. 1951, 6 pages
Subscriptions: Indv. $7

Portland Poynts   *Association*

Publishing Co: Atlantic Highlands Historical Society, PO Box 108, Atlantic Highlands, NJ 07716-0108 Tel # (908) 291-9454; Title Tel # (908) 291-1861
Personnel: Editor-Ruth Phillips
Editorial Description: Promotes & preserves history & keeps members aware of society activities.
General Info: (Formerly History Trails & Tales Old & New), Yr. Est. 1983, Bi-monthly, Trim Size-10 x 12½, Sheetfed press, 4 pages, No Color
Circulation: Total-650

The Prairie Rambler

Publishing Co: Jerry Baly, P.O. Box 505, Claremont, CA 91711
Editorial Description: Always a joy to pause and browse through the PR Filled with anecdotes and quotes from people throuhout history.
General Info: Monthly, Trim Size-8.5 x 11, 8 pages

Preservation New York   *Consumer, Association*

Publishing Co: Preservation League of New York State, 44 Central Ave, Albany, NY 12206-3002 Tel # (518) 412-5658 Fax # (518) 412-5684; Title Tel # (518) 462-5658 Title Fax # (518) 462-5684
Editorial Description: Discusses the preservation of historic New York architecture.
General Info: (Formerly Preservation League of New York State Newsletter), Yr. Est. 1974, Quarterly, Trim Size-8.5 x 11, 14 pages, Ind/Abs/Online: Avery, No Color
Subscriptions: Inst. $35, Free With Membership
Circulation: Total-2,000

Preservation Progress
See: ARCHITECTURE

Presidents' Journal   *Consumer*

Publishing Co: Cottontail Pubs., 79 Drakes Ridge Rd., Bennington, IN 47011-1802; Title Tel # (812) 427-3921
Personnel: Publisher, Editor-Ellyn R. Kern
Editorial Description: A newsletter that is educational & entertaining about our nation's presidents, their homes & families, facts and foibles; presidential places to visit, as well as presidential collectibles & profiles of the people who collect them.
General Info: Yr. Est. 1986, Quarterly, Trim Size-8½ x 11, Sheetfed press, 6 pages, ISSN: 8755-8939, No Color
Subscriptions: Indv. $14, $4/copy

Public History News   *Association*

Publishing Co: Natl. Council on Public History, 403 Richards Hall, Northeastern Univ., Boston, MA 02115; Title Tel # (617) 437-2627 Title Fax # (617) 437-2942
Personnel: Editor-Susan Keats, Production Mgr.-Joanne Madden
Editorial Description: PHN offers editorials, a regular update on NCPH activities, a report on legislative affairs of concern to public historians, information about upcoming conferences, fellowships, meetings, awards and recent publications, and report news of the publichistory field.
General Info: (Formerly NCPH Newsletter), Yr. Est. 1980, Quarterly, Trim Size-8½ x 11, 12 pages, 2 Color, Newsprint, Saddle-stitched
Acquistions: Publication Bought
Circulation: Total-2,000
Advertising: Inquire for rates.
List Rental: Rents Lists
Printing Co: Northeastern Printing Dept., Northeastern Univ., Boston, MA 02115

Public Works History

Publishing Co: Public Works Historical Society, 1525 East 53rd Street, Chicago, IL 60615-4530; Title Tel # (312) 667-2200
Personnel: Editor-Howard Rosen
General Info: Yr. Est. 1976, Bi-monthly
Circulation: Total-1,500

Pull Together
See: MILITARY & NAVAL

Putnam County Heritage   *Association*

Publishing Co: Putnam County Historical Society, 201 E. Main St., Box 264, Kalida, OH 45853; Title Tel # (419) 532-3041
Editorial Description: Newsletter that offers the history of Putnam County.
General Info: Yr. Est. 1978, Quarterly, Trim Size-8½ x 11, 8 pages
Subscriptions: Indv. $5, $1/copy
Circulation: Total-550
Printing Co: Unverferth Manufacturing Company, PO Box 357, Kalida, OH 45853-0357

Quaker Yeomen
See: GENEALOGY

Quarterdeck, The
See: MUSEUM PUBLICATIONS

Rail Indiana
See: RAILROADS

Rail Splitter, The
See: COLLECTIBLES

Rampant Lion
See: ETHNIC

Range History   *Association*

Publishing Co: Iron Range Historical Society, Gilbert City Hall, Box 786, Gilbert, MN 55741; Title Tel # (218) 749-3150
Editorial Description: Covers range history with Mesabi perspective.
Subscriptions: Indv. $10

Regional Archivist   *Association*

Publishing Co: Concordia Historical Institute, 801 De Mun Ave, St. Louis, MO 63105-3168 Parent Co.-Lutheran Church Missouri Synod, Saint Louis; Title Tel # (314) 721-5934 Title Fax # (314) 721-5902
Personnel: Editor-Marvin A. Huggins
Editorial Description: Archivist practice, Archives, preservation, news & notes.
General Info: Yr. Est. 1964, Quarterly, Trim Size-8½ x 11, Mimeo press, 4 pages, ISSN: 0364-2135, No Color, Other
Subscriptions: Free To Qualified Recipient
Circulation: Total-800

Renton Historical Society
Newsletter   *Association*

Publishing Co: Renton Historical Society, 235 Mill Ave. S, Renton, WA 98055-2133; Title Tel # (206) 255-2330
Personnel: Editor-Steve Anderson
Editorial Description: Society activities, projects, and short historical articles of the area.
General Info: Yr. Est. 1970, Quarterly, Trim Size-8½ x 11, Mimeo press, 6 pages, 2% ads, No Color
Subscriptions: Indv. $5, $1/copy
Circulation: Total-900
Advertising: Inquire for rates.

Research Reports from the
Rockefeller Archive
Center

Publishing Co: Rockefeller Archive Center, 15 Dayton Ave., Pocantico Hills, North Tarrytown, NY 10591-1598; Title Tel # (914) 631-4505
Personnel: Editor-Edwin Levoid, Editor-Kenneth Rose
Editorial Description: Reports by researchers on their projects at the Archive Center.
General Info: Yr. Est. 1990, Annually, 16 pages
Subscriptions: Free
Circulation: Total-5,000

Revue d'Histoire de
l'Amerique Francaise   *Association*   **CPM: $115**

Publishing Co: Institut d'Histoire de l'Amerique Francaise, 261 Avenue Bloomfield, Montreal, PQ H2V 3R6 Canada; Title Tel # (514) 278-2232 Title Fax # (514) 271-6369
Personnel: Publisher, Editor-Jacques Rouillard, Circ. Mgr.-Lise McNicoll
Editorial Description: Articles concerning the history of French civilization in America.
General Info: Yr. Est. 1947, Quarterly, Trim Size-6½ x 9¼, Letrpr. press, 160 pages, ISSN: 0035-2357, No Color, Perfect bound
Subscriptions: Indv. $54, Inst. $54, Can. $50, For. $54, $13/copy
Circulation: (ABC), Total-1,300
Advertising: $150.
Printing Co: Les Ateliers Marc Veilleux, 203 Ch. des Pionniers Ouest, C.P. 39, Cap St. Ignace, PQ G0R 1H0 Canada Tel # (418) 246-5666, Fax # (418) 246-5564

Ricardian Register   *Association*

Publishing Co: Richard III Society, Inc., c/o Word Catering, 4702 Dryades St., New Orleans, LA 70115 Tel # (508) 899-9673 Fax # (504) 897-0125; Title Tel # (504) 827-0161
Editorial Description: News for and about the American branch of the British Richard III Society, Inc.
General Info: Yr. Est. 1966, Quarterly, Trim Size-8½ x 11, Sheetfed press, 24 pages, No Color, Saddle-stitched
Subscriptions: Indv. $30, Can. $35
Acquistions: Publication Bought
Circulation: (100% controlled), Total-800
Advertising: Inquire for rates. Accepts Inserts.
Printing Co: Word Catering, 4702 Dryades St, New Orleans, LA 70115-5532 Tel # (504) 897-9673, Fax # (504) 897-0125

Ritchie County Historical Society Newsletter
See: GENEALOGY

River Yarns- National
Rivers Hall of Fame
Newsletter   *Consumer, Association*

Publishing Co: Dubuque County Historical Society, PO Box 266, Dubuque, IA 52004-0266; Title Tel # (319) 583-1241
Personnel: Publisher, Editor, Promotion Dir.-Jerry Enzler
General Info: Quarterly, Sheetfed press, 4 pages, No Color

Rockefeller Archive Center-Newsletter

Publishing Co: Rockefeller Archive Center, 15 Dayton Ave., Pocantico Hills, North Tarrytown, NY 10591-1598; Title Tel # (914) 631-4505
Personnel: Editor-Edwin Levoid, Editor-Kenneta W. Rose, Editor-Darwin Stapleton
Editorial Description: Research & acquisitions at the archives; center news.
General Info: Yr. Est. 1982, Annually, 16 pages, Saddle-stitched
Subscriptions: Free
Circulation: Total-12,000

Roesch House Report   *Association*

Publishing Co: Florida Historical Society, 1320 Highland Ave., Melbourne, FL 32935; Title Tel # (407) 259-0847 Title Fax # (407) 259-0847
Editorial Description: Reports on Florida historical preservation activities.
General Info: Irregular

Root Digger Newsletter
See: GENEALOGY

SAA Employment Bulletin

Publishing Co: Society of American Archivists, 600 S. Federal St., Ste. 504, Chicago, IL 60605-1898 Tel # (312) 922-0140; Title Tel # (312) 927-0140 Title Fax # (312) 347-1452
Personnel: Editor-Tara Shimandle
Editorial Description: Employment opportunities in the archival profession.
General Info: Bi-monthly, 4 pages, No Color, Matte
Subscriptions: Indv. $24
Circulation: Total-450
Advertising: Inquire for rates.

SHARP News
See: BOOKS & BOOK TRADE

SHOT Newsletter   *Association*   **CPM: $194**

Publishing Co: Society for the History of Technology, Auburn University, Dept of History, Auburn, AL 36849-5207 Tel # (906) 481-2459 Fax # (906) 487-2468; Title Tel # (334) 844-4360 Title Fax # (334) 844-6673
Personnel: Editor-Linda Biggs 1423, Production Mgr.-Susan Constant
Editorial Description: Provides information of interest to the members of the Society of the History of Technology.
General Info: Yr. Est. 1977, Quarterly, Sheetfed press, 16 pages, No Color, Looseleaf
Subscriptions: Indv. $10, Free With Membership
Circulation: Total-1,800
Advertising: $350.
List Rental: Actives: $65/M

S.L.A. Marshall Military History Collection-Newsletter
See: MILITARY & NAVAL

SMRC Newsletter
See: ANTHROPOLOGY

SPNEA News
See: ARCHITECTURE

San Angelo Genealogical & Historical Society Newsletter
See: GENEALOGY

San Diego Historical Society Times   *Consumer*

Publishing Co: San Diego Historical Society, PO Box 81825, San Diego, CA 92138-1825; Title Tel # (619) 232-6203 Title Fax # (619) 232-6297
Personnel: Editor-Christina Cameron
Editorial Description: To discover, collect, preserve, and interpret objects, documents, photographs, literary and artistic works and other articles or materials which are related to or illustrate the history of the county of San Diego and the south California region.
General Info: Quarterly
Printing Co: Carlsbad Printing Services, 5355 Avenida Encinas Ste F, Carlsbad, CA 92008-4360 Tel # (619) 438-9411, Fax # (619) 438-1349

Scholars of Early Modern Studies   *Association*   **CPM: $50**

Publishing Co: Sixteenth Century Publishers, NMSU LB 115, Kirksville, MO 63501; Title Tel # (816) 785-4665 Title Fax # (816) 785-4181
Personnel: Publisher, Editor-R.V. Schnucker
Editorial Description: Activities, research & addresses of scholars in early modern studies 1450-1648.
General Info: (Formerly Historians of Early Modern Europe), Yr. Est. 1961, Annually, Trim Size-8½ x 11, Sheetfed press, 163 pages, ISSN: 0883-3559, 10% ads, No Color, Newsprint
Subscriptions: Indv. $15, Inst. $20, For. $20, $10/copy
Circulation: Total-2,000
Advertising: $100.

Sea Letter
See: MILITARY & NAVAL

Searchlight
See: GENEALOGY

Seneca Searchers
See: GENEALOGY

Shavings
See: CONSTRUCTION & BUILDING

Showboat Centennials   *Consumer, Scholarly*

Publishing Co: Showboat Centennials, 76 Glen Dr, Worthington, OH 43085-4010; Title Tel # (614) 431-9422
Personnel: Publisher, Editor-Donald McDaniel
Editorial Description: History of showboats.
General Info: Yr. Est. 1979, Irregular, Trim Size-8½ x 11, Mimeo press, 8 pages, ISSN: 0749-9361, No Color, Newsprint, Looseleaf
Circulation: (100% controlled), Total-170

Slickens   *Association*

Publishing Co: Butte County Historical Society, PO Box 2195, Oroville, CA 95965-2195 Tel # (916) 533-5316; Title Tel # (916) 872-3363
Personnel: Editor-Bill Anderson
Editorial Description: News of historical society activities, local.
General Info: Monthly, Trim Size-8½ x 11, Offset press, 4 pages, No Color
Subscriptions: Free With Membership
Circulation: Total-800

Smithsonian Runner

Publishing Co: Smithsonian Institution, 900 Jefferson Dr., S.W., Washington, DC 20560-0001 Tel # (202) 357-2888; Title Tel # (202) 357-2627 Title Fax # (202) 786-2377
Personnel: Editor-Dan Agent
Editorial Description: For and about American Indians describing Smithsonian projects and programs about Native American subjects.
General Info: Yr. Est. 1990, Bi-monthly
Circulation: Total-8,700

Society for Historians of American Foreign Relations, Newsletter   *Association*

Publishing Co: Sponsor-Society for Historians of American Foreign Relations, Blackwell Publishers, 238 Main St., Cambridge, MA 02142 Tel # (617) 547-7110 Fax # (617) 547-0789
Personnel: Editor-William Brinker
Editorial Description: News items; brief articles of general interest to members of society.
General Info: Yr. Est. 1970, Quarterly

Society for Industrial Archeology Newsletter
See: ARCHAEOLOGY

Society for Italian Historical Studies-Newsletter

Publishing Co: Society for Italian Historical Studies, Boston College Historical Dept, Chestnut Hill, MA 02167; Title Tel # (617) 552-8000
Personnel: Editor-Alan Reinerman
General Info: Yr. Est. 1955, Annually, 21 pages
Subscriptions: Indv. $5
Circulation: Total-350

Sodus News, The
See: REGIONAL INTEREST

Southeast Asia Program Series: Monographs, Translations, Bibliographies
See: INTERNATIONAL AFFAIRS

Southeastern Historical Keyboard Society Newsletter
See: MUSIC & MUSIC TRADES

Southwestern Archivist
See: LIBRARY

Speedev
See: RAILROADS

Stamford Historical Society Newsletter   *Association*

Publishing Co: Stamford Historical Society, 1508 High Ridge Rd, Stamford, CT 06903-4107; Title Tel # (203) 329-1183
Personnel: Publisher, Editor-Russell Bastedo
Editorial Description: Inform members and public of Stamford historical society's activities.
General Info: Yr. Est. 1984, Quarterly, Trim Size-8½ x 11, Offset press, 8 pages, No Color
Circulation: (100% controlled), Total-500

Standard Bearer
Association

Publishing Co: National Flag Foundation, Flag Plaza, Pittsburgh, PA 15219; Title Tel # (412) 261-1776 Title Fax # (412) 261-9132
Personnel: Editor-Daniel R. Garwig
Editorial Description: Information, articles & editorials relating to the US flag and patriotism.
General Info: (Formerly Flag Plaza Standard/The New Constellation), Yr. Est. 1970, Bi-monthly, Trim Size-8½ x 11, Sheetfed press, 12 pages, ISSN: 0882-2220, 4 Color, Coated, Saddle-stitched
Subscriptions: Indv. $18, $3/copy
Circulation: Total-20,000

Stanford Historian

Publishing Co: Stanford Univ. History Dept., Publications, Stanford, CA 94305; Title Tel # (415) 723-2651

Strawbery Banke Newsletter
See: MUSEUM PUBLICATIONS

Strecker Museum News
See: MUSEUM PUBLICATIONS

Studebaker Family
See: GENEALOGY

Superstition Mountain Historical Society-Newsletter
Consumer, Association

Publishing Co: Superstition Mountain Historical Society, Inc., PO Box 3845, Apache Junction, AZ 85217-3845; Title Tel # (602) 983-4888
Personnel: Editor-Donna Reiner
Editorial Description: Historical society information and projects. Contains articles about the Superstition Mountain Region and surrounding areas.
General Info: Yr. Est. 1980, Quarterly, Trim Size-8½ x 11, Letrpr. press, 50 pages, No Color, Coated
Subscriptions: Indv. $15, $7/copy
Acquistions: Publication Sold
Circulation: Total-500
Advertising: Inquire for rates.

Surveillant: Acquisitions for Security & Intelligence Professionals
See: SECURITY & SURVEILLANCE

Swenson Center News
See: ETHNIC

Swiss-American Historical Society Review
Consumer

Publishing Co: Swiss American Historical Soc., 6440 N Bosworth Ave, Chicago, IL 60626-4921; Title Tel # (312) 262-8336
Personnel: Publisher-Ed Schmocker, Editor-Leo Schelbert
Editorial Description: Society news, information relating to Swiss-American history.
General Info: Yr. Est. 1964, 3x/yr.
Subscriptions: Indv. $25

Teiresias
Consumer

Publishing Co: McGill Univ. Dept. of Classics, 855 Sherbrooke St. W., Montreal, PQ H3A 2T7 Canada; Title Tel # (514) 392-5335
Personnel: Editor-A. Schachter
Editorial Description: Boeotian antiquity.
General Info: Yr. Est. 1971, Annually, Trim Size-8½ x 11, Mimeo press, 90 pages, ISSN: 0381-9361, No Color
Subscriptions: Indv. $8, $8/copy
Circulation: Total-380

Ten Broeck Newsletter

Publishing Co: Albany County Historical Assn., 9 Ten Broeck Pl, Albany, NY 12210-2524; Title Tel # (518) 436-9826
Personnel: Editor-Dorothy Billings
General Info: Yr. Est. 1975, Quarterly
Circulation: Total-1,000

Texas Catholic Historical Society Newsletter
Association

Publishing Co: Texas Catholic Historical Society, Box 704, St. Edward's Univ., Austin, TX 78767-0704; Title Tel # (512) 447-4132
Personnel: Publisher-Dr. Karl Schmidt, Editor-Brother William Dunn, C.S.C., Circ. Mgr., Production Mgr.-Joseph Sprug
Editorial Description: Texas Catholic Church history, related news items etc.
General Info: Yr. Est. 1976, Semi-annually, Trim Size-8½ x 11, Offset press, 6 pages, No Color
Subscriptions: Indv. $10, Inst. $15
Circulation: Total-550

Tomato Club, The
See: GARDENING & HORTICULTURE

Total Eclipse

Publishing Co: J. Taylor Block, P.O. Box 1055, Suisun City, CA 94585
Editorial Description: Its a unique zine, taking a rational approach to the magical sciences - full of history, social commentary.
General Info: Trim Size-8.5 x 11, 12 pages
Subscriptions: Indv. $2

Traces
See: GENEALOGY

Tracks
Consumer, Association

Publishing Co: Indiana Transportation Museum, Forest Park, Box 83, Noblesville, IN 46060-0083; Title Tel # (317) 773-6000 Title Fax # (317) 773-5530
Personnel: Publisher-Richard Howell, Editor-Michael Lennox, Art Dir.-James Vawter
Editorial Description: Covers restoration, exhibits, and rail excursions.
General Info: (Formerly I.T.M. News), Yr. Est. 1960, Bi-monthly, Trim Size-8½ x 11, Mimeo press, 4 pages, No Color, Matte
Subscriptions: Indv. $20, Inst. $50, Free
Circulation: Total-2,000
List Rental: Rents Lists
Printing Co: Indiana Printing, 121 E Pike St # 231, Crawfordsville, IN 47933-2513 Tel # (317) 362-4410

Tracks & Traces
See: GENEALOGY

Transfer, The
Association

Publishing Co: Oregon Electric Railway Historical Society, Inc., 1836 N Emerson St, Portland, OR 97217-3855 Tel # (503) 222-2226; Title Tel # (503) 357-3574
Personnel: Editor-Richard Thompson
General Info: (Formerly Trolley Park News), Yr. Est. 1958, Monthly, Trim Size-8½ x 11, Sheetfed press, 6 pages, No Color, Newsprint
Subscriptions: Indv. $15
Circulation: Total-200

Translation Series
See: INTERNATIONAL AFFAIRS

Treasures

Publishing Co: Reynolds Historical Library, 1700 University Blvd, Birmingham, AL 35233-1816; Title Tel # (205) 934-4475 Title Fax # (205) 939-0224
Personnel: Publisher, Editor-Marion McGuinn
Editorial Description: Publishes news & activities of Reynolds Historical Library UAB.
General Info: (Formerly Reynolds Library Assocs. Newsletter), Yr. Est. 1980, Annually, Sheetfed press, 4 pages, 2 Color, Matte
Circulation: (100% controlled), Total-3,700
Printing Co: UAB Print Shop, 1530 3rd Ave., S., Birmingham, AL 35294-0001 Tel # (205) 934-3790

Uncommon Sense

Publishing Co: Institute of Early American History, PO Box 8781, Williamsburg, VA 23187-8781 Fax # (804) 221-1047; Title Tel # (804) 221-1110
Personnel: Editor-Sally Mason
Editorial Description: Newsletter of activities in early American history.
General Info: (Formerly Institute of Eary American History and Culture News Letter), Yr. Est. 1952, Semi-annually, Trim Size-8½ x 11, Offset press, 6 pages
Subscriptions: Free With Membership
Circulation: (100% controlled), Total-2,000
List Rental: Rents Lists

U.S. Outdoor Drama
See: THEATRE

Utah State Historical Society Newsletter
Association

Publishing Co: Utah State Historical Society, 300 Rio Grande St, Salt Lake City, UT 84101-1182 Tel # (801) 533-3500; Title Tel # (801) 533-3514 Title Fax # (801) 533-3504
Editorial Description: News of Utah State Historical Society activity.
General Info: Yr. Est. 1950, Bi-monthly, Trim Size-7 x 10⅜, Offset press, 8 pages, No Color
Subscriptions: Free
Circulation: (100% controlled), Total-3,200

Vancouver Historical Society, Newsletter
Association

Publishing Co: Vancouver Historical Society, Box 3071, Vancouver, BC V6B 3X6 Canada; Title Tel # (604) 536-8849
Personnel: Editor-Christine Mullins
Editorial Description: History of City of Vancouver & British Columbia. Book lists.
General Info: (Formerly Vancouver History), Yr. Est. 1961, 9x/yr., Trim Size-8½ x 11, Mimeo press, 1 pages, ISSN: 0042-2487, No Color, Newsprint
Subscriptions: Indv. $17
Circulation: Total-250

Vincent of Beauvais
Newsletter — *Scholarly, Association*

Publishing Co: Bradley University, Department of History, Publications, Peoria, IL 61625-0001; Title Tel # (309) 677-2399 Title Fax # (309) 677-3687
Personnel: Editor-Gregory Guzman
Editorial Description: Focus on the manuscripts & work of this 13th century medieval author & encyclopedist.
General Info: Yr. Est. 1976, Annually, Trim Size-8½ x 11, Offset press, 20 pages
Subscriptions: Free
Circulation: Total-200

Violent Kin — *Consumer*

Publishing Co: Violent Kin, 5065 Westwood Lake Dr, Miami, FL 33165-6142
Personnel: Publisher, Editor-Paul Meredith
Editorial Description: Concerns the adventures & kinfolk of Jesse James & others touched by violence during the American past. Our purpose is not to glorify outlaws. We will search for the truth because your editor believes that our ancestors can only be understood if we know what sort of lives they led & something of the times in which they lived.
General Info: Yr. Est. 1989, Quarterly, Trim Size-8½ x 11, Offset press, 30 pages, ISSN: 1064-5071
Subscriptions: Indv. $12, Can. $12, For. $20, $3/copy

Virginia Historical Society
History Notes — *Association*

Publishing Co: Virginia Historical Society, PO Box 7311, Richmond, VA 23221-0311; Title Tel # (804) 358-4901 Title Fax # (804) 355-2399
Personnel: Editor-Nelson Lankford
Editorial Description: Brief articles on acquisitions of the Virginia Historical Society & membership activities.
General Info: (Formerly Virginia Historical Society Occassional Bulletin), Yr. Est. 1960, Quarterly, Letrpr. press, 12 pages, No Color, Newsprint
Subscriptions: $1/copy
Circulation: Total-5,100

Virginia Independent

Publishing Co: Virginia Commission on Bicentennial of the US Constitution, Univ. of Virginia, 207 Minor Hall, Charlottesville, VA 22903; Title Tel # (804) 924-0948
Personnel: Editor-Tracy Warren
Editorial Description: Historical articles, reprintings of Virginia documents, calendar listings, book reviews, all concerning Virginia's role in the creation of the Constitution.
General Info: Yr. Est. 1986, Quarterly, Sheetfed press, 8 pages, No Color, Coated
Circulation: Total-10,000

Voice in the Wilderness
See: CULTURE & HUMANITIES

Volunteer
See: MILITARY & NAVAL

Welland Historical Museum Newsletter
See: MUSEUM PUBLICATIONS

West Virginia & Regional
History Collection-
Newsletter — *Association*

Publishing Co: West Virginia University Libraries, Box 6069, Morgantown, WV 26506-6069 Tel # (304) 293-3640; Title Tel # (304) 293-3536 Title Fax # (304) 293-6638
Personnel: Editor-John Cuthbert
Editorial Description: News of West Virginia history & culture.
General Info: Yr. Est. 1985, Tri-annually, Sheetfed press, 10 pages, 2 Color, Newsprint
Subscriptions: Indv. $10
Circulation: Total-500
Printing Co: Fairmont Printing Co., PO Box 2000, Fairmont, WV 26555-2000 Tel # (304) 363-8500, Fax # (304) 363-8224

Westmorland Historical
Society, Newsletter — *Association*

Publishing Co: Westmorland Historical Society, RR 1, College Bridge, NB E0A 1L0 Canada; Title Tel # (506) 758-9355
Personnel: Editor-Edith Gillcash, Publisher, Circ. Mgr.-Wayne Gillcash
Editorial Description: Local events of historic interest & articles by membership & others. Research & pub.
General Info: Yr. Est. 1965, 3x/yr., Trim Size-8½ x 11, Mimeo press, 8 pages, No Color
Subscriptions: Indv. $10
Circulation: Total-250

Willard News — *Association*

Publishing Co: Willard Family Assn. of America, Inc., 185 Grant St, Lexington, MA 02173-2126
Editorial Description: Reunion Schedules & Reservations for Historical Associations.
General Info: Monthly

Wilson Museum Bulletin
See: MUSEUM PUBLICATIONS

Wisconsin Preservation — *Association*

Publishing Co: State Historical Society of Wisconsin, 816 State St., Madison, WI 53706-1488 Tel # (608) 264-6400; Title Tel # (608) 264-6501 Title Fax # (608) 264-6404
Personnel: Editor-Larry Reed
General Info: Yr. Est. 1977, Bi-monthly, Trim Size-8½ x 11, 12 pages, ISSN: 0276-4156, No Color, Newsprint
Subscriptions: Free
Circulation: Total-4,500

WyMonDak Messenger
See: GENEALOGY

Wyoming History News — *Association*

Publishing Co: Wyoming Historical Society-Dept. of Commerce, Third Floor, Barrett Building, 2301 Central Avenue, Cheyenne, WY 82002-0001; Title Tel # (307) 777-7015
Personnel: Editor-Judy West
Editorial Description: Carries current news of Wyoming State Historical Society and its 22 chapters, and news of activities in the historical profession.
General Info: Yr. Est. 1953, Monthly, Trim Size-8½ x 11, Offset press, 4 pages, No Color
Subscriptions: Indv. $9, Inst. $20
Acquistions: Publication Bought, Publication Sold
Circulation: Total-2,000

Yorker Palatine Newsletter
See: GENEALOGY

Yukon Historical &
Museums Association
Newsletter — *Association*

Publishing Co: Yukon Historical & Museums Assn., Box 4357, Whitehorse, YK Y1A 3T5 Canada; Title Tel # (403) 667-4704 Title Fax # (403) 668-7574
General Info: Yr. Est. 1977, Bi-monthly, Desktop press, 6 pages, Coated
Subscriptions: Indv. $20, Can. $20, Free With Membership
Acquistions: Publication Sold
Advertising: Accepts Inserts.

HOBBY

300 Star Letter
See: AUTOMOTIVE

ACCI Newsletter — *Association*

Publishing Co: Association of Crafts & Creative Industries, 1100 H. Brandywine Blvd., P.O. Box 2188, Zanesville, OH 43702-2188; Title Tel # (614) 452-4541 Title Fax # (614) 452-2552
Personnel: Publisher-Pam Palm, Editor-Julie Fox, Product Mgr.-Chuck Cihon, Mktg. Dir.-Jeff Beeler
Editorial Description: Covers Association News, board and committee activities, industry programs like news regarding the national craft month promo held , tour and travel information, etc. We also carry information about the Annual International Craft Expo. hel d each July in Chicago.
General Info: Yr. Est. 1976, Bi-monthly, Trim Size-17 x 11, Sheetfed press, 8 pages, 2 Color, Matte, Saddle-stitched
Subscriptions: Free With Membership
Circulation: (95% controlled), Total-6,000, International-250

ALPCA Newsletter — *Association*

Publishing Co: Automobile License Plate Collectors Assn., Box 77, Horner, WV 26372; Title Tel # (304) 842-3773
Personnel: Editor-Paul Maginnity, Circ. Mgr.-Gary Brent Kincade
Editorial Description: For the purpose of promoting interest in the collecting of motor vehicle license plates, fraternizing with fellow hobbyists, and exchanging information about the hobby with other members of the organization.
General Info: Yr. Est. 1954, Bi-monthly, Trim Size-8½ x 11, 32 pages, 1% ads, No Color
Subscriptions: Indv. $30, Can. $30, For. $30, $3/copy
Circulation: Total-3,000
Advertising: Inquire for rates.

ATHA Newsletter — *Association*

Publishing Co: Assn of Traditional Hooking Artists, 3209 Erwin Drive, Plano, TX 75074 Tel # (212) 423-8312; Title Tel # (508) 399-8230
Personnel: Circ. Mgr.-Nancy Martin, Editor, Production Mgr.-Judy Long, Adv. Dir.-Jill Hurd, Promotion Dir.-Cynthia Norwood
Editorial Description: Traditional rug hooking information; history, education and exchange of news from all states, Canada, Japan and England.
General Info: Yr. Est. 1979, Bi-monthly, Trim Size-8½ x 11, Offset press, 48 pages, Ind/Abs/Online: Canada, 2% ads, Color-cover, Matte
Subscriptions: Indv. $18, Can. $24, $4/copy
Circulation: Readership-2,200
Advertising: Inquire for rates.

Aerobics

Publishing Co: Aerobics Center, 12200 Preston Rd, Dallas, TX 75230-2223; Title Tel # (214) 661-3374
General Info: Monthly, 8 pages
Subscriptions: Indv. $15

Alles' Around the World Knitting Machine News & Views
CPM: $36

Publishing Co: Alles Knitting Publications, Inc., 1000 Jefferson Heights Rd, Pittsburgh, PA 15235-4707; Title Tel # (412) 795-1343
Personnel: Editor-Alles Hutchinson
General Info: Yr. Est. 1970, Monthly, Trim Size-8$\frac{12}{}$ x 11, Offset press, 52 pages, Matte, Saddle-stitched
Subscriptions: Indv. $310, $3/copy
Circulation: Total-8,500
Advertising: $310.

American Fish Decoy Association
Association

Publishing Co: American Fish Decoy Association, 624 Merritt, Fife Lake, MI 49633-9142; Title Tel # (616) 879-3912
Personnel: Publisher-John Shoffner, Editor-Art Kimball
Editorial Description: Exists to promote collecting fish decoys as a hobby.
General Info: Yr. Est. 1990, Quarterly
Subscriptions: Indv. $25, Free With Membership
Circulation: Total-175
Advertising: Inquire for rates.

American Lock Collectors Association Newsletter
See: COLLECTIBLES

American Star
See: AERONAUTICS/ASTRONAUTICS

American Typecasting Fellowship Newsletter
See: PRINTING/GRAPHIC ARTS

Annie's Crochet Newsletter Canadian
Consumer

Publishing Co: Annie's Attic, Inc., 222 Las Colinas Blvd W, Suite 1750, Irving, TX 75039-5437 Tel # (214) 488-1100 Fax # (214) 432-9555
Editorial Description: Canadian subscriber to a newsletter containing a variety of needlework project patterns.
List Rental: List Management Co.: Flynn Direct Response, 289 Davisville Avenue, Toronto, ON M4S 1H1 Canada Tel # (416) 322-8200, Fax # (416) 322-5200, Actives: 58,156

Antique Comb Collector
See: ANTIQUES & ART GOODS

Antique Outboard Motor Club Newsletter
Association

Publishing Co: Antique Outboard Motor Club, Inc., PO Box 09293, Milwaukee, WI 53209-0293; Title Tel # (414) 966-3697
General Info: 8x/yr.
Subscriptions: Free With Membership
Circulation: Total-1,260
Advertising: Inquire for rates.

Atlantic Inflight
Association

Publishing Co: Hang Gliding Assn. of Newfoundland, 16 Woodbine Avenue, Corner Brook, NF A2H 3N8 Canada; Title Tel # (709) 785-2697
Personnel: Editor-Allan Faulkner, Editor-Chris Walters
Editorial Description: Contains events and happenings, as well as personal articles from the general hang gliding population of Atlantic Canada.
General Info: Yr. Est. 1980, Quarterly, Trim Size-8½ x 11, Desktop press, 20 pages, 1% ads, No Color
Subscriptions: Indv. $10, Free With Membership
Advertising: $25. Accepts Inserts.
List Rental: Rents Lists

Auburn-Cord-Duesenberg Club Newsletter
Consumer, Association

Publishing Co: Auburn-Cord-Duesenberg Club, 9n089 Corron Rd, Elgin, IL 60123-8304; Title Tel # (708) 464-5767
Personnel: Editor-Jim Corbin, Production Mgr., Adv. Dir.-Jay Engler
Editorial Description: Activities of A-C-D Club, historical reprints, letters, classified advertisements.
General Info: Yr. Est. 1953, 10x/yr., Trim Size-8½ x 11, Offset press, 24 pages, 1% ads, 2 Color, Coated, Saddle-stitched
Subscriptions: $2/copy
Circulation: Total-1,800
Advertising: Inquire for rates. Accepts Inserts.
Printing Co: Engler Printing Co., 808 W State St, Fremont, OH 43420-2538 Tel # (419) 332-2181

B.C Contact!
See: AERONAUTICS/ASTRONAUTICS

Ballcard Collector

Publishing Co: George Robert Martin, Rr 2, Corryton, TN 37721-9802; Title Tel # (615) 933-5593
Personnel: Editor-George R. Martin
Editorial Description: Covers aspects of sport card collecting. Checklists, ads, auctions, and current values of cards and related items.
General Info: Yr. Est. 1966, Bi-monthly, Trim Size-6 x 8½, Mimeo press, 16 pages
Subscriptions: Indv. $3
Circulation: Total-750
Advertising: Inquire for rates.

Bang Board, The
Association

Publishing Co: Corn Item Collectors Assn., Inc., 613 N Long St, Shelbyville, IL 62565-1544; Title Tel # (217) 774-5002
Personnel: Editor-E. Eloise Alton
Editorial Description: Newsletter (THE BANG BOARD) is published 4 times a year and contains at least 36 pages each.
General Info: Yr. Est. 1986, Quarterly, Trim Size-8½ x 11, 36 pages
Subscriptions: Indv. $13, Free To Qualified Recipient
Circulation: Total-310

Bead and Button
Consumer

Publishing Co: Design House International, PO Box 14111, Reading, PA 19612-4111
Editorial Description: For bead and button enthusiasts.
General Info: Monthly
Circulation: Total-75,000
List Rental: List Management Co.: Media Marketplace, 140 Terry Drive, P.O. Box 500, Newtown, PA 18940-0500 Tel # (215) 968-5020, Fax # (215) 968-9410, Actives: 71,145, $90/M

Bill Nelson Newsletter
See: COLLECTIBLES

Brandstand
Consumer, Association

Publishing Co: Cigarette Pack Collectors Assn., 61 Searle St, Georgetown, MA 01833-2213; Title Tel # (508) 352-7377
Personnel: Editor-Richard Elliott
Editorial Description: Club newsletter for collectors of old cigarette advertising & packaging.
General Info: (Formerly Smoke Signals), Yr. Est. 1976, Bi-monthly
Subscriptions: Indv. $10, For. $10, $1/copy
Circulation: Total-250

Brewster Society News Scope
See: COLLECTIBLES

Bridge-Covered

Publishing Co: Lois Libbin, PO Box 710, Atwood, IL 61913-0710; Title Tel # (217) 578-3879
Personnel: Publisher, Editor-Lois Libbin
Editorial Description: Members interests only with emphasis on covered bridge postcards, covered bridges & preservation.
General Info: Yr. Est. 1977, Bi-monthly, Trim Size-8½ x 11, Mimeo press, 10 pages, Color
Subscriptions: Indv. $4
Acquistions: Publication Bought
Circulation: Total-310
Advertising: Inquire for rates.

CARD TALK
See: PRINTING/GRAPHIC ARTS

CN Lines
See: RAILROADS

Cambridge Crystal Ball
See: GLASS, STONE & CLAY

Canadian Military Medals & Insignia Journal
Association

Publishing Co: Canadian Society of Military Medals & Insignia, 1531 Bayview Ave, P.O Box 43536, Toronto, ON M4G 4G8 Canada
Personnel: Editor-James Steel, Circ. Mgr.-Frank Fluellon
Editorial Description: Collecting, study & research of medals, badges & insignia.
General Info: Yr. Est. 1965, Quarterly, Offset press, 16 pages, ISSN: 0701-0427, No Color
Subscriptions: Indv. $15
Circulation: Total-550

Candlelighter
See: BUSINESS & INDUSTRY

Candlewick Collector Newsletter, The
See: GLASS, STONE & CLAY

Cane Collector's Chronicle
See: COLLECTIBLES

Cardinal Club Newsletter
See: AERONAUTICS/ASTRONAUTICS

Chain Gang

Publishing Co: Key Collectors Intl., PO Box 9397, Phoenix, AZ 85068-9397;
Title Tel # (602) 942-0043
Personnel: Editor-Don Stewart
Editorial Description: History and study of key chains for collectors.
General Info: Yr. Est. 1978, Bi-monthly

Chainmail

Publishing Co: Intl. Fantasy Gaming Society, PO Box 3577, Boulder, CO 80307-3577
Personnel: Editor-Margo Toth
Editorial Description: Newsletter summarizes activities of the International Gaming Society (IFGS). The IFGS runs live-scale role playing games all over the U.S., along with a national convention.
General Info: Yr. Est. 1981, Monthly, Trim Size-8½ x 11, Letrpr. press, 16 pages, 1% ads, No Color, Saddle-stitched
Subscriptions: Indv. $10, Can. $13
Circulation: Total-500
Advertising: Accepts Inserts.
List Rental: Rents Lists
Printing Co: Printery, 1635 Folsom St, Boulder, CO 80302-6717 Tel # (303) 442-1032

Chauffeurs' Badges and Transportation Badges of the World
Consumer

Publishing Co: Dr. Edward H. Miles, 888 8th Ave., New York, NY 10019-5704;
Title Tel # (212) 765-2660
General Info: Yr. Est. 1992, Annually, Looseleaf
Subscriptions: Indv. $100, $8/copy

Chicago Playing Card Collectors, Membership Roster
Association

Publishing Co: Chicago Playing Card Collector, Inc., 1559 W. Pratt Blvd., Chicago, IL 60626-4228;
Title Tel # (312) 274-0250
Personnel: Circ. Mgr.-Bernie De Somer, Publisher, Editor, Adv. Dir.-Barbara Lunaburg, Art Dir.-Shirley Barak
Editorial Description: Articles on playing cards, history of card enclosures, reports, news of meetings & conventions, and instructions for collectors.
General Info: Yr. Est. 1955, Quarterly, Trim Size-8½ x 11, 50 pages, No Color, Matte
Subscriptions: Indv. $15, $2/copy
Circulation: Total-600
Advertising: Inquire for rates.

Circuit, The
See: PHILATELY & POSTAL AFFAIRS

Coin Machine Trader
See: VENDING MACHINES

Collectors' Item, The

Publishing Co: American Transit Collectors' Assn., C/O Bruce Gilson, 601 Silver Springs Ave #4, Silver Springs, MD 20910-4649; Title Tel # (703) 739-8855
Personnel: Editor-Bruce Gilson
General Info: Yr. Est. 1976, 8x/yr., 6 pages

Contest News-Letter

Publishing Co: Contest Partners, PO Box 25227, Arlington, VA 22202-9227;
Title Tel # (703) 685-7858
Personnel: Publisher-Bob Krefting, Editor-Deni Hamilton, Circ. Mgr.-Bill Anderson, Production Mgr.-Les Whiteley, Adv. Dir.-Mal McCluskey, Promotion Dir.-Rosalie Bruno
Editorial Description: Instructions, tips, and information on how to enter sweepstakes.
General Info: Yr. Est. 1975, Monthly, Trim Size-8½ x 11, Web press, 12 pages, ISSN: 0894-0207, No Color, Coated
Subscriptions: Indv. $15, $2/copy
Circulation: Total-900,000
Advertising: Accepts Inserts.
List Rental: List Management Co.: Manager: Mal McCluskey; List Services Corp., 6 Trowbridge Dr., PO Box 516, Bethel, CT 06801-2858 Tel # (203) 743-2600, Fax # (203) 743-0589, Actives: 575,000, $70/M, Hotline: 48,000, $77.50/M, Expires: 120,000, $50/M
Printing Co: Tempographics, 455 E North Ave, Carol Stream, IL 60188-2167 Tel # (708) 462-8200, Fax # (708) 462-0350

Contest News Wire
See: GAMBLING

Contestogram

Publishing Co: Contestogram, PO Box 2711, Paducah, KY 42002-2711; Title Tel # (502) 442-9202
Personnel: Editor-Bob Buchanan
General Info: Monthly, 12 pages
List Rental: List Management Co.: Venture Communications, 60 Madison Avenue, 3rd fl., New York, NY 10010 Tel # (212) 684-4800, Fax # (212) 545-1680, Actives: 38,725

Cooking Contest Chronicle
See: FOOD

Cormorant News Bulletin
See: AUTOMOTIVE

Coryell Newsletter
See: GENEALOGY

Country Press, The

Publishing Co: J.L. Walker, PO Box 5024, Durango, CO 81301-6813
Personnel: Publisher-Janet Walker
Editorial Description: Home business news, arts & crafts related, & outlets for products.
General Info: Yr. Est. 1984, Quarterly, Trim Size-8½ x 11, Desktop press, 12 pages, 7% ads, No Color, Newsprint
Subscriptions: Indv. $20
Advertising: Inquire for rates.

Craft Marketing News
Business, Consumer

Publishing Co: Front Room Publ., PO Box 1541, Clifton, NJ 07015-1541; Title Tel # (201) 773-4215
Title Fax # (201) 773-4215
Personnel: Publisher-Robert Patti, Editor-Adele Patti
Editorial Description: Craft marketing news for crafts people & craft shop owners.
General Info: (Formerly Front Room News), Yr. Est. 1984, Monthly, Trim Size-8½ x 11, Web press, 16 pages, ISSN: 1046-9699, No Color, Saddle-stitched
Subscriptions: Indv. $37, $4/copy
Circulation: Total-2,000
Printing Co: Marrakesh Express, 500 Anclote Rd, Tarpon Springs, FL 34689-6701 Tel # (813) 942-2218, Fax # (813) 937-4758

Craft Related Newsletters, Periodicals & Publications
Consumer

Publishing Co: Prosperity & Profits Unlimited, PO Box 416, Denver, CO 80201-0416;
Title Tel # (303) 575-5676
Personnel: Publisher, Editor-A.C. Doyle
Editorial Description: Listing of sources of craft newsletters, calendar date publications, patterns, etc.
General Info: Yr. Est. 1990, Annually, Trim Size-8½ x 11, Sheetfed press, 12 pages, ISSN: 1053-2013, No Color, Looseleaf
Subscriptions: Indv. $8, Inst. $8, Can. $10, For. $11, $8/copy

Creative Machine Newsletter
Consumer   **CPM: $179**

Publishing Co: Open Chain Publishing, Inc., PO Box 2634, Menlo Park, CA 94026-2634;
Title Tel # (415) 366-4440 Title Fax # (415) 366-4455
Personnel: Publisher, Editor-Robbie Fanning
Editorial Description: Newsletter for sewing machine and serger enthusiasts.
General Info: Yr. Est. 1990, Quarterly, Trim Size-8½ x 11, Desktop press, 48 pages, ISSN: 1060-0493, 2 Color, Recycled, Saddle-stitched
Subscriptions: Indv. $16, Can. $22, For. $22, $5/copy
Circulation: Total-6,000
Advertising: $1,075.
List Rental: Actives: 22,000
Printing Co: EBSCO Media, 801 5th Ave. S., Birmingham, AL 35233-1102 Tel # (205) 323-1508, Fax # (205) 226-8400

Cucurbits
See: GARDENING & HORTICULTURE

Current
See: BOATS & BOATING

Current Blackjack News
See: GAMBLING

Diamond Duds
See: BASEBALL

Director
Consumer, Association

Publishing Co: Frog Pond, The, PO Box 193, Beech Grove, IN 46107-0193
Personnel: Editor-Merelaine Haskett
Editorial Description: Devoted to collection of frog motifs in all forms (jewelry, figurines, toys, art, etc.) Contains contests, articles on frogs, and club information.
General Info: Yr. Est. 1985, Bi-monthly, Letrpr. press, 4 pages, No Color
Subscriptions: Indv. $17, Can. $17, For. $20, $3/copy
Circulation: Total-400

Dollmasters, The
See: ANTIQUES & ART GOODS

Doorknob Collector, The
Consumer, Association   **CPM: $222**

Publishing Co: Antique Doorknob Collectors of America, PO Box 126, Eola, IL 60519-0126;
Title Tel # (708) 357-2381 Title Fax # (708) 357-2391
Personnel: Publisher, Editor-Raymond J. Nemec, Production Mgr., Art Dir.-Loretta Nemec
Editorial Description: Published for collectors of antique hardware.
General Info: Yr. Est. 1981, Bi-monthly, Trim Size-8½ x 11, 8 pages, 2 Color, Coated
Subscriptions: Indv. $25, $4/copy
Circulation: (74% controlled), Total-270
Advertising: $60.

Double Clutch
See: AUTOMOTIVE

ERTL Replica
Consumer

Publishing Info: Ertl Co., The, PO Box 500, Dyersville, IA 52040-0500; Title Tel # (319) 875-2000
Personnel: Publisher, Editor-Karen Sands
Editorial Description: Informational clearinghouse about new & old collectible ERTL Replica toys.
General Info: Yr. Est. 1982, Bi-monthly, Offset press, 20 pages, 4 Color, Coated
Subscriptions: Indv. $10, For. $14, $2/copy
Acquistions: Publication Bought
Circulation: Total-40,000
Printing Co: Cedar Graphics, Inc., P.O. Box 185, Hiawatha, IA 52233-1458 Tel # (319) 393-3600, Fax # (319) 393-3934

Edges
See: COLLECTIBLES

Educated Traveler, The
See: TRAVEL

Egg Cup Collectors Corner
Consumer

Publishing Info: Paznmes, 67 Stevens Ave, Old Bridge, NJ 08857-2244; Title Tel # (908) 679-8924
Personnel: Publisher, Editor, Circ. Mgr., Production Mgr., Adv. Dir., Mktg. Dir.-Joan George
Editorial Description: Information about egg cups.
General Info: Yr. Est. 1986, Quarterly, Trim Size-8½ x 11, Offset press, 16 pages, Coated
Subscriptions: Can. $18, For. $22, $5/copy
List Rental: Rents Lists
Printing Co: Penbrooke Printers, Main Street, Sayerville, NJ

Emerald City Mirror
See: CHILDREN

Ephemera News
Association **CPM: $160**

Publishing Info: Ephemera Society of America, Inc., PO Box 95, Cazenovia, NY 13035; Title Tel # (315) 655-2810 Title Fax # (315) 655-1078
Personnel: Publisher-Ephemera Society, Editor-Michelle Megrath, Promotion Dir.-Carol Resnick
Editorial Description: Articles on Ephemera, calendar of events, book reviews.
General Info: Yr. Est. 1980, Quarterly, Trim Size-8½ x 11, Web press, 28 pages, ISSN: 0734-3337, 2 Color, Matte, Saddle-stitched
Subscriptions: Indv. $35, Inst. $35, $3/copy
Circulation: Total-1,000
Advertising: $160. Accepts Inserts.
List Rental: Actives: $75/M
Printing Co: Quartier Printing, 719 East Genesee Street, Syracuse, NY 13210 Tel # (315) 476-3630, Fax # (315) 476-3635

Ertl Blueprinter, The
See: COLLECTIBLES

Fan Club Monitor
See: FAN MAGAZINES-MOVIE, RADIO, TV

Fare Share-The Food Letter
See: FOOD

Flax Craft
See: TEXTILES

Front Striker Bulletin
See: COLLECTIBLES

Function Key, The
See: COMPUTERS & AUTOMATION

G.I. Joe Collectors Club
See: COLLECTIBLES

Gaming Confidential
See: GAMBLING

Gift Basket Idea Newsletter
See: GIFTS, GAMES, TOYS

Glove Collector Newsletter, The
Consumer

Publishing Info: The Glove Collector, 14057 Rolling Hills Ln, Dallas, TX 75240-3807 Fax # (214) 699-9851; Title Tel # (214) 699-1808
Personnel: Publisher, Editor-Joe Phillips
General Info: Yr. Est. 1989, Bi-monthly
Subscriptions: Indv. $17
Circulation: Total-400

Goren Bridge Letter
Consumer

Publishing Info: Tribune Media Services, 435 N. Michigan Avenue, Chicago, IL 60611-4008 Tel # (312) 222-4444 Fax # (312) 222-4328
Personnel: Publisher-Keith Williams, Editor-Tannah Hirsch
Editorial Description: Offers bridge playing tips and advice for game players at all skill levels.
General Info: Yr. Est. 1984, Monthly, Trim Size-8½ x 11, 8 pages, 2 Color
Subscriptions: Indv. $32
List Rental: Rents Lists

Green Country Quarterly
See: GENEALOGY

Guidon
See: CLUBS

Gulliver's Gazette

Publishing Info: Lilliputian Bottle Club, 5626 S Corning Ave, Los Angeles, CA 90056-1305; Title Tel # (213) 837-2823
Personnel: Editor-Lee Weiss, Circ. Mgr.-Gordon Brunk
Editorial Description: For collectors of miniature bottles.
General Info: Yr. Est. 1970, Bi-monthly, Trim Size-8½ x 11, 14 pages, Color
Subscriptions: Indv. $10, Can. $15, For. $15
Circulation: Total-300
Advertising: Inquire for rates. Accepts Inserts.
Printing Co: Lyngate Printing Co., 3643 Abbott Rd, Lynwood, CA 90262-2102 Tel # (213) 566-2166

Gunsite Gossip

Publishing Info: Gunsite Press, PO Box 401, Paulden, AZ 86334-0401; Title Tel # (602) 636-4565
Personnel: Publisher-Betty Wrath, Editor-Jeff Cooper, Circ. Mgr.-Diane Crawford, Production Mgr.-Jim Wrath
General Info: Yr. Est. 1981, Semi-monthly, Desktop press, 4 pages, No Color
Subscriptions: Indv. $15, $1/copy
Circulation: (48% controlled), Total-1,300, Subscriptions-600

HAC Techline
See: AERONAUTICS/ASTRONAUTICS

Happy Hobbies

Publishing Info: Happy Hobbies Pubs., PO Box 70, Claymont, DE 19703-0070; Title Tel # (314) 443-5325
Personnel: Editor-Pam Myers
Editorial Description: Contains patterns & designs for quilts, embroidery, crochet, cross-stitch & applique.
General Info: Yr. Est. 1965, Quarterly, 40 pages
Circulation: Total-1,100

Heather Notes
See: BOTANY

Higgins & Gage World Postal Stationery Catalog
See: PHILATELY & POSTAL AFFAIRS

Highland Highlights

Publishing Info: Southern Highland Handicraft Guild, PO Box 9545, Asheville, NC 28815-0545; Title Tel # (704) 298-7928
Personnel: Editor-Cornelia Graves
Editorial Description: For the membership of the Southern Highland Handicraft Guild.
General Info: Yr. Est. 1959, Monthly, 6 pages, No Color, Coated
Subscriptions: Indv. $25
Circulation: Total-1,000

Hobby/Business World
Consumer

Publishing Info: Cricket Communications, Inc., PO Box 527, Ardmore, PA 19003-0527; Title Tel # (215) 747-6684 Title Fax # (215) 747-7082
Personnel: Publisher-Mark Battersby, Editor-J. Crickett
Editorial Description: Devoted to the tax & financial aspects of hobby businesses.
General Info: Yr. Est. 1977, Monthly, Trim Size-8½ x 11, Offset press, 16 pages, No Color, Newsprint
Subscriptions: Indv. $24
Acquistions: Publication Bought
Circulation: Total-2,875

Ignitor
Association

Publishing Info: Spark Plug Collectors of America, PO Box 2229, Ann Arbor, MI 48106-2229; Title Tel # (313) 971-4229
Personnel: Publisher-William Bond, Editor-Rick Harris
Editorial Description: Member ads, old ad reprints, informative articles on antique spark plugs.
General Info: Yr. Est. 1976, Quarterly, Offset press, 20 pages, Color-cover
Subscriptions: Indv. $15, For. $20
Circulation: Total-300

In the Groove
See: COLLECTIBLES

Inky Trail News
Consumer

Publishing Info: Inky Trail News, 1054 Lakeview Drive, Cadiz, KY 42211-8654
Editorial Description: Helps introduce pen pals to one another.
General Info: Monthly

International Calculator
Collector
Association CPM: $100

Publishing Co: International Association of Calculator Co., 14561 Livingston Ave, Tustin, CA 92680-2618; Title Tel # (714) 730-6140 Title Fax # (714) 730-6140
Personnel: Publisher, Editor-Guy Ball
Editorial Description: Informative newsletter for the collector of portable electronic calculators.
General Info: Yr. Est. 1992, Quarterly, Trim Size-5½ x 8½, Offset press, 16 pages, No Color, Matte, Saddle-stitched
Subscriptions: Indv. $16, Can. $20, For. $20
Circulation: Total-450
Advertising: $45. Accepts Inserts.

Intl. Seal, Label & Cigar
Band Society, News
Bulletin
Association

Publishing Co: International Seal, Label & Cigar Band Society, 8915 E Bellevue St, Tucson, AZ 85715-5618; Title Tel # (602) 296-1048
Personnel: Editor-M.H. Freedmen
General Info: Yr. Est. 1957, Trim Size-8½ x 11, Mimeo press, 10 pages, No Color, Newsprint
Subscriptions: Indv. $7, $1/copy
Circulation: Total-200

Joan Walsh Anglund Collector's News
See: CHILDREN

Jonesboro Wind

Publishing Co: Tara Collectors Club, 10698 Sandpiper Rd, Jonesboro, GA 30236-6696
Personnel: Publisher-Jim Swords, Editor-Mason Eagan
General Info: Quarterly

Kanvention Xtra

Publishing Co: Tin Can Collectors Association, 11326 Ventura Blvd, Studio City, CA 91604-3137

LANSA
See: NUMISMATICS

Liberty Bell Crier
Association

Publishing Co: Liberty Bell Matchcover Club, 6048 N Water St, Philadelphia, PA 19120-2015 Tel # (512) 424-5218; Title Tel # (215) 424-5218
General Info: Yr. Est. 1982, 5x/yr., Desktop press, 8 pages, Other, Other
Subscriptions: Free With Membership
Circulation: Readership-200

Light Aircraft Manufacturers Assn. -Newsletter
See: AERONAUTICS/ASTRONAUTICS

Lincoln Owners Club,
Bulletin

Publishing Co: Lincoln Owners Club, 99 Drakestown Rd., Long Valley, NJ 07853-3298
General Info: Bi-monthly

Looming Arts, The
Business

Publishing Co: Pendleton Shop, PO Box 233, Sedona, AZ 86339-0233; Title Tel # (602) 282-3671
Personnel: Editor-Mary Pendleton
Editorial Description: Textbook type publication for handweavers with fabric samples.
General Info: Yr. Est. 1966, 5x/yr., Trim Size-8½ x 11, 8 pages
Subscriptions: Indv. $11, Can. $13, For. $13, $3/copy
Circulation: Total-750
Printing Co: Oak Creek Press, Sedona, AZ 86336

MIAA Industry News
Business, Association

Publishing Co: Miniatures Industry Assn. of America, 1100h Brandywine Blvd # 2188, Zanesville, OH 43702-2188; Title Tel # (614) 452-4541 Title Fax # (614) 452-2552
Personnel: Publisher-Patty Parrish, Circ. Mgr.-Tricia Ritchey, Adv. Dir.-Duane Meyers, Production Mgr., Art Dir.-Paula Morris, Editor, Editorial Page Ed., Feature Ed., Bk. Rev. Ed., Promotion Dir.-Debby Johnston
Editorial Description: Carries MIAA associations news & also industry news for the miniatures industry. Targets miniatures, dolls, dollhouses & collectible miniatures. Articles on business & marketing. Information on MIAA annual trade shows & National Dollhouse & Miniatures Month.
General Info: (Formerly MIAA News), Yr. Est. 1987, Quarterly, Trim Size-8½ x 11, Offset press, 16 pages, 2 Color, Matte, Saddle-stitched
Subscriptions: Indv. $30, $5/copy
Circulation: Total-4,200, Readership-4,200
Advertising: Inquire for rates.

MJF Baseball Card
Advisory

Publishing Co: MJF Publications, PO Box 3056, Stamford, CT 06905-0056; Title Tel # (203) 968-1461
Personnel: Editor-Michael Funke
General Info: Monthly
Subscriptions: Indv. $75

MOOsletter, The
See: DAIRY

Manhattan Chess Club News
See: SPORTS & SPORTING GOODS

Manuscript Society News
Business, Association

Publishing Co: Manuscript Society, 350 N Niagara St, Burbank, CA 91505-3648
Personnel: Editor-S.L. Carson
Editorial Description: Society news and info of interest to archivists librarians, manuscript collectors.
General Info: Yr. Est. 1980, Quarterly, ISSN: 0195-7813
Subscriptions: Indv. $35, Inst. $35, Can. $35, For. $35, $2/copy
Circulation: Total-1,800
List Rental: Actives: 1,800, $200/M

Marble Mania
Association

Publishing Co: Marble Collectors' Society of America, PO Box 222, Trumbull, CT 06611-0222; Title Tel # (203) 261-3223
Personnel: Publisher-Stanley Block
Editorial Description: Historical information as well as current events relating to the hobby of marble collecting.
General Info: Yr. Est. 1975, Quarterly, Trim Size-8½ x 11, 8 pages, No Color
Subscriptions: Indv. $12, $3/copy
Circulation: (100% controlled), Total-1,800
Printing Co: Anray Litho, Higgins Ave., Milford, CT 06460 Tel # (203) 877-1000

Marklin Club
Consumer

Publishing Co: Marklin, Inc., 16988 W Victor Rd # 51319, New Berlin, WI 53151-4135; Title Tel # (414) 784-0717 Title Fax # (414) 784-1095
Personnel: Editor-Tammy Schoen
Editorial Description: The Marklin Club is dedicated to serving the special interests of the Marklin enthusiast. It's goal is to help you to get the most from your Marklin trains.
General Info: Yr. Est. 1985, Bi-monthly
Subscriptions: Indv. $13, For. $20
Circulation: Total-5,000

Marklin Digital Club

Publishing Co: Marklin, Inc., 16988 W Victor Rd # 51319, New Berlin, WI 53151-4135; Title Tel # (414) 784-8854 Title Fax # (414) 784-1095
Personnel: Editor-Dr. Tom Catherall
Editorial Description: The Marklin Digital Club provides members with in-depth knowledge and insight into the Marklin Digital multi-train operating system.
General Info: Bi-monthly
Subscriptions: Indv. $12, For. $17
Circulation: Total-500

Mile Post
Association

Publishing Co: Milestone Car Society Inc., PO Box 24612, Indianapolis, IN 46224-0612; Title Tel # (317) 244-9778
Personnel: Publisher-Jack Martin
Editorial Description: To promote the preservation, understanding, enjoyment & restoration of domestic & foreign automobiles from 1945 through 1972.
General Info: Yr. Est. 1971, Bi-monthly, Trim Size-8½ x 11, Web press, 19 pages, No Color
Subscriptions: $3/copy
Circulation: Total-800
Advertising: Inquire for rates.
List Rental: Rents Lists

Mini License Plate & Key Chain Tag Newsletter
See: GOLF

Mini-Thistle
Association

Publishing Co: Pairpoint Cup Plate Collectors of America, Box A2058, New Bedford, MA 02741-2058; Title Tel # (508) 997-1813
Personnel: Editor-Priscilla Chasse
Editorial Description: Classified ad newsletter dealing with cup plates and related items.
General Info: Yr. Est. 1976, Bi-monthly, Offset press, 2 pages
Subscriptions: Indv. $10
Circulation: Total-1,500
Advertising: Inquire for rates.

Miniature Book News
See: BOOKS & BOOK TRADE

Mobilia
See: AUTOMOTIVE

The Modeler's Resource

Publishing Co: Fred DeRuvo, 1141 Holly Avenue, Clovis, CA 93611
Editorial Description: Catering to the vehicular and figure kit builder
General Info: Trim Size-8.5 x 11, 24 pages
Subscriptions: Indv. $3

Mystic Light of the
Aladdin Knights   *Association*

Publishing Co: Aladdin Knights of the Mystic Light, 3935 Kelley Rd, Kevil, KY 42053-9431; Title Tel # (502) 488-2116 Title Fax # (502) 488-2116
Personnel: Publisher, Editor-J. Courter
Editorial Description: Aladdin brand kerosene and electric lamps.
General Info: Yr. Est. 1973, Bi-monthly, Desktop press, 12 pages, No Color, Matte
Subscriptions: Indv. $20
Circulation: Total-1,500
Advertising: Inquire for rates.

NAVA News
See: HISTORY

National Federation of Flemish Giant Rabbit Breeders, Bulletin
See: LIVESTOCK

National Model Railroad
Association Bulletin   *Association*

Publishing Co: Natl. Model Railroad Assn., 4121 Cromwell Rd, Chattanooga, TN 37421-2119; Title Tel # (615) 892-2846
General Info: Monthly
Subscriptions: Indv. $10
Circulation: Total-27,000

National Valentine
Collectors Bulletin   *Association*

Publishing Co: National Valentine Collectors Association, PO Box 1404, Santa Ana, CA 92702-1404; Title Tel # (714) 547-1355
Personnel: Editor-Evalene Pulati
Editorial Description: Each issue concentrates on some special aspect of collecting with illustrations.
General Info: Yr. Est. 1977, Quarterly, Sheetfed press, 14 pages, ISSN: 1044-8896, No Color, Newsprint
Subscriptions: Indv. $16, Can. $20, For. $20, Free With Membership

Newsy Vents   *Association*

Publishing Co: Maher Studios, PO Box 420, Littleton, CO 80160-0420; Title Tel # (303) 798-6830
Personnel: Publisher, Editor-Clinton Detweiler, Circ. Mgr.-Adelia Detweiler, Art Dir.-David Miller
Editorial Description: Ventriloquists & Ventriloquism.
General Info: Yr. Est. 1944, Quarterly, Trim Size-5$^{1}/_{2}$ x 8$^{1}/_{2}$, Sheetfed press, 12 pages, 2 Color, Newsprint
Subscriptions: Indv. $8
Circulation: Total-1,825
Printing Co: Maher Studios, 800 W Littleton Blvd, Littleton, CO 80120-2302

Nova Scotia Designer
Crafts Council
Newsletter

Publishing Co: Nova Scotia Designer Crafts Council, 1809 Barrington Street, Suite 901, Halifax, NS B3J 3K8 Canada; Title Tel # (902) 423-3837
Personnel: Editor, Adv. Dir.-Robin Metcalfe
Editorial Description: Bimonthly membership newsletter of the NSDCC. Craft & organizational news, small business information, notices.
General Info: Yr. Est. 1974, Bi-monthly, Trim Size-7$^{3}/_{4}$ x 11, 24 pages, ISSN: 0834-3136, No Color, Newsprint, Saddle-stitched
Circulation: Total-500
Advertising: Inquire for rates.

Old Abe's News
See: COLLECTIBLES

On Cover
See: PHILATELY & POSTAL AFFAIRS

Oz Collector, The   *Consumer*

Publishing Co: Books of Wonder, 132 7th Avenue at 18th Street, New York, NY 10011-1803; Title Tel # (212) 989-3270 Title Fax # (212) 989-1203
Personnel: Editor-Peter Glassman
Editorial Description: A guide to everything Oz -a plethora of news and information about the world of Oz- including Oz items for sale:books toys,reference works, posters, movie memorabilia.
General Info: Yr. Est. 1985, Semi-annually, Trim Size-8$^{1}/_{2}$ x 11, Offset press, 16 pages, ISSN: 0886-8697, No Color, Matte, Saddle-stitched
Subscriptions: $2/copy
Printing Co: Downtown Offset, 216 W. 18th St., New York, NY 10011 Tel # (212) 807-1930

Oz Trading Post

Publishing Co: Sponsor-The International Wizard of Oz Club, International Wizard of Oz Club, The, PO Box 95, Kinderhook, IL 62345-0095
Personnel: Editor-Fred Meyer
Editorial Description: Lists material club members wish to buy, sell, or trade.
General Info: Yr. Est. 1965, Tri-annually
Circulation: Total-2,000

PATINAGRAM
See: ANTIQUES & ART GOODS

Paperweight Collectors'
Association, Bulletin

Publishing Co: Paperweight Collectors' Assn., 47 Windsor Rd, Scarsdale, NY 10583-4824
General Info: Annually

Peanut Papers
See: COLLECTIBLES

Pen Pal Post   *Business, Consumer*

Publishing Co: World Pen Pals, 1694 Como Ave, Saint Paul, MN 55108-2710; Title Tel # (612) 647-0191 Title Fax # (612) 647-9268
General Info: (Formerly Write in There), Annually, Recycled
Circulation: Total-40,000

Pennsylvania Crafts   CPM: $100

Publishing Co: Pennsylvania Guild of Craftsmen, Tyler Craft, Richboro, PA 18954; Title Tel # (215) 579-5997
Personnel: Editor-Lyn Jackson
General Info: 10x/yr., Trim Size-8$^{1}/_{2}$ x 11, Desktop press, 16 pages
Subscriptions: Indv. $40
Circulation: Total-2,000
Advertising: $200.

Photograph Collector
See: PHOTOGRAPHY

Poor Man's Sawdust
Plansletter

Publishing Co: Poor Man's Pubs., 7000 20th St Lot 930, Vero Beach, FL 32966-8878; Title Tel # (301) 776-3792
Personnel: Editor-J.S. Blackwell
Editorial Description: Contains u-build plans, projects, ideas, tips, guides, etc.
General Info: Yr. Est. 1985, Quarterly, 24 pages, ISSN: 0887-8889
Circulation: Total-2,500

Postcard Classics
See: COLLECTIBLES

Potpourri from Herbal Acres   *Business, Consumer*

Publishing Co: Pine Row Pubs., PO Box 428, Washington Crossing, PA 18977-0428; Title Tel # (215) 493-4259
Personnel: Publisher, Editor-Phyllis V. Shaudys
Editorial Description: A network of herb hobbyists sharing recipes, crafts & ideas.
General Info: Yr. Est. 1979, Quarterly, Sheetfed press, 20 pages, ISSN: 0197-4084, No Color
Subscriptions: Indv. $18
Circulation: Total-2,000

Potpourri Simple & Easy Update
See: GIFTS, GAMES, TOYS

Presidents' Journal
See: HISTORY

Quilter's Newsletter
Magazine   *Consumer*

Publishing Co: Leman Publications, Inc., P.o. Box 4101, Golden, CO 80401-0101 Parent Co.-Rodale Press, Emmaus; Title Tel # (303) 420-4272
Personnel: Editor in Chief-Bonnie Leman, Circ. Mgr.-Scott Ashley, Publisher, Art Dir.-Mary Leman Austin
Editorial Description: Information and articles for quilting enthusiasts, both experienced and beginners.
General Info: Yr. Est. 1969, 10x/yr., Trim Size-8$^{1}/_{2}$ x 11, ISSN: 0274-712X, 4 Color, Matte, Saddle-stitched
Subscriptions: Indv. $19
Circulation: Total-175,000
Advertising: Inquire for rates.

Rathkamp Matchcover
Society-Bulletin   *Consumer, Association*

Publishing Co: Rathkamp Matchcover Society, 25 Huntsmans Horn Cir Dept Dn, The Woodlands, TX 77380-0938 Tel # (713) 367-2109; Title Tel # (513) 367-2109
Personnel: Editor-Mike Prero
General Info: (Formerly Voice of the Hobby), Yr. Est. 1941, Bi-monthly, 24 pages, No Color
Subscriptions: Indv. $15, Inst. $15, Can. $20, For. $20, Free With Membership
Circulation: (100% controlled), Total-1,600

Reply Coupon Collector   *Consumer*

Publishing Co: Sponsor-International Society of Reply Coupon Collectors, Reply Coupon Collector, PO Box 165, Somers, WI 53171-0165; Title Tel # (414) 552-8740
Personnel: Editor-Allan Hauck
Editorial Description: Latest news on reply coupons of all countries & kinds.
General Info: Yr. Est. 1954, Semi-annually
Subscriptions: Indv. $15, For. $25

Rollin' Rock Club-News Letter

Publishing Co: Rollin' Rock Club, 15 Kennington Dr., Warrington, FL 32507-1026;
Title Tel # (904) 455-6424
Personnel: Editor-Simonne Wood
Editorial Description: Promotes fellowship in the hobby of gem & mineral collecting.
General Info: Yr. Est. 1956, Quarterly, 32 pages
Subscriptions: Indv. $8
Circulation: Total-500

Rough Rider
See: AUTOMOTIVE

Rugging Room Bulletin
See: NEEDLEWORK, KNITTING

SWCHA Newsletter   *Business, Association*

Publishing Co: Southwestern Craft & Hobby Association, 1100 H Brandywine Blvd., P.O. Box 2188, Zanesville, OH 43702-2188; Title Tel # (614) 452-4541 Title Fax # (614) 452-2552
Personnel: Editor-Denise Northrop
Editorial Description: Information related to Association events & members, as well as the craft industry.
General Info: Yr. Est. 1978, 3x/yr., Trim Size-17 x 11, Sheetfed press, 6 pages, 2 Color, Matte, Saddle-stitched
Subscriptions: $2/copy
Circulation: Total-5,000

SWL   *Consumer, Association*

Publishing Co: American Shortwave Listeners Club, 16182 Ballad Ln, Huntington Beach, CA 92649-2272; Title Tel # (714) 846-1685
Personnel: Publisher, Circ. Mgr., Adv. Dir.-Stewart MacKenzie
Editorial Description: Devoted to the enjoyment of long distance radio listening. 'Dedicated to the principal of world friendship through shortwave which means that our activities are directed toward advancement of the SWL hobby.'
General Info: Yr. Est. 1959, Monthly, Trim Size-8½ x 10, Offset press, 60 pages, ISSN: 0162-5934, 25% ads, Color-cover, Other, Saddle-stitched
Subscriptions: Indv. $24, Inst. $23, Can. $25, For. $28, $2/copy
Advertising: $50. Accepts Inserts.
Printing Co: Office Depot, 7742 Edinger Ave., Huntington Beach, CA 92347 Fax # (800) 685-5010

Sand Paper, The   *Association*

Publishing Co: International Sand Collectors Society, 43 Highview Ave, Old Greenwich, CT 06870-1703; Title Tel # (203) 637-0093
Personnel: Publisher-William S. Diefenbach
Editorial Description: News for collectors, techniques of sand collecting. Exchange/trading information.
General Info: Yr. Est. 1969, Quarterly, Trim Size-8 x 11½, Offset press, 6 pages, Matte, Other
Subscriptions: Indv. $10
Circulation: Total-150

Scenterpiece Update
See: GIFTS, GAMES, TOYS

Scentouri News
See: COSMETICS & PERFUMES

Scouter's Digest
See: YOUTH

Scrabble News
See: GIFTS, GAMES, TOYS

Sewing & Crafts Hotline
See: CRAFTS

Sharing Memories   *Consumer, Association*

Publishing Co: Enesco Corp. The Memories of Yesterday Collector's Society, PO Box 245, Elk Grove Village, IL 60009-0245 Tel # (708) 640-5200; Title Tel # (708) 228-3738
Personnel: Publisher-Diana Derbas
Editorial Description: Memories of Yesterday Collector Society member newsletter.
General Info: Yr. Est. 1991, Quarterly, Trim Size-8½ x 11, Sheetfed press, 6 pages, Recycled, Other
Subscriptions: Indv. $21, $1/copy
Circulation: Total-35,000

Shavings
See: CONSTRUCTION & BUILDING

Shooting the Breeze   *Consumer, Association*   **CPM: $233**

Publishing Co: Miniature Arms Society, 4910 Kilburn Ave., Rockford, IL 61101-1746; Title Tel # (815) 964-2569 Title Fax # (815) 964-7267
Personnel: Publisher-David Hall, Editor-Ralph Koebbeman
Editorial Description: Articles on miniature arms making, collecting, and club news.
General Info: Yr. Est. 1973, Quarterly, Trim Size-8½ x 11, Web press, 36 pages, No Color, Coated, Saddle-stitched
Subscriptions: $5/copy
Circulation: Total-300
Advertising: $70.

Sign of the Cat
See: AUTOMOTIVE

Size of Craft/Hobby Industry Survey
See: CRAFTS

Snow Biz
See: ANTIQUES & ART GOODS

Sound Waves   *Consumer*

Publishing Co: Vintage Radio & Phonograph Society, Inc., PO Box 165345, Irving, TX 75016-5345; Title Tel # (214) 315-2553
Personnel: Publications Director-George Potter
Editorial Description: Features articles, book reviews and technical reviews devoted to antique radio and phonograph collecting.
General Info: Monthly, Trim Size-8½ x 11, Mimeo press, 2 pages, Coated, Saddle-stitched
Subscriptions: Indv. $14, For. $17, Free With Membership
Circulation: Total-450
Printing Co: X-Press Colour Graphics, Inc., 932 W Airport Fwy, Irving, TX 75062-6201 Tel # (214) 438-8131

Space Autograph News
See: AERONAUTICS/ASTRONAUTICS

Stained Finger, The
See: COLLECTIBLES

Strategist
See: GIFTS, GAMES, TOYS

Subway Surfer

Publishing Co: Tim Paul, 5208 18 NE, Seattle, WA 98105
Editorial Description: While surban sports fans go out for a game of softball or touch football, hardcore city residents engage in (how should we put it?) Electric activities, skitching, which is the sport of hanging on the back of busses
General Info: Trim Size-5 x 7, 12 pages
Subscriptions: Indv. $1

Table Top Train News   *Consumer*   **CPM: $83**

Publishing Co: Railtech, Inc., PO Box 3280, Ann Arbor, MI 48106-3280 Tel # (313) 426-1516; Title Tel # (313) 426-1510 Title Fax # (313) 426-7516
Personnel: Publisher-Denise M. Taylor, Editor-Richard Taylor, Circ. Mgr.-Cindy Wagner, Adv. Dir.-Jeff Ream
Editorial Description: Designed for collectors and operators of table top trains.
General Info: (Formerly Table Topper Newsletter), Yr. Est. 1994, Quarterly, Trim Size-8½ x 11, Desktop press, 20 pages, 2 Color, Matte, Perfect bound
Subscriptions: Indv. $22, $13/copy
Circulation: (23% controlled), Total-3,000, Subscriptions-1,000
Advertising: $250.
List Rental: Rents Lists
Printing Co: Eco-Graphics, 2372 Abbott Street, Ann Arbor, MI 48103 Tel # (313) 769-5077, Fax # (313) 769-5818

Teddy Tribune

Publishing Co: Teddy Tribune, 254 Sidney St W, Saint Paul, MN 55107-3494; Title Tel # (612) 291-7571
Personnel: Editor-Barbara Wolters
Editorial Description: Everything about teddy bears.
General Info: Yr. Est. 1980, 10x/yr.
Subscriptions: Indv. $17, $2/copy

Tight Lines   *Association*

Publishing Co: Greater Delaware Valley Kite Society, PO Box 888, Newfield, NJ 08344-0888; Title Tel # (609) 697-2285
Personnel: Publisher, Editor-Leonard Conover
Editorial Description: Kites-How to make, Where to fly, & What to buy.
General Info: Yr. Est. 1981, Bi-monthly, Trim Size-8½ x 11, Sheetfed press, 10 pages, No Color, Newsprint
Subscriptions: Indv. $6, $1/copy
Acquistions: Publication Bought
Circulation: Total-600
Advertising: Inquire for rates. Accepts Inserts.
List Rental: Actives: $25/M

Toothpick Bulletin   *Association*

Publishing Co: Natl. Toothpick Holder Collectors Society, PO Box 204, Eureka, IL 61530-0204; Title Tel # (309) 467-2535
Personnel: Editor-Judy Knauer
General Info: Yr. Est. 1974, Monthly, Mimeo press
Subscriptions: Free With Membership
Circulation: (100% controlled), Total-500

Torsion Bar
See: AUTOMOTIVE

Town Pump
Association

Publishing Co: International Carnival Glass Assn., PO Box 306, Mentone, IN 46539-0306;
Title Tel # (219) 353-7678
General Info: Yr. Est. 1967, Quarterly
Circulation: Total-1,300

Traders' Horn
See: GIFTS, GAMES, TOYS

Transport World
CPM$50000

Publishing Co: Intl. Railroad & Transportation Postcard Collectors Club, PO Box 6782, Providence, RI 02940-6782
Personnel: Editor-Robert Andrews
Editorial Description: Articles & information on transportation. Related to post cards, checklist of different series of post cards of transportation subjects.
General Info: Yr. Est. 1978, Quarterly, Trim Size-8½ x 11, 24 pages, 2% ads
Subscriptions: Indv. $10, Can. $15, For. $20
Acquistions: Publication Bought
Circulation: Total-500
Advertising: $25,000.

Uncle HQ/Spycon
Consumer, Association

Publishing Co: U.N.C.L.E., HQ. /Spycon, 234 Washo Dr, Lake Zurich, IL 60047-7902;
Title Tel # (847) 925-9220
Personnel: Editor-Susan Cole, Photo Ed.-Vicki Holt, Bk. Rev. Ed.-Ellen Druda, Promotion Dir.-Darlene Kepner
General Info: Yr. Est. 1976, Quarterly
Subscriptions: Indv. $11, Can. $12, For. $15
Circulation: Total-400
Advertising: Inquire for rates.

Watergardening News
See: GARDENING & HORTICULTURE

West Coast Lock Collectors
See: COLLECTIBLES

Whoop 'N' Holler
See: OUTDOORS

Winning Sweepstakes Newsletter
Consumer

Publishing Co: Sebell Publishing Co., Inc., 965 Concord St, Framingham, MA 01701-4685;
Title Tel # (508) 820-1800 Title Fax # (508) 875-9645
Personnel: Publisher-Jeffrey Sklar
Editorial Description: Winning Sweepstakes newsletter features complete entry details for the hardest-to-find and easiest-to-win sweepstakes, and proven strategies for wining big-money sweepstakes prizes time and again.
General Info: Yr. Est. 1983, Monthly, Trim Size-8½ x 11, Web press, 16 pages, ISSN: 0738-0143, No Color
Subscriptions: Indv. $30, $3/copy
Circulation: Total-100,000
Advertising: Accepts Inserts.
List Rental: Rents Lists

Working Wine Guide, The
See: BEVERAGES - BREWING

World Postal Stationery New Issue Report
See: PHILATELY & POSTAL AFFAIRS

Yo-Yo Times
See: GIFTS, GAMES, TOYS

Your Season Ticket
See: BASEBALL

HOME & HOME ENTERTAINMENT

Decorator's Insider
See: INTERIOR DESIGN & DECORATION

Delogram
See: REAL ESTATE

Egg Cup Collectors Corner
See: HOBBY

Festivities
See: ENTERTAINMENT

Flooring Fax News
See: FURNITURE & HOME FURNISHINGS

Friends of Doctor Who Newsletter
See: SCIENCE FICTION & FANTASY

Home Automation News
See: ELECTRIC & ELECTRONIC EQUIPMENT

Laser Disc Newsletter, The
Business, Consumer **CPM: $100**

Publishing Co: Laser Disc Newsletter, The, PO Box 420, East Rockaway, NY 11518-0420;
Title Tel # (516) 594-9304 Title Fax # (516) 594-4307
Personnel: Publisher, Editor-Douglas Pratt
Editorial Description: Newsletter for laser video disc consumers.
General Info: Yr. Est. 1984, Monthly, Trim Size-8½ x 11, Sheetfed press, 24 pages, ISSN: 0749-5250, 10% ads, No Color
Subscriptions: Indv. $35, For. $50, $4/copy
Circulation: Total-6,000
Advertising: $600.
List Rental: Actives: 3,500, $100/M, Expires: 3,000, $100/M
Printing Co: Cambridge Graphics, 75 Varick St., New York, NY 10013 Tel # (212) 219-1077

Leased Access Report - Audience
See: TELEVISION & VIDEO

Living in Style
See: FURNITURE & HOME FURNISHINGS

NAHWW Newsletter
Association

Publishing Co: National Association of Home & Workshop Writers, PO Box 10, Palomar Mountain, CA 92060-0010
Personnel: Editor-Richard Day, Production Mgr.-Huck Devenzio
Editorial Description: Contains marketing & other information of interest to home & workshop writers who are members of the assn.
General Info: Yr. Est. 1973, Quarterly, Trim Size-8½ x 11, Offset press, 8 pages, No Color, Newsprint
Subscriptions: Free With Membership
Circulation: Readership-200

Nari Focus
See: CONSTRUCTION & BUILDING

Penny Pincher
See: FAMILY

Report - Height of Fashion
Association

Publishing Co: Armstrong World Industries, Employee Communications, Box 3001, Lancaster, PA 17604 Tel # (717) 397-0611
Editorial Description: Armstrong's newsletter of home design.
General Info: Yr. Est. 1991, Quarterly, Trim Size-8½ x 11, 4 pages, 4 Color, Coated, Saddle-stitched
Printing Co: Intelligencer Printing Co., 330 Eden Rd #1768, Lancaster, PA 17601-4218
Tel # (717) 291-3100, Fax # (717) 569-2643

Sadie's Chatter Newsletter
Consumer

Publishing Co: Sadie's Chatter Newsletter, PO Box 2061, Tulsa, OK 74101-2061;
Title Tel # (918) 756-8099
Personnel: Publisher, Editor-Doris Gist
Editorial Description: Recipes, patterns, etc. for the home.
General Info: Yr. Est. 1972, Monthly, Trim Size-8½ x 11, Offset press, 13 pages, No Color
Subscriptions: Indv. $6, $1/copy
Circulation: Total-500
Advertising: Inquire for rates.

Swimming Pool Today
Association

Publishing Co: Natl Swimming Pool Owner's Assoc., 1213 Ridgecrest Cir, Denton, TX 76205-5421;
Title Tel # (817) 273-2658
Personnel: Publisher, Editor-Tom Doron, Circ. Mgr.-Susan Byrd, Art Dir.-Jamie Pritchett
Editorial Description: Covers safety,water chemistry,maintenance & all other pool subjects.
General Info: Yr. Est. 1985, Quarterly, Trim Size-8½ x 11, Web press, 16 pages, 2 Color, Newsprint, Saddle-stitched
Subscriptions: Indv. $5, $1/copy
Circulation: Total-100,000

Tea Talk, A Newsletter on the Pleasures of Tea
See: BEVERAGES - BREWING

HOME ECONOMICS

AACF Action

Publishing Co: American Association of Family & Consumer Sciences, 1555 King St., Alexandria, VA 22314-2738; Title Tel # (703) 706-4600 Title Fax # (703) 706-4663
Editorial Description: Covers news of American Home Economics Assn. & includes relevant news items.
General Info: (Formerly AHEA Newletter), Yr. Est. 1974, 5x/yr., Trim Size-11 x 18, Web press, 12 pages, 3% ads, No Color, Newsprint, Other
Subscriptions: Indv. $15
Circulation: Total-17,000
Advertising: Inquire for rates.
List Rental: Rents Lists

AAHE Newsletter
See: ARCHITECTURE

American Home Sewing and Craft Association
See: TEXTILES

Baking Sheet, The
See: BAKING

Barter Update - Barter Basics Edition
See: BUSINESS & INDUSTRY

Clothing for Less Newsletter
See: CONSUMER INTERESTS

Cooking Contest Chronicle
See: FOOD

Cooks Corner, The
See: FOOD

Corporate Consumer Forum Trendletter

Publishing Co: Home Economists in Business, 5008-16 Pine Creek Dr., Westerville, OH 43081-4899; Title Tel # (614) 890-4342 Title Fax # (614) 895-3466
Personnel: Editor-Linda Smithson, Publisher, Production Mgr.-Shawna Hooser
Editorial Description: Contains information on four basic trends - aging, biotechnology, environment and activism. Also other fey trend information influencing the marketplace and consumers.
General Info: Yr. Est. 1991, Bi-monthly
Subscriptions: Indv. $54

Coupon Treasure Hunt Newsletter   *Consumer, Association*

Publishing Co: Update Publicare Co, P O Box 416, Denver, CO 80201 Tel # (308) 577-5567; Title Tel # (303) 575-5676
Personnel: Editor-A. Doyle
Editorial Description: Coupon how to & basic information
General Info: Yr. Est. 1990, Irregular, Trim Size-8.5 x 11, 4 pages, ISSN: 1053-6523
Subscriptions: Indv. $9, Inst. $4, Can. $6, For. $8, $4/copy

Curmudgeon's Home Companion, The
See: FOOD

Extension Line Lookout   *Association*

Publishing Co: Cooperative Extension Association, 21 S. Grove St., E. Aurora, NY 14052-2398; Title Tel # (716) 652-5401
Personnel: Editor-R. McCoy, Editor-J. Ward, Circ. Mgr.-B. Spanitz, Circ. Mgr.-K. Welsh, Production Mgr.-Ellen George, Prod. Coord.-M. Hand
Editorial Description: Home economics and home gardening information.
General Info: Monthly, Offset press, 16 pages, 2 Color
Subscriptions: Indv. $6
Circulation: Total-3,800

Food Free or Cheap Newsletter   *Consumer*

Publishing Co: Prosperity & Profits Unlimited, PO Box 416, Denver, CO 80201-0416; Title Tel # (303) 575-5676
Personnel: Publisher-A. Doyle, Editor-A.C. Doyle
Editorial Description: Ways to find food that is free or cheap.
General Info: Yr. Est. 1990, Every two years, Trim Size-8.5 x 11, 4 pages, ISSN: 1054-0768
Subscriptions: Indv. $4, Inst. $4, Can. $6, For. $8, $4/copy

Frugal Bugle, The
See: BANKING & FINANCE

Frugal Consumers Dollar Stretching Possibility Newsletter
See: CONSUMER INTERESTS

Get Organized! News, The
See: GENERAL INTEREST

Home Ec News   *Association*

Publishing Co: Alberta Teachers' Association, 11010-142 St., Edmonton, AB T5N 2R1 Canada Tel # (403) 453-2411
Personnel: Editor-Angie Roelofs
Editorial Description: To provide current information re: Home Economics Council, learning materials, professional development activities.
General Info: Yr. Est. 1961, Trim Size-8½ x 11, Mimeo press, 12 pages, ISSN: 0018-4004, No Color, Newsprint
Subscriptions: Indv. $30
Circulation: (100% controlled), Total-600

Home Economics Educator   *Association*

Publishing Co: Home Economics Education Assn., 122 Broadview Ave, Fairmont, WV 26554-1422
Personnel: Editor-Stephanie Price
Editorial Description: Better understanding of family & community life, broaden scope of curriculum & improve quality of H.E. instruction.
General Info: Yr. Est. 1927, Semi-annually, Trim Size-8½ x 11, 8 pages
Subscriptions: Indv. $15, Can. $20
Circulation: (100% controlled), Total-2,500

Home Economics Forum   *Association*

Publishing Co: Omicron Nu Home Economics Honor Society, PO Box 247, Haslett, MI 48840-0247; Title Tel # (517) 339-3324
Personnel: Editor-Dorothy Mitstifer
General Info: (Formerly Omicron Nu Newsletter), Yr. Est. 1971, Quarterly
Circulation: Total-50,000

Home Work
See: BUSINESS & INDUSTRY

NEHC Update

Publishing Co: Natl. Extension Homemakers Council, 835 W. 7th St., Loveland, OR 80537-5360; Title Tel # (303) 663-6458
Personnel: Editor-Hazel Leininger
Editorial Description: Reports by states of homemakers projects. Latest information of home economics, citizenship, cultural arts, family life, health, intl. affairs, public information.
General Info: (Formerly Natl. Notes/Homemaker Update), Yr. Est. 1986, Bi-monthly, Trim Size-8½ x 11, Web press, 24 pages, No Color, Coated, Saddle-stitched
Subscriptions: Indv. $5
Circulation: Total-2,200

Nutrition Funding Report, The
See: HEALTH

Practically Green
See: CONSUMER INTERESTS

Quick, Easy, Cheap and Simple..the Newsletter   *Consumer*

Publishing Co: QEC & S, 4057 North Drake, Chicago, IL 60618-2219; Title Tel # (312) 267-5269
Editorial Description: Money, time and effort saving tips, ideas and services sources.
General Info: Yr. Est. 1992, 10x/yr., 8 pages
Subscriptions: Indv. $13, $2/copy

RTW Review
See: APPAREL & ACCESSORIES

Refunding Update - Introduction to Refunding
See: CONSUMER INTERESTS

SHETA Newsletter
See: EDUCATION

Smorgasboard-Plenty to Eat Update
See: FOOD

Soups Cheap or Almost Free
See: FOOD

Supermarket Savvy Information Resource Service
See: FOOD

THESA Newsletter
See: EDUCATION

Tea Times
See: BEVERAGES - BREWING

Tightwad Gazette
See: CONSUMER INTERESTS

HORSES

AAEP Report   *Association*

Publishing Co: American Assn. of Equine Practitioners, 4075 Iron Works Rd, Lexington, KY 40511-8462; Title Tel # (606) 233-0147 Title Fax # (606) 233-1968
Personnel: Editor-David Foley
Editorial Description: Equine health.
General Info: 10x/yr., Trim Size-8½ x 11, Sheetfed press, 6 pages, No Color, Newsprint
Subscriptions: Indv. $20, Free With Membership
Circulation: Total-5,400
List Rental: Actives: $100/M

AHC News — *Association*

Publishing Co: American Horse Council, 1700 K St NW Ste 300, Washington, DC 20006-3805; Title Tel # (202) 296-4031 Title Fax # (202) 296-1970
Editorial Description: Info of interest to horse owners. Provides information on federal legislation affecting the horse industry.
General Info: (Formerly AHC Newsletter), Yr. Est. 1969, Bi-monthly, Trim Size-8½ x 11, Desktop press, 6 pages, Coated
Subscriptions: Free With Membership
Circulation: Total-18,000

AHPA Newsletter — *Association*

Publishing Co: American Horse Protection Association, 1000 29th St NW Apt T100, Washington, DC 20007-3820; Title Tel # (202) 965-0500
Personnel: Editor-Robin Lohnes
Editorial Description: News of the association's efforts to end the abuse of horses and burros.
General Info: Yr. Est. 1969, Quarterly, 8 pages, No Color
Subscriptions: Indv. $20, $25/copy
Circulation: (100% controlled), Total-15,000

American Mustang World — *Association*

Publishing Co: American Mustang Assn., PO Box 338, Yucaipa, CA 92399-0338
Personnel: Publisher, Editor-Lenore Negri
Editorial Description: Devoted to the world of horses, especially the Mustang.
General Info: (Formerly American Mustang Assn.-Newsletter), Yr. Est. 1972, Quarterly, Offset press, 8 pages, No Color
Subscriptions: Free With Membership
Circulation: (100% controlled), Total-150
Advertising: Inquire for rates.

American Shire Horse Association -Newsletter — *Association*

Publishing Co: American Shire Horse Assn., 9251 Lansing Ave N, Stillwater, MN 55082-8414; Title Tel # (515) 993-3113 Title Fax # (515) 993-5113
Personnel: Publisher, Editor, Adv. Dir.-Lowell Wagoner
Editorial Description: News for breeders & owners of Shire Draft horses.
General Info: Yr. Est. 1885, Quarterly, 16 pages, No Color
Circulation: Total-515
Advertising: Inquire for rates.

CHA Newsletter — *Association*

Publishing Co: Camp Horsemanship Assn., 5318 Old Bullard Rd, Tyler, TX 75703-3612
Editorial Description: Interested in riding safety.
General Info: Yr. Est. 1967, Quarterly, Offset press, 4 pages, No Color
Circulation: Total-5,400

Canadian Murray Grey News

Publishing Co: Canadian Murray Grey Assn., Box 605, Red Deer, AB T4N 5G6 Canada; Title Tel # (403) 343-1355
General Info: Yr. Est. 1974, Quarterly, Trim Size-11 x 15
Circulation: Total-500
Advertising: Inquire for rates.

Council Courier — *Business, Association*

Publishing Co: Council Courier, PO Box 26182, Oklahoma City, OK 73126-0182; Title Tel # (405) 942-2291
Editorial Description: Horse industry newsletter.
General Info: Yr. Est. 1978, Monthly

Curly Cues — *Association*

Publishing Co: American Bashkir Curly Registry, PO Box 246, Ely, NV 89301-0246; Title Tel # (702) 289-4228
Personnel: Editor, Production Mgr.-Sunny Martin
Editorial Description: Newsletter to inform & educate owners of curly-coated horses.
General Info: Yr. Est. 1971, Semi-annually, Trim Size-8½ x 11, 20 pages, ISSN: 0887-2406, No Color, Matte
Subscriptions: Free With Membership
Circulation: Total-1,500
Printing Co: Ely Daily Times, PO Box 1139, Ely, NV 89301-1139 Tel # (702) 289-4491

Equestrian Trails — *Association* — CPM: $50

Publishing Co: Equestrian Trails, Inc., 13741 Foothill Blvd., 2201, Sylmar, CA 91342-3133; Title Tel # (818) 362-6819 Title Fax # (818) 362-9443
Personnel: Circ. Mgr.-Dina Graboyes, Editor, Adv. Dir.-Holly Carson
Editorial Description: Publication of general horse information & organization news & information.
General Info: Yr. Est. 1970, Monthly, Trim Size-10¾ x 17, Offset press, 40 pages, ISSN: 013-9831, Color, Newsprint
Subscriptions: Free With Membership
Circulation: (100% controlled), Total-4,000
Advertising: $200.
Printing Co: American Foothill Publishing Co., 10001 Commerce Ave, Tujunga, CA 91042-2303 Tel # (818) 352-7878

Feed Facts
See: LIVESTOCK

Girls' Rodeo Association News

Publishing Co: Womans Professional Rodeo Association, Rr 5 Box 698, Blanchard, OK 73010-9351; Title Tel # (405) 485-2277
Personnel: Editor-Ludia Moore
General Info: Yr. Est. 1964, Monthly
Subscriptions: Indv. $5

Grayson Gram

Publishing Co: Grayson Foundation, Inc., 1718 Alexandria Drive, Box 4158, Lexington, KY 40544; Title Tel # (606) 278-5243
Personnel: Editor-Edward Ford
Editorial Description: Reports on Foundation activities & programs related to horses & equine medical research.
General Info: Yr. Est. 1984, Quarterly, 4 pages
Circulation: Total-3,500

Hall of Fame of the Trotter Newsletter

Publishing Co: Trotting Horse Museum, 240 Main St, Goshen, NY 10924-2157; Title Tel # (914) 294-6330
Personnel: Editor-Philip A. Pines
Editorial Description: Reports on historical and current articles -contributor's corner, message to members, brief reports.
General Info: Yr. Est. 1966, Quarterly, Trim Size-8 x 11½, Web press, 6 pages, No Color, Newsprint
Acquistions: Publication Bought
Circulation: (100% controlled), Total-1,200
Printing Co: Rama Printers, 25 Boxwood Ln, Buffalo, NY 14227-2707 Tel # (716) 692-2884

Handicapping Monthly
See: GAMBLING

Harness & Greyhound Racing Handicapping
See: GAMBLING

Horse! — *Consumer*

Publishing Co: Tufts University School of Veterinary Medicine, 200 Westboro Rd., North Grafton, MA 01536
Editorial Description: Information for horse owners about how to care for their animals.

Horse Cents — *Association* — CPM: $100

Publishing Co: Canadian Thoroughbred Horse Society, 255 17th Ave. SW, Ste. 401, Calgary, AB T2S 2T8 Canada; Title Tel # (403) 229-3609
Personnel: Editor-R. Gellner
General Info: Yr. Est. 1982, Monthly, Trim Size-8½ x 11, 12 pages, 4 Color, Coated, Other
Subscriptions: Indv. $12, Can. $12
Circulation: Total-2,500
Advertising: $250. Accepts Inserts.

Horse Report, The — *Scholarly*

Publishing Co: California Center for Equine Health and Performance, University of California, Davis, CA 95616-8589 Fax # (916) 752-9379; Title Tel # (916) 752-6433 Title Fax # (915) 752-9379
Personnel: Editor-Laurie Fio
General Info: Yr. Est. 1982, Quarterly, Trim Size-8½ x 11, Offset press, 4 pages, No Color, Matte, Saddle-stitched
Subscriptions: Free
Circulation: Total-25,000

Illinois Horse Report

Publishing Co: Univ. of Illinois at Urbana Champaign, 227 Illini Union, 1401 W. Green Street, Urbana, IL 61801 Tel # (217) 333-1477 Fax # (217) 333-7803; Title Tel # (217) 333-2666 Title Fax # (217) 333-1952
Personnel: Publisher-Kevin Kline
Editorial Description: Current information on nutrition, management, health, & breeding. Updates on research & educational activity. Four issues per year.
General Info: Quarterly
Subscriptions: Indv. $4

Journal of Equine Veterinary Science
See: VETERINARY

KTA Wire — *Association*

Publishing Co: Kentucky Thoroughbred Assn., PO Box 4040, Lexington, KY 40544-4040; Title Tel # (606) 277-1122
Personnel: Editor-Laura Schneider
Editorial Description: Racing and breeding.
General Info: Yr. Est. 1983, Bi-monthly, Offset press, 6 pages, 2 Color
Circulation: (100% controlled), Total-1,400

Ketch Pen
Consumer, Association

Publishing Co: Sponsor-National Cowboy Hall of Fame, Rodeo Historical Society, 1700 NE 63rd St, Oklahoma City, OK 73111-7906 Tel # (405) 478-6404; Title Tel # (405) 478-2250 Title Fax # (405) 478-4714
Personnel: Circ. Mgr.-Donna Dolf, Art Dir.-M. J. Van Deventer, Editor, Mktg. Dir.-M.J. Van Deventer
Editorial Description: Current & historical rodeo.
General Info: (Formerly Wild Bunch), Yr. Est. 1975, Semi-annually, Trim Size-8½ x 11, Sheetfed press, 16 pages, Matte, Saddle-stitched
Subscriptions: Indv. $25
Circulation: Total-1,020

Michigan United Thoroughbred Breeders
Business, Association

Publishing Co: Michigan United Thoroughbred Breeders & Owners Assn., PO Box 2752, Livonia, MI 48151-0752; Title Tel # (313) 422-2044
Editorial Description: Current board action, informative data, ads.
General Info: Yr. Est. 1981, Monthly, Trim Size-8½ x 11, Sheetfed press, 8 pages, 3% ads, No Color
Circulation: Total-800
Advertising: Accepts Inserts.
Printing Co: Sir Speedy, 31193 Plymouth Rd, Livonia, MI 48150-2103 Tel # (313) 422-3380

NARHA News
See: SPORTS & SPORTING GOODS

National Turf Writers Assn. Newsletter
See: JOURNALISM

New Hub, The
Association　　CPM: $62

Publishing Co: Carriage Association of America, Inc., 177 Pointers Auburn Road, Salem, NJ 08079-9742; Title Tel # (609) 935-1616 Title Fax # (609) 935-4955
Personnel: Editor-Jill Ryder
Editorial Description: Monthly newsletter of Carriage Assn. available with membership. Quarterly magazine, The Carriage Journal, also included with membership.
General Info: Yr. Est. 1983, Monthly, Trim Size-8½ x 11, 60 pages, 10% ads, Color
Subscriptions: Indv. $45, Inst. $25, Can. $45, For. $45, $5/copy
Circulation: Total-4,000
Advertising: $250.
Printing Co: Sheridan Press, 450 Fame Avenue, Hanover, PA 17331-9581 Tel # (717) 632-3535, Fax # (717) 633-8900

News of Cosca
Association

Publishing Co: News of Cosca, 4232 Poe Rd, Medina, OH 44256-9740; Title Tel # (216) 723-2125
Personnel: Editor-Shirley Nowak
Editorial Description: General Interest. Horse Shows
General Info: Monthly, 7 pages, 25% ads
Subscriptions: Free With Membership
Advertising: $77.
List Rental: Rents Lists
Printing Co: East Canton Printing, 200 Church St W, East Canton, OH 44730-1185 Tel # (216) 488-1266

Over the Fence

Publishing Co: Sponsor-Michigan Horse Council, Michigan Horse Council, PO Box 22008, Lansing, MI 48909-2008; Title Fax # (310) 842-8219
Editorial Description: Covers the state horse industry.
General Info: Yr. Est. 1987, Quarterly, Sheetfed press, 8 pages, 2 Color, Matte
Circulation: Total-300
Printing Co: Mason Printing, Cedar Street, Mason, MI 48864

Palomino Parade
Business

Publishing Co: The Palomino Horse Association, Star Route Box 24, Dornsife, PA 17823; Title Tel # (717) 758-3067
Personnel: Editor-Jean Plankenhorn
General Info: Yr. Est. 1936, Bi-monthly, Desktop press, 4 pages
Subscriptions: Indv. $15, Free With Membership
Circulation: Total-300
Advertising: Inquire for rates.

Promotions of Member Tracks
Association

Publishing Co: Harness Tracks of America, 4640 E. Sunrise Srive, Suite 200, Tucson, AZ 85718-4576 Tel # (520) 529-2525 Fax # (520) 529-3235
Editorial Description: Informs publicity and marketing directors and management of 35 member tracks in the racing industry
General Info: Irregular
Circulation: (93% controlled), Total-300, International-20, Readership-300

Racing Update

Publishing Co: Racing Update Inc., PO Box 11052, Lexington, KY 40512-1052; Title Tel # (606) 231-7966 Title Fax # (606) 259-1262
Personnel: Editor-Bill Oppenhiem
Editorial Description: Recognized for providing accurate, unbiased anlaysis & facts about racing, breeding, & the thoroughbred marketplace.
General Info: Yr. Est. 1978, Bi-weekly, 8 pages
Subscriptions: Indv. $200, Can. $200, For. $200

Registry News
Association

Publishing Co: Arabian Horse Registry of America, 12000 Zuni St., Westminster, CO 80234-2300; Title Tel # (303) 450-4748
Personnel: Editor-Ralph Clark
Editorial Description: Information pertaining to registry activities, rules and regulations; policies.
General Info: Yr. Est. 1908, Quarterly, Trim Size-8½ x 11, Sheetfed press, 8 pages, 2 Color, Coated
Circulation: (100% controlled), Total-25,000

Track Topics
Business, Association

Publishing Co: Harness Tracks of America, 4640 E. Sunrise Srive, Suite 200, Tucson, AZ 85718-4576 Tel # (520) 529-2525 Fax # (520) 529-3235
Personnel: Editor-Stanley F. Bergstein, Promotion Dir.-Tammy A Gantt
Editorial Description: Informs management of 35 member tracks of developments in the harness racing industry.
General Info: Yr. Est. 1962, Weekly, Trim Size-8½ x 11, Offset press, 4 pages, No Color
Subscriptions: Free To Qualified Recipient
Circulation: (100% controlled), Total-2,200, Readership-2,200

USET News

Publishing Co: U.S. Equestrian Team, Inc., Pottersville Rd., Gladstone, NJ 07934; Title Tel # (201) 234-1251 Title Fax # (201) 234-9417
Personnel: Editor-Marty Bauman, Art Dir.-Mickey Kirby
Editorial Description: Results of national and international competitions, dates of selections and screening trials.
General Info: Yr. Est. 1950, Bi-monthly, Trim Size-8½ x 11, Letrpr. press, 12 pages, Color-cover, Coated, Saddle-stitched
Circulation: (100% controlled), Total-13,000
Printing Co: Lehigh Litho, Inc., 2285 Ave. A, LVIP, Bethlehem, PA 18017 Tel # (610) 691-5050

Virginia Hay Clearing House
See: AGRICULTURE

Virginia Horse Council News
Association

Publishing Co: Virginia Horse Council, PO Box 72, Riner, VA 24149-0072; Title Tel # (703) 382-3071
Personnel: Publisher, Mag. Ed.-Alice Alley
Editorial Description: Promotes VA's horse industry informs members, lobbies state government recognizes 4-H And industry leaders achievements. Concerned with health, legislation and pride in VA's horse industry.
General Info: (Formerly Virginia Horse), Yr. Est. 1980, Bi-monthly, Trim Size-8½ x 11, Sheetfed press, 16 pages, No Color, Saddle-stitched
Subscriptions: Indv. $10, $2/copy
Acquistions: Publication Bought
Advertising: $60. Accepts Inserts.
Printing Co: Christiansburg Printing, P.O. Box 291, Christiansburg, VA 24073 Tel # (703) 382-9111, Fax # (703) 381-2490

Virginia Thoroughbred News
Business, Association

Publishing Co: Virginia Thoroughbred Assn., 38 Garrett St, Warrenton, VA 22186-3107; Title Tel # (703) 347-4313
Personnel: Editor-Leigh Myzk
Editorial Description: Breed.
General Info: Monthly, 24 pages, 4% ads
Circulation: Total-800

Welsh Pony & Cob Society of America Newsletter
Association　　CPM: $83

Publishing Co: Welsh Pony & Cob Soc. of Amer., Inc., PO Box 2977, Winchester, VA 22604-2177; Title Tel # (703) 667-6195
Personnel: Editor-Kerri Mustain
Editorial Description: Breed registry information & news.
General Info: Yr. Est. 1974, Quarterly, 20 pages, No Color
Subscriptions: Free With Membership
Circulation: Total-1,200
Advertising: $100.

Western Industry Report International
See: BUSINESS & INDUSTRY

HOSPITALS & NURSING HOMES

AAB Bulletin
See: SCIENCE

AAPT News
See: PSYCHOLOGY

AHME News   *Association*

Publishing Co: Assn. for Hospital Med. Education, 1101 Connecticut Ave NW Ste, 700, Washington, DC 20036-4303; Title Tel # (202) 857-1196
Personnel: Editor-Michael Hamm
Editorial Description: Concerned with medical education primarily in community hospitals.
General Info: Yr. Est. 1956, Bi-monthly, Letrpr. press, 5 pages, Newsprint
Circulation: Total-560
Advertising: Inquire for rates.
List Rental: Actives: $150/M
Printing Co: Tuxedo Press, 3501 Windom Rd, Brentwood, MD 20722-1095 Tel # (301) 864-6400

AHP Connect   *Association*

Publishing Co: Association for Healthcare Philanthropy, 313 Park Ave Ste 400, Falls Church, VA 22046-3303; Title Tel # (703) 532-6243 Title Fax # (703) 532-7170
Personnel: Publisher-William McGinly, Editor-Kathy Brady
Editorial Description: Features association events, developments in hospital and healthcare philantropy and fundraising, etc.
General Info: (Formerly NAHD News, AHP News), 10x/yr., Trim Size-8½ x 11, 8 pages, Coated, Saddle-stitched
Subscriptions: Indv. $50, Free With Membership
Circulation: Total-2,500, Readership-2,500
List Rental: Actives: $450/M
Printing Co: Alta Vista Printing Co., 503 3rd St., Alta Vista, VA 24517 Tel # (804) 369-6633

AHRA Link   *Association*

Publishing Co: American Healthcare Radiology Administrators, 111 Boston Post Rd. #215, PO Box 334, Sudbury, MA 01776-2403; Title Tel # (508) 443-7591 Title Fax # (508) 443-8046
Personnel: Editor-Paul Ferruri
Editorial Description: News and activities of AHRA, position ads and listings of educational events, management information on health care administration.
General Info: Yr. Est. 1982, Monthly, Trim Size-8½ x 11, Sheetfed press, 8 pages, 3% ads, 2 Color, Newsprint
Acquistions: Publication Bought
Circulation: Total-3,929
Advertising: Inquire for rates.

AOHA Today   *Association*

Publishing Co: American Osteopathic Hospital Association, 5301 Wisconsin Ave NW Ste 630, Washington, DC 20015-2015; Title Tel # (202) 686-1700 Title Fax # (202) 686-7615
Personnel: Publisher-David Kushner, Editor-Betty Lynn Sprinkle
Editorial Description: For osteopathic hospital administrators/CEOs, their staffs & trustees.
General Info: (Formerly Osteopathic Hospitals), Yr. Est. 1957, 8x/yr., Offset press, 12 pages, ISSN: 1044-1980, 1% ads, 2 Color, Matte, Saddle-stitched
Subscriptions: Indv. $28
Circulation: (100% controlled), Total-1,600
Advertising: Inquire for rates.
Printing Co: Print-A-Copy, 7315 Wisconsin Ave., Bethesda, MD 20814 Tel # (301) 656-4456

ASCA Quarterly
See: HEALTH

Action Kit for Hospital Law   *Business*

Publishing Co: Action Kit for Hospital Law, 4614 Fifth Ave., Pittsburgh, PA 15213-3663; Title Tel # (412) 687-8275 Title Fax # (412) 687-7692
Editorial Description: A looseleaf reference with monthly newsletter discussing legal issues of interest to hospital management.
General Info: Yr. Est. 1972, Monthly, Looseleaf
Subscriptions: Indv. $495, Inst. $495

Action Kit for Hospital Trustees   *Business*

Publishing Co: Action Kit for Hospital Law, 4614 Fifth Ave., Pittsburgh, PA 15213-3663; Title Tel # (412) 687-8275 Title Fax # (412) 687-7692
Editorial Description: A bi-monthly newsletter which discusses recent court cases & legal issues of interest to hospital governing board members.
General Info: Yr. Est. 1973, Bi-monthly
Subscriptions: Inst. $295

Adolescent Medicine
See: MEDICINE

Adult Day Care Letter   *Business*

Publishing Co: Health Resource Publishing, 3100 Hwy. 138, PO Box 1442, Wall Township, NJ 07719-1442; Title Tel # (908) 681-1133 Title Fax # (908) 681-0490
Personnel: Publisher-Robert Jenkins, Editor-Edward Miller
Editorial Description: Management information, trends & developments, linkage with others across country.
General Info: Yr. Est. 1985, Monthly, Trim Size-8½ x 11, Letrpr. press, 8 pages, ISSN: 0885-4572, No Color, Newsprint
Subscriptions: Indv. $147, $12/copy
Advertising: Inquire for rates. Accepts Inserts.
List Rental: Actives: $90/M
Printing Co: ACN Graphics, 1602 Birchwood Ln, Neptune, NJ 07753-6910 Tel # (908) 681-6083

Alexian Pulse

Publishing Co: St. Alexis Hospital, 5163 Broadway Ave, Cleveland, OH 44127-1532 Tel # (216) 429-8000
Personnel: Editor-Joseph Glorioso
Editorial Description: Interests: baby care; ecology; hobbies; new products; public service material.
General Info: Yr. Est. 1970, Trim Size-8½ x 11
Circulation: Total-2,500

Alexigram

Publishing Co: St. Alexis Hospital, 5163 Broadway Ave, Cleveland, OH 44127-1532 Tel # (216) 429-8000
Editorial Description: Circulated to medical staff of St. Alexis Hospital.

Allan Fine's Trends in Integrated Health Care   *Business*

Publishing Co: Aspen Publishers, Inc., 200 Orchard Ridge Dr., Ste 200, Gaithersburg, MD 20878-5440 Fax # (301) 417-7655 Parent Co.-Wolters Kluwer US Corporation, New York; Title Tel # (301) 417-7500 Title Fax # (301) 417-7550
Personnel: Editor-Allan Fine, Mktg. Mgr.-Trudi Graham
Editorial Description: Techniques on how to approach employers and business coalitions.. Regional variations in direct employer contracting.. Step to take now to avoid future legal risks.
General Info: (Formerly Hospital Managed Care and Direct Contracting), Yr. Est. 1991, Monthly, 8 pages, ISSN: 1061-7620
Subscriptions: Indv. $259, For. $311, $27/copy
Circulation: Readership-3,100
List Rental: List Management Co.: Stevens-Knox List Management, 304 Park Ave S., New York, NY 10010-5312 Tel # (212) 388-8800, Fax # (212) 388-8890, Actives: $650/M

Alpha

Publishing Co: Southwest Texas Methodist Hospital, 7700 Floyd Curl Dr, San Antonio, TX 78229-3902 Tel # (210) 692-4000
Editorial Description: Keeps public posted on what's happening, new equipment, goals met, etc.
General Info: Quarterly

American College of Medical Quality Newsletter Focus
See: MEDICINE

BBI Newsletter, The   *Business*

Publishing Co: American Health Consultants, Inc., 3525 Piedmont Rd., Building #6, Ste. 400, Atlanta, GA 30305-0056 Tel # (404) 262-7436 Fax # (404) 284-3291
Personnel: Publisher-Don Johnston, Editor-Mike Gibb, Editor-Dona Watson, Assoc. Ed.-Anna Lee, Circ. Mgr.-Cheryl Scaglione
Editorial Description: Market analysis, technology developments, market data, trends & forecasts for healthcare executives.
General Info: (Formerly Biomedical Business International), Yr. Est. 1978, Monthly, Trim Size-8½ x 11, Sheetfed press, 20 pages, ISSN: 1049-4316, Ind/Abs/Online: Predicast, PTS, No Color, Matte, Saddle-stitched
Subscriptions: Indv. $725, Can. $725, For. $725
Acquistions: Publication Bought, Publication Sold
Circulation: Total-3,000
List Rental: Actives: $145/M
Printing Co: Wright Litho, 125 W La Palma Ave, Anaheim, CA 92801-2538 Tel # (714) 778-4499

BBI's Monitor of Technology Assessment & Reimbursement
See: MEDICINE

BCHA News
See: HEALTH

Baroness

Publishing Co: Baroness Erlanger Hospital, 975 E. Third St., Chattanooga, TN 37403; Title Tel # (423) 778-7427 Title Fax # (423) 778-7615
Personnel: Editor-Paula Bean

Bedside Banner

Publishing Co: Rockingham Memorial Hospital, 235 Cantrell Ave, Harrisonburg, VA 22801-3248; Title Tel # (703) 564-5886 Title Fax # (703) 433-0992
Personnel: Editor-Debra Thompson
Editorial Description: Public service material, hospital news.
General Info: Yr. Est. 1975, Monthly, Trim Size-8½ x 11, Sheetfed press, 8 pages, 2 Color, Coated
Subscriptions: Free
Circulation: Total-12,000
Printing Co: Good Printers, 213 Dry River Rd, Bridgewater, VA 22812-1242 Tel # (703) 828-4663

Bellevue Bulletin

Publishing Co: Bellevue Hospital, First Ave. at 27th St., New York, NY 10016; Title Tel # (212) 561-6110
Personnel: Editor-Nancy Carlson
Editorial Description: Hospital news letter.
General Info: (Formerly Bellevue Report), Yr. Est. 1971, Trim Size-8½ x 11½, Offset press, 4 pages
Circulation: Total-6,000

Bethes-Data

Publishing Co: Bethesda Hospital, Oak St. & Reading Rd., Cincinnati, OH 45206; Title Tel # (513) 559-6131
Personnel: Editor-Marjorie L. Muh

Blue Cross of Wisconsin, News *Association*

Publishing Co: Blue Cross Blue Shield United of Wisconsin, 401 W Michigan St, Milwaukee, WI 53203-2804

Blue Review

Publishing Co: Hawaii Medical Services Assn., PO Box 860, Honolulu, HI 96808-0860
Tel # (808) 948-6111
General Info: Yr. Est. 1966, Monthly, Trim Size-8½ x 11
Circulation: Total-475

Briefings on Hospital Safety *Business*

Publishing Co: Opus Communications, Inc., Box 1168, 100 Hoods Lane, Marblehead, MA 01945; Title Tel # (617) 639-1872 Title Fax # (617) 639-2982
Personnel: Publisher-Jennifer Cofer, Editor-Michael Paskavitz
Editorial Description: For hospital safely management - discusses all the regulations and ways to get hospitals more involved in safety management and meet JCAHO standards.
General Info: Yr. Est. 1993, Monthly, Trim Size-8½ x 11, 12 pages, ISSN: 1076-5972, 2 Color, Saddle-stitched
Subscriptions: Indv. $187
List Rental: Rents Lists

Briefings on JCAHO *Business*

Publishing Co: Opus Communications, Inc., Box 1168, 100 Hoods Lane, Marblehead, MA 01945; Title Tel # (617) 639-1872 Title Fax # (617) 639-2982
Personnel: Publisher-Jennifer Cofer, Editor-Michael Paskavitz
Editorial Description: A guide for JCAHO survey coordinaotrs, administrators and quality managers. Interprets JCAHO standards & regulations and offers advice on how best to meet them.
General Info: Yr. Est. 1990, Monthly, Trim Size-8½ x 11, 12 pages, ISSN: 1054-6995, 2 Color, Saddle-stitched
Subscriptions: Indv. $292
List Rental: Rents Lists

Briefings on JCAHO-Home Care *Business*

Publishing Co: Opus Communications, Inc., Box 1168, 100 Hoods Lane, Marblehead, MA 01945; Title Tel # (617) 639-1872 Title Fax # (617) 639-2982
Personnel: Publisher-Jennifer Cofer, Editor-Michael Paskavitz
Editorial Description: A guide for home care administrators and professionals. Interprets JCAHO standards & regulations and how best to meet them.
General Info: Yr. Est. 1994, Monthly, Trim Size-8½ x 11, 12 pages, ISSN: 1079-2368, 2 Color, Matte, Saddle-stitched
Subscriptions: Indv. $177
List Rental: Rents Lists

Briefings on Laboratory Safety and Accreditation

Publishing Co: Opus Communications, Inc., Box 1168, 100 Hoods Lane, Marblehead, MA 01945; Title Tel # (617) 639-1872 Title Fax # (617) 639-2982
Editorial Description: Offers practical advice and interpretation for maintaining safety and compliance within the Laboratory.
General Info: Yr. Est. 1995, Trim Size-8½ x 11, 12 pages, ISSN: 1083-5865, 2 Color
Subscriptions: Indv. $157
List Rental: Rents Lists

Briefings on Long-Term Care Regulations *Business*

Publishing Co: Opus Communications, Inc., Box 1168, 100 Hoods Lane, Marblehead, MA 01945; Title Tel # (617) 639-1872 Title Fax # (617) 639-2982
Personnel: Publisher-Jennifer Cofer, Editor-Suzanne Perney
Editorial Description: Instructs the management team on how to meet the challenges of complying with a myriad of regulators and attain the highest reimbursement.
General Info: (Formerly Briefings on Long-Term Care), Yr. Est. 1993, Monthly, Trim Size-8½ x 11, 12 pages, ISSN: 1076-6014, 2 Color, Saddle-stitched
Subscriptions: Indv. $177
List Rental: Rents Lists

Briefings on Subacute Care: Regulations & Reimbursement *Business*

Publishing Co: Opus Communications, Inc., Box 1168, 100 Hoods Lane, Marblehead, MA 01945; Title Tel # (617) 639-1872 Title Fax # (617) 639-2982
Personnel: Publisher-Jennifer Cofer, Editor-Suzanne Perney
Editorial Description: Covers management, development and marketing of subacute care facilities and discusses how to get the maximum reimbursement for your facility. In addition, it covers all the regulators and offers practical advice on how to comply.
General Info: Yr. Est. 1994, Monthly, Trim Size-8½ x 11, 12 pages, ISSN: 1076-5999, 2 Color, Saddle-stitched
Subscriptions: Indv. $296
List Rental: Rents Lists

Brookdale Hospital Medical Center News-Scope *Association*

Publishing Co: Brookdale Hospital Medical Center, Linden Blvd at Brookdale Plaza, Brooklyn, NY 11212-3198; Title Tel # (718) 240-5345
Personnel: Editor-Mimi Grinker
Editorial Description: Brookdale Hospital facilities, services, patients, volunteers, staff.
General Info: (Formerly Brookdale Hospital Medical Center News), Yr. Est. 1972, Quarterly, Trim Size-11 x 14, Offset press, 10 pages, Color
Subscriptions: Free
Circulation: Total-11,000

Brookridge Forum

Publishing Co: Brookridge Institute, 1209 Palm Ave, San Mateo, CA 94402-2437; Title Tel # (415) 349-9675
Personnel: Editor-Leo Kiley
General Info: Yr. Est. 1985, Quarterly, Web press, 16 pages, No Color
Subscriptions: Indv. $15
Advertising: Accepts Inserts.
List Rental: Actives: $60/M
Printing Co: Xpress, 1303 Grandview Dr, South San Francisco, CA 94080-4909 Tel # (415) 583-5671

Bulletin

Publishing Co: Hospital Auxiliaries Assn. of Ontario, 150 Ferrand Dr., Don Mills, ON M3C 1H6 Canada
General Info: Yr. Est. 1969, Trim Size-8½ x 11, Sheetfed press, Matte, Saddle-stitched
Circulation: Total-200

CCH Monitor: The Newsletter of Managed Care
See: HEALTH

CHOC Talk *Consumer, Association*

Publishing Co: Children's Hospital of Orange County, Box5700, Orange, CA 92613; Title Tel # (714) 532-8680 Title Fax # (714) 532-8618
Personnel: Editor-Marilyn Fisher
Editorial Description: Informs & educates staff, volunteers, donors, & general public.
General Info: Yr. Est. 1964, Quarterly, Trim Size-8½ x 11, Sheetfed press, 32 pages, 2 Color, Coated, Saddle-stitched
Circulation: (100% controlled), Total-10,000
Printing Co: Columbia Lithograph Co., 12078 Fiorence Ave., Santa Fe Spring, CA 90670 Tel # (818) 442-8088

Canadian Society of Cytology Bulletin

Publishing Co: Canadian Society of Cytology, Health Sciences Ctre., Winnipeg, MB R3A 1A9 Canada; Title Tel # (204) 787-3657 Title Fax # (204) 787-4942
Personnel: Editor-Vicky Chen
Editorial Description: A non-profit publication to facilitate communication among cytopathologists and cytotechnologists on issues related to service, education, research and administration in cytopathology.
General Info: (Formerly Canadian Society of Cytology Newsletter), Yr. Est. 1984, Quarterly, 10 pages, No Color
Subscriptions: $5/copy
Circulation: Total-365
Advertising: Inquire for rates.
Printing Co: St. Joseph's Hospital, 50 Charlton Avenue E., Hamilton, ON L8N 4A6 Canada Tel # (416) 522-4941

Capitation & Medical Practice *Business*

Publishing Co: Aspen Publishers, Inc., 200 Orchard Ridge Dr., Ste 200, Gaithersburg, MD 20878-5440 Fax # (301) 417-7655 Parent Co.-Wolters Kluwer US Corporation, New York; Title Tel # (301) 417-7500 Title Fax # (301) 417-7550
Personnel: Mktg. Mgr.-Trudi Graham
Editorial Description: Practical guidance on how to reengineer for success under the new at risk payment environment. Control costs, maintain quality, assume risk safely, and ensure financial stability under capitated reimbursement.
General Info: Yr. Est. 1994, Monthly, 8 pages, ISSN: 1076-1047
Subscriptions: Indv. $199, For. $239, $21/copy
Circulation: Readership-1,200

Capitation Management Report
See: HEALTH

Capsule *Association*

Publishing Co: Bridgeport Hospital, 267 Grant St, Bridgeport, CT 06610-2870; Title Tel # (203) 384-3532
Personnel: Editor-Marci Mullikin
Editorial Description: Medical features about the hospital, new facilities, hospital policy, publicity on hospital staff.
General Info: Yr. Est. 1948, Monthly, Trim Size-8½ x 11, Offset press, 8 pages, 2 Color, Newsprint, Saddle-stitched
Circulation: (100% controlled), Total-3,000

Capsule *Business, Consumer*

Publishing Co: Wyandotte General Hospital, 2333 Biddle St, Wyandotte, MI 48192-4693; Title Tel # (313) 284-2400
Personnel: Editor-Michael Jenkins
General Info: (Formerly Capsule Comments), Yr. Est. 1961, Bi-monthly
Circulation: Total-3,000

Centerpiece — *Association*

Publishing Co: Fort Wayne State Developmental Center, 4900 Saint Joe Rd, Fort Wayne, IN 46835-3275; Title Tel # (219) 485-7554 Title Fax # (219) 485-2863
Personnel: Editor-Jeff Smith
Editorial Description: Prints important and timely information for FWSDC employees.
General Info: Yr. Est. 1958, Monthly, Trim Size-8½ x 11½, Offset press, 4 pages, No Color

Children's Hospital Times

Publishing Co: Children's Hospital of Philadelphia, 34th St. & Civic Ctr. Blvd., Philadelphia, PA 19104; Title Tel # (215) 590-1000 Title Fax # (215) 590-4090
Personnel: Editor-Karen Yoong
Editorial Description: Internal newsletter for employees of the Children's Hospital of Philadelphia.
General Info: Yr. Est. 1967, Bi-monthly, Trim Size-11 x 14, Sheetfed press, 4 pages, No Color, Coated
Circulation: (100% controlled), Total-3,350
Printing Co: Mangos Graphics, 10 S. Leopard Rd., Paoli, PA 19301

Clinical Data Management — *Business*

Publishing Co: Aspen Publishers, Inc., 200 Orchard Ridge Dr., Ste 200, Gaithersburg, MD 20878-5440 Fax # (301) 417-7655 Parent Co.-Wolters Kluwer US Corporation, New York; Title Tel # (301) 417-7500 Title Fax # (301) 417-7550
Personnel: Mktg. Dir.-Trudi Graham
Editorial Description: Case studies, analysis and news on clinical systems integration and management.
General Info: Yr. Est. 1994, Monthly, 8 pages, ISSN: 1073-6379
Subscriptions: Indv. $199, For. $239, $21/copy
Circulation: Readership-800

Clinical Lab Letter
See: MEDICINE

Clinical Laboratory PCS — *Business*

Publishing Co: ECRI, 5200 Butler Pike, Plymouth Meeting, PA 19462-1298; Title Tel # (610) 825-6000 Title Fax # (610) 834-1275
Personnel: Editor-Garrett Hayner, Circ. Mgr.-Diane Schwarztrauber, Promotion Dir.-Michele Carlin
Editorial Description: Product comparison information in binder system with monthly updates.
General Info: Yr. Est. 1984, Monthly, Looseleaf
Subscriptions: Indv. $695, For. $745

Coding Clinic for ICD-9-CM
See: MANAGEMENT

Commoner

Publishing Co: Bryan Memorial Hospital, 1600 S 48th St, Lincoln, NE 68506-1299; Title Tel # (402) 483-3675
Personnel: Editor-Paul Hadley
Editorial Description: Industry news; general stories with company tie-in.
General Info: Yr. Est. 1969, Semi-monthly, Trim Size-8½ x 11, Web press, 8 pages, Color, Newsprint
Circulation: Total-3,000

Contact
See: PHYSIOLOGY

DH Pulse — *Association*

Publishing Co: Deaconess Hospital, 311 Straight St, Cincinnati, OH 45219-1099; Title Tel # (513) 559-2760 Title Fax # (513) 475-5284
Personnel: Editor-Kyle Ketabchi
Editorial Description: Hospital's growth, development and activities of the employees, volunteers, doctors and others associated with the hospital.
General Info: (Formerly Deaconews), Bi-weekly, Trim Size-8½ x 11, Letrpr. press, 4 pages, 2 Color, Coated, Saddle-stitched
Subscriptions: Free To Qualified Recipient
Circulation: Total-3,000
Printing Co: Koehler Graphics, 2200 Dana Ave, Cincinnati, OH 45208-1025 Tel # (513) 351-4400, Fax # (513) 351-2802

Developing & Managing Physician Networks — *Business*

Publishing Co: Thompson Publishing Group, 747 Third Ave., New York, NY 10017 Tel # (212) 888-7220 Fax # (212) 486-3400; Title Fax # (800) 999-2320
Personnel: Publisher-Ken Gesser, Editor-Virginia McMorrow, Production Mgr.-R.D. Whitney
General Info: Yr. Est. 1995, Monthly, Looseleaf
Subscriptions: Indv. $295

Discharge Planning Update — *Business*

Publishing Co: American Hospital Publishing, Inc., 737 N. Michigan Ave., Ste. 700, Chicago, IL 60611-2431 Tel # (312) 280-6800 Fax # (312) 944-4232; Title Tel # (312) 280-3560
Personnel: Editor-Elizabeth McNulty
Editorial Description: Multi-disciplinary pub. focusing on discharge planning/follow-up care for hospitalized patients.
General Info: Yr. Est. 1980, Bi-monthly, 24 pages
Subscriptions: Indv. $57, $10/copy
Circulation: Total-2,000

Drug GMP Report
See: DRUGS & PHARMACEUTICALS

Drug Utilization Review
See: DRUGS & PHARMACEUTICALS

Economic Trends

Publishing Co: Sponsor-American Hospital Assn., American Hospital Publishing, Inc., 737 N. Michigan Ave., Ste. 700, Chicago, IL 60611-2431 Tel # (312) 280-6800 Fax # (312) 944-4232; Title Tel # (312) 280-6236
Personnel: Publisher-Karen McGannon, Editor-Louise Mirkin
Editorial Description: Reports on health care economic trends & indicators.
General Info: Yr. Est. 1985, Quarterly, ISSN: 0882-5807
Subscriptions: Indv. $135, $25/copy
Circulation: Total-2,500

Einstein Health Update

Publishing Co: Albert Einstein Medical Center, York and Tabor Roads, Philadelphia, PA 19141; Title Tel # (215) 456-7326
Personnel: Publisher-Robert Kimmel, Editor-Anne Madell, Circ. Mgr.-Production Mgr.-Laura Young, Art Dir.-Annemarie Fisher, Promotion Dir.-Annemarie Armstrong
Editorial Description: Focuses on health information for Einstein consumers.
General Info: (Formerly Einstein Monthly), Yr. Est. 1982, Bi-monthly, Sheetfed press, 12 pages, 2 Color, Newsprint, Perfect bound
Circulation: (100% controlled), Total-8,500
Printing Co: Waldman Graphics, 9100 Pennsauken Hwy, Pennsauken, NJ 08110-1293 Tel # (609) 662-9111, Fax # (609) 665-1789

Elderly Health Services Letter
See: HEALTH

Emergency Management Today
See: GOVERNMENT

Employee Assistance Program Management Letter
See: INDUSTRIAL RELATIONS/PERSONNEL

Europe Drug & Device Report
See: DRUGS & PHARMACEUTICALS

Focus — *Consumer, Association*

Publishing Co: Lansing General Hospital, 2727 S Pennsylvania Ave, Lansing, MI 48910-3488; Title Tel # (517) 377-8796
Personnel: Editor-Chris Henning, Asst. Ed.-Andrew Corner
Editorial Description: Highlights hospital services, employees departments.
General Info: (Formerly Little General), Bi-weekly, Trim Size-8½ x 11, Web press, 24 pages, 4 Color
Circulation: (100% controlled), Total-1,000

Focus

Publishing Co: Downstate Medical Center, 450 Clarkson Ave, Brooklyn, NY 11203-2012; Title Tel # (718) 270-1000
Personnel: Editor-Janis Owens-Staunton
Editorial Description: Emphasizes people at Downstate--the activities, programs, and events involving the Downstate community.
General Info: Yr. Est. 1978, Monthly, Trim Size-8½ x 11, Offset press, 8 pages, 2 Color
Circulation: Total-6,000

Forum News — *Business, Association*

Publishing Co: Forum for Health Care Planning, 314 Vista De Valle, Mill Valley, CA 94941-4017; Title Tel # (415) 381-1846 Title Fax # (415) 381-1104
Editorial Description: The Forum is a national organization of diverse health care professionals committed to high quality health care planning.
General Info: (Formerly American Assn. for Hospital Planning), Yr. Est. 1950, Quarterly
List Rental: Rents Lists

GMP Letter, The
See: HEALTH

Generally Speaking — *Association*

Publishing Co: Montreal General Hospital, 1650 Cedar Ave., Rm. E 6-227, Montreal, PQ H3G 1A4 Canada; Title Tel # (514) 937-6011
Personnel: Editor-Joan Lamontagne
Editorial Description: The focus of this quarterly is the employee. It is designed to inform & entertain. An editorial committee is chosen by the editor-these members are all employees representing a cross-section of hospital departments.
General Info: (Formerly Montreal Genl. Hosp. News), Yr. Est. 1960, Quarterly, Trim Size-8½ x 11, 24 pages, ISSN: 0027-0709, 2 Color
Subscriptions: Free To Qualified Recipient
Circulation: (100% controlled), Total-4,500

Good Samaritan Today

Publishing Co: Good Samaritan Hospital, Public Relations, 1111 E. McDowell, Phoenix, AZ 85203 Tel # (602) 239-2000; Title Tel # (602) 239-4412
General Info: (Formerly Samaritan), Annually

HAI News
See: SOCIAL SERVICES & WELFARE

HANYS News
See: HEALTH

HARA: Hospital Accounts
Receiving Analysis *Business*

Publishing Co: Zimmerman & Associates, Inc., 5307 South 92nd St., Hales Corners, WI 53130-1677
Parent Co.-Aspen Publishers, Inc., Gaithersburg; Title Tel # (414) 425-2189
Title Fax # (414) 425-4807
Personnel: Editor-Bruce Nelson, Publisher, Adv. Dir.-David Zimmerman, Art Dir.-Kathleen Hamm
Editorial Description: Quarterly analysis of hospital accounts receivable performance. Includes comparisons to peer groups and performance benchmarkers.
General Info: Yr. Est. 1986, Quarterly
Subscriptions: Indv. $397, $100/copy
Circulation: Total-1,000

HIRA News *Association*

Publishing Co: Health Industry Rep. Assn., 5818 Reeds Rd, Mission, KS 66202-2740;
Title Tel # (913) 262-4513
Personnel: Editor-Melody Fawl
Editorial Description: Medical equipment and other products in the health care field.
General Info: Yr. Est. 1978, Monthly, Trim Size-8½ x 11, Letrpr. press, 4 pages
Circulation: (100% controlled), Total-250

Health Care *Business*

Publishing Co: National Technical Information Service U.S., 5285 Port Royal Rd., Springfield, VA 22161-0001 Fax # (703) 487-4630; Title Tel # (703) 487-4630
Editorial Description: Covers planning methodology, health services, facilities utilization, health manpower requirements, & education.
General Info: (Formerly Health Planning), Weekly, Trim Size-8½ x 11, Offset press, ISSN: 0017-9086
Subscriptions: Indv. $135, Can. $135, For. $195

Health Care Antitrust
See: LAW

Health Care Biller
See: HEALTH

Health Care Capitation and Risk Contracting Manual
See: HEALTH

Health Care Collector
See: HEALTH

Health Care Marketing
and Public Relations *Association*

Publishing Co: American Society for Hospital Marketing & Public Relations D, 840 N. Lake Shore Dr., Chicago, IL 60611-2497; Title Tel # (312) 280-6359
Personnel: Editor-Betsy Rubin
Editorial Description: Trends and practical discussions of the business of healthcare PR & marketing.
General Info: (Formerly Hospital Marketing and Public Relations), Yr. Est. 1965, Bi-monthly, Trim Size-8½ x 11, Offset press, 12 pages, 2 Color, Newsprint
Circulation: (100% controlled), Total-3,000
List Rental: Rents Lists

Health Care Registrar
See: HEALTH

Health Care Strategic
Management *Business* **CPM: $458**

Publishing Co: Business Word, Inc., 5350 S. Roslyn St., Ste. 400, Englewood, CO 80111-2125;
Title Tel # (303) 290-8500 Title Fax # (303) 290-9025
Personnel: Publisher-Donald Johnson, Editor-Alan Kania, Production Mgr.-Todd Reid, Adv. Dir.-Dave Jeans, Circ. Mgr., Promotion Dir.-Linda Gamble
Editorial Description: The newsletter for hospital strategists.
General Info: Yr. Est. 1983, Monthly, Trim Size-8½ x 11, Sheetfed press, 24 pages, ISSN: 0742-1478, 2 Color, Matte, Saddle-stitched
Subscriptions: Indv. $187, Can. $193, For. $205, $20/copy
Circulation: Total-1,200
Advertising: $550.
List Rental: Actives: $325/M

Health Devices Alerts *Business*

Publishing Co: ECRI, 5200 Butler Pike, Plymouth Meeting, PA 19462-1298;
Title Tel # (610) 825-6000 Title Fax # (610) 834-1275
Personnel: Editor-Eileen Erinoff, Circ. Mgr.-Michele Carlin
Editorial Description: Reported problems, hazards, recalls, involving medical devices.
General Info: Yr. Est. 1977, Weekly, Trim Size-8½ x 11, Sheetfed press, 6 pages, ISSN: 0163-0458, Color-cover, Newsprint, Looseleaf
Subscriptions: Indv. $695, For. $725

Health Employment Law Update
See: LAW

Health Funds
Development Letter *Business*

Publishing Co: Health Resource Publishing, 3100 Hwy. 138, PO Box 1442, Wall Township, NJ 07719-1442; Title Tel # (908) 681-1133 Title Fax # (908) 681-0490
Personnel: Publisher-Robert Jenkins, Editor-Beth-Ann Kecher
Editorial Description: Information on federal and foundation grant trends for hospitals, medical centers and health care agencies.
General Info: Yr. Est. 1978, Monthly, Trim Size-8½ x 11, Desktop press, 8 pages, ISSN: 0193-7928, No Color, Newsprint
Subscriptions: Indv. $187, $16/copy
Advertising: Inquire for rates. Accepts Inserts.
List Rental: Actives: $95/M
Printing Co: ACN Graphics, 1602 Birchwood Ln, Neptune, NJ 07753-6910 Tel # (908) 681-6083

Health Systems Leader
See: MANAGEMENT

Health Victory Bulletin
See: HEALTH

HealthCare Systems NewsLetter
See: HEALTH

HealthPlus55 Calendar

Publishing Co: Scripps Memorial Hospital, 9888 Genesee Ave # 28, La Jolla, CA 92037-1200;
Title Tel # (619) 457-6892
Personnel: Publisher-Ian Temple, Editor-Barbara Ekberg
Editorial Description: Contains health & program information for seniors.
General Info: Yr. Est. 1987, Quarterly, Sheetfed press, 8 pages, 2 Color, Coated
Circulation: Total-10,000
Printing Co: Spectrum Printers, 4395 El Cajon Blvd, San Diego, CA 92105-1226
Tel # (619) 283-7205

Healthbeat
See: HEALTH

Healthcare Advocate *Association*

Publishing Co: Alberta Hospital Association, 10009 108th St., Edmonton, AB T5J 3C5 Canada
Tel # (403) 498-8400 Fax # (403) 498-8465; Title Tel # (403) 423-1776
Personnel: Editor-Gerry Warner
Editorial Description: News and events in the Alberta hospital and health care scene.
General Info: (Formerly Hospitalta), Yr. Est. 1962, Monthly, Trim Size-7½ x 9½, Offset press, 10 pages, ISSN: 0821-2015, Color
Subscriptions: Indv. $10, Can. $21
Circulation: Total-2,800

Healthcare Fund Raising
Newsletter *Business*

Publishing Co: Health Resource Publishing, 3100 Hwy. 138, PO Box 1442, Wall Township, NJ 07719-1442; Title Tel # (908) 681-1133 Title Fax # (908) 681-0490
Personnel: Publisher-Robert Jenkins, Editor-Beth-Ann Kecher
Editorial Description: Provides reliable and timely information plus all the latest news, ideas and tips in hospital fund raising from across the country.
General Info: (Formerly Hospital Fund Raising Newsletter), Yr. Est. 1979, Monthly, Trim Size-8½ x 11, Desktop press, 8 pages, ISSN: 0193-9939, No Color, Newsprint
Subscriptions: Indv. $107, $13/copy
Advertising: Inquire for rates. Accepts Inserts.
List Rental: Actives: $95/M
Printing Co: ACN Graphics, 1602 Birchwood Ln, Neptune, NJ 07753-6910 Tel # (908) 681-6083

Healthcare Investor
See: INVESTMENT

Healthcare Leadership
Review *Business*

Publishing Co: COR Healthcare Resources, PO Box 40959, Santa Barbara, CA 93140-0959;
Title Tel # (805) 564-2177 Title Fax # (805) 564-2146
Personnel: Publisher, Editor-Dean Anderson
Editorial Description: Informative summaries of articles from health care management publications.
General Info: (Formerly Hospital Management Review), Yr. Est. 1982, Monthly, Trim Size-8½ x 11, Sheetfed press, 16 pages, ISSN: 1082-6718, 2 Color, Newsprint, Saddle-stitched
Subscriptions: Indv. $97, Can. $97, For. $109, $10/copy
Acquisitions: Publication Bought
List Rental: Actives: 6,100, $150/M, Expires: $150/M

Healthcare Management
Team Letter *Business*

Publishing Co: Health Resource Publishing, 3100 Hwy. 138, PO Box 1442, Wall Township, NJ 07719-1442; Title Tel # (908) 681-1133 Title Fax # (908) 681-0490
Personnel: Publisher, Editor-Robert Jenkins
Editorial Description: Each issue contains information which you may wish to include on the agenda of your management team or department head meetings. You need to make decisions weeks, and in many cases, months, before it appears in the healthcare trade magazine.
General Info: Yr. Est. 1985, Monthly, Trim Size-8½ x 11, Offset press, 8 pages, ISSN: 0891-9267, No Color, Newsprint
Subscriptions: Indv. $167, $13/copy
Advertising: Inquire for rates. Accepts Inserts.
List Rental: Actives: $95/M
Printing Co: ACN Graphics, 1602 Birchwood Ln, Neptune, NJ 07753-6910 Tel # (908) 681-6083

Healthcare Marketing
Abstracts *Business*

Publishing Co: COR Healthcare Resources, PO Box 40959, Santa Barbara, CA 93140-0959
Fax # (805) 564-2146; Title Tel # (805) 564-2177
Personnel: Publisher-Dean Anderson, Editor-Therese Droste
Editorial Description: Informative abstracts of articles on healthcare marketing.
General Info: Yr. Est. 1986, Monthly, Trim Size-8½ x 11, Offset press, 12 pages, ISSN: 0891-5016, 2 Color, Newsprint, Saddle-stitched
Subscriptions: Indv. $96, Can. $96, For. $108, $10/copy
Acquistions: Publication Bought
List Rental: Actives: $150/M, Expires: $150/M

Healthcare Quality
Abstracts *Business*

Publishing Co: COR Healthcare Resources, PO Box 40959, Santa Barbara, CA 93140-0959;
Title Tel # (805) 564-2177 Title Fax # (805) 564-2146
Personnel: Publisher-Dean Anderson, Editor-Janet Glasheen
Editorial Description: Abstracts of articles on healthcare, quality, improvement, case management, benchmarking, critical pathways, and critical guidelines.
General Info: Yr. Est. 1993, Monthly, Trim Size-8½ x 11, Offset press, 16 pages, ISSN: 1073-0303, 2 Color, Newsprint, Saddle-stitched
Subscriptions: Indv. $98, Can. $98, For. $110, $10/copy
List Rental: Actives: $150/M, Expires: $150/M

Healthcare Systems
Strategy Report *Business*

Publishing Co: Capitol Publications, Inc., 1101 King St., Ste. 444, Alexandria, VA 22314-2968
Fax # (703) 739-6501; Title Tel # (703) 683-4100 Title Fax # (703) 739-6601
Personnel: Publisher-Cynthia Carter, Editor-Terry Rudd, Exec. Ed.-Russell Jackson, Circ. Mgr.-Peggy Dwyer, Production Mgr.-Billy Adams, Art Dir.-Linda McDonald, Mktg. Dir.-Mary Lou Probka, Promotion Dir.-Claudia Moran
Editorial Description: Provides healthcare execs with methods for repositioning and realigning their operations into streamlined systems that provide top quality care.
General Info: (Formerly Health Care Competition Week), Yr. Est. 1982, Bi-weekly, Trim Size-8½ x 11, Sheetfed press, 10 pages, ISSN: 0886-2095, Ind/Abs/Online: Predicasts, 2 Color
Subscriptions: Indv. $447, Inst. $447
Acquistions: Publication Bought
List Rental: Actives: $150/M
Printing Co: Capitol Publications, Inc., 1101 King St., Ste. 444, Alexandria, VA 22314-2968
Tel # (703) 683-4100, Fax # (703) 739-6501

Healthcare Technology &
Business Opportunities *Business*

Publishing Co: American Health Consultants, Inc., 3525 Piedmont Rd., Building #6, Ste. 400, Atlanta, GA 30305-0056 Tel # (404) 262-7436 Fax # (404) 284-3291
Personnel: Publisher-Don Johnston, Editor-Mike Gibb, Assoc. Ed.-Anna Lee, Circ. Dir.-Cheryl Scaglione, Product Mgr.-Dona Watson, Mktg. Mgr.-Paige Stanfield
Editorial Description: For research & development professionals in the healthcare field; patent transfer information, medical high-tech developments available for licensing.
General Info: (Formerly Medical Product Development), Yr. Est. 1979, Monthly, Trim Size-8½ x 11, Sheetfed press, 12 pages, ISSN: 1049-4499, Ind/Abs/Online: Predicast, PTS, 3% ads, No Color, Matte, Saddle-stitched
Subscriptions: Indv. $295, Can. $295, For. $295, $25/copy
Acquistions: Publication Bought, Publication Sold
Circulation: Total-1,000
List Rental: Actives: $145/M
Printing Co: McGinnis Printing, 320 S Main St, Santa Ana, CA 92701-5710

Healthcare Trends Report
See: HEALTH

Healthcaring *Business, Association*

Publishing Co: Mississippi Baptist Medical Center, 1225 N. State St., Jackson, MS 39202-2002
Tel # (601) 968-1000; Title Tel # (601) 968-5135 Title Fax # (601) 968-4137
Personnel: Editor-Jean B. May
Editorial Description: News for board members, contributors, employees, and medical staff.
General Info: (Formerly Reflector), Yr. Est. 1956, Quarterly, Trim Size-11 x 15, Sheetfed press, 8 pages, 2 Color, Coated, Saddle-stitched
Subscriptions: Free
Circulation: Total-45,000
Printing Co: Hederman Brothers Commercial Printers, 321 E Pearl St, Jackson, MS 39201-3407
Tel # (601) 961-7300

Hill Topic

Publishing Co: Glenwood State Hospital-School, 711 S Vine St, Glenwood, IA 51534-1927;
Title Tel # (712) 527-4811
Editorial Description: Describes programs for the mentally retarded.
General Info: Yr. Est. 1954, Trim Size-8½ x 11, 10 pages
Circulation: Total-1,000

Home Advantage
See: ADVERTISING & MARKETING

Horizons *Association*

Publishing Co: Sisters of Charity Hospital, 2157 Main St, Buffalo, NY 14214-2648;
Title Tel # (716) 862-2700
Personnel: Editor, Circ. Mgr., Art Dir.-Dennis McCarthy
Editorial Description: Hospital and staff news for employees.
General Info: (Formerly Sisters of Charity Hospital of Buffalo, Journal of The), Yr. Est. 1964, Bi-monthly, Trim Size-11 x 17, Offset press, 8 pages, Color
Circulation: Total-5,500

Horizons

Publishing Co: Hialeah Hospital, 651 E 25th St, Hialeah, FL 33013-3878; Title Tel # (305) 693-6100
Personnel: Publisher, Editor, Production Mgr.-JoLynn De La Torre
General Info: Yr. Est. 1961, Monthly, Trim Size-8½ x 11, Sheetfed press, 6 pages, 2 Color, Coated
Acquistions: Publication Bought
Circulation: (100% controlled), Total-1,500
List Rental: Rents Lists

Hospice Letter *Business*

Publishing Co: Health Resource Publishing, 3100 Hwy. 138, PO Box 1442, Wall Township, NJ 07719-1442; Title Tel # (908) 681-1133 Title Fax # (908) 681-0490
Personnel: Publisher-Robert Jenkins
Editorial Description: Monthly newsletter reporting the latest developments in the rapidly expanding hospice concept of caring for the terminally-ill. Read by administrators and directors who follow Medicare reimbursement and hospice accreditation. Explains how hospices are raising money by staging community events. Includes new legislation and regulations and the latest on nursing care, volunteers, and counseling progr
General Info: Yr. Est. 1979, Monthly, Trim Size-8½ x 11, Letrpr. press, 8 pages, ISSN: 0913-6816, No Color, Newsprint
Subscriptions: Indv. $137, $11/copy
Advertising: Inquire for rates. Accepts Inserts.
List Rental: Actives: $90/M
Printing Co: ACN Graphics, 1602 Birchwood Ln, Neptune, NJ 07753-6910 Tel # (908) 681-6083

Hospital Administration
Currents *Business*

Publishing Co: Ross Labs., 625 Cleveland Ave, Columbus, OH 43215-1754;
Title Tel # (614) 227-3315
Personnel: Editor-Esther Silverman, Adv. Dir.-Beman Pound
Editorial Description: Covers subjects of special interest to hospital administrators and other related subjects.
General Info: Yr. Est. 1957, Bi-monthly, Trim Size-8½ x 11, 4 pages, 2 Color
Circulation: Total-14,000
Advertising: Inquire for rates.

Hospital Admitting
Monthly *Business*

Publishing Co: American Health Consultants, Inc., 3525 Piedmont Rd., Building #6, Ste. 400, Atlanta, GA 30305-0056 Tel # (404) 262-7436 Fax # (404) 284-3291
Personnel: Publisher-Connie Austin, Editor-Glen Harris, Circ. Mgr.-Monica Brown, Production Mgr.-Mike Witter, Mktg. Mgr.-Robin Prows
Editorial Description: News of changing procedures/policies for hospital admission.
General Info: Monthly, Trim Size-8½ x 11, Offset press, 16 pages, Ind/Abs/Online: Mead Data Central, 2 Color
Subscriptions: Indv. $299, $28/copy
Circulation: Total-1,775
List Rental: Actives: $145/M

Hospital Benchmarks *Business*

Publishing Co: American Health Consultants, Inc., 3525 Piedmont Rd., Building #6, Ste. 400, Atlanta, GA 30305-0056 Fax # (404) 284-3291; Title Tel # (404) 262-7436
Personnel: Publisher-Lauren Oden, Editor-Allyson Harris, Circ. Mgr.-Monica Brown, Production Mgr.-Mike Witter, Mktg. Dir.-Michelle Titus
Editorial Description: Case studie of best hospital administrative practices.
General Info: Yr. Est. 1994, Monthly
Subscriptions: Indv. $259
List Rental: Actives: $145/M

Hospital Contracts Manual
See: LABOR

Hospital Cost
Management &
Accounting *Business*

Publishing Co: Aspen Publishers, Inc., 200 Orchard Ridge Dr., Ste 200, Gaithersburg, MD 20878-5440 Tel # (301) 417-7500 Fax # (301) 417-7655 Parent Co.-Wolters Kluwer US Corporation, New York; Title Tel # (410) 417-7500 Title Fax # (301) 417-7550
Personnel: Editor-Steven A. Finkler, PhD,CPA, VP Mktg.-Cynthia Smith, Mktg. Mgr.-Trudi Graham
Editorial Description: Top health care financial experts provide the latest accounting strategies to help monitor dept. costs, increase profits, improve accuracy of cost data, and improve a hospital's ability to control costs.
General Info: (Formerly Hospital Cost Accounting Advisor), Yr. Est. 1989, Monthly, Trim Size-8½ x 11, 8 pages, ISSN: 8756-7288
Subscriptions: Indv. $230, For. $276, $24/copy
List Rental: List Management Co.: Stevens-Knox List Management, 304 Park Ave S., New York, NY 10010-5312 Tel # (212) 388-8800, Fax # (212) 388-8890

Hospital Employee Health *Business*

Publishing Co: American Health Consultants, Inc., 3525 Piedmont Rd., Building #6, Ste. 400, Atlanta, GA 30305-0056 Tel # (404) 262-7436 Fax # (404) 284-3291; Title Tel # (404) 351-4523 Title Fax # (404) 352-1971
Personnel: Publisher-Lauren Oden, Editor-Richard Jarvis, Circ. Mgr.-Monica Brown, Production Mgr.-Mike Witter, Mktg. Dir.-David Price
Editorial Description: Technical and administrative aspects of protecting hospital employees from special rises.
General Info: Yr. Est. 1982, Monthly, Trim Size-8½ x 11, Offset press, 16 pages, Ind/Abs/Online: Mead Data Central, 2 Color
Subscriptions: Indv. $229
Circulation: Total-2,100
List Rental: Actives: $145/M

Hospital Ethics

Publishing Co: American Hospital Publishing, Inc., 737 N. Michigan Ave., Ste. 700, Chicago, IL 60611-2431 Tel # (312) 280-6800 Fax # (312) 944-4232; Title Tel # (312) 280-6236
Personnel: Editor-Donald Phillips
Editorial Description: Review of latest information/opinion in field of hospital ethics.
General Info: Yr. Est. 1985, Bi-monthly, ISSN: 8756-8519
Subscriptions: Indv. $135, $18/copy
Circulation: Total-2,000

Hospital Fast Payment Report

Publishing Co: St. Anthony Consulting Group, 11410 Isaac Newton Sq., N., Ste. 200, Alexandria, VA 22090-5012; Title Tel # (703) 549-0100
Personnel: Publisher-Eugene W. Lorenz, Editor-Janis Oppelt, Circ. Mgr.-Kathi Lawson, Production Mgr.-Lisa Woodward, Art Dir.-Laura Daras, Promotion Dir.-Lori Liggett
Editorial Description: Information on collections, A/R management, DRG management, Medicare, etc. for hospital personnel.
General Info: Yr. Est. 1986, Monthly, Trim Size-8½ x 11, Web press, 8 pages, 2 Color, Matte
Subscriptions: Indv. $198, $17/copy
Acquistions: Publication Bought
Advertising: Accepts Inserts.
List Rental: List Management Co.: PCS Mailing List Co., 85 Constitution La., Danvers, MA 01923 Tel # (508) 777-3332, Fax # (508) 777-9161, Actives: $100/M, Hotline: $110/M
Printing Co: St. Anthony Press, 3431 Carlin Springs Rd, Baileys Crossroads, VA 22041-2802

Hospital Food & Nutrition Focus *Business*

Publishing Co: Aspen Publishers, Inc., 200 Orchard Ridge Dr., Ste 200, Gaithersburg, MD 20878-5440 Parent Co.-Wolters Kluwer US Corporation, New York; Title Tel # (301) 417-7500 Title Fax # (301) 417-7655
Personnel: Publisher-Michael Brown, Editor-Darlene Dougherty, Production Mgr.-Ruth McKendry, Adv. Dir.-Frances Ray, Promotion Dir.-Janis Treacy
Editorial Description: Monthly publication featuring the latest news in hospital foodservice, ready-to-use forms and checklists, suggestions for revenue-building programs and efficient procedures, step-by-step guidelines, and much more.
General Info: Yr. Est. 1984, Monthly, ISSN: 0747-7367
Subscriptions: Indv. $152, For. $182, $16/copy
Circulation: Total-1,300
List Rental: List Management Co.: Stevens-Knox List Management, 304 Park Ave S., New York, NY 10010-5312 Tel # (212) 388-8800, Fax # (212) 388-8890, Actives: $80/M

Hospital Home Health

Publishing Co: American Health Consultants, Inc., 3525 Piedmont Rd., Building #6, Ste. 400, Atlanta, GA 30305-0056 Tel # (404) 262-7436 Fax # (404) 284-3291; Title Tel # (404) 351-4523 Title Fax # (404) 352-1971
Personnel: Publisher-Connie Austin, Editor-Cheli Brown, Exec. Ed.-Greg Freeman, Mng. Editor-Donald R. Johnston, Circ. Mgr.-Monica Brown, Production Mgr.-Mike Witterms, Mktg. Mgr.-Rebecca Swancott-Torres
Editorial Description: Covers legal, clinical, management aspects of hospital-affiliated home care.
General Info: Yr. Est. 1984, Monthly, Trim Size-8½ x 11, 14 pages, ISSN: 0884-8521, 2 Color
Subscriptions: Indv. $319, Inst. $259, Can. $269, For. $279, $29/copy
Circulation: Total-1,070
List Rental: Actives: $145/M

Hospital Infection Control *Consumer*

Publishing Co: American Health Consultants, Inc., 3525 Piedmont Rd., Building #6, Ste. 400, Atlanta, GA 30305-0056 Fax # (404) 284-3291; Title Tel # (404) 262-7436 Title Fax # (404) 262-7837
Personnel: Publisher-Lauren Oden, Editor-Gary Evans, Circ. Mgr.-Monica Brown, Circ. Mgr.-Robin Salet, Production Mgr.-Mike Witter, Mktg. Dir.-David Price
Editorial Description: Covers the subject of infections acquired by patients in hospitals and how to prevent acquisition of such infections.
General Info: Yr. Est. 1973, Monthly, Trim Size-8½ x 11, Offset press, 16 pages, ISSN: 0098-180X, Ind/Abs/Online: Mead Data Central, 2 Color
Subscriptions: Indv. $269
Circulation: Total-4,500
List Rental: Actives: $145/M

Hospital Insurance Litigation Reporter
See: LAW

Hospital Integrated Care Report *Business*

Publishing Co: American Health Consultants, Inc., 3525 Piedmont Rd., Building #6, Ste. 400, Atlanta, GA 30305-0056 Tel # (404) 262-7436 Fax # (404) 284-3291
Personnel: Publisher-Connie Austin, Editor-Glen Harris, Circ. Mgr.-Monica Brown, Production Mgr.-Mike Witter, Mktg. Dir.-Robin Prows
Editorial Description: Covers managed care for hospital professionals.
General Info: Yr. Est. 1993, Monthly
Subscriptions: Indv. $319, $30/copy
List Rental: Actives: $145/M

Hospital Law Manual & Newsletter
See: LAW

Hospital Law Newsletter *Business*

Publishing Co: Aspen Publishers, Inc., 200 Orchard Ridge Dr., Ste 200, Gaithersburg, MD 20878-5440 Fax # (301) 417-7655 Parent Co.-Wolters Kluwer US Corporation, New York; Title Tel # (301) 417-7500 Title Fax # (301) 417-7550
Personnel: Editor, Editor-Nathan Hershey, LLB
Editorial Description: Latest information on malpractice, credential requirements, hospital-physician relationships, financial issues, employee relations antitrust, and contracting.
General Info: Monthly, 8 pages, ISSN: 0738-0984
Subscriptions: Indv. $295, For. $354, $31/copy
Circulation: Readership-2,200
List Rental: List Management Co.: Stevens-Knox List Management, 304 Park Ave S., New York, NY 10010-5312 Tel # (212) 388-8800, Fax # (212) 388-8890

Hospital Litigation Reporter
See: LAW

Hospital Materials Management *Business* CPM: $343

Publishing Co: Business Word, Inc., 5350 S. Roslyn St., Ste. 400, Englewood, CO 80111-2125; Title Tel # (303) 290-8500 Title Fax # (303) 290-9025
Personnel: Publisher-Donald Johnson, Editor-Curt Werner, Production Mgr.-Todd Reid, Adv. Dir.-Dave Jeans, Circ. Mgr., Mktg. Dir., Promotion Dir.-Linda Gamble
Editorial Description: Covers group purchasing & materials management.
General Info: (Formerly Hospital Purchasing Management), Yr. Est. 1976, Monthly, Trim Size-8½ x 11, Sheetfed press, 24 pages, ISSN: 0163-1322, 2 Color, Matte, Saddle-stitched
Subscriptions: Indv. $207, Can. $193, For. $205, $20/copy
Circulation: Total-1,600, Source-IS
Advertising: $550.
List Rental: Actives: $325/M

Hospital Materials Management News *Association*

Publishing Co: American Soc. for Hospital Material Mgt., 840 N. Lake Shore Dr., Chicago, IL 60611-2497; Title Tel # (312) 280-6137
Personnel: Editor, Promotion Dir.-Shelly Johnson
Editorial Description: A newsletter for the society which features assn. news & important information on the field of hospital materials management.
General Info: Yr. Est. 1962, Bi-monthly, 8 pages, ISSN: 0749-6672, 2 Color, Coated, Saddle-stitched
Circulation: (100% controlled), Total-1,900

Hospital Network Insider *Business*

Publishing Co: United Communications Group, 11300 Rockville Pike, Ste. 1100, Rockville, MD 20852-3030 Tel # (301) 816-8950 Fax # (301) 816-8945
Editorial Description: Reimbursement/cost containment information for hospital CFOs.
General Info: Bi-weekly

Hospital Peer Review *Consumer*

Publishing Co: American Health Consultants, Inc., 3525 Piedmont Rd., Building #6, Ste. 400, Atlanta, GA 30305-0056 Fax # (404) 284-3291; Title Tel # (404) 262-7436 Title Fax # (800) 284-3291
Personnel: Publisher-Lauren Oden, Editor-Allyson Harris, Circ. Mgr.-Monica Brown, Production Mgr.-Mike Witterd, Mktg. Dir.-Michelle Titus
Editorial Description: News and advice on utilization review, quality assurance, legal issues.
General Info: Yr. Est. 1974, Monthly, Trim Size-8½ x 11, Offset press, 16 pages, Ind/Abs/Online: Mead Data Central, Color
Subscriptions: Indv. $219
Circulation: Total-3,900
List Rental: Actives: $145/M

Hospital Risk Control System *Business*

Publishing Co: ECRI, 5200 Butler Pike, Plymouth Meeting, PA 19462-1298; Title Tel # (610) 825-6000 Title Fax # (610) 834-1275
Personnel: Editor-Sharon Bayless, Circ. Mgr.-Diane Schwarztrauber, Promotion Dir.-Michele Carlin
Editorial Description: Risk management topics for hospitals; includes free consultation services.
General Info: Yr. Est. 1981, Monthly, Sheetfed press, Looseleaf
Subscriptions: Indv. $695, For. $595

Hospital Risk Management
Business

Publishing Co: American Health Consultants, Inc., 3525 Piedmont Rd., Building #6, Ste. 400, Atlanta, GA 30305-0056 Tel # (404) 262-7436 Fax # (404) 284-3291
Personnel: Publisher-Connie Austin, Editor-Linda Morningstar, Circ. Mgr.-Monica Brown, Production Mgr.-Mike Witter, Mktg. Mgr.-Robin Prows
Editorial Description: Loss prevention in hospitals, medical malpractice, liability for patient, staff and visitor injuries, etc.
General Info: Yr. Est. 1979, Monthly, Trim Size-8½ x 11, Offset press, 16 pages, ISSN: 0199-6312, Ind/Abs/Online: Mead Data Central, 2 Color
Subscriptions: Indv. $329, $31/copy
Circulation: (100% controlled), Total-2,650
List Rental: Actives: $145/M

Hospital Safety Information Service
See: SAFETY

Hospital Technology Alerts

Publishing Co: Ross Pubs., Inc., PO Box 80, Boston, MA 02113-0001
Editorial Description: Developments in hospital technology and related topics.
General Info: Monthly
Subscriptions: Indv. $125

Hospital Technology Series

Publishing Co: American Hospital Publishing, Inc., 737 N. Michigan Ave., Ste. 700, Chicago, IL 60611-2431 Tel # (312) 280-6800 Fax # (312) 944-4232; Title Tel # (312) 280-6236
Personnel: Publisher-Henry Alder, Editor-Dianne Spenner
Editorial Description: Comprehensive coverage of developments in medical technology.
General Info: Yr. Est. 1981, Monthly, ISSN: 0888-711X
Subscriptions: Indv. $295, $25/copy
Circulation: Total-1,300

Housing the Elderly Report
Business

Publishing Co: CD Publications, 8204 Fenton St., Silver Spring, MD 20910-4571; Title Tel # (301) 588-6380 Title Fax # (301) 588-6385
Personnel: Publisher-Mike Gerecht, Editor-Leah Thayer, Circ. Mgr.-Kurt Eisentraut, Mktg. Dir.-Joyce Meals
Editorial Description: News and advice for owners and managers of long-term care facilities on marketing and managing all types of elderly housing.
General Info: Yr. Est. 1982, Monthly, Trim Size-8½ x 11, Sheetfed press, 14 pages, ISSN: 1050-3234, No Color, Matte, Other
Subscriptions: Indv. $175, Can. $185, For. $215, $15/copy
List Rental: List Management Co.: Manager: Amy Seyler; Washington Advertising Service, 8204 Fenton St., Silver Spring, MD 20910 Tel # (301) 588-7920, Fax # (301) 588-6385, Actives: 4,262, $150/M, Expires: 4,301, $150/M

How to Get Paid
See: MANAGEMENT

Human Resources Administrator

Publishing Co: American Hospital Publishing, Inc., 737 N. Michigan Ave., Ste. 700, Chicago, IL 60611-2431 Tel # (312) 280-6800 Fax # (312) 944-4232; Title Tel # (312) 280-6236
General Info: (Formerly Hospital Personnel Administration), Yr. Est. 1964, Bi-monthly
Circulation: Total-2,500

Icarus File, The
Association   CPM: $46

Publishing Co: Phoenix Society for Burn Survivors, Inc., The, 11 Rust Hill Rd, Levittown, PA 19056-2311; Title Tel # (215) 946-2876 Title Fax # (215) 946-4788
Personnel: Publisher, Editor-Alan Brealau, Production Mgr.-Ruth Coriell, Art Dir.-Holly Vernon
Editorial Description: Society newsletter dealing with burn prevention, care and disfigurement; news of members.
General Info: Yr. Est. 1980, Quarterly, Trim Size-8 x 11, Roto. press, 16 pages, Color-cover
Subscriptions: Indv. $4, Can. $6, For. $6, $1/copy
Acquistions: Publication Bought
Circulation: Total-7,500
Advertising: $350. Accepts Inserts.
List Rental: Rents Lists
Printing Co: Nationwide Printing, 5906 N Jefferson St, Burlington, KY 41005-9772 Tel # (606) 586-9005

Infection Control Weekly
See: DRUGS & PHARMACEUTICALS

Info
See: ENVIRONMENT & ECOLOGY

Inside Ambulatory Care
Business

Publishing Co: Aspen Publishers, Inc., 200 Orchard Ridge Dr., Ste 200, Gaithersburg, MD 20878-5440 Fax # (301) 417-7655 Parent Co.-Wolters Kluwer US Corporation, New York; Title Tel # (301) 417-7500 Title Fax # (301) 417-7550
Personnel: Editor-Steve Larose, Mktg. Dir.-Trudi Graham
Editorial Description: Focuses on the day-to-day management concerns of all ambulatory care/outpatient services managers. Covers innovations and trends in ambulatory care at hospitals and freestanding centers nationwide.
General Info: Yr. Est. 1994, Monthly, 8 pages, ISSN: 1073-6506
Subscriptions: Indv. $199, For. $239, $21/copy

Inside Health Law
Business

Publishing Co: Aspen Publishers, Inc., 200 Orchard Ridge Dr., Ste 200, Gaithersburg, MD 20878-5440 Fax # (301) 417-7655 Parent Co.-Wolters Kluwer US Corporation, New York; Title Tel # (301) 417-7500 Title Fax # (301) 417-7550
Personnel: Mktg. Mgr.-Trudi Graham
Editorial Description: Legal developments in health care.
General Info: Yr. Est. 1996, Monthly, 8 pages

Inside Medicaid Managed Care
Business

Publishing Co: Aspen Publishers, Inc., 200 Orchard Ridge Dr., Ste 200, Gaithersburg, MD 20878-5440 Fax # (301) 417-7655 Parent Co.-Wolters Kluwer US Corporation, New York; Title Tel # (301) 417-7500 Title Fax # (301) 417-7550
Personnel: Editor-Jayne Walley, Mktg. Mgr.-Trudi Graham
Editorial Description: Especially created to serve as an always up-to-date source of how-to guidance for contractors, insurers and providers. Each monthly issue brings you tried and proven solutions for assuring success in every aspect of medicial managed care.
General Info: Yr. Est. 1995, Monthly, 8 pages, ISSN: 1081-1729
Subscriptions: Indv. $249, For. $299, $26/copy

Inside Preventive Care
Business

Publishing Co: Aspen Publishers, Inc., 200 Orchard Ridge Dr., Ste 200, Gaithersburg, MD 20878-5440 Fax # (301) 417-7655 Parent Co.-Wolters Kluwer US Corporation, New York; Title Tel # (301) 417-7500 Title Fax # (301) 417-7550
Personnel: Editor-Steve Larose, Mktg. Mgr.-Trudi Graham
Editorial Description: Learn proven strategies for demand management. Benefit from information on effective patient education, instructing physicians and nurses in techniques of good preventive health care.
General Info: Yr. Est. 1995, 8 pages, ISSN: 1077-9558
Subscriptions: Indv. $149, For. $179, $16/copy

Insider (Miami Valley Hospital)
Association

Publishing Co: Miami Valley Hospital, 1 Wyoming St, Dayton, OH 45409-2763; Title Tel # (513) 223-6192
Editorial Description: For MUH employees, volunteers & medical staff.
General Info: Yr. Est. 1980, Monthly, 12 pages
Circulation: Total-4,000

Integrated Health Care Delivery Systems
Business

Publishing Co: Thompson Publishing Group, 747 Third Ave., New York, NY 10017 Tel # (212) 888-7220 Fax # (212) 486-3400; Title Fax # (800) 999-2320
Personnel: Publisher-Ken Gesser, Editor-Allan Fine, Production Mgr.-R.D. Whitney, Mktg. Dir.-Kevin Mahon
Editorial Description: Successful strategies for hospital and physician collaboration. Subscription includes monthly newsletters and quarterly updates.
General Info: Yr. Est. 1993, Monthly, Looseleaf
Subscriptions: Indv. $295

Integrated Senior Care: Assisted Living and Long-Term Care Newsletter
See: SENIOR CITIZENS

Intercom

Publishing Co: St. Luke's Hospital, 1227 E Rusholme St, Davenport, IA 52803-2498; Title Tel # (319) 326-6896
Personnel: Editor-Blake Lewis, III, Circ. Mgr., Production Mgr.-Regina Howell
Editorial Description: General information on hospital activities for employees and others.
General Info: Yr. Est. 1968, Bi-weekly, Trim Size-8½ x 11, Mimeo press, 2 pages, No Color, Newsprint
Circulation: Total-800

JH News
See: HOUSE ORGANS

Journal

Publishing Co: St. Joseph Medical Center, Mktg. & Public Relations, 501 S. Buena Vista St., Burbank, CA 91505 Tel # (818) 843-5111

KIDStuff

Publishing Co: Children's Hospital of the King's Daughters, 601 Children's Lane, Norfolk, VA 23507; Title Tel # (804) 668-7043 Title Fax # (804) 668-7350
General Info: (Formerly News from the Land of the Little People)

Kashrus Faxletter
See: FOOD

LSAC News

Publishing Co: St. Jude Children's Research Hospital, 501 St. Jude Place, Memphis, TN 38105; Title Tel # (901) 524-0372 Title Fax # (901) 523-6600
Personnel: Editor-Shelia Bonaiuto
General Info: Quarterly
Subscriptions: Indv. $10

Laughter Prescription Newsletter
See: HUMOR & SATIRE

Laughter Works
See: HUMOR & SATIRE

Legal Guide for Physicians
See: LAW

Long-Term Care
Administrator   *Association*   **CPM: $91**

Publishing Co: American College of Health Care Administrators, 325 S. Patrick St., Alexandria, VA 22314-3571 Fax # (703) 739-7901; Title Tel # (703) 739-7900
Personnel: Editor-Jan Lamoglia
Editorial Description: Latest news about the long-term care field. Features the Capital Report, Great Ideas and Q & A on death and dying. Includes classified ads and education calendar.
General Info: Yr. Est. 1967, Semi-monthly, Trim Size-8½ x 11, Offset press, 16 pages, ISSN: 0146-275X, 2% ads, 2 Color, Matte, Saddle-stitched
Subscriptions: Indv. $45, Inst. $45, Can. $45, For. $55, $5/copy
Acquistions: Publication Bought
Circulation: Total-6,300
Advertising: $575. Accepts Inserts.
List Rental: List Management Co.: Manager: Vera Johnson; MGI-Marketing General Inc., 105 Oronoco St., Alexandria, VA 22314-2015 Tel # (703) 739-1000, Actives: $77/M
Printing Co: Custom Print, Inc., 2611 S. Shirlington Rd., Arlington, VA 22206-2529 Tel # (703) 979-6670

Lung Line Letter   *Consumer, Association*

Publishing Co: Natl. Jewish Ctr. for Immunology and Respiratory Medicine, 1400 Jackson St, Denver, CO 80206-2761 Tel # (303) 398-1080 Fax # (303) 270-2171; Title Tel # (303) 398-1000
Personnel: Editor-Janet Broner
Editorial Description: Designed to inform consumers about the latest developments in treating respiratory and immunologic diseases.
General Info: Yr. Est. 1970, Quarterly
Circulation: Total-14,200

MDR Watch
See: HEALTH

MGH News

Publishing Co: Massachusetts General Hospital, 32 Fruit St, Boston, MA 02114-2620; Title Tel # (617) 726-2206
Personnel: Editor-Martin S. Bander, Circ. Mgr.-Doris Schreckergaist, Art Dir.-Robert Galla
Editorial Description: An educational publication which attempts to place medical news in perspective.
General Info: Yr. Est. 1942, Monthly, Trim Size-8½ x 11, Offset press, 8 pages, 2 Color, Coated
Circulation: (100% controlled), Total-27,000

MLA News
See: LIBRARY

Managed Care Law Outlook
See: LAW

Managed Care Outlook   *Business*

Publishing Co: Capitol Publications, Inc., 1101 King St., Ste. 444, Alexandria, VA 22314-2968; Title Tel # (703) 683-4100 Title Fax # (703) 739-6501
Personnel: Publisher-Cynthia Carter, Editor-Carol Sardinha, Exec. Ed.-Russ Jackson, Circ. Mgr.-Peggy Dwyer, Production Mgr.-Billy Adams, Art Dir.-Linda McDonald, Mktg. Dir.-Mary Lou Probka, Promotion Dir.-Kelly Baptiste
Editorial Description: Concise updates and analysis on the latest mergers & acquisitions, new product development and pricing, case studies of competitors' strategic plans.
General Info: Yr. Est. 1988, Bi-weekly, Trim Size-8½ x 11, 12 pages, ISSN: 0896-6567, Ind/Abs/Online: Predicasts
Subscriptions: Indv. $439, Inst. $439
List Rental: Actives: $150/M
Printing Co: Capitol Publications, Inc., 1101 King St., Ste. 444, Alexandria, VA 22314-2968 Tel # (703) 683-4100, Fax # (703) 739-6501

Managed Pharmaceutical Report
See: DRUGS & PHARMACEUTICALS

Managing Integration and Operations: A Guide to Quality Health Care Systems   *Business*

Publishing Co: Thompson Publishing Group, 747 Third Ave., New York, NY 10017 Fax # (212) 486-3400; Title Tel # (212) 888-7220 Title Fax # (800) 999-2320
Personnel: Publisher-Ken Gesser, Editor-William Shaw, Production Mgr.-Mauro Vaisman, Mktg. Dir.-Barbara McGee
General Info: Yr. Est. 1995, Monthly, Looseleaf
Subscriptions: Indv. $395

Managing Senior Care   *Business*

Publishing Co: Business Publishers, Inc., 951 Pershing Dr., Silver Spring, MD 20910-4464 Tel # (301) 589-5103 Fax # (301) 589-8493
Personnel: Publisher-Leonard A. Eiserer, Editor-Sarah Spencer, Circ. Mgr.-Brenda Davenport
General Info: Monthly
List Rental: List Management Co.: BPI Direct, 951 Pershing Dr., Silver Spring, MD 20910-4464 Tel # (301) 585-5976, Fax # (301) 587-4530

Marian Newsletter

Publishing Co: Marian Health Center, 801 5 th Street, Sioux City, IA 51101-1399; Title Tel # (712) 279-2147
Circulation: Total-1,700

Material & Finance Strategy   *Business*

Publishing Co: Concepts in Healthcare, 171 Main St # 102, Ashland, MA 01721-1153; Title Tel # (508) 881-7722
Personnel: Publisher-Warren Blanding, Editor-Josephine Hughes
Editorial Description: Inventory & materials management, storage, finance, administration in health care.
General Info: Yr. Est. 1980, Monthly, Trim Size-8½ x 11, Offset press, 4 pages, 2 Color
Subscriptions: Indv. $65, $5/copy

Materiel Manager   *Association*

Publishing Co: Saskatchewan Assn of Health Organizations, 1445 Park St., Regina, SK S4N 4C5 Canada Tel # (306) 347-5500; Title Tel # (306) 347-5526 Title Fax # (306) 525-1960
Personnel: Publisher-Loretta Fritz, Editor-Suzanne Deck, Production Mgr.-Andrew Caswell
General Info: Yr. Est. 1993, Quarterly, Trim Size-8½ x 11, Offset press, 4 pages, 2 Color, Saddle-stitched
Subscriptions: Free To Qualified Recipient
Circulation: Total-1,000
Printing Co: Printwest Communications, 1150 8th Ave., Regina, SK Canada Tel # (306) 525-2304

McLean Bulletin
See: HOUSE ORGANS

Medical Center News

Publishing Co: St. Joseph Medical Center, Mktg. & Public Relations, 501 S. Buena Vista St., Burbank, CA 91505; Title Tel # (818) 843-5111

Medical Liability Advisory Service
See: LAW

Medical Network Strategy
Report   *Business*

Publishing Co: COR Healthcare Resources, PO Box 40959, Santa Barbara, CA 93140-0959 Fax # (805) 564-2146; Title Tel # (805) 564-2177
Personnel: Publisher-Dean Anderson, Editor-Therese Droste
Editorial Description: Strategies for building integrated medical delivery networks.
General Info: (Formerly Medical Staff Strategy Report), Yr. Est. 1992, Monthly, Trim Size-8½ x 11, Sheetfed press, 12 pages, 2 Color, Saddle-stitched
Subscriptions: Indv. $226, Can. $226, For. $238, $20/copy
List Rental: Actives: 2,400, $150/M, Expires: $150/M

Medical Records Briefing   *Business*

Publishing Co: Opus Communications, Inc., Box 1168, 100 Hoods Lane, Marblehead, MA 01945; Title Tel # (617) 639-1872 Title Fax # (617) 639-2982
Personnel: Publisher-Jennifer Cofer, Circ. Mgr.-Marje Radloff
Editorial Description: A practical guide for health information managers of medical records departments in acute care hospitals.
General Info: Yr. Est. 1986, Monthly, Trim Size-8½ x 11, 12 pages, ISSN: 1052-4924, 2 Color, Saddle-stitched
Subscriptions: Indv. $177, Can. $177, For. $177
List Rental: Rents Lists

Medical Staff Briefing   *Business*

Publishing Co: Opus Communications, Inc., Box 1168, 100 Hoods Lane, Marblehead, MA 01945; Title Tel # (617) 639-1872 Title Fax # (617) 639-2982
Personnel: Publisher-Jennifer Cofer, Editor-Cathy Rossi
Editorial Description: A practical guide for medical staff professionals and elected medical staff leaders. Discusses clinical privilege delineation and physician credentialing.
General Info: Yr. Est. 1990, Monthly, Trim Size-8½ x 11, Desktop press, 12 pages, ISSN: 1076-6022, 2 Color, Saddle-stitched
Subscriptions: Indv. $247

Medical Staff Law Manual   *Business*

Publishing Co: Action Kit for Hospital Law, 4614 Fifth Ave., Pittsburgh, PA 15213-3663; Title Tel # (412) 687-8275 Title Fax # (412) 687-7692
Editorial Description: A loose leaf reference book which includes a monthly newsletter for hospital managers & medical staff leaders addressing issues concerning medical staff appointment & clinical privileges.
General Info: Yr. Est. 1984, Monthly, Trim Size-8½ x 11, 4 pages, 2 Color
Subscriptions: Inst. $675

Medical Staff News

Publishing Co: Hahnemann Medical College, Hospital, 235 N 15th St, Philadelphia, PA 19102-1122; Title Tel # (215) 448-7690
Personnel: Editor-Mildred Plenty
General Info: 10x/yr., Trim Size-8½ x 11, Offset press, 4 pages
Circulation: Total-6,000

Medical Waste News
See: ENVIRONMENT & ECOLOGY

Medicare Advisor
Business

Publishing Co: Shannon Publications, Inc., 9441 L.B.J. Fwy, Ste. #510 Box #2, Dallas, TX 75243-4541; Title Tel # (214) 644-0159 Title Fax # (214) 644-1538
Personnel: Publisher-Brian Buchan, Publisher, Editor-Ellen Bradley, Circ. Mgr.-Tony Bradley
Editorial Description: Covers medicare issues and developments for Nursing Homes.
General Info: Yr. Est. 1986, Monthly, Trim Size-8½ x 11, Sheetfed press, 6 pages, ISSN: 0897-9634
Subscriptions: Indv. $125, For. $135
Advertising: Accepts Inserts.
List Rental: Rents Lists

Medicine on the Net
Business

Publishing Co: COR Healthcare Resources, PO Box 40959, Santa Barbara, CA 93140-0959; Title Tel # (805) 564-2177 Title Fax # (805) 564-2146
Personnel: Publisher-Dean H. Anderson, Editor-Paul Engstrom
Editorial Description: Medical resources available on the Internet & how healthcare professionals are using the Internet to access information & communicate with patients & colleagues.
General Info: Yr. Est. 1995, Monthly, Sheetfed press, ISSN: 1085-3502, 2 Color, Saddle-stitched
Subscriptions: Indv. $87, Can. $87, For. $99, $10/copy

Messenger, The
Consumer

Publishing Co: St. Patrick Hospital, 500 W Broadway St, Missoula, MT 59802-4008; Title Tel # (406) 542-0001 Title Fax # (406) 543-6836
Personnel: Publisher, Editor-Jeffrey Smith
Editorial Description: Monthly health newsletter with emphasis on western Montana people and issues.
General Info: Yr. Est. 1979, Monthly, 4 pages, 2 Color, Coated
Subscriptions: Free
Circulation: Total-6,000
Printing Co: Artcraft, 150 E Spruce St, Missoula, MT 59802-4504 Tel # (406) 543-8311

Messenger

Publishing Co: Tarrant County Hospital District, 1500 S Main St, Fort Worth, TX 76104-4917 Tel # (817) 921-3431

Mini Headliner
Business

Publishing Co: Memorial Hospital, 600 Northern Blvd, Albany, NY 12204-1004; Title Tel # (518) 471-3221
Editorial Description: General news of new hospital equipment, new appointments to the staff, social events, building fund progress.
General Info: (Formerly Memorial Hospital Newsletter), Yr. Est. 1960, Bi-weekly
Circulation: Total-3,000

Minnesota Nursing Accent
See: NURSING

Montefiore Medicine

Publishing Co: Montefiore Hospital, 3412 Bainbridge Ave, Bronx, NY 10467-2404

NAAP News
Business, Association

Publishing Co: National Association of Activity Professionals, 1225 Eye St. NW, #300, Washington, DC 20005; Title Tel # (202) 289-0722
Personnel: Editor-Charles Price, Production Mgr.-Paige Sifford
Editorial Description: For members activity directors & leaders in nursing homes, etc.
General Info: (Formerly NAAP Update), Yr. Est. 1981, Monthly, Trim Size-8½ x 11, Web press, 8 pages, 2% ads, No Color, Newsprint
Subscriptions: Indv. $45
Circulation: (100% controlled), Total-2,500
List Rental: Rents Lists
Printing Co: Balmar Graphics, 1021 15th St NW, Washington, DC 20005-2601 Tel # (202) 659-3610

NACHRI Newsletter
Association

Publishing Co: Natl. Assn. of Children's Hospitals, 401 Wythe St., Alexandria, VA 22314-1926; Title Tel # (703) 684-1355
Personnel: Editor-Louise Hutchinson
Editorial Description: Contains articles of interest to persons in Children's Hospital field.
General Info: Yr. Est. 1968, Quarterly, Trim Size-8½ x 11, 8 pages, 2 Color, Coated
Circulation: Total-4,500
Printing Co: Old Dominion Printing Co., 444 Swann Ave, Alexandria, VA 22301-1047

NRAA Journal
Association

Publishing Co: National Renal Administrators Association, 4046 Gratridt Ave., Pt. Huron, MI 48060-1202; Title Tel # (313) 987-3625 Title Fax # (810) 987-4120
Personnel: Publisher-J. Michael Allen, Editor-Mardee Hagen, Production Mgr.-Gloria Justice
Editorial Description: For renal patient care suppliers.
General Info: (Formerly NRAA Newsletter), Yr. Est. 1978, Annually, Trim Size-8½ x 11, Sheetfed press, 20 pages, Newsprint
Subscriptions: Indv. $6
Circulation: (100% controlled), Total-300

NYU Medical Center Staff News

Publishing Co: New York Univ. Medical Center, 550 1st Ave, New York, NY 10016-6481; Title Tel # (212) 263-5488 Title Fax # (212) 263-8425
Personnel: Editor-David Sachs
Editorial Description: An in-house publication that focuses on activities involving non-physicians at NYU Medical Center.
General Info: (Formerly Medical CenterNews), Yr. Est. 1960

National Intelligence Report on Clinical Labs, Blood Banks

Publishing Co: Washington G-2 Reports, 1111 14th St NW Ste 711, Washington, DC 20005-5603; Title Tel # (202) 789-1034
Personnel: Editor-Jim Curren, Publisher, Adv. Dir., Promotion Dir.-Dennis Weissmann
General Info: Yr. Est. 1979, Semi-monthly, 10 pages
Subscriptions: Indv. $198
Circulation: Total-1,500

National Report on Subacute Care
Business

Publishing Co: Harling Communications, 18-4 E. Dunde Rd., Ste. 202, Barrington, IL 60010 Tel # (708) 304-1011 Fax # (708) 304-1035
Personnel: Publisher-Mark Harling, Editor-Marjorie Lellis
Editorial Description: Covers the subacute transitional care industry.
General Info: Yr. Est. 1994, Bi-weekly
Subscriptions: Indv. $347

New Epidemiology Monitor, The
See: HEALTH

New York Hospital News

Publishing Co: Society of the New York Hospital, 528 E 68th St, New York, NY 10021-6342; Title Tel # (212) 472-6334

News

Publishing Co: St. Francis Xavier Hospital, 135 Rutledge Ave, Charleston, SC 29401-1338; Title Tel # (803) 577-1000

News-In-Brief

Publishing Co: St. Alexis Hospital, 5163 Broadway Ave, Cleveland, OH 44127-1532 Tel # (216) 429-8000

Newsline

Publishing Co: United Hospitals, 333 Smith Ave N, St. Paul, MN 55102-2389; Title Tel # (612) 292-5531
Personnel: Editor-George Ryan
Editorial Description: News & information for medical staff.
General Info: Yr. Est. 1978, Monthly, Trim Size-8½ x 11, Desktop press, 4 pages
Acquistions: Publication Bought
Circulation: Total-1,000

Nite Lite

Publishing Co: Rhode Island Hospital, 593 Eddy St, Providence, RI 02903-4923

Northwood Ermissaeren

Publishing Co: Northwood Deaconess Hospital, Northwood, ND 58267
Personnel: Editor-Rev. John Johanson
Editorial Description: Text: Eng & Norwegian.
General Info: Yr. Est. 1914, Monthly
Subscriptions: Indv. $1
Circulation: Total-1,510

Nursing Home Regulations
Business

Publishing Co: Thompson Publishing Group, 747 Third Ave., New York, NY 10017 Tel # (212) 888-7220 Fax # (212) 486-3400; Title Tel # (212) 888-1244 Title Fax # (800) 999-2320
Personnel: Editor-Robert Fogg, Production Mgr.-Mauno Vaisman, Mktg. Dir.-James Kawawagh
Editorial Description: Provides current information on survey and certification procedures, enforcement procedures, and slternative remedies for noncompliance. Subscription includes monthly newsletter and updates.
General Info: Yr. Est. 1993, Monthly, Looseleaf
Subscriptions: Indv. $295

OR Manager
See: HEALTH

OSHA Guide for Health Care Facilities
Business

Publishing Co: Thompson Publishing Group, 747 Third Ave., New York, NY 10017 Tel # (212) 888-7220; Title Tel # (212) 888-7295 Title Fax # (212) 486-3400
Personnel: Publisher-Kenneth R. Gesser, Editor-Rosalie L. Donlon, Production Mgr.-R.D. Whitney, Mktg. Dir.-Kevin Mahon
Editorial Description: One volume loseleaf service with monthly updates and bulletin to keep health care facilities up-to-date on OSHA requirements specifically targeted to the health care industry.
General Info: Yr. Est. 1994, Monthly, Looseleaf
Subscriptions: Indv. $397

Official Journal - American College of Medical Quality
See: MEDICINE

Ontario Hosptials Today

Publishing Co: Ontario Hospital Association, 150 Ferrand Dr., Don Mills, ON M3C 1H6 Canada;
   Title Tel # (416) 429-2661 Title Fax # (416) 429-1363
Personnel: Editor-Alan Orr
Editorial Description: Covers news & current issues of importance to Association members & health
   care providers throughout Ontario province.
General Info: (Formerly Hospital Highlights), Yr. Est. 1985, Monthly
Subscriptions: Can. $15

Operating Room Risk Management

Publishing Co: ECRI, 5200 Butler Pike, Plymouth Meeting, PA 19462-1298;
   Title Tel # (610) 825-6000 Title Fax # (610) 834-1275
Personnel: Editor-Sharon Bayless, Circ. Mgr.-Diane Schwarztrauber, Promotion Dir.-Michele Carlin
Editorial Description: Risk management topics that deal specifically with the operating room.
General Info: Bi-monthly, Coated, Looseleaf
Subscriptions: Indv. $395, Can. $395, For. $425

Outpatient Reimbursement Management   *Business*

Publishing Co: American Health Consultants, Inc., 3525 Piedmont Rd., Building #6, Ste. 400,
   Atlanta, GA 30305-0056 Tel # (404) 262-7436 Fax # (404) 284-3291
Personnel: Publisher-Connie Autin, Editor-Glen Harris, Circ. Mgr.-Monica Brown, Production Mgr.-
   Mike Witter, Mktg. Dir.-Robin Prows
Editorial Description: Helps reimbursement managers gain maximum reimbursement rate for
   outpatient services.
General Info: Yr. Est. 1994, Monthly
Subscriptions: Indv. $299, $30/copy
List Rental: Actives: $145/M

Outreach   *Association*

Publishing Co: American Hospital Publishing, Inc., 737 N. Michigan Ave., Ste. 700, Chicago, IL
   60611-2431 Tel # (312) 280-6800 Fax # (312) 944-4232; Title Tel # (312) 280-6236
Personnel: Publisher, Editor-Lynn Jones
Editorial Description: Bimonthly report on hospital ambulatory care services.
General Info: Yr. Est. 1980, Bi-monthly, 8 pages, ISSN: 0270-207X
Subscriptions: Indv. $85, $10/copy
Circulation: (100% controlled), Total-3,000

PPO Letter, The   *Business*

Publishing Co: Capitol Publications, Inc., 1101 King St., Ste. 444, Alexandria, VA 22314-2968;
   Title Tel # (703) 683-4100 Title Fax # (703) 739-6501
Personnel: Publisher-Cynthia Carter, Editor-Jim Gutman, Circ. Mgr.-Peggy Dwyer, Production Mgr.-
   Billy Adams, Art Dir.-Linda McDonald, Mktg. Dir.-Mary Lou Probka, Promotion Dir.-Kelly Baptiste
Editorial Description: Comprehensive coverage of the latest developments in the preferred provider
   arrangements industry. Which firms are joining forces, marketing strategies, & legislation &
   regulation.
General Info: Yr. Est. 1990, Bi-weekly, Trim Size-8½ x 11, 8 pages, ISSN: 1054-2396, Color
Subscriptions: Indv. $397, Inst. $397
Acquistions: Publication Bought
List Rental: Actives: $150/M
Printing Co: Capitol Publications, Inc., 1101 King St., Ste. 444, Alexandria, VA 22314-2968
   Tel # (703) 683-4100, Fax # (703) 739-6501

Pacemaker

Publishing Co: Akron City Hospital, 525 E Market St, Akron, OH 44304-1619;
   Title Tel # (216) 375-3000

Pacesetter

Publishing Co: Sister of Providence Hospital, Public Relations, Everett, WA 98206
   Tel # (206) 261-2000

Pager

Publishing Co: St. John Medical Center, 1923 S Utica Ave, Tulsa, OK 74104-6502;
   Title Tel # (918) 744-2820 Title Fax # (918) 744-2200
Personnel: Editor, Production Mgr.-Renee Michalopulos, Art Dir.-Debbie Taylor
Editorial Description: News about SJMC for employees & friends of the hospital.
General Info: (Formerly Scanner), Yr. Est. 1982, Monthly, Trim Size-8½ x 11, Sheetfed press, 4
   pages, ISSN: 0033-4197, 2 Color, Newsprint, Saddle-stitched
Circulation: (100% controlled), Total-3,000
Printing Co: St. John Medical Ctr., 1923 S Utica Ave, Tulsa, OK 74104-6502 Tel # (918) 744-2345

Patient Accounts   *Association*   **CPM$1077**

Publishing Co: Healthcare Financial Management Assn., Two Westbrook Corp. Ctr., #700,
   Westchester, IL 60154-5700; Title Tel # (708) 531-9600 Title Fax # (708) 531-0032
Personnel: Publisher-Ronald E. Keener, Publisher-Cherye T. Stachun, Editor-Bill Siwicki, Adv. Dir.-
   Dianne Lach
Editorial Description: Newsletter for business office managers, patient accounts managers, and
   receivables managers of healthcare facilities.
General Info: Yr. Est. 1978, Monthly, Trim Size-8½ x 11, Sheetfed press, 8 pages, 2 Color,
   Newsprint, Saddle-stitched
Subscriptions: Indv. $75
Circulation: Total-2,200
Advertising: $2,370.
Printing Co: Performance Graphics, Inc., 747 N Church Rd Ste A3, Elmhurst, IL 60126-1436
   Tel # (708) 832-1313

Patient Care Law   *Business*

Publishing Co: Action Kit for Hospital Law, 4614 Fifth Ave., Pittsburgh, PA 15213-3663
   Tel # (412) 687-8275; Title Tel # (412) 687-7677 Title Fax # (412) 687-7692
Editorial Description: A loose leaf reference book, which includes a bi-monthly newsletter which
   discusses legal issues of interest to nurse supervisor.
General Info: Yr. Est. 1982, Bi-monthly
Subscriptions: Inst. $275

Patient Education Management   *Business*

Publishing Co: American Health Consultants, Inc., 3525 Piedmont Rd., Building #6, Ste. 400,
   Atlanta, GA 30305-0056 Tel # (404) 262-7436 Fax # (404) 284-3291
Personnel: Publisher-Connie Austin, Editor-Linda Morningstar, Circ. Mgr.-Monica Brown, Production
   Mgr.-Mike Witter, Mktg. Dir.-Robin Prows
Editorial Description: How-to information for managing patient education programs.
General Info: Yr. Est. 1994, Monthly
Subscriptions: Indv. $239, $24/copy
List Rental: Actives: $145/M

Patients' Rights Reporter
   See: LAW

Pediatric Therapeutic Newsletter

Publishing Co: Children's Hospital of Michigan, 3901 Beaubien St, Detroit, MI 48201-2119;
   Title Tel # (313) 745-5826
Personnel: Editor-Dan Artman
Editorial Description: Review of current pharmaceuticals & usage with children.
General Info: Yr. Est. 1985, Quarterly, Trim Size-8½ x 11, Sheetfed press, 6 pages, 2 Color,
   Newsprint
Subscriptions: Indv. $20
Acquistions: Publication Sold
Circulation: Total-3,600
Printing Co: J. Motschall Printing Corp., 10090 W Chicago, Detroit, MI 48204-2696
   Tel # (313) 834-3303

People

Publishing Co: Sacred Heart Hospital, 421 Chew St., Allentown, PA 18102-3490;
   Title Tel # (215) 776-4690 Title Fax # (610) 776-5149
Personnel: Editor-Mary Venditta
Editorial Description: Employee activities, news, information, announcements, etc.
General Info: Yr. Est. 1985, Bi-monthly, Trim Size-8½ x 11, Offset press, 8 pages, 2 Color, Matte
Circulation: (100% controlled), Total-1,000
Printing Co: Christmas City Printing, 861 14th Ave, Bethlehem, PA 18018-2244 Tel # (215) 868-5844

Perspective

Publishing Co: St. Joseph's Hospital, 5000 W Chambers St, Milwaukee, WI 53210-1688;
   Title Tel # (414) 447-2000
Personnel: Editor-Liana Wayda
General Info: Monthly, Trim Size-8½ x 11, Offset press, 14 pages

Perspective

Publishing Co: Tarrant County Hospital District, 1500 S Main St, Fort Worth, TX 76104-4917
   Tel # (817) 921-3431
General Info: Bi-monthly
Circulation: Total-3,000

Pharmacy Cost Control News
   See: DRUGS & PHARMACEUTICALS

Portercare

Publishing Co: Porter Memorial Hospital, 2525 S Downing St, Denver, CO 80210-5876
   Tel # (303) 778-1955

Post Scripps

Publishing Co: Scripps Memorial Hospital, 9888 Genesee Ave # 28, La Jolla, CA 92037-1200;
   Title Tel # (619) 457-6892
Personnel: Publisher-James Bowers, Editor, Art Dir.-Ian Temple
Editorial Description: Contains applicable health information, technology & health column
   information on Scripps Memorial Hospitals services, programs, & physicians.
General Info: Yr. Est. 1974, Quarterly, Trim Size-8½ x 11, Offset press, 12 pages, 2 Color, Coated,
   Saddle-stitched
Circulation: Total-46,000
Printing Co: Conkin Litho, 3739 6th Ave, San Diego, CA 92103-4394 Tel # (619) 297-1696

Proactive Risk Management   *Business*

Publishing Co: Lippincott-Raven Press Publishers, 227 E. Washington Square, Philadelphia, PA
   19106 Tel # (215) 238-4200 Fax # (215) 238-4227 Parent Co.-Wolters Kluwer US Corporation,
   New York
Personnel: Publisher-Steve McCoy, Editor-Mark Ryan, Mktg. Dir.-Michele Duncan
General Info: Yr. Est. 1994, Monthly, ISSN: 1078-456X
Subscriptions: Indv. $170, For. $195
List Rental: Rents Lists

Professional Placement
Newsnotes *Association*

Publishing Co: Catholic Medical Mission Bd., Placement Desk, 10 W. 17th St., New York, NY 10011-5701; Title Tel # (212) 242-7757 Title Fax # (212) 807-9161
Personnel: Publisher-James Yannarell, S.J., Editor-Michael McCarthy
Editorial Description: Purpose: to describe for membership-experiences, reactions and impressions of medical volunteers.
General Info: Yr. Est. 1961, Quarterly, Trim Size-8½ x 11, Offset press, 4 pages, 2 Color, Coated
Circulation: (100% controlled), Total-5,000

Professional Staff Bulletin

Publishing Co: St. Joseph Medical Center, Mktg. & Public Relations, 501 S. Buena Vista St., Burbank, CA 91505; Title Tel # (818) 843-5111

Profiles

Publishing Co: Good Samaritan Hospital, 2222 Philadelphia Dr, Dayton, OH 45406-1891; Title Tel # (513) 278-2612

Progress -GWU Medical
Center *Consumer, Association*

Publishing Co: George Washington University Medical Center, 2300 I St NW, Washington, DC 20037-2337; Title Tel # (202) 994-3415 Title Fax # (202) 994-0926
Personnel: Editor-Heidi Rosvold-Brenhol
Editorial Description: Bi-monthly employee newsletter features news items of interest to both medical & non-medical staff. Program & personnel profiles as well as calendar-of-events items are included.
General Info: (Formerly Friday Report), Yr. Est. 1989, Bi-weekly, Desktop press, 8 pages, 2 Color, Coated
Circulation: Total-6,000

Psychogram

Publishing Co: Greystone Park Psychiatric Hospital, Greystone Park, NJ 07950
General Info: Semi-annually

Public Health/State Capitals
See: HEALTH

Pulse

Publishing Co: Roosevelt Hospital, 428 W 59th St, New York, NY 10019-1192

Pulsebeat

Publishing Co: Wake County Hospital System Inc., PO Box 14465, Raleigh, NC 27620-4465; Title Tel # (919) 755-8120
Editorial Description: Features on medical issues, equipment, personnel & policies, expansions of services.
General Info: Yr. Est. 1960, Quarterly, Offset press, 8 pages, No Color, Newsprint
Subscriptions: Free
Circulation: Total-2,500

Pulsette

Publishing Co: Roosevelt Hospital, 428 W 59th St, New York, NY 10019-1192

Quality Letter for Healthcare Leaders, The
See: MANAGEMENT

Quarterly

Publishing Co: Seton Medical Center, 1201 W 38th St, Austin, TX 78705-1056 Tel # (512) 323-1000

Queen's Connection *Business*

Publishing Co: Queen's Medical Center, 1301 Punchbowl St., Honolulu, Oahu, HI 96813-2499; Title Tel # (808) 547-4780
Personnel: Publisher, Editor-Paula Elizabeth
Editorial Description: Weekly employee newsletter.
General Info: (Formerly Staff Bulletin), Yr. Est. 1985, Weekly, Mimeo press, 2 pages, Color, Newsprint
Circulation: Total-1,600

Queen's Vision

Publishing Co: Queen's Medical Center, 1301 Punchbowl St., Honolulu, Oahu, HI 96813-2499; Title Tel # (808) 547-4780
Personnel: Publisher, Editor-Maggie Jarrett, Art Dir.-Momi Ojha
Editorial Description: Items on science, new products, public service and general hospital news.
General Info: (Formerly Queen's Hospital Newsletter), Quarterly, Sheetfed press, 8 pages, 2 Color, Newsprint
Acquistions: Publication Bought
Circulation: Total-20,000
Printing Co: Hawaii Hochi, Ltd., 917 Kokea St, Honolulu, HI 96817-4528 Tel # (808) 845-2255, Fax # (808) 847-7215

Rate Controls *Business*

Publishing Co: R. C. Publications, 10221 North 32nd Street, Suite J-1, Phoenix, AZ 85028-3849, Title Tel # (602) 995-9435 Title Fax # (602) 995-9458
Personnel: Publisher, Editor-Arnold Silver
Editorial Description: Newsletter for administrators and financial managers of health care facilities.
General Info: Yr. Est. 1976, Semi-monthly, Trim Size-8½ x 11, Sheetfed press, 8 pages, No Color
Subscriptions: Indv. $195
Circulation: Total-2,600

Receivables Report
See: ACCOUNTING

Reengineering the Hospital

Publishing Co: Zimmerman & Associates, Inc., 5307 South 92nd St., Hales Corners, WI 53130-1677 Parent Co.-Aspen Publishers, Inc., Gaithersburg; Title Tel # (414) 425-2189 Title Fax # (414) 425-4807
Personnel: Editorial Dir.-Jo Ann Petaschnick
General Info: Yr. Est. 1994, Monthly
Subscriptions: Indv. $197

Regan Report on Hospital
Law

Publishing Co: Medica Press Inc., 10 Dorrance St. - Rm. 500, Providence, RI 02903-2018; Title Tel # (401) 421-4747 Title Fax # (401) 421-4747
Personnel: Publisher, Editor-A. David Tammelleo, Circ. Mgr.-Elaine Bedrosian
Editorial Description: Reports the latest & most significant appellate court decisions on hospital law and medical malpractice. In a case and comment format with lessons on legal rights and responsiblities, risk management, and defense strategies.
General Info: Yr. Est. 1960, Monthly, Trim Size-8½ x 11, Offset press, 4 pages, ISSN: 0034-317X, 2 Color, Coated
Subscriptions: Indv. $48, Inst. $48, Can. $48, For. $48, $4/copy
Circulation: Total-30,000
List Rental: Rents Lists

Regan Report on Medical Law
See: MEDICINE

Regan Report on Nursing Law
See: NURSING

Report on Healthcare
Information
Management *Business*

Publishing Co: Capitol Publications, Inc., 1101 King St., Ste. 444, Alexandria, VA 22314-2968; Title Tel # (703) 683-4100 Title Fax # (703) 739-6501
Personnel: Publisher-Cynthia Carter, Editor-Pamela Vaupel, Circ. Mgr.-Peggy Dwyer, Production Mgr.-Billy Adams, Art Dir.-Linda McDonald, Mktg. Dir.-Mary Lou Probka, Promotion Dir.-Kim Fisher
Editorial Description: Keeps healthcare execs on top of what's working in info systems--and what's in store. Reports on standards info systems--and what's in store. Reports on standards for claims submission & EOI and what those developments mean.
General Info: Yr. Est. 1993, Monthly, Trim Size-8½ x 11, 12 pages
Subscriptions: Indv. $335, Inst. $335
List Rental: Actives: $175/M, Expires: $175/M
Printing Co: Capitol Publications, Inc., 1101 King St., Ste. 444, Alexandria, VA 22314-2968 Tel # (703) 683-4100, Fax # (703) 739-6501

Report on Healthcare
Management Solutions *Business*

Publishing Co: Business Publishers, Inc., 951 Pershing Dr., Silver Spring, MD 20910-4464 Tel # (301) 589-5103 Fax # (301) 589-8493
General Info: Monthly
List Rental: List Management Co.: BPI Direct, 951 Pershing Dr., Silver Spring, MD 20910-4464 Tel # (301) 585-5976, Fax # (301) 587-4530

Report on Institutional Foodservice
See: FOOD

Report on Medical
Guidelines and
Outcomes Research *Business*

Publishing Co: Capitol Publications, Inc., 1101 King St., Ste. 444, Alexandria, VA 22314-2968; Title Tel # (703) 683-4100 Title Fax # (703) 739-6501
Personnel: Publisher-Cynthia Carter, Editor-Mary Darby, Exec. Ed.-Russell Jackson, Circ. Mgr.-Peggy Dwyer, Production Mgr.-Billy Adams, Art Dir.-Linda McDonald, Mktg. Dir.-Mary Lou Probka, Promotion Dir.-Kim Fisher
Editorial Description: Developments in practice guidelines, outcomes measurement health status assessment & effectiveness research-info subscribers can use to improve care.
General Info: Yr. Est. 1990, Bi-weekly, Trim Size-8½ x 11, 12 pages, 2 Color
Subscriptions: Indv. $495, Inst. $495
List Rental: Actives: $150/M
Printing Co: Capitol Publications, Inc., 1101 King St., Ste. 444, Alexandria, VA 22314-2968 Tel # (703) 683-4100, Fax # (703) 739-6501

Report on Physician
Trends *Business*

Publishing Co: Capitol Publications, Inc., 1101 King St., Ste. 444, Alexandria, VA 22314-2968; Title Tel # (703) 683-4100 Title Fax # (703) 739-6501
Personnel: Publisher-Cynthia Carter, Editor-Pamel Taulbee, Circ. Mgr.-Peggy Dwyer, Production Mgr.-Billy Adams, Art Dir.-Linda McDonald, Mktg. Dir.-Mary Lou Probka, Promotion Dir.-Kim Fisher
Editorial Description: Guide to understanding & managing, physician relationships. Facts & data on who the best doctors are, where to get them & how to make them productive members of your team.
General Info: Yr. Est. 1992, Monthly, Trim Size-8½ x 11, 12 pages, ISSN: 1068-5219, 2 Color
Subscriptions: Indv. $295, Inst. $295
List Rental: Actives: $175/M, Expires: $175/M
Printing Co: Capitol Publications, Inc., 1101 King St., Ste. 444, Alexandria, VA 22314-2968 Tel # (703) 683-4100, Fax # (703) 739-6501

Respiratory Care Manager *Business*

Publishing Co: Opus Communications, Inc., Box 1168, 100 Hoods Lane, Marblehead, MA 01945; Title Tel # (617) 639-1872 Title Fax # (617) 639-2982
Personnel: Publisher-Jennifer Cofer, Editor-Cathy Rossi
Editorial Description: Relates current, professional news on respiratory care management, standards, and regulations for respiratory care professionals.
General Info: Yr. Est. 1992, Monthly, Trim Size-8½ x 11, 12 pages, ISSN: 1076-6030, 2 Color, Saddle-stitched
Subscriptions: Indv. $127, Inst. $117
List Rental: Rents Lists

Responses

Publishing Co: Hawthorne Community Hospital, 11711 Grevillea Ave, Hawthorne, CA 90250-2222

Round the Center

Publishing Co: Children's Hospital Medical Center, Elland & Bethesda Ave., Cincinnati, OH 45229-2899; Title Tel # (513) 559-4420
Personnel: Editor-Beatrice Rose
Editorial Description: Feature articles on dept. employees policies & programs at Children's Hospital Medical Ctr. Also announcements of new appointments, employee transfers, promotions, etc.
General Info: Yr. Est. 1970, Bi-weekly, Trim Size-9 x 16, Sheetfed press, 4 pages, 2 Color, Matte
Circulation: Total-4,300
Printing Co: Westerman Print Co., 2116 Colerain Ave, Cincinnati, OH 45214-1878 Tel # (513) 721-6492

Russ Coile's Health
Trends *Business*

Publishing Co: Aspen Publishers, Inc., 200 Orchard Ridge Dr., Ste 200, Gaithersburg, MD 20878-5440 Fax # (301) 417-7655 Parent Co.-Wolters Kluwer US Corporation, New York; Title Tel # (301) 417-7500 Title Fax # (301) 417-7550
Personnel: Editor-Russell Coile, Jr., Mktg. Mgr.-Trudi Graham
Editorial Description: Offers guidance, advice, valuable experiencess, and insight into the rapidly changing environment, focusing on the growing complexity of the marketplace and the interdependence of all types of provides and healthcare organizations.
General Info: (Formerly Hospital Strategy Report), Yr. Est. 1992, Monthly, 8 pages, ISSN: 1079-7726
Subscriptions: Indv. $210, For. $252, $22/copy
Circulation: Readership-2,000
List Rental: List Management Co.: Stevens-Knox List Management, 304 Park Ave S., New York, NY 10010-5312 Tel # (212) 388-8800, Fax # (212) 388-8890, Actives: $375/M

Ryan Advisory for Health, Facilities Governing Boards
See: HEALTH

St. Agnes News *Consumer, Association*

Publishing Co: St. Agnes Hospital, 900 S Caton Ave, Baltimore, MD 21229-5299; Title Tel # (410) 368-2170 Title Fax # (410) 368-2947
Personnel: Editor-Helen Becker
Editorial Description: Articles & photos of interest to hospital employees & medical staff.
General Info: Yr. Est. 1961, Bi-monthly, Trim Size-11¼ x 17½, Sheetfed press, 8 pages, 2 Color, Coated
Subscriptions: Free
Circulation: Total-5,500
Printing Co: Art Litho, 1500 W Patapsco Ave, Baltimore, MD 21230-3485 Tel # (301) 355-3200, Fax # (301) 355-3013

St. Luke's Insight
See: HEALTH

Silver Times
See: SENIOR CITIZENS

Skyline News

Publishing Co: Greater New York Hospital Assn, 555 W. 57th St., New York, NY 10019-2974; Title Tel # (212) 246-7100 Title Fax # (212) 262-6350
Personnel: Editor-Carolyn Yordan
Editorial Description: Summary/update on key health issues of concern to GNYHA members.
General Info: Bi-weekly, Trim Size-8½ x 11, Mimeo press, 2 pages, No Color, Newsprint
Subscriptions: Indv. $250
Circulation: Total-1,500

Small or Rural Hospital
Update *Business, Association*

Publishing Co: American Hospital Publishing, Inc., 737 N. Michigan Ave., Ste. 700, Chicago, IL 60611-2431 Tel # (312) 280-6800 Fax # (312) 944-4232; Title Tel # (312) 280-6395
Personnel: Editor-John Supplitt
Editorial Description: Covers news and issues relating especially to small or rural hospitals and their operations.
General Info: (Formerly Small or Rural Hospital Report), Yr. Est. 1977, Irregular
Circulation: Total-3,500

Specialty Capitation Manual: Rate Setting, Evaluation and Implementation
See: HEALTH

Spirit

Publishing Co: Presbyterian Hospital, Pacific Medical Ctr., 2333 Buchanan, San Francisco, CA 94115; Title Tel # (415) 563-4321

Strategic Advantage *Business*

Publishing Co: IMS America, 660 W. Germantown Pike #905, Plymouth Meeting, PA 19462-1048 Tel # (610) 834-5000 Fax # (610) 834-5018
Editorial Description: Information for companies in the healthcare industry.
General Info: Trim Size-8½ x 11, 6 pages, 2 Color, Matte

Strategic Health Care Marketing
See: HEALTH

Strategies for Healthcare
Excellence *Business*

Publishing Co: COR Healthcare Resources, PO Box 40959, Santa Barbara, CA 93140-0959; Title Tel # (805) 564-2177 Title Fax # (805) 564-2146
Personnel: Publisher-Dean Anderson, Editor-Susan Anthony
Editorial Description: Case studies of innovative healthcare organizations & commentaries from leading experts. Focuses on reengineering, effectiveness, and quality improvement.
General Info: (Formerly Healthcare Productivity Report), Yr. Est. 1987, Monthly, Trim Size-8½ x 11, Sheetfed press, 12 pages, ISSN: 1058-7829, Ind/Abs/Online: Hosp.Lit.Ind., 2 Color, Newsprint, Saddle-stitched
Subscriptions: Indv. $227, Can. $227, For. $239, $20/copy
Acquistions: Publication Bought
List Rental: List Management Co.: Cor Research Inc., P.O. Box 40959, Santa Barbara, OH 93140-0959 Tel # (805) 564-2177, Fax # (805) 564-2146, Actives: 1,900, $150/M, Expires: $150/M

Subacute Care: A Guide to
Development,
Implementation and
Management *Business*

Publishing Co: Thompson Publishing Group, 747 Third Ave., New York, NY 10017; Title Tel # (212) 888-7220 Title Fax # (212) 486-3400
Personnel: Editor-Frances Fowler, Production Mgr.-Mauro Vaisman, Mktg. Dir.-Barbara McGee
General Info: Yr. Est. 1995, Monthly, Looseleaf
Subscriptions: Indv. $347

Subacute Care
Management *Business*

Publishing Co: American Health Consultants, Inc., 3525 Piedmont Rd., Building #6, Ste. 400, Atlanta, GA 30305-0056 Tel # (404) 262-7436 Fax # (404) 284-3291
Personnel: Publisher-Connie Austin, Editor-Joy Daughtery, Circ. Mgr.-Monica Brown, Production Mgr.-Mike Witter, Mktg. Dir.-Rebecca Swancott-Torres
Editorial Description: Covers management and delivery of care to patients in transitional settings.
General Info: Yr. Est. 1994, Monthly
Subscriptions: Indv. $249, $23/copy
List Rental: Actives: $145/M

Substance Abuse Report
See: HEALTH

Surgical HPCS

Publishing Co: ECRI, 5200 Butler Pike, Plymouth Meeting, PA 19462-1298; Title Tel # (610) 825-6000 Title Fax # (610) 834-1275
Personnel: Editor-Garrett Hayner, Circ. Mgr.-Diane Schwarztrauber, Promotion Dir.-Michele Carlin
Editorial Description: Product comparison information in binder system with regular updates.
General Info: Monthly, Looseleaf
Subscriptions: Indv. $345, For. $395

Teamwork

Publishing Co: Provenant Health Partners, 4231 W 16th Ave, Denver, CO 80204-1374; Title Tel # (303) 629-3715
Personnel: Editor-Robert Grigsby, Art Dir.-Roger Radtke
Editorial Description: Specific hospital information.
General Info: Bi-weekly, Trim Size-8½ x 11, 4 pages
Circulation: (100% controlled), Total-2,500
Printing Co: Turbo Press, 1131 W Custer Pl, Denver, CO 80223-2316

Today

Publishing Co: St. John Hospital Inc., Marketing & Public Relations, 22101 Moross Rd., Detroit, MI 48236-2148 Tel # (313) 343-4000; Title Tel # (313) 343-7454 Title Fax # (343) 417-2950
General Info: (Formerly Voice)

Tower

Publishing Co: Tarrant County Hospital District, 1500 S Main St, Fort Worth, TX 76104-4917 Tel # (817) 921-3431
Personnel: Editor-William A. Russell
General Info: Monthly
Circulation: Total-1,000

UNMC News   *Association*

Publishing Co: Univ. of Nebraska Medical Ctr., 600 So. 42nd St., Omaha, NE 68198-0001; Title Tel # (402) 559-4353
Personnel: Editor-Barbara Newcomer
Editorial Description: Internal newsletter for medical center faculty, staff, students & volunteers.
General Info: Yr. Est. 1980, Bi-weekly, Trim Size-8½ x 11, Sheetfed press, 8 pages, 2 Color, Newsprint, Saddle-stitched
Subscriptions: Free To Qualified Recipient
Circulation: (100% controlled), Total-4,500

Universal Healthcare
Almanac   *Business*

Publishing Co: R. C. Publications, 10221 North 32nd Street, Suite J-1, Phoenix, AZ 85028-3849 Tel # (602) 995-9435 Fax # (602) 995-9458; Title Tel # (602) 996-2220 Title Fax # (602) 996-2330
Personnel: Editor-Linda Cherner
Editorial Description: Comprehensive resource that provides healthcare statistics through quarterly updates. International, National, State and MSA data trends are covered from 1929-2030.
General Info: Yr. Est. 1985, Quarterly, Trim Size-8½ x 11, Sheetfed press, 475 pages, ISSN: 1069-6725, No Color, Looseleaf
Subscriptions: Indv. $160, Inst. $160, Can. $170, $160/copy

University Hospitals
Lifelines

Publishing Co: Univ. of Wisconsin Hospitals, 1300 University Ave, Madison, WI 53706-1510

University Hospitals News
Review

Publishing Co: Univ. of Wisconsin Hospitals, 1300 University Ave, Madison, WI 53706-1510; Title Tel # (608) 262-6343
Personnel: Editor-Miss Lynn M. Kraeer
General Info: Monthly, Trim Size-8½ x 11, Letrpr. press, 8 pages
Circulation: Total-5,200

Update   *Association*

Publishing Co: United Hospitals, 333 Smith Ave N, St. Paul, MN 55102-2389; Title Tel # (612) 292-5531
Personnel: Editor-Mary Farr
Editorial Description: Hospital news, employee news, gen. health info.
General Info: Yr. Est. 1978, Weekly, Trim Size-8½ x 11, Offset press, 2 pages, No Color, Newsprint
Subscriptions: Free
Circulation: Total-1,300

Vic News

Publishing Co: Royal Victoria Hospital, 687 Pine Ave. W., Montreal, PQ H3A 1A1 Canada; Title Tel # (514) 843-1560
Personnel: Editor-Cecily Lawson-Smith
Editorial Description: Employee publication reporting on operations and activities of the Royal Victoria Hospital.
General Info: (Formerly RVH News), Yr. Est. 1951, Monthly, Offset press, 8 pages, 2 Color, Newsprint, Saddle-stitched
Circulation: Total-3,000
Advertising: Inquire for rates.

Vision   *Business*

Publishing Co: St. Joseph's Hospital, 350 W Thomas Rd, Phoenix, AZ 85013-4496; Title Tel # (602) 285-3053
Editorial Description: Inhouse employee newslettter; news and features.
General Info: (Formerly Tempo), Yr. Est. 1970, Semi-monthly, Trim Size-8½ x 11, Sheetfed press, 8 pages, 2 Color, Newsprint
Circulation: Total-4,000

Vital Signs

Publishing Co: Richmond Heights General Hospital, 27100 Chardon Rd, Richmond Heights, OH 44143-1198; Title Tel # (216) 585-6440
Personnel: Editor-Brenda Lightner
Editorial Description: In-house & community newsletter used as an educational tool.
General Info: Quarterly, Web press, 8 pages, 2 Color, Newsprint
Circulation: Total-20,500

Volunteer

Publishing Co: Hospital Auxiliaries Assn. of Ontario, 150 Ferrand Dr., Don Mills, ON M3C 1H6 Canada
General Info: Yr. Est. 1954, Quarterly, Trim Size-8½ x 11, Sheetfed press, 12 pages, Matte, Saddle-stitched
Circulation: Total-1,500

Volunteer Leader   *Association*   **CPM: $111**

Publishing Co: American Hospital Publishing, Inc., 737 N. Michigan Ave., Ste. 700, Chicago, IL 60611-2431 Tel # (312) 280-6800 Fax # (312) 944-4232; Title Tel # (312) 440-6800 Title Fax # (312) 951-8491
Personnel: Publisher-Daniel Schechter, Editor-Frank Sabatino, Circ. Mgr.-Kate Confer, Production Mgr.-Martin Weitzel, Adv. Dir.-Richard Dudley, Art Dir.-Marcia Kuhr
Editorial Description: Articles for those who participate in or direct activities of hospital volunteers.
General Info: Yr. Est. 1960, Quarterly, Trim Size-7 x 9½, Sheetfed press, 16 pages, ISSN: 0005-1861, 2 Color, Newsprint
Subscriptions: Indv. $8, $3/copy
Circulation: (59% controlled), Total-6,722, Subscriptions-2,138
Advertising: $750.

Whats Up Doc?
See: MEDICINE

Window

Publishing Co: New York Hospital-Cornell Medical Center, 525 E 68th St, New York, NY 10021-4873; Title Tel # (212) 746-5454
Personnel: Editor-Felicia Narvaez
Editorial Description: House organ for the New York Hospital-Cornell Medical Center.
General Info: Yr. Est. 1981, Bi-monthly, Trim Size-11 x 14, 8 pages, No Color
Circulation: Total-13,000
Printing Co: Cosmos Communications, 1105 44th Dr, Long Island City, NY 11101-5107 Tel # (718) 482-1800

Worker's Comp Managed
Care   *Business*

Publishing Co: Capitol Publications, Inc., 1101 King St., Ste. 444, Alexandria, VA 22314-2968; Title Tel # (703) 683-4100 Title Fax # (703) 739-6501
Personnel: Publisher-Cynthia Carter, Editor-Jim Gutman, Circ. Mgr.-Peggy Dwyer, Production Mgr.-Billy Adams, Art Dir.-Linda McDonald, Mktg. Dir.-Mary Lou Probka, Promotion Dir.-Kelly Baptiste
Editorial Description: Reports on new contracts, consolidations & startups that are paving the way for effective workers' comp managed care plans.
General Info: Yr. Est. 1992, Monthly, Trim Size-8½ x 11, Offset press, 12 pages, ISSN: 1066-2669, 2 Color
Subscriptions: Indv. $297, Inst. $297
Acquistions: Publication Bought
List Rental: Actives: $150/M
Printing Co: Capitol Publications, Inc., 1101 King St., Ste. 444, Alexandria, VA 22314-2968 Tel # (703) 683-4100, Fax # (703) 739-6501

Zimmerman Letter, The
See: HEALTH

HOTEL INDUSTRY

ACME Newsletter   *Business, Association*

Publishing Co: Assn. for Convention Marketing Executives, 1819 Peachtree St NE Ste 712, Atlanta, GA 30309-1849 Tel # (404) 355-7900 Fax # (404) 351-3348
Editorial Description: Current news and activities of interest to convention marketing executives.
General Info: Irregular
Subscriptions: Free With Membership

AH & MA Reports   *Association*

Publishing Co: American Hotel & Motel Association, 1201 New York Ave NW Ste 600, Washington, DC 20005-3917 Tel # (202) 289-3157 Fax # (202) 289-3110
Personnel: Editor-Catherine Cochran

Association for Convention
Operations Management
Newsletter   *Business, Association*

Publishing Co: Assn. for Convention Operations Management, 1819 Peachtree St NE Ste 712, Atlanta, GA 30309-1849 Tel # (404) 357-3220; Title Tel # (404) 351-3220 Title Fax # (404) 351-3348
Personnel: Publisher-William Just
Editorial Description: Current news and happenings of interest to convention service/operations managers.
General Info: Yr. Est. 1988, Quarterly, Desktop press, 8 pages, 2 Color, Matte
Subscriptions: Free With Membership
Circulation: Total-800

Atlantic City Action   *Business*

Publishing Co: Atlantic City Action, PO Box 5059, Atlantic City, NJ 08404-5059; Title Tel # (609) 347-1225 Title Fax # (609) 345-4168
Personnel: Publisher, Editor-Al Glasgow
Editorial Description: Statistical analysis of monthly gaming revenues for Atlantic City casino industry, with commentary & projections.
General Info: Yr. Est. 1978, Monthly, Trim Size-8½ x 11, Sheetfed press, 8 pages, No Color, Newsprint
Subscriptions: Indv. $125, For. $150, $13/copy
Acquistions: Publication Bought
Circulation: Total-2,000
Printing Co: Advance Printing, 6599 Delilah Rd, Pleasantville, NJ 08232-9532 Tel # (609) 645-3569, Fax # (609) 383-8737

Bed & Breakfast Shoptalk   *Association*

Publishing Co: American Bed & Breakfast Association, PO Box 1387, Midlothian, VA 23113-8387; Title Tel # (804) 379-2222
Personnel: Editor-Sarah Sonk
General Info: Yr. Est. 1981, Monthly, 2 Color
Subscriptions: Indv. $56
Circulation: Total-3,000

Briefing   *Business*

Publishing Co: Walter Mathews Assocs., Inc., 799 Broadway, New York, NY 10003; Title Tel # (212) 533-9445
Personnel: Editor-Scott Wagendorf
Editorial Description: Covers the hospitality industry.
General Info: Yr. Est. 1976, 10x/yr.
Subscriptions: Indv. $65

CKC Report, The Hotel Technology Newsletter   *Business*

Publishing Co: Chervenak, Keane & Co., 307 E. 44th St., New York, NY 10017-4400; Title Tel # (212) 986-8230 Title Fax # (212) 983-5275
Personnel: Publisher-Larry Chervenak, Mng. Editor-Joyce Christmas, Circ. Mgr.-Joanne Smith, Production Mgr.-J. Christmas
Editorial Description: Hotel technology (information processing, security, telecommunications, energy, fire safety, A/V).
General Info: Yr. Est. 1984, 10x/yr., Trim Size-8½ x 11, Offset press, 20 pages, ISSN: 0890-2135, No Color, Newsprint, Saddle-stitched
Subscriptions: Indv. $180, For. $230, $20/copy

Cameron's Foodservice Marketing Reporter
See: RESTAURANTS & CATERING

Casino Chronicle
See: ENTERTAINMENT

Center News

Publishing Co: Memorial Sloan-Kettering Cancer Ctr., 1275 York Av., Dept. of Public Affairs, New York, NY 10021-6007
General Info: 8 pages

Checking-In   *Business, Association*   **CPM: $227**

Publishing Co: Motel Assn. of Alberta, 10335 178th St., Ste. 202, Edmonton, AB T5S 1R5 Canada; Title Tel # (403) 944-1199 Title Fax # (403) 455-6675
Personnel: Editor-Valerie Sneltzer
Editorial Description: Covers products and services that better the motel industry.
General Info: (Formerly MAA News Bulletin), Yr. Est. 1955, Bi-monthly, Trim Size-8½ x 11, Mimeo press, 8 pages, No Color, Saddle-stitched
Subscriptions: Free With Membership
Circulation: Total-550
Advertising: $125.

Construction & Modernization Report
See: CONSTRUCTION & BUILDING

Dram Shop & Alcohol Reporter
See: LAW

Good Night News   *Business*

Publishing Co: Chalet Suisse Intl. Inc., Chalet Dr., Rt. 101, Wilton, NH 03086; Title Tel # (603) 654-2000
Personnel: Editor-Carl Bahn, Adv. Dir.-Scott Rathke, Art Dir.-Lisa Lynn
Editorial Description: Company business and information important and interesting to the business traveler.
General Info: (Formerly The Grapevine), Yr. Est. 1977, Quarterly, Trim Size-11 x 17, 4 pages, 2 Color
Circulation: (100% controlled), Total-22,000

HRI Buyers Guide   *Business*

Publishing Co: Urner Barry Publications, Inc., PO Box 389, Toms River, NJ 08754-0389; Title Tel # (908) 240-5330 Title Fax # (908) 341-0891
Personnel: Editor-Michael O'Shaughnessy, Production Mgr.-Bill Curro, Adv. Dir.-Lisa Sharkus, Promotion Dir.-Sheila Deane
Editorial Description: Weekly compilation of current food prices for hotels, restaurants, etc.
General Info: (Formerly Restaurant Buyer's Guide), Yr. Est. 1970, Weekly, Trim Size-11 x 17, Sheetfed press, 4 pages, ISSN: 0270-4161, No Color, Newsprint
Subscriptions: Indv. $82, Can. $92, For. $116, $15/copy
Circulation: Total-120

HRI Meat Price Report
See: MEAT & MEAT PROVISIONS

Hospitality Law   *Business*

Publishing Co: Magna Publications, Inc., 611 N Sherman Ave, Madison, WI 53704-4410 Fax # (608) 246-3597; Title Tel # (608) 246-3580 Title Fax # (608) 249-3597
Personnel: Publisher-Richard C. Perkins, Editor-Doris Green, Editorial Dir.-Mary Lou Santovec, Circ. Mgr.-Tom Crawford, Art Dir.-Tami Cook, Mktg. Dir.-Lisa Collins
Editorial Description: A briefing service exclusively for hotel managers who want to prevent lawsuits and keep their properties safe, secure, and profitable.
General Info: Yr. Est. 1986, Monthly, Trim Size-8½ x 11, Offset press, 8 pages, ISSN: 0889-5414, 2 Color, Coated
Subscriptions: Indv. $207, $14/copy
Acquistions: Publication Bought, Publication Sold
Circulation: Total-1,700
Advertising: Inquire for rates. Accepts Inserts.
List Rental: Actives: $125/M, Hotline: $150/M, Expires: $75/M
Printing Co: Quicksilver Press Inc., 2138 Pennsylvania Ave., Madison, WI 53704-4748 Tel # (608) 244-5040

Hospitality World   *Association*

Publishing Co: Intl. Food, Wine & Travel Writers Assn., 1556 Plateau Ave, Los Altos, CA 94024-5320; Title Tel # (619) 320-4271
Personnel: Editor-Will Hansen
General Info: Yr. Est. 1985, Monthly, Trim Size-8½ x 11, Letrpr. press, 10 pages, 2 Color, Newsprint
Subscriptions: Indv. $50
Circulation: (100% controlled), Total-400

Hotel, Resort, Cruise Ship and Spa Report
See: TRAVEL

Hotel Update   *Business*

Publishing Co: Entertainment Publications, Inc., 2125 Butterfield Dr, Troy, MI 48084-3423; Title Tel # (810) 637-8432 Title Fax # (810) 637-2035
Personnel: Editor-Robert McHenry, Production Mgr.-Cindy Detloff
Editorial Description: Trends and opportunities that give hospitality marketing professional information to increase occupancy rates and revenues.
General Info: Yr. Est. 1990, Monthly, Trim Size-8½ x 14, Sheetfed press, 4 pages, Matte
Subscriptions: Indv. $24
Acquistions: Publication Bought, Publication Sold
Circulation: Total-15,000

Industry Update

Publishing Co: Texas Hotel & Motel Assn., 900 Congress Ave Ste 310, Austin, TX 78701-2432; Title Tel # (512) 474-2996 Title Fax # (512) 480-0773
Personnel: Publisher-Melissa Carroll
General Info: Yr. Est. 1988, Bi-weekly, 4 pages

Inn Side Issues   *Association*

Publishing Co: Hotel & Motel Brokers of America, 10220 N. Executive Hills Blvd., Ste. 610, Kansas City, MO 64153-2327 Fax # (816) 981-7071; Title Tel # (816) 891-7070
Personnel: Editor-Robert Kralicek
Editorial Description: For hotel, motel owners and investors.
General Info: (Formerly Motel Topics), Yr. Est. 1984, Quarterly, Trim Size-8½ x 11, 4 pages, 2 Color
Circulation: Total-34,000
Printing Co: Federal Letter, PO Box 411667, Kansas City, MO 64141-1667 Tel # (816) 421-5164

Innkeeping   *Business*

Publishing Co: P.A.I.I., PO Box 90710, Santa Barbara, CA 93190-0710; Title Tel # (805) 569-1853 Title Fax # (805) 682-1016
Personnel: Publisher-JoAnn Bell, Editor-Pat Hardy
Editorial Description: Hotel industry news and developments.
General Info: Yr. Est. 1982, Monthly, 10 pages, 1% ads, No Color, Newsprint
Subscriptions: Indv. $65, Can. $65, For. $75, $5/copy
Circulation: Total-1,500
Advertising: Inquire for rates.

Inside Government

Publishing Co: American Hotel & Motel Association, 1201 New York Ave NW Ste 600, Washington, DC 20005-3917 Tel # (202) 289-3157 Fax # (202) 289-3110; Title Tel # (202) 289-3100
General Info: Yr. Est. 1910, Monthly

International Visitor
See: TRAVEL

MarketShare

Publishing Co: Source Strategies, Inc., PO Box 120055, San Antonio, TX 78212-9255; Title Tel # (210) 734-3434 Title Fax # (210) 735-7970
Personnel: Publisher-Bruce Walker, Editor-Cara Campos, Circ. Mgr.-Rob Strauss
Editorial Description: Tracks market shares of 45 Hotel brands/chains.
General Info: Yr. Est. 1987, Quarterly, Trim Size-8½ x 11, Sheetfed press, 16 pages, 2 Color, Coated, Saddle-stitched
Subscriptions: Indv. $95, $50/copy
Circulation: Total-300

Meeting Planners Alert

Publishing Co: Darrells Graphic & Print, 8554 Loretto Ave, Cotati, CA 94931-4471;
Title Tel # (415) 499-7674
Personnel: Publisher, Editor-Frank Stasiowski, Promotion Dir.-Richard Vendola, Jr.
Editorial Description: Management newsletter for meeting planners and suppliers.
General Info: Yr. Est. 1984, Monthly, Trim Size-8½ x 11, 6 pages, ISSN: 0743-3832, 2 Color
Subscriptions: Indv. $84, $7/copy
Circulation: Total-2,000
Printing Co: Media Forms Group, PO Box 27, Milton, MA 02186-0002

Motel News   *Association*

Publishing Co: Natl. Motel Brokers, 3 37th Ave Ste 5, San Mateo, CA 94403-4457;
Title Tel # (415) 349-1234
Personnel: Editor-Lynda Backman

Quicktrips Travel Letter
See: TRAVEL

Star Service
See: TRAVEL

Technomic Foodservice Digest
See: FOOD

Total Quality in
Hospitality   *Business*

Publishing Co: Magna Publications, Inc., 611 N Sherman Ave, Madison, WI 53704-4410
Tel # (608) 246-3580 Fax # (608) 246-3597
Personnel: Editor-Barbara Mulhern, Promotion Dir.-Lisa Collins
Editorial Description: Designed to help hospitality managers build profits through customer satisfaction.
General Info: Yr. Est. 1993, Monthly, Trim Size-8½ x 11, Offset press, 8 pages, ISSN: 1069-5591, 2 Color
Subscriptions: Indv. $198, $6/copy
Circulation: Total-500
Advertising: Accepts Inserts.
List Rental: Actives: $125/M, Hotline: $150/M, Expires: $75/M

Travel & Tourism Executive Report
See: TRAVEL

Travel Confidential
See: TRAVEL

Travel For Less
See: TRAVEL

Travel Publicity Leads
See: TRAVEL

Travel Scoop Consumer Newsletter
See: TRAVEL

Trends in the Hotel Industry
New York City   *Business*

Publishing Co: PKF Consulting, 420 Lexington Ave., Suite 2400, New York, NY 10170
Tel # (212) 867-8000; Title Tel # (713) 999-5134 Title Fax # (713) 820-6727
Personnel: Editor, Circ. Mgr.-John A. Fox
Editorial Description: Monthly newsletter (statistical) reporting occupancy and rate averages for NYC.
General Info: Yr. Est. 1961, Monthly, Sheetfed press, 6 pages, 2 Color, Coated
Acquistions: Publication Bought
Circulation: Total-700

Uncommon Lodgings

Publishing Co: Uncommon Lodgings, 12124 Midlake Dr, Dallas, TX 75218-1354;
Title Tel # (214) 343-9766
Personnel: Editor-Barry Gardner
Editorial Description: News on unusual lodging accomodations.
General Info: Yr. Est. 1988, 11x/yr.
Subscriptions: Indv. $16

What You Didn't Know   *Business*

Publishing Co: Hyatt Intl. Corp., 200 W. Madison, Chicago, IL 60606-3414;
Title Tel # (312) 750-8332
Personnel: Publisher, Editor-Donna Simmons
Editorial Description: Monthly newsletter containing new information on Hyatt Intl. Hotels.
General Info: Yr. Est. 1988, Monthly, 2 pages, 2 Color, Coated
Acquistions: Publication Bought
Circulation: Total-1,500
List Rental: Rents Lists
Printing Co: Val M. Kelly Mktng. Comm., 402 1/2 N Main St, Wauconda, IL 60084-1707
Tel # (708) 526-7414

HOUSE ORGANS

345

Publishing Co: Bristol-Myers Company, Products Div., 345 Park Ave Fl 9, New York, NY 10154-0004; Title Tel # (212) 546-4000
Personnel: Editor-Mary Evans
General Info: Monthly, Trim Size-7 x 7, Offset press, 12 pages
Circulation: Total-2,000

ABF By-Lines   *Business*

Publishing Co: ABF Freight System, Inc., PO Box 48, Ft. Smith, AR 72902-0048
Tel # (501) 785-8600; Title Tel # (501) 785-8946 Title Fax # (501) 785-6021
Personnel: Editor-Jan Cutsinger
Editorial Description: Information and news for employees.
General Info: Yr. Est. 1953, Monthly, Trim Size-8.5 x 11, Sheetfed press, 12 pages, No Color, Coated, Other
Circulation: (100% controlled), Total-12,000

AHP Vista   *Business*

Publishing Co: American Home Foods Division, American Home Products Corp., 5 Giralda Farms, Madison, NJ 07940-1027
Personnel: Editor-Sharon McCullen
General Info: (Formerly AHF Speed Up), Quarterly

AMAX News

Publishing Co: AMAX, Inc., 9100 E Mineral Cir, Englewood, CO 80112-3401;
Title Tel # (212) 856-4200
Personnel: Editor-Wendy Yang
Editorial Description: Distributed to employees at divisions company wide.
General Info: Bi-monthly, Trim Size-11 x 14, Sheetfed press, 4 pages, 2 Color
Circulation: Total-5,000
Printing Co: Beacon Press, 225 Varick St, New York, NY 10014-4395 Tel # (212) 691-5050

A/OD News   *Business, Association*

Publishing Co: ITT, Aerospace/Optical Div., PO Box 3700, Fort Wayne, IN 46801-3700;
Title Tel # (219) 487-6000
Personnel: Editor-Joan Lynn
Editorial Description: Employee news, awards.
General Info: (Formerly Aero Optic Topics Vision; A/OD Airwaves), Monthly, Trim Size-10½ x 14½, Offset press, 8 pages, 2 Color
Circulation: (100% controlled), Total-2,200

ATSCO News

Publishing Co: American Transfer, 4204 Lindberg Dr, Dallas, TX 75244-2401;
Title Tel # (214) 241-3581
Personnel: Editor-Anthony J. Hess
Editorial Description: General stories with company tie-in.
General Info: Yr. Est. 1959, Trim Size-9½ x 12, 4 pages
Circulation: Total-375

About the First

Publishing Co: First Natl. Bank of Boston, 100 Federal, Boston, MA 02110-1898;
Title Tel # (617) 434-2200
Personnel: Editor-Joyce L. Eldridge, Adv. Dir.-Arthur M. Jones
Editorial Description: Enlightens employees and friends of The First National Bank of Boston about organization's achievements and goals, fosters company pride and identification.
General Info: Yr. Est. 1940, Monthly, Offset press, 8 pages
Circulation: Total-7,000

About US

Publishing Co: United Olympic Life Insurance, 4601 Fairfax Dr., Arlington, VA 22203-1500;
Title Tel # (703) 875-3521 Title Fax # (703) 876-3677
Personnel: Editor-Maria Yannopoulos
Editorial Description: In-house employee publication.
General Info: Yr. Est. 1980, Bi-monthly, Trim Size-8½ x 11, Sheetfed press, 16 pages, 2 Color, Coated
Circulation: Total-2,000

About Your Health

Publishing Co: Equicor, 1801 W End Ave Fl 3, Nashville, TN 37203-2526; Title Tel # (615) 297-9644
Personnel: Publisher-Barrie Atkin
General Info: Yr. Est. 1987, Quarterly, 4 Color

Across Copperweld   *Business*

Publishing Co: Copperweld Corp., 4 Gateway Cemter, Suite 2200, Pittsburgh, PA 15222
Tel # (412) 263-3200 Fax # (412) 263-6995
Personnel: Editor-Kristine M. Blimmel
General Info: (Formerly Regal Reporter), Quarterly

Action

Publishing Co: AC Spark Plug, Rochester Div., 1300 N Dort Hwy, Flint, MI 48506-3956;
Title Tel # (313) 257-3900
Personnel: Editor-E. Garner Windham
Editorial Description: Company publication employee oriented.
General Info: Bi-monthly, Trim Size-8½ x 11, Offset press, 8 pages
Circulation: Total-16,000

Aerospace Facts

Publishing Co: Thiokol Corp., PO Box 524, Brigham City, UT 84302-0524; Title Tel # (801) 863-3511
Personnel: Adv. Dir.-James Brown
Editorial Description: Articles on Thiokol Corporation products and programs designed to enhance the image or the company and market company products.
General Info: Yr. Est. 1965, Quarterly, Trim Size-8½ x 11, Offset press, 16 pages, Color
Subscriptions: Free
Circulation: Total-6,000

Aeroviews

Publishing Co: Cooper Airmotive, 7555 Lemon Ave., P.O. Box 7086, Dallas, TX 75209-0086; Title Tel # (214) 956-5195 Title Fax # (214) 956-3379
Personnel: Publisher, Editor, Adv. Dir.-Evelyn Bowron
General Info: (Formerly Leader), Yr. Est. 1976, Quarterly, Trim Size-11 x 16, Web press, 24 pages, Coated, Saddle-stitched
Circulation: (100% controlled), Total-8,000

Aetna-Izer   *Business*

Publishing Co: Aeltus Managing, Inc., 242 Trumbull St., Hartford, CT 06156 Tel # (203) 273-4368; Title Tel # (203) 273-0123
Personnel: Editor-Mary DiLeo
General Info: Yr. Est. 1967, Monthly
Advertising: Inquire for rates.

AetnaSphere   *Business*

Publishing Co: Aeltus Managing, Inc., 242 Trumbull St., Hartford, CT 06156 Tel # (203) 273-4368
Personnel: Publications Director-Carol Atlas
Editorial Description: Information for and about Aetna employees.

Affiliated Advertising Agencies Intl. News
See: ADVERTISING & MARKETING

Agency News Items

Publishing Co: Equitable Life Assurance Society, 787 Seventh Avenue, New York, NY 10019-1201 Tel # (212) 554-2100; Title Tel # (212) 554-1234
Personnel: Editor-Tom Donnon
Editorial Description: A monthly newspaper for members of the equitable agency force.
General Info: Yr. Est. 1896, Monthly, Trim Size-11 x 17, Letrpr. press, 8 pages, Newsprint, Other
Circulation: Total-16,000

Agents News

Publishing Co: Indiana Farmers Mutual Ins., 10 W. 106th St., P.O. Box 527-, Indianapolis, IN 46206-0527; Title Tel # (317) 846-4211
Personnel: Editor-Susan Andrews
Editorial Description: Industry news; general news with company tie-in. Pictures, 35mm photos.
General Info: Bi-monthly, Trim Size-8½ x 11, 5 pages, 2 Color, Coated
Circulation: (100% controlled), Total-850

Akron Daily Digest   *Business*

Publishing Co: Goodyear Tire & Rubber Co., 1144 E. Market St., Akron, OH 44316-0001 Tel # (330) 796-2121; Title Tel # (330) 796-3236 Title Fax # (330) 796-1817
Editorial Description: Daily newspaper for Goodyear Associates.
General Info: Daily

Alaska Forest Perspective   *Association*

Publishing Co: Alaska Loggers Assn. Inc., 111 Stedman St Ste 200, Ketchikan, AK 99901-6549; Title Tel # (907) 225-6114 Title Fax # (907) 225-5920
Personnel: Editor-Larry Blasing
General Info: Yr. Est. 1963, Monthly, 6 pages
Circulation: Total-900

Aleutian Current

Publishing Co: Aleut Corp. The, 4000 Old Seward Hwy Ste 300, Anchorage, AK 99503-6068; Title Tel # (907) 561-4300
Personnel: Publisher-Julie Jones
Editorial Description: Newsletter for our shareholders regarding our activities and that of the region.
General Info: Yr. Est. 1971, Bi-monthly, Trim Size-8½ x 11, 6 pages
Circulation: Total-2,800

Along the Track   *Association*

Publishing Co: Long Island Rail Road, Jamaica Sta., Jamaica, NY 11432-5597; Title Tel # (718) 990-8228
Personnel: Editor-Don Malone, Art Dir.-Bernadette Clemons
Editorial Description: Long Island Rail Road and its employees, their jobs, interests, sometimes their private lives.
General Info: Yr. Est. 1974, Bi-monthly, Trim Size-10 x 15, Desktop press, 6 pages, 2 Color, Coated
Subscriptions: Free With Membership
Acquistions: Publication Bought
Circulation: (100% controlled), Total-7,000
Printing Co: LIRR Printshop, Jamaica Sta., New York, NY 11435 Tel # (718) 990-8344

Aluminator

Publishing Co: Kaiser Aluminum, PO Box 1031, Baton Rouge, LA 70821-1031; Title Tel # (504) 231-5111
Personnel: Editor-W. H. Moore
General Info: Yr. Est. 1956, Monthly, Trim Size-8½ x 11, 8 pages
Circulation: Total-1,200

American Fletcherline

Publishing Co: American Fletcher Corp., 111 Monument Cir. W., #701, Indianapolis, IN 46277-0001; Title Tel # (317) 321-3005
Personnel: Editor-Joan Sheridan
Editorial Description: Industry news; general stories with company tie-in.
General Info: Yr. Est. 1973, Monthly, Trim Size-8½ x 11, 5 pages, 2 Color
Circulation: Total-3,000

Anchor Line   *Business*

Publishing Co: Anchor Computer, Inc., 1900 New Hwy, Farmingdale, NY 11735-1509; Title Tel # (516) 293-6100
Editorial Description: The newsletter of Anchor Computer Inc.
General Info: Yr. Est. 1982, Quarterly

Apache Arrows

Publishing Co: Apache Corporation, 2000 Post Oak Blvd., Ste. 100, Houston, TX 77056-4400; Title Tel # (303) 837-5097 Title Fax # (303) 837-5688
Personnel: Publisher-Roger Plank, Editor, Production Mgr.-Becky Herlinger
Editorial Description: Company news, industry trends, workplace trends & issues.
General Info: Yr. Est. 1965, Bi-monthly, Trim Size-8½ x 11, Sheetfed press, 8 pages, 2 Color, Newsprint
Acquistions: Publication Bought
Circulation: Total-725
Printing Co: Americopy Printing, 1700 Lincoln, #140, Denver, CO 80203-4519 Tel # (303) 293-9083

Assembler

Publishing Co: General Motors Corp., GM Assembly Div., Lordstown Plant GMC, Lordstown, OH 44482; Title Tel # (216) 824-5000

Associates

Publishing Co: Assocs. Corp. of North America, 250 Carpenter Frwy., Dallas, TX 75222 Tel # (214) 541-4000

Atex Times   *Association*

Publishing Co: Atex, Inc., 15 Crosby Dr, Bedford, MA 01730-1401
Personnel: Editor-Bill Machovec
Editorial Description: For employees of the Atex Co.
General Info: Quarterly

Auto-Gram

Publishing Co: General Motors Corp., GM Assembly Div., 8000 Van Nuys Blvd, Van Nuys, CA 91402-6025; Title Tel # (818) 997-5000
Personnel: Adv. Dir.-Owen O'Conner

Auto Line

Publishing Co: General Motors Corp., GM Assembly Div., 1500 E. Route A, Wentzville, MO 63385-3630; Title Tel # (314) 327-5711
Personnel: Editor-Alfred Moellenhoff

B-G World

Publishing Co: Barber Greene World, 3000 Barber Greene Rd, De Kalb, IL 60115-9590
Personnel: Editor-Tony Finck
Editorial Description: Published for employees at company plants in Aurora, and DeKalb, Ill; Milwaukee, Wisc.; and Don Mills, Ontario.
General Info: Monthly

BFEC Update

Publishing Co: Bendix Field Engineering Corp., 1 Bendix Rd, Columbia, MD 21045-1832; Title Tel # (301) 730-3700
Personnel: Editor-Steve Daley
General Info: Bi-monthly, 4 pages
Circulation: Total-4,500

BMA Skylines

Publishing Co: Business Men's Assurance Co., BMA Tower, Box 419458, Kansas City, MO 64141; Title Tel # (816) 753-8000
Personnel: Editor-Mimi Mann
Editorial Description: Industry and company news and feature stories. Also publish daily news sheet.
General Info: Yr. Est. 1964, Semi-monthly, Trim Size-14 x 20, Offset press, 4 pages
Circulation: Total-1,800

Back Talk

Publishing Co: J.M. Kesslinger and Associates, 2444 Morris Avenue, Union, NJ 07083-5711; Title Tel # (201) 623-0007
Editorial Description: External house organ containing articles on advertising, marketing, PR, etc.
General Info: Yr. Est. 1946, Bi-monthly, 12 pages, 2 Color
Circulation: Total-2,500

BancAccount   *Business, Association*

Publishing Co: Bancohio Corp., 155 E. Broad St., Columbus, OH 43251-0001; Title Tel # (614) 463-8051
Personnel: Editor-Barbara Conley
Editorial Description: Informs employees of business matters.
General Info: Yr. Est. 1974, Monthly, Trim Size-8½ x 11, 16 pages, Color
Circulation: Total-7,500

Bank Lines

Publishing Co: Merchants Bank, 702 Hamilton Mall, Allentown, PA 18101-2419

Bank News

Publishing Co: Northern Trust Co., 50 S. La Salle St., Chicago, IL 60675-0001;
Title Tel # (312) 630-6000
Personnel: Editor-Judith Munson
Editorial Description: House organ with news regarding the organization and its employees.
General Info: Weekly
Circulation: Total-5,500

Bank Notes

Publishing Co: Wilmington Trust Co., Rodney Sq., N., Wilmington, DE 19801-1284;
Title Tel # (302) 651-1000
General Info: Monthly, Trim Size-8½ x 11, Offset press, 9 pages
Circulation: Total-1,000

Bank Notes   *Business*

Publishing Co: AmeriTrust Co., 900 Euclid Ave, Cleveland, OH 44115-1461;
Title Tel # (216) 687-6731
Personnel: Editor-Dennis Casey
Editorial Description: Forum for information of interest to AmeriTrust employees and retirees.
General Info: Monthly, Trim Size-9 x 12, Offset press, 8 pages, No Color, Coated, Saddle-stitched
Circulation: Total-5,500
Printing Co: Carpenter Reserve Printing, 7100 Euclid Ave, Cleveland, OH 44103-4016
Tel # (216) 431-0800

Bank Notes

Publishing Co: Toronto-Dominion Bank, Toronto Dominion Center, Box 1, Toronto, ON M5K 1A2
Canada; Title Tel # (416) 866-5696
Personnel: Editor-Gerry Chiasson
Editorial Description: General items with company tie-in.
General Info: Yr. Est. 1922, Monthly, Sheetfed press, 8 pages, 2 Color, Coated
Circulation: (100% controlled), Total-30,000
Printing Co: Arthurs Jones Lithographing, 1060 Tristar Dr., Mississauga, ON L5T 1H9 Canada
Tel # (416) 564-3333

Bank One

Publishing Co: Bank of New York, 1 Wall St Fl 13, New York, NY 10005-2501;
Title Tel # (212) 495-1784
Personnel: Editor-Joseph J. Pera
General Info: Yr. Est. 1923, Monthly, Trim Size-11 x 15½, Offset press, 10 pages
Circulation: Total-8,000

Bank Wire

Publishing Co: First Interstate Bank, PO Box 160, Seattle, WA 98111-0160;
Title Tel # (206) 292-3111
General Info: (Formerly Washingtonian)

Banker's Hours

Publishing Co: Sponsor-Texas Commerce Bancshares, Inc., Texas Commerce Bank, PO Box 2558,
Houston, TX 77252-8050 Fax # (713) 216-5486; Title Tel # (713) 236-5009
Editorial Description: Newsletter for the employees of the statewide Texas Commerce Bancshares.
General Info: Yr. Est. 1968, Monthly, Trim Size-8½ x 11, Offset press, 4 pages, No Color, Newsprint,
Saddle-stitched
Circulation: (100% controlled), Total-10,000
Printing Co: Hearn Lithographics, 600 Mcgowen St, Houston, TX 77006-2326 Tel # (713) 528-5391

Bankers Life

Publishing Co: Bankers Life, 4444 W Lawrence Ave, Chicago, IL 60630-2546;
Title Tel # (312) 777-7000
Personnel: Editor-Wilbert Foley, Jr.
General Info: Monthly, Trim Size-7⅞ x 9¾, Offset press, 32 pages
Circulation: Total-6,000

Bankers Notes   *Association*

Publishing Co: United Olympic Life Insurance, 4601 Fairfax Dr., Arlington, VA 22203-1500;
Title Tel # (703) 875-3521 Title Fax # (703) 876-3677
Personnel: Editor-Maria Yannopoulos
Editorial Description: Marketing publication for field force.
General Info: Bi-monthly, Trim Size-8½ x 11, Sheetfed press, 8 pages, Color, Coated
Acquistions: Publication Bought
Circulation: (100% controlled), Total-8,000

Banknotes   *Business*

Publishing Co: Bank of Oklahoma, PO Box 2300, Tulsa, OK 74192 Fax # (918) 588-6853;
Title Tel # (918) 588-6348
Personnel: Editor-Russ Florence
Editorial Description: Contains financial, human interest & employee information for & about
employees of the Bank of Oklahoma & its subsidiaries.
General Info: (Formerly Pace Phlash; Express), Yr. Est. 1984, Weekly, Trim Size-8½ x 11, Mimeo
press, 6 pages, No Color
Circulation: Total-1,500

Baystater

Publishing Co: NYNEX, 125 High St Ste 30, Boston, MA 02110-2704 Tel # (617) 743-9800;
Title Tel # (617) 743-3530
Personnel: Editor-Susana Thompson
General Info: Trim Size-8½ x 11

Baytown Briefs   *Business*

Publishing Co: Sponsor-Exxon Baytown Refinery Exxon U.S.A., Exxon Co., U.S.A., 800 Bell St.,
Houston, TX 77002 Tel # (713) 656-3636; Title Tel # (713) 425-3332
Personnel: Editor-G.R. Pfennig
Editorial Description: Industry news.
General Info: Yr. Est. 1953, Bi-monthly, Desktop press, 8 pages, Saddle-stitched
Acquistions: Publication Bought
Circulation: Total-6,700
Printing Co: Gulf Printing, 2210 W Dallas St, Houston, TX 77019-4397 Tel # (713) 529-4201

Beacon

Publishing Co: General Motors Corp., GM Assembly Div.-Fairfax GMC, Kansas City, KS 66115;
Title Tel # (913) 345-2211

Beacon Bulletin

Publishing Co: Chevrolet-Pontiac-Canada Group, 199 Beekman Ave, North Tarrytown, NY
10591-2403; Title Tel # (914) 524-1000 Title Fax # (914) 524-1630
Personnel: Editor-Shirley Crate, Publisher, Circ. Mgr.-James Kovacs, Production Mgr.-Albert Lopez,
Adv. Dir.-Rita Retoske, Art Dir.-Tom Lorenz, Promotion Dir.-Paul O'Sullivan
Editorial Description: Published for & about North Tarrytown employees. Story ideas & suggestions
are welcomed from employees & their families at any time.
General Info: (Formerly Hudson Viewer), Yr. Est. 1977, Monthly, Letrpr. press, 10 pages, 2 Color,
Newsprint
Circulation: (100% controlled), Total-4,000
Printing Co: Mackey Printers, 104 Central Ave, Tarrytown, NY 10591-3319

Beam

Publishing Co: Bristol-Myers Company, Products Div., 345 Park Ave Fl 9, New York, NY
10154-0004; Title Tel # (212) 644-2100
Personnel: Editor-J. Henderson
General Info: Monthly, Trim Size-8½ x 11, Offset press, 18 pages
Circulation: Total-4,500

Bellringer

Publishing Co: State Farm Mutual Auto Insurance Co., 1500 W. Highway 36, Saint Paul, MN
55161-0001; Title Tel # (612) 631-4246
Personnel: Editor-Carolyn Bailey-Sudduth
General Info: Monthly, Trim Size-8½ x 11, 28 pages
Circulation: Total-1,200

Benedictine Monks of
Florida   *Association*

Publishing Co: Order of St. Benedict of Florida, St. Leo Abbey, St. Leo, FL 33574-9999;
Title Tel # (904) 588-2881
Editorial Description: To communicate all events at the Monastery.
General Info: (Formerly Florida Benedictines), Yr. Est. 1975, Quarterly, 8 pages, 2 Color
Circulation: Total-4,000

Benenet Bulletin

Publishing Co: Johnson & Higgins, 125 Broad St, New York, NY 10004-2424
General Info: Weekly

Berkshire Life Newsletter   *Business*

Publishing Co: Berkshire Life Insurance Co., 700 South St, Pittsfield, MA 01201-8212;
Title Tel # (413) 499-4321
Personnel: Editor-Susan LeBourdais, Contrib. Ed.-Elizabeth Maynard, Art Dir.-John Broderick
Editorial Description: Employee news and information.
General Info: Yr. Est. 1957, Bi-weekly, Trim Size-8½ x 11, Sheetfed press, 4 pages, 2 Color, Matte
Subscriptions: Free To Qualified Recipient
Circulation: (82% controlled), Total-850
Printing Co: John C. Otto Co., PO Box 367, East Longmeadow, MA 01028-0367
Tel # (413) 525-4131

Best Foods Marketing
News

Publishing Co: CPC Intl. Inc., Intl. Plaza, Englewood Cliffs, NJ 07632; Title Tel # (201) 894-4000
Personnel: Editor-James Burke
General Info: Monthly, Trim Size-9½ x 12½, Offset press, 10 pages

Between Calls

Publishing Co: Dover Corp., Norris-O'Bannon Div., Box 2070, Tulsa, OK 74101-2070
Personnel: Editor-Pat Dillard
Editorial Description: For the amusement of our customers between calls from our sales
representatives.
General Info: Yr. Est. 1924, Monthly
Circulation: Total-11,000

Big Idea

Publishing Co: United Parcel Service, 643 W 43rd St, New York, NY 10036-1917;
Title Tel # (212) 695-7500
Personnel: Editor-Maurice A. Reece
General Info: Monthly, Trim Size-8½ x 11, Offset press, 8 pages
Circulation: Total-40,000

Blower Outlet

Publishing Co: Dresser Industries, Inc., 900 W Mount St, Connersville, IN 47331-1675;
Title Tel # (317) 827-9200
Personnel: Editor-Connie Chandler
General Info: Yr. Est. 1946, Quarterly, Trim Size-8½ x 11, Sheetfed press, 12 pages, 2 Color,
Coated
Circulation: Total-1,200
Printing Co: Exponent Publishers, Inc., 50 Paul R Foulke Pky, Hagerstown, IN 47346-1626
Tel # (317) 489-4588

Blue Chip Business   *Business*

Publishing Co: CM Alliance, 140 Garden St, Hartford, CT 06154-0001; Title Tel # (203) 727-6500
Title Fax # (203) 727-6939
Personnel: Editor-Rick Kontur
Editorial Description: Information & sales support for insurance company agents & field office
personnel.
General Info: Yr. Est. 1922, Bi-weekly, Trim Size-11 x 12, Letrpr. press, 8 pages, No Color
Circulation: (100% controlled), Total-5,000

Blue Streak Release   *Business, Association*

Publishing Co: W. H. Brady Co., 727 W Glendale Ave, Milwaukee, WI 53209-6509;
Title Tel # (414) 332-8100
Personnel: Editor-Laurie Bernardy
Editorial Description: Internal and external business news, features.
General Info: Yr. Est. 1955, Bi-monthly, Trim Size-11 x 17, Sheetfed press, 20 pages, 2 Color,
Coated, Saddle-stitched
Circulation: (100% controlled), Total-3,000
Printing Co: Account Manager: Mike Canfield; Universal, Sheboygan, WI

Book Authors Newsletter

Publishing Co: F & W Publications, 1507 Dana Ave., Cincinnati, OH 45207-1056;
Title Tel # (513) 531-2222 Title Fax # (513) 531-1843
Personnel: Publisher, Editor-Kirk Polking, Art Dir.-Carol Buchanan
Editorial Description: Writing and marketing tips for novel and nonfiction book writers who are
students in our courses.
General Info: Yr. Est. 1988, Semi-annually, Trim Size-8½ x 11, Sheetfed press, 6 pages, Newsprint
Circulation: Total-3,000

Brach Family News

Publishing Co: E.J. Brach, 4656 W Kinzie St, Chicago, IL 60644-2041; Title Tel # (312) 626-1200
Personnel: Editor-William W. Gould
General Info: Monthly, Trim Size-11 x 14, Letrpr. press, 5 pages
Circulation: Total-4,000

Braintree Express   *Business*

Publishing Co: Armstrong World Industries, Employee Communications, Box 3001, Lancaster, PA
17604 Tel # (717) 397-0611; Title Tel # (617) 843-3950
Personnel: Publisher-John Graham, Editor-Jack Lane
Editorial Description: Employee newsletter for Armstrong World Industries. Includes coverage of
company events, promotions, industry news.
General Info: Yr. Est. 1985, Weekly, Trim Size-8½ x 11, Desktop press, 2 pages, 2 Color, Matte
Circulation: Total-900
Printing Co: Ink Spot, The, 40 Oval Rd, Quincy, MA 02170-3813 Tel # (617) 273-7605,
Fax # (617) 471-8810

Breadwinner

Publishing Co: Arnold Bakers Inc., Hamilton Ave., Greenwich, CT 06830
Personnel: Editor-Robert F. Merritt
General Info: Bi-monthly, Trim Size-8½ x 11, Letrpr. press, 5 pages
Circulation: Total-1,250

Breezes   *Business*

Publishing Co: Fedl. Reserve Bank of Boston, PO Box 2076, Boston, MA 02106-2076;
Title Tel # (617) 973-3488
Personnel: Editor-Brenda Salyer
General Info: Monthly, Trim Size-8½ x 11, Offset press, 8 pages, 2 Color
Circulation: (100% controlled), Total-1,600

Bridge

Publishing Co: E.I. du Pont de Nemours, 10007 Market Street, Wilmington, DE 19898-0001;
Title Tel # (302) 774-1000

Bright Side

Publishing Co: Campus Crusade for Christ, 100 Sunport Ln., Ste 1600, Orlando, FL 32809-7871
Fax # (407) 826-2374; Title Tel # (407) 826-2390
Personnel: Editor-Judy Nelson
Editorial Description: News of Campus Crusade.
General Info: Yr. Est. 1967, Monthly, Offset press, 4 pages, 2 Color, Newsprint, Other
Subscriptions: Free With Membership
Circulation: (100% controlled), Total-6,750, Readership-6,750

Bristol-Myers New York

Publishing Co: Bristol-Myers Company, Products Div., 345 Park Ave Fl 9, New York, NY
10154-0004
Personnel: Editor-Sandra Washburn
General Info: Yr. Est. 1975, Monthly, Trim Size-9 x 12, 8 pages
Circulation: Total-2,000

British Columbia Ferries, Fleet Bulletin

Publishing Co: British Columbia Ministry of Transportation, 940 Blanshard St., Victoria, BC V8W 3E6
Canada; Title Tel # (604) 381-1401
General Info: Yr. Est. 1970, Bi-monthly

Brown Forum   *Association*

Publishing Co: Brown-Forman, Corp., 850 Dixie Hwy, Louisville, KY 40210-1038
Personnel: Editor-Alice McKinley
Editorial Description: For active & retired employees.
General Info: Quarterly, Trim Size-8½ x 11, Offset press, 16 pages
Circulation: Total-2,500

Bru-It

Publishing Co: Lone Star Bring Co., 600 Lone Star Blvd, San Antonio, TX 78204-1707
Personnel: Editor-Betty Wilson
General Info: Yr. Est. 1942, Bi-monthly

Brush Up

Publishing Co: Oral-B, 1 Lagoon Dr., Redwood City, CA 94065-1562; Title Tel # (415) 598-5000
Personnel: Editor-Paula Gordon
General Info: Yr. Est. 1986, Quarterly

Bucket

Publishing Co: KFC, PO Box 32070, Louisville, KY 40232-2070 Tel # (502) 456-8300

Bulldozer

Publishing Co: Finning Ltd., 555 Great Northern Way, Vancouver, BC V5T 1E2 Canada;
Title Tel # (604) 872-4444 Title Fax # (604) 691-6286
Personnel: Editor-Blair Nikiforuk
Editorial Description: General stories with company tie-in.
General Info: Yr. Est. 1953, Bi-monthly, Trim Size-8½ x 11, 8 pages, Coated
Acquistions: Publication Bought
Circulation: Total-3,000

Bulletin

Publishing Co: Pacific Power, 920 SW 6th Ave, Portland, OR 97204-1297
Personnel: Editor-Darby Collins
General Info: Monthly, Trim Size-11 x 17, Offset press, 8 pages, 2 Color, Coated
Circulation: Total-15,000

Bulletin

Publishing Co: Wisconsin Bell, Inc., 722 N Broadway, Milwaukee, WI 53202-4303;
Title Tel # (414) 678-2372 Title Fax # (414) 678-2756
Personnel: Editor-Lorna Sorenson
Editorial Description: Weekly update publication for active employees of Wisconsin Bell.
General Info: Weekly
Circulation: Total-7,000

Business Briefly

Publishing Co: Goodyear Canada, Inc., 10 Four Seasons Pl., Islington, ON M9B 6G2 Canada;
Title Tel # (416) 626-4611
Personnel: Editor-Erin Hayward
Editorial Description: For all Goodyear Canada employees. Subjects, production, product sales,
corporate, general interest, personal achievements of employees on & off the job.
General Info: Yr. Est. 1910, Monthly, Trim Size-10½ x 13, Sheetfed press, 6 pages, No Color,
Coated
Subscriptions: Free
Circulation: (100% controlled), Total-5,000

BusinessLine

Publishing Co: John Hancock Mutual Life Ins. Co., 200 Berkeley St., Boston, MA 02116-5023;
Title Tel # (617) 572-6407 Title Fax # (617) 572-6451
Personnel: Editor-Jack Conway, Art Dir.-Juliana Chan
Editorial Description: Published for all associates of John Hancock & its subsidary operations as a
periodic record of the business progress of the company & the insurance & financial services
industries in general.
General Info: Yr. Est. 1985, Bi-weekly, Sheetfed press, 6 pages, 4 Color, Coated
Circulation: Total-24,000
Printing Co: Nimrod Press, 170 Brookline Ave, Boston, MA 02215-3907 Tel # (617) 437-7900,
Fax # (617) 262-5228

Busy Signal

Publishing Co: Northern Telecom Ltd., 150 Montreal Toronto Blvd., Lachine, PQ H8S 1B6 Canada
Tel # (514) 634-3511

Butler Builder

Publishing Co: Butler Mfg. Co., 7400 E 13th St, Kansas City, MO 64126-2339
General Info: Monthly

Buzzer   *Consumer*

Publishing Co: BC Transit, 1200 W. 73rd Ave., #400, Vancouver, BC V6P 6M2 Canada; Title Tel # (604) 264-5000
Personnel: Publisher-George Stroppa, Circ. Mgr.-Jacki Ballerone, Art Dir.-Theresa Magee
Editorial Description: Covers information on bus schedules, routes, community events, transit topics.
General Info: Yr. Est. 1916, Bi-weekly, Trim Size-$3^7/_8$ x $7^1/_4$, Sheetfed press, 4 pages, 2 Color
Circulation: (100% controlled), Total-80,000

Byline

Publishing Co: Rockford Newspapers Inc., 99 E State St, Rockford, IL 61104-1004 Tel # (815) 987-1200 Fax # (815) 962-6578; Title Tel # (815) 987-1322
Editorial Description: Internal company newsletter covering personnel and company information.
General Info: (Formerly News Tower News Letter), Monthly, Offset press, 5 pages
Circulation: Total-500

C. Brewer Today   *Business*

Publishing Co: C. Brewer, PO Box 1826, Honolulu, HI 96805-1826; Title Tel # (808) 536-4461
Personnel: Editor-Kathy Oshiro, Circ. Mgr.-Nicole Buzynski
Editorial Description: Company & industry news; some general items with company tie-in.
General Info: Yr. Est. 1976, Bi-monthly, Trim Size-$11^1/_4$ x 14, 4 pages, No Color, Coated
Circulation: Total-2,000

CCLA News Notes

Publishing Co: Canadian Civil Liberties Assn., 229 Yonge St., #403, Toronto, ON M5B 1N9 Canada
General Info: Quarterly
Printing Co: Speed Copy, 209 Avenue Road, Toronto, ON M5R 2J3 Canada Tel # (416) 922-4122

CPL Hot Line   *Business*

Publishing Co: Central Power & Light Co., 120 N Chaparral St # 2121, Corpus Christi, TX 78401-2802; Title Tel # (512) 881-5500
Personnel: Editor-Andy Hines, Adv. Dir.-Patricia Covington, Art Dir.-Al Hesse
Editorial Description: Quick-breaking news that affects the company.
General Info: Yr. Est. 1960, Bi-weekly, Trim Size-$8^1/_2$ x 11, Offset press, 2 pages, Color
Circulation: (100% controlled), Total-3,100

CS News

Publishing Co: AG Communication Systems, PO Box 52179, Phoenix, AZ 85072-2179; Title Tel # (602) 581-4271 Title Fax # (602) 581-4282
Personnel: Editor-Barbara Walker
Editorial Description: Industry & company news for employees throughout United States.
General Info: Monthly, Trim Size-11 x $15^1/_2$, Letrpr. press, 12 pages, No Color, Coated
Circulation: Total-6,000

Camcar Camera

Publishing Co: Camcar Screw Mfg. Co., 600 18th Ave, Rockford, IL 61104-5159; Title Tel # (815) 961-5000
Personnel: Editor-Dean Lamb
Editorial Description: Family news, new equipment, activities and sports at Camcar.
General Info: Yr. Est. 1951, Annually, Trim Size-$8^1/_2$ x 11, 16 pages, 4 Color, Coated, Saddle-stitched
Circulation: (100% controlled), Total-2,400

Campbell's News, Front Page

Publishing Co: Campbell Soup Co., 375 Memorial Ave., Camden, NJ 08103; Title Tel # (609) 342-4800

Can-A-Gram

Publishing Co: Sherwin-Williams Co., Container Plant, Carolina & Myron Sts., Hubbard, OH 44425
Personnel: Editor-R. B. Stratton
Editorial Description: General stories with company tie-in.
General Info: Bi-monthly, Trim Size-$8^1/_2$ x 11, 4 pages
Circulation: Total-275

Can Line

Publishing Co: Ball Packing Group, PO Box 589, Broomfield, CO 80038-0589; Title Tel # (303) 469-5511
Personnel: Editor-Harold Sohn
General Info: (Formerly Ball Metal Container Grp.), Yr. Est. 1969, Monthly, Trim Size-11 x 14, 4 pages
Circulation: Total-1,000

Canadian Pension Conference, Newsletter

Publishing Co: Canadian Pension Conference, 800 Rene Levesque W., #1100, Montreal, PQ H3B 1X9 Canada; Title Tel # (514) 866-3687
Personnel: Editor-Gilles Trigane
General Info: (Formerly Ad Valorem), Yr. Est. 1984, Quarterly, 8 pages
Circulation: Total-1,200

Canadian Society for Colour, Newsletter

Publishing Co: Canadian Society for Colour, C/O Dr. T. Nilsson, Prince Edward Isl., Charlottetown, PE C1A 4P3 Canada; Title Tel # (902) 566-0489
Personnel: Editor-Dr. T. Nilsson
Editorial Description: Anything pertaining to color: standards, vision, physiology, physics, lighting, architecture, consumer, theater, printing, paints, fabrics, & art. Professional papers, letters, book reviews, news, proceedings of Canadian & Intl. Assns.
General Info: Yr. Est. 1973, Quarterly, Trim Size-$8^1/_2$ x 11, Sheetfed press, 12 pages, ISSN: 0317-1825, Newsprint, Saddle-stitched
Subscriptions: Indv. $25
Circulation: Total-250
Advertising: Inquire for rates. Accepts Inserts.
Printing Co: Clarke Printing, 220 Kent St., Charlottetown, PE C1A 1P2 Canada Tel # (902) 892-4557

Capsule   *Association*

Publishing Co: Pfizer Inc., Eastern Pt. Rd., Groton, CT 06340 Parent Co.-Pfizer Inc., New York; Title Tel # (203) 441-3144 Title Fax # (203) 441-4735
Personnel: Editor-John P. Stratton
Editorial Description: Industry news, general stories with or without company tie-in.
General Info: Yr. Est. 1955, Monthly, Trim Size-$8^1/_2$ x 11, Offset press, 12 pages, 2 Color
Subscriptions: Free To Qualified Recipient
Circulation: Total-4,800, Readership-8,000
Advertising: Inquire for rates.

Capsule

Publishing Co: Grossmont District Hospital, PO Box 158, La Mesa, CA 91944-0158; Title Tel # (619) 589-4151
Personnel: Editor-Kay Simpson
General Info: Yr. Est. 1956, Monthly, Trim Size-$8^1/_2$ x 11, Sheetfed press, 6 pages, No Color, Newsprint
Acquistions: Publication Bought
Circulation: Total-4,000

Carta del Presidente

Publishing Co: Fundacion Educativa Ana G. Mendey, Apartado AE, Rio Piedras, PR 00928
Editorial Description: Communications flowing from top management on matter pertaining to administrative policies, activities, planning.
General Info: Monthly, Trim Size-$8^1/_2$ x 11
Circulation: Total-800

Celo Education Notes
See: EDUCATION

Central Hudson Newsletter   *Business*

Publishing Co: Central Hudson Gas & Electric Corp., 284 South Ave, Poughkeepsie, NY 12601-4838; Title Tel # (914) 486-5858 Title Fax # (914) 486-5544
Personnel: Editor-Kim Knox
Editorial Description: A weekly newsletter for employees & retirees of Central Hudson Gas & Elec. Corp. The newsletter contains news stories features, profiles & regular columns relating to company & utility news.
General Info: (Formerly Report to Employees), Yr. Est. 1980, Weekly, Trim Size-$8^1/_2$ x 11, 8 pages, 2 Color, Coated
Subscriptions: Free To Qualified Recipient
Circulation: (100% controlled), Total-2,000, Readership-2,000

Cergram

Publishing Co: Certified Grocers of Calif., Ltd., 2601 S Eastern Ave, Los Angeles, CA 90040-1401; Title Tel # (213) 723-7476
Personnel: Editor-Shelley Machock
Editorial Description: Employee newsletter.
General Info: Monthly, Trim Size-$8^1/_2$ x 11, Sheetfed press, 6 pages, No Color, Coated
Circulation: Total-3,000

Channel
See: LIBRARY

Chapter News

Publishing Co: American Natl. Red Cross, Rocky Mountain Div., 444 Sherman St, Denver, CO 80203-3521; Title Tel # (303) 399-0550

Checkerlinks

Publishing Co: Ralston Purina Co., Checkerboard Square, Saint Louis, MO 63164-0001 Tel # (314) 982-1000
Personnel: Editor-Alyce Menkhus
General Info: Bi-monthly
Circulation: Total-10,000

Chemical Chronicle

Publishing Co: Chemical Bank, 270 Park Avenue, New York, NY 10017; Title Tel # (212) 770-1234
Personnel: Editor-Geraldine Kitay
General Info: Monthly, Trim Size-11 x $14^1/_2$, Offset press, 10 pages
Circulation: Total-13,500

Chemscope

Publishing Co: Chemtech Industries, Inc., PO Box 31000, Saint Louis, MO 63131-1000
Tel # (314) 530-1082
Personnel: Editor-L. Law
General Info: Yr. Est. 1960, Monthly, Trim Size-8½ x 11

Chevy Communicator

Publishing Co: General Motors Corp., Chevrolet-Detroit Assembly, 601 Piquette St, Detroit, MI 48202-3551; Title Tel # (313) 974-3553
Personnel: Editor-Jacqueline Hall

Chez BBL

Publishing Co: Beauchemin-Beaton-LaPointe, Inc., 2045 Stanley St., Montreal, PQ H3A 2V4 Canada; Title Tel # (514) 987-9844
Personnel: Editor-Denis Lajeunesse
Editorial Description: Informs employees of company objectives, projects, future expansion plans; social events; employee achievements.
General Info: Quarterly, Trim Size-8½ x 11, 4 pages
Circulation: Total-200

Chocolate Shake   *Consumer*

Publishing Co: World's Finest Chocolate, Inc., 4801 S Lawndale Ave, Chicago, IL 60632-3018; Title Tel # (312) 847-4600 Title Fax # (312) 847-4006
Personnel: Editor, Production Mgr.-Betty Lazo, Adv. Dir., Art Dir.-Michael Koss
Editorial Description: All subjects of general public interest from vacation guidelines to consumer benefits & social security-hunting, safety etc.
General Info: Yr. Est. 1960, Bi-weekly, Trim Size-8½ x 11, Sheetfed press, 4 pages, 2 Color, Coated
Acquistions: Publication Bought
Circulation: (100% controlled), Total-500
Printing Co: Kinney Printing, 3375 W Columbus Ave, Chicago, IL 60652-2594 Tel # (312) 436-7600

City Holler

Publishing Co: City of Boston, Office of Communications, 1 City Hall Plaza, New City Ha, Boston, MA 02201-0001
Editorial Description: Features & public service material concerning employees & services offered by many city agencies.
General Info: Yr. Est. 1972, Bi-monthly, Trim Size-10¾ x 15, 8 pages
Circulation: Total-9,000

Civil Service Sentinel

Publishing Co: Civil Service Retired Employees Assn., 267 Broadway, New York, NY 10007-2387; Title Tel # (212) 233-7541
Personnel: Publisher-Herbert Bauch, Editor-Kjell Kjellberg
Editorial Description: News of special interest to CSREA members.
General Info: Yr. Est. 1967, 10x/yr.

Clairol Highlights

Publishing Co: Clairol, Inc., Bristol-Myers Squibb, 345 Park Ave., New York, NY 10154-0192; Title Tel # (212) 546-5000
Personnel: Editor-Connie Kain
Editorial Description: Company news; aims to inform employees of company & industry news, to communicate management viewpoint to employees.
General Info: Yr. Est. 1958, Bi-monthly, Trim Size-10¼ x 13½, Web press, 12 pages, 4 Color, Coated, Saddle-stitched
Circulation: Total-3,600

Coachman

Publishing Co: General Motors Corp., Fisher Body Public Relations, 3007 Van Dyke Avenue, Warren, MI 48090 Fax # (313) 649-3614; Title Tel # (301) 762-9500

Coffee Break

Publishing Co: North Coast Advertising, 1601 Cottage St, Ashland, OH 44805-1235 Parent Co.-Heritage Press, Ashland; Title Tel # (419) 281-5554 Title Fax # (419) 289-9605
Personnel: Editor-Dick Tettlebach, Circ. Mgr., Production Mgr., Adv. Dir.-Cindi Kauffman, Publisher, Art Dir., Promotion Dir.-Bill Hooker
Editorial Description: A personalized corporate newsletter.
General Info: Yr. Est. 1986, Monthly, Trim Size-8½ x 11, 4 pages, 2 Color, Matte
Subscriptions: Indv. $250
Acquistions: Publication Bought
Printing Co: Heritage Press, 1601 Cottage St, Ashland, OH 44805-1235 Tel # (419) 289-9209

Colleague

Publishing Co: Grinnell Mutual Reinsurance Co., Int. 80 at Hwy. 146, Grinnell, IA 50112; Title Tel # (515) 236-6121
Personnel: Editor-Marilyn Deppe
Editorial Description: To disseminate information pertaining to company and staff; to educate, stimulate & inform.
General Info: Yr. Est. 1960, 13x/yr., Trim Size-8½ x 11, Offset press, 6 pages, 2 Color
Circulation: (100% controlled), Total-900

Columbia Hi-Lites

Publishing Co: Columbia Savings, 1740 Broadway, Denver, CO 80274-0001 Tel # (303) 831-9600

Columns   *Business, Association*

Publishing Co: Northwestern Natl. Life Ins. Co., 20 Washington Ave S, Minneapolis, MN 55401-1908; Title Tel # (612) 372-5432 Title Fax # (612) 342-3002
Personnel: Editor-Ruth Weber
Editorial Description: An employee publication providing information onthe company's direction, its divisions, human resources issues, and industry related topics.
General Info: (Formerly Lifelines), Yr. Est. 1947, Bi-monthly, Sheetfed press, 8 pages, No Color, Matte
Circulation: Total-3,000
Printing Co: Coremar, 7041 Boone Ave N, Minneapolis, MN 55428-1504

Comments

Publishing Co: FMC Corp., Agricultural Machinery Div., 103 E. Maple St., Hoopeston, IL 60942-1627; Title Tel # (501) 935-1970
Personnel: Editor-Marion Meredith
Editorial Description: Employee news.
General Info: Yr. Est. 1972, Bi-monthly, Trim Size-8½ x 11
Circulation: Total-800

Communicaid

Publishing Co: Allied Group Insurance Svcs., Box 974, 701 Fifth Ave., Des Moines, IA 50304-0974; Title Tel # (515) 280-4211
Personnel: Editor-Morel Stientjes
General Info: Monthly, Trim Size-11 x 17, Offset press, 6 pages
Circulation: Total-800

Communicator

Publishing Co: Hallicrafters Company, Northrop Corp., 600 Hicks Rd, Rolling Meadows, IL 60008-1015
Personnel: Editor-Robert P. Budler
General Info: Weekly, Trim Size-8½ x 11, Offset press, 3 pages
Circulation: Total-1,000

Communicator

Publishing Co: COM/Energy Services Co., PO Box 9150, Cambridge, MA 02139-9150; Title Tel # (617) 864-3100
Personnel: Publisher-Sal Miccichie, Editor-Sal Micciche
Editorial Description: Business & Human interest.
General Info: (Formerly Negea News), Yr. Est. 1950, Monthly, Trim Size-11¼ x 17, Offset press, 8 pages, 2 Color, Coated
Circulation: Total-3,800

Communicator

Publishing Co: State Chemical Mfg. Co., 3100 Hamilton Ave., Cleveland, OH 44114-3701; Title Tel # (216) 861-7114 Title Fax # (216) 861-5213
Personnel: Editor-Leonard Bergenstein
Editorial Description: Company oriented news.
General Info: Yr. Est. 1960, Weekly, Trim Size-8½ x 11
Circulation: Total-450

Communicator

Publishing Co: Nashua Corp., 44 Franklin St, Nashua, NH 03060-2686; Title Tel # (603) 880-2443
Editorial Description: Nashua Corporation Headquarters Facility newsletter.
General Info: Yr. Est. 1981, Weekly, Trim Size-8½ x 11, Mimeo press, 8 pages, No Color
Circulation: Total-2,000

Communicator   *Association*

Publishing Co: American Institute of Parliamentarians, 10535 Metropolitan Ave, Kensington, MD 20895-2627; Title Tel # (219) 422-3680
Personnel: Editor-Cleon Babcock, Circ. Mgr.-Bertha Lorenz
Editorial Description: News of activities in AIP and the Parlimentary World.
General Info: Yr. Est. 1978, Quarterly, Trim Size-8½ x 11, Letrpr. press, 8 pages, Color, Newsprint
Acquistions: Publication Bought
Circulation: Total-1,400
Printing Co: Advantage Printing and Packaging, 256 E Pettit Ave, Fort Wayne, IN 46806-3052 Tel # (219) 745-3028

Communique-United Telephone
See: TELECOMMUNICATIONS

Conductor   *Business*

Publishing Co: Diversey Corp., 1 Roberts Beck Parkway, Mississauga, ON L4Z 3S9 Canada; Title Tel # (905) 897-5600
General Info: (Formerly Diversey Doings), Quarterly, Trim Size-8½ x 11, Offset press, 12 pages
Circulation: Total-800

Connecticut Mutual Life
News   *Business*

Publishing Co: CM Alliance, 140 Garden St, Hartford, CT 06154-0001; Title Tel # (203) 727-6500
Personnel: Editor-David Conrad
Editorial Description: Industry news; general stories with company tie-in.
General Info: (Formerly CML News), Bi-weekly, Trim Size-11 x 15, 6 pages, No Color
Circulation: Total-1,800

Connections

Publishing Co: Lutheran Medical Ctr., 2609 Franklin Blvd., Cleveland, OH 44113-2992;
Title Tel # (216) 696-4300 Title Fax # (216) 363-2345
General Info: (Formerly Bright Corridors)

Connections

Publishing Co: Dallas Area Rapid Transit, PO Box 660163, Dallas, TX 75266-9299;
Title Tel # (214) 658-6212
Personnel: Editor-Haunani Shipper, Art Dir.-Carter Wilson
Editorial Description: Features job-related news, changes affecting employees and employee/retiree news.
General Info: (Formerly Hotline), Yr. Est. 1987, Monthly, Trim Size-6½ x 13½, Offset press, 12 pages, 2 Color, Coated
Circulation: (100% controlled), Total-3,000

Connections *Business, Association*

Publishing Co: Greyhound Lines, Inc., PO Box 660606, Dallas, TX 75266-0606;
Title Tel # (214) 789-7000
Personnel: Editor-Bill Kula
General Info: (Formerly Trailways Eagle; Lines), Yr. Est. 1980, Monthly, 4 Color
Circulation: Total-2,500

Contact *Business, Association*

Publishing Co: Crown Life Ins. Co., 1901 Scarth St., Regina, SK S4P 4L4 Canada
Tel # (306) 751-6000 Fax # (306) 751-6001
Personnel: Editor-Marilyn DuncanWebb, Circ. Mgr.-Elvira Brolley
Editorial Description: Published for insurance company personnel.
General Info: Monthly
Circulation: Total-24,000

Conveyor *Business, Consumer*

Publishing Co: Whirlpool Corp., 1300 Marion Agosta Rd., Marion, OH 43302-9577
Fax # (614) 383-7656; Title Tel # (614) 383-7335
Editorial Description: Employee activities, personnel benefits, operational developments, and economic factors affecting operations.
General Info: Quarterly, Trim Size-8½ x 11, Offset press, 20 pages, 4 Color
Circulation: Total-3,000

Conveyor

Publishing Co: Sterling Drug Inc., Pharmaceutical Production Grou, Myerstown, PA 17067

Conveyor *Business*

Publishing Co: Monterey Coal Co., Div. of Exxon, PO Box 496, Carlinville, IL 62626-0496;
Title Tel # (217) 854-4292
Editorial Description: Company newsletter to employees, annuitants, survivors providing information on business, benefits and personnel.
General Info: (Formerly News Conveyor), Yr. Est. 1971, Monthly, Trim Size-8⅝ x 10¾, Offset press, 10 pages, No Color
Circulation: Total-1,600

Copy

Publishing Co: Houston Chronicle, PO Box 4260, Houston, TX 77210-4260 Tel # (713) 220-7171
Parent Co.-Hearst Corp., New York
Personnel: Editor-Jane Griffing
General Info: Monthly, Trim Size-6 x 9, Offset press, 16 pages
Circulation: Total-1,800

Core Driller

Publishing Co: George E. Failing Co., PO Box 872, Enid, OK 73702-0872;
Title Tel # (405) 234-4141 Title Fax # (405) 233-6807
Personnel: Publisher-George Failing, Editor, Circ. Mgr., Adv. Dir., Promotion Dir.-Marilyn Foos
Editorial Description: To provide information relating to Failing Company products for Failing customers.
General Info: Yr. Est. 1935, Quarterly, Trim Size-8½ x 20¾, Sheetfed press, 4 pages, 2 Color, Coated
Circulation: Total-16,000

Count-Down

Publishing Co: Milgo Electric Corp., Box 407044, Sunrise, FL 33340-7044
Personnel: Editor-Richard N. Nathanson
General Info: Bi-monthly
Circulation: Total-400

Counterpoint

Publishing Co: Whitehall-Robins, PO Box 26609, Richmond, VA 23261-6609;
Title Tel # (804) 257-2112
Personnel: Editor-Joyce Dixon
General Info: (Formerly Round Robins), Yr. Est. 1953, Monthly, Trim Size-11 x 14½, Offset press, 5 pages, No Color, Coated
Circulation: (100% controlled), Total-4,200

Cover-All

Publishing Co: Tri-State Industrial Laundries, Inc., 1634 Lincoln Ave # 4145, Utica, NY 13502-5312;
Title Tel # (315) 732-4195
Personnel: Editor-Linda Stern
Editorial Description: Company Information-health-safety.
General Info: (Formerly Triangle), Yr. Est. 1967, Bi-monthly, Desktop press, 10 pages, No Color, Newsprint
Circulation: (100% controlled), Total-350
Printing Co: Beacon, 505 Roberts St, Utica, NY 13502-4515 Tel # (315) 732-1803

Craftsman, II *Business, Association*

Publishing Co: West Bend Co., 400 E Washington St, West Bend, WI 53095-2584
Tel # (414) 334-6911; Title Tel # (414) 334-6831 Title Fax # (414) 334-6800
Personnel: Publisher, Editor, Production Mgr., Art Dir.-Darcy Morrow
Editorial Description: Articles deal with co. happenings & events. Its goal is to keep employees informed of co. issues. & to give recognition for their services.
General Info: Bi-weekly, Trim Size-8½ x 11, Offset press, 4 pages, 2 Color, Coated
Circulation: Total-1,300
Printing Co: Valley Web, 1299 Stowe Avenue, Medford, OR 97504 Tel # (503) 772-7039

Cravens Dargan

Publishing Co: Cravens Dargan, PO Box 1660, Houston, TX 77251-1660
Personnel: Editor-Terry Edgar
Editorial Description: Circulated to home office employees and branch office employees.
General Info: Yr. Est. 1975, Monthly, Trim Size-8¼ x 10½, 6 pages
Circulation: Total-450

Currency

Publishing Co: Continental Bank, 231 S. La Salle St., Chicago, IL 60697-0001 Tel # (312) 974-5210;
Title Tel # (312) 923-5210
Personnel: Editor-Debby Storms
General Info: Bi-weekly, Trim Size-11 x 17, Sheetfed press, 4 pages, No Color, Recycled
Subscriptions: Free To Qualified Recipient
Circulation: Total-10,000
List Rental: Rents Lists
Printing Co: Wicklander Printing Co., 1550 S State St, Chicago, IL 60605-2805 Tel # (312) 225-1300

Curtis Ade

Publishing Co: American Business Products, Inc., 2100 RiverEdge Pkwy., Atlanta, GA 30328-4674
Tel # (404) 953-8300; Title Tel # (404) 951-1000
Personnel: Editor-Wynell M. Lauver
General Info: Monthly, Trim Size-8½ x 11, Offset press, 16 pages
Circulation: Total-1,100

Cutler-Hammer Record

Publishing Co: Cutler-Hammer Inc., 4201 N 27th St, Milwaukee, WI 53216-1807
Personnel: Editor-Frank Hayes
General Info: Quarterly, Trim Size-8½ x 11, Offset press, 16 pages
Circulation: Total-12,000

DP&L News

Publishing Co: Dayton Power, Courthouse Plaza S.W., Dayton, OH 45402;
Title Tel # (513) 224-6462
Personnel: Editor-Lester L. Vlahos
Editorial Description: Employee publication consisting of news and events about the company, its products and its employees.
General Info: (Formerly Forward Magazine), Yr. Est. 1922, Monthly, Trim Size-11 x 15, Web press, 6 pages
Circulation: Total-5,500

Daily, The *Business*

Publishing Co: Merck & Co., Inc., PO Box 4, West Point, PA 19486-0004 Tel # (215) 652-5000;
Title Tel # (215) 652-5628
Personnel: Editor-Madeleine Kaye
Editorial Description: Covers company news, medical advances, brief notes on birthdays, anniversairies, etc., and personnel changes.
General Info: (Formerly Noon Extract), Yr. Est. 1963, Daily, Offset press, 2 pages, No Color, Newsprint
Circulation: (100% controlled), Total-4,000

Daily Newsline

Publishing Co: General Motors Corp., PO Box 629, Janesville, WI 53547-0629;
Title Tel # (608) 756-7877 Title Fax # (608) 756-7089
Personnel: Editor-Richard Costerisan
Editorial Description: Up-to-date auto industry news mixed with in-plant info.
General Info: (Formerly Rock River Review), Yr. Est. 1985, Daily, Trim Size-8½ x 14, 2 pages, No Color, Newsprint
Circulation: Total-2,500

Dairy Foods Group *Business*

Publishing Co: Crowley Foods, Inc., PO Box 549, Binghamton, NY 13902-0549;
Title Tel # (607) 722-6441
Personnel: Editor-Jeanne Walter
Editorial Description: Company & employee news, new products features.
General Info: Bi-monthly, Trim Size-8½ x 11, Offset press, 6 pages, Color, Coated
Acquistions: Publication Bought
Circulation: (100% controlled), Total-2,550
Printing Co: Johnson City Publishing, 112 Hall St., Binghamton, NY 13903 Tel # (607) 772-0678

Dana Reading Communicator

Publishing Co: Dana Corp., PO Box 13445, Reading, PA 19612-3445; Title Tel # (215) 371-7000
General Info: Bi-monthly, Trim Size-8½ x 11, Offset press, 22 pages, Color
Circulation: Total-3,500

Data Systems News   *Business*

Publishing Co: Litton Industries, Data Systems Div., 29851 Agoura Rd, Agoura Hills, CA 91301-2511; Title Tel # (818) 902-4000
Personnel: Editor-Charlene Schueller
General Info: Bi-weekly

Davey Bulletin

Publishing Co: Davey Tree Expert Co., 1500 N Mantua St, Kent, OH 44240-2399; Title Tel # (216) 673-9511
Personnel: Editor-George W. Gallaway, Adv. Mgr.-Kurt Appleman
General Info: Monthly, Trim Size-8¼ x 11¼, Letrpr. press, 20 pages
Circulation: Total-2,900

Delco Doings

Publishing Co: Delco Products Division, 2000 Forrer Blvd Stop 1042, Dayton, OH 45420-1373; Title Tel # (513) 455-7456
Personnel: Publisher-Charles Kronbach
General Info: Monthly, Offset press, 6 pages
Circulation: Total-10,000

Diamond State Bulletin

Publishing Co: Bell Telelphone Co. of PA, One Parkway, 9th fl., Philadelphia, PA 19102-1589; Title Tel # (215) 466-9900

Dictaphone Ambassador

Publishing Co: Dictaphone Corp., 3191 Broadbridge Ave, Stratford, CT 06497-2566; Title Tel # (203) 381-7000
Personnel: Editor-A. R. Gower
Editorial Description: Company product news, promotions, service awards, employee activities.
General Info: Yr. Est. 1961, Quarterly
Circulation: Total-1,200

Dictaphone Record

Publishing Co: Dictaphone Corp., 3191 Broadbridge Ave, Stratford, CT 06497-2566; Title Tel # (203) 381-7000

Dimensions   *Business*

Publishing Co: Dentsply Intl. Inc., 570 W College Ave, York, PA 17404-3886; Title Tel # (717) 845-7511
Personnel: Editor-George Rhodes
Editorial Description: Devoted to employee and industry news, stories about dentistry of dental health, dental education, new developments in the field.
General Info: (Formerly The Crescent), Yr. Est. 1965, Quarterly, Trim Size-8½ x 11, Offset press, 32 pages, No Color
Circulation: (100% controlled), Total-4,000
Printing Co: Strine Printing Co., I-83 Industrial Pk., York, PA 17405 Tel # (717) 767-6602

Direct Connection   *Business*

Publishing Co: Packard Electric Div., GMC, PO Box 431, Warren, OH 44486-0001; Title Tel # (216) 373-3029 Title Fax # (216) 373-4185
Personnel: Publisher-Patricia Hawkins, Editor-Sharon Roncone
Editorial Description: Automotive and automotive electrical component industry news. Includes human interest features.
General Info: (Formerly Packard This Week), Yr. Est. 1938, Weekly, Sheetfed press, 4 pages, No Color, Matte
Circulation: Total-7,200
Printing Co: Warren Printing, 387 Chestnut Ave NE, Warren, OH 44483-5856 Tel # (216) 395-9538

Directions   *Business*

Publishing Co: TCI Marketing Inc., 1011 Centre Rd., Ste. 403, Wilmington, DE 19805-1266
Editorial Description: Information for stockholders and staff of TCI Direct Marketing Co.
General Info: Yr. Est. 1995, Irregular
List Rental: Rents Lists

Douglas Top-CS

Publishing Co: Douglas Furniture Corp., PO Box 97, Bedford Park, IL 60499-0097

Drackett Diamonds

Publishing Co: Drackett Div., Bristol-Myers Co., 8600 Governors Hill Dr. #300, Cincinnati, OH 45249-1388 Tel # (513) 632-1500; Title Tel # (513) 632-1841
Personnel: Editor-Susan Scardina
General Info: Yr. Est. 1991

DuPont Engineering News

Publishing Co: E.I. du Pont de Nemours, 10007 Market Street, Wilmington, DE 19898-0001 Tel # (302) 774-1000

Duffel Bag   *Association*

Publishing Co: Boy Scouts of America, St. Louis Area Council, 4568 W Pine Blvd, Saint Louis, MO 63108-2110; Title Tel # (314) 361-0600 Title Fax # (314) 361-3165
Personnel: Editor-Paul Brockland
General Info: Monthly, Trim Size-11 x 17, Offset press, 14 pages, 2 Color
Subscriptions: Indv. $5
Circulation: Total-8,000
Printing Co: John S. Swift Co., 1243 Research Blvd, Saint Louis, MO 63132-1713 Tel # (314) 991-4300

Duraclean Journal   *Association*

Publishing Co: Duraclean Intl., Duraclean Bldg., Deerfield, IL 60015; Title Tel # (708) 945-2000
Personnel: Editor-William Ondrratschek
Editorial Description: General information & sales promotional material for Duraclean franchise holders.
General Info: Yr. Est. 1956, Monthly, Trim Size-8½ x 11, Offset press, 8 pages, 2 Color, Coated, Saddle-stitched
Circulation: Total-1,100

Dyna-Mite

Publishing Co: Natl. Travelers Life Co., 820 Keosauqua Way, Des Moines, IA 50309-1599
Personnel: Editor-Mrs. Lois Flurkey
General Info: Weekly, Offset press, 3 pages
Circulation: Total-1,300

Dynamo

Publishing Co: Natl. Travelers Life Co., 820 Keosauqua Way, Des Moines, IA 50309-1599; Title Tel # (515) 283-0101
Personnel: Editor-Dave Danielson
Editorial Description: Communicate product information, corporate & industry developments to sales force.
General Info: Quarterly, Trim Size-8½ x 11, Sheetfed press, 20 pages, 2 Color, Coated
Circulation: (100% controlled), Total-1,500

E-M Diamond

Publishing Co: Electric Machinery Mfg. Co., 800 Central Ave NE, Minneapolis, MN 55413-2403

ED Newsletter

Publishing Co: General Dynamics/Electro Dynamics, 150th Ave., Avenel, NJ 07001; Title Tel # (201) 636-9100

Eagle

Publishing Co: Martin Marietta Eagle Electronics & Missiles Group, Box 5837, Orlando, FL 32855; Title Tel # (407) 356-2211 Title Fax # (407) 356-2080
Personnel: Editor-Kitty Day
Editorial Description: Items of interest to employees.
General Info: Bi-weekly, Offset press, 8 pages, 2 Color, Matte
Acquistions: Publication Bought
Circulation: Total-16,000
Printing Co: Moran Printing Company, 9125 Bachman Rd, Orlando, FL 32824-8020 Tel # (407) 632-0550, Fax # (407) 639-4069

Easter Seal Network News   *Association*

Publishing Co: Easter Seal Soc. of Wis. Inc., 101 Nob Hill Rd Rm 301, Madison, WI 53713-3969; Title Tel # (608) 277-8288
Personnel: Editor-Paul Maki
Editorial Description: Services and programs of the Easter Seal Society of Wisconsin.
General Info: (Formerly Easter Seal News), Quarterly, Trim Size-8½ x 11, Sheetfed press, 6 pages, No Color, Matte
Subscriptions: Indv. $2
Acquistions: Publication Bought
Circulation: (100% controlled), Total-3,000

Eaton Today   *Business*

Publishing Co: Eaton Corp., 1111 Superior Ave., Eaton Ctr., Cleveland, OH 44114-2584; Title Tel # (216) 523-4738
Personnel: Editor-Tim Weidner
Editorial Description: Corporate news, individual stories about employees, facilities.
General Info: Yr. Est. 1986, Monthly, Sheetfed press, 4 pages, 4 Color, Matte
Circulation: Total-30,000
Printing Co: Carpenter Reserve Printing, 7100 Euclid Ave, Cleveland, OH 44103-4016 Tel # (216) 431-0800

Echoes

Publishing Co: Lennox Industries, 200 S. 12th Ave., Marshall, IA 50158-3005; Title Tel # (515) 754-4583
Personnel: Editor-Terry Frederickson
Editorial Description: In-plant newspaper covering events of week.
General Info: Yr. Est. 1962, Weekly, Trim Size-8½ x 11, Mimeo press, 4 pages, No Color, Newsprint
Circulation: (100% controlled), Total-1,200

Editorial Eye
See: JOURNALISM

Edu/Gram

Publishing Co: Edu/Gram, Oregon Board Of Education 942, Salem, OR 97310-0001
  Tel # (503) 378-3569
Personnel: Editor-Ed Jacobson
General Info: 10x/yr., Offset press, 6 pages
Circulation: Total-27,500

Elco Extra   *Association*

Publishing Co: Elco Industries, Inc., 1111 Samuelson Rd # 7009, Rockford, IL 61109-3641;
  Title Tel # (815) 397-5155
Personnel: Editor, Art Dir.-Angela Larson
Editorial Description: Company news, employee activities and special events, community news, wellness information, employee recognition.
General Info: (Formerly Elco Newsletter), Semi-weekly, Trim Size-8½ x 14, Sheetfed press, 2 pages, 2 Color, Coated
Circulation: Total-1,200

Electric Leaguer

Publishing Co: Electric League of Chattanooga, PO Box 182255, Chattanooga, TN 37422-7255
Personnel: Editor-Hal Morris
Editorial Description: News of & for members of electric league.
General Info: Yr. Est. 1926, Quarterly, Web press, 4 pages, No Color
Printing Co: Chattanooga Printing Co., 110 Somerville Ave, Chattanooga, TN 37405-3266
  Tel # (615) 266-6166

Em-Pica

Publishing Co: Mack Printing Co., 1991 Northampton St, Easton, PA 18042-3189
Personnel: Editor-Helen MacDonald

Emblem Flashes

Publishing Co: Farmers Insurance Group, 4680 Wilshire Blvd, Los Angeles, CA 90010-3807;
  Title Tel # (213) 931-1961
Personnel: Editor-Rosemary D. Coney
General Info: Bi-monthly, Trim Size-8½ x 11, Letrpr. press, 20 pages
Circulation: Total-6,400

Emphasis

Publishing Co: United Olympic Life Insurance, 4601 Fairfax Dr., Arlington, VA 22203-1500
Personnel: Editor-Maria Yannopoulos
Editorial Description: Marekting publication for field force.
General Info: Bi-monthly, Trim Size-8½ x 11, Sheetfed press, 8 pages, 2 Color, Coated
Circulation: Total-1,200

Employee Bulletin

Publishing Co: Chrysler Corp., 1200 Chrysler Dr., Highland Pk., MI 48288-0001;
  Title Tel # (313) 956-2894
Personnel: Editor-Bob Moreillon
General Info: Monthly
Circulation: Total-1,800

Energy
See: PETROLEUM & NATURAL GAS

Equinews

Publishing Co: Equitable Life Assurance Society, 787 Seventh Avenue, New York, NY 10019-1201
  Tel # (212) 554-2100; Title Tel # (212) 554-1234
Personnel: Editor-William C. McGuire
General Info: Monthly, Trim Size-8 x 9½, Offset press, 24 pages
Circulation: Total-15,000

Eritrean Newsletter

Publishing Co: Eritrean Relief Assn. in Canada, Inc., 29 Prince Arthur Ave., Toronto, ON M5R 1B2 Canada; Title Tel # (416) 961-0994
Personnel: Editor-John Sorenson
Editorial Description: Contains information on the Horn of Africa related to relief & development, events in Canada concerning NGOs & Eritrean communities, interviews, book reviews, current events, historical background.
General Info: Yr. Est. 1984, Quarterly, 8 pages
Subscriptions: Indv. $7, Inst. $15
Circulation: Total-4,000

Ethicon News   *Business*

Publishing Co: Ethicon Inc., Johnson & Johnson, Somerville, NJ 08876; Title Tel # (908) 218-3174
Personnel: Editor-Liz Slavin
General Info: Bi-monthly, Trim Size-9 x 12, Offset press, 8 pages, No Color, Coated
Circulation: Total-6,700
Printing Co: Hatteras Press, PO Box 303, Manasquan, NJ 08736-0303 Tel # (908) 223-9888

Ewa Hurri-Cane

Publishing Co: Ewa Sugar Company, Inc., Box O, Waipahu, HI 96797
Personnel: Editor-Richard Lau
General Info: Weekly, Trim Size-10 x 12, Offset press, 2 pages
Circulation: Total-1,200

Exciter

Publishing Co: Central Maine Power Co., Edison Drive, Augusta, ME 04336-0001
Personnel: Editor-Peter G. Thompson
General Info: Trim Size-9 x 12, Offset press, 14 pages
Circulation: Total-2,600

Expander

Publishing Co: Warren Petroleum Corp., Gulf Oil Corp., PO Box 1589, Tulsa, OK 74102-1589;
  Title Tel # (918) 560-4000
Personnel: Editor-Maureen Van Dyke
General Info: (Formerly Stabilizer), Bi-monthly
Circulation: Total-1,850

Exploder

Publishing Co: E.I. du Pont de Nemours, Exploder Mag., Pompton Lakes, NJ 07442;
  Title Tel # (201) 835-6181
Personnel: Editor-Henry E. Allen
Editorial Description: Features plant and community items.
General Info: Yr. Est. 1943, Bi-monthly

Expro News/Expro Update

Publishing Co: Exxon Co., U.S.A., 800 Bell St., Houston, TX 77002 Tel # (713) 656-3636
Personnel: Editor-Ann Patton

Exxon Extra

Publishing Co: Exxon Co., U.S.A., 800 Bell St., Houston, TX 77002 Tel # (713) 656-3636
Personnel: Editor-Vin Corwin

Exxon Underway

Publishing Co: Exxon Co., U.S.A., 800 Bell St., Houston, TX 77002 Tel # (713) 656-3636

FSCA Bulletin

Publishing Co: Foreign Service Community Assn., L.B. Pearson Bldg., Sussex Dr., Ottawa, ON K1A 0G2 Canada
Editorial Description: Deals with issues of concern to foreign service membership.
General Info: Yr. Est. 1977, Quarterly, 24 pages
Circulation: (100% controlled), Total-600
Advertising: Inquire for rates.

FYI   *Consumer*

Publishing Co: Time Warner Publishing Inc., 1271 Ave. of the Americas, Rockefeller Center, New York, NY 10020-1300 Tel # (212) 522-1212 Fax # (212) 765-2699; Title Tel # (212) 522-2740 Title Fax # (212) 522-0017
Personnel: Publisher-Peter Costiglio, Editor-Belinda Luscombe, Production Mgr., Art Dir.-Beth Power
Editorial Description: Covers news of the Time, Inc. Magazine Co. & its employees.
General Info: Yr. Est. 1940, Bi-monthly, Trim Size-8½ x 11, Offset press, 8 pages, 3% ads, 2 Color, Coated, Saddle-stitched
Subscriptions: Indv. $12
Circulation: (97% controlled), Total-9,118, Subscriptions-200
Advertising: Inquire for rates.
Printing Co: First Impressions, 25 Adams Ct, Plainview, NY 11803-1601 Tel # (516) 333-3343

FYI
See: PETROLEUM & NATURAL GAS

FYI International   *Business*

Publishing Co: Equifax Inc., 1600 Peachtree St. NW, Atlanta, GA 30309; Title Tel # (404) 885-8482 Title Fax # (404) 888-3464
Personnel: Editor-Halle Holland
Editorial Description: Information about and affecting Equifax for its employees and retirees in the US, Canada, and UK.
General Info: (Formerly Intercom; Roundtable), Monthly, 4 Color, Matte
Subscriptions: Free To Qualified Recipient

Fedlink   *Business, Association*

Publishing Co: Electro Federation, 10 Carlson Court, #210, Rexdale, ON M9W 6L7 Canada Fax # (416) 674-7412; Title Tel # (416) 674-7410
Editorial Description: Updates members on assn. , industry activities.
General Info: (Formerly CEMA Newsletter; Scanner), Yr. Est. 1976, Monthly, Trim Size-8½ x 11, Offset press, 8 pages
Circulation: (100% controlled), Total-2,000

Fincastle Fabrications

Publishing Co: Louisville Textiles, Pennsylvania Furniture Co., 1318 Mchenry St, Louisville, KY 40217-1216

First Nat'l. Bank's Arizona
Times

Publishing Co: First Natl. Bank of Arizona, Western Bancorporation, 100 W. Washington, Phoenix, AZ 85003-1805; Title Tel # (602) 271-6000

First Union Network
Business, Consumer

Publishing Co: Ameribanc-First Union Natl. Bank, 301 S. Tryon St., 2 First Union Ctr., 15th fl., Charlotte, NC 28288-0570 Fax # (704) 374-4464; Title Tel # (704) 374-6444
Personnel: Editor-David Nanney
Editorial Description: News and information for First Union employees.
General Info: Monthly, Coated

Flash
Business, Association

Publishing Co: Southland Corp., 2828 N Haskell Ave, Dallas, TX 75204-2990
Personnel: Editor-Tony Katsulos
Editorial Description: Occasional newsletter listing events and activities of immediate interest.
General Info: Irregular

Flashes

Publishing Co: Jewel Food Stores, 1955 W North Ave, Melrose Park, IL 60160-1181; Title Tel # (708) 531-6932
Personnel: Editor-Brian Yeager
Editorial Description: Internal news.
General Info: Bi-weekly, Trim Size-7 x 8½, Mimeo press, 16 pages
Circulation: Total-10,000

Focus

Publishing Co: Natl. Steel Corp. - Great Lakes Division, 1 Quality Dr., Ecorse, MI 48229; Title Tel # (313) 297-2250
Personnel: Editor-John Jacksy
General Info: (Formerly Ingot), Yr. Est. 1955, Monthly, Trim Size-9 x 12, Letrpr. press, 12 pages, No Color
Circulation: Total-15,500

Focus: Eye on the Mailer

Publishing Co: USPS: Communications, J.A. Farley Bldg., New York, NY 10199-9641; Title Fax # (212) 330-3934
Personnel: Editor-Diane Todd, Art Dir.-Steve Queen
General Info: Yr. Est. 1987, Monthly, Trim Size-8½ x 11, 8 pages, 2 Color, Coated, Saddle-stitched
Acquistions: Publication Bought
Circulation: Total-3,000

Ford Sterling-Canton News

Publishing Co: Ford Motor Credit Co., The American Rd., Dearborn, MI 48121; Title Tel # (313) 322-3000

Formula
Business

Publishing Co: Rohm & Haas Co., Independence Mall West, Philadelphia, PA 19105 Tel # (215) 592-3480; Title Tel # (215) 592-3471
Personnel: Editor-Mary Shields, Art Dir.-Barbara Bosha
Editorial Description: Co. news & features.
General Info: Monthly, Trim Size-11 x 14, Offset press, 6 pages, 2 Color, Newsprint
Circulation: (100% controlled), Total-15,000

Forward

Publishing Co: Montgomery Ward, 1 Montgomery Ward Plz # 8-3, Chicago, IL 60671-0001; Title Tel # (312) 467-3165
Personnel: Publisher, Editor-Faith Wicklander, Production Mgr.-Judy Gustafson
Editorial Description: Forward is a quarterly in-house publication for active & retired Montgomery Ward associates. It reports the news of fellow associates & of the company's policies, plans & activities.
General Info: Yr. Est. 1904, Quarterly, Web press, 12 pages, No Color, Matte, Saddle-stitched
Subscriptions: Free
Circulation: Total-97,000
Printing Co: Wicklander Printing Co., 1550 S State St, Chicago, IL 60605-2805 Tel # (312) 225-1300

Foxtales
Association

Publishing Co: G. Fox & Company, 426 Washington St, Boston, MA 02108-5219
Personnel: Editor-Chris Berger
Editorial Description: In house newsletter that focuses on customer service and other various department store issues.
General Info: (Formerly Go-Getter), Bi-monthly, Sheetfed press, 10 pages, 2 Color, Saddle-stitched
Circulation: Total-3,600
Printing Co: Account Manager: Joe Visgilio; Old Windsor Press, 67 Old Windsor Rd, Bloomfield, CT 06002-1416

Frank-Ly Speaking

Publishing Co: Frank-Ly Speaking, 1310 Surf Ave, Brooklyn, NY 11224-2404; Title Tel # (212) 266-3161
Personnel: Editor-Charles S. Schmeck

Fraser Voyageur

Publishing Co: Fraser Paper, Ltd., 9 West Broad St., Box 10055, Stamford, CT 06904; Title Tel # (203) 359-2544
General Info: Quarterly
Circulation: Total-6,000

From the Rooftops

Publishing Co: Coop. Housing Fed. of Canada, 225 Metcalfe Street, #311, Ottawa, ON K2P 1P9 Canada; Title Tel # (613) 230-2201 Title Fax # (613) 230-2231
Personnel: Editor-Lyse Huot
Editorial Description: Policy & program news on Canadian non-profit cooperative housing.
General Info: Yr. Est. 1970, Quarterly, Trim Size-8½ x 11, Web press, 8 pages, 2 Color, Newsprint
Circulation: Total-3,000

GE News

Publishing Co: GE, 1285 Boston Ave, Bridgeport, CT 06610-2612; Title Tel # (203) 382-2456 Title Fax # (203) 382-4152
Personnel: Editor-Patrick Brennan
General Info: Weekly, Trim Size-8½ x 11, Letrpr. press, 4 pages
Circulation: Total-1,400

GF News

Publishing Co: General Foods Corp., 250 North St, White Plains, NY 10605-2236
Personnel: Editor-Jeane Maroney
General Info: 10x/yr., Trim Size-7½ x 9½, Letrpr. press, 28 pages
Circulation: Total-25,000

Gaslight Review

Publishing Co: New Jersey Natural Gas Co., PO Box 1464, Wall, NJ 07719-1464; Title Tel # (908) 938-1223
Personnel: Editor-Glenn Philips
Editorial Description: For company employees highlighting events. Also includes news about employees.
General Info: (Formerly Natural Gasser), Yr. Est. 1980, Bi-monthly, Trim Size-8½ x 11, 8 pages, No Color
Circulation: Total-1,000

Gem

Publishing Co: Gordon Jewelry Corp., PO Box 152777, Irving, TX 75015-2777 Tel # (214) 580-5574

General Libraries Newsletter
See: LIBRARY

Genius At Work

Publishing Co: Kano Labs, 1000 Thompson Ln, Nashville, TN 37211-2658; Title Tel # (615) 833-4101
Personnel: Editor-Peter Zimmerman
Editorial Description: Practical and inspirational matter of special interest to mechanical minded men.
General Info: Yr. Est. 1939, Quarterly, Looseleaf
Circulation: Total-32,000

Globe

Publishing Co: Pacific Valves, Inc., 3201 Walnut Ave, Long Beach, CA 90807-5225

Gold Coaster

Publishing Co: Sears Roebuck, 901 N. Fedl. Hwy., Fort Lauderdale, FL 33304-2787; Title Tel # (305) 779-1300

Goldberg Bulletin

Publishing Co: S. Goldberg, 20 E Broadway, Hackensack, NJ 07601-6820; Title Tel # (201) 342-1200
Personnel: Editor-Thomas Lewis
Editorial Description: Contains employee news, information about company activities, articles on safety.
General Info: Yr. Est. 1948, Monthly
Circulation: Total-600

Golden Pen
Business

Publishing Co: Golden State Mutual Life Ins. Co., 1999 W Adams Blvd, Los Angeles, CA 90018-3514; Title Tel # (213) 731-1131
Personnel: Editor-Harold Toliver, Adv. Dir.-William E. Pajaud
Editorial Description: Inform employees & policyowners about people, events in their community & how it may affect their insurance needs.
General Info: Yr. Est. 1972, Quarterly, Trim Size-8½ x 11, Offset press, 16 pages
Circulation: Total-2,000

Good Word
Business

Publishing Co: Aeltus Managing, Inc., 242 Trumbull St., Hartford, CT 06156 Tel # (203) 273-4368
Personnel: Publications Director-Carol Atlas
Editorial Description: Information and news for Aetna staff.

Goodall News

Publishing Co: Goodall Rubber Co., Grovers Mill Rd. #203, Trenton, NJ 08648-4708; Title Tel # (215) 574-8484
Personnel: Editor-Robert Shimer
Editorial Description: Emphasis is on the importance of good communications, qualities of salesmanship and other topics that can help everybody to do a better job. Written in a light, hopefully entertaining style.
General Info: Yr. Est. 1941, 8x/yr.
Circulation: Total-37,000

Goodtimers Newsletter

Publishing Co: Devilbiss Co., 1724 Indian Wood Circle, Maumee, OH 43537-4005; Title Tel # (414) 470-2169
Personnel: Editor-Charlie Markus
Editorial Description: For employees and retirees of DeVilbiss Company.
General Info: Yr. Est. 1978, Quarterly, Trim Size-8½ x 11, Offset press, 6 pages, No Color, Newsprint
Circulation: Total-1,000

Goodwill Dimensions
See: SOCIAL SERVICES & WELFARE

Grapevine   *Business*

Publishing Co: Forest Lawn Memorial Parks, 1712 S Glendale Ave, Glendale, CA 91205-3320; Title Tel # (213) 254-3131 Title Fax # (213) 344-9035
Personnel: Editor-Dick Fisher
Editorial Description: Emphasis on employer-employee relations, benefits, personalization of personnel.
General Info: Yr. Est. 1949, Monthly, Trim Size-8½ x 11, Offset press, 8 pages, 2 Color, Coated, Saddle-stitched
Circulation: Total-1,000
Printing Co: Hal Kline, 5711 Sheila Street, Commerce, CA 90040 Tel # (213) 726-2975, Fax # (213) 726-7100

Graphicopy

Publishing Co: Meredith Graphics, 1231 E. 286th St., Euclid, OH 44132-2194; Title Tel # (216) 261-6333
Personnel: Editor-M. E. Meredith
General Info: Yr. Est. 1947, Monthly, Trim Size-8½ x 11, Sheetfed press, 4 pages, 2 Color, Coated
Subscriptions: Free To Qualified Recipient
Circulation: Total-2,500

Great Centralizer

Publishing Co: Great Central Insurance Co., PO Box 807, Peoria, IL 61652-0807
Personnel: Editor-Harold S. Lang
General Info: Monthly, Trim Size-8½ x 11, Offset press, 4 pages
Circulation: Total-500

Guardian

Publishing Co: Guardian Life Insurance Co. of America, 201 Park Ave. S., New York, NY 10003-1699; Title Tel # (212) 473-3000

HF News

Publishing Co: Houston Fearless 76 Corp., 203 W Artesia Blvd, Compton, CA 90220-5550
General Info: Monthly, Trim Size-8½ x 11, Offset press, 6 pages
Circulation: Total-1,500

HTB Happenings   *Business*

Publishing Co: HTB Inc., Box 1845, 1411 Classen Bl, Oklahoma City, OK 73101-1845; Title Tel # (405) 525-7451
Personnel: Editor-Linda Blunt
Editorial Description: Marketing piece with employee supplement.
General Info: Quarterly, Trim Size-11 x 17, Web press, 10 pages, No Color, Coated
Circulation: Total-5,000

Half-Loaf

Publishing Co: Arnold Bakers Inc., Hamilton Ave., Greenwich, CT 06830
Personnel: Editor-Thomas J. McKenna
General Info: Monthly
Circulation: Total-1,200

Hanover Shoe News

Publishing Co: Hanover Shoe Co., Inc., 240 Kindig Lane, Hanover, PA 17331
Personnel: Editor-Bradley R. Cashman
General Info: Monthly, Trim Size-8½ x 11, Offset press, 12 pages
Circulation: Total-1,600

Head Office News

Publishing Co: Metropolitan Life Insurance Co., Pacific Coast Head Office, 425 Market St., San Francisco, CA 94105-2406; Title Tel # (415) 546-3000
Personnel: Editor-Charlotte Madison
General Info: Bi-weekly, Trim Size-10½ x 15, Letrpr. press, 4 pages
Circulation: Total-2,400

Heart to Heart
See: HEALTH

Heinz Line

Publishing Co: Heinz USA, PO Box 57, Pittsburgh, PA 15230-0057; Title Tel # (412) 237-5743
Personnel: Editor-Cheryl Stewart Miller
Editorial Description: Informs Heinz U.S.A. employees and retirees about the company, its programs and products.
General Info: (Formerly News Beat), Yr. Est. 1971, Quarterly, Trim Size-8½ x 11, Sheetfed press, 16 pages, No Color, Matte, Saddle-stitched
Circulation: (100% controlled), Total-9,000
Printing Co: Broudy Printing Inc., 223 Auburn St, Pittsburgh, PA 15206-3209 Tel # (412) 362-6700

Helm

Publishing Co: Pier 1 Imports Inc., 2520 W. Freeway, Fort Worth, TX 76119-4608

Hi-Lines   *Association*

Publishing Co: Illinois Power Co., 500 S 27th St, Decatur, IL 62521-2200; Title Tel # (217) 424-6794
Personnel: Publisher, Editor-J. McNamara
General Info: 10x/yr., 32 pages, Color

Highlights

Publishing Co: United Services Automobile Assn., Usaa Bldg., San Antonio, TX 78288-0001

Highlights

Publishing Co: Delco Systems Operations, 6767 Hollister Ave, Goleta, CA 93117-3086
Personnel: Editor-Sheila Warren
Editorial Description: Weekly news for and about Delco Systems operations employees.
General Info: Yr. Est. 1976, Weekly, 4 pages
Circulation: Total-2,000

Hilo Coast Processing News

Publishing Co: Hilo Coast Processing Co., PO Box 4190, Hilo, HI 96720 Tel # (808) 964-1600

Hobart Plant News

Publishing Co: Hobart Bros. Co., 701 Ridge Ave., Troy, OH 45374-0001 Tel # (513) 332-4000

Houston Lines

Publishing Co: Panhandle Eastern Pipeline Co., PO Box 2521, Houston, TX 77252-2521; Title Tel # (713) 759-3530 Title Fax # (713) 759-7334
Personnel: Editor-Kami Hevssner
Editorial Description: Houston Lines is published by PEC for active Houston office employees.
General Info: Monthly, Trim Size-9 x 12, Offset press, 24 pages
Circulation: Total-2,400

Hughesnews

Publishing Co: Hughes Aircraft Co., Box 45066, Bldg. C1/C114, Los Angeles, CA 90045-0066; Title Tel # (213) 568-6300

Huntington Highlights

Publishing Co: Huntington Bankshares, Inc., 17 S. High St., Columbus, OH 43215-3456; Title Tel # (614) 463-4342
Personnel: Editor-Paula Jurcenko
Editorial Description: Recognizes & promotes co., personnel & products.
General Info: (Formerly Bank Notes), Yr. Est. 1987, Monthly, Trim Size-8½ x 11, 4 pages
Circulation: Total-5,500

Hy-Lites

Publishing Co: Hydro-Aire, Crane, 3000 Winona Ave, Burbank, CA 91504-2540
Personnel: Editor-Virgil Jorgensen
General Info: Yr. Est. 1966, Monthly, Trim Size-8½ x 11, Offset press, 4 pages, Coated
Circulation: Total-665
Printing Co: Hydro-Airr Co., 3000 Winona Ave, Burbank, CA 91504-2540 Tel # (818) 842-6121

Hydrogram

Publishing Co: Manitoba Hydro, Box 815, Winnipeg, MB R3C 2P4 Canada; Title Tel # (204) 474-4133
Personnel: Editor-Susan Griffiths
Editorial Description: News about Manitoba hydro: work completed new policies, staff changes, retirements, obits, births, coming events, operating statistics, employee achievements (professional & personal), projects around the province.
General Info: Yr. Est. 1971, Weekly, Trim Size-8½ x 11, 4 pages, 2 Color, Newsprint
Acquistions: Publication Bought
Circulation: Total-5,600

Illinois Bell News

Publishing Co: Illinois Bell Tel. Co., 225 W Randolph St, Chicago, IL 60606-1824; Title Tel # (312) 727-9411
Personnel: Editor-John R. Bonee
General Info: Bi-monthly, Trim Size-8⅝ x 11½, Offset press, 32 pages
Circulation: Total-50,000

Illinois Reporter   *Association*

Publishing Co: Illinois League of Savings, 220 E Adams St, Springfield, IL 62701-1123; Title Tel # (217) 522-5575
Personnel: Editor-Norma Altman
General Info: Bi-monthly
Circulation: Total-1,500
Advertising: Inquire for rates.

Image

Publishing Co: Big Brothers of Grtr Los Angeles Inc., 1486 Colorado Blvd, Los Angeles, CA 90041-2340; Title Tel # (213) 258-3333
Personnel: Editor-Carol Smith
Editorial Description: The Image informs our volunteers (Big Brothers, Board of Directors et al) donors & staff of Agency speical events both fund raising & non-fund raising. The Image is also a vehicle to recognize donors & volunteers.
General Info: Quarterly, Trim Size-8½ x 11, 4 pages, 2 Color

Impact-A-Gram

Publishing Co: Union Planters Corp., 7130 Goodlett Farm Parkway, Cordova, TN 38018 Fax # (901) 937-2396; Title Tel # (901) 383-6000
Personnel: Editor, Circ. Mgr.-Becky Davis
Editorial Description: Volunteer information, projects: Membership accomplishments.
General Info: Yr. Est. 1983, Monthly, Trim Size-8½ x 11, Sheetfed press, 2 pages
Circulation: Total-480

Imperial Clevite, Inc.

Publishing Co: Imperial Eastman Div., 6300 W. Howard St., Chicago, IL 60648-3492; Title Tel # (708) 967-4530
Editorial Description: Keeps employees informed about the company, new processes, new products health hints and the activities of fellow workers.
General Info: Yr. Est. 1945, Bi-monthly
Circulation: Total-2,200

In Gear

Publishing Co: Power Transmission Products, 2750 NW 31st Ave, Portland, OR 97210-1718 Tel # (503) 227-1271

In the LimeLite   *Business*

Publishing Co: Century Life of America, Heritage Way, Waverly, IA 50677; Title Tel # (319) 352-4090
Personnel: Editor-Marcia Janssen
Editorial Description: News from home office, company announcements.
General Info: Yr. Est. 1966, Monthly, Trim Size-8½ x 11, Offset press, 4 pages, No Color
Circulation: Total-550
Printing Co: Waverly Publishing, 708 Industrial Rd, Waverly, IA 50677-1812 Tel # (319) 352-1534

In the News

Publishing Co: Northern Trust Co., 50 S. La Salle St., Chicago, IL 60675-0001; Title Tel # (312) 630-6000
Editorial Description: Reprints of newspaper articles regarding the bank.

In the News   *Business*

Publishing Co: Aeltus Managing, Inc., 242 Trumbull St., Hartford, CT 06156 Tel # (203) 273-4368
Editorial Description: News and information for staff at Aetna's corporate campus.
General Info: Irregular, Trim Size-8½ x 14, 2 pages

In Synch   *Business*

Publishing Co: General Motors Corp., 28400 Plymouth Rd, Livonia, MI 48150-2366; Title Tel # (313) 523-8343
Personnel: Editor-Kathy Quinn
General Info: Yr. Est. 1975, Weekly, Trim Size-8½ x 11, Offset press, 4 pages
Circulation: Total-3,000

In Touch

Publishing Co: Pioneer Clubs Canada, Box 5447, 2320 Fairview Ave., Burlington, ON L7R 4L2 Canada; Title Tel # (416) 681-2883
General Info: (Formerly Lampion), Yr. Est. 1982, Quarterly, Trim Size-8½ x 11, Offset press, 6 pages, Saddle-stitched
Circulation: Total-7,000

InGeneral

Publishing Co: American General Life & Accident, 2110 American Gen. Center, Nashville, TN 37250-0001; Title Tel # (615) 749-1404
Personnel: Circ. Mgr.-Sara Roberts, Publisher, Production Mgr.-Shirley Jenkins, Art Dir.-Jeannie Hardwick, Editor, Adv. Dir., Promotion Dir.-Mitchell Pettross
Editorial Description: To communicate employee news, activities & events.
General Info: Yr. Est. 1984, Bi-weekly, 6 pages
Circulation: Total-2,000

Information Bulletin

Publishing Co: Arnold Bakers Inc., Hamilton Ave., Greenwich, CT 06830

Information Letter

Publishing Co: General Motors Corp., Arlington Plant-GMC, Arlington, TX 76010; Title Tel # (817) 652-2085

Info News

Publishing Co: Computer Sciences Corp., 650 N Sepulveda Blvd, El Segundo, CA 90245-3419 Tel # (310) 615-0311

Ingalls News   *Business*

Publishing Co: Ingalls Shipbuilding Division, Litton, PO Box 149, Pascagoula, MS 39568-0149; Title Tel # (601) 935-3971 Title Fax # (601) 935-5766
Personnel: Publisher, Editor-Mark Sullivan, Adv. Dir.-RoAnna Robertson
Editorial Description: Weekly employee pub. - news & features.
General Info: Yr. Est. 1940, Weekly, Trim Size-8½ x 11, Sheetfed press, 4 pages, 3% ads, No Color, Newsprint
Circulation: Total-14,000
Advertising: Inquire for rates.

Ingersolletter

Publishing Co: Ingersoll Milling Machine Co., 707 Fulton Ave, Rockford, IL 61103-4092; Title Tel # (815) 987-6223
Personnel: Editor-J. R. Stanis
General Info: Bi-monthly, Trim Size-8½ x 11, Offset press, 9 pages
Circulation: Total-1,900

Ingram News

Publishing Co: Ingram Corp., 4100 One Shell Sq., New Orleans, LA 70139

Injections from Medrad

Publishing Co: Medrad Inc., 566 Alpha Dr, Pittsburgh, PA 15238-2912

Ink Spot

Publishing Co: Free Press Newspaper Group, Box 250 Western Ave., Crystal Lake, IL 60039

Inner Circle Newsletter

Publishing Co: Franklin Soc. Fed. Saving, 1274 Ave. of Americas, New York, NY 10020-1704

Innovator   *Business*

Publishing Co: Continental Grain Co., Wayne Feed Div., 10 S. Riverside Plaza, Chicago, IL 60606-3708; Title Tel # (312) 930-1050 Title Fax # (312) 876-1060
Personnel: Editor-Barbara Becker, Adv. Dir.-Mark DeMarte
Editorial Description: Purpose is to increase communications between Wayne Feeds sales and other groups within the division through sales tips, marketing ideas, meeting recaps, merchandising suggestions, etc.
General Info: Yr. Est. 1960, Quarterly, Sheetfed press, 12 pages, 2 Color, Coated, Saddle-stitched
Subscriptions: Free To Qualified Recipient
Circulation: Total-1,000

Innovator

Publishing Co: Eaton Corp., 26201 Northwestern Hwy, Southfield, MI 48076-3926; Title Tel # (313) 354-2700
Personnel: Editor-Carole Payne
General Info: Yr. Est. 1972, Quarterly, 8 pages
Circulation: Total-400

Inside

Publishing Co: The Southern Company, 270 Peachtree St NW, Suite 2100, Atlanta, GA 30303 Tel # (404) 506-0573
Personnel: Editor-Jay Osborne, Art Dir.-Lora Ho
General Info: Bi-weekly
Circulation: Total-3,400

Inside AHS-UMS

Publishing Co: Blue Cross-Blue Shield of Greater New York, 622 Third Ave., New York, NY 10017-6794; Title Tel # (212) 490-4141
General Info: Monthly
Circulation: Total-4,100

Inside Bearings

Publishing Co: Miniature Precision Bearings, Inc., Precision Park, Keene, NH 03431; Title Tel # (603) 352-0310 Title Fax # (603) 357-1593
Personnel: Editor-David Rarebe
Editorial Description: Technical periodical which discusses new bearing technologies & applications.
General Info: (Formerly Engineering News), Yr. Est. 1985, Quarterly, Trim Size-8½ x 11, 4 pages, 2 Color, Coated
Circulation: Total-5,500

Inside Bridgeton

Publishing Co: Hussmann Refrigerator Co., 12999 Saint Charles Rock Rd, Bridgeton, MO 63044-2419; Title Tel # (314) 291-2000 Title Fax # (314) 291-3873
Personnel: Publisher, Editor-Glenna Purcell
Editorial Description: Includes company events, world events, local news, educational material to maintain communications and inform employees.
General Info: Yr. Est. 1942, Monthly, Trim Size-11 x 17, Coated, Saddle-stitched
Circulation: Total-2,000

Inside ISO

Publishing Co: Insurance Services Office, 7 World Trade Center, New York, NY 10048 Tel # (212) 898-6000

Inside News

Publishing Co: Illinois Farm Bureau, 1701 N. Towanda Ave, Bloomington, IL 61701-2051
Tel # (309) 557-3140 Fax # (309) 998-6090; Title Tel # (309) 557-2208
General Info: (Formerly Aglite), Yr. Est. 1979, Weekly, Trim Size-8½ x 11, Offset press, 6 pages
Circulation: Total-2,946

Inside Reckitt & Colman
Inc. *Business, Consumer*

Publishing Co: Reckitt & Colman Inc., 1655 Valley Rd # 943, Wayne, NJ 07470-2044
Personnel: Editor-Renee Prasuhn
Editorial Description: For employees of this spice and seasoning company.
General Info: Quarterly, Trim Size-8½ x 11, 12 pages, Color-cover, Coated, Saddle-stitched
Printing Co: Intelligencer Printing Co., 330 Eden Rd #1768, Lancaster, PA 17601-4218
Tel # (717) 291-3100, Fax # (717) 569-2643

Inside SAS

Publishing Co: Scandinavian Airlines System, Inc., Public Relations, 9 Polito Ave., 10th Floor,
Lyndhurst, NJ 07071; Title Tel # (201) 896-3600 Title Fax # (201) 896-3725
Personnel: Editor-Thomas Hanrahan
General Info: Bi-weekly, Trim Size-7¼ x 10½, Offset press, 30 pages
Circulation: Total-12,000

Inside UPS *Business*

Publishing Co: United Parcel Service Corp. Office, 55 Glendale Parkway, Atlanta, GA 30328
Tel # (770) 828-6000
Personnel: Editor-Stephen Smoot
Editorial Description: National publication for all employees of the United Parcel Service
General Info: Bi-monthly, Trim Size-8½ x 11, Web press, 28 pages, Color, Coated, Saddle-stitched
Subscriptions: Free To Qualified Recipient
Circulation: Total-300,000

Insider

Publishing Co: General Motors Corp., General Motors Institute, 1700 W. Third Ave., Flint, MI
48504-4898; Title Tel # (313) 762-9500

Insider

Publishing Co: Search Group, Inc., 7311 Greenhaven Dr Ste 145, Sacramento, CA 95831-3572;
Title Tel # (916) 392-2550 Title Fax # (916) 392-8440
Personnel: Editor-Judith Ryder
General Info: Yr. Est. 1975, Quarterly, Trim Size-8½ x 11, Desktop press, 16 pages, No Color,
Newsprint
Circulation: Total-400

Insight *Business*

Publishing Co: Chubb Life America, 1 Granite Pl, Concord, NH 03301-3258;
Title Tel # (603) 224-7741
Personnel: Editor-Kay Harrison
Editorial Description: Marketing articles for life insurance field force.
General Info: (Formerly United Life Leader), Yr. Est. 1914, Monthly, Trim Size-8½ x 11, Sheetfed
press, 12 pages, Color, Coated
Circulation: Total-3,000
Printing Co: Bridge & Byron, N. State St., Concord, NH 03301 Tel # (603) 225-5221

Insight

Publishing Co: Mississippi Power & Light Co. (MP&L), PO Box 1640, Jackson, MS 39215-1640
Personnel: Editor-Beth Leech Moore
Editorial Description: Company publication for first-line supervisors and above.
General Info: Yr. Est. 1990, Bi-monthly, 8 pages, 2 Color, Matte, Saddle-stitched
Circulation: Total-350
Printing Co: Graphic Reproductions, 663 N State St, Jackson, MS 39202-3304 Tel # (601) 948-6478

Insight

Publishing Co: Branch Banking, PO Box 1847, Wilson, NC 27894-1847; Title Tel # (919) 399-4111
Personnel: Editor-Ken Hamerick
General Info: (Formerly Branch Notes), Yr. Est. 1960, Bi-monthly, Trim Size-8½ x 11, 16 pages, 2
Color
Circulation: Total-3,500

Insight

Publishing Co: Diversity Water Technology, Inc., 7145 Pine St., Chagrin Falls, OH 44022
Tel # (216) 247-4770 Fax # (216) 247-7175

Insight *Business*

Publishing Co: NCR Corp., 1700 S. Patterson Blvd., Dayton, OH 45479-0001 Tel # (513) 445-5000;
Title Tel # (513) 445-1156 Title Fax # (513) 445-0636
Personnel: Editor-Suzanne Liebenrood
General Info: (Formerly NCR Personal), Yr. Est. 1983, Weekly, 6 pages
Subscriptions: Free
Circulation: Total-2,600

Insights Today *Association*

Publishing Co: Blue Cross, Blue Shield of Delaware, One Brandywine Gateway, Box 1991,
Wilmington, DE 19899 Tel # (302) 421-3000 Fax # (302) 421-2058; Title Tel # (302) 421-3301
Personnel: Editor-Deborah Chase, Art Dir.-Sandra Mallett
Editorial Description: Employee information, motivation, Company plans, personnel practices/
policies, profiles.
General Info: (Formerly Gateway; Insights), Yr. Est. 1948, Quarterly, Trim Size-11 x 17, Offset press,
12 pages, 2 Color
Circulation: (100% controlled), Total-1,000

Inter-View

Publishing Co: Braille Institute of America, 741 N Vermont Ave, Los Angeles, CA 90029-3514;
Title Tel # (213) 663-1111
Personnel: Editor-Tim Schwartz
Editorial Description: For the staff and volunteers of Braille Institute.
General Info: Monthly, 8 pages

Intercom

Publishing Co: United Telecommunications Inc., 601 State St, Hood River, OR 97031-1871

Intercom

Publishing Co: Richman Gordman Stores, 12100 W. Center Rd., Omaha, NE 68144-3998
Tel # (402) 691-4000

Intercom *Business*

Publishing Co: Munson Medical Ctr., 1105 6th St, Traverse City, MI 49684-2386
Tel # (616) 935-5000
Personnel: Editor-Robert Downes
General Info: Weekly, Desktop press, 4 pages, Coated
Circulation: Total-1,500
Printing Co: Conventional Graphics, 571 Blue Star Ct, Traverse City, MI 49684-8776
Tel # (616) 943-4301

Interface *Association*

Publishing Co: Smiths Industries, 4141 Eastern Ave SE, Grand Rapids, MI 49508-3469
Tel # (616) 241-8643; Title Tel # (616) 241-7000 Title Fax # (616) 241-7858
Personnel: Editor, Circ. Mgr., Production Mgr.-Jennifer Villarreal
Editorial Description: News coverage is given to Smiths Industries & employees regarding major
corporate happenings & activities.
General Info: (Formerly LSI Log), Yr. Est. 1950, Monthly, Trim Size-9 x 12, Offset press, 24 pages, 2
Color, Saddle-stitched
Circulation: Total-3,500
Printing Co: D&D Printing, 342 Market, Grand Rapids, MI 49503 Tel # (616) 454-7710

Interstate News *Association*

Publishing Co: Interstate Power Co., PO Box 769, Dubuque, IA 52004-0769;
Title Tel # (319) 582-5421
Personnel: Editor-Jim Efmoil
Editorial Description: Company news, news of employees and retired employees.
General Info: Yr. Est. 1939, Monthly, Trim Size-11½ x 17, Offset press, 8 pages, No Color
Circulation: (100% controlled), Total-1,900

Intra Comm *Business*

Publishing Co: General Motors Power Train, PO Box 909, Toledo, OH 43697-0909;
Title Tel # (419) 470-5191
Personnel: Editor-Jeff Kuhlman
General Info: (Formerly Turbo Hy-Lites; Hydra-Matic), Bi-monthly, Trim Size-9½ x 12½, Offset press,
8 pages, Coated
Circulation: (100% controlled), Total-6,500

Iowa Highlights *Business, Association*

Publishing Co: GTE Telephone Ops., PO Box 330, Grinnell, IA 50112-0330
General Info: Quarterly

Item *Business*

Publishing Co: Itek Corp., 10 Maguire Rd, Lexington, MA 02173-3199; Title Tel # (617) 276-2951
Personnel: Editor-Charlotte Baker
General Info: (Formerly Item News), Yr. Est. 1962, Monthly, Trim Size-11 x 14, Offset press, 8
pages, No Color
Circulation: (ABC, As of 03/31/95), Total-23,901

J & H Infaline

Publishing Co: Johnson & Higgins, 125 Broad St, New York, NY 10004-2424;
Title Tel # (212) 574-7000

J-L-C News

Publishing Co: J.L. Clark Mfg. Co., 2300 S 6th St, Rockford, IL 61104-7117

JH News
Business, Consumer

Publishing Co: Jewish Hospital of Cincinnati, 3200 Burnet Ave, Cincinnati, OH 45229-3099
Tel # (513) 569-2000; Title Tel # (513) 569-3640 Title Fax # (513) 569-2555
Personnel: Publisher-Pat Seger, Editor-Todd Napier, Art Dir.-Pat Huey
Editorial Description: Contains news, photos, and features of interest to employees.
General Info: (Formerly Hospi-Tales), Yr. Est. 1948, Bi-weekly, Trim Size-11 x 14, Offset press, 1 pages, 2 Color
Subscriptions: Free
Circulation: (100% controlled), Total-2,000

Jax
Consumer, Association

Publishing Co: Jackson Laboratory, 600 Main St, Bar Harbor, ME 04609-1500;
Title Tel # (207) 288-3371
Editorial Description: Information on scientific, educational, employee activities of The Jackson Laboratory.
General Info: Yr. Est. 1952, Quarterly, Trim Size-8½ x 11, Sheetfed press, 6 pages
Circulation: (100% controlled), Total-10,000

Johnson Wax Weekly

Publishing Co: Johnson Wax, 1525 Howe St, Racine, WI 53403-2236; Title Tel # (414) 554-4179
Editorial Description: Employee new products, company, news philosophy, recreation news & benefits for employees only.
General Info: (Formerly Johnson Weekly), Yr. Est. 1958, Weekly, Trim Size-9 x 12, Sheetfed press, 12 pages, 2 Color, Coated
Circulation: (100% controlled), Total-6,300

Journal

Publishing Co: Blue Cross & Blue Shield of Ohio, 2066 E 9th St, Cleveland, OH 44115-1303
Personnel: Editor-Samantha Franck
Editorial Description: Employee newsletter.
General Info: (Formerly Cross Section), Monthly, Trim Size-8½ x 11, Web press, 12 pages, 2 Color, Coated, Saddle-stitched
Circulation: Total-3,000

Journal/Sentinel Ink
Consumer

Publishing Co: Journal/Sentinel Inc., 333 W State St, Milwaukee, WI 53203-1305 Parent Co.-Journal Communications, Milwaukee
Personnel: Editor-Renee Prink
Editorial Description: Employee publication of Journal/Sentinel Inc., a subsideary of Journal Communications.
General Info: Yr. Est. 1993, Weekly, Trim Size-8½ x 11, Desktop press, 4 pages
Subscriptions: Free To Qualified Recipient
Circulation: (100% controlled), Total-2,600

Journalist

Publishing Co: Ontario Reporters' Assn., Simcoe, ON N3Y 4L2 Canada
General Info: (Formerly Ontario Reporters' Assn., Newsletter), Monthly

KNX Trade Talk

Publishing Co: Radio Station KNX, CBS, 6121 W. Sunset Blvd., Hollywood, CA 90028-6455;
Title Tel # (213) 469-1212
Editorial Description: Radio industry news; some general interest articles.
General Info: 10x/yr.

Ka Waipuna

Publishing Co: Honolulu Board of Water Supply, 630 S Beretania St, Honolulu, HI 96843-0002;
Title Tel # (808) 527-6126
Personnel: Editor-Denise De Costa, Circ. Mgr.-Lisa Kim
Editorial Description: Employee newsletter regarding activities, operations and special events relating to the Honolulu Board of Water Supply.
General Info: Yr. Est. 1954, Bi-monthly, Web press, 4 pages, No Color
Circulation: (100% controlled), Total-1,100
Printing Co: Fisher Printing Co., 919 Kekaulike St, Honolulu, HI 96817-5006 Tel # (808) 537-3966

Kaleidoscope
Business

Publishing Co: Blue Cross, 20 At Alpine Rd., Columbia, SC 29219-0001; Title Tel # (803) 788-3860
Personnel: Editor-Kelly Grabowski, Production Mgr.-Tim Floyd, Art Dir.-Gary Smith
Editorial Description: Information related to corporation operations and policies, problems.
General Info: (Formerly Blueprint), Monthly, Offset press, 4 pages, 4 Color, Coated
Circulation: Total-3,000

Kazoo News

Publishing Co: General Motors Corp., 5200 E Cork St, Kalamazoo, MI 49001-9603;
Title Tel # (616) 384-1100

Kelly-Springfield Today

Publishing Co: Kelly-Springfield Tire Co., Rte. 20 E., Freeport, IL 61032; Title Tel # (815) 235-4185

Kemper Insurance Magazine
Business

Publishing Co: Kemper National Insurance Companies, Pub. Affairs & Commisions, F-3, 1 Kemper Dr., Long Grove, IL 60049-0001; Title Tel # (847) 320-2057
Personnel: Publisher-Carol Vander Mey
Editorial Description: Corporate publication for employees and retirees of Kemper National Insurance Companies.
General Info: Yr. Est. 1934, Monthly, Trim Size-8½ x 11, Offset press, 8 pages, 2 Color, Matte, Saddle-stitched
Circulation: Total-14,000
Printing Co: Kemper Natl. Printing Services, Lake Zurich, IL 60047

Key Bank Flashes
Business

Publishing Co: First Trust, 201 S Warren St, Syracuse, NY 13202-1606; Title Tel # (315) 470-5261
Editorial Description: To inform employees of bank functions, special events, promotions, etc.
General Info: (Formerly First Trust Flashes), Semi-weekly, Trim Size-8½ x 11, 1 pages, No Color
Circulation: Total-850

Kilowatt Komments

Publishing Co: Benton City Electric Cooperative Assn., 1006 W 4th St # 488, Vinton, IA 52349-1017

Lablife

Publishing Co: General Motors Research Laboratories, 30500 Mound Rd # 9055, Warren, MI 48092-2031; Title Tel # (313) 986-0276 Title Fax # (810) 986-2243
Personnel: Editor-Constance Bodi
Editorial Description: An employe pub. featuring articles highlighting the people & projects of the GM research laboratories.
General Info: (Formerly Lab Notes), Yr. Est. 1944, Bi-weekly, Trim Size-8½ x 11
Circulation: Total-1,800

Laminator

Publishing Co: Ralph Wilson Plastics Co., Box 6110, Temple, TX 76503-6110;
Title Tel # (817) 778-2711 Title Fax # (817) 770-2460
Personnel: Editor-Scott Ewing
General Info: Yr. Est. 1960, Weekly, Trim Size-8½ x 11, 8 pages, 2 Color, Saddle-stitched
Circulation: (56% controlled), Total-2,850
Printing Co: American Printing, 16 S 4th St, Temple, TX 76501-4336 Tel # (817) 771-2422

Leader Digest

Publishing Co: Leader Fedl. Savings, 158 Madison Ave, Memphis, TN 38103-2630;
Title Tel # (901) 578-2345

Letter of Recognition

Publishing Co: Recognition Equipment Inc., PO Box 660204, Dallas, TX 75266-0204;
Title Tel # (214) 579-5971
Personnel: Editor-Melinda Swift
Editorial Description: Employee pub.
General Info: Yr. Est. 1970, Offset press, 12 pages, Coated
Circulation: (100% controlled), Total-3,500
Printing Co: Millet the Printer, 1000 South Ervay Street, Dallas, TX 75201 Tel # (214) 741-3602

Life in General
Business

Publishing Co: Gulf Life Insurance Co., Mc0204 American Gen Ctr., Nashville, TN 37250-0001;
Title Tel # (904) 390-7945
Personnel: Editor-Lori Messina, Art Dir.-Jean Girouard
Editorial Description: For home office employees.
General Info: Yr. Est. 1985, Quarterly, Trim Size-11 x 15, Offset press, 4 pages, Coated, Saddle-stitched
Subscriptions: $1/copy
Circulation: (100% controlled), Total-1,300

Life at Bankers

Publishing Co: Bankers Life, 4444 W Lawrence Ave, Chicago, IL 60630-2546;
Title Tel # (312) 777-7000
Personnel: Editor-Adele M. Lebow
General Info: Monthly, Trim Size-11 x 14½, Offset press, 6 pages
Circulation: Total-3,200

Life at McCurdy's
Association

Publishing Co: McCurdy, Midtown Plaza, Rochester, NY 14645-0001; Title Tel # (716) 232-1000
Personnel: Editor-Leslie Koster
Editorial Description: Storewide news, promotions & changes.
General Info: Yr. Est. 1948, Monthly, Trim Size-8½ x 11, Offset press, 6 pages
Circulation: Total-1,700

Lifelines

Publishing Co: Kentucky Lung Assn., PO Box 9067, Louisville, KY 40209-0067

Lifetime
Business

Publishing Co: Kansas City Life Insurance Co., PO Box 419139, Kansas City, MO 64141-6139;
Title Tel # (816) 753-7000
Personnel: Editor-Eileen Jenkins, Adv. Dir.-Ron Malcolm
Editorial Description: Publication for field force with emphasis on insurance-related articles.
General Info: Yr. Est. 1945, Monthly, Trim Size-8½ x 11, Offset press, 12 pages, 2 Color
Acquistions: Publication Bought
Circulation: (100% controlled), Total-3,000

Lindens Lines
See: AUTOMOTIVE

Link
Business

Publishing Co: Litton Systems Inc. -G/CS Div., 5500 Canoga Ave, Woodland Hills, CA 91367-6621 Fax # (818) 715-2448; Title Tel # (818) 712-7225
Personnel: Editor-Ron Palmer
Editorial Description: Employee pub. produced by Litton.
General Info: Yr. Est. 1961, Monthly, Trim Size-11½ x 16½, Offset press, 8 pages, No Color
Circulation: (100% controlled), Total-4,500

Link

Publishing Co: Lincoln First Bank of Rochester, PO Box 20472, Rochester, NY 14602-0472; Title Tel # (716) 258-5000
Editorial Description: Communication to employees of new service, products, bank achievements, goals, programs. On occassion, present management philosophy re: employee benefits, programs, banking related activities.
General Info: (Formerly Linc-All News), Quarterly, Trim Size-8 x 12¼, Letrpr. press, 10 pages, Color
Circulation: Total-2,400

Link

Publishing Co: Blue Cross-Blue Shield, 636 Grand Ave, Des Moines, IA 50309-2551; Title Tel # (515) 245-4702
Personnel: Editor-Sheri Luken
General Info: (Formerly Scope), Monthly, Trim Size-8½ x 11, Offset press, 8 pages, 2 Color
Circulation: (100% controlled)

Link-Belt Today

Publishing Co: Link-Belt Div., FMC Corp., 220 S Belmont Ave, Indianapolis, IN 46222-4210; Title Tel # (317) 632-5411
Personnel: Editor-George F. Dunn
General Info: Yr. Est. 1942, Weekly
Circulation: Total-5,400

Lion's Roar

Publishing Co: Dollar Savings Bank, PO Box 987, Pittsburgh, PA 15230-0987

Lithocraft

Publishing Co: Taylor Publishing Co., 1550 W Mockingbird Ln, Dallas, TX 75235-5007
Personnel: Editor-Lyn Wilson
General Info: Monthly
Circulation: Total-2,000

Local Topics

Publishing Co: Cook-Waite Labs Inc., Sterling Drug Inc., 90 Park Ave., New York, NY 10016-1389; Title Tel # (212) 972-4141
Personnel: Editor-D.E. Latham, Jr.
General Info: Monthly, Trim Size-3 x 5¼, Letrpr. press, 20 pages
Circulation: Total-2,000

Lockheed Southern Star

Publishing Co: Lockheed Aircraft Svc. Co., PO Box 33, Ontario, CA 91761-0033 Tel # (909) 395-2411
Personnel: Editor-Joseph Dabney
General Info: Semi-monthly, Trim Size-11 x 16½, Offset press, 8 pages
Circulation: Total-35,000

Long Haul Letter

Publishing Co: Flying J, Inc., PO Box 678, Brigham City, UT 84302-0678; Title Tel # (801) 734-9416
General Info: Yr. Est. 1985, 8 pages

Lubrication Beyond Oil
Ideas

Publishing Co: Acheson Colloids Co, PO Box 611747, Port Huron, MI 48061-1747; Title Tel # (313) 984-5581
Personnel: Editor-John E. Lott
Editorial Description: External house organ featuring case histories of dry film lubricant applications aimed at design engeeners in all major industries.
General Info: Yr. Est. 1971, Quarterly, Trim Size-8½ x 11, Offset press, 4 pages, Color
Circulation: Total-25,000

Lung Line Letter
See: HOSPITALS & NURSING HOMES

M News
Association

Publishing Co: Metropolitan Dade County Transit Agency, 6601 NW 72nd Ave, Miami, FL 33166-3029; Title Tel # (305) 638-6781
Personnel: Editor-Michael DeCossio
Editorial Description: Company news for employees of the Metropolitan Dade County Transit Agency.
General Info: (Formerly MTA Today), Bi-monthly, Trim Size-8½ x 11, 8 pages

MCF

Publishing Co: Texas Gas Transmission Corp., 3800 Frederica St., Owensboro, KY 42301-6900; Title Tel # (502) 926-8686 Title Fax # (502) 683-5373

MD Today

Publishing Co: General Motors Corp., GM Technical Ctr., Warren, MI 48090 Tel # (313) 556-2051; Title Tel # (313) 556-5000

M.F.D. Register

Publishing Co: Milwaukee Fire Dept., 711 W Wells St, Milwaukee, WI 53233-1479; Title Tel # (414) 276-5656
Personnel: Editor-Carl W. Klitzke
Editorial Description: For members of Fire Department and their families.
General Info: Yr. Est. 1961, Monthly, Letrpr. press, 4 pages, No Color
Circulation: (100% controlled), Total-1,900
Printing Co: MPI Graphics, 633 S Hawley Rd, Milwaukee, WI 53214-1948

MH Systems Scene
Business

Publishing Co: FMC Corp., PO Box 904, Chalfont, PA 18914-0904; Title Tel # (215) 822-4300
General Info: Quarterly

MONY Today

Publishing Co: Mutual of New York, 1740 Broadway, New York, NY 10019-4315; Title Tel # (212) 708-2488
Editorial Description: For employees and its field force.
General Info: (Formerly MONY News), Yr. Est. 1959, Weekly, Trim Size-11 x 15½, Offset press, 8 pages
Circulation: Total-13,000

M&T Observer
Business

Publishing Co: M & T Bank, 1 M And T Plz, Buffalo, NY 14203-2399; Title Tel # (716) 842-5385
Personnel: Editor-Karla Rogers
Editorial Description: House organ for a commercial bank.
General Info: 10x/yr., Sheetfed press, 8 pages, 2 Color, Coated
Circulation: Total-2,600

MUO News

Publishing Co: Mutual of Omaha, 500 Univ. Ave., Toronto, ON M5G 1V8 Canada; Title Tel # (416) 598-4321
Personnel: Editor-Nicholas Paoulyn

Macwhyte Whyte Line

Publishing Co: MacWhyte Wire Rope Co., 2906 14th Ave, Kenosha, WI 53140-5028; Title Tel # (414) 654-5381
Personnel: Publisher, Editor, Adv. Dir.-C.V. Markin
Editorial Description: Employee activities in and around plant.
General Info: Yr. Est. 1912, Quarterly, Trim Size-8½ x 11, Offset press, 4 pages, No Color
Circulation: (100% controlled), Total-800

Macy-Go-Round

Publishing Co: R. H. Macy, 180 Peachtree St. NW, Atlanta, GA 30303-1725
Personnel: Editor-Gerri Smith
General Info: Monthly, Trim Size-8½ x 11, Offset press, 5 pages
Circulation: Total-3,000

Main line
Business

Publishing Co: CNG Transmission Corp., PO Box 2450, Clarksburg, WV 26302-2450; Title Tel # (304) 623-8326
Editorial Description: Management's message to employees about Company.
General Info: (Formerly Main Line News), Yr. Est. 1965, Bi-monthly, Trim Size-8½ x 11, Offset press, 16 pages, 4 Color, Coated, Saddle-stitched
Circulation: (100% controlled), Total-4,000
Printing Co: Fairmont Printing Co., PO Box 2000, Fairmont, WV 26555-2000 Tel # (304) 363-8500, Fax # (304) 363-8224

Mainelines

Publishing Co: NYNEX, 125 High St Ste 30, Boston, MA 02110-2704 Tel # (617) 743-9800; Title Tel # (617) 743-3530
Personnel: Editor-Angela Brothers
General Info: 4 pages

Mainline Newsletter
Business

Publishing Co: Colonial Pipeline Co., PO Box 18855, Atlanta, GA 31126-0855; Title Tel # (404) 261-1470 Title Fax # (404) 841-2883
Editorial Description: Employee publication of Colonial Pipeline Co., refined petroleum products transporter.
General Info: (Formerly Linefill Magazine), Yr. Est. 1962, Bi-weekly, Trim Size-8½ x 11, Web press, 2 pages, No Color
Circulation: Total-850

Management News (K Mart)
Association

Publishing Co: K Mart Corp., 3100 W Big Beaver Rd, Troy, MI 48084-3004; Title Tel # (810) 643-1000
Personnel: Publications Director-Angela Rogers
Editorial Description: Informative & helpful articles geared toward management level.
General Info: Bi-monthly, 16 pages, 4 Color
Circulation: Total-13,000

Management Newsletter

Publishing Co: General Motors Corp., Gm Parts Div. Gmc, Flint, MI 48554-0001;
Title Tel # (313) 635-5000

Management Newsletter

Publishing Co: Mountain Bell, PO Box 960, Denver, CO 80201-0960

Marine Midland Regional
  Bulletin

Publishing Co: Marine Midland Bank, 1 Marine Midland Plz, Rochester, NY 14604-2401

Marriott World   *Business, Consumer*

Publishing Co: Marriott International, Marriott Dr., Dept. 935.27, Washington, DC 20058;
Title Tel # (301) 380-1033
Personnel: Editor-Terry Weisz
Editorial Description: Newsletter for employees and their families; in-company news only.
General Info: Yr. Est. 1937, Bi-monthly, Trim Size-8½ x 11, Offset press, 24 pages, 4 Color, Coated,
Saddle-stitched
Subscriptions: Free To Qualified Recipient
Circulation: Total-52,000

Martinsburg Monitor

Publishing Co: General Motors Corp., 1000 Warm Springs Ave, Martinsburg, WV 25401-3800;
Title Tel # (304) 267-5600

Mas-Back-Talk

Publishing Co: Masback, Inc., 2400 83rd St, North Bergen, NJ 07047-1406;
Title Tel # (212) 255-1300

Maxwell House Messenger

Publishing Co: Maxwell House Div., General Foods Corp., 1125 Hudson St, Hoboken, NJ
07030-5305
Personnel: Editor-Marie Scotti
General Info: Bi-monthly, Trim Size-8½ x 11, Letrpr. press, 16 pages
Circulation: Total-5,600

McKone   *Business*

Publishing Co: McKone & Co., 1900 Westridge Dr, Irving, TX 75038-2901;
Title Tel # (214) 550-7433
Personnel: Editor-Sheila Durante
Editorial Description: Published for employees and clients.
General Info: Quarterly

McLean Bulletin

Publishing Co: McLean Hospital, Dept. of Scientific Pubs., 115 Mill St, Belmont, MA 02178-1048

McNess Farmer

Publishing Co: Furst-McNess Co., 120 E Clark St, Freeport, IL 61032-3300 Tel # (815) 235-6151

Medical Bulletin of St. John
  Hospital

Publishing Co: St. John Hospital Inc., Marketing & Public Relations, 22101 Moross Rd., Detroit, MI
48236-2148 Tel # (313) 343-4000; Title Tel # (313) 343-7454 Title Fax # (313) 417-2950

Memo to Management

Publishing Co: Southern California Gas Co., 555 W. 5th St., Los Angeles, CA 90013-1011
Tel # (213) 204-2557; Title Tel # (213) 689-3621

Merry-Go-Round

Publishing Co: Kroger Co., 1014 Vine St, Cincinnati, OH 45202-1100

Messenger

Publishing Co: Intl. Correspondence Schools, Oak & Pawnee St., Scranton, PA 18515-0001;
Title Tel # (202) 342-7701
Personnel: Editor-Alan Mazzei
General Info: Bi-monthly, Trim Size-8½ x 11, Letrpr. press, 10 pages
Circulation: Total-1,200

Messenger

Publishing Co: Pacific Health Resources, 1423 S Grand Ave, Los Angeles, CA 90015-3073

Met-Ed System

Publishing Co: Metropolitan Edison Co., General Public Utilities Corp., PO Box 542, Reading, PA
19603-0542; Title Tel # (717) 929-3601
Personnel: Editor-William R. Ehst
Editorial Description: Electric utility industry policies, progress, problems. Company management,
employee education and information material.
General Info: Yr. Est. 1958, Quarterly, Trim Size-11½ x 17, Offset press, 10 pages
Circulation: Total-3,400

Micro Switch News   *Association*

Publishing Co: Micro Switch, A Div. of Honeywell, 11 W. Spring St., Freeport, IL 61032-4353;
Title Tel # (815) 235-5415
Personnel: Circ. Mgr.-Joe Vaske
Editorial Description: Contains news about employees and the company.
General Info: Yr. Est. 1940, Bi-monthly, Trim Size-8½ x 11, Offset press, 16 pages, 2 Color, Coated
Circulation: (100% controlled), Total-5,270
Printing Co: Wagner Printing Co., 1 E Spring St, Freeport, IL 61032-4338 Tel # (815) 235-7656

Mid-Continent News

Publishing Co: Mid-Continent Supply Co., 2240 Morriss Rd Ste 110, Flower Mound, TX 75028-3587

Mid Net News   *Association*

Publishing Co: National Association for Female Executives, Inc., 30 Irving Pl., 5th Floor, New York,
NY 10003-2303 Tel # (212) 477-2200 Fax # (212) 477-8215; Title Tel # (212) 897-4882
Editorial Description: For members of the Midtown Network Group.

Mid-Valley Impeller

Publishing Co: Mid-Valley Pipeline Co., PO Box 2388, Longview, TX 75606-2388

Milacron Review

Publishing Co: Cincinnati Milacron, 4701 Marburg Ave, Cincinnati, OH 45209-1025;
Title Tel # (513) 841-8100

Miles Alkalizer

Publishing Co: Miles Inc., 1127 Myrtle St # 40, Elkhart, IN 46514-2201; Title Tel # (219) 264-7584
Personnel: Publisher-Donald N. Yates, Editor-Roger Snow
Editorial Description: Employee publication for internal distribution.
General Info: (Formerly The Alkalizer), Yr. Est. 1936, Monthly, Sheetfed press, 4 pages, 2 Color,
Recycled
Subscriptions: Free To Qualified Recipient
Circulation: Total-6,500
Printing Co: Petersen Printing, 2920 W Sample St, South Bend, IN 46619-3232

Mill   *Business*

Publishing Co: Natl. Steel Corp., 20th & State, Granite City, IL 62040-4622;
Title Tel # (618) 451-3615
Personnel: Publisher, Editor-Norma Jones
Editorial Description: Employee newsletter of co. related events, promotions & plans/policies/
employer relations & mgt. style.
General Info: Yr. Est. 1950, Bi-monthly, Trim Size-8½ x 11, Offset press, 8 pages, 2 Color, Coated,
Saddle-stitched
Circulation: Total-6,000

Miller Management Briefing
  See: BEVERAGES - BREWING

Milton Bradley News

Publishing Co: Milton Bradley Co., PO Box 3400, Springfield, MA 01101-3400

Mirror   *Business*

Publishing Co: United Telephone Co. of Missouri, 319 Madison St, Jefferson City, MO 65101-3108;
Title Tel # (314) 634-1630
Personnel: Editor-Sandy Buersmeyer
Editorial Description: Employee retiree newsletter providing co. & industry news.
General Info: (Formerly The Edition), Yr. Est. 1969, Bi-weekly, Offset press, 4 pages, No Color,
Coated
Circulation: (100% controlled), Total-1,250

Missilani

Publishing Co: Hercules Aerospace, Box 98-FH27, Magna, UT 84044-0120;
Title Tel # (801) 251-4736
Personnel: Editor-anne Magin
General Info: Weekly, Trim Size-8½ x 11, Offset press, 2 Color, Newsprint
Circulation: Total-5,500

Mixing Bowl

Publishing Co: Mirro Aluminum Co., 1512 Washington St, Manitowoc, WI 54220-5046;
Title Tel # (414) 684-4421

Modern Merchant

Publishing Co: Furst-McNess Co., 120 E Clark St, Freeport, IL 61032-3300 Tel # (815) 235-6151

Momentum

Publishing Co: American Honda Motor Co. Inc., Employee Relations, 1919 Torrance Blvd., Torrance,
CA 90501-2746; Title Tel # (310) 783-2000
General Info: (Formerly Mighty to Mini News)

Money Engineer　　　　　*Association*

Publishing Co: Union Bank, 445 S Figueroa St, Los Angeles, CA 90071-1655;
Title Tel # (213) 236-5709
Personnel: Editor-Janice Nelson
Editorial Description: Union bank employee magazine.
General Info: Yr. Est. 1958, Bi-monthly, Trim Size-8½ x 11, Offset press, 16 pages, 2 Color, Coated
Circulation: (100% controlled), Total-6,000
Printing Co: Horn Graphics, Inc., 1101 E 18th St, Los Angeles, CA 90021-3009 Tel # (213) 748-1000

Motor Vator

Publishing Co: General Motors Corp., Chevy-Flint Metal Fabricating, Flint, MI 48553-0001;
Title Tel # (313) 236-0470

Muncie Transmitter

Publishing Co: Owens-Illinois Inc., 3600 Alameda Ave, Oakland, CA 94601-3329
Tel # (510) 436-2000; Title Tel # (415) 436-2000

Murray Tube Bulletin

Publishing Co: A. B. Murray Co. Inc., 58 Cabot Blvd E, Langhorne, PA 19047-9101;
Title Tel # (215) 788-9221

Music-Theatre Group Newsletter

Publishing Co: Music Theatre Group, 29 Bethune St, New York, NY 10014-1724;
Title Tel # (212) 924-3108
Personnel: Production Mgr.-Diane Wondisford

NBI Today

Publishing Co: Nabisco Brands, Inc., Nabisco Brands Plaza, Parsippany, NJ 07054-4471;
Title Tel # (201) 898-7821
Editorial Description: Internal newsletter for headquarters employees of Nabisco Brands, Inc.
General Info: Monthly, Trim Size-11 x 14¾, Sheetfed press, 4 pages, Coated
Circulation: Total-4,100

NBTA News　　　　　*Association*

Publishing Co: New Brunswick Teachers' Assn., Box 752, Fredericton, NB E3B 5R6 Canada;
Title Tel # (506) 455-8921
Personnel: Publisher-J.S. Mackinnon, Editor-Rod Campbell, Art Dir.-Dawn Parousiadis
Editorial Description: Teacher information and service announcements.
General Info: Yr. Est. 1958, 15x/yr., Trim Size-8½ x 11, Offset press, 16 pages, ISSN: 0317-5227, No Color
Circulation: (100% controlled), Total-7,100

N.E.S. News　　　　　*Business*

Publishing Co: Nashville Electric Service, 1214 Church St, Nashville, TN 37246-0002
General Info: Monthly, Trim Size-8½ x 12, Offset press, 10 pages, No Color, Newsprint, Saddle-stitched
Circulation: Total-1,200

NSC Today

Publishing Co: Natl. Starch, PO Box 6500, Bridgewater, NJ 08807-0500

NTS News

Publishing Co: Reynolds Electrical, PO Box 14400, Las Vegas, NV 89114-4400
Tel # (702) 295-1000

N/W　　　　　*Business*

Publishing Co: Newsweek, Inc., 251 W 57th St, New York, NY 10019-1802 Tel # (212) 445-4000;
Title Tel # (212) 445-4866 Title Fax # (212) 445-4929
Personnel: Editor-Cliff Chase
Editorial Description: Weekly in-house newsletter serving Newsweek, Inc's., world-wide staff.
General Info: Yr. Est. 1946, Weekly, Trim Size-8½ x 11, Offset press, 4 pages, 2 Color
Circulation: (100% controlled), Total-2,000

Nabisco News

Publishing Co: Nabisco Inc., 7300 S Kedzie Ave, Chicago, IL 60629-3534 Tel # (312) 925-4300

Nabisco (year)　　　　　*Business, Consumer*

Publishing Co: Nabisco Canada, 10 Park Lawn Rd., Etobicoke, ON M84 3H8 Canada;
Title Tel # (416) 253-3313
Editorial Description: To inform employees about company developments.
General Info: (Formerly Contact), Yr. Est. 1977, Bi-monthly, Trim Size-8½ x 11, Offset press, 6 pages, 2 Color
Circulation: (100% controlled), Total-3,000

National City News

Publishing Co: Natl. City Bank of Cleveland, 1900 E. 9th St., Cleveland, OH 44114-3484;
Title Tel # (216) 575-2511
Personnel: Editor-Marianne Hornyak
General Info: Monthly, Trim Size-8½ x 11, Sheetfed press, 6 pages, No Color, Coated
Circulation: Total-3,600

Neespaper

Publishing Co: New England Electric System, 20 Turnpike Rd, Westborough, MA 01581-3903

Neptune on the Move

Publishing Co: Neptune World Wide Moving, 55 Weyman Ave, New Rochelle, NY 10805-1410

Nesbitt Newsbits

Publishing Co: John J. Nesbitt Inc., State Rd. & Rhawn St., Philadelphia, PA 19136;
Title Tel # (215) 332-2400

Network

Publishing Co: Seattle City Light, 1015 3rd Ave # 809, Seattle, WA 98104-1198;
Title Tel # (206) 684-3112
Personnel: Editor-Kim Jasek, Art Dir.-Sam McJunkin
Editorial Description: Management & administrative issues; employees work activities; features & photos.
General Info: (Formerly City Light News), Yr. Est. 1976, Bi-monthly, Trim Size-11 x 17, Sheetfed press, 8 pages, 2 Color, Newsprint
Circulation: Total-3,200

Network　　　　　*Business*

Publishing Co: Sovereign Life Insurance Co., 500 4th Ave. SW, #800, Calgary, AB T2P 2V6 Canada; Title Tel # (403) 298-5475
Personnel: Publisher, Editor, Circ. Mgr.-Art Dir.-L. Palmer
Editorial Description: Articles on marketing/field/product news (50% of content) and coprorate/home office employee news (50%).
General Info: (Formerly Compass), Yr. Est. 1986, Bi-monthly, Trim Size-8½ x 11, Offset press, 12 pages, No Color, Coated
Acquistions: Publication Bought
Circulation: (100% controlled), Total-2,000
Printing Co: Cascade Printing, Bay 10, 2219 35th Ave., N.E., Calgary, AB T2E 6W3 Canada
Tel # (403) 250-2202

Networker

Publishing Co: HRB Systems, Box 60, Science Pk., State College, PA 16804-0060;
Title Tel # (814) 238-4311
Personnel: Editor-Cindy Spencer, Art Dir.-Patrick Besong
Editorial Description: The Circuit features business articles & interviews.
General Info: (Formerly Telefax), Bi-monthly, Trim Size-8½ x 11, Offset press, 20 pages, No Color, Coated
Circulation: (100% controlled), Total-1,700

New Notes

Publishing Co: North York Public Library, 5120 Yonge Street, North York, ON M2N 5N9 Canada;
Title Tel # (416) 395-5515 Title Fax # (416) 395-5542
General Info: Yr. Est. 1981, Bi-monthly, Sheetfed press, 12 pages, ISSN: 0821-476X, Color-cover, Matte
Subscriptions: Free To Qualified Recipient
Circulation: Total-800

New Oiler

Publishing Co: Shell Oil Co., PO Box 60193, New Orleans, LA 70160-0193;
Title Tel # (504) 588-6161

New York Divisionnews

Publishing Co: Contel of New York, 850 Harrison St. Ext., Johnstown, NY 12095;
Title Tel # (518) 762-6202
Personnel: Editor-James Hinkle
Editorial Description: For employees & retirees of CTC- New York.
General Info: Yr. Est. 1983, Monthly, Trim Size-8½ x 11, Offset press, 8 pages, Color, Newsprint, Saddle-stitched
Circulation: Total-1,500

New York Life News

Publishing Co: New York Life Insurance Co., 51 Madison Ave., #152, New York, NY 10010-1655;
Title Tel # (212) 576-7000
Personnel: Editor-Thomas M. Maher
General Info: Semi-monthly, Trim Size-9½ x 14, Letrpr. press, 4 pages
Circulation: Total-10,000

New York Metro Area Update　　　　　*Business*

Publishing Co: U.S. Postal Service, Executive Offices, 8th Ave. and 33rd St., New York, NY 10001;
Title Tel # (212) 330-3167
Personnel: Editor-Pat McGovern
Editorial Description: Information and news for New York City and Metropolitan area postal employees.
General Info: (Formerly Postscript), Yr. Est. 1974, Monthly, Trim Size-8½ x 11, Web press, 24 pages, Color, Coated, Saddle-stitched
Subscriptions: Free To Qualified Recipient
Circulation: Total-85,000

Newarker

Publishing Co: Sherwin-Williams Co., Brown St. & Lister Ave., Newark, NJ 07105;
Title Tel # (201) 344-6448

News
Business

Publishing Co: Canadian Imperial Bank of Commerce, Commerce Ct. N., 10th Fl., Toronto, ON M5L 1A2 Canada Tel # (416) 980-5036; Title Tel # (416) 980-5362
Editorial Description: Employee newsletter: lots of employee profiles, bank policies, practices, industry news.
General Info: Yr. Est. 1966, Monthly, Trim Size-11 x 15¾, Desktop press, 8 pages, 2 Color, Newsprint
Acquistions: Publication Bought

News

Publishing Co: Firestone Tire, PO Box 699, Pottstown, PA 19464-0699; Title Tel # (215) 326-5120

News & Review
See: MINING & MINERALS

News & Views

Publishing Co: Roseburg Forest Products Co., PO Box 1088, Roseburg, OR 97470-0252; Title Tel # (503) 679-3311
Personnel: Editor-Frank T. Cartiso
Editorial Description: Contains info on issues & topics relating to Forest Products industry & co. business.
General Info: Monthly, Trim Size-8⅜ x 10⅞, Web press, 16 pages, No Color, Coated, Saddle-stitched
Circulation: Total-6,500
Printing Co: Koke Printing Co., 2895 Chad Dr, Eugene, OR 97408-7335 Tel # (503) 687-0103

News in Brief

Publishing Co: Ameritech, PO Box 6250, Cleveland, OH 44101-1250; Title Tel # (216) 622-2400
Personnel: Editor-Marvin Gisser
Editorial Description: Covers news about the communications industry, the Bell System, Ohio Bell, employees and their families.
General Info: Yr. Est. 1954, Bi-weekly
Circulation: Total-25,000

News Briefs

Publishing Co: General Motors Corp., Willow Run Airport, 2625 Tyler, Ypsilanti, MI 48197; Title Tel # (313) 481-5000

News Bulletin

Publishing Co: General Motors Corp., 200 Georgesville Rd, Columbus, OH 43228-2020; Title Tel # (614) 275-5000

News Capsule

Publishing Co: Southwest General Hospital, 18697 Bagley Rd, Middleburg Heights, OH 44130-3497; Title Tel # (216) 826-8000
General Info: Monthly, Trim Size-11 x 17, 4 pages, No Color, Newsprint
Circulation: Total-3,600

News Caster

Publishing Co: General Motors Corp., Central Foundry Div., 77 W Center St, Saginaw, MI 48602-1201; Title Tel # (517) 757-0479
Personnel: Editor-Joseph Lawrence
General Info: Yr. Est. 1976

News of the Engineering Dept.

Publishing Co: E.I. du Pont de Nemours, 10007 Market Street, Wilmington, DE 19898-0001 Tel # (302) 774-1000

News Lines on the Line
Consumer, Association

Publishing Co: Linn County Rural Electric Cooperative Assn., PO Box 69, Marion, IA 52302-0069; Title Tel # (319) 377-1587 Title Fax # (319) 377-5875
Personnel: Editor-Lisa Hoefer
Editorial Description: Information for member consumers regarding cooperative and energy use.
General Info: Yr. Est. 1950, Monthly, Trim Size-8½ x 11, Offset press, 8 pages, No Color, Matte
Circulation: (95% controlled), Total-11,500
Printing Co: Linn Litho, Inc., 3303 3rd Ave, Marion, IA 52302-3930 Tel # (319) 377-8258

News Pix

Publishing Co: New York News, Inc., 450 W. 33rd St., 3rd Fl., New York, NY 10001-2603 Tel # (212) 210-2100; Title Tel # (212) 210-2935
Personnel: Editor-Carolyn Hinsey
General Info: Yr. Est. 1922, Bi-monthly, Trim Size-8½ x 11, Offset press, 20 pages
Circulation: Total-7,000

News and Views

Publishing Co: City Natl. Bank of Detroit, City Natl. Bank Bldg., Detroit, MI 48226; Title Tel # (313) 965-1900
Personnel: Editor-Dave Armstrong
General Info: Monthly, Trim Size-9½ x 11, Offset press, 4 pages
Circulation: Total-850

News/Notes

Publishing Co: Texas Gas Transmission Corp., 3800 Frederica St., Owensboro, KY 42301-6900; Title Tel # (502) 926-8686 Title Fax # (502) 683-5373
General Info: (Formerly Line Walker)

NewsReal
Association

Publishing Co: Fraser Valley Real Estate Board, Box 99, 15463- 104th Ave., Surrey, BC V3T 4W4 Canada; Title Tel # (604) 588-6555
Personnel: Editor-Trudy Lancelyn, Production Mgr.-Deann Leboutillier
Editorial Description: Real estate news concerning members, legislation, committee reports, feature articles & social functions.
General Info: (Formerly Valley Interim), Yr. Est. 1973, Bi-weekly, Trim Size-8½ x 11, Sheetfed press, 8 pages, 2 Color, Coated
Circulation: Total-2,400

News/Views
Business

Publishing Co: AT&T Southwestern Region, 1111 Woods Mill Rd, Ballwin, MO 63011-2943; Title Tel # (314) 391-2110
General Info: Bi-monthly, Trim Size-11 x 17, 8 pages, No Color

Newsbreak

Publishing Co: Allied-Signal, Inc., Kansas City Division, Box 1159, Kansas City, MO 64141; Title Tel # (816) 997-2181
Personnel: Editor-Shannon Gallagher
General Info: (Formerly Newsfront), Yr. Est. 1977, Bi-weekly, Trim Size-8½ x 11, Offset press, 6 pages, 2 Color
Circulation: (100% controlled), Total-9,000

Newsbriefs

Publishing Co: First Natl. Bank, I S. Pinckney St., Madison, WI 53701; Title Tel # (608) 252-4000
Personnel: Editor-J.D. Gibson
General Info: Monthly

Newsletter

Publishing Co: General Motors Corp., 281 Mount Lion Rd. SW, Atlanta, GA 30354; Title Tel # (404) 761-2485

Newsletter

Publishing Co: General Motors Corp., 780 James P Casey Rd, Bristol, CT 06010-2200

Newsletter

Publishing Co: General Motors Corp., 1300 Raritan Rd, Clark, NJ 07066-1102; Title Tel # (908) 276-4300

Newsletter

Publishing Co: General Motors Corp., 6817 Stadium Dr, Kansas City, MO 64129-1815; Title Tel # (913) 281-7215

Newsletter

Publishing Co: General Motors Corp., Roosevelt Hwy., P.O. Box 460, Massena, NY 13662-0460; Title Tel # (315) 764-2000

Newsletter

Publishing Co: General Motors Corp., 400 W Dennis Ave, Olathe, KS 66061-4306; Title Tel # (913) 791-6600

Newsletter

Publishing Co: General Motors Corp., 1445 Parkway Ave, Trenton, NJ 08628-3012; Title Tel # (609) 771-6200

Newsletter

Publishing Co: General Motors Corp., GM Technical Ctr., Warren, MI 48090 Tel # (313) 556-2051

Newsletter
Business, Association

Publishing Co: Western-Southern Life Insurance, Public Relations, 400 Broadway, Cincinnati, OH 45202-3341 Tel # (513) 629-1127; Title Tel # (513) 629-1930
Personnel: Editor-Donna Jerner
Editorial Description: Recognizes leading salespeople and disseminates company information.
General Info: Yr. Est. 1990, Monthly, Sheetfed press, 20 pages, 2 Color, Matte, Saddle-stitched
Circulation: Total-7,200

Newsletter for Management

Publishing Co: Chrysler Corp., 1200 Chrysler Dr., Highland Pk., MI 48288-0001; Title Tel # (313) 956-2894

Nissan People

Publishing Co: Nissan Motor Corp. in USA, PO Box 191, Gardena, CA 90248-0191 Tel # (310) 532-3111

No. 1 Team Bulletin

Publishing Co: General Motors Corp., 23500 Mound Rd, Warren, MI 48091-2049; Title Tel # (313) 978-0880

Nodular Nugget

Publishing Co: General Motors Corp., 2100 Veterans Memorial Pky, Saginaw, MI 48601-1209; Title Tel # (517) 757-5000

Nomad

Publishing Co: Northern Telecom Ltd., 150 Montreal Toronto Blvd., Lachine, PQ H8S 1B6 Canada Tel # (514) 634-3511

Noon News   *Business*

Publishing Co: Harnischfeger Corp., PO Box 554, Milwaukee, WI 53201-0554; Title Tel # (414) 797-6625
Editorial Description: News about Harnischfeger's products, markets, people & overall business performance.
General Info: Yr. Est. 1970, Weekly, Trim Size-8½ x 11, Offset press, 2 pages
Circulation: Total-5,000

Noon Time Newsline

Publishing Co: General Motors Corp., 10800 S Saginaw St, Grand Blanc, MI 48439-8120; Title Tel # (313) 694-8904

Norris-O'Bannon Between Calls

Publishing Co: Dover Corp., Norris-O'Bannon Div., Box 2070, Tulsa, OK 74101-2070

Northrop News

Publishing Co: Northrop Corp., Aircraft Div., 1 Northrop Ave, Hawthorne, CA 90250-3277

Now

Publishing Co: State Street Boston Corp., PO Box 351, Boston, MA 02101-0351

Nylon News

Publishing Co: E.I. du Pont de Nemours, 10007 Market Street, Wilmington, DE 19898-0001 Tel # (302) 774-1000

O-K News

Publishing Co: Cincinnati Gas, 139 E 4th St, Cincinnati, OH 45202-4003; Title Tel # (513) 381-2000
Personnel: Editor-James A. Guthrie
General Info: Weekly, Trim Size-11 x 16, Letrpr. press, 4 pages
Circulation: Total-5,500

OKI Newsletter

Publishing Co: Ohio-KY-Indiana Regional Council of Governments, 801B W. 8th St., Ste. 400, Cincinnati, OH 45203-1601; Title Tel # (513) 621-7060 Title Fax # (513) 621-9325
Personnel: Editor-Lou Ethridge

ONLI Echoes   *Business*

Publishing Co: Ohio National Companies, PO Box 237, Cincinnati, OH 45201-0237; Title Tel # (513) 861-3600
Personnel: Editor-Karen Taravella, Art Dir.-Ken Lay
Editorial Description: Employee profiles, industry news, company news.
General Info: Yr. Est. 1951, Monthly, Trim Size-8½ x 11, Letrpr. press, 5 pages, 2 Color, Coated
Circulation: (100% controlled), Total-600

Observation

Publishing Co: General Motors Corp., 30001 Van Dyke Ave Rm 134, Warren, MI 48093-2350; Title Tel # (313) 492-7151

Oceana's Law Library Newsletter See: LAW

Offline   *Association*

Publishing Co: Tacoma Public Library, 1102 Tacoma Ave S, Tacoma, WA 98402-2098
Personnel: Editor-Dave Dumkowski
Editorial Description: Library science info for Tacoma Public Library staff members.
General Info: Monthly

Ohio Licensed Practical Nurse

Publishing Co: Licensed Practical Nurse Assn. of Ohio, Inc., 1310 Saint Paris Pike, Springfield, OH 45504-1615

Ohio Power Review

Publishing Co: American Electric Power Customer Service Center, Box 400, Canton, OH 44701 Tel # (216) 455-8931

Oklahoma Rep!

Publishing Co: Oklahoma State Dept. of Industrial Development, 2401 N Lincoln Blvd Dept 500, Oklahoma City, OK 73105-4402; Title Tel # (405) 521-2011

Oldsmobile Team

Publishing Co: Oldsmobile Div., G.M.C., Public Relations Dept., 920 Townsend St., Lansing, MI 48921-0001; Title Tel # (517) 377-5000 Title Fax # (517) 377-2706
Personnel: Editor-K. A. Wulsey
Editorial Description: Keep employees informed about GM Oldsmobile, the industry and one another.
General Info: Quarterly, Trim Size-9 x 12, Offset press, 16 pages, Color
Circulation: Total-23,000

On Board   *Consumer*

Publishing Co: PSI, 4820 W 15th St, Lawrence, KS 66049-3846 Tel # (913) 865-9302
Personnel: Editor-Pat Schrepf
Editorial Description: Covers technical topics and projects.
General Info: (Formerly PTL News), Yr. Est. 1981, Quarterly, Trim Size-3¾ x 8½, 10 pages, No Color
Circulation: Total-5,000

On the Level   *Business*

Publishing Co: Canadian Masonry Contractors' Association, 360 Superior Blvd., Mississauga, ON L5T-2N7 Canada; Title Tel # (416) 564-6622 Title Fax # (905) 564-5744
Personnel: Publisher-Larry Jeffries, Editor, Circ. Mgr., Art Dir.-Scott Zieske
Editorial Description: Feature oriented company newsletter.
General Info: (Formerly Sharp-Bits), Yr. Est. 1982, Quarterly, Trim Size-8½ x 11, Sheetfed press, 8 pages, 2 Color, Coated
Subscriptions: Free
Circulation: (100% controlled), Total-2,550
Printing Co: Clark Printing Co., 720 N 11th St, Spearfish, SD 57783-2246 Tel # (605) 642-4705

On the Scene

Publishing Co: St. Paul Dispatch, 55 4th St E, Saint Paul, MN 55101-1106; Title Tel # (612) 222-5011
Editorial Description: A quarterly 12 page newsletter published for employees and retired employees of the St. Paul Pioneer Press and Dispatch newspapers.
General Info: Yr. Est. 1921, Quarterly, Trim Size-9 x 11¾, Offset press, 12 pages, No Color
Circulation: Total-1,300
Printing Co: St. Paul Pioneer Press And Dispatch, 345 Cedar St., St. Paul, MN 55101 Tel # (612) 222-5011

On-Stream

Publishing Co: CIBA Geigy Corp., 444 Saw Mill River Rd, Ardsley, NY 10502-2600; Title Tel # (914) 478-3131
Personnel: Editor-Kathy Berkowitz
General Info: 9x/yr., Trim Size-11 x 15, Offset press, 6 pages
Circulation: Total-12,000

On Target

Publishing Co: F.E. Myers, 1101 Myers Pky, Ashland, OH 44805-1969; Title Tel # (419) 289-1144
Personnel: Editor-K.M. Buetow
General Info: Semi-annually, 6 pages, 2 Color, Coated
Printing Co: Brethren Printing Co., 524 College Ave, Ashland, OH 44805-3703 Tel # (419) 289-1708

Onan News   *Business*

Publishing Co: Onan Corp., 1400 73rd Ave NE, Minneapolis, MN 55432-3796 Parent Co.-Cummins Engine Co., Columbus; Title Tel # (612) 574-5921 Title Fax # (612) 574-8060
Personnel: Editor-Alan Guidry
Editorial Description: For employees, new products, news, products applications & co. plans & progress.
General Info: Yr. Est. 1944, Quarterly, Trim Size-8½ x 11, Offset press, 12 pages, 2 Color, Newsprint, Saddle-stitched
Subscriptions: Free
Circulation: Total-3,000
Advertising: Accepts Inserts.

One Vision   *Association*

Publishing Co: Bell-Northern Research, 2221 Lakeside Blvd, Richardson, TX 75082-4305; Title Tel # (214) 684-1000
Editorial Description: Employee newsletter for Bell-Northern Research, a telecommunications company.
General Info: Bi-monthly
Circulation: Total-3,500

Onewser

Publishing Co: Owens-Illinois Inc., 3600 Alameda Ave, Oakland, CA 94601-3329 Tel # (510) 436-2000

Online

Publishing Co: Jersey Central Power & Light Co., Public Relations, 300 Madison Avenue, Morristown, NJ 07962-1911 Tel # (201) 285-9155; Title Tel # (201) 455-8782
Personnel: Editor-Lucille Andaloro
General Info: Monthly, Offset press, 24 pages
Circulation: Total-4,300

Open Line, The   *Business*

Publishing Co: General Motors Acceptance Corp., 3044 W. Grand Blvd., Annex 14, Detroit, MI 48202-3080
Personnel: Editor-William Lyle
Editorial Description: Employee newsletter-GMAC financial services-auto financing, insurance.
General Info: Bi-weekly, Offset press, 6 pages
Circulation: Total-1,000

Otis Bulletin   *Association*

Publishing Co: Otis Elevator Co., 1 Farm Springs Rd, Farmington, CT 06032-2500; Title Tel # (860) 676-6000
Personnel: Editor-Ira Morrison
Editorial Description: Feature-oriented news, company programs, human interest, promotions, etc.
General Info: Quarterly, Trim Size-11 x 14, Offset press, 16 pages, Color, Coated
Circulation: Total-15,000

Our Yard

Publishing Co: Sun Shipbuilding, Morton Ave., Chester, PA 19013

Outlook   *Association*

Publishing Co: Copperweld, Shelby Div., 132 W. Main St., Shelby, OH 44875-1300; Title Tel # (419) 342-1420 Title Fax # (419) 342-1473
Personnel: Publisher, Editor-Bob Bland
Editorial Description: Company news for employees.
General Info: (Formerly Tuby Talk), Yr. Est. 1944, Weekly, Trim Size-8½ x 11, Offset press, 6 pages, No Color, Matte
Subscriptions: Free To Qualified Recipient
Circulation: Total-600
Printing Co: Shelby Printing, Inc., 17 Washington St, Shelby, OH 44875-1249 Tel # (419) 342-3171

P.E. News   *Business*

Publishing Co: Perkin-Elmer Corp., 761 Main Ave., Norwalk, CT 06859-0105 Tel # (203) 762-6023 Fax # (203) 764-2892; Title Tel # (203) 762-6316
Personnel: Editor-Carol Blaszczynski
Editorial Description: General corporate information.
General Info: (Formerly PEN, The, Perkin-Elmer News), Quarterly, Trim Size-11 x 15, Letrpr. press, 8 pages, Color
Circulation: Total-14,000

PNC Banknews   *Association*

Publishing Co: PNC Bank, 5th Ave. and Wood St., 28th fl, Pittsburgh, PA 15265; Title Tel # (412) 762-2477
Personnel: VP Pubs.-Jeff Worden
Editorial Description: Articles inform & educate employees on banking & company operations; provide human interest stories, news & employees promotions, accomplishments, etc.
General Info: (Formerly Banknotes), Monthly, Trim Size-11 x 16½, Web press, 6 pages, Color, Coated
Circulation: (100% controlled), Total-5,600

Pacesetter

Publishing Co: Southern States Cooperative, PO Box 26234, Richmond, VA 23260-6234 Tel # (804) 281-1210; Title Tel # (804) 281-1368
Personnel: Editor-Shirley Sullivan, Production Mgr.-Art Dixon
Editorial Description: For members of Southern States Cooperative's retail family.
General Info: Monthly, Trim Size-8½ x 11, Offset press, 16 pages, 2 Color, Coated
Circulation: Total-4,500

Paint Leader

Publishing Co: E.I. du Pont de Nemours, 10007 Market Street, Wilmington, DE 19898-0001 Tel # (302) 774-1000

Paper Mate Points

Publishing Co: Paper Mate Co., Mini Pru Bldg. , 23rd Flr., C/O B. DeStefano, Boston, MA 02199; Title Tel # (312) 352-9000
Personnel: Editor-Mrs. Eleanor Andros
General Info: Bi-monthly, Trim Size-8½ x 11, Offset press, 10 pages
Circulation: Total-1,100

Paramount World

Publishing Co: Paramount Pictures Corp., Gulf & Western Bldg., New York, NY 10023 Tel # (212) 654-1000 Parent Co.-Viacom, New York; Title Tel # (212) 846-4320
Editorial Description: Motion picture information and sales promotion techniques.
General Info: Monthly
Circulation: Total-4,500

Parascope   *Business*

Publishing Co: Paragon Electric Co., Inc., PO Box 28, Two Rivers, WI 54241-0028; Title Tel # (414) 793-1161 Title Fax # (414) 793-3736
Personnel: Publisher-Tracee Mochal, Editor-Jeff Heinzen, Art Dir.-Pat Beitzel
General Info: Monthly, Desktop press, 12 pages, 2 Color, Coated, Saddle-stitched
Circulation: Total-1,500
Printing Co: MTWC Engraving, Manitowoc, WI 54241

Park Notes   *Association*

Publishing Co: Chicago Park District, 425 E Mcfetridge Dr, Chicago, IL 60605-2801; Title Tel # (312) 294-2492
Personnel: Publisher-Shawnelle Richie, Editor-Glenn Alexander
Editorial Description: Employee publication.
General Info: (Formerly Park Ways), Quarterly, Trim Size-8 x 10, Offset press, 8 pages, No Color
Advertising: Inquire for rates. Accepts Inserts.

Parkridge Probe

Publishing Co: Parkridge Hospital, 2333 Mccallie Ave, Chattanooga, TN 37404-3258 Tel # (423) 698-6061

Peerless Coffee Company Coffee Break
See: BEVERAGES - BREWING

People to People

Publishing Co: Pay Less Drug Stores N.W. Inc., 9275 SW Peyton Ln, Wilsonville, OR 97070-9200; Title Tel # (503) 682-4100
Personnel: Editor-Dave Rickard
General Info: Yr. Est. 1973, Monthly, Trim Size-8½ x 11, 8 pages, No Color
Circulation: Total-8,000

People 'n Pride

Publishing Co: General Motors Corp., G3248 Van Slyke Rd, Flint, MI 48552-0001 Tel # (313) 236-4300; Title Tel # (313) 236-8980
Personnel: Editor-Tom Borton
General Info: Yr. Est. 1985, Monthly, Trim Size-8½ x 11, 8 pages
Circulation: Total-2,800

Pep Talk

Publishing Co: Wayne Pump Company, Symington Wayne Corp., 124 E College Ave, Salisbury, MD 21801-6467; Title Tel # (301) 546-6600
Personnel: Editor-Argus Leidy

Pep Talk

Publishing Co: Dresser Industries Inc., PO Box 718, Dallas, TX 75221-0718; Title Tel # (214) 740-6000

Perceptive Report   *Business*

Publishing Co: Perceptive Marketers Agency, Ltd., 1100 E Hector St Ste 301, Conshohocken, PA 19428-2374; Title Tel # (610) 825-8710 Title Fax # (610) 825-9186
Personnel: Publisher, Editor-Allen Solovitz
General Info: Yr. Est. 1980, Monthly, Trim Size-8½ x 11, 4 pages, 4 Color, Coated
Subscriptions: Free To Qualified Recipient

Personnelly Speaking
See: GOVERNMENT

Petro-Chem

Publishing Co: Firestone Tire, Firestone Syn Rubber, Latex Co, Box 1269, Orange, TX 77630; Title Tel # (409) 883-1724
Personnel: Editor-Johnette Jackson
General Info: (Formerly Petro-Chem), Monthly, 6 pages, Coated
Circulation: (100% controlled), Total-450

Pfizer Scene

Publishing Co: Chas. Pfizer, 235 East 42nd Street, New York, NY 10017-5703; Title Tel # (212) 573-2255
Personnel: Editor-Ellen Rockford
General Info: 10x/yr., Trim Size-9 x 12, Offset press, 24 pages
Circulation: Total-20,000

Phillip Morris Globe   *Business, Association*

Publishing Co: Phillip Morris, USA, 800 Westchester Ave., Rye Brook, NY 10573; Title Tel # (212) 679-1800
Personnel: Publications Director-William Gamble
Editorial Description: News and information for and about Phillip Morris and its employees.
General Info: (Formerly Focus on Phillip Morris People), Monthly, Trim Size-8 x 10, 4 pages, Coated
Circulation: Total-9,000

Phorum

Publishing Co: Research Institute of America, 90 5th Avenue, New York, NY 10011-7629 Tel # (212) 645-4800; Title Tel # (201) 592-2840
Personnel: Editor-Robert M. Shaw
Editorial Description: Employee publication.
General Info: Yr. Est. 1957, Monthly, Trim Size-8½ x 11, Offset press, 16 pages
Circulation: Total-4,500

Physio Control Monitor · *Business*

Publishing Co: Physio Control Corp., 11811 Willows Rd NE, Redmond, WA 98052-2015;
Title Tel # (206) 867-4000
Personnel: Editor-Lesa Lightbourne, Art Dir.-Allen Matsumoto
Editorial Description: House organization used to inform, motivate & recognize Team Members working at Physio-Control.
General Info: Monthly, Trim Size-11 x 16, Web press, 4 pages, Color, Coated
Circulation: Total-300
Printing Co: Frank Potter & Assocs., 504 Yale Ave N, Seattle, WA 98109-5532 Tel # (206) 623-8844

Pine-Aire

Publishing Co: State Farm Mutual Auto Insurance Co., 1500 W. Highway 36, Saint Paul, MN 55161-0001; Title Tel # (612) 631-4251
Personnel: Editor-Karen Anderson
Editorial Description: Regional office employee publication covering local and national company news, departmental news, individual honor, recognition and unusual activity.
General Info: Monthly, Trim Size-8½ x 11, Offset press, 32 pages
Circulation: Total-1,500

Pinellas Pen

Publishing Co: Pinellas County Government, Personnel Dept., 400 S. St. Harrison Ave., Clearwater, FL 33516-5113; Title Tel # (813) 464-4835 Title Fax # (813) 464-3949

Pipeline

Publishing Co: Mansanto Fibers, PO Box 2204, Decatur, AL 35602-2204; Title Tel # (205) 552-2592
Personnel: Publisher-Shirley Mullins, Editor-Peggy Jones
Editorial Description: A plant news publication.
General Info: Weekly, 2 pages
Circulation: Total-1,600

Pipeline

Publishing Co: Lansing Board of Water & Light, PO Box 13007, Lansing, MI 48901-3007; Title Tel # (517) 371-6032 Title Fax # (517) 371-6855
General Info: (Formerly Watts and Drops)

Pipeline to Seniors
See: SENIOR CITIZENS

Pizza Hut Today

Publishing Co: Pizza Hut Inc., 9111 E Douglas Ave, Wichita, KS 67207-1296; Title Tel # (316) 681-9251 Title Fax # (316) 687-8937
Personnel: Publisher-Dan Paxton, Editor-Teresa Marshall, Art Dir.-Tina Biles
Editorial Description: Pizza Hut today is a 4-color tabloid mailed to company & franchise management employees throughout the system.
General Info: (Formerly News Brief), Yr. Est. 1987, Trim Size-8½ x 11, Web press, 16 pages, 4 Color, Newsprint
Acquisitions: Publication Bought

Pledge

Publishing Co: Greater New York Fund Inc., The, 99 Park Ave., New York, NY 10016-1503; Title Tel # (212) 986-8100
Personnel: Editor-Ruth Abat
General Info: Quarterly
Circulation: Total-3,000

Pointer · *Business, Association*

Publishing Co: Green Point Savings Bank, 4160 Main St, Flushing, NY 11355-3800
Editorial Description: Published by and for employees to keep them informed as to the various business and social activities.
General Info: Monthly, Trim Size-8½ x 11, Offset press, 12 pages, No Color
Circulation: Total-1,500

Polly Hale Newsletter
See: PRODUCE

Pony Express · *Business*

Publishing Co: Trust Co. of Georgia, 25 Park Pl. NE, Atlanta, GA 30303-2900; Title Tel # (404) 588-7230
Personnel: Editor-Hugh Suhr
General Info: Yr. Est. 1958, Weekly, Trim Size-8½ x 14, Offset press, 2 pages
Circulation: Total-2,600

Pool People
See: AGRICULTURE

Post · *Business*

Publishing Co: Bank One, Bank One Plaza, Lexington, KY 40507-2002; Title Tel # (606) 231-1000
Personnel: Publisher-Steve Kocen, Editor-Steve Kries, Production Mgr.-Mark Williamson, Art Dir.-Paula Gold
General Info: Yr. Est. 1975, Bi-monthly, Trim Size-8½ x 11, Sheetfed press, 8 pages, 2 Color, Coated, Saddle-stitched
Circulation: (100% controlled), Total-1,400

Post Box

Publishing Co: General Foods Corp., 250 North St, White Plains, NY 10605-2236
General Info: 10x/yr., Trim Size-10 x 13, Letrpr. press, 10 pages
Circulation: Total-5,000

Postings

Publishing Co: Transamerica Life Co., 1150 S Olive St, Los Angeles, CA 90015-2271
Tel # (213) 742-2210; Title Tel # (213) 742-4321
Personnel: Editor-Richard Smith
General Info: 15x/yr., Letrpr. press, 6 pages
Circulation: Total-5,000

Power News, The

Publishing Co: Simplicity Manufacturing Co., 500 N. Spring St., Port Washington, WI 53074-1752; Title Tel # (414) 284-8669 Title Fax # (414) 377-8202
General Info: (Formerly Simplicity Sentinel)

Power Plant

Publishing Co: Pratt, 400 Main St, East Hartford, CT 06118-1873; Title Tel # (203) 565-7500
Personnel: Editor-Robert J. Morrissey
Editorial Description: Pratt & Whitney house organ.
General Info: Bi-weekly, Trim Size-9 x 12, Offset press, 8 pages
Circulation: Total-40,000

Power Protection

Publishing Co: Boiler Inspection, 8 King St., E., Toronto, ON M5C 1B5 Canada Tel # (416) 363-5491

Power System News
See: POWER & POWER PLANTS

Powergrams · *Business, Consumer*

Publishing Co: Alabama Power Co., PO Box 2641, Birmingham, AL 35291; Title Tel # (205) 250-1387
Personnel: Editor-Jane Henry, Art Dir.-Tim Towns
Editorial Description: News and information for and about employees.
General Info: Yr. Est. 1920, Weekly, Trim Size-8½ x 11, Offset press, 32 pages, 4 Color, Saddle-stitched
Circulation: (100% controlled), Total-15,500

Preferred Word · *Business*

Publishing Co: Preferred Risk Mutual Ins. Cos., 1111 Ashworth Rd, West Des Moines, IA 50265-3544; Title Tel # (515) 225-5303
Personnel: Publisher, Editor-Anna Bridgford
Editorial Description: Co-ordination of home office and field, reports, outstanding achievement, notices, changes, etc.
General Info: (Formerly Always Preferred Word), Monthly, Trim Size-8½ x 11, Offset press, 8 pages, 2 Color, Coated
Circulation: Total-2,400

Printer's Impressions

Publishing Co: Clarke Printing, PO Box 460, San Antonio, TX 78292-0460
Printing Co: R.R. Donnelley & Sons, 1600 N. Main St., Pontiac, IL 61764-1060 Tel # (815) 844-5181, Fax # (708) 390-2618

Printing Salesman's Herald · *Consumer*

Publishing Co: Champion International Corp., 1 Champion Plz, Stamford, CT 06921-6001; Title Tel # (203) 358-7000
General Info: Quarterly

ProFile · *Business*

Publishing Co: Union Insurance Group, 303 E Washington St, Bloomington, IL 61701-4052; Title Tel # (309) 829-1061 Title Fax # (309) 827-0303
Personnel: Publisher, Editor-Ted Horn
Editorial Description: Limited quarterly 8 page house organ to 1150 independent agencies in 3 states, & company employees.
General Info: Yr. Est. 1959, Quarterly, Trim Size-8½ x 11, Sheetfed press, 8 pages, 2 Color, Newsprint
Subscriptions: Free
Circulation: (85% controlled), Total-1,400

Procession

Publishing Co: Blair Corporation, 220 Hickory St, Warren, PA 16366-0001; Title Tel # (814) 723-3600
Personnel: Editor-Deborah Ward
Editorial Description: Employee activities.
General Info: Yr. Est. 1945, Monthly, Offset press, 12 pages, 2 Color
Circulation: Total-3,000
Printing Co: Keystone Printing, Oak St. & Lexington Ave., Warren, PA 16365 Tel # (814) 723-8870

Profit Builder

Publishing Co: Louisiana Power, 142 Delaronde St, New Orleans, LA 70114-2326

Project Profile

Publishing Co: Computer Sciences Corp., 650 N Sepulveda Blvd, El Segundo, CA 90245-3419 Tel # (310) 615-0311

Provider, The

Publishing Co: United Olympic Life Insurance, 4601 Fairfax Dr., Arlington, VA 22203-1500;
Title Tel # (703) 875-3521 Title Fax # (703) 875-3677
Personnel: Editor-Grace Mataya
Editorial Description: Marketing publication for field force of Provident Life Insurance Co.
General Info: Yr. Est. 1986, Bi-monthly, Sheetfed press, 8 pages, 2 Color
Circulation: Total-5,100

Pru-Echo

Publishing Co: Prudential Insurance Co. of America, Prudential Plz, Newark, NJ 07102-3777
Personnel: Editor-Ron Fiorelli
General Info: Monthly, Offset press, 4 pages
Circulation: Total-2,200

Pump Patter   *Business*

Publishing Co: Harbison-Fischer Mfg. Co., 901 N Crowley Rd, Crowley, TX 76036-3739;
Title Tel # (817) 297-2211
General Info: Yr. Est. 1963, 10 pages, 2 Color, Coated
Circulation: Total-500

Pumplines   *Business*

Publishing Co: Goulds Pumps Inc., 240 Fall St, Seneca Falls, NY 13148-1590;
Title Tel # (315) 568-2811 Title Fax # (315) 565-2418
Personnel: Adv. Mgr.-Bob Urwin
Editorial Description: Dissemination of company & employee information to workers & management.
General Info: Yr. Est. 1902, Bi-monthly, Trim Size-8¾ x 11¾, Offset press, 48 pages, 2 Color, Coated, Saddle-stitched
Circulation: Total-4,000
Printing Co: Finger Lakes Press, 185 Clark St, Auburn, NY 13021-2255 Tel # (315) 252-7583

Punch Lines   *Business, Consumer*

Publishing Co: Dayton Progress Corp., 500 Progress Rd, Dayton, OH 45449-2351
Fax # (513) 859-5353; Title Tel # (513) 859-5111
Personnel: Editor-Rosemary Domansky
Editorial Description: Employee activities, company benefits, policies. Sports department news, suggestion.
General Info: Yr. Est. 1963, Quarterly, Trim Size-8½ x 11, Offset press, 24 pages, No Color
Circulation: (100% controlled), Total-600

Q   *Business, Association*

Publishing Co: First Interstate Bank of California, 633 W. 5th St., Los Angeles, CA 90071-2005;
Title Tel # (213) 614-4111
Personnel: Editor-Pat Kemper
Editorial Description: News & events pertaining to FIBC personnel.
General Info: Quarterly, Trim Size-11 x 15

Quarterly

Publishing Co: Reed Tool Co., PO Box 998, Sherman, TX 75091-0998 Tel # (903) 813-4777

RSB Dollars

Publishing Co: Rochester Savings Bank, 40 Franklin St, Rochester, NY 14604-1413;
Title Tel # (716) 258-3000
Personnel: Publisher, Editor-Mary Pierce
Editorial Description: To establish a closer relationship among bank staff members and to foster a better understanding of the policies and objectives of the bank.
General Info: (Formerly RSB Mirror), Weekly, 2 pages, No Color
Circulation: Total-500

RSR Lead Press   *Association*

Publishing Co: RSR Corp., 2777 N Stemmons Fwy #1800, Dallas, TX 75207-2277
Tel # (214) 631-2277; Title Tel # (214) 631-6070
Personnel: Publisher, Editor, Circ. Mgr., Adv. Dir., Art Dir.-Diana Parsell
Editorial Description: Company business, employee profiles, general interest.
General Info: Quarterly, Trim Size-8½ x 11, Sheetfed press, 8 pages, 2 Color
Subscriptions: Free
Circulation: Total-1,200

RWA Reporter

Publishing Co: Roy W. Walter & Assoc., 744 Prescott Place, Paramus, NJ 07652-3720;
Title Tel # (201) 891-3344
General Info: Yr. Est. 1982, Quarterly

Radian

Publishing Co: Textron Lycoming, 550 S Main St, Stratford, CT 06497-7572;
Title Tel # (203) 378-8211

Rainbow Reporter   *Business*

Publishing Co: Binney & Smith, 1100 Church Ln, Easton, PA 18040-6638
Personnel: Editor-Eric Zebley
Editorial Description: Information and history of Binney and Smith's crayola products.
General Info: Quarterly, Trim Size-8½ x 11, 18 pages, 4 Color, Coated, Saddle-stitched
Printing Co: Intelligencer Printing Co., 330 Eden Rd #1768, Lancaster, PA 17601-4218
Tel # (717) 291-3100, Fax # (717) 569-2643

Raytheon Aircraft News, The

Publishing Co: Raytheon Aircraft, 9709 E Central Ave # 85, Wichita, KS 67206-2507;
Title Tel # (316) 681-7604
Personnel: Editor-Pat Zerbe
Editorial Description: Communication between management and employees; employee and product feature stories.
General Info: (Formerly Beech Log, The/Beechcrafter), Bi-monthly, Trim Size-8½ x 11, Web press, 8 pages, No Color, Coated, Saddle-stitched
Circulation: (100% controlled), Total-10,000
Printing Co: Beech Aircraft, PO Box 85, Wichita, KS 67201-0085 Tel # (316) 676-7111

Reaching Out   *Business*

Publishing Co: Giddings & Lewis, Inc., 142 Doty St., PO Box 590, Fond Du Lac, WI 54935-0590
Tel # (414) 921-7100 Fax # (414) 929-4417; Title Tel # (414) 929-4212 Title Fax # (414) 929-4537
Editorial Description: A publication for the employees of Giddings & Lewis & their families.
General Info: Quarterly, Trim Size-8⅜ x 11, 8 pages, No Color, Coated, Saddle-stitched
Subscriptions: Free
Circulation: Total-4,000

Record

Publishing Co: Shell Oil Co., PO Box 60193, New Orleans, LA 70160-0193
General Info: 11x/yr., Trim Size-11½ x 16, Letrpr. press, 7 pages
Circulation: Total-6,500

Record

Publishing Co: Exxon Co. USA, P.O. Box 551, Baton Rouge, LA 70821; Title Tel # (504) 359-8322

Record

Publishing Co: Exxon Co. USA, 6301 Ivy Lane, # 7000, Greenbelt, MD 20770-1402;
Title Tel # (301) 785-6660

Recorder

Publishing Co: Dresser Industries Inc., PO Box 6504, Houston, TX 77265-6504;
Title Tel # (713) 750-2000

Reflections

Publishing Co: Blue Cross-Blue Shield Communications Div., 801 Pine St, Chattanooga, TN 37402-2520; Title Tel # (615) 755-2020

Reflections

Publishing Co: Southwest Texas Methodist Hospital, 7700 Floyd Curl Dr, San Antonio, TX 78229-3902 Tel # (210) 692-4000

Reflector

Publishing Co: General Motors Corp., Fisher Body-Grand Rapids No. 2, Grand Rapids, MI 49504;
Title Tel # (616) 246-2000

Retiree Roundup   *Business*

Publishing Co: Goodyear Tire & Rubber Co., 1144 E. Market St., Akron, OH 44316-0001
Tel # (330) 796-2121; Title Tel # (330) 796-4672 Title Fax # (330) 796-1817
General Info: Monthly

ReveNews

Publishing Co: Georgia Dept. of Revenue, 270 Washington St SW #424 E, Atlanta, GA 30334-9009
Tel # (404) 656-0568 Fax # (404) 651-9490; Title Tel # (404) 656-4236
Personnel: Publisher-Marcus Collins, SR., Editor-Marta Crane
Editorial Description: Employee newsletter of the Georgia Department of Revenue.
General Info: Yr. Est. 1963, Monthly, Trim Size-8½ x 11, Web press, 8 pages, Color
Circulation: Total-1,400

Richards Reporter

Publishing Co: Richards Manufacturing Co. Inc., 1450 E Brooks Rd, Memphis, TN 38116-1804

Richardson Employee Newsletter   *Business, Association*

Publishing Co: City of Richardson Texas, 411 West Arataho, Richardson, TX 75080;
Title Tel # (214) 238-4100
Personnel: Editor-Jill Clary
Editorial Description: Information for employees.
General Info: Monthly, Trim Size-8½ x 11, Offset press, 6 pages, No Color
Circulation: (100% controlled), Total-1,000

Ritenour Reporter   *Association*

Publishing Co: Ritenour School District, 2420 Woodson Rd, Saint Louis, MO 63114-5499;
Title Tel # (314) 426-9513 Title Fax # (314) 426-7144
Personnel: Editor-Cindy Gibson
Editorial Description: News about staff members, district news, and information for employees.
General Info: (Formerly Intercom), Monthly, Trim Size-8½ x 11, Sheetfed press, 2 pages, No Color, Matte
Circulation: Total-1,200

Rockwell News   *Business*

Publishing Co: Rockwell Corp., 400 Collins Rd., Cedar Rapids, IA 52498; Title Tel # (319) 395-4998
Personnel: Editor-Lawrence Gillius
General Info: Bi-monthly

Rockwell-Standard News

Publishing Co: North American Rockwell Corp., Automotive Div., 2135 W Maple Rd, Troy, MI 48084-7121; Title Tel # (313) 435-1000
Personnel: Editor-William Toderan
General Info: Quarterly, Trim Size-8½ x 11, Offset press, 28 pages
Circulation: Total-30,000

Roosevelt Ramblings

Publishing Co: Hotel Roosevelt, 45th St. -Madison Ave., New York, NY 10017; Title Tel # (212) 661-9600

Roosevelt Review

Publishing Co: Roosevelt Savings Bank, 1122 Franklin Ave, Garden City, NY 11530-1694
Editorial Description: House Organ. Not available to the public.

Roto Rooter Exchange   *Association*

Publishing Co: Roto-Rooter Corp., 300 Ashworth Rd, West Des Moines, IA 50265-3737; Title Tel # (515) 223-1345
Personnel: Editor-Mel Setter
Editorial Description: Mail 12/yr. to our franchise organization. Features program developments, how to run a better business, owner success corp. plans, & goalls, current events.
General Info: Yr. Est. 1938, Monthly, Trim Size-8½ x 11, Letrpr. press, 8 pages, Coated
Circulation: Total-700
Printing Co: Acme Printing, 66 Washington Ave, Des Moines, IA 50314-3675 Tel # (515) 244-1723

Round-Up

Publishing Co: Henke, PO Box 1309, Houston, TX 77251-1309

RoundUPS
See: PHILATELY & POSTAL AFFAIRS

Roundup

Publishing Co: ACME Boot Company, Inc., PO Box 749, Clarksville, TN 37041-0749; Title Tel # (615) 552-2000
Personnel: Publisher-Leo A. Brookshire, Editor-Pam McCaslin
Editorial Description: Company & business related.
General Info: Yr. Est. 1967, Bi-monthly, Trim Size-9 x 12, Offset press, 4 pages, Color
Acquisions: Publication Bought
Circulation: (100% controlled), Total-5,500

Rubbermaid Review   *Business*

Publishing Co: Rubbermaid, 1147 Akron Rd, Wooster, OH 44691-2596; Title Tel # (216) 264-6464
Personnel: Editor-Margo Kramer
General Info: Yr. Est. 1948, Bi-monthly, Trim Size-9½ x 12½, Offset press, 12 pages, 2 Color
Subscriptions: $1/copy
Circulation: (100% controlled), Total-2,400
Printing Co: Wooster Graphics & Litho, Lincoln Way, Wooster, OH 44691 Tel # (216) 264-5540

Rug Raps

Publishing Co: Carthage Mills Inc., 1821 Summit Rd., Cincinnati, OH 45237-2868; Title Tel # (513) 242-2740
Personnel: Editor-Charlotte Franken
Editorial Description: Employee interest items.
General Info: Bi-monthly

Rural Network Advocate
See: LIFESTYLE

SAS Inc'Lings   *Business*

Publishing Co: Scandinavian Airlines System, Inc., Public Relations, 9 Polito Ave., 10th Floor, Lyndhurst, NJ 07071 Tel # (201) 896-3600 Fax # (201) 896-3725
Personnel: Editor-Albert ChiodaA
Editorial Description: Information and news for employees.
General Info: Irregular

SBRC News

Publishing Co: Santa Barbara Research Center, Subs Hughes Aircraft Co., 75 Coromar Dr, Goleta, CA 93117-3088 Tel # (805) 562-4944

SD Newsletter   *Association*

Publishing Co: General Motors Corp., 3900 E Holland Rd, Saginaw, MI 48601-9494; Title Tel # (517) 757-4004
Personnel: Editor-Sherri Stelmach
General Info: Yr. Est. 1976, Daily

SFBNS Tie Line

Publishing Co: U.S. Navy, S.F. Bay Naval Shipyard, Vallejo, CA 94590
Personnel: Editor-Norma Ross Walter
General Info: Weekly
Circulation: Total-22,000

SO CAL Gas News

Publishing Co: Southern California Gas Co., Pacific Lighting System, 800 S. Flower St., Los Angeles, CA 90017-4608; Title Tel # (213) 620-1440
Personnel: Editor-Marylynn Holder
General Info: Bi-weekly, Trim Size-11 x 14, Letrpr. press, 10 pages
Circulation: Total-8,700

SPS News

Publishing Co: SPS Technologies, Highland Avenue, Jenkintown, PA 19046; Title Tel # (215) 572-3408 Title Fax # (215) 572-3408
Personnel: Publisher, Editor-Jennifer Lukoff
Editorial Description: Employee newsletter covering Bucks & Montgomery Co. locations of SPS Technologies.
General Info: Yr. Est. 1963, Bi-weekly, Trim Size-11 x 17, Sheetfed press, 4 pages, No Color, Newsprint
Circulation: Total-3,000
Printing Co: Comtech Lithographics, Inc., 7300 Rt. 130 N., Bldg. 20, Pennsauken, NJ 08110 Tel # (609) 665-8350

St. Nicholas News   *Consumer*

Publishing Co: St. Nicholas School, 13510 1st Ave NE, Seattle, WA 98125-3021

Saks Fifth Avenue News

Publishing Co: Saks Fifth Avenue, 611 5th Ave, New York, NY 10022-6899 Fax # (800) 221-3297; Title Tel # (212) 753-4000
Personnel: Editor-Leigh Hibbard
General Info: Bi-monthly, Trim Size-8¾ x 11¼, Offset press, 32 pages
Circulation: Total-10,000
List Rental: Rents Lists

Sales Bulletin   *Business*

Publishing Co: E.R. Squibb, Box 609, Princeton, NJ 08543; Title Tel # (609) 921-4000
Personnel: Editor-Arlene Ferrante-Ford
Editorial Description: To communicate between the sales force & the home office.
General Info: Yr. Est. 1925, Monthly, Sheetfed press, 8 pages, 2 Color
Circulation: (100% controlled), Total-1,250
Printing Co: Alma Offset Co., Bakers Basin Rd., Trenton, NJ 08648 Tel # (609) 883-3659

Salesgram

Publishing Co: Texas Power, Box 6331, 1511 Bryan St., Dallas, TX 75201 Tel # (214) 812-4600

Salute
See: SHIPS & SHIPPING

San Jacinto Spirit

Publishing Co: Simpson Pasenda Paper Co., PO Box 872, Pasadena, TX 77501-0872; Title Tel # (713) 475-6313
Personnel: Editor-Peggy Kingsberry
General Info: (Formerly Champion News-Chips), Yr. Est. 1937, Monthly, Trim Size-7 x 11, Offset press, 6 pages, Color
Circulation: Total-2,500

Scientific-Atlanta World

Publishing Co: Scientific-Atlanta Inc., 3845 Pleasantdale Rd, Atlanta, GA 30340-4266

Scoops

Publishing Co: Baskin-Robbins Inc., 1201 S Victory Blvd, Burbank, CA 91502-2552 Tel # (818) 843-5500

Scope

Publishing Co: State Accident Insurance Fund, Saif Bldg., Salem, OR 97312-0001 Tel # (503) 373-8000

Scope

Publishing Co: Valspar Corp., 1101 S. 3rd St., Minneapolis, MN 55415-1211 Tel # (612) 332-7371; Title Tel # (612) 375-7342 Title Fax # (612) 375-7723
Personnel: Editor-Kathy Junkman

Scott World   *Business*

Publishing Co: Scott Paper Co., Scott Plaza 1, Philadelphia, PA 19113; Title Tel # (215) 522-5000
Personnel: Editor-Stan Howard
Editorial Description: The publication of record for employees and retirees of Scott Paper Company.
General Info: Yr. Est. 1968, Monthly, Trim Size-9½ x 13¼, Offset press, 8 pages, 2 Color, Coated, Saddle-stitched
Circulation: (100% controlled), Total-25,000
Printing Co: Innovation Printing, 2051 Byberry Rd, Philadelphia, PA 19116-3086 Tel # (215) 969-4600

Seagram Spotlight

Publishing Co: Seagram Distillers Co., 375 Park Avenue, New York, NY 10152-0152; Title Tel # (212) 572-7000
Personnel: Editor-Dominick Albi
General Info: Quarterly, Trim Size-8½ x 11, Offset press, 32 pages

Searle Circlet

Publishing Co: G.D. Searle, 4711 Golf Rd., Skokie, IL 60076-1224; Title Tel # (708) 982-7884
Personnel: Editor-Joseph Bartulis
General Info: Weekly, Trim Size-6½ x 8½, Offset press, 4 pages
Circulation: Total-1,000

Security News

Publishing Co: Security Pacific National Bank, Research Dept. H8-3, Box 2097, Los Angeles, CA 90051-0097
Personnel: Editor-Betsy Saunders
General Info: Monthly, Trim Size-11⅛ x 18¼, Offset press, 14 pages
Circulation: Total-15,000

Semaphore   *Association*

Publishing Co: Black Hawk Council of Girl Scouts, 2710 Ski Ln, Madison, WI 53713-3267; Title Tel # (608) 249-6661
Personnel: Editor-Susan Liebl
Editorial Description: Interests: book reviews; ecology; hobbies; how-to stories about troop programs.
General Info: (Formerly Black Hawk Bulletin), Yr. Est. 1965, Trim Size-8½ x 11, Web press, 8 pages, 2 Color, Coated, Saddle-stitched
Circulation: Total-2,600

Sentry News   *Business*

Publishing Co: Sentry Insurance, 1800 N Point Dr, Stevens Point, WI 54482-0001; Title Tel # (715) 346-6781 Title Fax # (715) 346-7516
Personnel: Editor-Nick Schultz
Editorial Description: Employee publication of Sentry Insurance.
General Info: Yr. Est. 1968, Quarterly, Trim Size-8½ x 11, Offset press, 16 pages, No Color, Saddle-stitched
Subscriptions: Free To Qualified Recipient
Circulation: Total-7,300

Serono Lagniappe

Publishing Co: Sears Roebuck, 4400 Veterans Blvd., Metairie, LA 70002
Personnel: Editor-Miss Anne Gause
General Info: Bi-monthly, Trim Size-8½ x 11, Letrpr. press, 20 pages
Circulation: Total-2,000

Service

Publishing Co: Guardian Life Insurance Co. of America, 201 Park Ave. S., New York, NY 10003-1699

Servicegraph   *Consumer*

Publishing Co: Kansas Gas & Electric Co., PO Box 208, Wichita, KS 67201-0208; Title Tel # (316) 261-6364
Personnel: Editor-Ricky Ayre
Editorial Description: Electric utility company (investor owned) employee newsletter.
General Info: Monthly, Trim Size-8½ x 11, Offset press, 4 pages, Color, Matte
Circulation: Total-2,100

Shaklee Spirit   *Business*

Publishing Co: Shaklee Corp., 444 Market St, San Francisco, CA 94111-5378 Tel # (415) 954-3000; Title Tel # (415) 954-2648
Editorial Description: Newsletter/Magazine for employees; also covers larger issues like childcare, etc.
General Info: (Formerly Shaklee Reporter), Yr. Est. 1969, Bi-monthly, Trim Size-8½ x 11, 8 pages, 2 Color, Coated
Circulation: Total-1,500

Shaklee Survey

Publishing Co: Shaklee Corp., 444 Market St, San Francisco, CA 94111-5378 Tel # (415) 954-3000

Sharecropper
See: AGRICULTURE

Shell Alumni News

Publishing Co: Shell Oil Co., PO Box 2463, Houston, TX 77252-2463
Personnel: Editor-Beth Cassidy
Editorial Description: For Shell pensioners.
General Info: Bi-monthly

Shell Manhattan

Publishing Co: Shell Oil Company, Shell Chemical Co., 50 W 50th St, New York, NY 10112-1507 Tel # (212) 261-5640; Title Tel # (212) 262-3000
Personnel: Editor-Gareth L. Steen
General Info: Yr. Est. 1970, Monthly

Shell Record

Publishing Co: Shell Oil Co., PO Box 60193, New Orleans, LA 70160-0193

Shoptalk

Publishing Co: Automobile Club of Southern California, 2601 S. Figueroa St., 3rd Fl., Los Angeles, CA 90007-3289 Tel # (213) 741-4765 Fax # (213) 741-3033

Short Circuits   *Association*

Publishing Co: Dairyland Power Cooperative, PO Box 817, La Crosse, WI 54602-0817; Title Tel # (608) 788-4000
Personnel: Editor-D. Walsh
Editorial Description: Employee recognition, motivation and awarness on a daily basis.
General Info: Yr. Est. 1967, Daily, Trim Size-8½ x 11, Sheetfed press, 2 pages, No Color
Circulation: (100% controlled), Total-2,300

Sid Cato's Newsletter on Annual Reports
See: BUSINESS & INDUSTRY

Sightings   *Consumer*

Publishing Co: Allmerica Financial, 440 Lincoln St, Worcester, MA 01653-0002; Title Tel # (508) 855-2880 Title Fax # (508) 855-3675
Personnel: Publisher-Mark Madden, Editor-Jak Miner
Editorial Description: Financial/investment information for policy holders.
General Info: Yr. Est. 1991, Quarterly, Offset press, 2 Color
Subscriptions: Free To Qualified Recipient
Circulation: (100% controlled), Total-125,000

Signetwork   *Consumer*

Publishing Co: Bank of Virginia Co., PO Box 25970, Richmond, VA 23260-5970; Title Tel # (804) 771-7214
Personnel: Publisher-J. Ward, Editor-Lisa Oliva, Art Dir.-C. Tobey
Editorial Description: To inform bank personnel, retirees and board members about current bank programs and achievements. Serves as a communication tool and means to foster employee morale.
General Info: (Formerly Credit & Debits), Yr. Est. 1933, Bi-monthly, Trim Size-11 x 17, Letrpr. press, 8 pages, 2 Color
Subscriptions: $1/copy
Circulation: (100% controlled), Total-9,000
Advertising: Accepts Inserts.

Simpson Timber Company-
   Newsletter

Publishing Co: Simpson Investment Information Services, 1301 5th Ave. #1200, Seattle, WA 98101-2613
General Info: Yr. Est. 1985

Skil Extra

Publishing Co: Skil Corp., 4300 W Peterson Ave, Chicago, IL 60646-5928; Title Tel # (312) 286-7330
General Info: (Formerly Skil Chips)

Slices   *Association*

Publishing Co: Sunkist Growers, Inc., PO Box 7888, Van Nuys, CA 91409-7888; Title Tel # (818) 986-4800
Personnel: Editor-Dona Uhrig
Editorial Description: Employee publication--items relating to Sunkist, employee benefits, consumer interest.
General Info: Bi-monthly, Trim Size-8½ x 11, Offset press, 8 pages, No Color, Newsprint
Circulation: (100% controlled), Total-1,500

Snap-On Field Manager
   News   *Business*

Publishing Co: Snap-On Tools Corp., 1405 Avenue T, Grand Prairie, TX 75050-1234; Title Tel # (414) 656-5561
Personnel: Editor-Rick Secor
Editorial Description: Marketing sales newsletter for field manager personnel.
General Info: Yr. Est. 1983, Monthly, Trim Size-8½ x 11, Sheetfed press, 4 pages, 2 Color, Coated
Circulation: (100% controlled), Total-1,000
Printing Co: Badger Press, 7325-30th Ave., Kenosha, WI 53140 Tel # (414) 658-1628

Society Now   *Business, Consumer*

Publishing Co: Society Corp., 127 Public Sq., Cleveland, OH 44114-1216; Title Tel # (216) 689-3636
Personnel: Editor-Janet Gaydash
Editorial Description: Features corporate news, new products and services, employee news, trends & issues affecting our employees and the financial services industry.
General Info: (Formerly Society Corporate News), Yr. Est. 1977, Monthly, Trim Size-8½ x 11, Sheetfed press, 8 pages, 2 Color, Matte
Circulation: (100% controlled), Total-13,500
Printing Co: Perlmutter Printing Co., 4437 E 49th St, Cleveland, OH 44125-1054 Tel # (216) 271-5300

Sound of the Blues

Publishing Co: Blue Cross, PO Box 3248, Omaha, NE 68103-0248; Title Tel # (402) 390-1800

South Texan — *Business*

Publishing Co: Exxon Co. USA, PO Box 4697, Houston, TX 77210-4697; Title Tel # (512) 887-2241
Personnel: Editor-Carmen Atkins
Editorial Description: Inhouse publication for employees & annuitants.
General Info: Monthly, 12 pages
Circulation: Total-1,900

Southern California Water Co. Bulletin

Publishing Co: Southern California Water Co., 630 E Foothill Blvd, San Dimas, CA 91773-1207; Title Tel # (213) 386-7800
General Info: Yr. Est. 1940, Quarterly
Circulation: Total-400

Southern Highlights — *Business*

Publishing Co: The Southern Company, 270 Peachtree St NW, Suite 2100, Atlanta, GA 30303 Tel # (404) 506-0573; Title Tel # (404) 668-4595
Personnel: Editor-Jim Barber, Circ. Mgr.-Wanda McDaniel, Art Dir.-Bonita Loden
Editorial Description: Staff and management publication for 28,000 people in our system.
General Info: Bi-weekly, Color
Circulation: Total-28,000

Southern Natural Resources

Publishing Co: Southern Natural Resources Inc., PO Box 2563, Birmingham, AL 35202-2563

Southern Statesman

Publishing Co: Southern States Cooperative, PO Box 26234, Richmond, VA 23260-6234; Title Tel # (804) 281-1210
Personnel: Editor-Kathy Dixon, Production Mgr.-Art Dixon
Editorial Description: Published for company employees only.
General Info: 9x/yr., Trim Size-9$\frac{1}{8}$ x 12, Offset press, 8 pages, 2 Color, Coated
Acquisitions: Publication Bought
Circulation: (90% controlled), Total-5,500

Southwester — *Business*

Publishing Co: Southwestern Life Insurance Co., PO Box 2699, Dallas, TX 75221-2699; Title Tel # (214) 954-7618
Personnel: Editor-Pat Griswold
Editorial Description: Home office activities, promotions, and general news.
General Info: Yr. Est. 1909, Weekly, Trim Size-9 x 12, Mimeo press, 4 pages
Circulation: Total-1,800

Southwesterner

Publishing Co: Sears Roebuck, 13319 Montfort Drive, Dallas, TX 75240-5116; Title Tel # (214) 386-5991

Spartan News — *Business*

Publishing Co: Spartan Stores, Inc., 850 76th St. , S. W., Grand Rapids, MI 49508; Title Tel # (616) 878-2672
Personnel: Editor-Gary Evey
Editorial Description: News about the co. & Spartan people.
General Info: Semi-weekly, Desktop press, 4 pages
Circulation: (100% controlled), Total-2,000

Spectrum

Publishing Co: Fedl. Home Life Ins. Co., 6277 Sea Harbor Dr, Orlando, FL 32887-0001
Personnel: Editor-Robert Holderbaum
Editorial Description: Employee newsletter.
General Info: (Formerly Federal News), Monthly, Trim Size-9 x 12, Offset press, 4 pages
Circulation: Total-600
Printing Co: Lawson Printers Inc., 685 Columbia Ave W, Battle Creek, MI 49015-3070 Tel # (616) 965-0525

Spectrum

Publishing Co: Iowa Power, 823 Walnut St, Des Moines, IA 50309-3604 Tel # (515) 240-5555

Spectrum

Publishing Co: United Virginia Bankshares Inc., PO Box 26665, Richmond, VA 23261-6665

Speed Notes

Publishing Co: Tinnerman Prod. Inc., PO Box 6688, Cleveland, OH 44101-1688; Title Tel # (216) 741-9300
Personnel: Editor-Jean E. Forrest
General Info: Yr. Est. 1940, Monthly
Circulation: Total-1,000

Sperry Remington News

Publishing Co: Sperry Remington Co., Sperry Rand Corp., 60 Main St., Bridgeport, CT 06611

Spirit!

Publishing Co: Pacific First Fedl. Savings, PO Box 91029, Seattle, WA 98111-9129 Tel # (206) 383-2511; Title Tel # (206) 224-3368 Title Fax # (206) 224-3356
Personnel: Editor-Robb Zerr, Art Dir.-Colleen Kelly
General Info: (Formerly Pacific First Family News), Quarterly, Trim Size-10$\frac{1}{2}$ x 14, Desktop press, 12 pages, No Color
Circulation: Total-2,700

Spirit

Publishing Co: United Way Inc. of the Dayton Area, PO Box 67, Dayton, OH 45401-0067
Personnel: Editor-Rex Broome
Editorial Description: News, features on United Way services, agencies, volunteers.
General Info: Yr. Est. 1979, Monthly, Trim Size-8$\frac{1}{2}$ x 11, Offset press, 4 pages, No Color, Newsprint
Circulation: Total-3,600

Spirit of 375

Publishing Co: Seagram Distillers Co., 375 Park Avenue, New York, NY 10152-0152; Title Tel # (212) 572-7000
Personnel: Editor-Irving Babbitt
General Info: Quarterly, Trim Size-8$\frac{1}{2}$ x 11, Offset press, 8 pages
Circulation: Total-1,200

Square and Crescent — *Business*

Publishing Co: Morgan Construction Co., 15 Belmont St, Worcester, MA 01605-2665 Fax # (508) 755-6140; Title Tel # (508) 755-6111
Personnel: Editor-Michael Federman
Editorial Description: Company news, personnel information.
General Info: Yr. Est. 1957, Monthly, 14 pages, No Color, Newsprint, Saddle-stitched
Circulation: (100% controlled), Total-1,200
Printing Co: Atlas Press, 51 Pullman St, Worcester, MA 01606-3310 Tel # (508) 792-9000

Squibb Clinical Research Notes

Publishing Co: E.R. Squibb, Box 609, Princeton, NJ 08543; Title Tel # (609) 921-4000
General Info: Yr. Est. 1958

Squibbline

Publishing Co: E.R. Squibb, Box 609, Princeton, NJ 08543; Title Tel # (609) 921-4000
Personnel: Editor-Ralph Graff
General Info: Monthly, Trim Size-11 x 17, Offset press, 8 pages
Circulation: Total-9,500

Stackpole News

Publishing Co: Stackpole Carbon Co., Stackpole St., St. Marys, PA 15857

Staff Bulletin

Publishing Co: Children's Hospital Medical Center, Elland & Bethesda Ave., Cincinnati, OH 45229-2899; Title Tel # (513) 559-4420
Personnel: Editor-Beatric Rose
Editorial Description: For medical/dental staff & alumni of pediatric residency training program at Children's Hospital Medical Ctr. . Focuses on policies & programs, ongoing research, clinical issues, people & accomplishments, continuing medical education, announcements, etc.
General Info: 10x/yr., Trim Size-8$\frac{1}{2}$ x 11, Sheetfed press, 7 pages, 2 Color, Matte
Circulation: Total-2,400
Printing Co: Advance Printing Co., 1900 Section Rd, Cincinnati, OH 45237-3308 Tel # (513) 531-2299

Standard Oil Co. of California, Bulletin

Publishing Co: Standard Oil Co. of California, 225 Bush St., San Francisco, CA 94104-4207; Title Tel # (415) 894-7700
Personnel: Editor-J.A. Hildreth
General Info: (Formerly Standard Oil Co. of California Bulletin), Yr. Est. 1913, Quarterly
Circulation: Total-300,000

State Life Bulletin
See: INSURANCE

Statement — *Business*

Publishing Co: First Interstate Bank of OR, PO Box 3131, Portland, OR 97208-3131; Title Tel # (503) 225-2203
Personnel: Editor-Chris Moore
Editorial Description: To inform employees and retirees of the bank about news and issues that concern them and their jobs most directly.
General Info: Yr. Est. 1934, Monthly, Trim Size-11 x 17, Offset press, 12 pages, 2 Color, Coated
Circulation: Total-4,500
Printing Co: Irwin-Hodson, 2838 SE 9th Ave, Portland, OR 97202-2597 Tel # (503) 231-9990

Steamliner

Publishing Co: Electric-Motive Div., 9301 E 55th St, La Grange, IL 60525-3214
Personnel: Editor-MaryEllen Hartigan
Editorial Description: Publication for employees & retirees of Electro-Motive Div., General Motors Corp.
General Info: Yr. Est. 1930, Monthly, Trim Size-8$\frac{1}{2}$ x 11, Offset press, 8 pages
Circulation: Total-10,000

Steering Columns

Publishing Co: General Motors Corp., 3900 E Holland Rd, Saginaw, MI 48601-9494;
  Title Tel # (517) 757-4008
Personnel: Editor-Sherri Stelmach
Editorial Description: Tabloid monthly business pub. for all hourly & salaried employees of Saginaw
  Div., General Motors Corp.
General Info: Yr. Est. 1982, Monthly, 4 pages, 2 Color, Coated
Circulation: Total-26,000

Steiger Tr-Action News

Publishing Co: Steiger Tractor Inc., 3101 1st Ave N, Fargo, ND 58102-3005

Sundstrand Today   *Business*

Publishing Co: Sunstrand Corp., 4747 Harrison Ave, Rockford, IL 61108-7929;
  Title Tel # (815) 226-7361
Personnel: Editor-Mary Avery
Editorial Description: Current news on Sundstrand Corporation's happenings.
General Info: (Formerly Noon News), Yr. Est. 1978, Bi-weekly, Trim Size-11 x 22, Web press, 6
  pages, 2 Color, Newsprint
Circulation: (100% controlled), Total-6,000

Syntex Reporter

Publishing Co: Syntex Labs. Inc., 3401 Hillview Ave, Palo Alto, CA 94304-1320

Syracuse China News

Publishing Co: Syracuse China Corp., 2900 Court St, Syracuse, NY 13208-3218;
  Title Tel # (315) 468-1681
Personnel: Editor-Marcia Smith
General Info: Yr. Est. 1942, Quarterly
Circulation: Total-2,500

T-Blade

Publishing Co: Turbine Support Div., Chromalloy American Corp., Box 20148, San Antonio, TX
  78220

T-W News

Publishing Co: Taylor-Winfield Corp., 1052 Mahoning Ave NW, Warren, OH 44483-4622
Personnel: Editor-N.L. Pernice
General Info: Monthly
Circulation: Total-700

TFC Service

Publishing Co: Transamerica Life Co., 1150 S Olive St, Los Angeles, CA 90015-2271
  Tel # (213) 742-2210

TTX Press   *Business*

Publishing Co: Trailer Train Co., 101 N Wacker Dr, Chicago, IL 60606-7391 Fax # (312) 984-3865;
  Title Tel # (312) 853-3223
Editorial Description: Employee news and information.
General Info: Yr. Est. 1972, Monthly, Trim Size-8½ x 11, Offset press, 8 pages, 2 Color
Circulation: (100% controlled), Total-475

Taitline

Publishing Co: Tait Tech, Inc., 500 Webster St, Dayton, OH 45404-1525 Tel # (513) 258-2113

Talman Talk

Publishing Co: Talman Fedl. Savings, 30 W. Monroe St., Chicago, IL 60603-2401;
  Title Tel # (312) 877-5163
Personnel: Editor-Joan Bonnett
Editorial Description: Employee & retiree newsletter.
General Info: Bi-monthly, Trim Size-11 x 15, Letrpr. press, 8 pages, 2 Color, Coated
Circulation: Total-2,500

Team Reporter

Publishing Co: General Motors Corp., Chevrolet-Bay City, 100 Fitzgerald, Bay City, MI 48706;
  Title Tel # (517) 757-5000

Teamwork

Publishing Co: Grinnell Mutual Reinsurance Co., Int. 80 at Hwy. 146, Grinnell, IA 50112;
  Title Tel # (515) 236-6121
Personnel: Editor-Bruce Bumgardner
Editorial Description: To disseminate information to member farm mutuals.
General Info: Yr. Est. 1936, Monthly, Trim Size-8½ x 11, Offset press, No Color
Circulation: (100% controlled), Total-3,800

Technical Bulletin

Publishing Co: Computer Sciences Corp., 650 N Sepulveda Blvd, El Segundo, CA 90245-3419
  Tel # (310) 615-0311

Teco News

Publishing Co: Tampa Electric Co., Corp. Communications Office, 172 N. Franklin St., Tampa, FL
  33602; Title Tel # (813) 228-4281 Title Fax # (813) 228-4259

Telenews

Publishing Co: Illinois Bell Tel. Co., 225 W Randolph St, Chicago, IL 60606-1824

Telephone Review

Publishing Co: New York Telephone Co., 140 West St, New York, NY 10007-2174;
  Title Tel # (212) 394-4141
Personnel: Editor-Edward Oxford
General Info: 9x/yr., Trim Size-9 x 12, Offset press, 36 pages
Circulation: Total-100,000

Teller

Publishing Co: Bank of Delaware, 222 Delaware Ave, Wilmington, DE 19801-1600;
  Title Tel # (302) 429-1024
Personnel: Editor-Kathleen Cross
Editorial Description: Employee newsletter.
General Info: Yr. Est. 1958, Bi-monthly, Trim Size-8½ x 11, Offset press, 8 pages, 2 Color,
  Newsprint, Saddle-stitched
Circulation: Total-1,400
Printing Co: Intergraphics Press, 105 Vandever Ave # 07, Wilmington, DE 19802-4221
  Tel # (302) 652-3507

Telstar   *Business*

Publishing Co: Boston Mutual Life Ins. Co., Royal St., Canton, MA 02021; Title Tel # (617) 828-7000
Personnel: Editor-Jim Chisholm
Editorial Description: Insurance programs, industry news, personnel.
General Info: Yr. Est. 1901, Monthly, Trim Size-8½ x 11, Offset press, 4 pages, 2 Color
Circulation: (100% controlled), Total-1,100

Tempo

Publishing Co: Georgia International Life Insurance Co., PO Box 7325, Atlanta, GA 30357-0325

Tempo   *Business*

Publishing Co: Kansas City Life Insurance Co., PO Box 419139, Kansas City, MO 64141-6139;
  Title Tel # (816) 753-7000
Personnel: Editor-Nancy Vilmer
Editorial Description: In-house publication containing articles dealing with insurance industry,
  company, associates.
General Info: (Formerly Lifelines), Bi-weekly, Trim Size-8½ x 11, Offset press, 4 pages, No Color
Circulation: (100% controlled), Total-950

Tennant Topics   *Business*

Publishing Co: Tennant Co., 701 Lilac Dr N, Minneapolis, MN 55422-4687 Fax # (612) 541-6196;
  Title Tel # (612) 540-1636
Personnel: Editor-Linda Deml
Editorial Description: Company activities, policies, people.
General Info: Yr. Est. 1945, Bi-monthly, Trim Size-8½ x 11, Sheetfed press, 12 pages, Color-cover,
  Matte
Circulation: Total-2,000

Texas Eastern News

Publishing Co: Texas Eastern Transmission Corp., PO Box 2521, Houston, TX 77252-2521
  Tel # (713) 627-5400

Texas Power

Publishing Co: Texas Power, Box 6331, 1511 Bryan St., Dallas, TX 75201 Tel # (214) 812-4600
Personnel: Editor-Miss Mayfair Macaulaya

Times Line

Publishing Co: Times Publishing Co., PO Box 1121, Saint Petersburg, FL 33731-1121
Personnel: Editor-Gary Wilson
General Info: Weekly, Trim Size-8½ x 11, Sheetfed press, 6 pages

Tips   *Business*

Publishing Co: Fiberlux, Inc., 3010 Westchester Avenue, Purchase, NY 10577-2524
Personnel: Editor-Fred Smith
General Info: Quarterly, 4 pages

Tire Tracks

Publishing Co: Cooper Tire, Lima & Western Aves., Findlay, OH 45840; Title Tel # (419) 427-4857
  Title Fax # (419) 427-4719
Personnel: Editor-Debbie Crow

Together   *Association*

Publishing Co: United Way of Tri-State, 160 Water St., New York, NY 10038-4922;
  Title Tel # (212) 907-0451
Personnel: Editor-Roberta Diakun
Editorial Description: Promotes United Way support.
General Info: Yr. Est. 1977, Quarterly, Web press, 18 pages, Color
Subscriptions: Free
Circulation: (100% controlled), Total-8,000

Toledo News Bulletin Board

Publishing Co: Owens-Corning Fiberglas Corp., Fiberglas Tower, #t21, Toledo, OH 43659-0001; Title Tel # (419) 248-8000
Personnel: Editor-Bill Hamilton
General Info: (Formerly Tower News), Weekly

Toledo System

Publishing Co: Toledo Scale Company, Toledo Scale Div., 350 W Wilson Bridge Rd, Worthington, OH 43085-2217; Title Tel # (419) 478-5811
Personnel: Editor-Roger Cox, Adv. Dir.-Robert Terry
General Info: Yr. Est. 1901, Bi-monthly
Circulation: Total-4,500

Torch Bearer
See: EDUCATION

Tower News

Publishing Co: Sears Roebuck, Sears Tower Dept. 703, Bsc, #40-09, Chicago, IL 60684-0001 Tel # (312) 875-3000; Title Tel # (312) 302-3444

Tower Talk

Publishing Co: Lamar Life Insurance Co., 317 E Capitol St, Jackson, MS 39201-3493; Title Tel # (601) 354-5481
Personnel: Publisher-Lamar Life, Editor-Maidi Christensen, Circ. Mgr.-Linda Burke
General Info: Yr. Est. 1967, Monthly, Trim Size-8½ x 11, Offset press, 4 pages, No Color
Circulation: Total-350
Printing Co: Graphic Reproductions, 663 N State St, Jackson, MS 39202-3304 Tel # (601) 948-6478

Town Crier

Publishing Co: Town of Hempstead Office of Communication & Public Affairs, 1 Washington St, Hempstead, NY 11550-4921; Title Tel # (516) 489-5000
Personnel: Editor-Alexandra Trias
Editorial Description: Features on outstanding personnel, reports from each government department on promotions, etc.
Circulation: Total-4,500

Train Line

Publishing Co: Dresser Industries Inc., PO Box 718, Dallas, TX 75221-0718 Tel # (214) 740-6000

Transcom

Publishing Co: Bridgestone-Firestone Tire, PO Box 3000, Lavergne, TN 37086-3000 Tel # (615) 793-7581

Transit Times — *Association*

Publishing Co: Marta, 2424 Piedmont Rd NE, Atlanta, GA 30324-3330; Title Tel # (404) 848-5157 Title Fax # (404) 848-5098
Personnel: Editor-Judith Weisberg
Editorial Description: Public transportation news and history, related topics. Also employee information, local government information & general information related to transportation safety.
General Info: Yr. Est. 1949, Monthly, Trim Size-8½ x 11, Desktop press, 16 pages, No Color, Matte, Saddle-stitched
Subscriptions: Free
Acquistions: Publication Bought, Publication Sold
Circulation: (100% controlled), Total-500, Readership-5,000
Printing Co: Marta, 2424 Piedmont Rd NE, Atlanta, GA 30324-3330

Transmissions

Publishing Co: Houston Lighting & Power Co., 611 Walker St, Houston, TX 77002-4917; Title Tel # (713) 229-7701
Editorial Description: An in-house pub. for employees at Houston Lighting & Power.
General Info: Yr. Est. 1967, Monthly, Offset press, 6 pages, 2 Color, Newsprint, Perfect bound
Circulation: Total-13,000

Treadway Co-Operator

Publishing Co: Treadway Inns Corp., 23 Holcroft Rd W, Rochester, NY 14612-5519
Personnel: Editor-David Warner
General Info: Yr. Est. 1940, Monthly
Circulation: Total-600

Trefoil — *Association*

Publishing Co: Western Reserve Girl Scout Council, 345 White Pond Dr, Akron, OH 44320-1119; Title Tel # (216) 376-6876
Personnel: Editor-Lauwana Oliva
Editorial Description: Girl Scout programs; highlight volunteers; feature special achievements; introduce staff.
General Info: Semi-annually, Trim Size-11⅜ x 13½, Web press, 8 pages, 2 Color, Coated
Circulation: (100% controlled), Total-15,000

Trend

Publishing Co: Wisconsin Bell, Inc., 722 N Broadway, Milwaukee, WI 53202-4303; Title Tel # (404) 678-2691
Personnel: Editor-Lorna Sorenson
Editorial Description: Monthly 2-color, 8-page publication for employees & retirees of Wisconsin Bell.
General Info: Yr. Est. 1966, Monthly, Trim Size-11 x 14, Offset press, 4 pages
Circulation: Total-15,000

Triangle Times

Publishing Co: Triangle Printing Co., PO Box 1782, York, PA 17405-1782
General Info: Bi-monthly
Circulation: Total-3,500

Trona Times

Publishing Co: FMC Corp., Industrial Chemical Div., PO Box 872, Green River, WY 82935-0872; Title Tel # (607) 875-2580

UGI Horizons

Publishing Co: UGI Corp., PO Box 858, Valley Forge, PA 19482-0858

UMCommunity

Publishing Co: United Methodist Communications, 810 12th Ave S, Nashville, TN 37203-4704; Title Tel # (615) 742-5428
Personnel: Publisher-Roger Burgess, Editor-Connie Monroe
Editorial Description: For employees & retired employees of United Methodist Communications.
General Info: (Formerly 15 Minutes at UMCom), Yr. Est. 1987, Monthly, Trim Size-8½ x 11, Desktop press, 8 pages, Color, Recycled
Circulation: Total-300
Printing Co: Johnson Graphics, 2963 Foster Creighton Dr, Nashville, TN 37204-3716 Tel # (615) 242-5892

UNITIL News — *Consumer*

Publishing Co: UNITIL Service Corp., 216 Epping Rd, Exeter, NH 03833-4575; Title Tel # (603) 772-0775 Title Fax # (603) 772-4651
Personnel: Editor-Karen Coltin-Patterso
Editorial Description: Publication for employees, retirees and board of directors of holding company and five subsidiaries.
General Info: Yr. Est. 1987, Quarterly, Trim Size-8½ x 11, Offset press, 8 pages, 2 Color, Coated
Circulation: Total-350
Printing Co: CGC Printing, 210 West Rd., Portsmouth, NH 03801 Tel # (603) 436-5520

UNMC News
See: HOSPITALS & NURSING HOMES

UPBeat — *Business*

Publishing Co: Union Planters Corp., 7130 Goodlett Farm Parkway, Cordova, TN 38018 Fax # (901) 937-2396; Title Tel # (901) 383-6000
Editorial Description: Employee news and information.
General Info: Bi-monthly
Subscriptions: Free To Qualified Recipient

Under Our Roof

Publishing Co: Meadow Gold Dairies, PO Box 1880, Honolulu, HI 96805-1880 Tel # (808) 944-5957 Parent Co.-Borden Company, Ltd., Don Mills, Canada; Title Tel # (808) 949-5957
Personnel: Publisher, Editor-Angie Cuyong
Editorial Description: Published for employees and retirees.
General Info: Yr. Est. 1949, Quarterly, 4 pages, 2 Color
Circulation: (76% controlled), Total-650

Union Electric News — *Business, Consumer*

Publishing Co: Union Electric Co., PO Box 149, St. Louis, MO 63166-0149 Fax # (314) 554-2888; Title Tel # (314) 621-3222
Personnel: Editor-Deborah Walther
Editorial Description: News and information for employees.
General Info: Monthly, Trim Size-11 x 11, Offset press, 8 pages, 2 Color
Circulation: Total-10,700

Union Forever

Publishing Co: Union Fork & Hoe Co., 500 Dublin Ave, Columbus, OH 43215-2382; Title Tel # (614) 222-4429
Personnel: Publisher, Editor-Pete Frampton
Editorial Description: To let workers know of company plans, benefits, etc.
General Info: Yr. Est. 1943, Bi-monthly, Trim Size-8½ x 11, Offset press, 8 pages, Color
Circulation: Total-1,000

Union Trust Topics — *Business*

Publishing Co: Union Trust Co., Public Relations, 300 Main Street, Stamford, CT 06904; Title Tel # (203) 348-6211
Personnel: Editor-Lynne Krupa
General Info: (Formerly Tower Topics), Yr. Est. 1969, Bi-monthly, Trim Size-8½ x 11, Offset press, 20 pages, Color
Circulation: Total-3,000

Uniroyal World

Publishing Co: Uniroyal Inc., PO Box 846, Middlebury, CT 06762-0846; Title Tel # (203) 573-2220
Personnel: Editor-Ray Andresen
General Info: Bi-monthly, Trim Size-11½ x 15, Offset press, 8 pages, No Color
Circulation: Total-50,000

United of Ohio News   *Business*

Publishing Co: United Telephone Co of Ohio, PO Box 3555, Mansfield, OH 44907-0555;
  Title Tel # (419) 755-8422 Title Fax # (419) 755-8118
Personnel: Publisher-Rick Yocum, Editor-Gregory Christ, Art Dir.-David Ruckman
General Info: Yr. Est. 1968, Bi-weekly, Trim Size-11¼ x 17½, Offset press, 8 pages, No Color
Subscriptions: Free To Qualified Recipient
Circulation: Total-4,500

United Way Newsletter

Publishing Co: United Way of the Natl. Capital Area, 95 M St SW, Washington, DC 20024-3622;
  Title Tel # (202) 488-2063
Personnel: Editor-Roger Baumgarten
General Info: Quarterly, Trim Size-11 x 15½, 8 pages, 2 Color, Coated
Circulation: Total-6,000
Printing Co: Custom Print, Inc., 2611 S. Shirlington Rd., Arlington, VA 22206-2529
  Tel # (703) 979-6670

Univac News

Publishing Co: Remington Rand, PO Box 500, Blue Bell, PA 19422-0500; Title Tel # (215) 542-4011

Up-To-Date

Publishing Co: Ford Motor Credit Co., The American Rd., Dearborn, MI 48121
Personnel: Editor-E.D. Lintz
General Info: Trim Size-8½ x 11, Offset press, 4 pages
Circulation: Total-7,000

UpDate   *Association*

Publishing Co: San Diego Gas, 101 Ash St, San Diego, CA 92101-3017; Title Tel # (619) 696-4308
Personnel: Editor-John Britton, Circ. Mgr.-Pauline McKnight
Editorial Description: For SDG&E employees.
General Info: Yr. Est. 1986, Weekly, 4 pages
Subscriptions: Free
Circulation: Total-7,000

Update

Publishing Co: Federal Express Corp., 2837 Sprankel Ave., AMF Box 30, Memphis, TN 38118-1587;
  Title Tel # (901) 369-3600

Update

Publishing Co: General Motors Corp., GM Assembly Div., 1500 E. Route A, Wentzville, MO
  63385-3630

Update   *Business*

Publishing Co: Canadian Masonry Contractors' Association, 360 Superior Blvd., Mississauga, ON
  L5T-2N7 Canada; Title Tel # (605) 584-1020
Personnel: Publisher-Larry Jeffries, Editor, Circ. Mgr.-Scott Zieske
Editorial Description: Supervisory newsletter.
General Info: Yr. Est. 1981, Quarterly, Trim Size-8½ x 11, Sheetfed press, 4 pages, No Color,
  Newsprint
Subscriptions: Free
Circulation: (43% controlled), Total-1,500
Printing Co: Clark Printing Co., 720 N 11th St, Spearfish, SD 57783-2246 Tel # (605) 642-4705

Upscale Report   *Business, Consumer*

Publishing Co: Atlantic Scale Co., 136 Washington Ave, Nutley, NJ 07110;
  Title Tel # (201) 661-7090
Editorial Description: Employee news and company information.
General Info: Yr. Est. 1987, Semi-annually, 6 pages

Utilbits

Publishing Co: Tacoma Dept. Public Utilities, PO Box 11007, Tacoma, WA 98411-0007;
  Title Tel # (206) 383-2471
Personnel: Editor-Sue T. Veseth
Editorial Description: Articles of interest to employees and retired employees.
General Info: (Formerly Pun), Yr. Est. 1970, Monthly, Trim Size-8½ x 11, Offset press, 8 pages
Circulation: Total-1,500

VL-Voice of Lance

Publishing Co: Lance Inc., PO Box 32368, Charlotte, NC 28232-2368; Title Tel # (704) 554-1421

Valley Pres

Publishing Co: Valley Presbyterian Hospital, 15107 Vanowen St, Van Nuys, CA 91405-4597
  Tel # (818) 782-6600

Vanguard

Publishing Co: Alpha Beta Acme Markets, Inc., Acme Markets Inc., 777 S Harbor Blvd, La Habra,
  CA 90631-6839; Title Tel # (714) 738-2000
Personnel: Editor-Don Lorenzi
General Info: Monthly, Trim Size-8½ x 11, Offset press, 16 pages
Circulation: Total-10,000

Vault Talk   *Business*

Publishing Co: Trustmark Natl. Bank, PO Box 539, Brookhaven, MS 39601-0539;
  Title Tel # (601) 833-4771
Personnel: Editor-Rebecca Vaughn
General Info: Yr. Est. 1969, Monthly, Trim Size-8½ x 11, Offset press, 8 pages, No Color
Circulation: Total-750

Via ITT   *Business*

Publishing Co: ITT World Communications Inc., 380 Madison Avenue, New York, NY 10017-2513;
  Title Tel # (212) 797-3300
Personnel: Editor-Edward J. Felesina
Editorial Description: Thoroughly covers news of the international communicatioms business,
  featuring ITT World Communications' employees.
General Info: Yr. Est. 1954, Monthly
Circulation: Total-8,500

Viewpoint   *Business*

Publishing Co: Secura Insurance, 2401 S Memorial Dr, Appleton, WI 54915-1429;
  Title Tel # (414) 739-3161
Personnel: Editor-Gary Wischer
Editorial Description: Published for agents licensed with company; covers educational and
  informative issues of the industry.
General Info: (Formerly Viewpoints), Yr. Est. 1986, Quarterly, Trim Size-8½ x 11, Web press, 8
  pages, Color, Coated
Acquistions: Publication Bought
Circulation: (100% controlled), Total-1,700

Viewpoint

Publishing Co: Sherwin-Williams Co., 101 Prospect Ave., N.W., Cleveland, OH 44115;
  Title Tel # (216) 861-3400

Vigo View

Publishing Co: Chas. Pfizer, PO Box 88, Terre Haute, IN 47808-0088; Title Tel # (812) 299-2121
Personnel: Editor-H.F. White
Editorial Description: News and features concerning the company, management and employees.
General Info: Yr. Est. 1958, Bi-weekly
Circulation: Total-700

Virginian   *Association*

Publishing Co: Virginia Credit Union League, PO Box 11469, Lynchburg, VA 24506-1469;
  Title Tel # (804) 237-9600 Title Fax # (804) 239-9149
Subscriptions: Indv. $12

Visions

Publishing Co: United Telecommunications Inc., United Telephone Co. of Kansas, 5454 W. 110 St.,
  Overland Park, KS 66211
Personnel: Editor-Victoria Nelsen
General Info: (Formerly Sunflower Sentinal)

Voice of Motorola

Publishing Co: Motorola Inc., 1301 E. Algonquin Rd., Roselle, IL 60196-1078;
  Title Tel # (708) 397-1000

Voiceways

Publishing Co: New York Telephone Co., 140 West St, New York, NY 10007-2174;
  Title Tel # (212) 394-4141
Personnel: Editor-Barbara Dana
Editorial Description: Communications magazine designed to help PBX and TWX operators and
  management in their work.
General Info: Yr. Est. 1944, Quarterly

Vortecnology News

Publishing Co: Vortec Corp., 10125 Carver Rd, Cincinnati, OH 45242-4798;
  Title Tel # (513) 891-7475
General Info: Quarterly

Wak-Facts

Publishing Co: W. A. Krueger Co., 12821 W Bluemound Rd, Brookfield, WI 53005-8038
Personnel: Editor-Bud Gross
General Info: Bi-monthly
Circulation: Total-1,200

Waterfront General

Publishing Co: General Mills Inc., 54 S Michigan Ave, Buffalo, NY 14203-3086;
  Title Tel # (716) 856-6060
Personnel: Editor-Ronald Smith
Editorial Description: Explains policy, operations, and people to all employees and their families.
General Info: Yr. Est. 1985, Quarterly, Trim Size-8½ x 11, Letrpr. press, 12 pages, 2 Color, Coated
Subscriptions: $1/copy
Acquistions: Publication Bought
Circulation: Total-1,500
Advertising: Accepts Inserts.

Watts Watt   *Association*

Publishing Co: Corn Belt Power Cooperative, PO Box 508, Humboldt, IA 50548-0508;
Title Tel # (515) 332-2571
Personnel: Editor-J. Lamker
Editorial Description: Rural Electric Cooperative internal organ.
General Info: Monthly, 6 pages
Circulation: Total-910

Waynews   *Business*

Publishing Co: American Cyanamid Co., 1 Cyanamid Plz, Wayne, NJ 07470-2076;
Title Tel # (201) 831-3153
Personnel: Editor-Ellen Crane
Editorial Description: Corporate events, employee features, company news.
General Info: Bi-monthly, Trim Size-11 x 14½, Offset press, 8 pages, 2 Color, Newsprint
Circulation: Total-3,500

We the People

Publishing Co: Merrill Lynch, North Tower, World Trade Center, New York, NY 10281-1215;
Title Tel # (212) 637-1960
Personnel: Editor-Paul Lenihan
Editorial Description: Employee newsletter.
General Info: Yr. Est. 1947, 10x/yr., Trim Size-8½ x 14, Web press, 10 pages, 2 Color, Newsprint
Circulation: Total-58,000

Weekly Bulletin

Publishing Co: Virginia Mutual Benefits Life Ins. Co., Agency Dept., PO Box 201, Durham, NC 27702-0201; Title Tel # (804) 643-0245
Personnel: Editor-C.L. Townes, Sr.
General Info: Weekly, Trim Size-8½ x 11, Offset press, 12 pages
Circulation: Total-200

Weekly Chaser   *Business*

Publishing Co: Fort Worth Star Telegram, 400 W 7th St, Fort Worth, TX 76102-4793;
Title Tel # (817) 390-7853
Editorial Description: Weekly news in house for employees.
General Info: Weekly, Trim Size-8½ x 11, Offset press, 4 pages, 2 Color
Circulation: Total-1,300

Weekly News Bulletin

Publishing Co: General Motors Corp., GM Assembly Div.-Baltimore Pla, Baltimore, MD 21203;
Title Tel # (301) 631-2000

Weekly Update

Publishing Co: Pacific Telephone, 1010 Wilshire Blvd Rm 501, Los Angeles, CA 90017-5601;
Title Tel # (213) 811-9000

Weldwood News

Publishing Co: U.S. Plywood-Champion Papers Inc., 885 Conklin St, Farmingdale, NY 11735-2400;
Title Tel # (212) 895-8000
Personnel: Editor-Lawrence Karabaic
General Info: Yr. Est. 1942, Bi-monthly
Circulation: Total-18,000

Wellcome News

Publishing Co: Burroughs Wellcome, 3030 Cornwallis Rd., Research Triangle, NC 27709-2700;
Title Tel # (919) 248-4597
Personnel: Editor-Jay Johnson
Editorial Description: B.W. Co. employees & retirees; pharmaceutical focus.
General Info: Yr. Est. 1944, Monthly, Trim Size-8½ x 11, Offset press, 20 pages, 2 Color, Coated
Circulation: (100% controlled), Total-4,700
Printing Co: Greensboro Printing Co., 3012 Patterson St., Greensboro, NC 27408
Tel # (919) 294-4300, Fax # (910) 855-7397

Wells Fargo Messenger

Publishing Co: Wells Fargo Bank, 464 California St, San Francisco, CA 94104-1287;
Title Tel # (415) 396-3606

Wheel

Publishing Co: New England, 501 Boylston St, Boston, MA 02116-3706; Title Tel # (617) 578-2892
Personnel: Editor-Linda Hilliard, Art Dir.-Robin King
General Info: Yr. Est. 1949, Bi-weekly, Trim Size-11 x 17, Letrpr. press, 4 pages, Color-cover, Matte
Acquistions: Publication Bought
Circulation: Total-5,400
Printing Co: Nimrod Press, 170 Brookline Ave, Boston, MA 02215-3907 Tel # (617) 437-7900, Fax # (617) 262-5228

Where the Action Is!

Publishing Co: Sherwin-Williams Co., 754 Kevin Ct, Oakland, CA 94621-4040;
Title Tel # (415) 832-9815

Whirlpool World

Publishing Co: Whirlpool Corp., 2000 N M 63, Benton Harbor, MI 49022-2692;
Title Tel # (616) 926-5000
Personnel: Editor-Greg Brooke
General Info: Weekly, Trim Size-8½ x 11, Offset press, 6 pages
Circulation: (100% controlled), Total-2,700

Whitecaps

Publishing Co: White Cap Company, Continental Can Co., 1819 N Major Ave, Chicago, IL 60639-4117; Title Tel # (312) 637-2000
Personnel: Editor-Anne Sirosky
General Info: Weekly, Trim Size-8 x 10, Offset press, 4 pages
Circulation: Total-1,700

Wildcat

Publishing Co: Exxon Co. USA, Southeastern Div., P.O. Box 60, New Orleans, LA 70160;
Title Tel # (504) 561-3636

Wix Folks and Facts   *Business*

Publishing Co: Wix Corp., PO Box 1967, Gastonia, NC 28053-1967; Title Tel # (704) 864-6711
Personnel: Editor-Becky Causby
Editorial Description: Oil and air filter industry news-company products and personnel.
General Info: Yr. Est. 1967, Monthly, Trim Size-9½ x 12¼, 14 pages, 2 Color
Circulation: Total-3,200

Wolverine News

Publishing Co: Wolverine World Wide, N Main St., Rockford, MI 49341; Title Tel # (616) 866-5500
Personnel: Editor-Emerson G. McCarty
General Info: Bi-weekly, Trim Size-9 x 12, Offset press, 6 pages
Circulation: Total-3,500

Work

Publishing Co: Gold Seal Co., PO Box 941, Wayne, NJ 07474-0941

Working Times   *Business*

Publishing Co: Goodwill Industries of Central Indiana, 1635 W Michigan St, Indianapolis, IN 46222-3852; Title Tel # (317) 636-2541 Title Fax # (317) 636-2574
Personnel: Publisher-Jim McClelland, Editor-Teri Duell
Editorial Description: Of interest to people who face barriers to employment & supporters of Goodwill Industries of Central Indiana.
General Info: (Formerly Goodwill Quarterly), Quarterly, Trim Size-8½ x 11, Offset press, 8 pages, 2 Color, Newsprint
Circulation: (100% controlled), Total-20,000

World, The

Publishing Co: Bell Telelphone Co. of PA, One Parkway, 9th fl., Philadelphia, PA 19102-1589;
Title Tel # (215) 466-2400
Personnel: Editor-Paul Werner
General Info: (Formerly Telephone News), Bi-monthly, Trim Size-9 x 12, Letrpr. press, 48 pages, Ind/Abs/Online: Newsnet
Circulation: Total-50,000

World of GAF

Publishing Co: GAF Corp., 1361 Alps Rd, Wayne, NJ 07470-3700; Title Tel # (201) 628-3393
Title Fax # (201) 628-3577
Personnel: Editor-Patricia Iacobelli
Editorial Description: News of the corporation and its employees.
General Info: (Formerly GAF News), Yr. Est. 1966, Quarterly, Trim Size-8½ x 11, 8 pages, 2 Color, Matte, Saddle-stitched
Circulation: Total-4,200

World of Metal Finishing

Publishing Co: OMI Intl. Corp., 21441 Hoover Rd, Warren, MI 48089-3161 Tel # (810) 497-9100

Wrangler

Publishing Co: Sears Roebuck, Sears Tower Dept. 703, Bsc, #40-09, Chicago, IL 60684-0001
Tel # (312) 875-3000

Writer's Forum   *Consumer*   CPM: $48

Publishing Co: F & W Publications, 1507 Dana Ave., Cincinnati, OH 45207-1056
Tel # (513) 531-2222; Title Tel # (513) 531-2690 Title Fax # (513) 531-1843
Personnel: Publisher, Editor, Circ. Mgr.-Bruce Woods, Art Dir.-Steph Redman
Editorial Description: Articles on writing technique and interviews with well-known writers, as inspiration to students in short story and magazine article writing.
General Info: (Formerly WDS Forum), Yr. Est. 1970, Quarterly, Trim Size-5½ x 8½, Offset press, 16 pages, ISSN: 0275-9748, 2 Color, Matte, Saddle-stitched
Subscriptions: Indv. $6, $2/copy
Circulation: (100% controlled), Total-13,000
Advertising: $625.
List Rental: Rents Lists

Xerox World

Publishing Co: Xerox Corp., Xerox Sq. 021, Rochester, NY 14644-0001 Tel # (716) 423-3255

Yellow Pages by Berry

Publishing Co: L. M. Berry, PO Box 6000, Dayton, OH 45401-6000 Tel # (513) 296-4903

You   *Business*

Publishing Co: Transamerica Life Co., 1150 S Olive St, Los Angeles, CA 90015-2271;
   Title Tel # (213) 742-2210
Personnel: Editor-Dave Gurzenski, Art Dir.-Paul Belza
Editorial Description: Employees news.
General Info: Yr. Est. 1973, Monthly, Trim Size-8½ x 13, Offset press, 8 pages, No Color
Subscriptions: Free
Circulation: Total-4,000

HUMOR & SATIRE

Absurd Inquirer   *Association*

Publishing Co: Henry Roll, 2419 Greensburg Pike, Pittsburgh, PA 15221-3665
General Info: Monthly
Subscriptions: Indv. $10, $1/copy

America's At Our Doorstep

Publishing Co: America's At Our Doorstep, PO Box 411, Churchton, MD 20733-0411;
   Title Tel # (301) 261-5338
Personnel: Publisher-Dennis Brezina
Editorial Description: A bi-monthly newsletter of irreverence, satire, seriousness & silliness related to
   life at a bed & breakfast manor in rural Maryland.
General Info: Yr. Est. 1988, Bi-monthly, No Color
Subscriptions: Indv. $6, Can. $6, For. $6, $1/copy

Bananas

Publishing Co: Scholastic Inc., 555 Broadway, New York, NY 10012-3999 Tel # (212) 343-6196
   Fax # (212) 343-6620 Parent Co.-National Reading Conference, Chicago
Personnel: Editor-Bob Stine
General Info: Yr. Est. 1975, 8x/yr.
Subscriptions: Indv. $10

Bufaloon Newsletter   *Consumer*

Publishing Co: Raisin Blowme, 31 West Northrup Pl., Buffalo, NY 14214-1162
Editorial Description: Collages of semi-clad men and (mostly) women mixed with funny newsclips
   from the mainstream press.
General Info: Irregular, 20 pages
Subscriptions: $2/copy

Capitol Comedy   *Consumer*

Publishing Co: Capitol Comedy, 8801 Jones Mill Rd, Chevy Chase, MD 20815-4726;
   Title Tel # (202) 966-0264
Editorial Description: Topical political humor.
General Info: Yr. Est. 1989, Monthly
Subscriptions: Indv. $105
Circulation: Total-750

Comedy Writers Assn. Newsletter

Publishing Co: Comedy Writers Assn., PO Box 023304, Brooklyn, NY 11202-3304;
   Title Tel # (718) 855-5057
Personnel: Editor-Robert Makinson
Editorial Description: Articles on writing & selling comedy material.
General Info: Yr. Est. 1989, Trim Size-8½ x 11, Mimeo press, 3 pages, No Color, Matte
Subscriptions: $6/copy
Circulation: Total-125
Advertising: Inquire for rates.

Comic Highlights   *Business, Consumer*   CPM: $625

Publishing Co: Tom Adams Productions, PO Box 10246, Honolulu, HI 96816-0246;
   Title Tel # (808) 373-9800 Title Fax # (808) 373-9801
Personnel: Publisher, Editor-Tom Adams
Editorial Description: Provides several services for the stand-up comic, actor or speaker: short quick
   gags, weekly periodicals/wierd stories with many and varied punchlines & observations.
General Info: Yr. Est. 1970, Weekly, Trim Size-8½ x 11, Sheetfed press, 15 pages, 4% ads, No
   Color
Subscriptions: Indv. $125, For. $137, $10/copy
Circulation: Total-800
Advertising: $500. Accepts Inserts.
List Rental: Actives: $125/M, Expires: 5,000, $125/M

County Line
See: HISTORY

Curmudgeon's Home Companion, The
See: FOOD

Current Comedy   *Business*

Publishing Co: Georgetown Publishing House, 1101 30th St., NW, Washington, DC 20007;
   Title Tel # (202) 337-5980 Title Fax # (202) 337-1512
Personnel: Publisher-Lammot Copeland, Jr., Editor-Daniel White, Circ. Mgr.-Lisa M. Zorn
Editorial Description: Joke services for those meeting the public. Emphasis on political & business
   topics.
General Info: Yr. Est. 1960, Semi-monthly, Trim Size-8½ x 11, Sheetfed press, 4 pages, Color,
   Coated
Subscriptions: Indv. $90, Can. $106, For. $106, $3/copy
Acquistions: Publication Bought
Circulation: Total-2,000
List Rental: Actives: 2,000, $95/M, Expires: 10,000, $75/M

Deadelvis Fan Club: 50,000,000 Elvis Fans Don't Have a Clue   *Consumer*

Publishing Co: Deadelvis Fan Club, PO Box 1903, Evanston, IL 60204-1903
Editorial Description: Lots of great comical bits tearing the dead king down to size.
General Info: Quarterly
Subscriptions: Indv. $12, $4/copy

Dickin' Around
See: CLUBS

Father Flood Lectionary Series
See: RELIGIOUS & THEOLOGICAL

Fillmore Bungle   *Association*

Publishing Co: Soc. for the Preservation & Enhancement of the Recognition, of Millard Fillmore, 37
   Hillside Rd., Stratford, NJ 08084; Title Tel # (609) 627-5118 Title Fax # (609) 627-2252
Personnel: Editor-Phil Arkow
Editorial Description: Offbeat look at mediocrity in American life, as epitomized by Millard Fillmore,
   and other Fillmorabilia.
General Info: Yr. Est. 1975, Annually, Trim Size-8½ x 11, Desktop press, 10 pages, No Color,
   Newsprint
Subscriptions: Indv. $10
Circulation: Total-300

Flush Rush Quarterly
See: POLITICS

GAG Recap   *Business, Consumer*

Publishing Co: GAG Recap Publications, 12 Hedden Place, New Povidence, NJ 07974;
   Title Tel # (908) 464-1158
Personnel: Publisher, Editor-Al Gottlieb
Editorial Description: Reviews cartoons, editorials, and cartoon markets.
General Info: Yr. Est. 1954, Monthly, Trim Size-8½ x 11, 14 pages, No Color
Subscriptions: Indv. $50, Inst. $30, Can. $60, For. $60, $6/copy
Advertising: Accepts Inserts.

Gene Perret's Round Table   *Consumer*

Publishing Co: Gene Perret's Round Table & Comedy Svces., 2135 Huntington Drive, San Marino,
   CA 91108-2045; Title Tel # (818) 796-4823 Title Fax # (818) 796-4823
Personnel: Publisher-Gene Perret, Editor-Linda Perret
Editorial Description: How-to for anyone interested in a career in comedy writing.
General Info: Yr. Est. 1981, Monthly, Trim Size-8½ x 11, Mimeo press, 10 pages, Ind/Abs/Online: &
   inside information.', No Color
Subscriptions: Indv. $50, Inst. $55, Can. $50, For. $62, $5/copy

Hard Hat Times
See: MEDIA & COMMUNICATIONS

Humor Defense

Publishing Co: Humor Defense Publ., PO Box 10944, Pleasanton, CA 94588-0944;
   Title Tel # (510) 462-5710
Personnel: Editor-Virginia Tooper
Editorial Description: Devoted to positive application of humor in everyday life.
General Info: (Formerly Laugh Lovers News), Yr. Est. 1981, Bi-monthly, Trim Size-8½ x 11, Sheetfed
   press, 4 pages, Newsprint
Subscriptions: Indv. $10, $2/copy
Circulation: Total-800
Printing Co: Accelerated Printing, 3525 1st St, Livermore, CA 94550-2201 Tel # (415) 443-3777

Humor Digest and Conversation Piece - Chuckles & Grins

Publishing Co: ME, 448 N Mitchner Ave, Indianapolis, IN 46219-5116; Title Tel # (317) 356-4616
General Info: Yr. Est. 1958, Monthly
Subscriptions: Indv. $20

Jack Benny Times
See: FAN MAGAZINES-MOVIE, RADIO, TV

Jokesmith, The   *Business*

Publishing Co: Jokesmith, The, 44 Queensview Rd, Marlborough, MA 01752-1501;
  Title Tel # (508) 481-0979 Title Fax # (508) 481-0979
Personnel: Publisher, Editor-Edward McManus
Editorial Description: Comedy newsletter for business & professional speakers & speechwriters.
  Speech Augmentation.
General Info: Yr. Est. 1984, Quarterly, Trim Size-8½ x 11, Web press, 12 pages, ISSN: 0749-4351,
  No Color, Newsprint
Subscriptions: Indv. $40, $10/copy
Acquistions: Publication Sold
Circulation: Total-950
Advertising: Accepts Inserts.
List Rental: Actives: $100/M

Joyful Noiseletter
  See: RELIGIOUS & THEOLOGICAL

Latest Jokes

Publishing Co: Comedy Writers Assn., PO Box 023304, Brooklyn, NY 11202-3304;
  Title Tel # (718) 855-5057
Personnel: Publisher, Editor-Robert Makinson
Editorial Description: Jokes for comedians, disk jockeys & public speakers.
General Info: Yr. Est. 1974, Monthly, Trim Size-8½ x 11, Mimeo press, 3 pages, ISSN: 0887-6991,
  No Color
Subscriptions: Indv. $24, $3/copy
Circulation: Total-200
Advertising: Inquire for rates.

Laugh It Up   *Association*

Publishing Co: American Association for Therapeutic Humor, 2218 Crabtree Ln, Northbrook, IL
  60062-3520; Title Tel # (708) 291-0211
General Info: Yr. Est. 1987, Bi-monthly
Subscriptions: Indv. $35

Laughter Prescription Newsletter   *Consumer*

Publishing Co: Laughter Prescription Newsletter, 3011 Quebrada Circle, Carlsbad, CA 92009-8338;
  Title Tel # (619) 633-3790 Title Fax # (619) 634-1405
Personnel: Publisher, Editor, Bk. Rev. Ed., Adv. Dir., Mktg. Dir.-Karen Lee
Editorial Description: Jokes, quotes and anecdotes dedicated to the healing art of humor.
General Info: Yr. Est. 1989, Semi-monthly, Trim Size-8½ x 11, 8 pages, ISSN: 1046-5588, No Color,
  Matte, Other
Subscriptions: Indv. $18, Inst. $18, Can. $25, For. $25, $3/copy
Circulation: Total-500
Advertising: Accepts Inserts.
Printing Co: Rocks X Press, 2101 Las Palmas Drive, Suite 6, Carlsbad, CA 92009
  Tel # (619) 438-2992, Fax # (619) 438-2842

Laughter Works   *Consumer*

Publishing Co: Laughter Works Seminars, PO Box 1076, Fair Oaks, CA 95628-1076;
  Title Tel # (916) 863-1592 Title Fax # (916) 863-5072
Personnel: Publisher-Sandy Pelley, Editor-Jim Pelley, Production Mgr.-Darin Dimas, Art Dir.-Doreen
  Fung
Editorial Description: Laughter Works is your guffaw guide, mirth manager, & humor helper. Eight
  great pages of humor news & current comedy.
General Info: Yr. Est. 1988, Quarterly, Web press, 8 pages, ISSN: 1061-0367, 2 Color, Matte
Subscriptions: Indv. $18, Can. $21, For. $30, $6/copy
Circulation: Total-10,000, Readership-35,000
Advertising: Accepts Inserts.
List Rental: Rents Lists

Linda Perret's Humor Files   *Business*

Publishing Co: Gene Perret's Round Table & Comedy Svces., 2135 Huntington Drive, San Marino,
  CA 91108-2045; Title Tel # (818) 796-4823 Title Fax # (818) 796-4823
Personnel: Publisher, Editor-Linda Perret, Production Mgr.-Carol Maurer
Editorial Description: Humor for offices, speeches and presentations.
General Info: Yr. Est. 1993, Bi-weekly, Trim Size-8½ x 11, Desktop press, 4 pages, No Color, Matte,
  Other
Subscriptions: Indv. $105, Can. $120, For. $120, $8/copy
Acquistions: Publication Bought, Publication Sold
Printing Co: Valley Web, 1299 Stowe Avenue, Medford, OR 97504 Tel # (503) 772-7039

Lone Star Comedy Monthly   *Business*

Publishing Co: Lone Star Publications of Humor, Ste. 103, Box 29000, San Antonio, TX 78229
Personnel: Publisher, Editor-Lauren Barnett
Editorial Description: For professional humorists,(DJ's, public speakers, comedians, P.R. Reps.).
General Info: Yr. Est. 1983, Monthly, Trim Size-8½ x 11, Mimeo press, 6 pages, ISSN: 0736-8453,
  Newsprint
Subscriptions: Indv. $200, $20/copy

MOOsletter, The
  See: DAIRY

Monthly. . . Bulletin

Publishing Co: Monthly. . . Bulletin, 1630 Allston Way, Berkeley, CA 94703-1457
Personnel: Publisher, Editor-T. S. Child, Production Mgr., Art Dir.-Denver Tucson
Editorial Description: Small independent humorous/surrealist magazine. Crazy, funny, well-made.
General Info: Yr. Est. 1983, Semi-annually, Trim Size-5½ x 7½, Web press, 8 pages
Subscriptions: Indv. $1, $1/copy
Circulation: Total-500

News of the Weird   *Consumer*

Publishing Co: Deadfromtheneckup Inc., PO Box 8306, St. Petersburg, FL 33738
Editorial Description: Four pages crammed with the wackiest stuff you've ever thought to be true.
  Weird sex, botched robberies, and freak accidents.
General Info: 8x/yr., 4 pages
Subscriptions: Indv. $15

Pentatette   *Association*

Publishing Co: Limerick Special Interest Group, Box 365, Moffet, CA 94035-0365
Personnel: Editor-Arthur Deex
Editorial Description: The Limerick Special Interest Group is a club of limerick lovers. The monthly
  newsletter includes book reviews, articles & contributions - naughty & nice.
General Info: Yr. Est. 1981, Monthly, 18 pages
Subscriptions: Indv. $20, $1/copy

Phantastic Phunnies

Publishing Co: Phantastic Phunnies, 1450 Loop N. Rd., Kent, OH 44240-4619;
  Title Tel # (216) 673-5095
Personnel: Editor-John Fultz
Editorial Description: Topical one-liners for humorists.
General Info: Yr. Est. 1978, Monthly, 10 pages
Subscriptions: Indv. $65, $5/copy
Circulation: Total-1,000

Pun American Newsletter

Publishing Co: Pun American Newsletter, 1165 Elmwood Pl, Deerfield, IL 60015-1209;
  Title Tel # (847) 945-1790
Editorial Description: A newsletter devoted to puns.
General Info: Yr. Est. 1989, Quarterly
Subscriptions: Indv. $10
Circulation: Total-1,000

Pundit, The   *Consumer*

Publishing Co: The International Save The Pun Foundation, Box 5040, Station A, Toronto, ON M5W
  1N4 Canada; Title Tel # (416) 696-8146 Title Fax # (416) 424-3016
Personnel: Publisher, Editor-John S. Crosbie, Production Mgr.-George Robinson
Editorial Description: Humor & worldwide exchange of best puns to encourage reading and
  stimulate interest in words.
General Info: Yr. Est. 1979, Monthly, Trim Size-8½ x 11, Desktop press, 4 pages, ISSN: 0712-1318
Subscriptions: Indv. $26, Can. $26, $3/copy

Quagmire   *Association*

Publishing Co: NOT SAFE, Box 5743NX, Montecito, CA 93150-5743; Title Tel # (805) 969-6217
Personnel: Editor-Dale Lowdermilk
Editorial Description: Collection of satirical solutions to bureaucratic over-regulation.
General Info: Yr. Est. 1980, Trim Size-8½ x 11, Mimeo press, 4 pages, No Color, Newsprint
Subscriptions: Indv. $25, $5/copy
Circulation: Total-1,400
Printing Co: Kinkos Graphics, 451 Lopez Rd, Goleta, CA 93117-3236 Tel # (805) 964-3522

Realist

Publishing Co: The Realist, PO Box 1230, Venice, CA 90294-1230; Title Tel # (310) 392-5848
Personnel: Editor-Paul Krassner
Editorial Description: Irreverent social & political satire mixed with bizarre news items.
General Info: Yr. Est. 1958, Monthly, Trim Size-8½ x 11, 8 pages
Subscriptions: Indv. $23, $2/copy

SCROOGE Newsletter   *Association*

Publishing Co: S.C.R.O.O.G.E., 1447 Westwood Rd, Charlottesville, VA 22903-5151;
  Title Tel # (804) 977-4645
Personnel: Editor-Charles Langham
Editorial Description: Society to Curtail Ridiculous, Outrageous & Ostentatious Gift Exchanges.
  Newsletter includes short items on the over commercialization of the Christmas season, hints for
  inexpensive gifts, and a poem.
General Info: Yr. Est. 1979, Annually, Desktop press, 4 pages, 2 Color
Subscriptions: Indv. $2
Circulation: Total-1,066

Secular Humanist Bulletin
  See: PHILOSOPHY

To Wit   *Consumer, Association*

Publishing Co: American Humor Studies Assn., James Madison Unversity, English Dept.,
  Harrisonburg, VA 22807-0001
Personnel: Editor-Cameron Nickels
Editorial Description: Newsletter of the American Humor Studies Assoc.
General Info: Semi-annually, Trim Size-8½ x 11, No Color
Subscriptions: Indv. $20

Trade Journal Recap   *Business, Consumer*

Publishing Co: GAG Recap Publications, 12 Hedden Place, New Povidence, NJ 07974;
  Title Tel # (908) 464-1158
Personnel: Publisher, Editor-Al Gottlieb
Editorial Description: Describes cartoons in trade journals and house organs.
General Info: Yr. Est. 1975, Monthly, Trim Size-8½ x 11, Offset press, 4 pages, No Color, Other
Subscriptions: Indv. $20, Can. $25, For. $25, $3/copy
Advertising: Accepts Inserts.

View from Ledge *Consumer*

Publishing Co: Deadfromtheneckup Inc., PO Box 8306, St. Petersburg, FL 33738
Editorial Description: A funny newsletter featuring absurdist newsclips from around the country.
General Info: 8x/yr.
Subscriptions: Indv. $15

Woddis Newsletter CPM: $62

Publishing Co: International Banana Club, 2524 El Molino Ave, Altadena, CA 91001-2318;
Title Tel # (818) 798-2272
Personnel: Publisher, Editor-Ken Bannister
Editorial Description: Membership news, fun ideas, & positive tips. Products available with registered trademark.
General Info: Yr. Est. 1976, Semi-annually, 2% ads
Subscriptions: Indv. $15, $10/copy
Circulation: Total-8,000
Advertising: $500.
List Rental: Rents Lists

HUNTING & FISHING

Anglers Art

Publishing Co: Anglers Art, PO Box 148n, Plainfield, PA 17081-0148; Title Tel # (800) 848-1020
Title Fax # (717) 243-8603
Editorial Description: Features news on fairs, auctions, conventions, new publications and other items of interest to anglers. Books on fishing and related skills such as fly tying can be ordered through the newsletter, which also functions as a brochure of new sportfishing publications.

Angling Report, The *Consumer*

Publishing Co: Hunting Report Inc., 9300 S Dadeland Blvd Ste 605, Miami, FL 33156-2721;
Title Tel # (305) 670-1361 Title Fax # (305) 670-1376
Personnel: Editor-Don Causey
General Info: Yr. Est. 1988, Monthly, Desktop press, 12 pages
Subscriptions: Indv. $39
Circulation: Total-3,300
List Rental: List Management Co.: Chilcutt Direct Marketing, 9301 Cedar Lake Ave., Oklahoma City, OK 73114-7803 Tel # (405) 478-7245, Fax # (405) 478-2984
Printing Co: Printing Services, Box 66-1152, Miami Springs, FL 33156-2721 Tel # (305) 633-2571

Bird Hunting Report, The *Consumer*

Publishing Co: Pasha Publications, Inc, 1616 N. Fort Myer Dr., #1000, Arlington, VA 22209-3103
Tel # (703) 528-1244 Fax # (703) 528-4926; Title Tel # (305) 598-0158 Title Fax # (305) 598-0196
Editorial Description: Newsletter that delivers where-to-go information for birdshooters & waterfowlers who travel.
General Info: (Formerly Hunting Report for Birdshooters & Waterfowlers, The), Yr. Est. 1989, Monthly, 8 pages, No Color, Matte
Subscriptions: Indv. $45, Can. $51, For. $66, $5/copy
Circulation: Total-1,300
Advertising: Inquire for rates.
List Rental: Rents Lists
Printing Co: Printing Services, Inc., FL

Bulletin of the Canadian Association for Humane Trapping *Association*

Publishing Co: Canadian Assn. for Humane Trapping, Box 934, Station F, Toronto, ON M4Y 2N9 Canada; Title Tel # (416) 324-8726
Personnel: Editor-Jane Vinet
Editorial Description: Reports on work of the C.A.H.T. encouraging the use of humane methods in taking wild animals; comment and items of interest regarding conservation.
General Info: Yr. Est. 1954, Trim Size-8½ x 11, Offset press, 16 pages, No Color
Subscriptions: Indv. $15
Acquistions: Publication Bought
Circulation: Total-5,000

Canadian Archer
See: SPORTS & SPORTING GOODS

Conserve
See: ENVIRONMENT & ECOLOGY

Fishing Hot Spots 'Newsline'

Publishing Co: Fishing Hot Spots, 1999 River St, Rhinelander, WI 54501-2457;
Title Tel # (715) 369-5555
Personnel: Editor-Russ Warye
General Info: Yr. Est. 1984, Monthly
Subscriptions: Indv. $30

Fly-Tackle Dealer *Business* CPM: $125

Publishing Co: Down East Enterprise Inc., PO Box 679, Camden, ME 04843-0679
Fax # (207) 594-5144; Title Tel # (207) 594-9544 Title Fax # (207) 594-7215
Personnel: Publisher-H. Allen Fernald, Editor-Jim Butler, Circ. Mgr.-Deb Dodge, Production Mgr.-Marcel Dagneau, Adv. Dir.-Bill Anderson, Art Dir.-Kat Rosard
Editorial Description: Trade publication for the fly-fishing industry.
General Info: Yr. Est. 1980, Bi-monthly, Web press, 40 pages, 6% ads, 4 Color, Coated, Saddle-stitched
Subscriptions: Can. $20, For. $40, Free To Qualified Recipient
Circulation: (100% controlled), Total-10,000
Advertising: $1,255. Accepts Inserts.

Game Manager *Business*

Publishing Co: Multiple Use Managers, PO Box 1330, West Point, CA 95255-1330;
Title Tel # (209) 293-7087 Title Fax # (209) 293-7105
Editorial Description: Features articles on game management issues.
General Info: Quarterly, ISSN: 1066-0577
Subscriptions: Indv. $20

Hunter Training and Conservation, Instructor Newsletter

Publishing Co: Alberta Environmental Protection, Operations Branch, Main Floor North Tower, Petroleum Plaza, 9945 108 St., Edmonton, AB P5K 2G6 Canada; Title Tel # (403) 427-6727
General Info: Quarterly

Hunting Report for Big Game Hunters, The *Consumer*

Publishing Co: Hunting Report Inc., 9300 S Dadeland Blvd Ste 605, Miami, FL 33156-2721;
Title Tel # (305) 670-1361 Title Fax # (305) 670-1376
Personnel: Publisher, Editor-Don Causey
Editorial Description: Newsletter that delivers where-to-go information for hunters who travel.
General Info: (Formerly World Wide Hunters), Yr. Est. 1981, Monthly, Desktop press, 14 pages, 1% ads, No Color, Newsprint
Subscriptions: Indv. $60, Can. $66, For. $81, $5/copy
Circulation: Total-3,200
Advertising: Inquire for rates.
List Rental: List Management Co.: Manager: Don Causey; Chilcutt Direct Marketing, 9301 Cedar Lake Ave., Oklahoma City, OK 73114-7803 Tel # (405) 478-7245, Fax # (405) 478-2984, Actives: $100/M
Printing Co: Printing Services, Box 66-1152, Miami Springs, FL 33156-2721 Tel # (305) 633-2571

International Angler *Association*

Publishing Co: International Game Fish Assn., 1301 East Atlantic Blvd., Pompano Beach, FL 33060;
Title Tel # (305) 941-3474 Title Fax # (305) 941-5868
Personnel: Editor-Ray Crawford
Editorial Description: Reports angling activites throughout the world, updates world record freshwater, saltwater & fly fishing catches, etc.
General Info: (Formerly International Marine Angler), Yr. Est. 1973, Bi-monthly, Trim Size-8½ x 11, Offset press, 16 pages, ISSN: 0257-1420, 2 Color, Coated, Saddle-stitched
Circulation: Total-17,500

International Light Tackle Tournament Association, Bulletin *Association*

Publishing Co: Intl. Light Tackle Tournament Assn., 2044 Fedl. Ave., Costa Mesa, CA 92627-4132;
Title Tel # (714) 548-4273
Editorial Description: Report on recent fishing tournament of ILTTA.
General Info: Yr. Est. 1947, Annually, 4 pages, No Color
Circulation: Total-300

PanAngler

Publishing Co: PanAngling Ltd., 180 N. Michigan Ave., Chicago, IL 60601-7480;
Title Tel # (312) 263-0328
Personnel: Publisher, Editor-Jim Chapralis, Circ. Mgr.-Claudia Levy, Art Dir.-Al Trungale, Promotion Dir.-Ken Gould
Editorial Description: International sport fishing outside continental U.S.
General Info: Yr. Est. 1975, Monthly, Trim Size-8½ x 11, Sheetfed press, 8 pages, ISSN: 0739-4632, No Color, Newsprint
Subscriptions: Indv. $20, $2/copy
Circulation: Total-6,500
Printing Co: Kline's Printing & Mailing Service, 7131 N Clark St, Chicago, IL 60626-2407
Tel # (312) 274-8244

HYPNOSIS

Alternative Health Therapies Newsletter
See: HEALTH

Hypnotherapy Today *Association*

Publishing Co: American Association of Professional Hypnotherapists, PO Box 29, Boones Mill, VA 24065-0029; Title Tel # (540) 334-3035
Personnel: Publisher-William Brink
Editorial Description: Geared to the practicing hypnotherapist's clinical & business interests.
General Info: Yr. Est. 1980, Quarterly, Trim Size-8½ x 11, Offset press, 6 pages, ISSN: 0882-8652, No Color
Subscriptions: Free With Membership
Circulation: (85% controlled), Total-2,000
List Rental: Actives: $85/M

International Society of Hypnosis Newsletter *Association*

Publishing Co: Society for Clinical & Experimental Hypnosis, 8335 Allison Pointe Trail, Ste. 250, Indianapolis, VA 46250-1686; Title Tel # (215) 748-2161
Editorial Description: Newsletter for ISH members.
General Info: Yr. Est. 1978, Semi-annually, Offset press, 4 pages, No Color
Subscriptions: $4/copy
Circulation: Total-2,100

Mind Quest *Consumer, Association*

Publishing Co: Lighword Publishing Company, National Bank Building, 525 S. Main St., Suite 308, Del Rio, TX 78840 Fax # (210) 775-9640; Title Tel # (210) 774-3141
Personnel: Publisher-Bernie Nelson
Editorial Description: Subjects related to mind control by cults, media, etc.
General Info: (Formerly MK Newsletter), Quarterly, Trim Size-8½ x 11, 3 pages, No Color
Subscriptions: Indv. $3, $1/copy
Circulation: Total-500

INDUSTRIAL DESIGN

Association of Canadian Industrial Designers, Newsletter

Publishing Co: Assn. of Canadian Industrial Designers, C/O Humber College, 205 Humber College Blvd., Rexdale, ON M9W 5L7 Canada; Title Tel # (416) 675-3111
General Info: Quarterly

Daily Construction Report
See: CONSTRUCTION & BUILDING

Design Drafting News
See: ENGINEERING

Design Perspectives *Association* CPM: $200

Publishing Co: Industrial Designers Society of America, 142 Walker Rd, Great Falls, VA 22066-1836; Title Tel # (703) 759-0100 Title Fax # (703) 759-7679
Personnel: Editor-Karen Berube
Editorial Description: Analyzes current issues affecting design; publishes designers' viewpoints and presents information on design resources. Also includes news about design competitions, meetings and employment opportunities.
General Info: Yr. Est. 1965, Monthly, Trim Size-8½ x 11, Sheetfed press, 10 pages, 15% ads, 2 Color, Recycled
Subscriptions: Indv. $30, For. $37, $3/copy
Circulation: Total-2,500
Advertising: $500.
List Rental: Rents Lists
Printing Co: Charter Printing Co., 4202 Wheeler Ave, Alexandria, VA 22304-6413 Tel # (703) 370-1010, Fax # (703) 370-2009

Employment Law Manual
See: LAW

Enhanced Energy Recovery News
See: ENERGY

Flame Retardancy News
See: FIRE PROTECTION

Flexible Packaging Assn. Update
See: PACKAGING

Global Packaging & Brand Identity
See: PACKAGING

Illinois Writers Monthly
See: LITERATURE & LINGUISTICS

Kendall College of Art and Design
See: COLLEGE STUDENT

Safety Management
See: SAFETY

Voice Coil Newsletter
See: SOUND ENGINEERING

INDUSTRIAL RELATIONS/PERSONNEL

401(k) Dimensions
See: INVESTMENT

401(k) Handbook
See: INVESTMENT

APS Spokesman *Association*

Publishing Co: Association of Productivity Specialists, 521 Fifth Ave., New York, NY 10175; Title Tel # (212) 286-0943
Personnel: Publisher-R. Jacobson, Editor-R. Morren
Editorial Description: Provides information on individuals & companies working in the productivity consulting industry.
General Info: Yr. Est. 1977, Quarterly, Trim Size-8½ x 11, Sheetfed press, No Color
Circulation: (100% controlled), Total-300
Advertising: Accepts Inserts.

Accommodating Disability Decisions
See: LAW

Affirmative Action/EEO Update
See: CIVIL RIGHTS

Arizona Employment Law Letter
See: LAW

BNA Pension & Benefits Reporter *Business*

Publishing Co: Bureau of National Affairs, Inc., 1231 25th St. NW, Bldg. N-200, Washington, DC 20037-1157 Tel # (202) 452-4200 Fax # (202) 822-8092; Title Tel # (202) 452-4471 Title Fax # (202) 452-4084
Personnel: Publisher-William A. Beltz, Exec. Ed.-Kathleen D. Gill, Mag. Ed.-David A. Sayre, Assoc. Ed.-Deanne E. Neuman, Circ. Mgr.-Gary C. Seltzer
Editorial Description: Covers latest pension developments stemming from the passage of ERISA & its amendments, plus pension & welfare benefit resolutions, standards, enforcement actions, court decisions, legislative & administrative actions, agency options, & employee benefit trust fund requirements.
General Info: (Formerly BNA Pension Reporter), Yr. Est. 1974, Weekly, Trim Size-8½ x 11, Web press, 32 pages, ISSN: 1069-5117, Ind/Abs/Online: Life Insurance Indx,Property & Liability Insurance Indx,Nexis,Lexis,Westlaw
Subscriptions: Indv. $835, $1/copy

BNA Policy & Practice Series
See: MANAGEMENT

BNA's Employee Relations Weekly *Business, Association*

Publishing Co: Bureau of National Affairs, Inc., 1231 25th St. NW, Bldg. N-200, Washington, DC 20037-1157; Title Tel # (202) 452-4200 Title Fax # (202) 822-8092
Personnel: Publisher-William A. Beltz, Mng. Editor-Jeff Day, Circ. Mgr.-Gary C. Seltzer
Editorial Description: Gives an overview of the latest developments influencing employee relations in both private & public sectors, with information on EEO policy, federal, & state legislative & regulatory actions, NLRB actions, & the impact of foreign competition.
General Info: Yr. Est. 1983, Weekly, Trim Size-8½ x 11, Letrpr. press, 32 pages, ISSN: 0739-3016, Ind/Abs/Online: HRIN, No Color, Saddle-stitched
Subscriptions: Indv. $796

Bank Wage-Hour & Personnel Report
See: EMPLOYMENT

Benefits Guide Newsletter

Publishing Co: Warren, Gorham & Lamont, 31 Saint James Ave., Boston, MA 02116-4112 Parent Co.-Thomson Professional Publications, Stamford; Title Tel # (617) 423-2020 Title Fax # (617) 423-1914
Personnel: Publisher-Andrew Boden, Production Mgr.-Paul Kelly, Mktg. Dir.-Sandra Fox
General Info: (Formerly Employee Benefit), Yr. Est. 1994, Monthly
Subscriptions: Indv. $130
List Rental: List Management Co.: Manager: Seena Benedek; WG & L List Management, 1 Penn Plz Fl 42, New York, NY 10119-0002 Tel # (212) 971-5000

Benefits Review Board Reporters *Business*

Publishing Co: Matthew Bender & Co., 11 Penn Plaza, New York, NY 10001-2006 Fax # (212) 244-3188; Title Tel # (212) 967-7707
Personnel: Editor-B. Chase
Editorial Description: The comprehensive monitoring service authorized by the Board.
General Info: Yr. Est. 1974, Bi-weekly, Looseleaf
Subscriptions: $525/copy

Better Supervision
See: MANAGEMENT

Blue Ribbon Service
See: MANAGEMENT

Bulletin to Management *Business*

Publishing Co: Bureau of National Affairs, Inc., 1231 25th St. NW, Bldg. N-200, Washington, DC 20037-1157; Title Tel # (202) 452-4200 Title Fax # (202) 822-8092
Personnel: Publisher-William A. Beltz, Mng. Editor-Bill L. Manville, Circ. Mgr.-Gary C. Seltzer
Editorial Description: Features summaries of current developments in human resource/personnel management & labor relation. Discusses 'real-life job situtations' & provides policy guides on how companies have successfully handled employee relations problems. Recurring features include statistics.
General Info: Yr. Est. 1947, Weekly, Trim Size-8½ x 11, Offset press, 8 pages, ISSN: 0525-2156, Ind/Abs/Online: Personnel Literature Index, HRIN
Subscriptions: Indv. $272

Business at Risk: Trends in Personal Injury Litigation
 See: LAW

CLV Reports *Business*

Publishing Co: Canada Labour Views Co. Ltd., 304-950 Yonge St., Toronto, ON M4W 2J4 Canada; Title Tel # (416) 967-1144 Title Fax # (416) 967-9432
General Info: Yr. Est. 1956, Weekly
Subscriptions: Indv. $299

COBRA Guide

Publishing Co: CCH, Inc., 2700 Lake Cook Rd., Riverwoods, IL 60015 Parent Co.-Kluwer Law & Taxation Publishers, Cambridge; Title Tel # (847) 267-7000 Title Fax # (800) 224-8299
Editorial Description: Provides in-depth explanatory coverage, and full text reporting when needed of both federal and state health benefit continuation requirements for employers, with special emphasis on administration and valuable guidance in the area of communication.
General Info: Monthly, Looseleaf
Subscriptions: Indv. $252
List Rental: Rents Lists

CPA Personnel Report
 See: EMPLOYMENT

CSFA News
 See: EDUCATION

CUPA News
 See: SCHOOL ADMINISTRATION

Cal-OSHA Reporter
 See: SAFETY

California Employer Advisor
 See: EMPLOYMENT

California Employers' Guide to Employee Handbooks and Personnel Policy Manuals *Business*

Publishing Co: Matthew Bender & Co., 11 Penn Plaza, New York, NY 10001-2006 Tel # (212) 967-7707 Fax # (212) 244-3188
Editorial Description: Complete guide to writing, revising and updating employee handbooks and personnel policy manuals. Includes checklists, sample clauses, authority and cross-references to California Employment Law.
General Info: Yr. Est. 1989, Annually, Looseleaf

California Employment Law *Business*

Publishing Co: Matthew Bender & Co., 11 Penn Plaza, New York, NY 10001-2006 Tel # (212) 967-7707 Fax # (212) 244-3188
Editorial Description: Includes indepth discussion of the law, practice tips from experienced employment law practitioners, factual illustrations, sample employment documents, and litigation forms.
General Info: Yr. Est. 1989, Irregular, Looseleaf

California Employment Law Reporter *Business*

Publishing Co: Matthew Bender & Co., 11 Penn Plaza, New York, NY 10001-2006 Tel # (212) 967-7707 Fax # (212) 244-3188
Editorial Description: Summarizes all legislative, judicial, & regulatory developments in California employment law, as well as significant developments in related federal law. Features expert commentary from experienced employment law attorneys.
General Info: Yr. Est. 1990, Monthly, Looseleaf

California Public Sector Labor Relations *Business*

Publishing Co: Matthew Bender & Co., 11 Penn Plaza, New York, NY 10001-2006 Tel # (212) 967-7707 Fax # (212) 244-3188
Editorial Description: Comprehensively discusses the statutes governing public sector labor relations, as well as the important court cases & Public Employment Relations Board decisions interpreting those statutes. Covers the employer-employee relationship at the state & localgovernment levels, public school, community college & state university levels.
General Info: Yr. Est. 1989, Irregular, Looseleaf

Canadian Employment Benefits and Pension Guide *Business*

Publishing Co: CCH Canadian Ltd., 6 Garamond Ct., North York, ON M3C 1Z5 Canada Fax # (416) 444-8011 Parent Co.-CCH, Inc., Riverwoods; Title Tel # (416) 441-2992 Title Fax # (416) 444-9011
Personnel: Editor-Lionel Goulet
Editorial Description: Covers pension plans, fringe benefits, group insurance, medicare and executive compensation.
General Info: Monthly, Trim Size-6 x 9, Web press, No Color, Looseleaf
Subscriptions: Can. $570

Canadian Industrial Relations and Personnel Developments *Business*

Publishing Co: CCH Canadian Ltd., 6 Garamond Ct., North York, ON M3C 1Z5 Canada Fax # (416) 444-8011 Parent Co.-CCH, Inc., Riverwoods; Title Tel # (416) 441-2992 Title Fax # (416) 444-9011
Personnel: Editor-David Iggulden
Editorial Description: Review and analysis of significant developments in the industrial relations and personnel fields.
General Info: Yr. Est. 1971, Weekly, Trim Size-6 x 9, Offset press, 8 pages, 2 Color
Subscriptions: Can. $425

Canadian Labour Law Reporter
 See: LAW

Career Outplacement

Publishing Co: Career Management Consultants, Inc., 37628 Swede Heaven Rd, Arlington, WA 98223-5217; Title Tel # (717) 233-2272
Personnel: Publisher-Louis Persico, Editor-M. Kathleen Duttro
Editorial Description: Publisher articles related to outplacement, career management, industrial relations, personnel & employment.
General Info: Yr. Est. 1989, Quarterly, 4 pages
Subscriptions: Indv. $18
Acquistions: Publication Bought

Common Sense Negotiations
 See: MANAGEMENT

Comparative Industrial Relations Newsletter *Association, Consumer*

Publishing Co: DeGroote School of Business, McMaster University, Hamilton, ON L8S 4C7 Canada Tel # (905) 525-9140 Fax # (905) 527-0100
Personnel: Publisher-Roy Adams
Editorial Description: For those interested in corparate labor research and teaching.
General Info: Yr. Est. 1990, Semi-annually, Trim Size-8½ x 11, 12 pages, ISSN: 1198-6131, No Color
Subscriptions: Indv. $20, Inst. $35

Compensation *Business*

Publishing Co: Bureau of National Affairs, Inc., 1231 25th St. NW, Bldg. N-200, Washington, DC 20037-1157; Title Tel # (202) 452-4200 Title Fax # (202) 822-8092
Personnel: Publisher-William Beltz, Editor-Bill Manville, Circ. Mgr.-Gary Seltzer
Editorial Description: Covers laws dealing with workers' compensation & guidelines for industry. Includes advice on how to establish & maintain a balance compensation program; Offers examples of wage, fringe benefit policies, & atternative work schedules; Covers state minimum wage/ maximum hours, garnishment, wage payment, holiday, unemployment, income tax withholding, & temporary disability laws & more.
General Info: (Formerly Payroll Compensation), Yr. Est. 1952, Weekly, Trim Size-8½ x 11, Web press, 7 pages, ISSN: 0279-5418, Ind/Abs/Online: HRIN
Subscriptions: Indv. $650
Circulation: Total-4,640

Compliance Guide for Plan Administrators *Business*

Publishing Co: CCH, Inc., 2700 Lake Cook Rd., Riverwoods, IL 60015 Parent Co.-Kluwer Law & Taxation Publishers, Cambridge; Title Tel # (847) 267-7000 Title Fax # (800) 224-8299
Editorial Description: All-explanatory, emphasizes ERISA reporting, disclosure & fiduciary liability rules for employee benefit, self-employed & IRA plans by type. Provides actual-size ERISA forms & sample filled-in forms. CD version has interactive forms.
General Info: Yr. Est. 1976, Bi-weekly, Trim Size-6 x 9, Web press, 75 pages, No Color, Looseleaf
Subscriptions: Indv. $747

Coordination of Benefits Handbook *Business*

Publishing Co: Thompson Publishing Group, 1725 K Street, NW, Washington, DC 20006 Tel # (202) 872-4000
Editorial Description: Presents information more making timely and accurate claim determinations for all types of health benefits plans. Subscription includes quarterly updtes and news bulletins.
General Info: Annually, Looseleaf
Subscriptions: Indv. $292

Creative Training Techniques
Business

Publishing Co: Lakewood Publications, Inc., 50 S. Ninth St., Minneapolis, MN 55402-3165 Parent Co.-K-III Communications, New York; Title Tel # (612) 333-0471 Title Fax # (612) 333-6526
Personnel: Publisher-Philip Jones, Editor-Robert Pike, Circ. Mgr.-Nancy Swanson, Promotion Dir.-Carol A. Swanson
Editorial Description: Tips, tactics & how-to's for delivering effective training. It delivers down to basics, quick results-oriented ideas, techniques and methods that work.
General Info: Yr. Est. 1988, Monthly, Trim Size-8½ x 11, Sheetfed press, 8 pages, 2 Color, Recycled, Saddle-stitched
Subscriptions: Indv. $89, Can. $99, For. $109
Acquistions: Publication Bought
Circulation: Total-11,000
List Rental: List Management Co.: Manager: Paul Kolars; Lakewood Lists, 50 S. 9th St., Minneapolis, MN 55402 Tel # (612) 333-0471, Fax # (612) 333-6526, Actives: 10,093, $95/M

Customer Communicator, The
See: MANAGEMENT

Dialogue: The Canadian Payroll Assn.
Association

Publishing Co: Canadian Payroll Assn., 1867 Yonge St., Ste. 801, toronto, ON M4S 1Y5 Canada; Title Tel # (416) 487-3380
Personnel: Publisher-Karen Lander, Editor-Pauline Coogan, Production Mgr.-Carol Ford
Editorial Description: Provide leadership for payroll professionals.
General Info: 10x/yr., Sheetfed press, 16 pages, 1% ads, Color-cover, Matte, Saddle-stitched
Acquistions: Publication Bought
Circulation: Total-2,500
Advertising: Inquire for rates.
Printing Co: AW Dicks Graphics, 22 Sackville St., Toronto, ON M5A 3E2 Canada Tel # (416) 368-8028

Drug Detection Report
Business

Publishing Co: Pace Publications, 443 Park Ave. South, New York, NY 10016 Tel # (212) 685-5450 Fax # (212) 679-4701; Title Tel # (202) 785-1456 Title Fax # (202) 835-1772
Personnel: Publisher-Sid Goldstein, Editor-Vincent Taylor
Editorial Description: Independent report on drug testing in the workplace.
General Info: Semi-monthly
Subscriptions: Indv. $295

EBRI Issue Brief
Business

Publishing Co: Employee Benefit Research Institute, 2121 K St NW Ste 600, Washington, DC 20037-1801; Title Tel # (202) 659-0670
Personnel: Publisher-Dallas Salisbury, Editor-Carolyn Piucci, Promotion Dir.-Laura Bos
Editorial Description: The institute's main purpose is to conduct research, particularly in the area of pension and health and welfare plans.
General Info: Yr. Est. 1978, Monthly, Trim Size-8½ x 11, Sheetfed press, 20 pages, ISSN: 0887-137X, Ind/Abs/Online: HRIN, 2 Color, Newsprint, Saddle-stitched
Subscriptions: Indv. $224, $25/copy
List Rental: Actives: $100/M

EEO Compliance
Business

Publishing Co: Research Institute of America, 90 5th Avenue, New York, NY 10011-7629 Tel # (212) 645-4800; Title Tel # (800) 562-0245 Title Fax # (800) 562-0245
Personnel: Publisher-Lisa Galjanic, Editor-Michael O'Toole, Promotion Dir.-Claudia Levine
Editorial Description: Tracks federal & state anti-discrimination laws, & offers guidance.
General Info: Yr. Est. 1977, Monthly, Trim Size-8½ x 11
Subscriptions: Indv. $390
List Rental: List Management Co.: WG & L List Management, 1 Penn Plz Fl 42, New York, NY 10119-0002 Tel # (212) 971-5000

EEO Review
Business

Publishing Co: John Wiley & Sons, Inc., 605 Third Avenue, New York, NY 10158-0012 Tel # (212) 850-6000 Fax # (212) 850-6088; Title Tel # (212) 645-7880 Title Fax # (212) 675-4883
Personnel: Editor-Sarah Magee
Editorial Description: Covers EEO & other personnel policy responsibilities. Contains practical approaches to avoiding EEO problems in: drug abuse & alcohol, firing, hiring, discipline, counseling, AIDS, performance appraisal, & physical/mental handicaps.
General Info: Yr. Est. 1968, Monthly, Trim Size-8½ x 11, Sheetfed press, 8 pages, ISSN: 0148-6934, Coated, Saddle-stitched
Subscriptions: Indv. $160, Can. $160, For. $232
Circulation: Total-1,500
List Rental: Rents Lists
Printing Co: Hessey Printing, Inc., 424 Lafayette St # 100226, Nashville, TN 37203-4255 Tel # (615) 244-7180, Fax # (615) 255-6911

EEOC Compliance Manual
See: LAW

EMA Reporter
See: EMPLOYMENT

Effective Business Writing
See: MANAGEMENT

Employee Assistance Program Management Letter
Business, Consumer

Publishing Co: Health Resource Publishing, 3100 Hwy. 138, PO Box 1442, Wall Township, NJ 07719-1442; Title Tel # (908) 681-1133 Title Fax # (908) 681-0490
Personnel: Publisher-Robert Jenkins, Editor-Beth-Ann Kecher
Editorial Description: A comprehensive monthly management briefing on the range of influences surrounding your employee assistance program.
General Info: Yr. Est. 1987, Monthly, Trim Size-8½ x 11, Offset press, 8 pages, ISSN: 0896-0941, No Color, Newsprint
Subscriptions: Indv. $167, $11/copy
Advertising: Accepts Inserts.
List Rental: Actives: 10,500, $125/M
Printing Co: ACN Graphics, 1602 Birchwood Ln, Neptune, NJ 77553-6910 Tel # (908) 681-6083

Employee Benefit Notes
Business

Publishing Co: Employee Benefit Research Institute, 2121 K St NW Ste 600, Washington, DC 20037-1801; Title Tel # (202) 659-0670
Personnel: Publisher-Dallas Salisbury, Editor-Carolyn Piucci, Promotion Dir.-Laura Bos
Editorial Description: Pensions & health & welfare, public policy & legislative developments.
General Info: Yr. Est. 1978, Monthly, Trim Size-8½ x 11, Sheetfed press, 16 pages, ISSN: 0887-1388, Ind/Abs/Online: HRIN, 2 Color, Newsprint, Saddle-stitched
Subscriptions: Indv. $240, $25/copy
List Rental: Actives: $100/M

Employee Benefits Alert
Business

Publishing Co: Research Institute of America, 117 E Stevens Ave, Valhalla, NY 10595-1264; Title Tel # (212) 645-4800 Title Fax # (212) 337-4280
General Info: Yr. Est. 1987, 26x/yr.
Subscriptions: Indv. $101
List Rental: List Management Co.: WG & L List Management, 1 Penn Plz Fl 42, New York, NY 10119-0002 Tel # (212) 971-5000

Employee Benefits Basics
Business

Publishing Co: International Foundation of Employee Benefit Plans, 18700 W Bluemound Rd #69, P O Box 69, Brookfield, WI 53008-0069; Title Tel # (414) 786-6700 Title Fax # (414) 786-8670
Personnel: Publisher-Dee Birschel, Editor-Mary Jo Brzezinski
Editorial Description: Offers an introduction to selected topics for those new to the benefits field. Available only by subscription to publications package or by membership in IFFRP.
General Info: Yr. Est. 1986, Quarterly, ISSN: 1061-995X, Ind/Abs/Online: employee benefits infosource
Subscriptions: Indv. $170, Inst. $170, Can. $170, For. $220, $10/copy
Circulation: Total-34,000

Employee Benefits Cases
Business

Publishing Co: Bureau of National Affairs, Inc., 1231 25th St. NW, Bldg. N-200, Washington, DC 20037-1157; Title Tel # (202) 452-4200 Title Fax # (202) 822-8092
Personnel: Publisher-William A. Beltz, Mng. Editor-David A. Sayre, Circ. Mgr.-Gary C. Seltzer
Editorial Description: A weekly decisional service that reports the full text of federal & state court opinions & selected descisions of arbitrators & the NLRB on employee benefits issues.
General Info: Yr. Est. 1981, Weekly, Trim Size-6 x 9, Web press, 30 pages, ISSN: 0273-236X, Ind/Abs/Online: Autocite, Looseleaf
Subscriptions: Indv. $934

Employee Benefits Counselor

Publishing Co: Business Laws, Inc., 11630 Chillicothe Rd., Chesterland, OH 44026-1928; Title Tel # (216) 729-7996 Title Fax # (216) 729-0645
General Info: Yr. Est. 1993, Monthly, ISSN: 1068-4204
Subscriptions: Indv. $245, $20/copy

Employee Benefits Digest
Association

Publishing Co: International Foundation of Employee Benefit Plans, 18700 W Bluemound Rd #69, P O Box 69, Brookfield, WI 53008-0069 Fax # (414) 786-8670; Title Tel # (414) 786-6700 Title Fax # (414) 786-8620
Personnel: Publisher-Dee Birschel, Editor-Mary Jo Brzezinski
Editorial Description: News items & articles regarding employee benefits; Assn. News. Available only with subscription to publication package or by membership in IFEBP.
General Info: Yr. Est. 1964, Monthly, Trim Size-8½ x 11, Web press, 12 pages, ISSN: 0146-1141, Ind/Abs/Online: employee benefits infosource, 2 Color, Matte, Saddle-stitched
Subscriptions: Indv. $170, Inst. $170, Can. $170, For. $220, Free With Membership
Circulation: Total-34,000

Employee Benefits Management

Publishing Co: CCH, Inc., 2700 Lake Cook Rd., Riverwoods, IL 60015 Parent Co.-Kluwer Law & Taxation Publishers, Cambridge; Title Tel # (847) 267-7000 Title Fax # (800) 224-8299
Editorial Description: Provides comprehensive coverage of the full spectrum of employee benefits, including pensions, health care plans, paid time off, & work/family issues. Includes benefit forms & sample plans as well as the most recent best case practices in the benefits field & interviews with benefits experts.
General Info: Yr. Est. 1990, Semi-monthly, Looseleaf
Subscriptions: Indv. $714

Employee Benefits for Non-Profits
See: EMPLOYMENT

Employee Benefits
Practices
Business

Publishing Co: International Foundation of Employee Benefit Plans, 18700 W Bluemound Rd #69, P O Box 69, Brookfield, WI 53008-0069; Title Tel # (414) 786-6700 Title Fax # (414) 786-8670
Personnel: Publisher-Dee Birschel, Editor-Mary Jo Brzezinski
Editorial Description: Presents an in-depth study of a single employee benefit topic in each issue. Available only with subscription publications package or membership in IFEEP.
General Info: Yr. Est. 1987, Quarterly, ISSN: 0896-0127, Ind/Abs/Online: employee benefits infosource
Subscriptions: Indv. $170, Inst. $170, Can. $170, For. $220, $10/copy

Employee Communication *Business*

Publishing Co: Management Resources. Inc., 861 Lafayette Rd. #5, Hampton, NH 03842-1232; Title Tel # (603) 929-1600
Personnel: Publisher-William Quirk, Editor-Robert Carpenter
Editorial Description: How-to articles for personel and PR exwcutives in charge of communicating with employees. 21.
General Info: Yr. Est. 1978, Monthly, Trim Size-8½ x 11, 8 pages
Subscriptions: Indv. $95
List Rental: List Management Co.: Walter Karl Business Lists, One American Lane, Greenwich, CT 06831 Tel # (203) 552-6700, Fax # (203) 552-6799

Employee Policy for the Private and Public Sectors/State Capitals *Business*

Publishing Co: Wakeman/Walworth, 300 N. Washington St., Alexandria, VA 22314-2530; Title Tel # (703) 549-8606 Title Fax # (703) 549-1372
Personnel: Publisher-Keyes Walworth
Editorial Description: Provides comprehensive nationwide perspective on sexual harassment policies, unemployment and workers compensation, retirement, health plans dismissal practices, drug testing and more.
General Info: (Formerly From the State Capitals, Public Employee Policy), Yr. Est. 1946, Weekly, ISSN: 1061-9674
Subscriptions: Indv. $2,265, Inst. $212, Can. $235, For. $255

Employee Relations Bulletin *Business*

Publishing Co: Bureau of Business Practice, 24 Rope Ferry Rd, Waterford, CT 06386-0001 Tel # (806) 442-4365 Fax # (860) 434-3341 Parent Co.-Prentice Hall, Waterford; Title Tel # (860) 442-4365 Title Fax # (860) 434-3078
Personnel: Publisher-Joyce Anne Grabel, Editor-Liz Michalskl
Editorial Description: Training periodical for high-level executives in the human resources field. Explores the latest trends in employee relations management and new strategies for human resource development. Emphasis is on programs, policies and procedures.
General Info: (Formerly Employee Relations and Human Resources Bulletin), Yr. Est. 1965, Semi-monthly, Sheetfed press, 12 pages, ISSN: 0744-7779, 2 Color
Subscriptions: Indv. $180

Employer's Guide to Controlling Sexual Harassment *Business*

Publishing Co: Thompson Publishing Group, 1725 K Street, NW, Washington, DC 20006 Tel # (202) 872-4000
Editorial Description: Explains specific practices that violate civil rights and lead to sexual harassment and how to stop them. Subscription includes monthly updates plus a news bulletin.
General Info: Annually, Looseleaf
Subscriptions: Indv. $349

Employer's Guide to the Fair Labor Standards Act *Business*

Publishing Co: Thompson Publishing Group, 1725 K Street, NW, Washington, DC 20006 Tel # (202) 872-4000
Editorial Description: Shows how to classify employees, compute overtime compensation, understand what constitutes hours worked, and maintain employee records. Subscription includes monthly updates and a newsletter.
General Info: Annually, Looseleaf
Subscriptions: Indv. $279

Employer's Guide to Self-Insuring Health Benefits *Business*

Publishing Co: Thompson Publishing Group, 1725 K Street, NW, Washington, DC 20006 Tel # (202) 872-4000
Editorial Description: Shows how to set-up and administer a successful self-funded health plan. Subscription includes a monthly news bulletin and monthly updates.
General Info: Annually, Looseleaf
Subscriptions: Indv. $279

Employer's Handbook: Complying with IRS Employee Benefits Rules
See: TAXES

Employer's Handbook: Mandated Health Benefits - The COBRA Guide

Publishing Co: Thompson Publishing Group, 1725 K Street, NW, Washington, DC 20006 Tel # (202) 872-4000
Editorial Description: Explains the law and regulations, presents model employee notices & election forms, recordkeeping tools, and suggested compliance procedures. Subscription includes monthly bulletins and updates.
General Info: Looseleaf

Employers' Health Benefits Management Letter *Business, Consumer*

Publishing Co: Health Resource Publishing, 3100 Hwy. 138, PO Box 1442, Wall Township, NJ 07719-1442; Title Tel # (908) 681-1133 Title Fax # (908) 681-0490
Personnel: Publisher-Robert Jenkins, Editor-Beth-Ann Kecher
Editorial Description: Receive the latest news on what other employers are doing to appropriately save on healthcare spending; information on realistic ways you can move to cut health care costs for your company; coverage of actions by lawmakers in Washington and in states that affect your health insurance program and plans for the future; news of action by Blue Cross-Blue Shield plans and the major insurers.
General Info: (Formerly Employers' Health Costs Savings Letter), Yr. Est. 1983, Monthly, Trim Size-8½ x 11, Offset press, 8 pages, ISSN: 0740-9087, 1% ads, No Color, Newsprint
Subscriptions: Indv. $197, $15/copy
Advertising: Inquire for rates.
List Rental: Actives: $95/M
Printing Co: ACN Graphics, 1602 Birchwood Ln, Neptune, NJ 07753-6910 Tel # (908) 681-6083

Employment Health Law & Benefits *Business*

Publishing Co: Employment Research Inst., Inc., 5009 W Windsor Ave, Chicago, IL 60630-3926; Title Tel # (312) 545-0585 Title Fax # (312) 545-0586
Personnel: Publisher, Editor-Bernard Farber
Editorial Description: Covers employment health law issues such as disability discrimination, AIDS, drug testing & abuse, alcoholism, sick leave, health insurance, pregnancy discrimination, workers compensation, etc.
General Info: (Formerly Public Employment Health Reporter), Yr. Est. 1986, Monthly, Trim Size-8½ x 11, Offset press, 16 pages, ISSN: 1050-1193, Color-cover, Matte, Other
Subscriptions: Indv. $148, Can. $138, For. $138, $15/copy
Circulation: Total-200

Employment Law Deskbook *Business*

Publishing Co: Matthew Bender & Co., 11 Penn Plaza, New York, NY 10001-2006 Tel # (212) 967-7707 Fax # (212) 244-3188
Editorial Description: Written by employee relations specialists, this handy deskbook will make employment law accessible to the human resources professional.
General Info: Yr. Est. 1989, Irregular, Looseleaf

Employment Relations Bulletin

Publishing Co: Employment Relations Bulletin, Florida State University, Tallahassee, FL 32306-1096; Title Tel # (904) 644-4287
General Info: 10x/yr., Trim Size-8½ x 11, ISSN: 0746-9683

Equal Employment Opportunity Compliance

Publishing Co: Research Institute of America, 90 5th Avenue, New York, NY 10011-7629 Tel # (212) 645-4800; Title Tel # (800) 562-0245 Title Fax # (800) 562-0245
Personnel: Publisher-Lisa Galjanic, Editor-Michael O'Toole, Promotion Dir.-Claudia Levine
Editorial Description: The information you need to protect your co. from labor practices that may invite bias charges, this two volume set discusses how your co. employment practices are affected by equal employment law. The service shows you how to implement an affirmative a tion program, & provides a complete sample program to point you in the right direction.
General Info: Monthly, Trim Size-8½ x 11, Web press, Looseleaf
Subscriptions: Indv. $390
List Rental: List Management Co.: WG & L List Management, 1 Penn Plz Fl 42, New York, NY 10119-0002 Tel # (212) 971-5000

Executive Recruiter News *Business*

Publishing Co: Kennedy Publications, Templeton Rd., Fitzwilliam, NH 03447; Title Tel # (603) 585-6544 Title Fax # (603) 585-6401
Personnel: Publisher-James Kennedy, Editor-Tom Rodenhauser, Circ. Mgr.-Janet Ray, Art Dir.-Melinda Taylor, Mktg. Dir.-Carolyn Edwards
Editorial Description: Covers trends, associations, fees, statistics, surveys, & who's who in the recruiting field.
General Info: Yr. Est. 1980, Monthly, Trim Size-8½ x 11, Letrpr. press, 4 pages, ISSN: 0271-0781, 2 Color
Subscriptions: Indv. $187, Can. $207, For. $232, $16/copy
Printing Co: Sterling Business Corp., 206 Concord St, Peterborough, NH 03458-1209 Tel # (603) 924-9401

Fair Employment Report
See: EMPLOYMENT

Family and Medical Leave Handbook
See: LAW

Federal Human Resources
Week
Business, Association

Publishing Co: LRP Publications, 747 Dresher Rd., P.O. Box 980, Horsham, PA 19044-0980
Tel # (215) 784-0910 Fax # (215) 784-0317; Title Tel # (215) 784-0860 Title Fax # (215) 784-9639
Personnel: Publisher-Ken Kahn, Editor-Ken Hughes
Editorial Description: Addresses government-wide changes and problems impacting the federal human resource community.
General Info: 12 pages, 2 Color
Subscriptions: Indv. $295

Fink and Bornstein Workers' Compensation Newsletter
See: LAW

First Rate Customer Service
See: MANAGEMENT

Flex Plan Handbook
Business

Publishing Co: Thompson Publishing Group, 1725 K Street, NW, Washington, DC 20006
Tel # (202) 872-4000
Editorial Description: Shows employers how to introduce and/or improve a flex plan. Subscription includes quarterly updates.
General Info: Annually, Looseleaf
Subscriptions: Indv. $312

Flexible Benefits
Business

Publishing Co: Aspen Publishers, Inc., 200 Orchard Ridge Dr., Ste 200, Gaithersburg, MD 20878-5440 Fax # (301) 417-7655 Parent Co.-Wolters Kluwer US Corporation, New York; Title Tel # (301) 417-7500 Title Fax # (301) 417-7550
Personnel: Editor-Gregory Matthews
Editorial Description: Published for employee benefit specialists.
General Info: Yr. Est. 1993, Monthly, ISSN: 0743-8079
Subscriptions: Indv. $216, For. $259

Florida Workers' Compensation Law Bulletin
See: LAW

Florida Worker's Compensation Reporter
See: LAW

From Nine to Five
Business

Publishing Co: Dartnell Corp., 4660 N. Ravenswood Ave., Chicago, IL 60640-4510; Title Tel # (312) 561-4000 Title Fax # (312) 561-3801
Personnel: Publisher-Clark Fetridge, Editor-Kim Andersen, Production Mgr.-Megan Mulligan, Art Dir.-Andrew Epstein, Mktg. Dir.-George Economos
Editorial Description: Increasing office personnel efficiency; career development; new product information.
General Info: Yr. Est. 1960, Bi-weekly, Trim Size-8$\frac{1}{2}$ x 11, 4 pages, 2 Color, Matte
Subscriptions: Indv. $59
List Rental: List Management Co.: Manager: Sue McDorman; Leland Company, 1801 W. Leland Ave., Chicago, IL 60640-4363 Tel # (312) 561-4005, Fax # (312) 561-4099, Actives: $90/M, Hotline: $125/M

Front Line Management
See: MANAGEMENT

Getting Along
Business

Publishing Co: Dartnell Corp., 4660 N. Ravenswood Ave., Chicago, IL 60640-4510; Title Tel # (312) 561-4000 Title Fax # (312) 561-3801
Personnel: Publisher-Clark Fetridge, Editor-Jim Nawrocki, Production Mgr.-Megan Mulligan, Art Dir.-Andrew Epstein, Mktg. Dir.-George Economos
Editorial Description: Designed to transform your workforce into a spirited, closely knit team of workers dedicated to quality. Getting Along shows your staff how to work with subordinates, superiors, and co-workers as individuals to get things done more effectively.
General Info: Yr. Est. 1990, Bi-weekly, Trim Size-8$\frac{1}{2}$ x 11, 4 pages, 2 Color, Matte
Subscriptions: Indv. $59, $62/copy
List Rental: List Management Co.: Manager: Sue McDorman; Leland Company, 1801 W. Leland Ave., Chicago, IL 60640-4363 Tel # (312) 561-4005, Fax # (312) 561-4099, Actives: 70,785, $90/M, Hotline: $125/M

Guide to Assigning & Loaning Benefit Plan Money
See: INVESTMENT

Guide to Employment
Law and Regulation

Publishing Co: Research Institute of America, 90 5th Avenue, New York, NY 10011-7629
Tel # (212) 645-4800; Title Tel # (800) 562-0245 Title Fax # (800) 562-0245
Personnel: Publisher-Lisa Galjanic, Editor-Michael O'Toole, Promotion Dir.-Claudia Levine
Editorial Description: All information you need to evaluate the legality of your cos. position on any critical labor issue, this service presents the full text of current federal labor laws, executive orders & regulations, as well as insightful explanations of each state's lab r laws.
General Info: (Formerly Labor and Employee Relations), Weekly, Trim Size-6 x 9$\frac{1}{4}$, Web press, Looseleaf
Subscriptions: Indv. $399
List Rental: List Management Co.: WG & L List Management, 1 Penn Plz Fl 42, New York, NY 10119-0002 Tel # (212) 971-5000

Guide to the Form 5500 Series
See: TAXES

HR Briefing
Business

Publishing Co: Bureau of Business Practice, 24 Rope Ferry Rd, Waterford, CT 06386-0001
Fax # (860) 434-3341 Parent Co.-Prentice Hall, Waterford; Title Tel # (806) 442-4365
Personnel: Publisher-Holly Hughes, Editor-Jill Whitney
Editorial Description: Covers developments, trends, policies, practices in personnel/human resources. Emphasis on hands-on applications & implementation.
General Info: (Formerly Personnel Manager's Letter; Personnel Advisory Bulletin), Yr. Est. 1972, Semi-monthly, 8 pages, ISSN: 0164-5811
Subscriptions: Indv. $150

HR Fact Finder
Business

Publishing Co: Jamestown Area Labor Management Committee, PO Box 819, Jamestown, NY 14702-0819; Title Tel # (716) 665-3654 Title Fax # (716) 665-8060
Personnel: Editor-Karen France, Circ. Mgr.-Kristan Fox
Editorial Description: Contains articles on a wide range of human resource topics.
General Info: (Formerly Fact Finder, The), Yr. Est. 1987, Monthly, Trim Size-8$\frac{1}{2}$ x 11, 8 pages, ISSN: 1053-2331, 2 Color
Subscriptions: Indv. $89, $7/copy
Circulation: Total-3,500, Readership-3,500
List Rental: List Management Co.: Jamestown Area Labor - Managment Committee, PO Box 819, Jamestown, NY 14702 Tel # (716) 665-3654, Fax # (716) 665-8060, Actives: 12,013, $100/M

HR Planning Newsletter
Business, Consumer

Publishing Co: Wargo & Co., Inc., 100 E. Wisconsin Ave., Suite #350, Milwaukee, WI 53202; Title Tel # (414) 347-7750
Personnel: Publisher, Editor-James Peters
Editorial Description: A review of the state of the art/practice of strategic human resource management.
General Info: (Formerly Manpower Planning), Yr. Est. 1977, 10x/yr., Trim Size-8$\frac{1}{2}$ x 11, Desktop press, 8 pages, ISSN: 0733-0332, 2 Color, Newsprint
Subscriptions: Indv. $150, $20/copy
Circulation: Total-600
List Rental: Actives: $125/M

HR Reporter
Business

Publishing Co: LRP Publications, 747 Dresher Rd., P.O. Box 980, Horsham, PA 19044-0980
Tel # (215) 784-0910 Fax # (215) 784-0317
Personnel: Publisher-Ken Kahn, Editor-Marilyn Schaefer, Production Mgr.-Kathleen Neely, Mktg. Dir.-Jana Shellington
Editorial Description: Executive view on human resource management.
General Info: Yr. Est. 1984, Monthly, Sheetfed press, 10 pages, ISSN: 0741-6997, 2 Color, Newsprint
Subscriptions: Indv. $325, For. $347, $23/copy
Acquistions: Publication Bought, Publication Sold

Health Employment Law Update
See: LAW

Health Labor Relations
Reports
Business

Publishing Co: Interwood Publications, 3 Interwood Pl., Box 20241, Cincinnati, OH 45220-1821; Title Tel # (513) 221-3715
Personnel: Publisher, Editor-Frank Bardack
Editorial Description: Employee and labor relations health care news.
General Info: Yr. Est. 1976, Bi-weekly, Trim Size-8$\frac{1}{2}$ x 11, Sheetfed press, 6 pages, ISSN: 0148-4761, No Color, Newsprint
Subscriptions: Indv. $159, For. $181

Health in the Workplace
See: HEALTH

Hourly Wage Survey

Publishing Co: Dir Des Entreprise, C.P. 1153, Quebec, PQ G1K 7C3 Canada Tel # (514) 873-5324; Title Tel # (514) 288-6104
Personnel: Publisher-A. Martineau
General Info: Annually, Mimeo press, 200 pages, No Color, Looseleaf

Human Resource Management Compensation
See: MANAGEMENT

Human Resource
Management News
Business

Publishing Co: Remy Publishing Co., 350 W Hubbard St # 440, Chicago, IL 60610-4011; Title Tel # (312) 464-0300 Title Fax # (312) 464-0166
Personnel: Publisher-Robert Root, Editor-John Hickey, Circ. Mgr.-Trish Bissell
Editorial Description: Contains information on trends & developments in human resource administration & labor management relations with detailed reporting on significant subjects.
General Info: (Formerly Industrial Relations News), Yr. Est. 1950, Weekly, Trim Size-8$\frac{1}{2}$ x 11, Offset press, 4 pages, No Color
Subscriptions: Indv. $240, Inst. $240, Can. $240, For. $300

Human Resource
Professional   *Business*

Publishing Co: LRP Publications, 747 Dresher Rd., P.O. Box 980, Horsham, PA 19044-0980
Tel # (215) 784-0910 Fax # (215) 784-0317
Personnel: Publisher-Kenneth F. Kahn, Editor-Samantha Drake, Production Mgr.-Kathleen P. Neely,
Mktg. Dir.-Jana Shellington, Promotion Dir.-Gary Ragin
Editorial Description: Explores ideas, issues, and future trends that will provide answers for human
resource professionals.
General Info: Bi-monthly
Subscriptions: Indv. $105

Human Resources
International

Publishing Co: Lafferty Publications, 420 Lexington Ave., Ste. 1745, New York, NY 10170
Tel # (212) 557-6729 Fax # (212) 557-7266; Title Tel # (404) 636-6610 Title Fax # (404) 636-6422
Personnel: Publisher-Paul Byrne, Editor-Gerard Lysaght
General Info: Yr. Est. 1993, Monthly
Subscriptions: Indv. $879

Human Resources
Policies & Practices

Publishing Co: Research Institute of America, 90 5th Avenue, New York, NY 10011-7629
Tel # (212) 645-4800; Title Tel # (800) 562-0245
Personnel: Publisher-Lisa Galjanic, Editor-Constance Kallback, Promotion Dir.-Claudia Levine
Editorial Description: The definitive source to keep you informed on allo the latest developments in
reaching policy decisions on issues such as: sexual harassment, employing handicapped workers,
employee termination, conducting performance appraisals, drug testing, AIDS, mate nity leave, and
much more.
General Info: (Formerly Personnel Policies & Practices), Bi-weekly, Trim Size-6 x 9$\frac{1}{4}$, Web press,
Looseleaf
Subscriptions: Indv. $360
List Rental: List Management Co.: WG & L List Management, 1 Penn Plz Fl 42, New York, NY
10119-0002 Tel # (212) 971-5000

IE News: Industrial &
Labor Relations   *Association*

Publishing Co: Institute of Industrial Engineers, 25 Technology Park/Atlanta, Norcross, GA
30092-2988 Tel # (770) 449-0461; Title Tel # (404) 449-0460 Title Fax # (770) 263-8532
Personnel: Production Mgr.-Dona Brown
Editorial Description: Newsletter for IIE Industrial & Labor Relations Division.
General Info: Quarterly, Trim Size-8$\frac{1}{2}$ x 11, Sheetfed press, 4 pages, 2 Color, Matte, Saddle-stitched
Circulation: (100% controlled)
Advertising: $475. Accepts Inserts.
List Rental: Rents Lists

IRA Compliance Manual

Publishing Co: Research Institute of America, 90 5th Avenue, New York, NY 10011-7629
Tel # (212) 645-4800; Title Tel # (800) 562-0245 Title Fax # (201) 816-3484
Editorial Description: Two volume service explaining the complex rules governing IRAs, KEOGHs, &
simplified Employee Pension Plans.
General Info: Monthly, Trim Size-8$\frac{1}{2}$ x 11, Looseleaf
Subscriptions: Indv. $245
List Rental: List Management Co.: WG & L List Management, 1 Penn Plz Fl 42, New York, NY
10119-0002 Tel # (212) 971-5000

IRRA Newsletter   *Association*

Publishing Co: Industrial Relations Research Association, University of Wisconsin, 1180 Observatory
Dr., Madison, WI 53706-1393 Tel # (608) 262-2767 Fax # (608) 265-4591;
Title Tel # (608) 262-2762
Personnel: Editor-Kay Hutchison
Editorial Description: Meetings and activities of IRRA.
General Info: Yr. Est. 1947, Quarterly, Trim Size-8$\frac{1}{2}$ x 11, 8 pages, ISSN: 0019-0500, No Color,
Coated
Subscriptions: Indv. $52, Inst. $56, Can. $66, For. $66
Circulation: Total-4,000
Advertising: Inquire for rates.
List Rental: Rents Lists

Illinois Workers' Compensation Law Bulletin
See: LAW

In Command
See: OFFICE METHODS & EQUIPMENT

In Depth   *Business*

Publishing Co: Management Resources. Inc., 861 Lafayette Rd. #5, Hampton, NH 03842-1232;
Title Tel # (603) 929-1600
Personnel: Publisher-William Quirk, Editor-Kenneth Swann
Editorial Description: Supplement to Fair Employment Compliance.
General Info: Semi-monthly, ISSN: 0885-7199
Subscriptions: Indv. $215

Individual Employment Rights
See: LAW

Industrial Health & Hazards Update
See: SAFETY

Ink! Ink! Ink!
See: BUSINESS & INDUSTRY

Iowa Employment Law Letter
See: LAW

Jot and Jolts
See: MANAGEMENT

Kansas Employment Law Letter
See: LAW

Labor Arbitration in Government
See: LABOR UNION

Labor Studies Forum
See: LABOR

Lakewood Publications   *Business*

Publishing Co: Lakewood Publications, Inc., 50 S. Ninth St., Minneapolis, MN 55402-3165 Parent
Co.-K-III Communications, New York; Title Tel # (612) 333-0471 Title Fax # (612) 333-6526
Personnel: Publisher-Philip Jones, Editor-Brian McDermott, Circ. Mgr.-Nancy Swanson, Promotion
Dir.-Carol A. Swanson
Editorial Description: Published for executives who want to improve service, quality, customer
satisfaction and ultimately the bottom line. Also covers leadership, teams, rewards & recognitions,
and change management.
General Info: (Formerly Lakewood Report, The), Yr. Est. 1995, Monthly, Trim Size-8$\frac{1}{2}$ x 11,
Sheetfed press, 12 pages, ISSN: 0095 5892, 2 Color, Recycled, Saddle-stitched
Subscriptions: Indv. $128, Can. $138, For. $148
Circulation: Total-6,500
List Rental: List Management Co.: Manager: Paul Kolars; Lakewood Lists, 50 S. 9th St., Minneapolis,
MN 55402 Tel # (612) 333-0471, Fax # (612) 333-6526, Actives: 6,438, $95/M

Legal-Legislative Reporter
See: LAW

Legislative Network for Nursing
See: NURSING

LifeLines
See: HEALTH

Management Journal
See: MANAGEMENT

Management Memo
See: MANAGEMENT

Management Policies & Personnel Law
See: MANAGEMENT

Manager/Motivator
See: MANAGEMENT

Managing Diversity   *Business*

Publishing Co: Jamestown Area Labor Management Committee, PO Box 819, Jamestown, NY
14702-0819; Title Tel # (716) 665-3654 Title Fax # (716) 665-8060
Personnel: Publisher, Editor-Leo Patterson, Circ. Mgr.-Karen France
Editorial Description: Covers diversity management for human resource managers.
General Info: Yr. Est. 1991, Monthly, Trim Size-8$\frac{1}{2}$ x 11, 8 pages, 2 Color
Subscriptions: Indv. $90, $7/copy
Circulation: Total-7,100, Readership-7,100
List Rental: Actives: 12,013, $100/M

Managing Employee
Benefits

Publishing Co: Research Institute of America, 90 5th Avenue, New York, NY 10011-7629
Tel # (212) 645-4800; Title Tel # (800) 562-0245 Title Fax # (800) 562-0245
Personnel: Publisher-Lisa Galjanic, Editor-Connie Kallback, Promotion Dir.-Cladia Levine
Editorial Description: The latest techniques for benefits cost control, federal government actions, &
court rulings in response to legal challenges--all with plenty of practical pointers, tips & cautions on
issues such as: life & health insurance, programs, & time off from wor .
General Info: Monthly, Trim Size-8$\frac{1}{2}$ x 11, Web press, Looseleaf
Subscriptions: Indv. $219
List Rental: List Management Co.: WG & L List Management, 1 Penn Plz Fl 42, New York, NY
10119-0002 Tel # (212) 971-5000, Actives: $85/M, Expires: $85/M

Manufacturers Hanover
Pension Bulletin

Publishing Co: Manufacturers Hanover Trust, 270 Park Ave., New York, NY 10017-2040;
Title Tel # (212) 350-3300
Editorial Description: Notes recent developments, basic principles and background information
about pensions and profit-sharing plans.
General Info: Monthly

Mercer Bulletin, The   *Business*

Publishing Co: William M. Mercer. Limited, 161 Bay Street, Toronto, ON M5J 2S5 Canada; Title Tel # (416) 868-2000 Title Fax # (416) 868-7555
Personnel: Editor-Robert Dowsett, Circ. Mgr., Production Mgr.-Shirley Clements, Promotion Mgr.-Carol Duncan
Editorial Description: Canadian news and authoritative articles on employee benefits. Features articles on pension plans, group insurance, income tax, social security, etc.
General Info: (Formerly Mercer Actuarial Bulletin), Yr. Est. 1951, Monthly, Trim Size-8½ x 11, Offset press, 2 pages, No Color, Newsprint
Subscriptions: Free To Qualified Recipient
Circulation: Total-10,000, Readership-10,000
Advertising: Inquire for rates.

Michigan Workers' Compensation Law Reporter
See: LAW

Mississippi Employment Law Letter
See: LAW

Missouri Workers' Compensation Law Reporter
See: LAW

NAEN Bulletin
See: SCHOOL ADMINISTRATION

NCOSH

Publishing Co: NC Occupational Safety & Health Project, PO Box 2514, Durham, NC 27715-2514; Title Tel # (919) 286-9249
Personnel: Editor-Mark Schulz
General Info: Yr. Est. 1980, Quarterly, Trim Size-8½ x 11, Sheetfed press, 8 pages, No Color
Subscriptions: Indv. $15, Inst. $25
Circulation: (100% controlled), Total-2,400

National Public Employment Reporter
See: LAW

New Mexico Employment Law Letter
See: LAW

New York Workers' Compensation Law Reporter
See: LAW

News & Notes   *Association*

Publishing Co: Intl. Society for Performance & Instruction, 1300 L St. NW, Ste. 1250, Washington, DC 20005-4107; Title Tel # (202) 408-7969 Title Fax # (202) 408-7972
Editorial Description: Covers Society news & current events.
General Info: Yr. Est. 1990, 10x/yr., ISSN: 1044-9752, No Color
Subscriptions: Free With Membership
Circulation: Total-6,200
Advertising: Inquire for rates.
List Rental: Rents Lists

Newsbriefs   *Association*

Publishing Co: Intl. Society of Certified Employee Benefit Specialists, 18700 W. Bluemound Road, PO Box 209, Brookfield, WI 53008-0209 Fax # (414) 786-8650; Title Tel # (414) 786-8771 Title Fax # (414) 786-2990
Personnel: Editor-Mary Brennan
Editorial Description: Newsbriefs is published bi-monthly for members of the Intl. Society of Certified Employee Benefit Specialists, Inc.
General Info: Yr. Est. 1982, Bi-monthly, Trim Size-11.00 x 8.50, Web press, 16 pages, ISSN: 0731-4531, 2 Color, Newsprint, Saddle-stitched
Circulation: Total-3,400

Nursing Staff Development Insider
See: NURSING

OSHA Week   *Business*

Publishing Co: Stevens Publishing Corp., 3630 J.H. Kultgen Frwy., Waco, TX 76706 Tel # (817) 662-1134; Title Tel # (817) 662-7100 Title Fax # (817) 662-7075
Editorial Description: Health and safety news, legislation and regulation.
General Info: Weekly, ISSN: 1057-1435
Subscriptions: Indv. $468, Can. $522, For. $513

Office Hours
See: OFFICE METHODS & EQUIPMENT

On Workers' Compensation-Michigan Edition

Publishing Co: Edward M. Welch, Northwind Office Park, 4990 Northwind Dr., Ste. 230, East Lansing, MI 48823; Title Tel # (517) 332-5266 Title Fax # (517) 332-5273
Personnel: Publisher-Eward M. Welch, Editor-Nancy L. Scott, Contrib. Ed.-Katherine J. Welch
Editorial Description: Workers' compensation in Michigan.
General Info: Yr. Est. 1991, 10x/yr.
Subscriptions: Indv. $255

On Workers' Compensation-National Edition

Publishing Co: Edward M. Welch, Northwind Office Park, 4990 Northwind Dr., Ste. 230, East Lansing, MI 48823; Title Tel # (517) 332-5266 Title Fax # (517) 332-5273
Personnel: Publisher-Edward M. Welch, Editor-Nancy L. Scott, Contrib. Ed.-Katherine J. Welch
Editorial Description: Workers' compensation on national level.
General Info: Yr. Est. 1992, 10x/yr.
Subscriptions: Indv. $205

Oregon Employment Law Letter
See: LAW

Organizations & Change
See: MANAGEMENT

PBC Employment Briefs
See: EMPLOYMENT

PPF Survey (Personnel Policies Forum)   *Business*

Publishing Co: Bureau of National Affairs, Inc., 1231 25th St. NW, Bldg. N-200, Washington, DC 20037-1157; Title Tel # (202) 452-4200 Title Fax # (202) 822-8092
Personnel: Publisher-William A. Beltz, Mng. Editor-J. Michael Reidy, Circ. Mgr.-Gary C. Seltzer
Editorial Description: In-depth reports on human resource topics derived from responses to questionnaires sent to BNA's Personnel Policies Forum. Topics included recruiting & selection policies, promotion & transfer, salary administration, employee benefits, communication programs, grievance procedures, performance evaluation, training, discipline & discharge policies.
General Info: (Formerly Personnel Policies Forum), Yr. Est. 1951, Irregular, Trim Size-8½ x 11, Offset press, 64 pages, ISSN: 0361-7467, Looseleaf
Subscriptions: Indv. $50, $50/copy

Payroll Administration Guide   *Business*

Publishing Co: Bureau of National Affairs, Inc., 1231 25th St. NW, Bldg. N-200, Washington, DC 20037-1157 Fax # (202) 822-8092; Title Tel # (202) 452-4200 Title Fax # (202) 452-4603
Personnel: Publisher-William A. Beltz, Mng. Editor-Michael Baer, Mng. Editor-Roslyn T. Rosenberg, Circ. Mgr.-Gary C. Seltzer
Editorial Description: A notification-and-reference service for payroll professionals. Covers federal & state employment tax wage-hour, & wage-payment.
General Info: Yr. Est. 1990, Bi-weekly, Trim Size-8½ x 11, Offset press, 230 pages, Ind/Abs/Online: HRIN, Coated, Other, Looseleaf
Subscriptions: Indv. $495
Circulation: Total-6,000

Payroll Inserts   *Business*

Publishing Co: Economics Press, Inc., 12 Daniel Rd., Fairfield, NJ 07004-2565; Title Tel # (201) 227-1224 Title Fax # (201) 227-9742
Personnel: Editor-Robert Guder, Circ. Mgr.-Ann Lanahan
Editorial Description: Motivational notes that stress the importance of each employee's contribution to the total team effort.
General Info: Yr. Est. 1986, Bi-weekly
Subscriptions: Indv. $75
Circulation: Total-89,000
List Rental: List Management Co.: Manager: Michael Korman; Names in the News, 411 Theodore Fremd Ave., Rye, NY 10580 Tel # (914) 925-2400, Actives: $85/M
Printing Co: Beckley Press, 2 Sperry Rd, Fairfield, NJ 07004-2056 Tel # (201) 227-6350

Payroll Management Guide   *Business*

Publishing Co: CCH, Inc., 2700 Lake Cook Rd., Riverwoods, IL 60015 Fax # (800) 224-8299 Parent Co.-Kluwer Law & Taxation Publishers, Cambridge; Title Tel # (847) 267-7000 Title Fax # (312) 224-8299
Editorial Description: Explains federal, state and local rules affecting payroll management, including income tax withholding, social security and medicare, unemployment insurance rates, etc.
General Info: Yr. Est. 1943, Weekly, Trim Size-6 x 9, Web press, 225 pages, No Color, Looseleaf
Subscriptions: Indv. $527

Payroll Management Journal   *Business*

Publishing Co: CCH, Inc., 2700 Lake Cook Rd., Riverwoods, IL 60015 Parent Co.-Kluwer Law & Taxation Publishers, Cambridge; Title Tel # (847) 267-7000 Title Fax # (800) 224-8299
General Info: Yr. Est. 1994, Bi-weekly
Subscriptions: Indv. $131

Payroll Practitioner's Compliance Handbook
See: MANAGEMENT

Pennsylvania Workers' Compensation Law Reporter
See: LAW

Pension Fund Litigation Reporter
See: LAW

Pension Plan Guide   *Business*

Publishing Co: CCH, Inc., 2700 Lake Cook Rd., Riverwoods, IL 60015 Fax # (800) 224-8299 Parent Co.-Kluwer Law & Taxation Publishers, Cambridge; Title Tel # (847) 267-7000 Title Fax # (312) 244-8299
Editorial Description: Help for complying with eligibility, vesting, funding, fiduciary, termination insurance, reporting and other requirements of Code & ERISA. Explanations and full text.
General Info: Yr. Est. 1953, Weekly, Trim Size-6 x 9, Web press, 100 pages, No Color, Looseleaf
Subscriptions: Indv. $1,077
Advertising: Inquire for rates.

Pension and Profit Sharing   *Business*

Publishing Co: Research Institute of America, 90 5th Avenue, New York, NY 10011-7629 Tel # (212) 645-4800; Title Tel # (800) 562-0245 Title Fax # (201) 816-3484
Editorial Description: A combined encyclopedic shelf reference and updating tool that allows users to research any federal tax/non-tax questions on qualified retirement plans and how to keep up-to-date on what is happening in the field on a weekly basis.
General Info: Weekly, Trim Size-6 x 9¼, Offset press, Looseleaf
Subscriptions: Indv. $619
List Rental: List Management Co.: WG & L List Management, 1 Penn Plz Fl 42, New York, NY 10119-0002 Tel # (212) 971-5000

Pension and Profit-Sharing Plans Compliance Guide   *Business*

Publishing Co: Matthew Bender & Co., 11 Penn Plaza, New York, NY 10001-2006 Tel # (212) 967-7707 Fax # (212) 244-3188
Editorial Description: Complete, step-by-step guidance & analysis on every aspect of pension & profit-sharing plan compliance.
General Info: Yr. Est. 1986, Bi-monthly, Looseleaf

Pension and Profit-Sharing Plans: Forms and Practice with Tax Analysis   *Business*

Publishing Co: Matthew Bender & Co., 11 Penn Plaza, New York, NY 10001-2006 Tel # (212) 967-7707 Fax # (212) 244-3188
Editorial Description: Consisting of the most complete range of forms with commentary & tax analysis, contains virtually everything you'll need to successfully create, amend or terminate a pension or profit-sharing plan.
General Info: Yr. Est. 1988, Irregular, Looseleaf

Pensions and Deferred Compensation

Publishing Co: CCH, Inc., 2700 Lake Cook Rd., Riverwoods, IL 60015 Parent Co.-Kluwer Law & Taxation Publishers, Cambridge; Title Tel # (847) 267-7000 Title Fax # (800) 224-8299
Editorial Description: All-explanatory guide answers questions about the variety of retirement benefit plans availalbe, including qualified & nonqualified deferred compensation plans, & the rules that apply to each type of plan. Also includes discussion of fiduciary responsibilities & liabilities, plan termination procedure, & more.
General Info: Yr. Est. 1987, Monthly, Web press, Looseleaf
Subscriptions: Indv. $384

People Trends   *Business*

Publishing Co: Strategy Group Inc., The, 290 Beckley Ln, Dublin, OH 43017-1346 Tel # (614) 761-0967 Fax # (614) 761-0967
Personnel: Publisher, Editor-Carl Crawford, Mng. Editor-Fleda Anderson, Research Editor-Kimberly Crawford, Production Mgr.-Lisa Fogle
Editorial Description: Known as the trend charter of the human resource field. This publication researches more than 50 HR sources for the best information. Contains a large number of charts and data.
General Info: Yr. Est. 1992, Monthly, Trim Size-8½ x 11, Sheetfed press, 12 pages, ISSN: 1065-0253, Ind/Abs/Online: NewsNet, 2 Color, Coated, Saddle-stitched
Subscriptions: Indv. $261, Inst. $261, Can. $281, For. $281, $15/copy
Circulation: Total-12,000
List Rental: Actives: 72,000, $125/M, Hotline: $125/M, Expires: 1,000, $125/M
Printing Co: Bindery & Specialities Inc., 351 W Bigelow Ave, Plain City, OH 43064-1152 Tel # (614) 766-1240, Fax # (614) 873-4625

Personnel Management   *Business*

Publishing Co: Bureau of National Affairs, Inc., 1231 25th St. NW, Bldg. N-200, Washington, DC 20037-1157 Fax # (202) 822-8092; Title Tel # (202) 452-4200 Title Fax # (202) 452-4603
Personnel: Publisher-William A. Beltz, Mng. Editor-Bill L. Manville, Circ. Mgr.-Gary C. Seltzer
Editorial Description: Reference service covering human resource management & administration; includes policy guidance & discussions of legal & nonlegal human resource issues & problems; practical advice & examples of company policies & programs.
General Info: Yr. Est. 1950, Weekly, Trim Size-8½ x 11, Web press, 8 pages, ISSN: 0149-2675, Ind/Abs/Online: HRIN, Looseleaf
Subscriptions: Indv. $650
Circulation: Total-46,000

Personnel Management Guideposts for Federal Supervisors   *Business, Association*

Publishing Co: LRP Publications, 747 Dresher Rd., P.O. Box 980, Horsham, PA 19044-0980 Tel # (215) 784-0910 Fax # (215) 784-0317; Title Tel # (215) 784-0860 Title Fax # (215) 784-9639
Personnel: Publisher-Ken Kahn
Editorial Description: Prevents federal supervisors with personnel issues and demonstrates legally sound manner to confront them.
General Info: Monthly, 8 pages, 2 Color
Subscriptions: Indv. $95

Personnel Manager's Encyclopedia of Prewritten Personnel Policies   *Business*

Publishing Co: Business & Legal Reports, Inc., 39 Academy St., PO Box 1513, Madison, CT 06443-2646 Tel # (860) 245-7448 Fax # (860) 245-2559; Title Tel # (203) 245-7448 Title Fax # (203) 245-2559
Editorial Description: Policies developed by America's leading companies.
General Info: Yr. Est. 1983, Bi-monthly, Looseleaf
Subscriptions: Indv. $160

Personnel Postscript   *Business, Association*

Publishing Co: Medical Group Management Association, 104 Inverness Terrace E., Englewood, CO 80112-5306 Fax # (303) 397-1824; Title Tel # (303) 799-1111 Title Fax # (303) 643-4427
Personnel: Editor, Circ. Dir.-Marilee Aust, Production Mgr.-Dennis Barnhardt
Editorial Description: Personnel issues for medical practice executives from workplace violence to employee handbooks to the ADA.
General Info: Yr. Est. 1985, Quarterly, Trim Size-8½ x 11, Sheetfed press, 16 pages, ISSN: 0886-2125, No Color, Matte, Saddle-stitched
Subscriptions: Indv. $95, Inst. $80, $25/copy
Circulation: Total-650, Readership-650
Printing Co: RM Printing, 2785 N Speer Blvd Ste 222, Denver, CO 80211-4220 Tel # (303) 458-8270

Personnel Practice Ideas
See: MANAGEMENT

Personnel Practices/ Communications   *Business*

Publishing Co: CCH, Inc., 2700 Lake Cook Rd., Riverwoods, IL 60015 Parent Co.-Kluwer Law & Taxation Publishers, Cambridge; Title Tel # (847) 267-7000 Title Fax # (800) 224-8299
Editorial Description: Features coverage of orientation and training, promotions and transfers, leaves and vacations, work rules and grievances, handbooks and employee communications, and performance, productivity and morale.
General Info: Yr. Est. 1982, Monthly, Looseleaf
Subscriptions: Indv. $417

Perspectives
See: COLLEGE STUDENT LIFESTYLE

Perspectives on Employee Benefits   *Business*

Publishing Co: Newkirk Products, Inc., 15 Corporate Cir, Albany, NY 12203-5154 Tel # (518) 452-1000
Editorial Description: Custom publication for distribution to clients by professional consultants.
General Info: Quarterly, Trim Size-8½ x 11, 4 pages, 2 Color

Police Officer Grievances Bulletin
See: LAW ENFORCEMENT & PENOLOGY

Principles of Payroll Administration
See: MANAGEMENT

Profit-Sharing and Pension Forms   *Business*

Publishing Co: Research Institute of America, 90 5th Avenue, New York, NY 10011-7629 Tel # (212) 645-4800; Title Tel # (800) 562-0245 Title Fax # (201) 816-3484
Editorial Description: Plans, clauses and guides needed to select the provisions required to set up a qualified profit-sharing or pension plan.
General Info: Quarterly, Trim Size-8½ x 11, Offset press, Looseleaf
Subscriptions: Indv. $339
List Rental: List Management Co.: WG & L List Management, 1 Penn Plz Fl 42, New York, NY 10119-0002 Tel # (212) 971-5000

Project Equality of Wisconsin-Newsletter & Buyers' Guide
See: LABOR

Public Employee Dismissals Bulletin
See: PUBLIC MANAGEMENT & PLANNING

Quality 1st.

Publishing Co: Dartnell Corp., 4660 N. Ravenswood Ave., Chicago, IL 60640-4510; Title Tel # (312) 561-4000 Title Fax # (312) 561-3801
Personnel: Publisher-Clark Fetridge, Editor-Kim Anderson, Production Mgr.-Megan Mulligan, Art Dir.-Andrew Epstein, Mktg. Dir.-George Economos
Editorial Description: Each bi-weekly bulletin instills & reinforces an unshakable commitment to quality products & services & dedication to excellence in ones own work. The main goal of quality 1st is to help you create quality-minded employees-quality obsessed employees.
General Info: Yr. Est. 1990, Bi-weekly, Trim Size-8½ x 11, 4 pages, 2 Color, Matte
Subscriptions: $62/copy
List Rental: List Management Co.: Manager: Sue McDorman; Leland Company, 1801 W. Leland Ave., Chicago, IL 60640-4363 Tel # (312) 561-4005, Fax # (312) 561-4099, Actives: 70,785, $90/M, Hotline: $125/M

Recruiting Trends
See: EMPLOYMENT

Repetitive Stress Injury Litigation Reporter
See: LAW

Safety Management
See: SAFETY

Sales Bullet, A
See: SALESMANSHIP & SELLING

Smart Buying
See: PURCHASING

Spencer's Compliance Guide for Health & Benefit Plans
See: TAXES

Spencer's Research Reports on Employee Benefits   *Business*

Publishing Co: Charles D. Spencer & Assocs., Inc., 250 S. Wacker Dr., Ste. 600, Chicago, IL 60606-5834; Title Tel # (312) 993-7900 Title Fax # (312) 993-7910
Personnel: Publisher-Charles D. Spencer, Editor-Seymour LaRock, Mktg. Dir.-Art Cohen
Editorial Description: Analysis of employee benefit plans--design, cost and administration.
General Info: (Formerly EBPR Research Reports), Yr. Est. 1953, Weekly, Desktop press, ISSN: 0740-1329, Matte, Looseleaf
Subscriptions: Indv. $650
Circulation: Total-2,500

Spencer's Retirement Plan Service   *Business*

Publishing Co: Charles D. Spencer & Assocs., Inc., 250 S. Wacker Dr., Ste. 600, Chicago, IL 60606-5834; Title Tel # (312) 993-7900 Title Fax # (312) 993-7910
Personnel: Publisher-Charles D. Spencer, Editor-Ross Spencer, Mktg. Dir.-Art Cohen
Editorial Description: Analysis of pension & profit sharing plans--design, cost & administration.
General Info: Yr. Est. 1960, Monthly, Desktop press, Looseleaf
Subscriptions: Indv. $315
Circulation: Total-1,000

Staffing Industry Report
See: EMPLOYMENT

Strategy & Management

Publishing Co: Research Institute of America, 90 5th Avenue, New York, NY 10011-7629 Tel # (212) 645-4800; Title Tel # (800) 562-0245 Title Fax # (800) 562-0245
Personnel: Publisher-Lisa Galjanic, Editor-Constance Kallback, Promotion Dir.-Claudia Levine
Editorial Description: This service helps you achieve your goal for a cost-effective, legal & attractive pay & benefits program. It keeps you abreast of the latest developments in wages, salaries & benefits & provides you with new ideas on such topics as: planning a compensati n program, job evaluation techniques, determining the wage structure, executive & sales compensation, special pay plans, & performance evaluation
General Info: (Formerly Compensation), Monthly, Trim Size-6 x 9¼, Web press, Looseleaf
Subscriptions: Indv. $360
List Rental: List Management Co.: WG & L List Management, 1 Penn Plz Fl 42, New York, NY 10119-0002 Tel # (212) 971-5000

Successful Job Accomodation Strategies
See: DISABILITY

Summary of Labor Arbitration Awards
See: LABOR

Summary of Labor Arbitration Awards
See: LABOR UNION

Supervisor's Guide to Employment Practices
See: MANAGEMENT

TSM Reports   *Business*

Publishing Co: Designed Resources, PO Box 53798, Cincinnati, OH 45253 Tel # (513) 741-3907 Fax # (513) 741-3907
Personnel: Publisher-Robert Neumann
Editorial Description: Covers the temporary staffing industry.
General Info: Yr. Est. 1984, Monthly
Subscriptions: Indv. $98

Teacher's Guide to Classroom Management
See: EDUCATION

Team Leader
See: MANAGEMENT

Teamwork   *Business*

Publishing Co: Dartnell Corp., 4660 N. Ravenswood Ave., Chicago, IL 60640-4510; Title Tel # (312) 561-4000 Title Fax # (312) 561-3801
Personnel: Publisher-Clark Fetridge, Editor-Kim Andersen, Production Mgr.-Megan Mulligan, Art Dir.-Andrew Epstein, Mktg. Dir.-George Economos
Editorial Description: Designed as a personal guide to working successfully with people, Teamwork offers insight, wisdom, and new concepts in an interesting format.
General Info: Yr. Est. 1987, Bi-weekly, Trim Size-8½ x 11, 4 pages, 2 Color, Matte
Subscriptions: Indv. $59, $62/copy
List Rental: List Management Co.: Manager: Sue McDorman; Leland Company, 1801 W. Leland Ave., Chicago, IL 60640-4363 Tel # (312) 561-4005, Fax # (312) 561-4099, Actives: 70,785, $90/M, Hotline: $125/M

Telecommuting Review   *Business*

Publishing Co: Telespan Publishing, 50 W Palm St, Altadena, CA 91001-4337 Tel # (818) 797-5482 Fax # (818) 797-2035; Title Tel # (908) 329-2266 Title Fax # (908) 329-2703
Personnel: Publisher, Editor-Gil Gordon
Editorial Description: Coverage of telecommuting (work-at-home) programs, technical, legal, supervisory, & policy aspects. Intended for employers & vendors.
General Info: (Formerly Telecommuting Review: The Gordon Report), Yr. Est. 1984, Monthly, Sheetfed press, 10 pages, ISSN: 8756-7431, Ind/Abs/Online: Newsnet, Matte
Subscriptions: Indv. $157, Can. $157, For. $177, $15/copy

Tennessee Health Law Update
See: LAW

TrainMaster   *Business*   CPM: $342

Publishing Co: CDS Associates, 926 Coachella Ave, Sunnyvale, CA 94086-3435; Title Tel # (408) 738-2434 Title Fax # (408) 738-3916
Personnel: Publisher, Editor-Shelby Candland
Editorial Description: Covers training, employment development, and Human Resource issues.
General Info: Yr. Est. 1988, Quarterly, Trim Size-8½ x 11, Desktop press, 4 pages, No Color, Recycled, Saddle-stitched
Subscriptions: Indv. $35, $5/copy
Circulation: Total-525
Advertising: $180.
List Rental: Rents Lists

Training Directors' Forum Newsletter   *Business*

Publishing Co: Lakewood Publications, Inc., 50 S. Ninth St., Minneapolis, MN 55402-3165 Parent Co.-K-III Communications, New York; Title Tel # (612) 333-0471 Title Fax # (612) 333-6526
Personnel: Publisher-Philip Jones, Editor-Brian McDermott, Promotion Dir.-Carol A. Swanson
Editorial Description: Networking vehicle where top training executives discuss issues, ideas, technologies, and events.
General Info: Yr. Est. 1985, Monthly, Trim Size-8½ x 11, Sheetfed press, 8 pages, 2 Color, Recycled, Saddle-stitched
Subscriptions: Indv. $118, Can. $128, For. $138
Acquistions: Publication Bought
Circulation: Total-2,500
List Rental: Rents Lists

Training Trends   *Business*

Publishing Co: TPC Training, 750 Lake Cook Rd., Buffalo Grove, IL 60089-5080; Title Tel # (708) 537-6610
Personnel: Editor-Charles Gessert
Editorial Description: Goes to industrial plants with in-house training programs.
General Info: Yr. Est. 1969, Quarterly, 4 pages
Circulation: Total-25,000

WG&L Human Resources Forms with Commentary   *Business*

Publishing Co: Warren, Gorham & Lamont, 31 Saint James Ave., Boston, MA 02116-4112 Parent Co.-Thomson Professional Publications, Stamford; Title Tel # (617) 423-2020 Title Fax # (617) 423-1914
Personnel: Publisher-Andrew Boden, Production Mgr.-Paul Kelly, Mktg. Dir.-Sandra Fox
Editorial Description: A comprehensive volume that brings hundreds of HR forms all compiled from the nations leading corporations- designed to help save time and effort.
General Info: Semi-annually, Looseleaf
Subscriptions: Indv. $129
List Rental: List Management Co.: Manager: Seena Benedek; WG & L List Management, 1 Penn Plz Fl 42, New York, NY 10119-0002 Tel # (212) 971-5000

WIRRA News
See: COLLEGE ALUMNI

Western Canada Water *Consumer, Association*

Publishing Co: Western Canada Water & Wastewater Association, Box 6168, Sta. A, Calgary, AB T2H 2L4 Canada; Title Tel # (403) 259-4041 Title Fax # (403) 258-1631
Personnel: Editor-Janis Taylor, Circ. Mgr., Adv. Dir.-Doreen Munsie, Art Dir.-Laurie Nowicki
Editorial Description: Concerns related to personnel in Water/Wastewater Industry.
General Info: Yr. Est. 1948, Bi-monthly, Trim Size-8½ x 11, Offset press, 20 pages, 3% ads, 2 Color
Subscriptions: Indv. $40, $10/copy
Circulation: Total-2,500
Advertising: Inquire for rates.

What to Do about Personnel Problems in (Your State) *Business*

Publishing Co: Business & Legal Reports, Inc., 39 Academy St., PO Box 1513, Madison, CT 06443-2646; Title Tel # (860) 245-7448 Title Fax # (860) 245-2559
Personnel: Publisher-John Brady, Editor-Robert Brady, Art Dir.-John Kallio
Editorial Description: Looseleaf service featuring national news update and state newsletter covering compliance issue in HR: court cases, state and national legislative developments, practical compliance assistance.
General Info: Yr. Est. 1985, Monthly, 8 pages, 2 Color, Newsprint, Looseleaf
Subscriptions: Indv. $295
List Rental: List Management Co.: Marketing List Professionals, 39 Academy St # 1513, Madison, CT 06443-2646 Tel # (860) 245-2076, Fax # (860) 245-2559, Actives: $75/M

What's Ahead in Human Resources *Business*

Publishing Co: Remy Publishing Co., 350 W Hubbard St # 440, Chicago, IL 60610-4011; Title Tel # (312) 464-0300 Title Fax # (312) 464-0166
Personnel: Publisher-Robert Root, Editor-John Hickey, Circ. Mgr.-Trish Bissell
Editorial Description: A newsletter that covers human resource trends, legal issues, survey, books, conferences and products of particular interest to the human resources professional.
General Info: (Formerly What's Ahead in Personnel), Yr. Est. 1971, Semi-monthly, 4 pages, No Color
Subscriptions: Indv. $145, Inst. $145, Can. $145, For. $185

What's New in Benefits & Compensation *Business*

Publishing Co: Progressive Business Publications, 370 Technology Dr., #3019, Malverne, PA 19355-9863 Parent Co.-American Future Systems, Inc., Bryn Mawr; Title Tel # (610) 695-8600 Title Fax # (610) 647-8089
Personnel: Publisher-Edward M. Satell, Editorial Dir.-Stephen Meyer, Editor-Richard Turitz, Mktg. Dir.-Ed Moore
Editorial Description: Helps benefits and compensation professionals address the cost concerns of senior management while meeting the needs of employees.
General Info: Bi-weekly, 8 pages
Subscriptions: Indv. $299
List Rental: List Management Co.: Mail Marketing, Inc., 171 Terrace St., Haworth, NJ 07641-1899 Tel # (201) 387-1023, Fax # (201) 387-2976

Wisconsin Employment Law Letters
See: LAW

Work Times *Association*

Publishing Co: New Ways to Work, 785 Market St Ste 950, San Francisco, CA 94103-2016; Title Tel # (415) 995-9860 Title Fax # (415) 995-9867
Personnel: Editor-Barney Olmsted
Editorial Description: Alternative work-time schedules.
General Info: Yr. Est. 1982, Quarterly, Trim Size-8½ x 11, 8 pages, ISSN: 0736-9166, Recycled
Subscriptions: Indv. $35, Inst. $75, Can. $35, For. $35, $8/copy
Circulation: Total-400

Workers' Comp Advisor *Business, Consumer*

Publishing Co: Genesis Publishing, Inc., 10455 Sorrento Valley Rd Ste, 103, San Diego, CA 92121-1621; Title Tel # (619) 453-0858
Personnel: Publisher-Donna Buys Hawkins, Editor-William L. Hodge, Assoc. Ed.-Bonnie Potter-Collis, Mktg. Dir.-Jay W. Hillis
Editorial Description: Covers worker's compensation & occupational medicine.
General Info: (Formerly Medical Legal Reporter), Yr. Est. 1986, Monthly, Trim Size-8½ x 11, Offset press, 12 pages, ISSN: 1054-7819, 2 Color, Matte, Saddle-stitched
Subscriptions: Indv. $197, $17/copy
Acquistions: Publication Bought
Advertising: Inquire for rates. Accepts Inserts.
List Rental: Actives: $150/M

Workers' Comp Practice Advisor
See: MEDICINE

Workers' Compensation Biweekly Bulletin
See: LAW

Workers Compensation Guide *Business*

Publishing Co: Warren, Gorham & Lamont, 31 Saint James Ave., Boston, MA 02116-4112 Parent Co.-Thomson Professional Publications, Stamford; Title Tel # (617) 423-2020 Title Fax # (617) 423-1914
Personnel: Publisher-Andrew Boden, Production Mgr.-Paul Kelly, Mktg. Mgr.-Sandra Fox
Editorial Description: Thoroughly addresses compensation strategy, compliance and cost issues. It features concise digests of legal considerations, detailed wage and salary, and more. It covers every aspect of compensation including, wage and hour laws, pay for performanc e,all types of benefits and more.
General Info: (Formerly Compensation & Strategy Management), Bi-weekly, Looseleaf
Subscriptions: Indv. $149
List Rental: List Management Co.: Manager: Seena Benedek; WG & L List Management, 1 Penn Plz Fl 42, New York, NY 10119-0002 Tel # (212) 971-5000

Worker's Compensation Law Bulletin
See: LAW

Workforce Strategies
See: EMPLOYMENT

Working Smart *Business*

Publishing Co: National Institute of Business Management, 1101 King St Ste 411, Alexandria, VA 22314-2966 Parent Co.-National Information Corp., Alexandria; Title Tel # (703) 739-3798 Title Fax # (703) 549-9705
Personnel: Publisher-Steve Sturm, Editorial Dir.-Anne Cheevers, Mktg. Mgr.-Donna Houseman
Editorial Description: Human relations/management advisory letter.
General Info: (Formerly Personal Report for the Executive), Yr. Est. 1970, Monthly
Subscriptions: Indv. $48, Can. $60
Circulation: Total-50,000
Advertising: Accepts Inserts.
List Rental: List Management Co.: Direct Media, Inc., 200 Pemberwick Rd., PO Box 4565, Greenwich, CT 06830 Tel # (203) 532-3713, Fax # (203) 531-1452, Actives: $95/M, Expires: $55/M

Working Together *Business*

Publishing Co: Dartnell Corp., 4660 N. Ravenswood Ave., Chicago, IL 60640-4510 Tel # (312) 561-4000; Title Tel # (312) 561-5463 Title Fax # (312) 561-3801
Personnel: Publisher-Clark Fetridge, Editor-Kim Andersen, Production Mgr.-Megan Mulligan, Art Dir.-Andrew Epstein, Mktg. Dir.-George Economos
Editorial Description: Improving employee/management relations and performance; personal career development.
General Info: Yr. Est. 1983, Semi-monthly, 4 pages, 2 Color, Matte
Subscriptions: $62/copy
List Rental: List Management Co.: Manager: Sue McDorman; Leland Company, 1801 W. Leland Ave., Chicago, IL 60640-4363 Tel # (312) 561-4005, Fax # (312) 561-4099, Actives: 70,785, $90/M, Hotline: $125/M

Your Retirement Advisor *Business*

Publishing Co: Hearst Business Communications, RAI Division, 645 Stewart Ave., Garden City, NY 11530-4709; Title Tel # (516) 227-1300 Title Fax # (516) 229-3636
Personnel: Publisher-W. Boyd Griffin, Assoc. Publ.-Susan Barbey, Editor-Elaine Laramee
Editorial Description: Company sponsored publication for retired workers.
General Info: Yr. Est. 1958, Quarterly, Trim Size-8½ x 11, Offset press, 4 pages

Your Telephone Personality
See: TELECOMMUNICATIONS

INSTRUMENTS

AA Newsletter
See: CHEMISTRY & CHEMICALS

AAMI News *Consumer, Association*

Publishing Co: Assn. for the Advancement of Medical Instrumentation, 3330 Washington Blvd., Ste 400, Arlington, VA 22201-4502; Title Tel # (703) 525-4890 Title Fax # (703) 276-0793
Personnel: Editor-Mary Beth Hatem
Editorial Description: Presents assn. activities including standard pubs., regulatory & legislative actions.
General Info: Yr. Est. 1964, Monthly, Trim Size-8½ x 11, Sheetfed press, 16 pages, ISSN: 0739-0270, 2 Color, Newsprint
Subscriptions: Indv. $95, For. $140
Circulation: Total-5,000
Advertising: Inquire for rates.
List Rental: Rents Lists
Printing Co: Hagerstown Bookbinding & Printing, 952 Frederick St, Hagerstown, MD 21740-6821 Tel # (301) 733-2000, Fax # (301) 733-6586

Amplifications -- A Forum for PCR Users
See: CHEMISTRY & CHEMICALS

Chemical Monitor
See: CHEMISTRY & CHEMICALS

Clinica-World Medical Device & Diagnostic News
Business, Association   CPM: $915

Publishing Co: Pharmabooks, 1775 Broadway Ste 511, New York, NY 10019-1903; Title Tel # (212) 262-8230 Title Fax # (212) 262-8234
Personnel: Publisher-Philip Brown, Editor-Peter Charlish, Adv. Dir.-Peter Coltart
General Info: Weekly, Trim Size-209mm x 294mm, Offset press, 28 pages, 4 Color, Newsprint, Saddle-stitched
Subscriptions: Indv. $595
Circulation: (PSS), Total-1,890
Advertising: $1,730. Accepts Inserts.

Health Industry Today
See: HEALTH

IEEE Instrumentation & Measurement Society Newsletter
Business, Association   CPM: $140

Publishing Co: Institute of Electrical & Electronics Engineers, Inc., 445 Hoes Lane, PO Box 1331, Piscataway, NJ 08855-1331 Tel # (908) 562-3992 Fax # (908) 981-9334 Parent Co.-Institute of Electrical & Electronics Engineers, New York
Personnel: Editor-Tom Carver, Production Ed.-Ann Skrupski, Production Mgr.-Robert Smrek, Adv. Dir.-W.R. Saunders, Adv. Mgr.-Susan Schneidermer, Sales Mgr.-Susan Schneiderman
General Info: Yr. Est. 1984, Quarterly, Trim Size-8½ x 11, 28 pages, ISSN: 0161-1038, Coated, Saddle-stitched
Subscriptions: Free With Membership
Circulation: Total-4,983
Advertising: $700.
List Rental: Rents Lists

ISWM News
See: EDUCATION

Living Music
See: MUSIC & MUSIC TRADES

Measurement Chain, The

Publishing Co: Market Intelligence Research Co., 2525 Charleston Rd, Mountain View, CA 94043-1626; Title Tel # (415) 961-9000 Title Fax # (415) 961-5042
Personnel: Publisher-Wyman Bravard, Editor-Sarah Collings, Circ. Mgr.-Jennifer Williams, Art Dir.-Russell Haswell
Editorial Description: Marketing and business news for the sensor industry, covers sensors, test & measurement, analyticaL instrumentation, ATE, VXI, and process control.
General Info: (Formerly Sensors and Instrumentation News), Yr. Est. 1987, Monthly, Trim Size-8½ x 11, 16 pages, ISSN: 1051-9432, Ind/Abs/Online: Newsnet, Color-cover, Saddle-stitched
Subscriptions: Indv. $295, $50/copy
Acquistions: Publication Bought
Advertising: Inquire for rates.
List Rental: Rents Lists

Radon News Digest
See: ENVIRONMENT & ECOLOGY

Sensor Business Digest
Business

Publishing Co: Vital Information Publications, 321 Carrera Dr, Mill Valley, CA 94941-3995; Title Tel # (415) 389-8671 Title Fax # (415) 389-8671
Editorial Description: Covers the sensors and instrumentation industry.
General Info: Monthly, ISSN: 1060-1902
Subscriptions: Indv. $325, For. $345

INSURANCE

APPA Digest
See: MEDICINE

ASCA Quarterly
See: HEALTH

About US
See: HOUSE ORGANS

Actuarial Review, The
Association

Publishing Co: Casualty Actuarial Society, 1100 N Glebe Rd Ste 600, Arlington, VA 22201-4798; Title Tel # (703) 276-3100 Title Fax # (703) 276-3108
Personnel: Editor-Ted Zubulake, Editorial Asst.-Brenda Huber
Editorial Description: News and comment on casualty/property insurance actuarial affairs.
General Info: Yr. Est. 1974, Quarterly, Trim Size-8½ x 11, Desktop press, 18 pages, ISSN: 1046-5081, 2 Color, Matte, Saddle-stitched
Subscriptions: Indv. $10, Can. $16, Free With Membership
Circulation: Total-7,500
Printing Co: Balmar Printing & Graphics, 5130 Wilson Blvd, Arlington, VA 22205-1100 Tel # (703) 875-9000

Actuarial Update
Association

Publishing Co: American Academy of Actuaries, 1100 17th St. NW, 7th Fl., Washington, DC 20036 Fax # (202) 872-1948; Title Tel # (202) 223-8196
Personnel: Editor-Eotoni Mulder
Editorial Description: Articles & editorials on broad range of actuarial issues.
General Info: Yr. Est. 1965, Monthly, Trim Size-8½ x 11, Sheetfed press, 2 Color, Newsprint
Subscriptions: Free With Membership
Circulation: Total-10,000

Actuary
Association

Publishing Co: Society of Actuaries/Casualty Actuarial Society, 475 N. Martingale Rd., Suite 800, Schaumburg, IL 60173-2226; Title Tel # (708) 706-3500 Title Fax # (708) 706-3599
Personnel: Editor-Mike Cowell, Editor-Cecilla Green
Editorial Description: Insurance: life, health, pension planning and other employee benefit products designed by actuaries.
General Info: Yr. Est. 1967, 10x/yr., Trim Size-8½ x 11, 16 pages, 2 Color
Subscriptions: Indv. $15, Free With Membership
Circulation: Total-20,000
Printing Co: ABS Graphics, 901 S. Route 53, Addison, IL 60101 Tel # (708) 495-2400, Fax # (708) 495-2400

Advanced Underwriting Service
Business

Publishing Co: Dearborn Financial Publishing, 520 N. Dearborn St., Chicago, IL 60610-4354
Personnel: Editor-Georgia Mann, Adv. Dir.-Marjorie Sher
Editorial Description: Information of the law, revenue rulings, & judicial decisions affecting estate planning, employee benefits, business insurance & advanced sales.
General Info: Yr. Est. 1935, Monthly, Trim Size-8½ x 11½, Offset press, 2 Color, Looseleaf
Subscriptions: Indv. $395
List Rental: Rents Lists

Aeltus Weekly
Business

Publishing Co: Aeltus Managing, Inc., 242 Trumbull St., Hartford, CT 06156 Tel # (203) 273-4368; Title Tel # (203) 273-0605
Personnel: Editor-Jim Griffin
Editorial Description: For major journalists, federal government officials, and large commercial customers of Aeltus.
General Info: (Formerly Aeconomics; Capital Markets Weekly), Monthly

Agency Briefs Newsletter
Business

Publishing Co: Rough Notes Company, Inc., 11690 Technology Dr., Carmel, IN 46032-5600 Tel # (317) 582-1600 Fax # (317) 816-1000
Editorial Description: Interviews with insurance industry pros with insights on agency automation, personnel management, and marketing.
General Info: Monthly, Trim Size-8½ x 11, 8 pages, Saddle-stitched
Subscriptions: Indv. $70

Aim
Business

Publishing Co: Commercial Union Assurance Cos., One Beacon St., Boston, MA 02108-3100; Title Tel # (617) 725-6053
Editorial Description: In-house pub. for insurance sales force.
General Info: Yr. Est. 1977, Bi-monthly, Trim Size-11 x 17, Offset press, 8 pages, 2 Color
Circulation: Total-12,000

Albert Advisor
Business

Publishing Co: Graham Communications, 72 River Park St, Needham Heights, MA 02194-2631; Title Tel # (617) 449-2866 Title Fax # (617) 449-5340
Personnel: Publisher-John Graham, Editor-Judy Foley, Circ. Mgr.-Paul Graham, Production Mgr.-Richard Barry, Art Dir.-Jan Byorkman
Editorial Description: Newsletter of J.H. Albert Insurance.
General Info: Yr. Est. 1990, Quarterly, 4 pages, 2 Color, Coated, Perfect bound
Circulation: Total-3,000
Printing Co: Ink Spot, The, 40 Oval Rd, Quincy, MA 02170-3813 Tel # (617) 273-7605, Fax # (617) 471-8810

American Institute of Marine Underwriters, Bulletins

Publishing Co: American Institute of Marine Underwriters, 14 Wall St., New York, NY 10005-2145; Title Tel # (212) 233-0550

Appraiser, The
See: ANTIQUES & ART GOODS

Asset Sales Report
See: BANKING & FINANCE

Assets
Consumer

Publishing Co: American Society of CLU & ChFC, 270 S Bryn Mawr Ave # 59, Bryn Mawr, PA 19010-2105 Tel # (610) 526-2500 Fax # (610) 526-2538; Title Tel # (215) 896-4300
Personnel: Publisher-John Driskill, Editor-Carl Hall, Jr., Production Mgr.-Robert Titus, Circ. Mgr., Art Dir.-Carl Hall
Editorial Description: Business, tax, and financial newsletter sent by members to clients.
General Info: Yr. Est. 1980, Bi-monthly, Trim Size-11 x 17, Sheetfed press, 4 pages, 2 Color, Newsprint
Circulation: Total-86,000
Printing Co: Boyertown Publishing Co., 48 S. Reading Ave., P.O. Box 548, Boyertown, PA 19512 Tel # (215) 367-2121, Fax # (215) 367-7093

Austin Insurance Report *Business*

Publishing Co: Report Publications, Inc., PO Box 12368, Austin, TX 78711-2368; Title Tel # (512) 478-5663
Personnel: Editor-Homer Olsen, Circ. Mgr.-Shirl Scott
Editorial Description: Summarizes significant news in the Texas insurance industry.
General Info: Yr. Est. 1957, Weekly, Trim Size-7 x 9, Offset press, 4 pages, No Color
Subscriptions: Indv. $76, $2/copy
Circulation: Total-200

Auto Insurance Report *Business*

Publishing Co: Risk Communications, 33 Lindall St., Laguna Niguel, CA 92677-4738; Title Tel # (714) 443-0330
Personnel: Publisher-Brian Sullivan
Editorial Description: For regulators and underwriters of the auto insurance industry.
General Info: Yr. Est. 1994, Weekly

Automated Medical Payments News *Business*

Publishing Co: Faulkner & Gray, Inc., 300 S. Wacker Dr., 18th Fl., Chicago, IL 60606 Tel # (312) 913-1334 Fax # (312) 913-1365 Parent Co.-Thomson Corp., Stamford; Title Tel # (312) 648-0261 Title Fax # (312) 648-9569
Editorial Description: Covers automated medical claims payment and processing.
General Info: Yr. Est. 1992, Monthly, Trim Size-8½ x 11, 8 pages, 2 Color
Subscriptions: Indv. $275
List Rental: List Management Co.: Aggressive List Management, 18-2 E Dundee Rd Ste 101, Barrington, IL 60010-5273 Tel # (708) 304-4030, Fax # (708) 304-4032, Actives: $95/M

Automobile Insurance Losses Collision Coverages Variations by Make and Series *Business*

Publishing Co: Highway Lost Data Institute, 1005 N Glebe Rd Ste 800, Arlington, VA 22201-4751; Title Tel # (703) 247-1600
General Info: Yr. Est. 1972, Semi-annually
Circulation: Total-2,500

BBI's Monitor of Technology Assessment & Reimbursement
See: MEDICINE

BNA Policy & Practice Series
See: MANAGEMENT

Bad Faith Law Report
See: LAW

Bad Faith Law Update
See: LAW

Bankers Notes
See: HOUSE ORGANS

Banks in Insurance Report

Publishing Co: John Wiley & Sons, Inc., 605 Third Avenue, New York, NY 10158-0012 Tel # (212) 850-6000 Fax # (212) 850-6088; Title Tel # (212) 645-7880 Title Fax # (212) 645-1160
Personnel: Publisher-James Slabe, Editor-Edward J. Stoner, Mng. Editor-Jean Stephenson
Editorial Description: What, who & how-to's of bank expansion into insurance. Covers legal, legislative, regulatory developments, business strategies, & selling tactics.
General Info: Yr. Est. 1985, Monthly, Trim Size-8½ x 11, Sheetfed press, 16 pages, ISSN: 8756-6079, Coated, Saddle-stitched
Subscriptions: Indv. $345, For. $395
Advertising: Inquire for rates.
List Rental: Rents Lists
Printing Co: Hessey Printing, Inc., 424 Lafayette St # 100226, Nashville, TN 37203-4255 Tel # (615) 244-7180, Fax # (615) 255-6911

Best of Your Money Matters with Ric Edelman, The
See: INVESTMENT

BestWeek Life/Health Edition *Business*

Publishing Co: A.M. Best Co., Inc., Ambest Rd., Oldwick, NJ 08858-0700 Tel # (908) 439-2200 Fax # (908) 439-3296
Personnel: Publisher-Arthur Snyder, Editor-Christopher Winans, VP & Exec. Ed.-Richard L. Hall
General Info: Weekly, Trim Size-8½ x 11, 20 pages, Matte, Saddle-stitched
Subscriptions: Indv. $425

BestWeek, Property/Casualty Edition *Business*

Publishing Co: A.M. Best Co., Inc., Ambest Rd., Oldwick, NJ 08858-0700 Fax # (908) 439-3296; Title Tel # (908) 439-2200
Personnel: Publisher-Arthur Snyder, Editor-Christopher Winans, VP & Exec. Ed.-Richard Hall
Editorial Description: A unique information service providing information on key areas of today's complex property casualty & life health insurance industries, focusing on financial aspects of the business.
General Info: (Formerly Best's Insurance Management Reports), Yr. Est. 1957, Weekly, Trim Size-8½ x 11, 20 pages, No Color, Matte, Saddle-stitched
Subscriptions: Indv. $425

Best's Casualty Loss Reserve Development Series *Business*

Publishing Co: A.M. Best Co., Inc., Ambest Rd., Oldwick, NJ 08858-0700 Tel # (908) 439-2200 Fax # (908) 439-3296
Personnel: Publisher-Arthur Snyder, Editor-John Snyder
Editorial Description: Guidelines for loss reserve decisions with 10 years of accident data.
General Info: Irregular, Looseleaf
Subscriptions: Indv. $600

Best's Experience By State *Business*

Publishing Co: A.M. Best Co., Inc., Ambest Rd., Oldwick, NJ 08858-0700 Tel # (908) 439-2200 Fax # (908) 439-3296
Personnel: Publisher-Arthur Snyder, Editor-Carl Carlson
Editorial Description: Premium and loss f0r over 2,200 propert-casual insurance companies and marketing results of over 1,200 life-health companies.
General Info: Annually, Looseleaf

Best's Intelligencer *Business*

Publishing Co: A.M. Best Co., Inc., Ambest Rd., Oldwick, NJ 08858-0700 Fax # (908) 439-3296; Title Tel # (908) 439-2200
Personnel: Publisher-Arthur Snyder, Editor-Patricia A. Forsythe
Editorial Description: A summary report of approved commercial & personal insurance filings by state and company. Includes new and revised policy/program rates, rules, and forms. Overall rate level effects published. Subscr. $305 per state, per year.
General Info: Monthly, Sheetfed press, 2 Color, Newsprint
Subscriptions: Indv. $350

Best's Loss Control Engineering Manual *Business*

Publishing Co: A.M. Best Co., Inc., Ambest Rd., Oldwick, NJ 08858-0700 Fax # (908) 439-3296; Title Tel # (908) 439-2200
Personnel: Publisher-Arthur Snyder, Editor-Christine Koehler
Editorial Description: Inspection and investigation checklists for safety engineers and field inspectors.
General Info: Yr. Est. 1968, Looseleaf
Subscriptions: Indv. $500
Printing Co: Independent Graphics, River Road, Pittson, PA 18640

Best's Underwriting Guide *Business*

Publishing Co: A.M. Best Co., Inc., Ambest Rd., Oldwick, NJ 08858-0700 Fax # (908) 439-3296; Title Tel # (908) 439-2200
Personnel: Publisher-Arthur Snyder, Editor-Mary Beth Iannaccone
General Info: Yr. Est. 1975, Looseleaf
Subscriptions: Indv. $500
Circulation: Total-7,000
Printing Co: Independent Graphics, River Road, Pittson, PA 18640

Bulletin *Business, Association*

Publishing Co: New York State Insurance Dept., 160 W Broadway, New York, NY 10013-3393; Title Tel # (212) 602-0472
Personnel: Editor-Wayne Cotter
Editorial Description: Highlights principal activities of department including new legislation, regulations and circular letters, changes in status of licensed insurers, rate fillings and disciplinary actions.
General Info: Yr. Est. 1961, Monthly, Trim Size-8½ x 11, 2 Color, Newsprint
Acquistions: Publication Bought
Circulation: Total-2,500

Bulletin de l'Assurance *Association*

Publishing Co: Regie de l'Assurance-Maladie du Quebec, 1125, chemin Saint-Louis, Quebec, PQ G1K 7T3 Canada; Title Tel # (418) 682-5168
Personnel: Editor-Raymonde Moran, Art Dir.-Yolande Chatillon
General Info: Yr. Est. 1970, Bi-monthly
Circulation: Total-11,000

Business Insurance Law and Practice Guide
See: LAW

CALUnderwriter   *Association*   CPM: $162

Publishing Co: California Assn. of Life Underwriters, 70 Washington St. #325, Oakland, CA 94607-3737; Title Tel # (510) 834-2258 Title Fax # (510) 834-1453
Personnel: Publisher-Betty Combs, Editor, Adv. Dir.-Dan Crouch
Editorial Description: Life & health insurance & CALU assn. news. Legislation, regulation.
General Info: Yr. Est. 1970, Monthly, Trim Size-8½ x 11, Sheetfed press, 24 pages, ISSN: 0199-2414, 40% ads, 4 Color, Coated, Saddle-stitched
Subscriptions: Indv. $5
Circulation: Total-9,700
Advertising: $1,575. Accepts Inserts.
List Rental: Rents Lists
Printing Co: Superior Press, 717 Whitney St, San Leandro, CA 94577-1117

CLU Comment   *Business, Association*

Publishing Co: Inst. of Chartered Life Underwriters & Financial Consultants, 41 Lesmill Rd., Don Mills, ON M3B 2T3 Canada Fax # (416) 494-8031; Title Tel # (416) 444-5251
Personnel: Editor-Rudy Halmo, Circ. Mgr.-Vi Cameron
Editorial Description: Text in English & French.
General Info: Yr. Est. 1967, Bi-monthly, 4 pages, ISSN: 0382-7038
Circulation: Total-30,000
Printing Co: Valley Web, 1299 Stowe Avenue, Medford, OR 97504 Tel # (503) 772-7039

CPCU News   *Association*

Publishing Co: Chartered Property Casualty Underwriters Society, 720 Providence Rd., PO Box 3009, Malvern, PA 19355-0709 Fax # (610) 251-2761; Title Tel # (610) 251-2728
Personnel: Editor-Jane Greiner, Product Mgr.-Michele Lanetti, Mktg. Dir.-Sheila Doffner
Editorial Description: Designed to provide a direct line of communications with its membership.
General Info: Yr. Est. 1973, 10x/yr., Trim Size-8½ x 11, Offset press, 8 pages, 2 Color, Matte, Saddle-stitched
Subscriptions: Indv. $3, Free With Membership
Circulation: (100% controlled), Total-28,000

C.S.T. Connection
See: BUSINESS & INDUSTRY

California Insurance Law & Regulation Report
See: LAW

California Insurance Law Report

Publishing Co: Data Research, Inc., 4635 Nicols Rd Ste 100, Eagan, MN 55122-3337; Title Tel # (612) 452-8267 Title Fax # (612) 452-8694
General Info: Yr. Est. 1986, Monthly, Trim Size-8½ x 11, Sheetfed press, 6 pages, ISSN: 0890-4871, No Color, Newsprint
Subscriptions: Indv. $217
Circulation: Total-300
Printing Co: Helgeson Press, 7600 14th Ave S, Richfield, MN 55423-4530 Tel # (612) 869-6828

Canadian Insurance Law Reporter
See: LAW

Canadian Insurance Law Service
See: LAW

Canadian Transportation Law Reporter
See: TRAFFIC & TRANSPORTATION

Capitation Management Report
See: HEALTH

Case Evaluation Manual
See: LAW ENFORCEMENT & PENOLOGY

Case Evaluation/Basic Settlement Value Software
See: BUSINESS & INDUSTRY

Christian Brotherhood Newsletter   *Consumer*

Publishing Co: Christian Brotherhood Newsletter, 127 Hazelwood Ave, Barberton, OH 44203-1316; Title Tel # (216) 848-1511
Personnel: Publisher-Bruce Hawthorn, Editor-John Hawthorn
Editorial Description: Helps its Fundamentalist Christian subscribers pay their medical expenses by publishing them and asking for other subscriber contributions.
General Info: Monthly, Trim Size-8½ x 11, Mimeo press, 8 pages, Coated
Subscriptions: Indv. $150
Acquistions: Publication Sold
Circulation: Total-24,600

Cibgny Month   *Association*

Publishing Co: Chase Communications Group Ltd., 25-35 Beechwood, Box 9001, Mt. Vernon, NY 10552-9001 Tel # (914) 699-2020; Title Tel # (718) 320-2727 Title Fax # (914) 699-2025
Personnel: Editor-Carole Acunto
Editorial Description: Insurance update for ins. brokers.
General Info: (Formerly Brooklyn Ins. Brokers Assn. Bulletin), Yr. Est. 1971, Monthly, Trim Size-8½ x 11, Sheetfed press, 12 pages, No Color, Coated, Saddle-stitched
Subscriptions: Indv. $20
Circulation: Total-1,000
Advertising: Inquire for rates.
Printing Co: Gazette Press, Inc., 16 School St., Yonkers, NY 10701 Tel # (914) 963-8300, Fax # (914) 476-1052

Claims Forum
See: LAW

Commentaires

Publishing Co: Institut Canadien des Assureurs-Vie Agrees et des Conseill, 41 Lesmill Rd., Don Mills, ON M3B 2T3 Canada; Title Tel # (416) 444-5251 Title Fax # (416) 444-8031
Personnel: Editor-Rudy Halmo, Circ. Mgr.-Sandra Protain, Circ. Mgr.-Susanne Sykes
Editorial Description: Current information on financial planning.
General Info: Yr. Est. 1967, Bi-monthly, 4 pages, ISSN: 0382-7046, Looseleaf
Circulation: Total-30,000
Printing Co: Valley Web, 1299 Stowe Avenue, Medford, OR 97504 Tel # (503) 772-7039

Commercial Liability Insurance- Executive Briefings

Publishing Co: International Risk Management Institute, 12222 Merit Dr Ste 1660, Dallas, TX 75251-3207; Title Tel # (214) 960-7693 Title Fax # (214) 960-6037
Personnel: Editor-Maureen McLendon, Circ. Mgr.-Cathy Roberts
General Info: Yr. Est. 1985, Quarterly, Looseleaf
Subscriptions: Indv. $265

Construction Risk Management

Publishing Co: International Risk Management Institute, 12222 Merit Dr Ste 1660, Dallas, TX 75251-3207; Title Tel # (214) 960-7693 Title Fax # (214) 960-6037
Personnel: Publisher-Jack Gibson, Editor-Jeffrey Woodward, Circ. Mgr.-Cathy Roberts
General Info: Yr. Est. 1984, Quarterly
Subscriptions: Indv. $215

Consumer Credit Insurance Association Newsletter   *Association*

Publishing Co: Consumer Credit Insurance Assn., 542 S Dearborn St Ste 400, Chicago, IL 60605-1522; Title Tel # (312) 939-2242
Personnel: Editor-Holly Vana, Publisher, Production Mgr., Adv. Dir.-Carmela Rago
Editorial Description: News of interest in the credit insurance field as well as the national insurance field; member company changes, insurance department personnel changes etc.
General Info: Yr. Est. 1951, Monthly, Trim Size-8½ x 11, Mimeo press, 16 pages, No Color
Circulation: (100% controlled), Total-300

Contact
See: HOUSE ORGANS

Crittenden Insurance Markets -Commercial Lines

Publishing Co: Crittenden Research, Inc., PO Box 1150, Novato, CA 94948 Tel # (415) 382-2400 Fax # (619) 437-4204; Title Tel # (415) 382-2477
General Info: Weekly, ISSN: 0899-6350
Subscriptions: Indv. $395

Crop Insurance Insider   *Business, Association*

Publishing Co: American Assn. of Crop Insurers, 1 Mass. Ave. NW, #800, Washington, DC 20001 Fax # (202) 408-7633; Title Tel # (202) 789-4100
General Info: (Formerly Washington Update), Quarterly

Dennis Barry's Reimbursement Advisor
See: HEALTH

Disease Management News
See: HEALTH

Dividend   *Association*

Publishing Co: Equitable Life Insurance Co. of Iowa, PO Box 1635, Des Moines, IA 50306-1635; Title Tel # (515) 245-6773
Editorial Description: Internal communications tool-news, anniversaries, features, honors, information, and facts.
General Info: Yr. Est. 1950, Monthly, Trim Size-10⅝ x 14¼, Offset press, 6 pages, 2 Color
Circulation: Total-1,000

Electronic Claims
Processing Report *Business*

Publishing Co: Phillips Business Information, Inc., 1201 Seven Locks Rd., Ste 300, Potomac, MD 20854-2958 Tel # (301) 340-1520 Fax # (301) 424-4297
General Info: Bi-weekly
Subscriptions: Indv. $495

Emphasis
See: HOUSE ORGANS

Employer's Guide to Self-Insuring Health Benefits
See: INDUSTRIAL RELATIONS/PERSONNEL

Employer's Health Benefits Bulletin
See: HEALTH

Enrolled Actuaries Report *Association*

Publishing Co: American Academy of Actuaries, 1100 17th St. NW, 7th Fl., Washington, DC 20036 Fax # (202) 872-1948; Title Tel # (202) 223-8196
Personnel: Editor-Silvio Ingui
Editorial Description: Technical articles & editorials on pensions & employee benefit topics.
General Info: Yr. Est. 1976, Quarterly, Trim Size-8½ x 11, Sheetfed press, 8 pages, 2 Color, Newsprint
Circulation: Total-3,500

Executive Report on Managed Care
See: HEALTH

FCIA News *Business*

Publishing Co: FCIA Management Co., Inc., 40 Rector St Fl 11, New York, NY 10006-1705; Title Tel # (212) 306-5000 Title Fax # (212) 306-5035
Personnel: Editor-Anne Loftus
Editorial Description: Covers international economics, finance, U.S. foreign trade, export credit insurance.
General Info: Quarterly, Trim Size-8½ x 11, Desktop press, 4 pages, 2 Color, Coated
Circulation: Total-26,000
Printing Co: Practical Graphics, Inc., 135 W 20th St Fl 3, New York, NY 10011-3628 Tel # (212) 463-7800

FMCA Newsletter *Association*

Publishing Co: Fire Mark Circle of the Americas (FMCA), 2859 Marlin Dr., Chamblee, GA 30341-5119 Tel # (404) 451-2651
Editorial Description: News of the association and information on collecting Fire Insurance signs. Subscription includes annual directory and journal.
General Info: Quarterly, Trim Size-8½ x 11, 6 pages, No Color
Subscriptions: Indv. $30

Facts *Consumer*

Publishing Co: Florida Department of Insurance, The Capitol; LL-25, Tallahassee, FL 32301; Title Tel # (904) 488-6085
Personnel: Editor-Donna Harris
Editorial Description: Report of the Florida Department of Insurance and the Treasurer's Office.
General Info: (Formerly Primescope), Yr. Est. 1971, Monthly, Trim Size-8½ x 11½, Offset press, 4 pages, No Color, Newsprint
Subscriptions: Free
Circulation: Total-1,000

Federal & State Insurance
Week

Publishing Co: J.R. Publishing, Inc., PO Box 6654, Mc Lean, VA 22106-6654; Title Tel # (703) 532-2235 Title Fax # (703) 532-2236
Personnel: Publisher, Editor-John Reistrup
Editorial Description: Report on political, legislative & regulatory actions affecting insurance.
General Info: Yr. Est. 1987, Weekly
Subscriptions: Indv. $347

Federal Taxation of Life Insurance Companies
See: TAXES

Financial & Estate Planning
See: TAXES

Flexible Benefits
See: INDUSTRIAL RELATIONS/PERSONNEL

Future Actuary, The
See: COLLEGE STUDENT

Governmental Risk Mgmt.
Manual

Publishing Co: Risk Management Society Publishing, Inc., 655 Third Ave., 2nd Floor, New York, NY 10017 Tel # (212) 286-9364; Title Tel # (602) 622-5174
Personnel: Editor-Nestor Roos, Circ. Mgr.-M. Hall
Editorial Description: Risk management concepts & practices for all levels of government.
General Info: Yr. Est. 1976, Bi-monthly, Trim Size-8½ x 11, Offset press, 10 pages, No Color, Looseleaf
Subscriptions: Indv. $125
Circulation: Total-2,000

Health Care Biller
See: HEALTH

Health Care Collector
See: HEALTH

Hospital Insurance Litigation Reporter
See: LAW

How to Recover for Loss Or
Damage to Goods in
Transit *Business*

Publishing Co: Matthew Bender & Co., 11 Penn Plaza, New York, NY 10001-2006 Fax # (212) 244-3188; Title Tel # (212) 967-7707
Personnel: Editor-N. Masliansky
Editorial Description: Deals with carrier litigation, jurisdiction and venue, limitation of actions, liability.
General Info: Yr. Est. 1976, Looseleaf
Subscriptions: $290/copy

IBAO News *Business*

Publishing Co: Insurance Brokers Assn. of Ontario, 90 Eglinton Ave. E., 2nd fl., Toronto, ON M4P 2Y3 Canada; Title Tel # (416) 488-7422
Personnel: Editor-Terry Talor
Editorial Description: General insurance and general insurance brokers' matters; independent brokers system.
General Info: (Formerly IIABO News), Yr. Est. 1920, Monthly, Trim Size-8½ x 11, Offset press, 8 pages, No Color
Circulation: Total-4,001
Advertising: Inquire for rates.

I.I.I. Insurance Daily *Business*

Publishing Co: Insurance Information Institute, 110 William St, New York, NY 10038-3970; Title Tel # (212) 669-9200 Title Fax # (212) 732-1916
Editorial Description: Abstracts from newspaper articles relating to insurance.
General Info: Yr. Est. 1985, Daily, Trim Size-8½ x 11, 4 pages
Subscriptions: Indv. $1,700, $7/copy

IMMS Weekly Marketeer *Business*

Publishing Co: Insurance Marketing & Management Services, 12424 Wilshire Blvd., Ste. 600, Santa Monica, CA 90025-1040; Title Fax # (310) 298-4828
Personnel: Publisher-George Nordhaus, Editor-Noel Glaser
General Info: (Formerly IMS Weekly Marketeer), Yr. Est. 1980, Weekly, Sheetfed press, 4 pages, Ind/Abs/Online: Newsnet, 2 Color
Subscriptions: Indv. $160
Circulation: (100% controlled), Total-6,000

Illinois Insurance *Business*

Publishing Co: Illinois Dept. of Insurance, 320 W. Washington, Springfield, IL 62767-0001; Title Tel # (217) 782-4515
Personnel: Editor, Circ. Mgr.-Nan Nases
Editorial Description: Feature articles of interest to insurance regulators, industry & consumers, departmental policy statements & interpretations of insurance legislation & rules & regulations.
General Info: Yr. Est. 1969, Bi-monthly, Trim Size-8½ x 11, Sheetfed press, 12 pages, ISSN: 0094-7660, 2 Color, Newsprint, Saddle-stitched
Circulation: (76% controlled), Total-5,500

In-SITE *Business, Association*

Publishing Co: Society of Insurance Trainers & Educators, 2120 Market Street, Suite 108, San Francisco, CA 94114; Title Tel # (415) 621-2830 Title Fax # (415) 621-0889
Personnel: Editor-Lois Markovich
Editorial Description: Short articles related to insurance, education and training; news of interest to members.
General Info: (Formerly Education Exchange), Yr. Est. 1954, Bi-monthly, Trim Size-8½ x 11, Offset press, 8 pages, 2 Color, Other, Other
Subscriptions: Free With Membership
Circulation: Total-800
Printing Co: Burns & Associates, 183 Jordan Ave, San Francisco, CA 94118

Insurance Accountant *Business*

Publishing Co: American Banker Newsletters, One State Plaza, New York, NY 10004-1505 Fax # (202) 843-9620; Title Tel # (212) 803-8300 Title Fax # (212) 843-9620
Personnel: Publisher-David G. Schutt, Editor-Miles Maguire, Circ. Dir.-Maria Pritchett, Adv. Dir., Mktg. Dir.-Hans Winberg
Editorial Description: Accounting policy issues affecting the insurance industry.
General Info: Weekly
Subscriptions: Indv. $750, Can. $750, For. $780, $20/copy
Advertising: $1,400.
List Rental: Rents Lists

Insurance Action Review *Business, Association*

Publishing Co: Washington State Insurance Commissioner's Office, Insurance Bldg., Aq-21, Olympia, WA 98504-0001; Title Tel # (206) 753-2418
Personnel: Publisher-Dick Marquardt, Editor-Ed Ives
Editorial Description: Periodic review of Insurance Department action.
General Info: Yr. Est. 1977, Bi-monthly, No Color
Circulation: (100% controlled), Total-5,000

Insurance Bad Faith Litigation
See: LAW

Insurance Department Directory
See: GOVERNMENT

Insurance Forum   *Business*

Publishing Co: Insurance Forum, Inc., PO Box 245, Ellettsville, IN 47429-0245;
Title Tel # (812) 876-6502
Personnel: Editor-Joseph M. Belth, Circ. Mgr.-Lois Braunlin
Editorial Description: Problems and issues of interest to persons and organizations with a keen interest in insurance.
General Info: Yr. Est. 1974, Monthly, Trim Size-8½ x 11, Offset press, 4 pages, ISSN: 0095-2923, No Color
Subscriptions: Indv. $60, Inst. $60, Can. $60, For. $60, $5/copy

Insurance Industry International

Publishing Co: Lafferty Publications, 420 Lexington Ave., Ste. 1745, New York, NY 10170
Tel # (212) 557-6729 Fax # (212) 557-7266; Title Tel # (404) 636-6610 Title Fax # (404) 636-6422
Personnel: Publisher-Frank Lawson, Editor-Aine Coney
Editorial Description: Insurance Industry International reports corporate performance and strategy with particular emphasis on personal lines in the insurance industry worldwide.
General Info: 10x/yr.
Subscriptions: Indv. $1,059

Insurance Industry Litigation Reporter
See: LAW

Insurance Institute of Southern Alberta, Newsletter   *Business, Association*

Publishing Co: Insurance Institute of Southern Alberta, 1015 4th St. SW, #801, Calgary, AB T2R 1J4 Canada Parent Co.-Insurance Institute of Canada, Toronto, Canada; Title Tel # (403) 266-3427 Title Fax # (403) 269-3199
Editorial Description: Contains information for members of the Insurance Institute of Southern Alberta.
General Info: Yr. Est. 1954, Bi-monthly, Trim Size-8½ x 11, 4 pages
Circulation: Total-2,100
Printing Co: Petrotech Printing, Calgary, AB

Insurance Law Reports: Life, Health & Health & Accident   *Business*

Publishing Co: CCH, Inc., 2700 Lake Cook Rd., Riverwoods, IL 60015 Parent Co.-Kluwer Law & Taxation Publishers, Cambridge; Title Tel # (847) 267-7000 Title Fax # (800) 224-8299
Editorial Description: Reporting of new decisions interpreting insurance contracts.
General Info: Monthly, Trim Size-6 x 9, Web press, 120 pages, No Color, Looseleaf
Subscriptions: Indv. $1,010

Insurance Litigation Reporter
See: LAW

Insurance Marketing Insider   *Business, Consumer*

Publishing Co: Shelby Publishing Corp, 155 Federal Street, Boston, MA 02110-1727 Parent Co.-Standard Publishing, Boston; Title Tel # (617) 423-0978 Title Fax # (617) 482-7820
Personnel: Publisher-John Cross, Editor-Diane Montgomery, Circ. Mgr.-Kelly Westover, Production Mgr.-Lauren Lombardi, Mktg. Dir.-Wendy Kenniston
General Info: Monthly, Trim Size-8½ x 11, 8 pages, No Color
Subscriptions: Indv. $132, Can. $172, For. $172, $11/copy
List Rental: Rents Lists

Insurance Pro

Publishing Co: Merritt Professional Publishing, 1661 9th St, Santa Monica, CA 90404-3703;
Title Tel # (310) 450-7234 Title Fax # (310) 396-4563
Personnel: Editor-Pat Sheppard
Editorial Description: A monthly review of insurance news and trends for the insurance professional.
General Info: Yr. Est. 1995, Monthly, Trim Size-8½ x 11, 8 pages
Subscriptions: Indv. $79

Insurance Regulation/State Capitals   *Business, Consumer*

Publishing Co: Wakeman/Walworth, 300 N. Washington St., Alexandria, VA 22314-2530;
Title Tel # (703) 549-8606 Title Fax # (703) 549-1372
Personnel: Publisher-Keyes Walworth
Editorial Description: Focuses on states' insurance regulation including, health, life, automobile, homeowner, and malpractice.
General Info: (Formerly Insurance Regulation from the State Capitals), Yr. Est. 1946, Weekly, ISSN: 0016-1748
Subscriptions: Indv. $265, Inst. $212, Can. $235, For. $255

Insurance Regulator   *Business*

Publishing Co: American Banker Newsletters, One State Plaza, New York, NY 10004-1505
Fax # (202) 843-9620; Title Tel # (212) 803-8300 Title Fax # (212) 843-9620
Personnel: Publisher-David G. Schutt, Editor-Miles Maguire, Circ. Dir.-Maria Pritchett, Adv. Dir., Mktg. Dir.-Hans Winberg
Editorial Description: Regulatory developments affecting the insurance markets.
Subscriptions: Indv. $750, Can. $750, For. $780, $20/copy
Advertising: $1,400.
List Rental: Rents Lists

Insurance Report

Publishing Co: Merritt Professional Publishing, 1661 9th St, Santa Monica, CA 90404-3703;
Title Tel # (310) 450-7234 Title Fax # (310) 396-4563
Personnel: Editor-Debora Chan
Editorial Description: A biweekly review of market news for the insurance professional.
General Info: Yr. Est. 1995, Bi-weekly, Trim Size-8½ x 11, 10 pages
Subscriptions: Indv. $129

Insurance Research Letter

Publishing Co: International Research Service, 345 Kear Street, Yorktown, NY 10598;
Title Tel # (914) 245-7600
Personnel: Publisher-George Nielson, Editor-Thomas Lewis
Editorial Description: Covers recent news and developments in insurance.
General Info: Yr. Est. 1966, Monthly
Subscriptions: Indv. $600

Insurance Tax Review
See: TAXES

Investment Bulletin   *Business*

Publishing Co: American Council of Life Insurance, 1001 Pennsylvania Ave., NW, Washington, DC 20004-2505; Title Tel # (202) 624-2000
Editorial Description: Results of life insurers mortgage activity.
General Info: (Formerly Investment Topics), Quarterly
Subscriptions: Indv. $60
Circulation: Total-1,100

John Liner Letter   *Business, Consumer*

Publishing Co: Shelby Publishing Corp, 155 Federal Street, Boston, MA 02110-1727 Parent Co.-Standard Publishing, Boston; Title Tel # (617) 457-0600 Title Fax # (617) 482-7820
Personnel: Publisher-John Cross, Editor-Robert Montgomery, Circ. Mgr.-Kelly Westover, Production Mgr.-Lauren Lombardi, Mktg. Dir.-Wendy Kenniston
Editorial Description: Financial news and information.
General Info: Yr. Est. 1963, Monthly, Trim Size-8½ x 11, 8 pages
Subscriptions: Indv. $138, Can. $179, For. $179, $12/copy
List Rental: Rents Lists

Journal of the New York Institute of Legal Research
See: LAW

Kansas City Insurance Report
See: BANKING & FINANCE

Kemper Insurance Magazine
See: HOUSE ORGANS

LIMAC Newsletter

Publishing Co: Life Insurance Managers Association of Canada, 1 Queen St. E., Suite 1700, Toronto, ON M5C 2X9 Canada; Title Tel # (416) 359-2000 Title Fax # (416) 359-9173
Personnel: Editor-Gordon Dunn
General Info: Yr. Est. 1976, Quarterly, 4 pages
Circulation: Total-900

Law of Liability Insurance, The
See: LAW

Law of Life and Health Insurance, The
See: LAW

Legal Notes for Insurance   *Business*

Publishing Co: Data Research, Inc., 4635 Nicols Rd Ste 100, Eagan, MN 55122-3337;
Title Tel # (612) 452-8267 Title Fax # (612) 452-8694
Editorial Description: Summaries of court decisions dealing with insurance law.
General Info: Yr. Est. 1982, Monthly, Trim Size-8½ x 11, Sheetfed press, 8 pages, ISSN: 0094-0623, No Color, Newsprint
Subscriptions: Indv. $116, $7/copy
Circulation: Total-2,000
Printing Co: Helgeson Press, 7600 14th Ave S, Richfield, MN 55423-4530 Tel # (612) 869-6828

Liability Week

Publishing Co: J.R. Publishing, Inc., PO Box 6654, Mc Lean, VA 22106-6654;
Title Tel # (703) 532-2235 Title Fax # (703) 532-2236
Personnel: Publisher, Editor-John Reistrup, Circ. Dir.-Catherine Wolhowe
Editorial Description: Reports on political, judicial, and regulatory developments affecting liability.
General Info: Yr. Est. 1986, Weekly, Ind/Abs/Online: Newsnet
Subscriptions: Indv. $495

Life in General
See: HOUSE ORGANS

Life Insurance International   *Business*
Publishing Co: Lafferty Publications, 420 Lexington Ave., Ste. 1745, New York, NY 10170
    Tel # (212) 557-6729 Fax # (212) 557-7266; Title Tel # (404) 634-6610 Title Fax # (404) 634-6422
Personnel: Publisher-Frank Lawson, Editor in Chief-Michael Lafferty, Editor-Aine Coney
Editorial Description: Life Insurance Intl. provides news, intelligence on trends, strategy, marketing &
    distribution, products & services, legislation, leading figures and case studies in the insurance
    industry worldwide.
General Info: 10x/yr.
Subscriptions: Indv. $1,079

LifeLine / Vitalite
Publishing Co: Empire Financial Group, 259 King St. East, Kingston, ON K7L 3A8 Canada;
    Title Tel # (613) 548-1881 Title Fax # (613) 548-3854
Personnel: Editor-Amy Fisher
Editorial Description: Publication for agents of Empire Financial Group.
General Info: (Formerly Builder), Yr. Est. 1936, Monthly, Trim Size-8½ x 11, Web press, 6 pages, 2
    Color, Coated
Circulation: Total-1,200
Printing Co: Brown & Martin Ltd., 624 Justus Dr., Kingston, ON K7M 4H4 Canada
    Tel # (613) 389-6611

Lifetime
See: HOUSE ORGANS

Lloyd's Insurance
International   *Business*
Publishing Co: Lloyd's of London Press, 611 Broadway Rm 308, New York, NY 10012-2608;
    Title Tel # (212) 529-9500 Title Fax # (212) 529-9826
Personnel: Publisher-Don Wall, Editor-Robert Cox
Editorial Description: A survey of the global insurance markets.
General Info: Yr. Est. 1987, Monthly
Subscriptions: Indv. $265, For. $280

Malvern Examiner   *Business, Association*
Publishing Co: American Inst. for Chartered Property Casualty Underwriters, 720 Providence Road,
    PO Box 3016, Malvern, PA 19355-0716; Title Tel # (610) 644-2100 Title Fax # (610) 644-7629
Personnel: Editor-Karen Burger
Editorial Description: Contains news of Institute programs, services, materials, and activities. For
    current institute students.
General Info: Yr. Est. 1982, Annually, Trim Size-8½ x 11, Web press, 12 pages, 2 Color, Matte,
    Saddle-stitched
Subscriptions: Free
Circulation: Total-160,000

Managed Dental Care
See: EMPLOYMENT

Market Health News   *Consumer*
Publishing Co: Blue Cross, Blue Shield of Delaware, One Brandywine Gateway, Box 1991,
    Wilmington, DE 19899 Tel # (302) 421-3000 Fax # (302) 421-2058; Title Tel # (302) 421-3301
Personnel: Editor-Deborah Chase, Art Dir.-Sandra Gordenstein
Editorial Description: Blue Cross & Blue Shield benefits, projects, markets, membership information,
    profiles.
General Info: (Formerly Blue Cross and Blue Shield Health News Report), Yr. Est. 1987, Monthly,
    Trim Size-11 x 15, Offset press, 6 pages, Color
Circulation: Total-7,000
Printing Co: General Learning Corp., 60 Revere Dr, Northbrook, IL 60062-8002 Tel # (708) 205-3000

Mealey's Insurance Supplement
See: LAW

Mealey's Litigation Report: Asbestos
See: LAW

Mealey's Litigation Report: Bad Faith
See: LAW

Mealey's Litigation Report: Insurance
See: LAW

Mealey's Litigation Report:
Insurance Fraud   *Business*
Publishing Co: Mealey Publications, Inc., PO Box 446, Wayne, PA 19087-0446;
    Title Tel # (610) 688-6566 Title Fax # (610) 688-7552
Personnel: Publisher-Michael Mealey, Editor-John Hayes, Mktg. Dir.-Kathy Roach
Editorial Description: Industry news on insurance fraud.
General Info: Yr. Est. 1994, Semi-monthly, Trim Size-8½ x 11, 90 pages, ISSN: 1075-380X
Subscriptions: Indv. $550, For. $670, $50/copy

Mealey's Litigation Report: Insurance Insolvency
See: LAW

Mealey's Litigation Report: Product Liability
See: LAW

Mealey's Litigation Report: Reinsurance
See: LAW

Medical Benefits
See: HEALTH

Medical Practice Risk Manager
See: MEDICINE

Medicare Advisor
See: HOSPITALS & NURSING HOMES

Medicare Manager
See: MEDICINE

Medicare Review
See: MEDICINE

Mercer Bulletin, The
See: INDUSTRIAL RELATIONS/PERSONNEL

Model Laws, Regulations
and Guidelines   *Business, Association*
Publishing Co: National Association of Insurance Commissioners, 120 W. 12th St., Ste. 1100,
    Kansas City, MO 64105-1925; Title Tel # (816) 842-3600 Title Fax # (816) 471-7004
Personnel: Editor-Carolyn Johnson
Editorial Description: All model laws adopted by NAIC & state action on each.Includes some
    legislative history and case history.
General Info: Yr. Est. 1984, Quarterly, Trim Size-8½ x 11, Mimeo press, 400 pages, No Color,
    Newsprint, Looseleaf
Subscriptions: Indv. $295, $250/copy
Circulation: Total-1,700

Mutual Piper, The
Publishing Co: Professional Ins. Comm. of America, C/O Natl. Assn. of Mutual Ins., 3601 Vincennes
    Rd. Box 68700, Indianapolis, IN 46268-0700; Title Tel # (317) 875-5250
Personnel: Editor-Janet Goyne
General Info: Yr. Est. 1970, Quarterly, 8 pages

NAIC News, The   *Business, Association*
Publishing Co: National Association of Insurance Commissioners, 120 W. 12th St., Ste. 1100,
    Kansas City, MO 64105-1925; Title Tel # (816) 842-3600 Title Fax # (816) 471-7004
Personnel: Editor-Eva Malecki
Editorial Description: Summarizes current NAIC and insurance regulation activities.
General Info: Yr. Est. 1984, Monthly, Trim Size-8½ x 11, 8 pages, 2 Color, Saddle-stitched
Subscriptions: Indv. $200
Circulation: Total-2,400, Readership-2,800

NAPIA Bulletin
Publishing Co: Natl. Assn. of Public Insurance Adjusters, 300 Water St., Baltimore, MD 21202
    Tel # (410) 539-4141; Title Tel # (301) 539-4141
Personnel: Editor-Paul L. Cordish
General Info: Bi-monthly

NAPSLO Newsletter
Publishing Co: Natl. Assn. of Professional Surplus Line Offices, 6405 N. Cosby Avenue #201,
    Kansas City, MO 64151-3963; Title Tel # (816) 455-3210 Title Fax # (816) 454-8068
Personnel: Publisher, Editor-Mark Graham
Editorial Description: Association & industry news.
General Info: Yr. Est. 1975, Bi-monthly, Trim Size-8½ x 11, Sheetfed press, 8 pages, 2 Color,
    Saddle-stitched
Circulation: Total-1,500
Printing Co: Arrow Press, 2nd & East St., Parkville, MO 64152 Tel # (816) 741-0241

NARI Stethoscope
See: MEDICINE

National Auditor, The   *Association*
Publishing Co: Natl. Society of Insurance Premium Auditors, PO Box 68401, Indianapolis, IN
    46268-0401; Title Tel # (317) 253-0943
Personnel: Publisher, Editor-Richard Knarr
Editorial Description: Professional society newsletter for insurance auditors.
General Info: Yr. Est. 1976, Bi-monthly, Sheetfed press, 4 pages, ISSN: 0748-3961, No Color,
    Newsprint
Subscriptions: Indv. $45
Circulation: Total-1,300

New Era/Nova Doba
See: CLUBS

New Jersey Insurance Law and Regulation Reporter
See: LAW

New York Insurance Law
See: LAW

New York No-Fault Arbitration Reports

Publishing Co: American Arbitration Assn., 140 W. 51 St., New York, NY 10020-1203
Tel # (212) 484-4000 Fax # (212) 541-4841; Title Tel # (212) 484-4013 Title Fax # (212) 765-4874
Personnel: Editor-Richard Wentzler, Circ. Dir.-Nadine Stevens
Editorial Description: Report of no-fault arbitration decisions in New York State. The decisions resolve disputes involving personal injuries arising through use of operation of automobiles.
General Info: Yr. Est. 1977, Monthly, Trim Size-8½ x 11, Sheetfed press, 8 pages, ISSN: 0193-7693, Looseleaf
Subscriptions: Indv. $95
Circulation: Total-800
Printing Co: Benchemark Printing, 31 Lafayette St, Schenectady, NY 12305-2007

New York Reporter

Publishing Co: Royal-Globe Insurance Cos., 1 Chase Manhattan Plz., 38th Fl., New York, NY 10005-1401 Tel # (212) 553-3000; Title Tel # (212) 732-8400
Personnel: Editor-Virginia McLeod
General Info: Semi-annually
Circulation: Total-3,000

Newsletter
See: HOUSE ORGANS

No-Fault and Uninsured Motorist Automobile Insurance
See: LAW

Outlook *Consumer*

Publishing Co: United Olympic Life Insurance, 4601 Fairfax Dr., Arlington, VA 22203-1500; Title Tel # (703) 875-3521 Title Fax # (703) 875-3677
Personnel: Editor-Sandra Roth
Editorial Description: General interest for insurance policyowners.
General Info: Yr. Est. 1975, Semi-annually, Trim Size-8½ x 11, Sheetfed press, 8 pages, 2 Color, Coated, Saddle-stitched
Circulation: (100% controlled), Total-90,000

PPO Letter, The
See: HOSPITALS & NURSING HOMES

PRISM *Business, Association*

Publishing Co: Public Risk Insurance Services & Management, Inc., 411 E 3rd Ave, Eugene, OR 97401-2403; Title Tel # (503) 686-0168
Personnel: Editor-Loretta Gale
Editorial Description: Covers issues in the public risk insurance industry.
General Info: Quarterly, Trim Size-8½ x 11, 4 pages, 2 Color, Matte

Pension Actuary, The *Business, Association*

Publishing Co: American Society of Pension Actuaries, 4350 Fairfax Dr Ste 820, Arlington, VA 22203-1621; Title Tel # (703) 516-9300 Title Fax # (703) 516-9308
Personnel: Editor-Chester Salkind, Production Mgr.-Lynn McGee
Editorial Description: Covers the private pension system.
General Info: Yr. Est. 1966, Monthly, Trim Size-8½ x 11, Web press, 16 pages, Ind/Abs/Online: PIX BBS, Color, Coated, Saddle-stitched
Subscriptions: Free With Membership
Circulation: Total-4,000
List Rental: Rents Lists
Printing Co: District Creative Printing, 6350 Fallard Dr, Upper Marlboro, MD 20772-3885 Tel # (301) 868-8610, Fax # (301) 868-1015

Personal Lines Letter

Publishing Co: Shelby Publishing Corp, 155 Federal Street, Boston, MA 02110-1727 Parent Co.-Standard Publishing, Boston; Title Tel # (617) 423-0778
General Info: Monthly
List Rental: Actives: $120/M, Expires: $65/M

Policies in Review

Publishing Co: Shelby Publishing Corp, 155 Federal Street, Boston, MA 02110-1727 Parent Co.-Standard Publishing, Boston; Title Tel # (617) 423-0978 Title Fax # (617) 482-7820
Personnel: Publisher-John Cross, Editor-Roger Pierce, Circ. Mgr.-Kelly Westover, Production Mgr.-Lauren Lombardi, Mktg. Dir.-Wendy Kenniston
Editorial Description: Non-standard, excess, & surplus lines.
General Info: Monthly, 44 pages
Subscriptions: Indv. $227, Can. $295, For. $295, $16/copy
List Rental: Rents Lists

Producer News *Business*

Publishing Co: Barlist Publishing Company, Box 948, Northbrook, IL 60065
Personnel: Publisher-Charles Kaltenthaler, Editor-George Smith, Circ. Mgr.-Doris Pifer
Editorial Description: Syndicated newsletter, marketing tool for MGAS in the prop-liab excess/surplus lines area.
General Info: Yr. Est. 1976, Monthly, Trim Size-8½ x 11, Sheetfed press, 4 pages, No Color, Newsprint
Subscriptions: Indv. $27
Circulation: Total-27,000
Printing Co: Insurance Field Co., 1812 Production Ct, Louisville, KY 40299-2102 Tel # (502) 491-5857, Fax # (502) 491-5905

Producers Pipeline *Association*

Publishing Co: Natl. Assn. of Surety Bond Producers, 5301 Wisconsin Ave NW Ste 450, Washington, DC 20015-2015; Title Tel # (202) 686-3700 Title Fax # (202) 686-3656
Personnel: Editor-J. Martin Huber
Editorial Description: Developments of interest to contract surety agents.
General Info: Monthly, Offset press, 4 pages
Circulation: Total-1,500

Professional Development Tips

Publishing Co: Insurance Institute of America, 720 Providence Rd, Malvern, PA 19355-3443 Fax # (610) 251-9995; Title Tel # (610) 644-2100 Title Fax # (610) 644-7629
Personnel: Publisher-Anne Swigait
General Info: Trim Size-8.5 x 11, Sheetfed press, 2 pages, No Color, Coated, Other
Subscriptions: Free
Circulation: Total-750

Professional Liability Insurance *Business*

Publishing Co: International Risk Management Institute, 12222 Merit Dr Ste 1660, Dallas, TX 75251-3207; Title Tel # (214) 960-7693 Title Fax # (214) 960-6037
Editorial Description: Identifies exposures of a wide range of professionals and explains policies and markets that cover them.
General Info: Yr. Est. 1991, Quarterly, Looseleaf
Subscriptions: Indv. $231

Provider, The
See: HOUSE ORGANS

Public Health/State Capitals
See: HEALTH

Query *Consumer*

Publishing Co: American Society of CLU & CFC, 270 S Bryn Mawr Ave, Bryn Mawr, PA 19010-2105; Title Tel # (215) 526-2500
Personnel: Publisher-Deanne Sherman, Editor-Fred Dopheide, Production Mgr.-Robert Titus, Circ. Mgr., Art Dir.-Carl Hall
Editorial Description: Financial and tax planning newsletter.
General Info: Yr. Est. 1952, Monthly, Offset press, 2 pages, ISSN: 0033-6270, No Color, Newsprint
Circulation: Total-75,000
Printing Co: Boyertown Publishing Co., 48 S. Reading Ave., P.O. Box 548, Boyertown, PA 19512 Tel # (215) 367-2121, Fax # (215) 367-7093

RBRVS Fee Schedule : A Plain-English Guide
See: HEALTH

RIC Insight
See: SCIENCE

RIMScope *Association*

Publishing Co: Risk Management Society Publishing, Inc., 655 Third Ave., 2nd Floor, New York, NY 10017 Tel # (212) 286-9364; Title Tel # (212) 286-9292 Title Fax # (212) 986-9716
Personnel: Editor-Tom Johnson
Editorial Description: Internal letter to RIMS membership carries news of risk management/employee benefits field. 100% staff generated. No advertising.
General Info: (Formerly RIMS), Bi-weekly, Trim Size-8½ x 11, 2 pages
Subscriptions: Indv. $200, Can. $210, For. $210
Circulation: Total-8,000

Responsibilities of Insurance Agents and Brokers *Business*

Publishing Co: Matthew Bender & Co., 11 Penn Plaza, New York, NY 10001-2006 Fax # (212) 244-3188; Title Tel # (212) 967-7707
Personnel: Editor-S. Weisenfeld
Editorial Description: Complete guidance on the legal responsibilities of insurance agents & brokers.
General Info: Yr. Est. 1974, Irregular, Looseleaf
Subscriptions: $325/copy

Risk and Insurance's Managing Risk for Loss Prevention & Cost Control *Business*

Publishing Co: LRP Publications, 747 Dresher Rd., P.O. Box 980, Horsham, PA 19044-0980 Tel # (215) 784-0910 Fax # (215) 784-0317
Personnel: Publisher-Ken Kahn, Editor-Marilyn Schaefer, Production Mgr.-Kathleen Neely, Mktg. Dir.-Jana Shellington
Editorial Description: Insurance, risk management, and loss prevention developments affecting business, government.
General Info: (Formerly Loss Prevention & Control; Insurance & Risk Management), Yr. Est. 1979, Bi-weekly, Sheetfed press, 8 pages, ISSN: 0892-5887, 2 Color, Newsprint
Subscriptions: Indv. $398, For. $420
Acquisitions: Publication Bought, Publication Sold
Printing Co: Plymouth Printing, 1200 Cushing Pl SE, Washington, DC 20003-3599 Tel # (202) 488-7777, Fax # (202) 863-1078

Risk Management for the Executive Woman
Business

Publishing Co: Cox Pubs., PO Box 20316, Billings, MT 59104-0316; Title Tel # (406) 256-8822
Personnel: Publisher, Editor-Meridith Cox
Editorial Description: Reports of court decisions affecting insurance, personnel, health records & safety issues which expand liability or set up new areas of risk, helps female executives make effective risk management decisions before developing new policies & procedures or ndertaking new ventures.
General Info: (Formerly Cal Risk Mgr. Report for Female Exec.), Yr. Est. 1982, Bi-monthly, Trim Size-8½ x 11, Sheetfed press, 4 pages, ISSN: 0732-2666, 2 Color
Subscriptions: Indv. $85
Circulation: Total-350
Advertising: Inquire for rates.

Risk Management News
Business

Publishing Co: James E. Mooney & Co., 262 Mountain Ave # 50, Springfield, NJ 07081-2215; Title Tel # (201) 376-3500
Personnel: Publisher-Georgia Woke, Editor-James Mooney
Editorial Description: Reports on risk management & insurance issues.
General Info: Yr. Est. 1975, Monthly, 6 pages, ISSN: 0194-1038
Subscriptions: Indv. $80

Risk Management News/ Risk Management Manual
Business

Publishing Co: Merritt Professional Publishing, 1661 9th St, Santa Monica, CA 90404-3703; Title Tel # (310) 450-7234 Title Fax # (310) 396-4563
Personnel: Editor-James Walsh
Editorial Description: News and developments in the risk management field.
General Info: Bi-weekly, Trim Size-8½ x 11, 4 pages, No Color, Newsprint
Subscriptions: Indv. $397
Circulation: Total-1,000

Risk Report
Business

Publishing Co: International Risk Management Institute, 12222 Merit Dr Ste 1660, Dallas, TX 75251-3207; Title Tel # (214) 960-7693 Title Fax # (214) 960-6037
Personnel: Editor-Jack Gibson, Circ. Mgr.-Cathy Roberts
Editorial Description: Addresses subjects pertaining to risk management.
General Info: Yr. Est. 1979, Monthly, Trim Size-8½ x 11, Web press, 12 pages, ISSN: 0197-7539, No Color, Coated, Saddle-stitched
Subscriptions: Indv. $149, Can. $174
Acquistions: Publication Bought

Riskwatch
Business

Publishing Co: Public Risk Management Assn., 1815 Ft. Myer Drive, 10th Floor, Arlington, VA 22209 Fax # (703) 528-7766; Title Tel # (703) 528-7701 Title Fax # (703) 528-7966
Personnel: Editor-Dawn Stapleton
Editorial Description: Current events bulletin for public sector risk managers.
General Info: Monthly, Trim Size-8½ x 11, 6 pages, 2 Color, Coated
Subscriptions: Indv. $125
Circulation: Total-2,300
Printing Co: Serif Press, Inc., 1331 H St. NW, #110LL, Washington, DC 20005 Tel # (202) 737-4650

Royal Arcanum Bulletin

Publishing Co: Supreme Council of the Royal Arcanum, 61 Batterymarch St., Boston, MA 02110-3206; Title Tel # (617) 426-4135
General Info: Bi-monthly

SWAAA Newsletter
Association

Publishing Co: Southwest Assn of Affiliated Agencies, 1601 Rio Grande St Ste 440, Austin, TX 78701-1149; Title Tel # (512) 479-0425
Personnel: Editor-Lisa Fry
Editorial Description: Official publication of the Southwest Association of Affiliated Agencies
General Info: Quarterly, Trim Size-8½ x 11, Offset press, 8 pages, No Color, Coated
Subscriptions: Free With Membership
Advertising: Inquire for rates.
Printing Co: Austex Printing Co., 501 W 3rd St, Austin, TX 78701-3807 Tel # (512) 476-7581

Sanus Healthy Update
See: HEALTH

Security Letter
See: SECURITY & SURVEILLANCE

Sextant
Association

Publishing Co: Gamma Iota Sigma, 1775 S College Rd, Columbus, OH 43210-1309; Title Tel # (614) 292-0083
Personnel: Editor-Dr. Alan Williams
Editorial Description: News and information about and for local chapters (student/insurance/professional).
General Info: Yr. Est. 1965, Semi-annually, Trim Size-8½ x 11, Letrpr. press, 6 pages, 2 Color
Circulation: Total-2,000

Smart's California Worker's Comp Bulletin
Business

Publishing Co: James Whitaker & Associates, 1 Waters Park Dr., Ste. 104, San Mateo, CA 94403-1137 Fax # (415) 341-3304; Title Tel # (415) 341-2432
Personnel: Publisher-James Whitaker, Editor-Frederick Pilot
Editorial Description: Covers news and events of California's workers comp industry.
General Info: (Formerly Smart's Insurance Bulletin: Worker's Comp Edition), Yr. Est. 1992, Weekly, Trim Size-8.5 x 11, 4 pages, ISSN: 1070-020X, No Color, Matte, Case bound
Subscriptions: Indv. $297
Circulation: Total-350, Readership-350

Smart's Insurance Bulletin
Business

Publishing Co: James Whitaker & Associates, 1 Waters Park Dr., Ste. 104, San Mateo, CA 94403-1137; Title Tel # (415) 341-2432 Title Fax # (415) 341-3304
Personnel: Publisher-James Whitaker, Editor-Frederick Pilot
Editorial Description: Property-casualty insurance industry developments and news.
General Info: Yr. Est. 1957, Weekly, Trim Size-8.5 x 11, Desktop press, 4 pages, ISSN: 0736-8348, No Color, Matte
Subscriptions: Indv. $297
Circulation: Total-400, Readership-400

Smart's National Comp & Health Bulletin
Business

Publishing Co: James Whitaker & Associates, 1 Waters Park Dr., Ste. 104, San Mateo, CA 94403-1137; Title Tel # (415) 341-2432 Title Fax # (415) 341-3304
Personnel: Publisher-James Whitaker, Editor-Frederick Pilot
Editorial Description: News and analysis on national worker's comp and health news.
General Info: Yr. Est. 1993, Weekly, Trim Size-8.5 x 11, 4 pages, ISSN: 1070-0226, No Color, Matte
Subscriptions: Indv. $327
List Rental: Rents Lists

Social Security Practice Guide
See: LAW

Society Page
Association

Publishing Co: American Society of CLU & ChFC, 270 S Bryn Mawr Ave # 59, Bryn Mawr, PA 19010-2105 Tel # (610) 526-2500 Fax # (610) 526-2538; Title Tel # (215) 526-2500
Personnel: Publisher, Editor-Deanne Sherman, Mng. Editor, Production Mgr.-Carl Hall
Editorial Description: News and articles of interest to members of the American Society of CLU & CLFC.
General Info: Yr. Est. 1961, Bi-monthly, Trim Size-8¼ x 10¾, Web press, 32 pages, 2 Color
Circulation: (100% controlled), Total-33,309
Printing Co: Mack Printing Group, 1991 Northampton St., Easton, PA 18042-3189 Tel # (610) 250-7261, Fax # (610) 250-7211

Solutions: an idea exchange for CPCU and IIA course leaders
Business

Publishing Co: American Inst. for Chartered Property Casualty Underwriters, 720 Providence Road, PO Box 3016, Malvern, PA 19355-0716; Title Tel # (610) 644-2100 Title Fax # (610) 644-7629
Personnel: Editor-Cynthia Candelaria, Editor-Anne Swigart
Editorial Description: Published for leaders of Institute courses. Contains practical ideas on classroom formats, teaching tips, motivation and solving teaching related problems.
General Info: Yr. Est. 1991, Semi-annually, Trim Size-8½ x 11, Sheetfed press, 6 pages, 2 Color, Matte, Saddle-stitched
Subscriptions: Free
Circulation: Total-6,000

Specialty Capitation Manual: Rate Setting, Evaluation and Implementation
See: HEALTH

Specialty Coverage Market Reports

Publishing Co: Rough Notes Company, Inc., 11690 Technology Dr., Carmel, IN 46032-5600 Tel # (317) 582-1600 Fax # (317) 816-1000; Title Tel # (317) 634-1541 Title Fax # (317) 634-1041
Personnel: Editor-Wallace Clapp, Jr.
Editorial Description: Insurance industry news and information.
General Info: Yr. Est. 1968, Monthly, 8 pages
Subscriptions: Indv. $65
Circulation: Total-1,500

Spencer's Compliance Guide for Health & Benefit Plans
See: TAXES

Spencer's Research Reports on Employee Benefits
See: INDUSTRIAL RELATIONS/PERSONNEL

Spotlight
Association

Publishing Co: Blue Cross Blue Shield United of Wisconsin, 401 W Michigan St, Milwaukee, WI 53203-2804
General Info: Monthly
Circulation: Total-1,750

Standard & Poor's Insurance Ratings   *Business*

Publishing Co: Standard & Poor's Corp., 25 Broadway, New York, NY 10004 Tel # (212) 208-8000
Parent Co.-McGraw-Hill, New York; Title Tel # (212) 208-1592
Personnel: Publisher-Robert Frump, Editor-Robert Keane
Editorial Description: Updated ratings of insurance groups and companies.
General Info: Monthly

State Life Bulletin   *Business*

Publishing Co: State Life Insurance Co, PO Box 406, Indianapolis, IN 46206-0406;
Title Tel # (317) 632-3551
Personnel: Editor-Cindy Graham
Editorial Description: To serve as a communication between home office and field agencies.
General Info: (Formerly Link, The), Monthly, Trim Size-8½ x 11, Letrpr. press, 10 pages, 2 Color
Subscriptions: $2/copy
Circulation: (100% controlled), Total-700

Strategies
See: INVESTMENT

Sur le Champ

Publishing Co: Les Cooperants, Societe Mutuelle d'Assurance-Vie, 600, boul. de Maisonneuve
Ques, Montreal, PQ H3A 3J9 Canada; Title Tel # (514) 287-6500 Title Fax # (514) 287-6514
Editorial Description: Sales division.

Tempo
See: HOUSE ORGANS

Tips & Trends

Publishing Co: Travelers Corp., 1 Tower Sq, Hartford, CT 06115-1501
General Info: Quarterly

Travelers Protective Association of America, Bulletin   *Association*

Publishing Co: Travelers Protective Association, 3755 Lindell Blvd, Saint Louis, MO 63108-3476
Tel # (314) 371-0533 Fax # (314) 371-0537
Personnel: Publisher-W.J Karle, Jr.
General Info: Yr. Est. 1890, Monthly
Circulation: (100% controlled), Total-2,500

Uniter, The

Publishing Co: United Olympic Life Insurance, 4601 Fairfax Dr., Arlington, VA 22203-1500;
Title Tel # (703) 875-3521 Title Fax # (703) 875-3677
Personnel: Editor-Grace Mataya
Editorial Description: Marketing publication ofor field force of United Services Life Insurance Co.
General Info: Yr. Est. 1948, Monthly, Trim Size-8½ x 11, Sheetfed press, 8 pages, 2 Color, Coated
Circulation: Total-715

Valuation Quarterly

Publishing Co: Marshall & Stevens, 707 Wilshire Blvd., Ste. 5200, Los Angeles, CA 90017-3614;
Title Tel # (213) 624-6451
Editorial Description: Guide to arriving at the replacement cost of building. Covers wide range of
typical buildings includes depreciation and insurance exclusion suggestions. Primarily commercial
properties.
General Info: Yr. Est. 1936, Quarterly, Trim Size-6 x 9, Offset press, 25 pages, Looseleaf

WAEPA Record

Publishing Co: Worldwide Assurance for Employees of Public Agencies, 7651 Leesburg Pike, Falls
Church, VA 22043-2520; Title Tel # (703) 790-8010
General Info: Quarterly

Workers' Comp Advisor
See: INDUSTRIAL RELATIONS/PERSONNEL

Workers' Comp Executive   *Business*

Publishing Co: Commanon Corp., PO Box 1100, Grass Valley, CA 95945-1100 Tel # (916) 268-3900
Fax # (916) 268-2200; Title Tel # (916) 477-8500 Title Fax # (916) 477-8600
Personnel: Publisher-J. Dale Debber, Editor-John P. McCann, Circ. Mgr.-Gary Nodine, Adv. Dir.-Ken
Page, Promotion Dir.-Mark Fukui
Editorial Description: For professionals in the workers comp industry.
General Info: Yr. Est. 1990, Semi-monthly, 12 pages
Subscriptions: Indv. $395

Worker's Comp Managed Care
See: HOSPITALS & NURSING HOMES

Workers' Comp Practice Advisor
See: MEDICINE

INTERIOR DESIGN & DECORATION

AGSA Newsletter
See: GLASS, STONE & CLAY

CAUS News
See: TEXTILES

Decorator's Insider   *Business, Consumer*

Publishing Co: Decorator's Insider, 38 Grove Street, New York, NY 10014;
Title Tel # (212) 620-0435
Personnel: Publisher-Lemeau Arrott-Watt
Editorial Description: Interior decorating and designer tips and information from designer Lemeau
Arrott-Watt.
General Info: 10x/yr.
Subscriptions: Indv. $40

FIO Covering Ontario

Publishing Co: Floorcovering Institute of Ontario, 25 Clairville Dr., Rexdale, ON M9W 5Z7 Canada;
Title Tel # (416) 675-4332
Personnel: Publisher, Editor, Art Dir.-Zoltan Vertes
Editorial Description: An educational digest of current floor covering information relative to pricing,
news products, sales techniques, trends, people, problems & concerns & events.
General Info: Yr. Est. 1962, Bi-monthly, Trim Size-8½ x 11, Sheetfed press, 8 pages, 1% ads, 2
Color, Coated, Saddle-stitched
Subscriptions: Indv. $50, $5/copy
Acquistions: Publication Bought, Publication Sold
Circulation: (100% controlled), Total-500
Advertising: Inquire for rates. Accepts Inserts.
List Rental: Actives: $125/M

IFMA News
See: CONSTRUCTION & BUILDING

IFTA Network

Publishing Co: Intl. Furnishings & Design Assn., 107 World Trade Ctr., Box 58045, Dallas, TX
75258; Title Tel # (214) 747-2406
Personnel: Editor-Eric Harschhorn
General Info: (Formerly NHFL), Yr. Est. 1966, Quarterly, 4 pages
Circulation: Total-2,000

Interior Concerns Newsletter
See: ENVIRONMENT & ECOLOGY

Interior Fashion News
See: FURNITURE & HOME FURNISHINGS

Kendall College of Art and Design
See: COLLEGE STUDENT

Nari Focus
See: CONSTRUCTION & BUILDING

Newsletter Seattle Design   *Business*

Publishing Co: Seattle Design, 2601 Elliott Ave Ste 4119, Seattle, WA 98121-1326;
Title Tel # (206) 328-2725
Personnel: Publisher-Barry Senter
General Info: Quarterly

Potpourri Simple & Easy Update
See: GIFTS, GAMES, TOYS

Scenterpiece Update
See: GIFTS, GAMES, TOYS

Southwest Cleaning

Publishing Co: Sunbelt, PO Box 796575, Dallas, TX 75379-6575; Title Tel # (214) 484-4474
Personnel: Editor-Howard Clark
Editorial Description: Presents current information on the drapery, upholstery and carpet cleaning
industry.
General Info: Bi-monthly, ISSN: 0279-6902

Streamline   *Business, Association*

Publishing Co: Art Deco Society of the Palm Beaches, 325 SW 29th Ave., Delray Beach, FL
33445-4409; Title Tel # (407) 276-9925 Title Fax # (407) 276-9925
Personnel: Editor-Sharon Koskoff, Production Mgr.-David Bittner
Editorial Description: Devoted to preservation, education, and awareness of twentieth century
design and architecture.
General Info: Yr. Est. 1987, Quarterly, Sheetfed press, 8 pages, 20% ads
Subscriptions: $4/copy
Advertising: $200.

Terrazzo Topics   *Association*

Publishing Co: Natl. Terrazo & Mosaic Association, 3166 Des Plaines Ave., Suite 132, Des Plaines,
IL 60018-4204
General Info: 10x/yr., ISSN: 0040-3806
Circulation: Total-1,500

INTERNATIONAL AFFAIRS

14-Point Program to Reform and Restructure the U.N. System
See: GOVERNMENT

AALC Reporter
See: LABOR UNION

ACOA Action News   *Association*

Publishing Co: American Committee on Africa, 17 John St Fl 12, New York, NY 10038-4010; Title Tel # (212) 962-1210
Personnel: Editor-Rachael Kagan
Editorial Description: Reports on the activities of the American Committee on Africa, anti-apartheid activities on the federal, state & local levels, divestment & resources.
General Info: Irregular, Trim Size-8½ x 11, 6 pages
Subscriptions: Indv. $15, Inst. $25
Circulation: Total-5,000

ADRIS Newsletter
See: COMPUTERS & AUTOMATION

ANERA Newsletter   *Association*

Publishing Co: American Near East Refugee Aid, 1522 K St NW Ste 202, Washington, DC 20005-1202; Title Tel # (202) 347-2558 Title Fax # (202) 682-1637
Personnel: Publisher, Editor-Paula Stinson
Editorial Description: Issues relating to the Palestinians & Lebanese, especially community & economic development in the West Bank & Gaza Strip.
General Info: Yr. Est. 1972, Quarterly, Trim Size-8½ x 11, Offset press, 4 pages, No Color
Circulation: Total-30,000

APLIC International Communicator
See: LIBRARY

ARZA Report   *Association*

Publishing Co: Assn. of Reform Zionists of America, 838 5th Ave, New York, NY 10021-7012; Title Tel # (212) 249-0100 Title Fax # (212) 517-7968
Personnel: Editor-Ammiel Hirsch
Editorial Description: Update of ARZA activities; promotes support for Israel and the Progressive Movement there.
General Info: Yr. Est. 1977, Quarterly, Trim Size-12 x 18, Sheetfed press, 8 pages, 2 Color
Circulation: Total-55,000

ASA News   *Consumer, Association*   **CPM:** $9

Publishing Co: ASA Communications,Inc., 222 Merchandise Mart #1360, Chicago, IL 60654 Tel # (312) 464-0090 Fax # (312) 464-0091; Title Tel # (404) 329-6410
Personnel: Publisher-Edna Bay, Editor in Chief-Inge Calderon, Circ. Mgr.-Alan Rucinski, Editor, Circ. Mgr.-Eric Wright
Editorial Description: Research in Africa, African studies in the U.S. and abroad; employment and fellowships available.
General Info: (Formerly ASA Newsletter), Yr. Est. 1968, Bi-monthly, Trim Size-6 x 9, Offset press, 36 pages, ISSN: 0278-2219, No Color
Subscriptions: Indv. $40, Inst. $48, $5/copy
Circulation: (BPA, 100% controlled As of 06/30/95), Total-13,262
Advertising: $125.

ASC Newsletter

Publishing Co: African Studies Center, Univ. of California, Los Angeles, 405 Hilgard Ave, Los Angeles, CA 90024-1301; Title Tel # (213) 825-3779
Personnel: Editor-Merrick Posnansky, Circ. Mgr., Production Mgr.-S. Clarke-Ekong
Editorial Description: Profiles of visiting scholars, description of research.
General Info: Yr. Est. 1970, Semi-annually
Subscriptions: Free
Circulation: Total-2,500

A.S.I.F (Americans Seeking International Franchises)
See: INTERNATIONAL TRADE

Abstract of International Economic Trend Analysis
See: ECONOMICS

African Insider

Publishing Co: African Insider, Box 53398, Temple Heights Station, Washington, DC 20009
Editorial Description: News and current developments in Africa.
General Info: Yr. Est. 1984, Semi-monthly, Trim Size-8½ x 11, 4 pages, 2 Color, Saddle-stitched
Subscriptions: Indv. $75, Inst. $150

Alternative Trading News   *Association*

Publishing Co: Friends of the Third World, Inc., 611 W Wayne St, Fort Wayne, IN 46802-2125; Title Tel # (219) 422-6821 Title Fax # (219) 422-1650
Personnel: Publisher-Marian Waltz, Editor-Jim Goetsch, Circ. Mgr.-Fred Shaheen
Editorial Description: Domestic & international voluntary action against poverty, focus on marketing.
General Info: (Formerly Friends in Action), Yr. Est. 1981, Quarterly, Trim Size-8½ x 11, Sheetfed press, 12 pages, 2 Color, Recycled, Other
Subscriptions: Indv. $10, Inst. $10, Free With Membership
Circulation: Total-10,000
Printing Co: Delta Communication Printing Co-op, 611 W Wayne St, Fort Wayne, IN 46802-2125 Tel # (219) 425-1650

America Update

Publishing Co: Latin American Working Group, 603 1/2 Parliament St., Toronto, ON M4X 1P9 Canada Fax # (416) 921-0071; Title Tel # (416) 966-4775 Title Fax # (416) 921-0081
Editorial Description: News & analysis of events in the Americas & Canadian policy towards the region. Focus on grassroots movements and critical analysis.
General Info: (Formerly Nicaragua Update / Central America Update), Yr. Est. 1978, Bi-monthly, Trim Size-8½ x 11, Desktop press, 12 pages, ISSN: 0823-7689, Ind/Abs/Online: NewsNet, DIALOG, Predicasts, No Color, Newsprint, Saddle-stitched
Subscriptions: Indv. $25, Inst. $40, $5/copy
Circulation: Total-1,000

American Foreign Policy Entrance

Publishing Co: Natl. Committee on American Foreign Policy, Inc., 320 Park Ave., New York, NY 10022; Title Tel # (212) 224-1120 Title Fax # (212) 224-2524
Personnel: Editor-George Schwab
Editorial Description: Pertinent high quality views on intl. relations.
General Info: Yr. Est. 1976, Bi-monthly, Offset press, 14 pages, ISSN: 0738-3169, No Color
Subscriptions: Indv. $10, $2/copy
Circulation: Total-1,200
Printing Co: Brooklyn Letter Service, 26 Court St., Brooklyn, NY 11217 Tel # (718) 624-4632

American Society of International Law Newsletter
See: LAW

Americans for the Univ. of UNESCO Newsletter

Publishing Co: Americans for the Univ. of UNESCO, PO Box 18418, Asheville, NC 28814-0418; Title Tel # (704) 253-5383 Title Fax # (704) 252-6930
Personnel: Publisher, Editor-John Fobes, Production Mgr.-Jeff Fobes
Editorial Description: Promotes US involvement in UNESCO & multilateral cooperation.
General Info: Yr. Est. 1985, Quarterly, Sheetfed press, 20 pages, No Color, Saddle-stitched
Subscriptions: Indv. $25
Circulation: Total-3,200

Anglofile
See: ENTERTAINMENT

Antarctica Project Newsletter, The
See: ENVIRONMENT & ECOLOGY

Arab-Asian Affairs   *Business*

Publishing Co: World Reports Ltd., 280 Madison Ave Rm 1209, New York, NY 10016-0801; Title Tel # (212) 689-7442 Title Fax # (212) 481-0915
Personnel: Publisher, Editor-Christopher Story
General Info: 10x/yr.
Subscriptions: Indv. $135
Acquistions: Publication Bought

Arab Voice
See: CULTURE & HUMANITIES

Arms Control Reporter

Publishing Co: Inst. for Defense & Disarmament Studies, 675 Massachusetts Ave., Cambridge, MA 02139-3309; Title Tel # (617) 354-4337 Title Fax # (617) 354-1450
Personnel: Publisher-Randall Forsberg, Editor-Gregory Webb, Circ. Dir.-Matteo Luccio
Editorial Description: Comprehensive reference on arms control negotiations, treaties & proposals.
General Info: Yr. Est. 1982, 11x/yr., Trim Size-6½ x 9, Offset press, 75 pages, ISSN: 0886-3490, 4 Color, Looseleaf
Subscriptions: Indv. $175, Inst. $375, Can. $385, For. $385
Circulation: Total-400
Advertising: Inquire for rates. Accepts Inserts.
List Rental: Rents Lists
Printing Co: Pressworks International, 26 Fox Rd, Waltham, MA 02154-1007 Tel # (617) 890-4433

AsiaPacific Briefing Paper

Publishing Co: East-West Center, 1777 East-West Rd., Honolulu, HI 96848-0001
Editorial Description: Reports on research of importance and issues critical to the Asia-Pacific region.
General Info: Yr. Est. 1991, Monthly

Asian Political News

Publishing Co: Kyodo News Intl., 50 Rockefeller Plaza #803, New York, NY 10020-1605; Title Tel # (212) 397-3723 Title Fax # (212) 397-3721
Editorial Description: Current political issues in Asian countries.
General Info: Yr. Est. 1989, Weekly

Aura Wealth Newsletter
See: INVESTMENT

Australia Report

Publishing Co: Australian High Commission, 50 O'Connor St., Ottawa, ON K1P 6L2 Canada; Title Tel # (613) 236-0841
Personnel: Editor-Robert Pounds
Editorial Description: Review of major news items from Australia.
General Info: Yr. Est. 1982, Bi-weekly, Trim Size-8½ x 11, Sheetfed press, 4 pages, No Color
Circulation: Total-1,200
Printing Co: Zippy Printers, 264 Albert St., Ottawa, ON K1P 5G8 Canada Tel # (613) 563-2175

Baltic Studies Newsletter
See: EDUCATION

Bates International Trade Update
See: INTERNATIONAL TRADE

Batnua
Publishing Co: Habonim Dror North America, 27 W. 20th St., New York, NY 10011-3707; Title Tel # (212) 255-1796
Personnel: Editor-S. Weiss
Editorial Description: Monthly newsletter for a labor zionist youth movement.
General Info: Yr. Est. 1970, Quarterly, Offset press, 20 pages, 2 Color
Subscriptions: Indv. $5
Circulation: Total-1,500

Bay Area CISPES   *Association*
Publishing Co: Bay Area CISPES, 3382 26th St., San Francisco, CA 94110 Fax # (416) 648-6529; Title Tel # (415) 648-8222
General Info: (Formerly Oakland/Berkeley CISPES), Monthly

Berkeley-Leon Sister City Newsletter
Publishing Co: Berkeley-Leon Sister City Assn., PO Box 1004, Berkeley, CA 94701-1004; Title Tel # (510) 549-1387
Personnel: Editor-Marc Shulman
General Info: (Formerly Bulletin of the Nicaragua Info. Ctr.), Yr. Est. 1983, Bi-monthly
Subscriptions: Indv. $10

Boletin Informativo Newsletter
See: BOOKS & BOOK TRADE

Boycott Law Bulletin
See: INTERNATIONAL TRADE

Brazil-Canada Newsletter
See: INTERNATIONAL TRADE

Brazil Watch   *Business*
Publishing Co: Orbis Publications, L.L.C., 3201 New Mexico Ave., NW, Ste. 249, Washington, DC 20016 Tel # (202) 237-0155 Fax # (202) 237-0596; Title Tel # (202) 625-2702 Title Fax # (202) 333-8740
Personnel: Publisher-Stephen Foster, Editor in Chief-Richard Foster
Editorial Description: Economic, political, business events in Brazil. Written and edited from the capital city of Brasilia.
General Info: Yr. Est. 1983, Bi-weekly, ISSN: 0897-3967
Subscriptions: Indv. $695, Can. $695, For. $695
List Rental: List Management Co.: Eleanor L. Stark Company, 515 Madison Ave Rm 2300, New York, NY 10022-5403 Tel # (212) 838-1935, Fax # (212) 751-2024, Actives: 13,594, $145/M

Breaking the Siege   *Consumer, Association*
Publishing Co: Middle East Justice Network, PO Box 495, Boston, MA 02112; Title Tel # (617) 542-5056 Title Fax # (617) 542-4947
Personnel: Publisher-Tim Bishopric
Editorial Description: Newsletter for the Middle East Justice Network.
General Info: Yr. Est. 1989, Bi-monthly, Trim Size-8½ x 11, 8 pages
Subscriptions: Indv. $20

Bridges
See: EDUCATION

Bulletin
See: LABOR UNION

Bulletin
See: RELIGIOUS & THEOLOGICAL

Bulletin Match
Publishing Co: Match Int'l. Centre, 200 Elgin St., #1102, Ottawa, ON K2P 1L5 Canada; Title Tel # (613) 238-1312
Editorial Description: Global feminism and development issues. Women's empowerment through organizing to develop and implement strategies to end violence, become literate, save the environment, etc.
General Info: (Formerly Match News), ISSN: 0229-5814
Acquistions: Publication Bought, Publication Sold
List Rental: Rents Lists

CAMERA Media Report   *Consumer, Association*
Publishing Co: Committee for Accuracy in Middle East Reporting in America, Box 428, Boston, MA 02258-0428; Title Tel # (617) 789-3672 Title Fax # (617) 787-7853
Personnel: Editor-Andrea Levin
Editorial Description: Dedicated to the promotion of fair and balanced coverage of the Middle East.
General Info: Yr. Est. 1989, Quarterly, 20 pages
Subscriptions: Free With Membership
Circulation: Total-20,000, Readership-60,000
List Rental: List Management Co.: Manager: Heidi Werther; Mail America / Wallin Group Inc, P.O Box 1030, Manchester, NH 03105 Tel # (603) 623-1212, Fax # (603) 647-0755, Actives: 23,000, $95/M

CARE World Report
See: SOCIAL SERVICES & WELFARE

CARECEN Speaks
Publishing Co: Central American Refugee Ctr., 3112 Mount Pleasant St NW, Washington, DC 20010-2710; Title Tel # (202) 328-9799
Personnel: Editor-Sharon O'Day
General Info: Yr. Est. 1984

CENSA's Strategic Report
Publishing Co: Center for Study of the Americas, 2288 Fulton St # 103, Berkeley, CA 94704-1449; Title Tel # (415) 540-5006
Personnel: Editor-Roger Burbach
General Info: Yr. Est. 1985, Quarterly
Subscriptions: Indv. $10, $3/copy

CFJ Clearinghouse on the Central & Eastern European Press Newsletter
See: MEDIA & COMMUNICATIONS

CHF Newsbriefs   *Association*
Publishing Co: Cooperative Housing Foundation, PO Box 91280, Washington, DC 20090-1280; Title Tel # (301) 587-4700 Title Fax # (301) 587-2626
Personnel: Editor-Alicia George
Editorial Description: Natl. & intl. developments in field of cooperative housing.
General Info: (Formerly FCH Newsbriefs), Yr. Est. 1964, Semi-annually, Trim Size-8½ x 11, Sheetfed press, 8 pages, ISSN: 0895-5735, 2 Color, Recycled
Subscriptions: Free
Circulation: Total-5,000
Printing Co: Automated Graphic Systems, 4590 Graphics Drive, White Plains, MD 20695 Tel # (301) 843-1800, Fax # (301) 843-6339

CLAG Communication
See: GEOGRAPHY

COHA's Washington Report on the Hemisphere   *Business, Scholarly*
Publishing Co: Council on Hemispheric Affairs, 724 9th St., NW, Washington, DC 20001-4505; Title Tel # (202) 393-3322 Title Fax # (202) 393-3423
Personnel: Publisher-Larry Birns, Editor-Josh Meck, Editor-Pere Zirite, Circ. Mgr.-Philip Jaeger, Adv. Dir.-Nicole Stevenson, Art Dir.-David Williams, Mktg. Dir.-Lisa Gross
Editorial Description: Monitors the full spectrum of U.S. & Canadian relations with Latin America, including politics, diplomacy, national security interests, human rights & economics & trade.
General Info: (Formerly Washington Report on the Hemisphere), Yr. Est. 1980, Bi-weekly, Trim Size-8½ x 11, Sheetfed press, 8 pages, No Color, Perfect bound
Subscriptions: Indv. $175, Inst. $325, Can. $340, For. $365, $12/copy
Circulation: Total-1,000
List Rental: Actives: $85/M
Printing Co: International Printing, Coakley Circle, Rockville, MD 20852 Tel # (301) 588-6205

CREES News   *Scholarly*
Publishing Co: Center for Russian & East European Studies, 204 Lane Hall, Univ. of Michigan-Ann Arbor, Ann Arbor, MI 48109; Title Tel # (313) 764-0351 Title Fax # (313) 763-4765
General Info: (Formerly Center for Russian & Eastern European Studies Newsletter), Bi-monthly, Trim Size-8½ x 11, Mimeo press, 10 pages, No Color, Saddle-stitched
Subscriptions: Free
Circulation: Total-2,200
Advertising: Accepts Inserts.

CUSO Forum
See: EDUCATION

CWAS Newsletter
See: WOMEN'S

California Statesman's Foreign Policy Review   **CPM: $117**
Publishing Co: William Shearer, 8158 Palm St, Lemon Grove, CA 91945-3028; Title Tel # (619) 460-4484
Personnel: Publisher, Editor-William Shearer
Editorial Description: News/comments on intl. affairs. Supports non-interventionist foreign policy.
General Info: Yr. Est. 1972, Monthly, 4 pages
Subscriptions: Indv. $15, Free To Qualified Recipient
Circulation: Total-1,700
Advertising: $200.

Canadian News Facts   *Business*
Publishing Co: MPL Communications, Inc., 133 Richmond St. W., Ste. 700, Toronto, ON M5H 3M8 Canada; Title Tel # (416) 869-1177 Title Fax # (416) 869-0456
Personnel: Publisher-Barrie Martland, Publisher-Steven Pepper, Editor-Elizabeth Etherington
Editorial Description: Index & digest of Canadian current events.
General Info: Yr. Est. 1967, Bi-monthly, Sheetfed press, 10 pages, ISSN: 0008-4565, No Color, Newsprint
Subscriptions: Indv. $289
List Rental: Rents Lists

Canadian Studies Update
See: EDUCATION

Caribbean Newsletter   *Association*

Publishing Co: Friends for Jamaica Collective, PO Box 20392, New York, NY 10025-1513
Editorial Description: Promotes struggles of Jamaican and other Caribbean people.
General Info: (Formerly Friends For Jamaica), Yr. Est. 1980, Quarterly, Offset press, 10 pages, ISSN: 0894-0223, No Color
Subscriptions: Indv. $15, Inst. $17, For. $20, $2/copy
Circulation: Total-500
Printing Co: Grass Roots Press, 401 1/2 W Peace St, Raleigh, NC 27603-1133 Tel # (919) 828-2364

Carnegie Council Newsletter   *Consumer*

Publishing Co: Carnegie Council on Ethics & Intl. Affairs, 170 E 64th St, New York, NY 10021-7478; Title Tel # (212) 838-4120 Title Fax # (212) 752-2432
Personnel: Publisher, Editor-E. Esslinger, Circ. Mgr.-Deborah Caroll, Publisher, Editor, Promotion Dir.-Olivia Wakeman
Editorial Description: Eight page newsletter keeps members and friends apprised of Carnegie Council activities. Includes calender of upcoming events and articles about meetings, seminars, conferences, and new publications.
General Info: Yr. Est. 1984, Quarterly, Trim Size-8½ x 11, Coated
Circulation: Total-3,000

Catalyst - ATI's Technical Bulletin

Publishing Co: A.T.I., 1828 L Street, Ste 1000, Washington, DC 20036-4706 Tel # (202) 293-4640; Title Tel # (202) 293-4600 Title Fax # (202) 293-4598
Personnel: Editor-Susan Drake Swift
Editorial Description: Reports on the design, technology focus, & implementation of individual ATI field projects. The Bulletin is published four to six times per year & distributed free of charge.
General Info: (Formerly Appropriate Technology Bulletin), Yr. Est. 1984, Quarterly, ISSN: 0276-7066
Circulation: Total-1,600

Catholic Lithuania Update

Publishing Co: Lithuanian Catholic Religious Aid, 351 Highland Blvd, Brooklyn, NY 11207-1910; Title Tel # (718) 647-2434 Title Fax # (718) 827-6696
Editorial Description: Concerned with religious freedom in Soviet-occupied Lithuania.
General Info: Semi-annually

Center for Asian Studies Newsletter

Publishing Co: Center for Asian Studies, Univ. of Texas at Austin, SSB Rm.4-126, Austin, TX 78712; Title Tel # (512) 471-3434
Personnel: Editor-Sarah Wimer
General Info: (Formerly Texpera Newsletter)

Center for Peace & Conflict Studies Newsletter   *Association*

Publishing Co: Wayne State Univ. -Center, 2319 Faculty/Admin. Bldg., Detroit, MI 48202; Title Tel # (313) 577-3453 Title Fax # (313) 577-8369
Personnel: Editor-Larry Rossinger, Production Mgr.-Marjorie Katz
Editorial Description: Global news and information for peace education and conflict resolution.
General Info: (Formerly Ctr. for Teaching About Peace), Yr. Est. 1965, Quarterly, Offset press, 4 pages, No Color
Subscriptions: Indv. $15, Inst. $25
Circulation: Total-1,500

Central America News Letter

Publishing Co: Natl. Lawyer's Guild, 55 6th Ave, New York, NY 10013-1679; Title Tel # (212) 966-5000
General Info: Yr. Est. 1983, 16 pages
Subscriptions: Indv. $15
Circulation: Total-2,000

Central America NewsPak

Publishing Co: Central America Resource Center, PO Box 2327, Austin, TX 78768-2327; Title Tel # (512) 476-9841
Personnel: Editor-Billy Pope
General Info: Yr. Est. 1986, Bi-monthly
Subscriptions: Indv. $38

Changemakers
See: SOCIAL SERVICES & WELFARE

Chile: Summary of Recent Events

Publishing Co: Embassy of Chile, Press Office, 1736 Mass. Ave. NW, Washington, DC 20036
General Info: Yr. Est. 1974, Bi-monthly

China Agribusiness Report   *Business*

Publishing Co: China Agribusiness Report, PO Box 92619, Los Angeles, CA 90009-2619 Parent Co.-Asia Letter Group, Los Angeles; Title Tel # (852) 526-2950
Personnel: Editor-Charles Smith
Editorial Description: Developmenmts and news relating to the Chinese agricultural industry.
General Info: Bi-weekly
Subscriptions: Indv. $595

China Focus

Publishing Co: Princeton China Initiative, PO Box 209, Princeton, NJ 08542-0209 Tel # (609) 924-9292 Fax # (609) 924-1445
Personnel: Publisher-Lorraine Spiess
Editorial Description: Comments on Chinese political, economic, social, and cultural issues from an uncensored 'insider' perspective. Intended to serve as a bridge between Western 'China Watchers' and the Chinese community.
General Info: Yr. Est. 1993, Bi-monthly

China Forum Newsletter   *Consumer*

Publishing Co: China Forum, PO Box 13781, Berkeley, CA 94712-4781; Title Tel # (510) 644-3817 Title Fax # (510) 644-3817
Personnel: Publisher-Moachun Yu
Editorial Description: Created by the China Forum, an outreach program run by Chinese students in conjunction with concerned Americans at the University of California.
General Info: Yr. Est. 1991, Monthly, Trim Size-8½ x 11, Desktop press, ISSN: 0304-355X, 2 Color
Subscriptions: Indv. $10, For. $20

China Information   *Business, Consumer*

Publishing Co: Golden Horse Culture Business Development, PO Box 772161, Coral Springs, FL 33077-2161
Personnel: Publisher-Zhu Yongkang, Editor in Chief-Xu Jingen
Editorial Description: Covers issues of politics, economy and society in China.
General Info: Yr. Est. 1994, Monthly, Trim Size-8½ x 11, 34 pages, Color-cover, Matte, Saddle-stitched
Subscriptions: Indv. $33

China Newsletter   *Business, Scholarly*

Publishing Co: Japan External Trade Organization, 1221 Ave. of the Americas, New York, NY 10020-1001; Title Tel # (212) 997-0418 Title Fax # (212) 997-0464
Editorial Description: Articles on China's economic and trade developments.
General Info: Bi-monthly
Subscriptions: Indv. $60
Circulation: Total-500

Citizen Exchange Communique

Publishing Co: Citizen Exchange Council, 12 W. 31st St., 4th Fl., Ste. 1004-1005, New York, NY 10001-4415; Title Tel # (212) 643-1985
Personnel: Editor-Mary Shea
Editorial Description: Articles on citizen-oriented private exchanges of an educational and cultural nature with peoples from Communist countries. Information on USA-USSR travel.
General Info: Yr. Est. 1962, Trim Size-7 x 8½, Offset press, 4 pages, Color
Circulation: Total-12,000

Clips
See: TELEVISION & VIDEO

Coastal Society Bulletin, The
See: ENVIRONMENT & ECOLOGY

Collected Legislation of Russia
See: LAW

Colombian Newsletter   *Business*

Publishing Co: Colombian American Assn., 150 Nassau St., New York, NY 10038-1516 Fax # (212) 233-7779; Title Tel # (212) 233-7776
Personnel: Editor-Peter Smith
General Info: Monthly
Subscriptions: Indv. $200

Comecon Reports
See: ECONOMICS

Community of Joy

Publishing Co: Global Community, 214 West 92nd Street, New York, NY 10025; Title Tel # (212) 874-2828 Title Fax # (212) 874-4305
Editorial Description: Focuses on community building, peace makeing, earth preserving, and spriritual awakening, and interrelatedness of all these issues.
General Info: Trim Size-8½ x 11, 8 pages, No Color, Matte
Subscriptions: Indv. $2, Free With Membership

Constantian, The
See: POLITICS

Contact
Consumer, Association

Publishing Co: Canadian Asian Stud. Assn-Centre D'etudes De L'asie De L'est, Universite De Montreal, C.P. 6128, Succ. Centre Ville, Montreal, PQ H3C 3J7 Canada Tel # (514) 343-6111; Title Tel # (514) 398-8129 Title Fax # (514) 398-1882
Personnel: Editor-Charles Burton
Editorial Description: Asian studies.
General Info: (Formerly CASA Newsletter for Scholars of Asia), Yr. Est. 1968, Semi-annually, Offset press, ISSN: 0835-3336, Color-cover, Coated, Saddle-stitched
Subscriptions: Indv. $50, Inst. $75, $8/copy
Circulation: Total-600
Advertising: Inquire for rates. Accepts Inserts.
List Rental: Rents Lists

Cornell Modern Indonesia Project:
Scholarly

Publishing Co: Southeast Asia Program- Cornell Univ., 640 Stewart Ave., Ithaca, NY 14850 Tel # (607) 225-4359; Title Tel # (607) 255-4359 Title Fax # (607) 277-1904
Personnel: Editor-Audrey Kahin, Circ. Mgr.-Hazel Prentice, Promotion Dir.-Dolina Millar
Editorial Description: Scholarly publications on Indonesia.
General Info: (Formerly Cornell Modern Indonesia Project: Monographs,Interim Reports), Yr. Est. 1955, Irregular, Trim Size-7 x 10, 150 pages, No Color, Perfect bound, Looseleaf
Acquistions: Publication Sold

Costa Rica Report
Business

Publishing Co: U.S. Import-Export Publications Co., PO Box 428, Bellflower, CA 90707-0428 Tel # (310) 925-2918; Title Tel # (213) 925-2918
General Info: Monthly, 6 pages

Council Spotlight Booknotes
Association

Publishing Co: World Affairs Council of North Califilornia, 312 Sutter St Ste 200, San Francisco, CA 94108-4311; Title Tel # (415) 982-2541 Title Fax # (415) 982-5028
Personnel: Editor-L. Beeson
Editorial Description: Book reviews of current titles on intl.
General Info: (Formerly Spotlight on New Books on World Affairs), Yr. Est. 1959, Monthly, 4 pages
Subscriptions: Indv. $5
Circulation: Total-11,000

Countertrade Outlook (CTO)
See: INTERNATIONAL TRADE

Courage in the Struggle for Justice & Peace
Consumer, Association

Publishing Co: United Church of Christ Office for Church & Society, 110 Maryland Ave., N.E., Suite #207, Washington, DC 20002; Title Tel # (202) 543-1517 Title Fax # (202) 543-5994
Personnel: Editor-Russell Claussen
Editorial Description: Published by the office for church in society, United Church of Christ.
General Info: (Formerly UCC Network), Yr. Est. 1985, 10x/yr., Trim Size-8½ x 11, Offset press, 8 pages
Acquistions: Publication Bought
Circulation: Total-20,000
Printing Co: Kutztown Publishing Co., 15076 Kutztown Rd, Kutztown, PA 19530-9275 Tel # (215) 683-7341

Courier

Publishing Co: Stanley Foundation, 216 Sycamore St # 500, Muscatine, IA 52761-3838; Title Tel # (319) 264-1500 Title Fax # (319) 264-0864
Personnel: Editor-Jeff Martin, Mng. Editor-Keith Porter, Contrib. Ed.-Mary Gray, Editorial Asst.-Margo Schneider, Editorial Asst.-Bonnie Tharp, Art Dir.-Amy Bakke
Editorial Description: Newsletter conveying information and perspective gained from foundation-supported or sponsored activities.
General Info: Yr. Est. 1989, Web press, 12 pages, ISSN: 1044-5900, 2 Color, Matte, Saddle-stitched
Subscriptions: Free
Circulation: (100% controlled), Total-16,000
Printing Co: Type 2/GR 1, 1137 J Ave NE, Cedar Rapids, IA 52402-3830 Tel # (319) 366-6411

Crosscurrents
See: MUSIC & MUSIC TRADES

Cuba Subcommittee Newsletter
Business, Association

Publishing Co: Natl. Lawyer's Guild-Cuba Subcommittee, 5513 Oakmont Ave, Bethesda, MD 20817-3527; Title Tel # (312) 236-6180
Personnel: Editor-Debra Evenson
General Info: Irregular
Subscriptions: Indv. $10

Cuba Update Newsletter
Association

Publishing Co: Center for Cuban Studies, 124 W. 23rd St., New York, NY 10011-2400 Fax # (212) 242-1937; Title Tel # (212) 242-0559
Personnel: Editor-Sandra Levinson, Promotion Dir.-Irving Kessler
Editorial Description: News about CCS activities with special emphasis on trips to Cuba, conferences, & seminars.
General Info: Yr. Est. 1986, 16 pages, No Color, Newsprint, Saddle-stitched
Subscriptions: Indv. $40, Inst. $50
Circulation: Total-2,500

Cuban in Brief
Association

Publishing Co: Cuban American Natl. Foundation, 1000 Thomas Jefferson St NW, Ste 503, Washington, DC 20007-3835 Fax # (202) 338-0308; Title Tel # (202) 265-2822
General Info: (Formerly Cuban Update), Irregular, 6 pages, 2 Color
Circulation: Total-10,000

Czech the News
Business, Association

Publishing Co: Embassy of the Czech Republic, 3900 Spring of Freedom St., NW, Washington, DC 20008; Title Tel # (202) 274-9100 Title Fax # (202) 966-8540
Editorial Description: Newsletter of the embassy of the Czech Republic.
General Info: Yr. Est. 1993, Monthly, Trim Size-8½ x 11, 10 pages, No Color
Subscriptions: Free

DACOR Bulletin
Association

Publishing Co: Diplomatic and Consular Officers, retired, 1801 F St. NW, Washington, DC 20006-4497; Title Tel # (202) 682-0500
Editorial Description: For retired foreign service officers.
General Info: Monthly

DPI Programme Update

Publishing Co: United Nations Dept. of Public Information, Centres Programme Section, Rm. S-1060, New York, NY 10017 Tel # (212) 963-6850 Fax # (212) 963-7330
General Info: Semi-monthly

Daily News Bulletin
See: RELIGIOUS & THEOLOGICAL

Dateline: Mexico Today
Business

Publishing Co: Dateline: Mexico Today, 9297 Siempre Viva Rd # 5-144, San Diego, CA 92173-3628
Personnel: Publisher, Editor-Hugh Schott
General Info: Monthly

Delaney Report
See: ADVERTISING & MARKETING

Democratic Values
Association

Publishing Co: World Without War Council, 5153 N. Ashland Ave., Chicago, IL 60640-2831; Title Tel # (312) 663-4250
Personnel: Editor-Robert Woito
General Info: (Formerly World Without War Council-Midwest), Yr. Est. 1965, Quarterly, Trim Size-8½ x 11, Sheetfed press, 4 Color, Newsprint
Subscriptions: Indv. $20
Acquistions: Publication Bought
Circulation: Total-700
List Rental: Actives: $60/M
Printing Co: Omega Graphics, 421 S Wabash Ave, Chicago, IL 60605-1208

Detroit Council for World Affairs Newsletter

Publishing Co: Center for Peace and Conflict Studies, Wayne State Univ., 2319 Faculty Adm. Wayne Univ., Detroit, MI 48202 Fax # (313) 577-8269; Title Tel # (313) 577-3453 Title Fax # (317) 577-8269
Personnel: Editor-H. Bishop, Editor-E. Sherman
Editorial Description: Programs organized/sponsored by the Center for Peace & Conflict Studies.
General Info: (Formerly Center for Teaching About Peace and War Newsletter), Yr. Est. 1965, Quarterly, Trim Size-8½ x 11, Desktop press, 4 pages, ISSN: 0008-9133, Color
Subscriptions: Indv. $15
Circulation: (100% controlled), Total-1,000

Development Connections
Association   **CPM: $112**

Publishing Co: Society for Intl. Dev., Washington Chapter, 1875 Connecticut Ave. NW, Ste. 900, Washington, DC 20009-5728; Title Tel # (202) 347-1800
Personnel: Editor-Lawrence Goldman
Editorial Description: Information on current issues in international economic, political and social development. Job listings, book reviews, listing of conferences and seminars.
General Info: (Formerly Washington Chapter Report), Yr. Est. 1959, Monthly, Trim Size-8½ x 11, 12 pages, No Color, Newsprint
Subscriptions: Indv. $65, Inst. $400, Free With Membership
Circulation: Total-1,600
Advertising: $180.
List Rental: Rents Lists
Printing Co: Texpress, 8003 Woodmont Ave. # 206, Bethesda, MD

Digest of Commercial Laws of the World
See: LAW

Director's Monthly
See: MANAGEMENT

Distant Drums
See: PHILOSOPHY

Donald R. Morris Newsletter
See: NEWSPAPER INDUSTRY

Draft Notices
See: POLITICS

Eco Newsletter
See: ENVIRONMENT & ECOLOGY

Eco-Profiteer, The
See: INVESTMENT

El Rescate

Publishing Co: Southern California Ecumenical Center, 1340 S Bonnie Brae St, Los Angeles, CA 90006-5416; Title Tel # (213) 387-0460
General Info: Yr. Est. 1980, Monthly

El Salvador On Line

Publishing Co: Washington Center for Central American Studies, PO Box 29355, Washington, DC 20017-0355
General Info: Weekly, ISSN: 1046-0039, Ind/Abs/Online: NewsNet

Electrostatic Precipitator
See: ENGINEERING

Embassy of Sri Lanka
Newsletter

Publishing Co: Embassy of Sri Lanka, 2148 Wyoming Ave NW, Washington, DC 20008-3906
Editorial Description: News of Sri Lanka people and events and Embassy news.
General Info: Bi-weekly

Embassy of Switzerland
Bulletin   *Association*

Publishing Co: Embassy of Switzerland, 2900 Cathedral Ave NW, Washington, DC 20008-3499

Entre Nous
See: RELIGIOUS & THEOLOGICAL

Environment Watch: Latin America
See: ENVIRONMENT & ECOLOGY

Environment Watch: Western Europe
See: ENVIRONMENT & ECOLOGY

Esperanto U.S.A.
See: LITERATURE & LINGUISTICS

Estimate

Publishing Co: Intl. Estimate, Inc., 3030 S Abingdon St, Arlington, VA 22206-1605; Title Tel # (703) 681-2997 Title Fax # (703) 671-2998
Personnel: Editor-Michael E. Dunn, Co-Editor-Michael Dunn
Editorial Description: Political & security intelligence analysis of N. Africa, the Middle East, South Asia, East Asia & the Pacific. Written for intelligence professionals, international marketing executives, officers of financial institutions, defense & national security pla ners, military staff officers & regional specialists.
General Info: Yr. Est. 1989, Bi-weekly, Trim Size-8½ x 11, ISSN: 1043-1667
Subscriptions: Indv. $295, Inst. $150, Can. $295, For. $330

Ethics & International
Affairs Newsletter

Publishing Co: Carnegie Council on Ethics & Intl. Affairs, 170 E 64th St, New York, NY 10021-7478; Title Tel # (212) 838-4120 Title Fax # (212) 752-2432
Personnel: Publisher-Robert J. Myers, Editor-Joel Rosenthal, Mng. Editor-Matthew Mathern, Circ. Mgr.-Deborah Carroll, Production Mgr.-Matthew Mattern
Editorial Description: Augments the Carnegie Council's College-level curriculum development program by enabling college and university professors to bring the Council's various lecture and seminar programs to their classrooms.
General Info: Yr. Est. 1986, Semi-annually, Trim Size-8½ x 11
Circulation: (24% controlled), Total-5,000

Euro Cable TV Programming
See: TELEVISION & VIDEO

EuroScope   *Business*

Publishing Co: EuroScope, Inc., 46679 Winchester Dr, Sterling, VA 20164-3553; Title Tel # (703) 430-5417
Personnel: Publisher, Editor-John Baird
Editorial Description: Covers European Union (EU) legislation, information and notices.
General Info: Monthly, ISSN: 1060-9105
Subscriptions: Indv. $200, Inst. $200, Can. $300

EuroWatch
See: BUSINESS & INDUSTRY

European Studies Newsletter
See: HISTORY

Executive International
Insight   *Business, Consumer*

Publishing Co: International Insight, Inc., 1200 18th St NW Ste 305, Washington, DC 20036-2506; Title Tel # (202) 466-2146 Title Fax # (202) 466-2147
Editorial Description: Covers international events and affairs.
General Info: Yr. Est. 1993, Weekly
Subscriptions: Indv. $350

Facts on File World News
Digest   *Business, Consumer*

Publishing Co: Facts on File, Inc., 11 Penn Plaza, New York, NY 10001-2006 Tel # (212) 967-8800 Parent Co.-Infobase Holdings Inc., New York; Title Tel # (212) 683-2244 Title Fax # (212) 683-3633
Personnel: Publisher-Remmel Nunn, Editor-Thomas Hitchings, Circ. Mgr.-Steve Orlotsky, Production Mgr.-Olivia McKean
Editorial Description: Current news: political, economic, diplomatic sports and arts.
General Info: Yr. Est. 1941, Weekly, Trim Size-8½ x 11, Web press, 20 pages, ISSN: 0014-6641, Ind/Abs/Online: Nexis, Mead Data Central, No Color, Matte, Saddle-stitched
Subscriptions: Indv. $665, Inst. $665
Acquistions: Publication Bought
List Rental: Rents Lists
Printing Co: Science Press, 300 W Chestnut St, Ephrata, PA 17522-2002 Tel # (717) 738-9300, Fax # (717) 738-9413

Focus on Iran   *Association, Consumer*

Publishing Co: Azadegan Foundation, PO Box 40152, Washington, DC 20016-0152; Title Tel # (202) 363-5985
Editorial Description: Focuses on the liberation and freedom of the Iranian people.
General Info: Monthly

Food First Books
See: FOOD

Food First News & Views
See: SOCIAL SERVICES & WELFARE

Foreign Military Markets
Middle East & Africa   *Business, Association*

Publishing Co: Forecast International/DMS, Inc., 22 Commerce Rd., Newtown, CT 06470-1643; Title Tel # (203) 426-0800 Title Fax # (203) 426-1964
Editorial Description: This report details regional military budgets, positive manufacturing capability, & future requirements.
General Info: (Formerly Middle East & Africa), Monthly, Trim Size-8½ x 11, 1,200 pages, Color-cover, Matte, Other, Looseleaf
List Rental: Rents Lists

Foreign Press News

Publishing Co: Foreign Press Assn., 110 E 59th St Lbby 2, New York, NY 10022-1304; Title Tel # (212) 826-4721
General Info: Monthly

Foreign Tax Law Bi-Weekly Bulletin
See: LAW

Forum

Publishing Co: U.S. Japan Foundation, 145 E. 32nd St., New York, NY 10016-6002; Title Tel # (212) 481-8753 Title Fax # (212) 481-8762
General Info: Yr. Est. 1986, Quarterly
Acquistions: Publication Bought

Free Trade Advisory   *Business*

Publishing Co: United Communications Group, 11300 Rockville Pike, Ste. 1100, Rockville, MD 20852-3030 Tel # (301) 816-8950 Fax # (301) 816-8945
Personnel: Publisher-Susan R. Goldberg, Editor-Robert Taylor, Circ. Mgr.-Loretta Netzer, Production Mgr.-Gail Solomon
General Info: Yr. Est. 1991, Bi-weekly, Trim Size-8½ x 11, 8 pages, ISSN: 1058-5745, 2 Color
Subscriptions: Indv. $550, Can. $550, For. $550
List Rental: Rents Lists

Freeperson Network
News

Publishing Co: FreeNetwork, PO Box 224, Long Beach, CA 90801-0224; Title Tel # (714) 957-8075
Personnel: Editor-Dagny Sharon
Editorial Description: Assn. of intl. groups & individuals promoting individual sovereignty.
General Info: Yr. Est. 1984, Trim Size-8 x 10, Web press, 104 pages, 2 Color, Coated
Subscriptions: Indv. $5
Circulation: Total-500
Advertising: Accepts Inserts.
List Rental: Actives: $80/M

French-American News *Business, Association*

Publishing Co: French-American Chamber of Commerce in the US Inc., 1350 Ave. of the Americas, 6th Fl., New York, NY 10019-4702; Title Tel # (212) 371-4466 Title Fax # (212) 371-5368
Personnel: Editor-Vicki Banne
Editorial Description: Chamber activities, business stories addressed to N.Y. members.
General Info: Yr. Est. 1896, Bi-monthly, Trim Size-7 x 10, Offset press, 16 pages, No Color, Newsprint
Subscriptions: Free With Membership
Circulation: Total-1,000
Advertising: Inquire for rates. Accepts Inserts.
Printing Co: Galvanic Printing & Plate Co., Inc., 50 Commercial Ave, Moonachie, NJ 07074-1705 Tel # (201) 939-3600

Friends of the Filipino People Bulletin

Publishing Co: Friends of the Filipino People, PO Box 2125, Durham, NC 27702-2125; Title Tel # (919) 489-0002
Personnel: Editor-Tim McGloin
General Info: Yr. Est. 1973
Subscriptions: Indv. $5, Inst. $10

Futures International Law Letter
See: LAW

Global Money Management
See: INVESTMENT

Global Report *Consumer, Association*

Publishing Co: Center for War, Peace & the News Media, NYU, 10 Washington Pl. 4th Fl., New York, NY 10003; Title Tel # (212) 475-1077 Title Fax # (212) 260-6384
Personnel: Editor-Richard Hudson
Editorial Description: Reports on U.N. developments toward a world of peace with justice.
General Info: Yr. Est. 1977, Quarterly, Offset press, 4 pages, ISSN: 0730-9112, No Color, Newsprint
Subscriptions: Indv. $20
Circulation: Total-3,500

Global Statesmanship Ratings of the U.S. House
See: GOVERNMENT

Global Statesmanship Ratings of the U.S. Senate *Consumer*

Publishing Co: Campaign for U.N. Reform, 713 D St SE, Washington, DC 20003-2153; Title Tel # (202) 546-3956
General Info: Annually, 3 pages, No Color, Coated
Subscriptions: Free

Global Survey
See: MILITARY & NAVAL

Global Talk! *Consumer*

Publishing Co: PLAN International USA, 155 Plan Way, Warwick, RI 02886-1099; Title Tel # (401) 738-5600
Personnel: Editor-Jaya Sarkar
Editorial Description: Newsletter describing activities of organization in intl. education, cross-cultural communications.
General Info: Semi-annually, Sheetfed press, 4 pages, No Color, Newsprint
Subscriptions: Indv. $1, $1/copy
Circulation: Total-300

GloboFax
See: ETHNIC

Good News *Consumer, Association*

Publishing Co: American Institute of Polish Culture, 1440 79th St. Causeway, Miami, FL 33141; Title Tel # (305) 864-2349
Personnel: Editor-Blanca Rosenspiel
General Info: Quarterly
Circulation: Total-350

Government Union Critique
See: LABOR UNION

HIAS Headlines & Highlights *Association*

Publishing Co: HIAS, Inc., 333 Seventh Avenue, New York, NY 10001-5004; Title Tel # (212) 967-4100 Title Fax # (212) 645-2961
Personnel: Editor-Roberta Elliott
Editorial Description: Organizational newsletter. Details activities of this international migration and its Board of Directors.
General Info: (Formerly HIAS Reporter; HIAS Bulletin), Yr. Est. 1983, Quarterly, 6 pages, ISSN: 0041-509X, 2 Color, Coated
Circulation: Total-11,000
Printing Co: Perfect Press, 180 Varick Street, New York, NY 10014

The Harriman Review

Publishing Co: Sponsor-Harriman Institute, Columbia University, Columbia Univ., Harriman Institute, 420 W 118th St Fl 12, New York, NY 10027-7213; Title Tel # (212) 854-6218 Title Fax # (212) 666-3481
Personnel: Publisher, Editor-Ronald Meyer
Editorial Description: In-depth analysis of politics, culture, society of the USSR states.
General Info: (Formerly Harriman Institute Forum), Yr. Est. 1988, Monthly, Trim Size-8½ x 11, Offset press, 34 pages, ISSN: 0896-114X, Ind/Abs/Online: PAIS, 2 Color, Newsprint, Saddle-stitched
Subscriptions: Indv. $35, Inst. $35, For. $45, $5/copy
Circulation: Total-1,500
Printing Co: Columbia University Press, 562 W 113th St, New York, NY 10025-8099 Tel # (212) 316-7100

Hearts of the Handmaidens
See: WOMEN'S

Holland Info.

Publishing Co: Netherlands Consulate General, Economic Information Service, One Rockefeller Plz., New York, NY 10020-2094
General Info: Semi-monthly

Human Rights Education: The Fourth R

Publishing Co: Amnesty Intl. USA's Natl. Steering Committee on Human Rights, 1603 Honeysuckle Ln, Jonesboro, AR 72401-5104
General Info: Quarterly

Human Rights Research and Education Bulletin
See: CIVIL RIGHTS

IAEE Newsletter
See: ENERGY

ICASALS Newletter
See: AGRICULTURE

ICBB Reports

Publishing Co: Hillel: the Foundation for Jewish Campus Life, 1640 Rhode Island Ave NW, Washington, DC 20036 Tel # (202) 857-6560 Fax # (202) 296-6693; Title Tel # (202) 857-6545
Personnel: Circ. Mgr.-D Levenfeld
Editorial Description: In-depth on current issues of Jewish concerns.
General Info: Yr. Est. 1970, Monthly, Offset press, 10 pages, No Color
Subscriptions: Indv. $12, $2/copy
Circulation: (100% controlled), Total-2,000

IDB *Business, Association*

Publishing Co: Inter-American Development Bank, 1300 New York Ave NW, Washington, DC 20577-0006; Title Tel # (202) 623-1374
Personnel: Editor-Roger Hamilton
Editorial Description: Review of Latin American development issues, including description of IDB loan & technical cooperation operations, feature stories on Bank programs & activities.
General Info: Yr. Est. 1973, Monthly, 12 pages, Color
Circulation: Total-35,000

IFPRI Report *Association*

Publishing Co: Intl. Food Policy Research Institute, 1200 Seventeenth St., N.W., Washington, DC 20036; Title Tel # (202) 862-5670 Title Fax # (202) 467-4439
Personnel: Editor-Barbara Rose
Editorial Description: Summarizes recent research results and activities of the Institute. Features the analysis of strategies and policies for improving the food situation of low-income peoples of the Third World.
General Info: Yr. Est. 1979, Quarterly, 4 pages
Circulation: (100% controlled), Total-7,000

IIRR Report

Publishing Co: Intl. Institute of Rural Reconstruction, 475 Riverside Dr Ste 1270, New York, NY 10115-0122; Title Tel # (212) 870-2992
Personnel: Editor-Eric Blitz
Editorial Description: Third world rural development including agriculture, health, education, civic organization.
General Info: Yr. Est. 1960, Semi-annually, 4 pages, ISSN: 1011-8721, 2 Color
Subscriptions: Free
Circulation: Total-3,000

ILSA Newsletter
See: LAW

ISA Comparative Interdisciplinary Studies Section Bulletin

Publishing Co: International Studies Assn., Univ. Of Hawaii Soc. Sci., Dept, C/O F.w. Riggs, Honolulu, HI 96844-0001; Title Tel # (808) 956-8930
General Info: Yr. Est. 1973, Quarterly

ISG Newsletter
See: LAW

ISLA
Business, Scholarly

Publishing Co: Information Services on Latin America, 464 19th St, Oakland, CA 94612-2297; Title Tel # (510) 835-0678 Title Fax # (510) 835-3017
Personnel: Publisher-Fred Goff, Editor-Elizabeth Patelke
Editorial Description: Copies of articles on Latin America from major English language newspapers, comprehensive coverage of sociopolitical, diplomatic & economic news.
General Info: Yr. Est. 1970, Monthly, Trim Size-8¹/₂ x 11, 350 pages, ISSN: 0046-8401, No Color, Looseleaf
Subscriptions: Indv. $720
Circulation: Total-250

Ideas & Action
See: LABOR

In & Around the United Nations

Publishing Co: Quaker UN Office, 777 UN Plaza, New York, NY 10017; Title Tel # (212) 682-2745
Personnel: Editor-Diana Quick
General Info: Yr. Est. 1952, Bi-monthly

In Our Hands
See: POLITICS

Independent Scholars of Asia Newsletter
Business, Association

Publishing Co: Independent Scholars of Asia, Inc., 2321 Russell St Apt 3a, Berkeley, CA 94705-1959; Title Tel # (510) 849-3791 Title Fax # (510) 849-3791
Personnel: Publisher, Editor, Promotion Mgr.-Ruth-Inge Heinze
Editorial Description: Disseminate information on research & conditions in Asian countries.
General Info: Yr. Est. 1981, 3x/yr., Trim Size-²¹¹/₂ x 27, 12 pages, 1% ads
Subscriptions: Indv. $15, Inst. $15, Can. $15, For. $15, $5/copy
Circulation: Total-200
Advertising: Inquire for rates.
List Rental: Rents Lists

India News

Publishing Co: Information Service of India, Embassy of India, 2107 Massachusetts Ave NW, Washington, DC 20008-2811; Title Tel # (202) 939-9806
General Info: Yr. Est. 1962, Weekly

Indochina Newsletter

Publishing Co: Indochina Newsletter, 2161 Massachusetts Ave., Cambridge, MA 02140-1336; Title Tel # (617) 497-5273 Title Fax # (617) 354-2832
Personnel: Editor-Paul Shannon
Editorial Description: Recent developments in Indochina & in-depth look at the legacy of the war & Post-war conflicts. Special coverage on cacubodia 1979-1992
General Info: Yr. Est. 1979, 5x/yr., Trim Size-8¹/₂ x 11, Sheetfed press, 6 pages
Subscriptions: Indv. $14, Inst. $14, Can. $17, For. $17, $1/copy
Circulation: Total-700
Printing Co: Porter Square Press, Massachusetts Ave., Cambridge, MA 02140 Tel # (617) 492-5343

Infact News

Publishing Co: INFACT, 256 Hanover St., Ste. 3, Boston, MA 02113-2337; Title Tel # (617) 742-4583
Editorial Description: Organization which fights abuses of transnational corps focus against nuclear weapons.
General Info: Yr. Est. 1978, 4 pages, No Color
Circulation: Total-10,000

Information Service on Latin America
See: BIBLIOGRAPHY

Insider's Alert
See: INVESTMENT

International Commission of Jurists Newsletter/ Quarterly Report

Publishing Co: American Association for the Intl. Commission of Jurists, 777 UN Plaza, 9th Fl., New York, NY 10017; Title Tel # (212) 972-0883
Personnel: Editor-Niall MacDermott
General Info: Yr. Est. 1979, Quarterly, 45 pages, ISSN: 0252-0346, No Color
Subscriptions: Indv. $12, $3/copy

International Documents Review
Business, Consumer

Publishing Co: International Documents Review, 318 Edgewood Ave, Teaneck, NJ 07666-3021; Title Tel # (201) 833-1881 Title Fax # (201) 833-1835
Personnel: Editor-Bhaskar Menon
Editorial Description: Covers news and issues from the United Nations.
General Info: Weekly, Trim Size-8¹/₂ x 11, 8 pages, ISSN: 1054-4933, No Color
Subscriptions: Indv. $200

International Leads
See: LIBRARY

International Living
See: LIFESTYLE

International Marketing Intelligence News
See: INTERNATIONAL TRADE

International Marketing Newsletter
See: ADVERTISING & MARKETING

International News
See: ADVERTISING & MARKETING

International Observer
Business

Publishing Co: Government Bus. Worldwide Rpts., PO Box 5997, Washington, DC 20016-1597; Title Tel # (202) 244-7050 Title Fax # (202) 244-5410
Personnel: Publisher, Editor-J. Wagner
Editorial Description: Monthly information on political, diplomatic & economic developments around the world, domestic conditions, government policy & programs.
General Info: (Formerly Govt. Bus. Worldwide Report), Yr. Est. 1969, Monthly, Trim Size-8¹/₂ x 11, Offset press, 12 pages, ISSN: 1061-0324, No Color, Looseleaf
Subscriptions: Indv. $320, For. $340
Acquistions: Publication Sold

International Protection of the Environment
See: LAW

International Report
Business, Consumer

Publishing Co: International Report, PO Box 4882, Irvine, CA 92716-4882; Title Tel # (714) 856-5272 Title Fax # (714) 725-2436
Personnel: Editor-Raul Fernandez
Editorial Description: Analysis of world news.
General Info: (Formerly Columbia Report), Yr. Est. 1983, 3x/yr., Trim Size-8¹/₂ x 11, Offset press, 14 pages, ISSN: 0740-669X
Subscriptions: Indv. $6, Inst. $15
Circulation: Total-500

International Securities Regulation Report
See: INVESTMENT

International Society of Islands

Publishing Co: AAMA Intl., 1350 S King St., Ste 104, Honolulu, HI 96814-2008; Title Tel # (808) 737-8115
Personnel: Editor-Frank Wandell
General Info: Yr. Est. 1977, Monthly
Subscriptions: Indv. $40

International Studies Newsletter

Publishing Co: International Studies Associaton, Brigham Young Univ., D.M. Kennedy Ctr., 216 HRCB, Provo, UT 84602; Title Tel # (801) 378-5459
Personnel: Editor-Kristin Otterbacher
General Info: Yr. Est. 1973, Monthly
Subscriptions: Indv. $20
Circulation: Total-6,000

International Terrorism Newsletter
Business

Publishing Co: International Terrorism Newsletter, PO Box 22425, Louisville, KY 40252-0425
Personnel: Editor-Charles Hellebusch
General Info: Yr. Est. 1978, Monthly, ISSN: 07389191
Subscriptions: Indv. $24

International University Collegiate Sports Report
See: SPORTS & SPORTING GOODS

International Workcamper
Consumer

Publishing Co: Volunteers for Peace, Tiffany Rd., Belmont, VT 05730; Title Tel # (802) 259-2759 Title Fax # (802) 259-2922
Editorial Description: Promotes peace through international exchange and voluntary service.
General Info: Yr. Est. 1981, Annually, 4 pages, ISSN: 1066-3541
Subscriptions: Free
Circulation: Total-20,000
Printing Co: Daamen Printing, West Rutland Industrial Pk., W. Rutland, VT 05777 Tel # (802) 438-5472

Internewsletter
Association

Publishing Co: Internews Media Services, 1060-C National Press Bldg.NW, Washington, DC 20045-0001; Title Tel # (202) 347-4575 Title Fax # (703) 734-6956
Personnel: Publisher-Marie-Benoite Allizon, Editor-Renaud Detalle, Production Mgr.-Amour Toura Gaba, Promotion Dir.-Dariene Moyer
Editorial Description: Newsletter in French on Africa.
General Info: (Formerly Internewsletter Afrique), Yr. Est. 1977, Semi-monthly, Offset press, 12 pages, No Color
Subscriptions: Indv. $599, Inst. $498
Advertising: Inquire for rates.
Printing Co: Panic Press, 1656 K St NW, Washington, DC 20006-2801

Investment Laws of the World
See: INVESTMENT

Investment Treaties
See: LAW

Iraq Views & News
Publishing Co: Iraqi Press Office, 1801 P St NW, Washington, DC 20036-1201

Israel Foreign Affairs
Publishing Co: Israel Foreign Affairs, PO Box 19580, Sacramento, CA 95819-0580
Personnel: Publisher, Editor-Jane Hunter
General Info: Yr. Est. 1984, Monthly, 8 pages, ISSN: 0883-9832
Subscriptions: Indv. $20, Inst. $35, $2/copy

Italian Civil Code and Complementary Legislation
See: LAW

It's Our World
See: RELIGIOUS & THEOLOGICAL

JEI Report
See: INTERNATIONAL TRADE

JTA Weekly News Digest
Publishing Co: Jewish Telegraphic Agency, Inc., 330 7th Ave., 11th Fl., New York, NY 10001-5010 Fax # (212) 643-8498; Title Tel # (212) 643-1890
Personnel: Publisher-Mark Seal, Editor-Mark Joffe
Editorial Description: Summary of week's international news of Jewish interest & concern.
General Info: Yr. Est. 1935, Weekly, Sheetfed press, 4 pages, ISSN: 0021-6763, No Color
Subscriptions: Indv. $100, Can. $115, For. $130
Circulation: Total-7,000

Japan Economic Survey   *Business*
Publishing Co: Japan Economic Institute of America, 1000 Connecticut Ave., N.W., Washington, DC 20036-5347; Title Tel # (202) 296-5633
Editorial Description: Covers the state of the economy of Japan.
General Info: Monthly, Trim Size-8$\frac{1}{2}$ x 11, 16 pages, ISSN: 0888-5710
Subscriptions: Indv. $30, Inst. $30, Can. $35, For. $35

Japan Policy and Politics
See: POLITICS

Japan Society Newsletter
See: CULTURE & HUMANITIES

Japan Trade Center Information Service Monthly Economic Report
Publishing Co: Ruder, Finn & Rotman, 301 E. 57th St., New York, NY 10022-2995
General Info: Yr. Est. 1975, Monthly

Japan Weekly
See: INTERNATIONAL TRADE

Judaica Society International   *Association, Consumer*   **CPM:** $25
Publishing Co: Judaica Society International, 16 Housman Ct, Maplewood, NJ 07040-3006; Title Tel # (201) 763-8880
Personnel: Editor-Hy Kusnetz
Editorial Description: Political and economic studies.
General Info: Yr. Est. 1985, Quarterly, Trim Size-8$\frac{1}{2}$ x 11, 16 pages, ISSN: 1076-0857, No Color, Coated, Saddle-stitched
Subscriptions: Indv. $36, $10/copy
Circulation: Total-4,000
Advertising: $100.

Korea Update
Publishing Co: Korean Church Coalition, 475 Riverside Dr, New York, NY 10115-0697 Tel # (212) 870-2123 Fax # (212) 870-2881; Title Tel # (202) 546-4304 Title Fax # (202) 546-0090
Personnel: Publisher-Michael Hamm, Editor-Paul Kim
Editorial Description: Analysis, translated documents & press articles on human rights in Korea (both North & South).
General Info: Yr. Est. 1980, Bi-monthly, Web press, 12 pages, Color-cover, Newsprint
Subscriptions: Indv. $20, Can. $30, For. $30, $3/copy
Circulation: Total-2,949

Korean Research Bulletin
Publishing Co: Korean Research Council, 1565 Miramar Ave., Seaside, CA 93955-3326
Personnel: Editor-Sea Woon Chang
General Info: Yr. Est. 1976, Semi-annually
Subscriptions: Free

LAI Notes
Publishing Co: Latin American Institute, University Of New Mexico 801, Yale N.e., Albuquerque, NM 87131-0001 Tel # (505) 277-5985 Fax # (505) 277-5989; Title Tel # (505) 277-2961
Personnel: Publisher, Editor-Gilbert Merkx, Circ. Mgr.-Vickie Madrid Nelson
Editorial Description: Paragraph listings of conferences, grants, jobs UNM activities for Latin Americanists.
General Info: Yr. Est. 1980, Trim Size-8$\frac{1}{2}$ x 11, Mimeo press, 2 pages, Newsprint
Circulation: Total-1,600

LASA Forum
See: REGIONAL INTEREST

LAWS Quarterly
See: POLITICS

LDC Debt Report
See: BANKING & FINANCE

Language Matters
See: LITERATURE & LINGUISTICS

Latin America News Update   *Business, Association*
Publishing Co: Latin America News Update, PO Box 257247, Chicago, IL 60625-7247; Title Tel # (312) 275-0587
Personnel: Publisher-Evan Douthit
Editorial Description: News and issues covering Latin American countries.
General Info: Monthly, Trim Size-8$\frac{1}{2}$ x 11, 42 pages, No Color
Subscriptions: Indv. $36

Latin America Update
Publishing Co: Washington Office on Latin America, 110 Maryland Avenue, NE, Suite 404, Washington, DC 20002; Title Tel # (202) 544-8045
Personnel: Editor-Rachel Neild, Circ. Mgr.-Ulanda Rippy
Editorial Description: Bi-monthly analysis of political & economic conditions in Latin America & U.S. foreign policy toward the region.
General Info: Yr. Est. 1974, Bi-monthly, Web press, 8 pages, ISSN: 0738-601X, 2 Color, Newsprint
Subscriptions: Indv. $20, Inst. $35, For. $23, $3/copy
Circulation: (60% controlled), Total-2,000, Subscriptions-800, International-400
List Rental: Rents Lists
Printing Co: McArdle Printing Co., 800 Commerce Dr, Upper Marlboro, MD 20772-8792 Tel # (301) 390-8500

Latin American Jewish Studies
See: ETHNIC

Latin American Law and Business Report
See: INTERNATIONAL TRADE

Lawyer's Committee on Nuclear Policy Newsletter
See: LAW

Lebanon Report, The
Publishing Co: The Lebanese Center for Policy Studies, 1700 17th St NW Apt 306, Washington, DC 20009-2419; Title Tel # (202) 232-8350
Personnel: Editor-Paul Salem, Circ. Mgr., Adv. Dir.-Michelle Kjorlien
Editorial Description: Covers current events and issues in Lebanon.
General Info: Yr. Est. 1990, Monthly, Trim Size-8$\frac{1}{2}$ x 11, 8 pages, No Color
Subscriptions: Indv. $38, Inst. $75
Circulation: Total-3,000

Letter to Members
See: LAW

Lifelines
See: POLITICS

Liftoff
See: EDUCATION

Listen Real Loud: News of Women's Liberation Worldwide
See: WOMEN'S

Lithuanian-American Bulletin
See: ETHNIC

MSN Newsletter   *Consumer*
Publishing Co: Mozambique Support Network, PO Box 2284, Chicago, IL 60690-2284; Title Tel # (312) 922-3286 Title Fax # (312) 922-6988
Personnel: Circ. Mgr.-L. January, Publisher, Editor, Art Dir.-Sessy Nyman
Editorial Description: Solidarity newsletter about events in Mozambique & Mozambique related activities in the U.S.
General Info: Yr. Est. 1987, Quarterly, Desktop press, 10 pages, ISSN: 1045-0254, No Color, Newsprint
Subscriptions: Indv. $20, Inst. $30
Circulation: (33% controlled), Single Copy/Newsstand-700, Subscriptions-300
List Rental: Rents Lists

Maghreb Report
Business, Consumer

Publishing Co: Maghreb Report, PO Box 1593, Princeton, NJ 08542-1593;
Title Tel # (609) 924-0182 Title Fax # (609) 924-8185
Personnel: Publisher-Susan Rivers
Editorial Description: Covers politics and economics in North Africa.
General Info: Yr. Est. 1992, Bi-monthly, Trim Size-8½ x 11, 12 pages, ISSN: 1071-7579, No Color, Matte
Subscriptions: Indv. $50

Maps on File
See: GEOGRAPHY

Mealey's International Arbitration Report
See: LAW

Mennonite Central Committee-Washington Memo
See: POLITICS

Mexico Report, The
Business

Publishing Co: Legal Research International, Inc., 3701 Connecticut Ave., NW, Ste. 200, Washington, DC 20008-4501 Tel # (202) 363-8168; Title Tel # (202) 625-2424
Personnel: Editor-Christopher Whalen
Editorial Description: Contains articles and abstracts from newspapers covering Mexican politics.
General Info: Weekly, Trim Size-8½ x 11, 8 pages, No Color, Matte
Subscriptions: Indv. $450

Mexico Watch
Business

Publishing Co: Orbis Publications, L.L.C., 3201 New Mexico Ave., NW, Ste. 249, Washington, DC 20016; Title Tel # (202) 237-0155 Title Fax # (202) 237-0596
Personnel: Publisher-Kim Holmes, Editor-Michael Wilson
Editorial Description: Examines political & economic development in Mexico and current condition of U.S.-Mexico relations.
General Info: Yr. Est. 1990, Monthly, Trim Size-8½ x 11, Looseleaf
Subscriptions: Indv. $395, Can. $395, For. $395

Middle East Insider

Publishing Co: Canada Israel Committee, 980 Yonge St., #402, Toronto, ON M4W 2J5 Canada; Title Tel # (416) 963-9463 Title Fax # (416) 920-2631
Personnel: Publisher, Editor-David Weinberg, Circ. Mgr.-Dora Smaza
Editorial Description: A confidential, bi-weekly news analysis & commentary focusing on the politics of Israel & the Middle East. Special focus on Canadian Middle East policy.
General Info: (Formerly Canadian Middle East Digest), Yr. Est. 1984, Bi-weekly, Trim Size-8½ x 11, 6 pages, 2 Color, Coated
Circulation: Total-1,000
Advertising: Accepts Inserts.
Printing Co: Bowden's Information Services, 2206 Eglinton Ave., E., Toronto, ON M1L 4S7 Canada Tel # (416) 750-2220

Middle East Insight
Consumer

Publishing Co: International Insight, Inc., 1200 18th St NW Ste 305, Washington, DC 20036-2506; Title Tel # (202) 466-2146 Title Fax # (202) 466-2147
Editorial Description: Covers events and affairs in the Middle East.
General Info: Yr. Est. 1993, Weekly
Subscriptions: Indv. $350

Middle East Labor Bulletin
Business, Association

Publishing Co: Labor Committee on the Middle East, PO Box 421546, San Francisco, CA 94142-1546 Tel # (415) 255-9182
Personnel: Editor-Jeffrey Blankfort
Editorial Description: Cover Middle Eastern labor news.
General Info: Quarterly, Trim Size-8½ x 11, 30 pages, No Color

Middle East Policy Survey

Publishing Co: Middle East Policy Group, Inc., 3405 Rodman St NW, Washington, DC 20008-3116; Title Tel # (202) 363-3495 Title Fax # (202) 362-4513
Personnel: Editor-Richard Straus
Editorial Description: Assessment of Middle East policies and policy makers.
General Info: Yr. Est. 1980, Monthly, 4 pages
Subscriptions: Indv. $150, Inst. $150, For. $150
Circulation: Total-350

Minnesota International Center
Business, Association

Publishing Co: Minnesota International Center, 711 E River Rd, Minneapolis, MN 55455-0369; Title Tel # (612) 625-4421 Title Fax # (612) 624-1984
Personnel: Editor-Barb Olson
Editorial Description: To increase and strengthen international exchange and understanding between Minnesotans and the World.
General Info: (Formerly World Affairs Center), Yr. Est. 1953, Monthly, Trim Size-8½ x 11, Desktop press, 8 pages
Subscriptions: Indv. $25, Inst. $40
Circulation: Total-1,700, Readership-2,700
Advertising: Inquire for rates.

Minsk Business News
Consumer

Publishing Co: Minsk Business News, 1000 West McNab, Road Pompano Beach, FL 33069
Personnel: Editor-Mikhail Volodin
Editorial Description: Newsletter on business affaairs of Minsk - between Moscow and Poland - in Republic of Belarus.
General Info: Yr. Est. 1992, Monthly
Subscriptions: Indv. $24
Advertising: Inquire for rates.

Modern Greek Society: A Social Science Newsletter
Consumer, Association

Publishing Co: Sponsor-Modern Greek Studies Assn., Modern Greek Society, Modern Greek Studies Ass., Box 9411, Providence, RI 02940-9411; Title Tel # (401) 274-2397 Title Fax # (401) 456-8379
Personnel: Editor-Nikiforos Diamandouros, Publisher, Circ. Mgr., Production Mgr.-Peter Allen
Editorial Description: Systematic study of Modern Greek Society by social scientists in the field. Bibliography on social science research in Modern Greece.
General Info: (Formerly Modern Greek Society), Yr. Est. 1973, Semi-annually, Trim Size-9½ x 11, Desktop press, 80 pages, ISSN: 0147-0779, No Color, Newsprint, Case bound
Subscriptions: Indv. $15, Inst. $20, Can. $15, For. $15, $8/copy
Circulation: Total-600
List Rental: Actives: $75/M
Printing Co: Rhode Island College Office Services, 600 Mount Pleasant Ave, Providence, RI 02908-1924 Tel # (401) 456-8000

Monday: a weekly newsletter on refugee and immigration issues
See: ETHNIC

Money Laundering, Asset Forfeiture & Intl. Financial Crimes Newsletter
See: LAW

Morningstar Japan
Business, Consumer

Publishing Co: Morningstar, Inc., 225 W. Wacker Dr., Chicago, IL 60604-3606 Tel # (312) 696-6000 Fax # (312) 696-6001
Personnel: Publisher-Don Philips, Editor-Nika Yoshida, Mktg. Dir.-Kurt Herrman
Editorial Description: Single page profiles on 800 leading Japanese companies.
General Info: Yr. Est. 1992, Bi-weekly, ISSN: 1061-1886
Subscriptions: Indv. $495, Can. $465, For. $525

NAFSA Newsletter
See: EDUCATION

National Conference on Soviet Jewry-Newsbreak
Association

Publishing Co: Natl. Conference on Soviet Jewry, 730 Broadway, 2nd Floor, New York, NY 10003-9511; Title Tel # (212) 679-6122 Title Fax # (212) 686-1193
Personnel: Editor-Deborah Hart-Strober, Publisher, Production Mgr.-Shoshana Cardin
General Info: Bi-weekly, 2 pages, 2 Color
Subscriptions: Indv. $25
Circulation: Total-4,000

National League of POW/ MIA Families
Association

Publishing Co: National League of Families of American Prisoners, 1001 Connecticut Ave NW Ste, 919, Washington, DC 20036-5504; Title Tel # (202) 223-6846
Personnel: Publisher, Editor-Ann Griffiths
Editorial Description: Provides update on efforts to return POW/MIAs from Southeast Asia.
General Info: Yr. Est. 1974, Bi-monthly, Offset press, 12 pages, No Color
Subscriptions: Free
Circulation: Total-7,000
Printing Co: Huff Duplicating, 1100 17th St NW Ste 8b, Washington, DC 20036-4601 Tel # (202) 833-2000, Fax # (202) 452-1307

National Policy Watch
See: POLITICS

Near East Report

Publishing Co: Near East Report, Inc., 440 1st St NW Ste 307, Washington, DC 20001-2028; Title Tel # (202) 639-5254 Title Fax # (202) 347-4916
Personnel: Editor-Raphael Danziger, Adv. Dir.-Danita Oliver
Editorial Description: Washington newsletter on American policy in the Middle East.
General Info: Yr. Est. 1957, Weekly, Trim Size-8½ x 11, Offset press, 4 pages, ISSN: 0028-176X, Ind/Abs/Online: BoundVols., No Color
Subscriptions: Indv. $50, For. $65
Circulation: (90% controlled), Total-55,000
Printing Co: McArdle Printing Co., 800 Commerce Dr, Upper Marlboro, MD 20772-8792 Tel # (301) 390-8500

Neighbors
Association

Publishing Co: World Neighbors, Inc., 4127 NW 122nd St, Oklahoma City, OK 73120-8882 Tel # (405) 752-9700 Fax # (405) 752-9393; Title Tel # (405) 946-3333
Personnel: Editor-Charlene Scott, Production Mgr.-Becky Rosa
Editorial Description: Reports to donors on World Neighbors self-help program in 26 developing nations through feature stories and photographs from overseas project areas.
General Info: Quarterly, Trim Size-6½ x 9, Sheetfed press, 28 pages, 2 Color, Coated
Circulation: (100% controlled), Total-15,000

New American View
See: GOVERNMENT

New Directions in Middle East Studies Newsletter
Publishing Co: Univ. of California History Dept., Santa Barbara, Dept. of Hist., Santa Barbara, CA 93106; Title Tel # (805) 961-2311
General Info: Yr. Est. 1978, ISSN: 0270-7012

New Forces
See: GOVERNMENT

New Hampshire Council on World Affairs Bulletin
Publishing Co: New Hampshire Council on World Affairs, 11 Rosemary Ln, Durham, NH 03824-2332; Title Tel # (603) 862-1683
General Info: Monthly
Circulation: Total-600

New Zealand Economic Bulletin
Consumer, Association
Publishing Co: New Zealand Consulate, 12400 Wilshire Blvd Ste 1150, Los Angeles, CA 90025-1030
General Info: Quarterly

New Zealand Update
Business
Publishing Co: Embassy of New Zealand, 37 Observatory Cir NW, Washington, DC 20008-3686; Title Tel # (202) 328-4800
Personnel: Editor-Mei Taare
Editorial Description: Political, cultural, economic, business & trade news from New Zealand.
General Info: (Formerly New Zealand News), Yr. Est. 1979, Monthly, Trim Size-8½ x 11, Sheetfed press, 4 pages, 2 Color
Subscriptions: Free
Circulation: Total-6,500

News from Americas Watch
See: CIVIL RIGHTS

News from Jerusalem
See: PHILANTHROPY

News of Norway
Association
Publishing Co: Royal Norwegian Embassy, 2720-34th St., NW, Washington, DC 20008; Title Tel # (202) 333-6000
Personnel: Editor-Trygve Olfarnes
Editorial Description: Current economic, political, cultural events of general interest in Norway.
General Info: Yr. Est. 1941, Monthly, Trim Size-8½ x 11½, Offset press, 8 pages, ISSN: 0028-9272, 2 Color
Circulation: (100% controlled), Total-16,000
Printing Co: Newsletter Services, Inc., 9700 Philadelphia Court, Lanham, MD 20706 Tel # (301) 731-5200, Fax # (301) 731-5201

News Report
Publishing Co: Univ. of Wisconsin, South Asian Area Ctr., 1242 Van Hise, 1220 Linden Dr., Madison, WI 53706; Title Tel # (608) 262-3012
Personnel: Editor-Pamela Kviz
General Info: Quarterly, Trim Size-8½ x 11, Offset press, 10 pages
Circulation: Total-2,000

News-Tibet
Consumer
Publishing Co: Office of Tibet, 801 Second Ave., New York, NY 10017; Title Tel # (212) 213-5010 Title Fax # (212) 779-9245
Personnel: Publisher-Rinchen Dharlo
Editorial Description: Current situation in Tibet, Tibetian refugee activities in exile, and all phases of Tibetan culture.
General Info: Yr. Est. 1964, Trim Size-8½ x 11, Letrpr. press, 16 pages, 1% ads, Color-cover
Circulation: Total-5,000
Advertising: Inquire for rates.
List Rental: Actives: $200/M

NewsLinks
See: EDUCATION

Ngoma: The Talking Drum
See: SOCIAL SERVICES & WELFARE

Nicaragua Network News
Publishing Co: Nicaragua Network, 1247 E St., S.E., Washington, DC 20003-2221; Title Tel # (202) 223-2328
Personnel: Editor-Linda Clements
General Info: Yr. Est. 1987, Bi-monthly

Nicaragua Update
Publishing Co: Sponsor-Northern California Ecumenical Council, Nicaragua Interfaith Committee for Action, 942 Market St Ste 411, San Francisco, CA 94102-4008; Title Tel # (415) 433-6057
Personnel: Editor-Janine Chagoya
Editorial Description: Information on the current situation in Nicaragua.
General Info: Yr. Est. 1979, Quarterly, Trim Size-8½ x 14, Sheetfed press, 6 pages
Subscriptions: Indv. $12
Circulation: Total-7,000

North Star Compass
Association
Publishing Co: Canadian Freinds of Soviet People, 280 Queen St., W., Toronto, ON M5V 2A1 Canada Tel # (416) 977-5819 Fax # (416) 592-0781; Title Tel # (416) 927-5819 Title Fax # (416) 593-0781
Personnel: Editor-Michael Lucas
Editorial Description: To present news from sources that are striving to rebuild socialism in former ussr. Materials gathered from over 84 newspapers leading this struggle.
General Info: (Formerly Focus on Friendship), Yr. Est. 1970, Bi-monthly
Subscriptions: Free With Membership
Circulation: Total-4,000
Advertising: Inquire for rates.

Notes from the National Committee
Publishing Co: Natl. Committee on U.S.-China Relations, 71 W. 23rd St., 19th Fl., New York, NY 10010-4102; Title Tel # (212) 922-1385 Title Fax # (212) 557-8258
Personnel: Publisher, Editor-Elizabeth Knup
Editorial Description: Reports on Committee exchanges, editorials on U.S.-China relations.
General Info: Yr. Est. 1974, Offset press, 12 pages, 2 Color
Subscriptions: Indv. $5
Circulation: (100% controlled), Total-1,600

Ohio Slavic and East European Newsletter
Consumer, Association
Publishing Co: Ohio State University, Center for Slavic Studies, 303 Oxley Hall, Columbus, OH 43210-1219; Title Tel # (614) 292-8770 Title Fax # (614) 292-4273
Personnel: Editor-Matthew Schwanek
Editorial Description: News & announcements of interest to students of Russia & Eastern Europe, with an emphasis on activities at Ohio State Univ. & other Ohio institutions.
General Info: Yr. Est. 1973, Bi-monthly, Trim Size-8½ x 11, Mimeo press, 10 pages, ISSN: 1048-6615, No Color
Subscriptions: Free
Acquistions: Publication Bought
Circulation: Total-1,000

Olive Branch
See: POLITICS

One Country
Publishing Co: Baha'i International Community, 866 United Nations Plaza, Suite 120, New York, NY 10017
General Info: Quarterly, ISSN: 1018-9300

Open Doors News Brief
Association
Publishing Co: Open Doors with Brother Andrew, PO Box 27001, Santa Ana, CA 92799-7001; Title Tel # (714) 531-6000 Title Fax # (714) 531-6228
Personnel: Publisher, Editor-Jeff Taylor, Art Dir.-Suzi Quinones
Editorial Description: Information on persecution of Christians in restricted countries.
General Info: Yr. Est. 1971, Monthly, Trim Size-8½ x 11, Web press, 8 pages, 2 Color, Newsprint
Subscriptions: Indv. $12
Circulation: Total-70,000

Organization of American States, Statistical Bulletin
Association
Publishing Co: Organization of American States, 19th Constitution Ave. N W, Suite #300, Washington, DC 20006 Tel # (202) 458-3000; Title Tel # (703) 941-1617
General Info: Yr. Est. 1979, Quarterly, ISSN: 0250-6289
Subscriptions: Indv. $12
Circulation: Total-1,000

Orientalia Journal
Consumer
Publishing Co: Orientalia Journal, PO Box 94, Little Neck, NY 11363-0094; Title Tel # (718) 229-6593
Personnel: Publisher, Editor-Sandra Andacht, Art Dir., Promotion Dir.-Carl Andacht
Editorial Description: A bimonthly covering all aspects of oriental antiques and collectibles.
General Info: Yr. Est. 1979, Bi-monthly, Trim Size-8½ x 11, Sheetfed press, 12 pages, ISSN: 0164-3398, 2 Color, Newsprint
Subscriptions: Indv. $12, Inst. $10, $3/copy
Printing Co: Ancraft, 133 W. 21st St., New York, NY 10011 Tel # (212) 243-1560

Other Israel, The
Association, Consumer
Publishing Co: Israel Council for Israeli-Palestinian Peace, 4816 Cornell Ave, Downers Grove, IL 60515-3323; Title Tel # (708) 969-7584
Personnel: Editor-Adam Keller
Editorial Description: Covers the Israeli peace movement; comments on events in Israel and the Middle East.
General Info: Yr. Est. 1983, Bi-monthly, 12 pages, ISSN: 0792-4615, Matte, Other
Subscriptions: Indv. $30, Inst. $50
Circulation: Total-4,000, Readership-4,000

Outlook
See: HEALTH

Outpost
Consumer, Association

Publishing Co: Americans for A Safe Israel, 147 E. 76th St., New York, NY 10021-2822
Fax # (212) 988-4065; Title Tel # (212) 628-9400
Personnel: Publisher-Herbert Zweibon, Editor-Ruth King
Editorial Description: Topics include: Israel; American-Israel relations; Arab-Israel conflict; American political organizations.
General Info: Yr. Est. 1972, Monthly, 18 pages, No Color
Subscriptions: Free With Membership
Circulation: Total-12,000

Overground Railroad:
Telegraph News

Publishing Co: Overground Railroad, 722 Monroe St, Evanston, IL 60202-2613;
Title Tel # (708) 328-0772
General Info: Yr. Est. 1983, Bi-monthly

PACA News
Association

Publishing Co: People's Alliance on Central America, 284 Illinois Union, Univ. of ILL., 1401 W. Green, Urbana, IL 61801-7321; Title Tel # (217) 333-7076
Personnel: Editor-Lisa Offult
Editorial Description: News, editorials, resources, calendar of events relating to Central America.
General Info: Yr. Est. 1982, Monthly, 8 pages
Subscriptions: Indv. $15, Inst. $20
Circulation: Total-1,000

PADF News
Association

Publishing Co: Pan American Development Foundation, 1889 F St., N.W., Washington, DC 20006-4499 Tel # (202) 458-3969; Title Tel # (202) 458-3972 Title Fax # (202) 458-6316
Personnel: Editor-Jeanine Hess
Editorial Description: Subjects pertinent to PADF development programs in Latin America, Carribean, United States.
General Info: Offset press, 8 pages, 2 Color
Subscriptions: Free
Circulation: Total-5,000

PIASA Bulletin, The

Publishing Co: Polish Institute of Arts, 208 E 30th St, New York, NY 10016-8202
General Info: Bi-monthly

PLO Watch

Publishing Co: Middle Eastern Affairs Dept. of the Anti-Defamation League o, 823 U.N. Plz., New York, NY 10017

PS: Intelligent Guide to Jewish Affairs
See: POLITICS

Pacific Rim Telecommunications
See: TELECOMMUNICATIONS

Palestine Digest
Association

Publishing Co: League of Arab States, Arab Information Center, 747 3rd Ave., New York, NY 10017-2803
General Info: Yr. Est. 1971, Bi-monthly

Palestine Issue

Publishing Co: Palestine Liberation Organization, 115 E 65th St, New York, NY 10021-7006;
Title Tel # (212) 686-3530
General Info: Yr. Est. 1966

Participatory Formation
See: EDUCATION

Partners
Association

Publishing Co: Partners of the Americas, 1424 K St NW Ste 700, Washington, DC 20005-2410;
Title Tel # (202) 628-3300
Personnel: Editor-Doreen Cubie
Editorial Description: Citizens in 44 U.S. states and 21 Latin American countries cooperate on health, education, agricultural projects.
General Info: Yr. Est. 1975, Semi-monthly, Trim Size-11 x 16, Offset press, 8 pages, 2 Color
Circulation: Total-13,000

Peace Gazette
See: POLITICS

Peace Reporter
Association

Publishing Co: National Peace Foundation, 1835 K St NW Ste 610, Washington, DC 20006-1203;
Title Tel # (202) 223-1770 Title Fax # (202) 223-1718
Personnel: Editor-Kathleen Lansing
Editorial Description: Information on National Peace Foundation, the U.S. Institute of Peace & other peace institutes, United Nations, & peace education.
General Info: Yr. Est. 1986, Quarterly, Trim Size-8½ x 11, Offset press, 8 pages, ISSN: 1049-0779, 2 Color
Subscriptions: Indv. $35, Inst. $50, Free With Membership
Circulation: Total-16,000
Printing Co: Baker-Webster Printing, 1121 5th St NW, Washington, DC 20001-3690
Tel # (202) 628-8061

Peaceful Pieces
Consumer

Publishing Co: Boise Peace Quilt Project, 1110 Warm Springs Ave, Boise, ID 83712-7949
Tel # (208) 378-0293 Fax # (208) 323-0848; Title Tel # (208) 345-6709
Personnel: Editor-Lyn McCollum
Editorial Description: Promotes the production of peace quilts used as gestures of intl. goodwill.
General Info: Yr. Est. 1983, Quarterly, Trim Size-7 x 8½, Desktop press, 48 pages, No Color
Subscriptions: Indv. $6, $3/copy
Circulation: Total-600

Periscope
Association

Publishing Co: Assn. of Former Intelligence Officers, 6723 Whittier Ave Ste 303a, Mc Lean, VA 22101-4533; Title Tel # (703) 790-0320 Title Fax # (703) 790-0264
Editorial Description: Concerned about the future of U.S. intelligence system in consequence of prevalent media reporting.
General Info: Yr. Est. 1975, Quarterly

Perspectives on
Contemporary Ukraine
Association

Publishing Co: Ukrainian Research Institute, Harvard University, 1583 Massachusetts Ave, Cambridge, MA 02138-2801; Title Tel # (617) 495-4053 Title Fax # (617) 495-8097
Personnel: Editor-Andrew Sorokowski
Editorial Description: Listings of the weekly seminar in Ukrainian studies at Harvard Univ., Ukrainian research institute news, commentary and essays on contemporary Ukraine.
General Info: (Formerly Minutes of the Seminar in Ukrainian Studies), Yr. Est. 1970, Bi-monthly, Trim Size-8½ x 11, Desktop press, 12 pages, ISSN: 0362-8078, No Color, Saddle-stitched
Subscriptions: $3/copy
Circulation: Total-200
Printing Co: Harvard Univ. Copy Services, Harvard Univ., Cambridge, MA 02138

Philippine Labor Alert
Consumer

Publishing Co: Maka'ainana Media, 2252 Puna St, Honolulu, HI 96817-1539;
Title Tel # (808) 595-7362
Personnel: Editor-John Witeck
Editorial Description: Focuses on news and analysis of the Philippine worker's movement and US-Philippine relations.
General Info: Yr. Est. 1984, Quarterly, Trim Size-8½ x 11, Offset press, 12 pages
Subscriptions: Indv. $10, Inst. $20, Can. $12, For. $20, $3/copy
Circulation: Total-1,500

Philippine Letter
Business

Publishing Co: Philippine Letter, PO Box 88189, Los Angeles, CA 90009-8189;
Title Tel # (852) 526-2950
Personnel: Publisher, Editor-C. R. Smith
Editorial Description: Provides interpretation & analysis of the economic, trade, political, and social development of the Philippines.
General Info: Yr. Est. 1978, 24x/yr., Trim Size-8½ x 11, Offset press, 4 pages
Subscriptions: Indv. $120
Acquistions: Publication Bought

Philippine Studies
Newsletter
Scholarly, Association

Publishing Co: Sponsor-Assn. for Asian Studies, Univ. of Hawaii at Manoa, 1890 East-West Rd., Moore Hall, #416, Honolulu, HI 96822; Title Tel # (808) 956-2315
Personnel: Editor-Alice W. Mak, Circ. Mgr.-Connie Cox-Bodner
Editorial Description: News on academic activities in Philippine studies throughout the world.
General Info: (Formerly Philippine Studies Bulletin), Yr. Est. 1973, Tri-annually, Desktop press, 12 pages, No Color, Saddle-stitched
Subscriptions: Indv. $8, Inst. $10
Circulation: Total-200

Point of View

Publishing Co: Vermont Council on World Affairs, Trinity College, Burlington, VT 05401-1496;
Title Tel # (802) 658-0337
Personnel: Publisher-Vern Lindquist, Editor-Ingel Schaeffer
Editorial Description: General and specific information on international education and American foreign policy activities throughout Vermont.
General Info: (Formerly Vermont Council on World Affairs, Newsletter), Yr. Est. 1953, Quarterly, Mimeo press
Circulation: Total-1,250

Points East

Publishing Co: Sino-Judaic Institute, 232 Lexington Dr, Menlo Park, CA 94025-2910
Editorial Description: Focus is on the history of Jews in China, from Kaifeng Jews of early times to refugees in Shanghai in 20th Century, as well as other China-related issues which affect Jews.
General Info: Yr. Est. 1985, 3x/yr., ISSN: 1063-6269
Subscriptions: Indv. $50, Inst. $50, $5/copy
Acquistions: Publication Bought
Circulation: Total-1,000

Popline
See: ENVIRONMENT & ECOLOGY

Post-Soviet Jewry Report   *Association*

Publishing Co: Action for Post Soviet Jewry, Inc., 24 Crescent St., Ste. 306, Waltham, MA 02154-4060; Title Tel # (617) 893-2331 Title Fax # (617) 647-9474
Personnel: Editor-Judy Patkin
Editorial Description: Current update of events and situations, as well as human rights violations against Jews and dissidents in the former Soviet Union.
General Info: (Formerly Soviet Jewry Report), Yr. Est. 1975, Bi-monthly, Trim Size-8½ x 11, Offset press, 6 pages, No Color, Newsprint
Subscriptions: Indv. $36
Circulation: Total-4,000
Printing Co: Discount Newsletter Printing, 1487 Persisterce Dr., PO Box 1487, Woodbridge, VA 22193-0487 Tel # (703) 690-1788, Fax # (703) 491-2563

Post-Soviet Prospects

Publishing Co: Center for Strategic and International Studies(CSIS), 1800 K St NW-Ste 400, Washington, DC 20006; Title Tel # (202) 775-3240 Title Fax # (202) 775-3132
Personnel: Editor-Gabriel Schoenfeld, Mag. Ed.-David Kramer
Editorial Description: Our goal is to capture the problems and possibilities of those countries that are in very different ways, making the transition to a post-communist order.
General Info: (Formerly Soviet Prospects), Yr. Est. 1990, 8x/yr., ISSN: 1052-8601
Subscriptions: Indv. $24, Inst. $24, Can. $36, For. $36

Postal Link   *Business, Consumer*

Publishing Co: Johnson & Hayward, 516 W 19th St # 22, New York, NY 10011-2807; Title Tel # (212) 675-4250
General Info: Trim Size-8½ x 11, 4 pages, 2 Color, Matte

Public Affairs Newsletter

Publishing Co: Society for Citizen Education in World Affairs, 2038 Freda Laney #G-106, Cardiff by the Sea, CA 92007-1419; Title Tel # (202) 333-0741
Personnel: Publisher, Editor-Albert Mark, Circ. Mgr.-Marta Berk, Production Mgr.-Bertram Kall, Art Dir.-Art Blaker, Adv. Dir., Promotion Dir.-Jorie Mark
General Info: (Formerly World Affairs Newsletter), Yr. Est. 1962, Monthly, Trim Size-8½ x 11, Sheetfed press, 12 pages, 2 Color, Newsprint
Subscriptions: Indv. $18

RFE/RL Research Report   *Consumer, Association*

Publishing Co: RFE/RL Research Institute, 1201 Connecticut Ave NW Ste, 410, Washington, DC 20036-2605 Tel # (202) 457-6900 Fax # (202) 457-6992 Parent Co.-Radio Free Europe/Radio Liberty, Inc., New York
Personnel: Editor-David Allis
Editorial Description: Provide topical analyses of political, economic, security, and social developments in the area extending from the Baltic to the Balkans, and from the Oder to the Pacific.
General Info: (Formerly Report on the USSR; Report on Eastern Europe), Yr. Est. 1989, Weekly, ISSN: 0941-505X
Subscriptions: Indv. $195, Can. $150

Refugee Reports   *Consumer, Association*

Publishing Co: U.S. Committee for Refugees, 1717 Massachusetts Ave. NW, Suite 701, Washington, DC 20036-2001 Tel # (202) 347-3507 Fax # (202) 347-3418
General Info: Yr. Est. 1979, Monthly, ISSN: 0884-3554
Subscriptions: Indv. $45, Inst. $45, Can. $45, For. $95
Circulation: Total-1,600

Regulation of Intl. Commercial Aviation: The Intl. Regulatory Structure & Treaties
See: LAW

Report on Guatemala   *Consumer*

Publishing Co: Guatemala News & Information Bureau, PO Box 28594, Oakland, CA 94604-8594; Title Tel # (510) 835-0810 Title Fax # (510) 835-0810
Personnel: Editor-David Loeb
Editorial Description: News & analysis on political, economic, social situation in Guatemala.
General Info: (Formerly Guatemala), Yr. Est. 1978, Quarterly, Trim Size-8½ x 11, Web press, 16 pages, ISSN: 1043-3856, No Color, Newsprint, Saddle-stitched
Subscriptions: Indv. $12, Inst. $18, Can. $18, For. $18, $2/copy
Circulation: Total-3,500
List Rental: Actives: 1,300, $50/M
Printing Co: Alonzo Printing Co., Investment Blvd., Hayward, CA 94080 Tel # (510) 293-0522

Report on Science and Human Rights   *Association*

Publishing Co: American Assn. for the Advancement of Science, 1333 H St. NW, Washington, DC 20005-4707; Title Tel # (202) 326-6790
Personnel: Editor-K. Hannibal
Editorial Description: Examines intl. human rights violations against scientists & pertinent scientific issues.
General Info: (Formerly Clearinghouse Report on Science & Human Rights), Yr. Est. 1978, Semi-annually, 8 pages, ISSN: 0895-5999, No Color
Circulation: Total-2,500

Republic of Iraq, Bulletin of The

Publishing Co: Embassy of the Republic of Iraq, 1801 P St NW, Washington, DC 20036-1201
General Info: Yr. Est. 1960, Monthly

Republic of the Phillipines Newsletter

Publishing Co: Embassy of the Republic of the Phillipines, 1617 Massachusetts Ave NW, Washington, DC 20036-2209; Title Tel # (202) 483-0092 Title Fax # (202) 328-7614
Personnel: Editor-Macarthur Corsino
Editorial Description: Contains news on the Phillipines from Manila and the United States. Also contains views from the standpoint of the Phillipine Embassy.
General Info: Bi-weekly, Trim Size-8½ x 11

Research Bulletin on Southern Africa

Publishing Co: Fernand Braudel Center, Binghamton University, Box 6000, Binghamton, NY 13902-6000; Title Tel # (607) 777-4924 Title Fax # (607) 777-4315
Personnel: Editor-Immanuel Wallerstein
General Info: Yr. Est. 1983, Irregular, Trim Size-8½ x 11, Offset press, 10 pages
Subscriptions: Free
Circulation: Total-200

Resource Center Bulletin   *Business*

Publishing Co: Interhemispheric Resource Center, PO Box 4506, Albuquerque, NM 87196-4506; Title Tel # (505) 842-8288 Title Fax # (505) 246-1601
Personnel: Editor-Tom Barry, Adv. Dir.-Nancy Guinn, Art Dir.-John Hawley
Editorial Description: This publication is a report on US relations with Third World countries, especially those in Central America. Economic and food issues are discussed, as well as military & nonmilitary intervention.
General Info: Yr. Est. 1985, Quarterly, Trim Size-8½ x 11, 16 pages, ISSN: 0891-2688, 2 Color, Matte, Saddle-stitched
Subscriptions: Indv. $5, Can. $8, For. $8, $2/copy
Circulation: (5% controlled), Total-3,500, Subscriptions-1,200

Review

Publishing Co: North-South Institute, 55 Murray, #200, Ottawa, ON K1N 5M3 Canada; Title Tel # (613) 241-3535 Title Fax # (613) 241-7435
Editorial Description: Newsletter on Canadian foreign policy trends and development issues.
General Info: Quarterly, 16 pages, ISSN: 1188-4347
Subscriptions: Free
Circulation: Total-4,000, Readership-4,000
Printing Co: Lowe-Martin Group, 363 Coventry Rd., Ottawa, ON K1K 2C5 Canada Tel # (613) 741-0962, Fax # (613) 741-2144

Romanian Business News   *Business*

Publishing Co: COSMOS Inc., PO Box 30437, Bethesda, MD 20824-0437; Title Tel # (301) 229-5875 Title Fax # (301) 229-5876
Editorial Description: Covers business news and information from Romania.
General Info: 11x/yr., Trim Size-8½ x 11, 12 pages, 2 Color
Subscriptions: Indv. $185

Russia and Commonwealth Business Law Report
See: LAW

Russia and Her Neighbors, Facts & Views on Daily Life   *Consumer*

Publishing Co: Highgate Road Social Science Research Station, 32 Highgate Rd, Berkeley, CA 94707-1141; Title Tel # (510) 525-3248 Title Fax # (510) 525-3313
Personnel: Publisher-Ethel Dunn, Editor-Eugenia Miller, Circ. Mgr.-Patty Ratliff, Art Dir.-Diana Wong
Editorial Description: Facts & views on daily life in the Commonwealth of Independent States with emphasis on hard-to-find details.
General Info: (Formerly Station Relay), Yr. Est. 1985, Quarterly, Trim Size-8½ x 11, Desktop press, 90 pages, ISSN: 1066-0127, No Color
Subscriptions: Indv. $25, Inst. $30, For. $35, $12/copy
Circulation: Total-500
Advertising: Inquire for rates.

Russian Far East Update
See: INTERNATIONAL TRADE

SANE World/Freeze Focus
See: POLITICS

SPSC Letter · *Association*

Publishing Co: Saharan Peoples Support Committee, 217 E Lehr Ave, Ada, OH 45810-1431; Title Tel # (419) 634-3666
Personnel: Editor-Anne Lippert
Editorial Description: Describes refuge camps,diplomatic events,etc.
General Info: Yr. Est. 1979, Quarterly, Sheetfed press, 8 pages
Subscriptions: Indv. $5, $1/copy
Circulation: Total-1,000

SWL
See: HOBBY

Service Committee News
See: RELIGIOUS & THEOLOGICAL

Shalom-Jewish Peace Newsletter
See: RELIGIOUS & THEOLOGICAL

Short Alert

Publishing Co: Concordia College, 275 Syndicate St N, Saint Paul, MN 55104-5494; Title Tel # (800) 333-5697
Personnel: Editor-Patrick Charuhas

Six Nations, One Soul · *Association*

Publishing Co: Celtic League, American Branch, Box 20153, Dag Hammarskjold Ctr., New York, NY 10017
Editorial Description: Contains features and articles about Celtic language and culture in Scotland, Ireland, Brittany, Wales, Cornwall, and the Isle of Man.
General Info: Quarterly
Subscriptions: Free With Membership

Society for Historians of American Foreign Relations, Newsletter
See: HISTORY

Solidarity/Solidaridad

Publishing Co: Committee in Solidarity with Latin American Nonviolent Movem, 1114 Noble St, Houston, TX 77009-8438; Title Tel # (215) 868-6271
Personnel: Editor-Joanna Swanger
General Info: Yr. Est. 1982, Quarterly
Subscriptions: Indv. $5

Soundings · *Consumer, Association*

Publishing Co: World Neighbors, Inc., 4127 NW 122nd St, Oklahoma City, OK 73120-8882; Title Tel # (405) 752-9700 Title Fax # (405) 752-9393
Editorial Description: An idea exchange in rural development communications.
General Info: (Formerly Soundings from Around the World), Yr. Est. 1970, Semi-annually
Subscriptions: Indv. $5, $1/copy
Circulation: (100% controlled), Total-1,500

South Carolina Committee Against Hunger
See: NUTRITION

Southeast Asia Program Series: Monographs, Translations, Bibliographies · *Scholarly*

Publishing Co: Southeast Asia Program- Cornell Univ., 640 Stewart Ave., Ithaca, NY 14850 Tel # (607) 225-4359; Title Tel # (607) 255-4359 Title Fax # (607) 277-1904
Personnel: Editor-Audrey Kahin, Circ. Mgr.-Hazel Prentice, Promotion Dir.-Dolina Millar
Editorial Description: History, politics, anthropology of Southeast Asia.
General Info: (Formerly Data Papers), Yr. Est. 1986, Looseleaf

Soviet World Outlook · *Association*

Publishing Co: Advanced Intl. Studies Institute, 1740 Massachusetts Ave NW, Washington, DC 20036-1984; Title Tel # (202) 663-5600
Personnel: Editor-Mose Harvey, Art Dir.-Susan Kulchar
Editorial Description: Examines Kremlin views on issues critical to U.S. interests. Content is based upon but not limited to careful reading and analysis of the complete gamut of official Soviet sources.
General Info: Yr. Est. 1976, Monthly, Trim Size-8$\frac{1}{2}$ x 11, Offset press, 8 pages, Color
Subscriptions: Indv. $18, $2/copy
Circulation: Total-15,000

Special Libraries Assn., Social Science Division Bulletin
See: LIBRARY

Spotlight on Africa · *Consumer, Association*

Publishing Co: American-African Affairs Assn., 1001 Connecticut Ave NW Ste, 1,135, Washington, DC 20036-5504; Title Tel # (202) 223-5110
Personnel: Editor-J.A. Packer
Editorial Description: Educational organization designed to circulate information about African countries with
General Info: Yr. Est. 1965, Annually, 4 pages, 2 Color
Subscriptions: Indv. $10
Circulation: Total-1,500

Studium Papers · *Consumer*

Publishing Co: Studium: N. American Study Center for Polish Affairs, 1281 Rugby Cir, Bloomfield, MI 48302-0945; Title Tel # (313) 662-7109
Personnel: Editor-Marek Nowak
Editorial Description: Serves as a Forum on Contemporary Poland.
General Info: Yr. Est. 1976, Quarterly, 24 pages, ISSN: 0741-9694, Color, Coated
Subscriptions: Indv. $25, $8/copy
Circulation: Total-2,200
Advertising: Inquire for rates.

Super Projects · *Business, Association*

Publishing Co: World Development Council, 40 Technology Park, Norcross, GA 30092-9934 Fax # (404) 263-8825; Title Tel # (404) 446-6996 Title Fax # (770) 263-8825
Personnel: Editor-Laura Lyne
Editorial Description: Reports on programs and events of the Wordl Development Council whose members are involved in large scale international projects.
General Info: Yr. Est. 1992, Quarterly, Trim Size-8$\frac{1}{2}$ x 11, 8 pages, Coated
Subscriptions: Free With Membership

Tax Laws of the World
See: LAW

Tidewater Nicaragua Project Fdn. Newsletter

Publishing Co: Tidewater Nicaragua Project Foundation, 3916 Shell Rd, Hampton, VA 23669-4228; Title Tel # (804) 723-7179
General Info: Yr. Est. 1984, Quarterly

Tokyo Insider

Publishing Co: Asia Pacific Communications, Inc., 60 Madison Ave Lbby 3, New York, NY 10010-1600
General Info: Monthly
Subscriptions: Indv. $240

Toward Freedom · *Scholarly, Association* · CPM: $75

Publishing Co: Toward Freedom Inc., 209 College St # 202a, Burlington, VT 05401-8306; Title Tel # (802) 658-2523 Title Fax # (802) 658-3738
Personnel: Publisher-Robin Lloyd, Editor-Greg Guma, Circ. Mgr., Adv. Dir., Mktg. Dir.-Mike Reilly
Editorial Description: Covers global news: analysis, and advocacy as well as politics human rights and culture issues.
General Info: Yr. Est. 1952, 8x/yr., Trim Size-8$\frac{1}{4}$ x 10$\frac{3}{4}$, Desktop press, 24 pages, ISSN: 00-48-989, Ind/Abs/Online: Alt.Pr. Ind., 10% ads, No Color, Newsprint
Subscriptions: Indv. $25, Can. $30, For. $35, $3/copy
Circulation: Total-4,000
Advertising: $300.
Printing Co: B.D. Press, Sales Office, Georgia, VT 05403 Tel # (802) 898-4214, Fax # (802) 893-6790

Transatlantic Perspectives · *Consumer*

Publishing Co: German Marshall Fund of the U.S., 11 Dupont Circle, NW, Washington, DC 20036-1207; Title Tel # (202) 745-3950 Title Fax # (202) 265-1662
Personnel: Editor-Nick Allen
Editorial Description: Articles in which grantees report on their German Marshall Fund supported work.
General Info: Yr. Est. 1979, Quarterly, Trim Size-8$\frac{1}{2}$ x 11, Sheetfed press, 16 pages, ISSN: 0192-477X, Ind/Abs/Online: SAGE, 2 Color, Coated, Saddle-stitched
Subscriptions: Free
Circulation: Total-9,000

Transition: The Newsletter About Reforming Economies · *Business, Association*

Publishing Co: World Bank, 1818 H St., NW N-9023, Washington, DC 20433-0001 Tel # (202) 477-1234 Fax # (202) 477-6391; Title Tel # (202) 473-7466 Title Fax # (202) 522-1151
General Info: Yr. Est. 1990, Monthly
Subscriptions: Free
Circulation: Total-10,000, Readership-10,000
Advertising: Accepts Inserts.

Translation Series · *Scholarly*

Publishing Co: Southeast Asia Program- Cornell Univ., 640 Stewart Ave., Ithaca, NY 14850 Tel # (607) 225-4359; Title Tel # (607) 255-8038 Title Fax # (607) 277-1904
Personnel: Editor-Audrey Kahin, Circ. Mgr.-Hazel Prentice, Promotion Dir.-Dolina Millar
Editorial Description: Translations of scholarship on Southeast Asia.
General Info: Yr. Est. 1992, Irregular, Trim Size-7 x 10, 200 pages, No Color, Perfect bound, Looseleaf
Acquistions: Publication Sold

Trialogue

Publishing Co: Trilateral Commission, 345 E 46th St, New York, NY 10017-3518
Personnel: Editor-Franscois Sauzey
Editorial Description: Bulletin of North American-European-Japanese affairs.
General Info: Yr. Est. 1973
Circulation: Total-5,500

Twentieth Century Fund
Newsletter *Business*

Publishing Co: Twentieth Century Fund, 41 E 70th St, New York, NY 10021-4972; Title Tel # (212) 535-4441
Editorial Description: Reports on all research projects being conducted by the Twentieth Century Fund, as well as projects completed and books published.
General Info: Yr. Est. 1919, Quarterly, Web press, 4 pages, Color
Circulation: Total-12,000

UNESCO Assn. /USA-
Newsletter

Publishing Co: UNESCO Assn. /USA, 5815 Lawton Ave, Oakland, CA 94618-1510; Title Tel # (510) 654-4638 Title Fax # (510) 658-3469
Personnel: Editor-Dorothy Hackbarth
Editorial Description: Intl. information on education, science, culture, communication; emphasizing american interests.
General Info: Yr. Est. 1974, Bi-monthly, Mimeo press, 4 pages, Ind/Abs/Online: AOL
Subscriptions: Indv. $20, Inst. $35

UNITE!

Publishing Co: Association to Unite the Democracies, 1506 Pennsylvania Ave SE, Washington, DC 20003-3116; Title Tel # (202) 544-5150 Title Fax # (202) 544-3742
Personnel: Editor-Christopher Unger, Assoc. Ed.-Erik Johnson
Editorial Description: Covers initiatives toward problems of political, economic & military cooperation & integration in the European, Atlantic, Trilateral (OECD) & Helsinki process (CSCE) regions. Provides federalist analysis, & an American link to the federalist trend in the European community (EC).
General Info: (Formerly Federator, The), Yr. Est. 1991, Bi-monthly
Subscriptions: Indv. $20, Can. $20, For. $30, Free With Membership
Circulation: Total-2,500

USACOR Newsletter

Publishing Co: U.S. Assn. for the Club of Rome, 1359 SW 22nd Ter # 2, Miami, FL 33145-3938
Personnel: Editor-Jeff Fobes
General Info: Yr. Est. 1977, Quarterly
Subscriptions: Indv. $35
Circulation: Total-500

USAID Developments

Publishing Co: Agency for International Development, 320 21 St. N.W., Ste 4889, Washington, DC 20523-0001 Fax # (202) 647-3945; Title Tel # (202) 647-4330
Editorial Description: Facts about the U.S. foreign aid program.
General Info: (Formerly A.I.D. Highlights), Yr. Est. 1984, Quarterly, 4 pages, Color
Circulation: Total-25,000

USET Monthly Bulletin *Business*

Publishing Co: United South & Eastern Tribes, Inc., 711 Stewarts Ferry Pike # 100, Nashville, TN 37214-2634
General Info: Monthly, Desktop press

USLA Reporter *Association*

Publishing Co: USLA Justice Committee, 535 W. 51st St. #4-0, New York, NY 10019-5068; Title Tel # (212) 254-6062
Editorial Description: Supports and reports on the struggle for human rights in Latin America.

Uganda Newsletter *Association*

Publishing Co: Embassy of the Republic of Uganda, 5909 16th St NW, Washington, DC 20011-2816; Title Tel # (202) 726-7100
Personnel: Editor, Circ. Mgr.-Jesse Mutenga
Editorial Description: Current events in Uganda and Uganda government statements.
General Info: Yr. Est. 1968, Monthly, 25 pages, 2 Color
Circulation: Total-1,000

Ultimate Issues
See: LIFESTYLE

Understanding Defense
See: MILITARY & NAVAL

Unitarian-Universalists in Support of Sanctuary Newsletter
See: POLITICS

United Nations Jobs Newsletter
See: EMPLOYMENT

United Nations Weekly
Report Newsletter *Business, Consumer*

Publishing Co: United Nations Publications, Two UN Plaza, Room DC2-853, New York, NY 10017 Tel # (212) 963-8302 Fax # (212) 963-3489; Title Tel # (212) 288-8505
Personnel: Publisher, Editor-Renate McCarter
Editorial Description: News summary about United Nations and other international bodies, worldwide and additional services to subscribers.
General Info: Yr. Est. 1982, Weekly, Trim Size-8½ x 11, Offset press, 4 pages, 2 Color
Subscriptions: Indv. $93, $5/copy
Circulation: Total-1,400
Advertising: Accepts Inserts.

U.S. & World Early Warning Report for Investors
See: INVESTMENT

U.S. Anti-Apartheid
Newsletter

Publishing Co: American Friends Service Comm (AFSC)-International Division, 1501 Cherry St, Philadelphia, PA 19102-1429; Title Tel # (215) 241-7168
Personnel: Editor-Jerry Herman
Editorial Description: The U.S. Anti-Apartheid letter is published to promote communication among organizations involved in efforts to end apartheid in S. Africa. The newsletter also publizes the activities of grassroot regional/national organizations, campaigns and organizes against apartheid in N. America.
General Info: Quarterly, Desktop press, 8 pages, ISSN: 1054-3487
Subscriptions: Indv. $10
Circulation: Total-50,000

U.S.-Iran Review *Association, Business* CPM: $160

Publishing Co: Forum for American-Iranian Relations, 2000 L St NW Ste 200, Washington, DC 20036-4907 Tel # (202) 457-8800 Fax # (202) 457-1459; Title Tel # (202) 416-1635 Title Fax # (202) 625-1361
Personnel: Publisher-Biran Sepasy, Ph.D., Editor-Joseph Schechla, Adv. Mgr.-Steve Mill, Mktg. Dir.-John Luke, Promotion Mgr.-Sam Gelman
Editorial Description: Covers relations between USA and Iran.
General Info: Yr. Est. 1992, Monthly, Trim Size-8½ x 11, 16 pages, ISSN: 1070-4973, 40% ads, 2 Color
Subscriptions: Inst. $260, For. $25, $5/copy
Circulation: Total-5,000
Advertising: $800.
List Rental: Actives: 12,500, $250/M, Hotline: 1,350, $500/M

U.S.-Kazakhstan Monitor *Business, Association* CPM: $100

Publishing Co: U.S.-Kazakhstan Council, 2000 L St NW, Ste 200, Washington, DC 20036-4907; Title Tel # (202) 416-1624 Title Fax # (202) 416-1865
Personnel: Publisher-Bijan Sepasy, Editor-Kur Volkan, Production Mgr.-Sam Gelman, Promotion Dir.-John Luke
General Info: Yr. Est. 1993, Monthly, Trim Size-8½ x 11, 24 pages, 40% ads, 2 Color
Subscriptions: Indv. $100, Inst. $260, For. $25, $10/copy
Circulation: Total-5,000
Advertising: $500.
List Rental: Actives: 10,000

United States Space Law: Natl. & Intl. Regulation
See: LAW

Univ. of Texas At Austin
Ctr. for Asian Studies
Newsletter

Publishing Co: Univ. of Texas at Austin Asian Studies Dept., Ctr. for Asian Studies, SSB, 4.126, Austin, TX 78712; Title Tel # (512) 471-5811 Title Fax # (512) 471-9639
Personnel: Editor-Sarah Wimer
General Info: Yr. Est. 1987, Semi-annually, 12 pages, 2 Color, Newsprint
Circulation: Total-5,000
List Rental: Rents Lists

Update *Association*

Publishing Co: Boston Mobilization for Survival, 11 Garden St, Cambridge, MA 02138-3617; Title Tel # (617) 354-0008
Personnel: Editor-Lee Farris
Editorial Description: Discusses peace & justice issues, news of peace movement, especially citizen action on disarmament, Palestinian rights, Southern Africa, & youth empowerment.
General Info: (Formerly Mobilizer), Yr. Est. 1977, Monthly, Trim Size-11 x 17, Web press, 16 pages, 1% ads, No Color
Subscriptions: Indv. $15, Inst. $25, For. $25, Free
Circulation: Total-2,000
List Rental: Expires: $50/M

The Urban Age *Business, Consumer*

Publishing Co: The Urban Age, Room S10-108, The World Bank, 1818 H Street NW, Washington, DC 20433-0001; Title Fax # (202) 473-1391
Personnel: Editor-Mary McNeil, Production Dir.-John Metzger
Editorial Description: Articles describing international issues effects on urban lifestyles.
General Info: Quarterly, Trim Size-8½ x 11
Subscriptions: Indv. $40

Venezuela News Bulletin *Business*

Publishing Co: Venezuelan American Assn. of the U.S., 150 Nassau St., New York, NY 10038-1516 Tel # (212) 233-7776 Fax # (212) 233-7779
Personnel: Editor-Peter Smith
General Info: Yr. Est. 1952, Monthly
Subscriptions: Indv. $200

Vietnam Bulletin

Publishing Co: Embassy of Vietnam, 12719 Robindale Dr, Rockville, MD 20853-3442
General Info: Yr. Est. 1968, Monthly

Vietnam Business InfoTrack
See: INTERNATIONAL TRADE

Viewpoint
Consumer

Publishing Co: Oxfam America, 26 West St, Boston, MA 02111-1206; Title Tel # (617) 482-1211 Title Fax # (617) 728-2596
Personnel: Editor-Laura Inouye
General Info: (Formerly Oxfam America Facts for Action), Semi-annually
Subscriptions: Free
Circulation: Total-85,000

Voice of Guatemala

Publishing Co: Embassy of Guatemala, 2220 R St NW, Washington, DC 20008-4081
General Info: Yr. Est. 1981, Monthly

Voices
See: WOMEN'S

Volunteer of Liberty

Publishing Co: Veterans of the Abraham Lincoln Brigade, 799 Broadway Ste 227, New York, NY 10003-6811; Title Tel # (212) 674-5552
General Info: Quarterly
Circulation: Total-350

Warships Forecast
See: AERONAUTICS/ASTRONAUTICS

Washington Letter on Puerto Rico
Business

Publishing Co: Newsletter Services, Inc., 9700 Philadelphia Ct., Lanham, MD 20706-4405; Title Tel # (301) 731-5202 Title Fax # (301) 731-5203
Personnel: Publisher-Lisha Anthony, Editor-Ed Konstant, Circ. Mgr.-Priscilla Arenas, Mktg. Dir.-Susan Pangman
Editorial Description: Political & legislative developments in Washington, D. C. , that affect economy of Puerto Rico.
General Info: Yr. Est. 1974, Bi-weekly, Offset press
Subscriptions: Indv. $199
List Rental: List Management Co.: Taybi Direct East, Inc., 13321 New Hampshire Ave., Ste. 202, Silver Spring, MD 20904-3450 Tel # (301) 680-3633, Fax # (301) 680-3635

Washington Notes on Africa
Consumer, Association

Publishing Co: Washington Office on Africa, 110 Maryland Ave NE, Washington, DC 20002-5699 Fax # (202) 546-1545; Title Tel # (202) 546-7961
Personnel: Editor-Imani Countess
General Info: Tri-annually
Subscriptions: Indv. $30

Washington Pacific Report , The
Business, Association

Publishing Co: Washington Pacific Pubs. Inc., PO Box 26142, Alexandria, VA 22313-6142; Title Tel # (703) 519-7757 Title Fax # (703) 548-0633
Personnel: Publisher-Fred Radewagen, Editor-Fred Radewagon, Circ. Mgr.-A. Coleman
Editorial Description: Coverage of political, diplomatic, & strategic issues in the Insular Pacific.
General Info: Yr. Est. 1982, Semi-monthly, Trim Size-8½ x 11, Offset press, 6 pages, ISSN: 0748-6539, 2 Color, Matte, Other
Subscriptions: Indv. $164, Inst. $164, Can. $189, For. $189, $7/copy
Circulation: Readership-2,000
Printing Co: State Services Organization, 444 N. Capitol St., Washington, DC 20001 Tel # (202) 624-5490

Washington Report
Business, Consumer

Publishing Co: Council of the Americas, 1310 G St. NW, Ste. 690, Washington, DC 20005-3000; Title Tel # (202) 659-1547
Personnel: Editor-W. Knepper, Jr.
General Info: Yr. Est. 1958, Monthly

Waste Management: Western Europe
See: WATER SUPPLY, POWER & WASTE

Week in Germany, The
Business, Consumer

Publishing Co: German Information Center, 950 3rd Ave., New York, NY 10022-2781; Title Tel # (212) 888-9840 Title Fax # (212) 752-6691
Personnel: Editor-Susan Steiner
Editorial Description: A roundup of political, economic and other news from Gerermany as well as a review of the German press.
General Info: 45x/yr., Trim Size-8½ x 11, Web press, 8 pages, Ind/Abs/Online: DIALOG, 4 Color, Other, Other
Circulation: Total-40,000

Weekly Terrorism Profile
See: SECURITY & SURVEILLANCE

Witness for Peace Newsletter

Publishing Co: Witness for Peace, 110 Maryland Ave. NE #311, Washington, DC 20002-5626 Tel # (202) 797-1160 Fax # (202) 797-1164; Title Tel # (919) 688-5049 Title Fax # (919) 682-9435
Personnel: Editor-Lisa Barczak
General Info: Yr. Est. 1983, Quarterly, Color-cover, Newsprint
Subscriptions: Free With Membership
Circulation: Total-35,000
Advertising: Accepts Inserts.
List Rental: Actives: $65/M

Workers' Solidarity
See: LABOR

World Affairs Councellor

Publishing Co: World Affairs Council of Boston, 22 Batterymarch St., Boston, MA 02109; Title Tel # (617) 482-1740

World Bank Publications Update
Business, Consumer

Publishing Co: World Bank, 1818 H St., NW N-9023, Washington, DC 20433-0001 Tel # (202) 477-1234 Fax # (202) 477-6391; Title Tel # (202) 473-7543 Title Fax # (202) 473-6391
Personnel: Editor-Kedar Bryan
Editorial Description: Periodic current awareness bulletin, listing & describing all new titles published by the World Bank.
General Info: Yr. Est. 1983, Bi-monthly, Sheetfed press, 8 pages, 2 Color, Saddle-stitched
Acquistions: Publication Bought
Circulation: Total-85,000
Printing Co: Progress Printing, 8401 Timberlake Rd # 4575, Lynchburg, VA 24502-3112 Tel # (804) 239-9213, Fax # (804) 237-1618

World Federalist News
Association

Publishing Co: World Federalist Movement, 777 UN Plaza, 12th Fl., New York, NY 10017; Title Tel # (212) 599-1320 Title Fax # (212) 599-1332
Personnel: Editor-Jack Yost
Editorial Description: Report on issues of global governance, the U.N., and international law.
General Info: Yr. Est. 1983, Quarterly, Trim Size-8½ x 11, Offset press, 16 pages, ISSN: 1022-0860, 2 Color
Subscriptions: Indv. $15
Circulation: Total-5,000

World Goodwill Commentary
Consumer, Association

Publishing Co: World Goodwill, Box 722, Cooper Station, New York, NY 10276-0722; Title Tel # (212) 982-8770
Personnel: Editor-Jan Nation
Editorial Description: A bulletin on current trends in world affairs.
General Info: Yr. Est. 1973, Letrpr. press, 32 pages, Color, Newsprint, Saddle-stitched
Subscriptions: Free
Circulation: Total-20,000
Printing Co: Fort Orange Press, Inc., 31 Sand Creek Rd, Albany, NY 12205-1822 Tel # (518) 489-3233

World Goodwill Newsletter
Consumer

Publishing Co: World Goodwill, Box 722, Cooper Station, New York, NY 10276-0722; Title Tel # (212) 982-8770
Personnel: Editor-Jan Nation
Editorial Description: Quarterly bulletin combining comment & information on world affairs.
General Info: Yr. Est. 1960, Quarterly, Offset press, 8 pages, 2 Color, Newsprint
Subscriptions: Free
Circulation: Total-20,000
Printing Co: Fort Orange Press, Inc., 31 Sand Creek Rd, Albany, NY 12205-1822 Tel # (518) 489-3233

World Neighbors in Action
Business, Association

Publishing Co: World Neighbors, Inc., 4127 NW 122nd St, Oklahoma City, OK 73120-8882 Tel # (405) 752-9700 Fax # (405) 752-9393; Title Tel # (405) 946-3333 Title Fax # (405) 946-9994
Editorial Description: Newsletter for overseas project personnel. Available in English, Spanish or French.
General Info: Yr. Est. 1957, Semi-annually, Ind/Abs/Online: Bibl.Charts Illus.
Subscriptions: Indv. $10, $1/copy
Circulation: (40% controlled), Total-5,000

World Opinion Update

Publishing Co: Survey Research Consultants International, Inc., PO Box 25, Williamstown, MA 01267-0025; Title Tel # (413) 458-4414
Personnel: Publisher, Editor-Phillip Hastings, Circ. Mgr.-Ann Upton, Art Dir.-Walter Kasheta
Editorial Description: Results of recent public opinion polls conducted in 100 countries on topics of international interest, subjects include pol; itics, economic affairs, social issues.
General Info: Yr. Est. 1977, Monthly, Trim Size-8 x 10, Sheetfed press, 12 pages, Color
Subscriptions: Indv. $60, Inst. $45, Can. $60, For. $65, $8/copy
Circulation: Total-1,400
Printing Co: McClelland Press, North St., Williamstown, MA 01267

World Wide

Publishing Co: Centre for Development & Population Activities, 1717 Massachusetts Ave NW Lowr, 202, Washington, DC 20036-2001; Title Tel # (202) 667-1142
Personnel: Publisher-Laura Hirsch, Editor-Katherine Nutt
Editorial Description: Focus is on Third World development issues, project management, & organization's activities.
General Info: Yr. Est. 1984, Quarterly, Trim Size-11 x 25, Web press, 6 pages, No Color, Newsprint
Circulation: Total-2,500

Worldlit
See: EDUCATION

INTERNATIONAL TRADE

AIB Newsletter   *Business*   CPM: $88

Publishing Co: Academy of International Business, Univ. of Hawaii Manoa-CBA, Honolulu, HI 96822 Tel # (808) 956-3665; Title Tel # (504) 956-3665 Title Fax # (808) 956-3261
Personnel: Editor-James Wills, Production Dir.-Laurel King
Editorial Description: Calls for papers, meeting notices & membership news of interest to professors of intl. business around the world.
General Info: (Formerly AEIB), Yr. Est. 1968, Quarterly, Trim Size-8½ x 11, Desktop press, 520 pages, 2% ads, 2 Color, Saddle-stitched
Subscriptions: Indv. $57
Circulation: Total-2,700
Advertising: $240. Accepts Inserts.
List Rental: Actives: $150/M

ALERTA   *Association*

Publishing Co: Inter-Church Committee on Human Rights in Latin America, 129 St. Clair Ave. W., Toronto, ON M4V 1N5 Canada
Editorial Description: Canadian churches reporting on human rights in Latin America.
General Info: Yr. Est. 1994, Bi-monthly, ISSN: 1188-875X
Subscriptions: Indv. $20, Inst. $35, For. $25, $4/copy

ASEAN Briefing   *Business*

Publishing Co: Asia Letter Group, PO Box 88189, Los Angeles, CA 90009-8189 Tel # (213) 523-0057; Title Tel # (852) 526-2950
General Info: Monthly
Subscriptions: Indv. $72

A.S.I.F (Americans Seeking International Franchises)   *Association*   CPM: $533

Publishing Co: Assn. for Americans Seeking Intl. Franchises, 2765 N. Scottsdale Rd., Ste. 104-D, Scottsdale, AZ 85257; Title Tel # (602) 949-7848 Title Fax # (602) 990-1958
Personnel: Publisher, Editor, Adv. Dir.-Thomas R. Cutler, Production Mgr., Art Dir.-Daniel Flynn
Editorial Description: Americans wishing to explore franchising opportunities internationally. Focus on the saturation of the domestic market versus exploding intl. franchising situations.
General Info: Yr. Est. 1995, Quarterly, Trim Size-8½ x 11, Web press, 16 pages, No Color
Subscriptions: Indv. $400, Inst. $400, Can. $500, For. $500, Free With Membership
Circulation: (33% controlled), Total-1,500, Subscriptions-1,000, International-250
Advertising: $800.

Abstract of International Economic Trend Analysis
See: ECONOMICS

Alternative Trading News
See: INTERNATIONAL AFFAIRS

American Society of International Law Newsletter
See: LAW

Antitrust and Trade Regulation Report
See: LAW

Asahi Shimbun Satellite Edition   *Business*

Publishing Co: Asahi Shimbun Publishing Company, 757 3rd Ave., 3rd fl., New York, NY 10017; Title Tel # (212) 755-3900 Title Fax # (212) 755-3908
General Info: (Formerly Japan Access), Yr. Est. 1990, Weekly
Subscriptions: Indv. $300

Asia Letter, The   *Business*

Publishing Co: Asia Letter Group, PO Box 88189, Los Angeles, CA 90009-8189 Tel # (213) 523-0057; Title Tel # (213) 526-2950 Title Fax # (213) 526-7131
General Info: Weekly
Subscriptions: Indv. $195

Asian Aviation News
See: AERONAUTICS/ASTRONAUTICS

Asian Economic News

Publishing Co: Kyodo News Intl., 50 Rockefeller Plaza #803, New York, NY 10020-1605; Title Tel # (212) 397-3723 Title Fax # (212) 397-3721
Editorial Description: Economic and business news of Asian countries and regions.
General Info: Yr. Est. 1989, Weekly

Association of South-East Asian Nations (ASEAN)   *Business*

Publishing Co: Oceana Publications, Inc., 75 Main St, Dobbs Ferry, NY 10522-1601 Tel # (914) 693-8100 Fax # (914) 693-0402
Personnel: Editor-Brian H.W. Hill, Editor-Kenneth R. Simmonds
Editorial Description: Provides documents relevant to trade relations of the Assn. of S.E. Asian Nations.
General Info: Yr. Est. 1991, Irregular, Looseleaf
Subscriptions: Indv. $150

Atlantic Trade Report & Global Defense Industry   *Business*

Publishing Co: Bergerac International, Ltd., Rr 1 Box 309, Gainesville, VA 22065-2501; Title Tel # (703) 349-2922 Title Fax # (703) 349-2922
Personnel: Publisher, Editor-J. Combemale
Editorial Description: Atlantic Trade Report concentrates on the effects that the economic unification of Europe will have on the worldwide economic community. Legal mechanisms being used to unify Europe, political response from the countries involved, &opinions from U.S.
General Info: (Formerly Atlantic Trade Report), Yr. Est. 1989, Bi-weekly, Ind/Abs/Online: NewsNet
Subscriptions: Indv. $495, $15/copy
Acquistions: Publication Bought

Aura Wealth Newsletter
See: INVESTMENT

Australian Business News
See: BUSINESS & INDUSTRY

BACC Trade Bulletin   *Business*

Publishing Co: British-American Chamber of Commerce, 52 Vanderbilt Ave Fl 20, New York, NY 10017-3808; Title Tel # (212) 889-0680
Editorial Description: Updates on issues affecting British-American trade; trade opportunities.
General Info: Yr. Est. 1983, Quarterly, Web press, 6 pages, No Color
Circulation: Total-4,000
Advertising: Inquire for rates.

BNA's Eastern Europe Reporter   *Business*

Publishing Co: Bureau of National Affairs, Inc., 1231 25th St. NW, Bldg. N-200, Washington, DC 20037-1157; Title Tel # (202) 452-4200 Title Fax # (202) 822-8092
Personnel: Publisher-William A. Beltz, Editor-Linda Botsford, Mng. Editor-Basco Eszeki, Circ. Mgr.-Gary C. Seltzer
Editorial Description: A biweekly notification service covering legislative regulatory, & legal developments affecting business, trade, & investment in Eastern Europe & the Soviet Union.
General Info: Yr. Est. 1991, Bi-weekly, Trim Size-8½ x 11, Offset press, ISSN: 1058-7365, Looseleaf
Subscriptions: Indv. $895

BNA's Employee Relations Weekly
See: INDUSTRIAL RELATIONS/PERSONNEL

Baltic Business Report   *Business*

Publishing Co: Baltic Ventures, 1075 Washington St, West Newton, MA 02165-2118; Title Tel # (617) 527-2550 Title Fax # (617) 527-2823
Personnel: Editor-Andris Straumanis, Exec. Ed.-Paul D. Kalnins, Asst. Ed.-Renata Kalnins
Editorial Description: Provides information on Baltic trade, iinvestment, and economy.
General Info: Monthly, ISSN: 1058-1057, Ind/Abs/Online: NewsNet
Subscriptions: Indv. $260, Can. $260, For. $300

Basic Oil Laws & Concession Contracts
See: PETROLEUM & NATURAL GAS

Bates International Trade Update

Publishing Co: International Features, Inc., 8 South J St., Ste. 3, Box 1349, Lake Worth, FL 33460-3742; Title Tel # (407) 582-8320 Title Fax # (407) 582-8320
Personnel: Publisher, Editor-Wiliam Bates, Circ. Mgr.-Rick Lanning, Production Mgr.-Kevin O'Connell
Editorial Description: Latest developments in international trade. New economic contacts. Continual update on changes in cabinet positions of foreign governments. Trade information for import/export companies and other international corporations.
General Info: Yr. Est. 1989, Bi-weekly, Sheetfed press, 12 pages, No Color, Coated
Subscriptions: Indv. $104, Can. $104, For. $185
Circulation: Total-5,267

Bluebook Update Newsletter
See: AGRICULTURE

Boletin de Precios Internacionales de Productos Basicos

Publishing Co: Organization of American States, 19th Constitution Ave. N W, Suite #300, Washington, DC 20006 Tel # (202) 458-3000; Title Tel # (202) 458-3533
Editorial Description: Monthly statistics on the price of commodities. Bilingual (Spanish-English).
General Info: Quarterly, Trim Size-8³/₈ x 10³/₄, Sheetfed press, 12 pages, No Color
Subscriptions: Indv. $12, $1/copy
Circulation: (100% controlled)

Boycott Law Bulletin   *Business*

Publishing Co: Nu-Tec Publishing, Inc., 4715 Strack Rd., Ste. 211, Houston, TX 77069-1617 Fax # (731) 444-6564; Title Tel # (713) 444-6562 Title Fax # (713) 444-6564
Personnel: Editor-Joe Kamalick
Editorial Description: Covers international boycott and anti-boycott laws, including legislation, government enforcement actions & penalties, court cases, and private lawsuits. Published by fax, the Bulletin provides clearly written, timely information and expert analysis for corporate executives, attorneys, and others whose firms or clients face
General Info: Yr. Est. 1977, Bi-monthly, Trim Size-8½ x 11, 4 pages, ISSN: 0162-1726, Ind/Abs/ Online: Indexed
Subscriptions: Indv. $495, For. $595, $50/copy

Brazil-Canada Newsletter   *Business, Consumer*

Publishing Co: Brazil-Canada Chamber of Commerce, 6-2400 Dundas St., W., Box 355, Mississauga, ON L5K 2R8 Canada Tel # (416) 364-3555
General Info: Yr. Est. 1974, Monthly, 4 pages, No Color, Recycled
Subscriptions: Free In Designated Area
Circulation: Total-800
Printing Co: The Printing House, 16 Cumberland St., Toronto, ON M4W 1J5 Canada Tel # (416) 924-1416

Brazil Service
See: BUSINESS & INDUSTRY

Brazil Watch
See: INTERNATIONAL AFFAIRS

Break, The
See: SPORTS & SPORTING GOODS

Building Products for Export   *Business*

Publishing Co: Sweet's Group - McGraw Hill, 1221 Avenue of the Americas, New York, NY 10020 Tel # (212) 512-4323 Fax # (212) 512-4207
Personnel: Editorial Dir.-Tom Koster
General Info: (Formerly Import/Export Report), Monthly
Subscriptions: Indv. $277

Bulldog   *Association*

Publishing Co: British-American Chamber of Commerce, 52 Vanderbilt Ave Fl 20, New York, NY 10017-3808; Title Tel # (212) 889-0680
Editorial Description: Maintains regular contact with members, associates, and other related trade bodies, and keep them regularly informed about Chamber activities.
General Info: (Formerly British American Trade News), Yr. Est. 1960, Quarterly, Trim Size-8½ x 11, Offset press, 8 pages, 2 Color
Circulation: Total-2,500
Advertising: Inquire for rates.

Business & Environment

Publishing Co: U.S. Council for International Business, 1212 Ave of the Americas, New York, NY 10036-1689; Title Tel # (212) 354-4480
Personnel: Editor-Norine Kennedy
Editorial Description: Newssheet on international developments regarding the environment & the business role in environmental protection.
Subscriptions: Indv. $50
Circulation: Total-2,800

Business Asia   *Business*

Publishing Co: Economist Intelligence Unit, 111 W. 57th St., New York, NY 10019 Tel # (212) 554-0600 Fax # (212) 586-1181; Title Tel # (212) 540-0600
Personnel: Editor-Marcel Toussaint
Editorial Description: Reports developments affecting investment & trade in Asian markets. Include quarterly supplement reporting on Asia's emerging regions.
General Info: Yr. Est. 1970, Semi-monthly, Trim Size-8½ x 11, Color
Subscriptions: Indv. $620
Circulation: Total-3,000

Business China   *Business*

Publishing Co: Economist Intelligence Unit, 111 W. 57th St., New York, NY 10019 Tel # (212) 554-0600 Fax # (212) 586-1181; Title Tel # (212) 540-0600
Editorial Description: Provides corporate case studies. Analyses financial issues in, and affecting, China. Offers practical, detailed advice.
General Info: Semi-monthly
Subscriptions: Indv. $620

Business Eastern Europe   *Business*

Publishing Co: Economist Intelligence Unit, 111 W. 57th St., New York, NY 10019 Tel # (212) 554-0600 Fax # (212) 586-1181; Title Tel # (212) 540-0600
Personnel: Publisher-John Haley, Editor-Lois Tretiak
Editorial Description: Delivers late-breaking news, assesses business opportunities, and provides in-depth analysis.
General Info: Weekly, Trim Size-8.5 x 11, 12 pages, 2 Color
Subscriptions: Indv. $1,175

Business and the Environment
See: BUSINESS & INDUSTRY

Business Latin America   *Business*

Publishing Co: Economist Intelligence Unit, 111 W. 57th St., New York, NY 10019 Tel # (212) 554-0600 Fax # (212) 586-1181; Title Tel # (212) 540-0600 Title Fax # (212) 995-8837
Personnel: Editor-Helen Cunningham
Editorial Description: Reports developments affecting trade and investment in Latin American markets.
General Info: Yr. Est. 1966, Weekly
Subscriptions: Indv. $945

Business Law Europe   *Business*

Publishing Co: Matthew Bender & Co., 11 Penn Plaza, New York, NY 10001-2006 Tel # (212) 967-7707 Fax # (212) 244-3188
Editorial Description: Prepared by a team of renowned experts on European & transactional business law, provides up-to-the-minute information on important European Community legislation & its impact on business transactions.
General Info: Yr. Est. 1990, Bi-weekly

Business News   *Business, Association*

Publishing Co: U.S. Business Council for Southeastern Europe, PO Box 3635, Warrenton, VA 22186-8235; Title Tel # (703) 527-0280 Title Fax # (703) 527-0282
Personnel: Circ. Dir.-Richard Johnson, Adv. Dir.-Nola Burkhard
Editorial Description: Provides information useful to U.S. businessmen interested in business with Croatia, Macedonia, and Slovenia.
General Info: Yr. Est. 1973, Monthly, Trim Size-8 x 11, Sheetfed press, 12 pages, No Color
Subscriptions: Free With Membership
Circulation: Total-200

Business Russia   *Business*

Publishing Co: Economist Intelligence Unit, 111 W. 57th St., New York, NY 10019 Tel # (212) 554-0600 Fax # (212) 586-1181
Editorial Description: Covers business, finance and investment in all areas of the former Soviet Union.
General Info: Yr. Est. 1995, Monthly
Subscriptions: Indv. $675
List Rental: Rents Lists

Business Transactions in Germany (FRG)   *Business*

Publishing Co: Matthew Bender & Co., 11 Penn Plaza, New York, NY 10001-2006 Tel # (212) 967-7707 Fax # (212) 244-3188
Personnel: Editor-Bernd Ruster
Editorial Description: A comprehensive guide to doing business with an integral member of the world business community. This teatise provides a basic understanding of the German legal system, & first-hand information on some thirty business-related topics, including the effects of German reunification.
General Info: Yr. Est. 1983, Irregular, Looseleaf

CAMERA on Campus   *Association*

Publishing Co: Committee for Accuracy in Middle East Reporting in America, Box 428, Boston, MA 02258-0428; Title Tel # (617) 787-3672 Title Fax # (617) 787-7853
Personnel: Editor-Andrea Levin
Editorial Description: Dedicated to the promotion of fair and balanced coverage of the Middle East.Special focus on campus Issues.
General Info: Quarterly
Subscriptions: Free To Qualified Recipient
Circulation: Total-15,000, Readership-40,000

CECON Trade News/ CECON Boletin Comercial

Publishing Co: Organization of American States, 19th Constitution Ave. N W, Suite #300, Washington, DC 20006 Tel # (202) 458-3000; Title Tel # (202) 331-1010
Editorial Description: Latest trade on tariffs; custom duties; & trade bills pending in Congress.
General Info: Monthly, Trim Size-8³/₈ x 10³/₄, Sheetfed press, 12 pages
Subscriptions: Indv. $12, $1/copy

COHA's Washington Report on the Hemisphere
See: INTERNATIONAL AFFAIRS

California Statesman's Foreign Policy Review
See: INTERNATIONAL AFFAIRS

Canada Courier

Publishing Co: Canadian Department of Regional Industrial Expansion, 235 Queen, Ottawa, ON K1A 0H5 Canada; Title Tel # (613) 954-2788
Personnel: Editor-Mrs. A. Armstrong
Editorial Description: Information concerning Canadian goods available for sale in international markets.
General Info: Yr. Est. 1961, Monthly, Offset press, 8 pages, Color
Circulation: Total-200,000

Canada Japan Trade Council, Newsletter *Business*

Publishing Co: Canada Japan Trade Council, 75 Albert St., Suite #903, Ottawa, ON K1P 5E7 Canada; Title Tel # (613) 233-4047
Personnel: Editor-K.H. Pringsheim
Editorial Description: Trends, changes, developments in economics and societies of Canada & Japan.
General Info: Yr. Est. 1968, Monthly, Trim Size-8½ x 11, 12 pages, No Color, Newsprint
Circulation: Total-3,500
Printing Co: Ottawa Laser Copy, 880 Wellington St., Ottawa, ON K1R 6K7 Canada Tel # (613) 563-3210

Capital Formation and Investment Incentives Around the World *Business*

Publishing Co: Matthew Bender & Co., 11 Penn Plaza, New York, NY 10001-2006 Tel # (212) 967-7707 Fax # (212) 244-3188
Editorial Description: A comprehensive survey of the organization of overseas business & the incentives most countries offer to attract foreign investment. Designed as an adjunct to Foreign Tax & Trade Briefs. Catalogs nearly 60 nations.
General Info: Yr. Est. 1981, Irregular, Looseleaf

Caribbean Trendwatch *Business*

Publishing Co: Boerner Communications, P.O. Box L, Manhasset, NY 11030; Title Tel # (516) 741-8887 Title Fax # (516) 741-3131
Personnel: Editor-Hank Boerner
General Info: (Formerly Carib/Basin Trade Update), Yr. Est. 1987, Quarterly
Subscriptions: Indv. $48
Advertising: Accepts Inserts.

Caribbean Update *Business*

Publishing Co: Caribbean Update, 52 Maple Ave, Maplewood, NJ 07040-2626; Title Tel # (201) 762-1565 Title Fax # (201) 762-9585
Personnel: Publisher, Editor-Kal Wagenheim
Editorial Description: Covers business & economic news in the Caribbean/Central American region.
General Info: Yr. Est. 1985, Monthly, Trim Size-8½ x 11, Web press, 24 pages, ISSN: 8756-324X, No Color, Newsprint, Saddle-stitched
Subscriptions: Indv. $216, Inst. $216, Can. $216, For. $216, $18/copy
List Rental: List Management Co.: Information Marketing Services, 8130 Boone Blvd., Ste 310, Vienna, VA 22182-2640 Tel # (703) 821-8130, Fax # (703) 821-8243

Central European Business Guide *Business*

Publishing Co: CEBIS, 100 S. King St., Ste. 410, Seattle, WA 98104 Tel # (206) 343-9970 Fax # (206) 343-0484
Editorial Description: Practical advice for doing business in Eastern Europe.
General Info: Yr. Est. 1994, Monthly, Trim Size-8½ x 11, ISSN: 1073-2918

Chile Economic Report *Business*

Publishing Co: Corporacion de Fomento de la Produccion, 1 World Trade Ctr Ste 5151, New York, NY 10048-0202; Title Tel # (212) 938-0550 Title Fax # (212) 938-0568
Personnel: Editor-Marco A. Vallejo, Asst. Ed.-Jorge A. Gana
Editorial Description: Summaries of economic developments in Chile, investments, indicators, official policies.
General Info: (Formerly Chile Economic News), Yr. Est. 1967, Monthly, Trim Size-8½ x 11, Offset press, 12 pages, ISSN: 0884-4488, Coated, Saddle-stitched
Subscriptions: Free To Qualified Recipient
Circulation: Total-8,800

China Business & Trade *Business*

Publishing Co: Welt Publishing Co., 1413 K St. NW, Ste. 800, Washington, DC 20005-3405; Title Tel # (202) 371-0555 Title Fax # (202) 408-9369
Personnel: Publisher-Leo G.B. Welt
Editorial Description: News of commerce, economic developments, legislation, regulation, exhibitions, industry analysis.
General Info: Yr. Est. 1977, Bi-weekly, Trim Size-8½ x 11, Sheetfed press, 4 pages, ISSN: 0731-7700, No Color
Subscriptions: Indv. $249, Inst. $237, Can. $259, For. $279, $9/copy
Acquistions: Publication Bought
Circulation: (20% controlled), Total-600, Subscriptions-475
Advertising: Accepts Inserts.

China Letter, The *Business*

Publishing Co: Asia Letter Group, PO Box 88189, Los Angeles, CA 90009-8189 Tel # (213) 523-0057; Title Tel # (852) 526-2950
General Info: Monthly
Subscriptions: Indv. $195

China Trade

Publishing Co: China Trade Corporation, 267 Windsor St, Cambridge, MA 02139-1512; Title Tel # (617) 868-0981 Title Fax # (617) 491-0476
General Info: Yr. Est. 1986, Monthly
Subscriptions: Indv. $225

Civil Aircraft Forecast
See: AERONAUTICS/ASTRONAUTICS

Commercial Laws of the World
See: LAW

Commersant Weekly *Business, Consumer*

Publishing Co: WorldTrade Executive, PO Box 761, Concord, MA 01742-0761; Title Tel # (508) 287-0301 Title Fax # (508) 287-0302
Personnel: Publisher-Kim Sherman, Editor in Chief-Mikhail Rogoshnikov, Adv. Dir.-Dwight Ingalsbe
Editorial Description: Russian business news and information. Text in Russian
General Info: (Formerly Commersant International), Weekly, 4 Color, Newsprint
Subscriptions: Indv. $420, Can. $470, For. $470

Commodity Futures Forecast (R) Service
See: INVESTMENT

Common Market Reporter *Business*

Publishing Co: CCH, Inc., 2700 Lake Cook Rd., Riverwoods, IL 60015 Parent Co.-Kluwer Law & Taxation Publishers, Cambridge; Title Tel # (847) 267-7000 Title Fax # (800) 224-8299
Editorial Description: Publishes and explains the law, regulations and court decisions necessary for the guidance of business operations in the EEC.
General Info: Yr. Est. 1962, Bi-weekly, Trim Size-6 x 9, Web press, 200 pages, No Color, Looseleaf
Subscriptions: Indv. $1,070

Commuter Regional Airline News Intl.
See: AERONAUTICS/ASTRONAUTICS

Competition Law of Canada *Business*

Publishing Co: Matthew Bender & Co., 11 Penn Plaza, New York, NY 10001-2006 Tel # (212) 967-7707 Fax # (212) 244-3188
Personnel: Editor-Julian O. von Kalinowski
Editorial Description: Comprehensive analysis & practical examination of the competition law of Canada. Provides expert treatment of fair trade law, mergers & acquisitions, regulated industries, & unfair sales & distribution practices.
General Info: (Formerly World Law of Competition, Unit A, Volume 3), Yr. Est. 1979, Irregular, Looseleaf

Competition Law of European Economic Community *Business*

Publishing Co: Matthew Bender & Co., 11 Penn Plaza, New York, NY 10001-2006 Tel # (212) 967-7707 Fax # (212) 244-3188
Personnel: Editor-Julian O. Kalinowski
Editorial Description: The complete explanation of the competition policy of the EEC. Provides thorough dicussion of the founding treaty, organization, law & regulation of decisions & agreement affecting commerce & economic activity.
General Info: (Formerly World Law of Competition, Unite B, Volumes B1 and B2), Yr. Est. 1979, Irregular, Looseleaf

Competition Laws of the Pacific Rim Countries *Business*

Publishing Co: Matthew Bender & Co., 11 Penn Plaza, New York, NY 10001-2006 Tel # (212) 967-7707 Fax # (212) 244-3188
Personnel: Editor-Julian O. von Kalinowski
Editorial Description: The comprehensive guide to the competition laws of Japan, the Republic of China (Taiwan), South Korea, the Philippines, Australia, Hong Kong & New Zealand.
General Info: (Formerly World Law of Competition, Unit D, Volume D1), Yr. Est. 1986, Irregular, Looseleaf

Competition Laws of United Kingdom and Republic of Ireland *Business*

Publishing Co: Matthew Bender & Co., 11 Penn Plaza, New York, NY 10001-2006 Tel # (212) 967-7707 Fax # (212) 244-3188
Personnel: Editor-Julian O. von Kalinowski
Editorial Description: Details legislation, case law & regulations governing competition & trade in the United Kingdom & Ireland. Provides detailed coverage of restrictive trade practices, monopolies, merger control, restraints, licensing & price maintenance.
General Info: (Formerly World Law of Competition, Unit B, Voumes B3 and B4), Yr. Est. 1979, Irregular, Looseleaf

Connections to Mail Order/World Trade and Homebased Business Info.
See: ADVERTISING & MARKETING

Construction Market Intelligence: Russia
See: CONSTRUCTION & BUILDING

Consumers for World Trade
Newsletter *Business, Consumer*

Publishing Co: Consumers for World Trade, 2000 L St NW Ste 200, Washington, DC 20036-4907
Fax # (202) 785-0175; Title Tel # (202) 785-4835
Editorial Description: International trade policy and the consumer interest.
General Info: Yr. Est. 1978, Quarterly, Trim Size-8$\frac{1}{2}$ x 11, 8 pages, 2 Color
Subscriptions: Indv. $100, Free With Membership
Acquistions: Publication Bought
Circulation: Total-1,000

Countertrade Outlook
(CTO) *Business*

Publishing Co: DP Pubs., PO Box 7188, Fairfax Station, VA 22039-7188 Tel # (703) 452-1322;
Title Tel # (703) 425-1322 Title Fax # (703) 425-7911
Personnel: Publisher-Judith Fischer, Editor-Michael Morrison, Promotion Dir.-Ed McCormack
Editorial Description: Reports on reciprocal and unconventional international trade and project finance.
General Info: Yr. Est. 1983, Semi-monthly, ISSN: 0743-0369, Ind/Abs/Online: NEWSNET
Subscriptions: Indv. $588, Can. $588, For. $648
List Rental: List Management Co.: Information Marketing Services, 8130 Boone Blvd., Ste 310, Vienna, VA 22182-2640 Tel # (703) 821-8130, Fax # (703) 821-8243

Country Report: Cameroon
See: POLITICS

Crafts News
See: ART & SCULPTURE

Croners Reference Book for
World Traders *Consumer*

Publishing Co: Croner Publications, Inc., 34 Jericho Tpke, Jericho, NY 11753-1042;
Title Tel # (516) 333-9085 Title Fax # (516) 338-4986
Personnel: Publisher-Ron Guggenheimer, Editor-Elizabeth Duffy, Circ. Mgr.-Regina Friel
Editorial Description: Lists trade agencies, credit information and collection agencies, banks, freight forwarders, custom brokers, lawyers, etc. for every country in the world.
General Info: Monthly, Trim Size-8$\frac{1}{2}$ x 5$\frac{1}{2}$, 1,400 pages, Looseleaf
Subscriptions: Indv. $142

CrossBorder Monitor *Business*

Publishing Co: Economist Intelligence Unit, 111 W. 57th St., New York, NY 10019
Tel # (212) 554-0600 Fax # (212) 586-1181; Title Tel # (212) 540-0600
Personnel: Editor-Shirley Dreifus
Editorial Description: Reports to top executives of corporations with capital investments in world markets; covers business news with practical interpretations in international trade and investment.
General Info: (Formerly Business International; Multinational Business), Weekly
Subscriptions: Indv. $675
Printing Co: Tabard Press, 75 Varick St Fl 9, New York, NY 10013-1917 Tel # (212) 925-0303

Crow's Weekly Market Report
See: LUMBER & WOOD

CryoGas International
See: CHEMISTRY & CHEMICALS

Cuba Business *Business*

Publishing Co: Cuba Business, PO Box 15020, Washington, DC 20003-0020;
Title Tel # (202) 543-5507
Personnel: Editor-Arlene Alligood
Editorial Description: Economic and trade information from Cuba.
General Info: Monthly, Trim Size-8$\frac{1}{2}$ x 11, 8 pages, 2 Color, Coated
Subscriptions: Indv. $575

Cuba News
See: INVESTMENT

Cuba Report, The *Business*

Publishing Co: Cuba Newsletter Inc., 501 Brickell Key Dr Ste 200, Miami, FL 33131-2608;
Title Tel # (305) 381-8685 Title Fax # (305) 372-1089
Personnel: Publisher-James D. Whisenand, Editor-J. D. W
Editorial Description: A non political business newsletter on business, finance, and economic activity affecting cuba,
General Info: Yr. Est. 1992, Monthly, Trim Size-8 x 11.5, 8 pages, ISSN: 1062-0672, Ind/Abs/Online: Newsnet
Subscriptions: Indv. $425, Can. $475, For. $475, $40/copy

Currency Quarterly
See: INVESTMENT

Czech Republic
Business & Investment
News *Business*

Publishing Co: Fandango, 1613 Escalero Rd, Santa Rosa, CA 95409-3909;
Title Tel # (707) 539-2722 Title Fax # (707) 539-2722
Editorial Description: Cover Czech business and investment news and information.
General Info: Yr. Est. 1992, Bi-monthly, Trim Size-8$\frac{1}{2}$ x 11, Offset press, 16 pages, No Color, Saddle-stitched
Subscriptions: Indv. $45, Inst. $45, For. $50, Free To Qualified Recipient
Circulation: Total-2,000, Readership-2,000
Advertising: Inquire for rates. Accepts Inserts.
List Rental: Rents Lists

Dateline: Mexico Today
See: INTERNATIONAL AFFAIRS

Dateline: World Jewry *Association, Business*

Publishing Co: World Jewish Congress, 501 Madison Ave Fl 17, New York, NY 10022-5602
Tel # (212) 753-5770
Personnel: Editor-Evelyne Kayess
Editorial Description: Covers political/international news affecting world Jewry.
General Info: Irregular

Development Bank
Business Report *Business*

Publishing Co: International Publications, P.O. Box 19529, Alexandria, VA 22320;
Title Tel # (703) 548-5497
Personnel: Publisher-William Hearn, Editor-Susan Smith
General Info: Yr. Est. 1981, 26x/yr.
Subscriptions: Indv. $467

Doing Business in Brazil *Business*

Publishing Co: Matthew Bender & Co., 11 Penn Plaza, New York, NY 10001-2006
Tel # (212) 967-7707 Fax # (212) 244-3188
Personnel: Editor-J.M. Pinheiro Neto
Editorial Description: A wide-ranging overview of Brazilian business laws.
General Info: Yr. Est. 1979, Monthly, Looseleaf

Doing Business in Canada *Business*

Publishing Co: Matthew Bender & Co., 11 Penn Plaza, New York, NY 10001-2006
Tel # (212) 967-7707 Fax # (212) 244-3188
Editorial Description: Written by a top Canadian law firm, the work supplies the comprehensive coverage & expert advice necessary to make informed decisions. Designed for use by both attorneys & businessmen, this practical guide untangles the complex web of national & provincial legislation & regulation.
General Info: Irregular, Looseleaf

Doing Business in China *Business*

Publishing Co: Matthew Bender & Co., 11 Penn Plaza, New York, NY 10001-2006
Tel # (212) 967-7707 Fax # (212) 244-3188
Personnel: Editor-William P. Streng, Editor-Allen D. Wilcox
Editorial Description: A guide to all major areas of business law in the People's Republic of China. Closely examines key issues & potential pitfalls involved in import-export transactions, technology transfers, banking & financial transactions, tax matters & joint ventures.
General Info: Yr. Est. 1989, Irregular, Looseleaf

Doing Business in France *Business*

Publishing Co: Matthew Bender & Co., 11 Penn Plaza, New York, NY 10001-2006
Tel # (212) 967-7707 Fax # (212) 244-3188
Editorial Description: Practice-oriented treatise to provide all the basic concepts of French business law & practice.
General Info: Irregular, Looseleaf

Doing Business in Ireland *Business*

Publishing Co: Matthew Bender & Co., 11 Penn Plaza, New York, NY 10001-2006
Tel # (212) 967-7707 Fax # (212) 244-3188
Personnel: Editor-Brian O'Connor, Editor-Patrick Ussher
Editorial Description: Covers all matters pertinent to the Irish business and legal situation.
General Info: Yr. Est. 1987, Irregular, Looseleaf

Doing Business in Japan *Business*

Publishing Co: Matthew Bender & Co., 11 Penn Plaza, New York, NY 10001-2006
Tel # (212) 967-7707 Fax # (212) 244-3188
Personnel: Editor-Zentaro Kitagawa
Editorial Description: Comprehensive & practical treatment focuses on all subpractical treatment focuses on all substantive areas, including: contracts, business organizations & regulation, employment law, securities, intellectual property, competition law & taxation.
General Info: Yr. Est. 1980, Irregular, Looseleaf

Doing Business in Mexico *Business*

Publishing Co: Matthew Bender & Co., 11 Penn Plaza, New York, NY 10001-2006
Tel # (212) 967-7707 Fax # (212) 244-3188
Personnel: Editor-Joseph J. Norton
Editorial Description: Covers legal aspects of trade, including export incentive & the 'Maquilador' program; U.S. tax aspects; taxation of foreign residents under Mexican law; legal aspects of importing goods into Mexico; & texts of U.S. & Mexican laws, teatities, & forms.
General Info: Yr. Est. 1980, Irregular, Looseleaf

Doing Business in Spain *Business*

Publishing Co: Matthew Bender & Co., 11 Penn Plaza, New York, NY 10001-2006
Tel # (212) 967-7707 Fax # (212) 244-3188
Editorial Description: A guide to the business and legal environment in the newest member nation of the EEC.
General Info: Yr. Est. 1987, Irregular, Looseleaf

Doing Business in the United Kingdom *Business*

Publishing Co: Matthew Bender & Co., 11 Penn Plaza, New York, NY 10001-2006
Tel # (212) 967-7707 Fax # (212) 244-3188
Editorial Description: All the necessary legal background for planning business transactions & dealing with problems arising from investments & trade in the United Kingdom. Covers the business, private, commercial & regulatory laws of England, Scotland, & Northern Ireland.
General Info: Yr. Est. 1985, Irregular, Looseleaf

East Asian Business Intelligence *Business*

Publishing Co: Intl. Executive Reports, 717 D St. NW, Ste. 300, Washington, DC 20004-2807; Title Tel # (202) 628-6900 Title Fax # (202) 628-6618
Personnel: Editor-Anne Phelan, Publisher, Circ. Mgr.-William Hearn, Promotion Dir.-Lloyd Gibson
Editorial Description: Provides current business information, contracting, sales leads, and contact information on East Asian business.
General Info: Yr. Est. 1986, Semi-monthly, Trim Size-8½ x 11, Sheetfed press, 8 pages, ISSN: 0888-580X, Ind/Abs/Online: Newsnet, No Color, Matte
Subscriptions: Indv. $345, Inst. $195, Can. $355, For. $355
Acquistions: Publication Bought
Circulation: Total-450
List Rental: List Management Co.: Manager: Lloyd Gibson; Information Marketing Services, 8130 Boone Blvd., Ste 310, Vienna, VA 22182-2640 Tel # (703) 821-8130, Fax # (703) 821-8243, Actives: 15,200, $145/M

East-West Technology Digest *Consumer*

Publishing Co: Welt Publishing Co., 1413 K St. NW, Ste. 800, Washington, DC 20005-3405; Title Tel # (202) 371-0555 Title Fax # (202) 408-9369
Personnel: Publisher-Leo G.B. Welt
Editorial Description: Technology developed in the Eastern Bloc available to the West.
General Info: Yr. Est. 1975, Monthly, Trim Size-8½ x 11, Desktop press, 2 pages, ISSN: 0145-1421, No Color
Subscriptions: Indv. $99, Can. $109, For. $129, $9/copy
Circulation: Total-210

East/West Business & Trade *Business*

Publishing Co: Welt Publishing Co., 1413 K St. NW, Ste. 800, Washington, DC 20005-3405; Title Tel # (202) 371-0555 Title Fax # (202) 408-9369
Personnel: Publisher-Leo G.B. Welt, Editor-Halter Smith
Editorial Description: News of commerce, economic developments, legislation, regulation, exhibitions, industry analysis.
General Info: (Formerly Soviet Business & Trade), Yr. Est. 1972, Semi-monthly, Offset press, ISSN: 0731-7727, No Color
Subscriptions: Indv. $249, Can. $259, For. $279, $10/copy
Acquistions: Publication Bought
Circulation: Total-800
Advertising: Accepts Inserts.

East/West Business Package *Business*

Publishing Co: Welt Publishing Co., 1413 K St. NW, Ste. 800, Washington, DC 20005-3405 Fax # (202) 408-9369; Title Tel # (202) 371-0555 Title Fax # (202) 682-5833
Personnel: Publisher-Leo G.B. Welt, Editor-Walter Smith, Adv. Dir.-Deidre White, Production Mgr., Promotion Dir.-Joni Rafalski
Editorial Description: Commercial news about negotiations, contracts and sales between western companies and foreign trade organizations in the Soviet Union, Eastern Europe and China.
General Info: (Formerly Soviet-Eastern Europe-China Business), Yr. Est. 1972, Semi-monthly, Trim Size-8½ x 11, Offset press, 10 pages, 2 Color
Subscriptions: Indv. $399, Can. $409, For. $429, $18/copy
Acquistions: Publication Bought
Circulation: Total-200

East/West Commersant *Business*

Publishing Co: WorldTrade Executive, PO Box 761, Concord, MA 01742-0761 Tel # (508) 287-0301 Fax # (508) 287-0302
Personnel: Publisher-Gary Brown, Mng. Editor-Charlotte Pierce
Editorial Description: Tracks late breaking business opportunities, the availability of funding, reliable local contacts, and other essential trade and investment information related to Russia and Eastern Europe.
General Info: (Formerly East/West Business & Finance Alert), 22x/yr., Trim Size-8½ x 11, 12 pages, No Color
Subscriptions: Indv. $425, Can. $475, For. $475

East/West Executive Guide *Business*

Publishing Co: WorldTrade Executive, PO Box 761, Concord, MA 01742-0761; Title Tel # (508) 287-0301 Title Fax # (508) 287-0302
Editorial Description: The definitive source for business and legal developments in Russia and Eastern Europe. Contains revealing analyses from people solving critical legal and practical issues in the region every day.
General Info: Monthly
Subscriptions: Indv. $596, Can. $646, For. $646

Economic and Legal Information from Poland *Business*

Publishing Co: Embassy of the Republic of Poland, Commercial Counsellor's Office, 100 Park Ave., 10th Fl., New York, NY 10017-5516; Title Tel # (212) 370-5300

Economic Newsletter *Association*

Publishing Co: U.S.-Korea Economic Council, PO Box 174, Saint James, NY 11780-0174; Title Tel # (212) 662-8610
Personnel: Editor-Dr. William Henderson
Editorial Description: Summary of the Korean business press. Korean economic news.
General Info: Yr. Est. 1974, Monthly, Trim Size-8½ x 11, 4 pages, No Color
Circulation: (100% controlled), Total-300

Empire State Development
See: BUSINESS & INDUSTRY

Energy Prices & Taxes
See: ENERGY

Enforcement of Money Judgements Abroad *Business*

Publishing Co: Matthew Bender & Co., 11 Penn Plaza, New York, NY 10001-2006
Tel # (212) 967-7707 Fax # (212) 244-3188
Personnel: Editor-Philip R. Weems
Editorial Description: Addresses each country's present attitute toward enforcing foreign money judgements, the procedural requirements for filing for enforcement, & additional considerations for enforcing a foreign moeny judgement, including jurisdiction, reciprocity, treaty provisions, currency regulations, & defenses.
General Info: Yr. Est. 1988, Irregular, Looseleaf

Environment Watch: Latin America
See: ENVIRONMENT & ECOLOGY

Estimated World Requirements of Narcotic Drugs

Publishing Co: United Nations Publications, Two UN Plaza, Room DC2-853, New York, NY 10017; Title Tel # (212) 963-8302 Title Fax # (212) 963-3489
Personnel: Sales Mgr.-Susanna H. Section
General Info: Annually, ISSN: 0082-8327
Subscriptions: Indv. $36
List Rental: Rents Lists

Euro-Turf
See: GARDENING & HORTICULTURE

Euromedia Acquisitions & Finance
See: BUSINESS & INDUSTRY

Euromedia Regulation
See: MEDIA & COMMUNICATIONS

European Community

Publishing Co: U.S. Council for International Business, 1212 Ave of the Americas, New York, NY 10036-1689; Title Tel # (212) 354-4480
Personnel: Editor-Cly Wallace
Editorial Description: Newssheet on developments in the European Community affecting business and on Council activities.
General Info: 4 pages
Subscriptions: Indv. $50
Circulation: Total-2,800

European Community: The Single Market *Business*

Publishing Co: Oceana Publications, Inc., 75 Main St, Dobbs Ferry, NY 10522-1601
Tel # (914) 693-8100 Fax # (914) 693-0402
Personnel: Editor-Brian Hill, Editor-Kenneth Simmonds, Production Mgr.-Mike Wortzman, Mktg. Dir.-John Downey
Editorial Description: Trade and releated documents affecting the European Community.
General Info: Yr. Est. 1990, Irregular, Looseleaf
Subscriptions: Indv. $300

European Home Video
See: TELEVISION & VIDEO

European Media Business & Finance
See: MEDIA & COMMUNICATIONS

European Offshore Petroleum Newsletter
See: PETROLEUM & NATURAL GAS

European Radio
See: BROADCASTING

European TV Sports
See: TELEVISION & VIDEO

Exhibit Mexico
See: ADVERTISING & MARKETING

Eximbank Letter
See: BANKING & FINANCE

Export Finance Weekly   *Business*
Publishing Co: Trade Reports International Group, 2104 National Press Bldg., Washington, DC 20045; Title Tel # (301) 946-0817 Title Fax # (301) 946-2631
Personnel: Publisher, Editor-Jim Berger
General Info: Yr. Est. 1992, Weekly, Trim Size-8½ x 11, 35 pages
Subscriptions: Indv. $475

Export Marketing Insights
See: ADVERTISING & MARKETING

Export News   *Business, Association*
Publishing Co: Canadian Export Assn., 99 Bank St., #250, Ottawa, ON K1P 6B9 Canada; Title Tel # (613) 238-8888 Title Fax # (613) 563-9218
Personnel: Editor-J.D. Moore
General Info: (Formerly Export Digest, Export U.S.A. & Export News), Yr. Est. 1943, Monthly, Desktop press, 8 pages, Saddle-stitched
Subscriptions: Indv. $115, Can. $115, Free With Membership

Export News/Digest   *Association*   CPM: $300
Publishing Co: Sponsor-Canadian Exporters' Assn., Canadian Exporters Association, 99 Bank St., Ste. 250, Ottawa, ON K1P 6B9 Canada Fax # (613) 563-9218; Title Tel # (613) 238-8888
Personnel: Editor-Katherine Came
Editorial Description: Information and activities important to exporters, and those engaged in international business.
General Info: (Formerly Canadian Export Association Review and Digest Bulletin), Yr. Est. 1943, Bi-monthly, Trim Size-8½ x 11, Sheetfed press, 12 pages, ISSN: 0713-0341, 7% ads, No Color, Newsprint
Subscriptions: Indv. $100
Circulation: Total-3,000
Advertising: $900.

Export Update
Publishing Co: Trade Communications, Inc., 733 15th St NW Ste 1100, Washington, DC 20005-2112 Fax # (202) 783-5966; Title Tel # (202) 737-1060
Personnel: Publisher-Stephen Pfeiderer, Editor-Merritt Bragdon, Circ. Mgr.-John Perkins, Production Mgr.-Cheryl Cromer, Adv. Dir., Promotion Dir.-Grace Finne
Editorial Description: Includes significant buying trends, specific sales leads, in-depth country market profiles, latest figures on trade activity, schedules for trade fairs & missions, & insights on the effects of intl. news on U.S. businesses.
General Info: Yr. Est. 1985, Weekly, Trim Size-8½ x 11, Sheetfed press, 8 pages, ISSN: 0889-2458, Newsprint
Subscriptions: Indv. $375
Printing Co: McFarland Printing Co., 200 Cresent St., P.O. Box 3645, Harrisburg, PA 17105 Tel # (717) 234-6235, Fax # (717) 234-1587

Exportation Nouvelles
Publishing Co: Canadian Exporters Association, 99 Bank St., Ste. 250, Ottawa, ON K1P 6B9 Canada; Title Tel # (613) 238-8888 Title Fax # (613) 563-9218
Personnel: Editor-Katherine Came
Editorial Description: Text in French. Information and activities important to exporters, and those engaged in international business.
General Info: Bi-monthly
Advertising: $900.

Exporter, The   *Business*
Publishing Co: U.S. Import-Export Publications Co., PO Box 428, Bellflower, CA 90707-0428 Tel # (310) 925-2918; Title Tel # (213) 925-2918
Editorial Description: Expert info. on export procedures, shipping, insurance, etc.
General Info: Monthly, 16 pages, Ind/Abs/Online: Newsnet
Subscriptions: Indv. $95
List Rental: List Management Co.: List Technology Systems Group, Inc., 1001 Ave. of the Americas, New York, NY 10018 Tel # (212) 719-3850, Fax # (212) 719-1878, Actives: 58,939, $95/M

Federal Express International Newsletter   *Consumer*
Publishing Co: Federal Express Corp., Us Export Mktg. Dept. Box 727, Memphis, TN 38194-0001
Personnel: Editor in Chief-Judy Green, Editor-Dianne Bewley, Editor-Nick Jordan, Editor-Barbara Potter, Editor-Dori Wilson
General Info: Monthly, Trim Size-8½ x 11, 8 pages, 4 Color, Coated

Finance & Treasury   *Business*
Publishing Co: WorldTrade Executive, PO Box 761, Concord, MA 01742-0761; Title Tel # (508) 287-0301 Title Fax # (508) 287-0302
Personnel: Editor-Tom Ehrbar
Editorial Description: The leading source of information for international treasury managers. Demonstrates cash management techniques used by leading firms to manage worldwide financial resources. Monthly, a consensus of 60 corporate treasurers forecast exchange rates in the near, medium, and long terms.
General Info: (Formerly Financing Foreign Operations), Weekly, Trim Size-8½ x 11, 8 pages, Ind/Abs/Online: Dialog, Lexis, 2 Color
Subscriptions: Indv. $995, Can. $1,045, For. $1,045
Acquistions: Publication Bought, Publication Sold

Finance Latin America   *Business*
Publishing Co: Economist Intelligence Unit, 111 W. 57th St., New York, NY 10019 Tel # (212) 554-0600 Fax # (212) 586-1181
Personnel: Publisher-Wong Chiu Yin, Editor-William Millar
Editorial Description: Financial information and news on Latin America.
General Info: Yr. Est. 1993, Monthly, Trim Size-8½ x 11, 8 pages

Financial Digest
See: BANKING & FINANCE

Foreign Military Markets Latin American & Australasia
See: AERONAUTICS/ASTRONAUTICS

Foreign Trade by Commodities -Series C
Publishing Co: Organization for Economic Cooperation & Development, 2001 L St NW Ste 650, Washington, DC 20036-4910; Title Tel # (202) 785-6323 Title Fax # (202) 785-0350
Editorial Description: Imports and exports of OECD countries by SITC code.
General Info: Yr. Est. 1963, 5x/yr., Trim Size-9⅜ x 12½, Offset press, 700 pages, No Color
Subscriptions: Indv. $490

Foreign Trade Fairs New Products Newsletter   *Business*
Publishing Co: International Intertrade Index, Box 636, Federal Square, Newark, NJ 07101-0636; Title Tel # (908) 686-2382
Personnel: Editor-John E. Felber
Editorial Description: Index of new imported products as displayed at foreign trade fairs.
General Info: Yr. Est. 1955, Monthly, Trim Size-8½ x 11, Web press, 12 pages, No Color
Subscriptions: Indv. $45, Can. $55, For. $55, $5/copy

Franchise Wise (Quarterly newsletter of the intl gay & lesbian franchise assoc.)
See: GAY & LESBIAN INTEREST

Free Trade Advisory
See: INTERNATIONAL AFFAIRS

Free Trade Law Reporter   *Business*
Publishing Co: CCH Canadian Ltd., 6 Garamond Ct., North York, ON M3C 1Z5 Canada Fax # (416) 444-8011 Parent Co.-CCH, Inc., Riverwoods; Title Tel # (416) 441-2992 Title Fax # (416) 444-9011
Editorial Description: Commentary on key trade issues such as the elimination of custom duties, tariff exemptions, etc.
General Info: Yr. Est. 1989, Quarterly, Looseleaf
Subscriptions: Can. $295

Frohlinger's Marketing Report
See: ADVERTISING & MARKETING

Futures International Law Letter
See: LAW

Gas Turbine Engines/Markets
See: MACHINERY

Gateway   *Business*
Publishing Co: Citibank, Business & Professional Sort, 7836, One Court Squar, Long Island City, NY 11120-0001
Editorial Description: Global trade ideas and news for small businesses.
General Info: Yr. Est. 1994, Bi-monthly, Trim Size-8½ x 11, 8 pages

German American Business Council   *Association*
Publishing Co: German American Business Council, 1413 K St NW Ste 800, Washington, DC 20005-3405; Title Tel # (202) 371-0555 Title Fax # (202) 408-9369
Personnel: Editor-Brooke Stoddard
Editorial Description: Commercial news about German-American business. Updates on Association activities and new members.
General Info: Yr. Est. 1990, Quarterly, Trim Size-8½ x 11, Desktop press, 4 pages, 2 Color
Circulation: Total-1,000

German American Commerce
See: CHAMBER OF COMMERCE

Global Glimpses   *Business*   CPM: $500
Publishing Co: Assist International, 60 Madison Ave., 2nd Fl., New York, NY 10010-1600; Title Tel # (212) 725-3311 Title Fax # (212) 725-3312
Personnel: Publisher-Peter Robinson
Editorial Description: Covers international trade resources and events.
General Info: Yr. Est. 1992, Bi-weekly, Trim Size-8½ x 11, Desktop press, 6 pages, 2 Color, Matte, Other
Subscriptions: Indv. $60
Circulation: Total-4,000
Advertising: $2,000. Accepts Inserts.
List Rental: Actives: 4,000, $150/M

Global Investment in
Canada   *Business*

Publishing Co: Prentice-Hall Canada, 1870 Birchmont Rd., Scarborough, ON M1P 2T1 Canada Parent Co.-Simon & Schuster, Waterford; Title Tel # (416) 293-3621 Title Fax # (416) 299-2529
Personnel: Publisher-Yolanda deRooy, Editor-Jeff Hill, Circ. Dir.-Joanne Zinck, Production Dir.-Anita Boyle, Mktg. Dir.-Jerry Smith
Editorial Description: Foreign investment information and legislation information.
General Info: Yr. Est. 1974, Monthly, Trim Size-5$\frac{1}{2}$ x 8$\frac{1}{2}$, Desktop press, 25 pages, No Color, Coated, Looseleaf
Subscriptions: Can. $570
Circulation: Total-238
Printing Co: Commerce Press, 2250 Midland Ave., #17, Scarborough, ON M1P 4R9 Canada Tel # (416) 291-8796, Fax # (416) 291-9950

Global Market Perspective
See: INVESTMENT

Global Packaging & Brand Identity
See: PACKAGING

Global Private Banking - International Investment Outlook
See: BANKING & FINANCE

Globalist, The
See: INVESTMENT

Guide to Export & Project
Financing   *Business*

Publishing Co: Thompson Publishing Group, 1725 K Street, NW, Washington, DC 20006 Tel # (202) 872-4000
Editorial Description: Covers major export credit agencies and development banks that can provide competitive financing. Subscription includes a monthly newsletter and monthly updates.
General Info: Annually, Looseleaf
Subscriptions: Indv. $449, For. $595

Gulf Business Report   *Business*

Publishing Co: Phillips Business Information, Inc., 1201 Seven Locks Rd., Ste 300, Potomac, MD 20854-2958 Tel # (301) 340-1520 Fax # (301) 424-4297
Personnel: Publisher-Harry Baisden, Editor-David Gump, Staff Writer-Miriam Amie, Staff Writer-Laurie Lande, Staff Writer-Josh Martin, Circ. Mgr.-Kathy Thorne, Mktg. Dir.-Katrine Hellauer
Editorial Description: Trade publication concerning business opportunities in Kuwait.
General Info: (Formerly Gulf Reconstruction Report), Yr. Est. 1991, Bi-weekly, Trim Size-8$\frac{1}{2}$ x 11, Sheetfed press, 10 pages, 2 Color, Matte
Subscriptions: Indv. $396, Inst. $396, Can. $396, For. $426
Advertising: Accepts Inserts.
List Rental: Rents Lists
Printing Co: Plymouth Printing, 1200 Cushing Pl SE, Washington, DC 20003-3599 Tel # (202) 488-7777, Fax # (202) 863-1078

Holland Flower
See: FLORIST

Hong Kong Revenue Law
See: TAXES

IBIS International Traders
Newsletter   *Business*

Publishing Co: International Business Information Service, First St. , Box 3271, Tustin, CA 92681-3271
Personnel: Asst. Pub.-Dale Leveles, Art Dir.-J. Vantury, Editor, Promotion Dir.-Marc Iro
Editorial Description: Summarized listings of available imports & current information for importers. Regulations, trade leads, tips & ideas.
General Info: (Formerly IBIS Importers Newsletter), Yr. Est. 1985, Semi-monthly, Trim Size-8 x 11, Offset press, 5 pages, ISSN: 0880-3779
Subscriptions: Indv. $90
Circulation: Total-1,200

I.C. Europe   *Business*

Publishing Co: Marketmakers/Dataquest, 26524 Golden Valley Rd Ste 401, Santa Clarita, CA 91350-2931
Editorial Description: News and analysis of semiconductor market in Europe.
Subscriptions: Indv. $840

I.I.I.: Intl. Intertrade Index

Publishing Co: Printing Consultants, Federal Sq., Box 636, Newark, NJ 07101; Title Tel # (908) 686-2382
Personnel: Editor-John Felber
Editorial Description: Lists new products being offered by foreign manufacturers direct to U.S. importers & wholesalers. Gives descriptions, prices & photos of new products yet to be seen in U.S.
General Info: Yr. Est. 1955, Monthly, ISSN: 0020-7004
Subscriptions: Indv. $45, Can. $55, For. $55

IMF Survey
See: ECONOMICS

ISRI Report
See: METALS & METALWORKING

Importweek   *Business, Association*   CPM: $305

Publishing Co: Canadian Importers Association, 210 Dundas St. W., #700, Toronto, ON M5G 2E8 Canada; Title Tel # (416) 595-5333 Title Fax # (416) 595-8226
Personnel: Publisher-Donald McArthur, Editor-Catherine Hodgson
Editorial Description: Weekly articles on international trade. Regulations affecting Canada's import trade as well as tariffs, etc.
General Info: Yr. Est. 1936, Weekly, Trim Size-8$\frac{1}{2}$ x 11, Web press, 6 pages, ISSN: 0702-8385, Color-cover
Circulation: Total-1,800
Advertising: $550.
Printing Co: Metroprint, 190 Nashville Rd., Kleinberg, ON L0S 1C0 Canada Tel # (416) 893-1744

India Business and
Investment Report   *Business*

Publishing Co: PSI, Inc., 75 Maiden Lane, 12th Fl., New York, NY 10038-4810; Title Tel # (212) 806-8840 Title Fax # (212) 269-0420
Personnel: Publisher-Ranjit Shastri, Editor-S. Ghosh
Editorial Description: Concise report of key developments in India trade and investment, including export opportunities, sourcing potential, joint ventures, technology transfer deals, economic developments, legislation, regulations, exhibitions, industry analyses, statistics and political risks.
General Info: (Formerly India Business News; India Sourcing Update), Yr. Est. 1989, Monthly
Subscriptions: Indv. $197, Inst. $197, Can. $197, For. $227

Indonesia Letter, The   *Business*

Publishing Co: Asia Letter Group, PO Box 88189, Los Angeles, CA 90009-8189 Tel # (213) 523-0057; Title Tel # (852) 526-2950
General Info: Monthly
Subscriptions: Indv. $195

Information Broker
See: MEDIA & COMMUNICATIONS

Inside NAFTA   *Business, Consumer*

Publishing Co: Inside NAFTA, PO Box 7167, Ben Franklin Station, Washington, DC 20044
Personnel: Publisher-Jutta Hennig
Editorial Description: Covers all aspects of the NAFTA trade agreement as well as trade negotiations in the Western hemisphere such as the effort to create a Free Trade Area of the Americas (FTAA) by 2005.
General Info: Yr. Est. 1994, Bi-weekly
Subscriptions: Indv. $595
List Rental: Rents Lists

Inside U.S. Trade   *Business, Consumer*

Publishing Co: Inside Washington Publishers, P.O. Box 7167, Ben Franklin Station, Washington, DC 20044 Tel # (703) 512-1800; Title Tel # (703) 892-8500 Title Fax # (203) 685-2606
Personnel: Publisher-John Brand, Editor-Jutta Hennig
Editorial Description: Covers major government and industry trade action.
General Info: Yr. Est. 1983, Weekly, Trim Size-8$\frac{1}{2}$ x 11, Sheetfed press, 14 pages
Subscriptions: Indv. $595
List Rental: Actives: 23,419, $85/M

Inside/Outside Japan   *Business*

Publishing Co: Japan External Trade Organization, 1221 Ave. of the Americas, New York, NY 10020-1001; Title Tel # (212) 997-0418 Title Fax # (212) 997-0464
Editorial Description: Research & planning, Japan external trade organization, etc.
General Info: Monthly
Circulation: Total-900

Intelligent Highway, The
See: TRAFFIC & TRANSPORTATION

Inter-Americas Business
Newsletter

Publishing Co: Inter-Americas Consulting Group, PO Box 42184, Houston, TX 77242-2184; Title Tel # (713) 961-3399
General Info: Yr. Est. 1978, Monthly
Subscriptions: Indv. $75

Interfaith Impact & Preparedness
See: RELIGIOUS & THEOLOGICAL

Interflo: Trade Monitor of
the Former Soviet
Republics   *Business*

Publishing Co: Interflo, PO Box 42, Maplewood, NJ 07040-0042; Title Tel # (201) 763-9493 Title Fax # (201) 763-9493
Personnel: Publisher, Editor-Paul Surovell
Editorial Description: Abstracts on trade, investment & joint ventures in Russia, Ukraine, Kazakhstan, Belaras, Azerbaikan, Turkmenistan, and all former Soviet Republics.
General Info: Yr. Est. 1981, Monthly, Trim Size-8$\frac{1}{2}$ x 11, Mimeo press, 36 pages, ISSN: 0748-4631, No Color, Looseleaf
Subscriptions: Indv. $142, Can. $142, For. $165, $20/copy
Circulation: Total-500

International Banking Regulator
See: BANKING & FINANCE

International Business   *Business*

Publishing Co: U.S. Import-Export Publications Co., PO Box 428, Bellflower, CA 90707-0428; Title Tel # (310) 925-2918
Personnel: Publisher, Editor-Mervyn Heaton, Adv. Dir.-Frances Leneker
Editorial Description: 250 import and export offers for consumer, business and industrial products, each issue.
General Info: (Formerly Int'l Business Opportunities News), Yr. Est. 1975, Monthly, Trim Size-8½ x 11, Offset press, 12 pages, No Color
Subscriptions: Indv. $48, $5/copy
Circulation: Total-2,300
Advertising: Inquire for rates.

International Business Planning: Law and Taxation (United State)   *Business*

Publishing Co: Matthew Bender & Co., 11 Penn Plaza, New York, NY 10001-2006 Tel # (212) 967-7707 Fax # (212) 244-3188
Editorial Description: A practical guide for the solution of common legal, tax, & financial problems relating to international transactions. Provides guidance in the planning of the international business transaction, as well as in the management of existing undertakings.
General Info: Yr. Est. 1981, Irregular, Looseleaf

International Cellular
See: TELECOMMUNICATIONS

International Commercial Arbitration
See: LAW

International Co-Productions
See: TELEVISION & VIDEO

International Copyright Law and Practice
See: PATENTS/COPYRIGHTS/TRADE MARKS

International Country Risk Guide
See: BANKING & FINANCE

International Exporting Agreements   *Business*

Publishing Co: Matthew Bender & Co., 11 Penn Plaza, New York, NY 10001-2006 Tel # (212) 967-7707 Fax # (212) 244-3188
Editorial Description: A practical guide to negotiating & drafting international contracts for export sales. Model contract clauses, practice tips & checklists are provided.
General Info: Yr. Est. 1985, Irregular, Looseleaf

International Information Report   *Business*

Publishing Co: Washington Researchers, Ltd., PO Box 19005, Washington, DC 20036-9005 Tel # (202) 333-3499; Title Tel # (202) 333-3533 Title Fax # (202) 625-0656
Personnel: Editor-Penny Hill Press, Promotion Dir.-Ellen O'Kane
Editorial Description: An alert to help track international markets and competitors; up-to-the minute critical data and insights.
General Info: (Formerly Intl. Industry Dossier), Yr. Est. 1983, Monthly, Trim Size-8½ x 11, Offset press, 8 pages, ISSN: 0748-206X, Ind/Abs/Online: NEWSNET, 2 Color
Subscriptions: Indv. $160

International Labor Affairs

Publishing Co: U.S. Council for International Business, 1212 Ave of the Americas, New York, NY 10036-1689; Title Tel # (212) 354-4480
Personnel: Editor-Kevin Cornacchio
Editorial Description: Newssheet on developments in international organizations (esp. ILO & othe U.N. bodies) with respect to labor relations.
Subscriptions: Indv. $50
Circulation: Total-2,800

International Law & Trade Perspective
See: LAW

International Legal Framework for Services
See: LAW

International Market Alert   *Business*

Publishing Co: United Communications Group, 11300 Rockville Pike, Ste. 1100, Rockville, MD 20852-3030 Tel # (301) 816-8950 Fax # (301) 816-8945
Personnel: Publisher-Susan R. Goldberg, Editor-Robert Taylor, Circ. Mgr.-Loretta Netzer
Editorial Description: Vital and immediate advice and comment on all aspects of international finance and foreign exchange. Analysis of day's developments and impact on interest and exchange rates.
General Info: (Formerly Daily Telex Alert), Yr. Est. 1975, Daily, ISSN: 1051-8061
Subscriptions: Indv. $3,935, Can. $3,935, For. $4,845
List Rental: Actives: $250/M

International Marketing Intelligence News

Publishing Co: Netherlands Chamber of Commerce in the USA, 1 Rockefeller Plz., 11th Fl., New York, NY 10020-2002; Title Tel # (212) 265-6460 Title Fax # (212) 265-6402
Personnel: Publisher-Kersen De Jong
Editorial Description: Intl. business news focusing on the Netherland & the USA trade and business environment.
General Info: Yr. Est. 1988, Weekly, 2 pages
Subscriptions: Indv. $1,000
Circulation: Total-200
List Rental: Rents Lists

International Pet Industry News
See: ANIMALS

International Petroleum Industry
See: PETROLEUM & NATURAL GAS

International Private Power Quarterly
See: ENERGY

International Product Safety News
See: SAFETY

International Quality
See: MANAGEMENT

International Reports Newsletter   *Business*

Publishing Co: United Communications Group, 11300 Rockville Pike, Ste. 1100, Rockville, MD 20852-3030 Tel # (301) 816-8950 Fax # (301) 816-8945
Personnel: Publisher-Susan R. Goldberg, Editor-Robert Taylor, Circ. Mgr.-Loretta Netzer, Production Mgr.-Gail Solomon
Editorial Description: Developments and analysis of economic, financial and investment environments in important worldwide markets. Coverage of foreign exchange, international debt, interest rates. Statistical section with parallel rates for 75 currencies, international liquidity positions, export credit collection conditions.
General Info: Yr. Est. 1947, Weekly, Trim Size-8½ x 11, Mimeo press, 32 pages, ISSN: 0020-8507, Color-cover, Newsprint, Saddle-stitched
Subscriptions: Indv. $1,190, Can. $1,190, For. $1,190
Acquistions: Publication Bought
Circulation: Total-1,500
List Rental: List Management Co.: PRS List Management, 222 Teal Ave., POB 6482, Syracuse, NY 13217-6482 Tel # (315) 472-1224, Fax # (315) 472-1235, Actives: 5,540, $250/M
Printing Co: Xerox Reproduction Center, 200 Madison Ave., New York, NY 10016 Tel # (212) 685-7252

International Software Report
See: COMPUTERS & AUTOMATION

International Taxation Series
See: TAXES

International Trade & Investment Letter

Publishing Co: International Business Affairs Corp., c/o Richard Barovick, 4938 Hampden Lane, Bethesda, MD 20814-2914; Title Tel # (301) 907-8647 Title Fax # (301) 907-8650
Personnel: Publisher, Editor-Richard Barovick, Circ. Mgr.-Patricia Anderson
Editorial Description: Trends in U.S. policies, trade finance, & trading operations.
General Info: Monthly, 18 pages, ISSN: 0890-4257
Subscriptions: Indv. $252, $18/copy

International Trade Alert   *Business*

Publishing Co: American Assn. of Exporters and Importers, 11 W 42nd St Fl 30, New York, NY 10036-8002; Title Tel # (212) 944-2230
Personnel: Editor-Kelly Bundy
Editorial Description: Impending changes in laws, regulations affecting international trade; and trade opportunities.
General Info: (Formerly Import Alert), Yr. Est. 1921, Weekly, Offset press, 16 pages
Circulation: Total-2,100

International Trade Reporter   *Business*

Publishing Co: Bureau of National Affairs, Inc., 1231 25th St. NW, Bldg. N-200, Washington, DC 20037-1157; Title Tel # (202) 452-4200 Title Fax # (202) 822-8092
Personnel: Publisher-William A. Beltz, Editor-Deanne Neuman, Mng. Editor-Linda G. Botsford, Circ. Mgr.-Gary C. Seltzer
Editorial Description: A comprehensive source that reports & analyzes legislative & regulatory developments as well as private sector activities affecting international trade (both export & import).
General Info: (Formerly Intl Trade Reporter Current Reports), Yr. Est. 1947, Weekly, Trim Size-8½ x 11, Web press, 32 pages, ISSN: 1075-833X, Ind/Abs/Online: Lexis, Westlaw, Mead Data Central, Nexis
Subscriptions: Indv. $1,035

International Trade
Reporter Decisions   *Business*

Publishing Co: Bureau of National Affairs, Inc., 1231 25th St. NW, Bldg. N-200, Washington, DC 20037-1157; Title Tel # (202) 452-4200 Title Fax # (202) 822-8092
Personnel: Publisher-William A. Beltz, Mng. Editor-Linda G. Botsford, Circ. Mgr.-Gary C. Seltzer
Editorial Description: Features digested, classified & indexed judicial & administrative decisions dealing with legal issues arising from US trade law (mostly import cases).
General Info: (Formerly International Trade Reporter's U.S. Import Weekly), Bi-weekly, Trim Size-6 x 9, Offset press, ISSN: 0748-0709, Looseleaf
Subscriptions: Indv. $1,058

International Trade
Reporter Export
Reference Manual   *Business*

Publishing Co: Bureau of National Affairs, Inc., 1231 25th St. NW, Bldg. N-200, Washington, DC 20037-1157; Title Tel # (202) 452-4200 Title Fax # (202) 822-8092
Personnel: Publisher-William A. Beltz, Mng. Editor-Linda G. Botsford, Circ. Mgr.-Gary C. Seltzer
Editorial Description: A comprehensive source for foreign import regulations, U.S. export controls, and related requirements for preparing U.S. exports for shipment abroad.
General Info: (Formerly Export Shipping Manual), Weekly, Trim Size-6 x 9, Offset press, ISSN: 1043-5670, Looseleaf
Subscriptions: Indv. $662

International Trade
Reporter Import
Reference Manual   *Business*

Publishing Co: Bureau of National Affairs, Inc., 1231 25th St. NW, Bldg. N-200, Washington, DC 20037-1157; Title Tel # (202) 452-4200 Title Fax # (202) 822-8092
Personnel: Publisher-William A. Beltz, Editor-Deanne Neuman, Mng. Editor-Linda G. Botsford, Circ. Mgr.-Gary C. Seltzer
Editorial Description: A complete guide to entire import process with analysis & full text of statutes, regulations, & executive orders on subjects such as customhouse brokers, dumping, countervailing duties, escape clauses, & presidential retaliation.
General Info: (Formerly Intl. Trade Reporter Reference File), Bi-monthly, Trim Size-8½ x 11, Offset press, ISSN: 1043-5662, Looseleaf
Subscriptions: Indv. $1,058

International Visitor
See: TRAVEL

International Withholding Tax Treaty Guide
See: TAXES

Israel High-Tech Report

Publishing Co: Israel Publications Inc., 47 Byron Pl, Scarsdale, NY 10583-1901; Title Tel # (914) 723-8321 Title Fax # (914) 723-8340
Editorial Description: Developments in Israel's high tech industries.
General Info: Yr. Est. 1987, Monthly
Subscriptions: Indv. $150

Israel MarketFax
See: INVESTMENT

JEI Report   *Business, Scholarly*

Publishing Co: Japan Economic Institute of America, 1000 Connecticut Ave., N.W., Washington, DC 20036-5347; Title Tel # (202) 296-5633 Title Fax # (202) 296-8333
Editorial Description: Concerned with economic relations between the U.S. and Japan.
General Info: Yr. Est. 1957, Weekly, Trim Size-8½ x 11, Offset press, 20 pages, ISSN: 0744-6489, Newsprint
Subscriptions: Indv. $80, Can. $115, For. $140
Circulation: Total-1,500

Japan Economic Survey
See: INTERNATIONAL AFFAIRS

Japan Financial Market
Report

Publishing Co: Japan Market Research, Inc., 609 Columbus Ave., New York, NY 10024; Title Tel # (212) 496-6760 Title Fax # (212) 724-4915
Personnel: Editor-Koto Akagi
Editorial Description: Reports on Japan's financial market.
General Info: Yr. Est. 1988, Weekly
Subscriptions: Indv. $397

Japan Letter, The   *Business*

Publishing Co: Asia Letter Group, PO Box 88189, Los Angeles, CA 90009-8189 Tel # (213) 523-0057; Title Tel # (852) 526-2950
General Info: 24x/yr.
Subscriptions: Indv. $120

Japan M & A Reporter

Publishing Co: Ulmer Brothers Research Institute, 80 Maiden Lane, New York, NY 10038; Title Tel # (212) 344-4411 Title Fax # (212) 344-8074
General Info: Yr. Est. 1987, Monthly
Subscriptions: Indv. $575

Japan Medical Review
See: MEDICINE

Japan-U.S. Business
Report   *Business, Scholarly*

Publishing Co: Japan Economic Institute of America, 1000 Connecticut Ave., N.W., Washington, DC 20036-5347; Title Tel # (202) 296-5633 Title Fax # (202) 296-8333
Editorial Description: Covers what Japanese companies are doing in the U.S. & what American companies are doing in Japan.
General Info: Yr. Est. 1957, Monthly, Trim Size-8½ x 11, Sheetfed press, 20 pages, ISSN: 0888-5702, No Color, Newsprint
Subscriptions: Indv. $160
Circulation: Total-550
List Rental: Rents Lists

Japan Weekly   *Business, Consumer*

Publishing Co: Kyodo News Intl., 50 Rockefeller Plaza #803, New York, NY 10020-1605; Title Tel # (212) 397-3723 Title Fax # (212) 397-3721
Personnel: Circ. Mgr., Adv. Dir.-James Buckner, Editor, Art Dir.-Goro Kamata, Mktg. Dir.-Toshi Mitsudome, Production Mgr., Promotion Dir.-Bill Barone
Editorial Description: A weekly newsletter for political, business, trade technology and social news on Japan and Asia.
General Info: Yr. Est. 1995, Weekly
Subscriptions: Indv. $195, Inst. $195

Japan Weekly Monitor   *Business*

Publishing Co: Kyodo News Intl., 50 Rockefeller Plaza #803, New York, NY 10020-1605; Title Tel # (212) 397-3723 Title Fax # (212) 397-3721
Personnel: Publisher, Editor-M. Suito, Circ. Mgr.-Toshiaki Mitsudome
Editorial Description: Summary of yen fluctuation, Japan-U.S. news & headline service.
General Info: Yr. Est. 1984, Weekly, 8 pages, Ind/Abs/Online: NewsNet, DIALOG, No Color

Japanese International Taxation
See: TAXES

Joint Venture News

Publishing Co: Transmart Company, 3581 Kachemak Cir, Anchorage, AK 99515-2337; Title Tel # (907) 349-5481 Title Fax # (907) 522-1489
Editorial Description: News on joint ventures.
General Info: Yr. Est. 1989, Monthly
Subscriptions: Indv. $49

Korean Trade News

Publishing Co: Korean Traders Assn., Inc., 460 Park Ave., New York, NY 10022-1906
General Info: Yr. Est. 1967, Weekly
Circulation: Total-897
Advertising: Inquire for rates.

Lagniape Monthly on
Latin American
Projects & Finance   *Business*

Publishing Co: Latin American Info Services, 159 W 53rd St # 28B, New York, NY 10019-6050; Title Tel # (212) 765-5520 Title Fax # (212) 765-2927
Personnel: Publisher, Editor-Rosemary Werrett
Editorial Description: Monthly report on business and finance opportunities arising out of project and infrastructure development in Latin America
General Info: (Formerly Americas Trade & Finance), Yr. Est. 1992, Monthly, Trim Size-8½ x 11, Roto. press, 10 pages, ISSN: 1062-8118, 2 Color, Other, Case bound
Subscriptions: Indv. $450, Inst. $450
List Rental: Actives: 16,000, $220/M
Printing Co: Globe Mail Agency, Inc., 541 W 25th St, New York, NY 10001-5501 Tel # (212) 675-4600

Lagniappe Letter   *Business*

Publishing Co: Latin American Info Services, 159 W 53rd St # 28B, New York, NY 10019-6050; Title Tel # (212) 765-5520 Title Fax # (212) 765-2927
Personnel: Publisher-Pedro Pick, Editor-Rosemary Werrett
Editorial Description: Report of issues affecting business, banking and trade in Latin America. Subscription includes Lagniappe Quarterly Monitor.
General Info: Yr. Est. 1984, Bi-weekly, Trim Size-8½ x 11, Offset press, 10 pages, ISSN: 1040-3175, Ind/Abs/Online: Mead Data Central/ Predicasts, No Color, Newsprint, Saddle-stitched
Subscriptions: Indv. $675, Inst. $675
Acquistions: Publication Bought
List Rental: Actives: $220/M, Expires: $220/M
Printing Co: Globe Mail Agency, Inc., 541 W 25th St, New York, NY 10001-5501 Tel # (212) 675-4600

Lagniappe Quarterly
Monitor *Business*

Publishing Co: Latin American Info Services, 159 W 53rd St # 28B, New York, NY 10019-6050; Title Tel # (212) 765-5520 Title Fax # (212) 765-2927
Personnel: Publisher-Pedro Pick, Editor-Rosemary Werrett
Editorial Description: Financial and production trend analysis for business operations in Latin America. Subscription includes Lagniappe Letter.
General Info: Yr. Est. 1984, Quarterly, Trim Size-8½ x 11, Offset press, 18 pages, ISSN: 1040-3183, Ind/Abs/Online: Predicast/Mead Data Central, 2 Color, Other, Other
Subscriptions: Indv. $675, Inst. $675
List Rental: Actives: 16,000, $220/M
Printing Co: Globe Mail Agency, Inc., 541 W 25th St, New York, NY 10001-5501 Tel # (212) 675-4600

Latin American Finance &
Capital Markets *Business*

Publishing Co: WorldTrade Executive, PO Box 761, Concord, MA 01742-0761 Tel # (508) 287-0301 Fax # (508) 287-0302
Editorial Description: Provides the best available coverage of opportunities, hazards, and important developments for the treasury manager or investor involved in Latin American markets. Up-to-date information on risk management techniques, economic performance, and financial sector developments in Latin America.
General Info: Semi-monthly
Subscriptions: Indv. $595, Can. $645, For. $645

Latin American Index

Publishing Co: Welt Publishing Co., 1413 K St. NW, Ste. 800, Washington, DC 20005-3405; Title Tel # (202) 371-0555 Title Fax # (202) 408-9369
Personnel: Publisher-Leo G.B. Welt, Editor-William Knepper
Editorial Description: Political & economic risk analysis of major Latin American economies.
General Info: Yr. Est. 1970, Semi-monthly, Trim Size-8½ x 11, 4 pages
Subscriptions: Indv. $249, Inst. $237, Can. $259, For. $279, $6/copy
Acquistions: Publication Bought
Circulation: (20% controlled), Total-725, Subscriptions-575
Advertising: Accepts Inserts.

Latin American Law and
Business Report *Business*

Publishing Co: WorldTrade Executive, PO Box 761, Concord, MA 01742-0761 Tel # (508) 287-0301 Fax # (508) 287-0302
Editorial Description: Provides detailed information on legal and regulatory developments in the region in a quick-reading executive report. Late-breaking news on capital markets, privatization, accounting, local sourcing, labor issues, and much more.
General Info: Monthly
Subscriptions: Indv. $497, Can. $547, For. $547

Law & Practice Under the GATT
See: LAW

Law & Practice of the United States Regulation of International Trade
See: LAW

Law of the European Economic Community-A Commentary on the EEC Treaty
See: LAW

Letters of Credit Report
See: BANKING & FINANCE

Market: Asia Pacific
See: ADVERTISING & MARKETING

Market: Europe *Business*

Publishing Co: W-Two Publications, 202 The Commons, #401, Ithaca, NY 14850-5578; Title Tel # (607) 277-0934 Title Fax # (607) 277-0935
Personnel: Publisher, Editor-Doris L. Walsh, Circ. Mgr.-Marjorie Waldman, Production Mgr.-Margaret Nichols, Art Dir.-Carol Terrizzi
Editorial Description: Demographic and lifestyle trends in Eastern and Western Europe.
General Info: Yr. Est. 1990, Monthly, Trim Size-8½ x 11, Sheetfed press, 16 pages, ISSN: 1050-9410, Ind/Abs/Online: Predicasts, 2 Color, Matte, Saddle-stitched
Subscriptions: Indv. $377, Inst. $175, Can. $377, For. $377, $32/copy
Circulation: Total-400
List Rental: Actives: $250/M
Printing Co: Graphics Printing Plus, 3736 Kellogg Rd, Cortland, NY 13045-8818 Tel # (607) 753-9815

Market: Latin America *Business*

Publishing Co: W-Two Publications, 202 The Commons, #401, Ithaca, NY 14850-5578; Title Tel # (607) 277-0934 Title Fax # (607) 277-0935
Personnel: Publisher-Doris L. Walsh, Editor-Paula Kephart, Circ. Mgr.-Marjorie Waldman, Production Mgr.-Margret Nichols
Editorial Description: Explores demograhic and lifestyle trends of Latin American countries and what they mean for businesses.
General Info: Yr. Est. 1993, Monthly, Trim Size-8½ x 11, Sheetfed press, 12 pages, ISSN: 1066-7024, Ind/Abs/Online: Information Access, CWN Newsnet, 2 Color, Saddle-stitched
Subscriptions: Indv. $289, Inst. $175, Can. $289, For. $289, $35/copy
Circulation: Total-350
List Rental: Actives: $200/M, Expires: $200/M

Mexican Business Law Alert
See: LAW

Mexico Business Monthly *Business*

Publishing Co: Mexico Business Monthly, 52 Maple Ave, Maplewood, NJ 07040-2626; Title Tel # (201) 762-1565 Title Fax # (201) 762-9585
Personnel: Publisher, Editor-Kal Wagenheim
Editorial Description: Covers business and economic news in Mexico.
General Info: Yr. Est. 1991, Monthly, Trim Size-8½ x 11, Web press, 24 pages, ISSN: 1054-2663, No Color, Newsprint, Saddle-stitched
Subscriptions: Indv. $216, Inst. $188, Can. $216, For. $216, $18/copy
List Rental: List Management Co.: Information Marketing Services, 8130 Boone Blvd., Ste 310, Vienna, VA 22182-2640 Tel # (703) 821-8130, Fax # (703) 821-8243

Mexico Service *Business*

Publishing Co: United Communications Group, 11300 Rockville Pike, Ste. 1100, Rockville, MD 20852-3030 Tel # (301) 816-8950 Fax # (301) 816-8945
Personnel: Publisher-Susan R. Goldberg, Editor-Robert Taylor, Circ. Mgr.-Loretta Netzer, Production Mgr.-Gail Solomon
Editorial Description: Information, analysis and forecasts of investment opportunities, credit risk, and political climate in Mexico.
General Info: Yr. Est. 1981, Bi-weekly, Trim Size-8½ x 11, Mimeo press, 24 pages, ISSN: 1044-6303, Color-cover
Subscriptions: Indv. $585, Can. $585, For. $585
Circulation: Total-375
List Rental: List Management Co.: PRS List Management, 222 Teal Ave., POB 6482, Syracuse, NY 13217-6482 Tel # (315) 472-1224, Fax # (315) 472-1235, Actives: $250/M
Printing Co: Xerox Reproduction Center, 200 Madison Ave., New York, NY 10016 Tel # (212) 685-7252

Mexico Update
See: INVESTMENT

Mexico Watch
See: INTERNATIONAL AFFAIRS

Middle East Business Intelligence
See: BUSINESS & INDUSTRY

Middle East Trade Letter *Business*

Publishing Co: Middle East Trade Letter, PO Box 472986, Charlotte, NC 28247-2986; Title Tel # (704) 543-6161 Title Fax # (704) 542-7668
Personnel: Editor-Leslie Cohen
Editorial Description: Business opportunities, trade, contracts, financial info for Middle East & North Africa.
General Info: Yr. Est. 1974, Bi-weekly, Trim Size-8½ x 11, Sheetfed press, 4 pages, No Color
Subscriptions: Indv. $154, $4/copy
Acquistions: Publication Bought
Advertising: Accepts Inserts.
List Rental: Actives: $175/M

Minnesota International Center
See: INTERNATIONAL AFFAIRS

Monthly Exports of Ducks & Geese
See: POULTRY & POULTRY PRODUCTS

Monthly Statistics of
Foreign Trade -Series A

Publishing Co: Organization for Economic Cooperation & Development, 2001 L St NW Ste 650, Washington, DC 20036-4910; Title Tel # (202) 785-6323 Title Fax # (202) 785-0350
Editorial Description: Overall picture of the foreign trade of OECD countries.
General Info: Yr. Est. 1962, Monthly, Trim Size-7⅞ x 10⅝, Offset press, 100 pages, ISSN: 0474-5388, No Color
Subscriptions: Indv. $190, $18/copy

Montreal Plus *Business, Association*

Publishing Co: Montreal Board of Trade, 5 Place Rue Marie, Plaza Level, Montreal, PQ H3P 4Y2 Canada; Title Tel # (514) 871-4000
Personnel: Publisher-Alex Harper, Editor-Kevin Saville, Production Mgr.-Olaf Silva
Editorial Description: Eng. & Fr. text, business practical info.
General Info: (Formerly Forum), Monthly, Trim Size-8½ x 11, Web press, 16 pages, 2 Color, Saddle-stitched
Circulation: (100% controlled), Total-8,500
Advertising: Inquire for rates.

Multinational Corporations Law: Mexico, Cntrl.America, Panama, Cntrl. American Common Mkt.
See: LAW

NABE Outlook, Industry Survey & Policy Survey
See: ECONOMICS

NQB Pink Sheets for Equities
See: INVESTMENT

NQB Yellow Sheets for Taxable Bonds
See: INVESTMENT

Netherlands News

Publishing Co: Tappan Group, Inc., PO Box 167, Harrington Park, NJ 07640-0167;
Title Tel # (201) 871-3333
General Info: Yr. Est. 1982, 8x/yr.
Subscriptions: Indv. $10

News Bulletin
Business

Publishing Co: Brazilian American Chamber of Commerce, 22 W. 48th St., Ste. 404, New York, NY 10036-1803 Fax # (212) 921-1078; Title Tel # (212) 575-9030
Personnel: Editor-Peter Smith
Editorial Description: Monthly review to promote trade and investment between the U.S. and Brazil as well as contributing to the growth of bilateral economic relations.
General Info: Yr. Est. 1968, Monthly, Offset press, 16 pages, No Color, Newsprint
Subscriptions: Free With Membership
Circulation: Total-600

North American Free Trade & Investment Report, The
Business

Publishing Co: WorldTrade Executive, PO Box 761, Concord, MA 01742-0761 Tel # (508) 287-0301 Fax # (508) 287-0302
Editorial Description: Provides all the important NAFTA developments in a fast-reading format, plus the latest information on trade, investment and related trans-border issues in Mexico, the United States, and Canada
General Info: (Formerly US/Mexico Free Trade Reporter), Semi-monthly
Subscriptions: Indv. $660, Can. $710, For. $710

North American Free Trade Agreements
Business

Publishing Co: Oceana Publications, Inc., 75 Main St, Dobbs Ferry, NY 10522-1601 Tel # (914) 693-8100 Fax # (914) 693-0402
Personnel: Editor-James R. Holbein, Editor-Donald Musch, Production Mgr.-Mike Wortzman, Mktg. Dir.-John Downey
Editorial Description: Covers all free trade agreements between the U.S., Canada, and Mexico.
General Info: Yr. Est. 1992, Irregular, Looseleaf
Subscriptions: Indv. $350

Offshore Field Development International
See: ENERGY

Offshore International Newsletter
See: PETROLEUM & NATURAL GAS

Offshore Rig Locator International
See: ENERGY

Offshore Rig Newsletter
See: ENERGY

Overseas Living

Publishing Co: Overseas Orientation Service, PO Box 1611, Cullowhee, NC 28723-1611; Title Tel # (704) 586-0148
Personnel: Editor-Adele Landsman
Editorial Description: Info on overseas living.
General Info: Yr. Est. 1984, Bi-monthly

Pacific Chapter Update
See: METALS & METALWORKING

Passenger Shipping International

Publishing Co: Lloyd's of London Press, 611 Broadway Rm 308, New York, NY 10012-2608; Title Tel # (212) 529-9500 Title Fax # (212) 529-9826
Editorial Description: News of the passenger shipping industry.
General Info: Yr. Est. 1989, Monthly
Subscriptions: Indv. $395

Perryman Report
See: ECONOMICS

Pipelines

Publishing Co: Louis-Ferdinand & Co., Inc., 206 Warren St, Harrison, NJ 07029-1738; Title Tel # (201) 482-3060
Editorial Description: Practical advice on handling imports & exports; U.S. Customs regulations.
General Info: Yr. Est. 1990, Trim Size-8$\frac{1}{2}$ x 11, Mimeo press, 5 pages, No Color, Matte

Plant Shutdowns Monitor
Business, Consumer

Publishing Co: Third World Resources, DataCenter, 464 19th St., Oakland, CA 94612-2297 Tel # (510) 835-4692 Fax # (510) 835-3017
General Info: Monthly
Subscriptions: Indv. $450

Platts International Petrochemical Report
See: PETROLEUM & NATURAL GAS

Political Risk Letter
Business

Publishing Co: Political Risk Services, 6320 Fly Road Suite #102, PO Box 248, East Syracuse, NY 13057-0248 Tel # (315) 431-0511 Fax # (315) 431-0200 Parent Co.-International Business Communications, Ashland; Title Tel # (315) 472-1224 Title Fax # (315) 472-1235
Personnel: Publisher-Mary Lou Walsh, Editor-William Coplin, Editor-Michael O'Leary, Circ. Mgr.-Patti Davis
Editorial Description: A monthly, 14-page summary of the latest forecasts from PRS's global network of country risk analysis.
General Info: (Formerly F&S Political Risk Letter), Yr. Est. 1979, Monthly, Trim Size-8$\frac{1}{2}$ x 11, Mimeo press, 14 pages, ISSN: 0887-7629, Ind/Abs/Online: NewsNet, Predicasts, DIALOG, 2 Color, Matte, Other
Subscriptions: Indv. $435
Circulation: Total-410
Advertising: Accepts Inserts.
List Rental: List Management Co.: Manager: Mary Lou Walsh; PRS List Management, 222 Teal Ave., POB 6482, Syracuse, NY 13217-6482 Tel # (315) 472-1224, Fax # (315) 472-1235, Actives: $200/M, Expires: $200/M
Printing Co: Dupli Envelopes & Printing Graphics, 360 W Jefferson St # 1318, Syracuse, NY 13202-2319 Tel # (315) 422-3343

Private Placement Reporter
See: INVESTMENT

Pulp & Paper Week
See: PAPER

Reference Book for World Traders
Business

Publishing Co: U.S. Import-Export Publications Co., PO Box 428, Bellflower, CA 90707-0428; Title Tel # (310) 925-2918
General Info: Annually, 800 pages, Looseleaf
Subscriptions: $102/copy

Royal Mail, The
See: DIRECT MAIL

Rundt's Weekly Intelligence
Business

Publishing Co: S.J. Rundt Assocs., 130 E. 63rd St., New York, NY 10021-7334; Title Tel # (212) 838-0141
Personnel: Publisher, Editor-Dr. Hans P. Belcsak
Editorial Description: International financial & business risks.
General Info: Yr. Est. 1952, Weekly, Trim Size-8$\frac{1}{2}$ x 11, Offset press, 24 pages, 2 Color
Subscriptions: Indv. $675, For. $767
Advertising: Inquire for rates.
List Rental: Rents Lists

Russian Business News Update
Business

Publishing Co: Josh Zander Consulting Services, 4286 Redwood Hwy., Ste. 376, San Rafael, CA 94903 Tel # (415) 492-3382
Editorial Description: Covers Russian business news and information.
General Info: Yr. Est. 1994, Monthly, Trim Size-8$\frac{1}{2}$ x 11, 5 pages, 2 Color, Matte
Subscriptions: Free
Circulation: Total-300
List Rental: Rents Lists

Russian Far East Update
Business

Publishing Co: Russian Far East Update, PO Box 22126, Seattle, WA 98122; Title Tel # (206) 447-2668 Title Fax # (206) 628-0979
Personnel: Publisher, Editor-Elisa Miller, Circ. Mgr., Adv. Dir., Mktg. Mgr.-Clay Berry
Editorial Description: Trade and economic information plus news analysis of Russia's Far East.
General Info: Yr. Est. 1991, Monthly, 16 pages, ISSN: 1061-5679, Ind/Abs/Online: Chamber World Network
Subscriptions: Indv. $295, Can. $295, For. $335, $20/copy
Advertising: Inquire for rates. Accepts Inserts.
List Rental: Actives: 2,000, $200/M

Russian Perspective
Business, Consumer

Publishing Co: Oceana Publications, Inc., 75 Main St, Dobbs Ferry, NY 10522-1601 Tel # (914) 693-8100 Fax # (914) 693-0402
Personnel: Editor-Alexander Fishkin, Editor-Anna Reid, Editor-Emmanuel Zeltser
Editorial Description: Covers economic, legal, environmental and social issues of Russia.
General Info: Yr. Est. 1993, 8x/yr., Trim Size-8$\frac{1}{2}$ x 11, 4 pages, ISSN: 1070-6496
Subscriptions: Indv. $195, For. $250

SBANE Enterprise
See: BUSINESS & INDUSTRY

Shopping Center Ad Trends
See: DEPARTMENT STORE & RETAIL

Shrimp Notes
See: FISH & FISHERIES

Standard & Poor's CreditWeek International
See: INVESTMENT

Tax Letter Europe
See: TAXES

Tax Management International Forum
See: TAXES

Tax Management International Portfolios
See: TAXES

Tile News
Business, Association

Publishing Co: Italian Trade Commission-Tile Center, 499 Park Ave., New York, NY 10022-1240; Title Tel # (212) 980-1500 Title Fax # (212) 758-1050
Personnel: Editor-Masimo Mamberti, Adv. Dir.-Jacqaueline Greaves
Editorial Description: Published quarterly by the Italian Tile Ctr., A div. of the Italian Trade Commission, Tile News tracks trends in Italian tile design & highlights new installation applications.
General Info: Yr. Est. 1979, Quarterly, 6 pages, 4 Color, Coated
Subscriptions: Free
Circulation: Total-25,000

Trade & Development Biweekly
Business

Publishing Co: Congressional Information Bureau, Inc., 3030 Clarendon Blvd., Ste. 202, Arlington, VA 22201-2845 Tel # (703) 516-4801 Fax # (703) 516-4804
General Info: Yr. Est. 1991, Bi-weekly
Subscriptions: Indv. $160

Trade Directories of the World
Business, Consumer

Publishing Co: Croner Publications, Inc., 34 Jericho Tpke, Jericho, NY 11753-1042 Tel # (516) 333-9085; Title Tel # (516) 333-4085 Title Fax # (516) 338-4986
Personnel: Publisher-Ron Guggenheimer, Editor-Elizabeth Duffy, Circ. Mgr.-Regina Friel
Editorial Description: Data on close to four thousand trade and business directories covering U.S. and all foreign countries. Cross-indexed by subjects and countries.
General Info: Monthly, Trim Size-8½ x 5½, Offset press, 880 pages
Subscriptions: Indv. $90

Trade and Expand Internationally
Business

Publishing Co: Cricket Communications, Inc., PO Box 527, Ardmore, PA 19003-0527; Title Tel # (215) 747-6684 Title Fax # (215) 747-7082
Personnel: Publisher, Editor-Mark Battersby
Editorial Description: Provides information to large and small U.S. businesses wishing to sell products in the international market.
General Info: Yr. Est. 1993, Monthly

Trade Lines
Business, Association **CPM: $400**

Publishing Co: National Assoc. of Export Companies, PO Box 1330, Murray Hill Station, NY 10156 Parent Co.-Assist International, New York; Title Tel # (212) 725-3311 Title Fax # (212) 725-3312
Personnel: Editor-Peter Robinson, Adv. Dir.-Ted Nicholson
Editorial Description: Publication of the National Association of Export Companies.
General Info: Yr. Est. 1994, Quarterly, Trim Size-8 x 11, Desktop press, 8 pages, 20% ads, 2 Color, Matte, Other
Circulation: Total-5,000
Advertising: $2,000. Accepts Inserts.
List Rental: Rents Lists
Printing Co: Expedi Printing Co., 415 W 13th St, New York, NY 10014-1187 Tel # (212) 741-0222, Fax # (212) 924-3544

Transnational Bulletin, The
See: LAW

Transnational Contracts: Applicable Law & Settlement of Disputes
See: LAW

Transport Laws of the World
See: LAW

Ukrainian Business Digest
See: BUSINESS & INDUSTRY

U.S. Council for International Business Newsletter
See: BUSINESS & INDUSTRY

U.S. Customs and International Trade Guide
Business

Publishing Co: Matthew Bender & Co., 11 Penn Plaza, New York, NY 10001-2006 Fax # (212) 244-3188; Title Tel # (212) 967-7707
Personnel: Editor-E. Greenfield
Editorial Description: An outstanding guide covering virtually every importing and trade-related topic.
General Info: Yr. Est. 1979, Quarterly, Looseleaf
Subscriptions: $325/copy

U.S. Export & Administrative Regulations

Publishing Co: National Technical Information Service U.S., 5285 Port Royal Rd., Springfield, VA 22161-0001 Tel # (703) 487-4630 Fax # (703) 487-4630; Title Tel # (202) 482-2000
Editorial Description: Annual report. Details licensing operations and actual shipments of commodities and security export conditions.
General Info: (Formerly Export Control), Annually

U.S. International Practice & Procedure
See: TAXES

U.S. International Trade Reports
See: LAW

U.S. Taxation of Intl. Operations
See: TAXES

Vietnam Business InfoTrack
Business, Association

Publishing Co: Vietnam Access, PO Box 1210, Port Hueneme, CA 93044-1210; Title Tel # (805) 985-7126 Title Fax # (805) 985-0839
Personnel: Publisher, Editor-Kahn Le
Editorial Description: Comprehensive coverage of Vietnam market. Focuses on Trade, Investment and sector reports. Gives you an immediate advantage in evaluating the potential of doing business in Vietnam and operating in a timely and cost-effective manner.
General Info: Yr. Est. 1995, Trim Size-8½ x 11, Desktop press, 10 pages, No Color
Subscriptions: Indv. $495, Inst. $495, Can. $525, For. $525

Vietnam Market Watch
Business

Publishing Co: Vietnam Market Resources, 1616 Post Rd Ste 1106, Fairfield, CT 06430-5912 Fax # (203) 256-9790; Title Tel # (203) 256-0370
Personnel: Publisher-Khuong T. Ho
Editorial Description: For companies and professionals doing business in Vietnam.
General Info: Yr. Est. 1994, Monthly
Subscriptions: Indv. $295

View, The
See: CHAMBER OF COMMERCE

Washington Export Letter

Publishing Co: International Business Affairs Corp., c/o Richard Barovick, 4938 Hampden Lane, Bethesda, MD 20814-2914; Title Tel # (301) 907-8647
Personnel: Publisher, Editor-Richard Barovick, Circ. Mgr.-Patricia Anderson
Editorial Description: Monthly reports on govt. resources & regulations.
General Info: Yr. Est. 1988, Monthly, 12 pages, ISSN: 0890-4251
Subscriptions: Indv. $120

Washington International Business Report
Business

Publishing Co: International Business Govt. Counsellors, 818 Conn Ave. NW, 2nd Fl., Washington, DC 20006; Title Tel # (202) 872-8181 Title Fax # (202) 872-8696
Personnel: Editor-S. Spielmann
Editorial Description: Review of U.S. government international trade, tax & investment policies.
General Info: Yr. Est. 1970, Monthly, Trim Size-11 x 17, Sheetfed press, 10 pages, ISSN: 0049-691X, Color
Subscriptions: Indv. $288

Washington Report on Africa
Business

Publishing Co: Welt Publishing Co., 1413 K St. NW, Ste. 800, Washington, DC 20005-3405; Title Tel # (202) 371-0555 Title Fax # (202) 408-9369
Personnel: Publisher-Leo G.B. Welt
Editorial Description: Political and economic risk analysis of the major sub-Saharan African economies.
General Info: (Formerly African Index, African Business), Yr. Est. 1982, Semi-monthly, Trim Size-8½ x 11, Offset press, 4 pages
Subscriptions: Indv. $249, Inst. $237, Can. $259, For. $279, $10/copy
Acquistions: Publication Bought
Circulation: (34% controlled), Total-1,075, Subscriptions-700
Advertising: Accepts Inserts.

Washington Report on Latin America & the Caribbean
Business, Consumer

Publishing Co: Gilston Communications Group, PO Box 467, Washington, DC 20044-0467; Title Tel # (301) 570-4544 Title Fax # (301) 570-4545
Personnel: Publisher, Editor-Sam Gilston, Circ. Dir.-Elayne Gilston
General Info: Yr. Est. 1986, Bi-weekly
Subscriptions: Indv. $365, For. $395
List Rental: Rents Lists

Washington Tariff and Trade Letter
Business

Publishing Co: Gilston Communications Group, PO Box 467, Washington, DC 20044-0467; Title Tel # (301) 570-4544 Title Fax # (301) 570-4545
Personnel: Publisher, Editor-Sam Gilston, Circ. Mgr.-Elayne Gilston
Editorial Description: Government & congressional actions affecting exporting, importing, & int'l. investment merged with export advisor.
General Info: Yr. Est. 1981, Weekly, Offset press, 4 pages, ISSN: 0276-8275
Subscriptions: Indv. $487, For. $517
Acquistions: Publication Bought
List Rental: Actives: $75/M

Washington Trade Daily
Business, Association

Publishing Co: Trade Reports International Group, 2104 National Press Bldg., Washington, DC 20045; Title Tel # (301) 946-0817 Title Fax # (301) 946-2631
Personnel: Publisher, Editor-Jim Berger
General Info: (Formerly Washington Trade Week), Yr. Est. 1988, Daily, Trim Size-8½ x 11, 8 pages
Subscriptions: Indv. $550

Weekly International Market Alert
Business

Publishing Co: United Communications Group, 11300 Rockville Pike, Ste. 1100, Rockville, MD 20852-3030 Tel # (301) 816-8950 Fax # (301) 816-8945
Personnel: Publisher-Susan R. Goldberg, Editor-Robert Taylor, Circ. Mgr.-Loretta Netzer
Editorial Description: Synthesis of past week's market developments and forecasts on all aspects of international finance and foreign exchange. Review of developments and assessment of impact on interest and exchange rates.
General Info: (Formerly Special Telex Service), Yr. Est. 1975, Weekly, ISSN: 1051-807X
Subscriptions: Indv. $1,235, Can. $1,235, For. $1,455
List Rental: Actives: $250/M, Expires: $250/M

Weekly Report of the Market

Publishing Co: Coffee, Sugar & Cocoa Exchange, Inc., Four World Trade Center, New York, NY 10048-0896; Title Tel # (212) 938-2892
General Info: (Formerly Weekly Review of the Market), Weekly, 5 pages
Subscriptions: Indv. $20

William Winter Comments

Publishing Co: William Winter, Publisher, 6025 El Escorpion Rd, Woodland Hills, CA 91367-2928; Title Fax # (818) 347-7417
Personnel: Editor-William Winter
General Info: Yr. Est. 1961, 24x/yr.

Workers' Solidarity
See: LABOR

World Accounting
Business

Publishing Co: Matthew Bender & Co., 11 Penn Plaza, New York, NY 10001-2006 Tel # (212) 967-7707 Fax # (212) 244-3188
Editorial Description: Covers international & U.S. accounting standards as well as accounting in 19 of our most important trading partners. It assists you in handling foreign business transactions & in understanding the financial results of foreign operations.
General Info: Yr. Est. 1986, Irregular, Looseleaf

World Bank Publications Update
See: INTERNATIONAL AFFAIRS

World Power Systems Intelligence
See: AERONAUTICS/ASTRONAUTICS

World Shipping Laws and Fact Finding Tools
See: LAW

World Trade Report
Business

Publishing Co: New York Chamber of Commerce & Industry, 1 Battery Park Plz, New York, NY 10004-1491 Tel # (212) 493-7559 Fax # (212) 344-3344; Title Tel # (212) 493-7400
Editorial Description: Provides trade leads, docmentation updates, import/export notes & news on intl. trade events.
General Info: (Formerly World Trade Bulletin), Yr. Est. 1944, Monthly, 8 pages, ISSN: 0884-495X, No Color
Subscriptions: Indv. $95
Circulation: Total-1,950

Worldwide Business Practices Report
Association, Business

Publishing Co: International Cultural Enterprises, Inc., 1241 Dartmouth Ln, Deerfield, IL 60015-4072
Personnel: Publisher, Editor in Chief-Yuri Kovalenko, Mng. Editor-Anne Marie Hagel, Production Mgr.-John Marcus
Editorial Description: Information for successful international business.
General Info: Yr. Est. 1993, Monthly, Trim Size-8½ x 11, 16 pages, ISSN: 1069-4447
Subscriptions: Indv. $195, For. $245

Worldwide Graphics
Business

Publishing Co: Worldwide Graphics, 3952 N. Southport, P.O. Box 143, Chicago, IL 60613 Tel # (312) 935-2135
Editorial Description: Information for printers, publishers and their suppliers, internationally.
General Info: Yr. Est. 1995
Subscriptions: Indv. $327

INVESTMENT

401(k) Dimensions
Business

Publishing Co: Hearst Business Communications, RAI Division, 645 Stewart Ave., Garden City, NY 11530-4709; Title Tel # (516) 227-1300 Title Fax # (516) 229-3636
Personnel: Publisher-W. Boyd Griffin, Assoc. Publ.-Susan Barbey, Editor-Bruce Carveth
Editorial Description: Employer sponsored newsletter to educate 401(k) participants and those eligible to participants about basic investment principles.
General Info: Yr. Est. 1993, Quarterly

401(k) Handbook
Business

Publishing Co: Thompson Publishing Group, 1725 K Street, NW, Washington, DC 20006 Tel # (202) 872-4000
Editorial Description: Contains detailed explanations of the complex 401(k) rules plus trouble-shooting strategies. Subscription includes monthly bulletin and updates.
General Info: Annually, Looseleaf
Subscriptions: Indv. $319

401(k) Reporter
Business

Publishing Co: Universal Pensions Inc., PO Box 979, Brainerd, MN 56401-0979; Title Tel # (218) 829-4781 Title Fax # (218) 829-2106
Personnel: Editor-Jennifer Norquist
Editorial Description: Information and developments relating to 401(k) plans for financial organizations.
General Info: Yr. Est. 1985, Monthly, Trim Size-8½ x 11, Sheetfed press, 8 pages, ISSN: 0884-7657, 2 Color, Matte
Subscriptions: Indv. $126, Inst. $126
Printing Co: Universal Printing of Brainerd, 213 NW 4th St, Brainerd, MN 56401-3219 Tel # (218) 829-1982

ABA Trust Letter
See: BANKING & FINANCE

AIC Investment Bulletin

Publishing Co: AIC Investment Advisors, Inc., 440 South St, Pittsfield, MA 01201-8217; Title Tel # (413) 499-1111
Personnel: Editor-Richard Maloney
General Info: Yr. Est. 1963, Semi-monthly, 4 pages
Subscriptions: Indv. $48

AIMR Newsletter
Association

Publishing Co: Association for Investment Management and Research, AIMR, Box 3668, Charlottesville, VA 22903-0668 Fax # (804) 980-9755; Title Tel # (804) 977-6600 Title Fax # (804) 980-3685
Personnel: Editor-Karen Suggs
Editorial Description: A publication for AIMR members & subscribers which covers topic of interest to investment professionals, such as regulatory actions, performance presentation standards along with ethic issues and seminar publications sponsored by AIMR
General Info: Yr. Est. 1990, Bi-monthly, Trim Size-8½ x 11, Sheetfed press, 20 pages, 2 Color, Matte, Saddle-stitched
Subscriptions: Indv. $25
Circulation: Total-28,000
List Rental: Rents Lists
Printing Co: Progress Printing, 8401 Timberlake Rd # 4575, Lynchburg, VA 24502-3112 Tel # (804) 239-9213, Fax # (804) 237-1618

APPA Digest
See: MEDICINE

A.S.I.F (Americans Seeking International Franchises)
See: INTERNATIONAL TRADE

Abstract of American Economic Trend Analysis
See: ECONOMICS

Abstract of American Industrial Trend Analysis
See: BUSINESS & INDUSTRY

Abstract of International Economic Trend Analysis
See: ECONOMICS

Action Advisory
Business

Publishing Co: Bache, 100 Gold St., New York, NY 10038-1605; Title Tel # (212) 791-1000

Acu Trend
Business

Publishing Co: Acu Trend, 1830 W Saint Germain St # 34, Saint Cloud, MN 56301-4015;
Title Tel # (612) 251-1584
Personnel: Publisher, Editor-Don Weisman
Editorial Description: Provides precise analysis of cyclical patterns in precious metals & U.S. Treasury Bond markets.
General Info: Bi-weekly, Mimeo press, 2 pages
Subscriptions: Indv. $150, $5/copy

Addison Report

Publishing Co: Addison Investment Management Co., PO Box 402, Franklin, MA 02038-0402;
Title Tel # (508) 528-8678
Personnel: Publisher, Editor-Andrew Addison, Circ. Mgr., Adv. Dir.-Deborah Racicot
Editorial Description: An advisory service utilizing bonds and commodities. Specific mutual fund switch advice for bond
General Info: Yr. Est. 1980, 17x/yr., Trim Size-8½ x 11, Web press, 6 pages, Ind/Abs/Online: gold, No Color
Subscriptions: Indv. $175, $10/copy

Aden Analysis
Business

Publishing Co: Daniel Rosenthal & Assoc., PO Box 84905, Phoenix, AZ 85071-4905;
Title Tel # (203) 798-7967
Editorial Description: Covers a broad range of investor interests.
General Info: Monthly
Subscriptions: Indv. $195
Circulation: Total-5,000
List Rental: List Management Co.: Carnegie Marketing Assocs., Koll Executive Plaza, 3878 Carson St., Suite 220, Torrance, CA 90503 Tel # (310) 540-4757, Fax # (310) 540-7407, Actives: 29,768, $145/M

Adrian Day's Investment Analyst
Consumer

Publishing Co: Agora, Inc., 105 W. Monoment St., Baltimore, MD 21202-4702 Tel # (410) 783-2647 Fax # (410) 223-2662; Title Tel # (410) 224-8885 Title Fax # (410) 224-8229
Personnel: Publisher-William Bonner, Editor-Adrian Day
Editorial Description: Economic outlook, investment advice for individuals.
General Info: Monthly, Trim Size-8½ x 11, 10 pages, 2 Color, Matte
Subscriptions: Indv. $87, $5/copy
Circulation: Total-33,000
List Rental: List Management Co.: Name Bank, 14 W. Monument St., Baltimore, MD 21201 Tel # (410) 783-8463, Fax # (410) 783-8464, Actives: 35,852, $135/M, Hotline: 5,323, $150/M, Expires: 6,080, $110/M
Printing Co: Plymouth Printing, 1200 Cushing Pl SE, Washington, DC 20003-3599 Tel # (202) 488-7777, Fax # (202) 863-1078

Advance Planning Letter
Business

Publishing Co: Advance Planning Letter, 14 Audubon Pl, New Orleans, LA 70118-5526;
Title Tel # (504) 861-7117
Editorial Description: Specific investment advice for a solid return in buying power after taxes and inflation.
General Info: (Formerly Advance Planning Consultants Investment Letter), Yr. Est. 1977, 8x/yr., 8 pages

AgBioTech Stock Letter
See: AGRICULTURE

Aid & Analysis
Business

Publishing Co: Publishers Management Co., PO Box 84900, Phoenix, AZ 85071-4900
Editorial Description: Information about silver & gold metals trading.

Al Owen's Newsletter Digest
Business

Publishing Co: Al Owen's Newsletter Digest, 2201 Big Cove Rd SE, Huntsville, AL 35801-1349
Personnel: Publisher, Editor-Al Owen
General Info: Semi-monthly, 8 pages
Subscriptions: Indv. $75, Can. $75, For. $87

Alexander Paris Report

Publishing Co: HMR Publishing Co., Box 3073, Barrington Hill, IL 60011-3073;
Title Tel # (708) 382-7857
Personnel: Editor-Alexander Paris
Editorial Description: Summaries on the economy & business cycles trends.
General Info: Monthly

American Stock Exchange Guide
See: BANKING & FINANCE

American Stock Exchange Reports
Business

Publishing Co: Standard & Poor's Corp., 25 Broadway, New York, NY 10004 Parent Co.-McGraw-Hill, New York; Title Tel # (212) 208-8000 Title Fax # (212) 208-1161
Personnel: Publisher-Ronald Oliver, Mng. Editor-Richard Albanese
Editorial Description: Details financial reports on all ASE listed cos.
General Info: Yr. Est. 1966, Weekly, Looseleaf
Subscriptions: Indv. $1,325, $14/copy

American Stock Exchange Weekly Bulletin
Business

Publishing Co: American Stock Exchange, 86 Trinity Place, New York, NY 10006-1881 Tel # (212) 306-1386; Title Tel # (212) 306-1445
Editorial Description: News of membership changes, listings, dividends, meetings, etc.
General Info: Weekly, 8 pages

Analyst
Business

Publishing Co: Garrison Publishing Co., PO Box 1378, Pleasant Valley, NY 12569-1378;
Title Tel # (914) 896-7360
Personnel: Editor-Duff Cooper Smith
Editorial Description: Tracks earnings & publicly owned cos. & institutional trading.
General Info: Bi-weekly

Armstrong Report
Business

Publishing Co: Princeton Economic Consultants, Inc., PO Box 7227, Princeton, NJ 08543-7227;
Title Tel # (609) 987-0600

Arnold Jeffcoat's Money Matters

Publishing Co: Arnold Jeffcoat, PO Box 25, Iola, WI 54945-0025; Title Tel # (715) 445-3922
Personnel: Editor-Arnold Jeffcoat
General Info: Bi-monthly
Subscriptions: Indv. $25

Art/Antiques Investment Report
See: ART & SCULPTURE

Asia Stock Sourcebook
Business

Publishing Co: Institute for International Health and Development, 1141 Custis Street, Alexandria, VA 22308; Title Tel # (703) 768-9780 Title Fax # (703) 768-9779
Personnel: Editor-Paul Dietrich
Editorial Description: Investments in (non-Japanese) Asian stocks.
General Info: (Formerly Asia Investment Survey), Yr. Est. 1994, Bi-weekly
Subscriptions: Indv. $875

Asset Sales Report
See: BANKING & FINANCE

Astro-Cycle Forecaster
Business

Publishing Co: Cycle Research Institute of Florida, Inc., PO Box 5220, Deltona, FL 32728-5220
Personnel: Editor-Jack Giller
Editorial Description: Predicts events such as stock market cycles, weather, energy shortages.
General Info: Monthly

Astro-Investor, The
Business

Publishing Co: Mull Pubs., PO Box 11133, Indianapolis, IN 46201-0133; Title Tel # (317) 357-6855 Title Fax # (317) 353-6246
Personnel: Editor-Carol Mull
Editorial Description: Stock market forecasts based on cycles & planetary configurations.
General Info: (Formerly Wall Street Astrologer; Carol Mull's Market Forecaster), Yr. Est. 1986, Monthly, Trim Size-8½ x 11, 7 pages, No Color
Subscriptions: Indv. $45, $5/copy
Circulation: Total-300

Astute Investor
Business, Consumer

Publishing Co: Astute Investor, 135 Beechwood Lane, Kingston, TN 37763-4708;
Title Tel # (423) 376-2732
Personnel: Publisher, Editor-Charles Cardwell
Editorial Description: Value-oriented stock screens, critical examinations of investment strategies & literature.
General Info: Yr. Est. 1982, Monthly, Trim Size-8½ x 11, Offset press, 6 pages, ISSN: 0736-7643, No Color
Subscriptions: Indv. $30, Can. $30, For. $38, $3/copy
Circulation: Total-1,500

Auditor-Trak
Association, Business

Publishing Co: Strafford Pubs., Inc., 590 Dutch Valley Rd., N.E., Postal Drawer 13729, Atlanta, GA 30324-0729; Title Tel # (404) 881-1141 Title Fax # (404) 881-0074
Personnel: Publisher-Richard M. Ossoff, Editor-Suzanne Verity, Production Ed.-C. Malone Tumlin, Circ. Mgr., Mktg. Mgr.-Marianne Mueller
Editorial Description: Quarterly resource for tracking SEC auditor changes. Presents data clearly in a variety of configurations. Includes comprehensive gains and losses analysic and commentary on many change, including the reason.
General Info: (Formerly Auditor Changes), Yr. Est. 1992, Quarterly, Trim Size-8½ x 11, Offset press, 60 pages, ISSN: 1063-4053, No Color, Other, Other
Subscriptions: Indv. $492, Inst. $492, Can. $517, For. $517, $137/copy

Aura Wealth Newsletter
Business, Consumer

Publishing Co: Aura Publishing Co., 441 Central Ave., Box 1367, Scarsdale, NY 10583-9367 Fax # (914) 833-0930; Title Tel # (914) 834-2322
Personnel: Publisher-Arnold Josevie, Editor-Dr. Richard Sandell, Circ. Mgr.-Norma Hillso, Production Mgr.-John Chute, Art Dir.-Laurie Sandell
Editorial Description: Wealth management in unstable economies.
General Info: (Formerly Wealth Management Newsletter), Yr. Est. 1976, Bi-weekly, Trim Size-8½ x 11, Web press, 64 pages, ISSN: 1064-3184, 2 Color
Subscriptions: Indv. $2,150, $200/copy
Circulation: (96% controlled), Total-2,500

Automotive Investor
See: AUTOMOTIVE

Ayco Investment Report   *Business, Consumer*

Publishing Co: Ayco Investment Report, PO Box 15073, Albany, NY 12212-5073
Editorial Description: Investment information for Ayco's clients.
General Info: Bi-monthly, Trim Size-8$\frac{1}{2}$ x 11, 8 pages, No Color, Matte, Saddle-stitched

BCA Interest Rate Forecast   *Business*

Publishing Co: BCA Publications Ltd., 1002 Sherbrook St. W., Montreal, PQ H3A 3L6 Canada; Title Tel # (514) 499-9550 Title Fax # (514) 874-1894
Personnel: Editor-Martin Barnes, Circ. Mgr.-H. Paulson, Production Mgr.-E. Lankinen
Editorial Description: Analysis of bond & money market trends, economic developments, currency movements, & foreign interest rate trends.
General Info: Yr. Est. 1979, Monthly, Trim Size-8$\frac{1}{2}$ x 11, 52 pages, Color-cover, Saddle-stitched
Subscriptions: Indv. $645, $50/copy

BI Research   *Business, Consumer*

Publishing Co: BI Research, PO Box 133, Redding, CT 06875-1133; Title Tel # (203) 438-9924
Personnel: Editor-Thomas Bishop
Editorial Description: Special situation stock market newsletter. Specializing in undervalued O.T.C. stocks likely to double in price over the next 2 to 3 years. Issues include thorough updates of all open recommendations until sale.
General Info: Yr. Est. 1981, 10x/yr., Trim Size-8$\frac{1}{2}$ x 11, Offset press, 8 pages, No Color, Matte
Subscriptions: Indv. $90, Inst. $90, Can. $105, For. $105
Circulation: Total-6,000
Advertising: Inquire for rates.
List Rental: List Management Co.: Name-Finders Lists, Inc., 3180 18th St Fl 2, San Francisco, CA 94110-2028 Tel # (510) 533-4177, Fax # (510) 553-8677, Actives: 6,000, $150/M, Expires: 8,000, $100/M
Printing Co: Globe Mail Agency, Inc., 541 W 25th St, New York, NY 10001-5501 Tel # (212) 675-4600

BNA's Eastern Europe Reporter
See: INTERNATIONAL TRADE

Bahamas Dateline   *Business*   **CPM: $454**

Publishing Co: Caribbean Dateline Pubs., L'Enfant Plz., Box 23276, Washington, DC 20026 Fax # (703) 404-0899; Title Tel # (703) 404-0894 Title Fax # (703) 404-0894
Personnel: Publisher, Editor-N. Poteat Day, Circ. Mgr.-Kathy Richards, Adv. Dir.-Kathy Defindi
Editorial Description: News of political and business trends in the Bahamas as they affect the foreign investor and business person. Special emphasis on tax havens, real estate investment, and tourism investment. Includes a periodic supplement that lists Bahamian properties for sale or lease.
General Info: Yr. Est. 1976, Monthly, Trim Size-8$\frac{1}{2}$ x 11, Offset press, 4 pages
Subscriptions: Indv. $46, Inst. $46, Can. $46, For. $50, $4/copy
Circulation: Total-1,100
Advertising: $500. Accepts Inserts.

Baltic Business Report
See: INTERNATIONAL TRADE

Bank Credit Analyst
See: BANKING & FINANCE

Bank Loan Report
See: BANKING & FINANCE

Bank MergerFax
See: BANKING & FINANCE

Bank Mergers & Acquisitions
See: BANKING & FINANCE

Bankruptcy Data Source
See: BANKING & FINANCE

Bartlett Letters   *Consumer*

Publishing Co: John W. Bartlett, PO Box 465, Aurora, IL 60507-0465; Title Tel # (708) 896-3143
Personnel: Editor-John Bartlett
Editorial Description: Investment advisory service, covering 2 model funds.
General Info: Yr. Est. 1953, Monthly, Trim Size-8$\frac{1}{2}$ x 11, Mimeo press, 1 pages, No Color
Subscriptions: Indv. $25, $2/copy

Baxter World Economic Service   *Business*

Publishing Co: William Baxter, 1030 E. Putnam Ave., Box 2200, Greenwich, CT 06836; Title Tel # (203) 637-4559
Personnel: Publisher, Editor-William Baxter
Editorial Description: Investment advisory newsletter with a conservative approach.
General Info: (Formerly Baxter Economic Service), Yr. Est. 1926, Bi-weekly, Trim Size-8$\frac{1}{2}$ x 12$\frac{1}{2}$, Web press, 8 pages, No Color
Subscriptions: Indv. $175

Berko's Valve Investing

Publishing Co: Madent Publishing Inc., 1280 Coast Village Cir Ste C, Santa Barbara, CA 93108-2738; Title Fax # (805) 565-3433
General Info: Yr. Est. 1988, Monthly
Subscriptions: Indv. $95

Best Investor

Publishing Co: Man Computer Systems, Inc., 8413 168th St, Jamaica, NY 11432-2027; Title Tel # (718) 739-4242
Personnel: Editor-Jerry Felsen
General Info: Yr. Est. 1978, Quarterly
Subscriptions: Indv. $100

Best U.S. Stocks for Canadian Investors   *Business, Consumer*

Publishing Co: MPL Communications, Inc., 133 Richmond St. W., Ste. 700, Toronto, ON M5H 3M8 Canada Fax # (416) 869-0456; Title Tel # (416) 869-1177 Title Fax # (416) 869-0616
Personnel: Publisher-S. Pepper, Editor-Carlyle Dunbar, Circ. Mgr.-David Berger
Editorial Description: Targeted to the investor interested in investing in the U.S. stock market.
General Info: Yr. Est. 1992, Bi-weekly, Trim Size-8$\frac{1}{2}$ x 11, Sheetfed press, 8 pages, 2 Color, Matte, Saddle-stitched
Subscriptions: Indv. $179
List Rental: Actives: $130/M

Best of Your Money Matters with Ric Edelman, The   *Consumer*

Publishing Co: Edelman Communications, Inc., 12450 Fair Lakes Circle, Ste. 200, Fairfax, VA 22033; Title Tel # (703) 818-0800 Title Fax # (703) 818-1910
Personnel: Editor-Kathy Renezetti, Art Dir.-Will Cusserly, Mktg. Dir.-Lisa Anderson
Editorial Description: Get the answers you need about savings & investments, reducing your taxes, best way to save for retirement or college, protection against the costs of long-term care, type of wills & trusts from Ric Edelman, nationally recognized money expert & host of the award-winning call-in show Your Money Matters on WMAL radio Washington DCs #1 AM station.
General Info: Yr. Est. 1995, Monthly, Trim Size-8$\frac{1}{2}$ x 11, Sheetfed press, 8 pages, 2 Color, Matte, Saddle-stitched
Subscriptions: Indv. $30, $5/copy
Circulation: Readership-1,700
Printing Co: Budget Printing, 14511-G Lee Jackson Memorial H, wy, Chantilly, VA 22021

Big Picture, The   *Business, Consumer*

Publishing Co: KCI Communications, Inc., 1101 King St., Ste. 400, Alexandria, VA 22314-2980 Tel # (703) 548-2400 Fax # (703) 683-6974 Parent Co.-National Information Corp., Alexandria; Title Tel # (201) 947-8800
Personnel: Publisher-Allie Ash, Editor-Stephen Leeb
Editorial Description: Information on growth-stock selection.
General Info: (Formerly Indicator Digest; Personal Finance), Yr. Est. 1961, Semi-monthly
Subscriptions: Indv. $127
List Rental: List Management Co.: Media Mart, 1101 King St Ste 400, Alexandria, VA 22314-2944 Tel # (703) 548-2400, Fax # (703) 683-6974, Actives: 21,262, $165/M

Billington's Stock Focus II   *Business, Consumer*

Publishing Co: Sponsor-Omni Capital Corporation, Billington Publications, inc, PO Box 184, Point Roberts, WA 98281-0184; Title Tel # (360) 945-1490 Title Fax # (360) 945-1089
Personnel: Editor-Margaret Mantyn, Feature Ed.-Dawn Jacobsen, Adv. Dir.-Dave Williams, Art Dir.-Mark Madison, Publisher, Editorial Page Ed., Circ. Mgr., Production Mgr., Mktg. Dir., Promotion Dir.-Lance Fortt
Editorial Description: Information on the Nasdaq , Vancouver & Toronto stock exchanges, plus worldwide stock exchanges covers emerging light industry & technology companies.
General Info: (Formerly Stock Focus II), Yr. Est. 1986, Quarterly, Trim Size-8 x 11, Web press, 12 pages, 100% ads, Newsprint, Saddle-stitched
Subscriptions: Can. $350, Free
Circulation: (8% controlled), Total-260,000, Single Copy/Newsstand-200,000, International-100,000
Advertising: Inquire for rates. Accepts Inserts.
List Rental: Rents Lists
Printing Co: Mitchell Press, 1706 W 1st Ave, PO BOX 6000, Vancouver, BC V6B 4B9 Canada Tel # (604) 731-5211, Fax # (604) 731-0312

BioVenture Stock Report   *Business*

Publishing Co: BioVenture Publishing, 32 W. 25th Ave., Ste. 203, San Mateo, CA 94403-2236 Tel # (415) 574-7128 Fax # (415) 574-8319
Personnel: Editor in Chief-Cynthia Robbins-Roth
Editorial Description: Lists and analyses the top 100 public biotechnology companies.
General Info: Yr. Est. 1993, Bi-monthly
Subscriptions: Indv. $149

Biomedical Market Newsletter
See: MEDICINE

Blue Book of CBS Stock Reports   *Business, Consumer*

Publishing Co: MPL Communications, Inc., 133 Richmond St. W., Ste. 700, Toronto, ON M5H 3M8 Canada; Title Tel # (416) 869-1177 Title Fax # (416) 869-0456
Personnel: Publisher-Steve Pepper, Editor-Marc. Johnson, Circ. Mgr.-David Berger
Editorial Description: Statistical financial analysis; buy, sell, hold advice on conservative stocks.
General Info: Yr. Est. 1941, Bi-weekly, Trim Size-8$\frac{1}{2}$ x 11, Sheetfed press, 38 pages, ISSN: 0384-7802, 2 Color, Newsprint, Looseleaf
Subscriptions: Indv. $279
List Rental: Actives: $100/M

Blue Book of Mutual Fund Reports

Publishing Co: Blue Book of Mutual Fund Reports, 1023 Glenvilla Dr, Glen Burnie, MD 21061-4178
Personnel: Editor-Stephen Savage
General Info: (Formerly IRA-Keogh Retirement Fund Report), Bi-weekly, 40 pages
Subscriptions: Indv. $157

Blue Chip Stocks   *Business, Association*

Publishing Co: Elton Stephens Investments, 4016 S Michigan St, South Bend, IN 46614-2544; Title Tel # (219) 291-3823 Title Fax # (219) 291-3823
Personnel: Editor-Elton Stephens
General Info: Yr. Est. 1972, Annually, Trim Size-8½ x 11, Web press, 1 pages, ISSN: 0896-4904, No Color, Looseleaf
Subscriptions: Indv. $45, $45/copy
Acquistions: Publication Sold
Circulation: Total-2,000
Advertising: Inquire for rates. Accepts Inserts.
List Rental: Rents Lists

Blue List   *Business*

Publishing Co: Standard & Poor's Corp., 25 Broadway, New York, NY 10004 Tel # (212) 208-8000 Parent Co.-McGraw-Hill, New York; Title Tel # (212) 770-4340
Personnel: Publisher, Editor-Marjorie Rampino
Editorial Description: Records 10,000 to 12,000 municipal bond offerings each day, disseminating this information to over 5,000 subscribers.
General Info: Yr. Est. 1935, Daily, Looseleaf
Subscriptions: Indv. $935
Advertising: $525.

Blue Sky Law Reports   *Business*

Publishing Co: CCH, Inc., 2700 Lake Cook Rd., Riverwoods, IL 60015 Parent Co.-Kluwer Law & Taxation Publishers, Cambridge; Title Tel # (847) 267-7000 Title Fax # (800) 224-8299
Editorial Description: State blue sky and legal investment laws, forms securities, and personnel.
General Info: Yr. Est. 1928, Semi-monthly, Looseleaf
Subscriptions: Indv. $1,058

Blue Sky Regulation   *Business*

Publishing Co: Matthew Bender & Co., 11 Penn Plaza, New York, NY 10001-2006 Fax # (212) 244-3188; Title Tel # (212) 967-7707
Personnel: Editor-L. Rubenzahl
Editorial Description: Completely covers the 'Blue Sky' statutes, regulations, case law, and administrative opinions in every state and the District of Columbia.
General Info: (Formerly Business Organizations), Yr. Est. 1977, Irregular, Looseleaf
Subscriptions: $370/copy

Bob Brinker's Marketimer   *Business*

Publishing Co: Marketimer Investment Letter, 2023 N. Atlantic Avenue, Suite 301, Cocoa Beach, FL 32931; Title Tel # (407) 784-5003
Personnel: Publisher, Editor-Bob Brinker
Editorial Description: Market timing & no-load mutual fund selection including recommender list of funds & model investment portfolios.
General Info: Yr. Est. 1986, Monthly
Subscriptions: Indv. $185

Bob Nurock's Advisory   *Business, Consumer*

Publishing Co: Investor's Analysis, Inc., PO Box 460, Santa Fe, NM 87504-0460; Title Tel # (505) 983-9366
Personnel: Publisher, Editor-Robert Nurock, Circ. Mgr.-Sandi White
Editorial Description: Provides comprehensive stock market strategy and specific investment ideas. also covers mutual and sector funds, bonds, gold & currencies. Includes twice weekly telephone hotline and regular updates on E$P, the Elves Short term predictor and TMI, the technical market index.
General Info: (Formerly The Astute Investor), Yr. Est. 1979, 17x/yr., Sheetfed press, 8 pages, ISSN: 1050-9011, 2 Color, Newsprint
Subscriptions: Indv. $247, Can. $247, For. $267
Circulation: Total-8,000
List Rental: List Management Co.: JAMI Marketing, 2 Blue Hill Plz, Pearl River, NY 10965-3101 Tel # (914) 620-0700, Fax # (914) 620-1885, Actives: 22,000, $125/M

Bond Fund Survey   *Business*

Publishing Co: Survey Publications, Box 20429, New York, NY 10028; Title Tel # (212) 988-2498
Personnel: Publisher-Arthur Lack, Editor-Judith Lack
Editorial Description: Comprehensive reports on nation's bond funds.
General Info: Yr. Est. 1983, Monthly, Trim Size-8½ x 11, 36 pages, ISSN: 0738-5579, Looseleaf
Subscriptions: Indv. $450
Acquistions: Publication Bought

Bond Teller

Publishing Co: Savings Bonds Division, Treasury Dept, Washington, DC 20226-0001; Title Tel # (202) 634-5389
Personnel: Editor-Sheila Nelson
Editorial Description: Issuing agents of U. S. Savings Bonds informed about Bond program developments.
General Info: Yr. Est. 1971, Quarterly, Offset press, 4 pages, No Color
Circulation: Total-225,000

Bondweek   *Business*

Publishing Co: Capital Cities/ABC, 488 Madison Ave., 16th Floor, New York, NY 10022-5751 Parent Co.-Capital Cities/ABC, Inc., New York; Title Tel # (212) 224-3233 Title Fax # (212) 224-3353
Personnel: Publisher-Linda Litner, Editor-Tom Lamont, Mng. Editor-Patricia Ruggerio Muller, Circ. Mgr.-Gladys Delgado, Production Dir.-Susan Drobney, Adv. Dir.-Pat Bertucci, Mktg. Dir.-Dahlia Weinman
Editorial Description: Focuses its editorial coverage exclusively on the taxable fixed-income markets, is designed for an audience of senior investment and finance professionals, as well as investment bankers & traders. Each weekly issue covers investment strategies, emerging trends, interest rate analysis & forecasts, economic regulatory developments & new technology.
General Info: Yr. Est. 1981, Weekly, Trim Size-8½ x 11, Sheetfed press, 10 pages, Ind/Abs/Online: Lexis/Nexis news service, 2 Color, Newsprint
Subscriptions: Indv. $1,195, For. $1,241, $30/copy
Advertising: Inquire for rates.

Boston Stock Exchange Guide   *Business*

Publishing Co: CCH, Inc., 2700 Lake Cook Rd., Riverwoods, IL 60015 Parent Co.-Kluwer Law & Taxation Publishers, Cambridge; Title Tel # (847) 267-7000 Title Fax # (800) 224-8299
Editorial Description: Covers directory, constitution and rules. Published for the Boston Stock Exchange.
General Info: Yr. Est. 1970, Bi-monthly, Trim Size-6 x 9, Web press, 50 pages, No Color, Looseleaf
Subscriptions: Indv. $378

Bottom Line/Personal
See: CONSUMER INTERESTS

Bowne Review for CFO's & Investment Bankers 00
See: BANKING & FINANCE

Bowser Report   *Business*

Publishing Co: Bowser Report, PO Box 6278, Newport News, VA 23606-0278; Title Tel # (804) 877-5979 Title Fax # (804) 595-0622
Personnel: Publisher, Editor-R. Max Bowser, Circ. Mgr., Production Mgr.-Diane Hoffman, Assoc. Publ., Adv. Dir., Promotion Dir.-Cindy Bowser
Editorial Description: Information on growth companies for the small investor.
General Info: Yr. Est. 1976, Monthly, Trim Size-8½ x 11, Web press, 10 pages, ISSN: 0738-7288, No Color
Subscriptions: Indv. $48, Can. $48, For. $57, $4/copy
Circulation: Total-10,000
List Rental: List Management Co.: JAMI Marketing, 2 Blue Hill Plz, Pearl River, NY 10965-3101 Tel # (914) 620-0700, Fax # (914) 620-1885

Broadcast Investor
See: BROADCASTING

Broadcast Investor Charts
See: BROADCASTING

Broadcast Stats
See: BROADCASTING

Browning Newsletter   *Business*

Publishing Co: Fraser Management Associates, PO Box 494, Burlington, VT 05402-0494; Title Tel # (802) 658-0322 Title Fax # (802) 658-0260
Personnel: Publisher-James Fraser, Editor-Evelyn Browning Garriss
Editorial Description: The theory that the earth's climate effects history, & business.
General Info: Yr. Est. 1977, Monthly, Trim Size-8½ x 11, Letrpr. press, 8 pages, ISSN: 0896-3045
Subscriptions: Indv. $225, For. $237
Circulation: Total-600

Bruce Gould on Commodities   *Business*

Publishing Co: Bruce Gould Pubs., PO Box 16, Seattle, WA 98111-0016
Personnel: Publisher, Editor-Bruce Gould, Circ. Mgr.-Harry Butcher, Adv. Dir.-Bob Spear, Art Dir.-Sally Cupaiuoli
Editorial Description: Current events in World of finance, stock & commodity market & makes recommendations concerning purchase & sale of commodity futures contracts.
General Info: Yr. Est. 1976, Bi-weekly, Trim Size-8½ x 11, Offset press, 16 pages, No Color
Subscriptions: Indv. $285, $10/copy
Circulation: (100% controlled), Total-3,000
Advertising: Inquire for rates.

Bullion Advisory

Publishing Co: Moneypower, PO Box 2240, Minneapolis, MN 55422; Title Tel # (612) 537-8096
Personnel: Editor-James Moore
General Info: Yr. Est. 1985, Monthly
Subscriptions: Indv. $36

Bullish Consensus   *Business*

Publishing Co: Market Vane Corporation, PO Box 90490, Pasadena, CA 91109-0490; Title Tel # (818) 441-8466 Title Fax # (818) 441-3964
Personnel: Publisher-Earl Hadady, Editor-Richard Ishida, Adv. Dir.-Susan Yonai
Editorial Description: Survey of what professional futures traders think.
General Info: Yr. Est. 1970, Weekly, 2 pages
Subscriptions: Indv. $395, $10/copy

Business News
See: INTERNATIONAL TRADE

Business Russia
See: INTERNATIONAL TRADE

Buy Low - Sell High
Publishing Co: Securities Investment Management, 1224 Vallecita Dr, Santa Fe, NM 87501-8803; Title Tel # (505) 989-9224
Editorial Description: Information on successful securities investment.
General Info: Yr. Est. 1977, 26x/yr.

Buyouts   *Business*
Publishing Co: Venture Economics, Inc./City Year Inc., 285 Columbus Ave., Boston, MA 02116-5114 Tel # (617) 345-2000; Title Tel # (617) 345-2824 Title Fax # (617) 330-1909
Personnel: Editor-Elizabeth Squeri, Circ. Mgr.-Adam Kopp, Production Mgr.-Leanne Cowley, Promotion Dir.-Jack Stone
Editorial Description: Newsletter about management buyouts, leveraged acquisitions, & special situations.
General Info: Yr. Est. 1987, 17x/yr., Trim Size-8 1/2 x 11, ISSN: 1040-0990, Ind/Abs/Online: DIALOG, Predicasts
Subscriptions: Indv. $395, Can. $395, For. $425, $35/copy

CDA Mutual Fund Report
Publishing Co: CDA Investment Technologies Inc., 1355 Piccard Dr., Ste. 220, Rockville, MD 20850-4315 Tel # (954) 384-1500 Fax # (954) 384-1540; Title Tel # (301) 975-9600 Title Fax # (301) 590-1350
Editorial Description: Tabular listing that analyzes the performance, risk posture, percentile rankings & CDA ratings of over 6,000 mutual funds.
General Info: Yr. Est. 1985, Monthly, Trim Size-8 1/2 x 11, Sheetfed press, 100 pages, No Color, Newsprint, Perfect bound
Subscriptions: Indv. $275, $75/copy
Circulation: Total-1,713
Printing Co: Kirby Lithographic Co., 2900 S. Eads St., Arlington, VA 22202-4099 Tel # (703) 684-7600, Fax # (703) 683-5918

CDA/Investnet Insiders' Chronicle   *Business, Consumer*
Publishing Co: CDA Investment Technologies Inc., 1355 Piccard Dr., Ste. 220, Rockville, MD 20850-4315; Title Tel # (954) 384-1500 Title Fax # (954) 384-1540
Personnel: Editor-Bob Gabele, Production Dir.-Sherry Ginsberg
General Info: Weekly, ISSN: 0153-5152
Subscriptions: Indv. $445

CDCU Report
Publishing Co: National Federation of Community Development Credit Unions, 120 Wall St Fl 10, New York, NY 10005-3902; Title Tel # (212) 513-7191
Personnel: Editor-Clifford Rosenthal
General Info: Yr. Est. 1977, Quarterly, 12 pages
Circulation: Total-1,000

CRB Futures Chart Service
Publishing Co: Commodity Research Bureau, 75 Wall St., New York, NY 10005 Tel # (212) 504-7754
Personnel: Editor-Stuart Shinbein
General Info: Yr. Est. 1934, Weekly
Subscriptions: Indv. $395

CRB Outlook   *Business*
Publishing Co: Commodity Research Bureau, 75 Wall St., New York, NY 10005 Tel # (212) 504-7754
Personnel: Editor-Stuart Shinbein
General Info: Monthly
Subscriptions: Indv. $175

C.S.T. Connection
See: BUSINESS & INDUSTRY

Cable TV Investor
See: TELEVISION & VIDEO

Cabot Market Letter   *Business*
Publishing Co: Cabot Heritage Corp., PO Box 3067, Cabot Farm, 176 North St., Salem, MA 01970-6344 Fax # (508) 745-1283; Title Tel # (508) 745-5532
Personnel: Publisher, Editor-Carlton Lutts, Production Mgr.-Sheila Lindeman, Art Dir.-Carol Curtin
Editorial Description: Stock marekt advisory service, recommending high relative strength stocks & using marekt timing to avoid losses & exchange profits. Recommends Heritage Stocks for investors. to buy & hold.
General Info: Yr. Est. 1970, Bi-weekly, Trim Size-8 1/2 x 11, Sheetfed press, 6 pages, No Color
Subscriptions: Indv. $215
Acquistions: Publication Bought, Publication Sold
Circulation: Total-5,000
List Rental: Rents Lists

Cabot's Mutual Fund Navigator
Publishing Co: Cabot Heritage Corp., PO Box 3067, Cabot Farm, 176 North St., Salem, MA 01970-6344 Tel # (508) 745-5532; Title Tel # (617) 745-5532 Title Fax # (508) 745-1283
Personnel: Publisher-Carlton Lutts, Editor-Timothy Lutts, Production Mgr.-Sheila Lindeman, Art Dir.-Carol Curtin
Editorial Description: Mutual fund advisory service, recommending top performing no-load mutual funds for investors desiring income &/or growth, & using market timing to avoid losses & enhance gains.
General Info: Yr. Est. 1988, Monthly, Trim Size-8 1/2 x 11, Sheetfed press
Subscriptions: Indv. $125
Acquistions: Publication Bought, Publication Sold
Circulation: Total-1,000
List Rental: Rents Lists

California Municipal Bond Advisor   *Business, Consumer*
Publishing Co: California Municipal Bond Advisor, 1037 S. Palm Canyon Dr., Palm Springs, CA 92264-8378 Tel # (619) 320-7202; Title Tel # (619) 320-7997 Title Fax # (619) 320-7202
Personnel: Publisher-Zane Mann, Editor-Gavin Murphy
Editorial Description: An investment newsletter focusing on California Municipal Bonds prepared for individual bond investors & tax free mutual fund owners.
General Info: Yr. Est. 1984, Monthly, Desktop press, 8 pages, ISSN: 0749-2375, 2 Color
Subscriptions: Indv. $125
Circulation: Total-1,000

California Technology Stock Letter   *Business*
Publishing Co: CTSL Publishing Partners, PO Box 308, Half Moon Bay, CA 94019-0308; Title Tel # (415) 726-8495
Personnel: Publisher-Michael Murphy, Editor-Lissa Morgenthaler, Circ. Mgr.-Pamela Floquet
Editorial Description: Stock recommendation and discussion of technology covering West Coast companies.
General Info: Yr. Est. 1982, Bi-weekly, 14 pages
Subscriptions: Indv. $295, For. $345
Circulation: Total-1,000

Called Bond Record   *Business*
Publishing Co: Standard & Poor's Corp., 25 Broadway, New York, NY 10004 Parent Co.-McGraw-Hill, New York; Title Tel # (212) 208-8000
Personnel: Editor-Vito Calbi
Editorial Description: Semi-weekly reports on calls, defaults and payments.
General Info: Semi-weekly, Looseleaf
Subscriptions: Indv. $880

Cambridge Financial Manager   *Business*
Publishing Co: Cambridge Commodities Corp., 55 Cambridge Parkway, Cambridge, MA 02142 Tel # (614) 621-8500; Title Tel # (617) 661-6600
Personnel: Publisher, Editor-James Kneafsey, Circ. Mgr.-P.A. Otis
Editorial Description: Fundamental & technical market comments on all commodity future markets; commentary. Includes nightly
General Info: Yr. Est. 1977, Monthly, 4 pages, 2 Color, Newsprint
Subscriptions: Indv. $349

Canadian Mutual Fund Adviser   *Consumer*
Publishing Co: MPL Communications, Inc., 133 Richmond St. W., Ste. 700, Toronto, ON M5H 3M8 Canada; Title Tel # (416) 869-1177 Title Fax # (416) 869-0456
Personnel: Publisher-Barrie Martland, Publisher-Steven Pepper, Editor-Peter Brewster, Circ. Mgr.-Mindy Tenenbaum
Editorial Description: A bi-weekly newsletter focusing on Canadian Mutual Funds. Includes index and mutual fund planning guides.
General Info: Yr. Est. 1994, Bi-weekly
Subscriptions: Indv. $127, Can. $127
List Rental: Actives: $130/M

Canadian Real Estate Income Tax Guide
See: TAXES

Canadian Securities Law Reporter   *Business*
Publishing Co: CCH Canadian Ltd., 6 Garamond Ct., North York, ON M3C 1Z5 Canada Fax # (416) 444-8011 Parent Co.-CCH, Inc., Riverwoods; Title Tel # (416) 441-2992 Title Fax # (416) 444-9011
Personnel: Editor-Ray Bryan
Editorial Description: Publishes developments affecting Canadian federal and Provincial rules governing the issuance and sales of securities, plus the rules of the Stock Exchange in Canada.
General Info: Yr. Est. 1966, Monthly, Trim Size-6 x 9, Web press, No Color, Looseleaf
Subscriptions: Can. $670

Capital Growth Letter   *Business*
Publishing Co: Capital Growth Letter, PO Box 3358, Manhattan Beach, CA 90266-1358
Personnel: Editor-John Bollinger
Editorial Description: Investment and stock market information.
General Info: Monthly
Subscriptions: Indv. $197

Capital Ideas
Consumer

Publishing Co: JJB Hilliard, W.L. Lyons, Inc., 501 S. 4th St., Louisville, KY 40202-2503; Title Tel # (502) 588-8400 Title Fax # (502) 588-8487
Personnel: Editor-J. Stephen Brown, Production Mgr.-Melinda Branstetter
Editorial Description: Timely investment ideas for investors.
General Info: Yr. Est. 1981, Bi-monthly, Trim Size-8½ x 11, Sheetfed press, 4 pages, 2 Color
Subscriptions: Free To Qualified Recipient
Circulation: Total-110,000

Cappiello's Fund Digest

Publishing Co: Madent Publishing Inc., 1280 Coast Village Cir Ste C, Santa Barbara, CA 93108-2738; Title Fax # (805) 565-3433
General Info: Yr. Est. 1987, Monthly
Subscriptions: Indv. $200

Caribbean Dateline
Business   **CPM: $454**

Publishing Co: Caribbean Dateline Pubs., L'Enfant Plz., Box 23276, Washington, DC 20026 Tel # (703) 404-0894 Fax # (703) 404-0899
Personnel: Publisher, Editor-N. Poteat-Day, Circ. Mgr.-Kathy Richards, Adv. Dir.-Kathy DeFendi
Editorial Description: News of political and business trend in the Caribbean and central America from the perspective of the foreign investor and business person in these areas. Includes information on tax havens, real estate, national investment codes, currencies, trade information, offshore banking, business climate for foreigners, etc.
General Info: Yr. Est. 1980, Monthly, Trim Size-8½ x 11, Web press, 8 pages, No Color
Subscriptions: Indv. $95, Inst. $95, Can. $95, For. $95, $5/copy
Acquistions: Publication Bought
Circulation: Total-1,100, Readership-1,100
Advertising: $500. Accepts Inserts.

Caribbean Dateline's Tax Haven Report

Publishing Co: Caribbean Dateline Pubs., L'Enfant Plz., Box 23276, Washington, DC 20026 Fax # (703) 404-0899; Title Tel # (703) 404-0894 Title Fax # (703) 404-0894
Personnel: Publisher, Editor-N. Poteat Day, Circ. Mgr.-Kathy Richards
Editorial Description: Tax haven news, information, and laws. Includes information on passive investment, banking, caribbean markets, financial privacy and real estate purchasing.
General Info: Yr. Est. 1994, Monthly, Trim Size-8½ x 11, 4 pages, No Color
Subscriptions: Indv. $90, Inst. $90, Can. $90, For. $90, $5/copy
Advertising: $500. Accepts Inserts.

Carolan's Spiral Calendar Research
Business, Consumer

Publishing Co: Calendar Research, Inc., PO Box 41, Gainesville, GA 30503-0041 Fax # (770) 536-2514; Title Tel # (770) 718-0032 Title Fax # (770) 536-2574
General Info: Yr. Est. 1993, Monthly, 10 pages
Subscriptions: Indv. $279, For. $299

Cash Rich Cos.
Business, Consumer

Publishing Co: Astute Investor, 135 Beechwood Lane, Kingston, TN 37763-4708 Tel # (423) 376-2732; Title Tel # (723) 376-2732
Personnel: Publisher, Editor-Charles Cardwell
Editorial Description: Searches 5000 stocks to find the top forty through comparison of net-net/quick assets to price.
General Info: Yr. Est. 1991, Monthly, Trim Size-8½ x 11, Offset press, 4 pages, ISSN: 1054-9994, No Color
Subscriptions: Indv. $24, Can. $24, For. $32, $2/copy
Circulation: Total-500

Chart Insight
Business, Consumer

Publishing Co: Oster Communications, Inc., 219 Parkade, PO Box 6, Cedar Falls, IA 50613; Title Tel # (319) 277-1278 Title Fax # (319) 277-7982
Personnel: Publisher-Michael Walsten, Editor-Ken Scehusen
Editorial Description: Provides sophisticated technical analysis of 10 key futures markets.
General Info: Yr. Est. 1993, Weekly
Subscriptions: Indv. $199

Chartcraft Futures Service
Business

Publishing Co: Chartcraft, Inc., 30 Church St # 2046, New Rochelle, NY 10801-6302; Title Tel # (914) 632-0422 Title Fax # (914) 632-0335
Personnel: Editor-Michael Burke
Editorial Description: Weekly investment report on all major commodities analyzed by point & figure charts.
General Info: Yr. Est. 1948, Weekly, Trim Size-8½ x 11, Offset press, 14 pages, No Color, Looseleaf
Subscriptions: Indv. $256
List Rental: Rents Lists

Chartcraft Monthly NYSE and ASE Chartbook
Business

Publishing Co: Chartcraft, Inc., 30 Church St # 2046, New Rochelle, NY 10801-6302; Title Tel # (914) 632-0422 Title Fax # (914) 632-0335
Personnel: Editor-Michael Burke
Editorial Description: Point & figure charts on all NYSE/ASE stocks.
General Info: Monthly, Trim Size-8½ x 11, Offset press, 330 pages, Looseleaf
Subscriptions: Indv. $402, $41/copy
List Rental: Rents Lists

Chartcraft Options

Publishing Co: Chartcraft, Inc., 30 Church St # 2046, New Rochelle, NY 10801-6302; Title Tel # (914) 632-0422 Title Fax # (914) 632-0335
Personnel: Editor-Michael Burke
General Info: Yr. Est. 1974, Weekly
Subscriptions: Indv. $168
List Rental: Rents Lists

Chartcraft Over-The-Counter Chartbook
Business

Publishing Co: Chartcraft, Inc., 30 Church St # 2046, New Rochelle, NY 10801-6302; Title Tel # (914) 632-0422 Title Fax # (914) 632-0335
Personnel: Editor-Michael Burke
Editorial Description: Point & figure charts an over 1800 OTC charts.
General Info: Yr. Est. 1974, Quarterly, Trim Size-8½ x 11, Offset press, 180 pages, No Color, Looseleaf
Subscriptions: Indv. $114, $34/copy
List Rental: Rents Lists

Chartcraft Quarterly Option Chartbook
Business

Publishing Co: Chartcraft, Inc., 30 Church St # 2046, New Rochelle, NY 10801-6302; Title Tel # (914) 632-0422 Title Fax # (914) 632-0335
Personnel: Editor-Michael Burke
Editorial Description: Used in conjunction with weekly options service to update charts.
General Info: Yr. Est. 1979, Quarterly, Trim Size-8½ x 11, Offset press, 170 pages, No Color, Looseleaf
Subscriptions: Indv. $160, $46/copy
List Rental: Rents Lists

Chartcraft Weekly NYSE
Business

Publishing Co: Chartcraft, Inc., 30 Church St # 2046, New Rochelle, NY 10801-6302; Title Tel # (914) 632-0422 Title Fax # (914) 632-0335
Personnel: Editor-Michael Burke
Editorial Description: Point & figure investment service covering all the actively traded NYSE, ASE and OTC stocks.
General Info: Yr. Est. 1948, Weekly, Trim Size-8½ x 11, Offset press, 16 pages, No Color
Subscriptions: Indv. $256
List Rental: Rents Lists

Chartcraft Weekly Options Service
Business

Publishing Co: Chartcraft, Inc., 30 Church St # 2046, New Rochelle, NY 10801-6302 Fax # (914) 632-0335; Title Tel # (914) 632-0422
Personnel: Editor-Michael Burke
Editorial Description: Point & figure data on all underlying stocks.
General Info: Weekly, Trim Size-8½ x 11, Offset press, 7 pages, No Color
Subscriptions: Indv. $168
List Rental: Rents Lists

Chartist
Business

Publishing Co: Chartist, PO Box 758, Seal Beach, CA 90740-0758; Title Tel # (310) 596-2385
Personnel: Publisher, Editor-Dan Sullivan
Editorial Description: Stock advisory for long-and short-term investments.
General Info: Semi-monthly
Subscriptions: Indv. $85

Cheap Investor, The

Publishing Co: Mathews & Associates, Inc., 2549 W Golf Rd # 350, Hoffman Estates, IL 60194-1165; Title Tel # (708) 830-5666 Title Fax # (708) 830-5797
Personnel: Editor-Bill Mathews
Editorial Description: A 12 page monthly newsletter which contains 3 or 4 buy recommendations & updates on previous recommendations.
General Info: Yr. Est. 1981, Monthly, 12 pages, ISSN: 0747-7236
Subscriptions: Indv. $98, Can. $123, For. $128
Circulation: Total-3,000

Chicago Board Options Exchange
Business

Publishing Co: CCH, Inc., 2700 Lake Cook Rd., Riverwoods, IL 60015 Parent Co.-Kluwer Law & Taxation Publishers, Cambridge; Title Tel # (847) 267-7000 Title Fax # (800) 224-8299
Editorial Description: Covers directory, constitution and rules, and listed securities. Published for the Chicago Board Options Exchange.
General Info: Yr. Est. 1973, Monthly, Trim Size-6 x 9, Web press, 80 pages, No Color, Looseleaf
Subscriptions: Indv. $497

Chicago Mercantile Exchange Newsletter
Business

Publishing Co: CME, 30 South Wacker, Chicago, IL 60606-7402; Title Tel # (312) 930-8200
General Info: Quarterly

Chile Economic Report
See: INTERNATIONAL TRADE

Chiropractor's Financial Advisor

Publishing Co: Wildwood Assocs., 66 Shelter Rock Rd, Stamford, CT 06903-3529;
Title Tel # (203) 322-1403
Personnel: Editor-M.J. Goldberg
General Info: Yr. Est. 1985, Monthly
Subscriptions: Indv. $67

Christian MoneyLetter, The   *Business, Consumer*

Publishing Co: Communications Media Group, Inc., Box 50188, Indianapolis, IN 46250;
Title Tel # (317) 576-8150 Title Fax # (317) 594-8311
Personnel: Publisher-Daniel D. Busby
Editorial Description: Covering finance and tax matters for Christians.
General Info: Monthly, Trim Size-8½ x 11, Sheetfed press, 8 pages
Subscriptions: Indv. $40
Printing Co: Wesley Press, PO Box 50434, Indianapolis, IN 46250-0434 Tel # (317) 842-4230

Clean Yield   *Business, Consumer*

Publishing Co: Clean Yield Pubs., 41 Old Pasture Rd., Greensboro Bend, UT 05842-2102;
Title Tel # (802) 533-7178 Title Fax # (802) 533-2907
Personnel: Publisher-Rian Fried, Editor-Doug Fleer, Art Dir.-J. Bodenweber
Editorial Description: A stock market newsletter that tracks socially responsible investments.
General Info: Yr. Est. 1985, Monthly, Trim Size-8½ x 11, 7 pages, ISSN: 0882-3820, Recycled
Subscriptions: Indv. $95, Inst. $125, $3/copy
Acquistions: Publication Sold
List Rental: List Management Co.: Manager: Doug Fleer; Direct Communications Corp., 24 Wales St. Box 6628, Rutland, VT 05702-6628 Tel # (802) 747-3322, Fax # (802) 747-3376, Actives: $70/M, Expires: $70/M
Printing Co: Leahy Press, Box 244, River Street, Montpelier, VT 05602 Tel # (802) 223-2100

Client Line
See: ADVERTISING & MARKETING

Coffee, Sugar & Cocoa Exchange   *Business*

Publishing Co: CCH, Inc., 2700 Lake Cook Rd., Riverwoods, IL 60015 Parent Co.-Kluwer Law & Taxation Publishers, Cambridge; Title Tel # (847) 267-7000 Title Fax # (800) 224-8299
Editorial Description: Directory, by-laws & rules of the Coffee Sugar & Cocoa Exchange. Published for the Exchange.
General Info: Monthly, Trim Size-6 x 9, 80 pages, No Color, Looseleaf
Subscriptions: Indv. $275

Coin Previewer
See: NUMISMATICS

Coined Freedom Report   *Business, Consumer*

Publishing Co: Hoisager & Laird, Inc., 101 S Jennings Ave Ste 204, Fort Worth, TX 76104-1149
Tel # (817) 335-5443 Fax # (817) 335-7909
Personnel: Editor-Gary North
Editorial Description: Special report on gold for investors and collectors.
Subscriptions: Indv. $49
List Rental: List Management Co.: Carnegie Marketing Assocs., Koll Executive Plaza, 3878 Carson St., Suite 220, Torrance, CA 90503 Tel # (310) 540-4757, Fax # (310) 540-7407, Actives: 26,096, $80/M

Comex Monthly News   *Business*

Publishing Co: Commodity Exchange, Inc., 4 World Trade Ctr Ste 7451, New York, NY 10048-0204
Tel # (212) 938-2900; Title Tel # (212) 938-2914
General Info: Annually

Comex Weekly Market Report for Copper, Silver and Gold

Publishing Co: Commodity Exchange, Inc., 4 World Trade Ctr Ste 7451, New York, NY 10048-0204
Tel # (212) 938-2900; Title Tel # (212) 938-2914
Personnel: Editor-Fabian Josephs
General Info: Yr. Est. 1976, Weekly
Subscriptions: Indv. $25

Commercial Mortgage Alert
See: BANKING & FINANCE

Commercial Paper Ratings Guide   *Business*

Publishing Co: Standard & Poor's Corp., 25 Broadway, New York, NY 10004 Parent Co.-McGraw-Hill, New York; Title Tel # (212) 208-8000
Personnel: Publisher-Byron Klapper, Editor-Kathleen Fallon
Editorial Description: Pocket-sized guide to credit-worthiness of over 600 commercial paper issuers.
General Info: Monthly, Looseleaf
Subscriptions: Indv. $875, $81/copy

Commodex (R) System, The   *Consumer*

Publishing Co: Commodex (R) System, 7000 Blvd E., Guttenberg, NJ 07093-4814;
Title Tel # (201) 868-2600
Personnel: Circ. Mgr.-Paula Goodis, Publisher, Editor, Adv. Dir.-Philip Gotthelf
Editorial Description: Oldest daily futures trading system in the world. Follows 45 commodity and financial futures- up to 100 contract months. Available by mail, telephone, Fax, computer, DTN, and Knight-Ridder Money Center or Futures Center.
General Info: Yr. Est. 1959, Daily, 1 pages, 4 Color, Matte
Subscriptions: Indv. $575, For. $725
Circulation: Total-7,200
List Rental: List Management Co.: Venture Communications, 60 Madison Avenue, 3rd fl., New York, NY 10010 Tel # (212) 684-4800, Fax # (212) 545-1680, Expires: $100/M
Printing Co: Master Printing, 2400 Kennedy Blvd, Union City, NJ 07087-2215 Tel # (201) 867-8787

Commodity Futures Forecast (R) Service   *Consumer*

Publishing Co: Commodex (R) System, 7000 Blvd E., Guttenberg, NJ 07093-4814;
Title Tel # (201) 868-2600
Personnel: Circ. Mgr.-Paula Goodis, Publisher, Editor, Adv. Dir.-Philip Gotthelf
Editorial Description: Commodity futures trading services; extensive circulation. Tracks all major futures. Oldest and most consistently profitable weekly futures publication. Uses fundamental and technical analysis. Available by mail, hot-line, computer, and fax.
General Info: Yr. Est. 1956, Weekly, Trim Size-8½ x 11, Web press, 4 pages, 2 Color
Subscriptions: Indv. $350, For. $390
Circulation: Total-4,500
List Rental: List Management Co.: JAMI Marketing, 2 Blue Hill Plz, Pearl River, NY 10965-3101 Tel # (914) 620-0700, Fax # (914) 620-1885, Expires: $100/M
Printing Co: Master Printing, 2400 Kennedy Blvd, Union City, NJ 07087-2215 Tel # (201) 867-8787

Commodity Futures Law Reports   *Business*

Publishing Co: CCH, Inc., 2700 Lake Cook Rd., Riverwoods, IL 60015 Parent Co.-Kluwer Law & Taxation Publishers, Cambridge; Title Tel # (847) 267-7000 Title Fax # (800) 224-8299
Editorial Description: Publishes the rules regulating commodity options trading, contract markets, futures associations and commission merchants, floor brokers, trading advisors, etc.
General Info: Yr. Est. 1974, Semi-monthly, Trim Size-6 x 9, 100 pages, Color, Looseleaf
Subscriptions: Indv. $842

Commodity Market Exchange   *Business*

Publishing Co: Barter News Report, 511 Royal Oak Rd, Webster, FL 33597-9560;
Title Tel # (904) 793-4244
Personnel: Publisher, Editor-Trader Drew
Editorial Description: The oldest published Barter Source. Newsletter any update reports.
General Info: Yr. Est. 1986, Monthly, Trim Size-8½ x 11, Web press, 4 pages, No Color
Subscriptions: Indv. $24
Acquistions: Publication Bought
Circulation: Total-10,000
Advertising: Inquire for rates.
Printing Co: Swift Publishing, 511 Royal Oak Rd, Webster, FL 33597-9560

Commodity Price Charts   *Business, Consumer*

Publishing Co: Oster Communications, Inc., 219 Parkade, PO Box 6, Cedar Falls, IA 50613
Tel # (319) 277-1278 Fax # (319) 277-7982; Title Tel # (319) 277-6341
Personnel: Publisher-Michael Walsten, Editor-Karla Kelly
Editorial Description: Provides current charts of 47 futures markets.
General Info: Yr. Est. 1977, Weekly
Subscriptions: Indv. $425

Commodity Traders Consumer Report   *Business, Consumer*

Publishing Co: Bruce Babcock, Jr., 1731 Howe Ave # 149, Sacramento, CA 95825-2210;
Title Tel # (916) 677-7562 Title Fax # (916) 672-0425
Personnel: Editor-Bruce Babcock, Jr.
Editorial Description: Active Investors in the Commodities Market,
General Info: Yr. Est. 1983, Bi-monthly, 40 pages
Subscriptions: Indv. $198, Can. $198, For. $228
List Rental: List Management Co.: WMI/Worldata, 5200 Town Center Circle, Boca Raton, FL 33486 Tel # (407) 393-8200, Fax # (407) 368-8345, Actives: 33,000, $155/M

Common Stocks Common Sense Newsletter   *Business*

Publishing Co: Common Stocks Common Sense Newsletter, PO Box 224, Concord, MA 01742-0224
Tel # (508) 371-3023 Fax # (508) 371-1677
Editorial Description: Stock research and evaluations on sound, well managed undervalued comapnies.
General Info: Yr. Est. 1991, Monthly
Subscriptions: Indv. $99
Circulation: Total-5,000
List Rental: List Management Co.: Marketing Services Intl., 625 N Michigan Ave Ste 1920, Chicago, IL 60611-3109 Tel # (312) 642-1620, Fax # (312) 642-0679, Actives: 5,152

CommonWealth Letters *Business, Consumer*

Publishing Co: National Capital Corp., PO Box 21172, Tampa, FL 33622-1172; Title Tel # (813) 287-1075 Title Fax # (813) 286-0366
Personnel: Publisher-D.S. Miller, Editor-Jack Miller, Circ. Mgr.-G.K. Fogle, Circ. Mgr., Adv. Dir.-G. Fogle
Editorial Description: Comprehensive do-it-yourself guidance for single family house investors.
General Info: (Formerly Jack Miller's Commonwealth Letters), Yr. Est. 1978, Monthly, Trim Size-8½ x 11, Sheetfed press, 4 pages, ISSN: 0893-9136, Color, Newsprint
Subscriptions: Indv. $70, $5/copy
Circulation: Total-2,000
Printing Co: R. & L. Quick Printing, W. Hillsborough Ave, Tampa, FL 33615 Tel # (813) 884-6679

Compassion Today
See: CHILDREN

Compleat Investor *Business*

Publishing Co: Jobel Financial Co., PO Box 2560, Carson City, NV 89702-2560; Title Tel # (702) 882-7455
Personnel: Publisher, Editor-Belmont Reid
General Info: Yr. Est. 1980, Monthly, Offset press, 6 pages, No Color
Subscriptions: Indv. $95
Circulation: Total-350
Printing Co: Sierra Nevada Printing, 301 Hot Springs Road, Carson City, NV 89706 Tel # (702) 882-2230

Computer Letter
See: COMPUTERS & AUTOMATION

Computerized Investing *Business, Consumer*

Publishing Co: American Association of Individual Investors, 625 N. Michigan Ave. Ste. 1900, Chicago, IL 60611-3109; Title Tel # (312) 280-0170
Personnel: Editor-John Bajkowski
Editorial Description: Articles & reviews on investment-related software for investors wishing to use a computer to aid their investing.
General Info: Yr. Est. 1982, Bi-monthly, 24 pages, ISSN: 0734-4597, 2 Color
Subscriptions: Indv. $40, Can. $50, For. $50, $5/copy
Circulation: Total-30,617
List Rental: Actives: 38,300, $160/M, Expires: 6,100, $85/M

Concerned Investor, The *Consumer*

Publishing Co: Sacha Millstone, 1720 Eye St., N.W., Washington, DC 22006
Editorial Description: Investment strategies for those who want their investments to meet social criteria.
Subscriptions: Free

Conservative Speculator *Business, Consumer*

Publishing Co: Guidera Publishing Corp., 3 Myrtle Bank Rd, Hilton Head Island, SC 29926-1809; Title Tel # (803) 681-3399
Personnel: Editor-Lawrence Oakley, Art Dir.-R.C. Chapo, Publisher, Production Mgr., Promotion Dir.-Rosanne Oakley
Editorial Description: Specific special situation growth recommendations. Goal: to help conservative investor make more money from the 5-10 percent allocated to speculative investments than he makes from the 90-95 percent in CD's, etc. Each issue also includes Dow 30 market timing.
General Info: Yr. Est. 1988, Monthly, Trim Size-8½ x 11, Offset press, 12 pages, 2 Color, Matte
Subscriptions: Indv. $198, Inst. $198, Can. $198, For. $218, $20/copy
Acquisitions: Publication Bought
Printing Co: Guidera Fine Printing, 11 Palmetto Pky, Hilton Head Island, SC 29926-3759 Tel # (803) 681-3399

Consultant Compendium

Publishing Co: Consultant Compendium, 125 High Street, Boston, MA 02110-2704; Title Tel # (800) 446-2810 Title Fax # (804) 979-9962
Editorial Description: Information on all types of investments.
General Info: Annually, Looseleaf
Subscriptions: Indv. $695

Contrary Investor, The *Business*

Publishing Co: Fraser Management Associates, PO Box 494, Burlington, VT 05402-0494; Title Tel # (802) 658-0322 Title Fax # (802) 658-0260
Personnel: Publisher, Editor-James Fraser
Editorial Description: Concentrates on value versus fashion, discovering unusual superior profit potential.
General Info: Yr. Est. 1962, Bi-weekly, Trim Size-8½ x 11, Letrpr. press, 2 pages, ISSN: 0010-793X
Subscriptions: Indv. $125, Can. $137, For. $140
Circulation: Total-1,000

Contrary Investor Follow-Up *Business*

Publishing Co: Fraser Management Associates, PO Box 494, Burlington, VT 05402-0494; Title Tel # (802) 658-0322 Title Fax # (802) 658-0260
Personnel: Publisher, Editor-James Fraser
Editorial Description: Analyses & regular reports on all contrary investor selections.
General Info: Yr. Est. 1963, Bi-weekly, Trim Size-8½ x 11, Letrpr. press, 2 pages, ISSN: 0015-6019
Subscriptions: Indv. $75, Can. $87, For. $91
Circulation: Total-700

Cooke Stock Newsletter

Publishing Co: Cooke Stock Newsletter, 1345 Anchor Dr, Wantagh, NY 11793-2323; Title Tel # (516) 781-9326
Personnel: Editor-Robert Cooke
Editorial Description: Stock news and developments.
General Info: 10x/yr.
Subscriptions: Indv. $75

Corn/Bean Profit Alert
See: AGRICULTURE

Corporate Acquisitions, Mergers & Divestiture's *Business*

Publishing Co: Research Institute of America, 90 5th Avenue, New York, NY 10011-7629 Tel # (212) 645-4800; Title Tel # (800) 562-0245 Title Fax # (201) 816-3484
Editorial Description: A practical desk reference that guides users through all transactions, from start to finish. Combines tax strategies and business considerations in showing how to plan and execute these transactions in line with federal, state and SEC requirements.
General Info: Monthly, Looseleaf
Subscriptions: Indv. $379
List Rental: List Management Co.: WG & L List Management, 1 Penn Plz Fl 42, New York, NY 10119-0002 Tel # (212) 971-5000

Corporate Growth Weekly Report
See: BUSINESS & INDUSTRY

Corporate Registered Bond Interest Record *Business*

Publishing Co: Standard & Poor's Corp., 25 Broadway, New York, NY 10004 Parent Co.-McGraw-Hill, New York; Title Tel # (212) 208-8000
Personnel: Editor-V.L. Calbi
Editorial Description: Contains important information relating to interest payments on corporate registered bonds.
General Info: Yr. Est. 1967, Weekly, No Color, Looseleaf
Subscriptions: Indv. $2,095, $250/copy

Corporate Shareholder

Publishing Co: Market Value, Inc., 300 W 108th St Apt 5a, New York, NY 10025-2701; Title Tel # (212) 662-0877
Personnel: Publisher, Editor-Edward Kulkosky
Editorial Description: For professionals in the investor relations field.
General Info: Yr. Est. 1972, 22x/yr., Sheetfed press, 4 pages, 2 Color, Newsprint
Subscriptions: Indv. $249
Acquistions: Publication Sold
Printing Co: Globe Mail Agency, Inc., 541 W 25th St, New York, NY 10001-5501 Tel # (212) 675-4600

Corporation Records *Business*

Publishing Co: Standard & Poor's Corp., 25 Broadway, New York, NY 10004 Parent Co.-McGraw-Hill, New York; Title Tel # (212) 208-8000
Personnel: Publisher-K.W. Lutz, Editor-M. Antinoro
Editorial Description: News of corporate activity on over 10,000 companies.
General Info: Yr. Est. 1914, Bi-weekly, No Color, Looseleaf
Subscriptions: Indv. $1,865, Inst. $1,400

Corporation Records with Daily News Supplement *Business*

Publishing Co: Standard & Poor's Corp., 25 Broadway, New York, NY 10004 Parent Co.-McGraw-Hill, New York; Title Tel # (212) 208-8000
Personnel: Publisher-K.W. Lutz, Editor-M. Antinoro
Editorial Description: Seven volumes of financial data on nearly 11,000 companies.
General Info: (Formerly Corporation Records), Yr. Est. 1906, Daily, Looseleaf
Subscriptions: Indv. $3,160, Inst. $2,380

Cotton Trade Report *Business*

Publishing Co: New York Cotton Exchange, 4 World Trade Ctr., S.E. Plz., New York, NY 10048-0137; Title Tel # (212) 742-5070
Personnel: Econ. Ed.-Tim Barry
General Info: (Formerly Weekly Trade Report), Yr. Est. 1927, Weekly, 6 pages
Subscriptions: Indv. $80
Circulation: Total-200

Crawford Perspectives *Business*

Publishing Co: Crawford Perspectives, 655 N. Canyon Crest, # 19101, Tuscan, AZ 85715; Title Tel # (510) 577-1158
Personnel: Editor-Arch Crawford
Editorial Description: Astrologic cycles & technical analysis applied to general market timing.
General Info: Yr. Est. 1977, Monthly, Trim Size-8½ x 11, Mimeo press, 4 pages, No Color, Matte
Subscriptions: Indv. $250, $25/copy
Circulation: Total-1,000

Cris Commentary

Publishing Co: Frederick Research Corp., 1441 Prospect Ave, Plainfield, NJ 07060-3197; Title Tel # (908) 753-4514
Personnel: Publisher-Carl Frederick, Editor-C. Frederick
General Info: Monthly

Crisis Investing
Consumer

Publishing Co: Agora, Inc., 105 W. Monoment St., Baltimore, MD 21202-4702 Tel # (410) 783-2647 Fax # (410) 223-2662; Title Tel # (410) 234-0515
Personnel: Publisher-William Bonner
Editorial Description: Financial advisory newsletter which has a global outlook focusing on precious metals and mining commodities and technological innovative forms.
General Info: Yr. Est. 1981, Monthly
Subscriptions: Indv. $98
Circulation: Total-5,000
List Rental: List Management Co.: Name Bank, 14 W. Monument St., Baltimore, MD 21201 Tel # (410) 783-8463, Fax # (410) 783-8464, Actives: 11,661, $135/M, Expires: 20,000, $100/M

Cuba News
Business, Consumer

Publishing Co: Miami Herald Publ. Co, 1 Herald Plz, Miami, FL 33132-1609; Title Tel # (305) 376-3202 Title Fax # (305) 376-3201
Personnel: Editor-Mark Seibel
Editorial Description: Information on the economic currents of Cuba.
General Info: Yr. Est. 1993, Monthly
Subscriptions: Indv. $350
Circulation: Total-500
List Rental: Rents Lists

Cumulative Stock Profits
Business

Publishing Co: CSP Advisor, PO Box 246, Forest Hills, NY 11375-0246; Title Tel # (212) 896-8760
Personnel: Publisher, Editor, Adv. Dir.-S.J. Rifkin
Editorial Description: This service attempts to build up capital by small but quick cumulative stock profits. Charts for four stocks contain hand drawn support & resistance lines plus put & call options.
General Info: Yr. Est. 1969, Semi-monthly, Offset press, 2 pages, No Color
Subscriptions: Indv. $160, $10/copy
Circulation: Total-150
Advertising: Accepts Inserts.
List Rental: List Management Co.: JAMI Marketing, 2 Blue Hill Plz, Pearl River, NY 10965-3101 Tel # (914) 620-0700, Fax # (914) 620-1885

Currency Confidential
Business

Publishing Co: Phillips Business Information, Inc., 1201 Seven Locks Rd., Ste 300, Potomac, MD 20854-2958 Tel # (301) 340-1520 Fax # (301) 424-4297; Title Tel # (301) 340-2100 Title Fax # (301) 340-0542
Editorial Description: Weekly report on currency movements. Features forex rate forecasts, offers investment strategies.
General Info: Yr. Est. 1979, Weekly, 8 pages, ISSN: 0955-5323, Ind/Abs/Online: DIALOG
Subscriptions: Indv. $595
Advertising: Accepts Inserts.
List Rental: List Management Co.: PRS List Management, 222 Teal Ave., POB 6482, Syracuse, NY 13217-6482 Tel # (315) 472-1224, Fax # (315) 472-1235, Actives: $250/M, Expires: 7,070, $200/M

Currency Quarterly

Publishing Co: Phillips Business Information, Inc., 1201 Seven Locks Rd., Ste 300, Potomac, MD 20854-2958 Tel # (301) 340-1520 Fax # (301) 424-4297; Title Tel # (301) 340-2100 Title Fax # (301) 340-0542
Editorial Description: Covers over 80 currencies - a source of reference and aid to decision making in international business.
General Info: Quarterly, ISSN: 0959-227X
Subscriptions: Inst. $312
Acquistions: Publication Sold
Advertising: Accepts Inserts.

Czeschin Mutual Funds

Publishing Co: Agora, Inc., 105 W. Monoment St., Baltimore, MD 21202-4702 Tel # (410) 783-2647 Fax # (410) 223-2662; Title Tel # (410) 234-0515
Personnel: Publisher, Editor-Robert Czeschin
Editorial Description: Focuses on mutual funds and investment opportunities.
General Info: Yr. Est. 1981, Monthly
Subscriptions: Indv. $57
List Rental: Rents Lists

DRIP Investor
Business

Publishing Co: DRIP Investor, 7412 Calumet Ave, Hammond, IN 46324-2622; Title Tel # (219) 931-6480 Title Fax # (219) 931-6487
Editorial Description: Highlights updates on companies who offer dividend reinvestment plans for their stock.
General Info: Yr. Est. 1992, Monthly
Subscriptions: Indv. $79
Circulation: Total-7,200

Daily Graphs, American Stock Exchange

Publishing Co: Daily Graphs, Inc., 12655 Beatrice St, Los Angeles, CA 90066-7300 Tel # (310) 448-6843 Fax # (310) 577-7373
Editorial Description: Daily Graphs reports historical data and exclusive up-to-the-minute comparative details on over 2600 stocks in NASDAQ (OTC)/American and NYSE editions each week.
List Rental: List Management Co.: Name-Finders Lists, Inc., 3180 18th St Fl 2, San Francisco, CA 94110-2028 Tel # (510) 533-4177, Fax # (510) 553-8677, Actives: 174,189, $125/M

Daily Graphs-Stock Option Guide
Business

Publishing Co: Daily Graphs, Inc., 12655 Beatrice St, Los Angeles, CA 90066-7300 Tel # (310) 448-6843 Fax # (310) 577-7373; Title Tel # (213) 820-2583
Personnel: Editor-D. Hildebrandt, Adv. Dir.-Robert Drislane
Editorial Description: Computer generated graphs on all underlying option stocks, plus statistical data on all call & put options as the close of Friday's market.
General Info: Yr. Est. 1976, Weekly, Trim Size-8½ x 11, Offset press, 64 pages
Subscriptions: Indv. $110
List Rental: List Management Co.: Name-Finders Lists, Inc., 3180 18th St Fl 2, San Francisco, CA 94110-2028 Tel # (510) 533-4177, Fax # (510) 553-8677, Actives: 174,189, $125/M

Daily Graphs/New York/ OTC
Business

Publishing Co: Sponsor-William O'Neil & Co., Daily Graphs, Inc., 12655 Beatrice St, Los Angeles, CA 90066-7300 Tel # (310) 448-6843 Fax # (310) 577-7373; Title Tel # (213) 820-2583
Personnel: Editor-William O'Neil, Promotion Dir.-Robert Drislane
Editorial Description: Computer generated graphics on New York and American listed computers 200 OTC stocks covered.
General Info: Yr. Est. 1972, Weekly, Trim Size-8½ x 11, Web press, 304 pages, No Color
Subscriptions: Indv. $325, $10/copy
List Rental: List Management Co.: Name-Finders Lists, Inc., 3180 18th St Fl 2, San Francisco, CA 94110-2028 Tel # (510) 533-4177, Fax # (510) 553-8677, Actives: 174,189, $125/M

Daily Market Report
Business

Publishing Co: Coffee, Sugar & Cocoa Exchange, Inc., Four World Trade Center, New York, NY 10048-0896; Title Tel # (212) 938-2800
Personnel: Editor-Janet Troy
Editorial Description: Trading prices, open interest, volume in coffee, sugar, and cocoa.
General Info: Daily, Trim Size-8½ x 11, Mimeo press, 5 pages, 2 Color

Daily Trader
Business

Publishing Co: Investment Research Institute, Inc., 1259 Kemper Meadows Dr. #100, Cincinnati, OH 45240 Tel # (513) 589-3800 Fax # (513) 589-3810; Title Tel # (800) 922-4869 Title Fax # (513) 772-9397
Personnel: Publisher-Robert Bergen, Editor-Bernard Schaeffer, Circ. Mgr., Adv. Dir.-Robert Beigh
Editorial Description: Daily market timing advice for stock, option & mutual fund traders. Daily telephone hotline & weekly market letter provide market timing advice for stock, option & mutual fund traders.
General Info: Yr. Est. 1984, Daily, Trim Size-8½ x 11, Mimeo press, 1 pages, No Color, Newsprint
Subscriptions: Indv. $600
Acquistions: Publication Bought

David Hall's Inside View
Business, Consumer

Publishing Co: David Hall's Rare Coins & Collectibles, 1936e E Deere Ave # 102, Santa Ana, CA 92705-5723; Title Tel # (714) 261-0509 Title Fax # (714) 252-0541
General Info: Yr. Est. 1979, Monthly
Subscriptions: Indv. $97

DeWitt Letter, The
Business

Publishing Co: Dewitt Letter, 11619 Gilsan St, Silver Spring, MD 20902-3122; Title Tel # (202) 833-8160
Personnel: Editor-Harry Dewitt
General Info: 4 pages
Subscriptions: Indv. $100

Debt-Free & Prosperous Living
See: CONSUMER INTERESTS

Defined Contribution News
Business

Publishing Co: Capital Cities/ABC, 488 Madison Ave., 16th Floor, New York, NY 10022-5751 Fax # (212) 224-3353 Parent Co.-Capital Cities/ABC, Inc., New York; Title Tel # (212) 224-3233 Title Fax # (212) 224-3111
Personnel: Publisher-LInda Litner, Editor-Tom Lamont, Circ. Mgr.-Gladys Delgado, Production Mgr.-Susan Drobney, Adv. Dir.-Pat Bertucci, Mktg. Dir.-Dahlia Weinman
Editorial Description: Reports which funds are hinring DC managers, record keepers, or consultants and why. Covers new educational products, the latest alliances, and plan sponsor profiles.
General Info: Bi-weekly, Trim Size-8½ x 11, Sheetfed press, 14 pages, 2 Color, Newsprint
Subscriptions: Indv. $1,295, Can. $1,325, For. $1,370
Advertising: Inquire for rates.

Deliberations: The Ian McAvity Market Letter
Business

Publishing Co: Deliberations Research Inc., Box 182, Adelaide St. Sta., Toronto, ON M5C 2J1 Canada; Title Tel # (416) 867-1100 Title Fax # (416) 867-1109
Personnel: Publisher, Editor-Ian McAvity, Circ. Mgr., Circ. Mgr., Adv. Dir., Promotion Dir.-Lisa Gaudier
Editorial Description: Market analysis based on technical trends, covers, stock markets partial to N.Y.-gold & currency.
General Info: Semi-monthly, 12 pages
Subscriptions: Indv. $225
Advertising: Accepts Inserts.
List Rental: Rents Lists

Derivatives Tactics
Business

Publishing Co: Derivatives Strategy & Tactics, 153 Waverly Place, New York, NY 10014
Tel # (212) 366-9518 Fax # (212) 366-5051; Title Tel # (212) 439-4911 Title Fax # (212) 366-0551
Personnel: Publisher-Joe Kolman
Editorial Description: Focuses on developments in derivatives products, investment opportunities, etc.
General Info: (Formerly Derivatives Strategy & Tactics), Monthly
Subscriptions: Indv. $695

Derivatives Week
Business

Publishing Co: Capital Cities/ABC, 488 Madison Ave., 16th Floor, New York, NY 10022-5751
Fax # (212) 224-3353 Parent Co.-Capital Cities/ABC, Inc., New York; Title Tel # (212) 224-3233
Title Fax # (212) 224-3111
Personnel: Publisher-Linda Litner, Editor-Tom Lamont, Circ. Dir.-Gladys Delgado, Production Mgr.-Susan Drobney, Adv. Dir.-Pat Bertucci, Mktg. Dir.-Dahlia Weinman
Editorial Description: The only weekly comprehensive coverage of who's using derivatives and how. Covering London, Tokyo, and New York, it provides competitive intelligence and reports on the instruments linked to equities, interest rates, commodities, and currencies.
General Info: Weekly, Trim Size-8½ x 11, Sheetfed press, 10 pages, 2 Color, Newsprint
Advertising: Inquire for rates.

Dessauer's Journal of Financial Markets
Business

Publishing Co: Limmat Pubs. Inc., PO Box 1718, Orleans, MA 02653-1718;
Title Tel # (508) 255-1651 Title Fax # (508) 255-9243
Personnel: Publisher-John Dessauer, Editor-John Whitmarsh, Circ. Mgr., Adv. Dir.-Karen Wallace, Production Mgr., Promotion Dir.-Joan Dessauer
Editorial Description: Covers U.S. stock market, international markets, & the gold market.
General Info: Yr. Est. 1980, Semi-monthly, 8 pages, 2 Color
Subscriptions: Indv. $195
Circulation: Total-6,000
Advertising: Inquire for rates.
List Rental: Actives: 19,875, $75/M
Printing Co: Thompson's Printing, 51 Finlay Rd, Orleans, MA 02653-3320 Tel # (508) 255-0099

Diamond Insight
See: JEWELRY & HOROLOGY

Diamond Registry Bulletin
See: JEWELRY & HOROLOGY

Dick Davis Digest
Business, Consumer

Publishing Co: Dick Davis Publishing, 1080 SE 3rd Ave., Fort Lauderdale, FL 33316-1108;
Title Tel # (954) 467-8500 Title Fax # (954) 467-6444
Personnel: Publisher-Steve Halpern, Editor-Steven Halpern, Adv. Dir., Mktg. Dir.-Jaye Abbate
Editorial Description: The Digest researches over 400 financial services & research reports and condenses the best information to a 12-page compendium of what leading financial advisors currently recommend. Its conservative, long-term focus has made it one of the nation's largest circulation investment newsletters, and its impact on the market has made it the newsletter of choice for brokers and investment professionals.
General Info: Yr. Est. 1982, Bi-weekly, Trim Size-8¼ x 10½, Web press, 12 pages, 2 Color, Newsprint
Subscriptions: Indv. $165, $9/copy
Acquistions: Publication Bought, Publication Sold
Circulation: Total-33,000
Advertising: Accepts Inserts.
List Rental: List Management Co.: Manager: Jaye Abbate; Dick Davis Digest, PO Box 350630, Fort Lauderdale, FL 33335-0630 Tel # (305) 771-7111, Fax # (954) 467-6444, Actives: 33,474, $175/M, Expires: 38,624, $115/M
Printing Co: Direct Graphics, 829 S Vandemark Rd, Sidney, OH 45365-8984 Tel # (513) 498-2194, Fax # (513) 492-1100

Dines Letter
Business

Publishing Co: James Dines & Co., PO Box 22, Belvedere, CA 94920-0022
Personnel: Editor-James Dines
Editorial Description: Investment advisory newsletter forecasting stocks, bonds & interest rates, precious metals & commodities, plus future economic & political predictions. Specific advice on stocks given.
General Info: Yr. Est. 1960, Semi-monthly, 8 pages
Subscriptions: Indv. $195
List Rental: Rents Lists

Dividend Record-Daily
Business

Publishing Co: Standard & Poor's Corp., 25 Broadway, New York, NY 10004 Parent Co.-McGraw-Hill, New York; Title Tel # (212) 208-8000
Personnel: Publisher-Carl Ratner, Editor-Anthony Onofrio
Editorial Description: Daily dividend information on over 10,000 issues.
General Info: Yr. Est. 1931, Daily, Trim Size-8½ x 11, Offset press, 16 pages, No Color, Looseleaf
Subscriptions: Indv. $670, $14/copy

Dividend Record-Quarterly
Business

Publishing Co: Standard & Poor's Corp., 25 Broadway, New York, NY 10004 Parent Co.-McGraw-Hill, New York; Title Tel # (212) 208-8000
Personnel: Publisher-Carl Ratner, Editor-Anthony Onofrio
Editorial Description: Quarterly dividend information on over 10,000 issues.
General Info: Yr. Est. 1925, Quarterly, Trim Size-8½ x 11, Offset press, 150 pages, No Color, Looseleaf
Subscriptions: Indv. $91, $40/copy

Dow Theory Forecasts
Business

Publishing Co: Dow Theory Forecasts, Inc., 7412 Calumet Ave, Hammond, IN 46324-2622;
Title Tel # (219) 931-6480 Title Fax # (219) 931-6487
Personnel: Editor-Charles Carlson, Mng. Editor-Richard Moroney
Editorial Description: Stock market advisory service with market commentary based on company's interpretation of Dow Theory.
General Info: Yr. Est. 1946, Weekly, 8 pages, ISSN: 0300-7324
Subscriptions: Indv. $233
Circulation: Total-25,000
List Rental: List Management Co.: Kleid Company, Inc., 530 5th Ave., 17 Floor, New York, NY 10036-5101 Tel # (212) 819-3406, Fax # (212) 719-9788, Actives: $125/M, Expires: $95/M

Dow Theory Letters
Business

Publishing Co: Dow Theory Letters, Inc., PO Box 1759, La Jolla, CA 92038-1759;
Title Tel # (619) 454-0481
Personnel: Editor-Richard Russell
Editorial Description: Contains analyses of market trends under the Dow Theory, plus numerous technical studies. Studies of gold, monetary, economic, individual stocks and editorial commenta ry.
General Info: Yr. Est. 1958, Bi-weekly, Trim Size-8½ x 11, 6 pages, No Color
Subscriptions: Indv. $250, For. $248, $6/copy
Circulation: (87% controlled), Total-8,000
List Rental: Rents Lists

Dowbeaters
Business

Publishing Co: Dow Beaters, Inc., PO Box 284, Ironia, NJ 07845-0284; Title Tel # (201) 543-4860
Personnel: Editor-Peter DeAngelis, Promotion Dir.-K. Theiss
Editorial Description: Investment advisory newsletter featuring stocks selected for capital gains.
General Info: Yr. Est. 1977, Monthly, Desktop press, 4 pages, No Color, Newsprint
Subscriptions: Indv. $100

Downscaling
Business, Consumer

Publishing Co: Babbitt & Associates, PO Box 7117, Evansville, IN 47719-7117;
Title Tel # (219) 566-2488
Personnel: Publisher-David Babbitt, Editor-Kathy Babbitt
Editorial Description: General interest on saving money and building relationships.
General Info: Yr. Est. 1992, Monthly, Trim Size-8½ x 11, Sheetfed press, 8 pages, ISSN: 1063-5890
Subscriptions: Indv. $12, $3/copy
Advertising: Inquire for rates.
List Rental: Hotline: 1,000
Printing Co: Dockside Printing, 386 N 3rd St., Rogers City, WI 49779

Drip Investor
Business

Publishing Co: Dow Theory Forecasts, Inc., 7412 Calumet Ave, Hammond, IN 46324-2622;
Title Tel # (219) 931-6480 Title Fax # (219) 931-6487
Personnel: Editor-Charles Carlson
Editorial Description: Reports and updates of developments in field of dividend reinvestment of common stocks.
General Info: Yr. Est. 1992, Monthly
Subscriptions: Indv. $79
Circulation: Total-9,000

Dunn & Hargitt Commodity Service
Business

Publishing Co: Dunn & Hargitt, 22 N. 2nd St., Ste. 620, Lafayette, IN 47902-0620;
Title Tel # (317) 423-2624 Title Fax # (317) 423-4495
Personnel: Publisher, Editor-Dennis Dunn, Art Dir.-Bruce Graves, Promotion Dir.-Rosemary Allen
Editorial Description: Daily/weekly bar charts, point/figure charts, volume, open interest & comments.
General Info: Yr. Est. 1965, Weekly, Trim Size-8½ x 11, Offset press, 36 pages, 2 Color
Subscriptions: Indv. $245, $3/copy
Circulation: Total-2,000

Dynamic Investor, The
Business, Consumer

Publishing Co: Dynamic Investor, 8010 S Highway 101, Ukiah, CA 95482-9342;
Title Fax # (707) 462-2905
Personnel: Publisher-William Seay
Editorial Description: Investment tips and information.
General Info: Yr. Est. 1992, Monthly
Subscriptions: Indv. $79
List Rental: List Management Co.: InfoMat, 1815 W 213th St Ste 210, Torrance, CA 90501-2839 Tel # (310) 212-5944, Fax # (310) 212-5773, Actives: 4,800, $150/M

Eco-Profiteer, The
Business, Consumer

Publishing Co: Soundview Publications, 7100 Peachtree Dunwoody Rd., Suite #100, Atlanta, GA 30328-4134 Tel # (770) 668-0432; Title Tel # (404) 668-0432 Title Fax # (770) 668-0692
Editorial Description: Published for those who wish to profit from emerging business opportunities the environmental movement presents.
General Info: (Formerly GEO Report, The), Yr. Est. 1990, Semi-monthly
Subscriptions: Indv. $295, $8/copy
List Rental: List Management Co.: Carnegie Marketing Assocs., Koll Executive Plaza, 3878 Carson St., Suite 220, Torrance, CA 90503 Tel # (310) 540-4757, Fax # (310) 540-7407, Actives: 3,641, $195/M

Economic Logic   *Consumer*

Publishing Co: Economic Logic, 23031 Britner Ct, Bingham Farms, MI 48025-4705;
Title Tel # (313) 642-6373
Personnel: Publisher, Editor-Richard Greene
Editorial Description: Concise, logical analysis of current investment opportunities and economic issues for investors.
General Info: Yr. Est. 1981, Bi-monthly, 4 pages
Subscriptions: Indv. $6

Economic Outlook
See: ECONOMICS

Einhorn Newsletter
See: CHEMISTRY & CHEMICALS

Elliott Wave Currency & Commodity Forecast   *Business*

Publishing Co: Elliott Wave International, PO Box 1618, Gainesville, GA 30503-1618;
Title Tel # (404) 536-0309
Personnel: Publisher-Robert Prechter, Jr., Co-Editor-J.P. Chorek, Co-Editor-Peter De Sario, Co-Editor-Robert Kelley
Editorial Description: Analyzes Elliott Wave patterns & technical data on currencies & physical commodities.
General Info: (Formerly Elliott Wave Commodity Forecast), Yr. Est. 1983, Monthly, Trim Size-8$\frac{1}{2}$ x 11, Sheetfed press, 10 pages, 2 Color
Subscriptions: Indv. $249, For. $270
Printing Co: Reed Press, 206 Bradford St N, Gainesville, GA 30501-3608 Tel # (404) 534-5595

Elliott Wave Theorist   *Business*

Publishing Co: Elliott Wave International, PO Box 1618, Gainesville, GA 30503-1618;
Title Tel # (404) 536-0309
Personnel: Publisher, Editor-Robert Prechter, Jr.
Editorial Description: Analyzes Elliott Wave patterns, mathematical relationships, cycles of stocks, bonds, interest rates, & gold.
General Info: Yr. Est. 1979, Monthly, Trim Size-8$\frac{1}{2}$ x 11, Sheetfed press, 10 pages, ISSN: 0742-5252, 2 Color
Subscriptions: Indv. $233, For. $250, $20/copy
Acquistions: Publication Bought, Publication Sold
Printing Co: Georgia Printing Co., 706 Oak St, Gainesville, GA 30501-3510 Tel # (404) 536-1321

Emerging Markets Week   *Business*

Publishing Co: Capital Cities/ABC, 488 Madison Ave., 16th Floor, New York, NY 10022-5751 Fax # (212) 224-3353 Parent Co.-Capital Cities/ABC, Inc., New York; Title Tel # (212) 224-3233 Title Fax # (212) 224-3111
Personnel: Publisher-Linda Litner, Editor-Tom Lamont, Circ. Mgr.-Gladys Delgado, Production Mgr.-Susan Drobney, Adv. Dir.-Pat Bertucci, Mktg. Dir.-Dahlia Weinman
Editorial Description: Covers the financing plans of corporations and governments in Latin America, southeast Asia, and Eastern Europe. Reports on emerging market investment strategies used by savvy money managers around the globe.
General Info: Weekly, Trim Size-8$\frac{1}{2}$ x 11, Sheetfed press, 10 pages, 4 Color, Newsprint
Subscriptions: Indv. $1,395, Can. $1,425, For. $1,470
Advertising: Inquire for rates.

Employer's Guide to Fringe Benefits Rules   *Business*

Publishing Co: Thompson Publishing Group, 1725 K Street, NW, Washington, DC 20006 Tel # (202) 872-4000
Editorial Description: Compliance handbook on IRS rules regarding fringe benefits.
General Info: Monthly

Emprise Investment Newsletter   *Business, Consumer*

Publishing Co: Emprise Bank, 20 W 2nd Ave, Hutchinson, KS 67501-5246;
Title Tel # (316) 662-0561
Personnel: Editor-Dale Page
Editorial Description: Review & comments & prosections on topics of concern to investment subjects.
General Info: (Formerly Hutchinson National I Newsletter), Yr. Est. 1981, Monthly, Web press, 3 pages, 4 Color, Coated
Subscriptions: Indv. $65, Inst. $65
Acquistions: Publication Bought

Encyclopedia of Stock Market Techniques   *Business*

Publishing Co: Investors Intelligence, 30 Church St, New Rochelle, NY 10801-6302;
Title Tel # (914) 632-0422 Title Fax # (914) 632-0335
Personnel: Editor-Michael Burke
Editorial Description: 50 famous analysts' theories, methods & thoughts on investment techniques.
General Info: Yr. Est. 1963, Annually, Trim Size-8$\frac{1}{2}$ x 11, Offset press, 700 pages, Looseleaf
Subscriptions: $60/copy

Enterprises Financial Letter

Publishing Co: Enterprises Unlimited, 400 E 59th St., Apt 9F, New York, NY 10022-2344;
Title Tel # (212) 755-4363
Personnel: Editor-J. Walman, Circ. Mgr.-Mary Price, Adv. Dir.-John Edwards
Editorial Description: Reviews financial systems, other newsletters and financial advisory services.
General Info: Yr. Est. 1969, Monthly, No Color
Subscriptions: Indv. $400, $25/copy
Circulation: (67% controlled), Total-140,000, Subscriptions-45,000
List Rental: Actives: $90/M

Entrepreneurial Investments

Publishing Co: Business Communications Group, 3727 N Oak Trfy, Kansas City, MO 64116-2778;
Title Tel # (816) 931-0381
Editorial Description: Covers investment opportunities for entrepreneurs.
General Info: Yr. Est. 1983, Monthly

Environmental Invester's Green Market Report   *Business, Consumer*

Publishing Co: Chasen & Luck, 410 N Bronson Ave, Los Angeles, CA 90004-1504;
Title Tel # (213) 466-3297 Title Fax # (213) 465-9361
Editorial Description: Tracks more than 400 public companies with technologies, products or services in the pollution control, alternative energy, recycling , biotechnology or other socially responsible fields.
General Info: Yr. Est. 1995, Semi-monthly, ISSN: 1081-1869
Circulation: Total-2,156, Readership-2,156

Environmental Investor's Newsletter   *Business, Consumer*

Publishing Co: Chasen & Luck, 410 N Bronson Ave, Los Angeles, CA 90004-1504;
Title Tel # (213) 466-3297 Title Fax # (213) 465-9361
Personnel: Editor in Chief-Donna Luck, Mktg. Dir.-Craig Rhoades
Editorial Description: Profiles public and private companies with technologies, products or services in the pollution control, alternative energy, recycling, biotechnology or other socially responsible fields for individual and institutional investors.
General Info: Yr. Est. 1991, Bi-monthly, Trim Size-8$\frac{1}{2}$ x 11, 6 pages, ISSN: 1077-0860, No Color, Matte
Subscriptions: Indv. $59, Inst. $59, Can. $99, For. $120
Circulation: Total-4,298, Readership-4,298
Advertising: Inquire for rates.

Ernst & Young Financial Planning Reporter

Publishing Co: Ernst & Young, 1225 Connecticut Ave. NW, Washington, DC 20036 Tel # (202) 327-6000
General Info: Yr. Est. 1988, 24x/yr.
Subscriptions: Indv. $96

European Community
See: INTERNATIONAL TRADE

Executive Wealth Advisory   *Business, Consumer*

Publishing Co: National Institute of Business Management, 1101 King St Ste 411, Alexandria, VA 22314-2966 Parent Co.-National Information Corp., Alexandria
Personnel: Publisher-Brian Smith, Editor-Phil Springer
Editorial Description: A personal wealth building advisory for executives who want to substantially increase their net worth. Stocks, bonds, tapes, real estate, network & other investment planning devices.
General Info: Yr. Est. 1978, Monthly
Subscriptions: Indv. $100
Acquistions: Publication Bought, Publication Sold
Circulation: Total-40,000
List Rental: List Management Co.: The Lake Group, 411 Theodore Freund Ave., Rye, NY 10580-1497 Tel # (914) 925-2400, Fax # (914) 925-2499, Actives: 20,766, $95/M, Expires: 10,391, $55/M

FXC Investors Corp.   *Business*

Publishing Co: FXC Investors Corp., 6219 Cooper Ave, Glendale, NY 11385-6138;
Title Tel # (718) 417-1330 Title Fax # (718) 417-1330
Personnel: Editor-Francis Curzio
Editorial Description: Stock market advisory publication.
General Info: Yr. Est. 1972, Monthly, Letrpr. press, 8 pages, 2 Color
Subscriptions: Indv. $290, $15/copy
Circulation: (100% controlled), Total-1,600

Fabian Domestic Investment Resource   *Consumer*

Publishing Co: Fabian Investment Resources, 2100 Main Street, Ste. 300, Huntington Beach, CA 92648; Title Tel # (714) 536-1931
Personnel: Publisher-Dick Fabian, Editor-Doug Fabian
Editorial Description: Investment advice and information.
General Info: (Formerly Fabians' Telephone Switch Newsletter), Yr. Est. 1976, Quarterly, Trim Size-10 x 14$\frac{1}{2}$, Letrpr. press, 12 pages, 4 Color, Matte, Saddle-stitched
Subscriptions: Indv. $99
List Rental: Actives: 42,146, $150/M, Expires: 132,329, $75/M

Facts on the Funds   *Business*

Publishing Co: Vickers Stock Research Corp., 226 New York Ave, Huntington, NY 11743-2748
  Fax # (516) 423-7715; Title Tel # (516) 423-7710
Personnel: Editor-Jim Van Dyke
Editorial Description: List of investment cos. & assets. Portfolios of top funds.
General Info: Quarterly, Looseleaf
Subscriptions: Indv. $195
List Rental: Actives: $125/M

Faithful Steward   *Business, Association*

Publishing Co: Stewardship Publishing Co., PO Box 2628, Monroe, LA 71207-2628;
  Title Tel # (318) 388-1149
Personnel: Editor-David Rockett
Editorial Description: Conservative Christian critique of current economic issues & fundamental
  stocks for 3-5 year returns.
General Info: Yr. Est. 1987, Monthly, Trim Size-8½ x 11, Desktop press, 8 pages, No Color
Subscriptions: Free With Membership
Acquistions: Publication Bought
Circulation: Total-2,000
List Rental: Rents Lists

Family Investor   *Business, Consumer*

Publishing Co: William Spencer Educational Foundation, 6701 Blanco Rd Apt 712, San Antonio, TX
  78216-6161; Title Tel # (512) 733-0051
Personnel: Editor-Richard Robbins
Editorial Description: Local & national current investments in Mutual Trends Real Estate & Stocks.
General Info: Yr. Est. 1988, Monthly, Trim Size-8½ x 11, Desktop press, 4 pages, No Color, Perfect
  bound
Subscriptions: Indv. $20, Inst. $15, Can. $30, For. $40, $3/copy
Circulation: Total-1,000
Advertising: Accepts Inserts.

Favorably Positioned
Stocks   *Business, Consumer*

Publishing Co: Barrow Investment Management, Inc., 3800 W Bay To Bay Blvd Ste 21, Tampa, FL
  33629-6844; Title Tel # (813) 254-7779
Personnel: Publisher-Alston Barrow, Editor-Kate Villiers
Editorial Description: Twin-focus advisory investing real portfolios for aggressive growth &
  conservative subscribers. Tracks & rates top mutual funds; evaluates subscribers' stocks; teaches
  long-term investing. Market Pulse Index gauges current investment climate.
General Info: Yr. Est. 1984, 16x/yr., 8 pages, ISSN: 8756-4769, 2 Color
Subscriptions: Indv. $119, Inst. $117, $18/copy
Circulation: Total-5,000
List Rental: Actives: 15,000, $100/M, Expires: $100/M

Fed Tracker, The
See: ECONOMICS

Fidelity Insight   *Business, Consumer*

Publishing Co: Mutual Fund Investors Assn., 20 William Street, #310, Box 9135, Wellesley, MA
  02181-9135 Tel # (617) 369-2000 Fax # (617) 369-2510; Title Tel # (617) 235-4432
  Title Fax # (617) 235-5467
Personnel: Publisher, Editor-Eric Kobren, Circ. Mgr.-Teri Milton, Promotion Dir.-Richard Musto
Editorial Description: News & information on mutural fund investments.
General Info: (Formerly Insight), Yr. Est. 1985, Monthly, Trim Size-8½ x 11, Web press, 8 pages, No
  Color
Subscriptions: Indv. $177
Acquistions: Publication Bought
Circulation: Total-25,000
List Rental: Actives: $125/M
Printing Co: Nimrod Press, 170 Brookline Ave, Boston, MA 02215-3907 Tel # (617) 437-7900,
  Fax # (617) 262-5228

Final Edition Newsletter   *Business*

Publishing Co: Capital Pubs., Box 2132, Hollywood, FL 33022; Title Tel # (305) 925-2346
Personnel: Editor-Judith Bizzigotti
General Info: Monthly

Finance Over Fifty   *Business*

Publishing Co: Ron Jackson Co., 22 Yankee Hill, Oakland, CA 94618-2332;
  Title Tel # (510) 704-9490
Personnel: Publisher-Ron Jackson, Editor-Jeff Carter, Editor-Dick Warshaw
Editorial Description: Features information for retirement planning.
General Info: Yr. Est. 1985, Monthly, Trim Size-11 x 17, Sheetfed press, 8 pages, 2 Color, Coated
Subscriptions: Indv. $79
Acquistions: Publication Bought, Publication Sold
Circulation: Total-7,000
List Rental: List Management Co.: Name Bank, 14 W. Monument St., Baltimore, MD 21201
  Tel # (410) 783-8463, Fax # (410) 783-8464, Actives: 6,063, $135/M
Printing Co: Paris Printing, 25 Leveroni Ct., Novato, CA 94949

Financial & Economic
Research   *Business*

Publishing Co: Optima Investment Research, Inc., 111 W. Jackson, 15th Fl., Chicago, IL 60604;
  Title Tel # (312) 427-3616 Title Fax # (312) 427-9840
Personnel: Publisher-Richard Asplund
Editorial Description: Fundamental analysis of the news affecting the financial futures markets & a
  technical analysis of the T-Bonds, Eurodollars, T-Bills, currencies & stock indexes.
General Info: (Formerly T-Bond Futures Update), Yr. Est. 1983, Daily, Trim Size-8½ x 11, Mimeo
  press, 10 pages
Subscriptions: Inst. $3,600
Circulation: Total-250

Financial Digest
See: BANKING & FINANCE

Financial Foresight   *Business*

Publishing Co: Financial Foresight, 8020 E Tuckey Ln, Scottsdale, AZ 85250-5652
Personnel: Editor-Martha Liefer
General Info: Monthly

Financial News Online   *Business*

Publishing Co: Research Press Inc., 4500 W 72nd Ter, Prairie Village, KS 66208-2824
  Tel # (913) 362-9667 Fax # (913) 362-4922
Personnel: Publisher-Vernon Jacobs
Editorial Description: Print version of electronic newsletter covering investment, taxes, insurance,
  business, and legal information.
General Info: Monthly
Subscriptions: Indv. $96
Advertising: Inquire for rates.

Financial Observer - Canadian Financial Industry Digest, The
See: BUSINESS & INDUSTRY

Financial Planning Update
See: ECONOMICS

Financial Privacy Report   *Consumer*

Publishing Co: Financial Privacy Report, 1129 Cliff Rd E, Burnsville, MN 55337-1514;
  Title Tel # (612) 895-8757 Title Fax # (612) 895-5526
Personnel: Publisher-Daniel Rosenthal, Editor-Michael H. Ketcher, Art Dir.-Diane Washburn
Editorial Description: Ways to protect investments from govt. and IRS.
General Info: Yr. Est. 1991, Monthly, Trim Size-5½ x 8, 8 pages, No Color
Subscriptions: Indv. $96, Inst. $156, $15/copy
Circulation: Readership-3,500
Advertising: Inquire for rates.
List Rental: List Management Co.: Carnegie Marketing Assocs., Koll Executive Plaza, 3878 Carson
  St., Suite 220, Torrance, CA 90503 Tel # (310) 540-4757, Fax # (310) 540-7407, Actives: 3,500,
  $8/M

Financial Services Daily Fax
See: BANKING & FINANCE

Finvestor Report: Stocks
Around Five Dollars

Publishing Co: Finvestor Report, 7322 Pinewood St, Falls Church, VA 22046-2726
Personnel: Publisher, Editor-Nlls Peterson
Editorial Description: Examines inexpensive stocks often overlooked by Wall Street brokerage
  houses.
General Info: Yr. Est. 1985, Monthly

Food Investment Report   *Business*

Publishing Co: Food & Nutrition Press Inc., 2 Corporate Drive, Box 374, Trumbull, CT 06611-1338
  Tel # (203) 261-8587 Fax # (203) 261-9724
Personnel: Editor-Gerald C. Melson
Editorial Description: In-depth market analysis, as well as the fundamentals and technical approach
  in investing in food and related industries.
General Info: 15x/yr.
Subscriptions: Indv. $79

Forbes Special Situation
Survey   *Business*

Publishing Co: Forbes Publishing, 60 5th Ave, New York, NY 10011-8882 Tel # (212) 620-2200;
  Title Tel # (212) 620-2210
Personnel: Editor-Lawrence DeMaria
Editorial Description: One special situation (usually high risk stock, with large potential gain)
  reported in-depth.
General Info: Yr. Est. 1954, Monthly
Subscriptions: Indv. $495

Ford Investment Management Report   *Business*

Publishing Co: Ford Investor Services, 11722 Sorrento Valley Rd., Suite 1, San Diego, CA 92121-1099; Title Tel # (619) 755-1327 Title Fax # (619) 455-6316
Personnel: Publisher-Frances Morse, Editor-David Morse
Editorial Description: Fundamental data on 2,680 common stocks plus commentary & selections.
General Info: Yr. Est. 1970, Monthly, Trim Size-8½ x 11, Offset press, 20 pages, No Color, Newsprint, Saddle-stitched
Subscriptions: Indv. $240, $20/copy
Circulation: Total-200

Ford Investment Review   *Business*

Publishing Co: Ford Investor Services, 11722 Sorrento Valley Rd., Suite 1, San Diego, CA 92121-1099; Title Tel # (619) 755-1327 Title Fax # (619) 455-6316
Personnel: Editor-David Morse
General Info: Yr. Est. 1970, Monthly, 2 pages
Circulation: Total-1,000

Ford Value Report   *Business*

Publishing Co: Ford Investor Services, 11722 Sorrento Valley Rd., Suite 1, San Diego, CA 92121-1099; Title Tel # (619) 755-1327 Title Fax # (619) 455-6316
Personnel: Publisher-Frances Morse, Editor-David Morse
Editorial Description: Fundamental data & analysis results (intrinsic value, earnings trend) for 2,680 common stocks.
General Info: Yr. Est. 1970, Monthly, Trim Size-8½ x 11, Offset press, 10 pages, No Color, Newsprint
Subscriptions: Indv. $120, $10/copy
List Rental: Expires: 7,000, $125/M

Forecaster Moneyletter, The
See: ECONOMICS

Forecasts & Strategies   *Consumer*

Publishing Co: Phillips Publishing, Inc., 7811 Montrose Rd., Potomac, MD 20854-3394 Parent Co.-Phillips Business Information, Inc., Potomac; Title Tel # (301) 340-2100 Title Fax # (301) 294-1307
Personnel: Publisher-Thomas Phillips, Editor-Mark Skousen, Mktg. Dir.-Any Conlan
Editorial Description: Covers investments, taxes, and financial privacy. Since its inception, editor Mark Skousen has put subscribers on the winning side of investment trends.
General Info: (Formerly Mark Skousen's Forecasts & Strategies), Yr. Est. 1979, Monthly, 8 pages, ISSN: 0272-0868, Newsprint
Subscriptions: Indv. $99
Acquistions: Publication Bought, Publication Sold
List Rental: List Management Co.: Manager: John Baldwin; Phillips Publishing List Marketing, 7811 Montrose Rd., Potomac, MD 20854-3394 Tel # (301) 340-2100, Fax # (301) 294-1307, Actives: 37,893, $195/M, Expires: 33,019, $95/M

Foreign Activity Report   *Business, Association*

Publishing Co: Securities Industry Assn., 120 Broadway, New York, NY 10271-0080 Fax # (212) 608-1604; Title Tel # (212) 608-1500
Editorial Description: Analyzes the purchases and sales of U.S. securities by foreign investors and U.S. purchases and sales of foreign securities.
General Info: Yr. Est. 1978, Quarterly
Subscriptions: Indv. $40

Foreign Markets Advisory   *Business, Consumer*

Publishing Co: Muller Associates, Inc., PO Box 75, Fairfax Station, VA 22039-0075; Title Tel # (703) 425-5961 Title Fax # (703) 425-6263
Personnel: Publisher, Editor-David G. Muller, Jr.
Editorial Description: Concise outlooks on 40 foreign stock markets. Contains nearly 50 tables and charts which present concrete, comparable data; directory of foreign stocks traded in the U.S
General Info: Yr. Est. 1992, Monthly, Trim Size-8½ x 11, 16 pages, ISSN: 1067-5981, No Color, Saddle-stitched
Subscriptions: Indv. $225, Inst. $225, Can. $250, For. $250
List Rental: Rents Lists

Fortune-Teller

Publishing Co: Carson City Publications, PO Box 36, Midland Park, NJ 07432-0036
General Info: Yr. Est. 1979, Monthly
Subscriptions: Indv. $34

Forum, The   *Business, Association*

Publishing Co: Social Investment Forum, PO Box 2234, Boston, MA 02107 Tel # (617) 451-3369; Title Tel # (612) 333-8338
General Info: (Formerly Social Investment Forum), Quarterly
Subscriptions: Free With Membership
List Rental: Rents Lists

Franklin's Insight   *Business*

Publishing Co: Franklin's Insight, 711 Atlantic Ave., 5th Fl., Boston, MA 02111-2809; Title Tel # (617) 423-6655 Title Fax # (617) 482-6179
Personnel: Publisher-Elliott Sclar, Editor-Patrick McVeigh
Editorial Description: Stock advice and recommendations.
General Info: (Formerly Advisory Letter for Concerned Investors), Yr. Est. 1983, Monthly, 16 pages, Matte
Subscriptions: Indv. $19, Inst. $195, For. $220
Circulation: Total-750

Fraser Opinion Letter
See: ECONOMICS

Freidberg's Commodity & Currency Comments

Publishing Co: Friedberg Commodity Management Inc., BCE Place, 181 Bay Street, Suite 250, P.O. Box 866, Toronto, ON M5J 2T3 Canada; Title Tel # (416) 364-1171
General Info: Yr. Est. 1979, 11x/yr.
Subscriptions: Indv. $295

Friedberg's Commodity & Currency Comments

Publishing Co: Friedberg Commodity Management Inc., BCE Place, 181 Bay Street, Suite 250, P.O. Box 866, Toronto, ON M5J 2T3 Canada; Title Tel # (416) 364-1171 Title Fax # (416) 364-5385
Personnel: Publisher, Editor-Albert Friedberg, Circ. Mgr.-I. Kuschnerait, Art Dir.-Henry Fenig
Editorial Description: Analysis of current commodity & currency futures markets with buy/sell strategies/recommendations.
General Info: Yr. Est. 1980, Monthly, Trim Size-8½ x 11, Sheetfed press, 12 pages, ISSN: 0229-4559, 2 Color
Subscriptions: Indv. $295, $25/copy

Fund Exchange

Publishing Co: Paul A. Merriman & Assocs., 1200 Westlake Ave N, Seattle, WA 98109-3500; Title Tel # (206) 285-8877 Title Fax # (206) 286-2079
Personnel: Publisher, Editor-Paul Merriman
Editorial Description: Monthly newsletter & daily telephone hotline devoted to mutual fund switching of stock, bond, gold & intl. funds.
General Info: Yr. Est. 1983, Monthly, Trim Size-8½ x 11, 8 pages, No Color
Subscriptions: Indv. $125

Fund Profit Alert   *Business, Consumer*

Publishing Co: Investment Research Institute, Inc., 1259 Kemper Meadows Dr. #100, Cincinnati, OH 45240 Tel # (513) 589-3800; Title Tel # (613) 584-3800 Title Fax # (513) 589-3810
Personnel: Publisher-Robert Bergan, Editor-Bernard Schaeffer, Circ. Dir.-Kevin Addington, Mktg. Dir.-Randi Rosenberg
Editorial Description: Mutual fund investment tips and information.
General Info: Monthly
Subscriptions: Indv. $200
List Rental: Actives: $175/M

Fund Watch

Publishing Co: Institute for Econometric Research, 3471 N. Federal Hwy., Ft. Lauderdale, FL 33306-1019; Title Tel # (305) 563-9000 Title Fax # (305) 563-9003
Editorial Description: Features high-precision charts on more than a hundred top-performing and widely-owned high-performance mutual funds, with Profit Projections and Risk Ratings.
General Info: Yr. Est. 1991, Monthly, ISSN: 1057-6703
Subscriptions: Indv. $80, Inst. $80, Can. $80, For. $110
List Rental: Rents Lists

FundLetter, The   *Consumer*

Publishing Co: Hume Publishing Company Ltd., Suite 515, 4100 Yonge St., Willowdale, ON M2P 2B9 Canada; Title Tel # (416) 221-4596 Title Fax # (416) 221-4968
Personnel: Editor-A. Michael Keerma, Circ. Mgr.-Robin Young, Mktg. Dir.-Barbara Ritchie
Editorial Description: Canada's leading investment fund advisory newsletter. Advice and recommendations on open-end and closed-end funds for every type of portfolio.
General Info: Yr. Est. 1994, Monthly, Trim Size-8½ x 11, 8 pages, 2 Color, Matte
Subscriptions: Indv. $89, $10/copy
List Rental: List Management Co.: Herbert A. Watts, 455 Horner Ave., Toronto, ON M8W 4W9 Canada Tel # (416) 252-7741

Fundline   *Business*

Publishing Co: David H. Menashe & Co., PO Box 663, Woodland Hills, CA 91365-0663; Title Tel # (818) 346-5637
Personnel: Publisher, Editor, Circ. Mgr., Adv. Dir., Art Dir.-David Menashe
Editorial Description: Charts and rankings on no-load mutual funds with recommendations as to when to buy and sell. Includes monthly update bulletin and telephone hotline.
General Info: (Formerly Menashe Timing Service, The), Yr. Est. 1968, Monthly, Trim Size-8½ x 11, Sheetfed press, 8 pages, ISSN: 1049-4332, 2 Color
Subscriptions: Indv. $127, $9/copy
Circulation: Total-2,000
List Rental: List Management Co.: Carnegie Marketing Assocs., Koll Executive Plaza, 3878 Carson St., Suite 220, Torrance, CA 90503 Tel # (310) 540-4757, Fax # (310) 540-7407, Actives: 20,528, $95/M

Future Charts

Publishing Co: Commodity Trend Service, PO Box 32309, Palm Beach Gardens, FL 33420-2309; Title Fax # (407) 622-7623
General Info: Weekly

Future Hotline   *Business*

Publishing Co: Zweig Securities Advisory Service, Inc., PO Box 2900, Wantagh, NY 11793-0926; Title Tel # (516) 785-1300
Personnel: Publisher-Martin E. Zweig, Editor-Ned Davis
Editorial Description: Short term market trading service following 65 stocks and call options-hot line message.
General Info: (Formerly Traders Hotline), Bi-weekly, 8 pages
Subscriptions: Indv. $150

Futures International Law Letter
See: LAW

Futures and Options
Factors   *Business, Consumer*

Publishing Co: Wasendorf & Son Co., 802 Main St # 849, Cedar Falls, IA 50613-2953
Tel # (319) 268-0441; Title Tel # (319) 277-5240 Title Fax # (319) 277-0880
Personnel: Circ. Mgr., Production Mgr.-Cyndi Pool, Publisher, Editor, Adv. Dir., Promotion Dir.-Russell Wasendorf, Sr.
Editorial Description: Market commentary on most futures markets. A highly rated newsletter by Commodity Traders Consumer Report. One of the oldest continuously published newsletters in the futures industry, 15 years.
General Info: (Formerly Futures Portfolio Advisor), Yr. Est. 1980, Weekly, Trim Size-17 x 11, Web press, 8 pages, ISSN: 0892-0869, 2 Color, Matte
Subscriptions: Indv. $239, $5/copy
Acqusitions: Publication Bought, Publication Sold
Circulation: Total-2,000, Readership-2,000
Advertising: Accepts Inserts.
List Rental: Actives: $75/M

Futures and Options News   *Business, Association*

Publishing Co: Montreal Exchange, 800 Victoria Sq., Stock Exchange Tower, Montreal, PQ H4Z 1A9 Canada; Title Tel # (514) 871-2424 Title Fax # (514) 871-3559
Personnel: Publisher-Jean LaFlamme, Editor, Circ. Mgr.-Patrick Gagnon, Production Mgr.-Sylvie Brousseau, Mktg. Dir.-Zita Banasinski
Editorial Description: News, information & strategies on using Montreal Exchange options on equity, bonds & gold & futures on bonds & Canadian banker's acceptances.
General Info: (Formerly Montreal Options Newsletter), Yr. Est. 1935, Quarterly, Trim Size-8½ x 11, Desktop press, 6 pages, ISSN: 1183-4242, 2 Color, Coated
Subscriptions: Free
Circulation: Total-1,100
Printing Co: Litho Presse, 1030 Cheneville, Montreal, PQ H2Z 1V8 Canada Tel # (514) 875-6327

Garside Forecast   *Business*

Publishing Co: Garside, 5200 Irvine Blvd Spc 370, Irvine, CA 92720-2060;
Title Tel # (714) 259-1670
Personnel: Publisher, Editor-Ben C. Garside
Editorial Description: Stock market forecast and advisory based on numerous proprietary indicators.
General Info: Yr. Est. 1971, Bi-weekly, 6 pages
Subscriptions: Indv. $145

Georgia Contrarian, The   *Business, Consumer*

Publishing Co: P & A Communications, Inc., PO Box 464731, Lawrenceville, GA 30246-4731;
Title Tel # (770) 995-7450
Personnel: Publisher-Patrick Carroll
Editorial Description: Attempts to identify companies which are undervalued due to market pessimism.
General Info: Yr. Est. 1993, Monthly, Trim Size-8½ x 11, 8 pages, No Color, Matte, Saddle-stitched
Subscriptions: Indv. $60

Global Investing   *Business*   CPM: $266

Publishing Co: Agorot Ltd., 1040 First Ave., Ste. 305, New York, NY 10022-2902
Fax # (212) 758-0407; Title Tel # (212) 758-9480 Title Fax # (800) 388-4237
Personnel: Publisher, Editor-Vivian Lewis, Production Mgr.-Carlos Novero, Promotion Dir.-Diane Chaykin
Editorial Description: Independent coverage of American Depository Receipt market and closed-end country funds for retail investors.
General Info: (Formerly World100Rpt; AssetIntl; Intl.FundsMonitor; EuropeanMarketRpt), Yr. Est. 1991, Monthly, Trim Size-8½ x 11, 8 pages, 6% ads
Subscriptions: Indv. $199, Inst. $237, Can. $224, For. $249
Acqusitions: Publication Bought
Circulation: Total-4,500, Readership-9,000
Advertising: $1,200.
List Rental: List Management Co.: Name Bank, 14 W. Monument St., Baltimore, MD 21201 Tel # (410) 783-8463, Fax # (410) 783-8464

Global Investment in Canada
See: INTERNATIONAL TRADE

Global Investment Technology
See: BANKING & FINANCE

Global Market Perspective   *Business, Consumer*

Publishing Co: Elliott Wave International, PO Box 1618, Gainesville, GA 30503-1618;
Title Tel # (404) 536-0309
Personnel: Publisher-Robert Prechter
General Info: Yr. Est. 1990, Monthly, Trim Size-6 x 8½, 100 pages
Subscriptions: Indv. $599, For. $645
Printing Co: Electric City, PO Box 1920, Anderson, SC 29622-1920 Tel # (803) 224-3339

Global Money
Management   *Business*

Publishing Co: Capital Cities/ABC, 488 Madison Ave., 16th Floor, New York, NY 10022-5751 Parent Co.-Capital Cities/ABC, Inc., New York; Title Tel # (212) 224-3233 Title Fax # (212) 224-3353
Personnel: Publisher-Linda Litner, Editor-Tom Lamont, Circ. Dir.-Gladys DelGado, Production Dir.-Susan Drooney, Adv. Dir.-Pat Bertucci, Mktg. Dir.-Dahlia Weinman
Editorial Description: Based in London & featuring fast-breaking news affecting international fund management. A primary information resource for investment professionals. Each issue reports on investment strategies; pension fund searches; managers & custodians; performance measurement; developing markets & significant personnel changes.
General Info: Yr. Est. 1990, Bi-weekly, Trim Size-8½ x 11, 12 pages, Ind/Abs/Online: Lexis/Nexis news service, 2 Color, Newsprint
Subscriptions: Indv. $1,295, Can. $1,295, For. $1,295, $50/copy
Advertising: Inquire for rates.

Global Private Banking - International Investment Outlook
See: BANKING & FINANCE

Global Vision Investor
Newletter Monthly   *Business*

Publishing Co: Global Vision, 375 Douglas Ave., Ste. 1012, Altamonte Springs, FL 32714
Editorial Description: Covering the latest developments in wireless investments in the US and worldwide, hottest deals available, looking ahead toward new IPO's, industry developments affecting stock prices, stock recommendations, company profiles and much more.
General Info: Monthly

Globalist, The   *Business, Consumer*

Publishing Co: Island Grown Publications, 1063 Alford Place, Bainbridge Island, WA 98110;
Title Tel # (206) 343-6212
Editorial Description: Information on investment opportunities around the world.
General Info: Yr. Est. 1992, Monthly, Trim Size-8½ x 11, 6 pages, 2 Color, Coated
Subscriptions: Indv. $150, $13/copy

Going Public: The IPO
Reporter   *Business*

Publishing Co: IDD Enterprises, 2 World Trade Ctr. 18th Fl., New York, NY 10048-0203
Fax # (212) 321-2336 Parent Co.-Dow Jones & Co., Inc., New York; Title Tel # (212) 227-1200 Title Fax # (212) 321-3805
Personnel: Editor-Clint Winstead, Circ. Mgr.-Philip M. Mc.Gee, Production Mgr.-Maxine Margolese, Adv. Dir.-Mattie reyes, Mktg. Dir.-Janice Fellagera
Editorial Description: An accurate and timely information source that reports who's going public, who's recently gone public and how their deals have done, and how industry analysts and other professionals rate upcoming deals.
General Info: Yr. Est. 1977, Weekly, Desktop press, 10 pages, ISSN: 0735-9950, Ind/Abs/Online: Predicasts
Subscriptions: Indv. $1,195
Acqusitions: Publication Bought, Publication Sold
Advertising: $2,300. Accepts Inserts.
Printing Co: Dealers Digest, 2 World Trade Ctr., New York, NY 10048 Tel # (212) 227-1200

Gold Mining Stock Report   *Consumer*

Publishing Co: Gold Mining Stock Report, PO Box 1217, Lafayette, CA 94549-1217;
Title Tel # (415) 463-2200
Personnel: Publisher, Editor-Robert Bishop
Editorial Description: Penny stock analysis with specific recommendations & updates.
General Info: Yr. Est. 1984, Monthly, 8 pages, 2 Color
Subscriptions: Indv. $139, $12/copy

Gold Newsletter   *Consumer*

Publishing Co: Blanchard & Co., 110 Veterans Blve. Suite #200, P.O. Box 61740, New Orleans, LA 70161-1740; Title Tel # (504) 837-3010 Title Fax # (504) 837-9852
Personnel: Editor-James U. Blanchard
Editorial Description: Covers gold, hard assets, cash equivalents (U.S. & foreign currencies) plus geo-political economic commentary.
General Info: Yr. Est. 1971, Monthly, Trim Size-8 x 10¼, 24 pages, 2 Color, Matte, Saddle-stitched
Subscriptions: Indv. $95, For. $80, $7/copy
List Rental: List Management Co.: Names & Addresses, 160 E. Marquadt Dr., Wheeling, IL 60090-6428 Tel # (708) 465-1500, Fax # (708) 465-1521, Actives: 4,585, $100/M, Expires: 54,296

Gold and Silver Newsletter

Publishing Co: Monex International Ltd., 4910 Birch St, Newport Beach, CA 92660-2113;
Title Tel # (714) 752-1400
Personnel: Editor-Louis Carabini
General Info: (Formerly Pacific Coast Coin Exchange Gold and Silver Newsletter), Yr. Est. 1973, Monthly
Subscriptions: Indv. $36
Circulation: Total-50,000

Gold Standard Review
See: BANKING & FINANCE

Gold Stock Alert   *Business*

Publishing Co: Soundview Publications, 7100 Peachtree Dunwoody Rd., Suite #100, Atlanta, GA 30328-4134 Tel # (770) 668-0432 Fax # (770) 668-0692
Editorial Description: Fax service regarding the best gold stock buys.
General Info: Monthly
Subscriptions: Indv. $1,000

Goldstock Letter   *Consumer*

Publishing Co: Troubadour, Inc., PO Box 1490, Hanalei, HI 96714-1490; Title Tel # (808) 826-6550
Personnel: Publisher-David Marantette
Editorial Description: Covers the gold investment industry.
General Info: Monthly
Subscriptions: Indv. $325

Good Money: The Newsletter for Socially Concerned Investors *Consumer*

Publishing Co: Good Money Publications, Inc., PO Box 363, Worcester, VT 05682-0363; Title Tel # (802) 223-3911
Personnel: Publisher, Editor-Ritchie Lowry, Circ. Mgr.-Carol Major, Production Mgr.-Peter Lowry, Promotion Dir.-Larry Lewack
Editorial Description: Helps concerned investors find & profit from socially responsible corps.
General Info: Yr. Est. 1982, Bi-monthly, Trim Size-8½ x 11, Sheetfed press, 12 pages, ISSN: 0742-4515, 3% ads, 2 Color, Saddle-stitched
Subscriptions: Indv. $49, Inst. $149, $3/copy
Circulation: Total-1,700
Advertising: Inquire for rates.
Printing Co: Northlight Studio Press, Rte. 14, Box 568, Barre, VT 05641-0568 Tel # (802) 479-0565

Good News *Business*

Publishing Co: Investment & Speculation SIG, MENSA, 11160 Glade Dr, Reston, VA 22091-4709; Title Tel # (703) 620-4480
Personnel: Publisher, Editor-Ben Perchik
Editorial Description: Information on investments, mainly stocks, funds, also real estate, precious metals, collectibles. Features question and answer column plus taxes, economics, investment strategies, sample portfolios, education for new and troubled investors.
General Info: Yr. Est. 1980, Bi-monthly, Trim Size-8½ x 11, 8 pages, No Color
Subscriptions: Indv. $15, Inst. $15, $2/copy
Circulation: Total-160
Advertising: Inquire for rates. Accepts Inserts.
Printing Co: L & G Lithographics, 6558 Backlick Rd, Springfield, VA 22150-2801

Graham-Rea Investment Analysis

Publishing Co: Graham-Rea Investment Analysis, 10966 Chalon Rd, Los Angeles, CA 90077-3208; Title Tel # (213) 471-1917
General Info: Monthly
Subscriptions: Indv. $300

Grant's Interest Rate Observer *Business*

Publishing Co: Interest Rate Publishing Corporation, 30 Wall St., New York, NY 10005-2201; Title Tel # (212) 608-7994 Title Fax # (212) 608-5925
Personnel: Publisher-Jeremy Diamond, Editor-James Grant, Circ. Mgr.-Caroline McLaughlin, Circ. Mgr.-Caroline McLoughlin, Production Mgr.-Susan Egan
Editorial Description: Covers global credit markets & interest rates as they affect all investments. An early spokesman against excessive leverage in the eighties & now aimed at the emerging risks & opportunities of the Nineties.
General Info: Yr. Est. 1983, Bi-weekly, 16 pages, ISSN: 0748-8424, 3% ads, No Color, Matte, Saddle-stitched
Subscriptions: Indv. $450, Can. $450, For. $510, $20/copy
Circulation: Total-3,050
Advertising: Inquire for rates. Accepts Inserts.
Printing Co: Walden Press, 216 W 18th St, New York, NY 10011-4595 Tel # (212) 691-9220

Grant's Municipal Bond Observer *Business*

Publishing Co: Interest Rate Publishing Corporation, 30 Wall St., New York, NY 10005-2201; Title Tel # (212) 608-7994
Editorial Description: Covers the 1 Trillion dollar municipal bond market.
General Info: Yr. Est. 1994, Bi-weekly, Trim Size-8½ x 11, 16 pages
Subscriptions: Indv. $625

Granville Market Letter *Business*

Publishing Co: Granville Market Letter, PO Box 412006, Kansas City, MO 64141-2006; Title Tel # (816) 474-5353
Personnel: Publisher, Editor-Joseph Granville
Editorial Description: Stock market advisory letter. Specializes in calling the market turning points.
General Info: Yr. Est. 1963, Weekly, Trim Size-8½ x 11, 6 pages
Subscriptions: Indv. $250
Circulation: Total-13,000

Greater Kansas City Community Foundation Newsletter *Business, Association*

Publishing Co: Kansas City Community Foundation, 1055 Broadway St Ste 130, Kansas City, MO 64105-1595; Title Tel # (816) 842-0944
Personnel: Editor-Sandra Vader
General Info: Trim Size-8½ x 11, Offset press, 6 pages, No Color
Circulation: (100% controlled), Total-1,200

GreenMoney Journal *Business, Consumer*   CPM: $125

Publishing Co: Greenmoney Journal, W.608 Glass Ave., Spokane, WA 99205; Title Tel # (509) 328-1741
Personnel: Publisher-Cliff Feigenbarin, Editor-Tom Kliewer, Production Mgr.-Ted Ketchin
Editorial Description: Ethical socially aware investing information.
General Info: Yr. Est. 1992, Quarterly, Trim Size-24 x 8½, 12 pages, No Color, Recycled
Subscriptions: Indv. $35, Inst. $25, Free To Qualified Recipient
Circulation: Total-4,000
Advertising: $500.
List Rental: Rents Lists

Growth Fund Guide *Business, Consumer*

Publishing Co: Growth Fund Research, Inc., PO Box 6600, Rapid City, SD 57709-6600; Title Tel # (605) 341-1971
Personnel: Publisher-Walter Rouleau, Editor-William Rouleau
Editorial Description: The nations oldest no-load fund pub. Analyses market trends, charts & rates top performing no-load funds. Includes America's #1 asset allocation programs & telephone hotline.
General Info: Yr. Est. 1968, Monthly, Trim Size-6 x 9, Web press, 24 pages, No Color, Saddle-stitched
Subscriptions: Indv. $99, Can. $101, For. $124, $5/copy

Growth Stock Outlook *Consumer*

Publishing Co: Growth Stock Outlook, Inc., 4405 East West Hwy Ste 305, Bethesda, MD 20814-4534; Title Tel # (301) 654-5205
Personnel: Publisher, Editor, Adv. Dir.-Charles Allmon
Editorial Description: Earnings, sales, dividends, price range, PE multiples & institutional shareholdings on America's fastest-growing companies.
General Info: Yr. Est. 1965, Semi-monthly, Trim Size-8½ x 11, Offset press, 8 pages, Color, Newsprint
Subscriptions: Indv. $195, $15/copy
Acquistions: Publication Bought, Publication Sold

Growth Stock Services *Business*

Publishing Co: Growth Stock Services, 135 Massachusetts Ave, Boston, MA 02115-2606; Title Tel # (617) 350-5052
Personnel: Editor-Samuel Talbot
Editorial Description: Growth stock advisory service focusing on above-average emerging companies. Long-term orientation, seeking long-term capital gains. Low turnover.
General Info: Yr. Est. 1980, Monthly
Subscriptions: Indv. $1,000

Guide to Assigning & Loaning Benefit Plan Money *Business*

Publishing Co: Thompson Publishing Group, 1725 K Street, NW, Washington, DC 20006 Tel # (202) 872-4000
Personnel: Editor-Paul Hamburger
Editorial Description: Custom publication designed for distribution to clients by professional consultants.
General Info: Quarterly, Looseleaf

Guide to Early Retirement *Business, Consumer*

Publishing Co: The Guide to Early Retirement, PO Box 6824, Laguna Niguel, CA 92607-6824; Title Tel # (714) 831-1115
Editorial Description: Contains financial information including tax and estate planning.
General Info: Yr. Est. 1992, Monthly, Trim Size-8½ x 11, 8 pages, 2 Color
Subscriptions: Indv. $149, Inst. $75
Circulation: Total-500
Printing Co: Aliso Creek Printing, 23867 Aliso Creek, Laguna Niguel, CA 92677 Tel # (714) 831-8211

Harmonic Research *Business*

Publishing Co: Harmonic Research, 650 5th Ave.,166fl., New York, NY 10019-6142; Title Tel # (212) 484-2065 Title Fax # (212) 484-2026
Personnel: Editor-Mason Sexton, Circ. Mgr.-Claudia Mendelsohn
Editorial Description: Technical analysis of U.S. stocks, S&P futures, bond futures and currencies using Gann and Elliott Wave aproaches. Features on how to manage stock and commodity trading accounts.
General Info: Yr. Est. 1984, Monthly, Trim Size-8½ x 11, 10 pages, ISSN: 0888-8574, 4 Color, Newsprint
Subscriptions: Indv. $360, Can. $360, For. $360, $15/copy
Circulation: Total-350
List Rental: List Management Co.: Carnegie Marketing Assocs., Koll Executive Plaza, 3878 Carson St., Suite 220, Torrance, CA 90503 Tel # (310) 540-4757, Fax # (310) 540-7407, Actives: 7,190, $125/M

Harry Browne's Special Reports

Publishing Co: Harry Browne's Special Reports, Inc., 207 Jefferson Sq, Austin, TX 78731-6211; Title Tel # (512) 453-7313
Personnel: Editor-Charles Smith
General Info: Yr. Est. 1974, 10x/yr.
Subscriptions: Indv. $225

Healthcare Investor *Business, Consumer*

Publishing Co: Irving Levin Associates, Inc., 72 Park Street, New Canaan, CT 06840 Tel # (203) 966-4343 Fax # (203) 966-8510
Personnel: Editor-Stephen Monroe, Circ. Mgr.-Rosemary Sandstrom
Editorial Description: Financial/corporate news for the long-term care, and senior care industry.
General Info: Monthly, Trim Size-8½ x 11, 6 pages, ISSN: 1075-9107, 2 Color, Matte
Subscriptions: Indv. $250

Heim Investment Letter *Consumer*

Publishing Co: Heim Investment Services, PO Box 19435, Portland, OR 97280-0435; Title Tel # (503) 624-4816
Personnel: Editor-Lawrence Heim
Editorial Description: Investment advice newsletter, predicting big gains in gold & silver.
General Info: Yr. Est. 1974, Semi-monthly, 6 pages
Subscriptions: Indv. $150, For. $165

High Technology and Other Growth Stocks

Publishing Co: High Technology Growth Stocks, 402 Border Rd, Concord, MA 01742-4605; Title Tel # (508) 871-0096
Editorial Description: Features info on a wide range of growth stocks.
General Info: Yr. Est. 1981, Monthly
Subscriptions: Indv. $175

High Yield Report *Business*

Publishing Co: American Banker Newsletters, One State Plaza, New York, NY 10004-1505 Fax # (202) 843-9620; Title Tel # (212) 803-8300 Title Fax # (212) 843-9620
Personnel: Publisher-David G. Schutt, Editor-Ken Hunter, Circulation, Adv. Dir., Mktg. Dir.-Hans Winberg
Editorial Description: Authorative source on high yield bonds, distressed securities, workouts, and bankruptcies.
General Info: (Formerly Distressed Debt Report; Junk Bond Reporter), Weekly, Ind/Abs/Online: Mead Data Central, NewsNet, Predicasts/Dialog
Subscriptions: Indv. $795, Can. $795, For. $825, $20/copy
Advertising: Inquire for rates.

How to Manage Your Money
See: CONSUMER INTERESTS

Hulbert Financial Digest *Business*

Publishing Co: Hulbert Financial Digest, 316 Commerce St, Alexandria, VA 22314-2802; Title Tel # (703) 683-5905
Personnel: Editor-Mark Hulbert, Circ. Mgr.-Sean Godfrey
Editorial Description: Rates the performance of other investment advisory services.
General Info: Yr. Est. 1980, Monthly, Trim Size-8½ x 11, 10 pages, 2 Color
Subscriptions: Indv. $135, For. $155
Circulation: Total-9,000
List Rental: List Management Co.: Marketing Services Intl., 625 N Michigan Ave Ste 1920, Chicago, IL 60611-3109 Tel # (312) 642-1620, Fax # (312) 642-0679, Actives: 26,180, $125/M, Expires: 14,414, $120/M

Hume MoneyLetter/ Hotsheet, The

Publishing Co: The Hume Group, PO Box 105627, Atlanta, GA 30348-5627; Title Tel # (404) 426-1920 Title Fax # (770) 423-7349
Personnel: Publisher-B. Ordover, Editor-Michael Harris, Circ. Mgr.-J.W. Baker, Production Mgr.-Deborah Rose, Circ. Mgr., Promotion Dir.-S. Shutt
Editorial Description: General investment/tax strategies and trading recommendations. Each issue features the stock market news and analysis, financial trends, international investor opportunities, investment updated, and much more.
General Info: Yr. Est. 1979, Bi-weekly, Trim Size-8½ x 11, Sheetfed press, 8 pages, 2 Color
Subscriptions: Indv. $95, $5/copy
Acquistions: Publication Bought
Circulation: Total-38,000
List Rental: List Management Co.: Watts List Management, 455 Horner Avenue, Toronto, ON M8W 4W9 Canada Tel # (416) 252-7741, Fax # (416) 252-0037, Actives: 16,662, $130/M, Expires: 24,907, $85/M
Printing Co: Stezzi Direct, Inc., 448 Armour Cir NE, Atlanta, GA 30324-4002 Tel # (404) 876-2600

IBC's Bond Fund Report *Business*

Publishing Co: IBC/Donoghue, Inc., 290 Eliot St., PO Box 9104, Ashland, MA 01721-9104; Title Tel # (508) 881-2800 Title Fax # (508) 881-0001
Personnel: Publisher-Ken Bohlin, Editor-Chip Norton, Feature Ed.-Tracy Burk, Circ. Mgr.-Dick Marden, Product Mgr.-Peter Grealish, Production Mgr.-Dianne Belemarich, Mktg. Dir.-Jessica Evers
Editorial Description: Weekly analysis & statistics on 900+ Bond Mutual Funds yield, duration, distribution rate, averages and trend analysis.
General Info: (Formerly Bond Fund Report), Yr. Est. 1993, Weekly, Trim Size-8½ x 11, Offset press, 24 pages, ISSN: 0-913755-, Color, Matte
Subscriptions: Inst. $1,095
Advertising: Accepts Inserts.
List Rental: List Management Co.: PBI List Marketing, 1201 Seven Locks Rd., Potomac, MD 20854 Tel # (301) 340-7788, Fax # (301) 738-7581

IBC's Money Fund Report *Business*

Publishing Co: IBC/Donoghue, Inc., 290 Eliot St., PO Box 9104, Ashland, MA 01721-9104; Title Tel # (508) 881-2800 Title Fax # (508) 881-0001
Personnel: Publisher-Kenneth B. Bohlin, Editor-Ralph Norton, Feature Ed.-Tracy Burk, Circ. Mgr.-Richard Marden, Product Mgr.-Peter Grealish, Production Mgr.-Diane Belemarich, Mktg. Dir.-Jessica Evers
Editorial Description: Weekly guide reporting on yields average maturity and portfolio data for more than 1,100 taxable and tax-free money market mutual funds.
General Info: (Formerly IBC/Donoghue's Money Fund Report), Yr. Est. 1975, Weekly, 20 pages, ISSN: 0197-7091
Subscriptions: Inst. $1,295
Circulation: Total-590
List Rental: List Management Co.: PBI List Marketing, 1201 Seven Locks Rd., Potomac, MD 20854 Tel # (301) 340-7788, Fax # (301) 738-7581, Actives: $125/M

IBC's Money Market Insight *Business*

Publishing Co: IBC/Donoghue, Inc., 290 Eliot St., PO Box 9104, Ashland, MA 01721-9104; Title Tel # (508) 881-2800 Title Fax # (508) 881-0001
Personnel: Publisher-Ken Bohlin, Editor-Ralph G. Norton, Feature Ed.-Tracy Burk, Circ. Mgr.-Richard Marden, Production Mgr.-Dianne Belamarich, Mktg. Dir.-Jessica V. Evers
Editorial Description: Publication featuring graphs & expert commentary dealing with the money market industry. Features monthly yields, assets, sales/redemptions & commentary on more than 1000 money funds.
General Info: (Formerly Donoghue's Money Fund Report, Exec. Ed./Money Market Insight), Yr. Est. 1988, Monthly, Offset press, 22 pages, ISSN: 1043-285X, 2 Color, Matte
Subscriptions: Inst. $625
Acquistions: Publication Bought
Circulation: Total-518
List Rental: List Management Co.: PBI List Marketing, 1201 Seven Locks Rd., Potomac, MD 20854 Tel # (301) 340-7788, Fax # (301) 738-7581, Actives: $125/M

IBC's Moneyletter *Business, Consumer*

Publishing Co: IBC/Donoghue, Inc., 290 Eliot St., PO Box 9104, Ashland, MA 01721-9104 Fax # (508) 881-0001; Title Tel # (508) 881-2800 Title Fax # (508) 881-0982
Personnel: Publisher-Ken Bohlin, Editor-John Haggerty, Circ. Mgr.-Dick Marden, Art Dir.-Linda Conley, Production Mgr., Mktg. Dir.-Brian Kelly, Mktg. Mgr.-Mary Katis
Editorial Description: Consumer guide to no-load money market & mutual fund investing. Also includes fund and asset allocation recommendations and performance tracking.
General Info: (Formerly Moneyletter; Donoghue's Moneyletter), Yr. Est. 1980, Semi-monthly, Trim Size-8½ x 11, Offset press, 8 pages, ISSN: 0197-7083, Color, Newsprint
Subscriptions: Indv. $152, For. $123, $6/copy
Acquistions: Publication Bought
Circulation: Total-28,000
List Rental: List Management Co.: PBI List Marketing, 1201 Seven Locks Rd., Potomac, MD 20854 Tel # (301) 340-7788, Fax # (301) 738-7581, Actives: 28,000, $155/M, Expires: 12,804

IBC's Quarterly Report on Money Fund Performance *Business*

Publishing Co: IBC/Donoghue, Inc., 290 Eliot St., PO Box 9104, Ashland, MA 01721-9104 Fax # (508) 881-0001; Title Tel # (508) 881-2800 Title Fax # (508) 881-0982
Personnel: Publisher-Kenneth Bohlin, Editor-Ralph Norton, Feature Ed.-Tracy Burk, Circ. Mgr.-Dick Marden, Art Dir.-Dianne Belamakich, Mktg. Dir.-Jessica V. Evers
Editorial Description: Tracks and analyzes money fund performance and expense ratios for 800+ money market funds. Provides each month's fund expenses incurred and charged along with gross and net total returns and averages.
General Info: (Formerly Quarterly Report on Money Fund Expense Ratios), Yr. Est. 1980, Quarterly, Trim Size-8½ x 11, Offset press, 20 pages, ISSN: 0897-2044, 2 Color, Newsprint
Subscriptions: Inst. $525
Circulation: Total-210
List Rental: List Management Co.: PBI List Marketing, 1201 Seven Locks Rd., Potomac, MD 20854 Tel # (301) 340-7788, Fax # (301) 738-7581, Actives: $125/M

IBC's Rated Money Fund Report *Business*

Publishing Co: IBC/Donoghue, Inc., 290 Eliot St., PO Box 9104, Ashland, MA 01721-9104; Title Tel # (508) 881-2800 Title Fax # (508) 881-0001
Personnel: Publisher-Ken Bohlin, Editor-Ralph Norton, Circ. Mgr.-Dick Marden, Production Mgr.-Dianne Belemarich, Mktg. Dir.-Jessica Evers
Editorial Description: Provides commentary and performance analysis on money market mutual funds rated by S&P, Moody's and other rating agencies.
General Info: Yr. Est. 1995, Monthly, 16 pages, ISSN: 1082-2569
Subscriptions: Inst. $625
Circulation: Total-120

I/B/E/S Monthly Comments
See: BANKING & FINANCE

INVESTigate

Publishing Co: Corporate Relations Group/Gulf Atlanti Publishing, 1801 Lee Rd Ste 301, Winter Park, FL 32789-2165 Tel # (407) 628-5200 Fax # (407) 628-0807
Personnel: Editor-Jim Cassidy, Editor-Patrick Charuhas, Art Dir.-Mike Brahosky, Mktg. Dir.-Jack Rodriguez
Editorial Description: Investigative reports on publicly traded companies, corporate officers, and the financial industry.
General Info: Yr. Est. 1985, Monthly
Subscriptions: Indv. $78
Circulation: Total-9,000
List Rental: List Management Co.: Applied List Management, 1801 Lee Rd Ste 301, Winter Park, FL 32789-2165 Tel # (407) 628-5200, Fax # (407) 628-0807

IQ Trends

Publishing Co: Investment Quality Trends, 7440 Girard Ave Ste 4, La Jolla, CA 92037-5157; Title Tel # (619) 459-3818
Personnel: Publisher, Editor-G. Weiss
General Info: Yr. Est. 1966, Bi-weekly
Subscriptions: Indv. $250

IRA-Individual Retirement
Account Stocks
Business, Association

Publishing Co: Elton Stephens Investments, 4016 S Michigan St, South Bend, IN 46614-2544; Title Tel # (219) 291-3823 Title Fax # (219) 291-3823
Personnel: Editor-Elton Stephens
Editorial Description: Sell NYSE Stock Reports-Stock for your retirement account IRA.
General Info: Yr. Est. 1972, Annually, Trim Size-8½ x 11, Web press, ISSN: 0892-6018, No Color, Looseleaf
Subscriptions: Indv. $45, $45/copy
Acquisitions: Publication Sold
Circulation: Total-2,000
Advertising: Inquire for rates. Accepts Inserts.
List Rental: Rents Lists

IRA Reference Service
Business

Publishing Co: Universal Pensions Inc., PO Box 979, Brainerd, MN 56401-0979; Title Tel # (218) 829-4781 Title Fax # (218) 829-2106
Personnel: Editor-Jennifer Norquist
Editorial Description: Up-to-date reference available for IRA operations. For financial organizations.
General Info: Yr. Est. 1975, Quarterly, Trim Size-8½ x 11, Sheetfed press, 750 pages, Looseleaf
Subscriptions: Indv. $119, Inst. $119
Printing Co: Universal Printing of Brainerd, 213 NW 4th St, Brainerd, MN 56401-3219 Tel # (218) 829-1982

IRA Reporter
Business

Publishing Co: Universal Pensions Inc., PO Box 979, Brainerd, MN 56401-0979; Title Tel # (218) 829-4781 Title Fax # (218) 829-2106
Personnel: Editor-Jennifer Norquist
Editorial Description: Covers IRA issues for financial organizations.
General Info: Yr. Est. 1983, Monthly, Trim Size-8½ x 11, Sheetfed press, 8 pages, ISSN: 0739-2168, 2 Color, Matte
Subscriptions: Indv. $115, Inst. $115
Printing Co: Universal Printing of Brainerd, 213 NW 4th St, Brainerd, MN 56401-3219 Tel # (218) 829-1982

IRA/Growth Stock Monthly

Publishing Co: Walsh Research & Investment Co., 9150 Tampa Ave., Apt. 326, Northridge, CA 91324-2740; Title Tel # (818) 363-6815
Personnel: Publisher, Editor-John Walsh
General Info: Yr. Est. 1985, Monthly
Subscriptions: Indv. $145

Impartial Global Mutual
Fund Investor
Business, Consumer

Publishing Co: GMFI, P.O. Box 25, Station H, Montreal, PQ H3G-2K5 Canada Fax # (514) 962-6707; Title Tel # (514) 989-8027 Title Fax # (514) 932-6707
Personnel: Editor in Chief-Eric Roseman
Editorial Description: Guide to global mutual fund investing. Banks top performing funds worldwide, including offshore funds and closed-end funds.
General Info: Yr. Est. 1992, Monthly, Trim Size-8½ x 11, 24 pages, 2 Color
Subscriptions: Indv. $149, Can. $149, For. $179, $15/copy
Acquisitions: Publication Sold
Circulation: Total-450
Advertising: Accepts Inserts.

Income Advisor
Business, Consumer

Publishing Co: Income Investment Advisory, P.O Box 882002, San Diego, CA 92168; Title Tel # (619) 291-4900 Title Fax # (619) 298-4920
Personnel: Publisher-John Dyrek, Editor-Doug Sheses
Editorial Description: Investment newsletter focusing on undervalued,high yielding securities.Our universe includes utilities reits,prefessed issues,convertibles, and all other high yield undervalued securities.
General Info: Yr. Est. 1994, Monthly, Trim Size-8½ x 11, Letrpr. press, 8 pages, 2 Color, Matte
Subscriptions: Indv. $150, $13/copy
Circulation: Total-2,000

Income Digest
Consumer

Publishing Co: Dick Davis Publishing, 1080 SE 3rd Ave., Fort Lauderdale, FL 33316-1108; Title Tel # (954) 467-8500 Title Fax # (954) 467-6444
Personnel: Publisher, Editor-Steve Halpern, Adv. Dir.-Jaye Abbate
Editorial Description: Income Digest researches over 400 publications and investment research reports, and singles out the most viable investment concepts for income oriented investors. It's the perfect investment tool for investors currently in retirement or those planning forretirement who need investment information with the best potential for serving the needs of people seeking high current income with safety and growth
General Info: Yr. Est. 1996, Bi-monthly, Trim Size-8½ x 11, Web press, 8 pages, 2 Color, Other
Subscriptions: Indv. $99, $5/copy
List Rental: Rents Lists
Printing Co: Direct Graphics, 829 S Vandemark Rd, Sidney, OH 45365-8984 Tel # (513) 498-2194, Fax # (513) 492-1100

Income Fund Outlook
Consumer

Publishing Co: Institute for Econometric Research, 3471 N. Federal Hwy., Ft. Lauderdale, FL 33306-1019; Title Tel # (305) 563-9000 Title Fax # (305) 563-9003
Personnel: Publisher-Glen Parker, Editor-Norman Fosback
Editorial Description: Safety ratings, yield forecasts, & recommendations for money market mutual funds, insured money market accounts, & all types of bond & income funds.
General Info: (Formerly Income & Safety), Yr. Est. 1981, Monthly, Trim Size-8½ x 11, Sheetfed press, 10 pages, ISSN: 0891-1215, Color-cover, Newsprint
Subscriptions: Indv. $100, Inst. $100, Can. $100, For. $100
Acquisitions: Publication Bought, Publication Sold
List Rental: List Management Co.: JAMI Marketing, 2 Blue Hill Plz, Pearl River, NY 10965-3101 Tel # (914) 620-0700, Fax # (914) 620-1885

Income Stocks
Business, Association

Publishing Co: Elton Stephens Investments, 4016 S Michigan St, South Bend, IN 46614-2544; Title Tel # (219) 291-3823 Title Fax # (219) 291-3823
Personnel: Editor-Elton Stephens
General Info: Yr. Est. 1972, Annually, Trim Size-8½ x 11, Web press, 1 pages, ISSN: 0895-2183, No Color, Looseleaf
Subscriptions: Indv. $45, $45/copy
Acquisitions: Publication Sold
Circulation: Total-2,000
Advertising: Inquire for rates. Accepts Inserts.
List Rental: Rents Lists

Independent Advisor for
Vanguard Investors,
The
Consumer

Publishing Co: Fund Family Shareholder Assn., Inc., 42 Pleasant St, Watertown, MA 02172-2316 Tel # (617) 782-6222 Fax # (617) 787-2879 Parent Co.-Phillips Publishing, Inc., Potomac; Title Tel # (617) 926-5552 Title Fax # (617) 926-5562
Personnel: Publisher-David Thorne, Editor-Daniel Wiener, Circ. Mgr.-Kim Scott, Art Dir.-John Hall, Mktg. Dir.-Nancy Cathey
Editorial Description: Independent advisory service dedicated to investors in Vanguard mutual funds.
General Info: (Formerly Vanguard Adviser), Yr. Est. 1991, Monthly, Trim Size-8½ x 11, Sheetfed press, 12 pages, ISSN: 1056-2338, 2 Color
Subscriptions: Indv. $99
List Rental: List Management Co.: Manager: John Baldwin; Phillips Publishing List Marketing, 7811 Montrose Rd., Potomac, MD 20854-3394 Tel # (301) 340-2100, Fax # (301) 294-1307, Actives: 15,662, $195/M

Independent T. Rowe Price
Advisor
Business, Consumer

Publishing Co: Fund Family Shareholder Assn., Inc., 42 Pleasant St, Watertown, MA 02172-2316 Tel # (617) 782-6222 Fax # (617) 787-2879 Parent Co.-Phillips Publishing, Inc., Potomac
Personnel: Editor-Dan Wiener
Editorial Description: Covers T. Rowe's 56 mutual funds.
General Info: Monthly

Individual Retirement Plans Guide-IRA, SEP, Keogh
See: U.S. (& CANADIAN) FED. GOV'T.

Industry Group Market
Values
Business

Publishing Co: Standard & Poor's Corp., 25 Broadway, New York, NY 10004 Parent Co.-McGraw-Hill, New York; Title Tel # (212) 208-8000
Personnel: Editor-Elliott Shurgin
Editorial Description: Market values of each industry in the S&P 500 Index.
General Info: Monthly, 1 pages, Looseleaf
Subscriptions: Indv. $260

Industry Surveys
Business

Publishing Co: Standard & Poor's Corp., 25 Broadway, New York, NY 10004 Parent Co.-McGraw-Hill, New York; Title Tel # (212) 208-8000
Personnel: Editor-Tom Nugent
Editorial Description: Two volumes of economic analysis and data on 65 leading industries.
General Info: Quarterly, Looseleaf
Subscriptions: Indv. $1,115, $40/copy

Inside Edge
Business, Consumer

Publishing Co: Inside Edge, 10151 University Blvd., Orlando, FL 32817
Editorial Description: Innovative ideas for investing.
General Info: Monthly, Trim Size-8½ x 11, 4 pages, 4 Color, Other

Inside Mortgage Securities
See: BANKING & FINANCE

Inside Wall Street
Business, Consumer

Publishing Co: Inside Wall Street, PO Box 940245, Maitland, FL 32794-0245
Editorial Description: Insights for investors.
General Info: Yr. Est. 1993, Monthly
List Rental: Rents Lists

Insiders, The   *Consumer*

Publishing Co: Institute for Econometric Research, 3471 N. Federal Hwy., Ft. Lauderdale, FL 33306-1019; Title Tel # (305) 563-9000 Title Fax # (305) 563-9003
Personnel: Publisher-Glen Parker, Editor-Norman Fosback, Circ. Mgr.-Helen Nichols
Editorial Description: What corporate insiders, America's most knowledgeable investors, are doing with their companies' stocks, including recommendations.
General Info: Yr. Est. 1980, Semi-monthly, Trim Size-8½ x 11, Sheetfed press, 8 pages, ISSN: 0730-2908, No Color, Newsprint
Subscriptions: Indv. $100, Inst. $100, Can. $100, For. $145, $5/copy
Acquisitions: Publication Bought, Publication Sold
List Rental: List Management Co.: JAMI Marketing, 2 Blue Hill Plz, Pearl River, NY 10965-3101 Tel # (914) 620-0700, Fax # (914) 620-1885, Actives: 5,100, $135/M, Expires: 18,928, $100/M

Insider's Alert   *Business, Consumer*

Publishing Co: Soundview Publications, 7100 Peachtree Dunwoody Rd., Suite #100, Atlanta, GA 30328-4134; Title Tel # (770) 668-0432 Title Fax # (770) 668-0692
Personnel: Publisher-Wallis W. Wood, Editor in Chief-Lewis Walker, Production Mgr.-Penny Lane, Art Dir.-Elizabeth Bame, Mktg. Dir.-Joyce Morris
Editorial Description: Inside track investment information.
General Info: Yr. Est. 1993, Monthly, 8 pages, 2 Color, Matte
Subscriptions: Indv. $87, For. $100, $5/copy
Advertising: Accepts Inserts.
List Rental: List Management Co.: Carnegie Marketing Assocs., Koll Executive Plaza, 3878 Carson St., Suite 220, Torrance, CA 90503 Tel # (310) 540-4757, Fax # (310) 540-7407, Actives: 23,687, $150/M

Insider's Chronicle   *Business*

Publishing Co: Transamerica Media Corp., PO Box 2626, Greenwich, CT 06836-2626; Title Tel # (203) 637-5900
Personnel: Publisher-Herbert Messing
Editorial Description: Insider trading, purchase and sale of corporate stock by corporate officers and directors, statistical tables, review of 2 companies per issue.
General Info: Yr. Est. 1839, Weekly, Trim Size-8½ x 11, Offset press, 12 pages
Subscriptions: $10/copy

Insiders Option Report

Publishing Co: Vickers Stock Research Corp., 226 New York Ave, Huntington, NY 11743-2748 Fax # (516) 423-7715; Title Tel # (516) 423-7710
General Info: Bi-monthly
Subscriptions: Indv. $85
List Rental: Actives: $125/M

Insider's Report: Tax & Financial Planning for Physicians

Publishing Co: Wildwood Assocs., 66 Shelter Rock Rd, Stamford, CT 06903-3529; Title Tel # (203) 322-1403
Personnel: Editor-M.J. Goldberg
General Info: Yr. Est. 1985, Monthly
Subscriptions: Indv. $97

Insight: The Advisory Letter for Concerned Investors

Publishing Co: Insight: The Advisory Letter for Concerned Investors, 711 Atlantic Ave., 5th Fl., Boston, MA 02111-2809; Title Tel # (617) 423-6655
Personnel: Publisher-Elliott Sclar, Editor-Patrick McVeigh, Circ. Mgr.-Kathy Famulari, Adv. Dir., Promotion Dir.-Phil Zuckerman
General Info: Yr. Est. 1983, Monthly
Subscriptions: Indv. $195, For. $220

Insights & Trends

Publishing Co: Greenleaf Partners, 110 W 40th St Rm 2404, New York, NY 10018-3616; Title Tel # (212) 921-8300
General Info: Yr. Est. 1987, Monthly
Subscriptions: Indv. $300

Institutional Portfolio Guide   *Business*

Publishing Co: Vickers Stock Research Corp., 226 New York Ave, Huntington, NY 11743-2748; Title Tel # (516) 423-7710 Title Fax # (516) 423-7715
Personnel: Editor-Jim Van Dyke
Editorial Description: Stocks held in the portfolios of major U.S. and Canadian investment companies, funds, etc.
General Info: Quarterly, Mimeo press, 1,400 pages, No Color, Newsprint, Perfect bound, Looseleaf
Subscriptions: Indv. $935
List Rental: Actives: $125/M

Intelligence Report   *Consumer*

Publishing Co: Phillips Publishing, Inc., 7811 Montrose Rd., Potomac, MD 20854-3394 Parent Co.-Phillips Business Information, Inc., Potomac; Title Tel # (301) 340-2100 Title Fax # (301) 294-1307
Personnel: Publisher-Thomas Phillips, Editor-Richard Young, Mktg. Dir. Annette Payne
Editorial Description: Dick Young's Intelligence report is a monthly advisory providing low risk investment opportunities in equities riding locked In trends and fixed incomes backed by the full faith and credit of Uncle Sam.
General Info: (Formerly Richard C. Young's Intelligence Report), Yr. Est. 1986, Monthly, 8 pages, ISSN: 0884-3031, 2 Color, Matte
Subscriptions: Indv. $197, $5/copy
Acquisitions: Publication Bought, Publication Sold
List Rental: List Management Co.: Manager: John Baldwin; Phillips Publishing List Marketing, 7811 Montrose Rd., Potomac, MD 20854-3394 Tel # (301) 340-2100, Fax # (301) 294-1307, Actives: 36,307, $195/M, Expires: 29,037, $95/M

Interactive Multimedia Communications   *Business*

Publishing Co: 21st Century Research, 41 Tappan Rd., Norwood, NJ 07648-1708; Title Tel # (201) 868-0881
Personnel: Mng. Editor-Bohdan Szuprowicz
Editorial Description: High Technology venture capital investment opportunites.
General Info: (Formerly Multimedia Intelligence), Yr. Est. 1993, Monthly, Trim Size-8½ x 11, Desktop press, 12 pages
Subscriptions: Indv. $750

Interest Rate Service   *Business*

Publishing Co: World Reports Ltd., 280 Madison Ave Rm 1209, New York, NY 10016-0801; Title Tel # (212) 689-7442 Title Fax # (212) 481-0915
Personnel: Publisher, Editor-Christopher Story
General Info: Monthly
Subscriptions: Indv. $750
Acquisitions: Publication Bought

Interinvest Review and Outlook   *Business*

Publishing Co: Interinvest Corp., 84 Stage St., 7th Fl., Boston, MA 02109-2202 Fax # (617) 723-1966; Title Tel # (617) 723-7870
Personnel: Publisher-Hans Black, Editor-Dr. Hans Black, Circ. Mgr.-Patti Torre
Editorial Description: Reviews international political strategy & relationship to investments.
General Info: (Formerly Interinvest Corp. Investment Review), Yr. Est. 1975, Monthly, Mimeo press, 5 pages, 2 Color
Subscriptions: Indv. $125
Circulation: Total-1,400

Intermarket Review   *Business*

Publishing Co: Intl. Institute for Economic Research, PO Box 624, Gloucester, VA 23061-0624; Title Tel # (804) 694-0415
Personnel: Publisher, Editor-Martin Pring, Circ. Mgr.-Renee Pike, Production Mgr.-Felicia Hoeniger
Editorial Description: Reviews the technical position of world financial markets with emphasis on U.S. debt & equitites.
General Info: (Formerly Pring Market Review), Yr. Est. 1984, Monthly, Trim Size-8½ x 11, Sheetfed press, 48 pages, ISSN: 0892-189X, No Color, Newsprint
Subscriptions: Indv. $395
Circulation: Total-600
List Rental: Rents Lists
Printing Co: J & J Printing, Danbury Rd., New Milford, CT 06776 Tel # (203) 355-9535

International Bank Credit Analyst
See: BANKING & FINANCE

International Business Opportunities   *Business*

Publishing Co: U.S. Import-Export Publications Co., PO Box 428, Bellflower, CA 90707-0428; Title Tel # (310) 925-2918 Title Fax # (310) 804-1234
General Info: Yr. Est. 1987, Monthly
Subscriptions: Indv. $89

International Currency Review   *Business*

Publishing Co: World Reports Ltd., 280 Madison Ave Rm 1209, New York, NY 10016-0801; Title Tel # (212) 689-7442 Title Fax # (212) 481-0915
Personnel: Editor-Christopher Story
General Info: Semi-monthly
Subscriptions: Indv. $200
Acquisitions: Publication Bought

International Insiders Report

Publishing Co: Alan Feinstein Associates, 37 Alhambra Cir., Cranston, RI 02905-3416; Title Tel # (401) 467-5155 Title Fax # (401) 941-0988
Personnel: Publisher, Editor-Alan Shawn Feinstein
Editorial Description: New and unique financial opportunities from research for ASF's syndicated newspaper column.
General Info: Yr. Est. 1973, Monthly, Trim Size-8½ x 11, 4 pages, ISSN: 0095-2931, Color
Subscriptions: Indv. $60
Circulation: Total-35,000

International Investor
Business, Consumer

Publishing Co: Ram Financial Consultants, PO Box 770190, Ocala, FL 34477-0190
Editorial Description: Helps counsel publicly owned corporations in security related activities through astrology.
General Info: Bi-weekly
Subscriptions: Indv. $200

International Regulation of Finance and Investment
See: LAW

International Securities
Regulation Report
Business

Publishing Co: LRP Publications, 747 Dresher Rd., P.O. Box 980, Horsham, PA 19044-0980
Tel # (215) 784-0910 Fax # (215) 784-0317
Personnel: Publisher-Ken Kahn, Editor-Joseph Sims
Editorial Description: Regulatory developments in key international securities markets for lawyers & others active in transactions which focus on rules set by securities commissions and new laws.
General Info: Yr. Est. 1987, Bi-weekly, Trim Size-8$\frac{1}{2}$ x 11, Offset press, 8 pages, ISSN: 0896-3010, 2 Color
Subscriptions: Indv. $795, For. $795
Acquistions: Publication Bought, Publication Sold

InvesTech Market Analyst
Business, Consumer

Publishing Co: InvesTech Research, 2472 Birch Glen Rd, Whitefish, MT 59937-3349;
Title Tel # (406) 862-7777 Title Fax # (406) 862-7707
Personnel: Publisher, Editor-James Stack, Circ. Mgr.-Stacy Tandy, Adv. Dir., Promotion Dir.-Marilyn Nelson
Editorial Description: Provides a unique blending of key technical & monetary indicators which has earned widespread recognition for reliable risk allocation strategy.
General Info: (Formerly InvesTech Market Letter), Yr. Est. 1981, 18x/yr., Trim Size-8$\frac{1}{4}$ x 11, 8 pages, ISSN: 0896-4157, Color
Subscriptions: Indv. $175, For. $189
List Rental: Expires: $125/M

InvesTech Mutual Fund
Advisor
Business, Consumer

Publishing Co: InvesTech Research, 2472 Birch Glen Rd, Whitefish, MT 59937-3349;
Title Tel # (406) 862-7777
Personnel: Publisher, Editor-James Stack, Circ. Mgr.-Stacy Tandy, Adv. Dir., Promotion Dir.-Marilyn Nelson
Editorial Description: Provides a unique blending of key technical & monetary indicators which has earned widespread recognition for reliable risk allocation strategy.
General Info: Yr. Est. 1987, 18x/yr., Trim Size-8$\frac{1}{4}$ x 11, 4 pages, ISSN: 0896-4165, Color
Subscriptions: Indv. $175, For. $189
Acquistions: Publication Bought, Publication Sold
List Rental: Expires: $125/M

Invest with the Masters
Consumer

Publishing Co: Phillips Publishing, Inc., 7811 Montrose Rd., Potomac, MD 20854-3394 Parent Co.- Phillips Business Information, Inc., Potomac; Title Tel # (301) 340-2100 Title Fax # (301) 294-1307
Personnel: Publisher-Thomas Phillips, Editor-Dan Bruce, Mktg. Dir.-Annette Payne
Editorial Description: Reports activities of successful investors along with stock analysis.
General Info: (Formerly Insightful Investor), Yr. Est. 1995, Monthly, Trim Size-8$\frac{1}{2}$ x 11, Web press, 8 pages, 2 Color, Coated
Subscriptions: Indv. $99
Circulation: Total-10,000
List Rental: List Management Co.: Manager: John Baldwin; InfoMat, 1815 W 213th St Ste 210, Torrance, CA 90501-2839 Tel # (310) 212-5944, Fax # (310) 212-5773

Investext Advisor
Business

Publishing Co: Technical Data Intl., 11 Farnsworth St, Boston, MA 02210-1250;
Title Tel # (617) 330-7878
Personnel: Editor-Ann Candura
Editorial Description: Investext plus client newsletter.
General Info: Yr. Est. 1985, Trim Size-8$\frac{1}{2}$ x 11, Sheetfed press, 4 pages, ISSN: 0893-4274, 2 Color, Coated
Circulation: Total-3,000
List Rental: Actives: $100/M

Investing with Barry Ziskin
Consumer

Publishing Co: Investing with Barry Ziskin, 824 E. Baltimore St., Baltimore, MD 21202
Personnel: Publisher-Rick Popowitz
Editorial Description: Investment advice and updates on companies.
General Info: Yr. Est. 1994, Monthly
Subscriptions: Indv. $77

Investing in Canada
Business, Association

Publishing Co: Investment Canada, C.P. 2800, Succursale D, Ottawa, ON K1P 6A5 Canada;
Title Tel # (613) 995-0465 Title Fax # (613) 996-2515
Personnel: Editor-Vincent Beauliey, Editor-Lilian Rukas, Production Mgr.-Bernard Cossais
Editorial Description: Covers Canada's investment climate. Published in English & French.
General Info: Quarterly, 16 pages
Subscriptions: Free
Circulation: Total-10,000

Investing for a Better
World
Business, Consumer

Publishing Co: Franklin's Insight, 711 Atlantic Ave., 5th Fl., Boston, MA 02111-2809;
Title Tel # (617) 423-6655
Personnel: Publisher-Elliott Sclar, Editor-Patrick McVeigh
Editorial Description: Investment information including company profiles and social responsibility in investing.
General Info: (Formerly Advisory Letter for Concerned Investors), Yr. Est. 1983, Monthly, 4 pages, 2 Color, Matte
Subscriptions: Indv. $20
Circulation: Total-1,000
List Rental: Rents Lists

Investment Advisors
Performance Survey

Publishing Co: CDA Investment Technologies Inc., 1355 Piccard Dr., Ste. 220, Rockville, MD 20850-4315 Tel # (954) 384-1500 Fax # (954) 384-1540; Title Tel # (301) 975-9600 Title Fax # (301) 590-1350
Editorial Description: Covers balanced. equity and fixed accounts managed by a broad cross-section of investment advisors. Data is collected by publisher via a survey, which is filled out directly by participating advisors. A letter code is assigned to a specific Data Type whi h best describes the rates of return.
General Info: Yr. Est. 1987, Annually, Trim Size-8$\frac{1}{2}$ x 11, Mimeo press, No Color, Newsprint, Looseleaf
Subscriptions: Indv. $600, $275/copy
Circulation: Total-206

Investment Bulletin
See: INSURANCE

Investment Digest
Business, Consumer

Publishing Co: Pinson & Assoc., 13575 58th St N, Clearwater, FL 34620-3704;
Title Tel # (813) 538-4111
Personnel: Publisher, Editor-J.M. Pinson, Production Mgr.-Cris Staffelo
Editorial Description: Guide for independent investors.
General Info: (Formerly Option Letter), Yr. Est. 1983, Monthly, Trim Size-8$\frac{1}{2}$ x 11, Desktop press, 8 pages, 2 Color, Newsprint
Subscriptions: Indv. $69, $5/copy
Circulation: (100% controlled), Total-4,800
Advertising: Inquire for rates. Accepts Inserts.
List Rental: List Management Co.: Manager: J. Michael Pinson; InfoMat, 1815 W 213th St Ste 210, Torrance, CA 90501-2839 Tel # (310) 212-5944, Fax # (310) 212-5773, Actives: 8,383, $100/M, Hotline: $100/M, Expires: $75/M

Investment Forecast
Business

Publishing Co: Heese & Assocs., 15957 Alta Vista Dr., #4, La Mirada, CA 90638-3244
General Info: Monthly

Investment Guide
Business

Publishing Co: American Investment Services, Inc., PO Box 1000, Great Barrington, MA 01230-1000; Title Tel # (413) 528-1216 Title Fax # (413) 528-0103
Personnel: Editor-Louis Moscatello
Editorial Description: Current investment opportunities analysis.
General Info: Yr. Est. 1979, Monthly, Sheetfed press, 8 pages, No Color
Subscriptions: Indv. $49, $4/copy
Circulation: Total-13,500

Investment Horizons
Business

Publishing Co: Investment Information Services, Inc., 680 North Lake Shore Drive, Ste. #2038, Chicago, IL 60611-4402; Title Tel # (312) 649-6940
Personnel: Publisher-Gerald Perritt, Circ. Mgr.-Julie Ann Johnson, Promotion Dir.-Michael Corbett
General Info: Bi-monthly, Trim Size-8$\frac{3}{8}$ x 10$\frac{7}{8}$, 16 pages
Subscriptions: Indv. $250
Printing Co: Merrill Corp., 650 W Washington Blvd, Chicago, IL 60661-2117

Investment Laws of the
World
Business

Publishing Co: Oceana Publications, Inc., 75 Main St, Dobbs Ferry, NY 10522-1601
Tel # (914) 693-8100 Fax # (914) 693-0402; Title Tel # (914) 693-5944
Personnel: Production Mgr.-Mike Wortzman, Mktg. Dir.-John Downey
Editorial Description: Constitutional, legislative & treaty material covering 80 countries.
General Info: Yr. Est. 1973, Irregular, Trim Size-7 x 10, No Color, Newsprint, Looseleaf
Subscriptions: Indv. $1,150
Circulation: Total-350

Investment Ltd.
Partnerships Law Report
Business, Scholarly

Publishing Co: Clark Boardman Callaghan, 375 Hudson St, New York, NY 10014-3685
Fax # (212) 807-6209; Title Tel # (212) 929-7500 Title Fax # (212) 924-0460
Personnel: Publisher-Jim Fegam, Editor-John Duxbury, Art Dir.-Gene Spinelli, Promotion Dir.-Steve Murtha
Editorial Description: Latest on tax investment for partnership.
General Info: (Formerly Tax Sheltered Investments Law Report), Yr. Est. 1981, 10x/yr., Trim Size-8$\frac{1}{2}$ x 11, Sheetfed press, 8 pages, ISSN: 0731-5759, 2 Color
Subscriptions: Indv. $250

Investment Management
Report

Publishing Co: Ford Investor Services, 11722 Sorrento Valley Rd., Suite 1, San Diego, CA 92121-1099; Title Tel # (619) 755-1327 Title Fax # (619) 455-6316
Personnel: Editor-David Morse
General Info: Yr. Est. 1979, Monthly
Subscriptions: Indv. $240

Investment Management
Weekly *Business*

Publishing Co: Investment Management Pubs., 1 Liberty Sq., 12th Fl., Boston, MA 02109-4825 Fax # (617) 422-0162; Title Tel # (617) 426-5450 Title Fax # (617) 422-0462
Personnel: Publisher-Melanie DeCarolis, Editor-Richard Chimberg, Adv. Dir.-David Robins
Editorial Description: For corporate & public officials overseeing the investment of trillions of dollars of employee benefits assets & the professionals advising &/or managing that money.
General Info: Yr. Est. 1988, Weekly, Trim Size-8½ x 11, Sheetfed press, 8 pages, ISSN: 0896-8500, 2 Color, Matte, Saddle-stitched
Subscriptions: Indv. $1,195, Inst. $1,195, Can. $1,275, For. $1,275, $25/copy
Advertising: $2,425. Accepts Inserts.

Investment Newsletter
See: COMPUTERS & AUTOMATION

Investment Notes

Publishing Co: Investment Notes, PO Box 14430, Minneapolis, MN 55414-0430; Title Tel # (612) 824-2852
Personnel: Publisher, Editor-K. Dewey
General Info: Yr. Est. 1982, Monthly
Subscriptions: Indv. $175

Investment Perspectives *Business*

Publishing Co: Morgan Stanley & Co., Equity Research Dept., 1585 Broadway, 14th fl., New York, NY 10036; Title Tel # (212) 703-4000
Editorial Description: For Morgan-Stanley clients.
General Info: Yr. Est. 1975, Weekly, 40 pages

Investment Quality
Trends *Business*

Publishing Co: I.Q. Trends, 7440 Girard Ave Ste 4, La Jolla, CA 92037-5157; Title Tel # (619) 459-3818 Title Fax # (619) 459-3819
Personnel: Publisher, Editor-Geraldine Weiss, Circ. Mgr., Art Dir.-K. Taylor
Editorial Description: Advisory information on Blue-Chip stocks; features 3 undervalued stocks, high-dividend stock, statistical information, features charts.
General Info: (Formerly I.Q. Trends), Yr. Est. 1966, Bi-weekly, Trim Size-8½ x 11, Offset press, 12 pages, 2 Color
Subscriptions: Indv. $275, $10/copy
Circulation: Total-5,200
List Rental: Actives: $75/M

Investment Reporter, The

Publishing Co: MPL Communications, Inc., 133 Richmond St. W., Ste. 700, Toronto, ON M5H 3M8 Canada; Title Tel # (416) 869-1177 Title Fax # (416) 869-0456
Personnel: Publisher-S. Pepper, Circ. Mgr.-Mindy Tenenbaum
Editorial Description: Canadian stock market investment advisory newsletter.
General Info: Yr. Est. 1941, Weekly, Trim Size-8½ x 11, Sheetfed press, 8 pages, ISSN: 0700-5539, 2 Color, Newsprint
Subscriptions: Indv. $279, Can. $279
List Rental: Actives: $130/M

Investment Reporter *Consumer*

Publishing Co: Investment Reporter, 4600 Campus Dr., Ste. 205, Newport Beach, CA 92660-1801; Title Tel # (714) 724-0444 Title Fax # (714) 548-1669
Editorial Description: Covers stock opportunities on the NASDAQ exchange.
General Info: Monthly
Subscriptions: Indv. $56

Investment Treaties
See: LAW

Investment Update
Newsletter *Business*

Publishing Co: Erik S. Nelson, Inc., PO Box 672223, Marietta, GA 30067; Title Tel # (770) 435-5854 Title Fax # (770) 435-7980
Personnel: Publisher-Erik S. Nelson
Editorial Description: Finding high growth companies that will provide investors with above average returns. Through intensive research and a strict set of financial criteria, provides investment ideas that have the potential of producing superior results.
General Info: Yr. Est. 1992, Monthly, Trim Size-8½ x 11, Desktop press, 4 pages, No Color, Other, Other
Subscriptions: Indv. $30, Free To Qualified Recipient
Circulation: Readership-400

Investor Advantage *Consumer, Association*

Publishing Co: Twentieth Century Services, PO Box 419200, Kansas City, MO 64141-6200
Editorial Description: Published for shareholders of Twentieth century mutual funds.
General Info: Quarterly, Trim Size-8½ x 11, 6 pages, 4 Color, Coated

Investor Alert *Business, Consumer*

Publishing Co: Investor Alert, PO Box 1160, Pacifica, CA 94044-6160
Personnel: Publisher-Bill Cate
Editorial Description: Investment news and information on the stock market.
General Info: Monthly

Investor News *Consumer, Association*

Publishing Co: Investors Alliance, 219 Commercial Blvd., PO Box 11209, Fort Lauderdale, FL 33339-1209; Title Tel # (305) 491-5100
Editorial Description: Information for this association of independent investors.
General Info: Yr. Est. 1987, Monthly, Trim Size-8½ x 11, 20 pages
Subscriptions: Free With Membership

Investor Relations Newsletter
See: BANKING & FINANCE

Investor, U.S.A. *Business*

Publishing Co: Investor U.S.A., PO Box 370, Remsenburg, NY 11960-0370; Title Tel # (516) 325-0507 Title Fax # (212) 686-8522
Personnel: Publisher-Ed Jorgensen, Production Mgr.-Francis Duffy
Editorial Description: Stock market newsletter for sophisticated personal investor & advisers.
General Info: Yr. Est. 1983, Monthly, Sheetfed press, 8 pages, ISSN: 0739-3026, No Color, Newsprint
Subscriptions: Indv. $195, $18/copy
Circulation: Total-300

Investor's Advisory Service *Business*

Publishing Co: Harris Bank, 111 W. Monroe St., Chicago, IL 60694-0001; Title Tel # (312) 461-6624
Personnel: Publisher, Editor-Rober Scott
Editorial Description: Financial advisory newsletter.
General Info: Yr. Est. 1973, Monthly, 2 Color

Investor's Digest *Business*

Publishing Co: Institute for Econometric Research, 3471 N. Federal Hwy., Ft. Lauderdale, FL 33306-1019; Title Tel # (305) 563-9000 Title Fax # (305) 563-9003
Editorial Description: Digest of stock market advice: best stock recommendations (including short sales) shrewdest market-timing advice, and winning portfolio strategies of Wall Street's best and brightest.
General Info: Yr. Est. 1990, Monthly, ISSN: 1057-6711
Subscriptions: Indv. $60, Inst. $60, Can. $60, For. $90
List Rental: Rents Lists

Investor's Digest of
Canada *Business, Consumer* CPM: $200

Publishing Co: MPL Communications, Inc., 133 Richmond St. W., Ste. 700, Toronto, ON M5H 3M8 Canada; Title Tel # (416) 869-1177 Title Fax # (416) 869-0456
Personnel: Publisher-B. Martland, Publisher-S. Pepper, Editor-Richard Morrison, Circ. Mgr.-David Berger, Adv. Dir.-Peter Vos
Editorial Description: The key investment information source for individual investors and investment professionals including broker's research reports, specific investment recommendations & portfolio planning strategies.
General Info: Yr. Est. 1968, 24x/yr., Web press, 4 Color, Newsprint, Saddle-stitched
Subscriptions: Indv. $137, $6/copy
Circulation: Total-20,500
Advertising: $4,100. Accepts Inserts.
List Rental: Actives: $130/M

Investor's Hotline *Business, Consumer*

Publishing Co: Investor's Hotline, Inc., 10616 Beaver Dam Rd., Hunt Valley, MD 21030-2232 Fax # (410) 584-1043; Title Tel # (410) 771-0064
Personnel: Publisher-F. Joseph Bradley, Circ. Mgr.-Cindy Blair, Editor, Circ. Mgr.-Joanne Schenk, Product Mgr.-Jennifer Kreshtool
Editorial Description: Each month subscribers receive 4 up-to-the-minute interviews (48 per year) on cassette with printed sumamaries, featuring the world's financial experts on topics ranging from investments to economic & business trends.
General Info: (Formerly Audio Alert), Yr. Est. 1976, Monthly, No Color
Subscriptions: Indv. $225
Advertising: Accepts Inserts.
List Rental: List Management Co.: Carnegie Marketing Assocs., Koll Executive Plaza, 3878 Carson St., Suite 220, Torrance, CA 90503 Tel # (310) 540-4757, Fax # (310) 540-7407, Actives: $195/M, Expires: $95/M

Investor's World *Consumer*

Publishing Co: Phillips Publishing, Inc., 7811 Montrose Rd., Potomac, MD 20854-3394 Tel # (301) 340-2100 Fax # (301) 294-1307 Parent Co.-Phillips Business Information, Inc., Potomac; Title Tel # (301) 340-1520 Title Fax # (301) 340-0542
Personnel: Publisher-Thomas L. Phillips, Editor-John Dessauer, Mktg. Dir.-Amy Conlan
Editorial Description: Investment information and tips from John Dessauer.
General Info: (Formerly John Dessauer's Investor's World), Yr. Est. 1993, Monthly
Subscriptions: Indv. $99
List Rental: List Management Co.: Manager: John Bladwin; Phillips Publishing List Marketing, 7811 Montrose Rd., Potomac, MD 20854-3394 Tel # (301) 340-2100, Fax # (301) 294-1307, Actives: 52,476, $195/M, Expires: 5,947, $95/M

Irving's Interest Rate
Spectator — *Business, Consumer*

Publishing Co: Weiss Publishing & Marketing, 4176 Burns Rd., Palm Beach Gardens, FL 33410-4606 Tel # (407) 627-3300 Fax # (407) 625-6685; Title Fax # (612) 895-5526
Personnel: Publisher-Irving Weiss, Editor-Martin Weiss
Editorial Description: Faxed service on interest rate investment.
General Info: Daily
Subscriptions: Indv. $5,000

Island Properties Report
See: REAL ESTATE

Israel MarketFax — *Business*

Publishing Co: MarketFax, 1498M Reistertown Rd., Ste. 327, Baltimore, MD 21208
Personnel: Mng. Editor-David Weiner, Contrib. Ed.-Bruce Lubich
Editorial Description: Covers Israeli businesses whose stocks are traded on US exchanges.
General Info: Bi-weekly, Trim Size-8½ x 11, 10 pages, No Color
Subscriptions: Indv. $69

Israeli Investor Network
See: ENERGY

It's Your Money: The
Jorgensen Report — *Business, Consumer*

Publishing Co: InfoCom Group, 1250 45th St., Ste 200, Emeryville, CA 94608-2924 Tel # (510) 596-9300 Fax # (510) 596-9331; Title Tel # (415) 924-1612
Personnel: Publisher-R. Crandall, Editor-Jim Jorgensen
Editorial Description: Provides financial planning advice.
General Info: (Formerly Jorgensen Report), Yr. Est. 1982, Monthly, Sheetfed press, 12 pages, 1% ads, No Color
Subscriptions: Indv. $38
Advertising: Inquire for rates.
List Rental: Rents Lists

J. Taylor's Gold & Gold
Stocks — *Business, Consumer*

Publishing Co: Taylor Hard Money Advisors, Inc., 3342 61st St # 871, Woodside, NY 11377-2234; Title Tel # (718) 457-1426 Title Fax # (718) 457-1426
Personnel: Editor-Jay Taylor, Circ. Mgr.-Teresa Taylor
Editorial Description: Features developing gold mining stocks & other small cap situations.
General Info: (Formerly North American Goldmining Stocks), Yr. Est. 1981, Monthly, Desktop press, 8 pages, No Color
Subscriptions: Indv. $99, $15/copy
Circulation: Total-500

JULUKA Newsletter
See: ETHNIC

Jacobs Report on Asset
Protection Strategies — *Business, Association*

Publishing Co: Research Press Inc., 4500 W 72nd Ter, Prairie Village, KS 66208-2824; Title Tel # (913) 362-9667 Title Fax # (913) 362-4922
Personnel: Publisher, Editor-Vernon Jacobs
Editorial Description: Explains benefits and problems of various asset protection methods.
General Info: Yr. Est. 1993, Monthly, Trim Size-8½ x 11, Letrpr. press, 10 pages, No Color
Subscriptions: Indv. $145, For. $175, $15/copy

Japan-U.S. Business Report
See: INTERNATIONAL TRADE

Jim Cook's Market
Update & Other Essays — *Business*

Publishing Co: Investment Rarities, Inc., 7850 Metro Pky Ste 106, Minneapolis, MN 55425-1521 Tel # (612) 853-0700
Personnel: Editor-Jim Cook, Production Mgr.-Carla Foley, Circ. Mgr., Adv. Dir.-Lonnie Kocina, Art Dir.-Deb Kelly
Editorial Description: Client newsletter.
General Info: Yr. Est. 1978, Monthly, 4 pages
Subscriptions: Indv. $39
Circulation: Total-70,000

John Bollinger's Capital
Growth Letter

Publishing Co: Bollinger Capital Management, Inc., PO Box 3358, Manhattan Beach, CA 90266-1358; Title Tel # (310) 798-8855 Title Fax # (310) 798-8858
Personnel: Editor-John Bollinger, Publisher, Production Mgr.-Dorit Kehr
Editorial Description: Contains information on investment portfolios, stocks, & bonds.
General Info: Yr. Est. 1986, Monthly, Trim Size-8½ x 11, Sheetfed press, 12 pages, 2 Color, Matte
Subscriptions: Indv. $225

John Pugsley's Journal
See: BANKING & FINANCE

John T. Reed's Real Estate Investor's Monthly
See: REAL ESTATE

Jon Strebler's Investment
Outlook — *Business, Consumer*

Publishing Co: Jon S. Strebler's Investment Outlook, 229 Citrus Ave, Imperial Beach, CA 91932-1012; Title Tel # (619) 424-7604
Personnel: Publisher, Editor, Circ. Mgr.-Jon Strebler, Production Mgr.-Judy Thompson, Art Dir.-Sandra Brandon, Adv. Dir., Promotion Dir.-Robert Moskowitz
Editorial Description: Technically oriented analysis of stocks, bonds, gold & silver.
General Info: Yr. Est. 1984, Monthly, Mimeo press, 6 pages, Color, Newsprint
Subscriptions: Indv. $95, $10/copy
Circulation: Total-460

Junior Growth Stocks/New
Issue Digest — *Business*

Publishing Co: Growth Stock Outlook, Inc., 4405 East West Hwy Ste 305, Bethesda, MD 20814-4534; Title Tel # (301) 654-5205
Personnel: Publisher, Editor, Art Dir.-Charles Allmon
Editorial Description: Earnings, sales book values, price ranges, P/E ratios list on America's fastest growing cos.
General Info: Yr. Est. 1971, Quarterly, Trim Size-8½ x 11, Offset press, 10 pages, 2 Color, Newsprint
Subscriptions: Indv. $50, $25/copy

K.D. Investment Notes — *Business*

Publishing Co: K.D. Information Notes, Inc., PO Box 14430, Minneapolis, MN 55414-0430; Title Tel # (612) 824-2852
Personnel: Publisher, Editor-Kim Dewey
Editorial Description: Educational service explains investment basics (market commentary, features, readers' questions).
General Info: Yr. Est. 1982, Monthly, Trim Size-8½ x 11, Desktop press, 4 pages
Subscriptions: Indv. $150, $20/copy

Key-Volume Strategies

Publishing Co: Key-Volume Strategies, Inc., PO Box 407, White Plains, NY 10602-0407; Title Tel # (914) 698-0694
General Info: Yr. Est. 1970, 24x/yr.
Subscriptions: Indv. $229

Kimball Letter — *Business*

Publishing Co: Kimball Assocs., 4640 Rummell Rd, Saint Cloud, FL 34771-1708; Title Tel # (407) 892-8555
Personnel: Publisher-L.M. Kimball, Editor-Ed Kimball
Editorial Description: Analyses the positions of large traders in commodity futures.
General Info: Yr. Est. 1960, Semi-monthly
Subscriptions: Indv. $60

Kirkpatrick's Market
Strategist — *Business*

Publishing Co: Kirkpatrick & Co., PO Box 1066, Exeter, NH 03833-1066; Title Tel # (603) 772-5551 Title Fax # (603) 772-6247
Personnel: Publisher, Editor-Charles Kirkpatrick
Editorial Description: Weekly (short term) & monthly (intermediate-term) technical commentary on markets for professionals.
General Info: Yr. Est. 1981, Weekly, Desktop press, 11 pages, No Color
Subscriptions: Indv. $195, Inst. $2,500
Circulation: (100% controlled), Total-200

Kon-Lin Letter — *Business*

Publishing Co: Kon-Lin Research & Analysis Corp., 5 Water Rd, Rocky Point, NY 11778-9331; Title Tel # (516) 744-8536 Title Fax # (516) 744-3096
Personnel: Publisher-Lora Kuhn, Editor-Konrad Kuhn, Production Mgr.-Linda Kuhn
Editorial Description: Offers low-priced stock selections including a featured stock of the month. Monitors technical indicators; reviews fundamental analysis on emerging growth stocks under $10.
General Info: Yr. Est. 1981, Monthly, Trim Size-8½ x 11, Web press, 5 pages, No Color
Subscriptions: Indv. $95, For. $120, $10/copy
Acquistions: Publication Bought
Circulation: Total-8,000
List Rental: Actives: $85/M, Expires: $85/M

LaLoggia Letter, The — *Business*

Publishing Co: LaLoggia Letter, PO Box 167, Rochester, NY 14601-0167; Title Tel # (716) 232-1240
Personnel: Editor-Charles LaLoggia
General Info: Semi-monthly
Subscriptions: Indv. $170

Lambda Financial Advisor — *Consumer*

Publishing Co: Lambda Financial Advisor, PO Box 3569, Jersey City, NJ 07303-3569; Title Tel # (201) 963-1357
Personnel: Publisher, Editor-Julius Spohn
Editorial Description: Financial advice for gay men & women.
General Info: Yr. Est. 1984, Monthly, 8 pages
Subscriptions: Indv. $36, $5/copy
Circulation: Total-470

Lancz Letter   *Business*

Publishing Co: Alan B. Lancz & Assocs., Inc., 2400 N Reynolds Rd, Toledo, OH 43615-2818; Title Tel # (419) 536-5200 Title Fax # (419) 536-5401
Personnel: Publisher, Editor-Alan Lancz, Circ. Mgr.-Alice Murphy, Production Mgr.-Jody Stoner
Editorial Description: Investment advisory newsletter linked with a prominent professional money manager. Best known by finding undiscovered, undervalued stocks via direct discussions with management. Analysis on interest rates, U.S. dollar, precious metals & bonds are also featured. All past and current recommendations are ranked in priority order as to timliness and confidence safety.
General Info: Yr. Est. 1981, Irregular, Letrpr. press, 14 pages, 2 Color
Subscriptions: Indv. $250, Can. $275, For. $300, $15/copy
Circulation: (8% controlled), Subscriptions-1,200

Larry Abraham's Insider
Report   *Business, Consumer*

Publishing Co: Hoisager & Laird, Inc., 101 S Jennings Ave Ste 204, Fort Worth, TX 76104-1149 Tel # (817) 335-5443 Fax # (817) 335-7909
Personnel: Circ. Mgr.-John Johnson, Production Mgr.-Velda Malock, Publisher, Adv. Dir.-W.W. Wood
Editorial Description: Focuses on Behind The Scenes activities & how they affect investments.
General Info: Yr. Est. 1983, Monthly, Sheetfed press, 2 Color, Newsprint
Subscriptions: Indv. $199, $8/copy
Advertising: Accepts Inserts.
List Rental: List Management Co.: Media Mart, 1101 King St Ste 400, Alexandria, VA 22314-2944 Tel # (703) 548-2400, Fax # (703) 683-6974, Actives: 16,201, Expires: 18,206
Printing Co: Runbeck Graphics, 3101 N Central Ave Ste 490, Phoenix, AZ 85012-2638 Tel # (602) 230-0510

LifeLine / Vitalite
See: INSURANCE

Limited Partnership
Investment Review

Publishing Co: WPI Communications, Inc., 55 Morris Ave, Springfield, NJ 07081-1496; Title Tel # (201) 467-8700
Personnel: Publisher-S.H. Klinghoffer, Editor-D.W. Kennedy, Circ. Mgr.-M. Lang, Production Mgr.-J. Petino
Editorial Description: Covers syndications & marketing.
General Info: (Formerly Tax Shelter Investment Review), Yr. Est. 1987, Monthly, Trim Size-8½ x 11, Sheetfed press, 12 pages, Ind/Abs/Online: Newsnet, 2 Color, Newsprint
Subscriptions: Indv. $197
Acquistions: Publication Bought
List Rental: List Management Co.: WMI/Worldata, 5200 Town Center Circle, Boca Raton, FL 33486 Tel # (407) 393-8200, Fax # (407) 368-8345, Actives: 29,825, $75/M

Lipper Convertible Analysis
Report   *Business*

Publishing Co: Lipper Analytical Svcs., Inc., 47 Maple St., Suite 101, Summit, NJ 07901-2571 Tel # (908) 273-2772; Title Tel # (212) 312-0300
Personnel: Publisher-A. Michael Lipper, Editor-Eli Tanenbaum
Editorial Description: Available to institutional clients only for directed commission business.
General Info: (Formerly KV Convertible Fact Finder), Weekly, 28 pages, Saddle-stitched, Looseleaf

Lipper Directors' Analytical
Data   *Business*

Publishing Co: Lipper Analytical Svcs., Inc., 47 Maple St., Suite 101, Summit, NJ 07901-2571 Tel # (908) 273-2772; Title Tel # (212) 312-0300
Personnel: Publisher-Geoffrey Bobroff, Editor-Bradford Richardson
Editorial Description: Available to institutional clients only for directed commission business.
General Info: Quarterly, Trim Size-8½ x 11, Offset press, 1,200 pages, No Color, Looseleaf

Lipper Fixed Income Fund
Performance Analysis   *Business*

Publishing Co: Lipper Analytical Svcs., Inc., 47 Maple St., Suite 101, Summit, NJ 07901-2571 Tel # (908) 273-2772; Title Tel # (212) 312-0300
Personnel: Publisher-A. Michael Lipper, Editor-Theodora Annis
Editorial Description: Available to institutional clients only for directed commission business.
General Info: Monthly, Trim Size-8½ x 11, Offset press, 52 pages, No Color, Saddle-stitched, Looseleaf

Lipper Mutual Fund
Performance Analysis   *Business*

Publishing Co: Lipper Analytical Svcs., Inc., 47 Maple St., Suite 101, Summit, NJ 07901-2571 Tel # (908) 273-2772; Title Tel # (212) 312-0300
Personnel: Publisher-A. Michael Lipper, Editor-Joanne Jeager
Editorial Description: Available to institutional clients only.
General Info: Weekly, Trim Size-8½ x 11, Offset press, 52 pages, No Color, Saddle-stitched, Looseleaf

Lipper Overseas Fund
Table   *Business*

Publishing Co: Lipper Analytical Svcs., Inc., 47 Maple St., Suite 101, Summit, NJ 07901-2571 Tel # (908) 273-2772; Title Tel # (212) 312-0300
Personnel: Publisher-A. Michael Lipper, Editor-Jim Fung, Promotion Dir.-Frank Harrison
Editorial Description: Available to institutional clients for directed brokerage commissions.
General Info: Weekly, Looseleaf

Lipper Portfolio Analysis
Report on Fixed Income
Funds   *Business*

Publishing Co: Lipper Analytical Svcs., Inc., 47 Maple St., Suite 101, Summit, NJ 07901-2571 Tel # (908) 273-2772; Title Tel # (212) 312-0300
Personnel: Publisher-A. Michael Lipper, Editor-Hylton Phillips-Page, Promotion Dir.-Frank Harrison
Editorial Description: Available to institutions only for directed commission business.
General Info: Quarterly, Trim Size-8½ x 11, Offset press, 52 pages, No Color, Saddle-stitched, Looseleaf

Lipper Securities Industry
Financial Analysis
Service   *Business*

Publishing Co: Lipper Analytical Svcs., Inc., 47 Maple St., Suite 101, Summit, NJ 07901-2571 Tel # (908) 273-2772; Title Tel # (212) 312-0300
Personnel: Publisher-A. Michael Lipper, Editor-Perrin Long, Promotion Dir.-Frank Harrison
Editorial Description: Available to institutional clients only.
General Info: Monthly, Trim Size-8½ x 11, Offset press, 50 pages, No Color, Saddle-stitched, Looseleaf

Lipper Variable Insurance
Products Performance
Analysis Service

Publishing Co: Lipper Analytical Svcs., Inc., 47 Maple St., Suite 101, Summit, NJ 07901-2571 Tel # (908) 273-2772; Title Tel # (212) 312-0300
General Info: (Formerly Lipper Annuity and Closed End Survey), Looseleaf

Liquidation Alert
See: REAL ESTATE

Long Term Investing   *Business*

Publishing Co: Concept Publishing, PO Box 500, York, NY 14592-0500; Title Tel # (716) 243-3148
Personnel: Publisher, Circ. Mgr., Adv. Dir.-Jim Dovan, Editor, Art Dir.-David Coleman
Editorial Description: An investment advisory service incl. a monthly letter, special advisories providing timing, special reports, review of situations on request by subscribers, a copy of For The Long Term.
General Info: Yr. Est. 1975, Monthly, Trim Size-8½ x 11, Sheetfed press, 12 pages, No Color, Newsprint
Subscriptions: Indv. $99
Circulation: (100% controlled)

Long Term Values   *Business*

Publishing Co: Daily Graphs, Inc., 12655 Beatrice St, Los Angeles, CA 90066-7300 Tel # (310) 448-6843 Fax # (310) 577-7373; Title Tel # (213) 820-2583
Personnel: Editor-William O'Neil
Editorial Description: Long Term Values reports on over 4,000 stocks. It gives fact-filled graphic displays containing histori
General Info: Semi-monthly
List Rental: List Management Co.: Name-Finders Lists, Inc., 3180 18th St Fl 2, San Francisco, CA 94110-2028 Tel # (510) 533-4177, Fax # (510) 553-8677, Actives: 4,519, $660/M

Louis Rukeyser's Mutual
Funds   *Business, Consumer*

Publishing Co: Financial Service Associates, L.P., 1101 King St., Ste 400, Alexandria, VA 22314-2944 Tel # (703) 739-2644
Personnel: Publisher-Brian W. Smith, Editor in Chief-Louis Rukeyser, Mng. Editor-Dan Moser, Exec. Ed.-Soula Stefanopoulos, Design Ed.-Christina Gibson
Editorial Description: Information for current and potential investors in mutual funds.
General Info: Monthly, Trim Size-8½ x 11, 12 pages, 2 Color, Matte, Other
Subscriptions: Indv. $96

Louis Rukeyser's Wall
Street   *Business*

Publishing Co: Financial Service Associates, L.P., 1101 King St., Ste 400, Alexandria, VA 22314-2944 Tel # (703) 739-2644
Personnel: Publisher-Brian Smith, Assoc. Publ.-James U. Blanchard, III, Editor in Chief-Louis Rukeyser, Mng. Editor-Mark Salzinger, Exec. Ed.-Soula Stefanopoulos, Design Ed.-Christina B. Gibson
Editorial Description: Wall Street predictions and information.
General Info: Monthly, Trim Size-8½ x 11, 12 pages, 2 Color, Matte
Subscriptions: Indv. $99
Circulation: Total-400,000
List Rental: List Management Co.: Media Mart, 1101 King St Ste 400, Alexandria, VA 22314-2944 Tel # (703) 548-2400, Fax # (703) 683-6974, Actives: 415,113, $195/M

Low Priced Stock Survey   *Business*

Publishing Co: Dow Theory Forecasts, Inc., 7412 Calumet Ave, Hammond, IN 46324-2622; Title Tel # (219) 931-6480 Title Fax # (219) 391-6487
Personnel: Editor-Randall Roeing
Editorial Description: Analysis of stocks primarily priced at under $20.
General Info: Yr. Est. 1980, Bi-weekly, Sheetfed press, 6 pages, ISSN: 0273-7752, 2 Color
Subscriptions: Indv. $82
Circulation: Total-7,500
List Rental: List Management Co.: Kleid Company, Inc., 530 5th Ave., 17 Floor, New York, NY 10036-5101 Tel # (212) 819-3406, Fax # (212) 719-9788, Actives: $125/M

Low Priced Stocks — *Business, Association*

Publishing Co: Elton Stephens Investments, 4016 S Michigan St, South Bend, IN 46614-2544; Title Tel # (219) 291-3823 Title Fax # (219) 291-3823
Personnel: Editor-Elton Stephens
General Info: Yr. Est. 1972, Annually, Trim Size-8½ x 11, Web press, 1 pages, ISSN: 0892-984X, No Color, Looseleaf
Subscriptions: Indv. $45, $45/copy
Acquistions: Publication Sold
Circulation: Total-2,000
Advertising: Inquire for rates. Accepts Inserts.
List Rental: Rents Lists

Lynch International Investment Survey — *Business, Consumer*

Publishing Co: Lynch-Bowes, Inc., 301 Main St., #206, Port Washington, NY 11050-2705; Title Tel # (516) 883-7094 Title Fax # (516) 883-4338
Personnel: Publisher, Editor-Walter A. Lynch, Production Mgr.-Francis Johnson, Circ. Mgr., Promotion Dir.-Kathryn Grimm
Editorial Description: Fundamental investment review specializing in stocks, bonds, precious metals, currencies.
General Info: Yr. Est. 1971, Weekly, Trim Size-8½ x 11, Letrpr. press, 4 pages, 2 Color, Newsprint
Subscriptions: Indv. $175, Can. $175, For. $214
Circulation: Total-3,000
List Rental: List Management Co.: Manager: Kathryn Grimm; Coolidge List Marketing, 25 W. 43rd St., New York, NY 10036-7491 Tel # (212) 274-0630, Fax # (212) 274-0650, Actives: 3,000, $125/M, Expires: 17,000, $100/M
Printing Co: Leebolt Printing, 271 Main St, Port Washington, NY 11050-2703 Tel # (516) 944-3333

Lynch Municipal Bond Advisory — *Business, Consumer*

Publishing Co: Lynch Municipal Bond Advisory, PO Box 20476, New York, NY 10025
Personnel: Editor-James Lynch
Editorial Description: Advice on bond purchasing and investment.
General Info: Yr. Est. 1986, Monthly
Subscriptions: Indv. $350

MBH Weekly Commodity Letter — *Business*

Publishing Co: MBH Commodity Advisors, Inc., Northbrook Pl., 60 Revere Dr., #888, Northbrook, IL 60062; Title Tel # (708) 291-1870 Title Fax # (708) 291-9435
Personnel: Publisher, Editor-Jake Bernstein, Production Mgr.-M.J. Kinney
Editorial Description: Futures market trading.
General Info: Yr. Est. 1972, Weekly, 8 pages, No Color
Subscriptions: Indv. $895

MMA Cycles Report — *Business*

Publishing Co: Merriman Market Analyst, PO Box 250012, West Bloomfield, MI 48325-0012; Title Tel # (810) 626-3034 Title Fax # (810) 626-5674
Personnel: Editor-Raymond Merriman, Circ. Mgr.-Debra Christy, Adv. Dir.-Gina Samhat
Editorial Description: Financial market investment timing information.
General Info: (Formerly Merriman Market Analyst), Yr. Est. 1988, 20x/yr., Trim Size-8½ x 11, Letrpr. press, 8 pages, No Color, Newsprint
Subscriptions: Indv. $249, Inst. $249, For. $300
Circulation: Total-400
List Rental: Actives: $75/M, Expires: $75/M
Printing Co: Quality Quick Print, 88 W Maple Rd, Troy, MI 48084-5427 Tel # (313) 362-3685

MPT Review — *Consumer*

Publishing Co: Navellier & Assocs., Inc., PO Box 10012, Incline Village, NV 89450-1012; Title Tel # (702) 831-1396 Title Fax # (702) 832-4909
Personnel: Editor-Louis Navellier, Circ. Mgr.-Jerry Rushing, Mktg. Dir.-J. Rushing
Editorial Description: Quantitative analysis of stocks.
General Info: Yr. Est. 1987, Monthly, 16 pages, 2 Color
Subscriptions: Indv. $225, For. $250
Circulation: Total-5,500

MSRB Manual — *Business*

Publishing Co: CCH, Inc., 2700 Lake Cook Rd., Riverwoods, IL 60015 Parent Co.-Kluwer Law & Taxation Publishers, Cambridge; Title Tel # (847) 267-7000 Title Fax # (800) 224-8299
Editorial Description: Rules of the Municipal Rule-Making Board.
General Info: Yr. Est. 1977, Bi-monthly, Trim Size-6 x 9, Web press, 112 pages, No Color, Looseleaf
Subscriptions: Indv. $297

Major Trends

Publishing Co: Major Trends, 250 W. Coventry Court, Milwaukee, WI 53217-3963; Title Tel # (414) 352-8460
Personnel: Publisher, Editor-Ronald Sadoff
General Info: Monthly
Subscriptions: Indv. $195

Making Ends Meet
See: BANKING & FINANCE

Managed Account Reports — *Business, Consumer*

Publishing Co: Managed Account Reports, 220 Fifth Ave., New York, NY 10001; Title Tel # (212) 213-6202 Title Fax # (212) 213-1870
Personnel: Publisher-Greg Newton, Editor-Lois Baratz, Circ. Mgr.-Lydia Soto
Editorial Description: Commodity money management reports on trading advisors & futures funds. Also covers current developments, studies, events.
General Info: Yr. Est. 1979, Monthly, Trim Size-8½ x 11, Offset press, 32 pages, ISSN: 0197-5282, No Color
Subscriptions: Indv. $299, For. $370, $30/copy
List Rental: Rents Lists
Printing Co: Concord Press, 4785 Dorsey Hall Dr., Ellicott City, MD 21042 Tel # (410) 997-5340, Fax # (410) 997-5574

Managing Your Future — *Business*

Publishing Co: Time Warner Publishing Inc., 1271 Ave. of the Americas, Rockefeller Center, New York, NY 10020-1300 Tel # (212) 522-1212 Fax # (212) 765-2699; Title Tel # (212) 522-2651 Title Fax # (212) 522-1802
Personnel: Publisher-William Myers, Editor-Eric Schurenberg, Mng. Editor-Frank Lalli
Editorial Description: Bought and distributed by businesses for their employees that are enrolled in 401(K) plans.
General Info: Yr. Est. 1993, Quarterly, Trim Size-8½ x 11, 6 pages, 4 Color, Coated
Subscriptions: Indv. $240
Circulation: Total-511,000

Managing Your Money Better — *Business*

Publishing Co: Meca Software Ltd., 55 Walls Drive, Fairfield, CT 06430-0912; Title Tel # (203) 256-5000
Personnel: Publisher-Andrew Tobias, Editor-Nancy Spitzer, Production Mgr.-Jodi Pontillo
General Info: Quarterly
Circulation: Total-40,000
List Rental: List Management Co.: AZ Marketing Services, Inc., 31 River Rd, Cos Cob, CT 06807-2745 Tel # (203) 629-8088, Fax # (203) 661-1068

Mansfield Stock Chart Service

Publishing Co: R. W. Mansfield Co, 2973 John F. Kennedy Blvd., Jersey City, NJ 07306-3884 Fax # (201) 795-5476; Title Tel # (201) 795-0630
Personnel: Editor-Ezra Aboodi
Editorial Description: Publishes stock charts, plus weekly market averages, group averages, technical indicators, business barometers, analytical comments.
General Info: Yr. Est. 1938, Weekly, Sheetfed press
Subscriptions: Indv. $565, $30/copy

Margo's Market Monitor — *Business, Consumer*

Publishing Co: Margo's Market Monitor, PO Box 642, Lexington, MA 02173-0006; Title Tel # (617) 861-0302 Title Fax # (617) 861-1489
Personnel: Editor-Margo Parrish
Editorial Description: Offers Common Stocks, Fidelity Select Portfolios, Bond and Gold/Silver investment recommendations.
General Info: Yr. Est. 1980, Bi-weekly, Trim Size-8½ x 11, Mimeo press, 6 pages, No Color
Subscriptions: Indv. $125, Free To Qualified Recipient
Circulation: Total-2,000

Market Advantage

Publishing Co: Security Pacific Corp., 333 S Hope St, Los Angeles, CA 90071-2701
General Info: Weekly

Market Alert — *Business, Consumer*

Publishing Co: Blanchard & Co., 110 Veterans Blve. Suite #200, P.O. Box 61740, New Orleans, LA 70161-1740; Title Tel # (504) 837-3010 Title Fax # (504) 837-4884
General Info: Bi-monthly
Subscriptions: Indv. $78

Market Express — *Business*

Publishing Co: Corporate Relations Group/Gulf Atlanti Publishing, 1801 Lee Rd Ste 301, Winter Park, FL 32789-2165; Title Tel # (407) 628-5200 Title Fax # (407) 628-0807
Personnel: Publisher-R.E. Veitia, Editor-P. Charuhas, Circ. Mgr.-Joan Johns, Adv. Dir.-Jim Cassidy, Art Dir.-Mike Brahosky, Mktg. Dir.-Jack Rodriguez
Editorial Description: Stock tips on small-cap companies worldwide.
General Info: Yr. Est. 1984, Irregular, Trim Size-8½ x 11, 4 pages, 2 Color, Matte
Subscriptions: Indv. $149
Circulation: Total-110,000
Advertising: Inquire for rates. Accepts Inserts.
List Rental: List Management Co.: Manager: Roland Outar; Applied List Management, 1801 Lee Rd Ste 301, Winter Park, FL 32789-2165 Tel # (407) 628-5200, Fax # (407) 628-0807, Actives: $115/M
Printing Co: Altamonte Printing

Market Guide
Business

Publishing Co: Market Guide, Inc., 49 Glen Head Rd # 106, Glen Head, NY 11545-1413;
Title Tel # (516) 759-1253
Personnel: Publisher-Scott Emerich, Editor-Edward Vallar, Circ. Mgr.-Lauren Furst, Promotion Dir.-Jack Kemeny
Editorial Description: Fundamental & narrative financial information on 500 OTC cos.
General Info: (Formerly Unlisted Market Guide), Yr. Est. 1983, Weekly, Sheetfed press, 1,000 pages, ISSN: 0882-0775, No Color, Newsprint, Looseleaf
Subscriptions: Indv. $245
Circulation: Total-2,000

Market Insider Bulletin

Publishing Co: Evasona Co., Box 541, Thornhill, ON L3T 2C0 Canada; Title Tel # (416) 883-4843
Personnel: Editor-A. Jasansky, Circ. Mgr.-P. Jasansky
Editorial Description: Based on monitoring insider trades and investor's sentiments.
General Info: Yr. Est. 1981, Bi-weekly, Trim Size-8½ x 11, Mimeo press, 10 pages, 2 Color
Subscriptions: $4/copy
Circulation: Total-450

Market Logic

Publishing Co: Institute for Econometric Research, 3471 N. Federal Hwy., Ft. Lauderdale, FL 33306-1019; Title Tel # (305) 563-9000 Title Fax # (305) 563-9003
Personnel: Publisher-Glen Parker, Editor-Norman Fosback
Editorial Description: Stock market advisory service covering technical, fundamental & monetary. Indicators, specific stock recommendations, market timing & general investment advice.
General Info: Yr. Est. 1975, Semi-monthly, Trim Size-8½ x 11, Sheetfed press, 8 pages, ISSN: 0162-6817, No Color, Matte
Subscriptions: Indv. $200, Inst. $200, Can. $200, For. $245
Acquistions: Publication Bought, Publication Sold
List Rental: List Management Co.: JAMI Marketing, 2 Blue Hill Plz, Pearl River, NY 10965-3101 Tel # (914) 620-0700, Fax # (914) 620-1885, Actives: 14,346, $150/M, Expires: 28,886, $110/M

Market Mania Newsletter
Business

Publishing Co: Market Mania, PO Box 1234, Pacifica, CA 94044-6234; Title Tel # (415) 952-8853 Title Fax # (415) 952-0844
Personnel: Publisher, Editor-Glenn Cutler
Editorial Description: Specializes in environmental industry stocks, low-priced growth stocks with explosive potential, market timing, market commentary & hot-line.
General Info: Yr. Est. 1983, Monthly, 8 pages
Subscriptions: Indv. $119, Inst. $119, Can. $119, For. $132
Acquistions: Publication Bought

Market Mirror

Publishing Co: Market Mirror, 147-22 77th Rd., #204, Kew Gardens Hills, NY 11367; Title Tel # (212) 969-3904
Personnel: Editor-Noah Goldstein
General Info: Monthly
Subscriptions: Indv. $60

Market Screen

Publishing Co: Market Guide, Inc., 49 Glen Head Rd # 106, Glen Head, NY 11545-1413; Title Tel # (516) 759-1253
Personnel: Publisher-Scott Emerich, Editor-Edward Vallar, Circ. Mgr.-Lauren Furst
Editorial Description: Electronic data base of fundamental & narrative financial information on 5,000 OTC Cos.
General Info: Yr. Est. 1985, Daily

Market Timing Report
Business

Publishing Co: Market Timing Report, PO Box 225, Tucson, AZ 85702-0225 Tel # (520) 795-9552; Title Tel # (520) 624-6364
Personnel: Publisher, Editor-Ted Earle
Editorial Description: Investment recommendations for stocks, bonds & gold using mutual funds & future contracts.
General Info: Yr. Est. 1979, Monthly, Trim Size-8½ x 11, Mimeo press, 6 pages
Subscriptions: Indv. $100
Printing Co: Chedan Reproductions, 812 N Tyndall Ave, Tucson, AZ 85719-4829 Tel # (602) 882-0410

Market Vision
Business

Publishing Co: Market Vision, 2625 S. Roosevelt, Ste. 101, Tempe, AZ 85282
Personnel: Editor-Robert Millstone
Editorial Description: Showcases investment opportunities inf US and Canadian based small-cap public companies.
General Info: Quarterly, Trim Size-8½ x 11, 12 pages, Color, Coated, Saddle-stitched
Subscriptions: Indv. $80

MarketBrief Ratings
Business, Consumer

Publishing Co: Lovejoy Corporation, Box 1442, Palmer Sq., Princeton, NJ 08542-1442; Title Tel # (609) 989-9484 Title Fax # (609) 989-9484
Personnel: Publisher-Marie Pataky, Editor-David Luciano
Editorial Description: MarketBrief Ratings provides buy, sell, hold, and avoid ratings on optionable stocks and client stocks.
General Info: (Formerly MarketBrief), Yr. Est. 1982, Monthly, Trim Size-8½ x 11, 8 pages, ISSN: 0898-0799, Other
Subscriptions: Indv. $195, Inst. $195, Can. $195, For. $207, $19/copy

Marketarian Letter
Business

Publishing Co: Marketarian Inc., PO Box 1283, Grand Island, NE 68802-1283; Title Tel # (308) 381-2121 Title Fax # (308) 881-0930
Personnel: Editor-Jeff Helleberg
General Info: Yr. Est. 1981, 18x/yr.
Subscriptions: Indv. $225

Marketing Timing Report

Publishing Co: Marketing Timing Report, PO Box 225, Tucson, AZ 85702-0225; Title Tel # (602) 795-9552
General Info: Yr. Est. 1979, Monthly
Subscriptions: Indv. $100

Master Indicator of the Stock Market
Business, Consumer

Publishing Co: Master Indicator of the Stock Market, 11371 Torchwood Ct, West Palm Beach, FL 33414-6040
Personnel: Editor-John Goddess
General Info: Yr. Est. 1966, Semi-monthly
Subscriptions: Indv. $100
Circulation: Total-4,000
List Rental: List Management Co.: InfoMat, 1815 W 213th St Ste 210, Torrance, CA 90501-2839 Tel # (310) 212-5944, Fax # (310) 212-5773, Actives: 11,793, $125/M

Master Subscription
Business

Publishing Co: Argus Research Corp., 17 Battery Pl., New York, NY 10004-1101; Title Tel # (212) 425-7500 Title Fax # (212) 509-5408
Personnel: Editor-John Eade
Editorial Description: Independent equity research reports.
General Info: (Formerly Professional Investor Program), Weekly
Subscriptions: Indv. $2,500
Printing Co: Argus Printing & Mailing, 226 New York Ave, Huntington, NY 11743-2748 Tel # (516) 423-7710

McAlvany Intelligence Advisor
Business

Publishing Co: Publishers Management Co., PO Box 84900, Phoenix, AZ 85071-4900; Title Tel # (602) 252-4477
Personnel: Editor-Don McAlvany, Circ. Mgr.-John Johnson, Production Mgr.-Pat Derr
Editorial Description: Analysis of global, economic and monetary trends impacting investments.
General Info: (Formerly Gold and Monetary Report), Yr. Est. 1977, Monthly, Trim Size-8½ x 11, Sheetfed press, 8 pages, No Color, Newsprint
Subscriptions: Indv. $95, $5/copy
Advertising: Accepts Inserts.
List Rental: List Management Co.: Carnegie Marketing Assocs., Koll Executive Plaza, 3878 Carson St., Suite 220, Torrance, CA 90503 Tel # (310) 540-4757, Fax # (310) 540-7407
Printing Co: Runbeck Graphics, 3101 N Central Ave Ste 490, Phoenix, AZ 85012-2638 Tel # (602) 230-0510

McClellan Market Report, The
Business, Consumer

Publishing Co: McClellan Financial Publications, Inc., P.O. Box 4126, Glendale, CA 91222-0126; Title Tel # (818) 243-7119 Title Fax # (213) 687-4298
Personnel: Publisher-Sherman McClellan, Editor-Tom McClellan
Editorial Description: Covers unique uses of technical analysis to forecast future stock market action.
General Info: Yr. Est. 1995, Semi-monthly, Trim Size-8½ x 11, 80 pages, No Color, Matte
Subscriptions: Indv. $195, Can. $195, For. $235

McShane Letter
Business

Publishing Co: Donald B. McShane, 155 E. 55th St., New York, NY 10022-4072; Title Tel # (212) 688-2387
Personnel: Publisher, Editor-Donald McShane
Editorial Description: International economic advisory letter with emphasis on banking credit & investments.
General Info: Yr. Est. 1970, Monthly, 4 pages, 2 Color
Subscriptions: Indv. $150, $8/copy
Circulation: Total-3,000
List Rental: Actives: $145/M

Medical Technology Stock Letter
Business, Consumer

Publishing Co: Piedmont Venture Group, PO Box 40460, Berkeley, CA 94704-4460 Tel # (510) 843-1842; Title Tel # (510) 843-1857 Title Fax # (510) 843-0901
Personnel: Publisher-John McCamant, Editor-Jim McCamant, Circ. Mgr.-Michelle Adams
Editorial Description: Stock recommendation & discussion of medical biotechnology.
General Info: Yr. Est. 1983, Bi-weekly, 8 pages, ISSN: 1065-996X
Subscriptions: Indv. $320, For. $350

Meeting Monitor
See: MANAGEMENT

Mergers & Acquisitions
Report
Business

Publishing Co: IDD Enterprises, 2 World Trade Ctr. 18th Fl., New York, NY 10048-0203
Fax # (212) 321-2336 Parent Co.-Dow Jones & Co., Inc., New York; Title Tel # (212) 227-1200
Personnel: Editor-Clint Winstead, Circ. Mgr.-Philip M. McGee, Production Mgr.-Maxine Margolese, Adv. Dir.-Mattie Reyes, Mktg. Dir.-Janice Fellagera
Editorial Description: Corporate mergers, buyouts, and business restructuring.
General Info: Yr. Est. 1988, Weekly, Offset press, 12 pages, Ind/Abs/Online: Predicasts, 2 Color, Saddle-stitched
Subscriptions: Indv. $980
Advertising: $2,300. Accepts Inserts.
Printing Co: Dealers Digest, 2 World Trade Ctr., New York, NY 10048 Tel # (212) 227-1200

Merrill Lynch Market Letter

Publishing Co: Merrill Lynch, North Tower, World Trade Center, New York, NY 10281-1215
Tel # (212) 637-1960; Title Tel # (212) 637-5196
Editorial Description: Investment advisory service, primarily stocks.
General Info: Yr. Est. 1976, Semi-monthly
Circulation: Total-60,000

Merrill Lynch Stockfinder
Research Service

Publishing Co: Merrill Lynch, North Tower, World Trade Center, New York, NY 10281-1215
Tel # (212) 637-1960; Title Tel # (212) 766-5196
Personnel: Mng. Editor-Jerry Fischer
General Info: Yr. Est. 1982, Monthly
Subscriptions: Indv. $98

Metal Cycles
Business

Publishing Co: Mull Pubs., PO Box 11133, Indianapolis, IN 46201-0133; Title Tel # (317) 357-6855
Title Fax # (317) 353-6246
Personnel: Editor-Carol Mull
Editorial Description: Short-term price forecasts of aluminum, tin, zinc, nickel, copper, silver, lead, palladium, gold, and platinum based on cycles.
General Info: Yr. Est. 1994, Monthly, Trim Size-$8\frac{1}{2}$ x 11, 2 pages, No Color
Subscriptions: Indv. $150, $15/copy
Printing Co: Mull Publishing, PO Box 11133, Indianapolis, IN 46201-0133 Tel # (317) 353-6246

Mexico Update
Business

Publishing Co: United Communications Group, 11300 Rockville Pike, Ste. 1100, Rockville, MD 20852-3030 Tel # (301) 816-8950 Fax # (301) 816-8945
Editorial Description: News relating to Mexican finance, economics and politics.
General Info: Bi-weekly
Subscriptions: Indv. $270

Middle/Fixed Income
Letter
Consumer

Publishing Co: MASTCA Publishing Corp., PO Box 55, Loch Sheldrake, NY 12759-0055;
Title Tel # (914) 794-5793
Personnel: Publisher, Editor-Joel Lerner
Editorial Description: For the middle income person who does not understand finances.
General Info: Yr. Est. 1981, Monthly, Letrpr. press, 4 pages, No Color, Coated
Subscriptions: Indv. $34
Advertising: Inquire for rates.
List Rental: List Management Co.: WMI/Worldata, 5200 Town Center Circle, Boca Raton, FL 33486 Tel # (407) 393-8200, Fax # (407) 368-8345, Actives: 25,000, $85/M

Mike Segal's Commodity
Advisory

Publishing Co: Mike Segal's Commodity Advisory, 11 E. 86th St., #19B, New York, NY 10028-0548;
Title Tel # (212) 406-0211
Editorial Description: Timely commodity market information.
General Info: Yr. Est. 1982, 24x/yr.
Subscriptions: Indv. $185

Mitchell Report, The

Publishing Co: Los Angeles Stamp Collector, Box 1387, Hollywood, CA 90078;
Title Tel # (213) 467-2215
Personnel: Editor-Gretchen Mitchell
General Info: Yr. Est. 1984, Monthly

Monetary & Economic
Review
Consumer

Publishing Co: First American Monetary & Economic Review, 3500 JFK Pkwy., Ft. Collins, CO 80525; Title Tel # (303) 223-4962 Title Fax # (303) 223-4996
Personnel: Publisher, Editor-Larry Bates, Circ. Mgr.-Cheryl Olthoff, Production Mgr.-Marilyn Brannon, Art Dir.-Lisa Cole
Editorial Description: Analyzes over 20 markets from economic & political perspective.
General Info: (Formerly First American Monetary & Economic Review), Yr. Est. 1984, Monthly, Trim Size-11 x 17, Mimeo press, 16 pages, 2 Color, Newsprint
Subscriptions: Indv. $150
Circulation: Total-5,000
List Rental: Expires: $70/M

Monetary Digest

Publishing Co: Certified Mint, 3550 N Central Ave Ste 705, Phoenix, AZ 85012-2109;
Title Tel # (602) 234-2300
Personnel: Editor-William Haynes
Editorial Description: Covers economic, political, and social developments that affect the prices of precious metals.
General Info: Yr. Est. 1974, Monthly
Subscriptions: Indv. $36
Circulation: Total-7,000

Monetary Outlook, The
Business

Publishing Co: Monetary Outlook, PO Box 476, Leonia, NJ 07605-0476
General Info: Monthly

Money Management
Letter
Business

Publishing Co: Capital Cities/ABC, 488 Madison Ave., 16th Floor, New York, NY 10022-5751 Parent Co.-Capital Cities/ABC, Inc., New York; Title Tel # (212) 224-3233 Title Fax # (212) 224-3353
Personnel: Publisher-Linda Litner, Editor-Tom Lamont, Circ. Dir.-Gladys Delgado, Production Dir.-Susan Drobney, Adv. Dir.-Pat Bertucci, Mktg. Dir.-Dahlia Weinman
Editorial Description: Serves as a vital information resource for professionals involved in U.S. pension fund management. Each issue reports on new strategies and investment products, pension fund searches, performance measurement, developing markets and important personnel changes.
General Info: Yr. Est. 1977, Bi-weekly, Trim Size-$8\frac{1}{2}$ x 11, Sheetfed press, 16 pages, Ind/Abs/Online: Lexis/Nexis news service, 2 Color, Newsprint
Subscriptions: Indv. $1,295, Can. $1,325, For. $1,370, $55/copy
Advertising: Inquire for rates.

Money Manager's
Compliance Advisor
Business

Publishing Co: Thompson Publishing Group, 1725 K Street, NW, Washington, DC 20006
Tel # (202) 872-4000
Editorial Description: Compliance guide to SEC regulations of investment.
General Info: Monthly

Money Paper, The
Business, Association

Publishing Co: Temper of the Times, 1010 Mamaroneck Ave, Mamaroneck, NY 10543-1632;
Title Tel # (914) 381-5400 Title Fax # (914) 381-7206
Personnel: Publisher, Editor-Vita Nelson, Editor-Adriana Perez, Circ. Mgr.-Lucy Bank, Promotion Dir.-Maria Blasi
General Info: Yr. Est. 1982, Monthly, Web press, 12 pages
Subscriptions: Indv. $72
Printing Co: Star Press, P.O. Box 748, Holyoke, MA 01040-4994 Tel # (413) 532-7091

Money Reporter
Business, Consumer

Publishing Co: MPL Communications, Inc., 133 Richmond St. W., Ste. 700, Toronto, ON M5H 3M8 Canada; Title Tel # (416) 869-1177 Title Fax # (416) 869-0456
Personnel: Publisher-Barrie Martland, Publisher-Steve Pepper, Editor-Marc Johnson, Circ. Mgr.-David Berger
Editorial Description: The insider's letter for people whose interest is earning more investment income and paying less tax.
General Info: Yr. Est. 1977, Bi-weekly, Trim Size-$8\frac{1}{2}$ x 11, Sheetfed press, 8 pages, ISSN: 0709-0579, 2 Color, Matte
Subscriptions: Indv. $197
List Rental: Actives: $130/M

Money Talks
See: BANKING & FINANCE

MoneyLetter, The
Consumer

Publishing Co: Hume Publishing Company Ltd., Suite 515, 4100 Yonge St., Willowdale, ON M2P 2B9 Canada; Title Tel # (416) 221-4596 Title Fax # (416) 221-4968
Personnel: Editor in Chief-Gordon Pape, Publisher, Editorial Dir.-A. Michael Keerma, Circ. Mgr.-Robin Young, Mktg. Dir.-Barbara Ritchie
Editorial Description: Canada's leading investment advisory newsletter with advice and recommendations on stocks, bonds, and mutual funds, RRSPs from some Canada's top investment experts.
General Info: Yr. Est. 1976, Semi-monthly, Trim Size-$8\frac{1}{2}$ x 11, Sheetfed press, 8 pages, ISSN: 0703-7613, 2 Color, Matte
Subscriptions: Indv. $97, $10/copy
List Rental: List Management Co.: Herbert A. Watts, 455 Horner Ave., Toronto, ON M8W 4W9 Canada Tel # (416) 252-7741

Moneychanger, The
Business, Consumer

Publishing Co: Moneychanger, PO Box 1753, Memphis, TN 38101-1753; Title Tel # (901) 853-6136
Personnel: Editor-Franklin Sanders
Editorial Description: Covers methods to help Christians prosper with their principles intact in an era of monetary & moral chaos.
General Info: (Formerly Gold & Silver Update), Yr. Est. 1980, Monthly, Trim Size-$11\frac{1}{2}$ x $14\frac{1}{2}$, Web press, 8 pages, No Color, Newsprint
Subscriptions: Indv. $95
Acquisitions: Publication Sold
Advertising: Accepts Inserts.
List Rental: Actives: $245/M, Expires: $245/M

Monthly Statistics/Open-End Investment Companies Trends
Business, Association

Publishing Co: Investment Company Institute, 1401 H St. NW, Ste. 1200, Washington, DC 20005-2148 Tel # (202) 326-5800; Title Tel # (202) 293-7700
Personnel: Editor-Betty Hart
Editorial Description: Statistics on mutual fund sales, exchanges, assets, cash holdings and total portfolio transactions for the current month, previous month and a year ago.
General Info: (Formerly Trends in Mutual Fund Activity), Monthly, Trim Size-8$\frac{1}{2}$ x 11, Mimeo press, 6 pages, No Color
Subscriptions: Indv. $120

Monthly Stock Charts Canadian Companies

Publishing Co: Independent Survey Co., Box 6000, Vancouver, BC V6B 4B9 Canada; Title Tel # (604) 689-5795
Personnel: Publisher-Michael Den Hertog
General Info: Yr. Est. 1984, Quarterly

Moody's Global Short-Term Market Record

Publishing Co: Moody's Investors Service, Inc., 99 Church St., New York, NY 10007-2787 Tel # (212) 553-0300 Fax # (212) 553-4700 Parent Co.-Dun & Bradstreet, Wilton; Title Tel # (212) 553-4778
Editorial Description: Presents up-to-date information on all short-term instruments rated by Moody's. Designed to facilitate investment decisions in such instruments, this service consists of a monthly reference & statistical issue, as well as a quarterly analytical supplemen . Coverage in the service extends to commercial paper, bank certificates of deposit, third-party supported & structured short-term instruments th
General Info: Monthly, ISSN: 0888-5915

Moody's Monthly Short-Term Market Record
Business

Publishing Co: Moody's Investors Service, Inc., 99 Church St., New York, NY 10007-2787 Fax # (212) 553-4700 Parent Co.-Dun & Bradstreet, Wilton; Title Tel # (212) 553-0300
Personnel: Publisher-Sheila Lambert, Adv. Dir.-Eve Kram
Editorial Description: Statistical data on domestic & foreign short-term issues rated by Moody's.
General Info: (Formerly Moody's Commercial Paper Record, Section 1), Monthly, Offset press, 80 pages, Looseleaf
Circulation: (100% controlled), Total-15,000
Printing Co: R.R. Donnelley & Sons Company, 216 Greenfield Rd., Lancaster, PA 17601-2612 Tel # (717) 392-4074

Morningstar Closed-End Funds
Business, Consumer

Publishing Co: Morningstar, Inc., 225 W. Wacker Dr., Chicago, IL 60604-3606 Tel # (312) 696-6000 Fax # (312) 696-6001
Personnel: Publisher-Don Phillips, Editor-Catherine Gillis, Mktg. Dir.-Kurt Herrman
Editorial Description: Provides data and analysis investors need to make informed decisions about closed-end funds.
General Info: Yr. Est. 1991, Bi-weekly, ISSN: 1059-1419
Subscriptions: Indv. $195, Can. $225, For. $275
Circulation: Total-7,000

Morningstar Investor
Consumer

Publishing Co: Morningstar, Inc., 225 W. Wacker Dr., Chicago, IL 60604-3606 Tel # (312) 696-6000 Fax # (312) 696-6001
Personnel: Publisher-Don Phillips, Editor-Kyle Purcell, Mktg. Dir.-Kurt Herrman
Editorial Description: Gives statistics, news and advice needed to build a winning fund portfolio.
General Info: (Formerly 5-Star Investor), Yr. Est. 1992, Monthly, Trim Size-8$\frac{1}{2}$ x 11, 40 pages, ISSN: 1065-3414
Subscriptions: Indv. $65
Circulation: Total-50,000

Morningstar Mutual Funds
Business

Publishing Co: Morningstar, Inc., 225 W. Wacker Dr., Chicago, IL 60604-3606; Title Tel # (312) 696-6000 Title Fax # (312) 696-6001
Personnel: Publisher-Don Phillips, Editor-John Rekenthaler, Mng. Editor-Patty Dutile, Mktg. Dir.-Kurt Herrman
Editorial Description: Provides the data and analysis investors need to make informed decisions about mutual funds.
General Info: Yr. Est. 1986, Bi-weekly, Trim Size-8$\frac{1}{2}$ x 11, 150 pages, ISSN: 0890-7153
Subscriptions: Indv. $395
Circulation: Total-40,000
List Rental: List Management Co.: Manager: Rick Snyder; Marketing Services Intl., 625 N Michigan Ave Ste 1920, Chicago, IL 60611-3109 Tel # (312) 642-1620, Fax # (312) 642-0679, Actives: 55,231

Mortgage-Backed Securities Letter
Business

Publishing Co: IDD Enterprises, 2 World Trade Ctr. 18th Fl., New York, NY 10048-0203 Fax # (212) 321-2336 Parent Co.-Dow Jones & Co., Inc., New York; Title Tel # (212) 227-1200
Personnel: Editor-Clint Winstead, Circ. Mgr.-Philip M. McGee, Production Mgr.-Maxine Margoles, Adv. Dir.-Mattie Reyes, Mktg. Dir.-Janice Fellagera
Editorial Description: Information on the structured finance markets.
General Info: Yr. Est. 1990, Weekly, Offset press, 12 pages, 2 Color, Matte, Saddle-stitched
Subscriptions: Indv. $1,395
Advertising: $2,300.

Mortgage Bank Weekly
See: BANKING & FINANCE

Motion Picture Investor
See: FILM

Muni Bond Fund Report
Business, Consumer

Publishing Co: Greystone Media Services, Inc., PO Box 2947, Woburn, MA 01888-1747; Title Tel # (617) 721-4511
Personnel: Editor-R.G. Norton
Editorial Description: Municipal Bond fund news.
General Info: Yr. Est. 1986, Monthly
Subscriptions: Indv. $95
List Rental: List Management Co.: Carnegie Marketing Assocs., Koll Executive Plaza, 3878 Carson St., Suite 220, Torrance, CA 90503 Tel # (310) 540-4757, Fax # (310) 540-7407, Actives: 9,215, $95/M

Mutual Fund Advisor
Business, Association

Publishing Co: Wall Street Digest, One Sarasota Tower, Ste. 602, 2 N. Tamiami Trail, Sarasota, FL 34236; Title Tel # (813) 954-5500 Title Fax # (813) 364-8447
Personnel: Publisher, Editor-Donald Rowe
Editorial Description: Mutual Fund information and strategies.
General Info: Yr. Est. 1989, Monthly, Trim Size-8$\frac{1}{2}$ x 11, 12 pages, ISSN: 1050-656X
Subscriptions: Indv. $150, $13/copy
Circulation: Total-25,000
List Rental: List Management Co.: Carnegie Marketing Assocs., Koll Executive Plaza, 3878 Carson St., Suite 220, Torrance, CA 90503 Tel # (310) 540-4757, Fax # (310) 540-7407, Actives: 33,346, $155/M
Printing Co: Andrick & Associates, 4152 Independence Court, Sarasota, FL 32434 Tel # (813) 351-6565

Mutual Fund Analyst

Publishing Co: Mutual Fund Analyst, 16212 Bothell-Everett Highway, #F147, Mill Creek, WA 98012; Title Tel # (206) 337-1195
Editorial Description: Analysis of mutual fund performance, etc.
General Info: Yr. Est. 1990, Monthly
Subscriptions: Indv. $99

Mutual Fund Buyer's Guide

Publishing Co: Institute for Econometric Research, 3471 N. Federal Hwy., Ft. Lauderdale, FL 33306-1019; Title Tel # (305) 563-9000 Title Fax # (305) 563-9003
Editorial Description: Comprehensive, low-cost source of information on more than 1,500 funds. Covers all major stock, bond, and tax-free funds, including all-star ratings, up and down ranking, safety and performance ratings, and much more.
General Info: Yr. Est. 1992, Monthly, ISSN: 1067-1358
Subscriptions: Indv. $80, Inst. $80, Can. $80, For. $110
List Rental: Rents Lists

Mutual Fund Forecaster
Business

Publishing Co: Institute for Econometric Research, 3471 N. Federal Hwy., Ft. Lauderdale, FL 33306-1019; Title Tel # (305) 563-9000 Title Fax # (305) 563-9003
Personnel: Publisher-Glen Parker, Editor-Norman Fosback
Editorial Description: Profit projections & risk ratings for over 500 mutual funds.
General Info: Yr. Est. 1984, Monthly, Trim Size-8$\frac{1}{2}$ x 11, Web press, 12 pages, ISSN: 8755-9889, Color-cover, Newsprint, Saddle-stitched
Subscriptions: Indv. $100, Inst. $100, Can. $100, For. $130, $10/copy
Acquisitions: Publication Bought, Publication Sold
List Rental: List Management Co.: JAMI Marketing, 2 Blue Hill Plz, Pearl River, NY 10965-3101 Tel # (914) 620-0700, Fax # (914) 620-1885, Actives: 170,078, $145/M, Expires: 167,772, $85/M

Mutual Fund Investing
Business

Publishing Co: Phillips Publishing, Inc., 7811 Montrose Rd., Potomac, MD 20854-3394 Parent Co.-Phillips Business Information, Inc., Potomac; Title Tel # (301) 340-2100 Title Fax # (301) 294-1307
Personnel: Publisher-Thomas Phillips, Editor-Jay Schabacker, Mktg. Dir.-Nancy Cathey
Editorial Description: Mutual Fund Investing provides monthly investment advice. Editor Jay Schabacker guides subscribers in building portfolios from low risk, high performance, no-load mutual funds.
General Info: (Formerly Jay Schabacker's Mutual Fund Investing), Yr. Est. 1985, Monthly, 8 pages, ISSN: 8756-5161, 2 Color, Matte
Subscriptions: Indv. $99
Acquistions: Publication Bought, Publication Sold
List Rental: List Management Co.: Manager: John Baldwin; Phillips Publishing List Marketing, 7811 Montrose Rd., Potomac, MD 20854-3394 Tel # (301) 340-2100, Fax # (301) 294-1307, Actives: 39,337, $195/M, Expires: 34,307, $95/M

Mutual Fund Letter
Business, Consumer

Publishing Co: Investment Information Services, Inc., 680 North Lake Shore Drive, Ste. #2038, Chicago, IL 60611-4402; Title Tel # (312) 649-6940 Title Fax # (312) 649-5537
Personnel: Publisher, Editor-Gerald Perritt, Circ. Mgr.-Julie Ann Johnson, Promotion Dir.-Michael Corbett
General Info: Yr. Est. 1984, Monthly, Trim Size-8$\frac{1}{2}$ x 11, 12 pages
Subscriptions: Indv. $125
Printing Co: Merrill Corp., 650 W Washington Blvd, Chicago, IL 60661-2117

Mutual Fund Performance and Review

Publishing Co: CAMFOR, PO Box 1423, Baltimore, MD 21203-1423; Title Tel # (410) 235-0983 Title Fax # (410) 558-1699
Personnel: Publisher-Fred Labyak, Editor-Robert Czeschin
General Info: (Formerly Mutual Funds Outlook & Recommendations), Yr. Est. 1986, Monthly, Trim Size-8½ x 11, 8 pages
Subscriptions: Indv. $149, $5/copy

Mutual Fund Specialist

Publishing Co: Royal R. LeMier & Co., S7720 State Rd. 37, Eau Claire, WI 54701-9075; Title Tel # (715) 834-7425
Personnel: Publisher, Editor-Royal Le Mier
Editorial Description: Emphasis on family of funds concept to mutual fund investing.
General Info: Yr. Est. 1978, Monthly, Trim Size-8½ x 11, 16 pages
Subscriptions: Indv. $95
List Rental: List Management Co.: JAMI Marketing, 2 Blue Hill Plz, Pearl River, NY 10965-3101 Tel # (914) 620-0700, Fax # (914) 620-1885, Actives: 17,274, $85/M

Mutual Fund Strategist   *Business*

Publishing Co: Mutual Fund Strategist, PO Box 446, Burlington, VT 05402-0446; Title Tel # (802) 658-3513
Personnel: Publisher, Editor-Charlie Hooper
Editorial Description: Provides market timing signals for U.S., Intl. & Bond Mutual Funds.
General Info: Yr. Est. 1982, Monthly
Subscriptions: Indv. $149

Mutual Fund Trends   *Business, Consumer*

Publishing Co: Growth Fund Research, Inc., PO Box 6600, Rapid City, SD 57709-6600; Title Tel # (605) 341-1971
Personnel: Publisher-Walter Rouleau, Editor-William Rouleau
Editorial Description: Each issue provides 52 pages of statistics & weekly basis charts with multiple moving averages & relative strength lines for about 200 leading no-load funds, major averages & top notch indicators. Plus a weekly telephone hotline.
General Info: (Formerly Mutual Fund Chartist), Yr. Est. 1985, Monthly, Trim Size-6 x 9, Web press, 52 pages, No Color, Saddle-stitched
Subscriptions: Indv. $139, Can. $144, For. $189, $15/copy

Mutual Funds Guide   *Business*

Publishing Co: CCH, Inc., 2700 Lake Cook Rd., Riverwoods, IL 60015 Parent Co.-Kluwer Law & Taxation Publishers, Cambridge; Title Tel # (847) 267-7000 Title Fax # (800) 224-8299
Editorial Description: Covers fedral and state rules governing mutual funds.
General Info: Yr. Est. 1969, Bi-weekly, Trim Size-6 x 9, Web press, 100 pages, No Color, Looseleaf
Subscriptions: Indv. $767

Mutual Funds Scoreboard

Publishing Co: Mutual Funds Scoreboard, 6 Deer Trl, Old Tappan, NJ 07675-7125
General Info: Quarterly
Subscriptions: Indv. $15

NAIC Investor Advisory Service   *Business*

Publishing Co: Natl. Assn. of Investors Corp., PO Box 220, Royal Oak, MI 48068-0220; Title Tel # (810) 583-6242 Title Fax # (810) 583-4880
Editorial Description: Reports on 3 stocks in the buy range.
General Info: Monthly
Subscriptions: Indv. $125
Circulation: Total-3,000

NARI Stethoscope
See: MEDICINE

NASAA Reports   *Business*

Publishing Co: CCH, Inc., 2700 Lake Cook Rd., Riverwoods, IL 60015 Parent Co.-Kluwer Law & Taxation Publishers, Cambridge; Title Tel # (847) 267-7000 Title Fax # (800) 224-8299
Editorial Description: Provides timely coverage of materials from the North American Securities Adminstrators Association, Inc.
General Info: Irregular, Looseleaf
Subscriptions: Indv. $319

NASD Regulatory & Compliance Alert   *Association*

Publishing Co: Natl. Assn. of Securities Dealers, Inc., 1735 K St., N.W., Washington, DC 20006-1500 Tel # (202) 728-8000 Fax # (202) 293-6260; Title Tel # (202) 728-8474 Title Fax # (202) 728-8882
Personnel: Publisher-Margo Porter, Editor-Richard DeLouise
Editorial Description: To help members avoid rule violations by publishing recent regulotory rules interpretations, decisions, legislation, and NASD disciplinary actions.
General Info: Yr. Est. 1987, Trim Size-8½ x 11, 20 pages
Subscriptions: Indv. $80, Free With Membership
Circulation: Total-40,000
Printing Co: Hennage Creative Printers, 500 N Henry St, Alexandria, VA 22314-2233 Tel # (703) 683-8282

NASDAQ   *Business, Association*

Publishing Co: Natl. Assn. of Securities Dealers, Inc., 1735 K St., N.W., Washington, DC 20006-1500 Tel # (202) 728-8000 Fax # (202) 293-6260; Title Tel # (202) 728-6900 Title Fax # (202) 728-8882
Personnel: Publisher-Margo Porter, Editor-Jean R. Curtiss, Production Mgr.-Sharonine Lippercott
Editorial Description: Informs NASDAQ subscribers (securities traders) of developments in the NASDAQ market & of enhancements to the NASDAQ system.
General Info: (Formerly NASDAQ Subscriber Bulletin), Yr. Est. 1984, Bi-monthly, Sheetfed press, 6 pages, 2 Color, Saddle-stitched
Subscriptions: Indv. $80, $15/copy
Printing Co: Hennage Creative Printers, 500 N Henry St, Alexandria, VA 22314-2233 Tel # (703) 683-8282

NIS Equity Research Service   *Business*

Publishing Co: Northfield Information Services, Inc., 184 High St., Boston, MA 02110-3001; Title Tel # (617) 536-5340
General Info: Yr. Est. 1988, 26x/yr.

NQB Pink Sheets for Equities   *Business*

Publishing Co: Natl. Quotation Bureau, Inc., 150 Commerce Rd., Cedar Grove, NJ 07009-1208; Title Tel # (201) 239-6100 Title Fax # (201) 239-0080
Personnel: VP Editorial-Evelyn Walsh, Mng. Editor-Joann Lorgan
Editorial Description: Lists foreign & domestic securities with bid & asked prices of dealer firms. Lists global ADRs. Sold jointly with NQB Yellow Sheets.
General Info: (Formerly National Daily Quotation Service), Daily, Looseleaf
Subscriptions: Indv. $852, $25/copy
Circulation: Total-2,000

NQB Yellow Sheets for Taxable Bonds   *Business*

Publishing Co: Natl. Quotation Bureau, Inc., 150 Commerce Rd., Cedar Grove, NJ 07009-1208; Title Tel # (201) 239-6100 Title Fax # (201) 239-0080
Personnel: VP Editorial-Evelyn Walsh, Mng. Editor-Joann Lorgan
Editorial Description: Lists domestic and foreign securities with bid and asked prices of dealer firms. Sold jointly with NQB Pink Sheets.
General Info: Daily, Looseleaf
Subscriptions: Indv. $852, $25/copy
Circulation: Total-2,000

NYSE-Weekly Stock Buys   *Business, Association*

Publishing Co: Elton Stephens Investments, 4016 S Michigan St, South Bend, IN 46614-2544; Title Tel # (219) 291-3823 Title Fax # (219) 291-3823
Personnel: Editor-Elton Stephens
Editorial Description: List of Blue Chip income & growth stocks.
General Info: Yr. Est. 1991, Weekly, Trim Size-8½ x 11, Offset press, 1 pages, ISSN: 1060-6629
Subscriptions: $10/copy
Acquistions: Publication Sold
Circulation: Total-4,000
Advertising: Inquire for rates. Accepts Inserts.
List Rental: Rents Lists

Nasdaq and Regiora Exchange Stock Reports   *Business*

Publishing Co: Standard & Poor's Corp., 25 Broadway, New York, NY 10004 Parent Co.-McGraw-Hill, New York; Title Tel # (212) 208-8000 Title Fax # (212) 206-1161
Personnel: Publisher-Ronald Oliver, Mng. Editor-Richard Albanese
Editorial Description: Details reports on Nasdaq most active issues.
General Info: (Formerly Over-The-Counter Stock Reports), Yr. Est. 1934, Daily, 2 pages, Looseleaf
Subscriptions: Indv. $1,325, $14/copy

Ned Davis Research - Stock Market Strategy   *Business*

Publishing Co: Ned Davis Research, PO Box 1287, Nokomis, FL 34274-1287
Personnel: Editor-Tim Hayes
Editorial Description: Stock market advice and information.
General Info: Weekly

Netback   *Business, Consumer*

Publishing Co: Good Money Publications, Inc., PO Box 363, Worcester, VT 05682-0363; Title Tel # (800) 535-3551 Title Fax # (802) 223-8949
Personnel: Publisher-Ritchie P. Lowry
General Info: Yr. Est. 1982, Bi-monthly, 8 pages, ISSN: 0742-4507
Subscriptions: Indv. $75, Can. $83, For. $90
Advertising: Inquire for rates.

New Issue Digest   *Business*

Publishing Co: Growth Stock Outlook, Inc., 4405 East West Hwy Ste 305, Bethesda, MD 20814-4534; Title Tel # (301) 654-5205
Personnel: Publisher, Editor-Charles Allmon
Editorial Description: Covers the new issue stock market.
General Info: Yr. Est. 1971, Quarterly, 12 pages
Subscriptions: Indv. $50

New Issues   *Business*

Publishing Co: Institute for Econometric Research, 3471 N. Federal Hwy., Ft. Lauderdale, FL 33306-1019; Title Tel # (305) 563-9000 Title Fax # (305) 563-9003
Personnel: Publisher-Glen Parker, Editor-Norman Fosback
Editorial Description: Investor's guide to initial public offerings. Calendar of all forthcoming offerings, specific buy and sell recommendations.
General Info: Yr. Est. 1978, Monthly, Trim Size-8½ x 11, Sheetfed press, 6 pages, ISSN: 0162-9050, Color-cover, Newsprint
Subscriptions: Indv. $200, Inst. $200, Can. $200, For. $230
Acquistions: Publication Bought, Publication Sold
List Rental: List Management Co.: JAMI Marketing, 2 Blue Hill Plz, Pearl River, NY 10965-3101 Tel # (914) 620-0700, Fax # (914) 620-1885, Actives: 2,272, $150/M, Expires: 14,945, $110/M

New York Futures
Exchange   *Business*

Publishing Co: CCH, Inc., 2700 Lake Cook Rd., Riverwoods, IL 60015 Parent Co.-Kluwer Law & Taxation Publishers, Cambridge; Title Tel # (847) 267-7000 Title Fax # (800) 224-8299
Editorial Description: Directory & rule of the NYFEX.
General Info: Monthly, Trim Size-6 x 9, 32 pages, No Color, Looseleaf
Subscriptions: Indv. $367

New York Mercantile
Exchange   *Business*

Publishing Co: CCH, Inc., 2700 Lake Cook Rd., Riverwoods, IL 60015 Parent Co.-Kluwer Law & Taxation Publishers, Cambridge; Title Tel # (847) 267-7000 Title Fax # (800) 224-8299
Editorial Description: Directory & rules of the NYME. Published for NYMEX.
General Info: Monthly, Trim Size-6 x 9, 64 pages, No Color, Looseleaf
Subscriptions: Indv. $286

New York Stock Exchange
Guide   *Business*

Publishing Co: CCH, Inc., 2700 Lake Cook Rd., Riverwoods, IL 60015 Parent Co.-Kluwer Law & Taxation Publishers, Cambridge; Title Tel # (847) 267-7000 Title Fax # (800) 224-8299
Personnel: Editor-Ed Hanlon
Editorial Description: Directory, constitution, rules and SEC related material.
General Info: Yr. Est. 1957, Monthly, Trim Size-6 x 9, Web press, 112 pages, No Color, Looseleaf
Subscriptions: Indv. $589

New York Stock Exchange
Reports   *Business*

Publishing Co: Standard & Poor's Corp., 25 Broadway, New York, NY 10004 Parent Co.-McGraw-Hill, New York; Title Tel # (212) 208-8000 Title Fax # (212) 412-0299
Personnel: Publisher-Ronald Oliver, Mng. Editor-Richard Albanese
Editorial Description: Details financial reports on all NYSE- listed companies.
General Info: Yr. Est. 1933, Daily, 2 pages, Looseleaf
Subscriptions: Indv. $1,418, $14/copy
Circulation: Total-1,540

News & Offerings   *Consumer*

Publishing Co: Gabriele Hueglin & Cashman, 44 Wall St, New York, NY 10005-2488; Title Tel # (212) 225-7167
Personnel: Editor-Lauren Eastwood
Editorial Description: Special emphasis on tax exempts for clients.
General Info: Yr. Est. 1980, Monthly, Trim Size-8½ x 11, 4 pages
Circulation: (100% controlled), Total-20,000

News from ICSID   *Business*

Publishing Co: International Centre for the Settlement of Investment Disput, 1818 H St NW, Washington, DC 20433-0001 Tel # (202) 458-1533; Title Tel # (202) 477-1234 Title Fax # (202) 477-1269
Personnel: Editor-Francis Hamilton
Editorial Description: Provides current nformation on ICSID's arbitration, conciliation & other activities.
General Info: Yr. Est. 1984, Semi-annually, Trim Size-8½ x 11, 15 pages, 2 Color, Saddle-stitched
Subscriptions: Free
Circulation: (100% controlled), Total-4,000

News for Investors   *Business*

Publishing Co: Investor Responsibility Research Ctr., 1350 Connecticut Ave. N.W., Suite 700, Washington, DC 20036-1701 Fax # (202) 833-3555; Title Tel # (202) 833-0700
Personnel: Editor-Carolyn Mathinson, Mktg. Dir.-John McMahon
Editorial Description: Developments affecting corporate social responsibility.
General Info: Yr. Est. 1974, 11x/yr.
Subscriptions: Indv. $200
Circulation: Total-1,500

Newsletter Digest   *Business*

Publishing Co: Newsletter Digest, 2201 Big Cove Rd SE, Huntsville, AL 35801-1349; Title Tel # (205) 534-1535 Title Fax # (205) 533-4871
Personnel: Editor-Dr. Al Owen
Editorial Description: Concise abstracts of the leading investment, economic newsletters, with commentary.
General Info: Yr. Est. 1979, Bi-monthly, Trim Size-8½ x 11, Offset press, 8 pages, No Color
Subscriptions: Indv. $75, $3/copy
Circulation: Total-3,000
List Rental: List Management Co.: Carnegie Marketing Assocs., Koll Executive Plaza, 3878 Carson St., Suite 220, Torrance, CA 90503 Tel # (310) 540-4757, Fax # (310) 540-7407, Actives: 12,440, $85/M

Newspaper Investor   *Business*

Publishing Co: Paul Kagan Associates Inc., 126 Clock Tower Pl., Carmel, CA 93923-8746; Title Tel # (408) 624-1536 Title Fax # (408) 625-3225
Personnel: Publisher-Paul Kagan, Circ. Mgr.-Judith Pinney, Adv. Dir.-Johanne Hardy
Editorial Description: Valuations of publishing & newspaper companies with analysis of acquisitions & asset sales. Data on growth, market shares & stocks.
General Info: Yr. Est. 1989, Monthly, Trim Size-7¼ x 12, Other press, 12 pages, ISSN: 1042-4326, No Color, Other, Saddle-stitched
Subscriptions: Indv. $675
Advertising: Inquire for rates.

Ney Report   *Business*

Publishing Co: Richard Ney, PO Box 92223, Pasadena, CA 91109-2223; Title Tel # (818) 441-2222
Editorial Description: Stock market.
General Info: Yr. Est. 1975, Bi-weekly, Trim Size-8½ x 11, Sheetfed press, 4 pages, 2 Color
Subscriptions: Indv. $295, $12/copy

No-Load Fund Analyst   *Business, Consumer*

Publishing Co: L/G Research Inc., 4 Orinda Way Ste 230d, Orinda, CA 94563-2522; Title Tel # (510) 284-9017 Title Fax # (510) 254-0335
General Info: Yr. Est. 1989, Monthly
Subscriptions: Indv. $169, $10/copy
Circulation: Total-1,500

No-Load Fund Investor   *Consumer*

Publishing Co: No-Load Fund Investor, Inc., Box 318, Irvington-on-Hudson, NY 10533; Title Tel # (914) 693-7420 Title Fax # (914) 693-8067
Personnel: Publisher, Editor-Sheldon Jacobs
Editorial Description: Complete performance statistics, news, views, recommendations & forecasts for no-load funds. .
General Info: Yr. Est. 1979, Monthly, Trim Size-8½ x 11, Sheetfed press, 20 pages, ISSN: 0736-6256, No Color
Subscriptions: Indv. $119, For. $144
Acquistions: Publication Bought, Publication Sold
List Rental: List Management Co.: Marketing Services Intl., 625 N Michigan Ave Ste 1920, Chicago, IL 60611-3109 Tel # (312) 642-1620, Fax # (312) 642-0679, Actives: 20,000, $115/M, Expires: 40,000, $100/M

No Load Fund X   *Business, Consumer*

Publishing Co: Dal Investment Co., 235 Montgomery St., Ste. 662, San Francisco, CA 94104-2994 Fax # (415) 986-1595; Title Tel # (415) 986-7979
Personnel: Publisher, Editor-Burton Berry, Circ. Mgr.-Don Patrick, Adv. Dir., Art Dir., Promotion Dir.-Janet Brown
Editorial Description: Monitors noload mutual funds industry of 550 funds; indentifies best funds monthly; rates performance. Includes noload funds; complete distribution record monthly.
General Info: Yr. Est. 1975, Monthly, Trim Size-11 x 17, Web press, 12 pages, ISSN: 0194-0104, 2 Color, Newsprint, Saddle-stitched
Subscriptions: Indv. $119, Inst. $75, Can. $119, For. $119, $7/copy
Acquistions: Publication Bought
Circulation: Total-10,000
List Rental: Actives: 10,000, $155/M, Expires: 15,000, $125/M

No Load Mutual Fund
Consensus   *Business*

Publishing Co: No Load Mutual Fund Consensus, 143 Seminole Ave., Palm Beach, FL 33480-3732
Editorial Description: Rate no load mutual funds.
General Info: Yr. Est. 1992, Monthly
Subscriptions: Indv. $149

Norwood Commodity Fund
Index   *Business*

Publishing Co: Norwood Securities, 6134 N Milwaukee Ave, Chicago, IL 60646-3894; Title Tel # (312) 763-1540
Editorial Description: Compares performances of publicly offered commodity funds.
General Info: Yr. Est. 1958, Monthly, 5 pages
Subscriptions: $10/copy
Circulation: Total-300

Norwood Index Report

Publishing Co: Stark Research, Inc., 141 S Whitehall Ct # 591, Palatine, IL 60067-5836; Title Tel # (708) 359-4508 Title Fax # (708) 359-4508
Personnel: Publisher, Editor-Daniel Stark
Editorial Description: Track performance of over 100 public commodity funds. Compile statistics on Commodity Trading Advisors & General Partners.
General Info: Yr. Est. 1978, Monthly, 10 pages
Subscriptions: Indv. $245, Can. $245, For. $260, $20/copy
Circulation: Total-300
List Rental: Rents Lists

Nutshell
See: EMPLOYMENT

OSC Bulletin   *Business*

Publishing Co: Ontario Securities Commission, 20 Queen St. W., #1800, Toronto, ON M5H 3S8 Canada; Title Tel # (416) 597-0681
Editorial Description: Ontario securities commission bulletin.
General Info: Yr. Est. 1981, Weekly, 150 pages, ISSN: 0226-9325, Ind/Abs/Online: Cum.
Subscriptions: Indv. $600
Circulation: Total-1,500

OTC Communications   *Business*

Publishing Co: OTC Research Corp., 1040 Great Plain Avenue, Needham, MA 02192-2517
Tel # (617) 444-6100 Fax # (617) 444-6101
Personnel: Mng. Editor-Cynthia A. Gramer
Editorial Description: Reports on over-the counter stocks.
General Info: Monthly, Trim Size-8½ x 11, 4 pages, No Color, Matte

O.T.C. Growth Stock Watch   *Business, Consumer*

Publishing Co: OTC Research Corp., 1040 Great Plain Avenue, Needham, MA 02192-2517;
Title Tel # (617) 444-6100 Title Fax # (617) 444-6101
Personnel: Publisher-Geoffrey Eiten, Mng. Editor-John McElligott, Circ. Mgr.-Jonathan P. Goldstein, Mktg. Dir.-Quentin George
Editorial Description: Investment advisory newsletter concentrating on emerging growth companies on NASDAQ that meet a rigid set of financial criteria.
General Info: Yr. Est. 1979, Monthly, Trim Size-8½ x 11, Sheetfed press, 6 pages, No Color, Newsprint
Subscriptions: Indv. $299, Inst. $299, Can. $314, For. $314, $25/copy
Circulation: Total-2,200
List Rental: List Management Co.: Manager: Nicholas Moccia; Marketing Services Intl., 625 N Michigan Ave Ste 1920, Chicago, IL 60611-3109 Tel # (312) 642-1620, Fax # (312) 642-0679, Actives: 65,381, $135/M
Printing Co: Belmont Printing, 46 Brighton Ave., Belmont, MA 02178-3621 Tel # (617) 484-0833, Fax # (617) 484-9707

Oberweis Report   *Business, Consumer*

Publishing Co: Oberweis Securities, Inc., 1 Constitution Dr., Aurora, IL 60506;
Title Fax # (708) 896-5282
Personnel: Editor-Jim Oberweis
Editorial Description: Two model portfolios-high quality growth selections & speculative growth selections.
General Info: (Formerly Oberweis Securities Monthly Review), Yr. Est. 1976, Monthly, 4 pages
Subscriptions: Indv. $95
Circulation: Total-10,000

Officers Call
See: MILITARY & NAVAL

Oil Gas Production Report   *Business*

Publishing Co: Ministry of Energy, Mines & Petroleum Resources, Mineral Resources Division, Parliament Bldgs., Victoria, BC V8V 1X4 Canada
Personnel: Editor-Douglas Mackenzie
General Info: Monthly
Subscriptions: Indv. $30

Opportunities in Options   *Business*

Publishing Co: Opportunities in Options, PO Box 2126, Malibu, CA 90265-7126
Fax # (310) 456-3703; Title Tel # (310) 456-9699 Title Fax # (310) 456-9703
Personnel: Publisher, Editor-David Caplan
Editorial Description: Describes option strategies to traders of futures & stocks. Includes book
General Info: Yr. Est. 1984, Monthly, 8 pages
Subscriptions: Indv. $350
List Rental: Actives: 50,000, $150/M, Expires: 50,000, $125/M

Option Advisor, The   *Business, Consumer*

Publishing Co: Investment Research Institute, Inc., 1259 Kemper Meadows Dr. #100, Cincinnati, OH 45240; Title Tel # (513) 589-3800 Title Fax # (513) 589-3810
Personnel: Publisher-Robert Bergen, Editor-Bernard Schaeffer, Circ. Dir.-Kevin Addington, Mktg. Dir.-Randi Rosenberg
Editorial Description: Investment advice & strategies for listed stock options. Includes telephone hotline.
General Info: Yr. Est. 1981, 18x/yr., Trim Size-8½ x 11, Sheetfed press, 6 pages, 2 Color, Newsprint
Subscriptions: Indv. $210
Acquistions: Publication Bought
List Rental: Actives: $175/M

Option Strategist, The   *Consumer*

Publishing Co: McMillan Analysis Corp., 39 Meadowbrook Rd, Randolph, NJ 07869-3808;
Title Fax # (201) 328-1303
Personnel: Publisher, Editor-Lawerence G. McMillan
Editorial Description: Published by Lawerence G. Mcmillan,author of the bestselling book: Options AS A Strategic Investment. Strategy recommendations & articles on stock, index, & futures options monitored portfolio. Telephone hotline.
General Info: Yr. Est. 1990, Semi-monthly, Trim Size-8½ x 11, 8 pages, No Color
Subscriptions: Indv. $250, Free To Qualified Recipient
Circulation: (90% controlled), Total-300
List Rental: Actives: $90/M
Printing Co: Alphagraphics, Speedwell Ave., Morristown, NJ 07960

Option Weekly   *Consumer*

Publishing Co: Option Weekly, 4838 Randolph Dr, Annandale, VA 22003-6222;
Title Tel # (703) 354-6579
Personnel: Publisher-W. Nehl
Editorial Description: Computer aided selections of stock option hedges & spreads.
General Info: Yr. Est. 1974, Weekly, 10 pages, No Color
Subscriptions: Indv. $110

Options Update   *Business*

Publishing Co: Chicago Board Options Exchange, 400 S La Salle St, Chicago, IL 60605-1090;
Title Tel # (312) 786-5600
Editorial Description: Information from the Chicago Board Options Exchange for use by brokers.
General Info: Yr. Est. 1985, Semi-annually, Trim Size-11 x 11, 8 pages, 2 Color, Coated, Saddle-stitched

Ostaro's Market Newsletter   *Business*

Publishing Co: Cardinal Star Corp., Box A76, New York, NY 10163-9506; Title Tel # (212) 686-4121
Personnel: Publisher, Editor-Mr. Ostaro, Circ. Mgr.-D. Goele
Editorial Description: Charts gold, silver, DJIA for the next two months.
General Info: Yr. Est. 1980, Bi-monthly, Trim Size-8½ x 11, Web press, 4 pages, ISSN: 0197-3592, No Color
Subscriptions: Indv. $195, $32/copy
Circulation: (100% controlled), Total-1,000

Ottawa Letter
See: LAW

Over-55 Financial Management Letter   *Business*

Publishing Co: Research Institute of America, 90 5th Avenue, New York, NY 10011-7629
Tel # (212) 645-4800
Personnel: Publisher-J.P. Kent
General Info: Bi-weekly, 8 pages
List Rental: List Management Co.: WG & L List Management, 1 Penn Plz Fl 42, New York, NY 10119-0002 Tel # (212) 971-5000

Overpriced Stock Service   *Business*

Publishing Co: Murenove, Inc., PO Box 308, Half Moon Bay, CA 94019-0308;
Title Tel # (415) 726-8495
General Info: Yr. Est. 1983, Monthly
Subscriptions: Indv. $495, For. $525

PSE Highlights   *Business*

Publishing Co: Pacific Coast Stock Exchange, 115 Sansome St., San Francisco, CA 94104-3601;
Title Tel # (415) 393-4253
Personnel: Editor-Jeannie Williams
Editorial Description: Statistical summary of trading activity in options and equities.
General Info: Monthly

Pearson Investment Letter   *Business, Consumer*

Publishing Co: Pearson Investment Letter, 1628 White Arrow Dr, Dover, FL 33527-5741;
Title Tel # (813) 659-2560
Personnel: Publisher-Walter Pearson, Editor-R. Scott Pearson
Editorial Description: Investment newsletter includes pertinent information about certain stock companies that appear to be good candidates for purchase at each monthly publication; also has some information about current trends and world affairs.
General Info: Yr. Est. 1982, Monthly, Trim Size-8½ x 11, 10 pages
Subscriptions: Indv. $175, $2/copy
Circulation: Total-500

Penny Fortune Newsletter   *Business*

Publishing Co: Penny Fortune Newsletter, 1837 South Navara, Colorado Spring, CO 80906
Fax # (719) 576-3036; Title Tel # (719) 576-9200
Personnel: Publisher-J.C. Katz, Editor-James Fortune
Editorial Description: Reports on special situations & low priced securities; especially options & NASDAQ stocks. Gives specific buy & sell recommendations. Includes charts & graphs.
General Info: Yr. Est. 1980, Monthly, Trim Size-8½ x 11, Letrpr. press, 8 pages, Coated
Subscriptions: Indv. $79
Acquistions: Publication Bought
Advertising: Accepts Inserts
List Rental: Actives: $95/M, Hotline: $110/M, Expires: $75/M

Penny Stock Future   *Business*

Publishing Co: Economic Advice, 3910 NE 26th Ave, Lighthouse Point, FL 33064-8044;
Title Tel # (305) 941-3836
Personnel: Publisher, Editor-James Rapholz, Circ. Mgr.-Phyllis Rapholz, Adv. Dir.-Victor Bellucci
Editorial Description: Advice, information, & opinions on penny stocks. Precious metal mining specialists.
General Info: Yr. Est. 1980, Monthly, Trim Size-8 x 11, Mimeo press, 26 pages, 1% ads, No Color, Newsprint
Subscriptions: Indv. $65
Circulation: Total-9,000

Penny Stocks Newsletter   *Business, Consumer*

Publishing Co: Penny Stocks Newsletter, 31731 Outer Highway 10, Redlands, CA 92373-8610
Personnel: Publisher-Vello Kulbin
General Info: Yr. Est. 1978, Irregular, Offset press, 3 pages, No Color
Subscriptions: Indv. $750
Acquistions: Publication Bought

Pension Plan Fix-It Handbook
See: SENIOR CITIZENS

Personal Finance   *Consumer*

Publishing Co: KCI Communications, Inc., 1101 King St., Ste. 400, Alexandria, VA 22314-2980
Tel # (703) 548-2400 Fax # (703) 683-6974 Parent Co.-National Information Corp., Alexandria
Personnel: Publisher-Walter Pearce, Editor-Stephen Leeb
Editorial Description: Investment tips and analysis.
General Info: Semi-monthly, Trim Size-8½ x 11, 12 pages, Color, Matte, Saddle-stitched
Subscriptions: Indv. $99

Personal Financial Planning Letter
See: BANKING & FINANCE

Personal Moneyplan   *Business*

Publishing Co: Felton Enterprises, 501 Palmetto Dr # 100, Pasadena, CA 91105-1608;
Title Tel # (818) 795-5115
Personnel: Editor-David Reed Felton
General Info: Monthly

Perspectives on Hard Assets   *Business*

Publishing Co: Linden Agency, PO Box 1319, Ashland, OR 97520-0044; Title Tel # (503) 488-2326
Personnel: Editor-Michael Linden
General Info: Monthly
Subscriptions: Indv. $75

Perspectives on Managing Personal Assets   *Consumer*

Publishing Co: United States Trust Co., 114 W. 47th St., New York, NY 10036
Personnel: Exec. Ed.-Allison Cooke Kellogg, Co-Editor-David Bates, Co-Editor-Glenn Hintze, Production Mgr.-Hiroe Gregor, Art Dir.-James Sciortino, Composition Mgr.-Hilda Millender
Editorial Description: Explains investment approach and provides information to clients and friends for planning and managing personal financial affairs.
General Info: Bi-monthly

Peter Dag Investment Letter

Publishing Co: Peter Dag Investment Letter, 65 Lake Front Dr, Akron, OH 44319-3660;
Title Tel # (216) 644-2782
Personnel: Publisher, Editor-George Dagnino, Circ. Mgr.-Kathy Johnson, Adv. Dir.-Jack Klingel, Art Dir.-Jack Higgins
Editorial Description: Practical investment recommendations aiming at outperforming broad stock mark averages: model portfolio using mutual funds reviewed in each issue. Discusses major business cycle developments, interest rates, inflation, monetary policy, economic outlook. It features the equity-10 portfolio for aggressive investors.
General Info: Yr. Est. 1977, 29x/yr., Trim Size-8½ x 11, Letrpr. press, 6 pages, ISSN: 0196-9323, 2 Color
Subscriptions: Indv. $250
Advertising: Accepts Inserts.

Peter Eliades' Stock Market Cycles   *Business*

Publishing Co: Peter Eliades Stock Market Cycles, PO Box 6873, Santa Rosa, CA 95406-0873
Fax # (707) 579-0274
Personnel: Editor-Peter Eliades
Editorial Description: Stock market timing service based on cycles and technical indications.
General Info: Yr. Est. 1975, Semi-monthly, 4 pages

Plain Talk Investor   *Business*

Publishing Co: Plain Talk Investor, Inc., 1500 Skokie Blvd Ste 203, Northbrook, IL 60062-4113;
Title Tel # (708) 564-1955
Personnel: Editor-Fred Gordon
Subscriptions: Indv. $115

Pocket Change Investor, The
See: CONSUMER INTERESTS

Portfolio Letter   *Business*

Publishing Co: Capital Cities/ABC, 488 Madison Ave., 16th Floor, New York, NY 10022-5751
Fax # (212) 224-3353 Parent Co.-Capital Cities/ABC, Inc., New York; Title Tel # (212) 224-3233
Title Fax # (212) 224-3111
Personnel: Publisher-Linda Litner, Editor-Tom Lamont, Circ. Dir.-Gladys Delgado, Production Dir.-Susan Drobney, Adv. Dir.-Pat Bertucci, Mktg. Dir.-Dahlia Weinman
Editorial Description: Focuses its editorial coverage on the equity markets and is designed for an audience of senior investment and financial professionals. Each weekly issue reviews leading money managers' investment strategies, predictions by key stock analysts and the response of corporate executives to the movement of their companies' stock prices.
General Info: Yr. Est. 1979, Weekly, Trim Size-8½ x 11, Sheetfed press, 10 pages, Ind/Abs/Online: Lexis/Nexis news service, 4 Color, Newsprint
Subscriptions: Indv. $1,295, Can. $1,325, For. $1,370, $30/copy
Advertising: Inquire for rates.

Portfolio Selector Viewpoint

Publishing Co: Argus Research Corp., 17 Battery Pl., New York, NY 10004-1101;
Title Tel # (212) 425-7500 Title Fax # (212) 509-5408
Personnel: Editor-John Eade
Editorial Description: Two reports, one addressing specific stock market strategy, including technical advice; & the other placing stock market performance in the context of the economy. Stock recommendations are offered.
General Info: Monthly
Printing Co: Argus Printing & Mailing, 226 New York Ave, Huntington, NY 11743-2748
Tel # (516) 423-7710

Portfolios Investment Advisory

Publishing Co: Portfolios Investment Advisory, PO Box 997, Lynchburg, VA 24505-0997;
Title Tel # (804) 846-4642
Personnel: Editor-Richard Hoskins
General Info: Yr. Est. 1973, Monthly
Subscriptions: Indv. $150

Powell Gold Industry Guide and International Mining Analyst
See: MINING & MINERALS

Powell Monetary Analyst   *Business, Consumer*

Publishing Co: Reserve Research Ltd., Box 4135, Stn. A, Portland, ME 04101-0335;
Title Tel # (207) 774-4971
Personnel: Publisher, Editor, Circ. Mgr., Adv. Dir.-Larson Powell
Editorial Description: Investment advisory emphasizing gold/silver mining shares, gold coins and currency developments.
General Info: Yr. Est. 1971, Bi-weekly, Trim Size-8½ x 11, Offset press, 8 pages, ISSN: 0146-7190, Color
Subscriptions: Indv. $285, Inst. $285, Can. $285, For. $305, $15/copy
List Rental: List Management Co.: Coolidge List Marketing, 25 W. 43rd St., New York, NY 10036-7491 Tel # (212) 274-0630, Fax # (212) 274-0650, Actives: $75/M, Expires: 30,000

Practical Stock Picker   *Business*

Publishing Co: Practical Stock Picker, 8 W Parish Ct, Haverhill, MA 01832-1166
Personnel: Editor-W.J. Fallon
Editorial Description: Recommends a portfolio of high capitalization stocks.
General Info: Yr. Est. 1983, Semi-monthly
Subscriptions: Indv. $150

Predictions   *Business, Consumer*

Publishing Co: Agora, Inc., 105 W. Monument St., Baltimore, MD 21202-4702 Tel # (410) 783-2647
Fax # (410) 223-2662; Title Tel # (410) 234-0515
General Info: Yr. Est. 1982, Monthly
Subscriptions: Indv. $78
List Rental: List Management Co.: Name Bank, 14 W. Monument St., Baltimore, MD 21201
Tel # (410) 783-8463, Fax # (410) 783-8464

Prespectives on Esatate and Financial Planning
See: BANKING & FINANCE

Price Perceptions   *Consumer*

Publishing Co: Commodity Information Systems, Inc., 210 Park Ave. Bldg 2970, Oklahoma City, OK 73102-5604; Title Tel # (405) 235-5687
Personnel: Editor-William Gary, Circ. Mgr.-Robert Howard, Production Mgr.-Sheron Gary
General Info: (Formerly Commodity Information Systems, Inc.), Yr. Est. 1969, Semi-monthly, Trim Size-8½ x 11, Web press, 12 pages, No Color, Coated
Subscriptions: Indv. $360, Can. $360, For. $400
Acquistions: Publication Bought, Publication Sold

Primary Trend   *Consumer*

Publishing Co: Arnold Investment Counsel, Inc., 700 N. Water St., Milwaukee, WI 53202-4255;
Title Tel # (414) 271-2726 Title Fax # (414) 271-2809
Personnel: Editor-Roger Stafford, Circ. Mgr.-Lilli Gust
Editorial Description: Investment professional gives value oriented views on stocks and bonds. Also discusses trends in precious metals, commodities.
General Info: Yr. Est. 1979, 18x/yr., 8 pages, 2 Color
Subscriptions: Indv. $180, $10/copy

Princeton Portfolios   *Business, Consumer*

Publishing Co: Gianturco, 301 N. Harrison Bldg., #229, Bldg. B, #229, Princeton, NJ 08540-3599;
Title Tel # (609) 497-0362
Personnel: Publisher, Editor-Michael Gianturco
Editorial Description: Covers entire spectrum of developing technology in electronics, lasers, etc. Recommends stock portfolios.
General Info: Yr. Est. 1978, Monthly, Trim Size-8½ x 11, Offset press, 10 pages, No Color
Circulation: Total-1,500

Private Asset Management   *Business*

Publishing Co: Capital Cities/ABC, 488 Madison Ave., 16th Floor, New York, NY 10022-5751
Fax # (212) 224-3353 Parent Co.-Capital Cities/ABC, Inc., New York; Title Tel # (212) 224-3233
Title Fax # (212) 224-3111
General Info: Bi-weekly, Trim Size-8½ x 11, Sheetfed press, 14 pages, 2 Color, Newsprint
Advertising: Inquire for rates.

Private Inc. Opportunities

Publishing Co: Winning Market Strategies, 1235 Coast Village Road, Suite G, Santa Barbara, CA 93108; Title Tel # (805) 969-8400 Title Fax # (805) 563-9706
Personnel: Mng. Editor-Christine Burns
General Info: Yr. Est. 1994, Bi-monthly

Private Placement Letter   *Business*

Publishing Co: IDD Enterprises, 2 World Trade Ctr. 18th Fl., New York, NY 10048-0203 Parent Co.-Dow Jones & Co., Inc., New York; Title Tel # (212) 227-1200 Title Fax # (212) 321-2336
Personnel: Publisher-Clint Winstead, Circ. Mgr.-Philip M. McGee, Production Mgr.-Maxine Margolese, Adv. Dir.-Mattie Reyes, Mktg. Dir.-Janice Fellagera
Editorial Description: In-depth coverage of the private placement and 144A markets. Reports where deals are done, who's doing them, and offers the details of the package.
General Info: Yr. Est. 1982, Weekly, Offset press, 12 pages, 2 Color, Matte, Saddle-stitched
Subscriptions: Indv. $995
Acquistions: Publication Bought, Publication Sold
Advertising: $2,300. Accepts Inserts.
Printing Co: Dealers Digest, 2 World Trade Ctr., New York, NY 10048 Tel # (212) 227-1200

Private Placement Reporter   *Business*

Publishing Co: American Banker Newsletters, One State Plaza, New York, NY 10004-1505 Fax # (202) 843-9620; Title Tel # (212) 803-8300 Title Fax # (212) 843-9620
Personnel: Publisher-David G. Schutt, Editor-Michael Sisk, Circ. Dir.-Maria Pritchett, Adv. Dir., Mktg. Dir.-Hans Winberg
Editorial Description: Buying, selling and trading unregistered securities.
General Info: Weekly, Ind/Abs/Online: Mead Data Cental, NewsNet, Predicasts/Dialog, DataTimes
Subscriptions: Indv. $850, Can. $850, For. $880, $20/copy
Advertising: $1,400.

Pro Farmer
See: AGRICULTURE

Professional Tape Reader   *Consumer*

Publishing Co: Radcap Inc., Box 2407, Hollywood, FL 33022-2407
Personnel: Publisher, Editor-Stan Weinstein, Circ. Mgr.-R. Berg
Editorial Description: Stock market advisory service. Pages of charts and advice, objective forecasts for long/short term trends, markets most promising and most vulnerable stocks, indicator analysis. Covers options, mutual funds, gold, bonds.
General Info: Yr. Est. 1972, Semi-monthly, Letrpr. press, 8 pages
Subscriptions: Indv. $350
List Rental: Actives: $110/M, Expires: $125/M

Professional Timing Service

Publishing Co: Professional Timing Service, PO Box 7483, Missoula, MT 59807-7483; Title Tel # (406) 543-4131
Personnel: Editor-Curtis Hesler
Editorial Description: Short, intermediate-and long term market forecasts, research reports & investment advice.
General Info: Yr. Est. 1967, Bi-weekly, 4 pages
Subscriptions: Indv. $185
List Rental: Rents Lists

Profit Letter, The   *Business, Consumer*

Publishing Co: Legacy Communications, Unit 271, Box 8110, Blaine, WA 98230-9966; Title Tel # (604) 264-9462 Title Fax # (604) 264-9496
Personnel: Editor-Tom Kinakin, Circ. Mgr.-Derele Kinakin
Editorial Description: Advice on investing in junior companies, with potential to at least double or triple in value.
General Info: Yr. Est. 1987, 24x/yr., Trim Size-8½ x 11, 8 pages, No Color, Matte
Subscriptions: Indv. $150, Inst. $150, Can. $187, For. $175
Circulation: Total-1,200, Readership-3,000
Advertising: Accepts Inserts.

Profitable Investing   *Consumer*

Publishing Co: Phillips Publishing, Inc., 7811 Montrose Rd., Potomac, MD 20854-3394 Parent Co.-Phillips Business Information, Inc., Potomac; Title Tel # (301) 340-2100 Title Fax # (301) 294-1307
Personnel: Publisher-Thomas Phillips, Editor-Richard Band, Mktg. Dir.-Annette Payne
Editorial Description: Contrarian investor reveals the only safe ways to build wealth.
General Info: (Formerly Richard E. Band's Profitable Investing), Yr. Est. 1990, Monthly, Trim Size-8½ x 11, 8 pages, ISSN: 1048-3667, 2 Color, Matte
Subscriptions: Indv. $99, $12/copy
Acquistions: Publication Bought, Publication Sold
List Rental: List Management Co.: Manager: John Baldwin; Phillips Publishing List Marketing, 7811 Montrose Rd., Potomac, MD 20854-3394 Tel # (301) 340-2100, Fax # (301) 294-1307, Actives: 45,740, $155/M, Expires: 43,174

Prudent Speculator, The   *Business*

Publishing Co: Al Frank Asset Management, Inc., PO Box 1767, Santa Monica, CA 90406-1767; Title Tel # (310) 587-2410 Title Fax # (310) 587-2407
Personnel: Publisher, Editor-Al Frank, Circ. Mgr.-Victoria Baldwin
Editorial Description: Market commentary & investment strategies, with fundamental stock selections. Reports trades in Al Frank's actual portfolio; lists current recommendations.
General Info: (Formerly Pinchpenny Speculator, The), Yr. Est. 1977, Monthly, Trim Size-8½ x 11, Sheetfed press, 8 pages, ISSN: 0743-0809
Subscriptions: Indv. $175, Can. $175, For. $199, $15/copy
Circulation: Total-1,000
Printing Co: Printing Connection, The, 7242 Valjean Ave., Van Nuys, CA 91406-3412 Tel # (818) 782-5490, Fax # (818) 782-5491

Public Investor   *Association*

Publishing Co: Government Finance Officers Assn., 180 N Michigan Ave Ste 800, Chicago, IL 60601-7401 Fax # (312) 974-4806; Title Tel # (312) 977-9700 Title Fax # (312) 977-4806
Personnel: Editor-Corinne Larson, Product Mgr.-Karen Utterback, Mktg. Dir.-Rebecca Russum
Editorial Description: Information for people responsible for public funds.
General Info: Monthly, 6 pages
Subscriptions: Indv. $55, Inst. $85
Circulation: Total-1,400

Q-Weather Forecast & Commodities Outlook

Publishing Co: Boyd E. Quate & Associates, Box 7065, Holland Station, Suffolk, VA 23437; Title Tel # (804) 539-3989
Personnel: Publisher-Boyd Quate, Editor-B. Edward Quate
Editorial Description: Information for commodities investors.
General Info: Yr. Est. 1962, Bi-monthly
Subscriptions: Indv. $95

Quantum Advantage Investment & Technology Report
See: SCIENCE

Quarterly Performance Report   *Business, Consumer*

Publishing Co: Managed Account Reports, 220 Fifth Ave., New York, NY 10001; Title Tel # (212) 213-6202 Title Fax # (212) 213-1870
Personnel: Publisher-Greg Newton, Editor-Lois Peltz, Circ. Mgr.-Lydia Solo
Editorial Description: Statistical supplement to Managed Account Reports on commodity money managers & funds. Also contains data on each OJA covering quarters of current year & for prior years.
General Info: Yr. Est. 1981, Quarterly, Trim Size-8½ x 11, Offset press, 200 pages, No Color, Looseleaf
Subscriptions: Indv. $299, For. $395, $95/copy
Printing Co: Concord Press, 4785 Dorsey Hall Dr., Ellicott City, MD 21042 Tel # (410) 997-5340, Fax # (410) 997-5574

Quarterly Studies/Review

Publishing Co: Barrow Investment Management, Inc., 3800 W Bay To Bay Blvd Ste 21, Tampa, FL 33629-6844 Tel # (813) 254-7779; Title Tel # (813) 273-0222
Personnel: Publisher-Alston Barrow, Editor-Holly Paula
Editorial Description: Devoted to stock research, supplement to favorably positioned stocks. Lists 200 closely followed companies with target ratios & target prices w-buy-sell-hold recommendation.
General Info: Offset press, ISSN: 2756-4769, 2 Color, Newsprint
Subscriptions: Indv. $117, Inst. $195, $9/copy

Radiological Inspection Reports
See: NUCLEAR ENERGY

Rapaport Diamond Report
See: JEWELRY & HOROLOGY

Real Estate Investing Letter   *Business*

Publishing Co: Management Resources. Inc., 861 Lafayette Rd. #5, Hampton, NH 03842-1232; Title Tel # (603) 929-1600
Personnel: Publisher-William Quirk, Editor-H. Mandelbaum
Editorial Description: Investing techniques & tips for the individual real estate investor.
General Info: Yr. Est. 1975, Monthly, ISSN: 0145-1002
Subscriptions: Indv. $96
List Rental: List Management Co.: Walter Karl Business Lists, One American Lane, Greenwich, CT 06831 Tel # (203) 552-6700, Fax # (203) 552-6799, Actives: 16,631, $85/M

Real Estate Investor's Monthly
See: REAL ESTATE

Realty Stock Review   *Business*

Publishing Co: Audit Investment Inc., 92 Kennedy Rd., Box 7, Tranquility, NJ 07879-0007 Tel # (908) 850-1155; Title Tel # (201) 358-2735
Personnel: Publisher, Editor-Kenneth Campbell
Editorial Description: Investors in real estate securities.
General Info: (Formerly Realty Trust Review), Yr. Est. 1970, Semi-monthly, Offset press, 8 pages, No Color
Subscriptions: Indv. $288, $15/copy

Reaper   *Business*

Publishing Co: Publishers Management Co., PO Box 84900, Phoenix, AZ 85071-4900; Title Tel # (602) 252-4477
Personnel: Publisher-Velda Malock, Editor-R.E. McMaster
Editorial Description: World affairs, domestic economics, commodities.
General Info: Yr. Est. 1977, Weekly, Trim Size-8½ x 11, Sheetfed press, 10 pages, 2 Color, Newsprint
Subscriptions: Indv. $195
Advertising: Accepts Inserts.
List Rental: List Management Co.: Carnegie Marketing Assocs., Koll Executive Plaza, 3878 Carson St., Suite 220, Torrance, CA 90503 Tel # (310) 540-4757, Fax # (310) 540-7407
Printing Co: Runbeck Graphics, 3101 N Central Ave Ste 490, Phoenix, AZ 85012-2638 Tel # (602) 230-0510

Resort Management Report
See: BUSINESS & INDUSTRY

Retirement Letter
See: SENIOR CITIZENS

Retirement Plans Bulletin
See: SENIOR CITIZENS

Review for CFOs & Investment Bankers
See: BANKING & FINANCE

Richard Russell's Dow Theory Letters

Publishing Co: Richard Russell's Dow Theory Letters, PO Box 1759, La Jolla, CA 92038-1759; Title Tel # (619) 454-0481
Personnel: Publisher, Editor-Richard Russell
General Info: Yr. Est. 1957, Semi-weekly
Subscriptions: Indv. $225

Richland Report   *Business*

Publishing Co: Richland Co., 7865 E Roseland Dr, La Jolla, CA 92037-4016; Title Tel # (619) 459-2611 Title Fax # (619) 459-2612
Personnel: Publisher, Editor-Kennedy Gammage
Editorial Description: Economy & markets: stocks, bonds, precious metals & money instruments.
General Info: Yr. Est. 1976, Bi-weekly, Trim Size-8½ x 11, Offset press, 8 pages, No Color
Subscriptions: Indv. $197
List Rental: Rents Lists

Risk Factor Method of Investing   *Business, Consumer*

Publishing Co: Invest/O-Registered Investment Advisors, PO Box 5996, Bend, OR 97708-5996; Title Tel # (541) 389-3676
Personnel: Editor-William Kuhn
General Info: Yr. Est. 1978, Monthly, Trim Size-8½ x 11, 8 pages, No Color
Subscriptions: Indv. $100

Robbins Report

Publishing Co: William Spencer Educational Foundation, 6701 Blanco Rd Apt 712, San Antonio, TX 78216-6161; Title Tel # (512) 733-0051
Personnel: Publisher, Editor-Richard Robbins
Editorial Description: Survival yield & wealth for the investor. Global economics for the 21st century &
General Info: Yr. Est. 1965, Semi-monthly, Desktop press, 8 pages, No Color
Subscriptions: Indv. $125, $9/copy
Circulation: Total-1,600

Roesch Market Memo   *Business*

Publishing Co: Roesch Market Memo, 6511 W. 80th St., Overland Park, KS 66204-3811
Editorial Description: Technical and fundamental analysis applied to common stocks, market turns.
General Info: Yr. Est. 1981, Monthly
Subscriptions: Indv. $42
Circulation: Total-500

Ron Paul Survival Report   *Business, Consumer*

Publishing Co: Ron Paul Investment Letter, PO Box 602, Lake Jackson, TX 77566-0602; Title Tel # (713) 333-4800 Title Fax # (713) 333-3625
Personnel: Editor-Ron Paul
Editorial Description: News and developments in economics, finance, banking, and politics for investors.
General Info: (Formerly Ron Paul Investment Letter), Yr. Est. 1985, Monthly, Trim Size-8½ x 11, 8 pages
Subscriptions: Indv. $99
List Rental: Actives: 9,000, $135/M, Expires: 23,000, $100/M

Ronald Sadoff's Major Trends   *Business*

Publishing Co: Ronald Sadoff's Major Trends, 250 W. Coventry, Milwaukee, WI 53217-3961; Title Tel # (414) 352-8460
Personnel: Publisher, Editor-Ronald Sadoff
Editorial Description: Describes the overall trend for the stock market & which stocks to buy or sell.
General Info: Yr. Est. 1978, Monthly, 8 pages
Subscriptions: Indv. $195

Rosten Intl. Commodities Report   *Business*

Publishing Co: Rosten Publishing Co., 1009 W. Balboa Blvd., #B, Balboa, CA 92661-1003; Title Tel # (213) 475-9617
Personnel: Editor-David Rosten
General Info: Yr. Est. 1980, Quarterly
Circulation: Total-1,000

Rouge et Noir Casino Securities Watch   *Business*

Publishing Co: Rouge et Noir Inc., PO Box 1146, Midlothian, VA 23113-8146; Title Tel # (804) 230-0736 Title Fax # (804) 230-4931
Editorial Description: Financial reports on publicly traded casinos.
General Info: Yr. Est. 1990, Weekly
Subscriptions: Indv. $520

Rule/Howard Oil and Gas Analyst   *Business*

Publishing Co: Rule/Howard, 7770 El Camino Rd., Carlsbad, CA 92009
Editorial Description: The junior oil and gas stock analyst.
General Info: Monthly
Subscriptions: Indv. $149

Russian Business News Update
See: INTERNATIONAL TRADE

Russian Far East Update
See: INTERNATIONAL TRADE

Ryals Investment Report   *Business, Consumer*

Publishing Co: Ryal Investment report, 16372 Chippewa Rd, Apple Valley, CA 92307-1512; Title Tel # (619) 242-8724
General Info: Yr. Est. 1978, Monthly
Subscriptions: Indv. $84

S.A. Advisory   *Business*

Publishing Co: S.A. Advisory, 2274 Arbor Ln Apt 3, Salt Lake City, UT 84117-5365; Title Tel # (801) 272-4761
Personnel: Editor-William Velmer
Editorial Description: Fundamentally priced stock; buy & sell recommendations.
General Info: Yr. Est. 1983, Monthly, 10 pages, No Color, Coated
Subscriptions: Indv. $50
Circulation: Total-9,500
Advertising: Inquire for rates. Accepts Inserts.
List Rental: List Management Co.: JAMI Marketing, 2 Blue Hill Plz, Pearl River, NY 10965-3101 Tel # (914) 620-0700, Fax # (914) 620-1885

SAC Award Review
See: LAW

SCI Policy Report   *Business*

Publishing Co: Sparks Companies Inc., 6708 Whittier Ave, Mc Lean, VA 22101-4529 Tel # (703) 734-8787 Fax # (703) 893-1065
Editorial Description: Varies with service level.
General Info: Daily

SCOR Report
See: BANKING & FINANCE

SEC Accounting Rules
See: ACCOUNTING

SEC Docket   *Business*

Publishing Co: CCH, Inc., 2700 Lake Cook Rd., Riverwoods, IL 60015 Parent Co.-Kluwer Law & Taxation Publishers, Cambridge; Title Tel # (847) 267-7000 Title Fax # (800) 224-8299
Editorial Description: Reproduce texts of SEC rulings, opinions & other official actions as prepared by the agency in a handy drilled booklet-format.
General Info: Weekly, Looseleaf
Subscriptions: Indv. $329

SEC New Registrations Report
See: LAW

SEC No-Action Letter Weekly   *Business*

Publishing Co: CCH Washington Service Bureau, Inc., 655 15th St NW Ste 275, Washington, DC 20005-5701 Tel # (202) 508-0600 Fax # (202) 508-0694
Personnel: Editor-Hugh Kennedy, Circ. Mgr.-Michelle McCaulley
Editorial Description: Abstracts of every No-Action letter released by the SEC including act, section, and rule cites; alphabetical index of all letters released the previous week and cover stories highlighting changes in SEC policy, proposed or final rule adoptions and letters of interest.
General Info: Yr. Est. 1994, Weekly
Subscriptions: Indv. $325

SEC No-Action Letters Index & Summaries

Publishing Co: CCH Washington Service Bureau, Inc., 655 15th St NW Ste 275, Washington, DC 20005-5701; Title Tel # (202) 508-0600 Title Fax # (202) 508-0694
Personnel: Editor-Hugh Kennedy, Circ. Dir.-Michelle McCaulley
Editorial Description: Weekly abstracts of every every no-action and interpretive letter released by the SEC, plus monthly supplements indexing letters by Act, Section, Rule and topic.
General Info: Weekly, ISSN: 0162-2838
Subscriptions: Indv. $1,275

SEC Today
See: LAW

SNL Conversion Watch *Business*

Publishing Co: SNL Securities, 410 E. Main St., P.O. Box 2124, Charlottesville, VA 22902
Tel # (804) 977-1600 Fax # (804) 977-4466
Personnel: Publisher-Reid Nagle, Circ. Mgr.-Pat Labua, Product Mgr.-Chris Smith, Adv. Dir.-Jenn Nagaj, Mktg. Dir.-Judy Lewis
Editorial Description: Reports the latest data and news available on announced, approved, pending, and completed conversions of mutual thrifts to stock ownership.
General Info: Irregular
Subscriptions: Indv. $1,200, Inst. $1,200

SNL Finance Company Weekly
See: BANKING & FINANCE

SNL REIT Weekly
See: REAL ESTATE

SNL Weekly BankFAX
See: BANKING & FINANCE

S&P 500 Information Bulletin *Business*

Publishing Co: Standard & Poor's Corp., 25 Broadway, New York, NY 10004 Parent Co.-McGraw-Hill, New York; Title Tel # (212) 208-8000
Personnel: Editor-Elliott Shurgin
Editorial Description: Monthly report detailing price performance & composition of the S&P 500 Stock Price Index.
General Info: Monthly, Looseleaf
Subscriptions: Indv. $185, $20/copy

S&P MidCap 400 Information Bulletin *Business*

Publishing Co: Standard & Poor's Corp., 25 Broadway, New York, NY 10004 Parent Co.-McGraw-Hill, New York; Title Tel # (212) 208-8000
General Info: Yr. Est. 1991, Monthly, Looseleaf
Subscriptions: Indv. $200, $20/copy

Scientific Investment *Business* **CPM: $300**

Publishing Co: Agora, Inc., 105 W. Monoment St., Baltimore, MD 21202-4702 Tel # (410) 783-2647 Fax # (410) 223-2662; Title Tel # (410) 234-0515
Personnel: Publisher-Lee Euler, Editor-William Chidester, Fulflmnt. Mgr.-Jenn Lewis, Circulation-Kelly Graham, Graphic Designer-Becky Mangus, Mktg. Dir.-Deeba Jafri
Editorial Description: Investment forecasts and recommendations from the world's top financial experts.
General Info: (Formerly Financial Predictions), Yr. Est. 1983, Monthly, Trim Size-8½ x 10¾, 8 pages, 33% ads, 2 Color, Matte
Subscriptions: Indv. $78
Circulation: Total-20,000
Advertising: $6,000.
List Rental: List Management Co.: Name Bank, 14 W. Monument St., Baltimore, MD 21201 Tel # (410) 783-8463, Fax # (410) 783-8464, Actives: 17,500, $135/M

Scott Letter: Closed End Fund Report, The *Business, Consumer*

Publishing Co: Cole Publishing, Inc., 8659 Rio Grande Rd., Richmond, VA 23229-7822 Fax # (804) 343-3300; Title Tel # (804) 741-8707 Title Fax # (804) 343-3308
Personnel: Editor-George Cole Scott, Adv. Dir.-George Col Scott, Publisher, Circ. Mgr., Production Mgr., Art Dir., Mktg. Dir., Promotion Dir.-George Cole Scott
Editorial Description: Educational information on closed-end investment funds.
General Info: Yr. Est. 1988, Monthly, Offset press, 8 pages, Coated, Case bound
Subscriptions: Indv. $150, Inst. $150, Can. $150, For. $150, $15/copy
Advertising: Accepts Inserts.
Printing Co: Newsletter Services, Inc., 9700 Philadelphia Court, Lanham, MD 20706 Tel # (301) 731-5200, Fax # (301) 731-5201

Sector Fund Connection *Business*

Publishing Co: Sector Fund Connection, 8949 La Riviera Dr, Sacramento, CA 95826-2159; Title Tel # (916) 363-2055
Personnel: Editor-Manning Webb
General Info: (Formerly Rating the Stock Selectors), Irregular

Sector Funds Newsletter *Business, Consumer*

Publishing Co: Sector Funds Newsletter, PO Box 270048, San Diego, CA 92198-2048; Title Tel # (619) 748-0805
Personnel: Publisher-Dorothy Ohrn, Editor-Cato Ohrn
Editorial Description: Mutual Funds trading advice using method similar to actual portfolio management (trend-following).
General Info: Yr. Est. 1985, Monthly, Trim Size-8½ x 11, 6 pages, No Color, Matte
Subscriptions: Indv. $117, For. $127
Acquistions: Publication Bought
Circulation: Total-1,000

Securities & Syndication Review *Business*

Publishing Co: Securities Sources, Box 85600, Univ. Station, Seattle, WA 98145-1600; Title Tel # (206) 284-5249
Personnel: Publisher-Robert Frey, CFP, Editor-Robert Frey
Editorial Description: Tax, legislative and regulatory items for financial planners, attorneys, syndicators, accountants, advisers.
General Info: Yr. Est. 1983, Bi-monthly, Trim Size-8½ x 11, Letrpr. press, 6 pages, ISSN: 0739-8689, No Color, Newsprint
Subscriptions: Indv. $75, $15/copy
Circulation: Total-500

Securities Arbitration Commentator
See: LAW

Securities Industry Trends *Business, Association*

Publishing Co: Securities Industry Assn., 120 Broadway, New York, NY 10271-0080 Fax # (212) 608-1604; Title Tel # (212) 608-1500
Personnel: Editor-George Monahan
Editorial Description: Information about trends in the U.S. securities industry. Profitability and financial statements of the securities industry are discussed, as well as economic developments affecting securities firms.
General Info: Irregular
Subscriptions: Indv. $60

Securities Regulations
See: MANAGEMENT

Securities Week *Business*

Publishing Co: McGraw-Hill, 1221 Ave. of the Americas, 36th Fl., New York, NY 10020-1095 Tel # (212) 512-2000 Fax # (212) 512-6590; Title Tel # (212) 512-3144
Personnel: Publisher-Jack Slater, Editor-Lynn Griffo, Assoc. Ed.-Joan Gralla, Assoc. Ed.-Kim Norris, Circ. Mgr.-Julie Ferante
Editorial Description: Latest events at brokerage houses, exchanges, and regulatory organizations.
General Info: Yr. Est. 1973, Weekly, 12 pages, Ind/Abs/Online: DIALOG, Dow Jones, NewsNet, Nexis, No Color
Subscriptions: Indv. $1,025, $20/copy

Security Investing *Business, Consumer*

Publishing Co: John Charles Mallon & Associates, 305 Madison Avenue, Suite 1166, New York, NY 10165; Title Tel # (212) 697-0028 Title Fax # (212) 697-1576
Personnel: Publisher-John Charles Mallon
Editorial Description: Covers investing in the global security industry.
General Info: Yr. Est. 1994, Monthly, Trim Size-8½ x 11, 8 pages, No Color
Subscriptions: Indv. $195
Circulation: Total-2,500

Selected Research *Business*

Publishing Co: Moore, 45 Broadway, New York, NY 10006-3090; Title Tel # (212) 483-1861
Personnel: Publisher, Editor-Henry Tishman
Editorial Description: Features selected research on stocks and bonds.
General Info: Quarterly, Trim Size-8½ x 11, Offset press, Color

Selectrend *Business*

Publishing Co: Selectrend Research, Inc., 4641 Don Zarembo Dr, Los Angeles, CA 90008-4122
General Info: Weekly

Selling Mutual Funds *Business*

Publishing Co: Dow Jones Financial Publishing Corp., 179 Ave. at the Common, Shrewsbury, NJ 07702 Tel # (908) 389-8700 Fax # (908) 389-8701; Title Tel # (201) 389-3600 Title Fax # (201) 544-0779
General Info: Yr. Est. 1990, Monthly
Subscriptions: Indv. $955

Seminar Schedule
See: MANAGEMENT

Sentinel Investment Letter *Business*

Publishing Co: Hanover Investment Management Corp., 853 Second St Pike, Suite A-2, Richboro, PA 18954; Title Tel # (215) 953-6960
Editorial Description: Reviews recent & anticipated stock market activity & investment opportunities.
General Info: Yr. Est. 1978, Monthly, Trim Size-8½ x 11, 6 pages
Subscriptions: Indv. $150

Shelburne Securities Forecast *Business*

Publishing Co: Shelburne Securities Forecast, PO Box 5566, Arlington, VA 22205-0066
Personnel: Publisher, Editor-Robert Shelburne
Editorial Description: Analysis and recommendation on natural resource and closely related securities.
General Info: Yr. Est. 1976, Bi-weekly, Trim Size-8½ x 11, Offset press, 4 pages, No Color
Subscriptions: Indv. $49
List Rental: List Management Co.: Carnegie Marketing Assocs., Koll Executive Plaza, 3878 Carson St., Suite 220, Torrance, CA 90503 Tel # (310) 540-4757, Fax # (310) 540-7407, Actives: 4,568, $90/M

Short Alert

Publishing Co: Corporate Relations Group/Gulf Atlanti Publishing, 1801 Lee Rd Ste 301, Winter Park, FL 32789-2165 Tel # (407) 628-5200 Fax # (407) 628-0807
Personnel: Publisher-R.E. Veitia, Editor-P. Charuhas, Production Mgr.-Robyn Barto, Adv. Dir.-Jim Cassidy, Art Dir.-Mike Brahosky, Mktg. Dir.-Jack Rodriguez
Editorial Description: Stock tips on short selling opportunities.
General Info: Yr. Est. 1987, 3x/yr., Trim Size-8½ x 14, 1 pages, 2 Color, Newsprint
Subscriptions: Indv. $29
Circulation: Total-14,000
Advertising: Inquire for rates. Accepts Inserts.
List Rental: List Management Co.: Manager: Roland Outar; Applied List Management, 1801 Lee Rd Ste 301, Winter Park, FL 32789-2165 Tel # (407) 628-5200, Fax # (407) 628-0807, Actives: $150/M

Siegel Weekly Newsletter   *Business*

Publishing Co: Siegel Trading Co, Inc., 118 N Clinton St Ste 200, Chicago, IL 60661-2308; Title Tel # (312) 236-6789
Personnel: Editor-Allan Semenchuk
Editorial Description: Analysis and specific recommendations for most actively traded commodities each Thursday night.
General Info: (Formerly Siegel Market Letter), Yr. Est. 1952, Weekly, 4 pages, No Color

Silver & Gold Report   *Business*

Publishing Co: Weiss Publishing & Marketing, 4176 Burns Rd., Palm Beach Gardens, FL 33410-4606 Fax # (407) 625-6685; Title Tel # (407) 627-3300 Title Fax # (407) 684-9039
Personnel: Editor-James DiGeorgia
Editorial Description: Explores the inner workings of the silver and gold markets and the forces that move prices.
General Info: Monthly
Subscriptions: Indv. $96
List Rental: List Management Co.: Manager: Angela Leonard; Cornerstone List Mgrs., 2300 Yonge St., Ste. 2005, Box 2465, Toronto, ON M4P 1E4 Canada Tel # (416) 932-9555, Fax # (416) 932-9566, Actives: 5,347

Slanker Report, The   *Consumer*

Publishing Co: Ted Slanker, RR 2, Box 175, Powderly, TX 75473-9740; Title Tel # (903) 732-4653 Title Fax # (903) 732-4151
Personnel: Publisher, Editor-Ted Slanker
Editorial Description: Covers a broad spectrum of markets, economics, and investment ideas.
General Info: Monthly, Trim Size-8½ x 11, 8 pages, No Color, Matte
Subscriptions: Indv. $195, $17/copy

Small Business Compliance Advisor   *Business*

Publishing Co: Business & Legal Reports, Inc., 39 Academy St., PO Box 1513, Madison, CT 06443-2646 Tel # (860) 245-7448 Fax # (860) 245-2559
Editorial Description: Compliance guide on government regulations affecting small business operations.
General Info: Monthly

Smart Investing Newsletter   *Business*

Publishing Co: Phillips Publishing, Inc., 7811 Montrose Rd., Potomac, MD 20854-3394 Tel # (301) 340-2100 Fax # (301) 294-1307 Parent Co.-Phillips Business Information, Inc., Potomac; Title Tel # (301) 424-3700 Title Fax # (301) 340-2647
Personnel: Publisher-Thomas Phillips, Editor-Ken Gerbino, Mng. Editor-Carin Quinn, Mktg. Dir.-Kathy Gaito
Editorial Description: Ken Gerbino's Smart investing is a terrific source of great stock advice combing very profitable picks with easy-to-understand economic and market analysis and forecast.
General Info: (Formerly Kenneth J. Gerbino Investment Letter), Yr. Est. 1991, Monthly, Trim Size-8½ x 11, Sheetfed press, 8 pages, 2 Color, Coated
Subscriptions: Indv. $139, $5/copy
List Rental: Rents Lists

Smart Money   *Business, Consumer*

Publishing Co: Hirsch Organization, 6 Deer Trl, Old Tappan, NJ 07675-7125; Title Tel # (201) 664-3400
Personnel: Publisher, Editor-Yale Hirsch, Circ. Mgr.-Betty Ross, Adv. Dir.-Richard Silverman
Editorial Description: Specializes in recommending America's most undiscovered companies.
General Info: Yr. Est. 1973, Monthly, Sheetfed press, 8 pages, Color
Subscriptions: Indv. $98, $3/copy
Circulation: (ABC, As of 06/30/95), Total-576,338
List Rental: List Management Co.: Name-Finders Lists, Inc., 3180 18th St Fl 2, San Francisco, CA 94110-2028 Tel # (510) 533-4177, Fax # (510) 553-8677, Actives: 27,048, $90/M

Society Programs   *Association*

Publishing Co: Association for Investment Management and Research, AIMR, Box 3668, Charlottesville, VA 22903-0668 Fax # (804) 980-9755; Title Tel # (804) 977-6600 Title Fax # (804) 980-3685
Personnel: Editor-Charlie Morris
Editorial Description: Quarterly newsletter to Society leaders & Intl. members. Covers society's educational programs, location & date of events.
General Info: Quarterly, Trim Size-8½ x 11, Letrpr. press, 12 pages, No Color, Newsprint
Subscriptions: Indv. $45
Circulation: Total-600
List Rental: Rents Lists
Printing Co: Wayside Press, 2100 Berkmar Dr, Charlottesville, VA 22901-1499 Tel # (804) 973-3368

Sound Investing Basics   *Business*

Publishing Co: Alan B. Lancz & Assocs., Inc., 2400 N Reynolds Rd, Toledo, OH 43615-2818; Title Tel # (419) 536-5200 Title Fax # (419) 536-5401
Personnel: Circ. Mgr.-Alice Murphy, Production Mgr.-Kelly Duhaime
Editorial Description: Analysis of both on load and closed end mutual funds, in additions to offering valuable investment ideas, strotezies and tips with every issue. Specific recommendatrous of the best mutual funds for retirement plans and individuals (taxable) for the current investment climate.
General Info: Yr. Est. 1995, Quarterly, 2 pages, 2 Color
Subscriptions: Indv. $100, Can. $105, For. $110, $35/copy

Sound Mind Investing

Publishing Co: Pryor & Associates, 2337 Glen Eagle Dr, Louisville, KY 40222-6435; Title Tel # (502) 426-7420 .
General Info: Monthly
Subscriptions: Indv. $59

South Africa Review Service Reporter   *Business, Consumer*

Publishing Co: Investor Responsibility Research Ctr., 1350 Connecticut Ave. N.W., Suite 700, Washington, DC 20036-1701 Fax # (202) 833-3555; Title Tel # (202) 833-0700
Personnel: Editor-Meg Voorhes, Mktg. Dir.-John McMahon
Editorial Description: Devoted to recent political & economic developments in S. Africa.
General Info: Yr. Est. 1983, Quarterly, 20 pages
Subscriptions: Indv. $100

Special Investment Situations   *Business, Consumer*

Publishing Co: George Southerland, PO Box 4254, Chattanooga, TN 37405-0254
Personnel: Publisher, Editor-George Southerland
Editorial Description: Recommends low priced common stocks possessing substantial capital gain potential.
General Info: Yr. Est. 1979, Monthly, 4 pages, No Color
Subscriptions: Indv. $120

Special Situations

Publishing Co: Argus Research Corp., 17 Battery Pl., New York, NY 10004-1101; Title Tel # (212) 425-7500 Title Fax # (212) 509-5408
Personnel: Editor-John Eade
Editorial Description: Monthly investment magazine that investigates smaller cap stocks. Also includes computerized study screen & analysis of stocks.
General Info: Monthly, 8 pages
Subscriptions: Indv. $390, $35/copy
List Rental: List Management Co.: Robert Rickard List Marketing, 5512 Merrick Rd, Massapequa, NY 11758-6216 Tel # (516) 795-6466
Printing Co: Argus Printing & Mailing, 226 New York Ave, Huntington, NY 11743-2748 Tel # (516) 423-7710

Special Situations Newsletter   *Business*

Publishing Co: C.H. Kaplan Research Assoc., 26 Broadway, #200, New York, NY 10004-1703; Title Tel # (212) 908-4168 Title Fax # (201) 418-5085
Personnel: Publisher, Editor-Charles Kaplan
Editorial Description: Focuses on identifying special situations including undervalued stories, takeover candidates & low P/E stories.
General Info: Yr. Est. 1977, Monthly, Trim Size-8½ x 11, Offset press, 5 pages, ISSN: 1081-129x, No Color
Subscriptions: Indv. $150, For. $175

Spectrum Convertibles   *Business*

Publishing Co: CDA Investment Technologies Inc., 1355 Piccard Dr., Ste. 220, Rockville, MD 20850-4315 Tel # (954) 384-1500 Fax # (954) 384-1540; Title Tel # (301) 975-9600 Title Fax # (301) 590-1350
Personnel: Promotion Dir.-Lisa Warren
Editorial Description: Alphabetically lists by convertible issue the quarterly holdings and changes of all institutions with equity assets exceeding $100 million. Available 9 weeks after quarter end.
General Info: Quarterly, Trim Size-8½ x 11, 70 pages, No Color, Matte, Looseleaf
Subscriptions: Indv. $425, $150/copy
Circulation: Total-112

Spencer's Stock Selections   *Business, Consumer*

Publishing Co: Spencer's Stock Selections, 1276 Blueberry Ct, Altamonte Springs, FL 32714-1256; Title Tel # (407) 297-1487
Personnel: Editor-D.S. Robinson
Editorial Description: Covers stock investing for spectacular gains.
General Info: Monthly
Subscriptions: Indv. $145

Spread Letter   *Business*

Publishing Co: Spread Scope, Inc., Box 5841, Mission Hills, CA 91395-0841; Title Tel # (818) 365-4579
Editorial Description: Advisory service giving specific commodity spread trading advice. All recommended trades are made in a model account.
General Info: Yr. Est. 1974, Weekly, 6 pages, No Color
Subscriptions: Indv. $195

Standard & Poor's
CreditWeek International   *Business*

Publishing Co: Standard & Poor's Corp., 25 Broadway, New York, NY 10004 Tel # (212) 208-8000
Parent Co.-McGraw-Hill, New York
General Info: Yr. Est. 1983, Monthly, ISSN: 0739-9057

Standard & Poor's
Emerging & Special
Situations   *Business*

Publishing Co: Standard & Poor's Corp., 25 Broadway, New York, NY 10004 Parent Co.-McGraw-Hill, New York; Title Tel # (212) 208-8000
Personnel: Publisher-Stephen Sanborn, Editor-Robert Natale, Circ. Mgr.-Ronald Plotkin
Editorial Description: Describes new issues of corporate securities.
General Info: Yr. Est. 1982, Monthly, Trim Size-6¼ x 9, 32 pages, Ind/Abs/Online: Dialog, Dow Jones, NewsNet, No Color
Subscriptions: Indv. $180

Standard & Poor's The
Outlook   *Business*

Publishing Co: Standard & Poor's Corp., 25 Broadway, New York, NY 10004 Tel # (212) 208-8000
Parent Co.-McGraw-Hill, New York; Title Tel # (212) 208-8786
Editorial Description: Stock market and finance research.
General Info: Weekly
Subscriptions: Indv. $268
Circulation: Total-19,587
List Rental: List Management Co.: NRL Direct, 100 Union Ave, Cresskill, NJ 07626
Tel # (201) 568-0707, Actives: 20,000, $150/M

Standard & Poor's Stock
Guide   *Business*

Publishing Co: Standard & Poor's Corp., 25 Broadway, New York, NY 10004 Tel # (212) 208-8000
Parent Co.-McGraw-Hill, New York; Title Tel # (212) 208-8772
Editorial Description: Statistical info and data on over 5,000 stocks.
General Info: Monthly, 48 pages, ISSN: 0737-4135
List Rental: List Management Co.: NRL Direct, 100 Union Ave, Cresskill, NJ 07626
Tel # (201) 568-0707, Actives: 18,000, $125/M

Standard & Poor's
Trendline Daily Action
Stock Charts   *Business*

Publishing Co: Standard & Poor's Corp., 25 Broadway, New York, NY 10004 Tel # (212) 208-8000
Parent Co.-McGraw-Hill, New York; Title Tel # (212) 208-8772
Editorial Description: Daily plotted charts on 728 leading stocks.
General Info: (Formerly Standard & Poor's Trendlines), Yr. Est. 1960, Daily, ISSN: 0277-4968, Looseleaf
Subscriptions: Indv. $676
List Rental: Rents Lists

Stanger Report: A Guide
to Partnership
Investing, The   *Business, Association*

Publishing Co: Robert Stanger & Co., 1129 Broad St., Box 7490, Shrewsbury, NJ 07702-4314; Title Tel # (201) 389-3600 Title Fax # (201) 544-0779
Personnel: Publisher-Robert Stanger, Editor-Keith Allaire, Feature Ed.-Nancy Matton, Production Mgr.-Susanne Grajek, Mktg. Dir.-Tara Watkins
Editorial Description: Offers in-depth analysis of the limited partnership industry.
General Info: Yr. Est. 1979, Monthly, Trim Size-8½ x 11, Sheetfed press, 36 pages, ISSN: 01956620, Ind/Abs/Online: Newsnet, 20% ads, 2 Color, Coated, Saddle-stitched
Subscriptions: Indv. $447
Circulation: Readership-1,000
Advertising: $2,000. Accepts Inserts.
List Rental: Actives: $100/M, Expires: $80/M

Stanger Review:
Partnership Sales   *Business*

Publishing Co: Robert Stanger & Co., 1129 Broad St., Box 7490, Shrewsbury, NJ 07702-4314; Title Tel # (908) 389-3600
Personnel: Publisher-Robert Stanger, Editor-Keith Allaire, Circ. Mgr.-Donna Aumach, Mktg. Dir.-Tara Watkins
Editorial Description: Limited partnership sales.
General Info: Monthly, Trim Size-14 x 8½, 25 pages
Subscriptions: Indv. $6,000, $900/copy
List Rental: Rents Lists

Stark Research CTA
Report

Publishing Co: Stark Research, Inc., 141 S Whitehall Ct # 591, Palatine, IL 60067-5836; Title Tel # (708) 359-4508
Personnel: Publisher-Caniel Stark
Editorial Description: Comprehensive performanc echarts & statistics on over 100 commodity, trading advisors. Also, names, addresses, & phone numbers.
General Info: Yr. Est. 1989, Quarterly, Looseleaf
Subscriptions: Indv. $225, Can. $225, For. $240, $75/copy
List Rental: Rents Lists

Statistical Abstract Service   *Business, Consumer*

Publishing Co: Commodity Research Bureau, 75 Wall St., New York, NY 10005
Tel # (212) 504-7754
General Info: 3x/yr.
Subscriptions: Indv. $65

Statistical Indicator Reports   *Business*

Publishing Co: S.I. Assocs., PO Box 107, North Egremont, MA 01252-0107; Title Tel # (413) 528-3280
Personnel: Editor-Leonard Lempert
Editorial Description: Where the economy has been, is, & is going.
General Info: Yr. Est. 1954, Weekly, Letrpr. press, 4 pages, No Color, Newsprint
Subscriptions: Indv. $210

Statistical Service   *Business*

Publishing Co: Standard & Poor's Corp., 25 Broadway, New York, NY 10004 Parent Co.-McGraw-Hill, New York; Title Tel # (212) 208-8000
Personnel: Editor-Elliott Shurgin
Editorial Description: A comprehensive statistical service for business and industry.
General Info: Monthly, Looseleaf
Subscriptions: Indv. $490, $75/copy

Stock Chart Service   *Business*

Publishing Co: R. W. Mansfield Co, 2973 John F. Kennedy Blvd., Jersey City, NJ 07306-3884
Tel # (201) 795-0630; Title Tel # (201) 795-0629 Title Fax # (201) 795-5476
Personnel: Editor-Ira Wilkow
Editorial Description: Earnings and dividends, relative strength, moving averages for each stock. 3 services-one for each exchange.
General Info: Yr. Est. 1938, Weekly, Looseleaf
Subscriptions: Indv. $175
Advertising: Accepts Inserts.

Stock Market Monitor   *Business*

Publishing Co: Stock Market Monitor, Inc., PO Box 3802, Lisle, IL 60532-8802
Personnel: Editor-Frank Havranek, Circ. Mgr.-Jana Susankova, Adv. Dir.-Doris Schlembach
Editorial Description: Technical analysis of stock market trends and specific investment recommendations.
General Info: Yr. Est. 1981, Bi-weekly, Offset press, 6 pages, No Color
Subscriptions: Indv. $115
Circulation: Total-1,100

Stock Market Semiotics

Publishing Co: Market Semiotics, PO Box 1457, Castleton, VT 05735-1457
General Info: Daily

Stock Market Trendex   *Business, Consumer*

Publishing Co: Trendex Research Corp., 6006 Forest Bnd, San Antonio, TX 78240-3330
General Info: Yr. Est. 1948, Weekly
Subscriptions: Indv. $275

Stock Picture   *Business*

Publishing Co: M.C. Horsey & Co., Inc., PO Box H, Salisbury, MD 21802-1130; Title Tel # (301) 742-3700
Personnel: Editor-Jerome Sterling
General Info: Bi-monthly
Subscriptions: Indv. $100

Stock Price & Ratio Indexes   *Business*

Publishing Co: Standard & Poor's Corp., 25 Broadway, New York, NY 10004 Parent Co.-McGraw-Hill, New York; Title Tel # (212) 208-8000
Personnel: Editor-Elliott Shurgin
Editorial Description: Over 100 industry group stock price indexes with ratios for comparison with the market as a whole.
General Info: Weekly, 2 pages, 2 Color, Looseleaf
Subscriptions: Indv. $400

Stockmarket Cycles   *Business*

Publishing Co: Stockmarket Cycles, PO Box 6873, Santa Rosa, CA 95406-0873; Title Tel # (213) 465-5543
Personnel: Publisher, Editor-Peter Ellades, Circ. Mgr.-Ruth Neumarker
Editorial Description: Stock market advisory letter with technical & cyclical emphasis and a daily telephone hotline giving shorter term projections for most market averages, gold, bonds, T-bills & stock index futures.
General Info: Yr. Est. 1975, 18x/yr., Trim Size-8½ x 11, Offset press, 4 pages, No Color
Subscriptions: Indv. $480
Circulation: Total-3,500
Printing Co: AJ Printing & Graohics, 1350 Central Ave Ste 5, Santa Rosa, CA 95401-4779

Strategic Investment   *Business, Consumer*

Publishing Co: Agora, Inc., 105 W. Monoment St., Baltimore, MD 21202-4702 Tel # (410) 783-2647 Fax # (410) 223-2662; Title Tel # (410) 234-0515
Editorial Description: Dispenses investment advice based on a worldwide geopolitical outlook.
General Info: Yr. Est. 1985, Monthly
Subscriptions: Indv. $59
Circulation: Total-33,103
List Rental: List Management Co.: Name Bank, 14 W. Monument St., Baltimore, MD 21201 Tel # (410) 783-8463, Fax # (410) 783-8464, Actives: 38,842, $135/M, Expires: 19,605, $100/M

Strategies   *Business, Consumer*

Publishing Co: Sponsor-Manulife Financial, Ariad Custom Publishing, 119 Spadina Ave., #1005, Toronto, ON M5V 2L1 Canada Tel # (416) 971-9294
Editorial Description: Provides investment and money management information for insurance policyholders.
General Info: (Formerly Manulife Strategies), Yr. Est. 1993, Quarterly

Street Noises   *Business, Consumer*

Publishing Co: Prospector Publications, B101-325 Howe Street, Vancouver, BC V6C 1Z7 Canada; Title Tel # (604) 684-8166
Personnel: Editor-David O'Keefe
Editorial Description: Independent look at a selection of VSE trading companies.
General Info: Yr. Est. 1993, Bi-monthly, Trim Size-8½ x 11, 4 pages, 2 Color, Matte
Subscriptions: Indv. $25
Advertising: Accepts Inserts.

Street Smart Investing   *Business*

Publishing Co: 13D Research, Inc., SE Executive Park, 100 Executive Drive, Brewster, NY 10509; Title Tel # (914) 278-6500 Title Fax # (914) 278-6797
Personnel: Publisher-Kiril Sokoloff, Editor-Liz Read, Circ. Mgr.-Karen Blackman, Adv. Dir., Promotion Dir.-Wendy Boehm
Editorial Description: Provides equity research. Focuses on a particular corporation in each issue, providing investment history of valuations and risks. Updates previous company reports. Stock selections based on buying activities of na'
General Info: Yr. Est. 1983, Bi-weekly, 12 pages, Ind/Abs/Online: ion's smartest investors via 13D, 13F and insider government filings., 2 Color
Subscriptions: Indv. $350, $15/copy

Strongest Stocks   *Business, Consumer*

Publishing Co: Strongest Stocks, PO Box 565, Sausalito, CA 94966-0565
Personnel: Publisher-Joseph Gillaspy
General Info: Yr. Est. 1965, 18x/yr.
Subscriptions: Indv. $100

Sturza's Medical Investment Letter   *Business, Consumer*

Publishing Co: Taurus Littrow Publishing, 424 West End Ave 7th flr, New York, NY 10024-5777; Title Tel # (212) 873-7200 Title Fax # (212) 873-7799
Personnel: Publisher, Editor-Evan Sturza
Editorial Description: Provides advice on investing in the health care industry in consultation with a team of medical experts. Emphasis is on biotechnology, pharmaceutical, and medical device companies.
General Info: Yr. Est. 1991, Weekly
Subscriptions: Indv. $295, Inst. $295, Can. $320, For. $345, $30/copy

Successful Investing   *Business*

Publishing Co: Successful Investing Co., 256 S Robertson Blvd # 711, Beverly Hills, CA 90211-2898; Title Tel # (310) 657-1151
Personnel: Editor-Martin Armstrong
General Info: Monthly
Subscriptions: Indv. $195

Survival Tomorrow

Publishing Co: Personal Survival Center Inc., PO Box 1050, Rogue River, OR 97537-1050; Title Tel # (503) 582-1520
Personnel: Publisher-Neil McCaffrey, III, Editor-Nancy Tappan
Editorial Description: Self-sufficiency & long-term survival.
General Info: Yr. Est. 1977, Monthly, 12 pages
Subscriptions: Indv. $60
List Rental: List Management Co.: Name-Finders Lists, Inc., 3180 18th St Fl 2, San Francisco, CA 94110-2028 Tel # (510) 533-4177, Fax # (510) 553-8677, Actives: 18,800, $65/M

Swaps Monitor   *Business*

Publishing Co: Swaps Monitor, 648 Broadway, Suite 705, New York, NY 10012; Title Tel # (212) 254-9500
Personnel: Publisher-Paul Spraos
Editorial Description: Investment industry newsletter that covers industry news and infornmation.
General Info: Bi-weekly
Subscriptions: Indv. $1,000

Switch Fund Advisory

Publishing Co: Schabacker Investment Management, 8945 Shady Grove Ct., Gaithersburg, MD 20877-1308; Title Tel # (301) 840-0301
General Info: Yr. Est. 1976, Monthly
Subscriptions: Indv. $140

Systems & Forecasts   *Consumer*

Publishing Co: Signalert Corp., 150 Great Neck Rd Ste 204, Great Neck, NY 11021-3309; Title Tel # (516) 829-6444 Title Fax # (516) 829-9366
Personnel: Publisher, Editor-Gerald Appel
Editorial Description: Investment advisory service which monitors stocks, bonds, options, mutual funds and the general stock market. Provides market commentary and timing advice.
General Info: Yr. Est. 1973, Bi-weekly, Offset press, 8 pages, No Color
Subscriptions: Indv. $225
Circulation: Total-1,500
List Rental: List Management Co.: WMI/Worldata, 5200 Town Center Circle, Boca Raton, FL 33486 Tel # (407) 393-8200, Fax # (407) 368-8345, Actives: 45,400, $80/M

Taipan   *Business*

Publishing Co: Agora, Inc., 105 W. Monoment St., Baltimore, MD 21202-4702 Tel # (410) 783-2647 Fax # (410) 223-2662; Title Tel # (410) 234-0515 Title Fax # (410) 837-3879
Personnel: Publisher-William Bonner, Editor-Christoph Amborger, Editor-Karim Rahemtulla, Co-Editor-J. Christoph Amberger, Co-Editor-Karin Rahentulla, Circ. Mgr.-Cynthia Rott, Product Mgr.-Sean Martin, Mktg. Dir.-Deeba Jafri
Editorial Description: Investments in securities, stocks, real estate, currencies and collectibles.
General Info: Yr. Est. 1984, 24x/yr., Trim Size-8½ x 11, 20 pages, 2 Color, Matte, Saddle-stitched
Subscriptions: Indv. $129
Circulation: Total-50,000
Advertising: Inquire for rates.
List Rental: List Management Co.: Manager: Elizabeth Dent; Name Bank, 14 W. Monument St., Baltimore, MD 21201 Tel # (410) 783-8463, Fax # (410) 783-8464, Actives: 36,282, $135/M, Hotline: 4,626, $150/M, Expires: 43,934, $100/M

Taurus   *Business*

Publishing Co: Taurus Corp., 133 W Boscawen St # 767, Winchester, VA 22601-4115; Title Tel # (703) 667-4827 Title Fax # (703) 667-7484
Personnel: Publisher, Editor-Michael Chisholm
Editorial Description: The Taurus newsletter is for futures & future options. Recommendations for both long-term & short-term trading. Service features nightly hotline.
General Info: Yr. Est. 1976, Weekly, Mimeo press, 4 pages, No Color
Subscriptions: Indv. $400
Advertising: Accepts Inserts.
List Rental: Actives: $75/M

Tax Avoidance Digest   *Consumer*   **CPM: $93**

Publishing Co: Agora, Inc., 105 W. Monoment St., Baltimore, MD 21202-4702 Tel # (410) 783-2647 Fax # (410) 223-2662; Title Tel # (410) 234-0515
Personnel: Publisher-William Bonner, Editor-Robert Carlson, Circ. Mgr.-Daryl Berver, Production Mgr.-Douglas Cook, Adv. Dir.-Lee Euler, Art Dir.-Alex Nosevitch, Promotion Dir.-Lynn Fredericks
Editorial Description: The latest legal ways to avoid taxes.
General Info: Yr. Est. 1981, Monthly, Trim Size-8½ x 11, Web press, 24 pages, ISSN: 0733-2254, 20% ads, 2 Color, Newsprint, Saddle-stitched
Subscriptions: Indv. $71
Acquistions: Publication Bought
Circulation: Total-40,000
Advertising: $3,750.
List Rental: List Management Co.: Manager: Dawn McGrath; Name Bank, 14 W. Monument St., Baltimore, MD 21201 Tel # (410) 783-8463, Fax # (410) 783-8464, Actives: 61,311, $135/M
Printing Co: Cascio-Color Corp., 8000 Corporate Ct, Springfield, VA 22153-3132 Tel # (703) 750-0001

Tax, Estate and Financial Planning for the Elderly
See: BANKING & FINANCE

Tax Hotline
See: TAXES

TaxLetter, The
See: TAXES

Technical Indicator Review   *Business*

Publishing Co: Chartcraft, Inc., 30 Church St # 2046, New Rochelle, NY 10801-6302; Title Tel # (914) 632-0422 Title Fax # (914) 632-0335
Personnel: Editor-Michael Burke
Editorial Description: Investment service pinpointing the market trend by technical indicator analysis.
General Info: Yr. Est. 1960, 26x/yr.
Subscriptions: Indv. $99
List Rental: Rents Lists

Technical Trends   *Business*

Publishing Co: Technical Trends, PO Box 792, Wilton, CT 06897-0792; Title Tel # (203) 762-0229 Title Fax # (203) 761-1504
Personnel: Editor-John McGinley
Editorial Description: Investment letter which presents tested stock market indicators in chart form, together with commentary.
General Info: Yr. Est. 1960, Weekly, Trim Size-4 x 9, Offset press, 24 pages, ISSN: 0889-9525, No Color, Saddle-stitched
Subscriptions: Indv. $147, Can. $147, For. $180
List Rental: Actives: $100/M, Expires: $75/M

Ted Slanker's Market Update   *Business, Consumer*

Publishing Co: Ted Slanker, RR 2, Box 175, Powderly, TX 75473-9740; Title Tel # (903) 732-4653 Title Fax # (903) 732-4151
Personnel: Publisher, Editor-Ted Slanker
Editorial Description: Directed towards investors, brokers, analysts, and others interested in gold and gold stocks.
General Info: (Formerly Market Update), Yr. Est. 1984, Irregular, Trim Size-8½ x 11, 10 pages, No Color, Matte
Subscriptions: Free To Qualified Recipient
Circulation: Readership-10,800

Telephone Growth Income Service
Business

Publishing Co: Kinsman & Assocs., 1901 Sobre Vista Rd, Sonoma, CA 95476-3237; Title Tel # (707) 935-6504
Personnel: Editor-Robert Kinsman, Circ. Mgr.-Bobbi Alexander, Production Mgr.-Holly Newman
Editorial Description: Conservative investment advice emphasizing interest rate trends and the economy.
General Info: (Formerly Robert Kinsman's Low Risk Advisory), Yr. Est. 1979, Monthly, Trim Size-8$\frac{1}{2}$ x 11, 10 pages, 2 Color
Subscriptions: Indv. $175
Circulation: Total-3,500

Texas Trader's Trendex
Business

Publishing Co: Trendex Research Corp., 6006 Forest Bnd, San Antonio, TX 78240-3330
General Info: Weekly
Subscriptions: Indv. $248

Tiger on Spreads
Business, Consumer

Publishing Co: Tiger on Spreads, PO Box 1414, Mc Lean, VA 22101-1414; Title Tel # (202) 463-8608
Personnel: Editor-Phillip Tiger
Editorial Description: Concerned with commodity futures with emphasis on Spread relationships. Features breakdown by market groups, fundamental, technical, cyclic & historical analysis.
General Info: Yr. Est. 1981, Bi-weekly, Sheetfed press, 8 pages
Subscriptions: Indv. $240, Can. $240, For. $240
Circulation: Total-300
Advertising: Inquire for rates.

Timer Digest
Business, Consumer

Publishing Co: Timer Digest, Inc., PO Box 1688, Greenwich, CT 06836-1688; Title Tel # (203) 629-3503
Personnel: Editor-James Schmidt
Editorial Description: Lists stock market and mutual fund timers and their track records.
General Info: Yr. Est. 1982, 18x/yr.
Subscriptions: Indv. $225
Circulation: Total-600

Timing
Business

Publishing Co: Timing Financial Services, Ltd., 3219 W Mescal St, Phoenix, AZ 85029-4123; Title Tel # (602) 942-3111 Title Fax # (602) 789-7883
Personnel: Publisher, Editor-William Jaeger
Editorial Description: Covers the commodities futures markets from a fundamental & technical perspective. Also predicks worldwide weather patterns & their effect on commodity prices.
General Info: Yr. Est. 1979, 24x/yr., Desktop press, 8 pages
Subscriptions: Indv. $144, $6/copy
Advertising: Accepts Inserts.

Timing Analysis Projection
Business

Publishing Co: Covato Research Corp., Manor Oak II, Ste. 333, 1910 Cochran Rd., Pittsburgh, PA 15220; Title Tel # (412) 341-3700 Title Fax # (412) 341-8922
Personnel: Editor-Mr. Covato
General Info: Yr. Est. 1971, Monthly, Trim Size-8$\frac{1}{2}$ x 11, 54 pages, 2 Color
Subscriptions: Inst. $15,000

Timing and Tactics
Business

Publishing Co: Wilson Foster, 4987 Olivas Park Dr Ste 100, Ventura, CA 93003-7667; Title Tel # (805) 644-8207
Personnel: Publisher-James Alpdher, Editor-Harvey Willson
Editorial Description: Investment advisory letter for the fiduciary and serious investor.
General Info: Semi-monthly, 7 pages
Subscriptions: Indv. $175

Today's Investor
Business, Consumer

Publishing Co: Forte Communications, 111 Broadway Rm 1900, New York, NY 10006-1901 Tel # (212) 406-4466; Title Tel # (212) 406-4964
Personnel: Editor in Chief-K.C. Grainger, Mng. Editor-Charles W. McLaughlin, Publisher, Bk. Rev. Ed.-Patricia Meding
Editorial Description: Newspaper which gives advice on stocks selling for $15 or less per share for institutions, brokers, other market professionals and individual investors.
General Info: (Formerly Penny Stock News), Yr. Est. 1980, Monthly, Trim Size-8$\frac{1}{2}$ x 11, 6 pages, ISSN: 1042-8127, 2 Color
Subscriptions: Indv. $59, Can. $89, For. $109
Circulation: Total-31,000
Advertising: Inquire for rates. Accepts Inserts.
List Rental: List Management Co.: JAMI Marketing, 2 Blue Hill Plz, Pearl River, NY 10965-3101 Tel # (914) 620-0700, Fax # (914) 620-1885, Actives: 25,000, $95/M

Today's Options
Business

Publishing Co: Techno-Fundamental Investments, Inc., PO Box 14111, Scottsdale, AZ 85267-4111; Title Tel # (602) 996-2908
Personnel: Editor-Bob Jubb
General Info: Yr. Est. 1975, Monthly
Subscriptions: Indv. $195
List Rental: List Management Co.: Carnegie Marketing Assocs., Koll Executive Plaza, 3878 Carson St., Suite 220, Torrance, CA 90503 Tel # (310) 540-4757, Fax # (310) 540-7407, Actives: 7,543, $90/M

Tomorrow's Commodities
Business

Publishing Co: Techno-Fundamental Investments, Inc., PO Box 14111, Scottsdale, AZ 85267-4111; Title Tel # (602) 996-2908
Personnel: Editor-Bob Jubb
Editorial Description: Informs investors about commodities.
General Info: Yr. Est. 1975, 12x/yr.
Subscriptions: Indv. $295
List Rental: List Management Co.: Carnegie Marketing Assocs., Koll Executive Plaza, 3878 Carson St., Suite 220, Torrance, CA 90503 Tel # (310) 540-4757, Fax # (310) 540-7407, Actives: 11,915, $90/M

Tomorrow's Stocks
Business

Publishing Co: Techno-Fundamental Investments, Inc., PO Box 14111, Scottsdale, AZ 85267-4111; Title Tel # (602) 996-2908
Personnel: Editor-Bob Jubb
General Info: Yr. Est. 1975, Semi-monthly
Subscriptions: Indv. $145
List Rental: List Management Co.: Carnegie Marketing Assocs., Koll Executive Plaza, 3878 Carson St., Suite 220, Torrance, CA 90503 Tel # (310) 540-4757, Fax # (310) 540-7407, Actives: 28,078, $90/M

Trader's Option
Consumer

Publishing Co: Trader's Option, PO Box 727, Quincy, IL 62306-0727; Title Tel # (217) 222-4827
Personnel: Publisher, Editor-Thomas Lavery
Editorial Description: Short-term market timer's financial advisory for stocks/options traders.
General Info: Yr. Est. 1985, Monthly, 4 pages
Subscriptions: $18/copy

Trading Trends

Publishing Co: Minneapolis Grain Exchange, 130 Grain Exchange Bldg., 400 S. 4th St., Minneapolis, MN 55415; Title Tel # (612) 338-6212 Title Fax # (612) 339-1155
Personnel: Editor-Colleen Smith
General Info: Weekly
Circulation: Total-2,200

Transactions & Intentions Report
Business

Publishing Co: Vickers Stock Research Corp., 226 New York Ave, Huntington, NY 11743-2748; Title Tel # (516) 423-7710 Title Fax # (516) 423-7715
Editorial Description: Lists 144's and 130's that have been released by the SEC.
General Info: Bi-monthly
Subscriptions: Indv. $495
List Rental: Actives: $125/M

Treasury Manager's Report
See: ACCOUNTING

Trendway Advisory Service

Publishing Co: Sachs Co., The, 1346 S 3rd St, Louisville, KY 40208-2151; Title Tel # (502) 893-7765
Personnel: Editor-Richard E. Dysart, Adv. Dir.-Calvin Anderson
Editorial Description: Investment advice based on technical and fundamental analysis.
General Info: Yr. Est. 1933, Weekly
Subscriptions: Indv. $95

Tucker's Letter
Consumer

Publishing Co: Tucker's Letter, 1840 Vermont Ave NW, Washington, DC 20001-5006; Title Tel # (202) 667-3678
Personnel: Circ. Mgr.-John Beamer, Jr., Adv. Dir.-Leona Lea, Publisher, Editor, Art Dir.-Eugene Tucker
Editorial Description: Investment newsletter with emphasis on listed securities, art, antiques.
General Info: Yr. Est. 1972, Monthly, Trim Size-8 x 10, Letrpr. press, 4 pages, No Color
Subscriptions: Indv. $48, $5/copy
Circulation: Total-5,000

Turnaround Letter
Business, Consumer

Publishing Co: New Generation Research, Inc., 225 Friend St Ste 801, Boston, MA 02114-1812 Fax # (617) 573-4554; Title Tel # (617) 573-9550 Title Fax # (617) 573-9554
Personnel: Publisher, Editor-George Putnam
Editorial Description: Investment advisory newsletter providing information on promising stocks.
General Info: Yr. Est. 1986, Monthly, Sheetfed press, 10 pages, No Color, Newsprint
Subscriptions: Indv. $195
List Rental: List Management Co.: WMI/Worldata, 5200 Town Center Circle, Boca Raton, FL 33486 Tel # (407) 393-8200, Fax # (407) 368-8345, Actives: 9,763, $125/M
Printing Co: Newsletter Services, Inc., 9700 Philadelphia Court, Lanham, MD 20706 Tel # (301) 731-5200, Fax # (301) 731-5201

Turning Points
Business

Publishing Co: Concept Publishing, PO Box 500, York, NY 14592-0500; Title Tel # (716) 243-3148
Personnel: Publisher-Jim Dovan, Editor-David Coleman
Editorial Description: Stock and bond market short and long termtiming service with specific investment recommendations.
General Info: (Formerly Long Term Investing), Yr. Est. 1975, Semi-monthly, Trim Size-8$\frac{1}{4}$ x 10$\frac{1}{2}$, Sheetfed press, 4 pages, No Color, Newsprint
Subscriptions: Indv. $98
Circulation: Total-400

UnDiscoverd Stocks   *Consumer*

Publishing Co: UnDiscoverd Stocks, P.O. Box 109665, Palm Beach, FL 33410
Personnel: Editor-Nancy Zambell
Editorial Description: Information on picking little known stocks for investment.
General Info: Monthly
Subscriptions: Indv. $99

Under $5 Stock Survey   *Business, Consumer*

Publishing Co: American Small Business & Investors Association, 375 Douglas Ave., Ste 1012, Altamonte Springs, FL 32714-3315 Tel # (407) 788-0123 Fax # (407) 788-3933
Personnel: Editor-David Robinson
Editorial Description: Dedicated to finding small, profitable companies to invest in.
General Info: Monthly, Trim Size-8½ x 11, 4 pages, 2 Color
Subscriptions: Indv. $69

United & Babson Inv.
Report   *Business*

Publishing Co: Babson-United, 101 Prescott St, Wellesley Hills, MA 02181-7528; Title Tel # (617) 235-0900 Title Fax # (617) 235-9450
Personnel: Editor-Donald Fox, Circ. Mgr.-Kevin Quinn
Editorial Description: Investment information and stock advice.
General Info: Yr. Est. 1919, Weekly, Trim Size-8½ x 11, 12 pages, No Color, Matte
Subscriptions: Indv. $238
List Rental: List Management Co.: UBCD Direct, 101 Prescott Street, Wellesley Hills, MA 02181 Tel # (617) 235-0900, Fax # (617) 235-9450

U.S. & World Early Warning
Report for Investors   *Consumer*

Publishing Co: Henry-Madison Research, PO Box 1616-xo, Rocklin, CA 95677-7616; Title Tel # (916) 624-5750 Title Fax # (916) 632-2501
Personnel: Editor in Chief-Richard Maybury, Mktg. Dir.-Marilyn Williams
Editorial Description: Covers world news and issues for investors. Emphasis an how wars in east europe, asia and north africa affect the economy and investments.
General Info: Yr. Est. 1991, 10x/yr., Trim Size-8 x 11, 8 pages, No Color, Matte
Subscriptions: Indv. $149, $15/copy
Circulation: (100% controlled), Total-3,000

U.S. Council for International Business Newsletter
See: BUSINESS & INDUSTRY

U.S. Investment Report   *Business, Consumer*

Publishing Co: Quickel International Corp., 25 5th Ave Apt 4c, New York, NY 10003-4308 Tel # (212) 460-9200; Title Tel # (212) 995-2963 Title Fax # (212) 477-6070
Personnel: Publisher, Editor-Stephen Quickel, Circ. Mgr.-Helen Howard, Production Mgr.-Robert Stewart, Art Dir.-Bruce Haag
Editorial Description: Independent investment advisory providing serious U.S. and Foreign investors with authoritative recommendations, Model portfolio's and strategies, principally in a U.S. stock market.
General Info: Yr. Est. 1985, Semi-monthly, Sheetfed press, 8 pages, Color-cover, Newsprint
Subscriptions: Indv. $228, Can. $252, For. $252
Printing Co: Globe Mail Agency, Inc., 541 W 25th St, New York, NY 10001-5501 Tel # (212) 675-4600

Unlimited Editions Preview
See: BANKING & FINANCE

Uptrend, the Canadian
Penny Market Newsletter   *Business*

Publishing Co: Uptrend Investment Services, Box 49333, Bentall Four, Vancouver, BC V7X 1L4 Canada; Title Tel # (604) 640-0360 Title Fax # (604) 640-0300
Personnel: Editor-Henry Huber
Editorial Description: For the speculator/investor, specializing in the Vancouver Stock Exchange penny market.
General Info: (Formerly Hubergram), Yr. Est. 1979, Monthly, Trim Size-8½ x 14, Sheetfed press, 2 pages, Color
Subscriptions: Indv. $149
Circulation: Total-1,000

Uptrender Stock Index
Advisory   *Business*

Publishing Co: Uptrender Stock Market Advisory, 909 Waukegan Rd, Deerfield, IL 60015-3014; Title Tel # (847) 945-8004
Personnel: Publisher, Editor-Jay Adler
Editorial Description: Bullish alerts to prompt just-in-time entry into the stock market when the market presses on Springboards. Default/fax.
General Info: Daily, 1 pages, No Color
Subscriptions: Indv. $195

Utility Forecaster   *Business, Consumer*

Publishing Co: Capitol Publications, Inc., 1101 King St., Ste. 444, Alexandria, VA 22314-2968 Tel # (703) 683-4100 Fax # (703) 739-6501
Personnel: Editor-Roger Conrad
Editorial Description: Safe, dependable utility investment information.
General Info: Monthly
Subscriptions: Indv. $87
List Rental: List Management Co.: Media Mart, 1101 King St Ste 400, Alexandria, VA 22314-2944 Tel # (703) 548-2400, Fax # (703) 683-6974, Actives: 24,540, $140/M

ValuTalk   *Business, Consumer*

Publishing Co: Investor's Hotline, Inc., 10616 Beaver Dam Rd., Hunt Valley, MD 21030-2232 Tel # (410) 771-0064 Fax # (410) 584-1043
Personnel: Publisher-Joseph Bradley, Editor-Joanne Schenk, Product Mgr.-Jennifer Kreshtool
Editorial Description: In-depth objective evaluation of ground floor investment values. Includes cassette featuring investment professionals.
General Info: (Formerly ValuTrac), Yr. Est. 1990, Monthly
Subscriptions: Indv. $225
List Rental: List Management Co.: Carnegie Marketing Assocs., Koll Executive Plaza, 3878 Carson St., Suite 220, Torrance, CA 90503 Tel # (310) 540-4757, Fax # (310) 540-7407, Actives: 3,583, $195/M

Value Investing   *Business*

Publishing Co: Value Line, Inc., 220 E 42nd St., 6th Fl., New York, NY 10017-5891 Tel # (212) 907-1500 Fax # (212) 818-9748
General Info: Monthly

Value Line Convertibles   *Business*

Publishing Co: Value Line, Inc., 220 E 42nd St., 6th Fl., New York, NY 10017-5891 Fax # (212) 818-9748; Title Tel # (212) 907-1500
Personnel: Publisher-Allan Lyons, Editor-F. Barry Nelson
Editorial Description: Evaluates & provides statistical data for 585 convertibles & 90 warrants.
General Info: Yr. Est. 1970, Weekly, Web press, 32 pages, ISSN: 0737-0717, No Color
Subscriptions: Indv. $475
Circulation: (100% controlled), Total-5,000
List Rental: Actives: $110/M

Value Line Investment
Survey   *Consumer*

Publishing Co: Value Line, Inc., 220 E 42nd St., 6th Fl., New York, NY 10017-5891 Fax # (212) 818-9748; Title Tel # (212) 907-1500
Personnel: Editor-Arnold Bernhard, Circ. Mgr.-John Scunziano, Adv. Dir.-John Snyder
Editorial Description: Provides ratings and analysis of 1,700 stocks in 67 industries. Each edition contains full-page reports on about 110 leading stock with Summary-Index to 1,700 stocks updated.
General Info: Yr. Est. 1931, Weekly, Trim Size-8½ x 11, Offset press, 120 pages, 2 Color
Subscriptions: Indv. $495, $10/copy
Circulation: Total-96,000

Value Line OTC Special
Situations Service   *Business*

Publishing Co: Value Line, Inc., 220 E 42nd St., 6th Fl., New York, NY 10017-5891 Fax # (212) 818-9748; Title Tel # (212) 907-1500
Personnel: Publisher, Editor-Peter Shraga, Circ. Mgr.-John Scunziano, Adv. Dir.-Pat Woll
Editorial Description: Analyzes and recommends two special situations monthly, maintaining all previous recommendations under supervision.
General Info: Yr. Est. 1951, Bi-monthly, Trim Size-8½ x 11, Offset press, 20 pages, No Color
Subscriptions: Indv. $390

Value Line Options   *Business*

Publishing Co: Value Line, Inc., 220 E 42nd St., 6th Fl., New York, NY 10017-5891 Fax # (212) 818-9748; Title Tel # (212) 907-1500
Personnel: Publisher, Editor-Allan Lyons
Editorial Description: Evaluates & provides price charts for equity & index options.
General Info: Yr. Est. 1970, Weekly, Trim Size-8½ x 11, Web press, 120 pages, ISSN: 0737-0709
Subscriptions: Indv. $445
Circulation: Total-5,000
List Rental: Actives: $110/M

Vancouver   *Business*

Publishing Co: George Cross News Letter Ltd., 1710-609 Granville St., Vancouver, BC V7Y 1G5 Canada; Title Tel # (604) 683-7265 Title Fax # (607) 683-5306
Personnel: Publisher-G.B. Cross, Editor-E.E. Dickson
Editorial Description: Reports on activities of firms active on the Vancouver Stock Exchange.
General Info: Yr. Est. 1948, Daily, 6 pages, No Color, Newsprint
Subscriptions: Indv. $420, Can. $337, For. $605, $1/copy

Vaughan Report   *Business*

Publishing Co: Vaughan Report, 277 West End Ave., New York, NY 10023-2604
Personnel: Publisher, Editor-David Vaughan
Editorial Description: Financial news & commentary.
General Info: Yr. Est. 1980, Bi-monthly
Subscriptions: Indv. $75

Venture Capital Journ.   *Business*

Publishing Co: Securities Data Publishing, Inc., 40 W. 57th St., Ste. 802, New York, NY 10019-4001 Tel # (212) 765-5311 Fax # (212) 765-6123 Parent Co.-Thomson Financial Publishing, Skokie
Editorial Description: Information regarding venture capital and private equity.
General Info: Monthly
Subscriptions: Indv. $845

Vietnam Business InfoTrack
See: INTERNATIONAL TRADE

Volume Reversal Survey *Business*

Publishing Co: Volume Reversal Survey, PO Box 1451, Sedona, AZ 86339-1451;
Title Tel # (602) 282-1275 Title Fax # (520) 282-6364
Personnel: Publisher, Editor-Mark Leibovit
Editorial Description: Stock market newsletter utilizing volume & other technical tools to predict market and individual stock direction.
General Info: Yr. Est. 1979, Monthly, Trim Size-8½ x 11, Sheetfed press, 6 pages, ISSN: 8755-3406, 2 Color, Coated
Subscriptions: Indv. $360, $15/copy
Acquistions: Publication Bought
Circulation: Total-500
List Rental: Actives: 19,000, $85/M

W.D. Gann Weekly Technical Stock & Commodity Letter *Business*

Publishing Co: W.D. Gann Research, Inc., PO Box 8508, Saint Louis, MO 63126-0508;
Title Tel # (314) 843-1810
Personnel: Editor-Joseph Lederer
Editorial Description: Selects stocks & futures with exceptional technical long term chart patterns for high profit low risk trades. Issues graphic annual stock & commodity forecasts.
General Info: Yr. Est. 1919, Weekly
Subscriptions: Indv. $210

Wall Street Digest *Business, Association*

Publishing Co: Wall Street Digest, One Sarasota Tower, Ste. 602, 2 N. Tamiami Trail, Sarasota, FL 34236; Title Tel # (813) 954-5500 Title Fax # (813) 364-8447
Personnel: Publisher, Editor-D. H. Rowe
Editorial Description: Digest of the best investment advice from leading financial advisors. Provides economic commentary as it affects your investments & specific recommendations on stocks & mutual funds. Includes market timing for stocks, bonds, & gold.
General Info: Yr. Est. 1977, Monthly, Trim Size-8½ x 11, Web press, 16 pages, ISSN: 0899-0530, No Color
Subscriptions: Indv. $150, $13/copy
Acquistions: Publication Bought, Publication Sold
Circulation: Total-30,000
List Rental: List Management Co.: Carnegie Marketing Assocs., Koll Executive Plaza, 3878 Carson St., Suite 220, Torrance, CA 90503 Tel # (310) 540-4757, Fax # (310) 540-7407, Actives: 49,495, $150/M
Printing Co: American Southern, 7555 Commerce Ct, Sarasota, FL 34243-3218
Tel # (813) 351-0002

Wall Street Generalist *Business*

Publishing Co: Market Metrics, 5048 Brywill Cir., Sarasota, FL 34234-3727;
Title Tel # (813) 366-5642
Personnel: Editor-Ray Hines
Editorial Description: Reviews their stock market timing models for decisions.
General Info: 15x/yr.
Subscriptions: Indv. $160

Wall Street Letter *Business*

Publishing Co: Capital Cities/ABC, 488 Madison Ave., 16th Floor, New York, NY 10022-5751 Parent Co.-Capital Cities/ABC, Inc., New York; Title Tel # (212) 224-3233 Title Fax # (212) 224-3353
Personnel: Publisher-Linda Litner, Editor-Tom Lamont, Circ. Dir.-Gladys Delgado, Production Dir.-Susan Drobney, Adv. Dir.-Pat Bertucci, Mktg. Dir.-Dahlia Weinman
Editorial Description: Arriving on the desks of the financial world's leading players every Monday morning, Wall Street Letter is considered 'must reading' by executives at investment banks and brokerage firms as well as their vendors and regulators.
General Info: Yr. Est. 1969, Weekly, Trim Size-8½ x 11, Sheetfed press, 10 pages, Ind/Abs/Online: Lexis/Nexis news service, 2 Color, Newsprint
Subscriptions: Indv. $1,450, Can. $1,470, For. $1,525, $35/copy
Advertising: Inquire for rates.

Wall Street Micro Investor *Business*

Publishing Co: Wall Street On-Line Publishing, Box 6, Riverdale, NY 10471-0006;
Title Tel # (212) 884-5408 Title Fax # (212) 543-9033
General Info: Yr. Est. 1983, Bi-monthly
Subscriptions: Indv. $60
List Rental: List Management Co.: Venture Communications, 60 Madison Avenue, 3rd fl., New York, NY 10010 Tel # (212) 684-4800, Fax # (212) 545-1680, Actives: 37,000

Wall Street Money Letter *Consumer*

Publishing Co: Institute of Wall Street Studies, 5301 N. Federal Highway, Boca Raton, FL 33434
Personnel: Publisher, Editor-Peter Bruno, Circ. Mgr.-Thomas Ardiff
Editorial Description: What to buy & what to sell on Wall St.
General Info: Yr. Est. 1980, Monthly, Offset press, 6 pages, Newsprint
Subscriptions: Indv. $195

Wall Street Reports *Business*

Publishing Co: Wall Street Reports, 99 Wall St., New York, NY 10005-4393;
Title Tel # (212) 747-9500
Personnel: Publisher-Richard A. Holman
Editorial Description: Company studies and industry surveys from investment brokers. news of interest to investors and potential investors.
General Info: Yr. Est. 1967, Monthly, Looseleaf
Subscriptions: $1/copy
Circulation: Total-60,000
Advertising: Inquire for rates.

Wall Street S.O.S. Options Alert

Publishing Co: Security Objective Services, Rr 4 Box 403, Bay Minette, AL 36507-9314
General Info: Ind/Abs/Online: Newsnet

Wall Street Underground *Business, Consumer*

Publishing Co: Wall Street Underground, 1129 E. Cliff Rd, Burnsville, MN 55337-1514
Personnel: Editor-Nick Guarino
Editorial Description: Covers Wall Street and politics from a conservative perspective.
General Info: Yr. Est. 1994, Monthly
Subscriptions: Indv. $100
Circulation: Total-26,455
List Rental: List Management Co.: Carnegie Marketing Assocs., Koll Executive Plaza, 3878 Carson St., Suite 220, Torrance, CA 90503 Tel # (310) 540-4757, Fax # (310) 540-7407, Actives: 26,455, $195/M

Wasatch Letter *Business, Consumer*

Publishing Co: Wasatch Planning and Publishing, 3495 Medford Dr, Bountiful, UT 84010-5823;
Title Tel # (801) 292-8328 Title Fax # (801) 292-6927
Personnel: Publisher-Mary Flood
Editorial Description: Retirement and planning issues in regards to investment.
General Info: Yr. Est. 1992, Monthly, Trim Size-8½ x 11, 12 pages, ISSN: 1068-1477, No Color, Matte, Saddle-stitched
Subscriptions: Indv. $72

Weekly Futures Research Report *Business, Consumer*

Publishing Co: Shearson Lehman Bros., 1 Penn Plz, New York, NY 10119-0082;
Title Tel # (212) 643-5700
Editorial Description: Timely, accurate information for investors.
General Info: Weekly

Weekly Letter *Business*

Publishing Co: Aubrey G. Lanston, 1 Chase Manhattan Plaza, 53rd Fl., New York, NY 10005
Tel # (212) 612-1600; Title Tel # (212) 943-1200
Personnel: Editor-David Jones
Editorial Description: Yields and discussion of U.S. Treasury issues.
General Info: Yr. Est. 1950, Weekly, Trim Size-8½ x 14, Desktop press, 2 pages
Circulation: Total-2,224

Weekly Market Alert *Business*

Publishing Co: United Communications Group, 11300 Rockville Pike, Ste. 1100, Rockville, MD 20852-3030 Tel # (301) 816-8950 Fax # (301) 816-8945
Editorial Description: Weekly foreign exchange and bond commentary.
General Info: Weekly
Subscriptions: Indv. $795

Weekly Staff Report

Publishing Co: Argus Research Corp., 17 Battery Pl., New York, NY 10004-1101;
Title Tel # (212) 425-7500 Title Fax # (212) 509-5408
Personnel: Editor-John Eade
Editorial Description: Argus Research Corp. flagship report, offering econimic analysis, synopses of recent company analysis & comments on specific stocks.
General Info: Weekly
Subscriptions: Indv. $390, $35/copy
Printing Co: Argus Printing & Mailing, 226 New York Ave, Huntington, NY 11743-2748
Tel # (516) 423-7710

Weekly Stock Charts - Industrial Companies *Business*

Publishing Co: Independent Survey Co., Box 6000, Vancouver, BC V6B 4B9 Canada;
Title Tel # (604) 731-5777
General Info: Yr. Est. 1965, Monthly

Weekly Stock Charts - Resource Companies *Business*

Publishing Co: Independent Survey Co., Box 6000, Vancouver, BC V6B 4B9 Canada;
Title Tel # (604) 731-5777
Personnel: Editor-Michael Denhertog
General Info: Yr. Est. 1965, Monthly

Weekly Stock Option Guide *Business*

Publishing Co: Daily Graphs, Inc., 12655 Beatrice St, Los Angeles, CA 90066-7300
Tel # (310) 448-6843 Fax # (310) 577-7373; Title Tel # (213) 820-7011
Personnel: Editor-William O'Neil, Circ. Mgr.-Paul Bujold, Promotion Dir.-Robert M. Drislane
Editorial Description: Computer generated graphs on all underlying option stocks, statistical data on all active call & put options as of close of Friday's market.
General Info: Yr. Est. 1976, Weekly
Subscriptions: Indv. $160, $4/copy

Wellington Letter — *Business*

Publishing Co: Wellington Financial Corp., Hawaii Kai Executive Plaza, 6700 Kalanianaole Hwy #218, Honolulu, HI 96825-1299; Title Tel # (808) 396-2220 Title Fax # (808) 396-8640
Personnel: Publisher, Editor-Bert Dohmen
Editorial Description: Investment analysis & forecast for major financial markets & fields, utilizing technical & fundamental analysis.
General Info: Yr. Est. 1976, Monthly, 16 pages, 2 Color, Newsprint
Subscriptions: Indv. $375, For. $410

Western Investor Newsletter — *Business*

Publishing Co: Willamette Publishing, Inc., 111 S.W. 5th Ave., #2150, Portland, OR 97204-3624; Title Tel # (503) 222-0577
General Info: Yr. Est. 1985, 26x/yr.
Subscriptions: Indv. $150

Whisper On Wall Street — *Business, Consumer*

Publishing Co: G.H. Brooks Associates Inc., 221 West Ave, Darien, CT 06820-4202; Title Tel # (203) 656-0261
General Info: Yr. Est. 1982
Subscriptions: Indv. $28

Whitfields Utility Letter — *Business, Consumer*

Publishing Co: Whitfields Utility Letter, 2472 Bolsover St Ste 240, Houston, TX 77005-2537; Title Tel # (713) 521-2536
Personnel: Publisher, Editor-J. Charles Whitfield
Editorial Description: We use the fundamental approach to stocks selection. We comment on market conditions & recomend both purchase & sale of individual public utility shares.
General Info: Yr. Est. 1984, Monthly, Trim Size-8½ x 11, 6 pages, No Color
Subscriptions: Indv. $49
Circulation: Total-500
Printing Co: Kinkos Copies, 2455 Rice Blvd, Houston, TX 77005-3202 Tel # (713) 521-9465

Wilsearch Investment Letter — *Business*

Publishing Co: Wilsearch Investments Management Corp., 620 S 42nd St, Boulder, CO 80303-5909; Title Tel # (303) 292-1400
Personnel: Publisher, Editor-William Moore
Editorial Description: Seeks special situation stocks for maximum growth.
General Info: Yr. Est. 1982, 17x/yr., Trim Size-8½ x 11, Offset press, 8 pages, Color
Subscriptions: Indv. $17, $4/copy
Circulation: Total-150

Wireless Cable Investor
See: MEDIA & COMMUNICATIONS

Wireless Telecom Investor
See: TELECOMMUNICATIONS

Wisconsin Securities Bulletin — *Business*

Publishing Co: Wisconsin Commissioner of Securities, PO Box 1768, Madison, WI 53701-1768; Title Tel # (608) 266-3431 Title Fax # (608) 256-1259
Personnel: Editor-Wesley Ringo
Editorial Description: Commissioner's comments, synopsis of staff enforcement and opinion activities, also staff notes and NASAA information.
General Info: Yr. Est. 1939, Quarterly, Trim Size-8½ x 11, Offset press, 20 pages, No Color
Subscriptions: Indv. $15
Circulation: (100% controlled), Total-1,200
Printing Co: State of Wisconsin, PO Box 1768, Madison, WI 53701-1768 Tel # (608) 266-3431

Wolanchuk Report — *Business*

Publishing Co: Wolanchuk Report, 28037 Gratiot Ave, Roseville, MI 48066-4204; Title Tel # (313) 776-7555
Personnel: Publisher-Don Wolanchuk
General Info: Yr. Est. 1985, Weekly
Subscriptions: Indv. $190

Women and Money
See: WOMEN'S

Women's Investment Newsletter — *Business, Consumer*

Publishing Co: Phoenix Communications Group Ltd., 1837 S Nevada Ave # 223, Colorado Springs, CO 80906-2516; Title Tel # (719) 576-9200
Personnel: Publisher-J.M. Fortune, Editor-Suzanne James
General Info: Yr. Est. 1987, Monthly, Trim Size-8½ x 11, Offset press, 8 pages
Subscriptions: Indv. $69

Women's Market Share
See: WOMEN'S

Worden's Optioneer — *Business*

Publishing Co: Worden Brothers, PO Box 3458, Chapel Hill, NC 27515-3458; Title Tel # (919) 490-5250
Personnel: Editor-Peter Worden
Editorial Description: Market analysis & commentary plus specific recommendations on individual stock options. Also includes twice weekly telephone hotline updates.
General Info: Yr. Est. 1961, 18x/yr., 4 pages
Subscriptions: Indv. $58, Can. $58, For. $78

World Fine Art
See: ANTIQUES & ART GOODS

World Investor — *Business, Consumer*

Publishing Co: Agora, Inc., 105 W. Monoment St., Baltimore, MD 21202-4702 Tel # (410) 783-2647 Fax # (410) 223-2662; Title Fax # (410) 539-7348
Personnel: Editor-Robert Czesch
Editorial Description: International investment advice.
General Info: Monthly
Subscriptions: Indv. $59

World Market Perspective — *Business*

Publishing Co: Corporate Relations Group/Gulf Atlanti Publishing, 1801 Lee Rd Ste 301, Winter Park, FL 32789-2165 Tel # (407) 628-5200 Fax # (407) 628-0807
Personnel: Publisher-R. E. Veitia, Editor-P. Charuhas, Circ. Mgr.-Joan Johns, Adv. Dir.-Jim Cassloy, Art Dir.-Mike Brahosky, Mktg. Dir.-Jack Rodriguez
Editorial Description: Research economic trends in world markets as they affect investing.
General Info: (Formerly Market Perspective), Yr. Est. 1967, Monthly, Trim Size-8½ x 11, Offset press, 8 pages, 2 Color
Subscriptions: Indv. $96, $8/copy
Circulation: Total-6,000
Advertising: Accepts Inserts.
List Rental: List Management Co.: Manager: Roland Outar; Applied List Management, 1801 Lee Rd Ste 301, Winter Park, FL 32789-2165 Tel # (407) 628-5200, Fax # (407) 628-0807, Actives: $125/M

World Money Analyst — *Business*

Publishing Co: Agora, Inc., 105 W. Monoment St., Baltimore, MD 21202-4702 Tel # (410) 783-2647 Fax # (410) 223-2662
Personnel: Editor-Robert Czeschin
Editorial Description: Investment strategies and investment programs.
General Info: Yr. Est. 1974, Monthly, Trim Size-8½ x 11, 16 pages, 2 Color, Matte, Saddle-stitched
Subscriptions: Indv. $99
Circulation: Total-2,000
List Rental: List Management Co.: Name Bank, 14 W. Monument St., Baltimore, MD 21201 Tel # (410) 783-8463, Fax # (410) 783-8464, Actives: 23,000, $200/M

WorldWide Business Exchange
See: BUSINESS & INDUSTRY

Worldwide Investment Notes — *Business*

Publishing Co: Worldwide Investment Notes, PO Box 16041, Saint Louis, MO 63105-0741; Title Tel # (314) 726-2731
General Info: Yr. Est. 1980, 24x/yr.
Subscriptions: Indv. $99

Wrap Fee Advisor
See: BANKING & FINANCE

Yamamoto Forecast — *Business*

Publishing Co: Yamamoto Forecast, PO Box 573, Kahului, HI 96732-0573; Title Tel # (808) 877-2690
Personnel: Editor-Irwin Yamamoto
Editorial Description: Provides in-depth analysis of low-priced overlooked stocks which could translate to profitable returns.
General Info: Yr. Est. 1983, Monthly
Subscriptions: Indv. $350

Your Window Into the Future — *Business, Consumer*

Publishing Co: Moneypower, PO Box 2240, Minneapolis, MN 55422; Title Tel # (612) 537-8096
Personnel: Publisher, Editor-James Moore
General Info: Yr. Est. 1982, Monthly
Subscriptions: Indv. $99

Zenith Financial Report

Publishing Co: Stock Fund Management, Inc., 1125 17th St Ste 1700, Denver, CO 80202-2032; Title Tel # (303) 296-2138
Personnel: Publisher- CO, Editor-James Waters, Production Mgr.-Warren Gauge, Art Dir.-Warren Lange, Circ. Mgr., Adv. Dir., Promotion Dir.-T. Ky Rutter
Editorial Description: A monthly forecast of high performance money management techniques using a sentiment
General Info: (Formerly Zenith Report), Yr. Est. 1984, Monthly, Trim Size-8½ x 11, Web press, 8 pages, Ind/Abs/Online: & monetary, No Color, Newsprint
Subscriptions: Indv. $205, $19/copy
Circulation: (90% controlled)
List Rental: Actives: $75/M, Hotline: $75/M, Expires: $50/M

Zweig Forecast — *Consumer*

Publishing Co: Zweig Securities Advisory Service, Inc., PO Box 2900, Wantagh, NY 11793-0926; Title Tel # (516) 785-1300
Personnel: Publisher-Martin Zweig
Editorial Description: Stock market timing and stock recommendations.
General Info: Monthly, 4 pages, 2 Color
Subscriptions: Indv. $265
Circulation: Total-14,000
List Rental: Actives: $150/M

JEWELRY & HOROLOGY

Antique Comb Collector
See: ANTIQUES & ART GOODS

Benchmark — *Association*

Publishing Co: Manufacturing Jewelers and Silversmiths of America, One State St., 6th Floor, Providence, RI 02908-5035, Title Tel # (401) 274-3840 Title Fax # (401) 274-0265
Personnel: Publisher-David Rocha, Editor-David Latteur
Editorial Description: Details of assn. activities & industry events for members.
General Info: Yr. Est. 1987, Bi-monthly, Trim Size-8½ x 11, Sheetfed press, 4 pages, No Color, Newsprint
Circulation: Total-2,200

Costume Jewelry Review

Publishing Co: Retail Reporting Corp., 302 5th Ave Fl 11, New York, NY 10001-3604 Tel # (212) 279-7000 Fax # (212) 279-7014
General Info: (Formerly Jewelry Clip Review), Yr. Est. 1936, Monthly
Subscriptions: Indv. $108

Craft News
See: GLASS, STONE & CLAY

Diamond Insight — *Business, Consumer*

Publishing Co: Tryon Mercantile Inc., 790 Madison Avenue, New York, NY 10021-6124; Title Tel # (212) 570-4180 Title Fax # (212) 772-1286
Personnel: Publisher, Editor-Guido Giovannini, Circ. Mgr., Production Mgr.-Leslie Tcheyan
Editorial Description: Information about the world's important diamonds. Previews and results of auctions with a perspective on the investment market. Interviews, letters and comments from leading experts on diamonds.
General Info: Yr. Est. 1988, Monthly, Letrpr. press, 12 pages, ISSN: 0954-5581, Ind/Abs/Online: year index, Color-cover, Coated, Saddle-stitched
Subscriptions: Indv. $325, Can. $325, For. $325
Acquistions: Publication Bought
Circulation: Total-500, Readership-500

Diamond Registry Bulletin — *Business*

Publishing Co: Diamond Registry, The, 580 5th Ave., Rm. 806, New York, NY 10036-4701; Title Tel # (212) 575-0444 Title Fax # (212) 575-0722
Personnel: Publisher-Joseph Schlussel, Circ. Mgr.-Rose Schlussel
Editorial Description: World-wide diamond market; price lists, graphs, news items. Mining to jewelry.
General Info: Yr. Est. 1969, Monthly, 8 pages, Color
Subscriptions: Indv. $97, For. $125
Advertising: $500.

Diamontologist — *Business, Association*

Publishing Co: Diamond Council of America, 9140 Ward Pky, Kansas City, MO 64114-3336; Title Tel # (816) 444-3500 Title Fax # (816) 444-0330
Personnel: Editor-Marian Thomas
Editorial Description: Conducts correspondence course in gemology, and diamondology.
General Info: Yr. Est. 1944, Bi-monthly, Desktop press, 12 pages, 2 Color
Subscriptions: Free With Membership
Printing Co: State Line Printer, 9140 Ward Pkwy., Kansas City, MO 64114 Tel # (816) 444-3536, Fax # (816) 444-0330

Fashion Jewelry Review

Publishing Co: Retail Reporting Corp., 302 5th Ave Fl 11, New York, NY 10001-3604 Tel # (212) 279-7000 Fax # (212) 279-7014; Title Tel # (212) 255-9595
Editorial Description: For jewelry retailers, manufacturers and designers.
Subscriptions: Indv. $108

Gem & Jewelry Fact Sheets
Quarterly Supplement — *Business, Association*

Publishing Co: American Gem Society, 8881 W. Sahara Ave., Las Vegas, NV 89117-5865 Tel # (702) 255-6500 Fax # (702) 255-7420; Title Tel # (213) 936-4367
Personnel: Editor-Patricia A. Fry, Mktg. Coord.-Angela B. White
General Info: Yr. Est. 1984, Quarterly, Trim Size-6 x 9½, 8 pages, 2 Color
Subscriptions: Indv. $45
Circulation: Total-1,000

ISA Newsletter
See: FURNITURE & HOME FURNISHINGS

JA Report — *Association*

Publishing Co: Jewelers of America, 1185 6 Ave., 30th Fl., New York, NY 10036; Title Tel # (212) 768-8777
Editorial Description: Association activities and items of interest to members.
General Info: (Formerly RJA Bulletin), Yr. Est. 1980, 10x/yr., Trim Size-8½ x 11, Web press, 16 pages, No Color, Coated, Saddle-stitched
Circulation: Total-10,400

JPR — *Business, Consumer*

Publishing Co: Jewelry Price Report, PO Box 35, Rockville, VA 23146-0035 Fax # (718) 887-9057; Title Tel # (804) 749-4367
Personnel: Publisher, Editor-Nina Woolford, Production Mgr., Promotion Dir.-Gail Levine
General Info: Yr. Est. 1990, Quarterly, 150 pages, No Color, Looseleaf
Subscriptions: Indv. $150, Inst. $150, Can. $150, For. $180, $50/copy

Jewelers Board of Trade
Service Bulletin

Publishing Co: Jewelers Board of Trade, 70 Catamore Blvd, East Providence, RI 02914-1289
General Info: Yr. Est. 1908, Weekly, Trim Size-8½ x 11½, Offset press, 4 pages
Subscriptions: $24/copy
Circulation: Total-2,000

Jewelry Appraiser, The — *Business, Association*

Publishing Co: National Association of Jewelry Appraisers, PO Box 6558, Annapolis, MD 21401-0558 Tel # (301) 261-8270; Title Tel # (602) 941-8088
Personnel: Publisher, Editor in Chief-James Jolliff
Editorial Description: Items of interest to jewelry appraisers.
General Info: Yr. Est. 1982, Quarterly, Offset press, 24 pages, No Color
Subscriptions: Free With Membership
Circulation: Total-850
List Rental: Rents Lists

Jewelry Newsletter
International — *Business*

Publishing Co: Newsletters International, 2600 South Gessner Rd., Houston, TX 77063-3297; Title Tel # (713) 783-0100
Personnel: Editor-Len Fox
Editorial Description: Advises jewelry manufacturers, wholesalers, and retailers how to run their business more successfully.
General Info: Yr. Est. 1973, Monthly, Trim Size-8½ x 11, Offset press, 4 pages, ISSN: 0738-7261, No Color
Subscriptions: Indv. $250, $25/copy
Acquistions: Publication Bought
Advertising: Accepts Inserts.

Margaretologist, The — *Association*

Publishing Co: Center for Bead Research, 4 Essex St, Lake Placid, NY 12946-1236; Title Tel # (518) 523-1794 Title Fax # (518) 523-0197
Personnel: Publisher, Editor-Peter Francis, Jr.
Editorial Description: Dedicated to bead research; reports on the latest work in history, archaeology, and ethnography on all types of beads from around the world.
General Info: Yr. Est. 1985, Semi-annually, Sheetfed press, 12 pages, ISSN: 0892-1989, No Color, Matte
Subscriptions: Indv. $30, Inst. $30, Can. $35, For. $35, $7/copy
Circulation: Total-150

National Jeweler Newsletter — *Business*

Publishing Co: Miller Freeman, Inc., 1 Penn Plaza, 10th Fl., New York, NY 10119-1198; Title Tel # (212) 615-2380 Title Fax # (212) 279-3972
Editorial Description: News for Natl. Jeweler Magazine advertisers.
General Info: Monthly, Desktop press, 2 pages, 2 Color, Matte

Rapaport Diamond Report

Publishing Co: Rapaport USA, Inc., 3557 S. Valley View Bldg. C, Los Vegas, NV 89103; Title Tel # (212) 354-0575 Title Fax # (212) 840-0243
Personnel: Publisher-Martin Rapaport, Editor-Rivka Rapaport
Editorial Description: Contains diamond price list, listing service, & diamond market news.
General Info: Yr. Est. 1978, Weekly, Mimeo press, 8 pages, No Color
Subscriptions: Indv. $180, $5/copy
Acquistions: Publication Bought
Advertising: Accepts Inserts.

Spectra — *Business, Association*

Publishing Co: American Gem Society, 8881 W. Sahara Ave., Las Vegas, NV 89117-5865 Tel # (702) 255-6500 Fax # (702) 255-7420
Personnel: Editor-Patricia A. Fry, Mktg. Coord.-Angela B. White
Editorial Description: Spectra is the newsletter for the American Gem Society, an assn. of N. American retail jewelers, suppliers, & sustaining firms.
General Info: (Formerly Guilds), Yr. Est. 1934, Bi-monthly, Trim Size-8½ x 11, 12 pages, 5% ads, 2 Color, Newsprint
Circulation: Total-4,500
List Rental: Actives: $125/M

JOURNALISM

5th Down
See: FOOTBALL

AAP Monthly Report — *Association*

Publishing Co: Assn. of American Publishers, Inc., 71 Fifth Avenue, New York, NY 10003-3004 Tel # (212) 255-0200 Fax # (212) 255-7007; Title Tel # (202) 232-3335
Personnel: Editor-Judith Platt
General Info: Yr. Est. 1984, Monthly, Web press, 4 pages, ISSN: 0748-8173, 2 Color, Newsprint
Circulation: Total-1,200
Printing Co: Corporate Press, 403 Brightseat Rd., Landover, MD 20785-4706 Tel # (301) 499-9200, Fax # (301) 499-5435

AEJMC News — *Association*

Publishing Co: Assn. for Educ. in Journalism & Mass Communication, 1621 College St, Univ. of South Carolina, Columbia, SC 29208-0251; Title Tel # (803) 777-2005 Title Fax # (803) 777-4728
Personnel: Publisher-Jennifer McGill, Editor-Lanaey Canchell, Production Mgr.-Laney Cantrell
Editorial Description: Assn. journalism & mass communication news, natl. journalism education placement service.
General Info: (Formerly AEJ Newsletter), Yr. Est. 1912, Bi-monthly, Trim Size-11 x 15, Sheetfed press, 10 pages, ISSN: 0747-8909, No Color, Newsprint
Subscriptions: Indv. $10, Inst. $10, Can. $10, For. $10
Circulation: Total-3,500
Advertising: Inquire for rates.
Printing Co: Mackohn Printing, PO Box 1016, Columbia, SC 29202-1016

AIM Report

Publishing Co: Academia, Inc., 4455 Connecticut Ave NW Ste, 330, Washington, DC 20008-2328; Title Tel # (202) 466-2998 Title Fax # (202) 371-9054
Personnel: Editor-Reed Irvine
Editorial Description: To combat the liberal bias of the media. Expose them through our newsletter.
General Info: Bi-weekly, Trim Size-8½ x 11, 6 pages, 2 Color, Newsprint
Subscriptions: Indv. $30, $1/copy
Circulation: Total-30,000
Advertising: Accepts Inserts.
List Rental: List Management Co.: Capstone Lists, 1315 Duke Street, Alexandria, VA 22314 Tel # (703) 683-4131, Expires: $75/M
Printing Co: CLB Publishers & Lithographers, 10580 Metropolitan Ave, Kensington, MD 20895-2606 Tel # (301) 933-5220, Fax # (301) 933-2498

ASBPE National Newshound — *Association*

Publishing Co: American Society of Business Press Editors, 376 E. Saint Charles Road, Lombard, IL 60148-2361 Tel # (708) 889-4141 Fax # (708) 889-4140
Personnel: Editor-Martha Spizziri
Editorial Description: Information relating to editorial staff disseminating pertinent association news.
General Info: Bi-monthly, 6 pages, No Color
Subscriptions: Indv. $60, Free With Membership
Circulation: (100% controlled), Total-350

ASJA Newsletter — *Association*

Publishing Co: American Society of Journalists & Authors, 1501 Broadway Ste 302, New York, NY 10036-5501; Title Tel # (212) 997-0947 Title Fax # (212) 768-7414
Personnel: Editor-Dodi Schultz, Circ. Mgr.-Alexandra Cantor
Editorial Description: Membership newsletter of American Society of Journalists & Authors; contains industry updates & market news.
General Info: Yr. Est. 1952, 11x/yr., Trim Size-8½ x 11, Offset press, 24 pages, Newsprint
Circulation: (100% controlled), Total-1,600
List Rental: Actives: $90/M
Printing Co: Trinity Group, Inc., 350 Hudson St., New York, NY 10014 Tel # (212) 366-0770

AWA Newsletter
See: AERONAUTICS/ASTRONAUTICS

Alone

Publishing Co: Becky Thorp, 12 Norcross St, Rockville Center, NY 11570
Editorial Description: Becky seems almost obsessed with death with her discussions about cemeteries, her quiz on death related words, her rant about the high costs of funeral expenses, and newsclip about a women who died but wasn't discovered for four years.
General Info: Trim Size-8.5 x 11, 8 pages

Between the Lines — *Association*

Publishing Co: The Canadian Assn. of Journalists, Journalism Dept., Carleton U., 1125 Colonel By Drive, Ottawa, ON K1S 5B6 Canada; Title Tel # (613) 788-7424 Title Fax # (613) 788-5604
Personnel: Adv. Dir., Art Dir.-John Stevens
Editorial Description: Covers the activities of the Canadian Assoc. of Journalism.
General Info: Yr. Est. 1990, 5x/yr.
Subscriptions: Free With Membership
Circulation: Total-1,500

Bliss

Publishing Co: Mindy - Sue, 1035 E. Vista Way #206, vista, CA 92084
Editorial Description: A simple design with the stories typed up, cut out, and then pasted over photographs.
General Info: Trim Size-8.5 x 11, 18 pages
Subscriptions: Indv. $2

Blueline — *Association*

Publishing Co: Assn. of Earth Science Editors, 616 East Peabody Dr., C/O Susan Doenges, Champaign, IL 61820; Title Tel # (217) 244-2760
Personnel: Editor-Thomas Rafter
General Info: Yr. Est. 1967, Quarterly, Trim Size-8½ x 11, Letrpr. press, 8 pages, No Color, Newsprint
Subscriptions: $5/copy
Circulation: Total-350

Bookviews
See: BOOKS & BOOK TRADE

BrixaBrak

Publishing Co: BrikaBrak, 438 Pennsylvania Avenue, Santa Cruz, CA 95026
Editorial Description: A zine of relentless terror
Subscriptions: Indv. $1

Byline — *Association*

Publishing Co: American Agricultural Editors Assn., 612 W 22nd St, Austin, TX 78705-5116 Tel # (512) 474-2041 Fax # (512) 474-7787; Title Tel # (202) 785-6710
Editorial Description: Newsletter for American Agricultural Editors Association members.
General Info: (Formerly American Agricultural Editors Assn. Newsletter), Yr. Est. 1920, Monthly, Trim Size-8½ x 11, 4 pages
Circulation: Total-600

CMA Newsletter — *Association*

Publishing Co: College Media Advisers, Inc., Mj-300 Memphis State Univ., Memphis, TN 38152-0001; Title Tel # (901) 678-2403
Personnel: Editor-Ken Rosenauer
Editorial Description: Keeps members up to date on CMA activities.
General Info: Yr. Est. 1954, Monthly, Trim Size-8½ x 11, Offset press, 8 pages, No Color
Subscriptions: Indv. $25
Circulation: Total-925
List Rental: Actives: $75/M

California Writer's Report

Publishing Co: California Writers Report, 3654 4th St., Sparks, NV 89431-1230
Personnel: Publisher, Editor-Patricia Seeley
Editorial Description: The CWR is designed for freelance writers who want to earn more money as well as improve their writing skills. Features market & resource information and interviews with local editors and writers.'
General Info: Yr. Est. 1989, Monthly, 6 pages, ISSN: 1043-9390, No Color
Subscriptions: Indv. $29, $3/copy
Circulation: (90% controlled), Total-500
Printing Co: M & M Printing, 112 Pacific Ave, Long Beach, CA 90802-4410 Tel # (213) 495-0085

Captn' Nola

Publishing Co: Jacqui Meadows, 9304 Claremont NE, Albuquerque, MN 87112
Editorial Description: A fun zine put together by four people stuck in eight grade who can't stand it.
General Info: Trim Size-5 x 7, 20 pages
Subscriptions: Indv. $1

Chips off the Writer's Block — *Consumer*

Publishing Co: Chips off the Writer's Block, PO Box 83371, Los Angeles, CA 90083-0371
Personnel: Editor-Wanda Windham
Editorial Description: Information and motivation for the writer trying to get published.
General Info: Quarterly
Subscriptions: $5/copy
Advertising: Inquire for rates.

Circumspect

Publishing Co: Kelli Fannon, 1317 Lovette Lane, Daphne, AL 36526
Editorial Description: A slapped together collection that features a few amusing bits. Kelli's life story, along with 25 uses for oatmeal.
General Info: Trim Size-5 x 7, 22 pages
Subscriptions: Indv. $2

Cole Papers, The
See: NEWSPAPER INDUSTRY

Collectible Newspapers
See: COLLECTIBLES

Computer Writer's Pulse Report — *Business, Consumer*

Publishing Co: CD Kloek & Associates, 843 E Main St Ste 100, Medford, OR 97504-7137 Fax # (503) 776-3429
Personnel: Publisher-Chris Kloek
Editorial Description: Information and ideas for writers that use computers.
General Info: Monthly, Trim Size-8½ x 11, 8 pages
Subscriptions: Indv. $30

Copy Editor Newsletter — *Business*

Publishing Co: Copy Editor, P.O. Box 604, Ansonia Station, New York, NY 10023-0604; Title Tel # (212) 757-2645 Title Fax # (212) 995-2147
Personnel: Publisher, Editor-Mary Beth Protomastro, Copy Editor-Patricia M. Godfrey
Editorial Description: The National Newsletter for Professional Copy Editors
General Info: Yr. Est. 1990, Bi-monthly, Trim Size-8½ x 11, Offset press, ISSN: 1049-3190, No Color, Matte, Perfect bound
Subscriptions: Indv. $69, Can. $74
Acquistions: Publication Sold
Circulation: Total-2,200, Readership-2,200
List Rental: Actives: 2,200, $100/M, Expires: 1,000, $100/M
Printing Co: Admiral Photo Offset, 47 West St., New York, NY 10006 Tel # (212) 422-6848

Covering the Education Beat
See: SCHOOL ADMINISTRATION

Davey's Journal

Publishing Co: David M. Coffman, P.O. Box 75, Castilla, OH 44824
Editorial Description: David's personal journal
General Info: Trim Size-5 x 7, 14 pages
Subscriptions: Indv. $1

Defense Media Review — *Business, Association*

Publishing Co: Boston University, Center for Defense Journalism, 67 Bay State Rd, Boston, MA 02215-1897; Title Tel # (617) 353-6186 Title Fax # (617) 353-8707
Personnel: Editor-H. Joachim Maitre, Editorial Page Ed., Feature Ed.-Mario Fante, Bk. Rev. Ed., Production Mgr.-William Corliss, Circ. Mgr., Mktg. Dir.-Keith Tavares
General Info: Yr. Est. 1987, Monthly, Trim Size-8½ x 11, 12 pages, 2 Color, Saddle-stitched
Subscriptions: Indv. $60, For. $68
Circulation: Total-875, Readership-1,000
Printing Co: Boston Univ. Print Shop, 985 Commwealth Ave., Boston, MA 02215 Tel # (617) 353-4557, Fax # (617) 353-6555

Eaten Alive

Publishing Co: Victor Vanek, 5757 Boone, Boise, ID 83705
Editorial Description: Victor just clips stuff out of the magazines, pasted it on notebook paper, and then added comments that project a certain quality of wisdom.
General Info: Trim Size-8.5 x 11, 17 pages
Subscriptions: Indv. $3

EdPress News
See: EDUCATION

Editorial Eye — *Business, Scholarly*

Publishing Co: EEI, 66 Canal Center Plz Ste 200, Alexandria, VA 22314-5507; Title Tel # (703) 683-0683 Title Fax # (703) 683-4915
Personnel: Publisher-Claire Kincaid, Editor-Linda Jorgensen, Circ. Mgr.-Everett Arnold, Production Mgr.-Amy Lenihan, Mktg. Dir.-Andrea Sutiliffe
Editorial Description: Focusing on publications standards and pracitces; for writers, editors, designers, and publication managers.
General Info: Yr. Est. 1978, Monthly, Trim Size-8½ x 11, Sheetfed press, 12 pages, ISSN: 0193-7383, 2 Color, Newsprint
Subscriptions: Indv. $99, Inst. $99, Can. $103, For. $119
Acquistions: Publication Bought
Circulation: Total-2,549
List Rental: Actives: $125/M
Printing Co: Masterprint, 8401 Terminal Road, Newington, VA 22122 Tel # (703) 550-9555

Editorial Network — *Business, Consumer*

Publishing Co: Quadriga Publishing, 1613 Chelsea Rd # 311, San Marino, CA 91108-2419; Title Tel # (818) 355-6847
Personnel: Publisher, Editor-William Reinshagen
Editorial Description: Network for editors and publishers of small companies.
General Info: Yr. Est. 1993, Bi-monthly, Trim Size-8½ x 11, 8 pages, No Color
Subscriptions: Indv. $24
Circulation: Total-125

Editors' Exchange, The
See: NEWSPAPER INDUSTRY

Editor's Workshop Newsletter — *Association, Business*

Publishing Co: Lawrence Ragan Communications, Inc., 212 W.Superior St,Ste 200, Chicago, IL 60610-3533 Tel # (312) 335-0037 Fax # (312) 335-9583; Title Tel # (312) 922-8245 Title Fax # (312) 922-3336
Personnel: Publisher-Lawrence Ragon, Editor-Janine Wood, Art Dir.-Sharon Giankos
Editorial Description: News, ideas and techniques for newsletter editors, writers, and publishers.
General Info: (Formerly Workshops Notebook Supplement), Yr. Est. 1984, Monthly, Trim Size-8½ x 11, Sheetfed press, 16 pages, No Color, Newsprint, Saddle-stitched
Subscriptions: Indv. $119, $5/copy
Circulation: Total-5,500
List Rental: List Management Co.: Taybi Direct East, Inc., 13321 New Hampshire Ave., Ste. 202, Silver Spring, MD 20904-3450 Tel # (301) 680-3633, Fax # (301) 680-3635

Education Reporter — *Business, Association*

Publishing Co: Education Writers Association, 1331 H St. NW, Ste. 307, Washington, DC 20005-4706 Fax # (202) 637-9707; Title Tel # (202) 637-9700
Personnel: Editor-Linda Jacobson
General Info: Yr. Est. 1947, Bi-monthly
Subscriptions: Indv. $50, Free With Membership
Circulation: Total-900

Enter Title Here

Publishing Co: Greg Jarvela, P.O. Box 14, Vienna, OH 44473
Editorial Description: Greg talks about anything that's on his mind in addition to the many reviews, stories, and satrical essays.
General Info: Trim Size-8.5 x 11, 18 pages
Subscriptions: Indv. $1

Fillers for Publications — *Business*

Publishing Co: Publications Company, 7015 Prospect Pl. NE, Albuquerque, NM 87110-4311; Title Tel # (505) 884-7636 Title Fax # (505) 888-0477
Personnel: Publisher-George Dubow, Editor-John Raydell, Production Mgr.-Pat Johnston
Editorial Description: Word games, cartoons, crossword puzzles, & clip-art plus editorial copy--20 to 400 words for insertion in publications.
General Info: Yr. Est. 1959, Monthly, Trim Size-8½ x 11, Offset press, 8 pages, ISSN: 0739-0033, No Color, Coated
Subscriptions: Indv. $83

Flash Market News
See: BUSINESS & INDUSTRY

Foreign Press News
See: INTERNATIONAL AFFAIRS

Free Focus
See: POETRY & CREATIVE WRITING

Freelance Success Newsletter — *Business, Consumer* CPM$3000

Publishing Co: Creative License, 42 Hicks St., Suite 4N, Brooklyn, NY 11201-6906; Title Tel # (718) 625-5577 Title Fax # (718) 625-3399
Personnel: Publisher, Editor-Judith Broadhurst
Editorial Description: The marketing and management newsletter for experiences journalist and nonfiction authors.
General Info: Yr. Est. 1993, Monthly, Trim Size-8½ x 11, Sheetfed press, 10 pages, ISSN: 1067-2524, No Color, Matte
Subscriptions: Indv. $97
Circulation: Total-300
Advertising: $900.
List Rental: Actives: $90/M

Freelance Writer's Report — *Business*

Publishing Co: CNW Publishing, PO Box A, North Stratford, NH 03590-0167; Title Tel # (603) 922-8338 Title Fax # (603) 922-8339
Personnel: Publisher, Editor-Dana Cassell, Production Mgr.-Vicki DeLalla
Editorial Description: Market information, news and how-to material of interest to freelance writers.
General Info: Yr. Est. 1982, Monthly, Trim Size-8½ x 11, Desktop press, 8 pages, ISSN: 0731-549X, No Color, Matte
Subscriptions: Indv. $39, $4/copy
Circulation: Total-800, Readership-1,000
Advertising: Inquire for rates. Accepts Inserts.
List Rental: List Management Co.: Direct Communications Corp., 24 Wales St. Box 6628, Rutland, VT 05702-6628 Tel # (802) 747-3322, Fax # (802) 747-3376, Actives: 30,000, $75/M
Printing Co: Thmub Print, PO Box 428, Ossipee, NH 03864-0428 Tel # (603) 539-4656

The Freelancer — *Association* CPM: $100

Publishing Co: Editorial Freelancers Assn., 71 West 23rd St Ste 1504, New York, NY 10159-2050; Title Tel # (212) 929-5400 Title Fax # (212) 929-5439
Personnel: Editor-Anita Mondello, Contrib. Ed.-Patrice Godfrey, Contrib. Ed.-Carolyn Smith, Production Mgr.-Danielle Ponsolle
Editorial Description: News, features, reports on matters of interest to writers, editors, indexers. Reviews books of interest to freelance editors and writers.
General Info: (Formerly EFA Newsletter), Yr. Est. 1977, Bi-monthly, Trim Size-8½ x 11, Desktop press, 8 pages, No Color
Subscriptions: Indv. $20, $4/copy
Circulation: Total-1,000
Advertising: $100.
Printing Co: Admiral Photo, 47 West St., New York, NY 10006

Gerald R. Ford Foundation Newsletter
See: GOVERNMENT

German Press Review

Publishing Co: Embassy of Fedl. Republic of Germany, 4645 Reservoir Rd NW, Washington, DC 20007-1918
General Info: Weekly, Trim Size-8½ x 11, Letrpr. press, 5 pages, No Color
Circulation: Total-2,500

Ginger's Rag

Publishing Co: Ginger's Rag, 117 E. Louisa St #348, Seattle, WA 98102
Editorial Description: Sarting things out small, this issue is primarily a letter reprinted from a friend.
General Info: Trim Size-8.5 x 11, 4 pages
Subscriptions: Indv. $1

Golf Writers Association of America Newsletter   *Association*

Publishing Co: Golf Writers Assn. of America, I-7 25882 Orchard Lake Rd., Farmington Hills, MI 48336; Title Tel # (810) 442-1481
Personnel: Publisher-Robert Rickey
General Info: Yr. Est. 1946

IAPA News   *Association*

Publishing Co: Inter American Press Association, Press Freedom Program, 2911 NW 39th Street, Miami, FL 33142-5148 Fax # (305) 635-2272; Title Tel # (305) 634-2465
Personnel: Publisher-W.P. Williamson, Jr., Editor-Julil Munoz, Production Mgr.-Michael Hayes
Editorial Description: Devoted to freedom of expression in North, Central & South America & the Caribbean. Distributed to newspapers members of the Assn. & other interested entities.
General Info: (Formerly Press of the Americas), Yr. Est. 1942, Bi-monthly
Circulation: (100% controlled), Total-2,500

ICA Newsletter   *Association*

Publishing Co: International Communication Associaton, PO Box 9589, Austin, TX 78766-9589; Title Tel # (512) 454-8299 Title Fax # (512) 454-4221
Personnel: Editor-Robert Cox, Adv. Dir.-Lori Webb
General Info: Quarterly, Trim Size-8½ x 11, 16 pages, Saddle-stitched
Subscriptions: Indv. $10
Circulation: Total-2,300

Ideas Unlimited for Canadian Editors   *Business*

Publishing Co: Newsletter Services, Inc., 9700 Philadelphia Ct., Lanham, MD 20706-4405; Title Tel # (301) 731-5202 Title Fax # (301) 731-5203
Personnel: Publisher-Lisa A. Anthony, Exec. VP/Group Publisher-Michael Nagan, Editor-Will McNamara, Circ. Mgr.-Priscilla Arenas, Mktg. Mgr.-Susan Pangman
Editorial Description: Pre-formatted editorial features, fillers, and camera-ready artwork for in-house editors of company publications in Canada.
General Info: Yr. Est. 1992, Monthly, Trim Size-8½ x 11, 16 pages, ISSN: 1054-4747, Color-cover, Matte
Subscriptions: Indv. $195
List Rental: List Management Co.: Manager: Will McNamara; Taybi Direct East, Inc., 13321 New Hampshire Ave., Ste. 202, Silver Spring, MD 20904-3450 Tel # (301) 680-3633, Fax # (301) 680-3635

Imperial Beach Times
See: POETRY & CREATIVE WRITING

Independent Writer   *Association*

Publishing Co: Washington Independent Writers, 733 15th St NW Ste 220, Washington, DC 20005-2112; Title Tel # (202) 347-4973 Title Fax # (202) 628-0298
Personnel: Editor-I. Chapin
Editorial Description: Information important to freelance writers in the Washington metropolitan area.
General Info: (Formerly WIW Newsletter), Yr. Est. 1975, 11x/yr., Desktop press, 8 pages, No Color
Circulation: (100% controlled), Total-2,200
Advertising: Inquire for rates.
List Rental: Rents Lists

Internet Newsroom, The   *Business*

Publishing Co: Editors' Service, P.O. Box 737, Glen Echo, MD 20812; Title Tel # (301) 365-8065 Title Fax # (301) 365-0639
Personnel: Publisher-R.J. Maloy, Editor-T.K. Maloy
Editorial Description: Information for journalists about using the Internet.
General Info: Yr. Est. 1994, Bi-weekly, Trim Size-8½ x 11, 8 pages, 2 Color, Matte
Subscriptions: Indv. $120
Circulation: Total-400
Printing Co: All Together Printing, Bethesda, MD

Journalism Association of Community Colleges, Newsletter   *Association*

Publishing Co: Journalism Assn. of Community Colleges, Los Angeles Pierce College, 6201 Winnetka Ave., Woodland Hills, CA 91371; Title Tel # (818) 719-6427
Editorial Description: Periodic newsletter of organization activities.
General Info: Yr. Est. 1958, Trim Size-8½ x 11, 3 pages
Circulation: (100% controlled), Total-150

Kappa Tau Alpha Newsletter   *Business, Association*

Publishing Co: Kappa Tau Alpha, School of Journalism, Univ. of Missouri, Columbia, MO 65211; Title Tel # (573) 882-7685 Title Fax # (573) 882-4823
Personnel: Editor-Keith Sanders
Editorial Description: Reports KTA activities to chapter & members.
General Info: Yr. Est. 1984, Semi-annually, Sheetfed press, 6 pages, No Color
Subscriptions: Free With Membership
Circulation: (100% controlled), Total-2,000

Laughing Bear Newsletter
See: BOOKS & BOOK TRADE

MPA Bulletin   *Association*

Publishing Co: Albert Barnes, 61 Woodville Rd, Falmouth, ME 04105-1105; Title Tel # (207) 772-2954
Personnel: Editor-Albert Barnes
General Info: Monthly

Media Reporter
See: GAY & LESBIAN INTEREST

Melrose Valhalla

Publishing Co: E. U., P.O. Box 23687, Atlanta, GA 30322
Editorial Description: A zine devoted to Melrose Place full of sophisticated fanaticism and honest humor by four women who studies grad students, from the perspecitve of a devoted fans and critical feminists.
General Info: Trim Size-8.5 x 11, 8 pages

Mystery Science Manifesto 3000

Publishing Co: Dyna Moe, 6703 Tennyson Drive, McLean, VA 22101
Editorial Description: The life, dreams and demented fantasies of a high-school big shot juvenile delinquent healthy obsessed by the only TV show worth watching.
General Info: Trim Size-5 x 7, 12 pages

NATAS News
See: TELEVISION & VIDEO

NSSA News   *Association*

Publishing Co: Natl. Sportscasters and Sportswriters Assn., PO Box 559, Salisbury, NC 28145-0559; Title Tel # (704) 633-4275

NWC Market Update   *Business, Association*

Publishing Co: Natl. Writers Assn./Associated Business Writers of America, 1450 S. Havana, Ste. 424, Aurora, CO 80012; Title Tel # (303) 751-7844 Title Fax # (303) 751-8593
Personnel: Editor-Sandy Whelchel
Editorial Description: Interviews & news of magazines & book publishers.
General Info: Yr. Est. 1984, Bi-monthly, Sheetfed press, 24 pages, 2 Color, Saddle-stitched
Subscriptions: Indv. $18, For. $21, $2/copy
Circulation: Total-4,000
Advertising: Inquire for rates.
List Rental: Expires: 2,000, $100/M

National Association of Agricultural Journalists Newsletter   *Business, Association*

Publishing Co: Natl. Assn of Agricultural Journalists, 312 Valley View Dr., Huron, OH 44839; Title Tel # (419) 433-5412
General Info: (Formerly Newspaper Farm Editors' Assn. Newsletter), 8x/yr.
Subscriptions: Indv. $40, Free With Membership
Circulation: (100% controlled), Total-180

National Association of Black Journalists Newsletter   *Association*

Publishing Co: National Association of Black Journalists, 11600 Sunrise Valley Dr, Reston, VA 22091-1412 Tel # (703) 648-1270
General Info: Irregular

National Press Club Record   *Association*

Publishing Co: Natl. Press Club, Natl. Press Bldg., 529 14th St. NW, Washington, DC 20045-0001; Title Tel # (202) 662-7500 Title Fax # (202) 879-6725
Personnel: Editor-Dennis Feldman
Editorial Description: Internal house organ for members of the National Press Club; covers club events.
General Info: Yr. Est. 1949, Weekly, Trim Size-8½ x 11, Sheetfed press, 4 pages, 2 Color, Newsprint
Subscriptions: Indv. $50
Circulation: (100% controlled), Total-5,000

National Press Foundation Update   *Business, Consumer*

Publishing Co: National Press Foundation, 1282 National Press Building, Washington, DC 20045-2200; Title Tel # (202) 662-7350
Personnel: Publisher-David Yount, Editor-Frank Holeman, Production Mgr.-Donna Washington
Editorial Description: News of programs to improve American journalism.
General Info: Bi-monthly, Trim Size-8½ x 11, 4 pages, 2 Color
Circulation: Total-1,000
Printing Co: Good Impressions, 1111 2nd St NE, Washington, DC 20002-3403 Tel # (202) 546-5000

National Turf Writers Assn. Newsletter
Business, Association

Publishing Co: Natl. Turf Writers Assn., 1314 Bentwood Way, Louisville, KY 40223
Fax # (502) 244-3895; Title Tel # (502) 245-3809
Personnel: Editor-Jim Bolus
Editorial Description: News and information for and about writers, editors, and columnists who cover Thoroughbred horse racing.
General Info: Quarterly

New England Press Association Bulletin
Business

Publishing Co: New England Press Assn., 360 Huntington Ave, Boston, MA 02115-5096;
Title Tel # (617) 373-5610 Title Fax # (617) 373-5615
Editorial Description: Professional journalistic information.
General Info: Monthly
Circulation: Total-1,500

Newsletter (Harness Writers)
Association

Publishing Co: U.S. Harness Writer's Association, PO Box 10, Batavia, NY 14021-0010;
Title Tel # (716) 343-5900 Title Fax # (716) 344-1187
Personnel: Editor-William Brown, Jr.
General Info: Yr. Est. 1947, Quarterly, 1 pages
Circulation: Total-400
List Rental: Actives: $20/M

Newswire
See: EDUCATION

Nook News Market Bulletin
See: POETRY & CREATIVE WRITING

Overseas Press Club Bulletin
Association

Publishing Co: Overseas Press Club of America, Inc., 320 E. 42nd St., New York, NY 10017-5900;
Title Tel # (212) 983-4655
Personnel: Editor-William J. Wilson
Editorial Description: Covers news and features on foreign correspondence; also news of the club.
General Info: (Formerly Overseas Press Bulletin), Yr. Est. 1973, Semi-monthly
Subscriptions: Indv. $10
Circulation: Total-1,700
Advertising: Inquire for rates.

PR Marcom Jobs East
See: EMPLOYMENT

PR Marcom Jobs Mid-America
See: EMPLOYMENT

PR Marcom Jobs West-No. Calif./Pacific Nothwest
See: EMPLOYMENT

PR Marcom Jobs West-So. Calif.
See: EMPLOYMENT

PWAContact
Business, Association

Publishing Co: Periodical Writers Association of Canada, 24 Ryerson Ave., Toronto, ON M5T 2P3 Canada; Title Tel # (416) 868-6913 Title Fax # (416) 860-0826
Personnel: Editor-Kathe Lieber, Production Dir.-Paulette Kelly
Editorial Description: Association newsletter for members, publishers, editors.
General Info: Yr. Est. 1976, Bi-monthly, Trim Size-8½ x 11, Offset press, 28 pages, ISSN: 0822-4706, No Color, Saddle-stitched
Subscriptions: Indv. $125, Can. $125, Free With Membership
Acquistions: Publication Bought
Circulation: (100% controlled), Total-400
Advertising: Inquire for rates. Accepts Inserts.
List Rental: Rents Lists

Political Finance & Lobby Reporter
See: POLITICS

Prove it Pretzel Boy

Publishing Co: Alice Borealis, 2802 Parkview Terrace, Baltimore, MD 21214
Editorial Description: This is a side project to Alice's Zine of Dreams focusing on mail art, artist stamps, and related flotsam.
General Info: Trim Size-8.5 x 11, 2 pages
Subscriptions: Indv. $1

Publishers Auxiliary
See: LAW

Pundit, The
See: HUMOR & SATIRE

Quarterly Review of Doublespeak
See: EDUCATION

RNA Newsletter
Association

Publishing Co: Cincinnati Enquirer, Inc., 312 Elm St, Cincinnati, OH 45202-2739 Parent Co.-Gannett Newspapers Group, Springfield; Title Tel # (201) 641-6636
Personnel: Editor-Charles Austin
Editorial Description: Items of interest to religion editors and reporters on secular newspapers, news magazines and press services 'to advance the professional standards of religious journalism in the secular press'.
General Info: Yr. Est. 1953, Bi-monthly, Trim Size-8 x 11, Mimeo press, 10 pages, No Color
Subscriptions: Indv. $5
Circulation: Total-145

Really, a Free Newsletter
See: BOOKS & BOOK TRADE

Reporter--Your Editorial Assistant
Consumer

Publishing Co: Publications Company, 7015 Prospect Pl. NE, Albuquerque, NM 87110-4311
Fax # (505) 888-0477; Title Tel # (505) 884-7636
Personnel: Publisher-George Dubow, Editor-John Raydell, Production Mgr.-Pat Johnston
Editorial Description: Editorial copy, crossword puzzles, clip art, and cartoons for schools, journalism teachers, etc.
General Info: Yr. Est. 1962, 10x/yr., Trim Size-8½ x 11, 4 pages, ISSN: 0739-3121, No Color, Coated
Subscriptions: Indv. $39

SPAN Connection
See: BOOKS & BOOK TRADE

Science Writers
Consumer, Association

Publishing Co: Natl. Assn. of Science Writers, Inc., PO Box 294, Greenlawn, NY 11740-0294;
Title Tel # (516) 757-5664
Personnel: Publisher-Howard Lewis, Editor-Barbara Culliton
Editorial Description: Fosters dissemination of accurate information regarding science through all media normally devoted to informing the public.
General Info: Yr. Est. 1952, Quarterly, 20 pages, No Color
Circulation: (90% controlled), Total-2,000
Advertising: Inquire for rates.
List Rental: List Management Co.: Nat. Assn. of Science Writers, Inc., PO Box 294, Greenlawn, NY 11740, Actives: 1,000, $150/M

Scrivener
Association

Publishing Co: Scribes-The American Society of Writers on Legal Subjects, Box 7206, Winston-Salem, NC 27109-7206 Tel # (919) 759-5440 Fax # (919) 759-6077; Title Tel # (910) 759-5440 Title Fax # (910) 759-4301
Personnel: Publisher-Thomas Steele, Editor-Glen-Peter Ahlers
Editorial Description: Promotes the exchange of ideas for law writers and editors.
General Info: Quarterly, Trim Size-8½ x 11, Sheetfed press, 8 pages, 1% ads
Subscriptions: Free With Membership
Circulation: (100% controlled), Total-1,000
Advertising: Inquire for rates.
List Rental: Rents Lists

Smith's Report
Consumer

Publishing Co: Smith's Report, PO Box 3267, Visalia, CA 93278-3267; Title Tel # (209) 627-8757 Title Fax # (209) 733-6353
Personnel: Publisher, Editor-Bradley Smith
Editorial Description: Survey of censorship and suppression of free inquiry relating to European Holocaust.
General Info: (Formerly Revisionist Letters), Yr. Est. 1984, Semi-monthly, Trim Size-8½ x 11, Offset press, 8 pages, No Color, Newsprint
Subscriptions: Inst. $30, $3/copy
Circulation: Total-500

Travelwriter Marketletter
Business

Publishing Co: Travelwriter Marketletter, Waldorf-Astoria, 301 Park Ave., Ste. 1850, New York, NY 10022; Title Tel # (212) 759-6744 Title Fax # (212) 872-7272
Personnel: Publisher, Editor-Robert Milne
Editorial Description: Newsletter for travel writers and photographers about markets for travel articles and photos and other related information. Also reviews reference books, lists free trips for writers, etc.
General Info: Yr. Est. 1977, Monthly, Trim Size-8½ x 11, Mimeo press, 10 pages, ISSN: 0738-9093, No Color, Matte
Subscriptions: Indv. $60, Inst. $60, Can. $60, For. $70, $6/copy
Circulation: Total-1,000
List Rental: Actives: $100/M
Printing Co: Apple Press, 32 Garth Rd, Scarsdale, NY 10583-3751 Tel # (914) 723-6660

Tyndall Report
Business

Publishing Co: ADT Research, 135 Rivington St., Rm.4, New York, NY 10002;
Title Tel # (212) 674-8913 Title Fax # (212) 979-7304
Personnel: Publisher-Andrew Tyndall, Editor-Bruno Pajaczkowski
Editorial Description: A non-partisan monitor of TV network newscasts. Measures time spent on each story. Analyzes headline stories. Tracks time spent in ten top topics: economy, transportation, health, environment, etc. Features comprehensive data tables.
General Info: Yr. Est. 1988, Bi-monthly, Trim Size-8½ x 11, Mimeo press, 12 pages, No Color
Subscriptions: Indv. $60
Circulation: Total-300
Printing Co: Copy Technologies, 5 W 8th St, New York, NY 10011-9001 Tel # (212) 254-5545

Well Spring

Publishing Co: Well Spring Publishing, P.O. Box 3594, Ashland, OR 97520
Editorial Description: A journal for exploring the unlimited self.
General Info: Trim Size-8.5 x 11, 8 pages
Subscriptions: Indv. $3

West Virginia Fourth Estatesman   *Association*

Publishing Co: West Virginia Univ. School of Journalism, Box 6010, Morgantown, WV 26506-6010; Title Tel # (304) 293-3505 Title Fax # (304) 293-3072
Personnel: Publisher, Editor-William Slater
Editorial Description: For journalism alumni.
General Info: Yr. Est. 1941, Quarterly, Trim Size-8½ x 11, Offset press, 4 pages, No Color
Circulation: (100% controlled), Total-3,800

William Wants A Doll

Publishing Co: Arielle Greenberg, P.O. Box 8040, Long Island, NY 11101-8040
Editorial Description: A zine for girlie boys and buoyant girls
General Info: Trim Size-5 x 7, 20 pages
Subscriptions: Indv. $1

Writers Information Network
See: POETRY & CREATIVE WRITING

Writer's Lifeline
See: POETRY & CREATIVE WRITING

Writer's Nook News
See: POETRY & CREATIVE WRITING

Writers' Rendezvous
See: POETRY & CREATIVE WRITING

Writing Concepts: The Business Communications Report   *Business*

Publishing Co: Communications Concepts, Inc., 7481 Huntsman Blvd., Ste. 720, Springfield, VA 22153-1648; Title Tel # (703) 643-2200 Title Fax # (703) 643-2329
Personnel: Publisher, Editor-John De Lellis
Editorial Description: Focuses on the changing needs of writers, editors and publication managers.
General Info: (Formerly Communications Manager), Yr. Est. 1990, Monthly, Trim Size-8½ x 11, 8 pages, ISSN: 1050-4788, Ind/Abs/Online: AOL, 2 Color, Matte
Subscriptions: Indv. $99, Inst. $49, For. $119

Writing for Money   *Consumer*

Publishing Co: Blue Dolphin Communications, 83 Boston Post Rd, Sudbury, MA 01776-2438; Title Tel # (508) 443-6363 Title Fax # (508) 443-9728
Personnel: Publisher-Donald L. Nicholas, Publications Director-Donna Kelly, Editor-Jay Winchester, Copy Editor-Kathleen M. Hayes
Editorial Description: Lists outlets for freelance writers.
General Info: Yr. Est. 1993, Bi-monthly, Trim Size-8½ x 11, 32 pages, ISSN: 1073-709X, 2 Color
Subscriptions: Indv. $78, Can. $88, For. $98, $10/copy
Circulation: Total-20,000
List Rental: List Management Co.: Direct Media, Inc., 200 Pemberwick Rd., PO Box 4565, Greenwich, CT 06830 Tel # (203) 532-3713, Fax # (203) 531-1452, Actives: 11,961, $90/M
Printing Co: Newsletter Services, Inc., 9700 Philadelphia Court, Lanham, MD 20706 Tel # (301) 731-5200, Fax # (301) 731-5201

Writing World
See: MEDIA & COMMUNICATIONS

LABOR

AACE Bonus Briefs
See: EDUCATION

AACE Careers Update
See: EDUCATION

AKCENS
See: GOVERNMENT

Advocate

Publishing Co: Prince Edward Island Union of Public Sector Employees, Box 1116, Charlottetown, PE C1A 7M8 Canada; Title Tel # (902) 892-5335
Personnel: Editor-Ron Kelly
General Info: Yr. Est. 1982, Quarterly, 12 pages
Circulation: Total-4,400

American Flint

Publishing Co: Keystone Press, 1440 S Byrne Rd, Toledo, OH 43614-2363; Title Tel # (419) 385-6687 Title Fax # (419) 385-8839
Personnel: Editor-Richard G. Morgan
Editorial Description: Current data & information on labor trends, supply & demand.
General Info: Yr. Est. 1900, Monthly
Circulation: Total-12,000
Printing Co: Keystone Press, Toledo, OH

American Labor

Publishing Co: American Labor Education Center, 2000 P St NW Ste 300, Washington, DC 20036-5915; Title Tel # (202) 828-5170
Personnel: Editor-Matt Witt, Circ. Mgr.-Debi Duke, Art Dir.-Charles Myers
Editorial Description: Reports on ideas and projects of practical interest to union activists.
General Info: Yr. Est. 1979, Bi-monthly, Offset press, 8 pages, No Color
Subscriptions: Indv. $10, Inst. $40, $2/copy
Circulation: Total-5,000
Advertising: Inquire for rates.
Printing Co: Custom Print, Inc., 2611 S. Shirlington Rd., Arlington, VA 22206-2529 Tel # (703) 979-6670

Arbitration in the Schools   *Association*

Publishing Co: American Arbitration Assn., 140 W. 51 St., New York, NY 10020-1203 Tel # (212) 484-4000; Title Tel # (212) 484-4011 Title Fax # (212) 541-4841
Personnel: Editor-Earl Baderschneider
Editorial Description: Summary of selected labor arbitration awards in all levels of education, both public and private.
General Info: Yr. Est. 1970, Monthly, Trim Size-8½ x 11, 8 pages, ISSN: 0003-7885, 2 Color, Coated, Looseleaf
Subscriptions: Indv. $120
Circulation: Total-3,800
Printing Co: Sheridan Printing, 1425 3rd Ave, Alpha, NJ 08865-4695 Tel # (908) 454-0700, Fax # (908) 454-2554

Archives of Labor

Publishing Co: Walter Reuther Library, Wayne State University, 5401 Cass Ave., Detroit, MI 48202-3613; Title Tel # (313) 577-4024
Editorial Description: Describes archival collections for research: UAW, AFT, AFSCME, CIO others.
General Info: (Formerly Archives of Labor and Urban Affairs Newsletter), Yr. Est. 1971, Trim Size-8½ x 11, Offset press, 6 pages, 2 Color
Subscriptions: Free
Circulation: Total-3,500

Area Labor Market Newsletter; Gastonia   *Business, Association*

Publishing Co: North Carolina State Employment Security Commission, 111 E 3rd Ave, Gastonia, NC 28052-4362; Title Tel # (704) 865-6281
Personnel: Editor-Carl Harrelson, Jr.
Editorial Description: Narrative description and statistics to depict labor market conditions in Gaston County including employment, unemployment, unemployment rates and labor supply & demand.
General Info: Bi-monthly, 2 pages, 2 Color
Circulation: Total-300

Area Manpower Newsletter; Greensboro   *Business, Association*

Publishing Co: North Carolina State Employment Security Commission, 2005b S Elm Eugene St, Greensboro, NC 27406-2824; Title Tel # (919) 379-1850
Editorial Description: Presents labor force data along with comments.

Australian Labour Law Reports
See: LAW

BNA's Workers' Compensation Report
See: EMPLOYMENT

Black Lung Reporter   *Business*

Publishing Co: Matthew Bender & Co., 11 Penn Plaza, New York, NY 10001-2006 Tel # (212) 967-7707 Fax # (212) 244-3188
Editorial Description: Full text of the federal Coal Mine Health & Safety Act of 1969, as amended by the Black Lung Acts, related regulations, & proposed rules & regulations.
General Info: Yr. Est. 1980, Bi-weekly, Looseleaf

Blue Chip Job Growth Update: Ranking the States and MSAs
See: ECONOMICS

Business Currents   *Business, Association*

Publishing Co: Natl. Alliance of Business, 1201 New York Ave NW Ste 700, Washington, DC 20005-3917 Tel # (202) 289-2845; Title Tel # (202) 289-2932 Title Fax # (202) 289-1303
Personnel: Editor-Tom Lindsley, Production Mgr.-Michele Cahn
Editorial Description: Covers natl. policy developments relating to human resource development, education reform, job training and workforce quality.
General Info: Yr. Est. 1981, Bi-weekly, 4 pages, No Color, Newsprint
Subscriptions: Indv. $100
Circulation: Total-1,350
Printing Co: Lettercomm, Inc., 310 Swann Ave, Alexandria, VA 22301-1042 Tel # (703) 683-3105

CORAspondent
See: RELIGIOUS & THEOLOGICAL

Cal-OSHA Reporter
See: SAFETY

California Employer Advisor
See: EMPLOYMENT

California Public Sector Labor Relations
See: INDUSTRIAL RELATIONS/PERSONNEL

Canadian Industrial Relations and Personnel Developments
See: INDUSTRIAL RELATIONS/PERSONNEL

Canadian Labour Law Reporter
See: LAW

Career Connections
See: EDUCATION

Career Planning & Adult Development Network Newsletter *Association*

Publishing Co: Career Planning & Adult Development Network, 4965 Sierra Rd., San Jose, CA 95132-3414; Title Tel # (408) 559-4946 Title Fax # (408) 559-8211
Personnel: Publisher, Editor-Richard Knowdell
Editorial Description: Information on seminars, workshops, conferences, books, tests & films of interest to career counselors & trainers.
General Info: Yr. Est. 1979, Monthly, Trim Size-8½ x 11, Sheetfed press, 8 pages, ISSN: 0898-1353, No Color, Newsprint, Saddle-stitched
Subscriptions: Indv. $49, Inst. $49, Can. $64, For. $64, $5/copy
Circulation: Total-1,000
List Rental: Actives: $75/M

Child Labor Monitor
See: CONSUMER INTERESTS

Clear Report

Publishing Co: Center for Labor Education, Univ. Station, Univ. Of A, Birmingham, AL 35294-0001
General Info: Yr. Est. 1974, Quarterly

Cockshaw's Construction Labor News + Opinion *Business*

Publishing Co: Communications Counselors, Inc., PO Box 427, Newtown Square, PA 19073-0427; Title Tel # (610) 353-0123 Title Fax # (610) 353-0111
Personnel: Publisher, Editor-Peter A. Cockshaw, Circ. Mgr.-Janet Martinelli, Production Mgr.-Eric Cockshaw, Mktg. Dir.-Kelly Hagarty, Promotion Dir.-C.C. Barkdoll
Editorial Description: In-depth analysis of labor-related construction developments and trends. Topics include: bargaining data, contractor pay practices, comparisons of union vs. non-union wages/performance, legislative/legal actions, productivity studies, skilled labor shortage solutions, workers compensation costs, etc. Does not accept news releases.
General Info: Yr. Est. 1971, Monthly, Trim Size-8½ x 11, Offset press, 8 pages, ISSN: 0094-0372, No Color
Subscriptions: Indv. $229, $19/copy
Circulation: Total-9,465
Printing Co: J.R. Finio & Sons, 555 Baily Road, Yeadon, PA 19050 Tel # (610) 623-5800

Collier Labor Law and the Bankruptcy Code
See: LAW

Commercial Laws of the World
See: LAW

CompFlash *Business, Association*

Publishing Co: American Management Association, 135 West 50th Street, New York, NY 10020-1201 Tel # (212) 586-8100 Fax # (212) 903-8083; Title Tel # (212) 903-8069
Personnel: Publisher-Rosemary Kane Carlough, Editor-Linda J. Bennett, Product Mgr.-Carole Thielman, Art Dir.-Seval Newton, Mktg. Dir.-Beverly A. Hart, Circ. Dir., Promotion Dir.-Inez Lambert
Editorial Description: Presents developments affecting executive compensation, salaries, wages, benefits, etc.
General Info: Yr. Est. 1977, Monthly, Sheetfed press, 12 pages, ISSN: 0147-1570, Newsprint, Saddle-stitched
Subscriptions: Indv. $125, Can. $140, For. $150, $15/copy
Circulation: Total-1,908
List Rental: Rents Lists

Compensation
See: INDUSTRIAL RELATIONS/PERSONNEL

Confederation of Canadian Unions, Bulletin

Publishing Co: Confederation of Canadian Unions, 1331 1/2A St. Clair Ave., W., Toronto, ON M6E 1C3 Canada
General Info: Bi-monthly, Trim Size-8½ x 11, Mimeo press, 4 pages, Color-cover
Circulation: Total-1,350

Conference Board's Human Resources Briefing *Business*

Publishing Co: Conference Board, Inc., 845 3rd Ave., New York, NY 10022-6679; Title Tel # (212) 759-0900
Personnel: Editor-Theresa Brothers
Editorial Description: Issues & trends in corporate organization, compensation benefits; labor relations, training, development, & quality of worklife.
General Info: (Formerly Mngmnt.Briefing:Human Res; Conf. Bd. Mngmnt. Briefing:H.R.), Yr. Est. 1985, Monthly, Trim Size-8½ x 11, Offset press, 4 pages, 4 Color, Matte, Saddle-stitched
Subscriptions: Indv. $85, Free To Qualified Recipient
Circulation: Total-6,800
Printing Co: Sheridan Printing, 1425 3rd Ave, Alpha, NJ 08865-4695 Tel # (908) 454-0700, Fax # (908) 454-2554

Connecticut Labor Dept. - Labor Market Review

Publishing Co: Connecticut Labor Dept., Business Management, 200 Folly Brook Blvd., Wethersfield, CT 06109-1114; Title Tel # (203) 566-4374

Connecticut Labor Dept. News

Publishing Co: Connecticut Labor Dept., Business Management, 200 Folly Brook Blvd., Wethersfield, CT 06109-1114; Title Tel # (203) 566-4374
Personnel: Editor-C. Richard Ficks
Editorial Description: Plans, progress and results of labor dept projects.
Circulation: Total-4,000

Detroit Labor Market Review *Business, Association*

Publishing Co: Michigan Employment Security Commission, 7310 Woodward Ave, Detroit, MI 48202-3152; Title Tel # (313) 876-5429
Personnel: Editor-Daljit Rangi
Editorial Description: Review of labor market conditions in the Detroit Metropolitan Area.
General Info: Yr. Est. 1946, Monthly, Trim Size-8½ x 11, Offset press, 4 pages, No Color
Circulation: Total-2,000

Drafting the Union Contract: A Handbook for the Management Negotiator *Business*

Publishing Co: Matthew Bender & Co., 11 Penn Plaza, New York, NY 10001-2006 Tel # (212) 967-7707 Fax # (212) 244-3188
Editorial Description: An indispensable guide to drafting & interpreting collective bargaining agreements, from strikes & lockouts to health & welfare benefits, seniority provisions & much more. Provides complete coverage showing the legal consequences of particular contract language.
General Info: Yr. Est. 1988, Annually, Looseleaf

ESOP Profile *Association*

Publishing Co: ESOP Association, The, 1726 M St NW Ste 501, Washington, DC 20036-4502; Title Tel # (202) 293-2971 Title Fax # (202) 293-7568
Personnel: Editor-J. Michael Keeling
Editorial Description: Information relating to employee stock ownership plans.
General Info: (Formerly ESOP Report), Yr. Est. 1979, Monthly, 4 pages

Economic Notes *Business, Consumer*

Publishing Co: Labor Research Assn., 145 W 28th St Fl 6, New York, NY 10001-6191; Title Tel # (212) 714-1677 Title Fax # (212) 714-1674
Personnel: Editor-Gregory Tarpinian
Editorial Description: Labor management reviews.
General Info: Yr. Est. 1932, Monthly, Trim Size-8½ x 11, Desktop press, ISSN: 0013-0184, 2 Color
Subscriptions: Indv. $30, Inst. $50, For. $60, $5/copy

Education Update
See: EDUCATION

Employee Benefit Notes
See: INDUSTRIAL RELATIONS/PERSONNEL

Employee, Business, and Professional Defamation
See: LAW

Employee Relations in Action
See: LABOR UNION

Employee Terminations Law Bulletin *Business*

Publishing Co: Quinlan Publishing, 23 Drydock Ave, Boston, MA 02210-2387 Tel # (617) 542-0048 Fax # (617) 345-9646
Editorial Description: Covers problems and unfair actions of employee terminations.
General Info: Monthly
Subscriptions: Indv. $59

Employer's Guide to the Fair Labor Standards Act
See: INDUSTRIAL RELATIONS/PERSONNEL

Employer's Handbook: Independent Contractor vs. Employee *Business*

Publishing Co: Thompson Publishing Group, 1725 K Street, NW, Washington, DC 20006 Tel # (202) 872-4000
Editorial Description: Resource for structuring relationships with alternative workers to avoid costly employer mandates and trouble with the IRS.
General Info: Annually, Looseleaf
Subscriptions: $297/copy

Employers' Immigration Compliance Guide
See: LAW

Employment & the Economy: Atlantic Coastal Region
See: EMPLOYMENT

Employment & the Economy: Northern Region
See: EMPLOYMENT

Employment & the Economy: Southern Region
See: EMPLOYMENT

Employment & Training Reporter
See: EMPLOYMENT

Employment Health Law & Benefits
See: INDUSTRIAL RELATIONS/PERSONNEL

Employment and Labor Lawcast
See: LAW

Employment Law Deskbook
See: INDUSTRIAL RELATIONS/PERSONNEL

Employment Law Update *Business*

Publishing Co: Rutkowski & Associates, Inc., PO Box 15250, Evansville, IN 47716-0250; Title Tel # (812) 476-4520
Personnel: Publisher-Arthur Rutkowski, Editor-Barbara Rutkowski
Editorial Description: Newsletter for human resources executives including critical legislation, important cases, current issues/trends, in-depth special features, sample policies and authoritative analysis.
General Info: Yr. Est. 1986, Monthly, 8 pages, ISSN: 0890-9253, Color
Subscriptions: Indv. $98, $8/copy

Employment Litigation Reporter *Business*

Publishing Co: Andrews Publications, Inc., 1646 West Chester Pike, PO Box 1000, Westtown, PA 19395 Tel # (610) 399-6600; Title Tel # (215) 399-6600 Title Fax # (610) 399-6610
Personnel: Publisher-John E. Backe, Editor-Linda Coady, Mktg. Dir.-Andrew Katz
Editorial Description: Provides timely, indepth coverage of a growing number of employment-related lawsuits and includes full-text reproductions of court opinions and major pleadings from jurisdictions nationwide.
General Info: Yr. Est. 1986, Bi-monthly, Trim Size-8½ x 11, Mimeo press, 70 pages, ISSN: 1055-6249, No Color, Newsprint
Subscriptions: Indv. $800, $38/copy
Advertising: Inquire for rates.
List Rental: Actives: 358, $110/M

Employment Safety and Health Guide
See: SAFETY

Equal Employer, The
See: EMPLOYMENT

Fair Employment Compliance *Business*

Publishing Co: Management Resources. Inc., 861 Lafayette Rd. #5, Hampton, NH 03842-1232; Title Tel # (603) 929-1600
Personnel: Publisher-W.J. Quirk, Editor-Ken Swann
Editorial Description: Confidential letter to management on EEO court rulings, laws, suits and what they mean to employees.
General Info: Yr. Est. 1975, Semi-monthly, Trim Size-8½ x 11, Offset press, 6 pages, ISSN: 0885-7172, No Color, Matte
Subscriptions: Indv. $245, $20/copy
List Rental: List Management Co.: Statlistics, 11 Lake Ave. Extensions, Danbury, CT 06811 Tel # (203) 778-8700, Fax # (203) 778-4839

Fair Labor Standards Handbook
See: GOVERNMENT

Fink and Bornstein Workers' Compensation Newsletter
See: LAW

Fire and Police Personnel Reporter

Publishing Co: Public Safety Personnel Research Institute, Inc., 5519 N Cumberland Ave Ste 1008, Chicago, IL 60656-1480; Title Tel # (312) 763-2800 Title Fax # (312) 763-3225
Personnel: Editor-Wayne Schmidt, Circ. Mgr.-Missy Taki
Editorial Description: Labor, personnel and disciplinary decisions in federal and state appellate courts.
General Info: Yr. Est. 1974, Monthly, Trim Size-8½ x 11, Sheetfed press, 16 pages, ISSN: 0164-6397, Color-cover
Subscriptions: Indv. $178
Circulation: Total-1,200

Fire Service Labor Monthly
See: FIRE PROTECTION

First Line Supervisor *Business*

Publishing Co: Dartnell Corp., 4660 N. Ravenswood Ave., Chicago, IL 60640-4510; Title Tel # (312) 561-4000 Title Fax # (312) 561-3801
Personnel: Publisher-Clark Fetridge, Editor-Linda Segall, Production Mgr.-Megan Mulligan, Art Dir.-Andrew Epstein, Mktg. Dir.-Tracy Butzkos, Mktg. Dir.-George Economos
Editorial Description: Bulletin for factory foremen/women.
General Info: (Formerly Foremanship), Yr. Est. 1966, Bi-weekly, Trim Size-8½ x 11, Sheetfed press, 4 pages, Color
Subscriptions: $62/copy
List Rental: List Management Co.: Manager: Sue McDorman; Leland Company, 1801 W. Leland Ave., Chicago, IL 60640-4363 Tel # (312) 561-4005, Fax # (312) 561-4099, Actives: $90/M, Hotline: $125/M

Forewarned
See: LABOR UNION

Fresno Labor Market Bulletin

Publishing Co: California State Employment Development Dept., 800 Capitol Mall, Sacramento, CA 95814-4807
General Info: Monthly

Georgia Labor Market Trends *Business, Association*

Publishing Co: Georgia State Dept. of Labor, 148 International Blvd NE, Atlanta, GA 30303-1751; Title Tel # (404) 656-3177
Personnel: Editor-Pascal McLain
Editorial Description: Current industry employment & trends for state of Georgia & Metropolitan Statistical Areas (MSAs); current economic developments; manufacturing hours & learnings; civilian labor force.
General Info: Yr. Est. 1975, Monthly, Trim Size-8½ x 11, Offset press, 12 pages, Coated
Circulation: Total-2,000

Government Employee Relations Report
See: GOVERNMENT

Grassroots Economic Organizing (GEO)
See: CONSUMER INTERESTS

HR Planning Newsletter
See: INDUSTRIAL RELATIONS/PERSONNEL

Health Care Labor Manual & Newsletter *Business*

Publishing Co: Aspen Publishers, Inc., 200 Orchard Ridge Dr., Ste 200, Gaithersburg, MD 20878-5440 Tel # (301) 417-7500 Fax # (301) 417-7655 Parent Co.-Wolters Kluwer US Corporation, New York; Title Tel # (301) 241-7500 Title Fax # (301) 417-7550
Personnel: Publisher-Paul Lasky, Production Mgr.-Patricia Younger
General Info: Yr. Est. 1975, Bi-monthly, Looseleaf
Subscriptions: Indv. $689, For. $780
List Rental: List Management Co.: Stevens-Knox List Management, 304 Park Ave S., New York, NY 10010-5312 Tel # (212) 388-8800, Fax # (212) 388-8890, Actives: $80/M

Health Employment Law Update
See: LAW

Hiring Compliance Update *Business*

Publishing Co: Quinlan Publishing, 23 Drydock Ave, Boston, MA 02210-2387 Tel # (617) 542-0048 Fax # (617) 345-9646
Editorial Description: Essentials updates on laws affecting the hiring process.
General Info: (Formerly Employee Hiring Law Bulletin), Monthly
Subscriptions: Indv. $66

Hospital Contracts
Manual
Business

Publishing Co: Aspen Publishers, Inc., 200 Orchard Ridge Dr., Ste 200, Gaithersburg, MD 20878-5440 Fax # (301) 417-7655 Parent Co.-Wolters Kluwer US Corporation, New York; Title Tel # (301) 417-7500 Title Fax # (301) 417-7550
Personnel: Production Mgr.-Patricia Younger, Promotion Dir.-Trudi Graham
Editorial Description: Descriptions and samples of various hospital contracts.
General Info: Yr. Est. 1982, Semi-annually, Looseleaf
Subscriptions: Indv. $450, For. $510
List Rental: List Management Co.: Stevens-Knox List Management, 304 Park Ave S., New York, NY 10010-5312 Tel # (212) 388-8800, Fax # (212) 388-8890, Actives: $95/M

Human Resource Management News
See: INDUSTRIAL RELATIONS/PERSONNEL

Human Resources Equal Employment Opportunity
See: EMPLOYMENT

Human Resources Labor
Relations Bulletin

Publishing Co: Canadian Construction Assn, 85 Albert St., Tenth Floor, Ottawa, ON K1P 6A4 Canada; Title Tel # (613) 236-9455 Title Fax # (613) 236-9526
General Info: Yr. Est. 1969, Monthly, 4 pages
Circulation: Total-2,300

Human Resources Management Employee Relations
See: LABOR UNION

IAIABC Newsletter

Publishing Co: International Assn. of Industrial Accident Boards & Comm., 1575 Aviation Center Pky Ste, 509, Daytona Beach, FL 32114-3863 Fax # (904) 258-9965; Title Tel # (904) 252-2915
Personnel: Publisher, Editor, Circ. Mgr.-Robert Collyer
Editorial Description: Improving workmen's compensation laws and their administration.
General Info: Yr. Est. 1914, Monthly

ILR Alumni News

Publishing Co: Cornell Univ. ILR, 198 Ives Hall, Ithaca, NY 14851-0952; Title Tel # (607) 255-6511
Personnel: Editor-Mary Cullen
General Info: Semi-annually, 16 pages

IRC Newsletter

Publishing Co: Univ. of Hawaii at Manoa, 2440 Dole St, Honolulu, HI 96822-2302 Tel # (808) 948-8111; Title Tel # (808) 948-8132
General Info: Yr. Est. 1949, Bi-monthly
Circulation: Total-605

Ideas & Action
Business

Publishing Co: Sponsor-Workers Solidarity Alliance, Workers Solidarity Alliance, 339 Lafayette St Rm 202, New York, NY 10012-2725 Tel # (212) 979-8353
Personnel: Circ. Mgr.-Tom Wetzel
Editorial Description: Advocates self-managed unionism for workers, management of economy, anarcho-syndicalist.
General Info: (Formerly Ideas & Action), Yr. Est. 1978, Bi-monthly, Web press, 12 pages, No Color, Newsprint
Subscriptions: Indv. $5, $1/copy
Circulation: Total-500

Illinois Labor Market
Review

Publishing Co: Illinois Dept. of Employment Security, 401 S. State St. - 2 South, Chicago, IL 60605-1225; Title Tel # (312) 793-2316 Title Fax # (312) 793-6245
Editorial Description: Monthly newsletter & summary of economic indicators for the State: labor force, unemployment, industry employment, Job Service applicant characteristics, Unemployment Insurance claimants, Unemployment Insurance Trust Fund, & list of current Labor Surplus Areas.
General Info: Yr. Est. 1940, Monthly
Circulation: Total-12,000

Illinois State Federation of
Labor
Business

Publishing Co: Illinois State AFL-CIO, 828 S 2nd St Ste 200, Springfield, IL 62704-2638
Personnel: Editor-Robert Gibson
General Info: Yr. Est. 1914, Bi-monthly
Circulation: Total-4,000

Inside Labor Relations
See: LABOR UNION

Insights
Business

Publishing Co: Espirit de Corps, 11 Hanover Square, New York, NY 10005; Title Tel # (212) 425-7033
Editorial Description: Employee benefits, subjects of interest to personnel directors.
General Info: Yr. Est. 1988, Irregular

JACS Volunteer
See: EMPLOYMENT

Jewish Labor Committee
Review
Association

Publishing Co: Jewish Labor Committee, 25 E. 21st St., 2nd Fl., New York, NY 10010-6297; Title Tel # (212) 477-0707 Title Fax # (212) 477-1918
Personnel: Editor-Arieh Lebowitz
Editorial Description: House organ, organizational activity in fields of civil rights, human rights and human relations in labor movement and Jewish community.
General Info: Yr. Est. 1963, Trim Size-8½ x 11, Sheetfed press, 8 pages, No Color, Matte, Saddle-stitched
Subscriptions: Free With Membership
Circulation: Total-8,500

Job Training and Placement Report
See: DISABILITY

Jobs Impact Bulletin
See: EMPLOYMENT

John Burton's Workers'
Compensation Monitor
Business

Publishing Co: LRP Publications, 747 Dresher Rd., P.O. Box 980, Horsham, PA 19044-0980 Tel # (215) 784-0910 Fax # (215) 784-0317
Personnel: Publisher-Kenneth F. Kahn, Editor-John Burton, Jr., Production Mgr.-Kathleen P. Neely, Mktg. Dir.-Jana Shellington, Promotion Dir.-Gary Ragin
Editorial Description: Expert insights on the current workers' compensation developments to keep up-to-date on changes in the field.
General Info: Bi-monthly
Subscriptions: Indv. $175
List Rental: List Management Co.: Axon Lists, 747 Dresher Rd. Ste. 500, Box 980, Horsham, PA 19044 Tel # (215) 784-0860, Fax # (215) 784-0870, Actives: $125/M

Labor Arbitration in Government
See: LAW

Labor Arbitration Information System
See: LAW

Labor Area Summary
Business

Publishing Co: North Carolina State Employment Security Commission, 414 Ray Ave, Fayetteville, NC 28301-4916; Title Tel # (910) 486-1010 Title Fax # (910) 484-5155
Personnel: Editor-Mary Fisher
Editorial Description: Labor market information for Fayetteville, N.C.
General Info: Bi-monthly, 4 pages, No Color
Subscriptions: Free
Circulation: (100% controlled), Total-300

Labor Cases

Publishing Co: CCH, Inc., 2700 Lake Cook Rd., Riverwoods, IL 60015 Parent Co.-Kluwer Law & Taxation Publishers, Cambridge; Title Tel # (847) 267-7000 Title Fax # (800) 224-8299
Editorial Description: Publishes federal and state decisions on labor relations, wage-hour issues in bound volumes.
General Info: Looseleaf
Subscriptions: Indv. $50

Labor Contract Law
Bulletin
Business

Publishing Co: Quinlan Publishing, 23 Drydock Ave, Boston, MA 02210-2387 Fax # (617) 345-9646; Title Tel # (617) 542-0048
Editorial Description: Court decisions on labor law disputes.
General Info: Monthly
Subscriptions: Indv. $59
List Rental: List Management Co.: Stevens-Knox List Management, 304 Park Ave S., New York, NY 10010-5312 Tel # (212) 388-8800, Fax # (212) 388-8890

Labor and Employment
Arbitration
Business

Publishing Co: Matthew Bender & Co., 11 Penn Plaza, New York, NY 10001-2006 Tel # (212) 967-7707 Fax # (212) 244-3188
Personnel: Editor-Tim Bornstein, Editor-Anne Gosline
Editorial Description: For the lawyer & non-lawyer alike, with contributions from more than 60 experts in the field--including several past Presidents of the National Academy of Arbitrators a former Chairman of the NLRB & former Chairman of the National Mediation Board.
General Info: Yr. Est. 1988, Irregular, Looseleaf

Labor and Employment Law News
See: LAW

Labor and Employment Law Newsletter
See: LAW

Labor Law Reports
Business

Publishing Co: CCH, Inc., 2700 Lake Cook Rd., Riverwoods, IL 60015 Parent Co.-Kluwer Law & Taxation Publishers, Cambridge; Title Tel # (847) 267-7000 Title Fax # (800) 224-8299
Editorial Description: Explains federal and state labor relations, wage-hour, union contracts and allied rules - laws, regulations, decisions, etc.
General Info: Yr. Est. 1934, Weekly, Trim Size-6 x 9, Web press, 200 pages, No Color, Looseleaf
Subscriptions: Indv. $2,672
Advertising: Inquire for rates.

Labor Law Reports-
Summary

Publishing Co: CCH, Inc., 2700 Lake Cook Rd., Riverwoods, IL 60015 Parent Co.-Kluwer Law & Taxation Publishers, Cambridge; Title Tel # (847) 267-7000 Title Fax # (800) 224-8299
Editorial Description: Reviews changes in law, regulations, court and NLRB decisions, etc., each week for 'Labor Law Reports' and 'Labor Relations' subscribers.
General Info: Looseleaf
Subscriptions: Indv. $98

Labor Letter

Publishing Co: Cast Metals Assn., 455 State St Ste 201, Des Plaines, IL 60016-2281; Title Tel # (708) 299-9160
General Info: Semi-monthly

Labor-Management
Relations Analysis/News
and Background   *Business*

Publishing Co: Bureau of National Affairs, Inc., 1231 25th St. NW, Bldg. N-200, Washington, DC 20037-1157; Title Tel # (202) 452-4200 Title Fax # (202) 822-8092
Personnel: Publisher-William A. Beltz, Mng. Editor-Nancy J. Sedmak, Circ. Mgr.-Gary C. Seltzer
Editorial Description: Summarizes developments & rulings in the field of labor law, covers major non-decisional developments & recent significant arbitration awards, & provides in-depth analysis & evaluation of the week's labor news.
General Info: Weekly, Trim Size-6 x 9, Offset press, 32 pages, ISSN: 1043-5506, Ind/Abs/Online: Westlaw, Lexis, HRIN, Looseleaf
Subscriptions: Indv. $245

Labor Market Letter   *Business, Association*

Publishing Co: Pennsylvania State Office of Employment, 135 Franklin Ave, Scranton, PA 18503-1935; Title Tel # (717) 826-2418
Personnel: Editor-Jim Mowad
Editorial Description: Narrative review of current employment developments and prospects. Statistical tables depict resident and establishment employment, hours and earnings and labor turnover.
General Info: Monthly, Trim Size-8½ x 11, Mimeo press
Circulation: (100% controlled), Total-1,500

Labor Market Letter, Clarion

Publishing Co: Pennsylvania State Employment Service, 420 Wood St., PO Box 724, Clarion, PA 16214-1336; Title Tel # (814) 226-1600 Title Fax # (814) 226-1703
Editorial Description: Labor market information - Clarion County.
General Info: Bi-monthly, No Color

Labor Market Letter, York
Area   *Business, Association*

Publishing Co: Pennsylvania State Employment Service, 140 North Duke St., York, PA 17401-1110; Title Tel # (717) 771-4416
Personnel: Editor-Larry Baugher
Editorial Description: Labor market information for this area such as unemployment rate, etc.
General Info: Yr. Est. 1949, Quarterly, Trim Size-8½ x 11, Mimeo press, 6 pages
Circulation: Total-1,150

Labor Market News,
Birmingham Area

Publishing Co: Alabama State Dept. of Industrial Relations, 3440 3rd Ave S, Birmingham, AL 35222-1712; Title Tel # (205) 251-1181
Personnel: Editor-Robert B. Brantley
Editorial Description: Depicts economic trends related to manpower.
General Info: Yr. Est. 1946, Monthly, Trim Size-8½ x 11, Offset press, 4 pages
Circulation: Total-1,800

Labor Market Trends, A
News Letter, Richmond
Metropolitan Area   *Business, Association*

Publishing Co: Virginia State Dept. of Labor, Box 1358, 7000 Federal Bldg., Richmond, VA 23211-1358; Title Tel # (804) 786-5881
Personnel: Editor-Jerry Harrison
General Info: Monthly

Labor Network News
See: CULTURE & HUMANITIES

Labor Notes   *Business*

Publishing Co: Labor Education, 7435 Michigan Ave, Detroit, MI 48210-2227; Title Tel # (313) 842-6262
Personnel: Editor-Jim Woodward
Editorial Description: Labor news, from a rank & file viewpoint.
General Info: Yr. Est. 1979, Monthly, Trim Size-8½ x 11, Sheetfed press, 16 pages, ISSN: 0275-4452, Ind/Abs/Online: Alt.PressIndex, No Color, Newsprint, Saddle-stitched
Subscriptions: Indv. $10, Inst. $30, Can. $25, For. $25
Circulation: Total-7,500
List Rental: Actives: $100/M
Printing Co: Goodwill Printing, 2000 W 8 Mile Rd, Ferndale, MI 48220-2215 Tel # (313) 547-7500

Labor Record

Publishing Co: Labor Record, 724 Railroad St, Joliet, IL 60436-9524; Title Tel # (815) 744-6120
Personnel: Editor-Charles Hanuf
General Info: Yr. Est. 1927, Weekly
Subscriptions: Indv. $3
Circulation: Total-10,000
Advertising: Inquire for rates.

Labor Relations   *Business*

Publishing Co: Bureau of National Affairs, Inc., 1231 25th St. NW, Bldg. N-200, Washington, DC 20037-1157; Title Tel # (202) 452-4200 Title Fax # (202) 822-8092
Personnel: Publisher-William A. Beltz, Mng. Editor-Bill L. Manville, Circ. Mgr.-Gary C. Seltzer
Editorial Description: Notification & reference service carrying summaries of federal & state labor laws, National Labor Relations Board & court rulings, & policy guide for employer-employee relations. Discusses the employer's legal rights & obligations concerning labor relations matters, with a separate chapter on occupational safety & health concerns.
General Info: Bi-weekly, Trim Size-8½ x 11, Web press, 8 pages, ISSN: 0149-2713, Ind/Abs/Online: HRIN
Subscriptions: Indv. $650

Labor Relations Bulletin:
Discipline & Grievances   *Business*

Publishing Co: Bureau of Business Practice, 24 Rope Ferry Rd, Waterford, CT 06386-0001 Tel # (806) 442-4365 Fax # (860) 434-3341 Parent Co.-Prentice Hall, Waterford; Title Tel # (860) 442-4365
Personnel: Publisher-David Deffley, Editor-Emily Mitchell
Editorial Description: A newsletter that provides information and insight to help both management and labor officials avoid- or resolve- conflicts. Contains report on current developments in labor law and labor relations, actual arbitration cases, and a column in which different arbitrators reflect on issues they have had to address ('Reflections of an Arbitrator').
General Info: (Formerly Discipline and Control Update), Monthly
Subscriptions: Indv. $85

Labor Safety Newsletter
See: SAFETY

Labor Studies Forum   *Association*

Publishing Co: University & College Labor Education Association, Indiana Univ., Poplars 630, Div. of Labor Studies, Bloomington, IN 47405 Tel # (812) 855-9082
Personnel: Editor-Margaret Gibbons Wilson
Editorial Description: Newsletter of the University & College Labor Education Association. Contains articles, resource & research information, professional association news, calls for papers, meeting announcements, employment announcements, and funding information.
General Info: Yr. Est. 1988, Quarterly, Trim Size-8½ x 11, 8 pages
Subscriptions: Free With Membership
Circulation: Total-2,000
Advertising: Inquire for rates.

Labor Trends
See: LABOR UNION

Labor/Maintence Update

Publishing Co: Natl. Erectors Assn., 1501 Lee Hwy Ste 202, Arlington, VA 22209-1109 Fax # (703) 524-3364; Title Tel # (703) 524-3336
General Info: Quarterly, Desktop press, 4 pages, No Color
Subscriptions: Free To Qualified Recipient

Labour Reporter   *Consumer, Association*

Publishing Co: Saskatchewan Fed. of Labour, 2709 12th Ave., #103, Regina, SK S4T 1J3 Canada; Title Tel # (306) 525-0197 Title Fax # (306) 525-8960
Personnel: Editor-Garnet Dishaw
Editorial Description: Pro-labour, socialist oriented news and information.
General Info: Yr. Est. 1985, Monthly, 8 pages
Subscriptions: Free To Qualified Recipient
Circulation: Total-6,000
Printing Co: Associated Printers, 1212 Scarth St., Regina, SK S4R 2E6 Canada

Let's Be Human

Publishing Co: Let's Be Human, 454 Prospect Ave. #111, West Orange, NJ 07052-4103; Title Tel # (516) 731-3069
Personnel: Editor-Harry Fleischman
General Info: Yr. Est. 1953, Quarterly
Subscriptions: Indv. $10

Local Labor Force Trends,
Hood River Office

Publishing Co: Oregon State Employment Service, 700 Union St., #105, The Dalles, OR 97058-1893; Title Tel # (503) 296-5435
Editorial Description: Describes employment and unemployment trends for Hood River County for each month.
General Info: Monthly, 2 pages
Subscriptions: Free

Local Labor Force Trends,
Klamath Falls Office

Publishing Co: Oregon State Employment Service, PO Box 68, Klamath Falls, OR 97601-0382; Title Tel # (503) 883-5630

Local Labor Force Trends, McMinnville Office, *Business, Association*

Publishing Co: Oregon Employment Div., Research, 875 Union St NE, Salem, OR 97311-0800; Title Tel # (503) 373-1817
Personnel: Publisher-Duane Ackerson
Editorial Description: Local Labor market employment/unemployment/economic developments and trends.
General Info: Monthly, Trim Size-8½ x 11, 3 pages, No Color
Circulation: Total-175

Local Labor Market Developments; Longview Office

Publishing Co: Washington State Employment Security Dept., PO Box 29, Kelso, WA 98626-0002; Title Tel # (206) 577-2250
General Info: Monthly

Longshore Reporter *Business*

Publishing Co: Matthew Bender & Co., 11 Penn Plaza, New York, NY 10001-2006 Tel # (212) 967-7707 Fax # (212) 244-3188
Editorial Description: Full text of the Longshore and Habor Workers' Compensation Act & other relevant statutes, regulations & proposed rules & regulations.
General Info: Yr. Est. 1974, Bi-weekly, Looseleaf

MOICC News - Net *Business, Association*

Publishing Co: Minnesota Occupational Information Coordinating Committee, Dept. of Economic Security, 390 N. Robert, St. Paul, MN 55101; Title Tel # (612) 296-2072
Personnel: Editor-Carole Fuller
General Info: Yr. Est. 1980, Irregular, 8 pages, Color, Newsprint
Circulation: (100% controlled), Total-2,300

Maine Labor Market Digest *Business, Association*

Publishing Co: Maine Dept. of Labor, 20 Union St, Augusta, ME 04330-6826; Title Tel # (207) 287-2271 Title Fax # (207) 287-2947
Personnel: Editor-D. Evans, Circ. Mgr.-B. Evans
Editorial Description: Monthly report on labor market developments for state includes data on employment by industry, unemployment, hours worked, and wages.
General Info: (Formerly Maine Manpower), Yr. Est. 1962, Monthly, Trim Size-8½ x 11, Offset press, 6 pages, 2 Color, Newsprint
Subscriptions: Free
Circulation: Total-3,600

Management Policies & Personnel Law See: MANAGEMENT

Management Report for Nonunion Organizations *Business*

Publishing Co: John Wiley & Sons, Inc., 605 Third Avenue, New York, NY 10158-0012 Tel # (212) 850-6000 Fax # (212) 850-6088
Personnel: Editor-Sarah Magee
Editorial Description: Covers how-to's of preventing & counteracting union organization drives. Contains information on tools & techniques to maintain nonunion status.
General Info: (Formerly Hughes Report), Yr. Est. 1977, Monthly, Trim Size-8½ x 11, Sheetfed press, 8 pages, ISSN: 0745-4880, Coated, Saddle-stitched
Subscriptions: Indv. $204, Can. $204, For. $254
Advertising: Inquire for rates.
List Rental: Rents Lists
Printing Co: Hessey Printing, Inc., 424 Lafayette St # 100226, Nashville, TN 37203-4255 Tel # (615) 244-7180, Fax # (615) 255-6911

Managing Laboratory Personnel See: MANAGEMENT

Maryland Workplace

Publishing Co: Univ. of Maryland College of Business & Management, University Of Maryland, College Park, MD 20742-0001; Title Tel # (301) 405-2189
Personnel: Editor-Mercy Coogan
General Info: Yr. Est. 1978, Bi-monthly, 4 pages
Circulation: Total-2,000

Massachusetts Employment Review

Publishing Co: Massachusetts Div. of Employment Security, C.F. Hurley Bldg., Boston, MA 02114; Title Tel # (617) 727-7412
Personnel: Editor-Elliot Winer
General Info: Yr. Est. 1974, Monthly, 12 pages
Circulation: Total-1,500

Metropolitan Washington D.C. Area Labor Summary *Business, Association*

Publishing Co: Dept. of Employment Services, 500 C St NW, Washington, DC 20001-2110; Title Tel # (202) 724-7213 Title Fax # (202) 724-7216
Personnel: Editor-Richard Groner
General Info: (Formerly Greater Washington Area Labor Summary), Monthly, Offset press, 16 pages, No Color, Saddle-stitched
Subscriptions: Free
Circulation: Total-1,200

Michigan State University, School of Labor and Industrial Relations, Newsletter

Publishing Co: Michigan State Univ., School of Labor & Industrial Relations, 403 S Kedzie Hall, East Lansing, MI 48824-1032; Title Tel # (517) 355-1800 Title Fax # (517) 355-7656
Personnel: Editor-Sally Pratt
Circulation: Total-3,100

Middle East Labor Bulletin See: INTERNATIONAL AFFAIRS

Minnesota Labor Market Review *Business*

Publishing Co: Minnesota Dept. of Jobs & Training, 390 Robert St N, Saint Paul, MN 55101-1812; Title Tel # (612) 296-6545
Personnel: Editor-M. Chottepanda, Circ. Mgr.-Hugh Heimdahl, Production Mgr.-Carole Fuller
Editorial Description: Contains analysis, labor force estimates, industry employment, hours, earnings, & job market information. A quarterly issue has a feature article, research summary, & graphics.
General Info: (Formerly Current Minnesota Labor Conditions), Yr. Est. 1974, Monthly, Trim Size-8½ x 11, 8 pages
Circulation: Total-2,000

NASEA News

Publishing Co: Natl. Assn. of Student Employment Administrators, PO Box 8214, Omaha, NE 68108-0214 Tel # (712) 322-5518; Title Tel # (716) 395-2468
Personnel: Editor-Rick Kincaid
General Info: Yr. Est. 1980, Quarterly
Circulation: Total-400

NEA Notes

Publishing Co: Natl. Erectors Assn., 1501 Lee Hwy Ste 202, Arlington, VA 22209-1109; Title Tel # (703) 524-3336 Title Fax # (703) 524-3364
Personnel: Editor-Melissa Delany
Editorial Description: Newsletter for latest developments in construction safety, OSHA ANSI Natl. Safety Council etc.
General Info: (Formerly NEA Safety Spotlight), Yr. Est. 1973, Quarterly, 4 pages, No Color
Circulation: Total-2,000

NFWM Newsletter *Association*

Publishing Co: National Farm Worker Ministry, 1337 W Ohio St, Chicago, IL 60622-6430; Title Tel # (312) 829-6436 Title Fax # (312) 829-8915
Personnel: Editor-Patricia Drydyk, Production Mgr.-Paul Chavez
Editorial Description: Update on activities to organize farm workers for self-determination.
General Info: (Formerly Migrant Ministry), Yr. Est. 1971, Quarterly, Trim Size-8½ x 11, Web press, 7 pages, No Color
Subscriptions: Indv. $15
Circulation: (100% controlled)
Printing Co: United Farm Workers, PO Box 62, Keene, CA 93531-0062

NLRB Advice Memorandum Reporter See: LAW

National Consumers League Bulletin See: CONSUMER INTERESTS

National Health & Welfare Union Information Bulletin

Publishing Co: National Health & Welfare Union, 233 Gilmour St., Ste. 904, Ottawa, ON K2P 0P1 Canada
Personnel: Editor-R.E. Armstrong
General Info: Yr. Est. 1977, Quarterly, 12 pages
Circulation: Total-6,000

New Jersey Labor and Employment Law Quarterly
Business, Association

Publishing Co: New Jersey State Bar Association, New Jersey Law Center, 1 Constitution Sq., New Brunswick, NJ 08901-1520 Fax # (908) 828-0034; Title Tel # (908) 249-5000 Title Fax # (908) 249-2815
Personnel: Publisher-Lois Winnberg, Editor-Arnold Cohen, Production Mgr., Art Dir.-Dawn Costa
Editorial Description: Substantive & practical information for members of the New Jersey State Bar Assn. or non-attorneys interested in Labor & Employment Law.
General Info: (Formerly Labor & Employment Law Section Newsletter), Yr. Est. 1966, Quarterly, Trim Size-8½ x 11, Offset press, 20 pages, No Color, Matte, Saddle-stitched
Subscriptions: Indv. $40, Free With Membership
Circulation: Total-800

New York Civil Service Update
See: EMPLOYMENT

New York Workers' Compensation Law Reporter
See: LAW

News for Independent Unions

Publishing Co: Natl. Fed. of Independent Unions, Midwest Independent Union, 1166 S 11th St, Philadelphia, PA 19147-4627; Title Tel # (215) 336-3300
General Info: Quarterly

Newsletter for the National Center for Collective Bargaining
Scholarly, Association

Publishing Co: National Center for Collective Bargaining - Higher Ed., Baruch College, 17 Lexington Ave., Box G-1050, New York, NY 10010; Title Tel # (212) 387-1510 Title Fax # (212) 387-1516
Personnel: Publisher-Joel Douglas, Editor-Frank Annunziato, Production Mgr.-Beth Johnson
Editorial Description: Analyzes current trends, new developments, major decisions of courts & regulatory bodies in higher education collective bargaining.
General Info: Yr. Est. 1973, Quarterly, Trim Size-8½ x 11, 8 pages, ISSN: 0737-9285, No Color, Matte
Subscriptions: Indv. $35, Can. $35, For. $35, $9/copy

Nova Scotia Government Employees Union Newsletter
Association

Publishing Co: Nova Scotia Government Employees Union, 100 Eileen Stubbs Ave., Dartmouth, NS B3B 1Y6 Canada; Title Tel # (902) 424-4063
Personnel: Editor-Reg Lownie
Editorial Description: In-House Labour Union pub. for 11,000 provincial government employees.
General Info: Yr. Est. 1966, Bi-monthly, Trim Size-8½ x 11, Web press, 24 pages, 2 Color, Newsprint, Saddle-stitched
Circulation: Total-14,000
Printing Co: Dartmouth Printing, 69 Lyme Rd., Hanover, NH 03755-1293 Tel # (603) 643-2220, Fax # (603) 643-5479

Numbers News
See: ADVERTISING & MARKETING

OSHA Guide for Health Care Facilities
See: HOSPITALS & NURSING HOMES

Oklahoma Labor Market Information
Business

Publishing Co: Oklahoma Employment Security Commission, Research Division, 2401 N. Lincoln Blvd., Rm. 302, Oklahoma City, OK 73105-4495 Tel # (405) 557-5407; Title Tel # (405) 557-5382
Personnel: Editor-Roger Jackson, Circ. Mgr.-Milton Tinney
Editorial Description: The LMI Newsletter contains a monthly synopsis of the activity taking place in the Oklahoma labor market.
General Info: Yr. Est. 1949, Monthly, Trim Size-8½ x 11, Desktop press, 30 pages, Color-cover
Circulation: (100% controlled), Total-2,000

Organizations & Change
See: MANAGEMENT

PEPI Update
Consumer, Association

Publishing Co: Positive Employee Practice Institute, 50 South Ninth Street, Minneapolis, MN 55402; Title Tel # (612) 333-0471 Title Fax # (612) 333-6526
Editorial Description: For members of the Positive Employee Pratices Institute.
General Info: Yr. Est. 1989, Bi-monthly, Trim Size-8½ x 11, 6 pages, No Color

PERB News
Association

Publishing Co: Public Employment Relations Board, 80 Wolf Rd Fl 5, Albany, NY 12205-2604; Title Tel # (518) 457-2676
Personnel: Editor-R. Vatalaro
Editorial Description: Public sector labor relations.
General Info: Yr. Est. 1968, Monthly, Trim Size-8½ x 11, Offset press, 4 pages, Color
Subscriptions: Indv. $15, $2/copy
Circulation: Total-7,600

PSAC Union Update

Publishing Co: Public Service Alliance of Canada, 233 Gilmour, Ottawa, ON K2P 0P1 Canada; Title Tel # (613) 560-4348 Title Fax # (613) 236-1654
Personnel: Editor-Francine Filion, Art Dir.-Janet Jorgensen
General Info: (Formerly PSAC Weekly Newsletter), Yr. Est. 1989, Bi-weekly
Subscriptions: Free To Qualified Recipient
Circulation: Total-43,000

Payroll Practitioner's Compliance Handbook
See: MANAGEMENT

Pennsylvania's Labor Force...A Monthly Statistical Analysis
See: EMPLOYMENT

Pensacola Labor Market Trends
Business, Association

Publishing Co: Job Svc. of Florida, 236 W Garden St # 1393, Pensacola, FL 32501-5729; Title Tel # (904) 432-7651
Personnel: Editor-Shannon McCrary
Editorial Description: Labor market information and economic forecasting newsletter.
General Info: Monthly, 4 pages, No Color
Circulation: (100% controlled), Total-2,000

People Trends
See: INDUSTRIAL RELATIONS/PERSONNEL

Personnel Law Update, California Edition
See: LAW

Personnel Law Update, National Editon
See: LAW

Personnel Law Update, Texas Edition
See: LAW

Personnel Practice Ideas
See: MANAGEMENT

Personnel/HR Assistant, The
Business

Publishing Co: Council on Education in Management, 321 Lennon Lane, Walnut Creek, CA 94598; Title Tel # (510) 944-9444 Title Fax # (510) 988-1888
Editorial Description: Human resources - practical tips.
General Info: Yr. Est. 1988, Monthly
Subscriptions: Indv. $119

Philippine Labor Alert
See: INTERNATIONAL AFFAIRS

Police Labor Monthly
See: LAW ENFORCEMENT & PENOLOGY

Principles of Payroll Administration
See: MANAGEMENT

Professional, The
See: LABOR UNION

Project Equality of Wisconsin-Newsletter & Buyers' Guide
Business, Association

Publishing Co: Project Equality of Wisconsin, Inc., 1442 N Farwell Ave Ste 210, Milwaukee, WI 53202-2913 Parent Co.-Project Equality, Kansas City; Title Tel # (414) 272-2642 Title Fax # (414) 272-2644
Personnel: Production Mgr., Promotion Dir.-Jenny Schlag
Editorial Description: Project Equality is a nationwide interfaith program supporting equal opportunity employers with training and other assistance relating to diversity issues.
General Info: (Formerly Project Equality Update), Yr. Est. 1969, Quarterly, Trim Size-8½ x 11, Web press, 9 pages, 2 Color, Coated
Subscriptions: Indv. $30, Inst. $50, $5/copy
Circulation: Total-3,500
Advertising: Inquire for rates. Accepts Inserts.

Projects with Industry Forum
See: DISABILITY

Public Employment Law Notes
See: LAW

Public Employment Reports
See: GOVERNMENT

Public Safety Personnel Updance
See: LAW ENFORCEMENT & PENOLOGY

Quarterly Labour Force Statistics
See: ECONOMICS

Reading Labor Market News Release
See: GOVERNMENT

Ready Or Not
See: EMPLOYMENT

Recruiting Trends
See: EMPLOYMENT

Resistor
Association

Publishing Co: IBM Workers United, PO Box 634, Johnson City, NY 13790-0634; Title Tel # (607) 797-6911
Personnel: Publisher, Editor-Lee Conrad
Editorial Description: Newsletter for organizing IBM employees into a union.
General Info: Yr. Est. 1976, Bi-monthly, Trim Size-8½ x 14½, 2 pages
Subscriptions: Indv. $10
Circulation: Total-2,000

SERB Official Reporter
See: LAW

Safety Compliance Letter with OSHA Highlights
See: SAFETY

Safety Signals
See: SAFETY

San Diego Labor Market Bulletin

Publishing Co: Employment Development Dept., 1350 Front St Ste 3010, San Diego, CA 92101-3610; Title Tel # (714) 237-7601
Editorial Description: Estimated monthly employment and unemployment data for San Diego County.
General Info: Yr. Est. 1950, Monthly, Trim Size-8½ x 11, 2 pages, No Color
Circulation: Total-750

School of Labor and Industrial Relations, Newsletter
Association

Publishing Co: Michigan State Univ., College of Social Science, South Kedzie Hall, East Lansing, MI 48824-0001; Title Tel # (517) 355-1800 Title Fax # (517) 355-7656
Personnel: Editor-Sally Pratt
Editorial Description: Covers all activities of school in academic graduate programs research, and service areas of government, business, and labor; with special articles by faculty, book reviews personnel changes.
General Info: Yr. Est. 1961, Semi-annually, Trim Size-8½ x 11½, Offset press, 8 pages, Color
Circulation: Total-2,000

Science & Engineering Newsletter

Publishing Co: Natl. Consortium for Black Professional Development, 2210 Goldsmith Ln Ste 228a, Louisville, KY 40218-1038; Title Tel # (502) 451-8199
General Info: Quarterly

Serf's Up

Publishing Co: A.F.Z. Enterprises, P.O. Box 34695, Detroit, MI 48234
Editorial Description: A unique publication with lots of intriguing essays and probing interviews about fringe ideas and the potentials for freedom.
General Info: Trim Size-8.5 x 11, 14 pages
Subscriptions: Indv. $2

Smart Workplace Practices
See: MANAGEMENT

Smart's California Worker's Comp Bulletin
See: INSURANCE

South Dakota Labor Bulletin
Business, Association

Publishing Co: South Dakota Dept. of Labor, 420 S Roosevelt St, Aberdeen, SD 57401-5131; Title Tel # (605) 622-2314
Editorial Description: Labor force, employment & unemployment trends in the state of South Dakota & Sioux Falls & Rapid City MSA's.
General Info: Yr. Est. 1949, Monthly, Sheetfed press, 12 pages, No Color
Circulation: Total-2,000

Staffing Industry Report
See: EMPLOYMENT

Stamford Labor Market Review
Business, Association

Publishing Co: Connecticut State Labor Department, Office o fResearch, Office of Research, 111 High Ridge Rd., 3rd Fl., Stamford, CT 06905 Tel # (203) 566-3462; Title Tel # (203) 356-1515
Personnel: Publisher-Roger Therrien, Editor-Maryann Przybysz
Editorial Description: Labor market information, tables, graph, narrative. This is a free government leaflet.
General Info: (Formerly Stamford Labor Market Letter), Yr. Est. 1977, Quarterly, 2 pages, No Color
Subscriptions: Free
Circulation: Total-300

State Labor Laws
Business

Publishing Co: Bureau of National Affairs, Inc., 1231 25th St. NW, Bldg. N-200, Washington, DC 20037-1157; Title Tel # (202) 452-4200 Title Fax # (202) 822-8092
Personnel: Publisher-William A. Beltz, Mng. Editor-Roberto Federigan, Circ. Mgr.-Gary C. Seltzer
Editorial Description: Provides texts, digests, & charts of state labor laws, covering their scope, jurisdiction, aministration, & enformcement. Also discusses how state labor law relates to federal laws affecting labor relations & employment regulation & provides directories of state agencies that administer & enforce these laws.
General Info: Yr. Est. 1956, Weekly, Trim Size-6 x 9, Web press, ISSN: 0148-7981, Looseleaf
Subscriptions: Indv. $959

Study Time
Association

Publishing Co: American Arbitration Assn., 140 W. 51 St., New York, NY 10020-1203 Tel # (212) 484-4000; Title Tel # (212) 484-4012 Title Fax # (212) 541-4841
Personnel: Editor-Earl Baderschneider
Editorial Description: Articles of interest to labor arbitrators.
General Info: Quarterly, Trim Size-8½ x 11, 8 pages, 2 Color, Matte, Looseleaf
Subscriptions: Free With Membership
Circulation: Total-3,800

Sugar World
Business

Publishing Co: Intl Commn for Coordination of Solidarity Among Sugar Worker, 2084 Danforth Ave., Suite 3, Toronto, ON M4C1J9 Canada; Title Tel # (416) 467-8621 Title Fax # (416) 467-9143
Personnel: Editor-Reginald McQuaid
Editorial Description: A newsletter on issues of concern to sugar workers.
General Info: Yr. Est. 1977, Bi-monthly, Trim Size-8½ x 11, 4 pages, ISSN: 0229-737X, No Color
Subscriptions: Indv. $15, Inst. $30, $1/copy
Circulation: Total-1,000

Summary of Labor Arbitration Awards
Association

Publishing Co: American Arbitration Assn., 140 W. 51 St., New York, NY 10020-1203 Tel # (212) 484-4000 Fax # (212) 541-4841; Title Tel # (212) 484-4014 Title Fax # (212) 765-4874
Personnel: Editor-Margaret Leibowitz
Editorial Description: Summary of selected labor arbitration awards in private sector.
General Info: Yr. Est. 1959, Monthly, Trim Size-8½ x 11, 12 pages, ISSN: 0039-5005, 2 Color, Coated, Looseleaf
Subscriptions: Indv. $120
Circulation: Total-5,000
Printing Co: Sheridan Printing, 1425 3rd Ave, Alpha, NJ 08865-4695 Tel # (908) 454-0700, Fax # (908) 454-2554

TSM Reports
See: INDUSTRIAL RELATIONS/PERSONNEL

Tiesa
See: CLUBS

Trade Trax
See: WOMEN'S

Transition: The Newsletter About Reforming Economies
See: INTERNATIONAL AFFAIRS

UAPD Report
Association

Publishing Co: Union of American Physicians & Dentists, 1330 Broadway Ste 730, Oakland, CA 94612-2506; Title Tel # (510) 839-0193
General Info: Yr. Est. 1972, Monthly
Circulation: Total-5,000

Unfair Labor Practices Law Bulletin
Business

Publishing Co: Quinlan Publishing, 23 Drydock Ave, Boston, MA 02210-2387 Tel # (617) 542-0048 Fax # (617) 345-9646
Editorial Description: Cases and issues of unfair employer labor practices.
General Info: Monthly
Subscriptions: Indv. $59

Unjust Dismissal
Business

Publishing Co: Matthew Bender & Co., 11 Penn Plaza, New York, NY 10001-2006 Tel # (212) 967-7707 Fax # (212) 244-3188
Editorial Description: Comprehensive coverage of the most explosive issues in labor law today. Analyzes workers' rights and employers' responsibilities.
General Info: Yr. Est. 1985, Irregular, Looseleaf

Upper Peninsula Labor Market Review

Publishing Co: Michigan Employment Security Commission, 7310 Woodward Ave, Detroit, MI 48202-3152; Title Tel # (313) 876-5368
Editorial Description: A review of labor market conditions in Michigan's upper peninsula.
General Info: Yr. Est. 1946, Monthly, Trim Size-8½ x 11, Offset press, 4 pages
Circulation: Total-1,000

Utah Dept. of Employment Security-Labor Market Information

Publishing Co: Utah Dept. of Employment Security, 140 E Broadway, Salt Lake City, UT 84111-2305; Title Tel # (801) 533-2345
Personnel: Editor-Ray Sargent
General Info: (Formerly Utah Employment Newsletter), Yr. Est. 1953, Monthly
Circulation: Total-3,100

Vermont Labor Market   *Business*

Publishing Co: Vermont Dept. of Employment & Training, PO Box 488, Montpelier, VT 05601-0488; Title Tel # (802) 828-4321 Title Fax # (802) 828-4050
Personnel: Editor-Joseph Bahr
Editorial Description: News about unemployment compensation program, Vermont Employment & Training operations, & labor force statistics, monthly statistics on employment, hours & earnings, & labor market conditions.
General Info: Yr. Est. 1963, Monthly, Trim Size-8⁵⁄₁₆ x 10¹⁵⁄₁₆, Offset press, 8 pages, 2 Color
Subscriptions: Free
Circulation: Total-3,000

Vital Signs
See: NURSING

WG&L Human Resources Forms with Commentary
See: INDUSTRIAL RELATIONS/PERSONNEL

Wages and Hours
See: LAW

Wages and Hours: Law and Practice   *Business*

Publishing Co: Matthew Bender & Co., 11 Penn Plaza, New York, NY 10001-2006 Tel # (212) 967-7707 Fax # (212) 244-3188
Editorial Description: Covers all aspects of federal & state laws governing minimum wage, overtime & child labor standards. Focuses on the federal wagehour statutory scheme, including laws regulating work under government procurement contracts & federal assisted.
General Info: Yr. Est. 1989, Irregular, Looseleaf

What Is to Be Read
See: BOOKS & BOOK TRADE

What's Ahead in Human Resources
See: INDUSTRIAL RELATIONS/PERSONNEL

Wisconsin Safety & Health
See: SAFETY

Work America   *Business*

Publishing Co: Natl. Alliance of Business, 1201 New York Ave NW Ste 700, Washington, DC 20005-3917 Tel # (202) 289-2845 Fax # (202) 289-1303; Title Tel # (202) 289-2888
Personnel: Editor-Trudi Risnikof, Circ. Mgr.-Myra Nicholas
Editorial Description: Promotes business involvement in education & job training human resources programs.
General Info: (Formerly NAB Clearinghouse Showcase), Yr. Est. 1983, Monthly, Trim Size-11 x 17, Sheetfed press, 10 pages, 2% ads, 2 Color, Newsprint
Subscriptions: Indv. $30, $3/copy
Circulation: (80% controlled), Subscriptions-412
Advertising: Inquire for rates.
List Rental: Actives: $70/M
Printing Co: Goetz Printing Co., 7939 Angus Ct., Springfield, VA 22153-2844 Tel # (703) 569-8232, Fax # (703) 569-9364

Work in America

Publishing Co: Work in America Institute, 700 White Plains Road, Scarsdale, NY 10583; Title Tel # (914) 472-9600 Title Fax # (914) 472-9606
Personnel: Editor-John V. Hickey, Mktg. Mgr.-Lisa Starkey
General Info: Yr. Est. 1987, Monthly

Work and Family Life   *Business, Consumer*

Publishing Co: Work & Family Life, 2301 Mound Rd., Jacksonville, IL 62650-2200; Title Tel # (800) 676-2838 Title Fax # (708) 647-6868
Personnel: Publisher, Editor-Susan Ginsberg
Editorial Description: Balancing job and personal responsibilities.
General Info: Yr. Est. 1985, Monthly
Subscriptions: Indv. $36, Inst. $6
List Rental: Rents Lists

Work Programs Special Interest Section Newsletter

Publishing Co: American Occupational Therapy Assn., 4720 Montgomery Lane, PO Box 31220, Bethesda, MD 20824-1220 Tel # (301) 652-2682 Fax # (301) 652-7711; Title Tel # (301) 948-9626 Title Fax # (301) 948-5512
Personnel: Editor-Carl Betancourt

Workers' Comp Executive
See: INSURANCE

Workers Compensation Guide
See: INDUSTRIAL RELATIONS/PERSONNEL

Workers' Compensation Monthly   *Consumer*

Publishing Co: SEAK, Inc., 13 Falmouth Heights, P.O. Box 590, Falmouth, MA 02541-0590 Fax # (508) 540-1606; Title Tel # (508) 540-1606
Personnel: Editor-Steven Babitsky
Editorial Description: Natl. coverage of workers' compensation issues.
General Info: Yr. Est. 1980, Monthly, 32 pages, No Color
Subscriptions: Indv. $220

Workers' Solidarity   *Association*

Publishing Co: Workers Solidarity Alliance, 339 Lafayette St Rm 202, New York, NY 10012-2725 Tel # (212) 979-8353
Editorial Description: Covers the world of labor, international events, and social movements in the US & world from an anarchist unionist perspective.
General Info: Bi-monthly, Sheetfed press, 8 pages, No Color
Advertising: Inquire for rates.

Workforce Strategies
See: EMPLOYMENT

Your Safety News
See: SAFETY

LABOR UNION

32E Events   *Association*

Publishing Co: SEIU, Local 32E, 4234 Bronx Blvd, Bronx, NY 10466-2611; Title Tel # (718) 324-6556 Title Fax # (718) 994-2932
Personnel: Editor-Diana DeGroat
Editorial Description: A quarterly publication of information about membership
General Info: Yr. Est. 1988, Quarterly, Trim Size-8½ x 11, Offset press, 6 pages, 2 Color, Coated, Other
Subscriptions: Free With Membership
Circulation: Total-12,000
Printing Co: Altag Press, 962 Washington Avenue, Bronx, NY Tel # (718) 665-2803

204 Reporter   *Association*

Publishing Co: Service Employees Intl. Union, 1 Credit Union Dr., Toronto, ON M4A 2S6 Canada; Title Tel # (416) 752-4770 Title Fax # (416) 752-1966
Personnel: Editor-Ellen Gardener
Editorial Description: Coverage of members activities, contract negotiations, & union initiatives within the local.
General Info: Quarterly, Web press, 12 pages, No Color, Matte
Circulation: (100% controlled), Total-17,000
Printing Co: Thistle Printing, 14 Coldwater Rd., Don Mills, ON M3B 1Y7 Canada Tel # (416) 447-6421

AALC Reporter   *Association*

Publishing Co: Sponsor-AFL-CIO, African-American Labor Center, 1925 K St NW Ste 300, Washington, DC 20006-1105; Title Tel # (202) 778-4600 Title Fax # (202) 778-4601
Personnel: Editor-Mary Ann Forbes
Editorial Description: Programs & policies of AALC in Africa. In English/French/Arabic.
General Info: Yr. Est. 1965, Irregular, Trim Size-8½ x 11, Desktop press, 8 pages, 2 Color
Subscriptions: Free
Circulation: (100% controlled), Total-4,000
Printing Co: Kelly Press, Inc., 1701 Cabin Branch Rd, Cheverly, MD 20785-3820 Tel # (301) 386-2800

AIFLD Outlook

Publishing Co: American Institute for Free Labor Development, 1015 20th St., NW, Washington, DC 20036-4908; Title Tel # (202) 659-6300
Personnel: Editor-David Jessup
Editorial Description: Labor news. It describes activities of AIFLD both in the U.S.A. and in the Latin American and Caribbean countries where it operates.
General Info: Yr. Est. 1962, Bi-monthly, Trim Size-8½ x 11½, Offset press, 4 pages, Color

ALERTA
See: INTERNATIONAL TRADE

Arbitration in the Schools
See: LAW

BNA's Collective Bargaining
Bulletin *Business*

Publishing Co: Bureau of National Affairs, Inc., 1231 25th St. NW, Bldg. N-200, Washington, DC 20037-1157; Title Tel # (202) 452-4200 Title Fax # (202) 822-8092
Personnel: Publisher-William Beltz, Editor-Mary Dunn, Circ. Mgr.-Gary Seltzer
Editorial Description: Presents the latest developments in collective bargaining, including contract settlements, bargaining techniques, trends, & contract interpretations by the courts, administrative agencies & arbitrators.
General Info: (Formerly What's New in Collective Bargaining Negotiations & Contracts), Yr. Est. 1945, Bi-weekly, Trim Size-8½ x 11, Offset press, 6 pages, ISSN: 1084-8584, Ind/Abs/Online: HRIN
Subscriptions: Indv. $225

Bargaining Bulletin
See: EDUCATION

Brooklyn Longshoreman

Publishing Co: Local 1814, Intl. Longshoremen's Assn., 70 20th St., Brooklyn, NY 11232-1101; Title Tel # (212) 834-7853
Personnel: Editor-Jon Visel
General Info: Yr. Est. 1960, Trim Size-11¼ x 16, Offset press, 8 pages, Color
Circulation: Total-16,500

Builder, The

Publishing Co: Building & Construction Trades Dept. AFL-CIO, 815 16th St., N.W., Washington, DC 20006-4189; Title Tel # (202) 347-1461 Title Fax # (202) 628-0724
General Info: (Formerly Building and Constructin Trades Bulletin), Monthly

Building Service Division
Update

Publishing Co: Service Employees Intl. Union, 1313 L St. , N. W., Washington, DC 20005-4100; Title Tel # (202) 452-8750
Personnel: Publisher-John Sweeney, Editor-Joyce Moscata, Art Dir.-Jeff Langkau
General Info: (Formerly Leadership News Update), Yr. Est. 1987, Quarterly, 24 pages, 2 Color, Saddle-stitched
Circulation: Total-50,000

Bulletin

Publishing Co: AFL-CIO, 815 16th St NW, Washington, DC 20006-4145; Title Tel # (202) 637-5000
Personnel: Intl. Editor-Tom Kahn
General Info: Monthly, Trim Size-8½ x 11, 8 pages, ISSN: 0890-6165, Color-cover
Subscriptions: Free To Qualified Recipient
Circulation: Total-100,000
Printing Co: Kelly Press, Inc., 1701 Cabin Branch Rd, Cheverly, MD 20785-3820 Tel # (301) 386-2800

CLUW News

Publishing Co: Coalition of Labor Union Women, 15 Union Sq W, New York, NY 10003-3308; Title Tel # (212) 242-0700
Personnel: Editor-Diane Curry
General Info: Yr. Est. 1974, Bi-monthly
Subscriptions: Indv. $15

Canadian Labour Law Reporter
See: LAW

Chicago Union Teacher *Business*

Publishing Co: Chicago Teachers Union, 222 Merchandise Mart Plaza, Chicago, IL 60654-1005 Tel # (312) 329-6251 Parent Co.-American Federation of Teachers, Washington; Title Tel # (312) 329-9100
Personnel: Editor-Ellen Schur, Adv. Dir.-Carolyn Fulton
Editorial Description: Covers educational methods, materials and techniques with emphasis on Chicago schools.
General Info: Monthly, Trim Size-11½ x 15, Offset press, 20 pages
Circulation: Total-30,000

Child Labor Monitor
See: CONSUMER INTERESTS

Collective Bargaining
Negotiations & Contracts *Business*

Publishing Co: Bureau of National Affairs, Inc., 1231 25th St. NW, Bldg. N-200, Washington, DC 20037-1157 Tel # (202) 452-4200; Title Tel # (202) 452-4317 Title Fax # (202) 822-8092
Personnel: Publisher-William A. Beltz, Editor-Mary Dunn, Mng. Editor-Leslie Goldman, Circ. Mgr.-Gary C. Seltzer
Editorial Description: A biweekly notification & reference service containing information designed to help unions & management prepare, negotiate & adminster contacts.
General Info: Yr. Est. 1945, Bi-weekly, Trim Size-8½ x 11, Web press, 4 pages, ISSN: 0010-079X
Subscriptions: Indv. $869

Communicator *Business, Association*

Publishing Co: Newfoundland Assn. of Public Employees, Box 8100, St. John's, NF A1B 3M9 Canada; Title Tel # (709) 754-0700 Title Fax # (709) 754-0726
Personnel: Editor-Trudi Brake
Editorial Description: For union members emphasizing legislation, negotiations, education, national news, etc.
General Info: Yr. Est. 1968, Bi-monthly, Trim Size-8½ x 11, Offset press, 24 pages, 2 Color, Saddle-stitched
Circulation: (100% controlled), Total-18,500, Readership-18,500

Craftsman

Publishing Co: Chicago Local 458-3M GCIU, 204 S Ashland Ave, Chicago, IL 60607-5302; Title Tel # (312) 738-4200
Personnel: Editor-Stanley Mucha, Production Mgr.-Charles Timmel
General Info: Yr. Est. 1967, Quarterly, Sheetfed press, No Color
Acquistions: Publication Bought
Circulation: (100% controlled), Total-9,000
Printing Co: Bradley Printing Co., 2170 Mannheim Rd, Des Plaines, IL 60018-2995 Tel # (708) 635-8000, Fax # (708) 635-5064

Daily Labor Report *Business*

Publishing Co: Bureau of National Affairs, Inc., 1231 25th St. NW, Bldg. N-200, Washington, DC 20037-1157; Title Tel # (202) 452-4200 Title Fax # (202) 822-8092
Personnel: Publisher-William A. Beltz, Editor-William Bank, Mng. Editor-Susan J. Sala, Circ. Mgr.-Gary C. Seltzer
Editorial Description: A daily notification service that comprehensively covers the latest labor developments in Congress, the courts, federal agencies, unions, management, the NLRB & more.
General Info: (Formerly Daily Economic Reports on Current Trends affecting Managemen), Yr. Est. 1941, Daily, Trim Size-8½ x 11, Web press, 30 pages, ISSN: 0148-2693, Ind/Abs/Online: BNA, HRINB, WESTLAW, Mead Data Central, Lexis, Nexis
Subscriptions: Indv. $5,347

Drive Reporter

Publishing Co: International Brotherhood of Teamsters, Chauffeurs, Warehous, 2801 Trumbull St, Detroit, MI 48216-1270
General Info: Semi-monthly

Education Update
See: EDUCATION

Employee Policy for the Private and Public Sectors/State Capitals
See: INDUSTRIAL RELATIONS/PERSONNEL

Employee Relations in
Action *Business*

Publishing Co: Research Institute of America, 1340 Braddock Pl., Ste. 400, Alexandria, VA 22314-1651 Tel # (703) 706-8260 Fax # (703) 683-4824; Title Tel # (202) 842-0520 Title Fax # (212) 475-1790
Personnel: Publisher-John Roche, Editor-Elmer Ellentuck, Editor-Rhodes Henderer
Editorial Description: Case studies of employee problems with events, & arbitrations, & rulings. Offers practical guidance on what goes wrong - and how to solve them.
General Info: Yr. Est. 1960, Semi-monthly, Trim Size-8½ x 11, Sheetfed press, 4 pages
Subscriptions: Indv. $225
List Rental: List Management Co.: Taybi Direct East, Inc., 13321 New Hampshire Ave., Ste. 202, Silver Spring, MD 20904-3450 Tel # (301) 680-3633, Fax # (301) 680-3635

Employment and Labor Lawcast
See: LAW

Equity News *Association*

Publishing Co: Actors' Equity Association, 165 W. 46th St., New York, NY 10036-2598; Title Tel # (212) 719-9570 Title Fax # (212) 921-8454
Personnel: Editor-Dick Moore
Editorial Description: Contains news regarding the professional theatre.
General Info: Yr. Est. 1913, 10x/yr., 4 pages, No Color
Subscriptions: Indv. $20, Free With Membership
Circulation: Total-35,000

Fednews

Publishing Co: National Association of Government Employees, 159 Burgin Parkway, Quincy, MA 02169-4213; Title Tel # (617) 268-5002
Personnel: Editor-Kenneth T. Lyons
Editorial Description: News concerning government employees.
General Info: Yr. Est. 1961, Monthly
Subscriptions: Indv. $7
Circulation: Total-77,000

Forewarned *Business, Association*

Publishing Co: Americans Against Union Control of Government, 527 MAple Avenue, East, 3rd Fl., Vienna, VA 22180-4713 Tel # (703) 242-3575 Fax # (703) 242-3579 Parent Co.-Public Service Research Council, Vienna; Title Tel # (703) 438-3966 Title Fax # (703) 438-3935
Personnel: Editor-David Denholm
Editorial Description: Concerned with reversing the trend toward compulsory public sector bargaining.
General Info: Yr. Est. 1973, Monthly, 4 pages, No Color, Newsprint
Subscriptions: Free With Membership
Circulation: Total-15,000
List Rental: List Management Co.: Advanced List Marketing, 12700 Fair Lakes Cir Ste 346, Fairfax, VA 22033-4905 Tel # (703) 803-9662, Fax # (703) 803-9669

GPPAW Horizons *Association*

Publishing Co: Glass, Pottery, Plastics, 608 E Baltimore Pike # 607, Media, PA 19063-1735; Title Tel # (215) 565-5051
Personnel: Editor-Richard Kline
Editorial Description: Indexing for the Christian Science Monitor, New York Times, Wall Street Journal, Washington Post & LA Times.
General Info: Yr. Est. 1982, Monthly

Government Union Critique *Business, Consumer*

Publishing Co: Public Service Research Council, 527 Maple Ave. East, 3rd Floor, Vienna, VA 22180-4713; Title Tel # (703) 242-3575 Title Fax # (703) 242-3579
Personnel: Publisher-David Denholm
Editorial Description: Fortnightly news report on politics, economics and public sector labor relations.
General Info: Yr. Est. 1980, Bi-weekly, Sheetfed press, 50 pages, ISSN: 0738-3312, Saddle-stitched
Subscriptions: Indv. $80, $3/copy
Circulation: Total-1,500

Guild Watch
See: NEWSPAPER INDUSTRY

Healthwire

Publishing Co: Federation of Nurses and Health Professionals, 555 New Jersey Ave., NW, Washington, DC 20001-2029; Title Tel # (202) 879-4491
Personnel: Editor, Production Mgr.-Priscilla Nemeth, Art Dir.-Charlie Glendinning
Editorial Description: To inform members of the Federation of Nurses & Health Professionals about activities of union & keep them up to date on professional union & health industry issues.
General Info: Yr. Est. 1978, Bi-monthly, Trim Size-8$\frac{1}{2}$ x 11, Sheetfed press, 8 pages, 2 Color, Matte
Subscriptions: Free
Acquisitions: Publication Bought
Circulation: Total-60,000
Printing Co: Delancey Printing, 444 Swann Ave, Alexandria, VA 22301-1085 Tel # (703) 836-4628, Fax # (703) 836-4628

Human Resources
Management Employee
Relations

Publishing Co: CCH, Inc., 2700 Lake Cook Rd., Riverwoods, IL 60015 Parent Co.-Kluwer Law & Taxation Publishers, Cambridge; Title Tel # (847) 267-7000 Title Fax # (800) 224-8299
Editorial Description: Covers collective bargaining; organizing campaigns; elections; negotiating, drafting & monitoring union contracts; union administration; rights of nonunion workers; strikes & picketing; & remedies.
General Info: (Formerly Employment Relations), Monthly, Looseleaf
Subscriptions: Indv. $417

I-Beam

Publishing Co: Natl. Erectors Assn., 1501 Lee Hwy Ste 202, Arlington, VA 22209-1109 Fax # (703) 524-3364; Title Tel # (703) 524-3336
Personnel: Editor-Melissa Delany
Editorial Description: General news for the Union Construction Industry.
General Info: Yr. Est. 1970, Quarterly, 4 pages, No Color

ILA Longshore News *Association*

Publishing Co: Intl. Longshoremen's Assn., 17 Battery Pl., Rm. 1530, New York, NY 10004-1261; Title Tel # (212) 425-1200
Personnel: Editor-James McNamara
General Info: Yr. Est. 1892, Irregular

IUD Action *Association*

Publishing Co: Industrial Union Dept., AFL-CIO, 815 16th St NW Ste 301, Washington, DC 20006-4104; Title Tel # (202) 842-7800
General Info: (Formerly Industrial Union Department Digest), Monthly, 6 pages, 2 Color, Newsprint
Circulation: (100% controlled), Total-10,000

IUPIWI - Views

Publishing Co: International Union of Petroleum & Industrial Workers, 8131 E. Rosecrans Ave., Paramount, CA 90723-2798; Title Tel # (213) 630-6232 Title Fax # (213) 408-1073
Personnel: Publisher-George Beltz, Editor-Robert Davidson
General Info: (Formerly Independent Oiler), Yr. Est. 1947, Bi-monthly, Trim Size-11$\frac{1}{2}$ x 17, Offset press, 8 pages, ISSN: 0199-5685
Subscriptions: Indv. $5
Acquisitions: Publication Bought
Circulation: Total-10,000

Ideas & Action
See: LABOR

Independent Union of Plant
Protection Employees
News

Publishing Co: Independent Union of Plant Protection Employees, PO Box 2163, Pittsfield, MA 01202-2163
General Info: Monthly

Individual Employment Rights
See: LAW

Inside Labor Relations *Business*

Publishing Co: Research Institute of America, 1340 Braddock Pl., Ste. 400, Alexandria, VA 22314-1651 Tel # (703) 706-8260 Fax # (703) 683-4824; Title Tel # (202) 842-0520 Title Fax # (212) 475-1740
Personnel: Publisher-Andrew Jacobson, Editor-Rhodes Henderer, Editor-Matthew Tallmer, Circ. Mgr.-Ellen Hartman, Production Mgr.-Amy Ryan, Mktg. Dir.-Conrqad Heibel
Editorial Description: Straight-from-the-source-reports on labor policy from NLRB, EEOC Labor Dept., congress and the courts. 'Inside' info on what's really going on.
General Info: Yr. Est. 1994, Bi-weekly, 16 pages, Ind/Abs/Online: Newsnet
Subscriptions: Indv. $496

Insiders Report *Consumer*

Publishing Co: Concerned Educators Against Forced Unionism, 8001 Braddock Rd., #500, Springfield, VA 22160-0001; Title Tel # (703) 321-8519
Personnel: Editor-Cathy Jones
Editorial Description: News covering compulsory unionism and the Right to Work issue.
General Info: (Formerly Recaps), Yr. Est. 1975, 3x/yr., Trim Size-8$\frac{1}{2}$ x 11, Letrpr. press, 4 pages, 2 Color, Matte
Subscriptions: Free
Circulation: Total-7,500

International Union of
Petroleum Workers
Views

Publishing Co: International Union of Petroleum & Industrial Workers, 8131 E. Rosecrans Ave., Paramount, CA 90723-2798; Title Tel # (805) 833-6285
General Info: Monthly

Label Letter *Association*

Publishing Co: Union Label & Services Trades, 815 16th St., N.W., Rm. 607, Washington, DC 20006; Title Tel # (202) 628-2131 Title Fax # (202) 638-1602
Personnel: Editor-Merilyn Toro
Editorial Description: Carries union news and information.
General Info: (Formerly Official News), Bi-monthly, Trim Size-8$\frac{1}{2}$ x 11, Offset press, 6 pages, 2 Color, Matte
Acquisitions: Publication Bought
Circulation: (100% controlled), Total-30,000
Printing Co: Kelly Press, Inc., 1701 Cabin Branch Rd, Cheverly, MD 20785-3820 Tel # (301) 386-2800

Labor Arbitration Awards *Business*

Publishing Co: CCH, Inc., 2700 Lake Cook Rd., Riverwoods, IL 60015 Parent Co.-Kluwer Law & Taxation Publishers, Cambridge; Title Tel # (847) 267-7000 Title Fax # (800) 224-8299
Editorial Description: Current awards settling labor relations disputes. Selected for practical application to everyday grievance situations.
General Info: Yr. Est. 1961, Weekly, Trim Size-6 x 9, Web press, 40 pages, No Color, Looseleaf
Subscriptions: Indv. $1,044

Labor Arbitration and
Disputes Settlements *Business*

Publishing Co: Bureau of National Affairs, Inc., 1231 25th St. NW, Bldg. N-200, Washington, DC 20037-1157; Title Tel # (202) 452-4200 Title Fax # (202) 822-8092
Personnel: Publisher-William A. Beltz, Editor-Nancy J. Sedmak, Circ. Mgr.-Gary C. Seltzer
Editorial Description: Contains the full-text of arbitration cases, & digests of court decisions involving arbitration.
General Info: (Formerly Labor Arbitration Reports), Yr. Est. 1937, Weekly, Trim Size-6 x 9, Web press, ISSN: 0148-7981, Ind/Abs/Online: DIALOG, HRIN, Lexis, Westlaw, Perfect bound, Looseleaf
Subscriptions: Indv. $936

Labor Arbitration in
Government *Association*

Publishing Co: American Arbitration Assn., 140 W. 51 St., New York, NY 10020-1203 Tel # (212) 484-4000; Title Tel # (212) 484-4011 Title Fax # (212) 541-4841
Personnel: Editor-Earl Baderschneider
Editorial Description: Summary of labor arbitration decisions on the Municipal, State and Federal level.
General Info: Yr. Est. 1971, Monthly, Trim Size-8$\frac{1}{2}$ x 11, 8 pages, ISSN: 0047-3839, 2 Color, Coated, Looseleaf
Subscriptions: Indv. $120
Circulation: Total-3,000
Printing Co: Sheridan Printing, 1425 3rd Ave, Alpha, NJ 08865-4695 Tel # (908) 454-0700, Fax # (908) 454-2554

Labor Case Comments *Association*

Publishing Co: Cast Metals Assn., 455 State St Ste 201, Des Plaines, IL 60016-2281; Title Tel # (708) 299-9160
General Info: Semi-monthly

Labor Contract Law Bulletin
See: LABOR

Labor Law *Business*

Publishing Co: Matthew Bender & Co., 11 Penn Plaza, New York, NY 10001-2006 Fax # (212) 244-3188; Title Tel # (212) 967-7707
Editorial Description: All aspects of labor management relations analyzed by a nationally known labor mediator.
General Info: Yr. Est. 1973, Quarterly, Looseleaf
Subscriptions: $650/copy

Labor Law Developments   *Business*

Publishing Co: Matthew Bender & Co., 11 Penn Plaza, New York, NY 10001-2006
Fax # (212) 244-3188; Title Tel # (212) 967-7707
Personnel: Editor-E. Carr
Editorial Description: Annual collection of papers presented at the SWLF Labor Law Institute, by outstanding practitioners, labor law professors & NLRB members.
General Info: Yr. Est. 1967, Annually, Looseleaf
Subscriptions: $100/copy

Labor News   *Business*

Publishing Co: N.Y.C. Central Labor Council AFL-CIO, 386 Park Ave., S., New York, NY 10016-8842; Title Tel # (212) 685-9552 Title Fax # (212) 685-9557
Personnel: Editor-Ted Jacobsen
Editorial Description: News of Council, local union affiliates, officers and members; reports of national AFL-CIO policies and actions; city and community affairs; labor library news; arts and leisure time notes.
General Info: (Formerly Labor Chronicle), Yr. Est. 1904, Monthly, Trim Size-8½ x 11, Offset press, 4 pages, 2 Color
Subscriptions: Indv. $2
Circulation: (100% controlled), Total-10,000

Labor News

Publishing Co: Labor News, PO Box 1184, Quincy, IL 62306-1184; Title Tel # (217) 223-0803
Personnel: Editor-Kathryn Spratt
Editorial Description: Endorsed by Quincy Trades & Labor Assembly.
General Info: Weekly
Advertising: Inquire for rates.

Labor Relations Reporter

Publishing Co: Bureau of National Affairs, Inc., 1231 25th St. NW, Bldg. N-200, Washington, DC 20037-1157; Title Tel # (202) 452-4200 Title Fax # (202) 822-8092
Personnel: Publisher-William A. Beltz, Mng. Editor-Nancy J. Sedmak, Circ. Mgr.-Gary C. Seltzer
Editorial Description: A multi-part notification & reference service covering labor-management relations, wages & hours, labor arbitration, fair employment practices, individual employment rights & more.
General Info: Yr. Est. 1937, Weekly, Trim Size-8½ x 11, Web press, ISSN: 0148-7981, Ind/Abs/Online: DIALOG, HRIN, LEXIS, WESTLAW
Subscriptions: Indv. $3,479

Labor Relations Week   *Business*

Publishing Co: Bureau of National Affairs, Inc., 1231 25th St. NW, Bldg. N-200, Washington, DC 20037-1157; Title Tel # (202) 452-4200 Title Fax # (202) 822-8092
Personnel: Publisher-William A. Beltz, Mng. Editor-Susan Sala, Circ. Mgr.-Gary C. Seltzer
Editorial Description: Provides a comprehensive overview of developments influencing labor relations in the private sector.
General Info: Yr. Est. 1987, Weekly, Trim Size-8½ x 11, Web press, 24 pages, ISSN: 0891-4141, Ind/Abs/Online: HRIN
Subscriptions: Indv. $853

Labor Studies Forum
See: LABOR

Labor Trends   *Business*

Publishing Co: Research Institute of America, 1340 Braddock Pl., Ste. 400, Alexandria, VA 22314-1651 Tel # (703) 706-8260 Fax # (703) 683-4824; Title Tel # (202) 842-0520 Title Fax # (212) 475-1790
Personnel: Publisher-John Roche, Editor-Rhodes Henderer, Editor-Matthew Tallmer, Circ. Mgr.-Loretta Netzer, Production Mgr.-Amy Ryan
Editorial Description: Labor-management relations, strikes and settlements, wage developments, unusual contract terms, administrative, judicial, and legislative moves involving labor relations since 1945.
General Info: Yr. Est. 1945, Weekly, Trim Size-8½ x 11, Offset press, 4 pages, ISSN: 0023-6659, 2 Color
Subscriptions: Indv. $254
List Rental: List Management Co.: Taybi Direct East, Inc., 13321 New Hampshire Ave., Ste. 202, Silver Spring, MD 20904-3450 Tel # (301) 680-3633, Fax # (301) 680-3635

Labor/Maintence Update
See: LABOR

L'Abordage   *Association*

Publishing Co: Syndicat du Personnel Non-Enseignant de l'Univ. du Quebec/Ri, 300 Allee des Ursulines, Rimouski, PQ J5L 3A1 Canada Tel # (418) 724-1582
Personnel: Editor-Ann Nelles
General Info: Yr. Est. 1974, 15x/yr., 8 pages
Circulation: Total-250

Lancaster Area Labor Market Letter

Publishing Co: Pennsylvania Bureau of Employment Security, Lancaster Job Center, 48-50 W. Chestnut St., Lancaster, PA 17603-3582; Title Tel # (717) 394-7291
Editorial Description: Employment, unemployment, wage, hour and labor turnover data for Lancaster County, Pa.
General Info: Monthly, Trim Size-8½ x 11, Mimeo press, 3 pages
Circulation: Total-1,200

Le V'La   *Association*

Publishing Co: Syndicat des Professeurs du College de Maisonneuve, 3800 est, rue Sherbrooke, Montreal, PQ J4B 3P8 Canada; Title Tel # (514) 254-3361
Editorial Description: Union publication for college professors.
General Info: Yr. Est. 1974, 10x/yr., Trim Size-8½ x 11, 25 pages, No Color
Subscriptions: Free
Circulation: (100% controlled), Total-500

Lifelines
See: HEALTH

Local 144 Courage   *Association*

Publishing Co: Local 144, Hotel, Hospital, Nursing Home & Allied Services U, 233 W 49th St, New York, NY 10019-7404; Title Tel # (212) 265-2366 Title Fax # (212) 265-2417
Personnel: Editor-Joe Walker
Editorial Description: Official organ. of union local.
General Info: (Formerly Local 144 News), Bi-monthly, Letrpr. press, 12 pages, 2 Color
Circulation: Total-35,000
Advertising: Accepts Inserts.

Los Angeles Citizen   *Association*

Publishing Co: Los Angeles County Fed. of Labor, AFL-CIO, 2130 W 9th St, Los Angeles, CA 90006-2202; Title Tel # (213) 381-5611
General Info: Weekly
Advertising: Inquire for rates.

M.E.A. Today
See: EDUCATION

M.O.N.A. Pulse
See: NURSING

Malcriado/Voice of the Farm Worker   *Association*

Publishing Co: United Farm Workers Organizing Committee, AFL-CIO, PO Box 62, Keene, CA 93531; Title Tel # (805) 822-5571
Editorial Description: Editions in English and Spanish.
General Info: Yr. Est. 1964, Irregular
Subscriptions: Indv. $4
Circulation: Total-18,000

Maritime Newsletter

Publishing Co: Maritime Trades Dept., 215 16th St. NW, Ste. 310, Washington, DC 20006; Title Tel # (202) 628-6300 Title Fax # (202) 347-1137
Personnel: Editor-Jean Intrao
General Info: (Formerly Maritime), Yr. Est. 1967, Monthly, Trim Size-8½ x 11, 5 pages, ISSN: 0161-9373, Color
Subscriptions: Indv. $3
Printing Co: Affiliated Graphics, 3342 Bladensburg Rd, Brentwood, MD 20722-1898 Tel # (301) 927-3800

Mine-Mill Union

Publishing Co: International Union of Mine, Mill, Five Gateway Ctr., Pittsburgh, PA 15222-1209; Title Tel # (412) 562-2666
Personnel: Editor-A. C. Skinner
Editorial Description: Primarily to inform membership of developments within union, the labor movement generally, the non-ferrous metals industry. Also covers legislative and political scene.
General Info: Yr. Est. 1942, Monthly
Subscriptions: Indv. $1
Circulation: Total-32,000

Musical News   *Association*

Publishing Co: Musicians Union Local 6, 230 Jones St, San Francisco, CA 94102-2691; Title Tel # (415) 775-8118
Personnel: Editor-Melinda Wagner
Editorial Description: Union business and information concerning AF of M members.
General Info: Yr. Est. 1915, Monthly, Offset press, 8 pages, Color
Circulation: (100% controlled), Total-4,800
Advertising: Inquire for rates.

NLRB Case Handling Manual   *Business*

Publishing Co: CCH, Inc., 2700 Lake Cook Rd., Riverwoods, IL 60015 Parent Co.-Kluwer Law & Taxation Publishers, Cambridge; Title Tel # (847) 267-7000 Title Fax # (800) 224-8299
Editorial Description: Reproduces guidelines developed by the NLRB General Counsel for Regional Office staff used in processing cases arising under the National Labor Relations Act.
General Info: Yr. Est. 1976, Irregular, Trim Size-6 x 9, Web press, No Color, Looseleaf
Subscriptions: Indv. $318

NTEU Bulletin   *Association*

Publishing Co: National Treasury Employees Union, 901 E. St., N.W. Ste.600, Washington, DC 20004 Tel # (202) 638-7760 Fax # (202) 783-4085; Title Tel # (202) 783-4444 Title Fax # (202) 785-4085
Personnel: Publisher, Editor, Adv. Dir.-Eve Berton
Editorial Description: Publication of 2nd largest independent union for federal workers.
General Info: Yr. Est. 1973, Monthly, Web press, 8 pages, ISSN: 0279-540X, 2 Color, Newsprint
Subscriptions: Indv. $1
Circulation: Total-80,000

National Association of Master Mechanics

Publishing Co: Natl. Assn. of Master Mechanics, 117 Beaumont Ave, Newtonville, MA 02160-2315
General Info: Monthly

National Right to Work Newsletter

Publishing Co: National Right to Work Committee, 8001 Braddock Rd. #500, Springfield, VA 22160-0001; Title Tel # (703) 321-9820 Title Fax # (703) 321-7143
Personnel: Publisher-Reed Larson, Editor-Stanley Greer
Editorial Description: About the Right to Work movement. Describing efforts on the state and federal level to outlaw compulsory union membership.
General Info: Yr. Est. 1955, Monthly, Trim Size-8½ x 11, Web press, 8 pages, 2 Color, Newsprint
Subscriptions: Indv. $15, Free With Membership
Circulation: (100% controlled), Total-150,000

New York Letter Carriers

Publishing Co: Natl. Assn. of Letter Carriers, NY Letter Carriers, Branch 36, 347 W. 41st St., New York, NY 10036; Title Tel # (212) 239-3901
Personnel: Editor-Lenny Goldman, Publisher, Production Mgr.-Arthur Ullman, Circ. Mgr., Adv. Dir.-Sid Klein
Editorial Description: Labor-news-management-letter carriers news items-by-laws, contracts.
General Info: Yr. Est. 1938, Monthly, Web press, ISSN: 0028-7342, Color-cover
Acquistions: Publication Bought
Circulation: Total-10,000
Advertising: Inquire for rates.
Printing Co: International Newspaper Printing Co., 1305 44th Ave, Long Island City, NY 11101-6919 Tel # (718) 729-5440

Newsletter for the National Center for Collective Bargaining
See: LABOR

Newsline   *Association*

Publishing Co: New Brunswick Public Employees Assn., P. O. Box 95, Fredericton, NB E3B 4Y2 Canada; Title Tel # (506) 458-8440
Personnel: Editor-Ross Ingram
General Info: (Formerly Public Employees Journal), Yr. Est. 1970, Semi-monthly, 4 pages
Circulation: Total-5,000

Number 6 Bulletin   *Association*

Publishing Co: New York Typographical Union No. 6, 817 Broadway, New York, NY 10003-4709; Title Tel # (212) 533-2000 Title Fax # (212) 475-0536
Personnel: Publisher-James Grottola, Editor-Gunnar Janger
Editorial Description: Union membership publication coveriong subjects of interest to workers in the typesetting industry.
General Info: Yr. Est. 1898, Trim Size-8½ x 11, Offset press, 12 pages, ISSN: 0049-4968, 2 Color
Subscriptions: Free
Circulation: Total-6,000

OHEU News

Publishing Co: Ontario Hydro Employees Union, 244 Eglinton Avenue East, Toronto, ON M4P 1K9 Canada; Title Tel # (416) 481-4491
Personnel: Editor-Jim Donaldson
Editorial Description: News for members of local chapters.
General Info: Monthly, Offset press, 4 pages, Color
Circulation: Total-14,000

Ohio AFL-CIO News and Views   *Association*

Publishing Co: Ohio AFL-CIO, 271 E State St, Columbus, OH 43215-4370
General Info: Yr. Est. 1958, Bi-weekly, Trim Size-8½ x 11, Offset press, 4 pages, 2 Color

Organization of Professional Employees of the U.S. Dept. of Agriculture Newsletter   *Business*

Publishing Co: Organization of Professional Employees of the U.S. Dept. of, Usda South Bldg. , Rm. 1414, Washington, DC 20250-0001; Title Tel # (202) 447-4898
Personnel: Editor-Otis Thompson
General Info: Monthly
Circulation: (100% controlled)

PED Forum   *Business, Consumer*

Publishing Co: AFL-CIO Public Employee Dept., 816 16th St. NW, PED Ste. 308, Washington, DC 20006-4102; Title Tel # (202) 393-2820 Title Fax # (202) 347-1825
General Info: (Formerly In Public Service), Quarterly
Subscriptions: Indv. $2
Circulation: Total-3,500

PSAC Union Update
See: LABOR

Payroll Practitioner's Compliance Handbook
See: MANAGEMENT

Pennsylvania AFL-CIO News   *Association*

Publishing Co: Pennsylvania AFL-CIO, 230 State St, Harrisburg, PA 17101-1138 Fax # (717) 238-8541; Title Tel # (717) 238-9351
Personnel: Editor-Jim Deegan
Editorial Description: News of interest to organized labor and its affiliates.
General Info: Yr. Est. 1960, Monthly
Subscriptions: Indv. $3
Circulation: Total-10,000

Pennsylvania Nurse
See: NURSING

Personnel Practice Ideas
See: MANAGEMENT

Plan Administrators Compliance Manual   *Business*

Publishing Co: Research Institute of America, 90 5th Avenue, New York, NY 10011-7629 Tel # (212) 645-4800; Title Tel # (800) 562-0245 Title Fax # (201) 816-3484
Editorial Description: Enables users to comply with government requirements regarding employee benefit plans by advising what reports or forms are required when they are due, how to complete these, and where they need to be filed.
General Info: Semi-monthly, Trim Size-8½ x 11, Offset press, Looseleaf
Subscriptions: Indv. $469
List Rental: List Management Co.: WG & L List Management, 1 Penn Plz Fl 42, New York, NY 10119-0002 Tel # (212) 971-5000

Principles of Payroll Administration
See: MANAGEMENT

Professional, The

Publishing Co: Professional Employees Assn., #201, 1001 Wharf St., Victoria, BC V8W 1T6 Canada; Title Tel # (604) 385-8791 Title Fax # (604) 385-6629
Personnel: Editor-Alan MacLeod
General Info: Yr. Est. 1974, Monthly, Trim Size-8½ x 11, 6 pages
Subscriptions: Free With Membership
Circulation: Total-1,900

Public Sector Arbitration Awards

Publishing Co: Industrial Relations Service Bureau, 2909 Wayz Blvd., Minneapolis, MN 55405-2182; Title Tel # (612) 374-9100
General Info: Monthly

Record

Publishing Co: Local 1-2, Utility Workers Union of America, AFL-CIO, 386 Park Avenue South, New York, NY 10016-8846; Title Tel # (212) 532-7110
Personnel: Editor-Richard Rohman
Editorial Description: Official labor publication.
General Info: Yr. Est. 1938, Bi-monthly, Trim Size-11½ x 16, Letrpr. press, 12 pages
Circulation: Total-25,000

Retiree Newsletter

Publishing Co: International Brotherhood of Teamsters, Chauffers, Warehouse, 25 Louisiana Ave NW, Washington, DC 20001-2130
Editorial Description: For retired members of the AFL-CIO.
General Info: Monthly

SPEEA Spotlite   *Association*

Publishing Co: Seattle Professional Engineering Employees Association, 15205 52nd Ave S, Seattle, WA 98188-2336; Title Tel # (206) 433-0991 Title Fax # (206) 248-3990
Personnel: Editor, Adv. Dir., Art Dir.-Robbi Alberts
Editorial Description: Articles written by staff and members of labor union for Boeing engineers & technical workers.
General Info: Monthly, Trim Size-8½ x 11, Sheetfed press, 2 Color
Subscriptions: Indv. $2, Free With Membership
Circulation: (100% controlled), Total-18,000

Spotlight   *Association*

Publishing Co: Local 285, Rubber Workers, 202 W Liberty St, Lancaster, PA 17603-2714; Title Tel # (717) 394-7544
Personnel: Editor-John Yost
Editorial Description: Anything within the labor movement social activity.
General Info: Yr. Est. 1952, Quarterly, Trim Size-8 x 11½, 6 pages
Circulation: Total-2,500

Stereotypers

Publishing Co: Stereotypers, 90 E 214th St, Cleveland, OH 44123-1073
Personnel: Editor-James J. Kelley
General Info: Monthly
Circulation: Total-14,150
Advertising: Inquire for rates.

Stewards News

Publishing Co: Marine, 350 Fremont St, San Francisco, CA 94105-2316; Title Tel # (415) 543-5885
Personnel: Editor-Don L. Rotan
General Info: Bi-weekly
Circulation: Total-10,000

Stove Furnace

Publishing Co: Stove Furnace, 2929 S Jefferson Ave, Saint Louis, MO 63118-1510
  Tel # (314) 664-3736
General Info: Yr. Est. 1902, Quarterly
Circulation: Total-9,000

Summary of Labor Arbitration Awards   *Business, Consumer*

Publishing Co: LRP Publications, 747 Dresher Rd., P.O. Box 980, Horsham, PA 19044-0980
  Tel # (215) 784-0910 Fax # (215) 784-0317
Personnel: Publisher-Kenneth F. Kahn, Production Mgr.-Kathleen P. Neely, Mktg. Dir.-Jana Shellington, Promotion Dir.-Gary Ragin
Editorial Description: Provides a digest of private-sector labor arbitration decisions, covering the latest topics in collective bargaining with non-government employers.
General Info: Monthly
Subscriptions: Indv. $120

Telling It Like It Is   *Association*

Publishing Co: Transportation Communications International Union, 3 Research Pl., Rockville, MD 20850-3213; Title Tel # (301) 948-4910 Title Fax # (301) 330-7661
Personnel: Publisher, Editor-R.A. Scardelletti, Production Mgr.-Diane Curry
Editorial Description: Explores collective bargaining, legislative goals, transportation industry trends, issues affecting workers as taxpayers & consumers.
General Info: (Formerly Leadership Action Lines), Yr. Est. 1991, Bi-monthly, Trim Size-8½ x 11, Sheetfed press, 6 pages, 2 Color, Matte
Circulation: (100% controlled), Total-2,400
Printing Co: Kelly Press, Inc., 1701 Cabin Branch Rd, Cheverly, MD 20785-3820
  Tel # (301) 386-2800

Trade Union Advisor   *Business*

Publishing Co: Labor Research Assn., 145 W 28th St Fl 6, New York, NY 10001-6191;
  Title Tel # (212) 714-1677 Title Fax # (212) 714-1674
Personnel: Editor-Greg Tarpinian, Production Mgr.-Chris Nowlar
Editorial Description: Strategy for labor unions.
General Info: Yr. Est. 1987, Bi-weekly, Trim Size-8½ x 11, Desktop press, ISSN: 0895-5220, 2 Color
Subscriptions: Indv. $225, Inst. $225, $10/copy

Trade Union News

Publishing Co: Trade Union News, 20 Branford Pl, Newark, NJ 07102-2725;
  Title Tel # (202) 623-3053
General Info: Yr. Est. 1961, Monthly
Subscriptions: Indv. $2
Advertising: Inquire for rates.

Tribuna
    See: WOMEN'S

UAW Washington Report

Publishing Co: United Automobile Workers, 1757 N St NW, Washington, DC 20036-2884;
  Title Tel # (202) 828-8500
Personnel: Editor-Don Stillman
Editorial Description: Domestic & international problems of working men & women, with particular focus on trade union issues. Covers legislative & governmental actions affecting workers.
General Info: Weekly, Trim Size-8½ x 11, Web press, 4 pages, Color
Circulation: Total-60,000

U.I.U. Journal   *Association*

Publishing Co: Upholsterers' Intl. Union, PO Box 660, Feasterville, PA 19053-0660;
  Title Tel # (215) 923-5700
Personnel: Editor-Martin Garber
General Info: Yr. Est. 1922, Quarterly, Letrpr. press, 8 pages, ISSN: 0041-5162, 2 Color
Circulation: Total-44,000

USA Record

Publishing Co: Uniformed Sanitationmen's Assn., 23 Cliff St # 25, New York, NY 10038-2820;
  Title Tel # (212) 964-8900
Personnel: Editor-Edward T. Ostrowski
General Info: Yr. Est. 1973, Monthly

Unfair Labor Practices Law Bulletin
    See: LABOR

Union Labor Report   *Business, Association*

Publishing Co: Bureau of National Affairs, Inc., 1231 25th St. NW, Bldg. N-200, Washington, DC 20037-1157 Fax # (202) 822-8092; Title Tel # (202) 452-4200 Title Fax # (202) 452-4603
Personnel: Publisher-William A. Beltz, Mng. Editor-Bill L. Manville, Circ. Mgr.-Gary C. Seltzer
Editorial Description: A notification & reference service that provides practical guidance on day-to-day labor relations questions & current reports on employee relations & union developments.
General Info: Yr. Est. 1947, Bi-weekly, Trim Size-8½ x 11, Offset press, 8 pages, ISSN: 0091-5459, Ind/Abs/Online: HRIN
Subscriptions: Indv. $701

Union Labor Report Weekly Newsletter   *Business, Association*

Publishing Co: Bureau of National Affairs, Inc., 1231 25th St. NW, Bldg. N-200, Washington, DC 20037-1157; Title Tel # (202) 452-4200 Title Fax # (202) 822-8092
Personnel: Publisher-William L. Beltz, Editor-Bill L. Manville, Circ. Mgr.-Gary C. Seltzer
Editorial Description: Provides a roundup of developments of concern to organized labor. Includes summaries of arbitration awards & court cases. Recurring features include section title Special Report, Labor Facts, & Grievance Guide.
General Info: Yr. Est. 1947, Weekly, Trim Size-8½ x 11, Offset press, 8 pages, ISSN: 0190-5260, Ind/Abs/Online: HRIN
Subscriptions: Indv. $149

Union Labor Report's On the Line   *Association*

Publishing Co: Bureau of National Affairs, Inc., 1231 25th St. NW, Bldg. N-200, Washington, DC 20037-1157; Title Tel # (202) 452-4200 Title Fax # (202) 822-8092
Personnel: Publisher-William A. Beltz, Mng. Editor-Bill L. Manville, Circ. Mgr.-Gary C. Seltzer
Editorial Description: Reports on shopfloor issues affecting union stewards. Includes summaries of arbitration awards and court cases.
General Info: Yr. Est. 1978, Quarterly, Trim Size-8½ x 11, Offset press, 4 pages, ISSN: 0731-0307
Subscriptions: Indv. $2, $2/copy

Union Matters   *Association*

Publishing Co: Saskatchewan Government Employees Union, 1440 Broadway Ave., Regina, SK S4P 1E2 Canada; Title Tel # (306) 522-8571
Personnel: Editor-S. Sorensen
Editorial Description: News bulletin on trade union issues and related stories.
General Info: (Formerly News News News), Yr. Est. 1974, Quarterly, Trim Size-8½ x 11, Offset press, 2 pages, ISSN: 0316-8433, 2 Color
Circulation: Total-17,500

United Teacher   *Association*

Publishing Co: United Federation of Teachers, 260 Park Ave S, New York, NY 10010-7272;
  Title Tel # (212) 777-7500
Personnel: Editor-Ted Bleeker
General Info: Monthly
Circulation: Total-40,000

Unity   *Association*

Publishing Co: New York State AFL-CIO, 100 S Swan St, Albany, NY 12210-1939;
  Title Tel # (518) 436-8516
Personnel: Publisher-Paul Cole, Editor-Michael Griffin
Editorial Description: Emphasis on labor news in N.Y. as well as state legislation that affects labor.
General Info: (Formerly Federation), Monthly, Trim Size-8½ x 11, Offset press, 8 pages, 2 Color, Coated
Circulation: Total-4,000

Update, The   *Business, Association*

Publishing Co: Graphic Artists Guild, 11 W. 20th St., Apt. 8, New York, NY 10011-3704
  Tel # (212) 463-7730; Title Tel # (212) 463-7759
Personnel: Editor-Erica Meinhardt, Circ. Mgr., Adv. Dir.-Jeanne Gibbons, Publisher, Art Dir.-Rick Barry
Editorial Description: Featuring articles, legislative updates, guild news & listing of NYC arts events for illustrators, graphic designers, cartoonists, surface designers, computer artists & staff artists.
General Info: Yr. Est. 1970, Bi-monthly, Web press, 12 pages, 2% ads, No Color, Newsprint
Subscriptions: Indv. $15
Acquistions: Publication Bought
Circulation: Total-2,500
Advertising: Accepts Inserts.
List Rental: Actives: $100/M
Printing Co: Dispatch Graphics, 307 W. 36th St., New York, NY 10018 Tel # (212) 760-0099

Uqaqta
    See: EDUCATION

Voice of Local 1   *Association*

Publishing Co: United Food, 106 Memorial Pky, Utica, NY 13501-4818; Title Tel # (315) 797-9600
Personnel: Publisher-Joseph Talarico, Editor-Jay Bloom
Editorial Description: Covers new trends within the industry, legislation, shop news, scheduling of meetings and elections etc., and financial reports.
General Info: Yr. Est. 1957, Bi-monthly, Web press, 24 pages
Circulation: (100% controlled), Total-30,000
Printing Co: Dodge Graphics Press, 1501 Broad St, Utica, NY 13501-1098 Tel # (315) 735-9266

Voice of Local 399

Publishing Co: Hospital & Service Employees Union, 1247 W 7th St, Los Angeles, CA 90017-2309;
  Title Tel # (213) 680-9567
Personnel: Publisher-James Zellers, Editor-Tom Ramsay, Circ. Mgr.-Lillian Wierzel
Editorial Description: Labor journal.
General Info: Yr. Est. 1976, Monthly, Web press, 4 pages, 2 Color
Circulation: Total-22,000
Printing Co: Rodgers & McDonald Graphics, 1141 Sandhill Ave # 6270, Carson, CA 90746-1314
  Tel # (310) 604-1012

Western Michigan AFL-CIO News

Publishing Co: Muskegon Labor Council, 490 W Western Ave, Muskegon, MI 49440-1041
Personnel: Editor-Walter Tyler
General Info: Weekly
Circulation: Total-12,000
Advertising: Inquire for rates.

Wireport   *Business*

Publishing Co: Wire Service Guild, Local 222, 133 W 44th St, New York, NY 10036-4012; Title Tel # (212) 869-9290
Personnel: Editor-Tad Goodwin
General Info: Yr. Est. 1970, Monthly

Workers Compensation Guide
See: INDUSTRIAL RELATIONS/PERSONNEL

Writers Guild of America East Newsletter   *Association*

Publishing Co: Writers Guild of America East, 555 W 57th St, New York, NY 10019-2967 Fax # (212) 382-1909; Title Tel # (212) 761-1800
Personnel: Editor-Martin Waldman
Editorial Description: Information for members; professional writers in motion pictures, television & radio.
General Info: Yr. Est. 1972, Monthly, Trim Size-8½ x 11, Offset press, 8 pages, 2 Color, Coated
Subscriptions: Indv. $22
Circulation: Total-4,000
Advertising: Inquire for rates.

LAUNDRY, CLEANING & DYEING

Cleanroom Technology Newsletter
See: MANUFACTURING

Management Guidelines   *Association*

Publishing Co: Coin Laundry Association, 1315 Butterfield Rd Ste 212, Downers Grove, IL 60515-5602; Title Tel # (708) 963-5547 Title Fax # (708) 963-5864
Personnel: Editor-Brian Wallace, Mng. Editor-Dawn DeSart
Editorial Description: Technical items of general interest to the coin operated laundry and dry cleaning industry, ie. management techniques, statistical surveys, advertising & P.R. advice, maintenance tips, etc.
General Info: Yr. Est. 1960, Monthly, Trim Size-8½ x 11, Offset press, 4 pages, 2 Color
Subscriptions: Free

Maytag Commercial Merchandiser   *Business*

Publishing Co: Maytag Co., 1 Dependability Sq, Newton, IA 50208-9239; Title Tel # (515) 791-8518
Personnel: Sr. Ed.-Mike Klosterman
Editorial Description: Self-service laundry industry news; company products.
General Info: 3x/yr., Trim Size-8½ x 11, 8 pages, 4 Color, Coated, Saddle-stitched
Subscriptions: Free To Qualified Recipient
Circulation: Total-20,000

LAW

11th Circuit Law Letter   *Business*

Publishing Co: Barclays Law Publishers, 400 Oyster Point Blvd., S. San Francisco, CA 94080 Tel # (415) 244-6677; Title Tel # (615) 242-7395 Title Fax # (615) 256-6601
Personnel: Publisher-M. Lee Smith, Editor-Elizabeth Lane
Editorial Description: Summarizes all opinions of the 11th Circuit Court of Appeals.
General Info: Bi-weekly, ISSN: 0892-7308
Subscriptions: Indv. $157

401(k) Handbook
See: INVESTMENT

A-G Report   *Association*

Publishing Co: National Association of Attorneys General, 444 N Capitol St NW Ste 339, Washington, DC 20001-1512 Tel # (202) 434-8034; Title Tel # (202) 628-0435
Personnel: Editor-Eric Ziegler
Editorial Description: Activities of state attorney generals, new appointments, unusual litigation.
General Info: Monthly, Mimeo press, 4 pages, No Color
Subscriptions: Indv. $55

AALJ Newsletter   *Association*

Publishing Co: Assn. of Administrative Law Judges, 117 Gemini Cir # 407, Birmingham, AL 35209-5840; Title Tel # (414) 297-1941
Personnel: Editor-Judge Bernowski
General Info: Yr. Est. 1960, Bi-monthly

AAMA Washington Newsletter   *Association*

Publishing Co: American Apparel Manufacturers Assn., 2500 Wilson Blvd Ste 301, Arlington, VA 22201-3834; Title Tel # (703) 524-1864 Title Fax # (703) 522-6741
Personnel: Editor-Joan McNeal
Editorial Description: Look at legislative/regulatory news that affects the apparel industry.
General Info: Yr. Est. 1979, Bi-weekly, Trim Size-8½ x 11, Desktop press, 4 pages, No Color, Newsprint
Circulation: Total-3,500

AAMVA Bulletin
See: AUTOMOTIVE

AASCO Newsletter
See: AGRICULTURE

ABA Trust Letter
See: BANKING & FINANCE

ABA Washington Letter   *Association*

Publishing Co: Sponsor-Public Education Division, American Bar Association, 740 15th St. NW, Washington, DC 20005-1009 Tel # (202) 662-1016 Fax # (202) 662-1032; Title Tel # (202) 662-1017 Title Fax # (202) 331-2220
Personnel: Editor-Rhonda McMillion, Production Ed.-Michael Zarrelli
Editorial Description: 8-12 page legislative analyis covering congressional action.
General Info: Yr. Est. 1975, Monthly, Trim Size-8½ x 10¾, Offset press, 12 pages, 2 Color, Newsprint, Saddle-stitched
Subscriptions: Indv. $30
Circulation: Total-5,000
Printing Co: McArdle Printing Co., 800 Commerce Dr, Upper Marlboro, MD 20772-8792 Tel # (301) 390-8500

ABA Washington Summary
See: U.S. (& CANADIAN) FED. GOV'T.

ABA/BNA Lawyer's Manual on Professional Conduct   *Business*

Publishing Co: Bureau of National Affairs, Inc., 1231 25th St. NW, Bldg. N-200, Washington, DC 20037-1157; Title Tel # (202) 452-4200 Title Fax # (202) 822-8092
Personnel: Publisher-William A. Beltz, Mng. Editor-Robert Robbins, Circ. Mgr.-Gary C. Seltzer
Editorial Description: A notification & reference service covering a broad range of issues dealing with legal ethics & professional responsibility.
General Info: Yr. Est. 1984, Bi-weekly, Trim Size-6 x 9, Web press, 24 pages, ISSN: 0740-4050, Looseleaf
Subscriptions: Indv. $692

ACLU News
See: CIVIL RIGHTS

ADA Compliance Guide   *Business*

Publishing Co: Thompson Publishing Group, 1725 K Street, NW, Washington, DC 20006 Tel # (202) 872-4000
Personnel: Editor-Barbara Anderson
Editorial Description: Comprehensive 'how-to' manual with step-by-step instruction for compliance with the American with disabilities Act. Subscription includes the ADA Monthly Bulletin.
General Info: Annually, Looseleaf
Subscriptions: Indv. $259

ADA Update
See: DISABILITY

A.E. Legal Newsletter   *Business*

Publishing Co: Victor O. Schinnerer, 2 Wisconsin Cir., Chevy Chase, MD 20815-7022; Title Tel # (301) 961-9800
Editorial Description: Attorneys dealing with claims against members of the design profession.
General Info: 10x/yr., Trim Size-8½ x 11, Sheetfed press, 4 pages, 2 Color, Matte
Subscriptions: Indv. $200
Circulation: Total-500
Printing Co: Linemark Printing, Inc., 1220 Caraway Ct., Landover, MD 20785 Tel # (301) 925-9000

AIDS Benchbook

Publishing Co: Natl. Judicial College, Univ. Of Nevada, Reno, NV 89557-0001; Title Tel # (702) 784-6747 Title Fax # (702) 784-4234
Editorial Description: Quick source for trial judges on hearings involving AIDS issues.
General Info: Yr. Est. 1991, Irregular, Looseleaf
Subscriptions: $12/copy

AIDS Literature & Law Review

Publishing Co: University Publishing Group, Inc., 12 South Market St., Suite 300, Frederick, MD 21701-5441 Tel # (301) 694-8561; Title Tel # (301) 694-8531
Personnel: Publisher-N. Quist
Editorial Description: Features abstracts on all aspects of AIDS. Reviews more than 500 professional, medical & legal publications each month. Complete abstracts & citations provided. Covers medicine, public policy, law, education, psychology & social sciences.
General Info: (Formerly AIDS Literature & News Review), Yr. Est. 1986, Monthly, Trim Size-8½ x 11, ISSN: 0893-1526
Subscriptions: Inst. $225, For. $250

AIDS Litigation Reporter *Business*

Publishing Co: Andrews Publications, Inc., 1646 West Chester Pike, PO Box 1000, Westtown, PA 19395; Title Tel # (610) 399-6600 Title Tel # (610) 399-6610
Personnel: Publisher-John E. Backe, Editor-Ronald Baker, Mktg. Dir.-Andrew Katz
Editorial Description: Contains concise summaries of the latest opinions and filings issued in AIDS-related cases involving health care, employment, civil rights, criminal issues, and many other topic areas.
General Info: Yr. Est. 1987, Bi-monthly, Trim Size-8½ x 11, Mimeo press, 80 pages, ISSN: 0899-1464, Ind/Abs/Online: News Net, No Color, Newsprint
Subscriptions: Indv. $725, $35/copy
Advertising: Inquire for rates.
List Rental: Actives: 66,686, $105/M

AIDS Policy & Law *Business*

Publishing Co: LRP Publications, 747 Dresher Rd., P.O. Box 980, Horsham, PA 19044-0980 Tel # (215) 784-0910 Fax # (215) 784-0317
Personnel: Publisher-Ken Kahn, Editor-Frank Baram, Production Mgr.-Kathy Neely, Mktg. Dir.-Jana Shellington
Editorial Description: Covers the practical & legal issues of AIDS--the latest developments on the federal, state & local levels, fair employment practices, litigation, legislation, regulation, policy guidelines, case studies, interviews, & more.
General Info: Yr. Est. 1986, Bi-weekly, Trim Size-8½ x 11, Sheetfed press, 8 pages, ISSN: 0887-1493, 2 Color, Matte
Subscriptions: Indv. $487, For. $509

AIPLA Bulletin

Publishing Co: American Intellectual Property Law Assn., 2001 Jefferson Davis Hwy Ste, 203, Arlington, VA 22202-3603; Title Tel # (703) 415-0780
Personnel: Editor-Michael Blommer
General Info: Bi-monthly

AJA Benchmark *Association*

Publishing Co: American Judges Assn., 300 Newport Ave., PO Box 8798, Williamsburg, VA 23185-8798 Tel # (803) 259-1841; Title Tel # (804) 253-2000
Personnel: Editor-Joseph Burtell, Circ. Mgr.-Shelley Rockwell, Production Mgr.-Bill Fishback, Art Dir.-Stevalynn Adams
Editorial Description: Association news, news briefs on issues of interest to judges.
General Info: (Formerly Benchers' Briefs: Benchmark), Yr. Est. 1959, Quarterly, Trim Size-8½ x 11, Sheetfed press, 6 pages, 2 Color, Newsprint
Subscriptions: Indv. $25
Circulation: Total-2,800
Advertising: Inquire for rates.
Printing Co: Sir Speedy, 240 McClaws Cir., Williamsburg, VA 23185 Tel # (804) 220-1191

ALI Reporter, The *Association*

Publishing Co: American Law Institute, 4025 Chestnut St., Philadelphia, PA 19104-3099 Tel # (215) 243-1600; Title Tel # (215) 243-1626 Title Fax # (215) 243-1664
Personnel: Editor-Michael Greenwald, Circ. Mgr.-Joseph Mendecino, Art Dir.-Peter McGrenaghan
Editorial Description: Newsletter containing information about American Law Institute projects & members.
General Info: Yr. Est. 1978, Quarterly, Trim Size-8½ x 11, Sheetfed press, 8 pages, ISSN: 0164-5757, 2 Color, Newsprint, Saddle-stitched
Subscriptions: Free With Membership
Circulation: (97% controlled), Total-3,600
List Rental: Actives: $60/M
Printing Co: Kennedy Printing, 5534 Baltimore Ave, Philadelphia, PA 19143-3195 Tel # (215) 474-5150

ALMA Searchlight
See: CIVIL RIGHTS

ATLA Advocate *Association*

Publishing Co: Association of Trial Lawyers of America, 1050 31st St., NW, Washington, DC 20007-4409 Fax # (202) 625-7084; Title Tel # (202) 965-3500 Title Fax # (202) 965-0030
Personnel: Editor-Donald Dilworth
Editorial Description: Keeps association members abreast of association news, politics.
General Info: 9x/yr., Trim Size-8½ x 11, Sheetfed press, 16 pages, ISSN: 0746-4177, 2 Color, Matte, Saddle-stitched
Subscriptions: Free With Membership
Circulation: Total-62,000
List Rental: Rents Lists

Accommodating Disability Decisions

Publishing Co: CCH, Inc., 2700 Lake Cook Rd., Riverwoods, IL 60015 Parent Co.-Kluwer Law & Taxation Publishers, Cambridge; Title Tel # (847) 267-7000 Title Fax # (800) 224-8299
General Info: Bi-monthly, Looseleaf
Subscriptions: Indv. $351

Accountancy Law Reports
See: ACCOUNTING

Accountants SEC Practice Manual
See: ACCOUNTING

Accounting for Law Firms
See: ACCOUNTING

Accounting Systems for Law Offices *Business*

Publishing Co: Matthew Bender & Co., 11 Penn Plaza, New York, NY 10001-2006 Fax # (212) 244-3188; Title Tel # (212) 967-7707
Editorial Description: Detailed guide to a practical law office accounting system.
General Info: Yr. Est. 1978, Every two years, Looseleaf
Subscriptions: $100/copy

Action Kit for Hospital Law
See: HOSPITALS & NURSING HOMES

Action Kit for Hospital Trustees
See: HOSPITALS & NURSING HOMES

Addendum

Publishing Co: Indiana State Bar Assn., 230 E. Ohio St., Indianapolis, IN 46204-2199; Title Tel # (317) 639-5465 Title Fax # (317) 266-2588
Personnel: Editor-Susan Ferrer
General Info: Yr. Est. 1985, Bi-monthly, Trim Size-8½ x 11, Sheetfed press, 7 pages, 1% ads
Subscriptions: Indv. $1
Circulation: Total-10,000
Printing Co: Graphics Ltd., Inc., 401 N College Ave, Indianapolis, IN 46202-3605 Tel # (317) 263-3456

Administration Law *Business*

Publishing Co: Matthew Bender & Co., 11 Penn Plaza, New York, NY 10001-2006 Fax # (212) 244-3188; Title Tel # (212) 967-7707
Personnel: Editor-Basil Mezines
Editorial Description: Treats all aspects of procedure, including judicial review.
General Info: Yr. Est. 1977, Every two years, Looseleaf
Subscriptions: $410/copy

Administrative Law News *Association*

Publishing Co: American Bar Association, 750 N. Lake Shore Dr., Chicago, IL 60611-4497 Tel # (312) 988-6115 Fax # (312) 988-6030; Title Tel # (312) 988-5522 Title Fax # (312) 988-5528
Personnel: Editor-David Pritzker
Editorial Description: Reports on developments in the area of administrative law and regulation.
General Info: Yr. Est. 1974, Quarterly, Trim Size-8½ x 11, Sheetfed press, ISSN: 0567-9494
List Rental: Rents Lists

Adoption Law and Practice *Business*

Publishing Co: Matthew Bender & Co., 11 Penn Plaza, New York, NY 10001-2006 Tel # (212) 967-7707 Fax # (212) 244-3188
Personnel: Editor in Chief-Joan H. Hollinger
Editorial Description: Covers all the legal and practical aspects of adoption.
General Info: Yr. Est. 1988, Irregular, Looseleaf

Advanced Underwriting Service
See: INSURANCE

Advertising Compliance Service *Business*

Publishing Co: JLCom Publishing Co., 571 Passaic Ave., Nutley, NJ 07110-1236; Title Tel # (201) 661-3469 Title Fax # (201) 661-3469
Personnel: Publisher, Editor in Chief-John Lichtenberger
Editorial Description: Covers all aspects of advertising rules, regulations, etc. for attorneys responsible for reviewing marketing and advertising for national companies.
General Info: Yr. Est. 1978, Bi-weekly, Trim Size-8½ x 11, 18 pages
Subscriptions: Indv. $495, For. $595, $35/copy
Acquistions: Publication Bought

Affiliate *Association*

Publishing Co: Young Lawyers Division-American Bar Association, 750 N. Lake Shore Dr., Chicago, IL 60611-4403; Title Tel # (312) 988-6068
Personnel: Publisher-J. Podell, Editor-Janae Novotny, Circ. Mgr.-Mario Guizar, Adv. Dir.-Nora Whitford, Art Dir.-Robert Wooley
Editorial Description: News of the ABA/YLD affiliate outreach project.
General Info: Yr. Est. 1975, Bi-monthly, Trim Size-8½ x 11, Sheetfed press, 8 pages, ISSN: 0360-5485, 2 Color, Saddle-stitched
Circulation: (100% controlled), Total-3,600

Affirmative Action Compliance Manual for Federal Contractors
See: CIVIL RIGHTS

Affirmative Action/EEO Update
See: CIVIL RIGHTS

Agency Law Quarterly Real Estate Intelligence Report
See: REAL ESTATE

Agricultural Law Update   *Business, Association*

Publishing Co: Sponsor-American Agricultural Law Assn., American Agricultural Law Association, Univ. of Arkansas, Leflar Law Center, Fayetteville, AR 72701 Tel # (501) 575-7389 Fax # (501) 575-5830
Personnel: Editor-Linda McCormick
General Info: Yr. Est. 1983, Monthly, 8 pages
Subscriptions: Indv. $58
Circulation: Total-800, Readership-800

Alabama Employment Law Letter   *Business*

Publishing Co: M. Lee Smith Publishers & Printers ,LCC, P.O. Box 198867, 162 Fourth Avenue North, Nashville, TN 37219-8867; Title Tel # (615) 242-7395 Title Fax # (615) 256-6601
Personnel: Publisher-M. Lee Smith, Editor-David Middlebrooks, Circ. Mgr.-Cathy Bradford, Mktg. Dir.-Dave Yates
Editorial Description: Review of employment law developments that effect Alabama employers.
General Info: Yr. Est. 1990, Monthly, Trim Size-8½ x 11, 8 pages, ISSN: 1049-9369, 2 Color
Subscriptions: Indv. $97
List Rental: Rents Lists

Alabama Environmental Compliance Update   *Business*

Publishing Co: M. Lee Smith Publishers & Printers ,LCC, P.O. Box 198867, 162 Fourth Avenue North, Nashville, TN 37219-8867; Title Tel # (615) 242-7395 Title Fax # (615) 256-6601
Personnel: Publisher-M. Lee Smith, Editor-Fournier Gale, Circ. Mgr.-Cathy Bradford, Mktg. Dir.-Dave Yates
Editorial Description: Review of environmental law developments that affect Alabama companies.
General Info: Yr. Est. 1993, Monthly, Trim Size-8½ x 11, 8 pages, ISSN: 1066-1131, 2 Color
Subscriptions: Indv. $117
List Rental: Rents Lists
Printing Co: M. Lee Smith Publishers & Printers ,LLC, PO Box 198867, 162 Fourth Avenue, Nashville, TN 37219-8867 Tel # (615) 242-7395, Fax # (615) 256-6601

Alaska Employment Law Letter   *Business*

Publishing Co: M. Lee Smith Publishers & Printers ,LCC, P.O. Box 198867, 162 Fourth Avenue North, Nashville, TN 37219-8867 Tel # (615) 242-7395 Fax # (615) 256-6601
Personnel: Publisher-M.Lee Smith, Editor-Tom Daniel, Circ. Mgr.-Cathy Bradford, Mktg. Dir.-David Yates
General Info: Yr. Est. 1996, Monthly, Trim Size-8½ x 11, 8 pages, 2 Color
Subscriptions: Indv. $97
List Rental: Rents Lists

Alberta Corporations Law Guide   *Business*

Publishing Co: CCH Canadian Ltd., 6 Garamond Ct., North York, ON M3C 1Z5 Canada Fax # (416) 444-8011 Parent Co.-CCH, Inc., Riverwoods; Title Tel # (416) 441-2992 Title Fax # (416) 444-9011
Editorial Description: Coverage on Alberta Companies Act and Regulations.
General Info: Yr. Est. 1983, Monthly, Trim Size-6 x 9, Web press, No Color, Looseleaf
Subscriptions: Can. $455

Alberta Decisions Civil & Criminal Cases   *Business*

Publishing Co: Western Legal Publications, 301-1 Alexander St., Vancouver, BC V6A 1B2 Canada; Title Tel # (604) 687-5671 Title Fax # (604) 687-2796
Personnel: Publisher-Nancy Cotter, Editor-Ronda McNabb
Editorial Description: Monthly digests of current case law filed by subject.
General Info: Yr. Est. 1974, Monthly, Mimeo press, 65 pages, ISSN: 0313-7980, Ind/Abs/Online: INFOMART, QL, No Color, Newsprint, Looseleaf
Subscriptions: Can. $335

Alberta, N.W.T. and Yukon Tax Reports
See: TAXES

Alcoholic Beverage Control/State Capitals
See: BEVERAGES - BREWING

Alimony, Child Support and Counsel Fees--Award, Modification and Enforcement   *Business*

Publishing Co: Matthew Bender & Co., 11 Penn Plaza, New York, NY 10001-2006 Tel # (212) 967-7707 Fax # (212) 244-3188
Editorial Description: Provides complete coverage of three key economic aspects of divorce, with substantive analysis of relevant case law & statutes, & valuable practical advice.
General Info: Yr. Est. 1988, Irregular, Looseleaf

Allegheny Lawyer   *Association*

Publishing Co: Allegheny County Bar Association, 400 Koppers Bldg., Pittsburgh, PA 15219 Tel # (412) 261-6255; Title Tel # (412) 261-6161 Title Fax # (412) 261-3622
Personnel: Editor-James Smith, Production Mgr.-Julie Vodde
General Info: Monthly
Subscriptions: Free With Membership
Circulation: Total-70,000

Alston Wilkes Society Newsletter
See: LAW ENFORCEMENT & PENOLOGY

American Academy of Matrimonial Lawyers Newsletter   *Association*

Publishing Co: American Academy of Matrimonial Lawyers, 150 N Michigan Ave Ste 2040, Chicago, IL 60601-7524; Title Tel # (312) 263-6477
Personnel: Editor-Martin Haines
Editorial Description: Seeks to elevate the standards of matrimonial law.
General Info: Quarterly

American College of Legal Medicine, Notes from the President
See: MEDICINE

American Foreign Law Association, Newsletter   *Association*

Publishing Co: American Foreign Law Assn., C/O Milton Schwartz, Pres., 645 Madison Ave,. 17th Floor, New York, NY 10166-0005 Tel # (212) 759-5400; Title Tel # (212) 759-2400
Personnel: Editor-James Maxelner
Editorial Description: Reports on programs sponsored by the Assn. & on other activities related to foreign, intl. & comparative law, & intl. affairs of interest to Assn. members & practioners.
General Info: Yr. Est. 1974, Trim Size-8½ x 11, 12 pages
Subscriptions: Indv. $20
Circulation: Total-650
List Rental: Rents Lists

American Grand Jury Foundation Newsletter

Publishing Co: American Grand Jury Foundation, PO Box 1690, Modesto, CA 95353-1690; Title Tel # (209) 527-0966
Personnel: Editor-Bruce Olson
Editorial Description: State-wide news of grand jury activities; investigation methods; laws affecting the California grand juriess; ethical conduct for grand juries; grand jury achievements; suggestions for writing investigative reports.
General Info: Sheetfed press, 4 pages
Circulation: Total-450

American Law of Mining

Publishing Co: Matthew Bender & Co., 11 Penn Plaza, New York, NY 10001-2006 Fax # (212) 244-3188; Title Tel # (212) 967-7707
Personnel: Editor-E. Carr
Editorial Description: Edited by Rocky Mountain Mineral Law Foundation. Modern question-multiple use of mineral lands, taxation, securities laws, labor and lien laws.
General Info: Irregular, Looseleaf
Subscriptions: $550/copy

American Law of Products Liability Newsletter   *Business*

Publishing Co: Clark Boardman Callaghan, 50 Broad St. E., Rochester, NY 14694-0001 Tel # (716) 546-1490
General Info: Monthly
Subscriptions: Indv. $160

American Notary   *Business, Association*

Publishing Co: American Society of Notaries, PO Box 7663, Tallahassee, FL 32314-7663
Personnel: Editor-Eugene Hines
Editorial Description: Legislation, court decisions, and other matters of interest to notaries.
General Info: Yr. Est. 1965, Bi-monthly, Trim Size-8½ x 11, Web press, 8 pages, ISSN: 0044-7773, No Color, Newsprint
Subscriptions: Indv. $9, $2/copy
Circulation: (100% controlled)
Advertising: Inquire for rates.
List Rental: Actives: $55/M, Expires: $45/M
Printing Co: Suburban Printing Service, 5380a Eisenhower Ave, Alexandria, VA 22304-4856 Tel # (703) 370-5800, Fax # (703) 751-8637

American Society of International Law Newsletter   *Scholarly, Association*

Publishing Co: American Society of International Law, 2223 Massachusetts Ave. NW, Washington, DC 20008-2864; Title Tel # (202) 939-6000 Title Fax # (202) 797-7133
Personnel: Publisher-Marilou Righini, Editor-Sandra Liebel, Adv. Dir.-Carlton Ray
Editorial Description: The newsletter provides updates of the Society's activities and brief articles on recent developments in international law.
General Info: Bi-monthly, Trim Size-8½ x 11, 6 pages, ISSN: 1049-7893
Subscriptions: Indv. $20, Can. $25, For. $25, $5/copy
Circulation: Total-4,500, Readership-4,500
List Rental: Actives: $140/M

Americans with Disabilites Cases
See: DISABILITY

Americans with Disabilities Act-An Instructional Guide for Judge & Court Admin.,The

Publishing Co: Natl. Judicial College, Univ. Of Nevada, Reno, NV 89557-0001 Tel # (702) 784-6747 Fax # (702) 784-4234
General Info: Yr. Est. 1993
Subscriptions: Indv. $50, $50/copy

Americans with Disabilities Newsletter
See: DISABILITY

Andrews' Bank & Lender Liability Litigation Reporter   *Business*

Publishing Co: Andrews Publications, Inc., 1646 West Chester Pike, PO Box 1000, Westtown, PA 19395; Title Tel # (610) 399-6600 Title Fax # (610) 399-6610
Personnel: Publisher-John E. Backe, Editor-Denise Breslin Kachin, Mktg. Dir.-Andrew Katz
Editorial Description: For bank executives and attorneys who need to follow developments banking law. National journal of record reporting failed bank & thrift litigation.
General Info: (Formerly Failed Bank&Thrift Lit. Rptr.; Lender Liability Lit. Rptr.), Yr. Est. 1986, Bi-monthly, Trim Size-8½ x 11, Mimeo press, 70 pages, Ind/Abs/Online: NEWSNET
Subscriptions: Indv. $825, $39/copy
List Rental: Actives: 1,251, $110/M

Andrews Professional Liability Litigation Reporter   *Business*

Publishing Co: Andrews Publications, Inc., 1646 West Chester Pike, PO Box 1000, Westtown, PA 19395 Tel # (610) 399-6600; Title Tel # (215) 399-6600 Title Fax # (610) 399-6610
Personnel: Publisher-John E. Backe, Editor-Michelle Sarnocinski, Mktg. Dir.-Andrew Katz
Editorial Description: For third party liability of attorneys, investment bankers, financial advisors, accountants and other professionals. Contains concise summaries of recent complaints, answers, motions and decisions, and reprints the full texts of important briefs and opinions.
General Info: Yr. Est. 1992, Monthly, Trim Size-8½ x 11, 70 pages, ISSN: 1059-3969, Ind/Abs/Online: NEWSNET
Subscriptions: Indv. $650, $59/copy
Advertising: Inquire for rates.
List Rental: Actives: 66,686, $125/M

Antarctica and International Law: A Collection of Interstate and Narional Documents   *Business*

Publishing Co: Oceana Publications, Inc., 75 Main St, Dobbs Ferry, NY 10522-1601; Title Tel # (914) 693-8100 Title Fax # (914) 693-0402
Personnel: Editor-W. Bush, Production Mgr.-Mike Wortzman, Mktg. Dir.-John Downey
Editorial Description: Includes all significant legal materials pertaining to Antartica.
General Info: Yr. Est. 191 , Annually, Looseleaf
Subscriptions: $175/copy

Antarctica Project Newsletter, The
See: ENVIRONMENT & ECOLOGY

Antitrust & Commerce Report

Publishing Co: National Association of Attorneys General, 444 N Capitol St NW Ste 339, Washington, DC 20001-1512 Tel # (202) 434-8034; Title Tel # (202) 628-0435
Personnel: Editor-Elena Boisvert
General Info: Bi-monthly
Subscriptions: Indv. $145

Antitrust Counseling and Litigation Techniques   *Business*

Publishing Co: Matthew Bender & Co., 11 Penn Plaza, New York, NY 10001-2006 Tel # (212) 967-7707 Fax # (212) 244-3188
Editorial Description: The practical guide to corporate antitrust counseling and successful antitrust litigation, with contributions from over 50 leading practitioners in the field.
General Info: Yr. Est. 1984, Irregular, Looseleaf

Antitrust Counselor, The

Publishing Co: Business Laws, Inc., 11630 Chillicothe Rd., Chesterland, OH 44026-1928; Title Tel # (216) 729-7996 Title Fax # (216) 729-0645
General Info: Monthly
Subscriptions: Indv. $195, $20/copy

Antitrust FOIA Log   *Business*

Publishing Co: Washington Regulatory Reporting Group, PO Box 356, Basye, VA 22810-0356; Title Tel # (703) 856-2216 Title Fax # (703) 856-8331
Personnel: Publisher-Arthur Amolsch
General Info: Yr. Est. 1986, Weekly, Desktop press, ISSN: 0891-8546
Subscriptions: Indv. $335, Inst. $335, Can. $335, For. $435

Antitrust Laws and Trade Regulations   *Business*

Publishing Co: Matthew Bender & Co., 11 Penn Plaza, New York, NY 10001-2006 Fax # (212) 244-3188; Title Tel # (212) 967-7707
Personnel: Editor-Julian O. Kalinowski
Editorial Description: Fully detailed treatise on subject areas.
General Info: Yr. Est. 1969, Monthly, Looseleaf
Subscriptions: $790/copy

Antitrust Litigation Reporter   *Business*

Publishing Co: Andrews Publications, Inc., 1646 West Chester Pike, PO Box 1000, Westtown, PA 19395; Title Tel # (610) 399-6600 Title Fax # (610) 399-6610
Personnel: Publisher-John E. Backe, Editor-Jay Steinberg, Mktg. Dir.-Andrew Katz
Editorial Description: Offers comprehensive coverage of significant litigation brought under the federal and state antitrust statutes.
General Info: Yr. Est. 1993, Monthly, Trim Size-8½ x 11, 38 pages, ISSN: 1070-8472, No Color
Subscriptions: Indv. $700, $67/copy
Advertising: Inquire for rates.
List Rental: Actives: 66,686, $105/M

Antitrust Report

Publishing Co: National Association of Attorneys General, 444 N Capitol St NW Ste 339, Washington, DC 20001-1512 Tel # (202) 434-8034; Title Tel # (202) 628-0435
Personnel: Editor-Elena Boisvert
General Info: (Formerly Antitrust & Commerce Report), Yr. Est. 1980, Bi-monthly, 12 pages
Subscriptions: Indv. $145
Circulation: Total-300

Antitrust and Trade Regulation Report   *Business*

Publishing Co: Bureau of National Affairs, Inc., 1231 25th St. NW, Bldg. N-200, Washington, DC 20037-1157; Title Tel # (202) 452-4200 Title Fax # (202) 822-8092
Personnel: Publisher-William A. Beltz, Mng. Editor-Sheldon B. Richman, Circ. Mgr.-Gary C. Seltzer
Editorial Description: Weekly comprehensive coverage of significant competition & deceptive trade practice law developments on the federal, state & intl. levels.
General Info: Yr. Est. 1961, Weekly, Trim Size-8½ x 11, Offset press, 50 pages, ISSN: 0003-6021, Ind/Abs/Online: Lexis, Nexis, Westlaw, Mead Data Central, Looseleaf
Subscriptions: Indv. $1,077

Arbitration in the Schools   *Business, Consumer*

Publishing Co: LRP Publications, 747 Dresher Rd., P.O. Box 980, Horsham, PA 19044-0980 Tel # (215) 784-0910 Fax # (215) 784-0317
Personnel: Publisher-Kenneth F. Kahn, Production Mgr.-Kathleen P. Neely, Mktg. Dir.-Jana Shellington, Promotion Dir.-Gary Ragin
Editorial Description: Summarizes significant awards involving union employees (both teachers and support staff) in public and private institutions.
General Info: Monthly
Subscriptions: Indv. $120

Arizona Employment Law Letter   *Business*

Publishing Co: M. Lee Smith Publishers & Printers ,LCC, P.O. Box 198867, 162 Fourth Avenue North, Nashville, TN 37219-8867 Tel # (615) 242-7395 Fax # (615) 256-6601
Personnel: Publisher-M. Lee Smith, Editor-Allen Clarke, Circ. Mgr.-Cathy Bradford, Mktg. Dir.-Dave Yates
Editorial Description: Reviews employment developments that affect Arizona employers.
General Info: Yr. Est. 1994, Monthly, Trim Size-8½ x 11, 8 pages, ISSN: 1075-9611, 2 Color, Matte
Subscriptions: Indv. $97
Circulation: Total-750
List Rental: Rents Lists

Arizona Environmental Law Update   *Business*

Publishing Co: M. Lee Smith Publishers & Printers ,LCC, P.O. Box 198867, 162 Fourth Avenue North, Nashville, TN 37219-8867; Title Tel # (615) 242-7395 Title Fax # (615) 256-6601
Personnel: Publisher-M Lee Smith, Editor-Steve Owens, Circ. Mgr.-Cathy Bradford, Mktg. Dir.-David Yates
Editorial Description: Review of environmental law developments that affect Arizona companies.
General Info: (Formerly Arizona Environmental Law Letter), Yr. Est. 1990, Monthly, Trim Size-8½ x 11, 8 pages, ISSN: 1070-4655, 2 Color
Subscriptions: Indv. $117
List Rental: Rents Lists
Printing Co: M. Lee Smith Publishers & Printers ,LLC, PO Box 198867, 162 Fourth Avenue, Nashville, TN 37219-8867 Tel # (615) 242-7395, Fax # (615) 256-6601

Arkansas Employment Law Letter   *Business*

Publishing Co: M. Lee Smith Publishers & Printers ,LCC, P.O. Box 198867, 162 Fourth Avenue North, Nashville, TN 37219-8867 Tel # (615) 242-7395 Fax # (615) 256-6601
Personnel: Publisher-M Lee Smith, Editor-Steve Jones, Circ. Mgr.-Cathy Bradford, Mktg. Dir.-David Yates
General Info: Yr. Est. 1995, Monthly, Trim Size-8½ x 11, 8 pages, 2 Color
Subscriptions: Indv. $97
List Rental: Rents Lists

Arrest Law Bulletin
Business

Publishing Co: Quinlan Publishing, 23 Drydock Ave, Boston, MA 02210-2387 Fax # (617) 345-9646; Title Tel # (617) 542-0048
Personnel: Publisher-E. Michael Quinlan
Editorial Description: For law enforcement officials with case summaries.
General Info: Yr. Est. 1975, Monthly, 8 pages
Subscriptions: Indv. $60
List Rental: List Management Co.: Stevens-Knox List Management, 304 Park Ave S., New York, NY 10010-5312 Tel # (212) 388-8800, Fax # (212) 388-8890

Art of Advocacy
Business

Publishing Co: Matthew Bender & Co., 11 Penn Plaza, New York, NY 10001-2006 Fax # (212) 244-3188; Title Tel # (212) 967-7707
Personnel: Editor-S. Weisenfeld
Editorial Description: Updated annually or as needed. 13 volumes providing guidance on the law, principles, issues, & phraseology of advocacy.
General Info: Yr. Est. 1978, Annually, Looseleaf
Subscriptions: $1,290/copy

ArtsUSA UpDate
See: CULTURE & HUMANITIES

Asbestos Litigation Reporter
Business

Publishing Co: Andrews Publications, Inc., 1646 West Chester Pike, PO Box 1000, Westtown, PA 19395; Title Tel # (610) 399-6600 Title Fax # (610) 399-6610
Personnel: Publisher-John E. Backe, Editor-Tom Hennessey, Mktg. Dir.-Andrew Katz
Editorial Description: Covers the most recent developments in asbestos personal injury litigation.
General Info: Yr. Est. 1990, Bi-monthly, Trim Size-8½ x 11, Mimeo press, 80 pages, ISSN: 0273-3048, No Color, Newsprint
Subscriptions: Indv. $950, $44/copy
Advertising: Inquire for rates.
List Rental: Actives: 5,966, $110/M

Asbestos MDL-875 Update
Business

Publishing Co: Andrews Publications, Inc., 1646 West Chester Pike, PO Box 1000, Westtown, PA 19395 Tel # (610) 399-6600 Fax # (610) 399-6610
Personnel: Publisher-John E. Backe, Editor-Tom Hennessey, Mktg. Dir.-Andrew Katz
General Info: Yr. Est. 1991, Bi-monthly, Trim Size-8½ x 11, Offset press, ISSN: 1059-6232, No Color
Subscriptions: Indv. $650, $31/copy
Advertising: Inquire for rates.
List Rental: Actives: $125/M

Asbestos Property Litigation Reporter
Business

Publishing Co: Andrews Publications, Inc., 1646 West Chester Pike, PO Box 1000, Westtown, PA 19395; Title Tel # (610) 399-6600 Title Fax # (610) 399-6610
Personnel: Publisher-John E. Backe, Editor-Nick Sullivan, Mktg. Dir.-Andrew Katz
Editorial Description: Covers all the latest developments in actions brought by building owners against asbestos manufacturers to recover the costs of removing or encapsulating asbestos-containing building materials.
General Info: Yr. Est. 1987, Bi-monthly, Trim Size-8½ x 11, Mimeo press, ISSN: 1041-5130, No Color, Newsprint
Subscriptions: Indv. $725, $34/copy
Advertising: Inquire for rates.
List Rental: Actives: 66,686, $105/M

Asset Based Financing: A Transactional Guide
See: BANKING & FINANCE

Asset Forfeiture Practice and Procedure: A Digest of Case Law
Business

Publishing Co: Oceana Publications, Inc., 75 Main St, Dobbs Ferry, NY 10522-1601 Tel # (914) 693-8100 Fax # (914) 693-0402
Personnel: Editor-Judith E. Secher, Production Mgr.-Mike Wortzman, Mktg. Dir.-John Downey
Editorial Description: Provides detailed case descriptions for issues including burden of proof, probable cause and more.
General Info: Yr. Est. 1994, Irregular, Looseleaf
Subscriptions: Indv. $195

Assets Protection
See: ACCOUNTING

Association of American Law Schools, Newsletter
Association

Publishing Co: Association of American Law Schools, 1201 Conn. Ave. NW, #800, Washington, DC 20036-2605; Title Tel # (202) 296-8851 Title Fax # (202) 296-8869
Personnel: Editor-Alice Gresham Bullock, Asst. Ed., Production Dir.-Kimberly Rusin
Editorial Description: Seeks to improve the legal profession through legal education.
General Info: Yr. Est. 1964, Quarterly, Trim Size-8½ x 11, Sheetfed press, 28 pages, ISSN: 0519-1025, 2 Color, Matte, Saddle-stitched
Subscriptions: Indv. $28, Inst. $28, Can. $28, For. $28, $7/copy
Circulation: (90% controlled), Total-9,600
Printing Co: Automated Graphic Systems, 4590 Graphics Drive, White Plains, MD 20695 Tel # (301) 843-1800, Fax # (301) 843-6339

Association of Family and Conciliation Courts Newsletter
Association

Publishing Co: Association of Family and Conciliation Courts, 329 W Wilson St Rm 241, Madison, WI 53703-3612; Title Tel # (608) 251-4001 Title Fax # (608) 251-2231
Personnel: Editor-Ann L. Milne
Editorial Description: Interested in settling domestic disputes through mediation.
General Info: Yr. Est. 1963, Quarterly
Circulation: Total-1,200
Advertising: Inquire for rates.
List Rental: Rents Lists

Attorney-CPA
Business, Association

Publishing Co: American Assn. of Attorney CPA's, 24196 Alicia Pky., Ste. K, Mission Viejo, CA 92691-3926; Title Tel # (714) 768-0336
Personnel: Editor-Ronald DeVore
Editorial Description: Promotes high ethical standards of dual licensed professionals. Presents articles of professional interest to attorneys and CPAs. Also focuses on the concerns and problems of dually qualified attorney-CPAs. Publishes Association news and information .
General Info: Yr. Est. 1964, Bi-monthly, Trim Size-8½ x 11, Sheetfed press, 16 pages, ISSN: 0571-8279, 2 Color, Matte, Saddle-stitched
Subscriptions: Indv. $30, For. $40, $8/copy
Circulation: (100% controlled), Total-1,800
Advertising: Inquire for rates.
List Rental: Actives: $135/M, Expires: $125/M

Attorneys' Dictionary of Medicine
Business

Publishing Co: Matthew Bender & Co., 11 Penn Plaza, New York, NY 10001-2006 Fax # (212) 244-3188; Title Tel # (212) 967-7707
Personnel: Editor-B. Lieberman
Editorial Description: Used to turn medical jargon into plain English.
General Info: Yr. Est. 1962, Looseleaf
Subscriptions: $350/copy

Attorney's Dictionary of Patent Claims
Business

Publishing Co: Matthew Bender & Co., 11 Penn Plaza, New York, NY 10001-2006 Tel # (212) 967-7707 Fax # (212) 244-3188
Editorial Description: For patent drafters, providing invaluable assistance in preparing patent applications. A lexicon of the language of modern patent claims, includes terms from all patents arts, culled from thousand of claims recently accepted by the U.S. Patent & Trademark Office, especially chemical claims.
General Info: Yr. Est. 1985, Irregular, Looseleaf

Attorney's Handbook of Accounting
See: ACCOUNTING

Attorneys' Textbook of Medicine
Business

Publishing Co: Matthew Bender & Co., 11 Penn Plaza, New York, NY 10001-2006 Fax # (212) 244-3188; Title Tel # (212) 967-7707
Personnel: Editor-B. Lieberman
Editorial Description: A medico-legal research aid.
General Info: Yr. Est. 1934, Looseleaf
Subscriptions: $1,350/copy

Attorneys' Textbook of Medicine: Manual of Traumatic Injuries
Business

Publishing Co: Matthew Bender & Co., 11 Penn Plaza, New York, NY 10001-2006 Tel # (212) 967-7707 Fax # (212) 244-3188
Editorial Description: For the attorney preparing a case involving physical injury, the rehabilitation specialist seeking background on the cause of injury of the the insurance company employee handling medical claims.
General Info: Yr. Est. 1989, Irregular, Looseleaf

Australian Corporations & Securities Law Reports

Publishing Co: CCH, Inc., 2700 Lake Cook Rd., Riverwoods, IL 60015 Parent Co.-Kluwer Law & Taxation Publishers, Cambridge; Title Tel # (847) 267-7000 Title Fax # (800) 224-8299
Editorial Description: Contains detailed, practical coverage of the new Australian Corporations Law and ancillary legislation.
General Info: 18x/yr., Looseleaf
Subscriptions: Indv. $695

Australian Labour Law Reports

Publishing Co: CCH, Inc., 2700 Lake Cook Rd., Riverwoods, IL 60015 Parent Co.-Kluwer Law & Taxation Publishers, Cambridge; Title Tel # (847) 267-7000 Title Fax # (800) 224-8299
Editorial Description: Provides a comprehensive coverage of labour law for each of the Federal and State/Territory jurisdictions.
General Info: Looseleaf
Subscriptions: Indv. $685

Australian and New Zealand Insurance Law Reports

Publishing Co: CCH, Inc., 2700 Lake Cook Rd., Riverwoods, IL 60015 Parent Co.-Kluwer Law & Taxation Publishers, Cambridge; Title Tel # (847) 267-7000 Title Fax # (800) 224-8299
Editorial Description: Provides the most comprehensive & up-to-date discussion of insurance law in Australia & New Zealand.
General Info: Monthly, Looseleaf
Subscriptions: Indv. $1,185

Auto Dealer Law Reporter   *Business*

Publishing Co: Lewis L. Laska, 901 Church St, Nashville, TN 37203-3411; Title Tel # (615) 255-6288 Title Fax # (615) 255-6289
Personnel: Publisher, Editor-Lewis L. Laska
Editorial Description: National newsletter covering new car dealer management and litigation.
General Info: Yr. Est. 1995, Monthly, Trim Size-8½ x 11, 16 pages
Subscriptions: Indv. $195

Automatome
See: LIBRARY

Automobile Accident Law and Practice   *Business*

Publishing Co: Matthew Bender & Co., 11 Penn Plaza, New York, NY 10001-2006 Tel # (212) 967-7707 Fax # (212) 244-3188
Personnel: Editor in Chief-Keith Miller
Editorial Description: For plaintiff & defense attorneys, expert guidance on all theories of recovery related to auto accident cases. Includes practical information for every stage of a case, from establishing grounds for liability to closing arguements.
General Info: Yr. Est. 1988, Irregular, Looseleaf

Automotive Litigation Reporter
See: AUTOMOTIVE

Aviation Accident Law
See: AERONAUTICS/ASTRONAUTICS

Aviation Law Reports
See: AERONAUTICS/ASTRONAUTICS

Aviation Litigation Reporter
See: AERONAUTICS/ASTRONAUTICS

BNA Civil Trial Manual   *Business*

Publishing Co: Bureau of National Affairs, Inc., 1231 25th St. NW, Bldg. N-200, Washington, DC 20037-1157; Title Tel # (202) 452-4200 Title Fax # (202) 822-8092
Personnel: Publisher-William Beltz, Editor-Larry Ritchie, Circ. Mgr.-Gary Seltzer
Editorial Description: A notification & reference service covering decisions on civil procedure & evidence, verdicts & settlements, & new procedures & practice technique .
General Info: Yr. Est. 1985, Bi-weekly, Trim Size-6 x 9, Offset press, 24 pages, Looseleaf
Subscriptions: Indv. $944

BNA Criminal Practice Manual   *Business*

Publishing Co: Pike & Fischer Inc., 4600 East-West Hwy., Ste. 200, Bethesda, MD 20814-1438 Tel # (301) 652-6262 Fax # (301) 654-6297 Parent Co.-Bureau of National Affairs, Inc., Washington; Title Tel # (202) 452-4200 Title Fax # (202) 822-8092
Personnel: Publisher-William Beltz, Editor-Judith Mroczka, Circ. Mgr.-Gary Seltzer
Editorial Description: A notification & reference service consisting of a desk reference binder covering the entire court process from arrest through sentencing, & a newsletter covering developments in criminal law, evidence & procedures, & practice techniques.
General Info: Yr. Est. 1987, Bi-weekly, Trim Size-8½ x 11, Offset press, 30 pages, ISSN: 0889-9312, Looseleaf
Subscriptions: Indv. $630

BNA/ACCA Compliance Manual: Prevention of Corporate Liability
See: BUSINESS & INDUSTRY

BNA's Americans with Disabilities Act Manual
See: DISABILITY

BNA's Americans with Disabilities Act Manual Newsletter
See: DISABILITY

BNA's Collective Bargaining Bulletin
See: LABOR UNION

BNA's Corporate Counsel Weekly   *Business*

Publishing Co: Bureau of National Affairs, Inc., 1231 25th St. NW, Bldg. N-200, Washington, DC 20037-1157 Fax # (202) 822-8092; Title Tel # (202) 452-4200
Personnel: Publisher-William A. Beltz, Editor-Larry Lempert, Mng. Editor-Sarah Stevens, Circ. Mgr.-Gary C. Seltzer
Editorial Description: A weekly roundup of the latest developments in law that affect business, including coverage of the courts, federal regulatory agencies, the executive branch, states & professional assns.
General Info: (Formerly BNA's Washington Memorandum), Yr. Est. 1978, Weekly, Trim Size-8½ x 11, Offset press, 8 pages, ISSN: 0886-0475
Subscriptions: Indv. $590

BNA's Employee Relations Weekly
See: INDUSTRIAL RELATIONS/PERSONNEL

BNA's Environmental Compliance Bulletin
See: ENVIRONMENT & ECOLOGY

BNA's Environmental Due Diligence Guide
See: ENVIRONMENT & ECOLOGY

BNA's Health Law Reporter
See: HEALTH

BRN Report
See: NURSING

Bad Faith Law Report   *Business*

Publishing Co: Stratton Press, PO Box 96, San Ramon, CA 94583-0096; Title Tel # (510) 735-1719 Title Fax # (415) 731-6613
Personnel: Publisher-Patricia Ashley, Editor-Stephen Ashley
Editorial Description: Provides timely, concise reporting of developments in the law of bad faith. Includes critical summaries of every reported appellate decision in the United States, insightful articles, tables of cases and a cumulative digest. A professional journal for attorneys and insurance professionals.
General Info: Yr. Est. 1985, 10x/yr., Trim Size-8½ x 11, Web press, 24 pages, ISSN: 8756-5374, No Color, Matte
Subscriptions: Indv. $240
Circulation: Total-850
Printing Co: Sapir Press, 523 Mayfair Ave, South San Francisco, CA 94080-4509 Tel # (415) 952-7886

Bad Faith Law Update   *Business*

Publishing Co: Matthew Bender & Co., 11 Penn Plaza, New York, NY 10001-2006 Tel # (212) 967-7707 Fax # (212) 244-3188
Editorial Description: A monthly report offering authoritative, up-to-the-minute coverage of the latest developments in insurance bad fiath, wrongful discharge from employment & other areas of the law in which a breach of the implied covenant of good faith & fair dealing may give rise to a tort cause of action.
General Info: Yr. Est. 1986, Monthly, Looseleaf

Baldwin's Ohio Tax Service
See: TAXES

Ballantine and Sterling California Corporation Laws   *Business*

Publishing Co: Matthew Bender & Co., 11 Penn Plaza, New York, NY 10001-2006 Fax # (212) 244-3188; Title Tel # (212) 967-7707
Personnel: Editor-G. Leatherman
Editorial Description: Detailed analysis of general and non-profit corporation law in California, combined with procedural guides.
General Info: Yr. Est. 1932, Irregular, Looseleaf
Subscriptions: $635/copy

Bank Bailout Litigation News
See: BANKING & FINANCE

Bank Compliance Guide
See: BANKING & FINANCE

Bank Digest
See: BANKING & FINANCE

Bank Holding Company Compliance Manual
See: BANKING & FINANCE

Bank Lawyer Liability   *Business*

Publishing Co: LRP Publications, 747 Dresher Rd., P.O. Box 980, Horsham, PA 19044-0980 Tel # (215) 784-0910 Fax # (215) 784-0317
Personnel: Publisher-Ken Kahn, Editor-Joanne Fiore
Editorial Description: Analysis of RTC, FDIC, OTS, and related actions against bank lawyers. Emphasizes full text of complaints, pleadings, and opinions.
General Info: (Formerly Buraff's Litigation Report: Bank Lawyer Liability), Yr. Est. 1992, Bi-weekly, ISSN: 1067-618X
Subscriptions: Indv. $745, For. $767

Bank Securities Advisor
See: BANKING & FINANCE

Bank Wage-Hour & Personnel Report
See: EMPLOYMENT

Bankers' Letter of the
Law   *Business*

Publishing Co: Warren, Gorham & Lamont, 31 Saint James Ave., Boston, MA 02116-4112 Parent Co.-Thomson Professional Publications, Stamford; Title Tel # (617) 423-2020 Title Fax # (617) 423-1914
Personnel: Publisher-Larry Selby, Mktg. Dir.-Sandra Fox
Editorial Description: Coverage includes credit legislation and regulation, collections, UCC, federal and state court decisions.
General Info: Yr. Est. 1973, Monthly, Trim Size-8½ x 11, Offset press, 6 pages, ISSN: 0005-5433, 2 Color
Subscriptions: Indv. $193, Inst. $202
Advertising: Inquire for rates.
List Rental: List Management Co.: Manager: Seena Benedek; WG & L List Management, 1 Penn Plz Fl 42, New York, NY 10119-0002 Tel # (212) 971-5000

Banking Law Briefs   *Business, Association*

Publishing Co: Banking Law Briefs, 521 W Main St Ste 200, Belleville, IL 62220-1533
Personnel: Publisher, Editor-Donald Faerber
Editorial Description: Analysis of recent developments in commercial banking law.
General Info: Yr. Est. 1983, Semi-monthly, Trim Size-8½ x 11, Letrpr. press, 6 pages, ISSN: 1065-1004, Color
Subscriptions: Indv. $67
Circulation: Total-1,500

Banking Law Manual: Legal Guide to Commerical Banks, Thrift Institutions and Credit Unions
See: BANKING & FINANCE

Bankruptcy Alert

Publishing Co: Lawyers Co-Operative Publishing Co., Aqueduct Bldg., Rochester, NY 14694-0001; Title Tel # (716) 546-5530
General Info: Yr. Est. 1980, Monthly
Subscriptions: Indv. $125

Bankruptcy Counsellor

Publishing Co: Counsellor Pubs., PO Box 19070, Alexandria, VA 22320-0070; Title Tel # (703) 684-9156
Personnel: Editor-Gregory Lee
Editorial Description: Covers cases and statutes affecting bankruptcy practice.
General Info: Yr. Est. 1988, Bi-weekly
Subscriptions: Indv. $345

Bankruptcy Court
Decisions

Publishing Co: LRP Publications, 747 Dresher Rd., P.O. Box 980, Horsham, PA 19044-0980 Tel # (215) 784-0910 Fax # (215) 784-0317
Personnel: Publisher-Kenneth Kahn, Editor-Michelle Johnson, Circ. Mgr.-John Ekberg, Production Mgr.-Joan Trentham, Adv. Dir.-David Light, Promotion Dir.-Lisa Zoks
Editorial Description: Insights into current happenings in the bankruptcy world. Includes practice pointers, statistics, legislative and supreme court updates.
General Info: Yr. Est. 1974, Weekly, Trim Size-8½ x 11, Sheetfed press, 150 pages, ISSN: 0098-7336, No Color
Subscriptions: Indv. $760, $8/copy
Acquistions: Publication Bought
Circulation: Total-1,400
List Rental: List Management Co.: Manager: Becky Yolton; Axon Lists, 747 Dresher Rd. Ste. 500, Box 980, Horsham, PA 19044 Tel # (215) 784-0860, Fax # (215) 784-0870, Actives: 12,100, $125/M

Bankruptcy Current
Awareness Alert   *Business*

Publishing Co: Clark Boardman Callaghan, 50 Broad St. E., Rochester, NY 14694-0001; Title Tel # (716) 546-1490
General Info: (Formerly Bankruptcy Alert), Yr. Est. 1980, Monthly
Subscriptions: Indv. $125

Bankruptcy Law Letter   *Business*

Publishing Co: Warren, Gorham & Lamont, 31 Saint James Ave., Boston, MA 02116-4112 Parent Co.-Thomson Professional Publications, Stamford; Title Tel # (617) 423-2020 Title Fax # (617) 423-1914
Personnel: Publisher-Larry Selby, Mktg. Dir.-Sandra Fox
Editorial Description: Includes modern bankruptcy practice and procedure designed for creditors, debtors and advisors.
General Info: Yr. Est. 1981, Monthly, Trim Size-8½ x 11, 8 pages, 2 Color
Subscriptions: Indv. $155
Advertising: Inquire for rates.
List Rental: List Management Co.: Manager: Seena Benedek; WG & L List Management, 1 Penn Plz Fl 42, New York, NY 10119-0002 Tel # (212) 971-5000

Bankruptcy Law Reports   *Business*

Publishing Co: CCH, Inc., 2700 Lake Cook Rd., Riverwoods, IL 60015 Parent Co.-Kluwer Law & Taxation Publishers, Cambridge; Title Tel # (847) 267-7000 Title Fax # (800) 224-8299
Editorial Description: Provides federal bankruptcy, reorganization and debt readjustment laws and decisions under both the Bankruptcy Reform Act and the earlier Bankruptcy Act.
General Info: Yr. Est. 1929, Bi-weekly, Trim Size-6 x 9, Web press, 120 pages, No Color, Looseleaf
Subscriptions: Indv. $915

Bankruptcy Strategist

Publishing Co: Leader Publications, Inc., 345 Park Avenue South, New York, NY 10010 Parent Co.-New York Law Publishing Co., New York; Title Tel # (212) 545-6170 Title Fax # (212) 696-1848
Personnel: Publisher-Stuart Wise, Editor-Herbert Schlagman, Circ. Mgr.-Josephine Dimino, Promotion Dir.-Rose-Ann Morangelli
Editorial Description: Reports on decisions, legislation, and strategy in bankruptcy law.
General Info: Yr. Est. 1983, Monthly, Trim Size-8½ x 11, Offset press, 8 pages, ISSN: 0747-8917, Color, Newsprint, Saddle-stitched
Subscriptions: Indv. $245, $20/copy
Printing Co: Columbus Bookbinding, 1343 Belfast Ave, Columbus, OH 31904 Tel # (206) 323-9313, Fax # (206) 323-2987

Bar Bulletin   *Association*

Publishing Co: State Bar of New Mexico, PO Box 25883, Albuquerque, NM 87125-0883; Title Tel # (505) 842-6132 Title Fax # (505) 843-8765
Personnel: Editor-Cheryl Bruce, Production Mgr.-Veronica Trujillo, Adv. Dir.-Lynne M. Lucero
Editorial Description: Provides Bar members and others with the text of recent New Mexico court decisions. Includes information on significant developments in the courts, legislature and other branches of state and federal government.
General Info: (Formerly News & Views), Yr. Est. 1960, Weekly, Trim Size-8½ x 11, Sheetfed press, 48 pages, ISSN: 0039-0038, 20% ads, No Color, Matte, Saddle-stitched
Subscriptions: Indv. $55
Circulation: (85% controlled), Total-5,500
Advertising: Inquire for rates.
List Rental: Rents Lists

Barclays U.S. Eighth Circuit
Service   *Business*

Publishing Co: Barclays Law Publishers, 400 Oyster Point Blvd., S. San Francisco, CA 94080 Tel # (415) 244-6677; Title Tel # (415) 588-1155 Title Fax # (415) 588-5778
Personnel: Editor-R. James
General Info: (Formerly Eighth Circuit Service Newsletter), Yr. Est. 1984, 26x/yr.
Subscriptions: Indv. $395

Barclays U.S. Tenth Circuit
Service   *Business*

Publishing Co: Barclays Law Publishers, 400 Oyster Point Blvd., S. San Francisco, CA 94080 Tel # (415) 244-6677; Title Tel # (415) 588-1155 Title Fax # (415) 588-5778
General Info: (Formerly Tenth Circuit Service Newsletter), Yr. Est. 1984, 26x/yr.
Subscriptions: Indv. $395

Barger & Walen Newsletter

Publishing Co: Barger & Walen, 530 W. 6th St., 9th Fl., Los Angeles, CA 90014-1203; Title Tel # (213) 680-2800

Bencher's Advisory

Publishing Co: Law Society of Alberta, 919 11th Ave., SW Ste 600, Calgary, AB T2R 1P3 Canada; Title Tel # (403) 229-4700
Personnel: Editor-Theresa Goulet
Circulation: Total-6,000

Bender's Federal Practice
Forms

Publishing Co: Matthew Bender & Co., 11 Penn Plaza, New York, NY 10001-2006 Fax # (212) 244-3188; Title Tel # (212) 967-7707
Personnel: Editor-B. Chase
Editorial Description: Comprehensive federal practice forms designed with the general practitioner in mind. Supplements issued irregularly.
General Info: Yr. Est. 1951, Irregular, Looseleaf
Subscriptions: $1,025/copy

Bender's Federal Practice
Manual

Publishing Co: Matthew Bender & Co., 11 Penn Plaza, New York, NY 10001-2006 Fax # (212) 244-3188; Title Tel # (212) 967-7707
Personnel: Editor-B. Chase, Adv. Dir.-T. F. Saal
Editorial Description: A manual of procedure and court rules for practice in the Federal Courts, with annotations, advisory committee notes, and comments. Covers all federal courts including the specialty courts.
General Info: Yr. Est. 1948, Irregular, Trim Size-7 x 10, Letrpr. press, 100 pages, Looseleaf
Subscriptions: $205/copy
Circulation: Total-1,750

Bender's Florida Forms--
Pleadings   *Business*

Publishing Co: Matthew Bender & Co., 11 Penn Plaza, New York, NY 10001-2006 Tel # (212) 967-7707 Fax # (212) 244-3188
Editorial Description: A definitive set of Florida pleading forms arranged according to subject matter--drawn from the files of successful Florida Attorneys.
General Info: Yr. Est. 1968, Irregular, Looseleaf

Bender's Forms of Pleading   *Business*

Publishing Co: Matthew Bender & Co., 11 Penn Plaza, New York, NY 10001-2006
Tel # (212) 967-7707 Fax # (212) 244-3188
Editorial Description: Provides complaints, defense pleadings, bills of particulars, counterclaims, third-party complaints & petitions for torts, negligence, contract actions, statutory actions, special proceedings such as Article 78, equity proceedings & Surrogate's court proceedings, in New York State.
General Info: Yr. Est. 1946, Irregular, Looseleaf

Bender's INS Regulations
Service   *Business*

Publishing Co: Matthew Bender & Co., 11 Penn Plaza, New York, NY 10001-2006
Tel # (212) 967-7707 Fax # (212) 244-3188
Editorial Description: A portable, up-to-date version of INS regulations that can be used as a quick desk reference or conveniently carried to court.
General Info: Yr. Est. 1989, Bi-monthly, Looseleaf

Bender's New York
Evidence-CPLR   *Business*

Publishing Co: Matthew Bender & Co., 11 Penn Plaza, New York, NY 10001-2006
Fax # (212) 244-3188; Title Tel # (212) 967-7707
Personnel: Editor-R. Kaye
Editorial Description: Complete analytical explanation of the application of the rules of evidence.
General Info: (Formerly Bender's New York Proof), Yr. Est. 1962, Irregular, Looseleaf
Subscriptions: $650/copy

Benedict on Admiralty

Publishing Co: Matthew Bender & Co., 11 Penn Plaza, New York, NY 10001-2006
Fax # (212) 244-3188; Title Tel # (212) 967-7707
Personnel: Editor-A. Jenner
Editorial Description: Standard, comprehensive work on the subject for the United States since 1850.
General Info: Yr. Est. 1940, Irregular, Looseleaf
Subscriptions: $1,075/copy

Bergman on New York
Mortgage Foreclosures   *Business*

Publishing Co: Matthew Bender & Co., 11 Penn Plaza, New York, NY 10001-2006
Tel # (212) 967-7707 Fax # (212) 244-3188
Editorial Description: A complete analysis of the law, combined with unparalleled practical guidance for performing residential & commercial property foreclosures in New York. The treatise is complete with a multitude of annotated forms & tips for successful practice.
General Info: Yr. Est. 1990, Irregular, Looseleaf

Bifocal   *Scholarly, Association*

Publishing Co: Am. Bar Assn. Commmision on Legal Problems of the Elderly, 740 15th St. NW, Washington, DC 20051-1009 Tel # (202) 662-8690 Fax # (202) 662-1032; Title Tel # (202) 331-2297 Title Fax # (202) 331-2220
Personnel: Editor-Norma B. Gregerman
Editorial Description: Bar associations in focus on aging and the law.
General Info: Yr. Est. 1977, Quarterly, Trim Size-8½ x 11, Desktop press, 10 pages, ISSN: 0888-1537, 2 Color, Other
Subscriptions: Indv. $18, Inst. $18
Circulation: Total-1,000
Printing Co: Master Print, Inc., 8401-A Terminal Rd., Box 1467, Newington, VA 22122
Tel # (703) 550-9555

Bilingual Dictionary of
Criminal Justice Terms -
English/Spanish

Publishing Co: Gould Publications, Inc, 1333 N US Highway 17-92, Longwood, FL 32750-3724
Tel # (407) 695-9500 Fax # (407) 695-2906; Title Tel # (607) 724-3000
Editorial Description: A current, comprehensive collection defined in both English and Spanish reflecting significant penal codes, criminal procedures.
General Info: Annually, 250 pages, Looseleaf
Subscriptions: $20/copy

Bill of Rights Newsletter
See: CIVIL RIGHTS

Bioethics Literature Review
See: MEDICINE

Biotechnology Law
Report

Publishing Co: Mary Ann Liebert, Inc., 1651 3rd Ave, New York, NY 10128-3649
Tel # (212) 289-2300; Title Tel # (215) 892-9580
Personnel: Editor-Gerry Elman, Production Mgr.-Judith Gunn Bronson, Promotion Dir.-Aston Heroe
Editorial Description: Litigation, legislation and regulation affecting biotechnology. Includes patent, food & drug, environmental and other matters.
General Info: Yr. Est. 1982, Bi-monthly, Trim Size-8½ x 11, 96 pages, ISSN: 0278-9728, Ind/Abs/Online: Dialog, No Color
Subscriptions: Indv. $375
Circulation: Total-512
Advertising: Inquire for rates.

Biz Law Update   *Business*

Publishing Co: Biz Law Association, Inc., PO Box 247, Springdale, UT 84767-0247
Tel # (801) 772-3276; Title Tel # (801) 635-9817 Title Fax # (801) 772-3433
Personnel: Publisher, Editor-Scott Fry
Editorial Description: Reports important developments in business law for business owners and managers.
General Info: Yr. Est. 1992, Monthly, 16 pages
Subscriptions: Indv. $125

Black Congressional Monitor
See: GOVERNMENT

Blue Bulletin
See: POWER & POWER PLANTS

Board of Contract Appeals Bid Protest Decisions
See: GOVERNMENT

Bowne Digest for
Corporate & Securities
Lawyers   *Business*

Publishing Co: Brumberg Publications, Inc., 124 Harvard St., Brookline, MA 02146-6432; Title Tel # (617) 734-1979 Title Fax # (617) 734-1989
Personnel: Publisher-Bruce Brumberg, Editor-Susan Koffman, Production Mgr.-Karen Axelrod
Editorial Description: Summarizes important new articles on corporate & securities law, such as M&A, finance, directors & officers, insider training. Articles selected from over 270 publications.
General Info: Yr. Est. 1987, Monthly, Offset press, 8 pages, Ind/Abs/Online: Newsnet, 2 Color, Newsprint
Subscriptions: Indv. $125, $12/copy
Acquistions: Publication Bought

Boycott Law Bulletin
See: INTERNATIONAL TRADE

Breast Implant Litigation
Reporter   *Business*

Publishing Co: Andrews Publications, Inc., 1646 West Chester Pike, PO Box 1000, Westtown, PA 19395; Title Tel # (610) 399-6600 Title Fax # (610) 399-6610
Personnel: Publisher-John Backe, Editor-Donna Higgens, Mktg. Dir.-Andrew Katz
Editorial Description: Provides up-to-date information on breast implant suits around the country.
General Info: Yr. Est. 1992, Bi-monthly, Trim Size-8½ x 11, Mimeo press, 80 pages, ISSN: 1067-1814, Ind/Abs/Online: Net News, No Color
Subscriptions: Indv. $750, $33/copy
Advertising: Inquire for rates.
List Rental: Actives: 1,172, $110/M

Briefing Papers   *Business*

Publishing Co: Federal Pubs., Inc., 1120 20th St., NW, Fifth Floor, South Building, Washington, DC 20036-3484; Title Tel # (202) 337-7000 Title Fax # (202) 659-2233
Personnel: Editor-Valerie Gross
General Info: Yr. Est. 1963
Subscriptions: Indv. $664

Briefly   *Association*

Publishing Co: Christian Legal Society, 4208 Evergreen Ln Ste 222, Annandale, VA 22003-3264; Title Tel # (703) 642-1070 Title Fax # (703) 642-1075
Personnel: Editor-Bradley Jacob, Production Mgr.-Dundee Zimpet, Art Dir.-Lisa Hartman, Art Dir.-Manny Torres
Editorial Description: Newsletter of membership activity.
General Info: Yr. Est. 1982, Bi-monthly, Trim Size-8½ x 11, Sheetfed press, 4 pages, 2 Color, Newsprint
Subscriptions: Free With Membership
Circulation: Total-6,000

British Columbia
Corporations Law Guide   *Business*

Publishing Co: CCH Canadian Ltd., 6 Garamond Ct., North York, ON M3C 1Z5 Canada
Fax # (416) 444-8011 Parent Co.-CCH, Inc., Riverwoods; Title Tel # (416) 441-2992 Title Fax # (416) 444-9011
Editorial Description: Coverage of British Columbia Companies Act, 1973, and Regulations. Forms and precedents. Commentary on extra-provincial corporations. Report letter summary included.
General Info: Yr. Est. 1945, Monthly, Trim Size-6 x 9, Web press, No Color, Looseleaf
Subscriptions: Can. $350

British Columbia Real Estate Law Guide
See: REAL ESTATE

British Columbia Tax Reports
See: TAXES

British Tax Reports and Legislation
See: TAXES

Broadcasting and the Law
See: BROADCASTING

Brown's Business Reporter
See: BUSINESS & INDUSTRY

Building Officials and Code Administrators International Bulletin
See: CONSTRUCTION & BUILDING

Building Permits Law Bulletin
See: CONSTRUCTION & BUILDING

Bulletin of Law Science and Technology   *Association*

Publishing Co: American Bar Association, 750 N. Lake Shore Dr., Chicago, IL 60611-4497
Tel # (312) 988-6115 Fax # (312) 988-6030; Title Tel # (312) 988-5522 Title Fax # (312) 988-5528
Personnel: Editor-Marla Hillery
Editorial Description: News of legal developments in cases on science & technology.
General Info: Yr. Est. 1976, Bi-monthly, Offset press, ISSN: 0362-3769, Newsprint, Saddle-stitched
Circulation: Total-4,000
List Rental: Rents Lists

Business Accounting for Lawyers Newsletter
See: ACCOUNTING

Business Counsel   *Business*

Publishing Co: Natl. Chamber Litigation Center, Inc., 1615 H St NW, Washington, DC 20006-4975; Title Tel # (202) 463-5337
Personnel: Editor-Cam Esser
Editorial Description: Summary of case involvement and other activity of NCLC.
General Info: Yr. Est. 1977, Quarterly, Trim Size-8½ x 11, 8 pages, ISSN: 0193-4414, 2 Color
Subscriptions: Indv. $15
Circulation: (100% controlled), Total-1,000

Business Crime: Criminal Liabilty of the Business Community   *Business*

Publishing Co: Matthew Bender & Co., 11 Penn Plaza, New York, NY 10001-2006
Tel # (212) 967-7707 Fax # (212) 244-3188
Editorial Description: The most complete guide to the many criminal questions that can arise in modern business practice. Provides hot-to guidance for: setting up compliance programs to prevent corporate liability: effectively conducting internal corporate, investigations, & parallel administrative, civil & criminal proceedings.
General Info: Yr. Est. 1981, Irregular, Looseleaf

Business Crimes Bulletin

Publishing Co: Leader Publications, Inc., 345 Park Avenue South, New York, NY 10010 Parent Co.- New York Law Publishing Co., New York; Title Tel # (212) 545-6170 Title Fax # (212) 696-1848
Personnel: Publisher-Stuart M. Wise, Editor-Jed S. Rakoff, Circ. Mgr.-Kerry Kyle, Mktg. Dir.-Rose-Ann Morangelei
General Info: (Formerly Law Office Employment Bulletin), Yr. Est. 1993, Trim Size-8½ x 11, Offset press, 8 pages, ISSN: 1073-6271, Color
Subscriptions: Indv. $135, $11/copy
Printing Co: Columbus Bookbinding, 1343 Belfast Ave, Columbus, OH 31904 Tel # (206) 323-9313, Fax # (206) 323-2987

Business Franchise Guide
See: BUSINESS & INDUSTRY

Business Insurance Law and Practice Guide   *Business*

Publishing Co: Matthew Bender & Co., 11 Penn Plaza, New York, NY 10001-2006
Tel # (212) 967-7707 Fax # (212) 244-3188
Editorial Description: A comprehensive guide for both insurance companies & attorneys who advise businesses of all sizes. Complete with legal analysis based on case law & statutes, & helpful practice tips throughtout.
General Info: Yr. Est. 1989, Irregular, Looseleaf

Business and the Law

Publishing Co: Carswell, 2075 Kennedy Road, One Corporate Plaza, Scarborough, ON M1T 3V4 Canada Tel # (416) 609-8000 Fax # (416) 298-5094; Title Tel # (416) 445-4940 Title Fax # (416) 445-5352
General Info: Yr. Est. 1984, Monthly
Subscriptions: Indv. $195

Business Law Europe
See: INTERNATIONAL TRADE

Business Law Update   *Business*

Publishing Co: Business Law Update, PO Box 247, Springdale, UT 84767-0247; Title Tel # (801) 635-9817 Title Fax # (801) 635-9818
Editorial Description: Legal information for business management.
General Info: Monthly, Trim Size-8½ x 11, 16 pages
Subscriptions: Indv. $125

Business Organizations: Corporate Acquisitions and Mergers   *Business*

Publishing Co: Matthew Bender & Co., 11 Penn Plaza, New York, NY 10001-2006
Fax # (212) 244-3188; Title Tel # (212) 967-7707
Personnel: Editor-H. Costikyan
Editorial Description: A thorough, easy-to-use guide to the antitrust, tax, corporate, securities & financial aspects of business combinations with extensive forms, charts & tables.
General Info: Yr. Est. 1968, Irregular, Looseleaf
Subscriptions: $475/copy

Business Organizations: Franchising   *Business*

Publishing Co: Matthew Bender & Co., 11 Penn Plaza, New York, NY 10001-2006
Fax # (212) 244-3188; Title Tel # (212) 967-7707
Personnel: Editor-L. Rubenzahl
Editorial Description: All legal, business and tax considerations of modern franchising are synthesized into one guide.
General Info: Yr. Est. 1969, Irregular, Looseleaf
Subscriptions: $450/copy

Business Torts
See: BUSINESS & INDUSTRY

Business at Risk: Trends in Personal Injury Litigation   *Business, Consumer*

Publishing Co: LRP Publications, 747 Dresher Rd., P.O. Box 980, Horsham, PA 19044-0980
Tel # (215) 784-0910 Fax # (215) 784-0317
Personnel: Publisher-Kenneth Kahn, Editor-Brian Shenker
Editorial Description: Analyzes personal injury cases against companies over the last 5 years involving accidents at work, wrongful termination, premises liability, vehicular liability, etc. Also contains, statistics, tables, graphs, and case examples.
General Info: Annually, 271 pages
Subscriptions: Can. $40

CBA Report   *Association*

Publishing Co: Cincinnati Bar Assn., 35 E 7th St, Cincinnati, OH 45202-2492; Title Tel # (513) 381-8213 Title Fax # (513) 381-0528
Personnel: Editor-Cathy Hitz, Production Mgr.-Ted Deutsch, Adv. Dir.-Sue Kountz
Editorial Description: Membership newsletter.
General Info: Yr. Est. 1972, Monthly, Trim Size-8½ x 11, Sheetfed press, 24 pages, 3% ads, No Color, Coated, Saddle-stitched
Circulation: Total-3,600
Advertising: Inquire for rates.
Printing Co: Feicke Web, Iowa St., Cincinnati, OH 45206 Tel # (513) 751-5517

CCAR Pool   *Business*

Publishing Co: National Clearinghouse for Legal Services, 205 W Monroe St Unit 2, Chicago, IL 60606-5013; Title Tel # (312) 263-3830 Title Fax # (312) 263-3846
Personnel: Publisher-Rita McLennon, Editor-Bob Serafin, Production Mgr.-Susan Sebok
Editorial Description: Summarizes recent articles in computer press and reports on new products. Focus is on poverty law.
General Info: Yr. Est. 1984, 8x/yr., Sheetfed press, 16 pages, Color-cover, Saddle-stitched
Subscriptions: Indv. $30
Circulation: Total-1,400
Printing Co: Phillips Brothers Printers, 1555 W Jefferson St, Springfield, IL 62702-4734 Tel # (217) 787-3014, Fax # (217) 787-9624

CCH Tax Day Report
See: TAXES

C.J. the Americas
See: LAW ENFORCEMENT & PENOLOGY

CJ Europe
See: LAW ENFORCEMENT & PENOLOGY

C.J. International
See: LAW ENFORCEMENT & PENOLOGY

CJSA Forum

Publishing Co: Criminal Justice Statistics Assn., 444 N Capitol St NW Ste 606, Washington, DC 20001-1512; Title Tel # (202) 624-8560
Personnel: Circ. Mgr.-Loyce Craft, Editor, Production Mgr.-Karen Gasson
Editorial Description: The CJSA Forum; the newsletter of the criminal justice statistics assn., reports on current policy analysis in the states. It also highlights research methods used to address criminal justice problems.
General Info: (Formerly CJSA Bulletin), Yr. Est. 1983, Quarterly, 16 pages, No Color
Subscriptions: Indv. $25
Circulation: Total-400

COFIC Newsletter   *Business, Association*

Publishing Co: National Food Processors Assn., 1401 New York Ave. NW, Washington, DC 20005-2154 Tel # (202) 639-5934 Fax # (202) 637-8068
Editorial Description: A quarterly legal update on products liability by NFPA's coalition of food industry counsel.
General Info: Quarterly
Subscriptions: Free With Membership

COGEL Guardian
See: GOVERNMENT

CPA Managing Partner
Report   *Business*

Publishing Co: Strafford Pubs., Inc., 590 Dutch Valley Rd., N.E., Postal Drawer 13729, Atlanta, GA 30324-0729; Title Tel # (404) 881-1141 Title Fax # (404) 881-0074
Personnel: Publisher-Richard M. Ossoff, Editor-Suzanne Verity, Circ. Mgr., Mktg. Dir.-Marianne Mueller
Editorial Description: Provides managing partners in public accounting firms with problem solving tactics and management methods that can help the firm maintain stability and enhance profitability as it strives to achieve short-term and long-range goals.
General Info: Yr. Est. 1986, 12x/yr., ISSN: 0894-1815
Subscriptions: Indv. $287, Can. $317, For. $342, $20/copy
Acquistions: Publication Bought, Publication Sold
List Rental: Expires: $105/M

CSBS Examiner
See: BANKING & FINANCE

Cable TV Law Reporter
See: BROADCASTING

Cable TV and New Media Law & Finance
See: TELECOMMUNICATIONS

Cable TV Regulation
See: TELEVISION & VIDEO

California Construction
Law Reporter

Publishing Co: Shepard's/McGraw-Hill, Inc., 555 Middle Creek Pky, Colorado Springs, CO 80921-3622; Title Tel # (719) 488-3000 Title Fax # (719) 481-7448
Personnel: Editor-James Acret, Adv. Dir.-Peggy Everitt, Art Dir.-Leigh Vidakovich
Editorial Description: Covers significant cases affecting the construction industry, plus articles and commentary from construction lawyer.
General Info: Yr. Est. 1991, Monthly
Subscriptions: Indv. $200
List Rental: List Management Co.: The Lake Group, 411 Theodore Freund Ave., Rye, NY 10580-1497 Tel # (914) 925-2400, Fax # (914) 925-2499, Actives: 40,212, $130/M

California Corporate
Securities Law of 1968   *Business*

Publishing Co: Matthew Bender & Co., 11 Penn Plaza, New York, NY 10001-2006 Fax # (212) 244-3188; Title Tel # (212) 967-7707
Editorial Description: Analysis of the corporate securities law.
General Info: (Formerly Practice Under the California Corporate Securities Law), Yr. Est. 1968, Looseleaf
Subscriptions: $300/copy

California Corporations
Code and Corporate
Securities Rules   *Business*

Publishing Co: Matthew Bender & Co., 11 Penn Plaza, New York, NY 10001-2006 Fax # (212) 244-3188; Title Tel # (212) 967-7707
Personnel: Editor-G. Leatherman
Editorial Description: All code sections affected by current legislation, indicating section amended, added or indicating section amended, added or repealed & enactment chapter number. Detailed legislative history of each section. Rules of the Corporations Commissioner.
General Info: Annually, Looseleaf
Subscriptions: $33/copy

California Deposition and
Discovery Practice   *Business*

Publishing Co: Matthew Bender & Co., 11 Penn Plaza, New York, NY 10001-2006 Fax # (212) 244-3188; Title Tel # (212) 967-7707
Personnel: Editor-D. Coffee
Editorial Description: Complete guide, with law, text, annotated forms, & procedural checklist to every phase of discovery procedure in civil cases. Thorough coverage of all methods of obtaining discovery under the Civil Discovery Act of 1986, as well as extensive discussion of privileges, motion procedure, & sanctions.
General Info: Yr. Est. 1958, Irregular, Looseleaf
Subscriptions: $300/copy

California Employer
See: EMPLOYMENT

California Employer Advisor
See: EMPLOYMENT

California Employment Law
See: INDUSTRIAL RELATIONS/PERSONNEL

California Employment Law
Monitor   *Business*

Publishing Co: M. Lee Smith Publishers & Printers ,LCC, P.O. Box 198867, 162 Fourth Avenue North, Nashville, TN 37219-8867; Title Tel # (615) 242-7395 Title Fax # (615) 256-6601
Personnel: Publisher-M Lee Smith, Mng. Editor-Glenn Totten, Circ. Mgr.-Kathy Bradford, Mktg. Dir.-David Yates
General Info: (Formerly BNA California Employee Relations Report), Yr. Est. 1991, Monthly
Subscriptions: Indv. $267
Printing Co: M. Lee Smith Publishers & Printers ,LLC, PO Box 198867, 162 Fourth Avenue, Nashville, TN 37219-8867 Tel # (615) 242-7395, Fax # (615) 256-6601

California Employment Law Reporter
See: INDUSTRIAL RELATIONS/PERSONNEL

California Environmental
Law and Land Use
Practice   *Business*

Publishing Co: Matthew Bender & Co., 11 Penn Plaza, New York, NY 10001-2006 Tel # (212) 967-7707 Fax # (212) 244-3188
Editorial Description: Written by a host of environmental & land use specialists who practice in the private & public sectors & represent all points of view. Offering a wealth of practical information, the authors cover the entire scope of the law.
General Info: Yr. Est. 1989, Irregular, Looseleaf

California Family Law
Monthly   *Business*

Publishing Co: Matthew Bender & Co., 11 Penn Plaza, New York, NY 10001-2006 Tel # (212) 967-7707 Fax # (212) 244-3188
Editorial Description: Complements California Family Law--Practice and Procedure, covering recent cases, legislation, rules of court, and other developments in California family law each month.
General Info: Yr. Est. 1984, Monthly, Looseleaf

California Family Law-
Practice and Procedure   *Business*

Publishing Co: Matthew Bender & Co., 11 Penn Plaza, New York, NY 10001-2006 Fax # (212) 244-3188; Title Tel # (212) 967-7707
Personnel: Editor-R. Kojima
Editorial Description: Up-to-the-minute law and procedure for contemporary family law problems covering both the issues that arise in case of dissolution, as well as those related to ongoing family situations.
General Info: Yr. Est. 1978, Irregular, Looseleaf
Subscriptions: $550/copy

California Fish & Game
Code

Publishing Co: Gould Publications, Inc, 1333 N US Highway 17-92, Longwood, FL 32750-3724 Tel # (407) 695-9500 Fax # (407) 695-2906; Title Tel # (607) 724-3000
Editorial Description: Complete text of California fish & game code with addenda of related statutes.
General Info: Annually, Trim Size-5½ x 8½, Sheetfed press, 600 pages, Looseleaf
Subscriptions: Indv. $15, $20/copy

California Forms of
Pleading and Practice-
Annotated   *Business*

Publishing Co: Matthew Bender & Co., 11 Penn Plaza, New York, NY 10001-2006 Fax # (212) 244-3188; Title Tel # (212) 967-7707
Personnel: Editor-J. Shea
Editorial Description: Provides the right forms for all stages of civil actions and proceedings. The forms have been checked against published authorities, and many were based on forms drawn from files of private practitioners, law firms and courts.
General Info: Yr. Est. 1962, Irregular, Looseleaf
Subscriptions: $2,450/copy

California Insurance
Law & Regulation
Report

Publishing Co: Shepard's/McGraw-Hill, Inc., 555 Middle Creek Pky, Colorado Springs, CO 80921-3622; Title Tel # (719) 488-3000 Title Fax # (719) 481-7448
Personnel: Editor-John DiMugno, Production Mgr.-Cheryl Everitt, Adv. Dir.-Peggy Ives, Art Dir.-Leigh Vidakovich
General Info: Yr. Est. 1989, Monthly
Subscriptions: Indv. $365
List Rental: List Management Co.: The Lake Group, 411 Theodore Freund Ave., Rye, NY 10580-1497 Tel # (914) 925-2400, Fax # (914) 925-2499, Actives: 40,212, $130/M

California Insurance Law Report
See: INSURANCE

California Legal Forms-
Transaction Guide   *Business*

Publishing Co: Matthew Bender & Co., 11 Penn Plaza, New York, NY 10001-2006 Fax # (212) 244-3188; Title Tel # (212) 967-7707
Personnel: Editor-P. Getchell
Editorial Description: Basic legal guide to business transactions in California.
General Info: Yr. Est. 1968, Irregular, Looseleaf
Subscriptions: $1,825/copy

California Penal Code

Publishing Co: Gould Publications, Inc, 1333 N US Highway 17-92, Longwood, FL 32750-3724 Tel # (407) 695-9500 Fax # (407) 695-2906; Title Tel # (607) 724-3000
Editorial Description: Complete text of California Penal Code with related statutes.
General Info: Annually, Trim Size-5$\frac{1}{2}$ x 8$\frac{1}{2}$, Sheetfed press, 1,400 pages, No Color, Looseleaf
Subscriptions: Indv. $16, $25/copy

California Penal Code Slide Rule

Publishing Co: Gould Publications, Inc, 1333 N US Highway 17-92, Longwood, FL 32750-3724 Tel # (407) 695-9500 Fax # (407) 695-2906; Title Tel # (607) 724-3000
Editorial Description: Offenses in the Penal Code are quickly referenced with this pocket slide rule.
General Info: Annually, Trim Size-3$\frac{3}{4}$ x 8, Color-cover, Coated
Subscriptions: $6/copy

California Points and Authorities   *Business*

Publishing Co: Matthew Bender & Co., 11 Penn Plaza, New York, NY 10001-2006 Fax # (212) 244-3188; Title Tel # (212) 967-7707
Personnel: Editor-D. Coffee
Editorial Description: Provides the necessary statutory & case law required in law and motion proceedings. Easily adaptable for use in trial & appellate briefs & researching jury instructions, the forms are designed to assist the attorney in arguing points of law at all states of litigation.
General Info: Yr. Est. 1965, Irregular, Looseleaf
Subscriptions: $995/copy

California Products Liability Actions
See: CONSUMER INTERESTS

California Real Estate Law and Practice
See: REAL ESTATE

California Real Estate Reporter
See: REAL ESTATE

California School Law Digest
See: EDUCATION

.

California Statesman's Legislative Survey   CPM: $117

Publishing Co: William Shearer, 8158 Palm St, Lemon Grove, CA 91945-3028; Title Tel # (619) 460-4484
Personnel: Publisher, Editor-William Shearer
Editorial Description: Covers federal & California legislation on various domestic issues.
General Info: Yr. Est. 1965, Monthly, 4 pages
Subscriptions: Indv. $15, Free To Qualified Recipient
Circulation: Total-1,700
Advertising: $200.

California Tort Reporter   *Business*

Publishing Co: Shepard's/McGraw-Hill, Inc., 555 Middle Creek Pky, Colorado Springs, CO 80921-3622; Title Tel # (719) 488-3000 Title Fax # (719) 481-7448
Personnel: Publisher-Jeanine Lincoln, Editor-Peggy Ives
General Info: Yr. Est. 1980, Monthly
Subscriptions: Indv. $290
List Rental: List Management Co.: The Lake Group, 411 Theodore Freund Ave., Rye, NY 10580-1497 Tel # (914) 925-2400, Fax # (914) 925-2499, Actives: 40,212, $130/M

California Vehicle Code

Publishing Co: Gould Publications, Inc, 1333 N US Highway 17-92, Longwood, FL 32750-3724 Tel # (407) 695-9500 Fax # (407) 695-2906; Title Tel # (607) 724-3000
Editorial Description: Complete text of California Vehicle Code with addenda of related statutes.
General Info: Annually, Trim Size-5$\frac{1}{2}$ x 8$\frac{1}{2}$, Sheetfed press, 1,120 pages, No Color, Looseleaf
Subscriptions: $19/copy

California Water Law & Policy Reporter

Publishing Co: Shepard's/McGraw-Hill, Inc., 555 Middle Creek Pky, Colorado Springs, CO 80921-3622; Title Tel # (719) 488-3000 Title Fax # (719) 481-7448
Personnel: Production Mgr.-Cheryl Everitt, Adv. Dir.-Peggy Ives, Art Dir.-Leigh Vidakovich
General Info: Yr. Est. 1990, Monthly
Subscriptions: Indv. $295
List Rental: List Management Co.: The Lake Group, 411 Theodore Freund Ave., Rye, NY 10580-1497 Tel # (914) 925-2400, Fax # (914) 925-2499, Actives: 40,212, $130/M

Callaghan Communicator

Publishing Co: Clark Boardman Callaghan & Co., 155 Pfingsten Rd., Deerfield, IL 60015
Acquistions: Publication Bought, Publication Sold

Canada Corporations Law Reporter   *Business*

Publishing Co: CCH Canadian Ltd., 6 Garamond Ct., North York, ON M3C 1Z5 Canada Fax # (416) 444-8011 Parent Co.-CCH, Inc., Riverwoods; Title Tel # (416) 441-2992 Title Fax # (416) 444-9011
Editorial Description: Federal and province corporation laws. Foreign investment controls, combines investigation, bankruptcy and winding-up laws. Relevant Acts in full text, court decision and forms.
General Info: (Formerly Dominion Companies Law Reports), Yr. Est. 1945, Monthly, Trim Size-6 x 9, Web press, No Color, Looseleaf
Subscriptions: Can. $480

Canada Income Tax Guide
See: TAXES

Canadian Commercial Law Guide   *Business*

Publishing Co: CCH Canadian Ltd., 6 Garamond Ct., North York, ON M3C 1Z5 Canada Fax # (416) 444-8011 Parent Co.-CCH, Inc., Riverwoods; Title Tel # (416) 441-2992 Title Fax # (416) 444-9011
Personnel: Editor-Manuel Berenguel
Editorial Description: Commentary and texts on federal and provincial laws relating to consumer protection, sales contracts, conditional sales, installment sales, chattel mortgages, bills of sale etc.
General Info: (Formerly Canadian Sales and Credit Law Guide), Yr. Est. 1967, Monthly, Trim Size-6 x 9, Web press, No Color, Looseleaf
Subscriptions: Can. $475

Canadian Computer Law Reporter

Publishing Co: Insight Press, 55 University Avenue, Suite 1700, Toronto, ON M5J 2V6 Canada; Title Tel # (416) 777-2020
Personnel: Publisher-Robert Ross, Editor-Susie Chin, Promotion Dir.-Jane Neveleff
General Info: Yr. Est. 1983, Monthly, Web press, 12 pages, ISSN: 0822-6709
Subscriptions: Indv. $357
List Rental: Rents Lists

Canadian Corporations Law Guide

Publishing Co: CCH Canadian Ltd., 6 Garamond Ct., North York, ON M3C 1Z5 Canada Tel # (416) 441-2992 Fax # (416) 444-8011 Parent Co.-CCH, Inc., Riverwoods
Editorial Description: Spans law and practice affecting corporations organized under Canada Business Corporations Act.
General Info: Monthly, Looseleaf

Canadian Current Income Tax Proposals
See: TAXES

Canadian Employment Law   *Business*

Publishing Co: M. Lee Smith Publishers & Printers ,LCC, P.O. Box 198867, 162 Fourth Avenue North, Nashville, TN 37219-8867 Tel # (615) 242-7395 Fax # (615) 256-6601
Personnel: Publisher-M. Lee Smith, Editor-Brian Smeenk, Circ. Mgr.-Cathy Bradford, Mktg. Dir.-Dave Yates
Editorial Description: Published for US companies with editorial by McCarthy Tetrault -- Canada's largest law firm.
General Info: Yr. Est. 1994, Monthly, Trim Size-8$\frac{1}{2}$ x 11, 8 pages, ISSN: 1073-5720, 2 Color
Subscriptions: Indv. $177
List Rental: Rents Lists

Canadian Employment Safety and Health Guide
See: SAFETY

Canadian Energy News
See: ENERGY

Canadian Energy Program Reporter
See: ENERGY

Canadian Environmental Control Newsletter
See: ENVIRONMENT & ECOLOGY

Canadian Estate Planning & Administration Reporter   *Business*

Publishing Co: CCH, Inc., 2700 Lake Cook Rd., Riverwoods, IL 60015 Parent Co.-Kluwer Law & Taxation Publishers, Cambridge; Title Tel # (847) 267-7000 Title Fax # (800) 224-8299
Editorial Description: Commentary on estate planning and administration in Canada, including co-ownership of property, inter-vivos transfers, tax havens, will planning, trusts, etc.
General Info: Yr. Est. 1945, Monthly, Trim Size-6 x 9, Offset press, No Color, Looseleaf
Subscriptions: Indv. $515, Can. $380

Canadian Family Law Guide
See: FAMILY

Canadian Health Facilities Law Guide
See: HEALTH

Canadian Income Tax Act, Regulations & Rulings
See: TAXES

Canadian Insurance Law
Reporter *Business*

Publishing Co: CCH Canadian Ltd., 6 Garamond Ct., North York, ON M3C 1Z5 Canada
Fax # (416) 444-8011 Parent Co.-CCH, Inc., Riverwoods; Title Tel # (416) 441-2992
Title Fax # (416) 444-9011
Editorial Description: Full text decisions from provincial and federal courts on insurance contracts,
life, health, accident, fire, casualty, automobile, etc.
General Info: Yr. Est. 1945, Monthly, Trim Size-6 x 9, Web press, No Color, Looseleaf
Subscriptions: Can. $415

Canadian Insurance Law
Service *Business*

Publishing Co: Stone & Cox Ltd., 111 Peter St., #202, Toronto, ON M5V 2H1 Canada;
Title Tel # (416) 599-0772 Title Fax # (416) 599-0867
Personnel: Editor-B. Fraser, Circ. Mgr.-John Wyndham
Editorial Description: Statute law of each Canadian province and the Dominion as it affects
insurance operations. Amendments regulations and orders modifying the law.
General Info: Yr. Est. 1929, 13x/yr., 750 pages, No Color, Looseleaf
Subscriptions: Can. $1,100, $165/copy
Circulation: Total-600

Canadian Labour Law
Reporter *Business*

Publishing Co: CCH Canadian Ltd., 6 Garamond Ct., North York, ON M3C 1Z5 Canada
Fax # (416) 444-8011 Parent Co.-CCH, Inc., Riverwoods; Title Tel # (416) 441-2992
Title Fax # (416) 444-9011
Personnel: Editor-Theodora Opie
Editorial Description: Canadian Federal and Provincial labour laws, umemployement insurance.
General Info: Yr. Est. 1946, Semi-monthly, Trim Size-6 x 9, Web press, No Color, Looseleaf
Subscriptions: Can. $675

Canadian Law Libraries
See: LIBRARY

Canadian Occupational Safety & Health Law Monthly Report
See: SAFETY

Canadian Patent Reporter
See: PATENTS/COPYRIGHTS/TRADE MARKS

Canadian Plains Bulletin
See: ENVIRONMENT & ECOLOGY

Canadian Sales Tax Reporter
See: TAXES

Canadian Securities Law Reporter
See: INVESTMENT

Canadian Small Business Guide
See: BUSINESS & INDUSTRY

Canadian Tax Forms
See: TAXES

Canadian Tax Objection & Appeal Procedures
See: TAXES

Canadian Tax Reporter
See: TAXES

Canadian Transportation Law Reporter
See: TRAFFIC & TRANSPORTATION

Canadian Weekly Law
Sheet

Publishing Co: Butterworths, 75 Clegg Rd., Markham, ON L6G 1A1 Canada Tel # (905) 479-2665
Fax # (905) 479-2826; Title Tel # (416) 479-2665
Editorial Description: Contains brief summaries of reported court cases from all across Canada, plus
selected cases from Tax Appeal Board.
General Info: Yr. Est. 1959, Weekly
Subscriptions: Indv. $85

Capital Cases Benchbook *Association*

Publishing Co: Natl. Judicial College, Univ. Of Nevada, Reno, NV 89557-0001 Tel # (702) 784-6747
Fax # (702) 784-4234
Editorial Description: It includes guidelines for dealing with aggravating or mitigating evidence
offered during the penalty phase, coping with the myriad of challenges and issues common to this
type of litigation, evaluating requests for extraordinary costs, controlling jury selection, ensuring
effective case management, ruling on post-conviction remedies, motions, and more.
Subscriptions: Indv. $35, $35/copy

Capital Sources in Real Estate
See: REAL ESTATE

Capital West

Publishing Co: Mason West Co., 610 A E Battlefield, Suite #246, Springfield, TX 65807-4865;
Title Tel # (303) 238-7786
Personnel: Editor-Mason West
General Info: Yr. Est. 1989, Monthly

Carolina Justice Policy Center News
See: LAW ENFORCEMENT & PENOLOGY

Case Evaluation Manual
See: LAW ENFORCEMENT & PENOLOGY

Case Evaluation/Basic Settlement Value Software
See: BUSINESS & INDUSTRY

Center on Social Welfare Policy and Law Library Bulletin
See: LIBRARY

Champion *Association* CPM: $141

Publishing Co: Natl. Assn. of Criminal Defense Lawyers, 1627 K Street NW, Suite 1200,
Washington, DC 20006; Title Tel # (202) 872-8688 Title Fax # (202) 331-8269
Personnel: Editor, Editorial Page Ed., Bk. Rev. Ed.-Richard Bing, Adv. Mgr.-Steven Fraziery, Art Dir.-
Cathy Johnson, Mktg. Dir.-Steven Frazier
Editorial Description: The Champion's purposes are: to serve as a natl. forum for exchange of
information of interest & benefit to criminal defense lawyers; to further the assns. scientific &
educational aims; to serve as a natl. news medium directly relating to the members & heir chosen
field.
General Info: Yr. Est. 1979, 10x/yr., Offset press, 48 pages, ISSN: 0744-9488, 25% ads, 4 Color,
Coated, Saddle-stitched
Subscriptions: Indv. $75, Inst. $75, $5/copy
Circulation: Total-9,000
Advertising: $1,275. Accepts Inserts.
List Rental: Actives: 9,000, $100/M

Chapter 11 Update *Business*

Publishing Co: Andrews Publications, Inc., 1646 West Chester Pike, PO Box 1000, Westtown, PA
19395; Title Tel # (610) 399-6600 Title Fax # (610) 399-6610
Personnel: Publisher-John E. Backe, Editor-Donna Higgins, Mktg. Dir.-Andrew Katz
Editorial Description: Monitors all the significant legal proceedings associated with the growing
number of corporate reorganizations under Chapter 11 in bankruptcy courts nationwide.
General Info: Yr. Est. 1991, Monthly, Trim Size-8½ x 11, 10 pages, ISSN: 1055-9477
Subscriptions: Indv. $450, $23/copy
Advertising: Inquire for rates.
List Rental: Actives: 1,069, $110/M

Checks, Drafts and Notes
See: BANKING & FINANCE

Chemical Regulation Reporter
See: CHEMISTRY & CHEMICALS

Chemical Waste Litigation
Reporter

Publishing Co: Chem. Waste Lit. Rep. Inc., 1519 Connecticut Ave., Ste. 20, 0, Washington, DC
20036-1115; Title Tel # (202) 462-5755
Personnel: Publisher-Neil Cohen, Editor-John Clewette
Editorial Description: Articles on and case pleadings in RICO litigation.
General Info: (Formerly Chemical & Radiation Waste Litigation Reporter), Yr. Est. 1984, Monthly,
Sheetfed press, 150 pages, No Color, Looseleaf
Subscriptions: Indv. $1,400

Chicago Municipal Code
Handbook

Publishing Co: Gould Publications, Inc, 1333 N US Highway 17-92, Longwood, FL 32750-3724
Tel # (407) 695-9500 Fax # (407) 695-2906; Title Tel # (607) 724-3000
Editorial Description: Concise presentation of chapter sections from Chicago Municipal Code.
General Info: Annually, Trim Size-5½ x 8½, Sheetfed press, 610 pages, No Color, Looseleaf
Subscriptions: $20/copy

Chicago Stock Exchange Guide
See: BANKING & FINANCE

Child Custody and
Visitation Law and
Practice *Business*

Publishing Co: Matthew Bender & Co., 11 Penn Plaza, New York, NY 10001-2006
Tel # (212) 967-7707 Fax # (212) 244-3188
Editorial Description: This national publication covers all custody and visitation matters handled by
the family law practitioner.
General Info: Yr. Est. 1983, Irregular, Looseleaf

China Laws for Foreign Business-Business Regulation

Publishing Co: CCH, Inc., 2700 Lake Cook Rd., Riverwoods, IL 60015 Parent Co.-Kluwer Law & Taxation Publishers, Cambridge; Title Tel # (847) 267-7000 Title Fax # (800) 224-8299
Editorial Description: Contains the People's Republic of China's laws affecting the conduct of foreign trade in mainland China. Laws are in official Chinese language with precise English translations.
General Info: Irregular, Looseleaf
Circulation: Total-1,200

Choices
See: HEALTH

Church Council on Justice & Corrections, Update
See: RELIGIOUS & THEOLOGICAL

Church Law & Tax Report

Publishing Co: Christian Ministry Resources, 617 Greenbrook Pky, Matthews, NC 28105-7745; Title Tel # (704) 841-8066 Title Fax # (704) 846-5923
Personnel: Publisher-James Cobble, Editor-Richard Hammar
Editorial Description: Review of legal and tax developments affecting ministers and churches.
General Info: Yr. Est. 1987, Bi-monthly, Trim Size-8½ x 11, 32 pages, Saddle-stitched
Subscriptions: Indv. $78
Circulation: Total-16,000
List Rental: List Management Co.: Bernice Bush Co./Springdale Lists, 15052 Springdale St., Huntington Beach, CA 92649-1178 Tel # (714) 891-3344, Fax # (714) 897-0650, Actives: 20,000, $90/M

Citation, The

Publishing Co: American Medical Association, 515 N. State St., Chicago, IL 60610 Tel # (312) 464-4512 Fax # (312) 464-5834; Title Tel # (708) 438-2020 Title Fax # (708) 438-2299
Personnel: Editor-Kay Schraml
Editorial Description: Summaries of recent court decisions and legal developments affecting physicians and other health professionals.
General Info: Yr. Est. 1958, Semi-monthly, Trim Size-8½ x 11, Offset press, 12 pages, ISSN: 0009-7446, No Color
Subscriptions: Indv. $130, $7/copy
Circulation: Total-2,000

Citation
Business, Consumer

Publishing Co: Citation Corporation, 3538 Willow Valley Rd., Long Grove, IL 60047 Tel # (708) 438-2020; Title Fax # (312) 464-5846
General Info: Yr. Est. 1958, 24x/yr.
Subscriptions: Indv. $145
Acquistions: Publication Sold

Citator
Business

Publishing Co: Select Press, PO Box 37, Corte Madera, CA 94976-0037; Title Tel # (415) 924-1612 Title Fax # (415) 924-7179
General Info: Yr. Est. 1982, Monthly
Subscriptions: Indv. $365, Inst. $365
List Rental: Rents Lists

Civil Justice Roundtable

Publishing Co: Institute for Civil Justice-Rand Corp., 1700 Main St # 2138, Santa Monica, CA 90401-3208; Title Tel # (213) 393-0411
Personnel: Editor-Ginny Kuchta
General Info: Yr. Est. 1984, 2 pages
Circulation: Total-6,800

Civil Liberties
See: CIVIL RIGHTS

Civil Liberties
See: CIVIL RIGHTS

Civil Liberties Alert
See: CIVIL RIGHTS

Civil Penalty Case Digest Service
See: AERONAUTICS/ASTRONAUTICS

Civil RICO
Business

Publishing Co: Matthew Bender & Co., 11 Penn Plaza, New York, NY 10001-2006 Tel # (212) 967-7707 Fax # (212) 244-3188
Editorial Description: Responding to the growing use of civil RICO by private litigants after the Supreme Court's decision in Sedima, this all-inclusive publication fills the need for knowledgeable discussion of the substantive law, while incorporating a close examiniation of the practical problems & procedural issues involved when litigating a case.
General Info: Yr. Est. 1987, Irregular, Looseleaf

Civil RICO Litigation Reporter
Business

Publishing Co: Andrews Publications, Inc., 1646 West Chester Pike, PO Box 1000, Westtown, PA 19395; Title Tel # (610) 399-6600 Title Fax # (610) 399-6610
Personnel: Publisher-John Backe, Editor-Jay Steinberg, Mktg. Dir.-Andrew Katz
Editorial Description: Offers comprehensive coverage of the issues raised by the application of the Racketeer Influenced and Corrupt Organizations Act's provisions for civil actions.
General Info: Yr. Est. 1984, Monthly, Trim Size-8½ x 11, Mimeo press, 70 pages, ISSN: 0887-7874, No Color, Newsprint
Subscriptions: Indv. $800, $75/copy
List Rental: Actives: 100, $110/M

Civil RICO Report
Business

Publishing Co: LRP Publications, 747 Dresher Rd., P.O. Box 980, Horsham, PA 19044-0980 Tel # (215) 784-0910 Fax # (215) 784-0317
Personnel: Publisher-Ken Kahn, Editor-Lisa Baertlein
Editorial Description: Provides summaries of the latest Racketeer-Influenced and Corrupt Organization Act (RICO) complaints & decisions, as well as developments in federal or state RICO statutes.
General Info: Yr. Est. 1985, Weekly, Trim Size-8½ x 11, Sheetfed press, 8 pages, ISSN: 0884-0032, 2 Color, Newsprint
Subscriptions: Indv. $795, For. $795
Acquistions: Publication Bought, Publication Sold
List Rental: Rents Lists
Printing Co: Plymouth Printing, 1200 Cushing Pl SE, Washington, DC 20003-3599 Tel # (202) 488-7777, Fax # (202) 863-1078

Civil Rights/State Capitals
See: CIVIL RIGHTS

Claims Forum

Publishing Co: American Arbitration Assn., 140 W. 51 St., New York, NY 10020-1203 Tel # (212) 484-4000 Fax # (212) 541-4841; Title Tel # (212) 484-4010 Title Fax # (212) 765-4874
Personnel: Editor-Ted Pons, Promotion Dir.-Douglas French
Editorial Description: The insurance industry's use of alternative dispute resolution, the legal services of the American Arbitration Assns. is covered by the quarterly newsletter.
General Info: Yr. Est. 1987, Quarterly, Trim Size-8½ x 11, 8 pages, 2 Color, Matte
Circulation: Total-6,500
Printing Co: Sheridan Printing, 1425 3rd Ave, Alpha, NJ 08865-4695 Tel # (908) 454-0700, Fax # (908) 454-2554

Clark's Bank Deposits and Payments Monthly
See: BANKING & FINANCE

Clear News

Publishing Co: Council on Licensure, Enforcement & Regulation, Iron Works Pike, Box 11910, Lexington, KY 40578; Title Tel # (606) 231-1960 Title Fax # (606) 231-1943
Personnel: Editor-Pam Brinegar
General Info: Yr. Est. 1984, Quarterly, 8 pages, Color-cover, Matte
Subscriptions: Can. $25
Circulation: Total-3,500
Advertising: Inquire for rates.

Client Information Bulletin
See: ACCOUNTING

Code and Regulations
Business

Publishing Co: CCH, Inc., 2700 Lake Cook Rd., Riverwoods, IL 60015 Parent Co.-Kluwer Law & Taxation Publishers, Cambridge; Title Tel # (847) 267-7000 Title Fax # (800) 224-8299
Editorial Description: Internal Revenue Code with final and proposed income, withholding estate and gift tax regulations.
General Info: Yr. Est. 1946, Monthly, Trim Size-6 x 9, Web press, 280 pages, No Color, Looseleaf
Subscriptions: Indv. $362

Coffee, Sugar & Cocoa Exchange
See: INVESTMENT

Collected Legislation of Russia
Business

Publishing Co: Oceana Publications, Inc., 75 Main St, Dobbs Ferry, NY 10522-1601 Tel # (914) 693-8100; Title Tel # (914) 693-1320 Title Fax # (914) 693-0402
Personnel: Editor-William E. Butler, Production Mgr.-Mike Wortzman, Mktg. Dir.-John Downey
General Info: (Formerly Collected Legislation of the USSR & Constituent Republics), Irregular, Trim Size-7 x 10, ISSN: 0-379-104, Looseleaf
Subscriptions: Indv. $150

Collection of Bibliographic & Research Resources
Business

Publishing Co: Oceana Publications, Inc., 75 Main St, Dobbs Ferry, NY 10522-1601 Tel # (914) 693-8100; Title Tel # (914) 693-1320 Title Fax # (914) 693-0402
Personnel: Production Mgr.-Mike Wortzman, Mktg. Dir.-John Downey
General Info: Yr. Est. 1984, Irregular, Trim Size-7 x 10, ISSN: 0886-6724, Looseleaf
Subscriptions: Indv. $300

College of Law
Enforcement Newsletter

Publishing Co: Eastern Kentucky Univ., 217 Wallace Bldg., Richmond, KY 40475
   Tel # (606) 622-1000; Title Tel # (606) 622-1155
Personnel: Editor-Bruce Wolford
General Info: Yr. Est. 1980, 8 pages
Circulation: Total-4,000

Collier on Bankruptcy   *Business*

Publishing Co: Matthew Bender & Co., 11 Penn Plaza, New York, NY 10001-2006
   Fax # (212) 244-3188; Title Tel # (212) 967-7707
Personnel: Editor in Chief-Lawrence P. King, Editor-M. Diamond
Editorial Description: Detailed discussion, by the leading bankruptcy authorities, of the Bankruptcy Code as amended.
General Info: Yr. Est. 1979, Irregular, Looseleaf
Subscriptions: $1,250/copy

Collier Bankruptcy Cases   *Business*

Publishing Co: Matthew Bender & Co., 11 Penn Plaza, New York, NY 10001-2006
   Fax # (212) 244-3188; Title Tel # (212) 967-7707
Personnel: Editor-M. Diamond
Editorial Description: Full reprints of cases decided under the Code, preceded by a summary of the Code, preceded by a summary of the case & points of law on which the court based its decision.
General Info: Yr. Est. 1974, Bi-weekly, 250 pages, Looseleaf
Subscriptions: $450/copy

Collier Bankruptcy
Compensation Guide   *Business*

Publishing Co: Matthew Bender & Co., 11 Penn Plaza, New York, NY 10001-2006
   Tel # (212) 967-7707 Fax # (212) 244-3188
Personnel: Editor in Chief-Lawrence P. King
Editorial Description: A complete examination of the Code provisions, case law & current practice trends relevant to the compensation of attorneys, trustees & other professionals involved in bankruptcy cases. Contains substantive analysis as well as stratregic & practical guidance.
General Info: Yr. Est. 1988, Irregular, Looseleaf

Collier Bankruptcy
Examption Guide   *Business*

Publishing Co: Matthew Bender & Co., 11 Penn Plaza, New York, NY 10001-2006
   Tel # (212) 967-7707 Fax # (212) 244-3188
Personnel: Editor in Chief-Lawrence P. King
Editorial Description: A compilation of exemptions available in every state and territory.
General Info: Yr. Est. 1982, Irregular, Looseleaf

Collier Bankruptcy Forms
Manual   *Business*

Publishing Co: Matthew Bender & Co., 11 Penn Plaza, New York, NY 10001-2006
   Fax # (212) 244-3188; Title Tel # (212) 967-7707
Personnel: Editor-M. Diamond
Editorial Description: Specific forms for specific situations in bankruptcy proceedings.
General Info: Yr. Est. 1963, Annually, Looseleaf
Subscriptions: $102/copy

Collier Bankrupcy Manual   *Business*

Publishing Co: Matthew Bender & Co., 11 Penn Plaza, New York, NY 10001-2006
   Fax # (212) 244-3188; Title Tel # (212) 967-7707
Personnel: Editor-M. Diamond
Editorial Description: The essential substantive analysis needed for handling a case under the Bankruptcy Code.
General Info: Yr. Est. 1948, Irregular, Looseleaf
Subscriptions: $300/copy

Collier Bankruptcy Practice
Guide   *Business*

Publishing Co: Matthew Bender & Co., 11 Penn Plaza, New York, NY 10001-2006
   Tel # (212) 967-7707 Fax # (212) 244-3188
Personnel: Editor in Chief-Asa S. Herzog, Editor in Chief-Lawrence P. King
Editorial Description: The first complete strategic & procedural guide for all cases instituted under the Code. Organized according to the sequence of day-to-day practice, with contributions from over 35 prominent bankruptcy attorneys.
General Info: Yr. Est. 1981, Irregular, Looseleaf

Collier Family Law and the
Bankruptcy Code   *Business*

Publishing Co: Matthew Bender & Co., 11 Penn Plaza, New York, NY 10001-2006
   Tel # (212) 967-7707 Fax # (212) 244-3188
Personnel: Editor in Chief-Lawrence P. King
Editorial Description: For both the general practitioner & the matrimonial specialist, a comprehensive, practice-oriented guide to the impact of bankruptcy on family law issues. Examines the Bankruptcy Code with emphasis on provisions directly related to family law.
General Info: Yr. Est. 1990, Irregular, Looseleaf

Collier Farm Bankruptcy   *Business*

Publishing Co: Matthew Bender & Co., 11 Penn Plaza, New York, NY 10001-2006
   Tel # (212) 967-7707 Fax # (212) 244-3188
Personnel: Editor in Chief-Lawrence P. King
Editorial Description: A thorough treatment of the substantive & procedural issues involved in representing agricultural clients in insolvency matters. Covers options available under the Code as well as intricacies of agricultural financing.
General Info: Yr. Est. 1989, Irregular, Looseleaf

Collier Labor Law and the
Bankruptcy Code   *Consumer*

Publishing Co: Matthew Bender & Co., 11 Penn Plaza, New York, NY 10001-2006
   Tel # (212) 967-7707 Fax # (212) 244-3188
Personnel: Editor in Chief-Lawrence P. King
Editorial Description: Offering both substantive & procedural material, provides guidance for handling labor matters once a bankruptcy case has been commenced. With numerous forms, sample collective bargaining agreements, sample plans & other practice aides throughtout.
General Info: Yr. Est. 1989, Irregular, Looseleaf

Collier Lending Institutions
and the Bankruptcy Code   *Business*

Publishing Co: Matthew Bender & Co., 11 Penn Plaza, New York, NY 10001-2006
   Tel # (212) 967-7707 Fax # (212) 244-3188
Personnel: Editor in Chief-Lawrence P. King
Editorial Description: A complete, practice-oriented guide to the impact of bankruptcy on lending transactions.
General Info: Yr. Est. 1986, Irregular, Looseleaf

Collier Real Estate Transactions and the Bankruptcy Code
See: REAL ESTATE

Colorado Employment
Law Letter   *Business*

Publishing Co: M. Lee Smith Publishers & Printers ,LCC, P.O. Box 198867, 162 Fourth Avenue North, Nashville, TN 37219-8867; Title Tel # (615) 242-7395 Title Fax # (615) 256-6601
Personnel: Publisher-M Lee Smith, Editor-John Husband, Circ. Mgr.-Cathy Bradford, Mktg. Dir.-David Yates
Editorial Description: Review of employment law developments that affect Colorado employers.
General Info: Yr. Est. 1992, Monthly, Trim Size-8½ x 11, 8 pages, ISSN: 1059-504X, 2 Color
Subscriptions: Indv. $97
List Rental: Rents Lists
Printing Co: M. Lee Smith Publishers & Printers ,LLC, PO Box 198867, 162 Fourth Avenue, Nashville, TN 37219-8867 Tel # (615) 242-7395, Fax # (615) 256-6601

Colorado Environmental
Compliance Update   *Business*

Publishing Co: M. Lee Smith Publishers & Printers ,LCC, P.O. Box 198867, 162 Fourth Avenue North, Nashville, TN 37219-8867 Tel # (615) 242-7395 Fax # (615) 256-6601
Personnel: Publisher-M. Lee Smith, Editor-Edward McGath, Circ. Mgr.-Cathy Bradford, Mktg. Dir.-Dave Yates
General Info: Yr. Est. 1993, Monthly, ISSN: 1072-057X
Subscriptions: Indv. $117
List Rental: Rents Lists
Printing Co: M. Lee Smith Publishers & Printers ,LLC, PO Box 198867, 162 Fourth Avenue, Nashville, TN 37219-8867 Tel # (615) 242-7395, Fax # (615) 256-6601

Commercial and Consumer
Warranties--Drafting,
Performing and Litigating   *Business*

Publishing Co: Matthew Bender & Co., 11 Penn Plaza, New York, NY 10001-2006
   Tel # (212) 967-7707 Fax # (212) 244-3188
Editorial Description: The first complete work on one of the most actively litigated areas of commercial law, offering in-depth analyses & practical discussions, supported by extensive case authority from all jurisdictions.
General Info: Yr. Est. 1987, Irregular, Looseleaf

Commercial Damages: A
Guide To Remedies in
Business Litigation   *Business*

Publishing Co: Matthew Bender & Co., 11 Penn Plaza, New York, NY 10001-2006
   Tel # (212) 967-7707 Fax # (212) 244-3188
Editorial Description: Written by prominent scholars and practitioners in commercial law.
General Info: Yr. Est. 1986, Irregular, Looseleaf

Commercial Damages
Reporter   *Business*

Publishing Co: Matthew Bender & Co., 11 Penn Plaza, New York, NY 10001-2006
   Tel # (212) 967-7707 Fax # (212) 244-3188
Personnel: Editor in Chief-Charles L. Knapp
Editorial Description: Features an article, written by a practitioner or scholar in the commercial law field, examining a current issue in the area of commercial damages. Also included are annotations of state & federal cases, providing a convenient means of keeping up-to-datewith recent case law & new developments.
General Info: Yr. Est. 1986, 8x/yr., Looseleaf

Commercial Finance
See: BANKING & FINANCE

Commercial Insolvency Reporter

Publishing Co: Butterworth Legal Publishers, 8 Industrial Way # C, Salem, NH 03079-2837
Fax # (603) 898-9858; Title Tel # (603) 898-9664
Personnel: Editor-E. Bruce Leonard
General Info: Bi-monthly, 2 Color, Newsprint
Subscriptions: Indv. $150
Circulation: Total-50,000

Commercial Law Handbook

Publishing Co: Gould Publications, Inc, 1333 N US Highway 17-92, Longwood, FL 32750-3724
Tel # (407) 695-9500 Fax # (407) 695-2906; Title Tel # (607) 724-3000
Editorial Description: Complete UCC with official comments & pertinent commercial statutes.
General Info: Annually, Trim Size-5½ x 8½, Sheetfed press, 1,100 pages, No Color, Looseleaf
Subscriptions: $25/copy

Commercial Law Manual *Business*

Publishing Co: Matthew Bender & Co., 11 Penn Plaza, New York, NY 10001-2006
Tel # (212) 967-7707 Fax # (212) 244-3188
Editorial Description: Provides comprehensive, substantive and transactional analysis of the Uniform Commerical Code.
General Info: Yr. Est. 1991, Irregular, Looseleaf

Commercial Laws of the World *Business*

Publishing Co: Foreign Tax Law Publishers, Inc., PO Box 2189, Ormond Beach, FL 32175-2189;
Title Tel # (904) 253-5785 Title Fax # (904) 257-3003
Editorial Description: Contains company laws, commercial codes and related laws for over 100 countries. Many full-text translations. Some countries include labor laws.
General Info: Yr. Est. 1947, Irregular, Trim Size-8½ x 11, Sheetfed press, 100 pages, No Color, Looseleaf
Subscriptions: Indv. $1,250, $100/copy

Commercial Lease Law Insider
See: REAL ESTATE

Commercial Leasing Law & Strategy *Business*

Publishing Co: Leader Publications, Inc., 345 Park Avenue South, New York, NY 10010 Parent Co.-New York Law Publishing Co., New York; Title Tel # (212) 545-6170 Title Fax # (212) 696-1848
Personnel: Publisher-Stuart Wise, Editor-Stephanie McEvily, Circ. Mgr.-Kerry Kyle, Promotion Dir.-Rose-Ann Morangelli
Editorial Description: Reports on laws & developments in the leasing of commercial property.
General Info: Yr. Est. 1988, Monthly, Trim Size-8½ x 11, Offset press, 8 pages, ISSN: 0898-5634, Color, Newsprint
Subscriptions: Indv. $195, $16/copy
Acquistions: Publication Sold
Printing Co: Columbus Bookbinding, 1343 Belfast Ave, Columbus, OH 31904 Tel # (206) 323-9313, Fax # (206) 323-2987

Commercial Loan Documentation Guide
See: BANKING & FINANCE

Commercial Paper Under the UCC *Business*

Publishing Co: Matthew Bender & Co., 11 Penn Plaza, New York, NY 10001-2006
Tel # (212) 967-7707 Fax # (212) 244-3188
Editorial Description: An in-depth treatise on Article 3 of the Uniform Commerical Code. Specific chapters cover forms of transfer, contractual obligations of parties, electractual obligations of parties, electronic fund transfer and more.
General Info: Yr. Est. 1972, Irregular, Looseleaf

Commerical Law Report *Business*

Publishing Co: Matthew Bender & Co., 11 Penn Plaza, New York, NY 10001-2006
Tel # (212) 967-7707 Fax # (212) 244-3188
Editorial Description: Provides timely analysis of notable commerical cases and trend arising under the UCC.
General Info: Yr. Est. 1987, Monthly

Commission Update *Business, Association*

Publishing Co: Commission on Accreditation for Law Enforcement Agencies, In, 10306 Eaton Pl Ste 320, Fairfax, VA 22030-2201; Title Tel # (703) 352-4225 Title Fax # (703) 591-2206
Personnel: Editor-Beth Denniston
Editorial Description: Reports of law enforcement agency accreditation activities & benefits.
General Info: Yr. Est. 1980, Quarterly, Trim Size-8½ x 11, Sheetfed press, 4 pages, 2 Color, Newsprint
Circulation: Total-9,500
Printing Co: Baker-Webster Printing, 1121 5th St NW, Washington, DC 20001-3690
Tel # (202) 628-8061

Committee
See: GOVERNMENT

Committee on Native American Struggles Newsletter
See: CIVIL RIGHTS

Committee Report *Business, Consumer*

Publishing Co: Lawyers' Committee for Civil Rights Under Law, 1450 G St NW Ste 400, Washington, DC 20005-2001; Title Tel # (202) 662-8600
Personnel: Editor-Nancy Perkins, Art Dir.-Joan Owings
Editorial Description: Articles & features discussing the development & application of Civil Rights Law & other areas of interest in Civil Rights.
General Info: Yr. Est. 1970, Quarterly, Trim Size-8½ x 11, 22 pages, Saddle-stitched
Subscriptions: Indv. $20, Inst. $20
Acquistions: Publication Bought
Circulation: Total-4,000

Commodity Futures Law Reports
See: INVESTMENT

Common Market Reporter
See: INTERNATIONAL TRADE

Communications Law *Business*

Publishing Co: Matthew Bender & Co., 11 Penn Plaza, New York, NY 10001-2006
Tel # (212) 967-7707 Fax # (212) 244-3188
Editorial Description: Examines the substantive, procedural & strategic aspects of the law affecting cable television & other video technologies.
General Info: Yr. Est. 1983, Irregular, Looseleaf

Communications Lawyer *Association*

Publishing Co: American Bar Association, 750 N. Lake Shore Dr., Chicago, IL 60611-4497
Tel # (312) 988-6115 Fax # (312) 988-6030; Title Tel # (312) 988-5522 Title Fax # (319) 988-5528
Personnel: Editor-Harvey Zuckman, Production Mgr.-Marla Hillery
Editorial Description: Provides a review of significant communications law activities & developments.
General Info: Yr. Est. 1983, Quarterly, ISSN: 0737-7622
Subscriptions: Indv. $15, $4/copy
Circulation: Total-2,500
List Rental: Rents Lists

Community Association Law Reporter
See: REAL ESTATE

Comparative Negligence *Business*

Publishing Co: Matthew Bender & Co., 11 Penn Plaza, New York, NY 10001-2006
Tel # (212) 967-7707 Fax # (212) 244-3188
Editorial Description: For both plaintiff's & defendant's counsel, expert detailed analysis of the current status of comparative negligence in every state, as well as complete discussion of the effect of the doctrine on such areas as products liability, workers' compensation, wrongful death actions, conflict of laws & multi-party litigation.
General Info: Yr. Est. 1984, Irregular, Looseleaf

Compleat Lawyer *Association*

Publishing Co: American Bar Association, 750 N. Lake Shore Dr., Chicago, IL 60611-4497
Tel # (312) 988-6115 Fax # (312) 988-6030; Title Tel # (312) 988-5522 Title Fax # (319) 988-5528
Personnel: Editor-Bruce Davis
General Info: (Formerly Docket Call), Yr. Est. 1974, Quarterly, Ind/Abs/Online: Leg.Per.
Subscriptions: Indv. $3, $2/copy
Circulation: Total-83,000
List Rental: Rents Lists

Compliance Guide for Plan Administrators
See: INDUSTRIAL RELATIONS/PERSONNEL

Comptroller General Procurement Decisions
See: GOVERNMENT

Computer Contracts *Business*

Publishing Co: Matthew Bender & Co., 11 Penn Plaza, New York, NY 10001-2006
Tel # (212) 967-7707 Fax # (212) 244-3188
Editorial Description: Covers the full range of contracts for buying, selling, leasing & licensing hardware, software & services, with legal analysis & step-by-step guidance to help you handle contracts for computer users & vendors, marketing arrangements, software development, maintenance, licensing arrangemnt & telecommunications contracts.
General Info: Yr. Est. 1987, Irregular, Looseleaf

Computer Industry Litigation Reporter *Business*

Publishing Co: Andrews Publications, Inc., 1646 West Chester Pike, PO Box 1000, Westtown, PA 19395; Title Tel # (610) 399-6600 Title Fax # (610) 399-6610
Personnel: Publisher-John Backe, Editor-Donna Higgins, Mktg. Dir.-Andrew Katz
Editorial Description: Legal issues and they relate to hardware, software electronic databases and the computer industry in general.
General Info: Yr. Est. 1983, Bi-monthly, Trim Size-8½ x 11, Mimeo press, 80 pages, ISSN: 0740-1469, Ind/Abs/Online: NEWSNET, No Color, Newsprint
Subscriptions: Indv. $850, $40/copy
Advertising: Inquire for rates.
List Rental: Actives: 1,049, $110/M

Computer Law *Business*

Publishing Co: Matthew Bender & Co., 11 Penn Plaza, New York, NY 10001-2006
Tel # (212) 967-7707 Fax # (212) 244-3188
Editorial Description: Covers the concepts & techniques of evidence & discovery procedures as they apply to computer-based information, & to the protection of computer software under intellectual property laws.
General Info: Yr. Est. 1978, Irregular, Looseleaf

Computer Law & Tax Report
See: COMPUTERS & AUTOMATION

Computer Law Reporter
See: COMPUTERS & AUTOMATION

Computer Law Strategist

Publishing Co: Leader Publications, Inc., 345 Park Avenue South, New York, NY 10010 Parent Co.-New York Law Publishing Co., New York; Title Tel # (212) 545-6170 Title Fax # (212) 696-1848
Personnel: Publisher-Stuart Wise, Editor-Julian Millstein, Esq., Editor-Edward Pisacreta, Circ. Mgr.-Kerry Kyle, Mktg. Dir.-Rose-Ann Morangelei
Editorial Description: Legislative and case decision developments in law governing computers.
General Info: Yr. Est. 1984, Monthly, Trim Size-8½ x 11, Offset press, 8 pages, ISSN: 0747-8933, Color, Newsprint, Saddle-stitched
Subscriptions: Indv. $255, $21/copy
Acquistions: Publication Sold
Printing Co: Columbus Bookbinding, 1343 Belfast Ave, Columbus, OH 31904 Tel # (206) 323-9313, Fax # (206) 323-2987

Computing & Communications: Law & Protection Report
See: COMPUTERS & AUTOMATION

Confession Standards

Publishing Co: Gould Publications, Inc, 1333 N US Highway 17-92, Longwood, FL 32750-3724 Tel # (407) 695-9500 Fax # (407) 695-2906; Title Tel # (607) 724-3000
Editorial Description: Book of significant work on the law of confessions and a penetrating analysis of the new rules and problems yet to be resolved.
General Info: Annually, 150 pages, Looseleaf
Subscriptions: $10/copy

Confrontation   *Association*

Publishing Co: Jewish Lawyers Guild, 110 Wall St., New York, NY 10005-3801; Title Tel # (212) 227-8075

Congressional Action
See: CHAMBER OF COMMERCE

Connecticut Builder
See: CONSTRUCTION & BUILDING

Connecticut Criminal Laws

Publishing Co: Gould Publications, Inc, 1333 N US Highway 17-92, Longwood, FL 32750-3724 Tel # (407) 695-9500 Fax # (407) 695-2906; Title Tel # (607) 724-3000
Editorial Description: This book is a complete, accurate and up-to-date presentation of Title 53-53a, Title 54, Chapter 4205 of the General Statues of Connecticut and a comprehensive index.
General Info: Annually, 450 pages, Looseleaf
Subscriptions: $10/copy

Connecticut Employment
Law Letter   *Business*

Publishing Co: M. Lee Smith Publishers & Printers ,LCC, P.O. Box 198867, 162 Fourth Avenue North, Nashville, TN 37219-8867; Title Tel # (615) 242-7395 Title Fax # (615) 256-6601
Personnel: Editor-Ann Byrd, Circ. Mgr.-Cathy Bradford, Mktg. Dir.-Dave Yates
Editorial Description: Review of employment law developments that affect Connecticut employers.
General Info: Yr. Est. 1993, Monthly, Trim Size-8½ x 11, 8 pages, ISSN: 1064-4903, 2 Color
Subscriptions: Indv. $97
List Rental: Rents Lists
Printing Co: M. Lee Smith Publishers & Printers ,LLC, PO Box 198867, 162 Fourth Avenue, Nashville, TN 37219-8867 Tel # (615) 242-7395, Fax # (615) 256-6601

Connecticut
Environmental
Compliance Update   *Business*

Publishing Co: M. Lee Smith Publishers & Printers ,LCC, P.O. Box 198867, 162 Fourth Avenue North, Nashville, TN 37219-8867; Title Tel # (615) 242-7395 Title Fax # (615) 256-6601
Personnel: Publisher-M. Lee Smith, Editor-James Thompson, Circ. Mgr.-Cathy Bradford, Mktg. Dir.-Dave Yates
Editorial Description: Review of environmental law developments that affect Connecticut companies.
General Info: Yr. Est. 1992, Monthly, Trim Size-8½ x 11, 8 pages, ISSN: 1064-2382, 2 Color
Subscriptions: Indv. $107
List Rental: Rents Lists
Printing Co: Valley Web, 1299 Stowe Avenue, Medford, OR 97504 Tel # (503) 772-7039

Connecticut Law
Enforcement Handbook

Publishing Co: Gould Publications, Inc, 1333 N US Highway 17-92, Longwood, FL 32750-3724 Tel # (407) 695-9500 Fax # (407) 695-2906; Title Tel # (607) 724-3000
Editorial Description: A compact book listing current U.S. Supreme Court cases and constitutional criminal proceeding as well as selected statutes reduced into a series of elements.
General Info: Annually, 260 pages, Looseleaf
Subscriptions: $8/copy

Connecticut Law Journal

Publishing Co: Commission on Official Legal Publications, 111 Phoenix Ave., Office of Prod. & Distr., Enfield, CT 06082-4453; Title Tel # (203) 741-3027 Title Fax # (203) 745-2178
Personnel: Publications Director-Richard Hemenway
Editorial Description: Supreme, appellate & superior court decisions, regulations of CT. state agencies, legal notices.
General Info: Weekly, Sheetfed press, No Color, Looseleaf
Subscriptions: Indv. $180, $7/copy
Circulation: Total-6,000

Connecticut Motor
Vehicle & Traffic Laws

Publishing Co: Gould Publications, Inc, 1333 N US Highway 17-92, Longwood, FL 32750-3724 Tel # (407) 695-9500 Fax # (407) 695-2906; Title Tel # (607) 724-3000
Editorial Description: A complete presentation of the Motor Vehicle Laws of Connecticut.
General Info: Annually, 250 pages, Looseleaf
Subscriptions: $10/copy

Conservation
See: ENVIRONMENT & ECOLOGY

Consolidated Index to Units
1-5 of Bender's UCC
Service   *Business*

Publishing Co: Matthew Bender & Co., 11 Penn Plaza, New York, NY 10001-2006 Tel # (212) 967-7707 Fax # (212) 244-3188
Editorial Description: Brings together refences to all the volumes of the UCC Service. Listings are arranged under general topics as well as terms of art.
General Info: Yr. Est. 1972, Irregular, Looseleaf

Constitutions of the Countries of the World
See: POLITICS

Constitutions of
Dependencies & Special
Sovereignties   *Business, Consumer*

Publishing Co: Oceana Publications, Inc., 75 Main St, Dobbs Ferry, NY 10522-1601 Tel # (914) 693-8100; Title Tel # (914) 693-1320 Title Fax # (914) 693-0402
Personnel: Editor-A. Blaustein, Production Mgr.-Mike Wortzman, Adv. Dir.-Bert Flanz, Mktg. Dir.-John Downey
General Info: Yr. Est. 1975, Semi-annually, Trim Size-7 x 10, Looseleaf
Subscriptions: Indv. $895

Constitutions of the United
States: National & State   *Business, Consumer*

Publishing Co: Oceana Publications, Inc., 75 Main St, Dobbs Ferry, NY 10522-1601 Tel # (914) 693-8100; Title Tel # (914) 693-1320 Title Fax # (914) 693-0402
Personnel: Editor-F. Grad, Production Mgr.-Mike Wortzman, Mktg. Dir.-John Downey
General Info: Yr. Est. 1974, Semi-annually, Trim Size-7 x 10, Looseleaf
Subscriptions: Indv. $750

Construction Briefings   *Business*

Publishing Co: Federal Pubs., Inc., 1120 20th St., NW, Fifth Floor, South Building, Washington, DC 20036-3484; Title Tel # (202) 337-7000 Title Fax # (202) 659-2233
Personnel: Editor-Diane Davis, Mktg. Dir.-Beth Bolger
General Info: Yr. Est. 1978, Monthly
Subscriptions: Indv. $544

Construction Claims Monthly
See: CONSTRUCTION & BUILDING

Construction Contractor,
The   *Business, Association*

Publishing Co: Federal Pubs., Inc., 1120 20th St., NW, Fifth Floor, South Building, Washington, DC 20036-3484 Tel # (202) 337-7000; Title Tel # (202) 377-7000 Title Fax # (202) 659-2233
Personnel: Editor-Richard L. Shea, Mktg. Dir.-Beth Bolger
General Info: Yr. Est. 1977, 26x/yr., ISSN: 0162-3168
Subscriptions: Indv. $640

Construction and Design
Law

Publishing Co: Michie Law Publishing co., 701 East Water Street, Charlottesville, VA 22902-5389 Parent Co.-Reed Business Publishing Company, New York; Title Tel # (804) 972-7600 Title Fax # (800) 643-1280
Personnel: Editor-C. Allen Foster
Editorial Description: Analyzes 1500-plus construction and design cases in U.S. each year.
General Info: Yr. Est. 1984, Monthly, Trim Size-6⅝ x 10, Offset press, No Color, Newsprint, Saddle-stitched, Looseleaf
Subscriptions: Indv. $550

Construction Injury Liability Monthly
See: CONSTRUCTION & BUILDING

Construction Litigation
Reporter *Business, Association*

Publishing Co: Shepard's/McGraw-Hill, Inc., 555 Middle Creek Pky, Colorado Springs, CO 80921-3622; Title Tel # (719) 488-3000 Title Fax # (719) 481-7448
Personnel: Editor in Chief-Mary Kaye LaRue, Editor-Mark Schneier, Production Mgr.-Cheryl Everitt, Adv. Dir.-Peggy Ives, Art Dir.-Leigh Vidakovich
Editorial Description: Summaries of judicial& agency decisions in construction law. Free binder included.
General Info: Yr. Est. 1979, Monthly, Trim Size-8½ x 11, Web press, 24 pages, ISSN: 0279-1102, 2% ads, No Color, Newsprint, Saddle-stitched
Subscriptions: Indv. $340
Advertising: Inquire for rates. Accepts Inserts.
List Rental: List Management Co.: The Lake Group, 411 Theodore Freund Ave., Rye, NY 10580-1497 Tel # (914) 925-2400, Fax # (914) 925-2499, Actives: 40,212, $130/M

Consumer Credit Guide
See: BANKING & FINANCE

Consumer Credit: Law, Transaction and Forms
See: BANKING & FINANCE

Consumer Product
Litigation Reporter

Publishing Co: Andrews Publications, Inc., 1646 West Chester Pike, PO Box 1000, Westtown, PA 19395; Title Tel # (610) 399-6600 Title Fax # (610) 399-6610
Personnel: Publisher-John Backe, Editor-Jay Steinberg, Mktg. Dir.-Andrew Katz
Editorial Description: Covers areas such as strict liability, assumption of risk, insurance coverage, adequacy of warning, merchantability punitive damages, component liability, foreseeability and more.
General Info: Yr. Est. 1990, Monthly, Trim Size-8½ x 11, Mimeo press, ISSN: 1052-9632, Ind/Abs/Online: New Net, No Color
Subscriptions: Indv. $650, $46/copy
List Rental: Actives: 66,686, $125/M

Consumer Product Safety Guide
See: CONSUMER INTERESTS

Consumer Protection Report
See: CONSUMER INTERESTS

Contemporary Criminal
Procedure

Publishing Co: Gould Publications, Inc, 1333 N US Highway 17-92, Longwood, FL 32750-3724 Tel # (407) 695-9500 Fax # (407) 695-2906; Title Tel # (607) 724-3000
Editorial Description: Contains court decisions in a distinctive question and answer format.
General Info: Annually, 700 pages, Looseleaf
Subscriptions: Indv. $40, $35/copy

Continental Franchise Review
See: BUSINESS & INDUSTRY

Contract Appeals Decisions *Business*

Publishing Co: CCH, Inc., 2700 Lake Cook Rd., Riverwoods, IL 60015 Parent Co.-Kluwer Law & Taxation Publishers, Cambridge; Title Tel # (847) 267-7000 Title Fax # (800) 224-8299
Editorial Description: New decisions of the ASBCA and other Contract Appeals Boards rulings on contract problems - with bound volumes.
General Info: Yr. Est. 1956, Bi-weekly, Trim Size-6 x 9, Web press, 150 pages, No Color, Looseleaf
Subscriptions: Indv. $1,070

Contributions in Legal
Studies

Publishing Co: Greenwood Publishing Group, Inc., 88 Post Rd. W., PO Box 5007, Westport, CT 06881-5007 Fax # (203) 226-6009 Parent Co.-Elsevier Business Press, Morris Plains; Title Tel # (203) 226-3571
Personnel: Editor-Paul Murphy
Editorial Description: A series of updated volumes dealing with a wide range of legal topics.
General Info: ISSN: 0147-1074, Looseleaf

Cooperative Housing Bulletin
See: REAL ESTATE

Copyright Law Reports
See: PATENTS/COPYRIGHTS/TRADE MARKS

Corporate Compliance: Internal Reviews, Audits, and Investigations
See: BUSINESS & INDUSTRY

Corporate Counsel, The *Business*

Publishing Co: Executive Press, Inc., PO Box 21639, Concord, CA 94521; Title Tel # (510) 685-5111 Title Fax # (510) 685-5402
Editorial Description: Law.
General Info: Yr. Est. 1975, Bi-monthly

Corporate Counsel
LAWCST *Business*

Publishing Co: Vox Juris, Inc., P.O. Box 389, Pennington, NJ 08534; Title Tel # (609) 737-6543 Title Fax # (609) 737-3860
Personnel: Publisher-Jason Meyer, Esq, Editor-Mark Cohen, Esq, Circ. Mgr.-Karen E. Anderson, Mktg. Mgr.-Kathy W. Gould
Editorial Description: The legal newscast & case digesting service on audio cassette for lawyers who help manage businesses and organizations. Each issue includes an audiocassette and companion outline. Includes legal developments in antitrust, securities, employment and labor, environmental, law department management.
General Info: Yr. Est. 1994, Bi-weekly
Subscriptions: Indv. $329, Inst. $450, $25/copy

Corporate Counsellor

Publishing Co: Leader Publications, Inc., 345 Park Avenue South, New York, NY 10010 Parent Co.-New York Law Publishing Co., New York; Title Tel # (212) 545-6170 Title Fax # (212) 696-1848
Personnel: Publisher-Stuart Wise, Editor-Herbert Schlagman, Circ. Mgr.-Kerry Kyle, Promotion Dir.-Rose-Ann Morangelli
Editorial Description: Legal & regulatory issues faced by corp. lawyer.
General Info: Yr. Est. 1986, Monthly, Trim Size-8½ x 11, Offset press, 8 pages, ISSN: 0888-5877, Newsprint
Subscriptions: Indv. $245, $20/copy
Printing Co: Columbus Bookbinding, 1343 Belfast Ave, Columbus, OH 31904 Tel # (206) 323-9313, Fax # (206) 323-2987

Corporate Counsel's
Commercial Law Advisor

Publishing Co: Business Laws, Inc., 11630 Chillicothe Rd., Chesterland, OH 44026-1928; Title Tel # (216) 729-7996
General Info: (Formerly Bankruptcy & Commercial Law Advisor), Yr. Est. 1988, Monthly, 20 pages
Subscriptions: Indv. $285, $20/copy

Corporate Counsel's Intl.
Adviser

Publishing Co: Business Laws, Inc., 11630 Chillicothe Rd., Chesterland, OH 44026-1928; Title Tel # (216) 729-7996 Title Fax # (216) 729-0645
Personnel: Editor-William Hancock
General Info: Yr. Est. 1984, Monthly, 20 pages, ISSN: 0898-9907
Subscriptions: Indv. $285, $25/copy

Corporate Counsel's
Monitor

Publishing Co: Business Laws, Inc., 11630 Chillicothe Rd., Chesterland, OH 44026-1928; Title Tel # (216) 729-7996
Personnel: Editor-W.A. Hancock
General Info: Yr. Est. 1986, Monthly, 20 pages, ISSN: 0898-9923
Subscriptions: Indv. $285, $25/copy

Corporate Crime Reporter
See: BUSINESS & INDUSTRY

Corporate Executive, The *Business*

Publishing Co: Executive Press, Inc., PO Box 21639, Concord, CA 94521; Title Tel # (510) 685-5111 Title Fax # (510) 685-5402
Editorial Description: Law.
General Info: Yr. Est. 1986, Bi-monthly

Corporate Officers &
Directors Liability
Litigation Reporter *Business*

Publishing Co: Andrews Publications, Inc., 1646 West Chester Pike, PO Box 1000, Westtown, PA 19395; Title Tel # (610) 399-6600 Title Fax # (610) 399-6610
Personnel: Publisher-John Backe, Editor-Frank Reynolds, Mktg. Dir.-Andrew Katz
Editorial Description: Provides nationwide coverage of every type of litigation and legislation involving the individual liability of corporate officers and directors and corporate governance issues.
General Info: Yr. Est. 1985, Bi-monthly, Trim Size-8½ x 11, Mimeo press, 70 pages, ISSN: 0887-7793
Subscriptions: Indv. $850, $40/copy
Advertising: Inquire for rates.
List Rental: Actives: 66,686, $125/M

Corporate Practice Series *Business*

Publishing Co: Bureau of National Affairs, Inc., 1231 25th St. NW, Bldg. N-200, Washington, DC 20037-1157; Title Tel # (202) 452-4200 Title Fax # (202) 822-8092
Personnel: Publisher-William A. Beltz, Editor-Larry Lempert, Mng. Editor-Sarah Stevens, Circ. Mgr.-Gary C. Seltzer
Editorial Description: A corporate law reference service organized into a series of portfolios written by legal experts, with a weekly newsletter. Each portfolio covers a different legal subject, with detailed analysis, working papers & bibliography.
General Info: Yr. Est. 1978, Weekly, Trim Size-8½ x 11, Web press, 8 pages, ISSN: 0162-5691, Perfect bound, Looseleaf
Subscriptions: Indv. $1,458

Corporation Forms   *Business*

Publishing Co: Research Institute of America, 90 5th Avenue, New York, NY 10011-7629
Tel # (212) 645-4800; Title Tel # (800) 562-0245 Title Fax # (201) 816-3484
Editorial Description: Reference that provides subscribers with a complete set of forms to use for drafting specific forms relating to the formation, operation and dissolution of a corporation.
General Info: Monthly, Trim Size-6 x 9, Looseleaf
Subscriptions: Indv. $339
List Rental: List Management Co.: WG & L List Management, 1 Penn Plz Fl 42, New York, NY 10119-0002 Tel # (212) 971-5000

Correctional Compass
See: LAW ENFORCEMENT & PENOLOGY

Corrections Digest
See: LAW ENFORCEMENT & PENOLOGY

Cost Accounting Standards Guide
See: ACCOUNTING

Cotton Talks
See: AGRICULTURE

Council of New York Law Associates Newsletter   *Association*

Publishing Co: Council of New York Law Assocs., 99 Hudson St., New York, NY 10013-2815; Title Tel # (212) 219-1800 Title Fax # (212) 941-7458
Personnel: Editor-A. Hoyt, Production Mgr.-Anne Hoyt
Editorial Description: Public interest cases and news for pro bono attorneys. Focus is on community development and non-profit issues.
General Info: Bi-monthly, 12 pages, No Color
Circulation: Total-1,500

Counselor's Dispatch   *Business*

Publishing Co: Counselors Writing Services, PO Box 190, Lawrenceville, GA 30246
Fax # (404) 513-7006; Title Tel # (404) 513-1118 Title Fax # (770) 513-7006
Editorial Description: Client newsletter service for attorneys.
General Info: Yr. Est. 1994, Bi-monthly

Court of Appeals for the Federal Circuit: Review of Patent & Trademark Cases
See: PATENTS/COPYRIGHTS/TRADE MARKS

Court Awarded Attorney Fees   *Business*

Publishing Co: Matthew Bender & Co., 11 Penn Plaza, New York, NY 10001-2006
Tel # (212) 967-7707 Fax # (212) 244-3188
Editorial Description: Includes everything you need to petition for or to oppose a fee.
General Info: Yr. Est. 1983, Irregular, Looseleaf

Court Call   CPM: $500

Publishing Co: American Society of Trial Consultants, Dept. of Speech & Mass Comm., Towson State Univ., Towson, MD 21204; Title Tel # (410) 830-2448
Personnel: Editor-Karen Lisko
Editorial Description: News & research projects by trial consultants for attys. & courts.
General Info: Yr. Est. 1984, Quarterly, Trim Size-8½ x 11, Desktop press, 8 pages, No Color, Recycled
Circulation: Total-200
Advertising: $100.
List Rental: Rents Lists

Court Management & Administration Report   *Association*

Publishing Co: Clifford Kirsch, 10 Hopkins Dr, Lawrenceville, NJ 08648-2018
Personnel: Editor in Chief-Clifford P. Kirsch
General Info: Yr. Est. 1990, 11x/yr.
Subscriptions: Indv. $145, Can. $185, For. $185, $15/copy

Court Technology Bulletin   *Business*

Publishing Co: National Center for State Courts, 300 Newport Ave, Williamsburg, VA 23185-4147; Title Tel # (804) 253-2000 Title Fax # (804) 220-0449
Editorial Description: Current projects and trends in court room technology.
General Info: Bi-monthly
List Rental: Rents Lists

Courtroom Toxicology   *Business*

Publishing Co: Matthew Bender & Co., 11 Penn Plaza, New York, NY 10001-2006
Tel # (212) 967-7707 Fax # (212) 244-3188
Editorial Description: An authoritative treatise on using complex toxicology findings in the courtroom.
General Info: Yr. Est. 1981, Irregular, Looseleaf

Credit Union Law Service
See: BANKING & FINANCE

Creditors Workout Report   *Business*

Publishing Co: Warren, Gorham & Lamont, 31 Saint James Ave., Boston, MA 02116-4112 Parent Co.-Thomson Professional Publications, Stamford; Title Tel # (617) 423-2020 Title Fax # (617) 423-1914
Personnel: Publisher-L. Selby, Mktg. Dir.-Sandra Fox
Editorial Description: Provides timely coverage of important bankruptcy cases and changes to the bankruptcy code that affect your institution.
General Info: (Formerly Creditors Workout Strategies), Yr. Est. 1992, Monthly
Subscriptions: Indv. $195
Advertising: Inquire for rates.
List Rental: List Management Co.: Manager: Seena Benedek; WG & L List Management, 1 Penn Plz Fl 42, New York, NY 10119-0002 Tel # (212) 971-5000

Crime & Drug Report
See: LAW ENFORCEMENT & PENOLOGY

Crime Investigation Quizzer

Publishing Co: Gould Publications, Inc, 1333 N US Highway 17-92, Longwood, FL 32750-3724
Tel # (407) 695-9500 Fax # (407) 695-2906; Title Tel # (607) 724-3000
Editorial Description: An indispensable tool in the study for law inforcement examinations.
General Info: (Formerly Criminal Investigation Quizzer), Annually, 150 pages, Looseleaf
Subscriptions: Indv. $22, $20/copy

Criminal Constitutional Law   *Business*

Publishing Co: Matthew Bender & Co., 11 Penn Plaza, New York, NY 10001-2006
Tel # (212) 967-7707 Fax # (212) 244-3188
Editorial Description: Examines all the complex constitutional issues involved in criminal law. Provides substantive discussion, as well as procedural guidelines on tactics & strategy. The tretise analyzes all important Supreme Court, federal & state decisions interpreting theConstitution.
General Info: Yr. Est. 1990, Irregular, Looseleaf

Criminal Evidence for Law Enforcement Officers

Publishing Co: Gould Publications, Inc, 1333 N US Highway 17-92, Longwood, FL 32750-3724
Tel # (407) 695-9500 Fax # (407) 695-2906
Editorial Description: A precise guide to understanding the basic principles, rules and constitutional provisions regulating the evidence in criminal courts. Also include complete unannotated Federal Rules of Evidence
General Info: Annually, Looseleaf
Subscriptions: $27/copy

Criminal Law Advocacy   *Business*

Publishing Co: Matthew Bender & Co., 11 Penn Plaza, New York, NY 10001-2006
Tel # (212) 967-7707 Fax # (212) 244-3188
Editorial Description: All the important techniques behind successful criminal law practice, with specific guidelines for using the proper procedures. Numerous checklists, forms, & real-life examples of testimony, with author commentary throughout.
General Info: Irregular, Looseleaf

Criminal Law Advocacy Reporter   *Business*

Publishing Co: Matthew Bender & Co., 11 Penn Plaza, New York, NY 10001-2006
Tel # (212) 967-7707 Fax # (212) 244-3188
Editorial Description: Analysis of the latest cases & trends in criminal law & procedure. Each issue consists of atricles discussing strategy & tactics of some of the country's leading criminal practitioners, & cases decided by the Supreme Court. Articles are followed by numerous state & federal case annotations.
General Info: Yr. Est. 1982, Monthly

Criminal Law Deskbook   *Business*

Publishing Co: Matthew Bender & Co., 11 Penn Plaza, New York, NY 10001-2006
Tel # (212) 967-7707 Fax # (212) 244-3188
Editorial Description: Concise discussions of the basic principles of criminal procedure, substantive law, & criminal trial strategy & tactics.
General Info: Yr. Est. 1984, Irregular, Looseleaf

Criminal Law News

Publishing Co: West Publishing, 620 Opperman Dr., Eagan, MN 55123-1340 Parent Co.-Thomson Corp., Stamford; Title Tel # (612) 687-7000 Title Fax # (612) 687-7302
Editorial Description: Summaries of significant cases & legislation & applicable regulations from all U.S. Courts concerning criminal law.
General Info: Semi-monthly
Subscriptions: Indv. $178
Printing Co: West Publishing Corp., 620 Opperman Drive, Eagan, MN 55123 Tel # (612) 687-8000

Criminal Law Reporter

Publishing Co: Bureau of National Affairs, Inc., 1231 25th St. NW, Bldg. N-200, Washington, DC 20037-1157 Tel # (202) 452-4200 Fax # (202) 822-8092; Title Tel # (202) 452-4356 Title Fax # (202) 253-0332
Personnel: Publisher-William A. Beltz, Mng. Editor-Robert L. Goebes, Circ. Mgr.-Gary C. Seltzer
Editorial Description: A weekly notification service providing coverage of court decisions, federal legislative activities, & administrative developments in the field of criminal law. Criminal Justice Periodical Index.
General Info: Yr. Est. 1967, Weekly, Trim Size-8½ x 11, Web press, ISSN: 0011-1341
Subscriptions: Indv. $694

Criminal Practice Law
Review

Publishing Co: Michie Law Publishing co., 701 East Water Street, Charlottesville, VA 22902-5389 Parent Co.-Reed Business Publishing Company, New York; Title Tel # (804) 972-7600 Title Fax # (804) 972-7656
Personnel: Editor-Ruth Knight
Editorial Description: Selections of hard-to-find, outstanding articles from leading law reviews that are useful to the criminal bar.
General Info: Yr. Est. 1989, Quarterly, 160 pages, ISSN: 1044-3770, Looseleaf
Subscriptions: Indv. $80
Printing Co: Michie Co., PO Box 7587, Charlottesville, VA 22906-7587

Current Legal Forms with
Tax Analysis   *Business*

Publishing Co: Matthew Bender & Co., 11 Penn Plaza, New York, NY 10001-2006 Tel # (212) 967-7707 Fax # (212) 244-3188
Editorial Description: The most wiedely used set of legal forms ever published. Completely updated to reflect continuing changes in tax law.
General Info: Yr. Est. 1948, Irregular, Looseleaf

Customs and International
Trade Bar Association
Newsletter   *Business*

Publishing Co: Customs & Intl. Trade Bar Assn., c/o Andrew P. Vance, 475 Park Ave. S., New York, NY 10016; Title Tel # (212) 725-0200
Personnel: Publisher, Editor-Andrew Vance
Editorial Description: Attorneys admitted to practice and specializing in customs and international trade law in the United States.
General Info: Yr. Est. 1917, Bi-monthly

Customs Law &
Administration   *Business*

Publishing Co: Oceana Publications, Inc., 75 Main St, Dobbs Ferry, NY 10522-1601 Tel # (914) 693-8100; Title Tel # (914) 693-1320 Title Fax # (914) 693-0402
Personnel: Editor-R. Sturm, Editor-Eugene Wypyski, Production Mgr.-Mike Wortzman, Mktg. Dir.-John Downey
General Info: Yr. Est. 1982, Irregular, Trim Size-7 x 10, Looseleaf
Subscriptions: Indv. $695

Customs Law Handbook

Publishing Co: Gould Publications, Inc, 1333 N US Highway 17-92, Longwood, FL 32750-3724 Tel # (407) 695-9500 Fax # (407) 695-2906; Title Tel # (607) 724-3000
Editorial Description: USC Titles 18, 19, 21, & portions of related statutes.
General Info: Annually, Trim Size-5½ x 8½, 1,400 pages, No Color, Looseleaf
Subscriptions: $28/copy

D & O Liability Litigation
News   *Business*

Publishing Co: Litigation Reporting Service, PO Box 248, Chalfont, PA 18914-0248; Title Tel # (215) 822-9158
General Info: Semi-monthly
Subscriptions: Indv. $797

DES Litigation Reporter   *Business*

Publishing Co: Andrews Publications, Inc., 1646 West Chester Pike, PO Box 1000, Westtown, PA 19395; Title Tel # (610) 399-6600 Title Fax # (610) 399-6610
Personnel: Publisher-John E. Backe, Editor-Bob Sullivan, Mktg. Dir.-Andrew Katz
Editorial Description: A comprehensive report of litigation and legislation concerning diethylstilbestrol and its effects.
General Info: Yr. Est. 1981, Monthly, Trim Size-8½ x 11, Mimeo press, 80 pages, ISSN: 0276-5675, No Color, Newsprint
Subscriptions: Indv. $800, $75/copy
Advertising: Inquire for rates.
List Rental: Actives: 1,172, $110/M

DNA Newsletter   *Association*

Publishing Co: DNA-People's Legal Services, Inc., PO Box 306, Window Rock, AZ 86515-0306; Title Tel # (602) 871-4151
Personnel: Editor-T.J. Holgate
Editorial Description: Navajo Indian Law, features on DNA programs across the Navajo Nation, updates on major cases pertinant to the Navajos.
General Info: Yr. Est. 1968, Quarterly, Trim Size-8½ x 11, 8 pages, No Color
Subscriptions: Free
Circulation: Total-3,000

DWI Journal, Law &
Science   *Business*

Publishing Co: Whitaker Newsletters, 313 South Ave., Box 340, Fanwood, NJ 07023-1350; Title Tel # (908) 889-6336 Title Fax # (908) 889-6339
Personnel: Publisher-Joel Whitaker, Editor-John Tarantino, Circ. Mgr.-Sandra Smith
Editorial Description: Written for attorneys who specialize in drunk driving defense.
General Info: Yr. Est. 1986, Monthly, 16 pages, ISSN: 0889-0234
Subscriptions: Indv. $260, Inst. $260, $25/copy
List Rental: List Management Co.: The Lake Group, 411 Theodore Freund Ave., Rye, NY 10580-1497 Tel # (914) 925-2400, Fax # (914) 925-2499, Actives: 29,196, $70/M

Daily Commercial Record

Publishing Co: Daily Commercial Record, 706 Main St, Dallas, TX 75202-3699 Tel # (214) 741-6366
Editorial Description: A legal publication dealing with attorneys, credit houses, real estate, business firms interested in legal notices & records filed in city & county.
General Info: Yr. Est. 1888, Daily
Subscriptions: Indv. $60
Circulation: Total-2,000
Advertising: Inquire for rates.

Daily Labor Report
See: LABOR UNION

Damages in Tort Actions   *Business*

Publishing Co: Matthew Bender & Co., 11 Penn Plaza, New York, NY 10001-2006 Tel # (212) 967-7707 Fax # (212) 244-3188
Editorial Description: In-depth legal & policy analyses of compensatory & punitive damages in personal injury, wrongful death, & property damage cases. Shows how to increase the opportunity to recover a substantial verdict throught effective preparation & trial performance.
General Info: Yr. Est. 1982, Irregular, Looseleaf

DataLaw Report   *Business*

Publishing Co: Clark Boardman Callaghan & Co., 155 Pfingsten Rd., Deerfield, IL 60015
Personnel: Editor in Chief-Amelia Boss
Editorial Description: Analyzes the changing global legal environment for electronic information.
General Info: Yr. Est. 1993, Bi-monthly, Trim Size-8½ x 11, 36 pages

Debtor-Creditor law   *Business*

Publishing Co: Matthew Bender & Co., 11 Penn Plaza, New York, NY 10001-2006 Tel # (212) 967-7707 Fax # (212) 244-3188
Personnel: Editor in Chief-Theodore Eisenberg
Editorial Description: Covers all aspects of the creation & enforcement of the debtor-creditor relationship.
General Info: Yr. Est. 1982, Irregular, Looseleaf

Decisions & Developments   *Business*

Publishing Co: Decision & Developments, 260 Bear Hill Rd., Waltham, MA 02154; Title Tel # (617) 890-5678
Personnel: Editor-Joseph Landiorio
General Info: Yr. Est. 1980, Bi-monthly, 4 pages
Subscriptions: Indv. $84

Defense of Drunk Driving
Cases: Criminal, Civil   *Business*

Publishing Co: Matthew Bender & Co., 11 Penn Plaza, New York, NY 10001-2006 Fax # (212) 244-3188; Title Tel # (212) 967-7707
Personnel: Editor-R. Kaye
Editorial Description: All legal and scientific information needed to protect the client.
General Info: Yr. Est. 1963, Irregular, Looseleaf
Subscriptions: $450/copy

Defense of Narcotics Cases   *Business*

Publishing Co: Matthew Bender & Co., 11 Penn Plaza, New York, NY 10001-2006 Fax # (212) 244-3188; Title Tel # (212) 967-7707
Personnel: Editor-N. Masliansky
Editorial Description: Expert, up-to-date coverage of all aspects of narcotics cases and related matters, such as: identification of drugs, search & seizure, motor vehicle and airport searches, and pre-trial proceedings.
General Info: Yr. Est. 1972, Irregular, Looseleaf
Subscriptions: $210/copy

Defense of Speeding,
Reckless Driving and
Vehicular Homicide   *Business*

Publishing Co: Matthew Bender & Co., 11 Penn Plaza, New York, NY 10001-2006 Tel # (212) 967-7707 Fax # (212) 244-3188
Editorial Description: The law, technical knowledge & litigation techniques required to successfully defend a speeding, reckless driving or vehicular homicide case. Also covers revocation & suspension of drivers' licenses.
General Info: Yr. Est. 1984, Irregular, Looseleaf

Delaware Corporate Law
Update   *Business*

Publishing Co: Andrews Publications, Inc., 1646 West Chester Pike, PO Box 1000, Westtown, PA 19395; Title Tel # (610) 399-6600 Title Fax # (610) 399-6610
Personnel: Publisher-John E. Backe, Editor-Frank Reynolds, Mktg. Dir.-Andrew Katz
Editorial Description: Provides detailed analysis all decisions--published and unpublished--from the Delaware Chancery, Superior and Supreme Courts and the U.S. District Court.
General Info: Yr. Est. 1985, Monthly, Trim Size-8½ x 11, Mimeo press, ISSN: 0888-434X, No Color, Newsprint
Subscriptions: Indv. $475, $40/copy
Advertising: Inquire for rates.
List Rental: Actives: 390, $110/M

Delaware Corporate Litigation Reporter
Business

Publishing Co: Andrews Publications, Inc., 1646 West Chester Pike, PO Box 1000, Westtown, PA 19395; Title Tel # (610) 399-9600 Fax # (610) 399-6610
Personnel: Publisher-John E. Backe, Editor-Frank Reynolds, Mktg. Dir.-Andrew Katz
Editorial Description: Offers summaries and reproductions of every opinion issued by the Delaware Supreme, Superior, and Chancery Courts and the U.S. District Court for the District of Delaware concerning corporate issues.
General Info: Yr. Est. 1986, Bi-monthly, Trim Size-8½ x 11, Mimeo press, ISSN: 1042-5756, Ind/Abs/Online: News Net, No Color
Subscriptions: Indv. $850, $40/copy
Advertising: Inquire for rates.
List Rental: Actives: 390, $110/M

Delaware Corporation Law and Practice
Business

Publishing Co: Matthew Bender & Co., 11 Penn Plaza, New York, NY 10001-2006
Tel # (212) 967-7707 Fax # (212) 244-3188
Editorial Description: In-depth analysis of the General Corporation Law of Delaware--the single most important corporation law statute in the country.
General Info: Yr. Est. 1988, Irregular, Looseleaf

Delaware Employment Law Letter
Business

Publishing Co: M. Lee Smith Publishers & Printers ,LCC, P.O. Box 198867, 162 Fourth Avenue North, Nashville, TN 37219-8867; Title Tel # (615) 242-7395 Title Fax # (615) 256-6601
Personnel: Publisher-M Lee Smith, Editor-Bill Bowser, Circ. Mgr.-Cathy Bradford, Mktg. Dir.-David Yates
General Info: Yr. Est. 1996, Monthly, Trim Size-8½ x 11, 8 pages, 2 Color
Subscriptions: Indv. $97
List Rental: Rents Lists
Printing Co: M. Lee Smith Publishers & Printers ,LLC, PO Box 198867, 162 Fourth Avenue, Nashville, TN 37219-8867 Tel # (615) 242-7395, Fax # (615) 256-6601

Deposition Strategy, Law and Forms
Business

Publishing Co: Matthew Bender & Co., 11 Penn Plaza, New York, NY 10001-2006
Tel # (212) 967-7707 Fax # (212) 244-3188
Personnel: Editor-Steven Bellman, Editor-Alexander Sann
Editorial Description: Discusses every aspect of deposition practice & covers every commonly litigated area of the law, with each topic written by an expert in the field.
General Info: Irregular, Looseleaf

Derivatives LItigation Reporter
Business

Publishing Co: Andrews Publications, Inc., 1646 West Chester Pike, PO Box 1000, Westtown, PA 19395 Tel # (610) 399-9600 Fax # (610) 399-6610
Personnel: Publisher-John E. Backe, Editor-Bob McSherry, Mktg. Dir.-Andrew Katz
General Info: Yr. Est. 1995, Bi-monthly, Trim Size-8.5 x 11, Offset press, No Color
Subscriptions: Indv. $600, $29/copy
Advertising: Inquire for rates.
List Rental: Actives: $125/M

Devices & Diagnostics Letter
See: HEALTH

Dicta Monthly
Association

Publishing Co: Knoxville Bar Assn., PO Box 2027, Knoxville, TN 37901-2027 Tel # (615) 522-7501
Personnel: Editor-Marsha Lace
Editorial Description: Newsletter to lawyers in Knoxville, Tennessee.
General Info: Monthly, Trim Size-8 x 12¼, Offset press, 4 pages, No Color
Circulation: Total-655

Dictionary of 1040 Deductions
See: TAXES

Dictionary of Criminal Justice Terms

Publishing Co: Gould Publications, Inc, 1333 N US Highway 17-92, Longwood, FL 32750-3724
Tel # (407) 695-9500 Fax # (407) 695-2906; Title Tel # (607) 724-3000
Editorial Description: A comprehensive compilation of terms with definitions and annotations.
General Info: Annually, 250 pages, Looseleaf
Subscriptions: Indv. $11, $10/copy

Digest of Attorney General Opinions
Association

Publishing Co: Digest of Attorney General, 112 State Capitol Building, 2300 N. Lincoln Blvd., Oklahoma City, OK 73105; Title Tel # (405) 521-3921 Title Fax # (405) 521-6246
Editorial Description: Summary/Conclusion paragraphs of Attorney Gerneral
General Info: Quarterly, Trim Size-8½ x 11, Offset press, 6 pages, No Color, Other, Other
Subscriptions: Indv. $8
Circulation: Total-750

Digest of Canadian Intellectual Property Law
Business

Publishing Co: Carswell, 2075 Kennedy Road, One Corporate Plaza, Scarborough, ON M1T 3V4 Canada Tel # (416) 609-8000; Title Tel # (416) 298-5094
Personnel: Publisher-Catherine McKeown, Editor-Marshall Reinhart, Production Mgr.-Grant Daly
Editorial Description: Includes digests of court cases as well as comment on one case of interest and abstracts of articles published elsewhere. Topics covered inlcude copyright, patents, trademarks and confidential information.
General Info: Monthly, 12 pages, No Color
Subscriptions: Indv. $235
Printing Co: Carswell, 245 Bartley Dr., Toronto, ON M4V 2V8 Canada

Digest of Commercial Laws of the World
Business

Publishing Co: Oceana Publications, Inc., 75 Main St, Dobbs Ferry, NY 10522-1601
Tel # (914) 693-8100; Title Tel # (914) 693-1320 Title Fax # (914) 693-0402
Personnel: Editor-Lester Nelson, Production Mgr.-Mike Wortzman, Mktg. Dir.-John Downey
Editorial Description: Latest changes in regulations of 90 countries. Eleven loose-leaf volumes with quarterly updates.
General Info: Yr. Est. 1968, Quarterly, Trim Size-7 x 10, 500 pages, ISSN: 0419-1285, Newsprint, Looseleaf
Subscriptions: Indv. $1,100

Digest of Commercial Laws of the World: State Variations of Commercial Law
Business

Publishing Co: Oceana Publications, Inc., 75 Main St, Dobbs Ferry, NY 10522-1601
Tel # (914) 693-8100; Title Tel # (914) 693-1320 Title Fax # (914) 693-0402
Personnel: Editor-Lester Nelson, Production Mgr.-Mike Wortzman, Mktg. Dir.-John Downey
General Info: (Formerly Forms/Commercial Agreements&State Variations/Commercial Law), Yr. Est. 1984, Irregular, Trim Size-7 x 10, Looseleaf
Subscriptions: $200/copy

Digest for Corporate & Securities Lawyers

Publishing Co: Brumberg Publications, Inc., 124 Harvard St., Brookline, MA 02146-6432; Title Tel # (617) 734-1979 Title Fax # (617) 734-1989
Personnel: Publisher-Bruce Brumberg, Editor-Susan Koffman
Editorial Description: Summaries of current corporate law articles.
General Info: Yr. Est. 1986, 11x/yr.
Subscriptions: Indv. $125

Digest of Environmental Law
Business

Publishing Co: Strafford Pubs., Inc., 590 Dutch Valley Rd., N.E., Postal Drawer 13729, Atlanta, GA 30324-0729; Title Tel # (404) 881-1141 Title Fax # (404) 881-0074
Personnel: Publisher-Richard M. Ossoff, Mng. Editor-Jennifer F. Vaughan, Production Mgr.-C. Marlone Tumlin, Circ. Mgr., Mktg. Dir.-Marianne Mueller
Editorial Description: Covers issues of environmental law.
General Info: Yr. Est. 1987, 12x/yr., ISSN: 1073-9521
Subscriptions: Indv. $294, Inst. $260, Can. $324, For. $349, $25/copy

Digest of Intellectual Property Laws of the World
Business

Publishing Co: Oceana Publications, Inc., 75 Main St, Dobbs Ferry, NY 10522-1601
Tel # (914) 693-8100 Fax # (914) 693-0402
Personnel: Editor-Lester Nelson, Production Mgr.-Mike Wortzman, Mktg. Dir.-John Downey
Editorial Description: Law of over 100 nations.
General Info: Yr. Est. 1990, Irregular, ISSN: 0-379-010, Looseleaf
Subscriptions: Indv. $495

Digest of Legal Activities of Intl. Organizations & Other Institutions
Business

Publishing Co: Oceana Publications, Inc., 75 Main St, Dobbs Ferry, NY 10522-1601
Tel # (914) 693-8100; Title Tel # (914) 693-1320 Title Fax # (914) 693-0402
Personnel: Production Mgr.-Mike Wortzman, Mktg. Dir.-John Downey
General Info: Yr. Est. 1975, Irregular, Trim Size-7 x 10, Looseleaf
Subscriptions: Indv. $150

Disabilities in the Workplace Alert
Business

Publishing Co: Warren, Gorham & Lamont, 31 Saint James Ave., Boston, MA 02116-4112 Parent Co.-Thomson Professional Publications, Stamford; Title Tel # (617) 423-2020 Title Fax # (617) 423-1914
Personnel: Publisher-Andrew Boden, Production Mgr.-Paul Kelly, Mktg. Dir.-Sandra Fox
Editorial Description: This comprehensive reference provides in-depth analysis of federal and state laws, regulations and court decisions governing treatment of the disabled in the workplace. Subscription includes main volume and monthly updates and monthly Disabilities in the Workplace Alert newsletter.
General Info: Yr. Est. 1992, Monthly, Looseleaf
Subscriptions: Indv. $111
List Rental: List Management Co.: Manager: Seena Benedek; WG & L List Management, 1 Penn Plz Fl 42, New York, NY 10119-0002 Tel # (212) 971-5000

Disability Advocates Bulletin
See: DISABILITY

Disability Law Compliance Report
See: DISABILITY

Dispute Resolution   *Association*

Publishing Co: Sponsor-American Bar Assn., American Bar Association, 740 15th St. NW, Washington, DC 20005-1009 Tel # (202) 662-1016 Fax # (202) 662-1032; Title Tel # (202) 331-2258
Personnel: Publisher, Editor, Circ. Mgr.-Ric Hyde, Circ. Mgr.-Megan Sylvester
Editorial Description: Alternatives to traditional adversarial litigation.
General Info: Yr. Est. 1979, Quarterly, Trim Size-8½ x 11, 16 pages, ISSN: 0271-2709, 2 Color
Acquisitions: Publication Bought, Publication Sold
Circulation: Total-12,000
Printing Co: McArdle Printing Co., 800 Commerce Dr, Upper Marlboro, MD 20772-8792 Tel # (301) 390-8500

Disputed Paternity Proceedings
See: FAMILY

District of Columbia Criminal Law and Motor Vehicle Handbook

Publishing Co: Gould Publications, Inc, 1333 N US Highway 17-92, Longwood, FL 32750-3724 Tel # (407) 695-9500 Fax # (407) 695-2906
Editorial Description: Criminal offenses, criminal procedure, motor vehicle and traffic laws of the district of columbia
General Info: Annually, Looseleaf
Subscriptions: $20/copy

Docket Call   *Business, Association*

Publishing Co: Sponsor-Young Lawyers Conference, Virginia State Bar, 707 E Main St Ste 1500, Richmond, VA 23219-2803; Title Tel # (804) 775-0500
Editorial Description: News items about Virginia State Bar Young Lawyers Conferences activities.
General Info: (Formerly Young Lawyers Conference Newsletter), Yr. Est. 1973, Quarterly, Trim Size-8½ x 11, Sheetfed press, 16 pages, 2 Color, Newsprint, Saddle-stitched
Subscriptions: $1/copy
Circulation: (100% controlled), Total-8,000

Doing Business in Eastern Europe
See: BUSINESS & INDUSTRY

Doing Business in Europe
See: BUSINESS & INDUSTRY

Doing Business in the United States
See: BUSINESS & INDUSTRY

Dominion Law Reports

Publishing Co: Canada Law Book Co., Inc., 240 Edward St., Aurora, ON L4G 3S9 Canada Tel # (416) 841-6472 Fax # (416) 841-5085; Title Tel # (416) 773-6300
Personnel: Editor-J. Bruce Dunlop
General Info: Yr. Est. 1912, Weekly, 125 pages
Subscriptions: Indv. $114, Can. $109, For. $114
Advertising: Inquire for rates.

Dominion Tax Cases
See: TAXES

Drafting New York Wills- Law and Forms   *Business*

Publishing Co: Matthew Bender & Co., 11 Penn Plaza, New York, NY 10001-2006 Fax # (212) 244-3188; Title Tel # (212) 967-7707
Personnel: Editor-R. Lopatin
Editorial Description: Provides three step drafting system. Includes: checklist of more than 150 items to consider; 'Key Questions' Section; & hundred of will clauses for specific purposes, keyed to the checklist.
General Info: Yr. Est. 1948, Irregular, Looseleaf
Subscriptions: $200/copy

Dram Shop & Alcohol Reporter   *Business*

Publishing Co: Dram Shop & Alcohol Reporter, PO Box 590, Falmouth, MA 02541-0590; Title Tel # (508) 540-1606
Personnel: Publisher, Editor-Ronald Beitman
Editorial Description: The newsletter carries stories, case decisions & settlement information concerning liquor liability. The Reporter is desseminated nationally to attorneys, bars, restaurants, package stores & insurance carriers who are concerned with liquor liability.
General Info: Yr. Est. 1984, Monthly
Subscriptions: Indv. $120

Drinking & Driving Law

Publishing Co: Carswell, 2075 Kennedy Road, One Corporate Plaza, Scarborough, ON M1T 3V4 Canada Tel # (416) 609-8000 Fax # (416) 298-5094; Title Tel # (416) 445-4940 Title Fax # (416) 445-5352
Personnel: Publisher-Barry Garnet, Editor-Alan Gold, Circ. Mgr.-Mike Moore, Adv. Dir.-Melanie Causton
General Info: Yr. Est. 1986, Monthly, Trim Size-8½ x 11, ISSN: 0830-0917
Subscriptions: Indv. $170

Drinking/Driving Law Letter

Publishing Co: Clark Boardman Callaghan & Co., 155 Pfingsten Rd., Deerfield, IL 60015; Title Tel # (708) 948-7000
Personnel: Editor-Donald Nichols
Editorial Description: Summary of the latest cases involving driving under the influence.
General Info: Yr. Est. 1985, Bi-weekly, Trim Size-8½ x 11, Offset press, 8 pages, ISSN: 0730-2568
Subscriptions: Indv. $155, $5/copy
Acquisitions: Publication Bought, Publication Sold

Driving DWI Journal Law & Science

Publishing Co: InfoCom Group, 1250 45th St., Ste 200, Emeryville, CA 94608-2924 Tel # (510) 596-9300 Fax # (510) 596-9331; Title Tel # (415) 549-4300 Title Fax # (415) 549-4331
General Info: Yr. Est. 1987, Monthly
Subscriptions: Indv. $277

Drug Enforcement

Publishing Co: U.S. Dept. Justice, Drug Enforcement Administration, 1405 Eye Street, N.w., Washington, DC 20537-0001; Title Tel # (202) 633-1230
Personnel: Editor-Horton Heath, Jr.
Editorial Description: News stories, features, contributed articles and items on drug law enforcement, drug abuse prevention, enforcement training, drug intelligence, on local, state, national, international levels.
General Info: (Formerly BNDD Bulletin), Yr. Est. 1968, Quarterly, Trim Size-8½ x 11, Offset press, 40 pages, Color
Circulation: Total-55,000

Drug Law Report
See: DRUGS & PHARMACEUTICALS

Drug Policy Report
See: LAW ENFORCEMENT & PENOLOGY

Drug Product Liability   *Business*

Publishing Co: Matthew Bender & Co., 11 Penn Plaza, New York, NY 10001-2006 Fax # (212) 244-3188; Title Tel # (212) 967-7707
Personnel: Contrib. Ed.-Marden Guy Dixon, M.D., J.D., Contrib. Ed.-Frank C. Woodside, III, M.D., J.D.
Editorial Description: All aspects of drugs: manufacturing, marketing, distribution, quality control multiple prescription problems, drug identification, FDA coverage, and more.
General Info: Yr. Est. 1974, Irregular, Looseleaf
Subscriptions: $310/copy

Drugs and the Law

Publishing Co: Gould Publications, Inc, 1333 N US Highway 17-92, Longwood, FL 32750-3724 Tel # (407) 695-9500 Fax # (407) 695-2906; Title Tel # (607) 724-3000 Title Fax # (607) 723-4285
Editorial Description: A valuable tool for anyone involved in law enforcement, drug counseling and awareness, parents, teachers, students.
General Info: Looseleaf
Subscriptions: Indv. $35, $30/copy

Drunk Driving Law Reporter

Publishing Co: InfoCom Group, 1250 45th St., Ste 200, Emeryville, CA 94608-2924 Tel # (510) 596-9300 Fax # (510) 596-9331; Title Tel # (415) 549-4300
Personnel: Publisher-Jim Sinkinson
Editorial Description: News & updating services for specialists in drunk driving law.
General Info: Monthly
Subscriptions: Indv. $197

Dunlap-Hanna, Pennsylvania Forms   *Business*

Publishing Co: Matthew Bender & Co., 11 Penn Plaza, New York, NY 10001-2006 Tel # (212) 967-7707 Fax # (212) 244-3188
Personnel: Editor in Chief-Paul C. Heintz
Editorial Description: Provides forms for all types of litigation, plus forms for estates, wills & trusts, commerical transactons, general business formations & much more, along with expanatory text & handy reminders.
General Info: Yr. Est. 1845, Irregular, Looseleaf

EEOC Compliance Manual   *Business*

Publishing Co: CCH, Inc., 2700 Lake Cook Rd., Riverwoods, IL 60015 Parent Co.-Kluwer Law & Taxation Publishers, Cambridge; Title Tel # (847) 267-7000 Title Fax # (800) 224-8299
Editorial Description: Reproduces the policies, procedures and standards the Equal Employment Opportunity Commission uses to guide investigative, conciliation and enforcement staff. Includes Regional Attorneys' Deskbook.
General Info: Irregular, Looseleaf
Subscriptions: Indv. $263

EMF Litigation News — *Business*

Publishing Co: Litigation Reporting Service, PO Box 248, Chalfont, PA 18914-0248; Title Tel # (215) 822-9158
General Info: Yr. Est. 1993, Monthly
Subscriptions: Indv. $797

EPA Enforcement Manual
See: ENVIRONMENT & ECOLOGY

Eco Newsletter
See: ENVIRONMENT & ECOLOGY

Eco/Log Canadian Pollution Legislation — *Business*

Publishing Co: Southam Business Communications, Inc., 1450 Don Mills Rd., Don Mills, ON M3B 2X7 Canada Fax # (416) 442-2200; Title Tel # (416) 445-6641
Personnel: Publisher-Mary Mancini, Sr. Ed.-Mark Sabourin, Circ. Mgr.-Jennepher Hunter, Promotion Dir.-Saundra Dobroski
Editorial Description: Environmental acts, regulations, guidelines, standards, objectives & policies for Canada and its ten provinces and two territories.
General Info: Yr. Est. 1972, Bi-monthly, Trim Size-8½ x 11, Letrpr. press, 170 pages, ISSN: 0704-4062, No Color, Newsprint, Looseleaf
Subscriptions: Can. $815, For. $925
Acquistions: Publication Bought
List Rental: List Management Co.: Cornerstone List Mgrs., 2300 Yonge St., Ste. 2005, Box 2465, Toronto, ON M4P 1E4 Canada Tel # (416) 932-9555, Fax # (416) 932-9566, Actives: $80/M

Ecological Illness Law Reports — *Business*

Publishing Co: Ecological Illness Law Report, PO Box 6099, Wilmette, IL 60091-6099; Title Tel # (708) 256-3730
Editorial Description: Covers developments in current law, etc.
General Info: Yr. Est. 1982, Quarterly
Subscriptions: Indv. $30

Economic Development/State Capitals
See: BUSINESS & INDUSTRY

Economic and Legal Information from Poland
See: INTERNATIONAL TRADE

Education Law — *Business*

Publishing Co: Matthew Bender & Co., 11 Penn Plaza, New York, NY 10001-2006 Tel # (212) 967-7707 Fax # (212) 244-3188
Personnel: Editor in Chief-James A. Rapp
Editorial Description: An indispensable reference for attorneys who represent persons having a grievance against educational institutions, & attorneys representing such institutions, as well as school board members & administrators.
General Info: Yr. Est. 1984, Irregular, Looseleaf

Education Personnel Notes
See: EDUCATION

Educator's Guide to Controlling Sexual Harassment — *Business, Scholarly*

Publishing Co: Thompson Publishing Group, 1725 K Street, NW, Washington, DC 20006 Tel # (202) 872-4000
Editorial Description: Explains what to include in policies and complaint procedures and how to communicate them. Subscription includes monthly updates and a news bulletin.
General Info: Annually, Looseleaf
Subscriptions: Indv. $287

Effective Client Communication

Publishing Co: West Publishing, 620 Opperman Dr., Eagan, MN 55123-1340 Fax # (612) 687-7302 Parent Co.-Thomson Corp., Stamford; Title Tel # (612) 687-7000
General Info: Irregular, Looseleaf

Eldercare
See: SENIOR CITIZENS

Electromagnetic Field Litigation Reporter — *Business*

Publishing Co: Andrews Publications, Inc., 1646 West Chester Pike, PO Box 1000, Westtown, PA 19395; Title Tel # (610) 399-6600 Title Fax # (610) 399-6610
Personnel: Publisher-John E. Backe, Editor-Ronald Baker, Mktg. Dir.-Andrew Katz
Editorial Description: Tracks developments in every important legal action involving electromatgnetic radiation from power lines, cellular phones, video display terminals and radar and microwave equipment.
General Info: Yr. Est. 1993, Monthly, Trim Size-8½ x 11, Mimeo press, 70 pages, ISSN: 1069-6695, Ind/Abs/Online: Net News, No Color
Subscriptions: Indv. $700, $58/copy
Advertising: Inquire for rates.
List Rental: Actives: 66,686, $125/M

Emergency Department Law — *Business*

Publishing Co: Business Publishers, Inc., 951 Pershing Dr., Silver Spring, MD 20910-4464 Tel # (301) 589-5103 Fax # (301) 589-8493; Title Tel # (301) 587-6300 Title Fax # (301) 587-1081
Personnel: Circ. Dir.-Allison Inglesby
Editorial Description: News & analysis of malpractice & other legal issues as they affect urgent care facilities.
General Info: Yr. Est. 1989, Bi-weekly, Trim Size-8½ x 11, Sheetfed press, 8 pages, ISSN: 1042-2978, 2 Color, Matte
Subscriptions: Indv. $300, Can. $300, For. $312, $12/copy
Acquistions: Publication Bought, Publication Sold
List Rental: List Management Co.: BPI Direct, 951 Pershing Dr., Silver Spring, MD 20910-4464 Tel # (301) 585-5976, Fax # (301) 587-4530
Printing Co: Plymouth Printing, 1200 Cushing Pl SE, Washington, DC 20003-3599 Tel # (202) 488-7777, Fax # (202) 863-1078

Employee Benefits for Non-Profits
See: EMPLOYMENT

Employee, Business, and Professional Defamation — *Business*

Publishing Co: Matthew Bender & Co., 11 Penn Plaza, New York, NY 10001-2006 Tel # (212) 967-7707 Fax # (212) 244-3188
Editorial Description: This important treatise focuses on suits that can be brought by businesses and employees when their reputations are damaged.
General Info: Yr. Est. 1990, Irregular, Looseleaf

Employee Policy for the Private and Public Sectors/State Capitals
See: INDUSTRIAL RELATIONS/PERSONNEL

Employee Relations in Action
See: LABOR UNION

Employee Testing & the Law
See: EMPLOYMENT

Employer's Guide to Controlling Sexual Harassment
See: INDUSTRIAL RELATIONS/PERSONNEL

Employer's Guide to the Fair Labor Standards Act
See: INDUSTRIAL RELATIONS/PERSONNEL

Employer's Handbook: Complying with IRS Employee Benefits Rules
See: TAXES

Employer's Handbook: Independent Contractor vs. Employee
See: LABOR

Employers' Immigration Compliance Guide — *Business*

Publishing Co: Matthew Bender & Co., 11 Penn Plaza, New York, NY 10001-2006 Tel # (212) 967-7707 Fax # (212) 244-3188
Editorial Description: Contains the sweeping changes brought about by the Immigation Reform and Control Act of 1986.
General Info: Yr. Est. 1987, Monthly, Looseleaf

Employment Alert
See: EMPLOYMENT

Employment Discrimination
See: CIVIL RIGHTS

Employment Health Law & Benefits
See: INDUSTRIAL RELATIONS/PERSONNEL

Employment and Labor Lawcast — *Business*

Publishing Co: Vox Juris, Inc., P.O. Box 389, Pennington, NJ 08534; Title Tel # (609) 737-6543 Title Fax # (609) 737-3860
Personnel: Publisher-Jason Meyer, Editor-Marc Harrison, Circ. Mgr.-Karen Anderson, Mktg. Dir.-Kathy Gould
Editorial Description: Legal newscast and case digesting service for labor or employment buyers. Includes federal labor and employment law from coast to coast, trends in state law, new causes of action, tactics and strategies and trial techniques. Audio cassette and accompanying outline.
General Info: Yr. Est. 1995, Bi-weekly
Subscriptions: Indv. $329, Inst. $450, $25/copy

Employment Law Manual   *Business*

Publishing Co: Warren, Gorham & Lamont, 31 Saint James Ave., Boston, MA 02116-4112 Parent Co.-Thomson Professional Publications, Stamford; Title Tel # (617) 423-2020 Title Fax # (617) 423-1914
Personnel: Publisher-Andrew Boden, Production Mgr.-Paul Kelly, Mktg. Dir.-Sandra Fox
Editorial Description: This reference shows employers as well as the attorneys who represent them-the steps they should take to avoid legal trouble in all types of employment transactions.
General Info: (Formerly Guide to Employment Law & Regulation), Annually, Looseleaf
Subscriptions: Indv. $126, Inst. $126, Can. $126, For. $126
List Rental: List Management Co.: Manager: Seena Benedek; WG & L List Management, 1 Penn Plz Fl 42, New York, NY 10119-0002 Tel # (212) 971-5000

Employment Law News

Publishing Co: Natl. Employment Law Project, 36 W 44th St Ste 1415, New York, NY 10036-8102; Title Tel # (212) 870-2121
Personnel: Editor-Alison Berry-Harding
Editorial Description: Reviews developments in labor & employment law.
General Info: Quarterly, 12 pages
Subscriptions: Indv. $30, $5/copy
Circulation: Total-1,500

Employment Law Report, The
See: EMPLOYMENT

Employment Law Report

Publishing Co: Data Research, Inc., 4635 Nicols Rd Ste 100, Eagan, MN 55122-3337; Title Tel # (612) 452-8267 Title Fax # (612) 452-8694
General Info: Yr. Est. 1991, Monthly, Trim Size-8½ x 11, 8 pages, ISSN: 1058-1308, No Color, Newsprint
Subscriptions: Indv. $103
Circulation: Total-1,500
Printing Co: Helgeson Press, 7600 14th Ave S, Richfield, MN 55423-4530 Tel # (612) 869-6828

Employment Law Strategist   *Business*

Publishing Co: Leader Publications, Inc., 345 Park Avenue South, New York, NY 10010 Fax # (212) 696-1848 Parent Co.-New York Law Publishing Co., New York; Title Tel # (212) 545-6170 Title Fax # (212) 896-1848
Personnel: Publisher-Stuart Wise, Editor-Stephen Sheinfeld, Circ. Mgr.-Kerry Kyle, Mktg. Dir.-Rose-ann Mornancelli
Editorial Description: Covers issues of employment law.
General Info: Yr. Est. 1993, Monthly, Trim Size-8½ x 11, Offset press, 8 pages, Color
Subscriptions: Indv. $165, $14/copy
Printing Co: Columbus Bookbinding, 1343 Belfast Ave, Columbus, OH 31904 Tel # (206) 323-9313, Fax # (206) 323-2987

Employment Litigation Reporter
See: LABOR

Employment Practices Decisions
See: EMPLOYMENT

Employment Practices Guide
See: EMPLOYMENT

Employment Safety and Health Guide
See: SAFETY

Employment and Total Wages Paid by Employers Subject to the Louisiana Employment Security   *Business, Association*

Publishing Co: Louisiana Dept. of Labor, Box 94094, Baton Rouge, LA 70804-9094 Tel # (504) 342-3111; Title Tel # (504) 342-3141 Title Fax # (504) 342-9193
Personnel: Editor-Oliver Robinson
Editorial Description: Tabulations compiled from employment and wage reports of employers subject to the Louisiana Employment Security Law, by parish (county) and by selected industries.
General Info: Yr. Est. 1949, Quarterly, Trim Size-8½ x 11, Offset press, 9 pages, No Color
Subscriptions: Free
Circulation: Total-600

En Garde

Publishing Co: En Garde, 1660 Lincoln St Ste 2525, Denver, CO 80264-2501; Title Tel # (303) 860-1400
Personnel: Editor-Sam Lusky
General Info: 26x/yr.
Subscriptions: Indv. $50

Energy Management and Federal Energy Guidelines
See: ENERGY

Entertainment Industry Contracts   *Business*

Publishing Co: Matthew Bender & Co., 11 Penn Plaza, New York, NY 10001-2006 Tel # (212) 967-7707 Fax # (212) 244-3188
Personnel: Editor-Donald C. Farber
Editorial Description: An authoritative form book with commentary designed to provide attorneys, producers, agents, & other involved in the entertainment industry with expert guidance on negotiating & drafting contracts in the five major areas of the entertainment industry: Motion Pictures, Music, Television, Book Publishing, & Theatre.
General Info: Yr. Est. 1986, Irregular, Looseleaf

Entertainment Law & Finance   *Business*

Publishing Co: Leader Publications, Inc., 345 Park Avenue South, New York, NY 10010 Parent Co.-New York Law Publishing Co., New York; Title Tel # (212) 545-6170 Title Fax # (212) 696-1848
Personnel: Publisher-Stuart M. Wise, Editor-Stan Soocher, Circ. Mgr.-Kerry Kyle, Promotion Dir.-Rose-Ann Moranbelli
Editorial Description: Legal & financial developments in entertainment industry.
General Info: Yr. Est. 1985, Monthly, Trim Size-8½ x 11, Offset press, 8 pages, ISSN: 0883-2455, Newsprint
Subscriptions: Indv. $195, $16/copy
Acquistions: Publication Sold
Printing Co: Columbus Bookbinding, 1343 Belfast Ave, Columbus, OH 31904 Tel # (206) 323-9313, Fax # (206) 323-2987

Entertainment and Sports Lawyer   *Business, Association*

Publishing Co: American Bar Association, 750 N. Lake Shore Dr., Chicago, IL 60611-4497 Tel # (312) 988-6115 Fax # (312) 988-6030; Title Tel # (312) 988-5522 Title Fax # (312) 988-5528
Personnel: Editor-John Fallahay
Editorial Description: Newsletter for the ABA Forum Committee on the entertainment & sports industries.
General Info: Yr. Est. 1982, Quarterly, Trim Size-8½ x 11, Sheetfed press, 12 pages, ISSN: 0732-1880, 2 Color
Subscriptions: Indv. $20
Circulation: Total-4,000
List Rental: Rents Lists

Environment Reporter
See: ENVIRONMENT & ECOLOGY

Environmental Compliance Litigation & Strategy

Publishing Co: Leader Publications, Inc., 345 Park Avenue South, New York, NY 10010 Parent Co.-New York Law Publishing Co., New York; Title Tel # (212) 545-6170 Title Fax # (212) 696-1848
Personnel: Publisher-Stuart Wise, Editor-John Scagnelli, Editor-Lori Tripoli, Circ. Mgr.-Kerry Kyle, Mktg. Dir.-Rose-Ann Morangelei
Editorial Description: Legislation, regulations & case decisions involving hazardous waste.
General Info: (Formerly Hazardous Waste & Toxic Torts Law & Strategy), Yr. Est. 1985, Monthly, Trim Size-8½ x 11, Offset press, 8 pages, ISSN: 0884-3775, Color
Subscriptions: Indv. $210, $18/copy
Acquistions: Publication Sold

Environmental Compliance Report, The
See: ENVIRONMENT & ECOLOGY

Environmental Compliance Tool Kit
See: ENVIRONMENT & ECOLOGY

Environmental Control News for Southern Industry
See: ENVIRONMENT & ECOLOGY

Environmental Counselor, The

Publishing Co: Business Laws, Inc., 11630 Chillicothe Rd., Chesterland, OH 44026-1928; Title Tel # (216) 729-7996 Title Fax # (216) 729-7996
General Info: Yr. Est. 1988, Monthly, 24 pages, ISSN: 1041-3863
Subscriptions: Indv. $285, $20/copy

Environmental Impact in New York
See: ENVIRONMENT & ECOLOGY

Environmental LAWCAST

Publishing Co: Vox Juris, Inc., P.O. Box 389, Pennington, NJ 08534; Title Tel # (609) 737-6543 Title Fax # (609) 737-3860
Personnel: Publisher-Jason Meyer, Esq, Circ. Mgr.-Karen E. Anderson, Mktg. Mgr.-Kathy W. Gould
Editorial Description: The legal newscast on audio cassette for environmental lawyers. Each issue will include an audio cassette and companion outline.
General Info: Yr. Est. 1996, Semi-monthly

Environmental Laboratory Washington Report *Business*

Publishing Co: LRP Publications, 747 Dresher Rd., P.O. Box 980, Horsham, PA 19044-0980
Tel # (215) 784-0910 Fax # (215) 784-0317; Title Tel # (215) 784-0941 Title Fax # (215) 784-9639
Personnel: Publisher-Ken Kahn, Editor-Audrey Ross
Editorial Description: Covers regulation of safety and new laws/cases for managers of environmental labs.
General Info: (Formerly Laboratory Regulation News), Yr. Est. 1990, Bi-weekly, Trim Size-8½ x 11, Sheetfed press, 8 pages, ISSN: 1048-0706, 2 Color, Matte
Subscriptions: Indv. $349, For. $349
Acquistions: Publication Bought, Publication Sold

Environmental Law *Association*

Publishing Co: American Bar Association, 740 15th St. NW, Washington, DC 20005-1009
Tel # (202) 662-1016 Fax # (202) 662-1032; Title Tel # (202) 331-2276 Title Fax # (202) 331-2220
Personnel: Editor-Elissa Lichtenstein, Production Mgr.-Anne Dunn
Editorial Description: Current developments in the field of environmental law. Updates on all ABA environmental law programs, publications & other activities.
General Info: Yr. Est. 1973, Semi-annually, Trim Size-8½ x 11, Desktop press, 10 pages, ISSN: 0748-8769, 2 Color, Matte, Saddle-stitched
Subscriptions: Inst. $15, For. $37, $5/copy
Circulation: (96% controlled), Total-6,200, Subscriptions-200
List Rental: List Management Co.: Manager: Emily Ryerson; ABA List Sales, 750 N. Lakeshore Dr., Chicago, IL 60611, Actives: 6,200, $57/M

Environmental Law Journal *Association*

Publishing Co: State Bar of Texas, PO Box 12487 Capitol Station, Austin, TX 78711-2487
Tel # (512) 463-1463; Title Tel # (512) 463-1515
Personnel: Editor-Jimmy Alan Hall, Assoc. Ed.-Mewon Azarmehjr
Editorial Description: Newsletter of the Environmental & Natural Resources Law Section. Articles & notes on recent developments in this area of law for Texas practitioners. Notice of section activities & CLE courses.
General Info: Yr. Est. 1970, Quarterly, Trim Size-8½ x 11, 52 pages, ISSN: 0163-545X, No Color, Matte, Saddle-stitched
Subscriptions: Indv. $20, Inst. $20, $5/copy
Circulation: (99% controlled), Total-2,076, Readership-2,076
List Rental: Rents Lists

Environmental Law Reporter

Publishing Co: Sponsor-Environmental Law Institute, Environmental Law Institute, 1616 P St NW Ste 200, Washington, DC 20036-1493 Fax # (202) 328-5002; Title Tel # (202) 328-5150
Personnel: Publisher-J. William Futrell, Editor-Barry Breen, Circ. Mgr.-Anthony Waring, Production Mgr.-Dale Adams, Promotion Dir.-Anne Phelan
Editorial Description: Loose-leaf service for environmental specialists and students of environmental law.
General Info: Yr. Est. 1971, Monthly, Trim Size-8½ x 11, Web press, 160 pages, ISSN: 0046-2284, Ind/Abs/Online: Mead Data Central, WESTLAW, 2 Color, Newsprint, Saddle-stitched, Looseleaf
Subscriptions: Indv. $795
Circulation: Total-1,000
Printing Co: Goodway Graphics, 16 'A' Street, Burlington, MA 01803 Tel # (617) 272-5263, Fax # (617) 272-1752

Environmental Liability Enforcement & Penalties Report

Publishing Co: Shepard's/McGraw-Hill, Inc., 555 Middle Creek Pky, Colorado Springs, CO 80921-3622 Tel # (719) 488-3000; Title Tel # (719) 484-3000 Title Fax # (719) 481-7448
Personnel: Editor-Gala Hrgent, Production Mgr.-Cheryl Everitt, Adv. Dir.-Peggy Ives, Art Dir.-Leigh Vidakovich
General Info: (Formerly Environmental Liability in Commercial Transactions Reporter), Yr. Est. 1990, Monthly
Subscriptions: Indv. $295
Advertising: Inquire for rates.
List Rental: List Management Co.: The Lake Group, 411 Theodore Freund Ave., Rye, NY 10580-1497 Tel # (914) 925-2400, Fax # (914) 925-2499, Actives: 40,212, $130/M

Environmental Manager's Compliance Advisor
See: ENVIRONMENT & ECOLOGY

Environmental Notice Bulletin
See: ENVIRONMENT & ECOLOGY

Environmental Regulation/State Capitals
See: ENVIRONMENT & ECOLOGY

Ernie Mills' Legislative Report
See: GOVERNMENT

Estate Planning *Business*

Publishing Co: Research Institute of America, 117 E Stevens Ave, Valhalla, NY 10595-1264; Title Tel # (212) 645-4800
Editorial Description: Seven-volume analytical service that shows ho to develop, implement and administer plans for virtually every estate planning situation-backed with reprints of all applicable rules.
General Info: Monthly
List Rental: List Management Co.: WG & L List Management, 1 Penn Plz Fl 42, New York, NY 10119-0002 Tel # (212) 971-5000, Actives: $95/M, Expires: $60/M

Estate Planning Review
See: TAXES

Estate and Tax Bulletin

Publishing Co: Trust Dept., Natl. Bank Of Woodward & Fo, Detroit, MI 48278-0001; Title Tel # (313) 225-1000
Editorial Description: Investments, estate planning, wills and trusts.
General Info: Monthly

Estate Tax Freeze: Tools and Techniques *Business*

Publishing Co: Matthew Bender & Co., 11 Penn Plaza, New York, NY 10001-2006
Tel # (212) 967-7707 Fax # (212) 244-3188
Editorial Description: A collection of planning techniques designed to 'freeze' the value of a client's estate at current levels with passing future appreciation to the next generation. Provides practical guidance, comprehensive income, estate & gift tax text & all the necessary forms.
General Info: Yr. Est. 1985, Irregular, Looseleaf

Estate Tax Techniques *Business*

Publishing Co: Matthew Bender & Co., 11 Penn Plaza, New York, NY 10001-2006
Fax # (212) 244-3188; Title Tel # (212) 967-7707
Personnel: Editor-Bernard Greisman
Editorial Description: A working guide to estate, gift, & fiduciary income taxes, written by experts in the field, focusing on planning, problem solving, & practical applications of the law.
General Info: Yr. Est. 1965, Irregular, Looseleaf
Subscriptions: $250/copy

Estates, Powers, & Trusts Law
See: TAXES

Ethics in Government Reporter
See: GOVERNMENT

European Patents Handbook *Business*

Publishing Co: Matthew Bender & Co., 11 Penn Plaza, New York, NY 10001-2006
Tel # (212) 967-7707 Fax # (212) 244-3188
Editorial Description: A guidebook for patent attorneys.
General Info: Yr. Est. 1988, Irregular, Looseleaf

Executive Compensation
See: TAXES

Executive Legal Summary

Publishing Co: Business Laws, Inc., 11630 Chillicothe Rd., Chesterland, OH 44026-1928; Title Tel # (216) 729-7996
Personnel: Editor-William Hancock
General Info: Yr. Est. 1987, Quarterly, 4 pages
Subscriptions: Indv. $225, $10/copy

Exempt Organizations Report
See: TAXES

Exercise Standards & Malpractice Reporter, The *Business*

Publishing Co: PRC Publishing, Inc., 4418 Belden Village St NW, Canton, OH 44718-2516; Title Tel # (216) 492-6063 Title Fax # (216) 492-6176
Personnel: Editor-David L. Herbert, Esq., Production Mgr., Adv. Dir.-Molly Romig
Editorial Description: Quarterly newsletter designed to keep exercise and fitness professionals up to date on legal issues, standards of care, and laws affecting their fields.
General Info: Yr. Est. 1987, Bi-monthly, Sheetfed press, 16 pages, ISSN: 0891-0278, 2 Color, Matte, Saddle-stitched
Subscriptions: Indv. $40, Can. $46, For. $50, $10/copy
Circulation: (31% controlled), Subscriptions-1,000
Advertising: Inquire for rates. Accepts Inserts.
List Rental: Rents Lists

Expert and the Law *Association*

Publishing Co: Natl. Forensic Center, 17 Temple Ter, Lawrenceville, NJ 08648-3254; Title Tel # (609) 883-0550 Title Fax # (609) 883-7622
Personnel: Publisher-Betty Lipscher, Editor-Mark Wieckowski
Editorial Description: Application of scientific, medical, & technical knowledge to litigation.
General Info: Yr. Est. 1981, Bi-monthly, Trim Size-8½ x 11, Sheetfed press, 14 pages, Ind/Abs/Online: Mead Data Central, Color-cover, Newsprint
Subscriptions: Indv. $55
Circulation: Total-2,000
Advertising: Accepts Inserts.
List Rental: Actives: $200/M

FAIR-Immigration Report   *Consumer, Association*

Publishing Co: Federation for American Immigration Reform, 1666 Connecticut Ave NW, Ste. 400, Washington, DC 20009-1039; Title Tel # (202) 328-7004 Title Fax # (202) 387-3447
Personnel: Editor-Laura Viani
Editorial Description: For educating American people about the need to stop illegal immigration.
General Info: Yr. Est. 1979, Monthly, Trim Size-8½ x 11, 4 pages, ISSN: 1067-3337, 2 Color, Matte
Subscriptions: Indv. $25
Circulation: Total-41,000

FCC Daily Release Service   *Business*

Publishing Co: CCH Washington Service Bureau, Inc., 655 15th St NW Ste 275, Washington, DC 20005-5701 Tel # (202) 508-0600 Fax # (202) 508-0694
Personnel: Editor-Michelle George, Circ. Mgr.-Trent Seibert
Editorial Description: Daily release service of the public notices, reports, and agendas issued by the Federal Communications Commission.
General Info: Yr. Est. 1982, Daily, Looseleaf

FCL Newsletter
See: CIVIL RIGHTS

FDA Advertising and Promotion Manual   *Business*

Publishing Co: Thompson Publishing Group, 1725 K Street, NW, Washington, DC 20006 Tel # (202) 872-4000
Personnel: Editor-Wayne L. Pines
Editorial Description: Explains FDA and FTC regulations and guidelines for the advertising and promotion of pharmaceutical, medical device, biological, food, veterinary medicine, and cosmetic products. Subscription includes monthly updates and bulletins.
General Info: Annually, Looseleaf
Subscriptions: Indv. $647

FDA Enforcement Manual   *Business*

Publishing Co: Thompson Publishing Group, 1725 K Street, NW, Washington, DC 20006 Tel # (202) 872-4000
Personnel: Editor-Arthur N. Levine
Editorial Description: An essential tool for professional in the drug, medical device, food, and cosmetic industries who are responsible for compliance with FDA enforcement strategies. Subscription includes monthly bulletins.
General Info: Annually, Looseleaf
Subscriptions: Indv. $637

FDA Outline
See: GOVERNMENT

F.E.A.R. Chronicles
See: CIVIL RIGHTS

FELA Reporter and Railroad Liability Monitor
See: RAILROADS

FFL Newsletter

Publishing Co: Bureau of Alchohol, Tobacco, & Firearms, 1200 Penn. Ave. NW Ste. #7240, Washington, DC 20226-0001; Title Tel # (202) 566-7268
Personnel: Editor-Dot Koester
Editorial Description: To inform federal firearms licensees of changes in firearms laws/regulations.
General Info: Yr. Est. 1979, Semi-annually, Offset press, 4 pages, No Color, Newsprint
Circulation: (100% controlled), Total-235,000

FTC FOIA Log
See: BUSINESS & INDUSTRY

FTC WATCH
See: BUSINESS & INDUSTRY

Fair Employment Compliance
See: LABOR

Fair Employment Practices   *Business*

Publishing Co: Bureau of National Affairs, Inc., 1231 25th St. NW, Bldg. N-200, Washington, DC 20037-1157 Fax # (202) 822-8092; Title Tel # (202) 452-4200 Title Fax # (202) 452-4603
Personnel: Publisher-William A. Beltz, Editor-Bill Manville, Mng. Editor-Nancy J. Sedmak, Circ. Mgr.-Gary C. Seltzer
Editorial Description: A guide to the regulation of fair employment practices, including federal laws, orders, & regulations; policy guides & ground rules; & state & local fair employment practice laws.
General Info: (Formerly Fair Employment Practices Weekly), Yr. Est. 1965, Weekly, Trim Size-6 x 9, Web press, ISSN: 0149-2683, Ind/Abs/Online: HRIN, Westlaw, Lexis, Nexis, Looseleaf
Subscriptions: Indv. $1,280

Fair Employment Practices Summary of Latest Developments   *Business*

Publishing Co: Bureau of National Affairs, Inc., 1231 25th St. NW, Bldg. N-200, Washington, DC 20037-1157 Tel # (202) 452-4200 Fax # (202) 822-8092; Title Tel # (202) 452-4358 Title Fax # (202) 452-4603
Personnel: Publisher-William A. Beltz, Editor-Bill L. Manville, Circ. Mgr.-Gary C. Seltzer
Editorial Description: Highlights developments in employment opportunity & affirmative action, federal & state court decisions, EEOC rulings, OFCCP decisions, new laws, regulations, & agency directives, special programs for minorities, the handicapped, women, & older workers.
General Info: Yr. Est. 1965, Bi-weekly, Trim Size-8½ x 11, Web press, 6 pages, ISSN: 0525-2156, Ind/Abs/Online: HRIN
Subscriptions: Indv. $118

Family, Law and Democracy Report
See: GOVERNMENT

Family Law Handbook
See: FAMILY

Family Law Reporter
See: FAMILY

Family Law: Texas Practice and Procedure   *Business*

Publishing Co: Matthew Bender & Co., 11 Penn Plaza, New York, NY 10001-2006 Tel # (212) 967-7707 Fax # (212) 244-3188
Editorial Description: Thoroughly detailed exposition of all aspects of family law practice in Texas.
General Info: Yr. Est. 1982, Irregular, Looseleaf

Family and Medical Leave Handbook   *Business*

Publishing Co: Thompson Publishing Group, 1725 K Street, NW, Washington, DC 20006 Tel # (202) 872-4000
Editorial Description: Information for compliance with the Family and Medical Leave Act with updates and news bulletins monthly.
General Info: Annually, Looseleaf
Subscriptions: Indv. $298

Family Relations/State Capitals   *Business*

Publishing Co: Wakeman/Walworth, 300 N. Washington St., Alexandria, VA 22314-2530; Title Tel # (703) 549-8606 Title Fax # (703) 549-1372
Personnel: Publisher-Keyes Walworth
Editorial Description: Reports on legislative and regulatory measures concerning domestic violence, women's rights, juvenile justice, marital rights, abortion laws, welfare reform, AIDS testing.
General Info: (Formerly Family Relations from the State Capitals), Yr. Est. 1946, Weekly, Trim Size-8½ x 11, Offset press, 5 pages, ISSN: 0741-3505, No Color
Subscriptions: Indv. $265, Inst. $212, Can. $235, For. $255

Federal Action Affecting the States/State Capitals
See: U.S. (& CANADIAN) FED. GOV'T.

Federal Administrative Law Judges Conference Newsletter   *Association*

Publishing Co: FALJC, 800 K St NW Ste 400, Washington, DC 20001-8000; Title Tel # (202) 653-5000
General Info: Quarterly

Federal Audit Guides
See: ACCOUNTING

Federal Banking Law Reports   *Business*

Publishing Co: CCH, Inc., 2700 Lake Cook Rd., Riverwoods, IL 60015 Parent Co.-Kluwer Law & Taxation Publishers, Cambridge; Title Tel # (847) 267-7000 Title Fax # (800) 224-8299
Editorial Description: Spans Federal Reserve System, Deposit Insurance, National Bank Acts, related federal banking and loan rules.
General Info: Yr. Est. 1914, Weekly, Trim Size-6 x 9, Web press, 200 pages, No Color, Looseleaf
Subscriptions: Indv. $1,323

Federal Banking Law Service of A.S. Pratt   *Business*

Publishing Co: A.S. Pratt & Sons, 1911 Fort Myer Dr., Ste 308, Arlington, VA 22209-1603 Tel # (703) 528-1045; Title Tel # (703) 528-0145
Personnel: Publisher-Alan Rice, Editor-David Stemler
Editorial Description: Federal banking laws, rules and regulations, including consumer protection laws.
General Info: 35x/yr., Trim Size-6 x 9, ISSN: 0744-8791, Looseleaf
Subscriptions: Indv. $335

Federal Bankruptcy
Handbook

Publishing Co: Gould Publications, Inc, 1333 N US Highway 17-92, Longwood, FL 32750-3724
Tel # (407) 695-9500 Fax # (407) 695-2906; Title Tel # (607) 724-3000
Editorial Description: Complete unannotated title II & other pertinent statutes.
General Info: Annually, Trim Size-5½ x 8½, Sheetfed press, 650 pages, No Color, Looseleaf
Subscriptions: $21/copy

Federal Carriers Reports
See: TRAFFIC & TRANSPORTATION

Federal Case News

Publishing Co: West Publishing, 620 Opperman Dr., Eagan, MN 55123-1340 Tel # (612) 687-7000
Fax # (612) 687-7302 Parent Co.-Thomson Corp., Stamford
Editorial Description: Features information on a variety of cases being heard in the federal courts.
General Info: Weekly

Federal Civil Procedure
Handbook

Publishing Co: Gould Publications, Inc, 1333 N US Highway 17-92, Longwood, FL 32750-3724
Tel # (407) 695-9500 Fax # (407) 695-2906; Title Tel # (607) 724-3000
Editorial Description: Complete statute, USC Title 28, committee notes & Appellate Procedure Rules.
General Info: Annually, Trim Size-5½ x 8½, Sheetfed press, 900 pages, No Color, Looseleaf
Subscriptions: $21/copy

Federal Consumer
Protection: Laws,
Rules, & Regulations   *Business, Consumer*

Publishing Co: Oceana Publications, Inc., 75 Main St, Dobbs Ferry, NY 10522-1601
Tel # (914) 693-8100; Title Tel # (914) 693-1320 Title Fax # (914) 693-0402
Personnel: Editor-B.D. Reams, Jr., Production Mgr.-Mike Wortzman, Mktg. Dir.-John Downey
General Info: Yr. Est. 1979, Irregular, Trim Size-7 x 10, Looseleaf
Subscriptions: Indv. $695

Federal Contract Disputes   *Business*

Publishing Co: Business Publishers, Inc., 951 Pershing Dr., Silver Spring, MD 20910-4464;
Title Tel # (301) 589-5103 Title Fax # (301) 589-8493
Personnel: Publisher-Leonard A. Eiserer, Editor-Bruce Jervis, Esq., Circ. Mgr.-Brenda Davenport, Mktg. Mgr.-Eric Easton
Editorial Description: Coverage designed to help readers avoid disputes and successfully resolve those that can't be avoided. Gives concise synopses of major decisions.
General Info: Yr. Est. 1984, Monthly, Trim Size-8½ x 11, Desktop press, 8 pages, ISSN: 0747-9700, No Color, Recycled
Subscriptions: Indv. $285, Can. $285, For. $291
Advertising: Accepts Inserts.
List Rental: Rents Lists

Federal Contracts Report
See: BUSINESS & INDUSTRY

Federal Court of Appeal
Decisions

Publishing Co: Western Legal Publications, 301-1 Alexander St., Vancouver, BC V6A 1B2 Canada;
Title Tel # (604) 687-5671 Title Fax # (604) 687-2796
Personnel: Publisher-Nancy Cotter, Editor-Ronda McNabb
Editorial Description: Features court of appeals decisions on a wide range of cases.
General Info: Yr. Est. 1981, Monthly, ISSN: 0227-0390, Ind/Abs/Online: QL, INFOMART, Looseleaf
Subscriptions: Indv. $165

Federal Court of Canada
Service

Publishing Co: Butterworths, 75 Clegg Rd., Markham, ON L6G 1A1 Canada Tel # (905) 479-2665
Fax # (905) 479-2826; Title Tel # (416) 479-2665
Personnel: Editor-R.T. Hughes
General Info: Quarterly, Looseleaf
Subscriptions: Can. $310

Federal Court Procurement Decisions
See: GOVERNMENT

Federal Criminal Law
Handbook

Publishing Co: Gould Publications, Inc, 1333 N US Highway 17-92, Longwood, FL 32750-3724
Tel # (407) 695-9500 Fax # (407) 695-2906; Title Tel # (607) 724-3000
Editorial Description: Complete title 18 & title 21 (chapter 13) & rules of criminal procedure.
General Info: Annually, Trim Size-5½ x 8½, Sheetfed press, 1,000 pages, Looseleaf
Subscriptions: $21/copy

Federal Election Campaign Financing Guide
See: POLITICS

Federal Estate and Gift Tax Reports
See: TAXES

Federal Ethics Report
See: GOVERNMENT

Federal Evidence Practice
Guide   *Business*

Publishing Co: Matthew Bender & Co., 11 Penn Plaza, New York, NY 10001-2006
Tel # (212) 967-7707 Fax # (212) 244-3188
Editorial Description: Some of the country's leading trial lawyers provide thoughtful, practical guidance on crucial evidentiary matters from pre-trial gathering of the evidence through summation.
General Info: Yr. Est. 1989, Irregular, Looseleaf

Federal Excise Tax Reports
See: TAXES

Federal Income, Gift and
Estate Taxation   *Business*

Publishing Co: Matthew Bender & Co., 11 Penn Plaza, New York, NY 10001-2006
Fax # (212) 244-3188; Title Tel # (212) 967-7707
Personnel: Editor-V. Lorenzo
Editorial Description: Combines the highest level tax scholarship with a practical approach.
General Info: Yr. Est. 1942, Monthly, Looseleaf
Subscriptions: $860/copy

Federal Litigation Guide   *Business*

Publishing Co: Matthew Bender & Co., 11 Penn Plaza, New York, NY 10001-2006
Tel # (212) 967-7707 Fax # (212) 244-3188
Editorial Description: Top federal litigators provide invaluable practical guidance on the strategy & tactics involved in handling a civil case in the federal courts.
General Info: Yr. Est. 1985, Irregular, Looseleaf

Federal Litigator

Publishing Co: Shepard's/McGraw-Hill, Inc., 555 Middle Creek Pky, Colorado Springs, CO 80921-3622; Title Tel # (719) 488-3000 Title Fax # (719) 481-7448
Personnel: Editor-Jeffrey Brand, Editor-Neil Levy, Production Mgr.-Cheryl Everitt, Adv. Dir.-Peggy Ives, Art Dir.-Leigh Vidakovich
Editorial Description: Covers federal litigation issues.
General Info: Yr. Est. 1985, 10x/yr.
Subscriptions: Indv. $295
List Rental: List Management Co.: The Lake Group, 411 Theodore Freund Ave., Rye, NY 10580-1497 Tel # (914) 925-2400, Fax # (914) 925-2499, Actives: 40,212, $130/M

Federal Register Abstracts-Master Edition
See: U.S. (& CANADIAN) FED. GOV'T.

Federal Register Report
See: U.S. (& CANADIAN) FED. GOV'T.

Federal Rules of Evidence

Publishing Co: Gould Publications, Inc, 1333 N US Highway 17-92, Longwood, FL 32750-3724
Tel # (407) 695-9500 Fax # (407) 695-2906; Title Tel # (607) 724-3000
Editorial Description: Complete rules of evidence, committee notes, forms, uniform rules & addenda of related statutes & rules.
General Info: Annually, Trim Size-5½ x 8½, Sheetfed press, 250 pages, No Color, Looseleaf
Subscriptions: $13/copy

Federal Rules of Evidence
News

Publishing Co: Callaghan & Company, 155 Pfingsten Rd., Deerfield, IL 60015-5293;
Title Tel # (708) 948-7000
General Info: Monthly
Subscriptions: Indv. $155

Federal Securities Act of 1933-Treatise and Primary Source Manual
See: BANKING & FINANCE

Federal Securities Exchange Act of 1934
See: BANKING & FINANCE

Federal Securities Law
Reports   *Association*

Publishing Co: CCH, Inc., 2700 Lake Cook Rd., Riverwoods, IL 60015 Parent Co.-Kluwer Law & Taxation Publishers, Cambridge; Title Tel # (847) 267-7000 Title Fax # (800) 224-8299
Editorial Description: Covers SEC activities in controlling the securities business, pertinent laws, regulations, court and administrative decisions, etc. The accompanying Summary is available separately.
General Info: Yr. Est. 1933, Weekly, Trim Size-6 x 9, Web press, No Color, Looseleaf
Subscriptions: Indv. $1,447

Federal Sentencing Manual   *Business*

Publishing Co: Matthew Bender & Co., 11 Penn Plaza, New York, NY 10001-2006
Tel # (212) 967-7707 Fax # (212) 244-3188
Editorial Description: The first complete step-by-step guide to the system of federal sentencing created under the Sentencing Reform Act & the United States Sentencing Guidelines.
General Info: Yr. Est. 1989, Irregular, Looseleaf

Federal Tax Articles
See: TAXES

Federal Tax Coordinator 2d
See: TAXES

Federal Tax Forms
See: TAXES

Federal Taxation of Trusts, Grantors and Beneficiaries   *Business*

Publishing Co: Warren, Gorham & Lamont, 31 Saint James Ave., Boston, MA 02116-4112 Fax # (617) 423-1914 Parent Co.-Thomson Professional Publications, Stamford; Title Tel # (617) 423-2020
Personnel: Publisher-Wayne Barr, Production Mgr.-Mavra Kiey, Mktg. Dir.-Jim Spillane
Editorial Description: Guidance for tax specialists attorneys, accountants, trust officers, etc.
General Info: Yr. Est. 1978, Annually, Looseleaf
Subscriptions: Indv. $160
List Rental: List Management Co.: American List Counsel, 88 Orchard Cir # Cn-5219, Princeton, NJ 08540-3026 Tel # (908) 874-4300, Fax # (908) 874-4433

Federal Tort Claims Act News   *Business*

Publishing Co: LRP Publications, 747 Dresher Rd., P.O. Box 980, Horsham, PA 19044-0980 Tel # (215) 784-0910 Fax # (215) 784-0317
Editorial Description: Covers rapid changes in Federal Tort Claims Act case interpretation.
General Info: Monthly

Fiduciary Tax Guide
See: TAXES

Financial & Estate Planning
See: TAXES

Fink and Bornstein Workers' Compensation Newsletter   *Business*

Publishing Co: Fink & Bornstein, 466 DuPont Street, Toronto, ON M5R 1W6 Canada; Title Tel # (416) 537-0108 Title Fax # (416) 926-0072
General Info: Quarterly, Trim Size-8$\frac{1}{2}$ x 11, 10 pages, No Color, Matte
Subscriptions: Indv. $75

Fire & Casualty   *Business*

Publishing Co: CCH, Inc., 2700 Lake Cook Rd., Riverwoods, IL 60015 Parent Co.-Kluwer Law & Taxation Publishers, Cambridge; Title Tel # (847) 267-7000 Title Fax # (800) 224-8299
Editorial Description: Covers current court decisions relating to Fire and Casualty.
General Info: (Formerly Insurance Law Reports: Fire), Yr. Est. 1938, Bi-weekly, Trim Size-6 x 9, Web press, 75 pages, Color, Looseleaf
Subscriptions: Indv. $1,042

Fire and Police Personnel Reporter
See: LABOR

Firehouse Lawyer Monthly   *Business*

Publishing Co: Quinlan Publishing, 23 Drydock Ave, Boston, MA 02210-2387 Fax # (617) 345-9646; Title Tel # (617) 542-0048
Editorial Description: Problems of legal nature facing firefighters.
General Info: Yr. Est. 1978, Monthly
Subscriptions: Indv. $57
List Rental: List Management Co.: Stevens-Knox List Management, 304 Park Ave S., New York, NY 10010-5312 Tel # (212) 388-8800, Fax # (212) 388-8890

Fletcher Corporation Law Adviser

Publishing Co: Clark Boardman Callaghan & Co., 155 Pfingsten Rd., Deerfield, IL 60015; Title Tel # (708) 948-7000 Title Fax # (708) 948-8955
Editorial Description: Case, statute and regulatory effects on corporate law.
General Info: Monthly, 8 pages
Subscriptions: Indv. $295
Acquistions: Publication Bought, Publication Sold

Florida Administrative Law Reports   *Business, Association*

Publishing Co: FALR, Inc., PO Box 2309, Gainesville, FL 32602-2309; Title Tel # (904) 375-8036
Personnel: Publisher, Editor-Jim Konish
Editorial Description: Official administrative law reporter for most Florida agencies.
General Info: Yr. Est. 1979, Bi-weekly, Trim Size-7 x 8$\frac{1}{2}$, 250 pages, Ind/Abs/Online: Mead Data Central, Looseleaf
Subscriptions: Indv. $425

Florida Civil Trial Guide   *Business*

Publishing Co: Matthew Bender & Co., 11 Penn Plaza, New York, NY 10001-2006 Tel # (212) 967-7707 Fax # (212) 244-3188
Editorial Description: Contains dietailed discussion of the Florida Evidence Code & judicial interpretations, plus actual scripts for objections, responses, & arguments of the admission of evidence. Also covers pre-trial matters. Jury selection is explained & opening remarks & question for use on voir dire provided.
General Info: Yr. Est. 1990, Irregular, Looseleaf

Florida Corporations--Law and Practice   *Business*

Publishing Co: Matthew Bender & Co., 11 Penn Plaza, New York, NY 10001-2006 Tel # (212) 967-7707 Fax # (212) 244-3188
Editorial Description: Experts provide in-depth coverage of litigation & non-litigation matters associated with Florida Corporation law & its related tax & securities considerations.
General Info: Yr. Est. 1985, Irregular, Looseleaf

Florida Criminal Law and Motor Vehicle Handbook

Publishing Co: Gould Publications, Inc, 1333 N US Highway 17-92, Longwood, FL 32750-3724 Tel # (407) 695-9500 Fax # (407) 695-2906; Title Tel # (607) 724-3000
Editorial Description: A complete presentation of selected sections which directly relate to crimes, criminal procedure and corrections, domestic relations, alcoholic beverage, public health, audience proceedings relating to juveniles, as well as statutes.
General Info: Annually, 1,150 pages, Looseleaf
Subscriptions: Indv. $20, $19/copy

Florida Criminal Laws

Publishing Co: Gould Publications, Inc, 1333 N US Highway 17-92, Longwood, FL 32750-3724 Tel # (407) 695-9500 Fax # (407) 695-2906; Title Tel # (607) 724-3000
Editorial Description: This book presents selected chapter of the Criminal Laws of the State of Florida, with an appendix including rules of criminal proceedure, rules of juvenille procedure, other selected pertinent sections from the Florida statutes.
General Info: Annually, 680 pages, Looseleaf
Subscriptions: Indv. $17, $15/copy

Florida Employment Law Letter   *Business*

Publishing Co: M. Lee Smith Publishers & Printers ,LCC, P.O. Box 198867, 162 Fourth Avenue North, Nashville, TN 37219-8867; Title Tel # (615) 242-7395 Title Fax # (615) 256-6601
Personnel: Publisher-M Lee Smith, Editor-G. Thomas Harper, Circ. Mgr.-Cathy Bradford, Mktg. Dir.-David Yates
Editorial Description: Review of Florida employment law developments.
General Info: Yr. Est. 1989, Monthly, Trim Size-8$\frac{1}{2}$ x 11, 8 pages, ISSN: 1041-3537, 2 Color
Subscriptions: Indv. $127
List Rental: Actives: $75/M
Printing Co: M. Lee Smith Publishers & Printers ,LLC, PO Box 198867, 162 Fourth Avenue, Nashville, TN 37219-8867 Tel # (615) 242-7395, Fax # (615) 256-6601

Florida Environmental Compliance Update   *Business*

Publishing Co: M. Lee Smith Publishers & Printers ,LCC, P.O. Box 198867, 162 Fourth Avenue North, Nashville, TN 37219-8867 Fax # (615) 256-6601; Title Tel # (615) 242-7395 Title Fax # (615) 296-6601
Personnel: Publisher-M Lee Smith, Circ. Mgr.-Cathy Bradford, Mktg. Dir.-David Yates
Editorial Description: Review of Florida environmental law developments.
General Info: (Formerly Florida Environmental & Land Use Letter), Yr. Est. 1990, Monthly, Trim Size-8$\frac{1}{2}$ x 11, 8 pages, ISSN: 1064-1874, 2 Color
Subscriptions: Indv. $117
List Rental: Actives: $90/M
Printing Co: M. Lee Smith Publishers & Printers ,LLC, PO Box 198867, 162 Fourth Avenue, Nashville, TN 37219-8867 Tel # (615) 242-7395, Fax # (615) 256-6601

Florida Estates Practice Guide   *Business*

Publishing Co: Matthew Bender & Co., 11 Penn Plaza, New York, NY 10001-2006 Fax # (212) 244-3188; Title Tel # (212) 967-7707
Personnel: Editor-S. Schiff
Editorial Description: Information for the estate practitioner in Florida.
General Info: Yr. Est. 1964, Irregular, Looseleaf
Subscriptions: $300/copy

Florida Family Law   *Business*

Publishing Co: Matthew Bender & Co., 11 Penn Plaza, New York, NY 10001-2006 Tel # (212) 967-7707 Fax # (212) 244-3188
Editorial Description: Complete, up-to-the-minute coverage of every aspect of Florida family law, including both litigation & non-litigation matters. Each chapter is written or reviewed by an experienced Florida attorney who provides analysis of the law, together with numerouscases, forms, & other practical illustrations.
General Info: Yr. Est. 1986, Irregular, Looseleaf

Florida Family Law
Reporter *Business*

Publishing Co: Matthew Bender & Co., 11 Penn Plaza, New York, NY 10001-2006
Tel # (212) 967-7707 Fax # (212) 244-3188
Editorial Description: Contians summaries & analysis of Florida supreme court & appellate court matrimonial decisions; significant Florida legislation affecting family law practice; U.S. Supreme Court & federal court decisions in all areas of family law; & relevant tax developments. Includes comments on major decisions, & cross-references to Florida Family Law for further research of relevant issues.
General Info: Yr. Est. 1986, Monthly, Looseleaf

Florida Forms of Jury
Instruction *Business*

Publishing Co: Matthew Bender & Co., 11 Penn Plaza, New York, NY 10001-2006
Tel # (212) 967-7707 Fax # (212) 244-3188
Editorial Description: Coverage includes basic concepts & procedures governing instructions for any state of a civil action, a comprehensive section on breach of contract & a plethora of material on tort actions.
General Info: Yr. Est. 1989, Irregular, Looseleaf

Florida Healthtrac *Business, Consumer*

Publishing Co: M. Lee Smith Publishers & Printers ,LCC, P.O. Box 198867, 162 Fourth Avenue North, Nashville, TN 37219-8867 Tel # (615) 242-7395 Fax # (615) 256-6601
Personnel: Publisher-M. Lee Smith, Editor-Creston Nelson-Morrill, Circ. Mgr.-Cathy Bradford, Mktg. Dir.-Dave Yates
Editorial Description: Covers Florida's health law news for health-care providers.
General Info: Yr. Est. 1994, Monthly, Trim Size-8½ x 11, 12 pages, ISSN: 1078-6996, 2 Color
Subscriptions: Indv. $187
Acquistions: Publication Bought, Publication Sold
List Rental: Rents Lists
Printing Co: M. Lee Smith Publishers & Printers ,LLC, PO Box 198867, 162 Fourth Avenue, Nashville, TN 37219-8867 Tel # (615) 242-7395, Fax # (615) 256-6601

Florida Jury Verdict
Reporter

Publishing Co: Florida Legal Periodicals, Inc., PO Box 3730, Tallahassee, FL 32315-3730; Title Tel # (904) 224-6649
General Info: Yr. Est. 1981, Monthly, Trim Size-5½ x 8, Offset press, 28 pages, 1% ads, No Color, Looseleaf
Subscriptions: $20/copy
Circulation: Total-500
Advertising: Inquire for rates.

Florida Motor Vehicle Laws

Publishing Co: Gould Publications, Inc, 1333 N US Highway 17-92, Longwood, FL 32750-3724 Tel # (407) 695-9500 Fax # (407) 695-2906; Title Tel # (607) 724-3000
Editorial Description: Florida Motor Vehicle Laws. Unannotated.
General Info: Annually, Trim Size-5½ x 8½, 520 pages, No Color, Looseleaf
Subscriptions: $17/copy

Florida Real Estate Transactions
See: REAL ESTATE

Florida Torts *Business*

Publishing Co: Matthew Bender & Co., 11 Penn Plaza, New York, NY 10001-2006
Tel # (212) 967-7707 Fax # (212) 244-3188
Editorial Description: Prepared by experienced Florida practitioners, this substantive & practical guide, covers all the vital litigation & non-litigation matters associated with Florida tort law.
General Info: Yr. Est. 1988, Irregular, Looseleaf

Florida Torts Reporter *Business*

Publishing Co: Matthew Bender & Co., 11 Penn Plaza, New York, NY 10001-2006
Tel # (212) 967-7707 Fax # (212) 244-3188
Editorial Description: A valuable companion to Florida Torts, or an independent monthly service publication, this reporter covers the most recent judicial, administrative & legislative activities affecting the full range of Florida tort law.
General Info: Yr. Est. 1988, Monthly, Looseleaf

Florida Workers'
Compensation Law
Bulletin *Business, Consumer*

Publishing Co: LRP Publications, 747 Dresher Rd., P.O. Box 980, Horsham, PA 19044-0980
Tel # (215) 784-0910 Fax # (215) 784-0317
Personnel: Publisher-Kenneth F. Kahn, Editor-Joanne Fiore, Production Mgr.-Kathleen P. Neely, Mktg. Dir.-Jana Shellington, Promotion Dir.-Gary Ragin
Editorial Description: Publishes summaries of final merit orders from the judges of compensation claims, as well as decisions from the First District Court of Appeals and the Supreme Court of Florida.
General Info: Yr. Est. 1994, Bi-weekly
Subscriptions: Indv. $245

Florida Worker's
Compensation Reporter *Business*

Publishing Co: M. Lee Smith Publishers & Printers ,LCC, P.O. Box 198867, 162 Fourth Avenue North, Nashville, TN 37219-8867 Tel # (615) 242-7395 Fax # (615) 256-6601
Personnel: Publisher-M. Lee Smith, Editor-Creston Nelson-Morrill, Circ. Mgr.-Cathy Bradford, Mktg. Dir.-Dave Yates
Editorial Description: Covers Florida's workers' Compensation developments.
General Info: Yr. Est. 1994, Monthly, Trim Size-8½ x 11, 12 pages, ISSN: 1078-7003, 2 Color
Subscriptions: Indv. $147
List Rental: Rents Lists
Printing Co: M. Lee Smith Publishers & Printers ,LLC, PO Box 198867, 162 Fourth Avenue, Nashville, TN 37219-8867 Tel # (615) 242-7395, Fax # (615) 256-6601

Food Drug Cosmetic Law Reports
See: DRUGS & PHARMACEUTICALS

For the Record *Business, Association*

Publishing Co: National Sports Law Institute, Marquette Univ. Law School, P.O Box 1881, Milwaukee, WI 53201-1881; Title Tel # (414) 288-5815 Title Fax # (414) 288-5818
Personnel: Publisher-James Gray
Editorial Description: Articles address sports law, sports business, and sports ethics.
General Info: Yr. Est. 1989, Bi-monthly, Trim Size-8½ x 11, 8 pages, 2 Color
Subscriptions: Indv. $100, Free With Membership
Acquistions: Publication Bought, Publication Sold
Circulation: Total-500
Advertising: Inquire for rates. Accepts Inserts.
List Rental: Rents Lists

For the Record EXTRA
See: SPORTS & SPORTING GOODS

Foreign Assets Litigation
Reporter *Business*

Publishing Co: Andrews Publications, Inc., 1646 West Chester Pike, PO Box 1000, Westtown, PA 19395 Tel # (610) 399-6600; Title Tel # (215) 399-6600 Title Fax # (610) 399-6610
Personnel: Publisher-John E. Backe, Editor-Michelle Sarnocinski, Mktg. Dir.-Andrew Katz
General Info: (Formerly Iranian Assets Litigation Reporter), Yr. Est. 1980, Monthly, Trim Size-8½ x 11, Mimeo press, 90 pages, ISSN: 0277-2922, No Color, Newsprint
Subscriptions: Indv. $1,500, $133/copy
Advertising: Inquire for rates.
List Rental: Actives: 66,686, $125/M

Foreign Investment in Canada
See: BANKING & FINANCE

Foreign Tax Law Bi-Weekly
Bulletin *Association*

Publishing Co: Foreign Tax Law Publishers, Inc., PO Box 2189, Ormond Beach, FL 32175-2189; Title Tel # (904) 253-5785 Title Fax # (904) 257-3003
Editorial Description: Selected texts of amending laws and decrees, bills, proposed amendments and regulations, on taxation, corporate and investment law, translated into english from countries worldwide.
General Info: Yr. Est. 1947, Bi-weekly, Trim Size-8½ x 11, Sheetfed press, 19 pages, Ind/Abs/ Online: owens on line, No Color, Newsprint
Subscriptions: Indv. $150, Can. $200, For. $200

Forensic Sciences *Business*

Publishing Co: Matthew Bender & Co., 11 Penn Plaza, New York, NY 10001-2006
Tel # (212) 967-7707 Fax # (212) 244-3188
Personnel: Editor-Cyril H. Wecht, M.D., J.D.
Editorial Description: More than 25 experts discuss the sciences relevant to criminal and civil litigation and the law concerning their use in the courtroom.
General Info: Yr. Est. 1981, Irregular, Looseleaf

Forensic Serology News

Publishing Co: Forensic Sciences Foundation, Inc., PO Box 669, Colorado Springs, CO 80901-0669; Title Tel # (303) 596-6006
Personnel: Editor-Robert Gaensslen
General Info: Yr. Est. 1975, Bi-monthly
Circulation: Total-200

Forms and Procdures
Under the UCC *Business*

Publishing Co: Matthew Bender & Co., 11 Penn Plaza, New York, NY 10001-2006
Tel # (212) 967-7707 Fax # (212) 244-3188
Editorial Description: Complete guidance & procedural analysis for all aspects of the UCC & related statutes such as the Federal Consumer Credit Protection Act (Truth-in-Lending) & the Magnuson-Moss Federal Warranty Act. Includes forms, checklists & illustrative examples to explain application of the UCC to specific commercial situations.
General Info: Yr. Est. 1963, Irregular, Looseleaf

Fortune News
See: LAW ENFORCEMENT & PENOLOGY

Fourth Circuit Review   *Business*

Publishing Co: Appellate Review, Inc., 500 Country Lane, Louisville, KY 40207 Tel # (502) 897-5079 Fax # (502) 899-7791
Personnel: Publisher-Patricia Owen
Editorial Description: Presents digests of federal court decisions.
General Info: Yr. Est. 1985, Semi-monthly, ISSN: 0889-3578
Subscriptions: Indv. $267

Franchising Business & Law Alert   *Business*

Publishing Co: Leader Publications, Inc., 345 Park Avenue South, New York, NY 10010 Parent Co.-New York Law Publishing Co., New York; Title Tel # (212) 545-6170 Title Fax # (212) 696-1848
Personnel: Publisher-Stuart Wise, Editor-Erik Wulff, Circ. Mgr.-Kerry Kyle
General Info: Monthly, Trim Size-8½ x 11, Offset press, 12 pages, Color
Subscriptions: Indv. $195, $16/copy
Printing Co: Columbus Bookbinding, 1343 Belfast Ave, Columbus, OH 31904 Tel # (206) 323-9313, Fax # (206) 323-2987

Free Enterprise Society News
See: TAXES

Free Trade Law Reporter
See: INTERNATIONAL TRADE

French Business Law Guide

Publishing Co: CCH, Inc., 2700 Lake Cook Rd., Riverwoods, IL 60015 Parent Co.-Kluwer Law & Taxation Publishers, Cambridge; Title Tel # (847) 267-7000 Title Fax # (800) 224-8299
Editorial Description: Explains French laws governing business activities, treating such topics as The Corporation and Other Business Enterprises.
General Info: 10x/yr., Looseleaf
Subscriptions: Indv. $555

Friends of the Court

Publishing Co: Judicial Dept., Administrative Office of the Courts, Justice Bldg., 625 Marshall, Little Rock, AR 72201; Title Tel # (501) 682-9400 Title Fax # (501) 682-9410
Personnel: Editor-Karolyn Bond
General Info: (Formerly Amicus Curiae), Bi-monthly, Desktop press, 4 pages, No Color, Matte
Circulation: Total-1,500

Fulton County Daily Report

Publishing Co: Daily Report Co., 190 Pryor St SW, Atlanta, GA 30303-3607; Title Tel # (404) 521-1227
Personnel: Publisher-Frances Beck, Editor-R. Garp
Editorial Description: Legal news & business interest.
General Info: Yr. Est. 1890, Daily, Web press, 12 pages, No Color
Circulation: Total-1,600
Advertising: Inquire for rates.
List Rental: List Management Co.: Conrad Direct, Inc., 300 Knickerbocker Road, Creskill, NJ 07626 Tel # (201) 567-3200, Fax # (201) 567-4959, Actives: 4,237, $110/M

Fun-Raising Regulation Report
See: PHILANTHROPY

Futures International Law Letter   *Business*

Publishing Co: Commodities Law Press Associates, 40 Broad St Fl 20, New York, NY 10004-2315; Title Tel # (212) 612-9545 Title Fax # (212) 425-0266
Personnel: Publisher-Richard Miller
Editorial Description: Covers United States & international legal and regulatory developments affecting futures and derivatives trading.
General Info: (Formerly Commodities Law Letter), Yr. Est. 1981, Monthly, Trim Size-8½ x 11, 8 pages, ISSN: 1083-8562, Ind/Abs/Online: Iri, 2 Color
Subscriptions: Indv. $285, Inst. $285

General Aviation/ Helicopter Accident Report   *Business*

Publishing Co: Andrews Publications, Inc., 1646 West Chester Pike, PO Box 1000, Westtown, PA 19395 Tel # (610) 399-6600; Title Tel # (610) 399-6610 Title Fax # (610) 399-6610
Personnel: Publisher-John E. Backe, Editor-Susan Armstrong, Mktg. Dir.-Andrew Katz
Editorial Description: Critical source of information and potential business for attorneys, aviation slavage operators, insurers and industry executives.
General Info: (Formerly General Aviation Accident Report), Yr. Est. 1979, Weekly, Trim Size-8½ x 11, Mimeo press, 20 pages, ISSN: 0887-7823, No Color, Newsprint
Subscriptions: Indv. $1,500, $29/copy
Acquistions: Publication Bought, Publication Sold
Advertising: Inquire for rates.
List Rental: Actives: 990, $110/M

Georgia Courts Journal

Publishing Co: Administrative Office of Courts, 244 Washington St SW # 550, Atlanta, GA 30334-9007; Title Tel # (404) 656-5171
Personnel: Editor-Nancy Kahnt
Editorial Description: Newsletter for courts & court staff in Georgia.
General Info: Yr. Est. 1973, Bi-monthly, Offset press, 16 pages, No Color, Matte, Saddle-stitched
Subscriptions: Free
Circulation: Total-2,950
Printing Co: Baker Printing, 3856 Oakcliff Industrial Ct, Doraville, GA 30340-3407 Tel # (404) 446-0014

Georgia Criminal Law and Motor Vehicle Handbook

Publishing Co: Gould Publications, Inc, 1333 N US Highway 17-92, Longwood, FL 32750-3724 Tel # (407) 695-9500 Fax # (407) 695-2906
Editorial Description: Crimes and offenses, criminal procedure, and motor vehicle and traffic laws of georgia.
General Info: Annually, Looseleaf
Subscriptions: $22/copy

Georgia Employment Law Letter   *Business*

Publishing Co: M. Lee Smith Publishers & Printers ,LCC, P.O. Box 198867, 162 Fourth Avenue North, Nashville, TN 37219-8867; Title Tel # (615) 242-7395 Title Fax # (615) 256-6601
Personnel: Publisher-M Lee Smith, Editor-David Hagaman, Circ. Mgr.-Cathy Bradford, Mktg. Dir.-Dave Yates
Editorial Description: Review of employment law developments that affect Georgia employers.
General Info: Yr. Est. 1988, Monthly, Trim Size-8½ x 11, 8 pages, ISSN: 1040-4813, 2 Color
Subscriptions: Indv. $127
List Rental: Rents Lists
Printing Co: M. Lee Smith Publishers & Printers ,LLC, PO Box 198867, 162 Fourth Avenue, Nashville, TN 37219-8867 Tel # (615) 242-7395, Fax # (615) 256-6601

Georgia Environmental Law Letter   *Business*

Publishing Co: M. Lee Smith Publishers & Printers ,LCC, P.O. Box 198867, 162 Fourth Avenue North, Nashville, TN 37219-8867; Title Tel # (615) 242-7395 Title Fax # (615) 256-6601
Personnel: Publisher-M. Lee Smith, Editor-A.J. Tolman, Circ. Mgr.-Cathy Bradford, Mktg. Dir.-Dave Yates
Editorial Description: Review of developments in environmental law that affect Georgia companies.
General Info: Yr. Est. 1989, Monthly, Trim Size-8½ x 11, 8 pages, ISSN: 1044-2324, 2 Color
Subscriptions: Indv. $187
List Rental: Actives: $75/M
Printing Co: M. Lee Smith Publishers & Printers ,LLC, PO Box 198867, 162 Fourth Avenue, Nashville, TN 37219-8867 Tel # (615) 242-7395, Fax # (615) 256-6601

Georgia Health Law Update
See: HEALTH

Georgia Real Estate Law Letter   *Business*

Publishing Co: M. Lee Smith Publishers & Printers ,LCC, P.O. Box 198867, 162 Fourth Avenue North, Nashville, TN 37219-8867; Title Tel # (615) 242-7395 Title Fax # (615) 256-6601
Personnel: Publisher-M Lee Snith, Editor-Seth Weissman, Circ. Mgr.-Cathy Bradford, Mktg. Dir.-Dave Yates
Editorial Description: Review of GA Real Estate Law developments.
General Info: Yr. Est. 1988, Monthly, Trim Size-8 12 x 11, 8 pages, ISSN: 1040-4805, 2 Color
Subscriptions: Indv. $137
List Rental: Rents Lists
Printing Co: M. Lee Smith Publishers & Printers ,LLC, PO Box 198867, 162 Fourth Avenue, Nashville, TN 37219-8867 Tel # (615) 242-7395, Fax # (615) 256-6601

German Tax & Business Law Guide
See: TAXES

Gilbert Criminal Law and Procedure of New York

Publishing Co: Matthew Bender & Co., 11 Penn Plaza, New York, NY 10001-2006 Fax # (212) 244-3188; Title Tel # (212) 967-7707
Personnel: Editor-N. Masliasky
Editorial Description: Criminal law and practice in New York State.
General Info: Annually, Looseleaf
Subscriptions: $93/copy

Goodloe Report

Publishing Co: Goodloe Report, PO Box 25736, Seattle, WA 98125-1236; Title Tel # (206) 364-8164 Title Fax # (206) 368-7863
Personnel: Publisher, Editor-William Goodloe
Editorial Description: Abuses in legal systems.
General Info: Monthly, Trim Size-8½ x 11, 1 pages, Recycled

Goods in Transit
See: TRAFFIC & TRANSPORTATION

Government Contract Costs
Pricing & Accounting
Report
Business

Publishing Co: Federal Pubs., Inc., 1120 20th St., NW, Fifth Floor, South Building, Washington, DC 20036-3484 Tel # (202) 337-7000 Fax # (202) 659-2233
Personnel: Editor-Lisa Everhart
General Info: Yr. Est. 1988, Monthly
Subscriptions: Indv. $468

Government Contract
Litigation Reporter
Business

Publishing Co: Andrews Publications, Inc., 1646 West Chester Pike, PO Box 1000, Westtown, PA 19395; Title Tel # (610) 399-6600 Title Fax # (610) 399-6610
Personnel: Publisher-John E. Backe, Editor-Marcy Kowalchuk, Mktg. Dir.-Andrew Katz
Editorial Description: Provides up-to-the minute coverage of suits involving the Fales Claims Act, certification, contract termination, equitable adjustment and breach of contract, as well as other suits arisng out of the Contract Disputes Act.
General Info: (Formerly Defense Contract Litigation Report), Yr. Est. 1989, Bi-monthly, Trim Size-8½ x 11, Mimeo press, ISSN: 1047-1758, Ind/Abs/Online: NEWSNET, No Color, Newsprint
Subscriptions: Indv. $825, $39/copy
Advertising: Inquire for rates.
List Rental: Actives: 66,686, $125/M

Government Contractor

Publishing Co: Federal Pubs., Inc., 1120 20th St., NW, Fifth Floor, South Building, Washington, DC 20036-3484; Title Tel # (202) 337-7000 Title Fax # (202) 659-2233
Personnel: Editor-Marvin Friedman
General Info: Yr. Est. 1959, Weekly
Subscriptions: Indv. $960

Government Contracts Citator
See: GOVERNMENT

Government Contracts:
Law, Administration and
Procedure
Business

Publishing Co: Matthew Bender & Co., 11 Penn Plaza, New York, NY 10001-2006 Fax # (212) 244-3188; Title Tel # (212) 967-7707
Personnel: Editor-J. Eldridge
Editorial Description: Complete step-by-step coverage of important aspects of government contracts. Deals with allowable and unallowable costs, responsibilities of the contractor and excusable delays.
General Info: Yr. Est. 1962, Monthly, Looseleaf
Subscriptions: $775/copy

Gower Federal Service-Mining
See: MINING & MINERALS

Gower Federal Service-
Miscellaneous Land
Decisions
Business, Consumer

Publishing Co: Rocky Mountain Mineral Law Foundation, 7039 E 18th Ave, Denver, CO 80220-1826; Title Tel # (303) 321-8100 Title Fax # (303) 321-7657
Editorial Description: Public land surveys, classifications, grazing permits, rights-of-way, etc.
General Info: Yr. Est. 1970, 8x/yr., Looseleaf
Subscriptions: Indv. $165

Gower Federal Service-Oil and Gas
See: PETROLEUM & NATURAL GAS

Gower Federal Service-Outer Continental Shelf
See: PETROLEUM & NATURAL GAS

Gower Federal Service-
Royalty Valuation and
Management
Business

Publishing Co: Rocky Mountain Mineral Law Foundation, 7039 E 18th Ave, Denver, CO 80220-1826; Title Tel # (303) 321-8100 Title Fax # (303) 321-7657
Editorial Description: Oil, gas, and mineral royalties on federal lands.
General Info: Yr. Est. 1987, 9x/yr., Looseleaf
Subscriptions: Indv. $500

Grapevine
See: LAW ENFORCEMENT & PENOLOGY

Graphing and Charting,
Simplified

Publishing Co: Gould Publications, Inc, 1333 N US Highway 17-92, Longwood, FL 32750-3724 Tel # (407) 695-9500 Fax # (407) 695-2906; Title Tel # (607) 724-3000
Editorial Description: Contains test materials with questions and answers on interpreting graphs and charts.
General Info: Annually, 105 pages, Looseleaf
Subscriptions: Indv. $12, $9/copy

Guardian, The

Publishing Co: Natl. Assn. of Counsel for Children, 1205 Oneida St, Denver, CO 80220-2944; Title Tel # (303) 322-2260
Personnel: Editor-Laura Michaels
Editorial Description: Concerned with legal rights of children.
General Info: Yr. Est. 1977, Quarterly, Desktop press, 16 pages, 2 Color
Subscriptions: Indv. $45, Inst. $55
Advertising: Inquire for rates.
List Rental: Actives: 11,054, $150/M

Guide to Assigning & Loaning Benefit Plan Money
See: INVESTMENT

Guide to Good Clinical Practice
See: MANAGEMENT

Handling Federal Tort
Claims: Administrative
and Judicial Remedies
Business

Publishing Co: Matthew Bender & Co., 11 Penn Plaza, New York, NY 10001-2006 Fax # (212) 244-3188; Title Tel # (212) 967-7707
Personnel: Editor-R. Kaye
Editorial Description: The former Chief of the Torts Section of the Justice Department examines all substantive & procedural law under the Federal Tort Claims Act.
General Info: Yr. Est. 1964, Irregular, Looseleaf
Subscriptions: $310/copy

Hawaii Employment Law
Letter
Business

Publishing Co: M. Lee Smith Publishers & Printers ,LCC, P.O. Box 198867, 162 Fourth Avenue North, Nashville, TN 37219-8867; Title Tel # (615) 242-7395 Title Fax # (615) 256-6601
Personnel: Publisher-M Lee Smith, Circ. Mgr.-Cathy Bradford, Mktg. Dir.-David Yates
General Info: Yr. Est. 1996, Monthly, Trim Size-8½ x 11, 8 pages, 2 Color
Subscriptions: Indv. $97
List Rental: Rents Lists
Printing Co: M. Lee Smith Publishers & Printers ,LLC, PO Box 198867, 162 Fourth Avenue, Nashville, TN 37219-8867 Tel # (615) 242-7395, Fax # (615) 256-6601

Hawkins Chief Counsel's Interpretations
See: AERONAUTICS/ASTRONAUTICS

Hazardous Materials Transportation
See: ENVIRONMENT & ECOLOGY

Hazardous Waste
Litigation Reporter

Publishing Co: Andrews Publications, Inc., 1646 West Chester Pike, PO Box 1000, Westtown, PA 19395; Title Tel # (610) 399-6600 Title Fax # (610) 399-6610
Personnel: Publisher-John E. Backe, Editor-Jay Steinberg, Mktg. Dir.-Andrew Katz
Editorial Description: Covers the most recent developments in litigation arising under federal and state environmental statutes, including the Superfund Act, the Resource Conservation and Recovery Act and the Superfund Amendments and Reauthorization Act.
General Info: Yr. Est. 1980, Bi-monthly, Trim Size-8½ x 11, Mimeo press, 80 pages, ISSN: 0275-0244, Ind/Abs/Online: Net News, No Color, Newsprint
Subscriptions: Indv. $850, $40/copy
Advertising: Inquire for rates.
List Rental: Actives: 3,086, $11/M

Health Advocate
Business

Publishing Co: National Health Law Program, 2639 S. La Cienega Blvd., Los Angeles, CA 90034-2675; Title Tel # (310) 204-6010 Title Fax # (310) 204-0891
Personnel: Editor-Laurence Lavin
Editorial Description: A quarterly journal of health law information for persons representing low income people & helping them to obtain equity and non-discrimination in health care.
General Info: Yr. Est. 1948, Quarterly, Trim Size-8½ x 11, Desktop press, 30 pages, No Color, Matte, Saddle-stitched
Subscriptions: Indv. $20, $5/copy
Circulation: Total-3,000
Printing Co: Peace Press, 4117 W Jefferson Blvd, Los Angeles, CA 90016-4124

Health Alliance Alert
Business

Publishing Co: Faulkner & Gray Healthcare Information Center, 1133 15th St NW, Ste. 450, Washington, DC 20005-2710 Tel # (202) 828-4148 Parent Co.-Faulkner & Gray, Inc., New York; Title Tel # (202) 822-1252 Title Fax # (202) 828-2352
Personnel: Editor-John Reichard
Editorial Description: Legal news on the healthcare debate.
General Info: Bi-weekly
Subscriptions: Indv. $375

Health Care Antitrust
Business

Publishing Co: Thompson Publishing Group, 747 Third Ave., New York, NY 10017 Tel # (212) 888-7220 Fax # (212) 486-3400; Title Tel # (212) 888-7292 Title Fax # (800) 949-2320
Personnel: Editor-John P. Sarna, Production Mgr.-R.D. Whitney, Mktg. Dir.-James Kavanagh
Editorial Description: Published for those who need to know antitrust rules, their interpretation and enforcement as well as strategies to deal with present requirements. Subscription includes monthly and quarterly updates.
General Info: Yr. Est. 1994, Monthly, 8 pages, 2 Color, Looseleaf
Subscriptions: Indv. $347

Health Care Capitation and Risk Contracting Manual
See: HEALTH

Health Care Fraud
Litigation Reporter   *Business*

Publishing Co: Andrews Publications, Inc., 1646 West Chester Pike, PO Box 1000, Westtown, PA 19395 Tel # (610) 399-6600 Fax # (610) 399-6610
Personnel: Publisher-John E. Backe, Editor-Tom Hennessey, Mktg. Dir.-Andrew Katz
General Info: Yr. Est. 1996, Monthly, Trim Size-8½ x 11, Offset press, No Color
Subscriptions: Indv. $500, $50/copy
Advertising: Inquire for rates.
List Rental: Rents Lists

Health Care Law: A
Practical Guide   *Business*

Publishing Co: Matthew Bender & Co., 11 Penn Plaza, New York, NY 10001-2006
Tel # (212) 967-7707 Fax # (212) 244-3188
Editorial Description: A comprehensive analysis & practical guide for handling the many legal issues facing all health care providers in today's dynamic health care environment.
General Info: Irregular, Looseleaf

Health Care Law Newsletter   *Business*

Publishing Co: Matthew Bender & Co., 11 Penn Plaza, New York, NY 10001-2006
Tel # (212) 967-7707 Fax # (212) 244-3188
Editorial Description: Authored by one of the largest health law firms in the country specializing in all aspects of health care law. Covers important legislative, regulatory, & judicial changes relating to the current major issues in the field.
General Info: Yr. Est. 1986, Monthly, Looseleaf

Health Employment Law
Update   *Business, Consumer*

Publishing Co: Rutkowski & Associates, Inc., PO Box 15250, Evansville, IN 47716-0250;
Title Tel # (812) 476-4520
Personnel: Editor-Barbara Rutkowski
Editorial Description: Practical, timely review of current cases & trends in labor & employment law. Includes critical legislation, in-depth special features.
General Info: Yr. Est. 1985, Monthly, 8 pages, ISSN: 0890-9245, Color
Subscriptions: Indv. $98, $8/copy

Health Law Digest   *Association*

Publishing Co: Natl. Health Lawyers Assn., 1120 Connecticut Ave NW Ste, 950, Washington, DC 20036-3902; Title Tel # (202) 833-1100
Editorial Description: Case briefs of current decisions in the health field.
General Info: Yr. Est. 1972, Monthly, Trim Size-8½ x 11, Web press, 80 pages
Circulation: Total-4,500

Health Law Litigation
Reporter   *Business*

Publishing Co: Andrews Publications, Inc., 1646 West Chester Pike, PO Box 1000, Westtown, PA 19395; Title Tel # (610) 399-6600 Title Fax # (610) 399-6610
Personnel: Publisher-John E. Backe, Editor-Chris Evans, Mktg. Dir.-Andrew Katz
Editorial Description: Provides comprehensive coverage of the latest developments in all aspects of the burgeoning field of health care law.
General Info: (Formerly Medical Malpractice-Ob/Gyn Litigation Reporter), Yr. Est. 1985, Monthly, Trim Size-8½ x 11, Mimeo press, 70 pages, ISSN: 1056-4098, No Color, Newsprint
Subscriptions: Indv. $800, $75/copy
Advertising: Inquire for rates. Accepts Inserts.
List Rental: Actives: 6,921, $110/M

Health Law Week   *Business*

Publishing Co: Strafford Pubs., Inc., 590 Dutch Valley Rd., N.E., Postal Drawer 13729, Atlanta, GA 30324-0729; Title Tel # (404) 881-1141 Title Fax # (404) 881-0074
Personnel: Publisher-Richard M. Ossoff, Mng. Editor-Jennifer Vaughan, Circ. Mgr., Mktg. Mgr.-Marianne Mueller, Mktg. Mgr.-Marla Rawls Hill
Editorial Description: Judicial decisions that affect healthcare.
General Info: Yr. Est. 1991, 48x/yr., ISSN: 1063-4061
Subscriptions: Indv. $647, Can. $677, For. $702, $17/copy
List Rental: Actives: 18,249, $105/M

Health Lawyers News Report
See: HEALTH

Health Legislation & Regulation
See: HEALTH

Healthcare System Reform Alert
See: HEALTH

Hispanic Newsletter

Publishing Co: Cuban American Legal Defense & Education Fund, 2119 Webster St, Fort Wayne, IN 46802-6433; Title Tel # (219) 745-5421
Personnel: Editor-J. Heinbaugh
General Info: Monthly

Hospital Insurance
Litigation Reporter   *Business*

Publishing Co: Strafford Pubs., Inc., 590 Dutch Valley Rd., N.E., Postal Drawer 13729, Atlanta, GA 30324-0729; Title Tel # (404) 881-1141 Title Fax # (404) 881-0074
Personnel: Publisher-Richard M. Ossoff, Editor-Jennifer F. Vaughaw, Product Mgr.-Michael Hunter, Circ. Mgr., Mktg. Dir.-Marianne Mueller
Editorial Description: Digest of judicial decisions concerning all areas of health insurance.
General Info: Yr. Est. 1995, 12 pages
Subscriptions: Indv. $284, Can. $314, For. $339, $27/copy

Hospital Law Manual &
Newsletter   *Business*

Publishing Co: Aspen Publishers, Inc., 200 Orchard Ridge Dr., Ste 200, Gaithersburg, MD 20878-5440 Fax # (301) 417-7655 Parent Co.-Wolters Kluwer US Corporation, New York; Title Tel # (301) 417-7500 Title Fax # (301) 417-7550
Personnel: Publisher-Paul Lasky, Editor-Patricia Younger
Editorial Description: Federal and state government laws and regulations as related to hospital and general health care delivery discussed in practical terms.
General Info: Yr. Est. 1959, Monthly, Trim Size-6⅛ x 9¼, Sheetfed press, 500 pages, No Color, Looseleaf
Subscriptions: Indv. $799, For. $930
List Rental: List Management Co.: Stevens-Knox List Management, 304 Park Ave S., New York, NY 10010-5312 Tel # (212) 388-8800, Fax # (212) 388-8890, Actives: $80/M

Hospital Law Newsletter
See: HOSPITALS & NURSING HOMES

Hospital Litigation
Reporter   *Business*

Publishing Co: Strafford Pubs., Inc., 590 Dutch Valley Rd., N.E., Postal Drawer 13729, Atlanta, GA 30324-0729; Title Tel # (404) 881-1141 Title Fax # (404) 881-0074
Personnel: Publisher-Richard Ossoff, Mng. Editor-Jennifer Vaughan, Production Mgr.-C. Malone Tumlia, Circ. Mgr., Mktg. Mgr.-Marianne Mueller, Mktg. Mgr.-Marla Rawls Hill
Editorial Description: Monthly digest of judicial decisions that concern or affect the hospital environment exclusively; cases are screened and selected to provide concise, comprehensive coverage of issues important to hospital attorneys & administrators, risk management professionals & others involved with hospital litigation.
General Info: Yr. Est. 1989, 12x/yr., Sheetfed press, 16 pages, ISSN: 1048-5201, Color-cover, Matte
Subscriptions: Indv. $334, Can. $364, For. $389, $28/copy
List Rental: Actives: 10,651, $127/M

Hospitality Law
See: HOTEL INDUSTRY

Housing and Development Reporter/Current Developments
See: REAL ESTATE

Housing Law Bulletin
See: PUBLIC MANAGEMENT & PLANNING

How to Manage Your Law
Office   *Business*

Publishing Co: Matthew Bender & Co., 11 Penn Plaza, New York, NY 10001-2006
Fax # (212) 244-3188; Title Tel # (212) 967-7707
Personnel: Editor-R. Lopatin
Editorial Description: Discusses solo practice, federations of firms, space sharing, partnership structures, professional corporations, use of committees, setting fees and billing procedures.
General Info: Yr. Est. 1973, Irregular, 500 pages, Looseleaf
Subscriptions: $95/copy

How to Recover for Loss Or Damage to Goods in Transit
See: INSURANCE

Howe & Hutton Report

Publishing Co: Howe & Hutton, Attorneys at Law, 20 N Wacker Dr Ste 3550, Chicago, IL 60606-3102; Title Tel # (312) 263-3001 Title Fax # (312) 372-6685
Personnel: Publisher-Jonathan T. Howe, Editor-Terrence Hutton, Circ. Mgr.-Maureen Bafati
General Info: Yr. Est. 1985, Monthly, Trim Size-8½ x 11, 6 pages, 2 Color
Subscriptions: Indv. $100
Circulation: Total-950

Human Resources Management OSHA Compliance
See: MANAGEMENT

Human Resources
Manager's Legal
Reporter

Publishing Co: Business & Legal Reports, Inc., 39 Academy St., PO Box 1513, Madison, CT 06443-2646 Tel # (860) 245-7448 Fax # (860) 245-2559; Title Tel # (203) 245-7448 Title Fax # (203) 245-2559
General Info: Yr. Est. 1977, Monthly
Subscriptions: Indv. $84

Human Rights Bulletin
See: CIVIL RIGHTS

Human Rights: The Inter-American System
Business, Consumer

Publishing Co: Oceana Publications, Inc., 75 Main St, Dobbs Ferry, NY 10522-1601
Tel # (914) 693-8100; Title Tel # (914) 693-1320 Title Fax # (914) 693-0402
Personnel: Editor-T. Buergenthal, Production Mgr.-Mike Wortzman, Mktg. Dir.-John Downey
General Info: Yr. Est. 1982, Irregular, Trim Size-7 x 10, Looseleaf
Subscriptions: Indv. $570

Huntington Calendar
See: MUSEUM PUBLICATIONS

I.A.F.W.A. Newsletter
See: ENVIRONMENT & ECOLOGY

IBIS Briefing Service
See: BUSINESS & INDUSTRY

ILSA Newsletter

Publishing Co: Intl. Law Students Assn., 2223 Massachusetts Ave., N.W., Tillar House, Washington, DC 20008 Tel # (202) 939-6030; Title Tel # (202) 265-4375
Personnel: Editor-Denise Hodge, Circ. Mgr.-Pamela Young
Editorial Description: Exchange of ideas/information on study of international law.
General Info: Yr. Est. 1962, Bi-monthly, Trim Size-8½ x 11, 15 pages, No Color
Circulation: (100% controlled), Total-2,000

IRS Letter Rulings Reports
See: TAXES

IRS Publications
See: TAXES

ISG Newsletter

Publishing Co: Sponsor-Inst. for the Study of Genocide, John Jay College of Criminal Justice, 899 10th Ave Rm 623, New York, NY 10019-1029; Title Tel # (212) 489-3284
Personnel: Editor-Helen Fein, Production Mgr.-Lee Pilcher
Editorial Description: Contains information on the study of genocide.
General Info: Yr. Est. 1988, Semi-annually, Desktop press, 16 pages, Saddle-stitched
Subscriptions: Indv. $30

Idaho Employment Law Letter
Business

Publishing Co: M. Lee Smith Publishers & Printers ,LCC, P.O. Box 198867, 162 Fourth Avenue North, Nashville, TN 37219-8867; Title Tel # (615) 242-7395 Title Fax # (615) 256-6601
Personnel: Publisher-M Lee Smith, Editor-Amanda Brailsford, Circ. Mgr.-Cathy Bradford, Mktg. Dir.-David Yates
General Info: Yr. Est. 1996, Monthly, Trim Size-8½ x 11, 8 pages, 2 Color
Subscriptions: Indv. $97
List Rental: Rents Lists
Printing Co: M. Lee Smith Publishers & Printers ,LLC, PO Box 198867, 162 Fourth Avenue, Nashville, TN 37219-8867 Tel # (615) 242-7395, Fax # (615) 256-6601

Illinois Conservation Law

Publishing Co: Gould Publications, Inc, 1333 N US Highway 17-92, Longwood, FL 32750-3724
Tel # (407) 695-9500 Fax # (407) 695-2906; Title Tel # (607) 724-3000
Editorial Description: A complete, accurate, up-to-date presentation of Chapter 56-the Fish Code, and Chapter 61-the Wildlife Code, of the Illinois Revised Statute.
General Info: Annually, 400 pages, Looseleaf
Subscriptions: Indv. $20, $18/copy

Illinois Courts Bulletin
Association

Publishing Co: Illinois Bar Assn., 424 S 2nd St, Springfield, IL 62701-1779;
Title Tel # (217) 525-1760 Title Fax # (217) 525-0712
Personnel: Editor-Dennis Rendleman
Editorial Description: Digest of decided cases from Supreme Court of Illinois, Illinois Appellate Courts and United States Circuit Court of Appeals (7th Circuit). Digests are of latest decisions.
General Info: Monthly, Trim Size-8½ x 11, Offset press, 8 pages, No Color, Newsprint
Subscriptions: Indv. $35, For. $38, $3/copy
Circulation: Total-3,000

Illinois Courts Rule Book

Publishing Co: Law Bulletin Publishing Co., 415 N. State St., Chicago, IL 60610-4674
Fax # (312) 644-4255; Title Tel # (312) 644-7800
Personnel: Publisher-Lanning Macfarland, Jr., Editor-Debbie Adamo, Circ. Mgr., Adv. Dir.-Alan Bergner
Editorial Description: Rules & orders of Illinois Supreme, Appelate, Cook County Circuit Courts, code of criminal procedure, attorney registration, code of civil procedure & more. Supplemented quarterly.
General Info: Annually, Trim Size-8½ x 11, Web press, 550 pages, No Color, Newsprint, Looseleaf
Subscriptions: Indv. $68
Circulation: Total-3,000
Advertising: Inquire for rates.

Illinois Criminal Law & Procedure Handbook

Publishing Co: Gould Publications, Inc, 1333 N US Highway 17-92, Longwood, FL 32750-3724
Tel # (407) 695-9500 Fax # (407) 695-2906; Title Tel # (607) 724-3000
Editorial Description: Criminal laws, procedures & relevant sections of changes 38 plus related statutes.
General Info: Annually, Trim Size-5½ x 8½, Sheetfed press, 1,000 pages, No Color, Looseleaf
Subscriptions: Indv. $10, $20/copy

Illinois Employment Law Letter
Business

Publishing Co: M. Lee Smith Publishers & Printers ,LCC, P.O. Box 198867, 162 Fourth Avenue North, Nashville, TN 37219-8867; Title Tel # (615) 242-7395 Title Fax # (615) 256-6601
Personnel: Publisher-M Lee Smith, Editor-Allan Gunn, Circ. Mgr.-Cathy Bradford, Mktg. Dir.-Dave Yates
Editorial Description: Review of employment law developments that affect Illinois employers.
General Info: Yr. Est. 1990, Monthly, Trim Size-8½ x 11, 8 pages, ISSN: 1049-9385, 2 Color
Subscriptions: Indv. $97
List Rental: Rents Lists
Printing Co: M. Lee Smith Publishers & Printers ,LLC, PO Box 198867, 162 Fourth Avenue, Nashville, TN 37219-8867 Tel # (615) 242-7395, Fax # (615) 256-6601

Illinois Environmental Law Letter
Business

Publishing Co: M. Lee Smith Publishers & Printers ,LCC, P.O. Box 198867, 162 Fourth Avenue North, Nashville, TN 37219-8867; Title Tel # (615) 242-7395 Title Fax # (615) 256-6601
Personnel: Publisher-M Lee Smith, Editor-Sanford Stein, Circ. Mgr.-Cathy Bradford, Mktg. Dir.-Dave Yates
Editorial Description: Review of environmental law developments that affect Illinois companies.
General Info: Yr. Est. 1992, Monthly, Trim Size-8½ x 11, 8 pages, ISSN: 1059-5074, 2 Color
Subscriptions: Indv. $117
List Rental: Rents Lists
Printing Co: M. Lee Smith Publishers & Printers ,LLC, PO Box 198867, 162 Fourth Avenue, Nashville, TN 37219-8867 Tel # (615) 242-7395, Fax # (615) 256-6601

Illinois Insurance
See: INSURANCE

Illinois Tax Service
See: TAXES

Illinois Vehicle Code

Publishing Co: Gould Publications, Inc, 1333 N US Highway 17-92, Longwood, FL 32750-3724
Tel # (407) 695-9500 Fax # (407) 695-2906; Title Tel # (607) 724-3000
Editorial Description: Concise presentation of chapter 95 1/2.
General Info: Annually, Trim Size-5½ x 8½, Sheetfed press, 700 pages, No Color, Looseleaf
Subscriptions: $20/copy

Illinois Workers' Compensation Law Bulletin
Business, Consumer

Publishing Co: LRP Publications, 747 Dresher Rd., P.O. Box 980, Horsham, PA 19044-0980
Tel # (215) 784-0910 Fax # (215) 784-0317
Personnel: Publisher-Kenneth F. Kahn, Editor-Joanne Fiore, Production Mgr.-Kathleen P. Neely, Mktg. Dir.-Jana Shellington
Editorial Description: Provides selected workers' compensation decisions and opinions from the Illinois Industrial Commission and state appellate courts.
General Info: Yr. Est. 1993, Bi-weekly
Subscriptions: Indv. $255

Immigration Briefings
Association, Business

Publishing Co: Federal Pubs., Inc., 1120 20th St., NW, Fifth Floor, South Building, Washington, DC 20036-3484; Title Tel # (202) 337-7000 Title Fax # (202) 659-2233
Personnel: Editor-Patricia Mariani, Mktg. Dir.-Beth Bolger
Editorial Description: Current law for immigration practitioners.
General Info: Yr. Est. 1988, Monthly
Subscriptions: Indv. $348
List Rental: List Management Co.: Affinity Marketing Group Inc., P.O. Box 2409, Fairfax, VA 22031 Tel # (703) 978-4927, Fax # (703) 425-4537, Actives: 8,700, $100/M

Immigration Law and Procedure
Business

Publishing Co: Matthew Bender & Co., 11 Penn Plaza, New York, NY 10001-2006
Fax # (212) 244-3188; Title Tel # (212) 967-7707
Personnel: Editor-B. Chase
Editorial Description: A complete guide to all facets of immigration and nationality law.
General Info: Yr. Est. 1959, Irregular, Looseleaf
Subscriptions: $895/copy

Immigration Law and Procedure: Desk Edition
Business

Publishing Co: Matthew Bender & Co., 11 Penn Plaza, New York, NY 10001-2006
Tel # (212) 967-7707 Fax # (212) 244-3188
Editorial Description: A practical abridgement of Immigration Law and Procedure, condensed to bring you the essence of immigration and nationality issues in one easy-to-use volume.
General Info: Yr. Est. 1980, Annually, Looseleaf

Immigration Law and Procedure Reporter *Business*

Publishing Co: Matthew Bender & Co., 11 Penn Plaza, New York, NY 10001-2006 Tel # (212) 967-7707 Fax # (212) 244-3188
Personnel: Editor in Chief-Roy J. Watson
Editorial Description: Current and prospective coverage of all developments that will impact on your immigration practice.
General Info: Yr. Est. 1985, Monthly, Looseleaf

Immigration Law Report
See: U.S. (& CANADIAN) FED. GOV'T.

Immigration Newsletter *Association*

Publishing Co: Natl. Lawyer's Guild, 55 6th Ave, New York, NY 10013-1679; Title Tel # (212) 966-5000
General Info: Bi-monthly
Subscriptions: Indv. $40, Inst. $50
Circulation: Total-600

Immigration Policy & Law *Business, Consumer*

Publishing Co: LRP Publications, 747 Dresher Rd., P.O. Box 980, Horsham, PA 19044-0980 Tel # (215) 784-0910 Fax # (215) 784-0317
Personnel: Publisher-Ken Kahn, Editor-Michelle Brown
Editorial Description: Reports and analysis of the Immigration Reform & Control Act of 1986; includes requirements and procedures, litigation, enforcement actions, and activities of the IRS and Congress.
General Info: Yr. Est. 1987, Bi-weekly, Trim Size-8½ x 11, Sheetfed press, 10 pages, ISSN: 0892-547X, Ind/Abs/Online: HRIN, 2 Color, Newsprint
Subscriptions: Indv. $497, For. $497, $21/copy
Acquistions: Publication Bought, Publication Sold

In Brief
See: ENVIRONMENT & ECOLOGY

In Re

Publishing Co: Bar Assn. of San Francisco, 685 Market St # 700, San Francisco, CA 94105-4200 Tel # (415) 764-1600
General Info: 10x/yr.
Subscriptions: Indv. $2
Circulation: Total-4,500

Independent Power Report *Business*

Publishing Co: McGraw-Hill, 1221 Ave. of the Americas, 36th Fl., New York, NY 10020-1095 Tel # (212) 512-2000 Fax # (212) 512-6590; Title Tel # (212) 512-2306
Personnel: Publisher-John Slater, Editor in Chief-Richard Schwartz, Mng. Editor-Ray Pospisil, Circ. Mgr.-Georgia Safos, Promotion Dir.-Suzanne Goodman
Editorial Description: Provides latest news on private power developments around the world. Contains valuable leads for those sellingequipment or services; financing projects or looking for partners.
General Info: (Formerly Cogeneration Report), Yr. Est. 1985, Bi-weekly, Trim Size-8½ x 11, 20 pages, ISSN: 8756-372X, Ind/Abs/Online: DIALOG, Dow Jones, NewsNet, Nexis, Matte
Subscriptions: Indv. $915, Can. $915, For. $940

Index and Digest of OCC Opinion Letters
See: BANKING & FINANCE

Index to Recent New Hampshire Cases

Publishing Co: Hale Ridge Publishing, PO Box 370, Windham, NH 03087 Tel # (603) 889-7231; Title Tel # (603) 934-5333
Personnel: Editor-Douglas Adamson, Adv. Dir.-Robert Gillmore
Editorial Description: Index, by topic, statute, & case of court opinions. NH Supreme Court, major US District Court, state trial court, 1st Circuit Court & agencies as received.
General Info: Yr. Est. 1974, Monthly, Sheetfed press, 8 pages, No Color, Newsprint, Looseleaf
Subscriptions: Indv. $96, $7/copy
Circulation: Total-290
Printing Co: Sant Bani Press, 178 Main St, Tilton, NH 03276-1114 Tel # (603) 286-3114

Indian Affairs
See: ETHNIC

Indian Report
See: U.S. (& CANADIAN) FED. GOV'T.

Indiana Criminal Law & Motor Vehicle Handbook

Publishing Co: Gould Publications, Inc, 1333 N US Highway 17-92, Longwood, FL 32750-3724 Tel # (407) 695-9500 Fax # (407) 695-2906; Title Tel # (607) 724-3000
Editorial Description: The complete text of the Indiana Code from Title 9-Motor Vehicle, 11-Corrections and 35-Criminal Proceedure; and selected sections covering such topics as the Lottery, Law enforcement, vehicles and taxes, alcoholic beverages.
General Info: Annually, 1,050 pages, Looseleaf
Subscriptions: Indv. $20, $18/copy

Indiana Employment Law Letter *Business*

Publishing Co: M. Lee Smith Publishers & Printers ,LCC, P.O. Box 198867, 162 Fourth Avenue North, Nashville, TN 37219-8867; Title Tel # (615) 242-7395 Title Fax # (615) 256-6601
Personnel: Publisher-M Lee Smith, Editor-Todd M. Nierman, Circ. Mgr.-Cathy Bradford, Mktg. Dir.-Dave Yates
Editorial Description: Review of employment law developments that affect Indiana employers.
General Info: Yr. Est. 1991, Monthly, Trim Size-8½ x 11, 8 pages, ISSN: 105361915, 2 Color
Subscriptions: Indv. $97
List Rental: Rents Lists
Printing Co: M. Lee Smith Publishers & Printers ,LLC, PO Box 198867, 162 Fourth Avenue, Nashville, TN 37219-8867 Tel # (615) 242-7395, Fax # (615) 256-6601

Indiana Environmental Compliance Update *Business*

Publishing Co: M. Lee Smith Publishers & Printers ,LCC, P.O. Box 198867, 162 Fourth Avenue North, Nashville, TN 37219-8867; Title Tel # (615) 242-7395 Title Fax # (615) 256-6601
Personnel: Publisher-M. Lee Smith, Editor-Lewis Beckwith, Circ. Mgr.-Cathy Bradford, Mktg. Dir.-Dave Yates
Editorial Description: Review of environmental law developments that affect Indiana companies.
General Info: (Formerly Indiana Environmental Law Letter), Yr. Est. 1991, Monthly, Trim Size-8½ x 11, 8 pages, ISSN: 1053-6183, 2 Color
Subscriptions: Indv. $117
List Rental: Rents Lists
Printing Co: M. Lee Smith Publishers & Printers ,LLC, PO Box 198867, 162 Fourth Avenue, Nashville, TN 37219-8867 Tel # (615) 242-7395, Fax # (615) 256-6601

Indiana Estate Planning and Probate Practice *Business*

Publishing Co: Matthew Bender & Co., 11 Penn Plaza, New York, NY 10001-2006 Tel # (212) 967-7707 Fax # (212) 244-3188
Editorial Description: Covers Indiana law & procedure for estate planning & administration. Written by Indiana practitioners.
General Info: Yr. Est. 1990, Semi-annually, Looseleaf

Indiana Forms of Pleading and Practice *Business*

Publishing Co: Matthew Bender & Co., 11 Penn Plaza, New York, NY 10001-2006 Fax # (212) 244-3188; Title Tel # (212) 967-7707
Personnel: Editor-A. Jenner
Editorial Description: Coverage of all the Indiana Rules of Pleading & Practice along with sophisticated forms tailored by Indiana practitioners. Provides all forms necessary for civil action under the Indiana Trial rules, with commentary on the issues surrounding each rule, the full text of each rule, & comparisons of each rule to its federal counterpart & as needed, to prior Civil Code practice.
General Info: Yr. Est. 1972, Irregular, Trim Size-8½ x 11, Looseleaf
Subscriptions: $475/copy

Indiana Law Reporter

Publishing Co: Law Reporter Co., 209 Michigan Ave # 270, Crystal Falls, MI 49920-1312; Title Tel # (906) 875-6970
Personnel: Publisher-P.G. Oakes, Editor-John Sundquist
Editorial Description: Summaries of Indiana state & federal court decisions.
General Info: Yr. Est. 1978, Semi-monthly, 25 pages, No Color
Subscriptions: Indv. $195
Circulation: Total-295

Individual Employment Rights *Business*

Publishing Co: Bureau of National Affairs, Inc., 1231 25th St. NW, Bldg. N-200, Washington, DC 20037-1157; Title Tel # (202) 452-4200 Title Fax # (202) 822-8092
Personnel: Publisher-William A. Beltz, Mng. Editor-Nancy J. Sedmak, Circ. Mgr.-Gary C. Seltzer
Editorial Description: Case reference on individual employment rights issues including employment at will, privacy, polygraph testing & other employee rights issues outside the traditional labor management relations context.
General Info: Yr. Est. 1986, Bi-weekly, Trim Size-8½ x 11, Web press, 4 pages, Ind/Abs/Online: HRIN, Westlaw, Lexis
Subscriptions: Indv. $663

Individuals with Disabilities Education Law Reporter
See: DISABILITY

Industrial Health & Hazards Update
See: SAFETY

Info Franchise Newsletter
See: BUSINESS & INDUSTRY

Information Returns Guide
See: TAXES

Inheritance, Estate and Gift Tax Reports Fed-All States
See: TAXES

Inheritance Estate and Gift Tax Reports, Home State
See: TAXES

Inside Health Law
See: HOSPITALS & NURSING HOMES

Inside Labor Relations
See: LABOR UNION

Inside the PTO
See: PATENTS/COPYRIGHTS/TRADE MARKS

Insurance Bad Faith
Litigation   *Business*

Publishing Co: Matthew Bender & Co., 11 Penn Plaza, New York, NY 10001-2006
Tel # (212) 967-7707 Fax # (212) 244-3188
Editorial Description: Complete treatment of tort liability of insurers for wrongful conduct.
General Info: Yr. Est. 1984, Irregular, Looseleaf

Insurance Industry
Litigation Reporter   *Business*

Publishing Co: Andrews Publications, Inc., 1646 West Chester Pike, PO Box 1000, Westtown, PA 19395; Title Tel # (610) 399-6600 Title Fax # (610) 399-6610
Personnel: Publisher-John E. Backe, Editor-Marcy Kowalchuk, Mktg. Dir.-Andrew Katz
Editorial Description: Reports on developing issues in the field of insurance litigation.
General Info: Yr. Est. 1985, Bi-monthly, Trim Size-8$\frac{1}{2}$ x 11, Mimeo press, 70 pages, ISSN: 0887-7858, Ind/Abs/Online: Net News, No Color, Newsprint
Subscriptions: Indv. $825, $39/copy
Advertising: Inquire for rates.
List Rental: Actives: 1,122, $110/M

Insurance Law Reports: Life, Health & Health & Accident
See: INSURANCE

Insurance Litigation
Reporter

Publishing Co: Shepard's/McGraw-Hill, Inc., 555 Middle Creek Pky, Colorado Springs, CO 80921-3622; Title Tel # (719) 488-3000 Title Fax # (719) 481-7448
Personnel: Editor in Chief-Mary Kaye LaRue, Editor-John DiMugno, Production Mgr.-Cheryl Everitt, Adv. Dir.-Peggy Ives, Art Dir.-Leigh Vidakovich
Editorial Description: Summaries & analysis of recent decisions in insurance litigation.
General Info: (Formerly Insurance Liability Reporter), Yr. Est. 1978, Monthly, Trim Size-8$\frac{1}{2}$ x 11, Web press, 28 pages, ISSN: 0195-1858, 2% ads, No Color, Newsprint, Saddle-stitched
Subscriptions: Indv. $345
Advertising: Accepts Inserts.
List Rental: List Management Co.: The Lake Group, 411 Theodore Freund Ave., Rye, NY 10580-1497 Tel # (914) 925-2400, Fax # (914) 925-2499, Actives: 40,212, $130/M

Insurance Regulation/State Capitals
See: INSURANCE

Integrated Health Care Delivery: Business and Legal Forms
See: HEALTH

Intellectual Property
LAWCAST   *Business*

Publishing Co: Vox Juris, Inc., P.O. Box 389, Pennington, NJ 08534; Title Tel # (609) 737-6543 Title Fax # (609) 737-3860
Personnel: Publisher-Jason Meyer, Esq, Editor-Mark Cohen, Esq, Circ. Mgr.-Karen E. Anderson, Mktg. Mgr.-Kathy W. Gould
Editorial Description: The legal newscast & case digesting service on audio cassette for intellectual property lawyers. Each issue includes audio cassette and companion outline. Covers legal developments in patents, trademarks, copyright, trade secrets, trade dress, related issues in computer and biotech law.
General Info: Yr. Est. 1995
Subscriptions: Indv. $329, Inst. $450, $25/copy

Intellectual Property
Litigation Reporter   *Business*

Publishing Co: Andrews Publications, Inc., 1646 West Chester Pike, PO Box 1000, Westtown, PA 19395 Tel # (610) 399-6600 Fax # (610) 399-6610
Personnel: Publisher-John E. Backe, Editor-Jodine Mayberry, Mktg. Dir.-Andrew Katz
General Info: Yr. Est. 1994, Bi-monthly, Trim Size-8.5 x 11, Offset press, ISSN: 1078-2796, No Color
Subscriptions: Indv. $600
Advertising: Inquire for rates.
List Rental: Actives: $125/M

Intellectual Property
Strategist, The   *Business*

Publishing Co: Leader Publications, Inc., 345 Park Avenue South, New York, NY 10010 Tel # (212) 545-6170 Fax # (212) 696-1848 Parent Co.-New York Law Publishing Co., New York
Personnel: Publisher-Stuart Wise, Editor-Marya Lenn Yee, Circ. Mgr.-Kerry Kyle, Mktg. Dir.-Roseann Moranbelli
General Info: Monthly, Trim Size-8$\frac{1}{2}$ x 11, Offset press, 12 pages, Color
Subscriptions: Indv. $155, $13/copy
Printing Co: Columbus Bookbinding, 1343 Belfast Ave, Columbus, OH 31904 Tel # (206) 323-9313, Fax # (206) 323-2987

Intellectural Property
Counseling and Litigation   *Business*

Publishing Co: Matthew Bender & Co., 11 Penn Plaza, New York, NY 10001-2006
Tel # (212) 967-7707 Fax # (212) 244-3188
Personnel: Editor-Ethan Horwitz, Editor-Lester Horwitz
Editorial Description: A comprehensive practice guide to both client counseling & dispute resolution in areas of intellectual property law. Written by a host of leading U.S. intellectual property attorneys.
General Info: Yr. Est. 1988, Irregular, Looseleaf

Inter-American Arbitration

Publishing Co: Canadian Arbitration & Conciliation Centre, Univ. of Ottawa, Civil Law Section, Ottawa, ON K1N 6N5 Canada; Title Tel # (613) 232-1476 Title Fax # (613) 564-9800
Personnel: Editor-L. Kos-Rabcewicz-Z
General Info: Yr. Est. 1981, Quarterly, 8 pages
Subscriptions: Indv. $10
Circulation: Total-400

Inter-American Bar
Association Quarterly
Newsletter   *Association*

Publishing Co: Inter-American Bar Association, 1211 Connecticut Ave., NW, Ste. 202, Washington, DC 20036 Fax # (202) 393-1241; Title Tel # (202) 393-1217
Personnel: Editor-Mary Jane Pedlow
Editorial Description: Promotes uniformity of commercial legislation and the study of comparative law.
General Info: Yr. Est. 1940, Trim Size-8$\frac{1}{2}$ x 11, 8 pages
Subscriptions: Indv. $30
Circulation: Total-3,500

Interim

Publishing Co: Montana Legislative Services Division, P.O Box 201706, Helena, MT 59620-1706
Fax # (406) 444-3056; Title Tel # (406) 444-3064
Personnel: Editor-Connie Erikson
Editorial Description: Reports between-sessions activities of legislative committees.
General Info: Monthly, Trim Size-5$\frac{1}{2}$ x 8$\frac{1}{2}$, 20 pages, Other
Subscriptions: $1/copy
Circulation: Total-350
Printing Co: Montana Dept. of Administration - Publications & Graphics, P.O Box 200132, Helena, MT 59620-0132 Tel # (406) 444-3053, Fax # (406) 443-2213

Internal Revenue Manual-Audit and Administration
See: TAXES

International Academy of
Trial Lawyers Bulletin   *Association*

Publishing Co: International Academy of Trial Lawyers, 4 N 2nd St Ste 175, San Jose, CA 95113-1306; Title Tel # (408) 275-6767
General Info: Yr. Est. 1960, Semi-annually, Trim Size-8$\frac{1}{2}$ x 11, 20 pages
Circulation: Total-1,500

International Business Planning: Law and Taxation (United State)
See: INTERNATIONAL TRADE

International Commercial
Arbitration   *Business*

Publishing Co: Oceana Publications, Inc., 75 Main St, Dobbs Ferry, NY 10522-1601
Tel # (914) 693-8100; Title Tel # (914) 693-5944 Title Fax # (914) 693-0402
Personnel: Editor-K. Simmonds, Production Mgr.-Mike Wortzman, Mktg. Dir.-John Downey
Editorial Description: Representative collection of documents used in modern commercial arbitrations.
General Info: Yr. Est. 1974, Looseleaf

International Computer Law   *Business*

Publishing Co: Matthew Bender & Co., 11 Penn Plaza, New York, NY 10001-2006
Tel # (212) 967-7707 Fax # (212) 244-3188
Editorial Description: Beginning with an introduction to high technology, the text goes on to examine everything from export regulations to the protection of software by copyright.
General Info: Irregular, Looseleaf

International Copyright Law and Practice
See: PATENTS/COPYRIGHTS/TRADE MARKS

International Law & Trade
Perspective   *Business*

Publishing Co: Intl. Law & Trade Perspective, 604 S. King St., Ste. 100B, Leesburg, VA 22075-3911; Title Tel # (703) 779-2721
Editorial Description: Covers significant & interesting developments in the field of intl. law & trade, including the Congress, the courts and legal periodicals.
General Info: Yr. Est. 1975, Monthly, Trim Size-8$\frac{1}{2}$ x 11, Offset press, 12 pages, No Color
Subscriptions: Indv. $150, $12/copy
Circulation: Total-250

International Law News   *Association*

Publishing Co: American Bar Association, 740 15th St. NW, Washington, DC 20005-1009
Tel # (202) 662-1016 Fax # (202) 662-1032; Title Tel # (202) 331-2239
Personnel: Editor-Beth Van Hanswyk
Editorial Description: Reports on activities of Section of Intl. Law & Practice.
General Info: Quarterly, Trim Size-8$\frac{1}{2}$ x 11$\frac{1}{2}$, Sheetfed press, 24 pages, 2 Color, Newsprint, Saddle-stitched
Subscriptions: Free With Membership
Circulation: Total-17,000

International Legal Framework for Services   *Business*

Publishing Co: Oceana Publications, Inc., 75 Main St, Dobbs Ferry, NY 10522-1601
Tel # (914) 693-8100 Fax # (914) 693-0402
Personnel: Editor-Karl P. Sauvant, Editor-Jorg Weber, Production Mgr.-Michael Wortzman, Mktg. Mgr.-John Downey
Editorial Description: A collection of the most importatn agreements and arrangements which currently govern international transactions in services in trade, foreign direct investment, labor, and technology.
General Info: Yr. Est. 1992, Irregular, Looseleaf
Subscriptions: Indv. $400

International Medical Device Regulatory Monitor
See: DRUGS & PHARMACEUTICALS

International Ombudsman Institute Newsletter

Publishing Co: International Ombudsman Institute, University of Alberta, Faculty of Law, Edmonton, AB T6G 2H5 Canada; Title Tel # (403) 492-3196 Title Fax # (403) 492-4924
Personnel: Editor-Linda Reif
General Info: Quarterly, 14 pages, ISSN: 0229-2181
Subscriptions: Indv. $10

International Protection of the Environment   *Business*

Publishing Co: Oceana Publications, Inc., 75 Main St, Dobbs Ferry, NY 10522-1601;
Title Tel # (914) 693-8100 Title Fax # (914) 693-0402
Personnel: Editor-B. Ruster, Production Mgr.-Mike Wortzman, Mktg. Dir.-John Downey
Editorial Description: Treaties and related documents.
General Info: Yr. Est. 1990, Irregular, Looseleaf

International Regulation of Finance and Investment   *Business*

Publishing Co: Oceana Publications, Inc., 75 Main St, Dobbs Ferry, NY 10522-1601
Tel # (914) 693-8100 Fax # (914) 693-0402
Personnel: Editor-K. Rabalais, Production Mgr.-Mike Wortzman, Mktg. Dir.-John Downey
General Info: Yr. Est. 1994, Irregular, Looseleaf
Subscriptions: Indv. $150

International Securities Regulation Report
See: INVESTMENT

International Securities Regulations   *Business*

Publishing Co: Oceana Publications, Inc., 75 Main St, Dobbs Ferry, NY 10522-1601
Tel # (914) 693-8100 Fax # (914) 693-0402; Title Tel # (914) 693-1320
Personnel: Editor-Robert Rosen, Production Mgr.-Mike Wortzman, Mktg. Dir.-John Downey
General Info: Yr. Est. 1987, Irregular, Trim Size-7 x 10, Looseleaf
Subscriptions: Indv. $650

International Taxation Series
See: TAXES

International Trade Alert
See: INTERNATIONAL TRADE

International Trade Reporter Decisions
See: INTERNATIONAL TRADE

International Trade Reporter Export Reference Manual
See: INTERNATIONAL TRADE

Interpreter Releases   *Business*

Publishing Co: Federal Pubs., Inc., 1120 20th St., NW, Fifth Floor, South Building, Washington, DC 20036-3484; Title Tel # (202) 337-7000 Title Fax # (202) 659-2233
Personnel: Publisher, Editor-Maurice Roberts, Mktg. Dir.-Beth Bolger
General Info: Yr. Est. 1923, Weekly
Subscriptions: Indv. $498
List Rental: List Management Co.: Affinity Marketing Group Inc., P.O. Box 2409, Fairfax, VA 22031
Tel # (703) 978-4927, Fax # (703) 425-4537, Actives: 12,200

Investigative and Operational Report Writing

Publishing Co: Gould Publications, Inc, 1333 N US Highway 17-92, Longwood, FL 32750-3724
Tel # (407) 695-9500 Fax # (407) 695-2906; Title Tel # (607) 724-3000
Editorial Description: This booklet offers a set of guidelines to aid in official reporting. Including examples and step-by-step proceedures and how to prepare incident, operational, investigative, and supplementary reports.
General Info: Annually, 50 pages, Looseleaf
Subscriptions: Indv. $9, $7/copy

Investment Laws of the World
See: INVESTMENT

Investment Treaties   *Business*

Publishing Co: Oceana Publications, Inc., 75 Main St, Dobbs Ferry, NY 10522-1601
Tel # (914) 693-8100; Title Tel # (914) 693-1320 Title Fax # (914) 693-0402
Personnel: Production Mgr.-Mike Wortzman, Mktg. Dir.-John Downey
General Info: Yr. Est. 1983, Irregular, Trim Size-7 x 10, Looseleaf
Subscriptions: Indv. $595

Iowa Employment Law Letter   *Business*

Publishing Co: M. Lee Smith Publishers & Printers ,LCC, P.O. Box 198867, 162 Fourth Avenue North, Nashville, TN 37219-8867 Tel # (615) 242-7395 Fax # (615) 256-6601
Personnel: Publisher-M. Lee Smith, Editor-Greg Naylor, Circ. Mgr.-Cathy Bradford, Mktg. Dir.-Dave Yates
Editorial Description: Reviews employment law developments that effect Iowa employers.
General Info: Yr. Est. 1994, Monthly, ISSN: 1075-962X
Subscriptions: Indv. $97
List Rental: Rents Lists

Issues & Solutions
See: MANAGEMENT

Italian Civil Code and Complementary Legislation   *Business*

Publishing Co: Oceana Publications, Inc., 75 Main St, Dobbs Ferry, NY 10522-1601
Tel # (914) 693-8100 Fax # (914) 693-0402
Personnel: Editor-Mario Beltramo, Editor-Giovanni Longo, Editor-John Henry Merryman, Production Mgr.-Mike Wortzman, Mktg. Dir.-John Downey
Editorial Description: Covers civil and commercial matters.
General Info: Yr. Est. 1991, Irregular, Looseleaf
Subscriptions: Indv. $250

Jail & Prisoner Law Bulletin
See: LAW ENFORCEMENT & PENOLOGY

Job Announcements
See: EMPLOYMENT

Job Safety and Health
See: SAFETY

John Howard Society of Alberta, Reporter
See: LAW ENFORCEMENT & PENOLOGY

Journal of Law Enforcement Report Writing

Publishing Co: American Grand Jury Foundation, PO Box 1690, Modesto, CA 95353-1690;
Title Tel # (209) 527-0966
Personnel: Editor-Bruce Olson
Editorial Description: Suggestions for the improvement of law enforcement reports, humorous quotations from law enforcement reports, the relationship between thinking & writing, resources to improve law enforcement report writing.
General Info: Yr. Est. 1985, Semi-annually, Sheetfed press, 4 pages
Subscriptions: Free To Qualified Recipient
Circulation: Total-750

Journal of the New York Institute of Legal Research   *Business*

Publishing Co: New York Institute of Legal Research, PO Box 398, Yorktown Heights, NY 10598-0398 Parent Co.-Christopher Financial Services Inc., Yorktown Heights;
Title Tel # (914) 245-8400 Title Fax # (914) 245-7660
Personnel: Publisher-Herman A. Stuhl, Editor-David H. Klein, Science Ed.-Judith Koskella, Asst. Ed.-Meryl Morgan, Circ. Mgr.-Marsha Bingamad
Editorial Description: Items of interest to the ligitagator
General Info: Yr. Est. 1991, Bi-monthly, Trim Size-8$\frac{1}{2}$ x 11, Offset press, 10 pages, ISSN: 1049-5304, No Color, Matte, Saddle-stitched
Subscriptions: Indv. $495

Judicial Conduct Reporter

Publishing Co: American Judicature Society, 25 E Washington St Ste 1600, Chicago, IL 60602-1899; Title Tel # (312) 558-9175
Editorial Description: Reports news, analyzes developments, reviews cases relating to judicial conduct.
General Info: Yr. Est. 1979, Quarterly, 8 pages, ISSN: 0193-7367, Ind/Abs/Online: WESTLAW
Subscriptions: $3/copy
Circulation: Total-6,000

Judicial Discretion

Publishing Co: Natl. Judicial College, Univ. Of Nevada, Reno, NV 89557-0001; Title Tel # (702) 784-6747 Title Fax # (702) 784-4234
Editorial Description: A guide to difficult & much misunderstood topic of considerable importance to the trial judge. It is a functional analysis of judicial discretion-the excising of judgement in the form of a decision or choice-under a variety of circumstances.
General Info: Yr. Est. 1990, Irregular, Perfect bound
Subscriptions: Indv. $18, $18/copy

Just Compensation   *Business*

Publishing Co: Just Compensation, PO Box 5133, Sherman Oaks, CA 91413-5133; Title Tel # (818) 848-6765
Personnel: Publisher, Editor-Gideon Kanner
Editorial Description: Law-abstracts of court decisions in eminent domain and inverse condemnation.
General Info: Yr. Est. 1957, Monthly, Trim Size-6 x 9, 12 pages, ISSN: 0738-6494, No Color
Subscriptions: Indv. $115

Justica

Publishing Co: Judicial Process Commission, 121 Fitzhugh St N, Rochester, NY 14614-1214; Title Tel # (716) 325-7727
Personnel: Editor-Clare Regan
Editorial Description: Analysis of criminal justice issues such as the death penalty, drugs & prison overcrowding. Focus on alternative sanctions & community control of disputes.
General Info: Yr. Est. 1973, 11x/yr., 10 pages, No Color
Subscriptions: Indv. $5
Circulation: Total-2,550

Justice Report   *Business, Consumer*

Publishing Co: Natl. Assn. for Public Interest Law, 1118 22nd Street NW, Washington, DC 20009; Title Tel # (202) 546-9707
General Info: Quarterly

Justice Weekly

Publishing Co: EKHE Advertising, PO Box 1, Brooklyn, NY 11231-0001
Personnel: Editor-Philip Daniels
General Info: Yr. Est. 1970, Weekly
Subscriptions: Indv. $9
Circulation: Total-10,000

Juvenile Law Reports   *Business, Association*

Publishing Co: Knehans-Miller Publications, PO Box 88, Warrensburg, MO 64093-0088; Title Tel # (816) 429-1102
Personnel: Publisher-Jaclyn Miller, Editor-Dane Miller
Editorial Description: In-depth summaries, often with verbatim excerpts, & thorough subject/jurisdictional indexing of all federal & state appellate court decisions dealing with all aspects of juvenile justice & welfare.
General Info: Yr. Est. 1979, Monthly, Trim Size-8½ x 11, 20 pages, ISSN: 0276-9603, No Color, Looseleaf
Subscriptions: Indv. $120, Inst. $120, Can. $120, For. $155
Acquistions: Publication Bought

KC News
See: CONSTRUCTION & BUILDING

Kansas Employment Law
Letter   *Business*

Publishing Co: M. Lee Smith Publishers & Printers ,LCC, P.O. Box 198867, 162 Fourth Avenue North, Nashville, TN 37219-8867 Tel # (615) 242-7395 Fax # (615) 256-6601
Personnel: Publisher-M Lee Smith, Editor-Kathleen Babock, Circ. Mgr.-Cathy Bradford, Mktg. Dir.-Dave Yates
Editorial Description: Reviews employment law developments that effect Kansas employers.
General Info: Yr. Est. 1994, Monthly, ISSN: 1074-0422
Subscriptions: Indv. $97
List Rental: Rents Lists

Kansas/Iowa
Environmental
Compliance Update   *Business*

Publishing Co: M. Lee Smith Publishers & Printers ,LCC, P.O. Box 198867, 162 Fourth Avenue North, Nashville, TN 37219-8867; Title Tel # (615) 242-7395 Title Fax # (615) 256-6601
Personnel: Publisher-M. Lee Smith, Editor-George Von Stamwitz, Circ. Mgr.-Cathy Bradford, Mktg. Dir.-Dave Yates
Editorial Description: Review of environmental law developments that affect Kansas/Iowa companies.
General Info: (Formerly Kansas/Iowa Environmental Law Letter), Yr. Est. 1991, Monthly, Trim Size-8½ x 11, 8 pages, ISSN: 1075-9581, 2 Color
Subscriptions: Indv. $117
List Rental: Rents Lists
Printing Co: M. Lee Smith Publishers & Printers ,LLC, PO Box 198867, 162 Fourth Avenue, Nashville, TN 37219-8867 Tel # (615) 242-7395, Fax # (615) 256-6601

Kentucky Attorney General
Opinions

Publishing Co: Banks-Baldwin Law Publishing Co., PO Box 318063, Cleveland, OH 44131-8063; Title Tel # (216) 721-7373 Title Fax # (216) 721-8055
Personnel: Publisher-P.J. Lucier, Production Mgr.-Virginia Stucko, Promotion Dir.-George Hallaman
Editorial Description: Each year, subscribers receive four quarterly issues comprising all formal opinions of the Attorney General during the period, in either full text or syllabus treatment, with cumulative research aids. A permanent binder is furnished annually or biennial , as needed.
General Info: Yr. Est. 1964, Trim Size-7½ x 10, Web press, 160 pages, ISSN: 0748-9080, No Color, Matte, Saddle-stitched, Looseleaf
Subscriptions: Indv. $85

Kentucky Bar News   *Association*   CPM: $72

Publishing Co: Kentucky Bar Association, 514 W Main St, Frankfort, KY 40601-1883; Title Tel # (502) 564-3795 Title Fax # (502) 564-3225
Personnel: Publisher-Bruce Davis, Editor-Kent Hendrickson, Adv. Dir.-Ellen Razor
Editorial Description: Contains news and features of interest to Kentucky's Bench and Bar. Designed to be more timely and less formal than the Bench & Bar journal.
General Info: Yr. Est. 1990, Quarterly, Trim Size-11 x 14, Sheetfed press, 8 pages, 2 Color, Matte
Circulation: Total-10,000
Advertising: $725.
Printing Co: Beechmont Press, 9951 Bunsen Way, Louisville, KY 40299-2584 Tel # (502) 491-1396

Kentucky Employment
Law Letter   *Business*

Publishing Co: M. Lee Smith Publishers & Printers ,LCC, P.O. Box 198867, 162 Fourth Avenue North, Nashville, TN 37219-8867; Title Tel # (615) 242-7395 Title Fax # (615) 256-6601
Personnel: Publisher-M Lee Smith, Editor-Richard Cleary, Circ. Mgr.-Cathy Bradford, Mktg. Dir.-Dave Yates
Editorial Description: Review of employment law developments that affect Kentucky employers.
General Info: Yr. Est. 1990, Monthly, Trim Size-8½ x 11, 8 pages, ISSN: 1052-4371, 2 Color
Subscriptions: Indv. $97
List Rental: Rents Lists
Printing Co: M. Lee Smith Publishers & Printers ,LLC, PO Box 198867, 162 Fourth Avenue, Nashville, TN 37219-8867 Tel # (615) 242-7395, Fax # (615) 256-6601

Keyes Encyclopedic
Dictionary of Contract &
Procurement Law   *Business*

Publishing Co: Oceana Publications, Inc., 75 Main St, Dobbs Ferry, NY 10522-1601 Tel # (914) 693-8100; Title Tel # (914) 693-1320 Title Fax # (914) 693-0402
Personnel: Editor-N. Keyes, Production Mgr.-Mike Wortzman, Mktg. Dir.-John Downey
General Info: Yr. Est. 1992, Irregular, Trim Size-7 x 10, Looseleaf
Subscriptions: Indv. $160

LAMA Manager
See: MANAGEMENT

LEAF Lines   *Consumer, Association*

Publishing Co: Women's Legal Education and Action Fund, 415 Yonge Street, Suite 1800, Toronto, ON M5B 2E7 Canada Tel # (416) 595-7170 Fax # (416) 595-7191; Title Tel # (416) 575-7170 Title Fax # (905) 575-7191
Editorial Description: The Women's Legal Education and Action Fund is a national organization which promotes equality for women through legal action and public education.
General Info: Yr. Est. 1987, Quarterly, 2 Color, Recycled
Subscriptions: Indv. $40, $5/copy
Circulation: Total-7,000

LFL Reports:
See: CIVIL RIGHTS

LLC Advisor
See: TAXES

LRE Report
See: EDUCATION

Labor Arbitration Awards
See: LABOR UNION

Labor Arbitration in Government
See: LABOR UNION

Labor Arbitration in
Government   *Business, Consumer*

Publishing Co: LRP Publications, 747 Dresher Rd., P.O. Box 980, Horsham, PA 19044-0980
Tel # (215) 784-0910 Fax # (215) 784-0317
Personnel: Publisher-Kenneth F. Kahn, Production Mgr.-Kathleen P. Neely, Mktg. Dir.-Jana Shellington, Promotion Dir.-Gary Ragin
Editorial Description: Covers selected awards involving city, state, and federal employees (other than those employed by schools.)
General Info: Monthly
Subscriptions: Indv. $120

Labor Arbitration
Information System   *Business, Consumer*

Publishing Co: LRP Publications, 747 Dresher Rd., P.O. Box 980, Horsham, PA 19044-0980
Tel # (215) 784-0910 Fax # (215) 784-0317
Personnel: Publisher-Kenneth F. Kahn, Editor-Sandy Johnson, Production Mgr.-Kathleen P. Neely, Mktg. Dir.-Jana Shellington, Promotion Dir.-Gary Ragin
Editorial Description: Publishes arbitration awards reported each month in LRP, BNA, AAA and CCH allowing you to research a dispute that is going to arbitration or to investigate an arbitrator's background.
General Info: Monthly
Subscriptions: Indv. $475

Labor Contract Law Bulletin
See: LABOR

Labor and Employment
Law News   *Business*

Publishing Co: American Bar Association, 750 N. Lake Shore Dr., Chicago, IL 60611-4497
Tel # (312) 988-6115 Fax # (312) 988-6030; Title Tel # (312) 988-5522 Title Fax # (312) 988-5528
Personnel: Publisher-Jack Podell, Editor-Lester Asher, Production Mgr.-Evan Spelfogel, Adv. Dir.-Robert Blindauer, Art Dir.-David Carruthers
Editorial Description: Legal trends of interest to labor lawyers.
General Info: (Formerly Labor Relations Law), Yr. Est. 1971, Quarterly, Trim Size-8½ x 11, 8 pages, ISSN: 0193-5739, 2 Color
Subscriptions: Indv. $25
Circulation: Total-14,000
List Rental: Rents Lists

Labor and Employment Law
Newsletter   *Business*

Publishing Co: Matthew Bender & Co., 11 Penn Plaza, New York, NY 10001-2006
Tel # (212) 967-7707 Fax # (212) 244-3188
Personnel: Editor-Andrea Christensen
Editorial Description: A monthly newsletter covering major judicial, legislative & regulatory developments in all areas of labor & employment law.
General Info: Yr. Est. 1984, Monthly

Labor Law
See: LABOR UNION

Labor Law Developments
See: LABOR UNION

Labor Law Reports
See: LABOR

Labor-Management   Relations   Analysis/News   and
Background
See: LABOR

Labor Relations Reporter
See: LABOR UNION

Labor Relations Week
See: LABOR UNION

Labor Trends
See: LABOR UNION

Laboratory Regulation Manual & Newsletter
See: MEDICINE

Lambda Update
See: CIVIL RIGHTS

Land Development Law Reporter/Land Trends
See: REAL ESTATE

Land Use Law Report   *Business*

Publishing Co: Business Publishers, Inc., 951 Pershing Dr., Silver Spring, MD 20910-4464; Title Tel # (301) 589-5103 Title Fax # (301) 589-8493
Personnel: Publisher-Leonard A. Eiserer, Editor-James Lawlor, Esq., Circ. Mgr.-Brenda Davenport, Mktg. Mgr.-Keith Payne
Editorial Description: Zoning and land use decisions at all levels of government; impact on business community and environment.
General Info: Yr. Est. 1973, Bi-weekly, Trim Size-8½ x 11, Desktop press, 8 pages, 2 Color, Matte
Subscriptions: Indv. $314, Can. $314, For. $327
Advertising: Accepts Inserts.
List Rental: List Management Co.: BPI Direct, 951 Pershing Dr., Silver Spring, MD 20910-4464
Tel # (301) 585-5976, Fax # (301) 587-4530
Printing Co: Business Publishers In-House Print Shop, 951 Pershing Drive, Silver Spring, MD 20910-4454 Tel # (301) 589-8493

Landlord Tenant Law Bulletin
See: REAL ESTATE

Landmark Litigation Report

Publishing Co: Landmark Legal Foundation, 1006 Grand, 8th Floor, Kansas City, MO 64106-2300; Title Tel # (816) 474-6600 Title Fax # (816) 474-6609
General Info: Yr. Est. 1978, Quarterly, Trim Size-8½ x 11, 6 pages, 2 Color, Newsprint
Subscriptions: Free
Circulation: Total-4,000

Latin American Law and Business Report
See: INTERNATIONAL TRADE

Law & Justice
See: RELIGIOUS & THEOLOGICAL

Law & the Land

Publishing Co: R & C, 1 Commercial Plz, Hartford, CT 06103-3512; Title Tel # (203) 275-8200

Law & Practice Under the
GATT   *Business*

Publishing Co: Oceana Publications, Inc., 75 Main St, Dobbs Ferry, NY 10522-1601
Tel # (914) 693-8100; Title Tel # (914) 693-1320 Title Fax # (914) 693-0402
Personnel: Editor-Kenneth Simmonds, Production Mgr.-Mike Wortzman, Mktg. Dir.-John Downey
General Info: Yr. Est. 1987, Irregular, Trim Size-7 x 10, Looseleaf
Subscriptions: Indv. $595

Law & Practice of the
United States Regulation
of International Trade   *Business*

Publishing Co: Oceana Publications, Inc., 75 Main St, Dobbs Ferry, NY 10522-1601
Tel # (914) 693-8100; Title Tel # (914) 693-1320 Title Fax # (914) 693-0402
Personnel: Editor-Charles Johnston, Production Mgr.-Mike Wortzman, Mktg. Dir.-John Downey
General Info: Yr. Est. 1987, Irregular, Trim Size-7 x 10, Looseleaf
Subscriptions: Indv. $175

Law of Advertising   *Business*

Publishing Co: Matthew Bender & Co., 11 Penn Plaza, New York, NY 10001-2006
Fax # (212) 244-3188; Title Tel # (212) 967-7707
Personnel: Editor-H. Costikyan
Editorial Description: Contains rules governing each party to the advertising contract: media, consumers, advertisers, and advertising agencies.
General Info: Yr. Est. 1973, Irregular, Looseleaf
Subscriptions: $360/copy

Law of Associations: An
Operating Legal Manual
for Exectives and
Counsel   *Business*

Publishing Co: Matthew Bender & Co., 11 Penn Plaza, New York, NY 10001-2006
Fax # (212) 244-3188; Title Tel # (212) 967-7707
Personnel: Editor-George Webster
Editorial Description: Complete coverage of all legal & tax aspects of non-profit associations. Provides specialized information regarding tax exemptions & liabilities, executive compensation plans, political action committees, antitrust liability, public relations, & accounting procedures.
General Info: Yr. Est. 1971, Looseleaf
Subscriptions: $90/copy

Law Department
Management Adviser

Publishing Co: Business Laws, Inc., 11630 Chillicothe Rd., Chesterland, OH 44026-1928; Title Tel # (216) 729-7996
Personnel: Editor-William Hancock
General Info: (Formerly Corporate Counsel's Managerial Advisor), Yr. Est. 1984, Monthly, 16 pages, ISSN: 1052-2972
Subscriptions: Indv. $195, $20/copy

Law Digest

Publishing Co: Office of the Attorney Genl., 101 N 8th St, Richmond, VA 23219-2305
General Info: Monthly

Law Enforcement Liability Reporter
See: LAW ENFORCEMENT & PENOLOGY

Law of the European Economic Community-A Commentary on the EEC Treaty
Business

Publishing Co: Matthew Bender & Co., 11 Penn Plaza, New York, NY 10001-2006
Fax # (212) 244-3188; Title Tel # (212) 967-7707
Personnel: Editor-J. O'Brien
Editorial Description: Clearly organized explanation of the legal aspects of the EEC.
General Info: Yr. Est. 1976, Irregular, Looseleaf
Subscriptions: $475/copy

Law of Federal Oil and Gas Leases
See: PETROLEUM & NATURAL GAS

Law Firm Partnership & Benefits Report
Business

Publishing Co: Leader Publications, Inc., 345 Park Avenue South, New York, NY 10010 Parent Co.-New York Law Publishing Co., New York; Title Tel # (212) 545-6170 Title Fax # (212) 696-1848
Personnel: Publisher-Stuart Wise, Editor-Martha Middleson, Circ. Mgr.-Kerry Kyle, Mktg. Dir.-Roseann Morangelei
Editorial Description: Focuses on ways law firms can provide more cost-effective benefits.
General Info: (Formerly Law Firm Benefits), Yr. Est. 1992, Monthly, Trim Size-8½ x 11, Offset press, 8 pages, ISSN: 1061-9410, Color
Subscriptions: Indv. $165, $13/copy
Printing Co: Columbus Bookbinding, 1343 Belfast Ave, Columbus, OH 31904 Tel # (206) 323-9313, Fax # (206) 323-2987

Law Group Docket
See: CIVIL RIGHTS

Law of Hazardous Waste: Management, Cleanup, Liability and Litigation, The
Business

Publishing Co: Matthew Bender & Co., 11 Penn Plaza, New York, NY 10001-2006
Tel # (212) 967-7707 Fax # (212) 244-3188
Editorial Description: Contains current laws, regulations, & cases on both the federal & state levels with respect to the management of hazardous wastes, whether newly generated or the result of past dumping.
General Info: Yr. Est. 1987, Irregular, Looseleaf

Law of Liability Insurance, The
Business

Publishing Co: Matthew Bender & Co., 11 Penn Plaza, New York, NY 10001-2006
Tel # (212) 967-7707 Fax # (212) 244-3188
Editorial Description: Explains the terms & phrases essential for a general understanding of liability insurance, & discusses injuries to both persons & property.
General Info: Yr. Est. 1988, Irregular, Looseleaf

Law Librarian's Bulletin Board
Business

Publishing Co: Legal Information Svcs., PO Box 67, Newton Highlands, MA 02161-0001; Title Tel # (508) 443-4087 Title Fax # (508) 443-0364
Personnel: Editor-Elyse Fox
Editorial Description: Reports news developments and stategies in law L ibraries, government, publishers, library associations, also provides job listings.
General Info: Yr. Est. 1989, 8x/yr.
Subscriptions: Indv. $40, Inst. $40, Can. $40, For. $45, $5/copy

Law Library Assn. of Maryland News
See: LIBRARY

Law of Life and Health Insurance, The
Business

Publishing Co: Matthew Bender & Co., 11 Penn Plaza, New York, NY 10001-2006
Tel # (212) 967-7707 Fax # (212) 244-3188
Editorial Description: Written from the perspective of both the insurer & the insured, this publication is analytical & practical in approach, providing substantive statutory & case analyses, plus a variety of practice aids throughout.
General Info: Yr. Est. 1988, Irregular, Looseleaf

Law Office Administrator
See: MANAGEMENT

Law Office Automation and Technology
Business

Publishing Co: Matthew Bender & Co., 11 Penn Plaza, New York, NY 10001-2006
Tel # (212) 967-7707 Fax # (212) 244-3188
Editorial Description: Practical guidance on how to select, manage, use & update the automated systems appropriate for your practice, whether in a small, medium or large law firm or organization.
General Info: Yr. Est. 1980, Irregular, Looseleaf

Law Office Technology Review
Business

Publishing Co: Altman & Weil Publications, PO Box 625, Newtown Square, PA 19073-0625; Title Tel # (610) 359-9900 Title Fax # (610) 359-0467
Personnel: Publisher-Charles F. Huxsaw, Editor-Barry D. Bayor, Product Mgr.-Nancy Blodgett
Editorial Description: An unbiased review and assesment of software and hardware products desgined for or marketed to attorney
General Info: Yr. Est. 1995, Monthly, Trim Size-8.5 x 11, Sheetfed press, 8 pages, 2 Color, Saddle-stitched
Subscriptions: Indv. $195, Can. $245, For. $220
Circulation: Total-1,200
Printing Co: Kase Printing, 13 Hampshire Drive #18, Hudson, NH 03051 Tel # (603) 883-9223, Fax # (603) 883-9232

Law Officer's Bulletin
See: LAW ENFORCEMENT & PENOLOGY

Law of Oil and Gas Leases
See: PETROLEUM & NATURAL GAS

Law of Pooling and Unitization
Business

Publishing Co: Matthew Bender & Co., 11 Penn Plaza, New York, NY 10001-2006
Fax # (212) 244-3188; Title Tel # (212) 967-7707
Personnel: Editor-E. Carr
Editorial Description: Discusses all aspects - legal, tax, anti-trust, regulatory, statutory, policy, procedural, operational and technical-of pooling and unitization.
General Info: Yr. Est. 1957, Irregular, Looseleaf
Subscriptions: $325/copy

Law of Real Estate Financing
See: REAL ESTATE

Law-Related CD-ROM Update
Business

Publishing Co: Infosources Publishing, 140 Norma Rd, Teaneck, NJ 07666-4234; Title Tel # (201) 836-7072
Personnel: Publisher, Editor-Arlene Eis
Editorial Description: Information on new CD-ROM products in the legal area. Updates the Directory of Law-Related CD-ROMs with complete entries for each CD-ROM. Only available to Directory subscribers.
General Info: Yr. Est. 1993, Tri-annually, Trim Size-8½ x 11, 12 pages, ISSN: 1065-9285
Subscriptions: Indv. $44, For. $54
Advertising: Inquire for rates.

Law Reports
Business

Publishing Co: Catholic Health Assn. of the US, 4455 Woodson Rd, Saint Louis, MO 63134-3797; Title Tel # (314) 427-2500 Title Fax # (314) 427-0029
Personnel: Editor-John Miles
Editorial Description: Reports and analyses law affecting Catholic health care facilities.
General Info: Yr. Est. 1974, Trim Size-8½ x 11, Sheetfed press, 10 pages, No Color
Circulation: Total-3,000

Law School Placement Bulletin
Consumer

Publishing Co: Overseas Academic Opportunities, P.O. Box 768, Merrick, NY 11566-0368
Tel # (908) 774-1040 Fax # (908) 774-1040; Title Tel # (908) 724-4040 Title Fax # (908) 724-1040
Personnel: Publisher-Thomas Towey, Editor, Circ. Mgr.-Susan Towey
Editorial Description: Information on teaching positions at foreign law schools. Also information on grants and scholarships for study and research at foreign law schools.
General Info: Yr. Est. 1986, Bi-monthly, Trim Size-8½ x 11, 4 pages, ISSN: 1044-0615
Subscriptions: Indv. $47, Can. $50, For. $54, $5/copy
Circulation: Total-860
Printing Co: Banner Associates, 1109 Banner Ave, Brooklyn, NY 11235-5214 Tel # (718) 934-7857

Law Society of Upper Canada Communique

Publishing Co: Law Society of Upper Canada, Osgoode Hall, Toronto, ON M5H 2N6 Canada; Title Tel # (416) 947-3335
Personnel: Editor-Teresa Stark
General Info: 10x/yr.

Law Technology
Business, Association

Publishing Co: World Peace Through Law Center, 1000 Connecticut Ave., N.W., Washington, DC 20036-5302; Title Tel # (202) 466-5428 Title Fax # (202) 452-8540
Personnel: Editor-Stephen Skelly
Editorial Description: Covers developments pertaining to electronic data processing, laws, and legal research throughout the world.
General Info: (Formerly Law and Computer Technology), Yr. Est. 1968, Quarterly, Sheetfed press, 72 pages, ISSN: 0278-3916, 2 Color
Subscriptions: Indv. $100, $15/copy
Circulation: (100% controlled), Total-800

Lawyer International   *Business, Association*

Publishing Co: Lafferty Publications, 420 Lexington Ave., Ste. 1745, New York, NY 10170
Tel # (212) 557-6729 Fax # (212) 557-7266; Title Tel # (404) 636-6610 Title Fax # (404) 636-6422
Personnel: Publisher-Frank Lawson, Editor-Sandra Burke
Editorial Description: Lawyer International is the business briefing for lawyers operating in the international market.
General Info: Yr. Est. 1992, 10x/yr.
Subscriptions: Indv. $729

Lawyer Referral Network   *Association*

Publishing Co: American Bar Association, 750 N. Lake Shore Dr., Chicago, IL 60611-4497
Tel # (312) 988-6115 Fax # (312) 988-6030; Title Tel # (312) 988-5522 Title Fax # (312) 988-5528
Editorial Description: Covers news & developments relating to the lawyer referral & information service.
General Info: (Formerly LRIS Newsletter), Yr. Est. 1986, Quarterly, ISSN: 0890-7765
List Rental: Rents Lists

Lawyers' Arbitration Letter

Publishing Co: American Arbitration Assn., 140 W. 51 St., New York, NY 10020-1203
Tel # (212) 484-4000 Fax # (212) 541-4841; Title Tel # (212) 484-4005 Title Fax # (212) 765-4874
Personnel: Editor-Vicki Young
Editorial Description: Each issue deals with a specific aspect of alternative dispute resolution, with a discussion of count decisions & legislation.
General Info: Yr. Est. 1960, Quarterly, Web press, 12 pages, Matte, Saddle-stitched, Looseleaf
Subscriptions: Indv. $30
Circulation: Total-4,500
Printing Co: Mohican Press, New York, NY 10010

Lawyer's Brief, The

Publishing Co: Business Laws, Inc., 11630 Chillicothe Rd., Chesterland, OH 44026-1928;
Title Tel # (216) 729-7996 Title Fax # (216) 729-0645
Personnel: Editor-William Hancock
General Info: Yr. Est. 1970, Bi-monthly, 16 pages, ISSN: 0898-9966
Subscriptions: Indv. $398, $25/copy

Lawyer's Committee on Nuclear Policy Newsletter   *Business*

Publishing Co: Lawyer's Committee on Nuclear Policy, 666 Broadway Rm 610, New York, NY 10012-2317; Title Tel # (212) 674-7790
Personnel: Editor-Brian D'Agostino
Editorial Description: LCNP is the largest lawyers group in the world devoted to the abolition of nuclear weapons under international law.
General Info: Yr. Est. 1981, Trim Size-8½ x 11, 8 pages
Circulation: Total-2,000
List Rental: Rents Lists

Lawyers' Guide to Medical Proof   *Business*

Publishing Co: Matthew Bender & Co., 11 Penn Plaza, New York, NY 10001-2006
Fax # (212) 244-3188; Title Tel # (212) 967-7707
Personnel: Editor-B. Lieberman
Editorial Description: Provides practical advice on the psychology of a personal injury trial, effective dramatic advocacy and impeachment of expert's testimony, demonstrated by cross-examinations drawn from actual cases.
General Info: Yr. Est. 1966, Irregular, Looseleaf
Subscriptions: $420/copy

Lawyers Job Bulletin Board
See: EMPLOYMENT

Lawyers' Micro Users Group Newsletter
See: COMPUTERS & AUTOMATION

Lawyer's PC   *Business*

Publishing Co: Shepard's/McGraw-Hill, Inc., 555 Middle Creek Pky, Colorado Springs, CO 80921-3622; Title Tel # (719) 488-3000 Title Fax # (719) 481-7448
Personnel: Editor-Robert Wilkins, Production Mgr.-Cheryl Everitt, Adv. Dir.-Peggy Ives, Art Dir.-Leigh Vidakovich
Editorial Description: Newsletter written by lawyers for lawyers using personal computers.
General Info: (Formerly Lawyer's Microcomputer), Yr. Est. 1983, Semi-monthly, Trim Size-8½ x 11, Web press, 24 pages, ISSN: 0740-0942, 3% ads, No Color, Newsprint, Saddle-stitched
Subscriptions: Indv. $105
Advertising: Accepts Inserts.
List Rental: List Management Co.: The Lake Group, 411 Theodore Freund Ave., Rye, NY 10580-1497 Tel # (914) 925-2400, Fax # (914) 925-2499, Actives: 40,212, $130/M

Lawyers Tax Alert   *Business*

Publishing Co: Research Institute of America, 117 E Stevens Ave, Valhalla, NY 10595-1264;
Title Tel # (212) 645-4800
Editorial Description: Specific tax topics relevant to lawyers.
General Info: Yr. Est. 1978, Monthly
List Rental: List Management Co.: WG & L List Management, 1 Penn Plz Fl 42, New York, NY 10119-0002 Tel # (212) 971-5000, Actives: $95/M, Expires: $60/M

Lawyer's Weekly Report
See: TAXES

Leader's Equipment Leasing Newsletter

Publishing Co: Leader Publications, Inc., 345 Park Avenue South, New York, NY 10010 Parent Co.-New York Law Publishing Co., New York; Title Tel # (212) 545-6170 Title Fax # (212) 696-1848
Personnel: Publisher-Stuart Wise, Editor-Herbert Schlagman, Circ. Mgr.-Kerry Kyle, Promotion Dir.-Rose-Ann Morangelli
Editorial Description: Reports on tax legal & financial aspects of equipment leasing industry.
General Info: Yr. Est. 1982, Monthly, Trim Size-8½ x 11, Offset press, 8 pages, ISSN: 9733-4304, Color, Newsprint
Subscriptions: Indv. $295, $25/copy
Acquistions: Publication Sold
Printing Co: Columbus Bookbinding, 1343 Belfast Ave, Columbus, OH 31904 Tel # (206) 323-9313, Fax # (206) 323-2987

Leader's Legal Tech Newsletter
See: COMPUTERS & AUTOMATION

Ledger

Publishing Co: American League of Financial Institutions, 900 19th Street N.W., Suite #400, Washington, DC 20006; Title Tel # (202) 628-5624
General Info: Bi-monthly

Legal Advisory

Publishing Co: WPI Communications, Inc., 55 Morris Ave, Springfield, NJ 07081-1496;
Title Tel # (201) 467-8700 Title Fax # (201) 467-0368
General Info: Monthly
List Rental: Rents Lists

Legal Alert

Publishing Co: Insight Press, 55 University Avenue, Suite 1700, Toronto, ON M5J 2V6 Canada;
Title Tel # (416) 777-2020
Personnel: Publisher-Robert Ross, Editor-Shaun Johnson, Promotion Dir.-Jane Neveleff
General Info: Yr. Est. 1980, Monthly, Web press, 12 pages
Subscriptions: Indv. $275

Legal Guide for Physicians   *Business*

Publishing Co: Matthew Bender & Co., 11 Penn Plaza, New York, NY 10001-2006
Tel # (212) 967-7707 Fax # (212) 244-3188
Editorial Description: A unique guide written especially for the physician, with thorough discussion of issues & the inclusion of forms that you can use in your day-to-day practice.
General Info: Yr. Est. 1987, Irregular, Looseleaf

Legal Information Alert: What's New in Legal Publications   *Business*   CPM: $333

Publishing Co: Alert Publications Inc., 401 W Fullerton Pky Apt 1403, Chicago, IL 60614-2805;
Title Tel # (312) 525-7594 Title Fax # (312) 525-7015
Personnel: Publisher, Editor-Donna Tuke Heroy, Bk. Rev. Ed.-Christine Brotherton, Adv. Dir.-Lael Bush
Editorial Description: What's new in legal publishing, databases, & legal research techniques.
General Info: (Formerly US Law Library Alert), Yr. Est. 1981, 10x/yr., Trim Size-8½ x 11, Sheetfed press, 16 pages, ISSN: 0883-1297, Ind/Abs/Online: LIMI, 25% ads, 2 Color, Matte
Subscriptions: Indv. $149, Inst. $149, Can. $169, For. $169
Acquisitions: Publication Sold
Circulation: Total-1,200
Advertising: $400. Accepts Inserts.
List Rental: Rents Lists
Printing Co: Graphic Copy, 415 N. State, Chicago, IL 60605 Tel # (312) 644-7800

Legal-Legislative Reporter   *Association*

Publishing Co: International Foundation of Employee Benefit Plans, 18700 W Bluemound Rd #69, P O Box 69, Brookfield, WI 53008-0069; Title Tel # (414) 786-6700 Title Fax # (414) 786-8670
Personnel: Publisher-Dee Birschel, Editor-William Curtin
Editorial Description: Reports government actions and court decisions relating to employee benefits.Available only with subscription to publications package or membership to IFEBP.
General Info: Yr. Est. 1968, Monthly, Trim Size-8½ x 11, Web press, 8 pages, ISSN: 0458-9599, Ind/Abs/Online: employee benefits infosource, 2 Color
Subscriptions: Indv. $170, Inst. $170, Can. $170, For. $220, Free With Membership
Circulation: Total-34,000

Legal Liability Update   *Business*

Publishing Co: American Institute of CPA's, Harborside Financial Center, 201 Plaza Three, Jersey City, NJ 07311-3881 Tel # (201) 938-3283 Fax # (201) 938-3329; Title Tel # (202) 434-9201 Title Fax # (202) 638-4312
Personnel: Publisher-Robert Rainer, Editor, Feature Ed.-Sheri Bango, Mktg. Dir.-Charles Cohn
Editorial Description: State tort reform issues affecting CPA's.
General Info: Yr. Est. 1992, Irregular
Subscriptions: Free With Membership
Circulation: Total-2,500

Legal Newsletter

Publishing Co: WPI Communications, Inc., 55 Morris Ave, Springfield, NJ 07081-1496;
Title Tel # (201) 467-8700 Title Fax # (201) 467-0368
General Info: Quarterly

Legal Notes for Education
See: EDUCATION

Legal Notes for Insurance
See: INSURANCE

Legal Periodicals in English
See: PERIODICAL INDUSTRY

Legal Plan Letter   *Association*

Publishing Co: National Resource Center for Consumers of Legal Services, 6596 Main St., PO Box 340, Gloucester, VA 23061; Title Tel # (804) 693-9330 Title Fax # (804) 693-7363
Personnel: Publisher, Editor-Bill Bolger, Circ. Mgr.-Euretta Sturgeon
Editorial Description: News & resources on legal service plans & other developments in the delivery of legal services.
General Info: (Formerly New Directions Action Line), Yr. Est. 1982, Bi-weekly, Trim Size-8½ x 11, Offset press, 6 pages, ISSN: 0886-6678, No Color
Subscriptions: Inst. $95, Can. $95, For. $95, $3/copy

Legal Publisher, The   *Business*

Publishing Co: JK Publishing Inc., PO Box 71020, Milwaukee, WI 53211-7120 Fax # (414) 964-0843; Title Tel # (414) 332-1625 Title Fax # (414) 969-0843
Personnel: Publisher, Editor-John Kenney, Circ. Dir.-Patricia Glynn
Editorial Description: Covers start-ups of journals, newsletters, books and electronic (on-line) products for all fields of the legal profession. Also includes mergers & acquisitions of legal publishing properties & companies.
General Info: Yr. Est. 1991, Monthly, Trim Size-8 x 11, 8 pages, ISSN: 1056-196X, Ind/Abs/Online: Newsnet; Predicasts; Mead Data Central-Lexis, 2 Color, Matte
Subscriptions: Indv. $149, $14/copy
Advertising: $490. Accepts Inserts.
Printing Co: Account Manager: Esther Anderson; Anderson Graphics, 254 N Emmber Ln, Milwaukee, WI 53233-2638 Tel # (414) 276-4115

Legal Quarterly Digest of Mine Safety & Health Decisions
See: MINING & MINERALS

Legal Services Bulletin

Publishing Co: Alabama Consortium of Legal Services Programs, 500 Bell Bldg., 207 Montgomery St., Montgomery, AL 36104-3304; Title Tel # (205) 264-1471
Personnel: Publisher, Editor-Penny Weaver, Circ. Mgr.-Joyce Manniken
Editorial Description: Information about legal & other events from Legal Services perspective.
General Info: Yr. Est. 1981, Bi-monthly, 8 pages, 2 Color, Newsprint, Saddle-stitched
Subscriptions: Free
Circulation: (100% controlled)

Legal Support Staff
Newsletter   *Business*

Publishing Co: Moore/Parry Ltd., 3390 W. 41st Ave., Vancouver, BC V6N 3E4 Canada; Title Tel # (604) 266-4510 Title Fax # (604) 266-6639
Personnel: Circ. Mgr.-R. Moore, Publisher, Editor, Adv. Dir.-Katherine Moore, Art Dir.-Daphene Brown
Editorial Description: Procedure materials, forms, court registry announcements, precedents for Legal Support Staff.
General Info: (Formerly Legal Secretary's Newsletter, The), Yr. Est. 1973, Bi-monthly, Trim Size-8½ x 11, Letrpr. press, 10 pages, Color
Subscriptions: Indv. $69, $4/copy
Circulation: Total-2,500
Advertising: Inquire for rates.

Legal-eyes
See: DRUGS & PHARMACEUTICALS

Lender Liability Law and Litigation
See: BANKING & FINANCE

Lender Liability Law
Report   *Business*

Publishing Co: Warren, Gorham & Lamont, 31 Saint James Ave., Boston, MA 02116-4112 Parent Co.-Thomson Professional Publications, Stamford; Title Tel # (617) 423-2020 Title Fax # (617) 423-1914
Personnel: Publisher-Larry Selby, Mktg. Dir.-Sandra Fox
Editorial Description: Federal and state court decisions.
General Info: Yr. Est. 1987, Monthly, ISSN: 1045-1463
Subscriptions: Indv. $185
List Rental: List Management Co.: Manager: Seena Benedek; WG & L List Management, 1 Penn Plz Fl 42, New York, NY 10119-0002 Tel # (212) 971-5000

Lender Liability News   *Business*

Publishing Co: LRP Publications, 747 Dresher Rd., P.O. Box 980, Horsham, PA 19044-0980 Tel # (215) 784-0910 Fax # (215) 784-0317
Personnel: Publisher-Ken Kahn, Editor-Richard Hoffman
Editorial Description: Reports on litigation in which lenders are exposed to losses on their loans, keeping readers abreast of what is going on now and what is likely to happen in the future.
General Info: Yr. Est. 1988, Bi-weekly, Sheetfed press, 12 pages, ISSN: 0898-7645, 2 Color, Newsprint
Subscriptions: Indv. $597, For. $597
Acquistions: Publication Bought, Publication Sold

Lesbian/Gay Law Notes
See: GAY & LESBIAN INTEREST

Letter to Members   *Association*

Publishing Co: Inter-American Bar Association, 1211 Connecticut Ave., NW, Ste. 202, Washington, DC 20036 Fax # (202) 393-1241; Title Tel # (202) 393-1217
Personnel: Editor-Ysbell Kerns
General Info: Quarterly, 6 pages
Circulation: Total-3,500

Letters of Credit
See: BANKING & FINANCE

Leveraged Buyout &
Acquisitions Litigation
Reporter   *Business*

Publishing Co: Andrews Publications, Inc., 1646 West Chester Pike, PO Box 1000, Westtown, PA 19395; Title Tel # (610) 399-6600 Title Fax # (610) 399-6610
Personnel: Publisher-John E. Backe, Editor-Linda Coady, Mktg. Dir.-Andrew Katz
Editorial Description: Provides summaries and full-text opinions and key briefs in step-by-step coverage of leveraged buyout and related business issues in bankruptcy, federal district and appellate courts.
General Info: (Formerly Failed Leverage Buyout Litigation Reporter), Yr. Est. 1990, Monthly, Trim Size-8½ x 11, Mimeo press, ISSN: 1055-9485, No Color
Subscriptions: Indv. $700, $67/copy
Advertising: Inquire for rates.
List Rental: Actives: 1,251, $110/M

Lex Collegii

Publishing Co: College Legal Information, Inc., PO Box 150541, Nashville, TN 37215-0541; Title Tel # (615) 383-3332
Personnel: Publisher, Editor-Kent Weeks
Editorial Description: A legal newsletter for independent higher education.
General Info: Yr. Est. 1978, Quarterly, 8 pages, ISSN: 0749-9078
Subscriptions: Indv. $42, $8/copy

Liability Update   *Business*

Publishing Co: Victor O. Schinnerer, 2 Wisconsin Cir., Chevy Chase, MD 20815-7022
General Info: Yr. Est. 1980, 10x/yr., Trim Size-8½ x 11, Sheetfed press, 4 pages, 2 Color
Subscriptions: Indv. $50
Circulation: Total-18,000
Printing Co: Linemark Printing, Inc., 1220 Caraway Ct., Landover, MD 20785 Tel # (301) 925-9000

Liberator, The
See: CIVIL RIGHTS

Licensing Law and
Business Report   *Association*

Publishing Co: Clark Boardman Callaghan, 375 Hudson St, New York, NY 10014-3685 Fax # (212) 807-6209; Title Tel # (212) 929-7500 Title Fax # (212) 924-0460
Personnel: Publisher-Jim Fegen, Editor- Willian, Brinks, Et, Editorial Page Ed.-Jeanine Politi, Adv. Dir., Promotion Dir.-Steve Murtha
Editorial Description: Comprehensive newsletter reporting on national and international licensing law matters.
General Info: Yr. Est. 1978, Bi-monthly, Trim Size-8½ x 11, Sheetfed press, 12 pages, ISSN: 0162-5764, No Color
Subscriptions: Indv. $245
List Rental: Rents Lists

Life Entitlements
See: HEALTH

Lightbulb Journal for Inventors
See: PATENTS/COPYRIGHTS/TRADE MARKS

Limited Liability Company Guide
See: TAXES

Lindey on Separation
Agreements and
Antenuptial Contracts   *Business*

Publishing Co: Matthew Bender & Co., 11 Penn Plaza, New York, NY 10001-2006 Fax # (212) 244-3188; Title Tel # (212) 967-7707
Personnel: Editor-N. Masliansky
Editorial Description: Examines all facets of these vital agreements, including the impact of equitable distribution and community property statutes.
General Info: Yr. Est. 1937, Irregular, Looseleaf
Subscriptions: $330/copy

Liquor Control Law Reports
See: BEVERAGES - BREWING

Liquor Liability Law   *Business*

Publishing Co: Matthew Bender & Co., 11 Penn Plaza, New York, NY 10001-2006 Tel # (212) 967-7707 Fax # (212) 244-3188
Editorial Description: Comprehensive coverage of civil liability of tavern owners, social hosts, employers, etc., for negligent service of alcohol to minors and intoxicated persons.
General Info: Yr. Est. 1987, Irregular, Looseleaf

Litigation News
Association

Publishing Co: American Bar Association, 750 N. Lake Shore Dr., Chicago, IL 60611-4497
Tel # (312) 988-6115 Fax # (312) 988-6030; Title Tel # (312) 988-5522 Title Fax # (312) 988-5528
Personnel: Editor-Janet Kole, Production Mgr.-Jack Wolewiec
Editorial Description: ABA section of litigation.
General Info: Yr. Est. 1975, Quarterly, Web press, 32 pages, ISSN: 0147-9970, 2 Color
Subscriptions: Indv. $2
Circulation: Total-49,000
List Rental: Rents Lists

Lloyd's Aviation Law
Newsletter
Business

Publishing Co: LLP Maritime, 611 Broadway Rm 308, New York, NY 10012-2608;
Title Tel # (212) 529-9500 Title Fax # (212) 529-9826
Personnel: Publisher-Don Wall, Editor-George Tompkins
Editorial Description: Summary of international legal cases in aviation law.
General Info: Yr. Est. 1982, Bi-weekly, 6 pages
Subscriptions: Indv. $435
Circulation: Total-300

Lloyd's Maritime Law

Publishing Co: Lloyd's of London Press, 611 Broadway Rm 308, New York, NY 10012-2608;
Title Tel # (212) 529-9500 Title Fax # (212) 529-9826
Personnel: Publisher-Don Wall, Editor-Joseph Sweeney
General Info: Yr. Est. 1984, Semi-monthly
Subscriptions: Indv. $370

Local Government Law
Business

Publishing Co: Matthew Bender & Co., 11 Penn Plaza, New York, NY 10001-2006
Fax # (212) 244-3188; Title Tel # (212) 967-7707
Editorial Description: Clearly states the principles of law for all types of local governments, and backs those principles with case citations from all jurisdictions. Examines the laws and their impact in three primary areas: municipal, local entities, & counties.
General Info: Yr. Est. 1955, Semi-annually, Looseleaf
Subscriptions: $540/copy

Lottery, Paramutual & Casino Regulations/State Capitals
See: GAMBLING

Louisiana Coastal Law
Business

Publishing Co: Louisiana State Univ., Sea Grant Legal Program, 170 Law Ct., Baton Rouge, LA 70803-0001; Title Tel # (504) 388-5931 Title Fax # (504) 388-5938
Personnel: Editor-M. Wascom, Circ. Mgr.-J. Wilkins
Editorial Description: Issues covering a broad range of environmental, coastal zone, natural resources, and fisheries law & mgmt.
General Info: Yr. Est. 1971, Irregular, Trim Size-8½ x 11, Desktop press, 8 pages, 2 Color, Newsprint
Subscriptions: Free
Acquistions: Publication Bought
Circulation: Total-1,200
Printing Co: Louisiana State University Graphic Services, 3555 River Rd., Baton Rouge, LA 70803-0001 Tel # (504) 388-2800

Louisiana Criminal Law &
Motor Vehicle Handbook

Publishing Co: Gould Publications, Inc, 1333 N US Highway 17-92, Longwood, FL 32750-3724
Tel # (407) 695-9500 Fax # (407) 695-2906; Title Tel # (607) 724-3000
Editorial Description: The complete Criminal Law (Title 14), Motor Vehicle & Traffic Regulations (Title 32), Safety (Title 40), chapter 4 - food and drugs, and criminal procedures (Title 15), and the Codes of Criminal and juvenile procedures.
General Info: Annually, 1,040 pages, Looseleaf
Subscriptions: Indv. $25, $17/copy

Louisiana Employment
Law Letter
Business

Publishing Co: M. Lee Smith Publishers & Printers ,LCC, P.O. Box 198867, 162 Fourth Avenue North, Nashville, TN 37219-8867; Title Tel # (615) 242-7395 Title Fax # (615) 256-6601
Personnel: Publisher-M Lee Smith, Editor-H Mark Adams, Co-Editor-H. Mark Adams, Co-Editor-Mary Ellen Jordan, Circ. Mgr.-Cathy Bradford, Mktg. Dir.-Dave Yates
Editorial Description: Review of employment low developments that affect Louisiana employers.
General Info: Yr. Est. 1992, Monthly, Trim Size-8½ x 11, 8 pages, ISSN: 1059-5058, 2 Color
Subscriptions: Indv. $89
List Rental: Rents Lists
Printing Co: M. Lee Smith Publishers & Printers ,LLC, PO Box 198867, 162 Fourth Avenue, Nashville, TN 37219-8867 Tel # (615) 242-7395, Fax # (615) 256-6601

Louisiana Environmental
Compliance Update
Business

Publishing Co: M. Lee Smith Publishers & Printers ,LCC, P.O. Box 198867, 162 Fourth Avenue North, Nashville, TN 37219-8867; Title Tel # (615) 242-7395 Title Fax # (615) 256-6601
Personnel: Publisher-M Lee Smith, Editor-Mike Chernekoff, Circ. Mgr.-Cathy Bradford, Mktg. Dir.-Dave Yates
Editorial Description: Review of environmental law developments that affect Louisiana companies.
General Info: Yr. Est. 1993, Monthly, Trim Size-8½ x 11, 8 pages, ISSN: 1066-1115, 2 Color
Subscriptions: Indv. $117
List Rental: Rents Lists
Printing Co: M. Lee Smith Publishers & Printers ,LLC, PO Box 198867, 162 Fourth Avenue, Nashville, TN 37219-8867 Tel # (615) 242-7395, Fax # (615) 256-6601

M. W. & C. Newsletter
Business, Association

Publishing Co: Mathews, Woodbridge & Collins, 100 Thanet Cir Ste 306, Princeton, NJ 08540-3674
Fax # (609) 924-3936; Title Tel # (609) 924-3773 Title Fax # (609) 924-3036
Editorial Description: Newsletter on legal news.
General Info: Quarterly, Trim Size-8½ x 11, Letrpr. press, 4 pages, Color, Matte
Subscriptions: Free

MALDEF Newsletter
See: CIVIL RIGHTS

MCPL Education Fund, Food and Population Newsletter
See: POLITICS

MSRB Manual
See: INVESTMENT

Maine Employment Law
Letter
Business

Publishing Co: M. Lee Smith Publishers & Printers ,LCC, P.O. Box 198867, 162 Fourth Avenue North, Nashville, TN 37219-8867 Tel # (615) 242-7395 Fax # (615) 256-6601
Personnel: Publisher-M Lee Smith, Editor-Phil Mess, Circ. Mgr.-Cathy Bradford, Mktg. Dir.-David Yates
General Info: Yr. Est. 1995, Monthly, Trim Size-8½ x 11, 8 pages, 2 Color
Subscriptions: Indv. $97
List Rental: Rents Lists
Printing Co: M. Lee Smith Publishers & Printers ,LLC, PO Box 198867, 162 Fourth Avenue, Nashville, TN 37219-8867 Tel # (615) 242-7395, Fax # (615) 256-6601

Managed Care Law
Outlook
Business

Publishing Co: Capitol Publications, Inc., 1101 King St., Ste. 444, Alexandria, VA 22314-2968;
Title Tel # (703) 683-4100 Title Fax # (703) 739-6501
Personnel: Publisher-Cynthia Carter, Editor-Janet Lewis-Greene, Exec. Ed.-Russell Jackson, Circ. Mgr.-Peggy Dwyer, Production Mgr.-Billy Adams, Art Dir.-Linda Mcdonald, Mktg. Dir.-Mary Lou Probka, Promotion Dir.-Kelly Baptiste
Editorial Description: Timely exclusive coverage of critical strategic planning issues such as antitrust & anti-managed care law, benefits mandates & utilization review liability.
General Info: Yr. Est. 1989, Monthly, Trim Size-8½ x 11, 16 pages, Ind/Abs/Online: Predicasts
Subscriptions: Indv. $427, Inst. $427
List Rental: Actives: $150/M
Printing Co: Capitol Publications, Inc., 1101 King St., Ste. 444, Alexandria, VA 22314-2968
Tel # (703) 683-4100, Fax # (703) 739-6501

Management Policies & Personnel Law
See: MANAGEMENT

Manager's Legal Bulletin
See: MANAGEMENT

Managing Laboratory Personnel
See: MANAGEMENT

Manitoba Decisions, Civil
and Criminal Cases

Publishing Co: Western Legal Publications, 301-1 Alexander St., Vancouver, BC V6A 1B2 Canada
Fax # (604) 687-2796; Title Tel # (604) 687-5671
Personnel: Publisher-Nancy Cotter, Editor-Ronda McNabb
Editorial Description: Monthly digests of current case law filed by subject.
General Info: Yr. Est. 1975, Monthly, Mimeo press, 50 pages, ISSN: 0380-0008, Ind/Abs/Online: INFOMART, QL, No Color, Newsprint, Looseleaf
Subscriptions: Can. $290

Manitoba and Saskatchewan Tax Reports
See: TAXES

Manual of Complex
Litigation
Business

Publishing Co: Matthew Bender & Co., 11 Penn Plaza, New York, NY 10001-2006
Fax # (212) 244-3188; Title Tel # (212) 967-7707
Editorial Description: An official publication, written by the Judicial Panel on Multi-District Litigation. Offers complete, authoritative coverage of: Pre-trial procedure in complex civil & criminal cases, multiple & multi-district civil litigation, & class actions.
General Info: Yr. Est. 1986, Irregular, Looseleaf
Subscriptions: $100/copy

Maritimes Tax Reports
See: TAXES

Marketing Law Reporting Service
See: ADVERTISING & MARKETING

Marketing for Lawyers

Publishing Co: Leader Publications, Inc., 345 Park Avenue South, New York, NY 10010 Parent Co.-New York Law Publishing Co., New York; Title Tel # (212) 545-6170 Title Fax # (212) 696-1848
Personnel: Publisher-Stuart Wise, Editor-Daniel White, Circ. Mgr.-Kerry Kyle, Promotion Dir.-Rose-Ann Morangelli
Editorial Description: Helps lawyers expand their practice through marketing.
General Info: Yr. Est. 1987, Monthly, Trim Size-8½ x 11, Offset press, 8 pages, ISSN: 0893-7788, Newsprint
Subscriptions: Indv. $185, $15/copy
Acquistions: Publication Sold
List Rental: Rents Lists
Printing Co: Columbus Bookbinding, 1343 Belfast Ave, Columbus, OH 31904 Tel # (206) 323-9313, Fax # (206) 323-2987

Maryland Criminal Law & Motor Vehicle Handbook

Publishing Co: Gould Publications, Inc, 1333 N US Highway 17-92, Longwood, FL 32750-3724 Tel # (407) 695-9500 Fax # (407) 695-2906; Title Tel # (607) 724-3000
Editorial Description: A complete presentation of crimes and punishment also vehicle laws, and related statutes.
General Info: Annually, 900 pages, Looseleaf
Subscriptions: Indv. $22, $20/copy

Maryland Employment Law Letter *Business*

Publishing Co: M. Lee Smith Publishers & Printers ,LCC, P.O. Box 198867, 162 Fourth Avenue North, Nashville, TN 37219-8867; Title Tel # (615) 242-7395 Title Fax # (615) 256-6601
Personnel: Publisher-M Lee Smith, Editor-John Kyle, Circ. Mgr.-Cathy Bradford, Mktg. Dir.-Dave Yates
Editorial Description: Review of employment law developments that affect Maryland employers.
General Info: Yr. Est. 1990, Monthly, Trim Size-8½ x 11, 8 pages, ISSN: 1049-9377, 2 Color
Subscriptions: Indv. $97
List Rental: Rents Lists
Printing Co: M. Lee Smith Publishers & Printers ,LLC, PO Box 198867, 162 Fourth Avenue, Nashville, TN 37219-8867 Tel # (615) 242-7395, Fax # (615) 256-6601

Maryland Environmental Law Letter *Business*

Publishing Co: M. Lee Smith Publishers & Printers ,LCC, P.O. Box 198867, 162 Fourth Avenue North, Nashville, TN 37219-8867; Title Tel # (615) 242-7395 Title Fax # (615) 256-6601
Personnel: Publisher-M Lee Smith, Editor-Deborah Jennings, Circ. Mgr., Mktg. Dir.-Cathy Bradford, Mktg. Dir.-Dave Yates
Editorial Description: Review environmental law developments that affect Maryland companies.
General Info: Yr. Est. 1992, Monthly, Trim Size-8½ x 11, 8 pages, ISSN: 1062-7960, 2 Color
Subscriptions: Indv. $117
List Rental: Rents Lists
Printing Co: M. Lee Smith Publishers & Printers ,LLC, PO Box 198867, 162 Fourth Avenue, Nashville, TN 37219-8867 Tel # (615) 242-7395, Fax # (615) 256-6601

Massachusetts Corporation Law with Federal Tax Analysis *Business*

Publishing Co: Matthew Bender & Co., 11 Penn Plaza, New York, NY 10001-2006 Fax # (212) 244-3188; Title Tel # (212) 967-7707
Personnel: Editor-M. Tenner
Editorial Description: For Massachusetts small business planners, provides step-by-step guidance on how to proceed from start-up through liquidation of a business.
General Info: Yr. Est. 1963, Annually, Looseleaf
Subscriptions: $100/copy

Massachusetts Criminal Law & Proceedures

Publishing Co: Gould Publications, Inc, 1333 N US Highway 17-92, Longwood, FL 32750-3724 Tel # (407) 695-9500 Fax # (407) 695-2906; Title Tel # (607) 724-3000
Editorial Description: The complete presentation of Part IV, crimes, punishment , and proceedings in criminal cases of the General Laws of Massachusetts.
General Info: Annually, 810 pages, Looseleaf
Subscriptions: Indv. $22, $20/copy

Massachusetts Employment Law Letter *Business*

Publishing Co: M. Lee Smith Publishers & Printers ,LCC, P.O. Box 198867, 162 Fourth Avenue North, Nashville, TN 37219-8867 Fax # (615) 256-6601; Title Tel # (615) 242-7395 Title Fax # (615) 236-6601
Personnel: Publisher-M Lee Smith, Editor-Ralph Abbott, Circ. Mgr.-Cathy Bradford, Mktg. Dir.-David Yates
Editorial Description: Review of employment law developments that affect Massachusetts employers.
General Info: Yr. Est. 1990, Monthly, Trim Size-8½ x 11, 8 pages, ISSN: 1049-2062, 2 Color
Subscriptions: Indv. $97
List Rental: Actives: $90/M
Printing Co: M. Lee Smith Publishers & Printers ,LLC, PO Box 198867, 162 Fourth Avenue, Nashville, TN 37219-8867 Tel # (615) 242-7395, Fax # (615) 256-6601

Massachusetts Environmental Compliance Update *Business*

Publishing Co: M. Lee Smith Publishers & Printers ,LCC, P.O. Box 198867, 162 Fourth Avenue North, Nashville, TN 37219-8867; Title Tel # (615) 242-7395 Title Fax # (615) 256-6601
Personnel: Publisher-M Lee Smith, Editor-Gregor I. McGregor, Circ. Mgr.-Cathy Bradford, Mktg. Dir.-Dave Yates
Editorial Description: Review of environmental law developments that affect Massachusetts companies.
General Info: Yr. Est. 1992, Monthly, Trim Size-8½ x 11, 8 pages, ISSN: 1064-2374, 2 Color
Subscriptions: Indv. $117
List Rental: Rents Lists
Printing Co: M. Lee Smith Publishers & Printers ,LLC, PO Box 198867, 162 Fourth Avenue, Nashville, TN 37219-8867 Tel # (615) 242-7395, Fax # (615) 256-6601

Massachusetts Environmental Law Handbook

Publishing Co: Gould Publications, Inc, 1333 N US Highway 17-92, Longwood, FL 32750-3724 Tel # (407) 695-9500 Fax # (407) 695-2906
Editorial Description: The various chapters of the general laws related to the environment.
General Info: Annually, Looseleaf
Subscriptions: Indv. $35

Massachusetts Lawyers Weekly *Business*

Publishing Co: Lawyers Weekly Publications, 41 West St, Boston, MA 02111-1233 Tel # (617) 451-7300 Fax # (617) 451-7323
Personnel: Publisher-Samuel Spencer, Editor-Dan Sharp, Circ. Mgr.-Sharon Hildebrandt, Production Mgr.-Catherine Flynn, Adv. Dir.-Fred Merkle, Eastern Adv. Mgr.-Jeff Bryan, Promotion Dir.-Al Pawlick
Editorial Description: Legal news of Massachusetts.
General Info: Yr. Est. 1972, Weekly, Trim Size-11½ x 17, Web press, 48 pages, ISSN: 0196-7509, 4% ads, 2 Color, Newsprint
Subscriptions: Indv. $225, $5/copy
Circulation: (ABC), Readership-30,000
Advertising: Inquire for rates.
List Rental: List Management Co.: Manager: Fred Merkle; JAMI Marketing, 2 Blue Hill Plz, Pearl River, NY 10965-3101 Tel # (914) 620-0700, Fax # (914) 620-1885
Printing Co: Mariner Graphics, 165 Enterprise Dr, Marshfield, MA 02050-2132

Massachusetts Motor Vehicle and Traffic Code

Publishing Co: Gould Publications, Inc, 1333 N US Highway 17-92, Longwood, FL 32750-3724 Tel # (407) 695-9500 Fax # (407) 695-2906; Title Tel # (607) 724-3000
Editorial Description: A complete up-to-date presentation of the statutes, rules, and regulations relating to Motor Vehicle and traffic Laws of Massachusettes.
General Info: Annually, 720 pages, Looseleaf
Subscriptions: $20/copy

Massachusetts Pleading and Practice-Forms and Commentary *Business*

Publishing Co: Matthew Bender & Co., 11 Penn Plaza, New York, NY 10001-2006 Fax # (212) 244-3188; Title Tel # (212) 967-7707
Personnel: Editor-A. Jenner
Editorial Description: Covers all aspects of civil practice in the Massachusetts courts, with special emphasis on the Massachusetts Rules of Civil Procedure.
General Info: Yr. Est. 1974, Annually, Looseleaf
Subscriptions: $510/copy

Matrimonial Strategist

Publishing Co: Leader Publications, Inc., 345 Park Avenue South, New York, NY 10010 Parent Co.-New York Law Publishing Co., New York; Title Tel # (212) 545-6170 Title Fax # (212) 696-1848
Personnel: Publisher-Stuart Wise, Editor-Lydia Fogelman, Circ. Mgr.-Kerry Kyle, Mktg. Dir.-Rose-Ann Morangelei
Editorial Description: Reports on law & strategy in matrimonial area.
General Info: Yr. Est. 1983, Monthly, Trim Size-8½ x 11, Offset press, 8 pages, ISSN: 0736-4881, Color, Newsprint, Saddle-stitched
Subscriptions: Indv. $165, $14/copy
Acquistions: Publication Sold
List Rental: Rents Lists
Printing Co: Columbus Bookbinding, 1343 Belfast Ave, Columbus, OH 31904 Tel # (206) 323-9313, Fax # (206) 323-2987

McQuillin Municipal Law Report *Business*

Publishing Co: Clark Boardman Callaghan & Co., 155 Pfingsten Rd., Deerfield, IL 60015; Title Tel # (708) 948-7000
Editorial Description: Summary & analysis of latest municipal law cases.
General Info: Monthly, 12 pages
Subscriptions: Indv. $195
Acquistions: Publication Bought, Publication Sold

Mealey's Emerging Insurance Disputes *Business*

Publishing Co: Mealey Publications, Inc., PO Box 446, Wayne, PA 19087-0446
Tel # (610) 688-6566; Title Tel # (410) 688-6566 Title Fax # (610) 688-7552
Personnel: Publisher-Michael Mealey, Editor-Mauren McGuire
General Info: Yr. Est. 1969, Semi-monthly, Trim Size-8.5 x 11
Subscriptions: Indv. $650, Can. $770, $50/copy

Mealey's Insurance Supplement *Business*

Publishing Co: Mealey Publications, Inc., PO Box 446, Wayne, PA 19087-0446
Tel # (610) 688-6566 Fax # (610) 688-7552
Personnel: Publisher-Michael Mealey, Editor-Ton Hanson, Editor-Maureen McGuire, Mktg. Dir.-Kathy Roach
Editorial Description: Provides updates and additional information on insurance litigation.
General Info: Yr. Est. 1995, Bi-monthly, ISSN: 1081-8707
Subscriptions: Indv. $575, For. $695

Mealey's International Arbitration Report

Publishing Co: Mealey Publications, Inc., PO Box 446, Wayne, PA 19087-0446;
Title Tel # (610) 688-6566 Title Fax # (610) 688-7552
Personnel: Publisher-Michael Mealey, Editor-Edie Scott, Mktg. Dir.-Kathy Roach
Editorial Description: Document & editorial coverage of int'l. arbitration & related litigation.
General Info: Yr. Est. 1986, Monthly, Trim Size-8½ x 11, 90 pages, ISSN: 0886-0114
Subscriptions: Indv. $795, For. $855, $50/copy

Mealey's Litigation Report: Asbestos

Publishing Co: Mealey Publications, Inc., PO Box 446, Wayne, PA 19087-0446;
Title Tel # (610) 688-6566 Title Fax # (610) 688-7552
Personnel: Publisher-Michael Mealey, Editor-Tom Moylan, Editor-Sue Sutter, Mktg. Dir.-Kathy Roach
Editorial Description: Document & editorial coverage of nationwide asbestos litigation.
General Info: Yr. Est. 1984, Semi-monthly, Trim Size-8½ x 11, 90 pages, ISSN: 0742-4647
Subscriptions: Indv. $995, For. $1,115, $50/copy

Mealey's Litigation Report: Bad Faith

Publishing Co: Mealey Publications, Inc., PO Box 446, Wayne, PA 19087-0446;
Title Tel # (610) 688-6566 Title Fax # (610) 688-7552
Personnel: Publisher-Michael Mealey, Editor-Stephen Edocombe, Mktg. Dir.-Kathy Roach
General Info: Yr. Est. 1987, Semi-monthly, Trim Size-8½ x 11, 90 pages, ISSN: 0893-1011
Subscriptions: Indv. $835, For. $955, $50/copy

Mealey's Litigation Report: Breast Implants
See: HEALTH

Mealey's Litigation Report: Drugs & Medical Devices

Publishing Co: Mealey Publications, Inc., PO Box 446, Wayne, PA 19087-0446;
Tel # (610) 688-6566 Fax # (610) 688-7552
Personnel: Publisher-Michael Mealey, Editor-Scott Jacobs, Mktg. Dir.-Kathy Roach
General Info: Yr. Est. 1995, Semi-monthly
Subscriptions: Indv. $795

Mealey's Litigation Report: Insurance *Business*

Publishing Co: Mealey Publications, Inc., PO Box 446, Wayne, PA 19087-0446;
Title Tel # (610) 688-6566 Title Fax # (610) 688-7552
Personnel: Publisher-Michael Mealey, Editor-Steve Berstler, Mktg. Dir.-Kathy Roach
Editorial Description: Document & editorial coverage of declaratory judgment actions concerning insurance coverage for latent property damage & personal injury claims.
General Info: Yr. Est. 1984, 48x/yr., Trim Size-8½ x 11, 90 pages, ISSN: 8755-9005
Subscriptions: Indv. $1,595, For. $1,835, $50/copy

Mealey's Litigation Report: Insurance Fraud
See: INSURANCE

Mealey's Litigation Report: Insurance Insolvency

Publishing Co: Mealey Publications, Inc., PO Box 446, Wayne, PA 19087-0446;
Title Tel # (610) 688-6566 Title Fax # (610) 688-7552
Personnel: Publisher-Michael Mealey, Editor-Teresa Zink, Mktg. Dir.-Kathy Roach
Editorial Description: Covers litigation surrounding insolvent insurers. Also tracks which companies are being ordered into receivership.
General Info: Yr. Est. 1989, Semi-monthly, Trim Size-8½ x 11, 90 pages, ISSN: 1043-8416
Subscriptions: Indv. $895, For. $1,015, $50/copy

Mealey's Litigation Report: Intellectual Property
See: BUSINESS & INDUSTRY

Mealey's Litigation Report: Lead

Publishing Co: Mealey Publications, Inc., PO Box 446, Wayne, PA 19087-0446;
Title Tel # (610) 688-6566 Title Fax # (610) 688-7552
Personnel: Publisher-Michael Mealey, Editor-John Hayes
Editorial Description: Editorial and document coverage of lead litigation nationwide.
General Info: Yr. Est. 1991, Semi-monthly, 70 pages, ISSN: 1059-4116
Subscriptions: Indv. $750, For. $870, $50/copy

Mealey's Litigation Report: Norplant
See: HEALTH

Mealey's Litigation Report: Patents *Business*

Publishing Co: Mealey Publications, Inc., PO Box 446, Wayne, PA 19087-0446;
Title Tel # (610) 688-6566 Title Fax # (610) 688-7552
Personnel: Publisher-Michael Mealey, Editor-Maureen McGuire, Mktg. Dir.-Kathy Roach
Editorial Description: Covers patent litigation news.
General Info: Yr. Est. 1993, Semi-monthly, ISSN: 1070-4043
Subscriptions: Indv. $495, For. $415, $50/copy

Mealey's Litigation Report: Pedicle Screws

Publishing Co: Mealey Publications, Inc., PO Box 446, Wayne, PA 19087-0446
Tel # (610) 688-6566 Fax # (610) 688-7552
Personnel: Publisher-Michael Mealey, Editor-Tom Moylan, Mktg. Dir.-Kathy Roach
Editorial Description: Focuses on product liability and medical malpractice claims arising from the alleged failure of pedicle screws and other orthopedic implants.
General Info: Yr. Est. 1995, Semi-monthly, ISSN: 1082-5819
Subscriptions: Indv. $650

Mealey's Litigation Report: Product Liability

Publishing Co: Mealey Publications, Inc., PO Box 446, Wayne, PA 19087-0446;
Title Tel # (610) 688-6566 Title Fax # (610) 688-7552
Personnel: Publisher-Michael Mealey, Editor-John Hayes, Mktg. Dir.-Kathy Roach
Editorial Description: Sumarizes and publishes the latest product liability rulings from state supreme courts, federal appeals courts, and the U.S. Supreme Court, plus significant trial court rulings .
General Info: (Formerly Mealey's Litigation Report: Punitive Damages & Tort Reform), Yr. Est. 1995, Semi-monthly, Trim Size-8½ x 11, 90 pages, ISSN: 1081-7859
Subscriptions: Indv. $695, For. $746, $50/copy

Mealey's Litigation Report: Reinsurance

Publishing Co: Mealey Publications, Inc., PO Box 446, Wayne, PA 19087-0446;
Title Tel # (610) 688-6566 Title Fax # (610) 688-7552
Personnel: Publisher-Michael Mealey, Editor-Teresa Zink, Mktg. Dir.-Kathy Roach
Editorial Description: Covers the rapidly growing area of reinsurance law, including issues related to insolvency and regulatory considerations.
General Info: Semi-monthly, Trim Size-8½ x 11, 90 pages, ISSN: 1049-5347
Subscriptions: Indv. $1,050, For. $1,170, $50/copy

Mealey's Litigation Report: Superfund *Business*

Publishing Co: Mealey Publications, Inc., PO Box 446, Wayne, PA 19087-0446;
Title Tel # (610) 688-6566 Title Fax # (610) 688-7552
Personnel: Publisher-Michael Mealey, Editor-Stephen Edgcumbe, Mktg. Dir.-Kathy Roach
Editorial Description: Document & editorial coverage of litigation involving all sites of Superfund's National Priority List.
General Info: Yr. Est. 1988, Semi-monthly, Trim Size-8½ x 11, 90 pages, ISSN: 0897-3407
Subscriptions: Indv. $795, For. $846, $50/copy

Mealey's Litigation Report: Tobacco

Publishing Co: Mealey Publications, Inc., PO Box 446, Wayne, PA 19087-0446
Tel # (610) 688-6566 Fax # (610) 688-7552
Personnel: Publisher-Michael Mealey, Editor-Jennifer Hahn, Mktg. Dir.-Kathy Roach
Editorial Description: Provides all the latest news and crucial documentation surrounding tobacco and nicotine litigation, tracking every detail of significant cases from initial filing to final appeal.
General Info: Semi-monthly, ISSN: 0886-0122
Subscriptions: Indv. $650

Mealey's Litigation Report: Toxic Torts *Business*

Publishing Co: Mealey Publications, Inc., PO Box 446, Wayne, PA 19087-0446;
Title Tel # (610) 688-6566 Title Fax # (610) 688-7552
Personnel: Publisher-Michael Mealey, Editor-Scott Jacobs, Mktg. Dir.-Kathy Roach
Editorial Description: Editorial and document coverage of toxic tort litigation nationwide
General Info: Yr. Est. 1992, Semi-monthly, Trim Size-8½ x 11
Subscriptions: Indv. $795, For. $915, $50/copy

Media and the Law
See: BROADCASTING

Media Law Reporter
See: MEDIA & COMMUNICATIONS

Medicaid Fraud Report   *Association*

Publishing Co: National Association of Attorneys General, 444 N Capitol St NW Ste 339, Washington, DC 20001-1512 Tel # (202) 434-8034; Title Tel # (202) 434-4020 Title Fax # (202) 434-8008
Editorial Description: State prosecutions of medicaid provider fraud-hospitals, nursing homes, physicians, pharmacies, etc.
General Info: 10x/yr., Mimeo press
Subscriptions: Indv. $150

Medical Devices Litigation
Reporter   *Business*

Publishing Co: Andrews Publications, Inc., 1646 West Chester Pike, PO Box 1000, Westtown, PA 19395 Tel # (610) 399-9600 Fax # (610) 399-6610
Personnel: Publisher-John E. Backe, Editor-Michelle Sarnocinski, Mktg. Dir.-Andrew Katz
General Info: Yr. Est. 1994, Bi-monthly, ISSN: 1078-2974
Subscriptions: Indv. $650, $31/copy
Advertising: Inquire for rates.
List Rental: Actives: $125/M

Medical Devices Reporter
See: DRUGS & PHARMACEUTICALS

Medical Legal Aspects of
Breast Implants   *Business*

Publishing Co: Leader Publications, Inc., 345 Park Avenue South, New York, NY 10010 Parent Co.-New York Law Publishing Co., New York; Title Tel # (212) 545-6170 Title Fax # (212) 696-1848
Personnel: Publisher-Stuart Wise, Editor-Stephanie McEvily, Circ. Mgr.-Kerry Kyle, Mktg. Dir.-Rose-Ann Morangelei
Editorial Description: Medical and legal information regarding breast implants.
General Info: Yr. Est. 1992, Monthly, Trim Size-8½ x 11, Offset press, 8 pages, ISSN: 1067-3741, Color
Subscriptions: Indv. $165, $13/copy

Medical Liability Advisory
Service   *Business*

Publishing Co: Business Publishers, Inc., 951 Pershing Dr., Silver Spring, MD 20910-4464 Tel # (301) 589-5103 Fax # (301) 589-8493; Title Tel # (301) 587-6300 Title Fax # (301) 587-1081
Personnel: Publisher-Eric Easton, Editor-Bonita Becker, Circ. Mgr.-Kathleen Harrow, Promotion Dir.-Pat Nussman
Editorial Description: Gives you practical information on just what triggers a lawsuit--information you can pass on to your staff to claim-proof your procedures.
General Info: Yr. Est. 1976, Monthly, Trim Size-8½ x 11, Desktop press, 8 pages, ISSN: 0199-1272, Ind/Abs/Online: Newsnet & Predicasts, No Color, Recycled
Subscriptions: Indv. $225, Can. $225, For. $231
Advertising: Accepts Inserts.
List Rental: List Management Co.: Manager: Donald Peterson; BPI Direct, 951 Pershing Dr., Silver Spring, MD 20910-4464 Tel # (301) 585-5976, Fax # (301) 587-4530

Medical Liability Reporter

Publishing Co: Shepard's/McGraw-Hill, Inc., 555 Middle Creek Pky, Colorado Springs, CO 80921-3622; Title Tel # (719) 488-3000 Title Fax # (719) 481-7448
Personnel: Editor in Chief-Mary Kaye LaRue, Editor-Kevin Bushnell, Production Mgr.-Cheryl Everitt, Adv. Dir.-Peggy Ives, Art Dir.-Leigh Vidakovich
Editorial Description: Summaries & analysis of recent decisions in medical liability field.
General Info: Yr. Est. 1979, Monthly, 24 pages, ISSN: 0199-1833, No Color
Subscriptions: Indv. $295
List Rental: List Management Co.: The Lake Group, 411 Theodore Freund Ave., Rye, NY 10580-1497 Tel # (914) 925-2400, Fax # (914) 925-2499, Actives: 40,212, $130/M

Medical Malpractice   *Business*

Publishing Co: Matthew Bender & Co., 11 Penn Plaza, New York, NY 10001-2006 Fax # (212) 244-3188; Title Tel # (212) 967-7707
Personnel: Editor-S. Weisenfeld
Editorial Description: An essential treatise and complete litigation guide to proving or defending against malpractice charges.
General Info: (Formerly Trial of Medical Malpractice Cases), Yr. Est. 1960, Annually, Looseleaf
Subscriptions: $600/copy

Medical Malpractice: Guide
to Medical Issues   *Business*

Publishing Co: Matthew Bender & Co., 11 Penn Plaza, New York, NY 10001-2006 Tel # (212) 967-7707 Fax # (212) 244-3188
Personnel: Editor in Chief-Lee S. Goldsmith, M.D.,LL.B.
Editorial Description: Contains a unique combination of detailed medical information and complete case studies.
General Info: Yr. Est. 1986, Irregular, Looseleaf

Medical Malpractice Law &
Strategy   *Consumer*

Publishing Co: Leader Publications, Inc., 345 Park Avenue South, New York, NY 10010 Tel # (212) 545-6170 Parent Co.-New York Law Publishing Co., New York; Title Tel # (212) 779-9200 Title Fax # (212) 696-1848
Personnel: Publisher-Stuart Wise, Editor-Leslie Nicholson, Circ. Mgr.-Josephine Dimino, Mktg. Dir.-RoseAnn Morangelei
Editorial Description: Reports on law, strategy, & medical news in medical malpractice.
General Info: Yr. Est. 1983, Monthly, Trim Size-8½ x 11, Offset press, 8 pages, Color
Subscriptions: Indv. $185, $15/copy
Acquistions: Publication Sold

Medical Malpractice
Verdicts, Settlements &
Experts

Publishing Co: Lewis L. Laska, 901 Church St, Nashville, TN 37203-3411; Title Tel # (615) 255-6288 Title Fax # (615) 255-6289
Personnel: Publisher, Editor-Lewis Laska, Editorial Asst.-Lorenda Sue Patterson, J.D., Circ. Mgr.-Cathy Bradford
Editorial Description: Nation's only medical malpractice jury verdict reporter.
General Info: Yr. Est. 1985, Monthly, Trim Size-8½ x 11, 60 pages, Saddle-stitched
Subscriptions: Indv. $247
Acquistions: Publication Bought
Advertising: Accepts Inserts.

Medical Staff Law Manual
See: HOSPITALS & NURSING HOMES

Medical Staff and Physician Organization Legel Advisor
See: MEDICINE

Medical legal Aspects of
Cancer Litagation   *Business*

Publishing Co: Leader Publications, Inc., 345 Park Avenue South, New York, NY 10010 Tel # (212) 545-6170 Fax # (212) 696-1848 Parent Co.-New York Law Publishing Co., New York
Personnel: Publisher-Stuart Wise, Editor-Stephanie McEvily, Circ. Mgr.-Kerry Kyle, Mktg. Dir.-Rosanne Moranbelli
General Info: Monthly, Trim Size-8½ x 11, Offset press, 12 pages, Color
Subscriptions: Indv. $155, $13/copy
Printing Co: Columbus Bookbinding, 1343 Belfast Ave, Columbus, OH 31904 Tel # (206) 323-9313, Fax # (206) 323-2987

Medicare and Medicaid Guide
See: SOCIAL SERVICES & WELFARE

Medina's Bostwick Practice
Manual   *Business*

Publishing Co: Matthew Bender & Co., 11 Penn Plaza, New York, NY 10001-2006 Fax # (212) 244-3188; Title Tel # (212) 967-7707
Personnel: Editor-J. Borvick
Editorial Description: Information and law manual. Coverage includes: CPLR, Real Property Law, Surrogate's Court practice, matrimonial and family law, commercial practice, negligence.
General Info: Yr. Est. 1907, Irregular, Looseleaf
Subscriptions: $380/copy

Mental Health Law
Reporter   *Business*

Publishing Co: Business Publishers, Inc., 951 Pershing Dr., Silver Spring, MD 20910-4464 Tel # (301) 589-5103 Fax # (301) 589-8493; Title Tel # (301) 587-6300 Title Fax # (301) 587-1081
Personnel: Publisher-Eric Easton, Editor-Bonita Becker, Circ. Mgr.-Kathleen Harrow, Promotion Dir.-Pat Nussman
Editorial Description: Covers key malpractice cases across the U.S., distilling salient elements and explaining why the law worked one way in one case and quite differently in another.
General Info: Yr. Est. 1983, Monthly, Trim Size-8½ x 11, Desktop press, 8 pages, ISSN: 0741-5141, Ind/Abs/Online: Newsnet & Predicasts, No Color, Recycled
Subscriptions: Indv. $234, Can. $234, For. $240
Advertising: Accepts Inserts.
List Rental: List Management Co.: Manager: Donald Peterson; BPI Direct, 951 Pershing Dr., Silver Spring, MD 20910-4464 Tel # (301) 585-5976, Fax # (301) 587-4530

Mertens Current Tax Highlights
See: EMPLOYMENT

Mexican Business Law
Alert
Business

Publishing Co: M. Lee Smith Publishers & Printers ,LCC, P.O. Box 198867, 162 Fourth Avenue North, Nashville, TN 37219-8867 Tel # (615) 242-7395 Fax # (615) 256-6601
Personnel: Publisher-M. Lee Smith, Editor-Dennis Peyton, Circ. Mgr.-Cathy Bradford, Mktg. Dir.-Dave Yates
Editorial Description: Reviews Mexican business law & regulations for companies doing business in and with Mexico.
General Info: Yr. Est. 1994, Monthly, Trim Size-8$\frac{1}{2}$ x 11, 8 pages, ISSN: 1077-7326, 2 Color
Subscriptions: Indv. $197
List Rental: Rents Lists
Printing Co: M. Lee Smith Publishers & Printers ,LLC, PO Box 198867, 162 Fourth Avenue, Nashville, TN 37219-8867 Tel # (615) 242-7395, Fax # (615) 256-6601

Miami Institute on Estate
Planning
Association

Publishing Co: Matthew Bender & Co., 11 Penn Plaza, New York, NY 10001-2006 Fax # (212) 244-3188; Title Tel # (212) 967-7707
Personnel: Editor-R. Ross
Editorial Description: Up-to-date treatment of the estate planning field including new laws and regulations.
General Info: (Formerly Institute on Estate Planning), Annually, Looseleaf
Subscriptions: $100/copy

Michigan Civil Rights Commission Newsletter
See: CIVIL RIGHTS

Michigan Corporation Law
with Federal Tax Analysis
Business

Publishing Co: Matthew Bender & Co., 11 Penn Plaza, New York, NY 10001-2006 Fax # (212) 244-3188; Title Tel # (212) 967-7707
Personnel: Editor-Robert Schmidt
Editorial Description: For Michigan small business planners, provides step-by-step guidance on how to proceed from start-up through sale or liquidation of a business.
General Info: Yr. Est. 1963, Annually, Trim Size-8$\frac{1}{2}$ x 11, No Color, Matte, Looseleaf
Subscriptions: $90/copy

Michigan Employment
Law Letter
Business

Publishing Co: M. Lee Smith Publishers & Printers ,LCC, P.O. Box 198867, 162 Fourth Avenue North, Nashville, TN 37219-8867; Title Tel # (615) 242-7395 Title Fax # (615) 256-6601
Personnel: Publisher-M Lee Smith, Editor-Robert Vercruysse, Circ. Mgr.-Cathy Bradford, Mktg. Dir.-David Yates
Editorial Description: Review of employment law developments that affect Michigan employers.
General Info: Yr. Est. 1990, Monthly, Trim Size-8$\frac{1}{2}$ x 11, 8 pages, ISSN: 1046-9109, 2 Color
Subscriptions: Indv. $97
List Rental: Actives: $75/M
Printing Co: M. Lee Smith Publishers & Printers ,LLC, PO Box 198867, 162 Fourth Avenue, Nashville, TN 37219-8867 Tel # (615) 242-7395, Fax # (615) 256-6601

Michigan Environmental
Compliance Update
Business

Publishing Co: M. Lee Smith Publishers & Printers ,LCC, P.O. Box 198867, 162 Fourth Avenue North, Nashville, TN 37219-8867; Title Tel # (615) 242-7395 Title Fax # (615) 256-6601
Personnel: Publisher-M. Lee Smith, Editor-Joseph Polito, Circ. Mgr.-Cathy Bradford, Mktg. Dir.-Dave Yates
Editorial Description: Review of new environmental law developments that affect Michigan companies.
General Info: (Formerly Michigan Environmental Law Letter), Yr. Est. 1990, Monthly, Trim Size-8$\frac{1}{2}$ x 11, 8 pages, ISSN: 1073-9459, 2 Color
Subscriptions: Indv. $117
List Rental: Actives: $75/M
Printing Co: M. Lee Smith Publishers & Printers ,LLC, PO Box 198867, 162 Fourth Avenue, Nashville, TN 37219-8867 Tel # (615) 242-7395, Fax # (615) 256-6601

Michigan Motor Vehicle
Laws

Publishing Co: Gould Publications, Inc, 1333 N US Highway 17-92, Longwood, FL 32750-3724 Tel # (407) 695-9500 Fax # (407) 695-2906; Title Tel # (607) 724-3000
Editorial Description: Concise presentation of Michigan Motor Vehicle Laws. (Chapter 257) including the Uniform Traffic Code.
General Info: Annually, Trim Size-5$\frac{1}{2}$ x 8$\frac{1}{2}$, Sheetfed press, 700 pages, No Color, Looseleaf
Subscriptions: $18/copy

Michigan Penal Code
Professional

Publishing Co: Gould Publications, Inc, 1333 N US Highway 17-92, Longwood, FL 32750-3724 Tel # (407) 695-9500 Fax # (407) 695-2906; Title Tel # (607) 724-3000
Editorial Description: A complete, accurate and up-to-date presentation of Chapter 750 of the Compiled Laws and Supplemental Chapter 752. plus settlement excerpts from Chapter 712A, 722, and 333 of the Compiled Laws, and the Code of Criminal Procedures
General Info: Annually, 560 pages, Looseleaf
Subscriptions: Indv. $18, $16/copy

Michigan Probate Code

Publishing Co: Gould Publications, Inc, 1333 N US Highway 17-92, Longwood, FL 32750-3724 Tel # (407) 695-9500 Fax # (407) 695-2906; Title Tel # (607) 724-3000
Editorial Description: Michigan Probate Laws. Unannotated.
General Info: Annually, Trim Size-5$\frac{1}{2}$ x 8$\frac{1}{2}$, Sheetfed press, 120 pages, No Color, Looseleaf
Subscriptions: $16/copy

Michigan Workers'
Compensation Law
Reporter
Business, Consumer

Publishing Co: LRP Publications, 747 Dresher Rd., P.O. Box 980, Horsham, PA 19044-0980 Tel # (215) 784-0910 Fax # (215) 784-0317
Personnel: Publisher-Kenneth F. Kahn, Editor-Joanne Fiore, Production Mgr.-Kathleen P. Neely, Mktg. Dir.-Jana Shellington, Promotion Dir.-Gary Ragin
Editorial Description: The most comprehensive source available for workers' comepensation and related law issued by the state agencies and courts.
General Info: Bi-monthly
Subscriptions: Indv. $490

Midwest Transaction Guide
Business

Publishing Co: Matthew Bender & Co., 11 Penn Plaza, New York, NY 10001-2006 Tel # (212) 967-7707 Fax # (212) 244-3188
Editorial Description: For Illinois, Indiana & Michigan practitioners, state-by-state guidance on business, wills & trusts, commericial, real estate, & personal transactions.
General Info: Yr. Est. 1980, Irregular, Looseleaf

Milgrim on Licensing
See: PATENTS/COPYRIGHTS/TRADE MARKS

Milgrim on Trade Secrets
See: PATENTS/COPYRIGHTS/TRADE MARKS

Miller's Copyright
Newsletter

Publishing Co: Copyright Information Services, PO Box 9728, Yakima, WA 98909-0728; Title Tel # (206) 378-5128
Personnel: Editor-Jerome Miller
General Info: Yr. Est. 1988, Quarterly
Subscriptions: Indv. $25

Mine Regulation Reporter
See: MINING & MINERALS

Mine Safety and Health News
See: MINING & MINERALS

Mineral Law Newsletter

Publishing Co: Rocky Mountain Mineral Law Foundation, 7039 E 18th Ave, Denver, CO 80220-1826 Fax # (303) 321-7657; Title Tel # (303) 321-8100
Personnel: Editor-John Lowe
Editorial Description: Describes current statutory, regulation & case law in mining & oil & gas.
General Info: Yr. Est. 1983, Quarterly, Trim Size-8$\frac{1}{2}$ x 11
Subscriptions: Indv. $60, Can. $67, For. $75, $15/copy
Circulation: Total-800

Minnesota Employment
Law Letter
Business

Publishing Co: M. Lee Smith Publishers & Printers ,LCC, P.O. Box 198867, 162 Fourth Avenue North, Nashville, TN 37219-8867; Title Tel # (615) 242-7395 Title Fax # (615) 256-6601
Personnel: Publisher-M Lee Smith, Editor-Stephen Burton, Circ. Mgr.-Cathy Bradford, Mktg. Dir.-Dave Yates
Editorial Description: Review of employment law developments that affect Minnesota employers.
General Info: Yr. Est. 1991, Monthly, Trim Size-8$\frac{1}{2}$ x 11, 8 pages, ISSN: 1054-6367, 2 Color
Subscriptions: Indv. $87
List Rental: Rents Lists
Printing Co: M. Lee Smith Publishers & Printers ,LLC, PO Box 198867, 162 Fourth Avenue, Nashville, TN 37219-8867 Tel # (615) 242-7395, Fax # (615) 256-6601

Minnesota Environmental
Compliance Update
Business

Publishing Co: M. Lee Smith Publishers & Printers ,LCC, P.O. Box 198867, 162 Fourth Avenue North, Nashville, TN 37219-8867 Tel # (615) 242-7395 Fax # (615) 256-6601
Personnel: Publisher-M. Lee Smith, Editor-Jonathan Bloomberg, Circ. Mgr.-Cathy Bradford, Mktg. Dir.-Dave Yates
Editorial Description: State environmental information and laws.
General Info: Yr. Est. 1994, Monthly, Trim Size-8$\frac{1}{2}$ x 11, 8 pages, ISSN: 1072-916X, 2 Color
Subscriptions: Indv. $117
List Rental: Rents Lists
Printing Co: M. Lee Smith Publishers & Printers ,LLC, PO Box 198867, 162 Fourth Avenue, Nashville, TN 37219-8867 Tel # (615) 242-7395, Fax # (615) 256-6601

Mississippi Employment
Law Letter *Business*

Publishing Co: M. Lee Smith Publishers & Printers ,LCC, P.O. Box 198867, 162 Fourth Avenue North, Nashville, TN 37219-8867 Tel # (615) 242-7395 Fax # (615) 256-6601
Personnel: Publisher-M. Lee Smith, Editor-Peyton Irby, Jr., Circ. Mgr.-Cathy Bradford, Mktg. Dir.-Dave Yates
Editorial Description: Reviews employment law developments that effect Mississippi employers.
General Info: Yr. Est. 1994, Monthly, Trim Size-8½ x 11, 8 pages, ISSN: 1074-0430, 2 Color
Subscriptions: Indv. $97
List Rental: Rents Lists
Printing Co: M. Lee Smith Publishers & Printers ,LLC, PO Box 198867, 162 Fourth Avenue, Nashville, TN 37219-8867 Tel # (615) 242-7395, Fax # (615) 256-6601

Missouri Bar Bulletin *Association*

Publishing Co: Missouri Bar, 326 Monroe, Box 119, Box 119, Jefferson City, MO 65101-3106; Title Tel # (315) 635-4128
Personnel: Editor-Gary Toohey
Editorial Description: News of courts and legal profession.
General Info: Quarterly, Trim Size-8½ x 11, Sheetfed press, 16 pages, No Color
Circulation: (100% controlled), Total-18,000

Missouri Employment
Law Letter *Business*

Publishing Co: M. Lee Smith Publishers & Printers ,LCC, P.O. Box 198867, 162 Fourth Avenue North, Nashville, TN 37219-8867; Title Tel # (615) 242-7395 Title Fax # (615) 256-6601
Personnel: Publisher-M Lee Smith, Editor-Vance Miller, Circ. Mgr.-Cathy Bradford, Mktg. Dir.-Dave Yates
Editorial Description: Review of employment law developments that affect Missouri employers.
General Info: Yr. Est. 1991, Monthly, Trim Size-8½ x 11, 8 pages, ISSN: 1054-6375, 2 Color
Subscriptions: Indv. $97
List Rental: Rents Lists
Printing Co: M. Lee Smith Publishers & Printers ,LLC, PO Box 198867, 162 Fourth Avenue, Nashville, TN 37219-8867 Tel # (615) 242-7395, Fax # (615) 256-6601

Missouri Environmental
Compliance Update *Business*

Publishing Co: M. Lee Smith Publishers & Printers ,LCC, P.O. Box 198867, 162 Fourth Avenue North, Nashville, TN 37219-8867; Title Tel # (615) 242-7395 Title Fax # (615) 256-6601
Personnel: Publisher-M. Lee Smith, Editor-George Von Stamwitz, Circ. Mgr.-Cathy Bradford, Mktg. Dir.-Dave Yates
Editorial Description: Review of environmental law developments that affect Missouri companies.
General Info: (Formerly Missouri Environmental Law Letter), Yr. Est. 1991, Monthly, Trim Size-8½ x 11, 8 pages, ISSN: 1075-959X, 2 Color
Subscriptions: Indv. $117
List Rental: Rents Lists
Printing Co: M. Lee Smith Publishers & Printers ,LLC, PO Box 198867, 162 Fourth Avenue, Nashville, TN 37219-8867 Tel # (615) 242-7395, Fax # (615) 256-6601

Missouri Workers'
Compensation Law
Reporter *Business, Consumer*

Publishing Co: LRP Publications, 747 Dresher Rd., P.O. Box 980, Horsham, PA 19044-0980 Tel # (215) 784-0910 Fax # (215) 784-0317
Personnel: Publisher-Kenneth F. Kahn, Editor-Joanne Fiore, Production Mgr.-Kathleen P. Neely, Mktg. Dir.-Jana Shellington, Promotion Dir.-Gary Ragin
Editorial Description: The most comprehensive source available for workers' compensation and related law issued by the state agencies and courts.
General Info: Bi-monthly
Subscriptions: Indv. $460

Model Laws, Regulations and Guidelines
See: INSURANCE

Modern Construction and Development Forms
See: CONSTRUCTION & BUILDING

Modern Federal Jury
Instructions *Business*

Publishing Co: Matthew Bender & Co., 11 Penn Plaza, New York, NY 10001-2006 Tel # (212) 967-7707 Fax # (212) 244-3188
Editorial Description: For both judges & lawyers, a comprehensive guide to the jury instruction phase of a federal trial. The work provides general charges & substantive instructions for use in virtually every federal civil or criminal trial.
General Info: Yr. Est. 1984, Irregular, Looseleaf

Modern UCC Litigation
Forms *Business*

Publishing Co: Matthew Bender & Co., 11 Penn Plaza, New York, NY 10001-2006 Tel # (212) 967-7707 Fax # (212) 244-3188
Editorial Description: Complete up-to-date litigation forms adapted from actual cases for the preparation & trial of a commercial law suit. Reflects the most recent terminology, concepts, causes of action & defenses mandated by the UCC. Full explanations, alternative procedures & helpful commentary.
General Info: Yr. Est. 1969, Irregular, Looseleaf

Money and Family Law
See: ACCOUNTING

Money Laundering Alert *Business, Association*

Publishing Co: Alert Publications Partners, 1401 Brickell Ave, Ste 570, Miami, FL 33131-3503; Title Tel # (305) 530-0500 Title Fax # (305) 530-9434
Personnel: Publisher-Charls Intriago, Editor-Nikolas Korba, Circ. Mgr.-Deborah Pelland, Art Dir.-Patricia Intriago
Editorial Description: Covers legal issues, including new laws, regulations, and cases related to money laundering & the bank secrecy act in the U.S. and worldwide
General Info: Yr. Est. 1989, Monthly, Trim Size-8½ x 11, Offset press, 8 pages, ISSN: 1046-3070, Ind/Abs/Online: Lexis/Nexis, Dow Jones NTS, 2 Color, Matte
Subscriptions: Indv. $345, Can. $425, For. $425, $29/copy
Circulation: Readership-1,700
Advertising: Accepts Inserts.
Printing Co: Enterprise Printing, 415 NW 28th St, Miami, FL 33127-4135 Tel # (305) 576-0963

Money Laundering, Asset
Forfeiture & Intl. Financial
Crimes Newsletter *Business*

Publishing Co: Oceana Publications, Inc., 75 Main St, Dobbs Ferry, NY 10522-1601 Tel # (914) 693-8100 Fax # (914) 693-0402
Personnel: Editor-Fletcher N. Baldwin, Editor-Robert J. Munro
Editorial Description: Presents new legislative, regulatory and judicial developments in money laundering and asset forfeiture law.
General Info: Yr. Est. 1993, Bi-monthly, ISSN: 1070-1486
Subscriptions: Indv. $300, For. $385

Money Laundering Law
Report

Publishing Co: Leader Publications, Inc., 345 Park Avenue South, New York, NY 10010 Parent Co.-New York Law Publishing Co., New York; Title Tel # (212) 545-6170 Title Fax # (212) 696-1848
Personnel: Publisher-Stuart Wise, Editor-John Villa, Circ. Mgr.-Kerry Kyle, Mktg. Dir.-Rose-Ann Morangelei
General Info: Yr. Est. 1990, Monthly, Trim Size-8½ x 11, Offset press, 8 pages, Color
Subscriptions: Indv. $225, $18/copy
Printing Co: Columbus Bookbinding, 1343 Belfast Ave, Columbus, OH 31904 Tel # (206) 323-9313, Fax # (206) 323-2987

Montana Employment
Law Letter *Business*

Publishing Co: M. Lee Smith Publishers & Printers ,LCC, P.O. Box 198867, 162 Fourth Avenue North, Nashville, TN 37219-8867 Tel # (615) 242-7395 Fax # (615) 256-6601
Personnel: Publisher-M Lee Smith, Editor-Jeanne Bender, Circ. Mgr.-Cathy Bradford, Mktg. Dir.-David Yates
General Info: Yr. Est. 1996, Monthly, Trim Size-8½ x 11, 8 pages, 2 Color
Subscriptions: Indv. $97
List Rental: Rents Lists
Printing Co: M. Lee Smith Publishers & Printers ,LLC, PO Box 198867, 162 Fourth Avenue, Nashville, TN 37219-8867 Tel # (615) 242-7395, Fax # (615) 256-6601

Montgomery County Law
Reporter *Association*

Publishing Co: Montgomery Bar Assn., 100 W. Airy St., Norristown, PA 19401-4724 Tel # (610) 279-9660 Fax # (610) 279-4621; Title Tel # (215) 279-9660
Personnel: Editor-Blake Dunbar, Jr.
Editorial Description: Official legal periodical for Montgomery County, Pennsylvania.
General Info: Yr. Est. 1885, Weekly, Looseleaf
Subscriptions: Indv. $40
Circulation: Total-966
Advertising: Inquire for rates.

Moore's Federal Practice *Business*

Publishing Co: Matthew Bender & Co., 11 Penn Plaza, New York, NY 10001-2006 Tel # (212) 967-7707 Fax # (212) 244-3188
Editorial Description: One of the most cited texts in the legal world. Accepted as the autority in Federal Court. Also relied on for guidance & precedents in the states that follow the Federal Rules.
General Info: Irregular, Looseleaf

Moore's Manual--Forms *Business*

Publishing Co: Matthew Bender & Co., 11 Penn Plaza, New York, NY 10001-2006 Tel # (212) 967-7707 Fax # (212) 244-3188
Editorial Description: This companion to the Practice & Procedure Manual & condensation of Bender's Federal Practice Forms is an indispensable, handy deskbook of forms for day-to-day use.
General Info: Yr. Est. 1964, Irregular, Looseleaf

Moore's Manual-Federal
Practice and Procedure *Business*

Publishing Co: Matthew Bender & Co., 11 Penn Plaza, New York, NY 10001-2006 Fax # (212) 244-3188; Title Tel # (212) 967-7707
Personnel: Editor-G. Grotheer
Editorial Description: Comprehensive coverage of all areas of civil practice in the federal courts.
General Info: Yr. Est. 1962, Irregular, Looseleaf
Subscriptions: $345/copy

Morality in Media
Newsletter
Publishing Co: Morality in Media, Inc., 475 Riverside Dr., New York, NY 10115-0056;
Title Tel # (212) 870-3222 Title Fax # (212) 870-2765
Personnel: Editor-Robert Peters, Art Dir.-Debbie Becker
Editorial Description: Reports on pornography traffic, and indecency/violence on TV, obscenity law, court decisions, and community action.
General Info: Yr. Est. 1962, Bi-monthly, Trim Size-8½ x 11, Web press, 6 pages, ISSN: 0027-1004, No Color
Subscriptions: Indv. $20, $1/copy
Circulation: Total-15,000

Movement Support Network
News
Publishing Co: Center for Constitutional Rights, 666 Broadway Fl 7, New York, NY 10012-2317
General Info: Quarterly, Trim Size-8½ x 11, Offset press, 14 pages, Newsprint
Subscriptions: Indv. $8
Circulation: Total-5,000

Multimedia & Technology
See: COMPUTERS & AUTOMATION

Multimedia Strategist   *Business*
Publishing Co: Leader Publications, Inc., 345 Park Avenue South, New York, NY 10010
Tel # (212) 545-6170 Fax # (212) 696-1848 Parent Co.-New York Law Publishing Co., New York
Personnel: Publisher-Stuart Wise, Editor-Julian Millstein, Circ. Mgr.-Kerry Kyle, Mktg. Dir.-Roseann Moranbelli
General Info: Monthly, Trim Size-8½ x 11, Offset press, 8 pages, Color
Subscriptions: Indv. $155, $13/copy
Printing Co: Columbus Bookbinding, 1343 Belfast Ave, Columbus, OH 31904 Tel # (206) 323-9313, Fax # (206) 323-2987

Multinational Corporations
Law: Mexico, Cntrl.America, Panama, Cntrl. American Common Mkt.   *Business*
Publishing Co: Oceana Publications, Inc., 75 Main St, Dobbs Ferry, NY 10522-1601
Tel # (914) 693-8100; Title Tel # (914) 693-1320 Title Fax # (914) 693-0402
Personnel: Editor-Kenneth Simmonds, Production Mgr.-Mike Wortzman, Mktg. Dir.-John Downey
General Info: Yr. Est. 1979, Irregular, Trim Size-7 x 10, Looseleaf
Subscriptions: Indv. $500

Multistate Sales Tax Guide
See: TAXES

Municipal Attorney
See: PUBLIC MANAGEMENT & PLANNING

Municipal Immunity Law
Bulletin   *Business*
Publishing Co: Quinlan Publishing, 23 Drydock Ave, Boston, MA 02210-2387 Tel # (617) 542-0048 Fax # (617) 345-9646
Editorial Description: Covers immunity issues for local officials.
General Info: Monthly
Subscriptions: Indv. $60

Municipal Law Docket
See: PUBLIC MANAGEMENT & PLANNING

Municipal Litigation
Reporter   *Business*
Publishing Co: Strafford Pubs., Inc., 590 Dutch Valley Rd., N.E., Postal Drawer 13729, Atlanta, GA 30324-0729; Title Tel # (404) 881-1141 Title Fax # (404) 881-0074
Personnel: Publisher-Richard Ossoff, Editor-Stephanie McEvily, Mng. Editor-Jennifer Vaughan, Circ. Mgr., Mktg. Mgr.-Marianne Mueller, Mktg. Mgr.-Marla Rawls Hill
Editorial Description: Monthly digest of key court decisions on litigation involving local governments; cases are screened and selected to provide concise, comprehensive coverage of issues important to municipal attorneys and others involved with local government litigation.
General Info: Yr. Est. 1981, 12x/yr., Trim Size-8½ x 11, Sheetfed press, 16 pages, ISSN: 0278-1501, No Color, Newsprint, Saddle-stitched
Subscriptions: Indv. $387, Can. $417, For. $442, $32/copy
Acquistions: Publication Bought, Publication Sold
List Rental: Rents Lists

Municipalities in the U.S. Supreme Court
See: CIVIL RIGHTS

Murphy's Will Clauses   *Business*
Publishing Co: Matthew Bender & Co., 11 Penn Plaza, New York, NY 10001-2006
Fax # (212) 244-3188; Title Tel # (212) 967-7707
Personnel: Editor-R. Lopatin
General Info: Annually, Looseleaf
Subscriptions: $425/copy

Murphy's Will Clauses:
Annotations and Forms with Tax Effects   *Business*
Publishing Co: Matthew Bender & Co., 11 Penn Plaza, New York, NY 10001-2006
Fax # (212) 244-3188; Title Tel # (212) 967-7707
Personnel: Editor-R. Lopatin
Editorial Description: Gives 1400 framed will clauses--modern, efficient, court-tested, annotated, and tax-saving.
General Info: Yr. Est. 1960, Irregular, Looseleaf
Subscriptions: $425/copy

NABP Newsletter
See: DRUGS & PHARMACEUTICALS

NACDS Executive Newsletter
See: DRUGS & PHARMACEUTICALS

NALP Bulletin
See: EMPLOYMENT

NARF Legal Review   *Association*
Publishing Co: Native American Rights Fund, 1506 Broadway, Boulder, CO 80302-6296;
Title Tel # (303) 447-8760 Title Fax # (303) 443-7776
Personnel: Editor, Circ. Mgr.-Ray Ramirez
Editorial Description: Summarizes important case developments handled by the Native American Rights Fund.
General Info: (Formerly Narf Announcements), Yr. Est. 1971, Semi-annually, Offset press, 12 pages, No Color
Subscriptions: Indv. $25
Circulation: Total-30,000
List Rental: Actives: $65/M

NASD Manual
See: BANKING & FINANCE

NASJE News
Publishing Co: National Association of State Judicial Educators, 300 Newport Ave, Williamsburg, VA 23185-4147; Title Tel # (804) 253-2000 Title Fax # (804) 220-0449
Personnel: Publisher-Bill Fishback, Editor-Kay Boothman, Art Dir.-Tina Beaven
Editorial Description: Legal issues & educational techniques & resources of interest to educators of state court judges are printed in the newsletter.
General Info: Yr. Est. 1984, Quarterly, 2 Color
Circulation: Total-1,200
Printing Co: Sir Speedy, 240 McClaws Cir., Williamsburg, VA 23185 Tel # (804) 220-1191

NASSP Legal Memorandum
See: SCHOOL ADMINISTRATION

NAWJ Counterbalance   *Association*
Publishing Co: Natl. Assn. of Women Judges, c/o Natl. Ctr. for State Courts, 300 Newport Ave, Williamsburg, VA 23185-4147; Title Tel # (804) 253-2000 Title Fax # (804) 220-0449
Personnel: Editor-Lucile Watts, Production Mgr.-Mary McCall, Art Dir.-Tina Beaven
Editorial Description: Newsletter of the National Association of Women Judges.
General Info: (Formerly NAWJ News & Announcements), Yr. Est. 1981, Trim Size-8½ x 11, Offset press, 8 pages, 2 Color, Newsprint
Subscriptions: Free With Membership
Circulation: (100% controlled), Total-1,200, Readership-1,200
Printing Co: Prestige Press, Inc., 610 Rotary St, Hampton, VA 23661-1323 Tel # (804) 826-5881

NCBA Reports   *Business, Association*
Publishing Co: Natl. Commodity & Barter Assn., PO Box 2255, Longmont, CO 80502-2255;
Title Tel # (303) 654-1111
Personnel: Editor-John Voss
Editorial Description: Legal do-it-yourself & taxes. Constitution issues, political action, home schooling.
General Info: Yr. Est. 1979, Monthly, Trim Size-8½ x 11, 18 pages
Subscriptions: Indv. $70, Free With Membership
Advertising: Accepts Inserts.

NCBL Notes
Publishing Co: National Conference of Black Lawyers, 2 W. 125 St., New York, NY 10027;
Title Tel # (212) 864-4000
General Info: Quarterly, 6 pages
Subscriptions: Indv. $25

NIMLO Congressional News
See: GOVERNMENT

NLADA Cornerstone   *Association*
Publishing Co: Natl. Legal Aid & Defender Assn., 1625 K St NW Ste 8, Washington, DC 20006-1604; Title Tel # (202) 452-0620
Editorial Description: Articles concerning legal services attorneys & public defenders & pro bono issues.
General Info: (Formerly NLADA Washington Memo), Yr. Est. 1980, Quarterly, Web press, 16 pages, No Color
Subscriptions: Indv. $20, Inst. $20, $5/copy
Circulation: Total-4,000

NLRB Advice Memorandum
Reporter *Business, Consumer*

Publishing Co: LRP Publications, 747 Dresher Rd., P.O. Box 980, Horsham, PA 19044-0980
Tel # (215) 784-0910 Fax # (215) 784-0317
Personnel: Publisher-Kenneth F. Kahn, Editor-Sandy Johnson, Production Mgr.-Kathleen P. Neely, Mktg. Dir.-Jana Shellington, Promotion Dir.-Gary Ragin
Editorial Description: Keeps the labor relations practitioner abreast of the latest legal strategy and reasoning behind the NLRB General Counsel's decisions in unfair labor practices charges.
General Info: Monthly
Subscriptions: Indv. $510

NLRB Case Handling Manual
See: LABOR UNION

NMRLS Notes

Publishing Co: North Mississippi Rural Legal Services, PO Box 767, Oxford, MS 38655-0767;
Title Tel # (601) 234-8732 Title Fax # (601) 236-3263
Personnel: Publisher, Editor-Joseph Delaney, Jr., Circ. Mgr.-Deborah Gipson
Editorial Description: Reports on health, housing, economics, education and other social and legal issues affecting clients of NMRLS.
General Info: Yr. Est. 1976, Bi-monthly, 6 pages
Circulation: Total-1,500

NOCALL Newsletter
See: LIBRARY

NOLPE Notes
See: EDUCATION

NOLPE School Law
Reporter *Association* CPM: $500

Publishing Co: Natl. Organization on Legal Problems of Education, 3601 SW 29th St., Ste. 223, Topeka, KS 66614-2047; Title Tel # (913) 273-3550 Title Fax # (913) 273-2001
Personnel: Publisher-Robert Wagner, Editor-Jerry Parkinson
Editorial Description: Provides citations and case digests for all education law decisions reported by state and federal courts of record in the US.
General Info: Yr. Est. 1959, Monthly, Trim Size-8½ x 11, ISSN: 1059-4094, Looseleaf
Subscriptions: Indv. $95, Can. $105, For. $115, Free With Membership
Circulation: Total-2,000
Advertising: $1,000.
List Rental: Actives: 1,800, $500/M, Expires: 700, $200/M

NSBA Newsletter *Association*

Publishing Co: Nebraska State Bar Assn., PO Box 81809, Lincoln, NE 68501-1809;
Title Tel # (402) 475-7091 Title Fax # (402) 485-7098
Personnel: Editor-Sharon Stephan
General Info: Bi-monthly, Trim Size-8½ x 11, Offset press, 16 pages, No Color, Coated, Saddle-stitched
Subscriptions: Indv. $10, Can. $10, For. $10
Printing Co: Boomer's Printing, PO Box 80668, 130 N. 10th St., Lincoln, NE 68501-0668
Tel # (402) 343-8501

NSCLC Washington Weekly
See: SENIOR CITIZENS

NSPA Washington Reporter
See: ACCOUNTING

N.Y. Civil Liberties
See: CIVIL RIGHTS

N.Y. County Lawyer *Association*

Publishing Co: New York County Lawyers' Association, 14 Vesey St, New York, NY 10007-2906;
Title Tel # (212) 267-6646
Personnel: Editor-Jan Levy
Editorial Description: Articles of practical use to members, news of the Association, news of the Bar in general.
General Info: (Formerly Versey St. Letter), Yr. Est. 1943, Monthly, Trim Size-11 x 17, Sheetfed press, 6 pages, ISSN: 0049-6030, 3% ads, Color, Coated
Circulation: Total-11,000
Advertising: Inquire for rates. Accepts Inserts.
List Rental: Rents Lists

NYC Fire Law Handbook

Publishing Co: Gould Publications, Inc, 1333 N US Highway 17-92, Longwood, FL 32750-3724
Tel # (407) 695-9500 Fax # (407) 695-2906; Title Tel # (607) 724-3000
Editorial Description: Title 15 & chapter 4 of Title 27 of NYC Administrative Code. Unannotated.
General Info: Annually, Trim Size-5½ x 8½, Sheetfed press, No Color, Looseleaf
Subscriptions: $18/copy

NYC Housing Maintenance
Code

Publishing Co: Gould Publications, Inc, 1333 N US Highway 17-92, Longwood, FL 32750-3724
Tel # (407) 695-9500 Fax # (407) 695-2906; Title Tel # (607) 724-3000
Editorial Description: Book. Supplemented annually at additional cost. Conforms to official NYC book.
General Info: Annually, Trim Size-5½ x 8½, 400 pages, No Color, Looseleaf
Subscriptions: $17/copy

NYC Laws Digest

Publishing Co: Gould Publications, Inc, 1333 N US Highway 17-92, Longwood, FL 32750-3724
Tel # (407) 695-9500 Fax # (407) 695-2906; Title Tel # (607) 724-3000
Editorial Description: Contains part of NYC Charter, Health Code, Administrative Code.
General Info: (Formerly Law Digest), Annually, Trim Size-5½ x 8½, Sheetfed press, 220 pages, No Color, Looseleaf
Subscriptions: $12/copy

NYC Traffic Rules &
Regulations

Publishing Co: Gould Publications, Inc, 1333 N US Highway 17-92, Longwood, FL 32750-3724
Tel # (407) 695-9500 Fax # (407) 695-2906; Title Tel # (607) 724-3000
Editorial Description: Complete regulations relating to traffic.
General Info: Annually, Trim Size-5½ x 8½, 100 pages, No Color, Looseleaf
Subscriptions: $7/copy

Narcotics Enforcement &
Prevention Digest *Business*

Publishing Co: Washington Crime News Services, 3918 Prosperity Ave Ste 318, Fairfax, VA 22031-3333; Title Tel # (703) 573-1600 Title Fax # (703) 573-1604
Personnel: Publisher-R.J. O'Connell, Editor-Robert H. Feldkamp, Circ. Mgr.-Nancy Van Wyen
Editorial Description: Narcotics law enforcement, treatment, and abuse prevention.
General Info: (Formerly Narcotics Control Digest; Narcotics Demand Reduction Digest), Yr. Est. 1971, Weekly, Trim Size-8½ x 11, Sheetfed press, 10 pages, Ind/Abs/Online: CJPI, No Color
Subscriptions: Indv. $345, Can. $351, For. $395

Narcotics Law Bulletin *Business*

Publishing Co: Quinlan Publishing, 23 Drydock Ave, Boston, MA 02210-2387 Fax # (617) 345-9646;
Title Tel # (617) 542-0048
Editorial Description: Cases and issues dealing with drugs and drug arrests.
General Info: Monthly, 8 pages
Subscriptions: Indv. $59
List Rental: List Management Co.: Stevens-Knox List Management, 304 Park Ave S., New York, NY 10010-5312 Tel # (212) 388-8800, Fax # (212) 388-8890

Nash & Cibinic Report, The *Business*

Publishing Co: Federal Pubs., Inc., 1120 20th St., NW, Fifth Floor, South Building, Washington, DC 20036-3484; Title Tel # (202) 337-7000 Title Fax # (202) 659-2233
General Info: Yr. Est. 1987, Monthly
Subscriptions: Indv. $692

National Bankruptcy
Litigation Reporter *Business*

Publishing Co: Andrews Publications, Inc., 1646 West Chester Pike, PO Box 1000, Westtown, PA 19395; Title Tel # (610) 399-6600 Title Fax # (610) 399-6610
Personnel: Publisher-John E. Backe, Editor-Rosemary MacDonald, Mktg. Dir.-Andrew Katz
Editorial Description: Focuses on in depth coverage of bankruptcy filings of companies with assets in excess of $150,000. Businesses involved in agricultural, manufacturing, retail/wholesale and other service related industries are profiled.
General Info: (Formerly National Bankruptcy Reporter), Yr. Est. 1980, Weekly, Mimeo press, ISSN: 0275-0252, Ind/Abs/Online: News Net, No Color
Subscriptions: Indv. $1,800, $37/copy
Acquistions: Publication Bought, Publication Sold
Advertising: Inquire for rates.
List Rental: Actives: 166, $110/M

National Bar Bulletin

Publishing Co: Natl. Bar Assn., 1225 11th St NW, Washington, DC 20001-4217;
Title Tel # (202) 842-3900
Personnel: Publisher-John Crump, Editor-Lisa Davis
Editorial Description: Quarterly newsletter of assns. activities.
General Info: Yr. Est. 1969, Quarterly, Trim Size-11 x 17, Offset press, 8 pages, 2 Color, Coated
Subscriptions: Indv. $20
Acquistions: Publication Bought
Circulation: Total-12,500
Advertising: Accepts Inserts.

National Bulletin on Police Misconduct
See: LAW ENFORCEMENT & PENOLOGY

National Center for State
Courts Report and
Master Calendar

Publishing Co: National Center for State Courts, 300 Newport Ave, Williamsburg, VA 23185-4147;
Title Tel # (804) 253-2000 Title Fax # (804) 220-0449
Personnel: Editor-Kim Swanson, Editor-Kriss Winchester
General Info: Monthly
Subscriptions: Indv. $12

National ClearingHouse on
Marital and Date Rape *Association*

Publishing Co: Women's History Research Center, 2325 Oak St, Berkeley, CA 94708-1628; Title Tel # (510) 524-1582
Personnel: Circ. Mgr.-Renia Ehrenfevcht
Editorial Description: Law, psychology, social work, health, mental health, family services, police.
General Info: Yr. Est. 1980, 8 pages
Subscriptions: Indv. $5, $3/copy
Circulation: Total-2,000

National Conference of
Appellate Court Clerks
Newsletter *Association*

Publishing Co: Natl. Conference of Appellate Court Clerks, 300 Newport Ave, Williamsburg, VA 23185-4147; Title Tel # (804) 253-2000
Editorial Description: Circulated to Conference members only, addressing issues of importance to appellate court clerks.
General Info: Quarterly, Trim Size-8½ x 11
Circulation: Total-8,000

National Disability Law
Reporter *Business*

Publishing Co: LRP Publications, 747 Dresher Rd., P.O. Box 980, Horsham, PA 19044-0980 Tel # (215) 784-0910 Fax # (215) 784-0317
Personnel: Publisher-Ken Kahn, Editor-Tom D'Agostino, Mktg. Dir.-Judy Giering
Editorial Description: A full-text case law reporter covering federal disability statistics and regulations.
General Info: Yr. Est. 1992, Bi-weekly, Looseleaf
Subscriptions: Indv. $655, Inst. $655

National Employment Law
Project Library Bulletin *Association*

Publishing Co: Natl. Employment Law Project, 36 W 44th St Ste 1415, New York, NY 10036-8102; Title Tel # (212) 870-2121
Personnel: Editor, Art Dir.-Deborah Hassan
Editorial Description: Lists library acquisitions for preceeding year in labor & employment law.
General Info: Yr. Est. 1970, Annually, Trim Size-8½ x 11, 10 pages, Looseleaf
Circulation: Total-3,000

National Environmental Enforcement Journal
See: ENVIRONMENT & ECOLOGY

National Federation of the
Blind, Legislative Bulletin

Publishing Co: National Federation of the Blind, 1800 Johnson St., Baltimore, MD 21230-4998
Editorial Description: Legislative issues relevant to the Blind and vision impaired.
General Info: Monthly

National Financing Law
Digest *Business*

Publishing Co: Strafford Pubs., Inc., 590 Dutch Valley Rd., N.E., Postal Drawer 13729, Atlanta, GA 30324-0729; Title Tel # (404) 881-1141 Title Fax # (404) 881-0074
Personnel: Publisher-Richard Ossoff, Editor-Jennifer F. Vaughan, Circ. Mgr., Mktg. Dir.-Marianne Mueller
Editorial Description: Covers issues of banhruptcy, lenders liability, and the changing economic climate.
General Info: Yr. Est. 1988, 12x/yr., 16 pages, ISSN: 1073-953X, Saddle-stitched
Subscriptions: Indv. $334, Can. $364, For. $389, $25/copy

National Lawyers Wives
Newsletter *Association*

Publishing Co: American Lawyers Auxilary, 750 N. Lake Shore Dr., Chicago, IL 60611-4497; Title Tel # (312) 988-6387
Personnel: Editor-Sue Hnedricks

National Products Liability
Database Report *Business*

Publishing Co: Lewis L. Laska, 901 Church St, Nashville, TN 37203-3411; Title Tel # (615) 255-6288 Title Fax # (615) 255-6289
Personnel: Publisher, Editor-Lewis Laska, Editorial Asst.-Lorenda Sue Patterson, J.D.
Editorial Description: National newsletter on products liability litigation.
General Info: Yr. Est. 1991, Monthly, Trim Size-8½ x 11, 24 pages
Subscriptions: Indv. $279

National Property Law
Digests *Business*

Publishing Co: Strafford Pubs., Inc., 590 Dutch Valley Rd., N.E., Postal Drawer 13729, Atlanta, GA 30324-0729; Title Tel # (404) 881-1141 Title Fax # (404) 881-0074
Personnel: Publisher-Richard M. Ossoff, Mng. Editor-Jennifer F. Vaughan, Production Mgr.-C. Malone Tumlin, Circ. Mgr., Mktg. Dir.-Marianne Mueller
Editorial Description: Monthly digest of the most significant property law cases in the U.S. court system. Cases are screened and selected to provide concise, comprehensive coverage of the latest issues concerning property law.
General Info: Yr. Est. 1975, 12x/yr., ISSN: 0363-8340
Subscriptions: Indv. $397, Inst. $380, Can. $410, For. $435, $35/copy

National Public
Employment Reporter *Business*

Publishing Co: LRP Publications, 747 Dresher Rd., P.O. Box 980, Horsham, PA 19044-0980 Tel # (215) 784-0910 Fax # (215) 784-0317
Personnel: Publisher-Kenneth F. Kahn, Editor-Sandy Johnson, Production Mgr.-Kathleen P. Neely, Production Mgr.-Gary Ragin, Mktg. Dir.-Jana Shellington
Editorial Description: Follows controversies over the scope of bargaining issues, unfair practices, agency fees, and negotiation process as they evolve.
General Info: Quarterly
Subscriptions: Indv. $465
List Rental: List Management Co.: Axon Lists, 747 Dresher Rd. Ste. 500, Box 980, Horsham, PA 19044 Tel # (215) 784-0860, Fax # (215) 784-0870, Actives: $125/M

National Report on
Employee Termination
Bulletin *Business*

Publishing Co: Quinlan Publishing, 23 Drydock Ave, Boston, MA 02210-2387 Fax # (617) 345-9646; Title Tel # (617) 542-0048
Personnel: Publisher-E. Michael Quinlan
General Info: (Formerly Discharged Worker), Monthly, 8 pages
Subscriptions: Indv. $40
List Rental: List Management Co.: Stevens-Knox List Management, 304 Park Ave S., New York, NY 10010-5312 Tel # (212) 388-8800, Fax # (212) 388-8890

National Reporter *Business*

Publishing Co: Maritime Law Book Co., Box 302, Fredericton, NB E3B 4Y9 Canada Tel # (506) 453-9921
General Info: Bi-monthly, Ind/Abs/Online: QL Systems Ltd.
Subscriptions: Indv. $40

National Security Law Report
See: SECURITY & SURVEILLANCE

National Transportation Safety Board Digest Service
See: AERONAUTICS/ASTRONAUTICS

National Wetlands Newsletter
See: WATER SUPPLY, POWER & WASTE

Nebraska Employment
Law Letter *Business*

Publishing Co: M. Lee Smith Publishers & Printers ,LCC, P.O. Box 198867, 162 Fourth Avenue North, Nashville, TN 37219-8867 Tel # (615) 242-7395 Fax # (615) 256-6601
Personnel: Publisher-M Lee Smith, Editor-Sam Jensen, Circ. Mgr.-Cathy Bradford
General Info: Yr. Est. 1995, Monthly, Trim Size-8½ x 11, 8 pages, 2 Color
Subscriptions: Indv. $97
List Rental: Rents Lists
Printing Co: M. Lee Smith Publishers & Printers ,LLC, PO Box 198867, 162 Fourth Avenue, Nashville, TN 37219-8867 Tel # (615) 242-7395, Fax # (615) 256-6601

Necessary Elements

Publishing Co: Gould Publications, Inc, 1333 N US Highway 17-92, Longwood, FL 32750-3724 Tel # (407) 695-9500 Fax # (407) 695-2906
Editorial Description: Concise fashion elements necessary to prove a PRIMA FACIE case in the most common causes of actions, together with some possible DEFENSE there to
General Info: Irregular, ISSN: 0-87526-2, Looseleaf
Subscriptions: $6/copy

Nevada Employment Law
Letter *Business*

Publishing Co: M. Lee Smith Publishers & Printers ,LCC, P.O. Box 198867, 162 Fourth Avenue North, Nashville, TN 37219-8867 Tel # (615) 242-7395 Fax # (615) 256-6601
Personnel: Publisher-M Lee Smith, Editor-Patrick Hicks, Circ. Mgr.-Cathy Bradford, Mktg. Dir.-David Yates
General Info: Yr. Est. 1995, Monthly, Trim Size-8½ x 11, 8 pages, 2 Color
Subscriptions: Indv. $97
List Rental: Rents Lists
Printing Co: M. Lee Smith Publishers & Printers ,LLC, PO Box 198867, 162 Fourth Avenue, Nashville, TN 37219-8867 Tel # (615) 242-7395, Fax # (615) 256-6601

New Directions in the Law
of the Sea: Documents,
Series II *Business*

Publishing Co: Oceana Publications, Inc., 75 Main St, Dobbs Ferry, NY 10522-1601 Tel # (914) 693-8100; Title Tel # (914) 693-1320 Title Fax # (914) 693-0402
Personnel: Editor-Kenneth Simmonds, Production Mgr.-Mike Wortzman, Mktg. Dir.-John Downey
General Info: Yr. Est. 1985, Irregular, Trim Size-7 x 10, Looseleaf
Subscriptions: Indv. $650, $400/copy

New Hampshire
Employment Law Letter   *Business*

Publishing Co: M. Lee Smith Publishers & Printers ,LCC, P.O. Box 198867, 162 Fourth Avenue North, Nashville, TN 37219-8867 Tel # (615) 242-7395 Fax # (615) 256-6601
Personnel: Publisher-M Lee Smith, Circ. Mgr.-Cathy Bradford, Mktg. Dir.-David Yates
General Info: Yr. Est. 1995, Monthly, Trim Size-8½ x 11, 8 pages, 2 Color
Subscriptions: Indv. $97
List Rental: Rents Lists
Printing Co: M. Lee Smith Publishers & Printers ,LLC, PO Box 198867, 162 Fourth Avenue, Nashville, TN 37219-8867 Tel # (615) 242-7395, Fax # (615) 256-6601

New Jersey Civil Practice &
Court Rules

Publishing Co: Gould Publications, Inc, 1333 N US Highway 17-92, Longwood, FL 32750-3724 Tel # (407) 695-9500 Fax # (407) 695-2906; Title Tel # (607) 724-3000
Editorial Description: Book. Unannotated statutes supplemented annually at additional cost.
General Info: Annually, Trim Size-5½ x 8½, 800 pages, No Color, Looseleaf
Subscriptions: $19/copy

New Jersey Criminal
Justice Code

Publishing Co: Gould Publications, Inc, 1333 N US Highway 17-92, Longwood, FL 32750-3724 Tel # (407) 695-9500 Fax # (407) 695-2906; Title Tel # (607) 724-3000
Editorial Description: Complete title 2C & effective sections title 2A plus related statutes.
General Info: Annually, Trim Size-5½ x 8½, Sheetfed press, 860 pages, No Color, Looseleaf
Subscriptions: Indv. $8, $19/copy

New Jersey Criminal Justice Code Quizzer
See: LAW ENFORCEMENT & PENOLOGY

New Jersey Criminal Law and Motor Vehicle Handbook
See: LAW ENFORCEMENT & PENOLOGY

New Jersey Department of the Treasury, Local Property and Public Utility Branch News
See: TAXES

New Jersey Education Law Report
See: EDUCATION

New Jersey Employment
Law Letter   *Business*

Publishing Co: M. Lee Smith Publishers & Printers ,LCC, P.O. Box 198867, 162 Fourth Avenue North, Nashville, TN 37219-8867; Title Tel # (615) 242-7395 Title Fax # (615) 256-6601
Personnel: Publisher-M Lee Smith, Editor-Joseph Fortunato, Circ. Mgr.-Cathy Bradford, Mktg. Dir.-Dave Yates
Editorial Description: Review of employment law developments that affect New Jersey employers.
General Info: Yr. Est. 1992, Monthly, Trim Size-8½ x 11, 8 pages, ISSN: 1064-2390, 2 Color
Subscriptions: Indv. $97
List Rental: Rents Lists
Printing Co: M. Lee Smith Publishers & Printers ,LLC, PO Box 198867, 162 Fourth Avenue, Nashville, TN 37219-8867 Tel # (615) 242-7395, Fax # (615) 256-6601

New Jersey Family Lawyer
See: FAMILY

New Jersey Insurance
Law and Regulation
Reporter   *Business*

Publishing Co: Shepard's/McGraw-Hill, Inc., 555 Middle Creek Pky, Colorado Springs, CO 80921-3622; Title Tel # (719) 488-3000 Title Fax # (719) 481-7448
Personnel: Publisher-Anthony Monoco, Circ. Mgr.-Cheryl Everitt, Adv. Dir.-Peggy Ives, Art Dir.-Leigh Vidakovich
Editorial Description: Covering N.J Insurance Law and cases.
General Info: Yr. Est. 1991, Monthly
Subscriptions: Indv. $345
List Rental: List Management Co.: The Lake Group, 411 Theodore Freund Ave., Rye, NY 10580-1497 Tel # (914) 925-2400, Fax # (914) 925-2499, Actives: 40,212, $130/M

New Jersey LAWCAST

Publishing Co: Vox Juris, Inc., P.O. Box 389, Pennington, NJ 08534; Title Tel # (609) 737-6543 Title Fax # (609) 737-3860
Personnel: Publisher-Jason Meyer, Esq, Editor-Marc Cohen, Esq, Circ. Mgr.-Karen E. Anderson, Mktg. Mgr.-Kathy W. Gould
Editorial Description: The legal newscast & case digesting service on audio cassette for lawyers.Each issue includes an audiocassette and companion outline. Comprehensive coverage of published NJ state opinions, selected federal cases, interviews, features and legal news from NJ.
General Info: Yr. Est. 1994, Semi-monthly
Subscriptions: Indv. $329, Inst. $450, $25/copy

New Jersey Labor and Employment Law Quarterly
See: LABOR

New Jersey Law
Enforcement Handbook

Publishing Co: Gould Publications, Inc, 1333 N US Highway 17-92, Longwood, FL 32750-3724 Tel # (407) 695-9500 Fax # (407) 695-2906; Title Tel # (607) 724-3000
Editorial Description: Question & answer format analyzing court decisions.
General Info: Annually, Trim Size-5½ x 8½, 1,050 pages, Looseleaf
Subscriptions: $45/copy

New Jersey Law with
Forms   *Business*

Publishing Co: Matthew Bender & Co., 11 Penn Plaza, New York, NY 10001-2006 Fax # (212) 244-3188; Title Tel # (212) 967-7707
Personnel: Editor-A. Jenner
Editorial Description: Full coverage of agency: bills, notes, checks; constitutional law; contracts, surety, guaranty; corporations; crimes; criminal procedure; domestic relations; equity; evidence; municipal corporations, partnerships & association; personal property; law division practice; real property; torts; wills probate practice.
General Info: Yr. Est. 1948, Irregular, Looseleaf
Subscriptions: $550/copy

New Jersey Motor
Vehicle & Traffic Laws

Publishing Co: Gould Publications, Inc, 1333 N US Highway 17-92, Longwood, FL 32750-3724 Tel # (407) 695-9500 Fax # (407) 695-2906; Title Tel # (607) 724-3000
General Info: Annually, Trim Size-5½ x 8½, 600 pages, No Color, Looseleaf
Subscriptions: $19/copy

New Jersey State Tax News
See: TAXES

New Jersey Transaction
Guide   *Business*

Publishing Co: Matthew Bender & Co., 11 Penn Plaza, New York, NY 10001-2006 Tel # (212) 967-7707 Fax # (212) 244-3188
Editorial Description: A general form & procedural guide for the New Jersey practitioner covering civil, non-litigation-oriented subject areas in five units: Business Entities, Commercial Transactions, Real Estate Transactions, Personal Transactions, & Estate Planning.
General Info: Yr. Est. 1984, Irregular, Looseleaf

New Mexico Employment
Law Letter   *Business*

Publishing Co: M. Lee Smith Publishers & Printers ,LCC, P.O. Box 198867, 162 Fourth Avenue North, Nashville, TN 37219-8867 Tel # (615) 242-7395 Fax # (615) 256-6601
Personnel: Publisher-M. Lee Smith, Editor-Robert Tinnin, Jr., Circ. Mgr.-Cathy Bradford, Mktg. Dir.-Dave Yates
Editorial Description: Reviews employment law updates that effect New Mexico employers.
General Info: Yr. Est. 1994, Monthly, Trim Size-8½ x 11, 8 pages, ISSN: 1079-6363, 2 Color
Subscriptions: Indv. $97
List Rental: Rents Lists
Printing Co: M. Lee Smith Publishers & Printers ,LLC, PO Box 198867, 162 Fourth Avenue, Nashville, TN 37219-8867 Tel # (615) 242-7395, Fax # (615) 256-6601

New York Alcoholic
Beverage Control Law

Publishing Co: Gould Publications, Inc, 1333 N US Highway 17-92, Longwood, FL 32750-3724 Tel # (407) 695-9500 Fax # (407) 695-2906; Title Tel # (607) 724-3000 Title Fax # (607) 723-4285
Editorial Description: This book contains a complete presentation of Chapter 3-B on the Consolidated Laws of New York, including a comprehensive index; 150 pages.
General Info: Annually, 130 pages, Looseleaf
Subscriptions: $6/copy

New York Banking Law

Publishing Co: Gould Publications, Inc, 1333 N US Highway 17-92, Longwood, FL 32750-3724 Tel # (407) 695-9500 Fax # (407) 695-2906; Title Tel # (607) 724-3000
Editorial Description: Book. Supplemented annually at additional cost. Chapter 2 of the consolidated laws.
General Info: Annually, Trim Size-6 x 9, Sheetfed press, 930 pages, No Color, Looseleaf
Subscriptions: $59/copy

New York Canudo on
Criminal Law

Publishing Co: Gould Publications, Inc, 1333 N US Highway 17-92, Longwood, FL 32750-3724 Tel # (407) 695-9500 Fax # (407) 695-2906; Title Tel # (607) 724-3000 Title Fax # (607) 723-4285
Editorial Description: All of the recent important United states Supreme Court and New York Court decisions involving constitutional rights of the accused are fully discussed.
General Info: Annually, 1,000 pages, Looseleaf
Subscriptions: $40/copy

New York Canudo on
Evidence Laws

Publishing Co: Gould Publications, Inc, 1333 N US Highway 17-92, Longwood, FL 32750-3724 Tel # (407) 695-9500 Fax # (407) 695-2906; Title Tel # (607) 724-3000
Editorial Description: An in-depth practical handbook covering burden of proof; judicial notice; presumptions; admissions; confessions; witnesses on the stand; competancy of witness; etc.
General Info: Annually, 390 pages, Looseleaf
Subscriptions: $37/copy

New York City Building
Code

Publishing Co: Gould Publications, Inc, 1333 N US Highway 17-92, Longwood, FL 32750-3724
Tel # (407) 695-9500 Fax # (407) 695-2906; Title Tel # (607) 724-3000
Personnel: Editor-Kathleen Pichette
Editorial Description: Book. Supplemented annually at additional cost. Laws pertaining to buildings in N.Y.C. (Article 26 of the Administrative Codes).
General Info: Annually, Trim Size-8 x 11, Sheetfed press, 720 pages, No Color, Looseleaf
Subscriptions: $50/copy

New York Civil Practice:
CPLR *Business*

Publishing Co: Matthew Bender & Co., 11 Penn Plaza, New York, NY 10001-2006
Fax # (212) 244-3188; Title Tel # (212) 967-7707
Personnel: Editor-N. Masliansky
Editorial Description: Section-by-section analysis and guide to New York's civil procedural law.
General Info: Yr. Est. 1963, Irregular, Looseleaf
Subscriptions: $1,768/copy

New York Civil Practice
Law & Rules Handbook

Publishing Co: Gould Publications, Inc, 1333 N US Highway 17-92, Longwood, FL 32750-3724
Tel # (407) 695-9500 Fax # (407) 695-2906; Title Tel # (607) 724-3000 Title Fax # (607) 723-4285
Editorial Description: This book presents the Civil Practice Law and Rules (CPLR), Chapter 8 of the Consolidated Laws of New York, plus official forms.
General Info: Annually, 650 pages, Looseleaf
Subscriptions: $22/copy

New York Civil Service Law

Publishing Co: Gould Publications, Inc, 1333 N US Highway 17-92, Longwood, FL 32750-3724
Tel # (407) 695-9500 Fax # (407) 695-2906; Title Tel # (607) 724-3000 Title Fax # (607) 723-4285
Editorial Description: Chapter 7 of the Consolidated Laws of New York. Includes laws on Appeals, Awards, Benefits, Compensation, Demotions, Disciplinary Proceedings, etc.
General Info: Annually, 200 pages, Looseleaf
Subscriptions: $10/copy

New York Civil Service Update
See: EMPLOYMENT

New York Consolidated
Laws

Publishing Co: Gould Publications, Inc, 1333 N US Highway 17-92, Longwood, FL 32750-3724
Tel # (407) 695-9500 Fax # (407) 695-2906; Title Tel # (607) 724-3000
Editorial Description: Complete presentation of NY Statutes. Unannotated.
General Info: Annually, Trim Size-7 x 10, Web press, 1,200 pages, No Color, Coated, Perfect bound, Looseleaf
Subscriptions: $179/copy

New York Corporation Law
Handbook

Publishing Co: Gould Publications, Inc, 1333 N US Highway 17-92, Longwood, FL 32750-3724
Tel # (407) 695-9500 Fax # (407) 695-2906; Title Tel # (607) 724-3000
Editorial Description: Business Corporation Law & related statutes. Unannotated.
General Info: Annually, Trim Size-5$\frac{1}{2}$ x 8$\frac{1}{2}$, 900 pages, No Color, Looseleaf
Subscriptions: Indv. $15, $25/copy

New York Correction Law
See: LAW ENFORCEMENT & PENOLOGY

New York Court Forms

Publishing Co: Gould Publications, Inc, 1333 N US Highway 17-92, Longwood, FL 32750-3724
Tel # (407) 695-9500 Fax # (407) 695-2906; Title Tel # (607) 724-3000
Editorial Description: Contains all forms necessary for courts & police in New York State.
General Info: Annually, Trim Size-8$\frac{1}{2}$ x 11, 175 pages, No Color, Looseleaf
Subscriptions: $40/copy

New York Courts Manual of
Procedure

Publishing Co: Gould Publications, Inc, 1333 N US Highway 17-92, Longwood, FL 32750-3724
Tel # (407) 695-9500 Fax # (407) 695-2906; Title Tel # (607) 724-3000 Title Fax # (607) 723-4285
Editorial Description: A comprehensive manual for New York courts including forms.
General Info: Annually, 330 pages, Looseleaf
Subscriptions: $30/copy

New York Criminal Law
Handbook

Publishing Co: Gould Publications, Inc, 1333 N US Highway 17-92, Longwood, FL 32750-3724
Tel # (407) 695-9500 Fax # (407) 695-2906; Title Tel # (607) 724-3000
Editorial Description: Book supplemented annually at additional cost. N.Y. State penal statutes & constitutional rights of the individual. Cases & analysis.
General Info: Annually, Trim Size-5$\frac{1}{2}$ x 8$\frac{1}{2}$, Sheetfed press, 1,160 pages, No Color, Looseleaf
Subscriptions: Indv. $16, $25/copy

New York Criminal Practice *Business*

Publishing Co: Matthew Bender & Co., 11 Penn Plaza, New York, NY 10001-2006
Fax # (212) 244-3188; Title Tel # (212) 967-7707
Personnel: Editor-N. Masliansky
Editorial Description: Coverage includes: analysis of the CPL & Penal Law & related New York & federal statutes & cases; citations & cross-references. Discusses pertinent constitutional & policy issues & contains text of CPL provisions & court-tested forms.
General Info: Yr. Est. 1973, Irregular, Looseleaf
Subscriptions: $675/copy

New York Criminal
Procedure Law

Publishing Co: Gould Publications, Inc, 1333 N US Highway 17-92, Longwood, FL 32750-3724
Tel # (407) 695-9500 Fax # (407) 695-2906; Title Tel # (607) 724-3000
Editorial Description: Criminal procedure law of NYS, complete statutes.
General Info: (Formerly Criminal Procedure Law of New York), Annually, Trim Size-5$\frac{1}{2}$ x 8$\frac{1}{2}$, Sheetfed press, 500 pages, No Color, Looseleaf
Subscriptions: $7/copy

New York Criminal
Procedure Law
Questions & Answers

Publishing Co: Gould Publications, Inc, 1333 N US Highway 17-92, Longwood, FL 32750-3724
Tel # (407) 695-9500 Fax # (407) 695-2906; Title Tel # (607) 724-3000
Editorial Description: Study guide. Section numbers for reference given with answers.
General Info: Annually, Trim Size-5$\frac{1}{2}$ x 8$\frac{1}{2}$, 200 pages, No Color, Looseleaf
Subscriptions: $10/copy

New York Defense of
Justification

Publishing Co: Gould Publications, Inc, 1333 N US Highway 17-92, Longwood, FL 32750-3724
Tel # (407) 695-9500 Fax # (407) 695-2906; Title Tel # (607) 724-3000 Title Fax # (607) 723-4285
Editorial Description: This booklet presents a review of the use of Physical Force and Deadly Physical Force, including definitions, and questions and answers on the subject.
General Info: Annually, 20 pages, Looseleaf
Subscriptions: $3/copy

New York Domestic
Relations Reporter *Business*

Publishing Co: Matthew Bender & Co., 11 Penn Plaza, New York, NY 10001-2006
Tel # (212) 967-7707 Fax # (212) 244-3188
Editorial Description: A monthly reporter that highlights the full range of domestic relations practice issues, from divorce, custody and support, through property, taxation, paternity, adoption & more.
General Info: Yr. Est. 1989, Monthly, Looseleaf

New York E.P.T.L. &
S.C.P.A.

Publishing Co: Gould Publications, Inc, 1333 N US Highway 17-92, Longwood, FL 32750-3724
Tel # (407) 695-9500 Fax # (407) 695-2906; Title Tel # (607) 724-3000
General Info: Annually, Trim Size-5$\frac{1}{2}$ x 8$\frac{1}{2}$, 450 pages, No Color, Looseleaf
Subscriptions: $22/copy

New York Education Law Report
See: EDUCATION

New York Environmental
Conservation Law

Publishing Co: Gould Publications, Inc, 1333 N US Highway 17-92, Longwood, FL 32750-3724
Tel # (407) 695-9500 Fax # (407) 695-2906; Title Tel # (607) 724-3000
General Info: Annually, Trim Size-5$\frac{1}{2}$ x 8$\frac{1}{2}$, 1,000 pages, No Color, Looseleaf
Subscriptions: $22/copy

New York Estates-Wills-
Trusts *Business*

Publishing Co: CCH, Inc., 2700 Lake Cook Rd., Riverwoods, IL 60015 Parent Co.-Kluwer Law & Taxation Publishers, Cambridge; Title Tel # (847) 267-7000 Title Fax # (800) 224-8299
Editorial Description: New York state laws and court decisions affecting estate administration.
General Info: Yr. Est. 1967, Monthly, Trim Size-6 x 9, Web press, 60 pages, No Color, Looseleaf
Subscriptions: Indv. $1,099

New York Family Law
Update *Business*

Publishing Co: New York Family Law Institute, Inc., 32 S Monsey Rd, P.O. Box 774, Monsey, NY 10952-0774; Title Tel # (914) 426-3930 Title Fax # (914) 426-3930
Personnel: Publisher, Editor-David Blumberg
Editorial Description: Provides brief summaries of recent cases & statutes dealing with issues such as child support, visitation rights, child abuse, foster care, child custody, equitable distribution, divorce, adoption, & changes in court procedure. Scope limited to NY. Designed for lawyers, judges & related professionals.
General Info: Yr. Est. 1990, 48x/yr., Trim Size-8$\frac{1}{2}$ x 11, Offset press, 2 pages, ISSN: 1049-6319, Matte
Subscriptions: Indv. $249
Advertising: Inquire for rates.
Printing Co: Copyprints Offset, 118 Chestnut Ridge Rd, Montvale, NJ 07645-1706

New York 'Gitlitz' on Divorces and Announcments

Publishing Co: Gould Publications, Inc, 1333 N US Highway 17-92, Longwood, FL 32750-3724
Tel # (407) 695-9500 Fax # (407) 695-2906; Title Tel # (607) 724-3000
Editorial Description: Guide to rules applicable to uncontested divorces & annulments. DRL included.
General Info: (Formerly New York Uncontested Divorces & Annulments), Annually, Trim Size-5½ x 8½, Sheetfed press, 430 pages, No Color, Looseleaf
Subscriptions: $40/copy

New York Health Law Update
See: HEALTH

New York Insurance Law   *Business*

Publishing Co: Matthew Bender & Co., 11 Penn Plaza, New York, NY 10001-2006
Tel # (212) 967-7707 Fax # (212) 244-3188
Personnel: Editor-Wolcott B. Dunham, Jr.
Editorial Description: Provides complete coverage of insurance law in New York. It covers the state's extensive regulation of the insurance industry as well as the New York Law relating to insurance policy coverage.
General Info: Yr. Est. 1991, Irregular, Looseleaf

New York Landlord & Tenant Handbook

Publishing Co: Gould Publications, Inc, 1333 N US Highway 17-92, Longwood, FL 32750-3724
Tel # (407) 695-9500 Fax # (407) 695-2906; Title Tel # (607) 724-3000
General Info: Annually, Trim Size-5½ x 8½, 300 pages, No Color, Looseleaf
Subscriptions: $37/copy

New York Law Digest

Publishing Co: Gould Publications, Inc, 1333 N US Highway 17-92, Longwood, FL 32750-3724
Tel # (407) 695-9500 Fax # (407) 695-2906; Title Tel # (607) 724-3000
Editorial Description: This book contains selected sections of various NY laws used by personnel in the Criminal Justice System.
General Info: Annually, 670 pages, Looseleaf
Subscriptions: $15/copy

New York Lawyer's Letter   *Business*

Publishing Co: Doran Pubs., Inc., PO Box 391, Clifton Park, NY 12065-0391;
Title Tel # (518) 877-7492
General Info: Weekly
Subscriptions: Indv. $105

New York Legal Forms and Proceedures Handbook

Publishing Co: Gould Publications, Inc, 1333 N US Highway 17-92, Longwood, FL 32750-3724
Tel # (407) 695-9500 Fax # (407) 695-2906; Title Tel # (607) 724-3000
Editorial Description: An excellent tool for anyone dealing with legal forms in New York. Chronicles forms and step-by-step instructions.
General Info: Annually, 250 pages, Looseleaf
Subscriptions: $50/copy

New York Magistrates Desk Book

Publishing Co: Gould Publications, Inc, 1333 N US Highway 17-92, Longwood, FL 32750-3724
Tel # (407) 695-9500 Fax # (407) 695-2906; Title Tel # (607) 724-3000
Editorial Description: Official Directory of the New York State Magistrates Association. Contains by-laws, court location codes, & listings of each certified sitting judge in New York Town & Village Courts by name, address, county, & town or village. Excellent reference tool.
General Info: Annually, Trim Size-5½ x 8½, Sheetfed press, 200 pages, No Color, Looseleaf
Subscriptions: Indv. $18, $40/copy

New York Multiple Dwelling Law

Publishing Co: Gould Publications, Inc, 1333 N US Highway 17-92, Longwood, FL 32750-3724
Tel # (407) 695-9500 Fax # (407) 695-2906; Title Tel # (607) 724-3000
Editorial Description: Conforms to the official NYC book.
General Info: Annually, Trim Size-5½ x 8½, Sheetfed press, 275 pages, No Color, Looseleaf
Subscriptions: $17/copy

New York Navigation Laws

Publishing Co: Gould Publications, Inc, 1333 N US Highway 17-92, Longwood, FL 32750-3724
Tel # (407) 695-9500 Fax # (407) 695-2906; Title Tel # (607) 724-3000
Editorial Description: Complete text NYS navigation law unannotated w/changes in text.
General Info: (Formerly Navigation Law of NY), Annually, Trim Size-5½ x 8½, Sheetfed press, 130 pages, No Color, Looseleaf
Subscriptions: $7/copy

New York Negligence Reporter   *Business*

Publishing Co: Matthew Bender & Co., 11 Penn Plaza, New York, NY 10001-2006
Tel # (212) 967-7707 Fax # (212) 244-3188
Personnel: Editor-Jonathan A. Dachs, Editor-Norman E. Dachs
Editorial Description: In a concise, easy-to-read format, this reporter brings you the most important developments in personal injury practice each month.
General Info: Yr. Est. 1989, Monthly, Looseleaf

New York No-Fault Arbitration Reports
See: INSURANCE

New York Penal Law

Publishing Co: Gould Publications, Inc, 1333 N US Highway 17-92, Longwood, FL 32750-3724
Tel # (407) 695-9500 Fax # (407) 695-2906; Title Tel # (607) 724-3000
Editorial Description: This book presents the Penal Law, chap. 40 of the Consolidated Laws of New York and includes the schedules and definitions to controlled substances, public health law.
General Info: Annually, 340 pages, Looseleaf
Subscriptions: $7/copy

New York Penal Law & Criminal Procedure Law
See: LAW ENFORCEMENT & PENOLOGY

New York Penal Law Questions & Answers

Publishing Co: Gould Publications, Inc, 1333 N US Highway 17-92, Longwood, FL 32750-3724
Tel # (407) 695-9500 Fax # (407) 695-2906; Title Tel # (607) 724-3000
Editorial Description: Study Guide. Section numbers for reference given with answers.
General Info: Annually, Trim Size-5½ x 8½, Sheetfed press, 150 pages, No Color, Looseleaf
Subscriptions: $10/copy

New York Practice Guide: Business and Commericial   *Business*

Publishing Co: Matthew Bender & Co., 11 Penn Plaza, New York, NY 10001-2006
Tel # (212) 967-7707 Fax # (212) 244-3188
Personnel: Editor-Eileen M. Lach
Editorial Description: This illustrative, how-to guide take you step-by-step through every New York business and commercial transactions--from the vantage point of attorneys on both sides of the transaction.
General Info: Yr. Est. 1987, Irregular, Looseleaf

New York Practice Guide: Domestic Relations   *Business*

Publishing Co: Matthew Bender & Co., 11 Penn Plaza, New York, NY 10001-2006
Tel # (212) 967-7707 Fax # (212) 244-3188
Editorial Description: Provides step-by-step guidance for handling matrimonial actions, including up-to-date coverage of New York's Child Support Standards Act.
General Info: Yr. Est. 1988, Irregular, Looseleaf

New York Practice Guide: Negligence   *Business*

Publishing Co: Matthew Bender & Co., 11 Penn Plaza, New York, NY 10001-2006
Tel # (212) 967-7707 Fax # (212) 244-3188
Editorial Description: Expert analysis of case and staturtory law, accompanied by practice material.
General Info: Yr. Est. 1989, Irregular, Looseleaf

New York Practice Guide: Probate and Estate Administration   *Business*

Publishing Co: Matthew Bender & Co., 11 Penn Plaza, New York, NY 10001-2006
Tel # (212) 967-7707 Fax # (212) 244-3188
Personnel: Editor-Joseph T. Arenson
Editorial Description: Expert guidance on the essentials of probate and estate administration in New York State.
General Info: Yr. Est. 1985, Irregular, Looseleaf

New York Real Estate Law Reporter
See: REAL ESTATE

New York Real Property Laws Handbook

Publishing Co: Gould Publications, Inc, 1333 N US Highway 17-92, Longwood, FL 32750-3724
Tel # (407) 695-9500 Fax # (407) 695-2906; Title Tel # (607) 724-3000
Editorial Description: Real Property Law & related statutes.
General Info: Annually, Trim Size-5½ x 8½, Sheetfed press, 840 pages, No Color, Looseleaf
Subscriptions: Indv. $15, $25/copy

New York School District Law Letter

Publishing Co: Doran Pubs., Inc., PO Box 391, Clifton Park, NY 12065-0391;
Title Tel # (518) 877-7492
Personnel: Editor-Patricia Fitzpatrick
General Info: 24x/yr.
Subscriptions: Indv. $72

New York Search & Seizure

Publishing Co: Gould Publications, Inc, 1333 N US Highway 17-92, Longwood, FL 32750-3724
Tel # (407) 695-9500 Fax # (407) 695-2906; Title Tel # (607) 723-3000
Editorial Description: Presents a comprehensive review of the New York law on the exclusionary rule, probable couse, arrest, search and seizure, warrent requirements, motor vehicle stops, and suppression motives.
General Info: Annually, 450 pages, Looseleaf
Subscriptions: $40/copy

New York Small Claims
Guide

Publishing Co: Gould Publications, Inc, 1333 N US Highway 17-92, Longwood, FL 32750-3724
Tel # (407) 695-9500 Fax # (407) 695-2906; Title Tel # (607) 724-3000 Title Fax # (607) 723-4285
Editorial Description: This booklet presents a complete review of the Small Claims Court for Town and Village in New York State.
General Info: Annually, 21 pages, Looseleaf
Subscriptions: $4/copy

New York State Law Digest   *Association*

Publishing Co: New York State Bar Association, 1 Elk St, Albany, NY 12207-1002;
Title Tel # (518) 463-3200 Title Fax # (518) 463-8844
Personnel: Editor-David Siegel
Editorial Description: Summary of recent important federal & New York court cases.
General Info: Yr. Est. 1960, Monthly, Trim Size-8$\frac{1}{2}$ x 11, 4 pages, ISSN: 0028-7636
Subscriptions: Free With Membership
Circulation: (97% controlled), Total-59,000
Printing Co: Letter Shop, 133 Madison Ave, Albany, NY 12202-1707 Tel # (518) 434-1172

New York Stock Exchange Guide
See: INVESTMENT

New York Suppression
Manual--Arrest, Search
and Seizure, Confession
and Indentification   *Business*

Publishing Co: Matthew Bender & Co., 11 Penn Plaza, New York, NY 10001-2006
Tel # (212) 967-7707 Fax # (212) 244-3188
Editorial Description: New York's position on the Fourth, Fifth, and Sixth Amendment rights of criminal suspects and defendants frequently diverges from that of the U.S. Supreme Court.
General Info: Yr. Est. 1991, Irregular, Looseleaf

New York Surrogate's Court
Procedure Act

Publishing Co: Gould Publications, Inc, 1333 N US Highway 17-92, Longwood, FL 32750-3724
Tel # (407) 695-9500 Fax # (407) 695-2906; Title Tel # (607) 724-3000
Editorial Description: Complete text NYS Surrogate's court procedure. Unannotated w/changes in text.
General Info: Yr. Est. 1970, Annually, Trim Size-5$\frac{1}{2}$ x 8$\frac{1}{2}$, Sheetfed press, 325 pages, No Color, Looseleaf
Subscriptions: $11/copy

New York Town Laws

Publishing Co: Gould Publications, Inc, 1333 N US Highway 17-92, Longwood, FL 32750-3724
Tel # (407) 695-9500 Fax # (407) 695-2906; Title Tel # (607) 724-3000
Editorial Description: Chapter 62 of New York Consolidated Laws. Comprehensive index.
General Info: Annually, Trim Size-5$\frac{1}{2}$ x 8$\frac{1}{2}$, Sheetfed press, 400 pages, Looseleaf
Subscriptions: $18/copy

New York Understanding
the Penal Law

Publishing Co: Gould Publications, Inc, 1333 N US Highway 17-92, Longwood, FL 32750-3724
Tel # (407) 695-9500 Fax # (407) 695-2906
Editorial Description: Presents the law in a manner that makes it easily understood and teaches you how to prepare an 'Accusatory Instrument' that is 'sufficient on its face,' meeting the requirements in the C.P.L.
General Info: Annually, Looseleaf
Subscriptions: $24/copy

New York Vehicle & Traffic Law
See: TRAFFIC & TRANSPORTATION

New York Village Law

Publishing Co: Gould Publications, Inc, 1333 N US Highway 17-92, Longwood, FL 32750-3724
Tel # (407) 695-9500 Fax # (407) 695-2906; Title Tel # (607) 724-3000
Editorial Description: Book. Supplemented annually at additional cost. Comprehensive index. Chapter 64 of the Consolidated Laws of New York.
General Info: Annually, Trim Size-5$\frac{1}{2}$ x 8$\frac{1}{2}$, 200 pages, No Color, Looseleaf
Subscriptions: $16/copy

New York Workers'
Compensation Law
Handbook

Publishing Co: Gould Publications, Inc, 1333 N US Highway 17-92, Longwood, FL 32750-3724
Tel # (407) 695-9500 Fax # (407) 695-2906; Title Tel # (607) 724-3000 Title Fax # (607) 723-4285
Editorial Description: This book contains the complete Workers' Compensation Law, The Volunteers Ambulance Workers' Benefit Law, The Volunteer Fire Fighters' Benefit Law, Rules and Regulations of the Workers' Compensation Board, and a complete, integrated up-to-date index.
General Info: (Formerly New York Workers' Comprehensive Law Handbook), Annually, 620 pages, Looseleaf
Subscriptions: $35/copy

New York Workers'
Compensation Law
Reporter   *Business*

Publishing Co: LRP Publications, 747 Dresher Rd., P.O. Box 980, Horsham, PA 19044-0980
Tel # (215) 784-0910 Fax # (215) 784-0317
Personnel: Publisher-Kenneth F. Kahn, Editor-Joanne Fiore, Production Mgr.-Kathleen P. Neely, Mktg. Dir.-Jana Shellington, Promotion Dir.-Gary Ragin
Editorial Description: The most comprehensive source available for workers compensation and related law issued by the state agencies and courts.
General Info: Yr. Est. 1987, Bi-monthly
Subscriptions: Indv. $605
List Rental: List Management Co.: Axon Lists, 747 Dresher Rd. Ste. 500, Box 980, Horsham, PA 19044 Tel # (215) 784-0860, Fax # (215) 784-0870, Actives: 27,586, $125/M

New York/New Jersey
Environmental Law
Letter   *Business*

Publishing Co: M. Lee Smith Publishers & Printers ,LCC, P.O. Box 198867, 162 Fourth Avenue North, Nashville, TN 37219-8867; Title Tel # (615) 242-7395 Title Fax # (615) 256-6601
Personnel: Publisher-M Lee Smith, Editor-Gail H. Allyn, Circ. Mgr.-Cathy Bradford, Mktg. Dir.-Dave Yates
Editorial Description: Review environmental law developments that effect New Jersey companies.
General Info: (Formerly New Jersey Environmental Compliance Update), Yr. Est. 1992, Monthly, Trim Size-8$\frac{1}{2}$ x 11, 8 pages, ISSN: 1060-9954, 2 Color
Subscriptions: Indv. $117
List Rental: Rents Lists
Printing Co: M. Lee Smith Publishers & Printers ,LLC, PO Box 198867, 162 Fourth Avenue, Nashville, TN 37219-8867 Tel # (615) 242-7395, Fax # (615) 256-6601

News from ACAP
See: AERONAUTICS/ASTRONAUTICS

News from MCLI
See: CIVIL RIGHTS

News of New York
See: MEDICINE

Newsbriefs

Publishing Co: Lawyers Committee for Human Rights, 330 7th Ave., #10N, New York, NY 10001-5010; Title Tel # (212) 629-6170
Personnel: Editor-Lili Brown
General Info: Yr. Est. 1986, Quarterly
Subscriptions: Indv. $30, $8/copy

Newsletter   *Association*

Publishing Co: Friends of the Superior Court, 500 Indiana Ave. NW, Room 1146, Washington, DC 20001-2131; Title Tel # (202) 879-1759
Personnel: Editor-Ellen Weir
Editorial Description: Inform the community of the FRIENDS support of the Superior Court volunteer & intern programs of the Court Social Service Div. , The Child Care Center & the Child Abuse program.
General Info: (Formerly Friends of the Superior Court Newsletter), Yr. Est. 1973, Semi-annually, Trim Size-8$\frac{1}{2}$ x 11, 4 pages, 2 Color
Subscriptions: Free
Circulation: Total-1,000, Readership-1,000

Newsletter of the American Academy of Psychiatry
See: PSYCHIATRY

Newsletter of the Bar
Association of
Montgomery County,
Md.   *Association*

Publishing Co: Bar Assn. of Montgomery County, 27 W. Jefferson St., Rockville, MD 20850-4200; Title Tel # (301) 424-3454
Personnel: Editor-Beverly Mondin
Editorial Description: Intraprofessional communication vehicle; legal information: court schedules, State's Attorney's schedule, meeting minutes (state and local).
General Info: Yr. Est. 1965, Monthly, Trim Size-8$\frac{1}{2}$ x 11, Roto. press, 120 pages, 2% ads, 2 Color
Circulation: (100% controlled), Total-1,800
Advertising: Inquire for rates.
List Rental: Rents Lists

Newsletter on Intellectual Freedom
See: EDUCATION

Nichols on Eminent Domain
See: REAL ESTATE

Nimmer on Copyright
See: PATENTS/COPYRIGHTS/TRADE MARKS

No-Fault and Uninsured Motorist Automobile Insurance   *Business*

Publishing Co: Matthew Bender & Co., 11 Penn Plaza, New York, NY 10001-2006
Tel # (212) 967-7707 Fax # (212) 244-3188
Editorial Description: For both plaintiff's and defendant's counsel, practical guide for handling no-fault and uninsured motorist insurance claims.
General Info: Yr. Est. 1984, Irregular, Looseleaf

Norman, Hanson & DeTroy Newsletter

Publishing Co: Norman, Hanson & DeTroy, PO Box 4600, Portland, ME 04112-4600;
Title Tel # (207) 774-7000
Personnel: Editor-Stephen Moriarty
Editorial Description: Information on recent developments in the law, particularly Maine law & how it may affect the legal & business community.
General Info: Yr. Est. 1987, Quarterly
Subscriptions: Free To Qualified Recipient

North American Free Trade Agreements
See: INTERNATIONAL TRADE

North Carolina Criminal Law & Motor Vehicle Handbook

Publishing Co: Gould Publications, Inc, 1333 N US Highway 17-92, Longwood, FL 32750-3724
Tel # (407) 695-9500 Fax # (407) 695-2906; Title Tel # (607) 724-3000
Editorial Description: A complete presentation of general law of North Carolina.
General Info: Annually, 900 pages, Looseleaf
Subscriptions: $22/copy

North Carolina Employment Law Letter   *Business*

Publishing Co: M. Lee Smith Publishers & Printers ,LCC, P.O. Box 198867, 162 Fourth Avenue North, Nashville, TN 37219-8867; Title Tel # (615) 242-7395 Title Fax # (615) 256-6601
Personnel: Publisher-M Lee Smith, Editor-Richard Rainey, Circ. Mgr.-Cathy Bradford, Mktg. Dir.-Dave Yates
Editorial Description: Review of employment law developments that affect North Carolina employers.
General Info: Yr. Est. 1991, Monthly, Trim Size-8½ x 11, 8 pages, ISSN: 1054-6359, 2 Color
Subscriptions: Indv. $97
List Rental: Rents Lists
Printing Co: M. Lee Smith Publishers & Printers ,LLC, PO Box 198867, 162 Fourth Avenue, Nashville, TN 37219-8867 Tel # (615) 242-7395, Fax # (615) 256-6601

North Dakota Employment Law Letter   *Business*

Publishing Co: M. Lee Smith Publishers & Printers ,LCC, P.O. Box 198867, 162 Fourth Avenue North, Nashville, TN 37219-8867 Tel # (615) 242-7395 Fax # (615) 256-6601
Personnel: Publisher-M Lee Smith, Circ. Mgr.-Cathy Bradford, Mktg. Dir.-David Yates
General Info: Monthly, 2 Color
Advertising: $97.
List Rental: Rents Lists
Printing Co: M. Lee Smith Publishers & Printers ,LLC, PO Box 198867, 162 Fourth Avenue, Nashville, TN 37219-8867 Tel # (615) 242-7395, Fax # (615) 256-6601

Northwest Mining Assn.- Bulletin   *Association*

Publishing Co: Northwest Mining Assn., 10 N Post St Ste 414, Spokane, WA 99201-0705;
Title Tel # (509) 624-1158 Title Fax # (509) 623-1241
Personnel: Editor-Rhonda Thurman
Editorial Description: To share information with legislators, educational institutions, the mining community and the public on the need for and value of mining. To create awareness and a better and unstanding of mining.
General Info: Monthly, Trim Size-8½ x 11, 8 pages, 2 Color, Saddle-stitched
Subscriptions: Indv. $75, Free With Membership
Acquistions: Publication Bought
Circulation: Total-2,700
List Rental: Rents Lists

Norton Bankruptcy Law Adviser

Publishing Co: Callaghan & Company, 155 Pfingsten Rd., Deerfield, IL 60015-5293;
Title Tel # (708) 948-7000 Title Fax # (708) 948-8955
General Info: Yr. Est. 1983, Monthly
Subscriptions: Indv. $150

Notary Bulletin   *Association*

Publishing Co: National Notary Association, 8236 Remmet Ave, Canoga Park, CA 91309-7184;
Title Tel # (818) 713-4000 Title Fax # (818) 713-9061
Personnel: Publisher-Milton Valera, Editor-Charles Faerber, Adv. Dir.-Gaia Winter
Editorial Description: Reviews notary-related legislation, provides forum for readers and others to comment on notarial issues, profiles notary laws in the various states.
General Info: (Formerly Notary Viewpoint/State Notary Bulletin), Yr. Est. 1972, Bi-monthly, Trim Size-8½ x 11, Offset press, 16 pages, 2 Color, Newsprint
Subscriptions: Indv. $29, $5/copy
Circulation: (100% controlled), Total-115,000

Nova Scotia Current Law   *Association*

Publishing Co: Nova Scotia Barrister's Society, 1645 Granville Street, Suite 1101, Halifax, NS B3J 1X3 Canada; Title Tel # (902) 422-1491 Title Fax # (902) 429-4869
Personnel: Editor-Helen MacDonnell, Circ. Mgr.-Michele Pittman
Editorial Description: Cumulative index to decisions of Nova Scotia Courts.
General Info: Monthly, Trim Size-8½ x 11, 14 pages, No Color, Looseleaf
Subscriptions: Can. $70
Circulation: Total-115

Nova Scotia Reports

Publishing Co: Maritime Law Book Co., Box 302, Fredericton, NB E3B 4Y9 Canada
Tel # (506) 453-9921; Title Tel # (902) 667-3889
General Info: Yr. Est. 1970, Ind/Abs/Online: QL Systems Ltd.

Nuclear Law Bulletin

Publishing Co: Organization for Economic Cooperation & Development, 2001 L St NW Ste 650, Washington, DC 20036-4910; Title Tel # (202) 785-6323 Title Fax # (202) 785-0350
Editorial Description: Legislative activities, case law, and administrative decisions of governments and international organizations.
General Info: Yr. Est. 1968, Semi-annually, Trim Size-7⅞ x 10⅝, Offset press, 80 pages, ISSN: 0304-341X, No Color
Subscriptions: Indv. $58

Nuclear Regulation Reports
See: NUCLEAR ENERGY

Nursing Home Law Letter
See: SENIOR CITIZENS

Nursing Home Regulations
See: HOSPITALS & NURSING HOMES

OSHA Guide for Health Care Facilities
See: HOSPITALS & NURSING HOMES

Obscenity Law Bulletin
See: CIVIL RIGHTS

Obtaining IRS Private Letter Rulings: A Manual of Forms & Procedures from Touche Ross & Co   *Business*

Publishing Co: Oceana Publications, Inc., 75 Main St, Dobbs Ferry, NY 10522-1601
Tel # (914) 693-8100; Title Tel # (914) 693-1320 Title Fax # (914) 693-0402
Personnel: Editor-G. Padwe, Production Mgr.-Mike Wortzman, Mktg. Dir.-John Downey
General Info: Yr. Est. 1984, Irregular, Trim Size-7 x 10, Looseleaf
Subscriptions: Indv. $150

Occupational Health and Safety Law
See: SAFETY

Occupational Safety & Health Reporter
See: SAFETY

Occupational Safety and Health Act
See: SAFETY

Oceana's Law Library Newsletter   *Business*

Publishing Co: Oceana Publications, Inc., 75 Main St, Dobbs Ferry, NY 10522-1601
Tel # (914) 693-8100; Title Tel # (914) 693-1733 Title Fax # (914) 693-0402
Personnel: Editor-Leigh Damkohier, Mktg. Dir.-John Downey
Editorial Description: About Oceana's pubs., sponsored events, its authors, editors, & employees.
General Info: Yr. Est. 1960, Monthly, Offset press, 4 pages, No Color, Newsprint

Ohio Attorney General Opinions

Publishing Co: Banks-Baldwin Law Publishing Co., PO Box 318063, Cleveland, OH 44131-8063;
Title Tel # (216) 721-7373 Title Fax # (216) 721-8055
Personnel: Publisher-P.J. Lucier, Production Mgr.-Virginia Stucko, Promotion Dir.-George Hallaman
Editorial Description: Published in cooperation with the Office of the Attorney General, with full text of opinions.
General Info: Yr. Est. 1963, Quarterly, Trim Size-7½ x 10, Web press, 160 pages, ISSN: 0748-6170, No Color, Matte, Saddle-stitched, Looseleaf
Subscriptions: Indv. $95
Acquistions: Publication Bought, Publication Sold

Ohio Corporation Law with
Federal Tax Analysis   *Business*

Publishing Co: Matthew Bender & Co., 11 Penn Plaza, New York, NY 10001-2006
Fax # (212) 244-3188; Title Tel # (212) 967-7707
Personnel: Editor-M. Tenner
Editorial Description: For Ohio small business planners, provides step-by-step guidance on how to proceed from start-up through sale or liquidation of a business.
General Info: Yr. Est. 1961, Annually, Looseleaf
Subscriptions: $100/copy

Ohio Criminal Code

Publishing Co: Gould Publications, Inc, 1333 N US Highway 17-92, Longwood, FL 32750-3724
Tel # (407) 695-9500 Fax # (407) 695-2906; Title Tel # (607) 724-3000
Editorial Description: Criminal laws, state of Ohio, not annotated.
General Info: Yr. Est. 1975, Annually, Trim Size-5$\frac{1}{2}$ x 8$\frac{1}{2}$, Sheetfed press, 700 pages, No Color, Looseleaf
Subscriptions: Indv. $11, $18/copy

Ohio Criminal Law & Motor
Vehicle Handbook

Publishing Co: Gould Publications, Inc, 1333 N US Highway 17-92, Longwood, FL 32750-3724
Tel # (407) 695-9500 Fax # (407) 695-2906; Title Tel # (607) 724-3000
Editorial Description: A complete, accurate, and up-to-date presentations of the Ohio Criminal Laws.
General Info: Annually, 1,290 pages, Looseleaf
Subscriptions: $23/copy

Ohio District Court Review

Publishing Co: Anadem, Inc., 3620 N High St Ste 310, Columbus, OH 43214-3643;
Title Tel # (614) 262-2539
Personnel: Publisher-Will Kuhlmann, Editor-Mike Cheadle, Circ. Mgr.-Julie Hawkins, Production Mgr.-Eva Gildee, Promotion Dir.-Faith Reidenbach
Editorial Description: Digests unreported Ohio district court decisions, notable reported district court decisions, & selected 6th circuit decisions.
General Info: Yr. Est. 1980, Monthly, ISSN: 0274-7294
Subscriptions: Indv. $225

Ohio Employment Law
Letter   *Business*

Publishing Co: M. Lee Smith Publishers & Printers ,LCC, P.O. Box 198867, 162 Fourth Avenue North, Nashville, TN 37219-8867; Title Tel # (615) 242-7395 Title Fax # (615) 256-6601
Personnel: Publisher-M Lee Smith, Editor-Dean Denlinger, Circ. Mgr.-Cathy Bradford, Mktg. Dir.-David Yates
Editorial Description: Review of employment law developments that affect Ohio employers.
General Info: Yr. Est. 1990, Monthly, Trim Size-8$\frac{1}{2}$ x 11, 8 pages, ISSN: 1046-9206, 2 Color
Subscriptions: Indv. $97
List Rental: Actives: $75/M
Printing Co: M. Lee Smith Publishers & Printers ,LLC, PO Box 198867, 162 Fourth Avenue, Nashville, TN 37219-8867 Tel # (615) 242-7395, Fax # (615) 256-6601

Ohio Environmental Law
Letter   *Business*

Publishing Co: M. Lee Smith Publishers & Printers ,LCC, P.O. Box 198867, 162 Fourth Avenue North, Nashville, TN 37219-8867; Title Tel # (615) 242-7395 Title Fax # (615) 256-6601
Personnel: Publisher-M Lee Smith, Editor-Martin Seltzer, Circ. Mgr.-Cathy Bradford, Mktg. Dir.-Dave Yates
Editorial Description: Review environmental law developments that affect Ohio companies.
General Info: Yr. Est. 1990, Monthly, Trim Size-8$\frac{1}{2}$ x 11, 8 pages, ISSN: 1052-4355, 2 Color
Subscriptions: Indv. $117
List Rental: Rents Lists
Printing Co: M. Lee Smith Publishers & Printers ,LLC, PO Box 198867, 162 Fourth Avenue, Nashville, TN 37219-8867 Tel # (615) 242-7395, Fax # (615) 256-6601

Ohio Forms of Pleading
and Practice   *Business*

Publishing Co: Matthew Bender & Co., 11 Penn Plaza, New York, NY 10001-2006
Fax # (212) 244-3188; Title Tel # (212) 967-7707
Personnel: Editor-B. Chase
Editorial Description: Contains every form needed for all aspects of pleading and practice, with total coverage on the Civil Rules, Appellate Procedure, Probate Practice, selected Special Proceedings, Criminal and Juvenile rules and the Rules of Evidence.
General Info: Yr. Est. 1970, Irregular, Looseleaf
Subscriptions: $885/copy

Ohio Forms of Pleading
and Practice Pamphlet
Edition: Probate   *Business*

Publishing Co: Matthew Bender & Co., 11 Penn Plaza, New York, NY 10001-2006
Fax # (212) 244-3188; Title Tel # (212) 967-7707
General Info: Annually, Looseleaf
Subscriptions: $700/copy

Ohio Forms of Pleading
and Practice Pamphlet
Editions: Criminal Law   *Business*

Publishing Co: Matthew Bender & Co., 11 Penn Plaza, New York, NY 10001-2006
Fax # (212) 244-3188; Title Tel # (212) 967-7707
General Info: Annually, Looseleaf
Subscriptions: $700/copy

Ohio Forms of Pleading
and Practice Pamphlet:
Rules   *Business*

Publishing Co: Matthew Bender & Co., 11 Penn Plaza, New York, NY 10001-2006
Fax # (212) 244-3188; Title Tel # (212) 967-7707
General Info: Annually, Looseleaf
Subscriptions: $670/copy

Ohio Health Law Update   *Business*

Publishing Co: M. Lee Smith Publishers & Printers ,LCC, P.O. Box 198867, 162 Fourth Avenue North, Nashville, TN 37219-8867 Tel # (615) 242-7395 Fax # (615) 256-6601
Personnel: Publisher-M Lee Smith, Editor-John Latsko, Circ. Mgr.-Cathy Bradford, Mktg. Dir.-Dave Yates
Editorial Description: Covers NY and federal health law developments. Published for DeForest & Duer.
General Info: Yr. Est. 1994, Monthly, Trim Size-8$\frac{1}{2}$ x 11, 8 pages, ISSN: 1075-9603, 2 Color
Subscriptions: Indv. $177
Printing Co: M. Lee Smith Publishers & Printers ,LLC, PO Box 198867, 162 Fourth Avenue, Nashville, TN 37219-8867 Tel # (615) 242-7395, Fax # (615) 256-6601

Ohio Monthly Record

Publishing Co: Banks-Baldwin Law Publishing Co., PO Box 318063, Cleveland, OH 44131-8063;
Title Tel # (216) 721-7373 Title Fax # (216) 721-8055
Personnel: Publisher-P.J. Lucier, Promotion Dir.-George Hallaman
Editorial Description: A monthly service, containing the full text of new administrative agency rules, with research aids including notes to recent Ohio & Federal court decisions & agency opinions.
General Info: Yr. Est. 1977, Monthly, ISSN: 0163-0008, Looseleaf
Subscriptions: Indv. $310

Ohio Motor Vehicle Laws

Publishing Co: Gould Publications, Inc, 1333 N US Highway 17-92, Longwood, FL 32750-3724
Tel # (407) 695-9500 Fax # (407) 695-2906; Title Tel # (607) 724-3000
General Info: Annually, Trim Size-5$\frac{1}{2}$ x 8$\frac{1}{2}$, Sheetfed press, 480 pages, No Color, Looseleaf
Subscriptions: $18/copy

Ohio Transaction Guide-
Legal Forms   *Business*

Publishing Co: Matthew Bender & Co., 11 Penn Plaza, New York, NY 10001-2006
Fax # (212) 244-3188; Title Tel # (212) 967-7707
Personnel: Editor-S. Schiff
Editorial Description: A range of transactions, including business entities, wills, trusts, commercial, real estate, personal and family transactions, and marital settlement agreements.
General Info: Yr. Est. 1975, Irregular, Looseleaf
Subscriptions: $975/copy

Oil and Gas Law
See: PETROLEUM & NATURAL GAS

Oil and Gas Reporter
See: PETROLEUM & NATURAL GAS

Oil Spill Law Information Service
See: ENVIRONMENT & ECOLOGY

Oil Spill Planning Manual, The
See: ENVIRONMENT & ECOLOGY

Oil Spill U.S. Law Report   *Business*

Publishing Co: Cutter Information Corp., 37 Broadway, Ste. 1, Arlington, MA 02174-5552
Tel # (617) 648-8700; Title Tel # (617) 641-5125 Title Fax # (617) 648-1950
Personnel: Publisher-Karen Coburn, Editor-Amy Stolls, Circ. Mgr.-Dennis Crowley
Editorial Description: Covering implementation of the Oil Pollution Act of 1990 as well as activity regarding oil pollution legislatilon and regulations in individual U.S. status.
General Info: (Formerly Oil Spill Litigation News), Yr. Est. 1991, Quarterly, Trim Size-8$\frac{1}{2}$ x 11, 14 pages, ISSN: 1055-9175, Ind/Abs/Online: NewsNet, Predacists, Looseleaf
Subscriptions: Indv. $997, Can. $997, For. $1,250, $33/copy
Printing Co: Benjamin Franklin Smith Printers, 320 Stuart St, Boston, MA 02116-5242
Tel # (617) 426-1160

Oklahoma Employment
Law Letter   *Business*

Publishing Co: M. Lee Smith Publishers & Printers ,LCC, P.O. Box 198867, 162 Fourth Avenue North, Nashville, TN 37219-8867; Title Tel # (615) 242-7395 Title Fax # (615) 256-6601
Personnel: Publisher-M Lee Smith, Editor-Charles Plumb, Circ. Mgr.-Cathy Bradford, Mktg. Dir.-Dave Yates
Editorial Description: Review of employment law developments that affect Oklahoma employers.
General Info: Yr. Est. 1993, Monthly, Trim Size-8½ x 11, 8 pages, ISSN: 1066-1123, 2 Color
Subscriptions: Indv. $97
List Rental: Rents Lists
Printing Co: M. Lee Smith Publishers & Printers ,LLC, PO Box 198867, 162 Fourth Avenue, Nashville, TN 37219-8867 Tel # (615) 242-7395, Fax # (615) 256-6601

On Watch   *Association*

Publishing Co: Fleet Reserve Association, 125 N West St, Alexandria, VA 22314-2754; Title Tel # (703) 683-1400 Title Fax # (703) 549-6610
General Info: Bi-monthly, 8 pages, 2 Color, Matte, Saddle-stitched
Subscriptions: Inst. $17, Free
Circulation: Readership-160,000

Ontario Appeal Cases

Publishing Co: Maritime Law Book Co., Box 302, Fredericton, NB E3B 4Y9 Canada; Title Tel # (506) 453-9921
General Info: Yr. Est. 1984, Ind/Abs/Online: QL Systems Ltd., Looseleaf

Ontario Corporations Law
Guide   *Business, Association*

Publishing Co: CCH Canadian Ltd., 6 Garamond Ct., North York, ON M3C 1Z5 Canada Fax # (416) 444-8011 Parent Co.-CCH, Inc., Riverwoods; Title Tel # (416) 441-2992 Title Fax # (416) 444-9011
Personnel: Editor-Azza Gorieb
Editorial Description: Coverage on Ontario Business Corporations Act, & regulations, forms & precedents, commentary & text of law on special corporations under the Corporations Act.
General Info: Yr. Est. 1945, Monthly, Trim Size-6 x 9, Web press, No Color, Looseleaf
Subscriptions: Can. $405

Ontario Family Law
Reporter   *Business*

Publishing Co: Butterworths, 75 Clegg Rd., Markham, ON L6G 1A1 Canada Tel # (905) 479-2665 Fax # (905) 479-2826; Title Tel # (416) 479-2665
Personnel: Editor-Malcolm Kronby, Circ. Mgr.-Jeffery Wilson
Editorial Description: Covers unreported family law cases.
General Info: Yr. Est. 1987, Monthly, ISSN: 0835-636X, 2 Color, Newsprint
Subscriptions: Indv. $190
Circulation: Total-400

Ontario Real Estate Law Guide
See: REAL ESTATE

Ontario Tax Reports
See: TAXES

Open House
See: REAL ESTATE

Opinions of the Attorney General of California
See: LAW ENFORCEMENT & PENOLOGY

Opinions: Committees on
Professional Ethics   *Business*

Publishing Co: Oceana Publications, Inc., 75 Main St, Dobbs Ferry, NY 10522-1601 Tel # (914) 693-8100; Title Tel # (914) 693-1320 Title Fax # (914) 693-0402
Personnel: Editor-E. Wypyski, Production Mgr.-Mike Wortzman, Mktg. Dir.-John Downey
General Info: Yr. Est. 1980, Irregular, Trim Size-7 x 10, Looseleaf
Subscriptions: Indv. $450

Oregon Employment Law
Letter   *Business*

Publishing Co: M. Lee Smith Publishers & Printers ,LCC, P.O. Box 198867, 162 Fourth Avenue North, Nashville, TN 37219-8867 Tel # (615) 242-7395 Fax # (615) 256-6601
Personnel: Publisher-M. Lee Smith, Editor-Calvin Keith, Circ. Mgr.-Cathy Bradford, Mktg. Dir.-Dave Yates
Editorial Description: Covers employment law issues and regulations in Oregon.
General Info: Yr. Est. 1994, Monthly, Trim Size-8½ x 11, 8 pages, ISSN: 1077-2081, 2 Color
Subscriptions: Indv. $97
List Rental: Rents Lists
Printing Co: M. Lee Smith Publishers & Printers ,LLC, PO Box 198867, 162 Fourth Avenue, Nashville, TN 37219-8867 Tel # (615) 242-7395, Fax # (615) 256-6601

Organizing Corporate and Other Business Enterprises
See: BUSINESS & INDUSTRY

Ottawa Letter   *Business*

Publishing Co: CCH Canadian Ltd., 6 Garamond Ct., North York, ON M3C 1Z5 Canada Fax # (416) 444-8011 Parent Co.-CCH, Inc., Riverwoods; Title Tel # (416) 441-2992 Title Fax # (416) 444-9011
Personnel: Editor-Andrew Pollock
Editorial Description: News and commentary on Federal government items of interest to businessmen plus progress of bills through Parliament.
General Info: (Formerly View From Ottawa), Weekly, Trim Size-8½ x 11, Web press, 8 pages, ISSN: 0702-8210, No Color
Subscriptions: Can. $370

Outlook/State Capitals, The
See: GOVERNMENT

P-H Federal Taxes
See: TAXES

PBC Immigration Briefs   *Business, Consumer*

Publishing Co: Publishing & Business Consultants, 101 W. 64th St. Unit #3, Inglewood, CA 90302-1255 Tel # (213) 732-3477 Fax # (213) 732-3477
General Info: Quarterly, ISSN: 1059-2008
Advertising: Inquire for rates.

PIREPS
See: AERONAUTICS/ASTRONAUTICS

PLEA

Publishing Co: Public Legal Education Assn. of Saskatchewan, 220 3rd Ave. South, Rm. 210, Saskatoon, SK S7K 1M1 Canada
Personnel: Editor-Richard McCormick
General Info: Yr. Est. 1980, Quarterly
Circulation: Total-1,200

PLL Perspectives
See: LIBRARY

PTC Newsletter
See: PATENTS/COPYRIGHTS/TRADE MARKS

Pacific Stock Exchange Guide
See: BANKING & FINANCE

Pan Hellenic Society Inventors of Greece in U.S.A.
Newsletter
See: PATENTS/COPYRIGHTS/TRADE MARKS

Partnership Tax Planning & Practice
See: TAXES

Patent Law Perspectives
See: PATENTS/COPYRIGHTS/TRADE MARKS

Patent Litigation: Procedure and Tactics
See: PATENTS/COPYRIGHTS/TRADE MARKS

Patent Office Rules and Practice
See: PATENTS/COPYRIGHTS/TRADE MARKS

Patent Trends
See: PATENTS/COPYRIGHTS/TRADE MARKS

Patient Care Law
See: HOSPITALS & NURSING HOMES

Patients' Rights Reporter   *Consumer*

Publishing Co: Cox Pubs., PO Box 20316, Billings, MT 59104-0316 Tel # (406) 256-8822
Personnel: Publisher, Editor-Meridith Cox
Editorial Description: Keeps patients, their families & those providing pastoral care in health care settings, aware of legislative & court decisions having an effect on patients' rights. Social Workers also use this information to explain new patient care issues.
General Info: (Formerly Patients Rights in California), Yr. Est. 1983, Monthly, Sheetfed press, 4 pages, ISSN: 0736-2544, 2 Color
Subscriptions: Indv. $60
Circulation: Total-255

Patriots for Liberty
See: TAXES

Pennsylvania Crimes Code

Publishing Co: Gould Publications, Inc, 1333 N US Highway 17-92, Longwood, FL 32750-3724 Tel # (407) 695-9500 Fax # (407) 695-2906; Title Tel # (607) 724-3000
Editorial Description: Title 18 of Pennsylvania Consolidated Statutes. Unannotated plus rules of criminal procedure & drug laws.
General Info: (Formerly Crime Code of Pennsylvania), Yr. Est. 1970, Annually, Trim Size-5½ x 8½, Sheetfed press, 430 pages, No Color, Coated, Looseleaf
Subscriptions: Indv. $9, $22/copy

Pennsylvania Criminal Law
Digest

Publishing Co: Gould Publications, Inc, 1333 N US Highway 17-92, Longwood, FL 32750-3724
Tel # (407) 695-9500 Fax # (407) 695-2906; Title Tel # (607) 724-3000
Editorial Description: Book. Supplemented annually at additional cost. Contains the text of certain Pennsylvania laws and text material pertaining to Criminal Laws.
General Info: Annually, Trim Size-5½ x 8½, Sheetfed press, 430 pages, No Color, Looseleaf
Subscriptions: Indv. $7, $22/copy

Pennsylvania Criminal Law
and Practice   *Business*

Publishing Co: Matthew Bender & Co., 11 Penn Plaza, New York, NY 10001-2006
Tel # (212) 967-7707 Fax # (212) 244-3188
Editorial Description: A comprehensive treatise on the substantive and procedural aspects of Pennsylvania criminal practice.
General Info: Yr. Est. 1990, Irregular, Looseleaf

Pennsylvania Discovery &
Evidence Reporter   *Business, Consumer*

Publishing Co: LRP Publications, 747 Dresher Rd., P.O. Box 980, Horsham, PA 19044-0980
Tel # (215) 784-0910 Fax # (215) 784-0317
Personnel: Publisher-Ken Kahn, Editor-Michael Sachs
Editorial Description: Latest word on discovery and evidence from Pennsylvania Supreme, Superior, Commonwealth, and trial courts, US Court of Appeals, and US District Courts.
General Info: Monthly, Looseleaf
Subscriptions: Indv. $195

Pennsylvania Divorce &
Domestic Relations
Reporter   *Business, Consumer*

Publishing Co: LRP Publications, 747 Dresher Rd., P.O. Box 980, Horsham, PA 19044-0980
Tel # (215) 784-0910 Fax # (215) 784-0317
Personnel: Publisher-Kenneth Kahn, Editor-Michael Sachs
Editorial Description: Presents latest developments in Pennsylvania family law. Includes full text of Appellate Court decisions; highlights section; statute and regulation tracker and a topical index.
General Info: Bi-monthly, Looseleaf
Subscriptions: Indv. $495

Pennsylvania
Employment Law Letter   *Business*

Publishing Co: M. Lee Smith Publishers & Printers ,LCC, P.O. Box 198867, 162 Fourth Avenue North, Nashville, TN 37219-8867; Title Tel # (615) 242-7395 Title Fax # (615) 256-6601
Personnel: Publisher-M Lee Smith, Editor-Jacques Wood, Circ. Mgr.-Cathy Bradford, Mktg. Dir.-Dave Yates
Editorial Description: Review of employment law developments that affect Pennsylvania employers.
General Info: Yr. Est. 1990, Monthly, Trim Size-8½ x 11, 8 pages, ISSN: 1052-4363, 2 Color
Subscriptions: Indv. $97
List Rental: Rents Lists
Printing Co: M. Lee Smith Publishers & Printers ,LLC, PO Box 198867, 162 Fourth Avenue, Nashville, TN 37219-8867 Tel # (615) 242-7395, Fax # (615) 256-6601

Pennsylvania
Environmental
Compliance Update   *Business*

Publishing Co: M. Lee Smith Publishers & Printers ,LCC, P.O. Box 198867, 162 Fourth Avenue North, Nashville, TN 37219-8867 Tel # (615) 242-7395 Fax # (615) 256-6601
Personnel: Publisher-M Lee Smith, Editor-George Miller, Circ. Mgr.-Cathy Bradford, Mktg. Dir.-Dave Yates
Editorial Description: State environmental law information.
General Info: Yr. Est. 1994, Monthly, Trim Size-8½ x 11, 8 pages, ISSN: 1072-9143, 2 Color
Subscriptions: Indv. $117

Pennsylvania Injuries &
Damages Reporter   *Business, Consumer*

Publishing Co: LRP Publications, 747 Dresher Rd., P.O. Box 980, Horsham, PA 19044-0980
Tel # (215) 784-0910 Fax # (215) 784-0317
Personnel: Publisher-Ken Kahn, Editor-Michael Sachs
Editorial Description: Latest decisions on medical malpractice, motor vehicle law, workers compensation and product liability handed down by Pennsylvania's Supreme, Superior, Commonwealth, and trial courts as well as the Third Circuit Federal court.
General Info: Bi-monthly, Looseleaf
Subscriptions: Indv. $225

Pennsylvania Judiciary &
Judicial Proceedures

Publishing Co: Gould Publications, Inc, 1333 N US Highway 17-92, Longwood, FL 32750-3724
Tel # (407) 695-9500 Fax # (407) 695-2906; Title Tel # (607) 724-3000
Editorial Description: A concise presentation of Title 42 of the Pennsylvania Consolidated Statutes, including proceedings in all judicial actions.
General Info: Annually, 720 pages, Looseleaf
Subscriptions: $22/copy

Pennsylvania LAWCAST

Publishing Co: Vox Juris, Inc., P.O. Box 389, Pennington, NJ 08534; Title Tel # (609) 737-6543 Title Fax # (609) 737-3860
Personnel: Circ. Mgr.-Karen E. Anderson, Mktg. Mgr.-Kathy W. Gould
Editorial Description: The legal newscast on audio cassette for Pennsylvania lawyers.
General Info: Yr. Est. 1994, Semi-monthly

Pennsylvania Law
Enforcement Handbook

Publishing Co: Gould Publications, Inc, 1333 N US Highway 17-92, Longwood, FL 32750-3724
Tel # (407) 695-9500 Fax # (407) 695-2906; Title Tel # (607) 724-3000
Editorial Description: This handbook dissects and analyzes the Court decisions through a distinctive question and answer format.
General Info: Annually, 740 pages, ISSN: 0-87526-3, Looseleaf
Subscriptions: $45/copy

Pennsylvania Orphan's
Court Practice   *Business*

Publishing Co: Matthew Bender & Co., 11 Penn Plaza, New York, NY 10001-2006
Fax # (212) 244-3188; Title Tel # (212) 967-7707
Editorial Description: Guide on practice and procedure.
General Info: Yr. Est. 1961, Irregular, Looseleaf
Subscriptions: $400/copy

Pennsylvania Police Criminal Law Bulletin
See: LAW ENFORCEMENT & PENOLOGY

Pennsylvania Rules of Civil
Procedure

Publishing Co: Gould Publications, Inc, 1333 N US Highway 17-92, Longwood, FL 32750-3724
Tel # (407) 695-9500 Fax # (407) 695-2906; Title Tel # (607) 724-3000
General Info: Annually, Trim Size-5½ x 8½, 500 pages, No Color, Looseleaf
Subscriptions: $19/copy

Pennsylvania School Boards Association, Information Legislative Service
See: SCHOOL ADMINISTRATION

Pennsylvania Transaction
Guide-Legal Forms   *Business*

Publishing Co: Matthew Bender & Co., 11 Penn Plaza, New York, NY 10001-2006
Fax # (212) 244-3188; Title Tel # (212) 967-7707
Personnel: Editor-S. Schiff
Editorial Description: Comprehensive guidance on wills and trusts, business, commercial, real estate and personal transactions.
General Info: Yr. Est. 1974, Irregular, Looseleaf
Subscriptions: $960/copy

Pennsylvania Vehicles Law

Publishing Co: Gould Publications, Inc, 1333 N US Highway 17-92, Longwood, FL 32750-3724
Tel # (407) 695-9500 Fax # (407) 695-2906; Title Tel # (607) 724-3000
Editorial Description: A concise presentation of Title 75 of the Pennsylvania Consolidated Statutes including an addenda, Title 67, chapter 75, driver's license examination, and a comprehensive index.
General Info: Annually, 420 pages, Looseleaf
Subscriptions: $22/copy

Pennsylvania Workers'
Compensation Law
Reporter   *Business, Consumer*

Publishing Co: LRP Publications, 747 Dresher Rd., P.O. Box 980, Horsham, PA 19044-0980
Tel # (215) 784-0910 Fax # (215) 784-0317
Personnel: Publisher-Kenneth F. Kahn, Editor-Joanne Fiore, Production Mgr.-Kathleen P. Neely, Mktg. Dir.-Jana Shellington, Promotion Dir.-Gary Ragin
Editorial Description: The most comprehensive source available for workers' compensation and related law issued by the state agencies and courts.
General Info: Bi-weekly
Subscriptions: Indv. $605

Pension Fund Litigation
Reporter   *Business*

Publishing Co: Andrews Publications, Inc., 1646 West Chester Pike, PO Box 1000, Westtown, PA 19395 Tel # (610) 399-6600 Fax # (610) 399-6610
Personnel: Publisher-John E. Backe, Editor-Chris Evans, Mktg. Dir.-Andrew Katz
General Info: Yr. Est. 1990, Bi-monthly, Trim Size-8½ x 11, Offset press, ISSN: 1052-9640, No Color
Subscriptions: Indv. $700, $33/copy
Advertising: Inquire for rates.
List Rental: Actives: $125/M

Perfect Lawyer   *Business*

Publishing Co: Shepard's/McGraw-Hill, Inc., 555 Middle Creek Pky, Colorado Springs, CO 80921-3622; Title Tel # (719) 488-3000 Title Fax # (719) 481-7448
Personnel: Editor-Robert Wilkins, Production Mgr.-Cheryl Everitt, Adv. Dir.-Peggy Ives, Art Dir.-Leigh Vidakovich
Editorial Description: Assists lawyers in word processing legal documents.
General Info: Yr. Est. 1990, Monthly
Subscriptions: Indv. $110
List Rental: List Management Co.: The Lake Group, 411 Theodore Freund Ave., Rye, NY 10580-1497 Tel # (914) 925-2400, Fax # (914) 925-2499, Actives: 40,212, $130/M

Personal Injury-Actions, Defenses, Damages

Publishing Co: Matthew Bender & Co., 11 Penn Plaza, New York, NY 10001-2006
Fax # (212) 244-3188; Title Tel # (212) 967-7707
Personnel: Editor-L. Bogaty
Editorial Description: The largest and most comprehensive case law compendium in legal literature provides encyclopedic treatment of the personal injury law of every American jurisdiction.
General Info: Yr. Est. 1957, Irregular, Looseleaf
Subscriptions: $1,050/copy

Personal Injury Defense Reporter   *Business*

Publishing Co: Matthew Bender & Co., 11 Penn Plaza, New York, NY 10001-2006
Tel # (212) 967-7707 Fax # (212) 244-3188
Editorial Description: Articles focusing on both substantive law issues & practical matters such as strategy & tactics written for the personal injury defense bar.
General Info: Yr. Est. 1985, Monthly, Looseleaf

Personal Injury Defense Techniques   *Business*

Publishing Co: Matthew Bender & Co., 11 Penn Plaza, New York, NY 10001-2006
Tel # (212) 967-7707 Fax # (212) 244-3188
Personnel: Editor in Chief-Mark A. Dombroff
Editorial Description: Expert discussion of a wide range of the substantive & practical legal problems you face daily, along with suggestions for the best ways to remedy them. Written by prominent members of the personal injury defense bar.
General Info: Yr. Est. 1987, Irregular, Looseleaf

Personal Injury Newsletter   *Business*

Publishing Co: Matthew Bender & Co., 11 Penn Plaza, New York, NY 10001-2006
Fax # (212) 244-3188; Title Tel # (212) 967-7707
Personnel: Publisher-Diana Exelrod, Editor-Lewis Bogaty
Editorial Description: Bi-weekly compilation of news and analysis of outstanding recent personal injury cases, with commentary in the significance of court decisions.
General Info: Yr. Est. 1958, Bi-weekly
Subscriptions: Indv. $150
Circulation: Total-2,300

Personnel Law Update, California Edition   *Business*

Publishing Co: Council on Education in Management, 321 Lennon Lane, Walnut Creek, CA 94598; Title Tel # (510) 944-9444 Title Fax # (510) 988-1888
Editorial Description: Employment law and human resources management.
General Info: Yr. Est. 1985, Monthly
Subscriptions: Indv. $119

Personnel Law Update, National Editon   *Business*

Publishing Co: Council on Education in Management, 321 Lennon Lane, Walnut Creek, CA 94598; Title Tel # (510) 944-9444 Title Fax # (510) 988-1888
Editorial Description: Employment law and human resources management.
General Info: Yr. Est. 1986, Monthly
Subscriptions: Indv. $119

Personnel Law Update, Texas Edition   *Business*

Publishing Co: Council on Education in Management, 321 Lennon Lane, Walnut Creek, CA 94598; Title Tel # (510) 944-9444 Title Fax # (510) 988-1888
Editorial Description: Employment law and human resources management.
General Info: Yr. Est. 1988, Monthly
Subscriptions: Indv. $119

Perspective   *Business, Association*

Publishing Co: Magna Publications, Inc., 611 N Sherman Ave, Madison, WI 53704-4410; Title Tel # (608) 246-3580 Title Fax # (608) 246-3597
Personnel: Publisher-Richard C. Perkins, Editor-Dennis Black, Editorial Dir.-Mary Lou Santovec, Circ. Mgr.-Tom Crawford, Art Dir.-Kayla White, Mktg. Dir.-Lisa Collins, Promotion Dir.-Karen Oshman
Editorial Description: The campus legal monthly.
General Info: Yr. Est. 1986, Monthly, Trim Size-8½ x 11, Offset press, 8 pages, ISSN: 0888-9732, 2 Color
Subscriptions: Indv. $168, $11/copy
Circulation: Total-1,400
Advertising: Accepts Inserts.
List Rental: Rents Lists

Perspectives on the Construction Industry
See: CONSTRUCTION & BUILDING

Perspectives on Law Firm Management
See: MANAGEMENT

Perspectives on Litigation Support Services   *Business*

Publishing Co: Newkirk Products, Inc., 15 Corporate Cir, Albany, NY 12203-5154
Tel # (518) 452-1000
Editorial Description: Custom publication designed for distribution to clients by legal professionals.
General Info: Quarterly, Trim Size-8½ x 11, 4 pages, 2 Color

Pertinent Commercial Statutes

Publishing Co: Gould Publications, Inc, 1333 N US Highway 17-92, Longwood, FL 32750-3724
Tel # (407) 695-9500 Fax # (407) 695-2906; Title Tel # (607) 724-3000
Editorial Description: Selected unannotated pertinent commercial statutes.
General Info: Annually, Trim Size-5½ x 8½, 450 pages, No Color, Looseleaf
Subscriptions: $15/copy

Petroleum Legislation   *Business*

Publishing Co: Barrows Co., Inc., 116 E 66th St, New York, NY 10021-6547; Title Tel # (212) 772-1199 Title Fax # (212) 288-7242
Personnel: Publisher, Editor-Gordon Barrows, Circ. Mgr.-L.M. Guerra, Production Mgr.-Kenneth Hussman, Adv. Dir., Art Dir.-Dominique Jeune, Promotion Dir.-D. Jeune
Editorial Description: Petroleum Legislation is designed to give an immediate overview of oil and gas regulation, with a summary and analysis by country. This is kept up to date by supplementary volumes. The initial purchase price includes the first year's supplementary service, plus all volumes published in the service to date of subscription.
General Info: Quarterly, Looseleaf
Subscriptions: Indv. $4,800

Petroleum Taxation/ Legislation Report   *Business*

Publishing Co: Barrows Co., Inc., 116 E 66th St, New York, NY 10021-6547; Title Tel # (212) 772-1199 Title Fax # (212) 288-7242
Personnel: Publisher, Editor-Gordon Barrows, Editor-Marta Guerra, Production Mgr.-Kenneth Hussman, Adv. Dir., Art Dir.-Dominique Jeune, Circ. Mgr.-L.M. Guerra
Editorial Description: Bimonthly review of changes in world oil and gas law/tax regulation by country. Includes annual volume at end of year summarizing information by country. Subscription includes all back volumes covering 1973 through present year, plus bi-monthly review.
General Info: (Formerly Petroleum Taxation Report), Yr. Est. 1957, Bi-monthly, Trim Size-8½ x 11, Offset press, 50 pages, No Color
Subscriptions: Indv. $1,500
Circulation: Total-6,000
Printing Co: Barrows Co. Wyoming, 700 Main St., Ralston, WY 82440 Tel # (307) 745-3759

Pharmaceutical Litigation Reporter

Publishing Co: Andrews Publications, Inc., 1646 West Chester Pike, PO Box 1000, Westtown, PA 19395; Title Tel # (610) 399-6600 Title Fax # (610) 399-6610
Personnel: Publisher-John E. Backe, Editor-Bob Sullivan, Mktg. Dir.-Andrew Katz
Editorial Description: Provides up-to-date information on developments in pharmaceutical cases around the country.
General Info: Yr. Est. 1985, Monthly, Trim Size-8½ x 11, Mimeo press, 70 pages, ISSN: 0887-7815, Ind/Abs/Online: NEWS NET
Subscriptions: Indv. $750, $71/copy
Advertising: Inquire for rates.
List Rental: Actives: 1,206, $110/M

Pharmacy Law Digest
See: DRUGS & PHARMACEUTICALS

Philadelphia Stock Exchange Guide
See: BANKING & FINANCE

Physician's Malpractice Advisor
See: MEDICINE

Placement Bulletin
See: EMPLOYMENT

Plan Administrators Compliance Manual
See: LABOR UNION

Planning & Conducting a Course on 'Managing Trials Effectively'   *Association*

Publishing Co: Natl. Judicial College, Univ. Of Nevada, Reno, NV 89557-0001 Tel # (702) 784-6747 Fax # (702) 784-4234
General Info: Yr. Est. 1994, Looseleaf
Subscriptions: Indv. $35, $35/copy

Police Civil Liability
See: CIVIL RIGHTS

Police Investigation
Handbook *Business*

Publishing Co: Matthew Bender & Co., 11 Penn Plaza, New York, NY 10001-2006
Tel # (212) 967-7707 Fax # (212) 244-3188
Editorial Description: This comprehensive guide give investigators the legal & technical background they need to solidify cases & save prosecutions.
General Info: Yr. Est. 1990, Irregular, Looseleaf

Police Science
Fundamentals

Publishing Co: Gould Publications, Inc, 1333 N US Highway 17-92, Longwood, FL 32750-3724
Tel # (407) 695-9500 Fax # (407) 695-2906; Title Tel # (607) 724-3000
Editorial Description: An indispensable tool in the study for law enforcement promotions examination.
General Info: Annually, 220 pages, Looseleaf
Subscriptions: $12/copy

Political Finance & Lobby Reporter
See: POLITICS

Pollution Law
See: ENVIRONMENT & ECOLOGY

Practical Guide to
Document Authentication *Business*

Publishing Co: Oceana Publications, Inc., 75 Main St, Dobbs Ferry, NY 10522-1601
Tel # (914) 693-8100; Title Tel # (914) 693-1320 Title Fax # (914) 693-0402
Personnel: Editor-John Sinnott, Production Mgr.-Mike Wortzman, Mktg. Dir.-John Downey
General Info: Yr. Est. 1993, Irregular, Trim Size-7 x 10, Looseleaf
Subscriptions: Indv. $165

Practical Issues of
Professional
Responsibility in the
Practice of Law *Association*

Publishing Co: Legal-Medical Studies, Inc., Box 8219, JFK Sta., Boston, MA 02114-0032;
Title Tel # (617) 742-7959
Editorial Description: Revised edition of practical ethical problems.
General Info: Yr. Est. 1985, Annually, Offset press, 300 pages, No Color, Looseleaf
Subscriptions: $150/copy

Practical Law Books Review
See: BOOKS & BOOK TRADE

Practice Before Federal
Magistrates *Business*

Publishing Co: Matthew Bender & Co., 11 Penn Plaza, New York, NY 10001-2006
Tel # (212) 967-7707 Fax # (212) 244-3188
Editorial Description: Prepared by the expert in the field, this publication details everything the federal practitioner needs to know when some or all of a case is being handled by a federal magistrate.
General Info: Yr. Est. 1984, Irregular, Looseleaf

Practicing Attorney's
Letter *Business*

Publishing Co: Research Institute of America, 90 5th Avenue, New York, NY 10011-7629
Tel # (212) 645-4800; Title Tel # (201) 767-5059
Editorial Description: Devoted to practical aspects of a practice.
General Info: Bi-weekly
Subscriptions: Indv. $179
List Rental: List Management Co.: WG & L List Management, 1 Penn Plz Fl 42, New York, NY 10119-0002 Tel # (212) 971-5000

Premises Liability Report *Business*

Publishing Co: Strafford Pubs., Inc., 590 Dutch Valley Rd., N.E., Postal Drawer 13729, Atlanta, GA 30324-0729; Title Tel # (404) 881-1141 Title Fax # (404) 881-0074
Personnel: Publisher-Richard M. Ossoff, Mng. Editor-Jennifer Vaughan, Production Ed.-C. Malone Tumlin, Circ. Mgr., Mktg. Mgr.-Marianne Mueller, Mktg. Mgr.-Maria Rawls Hill
Editorial Description: Monthly digest of important legal developments affecting the liability of property owners, managers, and users.
General Info: Yr. Est. 1990, 12x/yr., Trim Size-8½ x 11, 12 pages, ISSN: 1055-730X
Subscriptions: Indv. $187, Can. $217, For. $242, $15/copy
Acquistions: Publication Bought, Publication Sold
List Rental: Rents Lists

Preservation Law Reporter

Publishing Co: National Trust for Historic Preservation, 1785 Massachusetts Ave., NW, Washington, DC 20036-2117; Title Tel # (202) 673-4035
Personnel: Editor-Julia Miller, Circ. Mgr.-Kathleen Amatangelo, Promotion Dir.-Paul Edmondson
Editorial Description: Legal publication covering developments in historic preservation & related fields.
General Info: Yr. Est. 1982, Quarterly, Desktop press, 100 pages, No Color, Newsprint, Looseleaf
Subscriptions: Indv. $90, Inst. $90
Circulation: (ABC), Total-400
Printing Co: District Service, 5004 Jackson St, Hyattsville, MD 20781-1009 Tel # (301) 779-3040

Prevention and Prosecution
of Computer and High
Technology Crime *Business*

Publishing Co: Matthew Bender & Co., 11 Penn Plaza, New York, NY 10001-2006
Tel # (212) 967-7707 Fax # (212) 244-3188
Editorial Description: From improving internal corporate security to every aspect of handling a case, provides a sweeping study of law & practice in this growing field.
General Info: Yr. Est. 1988, Irregular, Looseleaf

Prevention at Work *Business*

Publishing Co: Workers' Compensation Board of BC, 6951 Westminster Hwy., Richmond, BC V7C 1C6 Canada; Title Tel # (604) 279-7572 Title Fax # (604) 279-7696
Personnel: Editor-K. Eccles
Editorial Description: Reports on significant policy and procedural changes at the Board and newsworthy compensation issues of interest to employers and workers in all industries, also focusing on health and safety issues.
General Info: (Formerly WCB News), Yr. Est. 1947, Quarterly, Trim Size-9 x 12, Offset press, 12 pages, ISSN: 0709-9428, 2 Color, Coated
Subscriptions: Free
Circulation: Total-26,000

Preview of U.S. Supreme
Court Cases

Publishing Co: Sponsor-Public Education Division, American Bar Association, 750 N. Lake Shore Dr., Chicago, IL 60611-4497 Tel # (312) 988-6115 Fax # (312) 988-6030; Title Tel # (312) 988-5522 Title Fax # (312) 988-5528
Personnel: Publisher-Charles White, Editor-Charles Williams
Editorial Description: Our mission is to explain every case going before the Supreme Court befor decisions are handed down. Indepth articles cover everything from analysis of facts, to the issues and background of the cases that are orally argued before the U.S. Supreme Court.
General Info: Yr. Est. 1964, 10x/yr., Trim Size-8½ x 11, 20 pages, ISSN: 0363-0048, Ind/Abs/Online: WESTLAW, LEXIS, No Color
Subscriptions: Indv. $120
Circulation: Total-3,500
List Rental: Rents Lists

Privacy & American Business
See: BUSINESS & INDUSTRY

Privacy Journal
See: PHILANTHROPY

Privacy Law and Practice *Business*

Publishing Co: Matthew Bender & Co., 11 Penn Plaza, New York, NY 10001-2006
Tel # (212) 967-7707 Fax # (212) 244-3188
Personnel: Editor in Chief-George B. Trubow
Editorial Description: Provides expert analysis of pertinent federal, state and constitutional law for a broad spectrum of privacy issues, combined with practical guidance and procedural considerations.
General Info: Yr. Est. 1987, Irregular, Looseleaf

Privacy Times

Publishing Co: Privacy Times, Inc., PO Box 21501, Washington, DC 20009-9501; Title Tel # (202) 829-3660
Personnel: Publisher, Editor-Evan Hendricks
Editorial Description: Privacy, freedom of information and information law.
General Info: Yr. Est. 1981, Bi-weekly
Subscriptions: Indv. $225, Inst. $250, Can. $250, For. $275

Private Education Law Report
See: EDUCATION

Private Investors Abroad
See: BANKING & FINANCE

Private Security Case Law Reporter
See: SECURITY & SURVEILLANCE

Proactive Risk Management
See: HOSPITALS & NURSING HOMES

Probate Practice Reporter

Publishing Co: Shepard's/McGraw-Hill, Inc., 555 Middle Creek Pky, Colorado Springs, CO 80921-3622; Title Tel # (719) 488-3000 Title Fax # (719) 481-7448
Personnel: Production Mgr.-Cheryl Everitt, Adv. Dir.-Peggy Ives, Art Dir.-Leigh Vidakovich
Editorial Description: Analysis of the most significant probate & estate cases from around the nation. Free binder & annual index included.
General Info: Yr. Est. 1989, Monthly
Subscriptions: Indv. $275
List Rental: List Management Co.: The Lake Group, 411 Theodore Freund Ave., Rye, NY 10580-1497 Tel # (914) 925-2400, Fax # (914) 925-2499, Actives: 40,212, $130/M

Product: H R Manager's Legal Reporter
See: MANAGEMENT

Product Liability Law & Strategy Newsletter

Publishing Co: Leader Publications, Inc., 345 Park Avenue South, New York, NY 10010 Parent Co.-New York Law Publishing Co., New York; Title Tel # (212) 545-6170 Title Fax # (212) 696-1848
Personnel: Publisher-Stuart M. Wise, Editor-Alberta Cook, Circ. Mgr.-Kerry Kyle, Mktg. Dir.-RoseAnn Morangelei
General Info: Yr. Est. 1982, Monthly, Trim Size-8½ x 11, Offset press, 8 pages, Color
Subscriptions: Indv. $195, $16/copy
Printing Co: Columbus Bookbinding, 1343 Belfast Ave, Columbus, OH 31904 Tel # (206) 323-9313, Fax # (206) 323-2987

Products Liability
See: CONSUMER INTERESTS

Products Liability: An International Manual of Practice *Business*

Publishing Co: Oceana Publications, Inc., 75 Main St, Dobbs Ferry, NY 10522-1601
Tel # (914) 693-8100; Title Tel # (914) 693-1320 Title Fax # (914) 693-0402
Personnel: Editor-W. Freedman, Production Mgr.-Mike Wortzman, Mktg. Dir.-John Downey
General Info: Yr. Est. 1987, Irregular, Trim Size-7 x 10, Looseleaf
Subscriptions: Indv. $250

Products Liability Reporter
See: CONSUMER INTERESTS

Professional Apartment Management
See: REAL ESTATE

Professional Corporation Advisor
See: BANKING & FINANCE

Professional Liability Reporter

Publishing Co: Shepard's/McGraw-Hill, Inc., 555 Middle Creek Pky, Colorado Springs, CO 80921-3622; Title Tel # (719) 488-3000 Title Fax # (719) 481-7448
Personnel: Editor in Chief-Mary Kaye LaRue, Editor-William Jordan, Production Mgr.-Cheryl Everitt, Adv. Dir.-Peggy Ives, Art Dir.-Leigh Vidakovich
Editorial Description: Reporting & analysis of legal developments in professional liability law.
General Info: Yr. Est. 1976, Monthly, 24 pages, ISSN: 0145-3505, No Color
Subscriptions: Indv. $330
List Rental: List Management Co.: The Lake Group, 411 Theodore Freund Ave., Rye, NY 10580-1497 Tel # (914) 925-2400, Fax # (914) 925-2499, Actives: 40,212, $130/M

Professional Liability Update

Publishing Co: American Medical Association, 515 N. State St., Chicago, IL 60610
Tel # (312) 464-4512 Fax # (312) 464-5834; Title Tel # (312) 645-5000
Editorial Description: Reports on state and federal legislative developments, medicolegal decisions, and related items of interest.
General Info: Bi-monthly
Subscriptions: Free

Promotional Test Questions

Publishing Co: Gould Publications, Inc, 1333 N US Highway 17-92, Longwood, FL 32750-3724
Tel # (407) 695-9500 Fax # (407) 695-2906; Title Tel # (607) 724-3000
Editorial Description: A practical, in-depth study guide consisting of qpproximately 2000 multiple choice.
General Info: Annually, 500 pages, Looseleaf
Subscriptions: $22/copy

Prop 65 Litigation Reporter *Business*

Publishing Co: American Environmental Institute, 45 Belden St., 3rd Fl., San Francisco, CA 94104-2808; Title Tel # (415) 544-0111 Title Fax # (415) 544-0112
Personnel: Publisher-Alejandro Levins, Editor-Lana Beckett, Product Mgr.-Drew Carpenter
Editorial Description: Contains Proposition 65 court documents, motions, pleadings and decisions.
General Info: Yr. Est. 1995, Monthly
Subscriptions: Indv. $995

Prop 65 News
See: ENVIRONMENT & ECOLOGY

Property Insurance Report *Business*

Publishing Co: Risk Communications, 33 Lindall St., Laguna Niguel, CA 92677-4738;
Title Tel # (714) 443-0330
Personnel: Publisher-Brian Sullivan
Editorial Description: For professionals in the property insurance industry.
General Info: Yr. Est. 1994, Bi-weekly
Subscriptions: Indv. $397

Prosecution and Defense of Criminal Conspiracy Cases *Business*

Publishing Co: Matthew Bender & Co., 11 Penn Plaza, New York, NY 10001-2006
Fax # (212) 244-3188; Title Fax # (212) 967-7707
Editorial Description: Covers complex evidentiary matters to constitutional issues and practical considerations.
General Info: Yr. Est. 1978, Irregular, Looseleaf
Subscriptions: $105/copy

Prosecution and Defense of Forfeiture Cases *Business*

Publishing Co: Matthew Bender & Co., 11 Penn Plaza, New York, NY 10001-2006
Tel # (212) 967-7707 Fax # (212) 244-3188
Editorial Description: Provides valuable practical suggestions & model forms, & covers all the key forfeiture statutes, including the Uniform Controlled Substances Act & the Comprehensive Crime Control Act of 1984.
General Info: Yr. Est. 1985, Irregular, Looseleaf

Prosecution and Defense of Sex Crimes
See: SEX

Provincial Judges Assn. of B. C. Newsletter

Publishing Co: Provincial Judges Assn. of B.C., 350 Barlow Ave., Quesnel, BC V2J 2C1 Canada; Title Tel # (604) 660-2864
Personnel: Editor-J.S. de Villiers
Editorial Description: Commentary upon legal issues and court decisions for B.C. judges.
General Info: Yr. Est. 1972, Quarterly, 20 pages, No Color
Circulation: (100% controlled), Total-150

Proving Medical Diagnosis and Prognosis
See: MEDICINE

Public Assistance & Welfare Trends/State Capitals
See: SOCIAL SERVICES & WELFARE

Public Contract Law News *Association*

Publishing Co: American Bar Association, 750 N. Lake Shore Dr., Chicago, IL 60611-4497
Tel # (312) 988-6115 Fax # (312) 988-6030; Title Tel # (312) 988-5522 Title Fax # (312) 988-5528
Personnel: Editor-Richard Bright, Art Dir.-David Corruthers
Editorial Description: Articles relating to federal, state & local contract and grant law.
General Info: Yr. Est. 1965, Quarterly, Trim Size-8½ x 11, Sheetfed press, 20 pages, ISSN: 0569-3314, 2 Color, Newsprint, Saddle-stitched
Subscriptions: Indv. $20
Circulation: Total-4,000
List Rental: Rents Lists

Public Employment Law Notes *Business, Association*

Publishing Co: NYPER Publications, PO Box 662, Latham, NY 12110-0662 Tel # (518) 786-1654
Fax # (518) 458-8582; Title Tel # (518) 456-8582 Title Fax # (518) 786-1654
Personnel: Publisher-Sheila Randall Terkell, Editor-Harvey Randall, Esq., Circ. Dir., Promotion Dir.-Margo Bittner
Editorial Description: Summarizes important court and administrative decisions of interest to administrators, union officials, and attorneys involved in public personnel administration.
General Info: Yr. Est. 1980, Monthly, ISSN: 0809-9789
Subscriptions: Indv. $295, Inst. $295, Can. $295, For. $350, $25/copy
Advertising: Accepts Inserts.
List Rental: Rents Lists

Public Employment Law Report

Publishing Co: Data Research, Inc., 4635 Nicols Rd Ste 100, Eagan, MN 55122-3337;
Title Tel # (612) 452-8267 Title Fax # (612) 452-8694
Editorial Description: Summaries of court decisions dealing with public employment law.
General Info: Yr. Est. 1989, Monthly, Trim Size-8½ x 11, Sheetfed press, 8 pages, ISSN: 1043-8211, No Color, Matte
Subscriptions: Indv. $105
Circulation: Total-2,000
Printing Co: Helgeson Press, 7600 14th Ave S, Richfield, MN 55423-4530 Tel # (612) 869-6828

Public Employment Reports
See: GOVERNMENT

Public Eye

Publishing Co: Center for Public Representation, 121 S. Pinckney St., Madison, WI 53703-3338;
Title Tel # (608) 251-4008 Title Fax # (608) 251-1263
Personnel: Publisher-Louise Trubek, Editor-Kathy Parks
Editorial Description: Wisconsin public interest law in areas of elderly, children & consumer, health, women, open government.
General Info: (Formerly The Public I), Yr. Est. 1974, Quarterly, Web press, 16 pages, 2 Color, Matte, Saddle-stitched
Subscriptions: Indv. $20
Circulation: (55% controlled), Subscriptions-900
List Rental: Rents Lists
Printing Co: Marek Lithographics, PO Box 904, Muskego, WI 53150-0904

Public Health/State Capitals
See: HEALTH

Public Interest Briefs   *Consumer, Association*
Publishing Co: Center for Law in the Public Interest, 5750 Wilshire Blvd Ste 561, Los Angeles, CA 90036-3697; Title Tel # (213) 470-3000
Personnel: Editor-Marian Samuels
Editorial Description: The publication summarizes important CLIPI litigations.
General Info: Yr. Est. 1974, Semi-annually, Trim Size-8½ x 11, Letrpr. press, 8 pages, Color
Subscriptions: Indv. $35
Circulation: (100% controlled), Total-2,000

Public Safety and Justice Policies/State Capitals
See: LAW ENFORCEMENT & PENOLOGY

Public Safety Personnel Updance
See: LAW ENFORCEMENT & PENOLOGY

Publishers Auxiliary   *Association*
Publishing Co: Natl. Newspaper Assn., 1525 Wilson Blvd Ste 550, Arlington, VA 22209-2411; Title Tel # (703) 907-7900
Editorial Description: Provides news briefs on events & court cases affecting the print & broadcast news media & publishers.
General Info: (Formerly News/Media Update), Yr. Est. 1981, Bi-weekly, 8 pages

Punch List
See: CONSTRUCTION & BUILDING

Purchaser's Legal Adviser
See: PURCHASING

Quaker Committee on Jails & Justice Newsletter
Publishing Co: Quaker Committee on Jails & Justice, 60 Lowther Ave., Toronto, ON M5R 1C7 Canada
General Info: Yr. Est. 1975, Semi-annually, 8 pages, ISSN: 0824-6521
Circulation: Total-900

Quality of Care
See: DISABILITY

Quarterly Counselor
Publishing Co: Vidas & Arrett, P.A., 920 2nd Ave S Ste 1540, Minneapolis, MN 55402-4014; Title Tel # (612) 339-8801
Personnel: Editor-Oliver Arrett
Editorial Description: Info re: Intellectual property law-patents, trademarks, copyright & trade.
General Info: Yr. Est. 1985, Quarterly, Desktop press, 3 pages, No Color
Circulation: Total-500

Quebec Tax Reports
See: TAXES

Queens County Bar Association, Queens Bar Bulletin
Publishing Co: Queens County Bar Assn., 9035 148th St, Jamaica, NY 11435-4097
Personnel: Editor-Paul Kerson, Editor-Barry Tivin, Adv. Dir.-David Adler
General Info: Yr. Est. 1973, 8x/yr.
Subscriptions: Indv. $5

RCRA Corrective Action
See: ENVIRONMENT & ECOLOGY

RID-USA National Newsletter   *Consumer, Association*
Publishing Co: Remove Intoxicated Drivers-USA, Inc., PO Box 520, Schenectady, NY 12301-0520; Title Tel # (518) 372-0034 Title Fax # (518) 370-4917
Personnel: Publisher-Bill Aiken, Editor-Doris Aiken
General Info: (Formerly RID-NYS Newsletter), Yr. Est. 1978, Quarterly, Trim Size-8½ x 11, Desktop press, 8 pages
Subscriptions: Indv. $10
Advertising: Accepts Inserts.

RTC Resource Book   *Business*
Publishing Co: Land Development Law Reporter, 1401 16th St NW, Washington, DC 20036-2201; Title Tel # (202) 232-2144 Title Fax # (202) 232-4757
General Info: Yr. Est. 1990, Quarterly, Looseleaf
Subscriptions: Indv. $495

Rabkin and Johnson's Federal Income Gift and Estate Taxation
Publishing Co: Matthew Bender & Co., 11 Penn Plaza, New York, NY 10001-2006 Fax # (212) 244-3188; Title Tel # (212) 967-7707
General Info: Yr. Est. 1942, Monthly, Looseleaf
Subscriptions: $860/copy

Radon News Digest
See: ENVIRONMENT & ECOLOGY

Rainmaker's Review, The   *Business*
Publishing Co: Andrews Publications, Inc., 1646 West Chester Pike, PO Box 1000, Westtown, PA 19395 Tel # (610) 399-6600 Fax # (610) 399-6610
Personnel: Publisher-John E. Backe, Mktg. Dir.-Andrew Katz
General Info: Yr. Est. 1995, Quarterly, Trim Size-8.5 x 11, Offset press, No Color
Subscriptions: Indv. $100
Advertising: Inquire for rates.
List Rental: Actives: $125/M

Real Estate Law Report   *Business*
Publishing Co: Warren, Gorham & Lamont, 31 Saint James Ave., Boston, MA 02116-4112 Parent Co.-Thomson Professional Publications, Stamford; Title Tel # (617) 423-2020 Title Fax # (617) 423-1914
Personnel: Publisher-Larry Selby, Mktg. Dir.-Sandra Fox
Editorial Description: Informed analysis and opinion on developments in real estate law, with emphasis on practical guidance and planning.
General Info: Yr. Est. 1971, Monthly, Trim Size-7½ x 10, Offset press, 8 pages, ISSN: 0162-752X, 2 Color
Subscriptions: Indv. $125
List Rental: List Management Co.: Manager-Seena Benedek; WG & L List Management, 1 Penn Plz Fl 42, New York, NY 10119-0002 Tel # (212) 971-5000

Real Estate Tax Ideas
See: REAL ESTATE

Real Estate Transaction Series
See: REAL ESTATE

Real Estate Workouts Report   *Business*
Publishing Co: Warren, Gorham & Lamont, 31 Saint James Ave., Boston, MA 02116-4112 Parent Co.-Thomson Professional Publications, Stamford; Title Tel # (617) 423-2020 Title Fax # (617) 423-1914
Personnel: Publisher-Larry Selby, Mktg. Dir.-Sandra Fox
Editorial Description: Presents the newest, most innovative workout strategies.
General Info: (Formerly Real Estate Workouts & Asset Management), Yr. Est. 1992, Monthly
Subscriptions: Indv. $165
List Rental: List Management Co.: Manager: Seena Benedek; WG & L List Management, 1 Penn Plz Fl 42, New York, NY 10119-0002 Tel # (212) 971-5000

Real Estate/Environmental Liability News   *Business*
Publishing Co: LRP Publications, 747 Dresher Rd., P.O. Box 980, Horsham, PA 19044-0980 Tel # (215) 784-0910 Fax # (215) 784-0317
Personnel: Publisher-Ken Kahn, Editor-Ilene Stackel
Editorial Description: Most recent legal regulatory & legislative developments in environmental law that have an impact on commercial real estate transactions.
General Info: Yr. Est. 1989, Bi-weekly, Trim Size-8½ x 11, Sheetfed press, 12 pages, ISSN: 1046-9966, 2 Color, Matte
Subscriptions: Indv. $547, For. $547
Acquistions: Publication Bought, Publication Sold

Reasonable Action
See: TAXES

Regan Report on Hospital Law
See: HOSPITALS & NURSING HOMES

Regan Report on Medical Law
See: MEDICINE

Regan Report on Nursing Law
See: NURSING

Regulation of Intl. Commercial Aviation: The Intl. Regulatory Structure & Treaties   *Business*
Publishing Co: Oceana Publications, Inc., 75 Main St, Dobbs Ferry, NY 10522-1601 Tel # (914) 693-8100; Title Tel # (914) 693-1320 Title Fax # (914) 693-0402
Personnel: Editor-James Fox, Production Mgr.-Mike Wortzman, Mktg. Dir.-John Downey
General Info: Yr. Est. 1992, Irregular, Trim Size-7 x 10, Looseleaf
Subscriptions: Indv. $350

Regulatory Compliance Watch
See: BANKING & FINANCE

Regulatory Report
See: BANKING & FINANCE

Remarks: Trademark News for Business
See: PATENTS/COPYRIGHTS/TRADE MARKS

Repetitive Stress Injury
Litigation Reporter *Business*

Publishing Co: Andrews Publications, Inc., 1646 West Chester Pike, PO Box 1000, Westtown, PA 19395 Tel # (610) 399-6600; Title Tel # (215) 399-6600 Title Fax # (610) 399-6610
Personnel: Publisher-John E. Backe, Editor-Chris Evans, Mktg. Dir.-Andrew Katz
Editorial Description: Reports on carpal tunnel syndrome and other cumulative trauma litigation. Its focus is on the explosion of products liability lawsuits aimed at manufacturers of keyboards, scanners and other products, particularly those involved in the information services industry.
General Info: Yr. Est. 1992, Monthly, Trim Size-8½ x 11, Mimeo press, 70 pages, ISSN: 1067-0483, Ind/Abs/Online: News Net, No Color
Subscriptions: Indv. $675, $58/copy
Advertising: Inquire for rates.
List Rental: Actives: 66,686, $125/M

Report from the Hill
See: SOCIAL SERVICES & WELFARE

Report to Legal
Management *Business*

Publishing Co: Altman Weil Pensa Publications Inc., 2 Campus Blvd., Newtown Square, PA 19073; Title Tel # (610) 359-9900 Title Fax # (610) 359-0467
Personnel: Publisher-Charles F. Huxsaw, Editor-James Wilber
Editorial Description: A management aid to law offices covering the full range of managements issues including strategic planning, client and business development, marketing, economic and firms
General Info: Yr. Est. 1974, Monthly, Trim Size-8.5 x 11, Offset press, 12 pages, ISSN: 0191-836X, 2 Color
Subscriptions: Indv. $195, Can. $245, For. $220, $19/copy
Circulation: Total-1,000
Printing Co: Donaldson Printing, 181 W Hillcrest Ave, Havertown, PA 19083-1198 Tel # (215) 449-5600

Reporter on Human
Reproduction & the Law *Association*

Publishing Co: Legal-Medical Studies, Inc., Box 8219, JFK Sta., Boston, MA 02114-0032; Title Tel # (617) 742-7959
Personnel: Publisher-Patricia Patterson, Editor-Charles Kindregan
Editorial Description: Covers perspectives & court decisions concerning abortion, eugenics, & surrogate motherhood.
General Info: Yr. Est. 1972, Bi-monthly, Trim Size-8½ x 11, Offset press, 150 pages, ISSN: 8756-2057, Color-cover, Looseleaf
Subscriptions: Indv. $75
Circulation: (100% controlled), Total-400
Printing Co: Andrew T. Johnson Co., 15 Tremont Pl, Boston, MA 02108-4096 Tel # (617) 742-1610

Reporter on the Legal
Profession *Association*

Publishing Co: Legal-Medical Studies, Inc., Box 8219, JFK Sta., Boston, MA 02114-0032; Title Tel # (617) 742-7959
Personnel: Editor-Charles Kindregan
Editorial Description: Review of recent developments affecting the legal profession.
General Info: Yr. Est. 1979, Annually, Trim Size-8½ x 11, Offset press, 150 pages, ISSN: 8755-7509, No Color, Looseleaf
Subscriptions: Indv. $120

Representing the Child
Client *Business*

Publishing Co: Matthew Bender & Co., 11 Penn Plaza, New York, NY 10001-2006 Tel # (212) 967-7707 Fax # (212) 244-3188
Editorial Description: Covers all the legal & startegic considerations involved in a wide variety of issues affecting the representation of children who are either neglected, dependent or charged with delinquent behavior.
General Info: Yr. Est. 1987, Irregular, Looseleaf

Research Advisor :
Information Solutions
for Today's Legal
Professionals *Business*

Publishing Co: Alert Publications Inc., 401 W Fullerton Pky Apt 1403, Chicago, IL 60614-2805; Title Tel # (312) 525-7594 Title Fax # (312) 525-7015
Personnel: Publisher, Editor-Donna Heroy, Sr. Ed.-Nina Wendt, Bk. Rev. Ed.-Christine Brotherton, Adv. Dir.-Lael Bush
Editorial Description: Interviews with practioners on how to do research, profiles of research companies; book reviews.
General Info: Yr. Est. 1995, Bi-monthly, Trim Size-8½ x 11, 8 pages
Subscriptions: Indv. $49
Advertising: Inquire for rates.
List Rental: Rents Lists
Printing Co: Graphic Copy, 415 N. State, Chicago, IL 60605 Tel # (312) 644-7800

Resolve
See: ENVIRONMENT & ECOLOGY

Responsibilities of Insurance Agents and Brokers
See: INSURANCE

Review for CFOs & Investment Bankers
See: BANKING & FINANCE

Review of Maryland Laws,
The *Business*

Publishing Co: Challenge Press, Inc., 5907 Key Ave., Baltimore, MD 21215-3820; Title Tel # (410) 466-3147 Title Fax # (410) 542-0665
Personnel: Production Mgr.-Sharon Novograd
Editorial Description: Review of all Maryland legal developments.
General Info: Yr. Est. 1993, Bi-weekly
Subscriptions: Indv. $227

Rhode Island
Employment Law Letter *Business*

Publishing Co: M. Lee Smith Publishers & Printers ,LCC, P.O. Box 198867, 162 Fourth Avenue North, Nashville, TN 37219-8867 Tel # (615) 242-7395 Fax # (615) 256-6601
Personnel: Publisher-M Lee Smith, Editor-Tom Keeney, Circ. Mgr.-Cathy Bradford
General Info: Yr. Est. 1996, Monthly, Trim Size-8½ x 11, 8 pages, 2 Color
Subscriptions: Indv. $97
List Rental: Rents Lists
Printing Co: M. Lee Smith Publishers & Printers ,LLC, PO Box 198867, 162 Fourth Avenue, Nashville, TN 37219-8867 Tel # (615) 242-7395, Fax # (615) 256-6601

Rhodes Real Estate Review *Business*

Publishing Co: Rhodes Press, 50 Broadway, Hawthorne, NY 10532-1245; Title Fax # (215) 465-6959
Personnel: Publisher, Editor-Christopher Maffucci, Circ. Dir.-Jean Conti, Adv. Dir.-Irving Martin
Editorial Description: Covers New York State zoning & planning and environmental laws. Contains digests of NY and Federal decisions, articles, book reviews, and law review summaries.
General Info: Yr. Est. 1989, 8x/yr., 16 pages, No Color, Saddle-stitched
Subscriptions: Indv. $56, Inst. $56, $8/copy
Circulation: Total-3,500
Printing Co: Rhodes Press, 1423 S 9th St, Philadelphia, PA 19147-5703

Rico Business Disputes
Guide *Business*

Publishing Co: CCH, Inc., 2700 Lake Cook Rd., Riverwoods, IL 60015 Parent Co.-Kluwer Law & Taxation Publishers, Cambridge; Title Tel # (847) 267-7000 Title Fax # (800) 224-8299
Editorial Description: Legal developments concerning federal & state anti-racketeering laws in a civil context. Statutes, court decisions, civil enforcement actions.
General Info: Monthly, Looseleaf
Subscriptions: Indv. $509

Risk Management for the Executive Woman
See: INSURANCE

Rodent, The *Business*

Publishing Co: Rodent Publications, 2531 Sawtelle Blvd # 30, Los Angeles, CA 90064-3163 Fax # (213) 383-4833; Title Tel # (213) 871-8579 Title Fax # (213) 857-1353
Editorial Description: Satirical, sarcastic, and humorous look at lawyers.
General Info: Yr. Est. 1991, Monthly
Subscriptions: Indv. $18, Inst. $25, Can. $20, For. $20
Circulation: Total-3,000

Rules of Criminal
Procedure *Business*

Publishing Co: Matthew Bender & Co., 11 Penn Plaza, New York, NY 10001-2006 Fax # (212) 244-3188; Title Tel # (212) 967-7707
Editorial Description: Unmatch coverage of every detail of procedure in federal criminal cases fully annotated and practice-oriented.
General Info: Yr. Est. 1965, Irregular, Looseleaf
Subscriptions: $450/copy

Russia and
Commonwealth
Business Law Report *Business*

Publishing Co: LRP Publications, 747 Dresher Rd., P.O. Box 980, Horsham, PA 19044-0980 Tel # (215) 784-0910 Fax # (215) 784-0317
Personnel: Publisher-Ken Kahn, Editor-Al Celmer
Editorial Description: Significant business-related legal developments in the former U.S.S.R. providing in-depth analysis of important new laws, devices, regulations or instructions.
General Info: (Formerly Soviet Business Law Report), Yr. Est. 1990, Bi-weekly, Trim Size-8½ x 11, 12 pages, ISSN: 1064-637X, 2 Color
Subscriptions: Indv. $970, For. $992
List Rental: Rents Lists

S & CNS Asbestos
Bankruptcies Litigation
Reporter   *Business*

Publishing Co: Andrews Publications, Inc., 1646 West Chester Pike, PO Box 1000, Westtown, PA 19395 Tel # (610) 399-6600 Fax # (610) 399-6610
Personnel: Publisher-John E. Backe, Editor-Bob Sullivan, Mktg. Dir.-Andrew Katz
General Info: Yr. Est. 1982, Monthly, Trim Size-8½ x 11, Offset press, ISSN: 1078-313X, No Color
Subscriptions: Indv. $1,300, $38/copy
Advertising: Inquire for rates.
List Rental: Rents Lists

S Corporations Guide
See: TAXES

SAC Award Review

Publishing Co: Securities Arbitration Commentator, 6 1/2 Highland Pl, PO Box 112, Maplewood, NJ 07040-0112 Fax # (201) 761-1504; Title Tel # (201) 761-5880 Title Fax # (201) 378-8747
Personnel: Publisher, Editor-Richard Ryder, Mktg. Dir.-Jane Byrnes
Editorial Description: Developments in the field of arbitration of disputes regarding securities & commodities trading.
General Info: (Formerly SAC Award Reporter), Yr. Est. 1993, Irregular, Trim Size-8½ x 11, 8 pages
Subscriptions: Indv. $98, $24/copy
Acquistions: Publication Sold
Circulation: Total-450, Readership-450

SCOR Report
See: BANKING & FINANCE

SEC Accounting Rules
See: ACCOUNTING

SEC Docket
See: INVESTMENT

SEC New Registrations
Report   *Business, Consumer*

Publishing Co: CCH Washington Service Bureau, Inc., 655 15th St NW Ste 275, Washington, DC 20005-5701 Tel # (202) 508-0600 Fax # (202) 508-0694
Personnel: Editor-Tim Hinkle, Circ. Mgr.-Michelle McCaulley
Editorial Description: Monthly reports of market share rankings, including the top 15 underwriters and counsels, abstracts of the top 5 IPOs and list of the top 20 registration YTD. In addition, each issue contains a detailed summary of all the new IPOs filed with the SEC.
General Info: Yr. Est. 1994, Monthly
Subscriptions: Indv. $295

SEC No-Action Letter Weekly
See: INVESTMENT

SEC No-Action Letters Index & Summaries
See: INVESTMENT

SEC Today

Publishing Co: CCH Washington Service Bureau, Inc., 655 15th St NW Ste 275, Washington, DC 20005-5701; Title Tel # (202) 508-0600 Fax # (202) 508-0694
Personnel: Editor-Jackie Lumb, Circ. Dir.-Michelle McCaulley
Editorial Description: The only daily newsletter with SEC News Digest, the official SEC summary of administrative actions, rulings, releases and more. Also lists registrations, proxies, Williams Act filings no-action letters, and initial public offerings.
General Info: Yr. Est. 1981, Daily, Trim Size-8½ x 11, 10 pages, ISSN: 0745-2667
Subscriptions: Indv. $665

SERB Official Reporter

Publishing Co: Banks-Baldwin Law Publishing Co., PO Box 318063, Cleveland, OH 44131-8063; Title Tel # (216) 721-7373 Title Fax # (216) 721-8055
Personnel: Publisher-P.J. Lucier, Production Mgr.-Virginia Stucko, Promotion Dir.-George Hallaman
Editorial Description: The only authorized source of opinions issued under SERB's system of official citation. A monthly service, it includes the full text of SERB opinions; new court decisions; relevant statutes & rules; official forms, practice outlines, charts & checklists; & research aids.
General Info: Yr. Est. 1987, Monthly, Trim Size-7½ x 10, Web press, 44 pages, ISSN: 0894-3486, No Color, Newsprint, Saddle-stitched, Looseleaf
Subscriptions: Indv. $180, $20/copy
Acquistions: Publication Bought, Publication Sold

SNL Weekly ComplianceFax
See: BANKING & FINANCE

SOCMA Newsletter
See: CHEMISTRY & CHEMICALS

SONREEL News   *Business, Association*

Publishing Co: American Bar Assn. Sect. of Nat. Res., Energy, & Env. Law, 750 N. Lake Shore Dr., Chicago, IL 60611-4497 Tel # (312) 988-5000; Title Tel # (312) 988-6070
Personnel: Editor-Deldra Hall-Holmes, Circ. Mgr.-Thomas Haas
Editorial Description: Contains news and information of Section of Natural Resources, Energy, and Environmental Law for members.
General Info: (Formerly Natrl. Resources Newsletter, Natrl. Resources Law Newsletter), Yr. Est. 1965, Bi-monthly, Trim Size-8½ x 11, 8 pages, 2 Color, Recycled, Saddle-stitched
Circulation: (100% controlled), Total-9,000
Printing Co: Congress Printing, 2136 S Peoria St, Chicago, IL 60608-4526 Tel # (312) 733-6599, Fax # (312) 733-4095

Safety Compliance Alert
See: SAFETY

Sales and Bulk Transfers
Under the UCC   *Business*

Publishing Co: Matthew Bender & Co., 11 Penn Plaza, New York, NY 10001-2006 Tel # (212) 967-7707 Fax # (212) 244-3188
Editorial Description: A widely respected analytical treatise providing complete coverage of reported decisions on sales and bulk transfers.
General Info: Yr. Est. 1966, Irregular, Looseleaf

Saskatchewan Decisions
Civil and Criminal Cases

Publishing Co: Western Legal Publications, 301-1 Alexander St., Vancouver, BC V6A 1B2 Canada; Title Tel # (604) 687-5671 Title Fax # (604) 687-2796
Personnel: Publisher-Nancy Cotter, Editor-Ronda McNabb
Editorial Description: Monthly digests of current case law filed by subject.
General Info: Yr. Est. 1975, Monthly, Mimeo press, 65 pages, ISSN: 0319-7999, Ind/Abs/Online: QL, INFORMART, No Color, Looseleaf
Subscriptions: Indv. $225, Can. $290

Scaffold Industry Association Newsletter
See: CONSTRUCTION & BUILDING

School Law Bulletin
See: EDUCATION

School Law News
See: EDUCATION

School Law Newsletter
See: COLLEGE STUDENT LIFESTYLE

School Violence Alert: Maintaining Safe Schools
See: EDUCATION

Scientific Automobile
Accident Reconstruction   *Business*

Publishing Co: Matthew Bender & Co., 11 Penn Plaza, New York, NY 10001-2006 Fax # (212) 244-3188; Title Tel # (212) 967-7707
Personnel: Editor-R. Kaye
Editorial Description: Unparalleled coverage emphasizing products liability.
General Info: Yr. Est. 1964, Irregular, Looseleaf
Subscriptions: $440/copy

Scrivener
See: JOURNALISM

Search & Seizure Bulletin   *Business*

Publishing Co: Quinlan Publishing, 23 Drydock Ave, Boston, MA 02210-2387 Fax # (617) 345-9646; Title Tel # (617) 542-0048
Editorial Description: Court decisions on search and seizure cases and issues.
General Info: Monthly, 8 pages
Subscriptions: Indv. $62
List Rental: List Management Co.: Stevens-Knox List Management, 304 Park Ave S., New York, NY 10010-5312 Tel # (212) 388-8800, Fax # (212) 388-8890

Secondary Mortgage Market Guide
See: BANKING & FINANCE

Section 504 Compliance
Guide   *Business*

Publishing Co: Thompson Publishing Group, 1725 K Street, NW, Washington, DC 20006; Title Tel # (202) 872-4000 Title Fax # (202) 296-1091
Personnel: Editor-Darla Fera, Circ. Mgr.-Robert Mello, Production Mgr.-Kathy Stein, Promotion Dir.-Lori Keller
Editorial Description: Designed to help federal funds recipients comply with the requirements of Section 504 of the Rehabilitation Act. Subscription includes monthly newsletter and monthly updates as well as optional agency chapters with specific federal agency requirements.
General Info: (Formerly Handicapped Requirements Handbook), Yr. Est. 1978, Monthly, ISSN: 0194-7818, Looseleaf
Subscriptions: Indv. $218, Inst. $218, $65/copy
Circulation: Total-4,275

Section of Taxation Newsletter
See: TAXES

Secured Transaction Guide
See: BANKING & FINANCE

Secured Transactions
Under the UCC   *Business*

Publishing Co: Matthew Bender & Co., 11 Penn Plaza, New York, NY 10001-2006
Tel # (212) 967-7707 Fax # (212) 244-3188
Personnel: Editor in Chief-Julian B. McDonnell
Editorial Description: Covers Article 9 in depth.
General Info: Yr. Est. 1963, Irregular, Looseleaf

Securities & Commodities
Litigation Reporter   *Business*

Publishing Co: Andrews Publications, Inc., 1646 West Chester Pike, PO Box 1000, Westtown, PA 19395; Title Tel # (610) 399-6600 Title Fax # (610) 399-6610
Personnel: Publisher-John E. Backe, Editor-Bob McSherry, Mktg. Dir.-Andrew Katz
Editorial Description: Provides coverage of major reparations and enforcement actions involving the scope of the Commodity Exchange Act.
General Info: (Formerly Securities&Insider Trading Lit. Rptr; Commodities Lit. Rptr.), Yr. Est. 1985, Bi-monthly, Trim Size-8½ x 11, Mimeo press, 70 pages, No Color, Newsprint
Subscriptions: Indv. $1,250, $56/copy
Advertising: Inquire for rates.
List Rental: Actives: 422, $110/M

Securities & Syndication Review
See: INVESTMENT

Securities Arbitration
Commentator   *Business*

Publishing Co: Securities Arbitration Commentator, 6 1/2 Highland Pl, PO Box 112, Maplewood, NJ 07040-0112; Title Tel # (201) 761-5880 Title Fax # (201) 761-1504
Personnel: Publisher, Editor-Richard Ryder, Promotion Dir.-Jane Byrnes
Editorial Description: Concentrates upon issues & developments in the field of securities/ commodities arbitration.
General Info: Yr. Est. 1988, Monthly, Trim Size-8½ x 11, 22 pages, ISSN: 1041-3057
Subscriptions: Indv. $294, $20/copy
Acquistions: Publication Sold
Circulation: Total-1,600, Readership-1,600

Securities Class Action
Alert

Publishing Co: Investors Research Bureau Inc., 10 Mountainview Road, Upper Saddle River, NJ 07458-1933 Tel # (201) 236-9777; Title Tel # (201) 236-9377 Title Fax # (201) 236-9738
Personnel: Publisher-James M. Newman
Editorial Description: Comprehensive & timely information on securities class action lawsuits involving all areas of investments, includes new cases important court decisions, details of settlements and update.
General Info: Yr. Est. 1988, Monthly, ISSN: 1045-9715
Subscriptions: Indv. $525, Can. $595, For. $595, $45/copy

Securities Regulation and
Law Report   *Business*

Publishing Co: Bureau of National Affairs, Inc., 1231 25th St. NW, Bldg. N-200, Washington, DC 20037-1157; Title Tel # (202) 452-4200 Title Fax # (202) 822-8092
Personnel: Publisher-William A. Beltz, Mng. Editor-Susan Raleigh-Jenkins, Circ. Mgr.-Gary C. Seltzer
Editorial Description: Covers the latest securities & commodities activity at the federal & state levels, Congress, the Administration, SEC, CFTC, banking regulations, FASB, professional assns., the courts & industry.
General Info: Yr. Est. 1969, Weekly, Trim Size-8½ x 11, Web press, 40 pages, ISSN: 0037-0665, Ind/Abs/Online: Lexis, WESTLAW,
Subscriptions: Indv. $1,067

Securities Regulations
See: MANAGEMENT

Security Law Newsletter
See: SECURITY & SURVEILLANCE

Security and Special Police Legal Update
See: SECURITY & SURVEILLANCE

Self Storage Legal Review   *Business*

Publishing Co: Self Storage Legal Review, 2203 Los Angeles Ave, Berkeley, CA 94707-2619
Personnel: Publisher, Editor-D. Carlos Kaslow
Editorial Description: Provides legal articles of interest to owners, managers, and operators of self storage facilities.
General Info: Yr. Est. 1993, Quarterly, Trim Size-8½ x 11, Letrpr. press, 8 pages, ISSN: 1073-4465, 2 Color
Subscriptions: Indv. $85, Inst. $85, Can. $85, For. $100, $20/copy
Circulation: Total-1,500
List Rental: Actives: 1,300, $300/M, Expires: 100
Printing Co: Publications Ink, 1250 45th Street, Suite 200, Emeryville, CA 94608-2924 Tel # (510) 596-9340, Fax # (510) 596-9318

Seniors in Sacramento
See: SENIOR CITIZENS

Separation/Divorce
Newsletter

Publishing Co: Separation/Divorce Newsletter, 18 Reade Pl., Poughkeepsie, NY 12601-4507; Title Tel # (914) 485-6320
Personnel: Editor-Sanford Cohen
General Info: Yr. Est. 1986, Bi-monthly, 6 pages
Subscriptions: Indv. $25
Circulation: Total-1,000

Sexual Harassment
Litigation Reporter   *Business*

Publishing Co: Andrews Publications, Inc., 1646 West Chester Pike, PO Box 1000, Westtown, PA 19395 Tel # (610) 399-6600 Fax # (610) 399-6610
Personnel: Publisher-John E. Backe, Editor-Linda Coady, Mktg. Dir.-Andrew Katz
General Info: Monthly, Trim Size-8.5 x 11, Offset press, No Color
Subscriptions: Indv. $425, $41/copy
Advertising: Inquire for rates.
List Rental: Actives: $125/M

Shepard's Expert &
Scientific Evidence
Quarterly

Publishing Co: Shepard's/McGraw-Hill, Inc., 555 Middle Creek Pky, Colorado Springs, CO 80921-3622; Title Tel # (719) 488-3000 Title Fax # (719) 481-7448
Personnel: Production Mgr.-Cheryl Everitt, Adv. Dir.-Peggy Ives, Mktg. Dir.-Leigh Vidakovich
Editorial Description: Discussions and reviews of recent cases and developments in scientific evidence, ongoing coverage of the impact of the U.S. supreme court case, daubert.
General Info: Yr. Est. 1993, Quarterly, 60 pages
Subscriptions: Indv. $195
List Rental: List Management Co.: The Lake Group, 411 Theodore Freund Ave., Rye, NY 10580-1497 Tel # (914) 925-2400, Fax # (914) 925-2499, Actives: 40,212, $130/M

Single Audit Information
Service   *Business*

Publishing Co: Thompson Publishing Group, 1725 K Street, NW, Washington, DC 20006 Tel # (202) 872-4000; Title Tel # (202) 872-1766
Personnel: Publisher-Richard Thompson, Editor-Robert M. Lloyd
Editorial Description: Single Audit Act of 1984 compliance handbook. Subscription includes monthly updates and a monthly newsletter covering recent developments.
General Info: Monthly
Subscriptions: Indv. $274

Sixth Circuit Review   *Business*

Publishing Co: Appellate Review, Inc., 500 Country Lane, Louisville, KY 40207 Tel # (502) 897-5079 Fax # (502) 899-7791
Personnel: Publisher-Patricia Owen
Editorial Description: Contains digests of federal court decisions.
General Info: Yr. Est. 1971, Semi-monthly, ISSN: 0889-356x
Subscriptions: Indv. $267

Slate, The   *Association*   CPM: $666

Publishing Co: Correctional Education Assn. Region VII, L.A. County Office of Ed., 9300 E. Imperial Hwy., Downey, CA 90242; Title Tel # (213) 803-8204
Personnel: Editor-Silvia Ruiz
General Info: Yr. Est. 1980, Quarterly, Trim Size-8½ x 11, Desktop press, 12 pages, 2 Color, Matte, Saddle-stitched
Circulation: Total-450
Advertising: $300.

Small Corporation Update
See: BUSINESS & INDUSTRY

Small Firm Profit Report -
Attorney Edition   *Business*

Publishing Co: Professional Newsletters, Inc, State Taxation Institute, PO Box 81143, Atlanta, GA 30366-1143; Title Tel # (770) 457-1000
Personnel: Publisher-Robert Palmer
Editorial Description: Practice management and marketing help for small law firms and solo practioners
General Info: Yr. Est. 1995, Monthly
Subscriptions: Indv. $89

Social Security Practice
Guide   *Business*

Publishing Co: Matthew Bender & Co., 11 Penn Plaza, New York, NY 10001-2006 Tel # (212) 967-7707 Fax # (212) 244-3188
Editorial Description: A complete, practical guide on all substantive & procedural aspects of Social Security practice, written under the supervision of the National Organization of Social Secuity Claimants' Representatives.
General Info: Yr. Est. 1984, Irregular, Looseleaf

Social Security/SSI Informational Mailing
See: SENIOR CITIZENS

Societe de Criminologie du Quebec
See: LAW ENFORCEMENT & PENOLOGY

Software Law Bulletin   *Business*

Publishing Co: Andrews Publications, Inc., 1646 West Chester Pike, PO Box 1000, Westtown, PA 19395; Title Tel # (610) 399-6600 Title Fax # (610) 399-6610
Personnel: Publisher-John E. Backe, Editor-Denise Breslin Kachin, Mktg. Dir.-Andrew Katz
General Info: Yr. Est. 1988, Monthly, ISSN: 0897-2680
Subscriptions: Indv. $297, $30/copy
List Rental: Actives: $125/M

Software Taxation Letter   *Business*

Publishing Co: Kutish Publications, PO Box 113, Wayne, PA 19087-0113; Title Tel # (610) 975-9619 Title Fax # (610) 975-9623
General Info: Yr. Est. 1990, 10x/yr., ISSN: 1048-521X
Subscriptions: Indv. $275

South Carolina Appellate Digest

Publishing Co: National Legal Research Group, 2421 Ivy Road, P.O. Box 7187, Charlottesville, VA 22903; Title Tel # (800) 446-1870 Title Fax # (804) 295-4667
Personnel: Editor-Chris Hudson, Circ. Mgr.-Agnes Turner
Editorial Description: Summaries of state & federal cases from South Carolina.
General Info: Yr. Est. 1984, Bi-weekly, ISSN: 0743-2453
Subscriptions: Indv. $85, Can. $100, For. $100, $4/copy

South Carolina Criminal & Motor Vehicle Handbook

Publishing Co: Gould Publications, Inc, 1333 N US Highway 17-92, Longwood, FL 32750-3724 Tel # (407) 695-9500 Fax # (407) 695-2906
Editorial Description: A concise presentation of the criminal and motor vehicle laws of South Carolina.
General Info: Annually, Looseleaf
Subscriptions: Indv. $25

South Carolina Employment Law Letter   *Business*

Publishing Co: M. Lee Smith Publishers & Printers ,LCC, P.O. Box 198867, 162 Fourth Avenue North, Nashville, TN 37219-8867; Title Tel # (615) 242-7395 Title Fax # (615) 256-6601
Personnel: Publisher-M Lee Smith, Editor-Edwin Johnson, II, Circ. Mgr.-Cathy Bradford, Mktg. Dir.-Dave Yates
Editorial Description: Review of employment law developments that affect South Carolina employers.
General Info: Yr. Est. 1992, Monthly, Trim Size-8½ x 11, 8 pages, ISSN: 1064-461X, 2 Color
Subscriptions: Indv. $97
List Rental: Rents Lists
Printing Co: M. Lee Smith Publishers & Printers ,LLC, PO Box 198867, 162 Fourth Avenue, Nashville, TN 37219-8867 Tel # (615) 242-7395, Fax # (615) 256-6601

South Carolina Environmental Compliance Update   *Business*

Publishing Co: M. Lee Smith Publishers & Printers ,LCC, P.O. Box 198867, 162 Fourth Avenue North, Nashville, TN 37219-8867; Title Tel # (615) 242-7395 Title Fax # (615) 256-6601
Personnel: Publisher-M Lee Smith, Editor-John Hodge, Circ. Mgr.-Cathy Bradford, Mktg. Dir.-Dave Yates
Editorial Description: Review of environmental law developments that affect South Carolina companies.
General Info: Yr. Est. 1993, Monthly, Trim Size-8½ x 11, 8 pages, ISSN: 1065-7975, 2 Color
Subscriptions: Indv. $117
List Rental: Rents Lists
Printing Co: Valley Web, 1299 Stowe Avenue, Medford, OR 97504 Tel # (503) 772-7039

South Dakota Employment Law Letter   *Business*

Publishing Co: M. Lee Smith Publishers & Printers ,LCC, P.O. Box 198867, 162 Fourth Avenue North, Nashville, TN 37219-8867 Tel # (615) 242-7395 Fax # (615) 256-6601
Personnel: Publisher-M Lee Smith, Circ. Mgr.-Cathy Bradford, Mktg. Dir.-David Yates
General Info: Monthly, 2 Color
Subscriptions: Indv. $97
List Rental: Rents Lists
Printing Co: M. Lee Smith Publishers & Printers ,LLC, PO Box 198867, 162 Fourth Avenue, Nashville, TN 37219-8867 Tel # (615) 242-7395, Fax # (615) 256-6601

Southeast Litigation Guide   *Business*

Publishing Co: Matthew Bender & Co., 11 Penn Plaza, New York, NY 10001-2006 Tel # (212) 967-7707 Fax # (212) 244-3188
Editorial Description: Prominent trial layers in Florida, Georgia & Alabama provide step-by-steop guidance through every aspect of litigation practice.
General Info: Irregular, Looseleaf

Southeast Transaction Guide   *Business*

Publishing Co: Matthew Bender & Co., 11 Penn Plaza, New York, NY 10001-2006 Fax # (212) 244-3188; Title Tel # (212) 967-7707
Personnel: Editor-S. Schiff
Editorial Description: For Florida, Georgia and Alabama practitioners: Methodical coverage of a wide variety of business and legal transactions.
General Info: Yr. Est. 1976, Irregular, Looseleaf
Subscriptions: $920/copy

Special Education Law Update
See: EDUCATION

Sports & Entertainment Litigation Reporter   *Business*

Publishing Co: Andrews Publications, Inc., 1646 West Chester Pike, PO Box 1000, Westtown, PA 19395; Title Tel # (610) 399-6600 Title Fax # (610) 399-6610
Personnel: Publisher-John E. Backe, Editor-Robert Sullivan, Mktg. Dir.-Andrew Katz
Editorial Description: Covers the latest news in the fast-changing world of entertainment litigation.
General Info: (Formerly Entertainment Litigation Reporter), Yr. Est. 1989, Monthly, Trim Size-8½ x 11, Mimeo press, 80 pages, ISSN: 1047-4137, No Color, Newsprint
Subscriptions: Indv. $700, $67/copy
List Rental: Actives: 66,686, $125/M

Sports Industry News
See: SPORTS & SPORTING GOODS

Sports Medicine in Primary Care
See: MEDICINE

Sports Medicine Standards & Malpractice Reporter, The   *Business*

Publishing Co: PRC Publishing, Inc., 4418 Belden Village St NW, Canton, OH 44718-2516; Title Tel # (216) 492-6063 Title Fax # (216) 492-6176
Personnel: Editor-David L. Herbert, Esq., Adv. Dir.-Molly Romig
Editorial Description: Quarterly newsletter designed to keep sports medicine professionals up to date on current trends and issues within their fields. Discussion of standards of care, liability and risk management.
General Info: Yr. Est. 1989, Quarterly, Trim Size-8½ x 11, Sheetfed press, 20 pages, ISSN: 1041-696X, Ind/Abs/Online: indexed annually free to subscribers, 2 Color, Matte, Saddle-stitched
Subscriptions: Indv. $40, Can. $46, For. $50, $10/copy
Circulation: (33% controlled), Subscriptions-1,200
Advertising: Accepts Inserts.

Sports, Parks & Recreation Law Reporter, The   *Business*

Publishing Co: PRC Publishing, Inc., 4418 Belden Village St NW, Canton, OH 44718-2516; Title Tel # (216) 492-6063 Title Fax # (216) 492-6176
Personnel: Editor-David L. Herbert, Eq., Production Mgr., Adv. Dir.-Molly Romig
Editorial Description: Quarterly newsletter designed for sports, park and recreation professionals.
General Info: Yr. Est. 1988, Quarterly, Trim Size-8½ x 11, Sheetfed press, 16 pages, ISSN: 0893-8210, Ind/Abs/Online: indexed annually, free to subscribers, Matte, Saddle-stitched
Subscriptions: Indv. $40, $10/copy
Circulation: (58% controlled), Total-850, Subscriptions-350, International-10
Advertising: Accepts Inserts.
List Rental: Rents Lists

Standard & Poor's Review of Securities & Commodities Regulation   *Business*

Publishing Co: Standard & Poor's Corp., 25 Broadway, New York, NY 10004 Tel # (212) 208-8000 Parent Co.-McGraw-Hill, New York; Title Tel # (212) 208-8650
Personnel: Publisher-Stephen Sanborn, Editor-Michael Finkelstein
Editorial Description: Develops authoritative articles on the latest developments in securities & commodities law.
General Info: Yr. Est. 1968, Semi-monthly, Trim Size-8½ x 11, Web press, 8 pages, Ind/Abs/Online: Dialog, Dow Jones, NewsNet, Nexis, 2 Color
Subscriptions: Indv. $412, $18/copy
Circulation: Total-1,250

Standard Federal Tax Reports
See: TAXES

State Advocate, The
See: U.S. (& CANADIAN) FED. GOV'T.

State Constitutional Law Bulletin

Publishing Co: National Association of Attorneys General, 444 N Capitol St NW Ste 339, Washington, DC 20001-1512 Tel # (202) 434-8034
Editorial Description: Summarizes major state constitutional law opinions and decisions.
General Info: Yr. Est. 1987, Monthly
Subscriptions: Indv. $50
Circulation: Total-450

State Court Report

Publishing Co: National Center for State Courts, 300 Newport Ave, Williamsburg, VA 23185-4147; Title Tel # (804) 253-2000 Title Fax # (804) 220-0449
Personnel: Editor-Kriss Winchester, Circ. Mgr.-Kim Swanson, Production Mgr.-Mary McCall
Editorial Description: Reports on activities of Natl. Center for State Courts.
General Info: (Formerly Report), Yr. Est. 1973, Monthly, Trim Size-8½ x 11, Sheetfed press, 8 pages, ISSN: 0195-5241, 2 Color, Newsprint, Perfect bound
Subscriptions: Indv. $12, $2/copy
Circulation: Total-3,300
Printing Co: Sir Speedy, 240 McClaws Cir., Williamsburg, VA 23185 Tel # (804) 220-1191

State Labor Laws
See: LABOR

State Legislative Matters   *Business*

Publishing Co: American Institute of CPA's, Harborside Financial Center, 201 Plaza Three, Jersey City, NJ 07311-3881 Tel # (201) 938-3283 Fax # (201) 938-3329; Title Tel # (202) 434-9201 Title Fax # (202) 638-4512
Personnel: Publisher-Robert Rainer, Editor, Feature Ed.-Sheri Bango, Mktg. Dir.-Charles Cohn
Editorial Description: Legislative issues & regulatory issues affecting CPA's
General Info: Yr. Est. 1986, Irregular
Subscriptions: Free With Membership
Circulation: Total-500, Readership-500

State Legislative Report   *Association*

Publishing Co: American Bar Association, 740 15th St. NW, Washington, DC 20005-1009 Tel # (202) 662-1016 Fax # (202) 662-1032; Title Tel # (202) 331-2236 Title Fax # (202) 331-2220
Personnel: Editor-Patrick Sheehan, Production Mgr.-Diane Gibson
Editorial Description: Four to eight page state legislative tracking.
General Info: (Formerly Quality Control), Yr. Est. 1987, Irregular, Trim Size-8.5 x 11, Desktop press, 8 pages, No Color, Matte, Saddle-stitched
Subscriptions: Indv. $50
Circulation: (100% controlled), Total-900
List Rental: Rents Lists

State Tax Cases Reports
See: TAXES

State Tax Guide
See: TAXES

State Tax Reports All-States
See: TAXES

Steinman's Bergerman and Roth, New York Real Property Forms Annotated
See: REAL ESTATE

Strategic Alliance Alert

Publishing Co: Leader Publications, Inc., 345 Park Avenue South, New York, NY 10010 Parent Co.-New York Law Publishing Co., New York; Title Tel # (212) 545-6170 Title Fax # (212) 696-1848
Personnel: Publisher-Stuart Wise, Editor-Ruthanne Kurtyka, Circ. Dir.-Kerry Kyle, Promotion Dir.-Rose-Ann Morangelli
General Info: (Formerly Legal Tech), Yr. Est. 1983, Monthly, Trim Size-8½ x 11, Offset press, 8 pages, ISSN: 0738-0186, Color
Subscriptions: Indv. $195, $16/copy
Acquisitions: Publication Sold
Printing Co: Columbus Bookbinding, 1343 Belfast Ave, Columbus, OH 31904 Tel # (206) 323-9313, Fax # (206) 323-2987

Successful Litigation
Techniques   *Business*

Publishing Co: Matthew Bender & Co., 11 Penn Plaza, New York, NY 10001-2006 Fax # (212) 244-3188; Title Tel # (212) 967-7707
Personnel: Editor-S. Weisenfeld
Editorial Description: Provides a unique combination of instructional text and illustrative trial proceedings; plus entire trial transcripts, interspersed throughout with practice commentary.
General Info: Yr. Est. 1964, Irregular, Looseleaf
Subscriptions: $475/copy

Summary of Labor Arbitration Awards
See: LABOR

Summary of Labor Arbitration Awards
See: LABOR UNION

Summons   *Association*

Publishing Co: Tau Epsilon Rho Law Society, 36 Kresson Rd Ste E, Cherry Hill, NJ 08034-3227; Title Tel # (609) 429-3901
Personnel: Editor-Robert Bowytz
Editorial Description: News of coming events, local chapter items of interest, legal essays and reviews.
General Info: Yr. Est. 1921, Quarterly, Trim Size-11 x 16, 6 pages, No Color
Circulation: Total-4,000

Superfund Report

Publishing Co: Inside Washington Publishers, P.O. Box 7167, Ben Franklin Station, Washington, DC 20044 Tel # (703) 512-1800; Title Fax # (703) 892-8500 Title Fax # (703) 685-2606
General Info: Yr. Est. 1987, 26x/yr.
Subscriptions: Indv. $390

Supervision Handbook

Publishing Co: Gould Publications, Inc, 1333 N US Highway 17-92, Longwood, FL 32750-3724 Tel # (407) 695-9500 Fax # (407) 695-2906; Title Tel # (607) 724-3000
General Info: Annually, 175 pages, Looseleaf
Subscriptions: $17/copy

Supreme Court Bulletin   CPM: $107

Publishing Co: Hale Ridge Publishing, PO Box 370, Windham, NH 03087; Title Tel # (603) 889-7231
Personnel: Publisher, Adv. Dir., Promotion Dir.-David Armstrong
Editorial Description: Brief summaries of all US Supreme Court opinions, while in session.
General Info: Yr. Est. 1979, 24x/yr., Trim Size-8½ x 11, Web press, 4 pages, No Color, Matte
Subscriptions: Indv. $29, $4/copy
Acquistions: Publication Sold
Circulation: Total-2,800
Advertising: $300.
List Rental: Actives: $65/M
Printing Co: Armstrong Graphics, PO Box 628, Windham, NH 03087-0628 Tel # (603) 889-7231

Supreme Court of Canada
Reports Service

Publishing Co: Butterworths, 75 Clegg Rd., Markham, ON L6G 1A1 Canada Tel # (905) 479-2665; Title Tel # (416) 479-2665 Title Fax # (905) 479-2826
Editorial Description: Complete index to all reported decisions.
General Info: Quarterly, Looseleaf
Subscriptions: Indv. $95, Can. $225

Supreme Court Record

Publishing Co: Hale Ridge Publishing, PO Box 370, Windham, NH 03087; Title Tel # (603) 889-7231
Editorial Description: Full texts of US Supreme Court opinions.
General Info: Yr. Est. 1979, 30x/yr., Trim Size-8½ x 11, Web press, No Color, Other, Other
Subscriptions: Indv. $96, $10/copy
Printing Co: Armstrong Graphics, PO Box 628, Windham, NH 03087-0628 Tel # (603) 889-7231

Supreme Court Reporter

Publishing Co: Armstrong Graphics, PO Box 628, Windham, NH 03087-0628; Title Tel # (603) 497-8154
Personnel: Publisher, Editor-Robert Gillmore
General Info: Yr. Est. 1984, 20x/yr.
Subscriptions: Indv. $68

Synopsis of Boiler & Pressure Vessel Laws, Rules & Regulations
See: SAFETY

TMA Issues Monitor
See: TOBACCO

Tax Action Coordinator
See: TAXES

Tax Administrators News
See: TAXES

Tax Court Decisions
See: TAXES

Tax Court Reports
See: TAXES

Tax Laws of the World   *Business*

Publishing Co: Foreign Tax Law Publishers, Inc., PO Box 2189, Ormond Beach, FL 32175-2189; Title Tel # (904) 253-5785 Title Fax # (904) 257-3003
Editorial Description: Income, corporate, and related tax laws for over 100 countries. Many full text translations.
General Info: Yr. Est. 1947, Irregular, Trim Size-8½ x 11, Sheetfed press, 100 pages, No Color, Looseleaf
Subscriptions: Indv. $1,400, $100/copy

Tax Letter Europe
See: TAXES

Tax Planning
See: TAXES

Tax Treaties
See: TAXES

Taxation and Revenue Policies/State Capitals
See: TAXES

Taxation of Securities Transactions
See: TAXES

Taxes on Parade
See: TAXES

Taylor Law Update   *Business, Association*

Publishing Co: NYPER Publications, PO Box 662, Latham, NY 12110-0662; Title Tel # (518) 786-1654 Title Fax # (518) 458-8582
Personnel: Editor-Harvey Randall
Editorial Description: Summarizes important court and administrative ruling of interest to employees, union officials and attorneys.
General Info: (Formerly Labor Law Personnel Notes), Yr. Est. 1988, Monthly, ISSN: 1071-7404
Subscriptions: Indv. $95, Inst. $95
Advertising: Accepts Inserts.

Tennessee Attorneys Memo   *Business*

Publishing Co: M. Lee Smith Publishers & Printers ,LCC, P.O. Box 198867, 162 Fourth Avenue North, Nashville, TN 37219-8867; Title Tel # (615) 242-7395 Title Fax # (615) 256-6601
Personnel: Publisher-M. Lee Smith, Editor-Bradford Forrister, Circ. Mgr.-Cathy Bradford, Mktg. Dir.-David Yates
Editorial Description: Summarizes TN Appellate Court opinions (published & unpublished), TN General Assembly Acts, selected opinions of TN Attorney General, 6th Circuit Court of Appeals.
General Info: Yr. Est. 1975, Weekly, Trim Size-8½ x 11, Sheetfed press, 8 pages, ISSN: 0194-1259, 2 Color, Newsprint
Subscriptions: Indv. $307, Inst. $357
Acquistions: Publication Bought
List Rental: Actives: $75/M
Printing Co: M. Lee Smith Publishers & Printers ,LLC, PO Box 198867, 162 Fourth Avenue, Nashville, TN 37219-8867 Tel # (615) 242-7395, Fax # (615) 256-6601

Tennessee Employment Law Update   *Business*

Publishing Co: M. Lee Smith Publishers & Printers ,LCC, P.O. Box 198867, 162 Fourth Avenue North, Nashville, TN 37219-8867; Title Tel # (615) 242-7395 Title Fax # (615) 256-6601
Personnel: Publisher-M. Lee Smith, Editor-John Phillips, Circ. Mgr.-Cathy Bradford, Mktg. Dir.-Dave Yates
Editorial Description: Review of Tennessee employment law developments that affect Tennessee employers.
General Info: Yr. Est. 1986, Monthly, Trim Size-8½ x 11, 8 pages, ISSN: 0886-8557, 2 Color
Subscriptions: Indv. $97
List Rental: Rents Lists
Printing Co: M. Lee Smith Publishers & Printers ,LLC, PO Box 198867, 162 Fourth Avenue, Nashville, TN 37219-8867 Tel # (615) 242-7395, Fax # (615) 256-6601

Tennessee Environmental Law Letter   *Business*

Publishing Co: M. Lee Smith Publishers & Printers ,LCC, P.O. Box 198867, 162 Fourth Avenue North, Nashville, TN 37219-8867; Title Tel # (615) 242-7395 Title Fax # (615) 256-6601
Personnel: Publisher-M. Lee Smith, Editor-J. Andrew Goddard, Circ. Mgr.-Cathy Bradford, Mktg. Dir.-Dave Yates
Editorial Description: Review of environmental law developments that affect Tennessee companies.
General Info: Yr. Est. 1989, Monthly, Trim Size-8½ x 11, 8 pages, ISSN: 1042-3168, 2 Color
Subscriptions: Indv. $187
List Rental: Rents Lists
Printing Co: M. Lee Smith Publishers & Printers ,LLC, PO Box 198867, 162 Fourth Avenue, Nashville, TN 37219-8867 Tel # (615) 242-7395, Fax # (615) 256-6601

Tennessee Family Law Letter   *Business, Consumer*

Publishing Co: M. Lee Smith Publishers & Printers ,LCC, P.O. Box 198867, 162 Fourth Avenue North, Nashville, TN 37219-8867; Title Tel # (615) 242-7395 Title Fax # (615) 256-6601
Personnel: Publisher-M Lee Smith, Editor-W. Walton Garrett, Circ. Mgr.-Cathy Bradford, Mktg. Dir.-David Yates
Editorial Description: Digest of Tennessee family law developments.
General Info: Yr. Est. 1986, Monthly, Trim Size-8½ x 11, 8 pages, ISSN: 0890-5355
Subscriptions: Indv. $80
List Rental: Rents Lists
Printing Co: M. Lee Smith Publishers & Printers ,LLC, PO Box 198867, 162 Fourth Avenue, Nashville, TN 37219-8867 Tel # (615) 242-7395, Fax # (615) 256-6601

Tennessee Health Law Update   *Business*

Publishing Co: M. Lee Smith Publishers & Printers ,LCC, P.O. Box 198867, 162 Fourth Avenue North, Nashville, TN 37219-8867 Tel # (615) 242-7395 Fax # (615) 256-6601
Personnel: Publisher-M. Lee Smith, Editor-Patricia Meador, Circ. Mgr.-Cathy Bradford, Mktg. Dir.-Dave Yates
Editorial Description: Reviews health law developments that affect Tennessee companies.
General Info: Yr. Est. 1994, Monthly, Trim Size-8½ x 11, 8 pages, 2 Color
Subscriptions: Indv. $177
List Rental: Rents Lists
Printing Co: M. Lee Smith Publishers & Printers ,LLC, PO Box 198867, 162 Fourth Avenue, Nashville, TN 37219-8867 Tel # (615) 242-7395, Fax # (615) 256-6601

Tennessee Journal   *Business*

Publishing Co: M. Lee Smith Publishers & Printers ,LCC, P.O. Box 198867, 162 Fourth Avenue North, Nashville, TN 37219-8867; Title Tel # (615) 242-7395 Title Fax # (615) 256-6601
Personnel: Publisher-M. Lee Smith, Editor-Bradford Forrister, Circ. Mgr.-Cathy Bradford, Mktg. Dir.-David Yates
Editorial Description: The weekly insiders newsletter on Tennessee government, politics and business.
General Info: Yr. Est. 1975, Weekly, Trim Size-8½ x 11, Sheetfed press, 4 pages, ISSN: 0194-1240, 2 Color, Newsprint
Subscriptions: Indv. $197
List Rental: Actives: $75/M
Printing Co: M. Lee Smith Publishers & Printers ,LLC, PO Box 198867, 162 Fourth Avenue, Nashville, TN 37219-8867 Tel # (615) 242-7395, Fax # (615) 256-6601

Tennessee Law Enforcement Bulletin

Publishing Co: M. Lee Smith Publishers & Printers ,LCC, P.O. Box 198867, 162 Fourth Avenue North, Nashville, TN 37219-8867; Title Tel # (615) 242-7395 Title Fax # (615) 256-6601
Personnel: Publisher-M Lee Smith, Editor-Bill Parker, Circ. Mgr.-Cathy Bradford, Mktg. Dir.-David Yates
Editorial Description: Summary of TN legal developments of concern to law enforcement officials.
General Info: Yr. Est. 1977, Bi-monthly
Subscriptions: Indv. $85
List Rental: Rents Lists
Printing Co: M. Lee Smith Publishers & Printers ,LLC, PO Box 198867, 162 Fourth Avenue, Nashville, TN 37219-8867 Tel # (615) 242-7395, Fax # (615) 256-6601

Tennessee Litigation Reporter   *Business*

Publishing Co: Lewis L. Laska, 901 Church St, Nashville, TN 37203-3411; Title Tel # (615) 255-6288 Title Fax # (615) 255-6289
Personnel: Publisher, Editor-Lewis Laska, Editorial Asst.-Lorenda Sue Patterson, J.D.
Editorial Description: Tennessee trial court news including verdicts & settlements.
General Info: Yr. Est. 1984, Bi-monthly, Trim Size-8½ x 11, 16 pages, Matte, Saddle-stitched
Subscriptions: Indv. $180

Tennessee Medico-Legal Reporter   *Business*

Publishing Co: Lewis L. Laska, 901 Church St, Nashville, TN 37203-3411; Title Tel # (615) 255-6288 Title Fax # (615) 255-6289
Personnel: Publisher, Editor-Lewis Laska, Editorial Asst.-Lorenda Sue Patterson, J.D.
Editorial Description: Legal news for the Tennessee health care lawyer.
General Info: Yr. Est. 1983, Monthly, Trim Size-8½ x 11, Sheetfed press, 8 pages
Subscriptions: Indv. $195

Tennessee Real Estate Law Letter   *Business*

Publishing Co: M. Lee Smith Publishers & Printers ,LCC, P.O. Box 198867, 162 Fourth Avenue North, Nashville, TN 37219-8867; Title Tel # (615) 242-7395 Title Fax # (615) 256-6601
Personnel: Publisher-M Lee Smith, Editor-C. Dewees Berry, IV, Circ. Mgr.-Cathy Bradford, Mktg. Dir.-David Yates
Editorial Description: Survey of TN & Federal Real Estate Law developments.
General Info: Yr. Est. 1983, Monthly, Trim Size-8½ x 11, 8 pages, ISSN: 1059-5090, 2 Color
Subscriptions: Indv. $92
List Rental: Rents Lists
Printing Co: M. Lee Smith Publishers & Printers ,LLC, PO Box 198867, 162 Fourth Avenue, Nashville, TN 37219-8867 Tel # (615) 242-7395, Fax # (615) 256-6601

Testifying Expert, The   *Business, Consumer*

Publishing Co: LRP Publications, 747 Dresher Rd., P.O. Box 980, Horsham, PA 19044-0980 Tel # (215) 784-0910 Fax # (215) 784-0317
Personnel: Publisher-Ken Kahn, Editor-Bob McSherry
Editorial Description: Develop a reputation or improve your present standing as an expert witness with ongoing coverage of relevant decisions, new techniques, and seminar listings.
General Info: Monthly
Subscriptions: Indv. $125

Texas Corporations--Law and Practice   *Business*

Publishing Co: Matthew Bender & Co., 11 Penn Plaza, New York, NY 10001-2006 Tel # (212) 967-7707 Fax # (212) 244-3188
Editorial Description: A treatise on the law governing the formation & management of corporations in Texas, containing articles that take a modern view of representing a corporation.
General Info: Yr. Est. 1984, Irregular, Looseleaf

Texas Criminal Law and Motor Vehicle Handbook

Publishing Co: Gould Publications, Inc, 1333 N US Highway 17-92, Longwood, FL 32750-3724 Tel # (407) 695-9500 Fax # (407) 695-2906; Title Tel # (607) 724-3000 Title Fax # (607) 723-4285
Editorial Description: A concise presentation of the criminal and motor vehicle laws of Texas.
General Info: Looseleaf
Subscriptions: Indv. $22, $25/copy

Texas Criminal Practice
Guide
Business

Publishing Co: Matthew Bender & Co., 11 Penn Plaza, New York, NY 10001-2006
Fax # (212) 244-3188; Title Tel # (212) 967-7707
Personnel: Editor-S. Ford
Editorial Description: The most comprehensive treatise available on criminal practice in Texas.
General Info: Yr. Est. 1979, Irregular, Looseleaf
Subscriptions: $520/copy

Texas Employment Law
Letter
Business

Publishing Co: M. Lee Smith Publishers & Printers ,LCC, P.O. Box 198867, 162 Fourth Avenue North, Nashville, TN 37219-8867; Title Tel # (615) 242-7395 Title Fax # (615) 256-6601
Personnel: Publisher-M. Lee Smith, Editor-Michael Maslanka, Co-Editor-David Ellis, Co-Editor-Mike Maslanka, Circ. Mgr.-Cathy Bradford, Mktg. Dir.-Dave Yates
Editorial Description: Review of employment law developments that affect Texas employers.
General Info: Yr. Est. 1990, Monthly, Trim Size-8½ x 11, 8 pages, ISSN: 1046-9214, 2 Color
Subscriptions: Indv. $97
List Rental: Actives: $75/M
Printing Co: M. Lee Smith Publishers & Printers ,LLC, PO Box 198867, 162 Fourth Avenue, Nashville, TN 37219-8867 Tel # (615) 242-7395, Fax # (615) 256-6601

Texas Environmental Law
Letter
Business

Publishing Co: M. Lee Smith Publishers & Printers ,LCC, P.O. Box 198867, 162 Fourth Avenue North, Nashville, TN 37219-8867; Title Tel # (615) 242-7395 Title Fax # (615) 256-6601
Personnel: Publisher-M Lee Smith, Editor-Douglas Caroom, Circ. Mgr.-Cathy Bradford, Mktg. Dir.-Dave Yates
Editorial Description: Review of environmental law developments that affect Texas companies.
General Info: Yr. Est. 1989, Monthly, Trim Size-8½ x 11, 8 pages, ISSN: 1056-7585, 2 Color
Subscriptions: Indv. $117
List Rental: Rents Lists
Printing Co: M. Lee Smith Publishers & Printers ,LLC, PO Box 198867, 162 Fourth Avenue, Nashville, TN 37219-8867 Tel # (615) 242-7395, Fax # (615) 256-6601

Texas Family Law Reporter
Business

Publishing Co: Matthew Bender & Co., 11 Penn Plaza, New York, NY 10001-2006
Tel # (212) 967-7707 Fax # (212) 244-3188
Editorial Description: A monthly Reporter covering recent legislative & case-law developments in Texas family law. Functions as a monthly supplement to Family Law: Texas Practice & Procedure.
General Info: Yr. Est. 1983, Monthly

Texas Family Law Trial
Guide
Business

Publishing Co: Matthew Bender & Co., 11 Penn Plaza, New York, NY 10001-2006
Tel # (212) 967-7707 Fax # (212) 244-3188
Editorial Description: Each topic is outlined alphabetically by major issues, with the controlling statutes & cases to resolve the question. Ideal for use during consultation, dictation, planning or while in the courtroom.
General Info: Yr. Est. 1983, Semi-annually, Looseleaf

Texas Lawyer's Weekly
Letter
Association

Publishing Co: State Bar of Texas, PO Box 12487 Capitol Station, Austin, TX 78711-2487
Tel # (512) 463-1463
General Info: Weekly

Texas Litigation Guide
Business

Publishing Co: Matthew Bender & Co., 11 Penn Plaza, New York, NY 10001-2006
Fax # (212) 244-3188; Title Tel # (212) 967-7707
Personnel: Editor-S. Ford
Editorial Description: Prominent Texas trial lawyers provide step-by-step guidance through all aspects of litigation practice. Covers civil trial procedures: Business Entity, Commercial Real Estate, and Personal Injury litigation; Family Code, Probate Code & Administrative proceedings.
General Info: Yr. Est. 1977, Irregular, Looseleaf
Subscriptions: $1,525/copy

Texas Torts and Remedies
Business

Publishing Co: Matthew Bender & Co., 11 Penn Plaza, New York, NY 10001-2006
Tel # (212) 967-7707 Fax # (212) 244-3188
Editorial Description: Complete & detailed treatment of the substantive Texas law of torts as well as remedies for tortious injury.
General Info: Yr. Est. 1987, Irregular, Looseleaf

Texas Torts Update
Business

Publishing Co: Matthew Bender & Co., 11 Penn Plaza, New York, NY 10001-2006
Tel # (212) 967-7707 Fax # (212) 244-3188
Editorial Description: Authoritative, up-to-the-minute reporting on all the latest developments affecting personal injury practice in Taxas.
General Info: Yr. Est. 1986, Monthly, Looseleaf

Texas Transaction Guide-
Legal Forms
Business

Publishing Co: Matthew Bender & Co., 11 Penn Plaza, New York, NY 10001-2006
Fax # (212) 244-3188; Title Tel # (212) 967-7707
Personnel: Editor-S. Ford
Editorial Description: Offers legal background, research aids, practice guides, and forms for Texas legal transactions. Covers: wills and trusts, business, commercial, real estate and personal transactions.
General Info: Yr. Est. 1972, Irregular, Looseleaf
Subscriptions: $1,325/copy

Texas Transportation
See: TRAFFIC & TRANSPORTATION

Third Circuit Digest
Business

Publishing Co: Appellate Review, Inc., 500 Country Lane, Louisville, KY 40207 Tel # (502) 897-5079
Fax # (502) 899-7791
Personnel: Publisher-Patricia Owen
Editorial Description: Provides digests of federal court decisions.
General Info: Yr. Est. 1987, Semi-monthly, ISSN: 1043-1470
Subscriptions: Indv. $277

Tidbits
See: EDUCATION

Timesharing Law Reporter
Business, Association

Publishing Co: Land Development Law Reporter, 1401 16th St NW, Washington, DC 20036-2201; Title Tel # (202) 232-2144 Title Fax # (202) 232-4757
Personnel: Publisher-Stuart Bloch, Editor-Steve Sullivan, Circ. Mgr.-Pat Hunter
Editorial Description: Monitors legislation & court cases related to resort timesharing and membership campgrounds.
General Info: Yr. Est. 1980, Bi-monthly, Web press, 10 pages, ISSN: 0738-6923
Subscriptions: Indv. $195
Circulation: (100% controlled), Total-250

Title Management Today
Business

Publishing Co: Lewis L. Laska, 901 Church St, Nashville, TN 37203-3411; Title Tel # (615) 255-6288 Title Fax # (615) 255-6289
Personnel: Publisher, Editor-Lewis Laska, Editorial Asst.-Lorenda Patterson, J.D.
Editorial Description: National independent newsletter of title insurance industry.
General Info: Yr. Est. 1991, Monthly, Trim Size-8½ x 11, 12 pages
Subscriptions: Indv. $189

Tobacco Industry
Litigation Reporter
Business

Publishing Co: Andrews Publications, Inc., 1646 West Chester Pike, PO Box 1000, Westtown, PA 19395; Title Tel # (610) 399-6600 Title Fax # (610) 399-6610
Personnel: Publisher-John E. Backe, Editor-Edie McFall, Mktg. Dir.-Andrew Katz
Editorial Description: Offers nationwide coverage of litigation involving and impacting upon the tobacco industry.
General Info: (Formerly Tobacco Litigation Reporter), Yr. Est. 1985, Bi-monthly, Trim Size-8½ x 11, Mimeo press, 70 pages, ISSN: 0887-7831, Ind/Abs/Online: News Net
Subscriptions: Indv. $675, $60/copy
Advertising: Inquire for rates.
List Rental: Actives: 66,686, $125/M

Tobacco Products Litigation Reporter
See: TOBACCO

Tobacco on Trial
See: TOBACCO

Today's Dads
See: FAMILY

Torts
Business

Publishing Co: Gould Publications, Inc, 1333 N US Highway 17-92, Longwood, FL 32750-3724
Tel # (407) 695-9500 Fax # (407) 695-2906; Title Tel # (607) 724-3000
Editorial Description: A comprehensive review of the law of torts with particular reference to New York law. The elements of each tort are given with case examples.
General Info: Annually, 171 pages, Looseleaf
Subscriptions: $10/copy

Toxic Chemicals
Litigation Reporter
Business

Publishing Co: Andrews Publications, Inc., 1646 West Chester Pike, PO Box 1000, Westtown, PA 19395; Title Tel # (610) 399-6600 Title Fax # (610) 399-6610
Personnel: Publisher-John E. Backe, Editor-Jodine Mayberry, Mktg. Dir.-Andrew Katz
Editorial Description: Covers litigation arising from these substances and topics such as PCB contamination, lead-paint ingestion, workplace exposure, Agent Orange litigation and other compelling issues.
General Info: Yr. Est. 1983, Bi-monthly, Trim Size-8½ x 11, Mimeo press, 70 pages, ISSN: 0737-8513, Ind/Abs/Online: NEWSNET, No Color, Matte
Subscriptions: Indv. $850, $40/copy
Advertising: Inquire for rates.
List Rental: Actives: 2,361, $110/M

Toxics Law Reporter   *Business*

Publishing Co: Bureau of National Affairs, Inc., 1231 25th St. NW, Bldg. N-200, Washington, DC 20037-1157; Title Tel # (202) 452-4200 Title Fax # (202) 822-8092
Personnel: Publisher-William Beltz, Editor-William Frank, Circ. Mgr.-Gary Seltzer
Editorial Description: Covers legal developments concerning toxic tort & hazardous waste lawsuits & related insurance issues. Includes litigation under the Comprehensive Environmental Response, Compensation, & Liability Act (Superfund), & the Resource Conservation & Recovery Act (RCRA), developments in tort law reform & pertinent state cases & legislation.
General Info: Yr. Est. 1986, Weekly, Trim Size-8½ x 11, Web press, 24 pages, ISSN: 0887-7394, Ind/Abs/Online: HRIN, Nexis, Lexis, Looseleaf
Subscriptions: Indv. $1,380

Trade Regulations Reports   *Business*

Publishing Co: CCH, Inc., 2700 Lake Cook Rd., Riverwoods, IL 60015 Parent Co.-Kluwer Law & Taxation Publishers, Cambridge; Title Tel # (847) 267-7000 Title Fax # (800) 224-8299
Editorial Description: Provides legal developments concerning federal & state antitrust & consumer protection laws. Court decisions, statutes, & federal trade commission developments.
General Info: Yr. Est. 1914, Weekly, Trim Size-6 x 9, Web press, 80 pages, No Color, Looseleaf
Subscriptions: Indv. $1,922

Trademark Protection and Practice
See: PATENTS/COPYRIGHTS/TRADE MARKS

Traffic Law Reports
See: TRAFFIC & TRANSPORTATION

Transnational Bulletin, The   *Business*

Publishing Co: Lewis, D'Amato, Brisbois & Bisgaard, 221 N Figueroa St Ste 1200, Los Angeles, CA 90012-2601; Title Tel # (213) 250-1800
Personnel: Editor-H. Bennett Arnberger
Editorial Description: Legal info for the international business community written by lawyers of the firm.
General Info: Monthly, Trim Size-8½ x 11, 8 pages, 2 Color, Matte

Transnational Contracts: Applicable Law & Settlement of Disputes   *Business*

Publishing Co: Oceana Publications, Inc., 75 Main St, Dobbs Ferry, NY 10522-1601 Tel # (914) 693-8100 Title Tel # (914) 693-1320 Title Fax # (914) 693-0402
Personnel: Editor-Georges R. Delaume, Production Mgr.-Mike Wortzman, Mktg. Dir.-John Downey
General Info: Yr. Est. 1983, Irregular, Trim Size-7 x 10, Looseleaf
Subscriptions: Indv. $900

Transport Laws of the World   *Business*

Publishing Co: Oceana Publications, Inc., 75 Main St, Dobbs Ferry, NY 10522-1601 Tel # (914) 693-8100 Fax # (914) 693-0402; Title Tel # (914) 693-1320
Personnel: Editor-Malcolm Evans, Editor-Martin Stanford, Production Mgr.-Mike Wortzman, Mktg. Dir.-John Downey
General Info: Yr. Est. 1978, Irregular, Trim Size-7 x 10, Looseleaf

Treatise on Environmental Law   *Business*

Publishing Co: Matthew Bender & Co., 11 Penn Plaza, New York, NY 10001-2006 Fax # (212) 244-3188; Title Tel # (212) 967-7707
Personnel: Editor-M. Tenner
Editorial Description: Clarifies issues, analyzes the statutes, and cites important cases in every environmental problem area.
General Info: Yr. Est. 1973, Irregular, Looseleaf
Subscriptions: $450/copy

Trial of Accident Case   *Business*

Publishing Co: Matthew Bender & Co., 11 Penn Plaza, New York, NY 10001-2006 Fax # (212) 244-3188; Title Tel # (212) 967-7707
Personnel: Editor-L. Bogaty
Editorial Description: Provides the medical know-how for skillfully presenting cases involving injuries most frequently assoicated with automobile & slip-and-fall accidents. Includes tested stategies & techniqaues as well as actual question-and-answer sequences.
General Info: Yr. Est. 1958, Semi-monthly, Looseleaf
Subscriptions: $730/copy

Trumpet, The

Publishing Co: Alderson Hospitality House, PO Box 579, Alderson, WV 25904-0579; Title Tel # (304) 445-2769
Personnel: Editor-Robert Shively
General Info: (Formerly Judgement), Yr. Est. 1977, Quarterly, 16 pages
Circulation: Total-1,000

Trust Administration and Taxation   *Business*

Publishing Co: Matthew Bender & Co., 11 Penn Plaza, New York, NY 10001-2006 Fax # (212) 244-3188; Title Tel # (212) 967-7707
Personnel: Editor-S. Diamond
Editorial Description: A well-documented practical text on establishment, administration, & taxation of trusts, completely updated to reflect current legislation.
General Info: Yr. Est. 1957, Annually, Looseleaf
Subscriptions: $310/copy

Trust Department Administration and Operations
See: BANKING & FINANCE

Tulane Tax Institute
See: TAXES

UCC Reporter-Digest   *Business*

Publishing Co: Matthew Bender & Co., 11 Penn Plaza, New York, NY 10001-2006 Fax # (212) 244-3188; Title Tel # (212) 967-7707
Editorial Description: Case digests, annotations, and student comments on all cases covered by the Uniform Commerical Code.
General Info: Yr. Est. 1965, Quarterly, Looseleaf
Subscriptions: $750/copy
Circulation: Total-2,200

UCI Broadcast
See: LAW ENFORCEMENT & PENOLOGY

Unclaimed Property Law and Reporting Forms   *Business*

Publishing Co: Matthew Bender & Co., 11 Penn Plaza, New York, NY 10001-2006 Tel # (212) 967-7707 Fax # (212) 244-3188
Editorial Description: The most comprehensive coverage available of the escheat laws & requirements for holders of unclaimed property, applicable in every state. Includes analysis of the Uniform Unclaimed Property Acts, relevant case law & state statutes.
General Info: Yr. Est. 1984, Irregular, Looseleaf

Underground Storage Tank Guide
See: ENVIRONMENT & ECOLOGY

Unfair Labor Practices Law Bulletin
See: LABOR

Uniform Commercial Code

Publishing Co: Gould Publications, Inc, 1333 N US Highway 17-92, Longwood, FL 32750-3724 Tel # (407) 695-9500 Fax # (407) 695-2906; Title Tel # (607) 724-3000
Editorial Description: Presentation of Uniform Commercial Code with official comments.
General Info: Annually, Trim Size-5½ x 8½, Sheetfed press, 740 pages, Looseleaf
Subscriptions: $19/copy

Uniform Commercial Code Law Letter   *Business*

Publishing Co: Warren, Gorham & Lamont, 31 Saint James Ave., Boston, MA 02116-4112 Parent Co.-Thomson Professional Publications, Stamford; Title Tel # (617) 423-2020 Title Fax # (617) 423-1914
Personnel: Publisher-Larry Selby, Mktg. Dir.-Sandra Fox
Editorial Description: Coverage of commercial law, including consumer credit, business law, and negotiable instruments. Includes a monthly Consumer Credit Report incorporating the Truth-in-Lending Review by Prof. Earl Phillips.
General Info: Yr. Est. 1966, Monthly, Trim Size-8½ x 11, Offset press, 8 pages, ISSN: 0503-1966, 2 Color
Subscriptions: Indv. $180
List Rental: List Management Co.: Manager: Seena Benedek; WG & L List Management, 1 Penn Plz Fl 42, New York, NY 10119-0002 Tel # (212) 971-5000

Uniform Commercial Code State Variations

Publishing Co: Gould Publications, Inc, 1333 N US Highway 17-92, Longwood, FL 32750-3724 Tel # (407) 695-9500 Fax # (407) 695-2906; Title Tel # (607) 724-3000
Personnel: Editor-Claire Flavell
Editorial Description: Variations for 15 states.
General Info: Annually, Trim Size-5½ x 8½, Sheetfed press, No Color, Looseleaf
Subscriptions: $26/copy

Union Labor Report Weekly Newsletter
See: LABOR UNION

Union Labor Report's On the Line
See: LABOR UNION

United States Code Unannotated

Publishing Co: Gould Publications, Inc, 1333 N US Highway 17-92, Longwood, FL 32750-3724 Tel # (407) 695-9500 Fax # (407) 695-2906; Title Tel # (607) 724-3000
Editorial Description: A compilation of all 50 titles of the Federal Statutes unannotated in 15 volumes. Approx 1300 pgs. per vol.
General Info: Annually, 1,300 pages, Looseleaf
Subscriptions: $449/copy

U.S. Customs and International Trade Guide
See: INTERNATIONAL TRADE

U.S. International Trade
Reports   *Business*

Publishing Co: Oceana Publications, Inc., 75 Main St, Dobbs Ferry, NY 10522-1601
Tel # (914) 693-8100 Fax # (914) 693-0402; Title Tel # (914) 693-1320
Personnel: Editor-Edwin S. Newman, Editor-Eugene Wypyski, Production Mgr.-Mike Wortzman, Mktg. Dir.-John Downey
General Info: Yr. Est. 1986, Irregular, Trim Size-7 x 10, Looseleaf
Subscriptions: Indv. $760

United States Law Week   *Business*

Publishing Co: Bureau of National Affairs, Inc., 1231 25th St. NW, Bldg. N-200, Washington, DC 20037-1157; Title Tel # (202) 452-4200 Title Fax # (202) 822-8092
Personnel: Publisher-William A. Beltz, Mng. Editor-Gregory R. Pease, Circ. Mgr.-Gary C. Seltzer
Editorial Description: Notification & reference service providing complete up-to-date information about all significant court decisions, rulings, regulations, & interpretations in state & federal law.
General Info: Yr. Est. 1933, Weekly, Trim Size-8½ x 11, Offset press, ISSN: 0148-8139, Ind/Abs/Online: Lexis, Nexis, Westlaw, No Color, Looseleaf
Subscriptions: Indv. $819

United States Law Week
Summary and Analysis   *Business*

Publishing Co: Bureau of National Affairs, Inc., 1231 25th St. NW, Bldg. N-200, Washington, DC 20037-1157; Title Tel # (202) 452-4200 Title Fax # (202) 822-8092
Personnel: Publisher-William A. Beltz, Mng. Editor-Gregory R. Pease, Circ. Mgr.-Gary R. Seltzer
Editorial Description: Weekly summary of the most important legal developments during the past week with an index and table of cases. It is Section 1 of BNA's U.S. Law Week.
General Info: Yr. Est. 1933, Weekly, Trim Size-8½ x 11, Offset press, 4 pages, ISSN: 0190-5252, Looseleaf
Subscriptions: $167/copy

United States Space Law:
Natl. & Intl. Regulation   *Business*

Publishing Co: Oceana Publications, Inc., 75 Main St, Dobbs Ferry, NY 10522-1601
Tel # (914) 693-8100; Title Tel # (914) 693-1320 Title Fax # (914) 693-0402
Personnel: Editor-Stephen Gorove, Production Mgr.-Mike Wortzman, Mktg. Dir.-John Downey
General Info: Yr. Est. 1982, Irregular, Trim Size-7 x 10, Looseleaf
Subscriptions: Indv. $595

U.S. Supreme Court
Bulletin   *Business*

Publishing Co: CCH, Inc., 2700 Lake Cook Rd., Riverwoods, IL 60015 Parent Co.-Kluwer Law & Taxation Publishers, Cambridge; Title Tel # (847) 267-7000 Title Fax # (800) 224-8299
Editorial Description: Publishes the full, official texts of opinions announced by the High Court, with prompt notice of all actions taken. Covers court term from October of one year until June of the following year.
General Info: Yr. Est. 1936, 45x/yr., Trim Size-6 x 9, Web press, No Color, Looseleaf
Subscriptions: Indv. $734

Unjust Dismissal
See: LABOR

Urban, State & Local Law News
See: GOVERNMENT

Utah Employment Law
Letter   *Business*

Publishing Co: M. Lee Smith Publishers & Printers ,LCC, P.O. Box 198867, 162 Fourth Avenue North, Nashville, TN 37219-8867 Tel # (615) 242-7395 Fax # (615) 256-6601
Personnel: Publisher-M Lee Smith, Editor-Mary Anne Wood, Circ. Mgr.-Cathy Bradfood, Mktg. Dir.-David Yates
General Info: Yr. Est. 1996, Monthly, Trim Size-8½ x 11, 8 pages, 2 Color
Subscriptions: Indv. $97
List Rental: Rents Lists
Printing Co: M. Lee Smith Publishers & Printers ,LLC, PO Box 198867, 162 Fourth Avenue, Nashville, TN 37219-8867 Tel # (615) 242-7395, Fax # (615) 256-6601

Utilities Law Reports
See: PUBLIC UTILITIES

Verdict Reviews   *Business, Consumer*

Publishing Co: LRP Publications, 747 Dresher Rd., P.O. Box 980, Horsham, PA 19044-0980
Tel # (215) 784-0910 Fax # (215) 784-0317; Title Tel # (215) 784-0860 Title Fax # (215) 784-9645
Personnel: Publisher-Kenneth Kahn, Editor-Brian Shenker
Editorial Description: Each issue contains a feature article backed by case examples which analyze significant trends in personal injury jury verdicts nationwide.
General Info: Yr. Est. 1983, Bi-monthly, Trim Size-8½ x 11, 4 pages, No Color
Subscriptions: Indv. $375, $23/copy
Circulation: Total-800

Verdicts & Settlements

Publishing Co: Shepard's/McGraw-Hill, Inc., 555 Middle Creek Pky, Colorado Springs, CO 80921-3622; Title Tel # (719) 488-3000 Title Fax # (719) 481-7448
Personnel: Editor-William Jordan, Production Mgr.-Cheryl Everitt, Adv. Dir.-Peggy Ives, Art Dir.-Leigh Vidakovich
General Info: Yr. Est. 1988, Monthly
Subscriptions: Indv. $350
List Rental: List Management Co.: The Lake Group, 411 Theodore Freund Ave., Rye, NY 10580-1497 Tel # (914) 925-2400, Fax # (914) 925-2499, Actives: 40,212, $130/M

Vermont Employment
Law Letter   *Business*

Publishing Co: M. Lee Smith Publishers & Printers ,LCC, P.O. Box 198867, 162 Fourth Avenue North, Nashville, TN 37219-8867 Tel # (615) 242-7395 Fax # (615) 256-6601
Personnel: Publisher-M Lee Smith, Circ. Mgr.-Cathy Bradford, Mktg. Dir.-David Yates
General Info: Yr. Est. 1996, Monthly, Trim Size-8½ x 11, 8 pages, 2 Color
Subscriptions: Indv. $97
List Rental: Rents Lists
Printing Co: M. Lee Smith Publishers & Printers ,LLC, PO Box 198867, 162 Fourth Avenue, Nashville, TN 37219-8867 Tel # (615) 242-7395, Fax # (615) 256-6601

Victims' Rights: Law and
Litigations   *Business*

Publishing Co: Matthew Bender & Co., 11 Penn Plaza, New York, NY 10001-2006
Tel # (212) 967-7707 Fax # (212) 244-3188
Editorial Description: With ligitation tips, strategies, checklists & planning notes throughout, covers all the vital aspects of obtaining compensation & litigation victims' claims.
General Info: Yr. Est. 1989, Irregular, Looseleaf

Virginia Criminal Law &
Motor Vehicle Handbook

Publishing Co: Gould Publications, Inc, 1333 N US Highway 17-92, Longwood, FL 32750-3724
Tel # (407) 695-9500 Fax # (407) 695-2906; Title Tel # (607) 724-3000
Editorial Description: The text of selected sections of the code of Virginia.
General Info: Annually, 1,100 pages, Looseleaf
Subscriptions: $22/copy

Virginia Employment Law
Letter   *Business*

Publishing Co: M. Lee Smith Publishers & Printers ,LCC, P.O. Box 198867, 162 Fourth Avenue North, Nashville, TN 37219-8867; Title Tel # (615) 242-7395 Title Fax # (615) 256-6601
Personnel: Publisher-M. Lee Smith, Editor-James Meath, Circ. Mgr.-Cathy Bradford, Mktg. Dir.-Dave Yates
Editorial Description: Review of employment law developments that affect Virginia employers.
General Info: Yr. Est. 1989, Monthly, Trim Size-8½ x 11, 8 pages, ISSN: 1042-461X, 2 Color
Subscriptions: Indv. $97
List Rental: Rents Lists
Printing Co: M. Lee Smith Publishers & Printers ,LLC, PO Box 198867, 162 Fourth Avenue, Nashville, TN 37219-8867 Tel # (615) 242-7395, Fax # (615) 256-6601

Virginia Environmental
Compliance Update   *Business*

Publishing Co: M. Lee Smith Publishers & Printers ,LCC, P.O. Box 198867, 162 Fourth Avenue North, Nashville, TN 37219-8867 Tel # (615) 242-7395 Fax # (615) 256-6601
Personnel: Publisher-M. Lee Smith, Editor-Timothy Hayes, Circ. Mgr.-Cathy Bradford, Mktg. Dir.-Dave Yates
Editorial Description: Reviews environmental law developments that affect Virginia companies.
General Info: Yr. Est. 1993, Monthly, Trim Size-8½ x 11, 8 pages, ISSN: 1068-9516, 2 Color
Subscriptions: Indv. $117
List Rental: Rents Lists
Printing Co: M. Lee Smith Publishers & Printers ,LLC, PO Box 198867, 162 Fourth Avenue, Nashville, TN 37219-8867 Tel # (615) 242-7395, Fax # (615) 256-6601

WADE Review   *Association*

Publishing Co: World Assn. of Document Examiners, 111 N. Canal St., Chicago, IL 60606-7252; Title Tel # (312) 930-9446
Personnel: Publisher-Lee Arnold, Editor-Keith Miller, Circ. Mgr.-Phil Melican, Art Dir.-Elaine Rill
Editorial Description: News about the field of forged and disputed documents.
General Info: (Formerly World Assn./Document Examiners Newsletter: WADE Newsletter), Yr. Est. 1971, Monthly, Offset press
Circulation: Total-5,000

Wages and Hours   *Business*

Publishing Co: Bureau of National Affairs, Inc., 1231 25th St. NW, Bldg. N-200, Washington, DC 20037-1157; Title Tel # (202) 452-4200 Title Fax # (202) 822-8092
Personnel: Publisher-William A. Beltz, Editor-Bill Manville, Mng. Editor-Nancy J. Sedmak, Circ. Mgr.-Gary C. Seltzer
Editorial Description: Full text, summaries, & explanations of federal laws & regulations in such areas as reporting, exemptions, wage-hour division inspections, minimum wages, equal pay, overtime, & child labor; includes enforcement policies, procedures, & precedent-setting decisions.
General Info: (Formerly Wage Hour Reporter), Yr. Est. 1938, Bi-weekly, Trim Size-6 x 9, Offset press, ISSN: 0149-2691, Ind/Abs/Online: Dialog, Westlaw, Lexis, Looseleaf
Subscriptions: Indv. $611

Warning Letter Bulletin   *Consumer*

Publishing Co: Washington Information Source, 8901 Battery Pl, Bethesda, MD 20814-2638; Title Tel # (301) 907-6668 Title Fax # (301) 913-9482
Personnel: Publisher-Kenneth Reid, Editor-Beth Meyers
Editorial Description: Sums up and discusses FDA citations on companies violating FDA rules.
General Info: Yr. Est. 1993, Bi-weekly, 12 pages, ISSN: 1069-4218, Color-cover, Saddle-stitched
Subscriptions: Indv. $359, For. $419, $17/copy
List Rental: Actives: 8,000, $500/M

Warrens Forms of Agreement
Business

Publishing Co: Matthew Bender & Co., 11 Penn Plaza, New York, NY 10001-2006
Fax # (212) 244-3188; Title Tel # (212) 967-7707
Personnel: Editor-L. Rubenzahl
Editorial Description: A compilation of contract forms & alternative clauses for everyday business transactions.
General Info: Yr. Est. 1954, Annually, Looseleaf
Subscriptions: $460/copy

Warren's Heaton on Surrogate's Court Practice
Business

Publishing Co: Matthew Bender & Co., 11 Penn Plaza, New York, NY 10001-2006
Tel # (212) 967-7707 Fax # (212) 244-3188
Editorial Description: Accepted by the courts as the leading text & authority on substantive & procedural practice.
General Info: Yr. Est. 1907, Irregular, Looseleaf

Warren's Negligence in the New York Courts
Business

Publishing Co: Matthew Bender & Co., 11 Penn Plaza, New York, NY 10001-2006
Fax # (212) 244-3188; Title Tel # (212) 967-7707
Personnel: Editor-R. Kaye
Editorial Description: Full analysis and annotation of every fact situation in all the latest New York cases; including all cases and relevant statutes.
General Info: Yr. Est. 1941, Every two years, Looseleaf
Subscriptions: $675/copy

Warren's Weed New York Real Property
See: REAL ESTATE

Washington Counseletter
See: EDUCATION

Washington Employment Law Letter
See: EMPLOYMENT

Washington Memo
See: HEALTH

Washington Newsletter
See: ADVERTISING & MARKETING

Washington Report
Business, Association

Publishing Co: Medical Group Management Association, 104 Inverness Terrace E., Englewood, CO 80112-5306; Title Tel # (303) 799-1111 Title Fax # (303) 397-1824
Personnel: Editor-Randy Teach
Editorial Description: Washington Report is a legislative & regulatory news service prepared by MGMA's Govt. Relations Dept. It is not a substitute for individual determinations of medical group compliance with various federal regulatory requirements.
General Info: (Formerly Inside the Arena), Yr. Est. 1983, Monthly, Trim Size-8½ x 11, 4 pages, ISSN: 1040-2306, Color, Newsprint
Subscriptions: Indv. $40
Circulation: Total-2,500
Printing Co: Signal Graphics, 1485 S. Colorado Blvd., Denver, CO 80222 Tel # (303) 757-0040

Washington Social Legislation Bulletin

Publishing Co: Sponsor-Child Welfare League of America, Social Legislation Information Service, 440 1st St NW Ste 310, Washington, DC 20001-2085; Title Tel # (202) 638-2952
Personnel: Editor-Marjorie Kopp, Circ. Mgr.-Cathye Thomas
General Info: Yr. Est. 1944, Semi-monthly, ISSN: 0129-2578
Circulation: Total-1,550

Water Law Newsletter

Publishing Co: Rocky Mountain Mineral Law Foundation, 7039 E 18th Ave, Denver, CO 80220-1826
Fax # (303) 321-7657; Title Tel # (303) 321-8100
Personnel: Editor-George A. Gould
Editorial Description: Coverage of legislative and judicial developments in water law at federal, state, and local levels.
General Info: Yr. Est. 1965, Trim Size-8½ x 11, Offset press, 16 pages
Subscriptions: Indv. $20, Can. $27, For. $32, $5/copy
Circulation: Total-700

Water Log

Publishing Co: Mississippi-Alabama Sea Grant Legal Program, Univ. of Miss. Law Ctr., University, MS 38677
General Info: Yr. Est. 1981, Quarterly
Circulation: Total-850

Weekly Terrorism Profile
See: SECURITY & SURVEILLANCE

Weinstein's Evidence Manual
Business

Publishing Co: Matthew Bender & Co., 11 Penn Plaza, New York, NY 10001-2006
Tel # (212) 967-7707 Fax # (212) 244-3188
Editorial Description: A practical desktop & courtroom answer guide. Includes incisive analysis by Judge Weinstein. Contains discussion of the reason behind the Rule, its philosophy & practice, & how to use it to your advantage. Contains authoritative federal case citations.
General Info: Yr. Est. 1987, Irregular, Looseleaf

Weinstein's Evidence, United States Rules
Business

Publishing Co: Matthew Bender & Co., 11 Penn Plaza, New York, NY 10001-2006
Fax # (212) 244-3188; Title Tel # (212) 967-7707
Personnel: Editor-S. Katz
Editorial Description: Contains the essential analytical work on the Federal Rules of Evidence. All federal and state cases having bearing on the rules are reported.
General Info: Yr. Est. 1975, Looseleaf
Subscriptions: $840/copy

West Coast Environmental Law Research Foundation Newsletter
See: ENVIRONMENT & ECOLOGY

West Virginia Employment Law Letter
Business

Publishing Co: M. Lee Smith Publishers & Printers ,LCC, P.O. Box 198867, 162 Fourth Avenue North, Nashville, TN 37219-8867 Tel # (615) 242-7395 Fax # (615) 256-6601
Personnel: Publisher-M Lee Smith, Editor-David Morrison, Circ. Mgr.-Cathy Bradford, Mktg. Dir.-David Yates
General Info: Yr. Est. 1995, Monthly, Trim Size-8½ x 11, 8 pages, 2 Color
Subscriptions: Indv. $97
List Rental: Rents Lists
Printing Co: M. Lee Smith Publishers & Printers ,LLC, PO Box 198867, 162 Fourth Avenue, Nashville, TN 37219-8867 Tel # (615) 242-7395, Fax # (615) 256-6601

West's Federal Case News

Publishing Co: West Publishing, 620 Opperman Dr., Eagan, MN 55123-1340 Fax # (612) 687-7302
Parent Co.-Thomson Corp., Stamford; Title Tel # (612) 687-7000
Personnel: Editor-Brian Johnson
General Info: Weekly, Trim Size-5½ x 8, 75 pages, No Color
Subscriptions: Indv. $205, Inst. $205
Printing Co: West Publishing Corp., 620 Opperman Drive, Eagan, MN 55123 Tel # (612) 687-8000

What to Do about Personnel Problems in (Your State)
See: INDUSTRIAL RELATIONS/PERSONNEL

White-Collar Crime Reporter
Business

Publishing Co: Andrews Publications, Inc., 1646 West Chester Pike, PO Box 1000, Westtown, PA 19395; Title Tel # (610) 399-6600 Title Fax # (610) 399-6610
Personnel: Publisher-John E. Backe, Editor-Edith McFall, Mktg. Dir.-Andrew Katz
Editorial Description: Major articles guest written by practitioners in the area of white collar crime and covering such topics as sentencing guidelines, corporate liability, banking & securities fraud and government contract fraud.
General Info: Yr. Est. 1991, Monthly, Trim Size-8½ x 11, Mimeo press, 15 pages, ISSN: 0891-6721
Subscriptions: Indv. $495, $43/copy
Advertising: Inquire for rates.
List Rental: Actives: 66,686, $125/M

White, New York Corporations
Business

Publishing Co: Matthew Bender & Co., 11 Penn Plaza, New York, NY 10001-2006
Fax # (212) 244-3188; Title Tel # (212) 967-7707
Personnel: Editor-M. Tenner
Editorial Description: Analysis of statutory provisions, & coverage of recent amendments & dicisions. Federal tax analysis covering everything from pre-incorporation planning to sale or liquidation & dissolution.
General Info: Yr. Est. 1963, Annually, Looseleaf
Subscriptions: $435/copy

Wills-Estate Planning Forms
Business

Publishing Co: Research Institute of America, 90 5th Avenue, New York, NY 10011-7629
Tel # (212) 645-4800; Title Tel # (800) 562-0245
Editorial Description: Executors-trustees provisions, estate tax conservation, gifts on condition, living trust provisions, etc.
General Info: Monthly, Trim Size-6 x 9¼, Offset press, Looseleaf
Subscriptions: Indv. $336
List Rental: List Management Co.: WG & L List Management, 1 Penn Plz Fl 42, New York, NY 10119-0002 Tel # (212) 971-5000

Wills Estates and Trusts   *Business*

Publishing Co: Research Institute of America, 90 5th Avenue, New York, NY 10011-7629
Tel # (212) 645-4800; Title Tel # (800) 562-0245
Editorial Description: Each subject has a general text discussing the law involved.
General Info: Monthly, Trim Size-6 x 9¼, Offset press, Looseleaf
Subscriptions: Indv. $714
List Rental: List Management Co.: WG & L List Management, 1 Penn Plz Fl 42, New York, NY 10119-0002 Tel # (212) 971-5000

Wills Laws of New York

Publishing Co: Gould Publications, Inc, 1333 N US Highway 17-92, Longwood, FL 32750-3724
Tel # (407) 695-9500 Fax # (407) 695-2906; Title Tel # (607) 724-3000
Editorial Description: A concise review of the New York law relating to decendents' estates and wills containing every possible estate question.
General Info: (Formerly New York Kass on Wills), Annually, 225 pages, Looseleaf
Subscriptions: $30/copy

Window on Canadian Tax
See: TAXES

Wisconsin Appellate
Reporter

Publishing Co: Law Reporter Co., 209 Michigan Ave # 270, Crystal Falls, MI 49920-1312;
Title Tel # (906) 875-6970
Personnel: Publisher-P.G. Oakes, Editor-John Sundquist
Editorial Description: Summaries of unpublished decisions of the Wisconsin Court of Appeals.
General Info: Yr. Est. 1984, Monthly, 35 pages, No Color
Subscriptions: Indv. $175

Wisconsin Employment
Law Letters   *Business*

Publishing Co: M. Lee Smith Publishers & Printers ,LCC, P.O. Box 198867, 162 Fourth Avenue North, Nashville, TN 37219-8867; Title Tel # (615) 242-7395 Title Fax # (615) 256-6601
Personnel: Publisher-M. Lee Smith, Editor-Jack Walker, Circ. Mgr.-Cathy Bradford, Mktg. Dir.-Dave Yates
General Info: Yr. Est. 1992, Monthly, Trim Size-8½ x 11, 8 pages, ISSN: 1059-5066, 2 Color
Subscriptions: Indv. $97
List Rental: Rents Lists
Printing Co: M. Lee Smith Publishers & Printers ,LLC, PO Box 198867, 162 Fourth Avenue, Nashville, TN 37219-8867 Tel # (615) 242-7395, Fax # (615) 256-6601

Wisconsin Environmental Law and Regulation Report
See: ENVIRONMENT & ECOLOGY

Wisconsin Law Reporter

Publishing Co: Law Reporter Co., 209 Michigan Ave # 270, Crystal Falls, MI 49920-1312;
Title Tel # (906) 875-6970
Personnel: Publisher-P.G. Oakes, Editor-John Sundquist
Editorial Description: Summaries of Wisconsin state & federal court decisions.
General Info: Yr. Est. 1978, Semi-monthly, 21 pages, No Color
Subscriptions: Indv. $195
Circulation: Total-400

Women around New York
See: WOMEN'S

Workers' Comp Advisor
See: INDUSTRIAL RELATIONS/PERSONNEL

Workers' Comp Practice Advisor
See: MEDICINE

Workers' Compensation
Biweekly Bulletin   *Business*

Publishing Co: Quinlan Publishing, 23 Drydock Ave, Boston, MA 02210-2387 Fax # (617) 345-9646;
Title Tel # (617) 542-0048
Editorial Description: Latest court decisions on when and how compensation will be awarded.
General Info: Bi-weekly
Subscriptions: Indv. $89
List Rental: List Management Co.: Stevens-Knox List Management, 304 Park Ave S., New York, NY 10010-5312 Tel # (212) 388-8800, Fax # (212) 388-8890

Workers' Compensation
Cost Control   *Business*

Publishing Co: Quinlan Publishing, 23 Drydock Ave, Boston, MA 02210-2387 Tel # (617) 542-0048
Fax # (617) 345-9646
Editorial Description: Issues dealing with employer-employee relationships that help reduce insurance costs.
General Info: Monthly
Subscriptions: Indv. $93

Worker's Compensation
Law Bulletin   *Business*

Publishing Co: Quinlan Publishing, 23 Drydock Ave, Boston, MA 02210-2387 Fax # (617) 345-9646;
Title Tel # (617) 542-0048
Personnel: Editor-Mike Quinlan
Editorial Description: Latest court decisions on how and when compensation is given.
General Info: Yr. Est. 1978, Monthly, Looseleaf
Subscriptions: Indv. $59
List Rental: List Management Co.: Stevens-Knox List Management, 304 Park Ave S., New York, NY 10010-5312 Tel # (212) 388-8800, Fax # (212) 388-8890

World Federalist News
See: INTERNATIONAL AFFAIRS

World Jurist   *Business, Association*

Publishing Co: World Peace Through Law Center, 1000 Connecticut Ave., N.W., Washington, DC 20036-5302; Title Tel # (202) 466-5428 Title Fax # (202) 452-8540
Personnel: Editor-M. Bertocchi, Circ. Mgr.-M. Henneberry
Editorial Description: Research for international development as a basis for future world peace.
General Info: Yr. Est. 1963, Bi-monthly, Trim Size-8½ x 11, Sheetfed press, 12 pages, No Color
Subscriptions: Indv. $150, $5/copy
Circulation: (100% controlled), Total-6,000

World Patent Law: Patent Statutes, Regulations and Treaties
See: PATENTS/COPYRIGHTS/TRADE MARKS

World Patent Law and Practice
See: PATENTS/COPYRIGHTS/TRADE MARKS

World Shipping Laws and
Fact Finding Tools   *Business*

Publishing Co: Oceana Publications, Inc., 75 Main St, Dobbs Ferry, NY 10522-1601
Tel # (914) 693-8100; Title Tel # (914) 693-1320 Title Fax # (914) 693-0402
Personnel: Editor-David Jackson, Production Mgr.-Mike Wortzman, Mktg. Dir.-John Downey
General Info: Yr. Est. 1979, Irregular, Trim Size-7 x 10, Looseleaf
Subscriptions: Indv. $850

Wrongful Discharge
Report

Publishing Co: Andrews Publications, Inc., 1646 West Chester Pike, PO Box 1000, Westtown, PA 19395; Title Tel # (610) 399-6600 Title Fax # (610) 399-6610
Personnel: Publisher-John E. Backe, Editor-Linda Coady, Mktg. Dir.-Andrew Katz
Editorial Description: Nationwide coverage of suits alleging tort and contract claims against employers, including breach of contract, retaliatory discharge, constructive discharge public policy violations, Title VII, ADEA, ADA, Rehabilitation Act, RICO and civil rights violations, hiring practices, and employee benefits.
General Info: Yr. Est. 1987, Monthly, Trim Size-8½ x 11, Mimeo press, 25 pages, ISSN: 1053-0274, No Color
Subscriptions: Indv. $350, $29/copy
Advertising: Inquire for rates.
List Rental: Actives: 237, $110/M

Wyoming Criminal Law &
Motor Vehicle Handbook

Publishing Co: Gould Publications, Inc, 1333 N US Highway 17-92, Longwood, FL 32750-3724
Tel # (407) 695-9500 Fax # (407) 695-2906; Title Tel # (607) 724-3000
Editorial Description: A concise presentation of the crimes and offenses and motor vehicle laws of Wyoming.
General Info: Annually, 600 pages, Looseleaf
Subscriptions: $22/copy

Wyoming Employment
Law Letter   *Business*

Publishing Co: M. Lee Smith Publishers & Printers ,LCC, P.O. Box 198867, 162 Fourth Avenue North, Nashville, TN 37219-8867 Tel # (615) 242-7395 Fax # (615) 256-6601
Personnel: Publisher-M Lee Smith, Editor-Brad Cave, Circ. Mgr.-Cathy Bradford, Mktg. Dir.-David Yates
General Info: Monthly, Trim Size-8½ x 11, 8 pages, 2 Color
Subscriptions: Indv. $97
List Rental: Rents Lists
Printing Co: M. Lee Smith Publishers & Printers ,LLC, PO Box 198867, 162 Fourth Avenue, Nashville, TN 37219-8867 Tel # (615) 242-7395, Fax # (615) 256-6601

York University Institute for Social Research Newsletter
See: SOCIOLOGY

You & the Law   *Business*

Publishing Co: National Institute of Business Management, 1101 King St Ste 411, Alexandria, VA 22314-2966 Parent Co.-National Information Corp., Alexandria; Title Tel # (703) 739-3798 Title Fax # (703) 549-9705
Personnel: Publisher-Brian Smith, Editor-Joy Correge
Editorial Description: Executive guide to legal issues.
General Info: Yr. Est. 1970, Monthly, Trim Size-8½ x 11, 14 pages, ISSN: 0731-1109, 2 Color, Matte
Subscriptions: Indv. $100
Acquisitions: Publication Bought, Publication Sold
Circulation: Total-10,000
List Rental: Actives: $95/M, Expires: $55/M

Youth Law News

Publishing Co: Natl. Ctr. for Youth Law, 114 Sansome St., #950, San Francisco, CA 94104-3820; Title Tel # (415) 543-3307 Title Fax # (415) 956-9024
Personnel: Editor-Marcia Henry
General Info: Yr. Est. 1982, Bi-monthly, Sheetfed press, 24 pages, ISSN: 0882-8520, No Color, Matte, Saddle-stitched
Subscriptions: Indv. $40, Inst. $95, $3/copy
Circulation: Total-2,500
Printing Co: V.I.P. Litho, 1 Newhall St, San Francisco, CA 94124-1420 Tel # (415) 695-8888

Zoning and Land Use Control
See: PUBLIC MANAGEMENT & PLANNING

Zoning and Planning Law
Report

Publishing Co: Clark Boardman Callaghan, 375 Hudson St, New York, NY 10014-3685 Fax # (212) 807-6209; Title Tel # (212) 929-7500 Title Fax # (212) 924-0460
Personnel: Publisher-Jim Fegen, Editor-Beth Rubin, Production Dir.-Wayne Smith
Editorial Description: Comprehensive newsletter on zoning and planning law.
General Info: Yr. Est. 1977, 11x/yr., Trim Size-8$\frac{1}{2}$ x 11, Sheetfed press, 8 pages, ISSN: 0161-8113, No Color
Subscriptions: Indv. $195
List Rental: Rents Lists

LAW ENFORCEMENT & PENOLOGY

APA Newsletter   *Association*

Publishing Co: American Polygraph Association, PO Box 1061, Severna Park, MD 21146-8061 Tel # (410) 647-0936 Fax # (410) 647-8526; Title Tel # (410) 647-8526
General Info: Yr. Est. 1972, Bi-monthly, Trim Size-8$\frac{1}{2}$ x 11, 32 pages
Subscriptions: Indv. $35, Can. $45, For. $45, $6/copy
Circulation: Total-2,400
Printing Co: Sheridan Press, 450 Fame Avenue, Hanover, PA 17331-9581 Tel # (717) 632-3535, Fax # (717) 633-8900

ASIS Dynamics
See: BUSINESS & INDUSTRY

Alabama Prison Project
Newsletter

Publishing Co: Alabama Prison Project, 410 S Perry St, Montgomery, AL 36104-4236; Title Tel # (205) 264-7416
Editorial Description: Death penalty, prisons, community actions, creative writing, graphics.
General Info: Yr. Est. 1980, Quarterly, Trim Size-8$\frac{1}{2}$ x 11, Mimeo press, 8 pages
Subscriptions: Indv. $5
Acquistions: Publication Bought
Circulation: Total-650

All Points Bulletin
Newsletter

Publishing Co: Utah Peace Officers Assn, 3135 S 3600 W, Salt Lake City, UT 84119-2529; Title Tel # (801) 968-6969
Personnel: Editor-Brigitte Dawson
Editorial Description: News of the Assn., advises members of upcoming training programs.
General Info: Yr. Est. 1986, Quarterly, Trim Size-8$\frac{1}{2}$ x 11, 8 pages
Circulation: Total-2,400
Advertising: Inquire for rates.

Alston Wilkes Society
Newsletter   *Association*

Publishing Co: AWS, 2215 Devine St, Columbia, SC 29205-2401; Title Tel # (803) 799-2490
Personnel: Editor-Linda Halton
Editorial Description: News of Society's work with inmates of prisons in South Carolina.
General Info: Yr. Est. 1966, Quarterly, Trim Size-11 x 17, 12 pages
Circulation: (100% controlled), Total-8,500

American Protestant Correctional Chaplains Association Newsletter
See: RELIGIOUS & THEOLOGICAL

Animal Sheltering Magazine
See: ANIMALS

Arson Prevention Idea File
See: FIRE PROTECTION

Assessment Center
Handbook

Publishing Co: Gould Publications, Inc, 1333 N US Highway 17-92, Longwood, FL 32750-3724 Tel # (407) 695-9500 Fax # (407) 695-2906
Editorial Description: Oral and written assessment center excercises includes scoring methodology.
General Info: Irregular, Looseleaf
Subscriptions: $18/copy

BNA Criminal Practice Manual
See: LAW

BNA/ACCA Compliance Manual: Prevention of Corporate Liability
See: BUSINESS & INDUSTRY

Bilingual Handbook for
Public Safety
Professionals

Publishing Co: Gould Publications, Inc, 1333 N US Highway 17-92, Longwood, FL 32750-3724 Tel # (407) 695-9500 Fax # (407) 695-2906
Editorial Description: Provides users with the means to obtain from and provide to Spanish speaking subject critical information related to a variety of situations ranging from vehicle stops to evacuation. Includes cassette!
General Info: Irregular
Subscriptions: $24/copy

C.J. the Americas

Publishing Co: Office of International Criminal Justice, 1333 S Wabash Ave # 53, Chicago, IL 60605-2504; Title Tel # (312) 996-0159 Title Fax # (312) 413-0458
Personnel: Publisher, Editor-Richard Ward, Circ. Mgr.-Jeff Builta, Production Mgr.-Beth Pacholski, Art Dir.-Dave Zemke
Editorial Description: Specializin in criminal justice from South America, United States perspective.
General Info: Yr. Est. 1988, Bi-monthly, Trim Size-8$\frac{1}{2}$ x 11, 28 pages, ISSN: 0896-9922, 2 Color, Other, Saddle-stitched
Subscriptions: Indv. $24, Inst. $22, Can. $24, For. $42, $4/copy
Advertising: $350. Accepts Inserts.

CJ Europe

Publishing Co: Office of International Criminal Justice, 1333 S Wabash Ave # 53, Chicago, IL 60605-2504 Fax # (312) 413-0458; Title Tel # (312) 996-0159 Title Fax # (312) 913-0458
Personnel: Publisher, Editor-Richard Ward, Circ. Mgr.-Jeff Builta, Product Mgr.-Beth Pacholski, Art Dir.-Dave Zemke
Editorial Description: Specializing in criminal justice from a European perspective.
General Info: Yr. Est. 1991, Bi-monthly, Trim Size-8$\frac{1}{2}$ x 11, 16 pages, ISSN: 1059-2423, 2 Color, Other, Saddle-stitched
Subscriptions: Indv. $24, Inst. $22, Can. $24, For. $42, $4/copy
Advertising: Accepts Inserts.

C.J. International   CPM: $116

Publishing Co: Office of International Criminal Justice, 1333 S Wabash Ave # 53, Chicago, IL 60605-2504; Title Tel # (312) 996-0159 Title Fax # (312) 413-0458
Personnel: Publisher, Editor-Richard Ward, Circ. Mgr.-Jeff Builta, Production Mgr.-Beth Pacholski, Art Dir.-Dave Zemke
Editorial Description: Specializing in criminal justice from intl.perspective.
General Info: Yr. Est. 1984, Bi-monthly, Trim Size-8$\frac{1}{2}$ x 11, 28 pages, ISSN: 0882-0252, 2 Color, Other, Saddle-stitched
Subscriptions: Indv. $24, Inst. $22, Can. $24, For. $42, $4/copy
Circulation: Total-3,000
Advertising: $350. Accepts Inserts.

CJ Management & Training
Digest   *Business*

Publishing Co: Washington Crime News Services, 3918 Prosperity Ave Ste 318, Fairfax, VA 22031-3333; Title Tel # (703) 573-1600 Title Fax # (703) 573-1604
Personnel: Publisher-R.J. O'Connell, Editor-Betty Bosarge, Circ. Mgr.-Nancy Van Wyen
Editorial Description: Resource bulletin for law enforcement/criminal justice training directors and managers.
General Info: (Formerly Criminal Justice Digest; Training Aids Digest), Yr. Est. 1976, Semi-monthly, Trim Size-8$\frac{1}{2}$ x 11, Sheetfed press, 10 pages, No Color
Subscriptions: Indv. $295, Can. $298, For. $320

Campus Crime   *Business*

Publishing Co: Business Publishers, Inc., 951 Pershing Dr., Silver Spring, MD 20910-4464 Tel # (301) 589-5103 Fax # (301) 589-8493
Editorial Description: Published for security officials on college and university campuses. Reports on relevant federal legislation.
General Info: Yr. Est. 1991, Monthly, ISSN: 1054-3821
Subscriptions: Indv. $240

Canadian Police Chief   *Business, Association*   CPM: $416

Publishing Co: Canadian Assn. of Chiefs of Police, Inc., 130 Albert Street, Suite 1710, Ottawa, ON K1P 5G4 Canada; Title Tel # (613) 233-1106 Title Fax # (613) 233-6960
Personnel: Editor, Adv. Dir.-S.H. Schultz
General Info: (Formerly Canadian Police Bulletin), Yr. Est. 1967, 10x/yr., 94 pages, ISSN: 0713-4517
Subscriptions: Can. $54, For. $70
Circulation: Total-1,200, Readership-1,200
Advertising: $500. Accepts Inserts.

Canine Courier   *Association*

Publishing Co: U.S. Police Canine Assn., Rr 2 Box 221j, Angier, NC 27501-9638; Title Tel # (919) 639-0490 Title Fax # (919) 639-6091
Personnel: Editor-R. O. Rogers
Editorial Description: Police dog handlers & trainers news.
General Info: Quarterly, Trim Size-10 x 12, Web press, 28 pages, 3% ads, 2 Color
Subscriptions: Free With Membership
Circulation: (100% controlled), Total-3,500
Advertising: Inquire for rates.

Carolina Justice Policy Center News

Publishing Co: Carolina Justice Polce Center, PO Box 309, Durham, NC 27702-0309; Title Tel # (919) 682-1149 Title Fax # (919) 688-1725
Personnel: Editor-Melanie M. Lim
Editorial Description: The Carolina Justice Policy Center (CJPC) seeks to promote effective, humane, and equitable solutions to North Carolina's criminal justice problems. Programs include community corrections, community penalties, violence prevention, and opposition to the death penalty.
General Info: (Formerly Prison & Jail Project Bulletin), Yr. Est. 1983, Semi-annually, Trim Size-8.5 x 11, Offset press, 8 pages, Color, Recycled
Subscriptions: Indv. $6, Free With Membership
Circulation: Total-1,000, Readership-1,000
List Rental: Rents Lists

Case Evaluation Manual   *Business*

Publishing Co: LRP Publications, 747 Dresher Rd., P.O. Box 980, Horsham, PA 19044-0980 Tel # (215) 784-0910 Fax # (215) 784-0317
Personnel: Publisher-Virginia Hermann, Editor-Don Marshall, Circ. Mgr.-David Dreimiller, Adv. Dir.-Jodi Yuhaz, Promotion Dir.-Gerda Burton
Editorial Description: Research of all personal injuries & liabilities from a nationwide database of cases.
General Info: Yr. Est. 1959, Monthly, Trim Size-5½ x 8½, Looseleaf
Subscriptions: Indv. $625
Circulation: Total-4,000

Catalyst Newsletter   *Consumer, Association*

Publishing Co: Natl. Crime Prevention Council, 1700 K St NW 2nd Floor, Washington, DC 20006-3817; Title Tel # (202) 466-6272 Title Fax # (202) 296-1356
Personnel: Editor-Mary Jo Marvin
General Info: Yr. Est. 1981, Monthly, Trim Size-8½ x 11, Desktop press, 6 pages, 2 Color
Subscriptions: Free
Circulation: Total-14,500
Printing Co: Colortone Press, 1017 Brightseat Rd, Landover, MD 20785-3738 Tel # (301) 350-0100

Champion
    See: LAW

Church Council on Justice & Corrections, Update
    See: RELIGIOUS & THEOLOGICAL

Community Policing Digest   *Consumer*

Publishing Co: Washington Crime News Services, 3918 Prosperity Ave Ste 318, Fairfax, VA 22031-3333; Title Tel # (703) 573-1600 Title Fax # (703) 573-1604
Personnel: Publisher, Editor-R.J. O'Connell, Circ. Mgr.-Nancy VanWyen
Editorial Description: News summary of community policing, crime prevention, and victim issues.
General Info: (Formerly Community Crime Prevention Digest; Crime Victims Digest), Yr. Est. 1973, Monthly, Offset press, 10 pages, No Color, Newsprint
Subscriptions: Indv. $295, Can. $298, For. $320
Circulation: Total-1,000
List Rental: Rents Lists

Compiler   *Scholarly, Association*

Publishing Co: Illinois Criminal Justice Info. Authority, 120 S Riverside Plz Fl 10, Chicago, IL 60606-3913 Fax # (312) 793-3997; Title Tel # (312) 793-8550 Title Fax # (312) 793-8422
Personnel: Editorial Page Ed., Sr. Ed.-Sharon Bond
Editorial Description: Covers criminal justice research, policy & information issues.
General Info: Yr. Est. 1979, Quarterly, Trim Size-8½ x 11, Sheetfed press, 20 pages, ISSN: 1059-6569, 2 Color, Matte, Saddle-stitched
Subscriptions: Free
Circulation: (100% controlled), Total-9,000

Computing & Communications: Law & Protection Report
    See: COMPUTERS & AUTOMATION

Confidential Air Letter
    See: AERONAUTICS/ASTRONAUTICS

Corhealth
    See: HEALTH

Correctional Compass

Publishing Co: Florida Dept. of Corrections, 2601 Blairstone Rd, Tallahassee, FL 32399-2500; Title Tel # (904) 488-0420 Title Fax # (904) 922-2848
Personnel: Publisher-Harry Singletary, Jr., Editor-Paula Bryant
Editorial Description: Features information on employee promotions.
General Info: Yr. Est. 1961, Monthly, Sheetfed press, 8 pages, 2 Color, Coated
Acquistions: Publication Bought
Circulation: Total-13,000
Printing Co: Judd's, Inc., 294 Front Royal Road, Strasburg, VA 22657

Correctional Industries Assn. Newsletter   *Association*

Publishing Co: Correctional Industries Assn., Box 11910, Iron Works Pike, Lexington, KY 40578-1910; Title Tel # (606) 231-1902 Title Fax # (606) 231-1943
Personnel: Editor-Yolanda Swinford, Asst. Ed.-Barbara Ramey
General Info: Yr. Est. 1942, Quarterly, Offset press, 24 pages, 5% ads, 2 Color, Other, Saddle-stitched
Subscriptions: Indv. $75
Circulation: Total-2,000
Advertising: Inquire for rates.

Correctional Service Federation-U.S.A. Newsletter

Publishing Co: Correctional Service Federation-U.S.A., 436 W. Wisconsin Ave., Milwaukee, WI 53203-2105; Title Tel # (414) 271-2512
General Info: Yr. Est. 1962, Quarterly

Corrections Digest   *Business*

Publishing Co: Washington Crime News Services, 3918 Prosperity Ave Ste 318, Fairfax, VA 22031-3333; Title Tel # (703) 573-1600 Title Fax # (703) 573-1604
Personnel: Publisher-R.J. O'Connell, Editor-Betty Bosarge, Circ. Mgr.-Nancy VanWyen
Editorial Description: Information for the rehabilitation & correction professional.
General Info: Yr. Est. 1969, Weekly, Trim Size-8½ x 11, Sheetfed press, 10 pages, ISSN: 0010-9045, Ind/Abs/Online: CJPI, No Color
Subscriptions: Indv. $345, Can. $351, For. $395

Corrections Legal Defense Quarterly   *Association*

Publishing Co: Public Safety Employment Institute, Inc., 5519 N Cumberland Ave Ste 1008, Chicago, IL 60656-1480 Fax # (312) 763-3225; Title Tel # (312) 763-2800
Personnel: Editor-Emory Plitt
Editorial Description: Each issue is a single topic legal research article, covering legal aspects of correctional and detention facilities.
General Info: Yr. Est. 1993, Quarterly, Trim Size-8½ x 11, Sheetfed press, 28 pages, ISSN: 1076-7312, Color-cover
Subscriptions: Indv. $88, Inst. $88, Can. $88, For. $88
Circulation: Total-300
Printing Co: Pyramid Grapics, 230 Miller, S. San Francisco, CA 94080

Corrections Professional, The   *Business*

Publishing Co: LRP Publications, 747 Dresher Rd., P.O. Box 980, Horsham, PA 19044-0980 Tel # (215) 784-0910 Fax # (215) 784-0317
Editorial Description: Presents issues and news relating to corrections professionals.
General Info: Monthly

Court Technology Bulletin
    See: LAW

Crime & Delinquency in California/Advance Release   *Association*

Publishing Co: Bureau of Criminal Statistics, 4949 Broadway Rm E231, Sacramento, CA 95820-1528 Tel # (916) 227-3552
General Info: Yr. Est. 1979, Annually, Sheetfed press, 20 pages, 2 Color, Matte
Circulation: Total-5,000

Crime & Drug Report   *Business, Association*

Publishing Co: Drug Policy Research Institute, PO Box 3423, Arlington, VA 22203-0423; Title Tel # (703) 533-2077 Title Fax # (703) 533-1669
Personnel: Publisher, Editor-Richard Baum
Editorial Description: Provides news of federal law enforcement assistance and grants to state and local law enforcement agencies.
General Info: (Formerly Crime Policy Report), Yr. Est. 1995, Monthly, 12 pages
Subscriptions: Indv. $159, Inst. $159, Can. $169, For. $179

Crime Control Digest   *Business*

Publishing Co: Washington Crime News Services, 3918 Prosperity Ave Ste 318, Fairfax, VA 22031-3333; Title Tel # (703) 573-1600 Title Fax # (703) 573-1604
Personnel: Publisher-Richard O'Connell, Editor-Betty Bosarge, Circ. Mgr.-Nancy Van Wyen
Editorial Description: A complete news service for the law enforcement professional.
General Info: Yr. Est. 1967, Weekly, Trim Size-8½ x 11, Sheetfed press, 10 pages, ISSN: 0011-1295, No Color
Subscriptions: Indv. $345, Can. $351, For. $395

Crime Prevention News   *Business*

Publishing Co: CD Publications, 8204 Fenton St., Silver Spring, MD 20910-4571; Title Tel # (301) 588-6380 Title Fax # (301) 588-6385
Personnel: Publisher-Mike Gerecht, Circ. Mgr.-Kurt Eisentraut, Mktg. Dir.-Joyce Meals
Editorial Description: Covers sources and statistics about funding of crime prevention programs.
General Info: (Formerly Crime Prevention Funding News), Yr. Est. 1993, Semi-monthly, Trim Size-8½ x 11, Sheetfed press, 16 pages, ISSN: 1081-9959, No Color, Matte
Subscriptions: Indv. $259, Can. $269, For. $299, $15/copy
List Rental: List Management Co.: Manager: Amy Seyler; Washington Advertising Service, 8204 Fenton St., Silver Spring, MD 20910 Tel # (301) 588-7920, Fax # (301) 588-6385, Actives: 6,566, $150/M, Expires: $150/M

Crime in Your Community

Publishing Co: Royal Canadian Mounted Police, 1200 Vanien Parkway, Ottawa, ON K1A 0R2 Canada

Criminal Defense Techniques   *Business*

Publishing Co: Matthew Bender & Co., 11 Penn Plaza, New York, NY 10001-2006 Fax # (212) 244-3188; Title Tel # (212) 967-7707
Personnel: Editor-Michael Eisenstein
Editorial Description: Latest and most effective defense methods, tactics and techniques.
General Info: Yr. Est. 1969, Irregular, Looseleaf
Subscriptions: $915/copy

Criminal Evidence for Law Enforcement Officers
See: LAW

Criminal Justice Newsletter   *Business*

Publishing Co: Pace Publications, 443 Park Ave. South, New York, NY 10016 Tel # (212) 685-5450 Fax # (212) 679-4701; Title Tel # (202) 835-1770 Title Fax # (202) 835-1772
Personnel: Publisher-Sid Goldstein, Editor-Craig Fischer
Editorial Description: An independent report on criminal justice issues.
General Info: Yr. Est. 1970, Semi-monthly, ISSN: 0045-9038, Ind/Abs/Online: CJPI
Subscriptions: Indv. $198

Criminal Justice Research Bulletin

Publishing Co: Sam Houston State Univ. Criminal Justice Dept., Criminal Justice Ctr., Huntsville, TX 77341; Title Tel # (409) 294-1635
Personnel: Editor-Margaret Farnworth
Editorial Description: Promotes criminal justice practice & teaching.
General Info: Bi-monthly
Subscriptions: Free
Acquistions: Publication Bought

Defensive Tactics for Law Enforcement, Public Safety and Corrections Officers

Publishing Co: Gould Publications, Inc, 1333 N US Highway 17-92, Longwood, FL 32750-3724 Tel # (407) 695-9500 Fax # (407) 695-2906
Editorial Description: Includes use of force, positioning, pressure points, cuffing, searching, takedowns, ground fighting, weapons, ground fighting, weapons defense
General Info: Irregular, Looseleaf

Digest of Attorney General Opinions
See: LAW

District of Columbia Criminal Law and Motor Vehicle Handbook
See: LAW

Drug Detection Report
See: INDUSTRIAL RELATIONS/PERSONNEL

Drug Enforcement
See: LAW

Drug Enforcement Report   *Business*

Publishing Co: Pace Publications, 443 Park Ave. South, New York, NY 10016 Tel # (212) 685-5450 Fax # (212) 679-4701; Title Tel # (202) 835-1770
Personnel: Publisher-Sid Goldstein, Editor-Dean Boyd
Editorial Description: Law enforcement oriented. Dealing with narcotics & dangerous drug control.
General Info: Yr. Est. 1984, Semi-monthly, 8 pages, ISSN: 0894-1300
Subscriptions: Indv. $197

Drug Policy Report   *Business, Association*

Publishing Co: Drug Policy Research Institute, PO Box 3423, Arlington, VA 22203-0423; Title Tel # (703) 533-2077 Title Fax # (703) 533-1669
Personnel: Publisher, Editor-Richard Baum, Art Dir.-Jeff Soifer, Mktg. Dir.-Linda Bloss
Editorial Description: Every issue includes features on grant-related announcements and 4 full pages of news briefs on: Local Law Enforcement, Federal Agencies, International Narcotics Control, and Drug Prevention & Treatment as well as an article by an expert in a relevant field.
General Info: Yr. Est. 1994, Monthly, Trim Size-8½ x 11, 12 pages, ISSN: 1073-8649, 2 Color, Coated, Saddle-stitched
Subscriptions: Indv. $159, Inst. $159, Can. $169, For. $179, $15/copy
Circulation: Total-700

F.E.A.R. Chronicles
See: CIVIL RIGHTS

FFL Newsletter
See: LAW

FLEOA Newsletter   *Business, Association*

Publishing Co: Federal Law Enforcement Officers Assn., 106 Cedarhurst Ave, Selden, NY 11784-2908; Title Tel # (516) 698-0179
Personnel: Editor-Alan Bernstein
Editorial Description: Members are criminal investigators in the 1811 series employed by the U.S. government.
General Info: Yr. Est. 1978, Monthly, 12 pages
Circulation: Total-6,500
Advertising: Inquire for rates. Accepts Inserts.

Family Relations/State Capitals
See: LAW

Fire Police
See: FIRE PROTECTION

Fire and Police Personnel Reporter
See: LABOR

Fire Problem and Its Solution

Publishing Co: Gould Publications, Inc, 1333 N US Highway 17-92, Longwood, FL 32750-3724 Tel # (407) 695-9500 Fax # (407) 695-2906
Editorial Description: A modern problem-solving publication dealing with the local and by inference, the national fire problem. Contains review questions and answers.
General Info: Irregular, Looseleaf
Subscriptions: $30/copy

Florida Security Officer's Handbook

Publishing Co: Gould Publications, Inc, 1333 N US Highway 17-92, Longwood, FL 32750-3724 Tel # (407) 695-9500 Fax # (407) 695-2906
Editorial Description: A multi-purpose service, referenc, and training manual
General Info: Irregular, Looseleaf
Subscriptions: $13/copy

Fortune News   *Association*

Publishing Co: Fortune Society, 39 W. 19th St., New York, NY 10011-4225; Title Tel # (212) 206-7070 Title Fax # (212) 675-7347
Personnel: Publisher-JoAnne Page, Editor-Celestine Cox, Circ. Mgr.-Joanne Page, Adv. Dir., Art Dir.-JoAnne Page
Editorial Description: Options and opportunities for ex-offenders and adolescents in trouble.
General Info: Yr. Est. 1967, Bi-monthly, 16 pages, No Color
Subscriptions: Indv. $25, Inst. $25, Free To Qualified Recipient
Circulation: Total-35,000

Friends of the FBI Natl. Newsletter   *Association*

Publishing Co: Friends of the FBI, 1001 Connecticut Ave NW, Ste. 1135, Washington, DC 20036; Title Tel # (202) 223-5113
Personnel: Editor-J.A. Paulce
Editorial Description: Educational and research projects for those outside the FBI who are interested in its programs.
General Info: Quarterly
Circulation: Total-12,000

Funding Law Enforcement Hotline   *Business*

Publishing Co: Quinlan Publishing, 23 Drydock Ave, Boston, MA 02210-2387 Tel # (617) 542-0048 Fax # (617) 345-9646
Editorial Description: Information for law enforcement agencies on how to save money and get more funds.
General Info: Monthly
Subscriptions: Indv. $129

GOAL Gazette
See: GAY & LESBIAN INTEREST

Georgia Conservation Law
Handbook

Publishing Co: Gould Publications, Inc, 1333 N US Highway 17-92, Longwood, FL 32750-3724 Tel # (407) 695-9500 Fax # (407) 695-2906
Editorial Description: Includes game and fish, conservation and natural resources, crimes and offense, torts and title, waters of the state, ports, and watercraft
General Info: Annually, Looseleaf
Subscriptions: $28/copy

Georgia Criminal Law and Motor Vehicle Handbook
See: LAW

Grapevine *Association*
Publishing Co: North American Assn. of Wardens, PO Box 128, Eddyville, KY 42038-0128; Title Tel # (502) 388-2211
Personnel: Editor-Gene Scroggy
Editorial Description: Concerns itself with problems and programs of penal and correctional institutions.
General Info: Sheetfed press
Circulation: Total-200

IAAOC Report *Association*
Publishing Co: Intl. Assn. of Addictions & Offender Counseling, 5999 Stevenson Ave., Alexandria, VA 22304-3300 Tel # (703) 823-9800 Fax # (703) 823-0252 Parent Co.-American Counseling Assn., Alexandria
Personnel: Editor-William Toller
General Info: (Formerly POCA Report, The), Yr. Est. 1978, Quarterly, Trim Size-8½ x 11, Sheetfed press, 8 pages
Circulation: Total-1,025

IACP Training Key
Publishing Co: International Association of Chiefs of Police, 515 N Washington St Ste 400, Alexandria, VA 22314-2340; Title Tel # (703) 243-6500
General Info: Monthly

Illinois Criminal Law and
Motor Vehicle Handbook

Publishing Co: Gould Publications, Inc, 1333 N US Highway 17-92, Longwood, FL 32750-3724 Tel # (407) 695-9500 Fax # (407) 695-2906
Editorial Description: Vehicles, Criminal Offenses, Criminal Procedure, Corrections of Illinois
General Info: Irregular, Looseleaf
Subscriptions: $32/copy

Indiana Public Safety Letter
See: PUBLIC MANAGEMENT & PLANNING

Insider
See: HOUSE ORGANS

Interface *Association*
Publishing Co: Search Group, Inc., 7311 Greenhaven Dr Ste 145, Sacramento, CA 95831-3572; Title Tel # (916) 392-2550 Title Fax # (916) 392-8440
Personnel: Editor-Judith Ryder
Editorial Description: Intl. criminal justice news magazine focusing on information management policy & technology.
General Info: Yr. Est. 1974, Semi-annually, Trim Size-8½ x 11, 24 pages, 2 Color, Coated
Circulation: Total-2,500

Jail & Prisoner Law Bulletin *Association*
Publishing Co: AELE, 5519 N Cumberland Ave Ste 1008, Chicago, IL 60656-1480; Title Tel # (312) 763-2800
Personnel: Publisher-Wayne Schmidt, Editor-Bernard Farber
Editorial Description: Recent court cases involving jails, prisons and law suits against police, sheriffs and corrections.
General Info: Yr. Est. 1975, Monthly, Trim Size-8½ x 11, ISSN: 0739-0998, Color-cover, Newsprint
Subscriptions: Indv. $168, Inst. $168
Circulation: Total-1,300

John Howard Society of
Alberta, Reporter

Publishing Co: John Howard Society of Alberta, 10136 100th St., #706, Edmonton, AB T5J 0P1 Canada; Title Tel # (403) 423-4878 Title Fax # (403) 429-0008
Personnel: Editor-Christine Leonard
Editorial Description: Provides articles of general interest on criminal justice issues.
General Info: Yr. Est. 1984, Trim Size-8½ x 11, 4 pages
Subscriptions: Free With Membership
Acquistions: Publication Bought, Publication Sold
Circulation: Total-1,000
Advertising: Accepts Inserts.

Juvenile Justice Digest *Business*
Publishing Co: Washington Crime News Services, 3918 Prosperity Ave Ste 318, Fairfax, VA 22031-3333; Title Tel # (703) 573-1600 Title Fax # (703) 573-1604
Personnel: Editor-Susan Kernus, Publisher, Editor-R.J. O'Connell, Circ. Mgr.-Nancy Van Wyen
Editorial Description: News service for the juvenile justice and delinquency professional.
General Info: Yr. Est. 1973, Semi-monthly, Trim Size-8½ x 11, Sheetfed press, 10 pages, ISSN: 0094-2413, No Color
Subscriptions: Indv. $195, Can. $198, For. $220

Juvenile Law Reports
See: LAW

Keepers' Voice *Association* CPM: $38
Publishing Co: Sponsor-International Association Of Correctional Officers, Intl. Association of Correctional Officers, 1333 S. Wabash Ave #53, Box 53, Chicago, IL 60605-2504; Title Tel # (312) 996-5401 Title Fax # (312) 413-0458
Personnel: Editor-Jess Maghan, Circ. Mgr.-Erika Maybon, Production Mgr.-Beth Stolberg
Editorial Description: Serving the correctional officers. Includes practical, day-to-day training topics, current legislation, resources, conference notices and job openings.
General Info: Yr. Est. 1977, Quarterly, Trim Size-8½ x 11, Offset press, 24 pages, ISSN: 0274-4872, 2 Color, Newsprint, Saddle-stitched
Subscriptions: Indv. $20
Circulation: Total-13,000
Advertising: $500.

Kentucky State Police,
Official Bulletin

Publishing Co: Kentucky State Police, 919 Versailles Rd, Frankfort, KY 40601-4740; Title Tel # (502) 695-6300

Knife Defense
Publishing Co: Gould Publications, Inc, 1333 N US Highway 17-92, Longwood, FL 32750-3724 Tel # (407) 695-9500 Fax # (407) 695-2906
Editorial Description: Use of force, readiness and skill, etc
General Info: Irregular, Looseleaf
Subscriptions: $16/copy

Law Enforcement Liability
Reporter *Association*

Publishing Co: AELE, 5519 N Cumberland Ave Ste 1008, Chicago, IL 60656-1480; Title Tel # (312) 763-2800
Personnel: Publisher-Wayne Schmidt, Editor-Bernard Farber
Editorial Description: Recent court cases that have an impact upon law enforcement personnel and their attorneys.
General Info: (Formerly AELE Law Enforcement Liability Reporter), Yr. Est. 1973, Monthly, Sheetfed press, 16 pages, ISSN: 0271-5481, Color-cover
Subscriptions: Indv. $168, Inst. $168
Circulation: Total-1,300

Law Enforcement-New
England *Business*

Publishing Co: Thomas Lopatosky, 19 Joslin Street, Providence, RI 02909-2599; Title Tel # (401) 751-6217
Personnel: Publisher, Editor-Thomas J. Lopatosky
Editorial Description: News and ideas for law enforcement officials.
General Info: Yr. Est. 1995, Monthly, Trim Size-8½ x 11, 8 pages
Subscriptions: Indv. $24, Inst. $24, $3/copy

Law Officer's Bulletin *Business*
Publishing Co: Bureau of National Affairs, Inc., 1231 25th St. NW, Bldg. N-200, Washington, DC 20037-1157 Tel # (202) 452-4200 Fax # (202) 822-8092; Title Tel # (202) 452-4500 Title Fax # (202) 253-0332
Personnel: Publisher-William A. Beltz, Mng. Editor-Robert L. Goebes, Circ. Mgr.-Gary C. Seltzer
Editorial Description: Provides an update of court decisions, Justice Dept. proposals & congressional actions involving law enforcement officers, describing the legal reasoning & explaining the impact on the law enforcement community.
General Info: Yr. Est. 1976, Bi-weekly, Trim Size-8½ x 11, Offset press, 6 pages, ISSN: 0145-6571, Ind/Abs/Online: Criminal Justice Periodical Index CJPI
Subscriptions: Indv. $147

Long Island Police News
Publishing Co: Long Island Police News, PO Box 36, Copiague, NY 11726-0036
Personnel: Editor-John Jenkins
General Info: Yr. Est. 1973, Weekly
Subscriptions: Indv. $5

Management and
Supervision of Law
Enforcement Personnel

Publishing Co: Gould Publications, Inc, 1333 N US Highway 17-92, Longwood, FL 32750-3724 Tel # (407) 695-9500 Fax # (407) 695-2906
Editorial Description: A must for anyone studying for promotion in law enforcement or recently promoted
General Info: Irregular, Looseleaf
Subscriptions: $20/copy

Mansfield Weekly
Publishing Co: Department of Mental Retardation, Region #3, 670 Main Street, Willimantic, CT 06226 Tel # (203) 465-6359; Title Tel # (203) 429-6451

Michigan Penal Code
See: LAW

Military & Police Uniform Association Newsletter
See: CLUBS

Minnesota Legal Register

Publishing Co: Minnesota Legal Register, PO Box 3645, Duluth, MN 55803-3645; Title Tel # (218) 724-0401
Personnel: Publisher, Editor-Philip Bradley
Editorial Description: Minnesota Attorney General opinions & Tax Court decisions.
General Info: Yr. Est. 1968, Monthly, Trim Size-8½ x 11, Sheetfed press, 18 pages, No Color, Saddle-stitched, Looseleaf

Money Laundering, Asset Forfeiture & Intl. Financial Crimes Newsletter
See: LAW

Municipal Immunity Law Bulletin
See: LAW

NAFI Newsletter
See: FIRE PROTECTION

NDLOA Newsletter   *Association*

Publishing Co: Natl. Disabled Law Officers Assoc., 75 New St, Nutley, NJ 07110-1601
Personnel: Editor-Peter Frazza
Editorial Description: For the benefit of all disabled law officers.
Circulation: Total-5,000

NJDA News   *Association*

Publishing Co: National Juvenile Detention Association, c/o Eastern Kentucky Univ., 301 Perkins Bldg., Richmond, KY 40475-3127; Title Tel # (606) 622-6259 Title Fax # (606) 622-2333
Personnel: Editor-Joe Christy
Editorial Description: Communications and training advice on juvenile detention.
General Info: (Formerly Counterpoint), Yr. Est. 1970, Quarterly, Trim Size-8½ x 11, Desktop press, 12 pages
Subscriptions: Indv. $20, Inst. $20
Circulation: (100% controlled), Total-600

Narcotics Enforcement & Prevention Digest
See: LAW

National Bulletin on
Police Misconduct   *Consumer*

Publishing Co: Quinlan Publishing, 23 Drydock Ave, Boston, MA 02210-2387 Fax # (617) 345-9646; Title Tel # (617) 542-0048
Personnel: Publisher-E. Michael Quinlan
Editorial Description: Covers issues and cases of police wrong-doings.
General Info: Monthly
Subscriptions: Indv. $60
List Rental: List Management Co.: Stevens-Knox List Management, 304 Park Ave S., New York, NY 10010-5312 Tel # (212) 388-8800, Fax # (212) 388-8890

National Character Laboratory-Newsletter
See: MEDICINE

National Council Against Health Fraud Newsletter
See: HEALTH

National Federation of
Paralegal Associations   *Association*

Publishing Co: National Federation of Paralegal Associations, PO Box 33108, Kansas City, MO 64114-0108 Tel # (816) 941-4000 Fax # (816) 941-2725; Title Tel # (609) 234-4898
Editorial Description: NFPA is the national voice and the standard for excellence for the paralegal profession through its work on the issues of regulation, ethics, and education.

National Organization for Victim Assistance-Newsletter
See: SOCIAL SERVICES & WELFARE

National Prison Project
Journal

Publishing Co: Sponsor-National Prison Project, American Civil Liberties Union - National Prison Project, 1875 Connecticut Ave. NW, Washington, DC 20009; Title Tel # (202) 234-4830
Personnel: Editor-Jan Elvin
Editorial Description: Features articles, reports, legislative analysis & other developments in corrections & criminal justice.
General Info: Yr. Est. 1984, Quarterly, Trim Size-8½ x 11, 20 pages, ISSN: 0748-2655, 2 Color, Saddle-stitched
Subscriptions: Indv. $30
Circulation: Total-2,000
Advertising: Inquire for rates.
Printing Co: Hundley Lithograph, Inc., 6503 Chillum Pl NW, Washington, DC 20012-2189 Tel # (202) 829-7800

Necessary Elements
See: LAW

New England Harbormaster
See: GOVERNMENT

New Jersey Correction
News   *Association*

Publishing Co: Dept of Corrections, PO Box 7387, Trenton, NJ 08628-0387
General Info: Yr. Est. 1965, Quarterly, ISSN: 0028-5595

New Jersey Criminal
Justice Code Quizzer

Publishing Co: Gould Publications, Inc, 1333 N US Highway 17-92, Longwood, FL 32750-3724 Tel # (407) 695-9500 Fax # (407) 695-2906
Editorial Description: A comprehensive review of the Criminal Justice Code containing questions and answers and true/false exercises.
General Info: Annually, Looseleaf
Subscriptions: $19/copy

New Jersey Criminal Law
and Motor Vehicle
Handbook

Publishing Co: Gould Publications, Inc, 1333 N US Highway 17-92, Longwood, FL 32750-3724 Tel # (407) 695-9500 Fax # (407) 695-2906
Editorial Description: Criminal and Motor Vehicles Laws of New Jersey
General Info: Annually, ISSN: 0-87526-4, Looseleaf
Subscriptions: $28/copy

New Jersey Law Enforcement Handbook
See: LAW

New York Correction Law

Publishing Co: Gould Publications, Inc, 1333 N US Highway 17-92, Longwood, FL 32750-3724 Tel # (407) 695-9500 Fax # (407) 695-2906; Title Tel # (607) 724-3000
Editorial Description: The book presents the Correction Law Chapter 43 of the Consolidated Laws of New York plus extracts of the other New York Laws for corrections.
General Info: Annually, Trim Size-5½ x 8½, Sheetfed press, 525 pages, No Color, Looseleaf
Subscriptions: Indv. $5, $13/copy

New York Penal Law &
Criminal Procedure Law

Publishing Co: Gould Publications, Inc, 1333 N US Highway 17-92, Longwood, FL 32750-3724 Tel # (407) 695-9500 Fax # (407) 695-2906; Title Tel # (607) 724-3000
Editorial Description: Complete Penal Law & Criminal Procedure Law.
General Info: Yr. Est. 1965, Annually, Trim Size-5½ x 8½, Sheetfed press, 840 pages, No Color, Looseleaf
Subscriptions: $10/copy

New York Practical Tips for
Law Enforcement

Publishing Co: Gould Publications, Inc, 1333 N US Highway 17-92, Longwood, FL 32750-3724 Tel # (407) 695-9500 Fax # (407) 695-2906
Editorial Description: Contains invaluable information for the law enforcement officer, who faces a multitude of court - made rules before can be made.
General Info: Annually, Looseleaf
Subscriptions: $6/copy

New York Security Officer
Training Manual

Publishing Co: Gould Publications, Inc, 1333 N US Highway 17-92, Longwood, FL 32750-3724 Tel # (407) 695-9500 Fax # (407) 695-2906
Editorial Description: Simplifies the 8 Hour pre-assignment course and the laws that apply for certification and registration and offers a guideline for the 16 hour on-the-job training course
General Info: Annually, ISSN: 0-87526-4, Looseleaf
Subscriptions: $6/copy

News Update   *Association*

Publishing Co: National Association of Police Community Relations Officers, 125 Columbus Blvd., New Britain Police Dept., New Britain, CT 06051; Title Tel # (203) 229-0321
Editorial Description: Police-public cooperation for block watches.
General Info: Semi-monthly

Oklahoma Law
Enforcement Bulletin

Publishing Co: State Bureau of Investigation, 2132 NE 36th St, Oklahoma City, OK 73111-5306; Title Tel # (405) 427-5421
General Info: Monthly

On the Beat   *Association*

Publishing Co: New York City Housing Patrolmen's Benevolent Assn., Inc., 4740 21st St, Long Island City, NY 11101-5407; Title Tel # (718) 784-4722 Title Fax # (718) 784-4912
Personnel: Editor-Frances Napolitano
Editorial Description: Devoted to law enforcement personnel and security of tenants and visitors to public Housing Authority facilities.
General Info: Yr. Est. 1972, Quarterly, Trim Size-8½ x 11, Offset press, 16 pages, 2 Color
Subscriptions: Free
Circulation: Total-4,000

On the Line   *Association*

Publishing Co: American Correctional Association, 4380 Forbes Blvd., Lanham, MD 20706-4322
Tel # (301) 918-1800 Fax # (301) 918-1933; Title Tel # (301) 206-5100
Personnel: Editor-Kurt Olsson, Adv. Dir.-Marge Restivo, Art Dir.-Dana Murray
Editorial Description: For wardens, psychologists, etc. involved in the correctional field.
General Info: Yr. Est. 1870, 5x/yr., Trim Size-8½ x 11, Sheetfed press, 12 pages, No Color, Newsprint, Saddle-stitched
Subscriptions: Indv. $35
Circulation: Total-20,000
Printing Co: Pioneer Press, 11852 Coakley Cir, Rockville, MD 20852-2598 Tel # (301) 881-2622

Opinions of the Attorney
General of California   *Business*

Publishing Co: Matthew Bender & Co., 11 Penn Plaza, New York, NY 10001-2006
Fax # (212) 244-3188; Title Tel # (212) 967-7707
Editorial Description: Official opinions from the highest non-judicial legal officer of California.
General Info: Yr. Est. 1961, Monthly, Looseleaf
Subscriptions: $143/copy

Organized Crime Digest   *Business*

Publishing Co: Washington Crime News Services, 3918 Prosperity Ave Ste 318, Fairfax, VA 22031-3333; Title Tel # (703) 573-1600 Fax # (703) 573-1604
Personnel: Publisher-R. J. O'Connell, Editor-Betty Bosarge, Circ. Mgr.-Nancy Van Wyen
Editorial Description: Law enforcement efforts to combat organized crime with emphasis on success investigations and prosecutions; federal, state and local legislative and agency actions.
General Info: Yr. Est. 1980, Bi-weekly, Trim Size-8½ x 11, Offset press, 10 pages, ISSN: 0889-5716, No Color
Subscriptions: Indv. $295, Can. $298, For. $325
List Rental: Rents Lists

Outlook/State Capitals, The
See: GOVERNMENT

Overcrowded Times

Publishing Co: Castine Research Corporation, PO Box 110, Castine, ME 04421;
Title Tel # (207) 326-9521 Title Fax # (207) 326-9528
Personnel: Editor-Michael Terry
General Info: Bi-monthly, ISSN-1077-8209
Subscriptions: Indv. $39, Inst. $75
Printing Co: New Markets Printing, Brewer, ME 04412

Patrol News   *Business*

Publishing Co: Missouri State Highway Patrol, 1510 E. Elm St., PO Box 568, Jefferson City, MO 65102-0568; Title Tel # (573) 751-3013 Title Fax # (573) 751-9419
Personnel: Editor-C.A. Greeno
Editorial Description: Includes educational and instructional material concerning law enforcement techniques and activities related to the Missouri State Highway Patrol and its employees.
General Info: Yr. Est. 1966, Monthly, Trim Size-8½ x 11, Offset press, 28 pages, 2 Color
Circulation: (100% controlled), Total-3,700

Pennsylvania Police
Criminal Law Bulletin

Publishing Co: Pennsylvania Police Criminal Law Bulletin, 2579 Warren Rd, Indiana, PA 15701-3219; Title Tel # (412) 465-5165
Editorial Description: U.S. Supreme and Pennsylvania Court decisions, rules of criminal procedure.
General Info: Yr. Est. 1972, Monthly, 4 pages, No Color
Subscriptions: Indv. $22, $2/copy
Circulation: Total-650

Pillar

Publishing Co: Minnesota Correctional Facility, PO Box B, Saint Cloud, MN 56302-1000;
Title Tel # (612) 251-3510
Personnel: Editor-Jim Wimbush
General Info: Monthly, 16 pages
Subscriptions: Indv. $3
Advertising: Inquire for rates.

Police Department
Disciplinary Bulletin   *Business*

Publishing Co: Quinlan Publishing, 23 Drydock Ave, Boston, MA 02210-2387 Tel # (617) 542-0048 Fax # (617) 345-9646
Personnel: Editor-Will Oliver
Editorial Description: Discusses the when's and how's of disciplining officers, and how to avoid disciplinary problems.
General Info: Monthly, Trim Size-8½ x 11, 8 pages
Subscriptions: Indv. $59

Police Labor Monthly

Publishing Co: Justex Systems, PO Box 6224, Huntsville, TX 77342-6224 Fax # (409) 294-0984;
Title Tel # (409) 291-7981
General Info: Monthly

Police Management Review

Publishing Co: Planning Bureau, Police Dept., City of New York, 1 Police Plz, New York, NY 10038-1403; Title Tel # (212) 374-5000
Personnel: Editor-Sgt. Joseph A. Nardoza
General Info: Monthly
Circulation: Total-4,000

Police Officer Grievances
Bulletin   *Business*

Publishing Co: Quinlan Publishing, 23 Drydock Ave, Boston, MA 02210-2387 Fax # (617) 345-9646;
Title Tel # (617) 542-0048
Personnel: Publisher-E. Michael Quinlan
Editorial Description: Discusses hiring/firing of law enforcement employees and other police labor issues.
General Info: Monthly
Subscriptions: Indv. $60
List Rental: List Management Co.: Stevens-Knox List Management, 304 Park Ave S., New York, NY 10010-5312 Tel # (212) 388-8800, Fax # (212) 388-8890

Policing by Consent   *Consumer, Association*

Publishing Co: National Coalition on Police Accountability, 59 E. Van Buren, #2418, Chicago, IL 60605 Tel # (312) 663-5392 Fax # (312) 663-5396; Title Tel # (315) 474-6603
Personnel: Editor-Nancy Rhodes
Editorial Description: Articles and news advocating police accountability.
General Info: Monthly, Trim Size-8½ x 11, 16 pages, ISSN: 1080-1308, Matte
Subscriptions: Indv. $35, Free With Membership
Printing Co: SPC Press, 924 Burnet Ave., Syracuse, NY 13203 Tel # (315) 472-5478

Preliminary Report-Crime in
Selected Jurisdictions   *Association*

Publishing Co: Bureau of Criminal Statistics, 4949 Broadway Rm E231, Sacramento, CA 95820-1528 Tel # (916) 227-3552
Editorial Description: This report compares preliminary counts of crimes reported by Califorina law enforcement agencies serving populations of 100,000 or more.
General Info: Yr. Est. 1965, Semi-annually, Sheetfed press, 7 pages, Matte
Circulation: Total-4,500

Prison-Ashram Project Newsletter
See: PHILOSOPHY

Prison Mirror   *Association*

Publishing Co: Minnesota Correctional Facility, PO Box 55, Stillwater, MN 55082-0055;
Title Tel # (612) 439-1910
Personnel: Mng. Editor-Alan R. Orfi
Editorial Description: Oldest continously published prison newspaper.
General Info: Yr. Est. 1887, Bi-weekly, Trim Size-8½ x 11, 12 pages, ISSN: 1072-1037, 2 Color, Matte
Subscriptions: Indv. $15, For. $25

Probation & Parole Law
Reports   *Business, Association*

Publishing Co: Knehans-Miller Publications, PO Box 88, Warrensburg, MO 64093-0088;
Title Tel # (816) 429-1102
Personnel: Publisher-Jaclyn Miller, Editor-Dane Miller
Editorial Description: In-depth summaries, often with verbatim excerpts, & thorough subject/ jurisdictional indexing of all federal & state appelate court decisions dealing with all aspects of probation & parole and related issues.
General Info: Yr. Est. 1979, Monthly, Trim Size-8½ x 11, 16 pages, ISSN: 0276-6965, No Color, Looseleaf
Subscriptions: Indv. $120, Inst. $120, Can. $120, For. $155

Public Safety and Justice
Policies/State Capitals   *Business, Association*

Publishing Co: Wakeman/Walworth, 300 N. Washington St., Alexandria, VA 22314-2530;
Title Tel # (703) 549-8606 Title Fax # (703) 549-1372
Personnel: Publisher-Keyes Walworth
Editorial Description: Reports on gun control, law enforcement, firfighting, curfews, arrest procedures, prison administration, and other topical issues
General Info: (Formerly Public Safety and Justice Policies from the State Capitals), Yr. Est. 1946, Weekly, Offset press, 8 pages, ISSN: 1061-9704
Subscriptions: Indv. $265, Inst. $212, Can. $235, For. $255

Public Safety Management
See: FIRE PROTECTION

Public Safety Personnel
Updance   *Business, Association*

Publishing Co: NYPER Publications, PO Box 662, Latham, NY 12110-0662 Fax # (518) 458-8582;
Title Tel # (518) 786-1654
Personnel: Publisher-Sheila J. Jerkill, Editor-Harvey Randall
Editorial Description: Summarizes important court and administrative decisions of interest to law enforcement administrators, unions and personnel.
General Info: (Formerly Law Enforcement Personal Notes), Yr. Est. 1985, Monthly, ISSN: 1071-7412
Subscriptions: Indv. $95, Inst. $95, Can. $105, For. $105
Advertising: Accepts Inserts.

Quaker Committee on Jails & Justice Newsletter
See: LAW

San Quentin News　　*Association*

Publishing Co: California State Prison, State Prison, San Quentin, CA 94964;
Title Tel # (415) 454-1460
Personnel: Publisher-Daniel Vasquez, Editor-Joe Morse, Feature Ed.-Forrest Tucker
Editorial Description: Prison events & news.
General Info: Yr. Est. 1920, Weekly, Trim Size-8½ x 11, Sheetfed press, 4 pages, No Color,
Newsprint
Subscriptions: Indv. $2
Circulation: (91% controlled)

School Emergencies
See: SCHOOL ADMINISTRATION

School Violence Alert: Maintaining Safe Schools
See: EDUCATION

Scientific Sleuthing
Newsletter

Publishing Co: Mid-Atlantic Assn. of Forensic Sciences, PO Box 196, Mc Lean, VA 22101-0196;
Title Tel # (301) 428-0237
Editorial Description: Reports legal decisions and scientific journal articles involving forensic
evidence.
General Info: (Formerly Science in Criminal Law), Yr. Est. 1976, Quarterly, Trim Size-8½ x 11, 10
pages, No Color
Subscriptions: Inst. $20
Circulation: Total-630

Search & Seizure Bulletin
See: LAW

Search Group Technical
Report　　*Association*

Publishing Co: Search Group, Inc., 7311 Greenhaven Dr Ste 145, Sacramento, CA 95831-3572;
Title Tel # (916) 392-2550
General Info: Yr. Est. 1975, Irregular

Search and Seizure Law
Report　　*Business*

Publishing Co: Clark Boardman Callaghan, 375 Hudson St, New York, NY 10014-3685
Fax # (212) 807-6209; Title Tel # (212) 929-7500 Title Fax # (212) 924-0460
Personnel: Publisher-David Doughty, Editor-Alan Weinstein, Art Dir.-William Rushford, Promotion
Dir.-Robert Arkin
Editorial Description: Comprehensive newsletter on search and seizure law--cases and
developments.
General Info: Yr. Est. 1973, 11x/yr., Trim Size-8½ x 11, Sheetfed press, 8 pages, ISSN: 0095-1005,
No Color
Subscriptions: Indv. $205
List Rental: Actives: $70/M
Printing Co: Port City Press, 1323 Greenwood Rd, Pikesville, MD 21208-3611 Tel # (410) 486-3000,
Fax # (410) 486-0706

Security Police Digest

Publishing Co: U.S. Air Force, Chief of Security Police, Washington, DC 20314-0001
Personnel: Editor-F. Heiss
General Info: (Formerly Provost Marshall Digest), Yr. Est. 1947
Circulation: Total-7,000

Security and Special Police Legal Update
See: SECURITY & SURVEILLANCE

Select Hostile Actions
Against Civil Aviation　　*Consumer, Association*

Publishing Co: Air Incident Research, PO Box 4745, East Lansing, MI 48826-4745;
Title Tel # (517) 336-9375 Title Fax # (517) 336-9375
Personnel: Publisher-Michael Morris, Editor-Maureen Maclaughin
Editorial Description: Extensively detailed description of select illegal &/ or untoward actions against
civil and V-I-P Aviation; constantly updated to ongoing/current subscribers file-holders
General Info: (Formerly Hostile Actions Against Civil Aviation), Yr. Est. 1991, Every two years, Trim
Size-8.5 x 11, Desktop press, 250 pages, 4 Color, Looseleaf

Selected Articles for Arson Investigators
See: FIRE PROTECTION

Societe de Criminologie
du Quebec　　*Association*

Publishing Co: Societe de Criminologie du Quebec, 3 Place Laval, Unit 210, Laval, PQ H7N 1A2
Canada; Title Tel # (514) 662-6041 Title Fax # (514) 967-3326
General Info: Yr. Est. 1981, Bi-monthly, Trim Size-8½ x 11, 10 pages
Subscriptions: Indv. $6, Inst. $10
Circulation: Total-900
Advertising: Accepts Inserts.

Surveillant: Acquisitions for Security & Intelligence Professionals
See: SECURITY & SURVEILLANCE

Techniques for Effective
Management of Program
Operations　　*Business*

Publishing Co: Natl. Child Support Enforcement Reference Ctr., 330 C St SW # 2094, Washington,
DC 20201-0001; Title Tel # (301) 443-5106

Tennessee Law Enforcement Bulletin
See: LAW

Traffic Law Reports
See: TRAFFIC & TRANSPORTATION

Training Key　　*Association*

Publishing Co: International Association of Chiefs of Police, 515 N Washington St Ste 400,
Alexandria, VA 22314-2340; Title Tel # (301) 948-0922
Personnel: Editor-Phillip Lynn
Editorial Description: For formal instruction and individual study by police officers. A wide range of
practical topics and one well researched article on a current subject of police concern per issue.
General Info: Yr. Est. 1964, Bi-weekly, Web press, 6 pages, Color
Subscriptions: Indv. $4
Circulation: Total-40,000

UCI Broadcast

Publishing Co: Union Correctional Institution, PO Box 221, Raiford, FL 32083-0221;
Title Tel # (904) 431-1212
Personnel: Editor-Hal Hubener
Editorial Description: Inmate publication dedicated to a better understanding of inmate, penal, and
public problems - for both entertainment and enlightenment.
General Info: (Formerly Railford Record), Yr. Est. 1977, Monthly, Trim Size-5½ x 8½, 23 pages,
Color

Weekly Terrorism Profile
See: SECURITY & SURVEILLANCE

White-Collar Crime Reporter
See: LAW

LEASING & RENTING

ARA Inside Track　　*Association*

Publishing Co: American Rental Association, 1900 19th St., Moline, IL 61265-4198;
Title Tel # (309) 764-2475 Title Fax # (309) 764-1533
Personnel: Editor-Sandy Howell
Editorial Description: Monthly update on projects & events of the American Rental Assn.
General Info: (Formerly ARA Action News), Monthly, Trim Size-8½ x 11, Sheetfed press, 4 pages, 2
Color, Newsprint
Subscriptions: Free With Membership
Circulation: Total-6,000
Printing Co: Fuller's Printery, 835 5th Ave, Moline, IL 61265-1237 Tel # (309) 762-5811

ARA Washington News　　*Association*

Publishing Co: American Rental Association, 1900 19th St., Moline, IL 61265-4198
Fax # (309) 764-1533; Title Tel # (309) 764-2475
Personnel: Editor-Sandy Howell, Co-Editor-William T. Stephens
Editorial Description: Monthly update on legislative issues pertinent to the rental industry.
General Info: Monthly, Trim Size-8½ x 11, Sheetfed press, 4 pages, 2 Color, Newsprint
Subscriptions: Free With Membership
Circulation: Total-4,000
Printing Co: Fuller's Printery, 835 5th Ave, Moline, IL 61265-1237 Tel # (309) 762-5811

CPM Aspects
See: REAL ESTATE

Carlson Report for Shopping Center Management
See: REAL ESTATE

CommonWealth Letters
See: INVESTMENT

Dallas Tenants' News

Publishing Co: Dallas Tenants Assn., 2906 Swiss Ave, Dallas, TX 75204-5962;
Title Tel # (214) 828-4244
Personnel: Editor-Dorothy Masterson
General Info: Yr. Est. 1978, Bi-monthly
Subscriptions: Indv. $10

Insider　　*Business*

Publishing Co: Trade Dimensions, 263 Tresser Blvd., Stamford, CT 06901 Tel # (203) 325-3500
Fax # (203) 325-8423; Title Tel # (203) 977-7600 Title Fax # (203) 977-7645
Personnel: Publisher-Garrett Van Siclen, Editor-Lynn Beatty, Circulation-Denise Gaccino
General Info: Weekly, Trim Size-8½ x 11, Offset press, 6 pages, No Color
Subscriptions: Indv. $263, $5/copy
Circulation: Total-1,500

Leasing Professional

Publishing Co: Leasing Professional, PO Box 5675, Scottsdale, AZ 85261-5675;
Title Tel # (602) 860-0659 Title Fax # (602) 451-7957
Personnel: Editor-Michael Chemodurow
Editorial Description: Negotiaation and drafting office information for retail and industrial real estate leases.
General Info: Yr. Est. 1984, 10x/yr., 8 pages
Subscriptions: Indv. $195, $16/copy

Managing Housing Letter   *Business*

Publishing Co: CD Publications, 8204 Fenton St., Silver Spring, MD 20910-4571;
Title Tel # (301) 588-6380 Title Fax # (301) 588-6385
Personnel: Publisher-Mike Gerecht, Editor-Phil Porado, Circ. Mgr.-Kurt Eisentraut, Mktg. Dir.-Joyce Meals
Editorial Description: Information for owners & managers of all kinds of rental housing.
General Info: Yr. Est. 1978, Monthly, Trim Size-8½ x 11, Sheetfed press, 8 pages, ISSN: 0193-6308, No Color, Matte, Other
Subscriptions: Indv. $149, Can. $159, For. $189, $15/copy
List Rental: List Management Co.: Manager: Amy Seyler; Washington Advertising Service, 8204 Fenton St., Silver Spring, MD 20910 Tel # (301) 588-7920, Fax # (301) 588-6385, Actives: 1,771, $150/M, Expires: 4,319, $150/M

Rail Mart, The
See: RAILROADS

Renter's Rag   *Consumer, Association*

Publishing Co: The Tenants Union, 3902 S Ferdinand St, Seattle, WA 98118-1740;
Title Tel # (206) 722-6848
Personnel: Editor-John Bartlett
General Info: (Formerly 30 Day Notice/Tenant Tattler), Yr. Est. 1975, Quarterly, Trim Size-11½ x 16, 8 pages, No Color
Subscriptions: Free With Membership
Circulation: Total-2,000

Self Storage Legal Review
See: LAW

Shopping Center Digest
See: DEPARTMENT STORE & RETAIL

Texas Chapter NSLA Newsletter
See: EMPLOYMENT

LEATHER & LEATHER PRODUCTS

Hide and Leather Bulletin

Publishing Co: Jacobsen Publishing Co., 300 W Adams St Ste 835, Chicago, IL 60606-5109;
Title Tel # (312) 726-6600
Personnel: Editor-Robert C. Weber
Editorial Description: Published for the tanning and shoe manufacturing industry.
General Info: Daily

LLGMA Association News   *Association*

Publishing Co: Luggage & Leather Goods Manufacturers Assoc., 350 5th Ave., Ste. 2624, New York, NY 10118-0058 Tel # (212) 695-2340 Fax # (212) 643-8021; Title Tel # (212) 532-3960
Personnel: Editor-Robert Ermatinger
General Info: Monthly

Leather Conservation
News   *Association*

Publishing Co: Minnesota Historical Society, 345 Kellogg Blvd W, St. Paul, MN 55102-1906
Tel # (612) 296-2264 Fax # (612) 297-1345; Title Tel # (612) 727-5774 Title Fax # (612) 296-9961
Personnel: Publisher, Editor-Paul Storch
Editorial Description: Newsletter for active conservators in the fields of fine arts, archaeology, conservation of leather & leather containing artifacts.
General Info: Yr. Est. 1983, Annually, Trim Size-8½ x 11, Sheetfed press, 18 pages, ISSN: 0898-0128, No Color, Matte
Subscriptions: Indv. $15, Inst. $15, Can. $15, For. $18
Circulation: Total-140
List Rental: Rents Lists

Leathercraft Newsletter

Publishing Co: Leathercraft Guild, PO Box 734, Artesia, CA 90702-0734; Title Tel # (310) 864-2420
Personnel: Editor-Al Moran
General Info: Yr. Est. 1949, Monthly, 4 pages
Circulation: Total-300

National Shoe Traveler's
Association News

Publishing Co: Natl. Shoe Traveler's Assn., PO Box 456, Abington, MA 02351-0456;
Title Tel # (314) 993-3141 Title Fax # (314) 993-6699
General Info: 8x/yr., Trim Size-8½ x 11, 6 pages
Printing Co: Modern Litho-Print, 411 Madison St, Jefferson City, MO 65101-3190
Tel # (314) 635-6119, Fax # (314) 636-2655

Shoe Retailing Today   *Business, Association*

Publishing Co: National Shoe Retailers Assn., 9861 Broken Land Pky Ste 255, Columbia, MD 21046-1170; Title Tel # (410) 381-8282 Title Fax # (410) 381-1167
Personnel: Publisher-Bill Boettge, Editor-Cynthia Mullaly
Editorial Description: New items and business ideas in footwear for shoe retailers.
General Info: (Formerly NSRA News), Yr. Est. 1970, Monthly, Trim Size-8½ x 11, Sheetfed press, 16 pages, 2% ads, 2 Color, Matte, Saddle-stitched
Subscriptions: Indv. $20
Acquistions: Publication Bought
Circulation: Total-3,600
Advertising: Inquire for rates.
List Rental: Rents Lists

LIBRARY

AABC Newsletter

Publishing Co: Archives Association of British Columbia, Box 78530, Univ. Post Office, Vancouver, BC V6T 1Z4 Canada
Editorial Description: Association news and info of interest to archivists.
General Info: Quarterly
Subscriptions: Indv. $20

AASL Presidential Hotline   *Association*

Publishing Co: American Library Association, 50 E Huron St, Chicago, IL 60611-2795
Fax # (312) 440-9374; Title Tel # (312) 944-6780 Title Fax # (312) 664-7459
Personnel: Publisher-Ann Weeks
Editorial Description: Assn. news for school library media specialists.
General Info: Semi-annually, Trim Size-8½ x 11, 6 pages, No Color
Circulation: Total-7,500
List Rental: Rents Lists

ACCESS

Publishing Co: Society of Alabama Archivists, Alabama Dept. Of Archives 624, Washington Ave., Montgomery, AL 36130-0001
Editorial Description: Society news and developments in archival science.
General Info: Semi-annually
Subscriptions: Indv. $10

ACDA Bulletin   *Association*

Publishing Co: Assn. of Catholic Diocesan Archivists, Archdiocese of Chicago Archive, 5150 Northwest Hwy., Chicago, IL 60630 Tel # (312) 736-5150 Fax # (312) 736-0488
Personnel: Editor-Nancy Sandleback
Editorial Description: News for Catholic diocesan archivists.
General Info: Quarterly, Trim Size-8 x 11, 15 pages
Subscriptions: Indv. $15

ACRL/NY   *Business, Association*

Publishing Co: Association of College & Research Libraries - NY, PO Box 8331, New York, NY 10116-8331
Editorial Description: Newsletter for college and research library professionals in NY.
General Info: Quarterly

ACWR News

Publishing Co: Archivists for Congregations of Women Religious, 10319 K Malcolm Circle, Cockeysville, MD 21030
Editorial Description: News for archivists of women's religious orders.

AIC Newsletter
See: ART & SCULPTURE

AJL Newsletter   *Association*

Publishing Co: Assn. of Jewish Libraries, 15 East 26th Street, Room 1034, New York, NY 10010-1579 Tel # (212) 678-8092 Fax # (212) 678-8998; Title Tel # (407) 732-8032
Personnel: Editor-Hazel Karp, Editor-Irene Levin Wixman, Adv. Dir.-Roslyn Grand
Editorial Description: News, reviews, information, sources, programs for Judaica Libraries/Librarians worldwide.
General Info: Yr. Est. 1974, Quarterly, Trim Size-8½ x 11, Desktop press, 24 pages, ISSN: 0747-6175, No Color
Subscriptions: Indv. $30, Inst. $30, For. $50, $3/copy
Circulation: (70% controlled)
Advertising: $150.
List Rental: Actives: $125/M

ALA-SRRT Newsletter   *Business, Association*

Publishing Co: American Library Association, 50 E Huron St, Chicago, IL 60611-2795
Tel # (312) 944-6780 Fax # (312) 440-9374; Title Tel # (312) 280-1545
Personnel: Editor-Chris Sohol
Editorial Description: News of small press and movement press for libraries.
General Info: Yr. Est. 1969, Quarterly, Trim Size-8½ x 11, Offset press, 8 pages, ISSN: 0065-9096, No Color, Newsprint, Saddle-stitched
Subscriptions: Indv. $10, Inst. $20
Circulation: Total-1,200

ALA Washington Newsletter   *Association*

Publishing Co: American Library Assn, Washington Office, 1301 Pennsylvania Ave. NW, Ste. 403, Washington, DC 20004-1701; Title Tel # (202) 547-4440
Personnel: Editor-Eileen Cooke
Editorial Description: To inform librarians and educators of the current state of all federal legislation that concerns libraries and librarians.
General Info: Yr. Est. 1949, Monthly, Trim Size-8½ x 11, Mimeo press, 9 pages, Color
Subscriptions: Indv. $25, $2/copy
Circulation: Total-1,600

ALCTS Network News   *Business, Association*

Publishing Co: American Library Association, 50 E Huron St, Chicago, IL 60611-2795
Tel # (312) 944-6780 Fax # (312) 440-9374; Title Tel # (312) 280-5035 Title Fax # (312) 280-3257
Personnel: Editor-Karen Muller
Editorial Description: To improve communication with the Association for Library Collections & Technical Services members and others interested in library technical services.
General Info: Yr. Est. 1991, Irregular, ISSN: 1056-6694
Subscriptions: Free
Circulation: Total-1,800

ALCTS Newsletter   *Business, Association*

Publishing Co: American Library Association, 50 E Huron St, Chicago, IL 60611-2795
Tel # (312) 944-6780 Fax # (312) 440-9374; Title Tel # (312) 280-5035 Title Fax # (312) 280-3257
Personnel: Editor-Ann Swartzell
Editorial Description: To improve communication with the Association for Library & Technical Services members regarding activities of the various units.
General Info: (Formerly RTSD Newsletter), Yr. Est. 1976, Bi-monthly, Trim Size-8½ x 11, Offset press, 12 pages, ISSN: 1047-949X, No Color, Newsprint, Saddle-stitched
Subscriptions: Indv. $25, $5/copy
Circulation: Total-9,000

ALI Reporter, The
See: LAW

ALSC Newsletter   *Business, Association*

Publishing Co: American Library Association, 50 E Huron St, Chicago, IL 60611-2795
Tel # (312) 944-6780 Fax # (312) 440-9374; Title Tel # (312) 280-2165 Title Fax # (312) 280-3257
Personnel: Editor-Anita Steele, Production Mgr.-Dianne Rooney
Editorial Description: Improvement and extension of library service to children in all types of libraries.
General Info: Yr. Est. 1979, Quarterly, Trim Size-8½ x 11, Sheetfed press, 8 pages, ISSN: 0162-6612, No Color, Matte, Saddle-stitched
Subscriptions: Free With Membership
Circulation: Total-3,108
List Rental: Rents Lists

AMA Newsletter

Publishing Co: Assn. of Manitoba Archivists, Provincial Archives Manitoba, 200 Vaughan St., Winnipeg, MB R3C 1T5 Canada
Editorial Description: Association news and information of interest to archivists.
General Info: 3x/yr.

AMIA Newsletter (Assn. of Moving Image Archivists)   *Business, Association*

Publishing Co: Sponsor-Assn. of Moving Image Archivists, Natl. Center for Film & Video Preservation, The American Film Institute, 2021 N. Western Ave., Los Angeles, CA 90027; Title Tel # (213) 856-7637 Title Fax # (213) 467-4578
Editorial Description: For archivists of film and video.
General Info: (Formerly F/TAAC Newsletter), Yr. Est. 1988, Quarterly, Trim Size-8½ x 11, Offset press, 24 pages, ISSN: 1075-6477
Subscriptions: Indv. $50, Free With Membership
Circulation: Total-500
Advertising: Accepts Inserts.
List Rental: Rents Lists

AMICI   *Association*

Publishing Co: American Friends of the Vatican Library, 157 Lakeshore Rd., Grosse Pointe, MI 48236-3760; Title Tel # (313) 885-8855
Personnel: Editor-Yvonne Tata, Adv. Dir.-Charlotte Versasi
Editorial Description: Scholarly, financial & social news concerning Vatican Library.
General Info: Yr. Est. 1982, Quarterly, 8 pages, 2 Color
Subscriptions: Indv. $25
Acquistions: Publication Bought
Circulation: Total-1,500
Advertising: Accepts Inserts.

APLIC International Communicator   *Association*

Publishing Co: Association of Population Libraries & Information Centers In, 9 Galen St Ste 217, Watertown, MA 02172-4521; Title Tel # (617) 924-7200
Personnel: Editor-Cheri Coe
General Info: (Formerly APLICommunicator), Yr. Est. 1968, Quarterly, Trim Size-8½ x 11, Offset press, 20 pages, ISSN: 0981-9847, Color
Subscriptions: Indv. $25, Inst. $75
Circulation: (100% controlled), Total-140

ARL Newsletter   *Association*

Publishing Co: Association of Research Libraries, 21 Dupont Cir NW Ste 800, Washington, DC 20036-1109; Title Tel # (202) 296-2296 Title Fax # (202) 872-0884
Personnel: Editor-Nicola Daval
Editorial Description: News of the Association, information and events of importance to the research library community.
General Info: Yr. Est. 1965, Bi-monthly, Trim Size-8½ x 11, Offset press, 16 pages, ISSN: 0066-9652, Color
Subscriptions: Indv. $15, $5/copy
Circulation: Total-1,100

ARLIS/NA Update   *Association*

Publishing Co: Art Libraries Society of North America, 4101 Lake Boone Trl Ste 201, Raleigh, NC 27607-7506
Personnel: Editor-Pamela Parry
Editorial Description: Society & art library world news plus classified job advertisements.
General Info: Yr. Est. 1984, Bi-monthly, Trim Size-8½ x 11, Offset press, 12 pages, ISSN: 0073-040X, No Color, Matte
Subscriptions: Indv. $55, Inst. $75
Circulation: Total-1,300
Advertising: Inquire for rates.
List Rental: Actives: $100/M

AZLA Newsletter   CPM: $208

Publishing Co: Arizona State Library Assn., 14449 N. 73rd. St., Scottsdale, AZ 85260-3133; Title Tel # (602) 998-1954 Title Fax # (602) 998-7838
Personnel: Editor-Louis C. Howley
Editorial Description: Trends and information relating to library service in Arizona. Book reviews for books by members only. Classified in July/August issue.
General Info: (Formerly Arizona Librarian), Yr. Est. 1940, 10x/yr., Trim Size-8½ x 11, 12 pages, ISSN: 0515-0272, 8% ads, 2 Color, Recycled, Saddle-stitched
Subscriptions: Indv. $4, $1/copy
Circulation: Total-1,200
Advertising: $250.
Printing Co: Fellowship Printing, 13825 N. 32nd Street, Suite 38, Phoenix, AZ 85032
Tel # (602) 482-2843, Fax # (602) 482-2639

Academic Archivist

Publishing Co: Society of American Archivists, Archives, Rutgers University, New Brunswick, NJ 08903
Editorial Description: News and information devoted to the interests of academic archivists.

Acquisitions & Appraisal Section News

Publishing Co: Society of American Archivists, Special Collections Dept., Univ. of North Carolina Lib., Charlotte, NC 28223
Editorial Description: For archivists involved in acquisitions and appraisal.

Advertising Marketing Bulletin
See: ADVERTISING & MARKETING

African-American and Third World Archivists Roundtable Newsletter

Publishing Co: Moorland-Spingarn Research Center, Howard University, Washington, DC 20059-0001
Editorial Description: For archivists of African American and Third World related materials.
General Info: Semi-annually

Africana Libraries Newsletter   *Association*

Publishing Co: Michigan State University Libraries, Publications, E. Lansing, MI 48824-1048; Title Tel # (517) 355-2366 Title Fax # (517) 432-1445
Personnel: Editor-Joseph Lauer
Editorial Description: Listings of new publications, notes on serials and projects, meetings and other events.
General Info: Yr. Est. 1975, Quarterly, Trim Size-8½ x 11, Offset press, 8 pages, ISSN: 0148-7868, No Color
Circulation: Total-600

Agricultural Libraries Information Notes   *Association*

Publishing Co: U.S. Natl. Agricultural Library, 10301 Baltimore Ave, Beltsville, MD 20705-2351; Title Tel # (301) 504-6778 Title Fax # (301) 504-5472
Personnel: Editor-Joseph Swab
Editorial Description: Descriptions of information activities and resources in the agri-research world.
General Info: Yr. Est. 1975, Monthly, Trim Size-8½ x 11, Offset press, 48 pages, ISSN: 0095-2699, 2 Color, Newsprint, Saddle-stitched
Circulation: (100% controlled), Total-4,000

Alumni Newsletter, School of Library & Info Studies
See: COLLEGE ALUMNI

American Indian Libraries
Newsletter *Association*

Publishing Co: American Library Association, 50 E Huron St, Chicago, IL 60611-2795
Fax # (312) 440-9374; Title Tel # (312) 944-6780
Editorial Description: Issued by the Office for Library Outreach Services.
General Info: Yr. Est. 1976, Offset press, 4 pages, ISSN: 0193-8207
Subscriptions: Indv. $5, Inst. $7
Circulation: (100% controlled), Total-1,500

American Theological
Library Association
Newsletter *Association*

Publishing Co: American Theological Library Association, 820 Church St., Suite 300, Evanston, IL 60201-5613; Title Tel # (847) 869-7788 Title Fax # (847) 869-8513
Personnel: Editor-Melody Chartier
Editorial Description: Covers Association news.
General Info: Yr. Est. 1947, Quarterly, Desktop press, 40 pages, ISSN: 0003-1399, No Color, Other
Subscriptions: Indv. $20, Inst. $20, Can. $27, For. $27, Free With Membership
Circulation: Total-785
Advertising: Inquire for rates.
List Rental: Rents Lists

Appalachian Alternatives
See: CONSUMER INTERESTS

Apple Library Users Group Newsletter
See: COMPUTERS & AUTOMATION

Aquaphyte
See: SCIENCE

Archivists Society of Alberta Newsletter
See: CULTURE & HUMANITIES

Armed Forces Libraries
Round Table of ALA
Newsletter *Business, Association*

Publishing Co: American Library Assn, Washington Office, 1301 Pennsylvania Ave. NW, Ste. 403, Washington, DC 20004-1701; Title Tel # (202) 547-4440 Title Fax # (202) 547-7363
Personnel: Editor-Dane E. Aguilar
General Info: Quarterly
Subscriptions: Free With Membership

Asian/Pacific American
Librarians Assn.
Newsletter *Association*

Publishing Co: Asian/Pacific American Librarians Assn., Ball State University Library, Muncie, IN 47306-0001; Title Tel # (317) 285-5722
Personnel: Assoc. Ed.-Jack Tsukamoto, Adv. Dir.-Anna Wong
General Info: Yr. Est. 1980, Quarterly, Trim Size-8$\frac{1}{2}$ x 11, Offset press, 8 pages, ISSN: 1040-8517
Subscriptions: Indv. $10, Inst. $25
Circulation: Total-300
Advertising: Accepts Inserts.

Association of Canadian
Map Libraries &
Archives Bulletin *Association*

Publishing Co: Association of Canadian Map Libraries and Archives, National Archives of Canada., 344 Wellington St., Ottawa, ON K1A 0N3 Canada Fax # (613) 955-6226; Title Tel # (613) 996-6009 Title Fax # (613) 995-6226
Personnel: Editor-Colleen Beard
Editorial Description: Text in English and French.
General Info: (Formerly Association of Canadian Map Libraries Bulletin), Yr. Est. 1969, 3x/yr., 45 pages, ISSN: 0840-9331, No Color
Subscriptions: Indv. $35, Inst. $50, Can. $35, $4/copy
Circulation: Total-300
Advertising: Inquire for rates. Accepts Inserts.
List Rental: Actives: $25/M

Association of
Newfoundland &
Labrador Archivists
Newsletter

Publishing Co: Assn. Newfoundland & Labrador Archivists, Colonial Bldg., Military Rd., St. Johns, NF A1C 2C9 Canada
Editorial Description: Association news and info of interest to archivists.
General Info: Quarterly

Assn. of Parliamentary
Librarians in Canada,
Bulletin

Publishing Co: Assn. of Parliamentary Librarians in Canada, Library of Parliament, Parliament Bldgs., Ottawa, ON K1A 0A9 Canada
Personnel: Editor-Richard Pare
General Info: Yr. Est. 1983, Semi-annually, Ind/Abs/Online: CPI

At Your Service *Scholarly*

Publishing Co: EBSCO Subscription Services, PO Box 1431, Birmingham, AL 35201-1431
Tel # (205) 991-1123 Fax # (205) 995-1586
Personnel: Editor-Laura A. Ralstin, Art Ed.-Patty Lovett, Asst. Ed.-Larry J. Busch, Jr., Staff Writer-Ronda Culver, Production Mgr.-Gina K. Armstrong
Editorial Description: Published for serials librarians and other information professionals.
General Info: Quarterly, Trim Size-8$\frac{1}{2}$ x 11, 20 pages, 2 Color, Matte, Saddle-stitched

Automatome *Business, Association*

Publishing Co: American Association of Law Libraries, 53 W Jackson Blvd Ste 940, Chicago, IL 60604-3612; Title Tel # (312) 939-4764
Personnel: Editor-Anna Belle Leiserson
Editorial Description: Automation of law libraries.
General Info: Yr. Est. 1980, Quarterly
Circulation: Total-650

BCLA Reporter *Association*

Publishing Co: Sponsor-British Columbia Library Assn., British Columbia Library Association, #110 - 6545 Bonsor Avenue, Burnaby, BC V5H 1H3 Canada; Title Tel # (604) 430-9633 Title Fax # (604) 430-8595
Personnel: Editor-Jim Herrington, Bk. Rev. Ed.-Robin Van Heck, Production Mgr.-Clare Kelly, Adv. Dir.-P. Haggerty
Editorial Description: Reports on current events that pertain to libraries in British Columbia. Features conference reports, book reviews and articles on information retrieval and technology, library architecture, literacy, management, finance, etc.
General Info: Yr. Est. 1956, 5x/yr., 32 pages, ISSN: 0005-2876, No Color
Circulation: Total-850
Advertising: Accepts Inserts.
Printing Co: College Printers, 865 Terminal Avenue, Vancouver, BC V6A 2N3 Canada
Tel # (604) 685-6322, Fax # (604) 685-0743

BIN
See: BOOKS & BOOK TRADE

BNA's Review of What's
New *Business*

Publishing Co: Bureau of National Affairs, Inc., 1231 25th St. NW, Bldg. N-200, Washington, DC 20037-1157 Tel # (202) 452-4200 Fax # (202) 822-8092; Title Tel # (202) 452-4233 Title Fax # (202) 452-4324
Personnel: Publisher-William Beltz, Editor-Sarita Cabrera
Editorial Description: A free quarterly newsletter for librarians featuring new BNA information resources: books, looseleafs, newsletters, conferences, reports, videos, software, info-paks & online products.
General Info: Yr. Est. 1988, Quarterly, Trim Size-8$\frac{1}{2}$ x 11, Offset press, 4 pages, ISSN: 0897-5167
Subscriptions: Free

Bakken, The

Publishing Co: Bakken Library & Museum of Electricity in Life, 3537 Zenith Ave S, Minneapolis, MN 55416-4623; Title Tel # (612) 927-6508 Title Fax # (612) 927-7265
Personnel: Editor-David Rhees, Circ. Mgr.-Tamara Kosbau, Mng. Editor, Production Mgr.-Elizabeth Ihrig
Editorial Description: Promotes understanding of the history of electromedicine, further the education of science educators, advertise activities of museum & library.
General Info: (Formerly Electric Quarterly), Yr. Est. 1979, Semi-annually, Trim Size-8$\frac{1}{2}$ x 11, Mimeo press, 12 pages, No Color
Subscriptions: Free With Membership
Circulation: Total-1,500

Base Line *Association*

Publishing Co: Sponsor-Map & Geography Round Table, American Library Assn./MAGERT, 50 E. Huron St., Chicago, IL 60611
Personnel: Editor-Pat Seavey, Production Mgr.-Jim Coombs
Editorial Description: Is an official publication of the American Library Assns. Map & Geography Round Table. Provides current information on cartographic materials, other publications of interest to map & geography librarians, meetings, related governmental activities, & map librarianship.
General Info: Yr. Est. 1980, Bi-monthly, Trim Size-5$\frac{1}{2}$ x 8$\frac{1}{2}$, Offset press, 16 pages, ISSN: 0272-8532, No Color, Other, Saddle-stitched
Subscriptions: Indv. $15, Inst. $15, Can. $15, For. $20, $3/copy
Circulation: Total-500, Readership-500

Baseline *Business, Association*

Publishing Co: American Library Association, 50 E Huron St, Chicago, IL 60611-2795
Tel # (312) 944-6780 Fax # (312) 440-9374; Title Tel # (217) 782-5823
General Info: Yr. Est. 1980, 24x/yr.
Subscriptions: Indv. $15

Beta Phi Mu News Letter *Association*

Publishing Co: Beta Phi Mu, School of Library, Univ. of Pittsburgh, Pittsburgh, PA 15260-0001; Title Tel # (412) 624-9435 Title Fax # (412) 648-7001
Personnel: Editor-Blanche Woolls
Editorial Description: News of interest to members, chapter news, etc.
General Info: Yr. Est. 1952, Semi-annually

Between the Lines

Publishing Co: Library, Jewish Theological Seminary of America, 3080 Broadway, New York, NY 10027-4650; Title Tel # (212) 678-8081
General Info: Ind/Abs/Online: RLIN

Biblio-Files *Association*

Publishing Co: Public Library of Youngstown, 305 Wick Ave, Youngstown, OH 44503-1003; Title Tel # (216) 744-8636
Personnel: Editor-Jeanne Dykins
Editorial Description: To inform staff & patrons of library news, books, services.
General Info: Yr. Est. 1980, Monthly, Trim Size-7 x 8½, Offset press, 8 pages, No Color
Subscriptions: Indv. $3
Circulation: Total-2,000

Bluford Notes and Quotes

Publishing Co: North Carolina A&T State Univ., F.d. Bluford Library, Greensboro, NC 27411-0001; Title Tel # (919) 334-7617 Title Fax # (910) 334-7783
Personnel: Editor-Euthena Newman
Editorial Description: Covering news and activites of the University library.
General Info: (Formerly Random Notes), Yr. Est. 1965, Semi-annually, Color
Circulation: (100% controlled), Total-500

Book Marks *Association*

Publishing Co: Sponsor-SD Lib. Assoc., Susan Braunstein, 610 Quincy St, Rapid City, SD 57701-3630; Title Tel # (605) 394-4171 Title Fax # (605) 394-6626
Personnel: Editor-Susan Braunstein
Editorial Description: Libraries in South Dakota.
General Info: (Formerly Catalyst), Yr. Est. 1950, Bi-monthly, Trim Size-8½ x 11, Letrpr. press, 12 pages, ISSN: 0197-0437, No Color, Recycled, Other
Subscriptions: Indv. $15, $2/copy
Circulation: Total-700
Advertising: Inquire for rates.
List Rental: Rents Lists
Printing Co: G/S Printing, 919 Main Street, Rapid City, SD 57701 Tel # (605) 394-4171, Fax # (605) 394-6626

Bookmark *Association*

Publishing Co: Seattle Public Library, 1000 4th Ave, Seattle, WA 98104-1193; Title Tel # (206) 386-4636
Personnel: Editor-Edith Ring
General Info: Yr. Est. 1948, Trim Size-8 x 10, 4 pages
Subscriptions: Indv. $1

Boston University Library Letter

Publishing Co: Boston University Library, 771 Commonwealth Ave, Boston, MA 02215-1401; Title Tel # (617) 353-2000
Personnel: Editor-Gus Harrer
General Info: Yr. Est. 1961, Monthly

Branching Out

Publishing Co: Baltimore County Public Library, 320 York Road, Towson, MD 21204-5179; Title Tel # (301) 887-6100
Personnel: Editor-Kathleen Reis, Art Dir.-Pat Erdman
Editorial Description: News of Baltimore County Public Library & its 24 branches.
General Info: Yr. Est. 1961, Monthly, Trim Size-8½ x 11½, Offset press, 8 pages, No Color
Circulation: (100% controlled), Total-1,000

Briefings

Publishing Co: California Library Assn., 717 K St Ste 300, Sacramento, CA 95814-3406; Title Tel # (916) 447-8541 Title Fax # (916) 447-8394
General Info: Quarterly
Subscriptions: Indv. $5

Brooklyn Public Library Bulletin *Association*

Publishing Co: Brooklyn Public Library, Grand Army Plaza, Brooklyn, NY 11238; Title Tel # (718) 780-7758 Title Fax # (718) 399-0985
Personnel: Editor-Ellen Rudley, Art Dir.-Bill Creevy
Editorial Description: Library newsletter.
General Info: Yr. Est. 1952, Quarterly, Trim Size-8½ x 14, 4 pages, 2 Color
Subscriptions: Free In Designated Area
Circulation: Total-10,000

Buffalo & Erie County Public Library Bulletin *Consumer, Association*

Publishing Co: Buffalo & Erie County Public Library, Lafayette Square, Buffalo, NY 14203; Title Tel # (716) 858-8900
Personnel: Publisher, Editor-Michael Mahaney, Circ. Mgr.-Marie Schmukal, Art Dir.-Sarah Prochownik
General Info: Yr. Est. 1969, Monthly, Trim Size-8½ x 11, Desktop press, 4 pages
Circulation: Total-750

Bulletin of the Edward G. Miner Library *Association*

Publishing Co: Univ. of Rochester School of Medicine, 601 Elmwood Ave, Rochester, NY 14642-0001; Title Tel # (716) 275-3364
Personnel: Editor-Lucretia McClure
General Info: Yr. Est. 1964, Monthly
Circulation: Total-350

Bulletin, Florida & Caribbean Chapter Special Libraries Assn. *Scholarly*

Publishing Co: Special Libraries Assn., Florida & Caribbean Chapter, Blue Cross Blue Shield of FL, Corp. Library, 532 Riverside, Jacksonville, FL 32231
Personnel: Editor-Terri Robar
Editorial Description: Chapter news and information for special librarians.
General Info: Quarterly
Subscriptions: Indv. $15

Bulletin General Theological Ctr. of Maine
See: RELIGIOUS & THEOLOGICAL

Business & Finance Division-Bulletin

Publishing Co: Special Libraries Assn., 1700 18th St NW, Washington, DC 20009-2508 Fax # (202) 265-9317; Title Tel # (202) 234-4700
Personnel: Editor-Mary Gaylord
Editorial Description: Provides info on business & finance libraries.
General Info: Yr. Est. 1962
Subscriptions: Indv. $12
Circulation: Total-2,400

Business & Technical Newsletter *Business, Consumer*

Publishing Co: Muncie Public Library, 301 E Jackson St, Muncie, IN 47305-1878; Title Tel # (317) 747-8200
Editorial Description: Short descriptions of new materials available in the library's business and technical collection.
General Info: Monthly, Mimeo press, 1 pages
Subscriptions: Free
Circulation: Total-600

Business Information Alert:Sources,Strategies & Signposts for Information Professionals *Business*

Publishing Co: Alert Publications Inc., 401 W Fullerton Pky Apt 1403, Chicago, IL 60614-2805; Title Tel # (312) 525-7594 Title Fax # (312) 525-7015
Personnel: Publisher, Editor-Donna Heroy, Sr. Ed., Bk. Rev. Ed.-Vera Emmons, Adv. Dir.-Lael Bush
Editorial Description: News and information on new developments in information services, databases and publications.
General Info: Yr. Est. 1988, 10x/yr., Trim Size-8½ x 11, 16 pages, ISSN: 1042-0746, 2 Color, Matte
Subscriptions: Indv. $142, $15/copy
Advertising: Inquire for rates. Accepts Inserts.
List Rental: Rents Lists
Printing Co: Graphic Copy, 415 N. State, Chicago, IL 60605 Tel # (312) 644-7800

Business Information from Your Public Library *Business*

Publishing Co: Administrator's Digest, Inc., PO Box 993, South San Francisco, CA 94083-0993; Title Tel # (415) 573-5474
Personnel: Publisher, Editor-Robert Alvarez
Editorial Description: Sold to public libraries in quantity for free distribution to the business firms in their area.
General Info: Yr. Est. 1972, 3x/yr., 4 pages, ISSN: 0892-6034, Color
Subscriptions: Inst. $54
Circulation: Total-22,000
Printing Co: P I P, 1063 Chess Drive Suite G, Foster City, CA 94404 Tel # (415) 570-7907

CANB Gazette

Publishing Co: Council of Archives of New Brunswick, Box 6000, Fredericton, NB E3B 5H1 Canada
Editorial Description: Council news and developments of interest to archivists.
General Info: Bi-monthly

CCLI Newsletter

Publishing Co: California Clearinghouse on Library Instruction, UCLA College Library, Los Angeles, CA 90024-1450; Title Tel # (213) 825-2138
Personnel: Publisher-Esther Grassian
Editorial Description: Covers library instruction activities of California libraries & librarians.
General Info: Yr. Est. 1975, Semi-annually, Offset press, 8 pages
Circulation: Total-850

CDS Connection   *Business*

Publishing Co: Library of Congress, Cataloging Distribution Svc., Washington, DC 20541-0001
Tel # (202) 707-6100 Fax # (202) 707-1334
Personnel: Editor-Terry Erb
Editorial Description: Information and news from the Cataloging Distribution Service.
General Info: Monthly, Trim Size-8$\frac{1}{2}$ x 11, 6 pages, ISSN: 0895-2485, 2 Color, Coated

CISTI News   *Consumer, Association*

Publishing Co: Canada Institute for Scientific & Technical Information, Natl. Research Council, Canada, Bldg. M55, Montreal Rd., Ottawa, ON K1A 0S2 Canada; Title Tel # (613) 993-3854
Title Fax # (613) 952-9112
Personnel: Editor-Elizabeth Katz
Editorial Description: Newsletter of the Canada Institute for Scientific & Technical Information.
General Info: Yr. Est. 1983, Quarterly, Trim Size-8$\frac{1}{2}$ x 11, Sheetfed press, 12 pages, ISSN: 0715-8661, 2 Color, Matte, Saddle-stitched
Circulation: (100% controlled), Total-3,500

CLENExchange   *Consumer, Association*

Publishing Co: American Library Association, 50 E Huron St, Chicago, IL 60611-2795
Fax # (312) 440-9374; Title Tel # (312) 944-6780
Personnel: Editor-Marie Bryan
General Info: Quarterly
Subscriptions: Indv. $20, For. $25

CLR Reports   *Association*

Publishing Co: Council on Library Resources, Inc., 1400 16th St NW Ste 510, Washington, DC 20036-2217; Title Tel # (202) 483-7474 Title Fax # (202) 483-6410
Personnel: Editor-Ellen Timmer
Editorial Description: Recent grants, new projects, publications, etc.
General Info: (Formerly CLR Recent Developments), Yr. Est. 1972, Irregular, Trim Size-8$\frac{1}{2}$ x 11, Sheetfed press, 6 pages, ISSN: 0892-0605, 2 Color, Recycled
Circulation: Total-4,000

CLSI Newsletter of Library Automation

Publishing Co: CLSI, Inc., 320 Nevada St, Newtonville, MA 02160-1435; Title Tel # (617) 965-6310
Personnel: Publisher-Richard Porter, Editor-Trudy Kontoff
Editorial Description: Concerns library automation systems, their technology and libraries' experiences with automation.
General Info: Yr. Est. 1976, Semi-annually, Trim Size-8$\frac{1}{2}$ x 11, Offset press, 20 pages, ISSN: 0363-9479, 2 Color, Newsprint, Saddle-stitched
Subscriptions: Free
Circulation: Total-5,000
Printing Co: Smith Print, Inc., Longwater Dr./Assinippi Park, Norwell, MA 02061
Tel # (617) 871-0640, Fax # (617) 878-2040

CMC News (Computers in the Media Center) See: COMPUTERS & AUTOMATION

CPL Newsletter   *Association*

Publishing Co: Council of Planning Libraries, 1313 E 60th St, Chicago, IL 60637-2897;
Title Tel # (312) 947-2163
Personnel: Editor-Lynne DeMerritt, Production Mgr.-Harry Mallace
Editorial Description: News, articles, suggestions, and sources for planners and planning librarians.
General Info: Yr. Est. 1957, Irregular, Trim Size-8$\frac{1}{2}$ x 11, 16 pages, ISSN: 0045-8791
Subscriptions: Indv. $25, Inst. $45
Circulation: Total-175

CRIARL Newsletter   *Business, Association*

Publishing Co: Univ. of Rhode Island Library, Promenade St., Kingston, RI 02881;
Title Tel # (401) 792-2672
Personnel: Editor-Martha Kellogg
Editorial Description: News and articles of interest to Rhode Island library community.
General Info: Yr. Est. 1982, 8 pages, ISSN: 0882-6846, Color
Circulation: Total-400

California Libraries   *Association*

Publishing Co: California Library Assn., 717 K St Ste 300, Sacramento, CA 95814-3406
Fax # (916) 447-8394; Title Tel # (916) 447-8541 Title Fax # (416) 447-8394
Personnel: Editor-Mary Sue Ferrell
General Info: Yr. Est. 1967, Monthly, Trim Size-8$\frac{1}{2}$ x 11, Letrpr. press, 16 pages, ISSN: 0199-1299, 3% ads, 2 Color, Newsprint, Saddle-stitched
Acquistions: Publication Bought
Circulation: (100% controlled), Total-3,000
Advertising: Inquire for rates.
List Rental: Actives: $100/M
Printing Co: Cal Central Press, 2629 5th St, Sacramento, CA 95818-2896 Tel # (916) 441-5392

California State Library Newsletter

Publishing Co: California State Library, 914 Capitol Mall, Box 942837, Sacramento, CA 94237-0001;
Title Tel # (916) 322-8476
Personnel: Editor-Catherine Lewis
General Info: (Formerly From the State Librarian's Desk), Yr. Est. 1981, Monthly, Trim Size-8$\frac{1}{2}$ x 11, Mimeo press, 6 pages, ISSN: 0276-6973
Circulation: Total-2,300

Canadian Law Libraries   *Association*

Publishing Co: Canadian Assn. of Law Libraries, Bibl. de Droit, PO Box 1570, 190 Railway St., Kingston, ON K7L 5C8 Canada; Title Tel # (613) 531-9338 Title Fax # (613) 531-0626
Personnel: Editor-Andrea Cambridge
Editorial Description: Eng/Fr text.
General Info: (Formerly Canadian Association of Law Libraries Newsletter), Yr. Est. 1970, 5x/yr., 40 pages, ISSN: 1180-176X, 3% ads
Subscriptions: Indv. $60, Can. $64, For. $60, $15/copy
Circulation: Total-550, Readership-550
Advertising: Inquire for rates. Accepts Inserts.
List Rental: Rents Lists

Catholic Archives Newsletter   *Consumer, Association*

Publishing Co: Maryknoll Fathers & Brothers, Box 305, Maryknoll, NY 10545-0305
Tel # (914) 941-7590
Editorial Description: News of interest to Catholic archivists.
General Info: Semi-annually

Centennial State Libraries   *Association*

Publishing Co: Colorado Dept. of Education/Colo.St. Lib. & Adult Educ. Off., 201 E. Colfax, Denver, CO 80203-1704; Title Tel # (303) 866-6900
Personnel: Editor-Kathleen Parent
Editorial Description: Covers library issues & events on a local, state & natl. level.
General Info: Yr. Est. 1968, Monthly, Trim Size-8$\frac{1}{2}$ x 11, Desktop press, 8 pages, ISSN: 0887-1116, 2 Color, Matte, Saddle-stitched
Subscriptions: Free
Circulation: (100% controlled), Total-3,500

Center on Social Welfare Policy and Law Library Bulletin   *Association*

Publishing Co: Center on Social Welfare Policy & Law, 275 7th Ave Fl 6, New York, NY 10001-6708; Title Tel # (212) 633-6967 Title Fax # (212) 633-6371
Personnel: Editor-Barbara Schiola
Editorial Description: Information on new or revised publications, case developments, Federal Agency Policy Materials concerning welfare law.
General Info: Yr. Est. 1965, Monthly, Trim Size-8$\frac{1}{2}$ x 11, Mimeo press, 6 pages
Subscriptions: Free
Circulation: Total-2,000

Channel   *Association*

Publishing Co: Sponsor-WI Division for Libraries and Community Learning, Wisconsin Dept. of Public Instruction, PO Box 7841, Madison, WI 53707-7841; Title Tel # (608) 266-9679
Title Fax # (608) 267-1052
Personnel: Publisher-William Wilson, Editor-Telise Johnsen, Circ. Mgr.-Jane Sulzer, Art Dir.-Victoria Horn
Editorial Description: News of the Wisconsin state library agency and other Wisconsin state-level library/media center interests; Calendar of meetings and continuing education opportunities in Wisconsin.
General Info: (Formerly Channel D L S), Yr. Est. 1966, 11x/yr., Trim Size-8$\frac{1}{2}$ x 11, Sheetfed press, 20 pages, ISSN: 0146-1095, No Color, Matte, Saddle-stitched
Subscriptions: Free In Designated Area
Circulation: (91% controlled), Total-3,700
List Rental: Rents Lists

Chapter News   *Association*

Publishing Co: Special Libraries Assn., 1700 18th St NW, Washington, DC 20009-2508
Tel # (202) 234-4700 Fax # (202) 265-9317
Personnel: Editor-Naomi Prall, Asst. Ed.-Martha Lazarevic, Asst. Ed.-Rick Reid, Production Mgr.-Jane Axelrod, Adv. Mgr.-Barbara Fody
General Info: Quarterly
Advertising: Inquire for rates.

Checklist

Publishing Co: Saskatchewan Archivists Society, Box 399, Substation 6, Saskatoon, SK S7N 0W0 Canada
Editorial Description: Society news and developments of interest to archivists.
General Info: 3x/yr.
Subscriptions: Indv. $10

Chicago Area Archivists Newsletter

Publishing Co: Northwestern University Archives, Deering Library, Evanston, IL 60201
Editorial Description: News and developments of interest to archival science professionals.
General Info: Irregular
Subscriptions: Indv. $4

Church and Synagogue
Libraries   CPM: $71

Publishing Co: Church & Synagogue Library Association, PO Box 19357, Portland, OR 97280-0357 Fax # (503) 977-3734; Title Tel # (503) 244-6919 Title Fax # (503) 548-8752
Personnel: Editor-Sarah Moore, Circ. Mgr.-Judy Janzen, Adv. Dir.-Judith Janzen
Editorial Description: News of Church & Synagogue Library Assn. Also contains educational features for congregational librarians including book & media reviews.
General Info: Yr. Est. 1967, Bi-monthly, Trim Size-8½ x 11, 20 pages, ISSN: 0009-6342
Subscriptions: Indv. $25, $3/copy
Circulation: Total-3,500
Advertising: $250.
Printing Co: Performance Printing, 400 South Main Street, Clawson, MI 48017 Tel # (810) 288-0680

CircumSpice   *Business, Consumer*

Publishing Co: City College Library, 138th Street and Convent Ave., New York, NY 10031; Title Tel # (212) 650-7155
Personnel: Editor-Judy Connorton, Graphic Designer-John R. Luciano
Editorial Description: Campus library news.
General Info: Quarterly

Clark & Center Newsletter, The

Publishing Co: Univ. of California-Los Angeles, Wm Andrews Clark Mem. Library, 2520 Cimarron St., Los Angeles, CA 90018; Title Tel # (213) 731-4881
General Info: Irregular

Collection of Bibliographic & Research Resources
See: LAW

College & Research
Libraries   *Business, Association*

Publishing Co: American Library Association, 50 E Huron St, Chicago, IL 60611-2795 Tel # (312) 944-6780 Fax # (312) 440-9374
Personnel: Editor-Glorina Clair
General Info: Bi-monthly
Subscriptions: Indv. $50, Can. $55, For. $60, $14/copy

Colorado Archivist

Publishing Co: Colorado Archivist, Colorado State Univ. Libraries, Fort Collins, CO 80523-0001
Editorial Description: News and information of interest to archivists.
General Info: Quarterly
Subscriptions: Indv. $7

Commission on
Preservation & Access
Newsletter

Publishing Co: Commission on Preservation & Access, 1400 16th St NW Ste 740, Washington, DC 20036-2217
Editorial Description: News for archivists.

Connecticut Libraries   *Association*

Publishing Co: Automatic Printing & Mailing Inc., 300 Shaw Rd, North Branford, CT 06471-1055; Title Tel # (203) 772-4000
Personnel: Editor-David Kapp
Editorial Description: News, calendar, features, people, jobs, in and about Connecticut libraries.
General Info: (Formerly CLA News & Views), Yr. Est. 1956, Monthly, Trim Size-8½ x 11, Offset press, 8 pages, Ind/Abs/Online: Lib.Lit., No Color, Newsprint
Subscriptions: Indv. $25, $3/copy
Circulation: Total-1,000
Printing Co: Automatic Printing, 300 Shore Rd., North Branford, CT 06471 Tel # (203) 484-0451

Conservation
Administration News   CPM: $285

Publishing Co: University of Tulsa, 600 S College Ave, Tulsa, OK 74104-3189 Tel # (918) 631-2557 Fax # (918) 613-2033; Title Tel # (918) 631-3800 Title Fax # (918) 631-3823
Personnel: Publisher, Editor-Robert Patterson, Circ. Mgr.-Michael Frazier, Circ. Mgr.-Scott McClung, Production Mgr., Adv. Dir., Art Dir.-Toby Murray
Editorial Description: Library and archival preservation, a quarterly newsletter for administrators.
General Info: Yr. Est. 1979, Quarterly, Trim Size-8½ x 11, 32 pages, ISSN: 0192-2912, Ind/Abs/Online: DIALOG, 2 Color, Saddle-stitched
Subscriptions: Indv. $24, $6/copy
Circulation: Total-700
Advertising: $200.

Corn Belt Library System,
Sum and Substance   *Association*

Publishing Co: Corn Belt Library System, PO Box 1744, Bloomington, IL 61702-1744; Title Tel # (309) 452-4485 Title Fax # (309) 454-8716
Personnel: Editor-Jay Wozny
Editorial Description: Focus on library events relevant to the local library community.
General Info: Yr. Est. 1967, 10x/yr., Trim Size-8½ x 11, Sheetfed press, 8 pages, ISSN: 1041-343X, Color
Circulation: (100% controlled), Total-575

Corporate Library Update   *Business*

Publishing Co: Cahners Publishing Co., 249 W. 17th St., New York, NY 10011-5300 Tel # (212) 337-6900 Fax # (212) 337-6922 Parent Co.-Reed Elsevier, New York
Personnel: Publisher-Fred Ciporen, Exec. VP/Group Publisher-Frank J. Sibley, Editor in Chief-John N. Berry III, Editor-Susan S. DiMattia, Production Mgr.-John V. Turner III, Adv. Dir.-David Nudo
Editorial Description: Covers information services for professionals in a corporate environment, info management techniques, etc.
General Info: Semi-monthly, ISSN: 1061-5288, Looseleaf
Subscriptions: Indv. $69

Cottonboll   *Association*

Publishing Co: Alabama Public Library Service, 6030 Monticello Dr., Montgomery, AL 36130-0001; Title Tel # (205) 213-3900
Personnel: Editor-Pat Warner
Editorial Description: Newsletter of the Alabama Public library service-Alabama's state library agency.
General Info: Yr. Est. 1976, Bi-monthly, Trim Size-8½ x 11, Offset press, 8 pages, 2 Color
Circulation: Total-2,700

Council of Nova Scotia
Archives, Newsletter   *Association*

Publishing Co: Council of Nova Scotia Archives, 6016 University Archives, Halifax, NS B3H 1W4 Canada; Title Tel # (902) 424-7093 Title Fax # (902) 424-0628
Personnel: Editor-Margaret McBride
General Info: Yr. Est. 1984, Semi-annually, Trim Size-8½ x 11, Sheetfed press, 28 pages, ISSN: 0829-7142, No Color, Matte
Subscriptions: Free With Membership
Circulation: Total-200

Courier   *Association*

Publishing Co: Special Libraries Assn., Toronto Chapter, 740 Huron St., Toronto, ON M4V 2W3 Canada
Editorial Description: The official bulletin of the Toronto chapter of the Special Libraries Assn.
General Info: Yr. Est. 1963, 6x/yr., Trim Size-8½ x 11, 16 pages, ISSN: 0319-8383, 15% ads, 2 Color, Saddle-stitched
Subscriptions: Free With Membership
Advertising: Inquire for rates.
Printing Co: Printing Mill, 241 Richamond St., w., Toronto, ON Canada Tel # (416) 598-1582

Crab   *Association*   CPM: $192

Publishing Co: Maryland Library Assn., 400 Cathedral St Fl 3, Baltimore, MD 21201-4401; Title Tel # (410) 727-7422 Title Fax # (410) 396-5856
Personnel: Editor-Herb Foerstel
Editorial Description: Topics of interest to members.
General Info: Yr. Est. 1970, Bi-monthly, Trim Size-11 x 16, Web press, 12 pages, ISSN: 0300-7561, Color
Subscriptions: Indv. $15, $3/copy
Circulation: Total-1,300
Advertising: $250.

Cracmer Cruhbs

Publishing Co: Central Mass. Regional Library System, Worcester Public Library, Salem Sq., Worcester, MA 01608-2074; Title Tel # (508) 799-1654 Title Fax # (508) 799-1652
Personnel: Editor-Janice Charbonneau, Production Mgr.-Maureen Boyda
General Info: (Formerly Craker Barrel), Quarterly, 22 pages
Circulation: Total-875

Crossings
See: HISTORY

Current News on File
See: GOVERNMENT

DLA Bulletin   *Business, Consumer*

Publishing Co: University of California, Office of the President, Division of Library Automation, 300 Lakeside Drive, 8th Floor, Oakland, CA 94612-3550; Title Tel # (510) 987-0564 Title Fax # (510) 839-3573
Personnel: Editor-Mary Jean Moore
Editorial Description: Focuses on topics in the field of library automation.
General Info: Yr. Est. 1981, Irregular, Trim Size-8½ x 11, 28 pages, ISSN: 0272-037X, 2 Color, Matte, Saddle-stitched
Subscriptions: Free
Circulation: Total-2,500

Descriptive Notes

Publishing Co: Society of American Archivists, New York State Archives C.E.C., Empire State Plaza, Albany, NY 12230-0001
Editorial Description: News for archival professionals.
General Info: Irregular

Directions for Utah Libraries *Association*

Publishing Co: Utah State Library, 2150 S 300 W Ste 16, Salt Lake City, UT 84115-2579; Title Tel # (801) 466-5888
Personnel: Editor-Chip Ward
Editorial Description: News of interest to librarians, media specialists, and trustees in Utah.
General Info: (Formerly Horsefeathers), Yr. Est. 1966, Monthly, Trim Size-8½ x 11, Sheetfed press, 8 pages, No Color
Circulation: Total-1,800

Disability Resources Monthly
See: DISABILITY

District Note   *Consumer*

Publishing Co: Scranton Public Library, N. Washington Ave. & Vine St., Scranton, PA 18503;
Title Tel # (717) 348-3000
Personnel: Editor-Mary Garm
General Info: Yr. Est. 1966, Mimeo press, 11 pages, No Color
Circulation: (100% controlled), Total-170

Document Center Update   *Business*

Publishing Co: Document Center, 1504 industrial Way, Unit 9, Belmont, CA 94002
Tel # (415) 591-7600 Fax # (415) 591-7617
Editorial Description: Information from distributor of standards documents.
General Info: Yr. Est. 1995, Monthly
Subscriptions: Free To Qualified Recipient

Duke University Libraries

Publishing Co: Duke Univ. Library, Publications, Durham, NC 27706; Title Tel # (919) 684-2034
Title Fax # (919) 684-2855
Personnel: Editor-Joline Ezzell
General Info: Yr. Est. 1987, Trim Size-8½ x 11, Sheetfed press, 24 pages, ISSN: 0895-4909, 2 Color, Coated, Saddle-stitched
Subscriptions: Indv. $15
Acquisitions: Publication Bought
Circulation: (80% controlled), Total-2,600, Single Copy/Newsstand-500, International-100
Printing Co: AmeriGraphix, Rr 8 Box 215-A, Burlington, NC 27215-9808 Tel # (919) 229-4404

Dusty Shelf   *Business, Association*

Publishing Co: Sponsor-Kansas City Area Archivists, Kansas City Area Archivists, Nazarene Archives, 6401 The Paseo, Kansas City, MO 64131 Fax # (816) 361-4983;
Title Tel # (816) 333-7000
Personnel: Editor-Stan Ingersol, News Ed.-Bryan McLaughlin, Art Dir.-Lon Dagley
Editorial Description: News of archives in Eastern Kansas and Western Missouri.
General Info: (Formerly Extra Format), Yr. Est. 1979, Tri-annually, Trim Size-8½ x 11, 24 pages
Subscriptions: Indv. $10, Inst. $15, Free With Membership
Circulation: Total-200, Readership-250
Advertising: Inquire for rates. Accepts Inserts.
Printing Co: Univ. of Missouri at Kansas City, Copy Dept., 5200 Rockhill Rd., Kansas City, MO 64131

ECOL News
See: ENVIRONMENT & ECOLOGY

EMIE Bulletin EMIERT   *Consumer, Association*

Publishing Co: American Library Association, 50 E Huron St, Chicago, IL 60611-2795
Tel # (312) 944-6780 Fax # (312) 440-9374
General Info: Quarterly
Subscriptions: Indv. $10, Inst. $15, Free With Membership

ERIC/CRESS Bulletin
See: EDUCATION

ERIC/IR Update
See: EDUCATION

Eastern Region News

Publishing Co: Eastern Massachusetts Regional Library System, 666 Boylston St, Boston, MA 02116-0247; Title Tel # (617) 536-4010
Personnel: Editor-Edward Montana, Jr.
Editorial Description: Covers regional news, new buildings, special projects, federal grants, awards, etc. of libraries: services of headquarters library, conference reports, continuing education news and descriptions.
General Info: Yr. Est. 1966, Bi-monthly, Trim Size-8½ x 11, Letrpr. press, 12 pages, ISSN: 0012-8899, Color-cover, Newsprint
Circulation: (100% controlled), Total-2,500

Easy Access   *Association*

Publishing Co: Northwest Archivists, Inc., c/o Montana Historical Society, 225 N. Roberts St., Helena, MT 59620-1201 Tel # (406) 444-4775 Fax # (406) 444-2696
Personnel: Editor-Kathryn Otto, Bk. Rev. Ed.-Jodie Foley
Editorial Description: News for professional archivists.
General Info: Quarterly, Trim Size-8½ x 11, Desktop press, 16 pages, No Color, Matte, Saddle-stitched
Subscriptions: Indv. $10, Inst. $15
Advertising: Inquire for rates.

Enoch Pratt Free Library

Publishing Co: Enoch Pratt Free Library, 400 Cathedral St, Baltimore, MD 21201-4484;
Title Tel # (301) 396-5494
Personnel: Editor-Averil Kadis
Editorial Description: Library professional news.
General Info: Yr. Est. 1933, Monthly, Trim Size-8½ x 11, Sheetfed press, 8 pages, ISSN: 0013-8495, 2 Color, Newsprint
Subscriptions: Indv. $3
Circulation: Total-475
Printing Co: Pratt Print Shop, 400 Cathedral St, Baltimore, MD 21201-4401

Ex Libris   *Association*

Publishing Co: Johns Hopkins Univ., Milton S. Eisenhower Library, Baltimore, MD 21218;
Title Tel # (410) 516-8355 Title Fax # (410) 516-5080
Personnel: Editor-M.J. Miller, Circ. Mgr.-Cheryl Wagner
Editorial Description: Information about the Johns Hopkins University libraries for friends of the libraries and others.
General Info: Yr. Est. 1931, Tri-annually, Trim Size-8½ x 11, Letrpr. press, 6 pages, 2 Color
Circulation: Total-6,000

Extensions - Newsletter of the High/Scope Curriculum
See: EDUCATION

FEDLINK Technical Notes

Publishing Co: Federal Library & Information Center Committee, Library Of Congress, Washington, DC 20540-5100 Tel # (202) 707-4800; Title Tel # (202) 707-4828 Title Fax # (202) 707-4818
Personnel: Editor-Darlene Dolan
Editorial Description: Contains technical information for members of the Federal Library & Information Network.
General Info: Yr. Est. 1983, Monthly, Trim Size-8½ x 11, Desktop press, 8 pages, ISSN: 0737-4178, 2 Color, Newsprint
Circulation: Total-1,800
Printing Co: Westland Enterprises, Inc., 3621 Stewart Rd, Forestville, MD 20747-4741
Tel # (301) 587-5200

FLICC Newsletter   *Business*

Publishing Co: Federal Library & Information Center Committee, Library Of Congress, Washington, DC 20540-5100; Title Tel # (202) 707-4800 Title Fax # (202) 707-4818
Personnel: Editor in Chief-Dee Dolan, Editor-Rich Cermak, Editorial Asst.-Ronald Owens
Editorial Description: News of the Federal Library & Information Center.
General Info: (Formerly FLC Newsletter), Yr. Est. 1965, Quarterly, Trim Size-8½ x 11, Offset press, 8 pages, ISSN: 0882-908X, 2 Color, Matte, Saddle-stitched
Subscriptions: Free To Qualified Recipient
Circulation: Total-2,800
List Rental: Rents Lists

Faculty Newsletter IUB
Libraries

Publishing Co: Indiana Univ. Libraries, Lib Admin. Library C-Z, Bloomington, IN 47405
Personnel: Editor-Jennifer Paustenbaugh

Faxletter

Publishing Co: Faxon Co., Inc., 15 S.W. Park, Westwood, MA 02090-1725;
Title Tel # (617) 329-3350
Personnel: Editor-Kathleen Klesh
Editorial Description: For the exchange of ideas between Linx users & friends.
General Info: (Formerly Linxletter), Yr. Est. 1982, Bi-monthly, 6 pages, ISSN: 0882-231X, Color, Newsprint
Circulation: Total-10,000

Federal Librarian   *Business, Association*

Publishing Co: American Library Assn, Washington Office, 1301 Pennsylvania Ave. NW, Ste. 403, Washington, DC 20004-1701; Title Tel # (202) 547-4440 Title Fax # (202) 547-7363
Editorial Description: To promote Federal librarianship and related information issues.
General Info: Yr. Est. 1972, Quarterly, ISSN: 0273-1061
Subscriptions: Indv. $20, Inst. $20, Free With Membership
Circulation: Total-550

Fiction Digest
See: BOOKS & BOOK TRADE

Finger Lakes Library
System Newsletter

Publishing Co: Finger Lakes Library System, 314 N Cayuga St, Ithaca, NY 14850-4209;
Title Tel # (607) 273-4074
Personnel: Editor-Loretta Heimbuch
Editorial Description: For member librarians & trustees of Finger Lakes Library Systems.
General Info: Yr. Est. 1979, Bi-monthly, Trim Size-8½ x 11, Mimeo press, 12 pages, ISSN: 0195-4016, 2 Color, Newsprint
Subscriptions: Free
Circulation: Total-450

Flickertale Newsletter   *Association*

Publishing Co: North Dakota State Library, Liberty Memorial Bldg., 604 E. Boulevard Ave., Bismarck, ND 58505-0800; Title Tel # (701) 224-2492 Title Fax # (701) 224-2040
Personnel: Editor-Lori Lindemann
Editorial Description: Articles and short news items of interest to N.D. librarians.
General Info: Yr. Est. 1969, Bi-monthly, Offset press, 8 pages, No Color
Subscriptions: Indv. $12, Inst. $12
Circulation: Total-1,000

Florida Archivist

Publishing Co: Florida Archivist, 4191 Bradfordville Rd, Tallahassee, FL 32308-6401
Editorial Description: News and developments of interest to archivists.
General Info: Quarterly
Subscriptions: Indv. $15

Focus — *Association*

Publishing Co: Saskatchewan Library Assn., Box 3388, Regina, SK S4P 3H1 Canada; Title Tel # (306) 780-9413
Personnel: Editor-Frank Kemp
General Info: Yr. Est. 1952, Bi-monthly, Trim Size-8½ x 11, Mimeo press, 20 pages, ISSN: 0015-5179, 1% ads, Color-cover, Saddle-stitched
Circulation: Total-5,000
Advertising: Inquire for rates. Accepts Inserts.

Focus on the Center for Research Libraries

Publishing Co: Center for Research Libraries, 6050 S Kenwood Ave, Chicago, IL 60637-2804 Fax # (312) 995-4339; Title Tel # (312) 955-4545 Title Fax # (312) 955-4339
Personnel: Editor-Linda Naru
Editorial Description: News of programs, policies, collections & new acquisitions for CRL members & staff.
General Info: (Formerly Center for Research Libraries Newsletter), Yr. Est. 1949, Bi-monthly, Trim Size-8½ x 11, 4 pages, ISSN: 0275-4924, No Color, Newsprint
Subscriptions: Indv. $10
Circulation: Total-4,000

Follet Automation News — *Business*

Publishing Co: Follet Corporation, 1391 Corporate Dr., McHenry, IL 60050 Parent Co.-Simon & Schuster, Inc., New York; Title Tel # (815) 344-8700 Title Fax # (815) 344-8774
Personnel: Editor-M. Nowland
Editorial Description: Provides the solutions to library problems.
General Info: Tri-annually, Trim Size-8½ x 11, 20 pages, 2 Color, Matte, Saddle-stitched

Food for Thought-SLA — *Association*

Publishing Co: Special Libraries Assn., 1700 18th St NW, Washington, DC 20009-2508 Tel # (202) 234-4700 Fax # (202) 265-9317; Title Tel # (914) 683-6783
Personnel: Publisher, Editor-Margaret Bell
Editorial Description: The latest developments in information concerning food librarians.
General Info: Yr. Est. 1975, Bi-monthly, Trim Size-8½ x 11, Mimeo press, 10 pages, No Color
Subscriptions: Indv. $10
Circulation: Total-225

Footnotes — *Business*

Publishing Co: State Library of Iowa, East 12 And Grand140-B, Des Moines, IA 50319-0001; Title Tel # (515) 281-4400 Title Fax # (515) 281-3384
General Info: (Formerly Aardvark), Yr. Est. 1970, Monthly, Offset press, 8 pages
Subscriptions: Free
Circulation: Total-2,000

Footnotes

Publishing Co: Northwestern Univ. Library Council, 1935 Sheridan Rd, Evanston, IL 60208-0821; Title Tel # (708) 491-4449
General Info: Quarterly, Trim Size-8½ x 11, 8 pages, 2 Color, Recycled

For Reference — *Association*

Publishing Co: New York Metropolitan Reference, 57 E 11th St Fl 4, New York, NY 10003-4605; Title Tel # (212) 228-2320 Title Fax # (212) 228-2598
Editorial Description: News of Metro's activities to members.
General Info: Yr. Est. 1966, 10x/yr., Trim Size-8½ x 11, Offset press, 12 pages, ISSN: 0015-685X
Subscriptions: Indv. $10, For. $14
Circulation: Total-2,000

For Your Information — *Business, Association*

Publishing Co: Western New York Library Resources Council, 4455 Genessee St., P.O. Box 400, Buffalo, NY 14225-0400; Title Tel # (716) 633-0705
Editorial Description: Communication vehicle to/for the 100 members of the library consortium, the Western New York Library Resources Council.
General Info: (Formerly Newsletter), Yr. Est. 1972, 10x/yr., Mimeo press, 15 pages
Circulation: Total-1,000

Free Materials for Schools & Libraries
See: EDUCATION

Friends of Libraries U.S.A. Natl. Notebook — *Association*

Publishing Co: American Library Association, 50 E Huron St, Chicago, IL 60611-2795 Fax # (312) 440-9374; Title Tel # (312) 944-6780
Personnel: Editor-James Houck
Editorial Description: Available to members only. Information exchange for library friends groups.
General Info: Yr. Est. 1978, Quarterly, Sheetfed press, 12 pages, Saddle-stitched
Subscriptions: Indv. $25
Circulation: Total-1,600

Friends of the Orlando County Library System — *Association*

Publishing Co: Orange County Library System, 101 E Central Blvd, Orlando, FL 32801-2462; Title Tel # (407) 425-4694
Personnel: Editor-Joan Erwin
Editorial Description: Friends of library activities and library services.
General Info: Yr. Est. 1949, Monthly, Trim Size-8 x 11, Offset press, 1 pages, Color, Newsprint
Subscriptions: Indv. $2, Free
Circulation: Total-2,500

Friendscript — *Association*

Publishing Co: Library Friends of the Univ. of Illinois at Urbana-Champaign, 227 Library, 1408 W. Gregory, Urbana, IL 61801; Title Tel # (217) 333-5682 Title Fax # (217) 333-2214
Personnel: Editor-Terry Maher
Editorial Description: Information about activities relating to the library at the University of Illinois at Urbana-Champaign. 3rd largest academic library in the country (8 million volumes)
General Info: Yr. Est. 1979, Quarterly, Trim Size-9 x 12, Offset press, 6 pages, ISSN: 0192-5539, 2 Color, Newsprint
Subscriptions: Free With Membership
Circulation: (100% controlled), Total-8,000

From My Bookshelf: Books Noted For You — *Consumer*

Publishing Co: George Bonavia, 3295 Southgate Road, Ottawa, ON KIV 7Y3 Canada; Title Tel # (613) 521-5285
Personnel: Editor-George Bonavia
Editorial Description: Newsletter that reviews books and forms of publications in ethnocultural affairs.
General Info: Yr. Est. 1972, Monthly, 4 pages, ISSN: 0829-4976
Subscriptions: Free

Front and Center
See: ADVERTISING & MARKETING

Fugitive Pope

Publishing Co: Raleigh Clayton Muns, 1178 Margaret Ln, Olivette, MO 63132-2319
Personnel: Publisher-Raleigh Clayton Muns, Editor-Anne L. Wagner, Editorial Asst.-Samuel Francis Hopkins, Editorial Asst.-Isaac Michael Wagner-Muns
Editorial Description: The free-speech zine which explores library bizarreness and wierd information.
General Info: Irregular, ISSN: 1054-8947
Subscriptions: $1/copy

GIS Newsletter
See: GEOLOGY

GLTF Newsletter
See: GAY & LESBIAN INTEREST

General Libraries Newsletter — *Association*

Publishing Co: Univ. of Texas at Austin Libraries, PO Box P, Austin, TX 78713-8916; Title Tel # (512) 471-3811
Personnel: Circ. Mgr.-Mary Pound
Editorial Description: Activities & work program of the General Libraries.
General Info: 8 pages, ISSN: 0362-854X
Subscriptions: Free
Circulation: Total-3,500

Gerald R. Ford Foundation Newsletter
See: GOVERNMENT

Golda Meir Library Newsletter — *Consumer, Association*

Publishing Co: Golda Meir Library, University of Wisconsin, Box 604, Milwaukee, WI 53201-0604; Title Tel # (414) 229-6980 Title Fax # (414) 229-3605
Personnel: Editor-Tim Ericson
Editorial Description: Library resources and activities.
General Info: (Formerly UWM Library Newsletter), Yr. Est. 1974, Semi-annually, Trim Size-8½ x 11, Sheetfed press, 8 pages, 2 Color
Subscriptions: Free
Circulation: (100% controlled), Total-4,000

Good Stuff — *Association*

Publishing Co: University of North Dakota Printing Centre, Box 133, Grand Forks, ND 58202 Fax # (701) 777-3319; Title Tel # (701) 777-4636 Title Fax # (701) 277-3319
Personnel: Editor-Michael Hurely
Editorial Description: News and information of North Dakota Library Association and of libraries in the state. Announcements of interest to membership welcomed.
General Info: Yr. Est. 1971, Quarterly, Trim Size-8.5 x 11, 20 pages, Color-cover, Matte
Subscriptions: Indv. $10, Inst. $25
Advertising: $100.
Printing Co: University of North Dakota Printing Centre, University of North Dakota, Box 133, Grand Forks, ND 58202 Tel # (701) 277-4636

Government Records News — *Association*

Publishing Co: Society of American Archivists, New York State Archives C.E.C., Empire State Plaza, Albany, NY 12230-0001
Editorial Description: Developments of interest to archival professionals.

Graduate School of Library and Information Science Newsletter   *Association*

Publishing Co: Univ. of Illinois, Graduate School of Library & Info Science, 112 LIS, 501 E. Daniel St., Champaign, IL 61820; Title Tel # (217) 333-3280 Title Fax # (217) 244-3302
Personnel: Editor, Circ. Mgr.-Curt McKay
Editorial Description: News and information about the School's faculty, alumni, sponsored activities and events, publications and programs.
General Info: (Formerly Graduate School of Library Science Newsletter), Yr. Est. 1980, Semi-annually, Trim Size-8½ x 11, Desktop press, 8 pages, ISSN: 0277-528X, No Color, Recycled, Other
Circulation: (100% controlled), Total-5,000

Granite State Libraries   *Association*

Publishing Co: New Hampshire State Library, 20 Park St, Concord, NH 03301-6314 Tel # (603) 271-2393; Title Tel # (603) 271-1393 Title Fax # (603) 271-6826
Personnel: Editor-Matthew Higgins
Editorial Description: News on innovative librarianship, national, regional and state associational activities, reviews of N.H. books and state publications, and information on N.H. libraries and librarians.
General Info: (Formerly Books and Libraries), Yr. Est. 1965, Bi-monthly, Trim Size-8½ x 11, Offset press, 18 pages, ISSN: 0046-6301, Color
Subscriptions: Free
Circulation: Total-2,500
Advertising: Inquire for rates.

Greater New Orleans Archivists Newsletter

Publishing Co: Notarial Archives, 421 Loyola Ave, New Orleans, LA 70112-1195
Editorial Description: News and information of interest to archival professionals.
General Info: Quarterly
Subscriptions: Indv. $5

HLABC Forum
See: HEALTH

Harriet Beecher Stowe House & Library
See: HISTORY

Harvard Librarian   *Association*

Publishing Co: Harvard University Library, Wadsworth House, Cambridge, MA 02138; Title Tel # (617) 495-7793
Personnel: Editor-Timothy Hanke
Editorial Description: News of Harvard libraries & professional activities of Harvard librarians; essays in librarianship.
General Info: Yr. Est. 1957, Tri-annually, Trim Size-8½ x 11, Offset press, 12 pages, ISSN: 0073-0564, No Color, Newsprint
Circulation: Total-3,000
Printing Co: Harvard Univ. Office of the University Publisher, 219 Western Ave, Allston, MA 02134-1039

Hawaii Library Association Newsletter   *Business*

Publishing Co: Hawaii Library Association, PO Box 4441, Honolulu, HI 96812-4441; Title Tel # (808) 944-7405
Editorial Description: Articles and announcements of current interest to Hawaii Library Association members.
General Info: Quarterly, Trim Size-8½ x 11, 4 pages, 4 Color
Circulation: Total-440

Heritage

Publishing Co: Southern California Library for Social Studies & Research, 6120 S Vermont Ave, Los Angeles, CA 90044-3718; Title Tel # (213) 759-6063
Personnel: Editor-Bill Doyle
General Info: Quarterly, 4 pages
Subscriptions: Indv. $25

Hitch Hiker   *Association*

Publishing Co: New Mexico State Library, 325 Don Gaspar, Santa Fe, NM 87501-2777 Tel # (505) 827-3813; Title Tel # (505) 827-3812 Title Fax # (505) 827-3888
Personnel: Editor-Robert Upton
Editorial Description: Library news of interest to New Mexico librarians...people events, ideas.
General Info: Yr. Est. 1972, Weekly, Trim Size-8½ x 11, Desktop press, 1 pages, No Color
Subscriptions: Free
Circulation: Total-1,500

IASL Newsletter   *Association*

Publishing Co: International Association of School Librarianship, PO Box 19586, Kalamazoo, MI 49019-0586 Tel # (616) 343-5728
Personnel: Editor-Peter Genco
Editorial Description: News of school library developments, publications, projects international.
General Info: Yr. Est. 1971, Quarterly, Trim Size-8½ x 11, Mimeo press, 14 pages, ISSN: 0085-2015, No Color, Recycled
Subscriptions: Indv. $20, Free With Membership
Circulation: Total-900

IASSIST Quarterly   *Association*

Publishing Co: International Association for Social Science Information Svc, Data Library, Simon Fraser University, Burnaby, BC V5A 1S6 Canada; Title Tel # (604) 291-4349
Personnel: Editor-Walter Piovesan
Editorial Description: Articles relevant to organization and management of data archives and libraries.
General Info: Yr. Est. 1975, Quarterly, Trim Size-8½ x 11, Sheetfed press, 40 pages, ISSN: 0739-1137, No Color, Coated
Subscriptions: Indv. $40, Inst. $70
Circulation: Total-500

ILA Reporter   *Association*   **CPM: $68**

Publishing Co: Sponsor-Illinois Library Association, Illinois Library Assn., 33 W Grand Ave # 301, Chicago, IL 60610-4306; Title Tel # (312) 644-1896 Title Fax # (312) 644-1899
Personnel: Editor-Barbara Cunningham
General Info: Yr. Est. 1980, Monthly, Trim Size-8½ x 11, Sheetfed press, 24 pages, ISSN: 0018-9979, Color, Perfect bound
Subscriptions: Free With Membership
Circulation: Total-4,400
Advertising: $300.
List Rental: Actives: 3,200, $350/M

Impressions   *Association*

Publishing Co: New Jersey State Library, 185 W. State St., CN 520, Trenton, NJ 08625-0520 Tel # (609) 292-7306 Fax # (609) 989-7898; Title Tel # (609) 633-3805
Personnel: Editor-Carol DuBois
Editorial Description: News of interest to the statewide library community.
General Info: Yr. Est. 1979, Irregular, Offset press, 4 pages, ISSN: 0890-8346, No Color, Newsprint
Circulation: (100% controlled), Total-5,000

Impulse   *Association*

Publishing Co: Fresno County Public Library, 2420 Mariposa St, Fresno, CA 93721-2204; Title Tel # (209) 488-3223
Personnel: Editor, Circ. Mgr.-Eirck Miller, Art Dir.-Diana Griffin
Editorial Description: Material of interest or concern to the staff, generally of local origin.
General Info: Yr. Est. 1923, Weekly, Trim Size-8½ x 11, Offset press, 4 pages, 2 Color
Subscriptions: Indv. $12
Circulation: (66% controlled), Total-300

Indiana Slant   *Association*

Publishing Co: Sponsor-Indiana Chapter Special Libraries Assn., Indiana Chapter Special Libraries Assn., C/o IU Sch. Med. Li, 635 Barnhill, Indianapolis, IN 46223-0001; Title Tel # (317) 264-7182
Personnel: Editor-Lynn Smith
General Info: Yr. Est. 1970, Quarterly, Mimeo press, 10 pages
Circulation: (100% controlled), Total-225

Infinity

Publishing Co: Preservation Section, Soc. of American Archivists, 2104 W Addison St, Chicago, IL 60618-6124
Editorial Description: Features news of interest to archival professionals.
General Info: (Formerly Consect News), 3x/yr.

InfoManage: The International Management Newsletter for the Information Services Executive
See: MANAGEMENT

Information Advisor   *Business*

Publishing Co: Information Advisory Services, 300 Mcleod Ave, Missoula, MT 59801-4302 Tel # (406) 728-1171
Personnel: Publisher, Editor-Robert Berkman
Editorial Description: Shows how business information users can select the best data sources; evaluates the quality & reliability of information sources including print and online.
General Info: Yr. Est. 1988, Monthly, Trim Size-8½ x 11, Web press, 8 pages, ISSN: 1050-1576, 2 Color, Newsprint
Subscriptions: Indv. $130, Can. $140, For. $140, $10/copy
Acquistions: Publication Bought
Circulation: Total-650
List Rental: Rents Lists

Information Broker
See: MEDIA & COMMUNICATIONS

Information Bulletin

Publishing Co: New York Univ. Elmer Holmes Bobst Library, 70 Washington Sq S, New York, NY 10012-1019; Title Tel # (212) 998-2633
Personnel: Editor-Dorothy Swanson
General Info: Yr. Est. 1981

Information Hotline
See: COMPUTERS & AUTOMATION

Information Management   *Business*   CPM: $90

Publishing Co: Idea Group Publishing, Olde Liberty Square, Suite 230, 4811 Jonestown Road, Harrisburg, PA 17109; Title Tel # (717) 541-9150 Title Fax # (717) 541-9159
Personnel: Publisher, Editor-Mehdi Khosrowpour, Mng. Editor-Jan Travers
Editorial Description: Devoted to professionals in the information resources management field.
General Info: (Formerly Information Management Bulletin), Yr. Est. 1987, Semi-annually, Trim Size-8½ x 11, Sheetfed press, 24 pages, ISSN: 1080-286X, 3% ads, No Color, Other, Saddle-stitched
Subscriptions: Indv. $40, Inst. $60, For. $50
Circulation: Total-5,000
Advertising: $450.
List Rental: List Management Co.: L.T.S.T., 320 Northern Blvd., Great Neck, NY 11021
  Tel # (516) 482-2345, Fax # (516) 487-7721
Printing Co: Kutco Printing & Products Inc., 6700 Allentown Blvd., Harrisburg, PA 17112
  Tel # (717) 652-0556

Information Retrieval & Library Automation
See: COMPUTERS & AUTOMATION

Information Searcher
See: EDUCATION

Information Standards Quarterly
See: BIBLIOGRAPHY

Information Technology
Newsletter   *Business*

Publishing Co: Idea Group Publishing, Olde Liberty Square, Suite 230, 4811 Jonestown Road, Harrisburg, PA 17109; Title Tel # (717) 541-9150 Title Fax # (717) 541-9159
Personnel: Editor-Karen Cullings, Mng. Editor-Jan Travers
Editorial Description: Especially designed for librarians who wish to keep up-to-date with the latest applications and issues of information technologies in library information resources management.
General Info: Yr. Est. 1990, Semi-annually, Trim Size-8½ x 11, 16 pages, ISSN: 1057-7939, No Color, Matte, Saddle-stitched
Subscriptions: Indv. $20, Inst. $35, Can. $26, For. $26
Circulation: Total-850
Printing Co: Kutco Printing & Products Inc., 6700 Allentown Blvd., Harrisburg, PA 17112
  Tel # (717) 652-0556

Informed Librarian:
Professional Reading for the Information Professional, The   *Business, Association*

Publishing Co: Infosources Publishing, 140 Norma Rd, Teaneck, NJ 07666-4234;
  Title Tel # (201) 836-7072
Personnel: Publisher, Editor-Arlene Eis
Editorial Description: Compilation of the most recent tables of contents from over 130 valuable domestic and foreign library and information-related journals. Contains new book contents also.
General Info: Yr. Est. 1992, Monthly, Trim Size-8½ x 11, 16 pages, ISSN: 1061-3609
Subscriptions: Indv. $99, For. $119

Inglewood Public Library
Quarterly Report

Publishing Co: Inglewood Public Library, 101 W Manchester Blvd, Inglewood, CA 90301-1753;
  Title Tel # (310) 412-5397
Personnel: Editor-John Perkins
Editorial Description: Statistical and narrative description of developments at Inglewood Public Library.
General Info: Yr. Est. 1962, Quarterly, Trim Size-8½ x 11, Mimeo press, 13 pages, ISSN: 0020-1308, No Color, Newsprint
Subscriptions: Free
Circulation: Total-200
Printing Co: City of Inglewood Print Shop, 1 W Manchester Blvd, Inglewood, CA 90301-1750
  Tel # (213) 412-5517

Inside OLA

Publishing Co: Ontario Library Assn., 100 Lombard St., Ste. 303, Toronto, ON M5C 1M3 Canada;
  Title Tel # (416) 363-3388 Title Fax # (416) 941-9581
Personnel: Publisher-L. Moore, Editor, Art Dir.-P. McGuinness
General Info: Yr. Est. 1986, Offset press, 8 pages, ISSN: 0832-9605, No Color, Newsprint, Saddle-stitched
Circulation: Total-3,700
List Rental: Actives: $75/M
Printing Co: King Print, 38 Lisgar St., Toronto, ON M6J 3T3 Canada Tel # (416) 588-6468

Insight   *Association*

Publishing Co: Akron-Summit County Public Library, 55 S Main St, Akron, OH 44326-0001;
  Title Tel # (216) 762-7621
Personnel: Editor-Patricia H. Latshaw
Editorial Description: Activities & accessions of the library for the information of the general public.
General Info: (Formerly Owlet), Yr. Est. 1960, Bi-monthly, Trim Size-11 x 17, Offset press, 6 pages, 2 Color
Circulation: Total-2,500

Insight   *Association*

Publishing Co: Illinois State Library- Communications, 474 Hewlett Bldg., Springfield, IL 62756-0001;
  Title Tel # (217) 785-6925
Personnel: Editor-Julie Beamer
Editorial Description: Timely news for all types of libraries.
General Info: (Formerly Illinois Nodes), Yr. Est. 1972, Bi-monthly, Trim Size-8½ x 11, 4 pages, No Color
Circulation: (50% controlled), Total-8,300

Insights: Library of
Congress Professional
Assn. Newsletter   *Association*

Publishing Co: U.S. Library of Congress Professional Association, Library Of Congress, Washington, DC 20540-0001; Title Tel # (202) 707-3635
Personnel: Editor, Art Dir.-Sarah Rouse
Editorial Description: Professional reading on issues affecting librarianship, the Library of Congress, staff developments, etc.
General Info: (Formerly LCPA Newsletter), Yr. Est. 1969, Bi-monthly, Trim Size-8½ x 11, Offset press, 24 pages, ISSN: 0898-1795, No Color
Subscriptions: Indv. $4
Circulation: Total-1,850

Inter-Com: Washington
Area Librarians   *Association*

Publishing Co: District of Columbia Library Assn., 7117 Poplar Ave, Takoma Park, MD 20912-4671;
  Title Tel # (301) 270-3217
Personnel: Editor-Mary Feldman
Editorial Description: Activities of DCLA, Washington area, nation-wide libraries and librarians.
General Info: Yr. Est. 1971, Monthly, Offset press, 8 pages, No Color
Subscriptions: Indv. $10
Circulation: Total-900

Interface   *Consumer, Association*

Publishing Co: Sponsor-Assn. of Specialized & Cooperative Agencies, American Library Association, 50 E Huron St, Chicago, IL 60611-2795 Fax # (312) 440-9374; Title Tel # (312) 944-6780
Personnel: Editor-Jeannette Smithee
General Info: (Formerly AHIL Q), Yr. Est. 1978, Quarterly, ISSN: 0740-9591
Subscriptions: Indv. $10, $3/copy
Circulation: Total-2,000
Printing Co: Scotsman Press, Inc., PO Box 4970, 250 Bear St. West, Syracuse, NY 13221-4970
  Tel # (315) 472-7825

Intl. Assn. of Orientalist
Libraries Bulletin

Publishing Co: East Asian Library, Univ. of Southern California, Los Angeles, IL 90089-0182
  Tel # (213) 740-1772 Fax # (213) 749-1221; Title Tel # (217) 333-2290
Personnel: Editor-Om Sharma
Editorial Description: Articles, news items, book reviews.
General Info: Yr. Est. 1967, Semi-annually, 80 pages, ISSN: 0161-7397, 1% ads
Subscriptions: Indv. $15, Inst. $20, $6/copy
Circulation: Total-330

International Leads   *Association*

Publishing Co: American Library Association, 50 E Huron St, Chicago, IL 60611-2795
  Fax # (312) 440-9374; Title Tel # (312) 944-6780 Title Fax # (312) 944-3897
Personnel: Editor-Robert P. Doyle
General Info: Quarterly, ISSN: 0892-4546, Ind/Abs/Online: Library Literature
Subscriptions: Indv. $12

International Preservation
News

Publishing Co: IFLA PAC Core Programme, Natl. Preservation Program Office, Library Of Congress, Washington, DC 20540-0001
Editorial Description: News and developments for archivists.
General Info: 3x/yr., Trim Size-8½ x 11, 16 pages, 2 Color, Matte, Saddle-stitched

Jewish Librarians Caucus
Newsletter

Publishing Co: Jewish Librarians Caucus c/o Sylvia Eisen, 1118 N Lombardo Ave, Lecanto, FL 34461-9505
General Info: Quarterly
Subscriptions: Indv. $8
Circulation: Total-228

Ka Ri Weh Ha Wi   *Association*

Publishing Co: Akwesanse Library, St. Regis Mohawk Indian Res., RR 1, Box 14C, Hogansburg, NY 13655-9705 Fax # (518) 358-2649; Title Tel # (518) 358-2240
Personnel: Editor-Carol White
Editorial Description: To keep the community informed of library, museum, and community events. Community includes all natives living on and off the St. Regis Mohawk Reserve.
General Info: Yr. Est. 1972, Monthly, Trim Size-8½ x 14, Mimeo press, 4 pages, Color-cover
Subscriptions: Free In Designated Area
Circulation: Total-1,076

Kansas Libraries

Publishing Co: Kansas State Library, State Capital, 3rd Fl., Topeka, KS 66612
Personnel: Editor-Roy Bird
General Info: Monthly
Advertising: Inquire for rates.

Kentucky Archivist
See: HISTORY

Keynote
Consumer, Association

Publishing Co: Dept. for Libraries & Archives, 300 Coffee Tree Rd # 537, Frankfort, KY 40601-9267;
Title Tel # (502) 875-7000 Title Fax # (502) 564-5773
Personnel: Editor-Kelly Scott Reed
Editorial Description: Newsletter describing Kentucky's library, archival, and records management activities.
General Info: Tri-annually, Trim Size-8½ x 11, Offset press, 8 pages, Saddle-stitched
Subscriptions: Free
Circulation: (100% controlled), Total-2,500

Keywords
Association   **CPM: $113**

Publishing Co: American Society of Indexers, PO Box 48267, Seattle, WA 98148-0267;
Title Tel # (206) 241-9196 Title Fax # (206) 727-6430
Personnel: Editor-Anne Leach, Editor-Nancy Mulvany
Editorial Description: Contains articles & columns of interest to professional indexers. Emphasis on computer-assisted indexing. Also includes news of the society.
General Info: (Formerly American Society of Indexers Newsletter), Yr. Est. 1969, Bi-monthly, Trim Size-8½ x 11, Offset press, 32 pages, ISSN: 1064-1211, Color-cover, Newsprint, Saddle-stitched
Subscriptions: Indv. $40, Free With Membership
Circulation: Total-1,100
Advertising: $125. Accepts Inserts.
List Rental: Rents Lists

LHRT Newsletter
Association

Publishing Co: American Library Association, 50 E Huron St, Chicago, IL 60611-2795
Fax # (312) 440-9374; Title Tel # (312) 944-6780
Personnel: Editor-David Hove
General Info: Semi-annually
Subscriptions: Free With Membership
Circulation: Total-390

LIAC Newsletter

Publishing Co: Long Island Archives Conference, History Dept. St. John's Univ., Jamaica, NY 11439-0001
Personnel: Editor-R. Harmond
Editorial Description: News and developments in the field of archival science.
General Info: Yr. Est. 1982, Quarterly

LITA Newsletter
Association

Publishing Co: American Library Association, 50 E Huron St, Chicago, IL 60611-2795
Tel # (312) 944-6780 Fax # (312) 440-9374
Personnel: Editor-Walt Crawford
Editorial Description: News about the plans & activities of LITA, & about developments concerning library technology, standards, & continuing education events.
General Info: Yr. Est. 1980, Quarterly, Trim Size-8½ x 11, Offset press, 24 pages, ISSN: 0196-1799, No Color, Matte, Saddle-stitched
Subscriptions: Indv. $25, Can. $30, For. $40, $8/copy
Circulation: (100% controlled), Total-5,000
List Rental: Rents Lists

LSU Medical Center Library
Bulletin

Publishing Co: Louisiana State Univ. Medical Center Lib., Medical Center Library, 1542 Tulane Ave., New Orleans, LA 70112-2274; Title Tel # (504) 568-6100
Personnel: Editor-Judith Caruthers
General Info: Yr. Est. 1945, Quarterly

La Chronique
Association

Publishing Co: Association des Archivistes du Quebec, C.P. 423, Sillery, PQ G1T 2R8 Canada
Editorial Description: Association news and developments of interest to archivists.
General Info: 10x/yr.

Lantern's Core

Publishing Co: Northwestern Univ. Library, Staff Association, 1935 Sheridan Rd, Evanston, IL 60201-2924; Title Tel # (708) 491-7633 Title Fax # (708) 491-8306
Personnel: Editor-Rolf Erickson
Editorial Description: Covers news & information of interest to library employees.
General Info: Yr. Est. 1970, Monthly, Trim Size-8½ x 11, 14 pages, ISSN: 0047-4053
Subscriptions: Free
Circulation: Total-563

Law Librarian's Bulletin Board
See: LAW

Law Library Assn. of
Maryland News   *Association*   **CPM: $444**

Publishing Co: Law Library Assoc. of Maryland, 20 N Paca St, Baltimore, MD 21201-1725;
Title Tel # (410) 706-3728 Title Fax # (410) 706-8354
Personnel: Editor-Maxine Grosshans
Editorial Description: News information of the law library community in the Maryland area.
General Info: (Formerly Bliss News), Yr. Est. 1980, Quarterly, Trim Size-7 x 8½, Mimeo press, 12 pages, No Color
Circulation: Total-180
Advertising: $80.

Legal Information Alert: What's New in Legal Publications
See: LAW

Level Talk
Association

Publishing Co: Johns Hopkins Univ., Milton S. Eisenhower Library, Baltimore, MD 21218
Tel # (410) 516-8355; Title Tel # (410) 516-8325 Title Fax # (410) 516-5080
Personnel: Circ. Mgr.-John Malloy
Editorial Description: Internal library newsletter for staff communication.
General Info: Monthly, Trim Size-8½ x 11, Offset press, 5 pages, No Color
Circulation: (100% controlled), Total-300

Librarian's Newsletter

Publishing Co: John Wiley & Sons, Inc., 605 Third Avenue, New York, NY 10158-0012
Tel # (212) 850-6000 Fax # (212) 850-6088; Title Tel # (212) 850-6705
Personnel: Publisher-Audrey Melkin
Editorial Description: Listing of new Wiley titles targeted toward library buyers.
General Info: Bi-monthly, 88 pages, 2 Color, Newsprint, Saddle-stitched
List Rental: List Management Co.: American List Counsel, 88 Orchard Cir # Cn-5219, Princeton, NJ 08540-3026 Tel # (908) 874-4300, Fax # (908) 874-4433

Library

Publishing Co: Univ. of Minnesota, 309 19th Ave S, Minneapolis, MN 55455-0438

Library & Archives News
Association

Publishing Co: Leo Baeck Institute, Inc., 129 E. 73rd Street, New York, NY 10021
Tel # (212) 744-6400; Title Tel # (212) 333-5222 Title Fax # (212) 315-1716
Personnel: Editor-Gabrielle Bamberger
Editorial Description: Acquisitions and important material in the library and archives relating to the history of German Jewry.
General Info: Yr. Est. 1975, Semi-annually, Trim Size-8½ x 11, Offset press, 8 pages, No Color
Circulation: (100% controlled), Total-2,500

Library & Information
Sciences   *Business*

Publishing Co: National Technical Information Service U.S., 5285 Port Royal Rd., Springfield, VA 22161-0001 Fax # (703) 487-4630; Title Tel # (703) 487-4630
Editorial Description: Information systems; new technologies (CD-ROM, etc.) marketing and user services; personnel; and other topics relevant to information and library science.
General Info: Weekly, Trim Size-8½ x 11, Offset press, ISSN: 0364-6467, No Color
Subscriptions: Indv. $135, Can. $135, For. $195

Library Administrator's
Digest   *Business*

Publishing Co: Administrator's Digest, Inc., PO Box 993, South San Francisco, CA 94083-0993;
Title Tel # (415) 573-5474
Personnel: Publisher, Editor-Robert Alvarez
Editorial Description: Designed to help keep library administrators abreast of new ideas and developments applicable to their institutions.
General Info: (Formerly Administrator's Digest), Yr. Est. 1965, 10x/yr., Trim Size-8½ x 11, 8 pages, ISSN: 0746-6129, 2 Color
Subscriptions: Indv. $27, Inst. $39, Can. $39, For. $39
Acquistions: Publication Sold
Circulation: Total-1,600
Printing Co: P I P, 1063 Chess Drive Suite G, Foster City, CA 94404 Tel # (415) 570-7907

Library Associate

Publishing Co: Indiana Univ. Bloomington Libraries, Main Library, C-2, Bloomington, IN 47405;
Title Tel # (812) 855-0100

Library Benchmarking
Newsletter   *Business*

Publishing Co: Library Benchmarking International, 231 W 4th St Apt 505a, Cincinnati, OH 45202-2679; Title Tel # (513) 684-9244
Editorial Description: Cases and information in library benchmarking.
General Info: Bi-monthly, ISSN: 1072-4966
Subscriptions: Indv. $60

Library Bulletin
Association

Publishing Co: University of Texas General Libraries, Publications, Austin, TX 78712;
Title Tel # (512) 471-3811
Personnel: Editor, Circ. Mgr.-Mary Pound
Editorial Description: Information necessary for General Libraries staff activities.
General Info: Yr. Est. 1972, Weekly, Trim Size-8½ x 11, Offset press, 8 pages, No Color
Circulation: (77% controlled), Total-1,030

Library Bulletin

Publishing Co: SUNY-Upstate Medical Ctr., 766 Irving Ave, Syracuse, NY 13210-1605
General Info: Monthly

Library Calendar

Publishing Co: Edmonton Public Library, 7 Sir Winston Churchill Sq., Edmonton, AB T5J 2V4 Canada
Personnel: Publisher, Editor, Production Mgr.-Iolani Domingo
Editorial Description: Programme guide to Library activities.
General Info: Tri-annually, ISSN: 1195-3381
Circulation: Total-20,000

Library Connection, The   *Scholarly, Association*

Publishing Co: Syracuse Univ. Library Assocs., 600 Bird Library, Syracuse, NY 13244-2001
   Tel # (315) 443-2697 Fax # (315) 443-2671
Editorial Description: Reports on news of the Syracuse University Library.
General Info: Yr. Est. 1994, Semi-annually, Trim Size-8½ x 11, Offset press, 8 pages, 4 Color
Subscriptions: Free
Circulation: Total-4,000

Library Currents   *Business*

Publishing Co: Practical Perspectives Inc., PO Box 202108, Austin, TX 78720-2108;
   Title Tel # (512) 218-8038
Personnel: Publisher-Edward Seidenberg, Editor-Neva Smith
Editorial Description: Abstracts of the current library literature, for the busy librarian seeking to stay abreast of the library profession.
General Info: Yr. Est. 1984, Monthly, Trim Size-8½ x 11, 8 pages, ISSN: 0741-4188
Subscriptions: Indv. $45, Inst. $45, Can. $51, For. $60, $5/copy
Circulation: Total-650

Library Developments   *Association*

Publishing Co: Texas State Library, PO Box 12927, Austin, TX 78711-2927;
   Title Tel # (512) 463-5465 Title Fax # (512) 463-5436
Personnel: Editor-Jeanette Larson
Editorial Description: Newsletter about statewide library development from state agency development division.
General Info: Yr. Est. 1974, Bi-monthly, Trim Size-8½ x 11, Offset press, 20 pages, ISSN: 0145-5397, No Color, Newsprint
Subscriptions: Free In Designated Area
Circulation: Total-1,000
List Rental: Rents Lists

Library Directions   *Association*

Publishing Co: University of Manitoba Libraries, University of Manitoba, Winnipeg, MB R3T 2N2 Canada; Title Tel # (204) 474-9881 Title Fax # (201) 261-1515
Editorial Description: Newsletter of the University of Manitoba libraries.
General Info: Semi-annually, Trim Size-8½ x 11, 6 pages, ISSN: 1183-8701
Subscriptions: Free To Qualified Recipient

Library Editions

Publishing Co: Univ. of Alberta, 89 Ave. & 113th St., Edmonton, AB T6G 2J4 Canada;
   Title Tel # (403) 492-0072
Personnel: Editor-Sylvia Dubrule
Editorial Description: Small magazine concerned with the Univ. of Alberta Library. Articles on people, history & collections.
General Info: (Formerly Library Information Bulletin), Yr. Est. 1988, Trim Size-8½ x 11, 8 pages, ISSN: 0838-2964, 2 Color, Matte, Saddle-stitched
Circulation: (100% controlled)
Printing Co: Univ. of Alberta Printing Svcs., Genl. Services Bldg., Edmonton, AB T6G 2H1 Canada Tel # (403) 492-4246

Library Hi Tech News   *Business, Scholarly   CPM: $370*

Publishing Co: Pierian Press, PO Box 1808, Ann Arbor, MI 48106-1808 Fax # (313) 434-6409;
   Title Tel # (313) 434-5530
Personnel: Publisher, Editor-C. Edward Wall, Circ. Mgr.-M.E. Wall, Adv. Dir.-Annette Ferguson
Editorial Description: News and features on the use of technology in libraries.
General Info: Yr. Est. 1984, 10x/yr., Trim Size-8½ x 11, Web press, 32 pages, ISSN: 0741-9058, Newsprint, Saddle-stitched
Subscriptions: Indv. $72, Inst. $98, Can. $115, For. $115, $13/copy
Circulation: Total-2,000
Advertising: $740.

Library Hotline   *Business*

Publishing Co: Cahners Publishing Co., 249 W. 17th St., New York, NY 10011-5300
   Tel # (212) 337-6900 Fax # (212) 337-6922 Parent Co.-Reed Elsevier, New York;
   Title Tel # (203) 322-9055 Title Fax # (203) 968-9396
Personnel: Publisher-Fred Ciporen, Editor-Susan DiMattia, Circ. Mgr.-Mark Walter, Adv. Dir.-Rivka Modiano
Editorial Description: Late breaking news from Library Journal News Dept.
General Info: Yr. Est. 1971, Weekly, Offset press, 12 pages, ISSN: 0707-736X, 7% ads, No Color
Subscriptions: Indv. $74, Can. $91, For. $91
Circulation: Total-2,700
Advertising: Accepts Inserts.

Library and Information Science UPDATE   *Association*

Publishing Co: University of Toronto Faculty of Library & Information Sci., 140 St. George St., Toronto, ON M5S 1A1 Canada; Title Tel # (416) 978-7060
Personnel: Editor-Diane Henderson
Editorial Description: Library and Information Science UPDATE is a monthly current awareness bulletin designed to meet the needs of information professionals. Each issue provides 30-35 abstracts of current periodical articles in the fields of library and information science.
General Info: (Formerly Library Science UPDATE), Yr. Est. 1976, Monthly, Trim Size-8½ x 11, Offset press, 8 pages, ISSN: 0820-0521, No Color
Subscriptions: Indv. $48, Inst. $48, Can. $24, For. $54, $3/copy
Circulation: Total-235

Library Instruction Round Table News   *Consumer, Association*

Publishing Co: American Library Association, 50 E Huron St, Chicago, IL 60611-2795
   Tel # (312) 944-6780 Fax # (312) 440-9374

Library Issues: Briefings for Faculty & Administrators   *Scholarly*

Publishing Co: Mountainside Publishing, Inc., 321 S. Main St., Ste. 300, P.O. Box 8330, Ann Arbor, MI 48107; Title Tel # (313) 662-3925 Title Fax # (313) 662-4450
Personnel: Editor-Richard Dougherty, Circ. Mgr.-Sally Paul, Production Mgr.-Ann Dougherty
Editorial Description: Library problems as they affect college & university campuses as a whole.
General Info: Yr. Est. 1980, Bi-monthly, 4 pages, ISSN: 0734-3035
Subscriptions: Indv. $40, Inst. $40, Can. $40, For. $40, $7/copy
Circulation: Total-850
List Rental: Actives: $165/M

Library Lines

Publishing Co: Church Library Assn. of Ontario, 1202 York Mills Rd., #1104, Don Mills, ON M3A 1Y2 Canada
Personnel: Editor-Emma Austin
General Info: Yr. Est. 1969
Subscriptions: Free With Membership
Circulation: Total-200

Library Link   *Association*

Publishing Co: Univ. of Rhode Island Library Friends of the Library, Kingston, RI 02881-0803;
   Title Tel # (401) 874-2666 Title Fax # (401) 874-4608
Personnel: Editor-Deborah Mongeau
Editorial Description: Library newsletter.
General Info: (Formerly Library Letter), Yr. Est. 1967, Annually, Trim Size-8½ x 11, Offset press, 8 pages, No Color
Circulation: (100% controlled), Total-1,200

Library Matters   *Consumer*

Publishing Co: Queens Borough Public Library, 8911 Merrick Blvd, Jamaica, NY 11432-5200
   Tel # (718) 990-0704; Title Tel # (718) 990-0705 Title Fax # (718) 291-2695
Personnel: Publications Director-Constance Cooke, Editor-Mimi Koren, Mng. Editor-Dianne Blancato
Editorial Description: News, photos of Queens Library activities, events. Systemwide events calendar.
General Info: (Formerly Library News), Yr. Est. 1972, Quarterly, Trim Size-17 x 22½, Offset press, 4 pages, 2 Color, Newsprint
Circulation: Total-25,000
Printing Co: Tangent Graphics Inc., 162 Lodi St, Hackensack, NJ 07601-3929

Library Notes

Publishing Co: Univ. of North Carolina Library, Undergraduate Library Cb# 3942, Chapel Hill, NC 27599-0001; Title Tel # (919) 962-1355
Personnel: Publisher-James Govan, Editor, Circ. Mgr.-David Taylor, Art Dir.-Celia Pratt
Editorial Description: Libraries, information sciences, communication technology, faculty & staff.
General Info: Yr. Est. 1954, Monthly, Trim Size-8½ x 11, Sheetfed press, 4 pages, ISSN: 0468-5725, No Color
Circulation: Total-1,425

Library PR News   *Business*

Publishing Co: Library Educational Institute, Rr 1 Box 219, New Albany, PA 18833-9799;
   Title Tel # (717) 746-1842 Title Fax # (717) 746-1114
Personnel: Editor-Phil Bradbury
Editorial Description: Publicity, display & public relations for libraries.
General Info: Yr. Est. 1975, Bi-monthly, Trim Size-8½ x 11, Offset press, 24 pages, ISSN: 0164-9566, 2 Color
Subscriptions: Indv. $30, Can. $32, For. $41, $5/copy
Circulation: Total-5,000

Library Personnel News

Publishing Co: American Library Association, 50 E Huron St, Chicago, IL 60611-2795
   Fax # (312) 440-9374; Title Tel # (312) 944-6780
Personnel: Co-Editor-Jeniece Guy, Co-Editor-Margaret Myers
Editorial Description: Trends, legislation, resources & issues.
General Info: Yr. Est. 1987, Bi-monthly, Trim Size-8½ x 11, Offset press, 8 pages, ISSN: 0891-2742, 2 Color, Newsprint, Saddle-stitched
Subscriptions: Indv. $20, $4/copy
Circulation: Total-1,000

Library Staff Newsletter   *Consumer, Scholarly*

Publishing Co: Univ. of Florida Libraries, 204 Library West, Univ. Florida, Gainesville, FL 32611
Fax # (352) 392-7251; Title Tel # (352) 392-0342
Personnel: Exec. Ed.-Lana Rodriguez
General Info: (Formerly Univ. of Florida Libraries), Yr. Est. 1951, Monthly, Offset press, 4 pages
Circulation: Total-380

Library Systems Newsletter   *Business*

Publishing Co: American Library Association, 50 E Huron St, Chicago, IL 60611-2795
Tel # (312) 944-6780 Fax # (312) 440-9374
Personnel: Editor-Richard Bass
Editorial Description: Devoted to timely information on turn key automated systems for circulation, acquisitions, cataloging, etc.
General Info: Monthly
Subscriptions: Indv. $25

Library of Virginia News   *Consumer, Association*

Publishing Co: Library of Virginia, 11th St. at Capitol Sq., Richmond, VA 23219-3491
Tel # (804) 786-2329 Fax # (804) 371-6909; Title Tel # (804) 786-7133 Title Fax # (804) 786-5855
Personnel: Editor-Jan Hathcock
General Info: (Formerly Virginia State Library-News), Bi-monthly, Trim Size-8½ x 11, 8 pages
Subscriptions: Free
Circulation: Total-3,500
List Rental: Rents Lists

Library Workers for Peace Newsletter   *Association*

Publishing Co: New York City Library, 5th Ave. & 42nd St., New York, NY 10018;
Title Tel # (212) 340-0849

Lincoln Library Bulletin   *Business*

Publishing Co: Lincoln Library, 326 S 7th St, Springfield, IL 62701-1691; Title Tel # (217) 753-4926
Personnel: Editor, Art Dir.-Corrine Frisch
Editorial Description: News about the library, book annotations, and calendar of local events.
General Info: Yr. Est. 1940, 10x/yr., Offset press, 4 pages, No Color
Circulation: Total-7,000

Link

Publishing Co: Univ. of Nebraska-Lincoln, Library, Love Library, Lincoln, NE 68588-0410
General Info: Quarterly, Desktop press, 4 pages, 2 Color

Linkage

Publishing Co: Univ. of Pittsburgh, 135 N Bellefield Ave, Pittsburgh, PA 15213-2609;
Title Tel # (412) 624-5230
Editorial Description: Encouraging debate & dissention between library & information science professionals.
General Info: (Formerly Pitt Imprint), Yr. Est. 1962, Weekly, Mimeo press, 1 pages, No Color

Listening Post   *Association*

Publishing Co: Madison Public Library Staff Assn., 201 W Mifflin St, Madison, WI 53703-2511;
Title Tel # (608) 266-6363
Personnel: Editor-Clark Smith
Editorial Description: Published by and for the staff association of the Madison Public Library.
General Info: Yr. Est. 1949, Monthly, Trim Size-8½ x 11½, Mimeo press, 6 pages
Circulation: Total-150

Literarian, The   *Association*

Publishing Co: Mercantile Library Assn., 17 E 47th St, New York, NY 10017-1980;
Title Tel # (212) 755-6710
Personnel: Publisher-Harold Augenbraum, Editor-Nina Biddle
Editorial Description: General information about the assn. & its members & corporate supporters. News of upcoming programs, special events & additions to the book collection.
General Info: (Formerly Mecantile Library Assn. Newsletter), Yr. Est. 1850, Semi-monthly, Trim Size-8½ x 11, Desktop press, 4 pages, No Color, Newsprint
Circulation: Total-1,200

Louisiana Archives & Manuscripts Association Newsletter   *Association*

Publishing Co: Louisiana Archives and Manuscripts Association, PO Box 51213, New Orleans, LA 70151-1213
Editorial Description: Association news and developments of note to archival professionals.
General Info: Semi-annually
Subscriptions: Indv. $10, Free

MAC Newsletter

Publishing Co: Western Historical Manuscript Association, UM - St. Louis, 8001 Natural Bridge Rd., St. Louis, MO 63121; Title Tel # (314) 553-5129 Title Fax # (314) 553-5853
Editorial Description: Conference news and developments of interest to archivists.
General Info: Quarterly
Subscriptions: Indv. $12

MALT Newsletter

Publishing Co: Manitoba Assn. of Library Technicians, Box 1872, Winnipeg, MB R3C 3R1 Canada;
Title Tel # (204) 786-5601
Personnel: Editor-Debby Thorbaldson
General Info: Yr. Est. 1971, Quarterly, Trim Size-8½ x 11, Mimeo press, 20 pages, ISSN: 0710-3417, No Color, Newsprint
Subscriptions: Indv. $18, Inst. $20
Circulation: Total-150
Advertising: Inquire for rates. Accepts Inserts.

MARC Formats for Bibliographic Data

Publishing Co: U.S. Library of Congress, Cataloging Distribution Services, Washington, DC 20541-0001 Tel # (202) 707-6100 Fax # (202) 707-5017
Editorial Description: Specifications for MARC formats for books, films, ms., maps, music, serials.
Subscriptions: For. $75, $75/copy

MBLC Notes

Publishing Co: Mass. Board of Library Commissioners, 648 Beacon St, Boston, MA 02215-2002;
Title Tel # (617) 267-9400 Title Fax # (617) 421-9833
Personnel: Editor-Louise Kanus, Production Mgr.-Patrick Lynch, Art Dir.-Richard Taplin
Editorial Description: Reports on the developments of public library services in Massachusetts and news of interest to its library community.
General Info: (Formerly Currents), Yr. Est. 1973, Bi-monthly, Offset press, 8 pages, 2 Color
Circulation: Total-800

MHLS News   *Association*

Publishing Co: Mid/Hudson Library System, 103 Market St, Poughkeepsie, NY 12601-4028;
Title Tel # (914) 471-6060
Personnel: Editor-Paul Sanker
Editorial Description: Newsletter of state and regional activities affecting libraries.
General Info: Yr. Est. 1960, Quarterly, Offset press, 8 pages, 2 Color
Circulation: (100% controlled), Total-1,200
Advertising: Inquire for rates. Accepts Inserts.

MLA News   *Association*   CPM: $213

Publishing Co: Medical Library Association, 6 N Michigan Ave Ste 300, Chicago, IL 60602-4805;
Title Tel # (312) 419-9094 Title Fax # (312) 419-8950
Personnel: Publisher-Carla Funk, Editor-Jean Demas, Production Mgr.-Kimberly Pierceall, Adv. Dir.-Barbara Redmond
Editorial Description: Up-to-date inforamtion for the health information professional on the association, industry, legislation, and international events. Regular features cover new information technology, publications trends, classified job ads, and educational opportunities.
General Info: Yr. Est. 1961, Monthly, Trim Size-8½ x 11, Sheetfed press, 28 pages, ISSN: 0541-5489, No Color, Matte, Saddle-stitched
Subscriptions: Indv. $49, Can. $49, For. $62, Free With Membership
Circulation: Total-5,050
Advertising: $1,077.
List Rental: Actives: 5,500

MLS-Marketing Library Services   *Business*

Publishing Co: Information Today, Inc., 143 Old Marlton Pike, Medford, NJ 08055-8758
Tel # (609) 654-6266 Fax # (609) 654-4309; Title Tel # (617) 871-6288
Personnel: Editor-Kathy Miller, Publisher, Promotion Dir.-Carol Galvin
Editorial Description: A 'How-To' marketing tool written specifically for librarians. Covers marketing techniques for library managers.
General Info: Yr. Est. 1987, 8x/yr., Trim Size-8½ x 11, Offset press, 8 pages, ISSN: 0896-3908, 2 Color, Newsprint
Subscriptions: Indv. $65, Can. $71, For. $79
Circulation: Total-1,000

MO Library Info   *Association*

Publishing Co: Sponsor-MO Libraby Assn., Missouri Library Assn., 1806 Business 63 S. #B, Columbia, MO 65201-8404; Title Tel # (314) 449-4627
Personnel: Publisher, Editor, Adv. Dir.-Jean McCartney
Editorial Description: Library science. State & member news; conference & workshop information.
General Info: (Formerly MLA Newsletter), Yr. Est. 1970, Bi-monthly, Trim Size-8½ x 10⅞, Letrpr. press, 8 pages, ISSN: 0884-2205, 2% ads, No Color
Subscriptions: Indv. $6, Can. $6, For. $10, $1/copy
Circulation: Total-1,500
Advertising: Inquire for rates.

MPL Now

Publishing Co: Muncie Public Library, 301 E Jackson St, Muncie, IN 47305-1878;
Title Tel # (317) 747-8200
Personnel: Editor-John Drumm
Editorial Description: Covers events planned by the library. Reviews new books of interest to patrons.
General Info: Yr. Est. 1970, Monthly, 6 pages, Color
Subscriptions: Free
Circulation: Total-600

MPLA Newsletter   *Association*

Publishing Co: Mt. Plains Library Association, I.D. Weeks Library, University of South Dakota, Vermillion, SD 57069-2390; Title Tel # (605) 677-6082 Title Fax # (605) 677-5488
Personnel: Circ. Mgr.-Joe Edelen, Editor, Adv. Dir.-Jim Dertien
Editorial Description: Official publication of the Mountain Plains Library Association.
General Info: (Formerly MPLA Quarterly), Yr. Est. 1958, Bi-monthly, Trim Size-8½ x 11, Offset press, 24 pages, ISSN: 0145-6180, 1% ads, 4 Color
Subscriptions: Indv. $20, Inst. $20, Can. $26, For. $26, $4/copy
Circulation: (100% controlled), Total-1,200
Advertising: Inquire for rates.
List Rental: Actives $50/M
Printing Co: Broadcaster Press, 201 W Cherry St, Vermillion, SD 57069-1109 Tel # (605) 624-4429

MSLAVA Journal/
MSLAVA Newsletter   *Association*   **CPM: $400**

Publishing Co: Manitoba School Library-Audio-Visual Assn., 191 Harcourt St., Winnipeg, MB R3J 3H2 Canada; Title Tel # (204) 888-7961
Personnel: Editor-Margaret Elliot-Whitelow, Production Mgr.-Alexander Campbell
Editorial Description: Information and resource materials for librarians in schools and other educational institutions.
General Info: Yr. Est. 1968, Quarterly, Trim Size-8½ x 11, Desktop press, 44 pages, ISSN: 0315-9124, Ind/Abs/Online: Can.Ed.In., Color-cover, Other
Subscriptions: Indv. $20, Inst. $24, Can. $20
Acquistions: Publication Bought, Publication Sold
Circulation: Total-250
Advertising: $100. Accepts Inserts.
List Rental: Rents Lists

MSRRT Newsletter   *Association*

Publishing Co: Minnesota Library Assn. Social Responsibilities Round Table, 4645 Columbus Ave, Minneapolis, MN 55407-3527; Title Tel # (612) 541-8572
Personnel: Publisher, Editor-Christopher Dodge
Editorial Description: Peace & justice news & commentary for the library community, with special emphasis on annotations of alternative periodicals, short reviews, & networking information.
General Info: Yr. Est. 1988, 10x/yr., Trim Size-8½ x 11, Desktop press, 16 pages, No Color
Subscriptions: Indv. $15, Free With Membership

Magnes News
See: MUSEUM PUBLICATIONS

Maine Entry   *Association*   **CPM: $71**

Publishing Co: Sponsor-Maine State Library, Maine Library Assn., Local Govt. Ctr., Community Dr, Augusta, ME 04333-0001 Tel # (207) 623-1634; Title Tel # (207) 287-5620 Title Fax # (207) 287-5624
Personnel: Editor-Edna Comstock, Editor-Pam Turner
Editorial Description: News of importance to Maine librarians and affiliates.
General Info: (Formerly Downeast Libraries), Yr. Est. 1956, Quarterly, Trim Size-8 x 10½, Offset press, 36 pages, 8% ads, 2 Color
Subscriptions: Indv. $5, Inst. $25, $5/copy
Circulation: Total-1,400, Readership-1,400
Advertising: $100.

Maine Memo   *Association*

Publishing Co: Maine Library Assn., Local Govt. Ctr., Community Dr, Augusta, ME 04333-0001 Tel # (207) 623-1634; Title Tel # (207) 263-1634
Personnel: Editor, Production Mgr.-Daphne Crocker
Editorial Description: Calendar of events, current Maine library news.
General Info: (Formerly Maine Library Association Monthly Memo), Yr. Est. 1979, Monthly, Trim Size-8½ x 14, Sheetfed press, 2 pages, No Color
Circulation: Total-1,200

McMaster University Library
Research News   *Scholarly, Association*

Publishing Co: McMaster University Library Press, Mills Memorial Library, Hamilton, ON L8S 4L6 Canada; Title Tel # (416) 525-9140 Title Fax # (905) 546-0625
Editorial Description: Library science newsletter of collections housed in the division of archives & research collections, Mills Memorial Library, McMaster University.
General Info: Yr. Est. 1968, Semi-annually, Offset press, 4 pages, ISSN: 0024-9270, No Color, Perfect bound
Subscriptions: Free
Circulation: Total-500

Media Matters   *Association*

Publishing Co: North Carolina Dept. of Public Instruction, Educational Media & Technica, Raleigh, NC 27611; Title Tel # (919) 733-3193
Personnel: Publisher-Elsie Brumback, Editor, Circ. Mgr.-Sue Scott, Art Dir.-Barbara Michos
Editorial Description: Keeps the in-service school library/media personnel current on state and national issues related to a vital school media program. Provides models for such a program.
General Info: (Formerly Educational Media Bulletin), Yr. Est. 1979, Trim Size-8½ x 11, Offset press, 8 pages, No Color
Circulation: Total-3,200

Media Notes   *Business, Scholarly*

Publishing Co: Media Notes, PO Box E, Avon, CT 06001-0305; Title Tel # (203) 677-7170
Personnel: Publisher-Norma Hansen, Editor-Jack Short
Editorial Description: Takes a lighthearted look at the school library media field.
General Info: Yr. Est. 1966, Irregular, 4 pages, No Color
Subscriptions: Indv. $10
Circulation: Total-1,032

Mel Gabler's Newsletter
See: EDUCATION

Michigan Librarian   *Association*

Publishing Co: Michigan Library Assn., 6810 S. Cedar St., Ste. 6, Lansing, MI 48911-6909; Title Tel # (517) 694-6615
Personnel: Editor-Marianne Gessner
Editorial Description: Information of interest to librarians in Michigan.
General Info: (Formerly Michigan Librarian), Yr. Est. 1935, Monthly, Trim Size-8½ x 11, Desktop press, 8 pages, ISSN: 0884-9919, Ind/Abs/Online: Lib.Lit., 2 Color, Newsprint
Subscriptions: Indv. $40, For. $50, $4/copy
Circulation: Total-2,500

Microfilming Projects
Newsletter   *Association*

Publishing Co: SALALM Secretariat, General Library University Of, New Mexico, Albuquerque, NM 87131-0001 Fax # (505) 277-0646; Title Tel # (505) 277-5102
Personnel: Editor-Basil Malish, Circ. Mgr.-Sharon Moynahan
Editorial Description: Lists new & continuing original microfilming projects of research material on Latin America.
General Info: Yr. Est. 1964, Annually, Mimeo press, 20 pages
Subscriptions: $9/copy
Circulation: (100% controlled), Total-450
List Rental: Actives: $250/M

Mid-Atlantic Archivist   *Association*

Publishing Co: Sponsor-Mid-Atlantic Regional Archives Conference, Mid-Atlantic Regional Archives Conference, c/o Marsha Trimble, Univ. of Virginia Law Library, Charlottesville, VA 22901 Tel # (804) 924-3023; Title Tel # (202) 924-7549 Title Fax # (202) 994-1340
Personnel: Editor-G. David Anderson, News Ed.-Roger W. Fromm, Technology Ed.-Kathy Jacob, Software Editor-Kathleen D. Roe, News Ed.-Susan G. Swatzburg, Bk. Rev. Ed.-Mary Boccaccio, Adv. Dir.-Bruce Abrams
Editorial Description: News and information relating to archives and manuscripts.
General Info: Yr. Est. 1972, Quarterly, Trim Size-8½ x 11, Sheetfed press, 20 pages, ISSN: 0738-9396, Ind/Abs/Online: Bitnet, 2% ads, No Color, Newsprint, Saddle-stitched
Subscriptions: Indv. $10, $1/copy
Advertising: Inquire for rates.
List Rental: Rents Lists
Printing Co: Pickwick Press, 125 Georges Rd # 36, New Brunswick, NJ 08901-3105 Tel # (908) 246-2151

Milwaukee Reader   *Association*

Publishing Co: Milwaukee Public Library, 814 W Wisconsin Ave, Milwaukee, WI 53233-2309 Fax # (414) 278-2137; Title Tel # (414) 278-3031
Personnel: Editor-Lorelei Starck, Art Dir.-Mary Slough
Editorial Description: Articles of current interest, especially books & authors.
General Info: Yr. Est. 1942, Monthly, Trim Size-10 x 17, Offset press, 2 pages, 2 Color
Subscriptions: Indv. $5
Circulation: Total-4,500

Minnesota Department of
Education, Public Library
Newsletter   *Association*

Publishing Co: Office of Library Development & Services, 440 Capital Square Bldg., 550 Cedar St., St. Paul, MN 55101; Title Tel # (612) 296-2821 Title Fax # (612) 296-3272
Personnel: Editor-Darlene M. Arnold
Editorial Description: News of interest to Minnesota librarians.
General Info: Yr. Est. 1970, Monthly, 2 pages
Circulation: Total-800

Minnesota Library Assn.
Newsletter   *Association*   **CPM: $155**

Publishing Co: Minnesota Library Assn., 1315 Lowry Ave. N., Minneapolis, MN 55411-1326; Title Tel # (612) 521-1735 Title Fax # (612) 529-5503
Editorial Description: Contains articles on library issues and association news.
General Info: 13x/yr., Trim Size-8½ x 11, Sheetfed press, 8 pages, Color-cover
Subscriptions: Indv. $20, Inst. $20, Can. $25, For. $25, $3/copy
Circulation: (13% controlled), Total-900, Subscriptions-783
Advertising: $140.
List Rental: Rents Lists
Printing Co: Northside Printing, 1219 Lowry Ave. N., Minneapolis, MN 55411 Tel # (612) 522-5224

Missouri Libraries   *Association*

Publishing Co: Missouri State Library, PO Box 387, Jefferson City, MO 65102-0387; Title Tel # (314) 751-2680 Title Fax # (314) 751-3612
Personnel: Editor-Madeline Matson
Editorial Description: Newsletter containing information of interest to Missouri library community.
General Info: Yr. Est. 1988, Bi-monthly, Trim Size-8½ x 11, Web press, 20 pages, ISSN: 0899-6458, 2 Color, Coated, Saddle-stitched
Subscriptions: Free To Qualified Recipient
Circulation: Total-2,500

Mobile Public Library Today

Publishing Co: Mobile Public Library, 700 Government St, Mobile, AL 36602-1499;
Title Tel # (205) 434-7097
Personnel: Editor-Christina Bowersox, Circ. Mgr., Art Dir.-Paula Wilson
Editorial Description: Publicizes library's services, programs, public image, and needs.
General Info: Yr. Est. 1983, Bi-monthly, Trim Size-8½ x 11, Offset press, 4 pages, Color, Newsprint
Circulation: Total-5,000

Montana State Library
News Update
Consumer

Publishing Co: Montana State Library, 1515 E 6th Ave, Helena, MT 59601-4542;
Title Tel # (406) 444-5353 Title Fax # (406) 444-5612
Personnel: Editor-Cathy Siegner, Circ. Mgr.-Diane Gunderson
Editorial Description: News affecting Montana libraries.
General Info: (Formerly Montana Newsletter), Yr. Est. 1966, Bi-monthly, Trim Size-8½ x 11, Sheetfed press, 4 pages, No Color, Matte
Acquistions: Publication Bought
Circulation: Total-1,800
Printing Co: Publications & Graphics, 920 Front St, Helena, MT 59601-3311 Tel # (406) 444-3053

Music Cataloging Bulletin

Publishing Co: Music Library Assn., PO Box 487, Canton, MA 02021-0487 Tel # (617) 828-8450
Fax # (617) 828-8915; Title Tel # (313) 761-6350
Personnel: Editor-Marguerite Iskenderian
Editorial Description: Reports additions and changes in Library of Congress cataloging for musical materials. Also includes news of interest to music catalogers.
General Info: Yr. Est. 1970, Monthly, Trim Size-8½ x 11, Offset press, 4 pages, ISSN: 0027-4283
Subscriptions: Indv. $12, $1/copy
Circulation: Total-600

Music Library Association
Newsletter

Publishing Co: Music Library Assn., PO Box 487, Canton, MA 02021-0487 Tel # (617) 828-8450
Fax # (617) 828-8915
General Info: Yr. Est. 1969, Quarterly

N-Compass
Association

Publishing Co: Nebraska Library Commission, 1200 N St Ste 120, Lincoln, NE 68508-2020;
Title Tel # (402) 471-2045 Title Fax # (402) 471-2083
Personnel: Editor-Mary Jo Ryan
Editorial Description: Covers library activities of Nebraska with selected items on natl. & regional events plus legislative information & features about the activities of the Nebraska Library Commission.
General Info: (Formerly Overtones From the Underground; Overtones), Yr. Est. 1974, Quarterly, Trim Size-8½ x 11, Web press, 8 pages, 2 Color, Coated, Saddle-stitched
Circulation: (96% controlled), Total-2,000
List Rental: Actives: $30/M
Printing Co: Nebraska State Printing, 501 S 14th St, Lincoln, NE 68508-2711

NAGARA Clearinghouse

Publishing Co: National Association of Government Archives and Records, 11th St. at Capitol Square, Richmond, VA 23219
Editorial Description: News and reports on government records.
General Info: Quarterly

NFAIS Newsletter
Business, Association

Publishing Co: National Federation of Abstracting & Information Services, 1518 Walnut St., Suite 307, Philadelphia, PA 19102-3403; Title Tel # (215) 893-1561 Title Fax # (215) 893-1564
Personnel: Publisher-Richard Kaser, Editor-Wendy Wicks
Editorial Description: Abstracting & indexing services; databases, thesaurus developments, online, bibliography; information industry news; government info policy, international developments, calendar of conferences & seminars.
General Info: Yr. Est. 1958, Monthly, Trim Size-8½ x 11, Offset press, 12 pages, ISSN: 0090-0893, Color-cover, Saddle-stitched
Subscriptions: Indv. $120, For. $135, $15/copy
Circulation: Total-500
Advertising: Accepts Inserts.
Printing Co: Hamilton Press, Inc., 1042 Industrial Dr., West Berlin Industrial Center, Berlin, NJ 08009 Tel # (609) 753-0900, Fax # (609) 753-0307

NOCALL Newsletter
Business, Association

Publishing Co: Northern California Association of Law Libraries, Santa Clara University, Santa Clara, CA 95053-0001; Title Tel # (916) 440-6011
Editorial Description: Newsletter for the Northern California Association of Law Libraries.
General Info: Bi-monthly

NVR Reports
See: TELEVISION & VIDEO

NYLA Bulletin
Association　　CPM: $120

Publishing Co: Sponsor-New York Library Assn., New York Library Assn., 252 Hudson Ave, Albany, NY 12210-1802 Fax # (518) 427-1697; Title Tel # (518) 432-6952
Personnel: Publisher-Susan Keitel, Editor-Paul S. Girsdansky
Editorial Description: A 16 page publication, which comes out 10 times a year devoted to New York Library Association news and other news of the library industry.
General Info: Yr. Est. 1953, Monthly, Trim Size-8½ x 11, Web press, 16 pages, ISSN: 0027-7134, 2% ads, 2 Color, Newsprint, Saddle-stitched
Subscriptions: Free With Membership
Circulation: (100% controlled), Total-3,500, Readership-5,000
Advertising: $420.
List Rental: List Management Co.: NYLA, 252 Hudson Avenue, Albany, NY 12210
Tel # (518) 432-6952, Actives: 3,500, $120/M
Printing Co: Vanguard Offset Printers, 470 Mundet Place, Hillside, NJ 07205-1115
Tel # (908) 851-2222

National Librarian: The
NLA Newsletter
Association

Publishing Co: Natl. Librarians Assn., PO Box 486, Alma, MI 48801-0486 Fax # (517) 463-8694;
Title Tel # (517) 463-7227
Personnel: Editor-Peter Dollard
Editorial Description: News and views relating to professional concerns of librarians.
General Info: (Formerly NLA Newsletter), Yr. Est. 1975, Quarterly, 8 pages, ISSN: 0191-359X, Ind/Abs/Online: LISA
Subscriptions: Indv. $15
Circulation: Total-600
Advertising: Inquire for rates.

National Preservation News

Publishing Co: Natl. Preservation Program Office, Library Of Congress, Lm G07, Washington, DC 20540-0001; Title Tel # (202) 707-1840
General Info: 24 pages, ISSN: 0882-4339, Saddle-stitched

Nebraska Library
Association Quarterly
Association　　CPM: $205

Publishing Co: Nebraska Library Association, 7500 Mercy Rd, Omaha, NE 68124-2319;
Title Tel # (402) 398-6002
Editorial Description: News items from local and regional libraries, committee reports, contributed articles.
General Info: Yr. Est. 1970, Quarterly, Trim Size-5½ x 8½, Offset press, 35 pages, ISSN: 0028-1883
Subscriptions: Indv. $20, $5/copy
Circulation: Total-900
Advertising: $185.

New Notes
See: HOUSE ORGANS

New York Public Library
News
Association

Publishing Co: New York Public Library, Fifth Avenue & 42nd St., New York, NY 10018;
Title Tel # (212) 221-7676 Title Fax # (212) 768-7439
Personnel: Editor-Esther Harriott
Editorial Description: Reports activities at the New York Public Library to its donors.
General Info: (Formerly Library Lines), Yr. Est. 1971, Quarterly, Trim Size-9 x 12, Sheetfed press, 8 pages, ISSN: 1060-8176, 2 Color, Matte
Subscriptions: Free With Membership
Circulation: Total-29,000

New York University,
Society for the Libraries
Bulletin
Association

Publishing Co: New York University, Society for the Libraries, 70 Washington Sq S, New York, NY 10012-1019; Title Tel # (212) 998-1212
General Info: Yr. Est. 1934

Newberry Newsletter
Association

Publishing Co: Newberry Library, Renaissance Center, 60 W. Walton St., Chicago, IL 60610-3380 Tel # (312) 255-3514; Title Tel # (312) 943-9090
Personnel: Editor-Judson Scruton
Editorial Description: News and articles on the library's activities.
General Info: Yr. Est. 1973, Quarterly, 12 pages, 2 Color, Newsprint
Subscriptions: Indv. $30
Circulation: Total-5,000

News from Chapel Hill
Association

Publishing Co: Univ. of North Carolina at Chapel Hill, Alumni Assn., School Of Info. & Library Sci., Chapel Hill, NC 27599-0001
General Info: 12 pages
Circulation: Total-1,100

News from Fondren
Consumer, Association

Publishing Co: Rice University/Fondren Library, 6100 Main St Stop 44, Houston, TX 77005-1827;
Title Tel # (713) 285-5133 Title Fax # (713) 285-5258
Personnel: Editor-Elizabeth Baber
General Info: Yr. Est. 1991, Tri-annually, Trim Size-8½ x 11, Desktop press, 8 pages, 2 Color
Circulation: Total-2,500
Printing Co: Intl. Printing & Publishing, 2748 Bingle Rd, Houston, TX 77055-1135
Tel # (713) 464-8484, Fax # (713) 464-7239

News Library News
See: NEWSPAPER INDUSTRY

News for South Carolina
Libraries

Publishing Co: South Carolina State Library, 1500 Senate St. #11469, Columbia, SC 29211-3815
Tel # (803) 737-9970; Title Tel # (803) 734-8666 Title Fax # (803) 734-8676
Personnel: Editor-JoAnn M. Olson
Editorial Description: Library-related activities in South Carolina.
General Info: (Formerly News for Public Libraries), Yr. Est. 1957, Bi-monthly, Trim Size-8½ x 11½, Sheetfed press, 12 pages, ISSN: 0146-1842, No Color
Subscriptions: Free To Qualified Recipient
Circulation: Total-2,150

Newsletter of the
Congressional Archives
Roundtable *Association*

Publishing Co: Society of American Archivists, 600 S. Federal St., Ste. 504, Chicago, IL 60605-1898
Tel # (312) 922-0140 Fax # (312) 347-1452; Title Tel # (803) 251-8470 Title Fax # (803) 251-8472
Editorial Description: News relating to the Congressional Archives Roundtable.
General Info: Semi-annually

Newsletter on Intellectual Freedom
See: EDUCATION

Newspoke *Business, Association*

Publishing Co: Alaska Library Assn., PO Box 81084, Fairbanks, AK 99708-1084;
Title Tel # (907) 465-2927 Title Fax # (907) 465-2665
Personnel: Editor-Patience Frederiksen
Editorial Description: Articles concerning the Alaskan library community.
General Info: Bi-monthly, Trim Size-8½ x 11, 8 pages
Subscriptions: Indv. $15, Inst. $15
Circulation: Total-1,100

Nicolet Compass

Publishing Co: Nicolet Federated Library System, 515 Pine St, Green Bay, WI 54301-5194;
Title Tel # (414) 497-3443 Title Fax # (414) 497-3108
Personnel: Circ. Mgr.-Edie Eau Claire, Publisher, Editor, Art Dir.-Sylvia Pratt
Editorial Description: News,features & ideas for public librarians in Nicolet system.
General Info: Yr. Est. 1976, Bi-monthly, Sheetfed press, 20 pages, No Color, Newsprint
Circulation: Total-425

North Carolina Archivist

Publishing Co: Society of North Carolina Archivists, PO Box 20448, Raleigh, NC 27619-0448
Editorial Description: Society news and information of interest to professionals in the archival field.
Subscriptions: Indv. $15

North Country Library News *Association*

Publishing Co: North Country Library System, Outer W. Main St., Box 99, Watertown, NY 13601;
Title Tel # (315) 782-5540
Editorial Description: Events of interest and up-coming programs.
General Info: Yr. Est. 1948, Quarterly, 14 pages, 2 Color
Circulation: Total-677

North Country Reference
Research *Association*

Publishing Co: North Country Reference Research, 7 Commerce Ln, Canton, NY 13617-9666;
Title Tel # (315) 386-4560
Personnel: Editor-Richard Kimball
Editorial Description: Library news in Northern N.Y. and N.Y. state.
General Info: Yr. Est. 1968, Quarterly, Mimeo press, 6 pages, ISSN: 0029-2699, 2 Color
Circulation: (100% controlled), Total-250

Northern Latitudes

Publishing Co: Univ. of Minnesota Map Library, S76 Wilson Library, Minneapolis, MN 55455-0414
Personnel: Editor-Brent Allison
General Info: Yr. Est. 1989

Northern New Jersey Unit
Newsletter

Publishing Co: Catholic Library Assn., Northern New Jersey Unit, Immaculate Conception H. S., 33
Cottage Pl., Montclair, NJ 07042-3497; Title Tel # (201) 433-8877
Personnel: Editor-Sister Francis Devlin, S.C.
General Info: Yr. Est. 1965, Semi-annually
Circulation: Total-125

Notes
See: GOVERNMENT

Nova Scotia Library Assn.
News *Association*

Publishing Co: Nova Scotia Library Assn., c/o Glenda Roacne, 32 Glendale Ave., Lower Sackville,
NS B4C 3M1 Canada; Title Tel # (902) 864-4414
General Info: Yr. Est. 1973, Quarterly, 20 pages, ISSN: 1182-0209
Subscriptions: Indv. $10

Nova Scotia School Library
Assn. Bulletin

Publishing Co: Nova Scotia School Library Assn., C/O Gatez Brook Junior High, RR #1, Head of
Chezzetcook, NS B0J 1N0 Canada; Title Tel # (902) 462-6907
Personnel: Editor-Shirley Coulter
General Info: Yr. Est. 1971, 28 pages, ISSN: 0707-2457
Subscriptions: Indv. $10
Circulation: Total-200

O L A C Newsletter

Publishing Co: Sponsor-On-Line Audiovisual Catalogers, Inc., On-Line Audiovisual Catalogers,
Catalog Dept., Univ. of Arizona Library, Tuscon, AZ 85721-0001
Personnel: Publisher, Editor-Cecilia Piccolo
Editorial Description: Deals with on-line cataloging of AV materials in all settings.
General Info: Yr. Est. 1981, Quarterly, Trim Size-5½ x 8½, Sheetfed press, 32 pages, ISSN: 0739-1153, No Color, Newsprint
Subscriptions: Indv. $10, Inst. $16, Can. $10, $2/copy
Circulation: (91% controlled), Total-691
List Rental: Rents Lists

OCLC Newsletter *Association*

Publishing Co: OCLC Online Computer Library Ctr., 6565 Frantz Rd, Dublin, OH 43017-5308;
Title Tel # (614) 764-6000 Title Fax # (614) 764-0740
Personnel: Editor-Nita Dean, Art Dir.-Lorna Williamson
Editorial Description: Nationwide computer network for libraries. Newsletter provides general news of OCLC and its products and services and coverage of issues that affect its participating libraries.
General Info: Yr. Est. 1967, Bi-monthly, Trim Size-8½ x 11, Offset press, 32 pages, ISSN: 0163-898x, 2 Color, Saddle-stitched
Subscriptions: Free To Qualified Recipient
Circulation: Total-17,000
Printing Co: Typographic Printing Co., 2900 Banwick Rd, Columbus, OH 43232-3838
Tel # (614) 239-9090

OGLC Exchange
See: GOVERNMENT

OIF Memorandum *Association*

Publishing Co: American Library Association, 50 E Huron St, Chicago, IL 60611-2795
Tel # (312) 944-6780 Fax # (312) 440-9374; Title Tel # (312) 280-4223
Personnel: Editor-Judith Krug
General Info: Monthly, ISSN: 0734-3086, No Color
Subscriptions: Indv. $20

Oceana's Law Library Newsletter
See: LAW

Off the Record *Association*

Publishing Co: Archives Association of Ontario, Box 46009, College Park P. O., 444 Yonge Street,
Toronto, ON M5B 2L8 Canada; Title Tel # (416) 778-0426 Title Fax # (416) 778-8362
Personnel: Co-Editor-John Jung, Co-Editor-Janice Simpson
Editorial Description: Information for archivists and library science professionals.
General Info: 5x/yr., Trim Size-8½ x 11, Desktop press, 16 pages, ISSN: 1182-0055, Matte
Subscriptions: Free With Membership
Advertising: $300. Accepts Inserts.

Offline
See: HOUSE ORGANS

Ohio Archivist
See: HISTORY

Ohioana Quarterly *Business, Association*

Publishing Co: Ohioana Library Assn., 65 S. Front St., Suite 1105, Columbus, OH 43215
Fax # (614) 728-6974; Title Tel # (614) 466-3831
Personnel: Editor-Barbara Masleoff
Editorial Description: News and information for the Ohioana Library Association.
General Info: (Formerly Ohiana Library Newsletter), Quarterly
Subscriptions: Indv. $20, $5/copy
Circulation: Total-1,300

Oklahoma Librarian *Association*

Publishing Co: Oklahoma Library Assn., 300 Hardy Dr, Edmond, OK 73013-5101;
Title Tel # (405) 348-0506
Personnel: Editor-Patti Gallad, Circ. Mgr.-Kay Boies
Editorial Description: Newsletter of current events and issues for members of state library association.
General Info: Yr. Est. 1950, Bi-monthly, Offset press, 12 pages, ISSN: 0030-1760, 2 Color
Subscriptions: Indv. $25, $3/copy
Circulation: Total-1,000
Advertising: Inquire for rates.
Printing Co: Norman Transcript, Norman, OK

One-Person Library: A Newsletter for Librarians & Management   *Business*

Publishing Co: SMR International, Box 948, Murray Hill Station, New York, NY 10156-0948
Fax # (212) 685-2987; Title Tel # (212) 683-6285 Title Fax # (212) 683-2987
Personnel: Publisher-Guy St. Clair, Editor, Production Mgr.-Andrew Berner
Editorial Description: Articles, reviews, interviews specifically for librarians who work alone, or with minimal assistance, as well as for all librarians and information specialists seeking to maximize results with existing resources.
General Info: Yr. Est. 1984, Monthly, Trim Size-8 x 11, Web press, 8 pages, ISSN: 0748-8831, No Color, Newsprint
Subscriptions: Indv. $75, Can. $80, For. $85, $10/copy
Circulation: Total-1,800
Advertising: Accepts Inserts.
List Rental: Actives: 2,000, $500/M
Printing Co: Aladdin Printing, 1012 E Gun Hill Rd, Bronx, NY 10469-3720 Tel # (212) 653-3303

Online Hotline News Service on CD-ROM
See: TELECOMMUNICATIONS

Online Libraries & Microcomputers   *Business*

Publishing Co: Information Intelligence, Inc., PO Box 31098, Phoenix, AZ 85046-1098;
Title Tel # (602) 996-2283
Personnel: Editor-George Machovec
Editorial Description: Aimed at N. American libraries & info centers for library applications in online field, micro computers & library automation.
General Info: Yr. Est. 1983, Monthly, Trim Size-8½ x 11, Sheetfed press, 14 pages, ISSN: 0737-7770, Ind/Abs/Online: NewsNet, DataStar, DIALOG, CARL, ESA, 1% ads, No Color, Newsprint
Subscriptions: Indv. $63, Inst. $63, For. $88, $6/copy
Advertising: Inquire for rates.

Open Entry

Publishing Co: Michigan Archival Assn., Walter Reuther Library, Wayne State Univ., 5401 Cass, Detroit, MI 48202
Editorial Description: Association news and info of interest to archival professionals.
General Info: Semi-annually

Orange Seed Technical Bulletin   *Consumer*

Publishing Co: Florida State Library, R.A. Gray Bldg., Tallahassee, FL 32399-0250;
Title Tel # (904) 487-2651
Personnel: Editor, Circ. Mgr.-Betty Scott
Editorial Description: Administrative and professional information for public librarians in Florida.
General Info: (Formerly Orange Seed), Yr. Est. 1973, Monthly, Trim Size-8½ x 11, Offset press, 14 pages, No Color, Newsprint
Subscriptions: $1/copy
Circulation: (44% controlled), Total-1,250

Osler Library Newsletter   *Association*

Publishing Co: McGill University, Osler Library, 3655 Drummond St., Montreal, PQ H3G 1Y6 Canada; Title Tel # (514) 398-4720 Title Fax # (514) 398-5747
Personnel: Publisher, Editor-F.E. Wallis
Editorial Description: News and articles about the Osler Library and William Osler.
General Info: Yr. Est. 1969, 3x/yr., Trim Size-8½ x 11, Offset press, 4 pages, ISSN: 0085-4557, No Color
Subscriptions: Free
Circulation: Total-1,400

Ottawa Public Library Bulletin

Publishing Co: Ottawa Public Library, 120 Metcalfe Street, Ottawa, ON K1P 5M2 Canada;
Title Tel # (613) 598-4002 Title Fax # (613) 567-4013
Personnel: Editor-Ann Lupiano
Editorial Description: Newsletter for staff.
General Info: Yr. Est. 1968, Monthly, Trim Size-8½ x 11, Offset press, 4 pages, Matte, Saddle-stitched
Subscriptions: Free
Circulation: Total-115

Outrider   *Association*

Publishing Co: Wyoming State Library, Supreme Court & State Library, Cheyenne, WY 82002-0001;
Title Tel # (307) 777-7281 Title Fax # (307) 777-6289
Personnel: Editor-Linn Rounds
Editorial Description: Newsletter of the Wyoming State Library, specifically directed to Wyoming librarians, with some articles of general interest in the library field.
General Info: Yr. Est. 1968, Monthly, Trim Size-8½ x 11, Offset press, 8 pages, ISSN: 0030-7319, No Color, Matte
Circulation: Total-1,550
Printing Co: Cheyenne Newspapers, Inc., 702 W Lincolnway, Cheyenne, WY 82001-4359 Tel # (301) 634-3361

PAIS International News   *Business*

Publishing Co: Public Affairs Information Service, Inc., 521 W 43rd St, 5th Floor, New York, NY 10036-4396 Tel # (212) 736-3329 Fax # (213) 643-2848
Personnel: Publisher-Barbara Preschel, Editor-Debra Brown-Spruil
Editorial Description: Information on PAIS products and services.
General Info: Monthly, Trim Size-8½ x 11, 4 pages, Matte

PLL Perspectives   *Association*   CPM: $352

Publishing Co: Sabrina I. Pacifici, 1722 Eye St. NW, Washington, DC 20006 Tel # (202) 736-8510;
Title Tel # (212) 736-8510
Personnel: Publisher, Editor-Sabrina I. Pacifici, Adv. Dir.-Jeff Bosh
Editorial Description: The newsletter is a forum for issues and subjects pertinent to private law firm librarians throughout the world.
General Info: (Formerly Private Law Librarian), Yr. Est. 1989, Quarterly, Trim Size-8½ x 11, Desktop press, 28 pages, ISSN: 1068-9346, Color, Saddle-stitched
Subscriptions: Indv. $25, Inst. $25, $5/copy
Circulation: Total-1,700
Advertising: $600.
Printing Co: Lesher Printers, Inc., 810 N Wilson Ave, Fremont, OH 43420-2271 Tel # (419) 332-8253

PR Activity Report   *Business, Association*

Publishing Co: American Library Association, 50 E Huron St, Chicago, IL 60611-2795
Tel # (312) 944-6780 Fax # (312) 440-9374; Title Tel # (312) 280-5041 Title Fax # (312) 944-8520
Personnel: Editor-Linda Wallace
Editorial Description: PR tips & opportunities for libraries.
General Info: 4x/yr., Trim Size-8½ x 11, Sheetfed press, 6 pages, ISSN: 1991-8004, 2 Color, Recycled, Saddle-stitched
Subscriptions: Indv. $25, Can. $30, For. $35, $7/copy
Circulation: Total-800
List Rental: Rents Lists

Packet   *Association*

Publishing Co: Mississippi Library Commission, PO Box 10700, Jackson, MS 39289-0700;
Title Tel # (601) 359-1036
Personnel: Editor, Art Dir.-Lisa Ruble
Editorial Description: Library development, trends in services and programs, etc.
General Info: Yr. Est. 1970, Monthly, Trim Size-11 x 17, Offset press, 8 pages, ISSN: 0195-9646, 2 Color
Circulation: Total-2,500

Pennsauken Library Newsletter   *Association*

Publishing Co: Barbara Silberstein, c/o W. Leslie Rogers Library, 5605 Crescent Blvd., Pennsauken, NJ 08110; Title Tel # (609) 665-5959
Personnel: Editor-Mike Phillips
General Info: 9x/yr., 6 pages
Subscriptions: Indv. $5
Circulation: (100% controlled), Total-250

Pennsylvania Library Association Bulletin   *Association*

Publishing Co: Pennsylvania Library Association, 1919 N Front St, Harrisburg, PA 17102-2214
Fax # (717) 233-3121; Title Tel # (717) 233-3113
Personnel: Editor-Glenn Miller
General Info: Yr. Est. 1945, Monthly, Trim Size-8½ x 11, 12 pages, 2% ads, 2 Color, Coated
Subscriptions: Indv. $40, $2/copy
Circulation: Total-2,000
Advertising: Inquire for rates.
List Rental: Actives $50/M

Polar Libraries Bulletin   *Association*

Publishing Co: Alaska State Library, PO Box 110571, Juneau, AK 99811-0571;
Title Tel # (907) 465-2925 Title Fax # (907) 465-2665
Personnel: Editor-Kathryn Shelton
Editorial Description: Focuses on polar libraries colloquy.
General Info: (Formerly Northern Libraries Bulletin), Yr. Est. 1972, Trim Size-8½ x 11, Mimeo press, 8 pages, ISSN: 1049-7765, No Color
Circulation: (100% controlled), Total-300

Preface, Your Guide to Library Programs and Services   *Consumer*   CPM: $38

Publishing Co: Saskatoon Public Library, 311 23rd Street E., Saskatoon, SK S7K 0J6 Canada
Fax # (306) 975-7766; Title Tel # (306) 975-7530 Title Fax # (306) 975-7542
Personnel: Advertising & Sales-Lise Henderson
Editorial Description: A listing of programs and services available at the main library and each branch.
General Info: (Formerly Saskatoon, Public Library, Preface), Yr. Est. 1969, 5x/yr., Trim Size-8 x 10½, Web press, 40 pages, ISSN: 1184-1125, 2 Color, Newsprint
Subscriptions: Free
Circulation: (100% controlled), Total-6,500
Advertising: $250.

Primary Source
Consumer, Association

Publishing Co: Soc. of Mississippi Archivists, PO Box 1151, Jackson, MS 39215-1151; Title Tel # (601) 359-6868 Title Fax # (601) 359-6905
Personnel: Editor-Mattie Sink
Editorial Description: Covers archival & library science topics.
General Info: Yr. Est. 1979, Quarterly, Trim Size-8½ x 11, 20 pages, ISSN: 0741-6563, Saddle-stitched
Subscriptions: Indv. $8, Inst. $15
Circulation: Total-260

Primate Library Report: Audio-Visual Acquisitions
See: ZOOLOGY

PsycINFO
See: PSYCHOLOGY

Public Bridge

Publishing Co: Boulder Public Library, PO Box H, Boulder, CO 80306-1326
Personnel: Editor-Nancy Morgan
Editorial Description: News of the library & special events.
General Info: Bi-monthly, 8 pages
Circulation: Total-2,000

Public Library Services Newsletter
Association

Publishing Co: Public Library Services, 1525 First St., Brandon, MB R7A 7A1 Canada; Title Tel # (204) 726-6590 Title Fax # (204) 726-6868
Editorial Description: Promotes information sharing between libraries and provide an awareness of events in libraries throughout Manitoba.
General Info: Yr. Est. 1978, Bi-monthly, Trim Size-8½ x 11, Mimeo press, 8 pages, ISSN: 0706-7798, No Color, Recycled
Circulation: Total-300
Printing Co: Leech Printing, 857 18th St., Brandon, MB R7A 5B7 Canada Tel # (204) 728-3037, Fax # (204) 727-3338

Publisher's Report
See: BOOKS & BOOK TRADE

Purdue University, Pharmacy, Nursing & Health Sciences Library Notes

Publishing Co: Purdue Univ. Pharmacy Library, Pharmacy Bldg., W. Lafayette, IN 47907; Title Tel # (317) 494-1417
Personnel: Editor-Theodora Andrews
Editorial Description: Recent acquisitions, news notes, and matters of professional interest.
General Info: Yr. Est. 1959, Quarterly, Trim Size-8½ x 11, Mimeo press, 10 pages
Circulation: Total-400

RASD Update
Business, Association

Publishing Co: American Library Association, 50 E Huron St, Chicago, IL 60611-2795 Tel # (312) 944-6780 Fax # (312) 440-9374; Title Tel # (312) 280-4398 Title Fax # (312) 944-8085
Personnel: Publisher-Cathleen Bourdon, Editor-Jane Kleiner
Editorial Description: News for reference/adult services librarians about RASD activities/concerns.
General Info: Yr. Est. 1980, Quarterly, Trim Size-8½ x 11, Sheetfed press, 16 pages, ISSN: 0198-8344, No Color, Newsprint, Saddle-stitched
Subscriptions: Indv. $15, $4/copy
Circulation: Total-5,480

RBMS Newsletter

Publishing Co: Association of College & Research Libraries, 100 Riverview Ctr., Middletown, CT 06457-3445; Title Tel # (203) 347-6933 Title Fax # (203) 346-8586
Editorial Description: News of interest to college and research librarians.
General Info: Semi-annually
Subscriptions: Indv. $4

RLIN Focus

Publishing Co: Research Libraries Group, Inc., 1200 Villa Street, Mountain View, CA 94041-1100
Editorial Description: A service for the Research Libraries Group, Inc.
General Info: ISSN: 1068-1507

Radon News Digest
See: ENVIRONMENT & ECOLOGY

Reader's Review, The
See: BOOKS & BOOK TRADE

Reading in Indianapolis
Association

Publishing Co: Indianapolis-Marion County Public Library, PO Box 211, Indianapolis, IN 46206-0211; Title Tel # (317) 269-1732
Personnel: Editor-Anna Rohrer, Circ. Mgr.-Debbie Williams
Editorial Description: Programs for adults & children in each library & library resources; bibliographic articles; book reviews; collection news.
General Info: Yr. Est. 1973, Bi-weekly, Trim Size-8½ x 11, Offset press, 6 pages, 2 Color, Newsprint
Circulation: (100% controlled), Total-18,000
Printing Co: White Arts, Inc., 1203 E Saint Clair St, Lafayette, IN 46202-3590 Tel # (317) 356-9970

Readmore Newsletter
Business, Association **CPM: $210**

Publishing Co: Readmore, 22 Cortlandt St., New York, NY 10007-3194; Title Fax # (212) 571-7328
Personnel: Editor-Lisa Bogutz
Editorial Description: New publications and CD-Rom updates.
General Info: Quarterly, Trim Size-8½ x 11, Sheetfed press, Matte, Saddle-stitched
Circulation: Total-2,500
Advertising: $525.

Readmore Reporter
Business

Publishing Co: Readmore, 22 Cortlandt St., New York, NY 10007-3194 Fax # (212) 571-7328; Title Fax # (212) 233-0746
Personnel: Editor-Lisa Bogutz
Editorial Description: Newsletter for libraries.
General Info: Yr. Est. 1993, Quarterly, Trim Size-8½ x 11, 24 pages, ISSN: 1060-5673, 2 Color, Coated, Saddle-stitched

Recent Additions to the Library

Publishing Co: American Jewish Committee, 165 E 56th St, New York, NY 10022-2709 Tel # (212) 571-4000; Title Tel # (212) 751-4000 Title Fax # (212) 750-0326
Personnel: Editor-Michele Anish
Editorial Description: Subject arranged listing of noteworthy books & pamphlets.
General Info: Yr. Est. 1940, Quarterly, Trim Size-8½ x 11, Offset press, 9 pages, No Color
Circulation: Total-150

Record
Association

Publishing Co: Washington State Univ. Libraries, Holland 221, Pullman, WA 99163-5610; Title Tel # (509) 335-8726 Title Fax # (509) 335-6721
Personnel: Editor-Walt Dryfoos
Editorial Description: WSU libraries, news & events.
General Info: Yr. Est. 1939, Quarterly, Trim Size-8½ x 11, Sheetfed press, 4 pages, No Color, Newsprint
Subscriptions: Indv. $25, $5/copy

Records and Retrieval Report
Business

Publishing Co: Greenwood Publishing Group, Inc., 88 Post Rd. W., PO Box 5007, Westport, CT 06881-5007 Parent Co.-Elsevier Business Press, Morris Plains; Title Tel # (203) 226-3571 Title Fax # (203) 226-6009
Personnel: Editor-Ann Balough, Production Mgr.-James R. Ice
Editorial Description: For professional information managers. Offers cost-efficient solutions to records management problems. Explores solutions to information storage & retrieval problems while keeping records & documents managers current with new practices & technology, as well as products available from both new & familiar suppliers.
General Info: Yr. Est. 1985, 10x/yr., Trim Size-8½ x 11, 16 pages, ISSN: 8756-0089, 2 Color, Saddle-stitched
Subscriptions: Indv. $145, Inst. $145, Can. $185, For. $185
Acquistions: Publication Bought

Reference Point

Publishing Co: Dun's Marketing Services, 3 Sylvan Way, Parsippany, NJ 07054-3805

Reflections
Association

Publishing Co: Lakeland Library Region, 10023 Thatcher Ave., Box 813, North Battleford, SK S9A 2Z3 Canada Fax # (306) 445-5717; Title Tel # (306) 445-6108
Personnel: Editor-Jane Zhang
Editorial Description: News of local library scene, mostly of interest to regional employees. Book reviews by librarians & library patrons.
General Info: (Formerly Reflections from Lakeland), Yr. Est. 1973, Semi-annually, Trim Size-8½ x 11, Offset press, 25 pages, ISSN: 0384-0697, No Color
Subscriptions: Free
Circulation: (100% controlled), Total-200
Advertising: Accepts Inserts.

Regional Archivist
See: HISTORY

Reporter--Your Editorial Assistant
See: JOURNALISM

Research Advisor : Information Solutions for Today's Legal Professionals
See: LAW

Research Libraries Group News
Association

Publishing Co: Research Inc., 1200 Villa St, Mountain View, CA 94041-1106

Rhode Island Department of State Library Services Newsletter *Association*

Publishing Co: Rhode Island Dept. of State Library Services, 300 Richmond St., Providence, RI 02903-4222; Title Tel # (401) 277-2726
Personnel: Editor-Frank Iacono
Editorial Description: State and local library news, events, and meetings.
General Info: Yr. Est. 1964, Bi-monthly, 6 pages, No Color
Circulation: Total-800

River City Library Times *Consumer*

Publishing Co: Evansville Vanderburgh County Public Library, 22 SE 5th St., Evansville, IN 47708-1604; Title Tel # (812) 428-8200 Title Fax # (812) 428-8397
Editorial Description: Keeps patrons of the Library informed of its activities.
General Info: Yr. Est. 1977, Monthly, Trim Size-7 x 8½, Offset press, 4 pages, Color
Circulation: Total-1,400

SAA Employment Bulletin See: HISTORY

SAA Manuscript Repository Newsletter

Publishing Co: Kentucky Historical Society, PO Box H, Frankfort, KY 40602-2108 Tel # (502) 564-3016 Fax # (502) 564-4701
Editorial Description: News and developments of interest to archivists.
General Info: 3x/yr.

SAA Muse

Publishing Co: Archives of the Peabody Institute, 1 E Mt Vernon Pl, Baltimore, MD 21202-2308
Editorial Description: For archivists specializing in the performing arts.
General Info: Quarterly

SAALS Newsletter

Publishing Co: San Antonio Area Library System, 203 St. Marys St., San Antonio, TX 78205; Title Tel # (512) 225-5322
Personnel: Editor-Lee LaCaff
Editorial Description: Information for 38 libraries in a 21 county area around San Antonio.
General Info: (Formerly SAMRC Newsletter), Bi-monthly, Mimeo press, 17 pages, No Color
Acquistions: Publication Bought
Circulation: Total-400

SALALM Newsletter *Consumer, Association* CPM: $166

Publishing Co: SALALM Secretariat, General Library University Of, New Mexico, Albuquerque, NM 87131-0001 Fax # (505) 277-0646; Title Tel # (505) 277-5102
Personnel: Editor-Laurence Hallewell, Circ. Mgr.-Sharon Moynahan
Editorial Description: Organ of the Seminar on the Acquisition of Latin American Library Materials (SALALM).
General Info: Yr. Est. 1973, Bi-monthly, Trim Size-8½ x 11, Offset press, 32 pages, ISSN: 0098-6275
Subscriptions: Indv. $25
Circulation: Total-600
Advertising: $100.
List Rental: Actives: $250/M
Printing Co: POP Printing, 10900 Manuel, N.E., Albuquerque, NM 87112 Tel # (505) 298-9001

SEES Newsletter

Publishing Co: Assn. of College of Research Libraries, American Libr. Assn., 50 E. Huron St., Chicago, IL 60611-2795; Title Tel # (312) 944-6780
Personnel: Production Mgr.-George Eberhart
Editorial Description: Newsletter of the Slavic & E. European section of ACRL.
General Info: (Formerly ACRL Newsletter), Annually
Subscriptions: Indv. $4
Circulation: (100% controlled), Total-500
List Rental: Rents Lists

SGA Newsletter *Association*

Publishing Co: Society of Georgia Archivists, Box 80631, University of Georgia, Athens, GA 30608
Personnel: Editor-E. Lee Eltzroth
Editorial Description: Society news and developments of interest to archivists.
General Info: Yr. Est. 1970, Quarterly, Desktop press, 15 pages, Coated
Subscriptions: Indv. $12
Circulation: Total-300
List Rental: Rents Lists
Printing Co: Iberian Publishing Co., 548 Cedar Creek Dr, Athens, GA 30605-3408 Tel # (706) 546-6740

SHARP News See: BOOKS & BOOK TRADE

SIA Newsletter

Publishing Co: Society of Indiana Archivists, Univ. Archives Indiana State, Univ., Terre Haute, IN 47809-0001
Editorial Description: Society news and items of interest to archivists.
General Info: 3x/yr.
Subscriptions: Indv. $5

S.L.A. Marshall Military History Collection-Newsletter See: MILITARY & NAVAL

SLG News *Association*

Publishing Co: Special Library Group, Maine Lib. Assn., Community Dr., Augusta, ME 04333-0001; Title Tel # (207) 289-1600
Personnel: Editor-Louise Hinkley
General Info: Yr. Est. 1980, Semi-annually, Trim Size-8½ x 11, Mimeo press, 16 pages, No Color
Circulation: Total-225

SMILEtter

Publishing Co: Southcentral Minnesota Inter-Library Exchange (SMILE), PO Box 3031, Mankato, MN 56002-3031; Title Tel # (507) 389-5108
Personnel: Editor-Lucy Lowry
Editorial Description: Includes information of interest to libraries of all types in the SMILE region (south central Minnesota).
General Info: Monthly, 4 pages
Circulation: Total-610

SORT Bulletin *Business, Association*

Publishing Co: American Library Association, 50 E Huron St, Chicago, IL 60611-2795 Tel # (312) 944-6780 Fax # (312) 440-9374; Title Tel # (312) 280-3213
Personnel: Editor-Gwendolyn Richards
Editorial Description: For members of the Staff Organization Round Table.
General Info: Semi-annually

SRRT Newsletter *Association*

Publishing Co: Social Responsibilities Round Table Clearinghouse, 50 E Huron St, Chicago, IL 60611-2729; Title Tel # (312) 944-6780
Editorial Description: News of the Social Responsibilities Round Table (of the Amer. Library Ass'n) & info. on social responsiblity issues related to library service.
General Info: Yr. Est. 1969, Quarterly, Trim Size-8½ x 11, 8 pages, ISSN: 0749-1670, No Color
Subscriptions: Indv. $10
Circulation: Total-1,300

SUL News Notes *Association*

Publishing Co: Stanford University Libraries, Green Library, Stanford, CA 94305; Title Tel # (415) 725-1112
Personnel: Editor-Thomas Holt
Editorial Description: Newsletter for stanford University Librarires staff.
General Info: Yr. Est. 1992, Weekly
Circulation: Total-250

San Bernardino County Library Newsletter *Association*

Publishing Co: San Bernardino County Library, 104 W. 4th St., San Bernardino, CA 92415-0001; Title Tel # (714) 383-1095
Editorial Description: Internal news, news of countywide friends group, coming events, general interest.
General Info: (Formerly Friends of the San Bernardino Co. Library Newsletter), Yr. Est. 1960, Monthly, Offset press, 8 pages, No Color
Subscriptions: Free
Circulation: Total-1,500

Saskatchewan Assn. of Library Technicians Newsletter

Publishing Co: Saskatchewan Assn. of Library Technicians, Box 9388, Saskatoon, SK S7K 7E9 Canada; Title Tel # (306) 933-7568
Personnel: Editor-June Flegg
General Info: Quarterly, Trim Size-8½ x 11, 10 pages, No Color, Matte, Saddle-stitched

Saskatchewan Library *Association*

Publishing Co: Saskatchewan Library Assn., Box 3388, Regina, SK S4P 3H1 Canada; Title Tel # (306) 780-9413 Title Fax # (306) 757-4422
Editorial Description: Articles of interest to Saskatchewan library employees, library trustees, library supporters, & suppliers to libraries.
General Info: Yr. Est. 1947, Bi-monthly, Trim Size-8½ x 11, Offset press, 40 pages, ISSN: 0036-4924, 1% ads, Color-cover
Subscriptions: Can. $25
Circulation: (100% controlled), Total-250
Advertising: Inquire for rates.

Savitz Reports

Publishing Co: Sponsor-Savitz Library, Bulletin of the Savitz Library, Glassboro State College, Glassboro, NJ 08028-1702; Title Tel # (609) 863-6101
Personnel: Editor-Dr. S. Szilassy
Editorial Description: Articles and commentary on library services for local campus community and other state colleges.
General Info: Yr. Est. 1971, Semi-annually, Mimeo press, No Color, Newsprint
Circulation: Total-750

School Librarian's Workshop

Publishing Co: Library Learning Resources, PO Box 87, Berkeley Heights, NJ 07922-0087; Title Tel # (201) 635-1833 Title Fax # (201) 635-2614
Personnel: Editor-R. Toor
Editorial Description: Devoted to the needs of school librarians.
Subscriptions: Indv. $40

School Libraries in Canada   *Association*

Publishing Co: Canadian School Libraries Assn., 602-200 Elgin St., Ottawa, ON K2P 1L5 Canada; Title Tel # (613) 232-9625
Personnel: Editor-Marilyn Ming, Adv. Dir.-Tim Elliott
Editorial Description: Covers issues in librarianship for Canadian librarians.
General Info: Yr. Est. 1974, Web press, 48 pages, ISSN: 0227-3780, Ind/Abs/Online: Can.Ed.In.,Lib.Lit., 2% ads, No Color, Coated
Subscriptions: Indv. $35, $10/copy
Circulation: Total-1,000
Advertising: Inquire for rates.
Printing Co: Cal/Oka Printing, 4, 2720 12th St., NE, Calgary, AB T2E 7N4 Canada Tel # (403) 250-9200

School of Library and Information Science Newsletter

Publishing Co: Univ. of Iowa, School of Library & Info. Science, Publications, Iowa City, IA 52242; Title Tel # (319) 335-5707 Title Fax # (319) 335-5374
Personnel: Editor-Ethel Bloesch
Editorial Description: Library school activities, coming events, alumni news.
General Info: Yr. Est. 1966, Annually, Trim Size-8$\frac{1}{2}$ x 11, Offset press, 6 pages, ISSN: 0041-9648, No Color
Subscriptions: Free
Circulation: Total-4,000

School Library/Audio Visual Council Newsletter   *Business*

Publishing Co: Newfoundland Labrador Teachers Association, 3 Kenmount Rd., St. John's, NF A1B 1W1 Canada Fax # (709) 726-4302; Title Tel # (709) 726-3223
General Info: Yr. Est. 1974

Sci-Tech News   *Association*

Publishing Co: Special Libraries Assn., Metals/Materials Div., 471 E. Mesa Ave., Teaneck, NJ 07666 Tel # (201) 836-1137; Title Fax # (201) 836-1682
Personnel: Editor-Ellis Mount
Editorial Description: Articles, reviews and division information for five Special Libraries Assn. divisions: Aerospace, Engineering, Metals/Materials, Science & Technology, and Nuclear Science.
General Info: (Formerly Metals/Materials News), Yr. Est. 1953, Quarterly, Trim Size-8$\frac{1}{2}$ x 11, 8 pages, No Color
Subscriptions: Can. $20, For. $23
Circulation: (100% controlled), Total-250

Scouting Literature for Libraries & Teachers

Publishing Co: Boy Scouts of America, 1325 W Walnut Hill Ln, Irving, TX 75038-3096 Tel # (214) 580-2350; Title Tel # (214) 580-2280
Personnel: Publisher-Donald Olson, Editor-Jimmye Anderson, Art Dir.-Mary Hager
Editorial Description: Listing of Scouting Literature available.
General Info: Annually, 4 pages, Looseleaf
Circulation: Total-2,500

Selected Acquisitions

Publishing Co: Selected Acquisitions, 2425 Campus Rd, Honolulu, HI 96822-2216; Title Tel # (808) 948-8132
General Info: Looseleaf

Seneca District Newsletter

Publishing Co: Warren Library Assn, Warren, PA 16365; Title Tel # (814) 723-4650
Personnel: Editor-Barbara Kane
General Info: Yr. Est. 1965, Quarterly

Serials Focus

Publishing Co: UMI, 300 N Zeeb Rd, Ann Arbor, MI 48103-1553 Tel # (313) 761-4700 Fax # (313) 973-1540; Title Tel # (800) 521-0600
Personnel: Editor-Ruth Gretzinger, Adv. Dir.-Carol Bamford
Editorial Description: Special interest articles & product information for secondary school educators & librarians.
General Info: Yr. Est. 1986, Trim Size-8$\frac{1}{2}$ x 11, Sheetfed press, 6 pages, 2 Color, Coated
Circulation: Total-12,000

Simmons Librarian

Publishing Co: Simmons College, School of Library Science, Alumni Assn., 300 The Fenway, Boston, MA 02115-5898
Personnel: Editor-Kate Jones-Randall
General Info: Yr. Est. 1968, Semi-annually
Circulation: Total-7,000

Slate   *Association*

Publishing Co: Special Libraries Assn., Greater St. Louis Chapter, PO Box 7090, Saint Louis, MO 63177-7090; Title Tel # (314) 349-0405
Personnel: Editor-Barbara Rehrop
General Info: Yr. Est. 1942, Quarterly, Trim Size-8$\frac{1}{2}$ x 11, Desktop press, 10 pages, 2% ads, No Color
Subscriptions: Indv. $5
Circulation: Total-200

Society of California Archivists Newsletter

Publishing Co: Society of California Archivists, Honnold-Mudd Library, Claremont Coll., 800 Dartmouth, Claremont, CA 91711
Editorial Description: Society news and developments in archival science.
General Info: Quarterly
Subscriptions: Indv. $20

Software Reviews on File
See: COMPUTERS & AUTOMATION

Southwestern Archivist   *Association*   CPM: $125

Publishing Co: Sponsor-Society of Southwest Archivists, Southwestern Archivist, Howard-Tilton Library, Tulane Univ., New Orleans, LA 70118-5682; Title Tel # (504) 865-5685 Title Fax # (504) 865-6773
Personnel: Editor-Leon Miller
Editorial Description: News and developments of interest to archivists.
General Info: Yr. Est. 1976, Quarterly, Trim Size-8$\frac{1}{2}$ x 11, Offset press, 48 pages, ISSN: 1056-1021, 2 Color, Matte, Saddle-stitched
Subscriptions: Indv. $10, Inst. $25, Free With Membership
Circulation: Total-800, Readership-800
Advertising: $100. Accepts Inserts.
List Rental: Actives: 650, $100/M

SpeciaList   *Association*

Publishing Co: Sponsor-Special Libraries Assn/Ins. & Employee Benefits Division, Special Libraries Assn., 1700 18th St NW, Washington, DC 20009-2508; Title Tel # (202) 234-4700 Title Fax # (202) 265-9317
Personnel: Publisher-David Bender, Editor-Maria Barry, Adv. Dir.-Steve Jones
Editorial Description: News regarding the Special Libraries Association. Features articles about the special library information field, meetings, technology, newsmakers, etc. Also contains listings of positions open.
General Info: Yr. Est. 1988, Monthly, Trim Size-8$\frac{1}{2}$ x 11, Offset press, 16 pages, ISSN: 0273-9399, 4% ads, 2 Color, Newsprint, Saddle-stitched
Subscriptions: $4/copy
Circulation: Total-16,043
Advertising: Inquire for rates.
List Rental: Rents Lists
Printing Co: CTF, 150 Varick Street, New York City, NY 10003 Tel # (212) 675-1791

Special Libraries Assn., Social Science Division Bulletin   *Association*   CPM: $266

Publishing Co: Special Libraries Assn., Social Science Div., 2000 15th St N Ste 701, Arlington, VA 22201-2627; Title Tel # (703) 524-7802 Title Fax # (703) 524-9335
Personnel: Editor-Olivia Pickett, Bk. Rev. Ed.-Ron Buchan, Adv. Dir.-Nancy Minter
Editorial Description: Provides information about division activities plus features and book reviews on social science topics including urban affairs ,peace and international conflict resolution, health and human services, international relations.
General Info: Yr. Est. 1959, Trim Size-8$\frac{1}{2}$ x 11, Offset press, 20 pages, 10% ads, No Color, Other, Saddle-stitched
Subscriptions: Indv. $20, Inst. $20, Free With Membership
Circulation: (93% controlled), Total-750
Advertising: $200.
List Rental: List Management Co.: Special Libraries Association, 1700 18th Street NW, Washington, DC 20009-2508 Tel # (202) 234-4700, Fax # (202) 265-9317
Printing Co: Letter Comm., 310 Swann Ave., Alexandira, VA 22301 Tel # (703) 683-3105

Special Libraries Association, Upstate New York Chapter Bulletin   *Association*

Publishing Co: Special Libraries Assn., Upstate New York Chapter, Stuyvesant Plaza, C/O Kate Storms, Albany, NY 12203-3790; Title Tel # (518) 457-8421
Personnel: Editor-Kate Storms, Adv. Dir.-Bruce Connolly
Editorial Description: Chapter news, meeting announcements, topics of interest to information managers.
General Info: Yr. Est. 1976, Quarterly, Trim Size-5$\frac{1}{2}$ x 8$\frac{1}{2}$, Sheetfed press, 20 pages, 2% ads, No Color, Newsprint
Circulation: (100% controlled), Total-325
Advertising: Inquire for rates.
List Rental: Rents Lists

Spotlight on Your Library   *Consumer*

Publishing Co: Dayton, 215 E 3rd St, Dayton, OH 45402-2103; Title Tel # (513) 227-9500
Editorial Description: Covers news and activities about the library. Published for the residents of Montgomery County, Ohio.
General Info: Yr. Est. 1955, Bi-monthly, Trim Size-11 x 17, Offset press, 4 pages, ISSN: 0040-6252, 2 Color, Newsprint
Circulation: Total-8,000

Staff Association
Association

Publishing Co: Mobile Public Library, 700 Government St, Mobile, AL 36602-1499; Title Tel # (205) 434-7097
Personnel: Editor-Christina Bowersox, Circ. Mgr., Art Dir.-Paula Wilson
Editorial Description: House organ to promote good relations among staff, keep them abreast of institutional developments, recognize superior performance, develop family feeling.
General Info: (Formerly Complement; Voices), Yr. Est. 1966, Irregular, Trim Size-8½ x 14, Sheetfed press, 3 pages, No Color, Newsprint
Circulation: (100% controlled), Total-135

Staff Notes
Association

Publishing Co: Staff Association, Public Library of Cincinnati, 800 Vine St, Cincinnati, OH 45202-2009; Title Tel # (513) 369-6900
Editorial Description: News about and of interest to the staff of the Public Library of Cincinnati and Hamilton County.
General Info: Yr. Est. 1925, 10x/yr., 8 pages, No Color
Circulation: Total-200, Readership-900

Story Bag: A National Storytelling Newsletter
See: EDUCATION

TCART Newsletter

Publishing Co: Twin Cities Archives Round Table, Minneapolis Public Library, 300 Nicollet Mall, Minneapolis, MN 55401
Editorial Description: News and developments in the area of archival science.
General Info: Semi-annually

T.P.L. News

Publishing Co: Toronto Public Library, 281 Front St., E., Toronto, ON M5A 4L2 Canada; Title Tel # (416) 393-7565
Personnel: Editor-Lillian Salmon
Editorial Description: Internal newsletter for Toronto Public Library staff.
General Info: Yr. Est. 1971, Monthly, Web press, 10 pages, No Color, Newsprint
Circulation: (100% controlled), Total-850

TSLA Newsletter

Publishing Co: Tennessee Library Association, PO Box 158417, Nashville, TN 37215-8417; Title Tel # (615) 741-2451
Editorial Description: Contains current news of interest to librarians
General Info: Yr. Est. 1988, Bi-monthly, 4 pages
Circulation: Total-1,500

Tamiment Library Bulletin

Publishing Co: New York Univ. Libraries, 70 Washington Sq S, New York, NY 10012-1019; Title Tel # (212) 998-2633
Personnel: Editor-Dorothy Swanson
Editorial Description: To acquaint the public with details of the library's collections on history of socialism, communism and working class movements.
General Info: Yr. Est. 1957, Irregular, Trim Size-8½ x 11, 25 pages, Ind/Abs/Online: PAIS

Tar Heel Libraries
Association

Publishing Co: North Carolina State Library, 109 E Jones St, Raleigh, NC 27601-2806; Title Tel # (919) 733-2570 Title Fax # (919) 733-8748
Personnel: Editor-Diana Young
Editorial Description: NC information in public, academic, school, special and community college libraries in North Carolina. Send to members NC Library Association and North Carolina Legislators.
General Info: Yr. Est. 1977, Bi-monthly, Trim Size-8½ x 11, Sheetfed press, 12 pages, ISSN: 0193-4309, 2 Color, Newsprint
Circulation: (100% controlled), Total-3,400

Teamwork
Association

Publishing Co: Southeastern Pennsylvania Theological Library Assn., Moravian College, Reeves Library, Bethlehem, PA 18018-6650; Title Tel # (215) 248-4616
Personnel: Editor-David Wantluft, Circ. Mgr.-Thomas Minor
Editorial Description: Newsletter of the Southeastern Pa. Theological Library Association, including minutes of meetings, articles of news and information, and reports on projects of the association.
General Info: Yr. Est. 1970, Quarterly, Trim Size-8½ x 11, Mimeo press, 6 pages, ISSN: 1661-2434, No Color
Subscriptions: Indv. $4

Tennessee Archivists Newsletter

Publishing Co: Tennessee Technological Univ., University Archives, Box 5066, Cookeville, TN 38505
Editorial Description: News and developments of import to archivists.

Texas, Natural Resources Information System, Newsletter
See: ENVIRONMENT & ECOLOGY

Thomas Cooper Library Reflections

Publishing Co: Univ. of South Carolina, Library, Columbia, SC 29208
General Info: Yr. Est. 1989

Topics

Publishing Co: Southern Tier Library System, 301 Civic Plaza, Corning, NY 14830; Title Tel # (607) 962-3141
Personnel: Editor-Paul Malecki, Publisher, Circ. Mgr.-Roseanna Harris
Editorial Description: Local and statewide news and information about public libraries; for librarians, library trustees, educators and govt. officials in the (N.Y.) Southern Tier.
General Info: (Formerly Tier Topics), Yr. Est. 1959, Trim Size-8½ x 14, Sheetfed press, 2 pages, ISSN: 0163-8459, No Color, Coated
Acquistions: Publication Bought
Circulation: (100% controlled), Total-825
Printing Co: STLS Print Shop, 301 Civic Plz., Corning, NY 14830-2898 Tel # (607) 962-3141

Tracings

Publishing Co: Univ. of Oklahoma School of Library & Information Studies, 401 W Brooks St # 120, Norman, OK 73069-8824; Title Tel # (405) 325-3921
General Info: Semi-annually
Circulation: Total-1,400

Trinity College Library Newsletter
Association

Publishing Co: Trinity College Library, Publications, Hartford, CT 06106; Title Tel # (203) 527-3151
Personnel: Editor-Ralph Emerick
Editorial Description: Library news, announcements.
General Info: Yr. Est. 1966, 8x/yr.
Circulation: Total-500

UBC Library News
Association

Publishing Co: Univ. of British Columbia Library, 1956 Main Mall, Vancouver, BC V6T 1Y3 Canada; Title Tel # (604) 228-2076
Personnel: Editor-Julie Stevens
Editorial Description: Library newsletter to UBC faculty and staff.
General Info: Yr. Est. 1968, Trim Size-8½ x 11, Offset press, 6 pages, ISSN: 0382-0661, No Color
Circulation: Total-3,000

UCLA Librarian

Publishing Co: Univ. of California At Los Angeles, Library, Los Angeles, CA 90024; Title Tel # (213) 825-1201
Personnel: Editor-Beverly Harris
Editorial Description: News about UCLA libraries, major collections, & acquisitions.
General Info: Yr. Est. 1947, Bi-monthly, Trim Size-8½ x 11, Offset press, 8 pages, Color-cover, Newsprint, Saddle-stitched
Subscriptions: Indv. $35
Circulation: (100% controlled)

UCR Library News

Publishing Co: Univ. of California At Riverside, Lib. Admin., Box 5900, Riverside, CA 92517; Title Tel # (714) 787-3221
General Info: Yr. Est. 1957, Bi-weekly, Trim Size-8½ x 11, Mimeo press, 6 pages, No Color
Circulation: Total-250

UDT Newsletter

Publishing Co: National Library of Canada, 395 Wellington Street, Ottawa, ON K1A 0N4 Canada Tel # (613) 995-7969 Fax # (613) 991-9871; Title Tel # (613) 996-7401
Personnel: Publisher-Margo Wiper, Circ. Mgr.-Denis Schryburt
Editorial Description: Bilingual newsletter describing activities in universal dataflow and telecommunications (UDT), especially as it pertains to library work.
General Info: Yr. Est. 1987, Trim Size-8½ x 11, Color-cover
Subscriptions: Free
Circulation: Total-1,600

URISA Marketplace
Consumer, Association

Publishing Co: Urban and Regional Information Systems Association (URISA), 900 Second Street, NE, Suite 304, Washington, DC 20002; Title Tel # (202) 289-1685 Title Fax # (202) 842-1850
Personnel: Adv. Dir.-Peter Henry
Editorial Description: Job opportunities in the information management workplace.
General Info: Yr. Est. 1989, Monthly, Trim Size-8½ x 11, No Color
Advertising: Inquire for rates.

URISA News
Consumer, Association

Publishing Co: Urban and Regional Information Systems Association (URISA), 900 Second Street, NE, Suite 304, Washington, DC 20002; Title Tel # (202) 289-1685 Title Fax # (202) 842-1850
Personnel: Editor-Angela Ziesler, Adv. Dir.-Peter Henry
Editorial Description: News from the association and the information management industry.
General Info: 10x/yr., Trim Size-8½ x 11, 12 pages, No Color
Circulation: Total-3,500
Advertising: Inquire for rates.

USBE News: For Members Only
Association

Publishing Co: USBE, 2969 W 25th St, Cleveland, OH 44113-5332; Title Tel # (216) 241-6960
Personnel: Publisher-John Zubal, Editor-Victoria Nann
Editorial Description: News about USBE's services and activities.
General Info: (Formerly USBE News), Yr. Est. 1949, Irregular, Trim Size-8½ x 11, Offset press, 4 pages, ISSN: 0364-5215, No Color, Perfect bound
Subscriptions: Free With Membership
Circulation: Total-700

USS Reports
See: SOCIAL SERVICES & WELFARE

UTK Librarian
Consumer, Scholarly

Publishing Co: Univ. of Tennessee Library, 1015 Volunteer Blvd., Knoxville, TN 37996-1000; Title Tel # (423) 974-4273 Title Fax # (423) 974-2708
Personnel: Circ. Mgr.-Martha Rudolph
Editorial Description: Published for faculty & staff of Univ. of Tennessee, Knoxville.
General Info: Semi-annually

Undercurrent: Memphis/ Shelby County Public Library and Information Center Staff Newsletter
Association

Publishing Co: Memphis/Shelby County Staff Organization, 1850 Peabody Ave, Memphis, TN 38104-4021; Title Tel # (901) 386-8968
Personnel: Editor-Ann Ulmer
Editorial Description: News, feature articles by and about staff members. Including humor.
General Info: Yr. Est. 1959, Monthly, Trim Size-8½ x 11, Sheetfed press, 5 pages, 2 Color, Newsprint
Circulation: Total-425
Printing Co: Memphis Public Library, 1850 Peabody, Memphis, IN 38104

U.S. National Library of Medicine News
Business

Publishing Co: U.S. National Library of Medicine, 8600 Rockville Pike, Bethesda, MD 20894-0001; Title Tel # (301) 496-6308
Personnel: Editor-Roger L. Gilkeson
Editorial Description: Newsletter covering various NLM publications and programs.
General Info: (Formerly Army Medical Library News), Yr. Est. 1945, Monthly, Trim Size-7⅞ x 10¼, Offset press, 8 pages, ISSN: 0027-965X, No Color
Circulation: (100% controlled), Total-5,000

University of California Library, Friends Newsletter

Publishing Co: Univ. of California Library, La Jolla, CA 92093; Title Tel # (619) 452-2533
Personnel: Editor-Lynda Claassen
General Info: Yr. Est. 1964, 8 pages
Circulation: (100% controlled), Total-3,500

University of Iowa, Libraries, Newsletter
Association

Publishing Co: Univ. of Iowa Libraries, Main Library, Iowa City, IA 52242-1420 Fax # (319) 335-5900; Title Tel # (319) 335-5937
Personnel: Editor-Wayne Rawley, Circ. Mgr.-Richard Kolbet
Editorial Description: Library news for faculty at the U. of Iowa, selected public and college libraries in Iowa, and all ARL libraries.
General Info: Yr. Est. 1972, Semi-annually, Trim Size-8½ x 11, Letrpr. press, 4 pages, ISSN: 0047-1402, No Color
Circulation: Total-2,500

Upstate Medical Center Library Bulletin

Publishing Co: State Univ. of New York, Publications, Syracuse, NY 13210; Title Tel # (315) 443-1870
Personnel: Editor-Evelyn Hoeg
General Info: Yr. Est. 1961, Monthly, Offset press
Subscriptions: Indv. $6

Urban Libraries Exchange

Publishing Co: Urban Libraries Council, 425 N. Michigan Ave., Chicago, IL 60611-4213; Title Tel # (312) 661-1493
Personnel: Editor-Roy Millenson
General Info: (Formerly Lamp, The), Yr. Est. 1984, Monthly

Utah Libraries/News
Business, Association

Publishing Co: Utah Library Assn., 2150 S. 300 W., Salt Lake City, UT 84115-2579; Title Tel # (801) 466-5888
Personnel: Editor-Dale Swensen
Editorial Description: News of the activities, administration and programs of the Utah Library Association.
General Info: (Formerly Utah Libraries), Yr. Est. 1986, Bi-monthly, Trim Size-8½ x 11, Sheetfed press, 12 pages, Color-cover
Subscriptions: Indv. $8, $2/copy
Circulation: Total-650
Advertising: Inquire for rates.
List Rental: Rents Lists

Vermont Department of Libraries News

Publishing Co: Vermont Dept. of Libraries, Pavillion Office Bldg. 109, State. St., Montpelier, VT 05609-0001; Title Tel # (802) 828-3261
Personnel: Editor-Marianne Cassell
Editorial Description: News of the Vermont Dept. of Libraries and Vt. public libraries.
General Info: (Formerly Vermont Libraries), Yr. Est. 1976, Bi-monthly, Trim Size-8½ x 11, Offset press, 20 pages, No Color
Circulation: (100% controlled), Total-2,100

Vibrations
Association

Publishing Co: Indiana Univ. School of Library and Information Science, Indiana Univ., Main Library, Bloomington, IN 47405; Title Tel # (812) 855-2018 Title Fax # (812) 855-6166
Personnel: Editor-Penelope Mathiesen
Editorial Description: News from the Indiana University School of Library and Information Science about alumni, faculty and school. Covers placement, curriculum, awards.
General Info: (Formerly Newsletter School of Library & Information Science), Yr. Est. 1969, Semi-annually, Trim Size-8½ x 11½, Offset press, 6 pages, Color, Recycled
Circulation: Total-1,000

Vigo County Public Library Staff Bulletin

Publishing Co: Vigo County Public Library, Reference, 1 Library Sq., Terre Haute, IN 47807; Title Tel # (812) 232-1113 Title Fax # (812) 232-3208
Personnel: Editor-Shar Minnette
General Info: Monthly
Circulation: Total-400

Virginia Librarian Newsletter
Association

Publishing Co: Virginia Library Assn., 669 S. Washington St., Alexandria, VA 22314; Title Tel # (703) 519-7853
Personnel: Editor-Allan Zoellner, Adv. Dir.-Deborah Iannitto, Art Dir.-Richard McClintock
General Info: (Formerly Virginia Librarian), Yr. Est. 1953, Bi-monthly, Web press, 20 pages, Saddle-stitched
Circulation: Total-1,500
Advertising: Inquire for rates.

WLA Newsletter
Association   **CPM: $142**

Publishing Co: Wisconsin Library Assn., Inc., 4785 Hayes Rd., Madison, WI 53704-7364; Title Tel # (608) 242-2040 Title Fax # (608) 242-2050
Personnel: Editor-James Gollata, Adv. Dir., Mktg. Dir.-Larry Martin
Editorial Description: Provide information regarding activities of Association and professional info of interest to the library community.
General Info: Yr. Est. 1960, Bi-monthly, Trim Size-8½ x 11, Sheetfed press, 12 pages, ISSN: 0746-5785, 2 Color, Newsprint, Saddle-stitched
Subscriptions: Indv. $28, Inst. $28, Free With Membership
Circulation: Total-2,100, Readership-2,500
Advertising: $300.
Printing Co: Odana Press, Madison, WI

Washington University School of Medicine Library, Library Newsletter

Publishing Co: Washington University, School of Medicine Library, PO Box 8132, Saint Louis, MO 63156-8132; Title Tel # (314) 362-7080
Personnel: Editor-Dr. Susan Crawford
General Info: (Formerly Library Notes), Yr. Est. 1961, Bi-monthly, Sheetfed press, 10 pages
Circulation: Total-250

West Virginia Library Commission-Film Services

Publishing Co: West Virginia Library Commission, Cultural Center, Charleston, WV 25305 Tel # (304) 348-2041; Title Tel # (304) 348-3976
Personnel: Editor, Circ. Mgr.-S.L. Fesenmaier, Production Mgr.-Frani Fesenmaier, Promotion Dir.-Patty Wills
Editorial Description: Current news on new films, film culture, & general ideas.
General Info: Yr. Est. 1976, Quarterly, Sheetfed press, 20 pages, No Color
Subscriptions: Indv. $4
Circulation: Total-500

West Virginia Library Commission, Newsletter

Publishing Co: West Virginia Library Commission, Cultural Center, Charleston, WV 25305; Title Tel # (304) 348-2041
Personnel: Publisher-Frederic Glazer, Editor, Circ. Mgr.-Shirley Smith, Art Dir.-David Martin
Editorial Description: Current news of West Virginia Library Commission, public libraries throughout the state.
General Info: Yr. Est. 1955, Irregular, Trim Size-8½ x 11, 4 pages, No Color
Subscriptions: Free
Circulation: Total-1,500

Western Plains Library System Newsletter

Publishing Co: Western Plains Library System, PO Box 1027, Clinton, OK 73601-1027; Title Tel # (405) 323-0974
Personnel: Editor-Diane Ray, Circ. Mgr., Art Dir.-Dee Delk
Editorial Description: Contains news of library services and programs. Includes feature article on either an Okla. author or book each month.
General Info: Yr. Est. 1966, Bi-monthly, Trim Size-8½ x 11½, Mimeo press, 3 pages, No Color
Circulation: Total-1,800

What's Line

Publishing Co: Alabama Public Library Service, 6030 Monticello Dr., Montgomery, AL 36130-0001; Title Tel # (205) 213-3900
General Info: Quarterly

Whistle Stop

Publishing Co: Harry S. Truman Library Institute, U.S. Hwy. 24 & Delaware St., Independence, MO 64050; Title Tel # (816) 833-1400
Personnel: Editor-Dr. Benedict Zobrist
General Info: (Formerly Harry S. Truman Library Institute Newsletter), Yr. Est. 1961, Quarterly, 8 pages
Subscriptions: Free With Membership
Circulation: Total-2,450

Wiley Librarians' Newsletter, The
See: BOOKS & BOOK TRADE

Windows   *Consumer, Association*

Publishing Co: University North Carolina at Chapel Hill, Davis Library, Campus Box 3920, Chapel Hill, NC 27599-0001
Editorial Description: Library information - especially on UNC's Academic Affairs Library.
General Info: Quarterly, Trim Size-7 x 11, 12 pages, 2 Color, Matte, Saddle-stitched

Women in Libraries   *Consumer, Association*

Publishing Co: Sponsor-ALA Social Responsibilities Round Table Feminist Task Force, American Library Association, 50 E Huron St, Chicago, IL 60611-2795; Title Tel # (312) 944-6780 Title Fax # (312) 440-9374
Personnel: Editor-Madelein Tainton, Circ. Mgr.-Diedre Conkling
Editorial Description: Information for women as librarians & library users; book reviews.
General Info: Yr. Est. 1970, 5x/yr., Trim Size-8½ x 11, Sheetfed press, 8 pages, No Color
Subscriptions: Indv. $5, Inst. $10, $2/copy

Women's Collection Newsletter

Publishing Co: Northwestern Univ. Library, Special Collections, 1935 Sheridan Rd, Evanston, IL 60201-2924; Title Tel # (708) 491-2894
Personnel: Editor-Judy Lowman
General Info: Yr. Est. 1974, Semi-annually
Subscriptions: Free
Circulation: Total-1,500

Your Library   *Consumer*

Publishing Co: Fiends of the Worcester Public Library, 3 Salem Sq, Worcester, MA 01608-2074; Title Tel # (508) 799-1655 Title Fax # (508) 799-1652
Personnel: Editor-Christine Kardokas
Editorial Description: News & events about the library.
General Info: Yr. Est. 1981, Quarterly, Trim Size-8½ x 11, Sheetfed press, 8 pages, 2 Color, Newsprint
Circulation: Total-2,000
Printing Co: Valley Web, 1299 Stowe Avenue, Medford, OR 97504 Tel # (503) 772-7039

LIFESTYLE

Abapa Freer   *Consumer*

Publishing Co: Correspan, Box 759 - xbr, Veneta, OR 97487-0759
Personnel: Editor-Pat Underhill
Editorial Description: Info on places with fewer taxes and restrictions. Lists other sources of lifestyle information.
General Info: (Formerly Anet Paradox), Yr. Est. 1983, Quarterly, Trim Size-5½ x 8½, Mimeo press, 16 pages
Subscriptions: Indv. $1
Circulation: Total-3,000

Abstract of Marital Relationship Analysis
See: PSYCHOLOGY

Acadia Club, The

Publishing Co: Harmony Intl., Inc., 901 S Ashland Ave Apt 218a, Chicago, IL 60607-4054; Title Tel # (312) 733-0662
Personnel: Editor-Fred Wilson, III
Editorial Description: Our newsletter centers around people who come from MULTIRACIAL backgrounds.
General Info: Yr. Est. 1990, 5% ads
Advertising: Inquire for rates.

Alcyone Journal

Publishing Co: Alcyone Light Centre, 910 Glendale Ave., Ashland, OR 97520-2521; Title Tel # (541) 482-6332
Personnel: Editor-Diane Rasmussen
General Info: (Formerly SOLLA Journal), Yr. Est. 1985, Bi-monthly
Circulation: Total-150

American Nudist Research Library   *Association*

Publishing Co: American Nudist Research Library, 4425 S. Pleasant Hill Rd., Kissimmee, FL 34746-2703; Title Tel # (407) 933-2866
Personnel: Editor-Pete Hadley
General Info: Yr. Est. 1979, Quarterly, Trim Size-8½ x 11, 2 pages
Subscriptions: Indv. $10
Acquistions: Publication Bought

Aquarian Alternatives   *Association*

Publishing Co: Aquarian Research Foundation, 5620 Morton St, Philadelphia, PA 19144-1330; Title Tel # (215) 849-3237
Personnel: Publisher, Editor-Art Rosenblum
Editorial Description: Research in implementation of new society of peace and love.
General Info: (Formerly Aquarian Research Foundation Newsletter), Yr. Est. 1969, Irregular, Trim Size-8½ x 11, Sheetfed press, 8 pages, No Color
Subscriptions: Indv. $25, Free
Circulation: (85% controlled), Total-1,200
Advertising: Accepts Inserts.

BACKROAD BICYCLING for backroads cyclist

Publishing Co: Randy Wyatt, P.O. Box 372, Clay Center, KS 67432
Editorial Description: A bicycling newsletter that writes biking tips and stories about small-town living.
General Info: Yr. Est. 1987, Quarterly, Trim Size-8 x 11, 14 pages

Barter Update - Barter Basics Edition
See: BUSINESS & INDUSTRY

Be Somebody Be Yourself Poetry Newsletter   *Consumer*

Publishing Co: Prosperity & Profits Unlimited, PO Box 416, Denver, CO 80201-0416; Title Tel # (303) 575-5676
Personnel: Publisher, Editor-A.C. Doyle
Editorial Description: Poetry on being yourself.
General Info: Yr. Est. 1990, Annually, Trim Size-8½ x 11, Letrpr. press, 4 pages, ISSN: 1053-6531, No Color
Subscriptions: Indv. $2, Inst. $2, Can. $5, For. $5, $2/copy
Circulation: Total-2,000

Beem

Publishing Co: H.C. Williams, P.O. Box 423653, San Francisco, CA 94142
Editorial Description: Different lifestyles & different types of recipes.
General Info: Trim Size-8.5 x 11, 5 pages
Subscriptions: Indv. $1

Blue Mountain

Publishing Co: Blue Mountain Center of Meditation, PO Box 256, Tomales, CA 94971-0256; Title Tel # (707) 878-2369 Title Fax # (707) 878-2375
Personnel: Editor-BethAnn O'Connell
Editorial Description: Practical ideas on spiritual living as presented by Eknath Easwaran and the books of Nilgiri Press.
General Info: (Formerly Blue Mountain Center News - A Journal for Spiritual Living), Yr. Est. 1990, Quarterly
Subscriptions: Free
Circulation: Total-18,000

Bookviews
See: BOOKS & BOOK TRADE

CWC Communicator
See: WOMEN'S

Center for Plain Living Newsletter   *Association*

Publishing Co: Center for Plain Living, PO Box 100, Chesterhill, OH 43728-0100
Editorial Description: Provides information on the Center and its efforts to promote simpler living.
General Info: Quarterly
Subscriptions: Free With Membership

Connoisseurs' Guide to California Wine
See: BEVERAGES - BREWING

Coupon Treasure Hunt Newsletter
See: HOME ECONOMICS

Creativity in Action *Business, Association*

Publishing Co: Creative Education Foundation, 1050 Union Rd., Buffalo, NY 14224-3402;
Title Tel # (716) 675-3181 Title Fax # (716) 675-3209
Personnel: Publisher-John Meyerhoff, Editor-Andy Van Gundy, Circ. Mgr., Promotion Dir.-Grace Guzzetta
Editorial Description: Creativity In Action (CIA) is a monthly newsletter whose goal and challenge is to point the way toward a more creative lifestyle for each one of its readers. It has become increasingly evident that we, as individuals have been stifling and blocking our creative instincts as we get older. It has become equally evident that it is decidedly possible to reverse this destructive process, and to unlearn our
General Info: Yr. Est. 1972, Monthly, Trim Size-8½ x 11, 6 pages
Subscriptions: Indv. $50, Can. $55, For. $60, $4/copy
Circulation: Total-380
Printing Co: Reilly Printing & Graphics, 1045 Elmwood Ave, Buffalo, NY 14222

Critical Angels

Publishing Co: Arts Criticism, 2402 University Avenue West, Suite 208, Saint Paul, MN 55110
Editorial Description: More than just a calendar of events, this newsletter includes a variety of reports and interviews.
General Info: Quarterly
Subscriptions: Indv. $15

Cruise & Freighter Travel Letter
See: TRAVEL

Cupid's Destiny *Consumer*

Publishing Co: Destiny Syndicate, PO Box 5637, Reno, NV 89513-5637
Personnel: Publisher, Editor, Adv. Dir.-Kelly Williams
Editorial Description: Pictures, descriptions & addresses of men & women seeking friendship, romance, marriage.
General Info: Yr. Est. 1937, Tri-annually, Trim Size-8½ x 11½, Sheetfed press, 16 pages, No Color
Subscriptions: Indv. $27, $10/copy
Circulation: Total-20,000

DOE
See: SCIENCE FICTION & FANTASY

Dread Times

Publishing Co: Jamaican Style, 4-771 Kuhio Hwy #7-C, Kapaa, HI 96746
Editorial Description: The reggaeheartbeat of Hawaii comes to you in this simple newsletter of Rastafarian news, music, culture, and religion.
Subscriptions: Indv. $1

Dwelling Portably
See: OUTDOORS

Earthstewards Network News
See: ENVIRONMENT & ECOLOGY

Elysium Living *Consumer, Association*

Publishing Co: Elysium Institute, 814 Robinson Rd, Topanga, CA 90290-3627 Tel # (310) 455-1000
Personnel: Editor-Betty Lesley, Graphic Designer-Shaun Snyder
Editorial Description: News, information and calendar of events for nudist, naturist community. Bound with The Journal of the Senses.
General Info: Bi-monthly, Trim Size-8¼ x 11, 8 pages, 2 Color, Matte, Perfect bound
Subscriptions: Free With Membership

Emerge Playcouple *Consumer, Association*

Publishing Co: Sponsor-NASCA, Inc. (North American Swing Club Assn.), Lifestyles Press, 2641 W La Palma # A, Anaheim, CA 92801-2602; Title Tel # (714) 821-9953 Title Fax # (714) 821-1465
Personnel: Publisher, Editor-Robert McGinley, Circ. Mgr., Promotion Dir.-Robert Hartman
Editorial Description: News & educational articles on swinging, relationships, & sexual behavior.
General Info: Yr. Est. 1971, Bi-monthly, Trim Size-8½ x 11, Sheetfed press, 4 pages, ISSN: 92-006702, No Color, Newsprint
Subscriptions: Indv. $15, $3/copy
Acquistions: Publication Bought, Publication Sold
Circulation: Total-2,000
Advertising: Inquire for rates. Accepts Inserts.
Printing Co: Carol Swim Printing, 3458 W Orange Ave, Anaheim, CA 92804-3006 Tel # (714) 821-8690

Enough Is Enough: Simpler Living in the Complex, Post Modern World *Consumer*

Publishing Co: Dennis W. Brezina, P.O. Box 683, Chesapeake, MD 21915; Title Tel # (410) 885-2887
Editorial Description: Discusses ways (and need) to reduce consumption.
General Info: Yr. Est. 1995, Monthly, Trim Size-8½ x 11, 8 pages, ISSN: 1084-7456, Matte
Subscriptions: Indv. $20, Inst. $20, $3/copy
Circulation: Total-400, Readership-500
Printing Co: LifeWorks, 3181 'R' Street, Lincoln, NE 68503

Environmental Life Newsletter
See: ENVIRONMENT & ECOLOGY

Esperantic Studies

Publishing Co: Esperantic Studies Foundation, 3900 Northampton St., Washington, DC 20015
Editorial Description: A short newsletter promoting research on international languages studies and the expansion of Esperanto.
General Info: Trim Size-8.5 x 11, 4 pages

Family in America
See: FAMILY

Father Rights News

Publishing Co: Single Father Advocate, PO Box 55443, Seattle, WA 98155-0443; Title Tel # (206) 363-7823
General Info: (Formerly Single Father Advocate), Yr. Est. 1981, Monthly, 8 pages
Circulation: Total-500

Fathers Brothers Sons
See: MEN'S

Festivities
See: ENTERTAINMENT

Food Free or Cheap Newsletter
See: HOME ECONOMICS

Freedom Network News
See: POLITICS

Friendship Letter, The
See: GENERAL INTEREST

Frugal Finances
See: CONSUMER INTERESTS

Get Organized! News, The
See: GENERAL INTEREST

Green City Calendar

Publishing Co: Green City Project, P.O. Box 31251, San Francisco, CA 94131
Editorial Description: A local newsletter devoted to improving the quality of urban living through improved environmental activism.
General Info: Trim Size-8.5 x 11, 12 pages

Heinous

Publishing Co: Steve Mandich, P.O. Box 10412, Portland, OR 97210
Editorial Description: Many different interest. Such as Evil Knievel, many tribute songs written by daredevil stuntman. Informative FAQ about Wheelies.
General Info: 32 pages
Subscriptions: Indv. $1

Hobo Times *Consumer*

Publishing Co: National Hobo Association, World Way Center, Box 90430, Los Angeles, CA 90009-0430; Title Tel # (310) 645-1500
Personnel: Publisher-Garth Bishop
Editorial Description: News of the world of hobos including music, poetry, and literature. Many historical stories.
General Info: (Formerly Hobo News), Yr. Est. 1908, Bi-monthly, ISSN: 1055-3967
Subscriptions: Indv. $18, $3/copy
Circulation: Total-5,000

International Living *Consumer* CPM: $24

Publishing Co: Agora, Inc., 105 W. Monoment St., Baltimore, MD 21202-4702 Tel # (410) 783-2647 Fax # (410) 223-2662; Title Tel # (410) 234-0515 Title Fax # (410) 837-3879
Personnel: Publisher-William Bonner, Circ. Mgr.-Dary Berver, Production Mgr.-Alex Nosevich, Editor, Adv. Dir.-Kathleen Peddicord, Mktg. Dir.-Sandy Franks, Promotion Dir.-Kathleen Petticord
Editorial Description: Current, concise information on traveling, living, retiring, buying property, investing, studying, working and starting a business in another country.
General Info: Yr. Est. 1981, Monthly, Trim Size-8½ x 11, Web press, 24 pages, 20% ads, 2 Color, Newsprint, Saddle-stitched
Subscriptions: Indv. $48, $5/copy
Acquistions: Publication Bought, Publication Sold
Circulation: Total-50,000
Advertising: $1,200. Accepts Inserts.
List Rental: List Management Co.: Manager: Elizabeth Dent; Name Bank, 14 W. Monument St., Baltimore, MD 21201 Tel # (410) 783-8463, Fax # (410) 783-8464, Actives: 69,740, $75/M, Hotline: 4,400, $85/M, Expires: 30,000, $65/M

Journal of the Senses
See: HEALTH

Kat Barf

Publishing Co: Emily Jean Hetrick, 4707 Delbrook Road, Mechanicsburg, PA 17055-3042
Editorial Description: Lots of poems and stories about life.
General Info: Trim Size-8.5 x 11, 14 pages
Subscriptions: Indv. $1

Le Calendrier

Publishing Co: French Cultural Svcs., 126 Mount Auburn St, Cambridge, MA 02138-5701; Title Tel # (617) 354-3464
Personnel: Editor-Noelle de Chambrun
Editorial Description: A compilation of French cultural events happening in New England.
General Info: Yr. Est. 1979, Monthly, Trim Size-11 x 17, Desktop press, 1 pages, No Color
Subscriptions: Indv. $3
Circulation: Total-900

Lesbian and Gay Archivist
See: GAY & LESBIAN INTEREST

Letters from Abraham Lincoln
See: ART & SCULPTURE

Life Enrichment   *Consumer*

Publishing Co: F.J. Mclaughlin Newsletter Network, 1346 Joan Dr, Southampton, PA 18966-4341; Title Tel # (215) 322-1346
Personnel: Publisher, Editor-Flo McLaughlin
Editorial Description: For people who support and encourage one another through an exchange of experiences and ideas via a newsletter that emphasises the positive and upbeat outlook on life.
General Info: (Formerly Women's National Network), Quarterly, Trim Size-8½ x 11, 8 pages
Subscriptions: Indv. $10, Can. $10, For. $14, $3/copy
Circulation: Total-1,000

Living Cheap News
See: CONSUMER INTERESTS

Living Free   *Consumer*

Publishing Co: Living Free, c/o Jim Stumm, Box 29, Hiler Branch, Buffalo, NY 14223
Editorial Description: Covers a wide range of lifestyle topics such as cheap survival aimed at maximizing personal freedom despite the government's escalating war on freedom.
General Info: Yr. Est. 1979, Irregular, Trim Size-8½ x 11, Offset press, 8 pages
Subscriptions: Indv. $12, For. $15, $2/copy
Circulation: Total-300
Advertising: Inquire for rates.

Living Off the Land, Subtropic Newsletter
See: AGRICULTURE

Log Cabin News
See: HISTORY

Loving Brotherhood Newsletter
See: GAY & LESBIAN INTEREST

Low Fat for Life
See: FOOD

Male Call
See: MEN'S

Manhattan Cheapskate   *Consumer*

Publishing Co: Manhattan Cheapskate, 61 E 8th St, New York, NY 10003-6494; Title Tel # (212) 330-0607
Personnel: Editor-Howard Seibel
Editorial Description: How to live less expensively in New York City.
General Info: 10x/yr.
Subscriptions: Indv. $15, $2/copy
List Rental: Rents Lists

Mastering Life
See: SEX

Men & Wife Newsletter
See: FAMILY

Metro Singles   *Consumer*

Publishing Co: Metro Publications, PO Box 28203, Kansas City, MO 64188-0203; Title Tel # (816) 436-8424
Personnel: Publisher-Robert Huffstutter, Circ. Mgr.-R. Smith, Adv. Dir.-Patti Johnson
Editorial Description: Serves singles in Kansas City metro area. Includes articles & personals. Photos, short features, short stories, poetry & many quality photos.
General Info: Yr. Est. 1984, Bi-monthly, Trim Size-8½ x 11, Web press, 36 pages, 2 Color, Newsprint
Subscriptions: $2/copy
Circulation: Total-25,000
Advertising: Inquire for rates.

Mid Life Woman
See: WOMEN'S

Mind-Expander
See: PHILOSOPHY

Modern Divorce   *Consumer*

Publishing Co: National Association for Female Executives, Inc., 30 Irving Pl., 5th Floor, New York, NY 10003-2303 Tel # (212) 477-2200 Fax # (212) 477-8215
Editorial Description: Information to help make life easier for the divorced or separated person.
General Info: Yr. Est. 1994, Bi-monthly
Subscriptions: Indv. $29

My Pen Pal   *Consumer*

Publishing Co: Yama International, 806 E Fairmont Ave, Modesto, CA 95350-6073
Personnel: Publisher, Editor-Craig Francis, Production Mgr.-Brenda Francis
Editorial Description: Newsletter for pen pals, a mixture of fun and friendship. Each issue includes a pen pal directory from which pen pal selections can be made.
General Info: Yr. Est. 1990, Quarterly, Trim Size-8½ x 11, Desktop press, 10 pages, No Color
Subscriptions: $4/copy
Circulation: Total-500
Advertising: Inquire for rates. Accepts Inserts.

NAPH National Newsletter
See: DISABILITY

NOBODY YOU KNOW

Publishing Co: James McGraw, P.O. Box, Portland, OR 97242
Editorial Description: Jason's personal journey around the world.
General Info: Trim Size-8.5 x 11, 14 pages
Subscriptions: Indv. $1

New Jersey Self-Help Clearinghouse-Network

Publishing Co: New Jersey Self-Help Clearinghouse, St. Clare's Riverside Med. Ctr, Pocono Rd., Denville, NJ 07834; Title Tel # (201) 625-9565 Title Fax # (201) 625-8848
Personnel: Editor-Gwen Roe
Editorial Description: Reports on new developments in self-help movement; highlights work of self-help groups in N.J.
General Info: Yr. Est. 1981, Semi-annually, Trim Size-8½ x 11, Desktop press, 8 pages, 2 Color, Newsprint
Circulation: Total-6,000

New Relationships

Publishing Co: Sponsor-Experimental Cities, Inc., Equal Relationships Institute, PO Box 731, Pacific Palisades, CA 90272-0731; Title Tel # (310) 276-0686 Title Fax # (310) 274-7401
Personnel: Publisher-Genevieve Marcus, Ph.D., Promotion Dir.-Robert Smith
Editorial Description: Examines and articulates the profound changes occurring in contemporary relationships.
General Info: Yr. Est. 1983, Trim Size-8½ x 11, Offset press, 8 pages, ISSN: 0738-0674, 2 Color, Newsprint, Perfect bound
Subscriptions: Indv. $20, $2/copy
Circulation: Total-10,000
Printing Co: Larson Litho, 5959 S Western Ave, Los Angeles, CA 90047-1124 Tel # (213) 750-2256

News & Views/Single Life Inst.

Publishing Co: Single Life Institute, PO Box 2832, Abilene, TX 79604-2832
Personnel: Publisher-Glenda Ravanelli, Editor-Jim Ravanelli
Editorial Description: Serves Christian singles' lifestyle.
General Info: Monthly, 6 pages
Subscriptions: Indv. $6, Free
Circulation: Total-600

Off The Air

Publishing Co: Syracuse Community Radio, P.O. Box 6365, Syracuse, NY 13217
Editorial Description: A station done by books, bypassing pirates techniques used in the Bay Area and getting a full power station that support the Syracuse community.
General Info: Trim Size-8.5 x 11, 8 pages
Subscriptions: Indv. $1

One Family   *Association*

Publishing Co: Planetary Citizens, PO Box 1509, Mount Shasta, CA 96067-1509; Title Tel # (415) 325-2939
General Info: Yr. Est. 1972, Quarterly, Trim Size-8½ x 11, Web press, 8 pages, No Color
Circulation: Total-12,000

Ontario Vacation Farms
See: TRAVEL

Our Widening Circle   *Association*

Publishing Co: Green Circle Program, 1300 Spruce St, Philadelphia, PA 19107-5812; Title Tel # (215) 893-8400 Title Fax # (215) 735-9718
Personnel: Editor-Michael Blum, Editor-Niyona Spann-Wilsm
Editorial Description: Cover human relations and self-awareness topics.
General Info: Quarterly, Trim Size-8½ x 11, 12 pages, No Color, Matte, Saddle-stitched
Subscriptions: Indv. $20
Circulation: Total-2,800

PETA News
See: ENVIRONMENT & ECOLOGY

Peoplenet   *Consumer*

Publishing Co: Peoplenet, PO Box 897, Levittown, NY 11756-0911; Title Tel # (516) 579-4043
Personnel: Publisher, Editor, Promotion Dir.-Robert Mauro
Editorial Description: Peoplenet is a networking personals/dating newsletter by & for the disabled. It carries poems, articles & fiction on dating, sociality & romance.
General Info: Yr. Est. 1987, Tri-annually, Trim Size-8½ x 11, 12 pages
Subscriptions: Indv. $28, Can. $31, For. $31
Circulation: Total-200
Advertising: Inquire for rates.

Perfect Partner Network   *Consumer*

Publishing Co: Channel Media, Inc., 250 W. 57th Street, Suite 1527-89, New York, NY 10107
Editorial Description: Publication to help men and women find their 'Perfect Partner'.
General Info: Bi-monthly, Trim Size-8½ x 11, 16 pages, No Color, Matte, Saddle-stitched

Practically Green
See: CONSUMER INTERESTS

Prime Line Bulletin

Publishing Co: National Association for Retired Credit Union People, 5910 Mineral Point Rd, Madison, WI 53705-4456; Title Tel # (608) 238-4286
Personnel: Publisher, Editor-Philip Tschudy, Circ. Mgr.-LaVonne Reschke, Adv. Dir.-Russell Grote, Art Dir.-Marla Brenner
Editorial Description: Contains, retirement, consumer & travel information, plus articles on NARCUP Services.
General Info: Yr. Est. 1978, Quarterly, Web press, 4 pages, 4 Color, Coated
Circulation: Total-75,000

Privacy & American Business
See: BUSINESS & INDUSTRY

Private Lives

Publishing Co: Hecht Rubber Corp., Box 1550 Madison Sq. Sta., New York, NY 10159-1550
Personnel: Editor-Gloria Sun
Editorial Description: For the sexually adventurous.
List Rental: List Management Co.: Mail Marketing, Inc., 171 Terrace St., Haworth, NJ 07641-1899 Tel # (201) 387-1023, Fax # (201) 387-2976, Actives: 62,595, $60/M, Expires: 11,152, $50/M

Quicktrips Travel Letter
See: TRAVEL

Reading Woman
See: FICTION

Refunding Update - Introduction to Refunding
See: CONSUMER INTERESTS

Rough Draft

Publishing Co: S.F.C.S, P.O. Box 426392, San Francisco, CA 94142
Editorial Description: The official organ of the San Francisco Cacophony society
General Info: Trim Size-8.5 x 11, 2 pages
Subscriptions: Indv. $1

Rural Network Advocate   *Association*

Publishing Co: Rural Network, Inc., 6236 Borden Rd, Boscobel, WI 53805-9715; Title Tel # (608) 375-4659
Personnel: Publisher, Editor-Lois Fields
Editorial Description: Newsletter for Rural Network, a membership organization for people (U.S.A. and Canada) who are country oriented and who value a healthy environment.
General Info: Yr. Est. 1980, Monthly, Trim Size-8½ x 11, Sheetfed press, 8 pages, 6% ads, No Color, Matte
Subscriptions: Indv. $12, Can. $12, $1/copy
Circulation: Total-300
Printing Co: Achenbach Printing, 903 Wisconsin Ave, Boscobel, WI 53805-1531

Serf's Up
See: LABOR

Seventh House, The

Publishing Co: Seventh House, Box OX-171263, Memphis, TN 38187-1263; Title Tel # (901) 682-0296
Personnel: Editor-Ann Roberts
Editorial Description: The newsletter for SOUL MATES, a correspondence club for singles. Astrology is used as a special interest & guide for compatibility. Managed by Masters Degree Social Worker & Professional Astrologer.
General Info: Yr. Est. 1982, Quarterly, Trim Size-7 x 8½, Desktop press, 40 pages, No Color, Newsprint
Subscriptions: Indv. $75

Simple Cooking
See: FOOD

Single Lifestyle   *Consumer*

Publishing Co: Single Lifestyle, PO Box 11692, Santa Ana, CA 92711-1692; Title Tel # (714) 978-1230
Personnel: Publisher, Editor-Jerry Browne
General Info: Yr. Est. 1980, Monthly
Subscriptions: Indv. $18

Singles & Leaders Newsletter
See: RELIGIOUS & THEOLOGICAL

Soulmate News
See: NEW AGE

Soundings

Publishing Co: Federation of Egalitarian Communities, Acorn - RT. 3 Box 486A, Mineral, VA 23117; Title Tel # (540) 894-0595 Title Fax # (540) 894-0597
Editorial Description: Quarterly publication of the Federation of Egalitarian Communities, a group of income-sharing intentional communities.
General Info: Yr. Est. 1977, Quarterly, 12 pages
Subscriptions: Indv. $3
Advertising: Inquire for rates.

Storefront Bar-B-Q

Publishing Co: Shawn Swagerty, P.O. Box 433, Portland, OR 97207
Editorial Description: A zine about the interesting weirdos who inhabit Portland
General Info: Trim Size-8.5 x 11, 16 pages
Subscriptions: Indv. $2

Successtrax

Publishing Co: Ed Helvey Productions, PO Box 1357, Winchester, VA 22604-7857; Title Tel # (703) 888-3350 Title Fax # (703) 888-3363
Personnel: Circ. Mgr., Production Mgr.-BJ Gardner, Publisher, Editor, Promotion Dir.-Ed Helvey
Editorial Description: An candid interviews with successful people from all walks of life.'
General Info: Yr. Est. 1981, Monthly
Subscriptions: Indv. $144, $10/copy

Sylvia Porter's Active Retirement Newsletter
See: SENIOR CITIZENS

Tales From The Zone

Publishing Co: The Zone, 7019 Melrose Avenue, #166, Los Angeles, CA 90038
Editorial Description: The official newsletter for the L.A. Cacophony Society
General Info: Trim Size-8.5 x 11, 2 pages
Subscriptions: Indv. $1

Teachers In Touch
See: EDUCATION

Tightwad Gazette
See: CONSUMER INTERESTS

Touchpoint   *Consumer*

Publishing Co: Touchpoint, P.O. Box 408, Chloride, AZ 86431
Editorial Description: Information on open relationships, group marriages and other non-monogamous lifestyles
General Info: Irregular

Travelin' Woman
See: TRAVEL

UAA Communication
See: PUBLIC MANAGEMENT & PLANNING

Ultimate Issues   *Consumer*

Publishing Co: Ultimate Issues, 10573 W Pico Blvd Ste 167, Los Angeles, CA 90064-2348; Title Tel # (310) 558-3958 Title Fax # (310) 558-4241
Personnel: Publisher, Editor-Dennis Prager, Circ. Mgr.-Pat Havins, Mktg. Dir.-Mark Wilcox
General Info: Yr. Est. 1985, Quarterly, Trim Size-8½ x 11, Offset press, 22 pages, ISSN: 0888-3440, 2 Color, Coated
Subscriptions: Indv. $25, Inst. $25, Can. $27, For. $29, $8/copy
Circulation: Total-9,000
List Rental: List Management Co.: Manager: Pat Havens; AB Data, 8050 N Port Washington Rd, Milwaukee, WI 53217-2600 Tel # (414) 352-4404, Fax # (414) 352-3994
Printing Co: Trackstar Printing, 9133 S La Cienega Blvd Ste 230, Inglewood, CA 90301-4409 Tel # (213) 216-1275

Wellness Newsletter, The
See: HEALTH

What Doctors Don't Tell You
See: MEDICINE

Whatever Works

Publishing Co: Susan Boren, P.O. Box 569, Iowa City, IA 52244
Editorial Description: A friendly little zine featuring comics and handwritten commentary about what's wrong with the world.
General Info: Trim Size-8.5 x 11, 8 pages

Women's Health Matters
See: HEALTH

Working Wine Guide, The
See: BEVERAGES - BREWING

World of A.S.P. *Consumer, Association*

Publishing Co: American Self-Protection Assn., 825 Greengate Oval, Sagamore Hills, OH 44067-2311; Title Tel # (216) 467-1750 Title Fax # (216) 467-1750
Personnel: Editor-Evan Baltazzi, Production Mgr.-Gary A. Cook
Editorial Description: System of self defense, holistic self-protection, body-mind coordination aerobics based on self-defense motion, self - defense for handicapped persons aikido (asp) kickboxing (asp)grappling (asp) stickfighting (asp), pyschosomatic exercises (asp) tai-chi(asp)
General Info: Yr. Est. 1966, Quarterly, Trim Size-8½ x 11, Desktop press, 4 pages, No Color, Coated
Subscriptions: Indv. $45, Inst. $35, Can. $50, For. $45, Free With Membership
Circulation: Total-200

World Links

Publishing Co: Wendy, P.O. Box 43036, Mt. Clements, MI 48043
Editorial Description: A friendly international pen pal zine that's totally connected to the huge network of related publications.
General Info: Trim Size-5 x 7, 24 pages
Subscriptions: Indv. $2

LIGHTING

Copper Topics *Business*

Publishing Co: Espirit de Corps, 11 Hanover Square, New York, NY 10005; Title Tel # (212) 425-7033
Editorial Description: Copper Development Association.
General Info: Yr. Est. 1993, 3x/yr.
Subscriptions: Free

Electrical Product News
See: ELECTRIC & ELECTRONIC EQUIPMENT

ICA UPdate *Business*

Publishing Co: Espirit de Corps, 11 Hanover Square, New York, NY 10005; Title Tel # (212) 425-7033
Editorial Description: International Copper Association.
General Info: Irregular
Subscriptions: Free

Lighting Quarterly *Business*

Publishing Co: Espirit de Corps, 11 Hanover Square, New York, NY 10005; Title Tel # (212) 425-7033
Editorial Description: Phillip's Lighting Co.-Lightbulbs.
General Info: Yr. Est. 1992, Quarterly
Subscriptions: Free

Lighting Update *Business*

Publishing Co: Espirit de Corps, 11 Hanover Square, New York, NY 10005; Title Tel # (212) 425-7033
Editorial Description: Lighting fixtures.
General Info: Yr. Est. 1993, Quarterly
Subscriptions: Free To Qualified Recipient

Neon News *Business, Consumer*

Publishing Co: The Neon News, PO Box 668, Volcano, HI 96785-0668; Title Tel # (809) 967-7648
Personnel: Editor-Val Crawford, Editor-Ted Pirsig
Editorial Description: Covers all aspects of working with neon for signs, art, and architecture. Reader contributions form the bulk of the material.
General Info: Yr. Est. 1989, Quarterly
Subscriptions: Indv. $16, Inst. $16, Can. $18, For. $20, $4/copy
Circulation: Total-400

Signals
See: ELECTRIC & ELECTRONIC EQUIPMENT

Technical Brief
See: THEATRE

LITERARY REVIEWS

AOL

Publishing Co: ATX, P.O. Box 382507, Cambridge, MA 02238
Editorial Description: A personal view & discussion rediagnosis medicine, treatment, and problems with racism in the hospital.
General Info: Trim Size-11 x 8, 2 pages

Archive Newsletter

Publishing Co: Univ. of California/Archive for New Poetry, Central Univ. Library, C-075-S, La Jolla, CA 92093
Personnel: Publisher-Carolyn Haynes, Editor-Rae Armantrout
Editorial Description: Covers samples of poetry, reviews & announcements of poetry events in San Diego area.
General Info: Yr. Est. 1973, Letrpr. press, 40 pages, Color-cover, Coated, Saddle-stitched
Printing Co: Univ. of California - San Diego, Graphics Dept., La Jolla, CA 92093 Tel # (619) 534-3020

Boletin Informativo Newsletter
See: BOOKS & BOOK TRADE

Book Passage
See: LITERATURE & LINGUISTICS

Books of Wonder
See: BOOKS & BOOK TRADE

Bookviews
See: BOOKS & BOOK TRADE

CLMPages
See: PERIODICAL INDUSTRY

Chaney Chronical
See: LITERATURE & LINGUISTICS

Color Wheel Review *Consumer*

Publishing Co: 700 Elves Press, RR 2 Box 806, Warner, NH 03278-9202
Editorial Description: Reviews small press books and magazines.
General Info: Yr. Est. 1992, Tri-annually
Subscriptions: Indv. $5

The Columbo Newsletter

Publishing Co: Sheldon P. Catz, P.O. Box 1703, Pittsburgh, PA 15230
Editorial Description: A newsletter which primarily features credits, plot synopses, and lengthy critiques for all the episodes of Columbo.
Subscriptions: Indv. $3

Dear Reader
See: LITERATURE & LINGUISTICS

English Resource, The
See: LITERATURE & LINGUISTICS

Fight Back
See: AFRICAN-AMERICAN INTEREST

Free Focus
See: POETRY & CREATIVE WRITING

Frostbite Falls FAr Flung Flier

Publishing Co: FFFFF, P.O. Box 39, Macedonia, OH 44056
Editorial Description: The unofficial newsletter devoted to Rocky Bullwinkle and other Jay Ward/Bill Scott products.
General Info: Trim Size-8.5 x 11, 12 pages

Fugitive Pope
See: LIBRARY

Goob, The
See: LITERATURE & LINGUISTICS

Hoosier Challenger

Publishing Co: MUNZ, 9423 Montgomery Rd, Cincinnati, OH 45242-7602
General Info: Yr. Est. 1956, Bi-monthly
Subscriptions: $1/copy

James Dickey Newsletter *Association*

Publishing Co: DeKalb College, 2101 Womack Rd, Dunwoody, GA 30338-4435; Title Tel # (404) 551-3161
Personnel: Publisher, Editor-Joyce Pair
Editorial Description: Publishes articles about the work of James Dickey & an on-going bibliography as well as a few never before published poems of high quality.
General Info: Yr. Est. 1984, Semi-annually, Trim Size-8½ x 11, 30 pages, ISSN: 0749-0291, Ind/Abs/Online: MLA, AHI
Subscriptions: Indv. $5, Inst. $10, Can. $8, For. $8, $4/copy
Circulation: Total-200
Advertising: Accepts Inserts.

Jerome Riker Intl. Study of Organized Persecution of Children Newsletter
See: CHILDREN

Jewish Vegetarians Newsletter
See: RELIGIOUS & THEOLOGICAL

Journal of the William Morris Society in the United States
Association

Publishing Co: Sponsor-William Morris Society, SUNY Maritime College Humanities Dept., Publications, Bronx, NY 10465
Editorial Description: Dedicated to the life, works & ideas of William Morris.
General Info: (Formerly Journal of the William Morris Society in North America), Quarterly
Subscriptions: Indv. $20, Inst. $25
Circulation: Total-1,600

Just Books
See: LITERATURE & LINGUISTICS

LAWG Letter
Association

Publishing Co: Latin American Working Group, 603 1/2 Parliament St., Toronto, ON M4X 1P9 Canada Tel # (416) 966-4775 Fax # (416) 921-0071; Title Tel # (416) 966-4773 Title Fax # (416) 921-0081
Editorial Description: IN-depth analysis of particular issues in Canadian relations with Central & South America.
General Info: Yr. Est. 1973, Irregular, Trim Size-8½ x 11, 40 pages, ISSN: 0316-3393
Subscriptions: Inst. $45
Circulation: Total-500

Laughing Bear Newsletter
See: BOOKS & BOOK TRADE

Linington Lineup
Association

Publishing Co: Elizabeth Linington Society, 1223 Glen Ter, Glassboro, NJ 08028-1315; Title Tel # (609) 589-1571
Personnel: Publisher, Editor-Rinehart Potts
Editorial Description: Studies literary works of Elizabeth Linington, (aka Lesley Egan, Dell Shannon, Anne Blaisdell, Egan O'Neill.)
General Info: Yr. Est. 1983, Bi-monthly, Trim Size-8½ x 11, Offset press, 16 pages, ISSN: 8756-5609, No Color, Other, Other
Subscriptions: Indv. $12, $3/copy
Circulation: Total-400
Advertising: Inquire for rates. Accepts Inserts.

Literary Sketches
Consumer

Publishing Co: Literary Sketches, PO Box 810571, Dallas, TX 75381-0571; Title Tel # (214) 243-8776
Personnel: Publisher, Editor-Olivia Murray Nichols
Editorial Description: Reviews, articles and short biographical oddities.
General Info: Yr. Est. 1961, Monthly, Trim Size-8½ x 11, Offset press, 4 pages, ISSN: 0024-4597, No Color
Subscriptions: Indv. $7, Can. $8, For. $8, $1/copy
Circulation: Total-550
Advertising: Inquire for rates.
Printing Co: Dodd's Printing, 2901 Valley View Ln, Farmers Branch, TX 75234

Midwest Chesterton News
Association

Publishing Co: Midwest Chesterton News, 740 Spruce St, Barrington, IL 60010-3142; Title Tel # (708) 381-4584
Personnel: Publisher, Editor-John Peterson
Editorial Description: Promotes an interest in the life and work of G.K. Chesterton. Includes discussion, quotes, reviews and events.
General Info: Yr. Est. 1988, Monthly, Trim Size-8½ x 11, Mimeo press, 10 pages, No Color, Matte
Subscriptions: Indv. $11, Can. $12, For. $18, $1/copy
Circulation: Total-350

Millennial Prophecy Report
See: RELIGIOUS & THEOLOGICAL

Millennium Pop
See: MUSIC & MUSIC TRADES

Murder is Academic
See: EDUCATION

Mystery Notebook
See: MYSTERY & HORROR

Mythprint
Association

Publishing Co: Sponsor-Mythopoeic Society, The, Mythopoeic Society, PO Box 6707, Altadena, CA 91003-6707
Personnel: Editor-David Bratman, Production Mgr.-Lisa Harrigan
Editorial Description: Fantasy literature news bulletin.
General Info: (Formerly Mythopoeic Society Bulletin), Yr. Est. 1968, Monthly, Trim Size-6¼ x 8½, Sheetfed press, 16 pages, ISSN: 0146-9347, No Color, Newsprint
Subscriptions: Indv. $13, Inst. $13, Can. $17, For. $20
Circulation: Total-1,000

Neihardt Foundation Newsletter

Publishing Co: John G. Neihardt Foundation, Inc., Attn: Publications, Bancroft, NE 68004; Title Tel # (402) 648-3388
Editorial Description: Advances literary legacy & memory of Nebraska poet Laureate John G. Neihardt. Reports activities of Foundation & lists books & other items for sale.
General Info: Yr. Est. 1970, Semi-annually, 8 pages
Subscriptions: Indv. $15
Circulation: Total-350
Printing Co: Wisner News Chronicle, PO Box 460, Wisner, NE 68791-0460

Newspacket
Association

Publishing Co: Stephen Leacock Assn., Box 854, Orillia, ON L3V 6K8 Canada; Title Tel # (705) 325-6546
Personnel: Circ. Mgr.-Jack Stewart, Editor, Production Mgr., Art Dir.-Kathy Hunt
Editorial Description: To promote the understanding of Stephen Leacock and to encourage the literary arts and writers with particular emphasis on humour by Canadians.
General Info: Yr. Est. 1970, Tri-annually, Trim Size-8½ x 11, Offset press, 4 pages, ISSN: 0384-1642, No Color, Matte, Other
Subscriptions: Indv. $10, Free To Qualified Recipient
Circulation: (12% controlled), Total-2,500
Advertising: Inquire for rates.

Nickleby's Bookstore
See: LITERATURE & LINGUISTICS

Noticias de Aztlan
See: POETRY & CREATIVE WRITING

Oberlin Other
Consumer

Publishing Co: Oberlin Other, 285 E College St, Oberlin, OH 44074-1354

Op. Cit.
See: LITERATURE & LINGUISTICS

Ozark Feminist Review
See: WOMEN'S

R.J. Julia Booksellers
See: LITERATURE & LINGUISTICS

RPCV Writers & Readers
See: LITERATURE & LINGUISTICS

Reader's Review
See: LITERATURE & LINGUISTICS

Reading Woman
See: FICTION

Romantic Notions
See: ROMANCE

Select Fiction
Consumer

Publishing Co: Select Fiction, P.O. Box 1041, Sharon, CT 06069
Personnel: Editor-Harris Dienstfrey, Editor-Jane Dienstfrey
Editorial Description: Reviews of currently available books of literary merit that have not made it to one of the better known best-seller lists/
General Info: Yr. Est. 1993, 5x/yr.
Subscriptions: Indv. $1,500

Simple Cooking
See: FOOD

Small Press News
Consumer

Publishing Co: Stony Hill Productions, Rr 1 Box 780, New Sharon, ME 04955-9716; Title Tel # (207) 778-4699
Editorial Description: Covers news & reviews of small press material with emphasis on fiction & poetry. Small Press News is included with a subscription to Stony Hill magazine.
General Info: 4x/yr., ISSN: 0146-2067

South Asia Forum Quarterly
See: ETHNIC

Surveillant: Acquisitions for Security & Intelligence Professionals
See: SECURITY & SURVEILLANCE

Up All Night
See: LITERATURE & LINGUISTICS

Vroman's
See: LITERATURE & LINGUISTICS

What's New About London, Jack?
See: LITERATURE & LINGUISTICS

Writers Ink Press *Consumer*

Publishing Co: Writer Unlimited Agency, Inc., PO Box 698, Centereach, NY 11720-0698; Title Tel # (516) 821-2945 Title Fax # (516) 821-2945
Personnel: Publisher, Editor-David Axecrod, Production Mgr.-Anthony Guilbert, Art Dir.-Jessica Robinson
Editorial Description: Articles, art, photos, cartoons, interviews, satire, criticism, reviews, collages. No unsolicited manuscripts, materials for review welcome.
General Info: Yr. Est. 1975, Trim Size-5 x 7, Sheetfed press, 8 pages, No Color, Saddle-stitched
Subscriptions: Indv. $8
Circulation: Total-2,000
Advertising: Inquire for rates. Accepts Inserts.
List Rental: Rents Lists

Writing World
See: MEDIA & COMMUNICATIONS

Yous

Publishing Co: Andreas Spiliadis, 3019 Abell Ave, Baltimore, MD 21218
Editorial Description: More then just a hodge-podge of stuff, they include reprints, reviews, and lots of personal writing.
General Info: 20x/yr., Trim Size-5 x 7, 20 pages

LITERATURE & LINGUISTICS

AATF National Bulletin
See: EDUCATION

ALTA Newsletter *Association*

Publishing Co: Sponsor-American Literary Translations Assn., American Library Association, 50 E Huron St, Chicago, IL 60611-2795 Tel # (312) 944-6780 Fax # (312) 440-9374; Title Tel # (312) 280-2162 Title Fax # (312) 280-3257
Personnel: Publisher, Editor-Elizabeth Miller
Editorial Description: American Literary Translators Association members information bulletin.
General Info: Yr. Est. 1978, Tri-annually, Trim Size-8½ x 11, 5 pages, No Color, Newsprint
Subscriptions: Indv. $30, Free With Membership
Circulation: Total-1,000
Printing Co: Southern Methodist University, Dallas, TX 75275-0001 Tel # (214) 692-2000

ARA Journal
See: POLITICS

ASAIL Notes

Publishing Co: New Mexico State Univ. English Dept., c/o Andrew Wiget, Las Cruces, NM 88003; Title Tel # (505) 646-3931
Personnel: Editor-Dr. Wiggett
Editorial Description: Covers ASAIL activities & Native American literature.

ATJ Newsletter *Association*

Publishing Co: Association of Teachers of Japanese, Hillcrest 9, Middlebury College, Middlebury, VT 05753 Tel # (802) 388-3711 Fax # (802) 368-4329; Title Tel # (608) 262-2291
Personnel: Editor-Carole Cavanaugh
Editorial Description: News of the profession, including job notices.
General Info: Yr. Est. 1963, Tri-annually, Offset press, 15 pages, No Color, Newsprint
Subscriptions: Indv. $25, Inst. $45, For. $52, Free With Membership
Circulation: Total-1,200
List Rental: Actives: $100/M

Alumeto *Association*

Publishing Co: Kanada Esperanto-Asocio, Box 2159, Sidney, BC V8L 3S6 Canada
Personnel: Editor-Paul Hopkins
Editorial Description: Activities of the Association and other Esperanto associations regionally active in Canada. The newsletter is edited entirely in Esperanto.
General Info: Yr. Est. 1984, 3x/yr., Trim Size-4½ x 8¼, Offset press, 20 pages, ISSN: 0823-2539, No Color, Matte, Saddle-stitched
Subscriptions: Can. $10, Free With Membership
Circulation: (80% controlled), Total-250, International-30, Readership-250
Printing Co: Esperanto Press, R.R. 1, Bailieboro, ON K0L 1B0 Canada Tel # (705) 939-6088

Amaryllis Review

Publishing Co: Amaryllis Press, 535 Parkview Dr, Park City, UT 84060-5204
Personnel: Editor-Carol Poster
General Info: Quarterly, ISSN: 0886-7844

American Association of Teachers of German Newsletter *Association*

Publishing Co: American Association of Teachers of German, 112 Haddontowne Ct Ste 104, Cherry Hill, NJ 08034-3662; Title Tel # (609) 795-5553 Title Fax # (609) 795-9398
Personnel: Editor-Helene Zimmer-Loew
Editorial Description: Items of interest to professionals in the field of German language teaching and research, professional and political issues.
General Info: Yr. Est. 1967, Quarterly, Desktop press, 12 pages, ISSN: 0001-0243, No Color
Subscriptions: Indv. $10, Free With Membership
Circulation: Total-7,500
List Rental: Actives: 8,500, $85/M
Printing Co: Anchor Printing, 315 Horsham Rd, Horsham, PA 19044-2098 Tel # (215) 672-6676

American Association of Teachers of Italian

Publishing Co: Italica, Rutgers Univ., New Brunswick, NJ 08903; Title Tel # (201) 932-7031
Editorial Description: Promotes the study of Italian language, literature, and culture in U.S.A. and Canada.
General Info: Quarterly, Trim Size-8½ x 11½, Letrpr. press, 100 pages
Subscriptions: Indv. $10, $3/copy
Circulation: Total-2,000
Advertising: Inquire for rates.
List Rental: Rents Lists

American Association of Teachers of Slavic & Eastern European Languages News *Association* CPM: $96

Publishing Co: University of Iowa Russian Lang. Dept., Dept. of Russian, Phillips Hall 674, Iowa City, IA 52242-1316; Title Tel # (319) 335-0170 Title Fax # (319) 335-0640
Personnel: Publisher-George Gutsche, Editor-Ray Parrott, Circ. Mgr.-Joe Malik
Editorial Description: News items for teachers of Slavic languages.
General Info: Yr. Est. 1959, Bi-monthly, Trim Size-8½ x 11, 28 pages, ISSN: 0001-0251, No Color
Subscriptions: Indv. $20
Circulation: Total-1,300
Advertising: $125.

American Comparative Literature Assn. Newsletter

Publishing Co: American Comparative Literature Assn., 3010 JKHB, Brigham Young University, Provo, UT 84602 Title Tel # (801) 378-5529 Title Fax # (801) 378-4649
Personnel: Editor-Larry Peer
General Info: Yr. Est. 1968, Semi-annually, Trim Size-6 x 9, Desktop press, 100 pages, ISSN: 0891-3277, No Color, Perfect bound
Subscriptions: Indv. $6, Inst. $6, Can. $8, For. $8
Circulation: Total-800
Printing Co: Brigham Young University Printing Services, 205 UPB, Brigham Young University, Provo, UT 84602-1045 Tel # (801) 378-2809

American Hungarian Foundation Report *Consumer, Association*

Publishing Co: American Hungarian Foundation, P.O. Box 1084, New Brunswick, NJ 08901-2248; Title Tel # (908) 846-5777 Title Fax # (908) 249-7033
Personnel: Mng. Editor-August Molnar
Editorial Description: Reports on the programs and grants of the foundation.
General Info: Yr. Est. 1955, Semi-annually, Trim Size-8½ x 11, Sheetfed press, ISSN: 0194-164X, 4 Color, Coated
Subscriptions: Indv. $10, Inst. $10, Can. $10, For. $12, $6/copy
Circulation: Total-27,000
Advertising: Inquire for rates.

American Studies Assn. Newsletter
See: CULTURE & HUMANITIES

Antenne

Publishing Co: Societe des Traducteurs du Quebec, 1140 de Maisonneuve, Suite 1060, Montreal, PQ H3A 1M8 Canada; Title Tel # (514) 845-4411 Title Fax # (514) 845-9903
Editorial Description: Informational Bulletin for members.
General Info: Yr. Est. 1969, Bi-monthly, Trim Size-8½ x 11, Sheetfed press, 4 pages, 2 Color, Coated
Subscriptions: $1/copy
Circulation: (100% controlled), Total-2,000

Beckett Circle *Association*

Publishing Co: Samuel Beckett Society, Dept. of English, Florida State Univ., Talahassee, FL 32306; Title Tel # (904) 644-4869 Title Fax # (904) 644-8817
Personnel: Editor-Karen Laughlin, Adv. Dir.-Lois Oppenheim
Editorial Description: Newsletter of the Samuel Beckett Society to exchange scholarly information.
General Info: Yr. Est. 1978, Semi-annually, Trim Size-8½ x 11, Offset press, 12 pages, ISSN: 0732-2224, 2% ads, No Color, Newsprint
Subscriptions: Indv. $12
Circulation: Total-400
Advertising: Inquire for rates.
List Rental: Actives: $150/M

Black Literary Players
See: BOOKS & BOOK TRADE

Bluegrass Bulletin *Association*

Publishing Co: Sponsor-KCTFL, Morehead State University, UPC 1212, Morehead, KY 40351; Title Tel # (606) 783-2746
Personnel: Editor-John Secor
Editorial Description: Provides information on foreign language & TESOL education.
General Info: (Formerly Kentucky Modern Foreign Language Newsletter), Yr. Est. 1974, Quarterly, Trim Size-8½ x 11, Sheetfed press, 24 pages, No Color, Newsprint
Subscriptions: Indv. $5
Circulation: (100% controlled)
Advertising: $90.
List Rental: Actives: $10/M
Printing Co: Minuteman Press, 771 W Main St, Lexington, KY 40508-2054

Book Gazette
Scholarly

Publishing Co: John Benjamins North America, PO Box 27519, Philadelphia, PA 19118-0519
Tel # (215) 836-1200 Fax # (215) 836-1204
Editorial Description: Newsletter and catalog of books on language.
General Info: Semi-annually

Book Passage
Consumer

Publishing Co: Book Passage Book Store, 51 Tamal Vista Blvd, Corte Madera, CA 94925-1145
Tel # (415) 927-0960
Personnel: Editor-Bill Petrocelli
Editorial Description: Features interviews with authors, book reviews and book information.
General Info: Bi-monthly, 16 pages
Circulation: Total-70,000

Book Peddler/der Pakn-Treger
See: BOOKS & BOOK TRADE

Bueno
Consumer   **CPM: $80**

Publishing Co: In ONE EAR Publications, 29481 Manzanita Dr, Campo, CA 91906-1128;
Title Tel # (619) 478-5619 Title Fax # (619) 478-5363
Personnel: Publisher, Editor-Elizabeth Reid
Editorial Description: Reviews and gives information and tips for learning Spanish. Also lists books and resources for sale to help teach languages and foreign culture.
General Info: Yr. Est. 1991, Quarterly, Trim Size-5$\frac{1}{2}$ x 8$\frac{1}{2}$, 16 pages, ISSN: 1080-9937, No Color, Matte, Saddle-stitched
Subscriptions: Indv. $8
Circulation: Total-10,000, Readership-22,000
Advertising: $800.
List Rental: Actives: 5,000, $65/M

Bulletin de Terminologie
Association

Publishing Co: Universite Laval Dept. Linguistiques, Comite de Terminologie, Ste. Foy, PQ G1K 1P4 Canada; Title Tel # (418) 656-3622
Editorial Description: Covers French terminology & linguistics.
General Info: (Formerly Bulletin du Comite de Terminologie), Yr. Est. 1968, Irregular, Trim Size-8$\frac{1}{2}$ x 11, Offset press, 2 pages, No Color
Subscriptions: Free To Qualified Recipient
Circulation: (25% controlled), Total-5,000

CETA Bulletin
Association

Publishing Co: Chinese-English Translation Assistance Group, 3910 Knowles Ave # 400, Kensington, MD 20895-2427; Title Tel # (301) 946-7006
Personnel: Editor-J. Mathias
Editorial Description: Information relating to Chinese-English dictionaries and computers in translation.
General Info: Yr. Est. 1972, 8 pages, No Color
Circulation: Total-500

CFH Bulletin FCEH
Consumer

Publishing Co: Canadian Fed. for the Humanities, 151 Slater St. , #407, Ottawa, ON K1P 5H3 Canada; Title Tel # (613) 236-4686 Title Fax # (613) 238-6114
Personnel: Editor-John Thorp
Editorial Description: Eng./Fr. text.
General Info: (Formerly HRCC/CCRH), Yr. Est. 1974, Quarterly, Trim Size-8$\frac{1}{2}$ x 11, 36 pages, Color
Circulation: Total-10,000

CSL Bulletin
Association

Publishing Co: New York C. S. Lewis Society, 419 Springfield Ave, Westfield, NJ 07090-1009; Title Tel # (908) 233-4032
Personnel: Editor-Jerry Daniel
Editorial Description: Study and discussion of the works of C. S. Lewis.
General Info: Yr. Est. 1969, Monthly, Trim Size-8$\frac{1}{2}$ x 11, Offset press, 12 pages, ISSN: 0883-9980, Ind/Abs/Online: M.L.A., No Color
Subscriptions: Indv. $10
Circulation: Total-530

Canadian Assn. of Univ. Teachers of German, Newsletter
See: EDUCATION

Cauda Pavonis: Studies in Hermeticism
Association

Publishing Co: Washington State University English Dept., Publications, Pullman, WA 99164-0001; Title Tel # (509) 335-3023
Personnel: Editor-Stanton Linden
Editorial Description: Cauda Pavonis publishes material on all aspects of alchemy & hermeticism , their influence on literature, philosophy, art, religion, and the history of Science & Medicine.
General Info: Yr. Est. 1974, Semi-annually, 16 pages, Ind/Abs/Online: PMLA, Coated
Subscriptions: Indv. $10, Inst. $10, For. $12
Circulation: Total-450
Printing Co: Washington State University Press, Washington State Univ. Cooper, Publications Bldg., Pullman, WA 99164-0001 Tel # (509) 335-3518

Cavda Pavonis: Hermetic Text Society Newsletter
Association

Publishing Co: Cavda Pavonis, Dept. of English, Washington State Univ., Pullman, WA 99164-0001; Title Tel # (509) 335-3564
Personnel: Editor-Stanton V. Linden

Chaney Chronical

Publishing Co: London Northwest, 929 S Bay Rd NE, Olympia, WA 98506-4808; Title Tel # (360) 352-8622
Personnel: Publisher, Editor-David H. Schottmann
Editorial Description: Study of William Chaney, Father of Jack London.
General Info: Yr. Est. 1972, Irregular, Trim Size-5$\frac{1}{2}$ x 8$\frac{1}{2}$, Sheetfed press, No Color, Newsprint
Subscriptions: $1/copy
Advertising: Inquire for rates.

Comp Lit

Publishing Co: New York Univ. Graduate School of Arts and Science, 25 W 4th St Fl 5, New York, NY 10012-1119; Title Tel # (212) 998-8797
Personnel: Editor-Joseph Caporale
General Info: (Formerly Comparative Literature), Annually, Trim Size-8$\frac{1}{2}$ x 11, 12 pages
Circulation: Total-1,000

Comparative Literature in Canada/Litterature Comparee au Canada
Association

Publishing Co: University of Alberta Language Dept., c/o Dept. of Modern Languages, McMaster Univ., Hamilton, ON L8S 4M2 Canada; Title Tel # (416) 525-9140 Title Fax # (905) 527-0100
Personnel: Editor-Gerald Chapple
Editorial Description: To record proceedings of Canadian Comparative Literature Association, and to communicate news of members scholarly activities, text in English, French; publication of occasional proceedings of colloquia.
General Info: Yr. Est. 1969, Semi-annually, Trim Size-5$\frac{1}{2}$ x 8$\frac{1}{2}$, Mimeo press, 20 pages, ISSN: 0045-7795, Saddle-stitched
Subscriptions: Indv. $5, Inst. $7, Can. $7, For. $10, $4/copy
Circulation: Total-400

Comparative Romance Linguistics Newsletter

Publishing Co: Sponsor-MLA, Univ. of Virginia, 402 Cabell Hall, Charlottesville, VA 22903; Title Tel # (919) 737-2475
Personnel: Editor-Joel Rini
Editorial Description: To serve the interests of scholars in romance linguistics.
General Info: Yr. Est. 1951, Semi-annually, Trim Size-8$\frac{1}{2}$ x 11, Mimeo press, 40 pages, ISSN: 0010-4167, No Color
Subscriptions: Indv. $6, Inst. $8, $3/copy
Circulation: Total-120

Computer Writer's Pulse Report
See: JOURNALISM

Copy Editor Newsletter
See: JOURNALISM

D.H. Lawrence Society of N. America Newsletter

Publishing Co: Buchtel College of Arts and Sciences, Department of English, 350 Blin Hall, Akron, OH 44325-0001 Tel # (216) 972-5194
Personnel: Editor-Eleanor Green
Editorial Description: For members of the D.H. Lawrence Society of North America giving news of interest to Lawrence readers & scholars.
General Info: Yr. Est. 1981, Semi-annually, Trim Size-8$\frac{1}{2}$ x 11, Letrpr. press, 8 pages, 2 Color, Coated
Subscriptions: Indv. $10
Acquistions: Publication Bought
Circulation: Total-250
Advertising: Accepts Inserts.
List Rental: Rents Lists
Printing Co: Ohio Northern Univ., Ada, OH 45810

Dear Reader
Consumer

Publishing Co: Square Books, 1126 Van Buren Ave, Oxford, MS 38655-3998
General Info: Bi-monthly, 6 pages

Decodings
Association

Publishing Co: Johns Hopkins University Press, 2715 N Charles St, Baltimore, MD 21218-4363
Tel # (410) 516-6964
Editorial Description: Newsletter of the Society for Literature and Science.
General Info: Tri-annually

Details Omitted for Clarity

Publishing Co: Rusty Sabre, 434 Daisy Ave, Imperial Beach, CA 91932-2006
Editorial Description: A relatively short, but quite enjoyable, collection of light commentary.
General Info: Trim Size-8.5 x 11, 8 pages
Subscriptions: Indv. $2

Dickens Quarterly
Association   CPM: $165

Publishing Co: Rutgers University, Suite 431, New Brunswick, NJ 08903; Title Tel # (908) 932-8029 Title Fax # (908) 932-1150
Personnel: Editor-David Paroissien, Circ. Mgr.-Bobbie Robinson, Production Mgr., Adv. Dir., Promotion Dir.-Mary Rosner
Editorial Description: Bibliographies, reviews, brief articles, and news of interest to Dickens scholars around the world.
General Info: (Formerly Dickens Studies Newsletter), Yr. Est. 1970, Quarterly, Trim Size-6 x 9, Sheetfed press, 70 pages, ISSN: 0742-5473, No Color
Subscriptions: Indv. $20, Can. $20, For. $25, $5/copy
Circulation: Total-544
Advertising: $90.
List Rental: Rents Lists
Printing Co: General Printing Co., 1700 S 5th St, Louisville, KY 40208-1795 Tel # (502) 637-6277

Doris Lessing Newsletter
Association

Publishing Co: Doris Lessing Society, English Dept., Michigan State Univ., East Lansing, MI 48824 Tel # (517) 351-8163
Personnel: Editor-Ruth Saxton, Circ. Mgr.-Katherine Fishburn
Editorial Description: Contains short essays; book reviews pertinent to the study of Lessing; biographical & bibliographical information; and news of MLA panels on Lessing.
General Info: Yr. Est. 1976, Semi-annually, Trim Size-8½ x 11, 16 pages, ISSN: 0882-486X, No Color
Subscriptions: Indv. $10, Inst. $12, Can. $10, For. $14, $6/copy
Circulation: Total-250

Ellen Glasgow Newsletter

Publishing Co: Ellen Glasgow Society, Randolph-Macon College, Ashland, VA 23005
Personnel: Editor-Edgar MacDonald
Editorial Description: Features articles about Ellen glasgow and her contemporaries on the Richmond literary scene.
General Info: Yr. Est. 1974, Semi-annually

English Resource, The

Publishing Co: Portside Publications, 19 Stanwick Avenue, Toronto, ON M4E 1Z2 Canada; Title Tel # (416) 690-8725
Personnel: Publisher, Editor-Paul Brandon, Production Mgr.-John Darling, Art Dir.-Mike Busija
Editorial Description: Edited for teachers of English ranging from junior high through community college and univesity level. Contains teaching tips and strategies as well as reviews of books and new materials.
General Info: Yr. Est. 1991, 8x/yr., Web press, 12 pages, Matte, Saddle-stitched
Subscriptions: Indv. $40, Inst. $45, Can. $40, For. $50, $5/copy
Circulation: Total-5,575
Advertising: Inquire for rates.

English Speaking E-SU
News   *Association*

Publishing Co: English-Speaking Union of the U.S., 16 E 69th St, New York, NY 10021-4906; Title Tel # (212) 879-6800 Title Fax # (212) 772-2886
Personnel: Publisher, Editor-Richard Hunnewell
Editorial Description: News for E-SU membership.
General Info: Yr. Est. 1920, Quarterly, Trim Size-8½ x 11, Web press, 8 pages, Color-cover
Advertising: Inquire for rates.
Printing Co: PhotoNews, 329 Broadway, Bethpage, NY 11714-3714 Tel # (516) 681-0440

Esperanto U.S.A.
Association

Publishing Co: Esperanto League for North America, PO Box 1129, El Cerrito, CA 94530-1129; Title Tel # (510) 653-0998 Title Fax # (510) 653-1468
Personnel: Editor-Donald Harlow
Editorial Description: Partly in English, partly in Esperanto, Esperanto USA keeps members of the Esperanto League for North America abreast of int'l developments in the language.
General Info: (Formerly ELNA Newsletter), Yr. Est. 1952, Semi-monthly, Trim Size-8½ x 11, 16 pages, ISSN: 0030-5065, No Color, Saddle-stitched
Subscriptions: Indv. $30, $30/copy
Circulation: (8% controlled), Total-1,200, Subscriptions-1,100, International-150
Advertising: Inquire for rates.
Printing Co: Leesburg Printing Co., 1100 North Blvd E, Leesburg, FL 34748-5350 Tel # (904) 787-3348, Fax # (904) 787-2210

Eudora Welty Newsletter
Association

Publishing Co: Univ. of Toledo English Dept., Dept. of English Lang & Lit, 2801 W. Bancroft St., Toledo, OH 43606; Title Tel # (419) 537-2318
Personnel: Editor-W.U. McDonald
Editorial Description: Newsletter/bibliographical journal for students and collectors of Eudora Welty's writings.
General Info: Yr. Est. 1977, Semi-annually, Trim Size-8½ x 11, Offset press, 16 pages, ISSN: 0146-7220, No Color, Other
Subscriptions: Indv. $2, Can. $2, For. $3, $2/copy
Circulation: Total-185

Evelyn Waugh
Newsletter & Studies   *Scholarly*   CPM: $476

Publishing Co: Sponsor-Evelyn Waugh Society, Nassau Community College, State Univ. of New York, Education Drive, English Dept., Garden City, NY 11530-5793 Tel # (516) 572-7186; Title Tel # (516) 572-7792
Personnel: Publisher, Editor-Paul Doyle, Adv. Dir.-Alfred Borello
Editorial Description: To encourage research and continue interest in the writings and life of British author Evelyn Waugh.
General Info: (Formerly Evelyn Waugh Newsletter), Yr. Est. 1967, Tri-annually, Trim Size-8½ x 11, Sheetfed press, 8 pages, ISSN: 0014-3693, Ind/Abs/Online: MLA, LCR, AHI, No Color
Subscriptions: Indv. $8, Inst. $8, Can. $8, For. $10, $4/copy
Acquistions: Publication Bought, Publication Sold
Circulation: (78% controlled), Total-210, International-46
Advertising: $100. Accepts Inserts.
Printing Co: Printing Mart of Long Island, 154 Mineola Blvd, Mineola, NY 11501-3937 Tel # (516) 746-3640

FLARR Foreign Language
Assoc. of the Red River   *Association*

Publishing Co: Foreign Language Assn. of the Red River, Dept. of Modern Languages, Fargo, ND 58105; Title Tel # (701) 237-8846
Personnel: Editor-Kathleen Meyer
Editorial Description: Information for foreign language teachers in high schools, colleges, universities.
General Info: Yr. Est. 1973, Semi-annually, 10 pages, No Color
Subscriptions: Indv. $5
Circulation: Total-200

Faulkner Newsletter
Consumer, Association

Publishing Co: Yoknapatawpha Press, Inc., PO Box 248, Oxford, MS 38655-0248; Title Tel # (601) 234-0909 Title Fax # (601) 234-0800
Personnel: Circ. Mgr.-Dean Wells, Editor, Production Mgr.-William Boozer, Adv. Dir.-Lawrence Wells
Editorial Description: Provides the scholarly community with news of critical work and seminars on the work of William Faulkner. Includes news of conferences, auctions, and forthcoming publications.
General Info: Yr. Est. 1981, Quarterly, Offset press, 4 pages, ISSN: 0733-6357, Matte, Saddle-stitched
Subscriptions: Indv. $13, Inst. $13, Can. $14, For. $15, $3/copy
Circulation: Total-500

Fence Painter
Association

Publishing Co: Mark Twain Boyhood Home Assocs., 208 Hill St, Hannibal, MO 63401-3316; Title Tel # (314) 221-9010
Personnel: Editor-Henry Sweets, III
Editorial Description: Membership newsletter Mark Twain related articles.
General Info: Quarterly, Sheetfed press, 4 pages, ISSN: 0891-4958, No Color, Coated
Subscriptions: Indv. $10
Printing Co: Klene Printing Co., 205 N Main St, Hannibal, MO 63401-3538 Tel # (314) 221-0035

First Draft
Business

Publishing Co: Lawrence Ragan Communications, Inc., 212 W.Superior St,Ste 200, Chicago, IL 60610-3533 Tel # (312) 335-0037 Fax # (312) 335-9583
Personnel: Publisher-Lawrence Ragan, Editor-Susan Kammeyer, Circ. Mgr.-Susan Weston, Mktg. Dir.-Melissa Eckhardt, Mktg. Dir.-Gretchen Eisenfelder
Editorial Description: Practical ideas for editors.
General Info: Monthly
Subscriptions: Indv. $139
Circulation: Total-1,400
List Rental: List Management Co.: Taybi Direct East, Inc., 13321 New Hampshire Ave., Ste. 202, Silver Spring, MD 20904-3450 Tel # (301) 680-3633, Fax # (301) 680-3635

Five Owls

Publishing Co: Five Owls, 2004 Sheridan Ave S, Minneapolis, MN 55405-2354; Title Tel # (612) 377-2004
Personnel: Editor-Susan Stan, Circ. Mgr.-Daniel Dailey
Editorial Description: A review of children's books for readers personally & professionally involved in children's literature.
General Info: Yr. Est. 1987, Bi-monthly, Trim Size-8½ x 11, Sheetfed press, 24 pages, ISSN: 0892-6735, 1% ads, 2 Color, Matte, Saddle-stitched
Subscriptions: Indv. $18, Can. $23, For. $32, $4/copy
Acquistions: Publication Bought, Publication Sold
Circulation: (76% controlled), Subscriptions-3,500
Advertising: $695.

Flash Market News
See: BUSINESS & INDUSTRY

The Freelancer
See: JOURNALISM

Goethe News & Notes
Scholarly, Association

Publishing Co: Goethe Society of N. America, German Dept., Univ of California, Irvine, Irvine, CA 92717-3150 Tel # (714) 824-6406 Fax # (714) 824-3248; Title Tel # (313) 747-0242 Title Fax # (313) 764-3521
Personnel: Editor-Frederick Amrine
Editorial Description: News of interest to the members of the Goethe Society of North America. Business & announcement of meetings.
General Info: Yr. Est. 1979, Semi-annually, Trim Size-8½ x 11, Mimeo press, 8 pages, No Color
Circulation: Total-250
List Rental: Rents Lists

Goob, The   *Consumer*

Publishing Co: Goob, The, P.O Box 148056, Toledo, OH 43614
Personnel: Editor-Kait Egelston
Editorial Description: Literary newsletter that offers a wide variety of writings from people of all ages, genders, and races.
Subscriptions: $1/copy

Green Dragon   *Association*

Publishing Co: Tolkien Society of America, RFD 1, Box 63, Center Harbour, NH 03226-9801; Title Tel # (603) 253-6207
Personnel: Editor-Edmund Meskys
Editorial Description: Newsletter for J.R.R. Tolkien Society.
General Info: Yr. Est. 1965, Trim Size-8½ x 14, Sheetfed press, No Color
Subscriptions: $2/copy
Circulation: Total-1,000

Gypsy Lore Society Newsletter
See: ANTHROPOLOGY

Haiku Canada Newsletter
See: POETRY & CREATIVE WRITING

Hungarian Studies Newsletter
See: ETHNIC

IAPL Newsletter
See: PHILOSOPHY

IEEE Professional Communication Society Newsletter   *Association*   CPM: $165

Publishing Co: Institute of Electrical & Electronics Engineers, Inc., 445 Hoes Lane, PO Box 1331, Piscataway, NJ 08855-1331 Tel # (908) 562-3992 Fax # (908) 981-9334 Parent Co.-Institute of Electrical & Electronics Engineers, New York
Personnel: Editor-Bruce Brocka, Production Ed.-Ann Skrupski, Adv. Mgr.-Suean Schneidermen
Editorial Description: Stresses the global nature of communications technology.
General Info: Trim Size-8½ x 11, 16 pages, ISSN: 0161-5718, Matte, Saddle-stitched
Circulation: Total-2,413
Advertising: $400.
List Rental: Rents Lists

Iggeret   *Association*

Publishing Co: Natl. Assn. of Professors of Hebrew, 1220 Linden Dr, Madison, WI 53706-1525; Title Tel # (608) 262-2968
Personnel: Editor-Zev Garber, Circ. Mgr., Promotion Dir.-Gilead Morahg
General Info: Yr. Est. 1950, Semi-annually, 8 pages, Coated
Circulation: Total-400

Illinois TESOL/BE Newsletter   *Association*

Publishing Co: Illinois State Univ., 6123 English Language Inst., Normal, IL 61790-0001; Title Tel # (312) 989-3520
Personnel: Editor-Kasia Stadnik, Adv. Dir.-Marsha Santelli
Editorial Description: Source of professional information for the organizations members.
General Info: Yr. Est. 1972, Quarterly, Trim Size-8½ x 11, Offset press, 24 pages, 3% ads, No Color, Newsprint, Saddle-stitched
Circulation: (100% controlled), Total-900
Advertising: Inquire for rates. Accepts Inserts.
Printing Co: Copymat, 503 S. Main, Normal, IL 61761 Tel # (309) 452-1392

Illinois Writers Monthly

Publishing Co: Illinois Writers, Inc., ISU English Department, Normal, IL 61701-6901 Tel # (309) 438-7705; Title Tel # (217) 429-0117
Personnel: Editor-Barbara Lau
Editorial Description: Covers membership news, submissions, writing competitions, conferences.
General Info: Bi-monthly
Subscriptions: Indv. $15

Information/the WAFLT Bulletin   *Association*

Publishing Co: Sponsor-Madison & Wisconsin Assoc. of Foreign Language Teachers, Univ. Wisconsin-Madison, New Student Services, 905 University Ave., Ste.1, Madison, WI 53715-1005; Title Tel # (608) 262-6439
Personnel: Editor, Circ. Mgr.-Lewis Bosworth
Editorial Description: For foreign lang. teachers in Wisconsin: conference proceedings articles; news of AAT groups; Univ. course descriptions & policies; regional & national news on FLs/International studies.
General Info: (Formerly Wisconsin Assn. of Modern Foreign Language Teachers Bulletin), Yr. Est. 1950, Trim Size-8½ x 11, Offset press, 50 pages, 2 Color
Circulation: (100% controlled), Total-2,500
Advertising: Inquire for rates.

Jack London Newsletter

Publishing Co: Skysail, Inc., 5435 S. Ellis Avenue, Chicago, IL 60615
General Info: ISSN: 0021-3837

James Dickey Newsletter
See: LITERARY REVIEWS

James Fenimore Cooper Society Newsletter   *Scholarly, Association*

Publishing Co: James Fenimore Cooper Society, 8 Lake Street, Cooperstown, NY 13326; Title Tel # (607) 547-2118
Personnel: Editor, Circ. Mgr.-Hugh MacDougall
Editorial Description: Articles & book reviews of interest to James Fenimore Cooper Society members.
General Info: Yr. Est. 1990, Tri-annually, Trim Size-8½ x 11, 6 pages, ISSN: 1073-0907, No Color, Matte, Saddle-stitched
Subscriptions: Inst. $10, Can. $10, For. $10, $2/copy
Advertising: Inquire for rates.

Joseph Conrad Today

Publishing Co: Joseph Conrad Society of America, C/O Prof. David R. Smith, California Inst. Of Techn, Pasadena, CA 91125-0001; Title Tel # (818) 356-3605
General Info: Yr. Est. 1975, ISSN: 0162-413X
Subscriptions: Inst. $7
Circulation: Total-300

Just Books   *Consumer*

Publishing Co: Just Books, 19 E Putnam Ave, Greenwich, CT 06830-5443 Tel # (203) 869-5023
General Info: Monthly

Kewpiesta Kourier   *Association*

Publishing Co: International Rose O'Neill Club, c/o L. Holman, 309 Walnut Lane, Branson, MO 65616; Title Tel # (417) 334-3273
Personnel: Editor-Sally Crotser, Art Dir.-Lois Holman
Editorial Description: News of club activities & the works & life of Rose O'Neill, including creation of the world famous Kewpie Doll.
General Info: Yr. Est. 1968, Quarterly, 8 pages, No Color
Subscriptions: Indv. $7, $1/copy
Circulation: Total-1,200

LSA Bulletin   *Association*   CPM: $53

Publishing Co: Linguistic Society of America, 1325 18th St. NW, Ste 211, Washington, DC 20036-6505 Fax # (202) 835-1717; Title Tel # (202) 835-1714
Editorial Description: Programs of LSA meetings, news, announcements of forthcoming linguistics conferences. Subscription includes Language, journal of the LSA.
General Info: Yr. Est. 1971, Quarterly, Trim Size-6¾ x 10, Offset press, 16 pages, ISSN: 0023-6365, No Color, Newsprint, Saddle-stitched
Subscriptions: Indv. $55, Inst. $75, Can. $65, For. $65
Circulation: Total-6,500
Advertising: $350.
List Rental: Actives: 6,500, $175/M
Printing Co: Good Printers, 213 Dry River Rd, Bridgewater, VA 22812-1242 Tel # (703) 828-4663

La Fransasque

Publishing Co: Assn. Jeunesse Fransaskoise, Inc., 440 2e Ave. Nord, #203, Saskatoon, SK S7K 2C3 Canada; Title Tel # (306) 653-7447 Title Fax # (306) 653-3987
Editorial Description: Organizes activities in French communities to promote French language and culture in Saskatchewan.
General Info: Yr. Est. 1982, 10x/yr., Letrpr. press, 13 pages, 3% ads, 2 Color, Matte, Saddle-stitched
Circulation: Total-1,400
Printing Co: Boss Graphics, 1131 Main St., Saskatoon, SK S7H 0K8 Canada

La Riverego   *Association*

Publishing Co: Societe Quebecoise d'Esperanto, 6358-A rue de Bordeaux, Montreal, PQ H2G 2R8 Canada; Title Tel # (514) 272-0151 Title Fax # (514) 495-8442
Personnel: Editor-Sylvain Auclair
Editorial Description: Activities of the Societe Quebecoise d'Esperanto. Language problems, poems, various articles. Bilingual in Esperanto and French.
General Info: Yr. Est. 1985, Quarterly, Trim Size-5½ x 8½, 16 pages, ISSN: 0830-9574, Color-cover
Subscriptions: Can. $10, $3/copy
Circulation: Total-220
Advertising: Inquire for rates.

Language Maintenance

Publishing Co: Patricia Maynard, 2745 Winnetka Ave N # 121, New Hope, MN 55427-2830; Title Tel # (612) 533-2427
Personnel: Publisher, Editor-Patricia Maynard
Editorial Description: Deals with usage and misuse of english language and decline of same; literacy; etymology; propaganda.
General Info: Yr. Est. 1990, Bi-monthly, 10 pages, No Color
Subscriptions: Indv. $16, Inst. $16, Can. $16, For. $16, $4/copy
Circulation: Total-110
Printing Co: Atlas Instant Printing, 4120 Lakeland Ave N, Robbinsdale, MN 55422-1832

Language Matters   *Business*

Publishing Co: Translation Co. of America, Inc., 10 W 37th St, New York, NY 10018-7491; Title Tel # (212) 563-7054 Title Fax # (212) 695-2385
Personnel: Editor-Dick Mazziotti
Editorial Description: Translation and language oddities and information.
General Info: Quarterly, Trim Size-8½ x 11, Desktop press, 8 pages, Color, Matte, Saddle-stitched
Subscriptions: Free
Circulation: Total-5,000

Linguistics Research
Quarterly Report

Publishing Co: Linguistics Research Center, Univ. of Texas, P.O. Box 74247, Austin, TX 78713; Title Tel # (512) 471-4566
Personnel: Editor-Mayrose Coyle
General Info: (Formerly LRC News), Quarterly

Literary Sketches
See: LITERARY REVIEWS

MLA Newsletter *Association*

Publishing Co: Modern Language Association of America, 10 Astor Pl Fl 5, New York, NY 10003-6935; Title Tel # (212) 475-9500 Title Fax # (212) 477-9863
Personnel: Editor-Phyllis Franklin, Circ. Mgr.-Pat Hanley, Production Mgr.-Judith Altreuter, Promotion Dir.-David Smith
Editorial Description: For scholars & teachers of literatures & languages.
General Info: Yr. Est. 1969, Quarterly, Trim Size-8½ x 11, Sheetfed press, 24 pages, ISSN: 0160-5720, No Color, Recycled, Saddle-stitched
Subscriptions: Indv. $6, Inst. $6, Free With Membership
Circulation: Total-33,250
Advertising: Inquire for rates.
List Rental: Actives: $90/M
Printing Co: Kent Associates, 480 Canal St., New York, NY 10013 Tel # (212) 226-8080

Macedonia, Curiosum Mundi
See: CULTURE & HUMANITIES

Manitoba Writers' Guild
Newsletter *Association*

Publishing Co: Manitoba Writers' Guild, 100 Arthur St., Rm. 206, Winnipeg, MB R38 1H3 Canada; Title Tel # (204) 943-9066
Personnel: Editor-Helen Norrie
General Info: Yr. Est. 1981, Monthly
Circulation: Total-500
Advertising: Inquire for rates.

Mari Sandoz Heritage

Publishing Co: Mari Sandoz Heritage Society, c/o Chadron State College, Chadron, NE 69337; Title Tel # (308) 432-6276 Title Fax # (308) 432-3561
General Info: Semi-annually
Subscriptions: Indv. $15, Free With Membership
Circulation: Total-300

Milton Society of America,
Bulletin *Association*

Publishing Co: Milton Society Of America, Ohio University, 378 Ellis Hall, Athens, OH 45701
General Info: Annually

Minnesota Literature *Association* CPM: $250

Publishing Co: Minnesota Literature, 1 Nord Circle Rd, Saint Paul, MN 55127-6513; Title Tel # (612) 483-3904
Personnel: Editor-Mary Bround Smith
Editorial Description: Presents opportunities, grant and award information, events calendar and Minnesota publication news.
General Info: Monthly, Trim Size-8½ x 11, Offset press, 8 pages, 15% ads, No Color, Matte
Subscriptions: Indv. $10, $1/copy
Circulation: Total-800
Advertising: $200. Accepts Inserts.
Printing Co: Copy-Right, 121 E. 7th Pl., St. Paul, MN 55101 Tel # (612) 228-0130

Modern Greek Studies Association Bulletin
See: HISTORY

Moody Street Irregulars:
A Jack Kerouac
Newsletter *Consumer*

Publishing Co: Moody Street Irregulars, PO Box 157, Clarence Center, NY 14032-0157
Personnel: Editor-Joy Walsh, Circ. Mgr., Adv. Dir.-E. Murray, Production Mgr., Art Dir.-Karen Gajewski
Editorial Description: Focuses on the works of Jack Kerouac and others of the Beat Generation.
General Info: Yr. Est. 1978, Irregular, ISSN: 0196-2604, Ind/Abs/Online: MLA
Subscriptions: Indv. $10, Inst. $15, $3/copy
Circulation: Total-1,000
List Rental: Rents Lists

NAOS *Consumer*

Publishing Co: University of Pittsburgh-Dept. Hispanic Languages, 1309 Cathedral Of Learning, Pittsburgh, PA 15260-6299
Personnel: Publisher-Juan Adolfo Vazquez
Editorial Description: Linguistic studies of sacred topics.
General Info: Quarterly, Trim Size-8½ x 11, 54 pages, 2 Color, Matte, Saddle-stitched
Subscriptions: Indv. $20

Nestor

Publishing Co: Univ. of Cincinnati., Dept. of Classics, Cincinnati, OH 45221-0226; Title Tel # (513) 556-2660
Personnel: Editor-Michael Fotiadis
Editorial Description: Bibliography of pre-Classical archaeology, linguistics, and other relevant fields, in Greece, the Aegean, and the eastern Mediterranean and southeast Europe.
General Info: Yr. Est. 1953, 9x/yr., Trim Size-8½ x 11, 10 pages, ISSN: 0228-2812, No Color
Subscriptions: Indv. $8, Inst. $13, For. $10
Circulation: Total-800
Advertising: Accepts Inserts.

New England Classical
Newsletter & Journal *Association*

Publishing Co: Fairfield University, Greek and Roman Studies, c/o Vincent Rosivach, Fairfield, CT 06430; Title Tel # (203) 254-4000 Title Fax # (203) 254-4119
Personnel: Publisher, Editor-Gilbert Lawall
Editorial Description: News & items of interest for Classics teachers & professors and now also includes substantive articles & book reviews.
General Info: (Formerly Bay State Classical Newsletter), Yr. Est. 1972, Quarterly, Trim Size-8½ x 11, Offset press, 48 pages, ISSN: 0739-1188, No Color, Saddle-stitched
Subscriptions: Indv. $15
Circulation: Total-700

Newsletter *Association* CPM: $136

Publishing Co: American Philological Assn., Holy Cross College, Dept. of Classics, Worcester, MA 01610-2391 Fax # (508) 793-3428; Title Tel # (508) 793-2203 Title Fax # (508) 793-3030
Personnel: Editor-William Ziobro
Editorial Description: Bi-monthly newsletter for learned society of classical studies.
General Info: Yr. Est. 1869, Bi-monthly, 24 pages, ISSN: 0569-6941, 1% ads
Subscriptions: Free With Membership
Circulation: Total-3,300
Advertising: $450.
List Rental: Actives: $90/M

Newsletter of the
American Dialect
Society *Association*

Publishing Co: American Dialect Society, MacMurray Coll. English Dept., Jacksonville, IL 62650; Title Tel # (217) 479-7049 Title Fax # (217) 245-5214
Personnel: Publisher-Allan Metcalf, Editor-Dr. Allan Metcalf
Editorial Description: Educators and others interested in the English language in North America.
General Info: Yr. Est. 1969, Trim Size-7½ x 8½, Sheetfed press, 20 pages, ISSN: 0002-8193, No Color, Newsprint
Subscriptions: Indv. $25, $3/copy
Circulation: Total-900
Advertising: Inquire for rates.
Printing Co: Woodward Printing Co., 607 S Main St, Jacksonville, IL 62650-2907 Tel # (217) 245-4414

Newsletter of the
Cervantes Society *Association*

Publishing Co: Cervantes Society of America, Dept. of Modern Languages, Denison University, Granville, OH 43023; Title Tel # (614) 587-6228 Title Fax # (614) 587-6417
Personnel: Editor-William H. Clamurro
Editorial Description: Quarterly activities in Cervantine studies.
General Info: Yr. Est. 1980, Quarterly, Trim Size-8½ x 11, 4 pages
Subscriptions: Free With Membership
Circulation: Total-300
Advertising: Accepts Inserts.

Nickleby's Bookstore *Consumer*

Publishing Co: Nickelby's Bookstore, 1425 Grandview Ave, Columbus, OH 43212-2853 Tel # (614) 488-2665
General Info: Monthly, Trim Size-8 x 11, 4 pages, 2 Color
Circulation: Total-19,000

Nook News Market Bulletin
See: POETRY & CREATIVE WRITING

Old English Newsletter *Association*

Publishing Co: Center for Medieval and Early Renaissance Studies, SUNY Binghamton, Box 6000, Binghamton, NY 13902-6000; Title Tel # (607) 777-2130 Title Fax # (607) 777-4000
Personnel: Publisher, Editor, Circ. Mgr.-Paul Szarmach
Editorial Description: Short items on old English language & literature & news of general interest, provide interdisciplinary coverage of Anglo-Saxon England as well.
General Info: Yr. Est. 1966, Quarterly, Trim Size-8½ x 11, Web press, 60 pages, ISSN: 0030-1973, Ind/Abs/Online: ISI, No Color, Saddle-stitched
Subscriptions: Indv. $8, Inst. $15, $5/copy
Circulation: Total-900
Advertising: Accepts Inserts.
List Rental: Rents Lists
Printing Co: SUNY-Binghamton Campus Print Shop, Vestal Pkwy East, Admin. Bldg., Binghamton, NY 13902-6000 Tel # (607) 777-2207

Op. Cit. *Consumer*

Publishing Co: Waterstone's, 26 Exeter St, Boston, MA 02116-2711 Tel # (617) 859-7300
Personnel: Editor-Jay Leutze, Editor-Bert Wright
Editorial Description: Is written in literary journal style.
General Info: Quarterly

Oral History of the American Left

Publishing Co: New York Univ. Elmer Holmes Bobst Library, 70 Washington Sq S, New York, NY 10012-1019; Title Tel # (219) 998-2630
Personnel: Editor-Paul Buhle
General Info: Yr. Est. 1981

Oxford Modern Languages & Literature   *Association*

Publishing Co: Oxford Publishing, Inc., 307 Jackson Ave W, Oxford, MS 38655-2154 Tel # (601) 236-5510
Personnel: Editor-A. Raitt
Editorial Description: Monographs on language and literature based on theses submitted for graduate degrees at Oxford University.
General Info: Annually, Looseleaf

PEN Newsletter   *Association*

Publishing Co: P.E.N. American Center, 568 Broadway Rm 401, New York, NY 10012-3225; Title Tel # (212) 334-1660 Title Fax # (212) 334-2181
Personnel: Editor-Lucy Komisar, Mng. Editor-John Morrone
Editorial Description: Interviews & articles on American and International PEN activities relating to freedom of expression and literary & professional issues.
General Info: Yr. Est. 1963, Quarterly, Trim Size-8½ x 11, Offset press, 24 pages, No Color
Subscriptions: Indv. $18, $2/copy
Circulation: Total-3,500

Pennsylvania Classical Association Bulletin

Publishing Co: Franklin & Marshall College, PO Box 3003, Lancaster, PA 17604-3003 Tel # (717) 291-3911
Personnel: Editor-J. Farber
General Info: Yr. Est. 1942, Semi-annually
Subscriptions: Indv. $6
Circulation: Total-500

Pennsylvania State Modern Languages Association Bulletin

Publishing Co: Temple University, Anderson Hall #921, Philadelphia, PA 19122 Tel # (215) 204-8505
General Info: Semi-annually
Subscriptions: Indv. $2
Circulation: Total-1,200

Permanent International Altaistic Conference Newsletter   *Association*

Publishing Co: Central Eurasian Studies, Indiana Univ., Bloomington, IN 47405; Title Tel # (812) 855-0959 Title Fax # (812) 855-7500
Personnel: Publisher, Editor, Adv. Dir.-Denis Sinor
Editorial Description: To keep Altaic scholars abreast of current research projects and to provide information about publications, pertinent conferences, and the activities of other Altaic scholars.
General Info: Yr. Est. 1966, Irregular, Trim Size-8½ x 11, Offset press, 40 pages, No Color
Subscriptions: Free With Membership
Circulation: Total-650

Piegan Storyteller   *Association*

Publishing Co: James Willard Schultz Society, 135 Wildwood Dr, New Bern, NC 28562-9560; Title Tel # (919) 637-5985
Personnel: Publisher-Dean Combs, Editor, Circ. Mgr.-David Andrews
Editorial Description: James Willard Schultz, his works and his times.
General Info: Yr. Est. 1976, Quarterly, Trim Size-8½ x 11, Offset press, 20 pages, No Color
Subscriptions: Indv. $8, $1/copy
Circulation: Total-300
Advertising: Inquire for rates.

Political Speaker
See: MEDIA & COMMUNICATIONS

Poppin' Zits!
See: SOCIOLOGY

Pundit, The
See: HUMOR & SATIRE

Qualelibet   *Association*

Publishing Co: International Society of Hildegard von Bingen Studies, Western Michigan Univ., Kalamazoo, MI 49008-3899; Title Tel # (616) 387-5415
Personnel: Editor-Barbara Jelen, Publisher, Circ. Mgr.-Audrey Davidson, Circ. Mgr.-Bruce Hozeski
Editorial Description: Contains information on presentations, research, publications, etc. relating to Hildegard Von Bingen, a 12th Century German mystic.
General Info: Yr. Est. 1985, Semi-annually, Trim Size-8½ x 11, Mimeo press, 7 pages, No Color, Newsprint
Subscriptions: Indv. $8
Circulation: Total-300

R.J. Julia Booksellers   *Consumer*

Publishing Co: R.J. Julia, 768 Boston Post Rd, Madison, CT 06443-3047 Tel # (203) 245-3959
General Info: Quarterly, 8 pages, 2 Color

RPCV Writers & Readers   *Consumer, Association*   CPM: $200

Publishing Co: RPCV Writers & Readers, 4 Lodge Pole Rd, Pittsford, NY 14534-4550; Title Tel # (716) 223-1155 Title Fax # (716) 223-1158
Personnel: Publisher-John Coyne, Editor, Production Mgr.-Marian Haley Bell, Circ. Mgr., Adv. Dir.-Marian Haley Bell
Editorial Description: A newsletter for returned Peace Corps volunteers who are writers (published & unpublished) who are interested in networking. Contains interviews, reviews, books recently published written by RPCVs, information on friendly agents & other opportunities forRPCVs to have their work published.
General Info: (Formerly RPCV Writers), Yr. Est. 1989, Bi-monthly, Trim Size-8½ x 11, Offset press, 16 pages, ISSN: 1062-4694, No Color, Matte, Saddle-stitched
Subscriptions: Indv. $12, Can. $19, For. $19, $3/copy
Circulation: Total-500
Advertising: $100.
Printing Co: Leesburg Printing Co., 1100 North Blvd E, Leesburg, FL 34748-5350 Tel # (904) 787-3348, Fax # (904) 787-2210

Reader's Review   *Consumer*

Publishing Co: Wellington's Books, 120 Kilmayne Dr, Cary, NC 27511-4465 Tel # (919) 467-0815
General Info: Yr. Est. 1986, Tri-annually, 8 pages

Records of Early English Drama Newsletter   *Association*

Publishing Co: McMaster Univ., 1280 Main St., W., Hamilton, ON L8S 4L8 Canada; Title Tel # (905) 525-9140 Title Fax # (905) 577-6930
Personnel: Editor-Helen Ostovich
Editorial Description: English drama and minstrelry from its beginnings to 1642.
General Info: Yr. Est. 1976, Semi-annually, Trim Size-5½ x 8, 24 pages, 2 Color, Matte, Saddle-stitched
Subscriptions: Indv. $8, Inst. $10, Can. $10, For. $10, $5/copy
Acquistions: Publication Bought, Publication Sold
Circulation: Total-600

Right of Aesthetic Realism to Be Known, The
See: GENERAL INTEREST

Robinson Jeffers Newsletter   *Consumer*

Publishing Co: Occidental College, 1600 Campus Rd, Los Angeles, CA 90041-3376 Tel # (213) 259-2500; Title Tel # (310) 985-4235
Personnel: Editor-Dr. Robert Brophy, Publisher, Circ. Mgr.-Tyrus Harmsen
Editorial Description: Notes on current publications, reviews, and short critical articles concerning Robinson Jeffers.
General Info: Yr. Est. 1962, Quarterly, Trim Size-8½ x 11, Mimeo press, 25 pages, ISSN: 0300-7936
Subscriptions: Indv. $10, $1/copy
Circulation: Total-200

SHARP News
See: BOOKS & BOOK TRADE

Sanskrit Today   *Consumer*

Publishing Co: American Sanskrit Institute, 73 Four Corners Rd., Warwick, NY 10990 Tel # (914) 986-8652 Fax # (914) 987-7097
Editorial Description: Information about sanskrit and sanskrit classes.
General Info: Quarterly

Saul Bellow Society Newsletter   *Consumer, Association*

Publishing Co: Saul Bellow Society, 6533 Post Oak Dr, West Bloomfield, MI 48322-3831
Editorial Description: Information on and from the Saul Bellow Society.
General Info: Semi-annually
Subscriptions: Indv. $16

Shakespeare Newsletter   *Association*   CPM: $210

Publishing Co: Iona College, Department of English, New Rochelle, NY 10801-1890; Title Tel # (914) 633-2061
Personnel: Co-Editor-John Mahon, Co-Editor-Thomas Pendleton
Editorial Description: Survey and abstracts of scholarly & popular Shakespeare, plus original articles, news, reviews, trends, festivals, teaching, etc.
General Info: Yr. Est. 1951, Quarterly, Trim Size-8½ x 11, Sheetfed press, 12 pages, ISSN: 0037-3214, Ind/Abs/Online: Shakespeare Q.Lit. Criticism Register, No Color, Newsprint, Saddle-stitched
Subscriptions: Indv. $12, Inst. $12, For. $14, $3/copy
Circulation: Total-2,000
Advertising: $420. Accepts Inserts.
List Rental: Actives: $175/M

Sherlockin Tidbits   *Consumer*

Publishing Co: Rejoyce Ink, 42 Melrose Pl, Montclair, NJ 07042-2028
Personnel: Publisher, Editor, Circ. Mgr.-Arnold Korotkin
Editorial Description: Information articles, reviews, graphics, etc. Pertaining to Sherlock Holmes.
General Info: Yr. Est. 1987, Quarterly, Trim Size-8½ x 11, ISSN: 1040-4937, Looseleaf
Subscriptions: Indv. $8, $2/copy
Circulation: (100% controlled), Total-221, Readership-221
Advertising: Inquire for rates.

Sidney Newsletter

Publishing Co: Univ. of Guelph English Dept., Publications, Guelph, ON N1G 2W1 Canada; Title Tel # (519) 824-4120
Personnel: Editor-Gerald Rubin
Editorial Description: Features articles relating to the life and work of Sir Philip Sidney.
General Info: Yr. Est. 1980, Semi-annually

Sigma Tau Delta Newsletter *Association*

Publishing Co: Sigma Tau Delta, Northern IL Univ., English Dep, DeKalb, IL 60115; Title Tel # (815) 753-1612
Personnel: Publisher, Editor-William Johnson
Editorial Description: Contains news of Sigma Tau Delta, Intl. English Honor Society.
General Info: Yr. Est. 1970, Semi-annually, Trim Size-8½ x 11, Letrpr. press, 12 pages, No Color, Newsprint
Subscriptions: Indv. $5
Circulation: (100% controlled), Total-5,500

Six Nations, One Soul
See: INTERNATIONAL AFFAIRS

Society for German-American Studies Newsletter *Consumer, Association*

Publishing Co: Society for German American Studies, 500 Belmont Rd, Bettendorf, IA 52722-5649; Title Tel # (319) 359-7531
Personnel: Editor-La Vern Rippley
Editorial Description: Covers society events and news.
General Info: Yr. Est. 1979, Quarterly, Trim Size-8½ x 11, 8 pages
Subscriptions: Indv. $20
Circulation: Total-1,000
Printing Co: Art Design, 4890 S Robert Trl, Eagan, MN 55123-2123 Tel # (612) 423-5115

Society for the Study of Midwestern Literature Newsletter

Publishing Co: Society for the Study of Midwestern Literature, Michigan State University, Ernst Bessey Hall, East Lansing, MI 48824 Tel # (517) 353-4370
General Info: Yr. Est. 1971
Circulation: Total-400
Advertising: Inquire for rates.

Society for the Study of Southern Literature Newsletter

Publishing Co: Society for the Study of Southern Literature, Box 50, New Orleans, LA 70118; Title Tel # (504) 865-2476
Personnel: Editor-Susan Snell
General Info: Yr. Est. 1968, Semi-annually, 30 pages, ISSN: 0197-8071
Subscriptions: Indv. $5, Inst. $5, For. $5
Circulation: Total-450
List Rental: Rents Lists

Speakers' Idea File *Business*

Publishing Co: Lawrence Ragan Communications, Inc., 212 W.Superior St,Ste 200, Chicago, IL 60610-3533 Tel # (312) 335-0037 Fax # (312) 335-9583
Personnel: Publisher-Lawrence Ragan, Editor-Susan Kammeyer, Circ. Mgr.-Susan Weston, Art Dir.-Sharon Giankos, Mktg. Dir.-Melissa Eckhardt, Mktg. Dir.-Gretchen Eisenfelder
Editorial Description: Information including timely quotes, anecdotes, humor and statistics for presentation givers.
General Info: Monthly
Subscriptions: Indv. $119
List Rental: List Management Co.: Taybi Direct East, Inc., 13321 New Hampshire Ave., Ste. 202, Silver Spring, MD 20904-3450 Tel # (301) 680-3633, Fax # (301) 680-3635

Spenser Newsletter
See: POETRY & CREATIVE WRITING

Steinbeck Newsletter, The *Association*

Publishing Co: Steinbeck Research Center, San Jose State Univ., San Jose, CA 95192-0001; Title Tel # (408) 924-4588
Personnel: Editor-Susan Shillinglaw, Art Dir.-Craig Kochersberger
Editorial Description: Contains articles about Steinbeck, reviews, notes, and announcements. Also articles on related topics and photographs.
General Info: Yr. Est. 1988, Semi-annually, Trim Size-8½ x 11, Sheetfed press, 20 pages, Matte
Subscriptions: Indv. $20, $10/copy
Circulation: Total-1,000
Advertising: Accepts Inserts.
Printing Co: Carpenter Printing, 2159 Bering Dr, San Jose, CA 95131-2014

Story Time Stories That Rhyme
See: CHILDREN

TQS News *Consumer*

Publishing Co: Tonatiuh-Quinto Sol Intl., Inc., PO Box 9275, Berkeley, CA 94709-0275; Title Tel # (510) 655-8036 Title Fax # (510) 601-6938
Personnel: Publisher, Editor-Octavio Romano
Editorial Description: A contemporary newsletter of eclectic Chicano thought.
General Info: (Formerly Grito del Sol), Yr. Est. 1967, Bi-monthly, Trim Size-8½ x 11, 12 pages, ISSN: 1045-8875, No Color
Subscriptions: Indv. $16, Inst. $16, Can. $16, For. $17, $3/copy
Printing Co: PIP, 943 Marina Village Pky, Alameda, CA 94501-1048 Tel # (415) 769-6133

Teaching Language Through Literature, Newsletter

Publishing Co: Fordham Univ., Box 707, 501 Philosophy Hall, Bronx, NY 10458-0702; Title Tel # (212) 579-2387
Personnel: Editor-Jeanette Beer
Editorial Description: Contains articles, classroom programs, language laboratory (audio-visual) programs, as well as reviews of textbooks & literary records in different languages.
General Info: Yr. Est. 1961, Semi-annually, Trim Size-7½ x 10, 50 pages, ISSN: 0362-2746
Subscriptions: Indv. $6, Inst. $7, $4/copy
Circulation: Total-1,000

Texas Teller Quarterly Newsletter *Association*

Publishing Co: Texas Storytellers Association, PO Box 2806, Denton, TX 76202-2806; Title Tel # (817) 387-8336
Personnel: Exec. Ed.-Finley Stewart, Adv. Dir.-Karen Morgan
Editorial Description: Articles and tips on how to tell and collect stories and related news of interest.
General Info: Yr. Est. 1986, Bi-monthly, Trim Size-8½ x 11, Offset press, 8 pages, ISSN: 0892-5186, 30% ads, 2 Color, Matte, Saddle-stitched
Subscriptions: Indv. $25, $2/copy
Advertising: $200.
List Rental: Actives: 420, $100/M, Expires: 160

Thackeray Newsletter *Consumer, Association*

Publishing Co: Mississippi State University, English Dept., Mississippi State, MS 39762; Title Tel # (601) 325-3644
Personnel: Circ. Mgr.-P.L. Shillingsburg
Editorial Description: Scholarship news, reviews, notes relating to William M. Thackeray.
General Info: Yr. Est. 1974, Semi-annually, Trim Size-5¼ x 8½, 8 pages, Saddle-stitched
Subscriptions: Indv. $3, $2/copy

Thoreau Research Newsletter

Publishing Co: Thoreau Society, Inc., c/o Bradley Dean, Rte. 2, Box 36, Ayden, NC 28513-9502; Title Tel # (919) 355-0620 Title Fax # (919) 355-5280
Personnel: Publisher, Editor-Bradley Dean
Editorial Description: Research on the life and writings of Thoreau.
General Info: Yr. Est. 1990, Quarterly, Trim Size-8½ x 11, Desktop press, 8 pages, ISSN: 1055-7326, No Color, Saddle-stitched
Subscriptions: Indv. $5, $2/copy

Thoreau Society Bulletin *Association*

Publishing Co: Thoreau Society, Inc., c/o Bradley Dean, Rte. 2, Box 36, Ayden, NC 28513-9502; Title Tel # (919) 355-0620 Title Fax # (919) 355-5280
Personnel: Publisher, Editor-Bradley Dean
Editorial Description: Devoted to the life, writings and fame of Henry David Thoreau.
General Info: Yr. Est. 1941, Quarterly, Trim Size-8½ x 11, Web press, 8 pages, ISSN: 0040-6406, No Color, Saddle-stitched
Subscriptions: Indv. $20
Circulation: Total-2,000
Advertising: Accepts Inserts.

Translation Series
See: INTERNATIONAL AFFAIRS

Up All Night *Consumer*

Publishing Co: Books & Co., 350a E Stroop Rd, Dayton, OH 45429-2828 Tel # (513) 298-6540
Personnel: Editor-Tim Wills, Design Director-Joann Jozwiak
General Info: Bi-monthly, Trim Size-8½ x 11, 8 pages
Circulation: Total-43,000

Virginia Woolf Miscellany

Publishing Co: Sponsor-Stanford Univ., Sonoma State Univ. English Dept., 1801 E Cotati Ave, Rohnert Park, CA 94928-3613; Title Tel # (707) 664-2140 Title Fax # (707) 664-2505
Personnel: Editor-J.J. Wilson, Circ. Mgr., Promotion Dir.-Karen Petersen
Editorial Description: To encourage new directions & network in Woolf studies.
General Info: Yr. Est. 1973, Semi-annually, Trim Size-9 x 11, Offset press, 6 pages, No Color, Recycled
Subscriptions: Free With Membership
Circulation: Total-1,300
List Rental: Actives: $120/M
Printing Co: Sonoma State Univ., 1801 E Cotati Ave, Rohnert Park, CA 94928-3609 Tel # (707) 664-2880

Vroman's   *Consumer*

Publishing Co: Vroman's Bookstore, 695 E Colorado Blvd, Pasadena, CA 91101-2116
Tel # (818) 449-5320
Personnel: Adv. Dir.-Mickey Touchette
General Info: Bi-monthly
Circulation: Total-50,000
Advertising: Inquire for rates.

West Word   *Association, Business*

Publishing Co: Writers Guild of Alberta, 10523 100th Ave., Edmonton, AB T5J OA8 Canada;
Title Tel # (403) 426-5892
Personnel: Editor-Jena Bamsey
General Info: (Formerly Writers Guild of Alberta), Yr. Est. 1980, Bi-monthly, 10 pages, No Color
Subscriptions: Indv. $55, Inst. $55, $2/copy
Circulation: Total-1,000
Advertising: Inquire for rates. Accepts Inserts.
Printing Co: Heron Printing, 8651 63rd Ave., Edmonton, AB T6E 0E8 Canada Tel # (403) 465-3936

What's New About London, Jack?   *Consumer, Scholarly*

Publishing Co: London Northwest, 929 S Bay Rd NE, Olympia, WA 98506-4808;
Title Tel # (360) 352-8622
Personnel: Publisher, Editor, Circ. Mgr.-David Schlottmann
Editorial Description: Articles, interviews, criticism, reviews, concerning author Jack London.
General Info: Yr. Est. 1971, Irregular, Trim Size-5½ x 8½, Sheetfed press, 20 pages, No Color, Newsprint
Subscriptions: Indv. $20, $2/copy
Acquistions: Publication Sold
Circulation: Total-120
Advertising: Inquire for rates.

Wild About Wilde Newsletter   *Consumer, Association*

Publishing Co: Carmel McCaffrey, 2542 Vance Dr, Mount Airy, MD 21771-8814;
Title Tel # (410) 875-0699
Personnel: Publisher, Editor-Carmel McCaffrey
Editorial Description: Covers the work of Oscar Wilde.
General Info: Yr. Est. 1986, Semi-annually, Color-cover, Matte, Saddle-stitched
Subscriptions: Indv. $5
Circulation: Total-450

Willa Cather Pioneer Memorial Newsletter See: EDUCATION

William Carlos Williams Review   *Business*

Publishing Co: University of Texas at Austin, Dept. of English Literature, PAR 108, Austin, TX 78712-1164; Title Tel # (512) 471-7842 Title Fax # (512) 471-4909
Personnel: Editor-Brian Bremen, Bk. Rev. Ed.-Richard Frye
General Info: (Formerly William Carlos Williams Newsletter), Yr. Est. 1975, Semi-annually, Trim Size-7 x 10, 56 pages, ISSN: 0196-6286, 1% ads
Subscriptions: Indv. $10, Inst. $15, $5/copy
Circulation: Total-400
Advertising: Accepts Inserts.
List Rental: Rents Lists
Printing Co: UT Printing, Univ. of Texas at Austin, Austin, TX 78712

Winesburg Eagle

Publishing Co: Sherwood Anderson Society, Univ. of Richmond, Richmond, VA 23173;
Title Tel # (804) 285-6225
Personnel: Editor-Welford D. Taylor
Editorial Description: Any topic concerning Sherwood Anderson: life, work, reputation, etc.
General Info: Yr. Est. 1975, Semi-annually, Trim Size-8½ x 11, Offset press, 8 pages, No Color
Subscriptions: $3/copy
Circulation: Total-120
Advertising: Inquire for rates.

Working Communicator, The   *Business, Consumer*

Publishing Co: Lawrence Ragan Communications, Inc., 212 W.Superior St,Ste 200, Chicago, IL 60610-3533 Tel # (312) 335-0037; Title Tel # (612) 335-0037 Title Fax # (312) 335-9583
Personnel: Publisher-Lawrence Ragan, Editor-John Cowan, Editorial Dir.-Janine Wood, Circ. Dir.-Susan Weston, Art Dir.-Sharon Giankos, Mktg. Dir.-Melissa Eckhardt, Mktg. Dir.-Gretchen Eisenfelder
Editorial Description: New ideas, trends, and techniques for the working communicator.
General Info: Yr. Est. 1983, Monthly, Trim Size-8½ x 11, 8 pages, 2 Color, Matte, Saddle-stitched
Subscriptions: Indv. $97
List Rental: List Management Co.: Taybi Direct East, Inc., 13321 New Hampshire Ave., Ste. 202, Silver Spring, MD 20904-3450 Tel # (301) 680-3633, Fax # (301) 680-3635

World of Translation

Publishing Co: Translation Co. of America, Inc., 10 W 37th St, New York, NY 10018-7491
Tel # (212) 563-7054 Fax # (212) 695-2385; Title Tel # (212) 594-8720
Personnel: Editor-Serge Raffet
Editorial Description: Topics concerning translation problems for industry, science, commerce and the corporate world.
General Info: (Formerly Translation Talk), Trim Size-8½ x 11½, Offset press, 16 pages, Color
Circulation: Total-20,000

Write Direction   *Consumer*

Publishing Co: John Skipper, 707 6th St. SE, Mason City, IA 50401-4155; Title Tel # (515) 423-2283
Editorial Description: Offers tips and solutions for befinning writers.
General Info: Yr. Est. 1992, Monthly
Subscriptions: Indv. $13

Writer's Nook News See: POETRY & CREATIVE WRITING

Writers' Union of Canada Newsletter   *Business, Association*

Publishing Co: Writers' Union of Canada, 24 Ryerson Ave., Toronto, ON M5T 2P3 Canada;
Title Tel # (416) 703-8982 Title Fax # (416) 703-0826
General Info: Monthly

Writing Lab Newsletter See: EDUCATION

Yiddish of Greater Washington Newsletter   *Consumer*

Publishing Co: Yiddish of Greater Washington, Inc., 6125 Montrose Rd, Rockville, MD 20852-4857;
Title Tel # (202) 363-1832
Personnel: Editor-R. Lea Singer
Editorial Description: Features Yiddish news and activities worldwide. In Yiddish and English.
General Info: Yr. Est. 1979, Bi-monthly
Circulation: Total-3,000

Yukon Historical & Museums Association Newsletter See: HISTORY

Zane Grey Review, The   *Association*

Publishing Co: Zane Grey's West Society, 708 Warwick Ave, Fort Wayne, IN 46825-5653;
Title Tel # (219) 484-2904
General Info: Yr. Est. 1985, Bi-monthly
Subscriptions: Indv. $25, $3/copy

LIVESTOCK

AASRP Newsletter See: VETERINARY

ADGA News & Events   *Association*

Publishing Co: American Dairy Goat Assn., PO Box 865, Spindale, NC 28160-0865;
Title Tel # (704) 286-3801
Personnel: Editor-Denise Wilson
Editorial Description: Breeders and fanciers of dairy goats.
General Info: Yr. Est. 1904, Annually, Web press, 12 pages
Circulation: Total-14,000

AFIA Safetygram See: AGRICULTURE

Ag Executive See: AGRICULTURE

Alberta Agrologist See: AGRICULTURE

American CattleWoman   *Association*

Publishing Co: American Natl. CattleWomen, Inc., PO Box 3881, Englewood, CO 80155-3881;
Title Tel # (303) 694-0313 Title Fax # (303) 694-2390
Personnel: Editor-Lisa Taylor, Production Mgr.-Jodie Hickman
Editorial Description: Association newsletter.
General Info: (Formerly AWCW Newsletter), Yr. Est. 1952, Bi-monthly, Trim Size-8½ x 11, Sheetfed press, 12 pages, ISSN: 1042-5233, 2 Color, Matte, Saddle-stitched
Subscriptions: Indv. $25
Circulation: Total-7,500

American Dexter Cattle Association, Bulletins   *Association*

Publishing Co: American Dexter Cattle Assn., RR I, Box 378, Concordia, MO 64020-9233
Personnel: Editor-Rosemary Fleharty
Editorial Description: Update members on Dexter news throughout country.
General Info: Bi-monthly

American Murray Grey
News   *Association*

Publishing Co: American Murray Grey Assn., PO Box 34590, North Kansas City, MO 64116-0990; Title Tel # (406) 248-1266
Personnel: Editor-Joan Turnquist
Editorial Description: Seeks developments, recording, registration & promotion of the Murray Grey breed of cattle in the U.S.
General Info: Yr. Est. 1970, Bi-monthly, Trim Size-11½ x 17½, 8 pages, 2 Color
Circulation: Total-5,000
Advertising: Inquire for rates.
Printing Co: Artcraft Printers, PO Box 2044, Billings, MT 59103-2044 Tel # (406) 248-1000

American Silkie Bantam
Club-Newsletter

Publishing Co: American Silkie Bantam Club, 2221 Blue Ridge Blvd, Independence, MO 64052-1658; Title Tel # (816) 254-8389
Editorial Description: News items on the American Silkie Bantam Chicken & the people involved in raising & showing them.
General Info: Yr. Est. 1923, Monthly
Circulation: Total-225
Advertising: Inquire for rates.

Animal Sciences Newsletter   *Business*

Publishing Co: Univ. of Hawaii Animal Science Dept., 1800 E West Rd, Honolulu, HI 96822-2318 Tel # (808) 956-8356; Title Tel # (808) 956-7594 Title Fax # (808) 956-4883
Personnel: Editor, Circ. Mgr.-H. Zaleski, Art Dir.-Sam Kam
Editorial Description: News for livestock industry personnel.
General Info: (Formerly Hawaii Swine Newsletter), Yr. Est. 1961, Quarterly, 6 pages
Subscriptions: Free To Qualified Recipient
Acquistions: Publication Bought
Circulation: Total-1,500

Animal Welfare in Focus   *Consumer, Association*

Publishing Co: Canadian Federation of Humane Societies, 102-30 Concourse Gate, Nepean, ON K2E 7V7 Canada; Title Tel # (613) 224-8072 Title Fax # (613) 723-0252
Personnel: Editor-Jackie Munroe
Editorial Description: Animal welfare issues.
General Info: Yr. Est. 1986, Semi-annually, Trim Size-8½ x 11, 8 pages, 2 Color
Subscriptions: $1/copy
Circulation: Total-7,000

Beef Business Bulletin   *Association*

Publishing Co: National Cattlemen's Beef Assn., 5420 S. Quebec St., PO Box 3469, Englewood, CO 80155-3469 Parent Co.-National Cattlemen's Beef Association, Chicago; Title Tel # (303) 694-0305 Title Fax # (303) 694-2851
Personnel: Editor-Kendal Frazier, Adv. Dir.-Brett Erickson
Editorial Description: Current events in the cattle business.
General Info: (Formerly Beef Producer), Yr. Est. 1898, Weekly, Trim Size-8½ x 11, Offset press, 4 pages, 2 Color
Circulation: Total-24,500

Beef Producer News   *Business*

Publishing Co: Kent Feeds, Inc., 1600 Oregon St, Muscatine, IA 52761-1404; Title Tel # (319) 264-4211
Personnel: Editor-Jack May
Editorial Description: For producers who use Kent feeds and animal care products.
General Info: (Formerly Beef Roundup), Quarterly

Beef Update

Publishing Co: Iowa Beef Industry Council, PO Box 1730, Ames, IA 50010-1730
General Info: Monthly

Black Sheep Newsletter   *Business, Consumer*   CPM: $58

Publishing Co: Black Sheep Press, 25455 NW Dixie Mountain Rd, Scappoose, OR 97056-9500; Title Tel # (503) 621-3063
Personnel: Publisher, Editor-Peggy Lundquist, Circ. Mgr.-Angeline Podraza, Production Mgr.-Richard Lundquist
Editorial Description: Published quarterly for growers, spinners and textile artists interested in black sheep, wool and other animal fibers.
General Info: Yr. Est. 1974, Quarterly, Trim Size-7¼ x 10⅝, Web press, 48 pages, 25% ads, No Color, Newsprint, Saddle-stitched
Subscriptions: Indv. $14, Can. $18, For. $18, $4/copy
Circulation: Total-2,500
Advertising: $145.
Printing Co: Nickel Ads, P.O. Box 5667, Portland, OR 97228-5667 Tel # (503) 251-7553

Boer Trader & Meat Goat
News   *Business*

Publishing Co: Scott Campbell, PO Box 2678, San Angelo, TX 76902-2678; Title Tel # (915) 655-4434 Title Fax # (915) 658-8250
Personnel: Publisher-Scott Campbell, Editor-Gary Cutrer, Circ. Mgr.-Karen Cutrer, Adv. Dir.-Sandra Lacy, Promotion Dir.-DeAnna Campbell
Editorial Description: A weekly publication on the Boer and meat goat business.
General Info: Yr. Est. 1994, Weekly, Trim Size-8¼ x 10½, 6 pages
Subscriptions: Indv. $16, Can. $26, For. $30
Circulation: Total-700
Advertising: Inquire for rates.

Broadwater Market Letter
See: AGRICULTURE

Browse
See: AGRICULTURE

Buffalo!
See: ANIMALS

California Wool Growers
Newsletter   *Association*   CPM: $172

Publishing Co: Calif. Wool Growers Assn., 1225 H St # 101, Sacramento, CA 95814-1910; Title Tel # (916) 444-8122 Title Fax # (916) 443-0601
Personnel: Editor-Ann Wilson, Circ. Mgr.-Jan Sherbo
General Info: (Formerly California Wool), Monthly, Trim Size-8½ x 11, Desktop press, 6 pages, No Color, Coated
Subscriptions: Free With Membership
Circulation: Total-870
Advertising: $150. Accepts Inserts.

Caring for Animals   *Consumer, Association*

Publishing Co: Canadian Federation of Humane Societies, 102-30 Concourse Gate, Nepean, ON K2E 7V7 Canada; Title Tel # (613) 224-8072 Title Fax # (613) 723-0252
Personnel: Editor-Stephanie Brown
Editorial Description: Issues related to the use of animals in research; update on alternatives.
General Info: Yr. Est. 1984, Semi-annually, Trim Size-8½ x 11, 4 pages
Circulation: Total-2,000

Center for Rural Affairs Newsletter
See: AGRICULTURE

Commercial Cattle Issue

Publishing Co: Nelson R. Crow Pubs., 650 S Lipan St, Denver, CO 80223-2307; Title Tel # (303) 722-7600
Personnel: Editor-Fred Wortham
Editorial Description: For livestock breeders and buyers.

Duroc News   *Association*

Publishing Co: United Duroc Swine Registry, 1769 Us Highway 52 W # 2347, West Lafayette, IN 47906-5308

Federal Veterinarian
See: VETERINARY

Feed Facts

Publishing Co: MoorMan's Inc., 1000 N 30th St, Quincy, IL 61305-3115 Tel # (212) 222-7100; Title Tel # (217) 222-7100 Title Fax # (217) 222-7560
Personnel: Editor-Joy Moore
Editorial Description: Covers livestock feeding & management.
General Info: Yr. Est. 1942, Monthly, Trim Size-8½ x 11, Sheetfed press, 8 pages, 2 Color, Newsprint
Subscriptions: Free To Qualified Recipient
Circulation: Total-50,000

Feedgram
See: AGRICULTURE

Finnsheep Short Tales   *Business*

Publishing Co: Finnsheep Breeders Association, PO Box 512, Zionsville, IN 46077-0512; Title Tel # (317) 873-3597
Personnel: Editor-Claire Carter
Editorial Description: Covers raising, breeding & marketing of Finnsheep.
General Info: Yr. Est. 1980, Semi-annually, 24 pages, 3% ads
Circulation: Total-1,200
Advertising: Inquire for rates.
List Rental: Rents Lists

Grain and Livestock Market
News   *Business*

Publishing Co: Federal State Market News Service, PO Box 19281, Springfield, IL 62794-9281; Title Tel # (217) 782-4925
Editorial Description: Livestock summary of direct auction and area terminal market receipts and prices, grain futures, area interior and barge prices, area feedstuff summary export inspection figures.
General Info: Yr. Est. 1971, Monthly, Trim Size-8½ x 11, Offset press, 4 pages, No Color
Circulation: Total-1,400

Herd Profit Ability   *Business*

Publishing Co: Winsor Publishing Company, 1919 14th St Ste 300, Boulder, CO 80302-5321; Title Tel # (303) 444-6879 Title Fax # (303) 443-1842
Personnel: Publisher-Tom Winsor, Editor-Ty Wyant, Circ. Mgr.-Lisa Newell
General Info: Yr. Est. 1995, Semi-monthly

Idaho Wool Growers
Association
Business, Association   CPM: $285

Publishing Co: Idaho Wool Growers Assn., PO Box 2596, Boise, ID 83701-2596; Title Tel # (208) 344-2271 Title Fax # (208) 336-9447
Personnel: Editor-Rochelle A. Little
General Info: (Formerly Idaho Wool Growers Bulletin), Yr. Est. 1921, Monthly, Trim Size-8½ x 11, 8 pages
Subscriptions: Indv. $20, $2/copy
Circulation: Total-1,000, Readership-1,000
Advertising: $285. Accepts Inserts.

International Meat Processors Assn. Newsletter

Publishing Co: International Meat Processors Association, 1211 Gerry St, Woodstock, IL 60098-3613; Title Tel # (602) 297-0903
General Info: Yr. Est. 1981

Iowa Livestock Report
Business, Association

Publishing Co: Iowa Agricultural Statistics, 833 Federal Bldg., 210 Walnut St., Des Moines, IA 50309-2195; Title Tel # (515) 284-4340
Personnel: Editor-Duane Skow
Editorial Description: Features major livestock reports.
General Info: 17x/yr.
Subscriptions: Indv. $11

LMA Businessletter

Publishing Co: Livestock Marketing Assn., 7509 NW Tiffany Springs Pky, Kansas City, MO 64153-1386; Title Tel # (816) 891-0502
Personnel: Editor-John McBride
General Info: (Formerly Livestock Marketing Business Letter), 12 pages, ISSN: 0164-4963

Lamb & Wool Market News
Association

Publishing Co: American Sheep Industry Assn., 6911 S Yosemite St, Englewood, CO 80112-1415 Fax # (303) 771-8200; Title Tel # (303) 771-3500
Personnel: Editor-Laura Gerhard, Mktg. Coord.-Steve Meyer
Editorial Description: External house organ of the American Sheep Industry Association.
General Info: (Formerly Insights), Yr. Est. 1956, Weekly, Trim Size-8½ x 11, Offset press, 4 pages, 2 Color
Subscriptions: Can. $45, For. $45
Circulation: Total-1,026

Livestock
Business

Publishing Co: Kentucky Dept. of Agriculture, Livestock & Agricultural Svces, 500 Nero, Frankfort, KY 40601; Title Tel # (502) 564-4896
Editorial Description: Summary of weekly prices, Kentucky livestock markets and grain elevators.
General Info: Weekly, No Color

Livestock - Sacramento
Business

Publishing Co: California Dept. of Food & Agriculture, Communications Dept., 1220 N St. Rm. 100, Sacramento, CA 95814 Tel # (916) 654-0466; Title Tel # (916) 654-0298 Title Fax # (916) 654-1046
Editorial Description: California auctions, direct sales, and midwest markets for cattle, hogs, and sheep.
General Info: Weekly, Trim Size-8½ x 14, 2 pages, Ind/Abs/Online: ATI-NET, No Color
Subscriptions: Indv. $75, Can. $75, For. $96, $4/copy

Livestock Marketing News
Business

Publishing Co: California Dept. of Food & Agriculture, Communications Dept., 1220 N St. Rm. 100, Sacramento, CA 95814 Tel # (916) 654-0466; Title Tel # (209) 446-0881 Title Fax # (209) 466-0616
Personnel: Editor-Geoffrey Dong
Editorial Description: Covers California auctions, direct sales and midwest markets of cattle, hogs and sheep.
General Info: Weekly, 4 pages
Subscriptions: Indv. $48, Can. $48, For. $96, $4/copy

Livestock, Meat, and Wool Market News
Business, Consumer

Publishing Co: Agricultural Marketing Service, U.S. Dept. of Agriculture, South Bldg., Rm. 2613, Washington, DC 20090-6456 Tel # (202) 720-8054; Title Tel # (202) 720-6231 Title Fax # (202) 690-3732
Personnel: Editor-Michael O'Connor
Editorial Description: News and statistics on the nation's livestock industry.
General Info: Yr. Est. 1932, Weekly, Trim Size-5 x 8½, Offset press, 30 pages, No Color, Saddle-stitched
Subscriptions: Indv. $70, Can. $75, For. $105, $2/copy
Circulation: (98% controlled), Total-670
List Rental: Rents Lists
Printing Co: U.S. Government Printing Office, Superintendent Of Documents, Washington, DC 20402-0001 Tel # (202) 512-1800, Fax # (202) 512-2233

Livestock Prices & Markets

Publishing Co: Univ. of Illinois at Urbana Champaign, 227 Illini Union, 1401 W. Green Street, Urbana, IL 61801 Tel # (217) 333-1477 Fax # (217) 333-7803; Title Tel # (217) 333-2666 Title Fax # (217) 333-1952
Personnel: Publisher-Chris Hurt
Editorial Description: Forecasts of prices & production for hogs & cattle following inventory reports. Includes inventory data, forecasting methods & discussion of pricing strategies.
General Info: Bi-monthly
Subscriptions: Indv. $12

Livestock Review
Business

Publishing Co: U.S. Department of Agriculture, California Ag. Stat. Service, PO Box 1258, Sacramento, CA 95812
Editorial Description: Livestock inventories, intentions, & values; pasture, slaughter, & on-feed data for cattle & sheep.
General Info: Monthly
Subscriptions: Indv. $15, For. $30

Livestock Statistics Binder & Updates
Business, Association

Publishing Co: Statistics Canada, Agriculture Div., Farm Income & Prices Se, Tunney's Pasture, Ottawa, ON K1A 0T6 Canada; Title Tel # (613) 951-8716 Title Fax # (613) 951-3868
Personnel: Editor-Robert Plourde, Adv. Dir.-Debbie Dupuis
Editorial Description: Historical and current livestock data.
General Info: Yr. Est. 1993, Quarterly, Trim Size-8½ x 11, Mimeo press, 295 pages
Subscriptions: Indv. $173, Can. $144, For. $202
Circulation: Total-400

MOOsletter, The
See: DAIRY

Michigan Beef Industry News
Business

Publishing Co: Michigan Cattlemen's Assn., 2145 University Park Dr Ste, 300, Okemos, MI 48864-3982; Title Tel # (517) 373-3101

National Federation of Flemish Giant Rabbit Breeders, Bulletin
Association

Publishing Co: Natl. Fed. of Flemish Giant Rabbit Breeders, 233 Aultman Ave NW, Canton, OH 44708-5524; Title Tel # (216) 477-1382
General Info: Yr. Est. 1915, Quarterly, Mimeo press, 34 pages
Subscriptions: Indv. $10, Can. $14, For. $25, Free With Membership
Circulation: Total-500

National Hereford Hog ASGN
Association

Publishing Co: National Hereford Hog Record Association, Rr 1 Box 37, Flandreau, SD 57028-9724; Title Tel # (605) 997-2116 Title Fax # (605) 997-2116
Personnel: Publisher-Ruby Schrecengost
General Info: (Formerly Annual Newsletter), Yr. Est. 1934, Annually, Trim Size-8½ x 11, 10 pages, No Color
Subscriptions: Free
Circulation: (100% controlled), Total-400
Printing Co: Area Shopper, Route 1, Conneautville, PA 16406 Tel # (814) 587-2032, Fax # (814) 587-3720

Nona Morelli's Press Release
See: RESTAURANTS & CATERING

North American Bull Buyers Guide
Business

Publishing Co: Nelson R. Crow Pubs., 650 S Lipan St, Denver, CO 80223-2307; Title Tel # (303) 722-7600
Personnel: Editor-Fred Wortham
Editorial Description: For breeders and purchasers of specialized livestock.
General Info: Yr. Est. 1980, Monthly, Trim Size-8⅜ x 10⅞, Web press, 4 Color
Circulation: Total-12,900
Advertising: Inquire for rates.

Ostriches
Business

Publishing Co: Blue Ridge Ostrich Ranch, PO Box 339, Blue Ridge, TX 75424-0339
Editorial Description: Comprehensive news and reports on the ostrich breeding industry.
General Info: Monthly

Outlook News
Business

Publishing Co: Ohio State Univ., 2120 Fyffe Rd., Columbus, OH 43210-1010; Title Tel # (614) 292-5926 Title Fax # (619) 292-4749
General Info: Monthly
Subscriptions: Free

Park Post

Publishing Co: White Park Cattle Association of America, 419 N Water St, Madrid, IA 50156-1057; Title Tel # (515) 795-2013
Personnel: Editor-Joyce Fisher
General Info: Yr. Est. 1975, Quarterly, 6 pages, No Color, Newsprint
Circulation: Total-1,550

Pigletter   *Business*

Publishing Co: Pig World Inc., 204 N. Oak Ave., #312, Owatonna, MN 55060 Tel # (507) 444-9520; Title Fax # (507) 444-9520
Personnel: Editor-Larm Keltto, Circ. Mgr.-Clare Uthke
Editorial Description: Information on pig production and health.
General Info: Yr. Est. 1981, Monthly, Trim Size-8.5 x 11, Offset press, 4 pages, 2 Color
Subscriptions: Indv. $85, Can. $85, For. $85, $6/copy
Circulation: Total-2,300
Printing Co: J-C Press, 134 Vine, Owatonna, MN 55060 Tel # (507) 451-8960

Pork Producer News   *Business*

Publishing Co: Kent Feeds, Inc., 1600 Oregon St, Muscatine, IA 52761-1404; Title Tel # (319) 264-4211
Personnel: Editor-Terry Main
Editorial Description: For producers who use Kent feeds and animal care products.
General Info: (Formerly Pork Roundup), Quarterly

Porkfolio   *Association*

Publishing Co: Pork Nova Scotia, Box 1341, Truro, NS B2N 5N2 Canada; Title Tel # (902) 895-0581 Title Fax # (902) 893-4236
Personnel: Editor-John Miller
General Info: Yr. Est. 1984, Weekly, Trim Size-8½ x 11, Desktop press, 4 pages
Subscriptions: Indv. $25, Free To Qualified Recipient
Circulation: Total-350

Producers Bulletin   *Association*

Publishing Co: Wyoming Wool Grower's Association, 811 N Glenn Rd # 115, Casper, WY 82601-1625; Title Tel # (307) 265-5250
Personnel: Editor-Carolyn Paseneaux, Production Mgr., Adv. Dir.-Gale Peterson
Editorial Description: Coverage of sheep industry in Wyoming and issues which affect it.
General Info: (Formerly Sheepherder Sheet), Yr. Est. 1980, Bi-monthly, Desktop press, 4 pages, No Color
Subscriptions: Indv. $10
Circulation: (100% controlled), Total-1,200
Advertising: Inquire for rates.
Printing Co: House of Printing, PO Box 1688, Casper, WY 82602-1688 Tel # (307) 266-3170

Range Notes   *Business, Association*

Publishing Co: Regional Range Manager/Public Lands Branch, Box 3014 2 Fl. Sun Center, 530 8th St., S., Lethbridge, AB T1J 4C7 Canada; Title Tel # (403) 381-5486 Title Fax # (403) 381-5792
Editorial Description: Shares findings and recommendations from applied research carried out by the Range Managemant Program. Primarily for managers of public grazing lands.
General Info: Yr. Est. 1986, Irregular, ISSN: 0831-487X

Saskatchewan   *Business*

Publishing Co: SPI Marketing Group, 502 45th W., 2nd Fl., Saskatoon, SK S7L 6H2 Canada; Title Tel # (306) 653-3014 Title Fax # (306) 244-2918
Personnel: Publisher, Editor-Jack McClung
Editorial Description: All material related to pork production.
General Info: Yr. Est. 1976, Weekly, Trim Size-8½ x 11, Offset press, 4 pages, No Color, Newsprint
Circulation: Total-3,000

Sheep Producer News   *Business*

Publishing Co: Kent Feeds, Inc., 1600 Oregon St, Muscatine, IA 52761-1404 Tel # (319) 264-4211; Title Tel # (319) 264-4525
Personnel: Editor-Max Churchill
Editorial Description: For producers who use Kent feeds and animal care products.
General Info: Bi-monthly

Sheepherder, The
See: ENVIRONMENT & ECOLOGY

Speaking of Columbias   *Association*

Publishing Co: Columbia Sheep Breeders Assn. of America, PO Box 272, Upper Sandusky, OH 43351-0272; Title Tel # (614) 482-2608
Personnel: Editor-R.L. Gerber
General Info: Semi-monthly, Offset press, 24 pages, Color
Circulation: Total-2,000
Advertising: Inquire for rates.

The Stewart Report

Publishing Co: Western Financial Communications, P.O. Box 3715, Dana Point, CA 92629; Title Tel # (714) 240-3852
Editorial Description: David Stewart is widely recognized as one of the nation's premier authorities on low-priced, emerging-growth stock investments.
General Info: Yr. Est. 1982, Bi-monthly

Texas Livestock Market
News   *Business, Association*

Publishing Co: Texas Dept. of Agriculture, Box 12847 Cap. Station, Austin, TX 78711-2847; Title Tel # (512) 463-7626
Personnel: Editor-Rick Wahrmund
Editorial Description: A summary of federal-state livestock market news (prices) in Texas.
General Info: Yr. Est. 1966, Weekly, Trim Size-7½ x 8¾, Sheetfed press, 6 pages, ISSN: 0199-7041, No Color
Subscriptions: Indv. $20, For. $25
Circulation: (100% controlled), Total-1,100
Printing Co: Texas Tax Dept. of Agriculture, Box 12847 Cap. Station, Austin, TX 78711

Texas Longhorn Journal   *Business, Association*   CPM: $283

Publishing Co: International Texas Longhorn, P.O. Box 1609, Monument, CO 80132-1609; Title Tel # (817) 283-8873 Title Fax # (817) 545-8430
Personnel: Publisher-Charles Searle, Assoc. Ed.-Linda Altoonian, Production Mgr.-Ernie Gill, Mktg. Dir.-Marlene Gard
Editorial Description: Covers the Texas Longhorn industry. Also publish directories, newsletters, phamplets and lists.
General Info: Yr. Est. 1976, Bi-monthly
Subscriptions: Indv. $22, Can. $35, For. $35, $5/copy
Circulation: (10% controlled), Total-3,000, Subscriptions-2,500, International-100
Advertising: $850.

Utah Cattleman
Association Newsletter   *Business*

Publishing Co: Utah Cattleman Association, 150 S 600 E Ste 10b, Salt Lake City, UT 84102-1961; Title Tel # (801) 355-5748
Personnel: Editor-Kris Berg
Editorial Description: Articles on breeding, feeding, selling of cattle in intermountain area.
General Info: (Formerly Utah Cattleman Magazine), Yr. Est. 1951, Monthly, Trim Size-8½ x 11, Sheetfed press, 24 pages, 4 Color
Subscriptions: Indv. $4
Circulation: Total-3,700
Advertising: Inquire for rates.
Printing Co: Paragon Press, 200 S West Temple, Salt Lake City, UT 84101-1909

Virginia Agriculture Commodity Newsletter
See: AGRICULTURE

Virginia Hay Clearing House
See: AGRICULTURE

Washington Feedline

Publishing Co: American Feed Industry Assn., 1501 Wilson Blvd # 1100, Arlington, VA 22209-2403 Tel # (703) 524-0810; Title Tel # (703) 524-0180 Title Fax # (703) 524-1921
Editorial Description: Covers news of legislation relevant to the feed industry. Keeps members apprised of actions taken in response to bills & potential effect of legislation.
General Info: 5x/yr.

Weight Report

Publishing Co: Manitoba Beef Cattle Performances Assn., Box 232, Douglas, MB R0K 0R0 Canada; Title Tel # (204) 763-4696
Personnel: Editor-Sharon Bickford
General Info: Yr. Est. 1964, Quarterly, 12 pages
Circulation: Total-2,200

Wyoming Wool Grower's
Association Newsletter   *Business, Association*

Publishing Co: Wyoming Wool Grower's Association, 811 N Glenn Rd # 115, Casper, WY 82601-1625; Title Tel # (307) 265-5250
Personnel: Editor-Carolyn Paseneaux, Production Mgr., Adv. Dir., Art Dir.-Darlene Neeff
General Info: Monthly, Trim Size-8½ x 11, 6 pages
Subscriptions: Free With Membership

LUMBER & WOOD

APA-The Engineered Wood
Assoc.

Publishing Co: APA - The Engineered Wood Assoc., PO Box 11700, Tacoma, WA 98411-0700
General Info: (Formerly American Plywood Assn. Weekly Production Report), Weekly

AWPI Newsletter   *Association*

Publishing Co: American Wood Preservers Inst, 1945 Old Gallows Rd Ste 550, Vienna, VA 22182-3931; Title Tel # (703) 893-4005
Personnel: Publisher-John Hall, Editor-Mary Sullivan
Editorial Description: Monthly newsletter on government relations & environmental issues for the Wood Preservers Industry.
General Info: Yr. Est. 1975, Monthly, Trim Size-8½ x 11, Offset press, 12 pages, Color
Subscriptions: Indv. $8, $75/copy
Circulation: Total-1,100
Advertising: Inquire for rates.

Barometer   *Business*

Publishing Co: Western Wood Products Assn., 522 SW 5th Ave., Yeon Bldg., Portland, OR 97204-2133; Title Tel # (503) 224-3930 Title Fax # (503) 224-3934
Editorial Description: Summary of western lumber production, orders, shipments & inventory.
General Info: Weekly, Trim Size-8½ x 11, Sheetfed press, 2 pages, ISSN: 0511-8255, 2 Color, Looseleaf
Subscriptions: Indv. $48, $1/copy
Circulation: (100% controlled)

Canadian Wood Pallet & Container Assn., Newsletter

Publishing Co: Canadian Wood Pallet & Container Assn., Box 640, Pickering, ON L1V 3T3 Canada; Title Tel # (416) 831-3477 Title Fax # (905) 831-3477
Personnel: Editor-Gordon Hughes
Editorial Description: Up-to-date information for the Wooden Pallet/Container/Box & Crate industry. Information also available for pallet recycling & wood waste utilization. Lobbying is also in effect.
General Info: Yr. Est. 1970, Monthly
Subscriptions: $5/copy
Acquistions: Publication Bought
Circulation: Total-200

Crow's Weekly Market Report   *Business*

Publishing Co: C.C. Crow Publications, Inc., PO Box 25749, Portland, OR 97225-0749; Title Tel # (503) 646-8075 Title Fax # (503) 646-9971
Personnel: Publisher-Frank Vetorino, Editor-Sam Sherrill, Editorial Page Ed.-Linda Barr, Circ. Mgr.-Jeff Van Sant, Production Mgr.-A. Hedrick, Mktg. Dir.-Richard Nelson
Editorial Description: Market Report and pricing of lumber and plywood, futures, transportation. Subscription includes Journal.
General Info: Yr. Est. 1921, Weekly, 12 pages, Color
Subscriptions: Indv. $225, Can. $245, For. $285
Printing Co: R.G. Wilkes, 700 SE Clay St, Portland, OR 97214-3511 Tel # (503) 233-7711

Executive Brief

Publishing Co: Hardwood Plywood and Veneer Association, 1825 Michael Faraday Dr, P.O Box 2759, Reston, VA 22090-5304; Title Tel # (703) 435-2900 Title Fax # (703) 435-2537
Personnel: Publisher, Editor-William Groah
General Info: Yr. Est. 1987, Quarterly, 4 pages, 2 Color, Coated
Subscriptions: Indv. $16
Acquistions: Publication Bought
Circulation: Total-550

FPRS Technical Newsletter Series: Timber Harvesting and Merchandising   *Business*

Publishing Co: Forest Products Society, 2801 Marshall Ct., Madison, WI 53705-2257; Title Tel # (608) 231-1361 Title Fax # (608) 231-2152
Personnel: Editor-Arthur B. Brauner
General Info: Quarterly

Flooring Fax News
See: FURNITURE & HOME FURNISHINGS

Forest Forum
See: FORESTRY

Gulf Coast Pulpwood News

Publishing Co: Gulfcoast Pulpwood Assn, PO Box 100, Forest Home, AL 36030-0100; Title Tel # (205) 346-2220
General Info: Bi-monthly

Hardwood, Plywood & Veneer News   *Business, Association*

Publishing Co: Hardwood Plywood and Veneer Association, 1825 Michael Faraday Dr, P.O Box 2759, Reston, VA 22090-5304; Title Tel # (703) 435-2900 Title Fax # (703) 435-2537
Personnel: Publisher-E.T. Altman, Editor-Sarah Griffin Peck
Editorial Description: Book reviews, features, financial news, general news briefs, government affairs, new product news, personnel changes, technical features.
General Info: (Formerly Members Bulletin), Yr. Est. 1989, Bi-weekly, Trim Size-8½ x 11, Offset press, 8 pages, 2 Color, Matte
Subscriptions: Indv. $39, Inst. $39, Free With Membership
Circulation: Total-550

Housing Market Report
See: CONSTRUCTION & BUILDING

IHPA Newsletter

Publishing Co: Intl. Hardwood Products Assn., 4214 King St. West, Alexandria, VA 22302; Title Tel # (703) 820-6696
Personnel: Editor-Cathy Looney
General Info: Yr. Est. 1956, Monthly, Trim Size-8½ x 11, Sheetfed press, 4 pages, 2 Color
Circulation: Total-300

Information Log

Publishing Co: Northeastern Lumber Mfgs. Assn., 272 Tuttle Rd., Box 87A, Cumberland, ME 04021-9321; Title Tel # (207) 829-6901 Title Fax # (207) 829-4293
Personnel: Publisher, Editor-Donna Reynolds
Editorial Description: Discusses the growth, harvesting, production & marketing of Northeastern lumber & other industry related activities.
General Info: Yr. Est. 1970, Monthly, 8 pages, Color-cover
Circulation: Total-300

Journal, The
See: CONSTRUCTION & BUILDING

Logging   *Business, Association*

Publishing Co: Statistics Canada, Holland Ave/RH Coats, Holland Ave/Tunney's Pasture, Ottawa, ON K1A O26 Canada Tel # (613) 951-8116 Fax # (613) 951-0581; Title Tel # (613) 990-8116
Editorial Description: Number of establishments, employees, salaries, cost of fuel & electricity. Catalog #25-201.
General Info: Annually, 31 pages, ISSN: 0701-645X
Subscriptions: Indv. $36, Can. $30, For. $42, $36/copy

Lumber Price Index-Coast Mills   *Business*

Publishing Co: Western Wood Products Assn., 522 SW 5th Ave., Yeon Bldg., Portland, OR 97204-2133; Title Tel # (503) 224-3930 Title Fax # (503) 224-3934
Personnel: Circ. Mgr.-Louise Albert
Editorial Description: Refelects the trend of weighted index prices for coast species.
General Info: Yr. Est. 1982, Monthly, 1 pages, ISSN: 0735-066X, 2 Color, Coated, Looseleaf
Subscriptions: Indv. $28, $3/copy
Circulation: Total-400

Lumber Price Index-Inland Mills   *Business*

Publishing Co: Western Wood Products Assn., 522 SW 5th Ave., Yeon Bldg., Portland, OR 97204-2133; Title Tel # (503) 224-3930 Title Fax # (503) 224-3934
Personnel: Circ. Mgr.-Louise Albert
Editorial Description: Reflects the trend of weighted index prices for Inland species.
General Info: Yr. Est. 1933, Monthly, Trim Size-8½ x 11, Sheetfed press, 1 pages, ISSN: 0195-9395, 2 Color, Coated, Looseleaf
Subscriptions: Indv. $28, $3/copy
Circulation: Total-800

Madison's Canadian Lumber Reporter   *Business*

Publishing Co: Madison's Canadian Lumber Reporter, PO Box 2486, Vancouver, BC V6B 3W7 Canada; Title Tel # (604) 681-6838 Title Fax # (604) 681-6585
Personnel: Publisher-Laurence Cater, Editor-Ward Johnson, Asst. Ed., Asst. Ed.-Zara Heartwood, Circ. Mgr.-Leah McNutt
Editorial Description: Lumber industry news & lumber market prices.
General Info: Yr. Est. 1952, Weekly, Trim Size-8 x 10½, 8 pages, ISSN: 0715-5468, No Color, Matte
Subscriptions: Indv. $165, Can. $195, For. $240, $5/copy
Advertising: $455. Accepts Inserts.
List Rental: Actives: $135/M, Expires: $135/M
Printing Co: Alpha Omega Printing Services, 181 West 6th Street, Vancouver, BC V5Y 1K1 Canada Tel # (604) 875-0192, Fax # (604) 875-0192

NHLA Export Directory   *Association*

Publishing Co: Natl. Hardwood Lumber Assn., PO Box 34518, Memphis, TN 38184-0518; Title Tel # (901) 377-1818 Title Fax # (901) 382-6419
Personnel: Editor-Ernest Stebbins
Editorial Description: Provides news of industry & assn. activities to assn. members. Includes training course schedules, new members & other information.
General Info: (Formerly Natl. Hardwood Lumber Assn. - News), Monthly, Trim Size-8½ x 11, Mimeo press, 8 pages, Color-cover
Circulation: Total-1,800

Paper Stock Report:News and Trends of the Paper recycling Markets
See: ENVIRONMENT & ECOLOGY

Poly Probe
See: METALS & METALWORKING

Primary Processor Newsletter   *Association*

Publishing Co: Maine Bureau of Forestry Station, State House Station 22, Augusta, ME 04333-0001; Title Tel # (207) 289-2791
Editorial Description: Maine forestry news.
General Info: Yr. Est. 1949, Bi-monthly, Mimeo press, 8 pages
Circulation: Total-600

Pulp & Paper Wood Report   *Business*

Publishing Co: Miller Freeman, Inc., 600 Harrison St., San Francisco, CA 94107-1391 Tel # (415) 905-2200 Fax # (415) 905-2232 Parent Co.-Miller Freeman, Inc., New York
Editorial Description: Covers supply, demand, and prices for wood used in the paper industry.
General Info: Yr. Est. 1995, Monthly
Subscriptions: Indv. $347

Pulpwood Highlights *Business, Association*

Publishing Co: American Pulpwood Association, 600 Jefferson Plaza, St 350, Rockville, MD 20852; Title Tel # (301) 838-9385 Title Fax # (301) 838-9481
Editorial Description: For consumers and suppliers of pulpwood.
General Info: Monthly, Trim Size-8½ x 11, No Color
Subscriptions: Indv. $100, Free With Membership
Circulation: Total-2,500

Random Lengths Export Report *Business*

Publishing Co: Random Lengths Publications, Inc., PO Box 867, Eugene, OR 97440-0867 Tel # (541) 686-9925 Fax # (541) 686-9629; Title Tel # (514) 686-9925 Title Fax # (514) 686-9629
Personnel: Publisher-Jon Anderson, Editor-Jessie Taylor, Circ. Mgr.-Nancy Jodoin, Production Mgr.-Nancy West
Editorial Description: A summary of world wide trading in N. American softwood lumber & plywood.
General Info: Yr. Est. 1968, Bi-weekly, Trim Size-8¼ x 10¾, Offset press, 4 pages, ISSN: 8756-288X, 2 Color, Matte
Subscriptions: Indv. $155, Can. $165, For. $185, $4/copy
Acquistions: Publication Bought
Circulation: Total-1,250
List Rental: Rents Lists
Printing Co: QSL Printing, 309 W 4th Ave, Eugene, OR 97401-2581 Tel # (541) 687-1184, Fax # (541) 687-0078

Random Lengths Locator *Business*

Publishing Co: Random Lengths Publications, Inc., PO Box 867, Eugene, OR 97440-0867; Title Tel # (541) 686-9925 Title Fax # (541) 686-9629
Personnel: Publisher-Jon Anderson, Production Mgr.-Nancy West, Circ. Mgr.-Adv. Dir.-Nancy Jodoin
Editorial Description: Monthly advertising supplement to Random Lengths weekly report.
General Info: Yr. Est. 1983, Monthly, Trim Size-8½ x 11, Sheetfed press, 6 pages, ISSN: 1044-4912, 90% ads, Newsprint
Subscriptions: Indv. $25, Can. $25, $4/copy
Acquistions: Publication Bought
Circulation: Total-13,000, Readership-26,000
Advertising: Inquire for rates. Accepts Inserts.
List Rental: Rents Lists
Printing Co: QSL Printing, 309 W 4th Ave, Eugene, OR 97401-2581 Tel # (541) 687-1184, Fax # (541) 687-0078

Random Lengths Market Report *Business*

Publishing Co: Random Lengths Publications, Inc., PO Box 867, Eugene, OR 97440-0867; Title Tel # (541) 686-9925 Title Fax # (541) 686-9629
Personnel: Publisher-Jon Anderson, Editor-Burrle Elmore, Circ. Mgr.-Drenna Bjork, Production Mgr., Promotion Dir.-Nancy West
Editorial Description: Report on North American wood products marketing; price guide for commedity lumber and a structual panel products.
General Info: Yr. Est. 1944, Weekly, Trim Size-8¼ x 10¾, Offset press, 12 pages, ISSN: 0483-9420, 2 Color, Matte, Saddle-stitched
Subscriptions: Indv. $205, Can. $214, For. $245, $5/copy
Acquistions: Publication Bought
Circulation: Total-13,000, Readership-45,000
List Rental: Rents Lists
Printing Co: QSL Printing, 309 W 4th Ave, Eugene, OR 97401-2581 Tel # (541) 687-1184, Fax # (541) 687-0078

Random Lengths Midweek Market Report *Business*

Publishing Co: Random Lengths Publications, Inc., PO Box 867, Eugene, OR 97440-0867; Title Tel # (541) 686-9925 Title Fax # (541) 686-9629
Personnel: Publisher-Jon Anderson, Editor-Burrle Elmore, Circ. Mgr.-Drenna Bjork
Editorial Description: Update of Random Lengths weekly report on wood products prices.
General Info: Yr. Est. 1974, Weekly, Trim Size-8¼ x 10¾, Mimeo press, 1 pages, ISSN: 0483-9420, 2 Color, Matte
Subscriptions: Indv. $160, Can. $160, $4/copy
Circulation: Total-1,600
List Rental: Rents Lists

Random Lengths Yardstick *Business*

Publishing Co: Random Lengths Publications, Inc., PO Box 867, Eugene, OR 97440-0867 Fax # (541) 686-9629; Title Tel # (541) 686-9925
Personnel: Publisher-Jon Anderson, Editor-Joe Heitz, Circ. Dir.-Drenna Bjork, Production Mgr.-Nancy West
Editorial Description: Report of statistics related to the N. American forest products industry.
General Info: Yr. Est. 1991, Monthly, Trim Size-8¼ x 10¾, Sheetfed press, 24 pages, ISSN: 1055-0895, 2 Color, Coated, Saddle-stitched
Subscriptions: Indv. $198, Can. $205, For. $240, $20/copy
Circulation: Total-900
Printing Co: QSL Printing, 309 W 4th Ave, Eugene, OR 97401-2581 Tel # (541) 687-1184, Fax # (541) 687-0078

SF Newsletter *Association*

Publishing Co: Southern Forest Products Assn, PO Box 641700, Kenner, LA 70064-1700; Title Tel # (504) 443-4464 Title Fax # (504) 443-6612
Personnel: Editor-David Kellogg
Editorial Description: News about & affecting Southern forestry & its lumber products.
General Info: Weekly, 4 pages, 2 Color
Subscriptions: Indv. $25
Circulation: Total-1,500

Scroll Saw News
See: CRAFTS

Scrollsaw Chatter
See: CRAFTS

Southern Pine Lumber Mill Activity Summary *Association*

Publishing Co: Southern Forest Products Assn, PO Box 641700, Kenner, LA 70064-1700; Title Tel # (504) 443-4464 Title Fax # (504) 443-6612
Editorial Description: Weekly orders, production, shipments & inventory.
General Info: Weekly, 2 Color
Subscriptions: Indv. $25
Circulation: Total-1,500

Statistical Roundup *Business, Association*

Publishing Co: American Forest & Paper Assn., 1111 19th Street NW, Suite 800, Washington, DC 20036-3603; Title Tel # (202) 463-2700
Personnel: Publisher-Kathy Shaffer
Editorial Description: Economic statistics on production & shipments of softwood/hardwood lumber; international trade statistics; U.S. lumber consumption; and data for seasonally adjusted annual rates.
General Info: (Formerly Monthly Statistics of the Wood Products Industry), Yr. Est. 1988, Monthly, Looseleaf
Subscriptions: Indv. $157, Inst. $57, $20/copy
Circulation: Total-3,000

Two Way Transmissions *Association*

Publishing Co: Forest Industries Telecomm., 871 Country Club Rd # A, Eugene, OR 97401-6009; Title Tel # (541) 485-8441 Title Fax # (541) 485-7556
Personnel: Publisher, Editor-Kenton Sturdevant
Editorial Description: Newsletter for two-way radio licenses licensed in the Forest Products Radio Service. Designed to keep two way licences informed and updated with information and FCC rules and regulations affecting their business.
General Info: Yr. Est. 1949, Monthly, Trim Size-8½ x 11, Sheetfed press, 2 pages, No Color
Subscriptions: Free With Membership
Circulation: (100% controlled), Total-2,500
Printing Co: Bourland Printing, 545 Monroe St, Eugene, OR 97402-5187 Tel # (541) 485-8022

Vital Link, The
See: CONSTRUCTION & BUILDING

Western Wood Products Association. Export Report *Business*

Publishing Co: Western Wood Products Assn., 522 SW 5th Ave., Yeon Bldg., Portland, OR 97204-2133; Title Tel # (503) 224-3930 Title Fax # (503) 224-3934
Editorial Description: Volumes of softwood lumber exports by species & major country.
General Info: Monthly, Sheetfed press, 2 pages, ISSN: 0730-5176, Color, Looseleaf
Subscriptions: Indv. $28, $3/copy
Circulation: Total-400

Wood Design Focus
See: ENGINEERING

Wood Leader *Association*

Publishing Co: Canadian Wood Council, 1730 St. Laurent Blvd., Suite 350, Ottawa, ON K1P 6L5 Canada Tel # (613) 731-7800 Fax # (613) 731-7899; Title Tel # (613) 235-7221
Personnel: Publisher, Editor-Don Griffith
Editorial Description: Building codes, product standards, fire research, & wood industry news.
General Info: (Formerly Wood Communique), Yr. Est. 1972, 9x/yr., Trim Size-8½ x 11, Offset press, 4 pages, No Color
Circulation: (100% controlled), Total-1,200

Wood Machining News *Business, Consumer*

Publishing Co: Wood Machining Institute, PO Box 476, Berkeley, CA 94701-0476; Title Tel # (510) 943-5240 Title Fax # (510) 945-0947
Personnel: Publisher, Editor, Circ. Mgr., Production Mgr.-Ryszard Szymani, Ph.D.
Editorial Description: The newsletter follows worldwide developments in cutting tools & equipment.
General Info: Yr. Est. 1984, Bi-monthly, Trim Size-8½ x 11, 5 pages, ISSN: 0473-5231, No Color, Coated, Other
Subscriptions: Indv. $72, Can. $72, For. $78, $12/copy
Circulation: Total-800, Readership-1,000
Printing Co: Concord Graphicarts, 2970 Cloverdale Ave, Concord, CA 94518

MACHINERY

Ada Letters *Business, Association*

Publishing Co: Association for Computing Machinery, 1515 Broadway, 17th Fl., New York, NY 10036-5701 Tel # (212) 869-7440 Fax # (212) 302-5826
Editorial Description: For members of the Association.
General Info: Bi-monthly
Subscriptions: Indv. $53
Circulation: Total-4,000

Adviser Update   *Association*

Publishing Co: Dow Jones Newspaper Fund, Inc., PO Box 300, Princeton, NJ 08543-0300; Title Tel # (609) 452-2820
Personnel: Editor-George E. Taylor
Editorial Description: National newsletter about high school journalism trends and news, and information that affects high school journalism education.
General Info: (Formerly Newspaper Fund Newsletter), Yr. Est. 1961, Quarterly, Desktop press, 16 pages, Color, Coated
Subscriptions: Free
Circulation: Total-1,500

Bluebook Update Newsletter
See: AGRICULTURE

CEMA Bulletin   *Association*

Publishing Co: Conveyor Equipment Manufacturers Assn., 9384D Forestwood Ln., Manassas, VA 22110-4702; Title Tel # (301) 738-2448 Title Fax # (301) 738-0076
Personnel: Publisher, Editor-Raymond Lloyd
Editorial Description: Association and conveyor industry news, technical information, and data on related issues.
General Info: Yr. Est. 1933, Quarterly, Trim Size-8½ x 11, Offset press, 6 pages, 2 Color
Circulation: (100% controlled), Total-500

Condition Monitor   *Business*

Publishing Co: Elsevier Science Inc., 655 Avenue of the Americas, New York, NY 10010-5107 Tel # (212) 633-3916 Fax # (212) 633-3913 Parent Co.-Reed Elsevier, New York; Title Tel # (212) 633-3750 Title Fax # (212) 633-3764
Personnel: Publisher-G. Kitteringham, Editor-David Sleemen, Production Mgr.-Cesoline Champney
Editorial Description: Essential readind for anyone concerned with increasing machine life,planning for effective maintenance scheduling and avoiding machine failure-no more expensive down-time!
General Info: Monthly, ISSN: 0268-8050
Subscriptions: Indv. $396

Crane Safety Report, The
See: SAFETY

Editor & M & E Appraiser
See: ENGINEERING

Equipment & Materials Update
See: MANAGEMENT

FPM & SA Focus
See: FOOD

Gas Turbine Engines/ Markets   *Business*

Publishing Co: Forecast International/DMS, Inc., 22 Commerce Rd., Newtown, CT 06470-1643; Title Tel # (203) 426-0800 Title Fax # (203) 426-1964
Editorial Description: Reports on engines in development or production. Includes Market Analysis.
General Info: Monthly, Trim Size-12 x 11, 1,200 pages, No Color, Looseleaf
Subscriptions: Indv. $1,200
List Rental: Rents Lists

ISA Newsletter
See: FURNITURE & HOME FURNISHINGS

Jet News
See: WATER SUPPLY, POWER & WASTE

MACS ACTION!
See: AUTOMOTIVE

MACS Service Reports
See: AUTOMOTIVE

Machinery Outlook   *Business*

Publishing Co: Machinery Outlook, 1110 W Lake Cook Rd Ste 295, Buffalo Grove, IL 60089-1968; Title Tel # (708) 215-2999
Personnel: Publisher, Editor-Frank Manfredi
Editorial Description: A newsletter for the construction, mining, farm & material handling machinery industry.
General Info: Yr. Est. 1984, Monthly, Mimeo press, 18 pages, ISSN: 8756-923X, Newsprint
Subscriptions: Indv. $325, For. $375
Advertising: Accepts Inserts.

Maintenance Management   *Business*

Publishing Co: Bureau of Business Practice, 24 Rope Ferry Rd, Waterford, CT 06386-0001 Tel # (806) 442-4365 Parent Co.-Prentice Hall, Waterford; Title Tel # (860) 444-4365 Title Fax # (860) 434-3341
Personnel: Publisher-Peter Hawkins, Editor-Elaine Stattler
Editorial Description: Management & operating techniques for maintenance supervisors.
General Info: (Formerly Maintenance Supervisor's Bulletin), Yr. Est. 1975, Semi-monthly, 8 pages, ISSN: 0194-5912
Subscriptions: Indv. $95
Advertising: Accepts Inserts.

Metalworking Insiders' Report
See: METALS & METALWORKING

MicroMarkets and Technologies   *Business*

Publishing Co: Vital Information Publications, 321 Carrera Dr, Mill Valley, CA 94941-3995 Tel # (415) 389-8671; Title Tel # (415) 345-7018 Title Fax # (415) 389-8671
Editorial Description: Covers the international micromachinery industry.
General Info: Yr. Est. 1994, Monthly, ISSN: 1077-1565
Subscriptions: Indv. $325, For. $345

NASFM NEWs
See: MANUFACTURING

Nozzle Chatter   *Business, Association*

Publishing Co: Assn. of Diesel Specialists, 9140 Ward Pkwy., Kansas City, MO 64114-3313; Title Tel # (816) 444-3500 Title Fax # (816) 444-0330
Personnel: Publisher-Martin Fromm, Editor-Robert Guy Stewart
Editorial Description: News of Assn. of Diesel Specialists and diesel industry.
General Info: Yr. Est. 1957, Bi-monthly, Offset press, 8 pages, Newsprint
Subscriptions: Free With Membership
Circulation: Total-800
List Rental: Rents Lists

Power Press & Forging
See: SAFETY

Productivity
See: BUSINESS & INDUSTRY

SC & RA Newsletter
See: TRAFFIC & TRANSPORTATION

SMA Weighlog   *Association*

Publishing Co: Scale Manufacturers Assn., 9384D Forestwood Ln., Manassas, VA 22110-4702; Title Tel # (301) 738-2448 Title Fax # (301) 738-0076
Personnel: Publisher, Editor-Raymond Lloyd
Editorial Description: To provide Association news and technical information on issues affecting scale manufacturers.
General Info: Yr. Est. 1945, Quarterly, Trim Size-8½ x 11, Offset press, 4 pages, 2 Color

Salvage Bids   *Business*

Publishing Co: Salvage Bids, PO Box 5, Laconia, NH 03247-0005; Title Tel # (603) 524-4121
Personnel: Publisher, Editor, Circ. Mgr.-John Tamke
Editorial Description: Listing of auctions worldwide on machine tools, heavy contractors equipment and industry equipment.
General Info: Bi-weekly, Trim Size-8½ x 11, Offset press, 4 pages, No Color
Subscriptions: Indv. $400
Circulation: (100% controlled), Total-2,200

Soletter
See: ENGINEERING

Stark's Off-Highway Ledger   *Business*

Publishing Co: J-C Communications Co., Inc, 176 W. Adams St., Ste. 1732, Chicago, IL 60603; Title Tel # (312) 236-5122 Title Fax # (312) 236-3297
Personnel: Publisher-John Stark, Editor-Jeanine T. Hoch, Circ. Mgr.-Mary H. Bieszk
Editorial Description: Production sales and inventories of light, medium, and heavy duty trucks, farm and construction machinery.
General Info: Yr. Est. 1982, 24x/yr., 8 pages
Subscriptions: Indv. $810, Can. $810, For. $860

Total Employee Involvement
See: BUSINESS & INDUSTRY

Total Productive Maintenance
See: BUSINESS & INDUSTRY

Turbomachinery Digest   *Consumer*

Publishing Co: Concepts ETI, Inc., PO Box 643, Norwich, VT 05055-0643; Title Tel # (802) 296-2321
Personnel: Editor-Sharon Wight, Circ. Mgr.-M.B. Bradshaw
Editorial Description: All current turbomachinery technology in concise form.
General Info: Yr. Est. 1980, 10x/yr.

Turbomachinery Maintenance Newsletter   *Business*

Publishing Co: Business Journals, Inc., 50 Day St. #5550, S. Norwalk, CT 06854-3127 Fax # (203) 852-8175; Title Tel # (203) 853-6015
Personnel: Publisher-G.R. Brighton, Editor-R. Hines, Circ. Mgr.-Arthur Heilman, Circ. Mgr.-Hilda Zepka, Promotion Dir.-Skip Ruch
Editorial Description: Maintenance,repair & operation of rotating equipment.
General Info: Yr. Est. 1983, Monthly, Trim Size-8¼ x 10⅞, Offset press, 8 pages, 2 Color, Newsprint, Saddle-stitched
Subscriptions: Indv. $95, Can. $95, For. $120, $10/copy
Circulation: Total-200
Printing Co: Holly Press, 823 Main Street, Stamford, CT 06902 Tel # (203) 324-5779

William Hardash Auction Newsletter
See: ART & SCULPTURE

Wood Machining News
See: LUMBER & WOOD

World Power Systems Intelligence
See: AERONAUTICS/ASTRONAUTICS

MANAGEMENT

AAMA Executive   *Association*

Publishing Co: American Academy of Medical Administration, 30555 Southfield Rd Ste 150, Southfield, MI 48076-7750; Title Tel # (313) 540-4310 Title Fax # (810) 645-0590
Personnel: Editor-Thomas R. O'Donovan
General Info: Yr. Est. 1957, Bi-monthly, Trim Size-8½ x 11, 32 pages, 2% ads, 2 Color
Subscriptions: Indv. $60, $12/copy
Advertising: Inquire for rates.
List Rental: Actives: $100/M

ABT INSIGHTS   *Business*

Publishing Co: ABT Associates, 55 Wheeler Street, Cambridge, MA 02138; Title Tel # (617) 349-2713 Title Fax # (617) 492-5427
Personnel: Mng. Editor-Larry Kerpelman
Editorial Description: Service quality,marketing strategy,and business management
General Info: Yr. Est. 1990, Quarterly
Subscriptions: Free

ACTION   *Association*   **CPM: $185**

Publishing Co: Senior Executives Association, PO Box 7610, Washington, DC 20044-7610; Title Tel # (202) 927-7000 Title Fax # (202) 927-5192
Editorial Description: Association news and related items as well as relevant Federal legislative, indicial, and administrative news.
General Info: Yr. Est. 1980, 11x/yr., Trim Size-8½ x 11, Sheetfed press, 20 pages, ISSN: 0899-7152, 2 Color, Matte, Saddle-stitched
Subscriptions: Free With Membership
Acquistions: Publication Sold
Circulation: Total-3,500
Advertising: $650.
List Rental: Actives: 3,000, $250/M

AIMC Newsletter   *Association*

Publishing Co: Assn. of Internal Management Consultants, PO Box 304, East Bloomfield, NY 14443-0304 Fax # (716) 924-4946; Title Tel # (716) 657-7878
Personnel: Editor-Margareth Custer
Editorial Description: Practice of internal management consulting.
General Info: Yr. Est. 1971, Quarterly

AQP Report   *Association*

Publishing Co: Assn. for Quality & Participation, 801b W 8th St # 501, Cincinnati, OH 45203-1601; Title Tel # (513) 381-1959 Title Fax # (513) 381-0070
Personnel: Publisher-Ned Hamson, Editor-Freda Hughes
Editorial Description: Short articles & news about quality & participation.
General Info: (Formerly IAQC Circle Report), Yr. Est. 1982, Bi-monthly, Trim Size-8½ x 11, Web press, 16 pages, Color-cover, Recycled, Saddle-stitched
Subscriptions: Indv. $45, Free With Membership
Circulation: Total-11,000
List Rental: Actives: 11,000, $125/M

A.S.A.P.   *Business*

Publishing Co: Business One Irwin, 1333 Burr Ridge Pky, Burr Ridge, IL 60521-6489 Tel # (708) 206-2700
Editorial Description: 'Answers, solutions, advice for Professionals.'
General Info: Yr. Est. 1992, Quarterly
Subscriptions: Indv. $20

Abstract of Management Services Analysis   *Business, Association*

Publishing Co: Maxiplan Financial Club, Box 5255 Stn. C, 12687 52nd Ave., Montreal, PQ H1E 2H6 Canada Tel # (514) 648-2953
Personnel: Editor-Marcel Wistaff
Editorial Description: Provides specific executive diagnosis; operations analysis; financial perspectives; business opportunities and market surveys.
General Info: Yr. Est. 1990, Quarterly, Trim Size-8½ x 11, No Color
Subscriptions: Indv. $60, $25/copy

Academy of Management News   *Business*

Publishing Co: Baugh Center for Entrepreneurship, Baylor University, BU Box 8011, Waco, TX 76798-8011; Title Tel # (817) 755-2265 Title Fax # (817) 755-2421
General Info: Quarterly

Academy of Management Newsletter

Publishing Co: Academy of Management, PO Box 3020, Briarcliff Manor, NY 10510-8020; Title Tel # (914) 923-2607 Title Fax # (914) 923-2615
Personnel: Production Mgr., Adv. Dir.-Terese Vivenzo
Editorial Description: Current information about members, announcements, and official membersh communications.
General Info: Yr. Est. 1971, Quarterly, Trim Size-8½ x 11, Sheetfed press, 16 pages, ISSN: 0161-5998, Ind/Abs/Online: Bibl., Color, Saddle-stitched
Subscriptions: Indv. $35
Circulation: Total-8,500
List Rental: Rents Lists
Printing Co: Sheridan Press, 450 Fame Avenue, Hanover, PA 17331-9581 Tel # (717) 632-3535. Fax # (717) 633-8900

Accommodating Disabilities: Business Management Guide
See: DISABILITY

Administration & Management   *Business*

Publishing Co: National Technical Information Service U.S., 5285 Port Royal Rd., Springfield, VA 22161-0001 Fax # (703) 487-4630; Title Tel # (703) 487-4630
Editorial Description: Subject - specific newsletters produced weekly from NTIS scientific/technical database.
General Info: Weekly, Trim Size-8½ x 11, Offset press
Subscriptions: Indv. $115, Can. $115, For. $155

Administration & Management Special Interest Section Newsletter
See: HEARING & SPEECH

Administrative Assistant Adviser
See: BUSINESS & INDUSTRY

Ag Executive
See: AGRICULTURE

Aid for Education Report
See: EDUCATION

American Management Association Flash   *Business, Association*

Publishing Co: American Management Association, 135 West 50th Street, New York, NY 10020-1201 Tel # (212) 586-8100 Fax # (212) 903-8083
Editorial Description: Information on best seminars and training sessions.
General Info: Monthly

American Management Association Presidents' Assn. Program   *Business, Association*

Publishing Co: American Management Association, 135 West 50th Street, New York, NY 10020-1201 Tel # (212) 586-8100 Fax # (212) 903-8083

Applied Management Newsletter   *Business*

Publishing Co: Natl. Assn. for Management, 5920 E. Central Ave., #205, Wichita, KS 67208-4241; Title Tel # (316) 721-4684
Personnel: Publisher-Hugh Magness, Editor-Dr. Gerald Graham
Editorial Description: Designed for the training director & individual manager. Each issue covers one area of supervisory expertise that consists of self-checklist, research summary, case problem, & instructor notes.
General Info: Yr. Est. 1977, Monthly, Letrpr. press, 4 pages, ISSN: 0889-8227, 2 Color
Subscriptions: Indv. $39, Can. $50, For. $50

Aquaculture Newsletter International
See: FISH & FISHERIES

Association Educator   *Association*

Publishing Co: American Society of Association Executives, 1575 'I' St., N.W., 11th Fl., Washington, DC 20005-1168 Tel # (202) 626-2711 Fax # (202) 408-9633; Title Tel # (202) 626-2739
Personnel: Editor-Joseph Cavarretta
Editorial Description: Published for executives who manage educational programming in associations.
General Info: (Formerly Education Director), Monthly, 6 pages
Subscriptions: Free With Membership
Circulation: Total-1,450, Readership-1,700

Authentication News
See: PACKAGING

BNA Policy & Practice Series
Business

Publishing Co: Bureau of National Affairs, Inc., 1231 25th St. NW, Bldg. N-200, Washington, DC 20037-1157; Title Tel # (202) 452-4200 Title Fax # (202) 822-8092
Personnel: Publisher-William A. Beltz, Editor-Bill L. Manville, Circ. Mgr.-Gary C. Seltzer
Editorial Description: A weekly notification & reference service covering five major areas of employer-employee relations. Covered are personnel management, labor relations, fair employment practices, compensation, & wages & hours; in ten binders with two newsletters & occasional surveys.
General Info: (Formerly Labor Policy & Practice, Manual of Labor Supervision), Yr. Est. 1945, Weekly, Trim Size-8½ x 11, Offset press, 7 pages, ISSN: 0005-3228, Ind/Abs/Online: DIALOG, HRIN
Subscriptions: Indv. $1,386

Benefactor
Business

Publishing Co: Bedford House, 1800 Ironstone Mnr.Pickering, Toronto, ON L1W 3T9 Canada Tel # (905) 831-3000; Title Tel # (416) 340-9809 Title Fax # (416) 340-9813
Personnel: Editor-Len Wolstenholme
Editorial Description: Newsletter of non-profit management in Canada targeted to non-profit organizations.
General Info: Yr. Est. 1990, Semi-monthly
Subscriptions: Indv. $145

Benefits Communicator
Business

Publishing Co: HR Communication Services, PO Box 671, Richmond, VA 23218-1671; Title Tel # (804) 751-5003
Personnel: Publisher, Editor-Ann Black
Editorial Description: Reports on trends and issues in benefits administration and employee communication techniques.
General Info: Yr. Est. 1992, Bi-monthly, Trim Size-8½ x 11, Offset press, 8 pages, ISSN: 1063-9217, Matte
Subscriptions: Indv. $98
Printing Co: Pine Tree Press, 2410 Ownby Lane, Richmond, VA 23220 Fax # (804) 359-5820

Benefits Watch
See: BUSINESS & INDUSTRY

Better Supervision
Business

Publishing Co: Economics Press, Inc., 12 Daniel Rd., Fairfield, NJ 07004-2565; Title Tel # (201) 227-1224 Title Fax # (201) 227-9742
Personnel: Editor-Robert Guder, Circ. Mgr.-Ann Lanahan
Editorial Description: Techniques for managing people successfully.
General Info: Bi-weekly, Trim Size-7½ x 13⅝, 12 pages, ISSN: 1974
Subscriptions: Indv. $35, $1/copy
Circulation: Total-43,000
List Rental: List Management Co.: Manager: Michael Korman; Names in the News, 411 Theodore Fremd Ave., Rye, NY 10580 Tel # (914) 925-2400, Actives: 200,000, $85/M, Expires: 60,000, $60/M
Printing Co: Beckley Press, 2 Sperry Rd, Fairfield, NJ 07004-2056 Tel # (201) 227-6350

Better Work Supervisor

Publishing Co: Clement Communications, Inc., Concord Industrial Park, Concordville, PA 19331-9987 Tel # (610) 459-1700 Fax # (610) 459-5092; Title Tel # (215) 459-4200
General Info: Bi-weekly
Subscriptions: Indv. $48, $2/copy
List Rental: Actives: $70/M

Bill Staton's Money Advisory
See: BUSINESS & INDUSTRY

Blue Ribbon Service
Business

Publishing Co: Economics Press, Inc., 12 Daniel Rd., Fairfield, NJ 07004-2565; Title Tel # (201) 227-1224 Title Fax # (201) 227-9742
Personnel: Editor-Robert Guder
Editorial Description: Shows employees the importance of giving good customer service and methods of providing that service.
General Info: Yr. Est. 1979, Bi-weekly
Subscriptions: Indv. $51
Circulation: Total-27,760
List Rental: List Management Co.: Manager: Michael Korman; Names in the News, 411 Theodore Fremd Ave., Rye, NY 10580 Tel # (914) 925-2400, Actives: $85/M
Printing Co: Beckley Press, 2 Sperry Rd, Fairfield, NJ 07004-2056 Tel # (201) 227-6350

Board & Administrator (Nonprofit Edition)
Business

Publishing Co: Aspen Publishers, Inc., 200 Orchard Ridge Dr., Ste 200, Gaithersburg, MD 20878-5440 Parent Co.-Wolters Kluwer US Corporation, New York; Title Tel # (301) 417-7500 Title Fax # (301) 417-7655
Personnel: Editor-Chuck Elliot
Editorial Description: Board & Administrator is a network of administrators who share their strategies for improving their relationships with board members-and therefore making their jobs easier.
General Info: Yr. Est. 1984, Monthly
Subscriptions: Indv. $119, For. $143, $13/copy
List Rental: List Management Co.: Stevens-Knox List Management, 304 Park Ave S., New York, NY 10010-5312 Tel # (212) 388-8800, Fax # (212) 388-8890

Board Briefs
Association

Publishing Co: Community Associations Institute, 1630 Duke Street, Alexandria, VA 22314; Title Tel # (703) 548-8600 Title Fax # (703) 684-1581
Personnel: Exec. VP/Group Publisher-Barbara Byrd-Lawler, Editor-Anne Calmes
Editorial Description: A newsletter for community association leaders.
General Info: Yr. Est. 1989, Bi-monthly, Sheetfed press, 4 pages, ISSN: 1042-7120, 2 Color, Other
Subscriptions: Indv. $29
Circulation: Total-16,000
Printing Co: Ameriprint, 300 Mill St NE, Vienna, VA 22180-4524 Tel # (703) 281-7800

Bootstrappin' Entrepreneur
See: BUSINESS & INDUSTRY

Bootstrappin' Entrepreneur Bulletin
See: BUSINESS & INDUSTRY

Bowman's Accounting Report
See: ACCOUNTING

Briefings on Assisted Living
See: HEALTH

Briefings on Hospital Safety
See: HOSPITALS & NURSING HOMES

Briefings on JCAHO
See: HOSPITALS & NURSING HOMES

Briefings on JCAHO-Home Care
See: HOSPITALS & NURSING HOMES

Briefings on Laboratory Safety and Accreditation
See: HOSPITALS & NURSING HOMES

Briefings on Long-Term Care Regulations
See: HOSPITALS & NURSING HOMES

Briefings on Practice Management
Business

Publishing Co: Opus Communications, Inc., Box 1168, 100 Hoods Lane, Marblehead, MA 01945; Title Tel # (617) 639-1872 Title Fax # (617) 639-2982
Personnel: Publisher-Jennifer Cofer, Editor-Claudia Hoffacker
Editorial Description: Published for medical practice managers. Discusses new regulations, health care reform, reimbursement, trends, and ideas to make the office manager's job easier.
General Info: Yr. Est. 1993, Monthly, Trim Size-8½ x 11, 12 pages, ISSN: 1076-6006, 2 Color, Saddle-stitched
Subscriptions: Indv. $97
List Rental: Rents Lists

Briefings on Subacute Care: Regulations & Reimbursement
See: HOSPITALS & NURSING HOMES

Business Breakthroughs
See: BUSINESS & INDUSTRY

Business Crimes Bulletin
See: LAW

Business Review
See: BUSINESS & INDUSTRY

CEF News

Publishing Co: Chief Executives Organization, 5430 Grosvenor Ln Ste 210, Bethesda, MD 20814-2100; Title Tel # (305) 689-1352
General Info: Yr. Est. 1958, Quarterly

CFO & Controller Alert
See: ACCOUNTING

CMA Update
See: ACCOUNTING

CNS Outlook
See: AERONAUTICS/ASTRONAUTICS

CPA Administrative Report
See: ACCOUNTING

CQSS Reporter

Publishing Co: Don Caruth Associates, 519 I-30, Suite 242, Rockwell, TX 75087; Title Tel # (214) 279-0041 Title Fax # (214) 722-9548
Personnel: Publisher-Don Caruth, Editor-Steven Austin Stovall
Editorial Description: Contains timely articles related to improving customer service, sales, marketing, etc. Regular features include odd, interesting and unusual facts.
General Info: Yr. Est. 1991, Bi-monthly, Sheetfed press, 4 pages, No Color
Subscriptions: Indv. $29
Circulation: (50% controlled), Total-500, Subscriptions-250
Printing Co: Account Manager: Pat Elling; Quick Print Shop, 1125 Ridge Rd, Rockwall, TX 75087-4217

CRA Review
See: ECONOMICS

Canadian Nursing Management
See: BUSINESS & INDUSTRY

Canadian Payroll Manager, The
Business

Publishing Co: Carswell, 2075 Kennedy Road, One Corporate Plaza, Scarborough, ON M1T 3V4 Canada Tel # (416) 609-8000 Fax # (416) 298-5094; Title Tel # (416) 445-4940 Title Fax # (416) 445-5352
Personnel: Publisher-Robert McElman
Editorial Description: This newsletter provides payroll practitioners & financial officers with current topical information to assist them in the management & compliance aspects of the payroll function. Includes analysis of provincial & federal legislation & commentary on pend ng legislation.
General Info: Yr. Est. 1989, Monthly
Subscriptions: Indv. $185

Capacity Management Review
See: COMPUTERS & AUTOMATION

Capital Adjustments
See: TAXES

Capitation Management Report
See: HEALTH

Carlson Report for Shopping Center Management
See: REAL ESTATE

Case Study
See: BUSINESS & INDUSTRY

Center for Creative Leadership
Business

Publishing Co: Center for Creative Leadership, One Leadership Place, PO Box 26300, Greensboro, NC 27438-6300; Title Tel # (910) 288-7210 Title Fax # (910) 288-3999
Personnel: Publisher-Wilfred H. Drath, Editor-Matin Wilcox, Production Mgr.-Marcia Horowitz, Art Dir.-Joann Forguson
Editorial Description: Contains articles about leadership and management and information about Center for Creative Leadership people and activities.
General Info: Yr. Est. 1980, Quarterly, Trim Size-8½ x 11, Sheetfed press, 16 pages, ISSN: 1065-464X, 2 Color, Matte, Saddle-stitched
Subscriptions: Free
Circulation: Total-65,000
Printing Co: Greensboro Printing Co., 3012 Patterson St., Greensboro, NC 27408 Tel # (919) 294-4300, Fax # (910) 855-7397

Chief Executive Newsletter
Business

Publishing Co: Center for Entrepreneurial Management, 180 Varick Street, Penthouse, New York, NY 10014-4606; Title Tel # (212) 633-0060 Title Fax # (212) 633-0063
Personnel: Publisher, Editor-Joseph Mancuso, Design Ed.-Zoran Markovic, Circ. Mgr.-Karla Schulz, Adv. Dir.-Tony Towl, Promotion Dir.-Fleeming Meeks
Editorial Description: Unique management insights and sources for presidents of growing businesses.
General Info: (Formerly Chief Executive Officer's; Entrepreneurial Manager's), Yr. Est. 1978, Monthly, Trim Size-8½ x 11, Sheetfed press, 12 pages, ISSN: 0272-0396, Ind/Abs/Online: NewsNet, No Color, Matte, Saddle-stitched
Subscriptions: Indv. $96, $8/copy
Circulation: Total-2,800
List Rental: Rents Lists

Chief Officer's Aide
See: FIRE PROTECTION

Clean Air News
See: ENVIRONMENT & ECOLOGY

Coding Clinic for ICD-9-CM
Consumer

Publishing Co: American Hospital Publishing, Inc., 737 N. Michigan Ave., Ste. 700, Chicago, IL 60611-2431 Tel # (312) 280-6800 Fax # (312) 944-4232; Title Tel # (312) 280-6236
Personnel: Editor-Faye Brown
Editorial Description: Medical record coding.
General Info: Yr. Est. 1984, Quarterly, Trim Size-6 x 9, 20 pages, ISSN: 0742-9800
Subscriptions: Indv. $160, $25/copy
Circulation: Total-4,300

Common Sense Negotiations
Business

Publishing Co: Economics Press, Inc., 12 Daniel Rd., Fairfield, NJ 07004-2565; Title Tel # (201) 227-1224 Title Fax # (201) 227-9742
Personnel: Editor-Robert Guder, Circ. Mgr.-Ann Lanahan
Editorial Description: Features clear strategies that give the edge in dealing for oneself or the benefit of the company.
General Info: Yr. Est. 1990, Weekly, Trim Size-8½ x 11, 4 pages, Looseleaf
Subscriptions: Indv. $117
Circulation: Total-413
List Rental: List Management Co.: Manager: Michael Korman; Names in the News, 411 Theodore Fremd Ave., Rye, NY 10580 Tel # (914) 925-2400, Actives: $85/M
Printing Co: Beckley Press, 2 Sperry Rd, Fairfield, NJ 07004-2056 Tel # (201) 227-6350

Communication Briefings
See: MEDIA & COMMUNICATIONS

Communications Insights
Business

Publishing Co: Comquest Inc, 112 Schubert Drive, Downingtown, PA 19335; Title Tel # (610) 269-2100 Title Fax # (610) 269-2275
Personnel: Publisher-Joseph Schubert, Editor-Brooke Shonk, Circ. Mgr.-Mark Schubert, Art Dir.-Tim Hantula, Adv. Dir., Mktg. Dir.-Barbara Doran
Editorial Description: Tips and techniques for successful communication, management, and marketing.
General Info: Yr. Est. 1995, Bi-weekly, 6 pages
Subscriptions: Indv. $127

Communique
Business, Association

Publishing Co: Canadian Society of Club Managers, 41 Shilton Rd., Agincourt, ON M1S 2J8 Canada; Title Tel # (416) 293-9527
General Info: Yr. Est. 1980, Bi-monthly, 8 pages
Circulation: Total-400
Advertising: Inquire for rates.

Community Living of Florida
See: CONSTRUCTION & BUILDING

Community Relations Report
Business

Publishing Co: Joe Williams Communications, PO Box 924, Bartlesville, OK 74005-0924; Title Tel # (918) 336-2267 Title Fax # (918) 336-2733
Personnel: Publisher, Editor-Joe Williams, Circ. Mgr.-Barb Weatherly
Editorial Description: Focuses on community relations from a corporate standpoint.
General Info: Yr. Est. 1981, Monthly, Trim Size-8½ x 11, Sheetfed press, 12 pages, ISSN: 0736-7147, 2 Color, Saddle-stitched
Subscriptions: Indv. $139, Can. $139, For. $179, $2/copy
Acquistions: Publication Bought

Community Service
Business

Publishing Co: MLP Enterprises, 4202 Chestnut St # 1, Philadelphia, PA 19104-3015; Title Tel # (215) 662-0601
Editorial Description: Feature articles relating to management issues facing non-profit & community-based organizations.
General Info: Yr. Est. 1978, 10x/yr.
Subscriptions: Indv. $10, $2/copy

CompFlash
See: LABOR

Competitive Advantage
See: SALESMANSHIP & SELLING

Conference Call Calendar
Business

Publishing Co: Calendar Planning Corporation, 237 Park Ave., Ste. 900, New York, NY 10017 Tel # (212) 270-5555 Fax # (212) 808-2464
Personnel: Publisher-Nicholas Parks
Editorial Description: Provides information on scheduled conference calls.
General Info: Yr. Est. 1994, Daily

Consultants News
Business

Publishing Co: Kennedy Publications, Templeton Rd., Fitzwilliam, NH 03447 Tel # (603) 585-6544; Title Tel # (603) 585-2200 Title Fax # (603) 585-6401
Personnel: Publisher-James Kennedy, Editor-Tom Rodenhauser, Circ. Mgr.-Janet Roy, Art Dir.-Melinda Taylor, Mktg. Dir.-Carolyn Edwards
Editorial Description: Covers trends, associations, fees, statistics, surveys, marketing ideas, and who's who in management consulting.
General Info: Yr. Est. 1970, Monthly, Trim Size-8½ x 11, Offset press, 8 pages, ISSN: 0045-8201, 2 Color, Matte
Subscriptions: Indv. $188, Can. $208, For. $233, $16/copy
Printing Co: Sterling Business Corp., 206 Concord St, Peterborough, NH 03458-1209 Tel # (603) 924-9401

Consultant's Newsletter   *Business, Association*

Publishing Co: Society of Medical-Dental Management Consultants, 6215 Larson, Kansas City, MO 64133 Tel # (816) 353-8485 Fax # (816) 353-3137; Title Tel # (816) 353-8488
Personnel: Editor-William Kidd
General Info: Yr. Est. 1968, Quarterly, 10 pages, 2 Color
Subscriptions: Free To Qualified Recipient
Advertising: Inquire for rates.
Printing Co: Advertiser's Litho, 1000 W 25th St, Kansas City, MO 64108-2305 Tel # (816) 421-2171

Cooperative News Intl.
See: AGRICULTURE

Corporate Acquisitions, Mergers & Divestiture's
See: INVESTMENT

Corporate Community Relations Letter
See: BUSINESS & INDUSTRY

Corporate Governance
Update   *Business*

Publishing Co: Rowan & Bleuitt, 1000 Vermont Ave, N.W., Washington, DC 20005
Personnel: Editor-H. Boerner
Editorial Description: Information on corporate ethics; trends in management and governance; environmental compliance; shareholder relations. Covers topics of interest to CEOs, CFOs, and Board members.
General Info: Yr. Est. 1993, Quarterly
Subscriptions: Indv. $200
Advertising: Accepts Inserts.

Corporation Forms
See: LAW

Court Management & Administration Report
See: LAW

Cowles Report on Database Marketing
See: ADVERTISING & MARKETING

Creative Selling
See: SALESMANSHIP & SELLING

Credit & Collection Manager's Letter
See: BUSINESS & INDUSTRY

Customer Communicator,
The   *Business*

Publishing Co: Alexander Research & Communications, Inc., 215 Park Ave S., Ste. 1301, New York, NY 10003-1603; Title Tel # (212) 228-0246 Title Fax # (212) 228-0376
Personnel: Publisher-Shirley Alexander, Editor-Leslie Hansen Harps, Mng. Editor-Susan Hash, Circ. Mgr.-Mary Pagliaroli, Mktg. Dir.-Margaret Dewitt
Editorial Description: Provides customer service representatives with the skills, techniques and motivation they need to be more productive. Included with each subscription is the managers' copy of The SkillSharpener. The SkillSharpener come complete with sample handouts, worksheets and role play scenarios.
General Info: Yr. Est. 1976, Monthly, Trim Size-8½ x 11, 4 pages, ISSN: 0145-8450
Subscriptions: Indv. $137, Can. $167, For. $187, $11/copy
List Rental: List Management Co.: Response Media Products Inc., 2323 Perimeter Park Dr., Ste. 200, Atlanta, GA 30341-1335 Tel # (404) 451-5478, Fax # (404) 451-4929

Customer Service Manager's Letter
See: BUSINESS & INDUSTRY

Customer Service Newsletter
See: BUSINESS & INDUSTRY

Customer Service Report   *Business*

Publishing Co: Stovall Group, The, 310 E. I-30, Suite M102a, Garland, TX 75043; Title Tel # (214) 203-1515
Personnel: Editor-Steven Austin Stovall
Editorial Description: Contains new ideas, trends, and techniques for improving customer service in today's growth oriented organization. Regular features include odd facts, quotes, and readers forum.
General Info: Yr. Est. 1991, Bi-monthly, Trim Size-8½ x 11, Offset press, 4 pages, Color
Subscriptions: Indv. $39, Inst. $39, Can. $39, $7/copy
Circulation: Total-900

Customers First
See: SALESMANSHIP & SELLING

Daily Report for Executives
See: ECONOMICS

Datalog

Publishing Co: Business Intelligence Program-SRI Intl., 333 Ravenswood Ave, Menlo Park, CA 94025-3453; Title Tel # (415) 859-4600
Personnel: Production Mgr.-Paula O'Sullivan
General Info: Yr. Est. 1976, Monthly
Circulation: Total-14,000

Dealers Edge
See: AUTOMOTIVE

Delphi Report, The   *Business*

Publishing Co: Delphi Consulting Group, 100 City Hall Plaza, Boston, MA 02108-2106; Title Tel # (617) 247-1025 Title Fax # (617) 247-4957
Personnel: Editor-Thomas M. Koulopoulos, Editor-Michael J. Muth, Mng. Editor-Carl Frappaolo, Feature Ed.-Mary Ann Kozlowski, Circ. Mgr.-Linda Wynott
Editorial Description: Up-to-date developments in the workflow & electronic document management systems market with technology, application, and methodology information.
General Info: (Formerly Delphi Workflow Report), Monthly, Trim Size-8.5 x 11, Sheetfed press, 12 pages, ISSN: 1076-9404, 2 Color, Matte, Other
Subscriptions: Indv. $195, Can. $195, For. $245
Advertising: Accepts Inserts.
Printing Co: S & D Printing & Mailing, 6 Norfolk Avenue, South Easton, MA 02375 Tel # (508) 238-9100, Fax # (508) 238-2679

Developing & Managing Physician Networks
See: HOSPITALS & NURSING HOMES

Development Director's Letter
See: PHILANTHROPY

Director's Monthly   *Association*

Publishing Co: National Association of Corporate Directors, 1707 L St NW Ste 560, Washington, DC 20036-4201; Title Tel # (202) 775-0509 Title Fax # (202) 775-4857
Personnel: Publisher-John Nash, Editor-Alexandra LaJoux, Mktg. Dir.-Jennifer Jardon
Editorial Description: Official newsletter of the National Association of Corporate Directors-Corp. Governance Issues.
General Info: Yr. Est. 1977, Monthly, Trim Size-8½ x 11, Desktop press, 16 pages, 2 Color, Newsprint, Saddle-stitched
Subscriptions: Indv. $425, $15/copy
Circulation: Total-7,000
Printing Co: Custom Print, Inc., 2611 S. Shirlington Rd., Arlington, VA 22206-2529 Tel # (703) 979-6670

Directorship
See: BUSINESS & INDUSTRY

Directory Digest
See: BOOKS & BOOK TRADE

Distribution Center Management
See: BUSINESS & INDUSTRY

Distributor Management
Digest   *Business*

Publishing Co: Business Marketing & Publishing, Inc., PO Box 7457, Wilton, CT 06897-7457; Title Tel # (203) 834-9959
Personnel: Publisher, Editor-George Young
Editorial Description: News about wholesale distributors and manufacturers... products, people, markets, and customers.
General Info: Yr. Est. 1987, Quarterly, 5% ads
Subscriptions: Indv. $20, $5/copy
Advertising: $825. Accepts Inserts.
List Rental: Rents Lists

Distributor's & Wholesaler's Advisor, The
See: BUSINESS & INDUSTRY

Doctor's Office, The   *Business*

Publishing Co: Wentworth Worldwide Media, 1866 Colonial Village Lane, PO Box 10488, Lancaster, PA 17605-0488 Fax # (717) 393-5752; Title Tel # (717) 393-1000 Title Fax # (717) 393-2732
Personnel: Publisher-Cynthia Young, Editor-Ann Mead Ash, Circ. Mgr.-Patrick Hattannio, Production Mgr.-Natalie Zuch, Art Dir.-Natalie Zuck, Mktg. Dir.-Donna Sauder
Editorial Description: Marketing/management newsletter for medical practices.
General Info: Yr. Est. 1982, Monthly, Trim Size-8½ x 11, Web press, 12 pages, ISSN: 0733-2262, 2 Color, Matte, Saddle-stitched
Subscriptions: Indv. $98, $15/copy
Circulation: Total-50,000
Advertising: Accepts Inserts.
List Rental: List Management Co.: Manager: Donna Sander; Direct Media, Inc., 200 Pemberwick Rd., PO Box 4565, Greenwich, CT 06830 Tel # (203) 532-3713, Fax # (203) 531-1452, Actives: 16,400, $90/M
Printing Co: Stauffer Printing, 505 Willow Ln., Lancaster, PA 17601-5696 Tel # (717) 393-9311

Dollars & Cents
Business, Association

Publishing Co: American Society of Association Executives, 1575 'I' St., N.W., 11th Fl., Washington, DC 20005-1168 Tel # (202) 626-2711 Fax # (202) 408-9633; Title Tel # (202) 626-2739
Personnel: Editor-Joseph Cavaretta
Editorial Description: For financial, MIS, and human resource managers of non-profit organizations.
General Info: Yr. Est. 1984, Monthly, 6 pages
Subscriptions: Free With Membership
Circulation: Total-4,200, Readership-8,000
List Rental: Actives: 4,001, $175/M

Drafting the Union Contract: A Handbook for the Management Negotiator
See: LABOR

Drugs in the Workplace
See: DRUGS & PHARMACEUTICALS

EEO Review
See: INDUSTRIAL RELATIONS/PERSONNEL

EMA Reporter
See: EMPLOYMENT

E.M.S. Officer's Notebook
See: MEDICINE

Effective Business Writing
Business

Publishing Co: Economics Press, Inc., 12 Daniel Rd., Fairfield, NJ 07004-2565; Title Tel # (201) 227-1224 Title Fax # (201) 227-9742
Personnel: Editor-Linda Bullock, Circ. Mgr.-Ann Lanahan
Editorial Description: Reveals methods and short cuts successful writiers use in their work.
General Info: Yr. Est. 1991, Weekly, Trim Size-8½ x 11, 4 pages, Looseleaf
Subscriptions: Indv. $136
Circulation: Total-500
List Rental: List Management Co.: Manager: Michael Korman; Names in the News, 411 Theodore Fremd Ave., Rye, NY 10580 Tel # (914) 925-2400, Actives: $85/M
Printing Co: Beckley Press, 2 Sperry Rd, Fairfield, NJ 07004-2056 Tel # (201) 227-6350

Electric Utility Week's Demand-Side Report
See: PUBLIC UTILITIES

Employee Terminations Law Bulletin
See: LABOR

Employer's Handbook: Independent Contractor vs. Employee
See: LABOR

Environmental Compliance Alert
See: ENVIRONMENT & ECOLOGY

Equal Employer, The
See: EMPLOYMENT

Equipment & Materials Update
Business

Publishing Co: Infoteam, Inc., PO Box 15640, Plantation, FL 33318-5640 Fax # (954) 472-0544; Title Tel # (954) 473-9560 Title Fax # (954) 473-0544
Personnel: Publisher-Merton Allen, Editor-Walter A. Treff
Editorial Description: Covers materials development & utilization as well as equipment design, fabrication, application, maintenance, and integrity.
General Info: Yr. Est. 1993, Monthly, Trim Size-8½ x 11, Sheetfed press, 16 pages, ISSN: 1069-6490, Ind/Abs/Online: NewsNet, DIALOG, Predicasts, No Color, Newsprint
Subscriptions: Indv. $269, Can. $309, For. $379

Ethical Management
Business, Association

Publishing Co: Business Strategies, PO Box 19358, Portland, OR 97280-0358; Title Tel # (503) 244-5710 Title Fax # (503) 244-5710
Personnel: Publisher, Editor-Kathleen Purdy
Editorial Description: Newsletter for managinq ethically and effectively. Contains original articles, interviews, profiles of companies, book reviews, resources, calendar of events, how-to tips. Covers all business ethics issues.
General Info: Monthly, ISSN: 1058-6571, Recycled
Subscriptions: Indv. $97, Inst. $127, For. $127
Advertising: Accepts Inserts.
List Rental: Rents Lists

Executive Compensation Report (ECR)
See: BUSINESS & INDUSTRY

Executive Edge
Business

Publishing Co: Select Press, PO Box 37, Corte Madera, CA 94976-0037; Title Tel # (415) 924-1612 Title Fax # (415) 924-7179
Personnel: Publisher-Rick Crandall
Editorial Description: Covers quality customer service and marketing techniques.
General Info: (Formerly Executive Fitness Newsletter), Yr. Est. 1973, Monthly, 16 pages, ISSN: 1048-2954, 2 Color, Saddle-stitched
Subscriptions: Indv. $70, Inst. $70, Can. $80, For. $90
List Rental: Actives: 10,000, $70/M

Executive Issues
Business

Publishing Co: Sponsor-Wharton Executive Education, Wharton School, Univ. of Pennsylvania, Executive Education Division, 255 S. 38th St., Philadelphia, PA 19104-6359; Title Tel # (215) 898-1776 Title Fax # (215) 386-4304
Personnel: Publisher-Neil Neveras, Editor-Robin Saleman, Circ. Mgr.-Philip Frank
Editorial Description: Discusses current business issues, business continuing education and organization and development.
General Info: Yr. Est. 1989, Quarterly, Trim Size-8.5 x 11, Offset press, 8 pages, 2 Color, Matte, Saddle-stitched
Subscriptions: Free To Qualified Recipient
Circulation: Total-40,000
List Rental: Rents Lists

Executive Report on Customer Satisfaction
See: BUSINESS & INDUSTRY

Executive Search Review
See: EMPLOYMENT

Executive Solutions
Business

Publishing Co: Dartnell Corp., 4660 N. Ravenswood Ave., Chicago, IL 60640-4510; Title Tel # (312) 561-4000 Title Fax # (312) 561-3801
Personnel: Publisher-Clark Fetridge, Editor-Linda Segall, Production Mgr.-Megan Mulligan, Art Dir.-Andrew Epstein, Mktg. Dir.-George Economos, Mktg. Mgr.-Tracy Butzko
Editorial Description: Modern management techniques for executive training.
General Info: (Formerly Effective Executive), Yr. Est. 1970, Semi-monthly, Trim Size-8½ x 11, 4 pages, 2 Color
Subscriptions: Indv. $89
List Rental: List Management Co.: Manager: Sue McDorman; Leland Company, 1801 W. Leland Ave., Chicago, IL 60640-4363 Tel # (312) 561-4005, Fax # (312) 561-4099, Actives: 70,785, $90/M, Hotline: $125/M

Executive Speaker
Business, Association

Publishing Co: Executive Speaker Co., PO Box 292437, Dayton, OH 45429-0437; Title Tel # (513) 294-8493 Title Fax # (513) 294-6044
Personnel: Publisher, Editor-Robert Skovgard
Editorial Description: Clearinghouse & digest of speeches by executives. Features openings, closings & select quotes from recent speeches.
General Info: Yr. Est. 1980, Monthly, Trim Size-8½ x 11, 12 pages, ISSN: 0271-3659, Ind/Abs/Online: Nexis/Lexis, No Color, Matte
Subscriptions: Indv. $120, Inst. $120, Can. $120, For. $145
Advertising: Accepts Inserts.
List Rental: Actives: $125/M

Executive Strategies
Business

Publishing Co: National Institute of Business Management, 1101 King St Ste 411, Alexandria, VA 22314-2966 Parent Co.-National Information Corp., Alexandria; Title Tel # (703) 548-3885 Title Fax # (703) 549-0182
Personnel: Publisher-Steve Sturm, Editorial Dir.-Anne Cheevers, Mktg. Mgr.-Donna Houseman
Editorial Description: Career guidance for managers and executives.
General Info: Yr. Est. 1986, Monthly, Trim Size-8½ x 11, Matte
Subscriptions: Indv. $48, Can. $60
Acquistions: Publication Bought, Publication Sold
Circulation: Total-100,000
Advertising: Inquire for rates. Accepts Inserts.
List Rental: List Management Co.: Direct Media, Inc., 200 Pemberwick Rd., PO Box 4565, Greenwich, CT 06830 Tel # (203) 532-3713, Fax # (203) 531-1452, Actives: $95/M, Expires: $55/M

Executives' Digest
Business

Publishing Co: SKO/Brenner America, 196 Merrick Rd, Oceanside, NY 11572-1420; Title Tel # (516) 764-4400

FMA Bulletin

Publishing Co: Fulfillment Management Assn, Hearst Magazines, 250 W 55th St, New York, NY 10019-5201
Personnel: Editor-Dorothea Forier
General Info: (Formerly SFMA Bulletin), Yr. Est. 1971, Semi-monthly
Circulation: Total-395

FMRA News
See: AGRICULTURE

Facility Manager's Alert
See: CONSTRUCTION & BUILDING

Farm and Ranch Tax Letter
See: AGRICULTURE

Fast Break
See: SPORTS & SPORTING GOODS

Federal Assistance Monitor
  See: PHILANTHROPY

Financial Advantage, The   *Business*

Publishing Co: DCD Management Resources, 3773 Cherry Creek N. Dr., Ste. 575, Denver, CO 80209 Tel # (303) 331-6422 Fax # (303) 331-6425
Personnel: Mktg. Dir.-Sheryl Briles
Editorial Description: Designed to help managers and business owners control costs and increase efficiency.
General Info: Yr. Est. 1994, Bi-monthly, Trim Size-8½ x 11, 8 pages, 2 Color, Matte
Subscriptions: Indv. $48

Fire Officer's Notebook
  See: FIRE PROTECTION

First Line Supervisor
  See: LABOR

First Rate Customer
Service   *Business*

Publishing Co: Economics Press, Inc., 12 Daniel Rd., Fairfield, NJ 07004-2565; Title Tel # (201) 227-1224 Title Fax # (201) 227-9742
Personnel: Editor-Robert Guder, Circ. Mgr.-Ann Lanahan
Editorial Description: Gives customer service personnel advice that lets them handle their jobs with an enthusiastic, service oriented attitude.
General Info: Yr. Est. 1990, Bi-weekly, Trim Size-8½ x 11, 4 pages
Subscriptions: Indv. $41
Circulation: Total-16,000
List Rental: List Management Co.: Manager: Michael Korman; Names in the News, 411 Theodore Fremd Ave., Rye, NY 10580 Tel # (914) 925-2400, Actives: $85/M
Printing Co: Beckley Press, 2 Sperry Rd, Fairfield, NJ 07004-2056 Tel # (201) 227-6350

Focus, the Business
Continuity Planning
Newsletter   *Business*

Publishing Co: Coopers & Lybrand, 203 N La Salle St, Chicago, IL 60601-1296; Title Tel # (312) 701-5500
Editorial Description: For CEO's, corporate managers and data processing managers.
General Info: Yr. Est. 1994, Quarterly

Forum
  See: THEATRE

Front Line Management   *Business*

Publishing Co: Economics Press, Inc., 12 Daniel Rd., Fairfield, NJ 07004-2565; Title Tel # (201) 227-1224 Title Fax # (201) 227-9742
Personnel: Editor-Robert Guder, Circ. Mgr.-Ann Lanahan
Editorial Description: Ideas and suggestions that provide a solid foundation in the key principles of supervisory management.
General Info: Yr. Est. 1975, Weekly, Trim Size-8½ x 11, 4 pages, Looseleaf
Subscriptions: Indv. $142
Circulation: Total-1,200
Advertising: Inquire for rates.
List Rental: List Management Co.: Manager: Michael Korman; Names in the News, 411 Theodore Fremd Ave., Rye, NY 10580 Tel # (914) 925-2400
Printing Co: Beckley Press, 2 Sperry Rd, Fairfield, NJ 07004-2056 Tel # (201) 227-6350

Funeral Service Insider
  See: FUNERAL SERVICE

FutureScan
  See: ADVERTISING & MARKETING

Futurescope

Publishing Co: Arthur D. Little, Acorn Park, Cambridge, MA 02140-2390; Title Tel # (617) 270-1200
Personnel: Editor-Grahame Smith
General Info: Yr. Est. 1987, Monthly, Looseleaf

George Whalin's Retail Management Letter
  See: ADVERTISING & MARKETING

Getting Along
  See: INDUSTRIAL RELATIONS/PERSONNEL

Guide to Good Clinical
Practice   *Business*

Publishing Co: Thompson Publishing Group, 1725 K Street, NW, Washington, DC 20006 Tel # (202) 872-4000
Editorial Description: Designed for quick, easy access to explanations of laws and regulations affecting sponsors, clinical investigators and monitors.
General Info: Irregular, Looseleaf
Subscriptions: Indv. $537

HARA: Hospital Accounts Receivable Analysis
  See: HOSPITALS & NURSING HOMES

Handbook of Communications Systems Management
  See: COMPUTERS & AUTOMATION

Health Care
  See: HOSPITALS & NURSING HOMES

Health Care Capitation and Risk Contracting Manual
  See: HEALTH

Health Care Strategic Management
  See: HOSPITALS & NURSING HOMES

Health Systems Leader   *Business*

Publishing Co: Bader & Associates, Inc., P.O. Box 2106, Rockville, MD 20847-2106 Tel # (301) 468-1610 Fax # (301) 770-4919
Personnel: Publisher-Barry Bader, Editor-Meg Matheny, Sr. Ed.-Reggi Veatch
Editorial Description: Published for managers of health systems.
General Info: Yr. Est. 1988, Monthly
Subscriptions: Indv. $319

HealthCare Systems NewsLetter
  See: HEALTH

Healthcare Business &
Legal Strategies

Publishing Co: Atlantic Information Svcs., Inc., 1100 17th St. NW, Ste. 300, Washington, DC 20036-5503; Title Tel # (202) 775-9008 Title Fax # (202) 331-9542
Personnel: Publisher-Richard Biehl, Circ. Mgr.-Gwen Arnold, Production Dir.-Garry Peterson, Mktg. Dir.-Donna Lawton, Mktg. Mgr.-Christine Burdell
Editorial Description: Timely, authoritative news on safe harbors, physician self-referrals, joint ventures, physician recruitment, fraud and abuse, antitrust and tax issues.
General Info: (Formerly Healthcare Financial Ventures Relationships), Yr. Est. 1992, Bi-weekly
Subscriptions: Indv. $371
List Rental: List Management Co.: Tony Murray & Assoc., P.O. Box 2409, Fairfax, VA 22031-3739 Tel # (703) 425-5356, Fax # (703) 425-4537

Healthcare Management Team Letter
  See: HOSPITALS & NURSING HOMES

Healthcare Systems Strategy Report
  See: HOSPITALS & NURSING HOMES

Hiring & Firing Newsletter
  See: EMPLOYMENT

Hiring Compliance Update
  See: LABOR

Holistic Resource Management Quarterly
  See: ENVIRONMENT & ECOLOGY

Home-Based Business Newsletter
  See: BUSINESS & INDUSTRY

Home Business Report   *Business*

Publishing Co: Kerner Group, 3231 Forks St, Easton, PA 18045-5970 Tel # (610) 253-3054; Title Fax # (610) 559-8553
Editorial Description: How-to articles on time management, marketing, phone skills and more.
General Info: Yr. Est. 1993, Monthly
Subscriptions: Indv. $24

Homebased Business News Report
  See: BUSINESS & INDUSTRY

Homecare Administrative Horizons
  See: HEALTH

Homecare Direction
  See: HEALTH

Hospital Fast Payment Report
  See: HOSPITALS & NURSING HOMES

How to Get Paid   *Business*

Publishing Co: Wentworth Worldwide Media, 1866 Colonial Village Lane, PO Box 10488, Lancaster, PA 17605-0488; Title Tel # (717) 393-1000 Title Fax # (717) 393-5752
Personnel: Publisher-Cynthia Young, Editor-Ann Mead Ash, Production Mgr.-Art Dir.-Eileen Mauskoft, Circ. Mgr., Mktg. Dir.-Donna Sauder
Editorial Description: Provides collection information for patient account managers at medical practices.
General Info: Yr. Est. 1989, Monthly, Trim Size-8½ x 11, Sheetfed press, 8 pages, ISSN: 1066-1565, 2 Color, Matte, Saddle-stitched
Subscriptions: Indv. $79, $10/copy
Printing Co: The Doctor's Press, Olde Homestead Rd., Lancaster, PA 17605

Human Resource Management Compensation *Business*

Publishing Co: CCH, Inc., 2700 Lake Cook Rd., Riverwoods, IL 60015 Parent Co.-Kluwer Law & Taxation Publishers, Cambridge; Title Tel # (847) 267-7000 Title Fax # (800) 224-8299
Editorial Description: Explains federal and state wage-hour requirements, including overtime pay and minimum wage. Covers employee benefit plans, such as pension and profit-sharing plans, insurance and HMO, and executive compensation arrangements.
General Info: (Formerly Compensation), Yr. Est. 1982, Monthly, Looseleaf
Subscriptions: Indv. $417

Human Resources Equal Employment Opportunity
See: EMPLOYMENT

Human Resources Management in Canada *Business*

Publishing Co: Prentice-Hall Canada, 1870 Birchmont Rd., Scarborough, ON M1P 2T1 Canada Parent Co.-Simon & Schuster, Waterford; Title Tel # (416) 293-3621 Title Fax # (416) 299-2529
Personnel: Publisher-Yolanda deRooy, Editor-Jeff Hill, Circ. Dir.-Joanne Zinck, Production Dir.-Anita Boyle, Mktg. Dir.-Jerry Smith
Editorial Description: Information for human resource professionals.
General Info: Yr. Est. 1983, Monthly, Trim Size-5½ x 8½, 60 pages, No Color, Coated, Looseleaf
Subscriptions: Can. $549
Circulation: Total-1,243
Printing Co: Commerce Press, 2250 Midland Ave., #17, Scarborough, ON M1P 4R9 Canada Tel # (416) 291-8796, Fax # (416) 291-9950

Human Resources Management Employee Relations
See: LABOR UNION

Human Resources Management Ideas and Trends Newsletter *Business*

Publishing Co: CCH, Inc., 2700 Lake Cook Rd., Riverwoods, IL 60015 Parent Co.-Kluwer Law & Taxation Publishers, Cambridge; Title Tel # (847) 267-7000 Title Fax # (800) 224-8299
Editorial Description: Human Resources contains news, features, best practices & helpful information for managers & HR staff.
General Info: Yr. Est. 1982, Bi-weekly
Subscriptions: Indv. $197

Human Resources Management OSHA Compliance *Business*

Publishing Co: CCH, Inc., 2700 Lake Cook Rd., Riverwoods, IL 60015 Parent Co.-Kluwer Law & Taxation Publishers, Cambridge; Title Tel # (847) 267-7000 Title Fax # (800) 224-8299
Editorial Description: Federal & State OSHA Laws, agency directives, administrative & judicial rulings, hands-on compliance guidance.
General Info: Monthly, Looseleaf
Subscriptions: Indv. $417

IFMA News
See: CONSTRUCTION & BUILDING

IMA Focus
See: ACCOUNTING

INFOCUS
See: BUSINESS & INDUSTRY

I.P.M.A. News *Association* CPM: $83

Publishing Co: International Personnel Management Association, 1617 Duke St., Alexandria, VA 22314-3406; Title Tel # (703) 549-7100 Title Fax # (703) 684-0948
Personnel: Editor-Sarah Shiffert, Product Mgr.-Karen Smith
Editorial Description: Newsletter for I.P.M.A.
General Info: Yr. Est. 1973, Monthly, Trim Size-8½ x 11, Sheetfed press, 24 pages, 10% ads, 2 Color, Matte, Saddle-stitched
Subscriptions: Indv. $21
Circulation: Total-6,000
Advertising: $500.
List Rental: Actives: $105/M

IRA Compliance Manual
See: INDUSTRIAL RELATIONS/PERSONNEL

IS Budget International
See: COMPUTERS & AUTOMATION

IS Capacity Management Handbook Series
See: COMPUTERS & AUTOMATION

InfoManage: The International Management Newsletter for the Information Services Executive *Business*

Publishing Co: SMR International, Box 948, Murray Hill Station, New York, NY 10156-0948 Fax # (212) 685-2987; Title Tel # (212) 683-6285 Title Fax # (212) 683-2987
Personnel: Publisher-Guy St. Clair
Editorial Description: The information management newsletter for the information service executive.
General Info: Yr. Est. 1993, Monthly, Trim Size-8½ x 11, 8 pages, ISSN: 1070-0013
Subscriptions: Indv. $138, Can. $153, For. $168, $15/copy
Circulation: Total-1,000
List Rental: Actives: 1,000, $500/M

Information Interchange
See: OFFICE METHODS & EQUIPMENT

Information Management
See: LIBRARY

Information Solutions: A newsletter of ideas & techniques on how to profit from info. *Business*

Publishing Co: Information Plus, 14 Lafayette Square, Suite 2000, Buffalo, NY 14203-1920 Fax # (716) 852-1653; Title Tel # (716) 852-2220 Title Fax # (716) 842-6049
Personnel: Publisher, Editor-D.C. Sawyer, Circ. Mgr.-M. Clavijo, Production Mgr.-S. Stucker
Editorial Description: Discusses how to use competitive and customer intelligence. Each issue is devoted to an intelligence theme. A valuable tool for managers in marketing and related occupations, as well as entrepeneurs and small business owners.
General Info: Yr. Est. 1983, Bi-monthly, 8 pages, ISSN: 0824-3514, 2 Color, Matte, Saddle-stitched
Subscriptions: Indv. $65, Inst. $115
Printing Co: Copy Store, 53 Court St, Buffalo, NY 14202-3102 Tel # (716) 847-6400

Ink! Ink! Ink!
See: BUSINESS & INDUSTRY

Ink on Paper
See: PRINTING/GRAPHIC ARTS

Innisbrook Conference Review

Publishing Co: Innisbrook Resort, PO Box 1088, Tarpon Springs, FL 34688-1088 Tel # (813) 942-2000
Personnel: Editor-Bob Nelson
General Info: Quarterly, 6 pages

Innovator's Digest *Business*

Publishing Co: Infoteam, Inc., PO Box 15640, Plantation, FL 33318-5640 Fax # (954) 472-0544; Title Tel # (954) 473-9560 Title Fax # (954) 473-0544
Personnel: Publisher, Editor-Merton Allen
Editorial Description: Innovations in science, technology, engineering, manufacturing, marketing, management, materials, etc. From worldwide business, government, univ., & private sources.
General Info: (Formerly Information for Innovators), Yr. Est. 1980, Bi-weekly, Trim Size-8½ x 11, Offset press, 8 pages, ISSN: 0890-300X, Ind/Abs/Online: NewsNet, Predicasts, DataStar, DIALOG
Subscriptions: Indv. $319, Can. $359, For. $469, $25/copy

Integrated Health Care Delivery Systems
See: HOSPITALS & NURSING HOMES

Interactive Marketing News
See: DIRECT MAIL

International Quality *Business*

Publishing Co: Underwriters Laboratories, Inc., 333 Pfingsten Rd, Northbrook, IL 60062-2096 Tel # (708) 272-8800 Fax # (708) 272-8129
Personnel: Editor-Holly J. Schubert
Editorial Description: Focuses on quality issues including ISO 9000, QS 9000, ISO 14000 and TEL 9000 standards and other quality management topics.
General Info: Yr. Est. 1993, Quarterly, Trim Size-8½ x 11, Sheetfed press, 8 pages, 2 Color, Coated, Saddle-stitched
Subscriptions: Free To Qualified Recipient
Circulation: (100% controlled), Total-18,000

Investment Management Technology

Publishing Co: Waters Information Services, PO Box 2248, Binghamton, NY 13902-2248 Tel # (607) 770-4075; Title Tel # (607) 770-8535 Title Fax # (607) 770-9435
General Info: Yr. Est. 1991, Bi-weekly
Subscriptions: Indv. $595

Issues & Observations *Business*

Publishing Co: Center for Creative Leadership, One Leadership Place, PO Box 26300, Greensboro, NC 27438-6300 Fax # (910) 288-3999; Title Tel # (910) 288-7210
General Info: Bi-monthly

Issues & Solutions

Publishing Co: Ezra Medical Pubs., 23 Manns Hill Rd, Sharon, MA 02067-2271;
Title Tel # (213) 594-8347
Personnel: Publisher-William Edelman
Editorial Description: I&S is a management pub. for the medical products industry. Focus is on case study analysis & issue reviews of industry problems.
General Info: Yr. Est. 1989, Monthly, ISSN: 1048-230X
Subscriptions: Indv. $199, Can. $250, For. $299, $18/copy
Circulation: Total-2,000

Item Processing Report
See: BANKING & FINANCE

Jot and Jolts *Business*

Publishing Co: Economics Press, Inc., 12 Daniel Rd., Fairfield, NJ 07004-2565;
Title Tel # (201) 227-1224 Title Fax # (201) 227-9742
Personnel: Publisher-John Beckley, Editor-Robert Guder, Circ. Mgr.-Ann Lanahan, Production Mgr.-Matt Farley, Art Dir.-Charles Palminteri, Promotion Dir.-Diane Cody
Editorial Description: Monthly planner for supervisors; contains management theory.
General Info: Yr. Est. 1966, Monthly, Sheetfed press, 24 pages, 2 Color, Newsprint
Subscriptions: Indv. $16, $1/copy
Circulation: Total-32,000
List Rental: List Management Co.: Manager: Michael Korman; Names in the News, 411 Theodore Fremd Ave., Rye, NY 10580 Tel # (914) 925-2400, Actives: $85/M
Printing Co: Beckley Press, 2 Sperry Rd, Fairfield, NJ 07004-2056 Tel # (201) 227-6350

Kane's Beverage Week
See: BEVERAGES - BREWING

Keller Letter, The *Business*

Publishing Co: Wentworth Worldwide Media, 1866 Colonial Village Lane, PO Box 10488, Lancaster, PA 17605-0488 Tel # (717) 393-1000 Fax # (717) 393-5752; Title Fax # (717) 393-2732
Personnel: Editor in Chief-David Keller
Editorial Description: Companion letter to the Whats Legal NOW Newsletter that discusses employee management law for CEO's.
General Info: Monthly, Trim Size-8½ x 11, 2 pages, 2 Color
Subscriptions: Indv. $150

Ken Blanchard's Profiles
of Success *Business*

Publishing Co: Select Press, PO Box 37, Corte Madera, CA 94976-0037; Title Tel # (415) 924-1612
Editorial Description: Case studies & reports on companies doing outstanding things from quality to empowerment.
General Info: (Formerly Ken Blancard's Leadership Letter), Yr. Est. 1994, Monthly, 12 pages, ISSN: 1085-0082, 4 Color
Subscriptions: Indv. $249
List Rental: Rents Lists

Kennedy's Career Strategist
See: EMPLOYMENT

L.A. Group, A.S.C.S.
Newsletter *Business, Association*

Publishing Co: Amer. Soc. of Corp. Secretaries, 9275 SW Peyton Ln., Wilsonville, OR 97070-9200
Parent Co.-American Society of Corporate Secretaries, New York
Personnel: Editor-James Haight
Editorial Description: Business and legal information for corporate secretaries in Southwest.
General Info: Yr. Est. 1981, Quarterly, Offset press, 4 pages, ISSN: 0894-0622, No Color
Circulation: Total-350

LAMA Manager **CPM: $705**

Publishing Co: Legal Assistant Management Association, 638 Prospect Ave., Hartford, CT 06105-4250; Title Tel # (203) 586-7507 Title Fax # (203) 586-7550
Personnel: Editor-Linda Shanks, Adv. Dir.-Marla Clayton
Editorial Description: Bi-monthly newsletter cantaining articles on current trends and issues in the field of legal assistant management.
General Info: Yr. Est. 1984, Bi-monthly, Trim Size-5 x 5, Desktop press, 20 pages, 25% ads, No Color, Matte, Saddle-stitched
Subscriptions: Indv. $45
Circulation: Total-425, Readership-450
Advertising: $300.

LAMA's Watch on Washington
See: BUSINESS & INDUSTRY

Labor-Management Relations Analysis/News and Background
See: LABOR

Lakewood Publications
See: INDUSTRIAL RELATIONS/PERSONNEL

Law Firm Partnership & Benefits Report
See: LAW

Law Office Administrator *Business*

Publishing Co: Ardmore Publishing Company, P.O. Box 52843, Atlanta, GA 30355;
Title Tel # (770) 319-8105 Title Fax # (770) 436-4618
Personnel: Publisher-Susan Crawford, Editor-Fran Worrall
Editorial Description: Covers all aspects of managing a law office, including personnel, finance, government regulations, billing, marketing, facility management, and equipment.
General Info: Yr. Est. 1992, Monthly, Trim Size-8½ x 11, Roto. press, ISSN: 1071-7242, 2 Color, Saddle-stitched
Subscriptions: Indv. $127, Can. $137, For. $137
Circulation: Total-1,700
Printing Co: Seiz Printing, 4525 Acworth Industrial Dr., Acworth, GA 30101 Tel # (770) 917-7000, Fax # (770) 917-7020

Leadership - for the Front Lines
See: BUSINESS & INDUSTRY

Legislative Network for Nursing
See: NURSING

Leisure Beverage Insider
See: BEVERAGES - BREWING

Lewis & Clark Research
Notes *Business*

Publishing Co: Lewis & Clark Research, 6040 A. Six Forks Rd., Suite 112, Raleigh, NC 27609;
Title Tel # (919) 676-2036 Title Fax # (919) 846-2041
Personnel: Publisher-Lewis Copulsky, Editor-Doreen Clark
Editorial Description: Items covering new developments in market research, mail surveys, customer satisfaction, etc.
General Info: Yr. Est. 1992, Monthly
Subscriptions: Indv. $50, Free To Qualified Recipient

Logistics Comment *Association*

Publishing Co: Council of Logistics Management, 2803 Butterfield Rd., Suite #380, Oak Brook, IL 60521-1156; Title Tel # (708) 574-0985 Title Fax # (708) 574-0989
Personnel: Editor-Andrea Manning, Editor-Elaine Winter
General Info: (Formerly NCPDM Comment), Yr. Est. 1967, 5x/yr., Trim Size-8½ x 11, Offset press, 16 pages, 2 Color, Coated, Saddle-stitched
Subscriptions: Free With Membership
Circulation: Total-9,500

Long-Term Care Administrator
See: HOSPITALS & NURSING HOMES

Long Term Care Monitor
See: HEALTH

Managed Care
Reimbursememt Advisor,
The

Publishing Co: Zimmerman & Associates, Inc., 5307 South 92nd St., Hales Corners, WI 53130-1677
Parent Co.-Aspen Publishers, Inc., Gaithersburg; Title Tel # (414) 425-2189
Title Fax # (414) 425-4807
Personnel: Editorial Dir.-Jo Ann Petaschnick
General Info: Yr. Est. 1993, Monthly
Subscriptions: Indv. $167

Management Briefs *Business, Association*

Publishing Co: Clinical Laboratory Management Assoc., 9 Old Lincoln Highway, #201, Malvern, PA 19355-2135; Title Tel # (215) 647-8970 Title Fax # (610) 889-9731
Personnel: Editor-Jean Nelson
Editorial Description: Assn. news, regulatory news, management articles.
General Info: Yr. Est. 1971, Monthly, Trim Size-8½ x 11, Sheetfed press, 12 pages, ISSN: 1048-5007, 1% ads, 2 Color, Newsprint
Subscriptions: Indv. $37, Can. $37, For. $60, Free With Membership
Circulation: Total-6,000
Advertising: Inquire for rates.
List Rental: Actives: $200/M
Printing Co: ANRO, Inc., 222 W. Lancaster Ave., Devon, PA 19333

Management Consultant
International *Business*

Publishing Co: Lafferty Publications, 420 Lexington Ave., Ste. 1745, New York, NY 10170
Tel # (212) 557-6729 Fax # (212) 557-7266; Title Tel # (404) 636-6610 Title Fax # (404) 636-6422
Personnel: Publisher-Frank Lawson, Editor in Chief-Michael Lafferty, Editor-Sandra Burke
Editorial Description: The newsletter tracks the successes & failures of the world's largest management consulting firms, from a decidedly global perspective.
General Info: 10x/yr.
Subscriptions: Indv. $1,079

Management Controls *Business*

Publishing Co: KPMG Peat Marwick, 767 Fifth Avenue, New York, NY 10153;
Title Tel # (212) 758-9700
Personnel: Editor-Benjamin Newman
General Info: Yr. Est. 1965, Monthly

Management Journal   *Business*

Publishing Co: London House, 9701 W Higgins Rd Ste 770, Rosemont, IL 60018-4720;
Title Tel # (708) 292-3301 Title Fax # (708) 292-3400
Personnel: Editor-Susan Broply
Editorial Description: Newsletter dealing with human resources issues.
General Info: Yr. Est. 1979, Quarterly, Web press, 24 pages, Color, Coated
Circulation: (100% controlled), Total-25,000

Management Matters   *Business*

Publishing Co: Infoteam, Inc., PO Box 15640, Plantation, FL 33318-5640 Fax # (954) 472-0544;
Title Tel # (954) 473-9560 Title Fax # (954) 473-0544
Personnel: Publisher-Merton Allen, Editor-David Allen
Editorial Description: Topics relating to effective management.
General Info: Yr. Est. 1990, Monthly, Trim Size-8½ x 11, Offset press, 16 pages, ISSN: 1054-4275,
Ind/Abs/Online: NewsNet, DIALOG, Predicasts
Subscriptions: Indv. $269, Can. $309, For. $379, $25/copy

Management Memo   *Business*

Publishing Co: Economics Press, Inc., 12 Daniel Rd., Fairfield, NJ 07004-2565;
Title Tel # (201) 227-1224 Title Fax # (201) 227-9742
Personnel: Editor-Robert Guder, Circ. Mgr.-Ann Lanahan
Editorial Description: Covers one management principle each issue, focusing on ideas that have
proven to be effective in business leadership.
General Info: Yr. Est. 1965, Bi-weekly
Subscriptions: Indv. $35
Circulation: Total-13,000
List Rental: List Management Co.: Manager: Michael Korman; Names in the News, 411 Theodore
Fremd Ave., Rye, NY 10580 Tel # (914) 925-2400
Printing Co: Beckley Press, 2 Sperry Rd, Fairfield, NJ 07004-2056 Tel # (201) 227-6350

Management Policies & Personnel Law   *Business*

Publishing Co: Research Institute of America, 1340 Braddock Pl., Ste. 400, Alexandria, VA
22314-1651 Tel # (703) 706-8260 Fax # (703) 683-4824; Title Tel # (202) 842-0520
Title Fax # (212) 475-1790
Personnel: Publisher-John Roche, Editor-Elmer Ellentuck, Editor-Rhodes Henderer, Circ. Mgr.-
Loretta Netzer, Production Mgr.-Amy Ryan, Adv. Dir.-Mathew Tallmer
Editorial Description: News, cases, policies, and legal briefs for the human resources professional.
General Info: (Formerly Your Bus.& Law), Yr. Est. 1992, Bi-weekly, Trim Size-8½ x 11, Sheetfed
press, 8 pages, 2 Color
Subscriptions: Indv. $395
List Rental: List Management Co.: Taybi Direct East, Inc., 13321 New Hampshire Ave., Ste. 202,
Silver Spring, MD 20904-3450 Tel # (301) 680-3633, Fax # (301) 680-3635, Actives: 2,200, $95/M,
Expires: 1,400, $95/M
Printing Co: Newsletter Services, Inc., 9700 Philadelphia Court, Lanham, MD 20706
Tel # (301) 731-5200, Fax # (301) 731-5201

Management Portfolio
See: PRINTING/GRAPHIC ARTS

Management Report for Nonunion Organizations
See: LABOR

Manager/Motivator   *Business*

Publishing Co: Economics Press, Inc., 12 Daniel Rd., Fairfield, NJ 07004-2565;
Title Tel # (201) 227-1224 Title Fax # (201) 227-9742
Personnel: Editor-Robert Guder, Circ. Mgr.-Ann Lanahan
Editorial Description: Ideas on communicating with and inspiring employees.
General Info: Yr. Est. 1987, Bi-weekly, Trim Size-3¾ x 7⅜, 8 pages
Subscriptions: Indv. $35
Circulation: Total-4,600
List Rental: List Management Co.: Manager: Michael Korman; Names in the News, 411 Theodore
Fremd Ave., Rye, NY 10580 Tel # (914) 925-2400
Printing Co: Beckley Press, 2 Sperry Rd, Fairfield, NJ 07004-2056 Tel # (201) 227-6350

Manager's Legal Bulletin   *Business*

Publishing Co: Alexander Hamilton Inst., 70 Hilltop Rd, Ramsey, NJ 07446-1119
Tel # (201) 825-8161 Fax # (201) 825-8696
Personnel: Editor-Brian Zevnik, Promotion Dir.-Beth Roeder
Editorial Description: Legal and function issues for business managers.
General Info: Yr. Est. 1986, Semi-monthly, Sheetfed press, 4 pages, 2 Color, Newsprint
Subscriptions: Indv. $46, $1/copy
Circulation: Total-18,000
List Rental: Actives: $75/M

Manager's Notebook   *Business*

Publishing Co: American Productivity & Quality Center, 123 N. Post Oak Ln., Ste. 300, Houston, TX
77024-7718 Tel # (713) 685-4642 Fax # (713) 681-8578; Title Tel # (713) 681-4020
Personnel: Publisher, Editor-Deirdre Mckee, Production Mgr.-Cheryl Hansen, Circ. Mgr.,
Promotion Dir.-Charlotte Scroggins
Editorial Description: How-to information on managing productivity & quality.
General Info: Yr. Est. 1984, Bi-monthly, 6 pages, ISSN: 0743-3387, 2 Color, Coated, Looseleaf
Subscriptions: $13/copy
Circulation: Total-2,500
Printing Co: Brandt & Lawson, 815 Live Oak St., Houston, TX 77003-3220 Tel # (713) 227-5173

Managing International Credit & Collections
See: ACCOUNTING

Managing Laboratory Personnel   *Business*

Publishing Co: Thompson Publishing Group, 747 Third Ave., New York, NY 10017
Tel # (212) 888-7220 Fax # (212) 486-3400; Title Fax # (800) 999-2330
Editorial Description: Covers latest personnel management guidelines plus regulatory guidance.
Subscription includes quarterly supplements and updates.
General Info: Yr. Est. 1994, Annually, Looseleaf
Subscriptions: Indv. $279

Managing Senior Care
See: HOSPITALS & NURSING HOMES

Managing System Development
See: COMPUTERS & AUTOMATION

Manufacturing News
See: MANUFACTURING

Marketing Report, The
See: ADVERTISING & MARKETING

Marketing Technology
See: ADVERTISING & MARKETING

Materiel Manager
See: HOSPITALS & NURSING HOMES

Medical Group Management Marketer's Guidepost   *Business, Association*

Publishing Co: Medical Group Management Association, 104 Inverness Terrace E., Englewood, CO
80112-5306 Fax # (303) 397-1824; Title Tel # (303) 799-1111 Title Fax # (303) 643-4427
Personnel: Editor, Circ. Dir.-Marilee Aust, Promotion Dir.-Dennis Barnhardt
Editorial Description: A bi-moonthly marketing newsletter for medical practice executives.
General Info: Yr. Est. 1990, Bi-monthly, Trim Size-8½ x 11, Sheetfed press, 8 pages, ISSN: 1049-
880X, 2 Color, Coated, Saddle-stitched
Subscriptions: Indv. $48, Inst. $58, $20/copy
Circulation: Total-500, Readership-500
Printing Co: RM Printing, 2785 N Speer Blvd Ste 222, Denver, CO 80211-4220 Tel # (303) 458-8270

Medical Office Manager   *Business*

Publishing Co: Ardmore Publishing Company, P.O. Box 52843, Atlanta, GA 30355;
Title Tel # (770) 319-8105 Title Fax # (770) 436-4618
Personnel: Editor-Susan Crawford
Editorial Description: Covers management issues confronting medical offices including managed
care, staff management, Medicare coding, finance, and government regulations.
General Info: Yr. Est. 1987, Monthly, Trim Size-8½ x 11, Offset press, 12 pages, ISSN: 1052-4894, 2
Color, Matte, Saddle-stitched
Subscriptions: Indv. $172, Can. $182, For. $182
Circulation: Total-3,500
Printing Co: Seiz Printing, 4525 Acworth Industrial Dr., Acworth, GA 30101 Tel # (770) 917-7000,
Fax # (770) 917-7020

Medical Records Briefing
See: HOSPITALS & NURSING HOMES

Medical Staff Briefing
See: HOSPITALS & NURSING HOMES

Medicare Manager
See: MEDICINE

Meeting Monitor   *Business*

Publishing Co: Calendar Planning Corporation, 237 Park Ave., Ste. 900, New York, NY 10017
Tel # (212) 270-5555 Fax # (212) 808-2464
Personnel: Publisher-Nicholas Parks
Editorial Description: Tracks New York City meetings for Wall Street professionals.
General Info: Yr. Est. 1993, Weekly
Subscriptions: Indv. $280

Mental Health Weekly
See: HEALTH

Mentor
See: GENERAL INTEREST

Mini Manager   *Business*

Publishing Co: Mini Co., Inc., 2531 W. Dunlap Ave., #201, Phoenix, AZ 85021-2715;
Title Tel # (602) 870-1711 Title Fax # (602) 861-1094
Personnel: Editor-Darcy Van Ousbree, Art Dir.-Pete LaSacco
Editorial Description: Customer storage insurance & self-storage information for self-storage
owners & managers.
General Info: Yr. Est. 1979, Bi-monthly, Sheetfed press, 7 pages, Coated
Circulation: (100% controlled), Total-10,000
Printing Co: IPC, 2180 Maiden Lane, St. Joseph, MI 49085 Tel # (616) 983-7105,
Fax # (616) 983-5736

Minorities in Business Insider
See: BUSINESS & INDUSTRY

NAAP News
See: HOSPITALS & NURSING HOMES

NAFE Member News
See: WOMEN'S

National Society of Professional Resident Managers-Newsletter

Publishing Co: National Society of Professional Resident Managers, 1518 K St NW Ste 503, Washington, DC 20005-1203; Title Tel # (202) 737-0204
Personnel: Editor-Frank Connors
General Info: Yr. Est. 1964, Monthly, 8 pages
Circulation: Total-1,500

Net News
See: SPORTS & SPORTING GOODS

Network _Business, Association_

Publishing Co: The Planning Forum, 435 N. Michigan Ave., Ste. 1700, Chicago, IL 60611-4008; Title Tel # (513) 523-4185 Title Fax # (513) 523-7539
Personnel: Editor-Marthann Heard
Editorial Description: Contains ideas for strategic management and executive briefing; includes case studies, news, calendar of events and more.
General Info: Yr. Est. 1988, Monthly
Subscriptions: Free With Membership
Circulation: Total-6,000

Network _Business, Association_

Publishing Co: Technology Associations Secretariat, Technology Innovation Centre, 1 Research Dr., Dartmouth, NS B2Y 4M9 Canada Tel # (902) 463-8324 Fax # (902) 463-2703; Title Tel # (902) 464-4492 Title Fax # (902) 466-6889
Editorial Description: Offers promotional support for technology-based non-profit associations involved in the emerging information and advanced technology industries in Nova Scotia.
General Info: Monthly
Circulation: Total-1,200

New Account Selling
See: SALESMANSHIP & SELLING

Non-Profit Administrators Master Guide _Business_

Publishing Co: Master Guide Pubs., PO Box 27203, Salt Lake City, UT 84127-0203; Title Tel # (801) 486-0322
Personnel: Publisher, Editor-Vince Harding
General Info: Yr. Est. 1981, Monthly

Nonprofit Board Report _Business_

Publishing Co: Progressive Business Publications, 370 Technology Dr., #3019, Malverne, PA 19355-9863 Parent Co.-American Future Systems, Inc., Bryn Mawr; Title Tel # (610) 695-8600 Title Fax # (610) 647-8089
Personnel: Publisher-Edward M. Satell, Editor-Kerry M. Fitzgerald, Editorial Dir.-Stephen Meyer, Mktg. Dir.-Ed Moore
Editorial Description: Industry news and analysis for directors of nonprofits and their board members, helping boards become more effective, in a fast paced format.
General Info: Yr. Est. 1991, Monthly, 8 pages
Subscriptions: Indv. $249
List Rental: List Management Co.: Mail Marketing, Inc., 171 Terrace St., Haworth, NJ 07641-1899 Tel # (201) 387-1023, Fax # (201) 387-2976

OR/MS Today _Consumer, Association_

Publishing Co: Lionheart Publishing Inc., 2555 Cumberland Pkwy. #299, Atlanta, GA 30339-3908 Tel # (770) 431-0867; Title Tel # (404) 431-0867 Title Fax # (770) 432-6969
Personnel: Editor, Adv. Dir.-John Llewellyn
Editorial Description: Covers developments, state-of-art advances, conferences, news, short courses, grants and scholarships in the fields of operations research, management science.
General Info: Yr. Est. 1971, Bi-monthly, Web press, 80 pages, ISSN: 0030-3658, 3% ads, 4 Color, Coated, Saddle-stitched
Subscriptions: Indv. $6, $2/copy
Acquistions: Publication Bought
Circulation: Total-12,000
Advertising: Inquire for rates.
Printing Co: Publisher's Press, 100 Frank E. Simon Avenue, Sheperdsville, KY 40165 Tel # (502) 955-6526, Fax # (502) 833-4513

OSRA Newsletter
See: COMPUTERS & AUTOMATION

On Buying or Selling a Business
See: BUSINESS & INDUSTRY

On the Human Side _Business_

Publishing Co: Human Side Press Ltd., 1800 Bering Dr Ste 690, Houston, TX 77057-3129; Title Tel # (713) 266-5388 Title Fax # (713) 266-5387
Personnel: Publisher-Richard Doss
General Info: Yr. Est. 1985, Quarterly, Trim Size-8½ x 11, Desktop press, 8 pages, 2 Color
Circulation: Total-350

Opera America Newsline
See: MUSIC & MUSIC TRADES

Operations Alert _Business_

Publishing Co: Savings & Community Bankers of America, 900 19th St. NW, Ste. 400, Washington, DC 20006-2105; Title Tel # (202) 857-3146 Title Fax # (202) 296-8716
Personnel: Publisher-Robert Bradner, Editor-Edward Maney
Editorial Description: Operations information & practices for savings institutions.
General Info: Bi-weekly, Trim Size-8½ x 11, 4 pages
Subscriptions: Indv. $210
Circulation: Total-6,400

Organizations & Change _Business_

Publishing Co: International Registry of Organization Dev. Professionals, 11234 Walnut Ridge Rd, Chesterland, OH 44026-1240; Title Tel # (216) 461-4333 Title Fax # (216) 729-9319
Personnel: Publisher, Editor-Donald Cole
Editorial Description: A monthly newsletter for organization development professionals, & those interested in learning more about organization development & organization effectiveness.
General Info: Yr. Est. 1968, Monthly, Trim Size-8½ x 11, Sheetfed press, 10 pages
Subscriptions: Indv. $110, Inst. $110, Can. $110, For. $110
Circulation: Total-600
Advertising: Inquire for rates.
List Rental: Actives: $100/M

Outlook _Association_

Publishing Co: Club Managers Assn. of America, 1733 King St, Alexandria, VA 22314-2720; Title Tel # (703) 739-9500 Title Fax # (703) 739-0124
Personnel: Production Mgr.-Sara Ewy, Editor, Promotion Dir.-Kathi Pernell
Editorial Description: Mgmt., legislative & general articles of concern to private club managers.
General Info: Yr. Est. 1927, Monthly, Web press, 20 pages, 2 Color, Newsprint
Subscriptions: Indv. $11
Circulation: Total-4,000
Printing Co: Newsletter Services, Inc., 9700 Philadelphia Court, Lanham, MD 20706 Tel # (301) 731-5200, Fax # (301) 731-5201

PBC Business Guide _Business_

Publishing Co: Publishing & Business Consultants, 101 W. 64th St. Unit #3, Inglewood, CA 90302-1255 Tel # (213) 732-3477 Fax # (213) 732-3477
Personnel: Publisher-Andeson Atia
General Info: Quarterly, ISSN: 1095-2075
Circulation: Total-50,000
Advertising: Inquire for rates.

PPF Survey (Personnel Policies Forum)
See: INDUSTRIAL RELATIONS/PERSONNEL

Payroll Inserts
See: INDUSTRIAL RELATIONS/PERSONNEL

Payroll Practitioner's Compliance Handbook _Business_

Publishing Co: Warren, Gorham & Lamont, 31 Saint James Ave., Boston, MA 02116-4112 Parent Co.-Thomson Professional Publications, Stamford; Title Tel # (617) 423-2020 Title Fax # (617) 423-1914
Personnel: Publisher-Andrew Boden, Production Mgr.-Paul Kelly, Mktg. Dir.-Sandra Fox
Editorial Description: Published in the fall of each year in time for year-end reporting, this exprt reference guides you step-by-step through increasingly complex requirements to help you file year-end quarterly forms, deal with tricky items such as third party sick pay,reconcile wage and tax data, and more.
General Info: Annually, Looseleaf
Subscriptions: Indv. $105
List Rental: List Management Co.: Manager: Seena Benedek; WG & L List Management, 1 Penn Plz Fl 42, New York, NY 10119-0002 Tel # (212) 971-5000

Pension and Profit Sharing
See: INDUSTRIAL RELATIONS/PERSONNEL

People Trends
See: INDUSTRIAL RELATIONS/PERSONNEL

Personnel Manager's Encyclopedia of Prewritten Personnel Policies
See: INDUSTRIAL RELATIONS/PERSONNEL

Personnel Policy Manual _Business_

Publishing Co: Personnel Policy Svc., Inc., PO Box 7697, Louisville, KY 40257-0715; Title Tel # (502) 897-6782 Title Fax # (502) 896-4162
Editorial Description: Developing & maintaining personnel policies.
General Info: Monthly
Subscriptions: Indv. $367

Personnel Postscript
See: INDUSTRIAL RELATIONS/PERSONNEL

Personnel Practice Ideas   *Business*

Publishing Co: Warren, Gorham & Lamont, 31 Saint James Ave., Boston, MA 02116-4112 Parent Co.-Thomson Professional Publications, Stamford; Title Tel # (617) 423-2020 Title Fax # (617) 423-1914
Personnel: Publisher-Andrew Boden, Production Mgr.-Paul Kelly, Mktg. Dir.-Sandra Fox
Editorial Description: It is designed to provide a comprehensive source of current ideas and tested solutions to help you bring the full range of human resource problems under control.
General Info: (Formerly Policies & Practices), Monthly, Looseleaf
Subscriptions: Indv. $132
List Rental: List Management Co.: Manager: Seena Benedek; WG & L List Management, 1 Penn Plz Fl 42, New York, NY 10119-0002 Tel # (212) 971-5000

Personnel Practices/Communications
See: INDUSTRIAL RELATIONS/PERSONNEL

Perspective
See: BUSINESS & INDUSTRY

Perspectives on Law Firm Management   *Business*

Publishing Co: Newkirk Products, Inc., 15 Corporate Cir, Albany, NY 12203-5154 Tel # (518) 452-1000
Editorial Description: Custom publication for distribution to clients by consultants to law firms.
General Info: Quarterly, Trim Size-8$\frac{1}{2}$ x 11, 4 pages, 2 Color

Perspectives on Medical Practice Management   *Business*

Publishing Co: Newkirk Products, Inc., 15 Corporate Cir, Albany, NY 12203-5154 Tel # (518) 452-1000
Editorial Description: Custom publication designed for distribution to clients by consultants to those in medical practice.
General Info: Quarterly, Trim Size-8$\frac{1}{2}$ x 11, 4 pages, 2 Color

Plan Administrators Compliance Manual
See: LABOR UNION

Pony Express

Publishing Co: Royal Canadian Mounted Police, 1200 Vanien Parkway, Ottawa, ON K1A 0R2 Canada; Title Tel # (613) 993-3600
Personnel: Editor-Daniel Hall, Art Dir.-M. V. Thompson
Editorial Description: Staff relations monthly newsletter which is circulated as an in-house publication.
General Info: Yr. Est. 1976, Monthly, Trim Size-8$\frac{1}{2}$ x 11, Offset press, 10 pages, No Color, Saddle-stitched
Circulation: Total-3,100

Power Press & Forging
See: SAFETY

Power Products Business   *Business*

Publishing Co: Power Systems Research, Inc., 1301 Corporate Center Dr Ste, 113, Saint Paul, MN 55121-1259; Title Tel # (612) 454-0144 Title Fax # (612) 454-0760
Personnel: Publisher-George Zirnhelt, Editor-Gordon Gilbert, Business Ed.-Linda Olson, Intl. Editor-Dennis Huibregtse, Circ. Dir.-Barbara Dick, Production Dir.-Diane Austin
General Info: (Formerly Engine Power Perspective), Yr. Est. 1981, Monthly, Trim Size-8$\frac{1}{2}$ x 11, Desktop press, 8 pages, ISSN: 1056-4063, No Color, Saddle-stitched
Subscriptions: Indv. $365, Can. $365, For. $395, $25/copy
Circulation: Total-140

Practical Supervision
See: OFFICE METHODS & EQUIPMENT

President   *Business, Association*

Publishing Co: American Management Association, 135 West 50th Street, New York, NY 10020-1201 Tel # (212) 586-8100 Fax # (212) 903-8083; Title Tel # (212) 903-7990 Title Fax # (212) 903-8168
Personnel: Publisher-Rosemary Carlough, Editor-Barbara Parker
Editorial Description: Articles of practical value to chief executive officers of small and mid-sized companies in the U.S. and Europe.
General Info: (Formerly President's Forum), Yr. Est. 1962, Quarterly, Trim Size-8$\frac{1}{2}$ x 11, Offset press, 16 pages, ISSN: 0052-007X, 2 Color, Matte, Saddle-stitched
Subscriptions: Indv. $97, Free To Qualified Recipient
Acquistions: Publication Bought
Circulation: Total-6,000
Printing Co: Commercial Printers, 3 Hilltop Rd, Norwich, CT 06360-1554 Tel # (203) 886-0541, Fax # (203) 886-5805

Principles of Payroll Administration   *Business*

Publishing Co: Warren, Gorham & Lamont, 31 Saint James Ave., Boston, MA 02116-4112 Parent Co.-Thomson Professional Publications, Stamford; Title Tel # (617) 423-2020 Title Fax # (617) 423-1914
Personnel: Publisher-Andrew Boden, Production Mgr.-Paul Kelly, Mktg. Dir.-Sandra Fox
Editorial Description: Contains a complete collection of payroll essentials, with clear explanations of applicable laws, accounting procedures, and more. Two, a quick answer desktop reference with detailed topic index, and three, a step-by-step training manual with examples, charts, tables and self-quizzes in a question-and-answer format to simplify learning.
General Info: Annually, Looseleaf
Subscriptions: Indv. $166, Inst. $166, Can. $166, For. $166
List Rental: List Management Co.: Manager: Seena Benedek; WG & L List Management, 1 Penn Plz Fl 42, New York, NY 10119-0002 Tel # (212) 971-5000

Procedures Review
See: NUCLEAR ENERGY

Product: H R Manager's Legal Reporter   *Business*

Publishing Co: Ransom & Benjamin Publishers LLC, P.O. Box 606, Old Greenwich, CT 06870-0417 Tel # (203) 637-0221 Fax # (203) 637-3594
Personnel: Editor-Maureen Greengher
Editorial Description: Latest legal changes affecting HR management. Court decisions, federal regulations and administration developments.
General Info: Yr. Est. 1978, Monthly, Trim Size-8.5 x 11, 8 pages
Subscriptions: Indv. $110
List Rental: List Management Co.: Direct Media, Inc., 200 Pemberwick Rd., PO Box 4565, Greenwich, CT 06830 Tel # (203) 532-3713, Fax # (203) 531-1452, Actives: 22,000, $85/M

Productivity
See: BUSINESS & INDUSTRY

Productivity Brief   *Business, Association*

Publishing Co: American Productivity & Quality Center, 123 N. Post Oak Ln., Ste. 300, Houston, TX 77024-7718 Tel # (713) 685-4642 Fax # (713) 681-8578; Title Tel # (713) 681-4020
Personnel: Editor-Stephen Stewart, Staff Writer-Steve Scheffler, Art Dir.-Eric Heiserer
Editorial Description: Productivity, management, and business articles.
General Info: Yr. Est. 1981, Bi-monthly, Trim Size-8$\frac{1}{2}$ x 11, Offset press, 8 pages, ISSN: 0741-644X, 2 Color, Coated, Looseleaf
Subscriptions: $13/copy
Circulation: Total-2,000
Printing Co: Brandt & Lawson, 815 Live Oak St., Houston, TX 77003-3220 Tel # (713) 227-5173

Productivity Letter   *Business, Association*

Publishing Co: American Productivity & Quality Center, 123 N. Post Oak Ln., Ste. 300, Houston, TX 77024-7718 Tel # (713) 685-4642 Fax # (713) 681-8578; Title Tel # (713) 681-4020
Personnel: Editor-Steve Stewart, Staff Writer-Steve Scheffler, Art Dir.-Cheryl Hoffman
General Info: Yr. Est. 1981, Monthly, Trim Size-8$\frac{1}{2}$ x 11, Offset press, 8 pages, 2 Color, Coated
Circulation: Total-2,500
Printing Co: Brandt & Lawson, 815 Live Oak St., Houston, TX 77003-3220 Tel # (713) 227-5173

Productivity Views: Newsletter of Service Quality
See: BUSINESS & INDUSTRY

Professional Consultant & Information Marketing Report   *Business*

Publishing Co: Howard L. Shenson, 123 NW 2nd Ave. #403, Portland, OR 97209-3927; Title Tel # (503) 224-8834 Title Fax # (818) 703-6295
Personnel: Publisher, Editor-Howard Shenson, Circ. Mgr.-Pat Jordan
Editorial Description: Includes semi-annual survey of the consulting industry; fees charged; marketing of consulting & professionalservices & information products (seminars, manuals, software & newsletters).
General Info: (Formerly Howard L. Shenson Report), Yr. Est. 1977, Monthly, Trim Size-8$\frac{1}{2}$ x 11, Sheetfed press, 10 pages, ISSN: 0272-8559, No Color, Matte, Saddle-stitched
Subscriptions: Indv. $96, $8/copy
Acquistions: Publication Bought
Advertising: Inquire for rates. Accepts Inserts.

Professional Practice Today   *Business*

Publishing Co: PM Group, 1109 Comerica Building, Battle Creek, MI 49016 Fax # (616) 962-7726
Editorial Description: News and information for physicians and dentists about managing their practices.
General Info: Yr. Est. 1990, Monthly
Subscriptions: Indv. $97

Professional Purchasing
See: PURCHASING

Professional Services Management Journal   *Business*

Publishing Co: Practice Management Associates Ltd., 10 Midland Ave., Newton, MA 02158-1021; Title Tel # (617) 965-0055 Title Fax # (617) 965-5152
Personnel: Editor-Frank Stasiowski
General Info: Yr. Est. 1974, Monthly, Trim Size-8$\frac{1}{2}$ x 11, 8 pages
Subscriptions: Indv. $195, Can. $195, For. $250
List Rental: Rents Lists

Profiles in PDM

Publishing Co: Hunt Personnel Ltd., 21 W. 38th St., New York, NY 10018-5506;
   Title Tel # (212) 997-2299 Title Fax # (212) 997-0161
Personnel: Editor-Alex Metz
Editorial Description: Subjects deal with transportation/distribution, ranging from trends to what one
   can do th excell in the field.
General Info: Yr. Est. 1977, Bi-monthly, Trim Size-8½ x 11, 2 pages, 2 Color, Newsprint, Looseleaf
Circulation: Total-3,300

Profit-Sharing and Pension Forms
See: INDUSTRIAL RELATIONS/PERSONNEL

Project Management
See: CONSTRUCTION & BUILDING

Pryor Report
See: BUSINESS & INDUSTRY

Psychotherapy Finances   *Business*

Publishing Co: Ridgewood Financial Inst., Inc., 1016 Clemmons St Ste 407, Jupiter, FL 33477-3303;
   Title Tel # (201) 447-0681 Title Fax # (201) 427-3644
Personnel: Publisher-Herbert Klein, Editor-Gayle Tuttle
Editorial Description: Practice and personal financial information for professionals in private practice:
   fees, management, taxes, pensions, insurance, new business opportunities.
General Info: Yr. Est. 1974, Monthly, Offset press, 12 pages, ISSN: 0163-1543
Subscriptions: Indv. $68, $6/copy
Circulation: Total-7,000, Readership-21,000
List Rental: List Management Co.: Venture Communications, 60 Madison Avenue, 3rd fl., New York,
   NY 10010 Tel # (212) 684-4800, Fax # (212) 545-1680, Actives: 21,236, $95/M

Purchasing Executive's Bulletin
See: PURCHASING

Quality 1st.
See: INDUSTRIAL RELATIONS/PERSONNEL

Quality Action Planner   *Business*

Publishing Co: National Association of Printers & Lithographers, 780 Palisade Ave., Teaneck, NJ
   07666-3129
Editorial Description: Presents feature articles on quality manufacturing and service management,
   synopses of conference proceedings, research, and other news. Quality Action Planner is published
   with the cooperation of The Rochester Inst. of Technology, the Pitman Co., and DuPont Printing
   and Publishing.
General Info: Yr. Est. 1994
Subscriptions: Indv. $40, Free To Qualified Recipient

Quality Executive   *Business*

Publishing Co: B & B Press Inc., Box 801, Radio City Station, New York, NY 10102-0001;
   Title Tel # (212) 582-3791 Title Fax # (212) 246-7916
Personnel: Editor-Jerry Bowles
General Info: Yr. Est. 1989, Monthly
Subscriptions: Indv. $145

Quality Improvement Quarterly
See: PRINTING/GRAPHIC ARTS

Quality Letter for Healthcare Leaders, The   *Business*

Publishing Co: Capitol Publications, Inc., 1101 King St., Ste. 444, Alexandria, VA 22314-2968
   Fax # (703) 739-6501; Title Tel # (703) 683-4100
Personnel: Sr. Ed.-Reggi Veatch
Editorial Description: Provides information on quality control for healthcare management.
General Info: Yr. Est. 1989, Monthly
Subscriptions: Indv. $279
Circulation: Total-2,000
List Rental: Rents Lists

R & D Innovator
See: TELECOMMUNICATIONS

RPT on Healthcare Mgnt. & Solutions
See: NURSING

Rate Controls
See: HOSPITALS & NURSING HOMES

Real Estate Investment Ideas
See: REAL ESTATE

Real Estate Marketing Management Alert
See: REAL ESTATE

Receivables Report
See: ACCOUNTING

Records Retention: Law & Practice

Publishing Co: Carswell, 2075 Kennedy Road, One Corporate Plaza, Scarborough, ON M1T 3V4
   Canada; Title Tel # (416) 609-8000 Title Fax # (416) 298-5094
Personnel: Publisher-Barry Garnet, Editor-R.A. Cartwright, Adv. Dir.-Melanie Causton
Editorial Description: Supplemented book is a revision of Records Retention, originally published in
   1975.
General Info: (Formerly Records Retention), Annually, Looseleaf
Subscriptions: Indv. $165

Reengineering Economics Letter
See: ECONOMICS

Reference Guide to Managing Addiction Programs
See: HEALTH

Relocation Report
See: REAL ESTATE

Report on Healthcare Management Solutions
See: HOSPITALS & NURSING HOMES

Report to Legal Management
See: LAW

Report on Literacy Programs
See: EDUCATION

Report on Physician Trends
See: HOSPITALS & NURSING HOMES

Rescue Officer's Notebook
See: FIRE PROTECTION

Respiratory Care Manager
See: HOSPITALS & NURSING HOMES

Restaurant Management Insider
See: RESTAURANTS & CATERING

Runzheimer Reports on Relocation   *Business*

Publishing Co: Runzheimer Intl., Runzheimer Park, Rochester, WI 53167 Fax # (414) 767-2254;
   Title Tel # (414) 767-2200 Title Fax # (414) 767-2476
Personnel: Publisher-Karen Batterman, Editor-Holly Carlson
Editorial Description: News & information about employee relocation.
General Info: Yr. Est. 1982, Monthly, Trim Size-8½ x 11, Sheetfed press, 12 pages, ISSN: 0731-
   9150, No Color, Newsprint
Subscriptions: Indv. $354, $38/copy
Acquistions: Publication Bought

SAM Focus on Management   *Business, Association*

Publishing Co: Society for Advancement of Management, 126 E Lee Ave Ste 11, Vinton, VA
   24179-2518; Title Tel # (703) 342-5563
General Info: (Formerly Society for Advancement of Management, Proceedings), Quarterly
Subscriptions: Indv. $25

SEC Compliance
See: BANKING & FINANCE

SIM Network

Publishing Co: Society for Information Management, 401 N. Michigan Ave., Chicago, IL 60611-4212;
   Title Tel # (312) 644-6610 Title Fax # (312) 321-6869
General Info: Bi-monthly
Circulation: Total-2,000

Safety Compliance Alert
See: SAFETY

Safety Management
See: SAFETY

Sale$Maker$
See: SALESMANSHIP & SELLING

Sales & Marketing Executive Report
Business

Publishing Co: Dartnell Corp., 4660 N. Ravenswood Ave., Chicago, IL 60640-4510;
Title Tel # (312) 561-4000 Title Fax # (312) 561-3801
Personnel: Publisher-Clark Fetridge, Editor-Christen Heide, Production Mgr.-Megan Mulligan, Art Dir.-Andrew Epstein, Mktg. Dir.-George Economos
Editorial Description: Innovative ideas on essential areas of management such as payroll, sales meetings, compensation, development and training.
General Info: (Formerly Sales & Marketing Exec. Report; Sales & Marketing Profit), Yr. Est. 1975, Bi-weekly
Subscriptions: $156/copy
List Rental: List Management Co.: Manager: Sue McDorman; Leland Company, 1801 W. Leland Ave., Chicago, IL 60640-4363 Tel # (312) 561-4005, Fax # (312) 561-4099, Actives: 70,785, $90/M, Hotline: $125/M

Sales Bullet, A
See: SALESMANSHIP & SELLING

Sales Productivity Review, The
See: SALESMANSHIP & SELLING

Sales Rep's Advisor, The
See: SALESMANSHIP & SELLING

Salesmanship
See: SALESMANSHIP & SELLING

Saskatchewan Research Council
Business

Publishing Co: Saskatchewan Research Council - Technology Transfer Branch, 15 Innovation Blvd., Saskatoon, SK S7N 2X8 Canada Tel # (306) 933-5400 Fax # (306) 933-1446 Parent Co.-Saskatchewan Energy & Mines, Petrol. & Natural Gas Division, Regina, Canada;
Title Tel # (306) 933-5411
Personnel: Publisher, Editor-Cindy Buchanan
Editorial Description: Covers research, development, and transfer of innovative scientific and technological solutions, applications, and services.
General Info: (Formerly Technology Transfer), Yr. Est. 1964, Quarterly, Trim Size-14 x 24, 30 pages
Subscriptions: Free
Circulation: Total-10,000

Securities Regulations
Business

Publishing Co: Research Institute of America, 90 5th Avenue, New York, NY 10011-7629
Tel # (212) 645-4800; Title Tel # (800) 562-0245 Title Fax # (201) 816-3484
Editorial Description: Complete coverage of laws administered by the Federal Securities and Exchange Commission regulating transactions involving securities.
General Info: Bi-weekly, Trim Size-6 x 9¼, Offset press, No Color, Looseleaf
Subscriptions: Indv. $740
List Rental: List Management Co.: WG & L List Management, 1 Penn Plz Fl 42, New York, NY 10119-0002 Tel # (212) 971-5000

Selling Advantage
See: SALESMANSHIP & SELLING

Seminar Schedule
Business

Publishing Co: Calendar Planning Corporation, 237 Park Ave., Ste. 900, New York, NY 10017
Tel # (212) 270-5555 Fax # (212) 808-2464
Personnel: Publisher-Nicholas Parks
Editorial Description: Provides information on conferences for investment professionals.
General Info: Yr. Est. 1993, Semi-monthly
Subscriptions: Indv. $88

Service Dealer's Newsletter
Business

Publishing Co: Shopper Pubs., Inc., 1400 Easton Rd, Roslyn, PA 19001-1606;
Title Fax # (215) 659-2199
Personnel: Publisher, Editor-Alvin Booker, Circ. Mgr.-Caryle Kile
Editorial Description: Management information for service departments in companies and small repair firms.
General Info: Yr. Est. 1984, Monthly, Offset press, 6 pages, ISSN: 0739-6236
Subscriptions: Indv. $54, $5/copy
Circulation: Total-5,100
Advertising: Accepts Inserts.

Service Level Newsletter
Business

Publishing Co: SLN Inc., PO Box 6523, Annapolis, MD 21401-0523 Fax # (410) 267-0962;
Title Tel # (410) 267-0422 Title Fax # (410) 267-0563
General Info: Yr. Est. 1987, Monthly, 20 pages, 2 Color
Subscriptions: Indv. $337

Service Management
See: MANUFACTURING

Service Report, The

Publishing Co: Anne Petite Associates Limited, 160 Guildwood Parkway, West Hill, ON M1E 1P4 Canada; Title Tel # (416) 267-2430 Title Fax # (416) 267-2537
Personnel: Publisher-Anne Petite, Editor-Ruth Haehnel, Art Dir.-M. Bettridge
Editorial Description: Service Strategies for senior managers. Interviews, practical examples, cutting edge information about service techniques & philosophies with a bottom line orientation.
General Info: Yr. Est. 1991, 10x/yr., Web press, 8 pages, 2 Color, Coated, Saddle-stitched
Subscriptions: Indv. $120, Can. $120, $10/copy

Service that Sells!
Business

Publishing Co: Pencom Inc., 511 16th St., Ste. 400, Denver, CO 80202; Title Tel # (303) 595-3991
Title Fax # (303) 595-0815
Personnel: Editor-Phil Roberts, Mng. Editor-Bill Asbury, Feature Ed.-Teri Merbach, Assoc. Ed.-Kristen Loop, Art Dir.-Kristin Kirkland, Mktg. Dir.-Laurie Uttich
Editorial Description: Management information training, marketing and service in restaurants and bars.
General Info: Yr. Est. 1993, Monthly, Trim Size-8.5 x 11, Offset press, 8 pages, ISSN: 1083-9739, 4 Color, Matte, Saddle-stitched
Subscriptions: Indv. $99, Can. $139, For. $169
Printing Co: V I P Communications, 11250 E. 40th Avenue, Denver, CO 80239 Tel # (303) 371-8400

Singer Report on Managed Care Systems and Technology, The
See: COMPUTERS & AUTOMATION

The Small Business Advisor
See: BUSINESS & INDUSTRY

Small Business Builder
See: BUSINESS & INDUSTRY

Small Business Executive Report
Business

Publishing Co: Charles Moore Associates, Inc., PO Box 6, Southampton, PA 18966-0006;
Title Tel # (215) 355-6084 Title Fax # (215) 364-2212
Personnel: Publisher-Charles Moore, Circ. Mgr.-Nancy Hannigan
Editorial Description: Commercial and economic data for small business.
General Info: Monthly, 8 pages
Subscriptions: Indv. $49

Small Corporation Update
See: BUSINESS & INDUSTRY

Small Market Radio Newsletter
See: BROADCASTING

Smart Buying
See: PURCHASING

Smart Workplace Practices
Association

Publishing Co: Independent Small Business Employers, 520 S. Pierce Ave., Ste. 224, Mason City, IA 50401-2751; Title Tel # (515) 424-3187
Personnel: Publisher-Jim Collison, Editor-Jane Knudsen
Editorial Description: Features warnings, recommendations, tips that help employers manage employees better.
General Info: (Formerly Employer Advocate), Yr. Est. 1981, Monthly
Subscriptions: Indv. $149

Softwatch
See: COMPUTERS & AUTOMATION

Sound Thinking
Business

Publishing Co: Jay Mitchell Associates, Rte. 2, Box 1285, Fairfield, IA 52556-1285;
Title Tel # (515) 472-4087 Title Fax # (515) 472-6457
Personnel: Publisher, Editor-Jay Mitchell, Production Mgr.-Lori Morgan
Editorial Description: Notes & comment on radio, marketing & related industries.
General Info: Yr. Est. 1984, Monthly, Trim Size-8½ x 11, Sheetfed press, 4 pages, No Color, Matte
Subscriptions: Indv. $65
Circulation: Total-1,000
List Rental: Actives: $100/M
Printing Co: Fairfield Printing, 100 N Court St, Fairfield, IA 52556-2811

Soundview Executive Book Summaries
See: BUSINESS & INDUSTRY

Staff Leader
Business

Publishing Co: Aspen Publishers, Inc., 200 Orchard Ridge Dr., Ste 200, Gaithersburg, MD 20878-5440 Parent Co.-Wolters Kluwer US Corporation, New York; Title Tel # (301) 417-7500
Title Fax # (301) 417-7655
Personnel: Editor-Elizabeth Goehring
Editorial Description: This practical, informal, up-to-the minute newsletter guides any nonprofit administrator through the toughest of personnel problems, and connects you with other successful nonprofit administrators across the U.S. and Canada.
General Info: Monthly
Subscriptions: Indv. $119, For. $143, $12/copy
List Rental: List Management Co.: Stevens-Knox List Management, 304 Park Ave S., New York, NY 10010-5312 Tel # (212) 388-8800, Fax # (212) 388-8890

Stern's HR Management Review   *Consumer*

Publishing Co: Michael Daniels Publishers, PO Box 3233, Culver City, CA 90231-3233
Tel # (310) 838-4437; Title Tel # (310) 838-0551 Title Fax # (310) 838-2344
Personnel: Publisher-Michael Daniels, Editor-Yvette Borcia, Editor-Gerry Stern
Editorial Description: Reviews new human resource management organization and leadership
issues and publications. Presents the latest concepts & developments in such areas as
organization strategy and design, motivation, reward systems, change process, employment law,
selection, and management.
General Info: Yr. Est. 1991, Quarterly, Trim Size-8½ x 11, Desktop press, 6 pages, 2 Color
Subscriptions: Indv. $24

Success Orientation   *Business, Consumer*

Publishing Co: Sponsor-Jordan International Enterprises, Success Publications Inc., PO Box 487,
Roswell, GA 30077-0487 Tel # (770) 992-4060 Fax # (770) 992-7722; Title Tel # (404) 261-1122
Personnel: Publisher, Editor-Dr. DuPree Jordan, Jr., Art Dir., Promotion Dir.-Margaret M. Jordan
Editorial Description: Ideas on management and motivation for personal and professional growth.
General Info: (Formerly Personal and Professional Development), Yr. Est. 1969, Monthly, 4 pages
Subscriptions: Indv. $40
Circulation: Total-3,000

Successful Closing Techniques
See: SALESMANSHIP & SELLING

Successful Supervisor   *Business*

Publishing Co: Dartnell Corp., 4660 N. Ravenswood Ave., Chicago, IL 60640-4510;
Title Tel # (312) 561-4000 Title Fax # (312) 561-3801
Personnel: Publisher-Clark Fetridge, Editor-Linda Segall, Production Mgr.-Megan Mulligan, Art Dir.-
Andrew Epstein, Mktg. Dir.-George Economos
Editorial Description: How-to-do it motivational material, productivity, safety, leadership, topics for
supervisors.
General Info: Yr. Est. 1970, Bi-weekly, Trim Size-8½ x 11, Sheetfed press, 4 pages, 2 Color
Subscriptions: $62/copy
List Rental: List Management Co.: Manager: Sue McDorman; Leland Company, 1801 W. Leland
Ave., Chicago, IL 60640-4363 Tel # (312) 561-4005, Fax # (312) 561-4099, Actives: 70,937, $90/M,
Hotline: $125/M

Successful Telephone Selling
See: SALESMANSHIP & SELLING

Supervisor's Guide to Employment Practices   *Business*

Publishing Co: Clement Communications, Inc., Concord Industrial Park, Concordville, PA
19331-9987 Tel # (610) 459-1700 Fax # (610) 459-5092
Personnel: Publisher-George Clement
Editorial Description: Contains advice, case studies, and employment news for supervisors.
General Info: Yr. Est. 1995, Bi-weekly, Trim Size-8½ x 11, 6 pages, 4 Color, Matte, Looseleaf

Systems
See: ENGINEERING

Tax & Business Adviser
See: ACCOUNTING

Tax Alert for Management
See: TAXES

Tax Management Estates, Gifts & Trusts Reference File
See: TAXES

Tax Management Primary Sources Series V
See: TAXES

Tax Management Real Estate
See: TAXES

Team Leader   *Business*

Publishing Co: Dartnell Corp., 4660 N. Ravenswood Ave., Chicago, IL 60640-4510;
Title Tel # (312) 561-4000 Title Fax # (312) 561-3801
Personnel: Publisher-Clark Fetridge, Editor-Linda Segall, Production Mgr.-Megan Mulligan, Art Dir.-
Andrew Epstein, Mktg. Dir.-George Economos
Editorial Description: Team Leader gives managers, supervisors, and other team leaders a regular
source of information on spearheading productive teams. Contains usable advice and ideas on
motivating their staff to work together that helps to develop teams that positively effect the firm's
image.
General Info: Bi-weekly
Subscriptions: $62/copy
List Rental: List Management Co.: Manager: Sue McDorman; Leland Company, 1801 W. Leland
Ave., Chicago, IL 60640-4363 Tel # (312) 561-4005, Fax # (312) 561-4099, Actives: 70,785, $90/M,
Hotline: $125/M

Teamwork
See: INDUSTRIAL RELATIONS/PERSONNEL

Technology Alert   *Business*

Publishing Co: Infoteam, Inc., PO Box 15640, Plantation, FL 33318-5640 Fax # (954) 472-0544;
Title Tel # (954) 473-9560 Title Fax # (954) 473-0544
Personnel: Publisher, Editor-Merton Allen
Editorial Description: Reviews technical reports & database reports on multidisciplinary subjects,
including: science, engineering, manufacturing, processing, products, materials, marketing, etc. Full
text reprints of reports are available.
General Info: (Formerly Technology Alert & Technology Alert Database Reports), Yr. Est. 1987, Bi-
monthly, Trim Size-8½ x 11, Offset press, 8 pages, ISSN: 1054-4267, Ind/Abs/Online: NewsNet,
DIALOG, Predicasts
Subscriptions: Indv. $139, Can. $169, For. $209, $25/copy

Time Management Report   *Business*

Publishing Co: Harold Taylor Time Consultants, 2175 Sheppard Ave., E. #310, Willowdale, ON M2J
1W8 Canada; Title Tel # (416) 491-0777 Title Fax # (416) 491-8233
Personnel: Publisher, Editor-Harold Taylor, Circ. Mgr.-Joan Patterson
Editorial Description: Contains ideas on the effective use of personal time.
General Info: Yr. Est. 1980, Monthly, Offset press, 6 pages, 2 Color, Newsprint
Subscriptions: Indv. $50, Can. $50
Circulation: Total-250

Today's Collector
See: CREDIT AND CREDIT UNIONS

Tom Peters: On Achieving Excellence   *Business*

Publishing Co: TPG Communications, 555 Hamilton Ave., Palo Alto, CA 94301-2015;
Title Tel # (415) 326-4496 Title Fax # (415) 326-7065
Personnel: Publisher-Tom Peters, Editor-Paul Cohen
General Info: Yr. Est. 1986, Monthly, 12 pages, ISSN: 0887-5332, 2 Color, Newsprint
Subscriptions: Indv. $197, $20/copy
Circulation: Total-7,000
List Rental: List Management Co.: Pacific Lists, 100 Tamal Plaza Ste 50, Corte Madera, CA 94925
Tel # (415) 945-9450, Fax # (415) 945-9451, Actives: $120/M
Printing Co: Kable News Co., 16 S Wesley Ave, Mount Morris, IL 61054-1473 Tel # (815) 735-4151

Total Compliance   *Business*

Publishing Co: Safety-Kleen Corporation, 1000 North Randall Road, Elgin, IL 60123
Fax # (708) 468-8515
Editorial Description: Regulatory newsletter covering OSHA, EPA and DOT.
General Info: Monthly
Subscriptions: Indv. $95

Total Employee Involvement
See: BUSINESS & INDUSTRY

Total Productive Maintenance
See: BUSINESS & INDUSTRY

Total Quality in Hospitality
See: HOTEL INDUSTRY

TrainMaster
See: INDUSTRIAL RELATIONS/PERSONNEL

Transport (De)Regulation Report
See: TRAFFIC & TRANSPORTATION

Universal Healthcare Almanac
See: HOSPITALS & NURSING HOMES

Valuation Consultant   *Business*

Publishing Co: Marshall & Stevens, 707 Wilshire Blvd., Ste. 5200, Los Angeles, CA 90017-3614;
Title Tel # (213) 385-1515
Personnel: Editor-Joan McKain
Editorial Description: Covers accounting, taxation, property management, property records,
insurance, real estate, hospital, feasibility studies.
General Info: Yr. Est. 1964, Quarterly, Trim Size-8½ x 11, Offset press, 4 pages, Color
Circulation: Total-120,000

Value Engineering & Management Digest
See: ENGINEERING

WG&L Human Resources Forms with Commentary
See: INDUSTRIAL RELATIONS/PERSONNEL

Warehouse Management and Control Systems
See: BUSINESS & INDUSTRY

Whats Legal NOW   *Business, Consumer*

Publishing Co: Wentworth Worldwide Media, 1866 Colonial Village Lane, PO Box 10488, Lancaster,
PA 17605-0488 Tel # (717) 393-1000 Fax # (717) 393-5752; Title Fax # (717) 393-5196
Editorial Description: Helps supervisors resolve problems before they escalate.
General Info: Bi-weekly, Trim Size-8½ x 11, 4 pages, 2 Color
Subscriptions: Indv. $150

What's New in Benefits & Compensation
See: INDUSTRIAL RELATIONS/PERSONNEL

What's Working in Sales Management
See: SALESMANSHIP & SELLING

Williams Report — *Business*

Publishing Co: Joe Williams Communications, PO Box 924, Bartlesville, OK 74005-0924; Title Tel # (918) 336-2267 Title Fax # (918) 336-2733
Personnel: Publisher, Editor-Joe Williams, Circ. Mgr.-Barb Weatherly
General Info: (Formerly Communication Illustrated), Yr. Est. 1982, Monthly, Trim Size-8½ x 11, Desktop press, 12 pages, ISSN: 0736-7635, 2 Color
Subscriptions: Indv. $137, Can. $137, For. $177, $2/copy
Acquistions: Publication Bought

Women as Managers — *Business*

Publishing Co: Economics Press, Inc., 12 Daniel Rd., Fairfield, NJ 07004-2565
Tel # (201) 227-1224; Title Fax # (201) 227-9742
Editorial Description: Discusses differences in male and female management styles and how to develop one's own strengths. Presents techniques effective techniques used by women in management.
General Info: Bi-weekly
Subscriptions: $2/copy

Workers' Comp Advisor
See: INDUSTRIAL RELATIONS/PERSONNEL

Workers' Comp Practice Advisor
See: MEDICINE

Workers Compensation Guide
See: INDUSTRIAL RELATIONS/PERSONNEL

Working Smart
See: INDUSTRIAL RELATIONS/PERSONNEL

Working Together
See: INDUSTRIAL RELATIONS/PERSONNEL

You & the Law
See: LAW

Your Telephone Personality
See: TELECOMMUNICATIONS

Zimmerman Letter, The
See: HEALTH

MANUFACTURING

AC Connections — *Business, Association*

Publishing Co: Natl. Assn. of Manufacturers, 1331 Pennsylvania Ave., NW, N. Lobby, Ste. 1500, Washington, DC 20004-1703; Title Tel # (202) 637-3103
Personnel: Editor-Susan Hogg
Editorial Description: Published for members of the Association Council of the NAM.
General Info: (Formerly AC Reports), Monthly, Desktop press, 4 pages, 2 Color
Subscriptions: Free With Membership

AIPE Newsline — *Association*

Publishing Co: American Institute of Plant Engineers, 8180 Corporate Park Dr., Suite 305, Cincinnati, OH 45242-3309 Fax # (513) 247-7422; Title Tel # (513) 489-2473
Personnel: Editor-Linda Niesz
Editorial Description: National and regional news concerning AIPE members.
General Info: Bi-monthly, Trim Size-8½ x 11, Sheetfed press, 6 pages, ISSN: 8750-2046, 2 Color, Newsprint
Subscriptions: Indv. $7
Circulation: Total-10,000
List Rental: Rents Lists
Printing Co: Gardner Graphics, 6925 Valley Ave, Cincinnati, OH 45244-3083 Tel # (513) 271-0486

APICS News — *Association*

Publishing Co: American Production and Inventory Control Society, 500 W Annandale Rd, Falls Church, VA 22046-4205; Title Tel # (703) 237-8344
Personnel: Publisher-Ray Feldman, Editor-Jane Howell, Art Dir.-Karen Rose
General Info: (Formerly P & IM Review), Yr. Est. 1973, Monthly, Trim Size-8½ x 11, Offset press, 12 pages, ISSN: 0274-9874, 4 Color, Coated
Subscriptions: Indv. $45
Circulation: Total-62,000

ASEP News and Views
See: PLASTICS

Adhesive Trends — *Business, Association*

Publishing Co: Adhesives Manufacturers Assn., 401 N. Michigan Avenue, Chicago, IL 60611-4267; Title Tel # (312) 644-6610 Title Fax # (312) 321-6869
Personnel: Editor-Barbara Wolf
Editorial Description: Members are makers of paper converting and packaging adhesives, glue, gum, hot melts, paste.
General Info: (Formerly Indicators), Yr. Est. 1933, Bi-monthly, Sheetfed press, 10 pages, 2 Color, Coated, Saddle-stitched
Subscriptions: Free
Circulation: (100% controlled), Total-450

Advanced Ceramics Report — *Business*

Publishing Co: Elsevier Science Inc., 655 Avenue of the Americas, New York, NY 10010-5107 Tel # (212) 633-3916 Fax # (212) 633-3913 Parent Co.-Reed Elsevier, New York
Personnel: Publisher-Guy Kitteringhem, Editor-A. Weawes, Circ. Mgr.-Karen Richardson
Editorial Description: Detailed coverage of new products and materials. Includes contact names and addresses.
General Info: Yr. Est. 1985, Monthly, ISSN: 0268-9847, Ind/Abs/Online: DIALOG, Newsprint
Subscriptions: Indv. $533

Advanced Coatings & Surface Technology
See: CHEMISTRY & CHEMICALS

Advanced Composites Bulletin — *Business*

Publishing Co: Elsevier Science Inc., 655 Avenue of the Americas, New York, NY 10010-5107 Tel # (212) 633-3916 Fax # (212) 633-3913 Parent Co.-Reed Elsevier, New York
Personnel: Publisher-G. Kitteringham, Editor-A. Weaver, Production Mgr.-F. Robinson, Promotion Dir.-S. Sydrey Smith
Editorial Description: Detailed coverage of new products and materials. Includes contact names and addresses.
General Info: Yr. Est. 1987, Monthly, Desktop press, ISSN: 0951-953X, Ind/Abs/Online: DIALOG, Data-Star, 2 Color, Newsprint, Other
Subscriptions: Indv. $457

Advanced Manufacturing Technology — *Business*

Publishing Co: Technical Insights, Inc., PO Box 1304, Fort Lee, NJ 07024-9967; Title Tel # (201) 568-4744 Title Fax # (201) 568-8247
Personnel: Publisher-Kenneth A. Kovaly, Editor-Pamela Frost, Circ. Mgr.-Barbara Chaffee, Mktg. Dir.-Lyn Schmidt
Editorial Description: All phases of technological advances that can ensure manufacturing competitiveness.
General Info: Yr. Est. 1980, Monthly, Trim Size-8½ x 11, Sheetfed press, 14 pages, ISSN: 0885-5684, 2 Color, Matte, Other
Subscriptions: Indv. $575, For. $635
List Rental: Actives: $180/M
Printing Co: Allied Lettercraft, 307 W. 36th St., New York, NY 10018 Tel # (212) 279-4800

Advanced Materials — *Business*

Publishing Co: Advanced Materials, PO Box 6249, Hilton Head Island, SC 29938-6249; Title Tel # (803) 842-4940 Title Fax # (803) 842-4940
Personnel: Publisher, Editor-Philip West, Circ. Mgr., Promotion Dir.-Susan West
Editorial Description: Technical info & news about high-performance metals,composites,plastics & ceramics.
General Info: Yr. Est. 1979, 23x/yr., Trim Size-8½ x 11, Offset press, 6 pages, ISSN: 0734-7146, No Color
Subscriptions: Indv. $238, For. $260, $20/copy

Affiliated Warehouse Companies Newsletter
See: TRUCKING

Akron Daily Digest
See: HOUSE ORGANS

American Gear Manufacturers Association News Digest — *Business, Association* CPM: $340

Publishing Co: American Gear Manufacturers, 1500 King St Ste 201, Alexandria, VA 22314-2730; Title Tel # (703) 684-0211 Title Fax # (703) 684-0242
Editorial Description: Digest containing technical, product and industry information for gear manufacturers.
General Info: Yr. Est. 1916, Bi-monthly, 24 pages, 20% ads, 2 Color, Coated, Saddle-stitched
Subscriptions: Indv. $50, Free With Membership
Circulation: Total-2,000
Advertising: $680.

American Law of Products Liability Newsletter
See: LAW

Associations Council Connections

Publishing Co: Natl. Assn. of Manufacturers, 1331 Pennsylvania Ave., NW, N. Lobby, Ste. 1500, Washington, DC 20004-1703; Title Tel # (202) 637-3103 Title Fax # (202) 637-3182
Personnel: Editor-Valette Piper
Editorial Description: Assn. activities newsletter, also includes meeting, legislative, & Council news.
General Info: (Formerly Points of Interest), Yr. Est. 1981, Monthly, 4 pages
Subscriptions: Indv. $200
Circulation: Total-400

Braintree Express
See: HOUSE ORGANS

CMP Newsletter
See: METALS & METALWORKING

Canada Dry Crown
See: BEVERAGES - BREWING

Canada Petroleum Industry
See: PETROLEUM & NATURAL GAS

Capacity Utilization Rates in Canadian Manufacturing   *Business, Association*

Publishing Co: Statistics Canada, Holland Ave/RH Coats, Holland Ave/Tunney's Pasture, Ottawa, ON K1A O26 Canada Tel # (613) 951-8116 Fax # (613) 951-0581; Title Tel # (613) 990-8116
Editorial Description: Analytical extension of the capital stocks series presented in pub. 13-211. Catalog #31-003.
General Info: Yr. Est. 1976, Quarterly, 57 pages, ISSN: 0700-1517
Subscriptions: Indv. $13, Can. $11, For. $16

Cleanroom Markets Newsletter   *Business*

Publishing Co: McIlvaine Co., The, 2970 Maria Ave., Northbrook, IL 60062-2024; Title Tel # (847) 272-0010 Title Fax # (847) 272-9673
Personnel: Publisher-Robert McIlvaine
Editorial Description: Information on cleanrooms markets worldwide.
General Info: (Formerly Cleanroom Design Newsletter), Monthly
Subscriptions: Indv. $460, Can. $460, For. $460
List Rental: Rents Lists

Cleanroom Technology Newsletter   *Business*

Publishing Co: McIlvaine Co., The, 2970 Maria Ave., Northbrook, IL 60062-2024; Title Tel # (847) 272-0010 Title Fax # (847) 272-9673
Personnel: Publisher-Robert McIlvaine, Editor-Marilyn McIlvoine
Editorial Description: Information on cleanroom technology.
General Info: (Formerly Cleanroom Operations Newsletter), Monthly
Subscriptions: Indv. $270, For. $300
List Rental: Rents Lists

Composites & Adhesives Newsletter
See: ENGINEERING

Composites Industry Monthly
See: PLASTICS

Computer Aided Design Report   *Business*

Publishing Co: CAD/CAM Publishing, Inc., 1010 Turquoise St., Ste. 320, San Diego, CA 92109-1159; Title Tel # (619) 488-0533 Title Fax # (619) 488-6052
Personnel: Publisher-L. Wolfe, Editor-Jeannette De Wyze, Circ. Mgr.-Pat Wright, Art Dir.-H. Rosen
Editorial Description: Uses of computers by engineers in manufacturing design.
General Info: (Formerly CAD/CIM Alert), Yr. Est. 1981, Monthly, Trim Size-8½ x 11, Sheetfed press, 16 pages, ISSN: 0276-749X, No Color, Newsprint, Saddle-stitched
Subscriptions: Indv. $190, Can. $190, For. $244
List Rental: Actives: $200/M

Consumption of Containers and Other Packaging Supplies by the Manufacturing Industries   *Business, Association*

Publishing Co: Statistics Canada, Holland Ave/RH Coats, Holland Ave/Tunney's Pasture, Ottawa, ON K1A O26 Canada Tel # (613) 951-8116 Fax # (613) 951-0581; Title Tel # (613) 990-8116
Editorial Description: Breakdown by industry. 31-212.
General Info: Yr. Est. 1962, Annually, 28 pages, ISSN: 0576-0186
Subscriptions: Indv. $31, Can. $26, For. $36, $31/copy

Continuous Improvement   *Business*

Publishing Co: Continous Improvement, 8460 Dygert Dr, Alto, MI 49302-9746; Title Tel # (616) 891-9114 Title Fax # (616) 891-9114
Personnel: Publisher, Editor-Richard Clements, Production Mgr.-Mary Bustraan
Editorial Description: Tutorial & news on new quality assurance technologies and ISO 9000.
General Info: Yr. Est. 1986, Monthly, Trim-8½ x 11, Sheetfed press, 8 pages, ISSN: 1071-2240, No Color, Newsprint
Subscriptions: Indv. $95, Inst. $95, Can. $95, For. $95, $10/copy
Acquistions: Publication Bought, Publication Sold
Circulation: Total-2,000

Cureletter   *Business, Association*

Publishing Co: Captan Associates, Inc., PO Box 504, 744 Durham Terrace, Brick, NJ 08723-0504; Title Tel # (908) 840-1244 Title Fax # (908) 840-1211
Personnel: Publisher-Claire Bluestein, Editor-Josephine Salser, Co-Editor-Joseph Plamondon
Editorial Description: Covers technical & business aspects of radiation curing of coatings, adhesives, inks, photopolymers.
General Info: Yr. Est. 1984, Monthly, Trim Size-8½ x 11, Desktop press, 16 pages, ISSN: 1075-3567, No Color, Saddle-stitched
Subscriptions: Indv. $225, Inst. $227, Can. $227, For. $250
Acquistions: Publication Bought
Circulation: Total-150
Advertising: Inquire for rates. Accepts Inserts.
List Rental: List Management Co.: Captan Associates Inc., PO Box 504, 744 Durham Terrace, Brick, NJ 08723-0504 Tel # (908) 840-1244, Fax # (908) 840-1211, Actives: 15,000, $125/M
Printing Co: J.M. Printing, Pt. Pleasant, NJ 08742

Davis Database
See: COMPUTERS & AUTOMATION

Editor & M & E Appraiser
See: ENGINEERING

Electric Utilities Industry - U.S. and Canada
See: PUBLIC UTILITIES

Electro Manufacturing   *Business*

Publishing Co: Worldwide Videotex Co., PO Box 3273, Boynton Beach, FL 33424-3273 Tel # (407) 738-2276 Fax # (407) 738-2276
Editorial Description: Computer and electronic technologies used to help improve manufacturing effeciency.
General Info: Yr. Est. 1988, Monthly, ISSN: 1041-052X, Ind/Abs/Online: DIALOG
Subscriptions: Indv. $150, Inst. $150, Can. $150, For. $165

Empire State Development
See: BUSINESS & INDUSTRY

Employment Trends
See: EMPLOYMENT

Exhibitor
See: ADVERTISING & MARKETING

FIERF Newsletter
See: EDUCATION

FMA News   *Association*

Publishing Co: Fabricators & Manufacturers Assn., Intl., 833 Featherstone Rd, Rockford, IL 61107-6301; Title Tel # (815) 399-8700
Personnel: Publisher-John Nandzik, Editor-Tina Sullivan, Circ. Mgr.-Mary Poirier, Production Mgr., Art Dir.-Debra Strout
Editorial Description: Industry & Assn. news for FMA members.
General Info: (Formerly FMA Update), Yr. Est. 1970, Monthly, Sheetfed press, 8 pages, 2 Color, Newsprint
Circulation: (100% controlled), Total-1,300

FPDA News   *Association*

Publishing Co: Fluid Power Distributors Association, 201 Barclay Pavilion W, Cherry Hill, NJ 08034-2129; Title Tel # (609) 795-6113 Title Fax # (609) 795-6362
Personnel: Editor-K. DeMarco
Editorial Description: Association meeting information industry trends, member news, Association news, statistical and management information.
General Info: Yr. Est. 1983, Bi-monthly, Trim Size-8½ x 11, Offset press, 10 pages, 2 Color, Coated, Saddle-stitched
Subscriptions: Free To Qualified Recipient
Circulation: Total-2,400

Facilities Forum

Publishing Co: American Institute of Plant Engineers, 8180 Corporate Park Dr., Suite 305, Cincinnati, OH 45242-3309 Tel # (513) 489-2473 Fax # (513) 247-7422; Title Tel # (513) 561-6000 Title Fax # (513) 527-5914
Personnel: Editor-Dave Mcauley
Editorial Description: An idea-exchange newsletter for leaders in plant engineering & facilities management.
General Info: Yr. Est. 1984, Bi-monthly, 4 pages, 2 Color, Matte
Circulation: Total-4,500
Printing Co: Edge Graphics, 2250 Gilbert Ave # 6163, Cincinnati, OH 45206-2531 Tel # (513) 221-3343

Gem & Jewelry Fact Sheets Quarterly Supplement
See: JEWELRY & HOROLOGY

Good Guys, The
See: AUTOMOTIVE

Government Prime Contracts Monthly
See: U.S. (& CANADIAN) FED. GOV'T.

Gunderson News
Publishing Co: Gunderson, Inc., 4350 NW Front Ave, Portland, OR 97210-1499; Title Tel # (503) 228-9281 Title Fax # (503) 242-0683
Personnel: Publisher-Bruce Harmon, Editor, Art Dir.-Julie Ward
Editorial Description: Employee magazine for Gunderson, Inc.
General Info: (Formerly Torch & Stinger), Yr. Est. 1942, Quarterly, Trim Size-8½ x 11, Sheetfed press, 16 pages, 2 Color, Coated, Saddle-stitched
Circulation: Total-1,800

Health Industry Today
See: HEALTH

High-Tech Materials Alert   *Business*
Publishing Co: Technical Insights, Inc., PO Box 1304, Fort Lee, NJ 07024-9967; Title Tel # (201) 568-4744 Title Fax # (201) 568-8247
Personnel: Publisher-Kenneth A. Kovaly, Editorial Dir.-Peter R. Savage, Circ. Mgr.-Barbara Chaffee, Mktg. Dir.-Lyn Schmidt
Editorial Description: Details significant developments in high-performance materials ranging from alloys & metallic whiskers to ceramic & graphite fibers, their fabrication & industrial applications. Special monthly supplement: HTMA market forecast.
General Info: Yr. Est. 1984, Monthly, Trim Size-8½ x 11, Sheetfed press, 10 pages, ISSN: 0741-0808, 2 Color, Matte, Other
Subscriptions: Indv. $625, For. $685
List Rental: Actives: $180/M

Houston Petroleum Industry
See: PETROLEUM & NATURAL GAS

IE News: Engineering Economy
See: ECONOMICS

IE News: Ergonomics
See: ENGINEERING

IE News: Facilities Planning & Design   *Association*   CPM: $143
Publishing Co: Institute of Industrial Engineers, 25 Technology Park/Atlanta, Norcross, GA 30092-2988 Tel # (770) 449-0461; Title Tel # (404) 449-0460 Title Fax # (770) 263-8532
Personnel: Production Mgr.-Dona Brown
Editorial Description: Newsletter for IIE Facilities Planning & Design Division.
General Info: Quarterly, Trim Size-8½ x 11, Sheetfed press, 4 pages, 2 Color, Matte, Saddle-stitched
Circulation: (100% controlled), Total-3,300
Advertising: $475. Accepts Inserts.
List Rental: Rents Lists

IE News: Industrial & Labor Relations
See: INDUSTRIAL RELATIONS/PERSONNEL

IE News: Operations Research
See: ENGINEERING

IE News: Quality Control and Reliability Engineering   *Association*   CPM: $190
Publishing Co: Institute of Industrial Engineers, 25 Technology Park/Atlanta, Norcross, GA 30092-2988 Tel # (770) 449-0461; Title Tel # (404) 449-0460 Title Fax # (770) 263-8532
Personnel: Production Mgr.-Dona Brown
Editorial Description: Newsletter for IIE Quality Control & Reliability Engineering Division.
General Info: Quarterly, Trim Size-8½ x 11, Sheetfed press, 6 pages, 2 Color, Matte, Saddle-stitched
Circulation: Total-2,500
Advertising: $475. Accepts Inserts.
List Rental: Rents Lists

IE News: Work Measurement & Methods Engineering   *Association*   CPM: $88
Publishing Co: Institute of Industrial Engineers, 25 Technology Park/Atlanta, Norcross, GA 30092-2988 Tel # (770) 449-0461; Title Tel # (404) 449-0460 Title Fax # (770) 263-8532
Personnel: Production Mgr.-Dona Brown
Editorial Description: Newsletter for IIE Work Measurement & Methods Engineering Division.
General Info: Quarterly, Trim Size-8½ x 11, Sheetfed press, 4 pages, 2 Color, Matte, Saddle-stitched
Circulation: (100% controlled), Total-5,350
Advertising: $475. Accepts Inserts.
List Rental: Rents Lists

ILMA Compoundings
See: PETROLEUM & NATURAL GAS

ISTI Newswire
Publishing Co: International Spa and Tub Institute, 240 S Feldner Rd, Orange, CA 92668-2716; Title Tel # (714) 978-2081
Editorial Description: Manufacturers of spas and hot tubs and their accessories, as well as chemical manufacturers, suppliers of now materials, etc.
General Info: Yr. Est. 1978, Monthly

Industries in Transition
See: BUSINESS & INDUSTRY

Innovator's Digest
See: MANAGEMENT

Input   *Business*
Publishing Co: National Decorating Products Assn., Inc., 1050 N Lindbergh Blvd, Saint Louis, MO 63132-2912; Title Tel # (314) 991-3470 Title Fax # (314) 991-5039
Personnel: Editor-Wayne Simmons
General Info: Yr. Est. 1972, Bi-monthly
Subscriptions: Free With Membership
Circulation: Total-4,000

Inside R&D   *Business*
Publishing Co: Technical Insights, Inc., PO Box 1304, Fort Lee, NJ 07024-9967; Title Tel # (201) 568-4744 Title Fax # (201) 568-8247
Personnel: Publisher-Kenneth Kovaly, Editor-Charles Joslin, Circ. Mgr.-Barbara Chaffee, Mktg. Dir.-Lyn Schmidt
Editorial Description: Concentrates on current research and development that will create news products and markets in the near term. Two supplements: Report on Managing Innovation and Trends, Forecasts and Analyses.
General Info: Yr. Est. 1972, Weekly, Trim Size-8½ x 11, Sheetfed press, 6 pages, ISSN: 0030-757X, Matte, Other
Subscriptions: Indv. $790, For. $890
List Rental: Actives: $180/M
Printing Co: Allied Lettercraft, 307 W. 36th St., New York, NY 10018 Tel # (212) 279-4800

Intelligent Manufacturing   *Business*
Publishing Co: Lionheart Publishing Inc., 2555 Cumberland Pkwy. #299, Atlanta, GA 30339-3908; Title Tel # (770) 431-0867 Title Fax # (770) 432-6969
Personnel: Publisher-John Llewellyn, Editor-David Blanchard
Editorial Description: Provides expert solutions for manufacturing personnel, as well as up-to-the-minute news stories. Looks at specific production issues, emerging technologies and trends.
General Info: Yr. Est. 1995, Monthly, Trim Size-8½ x 11, 12 pages, ISSN: 1080-2576
Subscriptions: Indv. $115, Can. $115, For. $125, $20/copy
Advertising: Accepts Inserts.
List Rental: Rents Lists

International Petroleum Industry
See: PETROLEUM & NATURAL GAS

International Product Safety News
See: SAFETY

Inventory Management Newsletter   *Association, Business*
Publishing Co: Center for Inventory Management, 900 Secret Cove Dr, Sugar Hill, GA 30518-5366; Title Tel # (404) 296-6020
Personnel: Editor-Henry Jordan
General Info: Yr. Est. 1969, Quarterly, Trim Size-11 x 17, Sheetfed press, 6 pages, 2 Color, Newsprint
Circulation: Total-26,000

Japan-U.S. Business Report
See: INTERNATIONAL TRADE

Legislative Review
Publishing Co: Can Manufacturers Institute, 1625 Massachussetts Ave., NW, Washington, DC 20036-2289; Title Tel # (202) 232-4677
Personnel: Editor-Theresa Termine
General Info: Weekly, 8 pages, 2 Color, Saddle-stitched
Circulation: Total-313

MACS ACTION!
See: AUTOMOTIVE

MACS Service Reports
See: AUTOMOTIVE

MHI News
See: ENGINEERING

Manufacturing Applications
See: COMPUTERS & AUTOMATION

Manufacturing Automation   *Business*
Publishing Co: Vital Information Publications, 321 Carrera Dr, Mill Valley, CA 94941-3995 Tel # (415) 389-8671; Title Tel # (415) 345-7018 Title Fax # (415) 389-8671
Editorial Description: Covers business developments in the manufacturing automation industry.
General Info: Yr. Est. 1991, Monthly, ISSN: 1060-2712
Subscriptions: Indv. $325, For. $345

Manufacturing Market Insider
Business

Publishing Co: JBT Communications, PO Box 782, Needham Heights, MA 02194-0006; Title Tel # (617) 444-2154 Title Fax # (617) 455-8409
Personnel: Publisher, Editor-John B. Tuck, Circ. Mgr.-Ann Connors
Editorial Description: Covers the electronics assembly business with emphasis on contract manufacturing of electronics. Includes acquisitions, expansions, financial results and contract awards announced by contract manufacturers of electronics. Also contains market data and technology trends.
General Info: Yr. Est. 1991, Monthly, Trim Size-8½ x 11, Sheetfed press, 8 pages, ISSN: 1072-8651, No Color, Matte
Subscriptions: Indv. $388, Can. $388, For. $448
Printing Co: Inkstone Co, 178 Crescent Rd, Needham, MA 02194 Tel # (617) 433-0331

Manufacturing News
Business, Association

Publishing Co: Publishers & Producers, P.O. Box 36, Annandale, VA 22003; Title Tel # (703) 750-2664 Title Fax # (703) 750-0064
Personnel: Publisher, Editor-Richard McCormack, Circ. Mgr.-Anne Anderson, Product Mgr.-Keith Carter, Promotion Dir.-David Konstantin
General Info: Yr. Est. 1994, Semi-monthly, Trim Size-8 x 11½, 17 pages, ISSN: 10782397, Ind/Abs/Online: newsnet
Subscriptions: Indv. $395, For. $445, $15/copy

Manufacturing Technology
Business

Publishing Co: National Technical Information Service U.S., 5285 Port Royal Rd., Springfield, VA 22161-0001 Tel # (703) 487-4630 Fax # (703) 487-4630; Title Tel # (703) 487-4929
Editorial Description: Covers CAD/CAM, robotics, robots, productivity, manufacturing, planning, processing & control, plant design, & computer software.
General Info: Weekly, Trim Size-8½ x 11
Subscriptions: Indv. $175, Can. $175, For. $245

Manufacturing Trends

Publishing Co: Natl. Assn. of Manufacturers, 1331 Pennsylvania Ave., NW, N. Lobby, Ste. 1500, Washington, DC 20004-1703 Tel # (202) 637-3103
Personnel: Publisher-Jerry Jasinowski
Editorial Description: Focuses on major force affecting manufacturing.
General Info: Monthly

Mid-Continent States Petroleum Industry
See: PETROLEUM & NATURAL GAS

Monthly Product Announcement
See: BUSINESS & INDUSTRY

NACS SCAN

Publishing Co: Natl. Assn. of Convenience Stores, 1605 King St., Alexandria, VA 22314-2726; Title Tel # (703) 684-3600
Personnel: Editor-Lindsay Hutter
Editorial Description: To inform & educate NACS members on every important event & emerging issue, the NACS SCAN goes out to the industry, to Capitol Hill, & to the communities members serve to bring readers the top stories.
General Info: (Formerly NACS Update), Yr. Est. 1981, Monthly, Sheetfed press, 16 pages, 2 Color
Circulation: Total-6,400
Printing Co: Goetz Printing Co., 7939 Angus Ct., Springfield, VA 22153-2844 Tel # (703) 569-8232, Fax # (703) 569-9364

NASFM NEWs
Business

Publishing Co: Natl. Assn. of Store Fixture Manufacturers, 1776 N. Pine Island Road, #102, Plantation, FL 33322; Title Tel # (954) 424-1443 Title Fax # (954) 473-8268
Personnel: Publisher-Klein Merriman, Editor-Karen Budlong
Editorial Description: Assn. & industry newsletter.
General Info: Yr. Est. 1956, Bi-monthly
Subscriptions: Free With Membership

NSRA News
See: COMPUTERS & AUTOMATION

New Plant Report
See: CONSTRUCTION & BUILDING

Northeast States Petroleum Industry
See: PETROLEUM & NATURAL GAS

Nye Lubeletter Newsletter
Business

Publishing Co: Nye Lubricants, Inc., PO Box 8927, New Bedford, MA 02742-8927; Title Tel # (508) 996-6721
Editorial Description: Discusses use of lubricants in the manufacturing environment.
General Info: Yr. Est. 1972, Monthly, Trim Size-8½ x 11, 34 pages, No Color, Coated, Saddle-stitched

OPEDA Outlook

Publishing Co: Outdoor Power Equipment Distributors Assn., 1900 Arch St, Philadelphia, PA 19103-1404; Title Tel # (215) 564-3484
Personnel: Editor-Wendy Romig
General Info: Quarterly, Offset press, 8 pages, No Color, Newsprint

Official Board Markets
See: PAPER

Ozone Depleter Compliance Guide
See: ENVIRONMENT & ECOLOGY

Permian Basin Petroleum Industry
See: PETROLEUM & NATURAL GAS

Perspective
Business, Association

Publishing Co: Greater Seattle Chamber of Commerce, 1301 Fifth Ste 2400, Seattle, WA 98101 Tel # (206) 389-7200 Fax # (206) 389-7288; Title Tel # (206) 389-7243
Personnel: Editor-Dave Skarr
Editorial Description: Updates on Chamber/business issues & events in Greater-Seattle area.
General Info: (Formerly Seattle Business Newsletter; Newsline), Bi-weekly, Sheetfed press, 5 pages, 8% ads, No Color, Newsprint
Subscriptions: Indv. $8
Circulation: Total-7,000
Advertising: Inquire for rates.
List Rental: Rents Lists
Printing Co: Pioneer Printing Co., 514 W 19th St, Cheyenne, WY 82001-4336 Tel # (307) 635-4114

Petrochemical Industry - Worldwide
See: PETROLEUM & NATURAL GAS

Pipeline - Worldwide
See: PETROLEUM & NATURAL GAS

Plant Shutdowns Monitor
See: INTERNATIONAL TRADE

Plastics Week (Incorporating Plastics & the Environment)
See: PLASTICS

Poly Probe
See: METALS & METALWORKING

Power Products Business
See: MANAGEMENT

Productivity
See: BUSINESS & INDUSTRY

Products Liability Reporter
See: CONSUMER INTERESTS

Products Shipped by Canadian Manufacturers
Business, Association

Publishing Co: Statistics Canada, Holland Ave/RH Coats, Holland Ave/Tunney's Pasture, Ottawa, ON K1A O26 Canada Tel # (613) 951-8116 Fax # (613) 951-0581; Title Tel # (613) 951-1581 Title Fax # (613) 951-1584
Editorial Description: Value and quantities of products shipped by Canadian manufacturers. 31-211.
General Info: Yr. Est. 1961, Annually, 158 pages, ISSN: 0575-9455
Subscriptions: Indv. $72, Can. $60, For. $84

Quality Management
Business

Publishing Co: Bureau of Business Practice, 24 Rope Ferry Rd, Waterford, CT 06386-0001 Tel # (806) 442-4365 Fax # (860) 434-3341 Parent Co.-Prentice Hall, Waterford; Title Tel # (860) 442-4365
Personnel: Publisher-Elaine Stattles, Editor-Peter Hawkins, Art Dir.-Deni Fedeli
Editorial Description: Case studies and comments on how companies can improve the quality of their processes, products and services to achieve maximum operation and market competitiveness.
General Info: (Formerly Quality Assurance Bulletin), Yr. Est. 1981, Semi-monthly, 8 pages, ISSN: 1040-0664, 4 Color
Subscriptions: Indv. $138

Rapid Prototyping Report
See: COMPUTERS & AUTOMATION

Retiree Roundup
See: HOUSE ORGANS

Risk Management Program Handbook
Business

Publishing Co: Thompson Publishing Group, 1725 K Street, NW, Washington, DC 20006 Tel # (202) 872-4000
Editorial Description: Source of guidance for compliance with Clean Air Act requirements. Subscription includes monthly newsletter and updates.
General Info: Irregular, Looseleaf
Subscriptions: Indv. $349

SGD Newsletter
See: CONSTRUCTION & BUILDING

SIA Circuit

Publishing Co: Semiconductor Industry Assn., 181 Metro Dr., Ste. 450, San Jose, CA 95110-1346; Title Tel # (408) 246-2711 Title Fax # (408) 246-2830
Personnel: Publisher, Circ. Mgr., Art Dir.-LuAnn Jenkins
Editorial Description: A quarterly newsletter covering SIA public policy, occupational health & safety, & statistics programs.
General Info: Yr. Est. 1978, Quarterly, 8 pages, 2 Color, Coated
Circulation: (100% controlled), Total-3,200

SIGMA Newsletter
See: CONSTRUCTION & BUILDING

SMT Trends   *Business*

Publishing Co: New Insights, 303 Vallejo St., Crockett, CA 94525 Tel # (510) 787-2273; Title Tel # (415) 389-8671 Title Fax # (415) 389-8671
Personnel: Publisher, Editor-Michael New
Editorial Description: Marketing and business news for the surface mount industry. Covers component and packaging trends, CAD, CAE, pick & place, robotics, and test inspection.
General Info: (Formerly SMTrends), Yr. Est. 1984, Monthly, 16 pages, ISSN: 0890-7900, Color-cover
Subscriptions: Indv. $325
Acquistions: Publication Sold

Safety Signals
See: SAFETY

Sales Leads
See: SALESMANSHIP & SELLING

San Jacinto Spirit
See: HOUSE ORGANS

Screening Industry   *Business, Association*

Publishing Co: Screen Manufacturers Assn., Fitzgerald Corp., 3950 Lake Shre Dr. #502-A, Chicago, IL 60613-3431; Title Tel # (312) 525-2644
Personnel: Publisher-Frank Fitzzwald, Editor-Ellis Murphy, Circ. Mgr.-Kathryn Fitzgerald, Production Mgr.-June Fitzgerald, Art Dir.-Alice Lupins
Editorial Description: Industry news for users of insect screens, solar screens, protection screens & their components.
General Info: (Formerly Screening Industry News), Yr. Est. 1974, Quarterly, Trim Size-8½ x 11, 6 pages, 2 Color, Coated
Circulation: Total-1,000
List Rental: Actives: $150/M

Semi News

Publishing Co: Semiconductor Equipment & Materials Intl., 805 E Middlefield Rd, Mountain View, CA 94043-4025; Title Tel # (415) 940-6940
Personnel: Editor-Lisa Anderson
General Info: Yr. Est. 1973, Bi-monthly, 12 pages, 2 Color
Circulation: Total-10,000

Sensor Business Digest
See: INSTRUMENTS

Sensor Technology
See: ENGINEERING, ELECTRICAL

Service Management   *Association*   CPM: $75

Publishing Co: Natl. Assn. of Service Managers, 1030 W. Higgins Rd., Ste. 109, Hoffman Estates, IL 60195-3248; Title Tel # (708) 310-9930 Title Fax # (708) 310-9934
Personnel: Editor-Don Buelow
Editorial Description: For after market product service/support personnel in all manufacturing industries.
General Info: Yr. Est. 1984, Monthly, Trim Size-8½ x 11¼, Sheetfed press, 12 pages, 4% ads, 2 Color, Matte, Saddle-stitched
Subscriptions: Indv. $36, $3/copy
Circulation: (BPA), Total-8,000
Advertising: $600. Accepts Inserts.
List Rental: Actives: 5,000
Printing Co: Commercial Communications Inc., 2325-K Bluemound Rd., Waukesha, WI 53186 Tel # (414) 798-1999, Fax # (414) 798-8689

Southeast States Petroleum Industry
See: PETROLEUM & NATURAL GAS

Southwestern Ice
Association Newsletter   *Business, Association*   CPM: $500

Publishing Co: Southwestern Ice Assn., 1601 Rio Grande St Ste 440, Austin, TX 78701-1149; Title Tel # (512) 479-0425
Personnel: Editor-Lisa Fry
Editorial Description: Official publication of the Southwestern Ice Association. SWIA is an association of firms who are engaged in the production or distribution of ice in the southwestern United States.
General Info: Quarterly, Offset press, 12 pages, 40% ads, 2 Color, Coated
Subscriptions: Free With Membership
Circulation: Total-200
Advertising: $100.
Printing Co: Austex Printing Co., 501 W 3rd St, Austin, TX 78703-3807 Tel # (512) 476-7581

Staveley NDTech News

Publishing Co: Staveley NDT Technologies, Inc., 421 N Quay St, Kennewick, WA 99336-7735 Tel # (509) 735-7550 Fax # (509) 735-4672; Title Tel # (609) 883-5030
General Info: Yr. Est. 1984, Quarterly, 6 pages
Circulation: Total-5,000

Steering Columns
See: HOUSE ORGANS

Supermarket Strategic Alert
See: GROCERY

Tate Andale Inc.   *Business*

Publishing Co: Tate Andale Inc., 1941 Lansdowne Rd, Baltimore, MD 21227-1707 Fax # (410) 247-9672; Title Tel # (410) 247-8700
Personnel: VP Sales-George Yancey
General Info: Trim Size-8½ x 11, 52 pages, 2 Color, Coated, Other

Tech Notes   *Business*

Publishing Co: National Technical Information Service U.S., 5285 Port Royal Rd., Springfield, VA 22161-0001 Fax # (703) 487-4630; Title Tel # (703) 487-4630
Personnel: Editor-Edward Lehmann
Editorial Description: Describes new processes, equipment, materials, & techniques developed by Federal laboratories.
General Info: (Formerly Tech Notes Manufacturing), Yr. Est. 1972, Monthly, Trim Size-8½ x 11, Offset press, 120 pages, Ind/Abs/Online: FAT, No Color
Subscriptions: Indv. $185, Can. $185, For. $370, $8/copy

TechPak Newsletter
See: PACKAGING

Texas Business Review
See: BUSINESS & INDUSTRY

Texas Industrial Expansion
See: REGIONAL INTEREST

Texas Petroleum Industry
See: PETROLEUM & NATURAL GAS

Total Employee Involvement
See: BUSINESS & INDUSTRY

Total Productive Maintenance
See: BUSINESS & INDUSTRY

Tremco News
See: CONSTRUCTION & BUILDING

Tribology News   *Business*

Publishing Co: Gavarti Assocs. Ltd., 9240 N Sleepy Hollow Rd, Milwaukee, WI 53217-1240; Title Tel # (414) 351-3875
General Info: Quarterly, 8 pages

UAMR Newsletter   *Business*

Publishing Co: United Assn. of Manufacturers Representatives, 34071 La Plaza, PO Box 986, Dana Point, CA 92629 Tel # (714) 240-4966 Fax # (714) 240-4966; Title Tel # (913) 268-9466
Personnel: Editor-H. Keith Kittrell
Editorial Description: News information of interest to manufacturers' reps & principals.
General Info: Yr. Est. 1956, Monthly, Trim Size-8 x 10½, Web press, No Color
Subscriptions: Indv. $24
Circulation: (100% controlled), Total-1,200
Printing Co: Howard Johnson Printing, 127 Terrace Trl W, Lake Quivira, KS 66106-9504 Tel # (913) 631-7781

Valve World

Publishing Co: Valve Manufacturers Assn. of America, 1050 17th St NW Ste 701, Washington, DC 20036-5503; Title Tel # (202) 331-8105
Editorial Description: Currents focuses on the U.S. valve industry, its customers & its assn., VMA. It contains information on meetings & events, as well as intl. trade opportunities.
General Info: (Formerly Currents), Yr. Est. 1982, Monthly, Desktop press, 8 pages, No Color
Circulation: (100% controlled), Total-1,000

Vision   *Consumer, Association*

Publishing Co: Society of Manufacturing Engineers, One SME Dr., Box 930, Dearborn, MI 48121; Title Tel # (313) 271-1500 Title Fax # (313) 271-2861
Personnel: Editor-John Coleman, Circ. Mgr.-Marleen Vann, Production Mgr.-Dale Michelson, Publisher, Adv. Dir.-Tom Drozda, Art Dir.-Kathy Lake, Promotion Dir.-Gloria Farr
Editorial Description: Report on applications, news for vision systems in manfacturing.
General Info: Yr. Est. 1984, Quarterly, Trim Size-8½ x 11, Web press, 58 pages, 2 Color, Coated
Subscriptions: Indv. $60, $15/copy
Acquisitions: Publication Bought
Circulation: Total-3,600
Advertising: Inquire for rates.

Washington Economic & Policy Trends

Publishing Co: Natl. Assn. of Manufacturers, 1331 Pennsylvania Ave., NW, N. Lobby, Ste. 1500, Washington, DC 20004-1703 Tel # (202) 637-3103; Title Tel # (202) 637-3000
Personnel: Publisher-Jerry Jasinowski
Editorial Description: Published for the manufacturing industry.
General Info: Monthly

Western States Petroleum Industry
See: PETROLEUM & NATURAL GAS

Woodwords   *Association*   **CPM: $266**

Publishing Co: Wood Truss Council of America, 5937 Meadowood Dr., Ste. 14, Madison, WI 53711-4125; Title Tel # (608) 274-4849 Title Fax # (608) 274-3329
Personnel: Publisher, Editor-Tom Knight, Circ. Mgr.-Mary Edmundson, Art Dir.-DeeAnne Moran
Editorial Description: Newsletter covering management, marketing, technological issues in the engineered wood products industry.
General Info: Yr. Est. 1983, Monthly
Circulation: Total-4,500
Advertising: $1,200.
List Rental: Actives: 2,000, $0.20/M

MATHEMATICS

AmStat News   *Association*

Publishing Co: American Statistical Assn., 1429 Duke St., Alexandria, VA 22314-3415 Tel # (703) 684-1221
General Info: Yr. Est. 1974, Monthly, ISSN: 0163-9617
Subscriptions: Indv. $40, Free With Membership
Circulation: Total-17,000
Advertising: Inquire for rates.
List Rental: List Management Co.: MGI-Marketing General Inc., 105 Oronoco St., Alexandria, VA 22314-2015 Tel # (703) 739-1000, Actives: 16,522, $95/M

BCAMT Newsletter
See: EDUCATION

Biometric Bulletin
See: BIOLOGY

By the Numbers

Publishing Co: Indiana University Northwest, 3400 Broadway, Gary, IN 46408-1101 Tel # (219) 980-6795; Title Tel # (219) 980-6500
Personnel: Publisher-Donald Coffin
Editorial Description: Baseball statistics done by the Statistical Analysis Committee of the Society for American Baseball Research.
General Info: 8 pages
Subscriptions: $1/copy

C.M.S. Notes   *Consumer, Association*

Publishing Co: Canadian Mathematical Society, 577 King Edward, Ste. 109, Box 450, Station A, Ottawa, ON K1N 6N5 Canada Tel # (613) 562-5702 Fax # (613) 565-1539; Title Tel # (613) 564-2223 Title Fax # (613) 789-1539
Personnel: Editor in Chief-S. Swaninathan, Copy Editor, Circ. Mgr.-Monique Bouchard
Editorial Description: Primary organ for the dissemination of information to CMS members. Includes problems section.
General Info: (Formerly Notes, News, and Comments), Yr. Est. 1969, 9x/yr., Trim Size-8½ x 11, Offset press, 28 pages, ISSN: 1193-9273, No Color, Newsprint, Saddle-stitched
Subscriptions: Inst. $36, Can. $36, Free With Membership
Circulation: Total-1,200
Advertising: Inquire for rates.
List Rental: Actives: $200/M
Printing Co: Synergy Print & Copy, 1155 Lola Street, Unit 4, Ottawa, ON K1K 4C1 Canada Tel # (613) 749-9382, Fax # (613) 749-9820

Connect
See: EDUCATION

ENC Update   *Consumer, Association*

Publishing Co: Eisenhower National Clearinghouse for Mathematics & Science, Ohio State University, 1929 Kenny Rd., Columbus, OH 43210-1079; Title Tel # (614) 292-7784 Title Fax # (614) 292-2066
Personnel: Editor-Gay Gordon
Editorial Description: Includes information on Clearinghouse products and services.
General Info: Yr. Est. 1994, Tri-annually, Trim Size-8½ x 11, 12 pages, 2 Color, Matte, Saddle-stitched
Subscriptions: Free
Circulation: Total-150,000, Readership-150,000

Focus, The   *Association*

Publishing Co: Mathematical Association of America, 1529 18th St NW, Washington, DC 20036-1358; Title Tel # (202) 387-5200
Personnel: Advertising Admin.-Amy Fabbri
Editorial Description: Contains articles of interest to the college mathematics community. Includes Association and other relevant news.
General Info: Yr. Est. 1981, Bi-monthly, Trim Size-8½ x 11, Web press, 32 pages, ISSN: 0731-2040, 2 Color, Matte, Saddle-stitched
Circulation: Total-29,000
Advertising: Inquire for rates.
List Rental: List Management Co.: MGI-Marketing General Inc., 105 Oronoco St., Alexandria, VA 22314-2015 Tel # (703) 739-1000, Actives: 34,268, $75/M

IT Metric Strategies   *Business*

Publishing Co: Cutter Information Corp., 37 Broadway, Ste. 1, Arlington, MA 02174-5552 Fax # (617) 648-1950; Title Tel # (617) 648-8700 Title Fax # (617) 648-8707
Personnel: Publisher-Karen Coburn, Editor-Howard Rubin, Circ. Mgr.-Beth O'Neill, Production Mgr.-Laura St. Clair
General Info: Monthly
Subscriptions: Indv. $485, Can. $485, For. $545

MSU Mathematics Letter   *Business*

Publishing Co: Montana State Univ. Alumni Assn., 1501 South 11, Foundation & Alumni Center, Bozeman, MT 59717-0001 Tel # (406) 994-2401 Fax # (406) 994-6081; Title Tel # (406) 994-3601
Personnel: Editor-David Thomas
Editorial Description: For public relations with state school teachers. Includes: current events, calendar, activities of staff, etc.
General Info: (Formerly MSC Mathematics Letter), Yr. Est. 1958, Trim Size-8½ x 11, Mimeo press, 4 pages, Color
Subscriptions: Indv. $5
Circulation: (100% controlled), Total-800

Maple Tech
See: COMPUTERS & AUTOMATION

Mathematical Log   *Association*

Publishing Co: Mu Alpha Theta, University Of Oklahoma 601 Elm, Ave., Room 423, Norman, OK 73019-0001; Title Tel # (405) 325-4489 Title Fax # (405) 325-7184
Personnel: Editor-Thomas Butts
Editorial Description: Topics of mathematical interest to high school and jr. college students.
General Info: Yr. Est. 1957, Quarterly, 5 pages, ISSN: 0025-5580
Subscriptions: Indv. $3, Can. $6, For. $6
Circulation: Total-30,000

Montana State Univ. Mathematics Univ.

Publishing Co: Montana State Univ. Dept. of Mathematical Sciences, Publications, Bozeman, MT 59717-0001; Title Tel # (406) 994-3601 Title Fax # (406) 994-2893
Personnel: Editor-David Thomas
General Info: Yr. Est. 1958, Bi-monthly, 6 pages, Color
Circulation: Total-1,120

Multiple Linear Regression Viewpoints
See: PSYCHOLOGY

School Science and Mathematics
See: EDUCATION

Sextant
See: INSURANCE

TI PPC Notes
See: COMPUTERS & AUTOMATION

MEAT & MEAT PROVISIONS

AAMPlifier/Capitol Line-Up   *Association*

Publishing Co: American Assn. of Meat Processors, 1 Meating Pl # 269, Elizabethtown, PA 17022-2883; Title Tel # (717) 367-1168 Title Fax # (717) 367-9096
Personnel: Co-Editor-Stephen Krut, Co-Editor-Anne Tantum, Production Mgr.-Jane Frey
Editorial Description: Capitol Line-Up gives information to small meat processors pertaining to government activities relating to meat processing.
General Info: Yr. Est. 1951, Bi-weekly, Trim Size-8½ x 11, Sheetfed press, 4 pages, No Color, Newsprint
Subscriptions: Indv. $50, $2/copy
Circulation: Total-2,300
List Rental: Actives: $60/M

Beefalo News

Publishing Co: American Beefalo World Registry, 116 Executive Pk., Louisville, NY 40207-4201; Title Tel # (502) 897-1650 Title Fax # (502) 897-6984
Personnel: Publisher, Editor, Circ. Mgr.-Bonnie Waddell
Editorial Description: Contains information for breeders of Beefalo Cattle.
General Info: Yr. Est. 1986, Bi-monthly, 7 pages, No Color, Newsprint

Beefalo Nickel *Association* CPM: $79

Publishing Co: S & S Bovine Images, PO Box 12315, North Kansas City, MO 64116-0315; Title Tel # (502) 897-1650
Personnel: Publisher-Stan Butt, Editor-Olbis Edwards, Circ. Mgr.-Darrell Edwards
General Info: Yr. Est. 1983, Bi-monthly, Trim Size-8½ x 11, 20 pages, 7% ads, Color
Subscriptions: Indv. $15, $2/copy
Acquistions: Publication Bought
Circulation: Total-2,500
Advertising: $199.
Printing Co: Oluis Publishing, PO Box 178, Lexington, OK 73051-0178 Tel # (405) 527-9252

Browse
See: AGRICULTURE

Daily Market & News Service *Business*

Publishing Co: Barry Urner Publications Inc, 730 N Franklin Street, Chicago, IL 60610; Title Tel # (312) 944-3380 Title Fax # (312) 944-3709
Personnel: Publisher-Jeffrey Jankowiak, Editor-Joseph Gentile, Circ. Mgr.-Ruby Jones, Production Mgr.-Rob Leone, Promotion Dir.-Betsy Leyerle
Editorial Description: Price reports on sales of unprocessed meats in open carlot market.
General Info: Yr. Est. 1923, Daily, Trim Size-8½ x 14, Sheetfed press, 4 pages
Subscriptions: Indv. $389, For. $444, $2/copy
Acquistions: Publication Bought
Advertising: Inquire for rates. Accepts Inserts.

Federal Veterinarian
See: VETERINARY

Guide to U.S. Food Safety Law
See: FOOD

HRI Meat Price Report *Business*

Publishing Co: Urner Barry Publications, Inc., PO Box 389, Toms River, NJ 08754-0389; Title Tel # (908) 240-5330 Title Fax # (908) 341-0891
Personnel: Editor-Joe Fackenthal, Circ. Mgr.-Susan Pinksaw, Production Mgr.-Bill Curro, Adv. Dir.-Lisa Sharkus, Mktg. Dir.-Sheila Deane
Editorial Description: Compilation of current meat prices for hotels, restaurants, and institutions.
General Info: Weekly, Trim Size-11 x 17, Sheetfed press, 2 pages, No Color, Newsprint
Subscriptions: Indv. $165, Can. $175, For. $199, $15/copy

Idaho Wool Growers Association
See: LIVESTOCK

Lean Trimmings *Association*

Publishing Co: Sponsor-Western States Meat Assoc., Western States Meat Assn., 1615 Broadway Ste 900, Oakland, CA 94612-2135; Title Tel # (415) 763-1533 Title Fax # (415) 763-6186
Personnel: Editor-Michelle Singer
Editorial Description: Newsletter of interest to meat industry.
General Info: (Formerly WSMA Bulletin), Yr. Est. 1946, Weekly, Trim Size-8½ x 11, Mimeo press, 8 pages, Color
Subscriptions: Free With Membership
Circulation: Total-1,200
Advertising: Inquire for rates.

Meat Sheet *Business*

Publishing Co: Meat Sheet, Inc., PO Box 124, Westmont, IL 60559-0124; Title Tel # (708) 963-2252 Title Fax # (708) 963-2980
Personnel: Publisher-William Albanos, Jr., Editor-Debbie Ash, Circ. Mgr.-Tiffany Albanos, Production Mgr.-Ann Fisher, Adv. Dir.-Dale Stone, Art Dir.-Heide Albanos, Mktg. Dir.-Tammy Albanos, Promotion Dir.-Bob Brown
Editorial Description: Daily meat prices on 450 items, plus unique statistical information on cattle & hog industry.
General Info: Yr. Est. 1974, Daily, Trim Size-8½ x 11, Sheetfed press, 1 pages, ISSN: 0889-3609, Color, Coated
Subscriptions: Indv. $400, Inst. $400, Can. $420, For. $470, $2/copy
Circulation: Total-2,000
Advertising: Accepts Inserts.

Pigletter
See: LIVESTOCK

Yellow Sheet *Business*

Publishing Co: Urner Barry Publications, Inc., PO Box 389, Toms River, NJ 08754-0389; Title Tel # (908) 240-5330 Title Fax # (908) 341-0891
Personnel: Editor-Joseph Muldowney, Circ. Mgr.-Susan Pinksaw, Production Mgr.-Bill Curro, Adv. Dir.-Lisa Sharkus, Mktg. Dir.-Sheila Deane
Editorial Description: Prices of beef, pork, lamb, veal, and by-products along with USDA prices for the same items.
General Info: Daily, Trim Size-8½ x 11, Sheetfed press, 6 pages, Ind/Abs/Online: COMTELL, No Color, Newsprint
Subscriptions: Indv. $428, Can. $483, For. $603, $15/copy
Circulation: Total-1,400

MEDIA & COMMUNICATIONS

411 Newsletter *Business*

Publishing Co: United Communications Group, 11300 Rockville Pike, Ste. 1100, Rockville, MD 20852-3030 Tel # (301) 816-8950 Fax # (301) 816-8945; Title Fax # (301) 961-9666
Personnel: Publisher-Doug O'Boyle, Editor-Jim Sweeney
General Info: Yr. Est. 1980, Bi-weekly, Ind/Abs/Online: Data-Star, DIALOG, NewsNet, Predicasts
Subscriptions: Indv. $259
List Rental: Rents Lists

ABC NewsBulletin *Business, Association*

Publishing Co: Audit Bureau of Circulations, 900 N. Meacham Rd., Schaumburg, IL 60173-4968 Tel # (708) 605-0909; Title Tel # (847) 605-0909 Title Fax # (847) 605-0483
Personnel: Publications Director-Betty-Lou Pellicore, Editor-Colleen O'Grady
Editorial Description: Newsletter directed to affairs & services of the Audit Bureau of Circulations.
General Info: Yr. Est. 1914, Quarterly, Trim Size-8½ x 11, Sheetfed press, 20 pages, 2 Color, Coated, Saddle-stitched

ADRIS Newsletter
See: COMPUTERS & AUTOMATION

AV Guide Newsletter *Business* CPM: $733

Publishing Co: Scranton Gillette Communications, Inc., 380 E. Northwest Hwy., Des Plaines, IL 60016-2282 Tel # (708) 391-1000; Title Tel # (708) 298-6622 Title Fax # (708) 390-0408
Personnel: Publisher-H.S. Gillette, Editor-Natalie Ferguson, Circ. Mgr.-Linda Lamdin
General Info: Yr. Est. 1922, Monthly, Web press, 4 pages, No Color, Newsprint
Subscriptions: Indv. $15, Can. $18, For. $18
Circulation: Total-600
Advertising: $440.
List Rental: Actives: $55/M

Action Agenda *Consumer, Association*

Publishing Co: Media Watch, PO Box 618, Santa Cruz, CA 95061-0618; Title Tel # (408) 423-6355 Title Fax # (408) 423-6355
Personnel: Co-Editor-Laura Kuhn, Co-Editor-Ann Simonton
Editorial Description: Challenges the glorification of violence, sexism, racism, classism, and homophobia. Encourages individuals to become more critical and informed consumers of mass media.
General Info: Yr. Est. 1984, Quarterly, Trim Size-8½ x 11, 20 pages, ISSN: 1083-8015, Matte, Perfect bound
Subscriptions: Indv. $20, Inst. $20, Can. $25, For. $30, $4/copy
Printing Co: Community Printers, 1827 Soquel Ave, Santa Cruz, CA 95062-1385 Tel # (408) 426-4682

Advanced Office Technologies Report
See: COMPUTERS & AUTOMATION

Airspeed *Business*

Publishing Co: Lehrfeld, 55 Northern Blvd Ste 300, Great Neck, NY 11021-4058 Tel # (516) 487-9200; Title Tel # (718) 631-0660
Personnel: Publisher-Andrew Lehrfeld, Editor-Fern Gereg
Editorial Description: Techniques of bypassing the U.S. Post Office overseas.
General Info: Yr. Est. 1984, Monthly, Offset press, 2 pages, No Color, Newsprint
Subscriptions: Indv. $60
Circulation: (100% controlled), Total-1,000

Ancillary Profits *Business*

Publishing Co: Ancillary Profits, PO Box 301, Rowayton, CT 06853-0301; Title Tel # (203) 357-9209 Title Fax # (203) 358-9709
Personnel: Publisher-Marlene Jensen
Editorial Description: In-depth coverage of spin-off businesses periodical publishers can launch for new profits.
General Info: Yr. Est. 1992, 10x/yr., Trim Size-8½ x 11, Sheetfed press, 8 pages, ISSN: 1065-8769, 2 Color, Matte
Subscriptions: Indv. $247, Can. $257, For. $277, $20/copy
Circulation: Total-1,000
List Rental: Actives: 1,000, $200/M, Expires: 1,000, $150/M
Printing Co: Newsletter Press, 76 Valley St, East Providence, RI 02914-4424 Tel # (401) 438-5352

Audio Week
See: ELECTRIC & ELECTRONIC EQUIPMENT

BRS Bulletin *Business*

Publishing Co: Bibliographic Retrieval Service, Inc., 5 Computer Dr S, Albany, NY 12205-1608; Title Tel # (703) 442-0900
Personnel: Editor-Dona McDermott
General Info: Yr. Est. 1979, Bi-monthly, 28 pages, ISSN: 0196-7223
Subscriptions: Indv. $22
Circulation: Total-10,000
Advertising: Inquire for rates.

Bandwidth Report
See: TELECOMMUNICATIONS

Beauty Spot: News You Can Use

Publishing Co: Bradford Creative, 24 Fifth Ave., New York, NY 10011-8817; Title Tel # (212) 614-9683
Personnel: Publisher-C.G. Bradford, Editor-LindaAnn Loshiavo, Circ. Mgr.-Lisa Carter
Editorial Description: This publication reaches employees of the Fortune 500 & other major corporations at work. We focus on many topics of interest to these employees: health, nutrition, personal grooming, corporate travel, and psychological subjects.
General Info: Yr. Est. 1989, Quarterly, Web press, Matte
Subscriptions: Free To Qualified Recipient

Bill Palmer's Word Watching   *Business*

Publishing Co: William Palmer Consultant Regd., PO Box 8158, Victoria, BC V8W 3R8 Canada; Title Tel # (604) 383-7146
General Info: Yr. Est. 1977, Quarterly
Subscriptions: Indv. $11, Can. $11

Book Marketing Update
See: BOOKS & BOOK TRADE

Book Promotion Hotline
See: ADVERTISING & MARKETING

Broadcasting and the Law
See: BROADCASTING

Bulldog Reporter: Western Edition
See: ADVERTISING & MARKETING

Bureau Talk   *Association*

Publishing Co: Intl. Group of Agencies & Bureaus, 6845 Parkdale Pl., Ste. A, Indianapolis, IN 46254-5605 Tel # (317) 297-0872; Title Tel # (818) 335-8069 Title Fax # (818) 335-6127
Personnel: Publisher-Jim Montoya, Circ. Mgr.-Becky Vanderkleot, Production Mgr.-Donna Caruso
Editorial Description: Newsletter for Int'l. Group of Agencies & Bureaus. Association of Speakers Bureaus.
General Info: (Formerly I.G.A.B. Newsletter), Yr. Est. 1988, Monthly, Trim Size-8½ x 11, 4 pages, 2 Color, Coated
Subscriptions: Free With Membership
Circulation: Total-400
Advertising: Accepts Inserts.

Business Publisher   *Business*

Publishing Co: JK Publishing Inc., PO Box 71020, Milwaukee, WI 53211-7120; Title Tel # (414) 332-1625 Title Fax # (414) 964-0843
Personnel: Publisher, Editor-John Kenney, Circ. Mgr.-Jean O'Brien
Editorial Description: Covers trade magazine & business publishing industry.
General Info: (Formerly Business Media Week), Yr. Est. 1985, Bi-weekly, Trim Size-8½ x 11, 8 pages, ISSN: 8756-0636, Ind/Abs/Online: Newsnet, Predicasts, 1% ads, No Color, Matte
Subscriptions: Indv. $335, For. $355, $14/copy
Acquistions: Publication Bought
Advertising: Inquire for rates. Accepts Inserts.
Printing Co: Anderson Graphics, 254 N Emmber Ln, Milwaukee, WI 53233-2638 Tel # (414) 276-4115

C4I News   *Business*

Publishing Co: Phillips Business Information, Inc., 1201 Seven Locks Rd., Ste 300, Potomac, MD 20854-2958 Tel # (301) 340-1520 Fax # (301) 424-4297
General Info: Bi-weekly, ISSN: 1071-1317
Subscriptions: Indv. $595

CAMERA on Campus
See: INTERNATIONAL TRADE

CAMERA Media Report
See: INTERNATIONAL AFFAIRS

CFJ Clearinghouse on the Central & Eastern European Press Newsletter   *Business, Consumer*

Publishing Co: Center for Foreign Journalists, 11690-A Sunrise Valley Drive, Reston, VA 22091; Title Tel # (703) 620-5984 Title Fax # (703) 620-6790
Personnel: Publisher-George A. Krimsky, Editor-Don Lippincott, Production Mgr.-Elbreta Kranowska
Editorial Description: Covers recent developments in media in Central & European Press with emphasis on a wide efforts to aid development of professional and independent media in former Soviet-Bloc countries. Includes extensive media conference and program calendar for region.
General Info: Yr. Est. 1991, Bi-monthly, Trim Size-8½ x 11, 16 pages, No Color, Other, Other
Subscriptions: Free To Qualified Recipient
Circulation: Total-3,500, Readership-10,000
Printing Co: Hands, Inc., 750 Center Street, Herndon, VA 22091 Tel # (703) 471-6808

CFJ Newsletter, The   *Business, Association*

Publishing Co: Center for Foreign Journalists, 11690-A Sunrise Valley Drive, Reston, VA 22091; Title Tel # (703) 620-5984 Title Fax # (703) 620-6790
Personnel: Publisher-George A. Krimsky, Editor-Whayne Dillehay, Production Mgr., Mktg. Dir.-C.P. Braestrup
Editorial Description: Quarterly newsleter of media training center's programs and activities.
General Info: Yr. Est. 1985, Quarterly, Trim Size-8½ x 11, Offset press, 12 pages, 2 Color, Saddle-stitched
Subscriptions: Free To Qualified Recipient
Circulation: Total-6,000, Readership-10,000
Printing Co: AGS, 188 DeMarr Rd., White Plains, MD 20695 Tel # (301) 843-1800, Fax # (301) 843-6339

C.L. Pace Report
See: U.S. (& CANADIAN) FED. GOV'T.

Cable TV Law Reporter
See: BROADCASTING

Cable TV and New Media Law & Finance
See: TELECOMMUNICATIONS

Cable TV Programming
See: TELEVISION & VIDEO

Cable TV Regulation
See: TELEVISION & VIDEO

California Cable Letter
See: TELEVISION & VIDEO

Campus Computing and Communications
See: COMPUTERS & AUTOMATION

Canadian News Facts
See: INTERNATIONAL AFFAIRS

Cantu's Newsletter   *Business, Consumer*

Publishing Co: Cantu's Comedy Newsletter, PO Box 590634, San Francisco, CA 94159-0634 Tel # (415) 668-2402; Title Tel # (415) 628-2402
Personnel: Publisher, Editor-John Cantu
Editorial Description: Articles of interest to public speakers, writers comedian, comedy writers.
General Info: (Formerly Cantu's Comedy Newsletter), Yr. Est. 1980, Tri-annually, Trim Size-8½ x 11, Desktop press, 6 pages, No Color, Other
Subscriptions: Indv. $3, Inst. $3, Can. $3, For. $5, $2/copy
Circulation: Total-3,000

Capell's Circulation Report
See: ADVERTISING & MARKETING

Catalyst Media Review

Publishing Co: Catalyst, 250 Park Ave S Fl 5, New York, NY 10003-1402; Title Tel # (212) 759-9700
Personnel: Editor-Kathe Weir
Editorial Description: Annotated bibliography of audio-visual materials relating to women and work.
General Info: Yr. Est. 1981, Bi-monthly, Trim Size-8½ x 11, 7 pages, 2 Color
Subscriptions: Indv. $8
Circulation: (100% controlled), Total-1,500

Cellular Sales & Marketing Newsletter
See: TELECOMMUNICATIONS

Censorshi#

Publishing Co: Mark Arnold, 1464 La Playa #105, San Francisco, CA 94122
Editorial Description: A publication covering censorship in the media.
General Info: Quarterly, Trim Size-8.5 x 11, 16 pages
Subscriptions: Indv. $2

Change
See: DIRECT MAIL

Channels   *Business*

Publishing Co: PR Publishing Co., Inc., PO Box 600, Exeter, NH 03833-0600; Title Tel # (603) 778-0514 Title Fax # (603) 778-1741
Personnel: Editor-June Barber, Circ. Mgr.-Laurie Eldridge
Editorial Description: Public relations ideas and strategies.
General Info: Yr. Est. 1923, Monthly, Offset press, 8 pages, ISSN: 0009-1510, No Color
Subscriptions: Indv. $50, $5/copy

Clio Among the Media

Publishing Co: Sponsor-Assn. for Ed. in Journalism & Mass Communications (AEJMC), Univ. of Utah Communication Dept., Publications, Salt Lake City, UT 84112; Title Tel # (801) 581-6888
Personnel: Editor-Nickieann Fleener
Editorial Description: For scholars & educators of History of Journalism & Mass Communications.
General Info: Quarterly, Desktop press, 24 pages, No Color
Circulation: Total-450

Cogent Communicator, The
See: BUSINESS & INDUSTRY

Collegiate Trends
See: ADVERTISING & MARKETING

Communication Booknotes
See: TELECOMMUNICATIONS

Communication Briefings   *Business*

Publishing Co: Encoders, Inc., 1101 King St., Ste. 110, Alexandria, VA 22314; Title Tel # (703) 548-3800 Title Fax # (703) 684-2136
Personnel: Publisher-Don Bagin, Editor-Jack Gillespie, Mng. Editor-Susan Marshall, Circ. Mgr.-Patty Schmidt, Production Mgr.-Ed Moore, Mktg. Dir., Promotion Dir.-Brian McCallum
Editorial Description: Provides subscribers with communications ideas and techniques to use to persuade clients, influence peers, and motivate employees.
General Info: Yr. Est. 1981, Monthly, Trim Size-8½ x 11, Web press, 8 pages, ISSN: 0730-7799, 2 Color
Subscriptions: Indv. $79, Can. $99, For. $119, $6/copy
Acquistions: Publication Bought, Publication Sold
Circulation: Total-54,000
List Rental: List Management Co.: Manager: Ed Moore; Direct Media, Inc., 200 Pemberwick Rd., PO Box 4565, Greenwich, CT 06830 Tel # (203) 532-3713, Fax # (203) 531-1452, Actives: 39,000, $90/M
Printing Co: C.R. Waldman Graphic Communications, 9100 Pennsauken Highway, CN-90239, Pennsauken, NJ Tel # (609) 662-9111, Fax # (609) 665-1789

Communication Standards
News   *Business*

Publishing Co: Phillips Business Information, Inc., 1201 Seven Locks Rd., Ste 300, Potomac, MD 20854-2958 Tel # (301) 340-1520 Fax # (301) 424-4297
General Info: Bi-weekly, ISSN: 0741-2851
Subscriptions: Indv. $497

Communications   *Business*

Publishing Co: Professional Institute of the Public Service of Canada, 53 Auriga Dr., Nepean, ON K2E 8C3 Canada; Title Tel # (613) 228-6310 Title Fax # (613) 228-9048
Editorial Description: Eng/Fr text.
General Info: Yr. Est. 1975, Bi-monthly, 8 pages, 2 Color
Circulation: Total-35,000

Communications

Publishing Co: Research Institute of America, 90 5th Avenue, New York, NY 10011-7629 Tel # (212) 645-4800; Title Tel # (800) 562-0245
Personnel: Editor-Constance Kallback, Promotion Dir.-Lisa Galjanic
Editorial Description: The single volume reference that covers all bases to get your point across on co. policies & goals to both new & current employees, this service includes these features: preparing employee handbooks, writing newsletters, conducting performance appraisals & much more.
General Info: Bi-weekly, Trim Size-6 x 9¼, Web press, Looseleaf
Subscriptions: Indv. $360
List Rental: List Management Co.: WG & L List Management, 1 Penn Plz Fl 42, New York, NY 10119-0002 Tel # (212) 971-5000

Communications
Alternatives

Publishing Co: Datapro Research Corp., 600 Delran Pky, Delran, NJ 08075-1255 Tel # (609) 764-0100 Fax # (609) 764-2815

Communications Business & Finance
See: BROADCASTING

Communications Daily
See: TELECOMMUNICATIONS

Communications
Industries Report   *Association, Business*

Publishing Co: International Communications Industries Assn., 3150 Spring St, Fairfax, VA 22031-2399 Tel # (703) 273-2399; Title Tel # (703) 273-7200 Title Fax # (703) 278-8082
Personnel: Publisher, Editor, Circ. Mgr., Adv. Dir.-Kim Williams, Art Dir.-Fran Troup
Editorial Description: A-V , video & computer news, trade trends, member news, assn. programs.
General Info: Yr. Est. 1939, Monthly, Trim Size-8½ x 11, Sheetfed press, 16 pages, 2% ads, 2 Color, Newsprint, Saddle-stitched
Subscriptions: Indv. $20
Circulation: (BPA, 100% controlled), Total-15,346
List Rental: Rents Lists

Communications Industry
Forecast

Publishing Co: Veronis, Suhler & Associates, Inc., 350 Park Avenue, New York, NY 10022; Title Tel # (212) 935-4990 Title Fax # (212) 935-0877
Personnel: Publications Director-Don Leeds
Editorial Description: Five year forecast of all sectors of the communications industry.
General Info: Yr. Est. 1987, Annually
Subscriptions: Indv. $500

Communications Industry
Report

Publishing Co: Veronis, Suhler & Associates, Inc., 350 Park Avenue, New York, NY 10022; Title Tel # (212) 935-4990 Title Fax # (212) 935-0877
Personnel: Publications Director-Don Leeds
Editorial Description: Five year historic view of publicly traded companies in the communications industry.
General Info: Yr. Est. 1983, Annually
Subscriptions: Indv. $500

Communications Lawyer
See: LAW

Communications Product Reports
See: COMPUTERS & AUTOMATION

Communications Report
See: TELECOMMUNICATIONS

Communicator's
Notebook   *Business*

Publishing Co: Robert Miko, PO Box 1312, New York, NY 10018-0727; Title Tel # (212) 979-7395 Title Fax # (212) 877-2213
Personnel: Publisher, Editor-Robert Miko
Editorial Description: Notes & how-to info for intl. communicators.
General Info: Yr. Est. 1981, Weekly, Trim Size-8½ x 11, 6 pages
Subscriptions: Indv. $196, $5/copy
Acquistions: Publication Sold
Circulation: Total-300
List Rental: Rents Lists

Communique
See: ADVERTISING & MARKETING

Compendium Newsletter 'Your Guide to the Worlds Environmental Crises'
See: ENVIRONMENT & ECOLOGY

Conferee   *Business*

Publishing Co: Gerosota Publications, 3530 Pine Valley Dr, Sarasota, FL 34239-4335; Title Tel # (813) 924-3251 Title Fax # (813) 371-4183
General Info: Yr. Est. 1990, Bi-monthly
Subscriptions: Indv. $40

Connections   *Business*

Publishing Co: Burson-Marsteller, 230 Park Ave S, New York, NY 10003-1566; Title Tel # (212) 614-4000
Personnel: Editor-Joseph Kennedy
Editorial Description: Discusses corporate public relations issues, current events and opinions that can be affected by public relations.
General Info: Yr. Est. 1965, Monthly, Trim Size-8½ x 11½, 4 pages, No Color, Newsprint, Saddle-stitched
Circulation: Total-6,500

Connections   *Association*

Publishing Co: Sponsor-Southern States Communication Association, Southern States Communication Association, Speech Communication Dept., Box 5131, Hattiesburg, MS 39406-5131; Title Tel # (601) 266-4271 Title Fax # (601) 266-4263
Personnel: Editor, Circ. Mgr.-Susan Siltanen
General Info: Yr. Est. 1990, 3x/yr.
Subscriptions: Indv. $25, Inst. $75, $8/copy
Circulation: Total-1,500

Consumer Media Tech   *Business*

Publishing Co: Paul Kagan Associates Inc., 126 Clock Tower Pl., Carmel, CA 93923-8746; Title Tel # (408) 624-1536 Title Fax # (408) 625-3225
Personnel: Publisher-Paul Kagan, Editor-Dwight Beach, Adv. Dir.-Johanne Hardy
Editorial Description: Analysis of latest trends in home entertainment and communication.
General Info: Yr. Est. 1991, Monthly, Trim Size-7¼ x 10, Other press, 12 pages, No Color, Other, Saddle-stitched
Subscriptions: Indv. $645
Advertising: $1,560.

Converge-The Multimedia Developer's Resources
See: COMPUTERS & AUTOMATION

Copy Editor Newsletter
See: JOURNALISM

Corporate Annual Report
See: BUSINESS & INDUSTRY

Cowles/SIMBA Media Daily
See: PERIODICAL INDUSTRY

Cybernautics Digest   *Business*

Publishing Co: KFH Pubs., Inc., 3530 Bagley Ave. N., Seattle, WA 98103-9113
Tel # (206) 547-4950 Fax # (206) 545-6591
Personnel: Publisher-Stan Kehl, Editor-Terry Hansen, Assoc. Ed.-John Shaw, Art Dir.-Ray Kehl
Editorial Description: Summarizes articles published in the business and technical press that provide insightful analysis of new information technologies and trends.
General Info: Yr. Est. 1994, Monthly, Trim Size-8½ x 11, Offset press, 20 pages, ISSN: 1079-2112, No Color, Matte, Saddle-stitched
Subscriptions: Indv. $24, Can. $30, For. $48, $2/copy

Cyberspace PR Newsletter
See: ADVERTISING & MARKETING

DBS Report   *Business*

Publishing Co: Paul Kagan Associates Inc., 126 Clock Tower Pl., Carmel, CA 93923-8746;
Title Tel # (408) 624-1536 Title Fax # (408) 625-3225
Personnel: Publisher-Paul Kagan, Circ. Mgr.-Judy Pinney, Adv. Mgr.-Johanne Hardy
Editorial Description: Analyzes direct-to-home satellite ventures.
General Info: Yr. Est. 1990, Monthly, Trim Size-7¼ x 10, Other press, 12 pages, No Color, Other, Saddle-stitched
Subscriptions: Indv. $645
Advertising: $1,560.

DOT. Com
See: COMPUTERS & AUTOMATION

Deadline

Publishing Co: Center for War, Peace & the News Media, NYU, 10 Washington Pl. 4th Fl., New York, NY 10003; Title Tel # (212) 998-7960
Personnel: Editor-Mr. Wepple
General Info: Yr. Est. 1985, Bi-monthly
Subscriptions: Indv. $25, $2/copy

Democratic Communique   *Association*

Publishing Co: Union for Democratic Communications, 1016 61st St, Oakland, CA 94608-2355; Title Tel # (415) 596-3589
Personnel: Editor-Janet Wasko, Circ. Mgr.-Karen Paulsell
Editorial Description: News of democratic & grassroots communications projects, issues & pubs.
General Info: Yr. Est. 1981, Bi-monthly, 12 pages
Circulation: Total-250

Digest of the Univ. Film & Video Assn.
See: FILM

Disaster Trends Update   *Business*

Publishing Co: QW Communications, Co., PO Box 6591, Concord, NH 03303-6591; Title Tel # (603) 648-2629
Personnel: Editor-Michael O'Bryant
General Info: Yr. Est. 1987, Monthly
Subscriptions: Indv. $99
Circulation: Total-4,900
List Rental: Actives: $100/M

Document Image Automation   *Business*

Publishing Co: Phillips Business Information, Inc., 1201 Seven Locks Rd., Ste 300, Potomac, MD 20854-2958 Tel # (301) 340-1520 Fax # (301) 424-4297; Title Tel # (203) 226-6967
Personnel: Publisher-Alan Meckler, Editor-Don Avedon, Circ. Mgr.-Mike Hicks, Production Mgr.-Sandra Higgard
Editorial Description: Offers comprehensive coverage of events in optical storage and electronic document imaging fields.
General Info: (Formerly Videodisc Update), Yr. Est. 1982, Quarterly, Trim Size-8½ x 11, Web press, 10 pages, ISSN: 1071-6130, Ind/Abs/Online: NewsNet, DIALOG, Predicasts, 4 Color, Coated
Subscriptions: Indv. $59
Circulation: Total-1,000
List Rental: Rents Lists

EPS Decisions
See: PRINTING/GRAPHIC ARTS

Editorial Eye
See: JOURNALISM

Education Reporter
See: JOURNALISM

Electrical Sales Builder
See: SALESMANSHIP & SELLING

Electronic Information Report   *Business*

Publishing Co: Simba Information, Inc., 213 Danbury Rd. PO Box 7430, Wilton, CT 06897-7430 Fax # (203) 834-1771 Parent Co.-Cowles Business Media, New York; Title Tel # (203) 834-0033 Title Fax # (203) 834-0729
Personnel: Publisher-Chris Elwell, Editor-Paulette Donnelley, Circ. Mgr.-Cara Paul, Production Mgr.-Kendra Kalben, Mktg. Dir.-Michael Genaro
Editorial Description: Monitorss, analyzes & reports on trends and developments in information services. Covers online, multimedia, electronic publishing, new storage & distribution media, databases & value-added fax. Offers interpretions on the underlying trends as well as a strategic view of major issues.
General Info: (Formerly IDP Report), Yr. Est. 1979, 46x/yr., Trim Size-8½ x 11, Offset press, 8 pages, ISSN: 1076-0490, Ind/Abs/Online: DIALOG, Predicasts, No Color
Subscriptions: Indv. $479, For. $529
Acquistions: Publication Bought, Publication Sold
Circulation: Total-3,000
Advertising: Accepts Inserts.
Printing Co: Success Printing, 10 Pearl Street, Norwalk, CT 06850 Tel # (203) 847-1112, Fax # (203) 846-2770

Electronic Mail & Micro Systems
See: TELECOMMUNICATIONS

Electronic Marketplace Report
See: TELECOMMUNICATIONS

Electronic Messaging News
See: TELECOMMUNICATIONS

Electronic Public Information Newsletter
See: PUBLIC MANAGEMENT & PLANNING

Electronic Shopping News   *Business, Consumer*

Publishing Co: Arlen Communications, Inc., 7315 Wisconsin Ave., Ste. 600E, Bethesda, MD 20814-3203; Title Tel # (301) 656-7940 Title Fax # (301) 656-3204
Personnel: Publisher, Editor-Gary Arlen
General Info: Yr. Est. 1987, Monthly
Subscriptions: Indv. $500

Emerging Media Report   *Business*

Publishing Co: Knight MediaCom International, 780 Piermont Ave, Piermont, NY 10968-1032
Personnel: Publisher, Editor in Chief-Ron Knight
Editorial Description: Covers VR, TV, CD, PC, and entertainment marketing.
General Info: Yr. Est. 1993, 8x/yr., Trim Size-8½ x 11, 14 pages
Subscriptions: Indv. $147

Ernie Mills' Legislative Report
See: GOVERNMENT

Euromedia Regulation   *Business*

Publishing Co: Kagan World Media Inc., 126 Clock Tower Pl., Carmel, CA 93923-8734 Parent Co.-Paul Kagan Associates Inc., Carmel; Title Tel # (408) 624-1536 Title Fax # (408) 625-3225
Personnel: Publisher-Paul Kagan, Circ. Mgr.-Judy Pinney, Adv. Mgr.-Johanne Hardy
Editorial Description: Covers government oversight of public and private media throughout Europe.
General Info: Yr. Est. 1990, Monthly, Trim Size-7¼ x 10, Other press, 12 pages, No Color, Other, Saddle-stitched
Subscriptions: Indv. $595
Advertising: $1,560.

European Media Business & Finance   *Business*

Publishing Co: Phillips Business Information, Inc., 1201 Seven Locks Rd., Ste 300, Potomac, MD 20854-2958 Tel # (301) 340-1520 Fax # (301) 424-4297
General Info: Bi-weekly, ISSN: 1071-1570
Subscriptions: Indv. $895

European Telecommunications
See: TELECOMMUNICATIONS

Executive Speaker
See: MANAGEMENT

Executive Speechwriter Newsletter   *Business*

Publishing Co: Words, Ink, Emerson Falls Business Park, St. Johnsbury, VT 05819; Title Tel # (802) 748-4472 Title Fax # (802) 748-1939
Personnel: Publisher, Editor-Joe Ford, Circ. Mgr.-Anne Leverette, Art Dir.-Lisa Shonia
Editorial Description: A newsletter of quotes, jokes, stories and ideas for the executive speechmaker.
General Info: Yr. Est. 1986, Bi-monthly, Trim Size-8½ x 11, 12 pages
Subscriptions: Indv. $79, Can. $91, For. $91, $14/copy
Circulation: Total-6,000
List Rental: List Management Co.: Direct Media, Inc., 200 Pemberwick Rd., PO Box 4565, Greenwich, CT 06830 Tel # (203) 532-3713, Fax # (203) 531-1452, Actives: 12,880

Exhibit Mexico
See: ADVERTISING & MARKETING

Express Exchange
See: FILM

FCC Daily Release Service
See: LAW

FCC Report
See: TELECOMMUNICATIONS

Fax Reporter
See: TELECOMMUNICATIONS

Fiberoptics Marketing/Intelligence
See: BUSINESS & INDUSTRY

Fillers for Publications
See: JOURNALISM

Focus
See: RELIGIOUS & THEOLOGICAL

Followup File *Business*

Publishing Co: Stone/Scott, 2222 Foothill Blvd. #E344, La Canada, CA 91011 Fax # (818) 957-7788; Title Tel # (818) 356-9866 Title Fax # (818) 405-9498
Personnel: Publisher, Editor-Roger Scott, Political Editor-Jerry Goldberg, Arts Editor-Merry Suluvan, Circ. Mgr.-Colin Baker
Editorial Description: News and information for those involved in communications.
General Info: Yr. Est. 1974, Weekly, 4 pages
Subscriptions: Indv. $185
Circulation: Total-300

Freelance Writer's Report
See: JOURNALISM

Frohlinger's Marketing Report
See: ADVERTISING & MARKETING

Function Key, The
See: COMPUTERS & AUTOMATION

GA-SK Newsletter
See: DEAF

Gauge, The *Business*

Publishing Co: Delahaye Group, The, 117 Bow Street, Portsmouth, NH 03801 Tel # (603) 431-0111 Fax # (603) 431-0669
Personnel: Publisher-Katharine D. Paine, Editor-William Teamis Pearlberg, Art Dir.-Jill Ury
General Info: Yr. Est. 1989, Bi-monthly, Trim Size-8½ x 11, 4 pages
Circulation: Total-2,000

Gilligan's Island News
See: CLUBS

Graphic News
See: PRINTING/GRAPHIC ARTS

HESCA Feedback
See: HEALTH

Hanford Update Newsletter
See: WATER SUPPLY, POWER & WASTE

Hard Hat Times

Publishing Co: K.D. Information Notes, Inc., PO Box 14430, Minneapolis, MN 55414-0430; Title Tel # (612) 824-2852
Personnel: Editor-K. Dewey
Editorial Description: A publication for the public relations industry dedicated to the question: When does one use a hard hat?.
General Info: Yr. Est. 1989, Quarterly, Trim Size-8½ x 11, Desktop press, 10 pages, No Color, Matte
Subscriptions: Free To Qualified Recipient

Headlines

Publishing Co: Newsletters Plus, 100 Crescent Center Pky Ste, 1200, Tucker, GA 30084-7039; Title Tel # (404) 248-9092 Title Fax # (404) 248-9870
Personnel: Circ. Mgr., Production Mgr.-Cynthia Tillis, Art Dir.-Blaek Packman, Publisher, Editor, Promotion Dir.-Mike Shaw
Editorial Description: Contains information on producing corporate marketing newsletters.
General Info: Yr. Est. 1987, Quarterly, Web press, 4 pages, 2 Color, Coated
Acquistions: Publication Bought, Publication Sold
Circulation: Total-3,000
Printing Co: Williams Printing, 1240 Spring St NW, Atlanta, GA 30309-2862 Tel # (404) 875-6611, Fax # (404) 872-4025

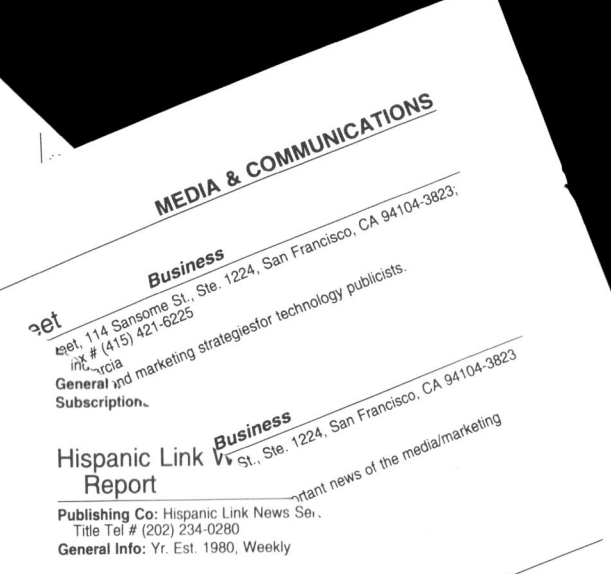

MEDIA & COMMUNICATIONS

Business

…et, 114 Sansome St., Ste. 1224, San Francisco, CA 94104-3823; in…# # (415) 421-6225
…rcia
General and marketing strategies for technology publicists.
Subscription…

Hispanic Link V… *Business*
Report
St., Ste. 1224, San Francisco, CA 94104-3823
…rtant news of the media/marketing
Publishing Co: Hispanic Link News Ser…. Title Tel # (202) 234-0280
General Info: Yr. Est. 1980, Weekly

Hispanic Media Update *Consumer,* 20005;

Publishing Co: Unimar, 980 N. Michigan Avenue, #1776, Chicago, IL.
Editorial Description: Information on the Hispanic media industry.
General Info: Yr. Est. 1983, Weekly
Subscriptions: Indv. $99
Circulation: Total-1,000

Home Business Idea Possibility Newsletter
See: BUSINESS & INDUSTRY

Hope Reports Industry
Quarterly *Business*

Publishing Co: Hope Reports, Inc., 58 Carverdale Dr, Rochester, NY 14618-4004 Tel # (716) 442-1310; Title Tel # (716) 552-1310 Title Fax # (716) 442-1725
Personnel: Publisher-Thomas Hope, Circ. Mgr.-Mabeth Hope
Editorial Description: Statistical revenue analysis of media suppliers: manufacturers, dealers, producers, etc.
General Info: Yr. Est. 1972, Quarterly, Trim Size-7½ x 11, Offset press, 110 pages, ISSN: 0749-8772, No Color, Looseleaf
Subscriptions: Indv. $2,700, Inst. $2,700, $1,000/copy

Hot Topics
See: EDUCATION

IQ Quarterly
See: COMPUTERS & AUTOMATION

ITVA News
See: TELEVISION & VIDEO

Ideas Unlimited for
Editors *Business*

Publishing Co: Newsletter Services, Inc., 9700 Philadelphia Ct., Lanham, MD 20706-4405; Title Tel # (301) 731-5202 Title Fax # (301) 731-5203
Personnel: Publisher-Lisa A. Anthony, Exec. VP/Group Publisher-Michael Nagan, Editor-Will McNamara, Circ. Mgr.-Priscilla Arenas, Mktg. Mgr.-Susan Pangman
Editorial Description: Pre-formatted editorial features, fillers, and camera-ready artwork for editors of company publications.
General Info: (Formerly Ideas Unlimited for Corporate Editors), Yr. Est. 1978, Monthly, ISSN: 1054-4747
Subscriptions: Indv. $195
List Rental: List Management Co.: Manager: Will McNamara; Taybi Direct East, Inc., 13321 New Hampshire Ave., Ste. 202, Silver Spring, MD 20904-3450 Tel # (301) 680-3633, Fax # (301) 680-3635

Impact *Business, Association*

Publishing Co: Public Affairs Council, 1019 19th St NW Ste 200, Washington, DC 20036-5105; Title Tel # (202) 872-1790
Personnel: Editor-Wes Pedersen
General Info: Bi-monthly, 8 pages

Independent Spirit *Consumer, Association*

Publishing Co: South Carolina Arts Commission Media Arts Center, 1800 Gervais St, Columbia, SC 29201-3504; Title Tel # (803) 734-8696 Title Fax # (803) 734-8526
Personnel: Editor-Susan Leonard
Editorial Description: Regional independent film/video reviews, festivals, works-in-progress.
General Info: Yr. Est. 1977, Web press, 10 pages, ISSN: 1076-9935, No Color
Subscriptions: Free
Circulation: Total-7,000
Printing Co: Sun Printing, 1367 John C Calhoun Dr SE, Orangeburg, SC 29115-6206

MEDIA & COMMUNICATIONS

Information Broker

Publishing Co: Bunwell Enterprises, Inc.,
Title Tel # (713) 537-9051 Title Fax # /
Personnel: Publisher, Editor-Helen Bur
information services.
Editorial Description: Covers fee-bas
General Info: (Formerly Journal of r
11, Offset press, 16 pages, ISSN
Subscriptions: Indv. $40, Can. $
Advertising: $250. Accepts ins
...ess

Information Indu...
   See: COMPU...

...he Americas, New York, NY 10010-5107
...it Co.-Reed Elsevier, New York

Information M...
Report
Publishing Co: Else
Tel # (212) 633-?
Personnel: Publis'
General Info: (F.
DIALOG, Da
Subscriptions

...STING
Inside ... on New

Insi...
...o: Inside Report on New Media, 901 Mariner's Blvd., San Mateo, CA 94404
...: Editor-Tony Bove
...al **Description:** Information on multimedia and interactive technologies.
...eral **Info:** Semi-monthly

Interactive Content
   See: COMPUTERS & AUTOMATION

Interactive Marketing Newsletter
   See: ADVERTISING & MARKETING

Interactive TV Strategies
   See: TELECOMMUNICATIONS

Intercom

Publishing Co: Society for Technical Communication, 901 N Stuart St Ste 904, Arlington, VA 22203-1854; Title Tel # (703) 522-4114 Title Fax # (703) 522-2075
Personnel: Publisher-William Stolgitis, Editor-H. Clark Mulligan
Editorial Description: Monthly newsletter providing Society members with information and articles on trends in the technical communication profession and on actvities within the Society. Inquire for ad rates.
General Info: Yr. Est. 1971, Monthly, Sheetfed press, 16 pages, 10% ads, Saddle-stitched
Subscriptions: Indv. $85
Advertising: Inquire for rates.
Printing Co: Weadon Printing, 6430 General Green Way, Alexandria, VA 22312-2413 Tel # (703) 750-0800, Fax # (703) 750-0807

Interface   *Association*

Publishing Co: Univ. of Connecticut, Ctr. for Instruct. Media, Box U-1, #3, 249 Glen Brook Rd., Storrs, CT 06269; Title Tel # (286) 486-2530 Title Fax # (860) 486-1766
Personnel: Editor-Pat Miller
Editorial Description: News of activities in media concerning the University of CT, Center for Instructional Media and Technology.
General Info: Yr. Est. 1974, Quarterly, Trim Size-8½ x 11, Offset press, 4 pages, No Color
Subscriptions: Free
Circulation: (100% controlled), Total-8,600
Printing Co: Hall & Bill, Bridge St., Willimantic, CT 06239

International
Communication Bulletin   *Association*

Publishing Co: University of Alabama School of Communication, Publications, Tuscaloosa, AL 35487-0172
Editorial Description: News and research items in the field of international communications; also, house organ for the international communications division of the AEJ.
General Info: Yr. Est. 1966, Quarterly, Trim Size-8½ x 11, Offset press, 4 pages, No Color
Subscriptions: Indv. $4, $1/copy
Circulation: Total-600

Investor Relations Update   **CPM: $666**

Publishing Co: National Investor Relations Institute, 8045 Leesburg Pike., Ste. 600, Vienna, VA 22182-2737 Tel # (703) 506-3570 Fax # (703) 506-3571; Title Tel # (703) 506-3578 Title Fax # (703) 506-3570
Personnel: Publisher-Louis Thompson, Editor-William Mahoney, Production Mgr.-Melissa Jones
Editorial Description: Articles & news to advance the practice of corporate investor relations.
General Info: Yr. Est. 1970, Monthly, Letrpr. press, 12 pages, 2 Color, Newsprint, Saddle-stitched
Subscriptions: Indv. $125
Circulation: Total-3,000
Advertising: $2,000.
List Rental: Rents Lists
Printing Co: Van Cortlandt Press, 10123 Senate Dr, Lanham, MD 20706-4808 Tel # (301) 577-7377, Fax # (301) 459-7768

Iowa Media Message   *Association*

Publishing Co: Iowa Educational Media Assn., 4401 6th St SW, Cedar Rapids, IA 52404-4432
Personnel: Editor-Patricia Severson, Circ. Mgr.-Michael Simonson, Adv. Dir.-Susan Zvacek
Editorial Description: News and professional articles for state media association.
General Info: Yr. Est. 1972, Quarterly, Trim Size-8½ x 11, Offset press, 4 pages, 2 Color, Newsprint, Saddle-stitched
Subscriptions: Indv. $15
Circulation: (100% controlled), Total-650
Advertising: Inquire for rates.
Printing Co: Heuss Printing, 911 N 2nd St, Ames, IA 50010-3336 Tel # (515) 232-6110

Issues Management Letter

Publishing Co: Conference on Issues & Media, 635 Slaters Ln Ste 102, Alexandria, VA 22314-1177; Title Tel # (703) 836-3105
Editorial Description: Covers issues in the national media.
General Info: Bi-weekly, ISSN: 0882-1798
Subscriptions: For. $225

Jack O'Dwyer's Newsletter   *Business*

Publishing Co: J.R. O'Dwyer Company, Inc., 271 Madison Ave Ste 600, New York, NY 10016-1001; Title Tel # (212) 679-2471 Title Fax # (212) 683-2750
Personnel: Publisher, Editor-Jack O'Dwyer, Sr. Ed.-Kevin McCauley, Sr. Ed.-Jerry Walker, Assoc. Publ., Research Mgr.-Maureen Wilson
Editorial Description: Public relations and media news.
General Info: Yr. Est. 1968, 50x/yr., Trim Size-8½ x 11, 8 pages, ISSN: 0047-1690, Ind/Abs/Online: NEXIS, No Color, Matte
Subscriptions: Indv. $225, For. $250, $5/copy

LNG Express Project
Survey

Publishing Co: Zeus Development Corporation, P.O. Box 272505, Houston, TX 77277-2505; Title Tel # (713) 952-9500 Title Fax # (713) 782-9594
Editorial Description: Survey provides summary of each fleet around the globe that is conducting, plans to conduct or is strongly considering conducting an LNG project.
General Info: Quarterly

Letter to Thinkers

Publishing Co: International Center for Creative Thinking/JMW Group, 1385 Boston Post Rd, Larchmont, NY 10538-3904; Title Tel # (914) 698-8600 Title Fax # (914) 698-8619
General Info: Yr. Est. 1984
Subscriptions: Indv. $95

Levin's Public Relations
Report   *Business*

Publishing Co: Levin Public Relations & Marketing, 30 Glenn St., White Plains, NY 10603-3213 Tel # (914) 992-0900; Title Tel # (914) 993-0900 Title Fax # (914) 993-9589
Personnel: Publisher-Donald Levin, Editor-Sylvia Moss
Editorial Description: Insight about public relations for corporate PR and Mgmt. and Marketing Executives.
General Info: Yr. Est. 1984, Quarterly, 2 pages
Subscriptions: Indv. $29, $8/copy
Circulation: Total-482

Lewis Letter on Cable Marketing
   See: TELEVISION & VIDEO

Lewis Letter on Energy Communication
   See: ENERGY

Lifestyle Media-Relations
Reporter   *Business*

Publishing Co: InfoCom Group, 1250 45th St., Ste 200, Emeryville, CA 94608-2924 Fax # (510) 596-9331; Title Tel # (510) 596-9300 Title Fax # (510) 593-9331
Personnel: Publisher-James Sinkinson, Editor-John Papageorge, Production Mgr.-Krista Gulbransen, Art Dir.-Cynthia Levitas, Mktg. Coord.-Courteney Lunt
Editorial Description: Media placement news with focus on lifestyle media.
General Info: Yr. Est. 1992, Monthly, Trim Size-8½ x 11, 8 pages, 2 Color, Matte
Subscriptions: Indv. $389, $10/copy
Circulation: Total-525
Advertising: Inquire for rates.

Luce Media Report
   See: ADVERTISING & MARKETING

MIN: Media Industry
Newsletter   *Business*

Publishing Co: Phillips Business Info., 305 Madison Ave., Ste. 4417, New York, NY 10165-0006 Parent Co.-Phillips Business Information, Inc., Potomac; Title Tel # (212) 983-5170 Title Fax # (212) 983-5144
Personnel: Publisher-Kismet Toksu Gould, Grp. Pub.-Ellen Stuhlmann, Editor-Steven Cohn, Group Editor, Media Editor-John Masterton, Production Mgr.-Teresa Fleisher, Mktg. Dir.-Lisa Kelley
Editorial Description: Reports developments in the media and advertising industries: financial reports, mergers, acquisitions, closings, personnel changes, etc.
General Info: (Formerly Magazine Industry Newsletter), Yr. Est. 1947, Weekly, Trim Size-8½ x 11, Web press, 8 pages, ISSN: 0024-9793, Ind/Abs/Online: Newsnet; Predicasts, No Color
Subscriptions: Indv. $395, For. $458, $17/copy
List Rental: Rents Lists

MSRRT Newsletter
See: LIBRARY

Macintosh Multimedia & Product Registry
See: COMPUTERS & AUTOMATION

Magazine Publishers of America International Newsletter
Business, Association

Publishing Co: Magazine Publishers of America, 919 Third Ave., 22nd Fl., New York, NY 10022; Title Tel # (212) 752-0055 Title Fax # (212) 888-4217
Personnel: Editor-Russell Melvin
Editorial Description: The newsletter tracks activities & trends in publishing worldwide; distributed primarily to international members.
General Info: Yr. Est. 1985, Bi-monthly, Trim Size-8½ x 11, 8 pages, No Color, Matte, Saddle-stitched
Subscriptions: Free With Membership

Managing the Human Climate
Business

Publishing Co: Philip Lesly Co., 155 N Harbor Dr Apt 5311, Chicago, IL 60601-7326; Title Tel # (312) 819-3590 Title Fax # (312) 819-3592
Personnel: Editor-Philip Lesly, Publisher, Circ. Mgr.-Virginia Lesly
Editorial Description: Public attitudes and forces for social change -- trends, causes, analyses, perceptions -- and how to deal with them.
General Info: Yr. Est. 1970, Bi-monthly, Trim Size-8½ x 11, Offset press, 4 pages, ISSN: 0277-7398, No Color
Subscriptions: Indv. $30, $5/copy
Circulation: Total-3,500

Marketing Pulse
Business

Publishing Co: Unlimited Positive Communications Inc., 11 N Chestnut St, New Paltz, NY 12561-1706; Title Tel # (914) 255-2222 Title Fax # (914) 255-2231
Personnel: Publisher, Editor-Bill Harvey, Mng. Editor-Jessica Blank
Editorial Description: Covers impact of new electronic media on communications industries.
General Info: Yr. Est. 1979, Monthly, Trim Size-8½ x 11, 8 pages, No Color, Matte
Subscriptions: Indv. $300, For. $330
Circulation: Total-500

Media Business & Finance
Business

Publishing Co: Phillips Business Information, Inc., 1201 Seven Locks Rd., Ste 300, Potomac, MD 20854-2958 Tel # (301) 340-1520 Fax # (301) 424-4297
Personnel: Publisher-Ellen Stuhlmann, Mng. Editor-Dave Bross, Circ. Mgr.-Ann Holland
Editorial Description: Covers multi-billion dollar European media marketplace.
General Info: (Formerly European Business Letter), Yr. Est. 1991, Bi-weekly, Trim Size-8½ x 11, 6 pages, ISSN: 1071-1570, Ind/Abs/Online: NEWSNET, Predicasts
Subscriptions: Indv. $795, $37/copy
Advertising: Accepts Inserts.
List Rental: Rents Lists

Media Business News

Publishing Co: Media Business Corp., 607 10th St Ste 103, Golden, CO 80401-1053; Title Tel # (303) 526-9633
Personnel: Publisher-Paul Maxwell, Editor-J.L. Freeman, Circ. Mgr.-Karen Chandler, Production Mgr.-Michael McCready, Art Dir.-Christine Henry, Adv. Dir., Promotion Dir.-Dave Topus
General Info: Yr. Est. 1987, Weekly, Trim Size-8½ x 11, Sheetfed press, 20 pages, 1% ads, Color-cover, Newsprint, Saddle-stitched
Subscriptions: Indv. $395
Circulation: Total-2,500
Advertising: Accepts Inserts.

Media Law Reporter
Business

Publishing Co: Bureau of National Affairs, Inc., 1231 25th St. NW, Bldg. N-200, Washington, DC 20037-1157; Title Tel # (202) 452-4200 Title Fax # (202) 822-8092
Personnel: Publisher-William A. Beltz, Editor-Cynthia Bolbach, Mng. Editor-Mary Anne McCoy-Pazanowski, Circ. Mgr.-Gary C. Seltzer
Editorial Description: A weekly reference service containing the full-text of federal & state court decisions & selected agency rulings affecting newspapers, magazines, radio, television, film & other media.
General Info: Yr. Est. 1977, Weekly, Trim Size-6 x 9, Offset press, ISSN: 0148-1045, Looseleaf
Subscriptions: Indv. $980

Media Matters
Business

Publishing Co: Media Dynamics, 18 E. 41st St., Ste. 1806, New York, NY 10017-6222; Title Tel # (212) 683-7895 Title Fax # (212) 683-7684
Personnel: Publisher-Ed Papazian, Editor-Carol Williams, Mktg. Mgr.-Sarah K. Ryan
Editorial Description: Provides original commentary, analyses, and forecasts on all aspects of media, including articles on rating methodology, upfront network buying & selling strategies, America's media consumption patterns and variables that influence TV show appeal, and more.
General Info: Yr. Est. 1986, Bi-monthly, Trim Size-8½ x 11, 10 pages, 2 Color, Other, Other
Subscriptions: Indv. $125, Inst. $63, Can. $150, For. $150, $35/copy
Circulation: Total-260
List Rental: List Management Co.: Uni-Mail, 1701 E Lake Ave Ste 480, Glenview, IL 60025-2097 Tel # (708) 998-8990, Fax # (708) 998-1801
Printing Co: Copy Garage, 3030 Northern Blvd Ste 1, Long Island City, NY 11101-2832 Tel # (718) 784-0388

Media Mergers & Acquisitions
Business

Publishing Co: Paul Kagan Associates Inc., 126 Clock Tower Pl., Carmel, CA 93923-8746; Title Tel # (408) 624-1536 Title Fax # (408) 625-3225
Personnel: Publisher, Editor-Paul Kagan, Circ. Mgr.-Judith Pinney, Adv. Mgr.-Johanne Hardy
Editorial Description: Exclusive analyses of values of major media deals, sales, & LBOs.
General Info: Yr. Est. 1987, Monthly, Trim Size-7¼ x 10, Other press, 16 pages, ISSN: 0895-4550, 5% ads, No Color, Other, Saddle-stitched
Subscriptions: Indv. $645
Advertising: Inquire for rates.

Media Monitor

Publishing Co: Center for Media & Public Affairs, 2100 L St NW Ste 300, Washington, DC 20037-1525; Title Tel # (202) 223-2942 Title Fax # (202) 872-4014
Personnel: Editor-Linda Lichter, Editor-Robert Lichter, Art Dir.-Mary Carroll Gunning
Editorial Description: Each issue provides scientific analysis of the media's coverage of current events or issues of ongoing interest.
General Info: Yr. Est. 1984, Monthly
Subscriptions: Indv. $75, $8/copy

Media News
See: EDUCATION

Media Report to Women
See: WOMEN'S

Media Sports Business
Business

Publishing Co: Paul Kagan Associates Inc., 126 Clock Tower Pl., Carmel, CA 93923-8746; Title Tel # (408) 624-1536 Title Fax # (408) 625-3225
Personnel: Publisher-Paul Kagan, Circ. Mgr.-Judith Pinney, Adv. Dir.-Johanne Hardy
Editorial Description: Economics of national & regional cable and pay TV sports.
General Info: Yr. Est. 1982, Monthly, Trim Size-7¼ x 10, Other press, 12 pages, ISSN: 0889-0951, No Color, Other, Saddle-stitched
Subscriptions: Indv. $645
Advertising: $1,560.

Media Update
Business   **CPM: $800**

Publishing Co: Marcus Schneck & Associates, 1328 Chestnut St., #393, Emmaus, PA 18049; Title Tel # (610) 481-9452 Title Fax # (610) 481-9453
Personnel: Publisher, Editor-Marcus Schneck
Editorial Description: Media placement opportunities in science, technology, education, and medicine.
General Info: Yr. Est. 1988, Semi-monthly, Trim Size-8½ x 11, Desktop press, 4 pages, No Color, Other, Other
Subscriptions: Indv. $120, $10/copy
Circulation: Total-250
Advertising: $200. Accepts Inserts.

Media Update Environment
Business

Publishing Co: Marcus Schneck & Associates, 1328 Chestnut St., #393, Emmaus, PA 18049 Tel # (610) 481-9452 Fax # (610) 481-9453
Personnel: Publisher, Editor-Marcus Schneck
Editorial Description: Media placement opportunities for environmental businesses and industries.
General Info: Yr. Est. 1993, Monthly, Trim Size-8½ x 11, 4 pages
Subscriptions: Indv. $180

Media Update Minority
Business

Publishing Co: Marcus Schneck & Associates, 1328 Chestnut St., #393, Emmaus, PA 18049; Title Tel # (610) 481-9452 Title Fax # (610) 481-9453
Personnel: Publisher, Editor-Marcus Schneck
Editorial Description: Media placement opportunities in minority issues and trends.
General Info: Yr. Est. 1991, Monthly, Trim Size-8½ x 11, Desktop press, 4 pages, No Color, Other, Other
Subscriptions: Indv. $100, Inst. $100, $10/copy
Advertising: $200.

Media Update Outdoors
Business

Publishing Co: Marcus Schneck & Associates, 1328 Chestnut St., #393, Emmaus, PA 18049; Title Tel # (610) 481-9452 Title Fax # (610) 481-9453
Personnel: Publisher-Marcus Schneck
Editorial Description: Media placement opportunities for the outdoor community
General Info: (Formerly Marcus Schneck & Associates), Yr. Est. 1992, Monthly, Trim Size-8½ x 11, Desktop press, 4 pages, No Color, Other, Other
Subscriptions: Indv. $100, Inst. $100, $10/copy
Advertising: $200. Accepts Inserts.

MediaWatch
Consumer

Publishing Co: Media Research Ctr., 113 S West St., 2nd Floor, Alexandria, VA 22314-2824; Title Tel # (703) 683-9733 Title Fax # (703) 683-9736
Personnel: Publisher-L.B. Bozell, III, Editor-Brent Baker, Circ. Mgr.-Jennifer Hardebeck, Circ. Mgr.-Kristin Kelly
Editorial Description: Attempts to document with examples, quotes, studies and analysis the liberal bias of major national news outlets, particularly the television networks.
General Info: Yr. Est. 1986, Monthly, Trim Size-8½ x 11, Web press, 8 pages, ISSN: 1053-8321, 2 Color
Subscriptions: Indv. $29, $2/copy
Circulation: Total-15,000
Printing Co: Valley Press, 6822 Navajo Dr, Baltimore, MD 21209-1518 Tel # (301) 484-2501

Millennium Pop
See: MUSIC & MUSIC TRADES

Mobile Phone News
See: TELECOMMUNICATIONS

Mobile Satellite News
See: TELECOMMUNICATIONS

Monitor   *Business*

Publishing Co: Information Today, Inc., 143 Old Marlton Pike, Medford, NJ 08055-8758;
Title Tel # (609) 654-6266 Title Fax # (609) 654-4309
Personnel: Publisher-Roger Bilboul, Editor-Harry Collier, Adv. Dir.-Michael Zarrello, Promotion Dir.-Lauree Padgett
Editorial Description: Analytical review of current events in online and electronic publishing industry. Reports on online and optical media, videotex, telecommunications policy, and micros, with updates and analyses of events and they occur in the field of electronic publishing.
General Info: (Formerly Monitor-Media), Yr. Est. 1981, Monthly, Trim Size-8½ x 11, Sheetfed press, 16 pages, ISSN: 0260-6666, 2 Color
Subscriptions: Indv. $290, Can. $300
Circulation: Total-150

Morality in Media Newsletter
See: LAW

Multimedia & Technology
See: COMPUTERS & AUTOMATION

Multimedia Business Report
See: COMPUTERS & AUTOMATION

Multimedia Daily
See: COMPUTERS & AUTOMATION

Multimedia Week   *Business*

Publishing Co: Phillips Business Information, Inc., 1201 Seven Locks Rd., Ste 300, Potomac, MD 20854-2958; Title Tel # (301) 340-1520 Title Fax # (301) 424-4297
Personnel: Publisher-Chris Scotton, Grp. Pub.-Megan St. John, Editor-Chris Sherman, Mng. Editor-Mary Crowley, Production Mgr.-Sherry Mitchell, Circ. Mgr., Mktg. Dir.-Ruth Zellers
Editorial Description: An executive report on the multimedia marketplace including timely news and in-depth analysis of business opportunities, contract awards, new products, mergers, and developments.
General Info: (Formerly Open Media Letter; S. Klein Newsletter on Computer Graphics), Yr. Est. 1992, Weekly, ISSN: 1064-6639
Subscriptions: Indv. $697, For. $760
Advertising: Inquire for rates. Accepts Inserts.
List Rental: Rents Lists

NAPBC Newsletter
See: BROADCASTING

NAPH National Newsletter
See: DISABILITY

News Library News
See: NEWSPAPER INDUSTRY

NewsNet Action Letter
See: TELECOMMUNICATIONS

Newsletter Communication   *Business*

Publishing Co: Newsletter Factory, 1000 Parkwood Cir. NW, Suite #823, Atlanta, GA 30339-2139; Title Tel # (770) 955-1600 Title Fax # (770) 555-3313
Personnel: Publisher-T. Hartman, Editor-Dianne Breen
General Info: Monthly
Subscriptions: Indv. $125

Newsletter Editor's Resource
See: PERIODICAL INDUSTRY

Newspaper Investor
See: INVESTMENT

Newswire
See: EDUCATION

Nook News Market Bulletin
See: POETRY & CREATIVE WRITING

OCS Video   *Consumer*

Publishing Co: Office des Communications Sociales, 1340 E. Blvd. Saint Joseph, Montreal, PQ H2J 1M3 Canada; Title Tel # (514) 524-8223 Title Fax # (514) 524-8522
Personnel: Publisher, Editor-Gilles Leblanc, Circ. Dir.-Denise Blondin, Production Mgr.-Jacques Paquette
Editorial Description: Evaluations of religions & social audiovisuals and video cassettes.
General Info: (Formerly Evaluation des productions audiovisuelles), Yr. Est. 1977, Tri-annually, Trim Size-7 x 8½, 16 pages, No Color, Matte, Saddle-stitched, Looseleaf
Subscriptions: Indv. $20, Can. $15
Circulation: Total-250

On Balance: Media
Treatment of Public
Policy Issues   *Business, Association*

Publishing Co: National Media Archive, 626 Bute St., Vancouver, BC V6E 3M1 Canada Parent Co.-Fraser Institute, Vancouver, Canada; Title Tel # (604) 688-0221 Title Fax # (604) 688-8539
Personnel: Publisher-Mike Walker, Editor-Lydia Miljan, Production Mgr.-Kristin McCahon, Promotion Dir.-Bev Horan
Editorial Description: Reports the results of research on media coverage of public policy issues.
General Info: Yr. Est. 1988, Monthly, Trim Size-8½ x 11, Desktop press, 8 pages, ISSN: 0840-612X, 2 Color, Matte, Saddle-stitched
Subscriptions: Indv. $95, $10/copy
Acquistions: Publication Bought, Publication Sold
Circulation: Total-1,500
Printing Co: Zippy Print, 1147 Melville St., Vancouver, BC V6F 2X5 Canada Tel # (604) 683-8688

Open Systems Communications
See: TELECOMMUNICATIONS

Organization for Research
on Women &
Communication-
Newsletter   *Association*

Publishing Co: Organization for Research on Women & Communication, Dept. of Speech Communication, SW Texas State Univ., San Marcos, TX 78666 Tel # (512) 245-2165 Fax # (512) 245-2165
Personnel: Editor-Karen Foss
General Info: Yr. Est. 1979, Semi-annually, 40 pages, 2% ads, No Color
Subscriptions: Indv. $12, Inst. $25, $5/copy
Circulation: Total-400

Origins, CNS Documentary Service
See: RELIGIOUS & THEOLOGICAL

PEP Talk   *Business*

Publishing Co: United Methodist Communications, 475 Riverside Dr Ste 1370, New York, NY 10115-0122
Editorial Description: Networking and sharing of ideas by producers of electronic media.
General Info: Yr. Est. 1983, Bi-monthly, Trim Size-8½ x 11, Offset press, 6 pages, No Color
Circulation: Total-1,100

PR Marcom Jobs Mid-America
See: EMPLOYMENT

PR Marcom Jobs West-No. Calif./Pacific Nothwest
See: EMPLOYMENT

PRC News
See: TELEVISION & VIDEO

Pacific Dialogue   *Business*

Publishing Co: Robert Miko, PO Box 1312, New York, NY 10018-0727; Title Tel # (212) 979-7395 Title Fax # (212) 877-2213
Personnel: Publisher, Editor-Robert Miko
Editorial Description: Monitor of Corporate communications of Pacific Region.
General Info: Yr. Est. 1982, Weekly, Trim Size-8½ x 11, Offset press, 4 pages
Subscriptions: Indv. $196, $5/copy
Circulation: Total-1,000
List Rental: Rents Lists

Perspective
See: ADVERTISING & MARKETING

Phone Sales Presentations for Service Type Businesses - A Newsletter
See: BUSINESS & INDUSTRY

Photo Marketing Newsline
See: PHOTOGRAPHY

Political Speaker   *Business*

Publishing Co: Lawrence Ragan Communications, Inc., 212 W.Superior St,Ste 200, Chicago, IL 60610-3533; Title Tel # (312) 335-0037 Title Fax # (312) 335-9583
Personnel: Publisher-Lawrence Ragan, Editor-Brad Zweck, Circ. Mgr.-Susan Weston, Art Dir.-Sharon Giankos, Mktg. Dir.-Melissa Eckhardt, Mktg. Dir.-Gretchen Eisenfelder
Editorial Description: Recent quotes, anecdotes, humor and advice from the statehouse to the white house.
General Info: Yr. Est. 1994, Monthly
Subscriptions: Indv. $119

Pro-Motion: A Quarterly Newsletter for the Media Escort Network   *Business*

Publishing Co: Beyond the Byte Co., 2501 Laurel Brook Rd. #388, Fallston, MD 21047-2336
Fax # (410) 872-7064; Title Tel # (410) 877-3524 Title Fax # (410) 877-7064
Personnel: Publisher, Editor-Emily Laisy
Editorial Description: News of interest to media escorts who take celebrities on tours.
General Info: Yr. Est. 1985, Quarterly, Trim Size-8½ x 11, Sheetfed press, 4 pages, ISSN: 0886-6104, No Color, Matte
Subscriptions: Indv. $12
Circulation: Total-250, Readership-500
Advertising: Accepts Inserts.
Printing Co: Horan Printing Co., 2530 Superior Ave., Cleveland, OH 44114 Tel # (216) 566-1388

Promotion Idea File
See: ADVERTISING & MARKETING

Proof   *Association*

Publishing Co: Florida Public Relations Assn., PO Box 7511, Winter Haven, FL 33883-7511; Title Tel # (813) 688-2730
Editorial Description: Covers all activities in the association.
General Info: Yr. Est. 1982, Monthly, Trim Size-8½ x 11

Public Relations News   *Business*

Publishing Co: Public Relations News, PO Box 1416, New York, NY 10021-1416; Title Tel # (212) 879-7090
Personnel: Publisher, Editor-Denny Griswold
Editorial Description: Case studies of successful programs, personnel and account changes and PR literature and materials. Information on successful public relations trends and techniques.
General Info: Yr. Est. 1944, Weekly, Trim Size-8½ x 11, 5 pages, ISSN: 0033-3697
Subscriptions: Indv. $277, Can. $317, For. $317, $15/copy
Acquistions: Publication Bought
List Rental: Actives: $55/M

Public Service Report

Publishing Co: Goodwill Communications, 9829 Summerday Dr., Burke, VA 22015-4026; Title Tel # (703) 866-3703 Title Fax # (703) 866-0850
General Info: Yr. Est. 1990, Quarterly
Subscriptions: Indv. $24

Publicity & Marketing Ideas
See: ADVERTISING & MARKETING

Quarterly Review of Doublespeak
See: EDUCATION

RFC News Service

Publishing Co: Resources for Comm. News Svc., 341 Mark West Station Rd, Windsor, CA 95492-9620; Title Tel # (707) 542-7819
General Info: 30x/yr.

Radio Promotion Bulletin
See: BROADCASTING

Ragan Report   *Business*

Publishing Co: Lawrence Ragan Communications, Inc., 212 W.Superior St,Ste 200, Chicago, IL 60610-3533 Tel # (312) 335-0037 Fax # (312) 335-9583; Title Tel # (312) 922-8245 Title Fax # (312) 922-3336
Personnel: Publisher-Lawrence Ragan, Editor-Steve Crescenzo, Circ. Mgr.-Susan Weston, Art Dir.-Q. E. Parker, Mktg. Dir.-Melissa Eckhardt, Mktg. Dir.-Gretchen Eisenfelder, Promotion Dir.-Betty Morse
Editorial Description: Survey of ideas and methods for communications executive.
General Info: Yr. Est. 1970, Weekly, Trim Size-8½ x 11, Offset press, 6 pages, ISSN: 0197-6060, No Color
Subscriptions: Indv. $267
Circulation: Total-5,200
List Rental: List Management Co.: Taybi Direct East, Inc., 13321 New Hampshire Ave., Ste. 202, Silver Spring, MD 20904-3450 Tel # (301) 680-3633, Fax # (301) 680-3635

Really, a Free Newsletter
See: BOOKS & BOOK TRADE

Remote Sensing Update   *Business*

Publishing Co: QW Communications, Co., PO Box 6591, Concord, NH 03303-6591; Title Tel # (603) 648-2629
General Info: Yr. Est. 1985, 24x/yr.
Subscriptions: Indv. $159
Circulation: Total-5,240
List Rental: Actives: $100/M

Report on AT&T
See: TELECOMMUNICATIONS

Reporter--Your Editorial Assistant
See: JOURNALISM

Reports on PC Communications
See: COMPUTERS & AUTOMATION

SIPIscope
See: SCIENCE

SPEX: Small Publishers Exchange
See: BOOKS & BOOK TRADE

Satellite Television Newsletter
See: TELEVISION & VIDEO

Se Habla Espanol Newsletter   *Business, Consumer*

Publishing Co: Hispanic Business, Inc., 360 S. Hope Ave., Ste. 300C, Santa Barbara, CA 93105-4017 Fax # (805) 687-4546; Title Tel # (805) 682-5843 Title Fax # (805) 563-1239
Editorial Description: Serving the Hispanic communications, media, marketing, and advertising industry.
General Info: Monthly, 2 pages
Subscriptions: Indv. $36
Circulation: Total-300

Self Employment Update - Business Idea Letters Edition
See: BUSINESS & INDUSTRY

Signals
See: CLUBS

Soundings
See: INTERNATIONAL AFFAIRS

Speechwriter's Newsletter

Publishing Co: Lawrence Ragan Communications, Inc., 212 W.Superior St,Ste 200, Chicago, IL 60610-3533 Tel # (312) 335-0037 Fax # (312) 335-9583; Title Tel # (312) 922-8245 Title Fax # (312) 922-3336
Personnel: Publisher-Lawrence Ragan, Editor-John M. Cowan, Circ. Mgr.-Susan Weston, Art Dir.-Q. E. Parker, Mktg. Dir.-Melissa Eckhardt, Mktg. Dir.-Gretchen Eisenfelder, Promotion Dir.-Betty Morse
Editorial Description: The weekly voice of the silent profession.
General Info: Yr. Est. 1980, Weekly, Trim Size-8½ x 11, Offset press, 4 pages, ISSN: 0272-8079, No Color
Subscriptions: Indv. $287
Circulation: Total-900
List Rental: List Management Co.: Taybi Direct East, Inc., 13321 New Hampshire Ave., Ste. 202, Silver Spring, MD 20904-3450 Tel # (301) 680-3633, Fax # (301) 680-3635

State Telephone Regulation Report
See: TELECOMMUNICATIONS

Step-By-Step Electronic Design
See: COMPUTERS & AUTOMATION

Success Track

Publishing Co: Intergalactic Enterprises, 28 Brookhaven Blvd., Port Jefferson Sta., NY 11776; Title Tel # (516) 331-3649 Title Fax # (516) 331-8645
Personnel: Editor-Michael Coleman
General Info: Yr. Est. 1988, Quarterly
Subscriptions: Indv. $59

TJFR Business News Reporter   *Business*

Publishing Co: TJFR Publishing, 545 N Maple Ave Fl 2, Ridgewood, NJ 07450-1612; Title Tel # (201) 444-6061 Title Fax # (201) 444-5919
Personnel: Editor-Thomas Grose, Mktg. Dir.-Thomas Elliott
Editorial Description: Business and financial news and developments.
General Info: Yr. Est. 1987, Semi-monthly
Subscriptions: Indv. $595, Can. $595, For. $625, $25/copy

TJFR Health News Reporter   *Business*

Publishing Co: TJFR Publishing, 545 N Maple Ave Fl 2, Ridgewood, NJ 07450-1612; Title Tel # (201) 444-6061 Title Fax # (201) 444-5919
Personnel: Publisher-Dean Rotbart, Editor-Erilyn Riley, Mktg. Dir.-Thomas Elloitt
Editorial Description: Healthcare media and healthcare newsmakers.
General Info: Yr. Est. 1993, Monthly
Subscriptions: Indv. $295, Can. $295, For. $350, $25/copy

Technology Applications Quarterly
See: EDUCATION

Technology for Communicators   *Business*

Publishing Co: Lawrence Ragan Communications, Inc., 212 W.Superior St,Ste 200, Chicago, IL 60610-3533 Tel # (312) 335-0037 Fax # (312) 335-9583
Editorial Description: Information on technology for speakers and writers.
General Info: Yr. Est. 1995, Monthly
Subscriptions: Indv. $189

Technology Pathfinder for Administrators
See: COMPUTERS & AUTOMATION

Telecommunications Advertising Report   *Business*

Publishing Co: Simba Information, Inc., 213 Danbury Rd. PO Box 7430, Wilton, CT 06897-7430
Tel # (203) 834-0033 Fax # (203) 834-1771 Parent Co.-Cowles Business Media, New York;
Title Tel # (203) 834-0330 Title Fax # (203) 834-0729
Personnel: Grp. Pub.-Chris Elwell, Editor-Matt Krusmen, Mktg. Dir.-Michael Genaro, Promotion Dir.-Michele Wolff
Editorial Description: News for telecommunications advertising and publishing industry executives.
General Info: (Formerly TA Report), Yr. Est. 1985, Bi-weekly, Trim Size-8½ x 11, Offset press, 8
pages, No Color, Newsprint
Subscriptions: Indv. $498, Can. $548, For. $548
List Rental: Rents Lists
Printing Co: Success Printing, 10 Pearl Street, Norwalk, CT 06850 Tel # (203) 847-1112,
Fax # (203) 846-2770

Telecommunications Reports
See: TELECOMMUNICATIONS

Telemedium   *Consumer*

Publishing Co: National Telemedia Council, 120 E Wilson St, Madison, WI 53703-3423;
Title Tel # (608) 257-7712 Title Fax # (608) 257-7714
Personnel: Editor-Marieli Rowe
Editorial Description: Media literacy education.
General Info: (Formerly Better Broadcast News), Yr. Est. 1953, Quarterly, Trim Size-8½ x 11, 6
pages, No Color

Television & Cable Action Update
See: TELEVISION & VIDEO

Ten Thousand Words   *Business, Consumer*

Publishing Co: Behavioral Images, Inc., 302 Leland, Bloomington, IL 61701-5646;
Title Tel # (309) 829-3931 Title Fax # (309) 829-9677
Personnel: Publisher-Stephen Johnson, Art Dir.-Sharon JOhnson
Editorial Description: Appraising Financial value of all Audx-visual recorded media for any purpose.
General Info: Yr. Est. 1976, Irregular, Trim Size-8½ x 11, Sheetfed press, 4 pages, ISSN: 1063-
9063, Newsprint
Subscriptions: Indv. $75, Inst. $75
Circulation: Total-3,000

Tools of the Trade: Books for Communicators
See: BOOKS & BOOK TRADE

Training Media Assn.

Publishing Co: Training Media Distributors Assn., 198 Thomas Johnson Dr Ste 206, Frederick, MD
21702-4317; Title Tel # (818) 995-7335
Personnel: Editor-Robert Gehrke
General Info: (Formerly News from TMDA), Yr. Est. 1978, Monthly, 2 pages
Circulation: Total-120

Trends in Communications Policy
See: TELECOMMUNICATIONS

Tyndall Report
See: JOURNALISM

U.S. Telecom Digest
See: TELECOMMUNICATIONS

Upon Further Muse   *Business*

Publishing Co: Centre for Professional Writing, 200 University Ave. W, Waterloo, ON N2L 3G1
Canada; Title Tel # (519) 725-0279 Title Fax # (519) 884-8995
General Info: Yr. Est. 1985, Quarterly

Video Investor
See: TELEVISION & VIDEO

Video-Rising to the Challenge
See: CHILDREN

Video Technology Newsletter
See: TELEVISION & VIDEO

Video Week
See: TELEVISION & VIDEO

Visual Literacy Review & Newsletter
See: EDUCATION

Voice Processing Newsletter
See: TELECOMMUNICATIONS

WRITE!
See: FILM

Warren's Telecom Regulation Monitor
See: TELECOMMUNICATIONS

Williams Report
See: MANAGEMENT

Windsor Report   *Business*

Publishing Co: Windsor Systems Dev., Inc., 11 W 42nd St Fl 12, New York, NY 10036-8002;
Title Tel # (212) 697-5390
Personnel: Publisher-Eric Murphy, Editor-Paul Martin
Editorial Description: Marketing trends in media sales. Computer use & analysis by media research.
General Info: Yr. Est. 1981, Bi-monthly, Trim Size-8½ x 11, Web press, 4 pages, No Color, Coated
Circulation: (100% controlled), Total-1,100

Wireless Cable Investor   *Business*

Publishing Co: Paul Kagan Associates Inc., 126 Clock Tower Pl., Carmel, CA 93923-8746;
Title Tel # (408) 624-1536 Title Fax # (408) 625-3225
Personnel: Publisher-Paul Kagan, Circ. Mgr.-Judy Pinney, Adv. Mgr.-Johanne Hardy
General Info: (Formerly Wireless Investor), Yr. Est. 1972, Monthly, Trim Size-7¼ x 10, Other press,
10 pages, No Color, Other, Saddle-stitched
Subscriptions: Indv. $595
Advertising: $1,560.

Working Communicator, The
See: LITERATURE & LINGUISTICS

Writer's Nook News
See: POETRY & CREATIVE WRITING

Writers' Rendezvous
See: POETRY & CREATIVE WRITING

Writing Concepts: The Business Communications Report
See: JOURNALISM

Writing World   *Consumer*

Publishing Co: Writing World, 44 Tarelton Road, Newton Center, MA 02159
Personnel: Publisher-Fern Reiss
Editorial Description: A frequently updated newsletter here to keep readers informed of all the latest
going-on, freebies, and opportunities.
General Info: Yr. Est. 1994, Bi-monthly, Desktop press, 10 pages, Other
Subscriptions: Indv. $60, Inst. $60, Can. $75, For. $75, $5/copy
Advertising: Inquire for rates.

Yankee Ingenuity   *Business*

Publishing Co: Yankee Group, 200 Portland St, Boston, MA 02114-1700; Title Tel # (617) 367-1000
Editorial Description: Communications and computing strategies.
General Info: Irregular

Yellow Pages & Directory Report
See: TELECOMMUNICATIONS

Yellowstone Multimedia Letter, The
See: COMPUTERS & AUTOMATION

MEDICINE

A Friend Indeed
See: WOMEN'S

AAB Bulletin
See: SCIENCE

AABB Weekly Report   *Association*

Publishing Co: American Association of Blood Banks, 8101 Glenbrook Rd., Bethesda, MD
20814-2749; Title Tel # (301) 907-6977 Title Fax # (301) 907-6895
Personnel: Editor-Eileen Church, Production Mgr.-John Saville
Editorial Description: News about blood banking transfusion medicine & related health issues.
General Info: (Formerly Blood Bank Week), Yr. Est. 1984, Weekly, Trim Size-8½ x 11, Desktop
press, 8 pages, ISSN: 0747-2420, 2 Color
Subscriptions: Indv. $128
Circulation: Total-1,500

AACPM Newsletter   *Association*

Publishing Co: American Assn. of Colleges of Podiatric Medicine, 1350 Piccard Dr Ste 322,
Rockville, MD 20850-4307 Tel # (301) 990-7400
Personnel: Editor-Suzanne Howard
Editorial Description: Information pertaining to podiatric medical education & the seven colleges of
podiatric medicine.
General Info: Yr. Est. 1978, 6 pages, Coated
Circulation: (100% controlled), Total-15,000

AADE News — *Association*

Publishing Co: P.M. Haeger & Assoc., 500 N Michigan Ave Ste 1400, Chicago, IL 60611-3703; Title Tel # (312) 661-1700
Personnel: Publisher-Melissa Pate, Mng. Editor-Mary Beach
Editorial Description: For members of the American Assn. of Diabetes Educators.
General Info: Yr. Est. 1983, 10x/yr., Trim Size-8½ x 11, Sheetfed press, 8 pages, 2 Color, Newsprint
Circulation: Total-7,000
Printing Co: Darby Graphics, 4015 N. Rockwell St., Chicago, IL 60618-3720 Tel # (312) 583-5090

AAMI News
See: INSTRUMENTS

AAMSI News — *Association*

Publishing Co: American Medical Informatics Association, 4915 Saint Elmo Ave Ste 302, Bethesda, MD 20814-6052; Title Tel # (301) 657-1291
Personnel: Publisher-Patricia Horner, Editor-Douglas Mackintosh, Circ. Mgr.-Susan Fletcher
Editorial Description: Computers/medical systems in health care with emphasis on clinical medicine.
General Info: Yr. Est. 1982, Quarterly, Trim Size-8½ x 11, Offset press, 15 pages
Subscriptions: Indv. $15, $2/copy
Circulation: Total-1,200

AAOA News — *Association*

Publishing Co: American Academy of Otolaryngic Allergy, 8455 Colesville Rd Ste 745, Silver Spring, MD 20910-3318 Fax # (301) 588-2454; Title Tel # (301) 588-1800
Personnel: Editor-Richard Madry
Editorial Description: News of interest to the ear, nose & throat allergist.
General Info: Yr. Est. 1981, Quarterly, Trim Size-8½ x 11, Offset press, 16 pages, 1% ads, No Color, Coated, Saddle-stitched
Circulation: (83% controlled), Total-12,000
List Rental: Actives: $500/M
Printing Co: Pallace

AAOA Record

Publishing Co: Auxiliary to the American Osteopathic Assn., 212 E Ohio St, Chicago, IL 60611-3203; Title Tel # (312) 280-5819
Editorial Description: Concerned with osteopathic medicine.
General Info: Yr. Est. 1941, Quarterly, 16 pages
Circulation: Total-7,000
Advertising: Inquire for rates.

A.A.O.S. Newsletter — *Association*

Publishing Co: American Assn. of Osteopathic Specialists, 804 Main St Ste F, Forest Park, GA 30050-1476; Title Tel # (404) 363-8263
Personnel: Editor-Floyd Pennington
Editorial Description: Quarterly update on Association and member activities.
General Info: Yr. Est. 1952, Quarterly, Trim Size-8½ x 11, Offset press
Subscriptions: Indv. $25, $6/copy
Circulation: (100% controlled), Total-1,000
Advertising: Inquire for rates.

AAOS Report

Publishing Co: American Academy of Orthopaedic Surgeons, 6300 N River Rd Ste 300, Rosemont, IL 60018-4232; Title Tel # (847) 823-7186
Personnel: Editor-Cinthia Oertal
Editorial Description: News on issues of interests to the practicing orthapaedic surgeon.
General Info: Yr. Est. 1975, Monthly, Trim Size-8.5 x 11, Desktop press, 4 pages, No Color, Other, Other
Circulation: Total-26,000
Printing Co: First Impressions, 700 Touhy Ave., Elk Grove, IL 06007 Tel # (708) 439-8600, Fax # (708) 439-8619

AAPA News — *Association*

Publishing Co: American Academy of Physician Assistants, 950 N. Washington St., Alexandria, VA 22314-1552; Title Tel # (703) 836-2272 Title Fax # (703) 684-1924
Personnel: Exec. Ed.-Jane Howard, Mng. Editor-Nancy Johnson, Adv. Dir.-Connie Szostak, Graphic Designer-Gayle Ely
General Info: Yr. Est. 1968, Semi-monthly, Desktop press, 20 pages, ISSN: 0894-0509, 2 Color, Matte, Saddle-stitched
Circulation: Total-22,000, Readership-22,000
Advertising: Inquire for rates.
List Rental: Rents Lists
Printing Co: CK Litho, 400 Prince George Blvd., Upper Marlboro, MD 20772-8734 Tel # (301) 390-7600

AAPS Newsletter — *Association*

Publishing Co: Assn. of American Physicians and Surgeons, 1601 N Tucson Blvd Ste 9, Tucson, AZ 85716-3405; Title Tel # (800) 635-1196 Title Fax # (602) 290-9674
Personnel: Editor-Jane Orient
Editorial Description: Socio-economic aspects of medical practice.
General Info: Yr. Est. 1943, Monthly, ISSN: 8750-9687
Subscriptions: Indv. $35
Circulation: Total-5,000

AARN Newsletter
See: NURSING

ACEP News — *Association*

Publishing Co: American College of Emergency Physicians, 1125 Executive Cir., Irving, TX 75038-2530; Title Tel # (214) 550-0911 Title Fax # (214) 580-2816
Personnel: Editor-Michael Weinstock, News Ed.-Teresa Huskey
Editorial Description: News of importance to physicians practicing emergency medicine.
General Info: Yr. Est. 1982, Monthly, Trim Size-8½ x 11, Sheetfed press, 16 pages, 2 Color, Matte
Subscriptions: Indv. $25
Circulation: Total-19,000
Advertising: Inquire for rates.
Printing Co: Mix Printing, 2441 Midway Rd, Carrollton, TX 75006-2526

ACLS Alert

Publishing Co: American Health Consultants, Inc., 3525 Piedmont Rd., Building #6, Ste. 400, Atlanta, GA 30305-0056 Tel # (404) 262-7436 Fax # (404) 284-3291; Title Fax # (404) 352-1971
Editorial Description: News and developments of interest to professional health consultants.
General Info: Monthly
Subscriptions: Indv. $88
List Rental: Actives: $100/M

ACMC Forum — *Association* — **CPM: $291**

Publishing Co: Assn. of Canadian Medical Colleges, 774 Echo Drive, Ottawa, ON K1S 5P2 Canada; Title Tel # (613) 730-0687 Title Fax # (613) 730-1196
Personnel: Editor-David Hawkins, Circ. Mgr., Production Mgr., Adv. Dir.-B. Stringer
Editorial Description: Matters of interest to Canadian medical educators.
General Info: (Formerly ACMC Newsletter), Yr. Est. 1967, Quarterly, Trim Size-8½ x 11, Web press, 24 pages, ISSN: 0317-5006, 2 Color, Matte, Saddle-stitched
Subscriptions: Indv. $35, Can. $30, For. $40, $5/copy
Circulation: (50% controlled), Total-1,200, Subscriptions-600
Advertising: $350.

A.C.M.D.P.Q. Bulletin — *Association*

Publishing Co: Assn. des Conseils des Medecins et Dentistes du Quebec Bulle, 308 est, boul. St. Joseph, Montreal, PQ H2T 1J2 Canada; Title Tel # (514) 842-5059
Personnel: Editor-Gerard Cournoyer, Production Mgr.-Armand Crevier
Editorial Description: Professional association news for dentists and doctors in Quebec. Text in French and English.
General Info: Yr. Est. 1975, Quarterly, Offset press, 8 pages, No Color
Circulation: Total-3,500

ACPA/CPF Newsletter — *Consumer, Association*

Publishing Co: ACPA/Cleft Palate Foundation, 1218 Grandview Ave, Pittsburgh, PA 15211-1239; Title Tel # (412) 481-1376
Editorial Description: Includes meeting announcements & highlights, news from the national office, news about members, board & committee meetings for membership only.
General Info: Yr. Est. 1976, Quarterly, 12 pages, No Color, Newsprint
Subscriptions: Free With Membership
Circulation: Total-2,500
Advertising: Inquire for rates.
List Rental: Actives: $50/M

ACPM News — *Association*

Publishing Co: American College of Preventive Medicine, 1660 L Street NW, Suite #206, Washington, DC 20036-5603 Fax # (202) 289-8274; Title Tel # (202) 466-2044 Title Fax # (202) 466-2662
Personnel: Editor-Christine Bilbrey
Editorial Description: Discusses topics related to preventive medicine, public health, aerospace medicine, & occupational medicine. Carries information on continuing medical education, legislative activities & programs of the College. Recurring features include news of members, news of research & a calendar of events.
General Info: (Formerly Preventive Medicine Newsletter), Yr. Est. 1954, Quarterly, Trim Size-8½ x 11, 10 pages, ISSN: 1044-4211, 2 Color, Matte, Saddle-stitched
Subscriptions: Indv. $25, Free With Membership
Acquistions: Publication Bought
Circulation: Total-2,000
List Rental: Rents Lists
Printing Co: Lettercomm, Inc., 310 Swann Ave, Alexandria, VA 22301-1042 Tel # (703) 683-3105

ADAA Reporter — *Consumer, Association*

Publishing Co: Anxiety Disorders Assn. of America, 6000 Executive Blvd Ste 513, Rockville, MD 20852-3803; Title Tel # (301) 231-9350
Personnel: Editor-Norman Klombers
Editorial Description: Published by the ADAA, an expansion of the Phobia Society of America, the newsletter reports new research treatment advances, self-help techniques & programs, public policy news & ADAA activities.
General Info: Yr. Est. 1990, Quarterly, Trim Size-8½ x 11, Web press, 8 pages, 2% ads, Coated
Subscriptions: Free With Membership
Circulation: Total-10,000
Advertising: Inquire for rates.
List Rental: Rents Lists
Printing Co: Newsletter Services, Inc., 9700 Philadelphia Court, Lanham, MD 20706 Tel # (301) 731-5200, Fax # (301) 731-5201

AIDS & Society: International Research Policy Bulletin

Publishing Co: African-Caribbean Institute, 4 W. Wheelock St., Hanover, NH 03755;
Title Tel # (802) 649-5296 Title Fax # (802) 649-2331
Personnel: Editor-Norman Miller, Mng. Editor-Kathy Cadow Parsonnet, Circ. Mgr.-Erika Stecklare, Production Mgr.-Ellen Kozak
Editorial Description: Directed to social & behavioral scientists, educators, and policymakers.
General Info: Quarterly, ISSN: 1055-0380
Subscriptions: Indv. $20, Inst. $35, $5/copy

AIDS & TB Weekly Abstracts from Conference Proceedings   *Business, Association*

Publishing Co: C.W. Henderson Publisher, Medical Center II, P.O. Box 5528, Atlanta, GA
31107-0528 Tel # (404) 507-7777 Fax # (404) 507-7788; Title Tel # (205) 995-1567
Title Fax # (404) 378-5411
Editorial Description: AIDS and Tuberculosis - related information developed at conferences.
General Info: (Formerly AIDS Abstracts from Conference Proceedings), Yr. Est. 1993, Monthly, ISSN: 1074-2891, Ind/Abs/Online: Newsnet, Univ., Microfilms, Inc.
Subscriptions: Indv. $995, Can. $995, For. $1,195

AIDS & TB Weekly Article Summaries   *Association*

Publishing Co: C.W. Henderson Publisher, Medical Center II, P.O. Box 5528, Atlanta, GA
31107-0528 Tel # (404) 507-7777 Fax # (404) 507-7788; Title Tel # (205) 995-1567
Title Fax # (404) 378-5411
Personnel: Editor-Alan D. Henderson
Editorial Description: Summaries of AIDS and Tuberculosis related articles from journals world-wide.
General Info: (Formerly AIDS Article Summaries), Yr. Est. 1994, Weekly, ISSN: 1074-2883, Ind/Abs/Online: Newsnet, Univ., Microfilms, inc.
Subscriptions: Indv. $995, Can. $995, For. $1,195

AIDS Clinical Care Newsletter   *Business*

Publishing Co: Sponsor-American Foundation for AIDS Research, Massachusetts Medical Society-Publ. Dir, 1440 Main St., Waltham, MA 02154-1649 Fax # (617) 893-8103;
Title Tel # (617) 893-3800 Title Fax # (617) 893-0413
Personnel: Publisher-Robert Bovenschulte, Editor-Deborah Cotton, MD, Circ. Mgr.-James Clifton, Production Mgr.-Alberta Fitzpatrick, Adv. Dir.-Art Wilschek
Editorial Description: Brings the latest developments on diagnosis and treatment of HIV-related diseases to the practicing clinician.
General Info: Yr. Est. 1989, Monthly, Trim Size-8½ x 11, Sheetfed press, 8 pages, ISSN: 1043-1543, 2 Color, Matte, Saddle-stitched
Subscriptions: Indv. $89, Inst. $89, Can. $117, For. $117, $9/copy
Circulation: (84% controlled), Total-32,000, Subscriptions-4,000, International-2,000
Advertising: Accepts Inserts.
List Rental: List Management Co.: Manager: Michelle Dinsmore; Response Media Products Inc., 2323 Perimeter Park Dr., Ste. 200, Atlanta, GA 30341-1335 Tel # (404) 451-5478, Fax # (404) 451-4929, Actives: 5,000, $500/M

AIDS Letter   *Association*

Publishing Co: Royal Society of Medicine, 150 E 58th St Fl 32, New York, NY 10155-0002;
Title Tel # (212) 371-1150
Personnel: Editor-Victor Daniels, Production Mgr.-Brian Weight, Publisher, Adv. Dir., Promotion Dir.-Howard Croft
General Info: Yr. Est. 1987, Bi-monthly, Trim Size-8½ x 11¾, Sheetfed press, 8 pages, ISSN: 0952-7427, 2 Color, Newsprint, Saddle-stitched
Subscriptions: Indv. $25, $6/copy
Acquisitons: Publication Bought
Circulation: Total-1,500
Advertising: Accepts Inserts.

AIDS Literature & Law Review See: LAW

AIDS Reference Guide: A Sourcebook for Planners & Decision Makers   *Business, Association*

Publishing Co: Atlantic Information Svcs., Inc., 1100 17th St. NW, Ste. 300, Washington, DC
20036-5503; Title Tel # (202) 775-9008 Title Fax # (202) 331-9542
Personnel: Publisher-Richard Biehl, Editor-Steven Goodwin, Circ. Mgr.-Kristin Mulcahy, Mktg. Dir.-Donna Lawton
Editorial Description: The AIDS Reference Guide is the only sourcebook of its kind for tracking the costs, financing & impact of the HIV epidemic. It documents the actions & results of public & private sector researchers & policy makers throughout the U.S.
General Info: Yr. Est. 1988, Monthly
Subscriptions: Indv. $392, Inst. $335, Can. $335, For. $458

AIDS Report   *Consumer*

Publishing Co: Food & Nutrition Press Inc., 2 Corporate Drive, Box 374, Trumbull, CT 06611-1338;
Title Tel # (203) 261-8587 Title Fax # (203) 261-9724
Personnel: Publisher-John O'Neil, Editor-Gerald Melson, Editor-Dean Pappas
Editorial Description: Provides timely, important developments in the medical social, economic, regulatory and political aspects of AIDS.
General Info: Yr. Est. 1987, Monthly, 8 pages, ISSN: 0893-5084
Subscriptions: Indv. $27, Inst. $23, Can. $23, For. $31, $2/copy

AIDS Report, The   *Consumer, Association*

Publishing Co: Harvard AIDS Institute, 8 Story St, Cambridge, MA 02138-4925 Tel # (617) 495-0478
Fax # (617) 495-2863
Personnel: Editor-Paula Brewer
Editorial Description: Covers international news about AIDS.
General Info: Quarterly
Subscriptions: Indv. $20

AIDS Therapies   *Association, Consumer*

Publishing Co: C.W. Henderson Publisher, Medical Center II, P.O. Box 5528, Atlanta, GA
31107-0528 Tel # (404) 507-7777 Fax # (404) 507-7788; Title Tel # (205) 995-1567
Personnel: Editor-Daniel J. Dendon
Editorial Description: Conventional and Experimental AIDS therapies.
General Info: Yr. Est. 1987, Monthly, Ind/Abs/Online: Newsnet, Univ., Microfilms, Inc.
Subscriptions: Indv. $995, Can. $995, For. $1,195

AIDS Treatment News   *Consumer*

Publishing Co: ATN Publications, PO Box 411256, San Francisco, CA 94141-1256;
Title Tel # (415) 255-0588 Title Fax # (415) 225-4659
Personnel: Publisher, Editor-Jonh S. James, Circ. Mgr.-Tom Fontaine
Editorial Description: AIDS treatment news reports on experimental and complimentary treatments, especially those available now. It collects information from scientists, physicians, health practitioners, health conferences and people with AIDS. It also examines ethical and public-policy issues around treatment research and access.
General Info: Yr. Est. 1986, Bi-weekly, Trim Size-8½ x 11, 8 pages, ISSN: 1052-4207
Subscriptions: Indv. $100, Inst. $230, Can. $230, $2/copy
Circulation: Total-5,000
Printing Co: Publications Ink, 1250 45th Street, Suite 200, Emeryville, CA 94608-2924
Tel # (510) 596-9340, Fax # (510) 596-9318

AIDS Weekly Plus   *Consumer, Association*

Publishing Co: C.W. Henderson Publisher, Medical Center II, P.O. Box 5528, Atlanta, GA
31107-0528 Tel # (404) 507-7777 Fax # (404) 507-7788; Title Tel # (205) 995-1567
Title Fax # (404) 378-5411
Personnel: Editor-Daniel J. Denoon, News Ed.-Keith Key
Editorial Description: Comprehensive worldwide coverage of all aspects of A.I.D.S.
General Info: (Formerly CDC AIDS Weekly; AIDS Weekly), Yr. Est. 1985, Weekly, ISSN: 0884-903X, Ind/Abs/Online: Newsnet, Univ., Microfilms, Inc.
Subscriptions: Indv. $1,895, Can. $1,895, For. $2,095

AIDS World Newsletter   *Association*

Publishing Co: AIDS Prevention Fund, PO Box 431, Wilbraham, MA 01095-0431;
Title Tel # (413) 734-1057
Personnel: Publisher-Paul Mozelski, Editor-Michelle Lunt
Editorial Description: Reveals latest AIDS information and statistics.
General Info: Yr. Est. 1993, Monthly

AIDS/STD News Report See: PHILANTHROPY

AIHP Notes See: HISTORY

AMCRA Newsletter, The Monitor   *Business, Association*   **CPM: $895**

Publishing Co: American Managed Care & Review Assn., 1200 19th St NW, Ste 200, Washington, DC 20036-2437; Title Tel # (202) 728-0506 Title Fax # (202) 728-0609
Personnel: Editor-Amanda Orr
Editorial Description: Focus on Managed Care, including HMOs, PPOs, IPAs, other health insurance organizations.
General Info: (Formerly American Assn. of Foundations for Medical Care-Newsletter), Yr. Est. 1971, Bi-monthly
Subscriptions: Indv. $125
Circulation: Total-1,000
Advertising: $895.

A.M.L.F.C. Bulletin   *Association*

Publishing Co: Assn. des Medecins de Langue Francaise du Canada, 8355 St. Laurent Blvd., Montreal, PQ H2P 2Z6 Canada; Title Tel # (514) 388-2228 Title Fax # (514) 388-5335
Personnel: Editor-Andre de Seve
Editorial Description: Interviews with doctors; AMLFC's activities; news on medicine.
General Info: (Formerly Bulletin), Monthly, Trim Size-8½ x 11, 4 pages, No Color
Circulation: Total-10,000

AMPRA Review   *Association*

Publishing Co: American Medical Peer Review Assn., 1140 Connecticut Ave NW Ste, 1050, Washington, DC 20036-4001; Title Tel # (202) 371-5610 Title Fax # (202) 371-8954
Personnel: Publisher-Julie Birkofer, Editor-Andrew Webber
Editorial Description: Broad issues in healthcare; innovations in the medical review field: private review activities; & updates on upcoming AMPRA events. This publicationa also provides a forum for guest writers.
General Info: Yr. Est. 1982, Quarterly, Letrpr. press, 10 pages, 2 Color, Coated
Subscriptions: Indv. $100
Acquisitions: Publication Bought
Circulation: (100% controlled), Total-1,300
Advertising: Inquire for rates.
Printing Co: Newsletter Services, Inc., 9700 Philadelphia Court, Lanham, MD 20706
Tel # (301) 731-5200, Fax # (301) 731-5201

AOE Network
Consumer

Publishing Co: American Health Information Management Association, 919 N Michigan Ave Fl 1400, Chicago, IL 60611-1601; Title Tel # (312) 787-2672
Editorial Description: Reviews developments in the field of medical record management & technology.
General Info: (Formerly AOE Newsletter), 3x/yr., Desktop press, 12 pages, No Color
Subscriptions: Indv. $25, Inst. $100

APAP Update

Publishing Co: Association of Physician Assistant Programs, 950 N Washington St, Alexandria, VA 22314-1534; Title Tel # (703) 836-2272
Personnel: Editor-Phaedra Ryder
General Info: (Formerly APAP Biweekly Report), Yr. Est. 1976, Monthly, Mimeo press, 6 pages, No Color, Newsprint
Circulation: Total-300

APF News
Association

Publishing Co: American Physicians Fellowship, Inc. for Medicine in Israel, 2001 Beacon St., Brookline, MA 02146-4227; Title Tel # (617) 232-5382
Personnel: Editor-Daniel Goldfarb
Editorial Description: The activities and accomplishments of the American Physicians Fellowship, Inc. in helping to make Israel a major medical center.
General Info: Yr. Est. 1951, Semi-annually, Trim Size-6 x 8
Circulation: Total-9,000
Advertising: Inquire for rates.

APLA Update
See: HEALTH

APPA Digest
Association

Publishing Co: American Professional Practice Assn., 292 Madison Ave., New York, NY 10017-6351; Title Tel # (212) 949-5900
Personnel: Editor-William Driscoll
Editorial Description: Association membership newsletter on financial planning for doctors.
General Info: Yr. Est. 1963, Quarterly, Trim Size-8¾ x 11½, Sheetfed press, 6 pages, 2 Color, Newsprint
Subscriptions: Free With Membership
Circulation: Total-65,000

APS Bulletin
See: HEALTH

AROCC Newsletter

Publishing Co: Assn. for Research of Childhood Cancer, Inc., PO Box 251, Buffalo, NY 14225-0251; Title Tel # (716) 684-8864
Editorial Description: Deals with pediatric cancer research news of interest to parents who have children with cancer.
General Info: Yr. Est. 1972, Bi-monthly, Trim Size-7 x 8½, 4 pages
Circulation: Total-1,000

ASA Refresher Courses in Anesthesiology
Consumer

Publishing Co: J.B. Lippincott Co., 227 E. Washington Sq., Philadelphia, PA 19106 Tel # (215) 238-4200
Personnel: Publisher-Marcia Serepy, Editor-S.H. Hershey, Circ. Mgr.-Kevin Fenton, Circ. Mgr.-Tish Packman, Production Mgr.-Earl Gerhart, Promotion Dir.-Virginia Kelly
General Info: Yr. Est. 1972, Annually, Sheetfed press, ISSN: 0363-471X, No Color, Looseleaf
Subscriptions: Indv. $19, Inst. $19

ASCLS Today
Association

Publishing Co: American Society for Clinical Laboratory Science, 7910 Woodmont Ave Ste 530, Bethesda, MD 20814-3015; Title Tel # (301) 657-2768 Title Fax # (301) 657-2909
Personnel: Editor-Kristen Lindemer, Adv. Dir.-Larry Lotridge
Editorial Description: Member newsletter.
General Info: (Formerly ASMT Today), Yr. Est. 1949, Monthly, Trim Size-8½ x 11, Web press, 8 pages, ISSN: 0895-3597, 2 Color, Other, Saddle-stitched
Subscriptions: Indv. $8, Free With Membership
Circulation: Total-20,000, Readership-20,000
Advertising: Inquire for rates.
List Rental: Rents Lists

ASDA News
Association   CPM: $204

Publishing Co: American Sleep Disorders Association, 1610 14th St NW Ste 300, Rochester, MN 55901; Title Tel # (507) 287-6006 Title Fax # (507) 287-6008
Personnel: Editor-Martin Cohn, Production Mgr.-Kathryn Brutinel
Editorial Description: Reports news of interest to members of the American Sleep Disorders Assn., the Sleep Research Society, and the Association of Polysomnographic Technology relating to sleep disorders medicine and clinical polysomnography.
General Info: (Formerly American Assn. of Sleep Disorders Centers/APSS Newsletter), Yr. Est. 1975, Quarterly, Trim Size-8½ x 11, Sheetfed press, 50 pages, ISSN: 0897-9375, 2% ads, 4 Color, Coated, Saddle-stitched
Subscriptions: Indv. $40, $10/copy
Circulation: Total-3,100
Advertising: $635.
List Rental: Rents Lists
Printing Co: Custom Printing Co., 1913 2nd St. SW, P O Box 519, Rochester, MN 55901 Tel # (507) 288-1851

ASET Newsletter
Association

Publishing Co: American Society of Electroneurodiagnostic Technologists, 204 W 7th St, Carroll, IA 51401-2317 Fax # (712) 792-6922; Title Tel # (712) 792-2978 Title Fax # (712) 792-6962
Personnel: Publisher, Editor, Circ. Mgr., Production Mgr., Art Dir.-Fran Pedelty
Editorial Description: Communicates with members-calendar, regional news, educational article.
General Info: Yr. Est. 1976, Bi-monthly, Trim Size-8½ x 11, Offset press, 36 pages, ISSN: 0886-5620, 2 Color, Matte
Subscriptions: Indv. $65, Inst. $260, Free With Membership
Advertising: Inquire for rates.
List Rental: Actives: 3,100, Expires: 1,100, $60/M

ASHP Newsletter
See: DRUGS & PHARMACEUTICALS

AVSC News
See: HEALTH

Abortion Report
See: POLITICS

Academy of Ambulatory Foot Surgery
Association

Publishing Co: Academy of Ambulatory Foot Surgery, PO Box 2730, Tuscaloosa, AL 35403-2730; Title Tel # (205) 758-3678
Personnel: Publisher-John Bell
Editorial Description: Newsletter on foot surgery.
General Info: Bi-monthly, Trim Size-11¼ x 17½, Web press, 12 pages, No Color
Circulation: Total-2,000
Advertising: Inquire for rates.

Academy Reporter
Business, Association

Publishing Co: American Pharmaceutical Assn., 2215 Constitution Ave NW, Washington, DC 20037-2975 Fax # (202) 713-2354; Title Tel # (202) 628-4410 Title Fax # (202) 723-2354
Personnel: Editor-Naomi Kaminsky, Circ. Mgr.-Joseph Martin, Production Mgr.-Jeffrey Ball, Art Dir.-Mary Jane Hickey
Editorial Description: News and comment by leaders of the three academics of APhA
General Info: Yr. Est. 1993, 3x/yr., Trim Size-8½ x 11, Offset press, 12 pages, 2 Color, Matte, Saddle-stitched
Subscriptions: Indv. $25, Free With Membership
Circulation: Total-22,500
List Rental: List Management Co.: Manager: Joseph Martin; Medical Marketing Service, 185 hansen Court, Ste. 110, Wood Dale, IL 60191-1146 Tel # (708) 350-1717
Printing Co: Master Print, Inc., 8401-A Terminal Rd., Box 1467, Newington, VA 22122 Tel # (703) 550-9555

Action-Texas Medical Association
Association

Publishing Co: Texas Medical Association, 401 W. 15th St., Austin, TX 78701-1680 Fax # (512) 370-1632; Title Tel # (512) 370-1300 Title Fax # (512) 370-1630
Personnel: Editor-Tammy Wishard, Adv. Dir.-Laurie Neece, Art Dir.-Gretchen Schultz
Editorial Description: Newsletter for Texas physicians and medical students. Non-scientific medical issue oriented.
General Info: (Formerly Action), Yr. Est. 1960, 10x/yr., Trim Size-8½ x 11, Sheetfed press, 4 pages, 2 Color, Matte
Subscriptions: Indv. $35
Circulation: Total-31,000

Adolescent Medicine
Business

Publishing Co: Adolescent Medicine, 821 Delaware Ave SW, Washington, DC 20024-4207; Title Tel # (202) 488-7533
Personnel: Publisher, Editor-Nathaniel Polster, Circ. Mgr.-Dale Zarb
Editorial Description: News useful for practicing physicians, nurses, coaches,social workers; hospitals.
General Info: Yr. Est. 1977, Monthly, Sheetfed press, 4 pages, ISSN: 0044-6335, 2 Color
Subscriptions: Indv. $69, $10/copy

Aesthetic Surgery

Publishing Co: American Society for Aesthetic Plastic Surgery, 3922 Atlantic Ave, Long Beach, CA 90807-3502; Title Tel # (213) 595-4275
Personnel: Publisher-Robert Stanton, Editor-Ronald Iverson, Production Mgr.-Sandra Gropp, Art Dir.-Julie Webber, Promotion Dir.-Edward Huggins
General Info: (Formerly Aesthetic Society News), Trim Size-8½ x 11, Sheetfed press, 24 pages, 4 Color, Coated
Subscriptions: $4/copy
Circulation: Total-2,800

Affiliates in Training
Association

Publishing Co: American College of Cardiology, 9111 Old Georgetown Rd, Bethesda, MD 20814-1699 Tel # (301) 897-2694; Title Tel # (301) 897-5400 Title Fax # (301) 897-9745
Personnel: Editor-Sharon Ballas
General Info: Yr. Est. 1984, Bi-monthly, Trim Size-8½ x 11, Offset press, 8 pages, 2 Color, Newsprint
Subscriptions: Indv. $10, Free With Membership
Circulation: Total-4,000
Advertising: Inquire for rates.
Printing Co: Goetz Printing Co., 7939 Angus Ct., Springfield, VA 22153-2844 Tel # (703) 569-8232, Fax # (703) 569-9364

Albert Einstein College of Medicine Faculty News

Publishing Co: Albert Einstein College of Medicine, 1308 Belfer Building, Bronx, NY 10461; Title Tel # (212) 430-2000
General Info: Yr. Est. 1956

Allergy & Clinical Immunology News

Publishing Co: Hogrefe & Huber Publishers, P.O. 2487, Kirkland, WA 98083; Title Tel # (416) 482-6339
Editorial Description: Examines research focusing on allergic mechanisms & diseases.
General Info: Bi-monthly, ISSN: 0838-1925

Allergy and Asthma Industry News   *Business*

Publishing Co: Good Communications, Inc., PO Box 10069, Austin, TX 78766; Title Tel # (512) 454-6090 Title Fax # (512) 454-3420
Personnel: Publisher, Editor-Ross Becker, Mng. Editor-Judi Sklar
Editorial Description: Monthly business letter senior executives in the pharmaceutical and allergy products industries. Provides sensitive information about upcoming new products, drugs in development , market information and new promotional efforts.
General Info: Yr. Est. 1995, Monthly, Trim Size-8½ x 11, 10 pages, ISSN: 1084-2721
Subscriptions: Indv. $295

Allergy Edge   *Consumer*

Publishing Co: Premier Allergy, 100 Crestent Center Park, Suite 1200, Tucker, GA 30084; Title Tel # (404) 414-2800 Title Fax # (770) 414-2810
Editorial Description: Allergy information written to consumers by doctors.
General Info: Monthly

Allergy Hotline   *Business, Consumer*

Publishing Co: Hotline Publishing, PO Box 161132, Altamonte Springs, FL 32716-1132; Title Tel # (407) 628-1377 Title Fax # (407) 628-9355
Editorial Description: Published for doctors and patients who suffer from allergies.
General Info: Yr. Est. 1992, Monthly
Subscriptions: Indv. $40, Can. $35, For. $35, $2/copy
Circulation: Total-1,000
Advertising: Inquire for rates.

Alumni Newsletter, Presbyterian   *Association*

Publishing Co: Presbyterian, 1753 W Congress Pky, Chicago, IL 60612-3809

Ambulatory Pediatric Association Newsletter   *Consumer*

Publishing Co: Ambulatory Pediatric Assn., 6728 Old Mclean Village Dr, Mc Lean, VA 22101-3906; Title Tel # (703) 556-9222
Personnel: Publisher-Marge Degnon, Editor-Dr. John Pascoe
Editorial Description: Newsletter for professional organization.
General Info: Yr. Est. 1964, 16 pages, No Color
Circulation: (100% controlled), Total-1,200

American Academy of Cosmetic Surgery   *Association*

Publishing Co: American Academy of Cosmetic Surgery, 401 N. Michigan Ave., Chicago, IL 60611-4212
Personnel: Editor-Richard Aronsohn, Production Mgr.-Russ Till, Adv. Dir.-Lynne Jeffes
General Info: Yr. Est. 1969, Quarterly, 4% ads
Subscriptions: Indv. $60, For. $70
Circulation: Total-7,000
Advertising: Inquire for rates.

American Academy of Podiatric Sports Medicine Newsletter   CPM$1500

Publishing Co: American Academy of Podiatric Sports Medicine, 1729 Glastonberry Rd, Potomac, MD 20854-2642; Title Tel # (301) 424-7440
Personnel: Publisher, Circ. Mgr.-Larry Shane
Editorial Description: Articles discussing injuries & treatments in the field of podiatry.
General Info: Yr. Est. 1970, Quarterly, Trim Size-8½ x 11, 12 pages, 1% ads, Color, Coated
Subscriptions: Indv. $40
Circulation: Total-1,000
Advertising: $1,500. Accepts Inserts.
List Rental: Actives: $125/M

American Academy of Podiatry Administration News-Letter   *Association*

Publishing Co: American Academy of Podiatry Administration, c/o John V. Cicero, 10 Meadow Lane, Bloomfield, NJ 07003
General Info: Quarterly
Subscriptions: Indv. $15

American Association of Senior Physicians- Newsletter   *Association*

Publishing Co: American Assn. of Senior Physicians, 515 N. State St., Chicago, IL 60610-4320; Title Tel # (312) 464-2460
Editorial Description: For physicians contemplating or in retirement.
General Info: (Formerly AASP Newsletter), Yr. Est. 1976, Bi-monthly, Trim Size-8½ x 11, Offset press, 4 pages, Color
Circulation: Total-5,000

American Association of Tissue Banks-Newsletter   *Consumer, Association*

Publishing Co: American Assn. of Tissue Banks, 1350 Beverly Rd Ste 220a, Mc Lean, VA 22101-3924; Title Tel # (703) 827-9582
Editorial Description: Disseminates information on transplant medicine and tissue banking.
General Info: Yr. Est. 1979, Quarterly, Trim Size-8½ x 11, Offset press, 12 pages, No Color, Newsprint
Circulation: Total-1,000

American College of Apothecaries-Newsletter

Publishing Co: American College of Apothecaries, 205 Daingerfield Rd, Alexandria, VA 22314-2833; Title Tel # (703) 684-8603
Personnel: Editor-Tracy Portner
General Info: Yr. Est. 1940, Monthly, 4 pages
Circulation: Total-1,100

American College of Legal Medicine, Notes from the President   *Association*   CPM: $362

Publishing Co: American College of Legal Medicine, 611 East Wells Street, Milwaukee, WI 53202 Tel # (414) 276-1881 Fax # (414) 276-3349; Title Tel # (800) 433-9137 Title Fax # (414) 276-1881
Personnel: Editor-David Baumann
Editorial Description: News and activities of the American College of legal medicine.
General Info: (Formerly Communique & Newsbriefs), Yr. Est. 1971, Quarterly, Trim Size-8½ x 11, Desktop press, 12 pages, No Color, Coated
Subscriptions: Free With Membership
Circulation: (62% controlled), Total-1,600
Advertising: $580.
List Rental: Rents Lists

American College of Medical Quality Newsletter Focus   *Business*

Publishing Co: American College of Medical Quality, 9005 Congressional Ct, Potomac, MD 20854-4608 Tel # (301) 365-3570 Fax # (301) 365-3202; Title Tel # (813) 497-3340 Title Fax # (813) 497-5573
Personnel: Editor-James Menges
Editorial Description: Practical & comprehensive evaluation of quality in healthcare- DRG's, QA-UR, Medicare & Medicaid, risk management & other areas of interest to physicians, allied health specialists, hospital & public health administrators & legislators.
General Info: Yr. Est. 1975, Bi-monthly, Desktop press, 12 pages, 3% ads, Newsprint
Subscriptions: Indv. $75, Inst. $70, $7/copy
Circulation: Total-2,000
Advertising: Inquire for rates.
List Rental: Rents Lists

American College of Osteopathic Pediatricians Newsletter

Publishing Co: American College of Osteopathic Pediatricians, 5301 Wisconsin Ave NW Ste 630, Washington, DC 20015-2015; Title Tel # (609) 393-3350
Personnel: Editor-Teresa Goeke
General Info: Yr. Est. 1940, Quarterly
Circulation: Total-300

American College of Radiology Bulletin

Publishing Co: American College of Radiology, 1891 Preston White Dr, Reston, VA 22091-4397; Title Tel # (703) 648-8911
Personnel: Editor-Marian Dinitz
Editorial Description: Articles concerning College activities, radiology and medical economics for members.
General Info: Yr. Est. 1942, Monthly, Trim Size-8½ x 11, Sheetfed press, 16 pages, 2 Color, Newsprint, Saddle-stitched
Subscriptions: Indv. $40
Circulation: (100% controlled), Total-21,000

American Geriatrics Society-Newsletter
See: SENIOR CITIZENS

American Institute for Cancer Research Newsletter
See: HEALTH

American Osteopathic College of Anesthesiologists Newsletter   *Association*

Publishing Co: American Osteopathic College of Anesthesiologists, 17201 E. U.S. Highway 40, Lees Summit, MO 64055; Title Tel # (816) 373-4700 Title Fax # (816) 373-1529
General Info: Yr. Est. 1952, Tri-annually

American Parkinson Disease Association Newsletter   *Association*

Publishing Co: American Parkinson Disease Association, 60 Bay St., Staten Island, NY 10301-2500; Title Tel # (718) 981-8001 Title Fax # (718) 981-4399
Personnel: Editor-Paul Maestrone
General Info: Yr. Est. 1979, Quarterly, Trim Size-8½ x 11, Sheetfed press, 8 pages, 2 Color
Subscriptions: Free
Circulation: Total-250,000

American Society of Anesthesiologists Newsletter   *Association*

Publishing Co: American Society of Anesthesiologists, 520 N Northwest Hwy, Park Ridge, IL 60068-2538; Title Tel # (847) 825-5586
Personnel: Editor-Dr. Erwin Lear
General Info: Monthly
Subscriptions: Indv. $12, Free With Membership

American Society of Bariatric Physicians Newsletter   *Association*

Publishing Co: American Society of Bariatric Physicians, 5600 S Quebec St Ste 109a, Englewood, CO 80111-2208; Title Tel # (303) 779-4833 Title Fax # (303) 779-4834
Personnel: Circ. Mgr., Production Mgr., Adv. Dir.-Beth Little, Editor, Mktg. Dir.-Jim Merker
Editorial Description: Official membership newsletter.
General Info: Yr. Est. 1986, Bi-monthly, Trim Size-8½ x 11, Sheetfed press, 12 pages, No Color
Subscriptions: Free With Membership
Advertising: Inquire for rates.
List Rental: Rents Lists
Printing Co: Sir Speedy, 9608 E Arapahoe Rd, Englewood, CO 80112-3703 Tel # (303) 799-4383, Fax # (303) 792-5140

American Society of Clinical Hypnosis-Newsletter   *Association*

Publishing Co: American Society of Clinical Hypnosis, 2200 E Devon Ave Ste 291, Des Plaines, IL 60018-4501; Title Tel # (708) 297-3317 Title Fax # (708) 297-7309
Personnel: Editor-William Wester, II
Editorial Description: Timely news of interest to members.
General Info: Yr. Est. 1957, Quarterly, Sheetfed press, 6 pages, 2 Color, Newsprint
Circulation: Total-3,200
Advertising: Inquire for rates.

Annotations
See: DENTAL

Antibiotic News and Report on Infectious Diseases

Publishing Co: Bristol-Myers Company, Products Div., 345 Park Ave Fl 9, New York, NY 10154-0004; Title Tel # (212) 644-2100

Antimicrobic & Infectious Diseases Newsletter
See: MICROBIOLOGY

Approved Bioequivalency Codes
See: DRUGS & PHARMACEUTICALS

Arthritis News
See: HEALTH

Assisted Reproduction Reviews   *Business*

Publishing Co: Williams & Wilkins, 351 W. Camden St., Baltimore, MD 21201-2436 Fax # (410) 528-4452; Title Tel # (410) 528-4068
Personnel: Editor-Alan H. DeCherney, MD
Editorial Description: Reporting on advanced treatment of infertility as well as the special needs of infertile couples, the journal is directed to ob/gyns, urologists, endocrinologists, embryologists, and biologists.
General Info: Yr. Est. 1991, Quarterly, ISSN: 1051-2446

Association of American Indian Physicians Newsletter   *Scholarly, Association*   CPM: $222

Publishing Co: Assn. of American Indian Physicians, 1235 Sovereign Row Ste C7, Oklahoma City, OK 73108-1833; Title Tel # (405) 946-7072 Title Fax # (405) 946-7651
Personnel: Editor-Margaret Knight
General Info: Irregular, 50% ads
Subscriptions: Free To Qualified Recipient
Circulation: Total-4,500
Advertising: $1,000.

Association of American Physicians and Surgeons Newsletter

Publishing Co: Assn. of American Physicians and Surgeons, 1601 N Tucson Blvd Ste 9, Tucson, AZ 85716-3405
Editorial Description: Represents physicians in the socio-economic aspects of medical practice.
General Info: Yr. Est. 1943, Monthly
Subscriptions: Indv. $35

Association for Biomedical Research-Update

Publishing Co: Association for Biomedical Research, 818 Connecticut Ave NW Ste 303, Washington, DC 20006-2702; Title Tel # (202) 857-0540
Personnel: Editor-Frankie Trull
General Info: (Formerly Research Animal Alliance-Update), 2 pages
Circulation: Total-600

Association of Health Facility Licensure & Certification Newsletter

Publishing Co: Assn. of Health Facility Licensure & Certification Directors, 1100 W 49th St # 309, Austin, TX 78756-3101; Title Tel # (512) 458-7611
Personnel: Editor-Diana Paterson
General Info: Semi-annually

Association for the History of Chiropractic-Bulletin

Publishing Co: Assn. for the History of Chiropractic, 207 S Grandview Dr, Pittsburgh, PA 15215-1822 Tel # (412) 782-0171; Title Tel # (319) 326-9897 Title Fax # (412) 784-8801
Personnel: Editor-Russell W. Gibbons
General Info: Yr. Est. 1980, 4 pages, ISSN: 0736-4377
Subscriptions: Indv. $50, $25/copy
Circulation: Total-850

Association of Medical Illustrators Newsletter
See: ART & SCULPTURE

Association of Pathology Chairmen Newsletter   *Association*

Publishing Co: Assn. of Pathology Chairmen, 9650 Rockville Pike, Bethesda, MD 20814-3998; Title Tel # (301) 571-1880 Title Fax # (301) 571-1879
Personnel: Editor-R.W. Prichard
Editorial Description: Provides news of the activities of departments of pathology in US medical schoosl to each of those departments thru the chairman.
General Info: Yr. Est. 1967, Quarterly, Trim Size-8½ x 11, Sheetfed press, 1 pages
Subscriptions: Free With Membership
Circulation: Total-150

Asthma & Allergy Advocate   *Consumer*

Publishing Co: American Academy of Allergy & Immunology, 611 E. Wells St., Milwaukee, WI 53202-3889; Title Tel # (414) 272-6071 Title Fax # (414) 276-3349
Personnel: Editor-Sarah Kaluzny-Petroff
Editorial Description: Information on allergy aids, news on asthma research and asthma/alergy treatments. Includes book reviews.
General Info: Yr. Est. 1985, Quarterly, Sheetfed press, 4 pages, ISSN: 0899-7470, 2 Color
Subscriptions: Indv. $70, $6/copy
Circulation: Total-40,000
List Rental: Rents Lists
Printing Co: Parker Printing /Hartland, 505 Industrial Dr., Hartland, WI 53029 Tel # (414) 367-3730, Fax # (414) 367-4185

Asthma Update   *Consumer, Association*

Publishing Co: Asthma Update, 123 Monticello Ave, Annapolis, MD 21401-3432; Title Tel # (410) 267-8329 Title Fax # (410) 267-0309
Personnel: Publisher, Editor-David Jamison
Editorial Description: Newsletter for parents & adult patients. Includes annotated abstracts from current medical medical journals and perspectives on asthma by health professionals.
General Info: Yr. Est. 1985, Quarterly, 4 pages, ISSN: 8756-4734
Subscriptions: Indv. $12, $3/copy

Atlantis, The Imagery Newsletter

Publishing Co: Atlantis, 4016 3rd Ave, San Diego, CA 92103-2102; Title Tel # (619) 298-7502
Personnel: Publisher-Dennis Gersten,M.D.
Editorial Description: Focuses on developments and techniques in imagery.
General Info: Yr. Est. 1988, Bi-monthly
Subscriptions: Indv. $50

B.A.S.H., Inc.
See: HEALTH

BBI's Monitor of Technology Assessment & Reimbursement *Business*

Publishing Co: American Health Consultants, Inc., 3525 Piedmont Rd., Building #6, Ste. 400, Atlanta, GA 30305-0056 Tel # (404) 262-7436 Fax # (404) 284-3291
Personnel: Publisher-Don Johnston, Editor-Dona Watson, Editorial Asst.-Paul Campbell, Assoc. Ed.-Mike Gibb, Asst. Ed.-Anna Lee, Circ. Mgr.-Cherly Seaglione
Editorial Description: Focuses on medical technology assessment patient outcomes research, and reimbursement issues that impact medical device, diagnostic, biotech and drug firms and markets.
General Info: Yr. Est. 1992, Monthly, Trim Size-8.5 x 11, Desktop press, 12 pages, ISSN: 1066-3037, 2 Color, Matte, Saddle-stitched
Subscriptions: Indv. $420
Acquistions: Publication Bought, Publication Sold
List Rental: Actives: $145/M

B.E.A.M. (Being Energetic About Multiplicity)
See: PSYCHOLOGY

Back Letter, The *Business*

Publishing Co: Lippincott-Raven Press Publishers, 227 E. Washington Square, Philadelphia, PA 19106 Tel # (215) 238-4200 Fax # (215) 238-4227 Parent Co.-Wolters Kluwer US Corporation, New York
Personnel: Publisher-Kathey Alexander, Editor-Mark Schoene, Mktg. Dir.-Michele Duncan
Editorial Description: Covering issues of health and orthopedic medicine.
General Info: Monthly
Subscriptions: Indv. $95, For. $105

Batting the Breeze
See: HEALTH

Being Alive *Consumer, Association*

Publishing Co: Being Alive, People with HIV/AIDS Coalition, 3626 W Sunset Blvd, Los Angeles, CA 90026-1059; Title Tel # (213) 667-3262 Title Fax # (213) 667-2735
Editorial Description: For people with HIV/AIDS.
General Info: Monthly, Trim Size-8½ x 11, 20 pages
Circulation: Total-11,000

Being Well
See: HEALTH

BioLaw *Business*

Publishing Co: University Publications of America, 121 Chanlon Rd, New Providence, NJ 07974-1541 Parent Co.-Reed Reference Publishing, New Providence; Title Fax # (908) 665-6688
Editorial Description: Serves those professionals who need both incisive analysis and the very lastest factual information on any bioethical subject including medical malpractice, death and dying, genetic counseling and engineering, living wills, health care costs, and more. Contains resource manual, monthly updates, and special sections.
General Info: Annually, Looseleaf
Subscriptions: Indv. $415

Bio/Med Technology Alert *Business*

Publishing Co: Technical Insights, Inc., PO Box 1304, Fort Lee, NJ 07024-9967; Title Tel # (201) 568-4744 Title Fax # (201) 568-8247
Personnel: Publisher-Kenneth A. Kovaly, Circ. Mgr.-Barbara Chaffee, Mktg. Dir.-Lyn A. Schmidt
Editorial Description: Tailored to companies searching for innovative technologies in the areas of medical devices, biomaterials healthcare. Field include: prosthetics, implants, drug delivery systems. Reports on strategic alliances, mergers & acquisitions, key patents listed.
General Info: Yr. Est. 1995, Weekly, 7 pages, ISSN: 1084-8746
Subscriptions: Indv. $890, For. $990
List Rental: Actives: $185/M

BioPeople
See: BIOCHEMISTRY

BioVenture Stock Report
See: INVESTMENT

BioVenture View
See: BIOCHEMISTRY

Bioethics Literature Review

Publishing Co: University Publishing Group, Inc., 12 South Market St., Suite 300, Frederick, MD 21701-5441 Tel # (301) 694-8561; Title Tel # (301) 694-8531
Personnel: Publisher-N. Quist
Editorial Description: Reviews literature on medical ethics, providing abstracts from more than 500 medical, legal, & professional journals each month.
General Info: Yr. Est. 1986, Monthly, ISSN: 0886-8913
Subscriptions: Indv. $45, Inst. $65

Bioethics Reporter

Publishing Co: Univ. Pubs. of America, Inc., 4520 East West Hwy Ste 800, Bethesda, MD 20814-3319; Title Tel # (301) 694-0100
Personnel: Publisher-Ruth Gaare
Editorial Description: Annual binder series containing comprehensive sourcebook & periodic updates.
General Info: Yr. Est. 1983, Bi-monthly, Trim Size-8½ x 11, Sheetfed press, 50 pages, No Color, Newsprint, Looseleaf

Biomaterials Forum

Publishing Co: Society for Biomaterials, 6518 Walker Street, Suite #150, Minneapolis, MN 55426-4244; Title Tel # (612) 927-8108 Title Fax # (612) 927-8127
Personnel: Publisher, Editor-P.E. Duncan, Circ. Mgr.-Rosealee Lee, Circ. Mgr., Adv. Dir.-Rosalee Lee
Editorial Description: Unique news & information for biomaterial scientists & medical device developers & users.
General Info: (Formerly Torch), Yr. Est. 1978, Bi-monthly, Trim Size-8½ x 11, Web press, 16 pages, 2% ads, No Color, Coated
Subscriptions: Indv. $40, Can. $45, $7/copy
Acquistions: Publication Bought
Circulation: Total-1,800
Advertising: Inquire for rates. Accepts Inserts.
List Rental: Rents Lists
Printing Co: England Press, 123 N 3rd St, Minneapolis, MN 55401-1693 Tel # (612) 338-8781

Biomedical Market Newsletter *Business* **CPM$1000**

Publishing Co: Biomedical Market Newsletter, Inc., 3237 Idaho Pl, Costa Mesa, CA 92626-2207 Fax # (714) 434-9755; Title Tel # (714) 434-9500 Title Fax # (714) 434-9500
Personnel: Publisher, Editor-David G. Anast, Mktg. Dir.-Steve Baker
Editorial Description: Comprehensive digest of medical marketing, business, financial and regulatory information on the medical manufacturing industry worldwide. Covers new product approvals, market analysis, stocks, venture capitals & much more.
General Info: Yr. Est. 1991, Monthly, Trim Size-8½ x 11, Offset press, 28 pages, ISSN: 1064-4180, Ind/Abs/Online: DATASTAR, COMPOSER, DIALOGUE, DOW JONES NEWS RETRIVAL, NEXUS, LEXUS., 2 Color, Matte, Saddle-stitched
Subscriptions: Indv. $695, Can. $790, For. $790, $55/copy
Circulation: Total-500
Advertising: $500. Accepts Inserts.
List Rental: Rents Lists
Printing Co: McGinnis Printing, 320 S Main St, Santa Ana, CA 92701-5710

Biomedical Optics
See: OPTICAL

Biomedical Safety & Standards *Business*

Publishing Co: Quest Publishing Co., 1351 Titan Way, Brea, CA 92621-3787 Fax # (714) 525-3787 Parent Co.-Lippincott-Raven Press Publishers, Philadelphia; Title Tel # (714) 738-6400 Title Fax # (714) 525-6258
Personnel: Publisher-Steve McCoy, Editor-Mark Ryan, Mktg. Dir.-Michele Duncan
Editorial Description: Covers hospital safety, equipment hazards & recalls, & relevant legislation.
General Info: Yr. Est. 1971, Semi-monthly, 8 pages, ISSN: 0048-0282, No Color, Newsprint, Saddle-stitched
Subscriptions: Indv. $265, Can. $265, For. $300
List Rental: Rents Lists

Biomedical Technology & Human Factors Engineering *Business*

Publishing Co: National Technical Information Service U.S., 5285 Port Royal Rd., Springfield, VA 22161-0001 Fax # (703) 487-4630; Title Tel # (703) 487-4630
Editorial Description: Covers biomedical facilities & supplies, human factors engineering, man-machine relations, bionics, artificial intelligence, & biomedical instrumentation.
General Info: Weekly, Trim Size-8½ x 11, Offset press, 4 pages, ISSN: 0163-1497, No Color
Subscriptions: Indv. $135, Can. $135, For. $195

Biomedical Technology Information Service *Consumer*

Publishing Co: Quest Publishing Co., 1351 Titan Way, Brea, CA 92621-3787 Fax # (714) 525-3787 Parent Co.-Lippincott-Raven Press Publishers, Philadelphia; Title Tel # (714) 738-6400 Title Fax # (714) 525-6258
Personnel: Publisher-Steve McCoy, Editor-Marty Matisoff, Mktg. Dir.-Michele Duncan
Editorial Description: Reports on latest advances in medical technology. Covers technical and professional topics.
General Info: Yr. Est. 1974, Semi-monthly, Trim Size-8½ x 11, Offset press, 12 pages, ISSN: 0147-2682, No Color, Newsprint, Saddle-stitched
Subscriptions: Indv. $290, Can. $290, For. $340
List Rental: Rents Lists

Biotechnology Software

Publishing Co: Mary Ann Liebert, Inc., 1651 3rd Ave, New York, NY 10128-3649; Title Tel # (212) 289-2300
Personnel: Publisher-Mary Liebert, Editor-Kevin Ahern
Editorial Description: Exploration of critical role played by computers in biotechnology advances.
General Info: Yr. Est. 1984, Bi-monthly, ISSN: 0749-0372
Subscriptions: Indv. $95, For. $125
Circulation: Total-4,000

Blood Weekly — *Business, Association*

Publishing Co: C.W. Henderson Publisher, Medical Center II, P.O. Box 5528, Atlanta, GA 31107-0528 Tel # (404) 507-7777 Fax # (404) 507-7788; Title Tel # (205) 995-1567 Title Fax # (404) 378-5411
Personnel: Publisher-C.W. Henderson, Editor-Cathy F. Clark, Calendar Ed.-Ken Kimsey
Editorial Description: Blood, Tissues; and organ banking; synthetic blood products; blood borne pathogens.
General Info: Yr. Est. 1993, Weekly, ISSN: 1065-6073
Subscriptions: Indv. $995, Can. $995, For. $1,195

Blue Sheet: Health Policy & Biomedical Research, The
See: DRUGS & PHARMACEUTICALS

Bresler Center News — *Association*

Publishing Co: Bresler Center, Inc., 115 S. Topanga Cyn. Blvd #158, Topanga, CA 90272-0967 Tel # (310) 317-4855 Fax # (310) 456-9055; Title Tel # (310) 455-3634
Personnel: Publisher-David Bresler
Editorial Description: Medical center newsletter.
General Info: Irregular, Trim Size-8½ x 11, 12 pages, 2 Color, Coated, Saddle-stitched
Circulation: Total-5,000
List Rental: Rents Lists

Briefings on Hospital Safety
See: HOSPITALS & NURSING HOMES

Briefings on Laboratory Safety and Accreditation
See: HOSPITALS & NURSING HOMES

Briefings on Long-Term Care Regulations
See: HOSPITALS & NURSING HOMES

Briefings on Subacute Care: Regulations & Reimbursement
See: HOSPITALS & NURSING HOMES

Bulletin — *Association*

Publishing Co: Assn. Pulmonaire du Quebec, 4837 Rue Boyer, Suite 100, Montreal, PQ H2J 3E6 Canada; Title Tel # (514) 596-0805 Title Fax # (514) 596-1173
Editorial Description: Christmas Seal Campaign-education to prevent respiratory disease such as: asthma-bronchitis-emphysema-tuberculosis, etc. smoking and health-air polution.
General Info: (Formerly Observation Opinion Orientation), Yr. Est. 1967, Quarterly, Trim Size-8½ x 11, Offset press, 16 pages, Color
Subscriptions: Indv. $25
Circulation: Total-10,000
Advertising: Inquire for rates.

Bulletin on Rheumatic Diseases

Publishing Co: Arthritis Foundation, 1314 Spring St. NW, Atlanta, GA 30309-2898; Title Tel # (404) 872-7100 Title Fax # (404) 872-0457
Personnel: Publisher-Cynthia Kahn, Editor-John O. Sergent, MD
Editorial Description: Concise reviews of current developments in rheumatology research & management.
General Info: Yr. Est. 1950, 8x/yr., Trim Size-8½ x 11, Web press, 8 pages, ISSN: 0007-5248, Ind/Abs/Online: InMd, Mead Data Central, 2 Color
Subscriptions: For. $15
Circulation: Total-42,000
Printing Co: Thomasson Printing Co., 720 Dixie St, Carrollton, GA 30117-3819

Burlington County Medical Society Newsletter — *Business, Association*

Publishing Co: Burlington County Medical Society, PO Box 1023, Mount Laurel, NJ 08054-7023; Title Tel # (609) 231-1515 Title Fax # (609) 231-1516
Personnel: Editor-Lee Buckwalter, M. D., Circ. Mgr.-Catherine Pegues
Editorial Description: Local medical profession news & articles of interest to society members.
General Info: Bi-monthly, Trim Size-6¾ x 8¾
Circulation: Total-390
Advertising: Inquire for rates.

CAMPS Newsletter — *Business, Association*

Publishing Co: California Association of Medical Product Suppliers, 1 Capitol Mall, Ste. 320, Sacramento, CA 95814; Title Tel # (916) 443-2115
Personnel: Publisher-J. Michael Allen, Editor-Robert Morthole, Circ. Mgr.-Susan Saunders
Editorial Description: Durable medical equipment suppliers.
General Info: Yr. Est. 1978, Bi-monthly, Trim Size-8½ x 11, Sheetfed press, 12 pages, 2 Color
Subscriptions: Indv. $7
Circulation: (96% controlled), Total-1,100
Advertising: Inquire for rates.

CCBC Newsletter — *Business, Association*

Publishing Co: Council of Community Blood Centers, 725 15th St NW Ste 700, Washington, DC 20005-2109; Title Tel # (202) 393-5725 Title Fax # (202) 393-1282
Personnel: Publisher-James MacPherson, Editor, Production Mgr.-Jane Starkey
Editorial Description: News of medical, regulatory & management developments in blood banking.
General Info: Yr. Est. 1962, Weekly, Trim Size-8½ x 11, Mimeo press, 12 pages, No Color, Other, Other
Subscriptions: Indv. $216, Inst. $216, Can. $216, For. $240, $5/copy
Circulation: (53% controlled), Total-560, Subscriptions-260, International-40

CHCG Pulse
See: NURSING

CIR News — *Association*

Publishing Co: Committee of Interns, 386 Park Ave., S., New York, NY 10016-8852; Title Tel # (212) 725-5500
Personnel: Editor-Michael Yellin
Editorial Description: For salaried doctors.
General Info: (Formerly CIR Bulletin), Bi-monthly, Web press, 12 pages, Color-cover, Newsprint
Subscriptions: Indv. $12
Circulation: Total-15,000
Advertising: Inquire for rates.

CNSW Newsletter

Publishing Co: Council of Nephrology Social Workers-Natl. Kidney Foundation, 30 E. 33rd St., New York, NY 10016-5337; Title Tel # (212) 889-2210
General Info: Yr. Est. 1975, Quarterly, 24 pages
Circulation: Total-1,000

COTH (Council of Teaching Hospitals) Report — *Association*

Publishing Co: Association of American Medical Colleges, 2450 N Street, N.W., Washington, DC 20037-1167 Tel # (202) 828-0400; Title Tel # (202) 828-0490
General Info: Yr. Est. 1967, Monthly, ISSN: 0146-2814
Subscriptions: Indv. $30

CPT Assistant

Publishing Co: American Medical Association, 515 N. State St., Chicago, IL 60610 Fax # (312) 464-5834; Title Tel # (312) 464-4512 Title Fax # (312) 464-5600
Personnel: Editor-Denise Andersen, Editor-Judy Coy, Editor-Charlotte Miller, Mktg. Mgr.-Tim Ryan, Mktg. Mgr.-Reg Schmidt
Editorial Description: News and developments of interest to CPT assistants.
General Info: Yr. Est. 1991, Quarterly
Subscriptions: Indv. $135

CSP Bulletin — *Association*

Publishing Co: California Soc. of Pathologists, 1 Capitol Mall, Ste. 320, Sacramento, CA 95814; Title Tel # (916) 446-6001 Title Fax # (916) 444-7462
Personnel: Publisher-Robert Achermann, Editor-Jennifer Blevins, Circ. Mgr.-Jennifer Baunach
General Info: Quarterly, Trim Size-8½ x 11, Sheetfed press, 8 pages, Color
Circulation: (100% controlled), Total-730
Advertising: Inquire for rates.

CUSAN
See: RELIGIOUS & THEOLOGICAL

California Society of Anesthesiologists, INC Bulletin — *Association*

Publishing Co: California Society of Anesthesiologists, Inc., 1065 E. Hillsdale Blvd., Ste. 806, Foster City, CA 94404-1613; Title Tel # (415) 345-3020
Personnel: Editor-Andie Wiedman, Circ. Mgr.-Norman Catron
Editorial Description: Advancement in anesthesiology; malpractice, legislation, president's page, programs of meetings.
General Info: Yr. Est. 1948, Quarterly, Trim Size-6 x 9, Offset press, 50 pages, No Color
Subscriptions: Indv. $8, $5/copy
Circulation: Total-2,500

Canadian Association of Pathologists, Newsletter — *Association*

Publishing Co: Canadian Assn. of Pathologists, Royal Alexandra Hosp., Edmonton, AB T5H 3V9 Canada; Title Tel # (403) 477-4366
Personnel: Editor-J. Jacques, Circ. Mgr.-Deborah Dyke
Editorial Description: Text in English, French.
General Info: Yr. Est. 1959, Bi-monthly, Trim Size-8½ x 11, Offset press, 25 pages, 2 Color
Circulation: (100% controlled), Total-700
Advertising: Inquire for rates.

Canadian Medical and Biological Engineering Society Newsletter *Association* **CPM$2000**

Publishing Co: Canadian Medical & Biological Engineering Society, Natl. Research Council, Montreal Rd., Bldg.M55, Rm393, Ottawa, ON K1A 0R8 Canada; Title Tel # (613) 993-1686 Title Fax # (613) 954-2216
Personnel: Editor-Brian Graham, Publisher, Circ. Mgr.-Art Dir.-Sally Chapman
Editorial Description: Covers items of interest to membership.
General Info: Yr. Est. 1981, Tri-annually, Trim Size-8½ x 11, 15 pages, ISSN: 0830-8845, 20% ads, 2 Color, Saddle-stitched
Circulation: Total-500
Advertising: $1,000.

Canadian ORT Reporter

Publishing Co: Canadian ORT Reporter, 5165 Sherbrooke St., Ste. 208, Montreal, PQ H4A 1T6 Canada
Editorial Description: Rehabilitation Through training.
General Info: Yr. Est. 1970, Semi-annually, 4 pages
Circulation: Total-8,000

Canadian Society for Immunology, Bulletin *Association*

Publishing Co: Canadian Society for Immunology, Univ. of Manitoba, Immunology Dept, 730 Wm. Ave., Winnipeg, MB R3E 0W3 Canada Fax # (204) 772-7924; Title Tel # (204) 789-3793
Personnel: Editor-Kent Hay Glass
General Info: Yr. Est. 1978, Quarterly
Circulation: Total-400
Advertising: Inquire for rates.

Cancer & Genetics Report *Business*

Publishing Co: McGraw-Hill, 1221 Ave. of the Americas, 36th Fl., New York, NY 10020-1095 Tel # (212) 512-2000 Fax # (212) 512-6590; Title Tel # (212) 512-6140 Title Fax # (212) 512-2723
Personnel: Editor-Mara Bovsun, Editor-Kevin Hamilton
Editorial Description: Covers biotechnology's role in the fight against cancer.
General Info: Yr. Est. 1993, Monthly
Subscriptions: Indv. $395

Cancer Challenge, The

Publishing Co: Cancer Guidance Institute, 1323 Forbes Ave., Pittsburgh, PA 15219-4725; Title Tel # (412) 521-2291
Personnel: Editor-Estelle Weissburg
Editorial Description: Supports cancer patients & their families.
General Info: Yr. Est. 1983, Quarterly, Letrpr. press, 4 pages
Subscriptions: Indv. $15
Circulation: Total-3,000
Printing Co: Raff Printing, 70 Allen St, Pittsburgh, PA 15210-1082 Tel # (412) 431-4044

Cancer Letter, The *Business*

Publishing Co: The Cancer Letter Inc., PO Box 15189, Washington, DC 20003-0189; Title Tel # (202) 543-7665 Title Fax # (202) 543-6879
Personnel: Publisher, Editor-Kirsten Goldberg
Editorial Description: Covers budget, policy & program development in the National Cancer Program; includes eight page supplement, and titled cancer economics.
General Info: Yr. Est. 1974, Weekly, Trim Size-8½ x 11, Sheetfed press, 8 pages, ISSN: 0096-3917, 2 Color, Newsprint
Subscriptions: Indv. $255, Can. $290, For. $290

Cancer Research News *Consumer, Association*

Publishing Co: Canadian Cancer Society-B.C. Div., 565 W. 10th Ave., Vancouver, BC V5Z 4J4 Canada; Title Tel # (604) 872-4400 Title Fax # (604) 870-4533
Personnel: Editor-Sandra Bishop
Editorial Description: Reports cancer research activities to general readership with focus on British Columbia. Its purpose is to educate health professionals and the public.
General Info: Yr. Est. 1981, Semi-annually, Trim Size-8½ x 11, Offset press, Recycled
Subscriptions: Free
Circulation: Total-3,500
Advertising: Accepts Inserts.

Cancer Researcher Weekly *Business, Association*

Publishing Co: CDC AIDS Weekly/NCI Cancer Weekly, PO Box 5528, Atlanta, GA 30307-0528; Title Tel # (404) 377-8895 Title Fax # (404) 378-5411
Personnel: Editor-WM. Edgar Boggan, Publisher, Adv. Dir.-Charles Henderson
Editorial Description: Comprehensive intl. pub. on cancer with subscribers in the U.S., Asia & Europe.
General Info: (Formerly NCI Cancer Weekly), Yr. Est. 1988, Weekly, Trim Size-8½ x 11, Sheetfed press, 28 pages, ISSN: 0896-7385, Ind/Abs/Online: NewsNet, DIALOG, Predicasts, 2 Color, Newsprint
Subscriptions: Indv. $995, Can. $995, For. $1,195
Acquistions: Publication Bought, Publication Sold
Advertising: Accepts Inserts.
List Rental: Rents Lists

Capitation Management Report
See: HEALTH

Cardiogram

Publishing Co: Reed & Carnick, 257 Cornelison Ave., Jersey City, NJ 07302-3198; Title Tel # (201) 981-0070
General Info: Bi-monthly, 8 pages

Cardiology Newsletter *Association*

Publishing Co: American College of Cardiology, 9111 Old Georgetown Rd, Bethesda, MD 20814-1699 Tel # (301) 897-2694; Title Tel # (301) 897-5400 Title Fax # (301) 897-9745
Personnel: Editor-Suzanne Howard
Editorial Description: Reports activities of the ACC as well as products, services and health policy issues.
General Info: Yr. Est. 1977, Monthly, Trim Size-11 x 14, Sheetfed press, 8 pages, 2 Color, Newsprint
Subscriptions: Indv. $59, Free With Membership
Circulation: Total-21,500

Cardiology Trends & Product News

Publishing Co: Medical Horizons Publishers, 240 Cedar Knolls Rd., #220, Cedar Knolls, NJ 07927-1621
Editorial Description: Covers new developments & products impacting on the field of cardiology.
General Info: (Formerly Cardiology Product News), Yr. Est. 1989, Monthly, ISSN: 1046-1558

Cardiothoracic and Vascular Anesthesia Update

Publishing Co: W.B. Saunders Co., Curtis Ctr., Independence Square West, Philadelphia, PA 19106 Tel # (215) 238-7800 Fax # (215) 238-6445 Parent Co.-Harcourt Brace Professional Publishing, Orlando
Personnel: Editor-Joel Kaplan, MD
Editorial Description: Concise reviews of a current problem or procedure in cardiothoracic and vascular anesthesia.
General Info: Annually, ISSN: 1046-1795, Looseleaf
Subscriptions: Inst. $136, For. $157, $105/copy

Career Services Bulletin *Consumer, Association*

Publishing Co: American College of Sports Medicine, 401 W Michigan St, Indianapolis, IN 46202-3233; Title Tel # (317) 637-9200 Title Fax # (317) 634-7817
Personnel: Publisher-D.M. Robertson, Editor-Virginia Gray
Editorial Description: Job openings, internships, & fellowships in or related to the field of exercise science & sports medicine.
General Info: Yr. Est. 1983, Monthly, Trim Size-8½ x 11, Mimeo press, 16 pages, ISSN: 1060-4219, Newsprint
Subscriptions: Indv. $20
Circulation: Total-15,000
Advertising: Inquire for rates.

Careers in Internal Medicine *Association*

Publishing Co: Assn. of Program Directors in Internal Medicine, 700 13th St NW Ste 250, Washington, DC 20005-3960 Tel # (202) 393-1658
Personnel: Editor-Barbara Schuster
General Info: Quarterly
Circulation: Total-740

Changing Medical Markets *Business*

Publishing Co: Theta Corp., 8 Old Indian Trl, Middlefield, CT 06455-1200 Parent Co.-Phillips Business Information, Inc., Potomac; Title Tel # (203) 349-1054 Title Fax # (203) 349-1227
Personnel: Publisher-Art Klaben, Editor-Phyllis Klaben
Editorial Description: Provides market analysis & forecasts, emerging technologies, new products, summaries of government rulings & regulations, corporate capsules, recaps of journal articles, meetings, abstract from market research reports.
General Info: Yr. Est. 1980, Monthly, Trim Size-8½ x 11, 10 pages, No Color, Coated
Subscriptions: Indv. $195, Can. $225, For. $225, $20/copy
Acquistions: Publication Bought
List Rental: Rents Lists

Children's Hospice International Newsletter
See: CHILDREN

Chinese American Medical Society Newsletter

Publishing Co: Chinese American Medical Society, 281 Edgewood Ave, Teaneck, NJ 07666-3023 Tel # (201) 833-1506 Fax # (201) 833-8252
Personnel: Publisher, Editor-Hsueh-liwa Wang, M.D.
Editorial Description: Listing of scientific meetings, educational tours, news of members, positions wanted and available. Excerpts of papers presented may be included as inserts.
General Info: Yr. Est. 1974, Quarterly, Sheetfed press, Newsprint
Circulation: Total-700
Printing Co: Bal's Offset Printing, 1438 Queen Anne Rd., Teaneck, NJ 07666 Tel # (201) 837-0411

Choices
See: HEALTH

Chronic Pain Letter
See: HEALTH

Chronicle

Publishing Co: Univ. of Osteopathic Med., 3200 Grand Ave, Des Moines, IA 50312-4198; Title Tel # (515) 271-1599
Personnel: Editor-Connie Galbraith
Editorial Description: Alumni newsletter.
General Info: (Formerly Nexus), Yr. Est. 1920, Quarterly, Trim Size-11 x 17, 12 pages, 2 Color
Circulation: (100% controlled), Total-7,000

Citation, The
See: LAW

Citation
See: LAW

Civil Abolitionist
See: HEALTH

Clin-Alert
See: DRUGS & PHARMACEUTICALS

Clinica-World Medical Device & Diagnostic News
See: INSTRUMENTS

Clinical Abstracts/Current Therapeutic Findings
See: DRUGS & PHARMACEUTICALS

Clinical Cancer Letter   *Consumer*

Publishing Co: The Cancer Letter Inc., PO Box 15189, Washington, DC 20003-0189; Title Tel # (202) 543-7665 Title Fax # (202) 543-6879
Personnel: Publisher, Editor-Kirsten Goldberg
Editorial Description: Advances in clinical cancer treatment research.
General Info: Yr. Est. 1978, Monthly, Trim Size-8½ x 11, Offset press, 16 pages, ISSN: 0164-985X, 2 Color
Subscriptions: Indv. $75, Can. $90, For. $90

Clinical Diabetes

Publishing Co: American Diabetes Association, 1660 Duke St, Alexandria, VA 22314-3447; Title Tel # (703) 549-1500 Title Fax # (703) 836-7439
Personnel: Publisher-Susan H. Coughlin, Editor-Marvin Levin, Circ. Mgr.-Gary Frisch, Production Mgr.-Don Jewler, Adv. Dir.-Peggy Donovan Abbott
Editorial Description: Newsletter covering practical diabetes information for the primary care physician.
General Info: Yr. Est. 1983, Bi-monthly, Web press, 24 pages, Ind/Abs/Online: BRS, 4 Color
Subscriptions: Indv. $30, Inst. $40, $7/copy
Circulation: Total-55,000
List Rental: Rents Lists

Clinical Lab Letter   *Consumer*

Publishing Co: Quest Publishing Co., 1351 Titan Way, Brea, CA 92621-3787 Fax # (714) 525-3787 Parent Co.-Lippincott-Raven Press Publishers, Philadelphia; Title Tel # (714) 738-6400 Title Fax # (714) 525-6258
Personnel: Publisher-Steve McCoy, Editor-Marty Matisoff, Mktg. Dir.-Michele Duncan
Editorial Description: For pathologists and clinical lab technologists in the hospital's clinical laboratory.
General Info: Yr. Est. 1980, Semi-monthly, Trim Size-8½ x 11, Offset press, 8 pages, ISSN: 0197-8454, No Color, Newsprint, Saddle-stitched
Subscriptions: Indv. $270, Can. $270, For. $310
List Rental: Rents Lists

Clinical Laser Monthly   *Consumer*

Publishing Co: American Health Consultants, Inc., 3525 Piedmont Rd., Building #6, Ste. 400, Atlanta, GA 30305-0056 Tel # (404) 262-7436 Fax # (404) 284-3291
Personnel: Publisher-Dr. Leslie Norins, Editor-Kim Klesty, Production Mgr.-Terri Sherrod, Adv. Dir.-David Wilson, Art Dir.-Robin Salet
Editorial Description: Practical news and expert advice for users of clinical lasers.
General Info: Yr. Est. 1983, Monthly, Trim Size-8½ x 11, Offset press, 16 pages, Ind/Abs/Online: Mead Data Central
Subscriptions: Indv. $159
Acquistions: Publication Bought, Publication Sold
Circulation: Total-1,750
List Rental: Actives: $100/M

Clinical Microbiology Reports

Publishing Co: W.B. Saunders Co., Curtis Ctr., Independence Square West, Philadelphia, PA 19106 Tel # (215) 238-7800 Fax # (215) 238-6445 Parent Co.-Harcourt Brace Professional Publishing, Orlando
Personnel: Editor-Irving Nachamkin, DrPH
Editorial Description: Presents critical evaluations of the most important new tests reported in the literature.
General Info: Monthly, ISSN: 1062-8150
Subscriptions: Indv. $89, Inst. $129, For. $139, $18/copy

Collected Letters in Obstetrics & Gynecology   *Business*

Publishing Co: DML Associates, Inc., 367 W. Main St., PO Box 1130, Northboro, MA 01532 Parent Co.-Adams/Laux Publishing Co., Inc., Maynard; Title Tel # (508) 393-1644 Title Fax # (508) 393-1594
Personnel: Publisher-Dean M. Laux, Editor-Miriam Laux
Editorial Description: Expert review and commentary on clinical cases in obstetrics and gynecology.
General Info: Yr. Est. 1960, Monthly, Trim Size-8½ x 11, Offset press, 12 pages, ISSN: 0443-9058, No Color
Subscriptions: Indv. $99, Can. $129, For. $129, $10/copy
Acquistions: Publication Bought
Circulation: Total-3,500
List Rental: Actives: $65/M

Collected Letters in Surgery   *Business, Association*

Publishing Co: Adams/Laux Publishing Co., Inc., 63 Great Road, Maynard, MA 01754 Tel # (508) 897-5552 Fax # (508) 897-6824; Title Tel # (508) 393-1644 Title Fax # (508) 393-1594
Personnel: Publisher-Dean Laux, Editor-Miriam Laux
Editorial Description: Expert review and commentary on clinical cases in surgery.
General Info: Yr. Est. 1978, Monthly, Trim Size-8½ x 11, 8 pages, ISSN: 0162-6477, No Color, Newsprint
Subscriptions: Indv. $99, Can. $129, For. $129, $10/copy
Acquistions: Publication Bought
Circulation: Total-1,000
List Rental: Actives: $65/M

Collier, Sarner & Associates Doctors Newsletter
See: BANKING & FINANCE

Community Alert   *Consumer, Association*

Publishing Co: Natl. Hemophilia Foundation, 110 Greene St Apt 303, New York, NY 10012-3832; Title Tel # (212) 219-8180 Title Fax # (212) 966-9247
Personnel: Editor-Jodie Corngold
Editorial Description: For members of the hemophilia community and its members.
General Info: (Formerly Hemophilia Newsnotes), Yr. Est. 1972, Monthly, Trim Size-8½ x 11, 24 pages, 2 Color, Coated, Saddle-stitched
Subscriptions: Free With Membership
Circulation: Total-15,000, Readership-15,000

Comparative Pathology Bulletin

Publishing Co: Registry of Comparative Pathology, Armed Forces Inst. Of Pathol., Washington, DC 20306-0001; Title Tel # (202) 576-2452 Title Fax # (202) 576-2164
Personnel: Editor-Linda K. Johnson
Editorial Description: Contains 1 feature article, 2 descriptions of animal models of human disease, and announcements of interest to the biomedical community.
General Info: Yr. Est. 1969, Quarterly, Trim Size-8½ x 11, 6 pages, No Color, Coated, Saddle-stitched
Subscriptions: Indv. $10, Inst. $10, Can. $10, For. $10
Circulation: Total-1,000
List Rental: Rents Lists
Printing Co: Information Services, Inc., 4733 Bethesda Ave Ste 700, Bethesda, MD 20814-5228 Tel # (301) 656-2942

Comprehensive Medline

Publishing Co: EBSCO, 83 Pine Street, PO Box 2250, Peabody, MA 01960-7250 Tel # (508) 535-8500 Fax # (508) 535-8545
General Info: (Formerly Comprehensive Medline)
Subscriptions: Indv. $900

Connections   *Association*

Publishing Co: Natl. Medical Fellowships, 110 W 32st St, New York, NY 10001; Title Tel # (212) 714-0933
Personnel: Editor-Brian Byrd
General Info: (Formerly National Medical Fellowships Newsletter; News Updates), Quarterly, Trim Size-8½ x 11, Offset press, 6 pages, 2 Color, Matte
Subscriptions: Free With Membership
Circulation: Total-11,000

Connective Issues

Publishing Co: Natl. Marfan Foundation, 382 Main St., Pt. Washington, NY 11050-3121; Title Tel # (516) 883-8712
Personnel: Publisher, Editor-Priscilla Ciccariello
Editorial Description: Provides communication between & information for people affected by the Marfan Syndrome, their families, the public and the medical profession.
General Info: Yr. Est. 1983, Quarterly, Trim Size-8 x 11, 14 pages, ISSN: 8756-9086
Subscriptions: Inst. $25
Circulation: Total-9,000

Conomikes Medicare
Hotline   *Business, Consumer*

Publishing Co: Conomikes Reports, Inc., 6033 W. Century Blvd. #990, Los Angeles, CA 90045-5309
   Tel # (610) 645-5100; Title Tel # (310) 645-5100 Title Fax # (310) 645-3224
Personnel: Publisher, Editor-George Conomikes, Circ. Dir., Promotion Dir.-Laura Pursell
Editorial Description: Information service helping physicians through the medicine maze.
General Info: Monthly, Trim Size-8½ x 11, Offset press, 8 pages, 2 Color
Subscriptions: Indv. $135, Inst. $135, Can. $135
Circulation: Total-1,841
Printing Co: CompuArtist, 2216 Federal Ave, Los Angeles, CA 90064-1404 Tel # (310) 477-0407

Conomikes Reports on
Medical Practice
Management

Publishing Co: Conomikes Reports, Inc., 6033 W. Century Blvd. #990, Los Angeles, CA 90045-5309
   Tel # (610) 645-5100; Title Tel # (310) 645-5100 Title Fax # (310) 645-3224
Editorial Description: Focuses on methods of medical practice management.
General Info: Yr. Est. 1981, Monthly
Subscriptions: Indv. $135, Inst. $135, Can. $135
Circulation: Total-3,023
Printing Co: CompuArtist, 2216 Federal Ave, Los Angeles, CA 90064-1404 Tel # (310) 477-0407

Conservative Orthopaedics
Intl. Assn.   *Association*

Publishing Co: Industrial Chemical Research Association, 1811 Monroe St, Dearborn, MI
   48124-2924; Title Tel # (313) 563-0360 Title Fax # (313) 563-0360
General Info: Yr. Est. 1982, Quarterly
Acquistions: Publication Bought
Circulation: Total-6,200

Consultant's Newsletter
See: MANAGEMENT

Consumer Reports on Health
See: HEALTH

Contact   *Association*

Publishing Co: World Council of Churches, 475 Riverside Dr., Ste 915, New York, NY 10115-0122
   Fax # (212) 870-2528; Title Tel # (212) 870-3340
Editorial Description: Christian Medical Commission news.
General Info: Bi-monthly

Contact
See: PHYSIOLOGY

Contact
See: HEARING & SPEECH

Contact Lens Update
See: OPTICAL

Contemporary Diagnostic
Radiology

Publishing Co: Williams & Wilkins, 351 W. Camden St., Baltimore, MD 21201-2436
   Tel # (410) 528-4068 Fax # (410) 528-4452; Title Tel # (410) 528-4000
Personnel: Publisher-Alma Wills, Editor-Robert Campbell, M. D., Circ. Mgr.-Maria Reid
Editorial Description: Contemporary Diagnostic Radiology keeps readers informed of complex
   developments, new procedures, and advances in technology. And with this continuing medical
   education program, practicing radiologists and residents to review and update their knowledge o
   basic radiologic concepts while earning CME credits.
General Info: Yr. Est. 1976, Bi-weekly, Trim Size-8½ x 11, 4 pages, ISSN: 0149-9007
Subscriptions: Indv. $260
Circulation: Total-1,709

Continuing Care Connection
See: HEALTH

Continuing Medical
Education Newsletter   *Association*

Publishing Co: American Medical Association, 515 N. State St., Chicago, IL 60610
   Tel # (312) 464-4512 Fax # (312) 464-5834; Title Tel # (312) 645-4952

Core Medline

Publishing Co: EBSCO, 83 Pine Street, PO Box 2250, Peabody, MA 01960-7250
   Tel # (508) 535-8500 Fax # (508) 535-8545
Editorial Description: A subject of Medline, this file includes more than 560 journals all indexed on
   one disc.
Subscriptions: Indv. $950

Creative Health Newsletter
See: HEALTH

Cureletter
See: MANUFACTURING

DATA - The Brown
University Digest of
Addiction Theory and
Application   *Business*

Publishing Co: Manisses Communications Group, Inc., PO Box 3357, Providence, RI 02906-0757
   Fax # (401) 861-6370; Title Tel # (401) 831-6020
Personnel: Publisher-Fraser Lang, Editor-David Lewis, M.D., Circ. Mgr.-Deb Zajas, Promotion Dir.-
   Betty Lang
Editorial Description: Digest of professional research journals from many disciplines covering
   addiction.
General Info: (Formerly Dig. of Add. Theo. & App.), Yr. Est. 1981, Monthly, 52 pages, ISSN: 1040-
   6328
Subscriptions: Indv. $127, Inst. $157, Can. $167, For. $177
Acquistions: Publication Bought, Publication Sold
Circulation: Total-4,000
List Rental: Actives: 5,000, $100/M
Printing Co: Newsletter Press, 76 Valley St, East Providence, RI 02914-4424 Tel # (401) 438-5352

DES Action Voice
See: HEALTH

Dean's Rounds

Publishing Co: Tufts Univ., Communications & Publ. Rel., 419 Boston Ave., Medford, MA 02155;
   Title Tel # (617) 956-5705
Editorial Description: News & research information from Tufts Univ. School of Medicine.
General Info: Yr. Est. 1973, Semi-annually, Trim Size-8½ x 11, Web press, 2 Color
Circulation: Total-10,000

Decisions   *Association*

Publishing Co: Medical Research Council of Canada, Holland Cross, 5th fl. Tower B, 1600 Scott St.,
   Ottawa, ON K1A 0W9 Canada; Title Tel # (613) 954-1806 Title Fax # (613) 954-6653
Personnel: Editor-Neil Morris
Editorial Description: Decisions made at meeting of the council.
General Info: Yr. Est. 1992, Tri-annually, 6 pages

Devices & Diagnostics Letter
See: HEALTH

Diagnostic Imaging Scan

Publishing Co: Miller Freeman, Inc., 1 Penn Plaza, 10th Fl., New York, NY 10119-1198
Personnel: Publisher-Vicki Masseria, Editor-Roger Lindahl, Circ. Mgr.-Michael Newton, Production
   Mgr.-Andy Mickus
Editorial Description: The Business Biweekly of Medical Imaging.
General Info: Yr. Est. 1986
Subscriptions: Indv. $497

Diagnostic Quarterly

Publishing Co: Scientific Newsletters, Rr 4 Box 7, Middletown, NY 10940-9685;
   Title Tel # (914) 355-9144 Title Fax # (914) 355-9147
Personnel: Publisher, Editor-Marc Duey, Circ. Mgr.-Maureen Duey
Editorial Description: Review of significant news & events in the world-wide in-vitro diagnostic
   industry, including reporting & analysis of new technology & products.
General Info: Yr. Est. 1989, Quarterly
Subscriptions: Indv. $995, For. $995

Diagnostics Intelligence
See: DRUGS & PHARMACEUTICALS

Dialogues in Pediatric
Urology

Publishing Co: William J. Miller Assoc., Inc., 45 Villa Rd., Pearl River, NY 10965-1440;
   Title Tel # (914) 735-7853 Title Fax # (914) 735-6628
Personnel: Publisher-William Miller, Editor-Richard Ehrlich, M. D., Circ. Mgr.-Tim Miller, Production
   Mgr.-Mark Mellilo
Editorial Description: Clinical articles in the area of pediatric urology/surgery for physician
   specialists.
General Info: Yr. Est. 1977, Monthly, Trim Size-8½ x 11, Offset press, 8 pages, ISSN: 0164-9507,
   No Color, Recycled, Saddle-stitched
Subscriptions: Indv. $58, Inst. $58, Can. $60, For. $65, $4/copy
Circulation: Total-680
Printing Co: Print Sprint, 160 W Nyack Rd, West Nyack, NY 10994-1709 Tel # (914) 358-1374

Dickinson's FDA Review
See: DRUGS & PHARMACEUTICALS

Dickinson's FDA Update by Fax
See: DRUGS & PHARMACEUTICALS

Dickinson's Pharmacy
See: DRUGS & PHARMACEUTICALS

Dining with Heart   *Consumer*

Publishing Co: Thomas Jefferson University Hospital, 11th and Chestnut Streets, Philadelphia, PA
   19107 Parent Co.-Thomas Jefferson University, Philadelphia
Editorial Description: Information about heart disease and treatment; also contains reviews of
   restaurants that offer 'heart smart' dining.
General Info: Trim Size-8½ x 11, 6 pages, 2 Color, Matte
Subscriptions: Free To Qualified Recipient

Disabilities Issues
See: DISABILITY

Doctor - Patient Studies   *Business*

Publishing Co: GSB/CHAS, 5627 S Drexel Ave, Chicago, IL 60637-1417; Title Tel # (312) 702-1453 Title Fax # (312) 702-0090
Personnel: Publisher-Mark Siegler, Editor-J. Hughes
Editorial Description: For doctors, ethicists, social scientists and others interested in research concerning doctor/patient relationships.
General Info: Yr. Est. 1990, Bi-monthly
Subscriptions: $1/copy
Circulation: (80% controlled), Total-250

Doctors for Disaster Preparedness
See: HEALTH

Doctor's Office, The
See: MANAGEMENT

Doctor's Office Lab News   *Consumer*

Publishing Co: Scientific Newsletters, Rr 4 Box 7, Middletown, NY 10940-9685; Title Tel # (714) 240-3579
Personnel: Publisher, Editor-Marc Duey, Circ. Mgr.-Maureen Duey
Editorial Description: Products, training tips, government regs, meetings, literature meetings, cost-executiveness.
General Info: (Formerly Doctor's In-Office Lab News), Yr. Est. 1985, 10x/yr., Trim Size-8½ x 11, Offset press, 10 pages, No Color
Subscriptions: Indv. $100, For. $115, $10/copy
Acquistions: Publication Bought, Publication Sold
Circulation: Total-1,500
List Rental: Actives: $75/M

Doctor's Tax Report
See: TAXES

Double Helix   *Association*

Publishing Co: Natl. Foundation for Infectious Diseases, 4733 Bethesda Ave Ste 750, Bethesda, MD 20814-5228; Title Tel # (301) 656-0003 Title Fax # (301) 907-0878
Personnel: Editor-Richard Duma, MD, PhD
Editorial Description: Supports education for the prevention of infectious diseases.
General Info: Yr. Est. 1975, Bi-monthly, Trim Size-8½ x 11, 6 pages, ISSN: 1064-1815, 2 Color
Subscriptions: Free
Circulation: Total-20,000
List Rental: Actives: $100/M

Down Syndrome News
See: GENETICS

Dramascope
See: PSYCHOLOGY

Drug & Market Development
See: DRUGS & PHARMACEUTICALS

Drug Facts and Comparisons Loose Leaf Edition
See: DRUGS & PHARMACEUTICALS

Drug GMP Report
See: DRUGS & PHARMACEUTICALS

Drug Interaction Facts Package
See: DRUGS & PHARMACEUTICALS

EMS Insider   *Business, Consumer*

Publishing Co: JEMS Communications Inc., PO Box 2789, Carlsbad, CA 92018-2789; Title Tel # (619) 431-9797 Title Fax # (619) 431-8176
Personnel: Publisher-Jim Page, Editor-Marion Gaeza, Circ. Mgr.-Pamela Stevenson, Production Mgr.-Janene Long-Forman, Art Dir.-Harriett Wilcox, Adv. Dir., Mktg. Dir.-Richard Bilger, Promotion Dir.-Gary Williams
Editorial Description: Newsletter providing emergency medical services managers and leaders with timely, useful information relative to the provision of emergency services.
General Info: Yr. Est. 1973, Monthly, Trim Size-8⅜ x 10⅞, Web press, 80 pages, 4 Color, Coated, Saddle-stitched
Subscriptions: Indv. $120, Can. $96, For. $100
Circulation: Total-1,600
List Rental: Actives: 1,500

E.M.S. Officer's Notebook

Publishing Co: Fire-Medic Services, 19 Joslin St., Providence, RI 02909-2599; Title Tel # (401) 751-6217
Personnel: Publisher, Editor-Thomas Lopatosky
Editorial Description: Ideas and information to assist officers of emergence medical service agencies with their supervisory and other duties.
General Info: Yr. Est. 1990, Bi-weekly, Looseleaf
Subscriptions: Indv. $35, $2/copy

Emergency Department Law
See: LAW

Emergency Medicine Reports

Publishing Co: American Health Consultants, Inc., 3525 Piedmont Rd., Building #6, Ste. 400, Atlanta, GA 30305-0056 Tel # (404) 262-7436 Fax # (404) 284-3291; Title Tel # (404) 351-4523 Title Fax # (404) 262-7837
Personnel: Publisher-David Wilson, Editor in Chief-Gideon Bosker, M.D., Mng. Editor-Gayle Childers, Circ. Mgr.-Monica Brown, Production Mgr.-Mike Witter, Mktg. Mgr.-Shawn Demario
Editorial Description: Educational materials in emergency medicine bi-weekly topics; credit available.
General Info: (Formerly E.R. Reports), Yr. Est. 1980, Bi-weekly, Trim Size-8½ x 11, Sheetfed press, 8 pages, ISSN: 0732-9628, Ind/Abs/Online: BRS, Color
Subscriptions: Indv. $229, $10/copy
Acquistions: Publication Bought, Publication Sold
List Rental: List Management Co.: Manager: Lawrence Cohen; AllMedia, Inc., 4965 Preston Park Blvd Ste 300, Plano, TX 75093-8397 Tel # (214) 985-4060, Fax # (214) 985-4061, Actives: $125/M

Emerging Pharmaceuticals
See: DRUGS & PHARMACEUTICALS

Endometriosis Assn. International Newsletter
See: HEALTH

Essex County Medical Society Bulletin   *Business, Association*

Publishing Co: Essex County Medical Society, 80 Compton Ave., Verona, NJ 07044; Title Tel # (201) 239-9392
Personnel: Publisher-Arthur Ellenburger, Editor-Mark Oleshinsky
Editorial Description: Covers local medical news of interest to assn. members.
General Info: 9x/yr., Trim Size-6 x 9
Circulation: Total-1,900
Advertising: Inquire for rates.

Ethics and Medics   *Business, Association*

Publishing Co: Pope John XXIII Ctr., 186 Forbes Rd., Braintree, MA 02184-2612; Title Tel # (617) 848-6965 Title Fax # (617) 849-1309
Personnel: Publisher-Russell Smith, Editor-Rev. Albert Moraczewski, Circ. Mgr.-Donald Powers, Mktg. Dir.-Margaret Mary Turner
Editorial Description: Ethics & Medics provides a Catholic perspective on medical ethics issues in the entire range of health & life sciences.
General Info: Yr. Est. 1976, Monthly, Trim Size-8½ x 11, Offset press, 4 pages, ISSN: 1071-3778, Color, Newsprint
Subscriptions: Indv. $18, For. $20, $1/copy
Circulation: Total-24,000
Printing Co: Jay-Way Graphics, Inc., 1227 Saint Louis Ave, Saint Louis, MO 63106-4034 Tel # (314) 241-7195

Europe Drug & Device Report
See: DRUGS & PHARMACEUTICALS

Executive Briefings on Hospital Regulation   *Business*

Publishing Co: Opus Communications, Inc., Box 1168, 100 Hoods Lane, Marblehead, MA 01945; Title Tel # (617) 639-1872 Title Fax # (617) 639-2982
Personnel: Publisher-Jennifer Cofer, Editor-William Wrinn
Editorial Description: A guide for hospital administrators. Interprets JCAHO standards & regulations and how best to meet them.
General Info: Yr. Est. 1994, Monthly, Trim Size-8½ x 11, 12 pages, ISSN: 1078-1900, 2 Color, Saddle-stitched
Subscriptions: Indv. $197
List Rental: Rents Lists

Executive Health's Good Health Report
See: HEALTH

FSMBNewsLine   *Association*

Publishing Co: Fed. of State Medical Boards of the U.S., Inc., 400 Fuller Wiser Road, Suite #300, Euless, TX 76039-3855; Title Tel # (817) 868-4000 Title Fax # (817) 686-4098
Personnel: Publisher-Linda C. Chandler, Editor-Linda Chandler
Editorial Description: A newsletter focused on current issues of interest to medical licensing and disciplinary authorities.
General Info: (Formerly FSMB Newsletter), Yr. Est. 1981, Monthly, Trim Size-8½ x 11, 2 pages, ISSN: 1062-5380, No Color
Subscriptions: Indv. $35, Inst. $35, Can. $35, For. $35, $4/copy
Circulation: Total-2,000
Printing Co: Cockrell Printing Co., 301 Galveston Ave, Fort Worth, TX 76104-1239 Tel # (817) 336-0571, Fax # (817) 654-3719

Facial Plastic Times

Publishing Co: American Academy of Facial Plastic & Reconstructive Surgery, 1110 Vermont Ave NW Ste 220, Washington, DC 20005-3522; Title Tel # (202) 842-4500
Personnel: Editor-Stacy Poliquin
General Info: Yr. Est. 1980, Bi-monthly, 8 pages

Fax-Stat on Drugs
See: DRUGS & PHARMACEUTICALS

Federal Air Surgeon's Medical Bulletin
See: AERONAUTICS/ASTRONAUTICS

Federal Physicians, The   *Association*   **CPM: $600**

Publishing Co: Financial Programs, Inc., 8621 Silver Oak Ct., Springfield, VA 22153-2129; Title Tel # (703) 455-5947 Title Fax # (703) 455-8282
Personnel: Publisher-Dennis Boyd, Editor-Jack Gribben, Production Mgr.-Nilk Cordovana
General Info: (Formerly Federal Physician Association), Yr. Est. 1979, Bi-monthly, 16 pages, ISSN: 1070-9029, 13% ads, 2 Color, Saddle-stitched
Subscriptions: Indv. $35, Free With Membership
Circulation: (100% controlled), Total-500
Advertising: $300.

Federation of American Health Systems Hotline

Publishing Co: Federation of American Hospitals, 1111 19th St NW Ste 402, Washington, DC 20036-3603; Title Tel # (202) 833-3090 Title Fax # (202) 861-0063
Personnel: Editor-Thomas Goodwin
General Info: Yr. Est. 1968, Bi-weekly

Fed. of Medical Specialists of Quebec, Bulletin

Publishing Co: Fed. of Medical Specialists of Quebec, CP 216 Succ. Desjardins, Montreal, PQ H5B 1G8 Canada
General Info: Monthly

Fed. of Medical Women of Canada, Newsletter   *Association*

Publishing Co: Fed. of Medical Women of Canada, 106, 1815 Alta Vista Dr., Ottawa, ON K1G 3Y6 Canada; Title Tel # (613) 731-1026 Title Fax # (613) 523-7736
Personnel: Editor-Catherine Lewis
Editorial Description: Information to members about Federation affairs & to publish material about issues, resources & opportunities of specific interest to medical women.
General Info: Quarterly, Trim Size-8 x 10, 12 pages, Matte
Subscriptions: Free With Membership
Acquisitions: Publication Bought
Circulation: Readership-800
Advertising: Accepts Inserts.

Fertility News   *Association*

Publishing Co: American Fertility Society for Reproductive Medicine, 1209 Montgomery Hwy., Birmingham, AL 35216-2809 Tel # (205) 978-5000 Fax # (205) 978-5005; Title Tel # (205) 933-8494
Personnel: Production Mgr.-Frances Crowe
Editorial Description: Promotes knowledge of all aspects of fertility, infertility, & mammalian reproduction. Documents the activities of the Society & its members in the field of reproductive medicine. Also includes a medical newsletter on reproductive endocrinology & fertili y.
General Info: Yr. Est. 1944, Quarterly, 20 pages, 2 Color, Coated, Saddle-stitched
Circulation: Total-10,500
List Rental: Rents Lists

Fighting Blindness News

Publishing Co: Foundation Fighting Blindness, The, Executive Plaza, 11350 McCormick Rd., Ste. 800, Hunt Valley, MD 21031; Title Tel # (410) 785-1414 Title Fax # (410) 771-9470
Personnel: Editor-Vivian Smith, Mktg. Dir.-Mike Conner
Editorial Description: National newsletter of The Foundation Fighting Blindness, featuring news on retinitis pigmentosa, mocular degeneration, usher syndrome & related retinal degenerative diseases. Includes research, fund raising news, some general items for visually impaired.
General Info: Yr. Est. 1972, Quarterly, Trim Size-8½ x 11, Web press, 16 pages, ISSN: 0899-7756, No Color, Matte
Circulation: Total-80,000

Flower Essence Society Newsletter
See: HEALTH

Focus   *Consumer*

Publishing Co: Harvard Univ. News Office for the Medical Area, 25 Shattuck St, Boston, MA 02115-6027; Title Tel # (617) 432-1590
Editorial Description: Basic and clinical research in medicine, public health and dentistry.
General Info: Yr. Est. 1976, Weekly, Trim Size-8 x 11, Letrpr. press, 12 pages
Subscriptions: Indv. $15
Circulation: Total-8,200

Focus on Geriatric Care & Rehabilitation
See: HEALTH

Forefront: The Newsletter for Optometric Staff
See: OPTICAL

Forensic Drug Abuse Advisor
See: DRUGS & PHARMACEUTICALS

Foundation for Biomedical Research-Newsletter

Publishing Co: Foundation for Biomedical Research, 818 Connecticut Ave NW Ste 303, Washington, DC 20006-2702; Title Tel # (202) 457-0654
Personnel: Editor-Eileen O'Donnell
General Info: Yr. Est. 1984, Bi-monthly, 4 pages

Frontiers in Immunoassay & Biotechnology
See: SCIENCE

Frontiers in Immunology & Biotechnology Scientific Newsletter
See: MICROBIOLOGY

Future Technology Intelligence Report
See: SCIENCE

GMP Letter, The
See: HEALTH

Gathered View, The
See: DISABILITY

Gaucher's Disease Registry Newsletter
See: HEALTH

Genetic Technology News
See: GENETICS

Geriatric Medicine Alerts   *Business*

Publishing Co: M.J. Powers, 374 Millburn Ave, Millburn, NJ 07041-1361 Tel # (201) 467-4556 Fax # (201) 912-8883
Personnel: Publisher-John Roche
Editorial Description: Covers latest news in geriatric medicine.
General Info: Yr. Est. 1994, Monthly, Trim Size-8½ x 11, 8 pages
Subscriptions: Indv. $59

Geriatric Psychiatry News
See: PSYCHOLOGY

Gerontology News   *Association*

Publishing Co: Sponsor-The Gerontological Society of America, Gerontological Society of America, The, 1275 K St NW Ste 350, Washington, DC 20005-4006 Fax # (202) 842-1150; Title Tel # (202) 842-1275
Personnel: Publisher-Carol A. Schutz, Editor, Production Mgr., Adv. Dir.-Shirley Brown, Promotion Dir.-Elizabeth Borgen
Editorial Description: Reports on policy issues, new resources & reports research highlights, grants awarded.
General Info: Yr. Est. 1978, Monthly, Offset press, 12 pages, No Color
Subscriptions: Indv. $50
Circulation: (94% controlled), Total-7,100
Advertising: Inquire for rates.
List Rental: Actives: $90/M
Printing Co: Corporate Press, 403 Brightseat Rd., Landover, MD 20785-4706 Tel # (301) 499-9200, Fax # (301) 499-5435

Gleams   *Business, Association*

Publishing Co: Glaucoma Research Fondation, 490 Post St Ste 830, San Francisco, CA 94102-1409 Fax # (415) 986-3162; Title Tel # (415) 986-3162 Title Fax # (415) 986-3763
Personnel: Editor-Lisa Wagreich
Editorial Description: Layperson's information on glaucoma diagnosis, treatment & research.
General Info: Yr. Est. 1982, Quarterly, Trim Size-8½ x 11, Sheetfed press, 6 pages, ISSN: 1072-7906, 2 Color, Newsprint
Subscriptions: Free
Circulation: Total-26,000, Readership-30,000
Printing Co: Schultz Printing, PO Box 2782, Sausalito, CA 94966-2782 Tel # (415) 331-3858

Global Missions
See: SOCIAL SERVICES & WELFARE

Gray Sheet: Medical Devices, Diagnostics & Instrumentation Reports   *Business*

Publishing Co: F-D-C Reports, Inc., 5550 Friendship Blvd, Chevy Chase, MD 20815-7278; Title Tel # (301) 657-9830 Title Fax # (301) 986-6467
Personnel: Publisher-Wallace Werble, Jr., Editor-Cole Palmer Werble, Circ. Dir.-Edward Picken, Adv. Dir.-Richard Messmer
Editorial Description: Reports on govt. regulatory and congressional actions affecting medical device industry, and review of the industry itself with financial analysis.
General Info: Yr. Est. 1974, Weekly, Trim Size-8½ x 11, Letrpr. press, 24 pages, ISSN: 0163-2426, Ind/Abs/Online: Mead Data, Data-Star, DIALOG, BRS, PNI, Color
Subscriptions: Indv. $630, Can. $630,570, For. $705, $18/copy

Grey Folder   *Association*

Publishing Co: New York Academy of Medicine, 2 E 103rd St, New York, NY 10029-5207; Title Tel # (212) 876-8200
Editorial Description: Program listing of activities of the academy.
General Info: Yr. Est. 1847, Monthly, Trim Size-6 x 9, Offset press, 30 pages
Circulation: Total-500

Group Practice

Publishing Co: Ontario Assn. of Medical Clinics, 2045 Dufferin St., Toronto, ON M6E 3R4 Canada; Title Tel # (416) 651-6633
General Info: Bi-monthly

Guide to Good Clinical Practice
See: MANAGEMENT

Guide to Medical Device Regulation
Business

Publishing Co: Thompson Publishing Group, 1725 K Street, NW, Washington, DC 20006
Tel # (202) 872-4000
Editorial Description: Guide to FDA regulation of medical devices.
General Info: Monthly
Subscriptions: Indv. $547

HANDI Information Center Update
See: HEALTH

HANDI Quarterly
See: HEALTH

HANYS News
See: HEALTH

HLB Newsletter
Business

Publishing Co: British Trading Co., 821 Delaware Ave SW, Washington, DC 20024-4207;
Title Tel # (202) 488-7533
Personnel: Publisher, Editor-Nathaniel Polster, Circ. Mgr.-Dale Zarb
Editorial Description: Heart, lung, blood and allied subjects research policy.
General Info: Yr. Est. 1985, Semi-monthly, ISSN: 0887-3712
Subscriptions: Indv. $296, Inst. $296, Can. $296, For. $346, $15/copy

Harvard AIDS Letter
Consumer

Publishing Co: Harvard AIDS Institute, 8 Story St, Cambridge, MA 02138-4925 Tel # (617) 495-0478
Fax # (617) 495-2863
Editorial Description: News from the AIDS community at Harvard.
General Info: Bi-monthly

Harvard Heart Letter
See: HEALTH

Health & Healing
Consumer

Publishing Co: Phillips Publishing, Inc., 7811 Montrose Rd., Potomac, MD 20854-3394
Fax # (301) 294-1307 Parent Co.-Phillips Business Information, Inc., Potomac;
Title Tel # (301) 340-2100 Title Fax # (301) 424-8202
Personnel: Publisher-Thomas L. Phillips, Editor-Julian Whitaker, Mktg. Dir.-Brendan Talty
Editorial Description: Dr. Julian Whitaker provides information on cutting edge medical research & alternative treatments such as healing foods, chelation therapy, beta carotene, vitamins, minerals & herbs.
General Info: Yr. Est. 1991, Monthly, Trim Size-8½ x 11, 8 pages, ISSN: 1057-9273
Subscriptions: Indv. $40, $7/copy
List Rental: List Management Co.: Manager: John Baldwin; Phillips Publishing List Marketing, 7811 Montrose Rd., Potomac, MD 20854-3394 Tel # (301) 340-2100, Fax # (301) 294-1307, Actives: 483,790, $125/M, Expires: 363,347, $85/M

Health Education Reports
See: HEALTH

Health Exchange
See: HEALTH

Health Facts
See: HEALTH

Health Law Litigation Reporter
See: LAW

Health News
See: HEALTH

Health Professions Report
See: EDUCATION

Health and Stress: The News Letter of the American Institute of Stress
Business, Association

Publishing Co: American Institute of Stress, Inc., 124 Park Ave, Yonkers, NY 10703-2904;
Title Tel # (914) 963-1200 Title Fax # (914) 965-6267
Personnel: Editor-Paul Rosch, MD
Editorial Description: Reviews & reports on all stress related matters.
General Info: (Formerly Practical Stress Management), Yr. Est. 1983, Monthly, Trim Size-8½ x 11, Letrpr. press, 8 pages, 2 Color, Coated, Saddle-stitched
Subscriptions: Indv. $35, Can. $45, For. $45
Circulation: Total-2,000
Printing Co: Gazette Press, Inc., 16 School St., Yonkers, NY 10701 Tel # (914) 963-8300, Fax # (914) 476-1052

HealthCare Systems NewsLetter
See: HEALTH

Healthcare Advocate
See: HOSPITALS & NURSING HOMES

Healthcare Investor
See: INVESTMENT

Healthcare Trends Report
See: HEALTH

HeartStyle
Association

Publishing Co: American Heart Association, 7272 Greenville Ave, Dallas, TX 75231-4596
Tel # (214) 706-1426 Fax # (214) 691-6342; Title Tel # (214) 706-1392
Personnel: Editor-Phil Kibak, Circ. Mgr.-Rosa Tamez
Editorial Description: Quarterly newsletter on research on heart & blood vessel disease.
General Info: (Formerly Cardiovascular Research Report), Yr. Est. 1978, Quarterly, Trim Size-8½ x 11, Offset press, 8 pages, 2 Color, Newsprint, Saddle-stitched
Circulation: Total-57,000

Helper
See: HEALTH

Hemlock Timelines
Consumer, Association **CPM: $71**

Publishing Co: Hemlock Society, 1551 Pearl St., Eugene, OR 97440-4030;
Title Tel # (503) 342-5748 Title Fax # (503) 345-2751
Personnel: Production Dir.-Robin Fletcher, Editor, Adv. Dir.-Kris Larson
Editorial Description: Provides background on questions associated with voluntary euthanasia.
General Info: (Formerly Hemlock Quarterly), Yr. Est. 1980, Quarterly, Trim Size-8½ x 11, Web press, 16 pages, ISSN: 0742-5376, 2 Color, Newsprint, Saddle-stitched
Subscriptions: Indv. $25, Can. $40, For. $40
Circulation: Total-35,000
Advertising: $2,500.
List Rental: List Management Co.: Manager: Robin Fletcher; Certified Mailing Lists, 4 Candlebush, Irvine, CA 92715-3727 Tel # (503) 342-5748
Printing Co: Northwest Web, 3592 W. 5th Ave., Eugene, OR 97402-5397 Tel # (503) 345-0552, Fax # (503) 484-0026

Hemophilia Today

Publishing Co: Canadian Hemophilia Society, 1450 City Councillors, #840, Montreal, PQ H3A 2E6 Canada; Title Tel # (514) 848-0503
Personnel: Editor-Dawn Rutherford
General Info: Yr. Est. 1964, Quarterly, Trim Size-8½ x 11, 6 pages, 2 Color, Newsprint, Saddle-stitched
Circulation: Total-4,500

Hepatitis B Coalition News
See: HEALTH

Hepatitis Weekly
Business

Publishing Co: C.W. Henderson Publisher, Medical Center II, P.O. Box 5528, Atlanta, GA 31107-0528 Tel # (404) 507-7777 Fax # (404) 507-7788
Editorial Description: Worlwide news and information on Hepatitis.
General Info: Yr. Est. 1995, Weekly
Subscriptions: Indv. $1,095, Can. $1,095, For. $1,295

Herbal Healer Academy Newsletter
See: HEALTH

High Performance Optometry

Publishing Co: Anadem, Inc., 3620 N High St Ste 310, Columbus, OH 43214-3643;
Title Tel # (614) 262-2539
Personnel: Publisher-Will Kuhlmann, Editor-Arol Augsburger, Production Mgr.-Cindy Taylor, Adv. Dir.-L. Joe Gaietto
Editorial Description: Digests medical & optometric journal articles about diagnosis & management of vision disorders & ocular disease.
General Info: Yr. Est. 1987, Bi-monthly, Trim Size-8½ x 11, ISSN: 0894-5810
Subscriptions: Indv. $76, Inst. $69, Can. $79, For. $84

Home Advantage
See: ADVERTISING & MARKETING

Homeopathic Research Reports

Publishing Co: Foundation for Homeopathic Education and Research, 2124 Kittredge St., Berkeley, CA 94704-1436; Title Tel # (510) 649-8930
Personnel: Editor-Dana Ullman
Editorial Description: Review of recent scientific research on homeopathic medicine.
General Info: Yr. Est. 1987, Semi-annually, 4 pages, 2 Color
Circulation: Total-35,000
List Rental: Rents Lists

Homeopathy Today
Association

Publishing Co: Natl. Center for Homeopathy, 801 N Fairfax St Ste 306, Alexandria, VA 22314-1757;
Title Tel # (703) 548-7790 Title Fax # (703) 548-7792
Personnel: Editor-Julian Winston
Editorial Description: Newsletter for members of center, professional & laypersons, interested in the practice of homeopathy.
General Info: Yr. Est. 1981, 11x/yr., Trim Size-8½ x 11, Desktop press, 16 pages, ISSN: 0886-1676, 4% ads, No Color, Newsprint
Subscriptions: Indv. $40, For. $55, $1/copy
Circulation: (37% controlled), Total-7,000

Homeostasis Quarterly *Association*

Publishing Co: Hypoglycemia Foundation, Inc., Adrenal Metabolic Resrch Soc., 32 Sunrise Terrace, Clifton Park, NJ 12065-2327
Personnel: Editor-Marilyn Light
General Info: Yr. Est. 1971, Quarterly, Offset press, 4 pages, No Color
Subscriptions: Indv. $5, $1/copy
Circulation: Total-5,000

Hospital Technology Alerts
See: HOSPITALS & NURSING HOMES

How to Get Paid
See: MANAGEMENT

Hydrocephalus News &
Notes *Consumer*

Publishing Co: National Hydrocephalus Foundation, 1670 Green Oak Circle, Lawrenceville, GA 30243 Tel # (770) 995-9570 Fax # (770) 995-8982; Title Tel # (815) 467-6548
Personnel: Editor-Warren Barshes
Editorial Description: A quaterly publication designed specifically for individuals affected by hydrocephalus, their families and the professionals who specialize in their care.
General Info: (Formerly Lifeline, National Hydrocephalus Foundation Newsletter), Yr. Est. 1979, Quarterly, Trim Size-8½ x 11, Desktop press, 6 pages, ISSN: 1068-8978, No Color
Subscriptions: Indv. $20
Circulation: Total-1,500, Readership-1,500

IABM Newsletter *Association*

Publishing Co: Intl. Academy of Behavioral Medicine/Counseling & Psychology, 13140 Coit Rd., Ste. 307, Dallas, TX 75240 Fax # (214) 437-1190; Title Tel # (214) 437-3370
Personnel: Editor-George Mount
Editorial Description: Covers general field of behavioral medicine & health care, & counseling & psychotherapy.
General Info: (Formerly Journal of the AABM), Yr. Est. 1979, Quarterly, Trim Size-8½ x 11, 4 pages
Subscriptions: Free With Membership
Circulation: Total-800
Advertising: Inquire for rates.

IAHP Newsletter

Publishing Co: International Association of Hygienic Physicians, 204 Stambaugh Bldg., Youngstown, OH 44503; Title Tel # (216) 746-5000 Title Fax # (216) 746-1836
Editorial Description: The IAHP promotes the clinical advancement of its profession, ethical responsibility, certification of other professionals and the accreditation of schools or training programs, and the health freedom of Assn. members. Members are limited to Primary CareDoctors specializing in the supervision of fasting as an integral of natural hygienic car.
General Info: (Formerly IAPNH Newsletter), Yr. Est. 1985, Quarterly
Subscriptions: Indv. $12

IAL News *Association*

Publishing Co: American Cancer Society, Inc., 1599 Clifton Rd NE, Atlanta, GA 30329-4250 Tel # (404) 329-7936; Title Tel # (404) 320-3333
Personnel: Editor-Jane Del Vecchio, Production Mgr.-Larry Silverman, Art Dir.-Susan Summers
Editorial Description: Latest developments pertaining to laryngectomees around the world.
General Info: Tri-annually, 4 pages
Circulation: Total-15,000

IDN-Infectious Diseases
Newsletter *Association*

Publishing Co: Elsevier Science Inc., 655 Avenue of the Americas, New York, NY 10010-5107 Tel # (212) 633-3916 Fax # (212) 633-3913 Parent Co.-Reed Elsevier, New York; Title Tel # (212) 867-9040
Personnel: Publisher-Glen Campbell, Editor-Charles Stratton, MD, Production Mgr.-Yvette Nora, Promotion Dir.-Cheryl Kahan
Editorial Description: Reports on newly characterized diseases, syndromes and treatment protocols and the latest techniques of diagnostic identification.
General Info: Yr. Est. 1982, Monthly, ISSN: 0278-2316, Ind/Abs/Online: Biol. Abst.
Subscriptions: Indv. $99, Inst. $175, Can. $99, For. $142
Circulation: Total-1,050
Printing Co: Vee Printing, 100 Dixon Rd., De Freestville, NY 12144

IMS International *Business, Consumer*

Publishing Co: IMS America, 660 W. Germantown Pike #905, Plymouth Meeting, PA 19462-1048 Tel # (610) 834-5000 Fax # (610) 834-5018; Title Tel # (215) 834-5104 Title Fax # (610) 834-5100
General Info: Trim Size-8½ x 11, 2 pages, No Color, Coated, Saddle-stitched

ISSD News
See: PSYCHOLOGY

Illinois Cancer News *Business, Association*

Publishing Co: American Cancer Society, Illinois Div., 77 E Monroe St, Chicago, IL 60603-5700; Title Tel # (312) 641-6150 Title Fax # (312) 641-6588
Personnel: Editor-Linda Haase, Asst. Ed.-Brooks Whitney
General Info: Quarterly, Trim Size-8½ x 14, 8 pages, 4 Color
Subscriptions: Free

ImmunoFacts
See: DRUGS & PHARMACEUTICALS

In Action
See: HEALTH

Infectious Disease Alert *Consumer*

Publishing Co: American Health Consultants, Inc., 3525 Piedmont Rd., Building #6, Ste. 400, Atlanta, GA 30305-0056 Tel # (404) 262-7436 Fax # (404) 284-3291; Title Tel # (404) 351-4523 Title Fax # (404) 352-1971
Personnel: Publisher-David Wilson, Editor-Jeffrey Galpin, Circ. Mgr.-Monica Brown, Production Mgr.-Kent Anderson, Mktg. Dir.-Debbie Zelnio
Editorial Description: A semi-monthly update of current developments in infectious disease and immunology.
General Info: Yr. Est. 1981, Semi-monthly, Trim Size-8½ x 11, 4 pages, 2 Color
Subscriptions: Indv. $159
List Rental: Actives: $125/M

Infectious Diseases
Newsletter *Consumer*

Publishing Co: Elsevier Science Inc., 655 Avenue of the Americas, New York, NY 10010-5107 Tel # (212) 633-3916 Fax # (212) 633-3913 Parent Co.-Reed Elsevier, New York; Title Tel # (212) 867-9040
Personnel: Editor-Charles Stratton

InfoPack
See: DRUGS & PHARMACEUTICALS

Inform Quarterly Newsletter *Business, Association*

Publishing Co: International Reference Organization in Forensic Medicine, 1877 Claudia Ave., Simi Valley, CA 93065-3642
Personnel: Editor-Thomas Noguchi
General Info: (Formerly Inform-Retter), Yr. Est. 1969, Quarterly
Subscriptions: Indv. $25
Circulation: Total-1,500

Information Exchange

Publishing Co: Natl. SIDS Resourec Center, 2070 Chain Bridge Rd., Ste. 450, Vienna, VA 22182-2536; Title Tel # (703) 821-8955 Title Fax # (703) 821-2098
Editorial Description: Encourages the exchange of information among SIDS groups nationwide. Covers topics including bereavement therapy, physicians accounts of aspects of SIDS, etc.
General Info: Tri-annually

Insight *Association*

Publishing Co: Eye Bank Assn. of America, 1001 Connecticut Ave NW Ste, 601, Washington, DC 20036-5504; Title Tel # (202) 775-4999 Title Fax # (202) 429-6036
General Info: (Formerly Eye Bank Assn. of America Newsletter/ Foresight), Yr. Est. 1961, Quarterly, Trim Size-8.5 x 11, 15 pages
Subscriptions: Free With Membership

InterPharmacy Forum
See: DRUGS & PHARMACEUTICALS

Internal Medicine Alert

Publishing Co: American Health Consultants, Inc., 3525 Piedmont Rd., Building #6, Ste. 400, Atlanta, GA 30305-0056 Tel # (404) 262-7436 Fax # (404) 284-3291; Title Tel # (404) 351-4523 Title Fax # (404) 352-1971
Personnel: Publisher-David Wilson, Circ. Mgr.-Monica Brown, Production Mgr.-Kent Anderson, Mktg. Dir.-Debbie Zelnio
General Info: Yr. Est. 1978, Semi-monthly, 4 pages, ISSN: 0195-315X
Subscriptions: Indv. $159
List Rental: Actives: $125/M

Internal Medicine Bulletin

Publishing Co: W.B. Saunders Co., Curtis Ctr., Independence Square West, Philadelphia, PA 19106 Tel # (215) 238-7800 Fax # (215) 238-6445 Parent Co.-Harcourt Brace Professional Publishing, Orlando
Personnel: Editor-Malcolm Thaler, MD
Editorial Description: Provides physicians in internal medicine and family practice with concise reviews of the most important articles in the current literature.
General Info: Yr. Est. 1993, 24x/yr., ISSN: 1065-9498
Subscriptions: Indv. $99, Inst. $99, For. $153, $18/copy

Intl. Assn. for the Study
of Pain-Newsletter

Publishing Co: International Association for the Study of Pain, 909 NE 43rd St Ste 306, Seattle, WA 98105-6020; Title Tel # (206) 547-6409 Title Fax # (206) 547-1703
Personnel: Editor-Louisa Jones
Editorial Description: Reports activities of Assn. (IASP) plus meetings & new books, technical articles.
General Info: Yr. Est. 1975, Bi-monthly, Trim Size-8½ x 11, Offset press, 8 pages, ISSN: 1017-0057, 2 Color, Newsprint
Acquistions: Publication Bought
Circulation: (92% controlled), Total-6,500, International-4,000
List Rental: Actives: 5,700, $150/M

International Guild of
Professional
Electrologists-Newsletter

Publishing Co: Intl. Guild of Professional Electrologists, 202 Boulevard St # B, High Point, NC 27262-4302; Title Tel # (919) 841-6631 Title Fax # (910) 841-5187
Personnel: Editor-Trudy Brown
General Info: Yr. Est. 1979, 6 pages

International Medical Device Regulatory Monitor
Business

Publishing Co: Newsletter Services, Inc., 9700 Philadelphia Ct., Lanham, MD 20706-4405; Title Tel # (301) 731-5202 Title Fax # (301) 731-5203
Personnel: Publisher-Lisa Anthony, Editor-Joanne Eglovistch, Circ. Mgr.-Priscilla Arenas, Mktg. Dir.-Susan Pangman
Editorial Description: Provides official, English-language texts of regualtions regarding approval and marketing of medical devices. Covers interantional standardization efforts, as well as regualations from individual countries.
General Info: Yr. Est. 1994, Monthly, ISSN: 1079-6940
Subscriptions: Indv. $495, Can. $495, For. $549
List Rental: List Management Co.: Taybi Direct East, Inc., 13321 New Hampshire Ave., Ste. 202, Silver Spring, MD 20904-3450 Tel # (301) 680-3633, Fax # (301) 680-3635

Internet Medicine
Consumer

Publishing Co: Lippincott-Raven Press Publishers, 227 E. Washington Square, Philadelphia, PA 19106 Tel # (215) 238-4200 Fax # (215) 238-4227 Parent Co.-Wolters Kluwer US Corporation, New York
Personnel: Publisher-Kathy Alexander, Editor-Alec Schwarz, Mktg. Dir.-Michele Duncan
Editorial Description: Covers internet resources for healthcare professionals. Offers critical reviews and feature articles on the medical sites and databases on the internet.
General Info: Yr. Est. 1996, Monthly
Subscriptions: Indv. $89, For. $110

Internist's Intercom
Association

Publishing Co: American Society of Internal Medicine, 2011 Pennsylvania Ave NW Ste, 800, Washington, DC 20006-1813 Tel # (202) 835-2746 Fax # (202) 835-0443; Title Tel # (202) 289-1700
Personnel: Editor-Barbara Lauter
Editorial Description: For ASIM members only; practical, timely legislative, socioeconomic, assn. information.
General Info: Yr. Est. 1956, Monthly, Trim Size-8½ x 11, Web press, 4 pages, ISSN: 0164-6419, 2 Color, Newsprint
Circulation: Total-30,000

Interventional Cardiology Newsletter
Business, Scholarly

Publishing Co: Elsevier Science Inc., 655 Avenue of the Americas, New York, NY 10010-5107 Parent Co.-Reed Elsevier, New York; Title Tel # (212) 633-3916 Title Fax # (212) 633-3913
Personnel: Publisher-Marci Tlusty, Editor-David Faxon, Promotion Dir.-Joe Barrett
General Info: Yr. Est. 1993, Bi-monthly, Web press, 8 pages, ISSN: 1063-4282
Subscriptions: Indv. $110, Inst. $110
Advertising: Inquire for rates.
List Rental: Actives: 293, $125/M

Intravenous Therapy News

Publishing Co: McMahon Publishing Co., 83 Peaceable St., W. Reading, CT 06896-3198; Title Tel # (203) 544-9343
Personnel: Publisher-Raymond McMahon, Editor-Sal Turco Pharmud
General Info: Yr. Est. 1974, Monthly
Subscriptions: Indv. $32
Circulation: Total-11,000

Ironic Blood
Consumer, Association

Publishing Co: Iron Overload Diseases Association, Inc., 433 Westwind Dr, North Palm Beach, FL 33408-5123; Title Tel # (407) 840-8512 Title Fax # (407) 842-9881
Personnel: Editor-Roberta Crawford
Editorial Description: Information on iron overload diseases for patients, doctors and public.
General Info: Yr. Est. 1981, Bi-monthly, Trim Size-11 x 17, Sheetfed press, 4 pages, ISSN: 0895-7762, Color
Subscriptions: Free
Circulation: Total-10,000

Jag
See: POLITICS

Japan Medical Review
Business, Association

Publishing Co: Japan Publications Inc., 41 Sutter St. #1112, San Francisco, CA 94104-4903; Title Tel # (415) 772-5555 Title Fax # (415) 772-5659
Personnel: Circ. Mgr., Mktg. Mgr.-Carol W. Kastner
Editorial Description: Contains the latest Ministry of Health regulations, policies, import & domestic product licenses and more for international health care executives.
General Info: Yr. Est. 1986, Monthly, 22 pages, ISSN: 0914-0255
Subscriptions: Indv. $600

Joint Letter, The
Consumer

Publishing Co: Lippincott-Raven Press Publishers, 227 E. Washington Square, Philadelphia, PA 19106 Tel # (215) 238-4200 Fax # (215) 238-4227 Parent Co.-Wolters Kluwer US Corporation, New York
Personnel: Publisher-Kathey Alexander, Editor-Colin Nelson, Mktg. Dir.-Michele Duncan
Editorial Description: Cover joint function, injury, and disease as well as orthopedic medicine in general.
General Info: Yr. Est. 1995, Monthly, ISSN: 1078-6260
Subscriptions: Indv. $130, Can. $130, For. $145

Journal of Hospital Occupational Health

Publishing Co: Journal of Hospital Occupational Health, PO Box 5241, Concord, CA 94524-0241; Title Tel # (916) 961-6579
Personnel: Editor-Louise Yinger
Editorial Description: Covers developments in hospital occupational health.
General Info: Yr. Est. 1981, Bi-monthly
Subscriptions: Indv. $25

Journal Watch
Business, Association

Publishing Co: Massachusetts Medical Society-Publ. Dir, 1440 Main St., Waltham, MA 02154-1649; Title Tel # (617) 893-3800 Title Fax # (617) 893-8103
Personnel: Publisher-Robert Bovenschulte, Editor-Alan Brett, M.D., Circ. Mgr.-Jed Clifton, Production Mgr.-Alberta Fitzpatrick, Adv. Dir.-Art Wilschek
Editorial Description: Contains 25-30 abstracts per issue from major medical journals covering latest research for practicing physicians.
General Info: Yr. Est. 1987, Bi-weekly, Trim Size-8½ x 11, Web press, 8 pages, ISSN: 0896-7210, Ind/Abs/Online: CD Plus, 2 Color, Matte, Saddle-stitched
Subscriptions: Indv. $87, Inst. $89, Can. $105, For. $105, $4/copy
Circulation: Total-30,000
List Rental: List Management Co.: Manager: Michelle Dinsmore; Response Media Products Inc., 2323 Perimeter Park Dr., Ste. 200, Atlanta, GA 30341-1335 Tel # (404) 451-5478, Fax # (404) 451-4929, Actives: 23,979, $90/M

Journal Watch for Psychiatry
See: PSYCHIATRY

KCMS Bulletin
Association　　**CPM: $86**

Publishing Co: Medical Society of the County of Kings, 1313 Bedford Ave, Brooklyn, NY 11216-2928; Title Tel # (718) 467-9000 Title Fax # (718) 778-0380
Personnel: Editor-Randall D. Bloomfield
General Info: Yr. Est. 1922, Bi-monthly, Offset press
Subscriptions: Indv. $15, $1/copy
Circulation: Total-3,000
Advertising: $260.
Printing Co: Alpert Press, 644 Pacific St, Brooklyn, NY 11217-2193 Tel # (718) 875-1058

K.V.P. News
Association

Publishing Co: Manitoba Assn. of Med. Radiation Technologists, Inc., 294 Duffield St., Winnipeg, MB R3J 2J9 Canada; Title Tel # (204) 888-6190
Personnel: Publisher, Editor, Circ. Mgr.-M.A. Lunn, R.T.
Editorial Description: News of meetings and functions of society, includes scientific articles.
General Info: Yr. Est. 1964, Quarterly, Trim Size-8½ x 11½, Offset press, 26 pages, ISSN: 0022-7439, No Color
Circulation: Total-680

LIMS News

Publishing Co: Laban/Bartenieff Institute of Movement Studies, Inc., 11 E 4th St, New York, NY 10003-6902; Title Tel # (212) 477-4299
General Info: (Formerly Laban/Bartenieff News), Yr. Est. 1978, Quarterly
Circulation: Total-500

LPI Newsletter
Consumer, Association

Publishing Co: Linus Pauling Institute of Science & Medicine, 440 Page Mill Rd, Palo Alto, CA 94306-2025; Title Tel # (415) 327-4064 Title Fax # (415) 327-8564
Personnel: Editor-Barbara Marinacci
Editorial Description: Institute research publications, personnel, honors, awards; related non-institute research. Helath information primarily related to nutrients.
General Info: (Formerly Linus Pauling Institute of Science & Medicine - Newsletter), Yr. Est. 1976, Semi-annually, Trim Size-8½ x 11, Offset press, 16 pages, 2 Color, Coated
Subscriptions: Free To Qualified Recipient
Circulation: Total-40,000, Readership-70,000
Printing Co: Pizazz, 1070 Commercial St Ste 110, San Jose, CA 95112-1420 Tel # (408) 453-1144

Lab Report

Publishing Co: G&R Pubs., Inc., 185 Devonshire St., Boston, MA 02110-1407; Title Tel # (617) 338-8860
Personnel: Editor-Dr. R. Gambino, Circ. Mgr., Production Mgr.-Tina Schryver
Editorial Description: Comprehensive laboratory newsletter reviewing significant developments in lab medicine & diagnostic lab testing; bibliographies with each article; cumulative index available with subscription.
General Info: (Formerly Lab. Medicine for Practicing Physicians), Yr. Est. 1979, Monthly, Trim Size-8 x 10½, Sheetfed press, 8 pages, ISSN: 1045-7313, Color, Newsprint
Subscriptions: Indv. $75, $8/copy
Acquistions: Publication Bought
Circulation: Total-2,300
List Rental: Rents Lists
Printing Co: Travers Printing Co., 32 Mission St, Gardner, MA 01440-2196

Laboratory Regulation Manual & Newsletter   *Business*

Publishing Co: Aspen Publishers, Inc., 200 Orchard Ridge Dr., Ste 200, Gaithersburg, MD 20878-5440 Fax # (301) 417-7655 Parent Co.-Wolters Kluwer US Corporation, New York; Title Tel # (301) 417-7500 Title Fax # (301) 417-7550
Personnel: Publisher-Paul Lasky, Editor-Patricia Younger
Editorial Description: Collection and explanation of the principal laws that effect the operation of clinical laboratories.
General Info: Yr. Est. 1976, Quarterly, Trim Size-6⅛ x 9¼, Offset press, 280 pages, No Color, Looseleaf
Subscriptions: Indv. $719, For. $810
List Rental: List Management Co.: Stevens-Knox List Management, 304 Park Ave S., New York, NY 10010-5312 Tel # (212) 388-8800, Fax # (212) 388-8890, Actives: $80/M

Latest Word, The

Publishing Co: W.B. Saunders Co., Curtis Ctr., Independence Square West, Philadelphia, PA 19106 Tel # (215) 238-7800 Fax # (215) 238-6445 Parent Co.-Harcourt Brace Professional Publishing, Orlando
Editorial Description: Ensures that medical transcriptionists, medical records administrators, and technicians keep abreast of advances in medicine and new terminology, especially in relation to pharmacology, instrumentation, procedures, and diagnostics.
General Info: Yr. Est. 1993, Bi-monthly, ISSN: 1067-716X
Subscriptions: Indv. $29, Inst. $39, For. $54, $7/copy

Laughter Prescription Newsletter
See: HUMOR & SATIRE

Life Entitlements
See: HEALTH

Life Sciences & Biotechnology Update
See: BIOLOGY

LifelineLetter
See: NUTRITION

Link   *Association*

Publishing Co: Ontario Society of Occupational Therapists, 55 Eglinton Ave. E., #210, Toronto, ON M4P 1G8 Canada; Title Tel # (416) 781-8290 Title Fax # (416) 782-4754
Personnel: Editor-Chris Farrell
General Info: (Formerly OSOT Newsletter), Yr. Est. 1990, Bi-monthly, 6 pages
Subscriptions: Can. $25
Circulation: Total-1,400
Advertising: Inquire for rates. Accepts Inserts.

Lupus Today   *Consumer, Association*

Publishing Co: American Lupus Society, 3914 Del Amo Blvd Ste 922, Torrance, CA 90503-2159; Title Tel # (310) 542-8891
Personnel: Editor-Vernon White
General Info: Yr. Est. 1978, Quarterly, 8 pages
Subscriptions: Free To Qualified Recipient

MDR Watch
See: HEALTH

MLA News
See: LIBRARY

MM News   *Association*

Publishing Co: Medical Soc. of the County of NY, 156 E 26th St, New York, NY 10010-1806; Title Fax # (212) 684-4741
Personnel: Editor-Cheryl Malone
General Info: (Formerly New York County Medical Society Newsletter), Monthly
Circulation: Total-6,200

MMA Inter-Com

Publishing Co: Manitoba Medical Assn., 125 Sherbrook St., Winnipeg, MB R3C 2B5 Canada
General Info: Monthly, 6 pages, 1% ads, Looseleaf
Circulation: Total-2,000
Advertising: Inquire for rates. Accepts Inserts.

MRO Update
See: HEALTH

Malaria Weekly   *Business*

Publishing Co: C.W. Henderson Publisher, Medical Center II, P.O. Box 5528, Atlanta, GA 31107-0528 Tel # (404) 507-7777 Fax # (404) 507-7788
Editorial Description: News and information on malaria treatment and prevention worldwide.
General Info: Yr. Est. 1995, Weekly
Subscriptions: Indv. $10,950, Can. $1,095, For. $1,295

Malloch Room Newsletter, The

Publishing Co: New York Academy of Medicine, 1216 Fifth Avenue, New York, NY 10029-5293; Title Tel # (212) 876-8200
General Info: Semi-annually

Managed Care Outlook
See: HOSPITALS & NURSING HOMES

Managed Care Week
See: HEALTH

Managing Your Medical Practice   *Business*

Publishing Co: Matthew Bender & Co., 11 Penn Plaza, New York, NY 10001-2006 Tel # (212) 967-7707 Fax # (212) 244-3188
Editorial Description: The complete guide to the business aspects of managing a medical practice.
General Info: Irregular, Looseleaf

Maryland Society for Medical Research, Bulletin of The

Publishing Co: Maryland Society for Medical Research, 522 W Lombard St, Baltimore, MD 21201-1636 Tel # (410) 539-0872

Mayo Clinical Update   *Business, Association*

Publishing Co: Mayo Foundation-Mayo Medical School, 200 1st St SW, Rochester, MN 55905-0001 Tel # (507) 284-2511; Title Tel # (507) 284-4660 Title Fax # (507) 284-5410
Personnel: Editor-Scott Litin
Editorial Description: Contains health information for physicians only.
General Info: Monthly, Trim Size-8½ x 11, 8 pages
Subscriptions: Free To Qualified Recipient
List Rental: List Management Co.: Kleid Company, Inc., 530 5th Ave., 17 Floor, New York, NY 10036-5101 Tel # (212) 819-3406, Fax # (212) 719-9788, Actives: 88,500, $75/M
Printing Co: Brown Brinting, 2300 Brown Avenue, US Hwy 14 W., PO Box 1549, Waseca, MN 56093-0517 Tel # (507) 835-2410, Fax # (507) 835-0420

Med Ed News
See: EDUCATION

Med News
See: HEALTH

Medical Abstracts Newsletter
See: HEALTH

Medical Alert
See: HEALTH

Medical Bulletin
See: DRUGS & PHARMACEUTICALS

Medical Bulletin: Montgomery County Medical Society   *Association*

Publishing Co: Montgomery County Medical Society, 40 S. Perry St., Dayton, OH 45402-1429; Title Tel # (513) 223-0990
Personnel: Editor-A. V. Black
General Info: Yr. Est. 1945, Monthly, Trim Size-6 x 9, Offset press, 24 pages, No Color
Circulation: Total-900

Medical Business Letter, The
See: HEALTH

Medical Device Approval Letter   *Business*

Publishing Co: Washington Information Source, 8901 Battery Pl, Bethesda, MD 20814-2638; Title Tel # (301) 907-6668 Title Fax # (301) 913-9482
Personnel: Publisher, Editor-Kenneth Reid
Editorial Description: Information on current medical device approval decisions.
General Info: Yr. Est. 1992, Bi-weekly, 22 pages, ISSN: 1060-8338, No Color, Saddle-stitched
Subscriptions: Indv. $417, For. $467, $35/copy
List Rental: Actives: 8,000

Medical Devices Litigation Reporter
See: LAW

Medical Devices Report   *Business, Association*

Publishing Co: Medical Devices Report, PO Box 1062, Manassas, VA 22110-1062; Title Tel # (703) 361-6472
Personnel: Publisher, Editor-Steve Butchock
Editorial Description: Independent national newsletter of the medical instrumentation industry. Covers FDA's regulatory activities affecting devices & diagnostic products. Also legislative & SEC updates. Stock Index, too.
General Info: Yr. Est. 1972, Weekly, ISSN: 0748-4852
Subscriptions: Indv. $420, Inst. $195, Can. $420, For. $470

Medical Devices Reporter
See: DRUGS & PHARMACEUTICALS

Medical Directory of Gtr. Kansas City *Business*

Publishing Co: Metropolitan Medical Society of Greater Kansas City, 3036 Gillham Rd, Kansas City, MO 64108-3119; Title Tel # (816) 531-8432
Personnel: Editor-John Renner, Adv. Dir.-Theresa Lansdon
Editorial Description: Comprehensive directory of medical, health, & related facilities of the greater Kansas City area. Office addresses, phone numbers & basic biographical information for members of participating medical societies.
General Info: Yr. Est. 1940, Annually, Trim Size-6 x 9, Letrpr. press, 400 pages, ISSN: 0894-5071, 5% ads, No Color, Coated, Looseleaf
Subscriptions: $35/copy
Circulation: (100% controlled), Total-4,000
Advertising: Inquire for rates.
Printing Co: Lowell Press, 115 E. 31st St., P.O. Box 411877, Kansas City, MO 64141-1877 Tel # (816) 753-4545, Fax # (816) 753-4057

Medical Ethics Advisor

Publishing Co: American Health Consultants, Inc., 3525 Piedmont Rd., Building #6, Ste. 400, Atlanta, GA 30305-0056 Fax # (404) 284-3291; Title Tel # (404) 262-7436 Title Fax # (800) 284-3291
Personnel: Publisher-Connie Austin, Editor-Linda Morningstar, Circ. Mgr.-Monica Brown, Production Mgr.-Mike Witter, Mktg. Mgr.-Robin Prows
Editorial Description: Gives physicians, nurses, clergy advice on handling medical-ethical dilemmas.
General Info: Yr. Est. 1985, Monthly, Trim Size-8½ x 11, 14 pages, ISSN: 0886-0653
Subscriptions: Indv. $279, $27/copy
Acquistions: Publication Bought, Publication Sold
Circulation: Total-900
List Rental: Actives: $145/M

Medical Group Management Marketer's Guidepost
See: MANAGEMENT

Medical Industry Employment Opportunities *Business* CPM: $800

Publishing Co: Biomedical Market Newsletter, Inc., 3237 Idaho Pl, Costa Mesa, CA 92626-2207; Title Tel # (714) 434-9500 Title Fax # (714) 434-9755
Personnel: Publisher, Editor-David Anast, Mktg. Dir.-Steve Bauer
Editorial Description: Covers possibilities for employment in the medical industry.
General Info: (Formerly Biomedical Employment Opportunities), Yr. Est. 1995, Bi-weekly, Trim Size-8½ x 11, Desktop press, 24 pages, 10% ads, 2 Color, Matte, Saddle-stitched
Subscriptions: Indv. $145, Can. $195, For. $195, $13/copy
Circulation: Total-500
Advertising: $400.
List Rental: Rents Lists

Medical Laser Report *Business*

Publishing Co: PennWell Publishing Company, Ten Tara Blvd., 5th Floor, Nashua, NH 03062-2801 Parent Co.-PennWell Publishing Co., Tulsa; Title Tel # (603) 891-9174 Title Fax # (603) 891-0574
Editorial Description: Devoted exclusively to the business of medical lasers. Provides latest information on new technologies, market opportunities, product trends and FDA decisions. Subscription includes Medical Laser Buyers Guide.
General Info: Monthly
Subscriptions: Indv. $345, For. $365, $25/copy

Medical Legal Aspects of Breast Implants
See: LAW

Medical Letter on Drugs and Therapeutics
See: DRUGS & PHARMACEUTICALS

Medical Liability Advisory Service
See: LAW

Medical Liability Reporter
See: LAW

Medical Malpractice
See: LAW

Medical Malpractice: Guide to Medical Issues
See: LAW

Medical Malpractice Law & Strategy
See: LAW

Medical Malpractice Verdicts, Settlements & Experts
See: LAW

Medical Materials Update *Business*

Publishing Co: Business Communications Co., 25 Van Zant St., Ste.13, Norwalk, CT 06855-1781; Title Tel # (203) 853-4266 Title Fax # (203) 853-0348
Personnel: Publisher-Louis Naturman, Editor-Mel Schlechter, Mktg. Dir.-Robert Butler
General Info: Yr. Est. 1977, Monthly, Trim Size-8½ x 11, 12 pages
Subscriptions: Indv. $350, Can. $400, For. $400, $35/copy
Advertising: Inquire for rates.
List Rental: Rents Lists

Medical-Moral Newsletter

Publishing Co: Ayd Medical Communications, 1130 E. Cold Spring Ln., Baltimore, MD 21239-3931 Tel # (410) 433-9220; Title Tel # (301) 433-9220 Title Fax # (301) 532-5419
Personnel: Editor-Frank Eyd, Jr., Circ. Mgr.-Ann Lovelace, Adv. Dir.-Bertram Morales
Editorial Description: Current thinking on medical-ethical issues.
General Info: (Formerly Medical Newsletter for Religious), Yr. Est. 1964, Monthly, Offset press, 4 pages, ISSN: 0002-7397, No Color, Newsprint
Subscriptions: Indv. $25, $3/copy
Circulation: Total-1,000

Medical Office Manager
See: MANAGEMENT

Medical Practice Letter

Publishing Co: Medical Practice Letter, 227 Everit St, New Haven, CT 06511-1335; Title Tel # (203) 776-5326
Personnel: Publisher, Editor-John Hoskins
Editorial Description: Management and finance in medical offices.
General Info: (Formerly The Practice Letter), Yr. Est. 1980, Monthly, Trim Size-8½ x 11, Web press, 8 pages, 2 Color
Subscriptions: $12/copy
Circulation: Total-600

Medical Practice Risk Manager *Business*

Publishing Co: American Medical Association, 515 N. State St., Chicago, IL 60610 Fax # (312) 464-5834; Title Tel # (312) 464-4512
Editorial Description: Helps physicians estasblish systems to enhance patient care and reduce liability risk.
General Info: Yr. Est. 1994, 10x/yr.
Subscriptions: Indv. $358

Medical Records Briefing
See: HOSPITALS & NURSING HOMES

Medical Reform *Consumer, Association*

Publishing Co: MRG, Box 158, Station D, Toronto, ON M6P 3J8 Canada; Title Tel # (416) 588-9167
Personnel: Editor-Haresh Kirpalani
Editorial Description: Promotes universal access to health care. Examines the social, economic, occupational & environmental causes of disease.
General Info: Yr. Est. 1979, Bi-monthly, Trim Size-8½ x 11, Sheetfed press, 16 pages, 1% ads, No Color, Perfect bound
Subscriptions: Indv. $25, Inst. $25
Acquistions: Publication Bought
Circulation: Total-300
Advertising: Accepts Inserts.

Medical Research Council of Canada, Newsletter *Association*

Publishing Co: Medical Research Council of Canada, Holland Cross, 5th fl. Tower B, 1600 Scott St., Ottawa, ON K1A 0W9 Canada Fax # (613) 954-6653; Title Tel # (613) 954-1806
Personnel: Editor-Neil Morris
Editorial Description: Keeps Canadian biomedical researchers informed of changes in policies and procedures of the Medical Research Council of Canada, membership of its committees, application closing dates, etc.
General Info: Yr. Est. 1970, Quarterly, 8 pages

Medical Scan

Publishing Co: Market Intelligence Research Co., 2525 Charleston Rd, Mountain View, CA 94043-1626
Editorial Description: Developing medical technologies and treatments.
General Info: Yr. Est. 1991, Monthly

Medical Scientific Update *Association*

Publishing Co: Natl. Jewish Ctr. for Immunology and Respiratory Medicine, 1400 Jackson St, Denver, CO 80206-2761 Tel # (303) 398-1080; Title Tel # (303) 398-1000 Title Fax # (303) 270-2171
Editorial Description: Designed to inform professional colleagues about our clinical programs & research activities.
General Info: Monthly

Medical Society Newsletter *Consumer*

Publishing Co: Vermont State Medical Society, 136 Main St, Montpelier, VT 05602-2913; Title Tel # (802) 223-7898
Personnel: Editor-D. Robert Vautier
Editorial Description: Informational newsletter distributed to Vermont member physicians.
General Info: Yr. Est. 1949, Monthly, Trim Size-8½ x 11, Offset press, 6 pages, No Color
Subscriptions: Indv. $15
Circulation: (100% controlled), Total-984

Medical Software Reviews *Business*

Publishing Co: Healthcare Computing Publications, 462 2nd St, Brooklyn, NY 11215-2503; Title Tel # (718) 499-5910 Title Fax # (718) 768-3260
Personnel: Editor-Sue Frisch, Production Dir.-Bruce Frisch
Editorial Description: Information on software pertaining to the medical industries.
General Info: Monthly, Trim Size-8½ x 11, 8 pages, ISSN: 1059-907X, 2 Color, Matte
Subscriptions: Indv. $75, Inst. $90, For. $19, $10/copy

Medical Staff Briefing
See: HOSPITALS & NURSING HOMES

Medical Staff and Physician Organization Legel Advisor   *Business*

Publishing Co: American Medical Association, 515 N. State St., Chicago, IL 60610 Fax # (312) 464-5834; Title Tel # (312) 464-4512
Editorial Description: Physicians perspective on medical staff issues.
General Info: 10x/yr.
Subscriptions: Indv. $358

Medical Utilization Management

Publishing Co: Faulkner & Gray Healthcare Information Center, 1133 15th St NW, Ste. 450, Washington, DC 20005-2710 Tel # (202) 828-4148 Parent Co.-Faulkner & Gray, Inc., New York; Title Tel # (202) 828-4150
Personnel: Publisher-L. Koizumi, Editor-Spencer Vibbert
Editorial Description: Covers Washington & national perspective on utilization & quality review of health service delivery.
General Info: Yr. Est. 1973, Semi-monthly, Trim Size-8½ x 11, Web press, 6 pages, ISSN: 0734-1970, 2 Color, Newsprint
Subscriptions: Indv. $365
Acquisions: Publication Bought, Publication Sold
List Rental: List Management Co.: Aggressive List Management, 18-2 E Dundee Rd Ste 101, Barrington, IL 60010-5273 Tel # (708) 304-4030, Fax # (708) 304-4032

Medicare Advisor
See: HOSPITALS & NURSING HOMES

Medicare Manager   *Business*

Publishing Co: Shannon Publications, Inc., 9441 L.B.J. Fwy, Ste. #510 Box #2, Dallas, TX 75243-4541; Title Tel # (214) 644-0159 Title Fax # (214) 644-1538
Personnel: Publisher-Ellen Brodley, Assoc. Publ., Editor-Brian Buchan, Copy Editor-Laureen Hill, Circ. Mgr.-Tony Bradley, Pack. Suppl.-Ellen Bradley
Editorial Description: Covers medicare reimbursement issues and practice management for physicians and office managers.
General Info: Yr. Est. 1991, Monthly, Trim Size-8½ x 11, Sheetfed press, 6 pages, ISSN: 1068-2465
Subscriptions: Indv. $117
Advertising: Accepts Inserts.
List Rental: Rents Lists

Medicare Review   *Business*

Publishing Co: Shannon Publications, Inc., 9441 L.B.J. Fwy, Ste. #510 Box #2, Dallas, TX 75243-4541; Title Tel # (214) 644-0159 Title Fax # (214) 644-1538
Personnel: Publisher-Ellen Bradley, Editor-Brian Buchan, Circ. Mgr.-Tony Bradley
Editorial Description: Focuses on medicare issues and developments. For physicians and/or office managers.
General Info: Yr. Est. 1985, Monthly, Trim Size-8½ x 11, Desktop press, 12 pages, ISSN: 085-0925, 2 Color
Subscriptions: Indv. $175, For. $185
Advertising: Accepts Inserts.
List Rental: Actives: $150/M

Medicine & Biology   *Business, Association*

Publishing Co: National Technical Information Service U.S., 5285 Port Royal Rd., Springfield, VA 22161-0001 Tel # (703) 487-4630 Fax # (703) 487-4630; Title Tel # (703) 487-4929
Editorial Description: Covers public health, industrial medicine, anatomy, biochemistry, botany, clinical chemistry & medicine, dentistry, electrophysiology, nutrition, occupational therapy, & parasitology.
General Info: Semi-monthly, Trim Size-8½ x 11, ISSN: 0364-6432
Subscriptions: Indv. $135, Can. $135, For. $195

Medicine & Health
See: HEALTH

Melanoma Letter   *Association*

Publishing Co: Skin Cancer Foundation, 245 Fifth Ave., Ste. 2402, New York, NY 10016; Title Tel # (212) 725-5176
Editorial Description: Published for the medical community focusing on vital issues concerning the most life-threatening form of skin cancer--malignant melanoma.
General Info: Yr. Est. 1982, Quarterly, Trim Size-8½ x 11, 4 pages, No Color, Newsprint
Subscriptions: Free With Membership
Circulation: Total-30,000

Membership Newsletter   *Association*

Publishing Co: Medical Society of Milwaukee County, 1126 S 70th St Ste S-507, Milwaukee, WI 53214-3151; Title Tel # (414) 271-9870 Title Fax # (414) 271-3348
Personnel: Editor, Adv. Dir.-Frank Bialek
Editorial Description: Informs membership of society activities and issues facing local medicine.
General Info: (Formerly Medical Society Times), Yr. Est. 1974, Monthly, Trim Size-8½ x 11, Desktop press, 24 pages, Color, Matte
Subscriptions: Indv. $13, Free With Membership
Circulation: (91% controlled), Total-2,400
Advertising: Inquire for rates. Accepts Inserts.
Printing Co: MA Graphics, 5455 S 108th St, Hales Corners, WI 53130-1353 Tel # (414) 425-1711

Men's Confidential
See: MEN'S

Mental Health Law Reporter
See: PSYCHOLOGY

Mental Medicine Update
See: PSYCHOLOGY

Messenger, The
See: HOSPITALS & NURSING HOMES

Miami Health Letter
See: HEALTH

Miami Health Letter en Espanol
See: HEALTH

Miami University School of Medicine Bulletin

Publishing Co: Miami Univ. School of Medicine, 1600 NW 10th Ave Rm 1149a, Miami, FL 33136-1015 Tel # (305) 547-6545 Fax # (305) 243-5681
General Info: Quarterly

Michigan Diabetes Research & Training Center-Newsletter

Publishing Co: Michigan Diabetes Research & Training Ctr., Univ. of Michigan, 3700 Upjohn Ctr., Ann Arbor, MI 48109-1189; Title Tel # (313) 763-5256
Personnel: Editor-Nili Tannenbaum
General Info: (Formerly DRTS Newsletter), Yr. Est. 1977, Monthly, 2 pages
Circulation: Total-650

Modern Nutrition News
See: NUTRITION

Monoclonal Antibody News   *Consumer*

Publishing Co: Mary Ann Liebert, Inc., 1651 3rd Ave, New York, NY 10128-3649; Title Tel # (212) 289-2300
Personnel: Publisher-Mary Ann Liebert, Editor-Zenon Steplewski
Editorial Description: Information on new hybrid cell lines, methodology and research on monoclonal antibodies.
General Info: Yr. Est. 1983, Quarterly, Trim Size-8½ x 11, Offset press, 20 pages, ISSN: 0272-4588, No Color, Newsprint, Saddle-stitched
Subscriptions: Indv. $131, Can. $171, For. $171
Circulation: Total-800
Advertising: Inquire for rates.

Myasthenia Gravis Foundation Newsletter

Publishing Co: Myasthenia Gravis Foundation, 222 S. Riverside Plaza, Ste. 1540, Chicago, IL 60606; Title Tel # (312) 258-0522
Personnel: Editor-Anna El-Qudsi
General Info: (Formerly Myasthenia Gravis Foundation Quarterly), Yr. Est. 1963, Quarterly
Circulation: Total-20,000
Advertising: Inquire for rates.

NAACLS News
See: EDUCATION

NARI Stethoscope   *Association*

Publishing Co: National Association of Residents & Interns, 292 Madison Ave., New York, NY 10017-6351 Fax # (212) 949-5910; Title Tel # (212) 949-5900
Personnel: Editor-William Driscoll
Editorial Description: Association membership newsletter for doctor-in-training. Covers financial planning topics.
General Info: Yr. Est. 1961, Quarterly, Trim Size-8¾ x 11½, Sheetfed press, 6 pages, 2 Color, Newsprint
Subscriptions: Free With Membership
Circulation: Total-45,500

NAS Newsletter
See: NURSING

NAVAPD News

Publishing Co: National Association of VA Physicians & Dentists, 101 N. Alfred St., Ste. 200, Alexandria, VA 22314-4005 Tel # (703) 548-0280; Title Tel # (703) 548-0281 Title Fax # (703) 548-8024
Personnel: Editor-Paul Schafer, MD
General Info: Yr. Est. 1976, Monthly, 8 pages
Circulation: Total-12,000

NBIE Newsletter *Association*

Publishing Co: National Institute of Burn Medicine, 909 E Ann St, Ann Arbor, MI 48104-1613; Title Tel # (313) 769-9000 Title Fax # (313) 769-9009
Personnel: Editor-I. Feller
Editorial Description: Data on prevention, treatment, outcome of the burn problem.
General Info: Yr. Est. 1964, Trim Size-8½ x 11, Offset press, 2 pages, No Color
Circulation: (100% controlled), Total-30,000

NBRC Horizons *Association*

Publishing Co: National Board for Respiratory Care, Inc., 8310 Nieman Rd, Lenexa, KS 66214-1562 Tel # (913) 599-4200; Title Tel # (913) 384-0282
Personnel: Editor-Gary Smith
General Info: (Formerly NBRC Newsletter)

NHF Headlines
See: HEALTH

NHO Newsline *Association*

Publishing Co: National Hospice Organization, 1901 N. Moore St., Ste. 901, Arlington, VA 22209-1714 Tel # (703) 243-5400 Fax # (703) 525-5712; Title Tel # (703) 243-5900 Title Fax # (703) 525-5762
Personnel: Editor, Adv. Dir.-Glenn Gillen
Editorial Description: National news on hospice legislation, management, state news, & calendar.
General Info: (Formerly NHO President's Letter; NHO Hospice News), Yr. Est. 1979, Semi-monthly, Trim Size-8½ x 11, Web press, 6 pages, 25% ads, No Color, Coated
Subscriptions: Free With Membership
Circulation: Readership-5,000
Advertising: $600. Accepts Inserts.
List Rental: Rents Lists
Printing Co: Corporate Press, 403 Brightseat Rd., Landover, MD 20785-4706 Tel # (301) 499-9200, Fax # (301) 499-5435

NKF Newsletter *Consumer, Association*

Publishing Co: National Kidney Foundation, 30 East 33 Street, New York, NY 10016 Fax # (212) 689-9261; Title Tel # (212) 889-2210
Editorial Description: Medical advances, legislative issues, available programs, services. For health care professionals, patients & the general public.
General Info: (Formerly Natl. Kidney Disease Found.), Bi-monthly, 8 pages
Circulation: Total-10,000

NOHA News
See: NUTRITION

NTIS Newsline
See: ENVIRONMENT & ECOLOGY

NYAM Notes

Publishing Co: New York Academy of Medicine, 1216 Fifth Avenue, New York, NY 10029-5293 Tel # (212) 876-8200; Title Tel # (212) 432-8200 Title Fax # (212) 423-0266

NYSSA Sphere *Association*

Publishing Co: New York State Society of Anesthesiologists, 41 E 42nd St Rm 1605, New York, NY 10017-5301; Title Tel # (212) 867-7140 Title Fax # (212) 867-7153
Personnel: Publisher-Kurt Becker, Editor-Alexander Gotta
General Info: (Formerly NYSSA Bulletin), Yr. Est. 1970, Bi-monthly, Trim Size-6 x 9, Sheetfed press, 40 pages, 2 Color, Coated, Saddle-stitched
Subscriptions: Indv. $20
Acquistions: Publication Bought
Circulation: Total-2,400
Printing Co: Washington Church Assn., 10146 Washington Church Rd, Miamisburg, OH 45342-4518 Tel # (513) 435-7336

National, The *Association*

Publishing Co: Canadian Assn. of Occupational Therapists, 110 Eglinton Ave W., 3rd Fl., Toronto, ON M4R 1A3 Canada Tel # (416) 487-5404; Title Tel # (604) 988-8747
Personnel: Editor-Mary Green, Adv. Dir.-John Bain
General Info: Yr. Est. 1974, Bi-monthly, Trim Size-8½ x 11, Offset press, 24 pages, 2 Color, Recycled, Saddle-stitched
Subscriptions: Indv. $18, Inst. $18, Can. $12, For. $18, $3/copy
Advertising: Inquire for rates.
Printing Co: College Printers, 865 Terminal Avenue, Vancouver, BC V6A 2N3 Canada Tel # (604) 685-6322, Fax # (604) 685-0743

National Board Examiner

Publishing Co: Natl. Board of Medical Examiners, 3930 Chestnut St, Philadelphia, PA 19104-3190; Title Tel # (215) 349-6400
General Info: Quarterly, 4 pages, 2 Color
Subscriptions: Free
Circulation: Total-65,000

National Character Laboratory-Newsletter

Publishing Co: Natl. Character Laboratory, 4635 Leeds Ave, El Paso, TX 79903-1211 Fax # (915) 562-3110; Title Tel # (915) 566-3675 Title Fax # (915) 562-5046
Personnel: Editor-A.J. Stuart, Jr.
General Info: Yr. Est. 1971, Quarterly, 18 pages, ISSN: 1067-1161
Subscriptions: Indv. $5
Circulation: Total-200

National Committee for Clinical Laboratory Standards-Update

Publishing Co: NCCLS, 940 West Valley Rd. Suite#1400, Wayne, PA 19087; Title Tel # (610) 688-0100 Title Fax # (610) 688-0700
Personnel: Editor-Margaret Gillock
General Info: Bi-monthly, Trim Size-8½ x 11, Sheetfed press, 8 pages, 2 Color, Matte, Saddle-stitched
Circulation: Total-4,000
List Rental: Rents Lists

National Council Against Health Fraud Newsletter
See: HEALTH

National Federation of Catholic Physicians Guilds Newsletter

Publishing Co: National Federation of Catholic Physicians Guilds, 850 Elm Grove Rd., Elm Grove, WI 53122-2527 Tel # (414) 784-3435
General Info: Quarterly

National Neurofibromatosis Foundation-Newsletter

Publishing Co: National Neurofibromatosis Foundation, Inc., 95 Pine St, New York, NY 10005-1611; Title Tel # (212) 460-8980
Personnel: Editor-Peter Bellermann
General Info: Quarterly, 8 pages, 2 Color, Newsprint
Subscriptions: Free
Acquistions: Publication Bought
Circulation: Total-26,000

National Psoriasis Foundation-Bulletin *Association*

Publishing Co: National Psoriasis Foundation/USA, 6600 SW 92nd Ave. #300, Portland, OR 97223-7195; Title Tel # (503) 244-7404 Title Fax # (503) 245-0626
Personnel: Editor-Sheri Decker, Feature Ed.-Susan Terry, Art Dir.-Robyn Baumbach
Editorial Description: Provides current information about psoriasis treatments, research & self-help. It also reports on the activities of the Natl. Psoriasis Foundation & its advocacy for those who have psoriasis.
General Info: Yr. Est. 1968, Bi-monthly, Trim Size-8½ x 11, Web press, 16 pages, ISSN: 1040-0060, 2 Color, Matte, Saddle-stitched
Subscriptions: $1/copy
Acquistions: Publication Bought
Circulation: Total-50,000, Readership-50,000
Printing Co: Times-Litho, 1829 Pacific Ave., PO Box 7, Forest Grove, OR 97116-2333 Tel # (503) 359-0300, Fax # (503) 357-3754

National Reye's Syndrome Foundation-In the News
See: HEALTH

Needle Tips & the Hepatitis B Coalition News
See: HEALTH

Neuroelectric News

Publishing Co: Neuroelectric Soc., Inc., Med. Col. of Wisconsin, 8700 W. Wisconsin Ave., Milwaukee, WI 53226
Personnel: Editor-Arsen Iwanovsky
General Info: Yr. Est. 1970, ISSN: 0047-942X
Subscriptions: Indv. $25
Circulation: Total-200

Neurofibromatosis Research Newsletter *Consumer, Association*

Publishing Co: National Neurofibromatosis Foundation, Inc., 95 Pine St, New York, NY 10005-1611; Title Tel # (212) 460-8980
Personnel: Editor-John Mulvihill
General Info: Semi-annually, 8 pages, No Color, Coated
Circulation: Total-3,500
Printing Co: Nadelstein Press, New York, NY 10013

Neurology Alert

Publishing Co: American Health Consultants, Inc., 3525 Piedmont Rd., Building #6, Ste. 400, Atlanta, GA 30305-0056 Tel # (404) 262-7436 Fax # (404) 284-3291; Title Tel # (404) 351-4523 Title Fax # (404) 352-1971
Personnel: Publisher-David Wilson, Production Mgr.-Kent Anderson, Mktg. Dir.-Debbie Zelnio
General Info: Monthly
Subscriptions: Indv. $159
List Rental: Actives: $125/M

Neurosurgical Consultations

Publishing Co: Williams & Wilkins, 351 W. Camden St., Baltimore, MD 21201-2436 Fax # (410) 528-4452; Title Tel # (410) 528-4068
Editorial Description: Series providing an ongoing forum for professional dialogue on current modes of diagnosis and treatment.
General Info: Yr. Est. 1990, Bi-weekly, ISSN: 1045-6694

New Brunswick Medical
Society Newsletter   *Business, Association*

Publishing Co: New Brunswick Medical Society, 176 York St., Fredericton, NB E3B 3N8 Canada;
Title Tel # (506) 458-8860
General Info: Monthly, Mimeo press, 4 pages, No Color
Circulation: (100% controlled), Total-950

New Developments in
Medicine & Drug Therapy   *Business, Consumer*

Publishing Co: Physician's & Scientists Publishing, PO Box 435, Glenview, IL 60025-0435;
Title Tel # (708) 559-0605 Title Fax # (708) 559-0699
Editorial Description: For healthcare consumers.
General Info: Bi-monthly, Trim Size-8½ x 11, ISSN: 1063-360X, Ind/Abs/Online: NLightN Database
(Library Service Corp.), 2 Color, Matte, Saddle-stitched
Subscriptions: Indv. $35, Can. $50, For. $55

New England Private
Ambulance Report

Publishing Co: Fire-Medic Services, 19 Joslin St., Providence, RI 02909-2599;
Title Tel # (401) 751-6217
Personnel: Publisher, Editor-Thomas Lopatosky
Editorial Description: News and features covering private ambulance services in 6 New England
States.
General Info: Yr. Est. 1990, Monthly, Trim Size-8½ x 11, Sheetfed press, 8 pages, No Color, Matte
Subscriptions: Indv. $30, Can. $30, For. $30, $3/copy

New Epidemiology Monitor, The
See: HEALTH

New Horizons for Medicine   *Consumer*

Publishing Co: Campaign for New York Hospital-Cornell Medical, 525 E 68th St # 123, New York,
NY 10021-4873 Tel # (212) 821-0500
Personnel: Editor in Chief-Mark Donato
Editorial Description: Medical news from New York Hospital-Cornell Medical.
General Info: Yr. Est. 1993, Semi-annually, Trim Size-8 x 17, 6 pages, 2 Color, Matte

New Orleans Physician   *Association*

Publishing Co: Orleans Parish Medical Society, 1800 Canal St, New Orleans, LA 70112-3014;
Title Tel # (504) 523-2474 Title Fax # (504) 522-3325
Personnel: Publisher-Susan D'Antoni, Editor-Russell C. Klein, MD
Editorial Description: Newsletter containing society activity information and news of physician
members.
General Info: Yr. Est. 1990, Monthly, 6 pages
Subscriptions: Indv. $10
Circulation: Total-2,000

News & Notes

Publishing Co: International College of Surgeons, 1516 N Lake Shore Dr, Chicago, IL 60610-1607
Tel # (312) 642-3555; Title Tel # (312) 787-6274 Title Fax # (312) 787-1624
Personnel: Editor-Jennifer Camano
Editorial Description: For the members of the U.S. section of the assn.
General Info: Quarterly, Trim Size-8½ x 11, 12 pages, 2 Color, Coated
Acquistions: Publication Bought, Publication Sold
Circulation: Total-7,000

News & Views   *Association*

Publishing Co: ALS Association, 1323 Forbes Ave., #200, Pittsburgh, PA 15219;
Title Tel # (412) 261-5940 Title Fax # (412) 471-2722
General Info: Yr. Est. 1982, Bi-monthly, Trim Size-11 x 17, Offset press, 8 pages
Subscriptions: Indv. $20
Circulation: Total-1,400
Printing Co: Suburban Printing Co., 720 Ohio River Blvd., Pittsburgh, PA 15202-3122
Tel # (412) 766-7227, Fax # (412) 766-0914

News of New York   *Association*

Publishing Co: Medical Society of the State of N.Y., 420 Lakeville Rd., Lake Success, NY
11042-1160; Title Tel # (516) 488-6100 Title Fax # (516) 488-1267
Personnel: Editor-Tom Donahue
Editorial Description: Nontechnical, socioeconomic aspects of medicine, including legal aspects,
legislation, society activities, news notes on various trends.
General Info: Yr. Est. 1945, Monthly, Trim Size-10½ x 13, Offset press, 20 pages, 4 Color, Coated,
Saddle-stitched
Subscriptions: Indv. $36
Circulation: Total-27,500
Advertising: Inquire for rates.

Newsletter of Medical Rehabilitation Administrators
See: HEALTH

Newsline   *Association*

Publishing Co: Leukemia Society of America, 600 3rd Ave Fl 4, New York, NY 10016-1900;
Title Tel # (212) 573-8484 Title Fax # (212) 856-9686
Personnel: Editor-Judy Sandford, Science Ed.-Mariann Jordan
Editorial Description: Fundraising news, medical updates, profiles of researchers and volunteers,
features.
General Info: (Formerly Society News), Yr. Est. 1983, Quarterly, Trim Size-8½ x 11, Offset press, 20
pages, 2 Color, Coated
Subscriptions: Free
Circulation: Total-51,000
Printing Co: King Lithographers, 245 S 4th Ave, Mount Vernon, NY 10550-3804
Tel # (914) 667-4200

North Dakota Society for
Clinical Laboratory
Sciences Newsletter   *Consumer, Association*

Publishing Co: North Dakota Society for Medical Technology, 2103 20th Ave S, Grand Forks, ND
58201-6162; Title Tel # (701) 780-1561 Title Fax # (701) 780-1473
Personnel: Editor-Eileen Nelson
General Info: Yr. Est. 1972, Quarterly, Web press, 28 pages, No Color
Subscriptions: Indv. $6
Circulation: (100% controlled), Total-400

Nutrition Research Newsletter
See: NUTRITION

OT Week   *Association*

Publishing Co: American Occupational Therapy Assn., 4720 Montgomery Lane, PO Box 31220,
Bethesda, MD 20824-1220 Tel # (301) 652-2682 Fax # (301) 652-7711; Title Tel # (301) 881-2740
Title Fax # (301) 881-2497
Editorial Description: Developments and news in the field of occupational therapy.
General Info: Yr. Est. 1986, Weekly
Subscriptions: Indv. $80
Circulation: Total-65,500
Advertising: Inquire for rates.

Ob/Gyn Clinical Alert

Publishing Co: American Health Consultants, Inc., 3525 Piedmont Rd., Building #6, Ste. 400,
Atlanta, GA 30305-0056 Tel # (404) 262-7436 Fax # (404) 284-3291; Title Tel # (404) 351-4523
Personnel: Publisher-David Wilson, Editor-Leon Speroff, MD, Circ. Mgr.-Monica Brown, Mktg. Dir.-
Debbie Zelnio
Editorial Description: Reviews medical literature & research related to gynecology & obstetrics.
General Info: Yr. Est. 1983, Monthly, ISSN: 0743-8354
Subscriptions: Indv. $159
List Rental: Actives: $125/M

Occupational &
Environmental Medicine
Report

Publishing Co: OEM Health Information, 181 Elliott St Ste 814, Beverly, MA 01915-3061;
Title Tel # (508) 921-7300 Title Fax # (508) 921-0304
Personnel: Publisher-Curtis Vouwie, Editor-Robert McCunney
Editorial Description: Covers occupational medicine.
General Info: Yr. Est. 1987, Monthly
Subscriptions: Indv. $110

Official Journal - American
College of Medical
Quality   *Business, Association*

Publishing Co: American College of Medical Quality, 9005 Congressional Ct, Potomac, MD
20854-4608 Tel # (301) 365-3570 Fax # (301) 365-3202; Title Tel # (813) 497-3340
Title Fax # (813) 497-5573
Personnel: Editor-David Jones, Adv. Dir.-Angela Hopkins
Editorial Description: Directed to continuing education of physicians in the areas of QA & UR.
General Info: Yr. Est. 1979, Quarterly, Offset press, 96 pages, Looseleaf
Subscriptions: Indv. $70
Circulation: Total-4,000
Printing Co: Cumberland Printing Co., 4 W Allen St, Mechanicsburg, PA 17055-6297
Tel # (717) 697-2204

On the Level
See: HEALTH

One-In-Ten

Publishing Co: Rehabilitation Intl., 25 E 21st St, New York, NY 10010-6298;
Title Tel # (212) 420-1500
Editorial Description: Focuses on their prevention & rehabilitation' in developing countries.'
General Info: Yr. Est. 1980, Quarterly

Optimist
See: HEALTH

Ortho Newsletter
See: HEALTH

Orthopedic Special Edition

Publishing Co: McMahon Group, 148 W. 24th St., 8th Floor, New York, NY 10011-1916; Title Tel # (212) 620-4600 Title Fax # (212) 620-5928
Personnel: Publisher-Raymond McMahon, Editor-James Prudden, Production Mgr.-Matt McMahono, Adv. Dir.-Lauren McMahon, Art Dir.-Michele McMahon
Editorial Description: Single subject 'newsletter' focusing on a single topic in orthopedics per issue.
General Info: (Formerly Orthopedic & Sports Medicine News), Monthly, Web press, 4 Color, Coated, Saddle-stitched
Subscriptions: Indv. $46, For. $78, $5/copy
Circulation: Total-20,384
Advertising: Accepts Inserts.
Printing Co: Democrat Printing & Lithographing Co., 6401 Lindsey Rd, Little Rock, AR 72206-3823 Tel # (501) 490-1575, Fax # (501) 490-2568

Osler Library Newsletter
See: LIBRARY

Osteopathic College of Ophthamology & Otorhinolaryngology-Newsletter

Publishing Co: Osteopathic College of Ophthalmology & Otorhinolaryngology, 405 W Grand Ave, Dayton, OH 45405-4720; Title Tel # (513) 222-4213
Personnel: Editor-Sharon Alexiades
General Info: Quarterly
Circulation: Total-485

Our Voice
See: HEALTH

Outpatient Reimbursement Management
See: HOSPITALS & NURSING HOMES

PDF Update

Publishing Co: Paget's Disease Foundation, Inc., 200 Varick Street, # 1004, New York, NY 10014-4810; Title Tel # (718) 596-1043
Personnel: Editor-Charlene Waldman
Editorial Description: Info about recent research on Paget's disease of bone & news of the Foundation.
General Info: Yr. Est. 1978, Semi-annually, 8 pages
Circulation: Total-34,000

PHO Update *Business*

Publishing Co: American Health Consultants, Inc., 3525 Piedmont Rd., Building #6, Ste. 400, Atlanta, GA 30305-0056 Tel # (404) 262-7436 Fax # (404) 284-3291
Personnel: Publisher-Connie Austin, Editor-Glen Harris, Circ. Mgr.-Monica Brown, Production Mgr.-Mike Witter, Mktg. Dir.-Robin Prows
Editorial Description: For physician hospital organizations.
General Info: Yr. Est. 1994, Monthly
Subscriptions: Indv. $379, $36/copy
List Rental: Actives: 145

PS: It Is News
See: PSYCHOLOGY

Parkinson Report

Publishing Co: National Parkinson Foundation, Inc., 1501 NW 9th Ave, Miami, FL 33136-1407; Title Tel # (305) 547-6666
Personnel: Editor-Lazarus Orkin, M.D., Production Mgr.-Linda Zuker
Editorial Description: Review of foundation news and research and treatment around the country.
General Info: (Formerly National Parkinson Foundation, Newsletter), Yr. Est. 1960, Quarterly, 16 pages, 2 Color, Coated, Saddle-stitched
Circulation: Total-70,000

Parkinson's Disease Foundation-Newsletter *Business, Association*

Publishing Co: Parkinson's Disease Foundation, 710 W 168th St, 10th FL., New York, NY 10032-9982; Title Tel # (212) 923-4700
Personnel: Editor-Dinah Tottenham Orr
Editorial Description: Updates on research & events of interest to people with Parkinson's family members & healthcare professionals. Tips for activities of daily living.
General Info: Yr. Est. 1957, Quarterly, Sheetfed press, 5 pages, 2 Color, Coated
Subscriptions: For. $10, Free
Circulation: Total-80,000

Parkinson's Disease Update *Association*

Publishing Co: Medical Publishing Co., Inc., PO Box 24622h, Philadelphia, PA 19111-0622; Title Tel # (215) 947-6638
Editorial Description: Contains information on Parkinson's Disease.
General Info: Yr. Est. 1992, Bi-monthly
Subscriptions: Indv. $40

Passaic County Medical Society Newsnotes *Association* CPM: $406

Publishing Co: Passaic County Medical Society, 999 Mcbride Ave Suite B-202, West Paterson, NJ 07424-2534; Title Tel # (201) 890-0700 Title Fax # (201) 890-2460
Personnel: Editor-William McGuire
Editorial Description: Local, state national and society news of interest to physician members.
General Info: (Formerly Bulletin), Yr. Est. 1966, 8x/yr., Trim Size-8½ x 11, Offset press, 16 pages, 25% ads, No Color, Newsprint
Subscriptions: Free With Membership
Circulation: Total-800
Advertising: $325.

Patient Drug Facts Package
See: DRUGS & PHARMACEUTICALS

Pediatric Alert *Business, Association*

Publishing Co: Pediatric Alert, PO Box 338, Newton Highlands, MA 02161-0004; Title Tel # (617) 237-3310
Personnel: Publisher-Allen Mitchell
Editorial Description: Surveys the world's current medical literature, lay press and news releases from private and governmental agencies to provide objective summaries of articles of interest to the pediatric practitioner.
General Info: Yr. Est. 1976, Bi-weekly, Trim Size-8½ x 11, ISSN: 0160-0184
Subscriptions: Indv. $65, Inst. $85, Can. $65, For. $85, $4/copy

Pediatric Currents

Publishing Co: Ross Labs., 625 Cleveland Ave, Columbus, OH 43215-1754; Title Tel # (614) 227-3264
Personnel: Editor-Dorothy Redfern, Adv. Dir.-Berman Pound, Art Dir.-Debbie Vajda
Editorial Description: Abstracts from the current medical literature in pediatrics, perinatology/neonatology, and adolescent medicine.
General Info: Yr. Est. 1965, 10x/yr., Trim Size-8½ x 11, Offset press, 6 pages, 2 Color
Circulation: (100% controlled), Total-83,000

Pediatric Report's Child Health Newsletter

Publishing Co: IGM Enterprises Inc., 71 Hope St. #155, Providence, RI 02906-2001; Title Tel # (401) 434-7390
Editorial Description: News and developments for medical professionals specializing in pediatrics.
General Info: Yr. Est. 1984, 11x/yr.
Subscriptions: Indv. $35

Pediatrics for Parents
See: FAMILY

People's Medical Society Newsletter *Consumer*

Publishing Co: People's Medical Society, 462 W Walnut St, Allentown, PA 18102-5488; Title Tel # (215) 770-1670 Title Fax # (610) 770-0607
Personnel: Editor-K. Patrick
General Info: Yr. Est. 1983, Bi-monthly, Trim Size-11 x 17, Letrpr. press, 8 pages, ISSN: 0736-4873, Ind/Abs/Online: DIALOG, 2 Color, Newsprint
Subscriptions: Indv. $20
Circulation: Total-80,000
List Rental: Actives: $75/M

Perinatal Addiction Research & Education Update *Business, Association*

Publishing Co: National Association for Perinatal Addiction Research & Ed., 200 N. Michigan Avenue, # Fl., Chicago, IL 60601-5909 Tel # (312) 389-2812; Title Tel # (312) 541-1272 Title Fax # (312) 541-1271
Personnel: Publisher-Judith Burnison
Editorial Description: Articles of interest to professionals in the field of perinatal addiction.
General Info: Yr. Est. 1988, Quarterly, Trim Size-8½ x 11, 10 pages, 2 Color, Saddle-stitched
Subscriptions: Free With Membership
Circulation: Total-2,000

Personnel Postscript
See: INDUSTRIAL RELATIONS/PERSONNEL

Perspective

Publishing Co: Arthritis Foundation, 1314 Spring St. NW, Atlanta, GA 30309-2898; Title Tel # (404) 872-7100 Title Fax # (404) 872-0457
Personnel: Publisher-Ruth Martin, Editor-Diana Anderson, Circ. Mgr.-Susan Charles, Production Mgr.-Cynthia Kahn, Adv. Dir.-Happy Tyree
Editorial Description: A newsletter for Arthritis Health professionals.
General Info: Yr. Est. 1967, Quarterly, Trim Size-8½ x 11, 12 pages, No Color, Coated, Saddle-stitched
Circulation: Total-2,000
List Rental: Rents Lists

Perspectives on Medical Practice Management
See: MANAGEMENT

Pharmacy News
See: DRUGS & PHARMACEUTICALS

Phi Chi Chronicles

Publishing Co: Phi Chi Chronicles, Central Office - Phi Chi, 1201 E. Spring St., New Albany, NY 47150
Personnel: Editor in Chief-Dan Cannon, M.D.
Editorial Description: Newsletter of the Phi Chi Medical Fraternity.
Subscriptions: Indv. $15
Printing Co: PDG Typesetting and Printing, 214 E. Main St., New Albany, NY 47150

Physiatrist, The   *Association*

Publishing Co: American Academy of Physical Medicine and Rehabilitation, One IRM Plaza Suite #250, Chicago, IL 60611-3604 Fax # (312) 464-0227; Title Tel # (312) 464-9700
Editorial Description: The official membership publication of the American Academy of Physical Medicine and Rehabilitation.
General Info: (Formerly PM&R News), Yr. Est. 1984, 10x/yr., Trim Size-8½ x 11, Sheetfed press, 16 pages, 2 Color, Newsprint
Subscriptions: Free With Membership
Circulation: Total-4,600
Advertising: Inquire for rates.
List Rental: Actives: $290/M

Physician Laboratory Regulations Manual
See: HEALTH

Physician Manager   *Business*

Publishing Co: Atlantic Information Svcs., Inc., 1100 17th St. NW, Ste. 300, Washington, DC 20036-5503; Title Tel # (202) 775-9008 Title Fax # (202) 331-9542
Personnel: Publisher-Rick Biehl, Editor-Laura Sachs, Circ. Mgr.-Kristen Mulcahy, Mktg. Dir.-Donna Lawton
Editorial Description: Practical news and valuable management tools to help achieve results as a medical manager.
General Info: Yr. Est. 1990, Bi-weekly, 8 pages
Subscriptions: Indv. $326
Acquistions: Publication Sold
List Rental: Rents Lists

Physician Marketplace Update

Publishing Co: American Medical Association, 515 N. State St., Chicago, IL 60610 Tel # (312) 464-4512 Fax # (312) 464-5834; Title Tel # (312) 645-5000 Title Fax # (312) 464-5600
Editorial Description: Articles and survey data on health care issues.
General Info: Bi-monthly
Subscriptions: Indv. $75

Physician's Malpractice Advisor

Publishing Co: Medlex Consulting, Inc., PO Box 748, Marblehead, MA 01945-0748; Title Tel # (617) 631-5226
Editorial Description: News, case histories & perspective on medical liability issues.
General Info: Yr. Est. 1989, Trim Size-8½ x 11, 12 pages, 2 Color, Matte, Saddle-stitched
Subscriptions: Indv. $120

Physicians Managed Care Report   *Business*

Publishing Co: American Health Consultants, Inc., 3525 Piedmont Rd., Building #6, Ste. 400, Atlanta, GA 30305-0056 Tel # (404) 262-7436 Fax # (404) 284-3291
Personnel: Publisher-Connie Austin, Editor-Eric Resultan, Circ. Mgr.-Monica Brown, Production Mgr.-Mike Witter, Mktg. Dir.-Robin Prows
Editorial Description: Managed care information for physicians.
General Info: Yr. Est. 1993, Monthly
Subscriptions: Indv. $269, $26/copy
List Rental: Actives: $145/M

Physician's Marketing & Management

Publishing Co: American Health Consultants, Inc., 3525 Piedmont Rd., Building #6, Ste. 400, Atlanta, GA 30305-0056; Title Tel # (404) 262-7436 Title Fax # (404) 284-3291
Personnel: Publisher-Connie Austin, Editor-Eric Resultan, Circ. Mgr.-Monica Brown, Production Mgr.-Mike Witter, Art Dir.-Chris Taylor, Mktg. Dir.-Robin Prows
Editorial Description: Marketing & management information for healthcare professionals in private practice.
General Info: Yr. Est. 1983, Monthly, Desktop press, 8 pages, ISSN: 0740-6983, Newsprint
Subscriptions: Indv. $189, $18/copy
Acquistions: Publication Bought, Publication Sold
Circulation: Total-5,000
List Rental: Actives: $145/M

Physician's Patient Newsletter
See: HEALTH

Physicians Payment

Publishing Co: American Health Consultants, Inc., 3525 Piedmont Rd., Building #6, Ste. 400, Atlanta, GA 30305-0056 Tel # (404) 262-7436 Fax # (404) 284-3291; Title Tel # (404) 351-4523
Personnel: Publisher-Connie Austin, Editor-Eric Resultan, Circ. Mgr.-Monica Brown, Production Mgr.-Mike Witter, Mktg. Mgr.-Robin Prows
General Info: (Formerly Physicians Payment Advisory), Monthly
Subscriptions: Indv. $299, $29/copy
List Rental: Actives: $145/M

Physiology Canada
See: PHYSIOLOGY

Physiotherapy Today
See: HEALTH

Pierce County Medical Society Newsleter   *Association*

Publishing Co: Pierce County Medical Society, 223 Tacoma Ave S, Tacoma, WA 98402-2513; Title Tel # (206) 572-3709
Personnel: Editor-Doug Jackson
Editorial Description: Covers local medical society & national medical news of interest to members.
General Info: Monthly, Trim Size-8½ x 11
Subscriptions: Indv. $20, Free With Membership
Circulation: Total-1,200

Pink Sheet: Prescription and OTC pharmaceuticals
See: DRUGS & PHARMACEUTICALS

Pirquet Bulletin of Clinical Medicine

Publishing Co: Pirquet Bulletin of Clinical Medicine, 310 E 14th St, New York, NY 10003-4200
Personnel: Editor-Gerhart Schwaz, M.D.
General Info: Yr. Est. 1953, 9x/yr.
Circulation: Total-900
Advertising: Inquire for rates.

Plastic Surgery Outlook

Publishing Co: Quality Medica Publishing, Inc, 2086 Craigshire Rd, Saint Louis, MO 63146-4010; Title Tel # (314) 878-7808 Title Fax # (314) 878-9937
Personnel: Publisher-Karen Berger, Editor-Ian Jackson
Editorial Description: Contains literature review & meeting highlights.
General Info: 10x/yr.
Subscriptions: Indv. $185

Polio Network News

Publishing Co: Gazette International Networking Institute, 4207 Lindell Boulevard, #110, St. Louis, MO 63108; Title Tel # (314) 534-0475 Title Fax # (314) 534-5070
Personnel: Editor-Joan Headley
Editorial Description: Information/network on late effects of poliomyelitis for physicians & survivors.
General Info: Yr. Est. 1985, Quarterly, Trim Size-8½ x 11, Offset press, 12 pages, ISSN: 1066-5331, No Color, Matte, Saddle-stitched
Subscriptions: Indv. $12, Inst. $20, Can. $16, For. $20
Circulation: Total-4,500

Porphyria News

Publishing Co: American Porphyria Foundation, PO Box 22712, Houston, TX 77227-2712; Title Tel # (713) 266-9617 Title Fax # (713) 871-1788
Personnel: Editor-Desiree Lyon
Editorial Description: Reviews current research & new treatments related to the disease porphyria.
General Info: Yr. Est. 1981, Quarterly, 1 pages
Subscriptions: Indv. $30, Free To Qualified Recipient
Circulation: Total-2,000

Post Anesthesia and Ambulatory Surgery Nursing Update

Publishing Co: W.B. Saunders Co., Curtis Ctr., Independence Square West, Philadelphia, PA 19106 Tel # (215) 238-7800 Fax # (215) 238-6445 Parent Co.-Harcourt Brace Professional Publishing, Orlando
Personnel: Editor-Nancy Burden, RN, CPAN
Editorial Description: Condenses current literature into a succinct yet comprehensive format for post anesthesia nurses, nurse anesthetists, and nurses in ambulatory surgery. Emphasizes assessment techniques, nursing interventions, documentation requirements, and complicationsassociated with specific procedures.
General Info: Yr. Est. 1993, Bi-monthly, ISSN: 1066-8977
Subscriptions: Indv. $49, Inst. $85, For. $100, $19/copy

Postgraduate Center for Mental Health-News

Publishing Co: Postgraduate Center for Mental Health, 124 E 28th St, New York, NY 10016-8402; Title Tel # (212) 689-7700
Personnel: Editor-Esther Smith
General Info: Yr. Est. 1983, Semi-annually, 6 pages
Circulation: Total-1,500

Practice Builder's What's Working in Practice Building , The
Business

Publishing Co: The Practice Builder, 18351 Jamboree Rd., Irvine, CA 92715-1011; Title Tel # (714) 253-7900 Title Fax # (714) 252-1002
Personnel: Publisher, Editor-Alan L. Bernstein, Circ. Mgr., Production Mgr.-Rick Lough
Editorial Description: Marketing strategies for professional practices.
General Info: Yr. Est. 1983, Monthly, Trim Size-8$\frac{1}{2}$ x 11, Offset press, 12 pages, ISSN: 0883-3036, 2 Color, Matte, Saddle-stitched
Subscriptions: Indv. $124, $11/copy
Circulation: Total-25,000
List Rental: List Management Co.: Manager: Lynette Coxey; WMI/Worldata, 5200 Town Center Circle, Boca Raton, FL 33486 Tel # (407) 393-8200, Fax # (407) 368-8345, Actives: 42,349, $90/M

President's Newsletter
Association

Publishing Co: Joint Council of Allergy & Immunology, PO Box 4620, Arlington Heights, IL 60006-4620 Tel # (708) 427-8100
Editorial Description: Promotes AACA events to membership.
General Info: Yr. Est. 1968, Semi-annually, Letrpr. press, 4 pages, 2 Color, Newsprint
Circulation: (100% controlled), Total-600

President's Weekly Activity Report

Publishing Co: Association of American Medical Colleges, 2450 N Street, N.W., Washington, DC 20037-1167; Title Tel # (202) 828-0400
Personnel: Editor-Joan Hartman-Moore
General Info: Yr. Est. 1954, Monthly

Pressure
Association

Publishing Co: Undersea & Hyperbaric Medical Society, 10531 Metropolitan Ave., Kensington, MD 20895-2627; Title Tel # (301) 942-2980 Title Fax # (301) 942-7804
Editorial Description: Courses, meetings, classifieds, general information on diving physiology & clincal hyperbaric medicine.
General Info: Yr. Est. 1972, Bi-monthly, Trim Size-8$\frac{1}{2}$ x 11, ISSN: 0889-0242, Saddle-stitched
Subscriptions: Indv. $25, $6/copy
Circulation: Total-2,500
Printing Co: Image Graphics, 1200 Indian Creek Ct., Beltsville, MD 20705 Tel # (301) 470-2700, Fax # (301) 470-2701

Prevention Report

Publishing Co: Rodale Press, 33 East Minor St., Emmaus, PA 18098-0001 Tel # (610) 967-5171 Fax # (610) 967-8963; Title Tel # (215) 967-5171
Personnel: Editor-Tom Dybdahl
Editorial Description: Promotes prevention & reduction of corporate health costs.
General Info: Monthly

Primary Care Medicine Drug Alerts
See: DRUGS & PHARMACEUTICALS

Primary Probe

Publishing Co: DUWEST Research/Scientific Newsletters, Rr 4 Box 7, Middletown, NY 10940-9685; Title Tel # (914) 355-9144 Title Fax # (914) 355-9147
Personnel: Publisher, Editor-Marc Duey, Circ. Mgr.-Maureen Duey
Editorial Description: Reporting, commentary, & analysis of the news & events affecting the in-vitro diagnostic & biotechnology industries.
General Info: Yr. Est. 1988, 8x/yr., ISSN: 0897-3164
Subscriptions: Indv. $450, For. $180, $25/copy
Circulation: Total-350
List Rental: Rents Lists

Probe Newsletter
See: SCIENCE

Professional Liability Update
See: LAW

Professional Placement Newsnotes
See: HOSPITALS & NURSING HOMES

Professional Practice Today
See: MANAGEMENT

Progress Against Cancer
Association

Publishing Co: Canadian Cancer Society-Ontario Div., 1639 Yonge St., Toronto, ON M4T 2W6 Canada; Title Tel # (416) 488-5400
Personnel: Editor-Barbara Kilvert
General Info: Yr. Est. 1948, Quarterly, Trim Size-8$\frac{1}{2}$ x 11, Offset press, 8 pages, 2 Color
Subscriptions: Free
Circulation: Total-40,000

Progress in Dermatology

Publishing Co: Dermatology Foundation, 1560 Sherman Ave., Evanston, IL 60201-3698; Title Tel # (708) 328-2256
General Info: Yr. Est. 1966, Quarterly, Trim Size-18$\frac{1}{2}$ x 26$\frac{1}{2}$, 12 pages, 2% ads
Circulation: Total-3,000
Advertising: Inquire for rates.

Progress Notes

Publishing Co: University of Louisville Alumni Assn., 2001 S. Brook St., Louisville, KY 40292-0001; Title Tel # (502) 852-6186
Editorial Description: Related information updates on research, faculty appointments and special events concerning the school of medicine.
General Info: (Formerly Medical News Notes), Semi-annually, 2 Color
Subscriptions: Free

Proving Medical Diagnosis and Prognosis

Publishing Co: Matthew Bender & Co., 11 Penn Plaza, New York, NY 10001-2006 Fax # (212) 244-3188; Title Tel # (212) 967-7707
Personnel: Editor-B. Lieberman
Editorial Description: Complete, authoritative guidance on orthopedic, neurological, and laboratory tests. In-depth discussion of medical records.
General Info: Yr. Est. 1970, Annually, Looseleaf
Subscriptions: $990/copy

Psychiatric Topics
See: PSYCHIATRY

Pulse
Business, Association

Publishing Co: Jefferson County Medical Society, 901 18th St. S., Birmingham, AL 35205-3733 Fax # (206) 939-0680; Title Tel # (205) 933-8601 Title Fax # (205) 939-0680
Personnel: Publisher-Jan B. Anderson, Editor-Jan Anderson
Editorial Description: Pulse is published 10 times yearly for 1,800 physicians who are members of the Jefferson County Medical Society.
General Info: (Formerly Bulletin Jeff. Co. Med. Soc.), Yr. Est. 1956, 10x/yr., Trim Size-8$\frac{1}{2}$ x 11, Web press, 8 pages, 2 Color, Newsprint, Saddle-stitched
Acquistions: Publication Bought
Circulation: Total-1,950
Advertising: Inquire for rates.
List Rental: Rents Lists
Printing Co: Lowry Printing, Inc., Box 876, Birmingham, AL 35256-0001 Tel # (205) 252-7103

QRC Advisor
Business

Publishing Co: Aspen Publishers, Inc., 200 Orchard Ridge Dr., Ste 200, Gaithersburg, MD 20878-5440 Fax # (301) 417-7655 Parent Co.-Wolters Kluwer US Corporation, New York; Title Tel # (301) 417-7500 Title Fax # (301) 417-7550
Personnel: Editor-Barbara Youngberg, VP Mktng.-Cynthia Smtih, Mktg. Mgr.-Trudi Graham
Editorial Description: This outstanding monthly offers sound, authoritative, state-of-the-art advice for effectively handling your official quality assurance, risk management, and cost control issues.
General Info: Yr. Est. 1985, Monthly, Trim Size-8$\frac{1}{2}$ x 11, 8 pages, ISSN: 0747-7384
Subscriptions: Indv. $210, For. $252, $22/copy
Circulation: Readership-7,300
List Rental: List Management Co.: Stevens-Knox List Management, 304 Park Ave S., New York, NY 10010-5312 Tel # (212) 388-8800, Fax # (212) 388-8890, Actives: $125/M, Expires: $125/M

Radioassay Ligand-Assay News

Publishing Co: DUWEST Research/Scientific Newsletters, Rr 4 Box 7, Middletown, NY 10940-9685; Title Tel # (914) 355-9144 Title Fax # (914) 355-9147
Personnel: Publisher, Editor-Marc Duey, Adv. Dir.-Maureen Duey
Editorial Description: Reports developments in technology, products & services in the field of immunodiagnostics, including RIA, EIA & related techniques.
General Info: (Formerly Radioassay Ligand-Assay News Scientific Newsletter), Yr. Est. 1974, 10x/yr., Trim Size-8$\frac{1}{2}$ x 12, Offset press, 10 pages, ISSN: 0098-0889, No Color
Subscriptions: Indv. $100, For. $115, $9/copy
Acquistions: Publication Bought, Publication Sold
Circulation: Total-1,900
List Rental: Actives: $65/M

Radiology & Imaging Letter
Consumer

Publishing Co: Quest Publishing Co., 1351 Titan Way, Brea, CA 92621-3787 Fax # (714) 525-3787 Parent Co.-Lippincott-Raven Press Publishers, Philadelphia; Title Tel # (714) 738-6400 Title Fax # (714) 525-6258
Personnel: Publisher-Steve McCoy, Editor-Linda Huang, Mktg. Dir.-Michele Duncan
Editorial Description: Independent newsletter in radiology including diagnostic imaging, radiation therapy, ultrasound, and nuclear medicine.
General Info: (Formerly Radiology Letter), Yr. Est. 1981, Semi-monthly, Trim Size-8$\frac{1}{2}$ x 11, Sheetfed press, 8 pages, ISSN: 0741-160X, No Color, Newsprint, Saddle-stitched
Subscriptions: Indv. $290, Can. $290, For. $340
List Rental: Rents Lists

Reaching Out
See: DISABILITY

Real Living with Diabetes
See: HEALTH

Real Living with Multiple Sclerosis
See: HEALTH

Refractive Surgery Outlook   *Scholarly, Association*

Publishing Co: American Academy of Ophthalmology, 655 Beach St, San Francisco, CA 94109-1336
Tel # (415) 561-8500; Tel # (415) 561-8539 Title Fax # (415) 561-8567
Personnel: Editor-Marguerite McDonald, MD, Mag. Ed.-John Hayes
Editorial Description: Physician-written articles about clinical and economic aspects of refractive surgery.
General Info: Yr. Est. 1995, 8 pages, 4 Color
Subscriptions: Free With Membership
Circulation: Total-900
Printing Co: Warren Waller Press, 339 Harbor Way, South San Francisco, CA 94080-6919
Tel # (415) 589-0578

Regan Report on Hospital Law
See: HOSPITALS & NURSING HOMES

Regan Report on Medical Law

Publishing Co: Medica Press Inc., 10 Dorrance St. - Rm. 500, Providence, RI 02903-2018;
Title Tel # (401) 421-4747
Personnel: Circ. Mgr.-Elaine Bedrosian, Publisher, Editor, Production Mgr.-David Tammelleo
Editorial Description: Reports the latest & most significant Appellate court decisions on Medical Law & Medical Malpractice. In a case and comment format with lessons on legal rights and responsibilities, risk management, and malpractice defense strategies.
General Info: Yr. Est. 1968, Monthly, Trim Size-8½ x 11, Offset press, 4 pages, ISSN: 0034-3188, 2 Color, Coated
Subscriptions: Indv. $48, Can. $48, For. $48, $4/copy
Acquistions: Publication Bought
Circulation: Total-20,000
List Rental: Rents Lists

Registry, The
See: HEARING & SPEECH

Rehab Update   *Business, Consumer*

Publishing Co: Psy-Ed Corp, 209 Harvard St Ste 303, Brookline, MA 02146-5005
Editorial Description: For professionals involved with rehab treatment of children and adults with disabilities.
General Info: Monthly
Circulation: Total-5,100
List Rental: List Management Co.: Wilson Marketing Group, 11924 W Washington Blvd, Los Angeles, CA 90066-5880 Tel # (213) 398-2754, Actives: 5,100, $100/M

Repetitive Stress Injury Litigation Reporter
See: LAW

Report on Healthcare Management Solutions
See: HOSPITALS & NURSING HOMES

Report on Medical Guidelines and Outcomes Research
See: HOSPITALS & NURSING HOMES

Report on Pediatric Infectuous Diseases   *Scholarly*

Publishing Co: Churchill Livingstone, Inc., 650 Ave. of the Americas, New York, NY 10011
Tel # (212) 727-7790; Title Tel # (212) 206-5040 Title Fax # (212) 727-7808
Personnel: Publisher-Jane Grochowski, Editor-George Peter
Editorial Description: A publication of the Pediatric Infectuous Diseases Society, this newsletter provides concise and contemporary information on issues of importance to practicing physicians responsible for the care of infants and children.
General Info: Yr. Est. 1991, 10x/yr., 8 pages, ISSN: 1050-9644, Color-cover, Newsprint
Subscriptions: Indv. $49, Inst. $59, Can. $95, For. $95

Report on Physician Trends
See: HOSPITALS & NURSING HOMES

Reporter on the Legal Profession
See: LAW

Reports

Publishing Co: Joint Council of Allergy & Immunology, PO Box 4620, Arlington Heights, IL 60006-4620 Tel # (708) 427-8100
Personnel: Editor-Joseph Lotharius
General Info: Yr. Est. 1975, Quarterly
Acquistions: Publication Bought
List Rental: Actives: $100/M

Reproductive Technology Update

Publishing Co: Reproductive Technology Update, 67 Peachtree Park Dr NE, Atlanta, GA 30309-1303; Title Tel # (404) 351-4523
Subscriptions: Indv. $189

Research Resources Reporter   *Consumer*

Publishing Co: National Center for Research Resources Information Ctr., Bldg. 31, Room 2B03, 9000 Rockville Pike, Bethesda, MD 20892 Tel # (301) 496-2125; Title Tel # (301) 496-5545
Personnel: Editor-Edward Post
Editorial Description: Reports on current bio medical research studies being conducted at research facilities. Supported by the NIH Division of Research Resources.
General Info: Yr. Est. 1977, Monthly, Trim Size-8½ x 11, Sheetfed press, 16 pages, ISSN: 0160-807X, No Color, Matte, Saddle-stitched
Subscriptions: Indv. $9, For. $11
Circulation: Total-13,500

Resolve National Newsletter
See: FAMILY

Respiratory Care Manager
See: HOSPITALS & NURSING HOMES

Review, The   *Consumer, Scholarly*

Publishing Co: House Ear Institute, 2100 W. 3rd, Los Angeles, CA 90057-2115;
Title Tel # (213) 483-4431 Title Fax # (213) 483-8789
Personnel: Editor-Dilys J. Jones
Editorial Description: Inform public of hearing and balance disorders and reports progress in ear research. Includes in-house news items.
General Info: (Formerly House Cochlear Implant Assn. Newsletter), Yr. Est. 1966, Tri-annually, Trim Size-8½ x 11, Web press, 8 pages, 2 Color, Newsprint, Saddle-stitched
Subscriptions: Indv. $10, Free
Circulation: Total-24,000

SIGBIO Newsletter   *Association*

Publishing Co: Association for Computing Machinery, 1515 Broadway, 17th Fl., New York, NY 10036-5701 Fax # (212) 302-5826; Title Tel # (212) 869-7440
Personnel: Production Mgr.-Donna Baglio
Editorial Description: Current developments and happenings in computer applications in biology and medicine, including education, research, administrative and health care applications.
General Info: Yr. Est. 1969, Quarterly, 20 pages, No Color
Subscriptions: Indv. $28, $10/copy
Circulation: Total-1,500

STFM Messenger   *Association*

Publishing Co: Society of Teachers of Family Medicine, 8880 Ward Pkwy., Box 8729, Kansas City, MO 64114-2756 Tel # (816) 333-9700 Fax # (816) 333-3884; Title Tel # (800) 274-2237
Personnel: Publisher, Editor-Diane Prout
Editorial Description: News of interest to family medicine educators.
General Info: (Formerly STFM Newsletter), Yr. Est. 1980, Bi-monthly, Sheetfed press, 6 pages, Newsprint
Circulation: Total-3,500
List Rental: Actives: $62/M
Printing Co: Boelte-Hall Litho, Inc., 4710 Roe Pky, Roeland Park, KS 66205-1114
Tel # (913) 432-5800

St. Anthony's Coding for OB/GYN Reimbursement Newsletter
See: HEALTH

St. Anthony's Coding for Orthopaedic Reimbursement
See: HEALTH

St. Anthony's Coding for Physician Reimbursement Newsletter
See: HEALTH

St. Anthony's Healthcare Resources Alert
See: HEALTH

St. Anthony's Physicians Resources Alert
See: HEALTH

St. John Ambulance, Instructor's Digest
See: HEALTH

Same-Day Surgery   *Business*

Publishing Co: American Health Consultants, Inc., 3525 Piedmont Rd., Building #6, Ste. 400, Atlanta, GA 30305-0056 Fax # (404) 284-3291; Title Tel # (404) 262-7436
Title Fax # (404) 262-7837
Personnel: Publisher-Connie Austin, Editor-Joy Daughtery, Circ. Mgr.-Monica Brown, Production Mgr.-Mike Witter, Mktg. Mgr.-Rebecca S. Torres
Editorial Description: Contains articles on administrative, financial, and medical aspects of ambulatory surgery.
General Info: Monthly, Trim Size-8½ x 11, Offset press, 16 pages, Ind/Abs/Online: Mead Data Central, 2 Color
Subscriptions: Indv. $339, $32/copy
Circulation: Total-2,680
List Rental: Actives: $145/M

Scalpel   *Association*

Publishing Co: Alpha Epsilon Delta, Jones Junior College, Ellisville, MS 39437;
 Title Tel # (601) 426-6019
General Info: Semi-annually
Circulation: Total-8,500

Scanner   *Association*

Publishing Co: American College of Nuclear Physicians, 1101 Connecticut Ave NW Ste, 700,
 Washington, DC 20036-4303; Title Tel # (202) 857-1135
Personnel: Publisher, Editor-Holly Anderson
Editorial Description: Physicians doing diagnostic work with radio-active pharmaceuticals.
General Info: (Formerly Scanner), Yr. Est. 1974, Monthly
Circulation: Total-1,500
List Rental: Rents Lists

Scientific American Medical Monthly Update

Publishing Co: Scientific American, Inc., 415 Madison Ave., New York, NY 10017-1179;
 Title Tel # (212) 754-0550
Personnel: Editor-Hilary Evans
General Info: Monthly
Subscriptions: Indv. $170

Scientific American Medicine

Publishing Co: Scientific American, Inc., 415 Madison Ave., New York, NY 10017-1179;
 Title Tel # (212) 754-0550 Title Fax # (212) 980-3062
Personnel: Editor-Edward Rubenstein
General Info: Yr. Est. 1978, Annually, Ind/Abs/Online: BRS, Looseleaf
Subscriptions: $5/copy
Circulation: Total-250,000
Advertising: Inquire for rates.
List Rental: List Management Co.: Business Mailers, Inc., 2000 York Rd., Oak Brook, IL 60521
 Fax # (708) 574-6121, Actives: 28,569, $90/M, Expires: 6,300, $75/M

Scleroderma Intl. Foundation-The Connector

Publishing Co: Scleroderma Intl. Foundation, 704 Gardner Center Rd, New Castle, PA 16101-6018;
 Title Tel # (412) 652-3109
Personnel: Editor-Sue Gramm
General Info: Quarterly
Circulation: Total-3,600

Scleroderma Spectrum   *Association*

Publishing Co: United Scleroderma Foundation, Inc., PO Box 399, Watsonville, CA 95077-0399;
 Title Tel # (408) 728-2202 Title Fax # (408) 728-3328
Personnel: Editor-Judy Frank, Editor-Cynthia Schelcher
General Info: (Formerly United Scleroderma Foundation-Newsletter), Yr. Est. 1977, Quarterly, 12
 pages, 2 Color
Subscriptions: Indv. $25
Circulation: Total-18,000
Printing Co: Watsonville Press, 325 Westridge Dr., Watsonville, CA 95076 Tel # (408) 722-7147

Scrip World Pharmaceutical News
  See: DRUGS & PHARMACEUTICALS

Second Opinion
  See: HEALTH

Self Publishing Update - How to Basics Edition
  See: BOOKS & BOOK TRADE

Sneeze the Day
  See: HEALTH

Society of Cardiovascular Anesthesiologists- Newsletter   *Association*

Publishing Co: Society of Cardiovascular Anesthesiologists, 1910 Byrd Avenue, #100, PO Box
 11086, Richmond, VA 23230-1086 Fax # (804) 282-0090; Title Tel # (804) 282-0084
Personnel: Editor-John Hinckley
General Info: Yr. Est. 1981, Bi-monthly, Sheetfed press, 16 pages, No Color, Newsprint
Circulation: (100% controlled), Total-2,000
List Rental: Actives: $100/M

Society of Toxicology of Canada Newsletter   *Association*

Publishing Co: Society of Toxicology of Canada, Box 517, Beaconsfield, PQ H9W 5V1 Canada;
 Title Tel # (514) 428-2676 Title Fax # (514) 428-2685
Personnel: Medical Ed.-Donal Ecobichon, Editor, Editorial Page Ed., Science Ed., Bk. Rev. Ed.-
 Donald Ecobichon
Editorial Description: Information on the field of toxicology.
General Info: Yr. Est. 1982, Quarterly, 10 pages, Ind/Abs/Online: CAN. BIOL. SOC., INT. UNION.
 TOXICOLOGY
Subscriptions: Indv. $10, Can. $10, Free
Circulation: (100% controlled), Total-450
Advertising: Inquire for rates. Accepts Inserts.
List Rental: Rents Lists

Society of Toxicology of Canada, Proceedings

Publishing Co: Society of Toxicology of Canada, Box 517, Beaconsfield, PQ H9W 5V1 Canada;
 Title Tel # (514) 398-3604
Personnel: Editor-D.J. Ecobichon
General Info: Yr. Est. 1979, Trim Size-8$\frac{1}{2}$ x 11, 12 pages, 1% ads, No Color
Circulation: (100% controlled), Total-300

Spina Bifida Insights

Publishing Co: Spina Bifida Association of America, 4590 Macarthur Blvd NW Ste 250, Washington,
 DC 20007-4226; Title Tel # (301) 770-7222 Title Fax # (301) 881-3392
Personnel: Editor-Tina Head
General Info: Bi-monthly, Web press, 16 pages, No Color
Subscriptions: Indv. $25
Acquistions: Publication Bought
Circulation: Total-12,000
Advertising: Inquire for rates.
List Rental: Rents Lists

Spinal Connection   *Association*

Publishing Co: Natl. Scoliosis Foundation, 72 Mt. Auburn St., Watertown, MA 02172-3930;
 Title Tel # (617) 926-0397 Title Fax # (617) 926-0398
Personnel: Editor-Joseph O'Brien
Editorial Description: Publication contains articles about treatment of scoliosis & activities of the
 Natl. Scoliosis Foundation.
General Info: Yr. Est. 1984, Semi-annually, Trim Size-8$\frac{1}{2}$ x 11, Offset press, 8 pages, 2 Color,
 Matte, Other
Circulation: Total-22,000

Spinal Cord Society- Newsletter

Publishing Co: Spinal Cord Society, Rr 5 Box 22a, Fergus Falls, MN 56537-9205;
 Title Tel # (218) 739-5252
Personnel: Editor-Charles Carson
Editorial Description: News of research pertaining to the cure of spinal cord injuries.
General Info: Yr. Est. 1980, Monthly, 20 pages
Circulation: Total-5,000

Sports Medicine Bulletin   *Association*

Publishing Co: American College of Sports Medicine, 401 W Michigan St, Indianapolis, IN
 46202-3233; Title Tel # (317) 637-9200 Title Fax # (317) 634-7817
Personnel: Publisher-D.M. Robertson, Editor-Anne T. Brown
Editorial Description: Member news.
General Info: Quarterly, Trim Size-8$\frac{1}{2}$ x 11, Offset press, 28 pages, ISSN: 0746-9306, 2 Color,
 Matte, Saddle-stitched
Subscriptions: Free With Membership
Circulation: Total-16,000
List Rental: Rents Lists

Sports Medicine Digest
  See: SPORTS & SPORTING GOODS

Sports Medicine Digest   *Business*

Publishing Co: Lippincott-Raven Press Publishers, 227 E. Washington Square, Philadelphia, PA
 19106 Tel # (215) 238-4200 Fax # (215) 238-4227 Parent Co.-Wolters Kluwer US Corporation,
 New York
Personnel: Publisher-Kathey Alexander, Editor-Mark Schoene, Mktg. Dir.-Michele Duncan
Editorial Description: Covering issues in sports medicine.
General Info: Yr. Est. 1979, Monthly
Subscriptions: Indv. $89, For. $100

Sports Medicine in Primary Care   *Consumer, Scholarly*

Publishing Co: Physical Education Fitness Ltd, 235 Mountainview Street, Decatur, GA 30030;
 Title Tel # (404) 377-0300 Title Fax # (404) 377-0604
Personnel: Publisher-Liz Medley, Editor-Rob Johnson, M.D
Editorial Description: Clinician's practical guide to diagnosis, treatment and prevention of injury &
 disease. Most current clinical developments in sports medicine relevant to primary care.
General Info: Yr. Est. 1995, Monthly, Trim Size-8$\frac{1}{2}$ x 11, 8 pages, ISSN: 1062-9297, 2 Color, Other
Subscriptions: Indv. $157, Can. $177, For. $197, $17/copy

State Health Legislation
Report

Publishing Co: American Medical Association, 515 N. State St., Chicago, IL 60610
Tel # (312) 464-4512 Fax # (312) 464-5834; Title Tel # (312) 645-4765
Personnel: Editor-Jeff Stokols, Circ. Mgr.-Lydia Oquendo
General Info: Quarterly
Subscriptions: Indv. $62, $20/copy

Strategic Health Care Marketing
See: HEALTH

Sturza's Medical Investment Letter
See: INVESTMENT

Substance Abuse Report
See: HEALTH

Support Group Newsletter

Publishing Co: ALS & Neuromuscular Research Foundation, California Pacific Med Center, 2351 Clay St., #419, San Francisco, CA 94115; Title Tel # (415) 981-5588
General Info: Monthly

TB Monitor   *Business*

Publishing Co: American Health Consultants, Inc., 3525 Piedmont Rd., Building #6, Ste. 400, Atlanta, GA 30305-0056 Fax # (404) 284-3291; Title Tel # (404) 262-7436
Personnel: Publisher-Lauren Oden, Editor-Richard Jarvis, Circ. Mgr.-Monica Brown, Production Mgr.-Mike Witter, Mktg. Dir.-David Price
Editorial Description: Addresses struggles of health care workers as they battle against tuberculosis.
General Info: Yr. Est. 1994, Monthly
Subscriptions: Indv. $219
List Rental: Actives: $145/M

TB Weekly   *Business, Association*

Publishing Co: C.W. Henderson Publisher, Medical Center II, P.O. Box 5528, Atlanta, GA 31107-0528 Tel # (404) 507-7777 Fax # (404) 507-7788; Title Tel # (205) 995-1567 Title Fax # (404) 378-5411
Personnel: Publisher-Charles Henderson, Editor-Salynn Boyles
Editorial Description: Comprehensive worldeide coverage of tuberculosis.
General Info: Yr. Est. 1993, Weekly, ISSN: 1065-982X
Subscriptions: Indv. $995, Can. $995, For. $1,195

TJFR Health News Reporter
See: MEDIA & COMMUNICATIONS

TMJ Update (Temporomandibular Joint Update)
See: DENTAL

Take a Breather...
See: HEALTH

Technology for Anesthesia   *Business*

Publishing Co: ECRI, 5200 Butler Pike, Plymouth Meeting, PA 19462-1298; Title Tel # (610) 825-6000 Title Fax # (610) 834-1275
Personnel: Editor-Elizabeth Bennet, Circ. Mgr.-Diane Schwarztrauber, Promotion Dir.-Michele Carlin
Editorial Description: Health care technology information for the specialist.
General Info: Monthly, 12 pages, ISSN: 8756-8578, No Color, Coated
Subscriptions: Indv. $95, For. $125

Technology for Cardiology   *Business*

Publishing Co: ECRI, 5200 Butler Pike, Plymouth Meeting, PA 19462-1298; Title Tel # (610) 825-6000 Title Fax # (610) 834-1275
Personnel: Editor-Elizabeth Bennet, Circ. Mgr.-Diane Schwarztrauber, Promotion Dir.-Michele Carlin
Editorial Description: Health care technology information for the specialist.
General Info: Yr. Est. 1981, Monthly, 12 pages, ISSN: 8756-8586, No Color, Coated
Subscriptions: Indv. $95, For. $125

Temple University Medical
Alumni Bulletin

Publishing Co: Temple Univ. Medical Center, Publications, Philadelphia, PA 19122; Title Tel # (215) 787-7000

Tennessee Medico-Legal Reporter
See: LAW

Topics in Pain Management

Publishing Co: Williams & Wilkins, 351 W. Camden St., Baltimore, MD 21201-2436
Fax # (410) 528-4452; Title Tel # (410) 528-4068
Editorial Description: Timesaving newsletter reviews dozens of journals and provides in-depth information needed to deal rapidly and effectively with pain disorders.
General Info: Monthly, ISSN: 0882-5645

Tourniquet, The

Publishing Co: Natl. Phlebotomy Assn., 5615 Landover Rd., Hyattsville, MD 20784-1228; Title Tel # (202) 636-4515
Personnel: Editor-Gary Campbell
Circulation: Total-5,000

Transplant

Publishing Co: Northern California Transplant Bank, Box 7999, San Francisco, CA 94120-7999; Title Tel # (415) 922-3100
Personnel: Editor-Sally Shapiro
General Info: Yr. Est. 1982, Quarterly
Circulation: Total-5,000

Transplant News   *Business, Association*

Publishing Co: Jim Warren Communications, 2030 Clarendon Ave., Suite #201, Arlington, VA 22201 Tel # (703) 525-4262
Editorial Description: Features news on organ, tissue and bone transplant procedures for physicians specializing in transplant surgery.
General Info: Yr. Est. 1990, 24x/yr.
Subscriptions: Indv. $259, For. $310, $12/copy
Circulation: Total-420, Readership-1,500
Advertising: Inquire for rates. Accepts Inserts.
List Rental: List Management Co.: Atlantic Information Services, 1050 17th St., NW, Washington, DC 20036

Treasures
See: HISTORY

Treatment Issues   *Consumer*

Publishing Co: Gay Men's Health Crisis, Medical Information, 129 W. 20th. St. 2nd Fl., New York, NY 10011-3629; Title Tel # (212) 337-3695 Title Fax # (212) 337-3656
Personnel: Editor-Kevin Armington
Editorial Description: Current research, experimental therapies and public health information on AIDS.
General Info: Yr. Est. 1987, 10x/yr., Sheetfed press, 12 pages, No Color, Newsprint
Subscriptions: Indv. $30, Inst. $50, Can. $60, For. $60, Free To Qualified Recipient
Circulation: Total-15,000

Triologistics   *Association*

Publishing Co: Sponsor-Triological Society, Triological Society, 10 S. Broadway, Ste. 1401, St. Louis, MO 63102-1741; Title Tel # (314) 621-6550 Title Fax # (314) 621-6688
Personnel: Editor-Victoria Harrison
Editorial Description: For society members.
General Info: Yr. Est. 1976, Tri-annually, Trim Size-8½ x 11, Web press, 4 pages, Newsprint
Circulation: Total-1,200
Printing Co: Valley Press, 5 E Montgomery Ave, Bala Cynwyd, PA 19004-2398 Tel # (215) 664-7770

Tufts Medical Alumni
Bulletin

Publishing Co: Tufts Medical School, 236 Harrison Ave, Boston, MA 02111-1835
General Info: Yr. Est. 1941
Subscriptions: $75/copy
Circulation: Total-6,200
Advertising: Inquire for rates.

UCLA Cancer Center
Bulletin

Publishing Co: UCLA Center for Health Sciences, Univ. of California-LA, 10-247 Louis Factor Bldg., Los Angeles, CA 90024
Personnel: Editor-Hali Wickner
General Info: Yr. Est. 1973
Circulation: Total-12,500

USPA Newsletter
See: PARAPSYCHOLOGY

Understanding Epilepsy   *Consumer, Association*

Publishing Co: Epilepsy Institute, 257 Park Avenue South, New York, NY 10010; Title Tel # (212) 677-8550
Editorial Description: Treatments and info about epilepsy.
General Info: Yr. Est. 1992, Quarterly, Trim Size-8½ x 11, 8 pages

Une Veritable Amie
See: WOMEN'S

Uniformed Services
Academy of Family
Physicians-Newsletter   *Association*

Publishing Co: Uniformed Services Academy of Family Physicians, PO Box 11086, Richmond, VA 23230-1086; Title Tel # (804) 358-3950
Personnel: Editor-Dean Kirkham
General Info: Quarterly, Trim Size-5½ x 8½, 12 pages
Circulation: Total-2,800
Advertising: Inquire for rates.

Urologe   *Consumer*

Publishing Co: Springer-Verlag Inc., 175 5th Ave., New York, NY 10010-7858 Tel # (212) 460-1500 Fax # (212) 473-6272

VCC Newsletter

Publishing Co: Vermont Cancer Center, Univ. Of Vermont 1 S. Prospect, St., Burlington, VT 05405-0001; Title Tel # (802) 656-4414
Personnel: Editor-Joan MacKenzie
Editorial Description: Information of a non-technical nature about Cancer Center programs of Cancer research prevention, education & state-of-the art medical care for members, scientific & medical professionals, donors, the public.
General Info: Yr. Est. 1978, Trim Size-8½ x 11, Desktop press, 4 pages, 2 Color, Newsprint
Circulation: Total-7,500

VHL Family Forum   *Association*   CPM: $85

Publishing Co: VHL Family Alliance, 171 Clinton Rd., Brookline, MA 02146-5815; Title Tel # (617) 232-5946 Title Fax # (617) 734-8233
Personnel: Publisher, Editor-Joyce W. Graff
Editorial Description: Newsletter of the VHL Family Alliance. Provides information on current research in diagnosis and treatment, resources, and coping skills. Forum for sharing information among families.
General Info: Yr. Est. 1993, 3x/yr., Trim Size-8½ x 11, Offset press, 16 pages, ISSN: 1066-4130, 2 Color, Coated, Saddle-stitched
Subscriptions: Indv. $25, Inst. $35, Can. $35, For. $35, $4/copy
Circulation: (72% controlled), Total-3,500, Readership-5,000
Advertising: $300. Accepts Inserts.
Printing Co: Marrakesh Express, 500 Anclote Rd, Tarpon Springs, FL 34689-6701 Tel # (813) 942-2218, Fax # (813) 937-4758

VHL News
See: GENETICS

Viewbox   *Consumer, Association*

Publishing Co: American Osteopathic College of Radiology, 1402 Cottage Lane Ave, Kirksville, MO 63501-4512; Title Tel # (816) 626-2121
Personnel: Publisher-Pamela Smith, Editor-Mark Finkelstein
General Info: (Formerly Am. Osteopathic Col. of Radiology. Newsletter), Quarterly
Circulation: Total-550
List Rental: Rents Lists

Vital Signs

Publishing Co: MD Resources, Inc., 9360 Sunset Dr Ste 250, Miami, FL 33173-3273; Title Tel # (305) 271-9213
Personnel: Editor-Carol Maxfield, Editor-Wendy Perlman
Editorial Description: News & information devoted to clients, physicians & companies affiliated with MD Resources.
General Info: Quarterly
Subscriptions: Indv. $25

WPH Medical Bulletin

Publishing Co: Western Pennsylvania Hospital, 4800 Friendship Ave, Pittsburgh, PA 15224-1722; Title Tel # (405) 578-5000
General Info: Yr. Est. 1968, Semi-annually

Washington Drug Letter
See: DRUGS & PHARMACEUTICALS

Washington Report
See: LAW

Weekly Epidemiological Record
See: HEALTH

Westchester Academy of Medicine Newsletter

Publishing Co: Westchester Academy of Medicine, 84 Purchase St, Purchase, NY 10577-2612; Title Tel # (914) 948-4100
General Info: Yr. Est. 1974, 10x/yr.

What Doctors Don't Tell You   *Consumer*

Publishing Co: Agora, Inc., 105 W. Monoment St., Baltimore, MD 21202-4702 Tel # (410) 783-2647 Fax # (410) 223-2662
Editorial Description: Covers natural alternative medicine therapies.
General Info: Monthly
Subscriptions: Indv. $49
List Rental: Actives: 26,200, $95/M

What's Happening in AMWA   *Business, Association*

Publishing Co: American Medical Women's Association, Inc., 801 N. Fairfax St., Ste. 400, Alexandria, VA 22314-1757; Title Tel # (703) 838-0500
Personnel: Editor-Sheri Singer
Editorial Description: Gives association activity information and relevant news for members.
General Info: Bi-monthly, Trim Size-8½ x 11, Sheetfed press, 8 pages, 2 Color, Saddle-stitched
Circulation: Total-13,000
List Rental: Rents Lists

Whats Up Doc?

Publishing Co: Canada Communication Group/Depository Services Program, 45 Sacre-Coeur Blvd., Room A2411E Natl. Printing Bur, Hull, PQ K1A 0S9 Canada Tel # (819) 956-7864 Fax # (819) 956-5134; Title Tel # (819) 997-5365 Title Fax # (819) 956-6341
Editorial Description: Newsletter of the depository services program.
General Info: Quarterly, ISSN: 0847-2149

Wilderness Medicine Letter   *Consumer, Association*

Publishing Co: Wilderness Medical Society, PO Box 2463, Indianapolis, IN 46206-2463 Fax # (317) 269-8150; Title Tel # (317) 631-1745 Title Fax # (317) 634-7817
Personnel: Editor-Karl Newmann, M.D
General Info: Yr. Est. 1984, Quarterly, 20 pages, Looseleaf
Subscriptions: Indv. $30, Inst. $30, Can. $30, For. $30
Circulation: Total-3,000
Printing Co: Pierson Printing, 333 S East St, Indianapolis, IN 46204-3712 Tel # (317) 639-2364

Women's Health Access Newsletter   *Consumer*

Publishing Co: Women's Health America, Inc., PO Box 9690, Madison, WI 53715; Title Tel # (608) 833-4767
Personnel: Publisher-Marla Ahlgrimm
Editorial Description: Women's health issues and Pre Menstrual Syndrome topics including research, diet, and exercise; also includes support group listings.
General Info: (Formerly PMS Access Newsletter), Yr. Est. 1985, Bi-monthly, Sheetfed press, 8 pages, 2 Color, Coated
Subscriptions: Indv. $15, $3/copy
Circulation: Total-3,000

Women's Health Matters
See: HEALTH

Women's Medicine Alerts   *Business*

Publishing Co: M.J. Powers, 374 Millburn Ave, Millburn, NJ 07041-1361 Tel # (201) 467-4556 Fax # (201) 912-8883
Personnel: Publisher-John Roche
Editorial Description: Covers newest biomedical news in women's medicine.
General Info: Yr. Est. 1994, Monthly, Trim Size-8½ x 11, 8 pages
Subscriptions: Indv. $59

Word & Deed

Publishing Co: ALM International (American Leprosy Missions), 1 Alm Way, Greenville, SC 29601-3060; Title Tel # (803) 271-7040 Title Fax # (803) 271-7062
Personnel: Publisher-Thomas Frist, Editor-Susan Renault, Circ. Mgr.-Susan Kastner, Art Dir.-Fred Galloway
Editorial Description: News & editorial matter on world-wide fight against Hansen's disease Leprosy with accent on ALM Intl. programs.
General Info: (Formerly Crossways), Quarterly, Web press, 8 pages, 2 Color, Newsprint
Subscriptions: Free
Circulation: Total-50,000

Workers' Comp Advisor
See: INDUSTRIAL RELATIONS/PERSONNEL

Workers' Comp Practice Advisor   *Business*

Publishing Co: Genesis Publishing, Inc., 10455 Sorrento Valley Rd Ste, 103, San Diego, CA 92121-1621 Tel # (619) 453-0858
Personnel: Publisher-Donna Buys Hawkins, Editor-William L. Hodge, Assoc. Ed.-Bonnie Potter-Collis, Mktg. Dir.-Jay W. Hillis
Editorial Description: Helps medical offices to process workers' compensation cases. Provides guidance and information on disability evaluation, report writing marketing, billing, and collection.
General Info: (Formerly Medical-Legal Practice Advisor), Yr. Est. 1993, 10x/yr., ISSN: 1068-9354
Subscriptions: Indv. $167, $17/copy
Advertising: Inquire for rates.
List Rental: Rents Lists

Your Health   *Consumer, Association*   CPM: $333

Publishing Co: International Academy of Nutrition & Preventive Medicine, PO Box 18433, Asheville, NC 28814-0433; Title Tel # (704) 258-3243
Personnel: Editor-Elizabeth Pavka, MS
Editorial Description: Reports advances in health care with emphasis on preventing illness, nutrition & health maintenance.
General Info: (Formerly Lay Newsletter), Yr. Est. 1980, Bi-monthly, Trim Size-8½ x 11, Desktop press, 10 pages, Color
Subscriptions: Indv. $30, Inst. $30, Can. $30, For. $30
Circulation: Total-600
Advertising: $200. Accepts Inserts.
List Rental: Actives: $75/M
Printing Co: Quick Copies of Asheville, N. Market St., Asheville, NC 28801 Tel # (704) 253-4007

MEN'S

Budg'y

Publishing Co: John Rob, P.O. Box 1407, Chambersburg, PA 17201
Editorial Description: An acronym for bisexual ultimtely dudely guy, basically a dude, but bisexual, very awesome.
General Info: Trim Size-8.5 x 11, 9 pages
Subscriptions: Indv. $1

CB
 See: RELIGIOUS & THEOLOGICAL

Celebrate the Self
 See: SEX

Fathers Brothers Sons   *Consumer*

Publishing Co: F.J. Mclaughlin Newsletter Network, 1346 Joan Dr, Southampton, PA 18966-4341;
 Title Tel # (215) 322-1346
Personnel: Publisher-Flo McLaughlin, Editor-Mark McLaughlin
Editorial Description: A forum about men - their relationships, expectations, and experiences shared via a network of writers.
General Info: Yr. Est. 1992, Quarterly, Trim Size-8½ x 11, Desktop press, 8 pages
Subscriptions: Indv. $10, Can. $10, For. $14, $3/copy
Circulation: Total-1,000
Advertising: Accepts Inserts.

Gay Airline & Travel Club Newsletter, The
 See: TRAVEL

Genuine Article, The   *Consumer*

Publishing Co: Source Publications, PO Box 654, Monroe, CT 06468-0654
Personnel: Publisher-Frank Wallis
Editorial Description: In praise of natural womanly beanty and in protest against surgical enhancements such as breast implants. Features continuing series of articles on the breast implant controversy; interviews with women who make their living as nude models; memoirs of pin-up legends, extensive letters section.
General Info: Yr. Est. 1995, Quarterly, Trim Size-8½ x 11, Sheetfed press, 8 pages, No Color, Coated, Case bound
Subscriptions: Indv. $7, Inst. $7, Can. $7, For. $7, $2/copy
Circulation: Total-500
Printing Co: Source Pub. Litho Dept., 3 Cross Hill Rd., Monroe, CT 06468-2436
 Tel # (203) 261-2469

Illustrator Collector's News, The
 See: COLLECTIBLES

Male Call

Publishing Co: Per Adams, PO Box 376, Cameron, WI 54822-0376; Title Tel # (715) 458-2443
Personnel: Publisher, Editor-Dan Adams
Editorial Description: Focuses on the male's place in today's society. Newsletter of the Mensa Mmale Call SIG.
General Info: Yr. Est. 1991, Monthly
Subscriptions: Indv. $14, Inst. $14, $2/copy

Men's Confidential   *Consumer*

Publishing Co: Rodale Press, 33 East Minor St., Emmaus, PA 18098-0001;
 Title Tel # (610) 967-5171 Title Fax # (610) 967-8963
Personnel: Circ. Mgr.-Keith Follweiler
Editorial Description: Addresses and explains the most recentmeidcal and health news and breakthroughs regarding male concerns and healthcare problems.
General Info: (Formerly Men's Health Newsletter), Yr. Est. 1986, Monthly, Trim Size-8½ x 11, 10 pages, 2 Color, Matte, Saddle-stitched
Subscriptions: Indv. $24, Can. $30, For. $36, $4/copy
Circulation: Total-65,000
List Rental: List Management Co.: Direct Media, Inc., 200 Pemberwick Rd., PO Box 4565, Greenwich, CT 06830 Tel # (203) 532-3713, Fax # (203) 531-1452, Actives: 40,537, $85/M

NAHWW Newsletter
 See: HOME & HOME ENTERTAINMENT

NAMSB News
 See: APPAREL & ACCESSORIES

National Men's Resource
Calendar   **CPM:** $69

Publishing Co: Mas Medium & Company, Box 80082, San Anselmo, CA 94979-0800;
 Title Tel # (415) 457-3389 Title Fax # (415) 453-2839
Personnel: Publisher, Editor, Production Mgr.-Gordon Clay
Editorial Description: Resource directory for men's events, groups and services nationally. Lists publications, book/video/movie/cassette reviews that involve a positive change in men's roles and relationships.
General Info: Yr. Est. 1985, Quarterly, Trim Size-8½ x 11, 40 pages, No Color, Matte, Saddle-stitched
Subscriptions: Indv. $10, Inst. $10, Can. $15, For. $15, $3/copy
Circulation: Total-720
Advertising: $50.

Survivor Activist, The
 See: PSYCHOLOGY

Today's Dads
 See: FAMILY

Torchlight
 See: RELIGIOUS & THEOLOGICAL

Transitions   *Consumer*

Publishing Co: National Coalition of Free Men, PO Box 129, Manhasset, NY 11030-0129;
 Title Tel # (516) 482-6378
Personnel: Publisher-Tom Williamson, Editor-Gerald Bissett
Editorial Description: Examines men's lives & sex discrimination issues that affect men.
General Info: (Formerly Options), Yr. Est. 1977, Bi-monthly, Trim Size-8½ x 11, Offset press, 12 pages, ISSN: 0886-862X, No Color, Newsprint
Subscriptions: Indv. $30, Inst. $30, Can. $30, For. $40, $2/copy
Advertising: $100. Accepts Inserts.
Printing Co: Top Copy-Quick Print, 1206 W Washington St, Stephenville, TX 76401-4137

METALS & METALWORKING

Advanced Materials
 See: MANUFACTURING

Aid & Analysis
 See: INVESTMENT

Alloy Digest   *Business*

Publishing Co: Village Press, 27 Canfield St, Orange, NJ 07050-3714 Tel # (201) 677-9160
 Fax # (201) 677-9331; Title Tel # (201) 746-7930
Personnel: Editor-Dennis Rahoi
Editorial Description: Individual alloy data sheet covering composition, properties, characteristics, fabricability and uses of commercial proprietory and standard alloys.
General Info: (Formerly Engineering Alloy Digest), Yr. Est. 1952, Monthly, Trim Size-8½ x 11, Offset press, 8 pages, Ind/Abs/Online: Metal Abstr., World Alum. Abstr., No Color
Subscriptions: Indv. $150

Aluminum Situation   *Business*

Publishing Co: Aluminum Assn., 900 19th St NW Ste 300, Washington, DC 20006-2105;
 Title Tel # (202) 862-5100
Editorial Description: Statistical update for aluminum industry.
General Info: Monthly
Subscriptions: Free

Around the Open Hearth   *Business, Association*

Publishing Co: Metal Treating Institute, 302 3rd St Ste 1, Neptune Beach, FL 32266-5138;
 Title Tel # (904) 249-0448
Personnel: Publisher, Editor-M. Lance Miller
Editorial Description: Monthly update of activities within the Metal Treating Institute & commercial heat treating industry.
General Info: Monthly, Offset press, 4 pages, No Color, Newsprint

Blacksmith Gazette

Publishing Co: Fred W. Holder, 950 S Falcon Rd, Camano Island, WA 98292-8411;
 Title Tel # (360) 387-0349 Title Fax # (360) 387-0349
Personnel: Publisher, Editor-Fred W. Holder
Editorial Description: News & techniques for Blacksmiths.
General Info: Yr. Est. 1980, Trim Size-11½ x 17, 12 pages
Subscriptions: Indv. $30, $3/copy
Circulation: Total-500

CBSA Capsules   *Association*

Publishing Co: Copper & Brass Servicenter Assn., 251 W. DeKalb Pike, King of Prussia, PA 19406-2433; Title Tel # (215) 265-6658 Title Fax # (610) 265-3419
Personnel: Editor-Franklin Brown, Jr.
Editorial Description: Association and Industry news affecting servicenters (distributors) brass mills and management personnel.
General Info: Yr. Est. 1957, Monthly, Trim Size-8½ x 11, Mimeo press, 6 pages, No Color
Subscriptions: Indv. $25
Circulation: Total-250

CMP Newsletter

Publishing Co: Center for Metals Production-Mellon Institute, 4400 5th Ave, Pittsburgh, PA 15213-2683; Title Tel # (412) 268-3496
Personnel: Editor-John Kollar
Editorial Description: For the electric utility industries marketing & management people. Also for materials producers production engineering & management people.
General Info: Yr. Est. 1985, 5x/yr., Trim Size-8½ x 11, Sheetfed press, 4 pages, 4 Color, Coated
Acquistions: Publication Bought
Circulation: Total-3,000
Printing Co: Geyer Printing Co., 3700 Bigelow Blvd, Pittsburgh, PA 15213-1102
 Tel # (412) 682-3633

Can Shipments Report   *Business, Association*

Publishing Co: Can Manufacturers Institute, 1625 Massachussetts Ave., NW, Washington, DC 20036-2289; Title Tel # (202) 232-4677
Personnel: Circ. Mgr.-Christa Lee
General Info: Yr. Est. 1972, Monthly, Trim Size-6 x 9, 8 pages, Color-cover, Saddle-stitched
Subscriptions: Indv. $250, Free With Membership
Circulation: Total-600

Casting Digest
Business, Association

Publishing Co: ASM International, Materials Information, 9639 Kinsman Rd., Materials Park, OH 44073-0002 Fax # (216) 338-4634; Title Tel # (216) 338-5151
Personnel: Editor-S. Chang, Editor-M. Finical, Circ. Mgr.-D. Barthelmes, Circ. Mgr., Prod. Coord.-N. Meadows
Editorial Description: Collection of abstracts listing published information sources worldwide on casting, including continuous, centrifugal, permanent mold, billet, ingot, vacuum, vibrational, slab, sand, shell mold, investment pressure, and die process.
General Info: Yr. Est. 1976, Monthly, Trim Size-8½ x 11, Offset press, 12 pages, No Color
Subscriptions: Indv. $120, $10/copy

Composites & Adhesives Newsletter
See: ENGINEERING

Craft News
See: GLASS, STONE & CLAY

Ductile Iron Data

Publishing Co: Ductile Iron Society, 28938 Lorain Rd Ste 202, North Olmsted, OH 44070-4014
General Info: Quarterly

Ductile Iron News
Business

Publishing Co: Ductile Iron Society, 28938 Lorain Rd Ste 202, North Olmsted, OH 44070-4014; Title Tel # (216) 734-8040 Title Fax # (216) 734-8182
Personnel: Editor-Dina Nichols, Adv. Dir.-Lee Randolph
General Info: Yr. Est. 1976, Trim Size-8½ x 11, Sheetfed press, 2% ads, 2 Color, Saddle-stitched
Circulation: Total-3,800

Ductile Iron Pipe News
Association

Publishing Co: Ductile Iron Pipe Research Assn., 245 Riverchase Pky E Ste O, Birmingham, AL 35244-1856; Title Tel # (205) 988-9870 Title Fax # (205) 988-9822
General Info: (Formerly Cast Iron Pipe News), Yr. Est. 1915

George Cross News Letter

Publishing Co: George Cross News Letter Ltd., 1710-609 Granville St., Vancouver, BC V7Y 1G5 Canada; Title Tel # (604) 683-7265 Title Fax # (604) 683-5306
Personnel: Editor-Allan Regier
General Info: Yr. Est. 1948, Daily

Gold News/Nouvelles de l'Or
Business, Consumer

Publishing Co: The Silver Institute, 1112 16th St NW Ste 240, Washington, DC 20036-4823; Title Tel # (202) 835-0185 Title Fax # (202) 835-0155
Personnel: Editor-John Lutley
Editorial Description: Technical and industrial information arm of leading producers of gold and gold products.
General Info: Yr. Est. 1976, Bi-monthly, Trim Size-8½ x 11, Offset press, 4 pages, No Color, Coated
Subscriptions: Indv. $35, Can. $45, For. $45
Circulation: Total-1,900
List Rental: Rents Lists

Handbook of Binary Phase Diagrams Updating Service
Consumer

Publishing Co: Genium Publishing Corp., 1 Genium Plz, Schenectady, NY 12304-4607; Title Tel # (518) 377-8854 Title Fax # (518) 377-1891
Personnel: Editor-Dr. William Moffatt, Publisher, Circ. Mgr., Production Mgr.-Robert Roy, Promotion Dir.-Paul Hans
Editorial Description: Collection of redrawn metal system diagrams.
General Info: Yr. Est. 1976, Trim Size-5½ x 8½, Sheetfed press, 30 pages, No Color, Newsprint, Looseleaf
Subscriptions: Indv. $95, Can. $95, For. $112
Circulation: Total-1,200
List Rental: Actives $85/M

High-Tech Materials Alert
See: MANUFACTURING

ILMA Compoundings
See: PETROLEUM & NATURAL GAS

IPMI News and Reviews

Publishing Co: International Precious Metals Inst., 4905 W Tilghman St Ste 160, Allentown, PA 18104-9133; Title Tel # (610) 395-9700 Title Fax # (610) 395-5855
Personnel: Editor-Roger Runck
Editorial Description: Precious metals: supply and demand, economics, applications, fabrication, properties. Personal and industry news of participants in the precious metals industry.
General Info: Yr. Est. 1977, Monthly, 8 pages, ISSN: 0730-1901, 4 Color, Coated, Saddle-stitched
Subscriptions: Indv. $24
Circulation: Total-1,200
Printing Co: Herald Printing, Inc., P.O. Box 367, New Washington, OH 44854-9769 Tel # (419) 492-2133, Fax # (419) 492-2128

ISRI Report
Business, Association

Publishing Co: Institute of Scrap Recycling Industries, 1325 G St., NW, Ste. 1000, Washington, L 20005-3104; Title Tel # (202) 737-1770 Title Fax # (202) 626-0900
Personnel: Publisher-James Fowler, Editor-Elise Browne
Editorial Description: Internal newsletter for the scrap processing & recycling industries (membership only).
General Info: (Formerly ISIS Report), Yr. Est. 1987, Bi-weekly, Trim Size-8½ x 11, Offset press, 4 pages, 2 Color, Recycled
Subscriptions: Free With Membership
Circulation: Total-1,800
Printing Co: Newsletter Services, Inc., 9700 Philadelphia Court, Lanham, MD 20706 Tel # (301) 731-5200, Fax # (301) 731-5201

Iron Age Scrap Price Bulletin
Business, Association

Publishing Co: Chilton Publications, One Chilton Way, Radnor, PA 19089-0001 Tel # (610) 964-4000 Fax # (610) 964-4978 Parent Co.-Capital Cities/ABC, Inc., New York; Title Tel # (212) 887-8532 Title Fax # (212) 887-8358
Personnel: Publisher-Larry Greenberg, Editor-Bryan Berry
Editorial Description: Pricing information on ferrous & nonferrous scrap metals; Pricing & production information on steel & nonferrous metals.
General Info: Yr. Est. 1985, Weekly
Subscriptions: Indv. $360, Can. $160, For. $225
Circulation: Total-200

Jet News
See: WATER SUPPLY, POWER & WASTE

Magnesium
Association

Publishing Co: International Magnesium Association, 1303 Vincent Pl Ste 1, McLean, VA 22101-3615; Title Tel # (703) 442-8888 Title Fax # (703) 821-1824
Personnel: Publisher-Byron Clow, Editor-Felicia Garber
Editorial Description: Magnesium industry statistics & trade information.
General Info: Yr. Est. 1975, 9x/yr., Letrpr. press, 7 pages, ISSN: 0891-6942, 2 Color, Coated
Subscriptions: Indv. $90
Circulation: Total-300

Magnesium Monthly Review
Business

Publishing Co: Magnesium Monthly Review, 106 Spring Forest Rd, Greenville, SC 29615-2241; Title Tel # (864) 244-5718
Personnel: Publisher-R. Brown, Editor-David Brown
Editorial Description: Comprehensive report of up-to-date information on all published activity in the magnesium field.
General Info: Yr. Est. 1971, Monthly, Trim Size-8½ x 11, Sheetfed press, 8 pages, ISSN: 0047-5491, Ind/Abs/Online: Metadex, No Color, Newsprint
Subscriptions: Indv. $60, Can. $60, For. $75, $5/copy
Circulation: Total-425, Readership-2,000

Members Exchange
See: ART & SCULPTURE

Metal Cycles
See: INVESTMENT

Metals Newsletter
See: SAFETY

Metals Week
Business

Publishing Co: McGraw-Hill, 1221 Ave. of the Americas, 36th Fl., New York, NY 10020-1095 Tel # (212) 512-2000 Fax # (212) 512-6590; Title Tel # (212) 512-2823
Personnel: Publisher, Editor in Chief-Patrick Ryan, Editor-Jeffrey Keiffe, Mng. Editor-Kenneth Jacobson, Circ. Mgr.-Marguerite Stanford
Editorial Description: Marketing and pricing news and analysis covering nonferrous metals industry on international basis. Extensive price listings in four currencies.
General Info: (Formerly E&MJ Metal), Yr. Est. 1930, Weekly, Trim Size-8½ x 11, Offset press, 8 pages, ISSN: 0026-0975, Ind/Abs/Online: DIALOG, Dow Jones, NewsNet, Nexis, Color
Subscriptions: Indv. $700

Metalworking Insiders' Report
Business

Publishing Co: Appleton Services, P.O. Box 107, Larchmont, NY 10538-0107 Parent Co.-Gardner Publications Inc., Cincinnati; Title Tel # (914) 834-2300 Title Fax # (914) 834-7035
Editorial Description: News for and about the metalworking industry.
General Info: Yr. Est. 1993, Bi-weekly, Ind/Abs/Online: Information Access Company
Subscriptions: Indv. $400

Metalworking Trends

Publishing Co: McGraw-Hill, 1221 Ave. of the Americas, 36th Fl., New York, NY 10020-1095 Tel # (212) 512-2000 Fax # (212) 512-6590
Personnel: Publisher-John E. Slater, Editor-William M. Stocker, Jr.
Editorial Description: Information pertinent to senior marketing/management decision makers in the metalworking manufacturing market place.
General Info: Yr. Est. 1975, Bi-weekly, Trim Size-8½ x 11, Offset press, 10 pages, Color
Subscriptions: Indv. $95

Modern Blacksmith
Business, Association

Publishing Co: Natl. Blacksmiths & Welders Assn., PO Box 123, Arnold, NE 69120-0123; Title Tel # (308) 848-2913
Personnel: Editor-James Holman
General Info: (Formerly Sparks off the Anvil), Yr. Est. 1885, Quarterly, Trim Size-8½ x 11, Sheetfed press, 24 pages, 15% ads, 2 Color, Coated
Subscriptions: Indv. $15, Free With Membership
Circulation: Total-500, Readership-1,000
Advertising: Inquire for rates.

NTMA Record
Association   **CPM: $291**

Publishing Co: Natl. Tooling & Machining Assn., 9300 Livingston Rd., Ft. Washington, MD 20744-4905; Title Tel # (301) 248-6200 Title Fax # (301) 248-7104
Personnel: Publisher-Matthew Coffey, Editor-Sandria Bailey
Editorial Description: Covers activities of 4,000 member companies of tool, die, and precision machining industry trade association. Heavy emphasis on government relations, business management.
General Info: (Formerly NTDPMA Record), Yr. Est. 1943, Monthly, Trim Size-11¼ x 15, Sheetfed press, 8 pages, 3% ads, 2 Color, Matte
Circulation: (100% controlled), Total-4,500
Advertising: $1,313. Accepts Inserts.

News & Views
Association

Publishing Co: Assn. of Steel Distributors, 401 N. Michigan, Chicago, IL 60611-4212; Title Tel # (312) 644-6610
Personnel: Editor-Steve Koppel
General Info: Yr. Est. 1943, Monthly

P/M Technology Newsletter
Business

Publishing Co: APMI International, 105 College Rd. E., Princeton, NJ 08540-6692; Title Tel # (609) 452-7700 Title Fax # (609) 987-8523
Personnel: Publisher-Donald White, Editor-Peter K. Johnson
Editorial Description: Covers metal powder producing and consuming industries from both economic and technical standpoints.
General Info: Yr. Est. 1962, Monthly, Trim Size-8½ x 11, Offset press, 4 pages, 2 Color, Coated
Subscriptions: Indv. $75, Inst. $150, Can. $150, For. $170, $15/copy
Circulation: Total-3,000
List Rental: Rents Lists

Pacific Chapter Update
Association

Publishing Co: American Inst. for International Steel, Pacific Chapter, 3808 W. Riverside Dr. Ste. 600, Burbank, CA 91505-4360 Tel # (818) 841-7477 Fax # (818) 841-7484; Title Tel # (213) 387-4595
Personnel: Publisher, Editor-Pat Penney
General Info: (Formerly West Coast Metal Importers Assn.-Newsletter), Yr. Est. 1958
Circulation: Total-400

Performance Materials
See: AERONAUTICS/ASTRONAUTICS

Petersen Aluminum Corp. News
Business

Publishing Co: Petersen Aluminum Corp., 965 Estes Ave, Elk Grove Village, IL 60007-4905
Personnel: Editor-Maury Petersen
General Info: Yr. Est. 1972, Semi-annually
Subscriptions: Free To Qualified Recipient
Circulation: Total-8,000

Poly Probe
Business, Association

Publishing Co: Polycrystalline Products Assn., 6089 Frantz Rd., Ste. 101, Dublin, OH 43017 Tel # (614) 766-3657 Fax # (614) 766-3605; Title Tel # (614) 798-2253 Title Fax # (614) 798-2255
Personnel: Editor-Pat O'Brien
Editorial Description: News about polycrystalline products (diamonds) and the Polycrystalline Products Assn.
General Info: Yr. Est. 1992, Quarterly, Desktop press, 4 pages, No Color, Coated
Subscriptions: Free To Qualified Recipient
Circulation: Total-700, Readership-1,500

Precious Metals News & Review
Business, Association

Publishing Co: International Precious Metals Institute, 705 Robinwood Ave, Columbus, OH 43213-1757; Title Tel # (614) 231-4767
Personnel: Editor-Roger Runck
Editorial Description: News & reviews about precious metals, supply & demand, economics, applications, fabrication, properties. Personal & industry news of participants in the precious metals industry.
General Info: Yr. Est. 1977, Monthly, Trim Size-8½ x 11, Sheetfed press, 8 pages, ISSN: 0730-1901, 4 Color, Coated, Saddle-stitched
Subscriptions: Indv. $18
Acquistions: Publication Bought
Circulation: Total-1,200
Printing Co: Herald Printing, Inc., P.O. Box 367, New Washington, OH 44854-9769 Tel # (419) 492-2133, Fax # (419) 492-2128

Precision
Business

Publishing Co: Sponsor-Natl. Tooling & Machining Assn., Hubecore Communications, Inc., 29100 Aurora Rd., Ste 200, Solon, OH 44139-1855 Tel # (216) 248-1125 Fax # (216) 248-0187; Title Tel # (301) 248-6200 Title Fax # (301) 248-7104
Personnel: Editor-Sandy Bailey
Editorial Description: Activities of the contract tooling & machining industry. Included in Tooling & Production magazine
General Info: Yr. Est. 1992, Bi-monthly, Trim Size-8½ x 11, 16 pages, 4 Color
Subscriptions: Free
Circulation: Total-25,000
Advertising: Inquire for rates.

Production and Shipments of Steel Pipe, Tubings and Fittings
Business, Association

Publishing Co: Statistics Canada, Holland Ave/RH Coats, Holland Ave/Tunney's Pasture, Ottawa, ON K1A O26 Canada Tel # (613) 951-8116 Fax # (613) 951-0581; Title Tel # (613) 990-8116
Editorial Description: Cat. #41-011.
General Info: Yr. Est. 1977, Monthly, 7 pages, ISSN: 0703-007X
Subscriptions: Indv. $6, Can. $5, For. $7, $6/copy

R & D Focus
Association

Publishing Co: Intl. Lead Zinc Research Organization, PO Box 12036, Rtp, NC 27709-2036; Title Tel # (919) 361-4647 Title Fax # (919) 361-1957
Personnel: Publisher, Editor-John Sharpe, III
Editorial Description: Reports on current research & development projects as well as corporate news. Research includes galvanizing, diecasting, alloy development, batteries, lead & zinc chemicals, & environmental health.
General Info: (Formerly Research Digest), Yr. Est. 1986, Trim Size-8½ x 11, Sheetfed press, 8 pages, 4 Color, Coated, Saddle-stitched
Circulation: Total-2,000

Repairing Metalware
Business

Publishing Co: Institute of Metal Repair, 1558 S Redwood St, Escondido, CA 92025-5643; Title Tel # (619) 747-5978
Personnel: Publisher, Editor-James Walker, Art Dir.-Margaret Walker
Editorial Description: Trade bulletin dedicated to repairing, restoring, preserving fine metalware.
General Info: Yr. Est. 1985, Monthly, Trim Size-8½ x 11, Sheetfed press, 10 pages, 2% ads, No Color, Newsprint
Subscriptions: Indv. $12, Can. $13, For. $16, $1/copy
Circulation: Total-500
Advertising: Inquire for rates.
List Rental: Actives: $25/M

Sci-Tech News
See: LIBRARY

Silver Institute Letter
Business

Publishing Co: The Silver Institute, 1112 16th St NW Ste 240, Washington, DC 20036-4823; Title Tel # (202) 835-0185 Title Fax # (202) 835-0155
Personnel: Editor-Larry Kahaner
Editorial Description: Articles on new uses of silver in industry and the arts, new silver coinage, etc.
General Info: Yr. Est. 1971, Bi-monthly, Offset press, 4 pages, No Color, Coated
Subscriptions: Indv. $20, Can. $25, For. $25
Circulation: Total-2,000
List Rental: Rents Lists

Steel Digest
Business

Publishing Co: Intersteel Technology, Inc., 8301 University Exec Park Dr, Ste 130, Charlotte, NC 28262-3355 Tel # (704) 549-4177
Personnel: Publisher, Editor-John Vallomy
Editorial Description: Editor addresses a subject of general interest to the steelmaking industry.
General Info: Yr. Est. 1984, Bi-monthly, Trim Size-8½ x 11, Sheetfed press, 6 pages, No Color
Subscriptions: Free To Qualified Recipient
Circulation: Total-700

Technology Transfer
See: MINING & MINERALS

Titanium
Business

Publishing Co: Titanium Development Association, 4141 Arapahoe Ave Ste 100, Boulder, CO 80303-1032 Tel # (303) 443-7515 Fax # (303) 443-4406; Title Tel # (513) 223-8432 Title Fax # (513) 223-6307
Personnel: Publisher-G.M. Hockaday, Editor-John Monsees
Editorial Description: Covers activities of interest to members of the titanium metal industry, plus: new product news, calendar, reference library.
General Info: (Formerly Tidbits), Yr. Est. 1984, Quarterly, Trim Size-8½ x 11, Offset press, 12 pages, 2 Color
Circulation: Total-900
Printing Co: Process Printing, 527 N Yellow Springs St, Springfield, OH 45504-2462 Tel # (513) 323-5786, Fax # (513) 323-4484

Tube Topics *Business, Association*

Publishing Co: Tube Council of North America, 740 Broadway, New York, NY 10003-9518; Title Tel # (212) 477-9007 Title Fax # (212) 460-9028
Personnel: Editor-Ted Klein
Editorial Description: Trends, processes, prods. and res. relating to the use of metal, plastic and tubes for dispensing products of all kinds.
General Info: Yr. Est. 1967, Quarterly, Trim Size-8½ x 11, Sheetfed press, 4 pages, 2 Color, Matte
Subscriptions: Free
Circulation: Total-3,000

U.S. Piper *Business*

Publishing Co: U.S. Pipe and Foundry Co., PO Box 10406, Birmingham, AL 35202-0406; Title Tel # (205) 254-7162 Title Fax # (205) 254-7170
Personnel: Publisher, Editor-George Bogs
Editorial Description: Articles deal with advantages of use of our products.
General Info: Yr. Est. 1928, Quarterly, Sheetfed press, 16 pages, 4 Color, Coated, Saddle-stitched
Circulation: Total-8,900
Printing Co: Ebsco Media, 801 5th Ave S, Birmingham, AL 35233-1102 Tel # (205) 323-1508, Fax # (205) 226-8400

WRC Bulletin *Association*

Publishing Co: Welding Research Council, 345 E 47th St Rm 1301, New York, NY 10017-2330; Title Tel # (212) 705-7956
Personnel: Editor-Dr. Martin Prager
General Info: 10x/yr., ISSN: 0043-2326
Subscriptions: Indv. $300

Welding Research News *Association, Business*

Publishing Co: Welding Research Council, 345 E 47th St Rm 1301, New York, NY 10017-2330; Title Tel # (212) 705-7956
Personnel: Editor-Dr. Martin Prager
Editorial Description: Highlights of articles published by the council.
General Info: Quarterly, 8 pages

Wire Industry News *Business*

Publishing Co: CRU International, 7500 Greenway Center Dr., Suite 480, Greenbelt, MD 20770-4430; Title Tel # (301) 441-8997 Title Fax # (301) 441-9091
Personnel: Publisher, Editor-Richard Callahan, Circ. Mgr.-Harriet Callahan
Editorial Description: Management newsletter for the worldwide wire industry.
General Info: Yr. Est. 1973, Bi-weekly, Trim Size-8½ x 11, Offset press, 8 pages, No Color
Subscriptions: Indv. $250, Can. $300, For. $300, $10/copy
Circulation: Total-2,000
Advertising: Inquire for rates. Accepts Inserts.
List Rental: Rents Lists

METEOROLOGY

AMS Newsletter

Publishing Co: American Meteorological Society, 45 Beacon St., Boston, MA 02108-3693 Tel # (617) 742-2425 Fax # (617) 742-8718
Editorial Description: Reports on issues and government actions affecting the meteorological community.
General Info: Yr. Est. 1980, Monthly
Subscriptions: Indv. $100

Arizona Climate Summary

Publishing Co: Office of Climatology, Arizona State Univ., Box 871508, Tempe, AZ 85287-1508; Title Tel # (602) 965-6265
Personnel: Editor-H. Verville & P Schaffer
Editorial Description: Maps & tables of previous month's weather data.
General Info: (Formerly Arizona's Weather Word), Yr. Est. 1974, Monthly, Trim Size-8½ x 11, Sheetfed press, 16 pages, No Color
Subscriptions: Indv. $15
Circulation: Total-150

Coastal Research
See: SCIENCE

Hourly Precipitation Data

Publishing Co: U.S. Natl. Climatic Data Ctr., Federal Bldg., MC-02, Asheville, NC 28801; Title Tel # (704) 259-0682
Editorial Description: Contains hourly & daily precipitation values for 3,000 stations in the U. S.
General Info: Yr. Est. 1951, Monthly, Offset press, 15 pages, No Color
Subscriptions: Indv. $19, $2/copy
Circulation: Total-5,000

National Weather Assn. Newsletter *Association*

Publishing Co: Natl. Weather Assn., 6704 Wolke Ct, Montgomery, AL 36116-2134; Title Tel # (334) 213-0388 Title Fax # (334) 213-0388
Personnel: Publisher-Kevin Lavin, Editor-Larry Burch
Editorial Description: Operational Meteorological Activity, Assn. News.
General Info: Yr. Est. 1976, Monthly, Trim Size-8½ x 11, Offset press, 7 pages, ISSN: 0271-1044, No Color, Newsprint
Subscriptions: Indv. $15, Inst. $18, Can. $18, For. $20, $2/copy
Circulation: Readership-2,400
Advertising: Accepts Inserts.

State Climatologist *Consumer, Association*

Publishing Co: Sponsor-Amer. Assn. of State Climatologists, National Climatic Data Center, N, NESDIS E/Ccx2, Federal Bldg. 151 Patton Ave, Asheville, NC 28801-5001; Title Tel # (704) 271-4475 Title Fax # (704) 271-4246
Personnel: Editor-Stephen Doty
Editorial Description: Established to provide information exchange to the state climatologists.
General Info: Yr. Est. 1977, Quarterly, Trim Size-8½ x 11, Sheetfed press, 8 pages, No Color, Newsprint, Saddle-stitched
Circulation: (72% controlled), Total-550
Printing Co: National Climatic Data Ctr., Federal Bldg., 151 Patton Ave, Asheville, NC 28801-5001 Tel # (704) 271-4226, Fax # (704) 271-4876

UCAR Newsletter *Consumer*

Publishing Co: Univ. Corp. for Atmospheric Research, Box 3000, Boulder, CO 80307-3000; Title Tel # (303) 497-8602
Personnel: Editor-Lucy Warner
Editorial Description: Directed at univ. atmospheric research community. Informs community of opportunities for research, collaboration, & use of NCAR facilities.
General Info: Yr. Est. 1973, Bi-monthly, Trim Size-8½ x 11, Offset press, 10 pages, No Color
Circulation: Total-2,300
Printing Co: Speedy Bee, 1750 30th St., Boulder, CO 80302 Tel # (303) 449-8990

Weekly Weather & Crop Bulletin
See: AGRICULTURE

Windswept *Association*

Publishing Co: Mount Washington Observatory, P.O. Box 2310, Main Street, North Conway, NH 03860 Tel # (603) 356-8345; Title Tel # (603) 466-3388
Personnel: Editor-Francis Belcher
Editorial Description: Features science, history, and information regarding Mt. Washington.
General Info: (Formerly mount Washington Observatory News Bulletin), Quarterly, Trim Size-5 x 7½, 28 pages
Subscriptions: Indv. $25
Circulation: Total-3,500

MICROBIOLOGY

AAB Bulletin
See: SCIENCE

American Type Culture Collection-Quarterly Newsletter
See: BIOLOGY

Antimicrobic & Infectious Diseases Newsletter *Consumer*

Publishing Co: Elsevier Science Inc., 655 Avenue of the Americas, New York, NY 10010-5107 Tel # (212) 633-3916 Parent Co.-Reed Elsevier, New York; Title Tel # (212) 633-3927 Title Fax # (212) 633-3913
Personnel: Publisher-Glen Campbell, Editor-Charles Stratton, Promotion Dir.-Joe Barrett
Editorial Description: Developments in antimicrobics and antimicrobial therapy.
General Info: Yr. Est. 1984, Monthly, Sheetfed press, 8 pages, ISSN: 0738-1751, No Color, Newsprint
Subscriptions: Indv. $48, $5/copy
Circulation: Total-1,068
List Rental: Actives: 1,250, $125/M
Printing Co: Vee Printing, 100 Dixon Rd., De Freestville, NY 12144

Biotechnology News
See: SCIENCE

Clinical Immunology Newsletter *Consumer*

Publishing Co: Elsevier Science Inc., 655 Avenue of the Americas, New York, NY 10010-5107 Parent Co.-Reed Elsevier, New York; Title Tel # (212) 633-3916 Title Fax # (212) 633-3913
Personnel: Publisher-Marci Tlusly, Editor-Henry Homurter, Adv. Dir.-Tino De Carlo, Promotion Dir.-Joseph Barrett
Editorial Description: Recent developments in immunopathology and serology.
General Info: Yr. Est. 1980, Monthly, Trim Size-8½ x 11, Sheetfed press, 8 pages, ISSN: 0197-1859, Color
Subscriptions: Indv. $58, $6/copy
Circulation: Total-1,100
List Rental: Actives: 327, $125/M

Clinical Investigator News
See: DRUGS & PHARMACEUTICALS

Clinical Microbiology Newsletter
Consumer

Publishing Co: Elsevier Science Inc., 655 Avenue of the Americas, New York, NY 10010-5107 Parent Co.-Reed Elsevier, New York; Title Tel # (212) 633-3916 Title Fax # (212) 633-3913
Personnel: Publisher-Marci Tlusty, Editor-Mary Jane Ferraro, Circ. Mgr.-Stephanie Dickson, Adv. Dir.-Tino De Carlo, Promotion Dir.-Joe Barrett
Editorial Description: Recent developments in diagnosis and treatment.
General Info: Yr. Est. 1979, Semi-monthly, Trim Size-8$\frac{1}{2}$ x 11, Sheetfed press, 8 pages, ISSN: 0196-4399, 2 Color
Subscriptions: Indv. $66, $7/copy
Circulation: Total-2,350
List Rental: Actives: 2,280, $125/M
Printing Co: Vee Printing, 100 Dixon Rd., De Freestville, NY 12144

Clinical Trials Monitor
See: DRUGS & PHARMACEUTICALS

Frontiers in Immunology & Biotechnology Scientific Newsletter

Publishing Co: Scientific Newsletters, Rr 4 Box 7, Middletown, NY 10940-9685; Title Tel # (914) 355-9144 Title Fax # (914) 355-9147
Personnel: Publisher, Editor-Marc Duey, Circ. Mgr.-Maureen Duey, Adv. Dir.-Kristy Lauria
Editorial Description: Latest developments in the non-isotopic immunoassay field--products, applications, etc.
General Info: (Formerly Combined & Biotech-Update), Yr. Est. 1980, 10x/yr., Trim Size-8$\frac{1}{2}$ x 11, Offset press, 10 pages, ISSN: 0270-0471, No Color
Subscriptions: Indv. $100, For. $115
Acquistions: Publication Bought, Publication Sold
Circulation: Total-1,700
List Rental: Actives: $65/M

Fungal Genetics Newsletter
See: BIOLOGY

GeneWATCH
See: GENETICS

IDN-Infectious Diseases Newsletter
See: MEDICINE

Microbiological Update

Publishing Co: Microbiological Applications, Inc., 132 San Remo Dr, Islamorada, FL 33036-3307; Title Tel # (305) 664-8513 Title Fax # (305) 664-8597
Personnel: Editor-Murray Cooper, Circ. Mgr.-Claire Sandberg, Production Mgr.-Matthew Cooper
General Info: Yr. Est. 1983, Monthly, 4 pages
Subscriptions: Indv. $160, Can. $175, For. $175

Mycological Society of America Newsletter
See: BIOLOGY

Primary Probe
See: MEDICINE

Radioassay Ligand-Assay News
See: MEDICINE

MILITARY & NAVAL

AFBA Transmitter
See: BROADCASTING

ALERT
Association

Publishing Co: Sponsor-Defense Credit Union Council, Defense Credit Union, 805 15th St NW Ste 300, Washington, DC 20005-2207; Title Tel # (202) 682-5993
Personnel: Editor-C.V. Toulme
Editorial Description: Rules, regulations affecting military credit unions & news regarding them.
General Info: Yr. Est. 1976, Monthly, Trim Size-8$\frac{1}{2}$ x 11, Offset press, 12 pages, 1% ads, No Color, Newsprint, Perfect bound
Subscriptions: Indv. $25
Circulation: (100% controlled)
Advertising: Inquire for rates.

AN Equipment Forecast
See: AERONAUTICS/ASTRONAUTICS

America's Spirit
See: SOCIAL SERVICES & WELFARE

Anchor Watch

Publishing Co: US Naval Academy Museum, 118 Maryland Ave, Annapolis, MD 21402-1316; Title Tel # (301) 267-2108
Personnel: Editor-James Cheevers
Editorial Description: News & information of historic naval ships.
General Info: Yr. Est. 1983, Quarterly, Trim Size-8$\frac{1}{2}$ x 11, Mimeo press, 6 pages
Subscriptions: Indv. $10, Free

Anti-Submarine Warfare

Publishing Co: Forecast International/DMS, Inc., 22 Commerce Rd., Newtown, CT 06470-1643 Fax # (203) 426-1964; Title Tel # (203) 426-0800 Title Fax # (203) 426-4262
Editorial Description: A guide to more than 130 non-warfare pact ASW programs detailing states & outlook, development, funding, contract history, & program analysis. Includes information on sonobuoys, torpedoes, ASW-systems & sonars.
General Info: Monthly, No Color, Looseleaf
Subscriptions: Indv. $1,295

Army Families

Publishing Co: Sponsor-Army Family Liaison Office, Department of the Army, Hqda (dape-Zxf), Washington, DC 20310-0001 Fax # (703) 695-3195; Title Tel # (703) 695-7714 Title Fax # (703) 695-7714
Personnel: Editor, Circ. Mgr., Promotion Dir.-Joe Wasserman
Editorial Description: To provide information on programs & policies that impact on the quality life of army families worldwide.
General Info: (Formerly News for Army Families), Yr. Est. 1982, Quarterly, Trim Size-8$\frac{1}{2}$ x 11, Letrpr. press, 6 pages, No Color, Newsprint
Circulation: Total-400,000
Printing Co: MacDonald & Eudy Printers, Inc., 4509 Geech Rd., Temple Hills, MD 20748 Tel # (301) 423-8900

At Ease
See: RELIGIOUS & THEOLOGICAL

BMD Monitor
Business

Publishing Co: Pasha Publications, Inc, 1616 N. Fort Myer Dr., #1000, Arlington, VA 22209-3103 Fax # (703) 528-4926; Title Tel # (703) 528-1244 Title Fax # (703) 528-1253
Personnel: Publisher-Tod Sedgwick, Grp. Pub.-Harry Baisden, Editor-Ann Roosevelt, Mng. Editor-Len Famiglietti, Circ. Mgr.-Kathy Thorne, Production-Russell Roberts, Mktg. Coord.-Clair Hill
Editorial Description: Covers the technical, budgetary, political and international developments in the ballistic and theater missile defense industry as well as related technologies.
General Info: (Formerly SDI Monitor), Yr. Est. 1986, Bi-weekly, Trim Size-8$\frac{1}{2}$ x 11, Web press, 12 pages, ISSN: 0886-7607, Ind/Abs/Online: NewsNet, DIALOG, No Color, Matte
Subscriptions: Indv. $787, For. $802, $31/copy
List Rental: Rents Lists

Black Vet

Publishing Co: Black Veterans for Social Justice, 680 Fulton St, Brooklyn, NY 11217-1609; Title Tel # (718) 935-1168
Personnel: Editor-Oronde Takuma
General Info: Yr. Est. 1988, Bi-monthly

C3I Forecast
Business

Publishing Co: Forecast International/DMS, Inc., 22 Commerce Rd., Newtown, CT 06470-1643 Fax # (203) 426-1964; Title Tel # (203) 426-0800 Title Fax # (203) 426-4262
General Info: 12x/yr., Looseleaf
Subscriptions: Indv. $1,295

C3I News
Consumer

Publishing Co: Washington Defense Reports, Inc., PO Box 34312, Bethesda, MD 20827-0312; Title Tel # (703) 573-1600
Personnel: Publisher-B. Thomas, Editor-David Sheehan, Circ. Mgr.-Donna Olin, Art Dir.-Bill Chadbourne, Promotion Dir.-B. Sheehan
Editorial Description: Summarizes latest technical marketing developments in command, control, communications system of the U.S. Dept. of Defense & Industry, with NATO & Third World data.
General Info: Yr. Est. 1984, Monthly, Letrpr. press, 10 pages, Color, Newsprint
Subscriptions: Indv. $195, $10/copy
Acquistions: Publication Bought, Publication Sold
Circulation: Total-2,500

CHI Dispatch
See: HISTORY

CPIA Bulletin
See: AERONAUTICS/ASTRONAUTICS

Campaign
See: PHILATELY & POSTAL AFFAIRS

Canadian Defense Update

Publishing Co: Baxter Publishing Co., 310 Dupont St., Toronto, ON M5R 1V9 Canada Fax # (416) 968-2377; Title Tel # (416) 968-7252
Personnel: Publisher-W.H. Baxter, Editor-Stuart Vallance, Circ. Mgr.-Guy Bolduc
Editorial Description: Contains information on military affairs and other related subjects.
General Info: Yr. Est. 1987, Monthly, Trim Size-8$\frac{1}{2}$ x 11, Sheetfed press, 8 pages, ISSN: 0835-7129, 2 Color, Newsprint, Saddle-stitched
Subscriptions: Indv. $180
Acquistions: Publication Bought

Canadian Military Medals & Insignia Journal
See: HOBBY

Cavalry Journal, The — *Consumer, Association*   CPM: $176

Publishing Co: U.S. Cavalry Association, PO Box 2325, Fort Riley, KS 66442-0325;
Title Tel # (913) 784-5797 Title Fax # (913) 784-5797
Personnel: Publisher, Editor-P.S. Bright
Editorial Description: News of association members, U.S. Cavalry Museum and Cavalry history.
General Info: (Formerly Crossed Sabers Newsletter), Yr. Est. 1976, Quarterly, Trim Size-8½ x 11,
Offset press, 26 pages, ISSN: 1074-0252, 40% ads, No Color, Saddle-stitched
Subscriptions: Indv. $25, Inst. $40, Can. $35, For. $35, Free With Membership
Acquistions: Publication Bought
Circulation: Total-3,000
Advertising: $530.
Printing Co: The Printery, 101 7th, Junction City, KS 66441 Tel # (913) 762-5112

Citizen Soldier — *Consumer*

Publishing Co: Citizen Soldier, 175 5th Ave Ste 808, New York, NY 10010-7703;
Title Tel # (212) 777-3470
Personnel: Editor-Tod Ensign
Editorial Description: Supports the rights of veterans and active duty servicepeople.
General Info: Yr. Est. 1969
List Rental: List Management Co.: Names in the News-California, 1 Bush St Bsmt 3, San Francisco,
CA 94104-4425 Tel # (415) 989-3350, Fax # (415) 433-7796, Actives: 6,864, $60/M

Civil War Round Table Digest
See: HISTORY

Coast Guard Reservist

Publishing Co: U.S. Gov't Printing Office, 2100 2nd St. S.W., Washington, DC 20593-0001;
Title Tel # (202) 267-1991 Title Fax # (202) 267-4553
Personnel: Editor-Paz Kruska
Editorial Description: Provides information of interest to Coast Guard Reservists.
General Info: Yr. Est. 1953, Monthly, Trim Size-8½ x 11, 2 Color, Newsprint, Saddle-stitched
Circulation: Total-25,000

Conscience and Military Tax Campaign
See: TAXES

Constitution Chronicle
See: MUSEUM PUBLICATIONS

Contracting and Acquisition
Newsletter — *Business, Association*

Publishing Co: U.S. Dept. of the Air Force, Hq Usaf/Rdcx, Washington, DC 20330-0001
Editorial Description: Catch D301, 6/4 - 2. Order from Supt. Doc., Wash. DC 20402.

Courier
See: INTERNATIONAL AFFAIRS

Covert Intelligence Letter — *Consumer*

Publishing Co: Horizone, PO Box 67, Saint Charles, MO 63302-0067; Title Tel # (314) 731-0993
Title Fax # (314) 731-0993
Personnel: Publisher, Editor-W. Waltzer, Circ. Mgr.-Col. Hooper, Adv. Dir.-J. Williams, Promotion
Dir.-Kim Soo
Editorial Description: Concise reports on counter terror activities & equipment & personnel. Analysis
of raids, terrorist & counter terror movements. News of Para Military activities.
General Info: (Formerly Horizon), Yr. Est. 1974, Bi-monthly, Trim Size-8½ x 11, Offset press, 2
pages, ISSN: 1076-8645, No Color
Subscriptions: Inst. $20, For. $18, $3/copy
Circulation: Total-350
Advertising: Inquire for rates.

DPF News Notes

Publishing Co: Disciples Peace Fellowship, PO Box 1986, Indianapolis, IN 46206-1986;
Title Tel # (317) 353-1491
Personnel: Editor-Garnett Day
General Info: Yr. Est. 1968
Circulation: Total-1,700

Defense & Aerospace Companies, Volume I
See: AERONAUTICS/ASTRONAUTICS

Defense & Aerospace
Companies, Volume II — *Business*

Publishing Co: Forecast International/DMS, Inc., 22 Commerce Rd., Newtown, CT 06470-1643
Fax # (203) 426-1964; Title Tel # (203) 426-0800 Title Fax # (203) 426-4262
Editorial Description: Covering Africa, Asia, Europe, Middle East & South America.
General Info: Monthly, Looseleaf
Subscriptions: Indv. $1,295

Defense Cleanup — *Business*

Publishing Co: Pasha Publications, Inc, 1616 N. Fort Myer Dr., #1000, Arlington, VA 22209-3103
Fax # (703) 528-4926; Title Tel # (703) 528-1244 Title Fax # (703) 528-1253
Personnel: Publisher-Tod Sedgwick, Editor-Bowman Cox, Mng. Editor-Jeff Schomisch, Assoc. Ed.-
Beth Herzberger, Circ. Mgr.-Kathy Thorne, Production-Rob Traister, Mktg. Coord.-Mary Anvari,
Mktg. Coord.-Julie Johnson
Editorial Description: Reports on Department of Defense's and Department of Energy's $140 billion
cleanup programs.
General Info: Yr. Est. 1990, Weekly, Trim Size-8½ x 11, Ind/Abs/Online: Predicasts, Matte
Subscriptions: Indv. $545, For. $575, $11/copy
List Rental: Rents Lists

Defense Contract Awards
See: GOVERNMENT

Defense Daily — *Business*

Publishing Co: Phillips Business Information, Inc., 1201 Seven Locks Rd., Ste 300, Potomac, MD
20854-2958 Tel # (301) 340-1520; Title Tel # (301) 340-2100 Title Fax # (301) 424-4297
Personnel: Publisher-Thomas Phillips, Editor-Norman Baker, Circ. Mgr.-Vanessa Henderson,
Production Mgr.-Bill Wynne, Adv. Dir., Promotion Dir.-Mark Ziebarth
Editorial Description: Exclusive coverage of all major defense & space programs daily.
General Info: (Formerly Space Business Daily; Aerospace Financial News), Yr. Est. 1959, Daily,
Sheetfed press, 8 pages, ISSN: 0889-0404, Ind/Abs/Online: DIALOG, NewsNet, Predicasts, No
Color, Newsprint
Subscriptions: Indv. $1,495, For. $1,320
Acquistions: Publication Bought, Publication Sold
Advertising: Inquire for rates. Accepts Inserts.
List Rental: Actives: $95/M
Printing Co: Phillips Publishing, Inc., 7811 Montrose Rd, Potomac, MD 20854-3394

Defense Media Review
See: JOURNALISM

Defense Technology News

Publishing Co: Phillips Business Information, Inc., 1201 Seven Locks Rd., Ste 300, Potomac, MD
20854-2958 Tel # (301) 340-1520; Title Tel # (301) 340-2100 Title Fax # (301) 424-4297
Personnel: Publisher-John Farley
General Info: Bi-weekly, 8 pages
Subscriptions: Indv. $445

Defense Week — *Association, Business*

Publishing Co: King Communications Group, 627 National Press Building, Washington, DC
20045-1601 Tel # (202) 638-4260 Fax # (202) 662-9719; Title Tel # (202) 638-7430
Title Fax # (202) 662-9744
Personnel: Publisher-Llewellyn King, Editor-David Lynch, Circ. Mgr.-Michele Bedard, Production
Mgr.-Clyde Pelzer, Art Dir.-Tony Campana, Promotion Dir.-Susan Pangman
Editorial Description: News on the developments of the U.S. military and defense industry. The
weekly publication reports on defense policy, DOD budget, acquisition issues, congressional
priorities and alliances, defense conversions, weapons R&D and others.
General Info: Yr. Est. 1979, Weekly, Trim Size-8½ x 11, Sheetfed press, 16 pages, ISSN: 0273-
3188, Ind/Abs/Online: NewsNet, DIALOG, Predicasts, 2 Color, Newsprint, Saddle-stitched
Subscriptions: Indv. $1,099, $22/copy
Acquistions: Publication Bought

Draft Notices
See: POLITICS

Electronic Warfare Digest — *Consumer*

Publishing Co: Washington National News Reports, 3918 Prosperity Ave Ste 318, Fairfax, VA
22031-3333; Title Tel # (703) 573-1600 Title Fax # (703) 573-1604
Personnel: Publisher-R. J. O'Connell, Editor-Brian Thomas, Circ. Mgr.-Nancy Van Wyen
Editorial Description: Defense Dept. Armed Services, Congress and the industry. Precise facts
about all new EW, ECM, ECCM, and RPV hardware and software systems, procurement, contracts
and R&D breakthroughs.
General Info: Yr. Est. 1977, Monthly, Trim Size-8½ x 11, Sheetfed press, 10 pages, ISSN: 0884-
4828, No Color
Subscriptions: Indv. $195, Can. $198, For. $206, $10/copy
Circulation: Total-5,000

Electronic Warfare
Forecast — *Business, Consumer*

Publishing Co: Forecast International /DMS, 22 Commerce Rd., Newtown, CT 06470-1643
Fax # (203) 426-4262; Title Tel # (203) 426-0800 Title Fax # (203) 426-1964
Editorial Description: Covers EW systems grouped by technology, airborne, sea-based & land-
based activities.
General Info: Monthly, Trim Size-8½ x 11, 1,200 pages, No Color, Looseleaf
Subscriptions: Indv. $1,295
List Rental: Rents Lists

Estimate
See: INTERNATIONAL AFFAIRS

Ex-P O W Bulletin
CPM: $17

Publishing Co: American Ex-Prisoners of War, 3201 E Pioneer Pky Ste 40, Arlington, TX 76010-5324; Title Tel # (817) 649-2979 Title Fax # (817) 649-0109
Personnel: Circ. Dir.-Clydie Morgan, Publisher, Editor, Production Mgr.-Sue Langseth
Editorial Description: Publication of the American Ex-Prisoners of War, it includes historical P O W accounts, current Ex-P O W news, legislation and medical research information.
General Info: Yr. Est. 1945, Monthly, Trim Size-8$\frac{1}{8}$ x 10$\frac{3}{4}$, Web press, 48 pages, 5% ads, Color-cover, Matte, Saddle-stitched
Subscriptions: Indv. $13, For. $20, Free
Circulation: Total-23,000
Advertising: $400.
Printing Co: Account Manager: Todd Johnson; Neff Printing, 7080 Martway St, Shawnee Mission, KS 66202-3267 Tel # (800) 255-0088, Fax # (913) 599-3299

Executive Briefing
Business, Association

Publishing Co: American Logistics Assn., 1133 15th St NW Ste 640, Washington, DC 20005-2710 Fax # (202) 296-4419; Title Tel # (202) 466-2520
Personnel: Publisher-A. Kolbet Schrichte, Editor-Carol Bok, Circ. Mgr.-Paul Pierpoint
Editorial Description: For international government, military resale, troop subsistence market.
General Info: Yr. Est. 1974, Bi-monthly, Trim Size-8$\frac{1}{2}$ x 11, Offset press, 6 pages, No Color, Newsprint
Circulation: (100% controlled), Total-2,500

Expediter

Publishing Co: Dept. of the Army, Military Traffic Mgt. Command, 5611 Columbia Pike, Falls Church, VA 22041-5000; Title Tel # (703) 756-1242
Editorial Description: Newspaper covering topics related to military traffic management.

Fiber Optics Business
See: TELECOMMUNICATIONS

For Your Eyes Only

Publishing Co: Tiger Publications, PO Box 8759, Amarillo, TX 79114-8759; Title Tel # (806) 655-2009
Personnel: Editor-Stephen Cole, Publisher, Circ. Mgr.-Leanna Cole
Editorial Description: Summary of current military activities.
General Info: Yr. Est. 1980, Bi-weekly, Trim Size-8$\frac{1}{2}$ x 11, Sheetfed press, 8 pages, ISSN: 0738-4203, Ind/Abs/Online: NewsNet, No Color, Matte
Subscriptions: Indv. $70, Can. $75, For. $88, $3/copy
Circulation: Total-1,000

Foreign Military Markets, Asia & Pacific Rim
Business

Publishing Co: Forecast International/DMS, Inc., 22 Commerce Rd., Newtown, CT 06470-1643 Fax # (203) 426-1964; Title Tel # (203) 426-0800 Title Fax # (203) 426-4262
General Info: Monthly, Looseleaf
Subscriptions: Indv. $1,295

Foreign Military Markets, Latin America & Caribbean
Business

Publishing Co: Forecast International/DMS, Inc., 22 Commerce Rd., Newtown, CT 06470-1643 Fax # (203) 426-1964; Title Tel # (203) 426-0800 Title Fax # (203) 426-4262
General Info: Monthly, Looseleaf
Subscriptions: Indv. $1,295

Foreign Military Markets Latin American & Australasia
See: AERONAUTICS/ASTRONAUTICS

Foreign Military Markets Middle East & Africa
See: INTERNATIONAL AFFAIRS

Foreign Military Markets NATO & Europe
See: AERONAUTICS/ASTRONAUTICS

Forge, The

Publishing Co: Valley Forge Military Academy & Junior College, 1001 Eagle Rd, Wayne, PA 19087-3694
Personnel: Editor-Maj. Larry Edwards, Photo Ed.-Bill Harris
Editorial Description: News and information for cadets, faculty, staff, alumni, parents and friends of Valley Forge Military Academy and Junior College.

Gamewarden Newsletter

Publishing Co: Gamewardens of Vietnam Assn., PO Box 5523, Virginia Beach, VA 23455-0523; Title Tel # (804) 464-2312
Personnel: Publisher-John Williams
Editorial Description: Publication of veterans of U.S. Navy's river patrol force (task force 116)
General Info: Yr. Est. 1968, Annually
Circulation: Total-2,000

General Orders
Association

Publishing Co: Legion of Valor of the U.S. of America, 92 Oak Leaf Ln, Chapel Hill, NC 27516-9440; Title Tel # (919) 933-0989
Personnel: Editor-M.G. Worley
Editorial Description: A journal of the nation's senior war veterans organization-750 members holding Medal of Honor, Distinguished Service Cross, Navy Cross, or Air Force Cross.
General Info: (Formerly Army & Navy Legion of Valor), Yr. Est. 1890, Bi-monthly, Trim Size-6 x 9, Web press, 24 pages, No Color, Coated
Subscriptions: Indv. $20, $3/copy
Circulation: (94% controlled), Total-850

George C. Marshall Foundation Topics
See: HISTORY

Global Survey
Business

Publishing Co: Government Bus. Worldwide Rpts., PO Box 5997, Washington, DC 20016-1597; Title Tel # (202) 244-7050 Title Fax # (202) 244-5410
Personnel: Publisher-J.H. Wagner
Editorial Description: Information on international governmental defense affairs.
General Info: (Formerly Defense Reference), Yr. Est. 1974, Monthly, Trim Size-8$\frac{1}{2}$ x 11, Offset press, 20 pages, ISSN: 1075-4644, No Color
Subscriptions: $50/copy

Government Business Worldwide Reports
See: GOVERNMENT

Guidon
See: CLUBS

Haversack, The
See: MUSEUM PUBLICATIONS

IUS Newsletter

Publishing Co: Inter-Univ. Seminar on Armed Forces & Society, Univ. of Chicago, 1126 E. 59th St., Chicago, IL 60611-1798; Title Tel # (312) 702-8694
Personnel: Editor-William Boltz
Circulation: Total-950
List Rental: Rents Lists

Inside the Air Force

Publishing Co: Inside Washington Publishers, P.O. Box 7167, Ben Franklin Station, Washington, DC 20044 Tel # (703) 512-1800; Title Tel # (703) 892-8500 Title Fax # (703) 685-2606
General Info: Yr. Est. 1990, Weekly
Subscriptions: Indv. $445

Inside Defense Electronics

Publishing Co: Inside Washington Publishers, P.O. Box 7167, Ben Franklin Station, Washington, DC 20044 Tel # (703) 512-1800; Title Tel # (703) 416-8500 Title Fax # (703) 685-2606
Personnel: Editor-Thomas Duffy
Editorial Description: Focuses on the defense electronics field.
General Info: Yr. Est. 1987, Weekly
Subscriptions: Indv. $485

Inside the Navy

Publishing Co: Inside Washington Publishers, P.O. Box 7167, Ben Franklin Station, Washington, DC 20044 Tel # (703) 512-1800; Title Tel # (703) 892-8500 Title Fax # (703) 685-2606
Personnel: Editor-Brendan McNally
General Info: Yr. Est. 1988, Weekly
Subscriptions: Indv. $435

Inside the Pentagon
Business, Consumer

Publishing Co: Inside Washington Publishers, P.O. Box 7167, Ben Franklin Station, Washington, DC 20044 Tel # (703) 512-1800; Title Tel # (703) 416-8500
Personnel: Publisher-John Grano, Editor-Richard Lardner
General Info: Yr. Est. 1985, Weekly
Subscriptions: Indv. $535

Inside the Pentagon's Electronic Combat Report

Publishing Co: Inside Washington Publishers, P.O. Box 7167, Ben Franklin Station, Washington, DC 20044 Tel # (703) 512-1800; Title Tel # (703) 892-8508
Personnel: Editor-Thomas Duffy
General Info: Yr. Est. 1987, Weekly
Subscriptions: Indv. $535

International Contractors, Volume II
Business

Publishing Co: Forecast International/DMS, Inc., 22 Commerce Rd., Newtown, CT 06470-1643 Fax # (203) 426-1964; Title Tel # (203) 426-0800 Title Fax # (203) 426-4262
Editorial Description: Covers weapons & electronics.
General Info: Monthly, Looseleaf
Subscriptions: Indv. $945

J.W.V.A. Bulletin
See: VETERANS

Kombatant W Ameryce
See: CLUBS

Land & Sea-Based Electronics Forcast   *Business*

Publishing Co: Forecast International/DMS, Inc., 22 Commerce Rd., Newtown, CT 06470-1643; Title Tel # (203) 426-0800 Title Fax # (203) 426-1964
Editorial Description: Detailed information on major retrofit & modernization programs for land & sea-based platforms; detailed estimates of probable updates through 2003.
General Info: (Formerly World Retrofit & Modernization Forecast: Land & Sea-Based Sy), Monthly, Looseleaf
Subscriptions: Indv. $1,200
List Rental: Rents Lists

Militarism Resource Project News

Publishing Co: Militarism Resource Project, 318 S 49th St, Philadelphia, PA 19143-1704; Title Tel # (215) 386-4875
General Info: Quarterly, 8 pages

Military & Police Uniform Association Newsletter
See: CLUBS

Military Aircraft Forecast   *Business*

Publishing Co: Forecast International/DMS, Inc., 22 Commerce Rd., Newtown, CT 06470-1643; Title Tel # (203) 426-0800 Title Fax # (203) 426-1964
Editorial Description: On combat and support aircraft & helicopters.
General Info: Monthly, No Color, Looseleaf
Subscriptions: Indv. $1,295
List Rental: Rents Lists

Military Aircraft Inventory Database License   *Business*

Publishing Co: Forecast International/DMS, Inc., 22 Commerce Rd., Newtown, CT 06470-1643 Fax # (203) 426-1964; Title Tel # (203) 426-0800 Title Fax # (203) 426-4262
General Info: Quarterly, Looseleaf
Subscriptions: Indv. $6,500

Military Force Structures of the World   *Business*

Publishing Co: Forecast International/DMS, Inc., 22 Commerce Rd., Newtown, CT 06470-1643 Fax # (203) 426-1964; Title Tel # (203) 426-0800 Title Fax # (203) 426-4262
General Info: Quarterly, Looseleaf
Subscriptions: Indv. $2,495

Military Living's R & R Report   *Association*

Publishing Co: Military Marketing Services, Inc., PO Box 2347, Falls Church, VA 22042-0347; Title Tel # (703) 237-0203 Title Fax # (703) 237-2233
Personnel: Publisher, Editor-Ann Crawford, Circ. Mgr., Production Mgr.-Anna Belle Causey, Adv. Dir.-Roy Crawford, Jr., Promotion Dir.-Roy Crawford
Editorial Description: Temporary military lodging, travel discounts, camping & rec. areas. Civilian travel opportunities.
General Info: Yr. Est. 1971, Bi-monthly, Trim Size-8½ x 11, Letrpr. press, 8 pages, No Color, Coated, Saddle-stitched
Subscriptions: Indv. $15, $3/copy
Circulation: Total-12,000
Advertising: Inquire for rates. Accepts Inserts.
Printing Co: Suburban Printing Service, 5380a Eisenhower Ave, Alexandria, VA 22304-4856 Tel # (703) 370-5800, Fax # (703) 751-8637

Military Robotics   *Business*

Publishing Co: L & B Ltd., 19 Rock Creek Church Rd NW, Washington, DC 20011-6005; Title Tel # (202) 723-1600 Title Fax # (202) 726-2979
Personnel: Publisher, Editor-Joseph Lovece, Production Mgr., Adv. Dir., Promotion Dir.-Gwen Benson-Walker
Editorial Description: News and information on military & government robotics systems.
General Info: Yr. Est. 1987, Bi-weekly, Desktop press, ISSN: 0896-0348, Ind/Abs/Online: DIALOG, Predicasts
Subscriptions: Indv. $350, Inst. $295, Can. $350, For. $375

Military Space   *Business*

Publishing Co: Pasha Publications, Inc, 1616 N. Fort Myer Dr., #1000, Arlington, VA 22209-3103; Title Tel # (703) 528-1244 Title Fax # (703) 528-4926
Personnel: Publisher-Tod Sedgwick, Grp. Pub.-Harry Baisden, Editor-Frank Seitzen, Mng. Editor-Len Famiglietti, Circ. Mgr.-Kathy Thorne, Production-Russell Roberts, Mktg. Coord.-Clair Hill
Editorial Description: Covers politics and technology of military space.
General Info: Yr. Est. 1984, Bi-weekly, Trim Size-8½ x 11, Web press, 8 pages, ISSN: 0743-7897, Ind/Abs/Online: NewsNet
Subscriptions: Indv. $575, For. $590, $23/copy
Acquistions: Publication Bought, Publication Sold
List Rental: Rents Lists

Military Travel News

Publishing Co: Connie Gibson Wehrman Connor, PO Box 9, Oakton, VA 22124-0009; Title Tel # (703) 281-9323
Personnel: Publisher-Connie Gibson Connor, Editor-Ed Wojtas, Adv. Dir.-Sharon Renalds
Editorial Description: Travel bargains and discounts for Department of Defense personnel,active duty, retired and families.
General Info: Yr. Est. 1970, Bi-monthly, Trim Size-8½ x 11, 4 pages, 2 Color
Subscriptions: Indv. $7, For. $9
Circulation: Total-7,500
Advertising: Inquire for rates.
Printing Co: Daystar Press, 151315 Lawn Ln., Rockville, MD 20850 Tel # (301) 424-0686

Military Vehicles Forecast   *Business*

Publishing Co: Forecast International/DMS, Inc., 22 Commerce Rd., Newtown, CT 06470-1643; Title Tel # (203) 426-0800 Title Fax # (203) 426-1964
Editorial Description: US, European, & international military vehicle programs are examined, covering main battle tanks, self-propelled artillery, infantry fighting vehicles, armored personnel carriers, & tactical vehicles.
General Info: Monthly, Trim Size-8½ x 11, 1,200 pages, Color-cover, Matte, Other, Looseleaf
Subscriptions: Indv. $1,295
List Rental: Rents Lists

Missile Forecast
See: AERONAUTICS/ASTRONAUTICS

NASOH Newsletter

Publishing Co: N.A. American Soc. for Oceanic History, Program in Maritime History, East Carolina University, Greenville, NC 27858-4353; Title Tel # (301) 267-6100
Personnel: Editor-William Roberts
Editorial Description: Provides information on history of the sea, especially N. America.
General Info: Yr. Est. 1975, 4 pages, Color
Subscriptions: Indv. $15
Circulation: Total-200
List Rental: Rents Lists

NAVAPD News
See: MEDICINE

NSIA Newsletter   *Association*

Publishing Co: Natl. Security Industrial Assn., 1025 Connecticut Ave NW Ste, 300, Washington, DC 20036-5405; Title Tel # (202) 775-1440 Title Fax # (202) 775-1309
Personnel: Editor-Dave Burpee
Editorial Description: Contains information concering activities of the assnis chapters and committees.
General Info: Yr. Est. 1944, Quarterly, Trim Size-8 x 10½, 12 pages, 2 Color, Matte, Other
Subscriptions: Free With Membership
Circulation: Total-8,000, Readership-8,000

National HQ Communicator

Publishing Co: Veterans of Foreign Wars of the U.S., 406 W. 34th St., Kansas City, MO 64111-2736; Title Tel # (816) 756-3390
Personnel: Editor-Richard Kolb
General Info: (Formerly PX: The VFW Post Exchange), Yr. Est. 1966, 9x/yr., Sheetfed press, 6 pages, 2 Color, Newsprint
Circulation: Total-15,000

Navy News and Undersea Technology   *Business*

Publishing Co: Pasha Publications, Inc, 1616 N. Fort Myer Dr., #1000, Arlington, VA 22209-3103; Title Tel # (703) 528-1244 Title Fax # (703) 528-4926
Personnel: Publisher-Tod Sedgwick, Grp. Pub.-Henry Baisden, Editor-Len Famiglietti, Assoc. Ed.-Thomas Jandl, Circ. Mgr.-Kathy Thorne, Production-Russell Roberts, Mktg. Coord.-Clair Hill
Editorial Description: Covers naval affairs worldwide. Topics include technology, policy, strategy, operations and industry. Also covers U.S. congressional activity as it affects U.S. and other navies.
General Info: Yr. Est. 1984, Weekly, Trim Size-8½ x 11, 14 pages, ISSN: 8756-1700, Ind/Abs/Online: NewsNet, DIALOG, Color-cover
Subscriptions: Indv. $545, For. $590, $11/copy
Acquistions: Publication Bought
Circulation: Total-2,000
List Rental: Rents Lists

New Technology Week
See: SCIENCE

Now Hear This   *Association*

Publishing Co: USS Callaway Assn., c/o Wallace Shipp, 5319 Manning Pl., NW, Washington, DC 20016-5311; Title Tel # (202) 363-3663
Personnel: Editor-Dorthy Shipp, Editor-Wallace E. Shipp
Editorial Description: News of shipmates & their families, deaths, marriages, births, problems, reunions, with pictures. News of other ships & their reunions. Information for veterans.
General Info: Yr. Est. 1965, Annually, Trim Size-8½ x 11, Offset press, 24 pages, ISSN: 1083-2246, No Color, Coated, Saddle-stitched
Subscriptions: Free To Qualified Recipient
Acquistions: Publication Bought, Publication Sold
Circulation: (100% controlled), Total-391
Printing Co: Stickley Printing Co., 2293 Lewis Ave, Rockville, MD 20851-2333 Tel # (301) 881-4121

Nuclear Arsenal Handbook

Publishing Co: Nuclear Arsenal Project, 2216 Race St, Denver, CO 80205-5640; Title Tel # (303) 377-7998
Personnel: Editor-Barbara Donachy
General Info: Yr. Est. 1982, Annually
Subscriptions: Indv. $4

Nuclear Resister
See: POLITICS

Nuclear Waste News
See: NUCLEAR ENERGY

Officers Call   *Association*   **CPM:** $13

Publishing Co: National Officers Assn., PO Box 4975, Reston, VA 22090-1464 Tel # (703) 438-3060 Fax # (703) 438-3049; Title Tel # (703) 438-3066 Title Fax # (708) 438-3049
Personnel: Editor-Bruce Pifel, Circ. Mgr., Adv. Dir.-Monica Worth
Editorial Description: Information on financial management and career opportunities for commissioned and warrant officers in all branches of the uniformed services; updates on entitlement issues.
General Info: (Formerly 1st Priority (1983)), Yr. Est. 1981, Quarterly, Trim Size-8½ x 11, Web press, 16 pages, ISSN: 1040-029X, 2 Color, Saddle-stitched
Subscriptions: Free With Membership
Circulation: Total-25,000, Readership-60,000
Advertising: $325. Accepts Inserts.
List Rental: Actives: 24,000, $65/M, Expires: 11,000, $50/M

On Watch
See: LAW

Ordnance & Munitions
Forecast   *Business*

Publishing Co: Forecast International/DMS, Inc., 22 Commerce Rd., Newtown, CT 06470-1643 Fax # (203) 426-1964; Title Tel # (203) 426-0800 Title Fax # (203) 426-4262
General Info: Monthly, Looseleaf
Subscriptions: Indv. $1,295

Peace Pac Newsletter

Publishing Co: Peace Pac, 110 Maryland Ave., NE, Washington, DC 20002-5626 Tel # (202) 544-0805; Title Tel # (202) 543-4100
Personnel: Editor-Suzy S. Kerr
General Info: (Formerly Congressional Update), Yr. Est. 1988, Quarterly
Subscriptions: Free

Periscope - Daily Defense News Capsules

Publishing Co: United Communications Group, 11300 Rockville Pike, Ste. 1100, Rockville, MD 20852-3030 Tel # (301) 816-8950 Fax # (301) 816-8945
Editorial Description: News capsules of worldwide military activities.
General Info: Yr. Est. 1990, Daily
List Rental: Rents Lists

Point
See: POLITICS

Pull Together   *Association*

Publishing Co: Naval Historical Center, Bldg. 157-1 WNY, Washington, DC 20374-0001 Tel # (202) 433-4407; Title Tel # (202) 433-2005
Editorial Description: Covers various aspects of naval history; announces upcoming events.
General Info: Semi-annually, Trim Size-8½ x 11, Offset press, 16 pages, No Color, Matte, Saddle-stitched
Circulation: Total-1,054

R.U.S.I. Newsletter   *Association*

Publishing Co: Royal United Services Inst. of Vancouver Island, Bay St. Armory, 715 Bay St., Victoria, BC V8T 1R1 Canada Fax # (604) 360-2472; Title Tel # (604) 384-1331
General Info: Yr. Est. 1927, Monthly, Trim Size-8½ x 10, Desktop press, 8 pages, Matte, Saddle-stitched
Printing Co: Tudor Printing Ltd., 101 Simcor St., Victoria, BC V8V 1K5 Canada Tel # (604) 382-2428, Fax # (604) 388-4633

Radar Forecast
See: AERONAUTICS/ASTRONAUTICS

Redstone Rocket

Publishing Co: Redstone Arsenal, U.S. Army Missle Command, Publ, Redstone, AL 35898-0001; Title Tel # (205) 876-1500

Routes to Roots

Publishing Co: Jewish War Veterans of the U.S., 1811 R St NW, Washington, DC 20009-1603; Title Tel # (202) 265-6280
General Info: Quarterly
Circulation: Total-8,000

Royal Regiment of Canada Newsletter

Publishing Co: Royal Regiment of Canada, Fort York Armoury, 660 Fleet St. West, Toronto, ON M5V 1A9 Canada; Title Tel # (416) 973-3677
General Info: Quarterly

S.L.A. Marshall Military History Collection-Newsletter   *Consumer*

Publishing Co: S.L.A. Marshall Military History Collection, University Library, University, Of Texas At El Paso, El Paso, TX 79968-0852; Title Tel # (915) 747-5697
Personnel: Editor-Thomas Burdett
Editorial Description: Announces developments in the Collection; contains articles of related interest.
General Info: Yr. Est. 1980, Irregular, Trim Size-8½ x 11, Sheetfed press, 4 pages, No Color, Matte
Subscriptions: Free
Circulation: (98% controlled), Total-500, International-10

Salute
See: SHIPS & SHIPPING

Sea Letter

Publishing Co: Natl. Maritime Museum Assn., PO Box 470 0310, San Francisco, CA 94147-0310; Title Tel # (415) 929-0202 Title Fax # (415) 673-5381
Personnel: Publisher-Russell Booth, Editor-Steve Haller, Production Mgr.-Tom Richardson, Art Dir.-Tony Mesler
Editorial Description: A forum for articles concerning Pacific Basin & West Coast Maritime history, including articles on technological, sociological, & economic aspects of our Maritime/Naval Past.
General Info: Yr. Est. 1960, Semi-annually, Sheetfed press, 30 pages, 4 Color, Coated
Circulation: (28% controlled), Total-3,500
Advertising: Inquire for rates.
List Rental: Rents Lists

Security Police Digest
See: LAW ENFORCEMENT & PENOLOGY

Sightseer   *Association*

Publishing Co: Natl. Assn. of the 6th Infantry Div., 5649 39th Ave S, Minneapolis, MN 55417-2917; Title Tel # (612) 727-2326
Personnel: Editor-Richard Flanders
Editorial Description: A newsletter for former members of the 6th Infantry Div. & the new 6th Infantry Div. (light) activated 3-26-86 & stationed Alaska.
General Info: Yr. Est. 1936, Quarterly, Trim Size-8½ x 11, Roto. press, 12 pages, 2 Color
Circulation: Total-1,100, Readership-1,100
Printing Co: Tandem Press, Inc., 7860 12 Ave S, Bloomgarden, MN 55425 Tel # (612) 854-6860, Fax # (612) 854-7155

Silent Wings

Publishing Co: William Horn, 7038 Northaven Rd, Dallas, TX 75230-3505; Title Tel # (214) 368-6097
Personnel: Publisher, Editor-William Horn
Editorial Description: For members & friends of World War II glider pilots.
General Info: Yr. Est. 1973, Quarterly, Sheetfed press, 16 pages, No Color, Newsprint
Subscriptions: Indv. $12, Can. $15, For. $18, $4/copy

Space Systems Forecast
See: AERONAUTICS/ASTRONAUTICS

Spacewatch
See: AERONAUTICS/ASTRONAUTICS

Study War No More
See: EDUCATION

Tactical Technology   *Business*

Publishing Co: Phillips Business Information, Inc., 1201 Seven Locks Rd., Ste 300, Potomac, MD 20854-2958 Tel # (301) 340-1520 Fax # (301) 424-4297
Editorial Description: Information on low intensity conflicts and the special operations on the war on drugs.
General Info: (Formerly Special Technologies), Bi-weekly, ISSN: 1059-0552
Subscriptions: Indv. $645, For. $680
Advertising: Accepts Inserts.

Technology Report   *Consumer*

Publishing Co: Sperry Corp., Mail Sta. 1W113, Marcus Ave., Great Neck, NY 11020; Title Tel # (516) 574-1591
Editorial Description: Review of defense and maritime technologies.
General Info: Yr. Est. 1982, Quarterly, Sheetfed press, 8 pages, 2 Color
Circulation: Total-12,000

Technology Transfer Week
Business

Publishing Co: Phillips Business Information, Inc., 1201 Seven Locks Rd., Ste 300, Potomac, MD 20854-2958 Tel # (301) 340-1520; Title Tel # (301) 340-2100 Title Fax # (301) 424-4297
Personnel: Publisher-Thomas Phillips, Editor-Eric DeRitis, Circ. Mgr.-Vanessa Henderson, Production Mgr.-Bill Wynne, Adv. Dir., Promotion Dir.-Mark Ziebarth
Editorial Description: Covers defense & aerospace marketing opportunities worldwide.
General Info: (Formerly Defense Marketing International), Yr. Est. 1989, Bi-weekly, Sheetfed press, 8 pages, ISSN: 1074-4363, Ind/Abs/Online: DIALOG, No Color, Matte
Subscriptions: Indv. $695, For. $760
Acquistions: Publication Bought, Publication Sold
Advertising: Inquire for rates. Accepts Inserts.
List Rental: Rents Lists
Printing Co: Phillips Publishing, Inc., 7811 Montrose Rd, Potomac, MD 20854-3394

USS Henrico APA-45 Newsletter
Association

Publishing Co: Sponsor-USS Henrico APA-45 Assoc., USS Henrico APA-45 Association, 15875 Interurban Rd., Platte City, MO 64079-9185; Title Tel # (816) 858-5411 Title Fax # (816) 858-5556
Personnel: Editor-Don Soper, Publisher, Circ. Mgr.-Betty Soper
Editorial Description: Newsletter for crew and officers who served on the USS Henrico APA-45 during the period from 1943-1968.
General Info: Yr. Est. 1973, Semi-annually, Trim Size-8$\frac{1}{2}$ x 11, Mimeo press, 14 pages, No Color, Newsprint
Subscriptions: Free With Membership
Circulation: (100% controlled), Total-754
Printing Co: Citizen Printing, PO Box 888, Platte City, MO 64079-0888

USS Liberty Newsletter

Publishing Co: USS Liberty Veterans Assn., 3 Burns Ave, Hicksville, NY 11801-2601; Title Tel # (516) 681-2268 Title Fax # (516) 681-2232
General Info: Yr. Est. 1981, Quarterly
Subscriptions: Indv. $15

Understanding Defense
Consumer

Publishing Co: Understanding Defense, 1574 Coburg Rd # 160, Eugene, OR 97401-4802; Title Tel # (503) 345-9379
Personnel: Circ. Dir.-Susan Peterson, Publisher, Editor, Production Mgr.-E.G. Ross
Editorial Description: Intelligence and analysis on defense and foreign policy.
General Info: Yr. Est. 1986, Monthly, Trim Size-8$\frac{1}{2}$ x 11, Desktop press, 8 pages, No Color, Matte
Subscriptions: Indv. $38, $3/copy
Circulation: Total-600

Underwater Letter
Business

Publishing Co: Callahan Pubs., PO Box 1173, McLean, VA 22101-1173; Title Tel # (703) 356-1925 Title Fax # (703) 356-9614
Personnel: Publisher, Editor-Vincent Callahan, Jr.
Editorial Description: Contracting opportunities, legislation & new developments in fields of oceanography and underwater defense.
General Info: (Formerly Underwater Defense Letter), Yr. Est. 1960, Semi-monthly, Trim Size-8$\frac{1}{2}$ x 11, Offset press, 8 pages, ISSN: 0041-6592, No Color
Subscriptions: Indv. $190, For. $200

U.S. Coast Guard-Safety Newsletter

Publishing Co: U.S. Coast Guard, 2100 2nd St SW, Washington, DC 20593-0001

U.S. Defense Budget Forecast
Business

Publishing Co: Forecast International/DMS, Inc., 22 Commerce Rd., Newtown, CT 06470-1643 Fax # (203) 426-1964; Title Tel # (203) 426-0800 Title Fax # (203) 426-4262
General Info: 7x/yr., Looseleaf
Subscriptions: Indv. $1,495

U.S. Handgunner
See: GUNS & FIREARMS

U.S. Navy Field Training Supervisors Association News Bulletin

Publishing Co: U.S. Navy Field Training Supervisors Assn., 84 Farrar Ave, Hyde Park, MA 02136-3223
General Info: Monthly

Vietnam War Newsletter

Publishing Co: Vietnam War Newsletter, PO Box 469, Collinsville, CT 06022-0469; Title Tel # (203) 582-9784
Personnel: Editor-Thomas Hebert
Editorial Description: An information clearinghouse for Vietnam Veterans; heavy emphasis on books.
General Info: Yr. Est. 1979, Monthly, Trim Size-5$\frac{1}{2}$ x 8$\frac{1}{2}$, Offset press, 28 pages, 2% ads
Subscriptions: Indv. $23, $2/copy
Circulation: Total-2,500
Advertising: Inquire for rates.
Printing Co: Lightning Press, 369 West Main St., Avon, CT 06001 Tel # (203) 677-2458

Volunteer
Association

Publishing Co: VALB, 799 Broadway Ste 227, New York, NY 10003-6811
Editorial Description: Organ of veterans of the Abraham Lincoln Brigade.
General Info: Quarterly, Trim Size-8$\frac{1}{2}$ x 11

War Letter

Publishing Co: Jerry Buchanan Advertising Agency, PO Box 2038, Vancouver, WA 98668-2038; Title Tel # (206) 574-3084
General Info: Yr. Est. 1991, Quarterly
Subscriptions: Indv. $15

Warships Forecast
See: AERONAUTICS/ASTRONAUTICS

World Retrofit & Modernization Forecast Airborne Systems
See: AERONAUTICS/ASTRONAUTICS

MINING & MINERALS

Alaska Geology
Business, Association

Publishing Co: Alaska Dept. of Natural Resources, Div./Geol. & Geophys. Surveys, 794 University Ave., Ste. 200, Fairbanks, AK 99709-3645 Tel # (907) 451-5000 Fax # (907) 451-5050; Title Tel # (907) 474-4779
Editorial Description: Newsletter on subjects of interest to typical Alaskan miner or earth scientist.
General Info: Yr. Est. 1960, Semi-annually, Trim Size-8$\frac{1}{2}$ x 11, Offset press, 16 pages, No Color, Newsprint, Saddle-stitched
Circulation: Total-4,000

American Law of Mining
See: LAW

Ash At Work
Association

Publishing Co: American Coal Ash Assn., Inc., 1913 I St NW Fl 6, Washington, DC 20006-2106; Title Tel # (703) 317-2400 Title Fax # (703) 317-2409
Personnel: Publisher, Editor-Samuel Tyson
Editorial Description: Activities of Association, technical and non-technical reviews of ash utilization projects and/or programs.
General Info: Yr. Est. 1968, Bi-monthly, Trim Size-8$\frac{1}{2}$ x 11, Mimeo press, 4 pages
Subscriptions: Free With Membership
Circulation: Total-2,800

Bulletin of the Mineralogical Society of Utah

Publishing Co: Mineralogical Society of Utah, 129 F St, Salt Lake City, UT 84103-2601; Title Tel # (801) 363-3392
Personnel: Editor-Leon S. Stanley
Editorial Description: Describes areas in Utah for the collection of minerals, rock specimens, fossils, gem materials, mining history, geology, botany, anthropology, ornithology, etc.
General Info: Yr. Est. 1957, Trim Size-8$\frac{1}{2}$ x 11, Offset press, 60 pages, Color
Subscriptions: $1/copy
Circulation: Total-2,000

CRA Review
See: ECONOMICS

CRS Perspectives
Business, Association

Publishing Co: Center for Resource Studies, Queens University, Kingston, ON K7L 3N6 Canada; Title Tel # (613) 545-2553 Title Fax # (613) 545-6651
Personnel: Publisher-G. Hood
Editorial Description: Mineral policy notes, reviews, CRS activities and new publications.
General Info: Yr. Est. 1978, Quarterly, Trim Size-11 x 17, 8 pages, ISSN: 0228-1821, No Color
Subscriptions: Indv. $30, Inst. $30, Can. $30, For. $30, $4/copy
Circulation: Total-1,000

Canadian Resources & PennyMines Analyst
Consumer

Publishing Co: MPL Communications, Inc., 133 Richmond St. W., Ste. 700, Toronto, ON M5H 3M8 Canada; Title Tel # (416) 869-1177 Title Fax # (416) 869-0456
Personnel: Publisher-Steve Pepper, Editor-Glen Tetu, Circ. Mgr.-David Berger, Circ. Mgr.-Diana Yeo
Editorial Description: To information source for investors in the Canadian resource and gold miningsector. It covers penny stocks as well as major companies.
General Info: Yr. Est. 1986, Monthly, Trim Size-8$\frac{1}{2}$ x 11, Sheetfed press, 8 pages, 2 Color, Matte
Subscriptions: Indv. $157
List Rental: Rents Lists

Coal & Synfuels Technology
See: ENERGY

Coal and Coke Statistics
Business, Association

Publishing Co: Statistics Canada, Holland Ave/RH Coats, Holland Ave/Tunney's Pasture, Ottawa, ON K1A O26 Canada Tel # (613) 951-8116 Fax # (613) 951-0581; Title Tel # (613) 990-8116
Editorial Description: Production, imports, exports & disposition of coal; supply & disposition of coke in Canada. Catalog #45-002.
General Info: Yr. Est. 1921, Monthly, 16 pages, ISSN: 0380-6847
Subscriptions: Indv. $12, Can. $10, For. $14, $8/copy

Coal Export Report

Publishing Co: King Publishing Corp., 6914 Office Park Cir # 52210, Knoxville, TN 37909-1161
Tel # (619) 584-6214; Title Tel # (615) 584-6294
Editorial Description: A ship by ship report of coal exports.
General Info: (Formerly Coal Export Week), Yr. Est. 1984, Weekly, Offset press, 12 pages, ISSN: 1047-4285, No Color, Newsprint
Subscriptions: Indv. $456

Coal Mining Women's Support Team-News!

Publishing Co: Coal Employment Project, 16221 Sunnyknoll Ct, Dumfries, VA 22026-1739; Title Tel # (703) 670-3416
Personnel: Editor-Betty Jean Hall
General Info: Yr. Est. 1977, 10x/yr.
Subscriptions: Indv. $25

Coal News · *Business*

Publishing Co: National Mining Association, 1130 17th St., N.W., Washington, DC 20036-4677
Tel # (202) 463-2624; Title Tel # (202) 463-2631 Title Fax # (202) 857-0135
General Info: Weekly

Coal Outlook · *Business*

Publishing Co: Pasha Publications, Inc, 1616 N. Fort Myer Dr., #1000, Arlington, VA 22209-3103; Title Tel # (703) 528-1244 Title Fax # (703) 528-4926
Personnel: Publisher-Tod Sedwick, Editor-Barry Cassell, Mng. Editor-Jeff Schomisch, Assoc. Ed.-Doug Beizer, Assoc. Ed.-David Massey, Circ. Mgr.-Kathy Thorne, Production-Rob Traister, Mktg. Coord.-Mary Anvari, Mktg. Coord.-Julie Johnson
Editorial Description: Coal markets, prices, regulations, legislation, corporate developments.
General Info: Yr. Est. 1975, Weekly, Trim Size-8½ x 11, Web press, 12 pages, ISSN: 0162-2714, Ind/Abs/Online: DIALOG, Mead Data Central, Predicasts, No Color, Matte
Subscriptions: Indv. $795, For. $825, $16/copy
List Rental: Actives: $95/M

Coal Tech International
See: ENERGY

Coal Week · *Business*

Publishing Co: McGraw-Hill, 1200 G St NW Ste 1100, Washington, DC 20005-3814
Tel # (202) 383-3700 Parent Co.-McGraw-Hill, New York; Title Tel # (202) 383-2190
Personnel: Publisher-John Slater, Editor-John Higgins, Mng. Editor-Paul Smith
General Info: Weekly, Ind/Abs/Online: DIALOG, Dow Jones, NewsNet, Nexis
Subscriptions: Indv. $216

Coal Week International · *Business*

Publishing Co: McGraw-Hill, 1200 G St NW Ste 1100, Washington, DC 20005-3814
Tel # (202) 383-3700 Parent Co.-McGraw-Hill, New York; Title Tel # (202) 383-2190
Personnel: Publisher-John Slater, Editor-Roseann Schwaderer, Mng. Editor-Paul Smith
General Info: Yr. Est. 1980, Weekly, Ind/Abs/Online: DIALOG, Dow Jones, NewsNet, Nexis
Subscriptions: Indv. $467

Coaldat Marketing Report
See: ENERGY

Coaldat Productivity Report · *Business*

Publishing Co: Pasha Publications, Inc, 1616 N. Fort Myer Dr., #1000, Arlington, VA 22209-3103
Fax # (703) 528-4926; Title Tel # (703) 528-1244 Title Fax # (703) 528-1253
Personnel: Publisher-Tod Sedgwick, Editor-Ron McMahon, Circ. Mgr.-Kathy Thorne, Promotion Dir.-Wade Martin
Editorial Description: Shows quarterly and year-to-date coal mine productivity.
General Info: Yr. Est. 1980, Quarterly, Mimeo press, 60 pages, Looseleaf
Subscriptions: Indv. $545, For. $585
List Rental: Rents Lists

Coaldat Quarterly
See: ENERGY

Concentrates · *Business, Association*

Publishing Co: Mining Club of the Southwest, PO Box 42317, Tucson, AZ 85733-2317; Title Tel # (602) 622-6257
General Info: Monthly
Circulation: Total-450

Diamond Insight
See: JEWELRY & HOROLOGY

Empire State Geogram-Research Issue
See: GEOLOGY

George Cross News Letter
See: METALS & METALWORKING

Gower Federal Service-Mining · *Business, Consumer*

Publishing Co: Rocky Mountain Mineral Law Foundation, 7039 E 18th Ave, Denver, CO 80220-1826; Title Tel # (303) 321-8100 Title Fax # (303) 321-7657
Editorial Description: Legal materials related to the location & maintenance of mining claims on public lands.
General Info: Yr. Est. 1962, 14x/yr., Looseleaf
Subscriptions: Indv. $315
Circulation: Total-150

Gower Federal Service-Miscellaneous Land Decisions
See: LAW

Gower Federal Service-Royalty Valuation and Management
See: LAW

Gypsum Products · *Business, Association*

Publishing Co: Statistics Canada, Holland Ave/RH Coats, Holland Ave/Tunney's Pasture, Ottawa, ON K1A O26 Canada Tel # (613) 951-8116 Fax # (613) 951-0581; Title Tel # (613) 951-1581 Title Fax # (613) 951-1584
Editorial Description: Text in English and French. Covers production, factory shipments and factory stocks. #44-003.
General Info: Yr. Est. 1972, Monthly, 3 pages, ISSN: 0380-7223
Subscriptions: Indv. $6, Can. $5, For. $7, $6/copy

Health and Safety Resource
See: FORESTRY

Industrial Specialties News · *Business*

Publishing Co: Blendon Information Services, 68 Longmore Street, Willowdale, ON M2N 6T8 Canada; Title Tel # (416) 223-5397 Title Fax # (416) 223-8532
Personnel: Publisher, Editor-Bob Orchard
Editorial Description: North American news about industrial minerals and their market.
General Info: Yr. Est. 1987, Semi-monthly, Trim Size-8½ x 11, 6 pages, ISSN: 0835-5134, Ind/Abs/Online: Predicasts/Dow Jones
Subscriptions: Indv. $557

International Coal Review · *Association*

Publishing Co: National Mining Association, 1130 17th St., N.W., Washington, DC 20036-4677
Tel # (202) 463-2624 Fax # (202) 857-0135; Title Tel # (202) 463-4780 Title Fax # (202) 833-9636
Editorial Description: Monthly newsletter containing v.s. coal export and import statistics by country of destimation and coal type.
General Info: Yr. Est. 1956, Monthly
Subscriptions: Indv. $100, Free With Membership

International Coal Trade

Publishing Co: King Publishing Corp., 6914 Office Park Cir # 52210, Knoxville, TN 37909-1161
Tel # (619) 584-6214; Title Tel # (615) 584-6294 Title Fax # (615) 558-6101
Editorial Description: International coal marketing information.
General Info: Yr. Est. 1984, Weekly, Offset press, 12 pages, ISSN: 0749-9043, No Color, Newsprint
Subscriptions: Indv. $790, For. $835

Investors' Update
See: NUMISMATICS

Jet News
See: WATER SUPPLY, POWER & WASTE

Kentucky Department of Mines and Minerals, Bulletin

Publishing Co: Kentucky Dept. of Mines, PO Box 14080, Lexington, KY 40512-4080; Title Tel # (605) 254-0367
General Info: Monthly

Legal Quarterly Digest of Mine Safety & Health Decisions · *Business, Association*

Publishing Co: Legal Publication Svces., 2008 N Emerson St., Arlington, VA 22207-1948; Title Tel # (703) 276-9796 Title Fax # (703) 243-3562
Personnel: Publisher, Editor-Ellen Smith
Editorial Description: Summarizes all recent legal decisions involving mine health and safety. Digests go back to 1970. full text of decisions are available by same day fax.
General Info: Yr. Est. 1970, Quarterly, Trim Size-8½ x 11, Desktop press, 100 pages, ISSN: 1051-53X, Looseleaf
Subscriptions: Indv. $325, For. $310
Circulation: Total-150
Advertising: Inquire for rates.
Printing Co: USA Print & Copy, Wilson Blvd., Arlington, VA 22201

Locating Gold, Gems and Minerals · *Business*

Publishing Co: United Prospectors Inc., 166 W H St, Benicia, CA 94510-3127
General Info: Yr. Est. 1947, Bi-monthly
Subscriptions: Indv. $6
Circulation: Total-200
Advertising: Inquire for rates.

Magnesium Monthly Review
See: METALS & METALWORKING

Metals Economics Group
Strategic Report   *Business, Association*

Publishing Co: Metals Economics Group, 1718 Argle St., Suite 300, Halifax, NS B3J 3N6 Canada; Title Tel # (902) 429-2880 Title Fax # (902) 429-6593
Personnel: Publisher-Michael Chender, Editor-Marilyn Beamish, Circ. Mgr.-Sandra Selva, Production Mgr.-Judy McKinnon, Promotion Dir.-Dominique Daniels
Editorial Description: Investigates financial & commercial issues in world-wide mine development.
General Info: (Formerly Mine Development Monthly), Yr. Est. 1981, Bi-monthly, 40 pages
Subscriptions: Indv. $1,150
Circulation: Total-150

Microscopial Society of Canada. Bulletin
See: OPTICAL

Mine Regulation Reporter   *Business*

Publishing Co: Pasha Publications, Inc, 1616 N. Fort Myer Dr., #1000, Arlington, VA 22209-3103; Title Tel # (703) 528-1244 Title Fax # (703) 528-4926
Personnel: Publisher-Tod Sedgwick, Editor-Ellen Smith, Mng. Editor-Jeff Schomisch, Circ. Dir.-Kathy Thorn, Production-Rob Traister, Mktg. Coord.-Mary Anvari, Mktg. Coord.-Julie Johnson
Editorial Description: A bi-weekly information service covering mine safety & health including federal programs, standards, enforcement activities, research, & legal decisions.
General Info: (Formerly Mine Safety & Health Reporter), Yr. Est. 1970, Bi-weekly, Trim Size-8½ x 11, Web press, 100 pages, ISSN: 0192-4745
Subscriptions: Indv. $785, For. $815, $31/copy
List Rental: Rents Lists
Printing Co: Buckley Offset, 1101 Pennsylvania Ave SE, Washington, DC 20003-2229

Mine Safety and Health
News   *Business, Association*

Publishing Co: Legal Publication Svces., 2008 N Emerson St., Arlington, VA 22207-1948 Tel # (703) 276-9796 Fax # (703) 243-3562
Personnel: Publisher, Mng. Editor-Ellen Smith, Law Ed.-Melanie Aclander
Editorial Description: Federal Mine Safety & Health Review Commission decisions. Articles on MSHA policies, proposed and final rules, feature stories on mine safety & health issues. Same day fax service available for all documents.
General Info: Yr. Est. 1994, Bi-weekly
Subscriptions: Indv. $475
Printing Co: USA Print & Copy, Wilson Blvd., Arlington, VA 22201

Mineral Law Newsletter
See: LAW

Minerals Research
Laboratory Newsletter

Publishing Co: North Carolina State Univ., Minerals Research Lab., 180 Coxe Ave., Asheville, NC 28801-4041; Title Tel # (704) 251-6155 Title Fax # (704) 251-6381
Personnel: Editor-John Schlonz
Editorial Description: Minerals Research Laboratory's new publications, news & current projects; MRL Advisory Committee meetings; news abstracts of mineral industry news.
General Info: (Formerly Minerals Research Laboratory Bulletin), Yr. Est. 1946, Quarterly
Circulation: Total-300

Mining Newsletter
See: SAFETY

Naddum News
See: ENVIRONMENT & ECOLOGY

News & Review

Publishing Co: Dresser Industries-Marion Div., 617 W Center St, Marion, OH 43302-3509; Title Fax # (614) 382-2052
Personnel: Editor-Peter Gilewicz
Editorial Description: News and technical articles on surface mining equipment produced by the Marion Division of Dresser Industries.
General Info: Yr. Est. 1989, Quarterly, 8 pages, 4 Color, Coated
Circulation: Total-8,000

Northern Coal

Publishing Co: King Publishing Corp., 6914 Office Park Cir # 52210, Knoxville, TN 37909-1161 Tel # (619) 584-6214; Title Tel # (615) 584-6294 Title Fax # (615) 558-6101
Editorial Description: Coal marketing information.
General Info: Weekly, Trim Size-8½ x 11, Offset press, 12 pages, ISSN: 0749-1719, No Color, Newsprint
Subscriptions: Indv. $547, For. $572

On the Level
See: HOUSE ORGANS

Past-Present Prints
See: HISTORY

Petroleum Coke Report

Publishing Co: King Publishing Corp., 6914 Office Park Cir # 52210, Knoxville, TN 37909-1161 Tel # (619) 584-6214; Title Tel # (615) 584-6294 Title Fax # (615) 558-6101
Editorial Description: Petroleum Coke marketing information.
General Info: Yr. Est. 1988, Trim Size-8½ x 11, 14 pages, ISSN: 1047-4285
Subscriptions: Indv. $1,440, $120/copy

Powell Gold Industry
Guide and International
Mining Analyst   *Business, Consumer*

Publishing Co: Reserve Research Ltd., Box 4135, Stn. A, Portland, ME 04101-0335; Title Tel # (207) 774-4971
Personnel: Publisher, Editor-Larson Powell
Editorial Description: Reviews & investment opinion of 100 leading mining companies.
General Info: (Formerly Powell Intl. Mining Analyst), Yr. Est. 1976, Quarterly, Trim Size-8½ x 11, Web press, 180 pages, ISSN: 0146-7204, Color-cover, Perfect bound
Subscriptions: Indv. $120, Inst. $120, Can. $120, For. $140, $35/copy
Acquistions: Publication Bought, Publication Sold
List Rental: Actives: $75/M, Expires: $75/M

Powell Monetary Analyst
See: INVESTMENT

Precious Metals News & Review
See: METALS & METALWORKING

Prospect Review
See: ENERGY

RIC News
See: SCIENCE

Rollin' Rock Club-News Letter
See: HOBBY

SONREEL News
See: LAW

Sand Paper, The
See: HOBBY

Southern Coal

Publishing Co: King Publishing Corp., 6914 Office Park Cir # 52210, Knoxville, TN 37909-1161 Tel # (619) 584-6214; Title Tel # (615) 584-6294 Title Fax # (615) 558-6101
Editorial Description: Coal Marketing Information.
General Info: Weekly, Trim Size-8 x 11, 12 pages, ISSN: 0749-1697, Newsprint
Subscriptions: Indv. $547, For. $572

Steel Industry Weekly
Review

Publishing Co: Steel Industry Weekly Review Ltd., 2 Uxbridge Rd, Scarsdale, NY 10583-2725; Title Tel # (716) 655-0218
Personnel: Publisher, Editor-Karl Keffer
General Info: Yr. Est. 1984, Weekly
Subscriptions: Indv. $75

Surview
See: GEOLOGY

Technology Transfer   *Business*

Publishing Co: Bureau of Mines, 810 7th St NW, Washington, DC 20241-0002; Title Tel # (202) 501-9323

Update
See: HOUSE ORGANS

Western Coal

Publishing Co: King Publishing Corp., 6914 Office Park Cir # 52210, Knoxville, TN 37909-1161 Tel # (619) 584-6214; Title Tel # (615) 584-6294 Title Fax # (615) 558-6101
Editorial Description: Coal marketing information.
General Info: Weekly, Trim Size-8½ x 11, Offset press, 12 pages, ISSN: 0749-1700
Subscriptions: Indv. $547, For. $572

MOBILE HOMES

Go Camping America!   *Consumer, Association*

Publishing Co: Recreational Vehicle Industry Assn., 1896 Preston White Dr, Reston, VA 22090 Tel # (703) 620-6003; Title Tel # (703) 734-3000
Editorial Description: Information for those in the camping industry.
General Info: Quarterly, Trim Size-8½ x 11, 4 pages, 4 Color, Coated

Mobile Home Living — *Consumer*

Publishing Co: Joe Sullivan, 300 E Arbor St Spc 57, Long Beach, CA 90805-6855; Title Tel # (310) 428-3567
Personnel: Publisher, Editor-Joe Sullivan
Editorial Description: Newsletter for mobile home owners by salesman Joe Sullivan.
General Info: Bi-monthly, Trim Size-7 x 8½, 4 pages, No Color, Matte, Saddle-stitched
Advertising: Inquire for rates.

Mobilehome Parks Report — *Business, Consumer*

Publishing Co: Parks Publishing Co., 3807 Pasadena Ave Ste 100, Sacramento, CA 95821-2863; Title Tel # (916) 971-0489
Personnel: Publisher, Editor-Thomas Kerr, Circ. Mgr.-Lalanna Tiomore
Editorial Description: Newsletter about mobilehome parks and manufactured housing legislation and issues.
General Info: (Formerly Kerr Report), Yr. Est. 1980, Monthly, Trim Size-11 x 17, Desktop press, 6 pages, ISSN: 0273-2726, No Color
Subscriptions: Indv. $135, $12/copy
Circulation: Total-350

RV Park & Campground Report
See: PARKS & RECREATION AREAS

RVDA News
See: OUTDOORS

Recreation Advisor — *Consumer, Association* — CPM: $24

Publishing Co: RLT Resource Group, PO Box 520, Gonzalez, FL 32560-0520; Title Tel # (904) 477-7992 Title Fax # (904) 479-8393
Personnel: Publisher, Editor-K.W. Stephens, Circ. Dir.-David Dykes, Adv. Dir.-Hugh C. McDaniel
Editorial Description: Covers RV recreation opportunities. General recreation, leisure and travel opportunities.
General Info: (Formerly Recreation World News), Yr. Est. 1983, Monthly, Trim Size-10½ x 13, Web press, 16 pages, 3% ads, No Color, Newsprint
Subscriptions: Indv. $15, Free With Membership
Circulation: Total-20,000
Advertising: $498. Accepts Inserts.

Rolling Ventures — *Consumer*

Publishing Co: Rolling Ventures, PO Box 2190, Henderson, NV 89041-2190; Title Tel # (206) 926-3946
Personnel: Editor-Kay Kennedy
Editorial Description: How to earn income while you travel in your RV.
General Info: Quarterly, 10 pages
Advertising: Inquire for rates.

Tracks RV News — *Consumer, Association*

Publishing Co: Tracks to Adventure, 2811 Jackson Ave Ste K, El Paso, TX 79930-3937
Editorial Description: RV/Mobile home tours through Alaska, Canada, USA and Mexico.
General Info: Yr. Est. 1975, Bi-monthly, Trim Size-8½ x 11, 8 pages, No Color, Matte

Western Mobile News

Publishing Co: Modern Housing Inc., 4043 Irving Pl, Culver City, CA 90232-2809
Personnel: Editor-Edward Ely
General Info: (Formerly Western Mobile Home News), Yr. Est. 1951, Weekly
Subscriptions: Indv. $5
Circulation: Total-26,000

MUSEUM PUBLICATIONS

ASI Posten
See: ETHNIC

ASTC Newsletter
See: SCIENCE

Academy Newsletter — *Association*

Publishing Co: California Academy of Sciences, Golden Gate Park, San Francisco, CA 94118-4599; Title Tel # (415) 221-5100 Title Fax # (415) 750-7346
Personnel: Editor-Sheri Ketchum, Graphic Designer-Nancy Campana
Editorial Description: Membership newsletter listing classes, meetings, lectures, cultural events, travel opportunities, and current exhibits. The Academy is a Natural History Museum, Planetarium, and Aquarium all under one roof.
General Info: (Formerly California Academy of Sciences Newsletter), Yr. Est. 1940, Monthly, Trim Size-8½ x 11, Offset press, 4 pages, 2 Color, Coated
Subscriptions: Free With Membership
Circulation: Total-25,000
Printing Co: Fruitridge Printing & Litho, 3258 Stockton Blvd., Sacramento, CA 95820-1418 Tel # (916) 452-9213

Air Power Museum Bulletin — *Association*

Publishing Co: Air Power Museum Inc., 22001 Bluegrass Road, Ottumwa, IA 52501-8569; Title Tel # (515) 938-2773
Personnel: Editor-Robert L. Taylor, Circ. Mgr.-Cindy Reis, Art Dir.-Brent Taylor
Editorial Description: Report on museum growth, also info on other air museums worldwide.
General Info: Yr. Est. 1965, Irregular, Trim Size-8½ x 11, Web press, 24 pages, ISSN: 0048-2358, Color, Saddle-stitched
Subscriptions: Indv. $35, $2/copy
Circulation: Total-6,000
Printing Co: Ottumwa Printing, 105 South Birch, Ottumwa, IA 52501

Alhfam Bulletin — *Association*

Publishing Co: Conner Prairie, 13400 Allisonville Rd, Fishers, IN 46038-3457; Title Tel # (317) 776-6000 Title Fax # (317) 776-6014
Personnel: Editor-Stephen Cox, Assoc. Ed.-Timothy Crumrin
Editorial Description: Activities of agricultural museums and living historical farms.
General Info: (Formerly Living Historical Farms Bulletin), Yr. Est. 1970, Bi-monthly, Trim Size-8½ x 11, Offset press, 14 pages, ISSN: 0047-4851, 1% ads
Subscriptions: Indv. $10, Inst. $25, $2/copy
Circulation: Total-1,200
Advertising: Inquire for rates.
Printing Co: Minuteman Press, 1094 Elden St, Herndon, VA 22070-3803

American Museum of Magic Newsletter

Publishing Co: American Museum of Magic, PO Box 5, Marshall, MI 49068-0005; Title Tel # (616) 781-7674
Personnel: Editor-Daniel Waldron, Publisher, Circ. Mgr.-Robert Lund
Editorial Description: Activities of American Museum of Magic.
General Info: Yr. Est. 1975, Irregular, Trim Size-8½ x 11, Sheetfed press, 2 pages, No Color, Newsprint
Subscriptions: Indv. $4

American Musical Instrument Society Newsletter
See: MUSIC & MUSIC TRADES

Appraiser, The
See: ANTIQUES & ART GOODS

Archaeological Newsletter
See: ARCHAEOLOGY

Artifacts — *Consumer, Association*

Publishing Co: Mizel Museum of Judaica, 560 S Monaco Pky, Denver, CO 80224-1227
Editorial Description: Newsletter of the Mizel Museum of Judaica.
General Info: Yr. Est. 1982, Quarterly

Arts Center News — *Consumer, Association*

Publishing Co: Robert W. Woodruff Arts Center, 1280 Peachtree St NE, Atlanta, GA 30309-3502 Tel # (404) 892-3600
Personnel: Editor-Bruce Galphin
Editorial Description: Information, news, and schedules of the Woodruff Arts Center in Atlanta, GA.
General Info: Quarterly, Trim Size-8½ x 11, 6 pages, No Color, Coated
Subscriptions: Free To Qualified Recipient

Artsfocus — *Association*

Publishing Co: Colorado Springs Fine Arts Center, 30 W Dale St, Colorado Springs, CO 80903-3210; Title Tel # (719) 634-5581 Title Fax # (719) 634-0570
Personnel: Editor-Margaret Lew, Circ. Mgr.-Marty Gaines
Editorial Description: Features museum exhibitions and performing arts, film series, art school & library articles, volunteer & membership activities. Includes events calendar.
General Info: Bi-monthly, Sheetfed press, 4 pages, 2 Color, Coated
Subscriptions: Indv. $20
Circulation: Total-4,000
Advertising: Inquire for rates.
List Rental: Rents Lists
Printing Co: Gowdy-Printcraft Press Inc., 22 N Sierra Madre St, Colorado Springs, CO 80903-3311 Tel # (719) 634-1593

Auction News from Christie's
See: ART & SCULPTURE

Aviso — *Association*

Publishing Co: American Assn. of Museums, 1225 Eye St. NW, Washington, DC 20004-1902; Title Tel # (202) 289-1818
Personnel: Editor-Bill Anderson, Production Mgr.- SusanWaterman, Adv. Dir.-Carlotta Eike
Editorial Description: Info on museum jobs, legislation, seminars, workshops & grant deadlines.
General Info: Yr. Est. 1924, Monthly, 16 pages, No Color
Subscriptions: $3/copy
Circulation: Total-10,500
Advertising: Inquire for rates.
List Rental: Rents Lists

BMA Today
Consumer

Publishing Co: Baltimore Museum of Art, Art Museum Drive, Baltimore, MD 21218-3898; Title Tel # (410) 396-6316 Title Fax # (410) 396-7153
Personnel: Editor-Audrey M. Frantz
Editorial Description: Listing of activities and exhibitions in the Baltimore Museum for members.
General Info: (Formerly BMA Members Calendar), Yr. Est. 1975, Monthly, Trim Size-8½ x 11⁷/₈, Sheetfed press, 20 pages, 2 Color, Coated, Saddle-stitched
Subscriptions: Free With Membership
Circulation: Total-12,000
Printing Co: Schneidereith & Sons, 2905 Whittington Ave, Baltimore, MD 21230-1419 Tel # (301) 525-0300

Bakken, The
See: LIBRARY

Blanden Memorial Art Museum-Bulletin

Publishing Co: Blanden Memorial Art Museum, 920 3rd Ave S, Fort Dodge, IA 50501-4723; Title Tel # (515) 573-2316
Personnel: Editor-Philip LaDouceur
General Info: (Formerly Blanden Memorial Art Gallery-Bulletin), Yr. Est. 1975, 4 pages
Circulation: Total-2,000

Bull & Branch
Association

Publishing Co: Friends of the Dard Hunter Paper Museum, 4517 Penn Ave N, Minneapolis, MN 55412-1132
Editorial Description: For members of the Friends of the dard Hunter Paper Museum.
General Info: Quarterly

Bulletin

Publishing Co: Museums Assn. of Saskatchewan, 1808 Smith St., Regina, SK S4P 2N3 Canada
General Info: Bi-monthly

Bulletin
Association

Publishing Co: Association of Museums in New Brunswick, 503 Queen St., Box 116 Station A, Fredericton, NB E3B 4Y2 Canada; Title Tel # (506) 452-2908 Title Fax # (506) 459-0481
Editorial Description: Technical information and general information on issues/events re: NB museums.
General Info: (Formerly Horizons; Alerte), Yr. Est. 1976, Quarterly, Trim Size-8½ x 11, Offset press, 4 pages, 2 Color, Recycled, Other
Acquisitions: Publication Bought, Publication Sold
Circulation: (100% controlled), Total-350
Advertising: Accepts Inserts.
Printing Co: Provincial Artisans, Fredericton, NB Canada

Bulletin-Association for Living Historical farms and Agricultural Museums
Business, Association

Publishing Co: Association for Living Historical Farms, Conner Prairie, 13400 Allisonville Rd., Fishers, IN 46038
Personnel: Editor-Stephen Cox
Editorial Description: Information on historical farms and agricultural museums in the USA.
General Info: Quarterly, ISSN: 0047-4851
Subscriptions: Indv. $15

Cahokian
See: ARCHAEOLOGY

Canadian Museum Of Flight And Transportation
See: AERONAUTICS/ASTRONAUTICS

Cavalry Journal, The
See: MILITARY & NAVAL

Charles MacNider Museum-Newsletter

Publishing Co: Charles H. MacNider Museum, 303 2nd St SE, Mason City, IA 50401-3925; Title Tel # (515) 421-3666
Personnel: Editor-Richard Leet
Editorial Description: News of Museum exhibitions, collection development, museum programs and special activities; illustrated.
General Info: Yr. Est. 1966, Bi-monthly, Trim Size-7 x 8, Offset press, 6 pages, 2 Color, Coated, Other
Subscriptions: Free With Membership
Circulation: (100% controlled), Total-1,000
Printing Co: Larson Printing Company, 714 S Delaware Ave, P.O Box 380, Mason City, IA 50402-0380 Tel # (515) 424-2623

Cheekwood Calendar
Association

Publishing Co: Cheekwood, Forrest Park Dr., Nashville, TN 37205; Title Tel # (615) 356-8000
Editorial Description: To inform the membership about exhibits (fine art and botanical), classes, concerts, special events. etc.
General Info: (Formerly Cheekwood Mirror), Yr. Est. 1961, Monthly, Trim Size-11 x 17, Letrpr. press, 2 pages, 2 Color
Subscriptions: $2/copy
Acquisitions: Publication Bought
Circulation: (100% controlled), Total-9,250

Collections
Consumer, Association

Publishing Co: Buffalo Society of Natural Sciences, Buffalo Museum of Scien, 1020 Humboldt Pkwy., Buffalo, NY 14211; Title Tel # (716) 896-5200 Title Fax # (716) 897-6723
Personnel: Editor-Barbara Park Leggett, Art Dir.-Joan Manias
Editorial Description: Articles on natural science subjects including anthropology; articles on museum activities, exhibits and on topics of interest to museum members.
General Info: (Formerly Science on the March), Yr. Est. 1920, Quarterly, Trim Size-8½ x 11, Web press, 8 pages, ISSN: 0016-0664, 2 Color, Newsprint, Saddle-stitched
Subscriptions: Indv. $5, $2/copy
Circulation: (100% controlled), Total-12,000

Column
Consumer, Association

Publishing Co: Arnot Art Museum, 235 Lake St, Elmira, NY 14901-3191; Title Tel # (607) 734-3697 Title Fax # (607) 734-5687
Personnel: Editor-Carolyn Warner
Editorial Description: Information for museum members on upcoming exhibitions & events.
General Info: Yr. Est. 1973, 5x/yr., Trim Size-9 x 12, 8 pages, 2 Color, Matte
Subscriptions: Free With Membership
Circulation: Total-1,400
Printing Co: Golos Printing, 110 E 9th St, Elmira Heights, NY 14903-1733 Tel # (607) 732-1896

Conservation: The Getty Conservation Institute Newsletter

Publishing Co: Getty Conservation Institute, 4503 Glencoe Ave, Marina Del Rey, CA 90292-6372 Tel # (310) 822-2299 Fax # (310) 821-9409; Title Tel # (213) 822-2299 Title Fax # (213) 821-9409
Personnel: Editor-Jane Siena, Production Mgr.-Irina Averkieff, Art Dir.-Jacki Gallagher
Editorial Description: Report on Getty Conservation Institute's projects on the conservation of cultural property.
General Info: (Formerly Getty Conservation Institue Newsletter), Yr. Est. 1986, Trim Size-11¾ x 11¾, 20 pages, ISSN: 0898-4808, 2 Color, Saddle-stitched
Subscriptions: Free
Acquisitions: Publication Bought
Circulation: Total-16,000

Constitution Chronicle
Consumer

Publishing Co: USS Constitution Museum Foundation, PO Box 1812, Boston, MA 02129-0001; Title Tel # (617) 426-1812
Editorial Description: Articles about the history of the USS Constitution, and activities of the USS Constitution Museum.
General Info: Yr. Est. 1976, Quarterly, Trim Size-11³/ x 12, Web press, 12 pages, 2 Color
Subscriptions: Free With Membership
Circulation: Total-11,000

Cooper-Hewitt Newsletter
Consumer

Publishing Co: Smithsonian Institution, 900 Jefferson Dr., S.W., Washington, DC 20560-0001 Tel # (202) 357-2888
Editorial Description: For members of the Cooper-Hewitt National Museum of Design, a branch of the Smithsonian.
General Info: Quarterly

Corral Dust
See: HISTORY

Crossings
See: HISTORY

Dacotah Prairie Times

Publishing Co: Dacotah Prairie Museum, PO Box 395, Aberdeen, SD 57402-0395 Tel # (605) 622-7117; Title Tel # (605) 229-1608
Personnel: Publisher, Editor-Merry Coleman, Circ. Mgr.-Sherri Rawstern
Editorial Description: Newsletter for museum friends and patrons.
General Info: Yr. Est. 1970, Quarterly, Trim Size-8½ x 11, Desktop press, 12 pages, No Color
Subscriptions: Free
Circulation: Total-1,400
Printing Co: Quality Quick Print, 112 N Main St, Aberdeen, SD 57401-3429 Tel # (605) 226-2541

Delaware State Museum, News

Publishing Co: Delaware State Museum, Court & Federal, Dover, DE 19901; Title Tel # (302) 736-4266

Dr. Samuel A. Mudd Society Newsletter
See: HISTORY

Education Program
Calendar

Publishing Co: Studio Museum, 144 W. 125th St., New York, NY 10027-4423;
Title Tel # (212) 864-4500
Editorial Description: African American art & the art of the African Diaspora.
General Info: Yr. Est. 1968, Quarterly, Trim Size-8½ x 14, Sheetfed press, 2 pages, 2 Color, Coated
Circulation: Total-3,000

Everhart Museum

Publishing Co: Nay Aug Park, Museum, Scranton, PA 18510; Title Tel # (717) 346-8370
Personnel: Editor-Leo Wojtanowski
General Info: Quarterly, 4 pages
Circulation: Total-1,600

Everson Museum of Art
Bulletin   *Association*

Publishing Co: Everson Museum of Art of Syracuse, 401 Harrison St, Syracuse, NY 13202-3019;
Title Tel # (315) 474-6064 Title Fax # (315) 474-6943
Personnel: Editor, Production Mgr.-Linda M. Herbert
Editorial Description: Highlights exhibitions; covers events, lectures, programs with articles and
photographs.
General Info: Yr. Est. 1975, Quarterly, Trim Size-11 x 17, Sheetfed press, 12 pages, No Color,
Coated
Acquistions: Publication Bought
Circulation: Total-4,000
Printing Co: Dellas Graphics, Inc., 835 Canal St, Syracuse, NY 13210-1177 Tel # (315) 474-4641

Federation News   *Association*

Publishing Co: Fed. of Nova Scotian Heritage, 1809 Barrington Street, #901, Halifax, NS B3J 3K8
Canada; Title Tel # (902) 423-4677 Title Fax # (902) 425-5606
Personnel: Editor-Don Hutchison
General Info: Yr. Est. 1976, Quarterly, ISSN: 0715-5190
Subscriptions: Indv. $15, Inst. $35, $4/copy
Circulation: Total-250

Forbes House Jottings

Publishing Co: Capt. Robert Bennet Forbes House, 215 Adams St, Milton, MA 02186-4215;
Title Tel # (617) 696-1815
Personnel: Editor-Dana Ricciardi, Circ. Mgr.-Nadine Leary
Editorial Description: Exhibits, acquisition and events.
General Info: (Formerly China Trade Register), Yr. Est. 1986, Quarterly, 6 pages
Subscriptions: Indv. $20, Inst. $30
Circulation: Total-1,500
Printing Co: Copy Stop Press, 39 Washington St., Quincy, MA 02186 Tel # (617) 471-5072

Fort Concho Guidon   *Association*

Publishing Co: Fort Concho National Historic Landmark, 213 E Avenue D, San Angelo, TX
76903-7020; Title Tel # (915) 657-4441
Personnel: Editor-John Neilson
Editorial Description: News of museum, restoration, and preseveration of Fort Concho.
General Info: Yr. Est. 1992, Quarterly, Trim Size-8½ x 11, Offset press, 8 pages, 2 Color, Coated
Subscriptions: Indv. $25
Circulation: Total-1,500

Genealogija
See: GENEALOGY

Gerald R. Ford Foundation Newsletter
See: GOVERNMENT

Good Earth Times   *Consumer*

Publishing Co: Good Earth Assn., Inc., Living Farm of the Ozarks, 202 E. Church St. at N. Bettis,
Pocahontas, AR 72455-2899; Title Tel # (501) 892-8329
Editorial Description: Historical farm operation.
General Info: Yr. Est. 1984, Irregular, Desktop press
Subscriptions: Indv. $5

Happenings Newsletter

Publishing Co: Manitoba Museum of Man & Nature, 190 Rupert Ave., Winnipeg, MB R3B 0N2
Canada; Title Tel # (204) 956-2830 Title Fax # (204) 942-3679
Personnel: Editor-Sue Caughlin
Editorial Description: Newsletter of the Manitoba Museum of Man and Nature.
General Info: Yr. Est. 1974, Bi-monthly, Trim Size-11 x 17, Offset press, 4 pages, ISSN: 0843-9133,
2 Color, Recycled
Subscriptions: Free With Membership
Circulation: Total-2,800
Printing Co: Esdale Printing Co, 232 Jarvis Avenue, Winnipeg, MB R2W 3A1 Canada
Tel # (204) 589-4371

Harvard University Art Museums Review
See: ART & SCULPTURE

Haversack, The   *Consumer, Association*

Publishing Co: Fort Ticonderoga Museum, PO Box 390, Ticonderoga, NY 12883-0390;
Title Tel # (518) 585-2821 Title Fax # (518) 585-2210
Personnel: Publisher-Nicholas Westbrook, Editor-Delight Gartlien, Circ. Mgr.-Linda Edson
Editorial Description: Informs members of museum activities.
General Info: Yr. Est. 1991, Semi-annually, Trim Size-8½ x 11, Offset press, 8 pages, ISSN: 1062-
340X, 2 Color, Saddle-stitched
Subscriptions: Free With Membership
Circulation: Total-2,500

Headway Recorder

Publishing Co: Natl. Capital Historical Museum of Transportation, Inc., PO Box 4007, Silver Spring,
MD 20914-4007; Title Tel # (301) 384-6352
Personnel: Editor-John Novack
General Info: (Formerly Electransite News), Yr. Est. 1941, Bi-monthly, 10 pages
Circulation: Total-300
Printing Co: Microform Service, Inc., PO Box 1067, Beltsville, MD 20704-1067

Heartbeat
See: GLASS, STONE & CLAY

Heritage Programs &
Museums Newsletter

Publishing Co: Heritage Programs & Museums, 22807 Easdt Woods Chapel Road, Blue Springs,
MO 64015-9747; Title Tel # (816) 881-4431 Title Fax # (816) 881-4626
Personnel: Editor-Gordon Julich, Art Dir.-Mary Koenig
Editorial Description: Promotes special events & programs for 6 Jackson County historic sites.
General Info: Yr. Est. 1986, Bi-monthly, Trim Size-8½ x 11, Web press, 8 pages, 2 Color, Newsprint
Subscriptions: Indv. $10
Acquistions: Publication Bought
Circulation: Total-2,500

Historic Deerfield Quarterly   *Association*

Publishing Co: Historic Deerfield, Inc., PO Box 321, Deerfield, MA 01342-0321;
Title Tel # (413) 774-5581
Personnel: Editor-Grace Friary
Editorial Description: New acquisitions in museum collections, interesting features and staff
activities.
General Info: Yr. Est. 1962, Quarterly, Trim Size-8½ x 11, Offset press, 6 pages, 2 Color, Coated
Circulation: Total-2,000
Printing Co: Excelsior Printing Co., 60 Roberts Dr., North Adams, MA 01247-3235
Tel # (413) 663-3771

Historic House News
See: HISTORY

Historical Gardener, The
See: GARDENING & HORTICULTURE

Historicalog
See: HISTORY

Hunter Museum of Art
Bulletin

Publishing Co: Hunter Museum of Art, 10 Bluff View St, Chattanooga, TN 37403-1111;
Title Tel # (615) 267-0968
Editorial Description: Lists exhibition and program schedules with descriptive narration relative to
both.
General Info: Yr. Est. 1960, Monthly, Trim Size-7 x 8½, Offset press, 14 pages, No Color
Circulation: Total-2,100

Huntington Calendar   *Association*

Publishing Co: Huntington Library Press, 1151 Oxford Rd, San Marino, CA 91108-1299
Tel # (818) 405-2172 Fax # (818) 585-0704; Title Tel # (818) 405-2147 Title Fax # (818) 405-0225
Personnel: Editor-Catherine Babcock, Art Dir.-Ava Moeller
Editorial Description: Reports on four divisions of the Huntington - its library, art gallery, botanical
gardens and research programs. Includes listing of exhibitions and public programs.
General Info: (Formerly Calendar of the Exhibitions), Yr. Est. 1936, Bi-monthly, Trim Size-8¼ x 11,
Offset press, 6 pages, ISSN: 0886-4683, 2 Color
Subscriptions: Free With Membership
Circulation: Total-8,500

Indian Awareness Center Newsletter
See: HISTORY

Insight

Publishing Co: J.B. Speed Art Museum, PO Box 2600, Louisville, KY 40201-2600;
Title Tel # (502) 636-2893
Personnel: Publisher-Peter Morrin, Editor-Mark Stuart, Art Dir.-Alan Pardee
General Info: Yr. Est. 1973, Bi-monthly, Trim Size-8 x 8, 16 pages
Circulation: Total-4,500

Institute of Diving Newsletter
See: OCEANOGRAPHY

J.B. Speed Art Museum
Bulletin   *Association*

Publishing Co: J.B. Speed Art Museum, PO Box 2600, Louisville, KY 40201-2600;
Title Tel # (502) 636-2893
Personnel: Publisher-Peter Morrin, Editor-K.S. Reed, Art Dir.-Alan Pardee
Editorial Description: Carrying articles dealing with museum accessions, it covers painting,
sculpture, and decorative arts of all periods and national origins.
General Info: Yr. Est. 1940, Semi-annually, Trim Size-7 x 10, 25 pages, 4 Color
Subscriptions: $1/copy
Circulation: (100% controlled), Total-3,000

Jib Gems

Publishing Co: Marine Museum of the Great Lakes-Kingston, 55 Ontario St., Kingston, ON K7L 2Y2
Canada Tel # (613) 542-2241; Title Tel # (613) 542-2261
Editorial Description: Focuses on marine news, museum events & museum collections.
General Info: Yr. Est. 1986, Quarterly, Desktop press, 4 pages, ISSN: 0839-105X
Subscriptions: Indv. $30, Free With Membership
Circulation: Total-600
Printing Co: Allan Graphics, 662 Princess St., Kingston, ON Canada Tel # (613) 546-6000

John & Mable Ringling Museum of Art-
Newsletter   *Association*

Publishing Co: Ringling Museum of Art, 5401 Bay Shore Rd, Sarasota, FL 34243-2161;
Title Tel # (813) 355-5101 Title Fax # (813) 351-7959
Personnel: Circ. Mgr.-Kate Monteith, Editor, Production Mgr.-Kathleen Chilson, Art Dir.-M. Chilson
Editorial Description: John and Mable Ringling Museum of Art showing ancient through
contempary art, emphasis on Baroque; Ringling Residence; Ringling Museum of the circus; Asolo
Theater.
General Info: Yr. Est. 1964, Quarterly, Trim Size-8½ x 11, Desktop press, 8 pages, 4 Color, Matte
Circulation: Total-5,000
Printing Co: Coastal Printing, 1730 Independence Blvd, Sarasota, FL 34234-2155
Tel # (813) 351-1515

Joslyn News

Publishing Co: Joslyn Art Museum, 2200 Dodge St, Omaha, NE 68102-1292;
Title Tel # (402) 342-3300 Title Fax # (402) 342-2376
Personnel: Editor-Linda Rajcevich
Editorial Description: Advertise museum activities.
General Info: Yr. Est. 1974, Bi-monthly, Trim Size-8½ x 11, Offset press, 12 pages, 2 Color, Matte,
Saddle-stitched
Subscriptions: Free With Membership
Circulation: Total-7,000

Journal   *Business, Association*

Publishing Co: Art Gallery of Ontario, 317 Dundas St., W., Toronto, ON M5T 1G4 Canada
Fax # (416) 977-8547; Title Tel # (416) 979-6648
Personnel: Editor-Aldona Satterthwaite, Production Mgr.-Sherri Somerville, Art Dir.-Marilyn Bouma-
Pyper, Mktg. Dir.-Frank Comella
Editorial Description: Gallery news briefs, exhibition features and events information.
General Info: (Formerly Gallery, AGO News), Yr. Est. 1979, Bi-monthly, Trim Size-9 x 11¾, Offset
press, 16 pages, 2 Color, Matte, Saddle-stitched
Subscriptions: Free With Membership
Circulation: Total-25,000

Ka Elele

Publishing Co: Bishop Museum, 1525 Bernice St # 19000-A, Honolulu, HI 96817-2704;
Title Tel # (808) 847-3511
General Info: (Formerly The Messenger), Yr. Est. 1963, Monthly
Circulation: Total-5,800

Latch String, The   *Consumer*

Publishing Co: C. M. Russell Museum, 400 13th St N, Great Falls, MT 59401-1498;
Title Tel # (406) 727-8787 Title Fax # (406) 727-2402
Personnel: Editor-Pam Yascavage
Editorial Description: Educational info. Museum attractions, events, exhibitions.
General Info: (Formerly C.M. Russell Museum Newsletter), Yr. Est. 1969, Monthly, Trim Size-17 x
22, Offset press, No Color, Matte, Saddle-stitched
Subscriptions: Free With Membership
Circulation: (37% controlled), Total-4,000, Subscriptions-2,500
Printing Co: Advanced Litho Printing, 300 9th Ave S, Great Falls, MT 59405-4034
Tel # (406) 453-0393

Lithuanian Museum Review   *Association*

Publishing Co: Balzekas Museum of Lithuanian Culture, 6500 S Pulaski Rd, Chicago, IL
60629-5136; Title Tel # (312) 582-6500
Personnel: Editor-Carole Miller, Art Dir.-Val Ramonis
Editorial Description: News on Lithuanians & Lithuania; current & upcoming activities, giftshop,
childrens museum.
General Info: Yr. Est. 1967, Bi-monthly, Web press, 8 pages, No Color
Subscriptions: Indv. $25, Free With Membership
Circulation: (100% controlled), Total-7,000

Longyear Museum
Quarterly News   *Association*

Publishing Co: Longyear Historical Society, 120 Seaver St, Brookline, MA 02146-5719;
Title Tel # (617) 277-8943 Title Fax # (617) 277-3385
General Info: (Formerly Longyear Historical Society and Museum), Quarterly
Subscriptions: Indv. $20
Circulation: Readership-5,000

Lookdown, The   *Association*

Publishing Co: Virginia Marine Science Museum, 717 General Booth Blvd, Virginia Beach, VA
23451-4811; Title Tel # (804) 437-4949 Title Fax # (804) 437-4976
Personnel: Editor-Mary Reid Barrow
Editorial Description: Marine education & museum activities.
General Info: (Formerly Virginia Marine Science Museum Newsletter), Yr. Est. 1980, Quarterly, Trim
Size-8½ x 11, Sheetfed press, 12 pages, 2 Color
Subscriptions: Free With Membership
Circulation: Total-4,000
Printing Co: Printcraft Press, 309 Columbia St, Portsmouth, VA 23704-3714 Tel # (804) 397-0759

MCZ Newsletter   *Association*

Publishing Co: Harvard University, Museum of Comparative Zoology, Cambridge, MA 02138;
Title Tel # (617) 495-2463 Title Fax # (617) 495-5667
Personnel: Editor-Gabrielle Whitehouse
Editorial Description: Popular level natural history.
General Info: Yr. Est. 1971, Semi-annually, Web press, 8 pages, No Color
Circulation: Total-2,500
Printing Co: Gangi Printing, Inc., 17 Kensington Ave, Somerville, MA 02145-2106
Tel # (617) 776-6071

MIT Museum Newsletter

Publishing Co: MIT Museum Shop, The, 265 Massachusetts Ave, Cambridge, MA 02139-4162
Tel # (617) 253-4462 Fax # (617) 253-8994; Title Tel # (617) 253-4444
Personnel: Editor-Marcia Conroy
General Info: Yr. Est. 1981, Offset press, 8 pages, No Color, Newsprint
Circulation: Total-3,000
Advertising: Accepts Inserts.
Printing Co: Arlington Litho, 6 Schouler Ct, Arlington, MA 02174-4789 Tel # (617) 646-8815

Magnes News   *Association*

Publishing Co: Judah Magnes Museum, 2911 Russell St, Berkeley, CA 94705-2333;
Title Tel # (510) 549-6950 Title Fax # (510) 849-3673
Personnel: Feature Ed.-Nalda Cassuto, Copy Editor, Copy Editor-Nelda Cassuto, Circ. Mgr.-Lisbeth
Schwab, Editor, Production Mgr.-Paula Friedman
Editorial Description: Reportage on museum events, exhibits, persons, scholarly material, curatorial
commentary, photographs.
General Info: Yr. Est. 1981, 3x/yr., Trim Size-11½ x 17, Desktop press, 4 pages, 2 Color, Matte,
Other
Subscriptions: Indv. $35, Free With Membership
Circulation: Total-3,000, Readership-6,000

Mansion Notes   *Business, Association*

Publishing Co: Centre County Historical Society, 1001 E College Ave, State College, PA
16801-6806; Title Tel # (814) 234-4779
Personnel: Publisher-Jacqueline Melander, Editor-Sara Phinney Kelley
General Info: Bi-monthly, Trim Size-8.5 x 11, Desktop press, 8 pages, Matte
Subscriptions: Free With Membership
Printing Co: Kinkos, 101 N. Atherton St., State College, PA 16801 Tel # (814) 238-2679

Mark Twain Memorial
Newsletter   *Consumer, Scholarly*

Publishing Co: Mark Twain Memorial Newsletter, 351 Farmington Ave., Hartford, CT 06105-4401;
Title Tel # (860) 247-0998 Title Fax # (860) 278-8148
Personnel: Editor-Jennifer Nuget
Editorial Description: News about Mark Twain activities and related events. Information about Mark
Twain Victorian architechture & decorative arts and related topics.
General Info: Yr. Est. 1955, Quarterly, Trim Size-8½ x 11, Offset press, 16 pages, No Color, Matte
Subscriptions: Free With Membership
Circulation: Total-1,400
Printing Co: Chatham Printing Company, 296 E. Robbins Ave., Newington, CT 06131
Tel # (860) 667-5610, Fax # (860) 667-5612

Members Bulletin

Publishing Co: Triton Museum of Art, 1505 Warburton Ave, Santa Clara, CA 95050-3712;
Title Tel # (408) 247-3754 Title Fax # (408) 247-3796
Personnel: Editor-Lisa Davoust
Editorial Description: Bi-monthly pub. which lists current exhibits & activities, new & renewing
memberships & related announcements.
General Info: Yr. Est. 1967, Bi-monthly, Trim Size-8½ x 11, Offset press, 6 pages, No Color, Coated
Circulation: Total-1,500

Members Calendar   *Association*

Publishing Co: Museum of Modern Art, 11 W 53rd St, New York, NY 10019-5498
Tel # (212) 708-9696; Title Tel # (212) 708-9671 Title Fax # (212) 708-9889
Personnel: Editor-Chris Lyon
Editorial Description: Monthly schedule of events, films, & exhibitions.
General Info: (Formerly Bulletin), Yr. Est. 1940, Monthly, Trim Size-4 x 9, Offset press, 22 pages, No Color
Subscriptions: Free With Membership
Circulation: Total-62,000
Printing Co: Eastern Press, PO Box 120280, East Haven, CT 06512-0280 Tel # (203) 467-6550, Fax # (203) 469-4364

Members Quarterly   *Association*

Publishing Co: Museum of Modern Art, 11 W 53rd St, New York, NY 10019-5498
Tel # (212) 708-9696; Title Tel # (212) 708-9671 Title Fax # (212) 708-9889
Personnel: Editor-Chris Lyon
Editorial Description: Interviews with curators of upcoming exhibitions, film schedules, special events, new publications & gift items.
General Info: (Formerly MOMA), Yr. Est. 1974, Quarterly, Offset press, 8 pages, 4 Color
Subscriptions: Free
Circulation: (100% controlled), Total-41,000
Advertising: Accepts Inserts.
Printing Co: R.R. Donnelley & Sons Company, PO Box 13654, Newark, NJ 07188-0001

Mirror   *Association*

Publishing Co: Lancaster Mennonite Historical Society, 2215 Millstream Rd, Lancaster, PA 17602-1499; Title Tel # (717) 393-9745
Personnel: Circ. Mgr.-Judith Stahly, Editor, Production Mgr.-Carolyn Wenger
Editorial Description: News of recent accessions to Society library, archives, and museum. Also news of seminars, field trips, public lectures, family reunion notices, bookshop discounts, publications notices, research activity, & Society developments.
General Info: Yr. Est. 1969, Bi-monthly, Trim Size-8½ x 11, Sheetfed press, 4 pages, ISSN: 0738-7237, No Color, Matte
Subscriptions: Indv. $5, Inst. $5, Can. $6, For. $6, $2/copy
Circulation: Total-9,100
Printing Co: Feldser Printing & Office Supplies, 21 E New St, Lancaster, PA 17602-2027 Tel # (717) 393-5841

Morris Arboretum Newsletter
See: BOTANY

Mosaic-News from the Museum of Fine Arts   *Association*

Publishing Co: Museum of Fine Arts, 255 Beach Dr. NE, St. Petersburg, FL 33701-3498; Title Tel # (813) 896-2667 Title Fax # (813) 894-4638
Personnel: Editor-Michael Milkovich, Circ. Mgr.-Donna Fletcher, Production Mgr.-Don Baldwin, Art Dir.-Diane Lesko
Editorial Description: Brief descriptive notes on current exhibitions, membership activities, fund-raising events. Mailed to all members & many museums. Recent accessions acknowledged, with critiques on the artists & their works; usually illustrated.
General Info: Yr. Est. 1966, Quarterly, Trim Size-8½ x 11, Sheetfed press, 16 pages, Color-cover, Coated, Saddle-stitched
Subscriptions: Free With Membership
Circulation: Total-4,000
Printing Co: Promocom Printing, Inc.

Mt. Holyoke College Art Museum-Newsletter   *Association*

Publishing Co: Mt. Holyoke College Art Museum, Mt. Holyoke College, South Hadley, MA 01075; Title Tel # (413) 538-2245
Personnel: Editor-Wendy Watson
Editorial Description: Articles about the museum, its collections & its exhibitions.
General Info: Yr. Est. 1978, Semi-annually, Sheetfed press, 8 pages, No Color, Coated
Subscriptions: Free With Membership
Circulation: Total-2,000
Printing Co: Hadley Printing, 58 Canal St, Holyoke, MA 01040-5880 Tel # (413) 536-8517

Munson-Williams-Proctor Institute Bulletin   *Business, Association*

Publishing Co: Munson-Williams-Proctor Institute, 310 Genesee St, Utica, NY 13502-4764 Fax # (315) 797-5608; Title Tel # (315) 797-0000
Personnel: Publisher-Timothy L. Trent, Editor-Joe Schmidt, Mktg. Dir.-David McHarg
Editorial Description: Institute events; year in review.
General Info: Yr. Est. 1941, Monthly, Trim Size-11 x 17, Offset press, 4 pages, No Color
Circulation: (100% controlled), Total-4,500
Printing Co: Steffen Printing & Publishing, Main St., Holland Patent, NY 13354 Tel # (315) 865-4100

Muse News   *Association*

Publishing Co: Vancouver Museums, 1100 Chestnut St., Vancouver, BC V6H 2L5 Canada; Title Tel # (604) 736-4431
Personnel: Editor-Karen Kelm
Editorial Description: Bulletin covering museum exhibits, special events
General Info: Yr. Est. 1975, Bi-monthly, 4 pages, No Color
Circulation: Total-7,000

Museogramme   *Association*   CPM: $211

Publishing Co: Canadian Museums Assn, 280 Metcalfe St., #400, Ottawa, ON K2P 1R7 Canada; Title Tel # (613) 567-0099 Title Fax # (613) 233-5438
Personnel: Editor in Chief-Aline Michaud, Editorial Asst.-Marie Louise Shields, Assoc. Ed.-Natalie Blais, Production-Linda McConnell
Editorial Description: Provides information on museum news events, assn. affairs, government cultural policies, and training in English & French.
General Info: Yr. Est. 1973, Bi-monthly, Trim Size-8¼ x 11, Sheetfed press, 12 pages, ISSN: 0380-4623, 20% ads, 2 Color, Recycled, Saddle-stitched
Subscriptions: Indv. $25, Inst. $32, Can. $25, For. $40, $2/copy
Circulation: Total-2,100
Advertising: $445. Accepts Inserts.
List Rental: Actives: $110/M
Printing Co: Print Action, 486 Gladstone Ave., Ottawa, ON K1R 5N8 Canada Tel # (613) 238-4782, Fax # (613) 238-3995

Museum Archivist   *Association*

Publishing Co: Amon Carter Museum, 3501 Camp Bowie Blvd, Fort Worth, TX 76107-2365; Title Tel # (817) 738-1933 Title Fax # (817) 738-4066
Personnel: Editor-Paula Stewart, Circ. Dir., Production Dir.-Alan Bain
Editorial Description: News for museum archivists.
General Info: Yr. Est. 1986, Semi-annually, Trim Size-8½ x 11, Desktop press, 20 pages, No Color, Other, Other
Subscriptions: Free To Qualified Recipient
Circulation: Total-450

Museum of Flight News   *Association*

Publishing Co: Museum of Flight, 9404 E Marginal Way S, Seattle, WA 98108-4097; Title Tel # (206) 764-5700 Title Fax # (206) 764-5707
Personnel: Editor-Hollis Palmer
Editorial Description: Dedicated to the promotion/preservation of the field of flight.
General Info: (Formerly Air Museum News), Yr. Est. 1979, Bi-monthly, Trim Size-8½ x 17½, Roto. press, 8 pages, 2 Color, Newsprint
Subscriptions: Indv. $35, Free With Membership
Circulation: Total-35,000
Advertising: Inquire for rates.
Printing Co: Valco Graphics, Inc., 480 Andover Park E, Seattle, WA 98188-7606 Tel # (206) 575-3500

Museum of the Great Plains Newsletter   *Association*

Publishing Co: Institute of the Great Plains, 601 NW Ferris Ave., P.O. Box 68, Lawton, OK 73502-0068; Title Tel # (405) 581-3460
Personnel: Editor-Steve Wilson
Editorial Description: An interdisciplinary publication devoted to the Great Plains, covers Museum of the Great Plains activities & programming. Newsletter received with a subscription to the Great Plains Journal.
General Info: Yr. Est. 1977, Annually, Trim Size-9 x 12, Web press, 8 pages, No Color, Coated
Subscriptions: Can. $18, For. $18, Free With Membership
Circulation: Total-815
Printing Co: Univ. of Oklahoma Printing Svcs., 1005 Asp Ave, Norman, OK 73019-6050 Tel # (405) 325-4176

Museum Insights   *Consumer*

Publishing Co: Museum Insights, 73 Juggler Meadow Rd, Amherst, MA 01002-9521; Title Tel # (413) 548-9561
Personnel: Publisher, Editor-Nancy Frazier
Editorial Description: Guide to small and unique museums and collections for potential visitors. Reviews exhibition catalogues, art videos.
General Info: Yr. Est. 1989, Bi-monthly, Trim Size-8½ x 11, Desktop press, 8 pages, No Color, Newsprint
Subscriptions: Indv. $24, Can. $28, For. $31, $5/copy
Circulation: Total-1,000

Museum Matters   *Consumer*

Publishing Co: Mississippi Museum of Art, 201 E. Pascagoula St., Jackson, MS 39201-4199 Fax # (601) 960-1505; Title Tel # (601) 960-1515
Editorial Description: Covers exhibitions & museum-related events.
General Info: (Formerly Mississippi Museum of Art-Perspective), Yr. Est. 1977, Bi-monthly, Trim Size-8½ x 11, Sheetfed press, 4 pages, 2 Color, Matte
Circulation: Total-2,000
Advertising: Inquire for rates.

Museum Monthly   *Association*

Publishing Co: Denver Museum of Natural History, 2001 Colorado Blvd, Denver, CO 80205-5798; Title Tel # (303) 370-8334
Personnel: Mng. Editor-Larry Sessions, Art Dir.-Keith Abernathy
Editorial Description: Program schedules and news for the Denver Museum of Natural History.
General Info: (Formerly Bear Pause), Yr. Est. 1970, Monthly
Circulation: Total-30,000
Printing Co: American Web Offset, 4040 Dahlia St., Denver, CO 80216-2420 Tel # (303) 321-2422, Fax # (303) 321-6636

Museum Newsletter   *Business, Association*

Publishing Co: Canadian Museum of Flight and Transportation, 13527 Crescent Rd, Surrey, BC V4A 1S5 Canada; Title Tel # (604) 535-1115 Title Fax # (604) 535-3292
Personnel: Publisher, Editor, Circ. Mgr.-Rose Zalesky
Editorial Description: Report of current museum activities; historic aviation articles.
General Info: Yr. Est. 1977, Quarterly, Trim Size-4¹⁄₄ x 7, Desktop press, 10 pages, ISSN: 0820-8336, 1% ads, No Color
Subscriptions: Free With Membership
Acquistions: Publication Bought
Advertising: Accepts Inserts.

Museum of Science
Magazine   *Association*

Publishing Co: Museum of Science, Science Park, Boston, MA 02114; Title Tel # (617) 589-0245
Personnel: Editor-Lorraine Welsh
Editorial Description: Promotes museum events & related activities for members, donors & schools.
General Info: Yr. Est. 1951, Monthly, Trim Size-9 x 11, Web press, 15 pages, 4 Color
Subscriptions: Indv. $5
Circulation: (100% controlled), Total-40,000

Museum of Staten Island
News

Publishing Co: Museum of Staten Island, 75 Stuyvesant Pl, Staten Island, NY 10301-1912

NAIMA Museum News

Publishing Co: Museum of the Cherokee Indian, PO Box 770a, Cherokee, NC 28719-0770
Personnel: Editor-Richard Hill
General Info: Quarterly

NBM News

Publishing Co: New Brunswick Museum, 277 Douglas Ave., Saint John, NB E2K 1E5 Canada; Title Tel # (506) 658-1842
Personnel: Circ. Mgr.-Art Robinson, Editor, Production Mgr.-Paul Castle
Editorial Description: Articles & Pictorial relating directly to New Brunswick Museum Collections.
General Info: (Formerly New Brunswick Museum News), Yr. Est. 1984, Bi-monthly, 24 pages, ISSN: 0822-6741, No Color, Coated, Saddle-stitched
Subscriptions: Indv. $20, Inst. $25
Circulation: Total-2,000

Newark Museum
Exhibitions & Events   *Association*

Publishing Co: Newark Museum, The, 49 Washington St # 450, Newark, NJ 07102-3109; Title Tel # (201) 596-6550
Editorial Description: Promotes exhibitions, activities & events sponsored by The Newark Museum.
General Info: Yr. Est. 1984, Bi-monthly, Sheetfed press, 6 pages, ISSN: 0028-9256, No Color, Newsprint
Subscriptions: Indv. $6
Circulation: Total-6,500
Printing Co: Harvard Printing Co., 550 Central Ave, Orange, NJ 07050-1403 Tel # (201) 672-0800

News Brief   *Association*

Publishing Co: Midwest Museums Conference, PO Box 11940, St. Louis, MO 63112-0040; Title Tel # (314) 454-3110 Title Fax # (314) 454-3162
Personnel: Publisher-Esther Hockett
Editorial Description: Articles and stories of interest to museums.
General Info: Yr. Est. 1930, 5x/yr., Trim Size-11 x 17, 4 pages, ISSN: 1073-0893, 2 Color
Subscriptions: Indv. $30, Inst. $50, Can. $40, For. $40, Free With Membership
Circulation: Total-1,000
Advertising: Accepts Inserts.

News Notes from the
Suggett House   *Association*

Publishing Co: Cortland County Historical Society, 25 Homer Ave, Cortland, NY 13045-2018; Title Tel # (607) 756-6071
General Info: Yr. Est. 1968, Tri-annually, Trim Size-8¹⁄₂ x 11, 4 pages, No Color
Subscriptions: Indv. $15
Circulation: Total-750

Newsletter   *Consumer, Association*

Publishing Co: Prince Edward Island Museum & Heritage Foundation, 2 Kent St., Charlottetown, PE C1A 1M6 Canada; Title Tel # (902) 368-6600 Title Fax # (902) 368-6608
Personnel: Editor-Nonie Fraser
General Info: Yr. Est. 1972, Tri-annually, Trim Size-8¹⁄₂ x 11, Sheetfed press, 4 pages, 2 Color, Matte
Subscriptions: Indv. $20, Inst. $30, Free With Membership
Circulation: Total-1,000
Printing Co: Williams & Crue Ltd., 4 Queen St., Summerside, PE C1N 4K5 Canada Tel # (902) 436-2125, Fax # (902) 436-3027

Newsletter East Asian Art & Archaeology
See: ART & SCULPTURE

Newsletter of the Society of Maine Archivists
See: HISTORY

Norfolklore   *Association*

Publishing Co: Norfolk Historical Society, 109 Norfolk St., S., Simcoe, ON N3Y 2W3 Canada; Title Tel # (519) 426-1583
Personnel: Editor-William Yeager
Editorial Description: Museum news for the Eva Brook Donly museum in Simcoe. Features on local history and genealogy.
General Info: (Formerly Eva Brook Donly Museum News), Yr. Est. 1980, Semi-monthly, Desktop press, 8 pages, 10% ads, No Color
Subscriptions: Indv. $20, Inst. $20, Can. $20, For. $20
Circulation: Total-650
Advertising: Inquire for rates. Accepts Inserts.

Norwegian-American
Museum Newsletter

Publishing Co: Vesterheim, the Norwegian-American Museum, 502 W Water St, Decorah, IA 52101-1734; Title Tel # (319) 382-9681
Personnel: Editor-Charles Langton
Editorial Description: The newsletter is a museum membership benefit.
General Info: Quarterly, Trim Size-8¹⁄₂ x 11, Offset press, 6 pages, No Color, Coated
Subscriptions: Indv. $10
Circulation: (100% controlled)

OHS Bulletin
See: HISTORY

OMNH Newsletter

Publishing Co: Oklahoma Museum of Natural History, Univ. Of Oklahoma 1335 Asp, Ave., Norman, OK 73019-0001; Title Tel # (405) 325-4712
Personnel: Editor-Jane Tague
Editorial Description: Carries news of special events, programs & exhibitions at the museum. Recurring features include a calendar of events, traveling exhibits schedule & column titled staff update.
General Info: Yr. Est. 1975, Quarterly, Trim Size-8¹⁄₂ x 11, 8 pages, No Color, Recycled
Subscriptions: Free With Membership
Circulation: (81% controlled), Total-800

PMA Members Newsletter

Publishing Co: Philadelphia Museum of Art, PO Box 7646, Philadelphia, PA 19101-7646; Title Tel # (215) 763-8100
Editorial Description: Articles and photos on loan exhibitions, acquisitions, and permanent collections.
General Info: Yr. Est. 1970, Monthly, Trim Size-9 x 19¹⁄₂, Sheetfed press, 2 Color, Coated
Circulation: Total-20,000

Pony Express Mail
See: HISTORY

Prehistoric Times
See: ARCHAEOLOGY

Quarterdeck, The

Publishing Co: Columbia River Maritime Museum, 1792 Marine Dr, Astoria, OR 97103-3525 Fax # (503) 224-2331; Title Tel # (503) 325-2323
Personnel: Editor-Karen Carpenter
Editorial Description: News of museum and illustrated historical articles.
General Info: (Formerly Quarterdeck Review), Yr. Est. 1973, Quarterly, Trim Size-8¹⁄₂ x 11, Web press, 16 pages, ISSN: 0891-2661, No Color, Matte, Saddle-stitched
Subscriptions: Indv. $15
Circulation: (100% controlled), Total-1,900
Printing Co: Anchor Graphics, 439-30th, Astoria, OR 97103 Tel # (503) 325-5841

Quarterly   *Association*

Publishing Co: Museum of the City of New York, 1220 5th Ave, New York, NY 10029-5287; Title Tel # (212) 534-1672
Personnel: Editor-Rosemarie Connors-McGalli, Circ. Mgr.-Beverly Bartow
Editorial Description: Update of museum activities, acquisitions, and exhibitions.
General Info: (Formerly Bulletin), Yr. Est. 1986, Quarterly, Trim Size-14 x 18¹⁄₄, Offset press, 6 pages, 2 Color
Circulation: (100% controlled), Total-3,200

ROS Bulletin   *Association*

Publishing Co: Reed Organ Society, The, The Musical Museum, Deansboro, NY 13328 Tel # (315) 841-8774
General Info: Yr. Est. 1982, Quarterly, ISSN: 0736-9549
Subscriptions: Indv. $18, For. $25, Free With Membership
Circulation: Total-950
Advertising: Accepts Inserts.

Rotunda   *Association*

Publishing Co: American Museum of Natural History, Museum Shop Catalog, Central Park West & 79th St., New York, NY 10024 Tel # (212) 769-5000; Title Tel # (212) 769-5606 Title Fax # (212) 769-5427
Personnel: Editor-Donna Bell
Editorial Description: Newsletter giving information on museum events, exhibitions, & activities.
General Info: Yr. Est. 1977, Monthly, Trim Size-11 x 17, Sheetfed press, 8 pages, ISSN: 0194-6110, No Color, Newsprint
Subscriptions: Free With Membership
Circulation: Total-50,000
Printing Co: Walden Press, 216 W 18th St, New York, NY 10011-4595 Tel # (212) 691-9220

S.I.I.A.S. News

Publishing Co: Staten Island Inst. of Arts & Sciences, 75 Stuyvesant Pl, Staten Island, NY 10301-1912; Title Tel # (718) 727-1135 Title Fax # (718) 273-5683
Personnel: Publisher, Editor, Circ. Mgr., Production Mgr.-Edward Gregory
Editorial Description: Newsletter featuring activities at the Staten Island Institute of Arts & Sciences, Staten Island's oldest cultural institution.
General Info: Yr. Est. 1984, Quarterly, No Color, Coated
Subscriptions: Indv. $25, Free
Circulation: (76% controlled), Total-17,000, Subscriptions-1,200

San Bernardino County Museum Association Newsletter — *Association*

Publishing Co: San Bernardino County Museum Assn., 2024 Orange Tree Ln, Redlands, CA 92374-2850; Title Tel # (909) 798-8570 Title Fax # (909) 798-8585
Personnel: Editor-Jennifer Reynolds, Circ. Mgr.-Candace McGloin
Editorial Description: Museum natural history and archaeological activities; public programming.
General Info: Yr. Est. 1952, Bi-monthly, Trim Size-8½ x 11, Letrpr. press, 16 pages, No Color, Saddle-stitched
Subscriptions: Indv. $20, $1/copy
Circulation: (100% controlled), Total-2,500
Advertising: Accepts Inserts.

Santa Barbara Museum of Natural History Museum Bulletin — *Consumer*

Publishing Co: Santa Barbara Museum of Natural History, 2559 Puesta Del Sol, Santa Barbara, CA 93105-2936; Title Tel # (805) 682-4711 Title Fax # (805) 569-3170
Personnel: Editor-Suzanne Farwell, Art Dir.-Teresa Rounds
Editorial Description: Provides knowledge & understanding of nature and indigenous peoples, especially the natural environment & American Indian cultures of California's central coast.
General Info: Yr. Est. 1916, Bi-monthly, Trim Size-8½ x 11, 12 pages, Coated
Subscriptions: Indv. $25, Free With Membership
Circulation: Total-5,000
Printing Co: Haagen Printing, 410 E Cota St, Santa Barbara, CA 93101-1624 Tel # (805) 962-7621

Science Museum News

Publishing Co: Carnegie Museum of Natural History, 4400 Forbes Ave, Pittsburgh, PA 15213-4007; Title Tel # (412) 622-3132 Title Fax # (412) 622-8837
Personnel: Editor-Elizabeth Mertz
Editorial Description: Articles of interest to directors of science and natural history museums.
General Info: Yr. Est. 1976, Semi-annually, Trim Size-8½ x 11, 6 pages, No Color, Matte
Subscriptions: Free To Qualified Recipient
Circulation: Total-250

Ships & Shipwrecks: The Newsletter of Nautical History & Discovery
See: ARCHAEOLOGY

Sirius — *Consumer, Association*

Publishing Co: Dog Museum, The, 1721 S Mason Rd, Saint Louis, MO 63131-1518; Title Tel # (314) 821-3647 Title Fax # (314) 821-7381
Personnel: Editor-Susan Brown
Editorial Description: Contains information on the Dog Museum as well as art and artists who use dogs as subjects.
General Info: Yr. Est. 1986, Quarterly, Trim Size-8½ x 11, Offset press, 12 pages, 2 Color, Coated, Saddle-stitched
Subscriptions: Indv. $35, Free With Membership

South Street Seaport Museum Development Beacon — *Consumer, Association*

Publishing Co: South Street Seaport Museum, 207 Front St, New York, NY 10038-2106; Title Tel # (212) 669-9464
Personnel: Editor-Elizabeth Hopkins
Editorial Description: Information and articles on the South Street Seaport Museum's development.
General Info: Semi-annually

Southwestern Archivist
See: LIBRARY

Speedev
See: RAILROADS

Stearns Newsletter, The
See: MUSIC & MUSIC TRADES

Strawbery Banke Newsletter — *Association*

Publishing Co: Strawbery Banke Museum, PO Box 300, Portsmouth, NH 03802-0300; Title Tel # (603) 433-1100
Personnel: Mktg. Dir.-Tony Wold
Editorial Description: Presents the programs, services, & developments of historic Strawbery Banke, first settled in 1630.
General Info: Yr. Est. 1971, Semi-annually
Subscriptions: Free With Membership
Circulation: Total-1,700

Strecker Museum News — *Association*

Publishing Co: John K. Strecker Museum, Baylor University, Box 97154, Waco, TX 76798 Fax # (817) 755-1321; Title Tel # (817) 755-1110
Personnel: Editor-David Lintz
Editorial Description: Informational piece on museum programs, staff, exhibitions; feature story, museum studies, current happenings, calendar, museum classes.
General Info: Yr. Est. 1970, Quarterly, Trim Size-8½ x 11, Sheetfed press, 8 pages, No Color, Matte
Subscriptions: Free
Circulation: Total-1,500

Texas Memorial Museum Bulletin — *Association, Consumer*

Publishing Co: Texas Memorial Museum, 2400 Trinity St., Univ. of Texas at Austin, Austin, TX 78705; Title Tel # (512) 471-1604 Title Fax # (512) 471-4794
Editorial Description: Reports of research in anthropology, paleontology, geology and history.
General Info: Yr. Est. 1960, Irregular, Offset press, ISSN: 0082-3074

Textile Museum Bulletin — *Consumer*

Publishing Co: Textile Museum, 2320 S Street N.W., Washington, DC 20008-4088; Title Tel # (202) 667-0441 Title Fax # (202) 483-0994
Personnel: Editor-Maury Sullivan
Editorial Description: Articles on current textile & carpet research-news of events at the Textile Museums Exhibitions, etc.
General Info: (Formerly Textile Museum Newsletter), Yr. Est. 1962, Quarterly, Trim Size-6 x 9, Web press, 16 pages, 2 Color, Coated, Saddle-stitched
Subscriptions: Indv. $50
Circulation: (100% controlled), Total-5,000
Printing Co: River Press, 135 Dixon Dr, Chestertown, MD 21620-1141 Tel # (301) 778-3487

Univ. Art Museum Newsletter — *Consumer, Association*

Publishing Co: University Art Museum, SUNY at Binghamton, Binghamton, NY 13901; Title Tel # (607) 777-2634
Personnel: Editor-Nancy Gonchar, Art Dir.-Roberta Scheer
Editorial Description: Art Museum Newsletter describing current & upcoming programs, exhibitions, etc. Reports on special exhibitions, collections & acquisitions.
General Info: Yr. Est. 1975, Semi-annually

Valentine News — *Association*

Publishing Co: Valentine Museum, 1015 E Clay St, Richmond, VA 23219-1590; Title Tel # (804) 649-0711 Title Fax # (804) 643-3510
Personnel: Editor-Margaret Tinsley
Editorial Description: Museum newsletter with special emphasis on exhibitions, & programs dealing with urban & social history of Richmond.
General Info: (Formerly Visitor), Quarterly, Trim Size-11 x 17, Offset press, 4 pages, 2 Color, Matte
Subscriptions: Indv. $50, Free With Membership
Circulation: Total-4,000

Virginia Museum Bulletin

Publishing Co: Virginia Museum of Fine Arts, 2800 Grove Ave, Richmond, VA 23221-2466 Fax # (804) 367-9393; Title Tel # (804) 367-0534 Title Fax # (804) 364-9393
Personnel: Editor-Monica Rumsey, Circ. Mgr.-Michelle Wilson, Art Dir.-Sarah Lavicka
Editorial Description: Calendar of events; includes news of recent additions to the collections and temporary loan exhibitions.
General Info: Yr. Est. 1940, Bi-monthly, Trim Size-7 x 10, Offset press, 20 pages, ISSN: 0363-3519, Ind/Abs/Online: RILA, 2 Color, Newsprint
Subscriptions: Indv. $5, For. $6, $1/copy
Circulation: Total-16,500

Welland Historical Museum Newsletter

Publishing Co: Welland Historical Museum, 65 Hooker, Welland, ON L3C 5G9 Canada Tel # (416) 732-2215; Title Tel # (905) 732-2215
Personnel: Editor-Mac Swackhammer
General Info: Yr. Est. 1987, Quarterly, Trim Size-8½ x 11, Offset press, 6 pages, Matte
Subscriptions: Free With Membership
Circulation: Total-400

West Point Museum Bulletin

Publishing Co: Association of Graduates USMA, 698 Mills Rd., Herbert Hall, West Point, NY 10996 Tel # (914) 938-2015 Fax # (914) 446-5800
General Info: Quarterly
Circulation: Total-1,250

Wilson Museum Bulletin — *Association*

Publishing Co: Castine Scientific Society, Box 196, Perkins St., Castine, ME 04421-0196; Title Tel # (207) 326-8545 Title Fax # (207) 326-8545
Personnel: Editor-E.W. Doudiet
Editorial Description: Features on exhibits, local history, folklore, geology.
General Info: Yr. Est. 1963, Tri-annually, Trim Size-8½ x 11, 4 pages
Subscriptions: Indv. $5
Circulation: Total-300
Printing Co: Furbush Roberts, 435 Odlin Rd, Bangor, ME 04401-6705 Tel # (207) 945-9409

Wolf Park News
See: ANIMALS

Yukon Historical & Museums Association Newsletter
See: HISTORY

MUSIC & MUSIC TRADES

70's Re-Visited, The
See: POLITICS

ACK!
Publishing Co: Mnemonic Box 115, #105-10277 35th Street, Surrey, BC V3T 4C3 Canada
Editorial Description: A short smack in the face about music, zines, and a whole bunch of interesting crap.
General Info: Trim Size-8.5 x 11, 8 pages

AGMA Newsletter   *Association*
Publishing Co: American Guild of Musical Artists, 1727 Broadway, New York, NY 10019-5284 Tel # (212) 265-3687
Personnel: Art Dir.-Kevin Hanek
Editorial Description: Association news and artists information.
General Info: Quarterly, Trim Size-8½ x 11, 4 pages, No Color
Subscriptions: Free With Membership

AMOA Location
See: ENTERTAINMENT

AMU Quarternote   *Association*
Publishing Co: Sponsor-American Musicians Union, American Musicians Union, 8 Tobin Ct, Dumont, NJ 07628-3329; Title Tel # (201) 384-5378
Editorial Description: Information and news of interest to AMU members.
General Info: Yr. Est. 1976, Quarterly, Trim Size-8½ x 11, Offset press, 4 pages, No Color
Subscriptions: $1/copy
Circulation: Total-300, Readership-300
Advertising: Inquire for rates.

ARSC Newsletter
See: SOUND ENGINEERING

Academy of Country Music Newsletter
Publishing Co: Academy of Country Music, 6255 Sunset Blvd., #923, Hollywood, CA 90028-7410; Title Tel # (213) 462-2351
Personnel: Editor-Fran Boyd
General Info: Yr. Est. 1964, Monthly, 8 pages
Circulation: Total-3,000
Advertising: Inquire for rates.

Accordion Teachers' Guild-Newsletter
Publishing Co: Accordion Teachers' Guild, Inc., 334 S Broadway, Pitman, NJ 08071-2405; Title Tel # (609) 854-6628
Personnel: Editor-Joanne Arnold
General Info: Yr. Est. 1941, Monthly, Sheetfed press, 8 pages, No Color, Newsprint
Subscriptions: Indv. $12
Acquistions: Publication Bought
Circulation: (100% controlled), Total-180

Alternance   *Consumer*
Publishing Co: Canadian Music Centre, 430 rue St. Pierre, #300, Montreal, PQ H2Y 2M5 Canada; Title Tel # (514) 849-9175
Editorial Description: Newsletter about the canadian composer on the national and international music scene.
General Info: (Formerly Compositeurs au Quebec), Tri-annually, Trim Size-8½ x 11, 12 pages
Subscriptions: Free
Circulation: (100% controlled), Total-500

Amateur Chamber Music Players-Newsletter   *Association*
Publishing Co: Amateur Chamber Music Players, Inc., 1123 Broadway Ste 304, New York, NY 10010-2007; Title Tel # (212) 645-7424 Title Fax # (212) 741-2672
Personnel: Co-Editor-Sally R. Bagg, Co-Editor-Susan McIntosh Lloyd
General Info: Yr. Est. 1948, 3x/yr., Trim Size-8½ x 11, Offset press, 8 pages, Matte, Saddle-stitched
Subscriptions: Free With Membership
Circulation: Total-4,200

Amateur Musician/ Musicien Amateur Cammac   *Association*
Publishing Co: Canadian Amateur Musicians, 1751 Richardson St., Ste. 2509, Montreal, PQ H3K 1G6 Canada Tel # (513) 932-8755 Fax # (514) 932-9811; Title Tel # (514) 932-8755
Personnel: Editor-Ralph Aldrich
Editorial Description: National newsletter of CAMMAC-Canadian Amateur Musicians.
General Info: Yr. Est. 1959, Semi-annually, Trim Size-11 x 17, Offset press, 24 pages, No Color
Subscriptions: Indv. $25, Inst. $35
Circulation: Total-3,000
Advertising: Inquire for rates.

American Brahms Society Newsletter   *Association*
Publishing Co: American Brahms Society, Univ. Of Washington School Of, Music, P.O Box 353450, Seattle, WA 98195-3450; Title Tel # (206) 543-0400
Personnel: Editor-Virginia Hancock, Publisher, Circ. Mgr., Production Mgr.-George Bozarth
Editorial Description: Essays, reports, reviews on research into life & works of Johannes Brahms.
General Info: Yr. Est. 1983, Semi-annually, Trim Size-8½ x 11, Offset press, 12 pages, ISSN: 8756-8357, No Color, Newsprint
Subscriptions: Indv. $25, Inst. $25, Can. $25, For. $25
Circulation: Total-1,500

American Brass Quintet Newsletter
Publishing Co: American Brass Chamber Music, 30 Lincoln Plaza, Suite 3N, New York, NY 10023

American Harmonica Newsletter   *Consumer, Association*
Publishing Co: American Harmonica Associates, 2362 Territorial Rd W, Battle Creek, MI 49015-4956; Title Tel # (616) 962-2989
Personnel: Music Editor, Entertainment Ed., Feature Ed.-Phillip W. Lloyd, Publisher, Editorial Page Ed., News Ed., Music Editor, Photo Ed., Production Mgr., Adv. Dir., Art Dir., Mktg. Dir.-Al Eichler, Editor, Circ. Mgr., Promotion Dir.-Al Eichter
Editorial Description: Articles and interviews concerning harmonica playing.
General Info: Yr. Est. 188 , Monthly, Trim Size-7¾ x 10¾, Web press, 48 pages, ISSN: 1050-7493, No Color, Newsprint, Saddle-stitched
Subscriptions: Indv. $21, Inst. $18, Can. $21, For. $28, $2/copy
Advertising: Inquire for rates. Accepts Inserts.
Printing Co: J-Ad Graphics, Inc., PO Box 188, 1952 N. Broadway, Hastings, MI 49058 Tel # (616) 945-9554

American Liszt Society, Inc., Newsletter   *Association*
Publishing Co: American Liszt Society, c/o Fernando Laires, 210 Devonshire Dr., Rochester, NY 14625 Tel # (716) 586-9922
Personnel: Editor-John Anderson
Editorial Description: For scholars, musicians, students interested in Liszt.
General Info: Yr. Est. 1984, Semi-annually, Trim Size-8½ x 11, Web press, 10 pages, ISSN: 0749-341X, No Color, Newsprint
Subscriptions: Indv. $25, Inst. $30
Circulation: Total-550
Printing Co: Minuteman Press, 1900 M St., NW, Washington, DC 20036

American Musical Instrument Society Newsletter   *Association*
Publishing Co: American Musical Instrument Society, RD#3 Box 205-B, Franklin, PA 16323-9804 Tel # (814) 374-4119 Fax # (814) 374-4563
Personnel: Editor-Harrison Poweley
Editorial Description: History, design, and use of musical instruments in all cultures.
General Info: Yr. Est. 1971, Tri-annually, Trim Size-8½ x 11, Offset press, 16 pages, ISSN: 0160-2365, Ind/Abs/Online: RILM, No Color, Matte
Subscriptions: Indv. $35, Inst. $35, Can. $40, For. $40, $5/copy
Circulation: Total-900
Advertising: Inquire for rates. Accepts Inserts.
List Rental: Rents Lists
Printing Co: Broadcaster Press, 201 W Cherry St, Vermillion, SD 57069-1109 Tel # (605) 624-4429

American Musicological Society Newsletter
Publishing Co: American Musicological Society, 201 S 34th St Rm 201, Philadelphia, PA 19104-6313; Title Tel # (215) 898-8698
Personnel: Editor-James Ladewig, Circ. Mgr.-Alvin Johnson
Editorial Description: Newsletter of the AMS.
General Info: Semi-annually, Web press, 16 pages, No Color, Saddle-stitched
Circulation: (100% controlled), Total-4,800
List Rental: Actives: $70/M
Printing Co: A-R Editions, Inc., 801 Deming Way, Madison, WI 53717-1918 Tel # (608) 836-9000

American Wagner Assn.
Newsletter   *Association*

Publishing Co: American Wagner Assn., 32 W 82nd St Apt 6c, New York, NY 10024-5622;
  Title Tel # (212) 874-4504
Personnel: Editor-Warren Michon
Editorial Description: Articles on educational & fund-raising events of AWA.
General Info: Yr. Est. 1984, Trim Size-8½ x 11, Desktop press, 12 pages, No Color, Other, Saddle-stitched
Subscriptions: Free With Membership
Circulation: Total-125

Archive of Contemporary
Music, The   *Consumer*

Publishing Co: Archive, 132 Crosby St, New York, NY 10012-3326; Title Tel # (212) 226-6967
  Title Fax # (212) 226-6540
Editorial Description: Infornnation on the largest popular music library in America.
General Info: Bi-monthly

Arts Center News
See: MUSEUM PUBLICATIONS

Atlanta Opera News   *Consumer*

Publishing Co: Atlanta Opera, 1800 Peachtree St. NW, Ste. 620, Atlanta, GA 30309-2507;
  Title Tel # (404) 355-3311 Title Fax # (404) 355-3259
Personnel: Editor-Erik M. Friedly, Art Dir.-Matt Belfi
Editorial Description: Information and schedules for The Atlanta Opera.
General Info: Quarterly, Trim Size-11 x 17, Sheetfed press, 8 pages, 2 Color, Matte, Other
Subscriptions: Free
Circulation: Readership-40,000

B.A.S. Speaker
See: SOUND ENGINEERING

BCMEA Newsletter
See: EDUCATION

Band Fan

Publishing Co: Detroit Concert Band, Inc., 7443 E. Butherus St., Ste. 100, Scottsdale, AR
  85260-2423; Title Tel # (602) 948-9870
Personnel: Publisher, Editor-John Stafford, Circ. Mgr.-M.L. Hornberger, Art Dir.-Mary Bingley
Editorial Description: Concert band research. Activities of Detroit Concert Band and Sousa.
General Info: Yr. Est. 1972, Trim Size-8½ x 11, Sheetfed press, 8 pages, No Color
Subscriptions: Indv. $15
Circulation: (100% controlled)

Bellmark Times, The   *Business, Consumer*

Publishing Co: Hard Core Marketing, 239 Ethan Allen Highway, Ridgefield, CT 06877
Editorial Description: News and information from the Bellmark record company.
General Info: Irregular, Trim Size-11 x 17, 4 pages, No Color, Matte

Bluegrass Reflections

Publishing Co: Southwest Bluegrass Club, 2704 Haley Ave, Fort Worth, TX 76117-4147
General Info: Monthly
Subscriptions: $1/copy

Bluesletter   *Consumer, Association*

Publishing Co: St. Louis Blues Society, PO Box 21652, St. Louis, MO 63109-0652
Editorial Description: Newsletter for those that support the blues.
General Info: Bi-monthly, 16 pages

Boogie

Publishing Co: John Bialas, 221 Venetian Ave., Gulfport, MI 39507-1636
Editorial Description: Rock.
General Info: Yr. Est. 1972, Quarterly
Subscriptions: Indv. $2
Advertising: Inquire for rates.

Boombah Herald
See: HISTORY

Boosey and Hawkes
Newsletter

Publishing Co: Boosey & Hawkes Inc., 24 E. 21st St., New York, NY 10010-7200;
  Title Tel # (212) 757-3332
Personnel: Editor-Steven Swartz, Circ. Mgr.-Richard Barrios, Art Dir.-Pat Jerina, Promotion Dir.-David Huntley
Editorial Description: News & information on contemporary Boosey & Hawkes composers & their music.
General Info: Yr. Est. 1965, Semi-annually, Trim Size-9 x 11, Sheetfed press, 8 pages, No Color, Matte, Saddle-stitched
Circulation: Total-10,000
List Rental: Rents Lists
Printing Co: A.J. Bart & Sons, Inc., 333 Johnson Ave, Brooklyn, NY 11206-2804
  Tel # (718) 417-1300

Brass Band Bridge   *Association*

Publishing Co: Sponsor-North American Brass Band Assn. , Inc., North American Brass Band Assn.,
  PO Box 2438, Cullowhee, NC 28723 Fax # (704) 293-9312; Title Tel # (704) 293-9312
Personnel: Editor-Karen Kneeburg
Editorial Description: For & about British -type brass bands throughout the U. S. & Canada.
General Info: Yr. Est. 1980, Quarterly, 6 pages
Subscriptions: Indv. $20
Circulation: Total-1,000
Advertising: Inquire for rates.

Brass Player   *Consumer, Association*   **CPM: $20**

Publishing Co: New York Brass Conference for Scholarships, 315 W 53rd St, New York, NY
  10019-5701 Tel # (212) 581-1480 Fax # (212) 489-5186
Personnel: Editor-Elizabeth Colin
Editorial Description: News and issues on scholarship activity of the NY Brass Conference.
General Info: Yr. Est. 1985, Quarterly, Trim Size-8½ x 11, 24 pages, No Color, Matte, Saddle-stitched
Subscriptions: Indv. $10
Circulation: Total-12,000
Advertising: $250. Accepts Inserts.
List Rental: Rents Lists

Bulletin   *Business*

Publishing Co: Gordon DeYoung, 6907 Rix St SE, Ada, MI 49301-9030
Editorial Description: Published to further the interests of collectors, restorers, musicians and historians regarding all types of reed organs.
General Info: Yr. Est. 1982, Quarterly, Trim Size-8½ x 11, 32 pages, ISSN: 0736-9549
Subscriptions: Indv. $13, Inst. $13, Can. $20, For. $20

CAMMAC Newsletter,
Southern Ontario
Region   *Association*

Publishing Co: CAMMAC, 283 Bogert Ave., Toronto, ON M2N 1L4 Canada;
  Title Tel # (416) 250-8527
Personnel: Editor-Claudia Morawetz, Circ. Dir.-David Briggs, Promotion Dir.-Nora Mular-Richards
Editorial Description: News, articles, announcements, personel ads of interest to amateur musicians.
General Info: Yr. Est. 1952, Monthly, Trim Size-8½ x 11, Sheetfed press, 10 pages, 10% ads, No Color, Saddle-stitched
Subscriptions: Indv. $35, Inst. $50, Free With Membership
Circulation: Total-450
Advertising: Inquire for rates.
Printing Co: Account Manager: Anwat Shariff; Q-Print, 61 Adelaide Strret East, Toronto, ON M5C
  1K6 Canada Tel # (416) 366-0374, Fax # (416) 366-5415

CBMR Digest   *Consumer, Association*

Publishing Co: Columbia College Center for Black Music Research, 600 S. Michigan Ave., Chicago,
  IL 60605-1966 Tel # (312) 663-1600; Title Tel # (312) 663-9462 Title Fax # (312) 663-9019
Personnel: Editor in Chief-Samuel A. Floyd, Jr., Mag. Ed.-Marsha J. Reisser
Editorial Description: A summary of information about current research in the field of Black music.
General Info: Yr. Est. 1988, Semi-annually, Trim Size-8½ x 11, 16 pages, ISSN: 1043-1241
Subscriptions: Free
Circulation: Total-6,000, Readership-6,000
List Rental: Rents Lists

CCM Update

Publishing Co: Contemporary Christian Communications, 107 Kenner Ave, Nashville, TN
  37205-2207; Title Tel # (615) 386-3011 Title Fax # (615) 386-3380
Personnel: Publisher, Editor-John Styll, Circ. Mgr.-Robert Schustedt, Production Mgr.-Ramona
  Wilkes, Adv. Dir.-DeDe Donatelli, Art Dir.-Brain Smith
Editorial Description: Contains the most up-to-the-minute news available on the Christian music business.
General Info: (Formerly Musicline Update), Yr. Est. 1983, Weekly, Trim Size-8½ x 11, Sheetfed
  press, 12 pages, ISSN: 0746-7656, 2 Color, Newsprint
Subscriptions: Indv. $120, $4/copy
Circulation: Total-1,400
Advertising: Inquire for rates. Accepts Inserts.

CIRPA Newsletter   *Association*

Publishing Co: CIRPA, 214 King Street W., Suite 614, Toronto, ON M5H 3S6 Canada;
  Title Tel # (416) 593-1665
Personnel: Editor-Richard Sutherland
General Info: Quarterly
Subscriptions: Indv. $40

CMEA Newsletter   *Association*   **CPM: $110**

Publishing Co: Canadian Music Educators Association, 16 Royaleigh Ave., Etobicoke, ON M9P 2J5
  Canada; Title Tel # (416) 244-3745 Title Fax # (416) 235-1833
Personnel: Editor-Jane Atkinson, Adv. Dir.-Frances Ford
Editorial Description: News, teaching materials, book reviews, calendar of musical events.
General Info: Yr. Est. 1968, 3x/yr., Trim Size-8½ x 11, Offset press, 24 pages, ISSN: 0008-4549,
  Color-cover, Saddle-stitched
Subscriptions: Indv. $25, Can. $35, For. $42, $3/copy
Circulation: Total-3,000
Advertising: $330.

Canadian Band Association
Newsletter   *Association*

Publishing Co: Canadian Band Association, Inc., 21 Tecumseh St., Brantford, ON N3S 2B3 Canada; Title Tel # (519) 753-1858
Personnel: Editor-Frank McKinnon
Editorial Description: News of bands & soloists, composers around the world. Papers on instruments of a technical nature, concerts, new members, news of meetings held. Purpose is to keep our members informed.
General Info: (Formerly Canadian Bandsman), Yr. Est. 1970, Quarterly, Trim Size-8½ x 11, Letrpr. press, 35 pages, No Color, Newsprint
Subscriptions: Indv. $30, Inst. $50
Circulation: (100% controlled), Total-175
Printing Co: Sir Speedy Printing Service & Copy Centre, 446 Grey St., Suite 107, Brantford, ON N3S 7L5 Canada Tel # (519) 756-0755

Canadian Opera Company
News

Publishing Co: Canadian Opera Co., 227 Front St. , E., Toronto, ON M5A 1E8 Canada; Title Tel # (416) 363-6671
Personnel: Editor, Art Dir.-Colin Eatock
Editorial Description: Feature articles on COC personalities, productions & activities.
General Info: (Formerly Overtures), Yr. Est. 1975, Trim Size-8½ x 11, Web press, 16 pages, ISSN: 0820-4896, No Color, Coated, Saddle-stitched
Subscriptions: Indv. $35
Circulation: (100% controlled), Total-14,000
Printing Co: Hartley Gibson Co. Ltd., 2533 Gerrard St., E., Scarborough, ON M1N 1W9 Canada Tel # (416) 690-6163, Fax # (416) 690-6203

Chatfield Brass Band-
Newsletter   *Consumer, Association*

Publishing Co: Chatfield Brass Band Library, 81 Library Lane, P.O Box 578, Chatfield, MN 55923; Title Tel # (507) 867-3275
Personnel: Editor-James Perkins
Editorial Description: Monthly newsletter which goes to bandmembers & music library members containing band activities & library activities, etc.
General Info: Yr. Est. 1969, Monthly, Trim Size-8½ x 11, Mimeo press, 3 pages, No Color
Subscriptions: Indv. $15
Acquistions: Publication Bought
Circulation: Total-2,200
Advertising: Accepts Inserts.

Choirboy Notes   *Consumer*

Publishing Co: Noteworthy Communications, 34518 Warren Road #315, Westland, MI 48185 Tel # (313) 721-5410 Fax # (313) 422-2628
Personnel: Publisher, Editor-James R. Koelsch
Editorial Description: Choirboy Notes is devoted exclusively to boys' choirs and their music. Covers secular and religious boys' choirs, their choristers, their directors, and the issues confronting them. Reviews records and concerts.
General Info: Bi-monthly, ISSN: 1080-8965
Subscriptions: Indv. $25, Can. $25, For. $35

Choirs Ontario   CPM: $133

Publishing Co: Ontario Choral Fed., 100 Richmond St. E., Suite 200, Toronto, ON M5C 2P9 Canada; Title Tel # (416) 363-7488 Title Fax # (416) 363-8236
Personnel: Editor-Bev Jahnke
Editorial Description: Has articles and choral listings of interest to choristers and conductors. Includes provincial and national topics such as festivals, concerts and competitions.
General Info: (Formerly Ontario Choral Fed. Newsletter), Trim Size-8½ x 11, Sheetfed press, 16 pages, 37% ads, 2 Color, Matte, Saddle-stitched
Acquistions: Publication Bought
Circulation: Total-1,500
Advertising: $200. Accepts Inserts.
Printing Co: Harmony Printing, 123 Eastside Dr., Toronto, ON M8Z 5S5 Canada Tel # (416) 232-1472

Chorale   *Consumer*

Publishing Co: Chorale, c/o Robert Schartoff, 30 Fifth Ave., Suite 15E, New York, NY 10011; Title Tel # (212) 473-0568
Personnel: Publisher-Robert Schartoff, Editor in Chief-Paul Epstein
Editorial Description: Newsletter for choral singers and enthusiasts.
General Info: Monthly
Subscriptions: $3/copy

College Band Directors
National Association
Newsletter

Publishing Co: College Band Directors Natl. Assn., Georgia State Univ., Atlanta, GA 30304
Personnel: Editor-Gary Corcoran
General Info: Yr. Est. 1941, Quarterly

Come-All-Ye
See: FOLKLORE

Composers' Forum Network
News   *Association*

Publishing Co: Composers' Forum, Inc., 260 W. Broadway, New York, NY 10013-2259; Title Tel # (212) 334-0216 Title Fax # (212) 941-9704
Editorial Description: Advocates authentic music creation.
General Info: Yr. Est. 1982, Quarterly
Subscriptions: Indv. $10
Circulation: Total-2,500

Conductors' Guild
Newsletter   *Association*

Publishing Co: Conductors Guild Inc., 103 South High Street, Room 6, West Chester, PA 19382-3262; Title Tel # (610) 430-6010 Title Fax # (610) 430-6010
Personnel: Editor-Steven Edwards
General Info: Quarterly
Circulation: Total-4,500
Advertising: Inquire for rates.

Connections   *Consumer, Association*   CPM: $56

Publishing Co: Music for People, 7 Middletown Road, Roxbury, NH 03431; Title Tel # (603) 352-4941 Title Fax # (603) 352-8377
Personnel: Publisher-David Darling, Editor-Bonnie Insull
Editorial Description: Connections is a vehicle for networking and communication for people interested in music and improvisation for self expression.
General Info: Yr. Est. 1988, Quarterly, Sheetfed press, 22 pages, ISSN: 1076-2485, 15% ads, No Color
Subscriptions: Indv. $30, Can. $35, For. $35, $5/copy
Circulation: Total-3,200
Advertising: $180.
Printing Co: Account Manager: Bev Worden; Wordens Quality Printing, Surry Village, NH 03431

Country Dance & Song Society News
See: CULTURE & HUMANITIES

Crawdaddy!   *Consumer*

Publishing Co: Crawdaddy!, PO Box 231155, Encinitas, CA 92023-1155
Personnel: Publisher-Paul Williams
Editorial Description: Articles and essays on musicians and the music industry.
General Info: Yr. Est. 1993, Quarterly, ISSN: 1079-0489
Subscriptions: Indv. $12, Can. $12, For. $12, $4/copy
Circulation: Total-1,200

Crosscurrents   *Consumer*

Publishing Co: Greenwich Press, 516 K South, Saskatoon, SK S7M 2E2 Canada; Title Tel # (306) 244-0679
Personnel: Publisher, Editor-Bob Fink
Editorial Description: Interdisciplinary: universal aspects of arts & politics illustrated with concrete events.
General Info: Yr. Est. 1975, Quarterly, Trim Size-7 x 8½, Desktop press, 4 pages, ISSN: 0704-6588, 2 Color, Newsprint
Subscriptions: Indv. $10, $1/copy
Acquistions: Publication Bought
Circulation: Total-500
Printing Co: Greenwich Press, 516 Ave. K, S., Saskatoon, SK S7M 2E2 Canada Tel # (306) 244-0679

Cue Sheet, The   *Association*

Publishing Co: Society for the Preservation of Film Music, 2930 El Caminito St, La Crescenta, CA 91214-2005; Title Tel # (818) 248-5775 Title Fax # (213) 474-2132
Personnel: Editor-Clifford McCarty, Publisher, Circ. Mgr., Production Mgr.-Leslie Zador, Adv. Dir.-Scherr Lillico
Editorial Description: Society newsletter concerning events, collections, composer profiles, interviews.
General Info: Yr. Est. 1982, Quarterly, Trim Size-5½ x 8½, Web press, 40 pages, ISSN: 0888-9015, No Color, Newsprint
Subscriptions: Indv. $30
Circulation: Total-400
Advertising: Accepts Inserts.
Printing Co: Quality Street Printing, 415 Santa Monica Blvd, Santa Monica, CA 90401-2306 Tel # (213) 395-8192

Curtain Call

Publishing Co: New York City Opera, New York State Theater, 20 Lincoln Center, New York, NY 10023

Darius Milhaud Society
Newsletter

Publishing Co: Darius Milhaud Society, 15715 Chadbourne Rd, Cleveland, OH 44120-3333
Editorial Description: Designed to encourage performance of Milhaud's music.
General Info: Yr. Est. 1985
Subscriptions: Indv. $25

Descarga Newsletter, The   *Consumer*

Publishing Co: Descarga, 328 Flatbush Ave Ste 180, Brooklyn, NY 11238-4302; Title Tel # (718) 693-2966 Title Fax # (718) 693-1316
Personnel: Editor-Bruce Polin
Editorial Description: For and by Latin music listeners.
General Info: Yr. Est. 1992, Monthly, Trim Size-8½ x 11, No Color, Matte, Perfect bound
Subscriptions: Indv. $17, Inst. $17, Can. $30, For. $40, $3/copy

DiscList   *Business*

Publishing Co: Informedia, PO Box 304, Novi, MI 48376-0304; Title Tel # (313) 348-2444
Personnel: Publisher, Editor-Terry Pochert, Production Mgr.-Darla Berdal
Editorial Description: Contains audio compact disc new release information.
General Info: (Formerly Compact DiscList), Yr. Est. 1984, Monthly, Trim Size-8½ x 11, Desktop press, 12 pages, ISSN: 0890-2415, No Color, Newsprint
Subscriptions: Indv. $40, $4/copy
Circulation: Total-2,500
List Rental: Actives: $100/M

Early Keyboard Studies
Newsletter   *Consumer*   CPM: $250

Publishing Co: Westfield Center for Early Keyboard Studies, Inc., 1 Cottage St., Easthampton, MA 01027-1658 Fax # (413) 527-7689; Title Tel # (413) 527-7664
Personnel: Publisher-Lynn Edwards, Editor-Gregory Hayes
Editorial Description: Promotes appreciation and understanding of keyboard music of all periods.
General Info: Yr. Est. 1989, Quarterly, Trim Size-8½ x 11, Sheetfed press, 12 pages, ISSN: 0882-0201, 2 Color, Newsprint
Subscriptions: Indv. $40, Inst. $40, Can. $45, For. $48, Free With Membership
Circulation: Total-500
Advertising: $125.

Early Music Newsletter   *Association*

Publishing Co: N.Y. Recorder Guild, 145 W. 93rd St., New York, NY 10025; Title Tel # (212) 662-2946
Personnel: Editor-Mariam Poser
Editorial Description: Calendar of concerts, reviews of concerts, book reviews, previews, interviews, essays.
General Info: 10x/yr., Trim Size-8½ x 11, Mimeo press, 10 pages, 2% ads, Newsprint
Subscriptions: Indv. $20, $2/copy
Circulation: Total-135
Advertising: Inquire for rates.
List Rental: Rents Lists

Electronotes

Publishing Co: Musical Engineering Group, 1 Pheasant Ln, Ithaca, NY 14850-6311
General Info: Monthly
Subscriptions: Indv. $20
Circulation: Total-1,000

Elvis Intl. Forum   *Consumer*   CPM: $33

Publishing Co: Herst Corp., The, PO Box 3373, Thousand Oaks, CA 91359-0373; Title Tel # (805) 379-4012
Personnel: Editor in Chief-Darwin Lamm, Music Editor-Judy Norwood, Feature Ed.-Leahw Ray, Circ. Mgr.-Eugene Semery
Editorial Description: Dedicated to life & music of Elvis Presley.
General Info: Yr. Est. 1987, Quarterly, Trim Size-8½ x 11, 80 pages, 4 Color, Coated, Saddle-stitched
Subscriptions: Indv. $15, Can. $30, For. $30, $4/copy
Circulation: Total-225,000
Advertising: $7,500.

Ernest Bloch Society
Bulletin

Publishing Co: Ernest Bloch Society, 34844 Old Stage Rd., Gualala, CA 95445; Title Tel # (707) 884-3473
Personnel: Editor-David Sills, Circ. Mgr.-Art Dir.-Lucienne Dimitroff
Editorial Description: About the late composer Ernest Bloch devoted to his notes, letters, pedagogy, music, recordings, concerts, bibliography.
General Info: (Formerly Ernest Bloch Society-Newsletter), Yr. Est. 1968, Trim Size-5½ x 8½, 26 pages, ISSN: 0071-1195, Color-cover, Newsprint
Subscriptions: Indv. $20

Focus on Festivals   *Consumer*   CPM: $31

Publishing Co: Associated Manitoba Arts Festivals, Inc., 424-100 Arthur St., Winnipeg, MB R3B 1H3 Canada; Title Tel # (204) 945-4578 Title Fax # (204) 948-2073
Personnel: Editor-Tanya Gregory Thomlinson
Editorial Description: This newsletter is primary a vehicle to distribute information / news about art festivals at the local, provincial or national level. It also contains other community arts information and articles relevant to festival volunteers and participants.
General Info: Yr. Est. 1981, Quarterly, Trim Size-8½ x 11, Mimeo press, 20 pages, 1% ads, No Color, Matte
Subscriptions: Can. $20, Free With Membership
Circulation: Total-3,200
Advertising: $100. Accepts Inserts.
Printing Co: Lasting Impressions, 1302 Notre Dame Avenue, Winnipeg, MB Tel # (204) 783-2755, Fax # (204) 772-4502

Gene Lees Jazzletter   *Consumer*

Publishing Co: Gene Lees Jazzletter, PO Box 240, Ojai, CA 93024-0240; Title Tel # (808) 640-8307 Title Fax # (805) 640-0253
General Info: Yr. Est. 1981, Monthly
Subscriptions: Indv. $60, Can. $60, For. $80

Girl Groups ('60's Rock N' Roll) Gazette
See: FAN MAGAZINES-MOVIE, RADIO, TV

Grateful Dead Almanac
See: FAN MAGAZINES-MOVIE, RADIO, TV

Hard n' Fast   *Consumer*   CPM: $40

Publishing Co: PS Inc., 1651 Dublin Rd, Dresher, PA 19025-1243; Title Tel # (215) 443-5160 Title Fax # (215) 443-5219
Personnel: Publisher, Editor-Alex Richter
Editorial Description: Rock and Roll news
General Info: Yr. Est. 1988, Monthly, Letrpr. press, 8 pages, No Color, Newsprint
Subscriptions: Indv. $15, $2/copy
Circulation: (PSS), Total-5,000
Advertising: $200.
Printing Co: Account Manager: Brian Francis; Fort Nassau Graphics, 3rd & Jersey Aves., Gloucester, NJ 08030

Historic Brass Society
Newsletter   *Association*

Publishing Co: Historic Brass Society, 148 W 23rd St Apt 2A, New York, NY 10011-2447; Title Tel # (212) 627-3820 Title Fax # (212) 627-3820
Personnel: Publisher-Jeffrey Nussbaum, Editor-Stewart Carter, Production-Karen Snowberg
Editorial Description: News, views, and notes for members and friends of the Historic Brass Society.
General Info: Yr. Est. 1989, Annually, Trim Size-8½ x 11, 70 pages, ISSN: 1045-4594, No Color, Saddle-stitched
Subscriptions: Indv. $20, Inst. $25, For. $20, $5/copy
Circulation: Total-800
List Rental: Actives: 800
Printing Co: McNaughton & Gunn, 960 Woodland Dr., PO Box 100, Saline, MI 48176 Tel # (313) 429-5411, Fax # (800) 677-2665

Hot Line News   *Business*

Publishing Co: Musicians National Hot Line Association, 277 E 6100 S, Salt Lake City, UT 84107-7302; Title Tel # (801) 268-2000
Personnel: Editor-Nancy Zitting, Circ. Mgr.-Marvin Zitting
Editorial Description: Newsletter on groups needing musicians/gigs & musicians available for work.
General Info: Yr. Est. 1980, Bi-monthly, Trim Size-8½ x 11, Sheetfed press, 4 pages, No Color, Newsprint
Subscriptions: Can. $25, For. $30
Acquistions: Publication Bought
Circulation: Total-1,000
Advertising: Inquire for rates. Accepts Inserts.

IMA Bulletin, The
See: COMPUTERS & AUTOMATION

In the Groove
See: COLLECTIBLES

Information Quarterly

Publishing Co: Center for Performing Arts Resources, 9582 Hamilton Avenue, Huntington Beach, CA 92646 Tel # (714) 964-6041
Editorial Description: Highlighting funding, promotion, publicity, programming and booking assistance avalabel for presenters and performers nationwide.
General Info: Quarterly
Subscriptions: Indv. $236

Insider, The   *Consumer*

Publishing Co: T.O.G. Music Enterprises, 2107 S Oakland St, Arlington, VA 22204-5413; Title Tel # (703) 685-0199
Editorial Description: Reviews independent music releases nationally.
General Info: Yr. Est. 1989, Monthly, Roto. press, 2 pages, 2% ads, No Color, Coated, Saddle-stitched
Subscriptions: Indv. $10, Inst. $25, Can. $15, For. $20
Circulation: Total-500
List Rental: Rents Lists

Intermission   *Association*

Publishing Co: New Orleans Jazz Club of Southern California, PO Box 15212, Long Beach, CA 90815-0212 Tel # (714) 838-5234; Title Tel # (310) 867-7501
Personnel: Editor-Norm Burnham
Editorial Description: Preservation of Dixieland Jazz.
General Info: Yr. Est. 1968, Bi-monthly, Trim Size-5½ x 8½, 18 pages, No Color, Matte, Saddle-stitched
Subscriptions: Indv. $6
Circulation: Total-400
Advertising: Inquire for rates.

International Horn Society-Newsletter

Publishing Co: Sponsor-Intl. Horn Society, International Horn Society, P O Box 1083, Hixson, TN 37343-1083; Title Tel # (405) 924-2271
Personnel: Publisher-Paul Mansur, Editor-Johnny Pherigo, Adv. Dir.-Katherine Thomson
Editorial Description: Provides Horn news of interest to its members.
General Info: Yr. Est. 1970, Quarterly, Trim Size-8½ x 11, 4 pages, No Color, Looseleaf
Circulation: (5% controlled), Total-3,000, Subscriptions-1,850, International-450
List Rental: Rents Lists
Printing Co: Prices Quality Printing, Durant, OK 74701 Tel # (801) 377-3026

International MIDI Users Group Newszine
See: COMPUTERS & AUTOMATION

International Piano Archives At Maryland Newsletter

Publishing Co: Univ. of Maryland, Music Library, Hombake 3210, College Park, MD 20742-0001
Personnel: Editor-Harold Diamond
Editorial Description: Includes articles about rare piano recordings.

Jazz Archivist

Publishing Co: Hogan Jazz Archive, Tilton Memorial Library, New Orleans, LA 70118; Title Tel # (504) 865-5688
Personnel: Editor-John Joyce
Editorial Description: Contains information on activities of the Hogan Jazz Archive at Tulane University - recent donations, processing of the collection, exhibits, and other special events. Feature articles on aspects of jazz history and research.
General Info: Yr. Est. 1986, Semi-annually, Trim Size-8.5 x 11, Desktop press, 16 pages, No Color
Circulation: Total-1,000

Jazz Newsletter

Publishing Co: New Orleans Jazz Club of California, PO Box 1225, Kerrville, TX 78029-1225; Title Tel # (210) 896-2285
Personnel: Publisher, Editor-Bill Bacin
Editorial Description: Current news of worldwide Jazz affairs and activities.
General Info: Yr. Est. 1963, Monthly
Subscriptions: Indv. $12, $1/copy

Julliard Journal   *Association*

Publishing Co: Julliard School, The, 60 Lincoln Center Plaza, New York, NY 10023-7498; Title Tel # (212) 799-5000 Title Fax # (212) 724-0263
Personnel: Publisher, Editor-Jane Rubinsky, Adv. Dir.-John Fountain
Editorial Description: Reports on activities of school, faculty, alumni, students and the arts, in general.
General Info: (Formerly Newspaper), Yr. Est. 1985, 8x/yr., Trim Size-11 x 17, Web press, 16 pages, No Color
Subscriptions: Indv. $15, Free With Membership
Circulation: (64% controlled), Total-15,500, Subscriptions-150, International-5,000
Advertising: Inquire for rates. Accepts Inserts.

Keyboard Teacher   *Association*

Publishing Co: Keyboard Teachers Association International, Inc., 361 Pin Oak Ln, Westbury, NY 11590-1941; Title Tel # (516) 333-3236
Personnel: Publisher, Editor-Albert DeVito
Editorial Description: Features professional music information/guidance and review of music by type.
General Info: Yr. Est. 1963, Quarterly, Trim Size-8½ x 11, Sheetfed press, 10 pages, ISSN: 1083-835X, No Color
Subscriptions: Indv. $25, Free With Membership

King Biscuit Times   *Consumer*

Publishing Co: KFFA AM/1360, PO Box 430, Helena, AR 72342-0430
Editorial Description: Newsletter on the American Blues scene.
General Info: Bi-monthly
Advertising: Inquire for rates.

Kodaly Musical Training Institute

Publishing Co: Univ. of Hartford/Hartt School of Music, 200 Bloomfield Ave., W. Hartford, CT 06117-1500
Personnel: Publisher-Laurdella Bodolay
Editorial Description: Covers institute activities.

Kurt Weill Newsletter   *Scholarly, Association*

Publishing Co: Kurt Weill Foundation for Music, 7 E. 20th St., New York, NY 10003-1106; Title Tel # (212) 505-5240 Title Fax # (212) 363-9663
Personnel: Editor-David Farneth, Production Mgr.-Edward Harsh
Editorial Description: All information related to the life & works of Kurt Weill & Lotte Lenya. Feature articles, reviews of books, performances & recordings. Scholarly emphasis.
General Info: Yr. Est. 1983, Semi-annually, Trim Size-8½ x 11, 32 pages, ISSN: 0899-6407, No Color, Matte, Saddle-stitched
Subscriptions: Free To Qualified Recipient
Circulation: Total-6,000
List Rental: Rents Lists
Printing Co: Edwards Brothers, Inc., 800 Edwards Dr., Lillington, NC 27546 Tel # (910) 893-2717

Laser Disc Newsletter, The
See: HOME & HOME ENTERTAINMENT

Laserlog

Publishing Co: Trade Service Publications, Inc., 10996 Torreyana Rd, San Diego, CA 92121-1105; Title Tel # (619) 457-5920
Personnel: Editor-Bonnie Dudley, Circ. Mgr.-Harry Weber, Adv. Dir.-Ed Nava, Promotion Dir.-Dan Henehan
Editorial Description: Lists all known CD's currently available, indexed & classified bi-weekly.
General Info: Yr. Est. 1987, Bi-weekly, Ind/Abs/Online: indexed, Looseleaf
Subscriptions: Indv. $216, Can. $240

Le Hit Parade   *Consumer*

Publishing Co: Le Hit Parade Co., 509 Penn Ayr Rd., Camp Hill, PA 17011-2056; Title Tel # (717) 691-7645
Personnel: Publisher, Editor-John Snoddy
Editorial Description: Interviews, album reviews and more covering today's music from France and Quebec.
General Info: Yr. Est. 1988, Quarterly, ISSN: 1044-5056
Subscriptions: Indv. $12, Can. $14, For. $16, $3/copy
Circulation: Total-600

Lead Belly Letter   *Consumer, Association*

Publishing Co: Lead Belly Society, PO Box 6679, Ithaca, NY 14851-6679; Title Tel # (607) 273-6615 Title Fax # (607) 844-4810
Personnel: Editor-Sean Killeen
Editorial Description: Historical information about the celebrated guitarist Huddie 'Lead Belly ' Ledbetter, and his music.
General Info: Yr. Est. 1990, Quarterly, Trim Size-8½ x 11, 12 pages, ISSN: 1056-5329, Saddle-stitched
Subscriptions: Indv. $17, Can. $20, For. $25, Free With Membership
Circulation: Total-3,000, Readership-10,000
Advertising: Accepts Inserts.
List Rental: Rents Lists

Leadsheet, The

Publishing Co: Nashville Songwriters Assn. Intl., 15 Music Sq W, Nashville, TN 37203-3203; Title Tel # (615) 321-5004 Title Fax # (615) 321-5027
General Info: Quarterly
Circulation: Total-2,400

Lee Lo's New York Jazz Newsletter   *Consumer*

Publishing Co: Lee Lo's New York Jazz Newsletter, 308 W 104th St Apt 2d, New York, NY 10025-4134
Personnel: Publisher-Lee Lowenfish
Editorial Description: Covers the NY jazz scene.
General Info: Monthly, Trim Size-8½ x 11, No Color
Subscriptions: Indv. $20

Lexington Philharmonic Society Newsletter

Publishing Co: Lexington Philharmonic Society, 161 N Mill St, Lexington, KY 40507-1125; Title Tel # (606) 233-4226
Personnel: Editor-Donna Childs
General Info: 5x/yr.
Circulation: Total-1,700

Living Music   *Business, Consumer*

Publishing Co: Minuscule University Press, PO Box 173, Desert Hot Springs, CA 92240-0173; Title Tel # (619) 329-8463
Personnel: Publisher, Editor in Chief-Dwight Winenger, Editor-Charles Norman Mason, Editorial Page Ed.-Grant Fletcher, Mng. Editor-Charles Mason, Feature Ed.-Lukas Foss, Music Editor-Alfred Reed, Bk. Rev. Ed.-Craig Hultgren, Circ. Mgr.-Marshall Bialosky, Production Mgr.-Dwight Andrews, Adv. Dir.-Neoma Knitten, Art Dir.-Dorothy Hindman, Mktg. Dir.-Aurelio de la Vega, Promotion Dir.-Max Lifchitz
Editorial Description: Articles, news, biography on new music, composers and performers.
General Info: Yr. Est. 1981, Quarterly, Trim Size-8½ x 11, Offset press, 8 pages, ISSN: 1775-092X, Ind/Abs/Online: Music information services information resource center, No Color, Other
Subscriptions: Indv. $15, Can. $17, For. $19, $4/copy
Circulation: Total-500, Readership-11,000
Advertising: Inquire for rates. Accepts Inserts.

Lyra
Consumer

Publishing Co: Steinway, Steinway Place, Long Island City, NY 11105; Title Tel # (718) 721-2600
Title Fax # (718) 932-4332
Personnel: Editor-Leo Apellman
Editorial Description: Editorial coverage of activities of Steinway & sons and Steinway concert artists.
General Info: (Formerly Steinways News), Yr. Est. 1935, Quarterly, Trim Size-8½ x 11
Subscriptions: Free
Circulation: Total-50,000

MACSEM Newsletter
Scholarly, Association

Publishing Co: Mid-Atlantic Chapter, Society for Ethnomusicology, 419 W. 119 St., Apt. 5E, New York, NY 10027; Title Tel # (212) 854-1247
Personnel: Editor-Niloofar Mina
Editorial Description: News of professional conferences,career opportunities,etc.,for ethnomusicologists.
General Info: Yr. Est. 1982, 8 pages
Subscriptions: Indv. $10
Circulation: Total-500

MUSENET
See: COLLEGE STUDENT

Millennium Pop
Consumer

Publishing Co: Millenium Pop, 173 Morrison Ave, Somerville, MA 02144-2016
Personnel: Publisher, Editor-Tim Riley, Exec. Ed.-Sara Laschever
Editorial Description: Covers issues of today's popular culture.
General Info: Yr. Est. 1994, Monthly
Subscriptions: Indv. $20, For. $30
Circulation: Total-500

Miller Notes

Publishing Co: Glenn Miller Birthplace Society, PO Box 61, Clarinda, IA 51632-0061; Title Tel # (712) 542-3881
Personnel: Editor-Wilda Martin
Editorial Description: News about Society activities, the annual festival, Miller books and recordings, and the Miller scholarship program.
General Info: Yr. Est. 1980, 5x/yr., Sheetfed press, 6 pages, No Color, Newsprint
Circulation: (50% controlled), Total-1,000, Single Copy/Newsstand-470

Minnesota Composers
Forum
Consumer, Association

Publishing Co: Minnesota Composers Forum, 332 Minnesota Street, #E145, St. Paul, MN 55101-1314; Title Tel # (612) 228-1407 Title Fax # (612) 223-8619
Personnel: Editor-Karen Nelson
Editorial Description: MCF is a non-profit organization that exists to encourage and provide for the creation, performance and appreciation of new music. This mission is accomplished by a wide range of programs through which living composers are able to create and present their music.
General Info: Yr. Est. 1976, Monthly, Trim Size-8½ x 11, 8 pages, Color-cover, Newsprint
Subscriptions: Indv. $30, Inst. $30, Can. $45, For. $45
Circulation: (33% controlled), Subscriptions-1,000
Advertising: Inquire for rates.
List Rental: Rents Lists
Printing Co: Account Manager: Steve Case; Penn Graphics, 1812 E 121st St, Burnsville, MN 55337-6801

Monthly Guide of Brooklyn
Academy of Music

Publishing Co: Brooklyn Academy of Music, 30 Lafayette Ave, Brooklyn, NY 11217-1486
Personnel: Publisher-John Latham, Editor-Miss Jan Henry
Editorial Description: Lists lectures, investments, world affairs, concerts, plays, musicals, operas, etc. under auspices of the Brooklyn Academy of Music.
General Info: 7x/yr.
Circulation: Total-20,000

Moravian Music Foundation
Newsletter
Scholarly, Association

Publishing Co: Moravian Music Foundation, 20 Cascade Ave., Winston-Salem, NC 27127-2904; Title Tel # (910) 725-0651 Title Fax # (910) 725-4514
General Info: Semi-annually, Trim Size-8 x 10, 16 pages
Circulation: Total-4,200

MuseLetter
Consumer

Publishing Co: MuseLetter, 859 N Hollywood Way # 324, Burbank, CA 91505-2833; Title Fax # (818) 599-3412
Personnel: Editor-Christopher Yavelow
General Info: Yr. Est. 1994, Bi-monthly
Subscriptions: Indv. $72

MusiCopyright
Intelligence
Business

Publishing Co: E.S. Proteus, 1657 The Fairway Ste 123, Jenkintown, PA 19046-1423; Title Tel # (215) 885-3154 Title Fax # (215) 885-0670
Personnel: Publisher-E.S. Proteus, Editor-Eric Nemeyer
Editorial Description: Provides music industry professionals and investors with news, perspectives, and research about copyrighted song and recording properties.
General Info: Yr. Est. 1992, Monthly, Trim Size-8½ x 11, Offset press, 16 pages, ISSN: 7067-876X, 2 Color, Saddle-stitched
Subscriptions: Indv. $595, Can. $620, For. $670, $50/copy
Circulation: Total-2,000
Advertising: Accepts Inserts.

Music Box

Publishing Co: Music Box, Inc., 3606 Edwin Ave, Cincinnati, OH 45204-1234; Title Tel # (513) 251-9382
Personnel: Publisher, Editor-Stephen M. Stroff
Subscriptions: Indv. $25, Can. $33, For. $33

Music Business Insight
Business

Publishing Co: Music Business File, PO Box 266, Astor Station, Boston, MA 02123-0266; Title Tel # (617) 639-1971
Personnel: Publisher, Editor-Peter Spellman
Editorial Description: Cutting-edge news, ideas and resources for busy music professionals.
General Info: Yr. Est. 1994, Quarterly, Trim Size-8½ x 11, Desktop press, 4 pages, No Color, Matte
Circulation: Total-350

Music Connoisseur, The
Consumer　　　　CPM: $90

Publishing Co: Barre Coe, PO Box 476, Peck Slip Station, New York, NY 10038; Title Tel # (212) 571-7636
Personnel: Publisher, Editor, Circ. Mgr., Production Mgr.-Barry Cohen
Editorial Description: Covers recordings and live rare music by today's finest classical artists.
General Info: Yr. Est. 1993, Quarterly, Trim Size-8½ x 11, 20 pages
Subscriptions: Indv. $5, Inst. $10
Circulation: Total-1,100
Advertising: $100. Accepts Inserts.
List Rental: Rents Lists

Music Critics Association
Newsletter
Association

Publishing Co: Music Critics Assoc., 6201 Tuckerman Ln, Rockville, MD 20852-3509; Title Tel # (301) 530-9527
Personnel: Editor-Richard Freed
General Info: (Formerly Critics Criteria), Yr. Est. 1969, Quarterly
Circulation: Total-1,000

Music From China

Publishing Co: Music From China, 170 Park Row Apt 12d, New York, NY 10038-1100
Personnel: Editor-Paul Shackman, Editor-Chen Yi, Production Dir.-Susan Cheng
Editorial Description: For encouraging interest in traditional and modern Chinese music.
General Info: Yr. Est. 1991, Quarterly, Trim Size-8½ x 11

Music Industry News
Business

Publishing Co: Mojave Music, Inc., 115 S. Topanga Canyon Blvd., Ste. 114, Topanga, CA 90290 Tel # (310) 455-0888 Fax # (310) 455-0894
Personnel: Publisher-Pat Nelson
Editorial Description: Covers the worldwide music industry.
General Info: Yr. Est. 1995, Weekly, Trim Size-8½ x 11, 2 pages
Subscriptions: Inst. $195, Can. $195, For. $245

Music for the Love of It
Consumer

Publishing Co: Music for the Love of It, 67 Parkside Drive, Berkeley, CA 94705; Title Tel # (510) 654-9134 Title Fax # (510) 654-4656
Personnel: Publisher-Ted Rust
Editorial Description: A bi-monthly newsletter about making one's own music.
General Info: Yr. Est. 1986, Bi-monthly, Trim Size-9½ x 11, 10 pages, ISSN: 0898-8757
Subscriptions: Indv. $20, Inst. $20, Can. $25, For. $25, $5/copy
Circulation: Total-500
Advertising: Inquire for rates.
Printing Co: Regent Press, 6020 Adelaine, Oakland, CA 94608

Music Notes
See: COLLEGE STUDENT

Music Research News

Publishing Co: Canadian Music Research Council, Simon Fraser University, Faculty of Education, Burnaby, BC V5A 1S6 Canada; Title Tel # (604) 291-3192
General Info: Yr. Est. 1976, Semi-annually, ISSN: 0700-3838

NARM Sounding Board   *Business*

Publishing Co: National Association of Recording Merchandisers, 3 Eves Dr Ste 307, Marlton, NJ 08053-3129; Title Tel # (609) 596-2221
Personnel: Editor, Adv. Dir.-Patrick Gorlick
Editorial Description: NARM news and trade report.
General Info: Bi-monthly, Trim Size-8½ x 11, 6 pages, 2% ads, 2 Color
Circulation: (100% controlled), Total-2,500
Printing Co: Donaldson Printing, 181 W Hillcrest Ave, Havertown, PA 19083-1198
Tel # (215) 449-5600

NCBA Newsletter   *Association*

Publishing Co: Natl. Catholic Band Assn., PO Box 1023, Notre Dame, IN 46556-1023; Title Tel # (219) 239-7136
Personnel: Editor-George Wiskirchen
General Info: Yr. Est. 1973, Monthly
Circulation: Total-200

National Association of Music Merchants News   *Business, Association*

Publishing Co: National Association of Music Merchants, 5140 Avenida Encinas, Carlsbad, CA 92008-4372; Title Tel # (619) 438-8001
Personnel: Editor-J. Derloshon
Editorial Description: Provides pertinent information on music retailing and association activity of interest to member music merchants, manufacturers, wholesalers, distributors, and music publishers.
General Info: Yr. Est. 1944, Monthly, Trim Size-8½ x 11, 16 pages
Subscriptions: Free With Membership
Circulation: Total-7,000

Network News   *Business, Association*   CPM: $175

Publishing Co: Los Angeles Music Network, PO Box 8934, Universal City, CA 91608-0934; Title Tel # (818) 769-6095
Personnel: Editor-Tess Taylor, Fulflmnt. Mgr.-Judyth Springer Thurman, Adv. Dir.-Cil Pereyra, Mktg. Dir., Promotion Dir.-Sandra Archer
Editorial Description: A record industry trade publication which promotes career advancement, communication, and information through networking within the industry.
General Info: Yr. Est. 1992, Bi-monthly, Trim Size-8½ x 11, 16 pages, Ind/Abs/Online: AOL, No Color, Matte, Saddle-stitched
Subscriptions: Indv. $39, Inst. $39, Free With Membership
Circulation: Total-3,500, Readership-16,000
Advertising: $615.
List Rental: Rents Lists

News-Can. Musical Heritage Soc./Nouvelles de la Soc. pour le Patrimoine Musical Can.   *Consumer, Association*

Publishing Co: Canadian Musical Heritage Society, Box 53161, Ottawa, ON K1N 1C5 Canada Tel # (613) 520-2600 Fax # (613) 520-6677
Personnel: Production Mgr.-Clifford Ford
General Info: Yr. Est. 1990, Irregular, ISSN: 1181-6023
Subscriptions: Inst. $100, Free With Membership

Newsletter of the American Handel Society   *Association*

Publishing Co: Sponsor-The American Handel Society, Inc., American Handel Society, Univ. Of Maryland Dept. Of, Music, College Park, MD 20742-0001; Title Tel # (301) 405-5523 Title Fax # (301) 314-9504
Personnel: Publisher-H. Serwer, Editor-C.S. Larve
Editorial Description: Covers life & music of Handel.
General Info: Yr. Est. 1986, Tri-annually, Sheetfed press, 8 pages, ISSN: 0888-8701, 2 Color, Newsprint
Subscriptions: Inst. $30
Circulation: Total-175
Printing Co: A-R Editions, Inc., 801 Deming Way, Madison, WI 53717-1918 Tel # (608) 836-9000

Newsletter, Institute for Studies in American Music   *Consumer, Association*

Publishing Co: Institute for Studies in American Music, Brooklyn College, Conservatory of Music, Brooklyn, NY 11210; Title Tel # (718) 951-5655 Title Fax # (718) 951-4858
Personnel: Editor-Carol Oja, Acting Ed.-Jeff Taylor, Assoc. Ed.-Ray Allen, Production-Kathleen Mason Krotman, Production-Larry Picard
Editorial Description: Articles, research reports, book and record reviews, news & information on all aspects of American music.
General Info: (Formerly ISAM Newsletter), Yr. Est. 1971, Semi-annually, Trim Size-8½ x 11, Desktop press, 16 pages, ISSN: 0145-8396, No Color, Matte, Saddle-stitched
Subscriptions: Free
Circulation: Total-4,000
Advertising: Inquire for rates. Accepts Inserts.
List Rental: Actives: $150/M

Newsletter of the International Women's Brass Conference   *Consumer, Association*

Publishing Co: International Women's Brass Conference, 540 S Geyer Rd, Saint Louis, MO 63122-5933
Personnel: Editor-Rebecca Bower
Editorial Description: For women brass instrument players.
General Info: Quarterly

Newsletter for Us

Publishing Co: United Serpents, PO Box 8915, Columbia, SC 29202-8915; Title Tel # (803) 254-2708
General Info: Annually, 6 pages
Circulation: Total-175

North Carolina Music Teacher   *Association*

Publishing Co: North Carolina Music Teachers Assn., Univ. Of North Carolina, Dept., Chapel Hill, NC 27599-0001; Title Tel # (919) 932-1096

Notes
See: COLLEGE STUDENT

Notes A Tempo   *Association*   CPM: $107

Publishing Co: West Virginia Music Educators Assn., Inc. Hall of Fine Arts, West Liberty State College, West Liberty, WV 26074-0335; Title Tel # (304) 336-8263 Title Fax # (304) 336-8285
Personnel: Editor-Edward Wolf
Editorial Description: Music and music education with emphasis on West Virginia.
General Info: Yr. Est. 1950, Monthly, Trim Size-8½ x 11, Web press, 10 pages, ISSN: 0029-3946, 4% ads, No Color
Subscriptions: Indv. $3
Circulation: Total-1,300
Advertising: $140. Accepts Inserts.
Printing Co: Lydic Printing Co., 33 Springfield Ave, Washington, PA 15301-5298 Tel # (412) 225-4120

Notes from the Songwriters Showcase   *Consumer*

Publishing Co: Notes from the Songwriters Showcase, PO Box 8098, 600 Franklin Ave., Garden City, NY 11530; Title Tel # (516) 572-7250 Title Fax # (516) 572-7497
Editorial Description: Insight of great American sogwriters into the creative process as well as interesting anecdotes behind the songs.
General Info: Monthly
Subscriptions: Indv. $10

Oak Ridge Boys Intl. Team Spirit

Publishing Co: Oak Ridge Boys Intl. Fan Club, 329 Rockland Rd, Hendersonville, TN 37075-3423; Title Tel # (615) 824-4924 Title Fax # (615) 822-7078
Personnel: Publisher, Editor, Production Mgr.-Kathy Harris, Circ. Mgr., Adv. Dir., Promotion Dir.-Linda Kirkpatrick
Editorial Description: Current news & photos pertaining only to the music group The Oak Ridge Boys & its members.
General Info: (Formerly Oak Ridge Boys), Yr. Est. 1976, Quarterly, Trim Size-8½ x 11, Letrpr. press, 4 pages, 2 Color, Coated
Circulation: (80% controlled), Total-15,000, International-250
Advertising: Inquire for rates. Accepts Inserts.

Opera America Newsline   *Business, Association*   CPM: $86

Publishing Co: Opera America, 1156 15th St. NW, Siute #810, Washington, DC 20005-1704 Tel # (202) 347-9262; Title Tel # (202) 293-4466 Title Fax # (202) 393-0735
Personnel: Editor-Arthur R. Smith
Editorial Description: A compendium of information from a variety of sources, including professional opera companies, Congress, the NEA, the American Arts Alliance, & other arts organizations. Covers opera company activities, legislation,non-profit & arts management issues, publications and conferences.
General Info: (Formerly Intercompany Announcements), Yr. Est. 1971, 10x/yr., Trim Size-8½ x 11, Sheetfed press, 32 pages, ISSN: 1062-7243, Color-cover, Coated, Saddle-stitched
Subscriptions: Free With Membership
Acquistions: Publication Bought, Publication Sold
Circulation: Total-2,900
Advertising: $250.
List Rental: Actives: $50/M

The Opera Journal

Publishing Co: National Opera Association, Dept of Music Univ. of Nevada, 4505 Maryland Pky., Las Vegas, NV 89154-5025; Title Tel # (702) 895-1665 Title Fax # (702) 895-4239
Personnel: Editor-Carol Kimball
Editorial Description: Opera & organizational information; members activities, opportunities for members & reports.
General Info: (Formerly National Opera Association Newsletter), Yr. Est. 1977, Quarterly, Web press, 16 pages, 3% ads, No Color
Subscriptions: Indv. $40, Inst. $50, Can. $56, For. $64
Circulation: (100% controlled), Total-575
Advertising: Inquire for rates.
List Rental: Actives: $50/M

Opera Scene
Consumer

Publishing Co: Opera Index, Inc., P.O. Box 492 Gracie Stn., New York, NY 10028
Tel # (212) 861-1651 Fax # (212) 861-1651; Title Tel # (212) 691-0552
Personnel: Editor-William Wells, Asst. Ed.-Roger Gross, Art Dir.-Grafton Moven
Editorial Description: Opera articles and reviews of performances, records and books, personal interviews.
General Info: (Formerly Opera Digest), Yr. Est. 1981, Bi-monthly, Offset press, 16 pages, No Color
Subscriptions: $2/copy
Circulation: Total-1,200
Advertising: Inquire for rates.

Operascene
Business, Consumer

Publishing Co: Opera Index, Inc., P.O. Box 492 Gracie Stn., New York, NY 10028;
Title Tel # (212) 861-1651 Title Fax # (212) 691-0552
Editorial Description: The Official Newsleter of Opera Index, Inc.
General Info: Monthly

Opus
Association   **CPM: $175**

Publishing Co: Saskatchewan Registered Music Teachers' Assn., 94 Green Meadow Rd., Regina, SK S4V 0A8 Canada Tel # (306) 789-8414 Fax # (306) 244-0580
Personnel: Editor-Janet McGonigle
General Info: (Formerly Saskatchewan Reg. Music Teachers' Assn Provincial Newsletter), Yr. Est. 1953, Quarterly, 8 pages
Subscriptions: Free With Membership
Circulation: Total-285
Advertising: $50.

Orchestra Canada/ Orchestres Canada
Consumer, Association   **CPM: $160**

Publishing Co: Assn. of Canadian Orchestras, 56 the Esplanade, #311, Toronto, ON M5E 1A7 Canada; Title Tel # (416) 366-8834 Title Fax # (416) 366-1780
Personnel: Editor-Ulla Colgrass
Editorial Description: Newsletter featuring information on action, advocacy, fundraising, marketing, education, & volunteers for supporting Canadian orchestras.
General Info: Yr. Est. 1973, Bi-monthly, 12 pages, 2 Color
Subscriptions: Indv. $22, Can. $22, For. $32
Circulation: Total-2,500
Advertising: $400.

P.M.O. Notes
Association

Publishing Co: Purdue Musical Organizations, Edward Elliott Hall of Music, Purdue Univ., W. Lafayette, IN 47906 Fax # (317) 496-1215; Title Tel # (317) 494-3941
Editorial Description: Alumni news magazine.
General Info: Yr. Est. 1968, Tri-annually, Trim Size-5½ x 8½, Sheetfed press, 28 pages, No Color, Newsprint
Subscriptions: Indv. $25
Circulation: Total-1,700
Printing Co: Lafayette Printing, 511 Fairy, Lafayette, IN 47901 Tel # (317) 423-2578

Pedal Steel Newsletter
Association

Publishing Co: Pedal Steel Guitar Assn., PO Box 248, Floral Park, NY 11002-0248
Personnel: Editor-Doug Mack, Adv. Dir.-Santo Equale
Editorial Description: Dedicated to the art of playing the pedal steel guitar and informing the public as to the merits of the instrument.
General Info: Yr. Est. 1973, 10x/yr., Trim Size-8½ x 11, Sheetfed press, 16 pages, Saddle-stitched
Subscriptions: Indv. $20, For. $27
Circulation: Total-1,200
Advertising: Inquire for rates.
Printing Co: Sir Speedy, 410 Jericho Tpke, New Hyde Park, NY 11040-4523 Tel # (516) 326-1000

Percussion News

Publishing Co: Percussive Arts Society, Inc., 701 NW Ferris Ave # 25, Lawton, OK 73507-5442; Title Tel # (405) 353-1955 Title Fax # (405) 353-1436
Personnel: Editor-Steve Beck
Editorial Description: Newsletter for membership activities.
General Info: Bi-monthly, Trim Size-11.5 x 14, Web press, 20 pages, Color, Newsprint, Other
Subscriptions: Indv. $40, Free With Membership
Circulation: Total-8,000, Readership-8,000
Advertising: Inquire for rates. Accepts Inserts.
List Rental: Rents Lists

Performance
See: ENTERTAINMENT

Peters Notes

Publishing Co: C.F. Peters Corp., 373 Park Ave., S., New York, NY 10016-8869;
Title Tel # (212) 686-4147
General Info: Quarterly

Phonolog

Publishing Co: Trade Service Publications, Inc., 10996 Torreyana Rd, San Diego, CA 92121-1105; Title Tel # (619) 457-5920
Personnel: Editor-Bonnie Dudley, Circ. Mgr.-Harry Weber, Adv. Dir.-Ed Nana, Promotion Dir.-Dan Henehan
Editorial Description: A catalog of tapes, records & CD's reporting new classical & rock releases.
General Info: Yr. Est. 1948, Weekly, Ind/Abs/Online: indexed, Looseleaf
Subscriptions: Indv. $468, Can. $522

Pi Kappa Lambda Newsletter
Association

Publishing Co: Pi Kappa Lamda Music Honor Society, Northwestern U. Music School, 711 Elgin Rd., Evanston, IL 60208-0001 Tel # (700) 491-5737; Title Tel # (708) 491-5737
Personnel: Editor-Lilias Circle
Editorial Description: An informational newsletter for members of Pi Kappa Lambda Music Honor Society.
General Info: Semi-annually, Trim Size-8½ x 11, 3 pages, Color
Circulation: (100% controlled), Total-8,500
Printing Co: The Printed Word, 827 Chicago Ave, Evanston, IL 60202-2307 Tel # (708) 328-1511

Pittsburgh Musician Magazine

Publishing Co: Skynote Publishing, 32510 Old Frankstown Road, Pittsburgh, PA 15239-2909; Title Tel # (412) 621-2209
Personnel: Publisher, Editor-Dennis Huber
Editorial Description: Entertainment & exhibitor contacts for major outdoor events-Mid Atlantic centennials, show production booking talent, opportunities.
General Info: (Formerly Fest Directory), Yr. Est. 1983, Quarterly, Trim Size-8½ x 11, Sheetfed press, 6 pages
Subscriptions: Indv. $20, $5/copy
Circulation: Total-1,200
List Rental: Actives: $60/M
Printing Co: University of Pittsburgh Central, Pittsburg, PA 15260 Tel # (412) 624-4141

Poco A Poco
Association

Publishing Co: Manhattan School of Music, 120 Claremont Ave, New York, NY 10027-4698; Title Tel # (212) 749-2802
Personnel: Publisher-Leslie Goldman, Editor-Victor Kioulaphides
Editorial Description: News of musical events, faculty, students, alumni of Manhattan School of Music.
General Info: Yr. Est. 1969, Weekly, Trim Size-8½ x 11, Offset press, 7 pages, No Color
Subscriptions: Free
Circulation: Total-1,200

Prelude, Fugue & Riffs
Consumer, Association

Publishing Co: Leonard Bernstein Society, 25 Central Park W Apt 1y, New York, NY 10023-7212; Title Tel # (212) 315-0643
Editorial Description: For fans of Leonard Bernstein.
General Info: Quarterly, Trim Size-8½ x 11, No Color

Producer Report
Business

Publishing Co: Mojave Music, Inc., 115 S. Topanga Canyon Blvd., Ste. 114, Topanga, CA 90290; Title Tel # (310) 455-0888 Title Fax # (310) 455-0894
Personnel: Publisher, Editor-Pat Nelson
Editorial Description: Producer Report covers record producer activity.
General Info: Yr. Est. 1993, Bi-weekly, 7 pages, ISSN: 1068-5391
Subscriptions: Indv. $500, For. $640

Promotional Programming
See: BROADCASTING

Quodlibet
Consumer, Association

Publishing Co: Intercollegiate Music Council, Inc., Wabash College, Dept of Music, Crawfordsville, IN 47933; Title Tel # (317) 364-4398
Personnel: Editor-Carl Stam
General Info: Yr. Est. 1954, Trim Size-8½ x 11, Sheetfed press, 16 pages, ISSN: 0885-9442, 4% ads, No Color, Matte, Saddle-stitched
List Rental: Rents Lists

ROS Bulletin
See: MUSEUM PUBLICATIONS

RPM: Review of Popular Music

Publishing Co: International Association for Study of Popular Music, SUNY/Dept. Of Music, Stony Brook, NY 11794-0001; Title Tel # (516) 689-6000
Personnel: Publisher, Editor-William Straw
Editorial Description: Covers association activities.
General Info: Yr. Est. 1986, Semi-annually, Trim Size-8½ x 11, 10 pages
Subscriptions: Indv. $35, Inst. $35
Circulation: Total-400

RTS Music Gazette

Publishing Co: RTS, PO Box 93897, Las Vegas, NV 89193-3897; Title Tel # (702) 896-1300
Personnel: Editor-I. Nii
Editorial Description: Newsletter about film music, collector soundtracks.
General Info: Yr. Est. 1973, Bi-monthly, Sheetfed press, 10 pages, No Color
Subscriptions: Indv. $25, Inst. $10, Can. $25, For. $35
Circulation: Total-500
List Rental: Actives: $25/M

Rag Times
Association

Publishing Co: Maple Leaf Club, 15222 Ricky Ct., Grass Valley, CA 95459
Personnel: Editor-Richard Zimmerman
Editorial Description: Devoted to the preservation of classic ragtime, past and present.
General Info: Yr. Est. 1967, Bi-monthly, Trim Size-8½ x 11, Sheetfed press, 10 pages, ISSN: 0090-4570, No Color, Newsprint
Subscriptions: Indv. $17, $2/copy
Circulation: Total-550
Advertising: Inquire for rates.

Record Research

Publishing Co: Record Research, 65 Grand Ave, Brooklyn, NY 11205-2593
Personnel: Editor-Len Kunstadt
Editorial Description: The magazine of record statistics and information.
General Info: Yr. Est. 1955, Bi-monthly
Subscriptions: Indv. $4

Records of Early English Drama Newsletter
See: LITERATURE & LINGUISTICS

Remember That Song
Consumer

Publishing Co: Remember That Song, 5623 N 64th Ave, Glendale, AZ 85301-5610
Tel # (602) 931-2835; Title Tel # (302) 435-2136
Personnel: Publisher, Editor, Circ. Mgr., Production Mgr., Production Mgr., Adv. Dir., Art Dir., Mktg. Dir., Promotion Dir.-Lois Cordrey
Editorial Description: Vintage sheet music collectors newsletter, interesting member written articles, illustrated old music reprints, buy-sell-trade-find music in world-spanning collections, music of interest 1850-1950.
General Info: Yr. Est. 1981, Monthly, Trim Size-7 x 8, Offset press, 24 pages, ISSN: 0889-8790, Other
Subscriptions: Indv. $17, Can. $19, For. $25
Circulation: Total-500
Advertising: Inquire for rates. Accepts Inserts.
List Rental: Rents Lists
Printing Co: Mail Box Services, 5821 N 67th Ave, Glendale, AZ 85301-8215 Tel # (602) 842-0033

Rhythm & Blues Foundation News
Consumer, Association

Publishing Co: Rhythm & Blues Foundation, 14th & Constitution Ave, NW, Rm. 4603, Mrc 657, Washington, DC 20560-0001 Tel # (202) 357-1654
Personnel: Editor in Chief-Suzan Jenkins
Editorial Description: News and information on rhythm and blues music.
General Info: Quarterly, Trim Size-8½ x 11, 12 pages, 2 Color

Rock & Rap Confidential
Consumer

Publishing Co: Rock & Rap Confidential, PO Box 341305, Los Angeles, CA 90034
Editorial Description: Filled with the latest gossip, politics, trends, and reviews.
General Info: Irregular, 8 pages

Rock & Roll Confidential
Consumer

Publishing Co: Rock & Roll Confidential, PO Box 341305, Los Angeles, CA 90034-9305
Personnel: Editor-Dave Marsh
Editorial Description: Exposes profit-making concerns and aims of the music industry.
General Info: Yr. Est. 1983, Monthly
Subscriptions: Indv. $24
Circulation: Total-6,500

Rockingchair
Consumer

Publishing Co: Cupola Productions, 966 N Randolph St, Philadelphia, PA 19123-1408;
Title Tel # (215) 925-6169
Personnel: Publisher-Stanley Nodvik, Editor-John Politis, Adv. Dir.-George Kiva
Editorial Description: A review newsletter for popular music fans & librarians who buy records.
General Info: Yr. Est. 1977, Monthly, Trim Size-6 x 8½, Offset press, 24 pages, ISSN: 0146-1885, No Color
Subscriptions: Indv. $25, $2/copy
Circulation: Total-579

SMEA Newsletter
See: EDUCATION

Sacred Music News & Review
Business

Publishing Co: TCMR Communications, PO Box 1179, Grapevine, TX 76099-1179;
Title Tel # (817) 488-0141 Title Fax # (817) 481-4191
Personnel: Publisher-William Rayborn, Editor-Timothy Sharp, Adv. Dir.-Deana Yarcott
Editorial Description: Product news and reviews of interest to church music directors performing traditional, non-evangelical music.
General Info: Yr. Est. 1992, Monthly, Trim Size-8½ x 11, 8 pages
Subscriptions: Indv. $40, Can. $45, For. $45, $3/copy
Circulation: Total-3,000
Advertising: Inquire for rates. Accepts Inserts.
List Rental: List Management Co.: Manager: Deana Yarcott; Response Unlimited, c/o The Old Plantation, Rte. 5, Box 251, Waynesboro, VA 22980-9111 Tel # (703) 943-6721, Fax # (703) 943-0841, Actives: 3,112, $70/M, Expires: $70/M

Saenger-Zeitung

Publishing Co: Federation of Workers Singing Socs. of USA, 1729 Springfield Ave, Maplewood, NJ 07040-2914
Personnel: Editor-Harold W. Tausch
General Info: Yr. Est. 1965, Monthly
Advertising: Inquire for rates.

Sanger-Hilsen/Singers Greetings
See: ETHNIC

Saskatchewan Band Assn. Newsletter

Publishing Co: Saskatchewan Band Assn., 1840 McIntyre St., Regina, SK S4P 2P9 Canada
Tel # (306) 652-2263; Title Tel # (306) 522-2263 Title Fax # (306) 565-2177
General Info: Quarterly

Saskatchewan Choral Federation Bulletin
Association

Publishing Co: Saskatchewan Choral Federation, 1870 Lorne St., Regina, SK S4P 2L7 Canada;
Title Tel # (306) 780-9230 Title Fax # (306) 781-6021
Personnel: Publisher-Yars Lozowchuk, Editor-Merle Bintner
General Info: Yr. Est. 1980, Bi-monthly, Trim Size-8½ x 11, Desktop press, 8 pages
Subscriptions: Free With Membership
Circulation: Total-1,550
Printing Co: Print 1, 2500 11th Ave., Regina, SK S4P 0K5 Canada Tel # (306) 757-0933, Fax # (306) 569-8151

Sassafras
See: SOCIAL SERVICES & WELFARE

Schirmer/News

Publishing Co: G. Schirmer Inc. /Assn. Music Publishers, Inc., 257 Park Ave. S., New York, NY 10011 Fax # (212) 254-2013; Title Tel # (212) 254-2100 Title Fax # (201) 254-2013
Personnel: Editor-Karen Campbell, Production Mgr.-Ed Matthew
Editorial Description: Newsletter of G.chirmer Inc. and Associated Music Publishers Inc. . Contains news of interest to orchestras, opera and ballet companies and ensembles, colleges, conductors, performers, record companies, radio stations and music libraries.
General Info: Semi-annually

Shake Rattle & Roll
Consumer

Publishing Co: Moonbeam Press, 1725 B Madison #3, Memphis, TN 38104;
Title Tel # (901) 276-1770
Personnel: Editor-Steve Walker
Editorial Description: Covers the Memphis music scene.
General Info: Bi-monthly

Sing! Jr.
Business, Consumer

Publishing Co: TCMR Communications, PO Box 1179, Grapevine, TX 76099-1179;
Title Tel # (817) 488-0141 Title Fax # (817) 481-4191
Personnel: Publisher, Editor-William Rayborn, Adv. Dir.-Deana Yarcott
Editorial Description: Contains information on products and services of particular interest to to church music directors as well as music industry news.
General Info: (Formerly Church Music Report, The), Monthly
Subscriptions: Indv. $40, Can. $45, For. $45, $3/copy
Circulation: Total-6,000
Advertising: Inquire for rates. Accepts Inserts.
List Rental: List Management Co.: Manager: Deana Yarcott; Response Unlimited, c/o The Old Plantation, Rte. 5, Box 251, Waynesboro, VA 22980-9111 Tel # (703) 943-6721, Fax # (703) 943-0841, Actives: 6,000, $80/M, Expires: $70/M

Slur

Publishing Co: John R. Scarano Jr, 3024 Duckworth Dr, Santoga, PA 19464
Editorial Description: A quite silly, featuring juvenile comments about sex and music.
General Info: Trim Size-5 x 7, 20 pages
Subscriptions: Indv. $1

Song Sheet, The
Consumer, Association

Publishing Co: Natl. Sheet Music Society, Inc., 1597 Fair Park Ave, Los Angeles, CA 90041-2255
Personnel: Editor-Linda Siegel
Editorial Description: From the National Sheet Music Society.
General Info: Monthly, Trim Size-8½ x 11, 2 Color

Song of Zion
Consumer

Publishing Co: Jackman Music Corp., PO Box 1900, Orem, UT 84059-1900;
Title Tel # (801) 225-0859
Personnel: Editor-Jerry Jackman
Editorial Description: Articles of interest to Mormon musicians & families.
General Info: Yr. Est. 1980, Bi-monthly, Trim Size-8½ x 11, Web press, 8 pages, ISSN: 0273-2920, 5% ads, 2 Color, Newsprint, Saddle-stitched
Subscriptions: Free To Qualified Recipient
Circulation: Total-17,000

Songwriters & Lyricist Club Newsletter

Publishing Co: Songwriters Club, C/O Robert Makinson, Box 023304, Brooklyn, NY 11202-0066; Title Tel # (718) 855-5057
Personnel: Editor-Robert Makinson
Editorial Description: For songwriters and lyricists.
General Info: (Formerly Lyric & Melody Newsletter), Semi-annually
Subscriptions: Indv. $30, $4/copy
Advertising: Inquire for rates.

Songwriters Guild News   *Association*

Publishing Co: Sponsor-Songwriters Guild Foundation, The, Songwriters Guild of America, 1500 Harbor Blvd., Weehawken, NJ 07087-6732; Title Tel # (201) 867-7603 Title Fax # (201) 768-9048
Personnel: Publisher, Editor-George Wurzbach
Editorial Description: Updating of guild activities and services (workshops, legislative lobbying, etc.).
General Info: (Formerly AGAC), Semi-annually, Trim Size-8½ x 11, 16 pages, 1% ads, No Color
Circulation: Total-5,500
Advertising: Inquire for rates.
Printing Co: Marquee Venture, 404 E. 14th St., New York, NY 10009

Songwriter's Monthly   *Consumer*

Publishing Co: Songwriter's Monthly, 322 Eastwood Avenue, Feasterville, PA 19053; Title Tel # (215) 953-0952 Title Fax # (215) 953-0952
Editorial Description: Information and tips for those trying to break into the songwriting industry.
General Info: Monthly
Subscriptions: Can. $25, For. $35, $20/copy
Advertising: $130.

Southeastern Historical Keyboard Society Newsletter   *Consumer, Association*

Publishing Co: Southeastern Historical Keyboard Society, PO Box 32022, Charlotte, NC 28232-2022 Tel # (704) 334-3468 Fax # (704) 334-3468
Personnel: Editor-Karen Hite Jacob
Editorial Description: Covers news and information of Society related to music before 1860.
General Info: Yr. Est. 1981, Semi-annually
Circulation: Total-275
Advertising: Inquire for rates.

Stanza

Publishing Co: Hymn Society in the United States & Canada, Texas Christian Univ., PO Box 30854, Fort Worth, TX 76129-0001; Title Tel # (817) 921-7608 Title Fax # (817) 921-7333
Personnel: Editor, Circ. Mgr.-W. Thomas Smith, Art Dir.-David Schaap
Editorial Description: Newsletter of practical information and news related to hymns.
General Info: Yr. Est. 1978, Semi-annually, Trim Size-8½ x 11, Offset press, 4 pages, No Color, Newsprint
Circulation: (100% controlled), Total-3,500
List Rental: Rents Lists

Stardift
See: POETRY & CREATIVE WRITING

Stearns Newsletter, The   *Consumer, Association*

Publishing Co: The Stearns Collection of Musical Instruments, School of Music, Univ. of Michigan, Ann Arbor, MI 48109; Title Tel # (313) 763-4389 Title Fax # (313) 763-5047
Personnel: Editor-William Malm
Editorial Description: News about musical instruments and Stearns events.
General Info: Yr. Est. 1986, Tri-annually, Offset press, 4 pages, Coated
Subscriptions: Indv. $30, Inst. $30, Free With Membership
Circulation: Total-300
Printing Co: Quality Copy Ctr., 3937 Jackson Ave, Ann Arbor, MI 48103-1823 Tel # (313) 769-5462, Fax # (312) 769-5467

Steel Guitar Intl. Newsletter   **CPM: $55**

Publishing Co: International Steel Guitar Convention, 9535 Midland Blvd, Saint Louis, MO 63114-3314; Title Tel # (314) 427-7794 Title Fax # (314) 427-0516
Personnel: Editor-DeWitt Scott, Sr.
Editorial Description: Steel guitar information, gossip, news, instruction, & articles.
General Info: Quarterly, 32 pages, No Color, Saddle-stitched
Subscriptions: Indv. $20, Can. $25, For. $25, $2/copy
Circulation: Total-1,800
Advertising: $100.
Printing Co: Krawll Printing, 2632 Woodson Rd, Saint Louis, MO 63114-4899 Tel # (314) 428-1234

String Instrument Craftsman   *Business, Consumer*

Publishing Co: PEN/LENS Press, 142 N Milpitas Blvd #280, Milpitas, CA 95035-4401; Title Tel # (408) 946-3282
Personnel: Publisher, Editor-Jim Hatlo
Editorial Description: Devoted to the string instrument craftsman & repair specialist. Techniques, materials, fixtures and tools. Coverage of both traditional and electric instruments.
General Info: Yr. Est. 1988, Bi-monthly, ISSN: 1044-3258
Subscriptions: Indv. $13, For. $28, $4/copy
Circulation: Total-2,750
Advertising: Inquire for rates.
List Rental: Rents Lists

Subway Entertainment Guide   *Consumer*

Publishing Co: F.M. Future Music, P.O. Box 4073, Hamden, CT 06514
Editorial Description: Music, film, and video news distributed at Subway fast food restaurants.
General Info: Monthly
Subscriptions: Free In Designated Area

Symphonium   *Business, Association*

Publishing Co: Symphonium, 1349 N Sheridan Ave, Pittsburgh, PA 15206-1759
Editorial Description: Newsletter for and about the Black symphony musician.
General Info: Yr. Est. 1988, Quarterly

Tempo

Publishing Co: Univ. of Miami University Center, University Center, Box 248121, Coral Gables, FL 33124
General Info: Monthly
Subscriptions: Indv. $3
Circulation: Total-7,000
Advertising: Inquire for rates.

Tempo

Publishing Co: New Jersey Music Educators Assn., Morris Hills High School, Rockaway, NJ 07866; Title Tel # (201) 627-9890
Personnel: Editor-Herman L. Dash, Adv. Dir.-Charles K. Pickering
General Info: Yr. Est. 1938
Subscriptions: Indv. $3, $1/copy
Circulation: Total-3,250
Advertising: Inquire for rates.

Third Street Music School Settlement Bulletin

Publishing Co: Third Street Music School Settlement, 235 E. 11th St., New York, NY 10003-7398; Title Tel # (212) 777-3240
Personnel: Publisher, Editor-Sally Mazor
Editorial Description: News of school events and calendar.
General Info: Yr. Est. 1980, Monthly, 2 pages, Color
Circulation: Total-6,000

Toronto Children's Chorus

Publishing Co: Toronto Children's Chorus, 931 College St., Toronto, ON M6H 1A1 Canada; Title Tel # (416) 516-3722 Title Fax # (416) 516-3724
Editorial Description: Covers news & events relating to the children's chorus.
General Info: Yr. Est. 1980, Tri-annually, ISSN: 0844-5818

Transoniq Hacker

Publishing Co: Transoniq Hacker, 1402 SW Upland Dr, Portland, OR 97221-2649; Title Tel # (503) 227-6848 Title Fax # (503) 227-6848
Personnel: Publisher, Circ. Mgr.-Eric Geislinger, Editor, Adv. Dir.-Jane Talisman
Editorial Description: User's newsletter for music digital samplers & synthesizers.
General Info: Yr. Est. 1985, Monthly, Web press, 36 pages, 1% ads, Color, Coated
Subscriptions: Indv. $23, $2/copy
Circulation: Total-5,000
Printing Co: Times-Litho, 1829 Pacific Ave., PO Box 7, Forest Grove, OR 97116-2333 Tel # (503) 359-0300, Fax # (503) 357-3754

Traverso   *Consumer, Association*

Publishing Co: Folkers & Powell, Rr 3 Box 56, Hudson, NY 12534-9508
Personnel: Editor-Ardal Powell
Editorial Description: For baroque flutists.
General Info: Quarterly, ISSN: 1041-7494
Subscriptions: Indv. $12, Can. $12, For. $15, $4/copy

Trebas Track
See: SOUND ENGINEERING

Treble Clef   *Association*

Publishing Co: Philadelphia Clef Club of the Performing Arts, 1231 N. Broad Street, Suite 209, Philadelphia, PA 19122
Editorial Description: Covers the club's performing arts/jazz news.
General Info: Quarterly

Tri-Son, News

Publishing Co: Tri-Son, Inc., PO Box 40328, Nashville, TN 37204-0328; Title Tel # (615) 371-9596 Title Fax # (615) 371-9597
Personnel: Circ. Mgr.-Kay Johnson, Publisher, Editor, Adv. Dir.-Loudilla Johnson, Art Dir.-Loretta Johnson
Editorial Description: Country music news, tour dates of artists (itineraries) radio stations, etc.
General Info: Yr. Est. 1963, Monthly, Trim Size-8½ x 11, Offset press, 8 pages, No Color
Subscriptions: Indv. $15, Can. $20, $1/copy
Circulation: Total-1,200

Turok's Choice
Business, Consumer

Publishing Co: Turok's Choice, Box 202, Old Chelsea Station, New York, NY 10113-0202; Title Tel # (212) 691-9229
Personnel: Publisher, Editor-Paul Turok
Editorial Description: Concise, informed criticism of classical recordings on both major & minor labels.
General Info: Yr. Est. 1990, 11x/yr., 4 pages, ISSN: 1052-3170, No Color
Subscriptions: Indv. $14, Can. $17, For. $20, $2/copy
Circulation: Readership-750
Advertising: Inquire for rates.

Ultimate Early Childhood Music Resource
See: EDUCATION

Upbeat: Youth Orchestra Newsletter

Publishing Co: American Symphony Orchestra League, 777 14th St NW Ste 500, Washington, DC 20005-3201
General Info: Quarterly
Circulation: Total-1,500

Update: New Music Seminar
Consumer

Publishing Co: New Music Seminar, 332 Bleecker St # G-29, New York, NY 10014-2980; Title Tel # (212) 473-4343
Editorial Description: New Music Seminar is an annual meeting of the intl. music business & showcase of music groups.
General Info: Semi-annually

Verdi Newsletter
Scholarly, Association

Publishing Co: American Institute for Verdi Studies, N.Y.U. Dept. of Music, 24 Waverly Pl., Rm. 268, New York, NY 10003-6687 Tel # (212) 998-8305; Title Tel # (212) 998-2587 Title Fax # (212) 995-4147
Personnel: Editor-Martin Chusid
General Info: (Formerly AIVS Newsletter), Yr. Est. 1976, Annually, Trim Size-8 x 11, Web press, 32 pages, No Color
Subscriptions: Indv. $15, Inst. $15, Can. $15, For. $15, $15/copy
Circulation: Total-500
Printing Co: APD Printing, 1325 Macklind Avenue, St. Louis, MD 63110 Tel # (313) 662-3291, Fax # (313) 662-1667

Videolog

Publishing Co: Trade Service Publications, Inc., 10996 Torreyana Rd, San Diego, CA 92121-1105; Title Tel # (619) 457-5920
Personnel: Editor-Bonnie Dudley, Circ. Mgr.-Harry Weber, Adv. Dir.-Ed Nava, Promotion Dir.-Dan Henehan
Editorial Description: Lists all known video films currently available, indexed & classified bi-weekly.
General Info: Yr. Est. 1948, Weekly, Web press, 90 pages, Ind/Abs/Online: indexed, No Color, Looseleaf
Subscriptions: Indv. $240, Can. $270
Advertising: Accepts Inserts.

Viol.

Publishing Co: DeKalb Musicians Supply Co., 115 Clairemont Ave., Decatur, GA 30030-2502; Title Tel # (404) 377-3419
General Info: Yr. Est. 1975, 5x/yr.
Subscriptions: Indv. $4

Viola da Gamba News
Association

Publishing Co: Viola da Gamba Soc. of America, 1308 Jackson Ave, Charleston, IL 61920-2242; Title Tel # (217) 348-8260
General Info: Quarterly

Viola d'Amore Society of America-Newsletter

Publishing Co: Viola d'Amore Society of America, 3923 47th St, Sunnyside, NY 11104-1419; Title Tel # (718) 729-3138
Personnel: Editor-Myron Rosenblum, Promotion Dir.-Daniel Thomason
Editorial Description: Information relating to history, performance, literature of the viola d'amore.
General Info: Yr. Est. 1977, Semi-annually, Sheetfed press, 15 pages, No Color
Subscriptions: Indv. $15, For. $15
Circulation: Total-200
Advertising: Inquire for rates.

Vitaphone News
Scholarly   CPM: $149

Publishing Co: The Vitaphone Project, 5 Meade Court, Piscataway, NJ 08854; Title Tel # (908) 463-8521 Title Fax # (908) 336-2603
Personnel: Editor, Adv. Dir.-David Goldenberg
Editorial Description: Updates readers on activities related to early sound-on-disc film preservation, 1925-30.
General Info: Yr. Est. 1991, Quarterly, Trim Size-8½ x 11, 8 pages, No Color, Recycled, Other
Subscriptions: Indv. $5
Circulation: Total-335, Readership-1,500
Advertising: $50.

Vocals
Business, Consumer

Publishing Co: PEN/LENS Press, 142 N Milpitas Blvd #280, Milpitas, CA 95035-4401; Title Tel # (408) 946-3282
Personnel: Publisher, Editor-Jim Hatlo
Editorial Description: Covering musicianship and technique for singers in all musical styles.
General Info: Bi-monthly
Subscriptions: Indv. $20, For. $28, $4/copy
Circulation: Total-3,250
Advertising: Inquire for rates.
List Rental: Rents Lists

Voice of Chorus America, The
Association   CPM: $66

Publishing Co: Chorus America, 1811 Chestnut St., Ste 401, Philadelphia, PA 19103-3721 Fax # (215) 563-2131; Title Tel # (215) 563-2430 Title Fax # (215) 563-2431
Personnel: Editor-Fred Leise, Adv. Dir.-Karen Ricther
Editorial Description: Information about national service organization for professional, independent and orchestral choruses.
General Info: (Formerly Voice), Yr. Est. 1977, Quarterly, Trim Size-8½ x 11, 28 pages, ISSN: 1074-0805, No Color
Subscriptions: Inst. $30, Can. $30, For. $35, Free With Membership
Circulation: Total-7,500
Advertising: $500.
List Rental: List Management Co.: Manager: Melvin R. Jones; Chorus America, 1811 Chestnut Street, Ste 401, Philadelplhia, PA 19103 Tel # (215) 563-2430, Fax # (215) 563-2431, Actives: 7,500

Voice Coil Newsletter
See: SOUND ENGINEERING

Wagner News

Publishing Co: Wagner Society of America, PO Box A3229, Chicago, IL 60690-3229
Personnel: Editor-Gerald Zimmerman
General Info: Yr. Est. 1974, 8x/yr.
Circulation: Total-175

Who: The Relay, The
Consumer

Publishing Co: Relay, Box 1670, Canal St. Station, New York, NY 10013-1670; Title Tel # (212) 732-0916
Personnel: Circ. Dir.-Shelby Gord, Art Dir.-Torben Nielsen, Publisher, Editor, Production Mgr., Adv. Dir., Promotion Dir.-Diane Hatz
Editorial Description: A fanzine devoted to the rock band The Who, and individual members. Issues consist of interviews, reviews, up-to-date news, retrospectives, trade sections, pen-pal listings, and much more. The Relay is published by fans for fans. Contributions are welcome.
General Info: Yr. Est. 1982, Semi-annually, 24 pages, No Color, Matte
Subscriptions: $3/copy

Willem Mengelberg Society Newsletter
Association

Publishing Co: Willem Mengelberg Society, 1408A Marshall St, Manitowoc, WI 54220-5140
Personnel: Publisher, Editor-Ronald Klett
Editorial Description: All aspects of the life, recordings, & concerts of the Dutch orchestral & choral conductor.
General Info: Yr. Est. 1970, Quarterly, Trim Size-8½ x 11, Offset press, 4 pages, ISSN: 1051-0788, No Color
Subscriptions: Indv. $7, Inst. $8, Can. $8, For. $9

Woods Hole Folk Music Society Newsletter
Consumer

Publishing Co: Woods Hole Folk Music Society, 174 Lake Shore Dr, East Falmouth, MA 02536-4792; Title Tel # (508) 540-0320
Editorial Description: News on folk performers, local folk festivals, club business and local folk radio.
General Info: Yr. Est. 1975, Irregular

Words About Music
Association

Publishing Co: National Academy of Pop Music, 885 2nd Ave Fl 26, New York, NY 10017-2201; Title Tel # (212) 319-1444
Editorial Description: Provides activities and service information for the national information for the national academy of popular music, custodian of the songwriter's Hall of Fame.
General Info: Yr. Est. 1969, Quarterly, Trim Size-8½ x 11, Letrpr. press, 6 pages, No Color
Circulation: Total-1,000
Printing Co: The Adams Group, 225 Varick Street, New York, NY 10014

Working Class Hero Beatles Club, The
See: FAN MAGAZINES-MOVIE, RADIO, TV

MYSTERY & HORROR

Afraid
Business, Consumer

Publishing Co: Afraid, 857 N Oxford Ave # 4, Los Angeles, CA 90029-3758
Editorial Description: Newsletter with advice and information for those in the horror story writing industry.
General Info: Monthly
Subscriptions: Indv. $25

Billington's Stock Focus II
See: INVESTMENT

Deadly Serious
Business, Scholarly

Publishing Co: Deadly Serious Press, PO Box 1045, Cooper Station, New York, NY 10276-1045; Title Tel # (212) 473-5723
Personnel: Publisher, Editor-Sharon Villines
Editorial Description: References for writers of mystery, detective and crime fiction.
General Info: Yr. Est. 1993, Bi-monthly, Trim Size-8½ x 11, Offset press, 8 pages, ISSN: 1070-0390, Matte
Subscriptions: Indv. $25, Can. $30, For. $35, $4/copy
Circulation: Total-700

Dracula News Journal
Association

Publishing Co: Dracula Press, 29 Washington Mews, New York, NY 10003-6608; Title Tel # (212) 982-6754
Personnel: Publisher-Dr. Jeanne Youngson, Editor-James Martin, Art Dir.-Wing Lee
Editorial Description: Poetry, showcase for writers, monographs, contests. We use members works only. 100% vampire material.
General Info: (Formerly COFC Newsletter Journal), Yr. Est. 1975, Quarterly, Trim Size-8½ x 8½, Offset press, 20 pages, Color-cover
Subscriptions: $4/copy
Circulation: Total-3,400
Advertising: Inquire for rates.

Genre Press Digest
See: SCIENCE FICTION & FANTASY

Murder is Academic
See: EDUCATION

Mystery Collectors' Bookline
Consumer

Publishing Co: BookLine Publishing Company, PO Box 150119, San Rafael, CA 94915; Title Tel # (415) 457-5463
Editorial Description: A newsletter for collectors of mystery and suspense fiction.
General Info: Yr. Est. 1995, 10x/yr.
Subscriptions: Indv. $75

Mystery Notebook
Consumer

Publishing Co: Stephen Wright, Box 1341, F.D.R. Station, New York, NY 10150-1341
Personnel: Publisher, Editor-Stephen Wright
Editorial Description: Essay-reviews on mystery and suspense literature.
General Info: Yr. Est. 1984, Quarterly, Trim Size-8½ x 11, Mimeo press, 16 pages, ISSN: 0740-8870
Subscriptions: $5/copy

New Jersey Graveline: Official Newsletter of the Garden Sate Horror Writers
Consumer

Publishing Co: Garden Sate Horror Writers, PO Box 696, Matawan, NJ 07747
Editorial Description: A newsletter for struggling New Jersey genre writers trying to make it in a tough market. Most valuable are their market listings.
General Info: Irregular

New Lovecraft Collector
Consumer

Publishing Co: Necronomicon Press, 101 Lockwood St, West Warwick, RI 02893-7622
Editorial Description: For collectors of HP Lovecraft's books and paraphanalia.
General Info: Quarterly, Trim Size-8½ x 11, No Color
Subscriptions: Indv. $5

Phantom of the Movies' VideoScope, The
See: TELEVISION & VIDEO

Scavenger's Newsletter
See: SCIENCE FICTION & FANTASY

Third Degree
Association

Publishing Co: Mystery Writers of America, Inc., 17 E. 47th St., 6th Fl., New York, NY 10017-1920; Title Tel # (212) 888-8171
Editorial Description: Focuses on MWA programs, speeches, publishing industry news, etc.
General Info: Yr. Est. 1946, 10x/yr., 8 pages
Subscriptions: Free With Membership
Circulation: Total-2,500

VRC Newsletter
Association

Publishing Co: Vampire Research Center, Box 252, Elmhurst, NY 11373
Editorial Description: Newsletter giving statistics on existing vampires.
General Info: Quarterly

Woman of Mystery
Consumer

Publishing Co: WOM'N, Box 1616, Canal St. Sta., New York, NY 10013-0869; Title Tel # (212) 226-3069
Personnel: Publisher, Editor-Amy Lubelski
Editorial Description: Annotates Agatha Christie novels in chronological order.
General Info: Yr. Est. 1986, Monthly, Trim Size-8½ x 11, Sheetfed press, 6 pages, ISSN: 1042-1491, No Color, Newsprint
Subscriptions: Indv. $30, $3/copy
Circulation: Total-600
Printing Co: Port City, 500 5th Ave Fl 1901, New York, NY 10110-0002 Tel # (212) 921-9166

NATURAL HISTORY

Academy Newsletter
See: MUSEUM PUBLICATIONS

American Paleontologist
See: GEOLOGY

Applied Orgonometry
See: CULTURE & HUMANITIES

B.C. Naturalist
Association CPM: $40

Publishing Co: Federation of British Columbia Nautralists, 321-1367 West Broadway, Vancouver, BC V6H 4A9 Canada; Title Tel # (604) 737-3057 Title Fax # (604) 738-7175
Personnel: Editor-Jude Grass
Editorial Description: Information about the outdoors and its preservation.
General Info: (Formerly Federation of British Columbia Naturalist Newsletter), Yr. Est. 1980, Quarterly, 32 pages, Newsprint
Subscriptions: Indv. $15
Circulation: Total-6,000
Advertising: $240.

Backyard Wildlife
Consumer CPM: $400

Publishing Co: Marcus Schneck & Associates, 1328 Chestnut St., #393, Emmaus, PA 18049; Title Tel # (610) 481-9452 Title Fax # (610) 481-9453
Personnel: Publisher, Editor-Marcus Schneck
Editorial Description: Developing, maintaining and enjoying a wildlife habitat in the backyard.
General Info: (Formerly Marcus Schneck & Associates), Yr. Est. 1993, Monthly, Trim Size-8½ x 11, Desktop press, 16 pages, ISSN: 1071-1961, No Color, Other, Other
Subscriptions: Indv. $30, Inst. $25, Can. $50, For. $50, $3/copy
Circulation: Total-500
Advertising: $200. Accepts Inserts.

Bulletin of the Global Volcanism Network
See: GEOPHYSICS

California Naturalist
Association

Publishing Co: Lupin Naturalist Club, PO Box 1274, Los Gatos, CA 95031-1274; Title Tel # (408) 353-2250
Personnel: Publisher-Molly Moore Sullivan
General Info: Quarterly
Subscriptions: Indv. $5
Circulation: Total-1,300

Connecticut Warbler
Consumer

Publishing Co: Connecticut Audubon Society, 2325 Burr St, Fairfield, CT 06430-1806; Title Tel # (203) 259-0416
Editorial Description: Covers Society news & natural history & environmental issues relating to the state of Connecticut.
General Info: Yr. Est. 1981, Quarterly

Conserve
See: ENVIRONMENT & ECOLOGY

Dawes Arboretum Newsletter
See: GARDENING & HORTICULTURE

Feuillets du Naturaliste

Publishing Co: Cercles Jeunes Naturalistes, 4101 rue Sherbrooke est, #124, Montreal, PQ H1X 2B2 Canada; Title Tel # (514) 252-3023
Personnel: Publisher-Therese Lanciault
Editorial Description: Study of nature on the elementary and secondary school level.
General Info: (Formerly Feuillets du Club), Yr. Est. 1970, Offset press, 4 pages, 2 Color, Looseleaf
Subscriptions: $1/copy
Circulation: Total-15,000
Printing Co: Regroupement Loisir Quebec, 4545 Pierre-de-Coubertin Ave., Montreal, PQ H1V 3R2 Canada Tel # (514) 252-3000

Fish & Wildlife Reference Service Newsletter
See: ENVIRONMENT & ECOLOGY

Forest Forum
See: FORESTRY

Guilfoyle Report
Business

Publishing Co: AG Editions, 41 Union Sq W Ste 523, New York, NY 10003-3208; Title Tel # (212) 929-0959 Title Fax # (212) 924-4796
Personnel: Editor-Ann Guilfoyle, Production Mgr.-Joanne Whitwell
Editorial Description: Marketing newsletter for natural history photographers. Researches publishers using such photography and lists current photo needs.
General Info: Yr. Est. 1982, 10x/yr.
Subscriptions: Indv. $125, For. $139, $5/copy
Printing Co: Admiral Photo Offset, 47 West St., New York, NY 10006 Tel # (212) 422-6848

Hawaiian Shell News
Association   **CPM: $390**

Publishing Co: Hawaiian Malacological Society, PO Box 22130, Honolulu, HI 96823-2130; Title Tel # (808) 734-3703
Personnel: Editor-Dwayne Minton, Circ. Mgr.-Ray McKinsey, Adv. Dir.-Olive Schoenberg
Editorial Description: Information on shells with emphasis on marine mollusca, shell collecting and collectors world-wide.
General Info: Yr. Est. 1952, Monthly, Trim Size-8$\frac{1}{2}$ x 11$\frac{1}{2}$, Offset press, 10 pages, ISSN: 0017-8624, Ind/Abs/Online: Bio.Abs., Color
Subscriptions: Indv. $25, Can. $31, For. $36, $1/copy
Circulation: (100% controlled), Total-1,600
Advertising: $625.
Printing Co: Fisher Printing Co., 919 Kekaulike St, Honolulu, HI 96817-5006 Tel # (808) 537-3966

Herbarium News
See: BOTANY

Illinois Natural History
Survey, Reports   *Association*

Publishing Co: Illinois Natural History Survey, Natural Resources Bldg., 607 E. Peabody, Champaign, IL 61820; Title Tel # (217) 333-6880 Title Fax # (217) 333-4949
Personnel: Editor-Charles Warwick
Editorial Description: Research in areas of aquatic biology, botany, economic entomology, entomology, ichthyology and wildlife research oriented to general public.
General Info: Yr. Est. 1962, Bi-monthly, Trim Size-8$\frac{1}{2}$ x 11, 8 pages, Coated, Saddle-stitched
Subscriptions: Free
Circulation: Total-2,200

Island Naturalist
Consumer, Association

Publishing Co: Natural History Society of Prince Edward Island, Box 2346, Charlottetown, PE C1A 8C1 Canada
Personnel: Editor-Dan MoAskill
Editorial Description: Information on how to conserve the flora and fauna of Prince Edward Island.
General Info: Yr. Est. 1974, Bi-monthly, Trim Size-8$\frac{1}{2}$ x 11, 16 pages, No Color
Subscriptions: Indv. $12, Can. $12
Circulation: Total-375

Jib Gems
See: MUSEUM PUBLICATIONS

Long Trail News, The
See: OUTDOORS

Mono Lake Newsletter
See: WATER SUPPLY, POWER & WASTE

Natural Science Newsletter
Consumer, Association

Publishing Co: Vermont Institute of Natural Science, Church Hill Rd., Woodstock, VT 05091; Title Tel # (802) 457-2779
Personnel: Editor-Sarah Laughlin
Editorial Description: Information for members.
General Info: Quarterly, No Color
Circulation: Total-6,000
Printing Co: Marus Printing Co., Hartland, VT 05048

Nature Views
Association

Publishing Co: Nature Saskatchewan, 206 - 1860 Lorne Street, Regina, SK S4P 2L7 Canada Fax # (306) 780-9263; Title Tel # (306) 780-9273 Title Fax # (306) 781-6021
Personnel: Editor-John Pollock
Editorial Description: Provincial natural history news, reports of meetings, field trips, environmental and conservation issues.
General Info: (Formerly Blue Jay News), Yr. Est. 1947, Quarterly, Trim Size-11 x 17, Web press, 12 pages, ISSN: 0581-8443, Color, Newsprint, Saddle-stitched
Subscriptions: Indv. $25, Inst. $25, Can. $25, For. $18, $1/copy
Advertising: $200.
Printing Co: Whitewood Press (Herald), Box 160, Whitewood, SK 5OG 5CO Canada Tel # (306) 735-2230, Fax # (306) 735-2899

New Hampshire Audubon
See: ORNITHOLOGY

Northbound
See: FORESTRY

Ohio Naturalist Newsletter, The
See: ENVIRONMENT & ECOLOGY

Pacific Seabird Group Bulletin
See: ORNITHOLOGY

Rotunda
See: MUSEUM PUBLICATIONS

Santa Barbara Museum of Natural History Museum Bulletin
See: MUSEUM PUBLICATIONS

Toronto Field Naturalist
Association

Publishing Co: Toronto Field Naturalists, 20 College St., #11, Toronto, ON M5G 1K2 Canada; Title Tel # (416) 968-6255
Editorial Description: Organization's activities, projects, news about projects.
General Info: Yr. Est. 1938, 8x/yr., Trim Size-8$\frac{1}{2}$ x 11, 30 pages, ISSN: 0820-636X, No Color, Recycled
Subscriptions: Indv. $25
Circulation: Total-1,500

Vancouver Aquascene
Aquarium Newsletter   *Association*

Publishing Co: Vancouver Public Aquarium Assn., Box 3232, Vancouver, BC V6B 3X8 Canada; Title Tel # (604) 685-3364
Personnel: Editor-Marissa Nichini
General Info: (Formerly Sea Pen), Yr. Est. 1956, 4x/yr., ISSN: 1203-1712
Subscriptions: Free With Membership
Circulation: Total-17,000, Readership-40,000

Winging It
See: ORNITHOLOGY

Wood Duck

Publishing Co: Hamilton Naturalists Club, Box 89052, Hamilton, ON L8S 4R5 Canada; Title Tel # (905) 634-3538
Personnel: Editor-Jean Stollard
General Info: Yr. Est. 1947, 9x/yr., Trim Size-8$\frac{1}{2}$ x 11, Mimeo press, 18 pages, ISSN: 0049-7886, No Color
Subscriptions: Free With Membership
Circulation: Total-600

NEEDLEWORK, KNITTING

AQS Update
Consumer, Association

Publishing Co: American Quilters Society, PO Box 3290, Paducah, KY 42002-3290 Tel # (502) 898-7903 Fax # (502) 898-8890 Parent Co.-Schroeder Publishing Co., Paducah
Personnel: Publisher-Meredith Schroeder, Editor-Charley Lynch
Editorial Description: Society news from the American Quilting Society.
General Info: Bi-monthly

American Home Sewing and Craft Association
See: TEXTILES

Annie's Crochet
Newsletter

Publishing Co: Annie's Attic, Inc., 222 Las Colinas Blvd W, Suite 1750, Irving, TX 75039-5437 Tel # (214) 488-1100 Fax # (214) 432-9555; Title Tel # (214) 636-4303
Personnel: Publisher, Editor-Anita Gentry, Production Mgr.-Ardis Nelson, Art Dir.-Andy Ashley, Circ. Mgr., Promotion Dir.-Chris Baker
Editorial Description: Patterns for crocheters, original crochet designs.
General Info: Yr. Est. 1983, Bi-monthly, Trim Size-5$\frac{1}{2}$ x 8$\frac{1}{2}$, Web press, 48 pages, ISSN: 0745-6360, 4 Color, Coated, Saddle-stitched
Subscriptions: Indv. $15, $4/copy
Circulation: Total-245,000
List Rental: List Management Co.: Total Media Concepts, 222 Cedar Ln Ste 201, Teaneck, NJ 07666-4312 Tel # (201) 692-0018, Fax # (201) 692-9817, Actives: 105,947, $60/M, Hotline: 21,852, $75/M
Printing Co: Ringier America, 12821 W Bluemound Rd, Brookfield, WI 53005-8038 Tel # (414) 786-6000

Annie's Crochet Newsletter Canadian
See: HOBBY

Annie's Pattern Club
Newsletter

Publishing Co: Annie's Attic, Inc., 222 Las Colinas Blvd W, Suite 1750, Irving, TX 75039-5437 Tel # (214) 488-1100 Fax # (214) 432-9555; Title Tel # (214) 636-4303
Personnel: Publisher, Editor-Anita Gentry, Production Mgr.-Ardis Nelson, Art Dir.-Andy Ashley, Circ. Mgr., Promotion Dir.-Chris Baker
Editorial Description: Patterns for crocheters & needle crafters, includes sewing, knitting, cross-stitch & crochet pattern designs.
General Info: Yr. Est. 1980, Bi-monthly, Trim Size-5$\frac{1}{2}$ x 8$\frac{1}{2}$, Web press, 48 pages, ISSN: 0199-7106, 4 Color, Coated, Saddle-stitched
Subscriptions: Indv. $15, $4/copy
Circulation: Total-165,000
List Rental: List Management Co.: Total Media Concepts, 222 Cedar Ln Ste 201, Teaneck, NJ 07666-4312 Tel # (201) 692-0018, Fax # (201) 692-9817, Actives: 110,633, $60/M, Hotline: 9,988, $80/M
Printing Co: Ringier America, 12821 W Bluemound Rd, Brookfield, WI 53005-8038 Tel # (414) 786-6000

Craft News
See: GLASS, STONE & CLAY

Draft & Design
See: CRAFTS

Flax Craft
See: TEXTILES

Needlepoint Bulletin *Consumer*

Publishing Co: Needlepoint, Inc., PO Box 13165, North Palm Beach, FL 33408-7165
Personnel: Publisher, Editor-Sharlene Weldon
Editorial Description: Needlepoint & all stitchery: news, products, market, trends, shoppin-by-mail, book reviews, events & people.
General Info: Yr. Est. 1973, Monthly, Web press, 6 pages, No Color
Subscriptions: Indv. $12, Can. $18, For. $24

Quilt Peddler *Consumer*

Publishing Co: Quilt Peddler, PO Box 1485, Valparaiso, IN 46384-1485
Editorial Description: What's new in quilting, with free patterns, offers and information on sources for quilting supplies.
General Info: Quarterly, Trim Size-8½ x 11, 12 pages

Rugging Room Bulletin *Business, Association*

Publishing Co: The Rugging Room, 10 Sawmill Dr # 824, Westford, MA 01886-2236;
Title Tel # (508) 692-8600
Editorial Description: Traditional American rug hooking news.
General Info: Quarterly, ISSN: 1043-2701
Subscriptions: Indv. $10

Sewing & Crafts Hotline
See: CRAFTS

Sewing Update

Publishing Co: PJS Publications, Inc., 2 News Plaza, PO Box 1790, Peoria, IL 61656
Tel # (309) 682-6626 Parent Co.-K-III Communications, New York
Personnel: Publisher, Editor-Tammy Young
Editorial Description: Fashion sewing.
General Info: (Formerly Palmer/Pletsch Sewing Update), Yr. Est. 1986, Bi-monthly
Subscriptions: Indv. $20
Advertising: Inquire for rates. Accepts Inserts.
List Rental: Rents Lists

Stumpwork Society Chronicle
See: ANTIQUES & ART GOODS

Thimbletter
See: COLLECTIBLES

Warp & Weft
See: CRAFTS

NEW AGE

Association for Past-Life Research & Therapies
See: PSYCHOLOGY

Chaotic Apochrypha

Publishing Co: Eric Davidson, 2183 Buckingham, #132, Richardson, TX 75081
Editorial Description: A publication devoted to exploring, promoting, and pushing the limits of free speech.
General Info: Trim Size-8.5 x 11, 40 pages

Christian New Age Quarterly
See: RELIGIOUS & THEOLOGICAL

Cosmic Voice

Publishing Co: Aetherius Society, 6202 Afton Place, Hollywood, CA 90028-8298;
Title Tel # (213) 465-9652
Personnel: Editor-Sir George King
Editorial Description: Dedicated to the dissemination of cosmic wisdom and practical metaphysics in furtherance of world peace and enlightenment.
General Info: Yr. Est. 1961, Monthly
Subscriptions: Indv. $16, Can. $16, For. $16, $2/copy

Creativa *Consumer*

Publishing Co: Creativa, 305 8th Ave., Apt. B7, Brooklyn, NY 11215-6618;
Title Tel # (212) 674-9006 Title Fax # (212) 674-9227
Editorial Description: NY holistic arts center letter.
General Info: Bi-monthly, Trim Size-8½ x 11, 16 pages, No Color, Matte
Advertising: Inquire for rates.

Deep Spring Newsletter
See: RELIGIOUS & THEOLOGICAL

EHE News
See: PARAPSYCHOLOGY

Flower Essence Society Newsletter
See: HEALTH

Friends of Omega *Consumer, Association*

Publishing Co: Omega Institute, 260 Lake Dr, Rhinebeck, NY 12572-3212 Tel # (914) 266-4444;
Title Tel # (914) 266-4301 Title Fax # (914) 266-4828
Editorial Description: Newsletter of the Omega Inst. for Holistic Studies.
General Info: Yr. Est. 1977, Quarterly

Indigo Sun *Consumer*

Publishing Co: Aquarian Publications, 1101 Post Oak Blvd Ste 312, Houston, TX 77056-3105;
Title Tel # (713) 599-5471 Title Fax # (713) 863-1353
Personnel: Editor-Carol Money
Editorial Description: New age and transformational issues.
General Info: Monthly
Circulation: Total-10,000

Iridis
See: PARAPSYCHOLOGY

Life Force News *Consumer*

Publishing Co: Meditation Center, PO Box 487, Fair Oaks, CA 95628-0487;
Title Tel # (916) 967-1911
Editorial Description: Covers meditation, yoga, vegetarianism and spiritual insights.
General Info: Monthly, Trim Size-8½ x 11, 12 pages, No Color, Matte, Saddle-stitched
Subscriptions: Free
Advertising: Inquire for rates.

Loving Brotherhood Newsletter
See: GAY & LESBIAN INTEREST

Memberletter
See: ASTROLOGY

Mind Quest
See: HYPNOSIS

New Environment Bulletin
See: ENVIRONMENT & ECOLOGY

New Frontiers

Publishing Co: New Frontiers Center. Inc., Rr 1, Oregon, WI 53575-9801; Title Tel # (608) 835-3795
Personnel: Editor-MaryJo Uphoff
Editorial Description: Unusual events, healing modalities, psyshic phenomena related education and research.
General Info: (Formerly New Frontiers Center Newsletter), Yr. Est. 1982, Quarterly, Trim Size-8½ x 11, 24 pages, No Color
Subscriptions: Indv. $10, For. $15, $4/copy
Circulation: Total-1,300

Parapsychology, Hypnosis, & Alternative Health
See: PARAPSYCHOLOGY

Perspective on Consciousness Bulletin

Publishing Co: A.R.E. Press, PO Box 595, Virginia Beach, VA 23451-0595;
Title Tel # (804) 428-3588
Personnel: Editor-Claire Grant
General Info: (Formerly Perspective on Consciousness & Psi Research), Bi-monthly, 4 pages
Subscriptions: Indv. $10

Psychic Guide Psychic Fair Network News *Consumer*

Publishing Co: Ad-Com, Inc., 1259 Rte. 46, Bldg. #1, Parsippany, NJ 07054-4909;
Title Tel # (201) 316-9511
Personnel: Publisher-Vincent Tabatneck, Circ. Mgr.-Christina Tabatneck, Production Mgr.-V. Tabatneck, Adv. Dir.-Teresa Handwerker, Editor, Art Dir.-Shirley Tabatneck
Editorial Description: Directed toward people interested in astrology, psychic, and paranormal occurrences.
General Info: Yr. Est. 1981, Quarterly, Trim Size-8½ x 15, Web press, 20 pages, 2 Color
Subscriptions: Indv. $5, $2/copy
Circulation: (100% controlled), Total-47,669

Revelations of Awareness *Consumer*

Publishing Co: Cosmic Awareness Communications, PO Box 115, Olympia, WA 98507-0115
Fax # (360) 956-1571
Editorial Description: Spiritual, economic, humanitarian newsletter from Edgar Cayce type source. Includes UFOs and mysteries.
General Info: Yr. Est. 1965, Bi-weekly, Trim Size-8½ x 11, Offset press, 20 pages, No Color, Matte, Other
Subscriptions: Indv. $42, $3/copy
Circulation: Total-2,000

SYZGY: The Journal of Contemporary Mentalism *Consumer*

Publishing Co: SYZGY: The Journal of Contemporary Mentalism, 2901 North 55th Avenue, Phoenix, AZ 85031 Tel # (602) 247-7323 Fax # (602) 247-4665
Editorial Description: Discusses the technique and craft for specialty entertainers.
General Info: Yr. Est. 1994, 18x/yr.
Subscriptions: Indv. $36

Soulmate News *Consumer*

Publishing Co: Soulmate News, PO Box 769, Ramah, NM 87321-0769
Personnel: Publisher-Jim Thompson, Jr.
Editorial Description: A singles network for those seeking spiritual partners.
General Info: Monthly, Trim Size-8½ x 11, 10 pages, No Color
Subscriptions: $2/copy
Circulation: Total-200

Sproutletter
See: NUTRITION

Star Beacon
See: UNIDENTIFIED FLYING OBJECTS

TMI Focus
See: PARAPSYCHOLOGY

Trager Newsletter
See: HEALTH

Triangles Bulletin
See: CLUBS

WE: Walk-ins for Evolution/A Newsletter for Conscious Connection *Consumer*

Publishing Co: WE Unlimited, PO Box 120633, Saint Paul, MN 55112-0021; Title Tel # (612) 783-0345
Personnel: Publisher, Editor-Liz Nelson, Manuscript Ed.-Deborah Field, Manuscript Ed.-Lily Frank
Editorial Description: Features services for and from walk-ins, their stories, activities or progress through interviews, reports, book reviews, columns to help walk-ins establish their own identities and paths.
General Info: Yr. Est. 1994, Quarterly, Offset press, 24 pages, ISSN: 1072-432X, 10% ads, No Color
Subscriptions: Indv. $13, Inst. $13, Can. $24, For. $24, $4/copy
Circulation: Total-500
Advertising: Inquire for rates. Accepts Inserts.

NEWS MAGAZINES

Food and Drink Weekly
See: FOOD

Global Mail

Publishing Co: SoapBox Juction, P.O. Box 597996, Chicago, IL 60659
Editorial Description: A newsletter of international mail art events.
General Info: Trim Size-8.5 x 11, 16 pages

IBF News

Publishing Co: International Bicycle Fund, 4887 Columbia Drive S, Seattle, WA 98108
Editorial Description: Newsletter that aims to de-emphasize the automobile in transportaion policy decisions.
General Info: Trim Size-8.5 x 11, 4 pages
Subscriptions: Indv. $1

Sodus News, The
See: REGIONAL INTEREST

Travelin' Woman
See: TRAVEL

NEWSPAPER INDUSTRY

Ancillary Profits
See: MEDIA & COMMUNICATIONS

Associated Court and Commercial Newspapers, Bulletin *Association*

Publishing Co: Associated Court, 2014 NW 24th Ave, Portland, OR 97210-2345; Title Tel # (503) 226-1311
General Info: Semi-annually

Canadian Daily Newspapers Blue Books *Consumer*

Publishing Co: Audit Bureau of Circulations, 900 N. Meacham Rd., Schaumburg, IL 60173-4968 Tel # (708) 605-0909; Title Tel # (847) 605-0909 Title Fax # (847) 605-0483
Editorial Description: Looseleaf volumes containing all Canadian Daily Newspaper members' publisher's statements.
General Info: Yr. Est. 1983, Semi-annually, Web press, Looseleaf
Subscriptions: $45/copy

Canadian Weekly Newspapers Blue Books *Consumer*

Publishing Co: Audit Bureau of Circulations, 900 N. Meacham Rd., Schaumburg, IL 60173-4968 Tel # (708) 605-0909; Title Tel # (847) 605-0909 Title Fax # (847) 605-0483
Editorial Description: Looseleaf volumes containing all Canadian Weekly Newspaper members' publisher's statements.
General Info: Semi-annually, Looseleaf
Subscriptions: $68/copy

Cartoonists Notebook *Association*

Publishing Co: Assn. of American Editorial Cartoonists, 4101 Lake Boone Trl Ste 201, Raleigh, NC 27607-7506; Title Tel # (405) 231-3283
Personnel: Publisher-Sally Nicholson
General Info: Quarterly
Subscriptions: Indv. $25

Cole Papers, The *Business*

Publishing Co: Cole Group, The, 2590 Greenwich St., Ste. 9, San Francisco, CA 94123-3333; Title Tel # (415) 673-2424 Title Fax # (415) 673-2449
Personnel: Publisher, Editor-David M. Cole, Circ. Mgr.-Marge Wetmore
Editorial Description: Covers technology of the publishing business - newspapers, magazines and information providers.
General Info: Yr. Est. 1989, Monthly, Trim Size-8½ x 11, Sheetfed press, 12 pages, ISSN: 1062-6727, Color, Coated, Saddle-stitched
Subscriptions: Indv. $139, Can. $149, For. $159, $11/copy
List Rental: Rents Lists
Printing Co: Account Manager: Gary Babb; Sierra Printers, 216 W Main St, Urbana, IL 61801-2622 Tel # (217) 344-4418, Fax # (217) 344-8164

Collectible Newspapers
See: COLLECTIBLES

Donald R. Morris Newsletter *Business, Consumer*

Publishing Co: Trident Syndicate, Inc., PO Box 19909, Houston, TX 77224-1909 Tel # (712) 781-7094 Fax # (713) 781-9594; Title Tel # (713) 781-7094 Title Fax # (713) 781-8584
Personnel: Publisher-Loran Sheffer, Editor-Donald Morris, Circ. Mgr.-Linda Pareno
Editorial Description: Commentary on world news & political events.
General Info: Yr. Est. 1989, Weekly, Trim Size-8½ x 11, Offset press, 4 pages, ISSN: 1053-5829, No Color, Matte
Subscriptions: Indv. $50, Can. $50, For. $75, $1/copy
Circulation: Total-750
List Rental: Rents Lists
Printing Co: Offshore Data Services, Inc., 3200 Wilcrest St., Suite #170, Houston, TX 77042 Tel # (713) 781-2713, Fax # (713) 781-9594

Editorials on File *Consumer*

Publishing Co: Facts on File, Inc., 11 Penn Plaza, New York, NY 10001-2006 Tel # (212) 967-8800 Parent Co.-Infobase Holdings Inc., New York; Title Tel # (212) 683-2244 Title Fax # (212) 683-3633
Personnel: Publisher-Remmel Nunn, Editor-Oliver Trager, Circ. Mgr.-Steve Orlofsky, Production Dir.-Olivia McKean
Editorial Description: Reprints of editorials from 140 leading newspapers of the US and Canada.
General Info: Yr. Est. 1970, Semi-monthly, Trim Size-8½ x 11½, Sheetfed press, 64 pages, ISSN: 0013-0966, No Color, Looseleaf
Subscriptions: Indv. $399, Inst. $399
Acquistions: Publication Bought
List Rental: Rents Lists
Printing Co: Science Press, 300 W Chestnut St, Ephrata, PA 17522-2002 Tel # (717) 738-9300, Fax # (717) 738-9413

Editors' Exchange, The *Business, Association*

Publishing Co: American Society of Newspaper Editors, PO Box 4090, Reston, VA 22090-1700; Title Tel # (703) 648-1147 Title Fax # (703) 620-4557
Personnel: Editor-Elise Burroughs
Editorial Description: Daily newspaper editors share readership ideas that have been successful at their newspapers.
General Info: Yr. Est. 1978, Trim Size-8½ x 11, 4 pages, No Color, Matte
Subscriptions: Indv. $11, Can. $11, For. $75
Circulation: Total-2,400
Printing Co: HBP, 952 Frederick St, Hagerstown, MD 21740-6821 Tel # (301) 733-2000

Education Reporter
See: JOURNALISM

Guild Watch *Business, Association*

Publishing Co: New York Times Newspaper Guild, 229 W 43rd St, New York, NY 10036-3913; Title Tel # (212) 556-1504
Editorial Description: Newsletter for the NY Times Newspaper Guild.
General Info: Bi-monthly

ISA Update
See: TELECOMMUNICATIONS

Intl. Society of Weekly Newspaper Editors, Newsletter *Association*

Publishing Co: Northern Illinois University Education Dept., Office of Public Affairs NIU, DeKalb, IL 60115 Tel # (815) 753-1681 Fax # (815) 753-3299; Title Tel # (815) 753-1925
Personnel: Editor-Donald Brod
Editorial Description: Monthly publication of organization news sent to members.
General Info: Yr. Est. 1976, Monthly, Mimeo press
Subscriptions: Indv. $25
Circulation: (100% controlled), Total-300

Journal/Sentinel Ink
See: HOUSE ORGANS

Maryland-Delaware-D.C. Press News *Association*

Publishing Co: Maryland-Delaware-D.C. Press Assn., Univ. Of Maryland College Of, Journalism, College Park, MD 20742-0001; Title Tel # (301) 454-0245 Title Fax # (301) 454-7912
Personnel: Editor-Patricia Marshall
Editorial Description: Newsletter containing information concerning newspaper industry and personnel changes and awards received by member newspapers.
General Info: Yr. Est. 1945, Monthly, Offset press, 4 pages, No Color
Subscriptions: Indv. $13, $5/copy
Circulation: Total-550
Advertising: Inquire for rates.

Monthly Newsprint Report
See: PAPER

News Library News *Association*

Publishing Co: Sponsor-Special Libraries Assn. Newspaper Div., News Division, SLA., 101 N. Fourth St., POB 798, Columbia, MO 65205; Title Tel # (314) 449-3811
Personnel: Editor-Christine Malesky, Circ. Mgr.-Jan Summers, Adv. Dir.-Kathy Trimble
Editorial Description: Articles on news libraries and new developments.
General Info: Quarterly, Trim Size-8½ x 11, Offset press, 8 pages, ISSN: 1047-417X, 2% ads, Color
Subscriptions: Indv. $30, Inst. $30, Free With Membership
Circulation: Total-800
Advertising: Inquire for rates.

NewsInc. *Business* CPM: $148

Publishing Co: Sponsor-American Newspaper Publishers Assn., Simba Information, Inc., 213 Danbury Rd. PO Box 7430, Wilton, CT 06897-7430 Fax # (203) 834-1771 Parent Co.-Cowles Business Media, New York; Title Tel # (203) 834-0033
Personnel: Publisher-Chris Elwell, Editor-Carl Mexurio, Mktg. Dir.-Michael Genaro, Promotion Dir.-Hillary Veeder
Editorial Description: The ultimate insider's guide to the newspaper industry you'll find writter news a opinion aon who's growing and who's not, who's grabbing ad pages and how they're doing it.
General Info: Yr. Est. 1989, Bi-weekly, Trim Size-8½ x 11, 10 pages, ISSN: 1043-7452, 2 Color, Matte
Subscriptions: Indv. $425, Can. $475, For. $475
Acquistions: Publication Sold
Circulation: (BPA, 55% controlled), Total-19,927, Subscriptions-4,000, Readership-45,000
Advertising: $2,950. Accepts Inserts.
List Rental: List Management Co.: Conrad Direct, Inc., 300 Knickerbocker Road, Creskill, NJ 07626 Tel # (201) 567-3200, Fax # (201) 567-4959, Actives: 14,250, $80/M

Newsday Connections *Consumer* CPM: $66

Publishing Co: Newsday, Electronic Publishing, 235 Pinelawn Rd., Melville, NY 11747-4250; Title Tel # (516) 843-2402
Editorial Description: Newsletter for Newsday newspaper on-line subscribers.
General Info: Quarterly, Trim Size-8½ x 10½, 6 pages, No Color
Circulation: Total-6,000
Advertising: $400.

Newslog *Association*

Publishing Co: Associated Church Press, PO Box 30215, Phoenix, AZ 85046-0215
Editorial Description: Published for members of the Associated Church Press.
General Info: (Formerly Editorial Council of the Religious Press), Yr. Est. 1916, Bi-monthly, Trim Size-8½ x 11, Offset press, 4 pages, No Color, Matte
Subscriptions: Free With Membership

PNPA Press *Association* CPM: $260

Publishing Co: Pennsylvania Newspaper Publishers' Association, 2717 N Front St, Harrisburg, PA 17110-1221; Title Tel # (717) 234-4067 Title Fax # (717) 234-0746
Personnel: Publisher-Timothy Williams, Circ. Mgr.-Joyce Shillingsford, Editor, Adv. Dir.-Amy Hiester
Editorial Description: Serves the newspaper printing and publishing industry of the Pennsylvania area. News on the latest technological developments, new equipment, and how-to-do-it items. Also news about Pennsylvania newspaper people and features, opinion pieces.
General Info: Yr. Est. 1929, Monthly, Trim Size-11⅜ x 14, Web press, 16 pages, 2 Color, Newsprint
Subscriptions: Indv. $18, $2/copy
Circulation: Total-1,000
Advertising: $260.

Plus Business
See: ADVERTISING & MARKETING

Sales and Idea Book *Association*

Publishing Co: International Newspaper Advertising Executives, 11600 Sunrise Valley Dr, Reston, VA 22091-1412; Title Tel # (217) 442-1068
Personnel: Publisher-Sid Bordedon, Editor-Roni English
Editorial Description: Member news, sales conference programs, sales training, survey compilations.
General Info: 10x/yr., Trim Size-7¾ x 8⅜, Web press, 16 pages, 4 Color
Subscriptions: Indv. $1
Circulation: (100% controlled), Total-3,400

Shrimp Notes
See: FISH & FISHERIES

Super Snack News *Consumer*

Publishing Co: Warren Publishing House, Inc., PO Box 2250, Everett, WA 98203-0250 Tel # (206) 353-3100; Title Tel # (206) 303-3100 Title Fax # (206) 355-7007
Personnel: Publisher-Jean Warren, Editor-Kathleen Cubley, Circ. Dir.-Melody Olney, Production Mgr.-JoAnna Brock, Art Dir.-Jill Lustig, Mktg. Dir.-David Warren
Editorial Description: Nutritious food, facts, and fun for children. Up to 200 copies permitted per subscription.
General Info: Yr. Est. 1991, Monthly, Trim Size-8½ x 11, 4 pages, Matte, Other
Subscriptions: Indv. $24, $2/copy
Circulation: Total-1,100
List Rental: Rents Lists
Printing Co: K & P Printing, 2927 Wetmore Ave, Everett, WA 98201-4016 Tel # (206) 259-4650, Fax # (206) 258-9422

U.S. Daily Newspapers Blue Books

Publishing Co: Audit Bureau of Circulations, 900 N. Meacham Rd., Schaumburg, IL 60173-4968 Tel # (708) 605-0909; Title Tel # (847) 605-0909 Title Fax # (847) 605-0483
Editorial Description: Looseleaf volumes of all U.S. Daily Newspaper members' publisher's statements.
General Info: Semi-annually, Looseleaf
Subscriptions: $395/copy

U.S. Weekly Newspapers Blue Books *Consumer*

Publishing Co: Audit Bureau of Circulations, 900 N. Meacham Rd., Schaumburg, IL 60173-4968 Tel # (708) 605-0909; Title Tel # (847) 605-0909 Title Fax # (847) 605-0483
Editorial Description: Looseleaf volumes containing all U.S. Weekly Newspaper members' publisher's statements.
General Info: Semi-annually, Looseleaf
Subscriptions: $95/copy

WNA Buletin *Association*

Publishing Co: Wisconsin Newspaper Assn., 702 N. Midvale Blvd., Madison, WI 53705-3261; Title Tel # (608) 238-7171
Personnel: Editor-Roman Brandt
General Info: Yr. Est. 1926, Quarterly, Offset press
Subscriptions: Indv. $2
Circulation: Total-750

NEWSPAPER MAGAZINE SUPPLEMENTS

Cypress, Texas

Bogus

Publishing Co: Bogus, 14227 Eventide, Cypress, TX 77429
Editorial Description: A collection of strange-but-true newsclips with the occasional comment by the editor.
General Info: Trim Size-8.5 x 11, 8 pages

New Berlin, Wisconsin

Father Flood Lectionary Series
See: RELIGIOUS & THEOLOGICAL

NEWSPAPERS

Mobile, Alabama

Vanguard , The
See: COLLEGE ALUMNI

San Francisco, California

Smart Basics *Consumer*

Publishing Co: Smart Basics, Inc., 1626 Union Street, San Francisco, CA 94123;
Title Tel # (415) 351-1515 Title Fax # (415) 351-1348
Editorial Description: Smart Basics goal is to nourish your mind as well as your health with the highest quality, cutting-edge supplements, backed by scientifically valid and accurate information so you can best choose which products suit your needs.
General Info: Monthly, Trim Size-8½ x 11, 8 pages, 2 Color, Matte
Subscriptions: $1/copy
Advertising: Inquire for rates.
List Rental: Rents Lists

Hinsdale, Illinois

Indian Head Park *Consumer*

Publishing Co: Doings Newspapers, Inc., 118 W 1st St, Hinsdale, IL 60521-4013;
Title Tel # (708) 887-0600 Title Fax # (708) 887-9646
Personnel: Assoc. Publ.-Jim Slonoff, Publisher, Editor-J. Peter Teschner, Exec. Ed.-Laurie Adams, Circ. Mgr.-Nancy Florio, Production Mgr.-Deb Murray, Adv. Dir.-Frieda Wolf
General Info: Yr. Est. 1985, Semi-weekly, Trim Size-10½ x 15, Other press, 96 pages, 6% ads, 4 Color, Newsprint, Saddle-stitched
Subscriptions: Indv. $42, $1/copy
Advertising: $840. Accepts Inserts.
Printing Co: Press Pubs., 112 S York St, Elmhurst, IL 60126-3432 Tel # (708) 834-0900

Oakbrook Terrace *Consumer*

Publishing Co: Doings Newspapers, Inc., 118 W 1st St, Hinsdale, IL 60521-4013;
Title Tel # (708) 887-0600 Title Fax # (708) 887-9646
Personnel: Assoc. Publ.-Jim Slonoff, Publisher, Editor-J. Peter Teschner, Exec. Ed.-Laurie Adams, Circ. Mgr.-Nancy Florio, Production Mgr.-Deb Murray, Adv. Dir.-Frieda Wolf
General Info: Yr. Est. 1985, Semi-weekly, Trim Size-10½ x 15, 96 pages, 4 Color, Newsprint, Saddle-stitched
Subscriptions: Indv. $42, $1/copy
Advertising: Accepts Inserts.
Printing Co: Press Pubs., 112 S York St, Elmhurst, IL 60126-3432 Tel # (708) 834-0900

Western Springs *Consumer*

Publishing Co: Doings Newspapers, Inc., 118 W 1st St, Hinsdale, IL 60521-4013;
Title Tel # (708) 887-0600 Title Fax # (708) 887-9646
Personnel: Assoc. Publ.-Jim Slonoff, Publisher, Editor-J. Peter Teschner, Exec. Ed.-Laurie Adams, Circ. Mgr.-Nancy Florio, Production Mgr.-Deb Murray, Adv. Dir.-Frieda Wolf
General Info: Yr. Est. 1985, Semi-weekly, Trim Size-10½ x 15, 96 pages, 6% ads, 4 Color, Saddle-stitched
Subscriptions: Indv. $41, $1/copy
Advertising: $840. Accepts Inserts.
Printing Co: Press Pubs., 112 S York St, Elmhurst, IL 60126-3432 Tel # (708) 834-0900

Silver Spring, Maryland

Minority Contract Opportunities *Business, Association*

Publishing Co: CD Publications, 8204 Fenton St., Silver Spring, MD 20910-4571;
Title Tel # (301) 588-6380 Title Fax # (301) 588-6385
Editorial Description: Minority Contract Opportunities is a weekly summarizing federal and private procurement notices and subcontracting opportunities for a wide range of products and services. It is designed to help minority business owmers find and win more contracts.
General Info: Yr. Est. 1987, Weekly, 12 pages
Subscriptions: Indv. $322, Inst. $322, $1/copy

Burlington, Massachusetts

HeadsUp *Business*

Publishing Co: Individual, Inc., 8 New England Executive Pk., Burlington, MA 01803
Editorial Description: Daily abstracts of custom selected articles and news releases delivered by Fax or E-mail.
General Info: Daily

Parsippany, New Jersey

DUN & BRADSTREET-DATALINE *Business, Association*

Publishing Co: Dun & Bradstreet Information Services, DATALINE, 3 Sylvan Way, Parsippany, NJ 07054; Title Fax # (201) 605-6921
Editorial Description: Dun & Bradstreet Dataline is a directory file containing basic company data, organizational status and additional marketing information on more than eight million U.S. business establishments. These include public and private companies as well as government agencies.
General Info: Annually

Brooklyn, New York

Fiction Digest
See: BOOKS & BOOK TRADE

Fulton, New York

Fulton Patriot, The

Publishing Co: Fulton Newspapers, Inc., Cor. 2nd & Oneida Sts., Fulton, NY 13069;
Title Tel # (315) 598-6397
Advertising: $180.

Cincinnati, Ohio

TW Cincinnati Enquirer *Consumer*

Publishing Co: TW Cincinnati Enquirer, 312 Elm Street, Cincinnati, OH 45202;
Title Tel # (513) 721-2700 Title Fax # (513) 768-8150
Personnel: Publisher-Harry M. Whipple, Editor-Lawrence Beaupre, Editorial Page Ed.-Peter Bronson, Feature Ed.-Sava Pearce, Circ. Mgr.-William Hunsbeuger, Production Mgr.-Mark Mikolagzyk, Adv. Dir.-David L. Hunke, Mktg. Dir.-Gerald T. Silvers
Editorial Description: Daily newspaper.
General Info: Yr. Est. 1841, Daily
Subscriptions: Indv. $322
Circulation: (ABC), Total-839,000
Advertising: $23. Accepts Inserts.

Madison, Wisconsin

Her Own Words *Consumer*

Publishing Co: Her Own Words, PO Box 5264, Madison, WI 53705; Title Tel # (608) 271-7083
Personnel: Publisher-Jocelyn Riley
Editorial Description: Covers women's history, literature, and art; non-traditional careers for women.
General Info: Trim Size-8½ x 11, 4 pages, ISSN: 0898-0241, No Color, Matte
Printing Co: Econoprint, Madison, WI

Perspective: The Campus Legal Monthly *Association, Scholarly*

Publishing Co: Magna Publications, Inc., 611 N Sherman Ave, Madison, WI 53704-4410
Tel # (608) 246-3580; Title Fax # (608) 246-3597
General Info: Monthly, Trim Size-8½ x 11, 8 pages, Color
Circulation: Total-1,200
Advertising: Inquire for rates.
List Rental: Rents Lists

CANADA

Charlottetown, Ontario

Carillon *Association*

Publishing Co: Veterans Affairs Canada, P.O Box 7700, Charlottetown, ON C1A 8M9 Canada
Tel # (905) 566-8459; Title Tel # (902) 566-8459 Title Fax # (902) 566-8508
Personnel: Editor-Teresa Maclean
Editorial Description: For & about Veterans Affairs Employees.
General Info: Yr. Est. 1968, 11x/yr., Trim Size-8½ x 11, Offset press, 20 pages, ISSN: 0825-7345, 2 Color, Newsprint
Subscriptions: Free To Qualified Recipient
Circulation: (100% controlled), Total-5,000, Readership-5,000

NUCLEAR ENERGY

ANS News *Association*

Publishing Co: American Nuclear Society, 555 N. Kensington Ave., La Grange Park, IL 60526
Tel # (708) 352-6611; Title Tel # (708) 579-8242 Title Fax # (708) 352-6464
Personnel: Publisher-Jon Payne, Production Mgr.-Wayne Witek
Editorial Description: Carries information on the activities of the Society and its members.
General Info: Yr. Est. 1983, Bi-monthly, Trim Size-11½ x 17, Offset press, 8 pages, ISSN: 0737-6812, 2 Color, Matte
Subscriptions: Indv. $82, Free With Membership
Circulation: (100% controlled), Total-15,000

Advocate
See: POLITICS

Atomic Data and Nuclear Data Tables *Association*

Publishing Co: Academic Press, Inc., 525 B St., Ste 1900, San Diego, CA 92101-4495 Parent Co.-Harcourt Brace Professional Publishing, San Diego; Title Tel # (619) 699-6825
Title Fax # (619) 699-6380
Personnel: Editor-Angela Li-Scholz, Promotion Coord.-Greta Simpson
Editorial Description: A journal devoted to compilations and evaluations of experimental and theoretical results in nuclear physics.
General Info: Yr. Est. 1966, Bi-monthly, Trim Size-8½ x 11, ISSN: 0092-640X, 4 Color, Looseleaf
Subscriptions: Indv. $321, Can. $321, For. $381
Advertising: $800. Accepts Inserts.
List Rental: Rents Lists

Atomic Energy
Clearinghouse   *Business*

Publishing Co: Congressional Information Bureau, Inc., 3030 Clarendon Blvd., Ste. 202, Arlington, VA 22201-2845 Tel # (703) 516-4801 Fax # (703) 516-4804; Title Tel # (202) 347-2275 Title Fax # (202) 347-2278
Personnel: Publisher-Robert Cazalas, Editor-Pamela Lessard
Editorial Description: Information on atomic energy legislation and federal agency reports on nuclear energy.
General Info: Yr. Est. 1955, Weekly, Trim Size-11½ x 14, Sheetfed press, 60 pages, ISSN: 0519-3389, No Color
Subscriptions: Indv. $525, Inst. $525, Can. $525, For. $750
Circulation: (CCAB)

CNS Bulletin   *Consumer, Association*

Publishing Co: Canadian Nuclear Assn. (CNA), 144 Front Street West Ste. 725, Toronto, ON M5J 2L7 Canada; Title Tel # (416) 977-6152
Personnel: Publisher-D. McArthur, Editor-Jim Weller
Editorial Description: CNS Membership newsletter: Articles on Canadian nuclear technology and CNS conferences and activities.
General Info: Yr. Est. 1980, Bi-monthly, ISSN: 0714-7074, Newsprint
Circulation: (100% controlled), Total-500

Critical Mass Energy Bulletin
See: ENERGY

Diablo

Publishing Co: Ray Fleming/Marilyn Apuzzo, 1530 1/2 Broad St, San Luis Obispo, CA 93401-4302; Title Tel # (805) 543-6614
Editorial Description: Watching Diablo Canyon nuclear reactor.
General Info: Trim Size-8½ x 14, 2 pages

Energy Prices & Taxes
See: ENERGY

Fusion Power Report
See: ENERGY

IAEE Newsletter
See: ENERGY

INFO Newsletter

Publishing Co: USCEA, 1776 I St NW Ste 400, Washington, DC 20006-3700; Title Tel # (202) 293-0770 Title Fax # (202) 785-4019
Personnel: Editor-Robert Livingston, Design Director-Susan Gum
Editorial Description: To serve as the voice of the nuclear energy industry.
General Info: (Formerly Press INFO, Nuclear INFO), Yr. Est. 1953, Monthly

Inside N.R.C.

Publishing Co: McGraw-Hill, 1221 Ave. of the Americas, 36th Fl., New York, NY 10020-1095 Tel # (212) 512-2000 Fax # (212) 512-6590; Title Tel # (212) 997-6410
Editorial Description: Reporting of news within the U.S. Nuclear Regulatory Commission.
General Info: Yr. Est. 1979, Bi-weekly, Offset press, 16 pages, ISSN: 0194-0252, Ind/Abs/Online: DIALOG, Dow Jones, NewsNet, Nexis, No Color
Subscriptions: $20/copy

New Manhattan Project
Newsletter

Publishing Co: American Friends Service Committee, NY City, 15 Rutherford Pl, New York, NY 10003-3705; Title Tel # (212) 598-0950
Editorial Description: Focuses on antinuclear issues & activities in the NY metro area.
General Info: 8x/yr., 6 pages
Subscriptions: Indv. $10

Nuclear Energy Info   *Business, Association*

Publishing Co: United States Council for Energy Awareness, 17761 I Street NW, Suite 400, Washington, DC 20006-3708 Tel # (202) 293-0770
Personnel: Editor-Leslie Lamkin
Editorial Description: Covers nuclear energy issues.
General Info: Bi-monthly, Trim Size-8½ x 11, 16 pages, 2 Color, Matte, Saddle-stitched

Nuclear Fuel   *Business*

Publishing Co: McGraw-Hill, 1200 G St NW Ste 1100, Washington, DC 20005-3814 Tel # (202) 383-3700 Parent Co.-McGraw-Hill, New York; Title Tel # (202) 383-2300
Personnel: Publisher-John Slater, Editor-Michael Knapik, Mng. Editor-Eric Linderman, Circ. Mgr.-Marguerite Stanford
General Info: Yr. Est. 1976, Bi-weekly, Ind/Abs/Online: DIALOG, Dow Jones, NewsNet, Nexis

Nuclear Law Bulletin
See: LAW

Nuclear Monitor   *Business, Consumer*

Publishing Co: Nuclear Information & Resource Service, 1424 16th St NW Ste 601, Washington, DC 20036-2211; Title Tel # (202) 328-0002 Title Fax # (202) 462-2183
Personnel: Publisher, Editor-Michael Mariotte
Editorial Description: Nuclear power safety, economics, and other topics of interest to the investment and regulatory communities.
General Info: Yr. Est. 1985, Monthly, Trim Size-8.5 x 11, Offset press, 6 pages, ISSN: 0889-3411, No Color, Newsprint
Subscriptions: Indv. $35, Inst. $250, Can. $250, For. $250, $10/copy
Circulation: Total-900
Printing Co: Press Room, 3608 Forest Dr, Alexandria, VA 22302-1005 Tel # (703) 998-4500

Nuclear Plant Maintenance Newsletter
See: POWER & POWER PLANTS

Nuclear Power Reactors in
the World

Publishing Co: UNIPUB, 4611-F Assembly Dr, Lanham, MD 20706-4370; Title Tel # (301) 459-7666 Title Fax # (301) 459-0056
Editorial Description: Listing of power reactors with information on operating reactors, those under construction, planned & shut down.
General Info: Yr. Est. 1969, Annually, 100 pages
Subscriptions: Indv. $17

Nuclear Regulation
Reports   *Business*

Publishing Co: CCH, Inc., 2700 Lake Cook Rd., Riverwoods, IL 60015 Parent Co.-Kluwer Law & Taxation Publishers, Cambridge; Title Tel # (847) 267-7000 Title Fax # (800) 224-8299
Editorial Description: Publishes the rules for development, production, licensing, processing and use of nuclear energy and its byproducts and waste disposal.
General Info: Yr. Est. 1975, Weekly, Trim Size-6 x 9, Web press, 70 pages, Color, Looseleaf
Subscriptions: Indv. $2,992
Advertising: Inquire for rates.

Nuclear Remediation
Week   *Business*

Publishing Co: King Communications Group, 627 National Press Building, Washington, DC 20045-1601 Tel # (202) 638-4260 Fax # (202) 662-9719
Editorial Description: Concentrates on the broad subject of cleaning up nuclear sites both civilian and military in the U.S. and aboard. It also reports on legistion, litigation, technology, funding, contracting & transportation.
General Info: (Formerly Nuclear Remediation Reports), Yr. Est. 1994, Weekly
Subscriptions: Indv. $695
Advertising: Accepts Inserts.

Nuclear Resister
See: POLITICS

Nuclear Standards News   *Association*

Publishing Co: American Nuclear Society, 555 N. Kensington Ave., La Grange Park, IL 60526 Tel # (708) 352-6611; Title Tel # (708) 579-8268 Title Fax # (708) 352-6464
Personnel: Editor-Marilyn Weber, Editorial Asst.-Roxanne Czimer
Editorial Description: Designated information on nuclear standards activities.
General Info: Yr. Est. 1970, Monthly, Trim Size-8½ x 11, Offset press, 6 pages, No Color
Subscriptions: Indv. $285
Circulation: Total-175

Nuclear Waste News   *Business*

Publishing Co: Business Publishers, Inc., 951 Pershing Dr., Silver Spring, MD 20910-4464 Tel # (301) 589-5103 Fax # (301) 589-8493; Title Tel # (301) 587-6300 Title Fax # (301) 587-1081
Personnel: Publisher-Leonard A. Eiserer, Editor-Thecla Fabian, Mktg. Dir.-Fay S. Gold
Editorial Description: As-it-happens coverage of political and legal developments in radioactive waste management; business opportunities and new technology also highlighted. Conference Calendar.
General Info: Yr. Est. 1981, Weekly, Trim Size-8½ x 11, Desktop press, 8 pages, ISSN: 0276-2897, Ind/Abs/Online: NewsNet, Predicasts, No Color, Recycled
Subscriptions: Indv. $737, Inst. $737, Can. $695, For. $762
Advertising: Accepts Inserts.
List Rental: List Management Co.: Manager: Jim Hauschild; BPI Direct, 951 Pershing Dr., Silver Spring, MD 20910-4464 Tel # (301) 585-5976, Fax # (301) 587-4530

Nucleonics Week   *Business*

Publishing Co: McGraw-Hill, 1200 G St NW Ste 1100, Washington, DC 20005-3814 Tel # (202) 383-3700 Parent Co.-McGraw-Hill, New York; Title Tel # (202) 383-2300
Personnel: Publisher-John Slater, Editor-Margaret Ryan, Mng. Editor-Brian Jordan, Circ. Mgr.-Peggy Collins
Editorial Description: Unbiased reporting of peaceful means of nuclear energy.
General Info: Yr. Est. 1960, 51x/yr., Trim Size-8½ x 11, Offset press, 14 pages, ISSN: 0048-105X, Ind/Abs/Online: DIALOG, Dow Jones, NewsNet, Nexis, No Color

Procedures Review
Business   CPM: $500

Publishing Co: Colby & Hyatt LLC, P.O Box 466, Dover, NJ 07802; Title Tel # (201) 989-5455
Title Fax # (201) 989-5455
Personnel: Publisher-Ted Colby & Sue Hyatt, Editor-Ted Colby
Editorial Description: Provides current information of value to procedure writers, editors, management and government regulation in the nuclear industry or other regulated industry.
General Info: Yr. Est. 1995, Monthly, Trim Size-8½ x 11, Letrpr. press, 12 pages, ISSN: 1082-0108, No Color, Matte
Subscriptions: Indv. $90, Can. $100, For. $112, $10/copy
Circulation: Total-1,000
Advertising: $500.

Professional Reactor Operator Society-The Communicator

Publishing Co: Professional Reactor Operator Society, PO Box 181, Mishicot, WI 54228-0181
Fax # (815) 741-0443; Title Tel # (815) 741-0443 Title Fax # (815) 941-0443
Personnel: Circ. Mgr.-Carl Gray, Editor, Production Mgr.-Greg Veith, Adv. Dir.-Dave Milner
Editorial Description: Articles related to Nuclear Power from an operator's perspective.
General Info: Yr. Est. 1980, Quarterly, Trim Size-8½ x 11, 44 pages, 1% ads, No Color, Newsprint
Subscriptions: Indv. $25
Circulation: (100% controlled), Total-1,000
Advertising: Inquire for rates. Accepts Inserts.

Progress Report

Publishing Co: Task Force Against Nuclear Pollution, PO Box 1817, Washington, DC 20013-1817
General Info: 4 pages

RSIC Newsletter
Consumer

Publishing Co: Oak Ridge National Library, PO Box 2008, Oak Ridge, TN 37831-2008;
Title Tel # (615) 574-6176 Title Fax # (615) 574-6182
Personnel: Editor-Alice Rice
Editorial Description: Radiation transport, biological shielding, radiation protection, neutrons and gamma rays.
General Info: Yr. Est. 1963, Monthly, Trim Size-8½ x 11, Offset press, 12 pages, No Color
Circulation: (100% controlled), Total-1,500

Radioactive Exchange
Business, Consumer

Publishing Co: Exchange Monitor Publications, PO Box 5757, Washington, DC 20016;
Title Tel # (202) 296-2814
Personnel: Publisher-Edward Helminski, Circ. Mgr.-Carole Helminski
Editorial Description: Views & information on radioactive high level, low level & intermediate level nuclear waste management.
General Info: Yr. Est. 1981, Bi-weekly, Desktop press, 16 pages, ISSN: 0891-3013, No Color
Subscriptions: Indv. $379, $25/copy
Acquistions: Publication Bought
Printing Co: IPI Graphics, 7925 Penn Randall Place, Upper Marlboro, MD 20772
Tel # (301) 736-3390

Radiological Inspection Reports

Publishing Co: Family Matters Press, PO Box 5674, Rockville, MD 20855-0674;
Title Tel # (301) 309-9329 Title Fax # (301) 762-6714
Personnel: Publisher-Steven Schulin
Editorial Description: Features radiation protection practices and pitfalls at commercial nuclear plants - technical and regulatory insights from government inspectors.
General Info: Yr. Est. 1991, Trim Size-8½ x 11, Desktop press, 40 pages, ISSN: 1054-8815
Subscriptions: Indv. $4,200

Whisper in the Woods
See: ENVIRONMENT & ECOLOGY

NUMISMATICS

ANSNewsletter
Association

Publishing Co: American Numismatic Society, Broadway at 155th St., New York, NY 10032;
Title Tel # (212) 234-3130 Title Fax # (212) 234-3381
Personnel: Editor-Marie H. Martin, Assoc. Ed.-Leslie A. Elam
Editorial Description: News of ANS activities; information for & about ANS members & ongoing numismatic research.
General Info: Yr. Est. 1979, Quarterly, Trim Size-8½ x 11, Offset press, 10 pages, No Color, Newsprint
Circulation: Total-2,400
Printing Co: Fischer Printing, 214 35th St, Union City, NJ 07087-5996 Tel # (201) 867-1630

Appraisers Standard
See: ANTIQUES & ART GOODS

Biomedical Technology Information Service
See: MEDICINE

Bunyan's Chips

Publishing Co: Intl. Organization of Wooden Money Collectors, PO Box 395, Goose Creek, SC 29445-0395
General Info: Monthly

COINfidential Report
Business

Publishing Co: Bale Books, PO Box 2727, New Orleans, LA 70176-2727
Personnel: Publisher, Editor-Don Bale
Editorial Description: Amazingly accurate coin and stock analysis recommendations since 1963. Market forecasts for coins and stocks. Inside coin and stock market information.
General Info: Yr. Est. 1963, Bi-monthly, Trim Size-6 x 9, Offset press, 4 pages, No Color
Subscriptions: Indv. $20, Can. $20, For. $20, $3/copy
Acquistions: Publication Bought
Circulation: Total-2,000
Advertising: Inquire for rates.
List Rental: Actives: $50/M

Certified Coin Dealer Newsletter
Business

Publishing Co: Coin Dealer Newsletter, PO Box 7939, Torrance, CA 90504-9339;
Title Tel # (310) 515-7369 Title Fax # (310) 515-7534
Personnel: Publisher-Ron Downing, Editor-Dennis Baker
Editorial Description: Dealer bid prices on actively traded U.S. coins certified by PCGS, NGC, ANACS, & NCI.
General Info: Yr. Est. 1986, Weekly, Trim Size-8½ x 11, 12 pages, No Color
Subscriptions: Indv. $117, $5/copy
Advertising: $750.

Coin Dealer Newsletter
Business

Publishing Co: Coin Dealer Newsletter, PO Box 7939, Torrance, CA 90504-9339;
Title Tel # (310) 515-7369 Title Fax # (310) 515-7534
Personnel: Publisher-Ron Downing, Editor-Dennis Baker
Editorial Description: Dealer-to-dealer bid & ask prices for all U.S. coins; market analysis of gold & silver bullion reports.
General Info: Yr. Est. 1963, Weekly, Trim Size-8½ x 11, 12 pages, No Color
Subscriptions: Indv. $98, $5/copy
Advertising: $1,000.

Coin Dealer Newsletter Monthly Supplement
Business

Publishing Co: Coin Dealer Newsletter, PO Box 7939, Torrance, CA 90504-9339;
Title Tel # (310) 515-7369 Title Fax # (310) 515-7534
Personnel: Publisher-Ron Downing, Editor-Dennis Baker
Editorial Description: Summary of activity not covered in the weekly letter; analyses of U.S. coin market by experts.
General Info: Yr. Est. 1976, Monthly, Trim Size-8½ x 11, 12 pages, No Color
Subscriptions: Indv. $98, $5/copy
Advertising: $1,000.

Coin Previewer

Publishing Co: Coin Previewer, PO Box 770396, Coral Springs, FL 33077-0396;
Title Tel # (305) 755-3012
Personnel: Publisher, Editor-Robert Leuchten, Circ. Mgr.-Joan Downing
Editorial Description: Numismatic investments-covers the current market with specific recommendations. Also precious metal market & current numismatic events.
General Info: Yr. Est. 1974, Monthly, Trim Size-8½ x 11, Sheetfed press, 8 pages, No Color
Subscriptions: Indv. $19, $2/copy
Acquistions: Publication Bought
Advertising: Inquire for rates. Accepts Inserts.

Coin Quote

Publishing Co: Numisco Rare Coins, 1423 W Fullerton Ave, Chicago, IL 60614-2011;
Title Tel # (312) 528-8800
Personnel: Publisher-Walter Perschke, Editor-Tom DeLorey
General Info: 10x/yr.
Subscriptions: Indv. $39

Currency Dealer Newsletter
Business

Publishing Co: Coin Dealer Newsletter, PO Box 7939, Torrance, CA 90504-9339;
Title Tel # (310) 515-7369 Title Fax # (310) 515-7534
Personnel: Publisher-Ron Downing, Editor-Dennis Baker
Editorial Description: Bid & ask prices for U.S. paper money, with informative articles.
General Info: Yr. Est. 1980, Monthly, Trim Size-8½ x 11, 8 pages, No Color
Subscriptions: Indv. $44, $5/copy
Advertising: Inquire for rates.

Fare Box
Association

Publishing Co: American Vecturist Association, PO Box 1204, Boston, MA 02104-1204;
Title Tel # (617) 277-8111
Personnel: Editor-John M. Coffee, Circ. Mgr., Production Mgr.-James D. Hemphill, Adv. Dir.-Robert Butler
Editorial Description: Historical data on transportation tokens and the firms that used them, including reports on new issues and discoveries and general news of interest to collectors.
General Info: Yr. Est. 1947, Monthly, Trim Size-8½ x 11, Mimeo press, 16 pages, 1% ads, No Color
Subscriptions: Indv. $16, $1/copy
Circulation: Total-850
Advertising: Inquire for rates. Accepts Inserts.

Forecaster Moneyletter, The
See: ECONOMICS

Investors' Update
Business, Consumer

Publishing Co: California Numismatic Investments, Inc., 525 W Manchester Blvd, Inglewood, CA 90301-1627; Title Tel # (310) 674-3330 Title Fax # (310) 330-3766
Personnel: Publisher, Editor-Richard Schwary, Circ. Mgr.-Scott Peterson, Production Mgr.-Jonathan Hefferlin, Promotion Dir.-Kenny Edwards
Editorial Description: Precious metals & rare coins.
General Info: Yr. Est. 1965, Monthly, Trim Size-8$\frac{1}{2}$ x 11, 8 pages, 2 Color, Matte
Subscriptions: Indv. $25, For. $35, $4/copy
Circulation: Total-12,000

LANSA
Business, Association

Publishing Co: Latin American Paper Money Society, 3304 Milford Mill Rd., Baltimore, MI 21244-2041; Title Tel # (410) 655-3109
Personnel: Publisher, Editor-Arthur Matz, Adv. Dir.-Yasha Beresiner, Promotion Dir.-Richard Miranda
Editorial Description: Paper money of Latin America and Iberian Peninsula.
General Info: Yr. Est. 1973, Trim Size-5$\frac{1}{2}$ x 8$\frac{1}{2}$, Mimeo press, 40 pages, ISSN: 0308-8677, 20% ads, No Color
Subscriptions: Indv. $8, $3/copy
Circulation: Total-400
Advertising: Inquire for rates. Accepts Inserts.
List Rental: Rents Lists

Members Exchange
See: ART & SCULPTURE

Numismatic Studies
Association

Publishing Co: American Numismatic Society, Broadway at 155th St., New York, NY 10032; Title Tel # (212) 234-3130 Title Fax # (212) 234-3381
Personnel: Editor-Marie H. Martin, Assoc. Ed.-Leslie A. Elam
Editorial Description: Monograph series with scholarly numismatic topics.
General Info: Yr. Est. 1938, Irregular, Trim Size-8$\frac{1}{2}$ x 12, Web press, ISSN: 0517-404x, No Color, Matte, Case bound, Looseleaf

Rosen Numismatic Advisory

Publishing Co: Numismatic Counseling Inc., PO Box 38, Plainview, NY 11803-0038; Title Tel # (516) 433-5800
General Info: Yr. Est. 1976, Monthly
Subscriptions: Indv. $79

SAENT

Publishing Co: Societe pour l'Etude de la Numismatique Francaise, 4304 Belden Village St NW, Canton, OH 44718-2514
Personnel: Editor-Philip Keller
Editorial Description: Text: Eng. & Fr.
General Info: Yr. Est. 1972, Semi-annually

Value Advisor
Business, Consumer

Publishing Co: Silver Dollars Collector Club, Ltd., 1760 S Escondido Blvd, Escondido, CA 92025-6520
Personnel: Editor-Steve Hirschhorn
Editorial Description: Advice on collecting & investing in all rare coins.
General Info: Yr. Est. 1977, Monthly, Trim Size-8$\frac{1}{2}$ x 11, No Color
Subscriptions: Indv. $36, $3/copy
Circulation: Total-15,000

Worldwide Treasure Bureau
Newsletter
Consumer

Publishing Co: Worldwide Treasure Bureau, 2230 W Sunnyside Ave Ste 2, Visalia, CA 93277-7269; Title Tel # (209) 732-2252 Title Fax # (209) 732-3930
Personnel: VP Mktng.-Ron Nieburgs
Editorial Description: Information on coins and artifacts from around the world for collectors.
General Info: 8x/yr.

NURSING

AAOHN News
Association   **CPM: $76**

Publishing Co: American Assn. of Occupational Health Nurses, 50 Lenox Pointe NE, Atlanta, GA 30324-3170; Title Tel # (404) 262-1162 Title Fax # (404) 262-1165
Personnel: Editor-Lauren Anderson, Adv. Dir.-Andrea Sumpter
Editorial Description: Covers news and issues of importance to Association members.
General Info: Yr. Est. 1942, Monthly, Trim Size-8$\frac{1}{2}$ x 11, Offset press, 8 pages, ISSN: 0746-620X, 2% ads, No Color, Coated, Saddle-stitched
Subscriptions: Indv. $12, Free With Membership
Circulation: (1% controlled), Total-13,000, Single Copy/Newsstand-250, Subscriptions-12,500
Advertising: $1,000.
List Rental: Actives: $65/M

AAPT News
See: PSYCHOLOGY

AARN Newsletter
Association   **CPM: $51**

Publishing Co: Alberta Association of Registered Nurses, 11620-168 St., Edmonton, AB T5M 4A6 Canada; Title Tel # (403) 451-0043 Title Fax # (403) 452-3276
Personnel: Editor-Evelyn Henderson
Editorial Description: Association news and developments of interest to nursing professionals.
General Info: Yr. Est. 1948, Monthly, Trim Size-8$\frac{1}{2}$ x 11, Sheetfed press, 32 pages, ISSN: 0001-0197, 4 Color, Coated, Saddle-stitched
Subscriptions: Indv. $35, Can. $50, $4/copy
Circulation: Total-25,250, Readership-25,250
Advertising: $1,300.
Printing Co: Quality Color Press, Inc., 17612 103rd Ave., Edmonton, AB T5S 1J9 Canada Tel # (403) 486-1199

ARN News
See: HEALTH

ARNN Access
Association

Publishing Co: Assn. of Registered Nurses of Newfoundland, PO Box 6116, 55 Military Rd., St. John's, NF A1C 5X8 Canada; Title Tel # (709) 753-6040 Title Fax # (709) 753-4940
Personnel: Exec. Ed.-Elizabeth Adey
Editorial Description: Informs nurses of issues and current developments in the profession.
General Info: (Formerly ARNN News), Yr. Est. 1975, Quarterly, Trim Size-8$\frac{1}{2}$ x 11, Sheetfed press, 16 pages, 2 Color, Matte, Saddle-stitched
Subscriptions: Can. $10
Circulation: (100% controlled), Total-6,000
Advertising: Inquire for rates.

ASCA Quarterly
See: HEALTH

ASNA Reporter

Publishing Co: Alabama State Nurses Assn., 360 N Hull St, Montgomery, AL 36104-3644; Title Tel # (205) 262-8321
Personnel: Editor-Elizabeth Barker, R.N.
Editorial Description: The latest information on continuing education programs throughout Alabama, professional meetings, etc.
General Info: Monthly, Trim Size-7 x 10, 4 pages, ISSN: 0024-5232, 2 Color
Subscriptions: Indv. $15, $2/copy
Circulation: (100% controlled), Total-3,200
Advertising: Inquire for rates.

Addictions Nursing Network

Publishing Co: Mary Ann Liebert, Inc., 1651 3rd Ave, New York, NY 10128-3649 Tel # (212) 289-2300
Personnel: Editor-Madeline Naegel
Editorial Description: Its focus is the most current, concise, and practical information available on the serious major health problems as well as the specialties of addictions nursing.
General Info: Yr. Est. 1988, Quarterly, ISSN: 0899-9112, Saddle-stitched
Subscriptions: Indv. $95, Can. $69, For. $109

Alaska Nurse
Association

Publishing Co: Alaska Nurses Association, 237 E. 3rd, Anchorage, AK 99501-2532; Title Tel # (907) 274-0827 Title Fax # (907) 272-0292
General Info: Yr. Est. 1953, Bi-monthly, Trim Size-8$\frac{1}{2}$ x 11
Subscriptions: Indv. $15, Can. $20, For. $20
Circulation: Total-500

Ambulatory Nursing
Administration

Publishing Co: American Academy of Ambulatory Nursing, 56 N Woodbury Rd # 56, Pitman, NJ 08071-1252; Title Tel # (609) 582-9617
Editorial Description: Members are registered nurses engaged in the care of ambulatory patients.
General Info: Yr. Est. 1972, Bi-monthly
Subscriptions: Indv. $75

Arizona Nurse
Association   **CPM: $300**

Publishing Co: Arizona Nurses' Assn., 1850 E Southern Ave # 1, Tempe, AZ 85282-5832; Title Tel # (602) 831-0404 Title Fax # (602) 839-4780
Editorial Description: Nursing; health related issues, state legislation, continuing education.
General Info: Yr. Est. 1947, Monthly, Trim Size-8$\frac{1}{2}$ x 11, Web press, 8 pages, ISSN: 0004-1599, Ind/Abs/Online: Cum.Ind.Nursing, 2 Color, Newsprint, Saddle-stitched
Subscriptions: Indv. $30, $3/copy
Circulation: Total-2,000
Advertising: $600.
List Rental: Actives: $75/M

Aspen's Advisor for
Nurse Executives
Business

Publishing Co: Aspen Publishers, Inc., 200 Orchard Ridge Dr., Ste 200, Gaithersburg, MD 20878-5440 Fax # (301) 417-7655 Parent Co.-Wolters Kluwer US Corporation, New York; Title Tel # (301) 417-7500 Title Fax # (301) 417-7550
Personnel: Publisher-Michael Brown, Publisher-Richard Kravitz, Editor-Cathleen Wilson
Editorial Description: Management info for the nurse executive.
General Info: Yr. Est. 1985, Monthly
Subscriptions: Indv. $155, $16/copy
List Rental: List Management Co.: Stevens-Knox List Management, 304 Park Ave S., New York, NY 10010-5312 Tel # (212) 388-8800, Fax # (212) 388-8890, Actives: $80/M

Association of Pediatric Oncology Nurses · *Association*

Publishing Co: Assn. of Pediatric Oncology Nurses, Box 7999, Pacific Med.Ctr., San Francisco, CA 94120-7999; Title Tel # (415) 563-8777
Editorial Description: Nurses caring for children with cancer.
General Info: Quarterly

BRN Report · *Association*

Publishing Co: California Board of Registered Nursing, PO Box 944210, Sacramento, CA 94244-2100; Title Tel # (916) 322-3350
Personnel: Editor-Fran Wright, Mng. Editor-Heidi Goodman
Editorial Description: Information pertaining to new laws, regulations policies concerning registered nursing.
General Info: (Formerly California Board of Registered Nursing), Semi-annually, 8 pages, 2 Color, Coated
Subscriptions: Free
Circulation: (100% controlled), Total-250,000
List Rental: Actives: $40/M
Printing Co: California Office of State Printing, 344 N. 7 th St., Sacramento, CA 95814

CAUSN Newsletter/Bulletin d'Information
See: EDUCATION

CHCG Pulse · *Association*

Publishing Co: Canadian Health Care Guild, #200 William Gray Building, 17410-107 Avenue, Edmonton, AB T5S 1E9 Canada; Title Tel # (403) 483-8126 Title Fax # (403) 484-3341
Personnel: Editor-Lynn Arbour
Editorial Description: Covers Guild news and events as well as healthcare/nursing industry news.
General Info: Yr. Est. 1976, Bi-monthly, Trim Size-8½ x 11, Letrpr. press, 1 pages, ISSN: 0706-2192, No Color, Coated
Subscriptions: Indv. $16
Acquistions: Publication Bought, Publication Sold
Circulation: Total-7,000

Carenotes

Publishing Co: College of Nursing Alumni Assn., Ohio State Univ., 1585 Neil Ave., Columbus, OH 43210-1289; Title Tel # (614) 292-2658
Personnel: Editor-Kathy Peppet
Editorial Description: This is an alumni newsletter mailed to all College of Nursing Alumni at Ohio State Univ.
General Info: Semi-annually, 12 pages
Circulation: Total-8,000
Printing Co: Zimmerman Publishing, 929 Harrison Ave, Columbus, OH 43215-1300 Tel # (614) 294-8881

Chicago District · *Business, Association* · CPM: $214

Publishing Co: Chicago Nurses Association, 203 N. Wabash Ave., Ste. 818, Chicago, IL 60601-2411; Title Tel # (312) 263-2708
Editorial Description: Covers nurses' image, better health care in Chicago; includes calendar of events.
General Info: (Formerly First), Yr. Est. 1946, Bi-monthly, Trim Size-8½ x 11, 4 pages, ISSN: 0199-2066, 2 Color
Subscriptions: $10/copy
Circulation: (100% controlled), Total-1,400
Advertising: $300.
Printing Co: Integrated Printing Group Inc., 800 E 31st St, La Grange Park, IL 60525-1223 Tel # (708) 354-3200

College of Nurses of Ontario College Communique

Publishing Co: College of Nurses of Ontario, 101 Davenport Rd., Toronto, ON M5R 3P1 Canada; Title Tel # (416) 928-0900 Title Fax # (416) 928-6507
General Info: Yr. Est. 1972, Bi-monthly
Subscriptions: Indv. $7, Can. $5, For. $7
Circulation: Total-145,000

Colorado Nurse · *Business* · CPM: $606

Publishing Co: Colorado Nurses Assn., 5453 E. Evans Pl., Denver, CO 80222-5206; Title Tel # (303) 757-7483 Title Fax # (303) 757-2679
Editorial Description: Serves all licensed nurses including RN's, LPN's, student nurses and advanced degree in Colorado.
General Info: Quarterly
Circulation: Total-49,000
Advertising: $29,700.
Printing Co: Arthur L. Davis Agency, 517 Washington St., Box 216, Cedar Falls, IA 50613-2842 Tel # (319) 277-2414, Fax # (319) 277-4055

Connecticut Nursing News · *Association*

Publishing Co: Connecticut Nurses Assn., 377 Research Pky Ste 2d, Meriden, CT 06450-7155; Title Tel # (203) 238-1207 Title Fax # (203) 238-3437
Personnel: Editor, Adv. Dir., Promotion Dir.-Karen S. Ponton
General Info: Yr. Est. 1904, Monthly, Trim Size-11½ x 14¼, Web press, 4 pages, ISSN: 0278-4092, 3% ads, No Color, Matte
Subscriptions: Indv. $20, $2/copy
Circulation: Total-2,000
List Rental: Actives: 1,600, $50/M
Printing Co: Marketing Design Group, Inc., 444 Main St # 1067, Deep River, CT 06417-2034

DNA Focus · *Association*

Publishing Co: Anthony Jannetti, Inc., E. Holly Ave. Box 56, Pitman, NJ 08071 Tel # (609) 256-2300; Title Tel # (609) 582-1915 Title Fax # (609) 589-7463
Personnel: Editor-P. Theringar, Adv. Dir.-Michael Cunningham
General Info: Yr. Est. 1982, Bi-monthly, 8 pages, 2 Color
Circulation: Total-600
Advertising: Inquire for rates.
Printing Co: Review Printing Co., 53 E Holly Ave, Pitman, NJ 08071-1198 Tel # (609) 589-7200

Delaware Nurses' Association Reporter

Publishing Co: Delaware Nurses Assn., 2634 Capitol TRL #C, Newark, DE 19711-7263; Title Tel # (302) 368-2333
Personnel: Editor-Brent Thompson
General Info: (Formerly Delaware Nurse), Yr. Est. 1968, 10x/yr., Trim Size-8½ x 11, 8 pages
Subscriptions: Indv. $10
Circulation: Total-800
List Rental: Actives: $40/M

Florida Nurse · *Association* · CPM: $77

Publishing Co: Florida Nurses Assn., PO Box 536985, Orlando, FL 32853-6985; Title Tel # (407) 896-3261
Personnel: Editor-Paula Massey, Advertising & Sales-Melissa Hutcherson, Adv. Dir., Mktg. Dir.-Debra Simko
General Info: Yr. Est. 1953, Monthly, Trim Size-11¼ x 14, Web press, 20 pages, ISSN: 0015-4199, 4 Color
Subscriptions: Indv. $15
Circulation: (100% controlled), Total-10,000
Advertising: $775.
List Rental: Rents Lists

Forum, The

Publishing Co: NAPNES, 1400 Spring St Ste 310, Silver Spring, MD 20910-2735; Title Tel # (301) 588-2491 Title Fax # (301) 588-2839
Personnel: Editor-Kathy Jentz, Circ. Dir.-Joyce Strong
Editorial Description: Latest news on practical nursing - education opportunities, conventions, scholarships, new regulations, etc.
General Info: 8x/yr.
Subscriptions: $1/copy
Printing Co: Newsletter Services, Inc., 9700 Philadelphia Court, Lanham, MD 20706 Tel # (301) 731-5200, Fax # (301) 731-5201

Geriatric Care · *Business*

Publishing Co: Eymann Publications, Inc., PO Box 3577, Reno, NV 89505-3577 Fax # (702) 323-2770; Title Tel # (702) 333-6651
Personnel: Publisher, Editor-Ken Eymann, Mng. Editor-Laurie Hall, Circ. Mgr.-Katie Pace
Editorial Description: Training for those who work with the elderly.
General Info: Yr. Est. 1969, Monthly, 4 pages, No Color
Subscriptions: Indv. $75
Circulation: Total-50,000

HANYS News
See: HEALTH

Health Professions Report
See: EDUCATION

Health Victory Bulletin
See: HEALTH

Home Advantage
See: ADVERTISING & MARKETING

Homecare Direction
See: HEALTH

ISNA Bulletin · *Association* · CPM: $156

Publishing Co: Indiana State Nurses Assn., 2915 N High School Rd, Indianapolis, IN 46224-2969 Fax # (217) 297-3525; Title Tel # (317) 299-4575 Title Fax # (317) 297-3525
Personnel: Editor-Naomi Patchin, Production Mgr.-Ernest Klein
Editorial Description: Covers Indiana nursing & the assn.
General Info: Yr. Est. 1974, 10x/yr., Trim Size-7½ x 10, Web press, 8 pages, 2% ads, 2 Color, Coated
Subscriptions: Indv. $30, Inst. $35
Circulation: Total-2,400
Advertising: $375.
List Rental: Actives: 3,000, $100/M

Iowa Board of Nursing Newsletter · *Association* · CPM: $675

Publishing Co: Arthur L. Davis Publishing Agency, 517 Washington Street, PO Box 216, Cedar Falls, IA 50613; Title Tel # (319) 277-2414 Title Fax # (319) 277-4055
Personnel: Publisher-Arthur L. Davis
Editorial Description: Serves all licensed nurses including RN's, LPN's, student nurses and advanced degree in Iowa.
General Info: Quarterly
Circulation: Total-44,000
Advertising: $29,700.
List Rental: Actives: 42,000

Journal Watch
See: MEDICINE

Journal Watch for Psychiatry
See: PSYCHIATRY

Kansas Board of Nursing
Newsletter   *Business*   **CPM: $781**

Publishing Co: Arthur L. Davis Publishing Agency, 517 Washington Street, PO Box 216, Cedar Falls, IA 50613; Title Tel # (319) 277-2414 Title Fax # (319) 277-4055
Personnel: Publisher-Arthur L. Davis
Editorial Description: Serves all licensed nurses including RN's, LPN's, student nurses and advanced degree in Kansas.
General Info: Quarterly
Circulation: Total-38,000
Advertising: $29,700.
List Rental: Actives: 35,000

Kentucky Nurse   *Business*   **CPM: $582**

Publishing Co: Kentucky Nurses Association, PO Box 2616, Louisville, KY 40201; Title Tel # (502) 637-2546 Title Fax # (502) 637-8236
Editorial Description: Serves all licensed nurses including RN's, LPN's, student nurses and advanced degree in Kentucky.
General Info: Quarterly
Circulation: Total-51,000
Advertising: $29,700.
Printing Co: Arthur L. Davis Agency, 517 Washington St., Box 216, Cedar Falls, IA 50613-2842 Tel # (319) 277-2414, Fax # (319) 277-4055

Laughter Prescription Newsletter
See: HUMOR & SATIRE

Legislative Network for
Nursing   *Business*

Publishing Co: Business Publishers, Inc., 951 Pershing Dr., Silver Spring, MD 20910-4464 Tel # (301) 589-5103 Fax # (301) 589-8493; Title Tel # (301) 587-6300 Title Fax # (301) 587-1081
Personnel: Publisher-Eric Easton, Editor-B.K. Morris, Circ. Mgr.-Kathleen Harrow, Promotion Dir.-Pat Nussman
Editorial Description: The only monthly publication dedicated to helping develop and improve nursing recruitment and retention programs.
General Info: (Formerly Nursing Recruitment and Retention), Yr. Est. 1988, Monthly, Trim Size-8½ x 11, Desktop press, 8 pages, Ind/Abs/Online: Newsnet & Predicasts, No Color, Recycled
Subscriptions: Indv. $330, Inst. $330, Can. $330, For. $336
Advertising: Accepts Inserts.
List Rental: List Management Co.: Manager: Donald Peterson; World Innovators, Inc., 72 Park St., New Canaan, CT 06840 Tel # (203) 966-0374, Fax # (208) 966-0926
Printing Co: Newsletter Press, 930-32 Bonifant St., Silver Spring, CT 20910

Long Term Care Monitor
See: HEALTH

MLN New Directions   *Association*

Publishing Co: Minnesota League for Nursing, PO Box 24713, Edina, MN 55424-0713 Tel # (612) 829-5891 Fax # (612) 920-0321
Personnel: Publisher-Marie Manthey, Editor-Julie Ditzler, Circ. Mgr., Art Dir.-Joan Carlson
Editorial Description: Member newsletter; update on the activities of the league.
General Info: (Formerly MLN Bulletin), Yr. Est. 1953, Quarterly, 4 pages, No Color
Subscriptions: Indv. $10
Circulation: Total-500
List Rental: Rents Lists

M.O.N.A. Pulse   *Association*

Publishing Co: Manitoba Organization of Nurses Assns., 502-275 Broadway, Winnipeg, MB R3C 4M6 Canada; Title Tel # (204) 632-6605
Personnel: Editor-Shirley Popadiuk, Circ. Mgr.-Laurel Jasper
Editorial Description: Contains articles related to the nursing profession, health care & labor relations.
General Info: Yr. Est. 1975, 5x/yr., Trim Size-8½ x 11, Web press, 12 pages, 2 Color, Newsprint, Saddle-stitched
Acquistions: Publication Bought
Circulation: (100% controlled), Total-10,000
Printing Co: Communigraphics, Inc., 41 May St., Winnipeg, MB R3B 0H1 Canada Tel # (204) 942-7351

Maine Nurse   *Association*

Publishing Co: Maine State Nurses Assn., PO Box 2240, Augusta, ME 04338-2240; Title Tel # (207) 622-1057
General Info: Yr. Est. 1966, Quarterly, Trim Size-11 x 14, Web press, 8 pages
Subscriptions: Indv. $25, $5/copy
Circulation: (100% controlled), Total-1,500
Advertising: Inquire for rates.

Michigan Nurse   *Association*

Publishing Co: Michigan Nurses Assn., 2310 Jolly Oak Rd, Okemos, MI 48864-4599; Title Tel # (517) 349-5640 Title Fax # (517) 349-5818
Personnel: Editor-Carol Franck, Circ. Mgr., Production Mgr., Adv. Dir., Promotion Dir.-Linda Wilkins-Brown
Editorial Description: MNA activities and news, current topics and trends in nursing.
General Info: Yr. Est. 1924, Monthly, Trim Size-8½ x 11, Web press, 16 pages, ISSN: 0026-2366, 2% ads, 2 Color, Newsprint, Saddle-stitched
Subscriptions: Indv. $15, For. $50, $5/copy
Circulation: (100% controlled), Total-7,200
Advertising: Inquire for rates.
Printing Co: Millbrook Printing Co., 3540 Jefferson Hwy, Grand Ledge, MI 48837-9750 Tel # (517) 627-4078

Minnesota Nursing
Accent   *Business, Association*

Publishing Co: Minnesota Nurses Assn., 1295 Bandana Blvd. N., Ste. 140, St. Paul, MN 55108-5115; Title Tel # (612) 646-4807 Title Fax # (612) 646-4807
Personnel: Editor-Hope Caldeen
Editorial Description: News about nursing in Minnesota and USA.
General Info: Yr. Est. 1925, Monthly, Trim Size-11 x 17, Offset press, 12 pages, 1% ads, Color, Newsprint, Saddle-stitched
Subscriptions: Indv. $25
Acquistions: Publication Bought
Circulation: Total-12,500
Advertising: Inquire for rates.
Printing Co: ABC Printers, 4101 Coon Rapids Blvd., Coon Rapids, MN 55433

N.A.H.C. Report
See: HEALTH

NAS Newsletter

Publishing Co: NAS Newsletter, 92 S Highland Ave, Ossining, NY 10562-5615; Title Tel # (914) 762-6498
Editorial Description: Covers news of the National Association of School Nurses. Focuses on issues of importance to school nurses nationwide.
General Info: 5x/yr.

NASNewsletter

Publishing Co: Sponsor-Natl. Assn. of School Nurses, Franklin Communications, 92 S Highland Ave, Ossining, NY 10562-5615; Title Tel # (914) 762-6498
Personnel: Publisher-Michael Franklin, Editor-Beverly Farguhar, Circ. Mgr.-Gloria Durgin, Adv. Dir.-Susan McCandless, Art Dir.-Marion Franklin
General Info: Monthly, Sheetfed press, 16 pages, 3% ads, 4 Color, Coated
Circulation: Total-5,000
Advertising: Accepts Inserts.
Printing Co: Canterbury Press, 301 Mill St, P.O. Box #4299, Rome, NY 13440-6952 Tel # (315) 337-5900, Fax # (315) 337-4070

NWTRNA Newsletter   *Association*

Publishing Co: Northwest Territories Registered Nurses Assn., Box 2757, Yellowknife, NT X1A 2R1 Canada; Title Tel # (403) 873-2745
General Info: (Formerly Northern Nurses News), Yr. Est. 1974, Quarterly, 16 pages
Circulation: Total-600
Advertising: Inquire for rates.

Nevada RNformation   *Association*   **CPM$2700**

Publishing Co: Nevada Nurses Association, 3660 Baker Lane, Reno, NV 89509-5409; Title Tel # (702) 825-3555 Title Fax # (702) 825-3555
Editorial Description: Serves all nurses including RN's, LPN's, student nurses and advanced degree in Nevada.
General Info: Quarterly
Circulation: Total-11,000
Advertising: $29,700.
List Rental: Actives: 11,000
Printing Co: Arthur L. Davis Agency, 517 Washington St., Box 216, Cedar Falls, IA 50613-2842 Tel # (319) 277-2414, Fax # (319) 277-4055

New Jersey Nurse   *Association*   **CPM: $135**

Publishing Co: New Jersey State Nurses Assn., 320 W State St, Trenton, NJ 08618-5704; Title Tel # (609) 392-4884 Title Fax # (609) 396-2330
Personnel: Editor-Dorothy Flemming, Production Mgr.-Andrea Aughenbaugh, Adv. Dir.-Julia Schneider
Editorial Description: Association program updates; continuing education information, state governmental updates, legislative information.
General Info: Yr. Est. 1902, Monthly, Trim Size-9¾ x 16, Web press, 16 pages, 3% ads, Color, Newsprint
Subscriptions: Indv. $20, For. $30, $3/copy
Circulation: (100% controlled), Total-5,000
Advertising: $675.

Nightingale *Association*

Publishing Co: National Association of Physicians' Nurses, 900 S Washington St Ste G13, Falls Church, VA 22046-4020; Title Tel # (703) 237-8616
Personnel: Publisher, Editor-R. Ludeman
Editorial Description: Medical information important to physicians and nurses. Personal information important to working women.
General Info: Yr. Est. 1973, Monthly, Trim Size-11 x 17, Offset press, 4 pages, ISSN: 0894-5780, 2 Color
Subscriptions: Indv. $15, Can. $20, For. $20, Free With Membership
Circulation: Total-3,500
List Rental: Actives: 3,500, $90/M, Expires: 2,000, $90/M

Nurses' Drug Alert
See: DRUGS & PHARMACEUTICALS

Nursing Educators
MicroWorld *Association*

Publishing Co: Nursing Educators MicroWorld, 1600 Saratoga Ave., Ste. 403, San Jose, CA 95129-5108; Title Tel # (408) 741-0156 Title Fax # (408) 741-5987
Personnel: Publisher, Editor-Christine Bolwell
Editorial Description: News, reviews & opinions for & about nurse educators using & planning to use microcomputers.
General Info: (Formerly Diskovery:computer-assisted healthcare education), Yr. Est. 1986, Bi-monthly, Trim Size-8½ x 11, Offset press, 8 pages, ISSN: 0893-1356, Ind/Abs/Online: CINAHL,Medline, Saddle-stitched
Subscriptions: Indv. $37, Inst. $74, Can. $47, For. $57

Nursing News *Association*

Publishing Co: Nurses Assn. of the Counties of Long Island, 99 Tulip Ave # 404, Floral Park, NY 11001-1959
Personnel: Editor-Barbara Malon
Editorial Description: Association news, meetings, educational conferences and programs, etc.
General Info: Yr. Est. 1936, Bi-monthly, Trim Size-8½ x 11, Sheetfed press, 8 pages, No Color
Subscriptions: Indv. $5, $1/copy
Circulation: Total-5,200
Advertising: Inquire for rates.

Nursing Quality Connection *Association*

Publishing Co: Mosby, 11830 Westline Industrial Dr., St. Louis, MO 63146-3313 Tel # (314) 872-8370 Fax # (314) 432-1380 Parent Co.-Times Mirror Company, Los Angeles
Personnel: Editor-Patricia Schroeder
Editorial Description: Reports on new developments, strategies, and regulations that all involved in quality must know.
General Info: Yr. Est. 1991, Bi-monthly
Subscriptions: Indv. $50, Inst. $65, Can. $75, For. $70

Nursing Staff Development
Insider *Association*

Publishing Co: Mosby, 11830 Westline Industrial Dr., St. Louis, MO 63146-3313 Tel # (314) 872-8370 Fax # (314) 432-1380 Parent Co.-Times Mirror Company, Los Angeles
Personnel: Editor-Donna Sheridan
Editorial Description: Offers trade secrets and proven ideas from a national network of experienced staff developers.
General Info: Yr. Est. 1992, Bi-monthly, Trim Size-8½ x 11, 8 pages
Subscriptions: Indv. $40, Inst. $55, Can. $50, For. $55

OR Manager
See: HEALTH

Oklahoma Nurse *Business* CPM: $690

Publishing Co: Arthur L. Davis Publishing Agency, 517 Washington Street, PO Box 216, Cedar Falls, IA 50613; Title Tel # (319) 277-2414 Title Fax # (319) 277-4055
Personnel: Publisher-Arthur L. Davis
Editorial Description: Serves all licensed nurses including RN's, LPN's, student nurses and advanced degree in Oklahoma.
General Info: Quarterly
Circulation: Total-43,000
Advertising: $29,700.

Ontario Nurses Association
Newsletter *Association*

Publishing Co: Ontario Nurses Assn., 85 Granville St., #600, Toronto, ON M5S 3A2 Canada; Title Tel # (416) 964-8833
General Info: 10x/yr.

Outpatient Reimbursement Management
See: HOSPITALS & NURSING HOMES

Parasol

Publishing Co: New Brunswick Nurses' Union, 750 Brunswick St., Fredericton, NB E3B 1H9 Canada; Title Tel # (506) 458-0118 Title Fax # (506) 459-2578
Personnel: Editor-Madeleine Steeves
General Info: Yr. Est. 1981, Quarterly, 12 pages, Color-cover
Circulation: Total-5,500
Printing Co: Wilson Printing, 410 Aberdeen St., P.O. Box 1373, Fredericton, NB E3B 5E3 Canada Tel # (506) 453-9909

Parent Care News Brief
See: BABY

Patient Education Management
See: HOSPITALS & NURSING HOMES

Pennsylvania Nurse *Association* CPM: $112

Publishing Co: Pennsylvania Nurses Assn., 2578 Interstate Dr., PO Box 68525, Harrisburg, PA 17110-9601; Title Tel # (717) 657-1222 Title Fax # (717) 657-3796
Personnel: Editor-Barry Ciccocioppo
Editorial Description: To inform members of association activities, report on conferences and meetings and issues in nursing.
General Info: Yr. Est. 1967, 11x/yr., Trim Size-10 x 14, Web press, 24 pages, ISSN: 0031-4617, 5% ads, 2 Color, Newsprint
Subscriptions: Indv. $15, Inst. $15, $1/copy
Circulation: Total-8,000
Advertising: $900.
List Rental: Rents Lists
Printing Co: Lewistown Sentinel, 375 Sixth St., PO Box 588, Lewistown, PA 17044 Fax # (717) 248-8317

Perspectives on Addictions Nursing
See: HEALTH

Perspectives in Respiratory Nursing
See: HEALTH

Psychosocial Nursing &
Mental Health Service

Publishing Co: Charles B. Slack, Inc., 6900 Grove Rd, Thorofare, NJ 08086-9447; Title Tel # (609) 848-1000 Title Fax # (609) 853-5991
Personnel: Publisher-Richard Roash, Editor-John Bond, Circ. Mgr.-Les Robeson, Adv. Dir.-P. Ford
General Info: Yr. Est. 1963, Monthly
Subscriptions: Indv. $44, Inst. $54, Can. $62, For. $80, $8/copy
Circulation: Total-12,000

RN Idaho *Association*

Publishing Co: Idaho State Nurses' Assn, 200 N. 4th, #M-20, Boise, ID 83702-6001; Title Tel # (208) 323-0103
Personnel: Editor-Nancy Leslie
General Info: Bi-monthly, Web press, 8 pages, ISSN: 0192-298X, No Color
Subscriptions: Indv. $10, $2/copy
Circulation: Total-750
Advertising: Inquire for rates.
Printing Co: Graphic Arts, 2285 Warm Springs Ave, Boise, ID 83712-8430 Tel # (208) 375-1010

RPT on Healthcare
Mgnt. & Solutions *Business, Association*

Publishing Co: Business Publishers, Inc., 951 Pershing Dr., Silver Spring, MD 20910-4464 Tel # (301) 589-5103 Fax # (301) 589-8493; Title Tel # (301) 587-6300 Title Fax # (301) 587-1081
Personnel: Publisher-Eric Easton, Editor-Carl Ayers, Circ. Mgr.-Kathleen Harrow, Promotion Dir.-Pat Nussman
Editorial Description: Covers immediate operational concerns and helps solve day-to-day problems, with case studies, interviews & innovative ideas that are working for other hospitals.
General Info: (Formerly Hospital Patient Relations Report), Yr. Est. 1980, Monthly, Trim Size-8½ x 11, Desktop press, 8 pages, Ind/Abs/Online: Newsnet & Predicasts, No Color, Recycled
Subscriptions: Indv. $276, Inst. $276, Can. $276, For. $282
Circulation: Total-250
Advertising: Accepts Inserts.
List Rental: List Management Co.: Manager: Donald Peterson; World Innovators, Inc., 72 Park St., New Canaan, CT 06840 Tel # (203) 966-0374, Fax # (208) 966-0926

Recruitment Directions *Association*

Publishing Co: National Association for Health Care Recruitment, PO Box 5769, Akron, OH 44372-5769 Fax # (216) 867-1630; Title Tel # (216) 867-3088
Personnel: Editor-Karen Hart
General Info: (Formerly NANR News), Yr. Est. 1975, Bi-monthly, Trim Size-8½ x 11, 12 pages, No Color
Subscriptions: Indv. $85
Circulation: Total-1,500
Advertising: Inquire for rates.
List Rental: Actives: 1,300, $500/M

Regan Report on Nursing
Law *Business*

Publishing Co: Medica Press Inc., 10 Dorrance St. - Rm. 500, Providence, RI 02903-2018; Title Tel # (401) 421-4747 Title Fax # (401) 421-4747
Personnel: Circ. Mgr.-Elaine Bedrosian, Publisher, Editor, Production Mgr.-David Tammelleo
Editorial Description: Reports the latest & most significant Appellate court decisions on Nursing, Law & Malpractice. In a case and comment format with lessons on legal rights and responsibilities, risk management and malpractice, and defense strategies.
General Info: Yr. Est. 1960, Monthly, Trim Size-8½ x 11, Offset press, 4 pages, ISSN: 0034-3196, Ind/Abs/Online: CINAHL, Color, Coated
Subscriptions: Indv. $48, Can. $48, For. $48, $4/copy
Circulation: Total-40,000
List Rental: Rents Lists

Saskatchewan Assn. of Certified Nursing Assistants Newsletter   *Association*

Publishing Co: Saskatchewan Assn. of Certified Nursing Assistants, 2310 Smith St., Regina, SK S4P 2P6 Canada; Title Tel # (306) 525-1436
Personnel: Editor-Ede Leeson
Editorial Description: News about the ass'n & about certified nsg. assistants in general.
General Info: Quarterly, 25 pages, 2 Color, Saddle-stitched
Subscriptions: Can. $5
Circulation: (100% controlled), Total-2,600

South Carolina Nurse   *Business*   CPM: $645

Publishing Co: Arthur L. Davis Publishing Agency, 517 Washington Street, PO Box 216, Cedar Falls, IA 50613 Fax # (319) 277-4055; Title Tel # (319) 277-2414 Title Fax # (219) 277-4055
Personnel: Publisher-Arthur L. Davis
Editorial Description: Serves all licensed nurses including RN's, LPN's, student nurses and advanced degree in South Carolina.
General Info: Quarterly
Circulation: Total-46,000
Advertising: $29,700.

South Dakota Nurse Newsletter   *Association*   CPM$2970

Publishing Co: Arthur L. Davis Publishing Agency, 517 Washington Street, PO Box 216, Cedar Falls, IA 50613; Title Tel # (319) 277-2414 Title Fax # (319) 277-4055
Personnel: Publisher-Arthur L. Davis
Editorial Description: Serves all licensed nurses including RN's, LPN's, student nurses and advanced degree in South Dakota.
General Info: Quarterly
Circulation: Total-10,000
Advertising: $29,700.
List Rental: Actives, 10,000

Stat   *Association*

Publishing Co: Wisconsin Nurses Assn., 6117 Monona Dr., Madison, WI 53716-3995; Title Tel # (608) 221-0383
Personnel: Editor-JoAnn Hanaway
Editorial Description: News & information: nursing issues, resources, practice, law, legislation, education.
General Info: Yr. Est. 1964, Semi-monthly, Offset press, 4 pages, ISSN: 0038-9986, No Color
Subscriptions: Indv. $45

Tar Heel Nurse   *Association*   CPM: $138

Publishing Co: North Carolina Nurses Assn., PO Box 12025, Raleigh, NC 27605-2025; Title Tel # (919) 821-4250 Title Fax # (919) 829-5807
Personnel: Editor-Sindy Barker, Circ. Mgr.-Melody Hocutt
Editorial Description: Nursing news of North Carolina, activities of North Carolina Nurses Association, issues and trends in nursing profession.
General Info: Yr. Est. 1943, Bi-monthly, Trim Size-8½ x 11, Sheetfed press, 32 pages, ISSN: 0039-9620, Ind/Abs/Online: Cum.In.Nursing, No Color, Matte, Saddle-stitched
Subscriptions: Indv. $25, $5/copy
Circulation: Total-3,600
Advertising: $500.
List Rental: Rents Lists
Printing Co: Universal Printing, 1407 Downtown Blvd., Raleigh, NC 27603 Tel # (919) 361-5809, Fax # (919) 361-5810

Utah Nurse   *Association*   CPM: $92

Publishing Co: Utah Nurses Association, 455 E 400 S Ste 402, Salt Lake City, UT 84111-3008; Title Tel # (801) 322-3439 Title Fax # (801) 822-3430
Personnel: Editor-Linda Deschner
Editorial Description: Official newsletter of the Utah Nurses' Assn. Contains nursing practice requirements, Board actions, Continuing Education, and other news.
General Info: (Formerly UNA Communique; One on One/Pro Re Nata), Yr. Est. 1975, Quarterly, 6 pages, 2 Color
Subscriptions: Inst. $12, Free To Qualified Recipient
Circulation: Total-18,000
Advertising: $1,656.

Utah Pro Re Nata   *Association*   CPM$1650

Publishing Co: Arthur L. Davis Publishing Agency, 517 Washington Street, PO Box 216, Cedar Falls, IA 50613; Title Tel # (319) 277-2414 Title Fax # (319) 277-4055
Personnel: Publisher-Arthur L. Davis
Editorial Description: Serves all licensed nurses including RN's, LPN's student nurses and advanced degree in Utah.
General Info: Quarterly
Circulation: Total-18,000
Advertising: $29,700.
List Rental: Actives, 17,000

VNAB Newsletter   *Association*

Publishing Co: Visiting Nurse Assn. of B'klyn., Public Relations Dept., 138 S. Oxford St., Brooklyn, NY 11217 Tel # (718) 230-6927 Fax # (718) 636-7972; Title Tel # (718) 636-7580 Title Fax # (718) 636-7572
Personnel: Editor-Elanor Brand
Editorial Description: Features information on the services provided by the VNA of Brooklyn & the activities of its board, staff & committee members. Covers news about home health care.
General Info: Yr. Est. 1970, 3x/yr., Offset press, 4 pages, 2 Color, Newsprint
Subscriptions: Free
Circulation: (91% controlled), Total-15,000
Printing Co: JNB Printing, 244 26th St, Brooklyn, NY 11232-1610 Tel # (718) 965-4700

Vital Signs   *Association*   CPM: $13

Publishing Co: National Nurses Association, 1765 Business Center Dr, Reston, VA 22090-5300 Fax # (703) 438-3072; Title Tel # (703) 438-3060 Title Fax # (703) 438-3049
Personnel: Publisher-Bruce Pifel, Editor-Monica Worth, Circ. Mgr.-Caroly Jones
Editorial Description: Information on nurses and the nursing profession.
General Info: Yr. Est. 1984, Quarterly, Trim Size-8½ x 11, 8 pages, ISSN: 1040-0281, 2 Color, Matte, Saddle-stitched
Subscriptions: Free With Membership
Circulation: Total-20,000, Readership-30,000
Advertising: $275. Accepts Inserts.
List Rental: Actives: 20,000, $65/M, Expires: 15,000, $55/M

Wyoming Nurse   *Association*

Publishing Co: Wyoming Nurses' Association, 1603 Capitol Ave., Ste. 305, Cheyenne, WY 82001-4561 Tel # (301) 635-3955; Title Tel # (307) 635-3955
Editorial Description: Quarterly newsletter to all RNs & LPNs licensed in Wyoming.
General Info: Yr. Est. 1926, Quarterly, Trim Size-0 x 16, 28 pages, No Color
Subscriptions: Indv. $15, Free With Membership
Circulation: Total-6,000
Advertising: Inquire for rates.
List Rental: Rents Lists
Printing Co: Arthur L. Davis Agency, 517 Washington St., Box 216, Cedar Falls, IA 50613-2842 Tel # (319) 277-2414, Fax # (319) 277-4055

Your Union Matters   *Association*

Publishing Co: Nova Scotia Nurses Union, 65 Queen St., Dartmouth, NS B2Y 1G4 Canada Tel # (902) 469-1474 Fax # (902) 466-6935
Personnel: Editor-Jim Guild
General Info: (Formerly Nova Scotia Nurses' Union Newsletter), Yr. Est. 1976, Quarterly
Subscriptions: Free With Membership

NUTRITION

American Institute for Cancer Research Newsletter
See: HEALTH

American Society of Bariatric Physicians Newsletter
See: MEDICINE

Border Connections
See: EDUCATION

Calorie Control Commentary
See: HEALTH

Celiac News
See: HEALTH

Consumer Reports on Health
See: HEALTH

Dairy Council Digest   *Consumer*

Publishing Co: National Dairy Council, 10255 W Higgins Rd Ste 900, Rosemont, IL 60018-5616; Title Tel # (708) 803-2000 Title Fax # (847) 803-2077
Personnel: Editor-Lois McBean
Editorial Description: Designed to review current research on food, nutrition & health for professionals.
General Info: Yr. Est. 1929, Bi-monthly, Trim Size-8½ x 11, Web press, 6 pages, ISSN: 0011-5568
Subscriptions: Indv. $12, Can. $16, For. $16
Circulation: Total-80,000

Diet Business Bulletin
See: HEALTH

Divinity School News & Notes
See: RELIGIOUS & THEOLOGICAL

Egg Producer
See: POULTRY & POULTRY PRODUCTS

Environmental Nutrition   *Consumer*

Publishing Co: Environmental Nutrition, Inc., 52 Riverside Dr., Apt 15A, New York, NY 10024-6558; Title Tel # (212) 362-0424 Title Fax # (212) 362-2066
Personnel: Publisher-Betty Goldblatt, BS MPH, Editor-Denise Webb, PhD RD, Production Mgr.-Larry S. Goldblaltus, Promotion Mgr.-Susan Boyle
Editorial Description: Wide range of nutrition topics. Written by registered dietitians.
General Info: (Formerly Environmental Nutrition Newsletter), Yr. Est. 1977, Monthly, Trim Size-8½ x 11, Web press, 8 pages, ISSN: 0893-4452, Ind/Abs/Online: DIALOG, 2 Color, Newsprint
Subscriptions: Indv. $30, $4/copy
Advertising: Accepts Inserts.
List Rental: List Management Co.: Coolidge List Marketing, 25 W. 43rd St., New York, NY 10036-7491 Tel # (212) 274-0630, Fax # (212) 274-0650, Actives: 75,000, $75/M
Printing Co: Account Manager: Orlerida Witchel; Newsletter Services, Inc., 9700 Philadelphia Court, Lanham, MD 20706 Tel # (301) 731-5200, Fax # (301) 731-5201

Executive Health's Good Health Report
See: HEALTH

Felix Letter

Publishing Co: Clara Felix, Publisher, PO Box 7094, Berkeley, CA 94707-0094
Editorial Description: Reviews and comments on current nutrtion research.
General Info: Yr. Est. 1981, Bi-monthly, ISSN: 0895-0040
Subscriptions: Indv. $11
Circulation: Total-2,000

Food & Nutrition
See: FOOD

Food & Nutrition Bulletin
See: FOOD

Food & Nutrition Letter
See: HEALTH

Food & Nutrition Newsletter   *Consumer*

Publishing Co: National Cattlemen's Beef Association, 444 N. Michigan Ave., Chicago, IL 60611-3978; Title Tel # (312) 467-5520 Title Fax # (312) 467-9729
Personnel: Editor-Maria Munoz
Editorial Description: Recent food and nutrition information and research.
General Info: (Formerly Food & Nutrition News), Yr. Est. 1930, 5x/yr., ISSN: 0015-6310
Circulation: Total-55,000

Food and Drink Weekly
See: FOOD

Food, Nutrition & Health

Publishing Co: Food & Nutrition Press Inc., 2 Corporate Drive, Box 374, Trumbull, CT 06611-1338; Title Tel # (203) 261-8587 Title Fax # (203) 261-9724
Personnel: Publisher-John O'Neil, Editor-Michele C. Fisher, Editor-Paul LaChance
Editorial Description: Coverage is provided on food, nutrition and health research including education and policy issues.
General Info: Monthly, Offset press, 6 pages
Subscriptions: Indv. $74, Inst. $71, Can. $71, For. $90, $6/copy

Food for Thought   *Association*

Publishing Co: Natl. Agricultural Library, Agriculture Dept., Washington, DC 20250-0001; Title Tel # (301) 344-3719
Editorial Description: Latest developments in information about agriculture & nutrition.
General Info: Yr. Est. 1975, Bi-monthly
Circulation: Total-300

Garlic Times   *Consumer*

Publishing Co: Harris Publishing, 1563 Solan Avenue, Suite 201, Berkeley, CA 94707-2116
Personnel: Editor-L.J. Harris
Editorial Description: Nutrition and food related items on garlic.
General Info: Yr. Est. 1976, Annually
Circulation: Total-5,000

Gathered View, The
See: DISABILITY

Gluten Intolerance Group's Newsletter   *Association*

Publishing Co: Gluten Intolerance Group, PO Box 23053, Seattle, WA 98102-0353; Title Tel # (206) 325-6980
Personnel: Editor-Elaine Hartsook
Editorial Description: Research abstracts, reviews, product information, recipes for celiac sprue persons & those with dermatitis herpetiformis.
General Info: Yr. Est. 1974, Quarterly, Trim Size-8½ x 11, Offset press, 12 pages, ISSN: 0890-507X, No Color
Subscriptions: Indv. $25, Can. $25, For. $30, $4/copy
Acquistions: Publication Bought
Circulation: Total-1,500, Readership-2,025

Good-News-Letter   *Consumer*

Publishing Co: American Institute for Cancer Research, 1759 R St NW, Washington, DC 20009-2583; Title Tel # (202) 328-7744 Title Fax # (202) 328-7226
Personnel: Editor-Christine Murray
Editorial Description: Entertaining games and puzzles which teach children the basics of good nutrition. For children ages 7-10.
General Info: Bi-monthly, Trim Size-8½ x 11, 4 pages, Matte
Subscriptions: Free
Circulation: Total-14,000

Guide to U.S. Food Labeling Law
See: ADVERTISING & MARKETING

Harvard Heart Letter
See: HEALTH

Health Alert
See: HEALTH

Health Exchange
See: HEALTH

Health Express   *Consumer*

Publishing Co: International Academy of Nutritional Consultants, 2375 Tropicana, Ste. 270, Las Vegas, NV 90109; Title Tel # (702) 454-1665
Editorial Description: Information on nutrition and health research, etc.
General Info: Monthly
Subscriptions: Indv. $12

Health Victory Bulletin
See: HEALTH

Healthways   *Association*

Publishing Co: Intl. Macrobiotic Shiatsu Society, 1122 M St, Eureka, CA 95501-2442; Title Tel # (707) 445-2290 Title Fax # (707) 445-2391
Personnel: Editor-Patrick McCarty
General Info: Trim Size-8½ x 11, 10 pages, ISSN: 0898-9251
Subscriptions: Indv. $25, For. $30
Circulation: Total-600

IAHP Newsletter
See: MEDICINE

Ironic Blood
See: MEDICINE

Jewish Vegetarians Newsletter
See: RELIGIOUS & THEOLOGICAL

KDA Sunflower   *Association*   CPM: $258

Publishing Co: Kansas Dietetic Assn., Dept. HRIMD Justin Hall 103, Kansas State University, Manhattan, KS 66506-1404; Title Tel # (913) 532-5521 Title Fax # (913) 532-5504
Personnel: Editor, Circ. Mgr.-Karen Miller
Editorial Description: Current events, section activities & legislative concerns of interest to the association.
General Info: (Formerly Sunflower), Yr. Est. 1946, 6x/yr., Trim Size-8½ x 11, 8 pages, ISSN: 0039-5382, No Color
Subscriptions: Indv. $20, For. $50
Circulation: Total-775, Readership-775
Advertising: $200.
List Rental: List Management Co.: Karen Miller RD ,LD, 11714 Hadley, Overland Park, KS 66210 Tel # (913) 451-5659, Actives: 775, $75/M
Printing Co: Midland Typesetting, 816 Wyandotte, Kansas City, MO 64105 Tel # (816) 842-2410

LPI Newsletter
See: MEDICINE

Life Extension Society News
See: HEALTH

LifelineLetter   *Association*

Publishing Co: Oley Foundation for Home Parenteral & Enteral Nutrition, 214 Hun Memorial, Albany Medical Ctr. A-23, Albany, NY 12208-3478; Title Tel # (518) 262-5079 Title Fax # (518) 262-5528
Personnel: Editor-Roslyn Dahl
Editorial Description: Written for HPEN consumer & their families to foster patient-to-patient sharing. The Letter contains articles contributed by HomePEN consumers, families, clinicians, researchers, & home care services.
General Info: (Formerly Lifeline Letter, The), Yr. Est. 1980, Bi-monthly, Trim Size-8½ x 11, 8 pages, 12% ads, Recycled, Saddle-stitched
Subscriptions: Indv. $35, Free To Qualified Recipient
Circulation: Total-4,500
Advertising: Inquire for rates.
Printing Co: New York Press & Graphics, Latham, NY Tel # (518) 786-6440

Lose Weight Naturally
Newsletter · *Consumer*

Publishing Co: Rodale Press, 33 East Minor St., Emmaus, PA 18098-0001 Tel # (610) 967-5171
Fax # (610) 967-8963; Title Tel # (215) 967-5171
Editorial Description: Information on natural methods to lose weight. Features on exercise, nutrition, body makeovers, etc.
General Info: Monthly
Subscriptions: Indv. $18

Low Fat for Life
See: FOOD

Make it Tasty with No/Low Salt--How To & Receipe Blends Edition
See: FOOD

Make it Tasty Spice Co. Blends Food Business Newsletter
See: FOOD

Meals for Millions/Freedom from Hunger Foundation Newsbriefs
See: SOCIAL SERVICES & WELFARE

Med News
See: HEALTH

Medical Update
See: HEALTH

Mind Garden Newsletter, The
See: FAMILY

Modern Nutrition News · *Consumer*

Publishing Co: Connaught Press Inc., 212 Hillside Ave, Hillside, NJ 07205-1824;
Title Tel # (201) 926-0816
Editorial Description: Focuses on new health and nutrition developments and research.
General Info: Quarterly
Subscriptions: Indv. $7

NIH Record
See: HEALTH

NNFA Today

Publishing Co: Natl. Nutritional Foods Assn., 150 Paularino Ave Ste 285, Costa Mesa, CA 92626-3302; Title Tel # (714) 966-6632 Title Fax # (714) 641-7005
Personnel: Publisher, Editor-Burton Kallman
Editorial Description: Articles of interest to members of the health food & natural products industry.
General Info: (Formerly NNFA Monitor), Yr. Est. 1986, Monthly, Trim Size-8½ x 11, 12 pages, Color, Coated
Subscriptions: Free With Membership
Circulation: Total-5,000

NOHA News · *Consumer, Association*

Publishing Co: Nutrition for Optimal Health Assn., PO Box 380, Winnetka, IL 60093-0380;
Title Tel # (708) 786-5326
Personnel: Editor-Marjorie Fisher, Co-Editor-Lynn Louison
Editorial Description: Reports nutritional information from scientific sources.
General Info: Yr. Est. 1976, Quarterly, Sheetfed press, 6 pages, No Color
Subscriptions: Indv. $8, $2/copy
Circulation: Total-700

National Council Against Health Fraud Newsletter
See: HEALTH

Natural Hygiene Soc. of
New Jersey Newsletter · *Association*

Publishing Co: Natural Hygiene of New Jersey Inc., PO Box 142, Pompton Plains, NJ 07444-0142;
Title Tel # (201) 839-5919
Personnel: Editor-Robert Lucia
Editorial Description: Features info on health, hygience, nutrition, exercise, etc.
General Info: Yr. Est. 1981, 8x/yr., Trim Size-7 x 8½, 4 pages, No Color
Subscriptions: Indv. $15
Printing Co: Lucia Graphics, 100 Valley Rd, Montclair, NJ 07042-2211 Tel # (201) 783-6761

Nutrition & the M.D. · *Consumer*

Publishing Co: Quest Publishing Co., 1351 Titan Way, Brea, CA 92621-3787 Tel # (714) 738-6400
Fax # (714) 525-3787 Parent Co.-Lippincott-Raven Press Publishers, Philadelphia
Personnel: Publisher-Steve McCoy, Editor-Gregg Nighswonger, Mktg. Dir.-Michele Duncan
Editorial Description: Covers issues of nutrition and healthcare.
General Info: Yr. Est. 1975, Monthly
Subscriptions: Indv. $52, For. $80

Nutrition Action
Healthletter · *Consumer, Association*

Publishing Co: Center for Science in the Public Interest, 1875 Connecticut Ave NW, Ste. 300, Washington, DC 20009-5728; Title Tel # (202) 332-9110 Title Fax # (202) 265-4954
Personnel: Editor in Chief-Stephen Schmidt, Exec. Ed.-Michael Jacobson, Circ. Mgr.-William Dugan, Production Mgr.-Debra Blink, Promotion Dir.-Dennis Bass
Editorial Description: Provides the latest research & practical advice on nutrition, diet, & related health issues, as well as the politics of nutrition. Includes recipes, reader questions, as well as books, and other products to purchase.
General Info: (Formerly Nutrition Action), Yr. Est. 1974, 10x/yr., Trim Size-8 x 10⅞, Web press, 16 pages, ISSN: 010885-77, 4 Color, Matte, Saddle-stitched
Subscriptions: Indv. $24, Can. $36, For. $32, $3/copy
Circulation: Total-841,784
List Rental: List Management Co.: Manager: William Dugan; Names in the News-California, 1 Bush St Bsmt 3, San Francisco, CA 94104-4425 Tel # (415) 989-3350, Fax # (415) 433-7796, Actives: 871,139, $85/M, Expires: 197,931, $50/M
Printing Co: Johnson & Hardin Co., 3600 Red Bank Rd, Cincinnati, OH 45227-4113
Tel # (513) 271-8834, Fax # (513) 527-2170

Nutrition Advocate · *Consumer*

Publishing Co: Advocacy Communications, 95 Brown Rd., Box 4716, Ithaca, NY 14852;
Title Tel # (607) 266-0313
Editorial Description: Focuses on the benefits of a vegetarian diet.
General Info: Monthly
Subscriptions: Indv. $30

Nutrition Forum · *Consumer*

Publishing Co: Nutrition Forum, 7111 60th Ave., Maspeth, NY 11378-2907 Tel # (718) 275-0414
Personnel: Co-Editor-Manfred Kroger, PhD, Co-Editor-Jack Raso, MS, RD
Editorial Description: Features developments and research in nutrition science. Focuses on nutrition and health fads, fallacies, and quackery
General Info: Yr. Est. 1984, Bi-monthly, Trim Size-8½ x 11, 8 pages, ISSN: 0748-8165
Subscriptions: Indv. $35, Inst. $50, For. $50
Acquistions: Publication Sold
Circulation: Total-2,000

Nutrition Funding Report, The
See: HEALTH

Nutrition Legislation
News · *Business, Association*

Publishing Co: Nutrition Legislation Services, PO Box 75035, Washington, DC 20013-0035;
Title Tel # (202) 488-8879 Title Fax # (202) 554-3116
Personnel: Publisher, Editor-Lenora Moragne, Ph.D., Circ. Mgr.-Nora Champion, Circ. Mgr.-Nora Champion, Ph.D., Production Mgr.-Nora Champion, PH.D
Editorial Description: Covers food and nutrition legislation and regulatory news covering all aspects of food and nutrition: nutrition research, nutrition education, international nutrition, nutrition manpower training, nutritio n surveillance and monitoring, food assistance or nutrition services, and food quality and safet, and provides a document retrieval services.
General Info: (Formerly Nutrition Legislation & Regulatory News), Yr. Est. 1985, Semi-monthly, Trim Size-8½ x 11, 8 pages, ISSN: 8756-6060, 2 Color, Matte
Subscriptions: Indv. $150, Inst. $150, Can. $150, For. $175, $10/copy
Acquistions: Publication Bought
List Rental: Actives: $65/M

Nutrition News · *Consumer, Association*

Publishing Co: National Dairy Council, 10255 W Higgins Rd Ste 900, Rosemont, IL 60018-5616
Fax # (847) 803-2077; Title Tel # (708) 803-2000
Personnel: Editor-Mary Garzino
Editorial Description: Nutrition-related research and developments. Techniques in teaching nutrition principles. Black-line master included in every issue.
General Info: Yr. Est. 1937, 3x/yr., Trim Size-8½ x 11, Offset press, 4 pages, ISSN: 0369-6464, 2 Color
Subscriptions: Indv. $6, Can. $9, For. $9, $2/copy
Circulation: Total-25,000

Nutrition Notes · *Association*

Publishing Co: American Institute of Nutrition, 9650 Rockville Pike, Bethesda, MD 20814-3998
Tel # (301) 530-7060; Title Tel # (301) 530-7050 Title Fax # (301) 571-1892
Personnel: Editor-Phyllis Moser-Veillon
Editorial Description: Features info on awards, reports, publications meetings, legislation and other topics of interest to nutrition scientists.
General Info: Yr. Est. 1965, Quarterly
Subscriptions: Indv. $24
Circulation: Total-3,200

Nutrition Report

Publishing Co: Health Media of America, 3309 4th Ave., San Diego, CA 92103-5703;
Title Tel # (619) 453-3887
Personnel: Publisher-Robert Garrison, Jr., Editor-Beth Somer, Circ. Mgr.-Caroline Moroney, Production Mgr.-Lisa Moye, Art Dir.-Kristi Paulson, Promotion Dir.-Tim Holsather
General Info: Yr. Est. 1983, Monthly, 8 pages, ISSN: 0740-8684, Color, Coated, Saddle-stitched
Subscriptions: Indv. $48, $4/copy
Circulation: Total-4,000

Nutrition Research Newsletter
Business, Scholarly

Publishing Co: LYDA Assocs., Inc., PO Box 700, Palisades, NY 10964-0700; Title Tel # (914) 359-8282 Title Fax # (914) 359-1229
Personnel: Publisher, Editor-Lillian Langseth, PH.D., Mng. Editor-Jennifer Shapiro, Circ. Mgr.-Karen Isaksen
Editorial Description: A literature survey service covering over 400 scientific journals. Provides summaries with full citations & author's addresses plus listing of pertinent reviews in nutrition & clinical nutrition.
General Info: Yr. Est. 1982, 10x/yr., Trim Size-8½ x 11, Offset press, 10 pages, ISSN: 0736-0037, Ind/Abs/Online: DIALOG, EBSCO, UMI, Information Access, Color-cover, Matte
Subscriptions: Indv. $96, Inst. $96, Can. $96, For. $106, $10/copy
Acquistions: Publication Bought
Circulation: Total-1,100
Printing Co: Minuteman Press, 260 Livington St., Northvale, NJ 07647 Tel # (201) 767-5604, Fax # (201) 767-6471

Nutrition Update

Publishing Co: Twin Laboratories, Inc., 2120 Smithtown Ave, Ronkonkoma, NY 11779-7327; Title Tel # (916) 756-3311
Personnel: Editor-Dr. Brian Leibovitz
Editorial Description: In depth analysis of the field of nutrition--with special emphasis on medical applications.
General Info: Yr. Est. 1985, Bi-monthly, Trim Size-8½ x 11, 15 pages, Color
Circulation: Total-30,000

Nutrition Week

Publishing Co: Community Nutrition Institute, 2001 S St NW Ste 530, Washington, DC 20009-1125; Title Tel # (202) 462-4700 Title Fax # (202) 462-5241
Personnel: Publisher, Editor-Rodney Leonard, Circ. Mgr.-Sheila Foley
Editorial Description: Provides comprehensive coverage of food programs & policies.
General Info: (Formerly CNI Weekly Report), Yr. Est. 1970, Weekly, Trim Size-8½ x 11, Web press, 8 pages, ISSN: 0736-0096, 2 Color
Subscriptions: Indv. $75, $2/copy
List Rental: Actives: $100/M

Nutritioning Parents
Business

Publishing Co: N.U.T.R.A. Program, PO Box 1217, Cashiers, NC 28717-1217; Title Tel # (404) 634-5264
Personnel: Publisher, Editor-Sara Sloan
General Info: Yr. Est. 1979, Monthly, Trim Size-8½ x 11, Offset press, 4 pages
Subscriptions: Indv. $15, $2/copy

Physician's Patient Newsletter
See: HEALTH

Pure Facts
See: HEALTH

Report on Institutional Foodservice
See: FOOD

Research Notes
See: FOOD

Running & FitNews
See: HEALTH

Second Opinion
See: HEALTH

Smorgasboard-Plenty to Eat Update
See: FOOD

South Carolina Committee Against Hunger
Consumer

Publishing Co: SPRUILL, 27 Oak Forest Dr, Charleston, SC 29407-7078; Title Tel # (803) 256-2749
Personnel: Editor-Genina Lewis
General Info: Yr. Est. 1978, Quarterly, Desktop press, 6 pages
Acquistions: Publication Bought
Circulation: (100% controlled), Total-2,000

Sproutletter
Business, Consumer   **CPM: $80**

Publishing Co: Sprouting Publications, PO Box 62, Ashland, OR 97520-0070 Tel # (503) 448-2326; Title Tel # (500) 445-5519 Title Fax # (503) 488-4429
Personnel: Publisher, Editor-Michael Linden
Editorial Description: Useful, unusual information on sprouting, live foods, nutritional algae, with emphasis on holistic health, nutrition, vegetarianism. Includes recipes, reviews, (books & products), new age & holistic networking, resources. Book and product reviews.
General Info: Yr. Est. 1990, Quarterly, Trim Size-8½ x 11, Web press, 8 pages, ISSN: 0744-9860, 12% ads, No Color, Recycled, Saddle-stitched
Subscriptions: Indv. $12, Inst. $10, Can. $16, For. $16, $4/copy
Acquistions: Publication Bought
Circulation: Total-2,000, Readership-4,000
Advertising: $160. Accepts Inserts.

Supermarket Savvy Information Resource Service
See: FOOD

Tiffin Topics Newsletter
Business

Publishing Co: New Hampshire Dept of Education, 101 Pleasant St, Concord, NH 03301-3860; Title Tel # (603) 271-3646
Editorial Description: Newsletter for school food service personnel concerning lunch programs.
General Info: Yr. Est. 1962, Quarterly, Trim Size-8½ x 11, 4 pages, 2 Color
Circulation: Total-700

Tufts University Diet and Nutrition Letter
Consumer

Publishing Co: Tufts Graduate School of Nutrition, 53 Park Pl., Fl. 8, New York, NY 10007; Title Tel # (212) 608-6516 Title Fax # (212) 608-5317
Personnel: Publisher-Deborah White, Asst. Pub.-Marie Johnson, Editor-Stanley Gershoff, Exec. Ed.-Lawrence Lindner, Circulation-Michelle Jones
Editorial Description: Newsletter featuring some of the leading specialists in diet, nutrition and health.
General Info: Yr. Est. 1983, Monthly, Trim Size-8.5 x 11, Web press, 8 pages, Ind/Abs/Online: DIALOG, Newsprint, Other
Subscriptions: Indv. $20
Circulation: Total-250,000
List Rental: List Management Co.: Kleid Company, Inc., 530 5th Ave., 17 Floor, New York, NY 10036-5101 Tel # (212) 819-3406, Fax # (212) 719-9788, Actives: 196,118, $80/M, Hotline: 10,000, $85/M, Expires: 55,447, $60/M
Printing Co: Newsletter Services, Inc., 9700 Philadelphia Court, Lanham, MD 20706 Tel # (301) 731-5200, Fax # (301) 731-5201

VHL Family Forum
See: MEDICINE

VHL News
See: GENETICS

Vegetarian Journal's Foodservice Update
See: FOOD

Wary Canary
See: ENVIRONMENT & ECOLOGY

Your Health
See: MEDICINE

OCEANOGRAPHY

American Shore & Beach Preservation Assn. -Newsletter
See: ENVIRONMENT & ECOLOGY

Appledore Times

Publishing Co: Shoals Marine Laboratory, Cornell Univ., G-14 Stimson Hall, Ithaca, NY 14853-7101; Title Tel # (607) 255-3717 Title Fax # (607) 255-0742
Personnel: Editor-Christine Bogdanowicz
Editorial Description: An informal and educational newsletter. Interested parties include Shoals Marine Lab participants, University students and faculty, school teachers and others curious about marine science and the Shoals Marine Lab. CT97280106.
General Info: Yr. Est. 1980, Desktop press, 8 pages, 2 Color, Saddle-stitched
Circulation: Total-6,000

C-CORE News
Association

Publishing Co: Centre for Cold Ocean Resources Engineering, Memorial Univ. of Newfoundland, St. John's, NF A1B 3X5 Canada; Title Tel # (709) 737-8354 Title Fax # (709) 737-4706
Personnel: Editor, Science Ed., News Ed., Photo Ed., Circ. Mgr., Production Mgr., Art Dir., Mktg. Dir., Promotion Dir.-E. Nesbitt
Editorial Description: Current research projects, people and events of interest to C-CORE, its associates and other research centers.
General Info: Yr. Est. 1976, 3x/yr., Trim Size-8½ x 11, Sheetfed press, 12 pages, ISSN: 0381-6486, 2 Color, Matte, Saddle-stitched
Subscriptions: Free
Circulation: Total-2,500
Advertising: Accepts Inserts.

CIB Daily Maritime Newsletter
See: SHIPS & SHIPPING

Coastal Reporter
See: ENVIRONMENT & ECOLOGY

Coastal Research
See: SCIENCE

Coastal Society Bulletin, The
See: ENVIRONMENT & ECOLOGY

Coastal Zone Management
Consumer

Publishing Co: Nautilus Press, Inc., 1054 National Press Building, Washington, DC 20045-2001; Title Tel # (202) 347-6643
Personnel: Publisher, Editor-John Botzum, Circ. Mgr.-Priscilla Capra
Editorial Description: Reports on the impact of energy developments, particularly offshore oil and gas in the coastal states.
General Info: 36x/yr., Trim Size-8½ x 11, Offset press, 6 pages, No Color
Subscriptions: Indv. $325

Earth System Monitor
Business, Association

Publishing Co: National Climatic Data Center, NOAA/NESDIS E/Ccx2, Federal Bldg. 151 Patton Ave, Asheville, NC 28801-5001
Editorial Description: Newsletter of the National Oceanic and Atmospheric Administration (NOAA).
General Info: Yr. Est. 1990, Bi-monthly, Trim Size-8½ x 11, 40 pages, No Color

Fathom

Publishing Co: Univ of Florida Sea Grant College, Univ. of Florida Bldg. 803, Gainesville, FL 32611-2003; Title Tel # (904) 392-2801 Title Fax # (904) 392-5113
Personnel: Editor-Jay Humphreys, Circ. Mgr.-Karen Owens, Production Mgr.-Art Dir.-Lori Kell
Editorial Description: Colorful magazine that highlights Sea Grant research, extension and education activities.
General Info: (Formerly Marine Log), Yr. Est. 1989, Quarterly, Web press, 8 pages, Color-cover, Coated, Saddle-stitched
Subscriptions: Indv. $5, Can. $6, For. $7, $1/copy
Acquistions: Publication Bought
Circulation: Total-190,000
Advertising: Accepts Inserts.
Printing Co: Colonial Press, 3690 NW 50th St, Miami, FL 33142-3987 Tel # (305) 633-1581

Gulf of Mexico Newsletter
See: ENERGY

Hawaiian Shell News
See: NATURAL HISTORY

Huntsman Marine Science News
See: FISH & FISHERIES

The ISC Newsletter
See: ZOOLOGY

Institute of Diving Newsletter
Business, Association　　CPM: $150

Publishing Co: Institute of Diving, 17314 Panama City Beach Pkwy, Panama City Beach, FL 32413-2020; Title Tel # (904) 235-4101 Title Fax # (904) 235-4101
Personnel: Editor-Dorothy Parkinson
Editorial Description: Professional, literary & scientific knowledge related to human-oriented activity in the undersea environment.
General Info: Yr. Est. 1977, Quarterly, Trim Size-8½ x 11, 10 pages, No Color, Coated
Subscriptions: Free With Membership
Circulation: Total-1,000
Advertising: $150.

Long Island Sound Study Update
Consumer

Publishing Co: Sponsor-EPA, Oceanic Society LI Chapter & the Long Island Sound Study, 185 Magee Ave., Stamford Marine Ctr., Stamford, CT 06902-5906; Title Tel # (203) 327-9786 Title Fax # (203) 967-2677
Personnel: Editor-Rick Schreiner
Editorial Description: Sound wide issues, events, & natural history; progress of EPA study.
General Info: Yr. Est. 1984, Quarterly, Trim Size-8½ x 11, Sheetfed press, 16 pages, 2 Color, Coated
Subscriptions: Indv. $25
Circulation: Total-5,100

Louisiana Coastal Law
See: LAW

MIT Sea Grant Quarterly Report
Association

Publishing Co: Sea Grant College Program, Bldg. E38-320, Cambridge, MA 02139; Title Tel # (617) 235-3461
Personnel: Editor-Karen Hartley
Editorial Description: A summary of Sea Grant sponsored ocean-related research; abstracts of earlier reports; articles range in interest from civil & ocean engineering to the biological sciences.
General Info: Yr. Est. 1979, Quarterly, 6 pages, 2 Color, Newsprint
Circulation: Total-2,500
Printing Co: MIT Graphic Arts, Massachusetts Ave., Cambridge, MA 02189

MSRC Bulletin Series
See: ENVIRONMENT & ECOLOGY

Makai

Publishing Co: Univ. of Hawaii Sea Grant Program, Sea Grant College Program, 1000 Pope Rd., #213, Honolulu, HI 96822; Title Tel # (808) 956-7410 Title Fax # (808) 956-2880
Personnel: Editor-Matthew Sanders, Circ. Mgr.-Joan Yamada
Editorial Description: For marine community in Hawaii & western pacific, & for general public to better use, enjoy, understand, & protect/conserve the ocean & coast.
General Info: (Formerly Marine Advisory Program Newsletter Sea Grant Newsletter), Yr. Est. 1979, Monthly, Trim Size-11 x 25, Offset press, 6 pages, ISSN: 0745-2896, 2 Color
Circulation: Total-2,600

Marine Briefs
Consumer

Publishing Co: Gulf Coast Research Lab., PO Box 7000, Ocean Springs, MS 39566-7000 Tel # (601) 872-4200; Title Tel # (601) 872-4273 Title Fax # (601) 872-4204
Personnel: Editor-Susan Griggs
Editorial Description: Oceanography & biology of the coastal zone fauna & flora, aquaculture, marine chemistry & geology, marine education all ages, seafood quality & technology, fisheries assistance.
General Info: Yr. Est. 1972, Bi-monthly, Trim Size-8½ x 11, Offset press, 8 pages, No Color
Circulation: (70% controlled), Total-1,200

Marine Mammal News

Publishing Co: Nautilus Press, Inc., 1054 National Press Building, Washington, DC 20045-2001; Title Tel # (202) 347-6643
Personnel: Publisher, Editor-John Botzum, Circ. Mgr., Promotion Dir.-Priscilla Capra
Editorial Description: Natl. & Intl. information & developments in marine mammals & the protection there of.
General Info: Yr. Est. 1973, Monthly
Subscriptions: Indv. $68

Marine Newsletter
See: SAFETY

Marine Sciences Research Center-Newsletter

Publishing Co: Marine Sciences Research Center, State Univ. Of Ny, Stony Brook, NY 11794-0001; Title Tel # (516) 632-8700 Title Fax # (516) 632-8820
Personnel: Editor-T. Bell, Art Dir.-L. Palmer
Editorial Description: Activities of the Marine Sciences Research Center.
General Info: Yr. Est. 1976, Quarterly, Trim Size-8½ x 11, 6 pages, 2 Color
Subscriptions: Free
Circulation: Total-1,500
Printing Co: Shannon & Sons, 1 Comac Loop, Ronkonkoma, NY 11799 Tel # (516) 981-1616

NAMS News

Publishing Co: Natl. Assn. of Marine Surveyors, Inc., PO Box 9306, Chesapeake, VA 23321-9306
Personnel: Publisher, Editor-Kim MacCartney
General Info: Yr. Est. 1960, Quarterly, 20 pages
Subscriptions: Indv. $25
Circulation: Total-400

NOAA Geodetic News

Publishing Co: National Geodetic Information Center, Rockville, MD 20852; Title Tel # (301) 443-8775
Personnel: Editor-John Love
General Info: (Formerly NOAA Geodetic Newssheet), Yr. Est. 1978, 8 pages
Circulation: Total-4,000

National Wetlands Newsletter
See: WATER SUPPLY, POWER & WASTE

Nova Scotia Reports
See: LAW

Ocean Science News

Publishing Co: Nautilus Press, Inc., 1054 National Press Building, Washington, DC 20045-2001; Title Tel # (202) 347-6643
Personnel: Publisher, Editor-John Botzum, Circ. Mgr.-Priscilla Capra
Editorial Description: National and international developments in science, mining, energy, environment, engineering, diving, law of the sea.
General Info: Yr. Est. 1957, Weekly, Trim Size-8½ x 11, Offset press, 8 pages, No Color
Subscriptions: Indv. $335

Ocean Technology & Engineering
Business

Publishing Co: National Technical Information Service U.S., 5285 Port Royal Rd., Springfield, VA 22161-0001 Fax # (703) 487-4630; Title Tel # (703) 487-4630
Editorial Description: Covers marine engineering, including harbors, port facilities, & marine navigation. Also contains information on dynamic, physical, & chemical oceanography.
General Info: Weekly, Trim Size-8½ x 11, Offset press, 8 pages, ISSN: 0364-6424, No Color
Subscriptions: Indv. $135, Can. $135, For. $195

Offshore Field Development International
See: ENERGY

Offshore Rig Locator International
See: ENERGY

Offshore Rig Newsletter
See: ENERGY

Quarterly CERCular
Information Bulletin — *Association*

Publishing Co: USAE Waterways Experiment Station, Attn: CEWES-CV-I, 3909 Halls Ferry Rd., Vicksburg, MS 39180; Title Tel # (601) 634-2012
Personnel: Editor-Bettye Stephens, Publisher, Circ. Mgr.-Fred Camfield
Editorial Description: Current activities of the Coastal Engineering Research Center. Includes annotated bibliography of recent CERC reports.
General Info: Yr. Est. 1976, Quarterly, Trim Size-8½ x 11, Letrpr. press, 6 pages, No Color, Newsprint
Subscriptions: Free
Circulation: (100% controlled), Total-2,700

Sea Grant Quarterly — *Consumer*

Publishing Co: Univ. of Hawaii Sea Grant Program, Sea Grant College Program, 1000 Pope Rd., #213, Honolulu, HI 96822 Tel # (808) 956-7410 Fax # (808) 956-2880; Title Tel # (808) 948-6921
Personnel: Editor-Rose Pfund, Circ. Mgr.-Joan Yamada
Editorial Description: Scientific/technical newsletter on marine topics for professional, technical, decisionmakers.
General Info: Yr. Est. 1979, Quarterly, Trim Size-8½ x 11, Offset press, 6 pages, 2 Color
Circulation: Total-1,350

Seacamp Association News

Publishing Co: Newfound Harbor Marine Institute, Rt. 3, Box 170, Big Pine Key, FL 33043; Title Tel # (305) 872-2331
Personnel: Editor-Leigh Williams
Editorial Description: Seacamp/Newfound Harbor Marine Institute is a non-profit marien science, environmental education facility. research
General Info: Yr. Est. 1975, 12 pages, Ind/Abs/Online: events
Circulation: Total-60,000

Spirit!
See: HOUSE ORGANS

Spoof Newsletter — *Association*

Publishing Co: Society for the Protection of Old Fishes, Inc., School Of Fisheries Wh-10, Univ. Of Washington, Seattle, WA 98195-0001 Tel # (206) 543-6194; Title Tel # (206) 778-7397
Personnel: Editor-Susan Brown
General Info: (Formerly Society for the Protection of Old Fishes-Newsletter), Yr. Est. 1967, Irregular, Trim Size-8.5 x 11, 6 pages
Subscriptions: Free With Membership
Circulation: Total-250

Tidings

Publishing Co: Belle W. Baruch Inst. for Marine Biology & Coastal Research, Univ. of South Carolina, Columbia, SC 29208-0001; Title Tel # (803) 777-3927
Personnel: Editor-Wendy Allen
General Info: Yr. Est. 1976
Circulation: Total-800

Tsunami Newsletter — *Association*

Publishing Co: International Tsunami Information Center, 737 Bishop Street, Suite #2200, Honolulu, HI 96813; Title Tel # (808) 532-6422 Title Fax # (808) 532-5576
Personnel: Editor-George Pararas-Carayan
Editorial Description: Informs interested individuals and agencies throughout the world news on tsunamis.
General Info: (Formerly ITIC Newsletter), Semi-annually, Offset press, 45 pages, No Color
Circulation: Total-695

Upwellings
See: ENVIRONMENT & ECOLOGY

Vancouver Aquascene Aquarium Newsletter
See: NATURAL HISTORY

Varex Reports

Publishing Co: Varex Corp., 4000 Blackthorn La., Burtonsville, MD 20866-1104; Title Tel # (301) 984-7760
Personnel: Editor-Dr. Jack Cazes
General Info: (Formerly Varex Chromat-O-Gram), Quarterly, 4 pages

Visibility
See: SPORTS & SPORTING GOODS

Washington Letter of
Oceanography

Publishing Co: Compass Publications, Inc., 1117 19th St N Ste 1000, Arlington, VA 22209-1790; Title Tel # (703) 524-3136 Title Fax # (703) 841-0852
Personnel: Publisher-Charles H. Bussmann, Editor-David Graham
Editorial Description: A newsletter circulated to those in ocean engineering, marine resources development, & undersea defense.
General Info: (Formerly UST/Washington Letter), Yr. Est. 1966, Bi-weekly, Desktop press, 4 pages, No Color, Newsprint
Subscriptions: Indv. $56, Can. $60, For. $78

OFFICE METHODS & EQUIPMENT

AOR Observer — *Business*

Publishing Co: Automated Office Resources, 812 Via Tornasol, Aptos, CA 95003-5624; Title Tel # (408) 688-4129
Personnel: Publisher, Editor-Paula Cecil, Production Mgr.-Michelle Cecil
Editorial Description: Research observation & news of present & future office systems technology.
General Info: (Formerly Word Processing News), Yr. Est. 1980, Bi-monthly, 8 pages

Administrative Assistant's Update
See: EMPLOYMENT

Advertising Via Telemarketing Script Presentations Newsletter
See: BUSINESS & INDUSTRY

Authorized OA Dealer
Report

Publishing Co: Camarro Research, 345 Carroll Rd # 691, Fairfield, CT 06430-3071; Title Tel # (203) 255-4100
Personnel: Publisher, Editor-Kenneth Cammaro
Editorial Description: New office products automaton trends & marketing issues. Covers portable office & video typewriters, WP's, PC's, FAX machines, desktop publishing systems, & channels of distribution.
General Info: Yr. Est. 1985, Bi-monthly, Trim Size-8½ x 11, Mimeo press, 16 pages, ISSN: 0889-9886, No Color, Newsprint
Subscriptions: Indv. $235
Acquistions: Publication Bought
Printing Co: Audubon Copy Shoppe, Post Rd., Fairfield, CT 06430 Tel # (203) 259-4311

BPIA Business Products
Industry Report — *Association*

Publishing Co: Business Products Industry Assn., The, 301 N. Fairfax St., Alexandria, VA 22314-2696; Title Tel # (703) 549-9040 Title Fax # (703) 683-7552
Personnel: Publisher-Simon DeGroot, Editor-Sandra Selva
Editorial Description: Timely topics of interest to the office products industry.
General Info: (Formerly NOPA Office Products Industry Report), Yr. Est. 1970, Bi-weekly, Trim Size-8¼ x 10¾, Web press, 12 pages, ISSN: 0746-5467, No Color, Recycled, Saddle-stitched
Subscriptions: Indv. $40, $3/copy
Circulation: Total-11,416
Printing Co: Charter Printing Co., 4202 Wheeler Ave, Alexandria, VA 22304-6413 Tel # (703) 370-1010, Fax # (703) 370-2009

Better Supervision
See: MANAGEMENT

Beyond the Bottom Line
See: BUSINESS & INDUSTRY

Blue Ribbon Service
See: MANAGEMENT

Business Review
See: BUSINESS & INDUSTRY

Business Technology
Hotline — *Business, Association*

Publishing Co: Business Technolgy Assn., 12411 Wornall Rd, Kansas City, MO 64145-1119; Title Tel # (816) 941-3100 Title Fax # (816) 941-8034
Personnel: Editor-Brent Hoskins, Assoc. Ed.-Peter Wilkinson, Circ. Mgr.-Gail Lacey, Adv. Dir.-Cheri Deverey
Editorial Description: News articles regarding the business equipment and systems industry, focusing on new products and technologies. Also news regarding the Business Technology Association.
General Info: (Formerly National Office Machine Dealers Hotline), Yr. Est. 1985, Semi-monthly, Trim Size-8.5 x 11, Offset press, 8 pages, 2 Color, Matte
Subscriptions: Indv. $15, Can. $22, For. $30, $15/copy
Circulation: Readership-5,000
Advertising: $2,280.
Printing Co: Mainline Printing, 818 SE Adams St, Topeka, KS 66601 Tel # (913) 233-2335

Buyers Laboratory Test
Reports — *Business, Consumer*

Publishing Co: Buyer's Laboratory, Inc., 20 Railroad Ave, Hackensack, NJ 07601-3309; Title Tel # (201) 488-0404 Title Fax # (201) 488-0464
Personnel: Editor-Anthony Polifrone, Circ. Mgr.-Marion Davidowicz, Art Dir.-Gil Hoffman, Publisher, Promotion Dir.-Burt Meerow
Editorial Description: Comparative test reports on competing makes and models of different types of office equipment and supplies.
General Info: Yr. Est. 1961, Monthly, Trim Size-8½ x 11, Offset press, No Color, Newsprint, Looseleaf
Subscriptions: Indv. $645
Circulation: Total-4,000

CAPs

Publishing Co: Boston Computer Society, Inc., 101 A First Ave. Suite #2, Waltham, MA 02154 Tel # (617) 290-5700 Fax # (617) 290-5744
General Info: Quarterly

CCAR Pool
   See: LAW

Church Secretary's Communique

Publishing Co: Christian Ministry Resources, 617 Greenbrook Pky, Matthews, NC 28105-7745; Title Tel # (704) 841-8066 Title Fax # (704) 846-5923
Editorial Description: Office newsletter for church secretaries.
General Info: Yr. Est. 1985, Monthly, Trim Size-8½ x 11, 4 pages, 2 Color
Subscriptions: Indv. $24
Circulation: Total-14,000
List Rental: List Management Co.: Bernice Bush Co./Springdale Lists, 15052 Springdale St., Huntington Beach, CA 92649-1178 Tel # (714) 891-3344, Fax # (714) 897-0650, Actives: 18,000, $80/M

Clerical   *Business*

Publishing Co: Dir Des Entreprise, C.P. 1153, Quebec, PQ G1K 7C3 Canada Tel # (514) 873-5324; Title Tel # (514) 288-6104
Personnel: Publisher-A. Martineau
General Info: Yr. Est. 1944, Annually, Mimeo press, 200 pages, No Color, Looseleaf

Clerical and Related Classifications   *Business*

Publishing Co: Dir Des Entreprise, C.P. 1153, Quebec, PQ G1K 7C3 Canada Tel # (514) 873-5324
Personnel: Publisher-A. Martineau
General Info: Annually, Mimeo press, 200 pages, No Color, Looseleaf

Color Businesss Report
   See: COMPUTERS & AUTOMATION

Communications Product Reports
   See: COMPUTERS & AUTOMATION

Copier FAXTS   *Business*

Publishing Co: Dataquest Div. Dun & Bradstreet Corp., 1290 Ridder Park Dr, San Jose, CA 95131-2304 Tel # (408) 437-8000; Title Tel # (805) 298-3263 Title Fax # (805) 298-4388
Personnel: Editor-Lynn Ritter
Editorial Description: New copier products, new fax products, pricing changes, distribution, competitive activity, trade shows.
General Info: (Formerly First Copy), Yr. Est. 1982, Monthly, 8 pages
Subscriptions: Indv. $195
Circulation: Total-1,200

Copier Review   *Consumer*

Publishing Co: Buyer's Laboratory, Inc., 20 Railroad Ave, Hackensack, NJ 07601-3309; Title Tel # (201) 488-0404 Title Fax # (201) 488-0461
Personnel: Editor-Anthony Polifrone, Circ. Mgr.-Marion Davidowicz, Publisher, Promotion Dir.-Burt Meerow
Editorial Description: Evaluates copiers, & comments on industry developments.
General Info: Yr. Est. 1978, Monthly, Trim Size-8½ x 11, Offset press, 4 pages, No Color, Newsprint, Looseleaf
Subscriptions: Indv. $365, $10/copy
Circulation: Total-1,000

Creative Secretary's Letter   *Business*

Publishing Co: Bureau of Business Practice, 24 Rope Ferry Rd, Waterford, CT 06386-0001 Tel # (806) 442-4365 Fax # (860) 434-3341 Parent Co.-Prentice Hall, Waterford; Title Tel # (860) 442-4365 Title Fax # (860) 434-3078
Personnel: Publisher-Elaine Stattler, Editor-Christine Greeley, Editor-Jo Ann Heyer, Art Dir.-Linda Cusano
Editorial Description: Helps office personnel to perform their tasks more quickly, easily and efficiently.
General Info: (Formerly P.S. for Professional Secretaries/Administrative Support Let), Yr. Est. 1960, Semi-monthly, Trim Size-8½ x 11, Offset press, 8 pages, ISSN: 1059-633X, 2 Color
Subscriptions: Indv. $119

Customer Communicator, The
   See: MANAGEMENT

Data Base Product Reports
   See: COMPUTERS & AUTOMATION

Data Entry Awareness Report
   See: COMPUTERS & AUTOMATION

Datapro Reports on Office Automation   *Business*

Publishing Co: Datapro Research Corp., 600 Delran Pky, Delran, NJ 08075-1255 Tel # (609) 764-0100 Fax # (609) 764-2815
General Info: Monthly
List Rental: List Management Co.: Mal Dunn & Associates, Inc., Hardscrabble Rd., Croton Falls, NY 10519 Tel # (914) 277-5558, Fax # (914) 277-5636

Discontinued Copier SpecCheck Guide   *Business*

Publishing Co: Dataquest Div. Dun & Bradstreet Corp., 1290 Ridder Park Dr, San Jose, CA 95131-2304 Tel # (408) 437-8000; Title Tel # (805) 298-3263 Title Fax # (805) 298-4388
Personnel: Editor-Richard Norton
Editorial Description: Contains detailed specifications and pricing information for more than 600 copiers discontinued since 1959.
General Info: Yr. Est. 1991, Annually, Perfect bound
Subscriptions: Indv. $75
Circulation: Total-11,000

Distributed Processing Product Reports
   See: COMPUTERS & AUTOMATION

ETCetera
   See: ANTIQUES & ART GOODS

Effective Business Writing
   See: MANAGEMENT

Exec-U-Tary   *Business, Association*

Publishing Co: National Association of Executive Secretaries, 900 S Washington St Ste G13, Falls Church, VA 22046-4020; Title Tel # (703) 237-8616
Personnel: Editor-S. Young
Editorial Description: Information pertinent to executive secretaries in their business and personal lives.
General Info: Yr. Est. 1975, Monthly, Trim Size-8½ x 11, Web press, 6 pages, ISSN: 0894-5748, 3% ads, 2 Color
Subscriptions: Indv. $20, Can. $30, For. $30
Circulation: (100% controlled), Total-5,500
Advertising: Inquire for rates.
List Rental: Actives: 5,500, $95/M, Expires: 6,000, $95/M

First Rate Customer Service
   See: MANAGEMENT

Forefront: The Newsletter for Optometric Staff
   See: OPTICAL

From Nine to Five
   See: INDUSTRIAL RELATIONS/PERSONNEL

Front Line Management
   See: MANAGEMENT

Get Organized! News, The
   See: GENERAL INTEREST

Home Office Connection   *Business, Consumer*

Publishing Co: KL Publications, 4003 Forest Dr, Aliquippa, PA 15001-4743; Title Tel # (412) 375-7331
Personnel: Publisher, Editor-Kay LaRocca
Editorial Description: Designed to assist the home-based resume writer/typing service operator in running a profitable & professional business.
General Info: Yr. Est. 1991, Monthly, Mimeo press, 5 pages, No Color, Matte
Subscriptions: Indv. $12

Imaging Technology Report
   See: COMPUTERS & AUTOMATION

In Command   *Business*

Publishing Co: Economics Press, Inc., 12 Daniel Rd., Fairfield, NJ 07004-2565; Title Tel # (201) 227-1224 Title Fax # (201) 227-9742
Personnel: Publisher-John Beckley, Editor-Robert Guder, Circ. Mgr.-Anne Lanahan, Production Mgr.-Matt Farley, Art Dir.-Charles Palminteri, Adv. Dir., Promotion Dir.-Diane Cody
Editorial Description: A series of 36 newsletters that refresh word processing training.
General Info: Yr. Est. 1984, Weekly, Sheetfed press, 4 pages, 2 Color, Newsprint, Looseleaf
Subscriptions: Indv. $146, $3/copy
List Rental: List Management Co.: Names in the News, 411 Theodore Fremd Ave., Rye, NY 10580 Tel # (914) 925-2400, Actives: $80/M
Printing Co: Beckley Press, 2 Sperry Rd, Fairfield, NJ 07004-2056 Tel # (201) 227-6350

Information Interchange

Publishing Co: Univ. of Illinois, Office of Business Affairs, (346 HAB), 506 S. Wright St., Urbana, IL 61801; Title Tel # (217) 244-0509 Title Fax # (217) 244-5821
Personnel: Technology Ed.-Melinda Carr
Editorial Description: A two-way source of communication between Business Affairs and the campus community. Informs departments of changes in policy or operations, explains significant features of financial systems and system operations, provides information on new programs, training sessions and reports which affect business operations.
General Info: Yr. Est. 1990, 3x/yr., Sheetfed press, 12 pages, Matte, Saddle-stitched
Circulation: Total-4,600

Jot and Jolts
   See: MANAGEMENT

Law Office Technology Review
   See: LAW

LifeLines
See: HEALTH

Mailing Equipment Hotline   *Business, Association*

Publishing Co: Business Technolgy Assn., 12411 Wornall Rd, Kansas City, MO 64145-1119;
Title Tel # (816) 941-3100 Title Fax # (816) 941-8034
Personnel: Editor-Brent Hoskins, Assoc. Ed.-Peter Wollinson, w
Editorial Description: News articles regarding mailing equipment & systems industry focusing on
new products & technologies. Also news regardin the business tech asso.
General Info: Yr. Est. 1995, 1x/yr.
Subscriptions: Indv. $15, Free With Membership
Printing Co: Mainline Printing, 818 SE Adams St, Topeka, KS 66601 Tel # (913) 233-2335

Management Memo
See: MANAGEMENT

Manager/Motivator
See: MANAGEMENT

Micro Alert: The Canadian Microcomputer Reference Guide
See: COMPUTERS & AUTOMATION

Micrographics Newsletter   *Business*

Publishing Co: Microfilm Publishing, Inc., PO Box 950, Larchmont, NY 10538-0950;
Title Tel # (914) 834-3044 Title Fax # (914) 834-3993
Personnel: Publisher, Editor-Mitchell M. Badler, Circ. Mgr., Production Mgr., Adv. Dir.-Dorothy Miceli
Editorial Description: News of micrographics news developments, products, applications, personnel
in the industry written for executives.
General Info: (Formerly Microfilm Newsletter), Yr. Est. 1969, Monthly, Trim Size-8½ x 11, Offset
press, 12 pages, ISSN: 0883-9808, No Color
Subscriptions: Indv. $178, Can. $178, For. $198, $25/copy
Advertising: $660. Accepts Inserts.
Printing Co: Minuteman Press, 1299 North Ave, New Rochelle, NY 10804-2604
Tel # (914) 576-0335

National Collegiate Association for Secretaries; Newsletter

Publishing Co: National Collegiate Association for Secretaries, Univ. of SC, College of Business,
Columbia, SC 29208-0001; Title Tel # (803) 777-6419

Newsletter Consultant, The
See: ADVERTISING & MARKETING

OSRA Newsletter
See: COMPUTERS & AUTOMATION

Office Developer
See: COMPUTERS & AUTOMATION

Office Hours   *Business*

Publishing Co: Economics Press, Inc., 12 Daniel Rd., Fairfield, NJ 07004-2565;
Title Tel # (201) 227-1224 Title Fax # (201) 227-9742
Personnel: Publisher-John Beckley, Circ. Mgr.-Anne Lanahan, Production Mgr.-Matt Farley, Art Dir.-
Charles Palminteri, Editor, Promotion Dir.-Diane Cody
Editorial Description: Tips on working in the office environment.
General Info: Yr. Est. 1987, Bi-weekly, Trim Size-8½ x 11, Sheetfed press, 4 pages, 2 Color, Coated
Subscriptions: Indv. $41, $2/copy
Circulation: Total-50,000
List Rental: List Management Co.: Manager: Michael Korman; Names in the News, 411 Theodore
Fremd Ave., Rye, NY 10580 Tel # (914) 925-2400, Actives: $80/M
Printing Co: Beckley Press, 2 Sperry Rd, Fairfield, NJ 07004-2056 Tel # (201) 227-6350

Office Machine Times   *Business*

Publishing Co: Sponsor-Keystone Business Machines, Promotional Pubs., Inc., 4232 Brownsville
Rd., Ste. 137, Pittsburgh, PA 15227 Tel # (412) 884-9445 Fax # (412) 884-7633
Editorial Description: Information about office machines and the distributor.
General Info: Irregular, Trim Size-11⅜ x 17½, 4 pages, Color, Newsprint

Office Newsletter

Publishing Co: Lowen Publishing, 2464 Rue Le Charlene, Rancho Palos Verdes, CA 90275-6361;
Title Tel # (213) 831-2770
Personnel: Editor-Tom Snodgrass
General Info: Yr. Est. 1986, Monthly, Trim Size-8½ x 11, 4 pages, ISSN: 0893-1224, 2 Color,
Newsprint
Subscriptions: Indv. $24, $2/copy
Acquistions: Publication Bought
List Rental: Rents Lists

Office Products Analyst   *Business*

Publishing Co: Industry Analyst, 50 Chestnut St, Rochester, NY 14604-2318;
Title Tel # (716) 232-5320 Title Fax # (716) 454-5760
Personnel: Editor-Louis Slawetsky
Editorial Description: A monthly newsletter devoted to the cost performance analysis of office
products.
General Info: Yr. Est. 1975, Monthly, Sheetfed press, 12 pages
Subscriptions: Indv. $195, Inst. $195, Can. $210, For. $210, $40/copy
Circulation: Total-221

Office Professional   *Business*

Publishing Co: Professional Training Assocs., Inc., 210 Commerce Blvd, Round Rock, TX
78664-2116; Title Tel # (512) 255-6006
Personnel: Publisher-Dennis Murphy, Editor-Marilyn Johnson, Circ. Mgr.-Jan Faubion, Promotion
Dir.-Sue Perry
Editorial Description: Secretarial methods, management thinking, & office systems, procedures, &
technology.
General Info: Yr. Est. 1981, Monthly, Trim Size-8½ x 11, 8 pages, ISSN: 0739-3156, 2 Color
Subscriptions: Indv. $48, For. $63, $4/copy
List Rental: Actives: $90/M

Officemation Product Reports
See: COMPUTERS & AUTOMATION

Packaged Software Reports
See: COMPUTERS & AUTOMATION

Payroll Inserts
See: INDUSTRIAL RELATIONS/PERSONNEL

PerfectOffice Newsletter
See: COMPUTERS & AUTOMATION

Personal Page and Ink Jet Printer Guide   *Business*

Publishing Co: Dataquest Div. Dun & Bradstreet Corp., 1290 Ridder Park Dr, San Jose, CA
95131-2304 Tel # (408) 437-8000
Personnel: Editor-Robert Fennell
Editorial Description: Contains detailed specifications and pricing information for more than 400 non-
impact printers.
General Info: Semi-annually, 450 pages, Perfect bound
Subscriptions: Indv. $95, $50/copy
Circulation: Total-3,000

Personal Report for the Professional Secretary
See: BUSINESS & INDUSTRY

Practical Supervision   *Business*

Publishing Co: Professional Training Assocs., Inc., 210 Commerce Blvd, Round Rock, TX
78664-2116; Title Tel # (512) 255-6006
Personnel: Publisher-Dennis Murphy, Editor-Mark Gozonsky, Circ. Mgr.-Jan Faubion, Promotion Dir.-
Sue Perry
Editorial Description: How to become an effective supervisor & solve daily supervisory problems.
General Info: Yr. Est. 1984, Monthly, Trim Size-8½ x 11, Offset press, 8 pages, ISSN: 0742-7859, 2
Color
Subscriptions: Indv. $48, For. $63, $4/copy
List Rental: Actives: $90/M

Printer Impressions
See: COMPUTERS & AUTOMATION

Productivity Views: Newsletter of Service Quality
See: BUSINESS & INDUSTRY

Report to Legal Management
See: LAW

Sale$Maker$
See: SALESMANSHIP & SELLING

Sales Bullet, A
See: SALESMANSHIP & SELLING

Sales Memory Jogger   *Business*

Publishing Co: Bureau of Business Practice, 24 Rope Ferry Rd, Waterford, CT 06386-0001
Tel # (806) 442-4365 Fax # (860) 434-3341 Parent Co.-Prentice Hall, Waterford;
Title Tel # (860) 442-4365
Personnel: Publisher-James E. Bradler, Editor-Paulette Kitchens, Art Dir.-Ellie Barber
Editorial Description: Time-organizer and pocket secretary, with editorial content.
General Info: Monthly, Trim Size-3¼ x 6½, Offset press, 72 pages, ISSN: 1077-9329, 2 Color, Matte,
Other
Subscriptions: Indv. $23
Circulation: Total-2,600

Small Business Builder
See: BUSINESS & INDUSTRY

Small Business Computer News
See: COMPUTERS & AUTOMATION

Smart Buying
See: PURCHASING

Staffing Industry Report
See: EMPLOYMENT

Telemarketing Update-Answering Service Business Script Presentations
See: ADVERTISING & MARKETING

Telemarketing Update-Catering Service Business Script Presentations
See: ADVERTISING & MARKETING

Telemarketing Update-Copier Service Business Script Presentations
See: ADVERTISING & MARKETING

Telemarketing Update-Secretarial Business Script Presentations
See: ADVERTISING & MARKETING

Telephone Angles   *Business*

Publishing Co: United Communications Group, 11300 Rockville Pike, Ste. 1100, Rockville, MD 20852-3030 Tel # (301) 816-8950 Fax # (301) 816-8945; Title Tel # (301) 961-8700
Personnel: Publisher-Doug O'Boyle, Editor-Jim Sweeney, Circ. Mgr.-Sharon Welch
Editorial Description: How to manage an efficient, cost effective business telephone system.
General Info: Yr. Est. 1980, Semi-monthly, Trim Size-8½ x 11, Offset press, 4 pages, ISSN: 0270-4269, Newsprint
Subscriptions: Indv. $239, $10/copy
Acquistions: Publication Bought, Publication Sold
List Rental: Rents Lists

Thayer Advertising Co.

Publishing Co: Thayer Corp Graphic International, PO Box 8465, Mankato, MN 56002-8465; Title Tel # (609) 853-0800
List Rental: Actives: 50,000, $75/M, Hotline: 5,170, $85/M

Times   *Association*

Publishing Co: Executive Women Intl., 515 South 700 32-E, Salt Lake City, UT 84102-2801 Tel # (801) 355-2800; Title Tel # (801) 263-3296
General Info: (Formerly Notebook), Quarterly, 12 pages, 2 Color
Circulation: (100% controlled), Total-5,000
Printing Co: Becker Printing Co., 840 Fannin St, Beaumont, TX 77701-2809 Tel # (409) 833-8618

Update: The Executives Purchasing Advisior   *Business*

Publishing Co: Buyer's Laboratory, Inc., 20 Railroad Ave, Hackensack, NJ 07601-3309; Title Tel # (201) 488-0404 Title Fax # (201) 488-0464
Personnel: Editor-Daria Hoffman, Circ. Mgr.-Marion Davidowitz, Publisher, Promotion Dir.-Burt Meerow
Editorial Description: Buying advice on business equipment & services.
General Info: (Formerly Update), Yr. Est. 1965, Semi-monthly, Trim Size-8½ x 11, Offset press, 8 pages, 2 Color, Newsprint, Saddle-stitched
Subscriptions: Indv. $95, $10/copy
Circulation: Total-2,000
List Rental: Rents Lists

Your Telephone Personality
See: TELECOMMUNICATIONS

OILS & FATS

Bluebook Update Newsletter
See: AGRICULTURE

Canola Digest
See: FEED, GRAIN & MILLING

Guide to Used Oil Regulations   *Business*

Publishing Co: Thompson Publishing Group, 1725 K Street, NW, Washington, DC 20006 Tel # (202) 872-4000
Editorial Description: Comprehensive state and federal coverage of EPAs management standards for used oil handling at all levels.
General Info: Monthly

Oils and Fats   *Business, Association*

Publishing Co: Statistics Canada, Holland Ave/RH Coats, Holland Ave/Tunney's Pasture, Ottawa, ON K1A 0Z6 Canada Tel # (613) 951-8116 Fax # (613) 951-0581; Title Tel # (613) 990-8116
Editorial Description: Text in English, French. Covers domestic purchases and production. (#32-006)
General Info: Yr. Est. 1950, Monthly, 5 pages, ISSN: 0527-5911
Subscriptions: Indv. $6, Can. $5, For. $7, $6/copy

Washington Correspondence   *Business*

Publishing Co: Natl. Institute of Oilseed Products, 412 1st St. SE, #100, Washington, DC 20003-1804; Title Tel # (202) 484-2773
Personnel: Publisher, Editor-Larry Meyers
Editorial Description: Fats and oils and allied fields, particularly imports and exports.
General Info: Yr. Est. 1947, Weekly, Desktop press, 8 pages, No Color
Subscriptions: Indv. $600, Free
Circulation: Total-500

OPTICAL

BACUS News
See: ENGINEERING, ELECTRICAL

Biomedical Optics   CPM: $250

Publishing Co: SPIE International Society for Optical Engineering, 1000 20th St., Bellingham, WA 98225-6705 Tel # (360) 676-3290; Title Tel # (206) 676-3290 Title Fax # (360) 647-1445
Personnel: Editor-Rich Donnelly, Adv. Dir.-Stacy Henry
Editorial Description: Contains short technical and opinion articles on the title subject.
General Info: Yr. Est. 1991, Quarterly, 30% ads
Subscriptions: Free With Membership
Circulation: (71% controlled), Total-3,500, Single Copy/Newsstand-500, Subscriptions-500
Advertising: $876.

Contact Lens Update

Publishing Co: Anadem, Inc., 3620 N High St Ste 310, Columbus, OH 43214-3643; Title Tel # (614) 262-2539
Personnel: Publisher-Will Kuhlmann, Editor-John Schoessler, Production Mgr.-Cindy Taylor, Adv. Dir.-L. Joe Gaietto, Promotion Dir.-Karla Gayle
Editorial Description: Digests medical & optometric journal articles about contact lens practice.
General Info: Yr. Est. 1982, Bi-monthly, ISSN: 0885-9264
Subscriptions: Indv. $69, Inst. $69, Can. $79, For. $84

Electronic Imaging
See: ENGINEERING, ELECTRICAL

Eye to Eye   *Association*

Publishing Co: Intl. Eye Foundation, Sibley Memorial Hospital, 7801 Norfolk Ave., Bethesda, MD 20814-6015; Title Tel # (301) 986-1830
Editorial Description: Descriptions of program activities of the Intl. Eye Foundation.
General Info: (Formerly Eyelights), Semi-annually, 8 pages
Circulation: Total-1,000

Forefront: The Newsletter for Optometric Staff

Publishing Co: Anadem, Inc., 3620 N High St Ste 310, Columbus, OH 43214-3643; Title Tel # (614) 262-2539 Title Fax # (614) 262-6630
Personnel: Publisher-Will Kuhlmann, Editor-Mike Cheadle, Production Mgr.-Cindy Taylor, Adv. Dir.-L. Joe Gaietto, Promotion Dir.-Karla Gayle
Editorial Description: Digests medical & business pubs. to present tips about patient relations & optometric practice management.
General Info: Yr. Est. 1988, Bi-monthly, ISSN: 1040-8495
Subscriptions: Indv. $36, Inst. $36, Can. $46, For. $51

Gift of Sight

Publishing Co: Co-Optics of America, Box 398, Box 393, Oneonta, NY 13820-0398; Title Tel # (607) 432-0557 Title Fax # (607) 432-1668
Personnel: Publisher, Editor, Circ. Mgr.-Barbara Lasher
General Info: (Formerly Your Eyes in Focus), Yr. Est. 1978, Semi-annually, Trim Size-8½ x 11, Letrpr. press, 4 pages, 1% ads, 2 Color, Newsprint
Subscriptions: Indv. $350
Circulation: Total-50,000
Advertising: Accepts Inserts.

Gift of Sight

Publishing Co: Operation Eyesight Universal, 4 Parkdale Crest N.W., Calgary, AB T2N 3T8 Canada; Title Tel # (403) 283-6323 Title Fax # (403) 270-1899
Personnel: Editor-Maureen McManus, Promotion Dir.-Barry Boyack
Editorial Description: To develop, encourage, and fund sight restoration and blindness prevention programs in the developing world. 'Sight' newsletter is published for the donor database.
General Info: (Formerly Operation Eyesight Universal Newsletter), Yr. Est. 1963, Quarterly, 2 pages, No Color, Coated
Circulation: Total-30,000
Printing Co: Windmill Printing, 4002 Fourth St., SE, Calgary, AB T2G 2W3 Canada Tel # (403) 287-2152

Holography
See: ENGINEERING, ELECTRICAL

Holography News
See: PRINTING/GRAPHIC ARTS

In Focus
Business, Association   CPM: $116

Publishing Co: Opticians Assn. of New Jersey, 150 W. State St., Trenton, NJ 08608;
Title Tel # (609) 695-0030 Title Fax # (609) 396-5361
Personnel: Publisher-John Patterson, Editor-Sam Morgenstern
Editorial Description: News and information for New Jersey opticians and others with related interests.
General Info: Yr. Est. 1993, Quarterly, Trim Size-8½ x 11, Offset press, 12 pages, 40% ads, 2 Color, Coated, Saddle-stitched
Subscriptions: Indv. $25, Inst. $25, $7/copy
Circulation: Total-6,000
Advertising: $700.
Printing Co: Hermitage Press Inc., 1595 Fifth Ave., Ewing, NJ 08638 Tel # (609) 882-3600, Fax # (609) 882-1137

Insight Washington; Insight Focus
Business

Publishing Co: Insight Communications, 5870 Hubbard Dr, Rockville, MD 20852-4818
Personnel: Editor-Charles Sonneborn
Editorial Description: Contains information on opthalmics.
General Info: Monthly
Subscriptions: Indv. $250

Issues & Solutions
See: MANAGEMENT

Microscopial Society of Canada. Bulletin
Consumer, Association   CPM: $613

Publishing Co: Microscopical Society of Canada, 1712 Avenue Rd., Box 54560, Toronto, ON M5M 4N5 Canada Parent Co.-Microscopical Society of Canada, Hamilton, Canada;
Title Tel # (416) 483-3712 Title Fax # (416) 483-3712
Personnel: Editor-C.J. Emerson, Bk. Rev. Ed.-G.T. Simon, Circ. Mgr.-Marie Colbert, Production Mgr., Adv. Dir.-F. Doane
Editorial Description: Information on instrumentation and applications of all aspects of the microscopical sciences, especially electron microscopy, in biology, materials sciences, physics.
General Info: Yr. Est. 1973, Quarterly, Trim Size-6 x 9, Offset press, 40 pages, ISSN: 0383-1825, 30% ads, Color-cover, Coated, Saddle-stitched
Subscriptions: Indv. $31, Can. $33, For. $35, Free With Membership
Acquisitions: Publication Bought
Circulation: Total-650
Advertising: $399. Accepts Inserts.
Printing Co: Imperial Press Ltd., 385 Brunel Rd., Mississauga, ON L4Z 1Z5 Canada Tel # (905) 890-1083, Fax # (905) 890-7144

Newfoundland Assn. of Optometrists Newsletter

Publishing Co: Newfoundland Assn. of Optometrists, Box 2284, Station C, St. John's, NF A1C 6E6 Canada
Personnel: Editor-Kathleen Simms
General Info: Quarterly, 12 pages

Ontario Assn. of Optometrists News

Publishing Co: Ontario Assn. of Optometrists, 290 Lawrence Ave.,W., Toronto, ON M5M 1B3 Canada; Title Tel # (416) 256-4411
Personnel: Editor-Linda Samek
General Info: Bi-monthly, 8 pages
Circulation: Total-800

Optical Computing
See: ENGINEERING, ELECTRICAL

Optical Materials and Engineering News
Business

Publishing Co: Business Communications Co., 25 Van Zant St., Ste.13, Norwalk, CT 06855-1781;
Title Tel # (203) 853-4266 Title Fax # (203) 853-0348
Personnel: Publisher-Louis Naturman, Editor-Anna Crull, Editor-Dick Hilton, Mktg. Dir.-Robert Butler
Editorial Description: Analyzes and reports on advanced optical materials, detectors and detector materials, including coatings and solid state laser media used in many advanced components and systems.
General Info: Yr. Est. 1990, Monthly, Trim Size-8½ x 11, 12 pages, ISSN: 1045-6570, No Color, Matte
Subscriptions: Indv. $350, Can. $400, For. $400, $35/copy
List Rental: List Management Co.: W.I. Mail Marketing, 470 Main St. #317, Ridgefield, CT 06877-4516 Tel # (203) 438-6822, Fax # (203) 438-7756, Actives: $120/M

Optical Memory News
Business

Publishing Co: Phillips Business Information, Inc., 1201 Seven Locks Rd., Ste 300, Potomac, MD 20854-2958 Tel # (301) 340-1520; Title Tel # (301) 340-2100 Title Fax # (301) 424-4297
Personnel: Publisher-Christopher Scotton, Grp. Pub.-Megan St. John, Editor-Marc Osgood Smith, Mng. Editor-Mary Crowley, Production Mgr.-Sherry Mitchell, Circ. Mgr., Mktg. Dir.-Ruth Zellers
Editorial Description: Optical memory drivers, media, etc. news for system integrators, vendors, users. Each issue contains detailed user case studies, sample business strategies, and analysis of the industry's key issues.
General Info: (Formerly Optical and Magnetic Report), Yr. Est. 1982, Bi-weekly, Trim Size-8½ x 11, 48 pages, ISSN: 0741-5869
Subscriptions: Indv. $547, For. $580
Advertising: Inquire for rates.
List Rental: Rents Lists

Optical Signal & Image Processing
See: ENGINEERING, ELECTRICAL

Optometrist's Patient Newsletter, The
Consumer

Publishing Co: Doctor's Press, The, 1866 Colonial Village Lane, Lancaster, PA 17605-0488
Tel # (717) 393-1000 Fax # (717) 393-5752; Title Tel # (717) 393-1010
Personnel: Publisher-Cynthia Young, Editor-Kim Conlin, Adv. Dir.-Rem Jackson, Art Dir.-Daniel Hill
Editorial Description: Newsletter for eye care professionals to use to market their practice by providing vision, eye health information that educates patients and encourages regular use of the services offered by the practice.
General Info: Yr. Est. 1988, Quarterly

Robotics
See: ENGINEERING, ELECTRICAL

World Aerospace & Defense Intelligence
See: AERONAUTICS/ASTRONAUTICS

ORNITHOLOGY

American Dove Association Newsletter
Association

Publishing Co: American Dove Assoc., PO Box 21, Milton, KY 40045-0021;
Title Tel # (502) 268-3240
Personnel: Publisher, Editor, Circ. Mgr.-Rita Courtney
Editorial Description: To promote and inform the dove fancy and those interested in the breed.
General Info: Yr. Est. 1955, Bi-monthly, Trim Size-8½ x 11, Offset press, 6 pages, No Color
Subscriptions: Indv. $8, Free
Circulation: (100% controlled)

American Hawkwatcher

Publishing Co: American Hawkwatcher, 629 W Green St, Allentown, PA 18102-1601;
Title Tel # (215) 434-1637
Personnel: Publisher, Editor-Donald Heintzelman
Editorial Description: Presents original raptor research conducted in the Americas.
General Info: Yr. Est. 1982, Trim Size-8½ x 11, Offset press, 4 pages, ISSN: 0748-8319, No Color

Audubon Happenings
Consumer, Association

Publishing Co: Chattanooga Audubon Society, 900 N Sanctuary Rd, Chattanooga, TN 37421-4105;
Title Tel # (615) 892-1499
General Info: Monthly

Birdscope
Association

Publishing Co: Cornell Univ. Ornithology Lab, 159 Sapsucker Woods Rd, Ithaca, NY 14850-1923;
Title Tel # (607) 255-2451
Personnel: Editor-Cynthia Berger
Editorial Description: Research newsletter of Cornell Laboratory of Ornithology.
General Info: (Formerly Cooperative Research Newsletter), Yr. Est. 1987, Tri-annually, Trim Size-8½ x 11, 4 pages, ISSN: 1041-6676
Subscriptions: Free With Membership
Circulation: Total-14,500

Books About Birds
See: BOOKS & BOOK TRADE

Curlew
Association

Publishing Co: Willow Beach Field Naturalists, Box 421, Port Hope, ON L1A 3W4 Canada;
Title Tel # (416) 885-5552
Personnel: Editor-Ulla Elliott, Editor-Norma Wallace
Editorial Description: Articles notes on botanical, ornithological observations in the area and related topics.
General Info: Yr. Est. 1954, 8x/yr., Trim Size-8½ x 11, Offset press, 7 pages, ISSN: 0011-3093, No Color, Other
Subscriptions: Indv. $13, Can. $17, Free With Membership
Circulation: Total-140
Advertising: Accepts Inserts.
Printing Co: Arc Industries, 275 Cottesmore Ave., Cobourg, ON K9A 4E3416 Canada Tel # (905) 372-3161

El Tecolote
Consumer, Association

Publishing Co: Audubon Society, Santa Barbara Chapter, 5679 Hollister Ave., 5B, Goleta, CA 93117; Title Tel # (805) 964-1468
Personnel: Editor-Dorin Mayes
General Info: Yr. Est. 1963, Monthly, Trim Size-8½ x 11, Offset press, 4 pages, No Color
Subscriptions: Indv. $10
Circulation: Total-1,200

Field Notes of Rhode Island Birds

Publishing Co: Audubon Society of Rhode Island, 12 Sanderson Rd, Smithfield, RI 02917-2606; Title Tel # (401) 231-6444
Personnel: Publisher, Editor-David Emerson
Editorial Description: Listing of bird sightings & numbers throughout RI, also summary of months weather & bird activity.
General Info: Yr. Est. 1969, Monthly
Subscriptions: Indv. $5
Circulation: Total-300

Hawk Migration Assn. of North America-Newsletter *Association*

Publishing Co: Hawk Migration Assn. of North America, PO Box 3482 Rivermont Stn., Lynchburg, VA 24503; Title Tel # (804) 847-7811
Editorial Description: Disseminates information about raptor migration in North America.
General Info: Yr. Est. 1974, Semi-annually, 60 pages, No Color
Subscriptions: Indv. $10, $4/copy
Circulation: Total-1,000
List Rental: Actives: $25/M

Hawk Mountain News *Association*

Publishing Co: Hawk Mountain Sanctuary Assn., Rt. 2, Kempton, PA 19529-9802 Tel # (610) 756-6961 Fax # (610) 756-4468; Title Tel # (215) 756-6961
Personnel: Editor-Nancy Keller
Editorial Description: Hawk migrations, conservation, events and affairs of sanctuary and association.
General Info: Yr. Est. 1938, Semi-annually, Trim Size-6 x 8¾, Sheetfed press, 32 pages, No Color, Coated
Subscriptions: Indv. $20, Free With Membership
Circulation: Total-10,000
Printing Co: Kutztown Publishing Co., 15076 Kutztown Rd, Kutztown, PA 19530-9275 Tel # (215) 683-7341

ICF Bugle *Association*

Publishing Co: International Crane Foundation, E11376 Shady Lane Rd, Baraboo, WI 53913-9778; Title Tel # (608) 356-9462 Title Fax # (608) 356-9465
Personnel: Editor-David Thompson
Editorial Description: Research, conservation news and propagation successes with cranes world-wide.
General Info: Yr. Est. 1974, Quarterly, Trim Size-8½ x 11, 8 pages, 4 Color
Subscriptions: Indv. $20, $1/copy
Circulation: Total-5,600
Printing Co: Mayland Printing, S. Park St., Madison, WI 53715 Tel # (608) 257-4656

International Council for Bird Preservation U.S. Section Newsletter

Publishing Co: Intl. Council for Bird Preservation, Dept. of Wildlife Ecology, Uni, Madison, WI 53706; Title Tel # (608) 262-2671

Linnean Newsletter

Publishing Co: Linnaean Society of New York, 15 W 77th St, New York, NY 10024-5153; Title Tel # (212) 769-5000
Personnel: Editor-Joseph DiCostanzo
General Info: Yr. Est. 1947, Monthly, Offset press, 2 Color, Recycled
Subscriptions: Indv. $4, Free With Membership
Circulation: Total-700

Mail Bag

Publishing Co: Brooks Bird Club, 707 Warwood Ave, Wheeling, WV 26003-6958; Title Tel # (304) 547-5253
Personnel: Editor-Robert Rine
Editorial Description: Newsletter of club events, environmental issues, member correspondence.
General Info: Yr. Est. 1943, Quarterly, Trim Size-8½ x 11, Mimeo press, 10 pages, No Color, Recycled
Subscriptions: Indv. $14
Circulation: Total-640
Printing Co: Copies Inc., 1618 Jacob St, Wheeling, WV 26003-3689 Tel # (304) 232-1166

Maine Audubon Quarterly

Publishing Co: Maine Audubon Society, PO Box 6009, Falmouth, ME 04105-6009; Title Tel # (207) 781-2330
Personnel: Editor-Peggy Milardo
Editorial Description: Wildlife and energy conservation, alternative sources of energy.
General Info: Quarterly, Offset press, 20 pages
Subscriptions: Indv. $20
Circulation: Total-4,200

Migrant *Association*

Publishing Co: Tennessee Ornithological Society, Rr 7 Box 338, Elizabethton, TN 37643-9145; Title Tel # (615) 542-8612
Editorial Description: Info on Tennessee birdlife.
General Info: Yr. Est. 1930, Quarterly
Subscriptions: Indv. $4
Circulation: Total-1,000

Nature Views
See: NATURAL HISTORY

New Hampshire Audubon *Association*

Publishing Co: Audubon Society of New Hampshire, 3 Silk Farm Rd., Concord, NH 03301-8200; Title Tel # (603) 224-9909 Title Fax # (603) 226-0902
Personnel: Publisher-Iain MacLeod, Editor-Susan Macleod, Editor, Production Mgr., Adv. Dir., Promotion Dir.-Iain Macleod
Editorial Description: Articles on conservation, natural history, & environmental issues, plus news on N.H. Audubon activities.
General Info: Yr. Est. 1966, Bi-monthly, Trim Size-8½ x 11, Offset press, 24 pages, 2 Color, Newsprint, Saddle-stitched
Subscriptions: Indv. $25, Inst. $50
Circulation: Total-5,500
Printing Co: Capital Offset Co., 181 N. Main St., Drawer #B, Concord, NH 03301 Tel # (603) 225-3308

North Star
See: ENVIRONMENT & ECOLOGY

Pacific Seabird Group Bulletin

Publishing Co: Pacific Seabird Group, 15 Central Way # 197, Kirkland, WA 98033-6116; Title Tel # (206) 821-2722
Personnel: Editor-Martha Springer, Circ. Mgr.-Ellen Chu, Circ. Mgr.-Kenneth Washeit
Editorial Description: Concerned with the natural history, biology, & conservation of seabirds of the Pacific Basin.
General Info: Yr. Est. 1973, Semi-annually, Trim Size-8½ x 11, Offset press, 50 pages, ISSN: 0740-3771, No Color, Matte, Saddle-stitched
Subscriptions: Indv. $15, Inst. $20, Can. $25, For. $25, $5/copy
List Rental: Actives: 350, Expires: 200

Peregrine Fund Newsletter

Publishing Co: Peregrine Fund, Inc., 5666 W Flying Hawk Ln, Boise, ID 83709-7289; Title Tel # (208) 362-3716 Title Fax # (208) 362-2376
Personnel: Editor-Bill Burnham, Editor-Tom Cade
Editorial Description: Reports year-by-year progress in research & efforts towards conservation of birds of prey of the world and the environment they require.
General Info: Yr. Est. 1973, Annually, 16 pages
Subscriptions: Free With Membership
Circulation: Total-6,000

Raptor Report, The *Scholarly, Association*

Publishing Co: Society for the Preservation of Birds of Prey, PO Box 66070, Los Angeles, CA 90066-0070; Title Tel # (310) 636-1662
Personnel: Editor-J. Richard Hilton
Editorial Description: Topical conservation issues with discussion & commentary. Strictly birds of preys, falconry & protection.
General Info: (Formerly The California condor (1966-1968)), Yr. Est. 1966, Annually, Trim Size-8½ x 11, Offset press, ISSN: 1048-8030, No Color
Subscriptions: Indv. $10, Free To Qualified Recipient
Circulation: Total-900

Trumpeter Swan Society Newsletter *Association*

Publishing Co: TTSS, 3800 County Road 24, Maple Plain, MN 55359-9652; Title Tel # (612) 476-4663 Title Fax # (612) 476-1514
Personnel: Editor-David Weaver
Editorial Description: Population status; habitat requirements; research conclusions; ecology and management; propagation techniques; restoration.
General Info: Yr. Est. 1968, Quarterly, Offset press, 12 pages, ISSN: 0742-2792, No Color
Subscriptions: Indv. $15, Inst. $25
Circulation: Total-500
Printing Co: Tonka Printing Co., 287 Water St, Excelsior, MN 55331-1882

Vocal Roll

Publishing Co: Central States Roller Canary Breeders Assn., C/O Robert Wild, 305 Grosvenor Ct., Bolingbrook, IL 60440; Title Tel # (708) 985-4416
Personnel: Editor-Robert Wild
General Info: Semi-annually

Winging It *Association*

Publishing Co: American Birding Association, PO Box 6599, Colorado Springs, CO 80934-6599; Title Tel # (719) 634-7736 Title Fax # (719) 471-4722
Personnel: Publisher-George Daniels, Circ. Mgr.-Lang Stevenson, Editor, Production Mgr., Adv. Dir.-Virginia Maynard
Editorial Description: For birding enthusiasts who need information about publications, services, equipment & programs that are available.
General Info: Yr. Est. 1989, Monthly, Trim Size-8½ x 11, Offset press, 16 pages, ISSN: 1042-511X, No Color, Matte, Saddle-stitched
Subscriptions: Indv. $36, Can. $45, For. $45
Circulation: Total-14,000
Advertising: Inquire for rates. Accepts Inserts.
List Rental: Rents Lists

Wood Duck
See: NATURAL HISTORY

OUTDOORS

American Rivers
See: ENVIRONMENT & ECOLOGY

American Wildlands
See: ENVIRONMENT & ECOLOGY

Arkansas Outdoors
Consumer, Association

Publishing Co: Arkansas Game & Fish Commission, 2 Natural Resources Dr., Little Rock, AR 72205-1501 Tel # (501) 223-6351; Title Tel # (501) 223-6342 Title Fax # (501) 223-6447
Personnel: Editor-Joe Mosby
Editorial Description: Activities of Ark. G & FC and outdoor-related groups, including wildlife & fisheries mgt., hunting seasons.
General Info: Yr. Est. 1955, Weekly, Trim Size-8½ x 14, Letrpr. press, 4 pages, No Color, Matte
Subscriptions: Free To Qualified Recipient
Circulation: Total-1,500

Backpacking Newsletter
Consumer

Publishing Co: Frank Ashley, Box 79, Spickard, MO 64679-0079
Personnel: Publisher, Editor-Frank Ashley
General Info: Yr. Est. 1976, Monthly, Offset press
Subscriptions: Indv. $20, $2/copy

Backyard Wildlife
See: NATURAL HISTORY

Breeze
Association

Publishing Co: Alpine Club of Canada, Edmonton Section, PO Box 2040, Canmore, AB T0L 0M0 Canada; Title Tel # (403) 439-5368
Personnel: Editor-Doug Konrad
Editorial Description: Information exchange for Edmonton Section, Alpine Club of Canada, trip reports, safety column, etc.
General Info: 10x/yr., Trim Size-8½ x 10, Mimeo press, 10 pages, 2% ads, Color-cover, Matte
Circulation: (84% controlled), Total-400, International-15
Advertising: Inquire for rates.

British Columbia Camping Association, Newsletter

Publishing Co: British Columbia Camping Assn., 3302 Senkler Road, Belcarra, BC V3H 4S3 Canada Tel # (604) 875-6760
Personnel: Editor-Susan Adair
General Info: 3x/yr.

Camping Assn. of Nova Scotia, Newsletter

Publishing Co: Camping Assn. of Nova Scotia, Box 3243, S. Halifax, NS B3J 3H5 Canada
General Info: Quarterly, 20 pages
Circulation: Total-150

Camping Update
Association

Publishing Co: American Camping Assn., 5000 State Road 67 N, Martinsville, IN 46151-7903 Fax # (317) 342-2065; Title Tel # (317) 342-8456
Personnel: Editor-Mary Ennis
Editorial Description: Information to assist local affiliate boards of the American Camping Assn.
General Info: Yr. Est. 1977, Trim Size-8½ x 11, 4 pages, No Color
Subscriptions: Indv. $5
Circulation: Total-700

Camping Women Trails

Publishing Co: Camping Women, 7623 Southbreeze Dr, Sacramento, CA 95828-5107; Title Tel # (408) 335-2210
Personnel: Editor-Pat Smith
Editorial Description: Short articles on camping & the outdoors. Chapter & organization activities.
General Info: Yr. Est. 1976, 10x/yr., Trim Size-11 x 17, 6 pages, No Color
Subscriptions: Indv. $8, $1/copy
Circulation: Total-250
Advertising: Inquire for rates. Accepts Inserts.

Camps Canada
See: PARKS & RECREATION AREAS

Canadian Archer
See: SPORTS & SPORTING GOODS

Caretaker Gazette, The
See: EMPLOYMENT

Conserve
See: ENVIRONMENT & ECOLOGY

Cruise & Freighter Travel Letter
See: TRAVEL

Dwelling Portably
Consumer

Publishing Co: Portable Dweling Info Letter, PO Box 190, Philomath, OR 97370-0190
Personnel: Editor-Holly Davis, Circ. Mgr.-Bert Davis
Editorial Description: Nomadic shelters, tools, techniques, lifeways; past & future. Reports, contacts.
General Info: (Formerly Message Post, About Dwelling Portably), Yr. Est. 1980, Tri-annually, Trim Size-5½ x 8½, Offset press, 16 pages
Subscriptions: Indv. $1, $1/copy
Circulation: Total-1,300
Advertising: Inquire for rates.

ERIC/CRESS Bulletin
See: EDUCATION

Ecolacy
See: EDUCATION

Expedition News
Consumer, Scholarly

Publishing Co: Blumenfeld and Associates, 397 Post Road, Ste. 202, Darien, CT 06820 Tel # (203) 656-3300 Fax # (203) 655-7710
Personnel: Editor-Jeff Blumenfeld, Asst. Ed.-John Lesser, Circ. Mgr.-Joan Kirbach
Editorial Description: Covers major expeditions, research projects, and notable adventures.
General Info: Yr. Est. 1995, Monthly, Trim Size-8.5 x 11, Desktop press, 3 pages, Ind/Abs/Online: CompuServe, AOL, MCI, Internet, No Color
Subscriptions: Indv. $36

Fish & Game Highlights
Consumer, Association

Publishing Co: NH Fish & Game Dept., 2 Hazen Dr, Concord, NH 03301-6507; Title Tel # (603) 271-3211
Personnel: Publisher, Editor-Dixie Sherrod
Editorial Description: Articles pertaining to hunting, fishing, non-game wildlife, snowmobiling, environment and conservation.
General Info: (Formerly Field Notes), Yr. Est. 1952, Monthly, Trim Size-8½ x 11, Sheetfed press, 6 pages, 2 Color
Subscriptions: Indv. $8
Circulation: Total-5,000
List Rental: Actives: $95/M
Printing Co: Town Line Printing, 102 Main St, Suncook, NH 03275-1236 Tel # (603) 485-8850

Fishing Hot Spots 'Newsline'
See: HUNTING & FISHING

Footprint, The

Publishing Co: Florida Trail Assn., PO Box 13708, Gainesville, FL 32604-1708; Title Tel # (904) 378-8823
General Info: (Formerly Florida Trail Assn. Newsletter), Yr. Est. 1966
Circulation: Total-2,500

Game Manager
See: HUNTING & FISHING

Go Camping America!
See: MOBILE HOMES

Hitch

Publishing Co: Jafari Intl., PO Box 192, Osceola, IN 46561-0192; Title Tel # (219) 258-0591
Personnel: Editor-Sherry Dranhan
General Info: Bi-monthly
Circulation: Total-1,200

Interlocken Globe
See: YOUTH

Islands Escapes
See: TRAVEL

Keystone Trails Association Newsletter

Publishing Co: Keystone Trails Association, PO Box 251, Cogan Station, PA 17728-0251
Personnel: Editor-Hugh Downing
General Info: Yr. Est. 1956, Quarterly, Trim Size-8½ x 11, Sheetfed press, 8 pages
Subscriptions: Indv. $6
Circulation: Total-1,500

Long Trail News, The
Consumer, Association　　CPM: $35

Publishing Co: Green Mountain Club, Inc., Route 100, RR 1 Box 650, Waterbury Center, VT 05677; Title Tel # (802) 244-7037 Title Fax # (802) 244-5867
Personnel: Editor, Circ. Mgr., Product Mgr., Adv. Dir.-Sylvia Plumb
Editorial Description: Quarterly membership publication of the Green Mountain Club. The Club founded & now maintains & protects the Long Trail-the nation's oldest long distance hiking trail.
General Info: Yr. Est. 1922, Quarterly, Trim Size-8½ x 11, Offset press, 16 pages, 2% ads, 2 Color, Newsprint, Saddle-stitched
Subscriptions: Indv. $24, Inst. $30, Free
Circulation: (100% controlled), Total-6,300
Advertising: $225.
Printing Co: Northlight Studio Press, Rte. 14, Box 568, Barre, VT 05641-0568 Tel # (802) 479-0565

MCM Newsletter *Association*

Publishing Co: Mountain Club of Maryland, 802 Kingston Rd, Baltimore, MD 21212-1908; Title Tel # (301) 377-6266
Personnel: Editor-Lester Miles

Media Update Outdoors
See: MEDIA & COMMUNICATIONS

NCWA Letter
See: ENVIRONMENT & ECOLOGY

News Notes of Outdoors Unlimited

Publishing Co: Outdoors Unlimited Inc., PO Box 373, Kaysville, UT 84037-0373; Title Tel # (801) 544-0960
Personnel: Editor-Patricia Hirschi
Editorial Description: Articles advocating wise multiple use and management of public lands.
General Info: Yr. Est. 1961, Monthly, Trim Size-8½ x 11, 8 pages, 2 Color
Subscriptions: Indv. $15
Circulation: Total-800
Printing Co: Carlsen Printing & Publishing, 419 22nd St, Ogden, UT 84401-1516 Tel # (801) 392-0022

North Star
See: ENVIRONMENT & ECOLOGY

Obsidian, The

Publishing Co: Obsidians, Inc., 840 Martin St, Eugene, OR 97405-4661
Personnel: Publisher, Editor-John Cecil
Editorial Description: Reports conservation news, activities of Club members, forth coming activities (hikes, climbs, etc.), actions of Governing Board.
General Info: Yr. Est. 1936, 11x/yr., Trim Size-8½ x 11, Mimeo press, 12 pages, No Color, Matte
Subscriptions: Indv. $5
Circulation: Total-420

Outdoor Crest *Association*

Publishing Co: Toronto Sportsmen's Association, 17 Mill St., Willowdale, ON M2P 1B3 Canada; Title Tel # (416) 487-4477
Personnel: Publisher, Editor-Peter Edwards
Editorial Description: Outdoor education, conservation, fishing, hunting, rock collecting, archery.
General Info: (Formerly Outdoor Crest Newsletter), Yr. Est. 1975, Irregular, Trim Size-8½ x 14, Mimeo press, 8 pages, ISSN: 0700-9909, Color
Subscriptions: Free
Circulation: Total-1,200

Outdoor Report

Publishing Co: Outdoor Recreation Council of B.C., 334-1367 W. Broadway, Vancouver, BC V6H 4A9 Canada Fax # (604) 738-7175; Title Tel # (604) 737-3058
General Info: (Formerly Outdoor Reports), Yr. Est. 1984, Quarterly, Trim Size-8½ x 11, Offset press, 4 pages, ISSN: 0826-3019, 2 Color, Recycled
Circulation: Total-2,400
Advertising: Accepts Inserts.

Outdoors Unlimited *Association*

Publishing Co: Outdoor Writers Association of America, Inc., 2017 Cato Ave Ste 101, State College, PA 16801-2765; Title Tel # (814) 234-1011
Personnel: Editor-Carol Kersavage
Editorial Description: Membership information, markets, craft improvement.
General Info: Yr. Est. 1940, Monthly, Trim Size-8½ x 11, Desktop press, 48 pages, ISSN: 0030-7181, No Color
Subscriptions: Indv. $100, Inst. $250, Can. $300
Circulation: (96% controlled), Total-2,600
Printing Co: Commercial Printing, 1224 N Atherton St, State College, PA 16803-2928 Tel # (814) 238-3025

Pathways Across America

Publishing Co: American Hiking Society, PO Box 20160, Washington, DC 20041-2160 Tel # (703) 754-4321; Title Tel # (703) 385-3252 Title Fax # (703) 754-9008
Personnel: Editor-Ellen Dudley
Editorial Description: Articles of interest to hiking enthusiasts.
General Info: Yr. Est. 1988, Quarterly

President's Commission on Americans Outdoors

Publishing Co: P.C.A.O., 18th & C St., NW Ms-3152-Mib, Washington, DC 20240-0001
General Info: Yr. Est. 1986

Questing
See: TRAVEL

RECorder *Association*

Publishing Co: Recreation & Park Assn. of New Brunswick, 440 Wilsey Rd., Ste. 105, Frederickton, NB E3B 7C5 Canada; Title Tel # (506) 459-1929
Personnel: Publisher-Susan Hebert
General Info: (Formerly Newsletter), Yr. Est. 1987, Quarterly
Advertising: Inquire for rates.

RV Park & Campground Report
See: PARKS & RECREATION AREAS

RVDA News *Business, Association* CPM: $281

Publishing Co: Recreation Vehicle Dealers Association, 3930 University Drive #500, Fairfax, VA 22030-2515; Title Tel # (703) 591-7130
Editorial Description: Reports RV industry news and association activities to members.
General Info: Yr. Est. 1970, Monthly, 40 pages, ISSN: 0891-6179, 25% ads
Subscriptions: Indv. $24
Circulation: Total-1,600
Advertising: $450.

Rec BC *Consumer, Association*

Publishing Co: Recreation and Parks Association, 10551 Shellenbridge Way, #30, Richmond, BC V6X 2W9 Canada Tel # (604) 273-8055
General Info: (Formerly Our Legacy), Yr. Est. 1987, Bi-monthly, Trim Size-8½ x 11, 12 pages, 4 Color, Coated
Subscriptions: Indv. $18
Circulation: Total-1,500
Advertising: Inquire for rates.

Recreation Assn. of Nova Scotia Tidings

Publishing Co: Recreation Assn. of NS, Box 3010 South, Halifax, NS B3J 3G6 Canada
Personnel: Editor-Linda Atkinson
General Info: Yr. Est. 1983, Quarterly, Trim Size-8½ x 11, 16 pages, Color
Subscriptions: Indv. $10, Inst. $10
Circulation: Total-2,000
Advertising: Inquire for rates.
Printing Co: Kentville Publishing, Box 430, Kentville, NS B4N 3X3 Canada

Recreation Executive Report
See: SPORTS & SPORTING GOODS

Scouter's Digest
See: YOUTH

Seedling News
See: ENVIRONMENT & ECOLOGY

Ski Tripper
See: SKIING & SNOWMOBILING

Sky Calendar
See: EDUCATION

Talking Leaves Newsletter *Consumer*

Publishing Co: Survival News Service, PO Box 41834, Los Angeles, CA 90041-0834; Title Tel # (213) 255-9502
Personnel: Publisher-Christopher Nyerges, Editor-Dolores Lynn Nyerges
Editorial Description: Articles, art photos, etc.
General Info: Yr. Est. 1981, Bi-monthly, Trim Size-8½ x 11, 8 pages, 25% ads, Newsprint
Subscriptions: Indv. $3
Circulation: Total-4,000
Advertising: Inquire for rates. Accepts Inserts.
List Rental: Actives: 2,000, $100/M

Trailhead

Publishing Co: Idaho Trails Council, Inc., PO Box 1629, Sun Valley, ID 83353-1629; Title Tel # (208) 622-3046
Personnel: Editor-Bernice Paige
Editorial Description: Stories & news of trails, trail users, & trail providers.
General Info: Yr. Est. 1974, Bi-monthly, Mimeo press, 16 pages, No Color, Newsprint
Subscriptions: Indv. $10, Inst. $20, $2/copy
Acquistions: Publication Bought
Circulation: Total-200
Advertising: Inquire for rates.
Printing Co: Zip-Print, Inc., F St., Idaho Falls, ID 83401 Tel # (208) 523-8831

Undercurrent
See: TRAVEL

U.S. Handgunner
See: GUNS & FIREARMS

U.S. Outdoor Drama
See: THEATRE

Whoop 'N' Holler *Consumer, Association*

Publishing Co: West Virginia Scenic Trails Assn., 633 West Virginia Ave, Morgantown, WV 26505-6764; Title Tel # (304) 296-5158
Personnel: Editor-George Rosier
Editorial Description: Newsletter for membership.
General Info: Yr. Est. 1972, Quarterly, Trim Size-8½ x 11, 12 pages, No Color
Subscriptions: Free With Membership
Circulation: Total-200

WindStar Wildlife Institute Journal

Publishing Co: Windstar Enterprises, Inc., 3603 Fry Road, Jefferson, MD 21755; Title Tel # (301) 834-9238 Title Fax # (301) 834-9064
Personnel: Editor-Thomas D. Patrick
Editorial Description: Assists individuals and families in establishing or enhancing the wildlife habitat on their properties.
General Info: Yr. Est. 1993, Bi-monthly
Subscriptions: Indv. $30

Winging It
See: ORNITHOLOGY

Workamper News
See: TRAVEL

PACKAGING

Authentication News
Business, Association

Publishing Co: Reconnaissance Holographics Ltd., 825 East Tufts Avenue, Cherry Hills, CO 80110; Title Tel # (303) 274-9874 Title Fax # (303) 274-4010
Personnel: Publisher-Lewis T. Kontnik, Editor-Ian M. Lancaster
Editorial Description: the international business newsletter of the anticounterfeiting authentication industry including valuable documents, branded products. currency, cards and other international products.
General Info: Yr. Est. 1995, 6 pages, No Color
Subscriptions: Indv. $494
Advertising: Inquire for rates. Accepts Inserts.
List Rental: Rents Lists

Board Converting News
Business   **CPM: $169**

Publishing Co: N.V. Business Publishers Corp., 43 Main St., Avon by the Sea, NJ 07717; Title Tel # (908) 502-0500 Title Fax # (908) 502-9606
Personnel: Publisher-Ted Vilardi, Co-Editor-Jim Curley, Circ. Mgr.-Gail Kalina, Co-Editor, Production Mgr.-Howard Neft, Adv. Dir.-Tom Vilardi
Editorial Description: Current trends in board converting, plus pricing information.
General Info: Yr. Est. 1984, Weekly, Trim Size-8 x 11, Sheetfed press, 32 pages, 4 Color, Perfect bound
Subscriptions: Indv. $120, Can. $130, For. $140, $11/copy
Circulation: (VAC, 5% controlled), Total-4,725, Subscriptions-4,477
Advertising: $800. Accepts Inserts.

Bottle/Can Recycling Update
See: ENVIRONMENT & ECOLOGY

Can Shipments Report
See: METALS & METALWORKING

Canadian Wood Pallet & Container Assn., Newsletter
See: LUMBER & WOOD

Converting Business Register
Business

Publishing Co: Quoin Publishing, 800 W Huron St Ste 3n, Chicago, IL 60622-5973 Parent Co.-PTN Publishing Co., Melville; Title Tel # (312) 226-5600 Title Fax # (312) 226-4640
Personnel: Publisher, Editor-Rod Piechowski
General Info: Yr. Est. 1988, Bi-monthly, Trim Size-8½ x 11, 4 pages
Subscriptions: Indv. $217, Inst. $217, For. $299, $10/copy
Circulation: Total-123
Advertising: Accepts Inserts.
Printing Co: Ability Ad Co., 806 N. Peoria St., Chicago, IL 60622 Tel # (312) 226-5353, Fax # (312) 226-3821

Environmental Packaging: U.S. Guide to Green Labeling, Packaging and Recycling
Business

Publishing Co: Thompson Publishing Group, 1725 K Street, NW, Washington, DC 20006 Tel # (202) 872-4000
Editorial Description: Provides environmental regulatory specialists, package designers, purchasing managers, R&D engineers, legal counsel, and product development managers with information through continually updated manual and monthly newsletter.
General Info: Annually, Looseleaf
Subscriptions: Indv. $398

European Packaging Newsletter and World Report

Publishing Co: EPN Inc., 669 S. Washington St., Alexandria, VA 22314-4109; Title Tel # (703) 519-3907 Title Fax # (703) 519-7732
Personnel: Publisher-Jack Cameron, Editor-Pierre Louis, Circ. Mgr.-Marilyn Berry
Editorial Description: News of packaging industry from Europe and around the world.
General Info: (Formerly European Packaging Digest), Yr. Est. 1961, Monthly, Trim Size-8½ x 11, 6 pages, Color, Coated
Subscriptions: Indv. $240, Can. $240, For. $255
List Rental: List Management Co.: Manager: Don Peterson; World Innovators, Inc., 72 Park St., New Canaan, CT 06840 Tel # (203) 966-0374, Fax # (208) 966-0926
Printing Co: The Copy Company, 2801-B Merriles Drive, Fairfax, VA 22031 Tel # (703) 698-5161, Fax # (703) 698-1760

Exchange Packet

Publishing Co: Natl. Assn. of Container Distributors, 1900 Arch St, Philadelphia, PA 19103-1404; Title Tel # (215) 564-3484
General Info: Bi-monthly

Executive Focus
Business, Association

Publishing Co: Can Manufacturers Institute, 1625 Massachussetts Ave., NW, Washington, DC 20036-2289; Title Tel # (202) 232-4677
General Info: Yr. Est. 1939, Quarterly, 12 pages, 2 Color, Saddle-stitched

Flexible Packaging Assn. Update
Business, Association

Publishing Co: Flexible Packaging Assn., 1090 Vermont Ave NW, Suite 500, Washington, DC 20005-4960; Title Tel # (202) 842-3880 Title Fax # (202) 842-3841
Personnel: Publisher-Glenn Braswell, Editor-Catherine Hyde
Editorial Description: Covers issues and activities affecting the flexible packaging industry.
General Info: Yr. Est. 1980, Monthly, Trim Size-8½ x 11, Offset press, 20 pages, 2 Color, Matte, Saddle-stitched
Subscriptions: Free With Membership
Circulation: Total-1,100
List Rental: Rents Lists
Printing Co: CLB Publishers & Lithographers, 10580 Metropolitan Ave, Kensington, MD 20895-2606 Tel # (301) 933-5220, Fax # (301) 933-2498

Food & Drink Daily
See: FOOD

Food, Cosmetics & Drug Packaging
Consumer

Publishing Co: Elsevier Science Inc., 655 Avenue of the Americas, New York, NY 10010-5107 Tel # (212) 633-3916 Fax # (212) 633-3913 Parent Co.-Reed Elsevier, New York
Personnel: Publisher-G. Kitteringham, Editor-A.. Weawes, Promotion Dir.-S. Syelrey Smith
Editorial Description: Technical & regulatory news on food, cosmetics, & drugs packaging.
General Info: (Formerly FCD Packaging), Monthly, Desktop press, 16 pages, ISSN: 0951-4554, Ind/Abs/Online: DIALOG, Predicasts, 2 Color, Newsprint, Other
Subscriptions: Indv. $538
Advertising: Accepts Inserts.

Food Industry Futures-A Strategy Service
See: FOOD

Global Packaging & Brand Identity
Business

Publishing Co: Global Packaging & Brand Identity Report, 1562 1st Ave Ste 344, New York, NY 10028-4004; Title Tel # (212) 734-7841 Title Fax # (212) 734-4964
Personnel: Assoc. Publ.-Phyllis Levy, Publisher, Editor-Murray Lubliner
Editorial Description: Discusses latest trends and news in packaging and brand idientity with a global perspective. Directed towards professionals in package design, brand managers and marketing executives.
General Info: Yr. Est. 1984, Monthly, Trim Size-8½ x 11, 6 pages, ISSN: 1078-5922, No Color, Matte
Subscriptions: Indv. $145, Can. $145, For. $160
Circulation: Total-1,500

Healthcare Packaging
Business

Publishing Co: Packaging Strategies, 122 S Church St, West Chester, PA 19382-3223 Tel # (610) 436-4220
Personnel: Publisher-William LeMaire, Editorial Dir.-Ben Miyares, Exec. Ed.-Mike Pehanich, Circ. Mgr.-Aurora Woodruff
Editorial Description: News and information for healthcare product packagers.
General Info: Yr. Est. 1992, Monthly, ISSN: 1068-0802, Looseleaf
Subscriptions: Indv. $295

Holography News
See: PRINTING/GRAPHIC ARTS

Marketing Law Reporting Service
See: ADVERTISING & MARKETING

New Product News
See: GROCERY

Official Board Markets
See: PAPER

Other Converted Paper Products Industries Including Asphalt Roofing Industry
Business, Association

Publishing Co: Statistics Canada, Holland Ave/RH Coats, Holland Ave/Tunney's Pasture, Ottawa, ON K1A O26 Canada Tel # (613) 951-8116 Fax # (613) 951-0581; Title Tel # (613) 951-1581 Title Fax # (613) 951-1584
Editorial Description: Catalog #36-250.
General Info: Yr. Est. 1975, Annually, 2 pages
Subscriptions: Indv. $42, Can. $35, For. $49, $42/copy

PHL Bullein
Association

Publishing Co: National Institute of Packaging, Handling, 6902 Lyle St, Lanham, MD 20706-3454; Title Tel # (301) 459-9105 Title Fax # (301) 459-4923
Personnel: Editor-Barbara Johnson
General Info: Yr. Est. 1956, Monthly, 10 pages, No Color
Subscriptions: Indv. $50, $5/copy
Circulation: (100% controlled), Total-800
Advertising: Accepts Inserts.

Packaging Strategies
Business

Publishing Co: Packaging Strategies, 122 S Church St, West Chester, PA 19382-3223 Tel # (610) 436-4220; Title Tel # (215) 436-4220 Title Fax # (610) 436-6277
Personnel: Publisher, Editor-W. H. LeMaire, Circ. Mgr.-Hilary Kennedy, Production Mgr., Promotion Dir.-Annette LeMaire
Editorial Description: Intelligence service on trends/developments in packaging materials, containers, machinery.
General Info: Yr. Est. 1983, Semi-monthly, Sheetfed press, 8 pages, ISSN: 8755-6189, No Color
Subscriptions: Indv. $397, Can. $297, For. $339, $35/copy
Acquistions: Publication Bought
Printing Co: CCA Graphics, 23 Wilson Ave # 3069, West Chester, PA 19382-4815 Tel # (215) 430-3438

Packet, The
Business, Association

Publishing Co: National Paperbox Association, 1201 E. Abingdon Dr., Ste. 203, Alexandria, VA 22314-1420; Title Tel # (703) 684-2212 Title Fax # (703) 683-6920
Personnel: Publisher-R. Mickey Gorman, Editor-Scott Miller
Editorial Description: Information & facts useful to the growth of the packaging industry.
General Info: (Formerly NP&PA Newsletter), Yr. Est. 1918, Bi-monthly, Trim Size-8½ x 11, Sheetfed press, 24 pages, 3% ads, 2 Color, Coated, Saddle-stitched
Subscriptions: Indv. $50, Free With Membership
Circulation: Total-500
Advertising: Inquire for rates.
List Rental: Actives: $125/M

Paper Stock Report:News and Trends of the Paper recycling Markets
See: ENVIRONMENT & ECOLOGY

Pulp & Paper Forecaster
Business

Publishing Co: Miller Freeman Publications, 411 Borel Ave., Ste. 100, San Mateo, CA 94402 Tel # (415) 358-9500 Fax # (415) 358-8725; Title Tel # (415) 905-2200 Title Fax # (415) 905-2240
Personnel: Publisher-Will Mies, Editor-Ken Lowe
General Info: (Formerly P & P Forecaster), Yr. Est. 1988, Bi-monthly
Subscriptions: Indv. $1,175

Shelf Presence
Business

Publishing Co: Shelf Presence, 740 Shady Grove Ln, Buffalo Grove, IL 60089-1425; Title Tel # (708) 215-8910 Title Fax # (708) 215-8914
Personnel: Publisher, Editor-Greg Erickson
Editorial Description: Ideas, news and issues concerning consumer goods packaging for designers, marketers and ad pros.
General Info: Yr. Est. 1994, Monthly, Trim Size-8½ x 11, 8 pages, ISSN: 1074-4738, 2 Color
Subscriptions: Indv. $259, Inst. $259, Can. $259, For. $259, $25/copy

Showcase

Publishing Co: Specialty Papers Co., PO Box 1031, Dayton, OH 45401-1031
Editorial Description: Packaging industry news and developments featuring company products.
General Info: Monthly
Circulation: Total-400

TechPak Newsletter
Business

Publishing Co: Market Search, Inc., 2727 N Holland Sylvania Rd Ste, A, Toledo, OH 43615-1800 Tel # (419) 535-7899 Fax # (419) 535-1243; Title Tel # (212) 512-4462 Title Fax # (212) 512-2989
Personnel: Publisher-Bob Martino, Editor-Peter Savage, Circ. Mgr.-Maurice N. Persiani
Editorial Description: Financial, political, technical news for packaging management.
General Info: (Formerly Packaging Letter), Yr. Est. 1956, Bi-weekly, Trim Size-8½ x 11, Sheetfed press, 10 pages, ISSN: 0892-7146, No Color
Subscriptions: Indv. $417, Can. $417, For. $457
Acquistions: Publication Sold
List Rental: List Management Co.: Performance Marketing, P.O Box 32699, Laughlin, NV 89028 Tel # (702) 299-0011, Fax # (702) 299-0224, Actives: 26,875, $125/M

Tube Topics
See: METALS & METALWORKING

PAINT

Chapter Bulletins

Publishing Co: Painting, 3913 Old Lee Hwy., #33B, Fairfax, VA 22030-2401; Title Tel # (703) 534-1201

Drop Cloth, The
See: CONSTRUCTION & BUILDING

Finishing Line
Business, Association   CPM: $326

Publishing Co: Sponsor-Soc. of Manufacturing Engineers, Assn. for Finishing Processes of SME, 1 Sme Dr # 930, Dearborn, MI 48128-2408 Parent Co.-Society of Manufacturing Engineers, Dearborn; Title Tel # (313) 271-1500 Title Fax # (313) 271-2861
Personnel: Editor-Gene Korte, Production Mgr.-Dale Michelson
Editorial Description: For manufacturing practitioners who develop or use industrial finishes.
General Info: (Formerly AFP Newsletter), Yr. Est. 1985, Quarterly, Trim Size-8½ x 11, 8 pages, 2 Color, Coated
Subscriptions: Indv. $70, Can. $80, For. $95
Acquistions: Publication Bought
Circulation: Total-3,000
Advertising: $980.

Legislative Bulletins

Publishing Co: Painting, 3913 Old Lee Hwy., #33B, Fairfax, VA 22030-2401; Title Tel # (703) 534-1201

Steel Structures Painting Bulletin
Association

Publishing Co: Steel Structures Painting Council, 2100 Wharton St Ste 310, Pittsburgh, PA 15203-1942; Title Tel # (412) 268-3327
Personnel: Editor-J. Rex
Editorial Description: Announces new publications, SSPC National Convention, other meetings, etc.
General Info: Yr. Est. 1951, 6 pages, No Color, Newsprint
Circulation: Total-50,000

PAPER

Abstract Bulletin of the Institute of Paper Science & Technology
Business

Publishing Co: Institute of Paper Science & Technology, 500 Tenth St. NW, Atlanta, GA 30318; Title Tel # (404) 894-5900 Title Fax # (404) 894-4778
Personnel: Editor-Rosanna M. Bechtel
Editorial Description: Abstracts of technical literature pertaining to pulp and paper processes, products, raw materials, and related science and technology.
General Info: (Formerly Abstract Bulletin of the Institute of Paper Chemistry), Yr. Est. 1929, Monthly, Trim Size-8½ x 11, Offset press, 1,800 pages
Circulation: Total-1,100

Canadian Paper Analyst
Business

Publishing Co: VDR Publications, Box 300, Victoria Station, Westmount, PQ H37 2U5 Canada; Title Tel # (514) 933-8749 Title Fax # (514) 849-8367
Personnel: Publisher, Editor-Jim Rowland
General Info: Yr. Est. 1979, 9x/yr.
Subscriptions: Indv. $195

Confidential. . . Newsletter

Publishing Co: Rolland, Inc., 140 McLevin, Unit 7, Scarborough, ON M1B 3V1 Canada; Title Tel # (416) 297-9511
General Info: Yr. Est. 1987, Quarterly, 4 pages

Converting Business Register
See: PACKAGING

Fibre Market News
Business   CPM: $406

Publishing Co: GIE Publishing, Inc. (Group Interest Enterprises), 4012 Bridge Ave., Cleveland, OH 44113-3320; Title Tel # (216) 961-4130 Title Fax # (216) 961-0364
Personnel: Publisher-Richard Foster, Editor-Dan Sandoval, Research Mgr., Circ. Dir.-Mark Fosse, Circ. Mgr.-Rosalie Slusher, Product Mgr.-Jami Childs, Adv. Dir.-Jim Keefe, Art Dir.-Helen Duerr
Editorial Description: For dealers, processors, brokers, and consumers of the secondary fibre (paper and paperboard) recycling market.
General Info: Yr. Est. 1963, Bi-weekly, Trim Size-8¼ x 11, Offset press, 16 pages, 2 Color
Subscriptions: Indv. $110, Can. $135, For. $170, $3/copy
Circulation: Total-1,500
Advertising: $609. Accepts Inserts.

Health and Safety Resource
See: FORESTRY

IPC-Reporter

Publishing Co: Institute of Paper Science & Technology, Inc., 500 10th St NW, Atlanta, GA 30318-5794 Tel # (404) 853-9500 Fax # (404) 853-9510; Title Tel # (414) 734-9251
General Info: Yr. Est. 1979, Semi-weekly, Offset press, 8 pages, No Color
Circulation: Total-250

ISRI Report
See: METALS & METALWORKING

Monthly Newsprint Report

Publishing Co: Canadian Pulp & Paper Association, 1155 Metcalfe St., Suite 1900, Montreal, PQ H3B 4T6 Canada; Title Tel # (514) 866-6621 Title Fax # (514) 866-3035
Personnel: Editor-Catherine Finley
General Info: Monthly, 4 pages

Newspaper   *Business*

Publishing Co: Paper Industry Information Office, PO Box 5670, Augusta, ME 04332-5670; Title Tel # (207) 622-3166 Title Fax # (207) 623-2198
Personnel: Editor-David Sargent
Editorial Description: Paper industry.
General Info: Bi-monthly, 4 pages
Circulation: Total-2,400

Nonwoven Markets
See: TEXTILES

Official Board Markets   *Business*   CPM: $107

Publishing Co: Advanstar Communications, Inc., 7500 Old Oak Blvd., Cleveland, OH 44130-3369 Tel # (216) 243-8100 Fax # (216) 891-2675; Title Tel # (312) 553-8922 Title Fax # (312) 553-8926
Personnel: Publisher-Robyn Smith, Editor-Mark Arzoumanian, Circ. Dir.-Robert A. Dahl, Circ. Mgr.-Karen Edgerton, Product Mgr.-Barb Johnson, Art Dir.-Clare Parfitt
Editorial Description: Includes currently revised price levels for both new liner & medium board and reclaimed paper stock. Also includes notices of impending changes in commodity prices, news, and features covering the board converting industry.
General Info: Yr. Est. 1924, Weekly, Trim Size-$7\frac{3}{4}$ x $10\frac{3}{4}$, Roto. press, 20 pages, 40% ads, No Color
Subscriptions: Indv. $135, Can. $135, For. $190, $4/copy
Circulation: (ABC, As of 06/30/95), Total-6,500, Readership-6,600
Advertising: $700. Accepts Inserts.
List Rental: List Management Co.: Taybi Direct East, Inc., 13321 New Hampshire Ave., Ste. 202, Silver Spring, MD 20904-3450 Tel # (301) 680-3633, Fax # (301) 680-3635, Actives: 5,640, $85/M
Printing Co: Davidson Printing Co., 4631 Mike Colalillo Dr, PO Box 16990, Duluth, MN 55807-2733 Tel # (218) 628-1016

Paper, Paperboard, and Wood Pulp, Monthly Statistical Summary   *Association*

Publishing Co: American Forest & Paper Assn., 1111 19th Street NW, Suite 800, Washington, DC 20036-3603 Tel # (202) 463-2700; Title Tel # (202) 463-5188
Personnel: Editor-B. Slatin
Editorial Description: Current statistics on the paper industry, special articles on economic and statistical trends.
General Info: Yr. Est. 1930, Monthly, 12 pages, No Color, Looseleaf
Subscriptions: Indv. $435, Can. $465, For. $465
Circulation: Total-1,500

Paper Pile Quarterly

Publishing Co: Paper Pile Quarterly, PO Box 337, San Anselmo, CA 94979-0337; Title Tel # (415) 454-5552
Personnel: Editor-Ada Fitzsimmons
General Info: Yr. Est. 1980, Quarterly
Subscriptions: $4/copy

Paper Recycler   *Business*

Publishing Co: Miller Freeman Publications, 411 Borel Ave., Ste. 100, San Mateo, CA 94402 Tel # (415) 358-9500 Fax # (415) 358-8725; Title Tel # (415) 905-2200 Title Fax # (415) 905-2240
General Info: Yr. Est. 1982, Monthly
Subscriptions: Indv. $337

Paper Stock Report:News and Trends of the Paper recycling Markets
See: ENVIRONMENT & ECOLOGY

Paper Tree Letter   *Business*

Publishing Co: Miller Freeman Publications, 411 Borel Ave., Ste. 100, San Mateo, CA 94402 Tel # (415) 358-9500 Fax # (415) 358-8725; Title Tel # (415) 905-2200
Personnel: Publisher, Editor-Will Mies, Circ. Mgr.-Michael Newton, Production Mgr.-Andy Mickus, Promotion Dir.-Paula Irons
Editorial Description: Analysis of topical issues in pulp,paper & wood products industries.
General Info: Yr. Est. 1981, Monthly, Trim Size-$8\frac{1}{2}$ x 11, Sheetfed press, 6 pages, ISSN: 0822-8094, No Color, Newsprint
Subscriptions: Indv. $349
Acquistions: Publication Bought, Publication Sold
Circulation: Total-1,200

Papetier   *Business, Association*

Publishing Co: Quebec Forest Industries Assn., 1200 Germain-Des-Pres, #102, Ste-Foy, PQ G1V 3M7 Canada; Title Tel # (418) 651-9352
General Info: Yr. Est. 1964, 8 pages
Subscriptions: Free
Circulation: Total-18,000

Printips
See: PRINTING/GRAPHIC ARTS

Pulp & Paper Forecaster
See: PACKAGING

Pulp & Paper Project Report   *Business*

Publishing Co: Miller Freeman Publications, 411 Borel Ave., Ste. 100, San Mateo, CA 94402 Tel # (415) 358-9500 Fax # (415) 358-8725; Title Tel # (415) 905-2200 Title Fax # (415) 905-2240
Personnel: Publisher-Leonard Haas, Editor-Carl Espe, Circ. Mgr.-Michael Newton, Production Mgr.-Andrew Mickus
Editorial Description: Tracks capital spending projects in the pulp and paper industry.
General Info: Yr. Est. 1982, Monthly, Trim Size-$8\frac{1}{2}$ x 11, Sheetfed press, 8 pages, No Color, Newsprint
Subscriptions: Indv. $389
Circulation: Total-800

Pulp & Paper Week   *Business*

Publishing Co: Miller Freeman Publications, 411 Borel Ave., Ste. 100, San Mateo, CA 94402 Tel # (415) 358-9500 Fax # (415) 358-8725; Title Tel # (415) 905-2200 Title Fax # (415) 905-2240
Personnel: Publisher-Leonard Haas, Editor-Will Mies, Circ. Mgr.-Michael Newton, Production Mgr.-Andrew Mickus
Editorial Description: News on markets, regulation, finance, capacity, labor; US and worldwide.
General Info: Yr. Est. 1978, Weekly, Trim Size-$8\frac{1}{2}$ x 11, Sheetfed press, 8 pages, No Color, Newsprint
Subscriptions: Indv. $657
Circulation: Total-2,100
List Rental: Rents Lists

Pulp & Paper Wood Report
See: LUMBER & WOOD

Report   *Business*

Publishing Co: Mead Publishing Paper Div., PO Box 757, Escanaba, MI 49829-0757; Title Tel # (906) 786-1660
Personnel: Editor-Doris Holmstrom
Editorial Description: Facilitate profitable operation of company and promote employee understanding support.
General Info: (Formerly Hiawathian), Yr. Est. 1949, Quarterly, Sheetfed press, 6 pages, 2 Color, Coated
Circulation: (100% controlled), Total-1,900

St. Croix Observer

Publishing Co: St. Croix Paper Co., Woodland, ME 04694
Personnel: Editor-R.F. Kozen
Editorial Description: Paper industry news and general interest articles featuring company products.
General Info: Bi-monthly
Circulation: Total-4,000

Sales Association of the Paper Industry, Bulletin   *Business, Association*

Publishing Co: Crosspoint Paper Corp., Marketing Dept., Chicago, IL 60680
General Info: Weekly

Seaboard Bulletin

Publishing Co: St. Regis Paper Co., Box 1200, Bucksport, ME 04416-1200
Editorial Description: Paper industry news and general items featuring company products.
General Info: 8x/yr.
Circulation: Total-2,000

Super Riegal Custom   *Consumer*

Publishing Co: Custom Papers Group, P.O. Box 1140, Alpha, NJ 08865-1140
Editorial Description: CPG makes filter papers for the automotive industry, security papers, art board, office papers and a host other products too numerous to list in this bulletin.
General Info: Trim Size-8.5 x 11, Other press, 16 pages, 2 Color, Matte, Other
Printing Co: Riegel Printing, 1 Graphics Dr # 7430, Trenton, NJ 08628-1547 Tel # (609) 771-0555

TOPLINE   *Business*

Publishing Co: American Forest & Paper Assn., 1111 19th Street NW, Suite 800, Washington, DC 20036-3603 Tel # (202) 463-2700; Title Tel # (202) 463-2420
Personnel: Editor-Kathy Hensley
Editorial Description: Covers stories and events of interest to the forest products and paper industry.
General Info: (Formerly AF & PA Report), Yr. Est. 1980, Monthly, Trim Size-$8\frac{1}{2}$ x 11, Mimeo press, 2 pages, 2 Color, Newsprint
Subscriptions: Free To Qualified Recipient
Circulation: (100% controlled), Total-1,000

Walden's Fiber & Board Report *Business*

Publishing Co: Walden-Mott Corp., 225 N. Franklin Trnpke., Ramsey, NJ 07446-1600; Title Tel # (201) 818-8630 Title Fax # (201) 818-8720
Personnel: Publisher-Alfred Walden, Editor-Gregg Fales
Editorial Description: Marketing and sales-oriented reporting of North American pulp, waste paper corrugated containerboard, box and carton markets. Includes news and analyses, prices, personnel and production data. Paper recycling an increasing topic.
General Info: Yr. Est. 1979, Bi-weekly, Trim Size-8½ x 11, 8 pages, No Color, Newsprint
Subscriptions: Indv. $210, Can. $210, For. $235
Circulation: Total-500
List Rental: Rents Lists
Printing Co: Copy Prints Offset, 118 Chestnut Ridge Road, Montvale, NJ 07645 Tel # (201) 391-8387, Fax # (201) 391-4562

Walden's Paper Report *Business*

Publishing Co: Walden-Mott Corp., 225 N. Franklin Trnpke., Ramsey, NJ 07446-1600; Title Tel # (201) 818-8630 Title Fax # (201) 818-8720
Personnel: Publisher-Alfred Walden, Editor-Sylvia Peremes
Editorial Description: Concise review of news on the North American paper industry.
General Info: Yr. Est. 1971, Bi-weekly, Trim Size-8½ x 11, Sheetfed press, 8 pages, 1% ads, 2 Color, Newsprint, Other
Subscriptions: Indv. $185, Can. $185, For. $215
Circulation: Total-750
Printing Co: Copy Prints Offset, 118 Chestnut Ridge Road, Montvale, NJ 07645 Tel # (201) 391-8387, Fax # (201) 391-4562

Warren Standard, The *Business, Consumer*

Publishing Co: S.D. Warren, 225 Franklin St., Boston, MA 02110 Tel # (617) 423-7300
Editorial Description: Provides customers with information on paper products, new technologies, and other news about the company.
General Info: Irregular, Trim Size-8½ x 11, 4 Color
Subscriptions: Free To Qualified Recipient

PARAPSYCHOLOGY

ASPR Newsletter *Association*

Publishing Co: American Society for Psychical Research, Inc., 5 W 73rd St, New York, NY 10023-3101; Title Tel # (212) 799-5050 Title Fax # (212) 496-2497
Editorial Description: News and articles about research and other developments in parapsychology, for laymen.
General Info: Yr. Est. 1968, Quarterly, Trim Size-8½ x 11, 10 pages, 2 Color
Subscriptions: Indv. $15, Free With Membership
Circulation: Total-2,000
List Rental: Actives: $85/M

American Association-Electronic Voice Phenomena *Association*

Publishing Co: American Assn. Electronic Voice Phenomena, 816 Midship Ct, Annapolis, MD 21401-7387; Title Tel # (301) 647-8742
Personnel: Publisher, Editor-Sarah Estep
Editorial Description: Interested inevidence for postmortem survival. Focus is on electronic evidence such as tape recorders, TV, computers.
General Info: (Formerly American Assn.-Electronic Voice Phenomena Quarterly Newslett), Yr. Est. 1982, Quarterly, Offset press, 6 pages, No Color
Subscriptions: Indv. $20
Circulation: Total-375
List Rental: Rents Lists

Association for Past-Life Research & Therapies
See: PSYCHOLOGY

Continuum *Consumer*

Publishing Co: ParaNet Information Services, Inc., PO Box 172, Denver, CO 80034-0172; Title Tel # (303) 429-2564
Personnel: Publisher-Michael Corbin
Editorial Description: Information on paranormal and UFO claims.
General Info: Yr. Est. 1989, Quarterly
Subscriptions: Indv. $18, $5/copy
Advertising: Accepts Inserts.

Dark Shadows Announcement
See: FAN MAGAZINES-MOVIE, RADIO, TV

Deep Spring Newsletter
See: RELIGIOUS & THEOLOGICAL

EHE News *Scholarly, Association*

Publishing Co: Exceptional Human Experience Network, Inc., 414 Rockledge Road, New Bern, NC 28562; Title Tel # (919) 636-8734 Title Fax # (919) 636-8371
Personnel: Editor-Rhea A. White
Editorial Description: Brief articles, book reviews, news items, & information on persons/ organizations concerned with psychical, mystical, death-related, transformative, & other anomalous/ inexplicable experiences, with the emphasis on the meaning of these 'exceptional human experiences.'
General Info: Yr. Est. 1994, Semi-annually, Trim Size-8½ x 11, Offset press, 16 pages
Subscriptions: Indv. $15, Inst. $180, Can. $20, For. $20, $10/copy
Circulation: Total-150

Future Technology Intelligence Report
See: SCIENCE

Georgian Newsletter

Publishing Co: Georgian Church, 1908 Verde St, Bakersfield, CA 93304-2841; Title Tel # (805) 323-3309
Personnel: Editor-Lady Fauna
Editorial Description: Comments on witchcraft, paganism, magick.
General Info: Yr. Est. 1973, Annually, Trim Size-8½ x 11, Mimeo press, 35 pages, No Color
Subscriptions: $35/copy
Advertising: Inquire for rates.

Ghost Trackers Newsletter *Consumer, Association* CPM: $371

Publishing Co: Ghost Research Society, PO Box 205, Dept. OC, Oak Lawn, IL 60454-0205; Title Tel # (708) 425-5163 Title Fax # (708) 425-3969
Personnel: Publisher, Editor-Dale Kaczmarek, Bk. Rev. Ed.-W. Ritchie Benedict
Editorial Description: Devoted to ghosts, hauntings, poltergeists and life after death. Articles from readers and contributors highlight the newsletter. Book reviews, movie critiques and a classified section complement each issue.
General Info: Yr. Est. 1982, Tri-annually, Trim Size-8½ x 11, Mimeo press, 26 pages, 5% ads, No Color
Subscriptions: Indv. $12, Inst. $20, Can. $20, For. $28, $4/copy
Circulation: Total-175, Readership-200
Advertising: $65. Accepts Inserts.
List Rental: Actives: $50/M

Hefley Psychic Report

Publishing Co: U.S. Research, Inc., PO Box 7242, Burbank, CA 91510-7242; Title Tel # (213) 841-2733
Personnel: Editor-Carl Hefley, Art Dir.-Andre Page
General Info: Bi-monthly
Subscriptions: $1/copy
Advertising: Inquire for rates.

Hypnotherapy Today
See: HYPNOSIS

Insider, The *Consumer, Association*

Publishing Co: Parapsychological Services Institute, 5575 B. Chamblee Dunwoody Rd., Atlanta, GA 30338 Tel # (404) 391-0991
Personnel: Editor-Judith Winters
Editorial Description: News and issues facing the parapsychological world.
General Info: Monthly
Subscriptions: Indv. $24

Insights *Association*

Publishing Co: Jersey Society of Parapsychology, PO Box 2071, Morristown, NJ 07962-2071; Title Tel # (201) 539-1466
Personnel: Editor-Phyllis Kimec-Wilhelm
General Info: Yr. Est. 1969, Monthly, Mimeo press, 6 pages
Subscriptions: Indv. $10
Circulation: Total-150
Printing Co: Chatham Minuteman, 7 Post Office Plz, Chatham, NJ 07928-2344 Tel # (201) 635-1880

Iridis

Publishing Co: California Society for Psychical Study, PO Box 844, Berkeley, CA 94701-0844
Personnel: Editor-Grace Furst
General Info: Yr. Est. 1957, Monthly, 10 pages
Subscriptions: Indv. $10, Free With Membership

Light Lines *Consumer*

Publishing Co: Sponsor-L/L Research, L/L Research, PO Box 5195, Louisville, KY 40255-0195; Title Tel # (502) 245-6495 Title Fax # (502) 245-6495
Personnel: Publisher-Carla Rueckert, Editor-Jim McCarty, Circ. Mgr., Adv. Dir.-James McCarty
Editorial Description: Messages from spiritual beings; concerning the process of metaphysical evolution.
General Info: Yr. Est. 1981, Quarterly, Trim Size-8½ x 11, 4 pages, No Color, Matte
Subscriptions: Indv. $6, $2/copy
Circulation: Total-5,000
Printing Co: ABC Printing, 3520 College Dr, Louisville, KY 40299-3682 Tel # (502) 267-8142

Memberletter
See: ASTROLOGY

Metaphysical Fellowship
Church Newsletter   *Association, Consumer*

Publishing Co: Metaphysical Fellowship Church Newsletter, 10591 Flower Ave, Stanton, CA 90680-2326; Title Tel # (714) 821-3984
General Info: Monthly, 6 pages
Advertising: Inquire for rates.

Mind Science Foundation News
See: PSYCHOLOGY

Munsters & the Addams Family Reunion
See: FAN MAGAZINES-MOVIE, RADIO, TV

New Eyes

Publishing Co: Center for Applied Intuition, 333 Ruth Ave, Mountain View, CA 94043-4114
General Info: Quarterly

OPRA Newsletter

Publishing Co: Organization of Psychic Research Associates, PO Box 720366, Norman, OK 73070; Title Tel # (405) 557-8048
Editorial Description: The study of the art & science of the energies & universal laws governing the holistic relation of mind, emotion, body & spirit.
General Info: Yr. Est. 1975, Monthly
Subscriptions: Indv. $10, $1/copy
Advertising: Inquire for rates.

OSMA Beacon

Publishing Co: Occidental Society of Metempiric Analysis, PO Box 308, Simla, CO 80835-0308; Title Tel # (303) 541-2544
Personnel: Editor-Bob Rondell
General Info: Bi-monthly, Trim Size-8$\frac{1}{2}$ x 14, 8 pages
Subscriptions: Indv. $12

Parapsychology,
Hypnosis, & Alternative
Health   *Consumer*

Publishing Co: Enterprises Unlimited, 400 E 59th St., Apt 9F, New York, NY 10022-2344; Title Tel # (212) 755-4363
Personnel: Publisher, Editor-Bill Thompson
Editorial Description: Covers all aspects of hyphosis & hypnotherapy.

Revelations of Awareness
See: NEW AGE

Seedling News
See: ENVIRONMENT & ECOLOGY

Skeptical Briefs   *Consumer*

Publishing Co: Committee/Scientific Investigation of Claims of Paranormal, PO Box 703, Amherst, NY 14226-0703; Title Tel # (716) 636-1425 Title Fax # (716) 636-1733
Personnel: Editor-Barry Karr, Production Mgr.-Tom Genoni
General Info: Yr. Est. 1984, Quarterly
Subscriptions: Indv. $18, $5/copy
Circulation: Total-3,000

Spiritual Advisory
Council-Newsletter

Publishing Co: Spiritual Advisory Council, 14345 SE 103rd Ter, Summerfield, FL 34491-3724; Title Tel # (352) 288-6607 Title Fax # (352) 288-6744
Personnel: Editor-Paul V. Johnson
Editorial Description: Acts as an intermediary between religion, science & personal revelations of mystics, clairvoyants, etc., to review, evaluate and update information about life after death to bring religion and spiritual sciences into proper perspective.
General Info: Yr. Est. 1976, Monthly, Trim Size-8$\frac{1}{2}$ x 11, 4 pages
Subscriptions: Free With Membership
Circulation: Total-3,200
List Rental: Actives: $60/M

Spiritual Frontiers
Fellowship International
Newsletter

Publishing Co: Spiritual Frontiers Fellowship Intl., PO Box 7868, Philadelphia, PA 19101-7868 Tel # (215) 222-1991; Title Tel # (816) 254-8585
Personnel: Publisher, Editor-Elizabeth Fenske, Ph.D.
Editorial Description: News of the Fellowship, articles by members relating to experiences in parapsychology, spirituality, consciousness studies.
General Info: Bi-monthly, 8 pages
Subscriptions: Indv. $35

Spiritual Frontiers
Fellowship Journal

Publishing Co: Sponsor-Spiritual Frontiers Fellowship International, Princeton Academic Press, 3175 Princeton Pike., Princeton, NJ 08648 Tel # (609) 896-2111; Title Tel # (215) 222-1991
General Info: Yr. Est. 1956, Semi-monthly

Spiritual Sciences Institute
Newsletter

Publishing Co: Spiritual Sciences Institute Newsletter, PO Box 22714, Santa Barbara, CA 93121-2714; Title Tel # (805) 969-3778
Personnel: Editor-Penelope Salinger
General Info: Bi-monthly, 6 pages
Subscriptions: Indv. $10

Star Beacon
See: UNIDENTIFIED FLYING OBJECTS

Still Waters Digest

Publishing Co: Still Waters Center, 615 Stafford Ln, Pensacola, FL 32506-4305; Title Tel # (904) 455-9511
Editorial Description: Promotes individual visionary thinking, exellerated transpersonal growth and appropriate planetary citizenship.
General Info: Monthly, Trim Size-7 x 10, 12 pages

TMI Focus   *Consumer, Association*

Publishing Co: Monroe Institute, Rr 1 Box 175, Faber, VA 22938-9751 Tel # (804) 361-9132 Fax # (804) 361-1611; Title Tel # (804) 361-1252
Personnel: Editor-Shirley Bliley
General Info: Quarterly, Trim Size-8$\frac{1}{2}$ x 11, Web press, 8 pages
Subscriptions: Indv. $25
Circulation: Total-1,700

USPA Newsletter   *Association*

Publishing Co: United States Psychotronics Assn., PO Box 354, Wilmette, IL 60091-0354; Title Tel # (708) 733-0116 Title Fax # (708) 733-0117
Personnel: Editor-Rita Fryer
Editorial Description: Deals with measurement of psychic phenomena; new paradigms; instrumentation. An open forum for science & the esoteric.
General Info: Yr. Est. 1976, Quarterly, 30 pages, No Color, Newsprint, Perfect bound
Subscriptions: Indv. $25, $5/copy
Circulation: Total-1,000

Winged Chariot, The
See: ASTROLOGY

PARKS & RECREATION AREAS

AALR Reporter   *Association*

Publishing Co: American Assn. for Leisure and Recreation, 1900 Association Dr, Reston, VA 22091-1502; Title Tel # (703) 476-3400 Title Fax # (703) 476-9527
Personnel: Editor-Christin Smith
Editorial Description: Members are teachers of leisure studies, recreation, park administration and the like.
General Info: Yr. Est. 1938, Quarterly, Trim Size-11 x 15, Sheetfed press, 4 pages, No Color, Newsprint, Other
Circulation: Total-40,000
Advertising: Inquire for rates.
List Rental: Rents Lists
Printing Co: Comprint, 9030 Comprint Ct, Gaithersburg, MD 20877-1313 Tel # (301) 921-2822, Fax # (301) 948-1967

Akwa Letter
See: HEALTH

Camps Canada   *Association*

Publishing Co: Canadian Camping Assn., 1810 Avenue Rd., Ste. 303, Toronto, ON M5M 3Z2 Canada; Title Tel # (416) 781-4717 Title Fax # (416) 781-7875
Personnel: Publisher-Margaret Seel, Editor, Editorial Page Ed., Feature Ed., Bk. Rev. Ed., Circ. Mgr., Production Mgr., Adv. Dir., Art Dir., Mktg. Dir., Promotion Dir.-Dawn Hunter
Editorial Description: Covers organized children's camps, with articles on safety, health, program ideas, environmental concerns, winter camping, and legislation.
General Info: (Formerly canadian Camping), Yr. Est. 1991, 6x/yr., Trim Size-8$\frac{1}{2}$ x 11, Desktop press, 8 pages, ISSN: 1185-3603, 1% ads, Color, Matte, Saddle-stitched
Subscriptions: Indv. $20, Can. $20, For. $25, $4/copy
Circulation: Total-1,200, Readership-2,500
Advertising: Inquire for rates. Accepts Inserts.
Printing Co: V & W Printers, 220 Industrial Parkway South, Unit 17, Aurora, ON L4G 3V6 Canada

Conserve
See: ENVIRONMENT & ECOLOGY

Dateline: NRPA

Publishing Co: Natl. Recreation & Park Assn., 2775 S. Quincy St., Ste. 300, Arlington, VA 22206-2236 Tel # (703) 820-4990 Fax # (703) 671-6772; Title Tel # (703) 820-4940
Personnel: Editor-Melissa Lanning, Production Mgr.-Ziggy Ziegenfuss, Adv. Dir.-Terrie Taylor
Editorial Description: Association news; park and recreation trends; timely legislative news.
General Info: (Formerly National Recreation and Park Association), Yr. Est. 1978, Monthly, Trim Size-8$\frac{1}{2}$ x 11, Sheetfed press, 12 pages, 2 Color
Subscriptions: Free With Membership
Circulation: Total-20,000

Employ
Association

Publishing Co: Natl. Recreation & Park Assn., 2775 S. Quincy St., Ste. 300, Arlington, VA 22206-2236 Tel # (703) 820-4990 Fax # (703) 671-6772; Title Tel # (703) 820-4940
Editorial Description: Assist individuals in preparing for their own job search in parks and recreation.
General Info: Yr. Est. 1974, 9x/yr., Trim Size-8½ x 11, 8 pages, No Color
Subscriptions: Indv. $25, $3/copy
Circulation: (100% controlled), Total-800

Federal Parks and Recreation

Publishing Co: Resources Publ. Co., 1010 Vermont Ave NW Ste 708, Washington, DC 20005-4995; Title Tel # (202) 638-7529
Personnel: Publisher, Editor-James Coffin, Circ. Mgr.-Chris Crandell
Editorial Description: Reports on park and recreation legislation/regulations from Washington.
General Info: Yr. Est. 1983, Bi-weekly, Trim Size-8½ x 11, Offset press, 10 pages, No Color
Subscriptions: Indv. $187
List Rental: Rents Lists

Historic House News
See: HISTORY

Ice Skating Institute of America Newsletter
Business, Association   **CPM: $80**

Publishing Co: Ice Skating Institute of America, 355 W. Dundee, Buffalo Grove, IL 60089-3500 Tel # (708) 808-7528; Title Tel # (708) 800-7528 Title Fax # (708) 808-8329
Personnel: Editor-Justine Smith, Adv. Dir.-Craig Cichy
Editorial Description: News of ice skating industry for rink owners, operators & instructors.
General Info: Yr. Est. 1960, Bi-monthly, Trim Size-8½ x 11, No Color, Newsprint, Saddle-stitched
Subscriptions: Indv. $36, Free With Membership
Circulation: (100% controlled), Total-2,500
Advertising: $200.

Leisure Lines
Association

Publishing Co: California Park & Recreation Society, Inc., 3031 F St Ste 202, Sacramento, CA 95816-3809; Title Tel # (916) 446-2777
Personnel: Editor, Production Mgr.-Anna Poole
Editorial Description: Issues, information on parks & recreation in California.
General Info: Monthly, Sheetfed press
Subscriptions: Indv. $2
Circulation: Total-5,000
List Rental: Rents Lists

Long Trail News, The
See: OUTDOORS

NCA Cave Talk
See: GEOLOGY

N.F.R.A. Newsletter
Association

Publishing Co: National Forest Recreation Assn., PO Box 409, Mammoth Lakes, CA 93546-0409 Tel # (619) 934-2887 Fax # (619) 934-9570
General Info: (Formerly NFRA News), Yr. Est. 1948, Quarterly, Trim Size-8½ x 11, Sheetfed press, 8 pages
Subscriptions: Indv. $8, $2/copy
Circulation: Total-6,000

North Star
See: ENVIRONMENT & ECOLOGY

OABA News
Association

Publishing Co: Outdoor Amusement Business Assn., 4600 W. 77th St., Minneapolis, MN 55435; Title Tel # (612) 831-4643 Title Fax # (612) 831-4642
Personnel: Editor-Roland Larson
Editorial Description: Amusement industry news.
General Info: Monthly, Trim Size-8½ x 11

OCAsional News
Association

Publishing Co: Ontario Camping Assn., 1810 Avenue Rd, # 302, Toronto, ON M5M 3Z1 Canada Fax # (416) 781-7875; Title Tel # (416) 781-0525
Personnel: Editor-Janet Adamson
Editorial Description: For members-general news and educational items re children's camps.
General Info: Yr. Est. 1965, Monthly, Trim Size-8½ x 11, Offset press, 6 pages, No Color
Subscriptions: Free With Membership
Circulation: (100% controlled), Total-600
Advertising: Inquire for rates.
List Rental: Rents Lists

Outdoor Report
See: OUTDOORS

Parks

Publishing Co: U.S. Natl. Park Service, Interior Bldg., Washington, DC 20240-0001
General Info: Quarterly

RV Park & Campground Report
Business, Association   **CPM: $230**

Publishing Co: National Association of RV Parks & Campgrounds, 8605 Westwood Center Dr Ste, 201, Vienna, VA 22182-2231; Title Tel # (703) 734-3000 Title Fax # (703) 734-3004
Personnel: Publisher-David Gorin, Editor, Adv. Dir.-Christine Beam
Editorial Description: Commercial campground industry reports and developments in state campground associations.
General Info: (Formerly NCOA NEWS), Yr. Est. 1967, Monthly, Trim Size-11 x 15, Sheetfed press, 8 pages, 20% ads, 2 Color, Matte
Subscriptions: Indv. $30, Can. $40, For. $60
Circulation: (100% controlled), Total-3,500
Advertising: $808. Accepts Inserts.
List Rental: List Management Co.: Manager: Micki Leak; Marketry, Inc., 2020 116th NE Ste 100, Bellevue, WA 98004-3017 Tel # (800) 346-2013, Fax # (206) 451-1941, Actives: 3,500, $85/M, Hotline: 80,000, $75/M
Printing Co: Presstar Printing, 12201 Old Columbia Pike, Silver Spring, MD 20904-1968 Tel # (301) 622-5000, Fax # (301) 622-5403

Rec BC
See: OUTDOORS

Recreation Executive Report
See: SPORTS & SPORTING GOODS

Recreation News
See: EDUCATION

Sand Paper

Publishing Co: Anza-Borrego Desert Natural History Assn., PO Box 311, Borrego Springs, CA 92004-0311; Title Tel # (619) 767-3760
Personnel: Publisher-Anza Borrego, Editor-Charles Stone
Editorial Description: Informs members of news about Ansa-Borrego Desert State Park, Association-sponsored lectures & 4-wheel-drive back-country tours in the Park, led by State Park Rangers. Also news about new publishing projects & park historical articles.
General Info: Yr. Est. 1971, 8x/yr., Trim Size-8½ x 11, 6 pages, No Color
Circulation: Total-1,300
Printing Co: Owl Printers, PO Box 669, Borrego Springs, CA 92004-0669

Save-The-Redwoods League Bulletin
See: ENVIRONMENT & ECOLOGY

Trail Tracks-American Trails Newsletter

Publishing Co: American Trails, 1400 16th St NW Ste 300, Washington, DC 20036-2217; Title Tel # (202) 797-5418
Personnel: Editor-Nancy Levine
Editorial Description: A newsletter for trail user groups with information on trail-related issues, specific information on trails, conferences, legislation & activities within the trail community. Newsletter is for all trail users.
General Info: Yr. Est. 1971, Bi-monthly, Trim Size-8½ x 11, Desktop press, 4 pages, 2 Color, Coated
Subscriptions: Indv. $50
Circulation: Total-1,000
List Rental: Actives: $65/M

Travel Scoop Consumer Newsletter
See: TRAVEL

West Coast Lifeliner
See: HEALTH

Workamper News
See: TRAVEL

Yosemite
Association

Publishing Co: Yosemite Association, PO Box 545, Yosemite Ntpk, CA 95389-0545; Title Tel # (209) 379-2646
Personnel: Publisher, Editor-Steve Medley
General Info: (Formerly Yosemite Members Journal), Yr. Est. 1922, Quarterly, Trim Size-7 x 10, Offset press, 16 pages, No Color
Subscriptions: Indv. $20
Circulation: Total-5,000

PATENTS/COPYRIGHTS/TRADE MARKS

A.S.I.F (Americans Seeking International Franchises)
See: INTERNATIONAL TRADE

Attorney's Dictionary of Patent Claims
See: LAW

BNA's Patent, Trademark & Copyright Journal — *Business*

Publishing Co: Bureau of National Affairs, Inc., 1231 25th St. NW, Bldg. N-200, Washington, DC 20037-1157; Title Tel # (202) 452-4200 Title Fax # (202) 822-8092
Personnel: Publisher-William A. Beltz, Editor-Jeffrey Samuels, Mng. Editor-James D. Crowne, Circ. Mgr.-Gary C. Seltzer, Adv. Dir.-Herbert Beard, Promotion Dir.-Gerry Egan
Editorial Description: Provides an in-depth review of significant current developments in the intellectual property field. Covers congressional activity, court decisions, relevant conferences, professional associations, international developments, plus actions of the Patent & Trademark Office & the Copyright Office.
General Info: Yr. Est. 1970, Weekly, Trim Size-8½ x 11, Offset press, 20 pages, ISSN: 0148-7965, Ind/Abs/Online: Lexis, Westlaw, Mead Data Central, No Color
Subscriptions: Indv. $1,101
Circulation: Total-2,400
Printing Co: McGardle, 1231 25th St NW, Washington, DC 20037-1157 Tel # (202) 452-4200

Canadian Patent Reporter

Publishing Co: Canada Law Book Co., Inc., 240 Edward St., Aurora, ON L4G 3S9 Canada Fax # (416) 841-5085; Title Tel # (416) 841-6472
Personnel: Editor-Gordon F. Henderson, Q.C.
Editorial Description: Covers cases on patents, copyrights, trade marks, trade names and industrial designs, together with points of practice and rulings of Commissioner of Patents and Registrar of Trademarks.
General Info: Yr. Est. 1942, Bi-weekly
Subscriptions: Indv. $250, Can. $244, For. $244

Copyright Law Reports — *Business*

Publishing Co: CCH, Inc., 2700 Lake Cook Rd., Riverwoods, IL 60015 Parent Co.-Kluwer Law & Taxation Publishers, Cambridge; Title Tel # (847) 267-7000 Title Fax # (800) 224-8299
Editorial Description: Sets out and explains today's rules under the copyright Revision act and reports new and proposed regulations, current case law activities and views of the regulators.
General Info: Yr. Est. 1978, Monthly, Trim Size-6 x 9, Web press, 30 pages, No Color, Looseleaf
Subscriptions: Indv. $643

Court of Appeals for the Federal Circuit: Review of Patent & Trademark Cases — *Business*

Publishing Co: Matthew Bender & Co., 11 Penn Plaza, New York, NY 10001-2006 Fax # (212) 244-3188; Title Tel # (212) 967-7707
Personnel: Editor-C. Knvll
Editorial Description: Procedure for patent & trademark cases on review in the Court of Appeals for the Federal Circuit from the U.S. Patent & Trademark Office & the U.S. District Courts. Discusses the applicable Rules for practice before the Federal Circuit & provides the necessary practice forms.
General Info: Yr. Est. 1973, Irregular, Looseleaf
Subscriptions: $200/copy

Digest of Canadian Intellectual Property Law
See: LAW

Entertainment Industry Contracts
See: LAW

European Patents Handbook
See: LAW

Franchise Wise (Quarterly newsletter of the intl gay & lesbian franchise assoc.)
See: GAY & LESBIAN INTEREST

Gene Therapy Newsletter
See: GENETICS

Healthcare Technology & Business Opportunities
See: HOSPITALS & NURSING HOMES

Inside the PTO — *Business*

Publishing Co: Questel Publishing, 8000 Westpark Dr., McLean, VA 22102 Tel # (703) 442-0900
Personnel: Editor in Chief-John A. Jenkins, Mng. Editor-Hank Burgoyne, Sr. Ed.-D. Ward Pimley
Editorial Description: Information on the Patent & Trade Office.
General Info: Yr. Est. 1995, Semi-monthly
Subscriptions: Indv. $425

Intellectual Property LAWCAST
See: LAW

Intellectual Property Litigation Reporter
See: LAW

Intellectual Property Counseling and Litigation
See: LAW

International Copyright Law and Practice — *Business*

Publishing Co: Matthew Bender & Co., 11 Penn Plaza, New York, NY 10001-2006 Tel # (212) 967-7707 Fax # (212) 244-3188
Editorial Description: Covers copyright laws, regulations & procedures of over 20 countries, with material arranged in an easy-to-use, country-by-country format.
General Info: Yr. Est. 1988, Irregular, Looseleaf

Lightbulb Journal for Inventors — *Consumer, Association* **CPM: $200**

Publishing Co: Inventor's Workshop Intl., 7332 Mason Ave, Canoga Park, CA 91306-2822; Title Tel # (818) 340-4268 Title Fax # (818) 884-8312
Personnel: Editor-Maggie Weisberg, Adv. Dir.-Stephanie Medvin
Editorial Description: Contains news and articles of interest to inventors and other creative people.
General Info: (Formerly Invent; Inventor's Journal), Yr. Est. 1971, Bi-monthly, Trim Size-8 x 12, Sheetfed press, 24 pages, Matte, Saddle-stitched
Subscriptions: Indv. $25, Inst. $24, Can. $35, For. $50, $5/copy
Circulation: Total-2,500
Advertising: $500. Accepts Inserts.

M. W. & C. Newsletter
See: LAW

McGraw-Hill's Tech Transfer Report
See: U.S. (& CANADIAN) FED. GOV'T.

Medical Devices Report
See: MEDICINE

Milgrim on Licensing — *Business*

Publishing Co: Matthew Bender & Co., 11 Penn Plaza, New York, NY 10001-2006 Tel # (212) 967-7707 Fax # (212) 244-3188
Personnel: Editor-Roger M. Milgrim
Editorial Description: A complete guide to the intellectual property licensing transaction. Milgrim covers licensing in all substantive areas of intellectual property. Also provided practical guidance on drafting agreements & contracts.
General Info: Yr. Est. 1990, Annually, Looseleaf

Milgrim on Trade Secrets — *Business*

Publishing Co: Matthew Bender & Co., 11 Penn Plaza, New York, NY 10001-2006 Fax # (212) 244-3188; Title Tel # (212) 967-7707
Personnel: Editor-C. Knull
Editorial Description: A complete guide to the protection and utilization of trade secrets and other intangible property.
General Info: Yr. Est. 1967, Annually, Looseleaf
Subscriptions: $325/copy

Mini Lab Focus
See: PHOTOGRAPHY

Multimedia & Technology
See: COMPUTERS & AUTOMATION

Nimmer on Copyright — *Business*

Publishing Co: Matthew Bender & Co., 11 Penn Plaza, New York, NY 10001-2006 Fax # (212) 244-3188; Title Tel # (212) 967-7707
Personnel: Editor-C. Knull
Editorial Description: An analytical and practical guide on the law of literary, musical, and artistic property, fully reflecting the 1976 Act and all recent changes in copyright law.
General Info: Yr. Est. 1963, Irregular, Looseleaf
Subscriptions: $460/copy

PTC Newsletter — *Association*

Publishing Co: American Bar Association, 750 N. Lake Shore Dr., Chicago, IL 60611-4497 Tel # (312) 988-6115 Fax # (312) 988-6030; Title Tel # (312) 988-5522 Title Fax # (312) 988-5528
Personnel: Editor-Thomas I. O'Brien, Production Mgr.-Rick Bright
Editorial Description: News of section of patent, trademark & copyright law.
General Info: Yr. Est. 1982, Quarterly, Sheetfed press, 12 pages, ISSN: 0736-8232, 2 Color, Matte, Saddle-stitched
Subscriptions: Free To Qualified Recipient
Circulation: (100% controlled), Total-8,000
List Rental: Rents Lists

Pan Hellenic Society Inventors of Greece in U.S.A. Newsletter — *Association*

Publishing Co: Pan Hellenic Society Inventors of Greece in U.S.A., 2053 Narwood Ave., South Merrick, NY 11566-3927; Title Tel # (516) 223-5958
Personnel: Editor-Kimon Louvaris, Circ. Mgr.-Milton Louvaris, B.SC, Art Dir.-Dr. Thomas Louvaris, B.SC, M.S
Editorial Description: Assists the Greek-American with the patenting, protecting and marketing of inventions.
General Info: Monthly
Circulation: Total-12,000

Patent Digest　　　　*Business, Association*

Publishing Co: Gas Appliance Manufacturers Assn, 1901 N. Moore St., #1100, Arlington, VA 22209;
Title Tel # (703) 525-9565 Title Fax # (703) 525-0718
Editorial Description: Descriptions of construction and design patents and trademark registrations in the gas appliance industry.
General Info: Yr. Est. 1946, Monthly, Trim Size-8½ x 11, Offset press, 15 pages, No Color
Subscriptions: $60/copy

Patent Law Perspectives　　*Business*

Publishing Co: Matthew Bender & Co., 11 Penn Plaza, New York, NY 10001-2006
Fax # (212) 244-3188; Title Tel # (212) 967-7707
Personnel: Editor-C. Knull
Editorial Description: Analysis of developments in patent law and the effects of these developments on current and future practice.
General Info: Yr. Est. 1970, Bi-monthly, Looseleaf
Subscriptions: $620/copy

Patent Litigation: Procedure and Tactics　　*Business*

Publishing Co: Matthew Bender & Co., 11 Penn Plaza, New York, NY 10001-2006
Fax # (212) 244-3188; Title Tel # (212) 967-7707
Personnel: Editor-C. Knull
Editorial Description: Discusses the impact on patent litigation of the Court of Appeals for the Federal Circuit. Completely covers patent litigation procedures under the Federal Rules of Civil Procedure. Offers tactical strategies for infringement suits.
General Info: Yr. Est. 1971, Irregular, Looseleaf
Subscriptions: $120/copy

Patent Office Rules and Practice　　*Business*

Publishing Co: Matthew Bender & Co., 11 Penn Plaza, New York, NY 10001-2006
Fax # (212) 244-3188; Title Tel # (212) 967-7707
Personnel: Editor-C. Knull
Editorial Description: Information needed to practice before the U.S. Patent Office.
General Info: Yr. Est. 1949, Irregular, Looseleaf
Subscriptions: $820/copy

Patent Trends　　　　*Association*

Publishing Co: Natl. Patent Council, c/o Schellin, 2121 Crystal Dr., Arlington, VA 22202-3706;
Title Tel # (703) 521-1669
General Info: Monthly

Patents　　　　*Business*

Publishing Co: Matthew Bender & Co., 11 Penn Plaza, New York, NY 10001-2006
Fax # (212) 244-3188; Title Tel # (212) 967-7707
Personnel: Editor-C. Knull
Editorial Description: Analyzes the substantive law of patents in the U.S.-the principles, doctrines, rules and cases on patentability, validity, infringement, application procedure, and perfecting rights to an invention.
General Info: Yr. Est. 1978, Annually, Looseleaf
Subscriptions: $710/copy

Remarks: Trademark News for Business　　*Association*

Publishing Co: International Trademark Association, 1133 Avenue of the Americas, New York, NY 10036-6710 Fax # (212) 768-7796; Title Tel # (212) 768-9887
Personnel: Editor-Mary McGrane
Editorial Description: Feature articles, columns & general news on marketing, advertising, design, & law as they relate to trademarks.
General Info: Yr. Est. 1988, Quarterly, Trim Size-8½ x 11, Sheetfed press, 8 pages, Coated, Saddle-stitched
Circulation: Total-6,000

Subrights Letter
See: BOOKS & BOOK TRADE

Technology Access Report
See: SCIENCE

Trademark Checklist　　*Business*

Publishing Co: International Trademark Association, 1133 Avenue of the Americas, New York, NY 10036-6710 Fax # (212) 768-7796; Title Tel # (212) 768-9887
Editorial Description: Correct spelling & usage of trademarks.
General Info: Irregular
Subscriptions: $5/copy

Trademark Protection and Practice　　*Business*

Publishing Co: Matthew Bender & Co., 11 Penn Plaza, New York, NY 10001-2006
Fax # (212) 244-3188; Title Tel # (212) 967-7707
Personnel: Editor-C. Knull
Editorial Description: Analysis of substantive law including the Trademark Law Revision Act of 1988. Coverage of Trademark Trial and Appeals Board practice, pharmaceutical trademarks, parties to infringement actions, and trademark tarnishment.
General Info: Yr. Est. 1974, Irregular, Looseleaf
Subscriptions: $440/copy

Trademark Trends　　　　*Business, Consumer*

Publishing Co: Board Report Publishing Co., Inc., Box 300789, Denver, CO 80203
Fax # (303) 839-1272; Title Tel # (303) 839-9058
Personnel: Publisher, Editor-Drew Miller
Editorial Description: Displays drawing and basic data on creative trademarks currently being registered.
General Info: Yr. Est. 1978, Monthly, Trim Size-8½ x 11, Offset press, 4 pages, No Color
Subscriptions: Indv. $59
List Rental: Actives: 3,000, $125/M, Expires: 2,000, $125/M

World Patent Law: Patent Statutes, Regulations and Treaties　　*Business*

Publishing Co: Matthew Bender & Co., 11 Penn Plaza, New York, NY 10001-2006
Fax # (212) 244-3188; Title Tel # (212) 967-7707
Editorial Description: Provides an up-to-date collection of carefully translated patent statues, rules & regulations for more than 200 countries. All major patent treaties, including the Paris Convention, European Patent Convention & Patent Corperation.
General Info: Yr. Est. 1974, Quarterly, Looseleaf
Subscriptions: $515/copy

World Patent Law and Practice　　*Business*

Publishing Co: Matthew Bender & Co., 11 Penn Plaza, New York, NY 10001-2006
Fax # (212) 244-3188; Title Tel # (212) 967-7707
Personnel: Editor-E. Greenfield
Editorial Description: The complete guide to world trademark law and practice, with detailed coverage of 35 major jurisdictions, and summary coverage of over 100.
General Info: Yr. Est. 1982, Quarterly, Looseleaf
Subscriptions: $325/copy

World Technology/Patent Licensing Gazette　　*Consumer*

Publishing Co: Techni Research Associates, Inc., PO Box T, Willow Grove, PA 19090;
Title Tel # (215) 657-1753
Personnel: Publisher-Louis Schiffman, Ph.D.
Editorial Description: Information on patents, licensing opportunities & technology transfer, lists abstracts & sources.
General Info: Yr. Est. 1968, Bi-monthly, Trim Size-8½ x 11, 20 pages, ISSN: 0278-8047
Subscriptions: Indv. $145

PERIODICAL INDUSTRY

ABC Bylaws and Rules Bulletin

Publishing Co: Audit Bureau of Circulations, 900 N. Meacham Rd., Schaumburg, IL 60173-4968
Tel # (708) 605-0909; Title Tel # (847) 605-0909 Title Fax # (847) 605-0483
Editorial Description: Announcements of bylaws and rules amendments, changes and similar information.
General Info: Trim Size-8½ x 11, 7 pages, No Color, Matte

American Native Press　　*Association*

Publishing Co: American Indian & Alaska Native Newspapers & Periodicals Res, 2801 S. University, 3301 S. University, Little Rock, AR 72204-1000; Title Tel # (501) 569-3160
Personnel: Editor-Dan Littlefield
General Info: Yr. Est. 1983, Quarterly, 4 pages, ISSN: 0882-2522
Circulation: Total-1,100

Ancillary Profits
See: MEDIA & COMMUNICATIONS

BPA International Forum　　*Business*

Publishing Co: BPA International, 270 Madison Ave., New York, NY 10016-0699
Editorial Description: Organization news and information on member publications.
General Info: Yr. Est. 1995, Quarterly, Trim Size-10 x 14, 6 pages, 2 Color, Matte
Subscriptions: Free With Membership

Bam! Bam!　　　　*Business*

Publishing Co: Fine Print Distributors, 500 Pampa Drive, Austin, TX 78752
Editorial Description: Information on distribution and other tips for small press magazine publishers.
General Info: Irregular

Blue Pencil

Publishing Co: Florida Magazine Association, 1133 W Morse Blvd Ste 201, Winter Park, FL 32789-3743 Tel # (407) 647-8839; Title Tel # (904) 392-1686

Business Publications Blue Books

Publishing Co: Audit Bureau of Circulations, 900 N. Meacham Rd., Schaumburg, IL 60173-4968
Tel # (708) 605-0909; Title Tel # (847) 605-0909 Title Fax # (847) 605-0483
Editorial Description: Looseleaf volumes containing all Business Publication members' publisher's statements.
General Info: Semi-annually, Looseleaf
Subscriptions: $115/copy

CLMPages
Business, Association

Publishing Co: Council of Literary Magazines & Presses, 154 Christopher St. #3C, New York, NY 10014-2839; Title Tel # (212) 741-9110 Title Fax # (212) 741-9112
Editorial Description: Information for literary magazines, publishers, presses, writers.
General Info: (Formerly CCLM Newsletter; CCLM News), Yr. Est. 1991, Quarterly, Trim Size-8$\frac{1}{2}$ x 11, Offset press, 6 pages, No Color, Matte
Subscriptions: Free With Membership
Circulation: Total-1,900
List Rental: Actives: 450, $50/M
Printing Co: Raymar Printing Co., 333 Hudson St., New York, NY 10013 Tel # (212) 255-1500

Canadian Magazine Publishers Assn.
Association

Publishing Co: Canadian Magazine Publishers Assn., 2 Stewart St., Toronto, ON M5V 1H6 Canada; Title Tel # (416) 362-2546 Title Fax # (416) 362-2547
Personnel: Editor-Cindy Goldrick
Editorial Description: Informs members of assn. activities & industry issues.
General Info: Yr. Est. 1973, 8x/yr., 8 pages, ISSN: 0826-9572, 2 Color, Newsprint, Saddle-stitched
Subscriptions: $1/copy
Circulation: Total-450
Advertising: Inquire for rates.
List Rental: Actives: $125/M

Canadian Periodicals Blue Books

Publishing Co: Audit Bureau of Circulations, 900 N. Meacham Rd., Schaumburg, IL 60173-4968 Tel # (708) 605-0909; Title Tel # (847) 605-0909 Title Fax # (847) 605-0483
Editorial Description: Looseleaf volumes containing all Canadian periodical members' publisher's statements.
General Info: Semi-annually, Looseleaf
Subscriptions: $105/copy

Capell's Circulation Report
See: ADVERTISING & MARKETING

Computer Publishing & Advertising Report
Business

Publishing Co: Simba Information, Inc., 213 Danbury Rd. PO Box 7430, Wilton, CT 06897-7430 Fax # (203) 834-1771 Parent Co.-Cowles Business Media, New York; Title Tel # (203) 834-0033 Title Fax # (203) 834-0729
Personnel: Publisher-Chris Elwell, Editor-Peter Breen, Mktg. Dir.-Michael Genaro, Promotion Dir.-Hillary Veeder
Editorial Description: For publishers of computer magazines and books and computer advertisers/marketers.
General Info: Yr. Est. 1983, Bi-weekly, Trim Size-8$\frac{1}{2}$ x 11, Offset press, 10 pages, ISSN: 0740-6231, No Color
Subscriptions: Indv. $525, Can. $575, For. $575
Printing Co: Success Printing, 10 Pearl Street, Norwalk, CT 06850 Tel # (203) 847-1112, Fax # (203) 846-2770

Copy Editor Newsletter
See: JOURNALISM

Cornerstone, The
Business

Publishing Co: R.R. Bowker, 121 Chanlon Rd, New Providence, NJ 07974-1541 Tel # (908) 665-2881 Fax # (908) 665-6688 Parent Co.-Reed Reference Publishing, New Providence; Title Tel # (212) 337-7123 Title Fax # (212) 337-6976
Personnel: Publisher-Liegh Yuster, Editor-Judy Salk
Editorial Description: Updates on reports & resources from RR Bowker and its affiliates.
General Info: (Formerly Ulrich's News), Yr. Est. 1988, Quarterly, Desktop press, 4 pages, ISSN: 0000-1392
Subscriptions: Free To Qualified Recipient

Cowles/SIMBA Media Daily
Business

Publishing Co: Simba Information, Inc., 213 Danbury Rd. PO Box 7430, Wilton, CT 06897-7430 Tel # (203) 834-0033 Fax # (203) 834-1771 Parent Co.-Cowles Business Media, New York
Editorial Description: Online information from the media and publishing industries via Online America.
General Info: Yr. Est. 1993, Daily

Directory Journal

Publishing Co: Association of North American Directory Publishers, 105 Summer St, Wrentham, MA 02093-1875; Title Tel # (508) 624-7688 Title Fax # (719) 528-1857
Personnel: Publisher-Carol Hill, Editor-Michael Pederson
General Info: Quarterly, Trim Size-8$\frac{1}{2}$ x 11, Web press, 16 pages, 2 Color, Newsprint, Saddle-stitched
Printing Co: College Publishing, 2415 Avenue J Ste 111, Arlington, TX 76006-6119 Tel # (817) 640-6633

Editorial Network
See: JOURNALISM

Editors Only
Business, Association

Publishing Co: Editors Only, PO Box 17108, Fountain Hills, AZ 85269-7108; Title Tel # (602) 837-6492 Title Fax # (602) 837-6872
Personnel: Publisher-Robert Myers, Editor-William Dunkerley, Circ. Mgr.-Barbara Myers
Editorial Description: Monthly newsletter for magazine editors featuring editing advice and news.
General Info: Yr. Est. 1982, Monthly, Trim Size-8$\frac{1}{2}$ x 11, Sheetfed press, 8 pages, ISSN: 0735-849\
Ind/Abs/Online: NewsNet, No Color, Newsprint
Subscriptions: Indv. $89, Can. $95, For. $105, $8/copy
Acquistions: Publication Bought

Editor's Workshop Newsletter
See: JOURNALISM

Electronic Publishing Forum
Association

Publishing Co: Electronic Publishing Special Working Group, 150 5th Ave Ste 302, New York, NY 10011-4311
Personnel: Editor-Fay Shapiro
Editorial Description: Covers electronic publishing issues for the Electronic Publishing Special Working Group.
General Info: Yr. Est. 1994, Irregular, Trim Size-8$\frac{1}{2}$ x 11, 8 pages, No Color, Matte

Farm Publications Blue Books

Publishing Co: Audit Bureau of Circulations, 900 N. Meacham Rd., Schaumburg, IL 60173-4968 Tel # (708) 605-0909; Title Tel # (847) 605-0909 Title Fax # (847) 605-0483
Editorial Description: Looseleaf volumes containing all Farm Publication members' publisher's statements.
General Info: Semi-annually, Looseleaf
Subscriptions: $23/copy

Folio: First Day
Business

Publishing Co: Cowles Magazine, Inc., 4 High Ridge Park, Stamford, CT 06905 Tel # (203) 322-2900 Fax # (203) 322-1966; Title Tel # (212) 683-3540
Personnel: Publisher-Hershel Sarbin, Editor-Keith Kelly, Mng. Editor-Martin Singer
Editorial Description: Faxed newsservice which reports breaking stories on the consumer and trade magazine industry.
General Info: Yr. Est. 1992
Subscriptions: Indv. $310
Circulation: Total-1,000

Hotline
Business, Association

Publishing Co: Newsletter Publishers Association, 1401 Wilson Blvd., Suite 207, Arlington, VA 22209-2341; Title Tel # (703) 527-2333 Title Fax # (703) 841-0629
Personnel: Editor-Frederick D. Goss, Production Mgr.-Mike Kibler
Editorial Description: Newsletter publishing business and news.
General Info: Yr. Est. 1977, Bi-weekly, Trim Size-8$\frac{7}{8}$ x 11, Web press, 8 pages, ISSN: 0749-1255, 2 Color, Matte
Subscriptions: Free With Membership
Circulation: Total-950

IEEE Publications Bulletin
Business, Scholarly

Publishing Co: Institute of Electrical & Electronics Engineers, Inc., 445 Hoes Lane, PO Box 1331, Piscataway, NJ 08855-1331 Parent Co.-Institute of Electrical & Electronics Engineers, New York; Title Tel # (908) 562-3992 Title Fax # (908) 981-9334
Personnel: Mktg. Dir.-Michelle Curtis, Sales Mgr.-Elyse Haratz
Editorial Description: Lists all new releases for IEEE publications with bibliographic information and descriptions of each title for librarians.
General Info: Yr. Est. 1971, Quarterly, Trim Size-8$\frac{1}{2}$ x 11, 138 pages, 2 Color, Matte, Perfect bound
Subscriptions: Free

Indexing & Abstracting Society of Canada, Bulletin

Publishing Co: Indexing & Abstracting Society of Canada, Box 744, Station F, Toronto, ON M4Y 2N6 Canada
Personnel: Publisher-Ann Taylor
General Info: Yr. Est. 1978, Quarterly, ISSN: 0227-1338
Circulation: Total-110
Advertising: Accepts Inserts.

Inkslinger's Review

Publishing Co: Continental Features/Continental News Service, 341 W Broadway # 265, San Diego, CA 92101-3802; Title Tel # (619) 492-8696
Personnel: Publisher, Editor-Gary Salamone
Editorial Description: Current events, interviews, fillers.
General Info: Yr. Est. 1981, Monthly, Trim Size-8$\frac{1}{2}$ x 11, Mimeo press, 2 pages, No Color, Other
Subscriptions: Indv. $19, Can. $25
List Rental: Actives: $30/M

Legal Periodicals in English   *Business*

Publishing Co: Glanville Publishers, Inc., 75 Main St, Dobbs Ferry, NY 10522-1601; Title Tel # (914) 693-8100 Title Fax # (914) 693-0402
Personnel: Editor-Eugene Wypyski, Circ. Mgr.-Alden Domizio, Production Mgr.-Mike Wortzman, Promotion Dir.-John Downey
Editorial Description: Photocopy of LC card per title & other data, frequency, etc. for English language legal periodicals.
General Info: Yr. Est. 1976, Annually, Trim Size-7 x 10, Sheetfed press, No Color, Matte, Looseleaf
Subscriptions: $125/copy
Circulation: Total-150
Printing Co: Boyd Printing Co., Inc., 49 Sheridan Ave, Albany, NY 12210-2735 Tel # (518) 436-9686, Fax # (518) 436-7433

Legal Publisher, The
See: LAW

Library Notes
See: LIBRARY

MPA Washington
Newsletter

Publishing Co: Magazine Publisher's Assn., 1211 Connecticut Ave NW Ste, 406, Washington, DC 20036-2701; Title Tel # (202) 296-7277
Personnel: Editor-George Gross
General Info: Monthly
Circulation: Total-800

Magazine Newsletter of
Research   *Association*

Publishing Co: Magazine Publishers of America, 919 3rd Avenue, 22nd Floor, New York, NY 10022-3801; Title Tel # (212) 872-3700
Personnel: Editor-Marian Confer
Editorial Description: Research interpretations and applications for magazine advertising and the market place.
General Info: Irregular, Web press, 8 pages, Color, Newsprint
Acquistions: Publication Bought
Circulation: (100% controlled), Total-18,000

Magazine Publishers of
America Research
Newsletter   *Business, Association*

Publishing Co: Magazine Publishers of America, 919 3rd Avenue, 22nd Floor, New York, NY 10022-3801 Tel # (212) 872-3700
Editorial Description: Each issue covers research on a magazine industry topic.
General Info: Irregular, Trim Size-8½ x 11, 8 pages, 4 Color, Matte, Saddle-stitched
Subscriptions: Indv. $4, Free With Membership

Media and the Law
See: BROADCASTING

Media Monitor   *Consumer*

Publishing Co: Plastic Cow Productions, PO Box 3081, Danville, CA 94526-8081
Editorial Description: Lists fanzines for sale.
General Info: Quarterly

Multimedia Publisher   *Business*

Publishing Co: Worldwide Videotex Co., PO Box 3273, Boynton Beach, FL 33424-3273 Fax # (407) 738-2276; Title Tel # (407) 738-2276 Title Fax # (407) 738-2275
Editorial Description: News and information on different means for distributing various publishing products.
General Info: (Formerly Infomedia Publisher), Yr. Est. 1991, Monthly
Subscriptions: Indv. $150, Inst. $150, Can. $150, For. $165

New York Wine Companion
See: BUSINESS & INDUSTRY

Newsletter Design   *Business*

Publishing Co: Hudson Associates, Inc., 44 W. Market St., PO Box 311, Rhinebeck, NY 12572-1403; Title Tel # (914) 876-2081 Title Fax # (914) 876-2561
Personnel: Publisher-Howard Penn Hudson, Editor-Paul Swift
General Info: Yr. Est. 1987, Monthly
Subscriptions: Indv. $125
List Rental: List Management Co.: Kleid Company, Inc., 530 5th Ave., 17 Floor, New York, NY 10036-5101 Tel # (212) 819-3406, Fax # (212) 719-9788, Actives: $55/M
Printing Co: Newsletter Services, Inc., 9700 Philadelphia Court, Lanham, MD 20706 Tel # (301) 731-5200, Fax # (301) 731-5201

Newsletter Editor's
Resource   *Business*

Publishing Co: Direct Marketing Association, PMDS Book Distribution Co., PO Box 391, Annapolis Junction, MD 20701-0391 Tel # (301) 604-0187 Fax # (301) 206-9789
Editorial Description: For direct marketing newsletter editors and writers.
General Info: Yr. Est. 1994, Bi-monthly

Newsletter on Newsletters   *Business*

Publishing Co: Hudson Associates, Inc., 44 W. Market St., PO Box 311, Rhinebeck, NY 12572-1403; Title Tel # (914) 876-2081 Title Fax # (914) 876-2561
Personnel: Publisher, Editor-Howard Penn Hudson, Mng. Editor-Paul Swift, Art Dir.-Richard Wambach
Editorial Description: Reports on entire newsletter industry including management, graphics, editorial, and promotion.
General Info: Yr. Est. 1964, Semi-weekly, Trim Size-8½ x 11, Offset press, 8 pages, ISSN: 0028-9507, No Color
Subscriptions: Indv. $144, For. $164, $8/copy
List Rental: List Management Co.: Kleid Company, Inc., 530 5th Ave., 17 Floor, New York, NY 10036-5101 Tel # (212) 819-3406, Fax # (212) 719-9788, Actives: $55/M

Newsletter Trends   *Business, Association*

Publishing Co: Sterling Communications, 1920 Ellesmere Road, Suite 104, Scarborough, ON M1H 2WY Canada Tel # (416) 513-2218; Title Tel # (416) 512-2218 Title Fax # (416) 512-6493
Personnel: Editor-Barbara A. Fanson
Editorial Description: A subscription 'how to' newsletter about newsletters - planning, writing, editing, designing, production, photography, printing and distribution. Inspirational guide to writing and producing a newsletter.
General Info: Yr. Est. 1991, Monthly, 8 pages, ISSN: 1185-5088, 2 Color, Matte
Subscriptions: Indv. $97, Can. $97
Printing Co: Sterling Copy, 144 Sheppard Ave. W., North York, ON M2N 1M8 Canada

Recycling Related Newsletters, Publications, Etc; A Reference
See: ENVIRONMENT & ECOLOGY

Recycling Update
See: ENVIRONMENT & ECOLOGY

SIMBA Report on
Directory Publishing   *Business*

Publishing Co: Simba Information, Inc., 213 Danbury Rd. PO Box 7430, Wilton, CT 06897-7430 Fax # (203) 834-1771 Parent Co.-Cowles Business Media, New York; Title Tel # (203) 834-0033 Title Fax # (203) 834-0729
Personnel: Editor-Victor Rubell, Editorial Dir.-Claire Schoen, Mng. Editor-Michael Hayes, Circulation-Joyce Brigish, Adv. Mgr.-Rosalind Flans, Mktg. Mgr.-Michael Genaro
Editorial Description: The SIMBA Report on Directory Publising provides directory publishers, distributors and suppliers with the problem-solving information and news they need to make profitable business decisions. Areas of coverage include CD ROM directory publishing opportunities, online services, production and circulation issues, marketing methods, desktop publishing, fulfillment and distributing trends, mergers and ac
General Info: (Formerly Morgan Report on Directory Publishing), Yr. Est. 1987, Monthly, Trim Size-8½ x 11, Sheetfed press, 16 pages, ISSN: 0890-9512, Ind/Abs/Online: NewsNet, DIALOG, Data-Star, 2 Color, Matte, Saddle-stitched
Subscriptions: Indv. $159, Can. $159, For. $184
Advertising: Inquire for rates.
List Rental: Rents Lists
Printing Co: Hamilton Press, Inc., 1042 Industrial Dr., West Berlin Industrial Center, Berlin, NJ 08009 Tel # (609) 753-0900, Fax # (609) 753-0307

SPANzine   *Association*

Publishing Co: Small Press Action Network, #19-155 W. 12th St., Box 47068, Vancouver, BC V5Z 4L6 Canada
Editorial Description: Covers doings of Small Press Action Network.
General Info: Quarterly
Subscriptions: Indv. $25

Self-Publisher's Business Letter
See: BOOKS & BOOK TRADE

Shortruns
See: PRINTING/GRAPHIC ARTS

Subrights Letter
See: BOOKS & BOOK TRADE

Subscription Marketing   *Business*

Publishing Co: Blue Dolphin Communications, 83 Boston Post Rd, Sudbury, MA 01776-2438 Tel # (508) 443-6363; Title Tel # (508) 443-8214 Title Fax # (508) 443-9728
Personnel: Publications Director-Donna Kelly, Publisher, Editor-Donald L. Nicholas, Exec. Ed.-Jack Edmonston, Mng. Editor-Laura Logan
Editorial Description: Helps publishers maximize subscription profits.
General Info: Yr. Est. 1994, Monthly, Trim Size-8½ x 11, 8 pages, ISSN: 1077-1557, 2 Color
Subscriptions: Indv. $195, Can. $295, For. $295, $25/copy
Circulation: Total-500
List Rental: List Management Co.: Direct Media, Inc., 200 Pemberwick Rd., PO Box 4565, Greenwich, CT 06830 Tel # (203) 532-3713, Fax # (203) 531-1452
Printing Co: Newsletter Services, Inc., 9700 Philadelphia Court, Lanham, MD 20706 Tel # (301) 731-5200, Fax # (301) 731-5201

Supermarket Savvy Information Resource Service
See: FOOD

U.S. & Canadian
Magazines Blue Books   *Consumer*

Publishing Co: Audit Bureau of Circulations, 900 N. Meacham Rd., Schaumburg, IL 60173-4968
Tel # (708) 605-0909; Title Tel # (847) 605-0909 Title Fax # (847) 605-0483
Editorial Description: Looseleaf volumes containing all U.S. & Canadian magazine members' publisher's statements.
General Info: Semi-annually, Looseleaf
Subscriptions: $210/copy

WPA News   *Business, Association*   CPM: $266

Publishing Co: Western Publications Association, 2401 Pacific Coast Highway, Hermosa Beach, CA 90254; Title Tel # (310) 318-9697
Personnel: Editor-Jane Silbering
Editorial Description: Newsletter for association of magazine publishers.
General Info: (Formerly Issue), Bi-monthly, Trim Size-8½ x 11, Sheetfed press, 16 pages, 4 Color, Coated, Saddle-stitched
Subscriptions: Free To Qualified Recipient
Circulation: Total-3,000
Advertising: $800.
List Rental: Actives: 5,001, $300/M
Printing Co: Southern California Graphics, 8432 Steller Dr, Culver City, CA 90232-2489
Tel # (310) 559-3600, Fax # (310) 558-3127

Worldwide Databases   *Business*

Publishing Co: Worldwide Videotex Co., PO Box 3273, Boynton Beach, FL 33424-3273
Fax # (407) 738-2276; Title Tel # (407) 738-2276 Title Fax # (407) 738-2275
Editorial Description: Online computer database information for publishers.
General Info: Yr. Est. 1990, Monthly
Subscriptions: Indv. $150, Inst. $150, Can. $150, For. $165

Worldwide Graphics
See: INTERNATIONAL TRADE

Zines!   *Consumer*

Publishing Co: Zines!, 221 North Blvd., Richmond, VA 23220
Personnel: Publisher, Editor-Christopher Martin
Editorial Description: Reviews various fanzines.
General Info: Yr. Est. 1993, Quarterly, Trim Size-8½ x 11, 12 pages
Subscriptions: Indv. $5

PETROLEUM & NATURAL GAS

A.G.A. Rate Service   *Business, Association*

Publishing Co: American Gas Association, 1515 Wilson Blvd., Arlington, VA 22209-2469
Fax # (703) 841-8406; Title Tel # (703) 841-8400
Personnel: Editor-Sheila Rana
Editorial Description: Current natural gas distribution rates compiled by area and latest purchased gas adjustment clauses.
General Info: Semi-annually, Trim Size-8½ x 11, No Color
Subscriptions: Indv. $300

Advanced Fuel
Technologies   *Business*

Publishing Co: McIlvaine Co., The, 2970 Maria Ave., Northbrook, IL 60062-2024;
Title Tel # (847) 272-0010 Title Fax # (847) 272-9673
Personnel: Publisher-R.W. McIlvaine, Editor-Margaret Cornell
Editorial Description: A complete information system with Manual, Newsletter, Catalog, Fact Finder, and 300 service units for reprints, advice, tapes and online fax answers.
General Info: Monthly, 8 pages
Subscriptions: Indv. $690, Can. $750, For. $750
List Rental: Rents Lists

Alaska Report   *Business*

Publishing Co: Petroleum Information Corp., PO Box 2612, Denver, CO 80201-2612
Tel # (303) 740-7100; Title Tel # (303) 545-7505
Personnel: Editor-Cameron Edmondson
Editorial Description: Weekly coverage of Alaska oil, gas, mining and leasing activity.
General Info: Yr. Est. 1955, Weekly, Trim Size-8½ x 11, 30 pages, No Color, Looseleaf
Subscriptions: Indv. $984

Alcohol Week   *Business*

Publishing Co: Phillips Business Information, Inc., 1201 Seven Locks Rd., Ste 300, Potomac, MD 20854-2958 Tel # (301) 340-1520 Fax # (301) 424-4297
General Info: Weekly
Subscriptions: Indv. $495
Acquistions: Publication Sold
List Rental: Rents Lists

Appalachian Basin Rotary
Report   *Business*

Publishing Co: Petroleum Information Corp., PO Box 2612, Denver, CO 80201-2612;
Title Tel # (303) 740-7100
Editorial Description: Petroleum Information report on NY, PA, OH, KY, WV and adjacent Appalachian states.
General Info: Weekly, Looseleaf
Subscriptions: Indv. $1,032

Asia/Pacific Oil Weekly
Report

Publishing Co: PennWell Publishing Co., 1421 South Sheridan Rd., Tulsa, OK 74112-6600
Tel # (918) 853-3161 Fax # (918) 831-9497; Title Tel # (918) 831-9701 Title Fax # (918) 832-9295
General Info: Weekly, No Color, Matte
Subscriptions: Indv. $395, Can. $465, For. $465
Advertising: Accepts Inserts.

Auto Service Profit
Report   *Business*

Publishing Co: United Communications Group, 11300 Rockville Pike, Ste. 1100, Rockville, MD 20852-3030 Tel # (301) 816-8950 Fax # (301) 816-8945; Title Tel # (301) 961-8700
Personnel: Publisher-David Rohde, Editor-William Donovan, Circ. Mgr.-Sharon Welch
Editorial Description: For independent shop & service stations.
General Info: Monthly
Subscriptions: Indv. $137, $11/copy
List Rental: Actives: $125/M

Basic Oil Laws &
Concession Contracts   *Business*

Publishing Co: Barrows Co., Inc., 116 E 66th St, New York, NY 10021-6547;
Title Tel # (212) 772-1199 Title Fax # (212) 288-7242
Personnel: Editor-Gordon Barrows, Promotion Dir.-Dominique Jeune
Editorial Description: This service contains the complete texts, in english translation, of oil laws, contracts, and concessions in all countries. Kept up to date by regular supplements. It is divided into regions. 1. MIDDLE EAST 2. EUROPE 3. NORTH AFRICA 4. SOUTH & CENTRAL AFRICA 5. CENTRAL AMERICA & CARIBBEAN 6. SOUTH AMERICA 7. ASIA & AUSTRALASIA Initial purchase price is $6200 for each region but renewals are $1450.
General Info: (Formerly Far East Oil Laws), Quarterly, Looseleaf

Bechtel Briefs
See: ENGINEERING

Bottom of the Barrel   *Business*

Publishing Co: Tele-Drop Inc., PO Box 3996, North Hollywood, CA 91609-0996;
Title Tel # (818) 768-5111 Title Fax # (818) 768-0537
Personnel: Publisher, Editor-Trilby Lundberg
Editorial Description: Asphalt, crude, and heavy fuel info including import information by country,
General Info: Yr. Est. 1986, Quarterly, Sheetfed press, 16 pages
Subscriptions: Indv. $600, $50/copy

Bulletin

Publishing Co: Standard Oil Co. of California, 225 Bush St., San Francisco, CA 94104-4207;
Title Tel # (415) 894-7700
Editorial Description: Petroleum industry news: general interest articles featuring company products and activities.
General Info: Quarterly
Circulation: Total-250,000

Canada Petroleum
Industry   *Business*

Publishing Co: Midwest Register Inc., 1120 E. 4th St., Tulsa, OK 74120-3220;
Title Tel # (918) 582-2000 Title Fax # (918) 587-9349
Personnel: Publisher/President/Advisor-Will L. HAmmack
General Info: (Formerly Canada Petroleum Directory), Yr. Est. 1945, Annually, 650 pages
Subscriptions: Can. $85, For. $85, $85/copy
Advertising: Inquire for rates.
List Rental: Rents Lists

Canadian Gas Rates   *Association*

Publishing Co: Canadian Gas Assn., 243 Consumers Rd., Suite 1200, North York, ON M2J 5E3 Canada Tel # (416) 498-1994 Fax # (416) 498-7465; Title Tel # (416) 447-6465
General Info: 90 pages, Looseleaf
Subscriptions: Indv. $60

Central Texas Coast Report   *Business*

Publishing Co: Petroleum Information Corp., PO Box 2612, Denver, CO 80201-2612;
Title Tel # (303) 740-7100
General Info: Weekly, Looseleaf
Subscriptions: Indv. $600

Daily Oil Bulletin

Publishing Co: C.O. Nickle Pubs., 999 8 St. SW, #300, Calgary, AB T2R 1N7 Canada Parent Co.-Southam Information & Technology Group, Calgary, Canada; Title Tel # (403) 244-6111
Personnel: Publisher, Editor-R. Charland
Editorial Description: News and devewlopments in the oil industry.
General Info: Yr. Est. 1937, Daily
Subscriptions: Indv. $588
List Rental: Rents Lists

Daily Permit Service (Permian Basin) *Business*

Publishing Co: Petroleum Information Corp., PO Box 2612, Denver, CO 80201-2612; Title Tel # (303) 740-7100
Editorial Description: Permian basin.
General Info: Daily, Looseleaf
Subscriptions: Indv. $504

Doig's Digest

Publishing Co: Ian M. Doig & Assoc. Ltd., 1512 Evergreen Hill SW, Calgary, AB T2Y 2V8 Canada; Title Tel # (403) 254-8057
Personnel: Publisher, Editor-Ian Doig
General Info: Yr. Est. 1983, Monthly, ISSN: 0827-4290
Subscriptions: Indv. $325

Drilling & Well Servicing Worldwide *Business*

Publishing Co: Midwest Register Inc., 1120 E. 4th St., Tulsa, OK 74120-3220; Title Tel # (918) 582-2000 Title Fax # (918) 587-9349
Personnel: Publisher/President/Advisor-Will L. Hammack
General Info: Yr. Est. 1945, Annually, 750 pages
Subscriptions: Can. $75, For. $75, $75/copy
Advertising: Inquire for rates.
List Rental: Rents Lists

Drilling Activity Report *Business*

Publishing Co: Saskatchewan Energy & Mines, Petroleum & Natural Gas, 1914 Hamilton St., Regina, SK S4P 4V4 Canada; Title Tel # (306) 787-2528 Title Fax # (306) 787-2527
Editorial Description: Lists by producing area information related to well licenses issued, well location & co-ordinates, well spud date & finish drilling date, well status & total depth, producing horizon of new wells & status update of existing wells.
General Info: Monthly, Trim Size-8½ x 11, Offset press, 45 pages, ISSN: 0228-5630, No Color
Subscriptions: Indv. $150, $13/copy

E & P Environment See: ENVIRONMENT & ECOLOGY

East Texas Report *Business*

Publishing Co: Petroleum Information Corp., PO Box 2612, Denver, CO 80201-2612; Title Tel # (303) 740-7100
General Info: Weekly, Looseleaf
Subscriptions: Indv. $1,380

Eastern Kentucky, West Virginia Report *Business*

Publishing Co: Petroleum Information Corp., PO Box 2612, Denver, CO 80201-2612; Title Tel # (303) 740-7100
General Info: Weekly, Looseleaf
Subscriptions: Indv. $960

Empire State Geogram-Research Issue See: GEOLOGY

Energy

Publishing Co: Exxon Co., U.S.A., 800 Bell St., Houston, TX 77002 Tel # (713) 656-3636
Personnel: Editor-Susan Berniard

Energy Exchange *Business*

Publishing Co: Brooklyn Union, 1 Metrotech Ctr, Brooklyn, NY 11201-3850 Tel # (718) 403-2000
Personnel: Publications Director-Patrick Gooney
Editorial Description: Published for architects and others using gas in developing properties.
General Info: (Formerly Dealers Choice), Bi-monthly
Circulation: Total-1,650

Energy Law and Transactions See: ENERGY

Energy Prices & Taxes See: ENERGY

Ernst & Young's Oil and Gas Tax Reporter *Business*

Publishing Co: CCH, Inc., 2700 Lake Cook Rd., Riverwoods, IL 60015 Parent Co.-Kluwer Law & Taxation Publishers, Cambridge; Title Tel # (847) 267-7000 Title Fax # (800) 224-8299
Editorial Description: Covering such topics as lease & purchase arrangements, royalties, intangible drilling & development costs, losses & abandonments, & the depletion deduction. There are quarterly updates to the loose-leaf reporter, a newsletter that accompanies the quarterly updates & a yearly revision.
General Info: Quarterly, Looseleaf
Subscriptions: Indv. $329
List Rental: Rents Lists

Estimate See: INTERNATIONAL AFFAIRS

European Offshore Petroleum Newsletter *Business*

Publishing Co: Hart Publications, 7811 Montrose Rd., Potomac, MD 20854 Tel # (301) 340-2100 Parent Co.-Phillips Business Information, Inc., Potomac

Exploration Daily *Business*

Publishing Co: Petroleum Information Corp., PO Box 2612, Denver, CO 80201-2612; Title Tel # (303) 740-7100
Personnel: Publisher-T. C. Cheney, Editor-Wm. Cobban
Editorial Description: Presents the most important exploration stories daily.
General Info: (Formerly National Exploration Daily), Yr. Est. 1978, Daily
Subscriptions: Indv. $600

Expro News/Expro Update See: HOUSE ORGANS

Exxon Extra See: HOUSE ORGANS

Exxon Underway See: HOUSE ORGANS

FERC Daily Release Service See: ENERGY

FYI *Association*

Publishing Co: Trans Mountain Pipeline Co., Ltd., Suite 900, 1333 W. Broadway, Vancouver, BC V6H 4C2 Canada; Title Tel # (604) 739-5000
Personnel: Editor-G. Wray
Editorial Description: Employee newsletter publishing internal changes, major corporate business & personal items of interests.
General Info: (Formerly For Your Information), Yr. Est. 1966, Bi-monthly, Trim Size-8½ x 11, Offset press, 8 pages, 2 Color
Circulation: (100% controlled), Total-500
Printing Co: SCP Printers, 2400 Viscount Way, Richmond, BC V6V 1N1 Canada Tel # (604) 270-9464

Federal Taxation of Oil and Gas Transactions *Business*

Publishing Co: Matthew Bender & Co., 11 Penn Plaza, New York, NY 10001-2006 Fax # (212) 244-3188; Title Tel # (212) 967-7707
Personnel: Editor-E. Carr
Editorial Description: The most extensive & comprehensive treatment of federal taxation of oil & gas available today. Exhaustively researched & comprehensively written.
General Info: Yr. Est. 1958, Annually, Looseleaf
Subscriptions: $195/copy

Field Reports See: BUSINESS & INDUSTRY

Foster Natural Gas Report *Association, Business*

Publishing Co: Foster Associates, Inc., 1015 15th St NW Ste 1100, Washington, DC 20005-2605; Title Tel # (202) 408-7710
Personnel: Editor-M.W. Rockefeller, Circ. Mgr.-Ann Frutchey
General Info: Yr. Est. 1956, Weekly, Mimeo press, 40 pages, ISSN: 0095-1587, Ind/Abs/Online: Mead Data Central, NewsNet, Fosters Bulletin Board, No Color
Subscriptions: Indv. $695
Circulation: Total-1,100

Four Corners Intermountain Edition *Business*

Publishing Co: Petroleum Information Corp., PO Box 2612, Denver, CO 80201-2612; Title Tel # (303) 740-7100
Editorial Description: W. Colo., UT, N. New Mex., AZ, NV.
General Info: Daily, Looseleaf
Subscriptions: Indv. $960

Fuel Price Analysis *Business*

Publishing Co: McGraw-Hill, 1221 Ave. of the Americas, 36th Fl., New York, NY 10020-1095 Tel # (212) 512-2000 Fax # (212) 512-6590

Gas Buyer's Guide *Business*

Publishing Co: Pasha Publications, Inc, 1616 N. Fort Myer Dr., #1000, Arlington, VA 22209-3103 Fax # (703) 528-4926; Title Tel # (703) 528-1244 Title Fax # (703) 528-1244
Personnel: Publisher-Joan Lindsey, Editor-Danny Macey, Circ. Mgr.-Kathy Thorne, Production Mgr.-Lois Wagner, Promotion Dir.-Delores Baisden
Editorial Description: Covers gas markets.
General Info: Yr. Est. 1984, Weekly, ISSN: 0742-3055
Subscriptions: Indv. $377, For. $407, $8/copy
Circulation: Total-1,300

Gas Daily See: ENERGY

Gas Markets Week   *Business*

Publishing Co: Pasha Publications, Inc, 1616 N. Fort Myer Dr., #1000, Arlington, VA 22209-3103
Fax # (703) 528-4926; Title Tel # (703) 528-1244 Title Fax # (703) 528-1253
Personnel: Publisher-Tod Sedgwick, Grp. Pub.-Joan Henderson, Editor-Robert Barton, Circ. Mgr.-Kathy Thorne, Production-Eva Absher, Mktg. Coord.-Delores Baisden
Editorial Description: Compiles and summarizes information from Gas Daily. Reports on the latest prices paid for natural gas, market trends, industry rumors, and other topics.
General Info: Weekly
Subscriptions: Indv. $497, For. $527, $10/copy

Gas Storage Report   *Business*

Publishing Co: Pasha Publications, Inc, 1616 N. Fort Myer Dr., #1000, Arlington, VA 22209-3103
Fax # (703) 528-4926; Title Tel # (703) 528-1244 Title Fax # (703) 528-1253
Personnel: Publisher-Tod Sedgwick, Grp. Pub.-Joan Henderson, Editor-Mark Hand, Production-Eva Absher, Mktg. Coord.-Delores Baisden
Editorial Description: Focuses on news about gas storage.
General Info: Monthly
Subscriptions: Indv. $495, For. $510, $41/copy

Gas Transactions Report   *Business*

Publishing Co: Hart Publications, 7811 Montrose Rd., Potomac, MD 20854 Tel # (301) 340-2100
Parent Co.-Phillips Business Information, Inc., Potomac
Editorial Description: Covers new gas contracts for transportation of natural gas.
General Info: Yr. Est. 1993, Bi-weekly
Subscriptions: Indv. $547

Gas Transportation
Marketing Service   *Business*

Publishing Co: Federal Programs Advisory Service, 1725 K St NW Ste 200, Washington, DC 20006-1401 Parent Co.-Thompson Publishing Group, Washington; Title Tel # (202) 872-4000 Title Fax # (410) 543-2921
Personnel: Publisher-Richard Thompson, Editor-Tanya Jackson, Editor-Carita Simons, Circ. Mgr.-Dale Miller, Mktg. Dir.-Conrad Hebel, Promotion Dir.-Lisa Granderson
General Info: Yr. Est. 1987, Monthly, Sheetfed press, No Color, Newsprint, Looseleaf
Subscriptions: Indv. $595
Circulation: Total-1,850

Gas Transportation Report   *Business*

Publishing Co: Pasha Publications, Inc, 1616 N. Fort Myer Dr., #1000, Arlington, VA 22209-3103
Tel # (703) 528-1244 Fax # (703) 528-4926; Title Tel # (703) 428-1244 Title Fax # (703) 528-1253
Personnel: Publisher-Tod Sedgwick, Grp. Pub.-Joan Henderson, Editor-Tom Castleman, Assoc. Ed.-Ron Zizmor, Circ. Mgr.-Kathy Thorne, Production-Eva Absher, Mktg. Coord.-Delores Baisden
Editorial Description: Covers the transportation of natural gas.
General Info: (Formerly Natural Gas Market Report (incorp.)), Yr. Est. 1992, Bi-weekly, 8 pages
Subscriptions: Indv. $397, For. $427, $8/copy

Gas Utilities Industry - Worldwide
See: PUBLIC UTILITIES

Gower Federal Service-Miscellaneous Land Decisions
See: LAW

Gower Federal Service-Oil
and Gas   *Business*

Publishing Co: Rocky Mountain Mineral Law Foundation, 7039 E 18th Ave, Denver, CO 80220-1826;
Title Tel # (303) 321-8100 Title Fax # (303) 321-7657
Editorial Description: Legal materials relative to the acquisition & maintenance of federal onshore oil & gas leases.
General Info: Yr. Est. 1955, 14x/yr., Looseleaf
Subscriptions: Indv. $215
Circulation: Total-230

Gower Federal Service-
Outer Continental Shelf   *Business*

Publishing Co: Rocky Mountain Mineral Law Foundation, 7039 E 18th Ave, Denver, CO 80220-1826;
Title Tel # (303) 321-8100 Title Fax # (303) 321-7657
Editorial Description: Federal oil and gas leasing of the Outer Continental Shelf.
General Info: Yr. Est. 1954, 6x/yr., Looseleaf
Subscriptions: Indv. $150, For. $200
Circulation: Total-150

Gower Federal Service-Royalty Valuation and Management
See: LAW

Gulf Coast East Texas
Rotary Report   *Business*

Publishing Co: Petroleum Information Corp., PO Box 2612, Denver, CO 80201-2612;
Title Tel # (303) 740-7100
Editorial Description: RRC dists. 1-6.
General Info: Weekly, Looseleaf
Subscriptions: Indv. $1,248

Gulf of Mexico Newsletter
See: ENERGY

Gulf of Mexico Report   *Business*

Publishing Co: Petroleum Information Corp., PO Box 2612, Denver, CO 80201-2612;
Title Tel # (303) 740-7100
Editorial Description: Gulf coast offshore.
General Info: Daily, Looseleaf
Subscriptions: Indv. $1,680

Gulf of Mexico Rotary
Report   *Business*

Publishing Co: Petroleum Information Corp., PO Box 2612, Denver, CO 80201-2612;
Title Tel # (303) 740-7100
General Info: (Formerly Gulf of Mexico Rotary Service), Weekly, Looseleaf
Subscriptions: Indv. $600

Hart's Pipeline Digest
Update Newsletter

Publishing Co: Hart Publications. Inc., 4545 Post Oak Place Drive, Suite 210, Houston, TX 77027-3105; Title Tel # (713) 499-3432 Title Fax # (713) 840-8585
Personnel: Publisher-H.M. Stemmer, Editor-Judy Clark, Adv. Dir.-Norma Babbitt, Production Mgr., Art Dir.-Rosalie Milton, Circ. Mgr., Promotion Dir.-Shirley Betts
Editorial Description: Update newsletter with latest pipelines planned, latest pipeline construction contracts awarded since last issue of Hart's Pipeline Digest magazine and updates, briefs on late breaking news items affecting the pipeline construction industry.
General Info: Monthly, 8 pages, ISSN: 0197-1506, No Color, Matte
Subscriptions: Can. $67, For. $67, $5/copy
Circulation: Total-6,900
Printing Co: Southwest Precision Printers, 7205 Ashcroft Dr, Houston, TX 77081-6399
Tel # (713) 777-3333

Houston New Locations   *Business*

Publishing Co: Petroleum Information Corp., PO Box 2612, Denver, CO 80201-2612;
Title Tel # (303) 740-7100
General Info: Daily, Looseleaf
Subscriptions: Indv. $1,140

Houston Petroleum
Industry   *Business*

Publishing Co: Midwest Register Inc., 1120 E. 4th St., Tulsa, OK 74120-3220;
Title Tel # (918) 582-2000 Title Fax # (918) 587-9349
Personnel: Publisher/President/Advisor-Will L. Hammack
General Info: Yr. Est. 1945, Annually, 750 pages
Subscriptions: Can. $65, For. $65, $65/copy
Advertising: Inquire for rates.
List Rental: Rents Lists

Houston Report   *Business*

Publishing Co: Petroleum Information Corp., PO Box 2612, Denver, CO 80201-2612;
Title Tel # (303) 740-7100
General Info: Daily, Looseleaf
Subscriptions: Indv. $2,520

ILMA Compoundings   *Business, Association*   CPM$1182

Publishing Co: Independent Lubricant Manufacturers Association, 651 S Washington St, Alexandria, VA 22314-4109; Title Tel # (703) 684-5574 Title Fax # (703) 836-8503
Personnel: Publisher-Nancy DeMarco, Editor-Lisa Tocci, Adv. Dir.-Gloria Briskin
Editorial Description: Business & government affairs news for independent blenders & compounders of lubricants, metalworking fluids & greases.
General Info: Yr. Est. 1948, Monthly, Trim Size-11$\frac{3}{8}$ x 15, Sheetfed press, 20 pages, ISSN: 1042-508X, 45% ads, 4 Color, Matte
Subscriptions: Indv. $800
Circulation: Total-1,950
Advertising: $2,305. Accepts Inserts.
List Rental: Actives $500/M
Printing Co: Corporate Press, 403 Brightseat Rd., Landover, MD 20785-4706 Tel # (301) 499-9200, Fax # (301) 499-5435

INGAA Washington
Report   *Association*   CPM: $375

Publishing Co: Interstate Natural Gas Assn. of America, 555 13th St NW Ste 300w, Washington, DC 20004-1109; Title Tel # (202) 626-3209
Personnel: Editor-Cheryl Hoffman
Editorial Description: Covers news of the interstate natural gas pipeline industry, especially federal legislative, judicial, regulatory & administrative developments.
General Info: Yr. Est. 1962, Bi-weekly, Trim Size-8$\frac{1}{2}$ x 11, Desktop press, 10 pages, No Color
Subscriptions: Indv. $379
Circulation: Total-800
Advertising: $300.

Illinois Basin Report   *Business*

Publishing Co: Petroleum Information Corp., PO Box 2612, Denver, CO 80201-2612;
Title Tel # (303) 740-7100
Editorial Description: IL, W. KY, Indiana, W. TN.
General Info: Weekly, Looseleaf
Subscriptions: Indv. $552

Illinois Basin Rotary Report   *Business*

Publishing Co: Petroleum Information Corp., PO Box 2612, Denver, CO 80201-2612;
   Title Tel # (303) 740-7100
General Info: Weekly, Looseleaf
Subscriptions: Indv. $696

Illinois Report   *Business*

Publishing Co: Petroleum Information Corp., PO Box 2612, Denver, CO 80201-2612;
   Title Tel # (303) 740-7100
General Info: Weekly, Looseleaf
Subscriptions: Indv. $444

Illustrator Magazine & Paper Collector's News
   See: COLLECTIBLES

Improved Recovery Week
   See: ENERGY

Independent Liquid Terminals Assn. -Newsletter
   See: CHEMISTRY & CHEMICALS

Inside CAODC   *Association*

Publishing Co: Canadian Assn. of Oilwell Drilling Contractors, #800-540 5th Ave., SW, Calgary, AB
   T2P 0M2 Canada; Title Tel # (403) 264-4311 Title Fax # (403) 263-3796
Personnel: Publisher-Diana Dennis, Production Mgr.-Leslie Diegel
General Info: (Formerly Drilling Rig Newsletter), Bi-monthly, 1 pages
Subscriptions: Indv. $100, Inst. $100, Can. $100
Circulation: Total-600

International Butane-
   Propane Newsletter   *Business*

Publishing Co: Butane-Propane News, Inc., 338 E Foothill Blvd # 660698, Arcadia, CA 91006-2542;
   Title Tel # (818) 357-2168 Title Fax # (818) 303-2854
Personnel: Publisher-Natalie Peal, Editor-Ann Rey, Circ. Mgr.-Ellie Fetchik
Editorial Description: Supply, demand, prices, new production facilities, product movements, and
   shipping developments around the world.
General Info: Yr. Est. 1977, Bi-weekly, 8 pages, No Color
Subscriptions: Indv. $215

International Fluidized Bed Review
   See: ENERGY

International Gas
   Technology Highlights   *Business*

Publishing Co: Institute of Gas Technology, 1700 S. Mt. Prospect Road, Des Plaines, IL 60018
   Tel # (708) 768-0500 Fax # (708) 768-0501; Title Tel # (312) 949-3970 Title Fax # (312) 949-3776
Personnel: Editor-Colleen Sen
Editorial Description: New developments of interest to natural gas industry. Management oriented.
General Info: Yr. Est. 1971, Bi-weekly, Trim Size-8½ x 11, Letrpr. press, 4 pages, ISSN: 0276-4040,
   No Color
Subscriptions: Indv. $90, For. $100
Circulation: (96% controlled), Total-2,500, International-300

International Oil
   Developments; Statistical
   Survey

Publishing Co: U.S. Central Intelligence Agency, Washington, DC 20505-0001;
   Title Tel # (703) 351-1100
General Info: (Formerly Intl. Oil Developments; Statistical Survey), Yr. Est. 1978, Bi-weekly, ISSN:
   0163-3724

International Oil News   *Business*

Publishing Co: William F. Bland Co., 111 Cloister Court, Suite 114, PO Box 16666, Chapel Hill, NC
   27516-6666; Title Tel # (919) 490-0700 Title Fax # (919) 490-3002
Personnel: Publisher, Editor-William Bland, Editor-Susan D. Kensil, Editor-Christopher R. Schultz,
   Circ. Dir.-Mollie B. Sandor, Promotion Mgr.-David M. Bland
Editorial Description: Reports on current developments in the worldwide oil & gas business--
   government actions, international agency moves, corporate changes, major exploration/
   development contracts & permits, significant finds, new regulations, supply-demand forecasts, etc.
General Info: (Formerly Intl Oil News Mgmnt Edtn; Intl Oil News Suppliers Edtn), Yr. Est. 1954,
   Weekly, Trim Size-8½ x 11, Sheetfed press, 6 pages, No Color, Looseleaf
Subscriptions: Indv. $517, $12/copy
List Rental: List Management Co.: Manager: Mollie Sandor; Media Marketplace, 140 Terry Drive,
   P.O. Box 500, Newtown, PA 18940-0500 Tel # (215) 968-5020, Fax # (215) 968-9410, Actives:
   16,387, $80/M

International Petroleum
   Finance   *Business*

Publishing Co: Petroleum Intelligence Weekly, Inc., 575 Broadway 4th Fl., New York, NY 10012
   Tel # (212) 941-5500 Fax # (212) 941-5509
Personnel: Publisher-Dillard Spriggs, Assoc. Publ.-A.J. Conley, Editor-Carol Epstein, Circ. Mgr.-Josh
   Kiernan
Editorial Description: Analytical reporting of earnings, finances, and management strategies, in the
   petroleum industry.
General Info: Yr. Est. 1978, Bi-weekly, 8 pages, ISSN: 0193-9270
Subscriptions: Indv. $580, Can. $58, For. $595, $35/copy
Acquistions: Publication Bought, Publication Sold

International Petroleum
   Finance

Publishing Co: Petroleum Intelligence Weekly, Inc., 575 Broadway 4th Fl., New York, NY 10012;
   Title Tel # (212) 941-5500 Title Fax # (212) 941-5509
Personnel: Publisher-Edward L. Morse, Editor-Cristina Haus, Circ. Mgr.-Anastasia Tasoulis
Editorial Description: A comprehensive price report on world aviation price trends, giving in-depth
   analysis on global markets and supplies airport-by-airport pricing. Includes airport features and
   regional updates.
General Info: (Formerly Jet Fuel Intelligence), Weekly, 6 pages
Subscriptions: Indv. $1,975

International Petroleum
   Industry   *Business*

Publishing Co: Midwest Register Inc., 1120 E. 4th St., Tulsa, OK 74120-3220;
   Title Tel # (918) 582-2000 Title Fax # (918) 587-9349
Personnel: Publisher/President/Advisor-Will L. Hammack
General Info: Yr. Est. 1945, Annually, 800 pages
Subscriptions: Can. $85, For. $85, $85/copy
Advertising: Inquire for rates.
List Rental: Rents Lists

International Taxation Series
   See: TAXES

International Trends in
   Oil & Gas   *Business*

Publishing Co: Petroleum Information Corp., PO Box 2612, Denver, CO 80201-2612
   Tel # (303) 740-7100; Title Tel # (713) 961-5660
Personnel: Editor-James Tanner
General Info: (Formerly Petroleum Information Intl.), Yr. Est. 1981, Annually, 4 pages, ISSN: 0730-
   7632
Subscriptions: Indv. $300, For. $360

Kansas New Location
   Service   *Business*

Publishing Co: Petroleum Information Corp., PO Box 2612, Denver, CO 80201-2612;
   Title Tel # (303) 740-7100
Editorial Description: KS, IA, MO, central & eastern Nebraska.
General Info: Daily, Looseleaf
Subscriptions: Indv. $480

Kansas Oil Marketer   *Business, Association*

Publishing Co: Kansas Oil Marketeers Association, PO Box 8479, Topeka, KS 66608-0479;
   Title Tel # (913) 233-9655
General Info: Bi-monthly
Circulation: Total-700

Kansas Report   *Business*

Publishing Co: Petroleum Information Corp., PO Box 2612, Denver, CO 80201-2612;
   Title Tel # (303) 740-7100
Editorial Description: KS, IA, central & eastern Nebraska.
General Info: Daily, Looseleaf
Subscriptions: Indv. $840

The LNG Observer   *Association*

Publishing Co: Institute of Gas Technology, 1700 S. Mt. Prospect Road, Des Plaines, IL 60018
   Tel # (708) 768-0500 Fax # (708) 768-0501; Title Tel # (312) 949-3970 Title Fax # (312) 949-3776
Personnel: Editor-Colleen Taylor Sen
Editorial Description: A quarterly publication surveying economic, political and technical
   developments in the U.S. and international liquefied natural gas industry.
General Info: Yr. Est. 1990, Quarterly, Letrpr. press, 12 pages, ISSN: 1053-6949, No Color, Matte
Subscriptions: Indv. $100, For. $100
Circulation: (98% controlled), Total-2,500, International-300

LOMA Bulletin   *Association*

Publishing Co: Louisiana Oil Marketers Assn., PO Box 80357, Baton Rouge, LA 70898-0357;
   Title Tel # (504) 344-6968
Personnel: Editor-Julius Mire, Jr.
Editorial Description: All matters concerned with marketing of petroleum products.
General Info: Monthly, Trim Size-8½ x 11, Mimeo press, 6 pages
Circulation: Total-550
Advertising: Inquire for rates.

LP Gas Priceline

Publishing Co: United Communications Group, 11300 Rockville Pike, Ste. 1100, Rockville, MD
   20852-3030 Tel # (301) 816-8950 Fax # (301) 816-8945; Title Tel # (301) 656-6666
Personnel: Editor-Ed Peskowitz
Editorial Description: LP gas pricing.
General Info: Daily
Subscriptions: Indv. $495
List Rental: Rents Lists

Land Rig Newsletter, The

Publishing Co: RJM Communications, PO Box 6645, Lubbock, TX 79493-6645
Fax # (806) 741-1553; Title Tel # (806) 741-1531
Personnel: Publisher-Richard J. Mason, Editor-Michael Slaton
Editorial Description: Publication covers trends in north American and international on shore contract drilling segment of the oil and gas industry.
General Info: Yr. Est. 1978, Monthly, Trim Size-8$\frac{1}{2}$ x 11, 10 pages, ISSN: 1043-7312
Subscriptions: Indv. $200

Law of Federal Oil and Gas Leases   *Business*

Publishing Co: Matthew Bender & Co., 11 Penn Plaza, New York, NY 10001-2006
Fax # (212) 244-3188; Title Tel # (212) 967-7707
Personnel: Editor-E. Carr
Editorial Description: Experts in industry, government, and private practice comment on the law of leases on the Outer Continental Shelf, public domain, etc.
General Info: Yr. Est. 1964, Irregular, Looseleaf
Subscriptions: $195/copy

Law of Oil and Gas Leases

Publishing Co: Matthew Bender & Co., 11 Penn Plaza, New York, NY 10001-2006
Fax # (212) 244-3188; Title Tel # (212) 967-7707
Personnel: Editor-E. Carr
Editorial Description: Reports of opinions by courts of all jurisdictions. Thorough annotations, various state laws are formulated and compared.
General Info: Yr. Est. 1958, Irregular, Looseleaf
Subscriptions: $220/copy

Location Plat Service-Gulf of Mexico   *Business*

Publishing Co: Petroleum Information Corp., PO Box 2612, Denver, CO 80201-2612;
Title Tel # (303) 740-7100
Editorial Description: Gulf of Mexico.
General Info: Daily, Looseleaf
Subscriptions: Indv. $1,080

Location Plat Service-S. Louisiana   *Business*

Publishing Co: Petroleum Information Corp., PO Box 2612, Denver, CO 80201-2612;
Title Tel # (303) 740-7100
Editorial Description: S. Louisiana.
General Info: Daily, Looseleaf
Subscriptions: Indv. $480

Location Plat Service-Southeast U.S.   *Business*

Publishing Co: Petroleum Information Corp., PO Box 2612, Denver, CO 80201-2612;
Title Tel # (303) 740-7100
Editorial Description: MS, AL, GA, FL.
General Info: Weekly, Looseleaf
Subscriptions: Indv. $720

Location Plat Service-Texas 1-4   *Business*

Publishing Co: Petroleum Information Corp., PO Box 2612, Denver, CO 80201-2612;
Title Tel # (303) 740-7100
Editorial Description: Texas RRC dists. 1-4.
General Info: Daily, Looseleaf
Subscriptions: Indv. $1,404

Location Plat Service-Texas 5,6   *Business*

Publishing Co: Petroleum Information Corp., PO Box 2612, Denver, CO 80201-2612;
Title Tel # (303) 740-7100
Editorial Description: Texas RRC dists. 5 & 6.
General Info: Daily, Looseleaf
Subscriptions: Indv. $648

Location Plat Service-Texas, One District   *Business*

Publishing Co: Petroleum Information Corp., PO Box 2612, Denver, CO 80201-2612;
Title Tel # (303) 740-7100
Editorial Description: For a single Texas district.
General Info: Daily, Looseleaf
Subscriptions: Indv. $492

Louisiana Offshore Report   *Business*

Publishing Co: Petroleum Information Corp., PO Box 2612, Denver, CO 80201-2612;
Title Tel # (303) 740-7100
General Info: Daily, Looseleaf
Subscriptions: Indv. $960

MLPGA News   *Business*

Publishing Co: MLPGA, Inc., 4100 Country Club Dr, Jefferson City, MO 65109-0302;
Title Tel # (314) 893-7655
Personnel: Editor-Emma Bommel, Adv. Dir.-Cindy Hale
General Info: Yr. Est. 1980, Bi-monthly, Web press, 20 pages, No Color, Newsprint, Saddle-stitched
Subscriptions: Indv. $10
Circulation: Total-675
Advertising: Inquire for rates.

Marketers, Purchasers & Trading Companies - Worldwide   *Business*

Publishing Co: Midwest Register Inc., 1120 E. 4th St., Tulsa, OK 74120-3220;
Title Tel # (918) 582-2000 Title Fax # (918) 587-9349
Personnel: Publisher/President/Advisor-Will L. Hammack
General Info: (Formerly Marketing - Worldwide Petroleum Industry), Yr. Est. 1945, Annually, 650 pages
Subscriptions: Can. $75, For. $75, $75/copy
Advertising: Inquire for rates.
List Rental: Rents Lists

Michigan Basin Report   *Business*

Publishing Co: Petroleum Information Corp., PO Box 2612, Denver, CO 80201-2612;
Title Tel # (303) 740-7100
Editorial Description: MI, N.W. Ohio, N. Indiana.
General Info: Weekly, Looseleaf
Subscriptions: Indv. $1,140

Michigan Basin Rotary Report   *Business*

Publishing Co: Petroleum Information Corp., PO Box 2612, Denver, CO 80201-2612;
Title Tel # (303) 740-7100
General Info: Weekly, Looseleaf
Subscriptions: Indv. $420

Mid-Continent Newsletter   *Business*

Publishing Co: Petroleum Information Corp., PO Box 2612, Denver, CO 80201-2612;
Title Tel # (303) 740-7100
General Info: Daily
Subscriptions: Indv. $780

Mid-Continent Region Report   *Business*

Publishing Co: Petroleum Information Corp., PO Box 2612, Denver, CO 80201-2612;
Title Tel # (303) 740-7100
Editorial Description: OK, KS, Texas Panhandle, NE, New Mexico, S.E. Colo., IA, MO.
General Info: Daily, Looseleaf
Subscriptions: Indv. $3,000

Mid-Continent Region Rotary Report   *Business*

Publishing Co: Petroleum Information Corp., PO Box 2612, Denver, CO 80201-2612;
Title Tel # (303) 740-7100
General Info: Weekly, Looseleaf
Subscriptions: Indv. $960

Mid-Continent States Petroleum Industry   *Business*

Publishing Co: Midwest Register Inc., 1120 E. 4th St., Tulsa, OK 74120-3220;
Title Tel # (918) 582-2000 Title Fax # (918) 587-9349
Personnel: Publisher/President/Advisor-Will L. Hammack
General Info: (Formerly Mid-Continent Petroleum Industry), Annually, 900 pages
Subscriptions: Can. $65, For. $65, $65/copy
Advertising: Inquire for rates.
List Rental: Rents Lists

Midland Report   *Business*

Publishing Co: Petroleum Information Corp., PO Box 2612, Denver, CO 80201-2612;
Title Tel # (303) 740-7100
Editorial Description: RRC Dists. 7B, 7C, 8, 8A, 9, S.E. New Mexico.
General Info: Daily, Looseleaf
Subscriptions: Indv. $2,700

Midland Report New Locations   *Business*

Publishing Co: Petroleum Information Corp., PO Box 2612, Denver, CO 80201-2612;
Title Tel # (303) 740-7100
Editorial Description: RRC Dists. 7B, 7C, 8, 8A, 9, S.E. New Mexico.
General Info: Daily, Looseleaf
Subscriptions: Indv. $960

Midwest and Northeast
Region Report   *Business*

Publishing Co: Petroleum Information Corp., PO Box 2612, Denver, CO 80201-2612; Title Tel # (303) 740-7100
Editorial Description: IL, MI, and Appalachian basins.
General Info: Weekly, Looseleaf
Subscriptions: Indv. $3,360

Mineral Law Newsletter
See: LAW

Monthly Completion Report   *Business*

Publishing Co: American Petroleum Inst., 1220 L St. , N. W., Dept. Publication, Washington, DC 20005-4070; Title Tel # (202) 682-8378 Title Fax # (202) 682-8154
Personnel: Circ. Mgr.-Geneva Redder
Editorial Description: Summary of oil wells, gas wells, dry holes, exploratory wells, etc.
General Info: (Formerly Monthly Report on Drilling Activity in the U.S.), Yr. Est. 1956, Monthly, 4 pages
Subscriptions: Indv. $65, Can. $72, For. $81

NGI's Daily Gas Price Index   *Business*

Publishing Co: Intelligence Press, PO Box 70587, Washington, DC 20024-0587; Title Tel # (703) 318-8848 Title Fax # (703) 318-0597
Editorial Description: Up-to-the-minute cash and futures price and market information.
General Info: Yr. Est. 1993, Daily

NGI's Gas Price Index   *Business*

Publishing Co: Intelligence Press, PO Box 70587, Washington, DC 20024-0587; Title Tel # (703) 318-8848 Title Fax # (703) 318-0597
Personnel: Publisher, Editor-Ellen Beswick
Editorial Description: Features gas price information.
General Info: Yr. Est. 1988, Weekly
Subscriptions: Indv. $525, For. $525

National Wildcat Monthly   *Business*

Publishing Co: Petroleum Information Corp., PO Box 2612, Denver, CO 80201-2612; Title Tel # (303) 740-7100
Personnel: Publisher-T. C. Cheney
Editorial Description: Oil & gas exploration in the U. S. & its waters.
General Info: Yr. Est. 1981, Monthly
Subscriptions: Indv. $480

Natural Gas Intelligence   *Business*

Publishing Co: Intelligence Press, PO Box 70587, Washington, DC 20024-0587; Title Tel # (703) 318-8848 Title Fax # (703) 318-0597
Editorial Description: Natural gas industry market news.
General Info: Yr. Est. 1981, Weekly
Subscriptions: Indv. $825, Can. $790, For. $870

Natural Gas Marketing   *Business*

Publishing Co: Pasha Publications, Inc, 1616 N. Fort Myer Dr., #1000, Arlington, VA 22209-3103 Tel # (703) 528-1244 Fax # (703) 528-4926
Personnel: Publisher-Tod Sedgwick, Grp. Pub.-Joan Henderson, Editor-Robert Lebling, Production-Eva Absher, Mktg. Coord.-Delores Baisden
Editorial Description: Focuses on marketing of natural gas.
General Info: Yr. Est. 1987, Monthly
Subscriptions: Indv. $512

Natural Gas Policy Act
Information Service

Publishing Co: Thompson Publishing Group, 1725 K Street, NW, Washington, DC 20006 Tel # (202) 872-4000; Title Tel # (202) 872-1766
Personnel: Publisher-Richard Thompson, Editor-Bill Reilly, Circ. Mgr.-Dale Milla, Production Mgr.-Martha Dahlman, Promotion Dir.-Lucy Caldwell-Stair
General Info: Bi-weekly, Sheetfed press, Newsprint, Looseleaf
Subscriptions: Indv. $1,560

Natural Gas Report   *Business*

Publishing Co: Bloomberg Financial Markets, 499 Park Ave, New York, NY 10022 Tel # (212) 318-2200 Fax # (212) 940-1980
Personnel: Publisher-Michael Bloomberg
Editorial Description: News and pricing on the energy market.
General Info: Bi-weekly, Trim Size-8½ x 11, 16 pages, No Color
Subscriptions: Indv. $100

Natural Gas Transportation
Information Service   *Business*

Publishing Co: Thompson Publishing Group, 1725 K Street, NW, Washington, DC 20006 Tel # (202) 872-4000; Title Tel # (202) 872-1766
Personnel: Publisher-Richard Thompson, Editor-Roger Smith, Circ. Mgr.-Dale Miller, Production Mgr.-Martha Dahlman, Promotion Dir.-Lucy Caldwell-Stair
Editorial Description: Subscription includes monthly update and details topics such as pipeline access, capacity brokering, service restructuring and more.
General Info: Monthly, Sheetfed press, No Color, Looseleaf
Subscriptions: Indv. $654

Natural Gas Week   *Business*

Publishing Co: Oil Daily Co., 1401 New York Ave. NW, Ste. 500, Washington, DC 20005-2102 Fax # (202) 347-8090; Title Tel # (202) 662-0700 Title Fax # (202) 347-8089
Personnel: Publisher, Editor-John Jennrich, Promotion Dir.-Luis Betancourt
Editorial Description: Economics newsletter covering natural gas from wellhead to burner tip.
General Info: Yr. Est. 1985, Weekly, Trim Size-8½ x 11, Web press, 24 pages, ISSN: 8756-3037, No Color
Subscriptions: Indv. $797, Inst. $350, Can. $697, For. $797, $10/copy
Acquistions: Publication Bought
Printing Co: McArdle Printing Co., 800 Commerce Dr, Upper Marlboro, MD 20772-8792 Tel # (301) 390-8500

New Locations Report-
Northern Rockies   *Business*

Publishing Co: Petroleum Information Corp., PO Box 2612, Denver, CO 80201-2612; Title Tel # (303) 740-7100
Editorial Description: New oil locations in Montana, N. Dakota, Wyoming, Idaho, and S. Dakota.
General Info: Daily, Looseleaf
Subscriptions: Indv. $288

New Locations Report-
Southern Rockies   *Business*

Publishing Co: Petroleum Information Corp., PO Box 2612, Denver, CO 80201-2612; Title Tel # (303) 740-7100
Editorial Description: New oil locations in Utah, Colorado, Neveda, New Mexico, Arizona, and western Nebraska.
General Info: Daily, Looseleaf
Subscriptions: Indv. $456

New Well Licenses Issued-
Alberta   *Business*

Publishing Co: Petroleum Information Canada Ltd., Suite 500 Bow Valley Sq. III, 255 5th Ave., S.W., Calgary, AB T2P 3G6 Canada; Title Tel # (403) 263-3822
General Info: Daily, Looseleaf

New Well Licenses Issued-
Saskatchewan/Mantiboa   *Business*

Publishing Co: Petroleum Information Canada Ltd., Suite 500 Bow Valley Sq. III, 255 5th Ave., S.W., Calgary, AB T2P 3G6 Canada; Title Tel # (403) 263-3822
General Info: Daily, Looseleaf

New Well Licenses issued-
British Columbia/Frontier   *Business*

Publishing Co: Petroleum Information Canada Ltd., Suite 500 Bow Valley Sq. III, 255 5th Ave., S.W., Calgary, AB T2P 3G6 Canada; Title Tel # (403) 263-3822
Editorial Description: Includes British Columbia, yukon, Artic islands, Northwest Territories, and offshore.
General Info: Daily, Looseleaf

New York, Pennsylvania
Report   *Business*

Publishing Co: Petroleum Information Corp., PO Box 2612, Denver, CO 80201-2612; Title Tel # (303) 740-7100
Editorial Description: Covers the oil industry in New York and Pennsylvania.
General Info: Weekly, Looseleaf
Subscriptions: Indv. $960

Nickle's CAODC Rig
Locator

Publishing Co: C.O. Nickle Pubs., 999 8 St. SW, #300, Calgary, AB T2R 1N7 Canada Parent Co.-Southam Information & Technology Group, Calgary, Canada; Title Tel # (403) 244-6111 Title Fax # (403) 245-8666
Personnel: Publisher-Rick Charland
General Info: Yr. Est. 1957, Weekly
Subscriptions: Indv. $204

Nickle's Daily Oil Bulletin   *Business*

Publishing Co: C.O. Nickle Pubs., 999 8 St. SW, #300, Calgary, AB T2R 1N7 Canada Parent Co.-Southam Information & Technology Group, Calgary, Canada; Title Tel # (403) 244-6111 Title Fax # (403) 245-8666
Personnel: Editor-Rick Charland, Circ. Mgr.-Kay Isaac
Editorial Description: Daily report on all aspects of the Canadian oil & gas industry.
General Info: Yr. Est. 1937, Daily, Offset press, 24 pages, No Color
Subscriptions: Indv. $696, $3/copy
Circulation: Total-2,600

Nickle's Geo-Plat Bulletin   *Business*

Publishing Co: C.O. Nickle Pubs., 999 8 St. SW, #300, Calgary, AB T2R 1N7 Canada Parent Co.-Southam Information & Technology Group, Calgary, Canada; Title Tel # (403) 244-6111
Personnel: Publisher, Editor-Richard Charland, Circ. Mgr.-Marnie Cardell
Editorial Description: Supplement to Daily Oil Bulletin.
General Info: Yr. Est. 1985, Bi-weekly, Offset press, 24 pages, No Color
Subscriptions: Indv. $300, $6/copy

North & West Central
Texas Report *Business*

Publishing Co: Petroleum Information Corp., PO Box 2612, Denver, CO 80201-2612;
Title Tel # (303) 740-7100
Editorial Description: RRC Dists. 7B & 9.
General Info: Semi-weekly, Looseleaf
Subscriptions: Indv. $1,512

North Dakota-South Dakota
Edition *Business*

Publishing Co: Petroleum Information Corp., PO Box 2612, Denver, CO 80201-2612;
Title Tel # (303) 740-7100
Editorial Description: The oil industry industry in North & South Dakota.
General Info: Daily, Looseleaf
Subscriptions: Indv. $960

North Gulf of Mexico Report *Business*

Publishing Co: Petroleum Information Corp., PO Box 2612, Denver, CO 80201-2612;
Title Tel # (303) 740-7100
Editorial Description: Covers the Gulf coast and Atlantic offshore oil industry.
General Info: Daily, Looseleaf
Subscriptions: Indv. $720

North Louisiana, Arkansas
Report *Business*

Publishing Co: Petroleum Information Corp., PO Box 2612, Denver, CO 80201-2612;
Title Tel # (303) 740-7100
General Info: Looseleaf
Subscriptions: Indv. $1,380

North Louisiana Report *Business*

Publishing Co: Petroleum Information Corp., PO Box 2612, Denver, CO 80201-2612;
Title Tel # (303) 740-7100
General Info: Weekly, Looseleaf
Subscriptions: Indv. $1,200

North Texas Report *Business*

Publishing Co: Petroleum Information Corp., PO Box 2612, Denver, CO 80201-2612;
Title Tel # (303) 740-7100
Editorial Description: RRC Dist. 9.
General Info: Weekly, Looseleaf
Subscriptions: Indv. $1,056

Northeast States
Petroleum Industry *Business*

Publishing Co: Midwest Register Inc., 1120 E. 4th St., Tulsa, OK 74120-3220;
Title Tel # (918) 582-2000 Title Fax # (918) 587-9349
Personnel: Publisher/President/Advisor-Will L. Hammack
General Info: Yr. Est. 1945, Annually, 785 pages
Subscriptions: Can. $65, For. $65, $40/copy
Advertising: Inquire for rates.
List Rental: Rents Lists

Northern Rockies Report *Business*

Publishing Co: Petroleum Information Corp., PO Box 2612, Denver, CO 80201-2612;
Title Tel # (303) 740-7100
Editorial Description: MT, ND, SD, ID.
General Info: Daily, Looseleaf
Subscriptions: Indv. $1,320

Northern Rockies and
Southern Rockies *Business*

Publishing Co: Petroleum Information Corp., PO Box 2612, Denver, CO 80201-2612;
Title Tel # (303) 740-7100
General Info: Daily, Looseleaf
Subscriptions: Indv. $1,440

Northern Rockies and
Wyoming *Business*

Publishing Co: Petroleum Information Corp., PO Box 2612, Denver, CO 80201-2612;
Title Tel # (303) 740-7100
General Info: Daily, Looseleaf
Subscriptions: Indv. $1,440, Can. $1,440

OPI Newsletter

Publishing Co: Ontario Petroleum Institute, Inc., 555 Southdale Road East, Suite 104, London, ON N6E 1A2 Canada; Title Tel # (519) 680-1620 Title Fax # (519) 680-1621
Personnel: Editor-Doug Gilbert
General Info: Bi-monthly, Trim Size-8½ x 11, Desktop press, 6 pages, Coated
Circulation: Total-400

Ocean Oil Weekly Report *Business*

Publishing Co: PennWell Publishing Co., 1421 South Sheridan Rd., Tulsa, OK 74112-6600
Tel # (918) 853-3161 Fax # (918) 831-9497; Title Tel # (918) 831-9701 Title Fax # (918) 832-9295
Personnel: Publisher-John Schirra, Editor-Michael Crowden, Circulation-Tracy Green
Editorial Description: Latest information on offshore petroleum and supporting Marine industries. Includes monthly list of worldwide hydrocarbon discoveries, plus a report on all mobile rigs under construction.
General Info: Yr. Est. 1967, Weekly, 8 pages, No Color, Matte
Subscriptions: Indv. $495, Can. $585, For. $585
Advertising: Accepts Inserts.

Octane Week *Business*

Publishing Co: Hart Publications, 7811 Montrose Rd., Potomac, MD 20854 Tel # (301) 340-2100
Parent Co.-Phillips Business Information, Inc., Potomac
Personnel: Publisher-Frederick Potter, Asst. Pub.-Brian Crotty, Editor-Kevin Adler, Mktg. Dir.-Paul Caplan
Editorial Description: Covers trends in refining technology, octane components & global oil & environmental developments.
General Info: Weekly
Subscriptions: Indv. $10, Can. $1,095, For. $1,095
Acquistions: Publication Sold
List Rental: Rents Lists

Offshore Field Development International
See: ENERGY

Offshore International
Newsletter *Business*

Publishing Co: Offshore Data Services, Inc., PO Box 19909, Houston, TX 77224-1909;
Title Tel # (713) 781-2713 Title Fax # (713) 781-9594
Personnel: Publisher-Loran Sheffer, Editor-Susanne Pagano, Circ. Mgr.-Linda Parreno, Promotion Dir.-Marie Sheffer
Editorial Description: Synopsis of major offshore oil & gas contracts (platforms, rigs, pipelines, etc.) and coverage of international events, company news affecting offshore oil & gas exploration and field development.
General Info: (Formerly Ocean Construction Report; Offshore Fleet Economics), Yr. Est. 1974, Weekly, Trim Size-8½ x 11, Offset press, 8 pages, ISSN: 1058-5842, No Color, Matte
Subscriptions: Indv. $525, Can. $525, For. $560, $12/copy
Acquistions: Publication Bought, Publication Sold
Circulation: Total-800
Advertising: Accepts Inserts.
List Rental: Actives: $75/M
Printing Co: Offshore Data Services, Inc., PO Box 19909, Houston, TX 77224-1909
Tel # (713) 781-7213, Fax # (713) 781-9594

Offshore Petroleum Industry

Publishing Co: Barrows Co., Inc., 116 E 66th St, New York, NY 10021-6547;
Title Tel # (212) 772-1199 Title Fax # (212) 288-7242
Personnel: Publisher-Gordon Barrows, Editor-M. Guerra, Production Mgr.-R. Hussman, Adv. Dir., Art Dir., Promotion Dir.-D. Jeune
Editorial Description: This service follows world oil and gas offshore operations in all countries. Major divisions of the service include world offshore investment, geographical favorability, offshore production, offshore technology, and offshore economics. Revised quarterly.
General Info: Yr. Est. 1960, Quarterly, Looseleaf
Subscriptions: Indv. $1,900

Offshore Rig Locator International
See: ENERGY

Offshore Rig Newsletter
See: ENERGY

Ohio Report *Business*

Publishing Co: Petroleum Information Corp., PO Box 2612, Denver, CO 80201-2612;
Title Tel # (303) 740-7100
General Info: Weekly, Looseleaf
Subscriptions: Indv. $600

Oil & Gas Interest
Newsletter *Business*

Publishing Co: Hart Publications, Inc., 1900 Grant St., Ste. 720, Denver, CO 80203
Tel # (303) 837-1917 Fax # (303) 837-8585 Parent Co.-Phillips Business Information, Inc., Potomac; Title Tel # (713) 579-2782 Title Fax # (713) 579-8895
Personnel: Editor-J. Stevenson
Editorial Description: Oil & gas business financial transactions.
General Info: (Formerly Oil-Gas Investments Newsletter), Yr. Est. 1986, Monthly, Trim Size-8½ x 11, 28 pages, Color-cover, Saddle-stitched
Subscriptions: Indv. $265, Can. $267, For. $320

Oil Buyers Guide *Business*

Publishing Co: Bloomberg Financial Markets, 499 Park Ave, New York, NY 10022
Tel # (212) 318-2200 Fax # (212) 940-1980; Title Tel # (609) 279-4263 Title Fax # (609) 683-7523
Personnel: Publisher-Michael Bloomberg, Editor in Chief-Matthew Winkler
Editorial Description: Pricing and news on the energy industry.
General Info: Weekly, Trim Size-8½ x 11, 16 pages, No Color
Subscriptions: Indv. $795

Oil Express   *Business*

Publishing Co: United Communications Group, 11300 Rockville Pike, Ste. 1100, Rockville, MD 20852-3030 Fax # (301) 816-8945; Title Tel # (301) 816-8950
Personnel: Publisher-David Rohde, Editor-Carole Donoghue, Circ. Mgr.-Sharon Welch
Editorial Description: Information for gasoline marketers on news and trends affecting them and the oil industry.
General Info: Yr. Est. 1977, Weekly, Trim Size-8½ x 11, Offset press, 8 pages, ISSN: 0195-0576
Subscriptions: Indv. $247, $4/copy
List Rental: Actives: $125/M

Oil and Gas Law   *Business*

Publishing Co: Matthew Bender & Co., 11 Penn Plaza, New York, NY 10001-2006 Fax # (212) 244-3188; Title Tel # (212) 967-7707
Personnel: Editor-E. Carr
Editorial Description: The most comprehensive and systematic study available on the creation, existence and transfer of property rights in the oil and gas industry.
General Info: Yr. Est. 1959, Irregular, Looseleaf
Subscriptions: $845/copy

Oil and Gas Law Abridged
Edition   *Business*

Publishing Co: Matthew Bender & Co., 11 Penn Plaza, New York, NY 10001-2006 Tel # (212) 967-7707 Fax # (212) 244-3188
Editorial Description: Handy desk edition, keyed to the master treatise. Full treatment of property interests, conveyancing, oil & gas leases, implied covenants, pooling & unitization.
General Info: Yr. Est. 1973, Irregular, Looseleaf

Oil and Gas Reporter   *Business*

Publishing Co: Matthew Bender & Co., 11 Penn Plaza, New York, NY 10001-2006 Fax # (212) 244-3188; Title Tel # (212) 967-7707
Personnel: Editor-Carol Holgren
Editorial Description: Monthly report of state and federal cases and administrative rulings in oil and gas law and taxation. Headnoted, with digest.
General Info: Yr. Est. 1952, Looseleaf
Subscriptions: Indv. $540, $530/copy

Oil and Gas Tax Quarterly

Publishing Co: Matthew Bender & Co., 11 Penn Plaza, New York, NY 10001-2006 Fax # (212) 244-3188; Title Tel # (212) 967-7707
Personnel: Editor-E. Carr
Editorial Description: Provides tax men, attorneys, and oil industry executives with the latest information in the field of oil and gas taxation. Recent court decisions and appeals are reported.
General Info: Yr. Est. 1951, Quarterly, Looseleaf
Subscriptions: $150/copy

Oil Marketing Bulletin   *Business*

Publishing Co: United Communications Group, 11300 Rockville Pike, Ste. 1100, Rockville, MD 20852-3030 Fax # (301) 816-8945; Title Tel # (301) 816-8950
Personnel: Publisher-David Rohde, Editor-Tom Kloza, Circ. Mgr.-Sharon Welch
Editorial Description: News & analysis of price & supply trends for refiners & marketers.
General Info: (Formerly First Monday), Yr. Est. 1984, Weekly, 6 pages
Subscriptions: Indv. $695, $10/copy
List Rental: Actives: $125/M

Oil Price Information
Service

Publishing Co: United Communications Group, 11300 Rockville Pike, Ste. 1100, Rockville, MD 20852-3030 Tel # (301) 816-8950 Fax # (301) 816-8945; Title Tel # (301) 961-8700
Personnel: Publisher-David Rohde, Editor-Ben Brockwell, Circ. Mgr.-Sharon Welch
Editorial Description: Wholesale prices & analysis ot gasoline, heating oil, diesel fuel, propane, etc.
General Info: Yr. Est. 1980, Weekly, ISSN: 0279-7801
List Rental: Actives: $125/M

Oil in the Rockies   *Business*

Publishing Co: Petroleum Information Corp., PO Box 2612, Denver, CO 80201-2612; Title Tel # (303) 740-7100
Personnel: Publisher-T. C. Cheney
Editorial Description: Oil and gas activity. Includes Wildcat Activity Map.
General Info: Yr. Est. 1953, Monthly
Subscriptions: Indv. $402

Oil Spill Intelligence Report
See: ENVIRONMENT & ECOLOGY

Oil Spill Planning Manual, The
See: ENVIRONMENT & ECOLOGY

Oil Spill U.S. Law Report
See: LAW

Oil/Energy Statistics Bulletin

Publishing Co: Oil Statistics Co., PO Box 189, Whitman, MA 02382-0189; Title Tel # (617) 447-6407
Personnel: Publisher, Editor-Jack McGilvray, Promotion Dir.-Jennifer McGilvrey
Editorial Description: Features up to date oil and energy statistics.
General Info: Yr. Est. 1925, 26x/yr., Trim Size-8½ x 11, 14 pages
Subscriptions: Indv. $185

Oilman's Weekly News
Letter   *Business*

Publishing Co: PennWell Publishing Co., 1421 South Sheridan Rd., Tulsa, OK 74112-6600 Tel # (918) 853-3161 Fax # (918) 831-9497; Title Tel # (918) 835-3161 Title Fax # (918) 832-9295
Personnel: Publisher-David Betham-Rogers, Editor-Neil Potter, Circulation-Tracy Green
Editorial Description: Serving Europe & the North Sea with news & technology in exploration, production, construction & marine transportation.
General Info: Weekly, 16 pages, No Color, Matte
Subscriptions: Indv. $895, Can. $895, For. $895
Advertising: Accepts Inserts.

Oklahoma New Location
Service   *Business*

Publishing Co: Petroleum Information Corp., PO Box 2612, Denver, CO 80201-2612; Title Tel # (303) 740-7100
General Info: Daily, Looseleaf
Subscriptions: Indv. $480

Oklahoma Report   *Business*

Publishing Co: Petroleum Information Corp., PO Box 2612, Denver, CO 80201-2612; Title Tel # (303) 740-7100
General Info: Daily, Looseleaf
Subscriptions: Indv. $960

Oliphant Washington Svc.

Publishing Co: Oliphant Washington News Service, PO Box 9808, Washington, DC 20016-8808 Tel # (202) 298-7226; Title Tel # (202) 338-3616
Personnel: Publisher, Editor-John Oliphant
General Info: Yr. Est. 1930, Daily
Subscriptions: Indv. $2,400

Oscar Report   *Business, Association*

Publishing Co: Canadian Assn. of Petroleum Producers, 2100-350 Seventh Ave., SW, Calgary, AB T2P 3N9 Canada Tel # (403) 267-1100; Title Fax # (403) 261-4622
Editorial Description: The focus is on oil spill containment & recovery.
General Info: Yr. Est. 1990, Semi-annually, Trim Size-8½ x 11, 12 pages, 4 Color, Recycled, Saddle-stitched
Subscriptions: Free

Oxy-Fuel News   *Business*

Publishing Co: Hart Publications, 7811 Montrose Rd., Potomac, MD 20854 Tel # (301) 340-2100 Parent Co.-Phillips Business Information, Inc., Potomac
Personnel: Publisher-Frederick Potter, Editor-Shannon Schaffer, Mktg. Dir.-Paul Caplan
Editorial Description: Weekly news and analysis on business, technology and legislation affecting gasoline refining and marketing; extensive price charts and price strategy.
General Info: Weekly
Subscriptions: Indv. $795, Can. $895, For. $895
Acquistions: Publication Sold
List Rental: Rents Lists

PIW's Global Oil Stocks &
Balances

Publishing Co: Petroleum Intelligence Weekly, Inc., 575 Broadway 4th Fl., New York, NY 10012; Title Tel # (212) 941-5500 Title Fax # (212) 941-5509
Personnel: Publisher-Edward Morse, Editor-Jay Bhutani, Circ. Dir.-Anastasia Tasoulis
Editorial Description: Sets the standard for reporting and analysis on the basic building blocks of the world oil market. S&B provides vital transparency, timeliness and insights to the tracking of supply, demand and inventory trends.
General Info: Yr. Est. 1990, Monthly
Subscriptions: Indv. $745, $62/copy
Circulation: Total-300

Permian Basin Petroleum
Industry   *Business*

Publishing Co: Midwest Register Inc., 1120 E. 4th St., Tulsa, OK 74120-3220; Title Tel # (918) 582-2000 Title Fax # (918) 587-9349
Personnel: Publisher/President/Advisor-Will L. Hammack
General Info: Yr. Est. 1945, Annually, 575 pages
Subscriptions: Can. $65, For. $65
Advertising: Inquire for rates.
List Rental: Rents Lists

Permian Basin Report   *Business*

Publishing Co: Petroleum Information Corp., PO Box 2612, Denver, CO 80201-2612; Title Tel # (303) 740-7100
Editorial Description: RRC dists. 7C, 8, 8A, S.E. New Mexico.
General Info: Semi-weekly, Looseleaf
Subscriptions: Indv. $1,680

Permian Basin Rotary
Report   *Business*

Publishing Co: Petroleum Information Corp., PO Box 2612, Denver, CO 80201-2612; Title Tel # (303) 740-7100
Editorial Description: Permian Basin.
General Info: (Formerly West Texas-S.E. New Mexico Rotary Report), Weekly, Looseleaf
Subscriptions: Indv. $480

PetroChemical News
See: CHEMISTRY & CHEMICALS

Petrochemical Industry - Worldwide   *Business*

Publishing Co: Midwest Register Inc., 1120 E. 4th St., Tulsa, OK 74120-3220;
Title Tel # (918) 582-2000 Title Fax # (918) 587-9349
Personnel: Publisher/President/Advisor-Will L. Hammack
General Info: Yr. Est. 1945, Annually, 800 pages
Subscriptions: Can. $75, For. $75, $75/copy
Advertising: Inquire for rates.
List Rental: Rents Lists

Petroconsultants International Oil Letter   *Business*

Publishing Co: Petroconsultants, Inc., 6600 Sands Point Dr # 740619, Houston, TX 77074-3726;
Title Tel # (713) 995-1764 Title Fax # (713) 995-8593
Personnel: Editor-Jay Gallagher
Editorial Description: International oil industry news and developments.
General Info: Yr. Est. 1984, Weekly
Subscriptions: Indv. $1,050, Can. $1,050, For. $1,150

Petroleum Concession Handbook   *Business*

Publishing Co: Barrows Co., Inc., 116 E 66th St, New York, NY 10021-6547;
Title Tel # (212) 772-1199 Title Fax # (212) 288-7242
Personnel: Publisher-G. Barrows, Editor-Gordon Barrows, Circ. Mgr.-L.M. Guerra, Production Mgr.-Kenneth Hussman, Adv. Dir., Art Dir.-Dominique Jeune
Editorial Description: Text of oil laws and concession contracts of various countries. Each country has a separate edition. Maps are included.
General Info: Yr. Est. 1957, Quarterly, Trim Size-8½ x 11, Offset press, 98 pages, No Color, Perfect bound, Looseleaf
Subscriptions: Indv. $4,400
Circulation: Total-10,000
Printing Co: Barrows Co. Wyoming, 700 Main St., Ralston, WY 82440 Tel # (307) 745-3759

Petroleum Information International: Global Coverage   *Business*

Publishing Co: Petroleum Information Corp., PO Box 2612, Denver, CO 80201-2612
Tel # (303) 740-7100
Personnel: Editor-Tom Cheney
Editorial Description: Reports global oil and gas activity.
General Info: Yr. Est. 1994, Monthly, Trim Size-8½ x 11, Color
Subscriptions: Indv. $1,000
Advertising: Inquire for rates.

Petroleum Intelligence Weekly

Publishing Co: Petroleum Intelligence Weekly, Inc., 575 Broadway 4th Fl., New York, NY 10012;
Title Tel # (212) 941-5500 Title Fax # (212) 941-5509
Personnel: Publisher-Edward Morse, Editor-Sarah Miller, Circ. Mgr.-Anastasia Tasoulis
Editorial Description: Recognized as the 'Bible' of the oil industry, PIW features a weekly analysis of major developments, issues and trends of oil and natural gas. For over 25 years, PIW's passion for accuracy has made it the industry standard for those who want the single best source of oil market insights.
General Info: Yr. Est. 1961, Weekly, Trim Size-7¾ x 10¼, 12 pages, Ind/Abs/Online: Petroleum/Energy Business News Index, Color
Subscriptions: Indv. $1,475, $30/copy
List Rental: Rents Lists

Petroleum Legislation
See: LAW

Petroleum Market Intelligence

Publishing Co: Petroleum Intelligence Weekly, Inc., 575 Broadway 4th Fl., New York, NY 10012;
Title Tel # (212) 941-5500 Title Fax # (212) 941-5509
Personnel: Publisher-Edward Morse, Editor-Ira Joseph, Circ. Mgr.-Anastasia Tasoulis
Editorial Description: Provides accurate analysis of regional pricing and production figures and key statistics on the oil market. Included are overviews of regional markets, crude output, spot prices and netbacks.
General Info: Yr. Est. 1987, Monthly, Trim Size-7¾ x 10¼, 12 pages, Color
Subscriptions: Indv. $645, $50/copy

Petroleum Outlook

Publishing Co: Filigree Inc., 25 Diaz St, Stamford, CT 06902-5608; Title Tel # (203) 869-2585
Personnel: Editor-Peter Hunsberger
Editorial Description: Reports on the progress-prospects for 50 fast growing oil production and service companies and on alternate months the outlook for 50 of the largest oil companies.
General Info: Yr. Est. 1948, Monthly, Trim Size-7 x 10, Offset press, 40 pages, ISSN: 0031-6490, No Color
Subscriptions: Indv. $76
Circulation: Total-3,500

Petroleum Taxation/Legislation Report
See: LAW

Pipeline - Worldwide   *Business*

Publishing Co: Midwest Register Inc., 1120 E. 4th St., Tulsa, OK 74120-3220;
Title Tel # (918) 582-2000 Title Fax # (918) 587-9349
Personnel: Publisher/President/Advisor-Will L. Hammack
General Info: Yr. Est. 1945, Annually, 800 pages
Subscriptions: Can. $75, For. $75, $75/copy
Advertising: Inquire for rates.
List Rental: Rents Lists

Platts International Petrochemical Report   *Business*

Publishing Co: McGraw-Hill, 1221 Ave. of the Americas, 36th Fl., New York, NY 10020-1095
Tel # (212) 512-2000 Fax # (212) 512-6590
General Info: Weekly, Ind/Abs/Online: Dialog, Dow Jones, NewsNet, Nexis

Platt's LP Gaswire

Publishing Co: McGraw-Hill, 1221 Ave. of the Americas, 36th Fl., New York, NY 10020-1095
Tel # (212) 512-2000 Fax # (212) 512-6590
General Info: Semi-weekly

Platt's Oil Export/Import Report

Publishing Co: McGraw-Hill, 1221 Ave. of the Americas, 36th Fl., New York, NY 10020-1095
Tel # (212) 512-2000 Fax # (212) 512-6590; Title Tel # (212) 512-6220
Personnel: Publisher-David Smith, Editor in Chief-Joseph Link, Assoc. Ed.-Beth Evans, Circ. Mgr.-Marguerite Stanford
Subscriptions: Indv. $425, For. $560

Platt's Oil Marketing Bulletin

Publishing Co: McGraw-Hill, 1221 Ave. of the Americas, 36th Fl., New York, NY 10020-1095
Tel # (212) 512-2000 Fax # (212) 512-6590; Title Tel # (202) 624-7534
Personnel: Editor-Paula Dwyer
General Info: (Formerly NPN Bulletin), Yr. Est. 1960, Weekly, 8 pages, ISSN: 0277-0415, Ind/Abs/Online: Mead Data Central
Circulation: Total-1,000

Platt's Oilgram Bunkerwire   *Business*

Publishing Co: McGraw-Hill, 1221 Ave. of the Americas, 36th Fl., New York, NY 10020-1095
Tel # (212) 512-2000 Fax # (212) 512-6590
General Info: Semi-weekly

Platt's Oilgram Marketscan European Edition   *Business*

Publishing Co: McGraw-Hill, 1221 Ave. of the Americas, 36th Fl., New York, NY 10020-1095
Tel # (212) 512-2000 Fax # (212) 512-6590
General Info: Daily

Platt's Oilgram Marketscan U.S. Edition

Publishing Co: McGraw-Hill, 1221 Ave. of the Americas, 36th Fl., New York, NY 10020-1095
Tel # (212) 512-2000 Fax # (212) 512-6590
General Info: Daily

Platt's Oilgram News   *Business*

Publishing Co: McGraw-Hill, 1221 Ave. of the Americas, 36th Fl., New York, NY 10020-1095
Fax # (212) 512-6590; Title Tel # (212) 512-2000
Personnel: Publisher-Robert Christie, Editor-Onnic Marashian, Mng. Editor-Robert DiNardo, Circ. Mgr.-Marguerite Stanford
Editorial Description: Daily reporting on oil and gas developments of international significance.
General Info: (Formerly Platt's Oilgram News Service), Yr. Est. 1934, Daily, Trim Size-8½ x 11½, Offset press, 6 pages, ISSN: 0163-1284, Ind/Abs/Online: DIALOG, Dow Jones, NewsNet, Nexis, No Color
Subscriptions: $5/copy

Platt's Oilgram Price Report

Publishing Co: McGraw-Hill, 1221 Ave. of the Americas, 36th Fl., New York, NY 10020-1095
Fax # (212) 512-6590; Title Tel # (212) 512-2000
Personnel: Publisher-Robert Christie, Editor in Chief-Joseph Link, Editor-C. Peckworth, Circ. Mgr.-Marguerite Stanford
Editorial Description: Prices and marketing data worldwide-information on buys, sales, trades.
General Info: Yr. Est. 1923, Daily, ISSN: 0162-1292, Ind/Abs/Online: DIALOG, Dow Jones, NewsNet, Nexis
Subscriptions: Indv. $1,117

Platt's Petrochemicalscan   *Business*

Publishing Co: McGraw-Hill, 1221 Ave. of the Americas, 36th Fl., New York, NY 10020-1095
Tel # (212) 512-2000 Fax # (212) 512-6590
General Info: Weekly

Platt's Polymerscan   *Business*

Publishing Co: McGraw-Hill, 1221 Ave. of the Americas, 36th Fl., New York, NY 10020-1095
Tel # (212) 512-2000 Fax # (212) 512-6590
General Info: Weekly

Prospect Review
  See: ENERGY

Quad Report, The
  See: ENERGY

Quad Special Reports, The
  See: ENERGY

Rebounder

Publishing Co: Asphalt Rubber Producers Group, 312 Massachusetts Ave NE, Washington, DC 20002-5702; Title Tel # (602) 955-1141
Personnel: Editor-Al France
Editorial Description: Educational newsletter about asphalt-rubber products.
General Info: Yr. Est. 1985, Quarterly

Refining & Gas Processing Worldwide   *Business*

Publishing Co: Midwest Register Inc., 1120 E. 4th St., Tulsa, OK 74120-3220; Title Tel # (918) 582-2000 Title Fax # (918) 587-9349
Personnel: Publisher/President/Advisor-Will L. Hammack
General Info: Yr. Est. 1945, Annually, 800 pages
Subscriptions: Can. $75, For. $75, $75/copy
Advertising: Inquire for rates.
List Rental: Rents Lists

Regulation of the Gas Industry   *Business*

Publishing Co: Matthew Bender & Co., 11 Penn Plaza, New York, NY 10001-2006 Tel # (212) 967-7707 Fax # (212) 244-3188
Editorial Description: A vital work for gas industry officials, attorneys, regulators or administrators.
General Info: Yr. Est. 1981, Irregular, Looseleaf

Rocky Mountain Newsletter   *Business*

Publishing Co: Petroleum Information Corp., PO Box 2612, Denver, CO 80201-2612; Title Tel # (303) 740-7100
Personnel: Editor-J. M. Anderson
General Info: Daily
Subscriptions: Indv. $888

Rocky Mountain Region Report   *Business*

Publishing Co: Petroleum Information Corp., PO Box 2612, Denver, CO 80201-2612; Title Tel # (303) 740-7100
Personnel: Editor-J. M. Anderson
Editorial Description: Regional oil industry information.
General Info: Daily, Looseleaf
Subscriptions: Indv. $1,560

Rocky Mountain Region Rotary Report   *Business*

Publishing Co: Petroleum Information Corp., PO Box 2612, Denver, CO 80201-2612; Title Tel # (303) 740-7100
General Info: Weekly, Looseleaf
Subscriptions: Indv. $732

Rule/Howard Oil and Gas Analyst
  See: INVESTMENT

SW Texas Coast Report   *Business*

Publishing Co: Petroleum Information Corp., PO Box 2612, Denver, CO 80201-2612; Title Tel # (303) 740-7100
Editorial Description: RRC District 1.
General Info: Weekly, Looseleaf
Subscriptions: Indv. $960

Scan

Publishing Co: Shell Oil Company, Shell Chemical Co., 50 W 50th St, New York, NY 10112-1507 Tel # (212) 261-5640; Title Tel # (212) 581-0380
Editorial Description: Petroleum industry and agricultural chemistry news and developments.
General Info: Monthly
Circulation: Total-25,000

Shreveport New Locations   *Business*

Publishing Co: Petroleum Information Corp., PO Box 2612, Denver, CO 80201-2612; Title Tel # (303) 740-7100
General Info: Daily, Looseleaf
Subscriptions: Indv. $1,104

Shreveport Report   *Business*

Publishing Co: Petroleum Information Corp., PO Box 2612, Denver, CO 80201-2612 Tel # (303) 740-7100; Title Tel # (313) 740-7100
Editorial Description: RRC Districts 5 & 6--Northern LA, MS, AR, AL, GA, FL, & SC
General Info: Daily, Looseleaf
Subscriptions: Indv. $2,460

South, Central Coast & Southwest Texas Report   *Business*

Publishing Co: Petroleum Information Corp., PO Box 2612, Denver, CO 80201-2612; Title Tel # (303) 740-7100
Editorial Description: RRC Districts 1, 2, 4.
General Info: Looseleaf
Subscriptions: Indv. $1,608

South Texas Report   *Business*

Publishing Co: Petroleum Information Corp., PO Box 2612, Denver, CO 80201-2612; Title Tel # (303) 740-7100
Editorial Description: RRC District 4.
General Info: Weekly, Looseleaf
Subscriptions: Indv. $900

Southeast New Mexico Report   *Business*

Publishing Co: Petroleum Information Corp., PO Box 2612, Denver, CO 80201-2612; Title Tel # (303) 740-7100
General Info: Weekly, Looseleaf
Subscriptions: Indv. $1,056

Southeast States Petroleum Industry   *Business*

Publishing Co: Midwest Register Inc., 1120 E. 4th St., Tulsa, OK 74120-3220; Title Tel # (918) 582-2000 Title Fax # (918) 587-9349
Personnel: Publisher/President/Advisor-Will L. Hammack
General Info: (Formerly Southeast US Petroleum Industry), Annually, 800 pages
Subscriptions: Can. $65, For. $65, $65/copy
Advertising: Inquire for rates.
List Rental: Rents Lists

Southeastern Edition   *Business*

Publishing Co: Petroleum Information Corp., PO Box 2612, Denver, CO 80201-2612; Title Tel # (303) 740-7100
Editorial Description: Eastern Colo., W. Neb.
General Info: Daily, Looseleaf
Subscriptions: Indv. $960

Southeastern States Report   *Business*

Publishing Co: Petroleum Information Corp., PO Box 2612, Denver, CO 80201-2612; Title Tel # (303) 740-7100
Editorial Description: MS, AL, GA, FL, SC.
General Info: Semi-weekly, Looseleaf
Subscriptions: Indv. $1,380

Southern Region Rotary Report   *Business*

Publishing Co: Petroleum Information Corp., PO Box 2612, Denver, CO 80201-2612; Title Tel # (303) 740-7100
Editorial Description: Covers Mississippi, Louisiana, Arkansas, Alabama, Florida, and Georgia.
General Info: Weekly, Looseleaf
Subscriptions: Indv. $1,248

Southern Rockies Report   *Business*

Publishing Co: Petroleum Information Corp., PO Box 2612, Denver, CO 80201-2612; Title Tel # (303) 740-7100
Editorial Description: CO, W. Neb., AZ, UT, N. New Mex., NV.
General Info: Daily, Looseleaf
Subscriptions: Indv. $1,320

Southern Rockies and Wyoming   *Business*

Publishing Co: Petroleum Information Corp., PO Box 2612, Denver, CO 80201-2612; Title Tel # (303) 740-7100
General Info: Daily, Looseleaf
Subscriptions: Indv. $1,440

Supply, Distribution, Manufacturing & Service — Business

Publishing Co: Midwest Register Inc., 1120 E. 4th St., Tulsa, OK 74120-3220;
Title Tel # (918) 582-2000 Title Fax # (918) 587-9349
Personnel: Publisher/President/Advisor-Will L. Hammack
General Info: (Formerly Supply and Distribution-Worldwide Petroleum Indusry), Yr. Est. 1945, Annually, 1,000 pages
Subscriptions: Can. $115, For. $115, $115/copy
Advertising: Inquire for rates.
List Rental: Rents Lists

Taxation of Mining Operations
See: TAXES

Texas Offshore Report — Business

Publishing Co: Petroleum Information Corp., PO Box 2612, Denver, CO 80201-2612;
Title Tel # (303) 740-7100
General Info: Daily, Looseleaf
Subscriptions: Indv. $780

Texas Panhandle Hi-Plains New Location Service — Business

Publishing Co: Petroleum Information Corp., PO Box 2612, Denver, CO 80201-2612;
Title Tel # (303) 740-7100
General Info: Daily, Looseleaf
Subscriptions: Indv. $600

Texas Panhandle Hi-Plains Report — Business

Publishing Co: Petroleum Information Corp., PO Box 2612, Denver, CO 80201-2612;
Title Tel # (303) 740-7100
Editorial Description: Texas and OK panhandles, N.E. New Mexico, S.E. Colo., W. Kansas.
General Info: Daily, Looseleaf
Subscriptions: Indv. $1,320

Texas Petroleum Industry — Business

Publishing Co: Midwest Register Inc., 1120 E. 4th St., Tulsa, OK 74120-3220;
Title Tel # (918) 582-2000 Title Fax # (918) 587-9349
Personnel: Publisher/President/Advisor-Will L. Hammack
General Info: Yr. Est. 1945, Annually, 1,100 pages
Subscriptions: Indv. $65, Can. $65, For. $65, $65/copy
Advertising: Inquire for rates.
List Rental: Rents Lists

Texas Petroleum Retailer

Publishing Co: Texas Petroleum Retailer, PO Box 9445, Austin, TX 78766-9445
Tel # (512) 453-9787
General Info: Yr. Est. 1949, Monthly
Subscriptions: Indv. $6
Circulation: Total-1,600
Advertising: Inquire for rates.

Tulsa Letter

Publishing Co: Petroleum Equipment Inst., 6514 E. 69th St., Tulsa, OK 74133-1729
Tel # (918) 494-9696 Fax # (918) 491-9895; Title Tel # (918) 743-9941

Underground Storage Tank News — Business

Publishing Co: Arizona Dept. of Environmental Quality, OCSEA Section, 3033 N. Central Ave, Phoenix, AZ 85012 Tel # (602) 207-2300 Fax # (602) 207-4872; Title Tel # (602) 207-4857 Title Fax # (602) 207-4346
Personnel: Publisher-Royce Flora, Feature Ed.-Tara Roesler, Editor, Circ. Mgr.-Staci Munday
Editorial Description: Articles relating to underground storage tank regulations; environmental legislation(Arizona & Federal); case studies.
General Info: Yr. Est. 1992, Quarterly, Trim Size-8½ x 11, Desktop press, 8 pages, 2 Color, Coated, Saddle-stitched
Subscriptions: Free
Circulation: Total-3,500, Readership-3,500
Printing Co: K & M Printing, 75 Baseline Road, Suite D-27, Gilbert, AZ 85233 Tel # (602) 926-0123, Fax # (602) 926-3097

U.S. Oil Week — Business

Publishing Co: Capitol Publications, Inc., 1101 King St., Ste. 444, Alexandria, VA 22314-2968
Fax # (703) 739-6501; Title Tel # (703) 683-4100 Title Fax # (703) 739-6437
Personnel: Publisher-Chris Vestal, Editor-Jack Peckham, Circ. Mgr.-Liz Soper, Art Dir.-Judy Denton, Production Mgr., Mktg. Dir., Promotion Dir.-Richard Rosenthal
Editorial Description: Industry developments & the latest marketing strategies for oil marketers.
General Info: Yr. Est. 1967, Weekly, Trim Size-8½ x 11, Sheetfed press, 16 pages, ISSN: 0502-9767, Ind/Abs/Online: Newsnet, 2 Color, Newsprint
Subscriptions: Indv. $267, Can. $267, For. $319, $10/copy
Acquisitions: Publication Bought
List Rental: Actives: $185/M, Expires: $185/M
Printing Co: Capitol Publications, Inc., 1101 King St., Ste. 444, Alexandria, VA 22314-2968
Tel # (703) 683-4100, Fax # (703) 739-6501

Upper Texas Coast Report — Business

Publishing Co: Petroleum Information Corp., PO Box 2612, Denver, CO 80201-2612;
Title Tel # (303) 740-7100
Editorial Description: RRC District 3.
General Info: (Formerly Upper Texas GC Report), Weekly, Looseleaf
Subscriptions: Indv. $1,368

Weekly Bulletin — Business

Publishing Co: American Petroleum Inst., 1220 L St. , N. W., Dept. Publication, Washington, DC 20005-4070; Title Tel # (202) 682-8378 Title Fax # (202) 962-4776
Personnel: Circ. Mgr.-Geneva Redder-McKinney
Editorial Description: Statistics on production, stocks & imports of crude oil & major petroleum products.
General Info: Yr. Est. 1920, Weekly, Trim Size-8½ x 11, Offset press, 8 pages, No Color
Subscriptions: Indv. $110, Can. $121, For. $138
Circulation: (100% controlled), Total-500

Weekly Canadian Progress Report — Business

Publishing Co: Petroleum Information Canada Ltd., Suite 500 Bow Valley Sq. III, 255 5th Ave., S.W., Calgary, AB T2P 3G6 Canada; Title Tel # (403) 263-3822
General Info: Weekly, Mimeo press, 130 pages, Ind/Abs/Online: Arctic Islands in one report.', Looseleaf
Subscriptions: $130/copy

Weekly Progress Report-Alberta — Business

Publishing Co: Petroleum Information Canada Ltd., Suite 500 Bow Valley Sq. III, 255 5th Ave., S.W., Calgary, AB T2P 3G6 Canada; Title Tel # (403) 263-3822
General Info: Weekly, Looseleaf

Weekly Progress Report-British Columbia/Frontier — Business

Publishing Co: Petroleum Information Canada Ltd., Suite 500 Bow Valley Sq. III, 255 5th Ave., S.W., Calgary, AB T2P 3G6 Canada; Title Tel # (403) 263-3822
General Info: Weekly, Looseleaf

Weekly Progress Report-Saskatchewan and Manitoba — Business

Publishing Co: Petroleum Information Canada Ltd., Suite 500 Bow Valley Sq. III, 255 5th Ave., S.W., Calgary, AB T2P 3G6 Canada; Title Tel # (403) 263-3822
General Info: Weekly, Looseleaf

Weekly Status List-Alberta — Business

Publishing Co: Petroleum Information Canada Ltd., Suite 500 Bow Valley Sq. III, 255 5th Ave., S.W., Calgary, AB T2P 3G6 Canada; Title Tel # (403) 263-3822
General Info: Weekly, Looseleaf

Weekly Status List-All Regions Canada — Business

Publishing Co: Petroleum Information Canada Ltd., Suite 500 Bow Valley Sq. III, 255 5th Ave., S.W., Calgary, AB T2P 3G6 Canada; Title Tel # (403) 263-3822
Editorial Description: Doesn't include Ontario.
General Info: Weekly, Looseleaf

Weekly Status List-British Columbia — Business

Publishing Co: Petroleum Information Canada Ltd., Suite 500 Bow Valley Sq. III, 255 5th Ave., S.W., Calgary, AB T2P 3G6 Canada; Title Tel # (403) 263-3822
General Info: Weekly, Looseleaf

Weekly Status List-Frontier Areas — Business

Publishing Co: Petroleum Information Canada Ltd., Suite 500 Bow Valley Sq. III, 255 5th Ave., S.W., Calgary, AB T2P 3G6 Canada; Title Tel # (403) 263-3822
Editorial Description: Including Yukon, Arctic Islands, N.W. Territories, and offshore.
General Info: (Formerly Weekly Status List Northwest Territories), Weekly, Looseleaf

Weekly Status List-Saskatchewan and Manitoba — Business

Publishing Co: Petroleum Information Canada Ltd., Suite 500 Bow Valley Sq. III, 255 5th Ave., S.W., Calgary, AB T2P 3G6 Canada; Title Tel # (403) 263-3822
General Info: Weekly, Looseleaf

Well Service Market Report   *Business*

Publishing Co: RJM Communications, PO Box 6645, Lubbock, TX 79493-6645 Tel # (806) 741-1531 Fax # (806) 741-1553
Editorial Description: Focuses on business and marketing coverage of oil and gas well service markets worldwide.
General Info: Yr. Est. 1991, Monthly, Trim Size-8½ x 11, 8 pages, ISSN: 1058-0646
Subscriptions: Indv. $200, For. $240

West Central and North Texas Rotary Reports   *Business*

Publishing Co: Petroleum Information Corp., PO Box 2612, Denver, CO 80201-2612; Title Tel # (303) 740-7100
Editorial Description: RRC dists. 7B29.
General Info: (Formerly Abilene, Wichita Falls District Rotary Reports), Weekly, Looseleaf
Subscriptions: Indv. $420

West Central Texas Report   *Business*

Publishing Co: Petroleum Information Corp., PO Box 2612, Denver, CO 80201-2612; Title Tel # (303) 740-7100
Editorial Description: RRC dist. 7B.
General Info: Weekly, Looseleaf
Subscriptions: Indv. $1,056

West Coast Region Report   *Business*

Publishing Co: Petroleum Information Corp., PO Box 2612, Denver, CO 80201-2612; Title Tel # (303) 740-7100
Editorial Description: California, Oregon, Washington & Pacific Offshore.
General Info: Daily, Looseleaf
Subscriptions: Indv. $588

West Coast Region Rotary Report   *Business*

Publishing Co: Petroleum Information Corp., PO Box 2612, Denver, CO 80201-2612; Title Tel # (303) 740-7100
Editorial Description: Calif., Ore., Wash. and offshore.
General Info: Weekly, Looseleaf
Subscriptions: Indv. $420

West Kentucky, Indiana Report   *Business*

Publishing Co: Petroleum Information Corp., PO Box 2612, Denver, CO 80201-2612; Title Tel # (303) 740-7100
General Info: Weekly, Looseleaf
Subscriptions: Indv. $480

West Texas Report   *Business*

Publishing Co: Petroleum Information Corp., PO Box 2612, Denver, CO 80201-2612; Title Tel # (303) 740-7100
Editorial Description: RRC dists. 7C, 8, 8A.
General Info: Weekly, Looseleaf
Subscriptions: Indv. $1,188

Western States Petroleum Industry   *Business*

Publishing Co: Midwest Register Inc., 1120 E. 4th St., Tulsa, OK 74120-3220; Title Tel # (918) 582-2000 Title Fax # (918) 587-9349
Personnel: Publisher/President/Advisor-Will L. Hammack
General Info: Yr. Est. 1945, Annually, 650 pages
Subscriptions: Can. $65, For. $65, $65/copy
Advertising: Inquire for rates.
List Rental: Rents Lists

World Gas Intelligence

Publishing Co: Petroleum Intelligence Weekly, Inc., 575 Broadway 4th Fl., New York, NY 10012; Title Tel # (212) 941-5500 Title Fax # (212) 941-5509
Personnel: Publisher-Edward Morse, Editor-Alan Townsend, Circ. Mgr.-Anastasia Tasoulis
Editorial Description: Offers incisive and authoratative news and analysis of the gas industry developments worldwide. WGI explores in detail the pipeline gas supply and use, along with current historical information for eight key markets.
General Info: Yr. Est. 1990, Monthly
Subscriptions: Indv. $755, $63/copy

World Geophysical News
See: GEOPHYSICS

Wyoming Geological Association Oil & Gas Fields Guide Book/Symposium
See: ENERGY

Wyoming Report   *Business*

Publishing Co: Petroleum Information Corp., PO Box 2612, Denver, CO 80201-2612; Title Tel # (303) 740-7100
General Info: Daily, Looseleaf
Subscriptions: Indv. $1,320

PHILANTHROPY

AHP Connect
See: HOSPITALS & NURSING HOMES

AIDS/STD News Report   *Business*

Publishing Co: CD Publications, 8204 Fenton St., Silver Spring, MD 20910-4571; Title Tel # (301) 588-6380 Title Fax # (301) 588-6385
Personnel: Publisher-Mike Gerecht, Editor-Jim Arvantes, Circ. Mgr.-Kurt Eisentraut, Mktg. Dir.-Joyce Meals
Editorial Description: Disseminates information about funding for AIDS programs.
General Info: (Formerly AIDS Funding Report; AIDS News Alert), Yr. Est. 1993, Semi-monthly, Trim Size-8½ x 11, Sheetfed press, 16 pages, ISSN: 1083-3064, No Color, Matte, Other
Subscriptions: Indv. $259, Can. $269, For. $299, $15/copy
List Rental: List Management Co.: Manager: Amy Seyler; Washington Advertising Service, 8204 Fenton St., Silver Spring, MD 20910 Tel # (301) 588-7920, Fax # (301) 588-6385, Actives: 4,953, $150/M, Expires: 1,082, $150/M

Aid for Education Report
See: EDUCATION

American Marketplace
See: ADVERTISING & MARKETING

Beyond the Counter
See: BUSINESS & INDUSTRY

Board & Administrator (Nonprofit Edition)
See: MANAGEMENT

CBE Report
See: EDUCATION

CJF Endowment Review

Publishing Co: Council of Jewish Federations, 730 Broadway, 2nd Fl., New York, NY 10003; Title Tel # (212) 475-5000
General Info: Yr. Est. 1983, Quarterly, Offset press, 8 pages, 2 Color
Circulation: Total-25,000

CSFA News
See: EDUCATION

Center for Self Sufficiency Update   *Consumer*

Publishing Co: Prosperity & Profits Unlimited, PO Box 416, Denver, CO 80201-0416; Title Tel # (303) 575-5676
Personnel: Publisher-A. Doyle
Editorial Description: Ideas and recipes for self sufficiency.
General Info: Yr. Est. 1985, Annually, ISSN: 0736-3044
Subscriptions: Indv. $2, Inst. $2, Can. $3, For. $5, $2/copy

Charitable Gift Planning News   *Business*

Publishing Co: Charitable Gift Planning News, 41 Sutter St Ste 1129, San Francisco, CA 94104-4903; Title Tel # (214) 978-3326 Title Fax # (214) 978-3395
General Info: Yr. Est. 1983, Monthly
Subscriptions: Indv. $132

Charitable Giving Tax Service   *Business*

Publishing Co: R&R Newkirk, 8695 Archer Ave Ste 10, Willow Springs, IL 60480-1260; Title Tel # (312) 306-9531
Personnel: Publisher-Marc Carmichael
Editorial Description: 3-volume reference library with updates. Sales oriented. Covers all aspects of planned giving & charitable estate planning.
General Info: Yr. Est. 1977, Bi-monthly, Looseleaf

Charity Rating Guide & Watchdog Report   *Business, Consumer*

Publishing Co: American Institute of Philanthropy, 393 N. Euclid Ave., Ste. 236, St. Louis, MO 63108; Title Tel # (314) 454-3040 Title Fax # (314) 454-9544
Editorial Description: Ratings of over 300 charities and useful consumer alerts for charitable donors.
General Info: Yr. Est. 1993, Quarterly
Subscriptions: Indv. $35, Inst. $100

Children & Youth Funding
Report — *Business*

Publishing Co: CD Publications, 8204 Fenton St., Silver Spring, MD 20910-4571;
Title Tel # (301) 588-6380 Title Fax # (301) 588-6385
Personnel: Publisher-Mike Gerecht, Editor-Mark Kuhn, Circ. Mgr.-Kurt Eisentraut, Mktg. Dir.-Joyce Meals
Editorial Description: Reports of sources and statistics on funding for children's and youth programs.
General Info: Yr. Est. 1992, Semi-monthly, Trim Size-8½ x 11, Sheetfed press, 18 pages, ISSN: 1063-892X, No Color, Matte, Perfect bound
Subscriptions: Indv. $259, Can. $269, For. $299, $15/copy
List Rental: List Management Co.: Manager: Amy Seyler; Washington Advertising Service, 8204 Fenton St., Silver Spring, MD 20910 Tel # (301) 588-7920, Fax # (301) 588-6385, Actives: 12,984, $150/M, Expires: 2,818, $150/M

Commentary — *Business, Consumer*

Publishing Co: Columbus Foundation, 1234 E Broad St, Columbus, OH 43205-1453;
Title Tel # (614) 251-4000 Title Fax # (614) 251-4009
Personnel: Editor-Carol Harmon
Editorial Description: To inform about ways of giving & show impact of grant-making activities.
General Info: Yr. Est. 1943, Quarterly, Trim Size-8½ x 11, Sheetfed press, 8 pages, 2 Color, Newsprint, Saddle-stitched
Circulation: (100% controlled), Total-12,500
Printing Co: Century Graphics, 5178 Sinclair Rd, Columbus, OH 43229-5458 Tel # (614) 431-1111

Community Health
Funding Report — *Business*

Publishing Co: CD Publications, 8204 Fenton St., Silver Spring, MD 20910-4571;
Title Tel # (301) 588-6380 Title Fax # (301) 588-6385
Personnel: Publisher-Mike Gerecht, Editor-Aaron Leibel, Circ. Mgr.-Kurt Eisentraut, Art Dir.-Joyce Meals
Editorial Description: Focuses on community health funding issues.
General Info: Yr. Est. 1990, Semi-monthly, Trim Size-8½ x 11, Sheetfed press, 16 pages, ISSN: 1050-3250, No Color, Matte
Subscriptions: Indv. $259, Can. $269, For. $299, $15/copy
List Rental: Actives: $150/M, Hotline: 17,886, Expires: 2,727, $150/M

Community Spirit — *Consumer*

Publishing Co: Community Spirit, 34-12 113th St., Apt. 12-E, Corona, NY 11368;
Title Tel # (718) 672-0976
Editorial Description: Covering people who are contributing to the community--looking for nominations in this field, as well.
General Info: Monthly

Corporate Community Relations Letter
See: BUSINESS & INDUSTRY

Corporate Giving Watch

Publishing Co: Taft Group, 835 Penobscot Bldg., Detroit, MI 48226-4094 Tel # (313) 961-2242
Parent Co.-Gale Research, Inc., Detroit; Title Tel # (301) 816-0210 Title Fax # (301) 816-0811
Personnel: Publisher-Robert Elster, Editor-Taghrid Hanna, Editor-Karin Koek, Editorial Asst.-Linda Thurn
Editorial Description: News & ideas for nonprofit organizations seeking corporate funds.
General Info: Yr. Est. 1981, Monthly, Trim Size-8½ x 11, Sheetfed press, 16 pages, ISSN: 1061-1258, 2 Color, Newsprint, Saddle-stitched
Subscriptions: Indv. $139
Circulation: Total-3,500
List Rental: Actives: $85/M

Corporate Philanthropy
Report — *Business*

Publishing Co: Capitol Publications, Inc., 1101 King St., Ste. 444, Alexandria, VA 22314-2968;
Title Tel # (703) 683-4100 Title Fax # (703) 739-6501
Personnel: Publisher-Cynthia Carter, Circ. Mgr.-Peggy Dwyer, Production Mgr.-Billy Adams, Art Dir.-Linda McDonald, Mktg. Dir.-Mary Lou Probka, Promotion Dir.-Yvette Giller
Editorial Description: Essential funding information for non-profit and corporate professionals. News on who's funding what & why.
General Info: 10x/yr., Trim Size-8½ x 11, 12 pages, ISSN: 0885-8365, 2 Color
Subscriptions: Indv. $200, Inst. $165
Circulation: Total-1,800
List Rental: Actives: $150/M
Printing Co: Capitol Publications, Inc., 1101 King St., Ste. 444, Alexandria, VA 22314-2968 Tel # (703) 683-4100, Fax # (703) 739-6501

Council Columns — *Association*

Publishing Co: Council on Foundations, Inc., 1828 L St NW Ste 300, Washington, DC 20036-5104;
Title Tel # (202) 466-6512 Title Fax # (202) 785-3926
Personnel: Editor, Assoc. Ed.-Margaret Schmid Odell
Editorial Description: Council columns reports on council initiatives, provides hands on grantmaking information and promotes activities of member foundations and corporate giving programs. Reports on issues affecting the field of organized philanthropy.
General Info: (Formerly Council on Foundations Newsletter), Yr. Est. 1949, Bi-weekly, Offset press, 4 pages, 2 Color, Newsprint
Subscriptions: Indv. $60, Free With Membership
Circulation: Total-8,100
Printing Co: Corporate Press, 403 Brightseat Rd., Landover, MD 20785-4706 Tel # (301) 499-9200, Fax # (301) 499-5435

Coupon Treasure Hunt Newsletter
See: HOME ECONOMICS

Crime Prevention News
See: LAW ENFORCEMENT & PENOLOGY

Development Director's
Letter — *Business*

Publishing Co: CD Publications, 8204 Fenton St., Silver Spring, MD 20910-4571;
Title Tel # (301) 588-6380 Title Fax # (301) 588-6385
Personnel: Publisher-Mike Gerecht, Editor-Dave Kittross, Circ. Mgr.-Kurt Eisentraut, Mktg. Dir.-Joyce Meals
Editorial Description: Proven grantseeking tips and fundraising strategies for nonprofit/government administrators.
General Info: Yr. Est. 1995, Monthly, Trim Size-8½ x 11, Sheetfed press, 10 pages, ISSN: 1084-6204, No Color, Matte, Other
Subscriptions: Indv. $129, Can. $139, For. $169, $15/copy
List Rental: Rents Lists

Dimensions — *Association*

Publishing Co: National Catholic Development Conference, 86 Front St, Hempstead, NY 11550-3617; Title Tel # (516) 481-6000 Title Fax # (516) 489-9287
Personnel: Editor-Sean Patrick Dolan
Editorial Description: Newsletter on Association News & News in Fund Raising.
General Info: Yr. Est. 1968, Monthly, Trim Size-8½ x 11, Letrpr. press, 16 pages, 2 Color, Matte, Saddle-stitched
Subscriptions: Free With Membership
Circulation: Total-1,000
Advertising: Inquire for rates.

Disability Funding News — *Business*

Publishing Co: CD Publications, 8204 Fenton St., Silver Spring, MD 20910-4571;
Title Tel # (301) 588-6380 Title Fax # (301) 588-6385
Personnel: Publisher-Mike Gerecht, Editor-Tim Breen, Circ. Mgr.-Kurt Eisentraut, Mktg. Dir.-Joyce Meals
Editorial Description: Information on funding programs for disabled persons.
General Info: Yr. Est. 1993, Semi-monthly, Trim Size-8½ x 11, Sheetfed press, 16 pages, ISSN: 1069-1359, No Color, Matte
Subscriptions: Indv. $259, Can. $269, For. $299, $15/copy
List Rental: List Management Co.: Manager: Amy Seyler; Washington Advertising Service, 8204 Fenton St., Silver Spring, MD 20910 Tel # (301) 588-7920, Fax # (301) 588-6385, Actives: 9,415, $150/M, Expires: 1,410, $150/M

Dollar Stretching Ideas — *Consumer*

Publishing Co: Economics Press, Inc., 12 Daniel Rd., Fairfield, NJ 07004-2565
Fax # (201) 227-9742; Title Tel # (201) 227-1224 Title Fax # (201) 227-9742
Personnel: Publisher-John Beckley, Editor-Robert Guder, Circ. Mgr.-Anne Lanahan, Production Mgr.-Matt Farley, Art Dir.-Charles Palminteri, Promotion Dir.-Diane Cody
Editorial Description: Practical advice for saving and spending wisely.
General Info: Yr. Est. 1974, 13x/yr., Trim Size-7 x 8½, Sheetfed press, 4 pages, 2 Color, Newsprint
Subscriptions: Indv. $38
Circulation: Total-35,000
List Rental: List Management Co.: Manager: Michael Korman; Names in the News, 411 Theodore Fremd Ave., Rye, NY 10580 Tel # (914) 925-2400
Printing Co: Beckley Press, 2 Sperry Rd, Fairfield, NJ 07004-2056 Tel # (201) 227-6350

Education Grants Alert — *Business*

Publishing Co: Capitol Publications, Inc., 1101 King St., Ste. 444, Alexandria, VA 22314-2968
Fax # (703) 739-6501; Title Tel # (703) 683-4100 Title Fax # (703) 739-6437
Personnel: Publisher-Cynthia Carter, Exec. Ed.-Joe McGavin, Circ. Mgr.-Peggy Dwyer, Production Mgr.-Billy Adams, Art Dir.-Linda McDonald, Mktg. Dir.-Mary Lou Probka, Promotion Dir.-Yvette Giller
Editorial Description: Info on federal and private funding opportunities for K-12 programs. Subscribers get funding alerts weeks--even months--before they're announced.
General Info: Yr. Est. 1991, Weekly, Trim Size-8½ x 11, 6 pages, ISSN: 1056-2656, Color-cover
Subscriptions: Indv. $299, Inst. $299
List Rental: Actives: $150/M
Printing Co: Capitol Publications, Inc., 1101 King St., Ste. 444, Alexandria, VA 22314-2968 Tel # (703) 683-4100, Fax # (703) 739-6501

FRI Monthly Portfolio — *Association*

Publishing Co: Taft Group, 835 Penobscot Bldg., Detroit, MI 48226-4094 Tel # (313) 961-2242
Parent Co.-Gale Research, Inc., Detroit; Title Tel # (301) 816-0210
Personnel: Publisher-Mark Scott, Editor-Jill Johnson
Editorial Description: Professional fund-raising techniques for development officers of nonprofit institutions.
General Info: Yr. Est. 1962, Monthly, Trim Size-8½ x 11, Offset press, 8 pages, ISSN: 0014-6137, 2 Color
Subscriptions: Indv. $75, $5/copy
List Rental: Rents Lists

FRM Weekly — *Business*

Publishing Co: Hoke Communications, Inc., 224 Seventh St., Garden City, NY 11530-5771;
Title Tel # (516) 746-6700 Title Fax # (516) 294-8141
Personnel: Publisher-Henry Hoke, III, Editor-William Olcott, City Ed.-Stu Boysen, Entertainment Ed.-Rosemarie Varonier, Promotion Dir.-Liz Gabriel
Editorial Description: News affecting fund raising by non-profits, including legislation, postal matters.
General Info: Yr. Est. 1977, Weekly, Offset press, 6 pages
Subscriptions: Indv. $115
Circulation: Total-439

Families in Crisis Funding Report
See: FAMILY

Federal Assistance Monitor
Business

Publishing Co: CD Publications, 8204 Fenton St., Silver Spring, MD 20910-4571; Title Tel # (301) 588-6380 Title Fax # (301) 588-6385
Personnel: Publisher-Mike Gerecht, Editor-Dave Kittross, Promotion Dir.-Joyce Meals
Editorial Description: Covers federal regulations, funding availability, legislative developments affecting funding of social/economic programs.
General Info: Yr. Est. 1986, Semi-monthly, Trim Size-8½ x 11, Sheetfed press, 18 pages, ISSN: 1050-3242, No Color, Matte, Other
Subscriptions: Indv. $259, Can. $269, For. $299, $15/copy
List Rental: List Management Co.: Manager: Amy Seyler; Washington Advertising Service, 8204 Fenton St., Silver Spring, MD 20910 Tel # (301) 588-7920, Fax # (301) 588-6385, Actives: 20,474, $150/M, Expires: 6,011, $150/M

Federal Grants & Contracts Weekly
Business

Publishing Co: Capitol Publications, Inc., 1101 King St., Ste. 444, Alexandria, VA 22314-2968; Title Tel # (703) 683-4100 Title Fax # (703) 739-6501
Personnel: Publisher-Cynthia Carter, Editor-Susan Wade, Exec. Ed.-Joe McGavin, Circ. Mgr.-Peggy Dwyer, Production Mgr.-Billy Adams, Art Dir.-Linda Mcdonald, Mktg. Dir.-Mary Lou Probka, Promotion Dir.-Yvette Giller
Editorial Description: The lastest funding announcements of federal grants for project opportunitites in research, training & services.
General Info: Yr. Est. 1977, Weekly, Trim Size-8½ x 11, 10 pages, ISSN: 0194-2247, Ind/Abs/Online: NewsNet, Color-cover
Subscriptions: Indv. $369, Inst. $369
Acquistions: Publication Bought
List Rental: Actives: $150/M
Printing Co: Capitol Publications, Inc., 1101 King St., Ste. 444, Alexandria, VA 22314-2968 Tel # (703) 683-4100, Fax # (703) 739-6501

Foundation & Corporate Grants Alert
Business

Publishing Co: Capitol Publications, Inc., 1101 King St., Ste. 444, Alexandria, VA 22314-2968; Title Tel # (703) 683-4100 Title Fax # (703) 739-6501
Personnel: Publisher-Cynthia Carter, Exec. Ed.-Joe McGarin, Circ. Mgr.-Peggy Dwyer, Production Mgr.-Billy Adams, Art Dir.-Linda McDonald, Mktg. Dir.-Mary Lou Probka, Promotion Dir.-Yvette Giller
Editorial Description: A complete guide for non-profit organizations. Tracks developments & trends in funding & provides notification of changes in foundations' funding priorities.
General Info: Yr. Est. 1992, Monthly, Trim Size-8½ x 11, 12 pages, ISSN: 1062-4686, Color-cover
Subscriptions: Indv. $245
List Rental: Actives: $150/M
Printing Co: Capitol Publications, Inc., 1101 King St., Ste. 444, Alexandria, VA 22314-2968 Tel # (703) 683-4100, Fax # (703) 739-6501

Foundation Giving Watch
Business

Publishing Co: Taft Group, 835 Penobscot Bldg., Detroit, MI 48226-4094 Tel # (313) 961-2242 Parent Co.-Gale Research, Inc., Detroit; Title Tel # (301) 816-0210 Title Fax # (301) 816-0811
Personnel: Publisher-Mark Scott, Editor-Taghrid Barron
Editorial Description: Comprehensive analysis of foundation funding priorities & grantmaking organizations.
General Info: Yr. Est. 1981, Monthly, Trim Size-8½ x 11, Sheetfed press, 20 pages, ISSN: 0741-7004, 2 Color, Newsprint
Subscriptions: Indv. $149
List Rental: Rents Lists

Fun-Raising Regulation Report
Business

Publishing Co: John Wiley & Sons, Inc., 605 Third Avenue, New York, NY 10158-0012 Tel # (212) 850-6000 Fax # (212) 850-6088
Personnel: Editor-Bruce R. Hopkins
Editorial Description: Covers changes in law on fund-raising and charitable giving.
General Info: Yr. Est. 1994, Bi-monthly, ISSN: 1077-2405
Subscriptions: Indv. $96

Fund Raising Forum
Association

Publishing Co: National Catholic Development Conference, 86 Front St, Hempstead, NY 11550-3617; Title Tel # (516) 481-6000 Title Fax # (516) 489-9287
Personnel: Editor-Sean Patrick Dolan
Editorial Description: Monthly journal of fund raising techniques.
General Info: Yr. Est. 1968, 10x/yr., Trim Size-8½ x 11, Letrpr. press, 4 pages, 2 Color, Coated
Circulation: Total-1,500

Funding Private Schools
See: SCHOOL ADMINISTRATION

Giraffe News
Consumer, Association

Publishing Co: Giraffe Project, 197 2nd Street, P O Box 759, Langley, WA 98260-0759; Title Tel # (360) 221-7989 Title Fax # (360) 221-7817
Editorial Description: Covers activities of organization the finds role-model 'giraffes' (people who stick their necks out) and tells their stories through mass media.
General Info: Yr. Est. 1983, Semi-annually
Subscriptions: Indv. $35

Giving USA Update
Business, Association

Publishing Co: AAFRC Trust for Philanthropy, 25 W 43rd St Fl 820, New York, NY 10036-7406 Tel # (712) 354-5799 Fax # (712) 768-1795; Title Tel # (212) 354-5799 Title Fax # (212) 768-1795
Personnel: Publisher-Joanne Hayes, Editor-Ann Kaplan, Circ. Mgr., Production Mgr.-Georgette Temple, Adv. Dir.-Donna Osterwail
Editorial Description: Quarterly newsletter of legal, economic and social developments affecting philanthropy.
General Info: (Formerly Fund Raising Review), Yr. Est. 1935, Quarterly, Trim Size-8½ x 11, Offset press, 8 pages, ISSN: 0899-3793
Subscriptions: Indv. $35, $10/copy
Acquistions: Publication Sold
Circulation: (100% controlled), Total-4,500

Grant$eeker, The
Consumer

Publishing Co: Government Information Services, Inc., 4301 Fairfax Dr., Ste. 875, Arlington, VA 22203-1627 Tel # (703) 528-1000 Fax # (703) 528-6060
Editorial Description: Shows grant seekers how to improve their proposal writing skills and other methods for bettering their chances to receive grants.
General Info: Monthly
Subscriptions: Indv. $98

Grants for Cities and Towns Biweekly Hotline
See: PUBLIC MANAGEMENT & PLANNING

Grants for School Districts Biweekly Hotline
See: SCHOOL ADMINISTRATION

Health Grants & Contracts Weekly
Business

Publishing Co: Capitol Publications, Inc., 1101 King St., Ste. 444, Alexandria, VA 22314-2968; Title Tel # (703) 683-4100 Title Fax # (703) 739-6501
Personnel: Publisher-Cynthia Carter, Editor-Susan Wade, Circ. Mgr.-Peggy Dwyer, Production Mgr.-Billy Adams, Art Dir.-Linda McDonald, Mktg. Dir.-Mary Lou Probka, Promotion Dir.-Yvette Giller
Editorial Description: Alerts health researchers, administrators & other fund-seekers to the latest federal grant opportunities. Includes scope of project, eligibility, funds amount, deadlines & contact officers.
General Info: Yr. Est. 1978, Weekly, Trim Size-8½ x 11, ISSN: 0194-2350, Ind/Abs/Online: Newsnet, Color-cover
Subscriptions: Indv. $349, Can. $349, For. $401, $10/copy
List Rental: Actives: $150/M
Printing Co: Capitol Publications, Inc., 1101 King St., Ste. 444, Alexandria, VA 22314-2968 Tel # (703) 683-4100, Fax # (703) 739-6501

In Contact
See: RELIGIOUS & THEOLOGICAL

International Guild of Professional Electrologists-Newsletter
See: MEDICINE

Italian Charities of America Bulletin

Publishing Co: Italian Charities of America, 83-20 Queens Blvd., Queens, NY 11373-4245
General Info: Monthly

Kiwanis International Foundation Newsletter
See: CLUBS

Liaison
See: ADVERTISING & MARKETING

Magnifier, The
See: ART & SCULPTURE

Market: Europe
See: INTERNATIONAL TRADE

Medical Abstracts Newsletter
See: HEALTH

Medical Research Funding Bulletin
Consumer, Association

Publishing Co: Science Support Center, Box 7507, FDR Station, NY, NY 10150-7507; Title Tel # (212) 371-3398
Personnel: Editor-Gabriel Studiman, Mktg. Dir.-John Connolly
Editorial Description: Funding for health research and training programs.
General Info: Yr. Est. 1972, 36x/yr., Trim Size-5½ x 8, Offset press, 20 pages, 2 Color, Saddle-stitched
Subscriptions: Indv. $75, Can. $80, For. $96
Circulation: Total-2,200

Mental Health News Alert   *Business*

Publishing Co: CD Publications, 8204 Fenton St., Silver Spring, MD 20910-4571;
Title Tel # (301) 588-6380 Title Fax # (301) 588-6385
Personnel: Publisher-Mike Gerecht, Editor-Pamela King, Circ. Mgr.-Kurt Eisentraut, Mktg. Dir.-Joyce Meals
Editorial Description: Information on sources and statistics on mental health funding.
General Info: (Formerly Mental Health Funding News), Yr. Est. 1992, Semi-monthly, Trim Size-8½ x 11, Sheetfed press, 16 pages, ISSN: 1062-7235, No Color, Matte, Other
Subscriptions: Indv. $259, Can. $269, For. $299, $15/copy
List Rental: Actives: 8,163, $150/M, Expires: 1,410, $150/M

Mini Lab Focus
See: PHOTOGRAPHY

Minority Funding Report
See: SOCIAL SERVICES & WELFARE

NAEIR Advantage
See: EDUCATION

NPA Bulletin
See: BABY

NSFRE News   *Association*

Publishing Co: Natl. Society of Fund Raising Executives, 1101 King St Ste 700, Alexandria, VA 22314-2944; Title Tel # (703) 684-0410 Title Fax # (703) 684-0540
Personnel: Editor-Deb Taylor, Circ. Dir.-Julie Ann Humphrey, Adv. Dir.-Alisa Nesmith
General Info: 8x/yr., Trim Size-8½ x 11, Desktop press, 16 pages, ISSN: 08902828, 1% ads, 2 Color, Matte
Subscriptions: Indv. $25, Can. $25, For. $25, $2/copy
Acquistions: Publication Bought
Circulation: Total-15,000
Advertising: Inquire for rates.
List Rental: Actives: $50/M
Printing Co: PMR Printing, Indian Creek Lane, Sterling, VA 22170

National Fund Raiser   *Business*

Publishing Co: Barnes Assocs., Inc., 735 Sunrise Ave., Suite #155, Roseville, CA 95661; Title Tel # (916) 786-7471
Personnel: Publisher, Editor-W. David Barnes, Circ. Mgr.-Sharon Barnes
Editorial Description: Covers in detail, the how-tos of fund raising for non-profit organizations.
General Info: (Formerly Barnes Fund Raiser), Yr. Est. 1974, Monthly, Sheetfed press, 6 pages, ISSN: 0272-0825, 2 Color, Newsprint
Subscriptions: Indv. $79, For. $95, $7/copy
Circulation: Total-2,000
List Rental: Actives: $100/M

New Jersey Notes of Grants and Funding

Publishing Co: Mitchell Guide Pubs., 23997 Cliff Dr Ext, Worton, MD 21678-1322; Title Tel # (908) 359-2215
Personnel: Publisher, Editor-Wendy Littman
Editorial Description: News summary of grants and funding/ for nonprofits.
General Info: Yr. Est. 1979, Bi-monthly, 8 pages, No Color, Newsprint
Subscriptions: Indv. $25
Circulation: Total-350

News from Jerusalem   *Association*

Publishing Co: Jerusalem Foundation, Inc., 60 E 42nd St Rm 1936, New York, NY 10165-1999; Title Tel # (212) 840-1101 Title Fax # (212) 869-0339
Personnel: Publisher, Editor, Circ. Mgr.-Sandra Rubin
Editorial Description: Distributed to donors, prospective donors and other interested parties. Designed to describe activities of the Jerusalem Foundation in the United States; provide news from Jerusalem; report on new and ongoing projects and programs of the Jerusalem Founda ion in Jerusalem.
General Info: Yr. Est. 1988, Semi-annually, Trim Size-8½ x 11, 8 pages, 2 Color, Coated
Subscriptions: Free To Qualified Recipient
Circulation: Total-8,000

Nonprofit Counsel   *Business*

Publishing Co: John Wiley & Sons, Inc., 605 Third Avenue, New York, NY 10158-0012
Tel # (212) 850-6000 Fax # (212) 850-6088
Personnel: Editor-Bruce R. Hopkins
Editorial Description: Articles on tax exemption, lobbying restrictions, emerging opportunities for nonprofits and more.
General Info: Yr. Est. 1994, Monthly, ISSN: 0742-3497
Subscriptions: Indv. $108

Outline
See: COLLEGE ALUMNI

Perspectives
See: COLLEGE STUDENT LIFESTYLE

Perspectives on Not-for-Profit Organizations   *Business*

Publishing Co: Newkirk Products, Inc., 15 Corporate Cir, Albany, NY 12203-5154
Tel # (518) 452-1000
Editorial Description: Custom publication designed for distribution to clients by professionals.
General Info: Quarterly, Trim Size-8½ x 11, 4 pages, 2 Color

Philanthropic Digest   *Consumer, Association*

Publishing Co: Philanthropic Digest, PO Box 380252, Cambridge, MA 02238-0252; Title Tel # (617) 661-8146
Personnel: Editor-Ann Castle
Editorial Description: Monthly listing of gifts & grants from individuals, foundations and corporations to philanthropy & charities.
General Info: Yr. Est. 1954, Monthly, Trim Size-8½ x 11, 16 pages, No Color
Subscriptions: Indv. $80, $10/copy
Circulation: Total-600

Philanthropy Trends That Count   *Business*

Publishing Co: Capitol Publications, Inc., 1101 King St., Ste. 444, Alexandria, VA 22314-2968 Fax # (703) 739-6501; Title Tel # (703) 683-4100 Title Fax # (703) 739-6437
Personnel: Publisher-Cynthia Carter, Circ. Mgr.-Liz Soper, Production Mgr.-Rosette Graham, Art Dir.-Linda McDonald, Promotion Dir.-Yvette Giller
Editorial Description: Easy to read briefs on demographic trends that affect program strategies.
General Info: 4x/yr., Trim Size-8½ x 11, 12 pages
Subscriptions: Indv. $90, For. $105, $23/copy
Acquistions: Publication Bought
List Rental: Actives: $175/M, Expires: $175/M
Printing Co: Capitol Publications, Inc., 1101 King St., Ste. 444, Alexandria, VA 22314-2968 Tel # (703) 683-4100, Fax # (703) 739-6501

Planned Gifts Counselor, The   *Business*

Publishing Co: Taft Group, 835 Penobscot Bldg., Detroit, MI 48226-4094 Tel # (313) 961-2242 Parent Co.-Gale Research, Inc., Detroit; Title Tel # (301) 816-0210 Title Fax # (301) 816-0811
Personnel: Publisher-Mark Scott, Editor-Alden Tueller
Editorial Description: Successful strategies for Planned Giving Programs.
General Info: Yr. Est. 1987, Monthly, Trim Size-8½ x 11, Sheetfed press, 8 pages, ISSN: 0891-4443, 2 Color, Newsprint
Subscriptions: Indv. $150

Privacy Journal   *Business, Consumer*

Publishing Co: Privacy Journal, PO Box 28577, Providence, RI 02908-0577; Title Tel # (401) 274-7861
Personnel: Publisher, Editor-Robert Smith, Circ. Mgr.-James Sulanowski
Editorial Description: Reports on new laws, public attitudes, and technology affecting the confidentiality of personal information.
General Info: Yr. Est. 1974, Monthly, Trim Size-8½ x 11, Offset press, 8 pages, ISSN: 0145-7659, Ind/Abs/Online: NewsNet, No Color, Matte
Subscriptions: Indv. $35, Inst. $118, Can. $118, For. $145, $10/copy
Printing Co: Newsletter Press, 76 Valley St, East Providence, RI 02914-4424 Tel # (401) 438-5352

Report to Donors   *Association*

Publishing Co: Church World Service, 28606 Phillips St, Elkhart, IN 46514-1239; Title Tel # (219) 264-3102 Title Fax # (219) 262-0966
Personnel: Editor-Ron Kaser
Editorial Description: For donors to the Church World Service.
General Info: Yr. Est. 1992, Tri-annually, Trim Size-11 x 16½, Letrpr. press, 4 pages, 2 Color, Coated
Subscriptions: Free To Qualified Recipient
Circulation: Total-30,000

Responsive Philanthropy   *Consumer, Association*   CPM: $100

Publishing Co: National Committee for Responsive Philanthropy, 2001 S. St. N.W., Suite 620, Washington, DC 20009-1125; Title Tel # (202) 387-9177 Title Fax # (202) 332-5084
Personnel: Publisher-Bob Bothwell, Editor-Beth Baker, Circ. Mgr., Promotion Dir.-Kate Conovey
Editorial Description: Current information on issues & reforms in private philanthropy, particularly as to how social justice and progressive public interest charities are affected.
General Info: Yr. Est. 1976, Quarterly, Trim Size-8½ x 11, 16 pages, ISSN: 1065-0008, Color, Saddle-stitched
Subscriptions: Indv. $25, Can. $30, For. $35
Circulation: (80% controlled), Total-5,000, Subscriptions-1,000, International-100
Advertising: $500.
List Rental: Actives: $134/M

Rural Property Investor
See: REAL ESTATE

Simple Cooking
See: FOOD

Special Libraries Assn., Social Science Division Bulletin
See: LIBRARY

Sponsors Report   *Business*

Publishing Co: Joyce Julius & Assocs., 3785 Varsity Dr, Ann Arbor, MI 48108-2223; Title Tel # (313) 971-1900 Title Fax # (313) 971-2059
Personnel: Editor-Eric Wright
General Info: Irregular

Substance Abuse
Funding News   *Business*

Publishing Co: CD Publications, 8204 Fenton St., Silver Spring, MD 20910-4571;
Title Tel # (301) 588-6380 Title Fax # (301) 588-6385
Personnel: Publisher-Mike Gerecht, Editor-Lee Byrd, Circ. Mgr.-Kurt Eisentraut, Mktg. Dir.-Joyce Meals
Editorial Description: Explores issues in funding of Substance Abuse programs.
General Info: Yr. Est. 1992, Semi-monthly, Trim Size-8½ x 11, Sheetfed press, 16 pages, ISSN: 1067-0165, No Color, Matte
Subscriptions: Indv. $259, Can. $269, For. $299, $15/copy
List Rental: List Management Co.: Manager: Amy Seyler; Washington Advertising Service, 8204 Fenton St., Silver Spring, MD 20910 Tel # (301) 588-7920, Fax # (301) 588-6385, Actives: 10,282, $150/M, Expires: 1,804, $150/M

TF Newsletter   *Association*

Publishing Co: Tolstoy Foundation, Inc., 104 Lake Rd., Valley Cottage, NY 10989;
Title Tel # (914) 268-6722 Title Fax # (914) 268-6937
Personnel: Editor-Leon Marion
Editorial Description: Text: Eng. & Russian, current programs & progress reports, re: refugees, Russian welfare assistance.
General Info: Yr. Est. 1939, Irregular, Trim Size-8½ x 14, Sheetfed press, 4 pages, No Color, Newsprint
Circulation: Total-2,000
Printing Co: Guaranteed Printing, 216 W. 18th St., New York, NY 10011 Tel # (212) 929-2410

United Way Newsletter
See: HOUSE ORGANS

Wise Giving Guide

Publishing Co: Natl. Charities Info Bureau, Inc., 19 Union Sq., W., New York, NY 10003-3395;
Title Tel # (212) 929-6300
Personnel: Editor-Frank Driscoll
Editorial Description: Lists the not-for-profit organizations about which NCIB reports & gives current evaluations against NCIB standards.
General Info: Yr. Est. 1976, ISSN: 0275-0031, 2 Color
Subscriptions: Indv. $25, $1/copy

PHILATELY & POSTAL AFFAIRS

Album Page   *Consumer, Association*

Publishing Co: Oregon Stamp Soc., PO Box 18165, Portland, OR 97218-0165;
Title Tel # (503) 254-7093
Personnel: Editor-Vance Terrall
Editorial Description: Philatelic newsletter to society members.
General Info: Yr. Est. 1959, Monthly, Offset press, 10 pages, 2% ads
Circulation: Total-350
Printing Co: Metro Printing, 340 NE 122nd Ave, Portland, OR 97230-2106

Alternative Delivery Today   *Business*

Publishing Co: National News, PO Box 37, Kensington, MD 20895-0037 Tel # (800) 547-0040;
Title Fax # (301) 985-6296
Personnel: Editor-Rick Barse, Editor-Cathy Sattler
Editorial Description: National News' newsletter covering advantages to alternative periodical delivery.
General Info: Quarterly, Trim Size-8½ x 11, 4 pages, No Color

American Philatelic News   *Association*

Publishing Co: Amer. Unit of ATA, PO Box 179, Washington, DC 20044-0179;
Title Tel # (202) 289-5260
Editorial Description: Articles and checklists about stamps concerning USA history and industry.
General Info: Yr. Est. 1951, Bi-monthly, 28 pages
Subscriptions: $1/copy
Circulation: Total-420

American Philatelic
Society Chapter
Activities Committee
Newsletter   *Association*

Publishing Co: Sponsor-American Philatelic Society, American Philatelic Society, PO Box 8000, State College, PA 16803-8000; Title Tel # (814) 237-3803 Title Fax # (814) 237-6128
Personnel: Editor-Diana Manchester
Editorial Description: Service newsletter to stamp clubs affiliated with the American Philatelic Society worldwide.
General Info: Yr. Est. 1886, Quarterly, Trim Size-8½ x 11, Offset press, 20 pages, No Color, Matte, Other
Subscriptions: Indv. $6, Free With Membership
Circulation: (94% controlled), Total-790, International-30, Readership-790
List Rental: Actives: $30/M
Printing Co: Express Tech, 1006 West College Ave, State College, PA 16801 Tel # (814) 237-7600, Fax # (814) 237-7574

Americana Philatelic News

Publishing Co: Americana Unit-American Topical Assn., PO Box 127, New Britain, CT 06050-0127;
Title Tel # (203) 667-1400
Personnel: Editor-August Mark Vaz
General Info: Yr. Est. 1951, Bi-monthly
Circulation: Total-400

Appraisers Standard
See: ANTIQUES & ART GOODS

Artistamp News
See: ART & SCULPTURE

Association of Private
Postal Systems Update   *Association*

Publishing Co: Association of Private Postal Systems, 5580 Power Inn Rd Ste F, Sacramento, CA 95820-6748; Title Tel # (916) 929-3300 Title Fax # (916) 929-3306
Editorial Description: Companies delivering third class mail, mostly door to door.
General Info: Yr. Est. 1975, Monthly

Autograph Research
See: COLLECTIBLES

Bay Phil   *Association*

Publishing Co: Friends of the Western Philatelic Library Inc., PO Box 2219, Sunnyvale, CA 94087-0219; Title Tel # (408) 733-0336
Personnel: Editor-Harold Short
Editorial Description: Stimulation to use philatelic research library.
General Info: Yr. Est. 1969, Semi-monthly, Web press, 8 pages, No Color
Subscriptions: Indv. $8
Circulation: Total-400

Bright Ideas Dealer
Newsletter

Publishing Co: Will Moss, 15705 Presswick Ln, Mitchellville, MD 20716-1714;
Title Tel # (301) 249-6097
Personnel: Publisher, Editor-Will Moss
Editorial Description: Latest in sources,techniques & equipment to help dealers make money.
General Info: Yr. Est. 1971, Semi-monthly, Web press, 4 pages, No Color, Newsprint
Subscriptions: Indv. $18

C.A.F.I.P. Bulletin   *Association*

Publishing Co: Canadian Assn. for Israel Philately, 260 Adelaide St. E., Box 33, Toronto, ON M5A 1N0 Canada; Title Tel # (416) 635-1749 Title Fax # (416) 635-1749
Personnel: Editor-Clif Fielder, Circ. Mgr.-Joseph Berkovits
Editorial Description: Features Palestine, Israel, Holy Land and Judaic philately.
General Info: Yr. Est. 1957, Bi-monthly, Trim Size-8½ x 11, Mimeo press, 5 pages, ISSN: 0007-7747, No Color
Subscriptions: Indv. $35, Can. $35
Acquistions: Publication Bought
Advertising: Inquire for rates. Accepts Inserts.

Campaign   *Association*

Publishing Co: Sponsor-Napoleonic Age Philatelists, Napoleonic Age Philatelists, 7513 Clayton Dr., Oklahoma City, OK 73132-5636; Title Tel # (405) 721-0044
Personnel: Publisher, Editor-Kenneth Berry
Editorial Description: Napoleon Bonaparte and his times as portrayed on postage stamps. History of the events and people associated with the French Revolution and French Empire 1789-1815.
General Info: Yr. Est. 1983, Quarterly, Trim Size-8½ x 11, Sheetfed press, 20 pages, No Color, Newsprint
Subscriptions: Indv. $8, Can. $8, For. $12

Channel Islands Reporter   *Association*

Publishing Co: Club of Channel Islands Collectors, PO Box 579, New York, NY 10028-0019;
Title Tel # (212) 228-4365
Personnel: Publisher, Circ. Mgr.-Matthew Trachinsky, Editor, Art Dir.-Robert Ausubel
Editorial Description: The stamps and postal history of Channel Islands philately.
General Info: Yr. Est. 1975, Quarterly, Trim Size-8½ x 11, Offset press, 20 pages, No Color
Subscriptions: Indv. $10, Can. $13, For. $16, $3/copy
Circulation: Total-500
Advertising: Inquire for rates.

Circuit, The   *Consumer, Association*   **CPM: $40**

Publishing Co: International Society of Worldwide Stamp Collectors, The, Rr 1 Box 69a/2505 Second St, Caddo Mills, TX 75135-9704; Title Tel # (903) 527-3957
Personnel: Circ. Dir.-Carol Cervenka, Publisher, Editor, Production Mgr., Art Dir.-Rita Kallal, Adv. Dir., Promotion Dir.-Thomas Fortunato
Editorial Description: This newsletter covers all aspects of worldwide stamp collecting with articles written by collectors for collectors. It also contains dealer ads and offers from fellow members interest in exchanges. Membership includes the newsletter, exchanges, stamp approval sales, auctions, youth programs and more. Send SASE for an application and further information.
General Info: Yr. Est. 1984, Bi-monthly, Trim Size-8½ x 11, Letrpr. press, 15 pages, 15% ads, No Color, Matte
Subscriptions: Indv. $8, Free
Circulation: Total-1,000
Advertising: $40.
List Rental: List Management Co.: Twin Peaks Press, PO Box 129, Vancouver, WA 98666-0129 Tel # (206) 694-2462, Fax # (206) 696-3210
Printing Co: Southern Graphics, 407 Natechitoches St, W. Monroe, LA 71291

Codex Filatelica — *Association*

Publishing Co: Sponsor-American Topical Assn., Mesoamerican Archaeology Study Unit, PO Box 1442, Riverside, CA 92502-1442
Personnel: Editor-Chris Moser
Editorial Description: Topical stamp collectors newsletter for New World Archeology & Indians on stamps.
General Info: Yr. Est. 1974, Bi-monthly, Trim Size-8½ x 11, Offset press, 10 pages, ISSN: 0896-3533, No Color
Subscriptions: Indv. $8, Can. $9, For. $22, $2/copy
Printing Co: PIP, Printers, Riverside, CA 92501

Dragon's Digest, The

Publishing Co: Ryukyu Philatelic Specialty Society, C/O Howard Wallace, Box 653, South Bend, IN 46624; Title Tel # (219) 288-3751
Personnel: Editor-Howard Wallace
General Info: Yr. Est. 1978, Bi-monthly
Circulation: Total-350

Europa News

Publishing Co: Europa Study Unit, 512 Church Rd., #4N, Bensenville, IL 60106; Title Tel # (708) 766-0349
Personnel: Publisher, Editor-Stephen Luster, Circ. Mgr.-John Jezek, Jr.
Editorial Description: In depth treatment of philatelic items issued in recognition of Europa-United Europe or a United States of Europe.
General Info: Yr. Est. 1959, Bi-monthly, Trim Size-8½ x 11, Mimeo press, 10 pages, No Color
Subscriptions: Indv. $8
Circulation: (100% controlled), Total-300

Fakes and Forgeries — *Association*

Publishing Co: Fakes and Forgeries Study Group, 107 Hoover Rd, Rochester, NY 14617-3611; Title Tel # (716) 544-0304 Title Fax # (716) 477-1128
Personnel: Editor-Anthony Torres
Editorial Description: Provide a forum for the sharing compilation & discussion of information regarding the entire range of non-genuine world- wide philatelic material.
General Info: Yr. Est. 1992, Quarterly, Trim Size-8½ x 11, Other press, 24 pages, 25% ads, No Color, Other, Other
Subscriptions: Indv. $10, Can. $11, For. $16, $3/copy
Circulation: Total-150
Advertising: Inquire for rates.

Fine & Performing Arts Philately Journal — *Association*

Publishing Co: Fine Arts Philatelists, 7234 River Rd., Conestoga, PA 17516-9761 Tel # (717) 872-4592
Personnel: Editor-Beatrice M. Killough
Editorial Description: Articles, features relating to the fine and performing arts on postage stamps.
General Info: (Formerly FAP Journal), Yr. Est. 1955, Quarterly, Trim Size-8½ x 11, Offset press, 12 pages, No Color, Saddle-stitched
Subscriptions: Indv. $12, $3/copy
Circulation: Total-500
Advertising: Inquire for rates.

Higgins & Gage World Postal Stationery Catalog — *Business, Association*

Publishing Co: Classic Philatelics, PO Box 5637, Huntington Beach, CA 92615-5637 Fax # (714) 968-6704; Title Tel # (714) 968-1717
Personnel: Editor-Mel Feiner
Editorial Description: Covers postal stationery worldwide, listed alphabetically in 19 volumes.
General Info: Yr. Est. 1965, Irregular, Trim Size-5½ x 8½, Mimeo press, 3,000 pages, No Color
Subscriptions: $230/copy
Circulation: Total-300

Liberian Philatelic Society Journal — *Association*

Publishing Co: Liberian Philatelic Society, 9027 S Oakley Ave, Chicago, IL 60620-6131; Title Tel # (312) 962-3416
Personnel: Publisher-Roy Mackal, Editor-Henry Chlanda
Editorial Description: Information about Liberian postage stamps.
General Info: Yr. Est. 1962, Bi-monthly, Trim Size-8½ x 11, Mimeo press, 10 pages, Ind/Abs/Online: Roy Mackal, 1% ads, No Color, Newsprint
Subscriptions: Indv. $8, $2/copy

Luren — *Association*

Publishing Co: Scandinavian Philatelic Library of Southern California, Inc., PO Box 310, Claremont, CA 91711-0310; Title Tel # (909) 626-1764
Personnel: Publisher, Editor-Paul Nelson
Editorial Description: Scandinavian philatelic info in English.
General Info: Yr. Est. 1958, Monthly, Trim Size-8½ x 11, Sheetfed press, 10 pages, ISSN: 0739-0025, 1% ads, No Color
Subscriptions: Indv. $10, Can. $10, For. $12, $1/copy
Circulation: Total-300
Advertising: Accepts Inserts.

Massachusetts Spy — *Association*

Publishing Co: Massachusetts Postal Research Society, Box 202, N. Abington, MA 02351-0202; Title Tel # (617) 878-4446
Personnel: Publisher, Editor, Adv. Dir.-Robert Borden
Editorial Description: Postal history of Mass.
General Info: Yr. Est. 1975, Bi-monthly, Trim Size-8½ x 11, Sheetfed press, 8 pages, 1% ads, No Color, Newsprint, Looseleaf
Subscriptions: Indv. $7, Can. $8, For. $9, $1/copy
Advertising: Inquire for rates.

NAPS Letter — *Association*

Publishing Co: National Association of Postal Supervisors, 1727 King St # 400, Alexandria, VA 22314-2753 Fax # (703) 836-9665; Title Tel # (703) 836-9661 Title Fax # (703) 836-8369
Editorial Description: News of interest to postal supervisors.
General Info: Yr. Est. 1908, Bi-weekly

New York Metro Area Update
See: HOUSE ORGANS

News of Hungarian Philately — *Association*

Publishing Co: Society for Hungarian Philately, Box 1162, Samp-Mortar Station, Fairfield, CT 06430-1162
Personnel: Editor-Csaba Kohalmi
General Info: Yr. Est. 1970, Quarterly, 20 pages
Subscriptions: Indv. $12, For. $16
Circulation: Total-250

Ohio Rural Carriers — *Association*

Publishing Co: Ohio Rural Letter Carriers' Assn, S. Twp. Rd. 187, Attica, OH 44807; Title Tel # (419) 925-4600
Personnel: Editor-Paul J. Moeller
Editorial Description: For members and families. To keep Ohio Rural Carriers informed about job developments.
General Info: Monthly, Trim Size-8½ x 11, Letrpr. press, 20 pages
Subscriptions: Indv. $4
Circulation: Total-3,500
Advertising: Inquire for rates.

On Cover — *Association*

Publishing Co: Sponsor-Motor CSCC, Motor City Stamp & Cover Club, 22608 Poplar Ct, Hazel Park, MI 48030-1928; Title Tel # (810) 546-0038
Personnel: Publisher, Editor-Robert Quintero
General Info: Yr. Est. 1957, Monthly, Trim Size-8½ x 11, Mimeo press, 8 pages, No Color
Subscriptions: Free With Membership
Advertising: Inquire for rates.

Passport — *Business*

Publishing Co: Worldpost Services, United States Postal Service, PO Box 23793, Washington, DC 20026-3793 Tel # (202) 832-5871
Personnel: Editor-Jo Anne Parke, Product Mgr.-Frank Richards
Editorial Description: A quarterly international marketing newsletter. Packed full of tips and information international business mailers can use to reach and serve customers in every corner of the globe effectively and economically.
General Info: Yr. Est. 1995, Quarterly, Trim Size-8½ x 11, 4 pages, 2 Color, Coated, Other

Perfins Bulletin

Publishing Co: Perfins Bulletin, PO Box 82, Grandview, MO 64030-0082; Title Tel # (816) 763-0590
Editorial Description: Promotes research into use of perforated insignia (Perfins) on postage stamps.
General Info: Yr. Est. 1945, Monthly, Trim Size-8½ x 11, Offset press, 12 pages, No Color
Subscriptions: Indv. $5, $1/copy
Circulation: (100% controlled), Total-1,000

Philagems Intl.

Publishing Co: Gems, Minerals & Jewelry Study Unit-American Topical Assn., PO Box 632, Tewksbury, MA 01876-0632; Title Tel # (508) 851-8283
Personnel: Editor-Patricia Mummert
Editorial Description: Contains articles on philatelic material related to gems, minerals & jewelry.
General Info: Yr. Est. 1976, Quarterly
Subscriptions: Indv. $10, Can. $10, For. $15
Circulation: Total-144

Philatelic Freemason — *Association*

Publishing Co: Masonic Study Unit, 59 Greenwood Rd, Andover, MA 01810-3311; Title Tel # (508) 470-0583
Personnel: Publisher-Robert Dominque, Editor-Robert Dominque, Circ. Mgr.-Otto Steding
Editorial Description: Articles on Masonic philately.
General Info: Yr. Est. 1977, Bi-monthly, Trim Size-8½ x 11, 12 pages, No Color, Matte
Subscriptions: Indv. $8, Can. $8, For. $14
Circulation: (100% controlled), Total-350

Philatex
Association

Publishing Co: Sponsor-San Antonio Philatelic Assn., Philatex, PO Box 1197, San Antonio, TX 78294-1197; Title Tel # (512) 223-8683
Personnel: Editor, Circ. Mgr.-Vince Williams
Editorial Description: Newsletter information for club members.
General Info: Yr. Est. 1982, Bi-monthly, Trim Size-8½ x 14, Letrpr. press, 4 pages, Color
Circulation: (100% controlled), Total-210

Pony Express Mail
See: HISTORY

Postal Link
See: INTERNATIONAL AFFAIRS

Postal Watch
Business

Publishing Co: Intertec Publishing Corporation, 9800 Metcalf Ave., PO Box 12901, Overland Park, KS 66212-2215 Tel # (913) 341-1300 Fax # (913) 967-1898 Parent Co.-K-III Communications, New York
Personnel: Publisher-Sandra Stewart, Assoc. Publ., Editor-Lori Billington, Assoc. Ed.-Susan Smith
Editorial Description: Addresses common concerns of those that deal with postal regulations.
General Info: Yr. Est. 1990, Semi-monthly, Sheetfed press, 8 pages, ISSN: 1052-3944, 2 Color, Coated
Subscriptions: Indv. $284
Advertising: Inquire for rates. Accepts Inserts.
Printing Co: Western Robidoux, 4006 Highway A, St. Joseph, MO 64503

Postal World
Business

Publishing Co: United Communications Group, 11300 Rockville Pike, Ste. 1100, Rockville, MD 20852-3030 Fax # (301) 816-8945; Title Tel # (301) 816-8950 Title Fax # (301) 819-8945
Personnel: Publisher, Editor-Marcus Smith, Circ. Mgr.-Monica Brown
Editorial Description: Information for volume mail users.
General Info: Yr. Est. 1975, Bi-weekly, Trim Size-8½ x 11, 4 pages, Newsprint
Subscriptions: Indv. $349
Acquistions: Publication Bought, Publication Sold
List Rental: List Management Co.: PBI List Marketing, 1201 Seven Locks Rd., Potomac, MD 20854 Tel # (301) 340-7788, Fax # (301) 738-7581, Actives: $125/M

Postcard Classics
See: COLLECTIBLES

Rapid Notice News Service

Publishing Co: Space Philatelists Intl. Society, C/O Martin Michaelson, Box 771, West Nyack, NY 10994
General Info: Monthly
Circulation: Total-175

Report to Members
Business, Association

Publishing Co: International Philatelic Press Club, PO Box 127, New Britain, CT 06050 Tel # (203) 667-1400
Personnel: Editor-Linda Stansfield
Editorial Description: News and information for writers and editors working in the area of philately.
General Info: Irregular, Trim Size-8½ x 11, 8 pages, No Color, Matte
Subscriptions: Free With Membership

RoundUPS
Business

Publishing Co: United Parcel Service, 643 W 43rd St, New York, NY 10036-1917
Editorial Description: Regional publication for employees, customers and affiliates.
General Info: (Formerly Pick UPS), Quarterly, Trim Size-8½ x 11, 8 pages, 4 Color, Coated

Royal Mail, The
See: DIRECT MAIL

St. Helena
Business, Association

Publishing Co: Sponsor-St. Helena & Dependencies Philatelic Soc., St. Helena, PO Box 1306, Greenville, ME 04441-1306; Title Tel # (207) 695-3077
Personnel: Editor-Everett Parker
Editorial Description: Official journal of society.
General Info: Yr. Est. 1977, Quarterly, Trim Size-8½ x 11, Offset press, 24 pages, No Color
Subscriptions: Indv. $10
Circulation: Total-250

Seaposter
Consumer, Association

Publishing Co: Maritime Postmark Society, 141 Gordon Ave, Wadsworth, OH 44281-2310 Tel # (216) 336-8227
Personnel: Editor-Thomas Hirschinger
Editorial Description: Features the latest information as to the postal markings applies to mail posted on board merchant ships while at sea. Information is both current and material not previously published.
General Info: Yr. Est. 1939, Bi-monthly, Offset press, 18 pages, ISSN: 0048-9891
Subscriptions: Indv. $10
Circulation: Total-200
Advertising: Inquire for rates.

Space Autograph News
See: AERONAUTICS/ASTRONAUTICS

Spec Sheet
Association

Publishing Co: Building Series Study Group of the Germany Philatelic Soc., 107 Hoover Rd, Rochester, NY 14617-3611; Title Tel # (716) 544-0304 Title Fax # (716) 477-1128
Personnel: Editor-Anthony Torres
Editorial Description: Study of the buildings series stamps of West Germany, 1948.
General Info: Yr. Est. 1962, Quarterly, Trim Size-8½ x 11, Other press, 20 pages, 25% ads, No Color, Other, Other
Subscriptions: Indv. $10, Can. $12, For. $15, $4/copy
Circulation: Total-115
Advertising: Inquire for rates.

Stamp Pals International Newsletter
Consumer, Association

Publishing Co: Gray House Publishing, 2201 Wayne St, Copperas Cove, TX 76522-4185; Title Tel # (817) 547-3977
Personnel: Publisher-Gerald Gray, Editor-Jim Danziger
Editorial Description: Listings of potential pen pals and stamp traders, buyers and sellers.
General Info: Yr. Est. 1989, Monthly
Subscriptions: Indv. $12
Circulation: Total-1,000
Advertising: Inquire for rates.
Printing Co: Printing Call, PO Box 9, Milledgeville, IL 61051-0009 Tel # (815) 225-7325

Stamps, Old Letters & History

Publishing Co: Cheswick Historical Society, 208 Allegheny Ave, Cheswick, PA 15024-1604; Title Tel # (412) 274-9106
Personnel: Editor-Steve Pavlina
General Info: Bi-monthly
Circulation: Total-500

Star Carrier
Association

Publishing Co: Natl. Star Route Mail Carriers Assn, 324 E Capitol St SE, Washington, DC 20003-3809; Title Tel # (202) 543-1661
Personnel: Editor-John Maraney
Editorial Description: Transportation of mail over highways under contract with the Postal Service.
General Info: Yr. Est. 1933, Monthly, Trim Size-8½ x 11, Offset press, 8 pages, No Color
Subscriptions: Indv. $25
Circulation: Total-6,000
Advertising: Inquire for rates.

Third Reich Study Group-Bulletin

Publishing Co: Third Reich Study Group-Germany Philatelic Society, PO Box 283, Needham Heights, MA 02194-0904
Personnel: Editor-James Lewis
Editorial Description: Research on postal history of Nazi Germany.
General Info: Yr. Est. 1962, Quarterly, Trim Size-8½ x 11, 30 pages, No Color
Subscriptions: Indv. $7, Can. $13
Circulation: Total-300

Transit Postmark Collector
Association

Publishing Co: Mobile Post Office Society, 2434 W 103rd St, Chicago, IL 60655-1002; Title Tel # (312) 779-4962
Personnel: Publisher, Editor-Warren Kimball, Jr.
Editorial Description: Devoted to collectors of covers, cachets, postmarks, history and data of U.S. and foreign highway post office and railway post office routes.
General Info: (Formerly HPO Notes), Yr. Est. 1950, Bi-monthly, Trim Size-8½ x 11, Offset press, 20 pages, No Color
Subscriptions: Indv. $6, $1/copy
Circulation: Total-650

Vermont Philatelist
Association

Publishing Co: Vermont Philatelic Society, 18 Fuller St, Montpelier, VT 05602-2405; Title Tel # (802) 223-2896
Personnel: Publisher-Peter Huntsman, Editor-Michael McMorrow, Circ. Mgr.-Paul Abajian
Editorial Description: Vermont philatelic information to members.
General Info: Yr. Est. 1956, Quarterly, Trim Size-5½ x 8½, Letrpr. press, 8 pages, No Color
Subscriptions: Indv. $4
Circulation: (100% controlled), Total-300

World Postal Stationery New Issue Report
Business, Association

Publishing Co: Classic Philatelics, PO Box 5637, Huntington Beach, CA 92615-5637; Title Tel # (714) 968-1717 Title Fax # (714) 968-6704
Personnel: Editor-Pat Feiner
Editorial Description: New issues of world postal stationery.
General Info: (Formerly Entire Truth, The), Yr. Est. 1983, Tri-annually, Trim Size-8½ x 11, Desktop press, 8 pages, No Color
Subscriptions: Indv. $10, For. $13
Circulation: Total-150

PHILOSOPHY

APA Newsletters, The   *Scholarly, Association*   CPM: $37

Publishing Co: American Philosophical Association, University of Delaware, Newark, DE 19716; Title Tel # (302) 831-1112 Title Fax # (302) 831-8690
Personnel: Editor-Eric Hoffman, Circ. Mgr.-Nova McKernan
Editorial Description: Contains articles, book reviews, course outlines, and announcements. Seven separate newsletters included in each issue: The Black Experience, Computer Use, Feminism, Law, Medicine, Teaching, International Cooperation.
General Info: Semi-annually, Trim Size-8½ x 11, 150 pages, Perfect bound
Subscriptions: Indv. $20, Inst. $20, $10/copy
Circulation: Total-4,000
Advertising: $150.
List Rental: Rents Lists
Printing Co: Lancaster Press, 3575 Hempland Rd., P.O Box 3657, Lancaster, PA 17604-3657 Tel # (717) 285-9095, Fax # (717) 285-7261

Alaska Metaphysical Council Newsletter   *Association*

Publishing Co: Alaska Metaphysical Newsletter, 3701 Eureka St Lot 21c, Anchorage, AK 99503-5838; Title Tel # (907) 279-8641
Editorial Description: New Age networking journal which correlates the listings and activities of metaphysical organizations in the Anchorage area. Features different views and thoughts of diverse belief systems.
General Info: Monthly
Subscriptions: Indv. $12, $1/copy
Acquistions: Publication Bought
Circulation: Total-250
Advertising: Accepts Inserts.

American Record
See: POLITICS

AngelWatch
See: RELIGIOUS & THEOLOGICAL

Applied Orgonometry
See: CULTURE & HUMANITIES

Bertrand Russell Society-Newsletter   *Association*

Publishing Co: Bertrand Russell Society, Inc., 3802 N Kenneth Ave, Chicago, IL 60641-2814; Title Tel # (312) 286-0676
Personnel: Editor-Don Jackanice
Editorial Description: Providing information by and about Bertrand Russell and this society.
General Info: Yr. Est. 1974, Quarterly, 32 pages
Subscriptions: Inst. $12
Circulation: Total-300

Bioethics Literature Review
See: MEDICINE

Book Newsletter & Catalog
See: BOOKS & BOOK TRADE

Bridging The Gap   *Business, Association*

Publishing Co: Moose Ear Press, 2722 County Park Road, P.O. Box 335, Chete, WI 54728; Title Tel # (715) 924-4906 Title Fax # (715) 924-4738
Personnel: Editor-Jackie Stocking, Art Dir.-Jerry Stocking, Mktg. Dir.-Karen Bates
Editorial Description: Bridging The Gap uses cognitive harmony to close or bridge people's problematic gaps in a respectful, wholistic & permanent way. It consists stories and ideas designed to help one bridge the gaps in one's life. Funded by donations to a non-profit educational of corp. A Choice Experience, Inc.
General Info: Yr. Est. 1993, Quarterly, Trim Size-8½ x 11, Desktop press, 16 pages, 2 Color, Matte, Saddle-stitched
Subscriptions: Indv. $14
Circulation: Total-5,000, Readership-60,000
List Rental: Actives: 5,000
Printing Co: Chetek Alert, Chetek, WI 54728

Carnegie Council Newsletter
See: INTERNATIONAL AFFAIRS

Cauda Pavonis: Studies in Hermeticism
See: LITERATURE & LINGUISTICS

Celebration News   *Consumer, Scholarly*

Publishing Co: Celebration Productions, 2207 W Colorado Ave, Colorado Springs, CO 80904-3324; Title Tel # (719) 634-1810 Title Fax # (719) 634-1810
Personnel: Editor-K.C. Costa, Publisher, Production Mgr., Adv. Dir.-Shanti Toll, Circ. Mgr., Art Dir.-Coreen Toll
General Info: Yr. Est. 1981, Quarterly, Trim Size-8½ x 11, Web press, 8 pages, 4% ads, No Color, Newsprint
Subscriptions: Free In Designated Area
Circulation: Total-4,000
Advertising: Inquire for rates.
List Rental: Rents Lists

Center for Icarian Studies-Newsletter

Publishing Co: Center for Icarian Studies, Western Ill. Univ., 438 Morgan Hall, Macomb, IL 61455-1396; Title Tel # (309) 298-1053
Personnel: Editor-Dr. Robert Sutton
General Info: Yr. Est. 1978, Semi-annually, 8 pages
Circulation: Total-500

Christian New Age Quarterly
See: RELIGIOUS & THEOLOGICAL

Cosmic Awareness News

Publishing Co: Cosmic Awareness Communications, PO Box 115, Olympia, WA 98507-0115 Fax # (360) 956-1571
Editorial Description: New Age philosophy and current events from Edgar Cayce-type trance state. Covers UFOs and the alien presence on Earth and the conspiracy for a New World Order.
General Info: Yr. Est. 1965, Monthly, 12 pages, Saddle-stitched
Subscriptions: Indv. $42, Can. $57, $3/copy
Circulation: Total-6,750

Dallas Institute Newsletter, The
See: PUBLIC MANAGEMENT & PLANNING

Distant Drums   *Association*

Publishing Co: Ronald S. Miller, 4106 Degardner Cir NW, Saint Francis, MN 55070-9705; Title Tel # (612) 753-6107
Personnel: Publisher, Editor-Ronald Miller
Editorial Description: Provides historical/contemporary research of modern syncretistic movements. Polemic & apologetic techniques are employed, as well as the juxtaposing of events.
General Info: Yr. Est. 1979, Quarterly, Mimeo press, 20 pages
Subscriptions: Indv. $18, $4/copy
Advertising: Accepts Inserts.

Doctor - Patient Studies
See: MEDICINE

Emshock Letter
See: POETRY & CREATIVE WRITING

Esoteric Newsletter

Publishing Co: Benjamin Shimon, 457 FDR Dr.(1604), New York, NY 10002-5954; Title Tel # (212) 777-4038
Personnel: Publisher, Editor-Benjamin Shimon
General Info: Yr. Est. 1988, Mimeo press, 4 pages, No Color, Newsprint
Circulation: Total-200

Ethics & International Affairs Newsletter
See: INTERNATIONAL AFFAIRS

Ethics & Perspectives   *Association*

Publishing Co: International Association of Ethicists, 117 W. Harrison Bldg., 6th Fl. #I-104, Chicago, IL 60605-1709
Editorial Description: General information on ethical activities around the world.
General Info: Yr. Est. 1986, Semi-annually, ISSN: 1011-3878, Looseleaf
Subscriptions: Indv. $50
Advertising: Inquire for rates.
List Rental: Rents Lists

Ethics and Policy

Publishing Co: Center for Ethics & Social Policy, Graduate Theological Union, 2400 Ridge Rd., Berkeley, CA 94709; Title Tel # (510) 649-2560 Title Fax # (510) 649-2565
Personnel: Editor-Chris Adams
General Info: (Formerly Center for Ethics and Policy Newsletter), Yr. Est. 1974, Quarterly, 7 pages
Subscriptions: Indv. $35, Free With Membership
Circulation: Total-3,500

Foundation for Philosophy of Creativity Newsletter   *Association*

Publishing Co: Foundation for Philosophy of Creativity, Publ. Adm. Dept., Slippery Rock Univ., Slippery Rock, PA 16057; Title Tel # (412) 738-2416 Title Fax # (412) 738-2098
Personnel: Editor-Larry Cobb
Editorial Description: Carries news of Foundation & Society plus reviews, short articles.
General Info: Yr. Est. 1960, Semi-annually, Trim Size-8½ x 11, Mimeo press, 7 pages, No Color
Subscriptions: Indv. $10
Circulation: (100% controlled), Total-150
List Rental: Rents Lists

Free Mind

Publishing Co: American Humanist Association, 7 Harwood Dr, PO Box 1188, Amherst, NY 14226-7188; Title Tel # (716) 839-5080 Title Fax # (716) 839-5079
Personnel: Editor-Bette Chambers
General Info: Yr. Est. 1957, Bi-monthly, Trim Size-11 x 8.50, 12 pages
Circulation: Total-4,600
Advertising: Inquire for rates.
List Rental: Rents Lists

Hearts of the Handmaidens
See: WOMEN'S

Huna Work
See: RELIGIOUS & THEOLOGICAL

IAPL Newsletter — *Association*

Publishing Co: Sponsor-Intl. Assn. for Philosophy & Literature, SUNY at Stony Brook Dept. Philosophy, Publications, Stony Brook, NY 11794-0001; Title Tel # (516) 632-7592
Personnel: Editor-Hugh Silverman
Editorial Description: Annual conference call for papers & spring program.
General Info: Yr. Est. 1976, Annually
Subscriptions: Indv. $10, Free With Membership
Circulation: Total-1,500
List Rental: Actives: $150/M

Immortal News

Publishing Co: Immortal News, 1027 69th Ave, Philadelphia, PA 19126-2911
Personnel: Publisher-Tony Lomastro
General Info: Yr. Est. 1983, Monthly, 8 pages
Subscriptions: Indv. $15
Acquisitions: Publication Bought, Publication Sold
Circulation: Total-800
Advertising: Inquire for rates. Accepts Inserts.

International Christian Studies Association Newsletter (ICSA Newsletter)
See: RELIGIOUS & THEOLOGICAL

International Society for Neoplatonic Studies-Newsletter

Publishing Co: International Society for Neoplatonic Studies, Coppin State College, 2500 W. North Ave., Baltimore, MD 21216-3698; Title Tel # (410) 333-7840
Personnel: Editor-Dr. William Carrol
Editorial Description: Focuses on issues & concerns of individuals involved in the study of Neoplatonism.
General Info: Yr. Est. 1987, Trim Size-8½ x 11, Desktop press, 8 pages, No Color, Newsprint
Circulation: Total-2,000

Issues in Ethics

Publishing Co: Center for Applied Ethics, Santa Clara University, Santa Clara, CA 95053-0001; Title Tel # (408) 554-5319 Title Fax # (408) 554-2700
Personnel: Editor-Manuel Velasquez, Circ. Mgr.-Jim Wake
General Info: Yr. Est. 1987, Trim Size-8½ x 11, Desktop press, 8 pages, No Color
Acquisitions: Publication Bought
Circulation: Total-4,000

Krotonian

Publishing Co: Krotona Institute of Theosophy, Ojai, CA 93023; Title Tel # (805) 646-2653
Personnel: Editor-Felix Layton
General Info: Quarterly, 4 pages
Subscriptions: Indv. $20

LFL Reports:
See: CIVIL RIGHTS

Light of the Logos

Publishing Co: Institute of Metaphysics, PO Box 640, Yucca Valley, CA 92286-0640; Title Tel # (619) 365-8371
Personnel: Editor-Marlene Tomasek
General Info: Trim Size-5½ x 8½, 16 pages

Live and Let Live
See: POLITICS

Logos — *Association*

Publishing Co: Swedenborg Foundation, PO Box 549, West Chester, PA 19381-0549; Title Tel # (212) 673-7310 Title Fax # (212) 254-0012
Personnel: Editor, Production Mgr.-Kristine Jordahl
Editorial Description: To announce events of the foundation, inform readers of our programs, and publicize our publications, films and books.
General Info: (Formerly Swedenborg Foundation Newsletter), Yr. Est. 1974, Semi-annually, Trim Size-8½ x 11, Sheetfed press, 12 pages, 2 Color
Circulation: (100% controlled), Total-32,000

Lonergan Studies Newsletter — *Association*

Publishing Co: Lonergan Research Institute, 10 St. Mary, #500, Toronto, ON M4Y 1P9 Canada; Title Tel # (416) 922-8374
Personnel: Editor-F.E. Crowe
Editorial Description: News of workshops and meetings exploring the ideas of Lonergan. Includes bibliography of works by and about Lonergan.
General Info: Yr. Est. 1980, Quarterly, Trim Size-8½ x 11, 8 pages, ISSN: 0845-2849
Subscriptions: Indv. $5, Can. $6
Circulation: Total-300

Memberletter
See: ASTROLOGY

Mind-Expander — *Consumer, Association*

Publishing Co: Phenix Society, PO Box 351, Cheshire, CT 06410-0351; Title Tel # (203) 387-6913
Personnel: Editor-Virginia Cone
Editorial Description: Contains articles on meditation, relaxation and related topics.
General Info: Quarterly, 4 pages
Subscriptions: Indv. $6

Museletter
See: SCIENCE

Newsletter of Center for Process Studies — *Association*

Publishing Co: Center for Process Studies, 1325 N College Ave, Claremont, CA 91711-3154; Title Tel # (909) 621-5330
Personnel: Publisher-John B. Cobb, Editor-Laurel Huff
Editorial Description: News & announcements of Center conferences, activities, pubs. & visitors.
General Info: Yr. Est. 1975, 3x/yr., Trim Size-8½ x 11, Offset press, 12 pages, ISSN: 0360-618X, No Color, Matte, Other
Subscriptions: Indv. $5, $2/copy
Circulation: Total-800
Printing Co: Claremont Copy Center, 250 W. First Sreet Suite 116, Claremont, CA 91711 Tel # (714) 624-4615

Noetic Sciences Bulletin — *Consumer, Association*

Publishing Co: Institute of Noetic Sciences, 475 Gate 5 Rd Ste 300, Sausalito, CA 94965-2835; Title Tel # (415) 331-5650
Personnel: Editor-Carol Guion, Circ. Mgr.-Ron Fine, Production Mgr.-James Minkin, Art Dir.-Leona Jamison
Editorial Description: News & events related to activities of the Institute of Noetic Sciences.
General Info: Yr. Est. 1986, Quarterly, Web press, 8 pages, ISSN: 0897-1013, No Color, Newsprint
Subscriptions: Indv. $35, $1/copy
Circulation: Total-19,000
List Rental: List Management Co.: Pacific Lists, 100 Tamal Plaza Ste 50, Corte Madera, CA 94925 Tel # (415) 945-9450, Fax # (415) 945-9451, Actives: $80/M
Printing Co: Alonzo Printing Co., Investment Blvd., Hayward, CA 94080 Tel # (510) 293-0522

One Spirit — *Consumer*

Publishing Co: One Spirit, Circulation, Camp Hill, PA 17012-0001
Editorial Description: Books, cassettes, videos, CDs and CD-ROMs on spirituality, health and psychology.
General Info: Yr. Est. 1995, 15x/yr.

Ozark Feminist Review
See: WOMEN'S

Pantheist Vision

Publishing Co: Universal Pantheist Society, PO Box 265, Big Pine, CA 93513-0265; Title Tel # (209) 739-8527
Personnel: Editor-Harold Wood
Editorial Description: Pantheist Vision is an idea interchange among Pantheists.
General Info: Quarterly, Trim Size-5½ x 8½, 9 pages, ISSN: 0745-5368
Subscriptions: Indv. $8

Perspective
See: EDUCATION

Phil Facts — *Scholarly*

Publishing Co: Philosophy Documentation Center, Bowling Green State Univ., Bowling Green, OH 43403-0001; Title Tel # (419) 372-2419 Title Fax # (419) 372-6987
Personnel: Editor-R.H. Lineback, Circ. Mgr.-Janet Wilhelm, Adv. Dir.-Lori Fells
Editorial Description: Publishes information about the Philosophy Documentation Center & its products & services. The newsletter also includes information on outside philosophical activities that is of interest to our customers.
General Info: Yr. Est. 1984, Semi-annually, Trim Size-8½ x 11, 6 pages, 2 Color
Subscriptions: Free
Circulation: Total-9,000
Advertising: Inquire for rates.
List Rental: Rents Lists

Positive Economist Bulletin Supplement for Objectivists — *Consumer*

Publishing Co: Code of the West Publishing, 1633 Best Ln, Eugene, OR 97401-5030
Editorial Description: Focuses on reality, reason, freedom, and self-responsiblity.
General Info: Yr. Est. 1991, Bi-monthly, Trim Size-8½ x 11, Desktop press, 8 pages, No Color, Matte
Subscriptions: Indv. $30, $5/copy

Prison-Ashram Project
Newsletter *Consumer, Association*

Publishing Co: Human Kindness Foundation, Rt. 1, Box 201-N, Durham, NC 27705-9801; Title Tel # (919) 942-2138 Title Fax # (919) 942-0830
Personnel: Circ. Mgr.-Sita Lozoff, Editor, Art Dir.-Bo Lozoff
Editorial Description: Spiritual (not religious) self-help for prisoners and others.
General Info: Yr. Est. 1973, 3x/yr., Trim Size-5½ x 8½, Sheetfed press, 8 pages, 2 Color, Matte
Circulation: Total-16,000

Report from the Institute for Philosophy & Public Policy *Scholarly*

Publishing Co: Institute for Philosophy & Public Policy, University Of Maryland Rm 3111, Van Munching Hall 31110, College Park, MD 20742-0001; Title Tel # (301) 405-4753 Title Fax # (301) 314-9346
Personnel: Editor-Arthur Evenchik
Editorial Description: Articles intended to advance philosophically informed debate on current policy choices.
General Info: Yr. Est. 1981, Quarterly, Trim Size-8½ x 11, Offset press, 24 pages, ISSN: 1067-2478, 2 Color, Matte, Saddle-stitched
Subscriptions: Free
Circulation: (100% controlled), Total-10,000, Readership-10,000

Response *Consumer, Association*

Publishing Co: Simon Wiesenthal Center, 9760 W Pico Blvd, Los Angeles, CA 90035-4792 Fax # (310) 553-4521; Title Tel # (310) 553-9036 Title Fax # (303) 553-4521
Personnel: Editor in Chief-Abraham Cooper
Editorial Description: Contains articles on contemporary issues, Nazi war criminals, global antisemitism, world Jewry, human rights.
General Info: Yr. Est. 1978, Quarterly, 16 pages, 4 Color
Subscriptions: Free With Membership
Circulation: Total-400,000

Revelations of Awareness
See: NEW AGE

Right of Aesthetic Realism to Be Known, The
See: GENERAL INTEREST

SPEP Newsletter *Association*

Publishing Co: Society for Phenomenology and Existential Philosophy, Villanova University, Dept. of Philosophy, Villanova, PA 19085 Tel # (610) 519-4690
Personnel: Editor-John Caputo
Editorial Description: Annual conferences & information concerning contemporary continental philosophy & the human sciences.
General Info: Yr. Est. 1961, Semi-annually, Trim Size-5½ x 8½, Offset press, 12 pages
Subscriptions: Indv. $20
Circulation: Total-1,200
List Rental: Rents Lists

Sea Wind Letter

Publishing Co: Sea Wind Press, PO Box 222964, Carmel, CA 93922-2964; Title Tel # (408) 624-4760
Personnel: Editor-Gail Pierce
General Info: Quarterly, 6 pages
Subscriptions: Indv. $6
Advertising: Inquire for rates.

Secular Humanist Bulletin *Consumer, Association*

Publishing Co: Codesh Inc., PO Box 664, Buffalo, NY 14226-0664; Title Tel # (716) 636-7571 Title Fax # (716) 636-1733
Personnel: Publisher-Paul Kurtz, Editor-Tom Flynn, Production Mgr.-Timothy Madigan, Promotion Dir.-Steve Karr
Editorial Description: News, humor and opinion regarding secular humanism, church-state separation, biblical criticism, atheism, etc.
General Info: (Formerly The Secular Humanist Bulletin), Yr. Est. 1985, Quarterly, Trim Size-8½ x 11, 16 pages, ISSN: 1063-2611, Matte
Subscriptions: Indv. $18, Inst. $18, $2/copy
Acquistions: Publication Bought
Circulation: Total-5,000
Printing Co: Account Manager: Mary Hennesy; Printers Press, 1881 Kenmore Ave, Kenmore, NY 14217-2523 Tel # (716) 876-2284

Selden Millennium *Association*

Publishing Co: Selden Assn., 1223 Glen Ter, Glassboro, NJ 08028-1315
Personnel: Editor-R. P. Skeen
Editorial Description: Theoretical studies in philosophy of history as organized by Hari Seldon & research faculty of the Trantor Foundation.
General Info: Yr. Est. 1950, Quarterly, Offset press, 24 pages, No Color
Circulation: Total-500

Snow Lion Newsletter & Catalog
See: RELIGIOUS & THEOLOGICAL

Society for Business Ethics
Newsletter *Association*

Publishing Co: Society for Business Ethics, American College, 270 Bryn Mawr Ave., Bryn Mawr, PA 19010-2196 Tel # (610) 526-1387; Title Tel # (408) 554-5319
Personnel: Editor-Manuel Velasquez, Circ. Mgr.-Claire Andre
Editorial Description: To promote study & discussion of business ethics.
General Info: Yr. Est. 1980, Trim Size-8½ x 11, Desktop press, 6 pages, No Color
Subscriptions: Indv. $5
Circulation: Total-660

Society for Values in Higher Education-Newsletter
See: EDUCATION

Sparrow Hawk Villager

Publishing Co: Light of Christ Community Church, 22 Summit Ridge Dr, Tahlequah, OK 74464-9260; Title Tel # (918) 456-3421
Personnel: Editor-Debbie Dice, Editor-Mary Beth Marvin, Circ. Mgr.-Finbarr Ross, Production Mgr.-Marianne Sansing
Editorial Description: Church & seminary schedules & classes, activities of this intl. spiritual community whose philosophy is based on Esoteric Christianity, world religions & metaphysical subjects.
General Info: Monthly, Sheetfed press, 10 pages, No Color, Newsprint
Subscriptions: Indv. $15
Printing Co: Heritage Printing Co., 124 N Water Ave, Tahlequah, OK 74464-2824 Tel # (918) 456-5612

Star Beacon
See: UNIDENTIFIED FLYING OBJECTS

The Temptation of Saint Anthony
See: POETRY & CREATIVE WRITING

Thoughtline *Consumer, Scholarly*

Publishing Co: Arcana Workshops, PO Box 506, Manhattan Beach, CA 90267-0506 Tel # (213) 379-9990; Title Tel # (310) 379-9990
Personnel: Editor-Tom Carney
Editorial Description: Meditation training center commentary on esoteric psychology, healing & meditation.
General Info: Yr. Est. 1956, Monthly, Mimeo press, 6 pages, No Color
Subscriptions: Free
Circulation: Total-350

Transformers Notebook

Publishing Co: Eupsychian Press, PO Box 3090, Austin, TX 78764-3090; Title Tel # (512) 327-2795 Title Fax # (512) 327-6043
Personnel: Publisher-Gregory Zelonka, Editor-Jacquelyn Small
Editorial Description: Jacquelyn Small writes for the transformational people helpers, giving information on 'transformer consciousness' and an itinerary of workshops.
General Info: Yr. Est. 1983, Quarterly, Offset press, 8 pages, 2 Color, Matte
Subscriptions: Inst. $18, $5/copy
Circulation: Total-8,500
List Rental: Rents Lists

Triangles Bulletin
See: CLUBS

USPA Newsletter
See: PARAPSYCHOLOGY

University for Humanistic Studies Quarterly Newsletter

Publishing Co: University for Humanistic Studies, 380 Stevens Ave., Ste. 210, Solana Beach, CA 92075-2068; Title Tel # (619) 259-9733
General Info: Quarterly, 14 pages

Vibrations

Publishing Co: Open Mind Book Store, 119 Harverd SE, P.O. Box 4722, Albuquerque, NM 87196; Title Tel # (505) 262-0066
Personnel: Editor-Rich Cramer
General Info: Monthly, 8 pages
Subscriptions: Indv. $5

Voluntaryist, The
See: POLITICS

Walk Away
See: RELIGIOUS & THEOLOGICAL

Way Fourth
See: RELIGIOUS & THEOLOGICAL

West Coast Libertarian
See: POLITICS

Wisdom Conservancy
Newsletter, The
Consumer, Association

Publishing Co: Wisdom Conservancy at Merriam Hilll Education Ctr., 148 Merriam Hill Rd, Greenville, NH 03048-3300 Fax # (603) 878-2018; Title Tel # (603) 878-0538
Personnel: Publisher, Editor-Steven McFadden
Editorial Description: Conserves, communicates and encourages wisdom. Includes interviews and profiles of learned and compassionate elders from around the world.
General Info: (Formerly Wisdom Chronicle), Yr. Est. 1994, Quarterly, Trim Size-8½ x 11, Offset press, 8 pages, ISSN: 1077-5064
Subscriptions: Indv. $30, Can. $45, For. $45
Circulation: Total-800
Advertising: Inquire for rates.
List Rental: Rents Lists
Printing Co: Atlantic Press, 2 Marshall St, Milford, NH 03055-3714 Tel # (603) 673-0645

World Freedom Bulletin
See: CIVIL RIGHTS

PHOTOGRAPHY

APCDI ImagePack
Business, Association

Publishing Co: Photo Marketing Association International, 3000 Picture Pl, Jackson, MI 49201-8853 Tel # (517) 788-8100 Fax # (517) 788-8371
Personnel: Exec. Ed.-Gary Pageau
Editorial Description: Information for and about the Assn. of Photo CD Imagers.
General Info: Monthly, Trim Size-8½ x 11, 4 pages

APCL Colorgram
Business, Association

Publishing Co: Photo Marketing Association International, 3000 Picture Pl, Jackson, MI 49201-8853 Tel # (517) 788-8100 Fax # (517) 788-8371
Personnel: Exec. Ed.-Gary Pageau
Editorial Description: Reports on the activities of the Assn. of Professional Color Lab members.
General Info: Monthly, Trim Size-8½ x 11, 8 pages

APNY Newsletter
Association

Publishing Co: Advertising Photographers of New York, 27 W. 20th St., New York, NY 10011-3707; Title Tel # (212) 807-0399 Title Fax # (212) 727-8120
Personnel: Publisher-Myina Masuci, Publisher-Lauren Wenle, Editor, Adv. Dir., Art Dir.-Michael O'Connor
General Info: (Formerly APA Magazine), Yr. Est. 1980, Bi-monthly, Trim Size-8½ x 11, Sheetfed press, 32 pages, 50% ads, 4 Color, Coated, Saddle-stitched
Subscriptions: $4/copy
Circulation: (100% controlled), Total-1,200
Advertising: Inquire for rates. Accepts Inserts.
List Rental: Rents Lists

ASP Newsletter
Association

Publishing Co: American Society of Photographers, PO Box 3191, Spartanburg, SC 29304-3191; Title Tel # (803) 585-5688
Personnel: Publisher, Editor-Jerry Cornelius
General Info: Yr. Est. 1937, Quarterly, Sheetfed press, 12 pages, No Color, Newsprint, Saddle-stitched
Circulation: Total-550

American Society of
Media Photographers,
Bulletin
Business, Association

Publishing Co: American Society of Media Photographers, 14 Washington Rd Ste 502, Princeton Junction, NJ 08550-1028; Title Tel # (609) 799-8300 Title Fax # (609) 799-2233
Personnel: Editor-Peter Skinner, Production Mgr.-Cilla Skinner
Editorial Description: Addresses the interests & preoccupations of the photography professional.
General Info: Yr. Est. 1970, Monthly, Sheetfed press, 24 pages, 4 Color, Coated, Saddle-stitched
Subscriptions: Indv. $12
Circulation: (100% controlled), Total-6,000
Advertising: Inquire for rates. Accepts Inserts.
List Rental: Rents Lists

Calumet View

Publishing Co: Calumet Photographic, Inc., 890 Supreme Dr, Bensenville, IL 60106-1181; Title Tel # (708) 860-7447
Personnel: Editor-David Gremp, Art Dir.-Sue Schwerin
Editorial Description: Essays pertaining to professional & fine art photographic interests.
General Info: Yr. Est. 1983, Semi-annually, Trim Size-8½ x 11, Web press, 32 pages, ISSN: 0737-3295, 2 Color, Coated, Saddle-stitched
Circulation: (100% controlled), Total-75,000
Printing Co: Strathmore Printing, 200 Gary Lane, Geneva, IL 60134 Tel # (708) 232-9677, Fax # (708) 232-0198

EPS Decisions
See: PRINTING/GRAPHIC ARTS

Electronic Photography
News
Business

Publishing Co: Photofinishing News, Inc., 10915 Bonita Beach Rd Ste 1091, Bonita Springs, FL 33923-9049; Title Tel # (941) 992-4421 Title Fax # (941) 992-6328
Personnel: Publisher-Don Franz
General Info: Yr. Est. 1986, Monthly, Trim Size-8½ x 11, Desktop press, 8 pages, ISSN: 0896-0976, Newsprint
Subscriptions: Indv. $90, Can. $90, For. $112
Circulation: Total-300

Foto Flash
Association

Publishing Co: Natl. Assn. for Photographic Art, 23 Latham Ave., Scarborough, ON M1H 1Y3 Canada; Title Tel # (416) 261-1626
Personnel: Circ. Mgr.-Bruce Blackburn
Editorial Description: Information about N.A.P.A. activities, photographic exhibitions, tips on photography for N.A.P.A. members.
General Info: Yr. Est. 1969, Quarterly, Offset press, 16 pages, ISSN: 0318-7500, No Color

Genuine Article, The
See: MEN'S

Guilfoyle Report
See: NATURAL HISTORY

Images
Business, Consumer **CPM: $57**

Publishing Co: Noble Publishing Co., PO Box 1509, Candler, NC 28715-1509 Tel # (704) 696-3269 Parent Co.-Unlimited Editions International, Candler
Personnel: Publisher, Editor-Gregory Hugh Leng
Editorial Description: Published for both amateur and professional photographers. Includes information onmarketing photos, competition, and improving skills.
General Info: Yr. Est. 1982, Quarterly, Trim Size-8½ x 11, Web press, 8 pages, 20% ads, No Color, Matte
Subscriptions: Indv. $20, $5/copy
Circulation: Total-21,000
Advertising: $1,200.
List Rental: Actives: $45/M, Hotline: $90/M

In Focus
Association

Publishing Co: American Photographic Historical Society, 1150 6th Ave., New York, NY 10036-2701; Title Tel # (212) 575-0483
Personnel: Editor-George Gilbert, Production Mgr.-Jerry Fine
Editorial Description: Newsletter format for items relevant to study of history of photography.
General Info: Yr. Est. 1983, Monthly, Trim Size-8½ x 11, Desktop press, 4 pages, Matte
Subscriptions: Indv. $30, Inst. $25, Can. $40, For. $40, $3/copy
Circulation: Total-500, Readership-500
Advertising: Inquire for rates. Accepts Inserts.

International Association of
Panoramic
Photographers
Consumer, Association

Publishing Co: International Association of Panoramic Photographers, 2725 Sutton Blvd, Saint Louis, MO 63143-3007 Tel # (314) 781-3600
Personnel: Editor-Warren Wight, Circ. Mgr.-Richard Fowler
Editorial Description: For amateur and professional panoramic photographers.
General Info: Monthly, Trim Size-8½ x 11, 16 pages, ISSN: 1063-7478, 2 Color

International Museum of
Photography At George
Eastman House
Newsletter
Consumer

Publishing Co: George Eastman House International Museum of Photography and, 900 East Ave, Rochester, NY 14607-2219; Title Tel # (716) 271-3361 Title Fax # (716) 271-3970
Personnel: Editor-Elizal Benington, Production Mgr.-Ann H. Stevens, Art Dir.-Windsor St. Design Assoc., Mktg. Dir.-Patricia S. Muself
Editorial Description: News events and calendar of museum's activities. Produced 10 times per year.
General Info: Yr. Est. 1979, 10x/yr., Trim Size-7 x 11, Offset press, 14 pages, ISSN: 1055-3886, Color, Coated, Saddle-stitched
Subscriptions: Free With Membership
Circulation: Total-3,600
Printing Co: Ayer & Streb, 148 Hollenbeck St, Rochester, NY 14621-3234 Tel # (716) 544-0900

Leased Access Report - Audience
See: TELEVISION & VIDEO

Light and Shade
Business, Association

Publishing Co: Pictorial Photographers of America, 299 W. 12th St., New York, NY 10014-1824; Title Tel # (212) 242-1117
Personnel: Publisher, Editor-Sylvia Mavis
Editorial Description: Published monthly, October through June.
General Info: Yr. Est. 1916, Monthly, Web press, 6 pages
Subscriptions: Indv. $40

Mini Lab Focus
Business, Association

Publishing Co: Sponsor-PMA, Photo Marketing Association International, 3000 Picture Pl, Jackson, MI 49201-8853; Title Tel # (517) 788-8100 Title Fax # (517) 788-8371
Personnel: Exec. Ed.-Gary Pageau
Editorial Description: For Mini Lab owners & managers.
General Info: (Formerly Focus), Yr. Est. 1984, Monthly, Trim Size-17 x 11, Offset press, 4 pages, 2 Color
Subscriptions: Free With Membership
Circulation: Total-3,000

Minolta Contact Sheet

Publishing Co: Minolta Corp., 101 Williams Dr, Ramsey, NJ 07446-1293
Personnel: Editor-John Jonny
General Info: Semi-annually

NAPET News
Business, Association

Publishing Co: Photo Marketing Association International, 3000 Picture Pl, Jackson, MI 49201-8853 Fax # (517) 788-8371; Title Tel # (517) 788-8100
Personnel: Exec. Ed.-Gary Pageau
Editorial Description: Published for members of the Natl. Assn. of Photo Equipment Technicians (repair firms).
General Info: Monthly, Desktop press, 2 pages, 2 Color, Coated
Circulation: Total-750

Natural Image
Business, Consumer

Publishing Co: Lepp & Assocs., PO Box 6240, Los Osos, CA 93412-6240; Title Tel # (805) 528-7385
Personnel: Editor-George Lepp
Editorial Description: How-to articles for photography techniques and equipment usage.
General Info: Yr. Est. 1985, Quarterly, Trim Size-5$\frac{1}{2}$ x 8$\frac{1}{2}$, Desktop press, 24 pages
Subscriptions: Indv. $18, Can. $18, For. $24
Circulation: Total-1,500
Printing Co: A-1 Printers, 525 Harbor St, Morro Bay, CA 93442-1903 Tel # (805) 772-3200

Nikkei Weekly
Business

Publishing Co: Nikkei Weekly, 1325 Ave. of the Americas, New York, NY 10019
General Info: Weekly
Subscriptions: Indv. $108

Open Space
Consumer

Publishing Co: Open Space Art Society, 5100 Fort Street, Victoria, BC V8W 1E6 Canada; Title Tel # (604) 383-8833
Personnel: Editor-Tom Gore
Editorial Description: Reviews criticism, letters & excerpts from the literature of photography.
General Info: Yr. Est. 1975, Trim Size-8$\frac{1}{2}$ x 11, 8 pages
Subscriptions: Indv. $10
Circulation: Total-200

PRC Newsletter
Business, Consumer

Publishing Co: Photographic Resource Center, Boston University, 602 Commonwealth Ave., Boston, MA 02215-1300; Title Tel # (617) 353-0700
Personnel: Editor-Darsie Alexander
Editorial Description: Guide to photo exhibitions, lectures, conferences, publications, contests, workshops, etc.
General Info: Monthly, Trim Size-8$\frac{1}{2}$ x 11, Matte
Subscriptions: Free With Membership
List Rental: Rents Lists

PWP Newsletter
Business, Association

Publishing Co: Photographics Unlimited, 17 W. 17th St., New York, NY 10011-5510; Title Tel # (212) 255-9676
Editorial Description: Open to all women & men photographers.
General Info: (Formerly Professional Women's Photographers Newsletter), Yr. Est. 1984, Bi-monthly, No Color
Subscriptions: Indv. $15
Circulation: Total-500
Advertising: Inquire for rates.

Photo Daily
Business

Publishing Co: PhotoSource Intl., Pine Lake Farm, 1910 35th Rd., Osceola, WI 54020-5602; Title Tel # (715) 248-3800 Title Fax # (715) 248-7394
Personnel: Publisher-Rohn Engh, Editor-Lori Johnson, Circ. Mgr.-Kathy Kloetzke, Production Mgr.-Alice Dee
Editorial Description: Provides photo marketing information through electronic delivery. Photo Daily lists the specific photographic needs of advertising agencies, public relation firms, corporations, & major book & magazine publishers.
General Info: (Formerly Photobulletin Daily), Yr. Est. 1989, Weekly, Trim Size-8$\frac{1}{2}$ x 11, 3 pages, Ind/Abs/Online: GEnie, NewsNet, No Color
Subscriptions: Indv. $660, For. $515, $15/copy
List Rental: List Management Co.: Carnegie Marketing Assocs., Koll Executive Plaza, 3878 Carson St., Suite 220, Torrance, CA 90503 Tel # (310) 540-4757, Fax # (310) 540-7407, Actives: 43,743, $80/M

Photo Marketing Newsline
Association

Publishing Co: Photo Marketing Association International, 3000 Picture Pl, Jackson, MI 49201-8853; Title Tel # (517) 788-8100 Title Fax # (517) 788-8371
Personnel: Exec. Ed.-Gary Pageau
Editorial Description: News of interest to photo businesses. Trade pub.
General Info: Yr. Est. 1970, Bi-weekly, Trim Size-8$\frac{1}{2}$ x 11, Sheetfed press, 4 pages, 2 Color
Subscriptions: Indv. $36
Circulation: Total-13,200
List Rental: Actives: $150/M

Photo Review Newsletter, The
Consumer

Publishing Co: Photo Review, The, 301 Hill Ave, Langhorne, PA 19047-2819; Title Tel # (215) 757-8921 Title Fax # (215) 757-6421
Personnel: Editor-Stephen Perloff
Editorial Description: News on photographic activities in the Mid-Atlantic area.
General Info: (Formerly Phila. Photo Review Newsletter, The), Yr. Est. 1976, 8x/yr., Trim Size-8$\frac{1}{2}$ x 11, Sheetfed press, 8 pages, ISSN: 0363-0488, No Color, Matte
Subscriptions: Indv. $28, Can. $35, For. $42
Circulation: Total-2,300
Advertising: Inquire for rates.
Printing Co: Consolidated/Drake, 5050 Parkside Ave, Philadelphia, PA 19131-4794 Tel # (215) 879-1400

Photo Scientist

Publishing Co: Rochester Institute of Technology Alumni Relations, Box 9887, Alumni Relations Dept., Rochester, NY 14623-0887 Tel # (716) 475-2400
General Info: Quarterly
Circulation: Total-1,000

PhotoStockNotes
Business

Publishing Co: PhotoSource Intl., Pine Lake Farm, 1910 35th Rd., Osceola, WI 54020-5602; Title Tel # (715) 248-3800 Title Fax # (715) 248-7394
Personnel: Publisher-Rohn Engh, Editor-Lori Johnson, Circ. Mgr.-Kathy Kay
Editorial Description: Information that keeps stock photographers up to date on what's working in the industry.
General Info: Yr. Est. 1993, Monthly, Trim Size-8$\frac{1}{2}$ x 11, 8 pages, 2 Color, Matte
Subscriptions: Indv. $60, $5/copy
Advertising: Accepts Inserts.

Photofinishing Newsletter
Business, Consumer

Publishing Co: Photofinishing News, Inc., 10915 Bonita Beach Rd Ste 1091, Bonita Springs, FL 33923-9049; Title Tel # (941) 992-4421 Title Fax # (941) 992-6328
Personnel: Editor-Donald Franz
Editorial Description: Covers marketing, technical developments worldwide in amateur & professional photo processing.
General Info: Yr. Est. 1983, Bi-weekly, Trim Size-8$\frac{1}{2}$ x 11, Desktop press, 8 pages, ISSN: 0889-2393, Newsprint
Subscriptions: Indv. $125, Can. $125, For. $150
Acquistions: Publication Bought
Circulation: Total-400

Photofolio
Business, Consumer

Publishing Co: Photocollect, 740 West End Ave., New York, NY 10025-6246; Title Tel # (212) 222-7381
Personnel: Publisher, Editor-Alan Klotz, Circ. Mgr.-Tania Hryuyszyn
Editorial Description: Photographic history, conservation, photograph collecting, market analysis, auction summary.
General Info: Quarterly, Trim Size-8$\frac{1}{2}$ x 11, Sheetfed press, 10 pages
Subscriptions: Indv. $20, $5/copy
Circulation: Total-500

Photograph Collector
Business, Consumer

Publishing Co: Photographic Arts Center, 163 Amsterdam Ave #201, New York, NY 10023-5001 Parent Co.-The Consultant Press, New York; Title Tel # (212) 838-8640 Title Fax # (212) 873-7065
Personnel: Publisher-Robert Persky, Editor-Joshua Persky, Circ. Mgr.-Bob Persky
Editorial Description: Information for the serious photograph collector, the curator & dealer.
General Info: Yr. Est. 1980, Monthly, Trim Size-8$\frac{1}{2}$ x 11, Sheetfed press, 8 pages, ISSN: 0271-0838, No Color, Other
Subscriptions: Indv. $125, Can. $125, For. $149, $10/copy
Circulation: Total-1,000
Advertising: Accepts Inserts.
List Rental: Actives: $85/M

Photographs: A Collector's Newsletter

Publishing Co: Allen Arpadi, 5846 Waterman Blvd, Saint Louis, MO 63112-1516; Title Tel # (212) 966-4185
Personnel: Editor-John Crittenden
General Info: Bi-monthly
Subscriptions: Indv. $65

Photography   *Business*

Publishing Co: Photography Assocs., PO Box A, Old Greenwich, CT 06870-0601;
Title Tel # (203) 531-7807 Title Fax # (203) 622-6688
Personnel: Publisher-C. De La Belle Issue, Production Mgr.-D. Wheeler, Editor, Circ. Mgr., Promotion Dir.-R.H. Lourie
Editorial Description: Text & photography oriented to current market themes. Also book reviews, gallery & exposition information, international photography events.
General Info: Yr. Est. 1987, Quarterly, 32 pages, Coated, Saddle-stitched
Subscriptions: Indv. $500
Acquistions: Publication Bought, Publication Sold
Circulation: Total-1,150

Photoletter   *Consumer*

Publishing Co: PhotoSource Intl., Pine Lake Farm, 1910 35th Rd., Osceola, WI 54020-5602;
Title Tel # (715) 248-3800 Title Fax # (715) 248-7394
Personnel: Publisher-Rohn Engh, Editor-Lynette Layer, Circ. Mgr.-Kathy Kay, Production Mgr.-Alice Dee, Promotion Dir.-Lori Johnson
Editorial Description: Information source for independent photographers. Contains new and useful marketing information and trends in the field.
General Info: Yr. Est. 1976, Monthly, Trim Size-8½ x 11, Offset press, 4 pages, ISSN: 0190-1400, Ind/Abs/Online: NewsNet, GEnie, MCI, No Color
Subscriptions: Indv. $108, $9/copy
Circulation: Total-634
Advertising: Accepts Inserts.
List Rental: List Management Co.: Manager: Rohn Engh; Carnegie Marketing Assocs., Koll Executive Plaza, 3878 Carson St., Suite 220, Torrance, CA 90503 Tel # (310) 540-4757, Fax # (310) 540-7407, Actives: 43,743, $60/M, Hotline: $60/M

Picture Buyer and F.P.G.
Newsletter to
Photographers   *Business*

Publishing Co: Picture Buyer, 32 Union Square, New York, NY 10003; Title Tel # (212) 777-4210
Personnel: Editor-Arthur Brackman
Editorial Description: Market information for photographers and prospective buyers.
General Info: Yr. Est. 1936, Quarterly

Re:view   *Association*

Publishing Co: Friends of Photography, 250 4th St, San Francisco, CA 94103-3117;
Title Tel # (415) 495-7000 Title Fax # (415) 495-8517
Personnel: Editor-Michael Read
Editorial Description: Review of photography books, and information about activities of The Friends and the field of photography.
General Info: (Formerly Friends of Photography Newsletter), Yr. Est. 1978, Bi-monthly, Trim Size-8½ x 11, Web press, 16 pages, ISSN: 0891-5326, No Color, Newsprint, Saddle-stitched
Subscriptions: Indv. $50, $2/copy
Circulation: Total-15,000
Printing Co: Alonzo Printing Co., Investment Blvd., Hayward, CA 94080 Tel # (510) 293-0522

Rotkin Review   *Business*

Publishing Co: Photography for Industry (PFI) Books, 38 Rick Lane, W., RR4, Peekskill, NY 10566-9804 Tel # (914) 736-7693 Fax # (914) 736-7694; Title Tel # (212) 757-9255
Personnel: Publisher, Editor-Charles Rotkin
Editorial Description: Reviews & direct-markets photographic, art, and communications books only.
General Info: Yr. Est. 1985, Quarterly, Trim Size-8½ x 11, Sheetfed press, 36 pages, ISSN: 0883-735X, 2% ads, No Color, Saddle-stitched
Subscriptions: Indv. $25, $8/copy
Circulation: (95% controlled), Subscriptions-250
Advertising: Accepts Inserts.

SPE Newsletter

Publishing Co: Society for Photographic Education, Campus Box Univ. Colo., #318, Boulder, CO 80309-0001; Title Tel # (505) 268-4073
Personnel: Editor-Judith Thorpe, Production Mgr., Adv. Dir.-Janet Pritchard
General Info: Yr. Est. 1963, 5x/yr., Offset press, 6 pages, ISSN: 0748-6413, No Color
Subscriptions: Indv. $50
Circulation: Total-1,700
Advertising: Inquire for rates. Accepts Inserts.
List Rental: Actives: $150/M

SPFE Newsletter   *Business, Association*

Publishing Co: Sponsor-Society of Photo Finishing Engineers (SPFE), Photo Marketing Association International, 3000 Picture Pl, Jackson, MI 49201-8853 Fax # (517) 788-8371; Title Tel # (517) 788-8100
Personnel: Exec. Ed.-Gary Pageau, Art Dir.-Melissa Genco
Editorial Description: Published for SPFE members (wholesale photofinishers qualifying by exam).
General Info: Bi-monthly, Desktop press, 4 pages, 2 Color
Circulation: Total-1,034

Sales Counter   *Business, Association*

Publishing Co: Sponsor-Society of Photographic Counselors (CPC), Photo Marketing Association International, 3000 Picture Pl, Jackson, MI 49201-8853; Title Tel # (517) 788-8100 Title Fax # (517) 788-8371
Personnel: Exec. Ed.-Gary Pageau
Editorial Description: Published for CPC members (photo/video retailers qualifying by exam to become a CPC).
General Info: Monthly, Trim Size-8½ x 11, Desktop press, 4 pages, 2 Color, Coated
Circulation: Total-1,100

School Photographer   *Business, Association*

Publishing Co: Sponsor-PSPA-Prof. School Photogr. of America, Photo Marketing Association International, 3000 Picture Pl, Jackson, MI 49201-8853; Title Tel # (517) 788-8100 Title Fax # (517) 788-8371
Personnel: Publisher-Lora Helou, Exec. Ed.-Gary Pageau
Editorial Description: Published for PSPA members (Professional School Photographers of America).
General Info: Monthly, Trim Size-8½ x 11, Desktop press, 4 pages, 2 Color, Coated
Circulation: Total-600

Specialty Lab Update   *Business, Association*

Publishing Co: Photo Marketing Association International, 3000 Picture Pl, Jackson, MI 49201-8853 Fax # (517) 788-8371; Title Tel # (517) 788-8100
Personnel: Exec. Ed.-Gary Pageau, Art Dir.-Melissa Genco
Editorial Description: Published for commercial & in-house photo labs.
General Info: Monthly, Desktop press, 4 pages, 2 Color, Coated
Circulation: Total-1,300

Step-By-Step Electronic Design
See: COMPUTERS & AUTOMATION

Stock Shooter

Publishing Co: Redstone Publishing, 8 Thomas St., New York, NY 10007-1197;
Title Tel # (212) 964-8027
Personnel: Publisher-Raeanne Rubinstein
General Info: Yr. Est. 1987, 10x/yr., 18 pages, ISSN: 0896-1387
Subscriptions: Indv. $57

Thin Film Directions

Publishing Co: Materials Research Corp., Rte. 303, Orangeburg, NY 10962
General Info: 4 pages

Visual Literacy Review & Newsletter
See: EDUCATION

Wedding Photographer,
The   *Association*

Publishing Co: Wedding Photographers Intl., 1312 Lincoln Blvd # 2003, Santa Monica, CA 90401-1706; Title Tel # (213) 451-0090
Personnel: Publisher-Steve Sheanin, Editor-Sandi Messana, Art Dir.-Gennie Kiuchi
Editorial Description: Monthly membership newsletter for professional wedding photographers.
General Info: Yr. Est. 1975, Monthly, 10 pages, 2 Color, Newsprint
Subscriptions: Indv. $75
Circulation: Total-3,000
List Rental: Rents Lists

Wolfman Report   *Business*

Publishing Co: Hachette Filipacchi Magazines, Inc., 1633 Broadway, New York, NY 10019-6741 Tel # (212) 767-6000 Fax # (212) 489-4577
Personnel: Publisher-Lydia Wolfman, Editor-Harold Martin
Editorial Description: Wolfman Report on the photographic & imaging industry in the United States.
General Info: Annually, ISSN: 0084-103X, 4 Color, Coated, Saddle-stitched
Subscriptions: Indv. $135, $175/copy
Circulation: Total-9,000
Advertising: Inquire for rates.

Zone VI Newsletter   *Business, Consumer*

Publishing Co: Zone VI Studios, Inc., 22 High St, Brattleboro, VT 05301-3001;
Title Tel # (802) 257-5161
Personnel: Editor-Fred Picker
Editorial Description: A quarterly reviews of concepts, techniques, & products in the photographic field. Written by Fred Picker author of five photography books & renowned teacher.
General Info: Yr. Est. 1972, Quarterly
Subscriptions: Indv. $19, $3/copy
List Rental: Actives: $70/M

PHYSICS

AAPT Announcer   *Association*

Publishing Co: American Association of Physics Teachers Publications, 1 Physics Ellipse, College Park, MD 20740; Title Tel # (301) 345-4200
Personnel: Editor-Bernard Khoury, Circ. Mgr.-Ruth Spong, Production Mgr.-Donna Willis, Adv. Dir.-Delores Mason
Editorial Description: Information about AAPT meetings and other activities to AAPT members.
General Info: Yr. Est. 1971, Quarterly, Web press, 100 pages, ISSN: 0275-5691, 1% ads, 2 Color
Subscriptions: Indv. $35, Free
Circulation: Total-9,500
Advertising: Inquire for rates.
List Rental: Actives: $85/M
Printing Co: Sheridan Press, 450 Fame Ave, Hanover, PA 17331-9581 Tel # (717) 632-3535, Fax # (717) 633-8900

AIP History of Physics Newsletter

Publishing Co: American Institute of Physics, One Physics Ellipse, College Park, MD 20740-3843 Tel # (301) 209-3000 Fax # (516) 394-9704; Title Tel # (212) 661-9404
Personnel: Editor-Spencer Weart
General Info: (Formerly AIP Newsletter), Yr. Est. 1964, Semi-annually
Circulation: Total-6,000

APS News   *Scholarly, Association*

Publishing Co: American Institute of Physics, One Physics Ellipse, College Park, MD 20740-3843 Tel # (301) 209-3000 Fax # (516) 394-9704; Title Tel # (301) 209-3200
Personnel: Editor in Chief-Benjamin Bederson, Editor-Brian B. Schwartz
Editorial Description: Contains news of the society and of its Divisions, Topical Groups, Sections, and Forums; advance information on meetings of the Society; and reports to the Society by its committees and task force.
General Info: Monthly, ISSN: 1058-8132
Subscriptions: Inst. $120, Can. $130, For. $140

BACUS News
See: ENGINEERING, ELECTRICAL

Biomedical Optics
See: OPTICAL

CryoGas International
See: CHEMISTRY & CHEMICALS

Diamond Industry Week
See: SCIENCE

Electrical Sensitivity News
See: ENVIRONMENT & ECOLOGY

Electronic Imaging
See: ENGINEERING, ELECTRICAL

F-IR Update   *Business*

Publishing Co: Perkin-Elmer Corp., 761 Main Ave., Norwalk, CT 06859-0105 Tel # (203) 762-6023 Fax # (203) 764-2892
Editorial Description: Covers latest news in infra-red spectroscopy.
General Info: Quarterly

Future Technology Intelligence Report
See: SCIENCE

Holography
See: ENGINEERING, ELECTRICAL

Inspec Matters
See: ENGINEERING, ELECTRICAL

Institute for Fusion Studies Newsletter   *Scholarly*

Publishing Co: Institute for Fusion Studies, Univ. of Texas at Austin, RLM 11 234, Austin, TX 78712-1060; Title Tel # (512) 471-4378 Title Fax # (512) 471-6715
Personnel: Editor-Frank Waelbroeck, Circ. Mgr.-Saralyn Stewart
General Info: Yr. Est. 1982, Annually, Trim Size-8½ x 11, 10 pages, ISSN: 1076-9080, Color, Matte, Perfect bound
Subscriptions: Free To Qualified Recipient
Circulation: Total-400, Readership-700
Advertising: Inquire for rates.
Printing Co: Austex Printing Co., 501 W 3rd St, Austin, TX 78701-3807 Tel # (512) 476-7581

Laserline

Publishing Co: Litton Laser Systems, PO Box 547300, Orlando, FL 32854-7300 Tel # (407) 295-4010; Title Tel # (305) 295-4010
Personnel: Editor-Phillis Heatley
General Info: Yr. Est. 1972, Monthly
Subscriptions: Indv. $45
Circulation: Total-500

Microscopial Society of Canada. Bulletin
See: OPTICAL

NanoNews
See: SCIENCE

Occultation Newsletter
See: ASTRONOMY

Optical Computing
See: ENGINEERING, ELECTRICAL

Optical Signal & Image Processing
See: ENGINEERING, ELECTRICAL

Physicians' Medicare Guide

Publishing Co: CCH, Inc., 2700 Lake Cook Rd., Riverwoods, IL 60015 Parent Co.-Kluwer Law & Taxation Publishers, Cambridge; Title Tel # (847) 267-7000 Title Fax # (800) 224-8299
Editorial Description: Contains information that physicians, their billing clerk and billing agencies need to understand the Medicare (RVS) fee schedule under the Medicare part b program and to calculate the amount paid under the fee schedule.
General Info: Bi-monthly, Looseleaf
Subscriptions: Indv. $365

Physics   *Business*

Publishing Co: National Technical Information Service U.S., 5285 Port Royal Rd., Springfield, VA 22161-0001 Tel # (703) 487-4630 Fax # (703) 487-4630; Title Tel # (703) 487-4650
Editorial Description: Covers acoustics, fluid mechanics, optics, lasers, solid state physics, crystallography, cryogenics, structural mechanics, plasma physics, electricity, & magnetism.
General Info: Weekly, Trim Size-8½ x 11, Offset press, 16 pages, ISSN: 0163-1446, No Color
Subscriptions: Indv. $105, Can. $145

RLE Currents
See: ENGINEERING, ELECTRICAL

Rheology Bulletin

Publishing Co: Society of Rheology, c/o Dr. Arthur Metzner, Chemical Engineering, Univ. of Delaware, Newark, DE 19716
Personnel: Editor-Raymond R. Myers
Editorial Description: News of interest to members.
General Info: Yr. Est. 1937

Robotics
See: ENGINEERING, ELECTRICAL

SPS Newsletter   *Consumer*

Publishing Co: Sponsor-American Institute of Physics, Society of Physics Students, 1825 Connecticut Ave NW Ste, 213, Washington, DC 20009-5708 Parent Co.-American Institute of Physics, College Park; Title Tel # (202) 232-6688
Personnel: Editor-Donald Kirwan
Editorial Description: News of interest to the members of the Society of Physics Students.
General Info: Yr. Est. 1968, 5x/yr., Sheetfed press, 8 pages, No Color, Newsprint, Saddle-stitched
Circulation: Total-9,000

Sigma Pi Sigma Radiations   *Association*

Publishing Co: American Institute of Physics, One Physics Ellipse, College Park, MD 20740-3843 Tel # (301) 209-3000 Fax # (516) 394-9704
Personnel: Editor-Donald Kirwan
Editorial Description: Information on Sigma Pi Sigma, the physics honor society, and on physics news.
General Info: (Formerly Radiations of Sigma Pi Sigma, The), Yr. Est. 1930, Annually, Trim Size-8½ x 11, Sheetfed press, 8 pages, No Color
Circulation: (100% controlled), Total-25,000

Superconductivity News
See: SCIENCE

Thermophysics and Electronics Newsletter   *Consumer*

Publishing Co: CINDAS, 2595 Yeager Rd, West Lafayette, IN 47906-1398; Title Tel # (317) 494-6300
Personnel: Editor-C.Y. Ho
Editorial Description: Editorial, Calendar of Events, News of CINDAS/TEPIAC, Technical Digest.
General Info: Yr. Est. 1972, Quarterly, Trim Size-8½ x 11, Offset press, 6 pages, ISSN: 0194-6455, Color
Circulation: (100% controlled), Total-11,000

USPA Newsletter
See: PARAPSYCHOLOGY

PHYSIOLOGY

American Academy of Esthetic Dentistry Newsletter
See: DENTAL

Contact   *Association*   CPM: $128

Publishing Co: Canadian Physiotherapy Assn., 890 Yonge St., 9th Fl., Toronto, ON M4W 3P4 Canada; Title Tel # (416) 924-5312 Title Fax # (416) 924-7335
Personnel: Editor-Dale James, Adv. Dir.-Robin Hurst, Mktg. Dir.-Giuliano Tolusso
Editorial Description: News and information on trends and issues of interest to CPA members.
General Info: Yr. Est. 1980, Monthly, Trim Size-8½ x 11, Web press, 12 pages, 3% ads, 2 Color, Recycled, Saddle-stitched
Subscriptions: Free With Membership
Circulation: (100% controlled), Total-7,500
Advertising: $965.
List Rental: Rents Lists

Creative Health Newsletter
See: HEALTH

Kinnection
Business, Association

Publishing Co: Ontario Association of Applied Kinesiology, 6519B Mississauga Rd., Mississauga, ON L5N 1A6 Canada Fax # (416) 567-7191; Title Tel # (416) 567-7194 Title Fax # (905) 567-7191
Personnel: Editor-Rick Roach
Editorial Description: The Ontario Association of Applied Kinesiology exists to promote the application of the science of human movement to other professionals and to the community; to uphold the standards of the profession of Kinesiology; and to assist Kinesiologists in the performance of their duties and responsibilities.
General Info: Yr. Est. 1983, Bi-monthly, Trim Size-8½ x 11, Desktop press, 8 pages, ISSN: 0823-0536, No Color, Matte
Circulation: Total-350
Advertising: Inquire for rates. Accepts Inserts.
List Rental: Actives: $150/M

LPI Newsletter
See: MEDICINE

Physiologist
Consumer

Publishing Co: American Physiological Society, 9650 Rockville Pike, Bethesda, MD 20814-3998 Tel # (301) 530-7071; Title Tel # (301) 530-7164 Title Fax # (301) 571-1814
Personnel: Editor-M. Frank, Circ. Mgr.-Sam Masri, Production Mgr.-Laurie Chambers, Adv. Dir.-Charles Hirsch, Art Dir.-Susie Mann, Publisher, Promotion Dir.-Brenda Rauner
Editorial Description: Articles on Society affairs & announcements, as well as articles of impotances to physiologists but not suitable for other Society publications. Supplements are published on an annual basis.
General Info: Yr. Est. 1957, Bi-monthly, Trim Size-8½ x 11, Sheetfed press, 16 pages, ISSN: 0031-9376, 2 Color, Matte, Saddle-stitched
Subscriptions: Indv. $25, For. $35, $15/copy
Circulation: Total-6,800
Advertising: Inquire for rates.
List Rental: Rents Lists
Printing Co: FASEB Printing, 9650 Rockville Pike, Bethesda, MD 20814-3998 Tel # (301) 530-7000

Physiology Canada
Association   **CPM: $461**

Publishing Co: Sponsor-Canadian Physiological Soc., Canadian Physiological Society, University of Western Ontario, Department of Physiology, London, ON N6A 5C1 Canada; Title Tel # (519) 661-3480
Personnel: Editor-D.L. Jones
Editorial Description: Physiology and medical science in Canada.
General Info: Yr. Est. 1969, 3x/yr., Trim Size-4 x 5½, Offset press, 60 pages, ISSN: 0822-9058, Color-cover, Saddle-stitched
Subscriptions: Indv. $12, Can. $12, $7/copy
Circulation: Total-650
Advertising: $300. Accepts Inserts.

Sports Medicine in Primary Care
See: MEDICINE

PLASTICS

ACM Monthly
Business

Publishing Co: Composite Market Reports, 1345 E. Main St., Suite 100, Mesa, AZ 85203-8950; Title Tel # (602) 461-9445 Title Fax # (602) 461-8177
Personnel: Publisher, Editor-Bill Benjamin
Editorial Description: Market and technology intelligence for materials suppliers. Covers advanced composite materials, processes, markets, applications, and acquisition/divestiture information in the sectors of military, industrial, sports/recreation, transport, civil engineering, and more.
General Info: Yr. Est. 1971, Monthly, Offset press, 8 pages, ISSN: 1058-9031, No Color
Subscriptions: Inst. $2,325

ASEP News and Views
Consumer, Association

Publishing Co: American Society of Electroplated Plastics, 1767 Business Center Dr., Reston, VA 22090-5332; Title Tel # (202) 371-1323 Title Fax # (202) 371-1090
Personnel: Editor-Peter Rolph, Publisher, Adv. Dir.-David Barrack, Production Mgr., Art Dir.-Jennifer Baugh
Editorial Description: Association news & technical information affecting the electroplated plastics industry.
General Info: (Formerly ASEP Newsletter), Yr. Est. 1966, Quarterly, Trim Size-8½ x 11, Mimeo press, 6 pages, 2 Color
Circulation: (100% controlled), Total-500
Advertising: Inquire for rates.
List Rental: Rents Lists

Additives for Polymers
Business

Publishing Co: Elsevier Science Inc., 655 Avenue of the Americas, New York, NY 10010-5107 Tel # (212) 633-3916 Fax # (212) 633-3913 Parent Co.-Reed Elsevier, New York; Title Tel # (212) 633-3750 Title Fax # (212) 633-3764
Personnel: Publisher-Guy Kitteringham, Editor-A. Weawer, Promotion Dir.-F. Robinson
Editorial Description: Each issue identifies and details relevant materials and products, new applications, new research and technical developments, newly issued US and British patents.
General Info: Monthly, ISSN: 0306-3747
Subscriptions: Indv. $589

Advanced Materials
See: MANUFACTURING

Antique Comb Collector
See: ANTIQUES & ART GOODS

Composites & Adhesives Newsletter
See: ENGINEERING

Composites Industry
Monthly   *Business*

Publishing Co: Composite Market Reports, 1345 E. Main St., Suite 100, Mesa, AZ 85203-8950; Title Tel # (602) 461-9445 Title Fax # (602) 461-8177
Personnel: Publisher, Editor-William Benjamin
Editorial Description: Market and technology intelligence for users, prime & sub-contractors, universities, government, and others. covers advanced composite materials, processes, applications, and acquisition/divestiture information in the sectors of military, industrial, sports/recreation, transport, medical, and more.
General Info: Yr. Est. 1989, Monthly, Offset press, 8 pages, ISSN: 1058-904X, No Color, Matte
Subscriptions: Inst. $1,495

Composites News:
Infrastructure   *Business*

Publishing Co: Composites Worldwide Inc., 991 Lomas Santa Fe Dr # C469, Solana Beach, CA 92075-2125; Title Tel # (619) 755-1372 Title Fax # (619) 755-5271
Personnel: Publisher, Editor, Mag. Ed., Circ. Mgr.-Steve Loud, Adv. Dir.-Susan Loud
Editorial Description: Focuses on the processes, applications markets, design, international activities and more related to composite materials, particularly for civil engineering and construction, but for all markets and structural applications.
General Info: Yr. Est. 1993, Bi-weekly, Trim Size-11 x 17, Offset press, 8 pages, ISSN: 1074-519X, Ind/Abs/Online: dialog,dow jones news retrieval, Matte
Subscriptions: Indv. $287, Inst. $287, For. $317, $13/copy
Circulation: Total-1,000, Readership-4,500
Advertising: Inquire for rates. Accepts Inserts.
List Rental: Rents Lists
Printing Co: Complex Graphics, 7188 Clairemont Mesa Blvd, San Diego, CA 92111-1005 Tel # (619) 467-0474, Fax # (619) 467-0301

Cureletter
See: MANUFACTURING

DLPA News
Business, Association

Publishing Co: Decorative Laminate Products Assn., 13924 Braddock Rd # 100, Centreville, VA 22020-1910; Title Tel # (312) 922-6222 Title Fax # (312) 922-2734
Personnel: Publisher, Editor, Adv. Dir.-Charles Stolberg
Editorial Description: Technical articles, news items, & new product information for fabricators of plastic laminate.
General Info: Quarterly, Trim Size-8½ x 11, Sheetfed press, 8 pages, 30% ads, 2 Color, Coated
Subscriptions: Indv. $12, $3/copy
Circulation: Total-1,000
Advertising: Inquire for rates. Accepts Inserts.

Flexible Packaging Assn. Update
See: PACKAGING

Great Lakes Basin Report
See: FISH & FISHERIES

High Performance Plastics
Business

Publishing Co: Elsevier Science Inc., 655 Avenue of the Americas, New York, NY 10010-5107 Tel # (212) 633-3916 Fax # (212) 633-3913 Parent Co.-Reed Elsevier, New York
Personnel: Publisher-Guy Katteringham, Editor-A. Weawer, Circ. Mgr.-Karen Richardson, Production Mgr.-F. Robinson
Editorial Description: Monthly report on manufacture & uses of high performance plastics in industry.
General Info: Yr. Est. 1983, Monthly, 16 pages, ISSN: 0264-7753, Ind/Abs/Online: DIALOG
Subscriptions: Indv. $474

Holography News
See: PRINTING/GRAPHIC ARTS

ISRI Report
See: METALS & METALWORKING

Nonwoven Markets
See: TEXTILES

Performance Materials
See: AERONAUTICS/ASTRONAUTICS

PetroChemical News
See: CHEMISTRY & CHEMICALS

Plastic Optical Fiber
(POF) Newsletter   *Business, Consumer*

Publishing Co: Information Gatekeepers, Inc., 214 Harvard Ave., Boston, MA 02134-4651 Fax # (617) 782-8562; Title Tel # (617) 232-3111 Title Fax # (617) 734-8562
Editorial Description: Covers recent developments in POF Components, systems and applications. New development in graded index filers, sources, & other components promise new opportunities. Covers data, communications & applications such as illumination, signage, & imaging.
General Info: Semi-monthly, ISSN: 1064-1068
Subscriptions: Indv. $275, Can. $275, For. $315, $50/copy
Advertising: Accepts Inserts.
List Rental: Rents Lists

Plastics Brief Newsletter   *Business*

Publishing Co: Market Search, Inc., 2727 N Holland Sylvania Rd Ste, A, Toledo, OH 43615-1800; Title Tel # (419) 535-7899 Title Fax # (419) 535-1243
Personnel: Publisher, Editor-James Best
Editorial Description: For plastics sales and marketing executives. Covers new materials, new applications, market trends, price changes.
General Info: (Formerly Plastics Marketing News Brief), Yr. Est. 1972, Weekly, Trim Size-8½ x 11, Offset press, 4 pages, ISSN: 0745-0168, No Color
Subscriptions: Indv. $298
Circulation: Total-2,000

Plastics in Building Construction   *Business*

Publishing Co: Technomic Publishing Co., Inc., 851 New Holland Ave. #3535, Lancaster, PA 17601-5644; Title Tel # (717) 291-5609 Title Fax # (717) 295-4538
Personnel: Editor-James Harrington, Production Mgr.-Tony Deraco
Editorial Description: Report on new plastic materials, applications & markets in building, construction & civil engineering worldwide.
General Info: Yr. Est. 1976, Monthly, Offset press, 8 pages, ISSN: 0147-2429
Subscriptions: Indv. $195, $17/copy
Circulation: Total-150
List Rental: Rents Lists

Plastics Business News   *Business*

Publishing Co: Market Search, Inc., 2727 N Holland Sylvania Rd Ste, A, Toledo, OH 43615-1800 Tel # (419) 535-7899 Fax # (419) 535-1243; Title Tel # (703) 247-3425 Title Fax # (703) 247-3421
Personnel: Publisher-David Swit, Editor-Elaine Zablocki, Circ. Mgr.-Chris Rogers, Production Mgr.-Jeffrey Williams, Promotion Dir.-Marjorie Weiner
General Info: Yr. Est. 1982, Bi-weekly, Trim Size-8½ x 11, Sheetfed press, 8 pages, ISSN: 0734-1784, Ind/Abs/Online: Newsnet, Color-cover, Recycled
Subscriptions: Indv. $327, Inst. $327, Can. $327, For. $382
Acquisions: Publication Bought, Publication Sold
List Rental: Rents Lists

Plastics Focus   *Business*

Publishing Co: Plastics Connection, PO Box 814, Amherst, MA 01004-0814; Title Tel # (413) 549-5020 Title Fax # (413) 549-9955
Personnel: Publisher, Editor-Michael Berins
Editorial Description: Bi-weekly interpretive news report for the plastics industry.
General Info: Yr. Est. 1968, Bi-weekly, Sheetfed press, 6 pages, ISSN: 0554-2952, No Color
Subscriptions: Indv. $275, Can. $275, For. $315

Plastics Recycling Update
See: ENVIRONMENT & ECOLOGY

Plastics Week (Incorporating Plastics & the Environment)   *Business*

Publishing Co: Market Search, Inc., 2727 N Holland Sylvania Rd Ste, A, Toledo, OH 43615-1800 Tel # (419) 535-7899 Fax # (419) 535-1243; Title Tel # (212) 512-6779 Title Fax # (212) 512-2989
Personnel: Publisher-Peter Savage, Editorial Dir.-Richard Zanetti, Assoc. Ed.-Joseph Innace
Editorial Description: Weekly newsletter on plastics. Focusing on strategies, markets, technology, recycling & environmental issues.
General Info: (Formerly Plastics Week), Yr. Est. 1989, Weekly, Trim Size-8½ x 11, 6 pages, ISSN: 1044-9603
Subscriptions: Indv. $480, Can. $480, For. $530
Acquisions: Publication Sold

Regulatory Update   *Business*

Publishing Co: Lewis B. Weisfeld, 1 Franklin Town Blvd Apt 1204, Philadelphia, PA 19103-1246; Title Tel # (215) 567-7235
Personnel: Publisher, Editor-Lewis Weisfeld
Editorial Description: Government regulations related to plastics industry.
General Info: Yr. Est. 1983, Monthly, Desktop press, 8 pages, ISSN: 1065-1896, No Color, Newsprint
Subscriptions: Indv. $95, For. $105, $12/copy

TechPak Newsletter
See: PACKAGING

Tube Topics
See: METALS & METALWORKING

U.S.I. News
See: CHEMISTRY & CHEMICALS

Urethane Plastics and Products   *Business*

Publishing Co: Technomic Publishing Co., Inc., 851 New Holland Ave. #3535, Lancaster, PA 17601-5644; Title Tel # (717) 291-5609 Title Fax # (717) 295-4538
Personnel: Editor-Michael Margotta, Production Mgr.-Tony Deraco
Editorial Description: The newsletter of the urethane industry.
General Info: Yr. Est. 1970, Monthly, Offset press, 20 pages, ISSN: 0049-5700
Subscriptions: Indv. $195, $17/copy
Circulation: Total-150
List Rental: Rents Lists

Windsor Association of Mold Makers, News

Publishing Co: Windsor Association of Mold Makers, 220 Eastland Blvd., Windsor, ON N8S 3G9 Canada; Title Tel # (519) 972-8922
Personnel: Editor-Dianne Moore
General Info: Yr. Est. 1983, 7x/yr., 10 pages
Circulation: Total-150

POETRY & CREATIVE WRITING

AAHA Newsletter   *Association*

Publishing Co: American Assn. of Handwriting Analysts, 820 W Maple St, Hinsdale, IL 60521-3043; Title Tel # (708) 325-2266
Personnel: Editor-Rose Matousek
Editorial Description: Seeks public recognition of usefulness of handwriting analysis in identification and description of the personality of a writer.
General Info: Bi-monthly

ABACUS   *Consumer*

Publishing Co: Potes & Poets Press, 181 Edgemont Ave., Elmwood, CT 06110-1005; Title Tel # (203) 233-2023
Personnel: Editor-Peter Ganick
Editorial Description: A single author magazine issued 8 time a year. Specialty: L-A-N-G-U-A-G-E poetry.
General Info: Yr. Est. 1983, ISSN: 0886-4047
Subscriptions: Indv. $21, Inst. $21, Can. $25, For. $40, $3/copy
Printing Co: Cricket Press, 19 Sedgwick Rd., W. Hartford, CT 06107 Tel # (203) 521-9279

Actuary of the Abstract
See: SCIENCE FICTION & FANTASY

Appearances

Publishing Co: Appearances, 165 W. 26th St., New York, NY 10001-6802; Title Tel # (212) 675-3026
General Info: Yr. Est. 1977, Annually, Trim Size-8½ x 11, 76 pages
Subscriptions: Indv. $5, $4/copy
Circulation: Total-900

Art in Wisconsin
See: ART & SCULPTURE

Azorean Express   *Consumer*

Publishing Co: Seven Buffaloes Press, Box 249, Big Timber, MT 59011-0249
Personnel: Publisher, Editor-Art Cuelho
Editorial Description: Short stories, poems & some non-fiction, all relating to rural life.
General Info: Yr. Est. 1985
Subscriptions: $7/copy
Circulation: Total-500

B.E.A.M. (Being Energetic About Multiplicity)
See: PSYCHOLOGY

Badger Stone Chronicles   *Consumer*

Publishing Co: Seven Buffaloes Press, Box 249, Big Timber, MT 59011-0249
Personnel: Publisher, Editor-Art Cuelho
Editorial Description: Presents new poetry. Each issue geared to a specific theme.
General Info: Yr. Est. 1987, Semi-annually
Subscriptions: $7/copy

Be Somebody Be Yourself Poetry Newsletter
See: LIFESTYLE

Boletin Informativo Newsletter
See: BOOKS & BOOK TRADE

Bread & Butter Chronicles   *Consumer*

Publishing Co: Seven Buffaloes Press, Box 249, Big Timber, MT 59011-0249
Personnel: Publisher, Editor-Art Cuelho
General Info: Yr. Est. 1985, Semi-annually, 8 pages
Subscriptions: $7/copy
Circulation: Total-500

C.A.L. Newsletter   *Business*

Publishing Co: Conservatory of American Letters, PO Box 7, North Waterford, ME 04267-0007; Title Tel # (207) 583-4143
Personnel: Circ. Mgr.-Debbie Benner, Adv. Dir.-Elaine Bennett, Publisher, Editor, Art Dir.-Bob Olmsted
Editorial Description: Articles, news of interest to writers.
General Info: Yr. Est. 1986, Quarterly, Trim Size-8½ x 11, Desktop press, 8 pages, 2% ads, No Color, Recycled
Subscriptions: Indv. $4, $2/copy
Acquisions: Publication Bought
Advertising: $98. Accepts Inserts.
List Rental: Actives $40/M

CLMPages
See: PERIODICAL INDUSTRY

California Writer's Report
See: JOURNALISM

Cantu's Newsletter
See: MEDIA & COMMUNICATIONS

Carta Abierta
See: ETHNIC

Char-Koosta
See: ETHNIC

Chips off the Writer's Block
See: JOURNALISM

Computer Writer's Pulse Report
See: JOURNALISM

Cross & Quill, the Christian Writers Newsletter
See: EDUCATION

Dis-Connections   Consumer, Association
Publishing Co: Writers Studio, 78 Charles St., New York, NY 10014; Title Tel # (212) 255-7075
Personnel: Publisher-Philip Schultz, Editor-Leslie Findlen
Editorial Description: Prose, poetry and information from and for writers studying at the Writers Studio.
General Info: Quarterly

El Machete Mecha
Publishing Co: Los Angeles City College, 855 N Vermont Ave, Los Angeles, CA 90029-3588 Tel # (213) 669-4000; Title Tel # (213) 663-9141
Editorial Description: Chicano literature.

Emshock Letter
Publishing Co: Emshock Letter, Box 411, Randall Flat Rd., Troy, ID 83871-0411; Title Tel # (208) 835-4902
Personnel: Publisher, Editor-Steve Erickson
Editorial Description: Features, poetry, philosophy, metaphysics, spirituality & how these express human ideas & events.
General Info: Yr. Est. 1977, Irregular
Subscriptions: Indv. $25, Can. $35, For. $45

Fashion Poetry Patterns
Publishing Co: Prosperity & Profits Unlimited, PO Box 416, Denver, CO 80201-0416; Title Tel # (303) 575-5676
Personnel: Publisher-A. Doyle
Editorial Description: Patterns and fashion tips in poetry form.
General Info: Yr. Est. 1984, Annually, Offset press, 4 pages, No Color
Subscriptions: Indv. $25, Inst. $25, Can. $28, For. $30, $25/copy
Circulation: Total-4,000

Free Focus   Business, Association   CPM: $5
Publishing Co: Sponsor-Thursday's Press and Wednesday's Press, Bowbridge Press, PO Box 7415, New York, NY 10116-7415
Personnel: Publisher, Editor-Patricia Coscia, Circ. Mgr., Adv. Dir.-Edward E. Janz
Editorial Description: Free Focus is a small press magazine which free focuses on the educated women of today and needs stories and poems. Patricia D. Coscia says 'I think that the poet who is unknown will never be known unless she or he sends out their poems to a publisher orgets involved in a literary magazine such as this one.'
General Info: Yr. Est. 1985, Quarterly, Trim Size-8 x 14, Desktop press, 12 pages, 2 Color
Subscriptions: Indv. $5, $3/copy
Circulation: Total-2,000, Readership-2,000
Advertising: $10. Accepts Inserts.
List Rental: Actives, 2,000, $5/M

Function Key, The
See: COMPUTERS & AUTOMATION

Haiku Canada Newsletter
Publishing Co: Haiku Canada Newsletter, Apt. 2609A, 500 Laurier W., Ap, Ottawa, ON K1R 5E1 Canada; Title Tel # (613) 237-8833
Personnel: Editor-Ruby Spriggs
Editorial Description: Haiku selections; forum of members' recent work; fact-oriented exchange on events, markets and publications; occasional articles. Subscription includes haiku sheets and annual members' anthology.
General Info: Yr. Est. 1985, 36 pages, No Color, Matte
Subscriptions: Can. $20, $5/copy
Circulation: Total-250

Handicap News
See: DISABILITY

Hard Row to Hoe
See: CULTURE & HUMANITIES

Hearts of the Handmaidens
See: WOMEN'S

Hobo Times
See: LIFESTYLE

Hollywood Scriptwriter   Business
Publishing Co: Hollywood Scriptwriter, 1626 N. Wilcox, #385, Hollywood, CA 90028-6273; Title Tel # (818) 991-3096
Personnel: Publisher-Kerry cox, Editor-Kerry Cox, Circ. Mgr.-Leah Cox
Editorial Description: Interviews, articles & market listings for motion picture/TV screenwriters. Also includes software & book reviews and survey of agents.
General Info: (Formerly Hollywood Scriptletter), Yr. Est. 1980, Monthly, Offset press, 10 pages
Subscriptions: Indv. $44, Can. $44, For. $50, $3/copy
Circulation: Total-900
Advertising: Inquire for rates.

Hoofstrikes Newsletter
Publishing Co: Gweetna Press, PO Box 106, Mount Pleasant, MI 48804-0106
Personnel: Editor-Cathy Ford
Editorial Description: Poetry, fiction, artwork, cartoons & non-fiction relating to animals.
General Info: Yr. Est. 1983, Bi-monthly

Hwup!: The Wordshop For Poets   Consumer
Publishing Co: HWUP!, PO Box 12743, Tallahassee, FL 32317-3743
Editorial Description: A lively newsletter devoted to those writing & marketing poetry. Poetry contests, writing tips, reader feedback, markets, & reviews of poetry journals.
General Info: 10x/yr., 16 pages
Subscriptions: Indv. $17, $2/copy

Imperial Beach Times   Consumer
Publishing Co: Imperial Beach Times, Inc., PO Box 1208, Imperial Beach, CA 91933-1208; Title Tel # (619) 429-5533 Title Fax # (619) 429-5556
Personnel: Publisher, Editor-Tania Wisbar, Circ. Mgr., Production Mgr.-Genie Meade, Adv. Dir.-Dorothy Poggi
Editorial Description: Monthly news review of Imperial Beach.
General Info: Yr. Est. 1985, Monthly, Trim Size-11½ x 15, Web press, 24 pages, 4% ads, Color-cover, Newsprint
Subscriptions: $2/copy
Circulation: Total-10,800

International Pen Club-Newsletter   Consumer
Publishing Co: Writers in Exile Center, 42 Derby Ave, Orange, CT 06477-1433; Title Tel # (203) 397-1479 Title Fax # (203) 737-4233
Personnel: Editor-Clara Gyorgyey
General Info: Yr. Est. 1952, Quarterly, Offset press
Subscriptions: Free With Membership
Circulation: Total-150, Readership-200
List Rental: Rents Lists

Iowa Woman
See: WOMEN'S

James Dickey Newsletter
See: LITERARY REVIEWS

Keep, The   Consumer
Publishing Co: Midwest Center for the Literary Arts, The Writers Place, 3607 Pennsylvania, Kansas City, MO 64111
Personnel: Editor-Roderick/Wyatt Townley
Editorial Description: Newsletter for writers about writers.
General Info: Yr. Est. 1992, Quarterly, Trim Size-8½ x 11

Kestrel
Publishing Co: Robin Hadley, P.O. Box 424, Sea Cliff, NY 11579
Editorial Description: An impressive zine produced by a collective of high school students. Original writing and reprints about political issues, mixed with some poetry and unique short stories.
General Info: Trim Size-8.5 x 11, 23 pages
Subscriptions: Indv. $2

Kids Rhyme Newsletter - Stories, Games & More
See: CHILDREN

LCP Newsletter   Association
Publishing Co: League of Canadian Poets, 54 Wolseley St., 3rd Floor, Toronto, ON M5T 1A5 Canada; Title Tel # (416) 504-1657 Title Fax # (416) 947-0159
Personnel: Editor-Richard Lush
Editorial Description: Features information of interest to Canadian poets including contests, awards, academic postings, etc.
General Info: Yr. Est. 1970, 6x/yr., Trim Size-8½ x 11, 8 pages, No Color
Subscriptions: Indv. $20, Inst. $20, Can. $20, $1/copy
Circulation: (80% controlled), Total-500
Advertising: Inquire for rates. Accepts Inserts.
Printing Co: DALCO Print, 24 Ryerson Ave., Toronto, ON M5T 2P3 Canada

Museletter

Publishing Co: League of Canadian Poets, 54 Wolseley St., 3rd Floor, Toronto, ON M5T 1A5 Canada; Title Tel # (416) 504-1657 Title Fax # (416) 947-0159
Personnel: Publisher-Angela Rebeiro, Editor-Richard Lush, Circ. Mgr.-A. Rebeiro, Production Mgr.-John Oughton
Editorial Description: Contains articles on poetry & poetics, as well as poems (primarily by members.)
General Info: (Formerly Newsletter), Yr. Est. 1970, 6x/yr., Trim Size-8½ x 11, Sheetfed press, 32 pages, No Color
Subscriptions: Indv. $20, Can. $20, $1/copy
Circulation: (80% controlled), Total-500
Advertising: Inquire for rates.
Printing Co: DALCO Print, 24 Ryerson Ave., Toronto, ON M5T 2P3 Canada

N.P.D.C. Newsletter   *Association*

Publishing Co: Florida State Poetry Soc., Inc., 1110 N Venetian Dr, Miami Beach, FL 33139-1019; Title Tel # (305) 373-9790
Personnel: Publisher, Editor-Frances Handler
General Info: Yr. Est. 1965, Bi-monthly
Circulation: Total-17,000

Nathaniel Hawthorne Society-Newsletter

Publishing Co: Nathaniel Hawthorne Society, Clemson Univ. Dept. Of English, Clemson, SC 29634-0001; Title Tel # (803) 656-3041
Personnel: Editor-John Idol, Jr.
General Info: Yr. Est. 1975, Semi-annually, ISSN: 0890-4197
Subscriptions: Indv. $10, $3/copy
Circulation: Total-400
Advertising: Accepts Inserts.
List Rental: Rents Lists

The National Library of Poetry

Publishing Co: The National Library of Poetry, 11419-10 Cronridge Drive, P.O. Box 704, Owings Mills, MD 21117; Title Tel # (410) 356-2000
Editorial Description: The National Library of Poetry, founded in 1982, is the largest poetry organization in the world
General Info: Yr. Est. 1982
Advertising: Inquire for rates.

Network
See: WOMEN'S

Night Owl's Newsletter

Publishing Co: Julian Associates, 6831 Spencer Hwy. Suite 203, Pasadena, TX 77505-1772; Title Tel # (404) 889-2597
Personnel: Editor-Robin Parker, Publisher, Mng. Editor-Debbie Jordan, Poetry Ed.-Anita Sargent
Editorial Description: Publication for people who can't sleep at night and want to use that time productively. No pornography! We give positive support to Owls (Night People) who live and work in a world run by Larks (Day People).
General Info: Yr. Est. 1990, Quarterly, Trim Size-8½ x 11, Desktop press, 16 pages, ISSN: 1051-2152
Subscriptions: Indv. $12, Inst. $10, Can. $13, For. $14, $4/copy
Advertising: Inquire for rates. Accepts Inserts.

Nook News Market Bulletin   *Business, Consumer*

Publishing Co: Writer's Nook Press, 38114 3rd St Ste 181, Willoughby, OH 44094-6140; Title Tel # (216) 762-9128 Title Fax # (216) 354-6403
Personnel: Publisher, Editor-Eugene Ortiz
Editorial Description: Latest listings of markets, large & small, for freelance writers.
General Info: Yr. Est. 1989, Quarterly, Desktop press, 12 pages, Matte, Saddle-stitched
Subscriptions: Indv. $14, For. $36, $5/copy
Circulation: Total-500
Advertising: Inquire for rates.

North Pacific Women Writers Retreat
See: WOMEN'S

Noticias de Aztlan   *Consumer, Association*

Publishing Co: Univ. of California at Los Angeles, 405 Hilgard Ave., 3121 Campbell Hall, Los Angeles, CA 90024-1301; Title Tel # (213) 825-2363
Personnel: Editor, Circ. Mgr.-Tomas Gasper
Editorial Description: Short essays, reviews, research in progress, conferences, job-announcements, on Chicano studies.
General Info: (Formerly Mirlo Canta-Chicano Studies), Yr. Est. 1973, Trim Size-8½ x 11, Offset press, 16 pages, ISSN: 0739-3334, No Color, Newsprint, Perfect bound
Subscriptions: Indv. $5, Inst. $12
Circulation: Total-500
Printing Co: UCLA Publication Svcs., 405 Hilgard Ave, Los Angeles, CA 90024-1561 Tel # (213) 825-7040

O'Neill, The
See: THEATRE

Our Write Mind

Publishing Co: Julian Associates, 6831 Spencer Hwy. Suite 203, Pasadena, TX 77505-1772; Title Tel # (713) 470-8748
Personnel: Publisher-Debbie Jordan, Editor-Robin Parker, Poetry Ed.-Anita Sargent
Editorial Description: Publication on the art and business of writing, treating the writer as a human being, with human foibles. Gives writers positive support in their struggle to set and reach their writing goals.
General Info: (Formerly Southeast Writer's Voice), Yr. Est. 1989, Monthly, Trim Size-8½ x 11, Desktop press, 60 pages, ISSN: 1055-4130
Subscriptions: Indv. $10, Can. $11, For. $12
Circulation: Total-175
Advertising: Inquire for rates.

Outlines, Synopses, Proposals that Sold
See: BOOKS & BOOK TRADE

Ozark Feminist Review
See: WOMEN'S

PEN Newsletter
See: LITERATURE & LINGUISTICS

P.R.C. Newsletter and Calendar   *Association*

Publishing Co: Poetry Resource Center of Michigan, Wayne State Unv., Eng. Dept., 51 Warren, Detroit, MI 48202 Tel # (810) 754-9645; Title Tel # (313) 754-9645
Personnel: Editor-Cindi St. Germain
General Info: (Formerly Third Coast Poetry Resource Center Newsletter & Calendar), Yr. Est. 1979, Monthly, Offset press, 4 pages
Subscriptions: Indv. $20
Circulation: Total-3,000
Advertising: Inquire for rates.

Poetidings   *Association*

Publishing Co: New Jersey Poetry Soc. Inc., RTE 1, POB 720, Franklinville, NJ 08322; Title Tel # (609) 875-8122
Personnel: Editor, Circ. Mgr.-Edith Kaltovich
Editorial Description: Seminars, anthologies, public readings, contests, banquest.
General Info: Yr. Est. 1965, Monthly, Offset press, 8 pages, No Color
Subscriptions: Indv. $13, $1/copy
Circulation: Total-300

Poetry Explosion Newsletter (PEN)   *Consumer*   CPM: $266

Publishing Co: Poet Band Co., PO Box 2648, Newport News, VA 23609-0648; Title Tel # (804) 722-7127
Personnel: Publisher, Editor-Arthur Ford, Circ. Mgr.-Christine Jones, Production Mgr.-Marjorie Booker
Editorial Description: Various styles and contents of poetry.
General Info: Yr. Est. 1985, Quarterly, Trim Size-8½ x 11, 12 pages, 2 Color, Matte, Saddle-stitched
Subscriptions: Indv. $12
Circulation: Total-300
Advertising: $80.

Poetry Society of America Newsletter   *Association*   CPM: $129

Publishing Co: Poetry Society of America, 15 Gramercy Park S, New York, NY 10003-1705; Title Tel # (212) 254-9628 Title Fax # (212) 673-2352
Personnel: Editor, Adv. Dir.-Monica De La Torre
Editorial Description: Contains book reviews, original prose on poetry interviews with poets, news of members, & information on grants & conferences.
General Info: (Formerly PSA Bulletin), Yr. Est. 1950, Annually, Trim Size-5½ x 8½, Offset press, 20 pages, No Color, Newsprint, Saddle-stitched
Subscriptions: Indv. $40, Free With Membership
Acquistions: Publication Bought
Circulation: (70% controlled), Total-2,700, Readership-5,000
Advertising: $350.
List Rental: Actives: $100/M

Poets' Digest   *Consumer*

Publishing Co: Cooper House Publishing, Inc., PO Box 54947, Oklahoma City, OK 73154-1947 Tel # (405) 949-2020
Personnel: Editor-Peggy Cooper
Editorial Description: Information for poets and others; supplements Poet Magazine.
General Info: Quarterly, Trim Size-8½ x 11, 4 pages, No Color, Matte
Subscriptions: Free
Advertising: Inquire for rates.

Portfolio   *Consumer*

Publishing Co: Freelance Studios, 139 Old South River Rd., Jackson, GA 30233
Editorial Description: This is the group newsletter of a relative new organization called Amateur Creator's Union. They help unknown writers & artists break into the industry by giving them advice & need experience.
General Info: Irregular, 16 pages
Subscriptions: $3/copy

Promises, Pro-Mss
See: SCIENCE FICTION & FANTASY

Pundit, The
See: HUMOR & SATIRE

Ralph: Coffee, Jazz, &
Poetry *Consumer* **CPM: $60**

Publishing Co: Ralph, PO Box 505, 1288 Broughton Street, Vancouver, BC V6G 2B5 Canada; Title Tel # (604) 654-2929 Title Fax # (604) 654-1993
Personnel: Editor-Ralph Alfonso
Editorial Description: Contains poetry, music and literature reviews.
General Info: Yr. Est. 1992, Monthly, Trim Size-5½ x 8½, Mimeo press, 4 pages, ISSN: 1203-0287, 30% ads, 4 Color, Matte
Subscriptions: Indv. $6, Inst. $6, Can. $6, For. $12, Free In Designated Area
Circulation: Total-3,000, Readership-3,000
Advertising: $180. Accepts Inserts.

Reading Programs with Stories that Educate, Inform, Entertain and Rhyme
See: CHILDREN

Reading Woman
See: FICTION

Recipe Greetings Update *Consumer*

Publishing Co: Prosperity & Profits Unlimited, PO Box 416, Denver, CO 80201-0416; Title Tel # (303) 575-5676
Personnel: Publisher, Editor-A.C. Doyle
Editorial Description: Poetry for making your own greeting cards.
General Info: Yr. Est. 1990, Annually, Trim Size-8½ x 11, Letrpr. press, 4 pages, ISSN: 1053-7171, No Color
Subscriptions: Indv. $5, Inst. $5, Can. $8, For. $8, $5/copy

Residential Garbage

Publishing Co: Andrea Fernandez, 624 E. 15th Street, North Vancouver, BC V7L 2S2 Canada
Editorial Description: Filled with plenty of poems, rants, confessions, and clips.
General Info: Trim Size-8.5 x 11, 22 pages
Subscriptions: Indv. $1

Rollmag *Consumer*

Publishing Co: Rollmag, PO Box 5001, Mill Valley, CA 94942-5001
Personnel: Publisher-Kenneth Maue
Editorial Description: The newsletter on common sense.
General Info: Yr. Est. 1987, 10x/yr., 4 pages
Subscriptions: Indv. $20

Script-Central
See: COMPUTERS & AUTOMATION

Soundings
See: PSYCHOLOGY

Southern Rose Review

Publishing Co: Shamrock Publishing, RR 3 Box 272-D, Ripley, MS 38663-9803
General Info: Bi-monthly

Spenser Newsletter

Publishing Co: Kansas State University English Dept., 122 Denison Hall, Manhattan, KS 66506-0700; Title Tel # (913) 532-6716 Title Fax # (913) 532-7004
Personnel: Publisher, Editor-Jerome S. Dees
Editorial Description: Reviews abstracts, etc. of critical materials relating to Edmund Spenser.
General Info: Yr. Est. 1970, Trim Size-6¾ x 8½, Sheetfed press, 28 pages, ISSN: 0038-7347, No Color, Newsprint, Saddle-stitched
Subscriptions: Indv. $7, Can. $7, For. $11, $3/copy
Circulation: Total-600

Stardift

Publishing Co: Jen, LPO 16261, P.O. Box 5064, New Brunswick, NJ 08903-5064
Editorial Description: A music commentary, poetry, and comments about her favorite band Lush.
General Info: Trim Size-5 x 7, 18 pages
Subscriptions: Indv. $1

Stories that Rhyme, Every Time Kids Pages
See: CHILDREN

Story Rhyme Reproducible Newsletter
See: EDUCATION

Story Rhyme Word Mapping
See: CROSS-WORD PUZZLES

Story Time Stories That Rhyme
See: CHILDREN

The Street Irregular *Business, Consumer*

Publishing Co: The Writers Alliance, 12 Skylark Ln, Stony Brook, NY 11790-3121; Title Tel # (516) 751-7080
Personnel: Publisher-Kiel Stuart, Editor-Howard Austerlitz
Editorial Description: Features how-to articles for writers of fiction and non-fiction, poetry, and criticism pieces as well as articles about computers and writing.
General Info: (Formerly Keystrokes), Yr. Est. 1980, Irregular
Subscriptions: Indv. $10, $4/copy
Advertising: Inquire for rates.

Strophes

Publishing Co: Natl. Fed. of State Poetry Societies, C/O Kinnaman, RR 3, Box 348, Alexandria, IN 46001; Title Tel # (317) 754-7082
Personnel: Editor-Kay Hight Kinnaman
Editorial Description: Strophes is the official newsletter of the Natl. Fed. of State Poetry Societies. We advertize poetry contents that are open to all poets. Interested only in poets & poetry.
General Info: Quarterly
Subscriptions: Indv. $2, $1/copy
Circulation: Total-9,000

Studio City for the IIGS
See: COMPUTERS & AUTOMATION

Talisman

Publishing Co: Talisman, 719 Swift, Santa Cruz, CA 95060-5853; Title Tel # (408) 425-7847
Personnel: Editor-Blythe Ayne
Editorial Description: Poetry, fiction, art, photos.
General Info: Yr. Est. 1973, Trim Size-3½ x 4¼, 32 pages
Subscriptions: Indv. $3
Circulation: Total-300

The Temptation of Saint Anthony

Publishing Co: Martin Bormann's Cranial Splints, PO Box 8166, Philadelphia, PA 19101-8166; Title Fax # (215) 898-0587
Personnel: Publisher, Editor-Mark-Jason Dominus, Production Dir.-Ranjit Bhatnagat
Editorial Description: Emphasis on life as a work of art - humor, surrealism, fiction, and speculation.
General Info: Yr. Est. 1991, Monthly, 5 pages, ISSN: 1062-3981, No Color, Matte
Subscriptions: Indv. $10, $1/copy

Third Degree
See: MYSTERY & HORROR

Tidepools

Publishing Co: Penninsula College, Publications, Port Angeles, WA 98362; Title Tel # (206) 452-9277
Personnel: Editor-Alice Hammer
Editorial Description: Peninsula Colleges art & literary magazine, published yearly.
General Info: Yr. Est. 1972, Trim Size-5½ x 8½, Offset press, 100 pages, 4 Color, Saddle-stitched
Subscriptions: Indv. $5, $4/copy
Circulation: (100% controlled), Total-500
Printing Co: Pen Print, Port Angeles, WA 98362

WRITE!
See: FILM

Women Who Write
See: WOMEN'S

Workshop
See: SCIENCE FICTION & FANTASY

Writers Information
Network *Business, Association*

Publishing Co: Writers Information Network, PO Box 11337, Bainbridge Island, WA 98110-5337; Title Tel # (206) 842-9103 Title Fax # (206) 842-0536
Editorial Description: Provides market information, industry news and trends, writing conference announcements, book reviews and inspirational material for Christian writers.
General Info: Yr. Est. 1980, Bi-monthly, Trim Size-8½ x 11, Offset press, 24 pages, Other, Other
Subscriptions: Indv. $25, Can. $35, For. $35
Circulation: Total-1,000
Advertising: Inquire for rates.
List Rental: Actives: 15,000, $100/M

Writer's Lifeline *Consumer*

Publishing Co: Writer's Lifeline, Box 1641, Cornwall, ON K6H 5V6 Canada; Title Tel # (613) 932-2135
Personnel: Editor-Stephen Gill
Editorial Description: News and items of interest to writers, poets, publishers and librarians.
General Info: Yr. Est. 1974, Quarterly
Subscriptions: Indv. $18

Writer's Nook News *Business*

Publishing Co: Writer's Nook Press, 38114 3rd St Ste 181, Willoughby, OH 44094-6140; Title Tel # (216) 762-9128 Title Fax # (216) 354-6403
Personnel: Publisher, Editor-Eugene Ortiz
Editorial Description: Conferences, contests, markets, legislative/tax news, writing tips, much more!.
General Info: Yr. Est. 1985, Quarterly, Trim Size-8½ x 11, Offset press, 12 pages, ISSN: 0890-9504, 2% ads, No Color, Matte, Saddle-stitched
Subscriptions: Indv. $18, For. $36, $5/copy
Circulation: Total-5,000
Advertising: Inquire for rates.

Writers' Rendezvous *Consumer*

Publishing Co: Writers' Rendezvous, PO Box 105, Sacramento, CA 95812-0105
Personnel: Publisher, Editor, Adv. Dir.-Karen M. Campbell
Editorial Description: Newsletter for, by, and about freelance writers, everthing published relates to writing, penpal column helps writers find support and encouragement. SASE for more info. (includes lists of publications seeking articles, short stories and poetry.
General Info: Yr. Est. 1986, Quarterly, 24 pages, 9% ads, No Color
Subscriptions: Indv. $12, Can. $15, For. $25, $4/copy
Advertising: $15.

Writing Concepts: The Business Communications Report
See: JOURNALISM

Writing World
See: MEDIA & COMMUNICATIONS

POLITICS

70's Re-Visited, The

Publishing Co: Richie Cunningham, 227 Hampshire Drive, Chalfont, PA 18914
Editorial Description: Both politics and pop culture are explore in this '70s zine.
General Info: Trim Size-8.5 x 11, 10 pages
Subscriptions: Indv. $1

A Monetary Time Bomb is Ticking, Ticking, Ticking
See: ECONOMICS

ACLU News
See: CIVIL RIGHTS

ADA Today *Association*

Publishing Co: Americans for Democratic Action, 1625 K St NW Ste 210, Washington, DC 20006-1604; Title Tel # (202) 785-5980 Title Fax # (202) 785-5969
Personnel: Editor-Valerie Dulk, Production Mgr.-Vale Dulk
Editorial Description: For liberal activists, dealing with social issues in foreign & domestic policy.
General Info: (Formerly ADA World), Yr. Est. 1947, Quarterly, Trim Size-8½ x 11, Offset press, 4 pages, No Color, Newsprint
Subscriptions: Indv. $20, Free
Circulation: Total-30,000
List Rental: Actives: $60/M
Printing Co: Doyle Printing & Offset, 6911 Old Landover Rd, Landover, MD 20785-1503 Tel # (301) 322-4800, Fax # (301) 372-2860

ADAction News and Notes

Publishing Co: Americans for Democratic Action, 1625 K St NW Ste 210, Washington, DC 20006-1604; Title Tel # (202) 785-5980 Title Fax # (202) 785-5969
Personnel: Editor-Amy Isaacs
Editorial Description: Organization news and coverage of political issues.
General Info: Weekly
Subscriptions: Indv. $20
List Rental: Rents Lists

ADPSR News *Association*

Publishing Co: Architects/Designers/Planners for Social Responsibility, 175 Fifth Ave. Ste., #2210, New York, NY 10010; Title Tel # (212) 924-7893
General Info: Yr. Est. 1984, Semi-annually, 8 pages

AIM Report
See: JOURNALISM

ALF News
See: WOMEN'S

ARA Journal *CPM$2000*

Publishing Co: American Romanian Academy, 3328 Monte Vista Ave, Davis, CA 95616-4929; Title Tel # (916) 758-7720 Title Fax # (916) 758-7720
Personnel: Editor-Ion Manea
Editorial Description: Covers news relating to activities of the Academy. Publish papers presented to the annual convention.
General Info: (Formerly ARA Bulletin), Yr. Est. 1980, Annually, Mimeo press, 320 pages, ISSN: 0896-1018, Color-cover, Perfect bound
Subscriptions: Indv. $20, Inst. $30, For. $30, $20/copy
Circulation: (30% controlled), Total-500, Subscriptions-300, Readership-500
Advertising: $1,000.
Printing Co: Account Manager: Gareth K. Perkins; Scythian Book, PO Box 3647, Oakland, CA 94609-0647 Tel # (510) 653-8048

Abortion Report *Business*

Publishing Co: American Political Network, 3129 Mt. Vernon Ave., Alexandria, VA 22305-2640; Title Tel # (703) 237-5130 Title Fax # (703) 237-5141
Personnel: Publisher-Doug Bailey, Mktg. Dir.-Val Syme
Editorial Description: Non-partisan, daily news briefing covering abortion reform politics.
General Info: Daily
Subscriptions: Indv. $2,400

Action Agenda
See: MEDIA & COMMUNICATIONS

Action on Colombia
See: CIVIL RIGHTS

Advocate *Association*

Publishing Co: Peace Farm, Hc 2 Box 25, Panhandle, TX 79068-9603; Title Tel # (806) 335-1715
Personnel: Editor-Mavis Belisle
Editorial Description: News relating to anti-war & no-nukes activism. Promotes the objective of achieving peace through non-violent peaceful news.
General Info: Yr. Est. 1986, Quarterly, Trim Size-8½ x 11, Offset press, 6 pages, Recycled
Subscriptions: Indv. $5
Circulation: Total-850

Agenda *Consumer*

Publishing Co: Agenda Publications, 220 S Main St, Ann Arbor, MI 48104-2106; Title Tel # (313) 996-8018
Personnel: Editor, Adv. Dir.-Ted Sylvester, Publisher, Production Mgr., Art Dir.-Laurie Wechter
Editorial Description: Agenda is a grassroots, altenative newspaper which covers local, national, and international issues from a center to left of center viewpoint. Topics include human rights, women, racism, labor Central America, S. Africa, and other concerns.
General Info: Yr. Est. 1986, Monthly, Trim Size-11 x 17, Web press, 12 pages, ISSN: 1047-0727, 5% ads, 2 Color, Newsprint
Subscriptions: Indv. $15, For. $30, $2/copy
Circulation: Total-20,000
Advertising: Accepts Inserts.
Printing Co: Ypsilanti Press, 20 E Michigan Ave # 280, Ypsilanti, MI 48198-5610 Tel # (313) 487-8311

Alaska Legislative Digest

Publishing Co: Alaska Information & Research, 3037 South Circle, Anchorage, AK 99507-3956; Title Tel # (907) 349-7711
Personnel: Editor-Mike Bradner
Editorial Description: Covers Alaskan legislative news and developments.
General Info: Yr. Est. 1970, 23x/yr.
Subscriptions: Indv. $200

Albany Report *Business*

Publishing Co: Sawchuk, Brown Associates, 41 State St., Ste. 500, Albany, NY 12207-2833 Tel # (518) 462-0688; Title Tel # (518) 462-0318 Title Fax # (518) 462-0688
Personnel: Publisher, Editor-David P. Brown, Contrib. Ed.-Tina Lincer First, Contrib. Ed., Adv. Dir.-William Schwarz
Editorial Description: Covers legislative and political news.
General Info: Yr. Est. 1991, Bi-monthly, Trim Size-8½ x 11, Desktop press, 4 pages, 2 Color, Matte, Saddle-stitched
Subscriptions: Indv. $125
Circulation: Total-500, Readership-500

Alcoholic Beverage Control/State Capitals
See: BEVERAGES - BREWING

Alternatives
See: PUBLIC MANAGEMENT & PLANNING

America Update
See: INTERNATIONAL AFFAIRS

American Independent *Association* *CPM: $105*

Publishing Co: William Shearer, 8158 Palm St, Lemon Grove, CA 91945-3028; Title Tel # (619) 460-4484
Personnel: Publisher, Editor-William Shearer
Editorial Description: Provides coverage of American independent party. State & national.
General Info: Yr. Est. 1974, Monthly, 6 pages
Subscriptions: Indv. $15, Free To Qualified Recipient
Circulation: Total-1,900
Advertising: $200.

American Political Report   *Business*

Publishing Co: American Political Research Corp., 7316 Wisconsin Ave Ste 215, Bethesda, MD 20814-2925; Title Tel # (301) 654-4990
Personnel: Publisher-Kevin P. Phillips, Editor-Kevin Phillips
Editorial Description: Monitors elections, political developments business-related political situations/trends.
General Info: Yr. Est. 1971, Bi-weekly, Offset press, 8 pages
Subscriptions: Indv. $195, For. $205
Circulation: Total-1,200
Printing Co: McArdle Printing Co., 800 Commerce Dr, Upper Marlboro, MD 20772-8792 Tel # (301) 390-8500

American Record

Publishing Co: American Communications Network, 100 N Woodpecker Rd, Hagerstown, IN 47346-1431; Title Tel # (317) 489-5566
Personnel: Publisher, Editor-Brian Bex
Editorial Description: Focuses on questions regarding liberty, limited government, dignity, etc.
General Info: Yr. Est. 1966, Monthly

American Sentinel   *Consumer*

Publishing Co: Sentinel Communications, Inc., 15113 Steele Creek Rd, Charlotte, NC 28273-6855 Tel # (704) 587-0898 Fax # (704) 587-0195
Editorial Description: Report on left-wing activities.
General Info: (Formerly Pink Sheet on the Left), Yr. Est. 1971, Bi-weekly, ISSN: 0278-0585
Subscriptions: Indv. $87
List Rental: Actives, 28,000, $125/M

American Society of International Law Newsletter
See: LAW

America's At Our Doorstep
See: HUMOR & SATIRE

America's Future

Publishing Co: America's Future, 7800 Bonhomme Ave., St. Louis, MO 63105 Tel # (314) 725-6003 Fax # (314) 721-3373; Title Tel # (717) 296-2800 Title Fax # (717) 296-2811
Personnel: Publisher-Robert Morris, Editor-F.R. Duplantier
Editorial Description: Conservative commentary on current events, emphasizing the benefits of free enterprise & constitutional government.
General Info: Yr. Est. 1959, Bi-monthly, Trim Size-8½ x 11, Sheetfed press, 8 pages, ISSN: 0003-1593, No Color
Subscriptions: Indv. $10, $1/copy
Circulation: Total-13,500

Anti-Apartheid Alert

Publishing Co: San Francisco Anti-Apartheid Committee, 916 Laguna St, San Francisco, CA 94115-4815; Title Tel # (415) 552-8123
General Info: Monthly, 4 pages

Anti-Draft   *Consumer, Association*

Publishing Co: Committee Against Registration & Draft, PO Box 262, Madison, WI 53701-0262; Title Tel # (608) 257-7562
Personnel: Publisher, Editor-Gillam Kerley
Editorial Description: Newsletter of the anti-draft movement.
General Info: Yr. Est. 1979, Irregular, Trim Size-8½ x 11, Sheetfed press, 8 pages
Subscriptions: Indv. $5, Inst. $10, $2/copy
Circulation: Total-7,000

ArtsUSA UpDate
See: CULTURE & HUMANITIES

Asian & Pacific Newsletter

Publishing Co: American Friends Service Committee, Hawaii, 2426 Oahu Ave, Honolulu, HI 96822-1967; Title Tel # (808) 988-6266
Personnel: Editor-H. DeCambra
General Info: Quarterly, Trim Size-11 x 17, Desktop press, 8 pages
Subscriptions: Indv. $4
Circulation: Total-1,000

Asian Political News
See: INTERNATIONAL AFFAIRS

Austin Report   *Consumer*

Publishing Co: Report Publications, Inc., PO Box 12368, Austin, TX 78711-2368; Title Tel # (512) 478-5663
Personnel: Editor-Bill Kidd, Circ. Mgr.-Shirl Scott
Editorial Description: A summary of all significant news events in and out of the State Capitol.
General Info: Yr. Est. 1949, Weekly, Trim Size-7 x 9, Offset press, 4 pages, No Color
Subscriptions: Indv. $29, $2/copy
Circulation: Total-1,500

BCUN Briefing

Publishing Co: Business Council for the United Nations, 60 E 42nd St Rm 2925, New York, NY 10165-2999; Title Tel # (212) 661-1772
General Info: Yr. Est. 1987, Quarterly
Circulation: Total-4,000

Backchannel

Publishing Co: Foreign Policy Research Institute, 3615 Chestnut St., Philadelphia, PA 19104-2671 Fax # (215) 382-0131; Title Tel # (215) 382-0685
Personnel: Editor-Kevin McNamara
Editorial Description: Report on activities of the Foreign Policy Research Institute.
General Info: (Formerly FPRI Newsletter), Quarterly, Trim Size-8½ x 11, Desktop press, 1 pages
Circulation: Total-1,500

Ballot Access News

Publishing Co: Coalition for Free & Open Elections, POB 470296 St., San Francisco, CA 94147-0296; Title Tel # (415) 922-9779 Title Fax # (415) 441-4268
Personnel: Publisher, Editor-Richard Winger
Editorial Description: Covers developments in the law relating to political parties, especially political parties other than the two major parties.
General Info: Yr. Est. 1985, 13x/yr., Trim Size-8½ x 11, Sheetfed press, ISSN: 1043-6898, No Color, Matte
Subscriptions: Indv. $8, Inst. $8, Can. $10, For. $12, $1/copy
List Rental: Actives: $75/M
Printing Co: United Printing, 573 Ofarrell St, San Francisco, CA 94102-1931 Tel # (415) 776-5799

Banner   *Association*

Publishing Co: Coalition to Stop Gun Violence, 100 Maryland Ave NE # 402, Washington, DC 20002-5625; Title Tel # (202) 544-7190 Title Fax # (202) 544-7213
Personnel: Editor-Marjolyn Bylefeld
General Info: (Formerly News and Views), Quarterly, 2 Color, Newsprint
Circulation: Total-20,000

Beacon Hill Roll Call
See: GOVERNMENT

Bill Shipp's Georgia
See: GOVERNMENT

Black Vet
See: MILITARY & NAVAL

Boycott Action News
See: CONSUMER INTERESTS

Breaking the Siege
See: INTERNATIONAL AFFAIRS

Briefly
See: RELIGIOUS & THEOLOGICAL

Business & Public Affairs Fortnightly

Publishing Co: American Political Research Corp., 7316 Wisconsin Ave Ste 215, Bethesda, MD 20814-2925; Title Tel # (301) 654-4990
Personnel: Publisher, Editor-Kevin Phillips
General Info: Yr. Est. 1979, Semi-monthly
Subscriptions: Indv. $148
Printing Co: McArdle Printing Co., 800 Commerce Dr, Upper Marlboro, MD 20772-8792 Tel # (301) 390-8500

CALC Report   *Association*

Publishing Co: Atlanta CALC, 92 Piedmont Ave., N.E., Atlanta, GA 30303-2528 Tel # (404) 688-7407; Title Tel # (404) 377-1983
Personnel: Editor-Marc Reeve
Editorial Description: Current events on international & domestic scene.
General Info: (Formerly CALC Report/Satygrapha), Yr. Est. 1972, Bi-monthly, Offset press, 8 pages, No Color
Subscriptions: Indv. $5, $1/copy
Circulation: (100% controlled), Total-1,500
Advertising: Inquire for rates.

CARAL Newsletter
See: WOMEN'S

CARD News Service   *Consumer*

Publishing Co: Committee Against Registration & Draft, PO Box 262, Madison, WI 53701-0262; Title Tel # (608) 257-7562
Personnel: Publisher, Editor-Gillam Kerley
Editorial Description: Clippings service on draft & military personnel issues.
General Info: Yr. Est. 1986, Irregular, Mimeo press, 16 pages, No Color, Newsprint
Subscriptions: Indv. $10, $2/copy

CATO Policy Report

Publishing Co: CATO Institute, 1000 Massachusetts Ave. NW, #6, Washington, DC 20001-5403 Tel # (202) 546-0200; Title Tel # (202) 842-0200 Title Fax # (202) 546-0728
Personnel: Publisher-Edward Crane, III, Editor-David Boaz, Production Mgr.-David Lampo
Editorial Description: Free market analysis of government intervention in the economy.
General Info: (Formerly Policy Report), Yr. Est. 1979, Bi-monthly, Trim Size-8½ x 11, Sheetfed press, 16 pages, ISSN: 0743-605X, Ind/Abs/Online: PAIS, 2 Color, Coated, Saddle-stitched
Circulation: (100% controlled), Total-10,000
List Rental: Actives: $95/M
Printing Co: Corporate Press, 403 Brightseat Rd., Landover, MD 20785-4706 Tel # (301) 499-9200, Fax # (301) 499-5435

CAWP News & Notes   *Association*

Publishing Co: Center for the American Woman and Politics, Eagleton Institute of Politics, Rutgers University, New Brunswick, NJ 08901 Tel # (908) 828-2210
General Info: Tri-annually
Subscriptions: Indv. $25, Can. $30, For. $35

CCCO News Notes   *Association*

Publishing Co: Central Committee for Conscientious Objectors, 655 Sutter Street, Suite 514, San Francisco, CA 94102-1034 Tel # (415) 545-4620; Title Tel # (908) 246-3156
Personnel: Circ. Mgr.-Lisa Price, Editor, Adv. Dir.-Robert Seeley
Editorial Description: Covers conscientious objection, war and peace.
General Info: Yr. Est. 1949, Quarterly, Trim Size-8½ x 11, Web press, 16 pages, 2 Color
Circulation: Total-35,000

CCP Research Newsletter   *Consumer*

Publishing Co: Colorado College History Dept., Publications, Colorado Springs, CO 80903; Title Tel # (719) 473-2233
Personnel: Editor-Timothy Cheek
Editorial Description: For the Chinese Communism Research Group.
General Info: Tri-annually
Subscriptions: Indv. $12

CEASE News

Publishing Co: Concerned Educators Allied for A Safe Environment, 17 Gerry St, Cambridge, MA 02138-5745; Title Tel # (617) 864-0999
Personnel: Editor-Peggy Schirmer
Editorial Description: Newsletter purpose: Education of the early childhood community on issues of peace, environmental hazards & violence in the lives of children goals: the redirection of funds from the military to human needs.
General Info: Trim Size-7 x 7½, 7 pages
Subscriptions: Indv. $5

CFJ Clearinghouse on the Central & Eastern European Press Newsletter
See: MEDIA & COMMUNICATIONS

C.J. Weekly   *Business*

Publishing Co: Information for Public Affairs, Inc., State Net, 2101 K Street, Sacramento, CA 95816-4920; Title Tel # (916) 444-2840 Title Fax # (916) 444-2339
Personnel: Publisher-Thomas Hoeber, Circ. Mgr.-Sheryl Lilly, Product Mgr.-Lise Vernasco
Editorial Description: Insider info & listing of officials & lobbyists.
General Info: (Formerly California Journal Newsfile), Yr. Est. 1983, Weekly, Trim Size-8½ x 11, Sheetfed press, 10 pages, 2 Color, Coated, Saddle-stitched
Subscriptions: Indv. $295
Circulation: Total-550
List Rental: Actives: 500, $75/M

COHA's Washington Report on the Hemisphere
See: INTERNATIONAL AFFAIRS

COPRED Peace Chronicle

Publishing Co: Consortium on Peace Research, Education & Development, George Mason Univ., 4400 University Dr., Fairfax, VA 22030-4444; Title Tel # (703) 993-3639 Title Fax # (703) 993-1302
Personnel: Editor-Maire Dugan
General Info: Yr. Est. 1975, Bi-monthly, 24 pages
Subscriptions: Indv. $45, Inst. $125
Circulation: Total-800
Advertising: Inquire for rates.
List Rental: Rents Lists

COSSA Washington Update

Publishing Co: Consortium of Social Science Assocs., 1522 K St NW Ste 836, Washington, DC 20005-1202; Title Tel # (202) 842-3525 Title Fax # (202) 842-2788
Personnel: Publisher-Howard Silver, Editor-Michael Buckley
General Info: Bi-weekly, 8 pages
Subscriptions: Indv. $60, Inst. $130, Can. $130, For. $130, $65/copy
Circulation: Total-1,500

CQ Researcher   *Consumer*

Publishing Co: Congressional Quarterly, Inc., 1414 22nd St. NW, Washington, DC 20037-1096 Fax # (202) 728-1863; Title Tel # (202) 887-8500
Personnel: Publisher-Neil Skene, Editor-Sandra Stencel, Circ. Mgr.-Judy Stachnik, Production Mgr.-I. D. Fuller
Editorial Description: Covers any subject that is in the news.
General Info: (Formerly Editorial Research Reports), Yr. Est. 1923, Weekly, Trim Size-6 x 9, Offset press, 17 pages, ISSN: 0013-0958, Ind/Abs/Online: PAIS, No Color
Subscriptions: Indv. $314

California Eye, The

Publishing Co: Political Animal Co., 1100 Montecito Dr., Los Angeles, CA 90031-1637 Tel # (213) 481-3809 Fax # (213) 481-0212
Personnel: Publisher-Robert Bush, Editor-Joseph Scott, Circ. Mgr.-Gretchen Stockdale
Editorial Description: Non-partisan coverage of California politcs.
General Info: Yr. Est. 1979, Bi-weekly, Trim Size-11 x 17, Sheetfed press, 4 pages, No Color
Subscriptions: Indv. $150
Acquistions: Publication Bought
Printing Co: King House Printing & Publishing Co., 8854 Southwestern Ave., Los Angeles, CA 90047 Tel # (213) 759-7960

California Political Week   *Business, Association*

Publishing Co: California Political Week, Inc., PO Box 1468, Beverly Hills, CA 90213-1468; Title Tel # (310) 659-0205 Title Fax # (310) 657-4340
Personnel: Publisher, Editor-Dick Rosengarten
Editorial Description: California state & local government & California politics.
General Info: Yr. Est. 1979, Weekly, Trim Size-7½ x 10, Offset press, 4 pages, ISSN: 0195-6175
Subscriptions: Indv. $90, Inst. $90
Acquistions: Publication Sold
Circulation: Total-3,000

California Statesman
See: GOVERNMENT

California Statesman's Foreign Policy Review
See: INTERNATIONAL AFFAIRS

California Statesman's Legislative Survey
See: LAW

California Wool Growers Newsletter
See: LIVESTOCK

Campus Watch

Publishing Co: Bill of Rights Foundation, 523 S Plymouth Ct Fl 800, Chicago, IL 60605-1511; Title Tel # (212) 569-0069
Personnel: Editor-Phil Agee, Jr.
Editorial Description: Seeks to raise awareness of intelligence activities concerning the academic community. Specific areas of coverage include officer & scholar in residence programs, recruitment, research, special operations, & CIA related student activism.
General Info: Yr. Est. 1989, Semi-annually, 12 pages, ISSN: 1050-5644, No Color
Subscriptions: Indv. $6, Inst. $10, $3/copy

Canadian Political Science Association Bulletin   *Association*

Publishing Co: Canadian Political Science Association, 1 Stewart St. #205, Ottawa, ON K1N 6H7 Canada; Title Tel # (613) 564-4026 Title Fax # (613) 230-2746
Personnel: Editor-David Seigel, Circ. Mgr., Adv. Dir., Promotion Dir.-Michelle Hopkins
General Info: Yr. Est. 1976, Semi-annually, 60 pages, Saddle-stitched
Subscriptions: Can. $15, For. $15, Free With Membership
Advertising: $300. Accepts Inserts.
List Rental: List Management Co.: Canadian Political Science Association Bulletin, 1 Stewart St. #205, Ottawa, ON K1N 6H7 Canada

Canadian Studies Update
See: EDUCATION

Canadian World Federalist   *Association*

Publishing Co: World Federalist of Canada & World Federalist Foundation, 207-145 Spruce St., Ottawa, ON K1R 6P1 Canada; Title Tel # (613) 232-0647
Personnel: Editor-Fergus Watt
Editorial Description: Coverage of WFC activities, natl. & intl. events pertaining to United Nations, world law & the evolution of world community.
General Info: Yr. Est. 1961, Bi-monthly, Trim Size-8½ x 11, Offset press, 8 pages, ISSN: 0382-8662, No Color
Subscriptions: Indv. $8, $2/copy
Circulation: (100% controlled)

Canadian Zionist   *Consumer*

Publishing Co: Canadian Zionist Fed., 5250 Decarie Blvd., Ste. 550, Montreal, PQ H3X 2H9 Canada; Title Tel # (514) 486-9526 Title Fax # (514) 483-6392
Editorial Description: Deals with the Middle East and Jewish interests.
General Info: Yr. Est. 1934, Tri-annually, Trim Size-11½ x 15, Web press, 6 pages, 2 Color
Subscriptions: Free In Designated Area
Circulation: Total-3,000

Caribbean Newsletter
See: INTERNATIONAL AFFAIRS

Catholic Study Council
Bulletin   *Consumer*

Publishing Co: Natl. Center for Public Policy Research, 300 Eye St. NE, #3, Washington, DC 20002
Fax # (202) 543-1286; Title Tel # (202) 543-1286 Title Fax # (202) 543-4779
Personnel: Publisher-Amy Moritz, Editor-Michael Pauley, Production Mgr.-Nicholas Damask
Editorial Description: Covers U.S. foreign & domestic policies from a Catholic viewpoint.
General Info: Yr. Est. 1985, Irregular, Offset press, 2 pages, 2 Color, Newsprint
Subscriptions: Indv. $15
Circulation: Total-1,100

Cement Squeeze

Publishing Co: Cement Squeeze, P.O. Box 2112, Tempe, AZ 85280
Editorial Description: A noble effort from this group of writers trying to create a liberal voice in the conservative greater Phoenix area.
General Info: Trim Size-8.5 x 11, 16 pages
Subscriptions: Indv. $2

Challenge (year)   *Association*

Publishing Co: National Federation of Republican Women, 310 1st St SE, Washington, DC
20003-1801; Title Tel # (202) 547-9341
Personnel: Publisher, Editor-Linde Leinbach, Circ. Mgr.-Linda Moore
General Info: Yr. Est. 1979, Bi-monthly, Trim Size-8½ x 11, Web press, 16 pages, 2 Color, Coated
Subscriptions: Indv. $15
Circulation: (100% controlled), Total-160,000

Christian Civic League Record
See: RELIGIOUS & THEOLOGICAL

Citizen Soldier
See: MILITARY & NAVAL

Citizenship Education News

Publishing Co: Council for the Advancement of Citizenship, 44 Canal Center Plz., Alexandria, VA
22314-1593; Title Tel # (202) 857-0580 Title Fax # (202) 857-9160
Personnel: Editor-Nancy Warzer
General Info: Yr. Est. 1981, Quarterly
Subscriptions: Indv. $25, $5/copy

Civil Libertarian

Publishing Co: Libertarians for Gay & Lesbian Concerns, 1800 Market St # 210, San Francisco, CA
94102-6227; Title Tel # (415) 552-0838
Editorial Description: Covers government violations of individual rights, censorship, AIDS & other current topics of importance.
General Info: Yr. Est. 1981, Bi-monthly
Subscriptions: Indv. $15, $2/copy

Clinton Watch   *Consumer*

Publishing Co: Eagle Publishing, Inc., 422 First Street SE, Suite 300, Washington, DC 20003
Tel # (202) 546-5005 Parent Co.-Phillips Business Information, Inc., Potomac
Editorial Description: Skeptical view of President Clinton's activities.
General Info: Monthly
Circulation: Total-9,300
List Rental: Actives: 9,300, $125/M

Cold War International
History Project Bulletin   *Consumer, Association*

Publishing Co: Woodrow Wilson International Center for Scholars, 100 Jefferson Dr., S.w.,
Washington, DC 20560-0001; Title Tel # (202) 357-2967 Title Fax # (202) 357-4439
Personnel: Editor-James Hershberg
Editorial Description: Information from both sides about the Cold War that existed between USA and USSR after WWII.
General Info: Yr. Est. 1992, Quarterly, Trim Size-8½ x 11, 36 pages

Comments & Corrections

Publishing Co: Robert W. Lee, PO Box 65902, Salt Lake City, UT 84165-0902;
Title Tel # (801) 466-5506
Personnel: Publisher, Editor-Robert Lee
Editorial Description: Commentary on political, economic, and ethical issues.
General Info: (Formerly Wasatch Watchdog), Yr. Est. 1981, Trim Size-8½ x 11, Mimeo press, 10 pages, No Color, Newsprint
Subscriptions: Indv. $27, $3/copy

Committee on Native American Struggles Newsletter
See: CIVIL RIGHTS

Common Sense   *Association*   CPM: $96

Publishing Co: Libertarian Info. Services, PO Box 817802, Hollywood, FL 33081-1802
Tel # (305) 471-0103; Title Tel # (305) 221-0154 Title Fax # (305) 471-0113
Personnel: Editor-Claude Pinsonneault, Circ. Mgr.-John Thenchard, Production Mgr.-T. Gordon,
Production Mgr.-C. Pinsonneault, Adv. Dir.-Anthony Collins, Art Dir.-Thomas Gordon
Editorial Description: Newsletter for libertarians & other friends of liberty.
General Info: Yr. Est. 1971, Bi-monthly, Trim Size-6½ x 8, Desktop press, 12 pages, 5% ads
Subscriptions: Indv. $12, Inst. $10, Can. $12, For. $15, $1/copy
Circulation: Total-500
Advertising: $48.
Printing Co: Ace Printing Co., 95th Ave. & Bird Rd., Miami, FL 33172 Tel # (305) 221-7761

Commonsense   *Association*

Publishing Co: Republican Natl. Committee, Publications, 310 First St SE, Washington, DC
20003-1801 Tel # (202) 863-8500

Confidential Air Letter
See: AERONAUTICS/ASTRONAUTICS

Connection

Publishing Co: Peace Links, 747 8th St SE, Washington, DC 20003-2802; Title Tel # (202) 544-0805
Personnel: Editor-Mary Leopold
Editorial Description: Information for peace activist networking.
General Info: Yr. Est. 1982, Quarterly, 4 pages
Circulation: Total-23,000

Conscience and Military Tax Campaign
See: TAXES

Conservation Voter
See: ENVIRONMENT & ECOLOGY

Constantian, The   *Association*   CPM: $83

Publishing Co: Constantian Society, The, 123 Orr Rd, Pittsburgh, PA 15241-2219;
Title Tel # (412) 831-8750
Personnel: Publisher, Editor-Randall Dicks
Editorial Description: Contains information on monarchy & royalty of all countries, current events,
biography, analysis, & book reviews.
General Info: Yr. Est. 1970, Quarterly, Trim Size-8½ x 11, Desktop press, 12 pages, ISSN: 0270-
532X, No Color
Subscriptions: Indv. $10, Inst. $7, Can. $11, For. $11, $4/copy
Circulation: Total-600
Advertising: $50. Accepts Inserts.

Constitution
See: GOVERNMENT

Constitutions of the
Countries of the World   *Business, Consumer*

Publishing Co: Oceana Publications, Inc., 75 Main St, Dobbs Ferry, NY 10522-1601
Tel # (914) 693-8100 Fax # (914) 693-0402; Title Tel # (914) 693-1320
Personnel: Editor-Albert Blaustein, Editor, Editor-Bert Flanz, Product Mgr.-Mike Wortzman, Mktg.
Dir.-John Downey
Editorial Description: Up-to-date texts of national constitutions in English.
General Info: Yr. Est. 1971, Irregular, Trim Size-7 x 10, No Color, Newsprint, Looseleaf
Subscriptions: Indv. $2,500
Circulation: Total-350

Convergence

Publishing Co: Christic Institute, PO Box 845, Malibu, CA 90265-0845; Title Tel # (310) 287-1556
Personnel: Publisher-Sara Nelson, Editor-Andrew Lang, Production Mgr.-Tia Lessin
General Info: Yr. Est. 1980, Quarterly, Web press, 24 pages, Ind/Abs/Online: PeaceNet, 2 Color,
Saddle-stitched
Subscriptions: Indv. $25, Inst. $40, $1/copy
Circulation: Total-50,000
Printing Co: Valley Offset, 422 Colorado Ave, La Junta, CO 81050-2336 Tel # (719) 384-4475

Cornell Modern Indonesia Project:
See: INTERNATIONAL AFFAIRS

Corporate Responsibility Monitor
See: BUSINESS & INDUSTRY

Council for a Livable
World Newsletter

Publishing Co: Council for a Livable World, 110 Maryland Ave. NE, Suite 409, Washington, DC
20002; Title Tel # (202) 543-4100 Title Fax # (202) 543-6297
Personnel: Editor-John Isaacs, Editor-Wayne Jaquith
Editorial Description: Analysis of candidates & issues involved in election for U.S. Senate with
special emphasis on nuclear disarmament.
General Info: Yr. Est. 1962, Monthly, Trim Size-8½ x 11, Offset press, 6 pages, 2 Color, Recycled
Subscriptions: Free
List Rental: Actives: 23,000, $65/M, Expires: $30/M

Country Report:
Cameroon   *Business*

Publishing Co: Political Risk Services, 6320 Fly Road Suite #102, PO Box 248, East Syracuse, NY
13057-0248 Tel # (315) 431-0511 Fax # (315) 431-0200 Parent Co.-International Business
Communications, Ashland; Title Tel # (315) 472-1224 Title Fax # (315) 472-1235
Personnel: Publisher-Mary Lou Walsh, Editor-Michael O'Leary, Circ. Mgr.-Patti Davis, Editor,
Production Mgr.-William Coplin
General Info: (Formerly Country Report: Algeria), Yr. Est. 1979, Annually, Trim Size-8½ x 11, Mimeo
press, 50 pages, ISSN: 1054-5301, Matte, Other
Subscriptions: $325/copy
List Rental: List Management Co.: Manager: Mary Lou Walsh; PRS List Management, 222 Teal Ave.,
POB 6482, Syracuse, NY 13217-6482 Tel # (315) 472-1224, Fax # (315) 472-1235

Courier
See: INTERNATIONAL AFFAIRS

Crime & Justice Network Newsletter

Publishing Co: MCC Office on Crime Justice, PO Box 500, Akron, PA 17501-0500; Title Tel # (717) 859-3889
Personnel: Editor-Howard Zehr
Editorial Description: Addresses victim/offender concerns.
General Info: Yr. Est. 1979, Quarterly, Trim Size-8½ x 11, Sheetfed press, 12 pages, 2 Color
Subscriptions: Indv. $5

Crosscurrents
See: MUSIC & MUSIC TRADES

Cutting Edge

Publishing Co: World Peace University, 400 2nd St # 77, Lake Oswego, OR 97034-3127; Title Tel # (503) 697-1205
General Info: Yr. Est. 1985, 8 pages
Subscriptions: Indv. $15

Deficit Letter, The
See: U.S. (& CANADIAN) FED. GOV'T.

Democratic Commitment   *Association*

Publishing Co: British Columbia Civil Liberties Assn., 815 W. Hastings St., #425, Vancouver, BC V6C 1B4 Canada; Title Tel # (604) 687-2919
Editorial Description: Briefs on Civil Liberties & Human Rights topics.
General Info: Yr. Est. 1967, 4 pages
Subscriptions: Indv. $20

Digest of Attorney General Opinions
See: LAW

Discussion Bulletin

Publishing Co: Natl. Committee for Independent Political Action, PO Box 170610, Brooklyn, NY 11217-0610; Title Tel # (718) 643-9603
Personnel: Editor- Committee
General Info: Yr. Est. 1984, Quarterly
Subscriptions: Indv. $10, Inst. $25, $4/copy

Don Bell Reports

Publishing Co: Don Bell Reports, 544 Ferguson Lane, Palm Beach, FL 33415-3527
Editorial Description: Analysis and commentary on trends toward expanding non-elected government.
General Info: Bi-weekly
Subscriptions: Indv. $40

Donald R. Morris Newsletter
See: NEWSPAPER INDUSTRY

Draft Notices   *Association*

Publishing Co: Committee Opposed to Militarism and the Draft, PO Box 15195, San Diego, CA 92175-5195; Title Tel # (619) 282-9968
Editorial Description: Anti-militarist; legislative & legal updates; analysis.
General Info: Yr. Est. 1979, Bi-monthly, Trim Size-8½ x 11, Sheetfed press, 10 pages, No Color, Matte
Subscriptions: Indv. $12, $2/copy
Circulation: Total-1,000

East European News   *Association*

Publishing Co: Workers Solidarity Alliance, 339 Lafayette St Rm 202, New York, NY 10012-2725 Tel # (212) 979-8353; Title Tel # (212) 979-8385
Editorial Description: General analysis of world affairs and labor, and community struggles. Primary emphasis is anarcho-syndicalist education and propaganda.
General Info: (Formerly Black Flag of Anarchism, On the Line), Yr. Est. 1978, Quarterly, Trim Size-8½ x 11, Offset press, 8 pages, No Color
Subscriptions: Indv. $5
Circulation: (100% controlled), Total-1,000

Eco-Profiteer, The
See: INVESTMENT

Economic Development/State Capitals
See: BUSINESS & INDUSTRY

Economic Issues
See: ECONOMICS

Editorials on File
See: NEWSPAPER INDUSTRY

El Salvador On Line
See: INTERNATIONAL AFFAIRS

Employee Policy for the Private and Public Sectors/State Capitals
See: INDUSTRIAL RELATIONS/PERSONNEL

Ernie Mills' Legislative Report
See: GOVERNMENT

Estimate
See: INTERNATIONAL AFFAIRS

Ethics & International Affairs Newsletter
See: INTERNATIONAL AFFAIRS

Ethics & Public Policy Center Newsletter
See: RELIGIOUS & THEOLOGICAL

European Studies Newsletter
See: HISTORY

Evans-Novak Political Report   *Business*

Publishing Co: Eagle Publishing, Inc., 422 First Street SE, Suite 300, Washington, DC 20003 Tel # (202) 546-5005 Parent Co.-Phillips Business Information, Inc., Potomac
Personnel: Mktg. Dir.-Martha Seitchek
Editorial Description: Latest information on national politics.
General Info: Yr. Est. 1967, Bi-weekly, Mimeo press, ISSN: 0014-3650, No Color, Newsprint
Subscriptions: Indv. $247
Circulation: Total-2,000
List Rental: Rents Lists

Executive Newsweek   *Consumer*

Publishing Co: Newsweek, Inc., 251 W 57th St, New York, NY 10019-1802 Tel # (212) 445-4000
Personnel: Editor-Edward Kosner
General Info: Monthly

F.E.A.R. Chronicles
See: CIVIL RIGHTS

Facts for Action

Publishing Co: Methodist Peace Fellowship, 206 W Main St, Crisfield, MD 21817-1327; Title Tel # (302) 368-7449
Editorial Description: Reviews developments in the peace movement.
General Info: Monthly
Circulation: Total-1,500

Facts on File World News Digest
See: INTERNATIONAL AFFAIRS

Family, Law and Democracy Report
See: GOVERNMENT

Federal Action Affecting the States/State Capitals
See: U.S. (& CANADIAN) FED. GOV'T.

Federal Budget Report
See: GOVERNMENT

Federal Election Campaign Financing Guide   *Business*

Publishing Co: CCH, Inc., 2700 Lake Cook Rd., Riverwoods, IL 60015 Parent Co.-Kluwer Law & Taxation Publishers, Cambridge; Title Tel # (847) 267-7000 Title Fax # (800) 224-8299
Editorial Description: Interprets and updates laws covering political contributions for federal elections; Court decisions and regulations interpreting and implementing the federal laws.
General Info: Yr. Est. 1976, Monthly, Trim Size-6 x 9, Web press, 60 pages, No Color, Looseleaf
Subscriptions: Indv. $465

Federal Election Commission Record   *Association*

Publishing Co: U.S. Federal Election Commission, 999 E St NW, Washington, DC 20463-0002; Title Tel # (202) 376-3120
Editorial Description: Factual summary of all official decisions by FEC.
General Info: Yr. Est. 1975, Monthly, Trim Size-8½ x 11, Sheetfed press, 10 pages, Ind/Abs/Online: Annual Ind., Color
Circulation: Total-12,000
List Rental: List Management Co.: PRS List Management, 222 Teal Ave., POB 6482, Syracuse, NY 13217-6482 Tel # (315) 472-1224, Fax # (315) 472-1235, Actives: 5,497, $65/M

Feminists for Animal Rights
See: WOMEN'S

Fernand Braudel Center-Newsletter
See: SOCIOLOGY

Fight Back
See: AFRICAN-AMERICAN INTEREST

The Fire Fly

Publishing Co: The Fire Fly, P.O. Box 133, Angle Inlet, MN 56711
Editorial Description: A freindly little newletter with an empowered smalltown spirit featuring a variety of pesonal politicl writing.
General Info: Trim Size-8.5 x 11, 8 pages

Florida Insight
See: GOVERNMENT

Flush Rush Quarterly   *Consumer*

Publishing Co: Flush Rush Quarterly, PO Box 270525, San Diego, CA 92198-2525; Title Tel # (619) 599-7805
Editorial Description: Satire and opinions on and about Rush Limbaugh.
General Info: Quarterly, Trim Size-8½ x 11, 2 Color
Subscriptions: Indv. $14

Focus   *Consumer, Association*

Publishing Co: Sponsor-Joint Ctr. for Political Studies, Joint Center for Political Studies, 1090 Vermont Ave. NW Ste. 1100, Washington, DC 20005-4905; Title Tel # (202) 789-3500
Personnel: Editor-Jane Lewin, Promotion Dir.-Carl Cook
Editorial Description: Political and policy matters of interest to blacks and other minorities.
General Info: Yr. Est. 1972, Monthly, Offset press, 8 pages, ISSN: 0740-0195, Ind/Abs/Online: PAIS,CIS, 2 Color, Newsprint, Saddle-stitched
Subscriptions: Indv. $12, $1/copy
Circulation: Total-11,000

Focus-Off. of Americas

Publishing Co: Office of the Americas, 8124 W 3rd St Ste 201, Los Angeles, CA 90048-4328; Title Tel # (213) 451-2428
Personnel: Editor-Joyce Fiske
General Info: Yr. Est. 1983, Quarterly, 8 pages
Circulation: Total-9,000

Food First Books
See: FOOD

Food First News & Views
See: SOCIAL SERVICES & WELFARE

Foreign Intelligence Literary
Scene (FILS)

Publishing Co: Natl. Intelligence Study Center, 1800 K St NW Ste 1102, Washington, DC 20006-2202; Title Tel # (202) 466-6029 Title Fax # (202) 331-0109
Personnel: Editor-Marjorie Cline
General Info: Yr. Est. 1982, Bi-monthly, Trim Size-8 x 11, Sheetfed press, 12 pages, ISSN: 0749-9132, No Color, Newsprint
Subscriptions: Indv. $50, $6/copy
Printing Co: DuBois Co., 7414 Leahy Rd, New Carrollton, MD 20784-3662 Tel # (301) 552-3600

Former Presidents
Quarterly   *Consumer*

Publishing Co: RHL Enterprises, PO Box 6443, Fullerton, CA 92634-6443; Title Tel # (714) 738-4386
Personnel: Editor-Robert Lewandowski
Editorial Description: Covers activities of retired US presidents.
General Info: Yr. Est. 1993, Quarterly, Trim Size-8½ x 11, 8 pages, ISSN: 1070-0374
Subscriptions: Indv. $12, $4/copy

Fourth World Journal

Publishing Co: Fourth World Movement, 7600 Willow Hill Dr, Landover, MD 20785-4658; Title Tel # (301) 336-9489 Title Fax # (301) 336-0092
Personnel: Editor-Susan Devins
Editorial Description: Bringing people together around the poorest.
General Info: Yr. Est. 1968, Bi-monthly, Trim Size-8½ x 11, Offset press, 4 pages, ISSN: 0882-3723, No Color, Newsprint
Subscriptions: Indv. $7
Circulation: Total-8,500

Freak Man Freak
See: REGIONAL INTEREST

Freedom Network News   *Consumer, Association*

Publishing Co: International Society for Individual Liberty, 1800 Market St, San Francisco, CA 94102-6227 Tel # (415) 864-0952
Editorial Description: Information about groups and activities world-wide working for libertarian solutions.

Freedom Writer
See: CIVIL RIGHTS

From the Right

Publishing Co: American Position, 115 Lords Hwy, Weston, CT 06883-1715; Title Tel # (203) 226-4346
General Info: Yr. Est. 1990, 18x/yr.
Subscriptions: Indv. $98

Future Watch

Publishing Co: Robert W. Golobish, 64 King Dr., Indianapolis, IN 46260; Title Tel # (317) 251-6135
Personnel: Publisher, Editor-Robert Golobish
Editorial Description: A newsletter on the future for public relations professionals.
General Info: Yr. Est. 1990, Bi-monthly, 4 pages
Subscriptions: Indv. $24, $6/copy

FutureScan
See: ADVERTISING & MARKETING

Gallup Poll, The   *Business, Association*

Publishing Co: Gallup Canada, Inc., 180 Bloor St. W., 10th Fl., Toronto, ON M5S 2V6 Canada; Title Tel # (416) 961-2811 Title Fax # (416) 961-3662
Personnel: Editor-Gary Edwards, Editor, Circ. Mgr.-Jon Hughes, Production Mgr.-Dorothy Hu
Editorial Description: Canadian public opinion surveys.
General Info: (Formerly Gallup Report, The), Yr. Est. 1941, Semi-weekly, Trim Size-8½ x 11, Desktop press, 2 pages, ISSN: 1197-4303, Ind/Abs/Online: Micromedia limited(Toronto),Information Access Ltd(California)
Subscriptions: Indv. $425, For. $450, $50/copy

GeneWATCH
See: GENETICS

Goodkin Report

Publishing Co: Goodkin Group, 501 Pine Needles Dr, Del Mar, CA 92014-3333; Title Tel # (609) 452-5331
General Info: Yr. Est. 1965, Monthly

Government WasteWatch
See: GOVERNMENT

Grass Roots
Campaigning   *Consumer*

Publishing Co: Campaign Consultants, PO Box 7281, Little Rock, AR 72217-7281 Fax # (510) 225-5167; Title Tel # (501) 225-3996 Title Fax # (501) 225-5167
Personnel: Publisher, Editor-Jerry L. Russell
Editorial Description: Nuts-and-bolts articles on political campaign techniques-all levels.
General Info: Yr. Est. 1979, Monthly, Mimeo press, 8 pages, No Color
Subscriptions: Indv. $36, $4/copy
Circulation: Total-480
Advertising: Inquire for rates.

Grassroots

Publishing Co: Grassroots Leadership, 1300 Baxter St. 200, Box 36006, Charlotte, NC 28204-3053; Title Tel # (704) 332-3090
Personnel: Editor-Michelle Handler
General Info: Yr. Est. 1986, Semi-annually

Green Party News
See: ENVIRONMENT & ECOLOGY

Green Party Newsletter

Publishing Co: Green Party USA, PO Box 9693, Downers Grove, IL 60515-9693; Title Tel # (708) 898-5122
Personnel: Editor-Lowell Mathes
Editorial Description: Offical national newsletter Green Party USA-Federal Election Commission I.D.#C00170050 of green philosophy-to create jobs without pollution; primary coverage-movers and shakers of national green movement; green politicians in particuar.
General Info: Yr. Est. 1973, Quarterly, Trim Size-8½ x 14, Desktop press, 1 pages, No Color
Subscriptions: Indv. $25

Greenpeace
See: ENVIRONMENT & ECOLOGY

HHH Institute News

Publishing Co: Hubert H. Humphrey Institute of Public Affairs, 301 19th Ave., Public Affairs, Univ. of Minnesota, Minneapolis, MN 55455-0429; Title Tel # (612) 625-1326
Personnel: Editor-Dana Schroeder
Editorial Description: HHH Institute News is the newsletter about projects, events, people of the Humphrey institute's graduate school of public affairs at the Univ. of Minnesota.
General Info: (Formerly A Capital Idea), Yr. Est. 1984, Semi-annually, Trim Size-8½ x 11, Sheetfed press, 24 pages, No Color, Coated
Circulation: Total-6,000

The Harriman Review
See: INTERNATIONAL AFFAIRS

Hill Report, The

Publishing Co: Neva Hill & Company, PO Box 6388, Oklahoma City, OK 73153-0388; Title Tel # (405) 692-2225 Title Fax # (405) 692-2454
Personnel: Publisher/President/Advisor, Editor-Neva Hill, Publisher/President/Advisor, Editor-Mike McCarville
Editorial Description: Insider's report on Oklahoma politics & government.
General Info: (Formerly McCarville/Hill Report; McCarville Report), Yr. Est. 1980, Weekly, 4 pages, ISSN: 0732-0205
Subscriptions: Indv. $195
Circulation: Total-214

Hudson Institute Report   *Business*

Publishing Co: Hudson Institute, Herman Kahn Center, 5395 Emerson Way, Box 26-919, Indianapolis, IN 46226; Title Tel # (317) 545-1000
Personnel: Editor-Robert Collins
Editorial Description: Describes ongoing projects, staff biographies and a listing of available reports, seminars etc.
General Info: (Formerly Communique), Yr. Est. 1961, Quarterly, Trim Size-8½ x 11, 12 pages, Color-cover, Matte, Saddle-stitched
Subscriptions: Indv. $50
Circulation: Total-9,200
Printing Co: White Arts, Inc., 1203 E Saint Clair St, Lafayette, IN 46202-3590 Tel # (317) 356-9970

Human Rights Education: The Fourth R
See: INTERNATIONAL AFFAIRS

Human Rights Research and Education Bulletin
See: CIVIL RIGHTS

IPPNW Report

Publishing Co: International Physicians for the Prevention of Nuclear War, 126 Rogers St, Cambridge, MA 02142-1024; Title Tel # (617) 868-5050
Personnel: Editor-Lynn Martin
General Info: Yr. Est. 1982
Subscriptions: Indv. $15

ISLA
See: INTERNATIONAL AFFAIRS

Ideas & Action
See: LABOR

Illinois Libertarian   CPM: $100

Publishing Co: Libertarian Party of Illinois, PO Box 313, Chicago, IL 60690-0313; Title Tel # (708) 810-1974
Personnel: Editor-Kenneth Prazak
Editorial Description: News and commentary on libertarian activities, politics, and public policy.
General Info: Yr. Est. 1975, Monthly, Trim Size-8½ x 11, Letrpr. press, 4 pages, No Color, Newsprint
Subscriptions: Indv. $15
Acquistions: Publication Bought
Circulation: Total-400
Advertising: $40.
List Rental: Rents Lists
Printing Co: Quik Print, Oakbrook Terrace, IL 60181

Illinois Voter   *Consumer, Association*

Publishing Co: League of Women Voters of Illinois, 332 S Michigan Ave Ste 1142, Chicago, IL 60604-4305 Tel # (312) 939-5935; Title Tel # (312) 939-5985 Title Fax # (312) 939-6887
Editorial Description: Reports on league governmental studies, legislative activities and programs.
General Info: Quarterly
Subscriptions: Indv. $8, Inst. $8, Free With Membership
Circulation: Total-5,700

Imprimis   *Business, Consumer*

Publishing Co: Hillsdale College, 33 E College St, Hillsdale, MI 49242-1298; Title Tel # (517) 439-1524 Title Fax # (517) 437-0190
Personnel: Mng. Editor-Lissa Roche, Publisher, Exec. Ed.-Ronald Trowbridge
Editorial Description: Conservative views on topical issues.
General Info: Yr. Est. 1972, Monthly, Trim Size-6 x 11, Web press, 6 pages, ISSN: 0277-8432, 2 Color, Matte, Saddle-stitched
Subscriptions: Free
Circulation: Total-620,000
Printing Co: Cyril Scott Company, PO Box 310, Lancaster, OH 43130-0310

In Our Hands   *Consumer*

Publishing Co: Wisconsin Nuclear Weapons Freeze Campaign, 2122 Luann Lane, Madison, WI 53713-4526; Title Tel # (608) 258-4880
Editorial Description: Info & commentary on the peace movement in Wisconsin.
General Info: (Formerly Freeze Update), 8 pages
Subscriptions: Indv. $15
Circulation: Total-8,000

Independent Action News

Publishing Co: Independent Action, 645 Pennsylvania Ave. SE, Ste. 2, Washington, DC 20003-4317; Title Tel # (202) 543-2500
Personnel: Editor-Cheryl Kagan
Editorial Description: Political (progressive) newsletter.
General Info: Yr. Est. 1981, Quarterly, Trim Size-8½ x 11, 4 pages, 2 Color
Subscriptions: Indv. $25
Circulation: Total-25,000

Independent Thinking Review
See: EDUCATION

Indochina Newsletter
See: INTERNATIONAL AFFAIRS

Inform

Publishing Co: Inform, PO Box 489, Elizabeth, NJ 07207-0489
Editorial Description: Aims to uncover and combat subversive organizations in the U.S.
General Info: Yr. Est. 1918, Monthly

Initiative & Referendum: The Power of the People!

Publishing Co: Initiative Resource Center, 235 Douglass St, San Francisco, CA 94114-2424; Title Tel # (415) 431-4765
Personnel: Editor-David Schmidt
Editorial Description: Covers Initiative & Referendum campaigns & procedures nationwide.
General Info: (Formerly Initiative News Report), Yr. Est. 1980, Quarterly, Trim Size-8½₂ x 11, 10 pages, No Color
Subscriptions: Indv. $35, $5/copy
Circulation: Total-1,000
List Rental: Actives: $100/M
Printing Co: Direct Mail Press Eco Print, 9335 Fraser Ave, Silver Spring, MD 20910-1228 Tel # (301) 585-7077

Inside Alabama Politics

Publishing Co: Inside Alabama Politics, PO Box 66200, Mobile, AL 36660-1200; Title Tel # (205) 473-6269 Title Fax # (334) 479-8822
Personnel: Editor-Bessie Ford
Editorial Description: Covers the political scene in Alabama.
General Info: Yr. Est. 1985, 39x/yr.
Subscriptions: Indv. $83

Inside Labor Relations
See: LABOR UNION

Inside Michigan Politics

Publishing Co: Inside Michigan Politics, 2029 S Waverly Rd, Lansing, MI 48917-4263; Title Tel # (517) 487-6665 Title Fax # (517) 487-3830
Personnel: Editor-W.S. Ballenger
Editorial Description: Covers the Michigan political scene.
General Info: Yr. Est. 1987, 24x/yr.
Subscriptions: Indv. $160
Circulation: Total-1,200

Inside the White House

Publishing Co: Inside Washington Publishers, P.O. Box 7167, Ben Franklin Station, Washington, DC 20044 Tel # (703) 512-1800; Title Tel # (703) 892-8500
Personnel: Editor-Joe Burey
General Info: (Formerly Inside O.M.B.), Yr. Est. 1982, Weekly
Subscriptions: Indv. $495

Insider's Alert
See: INVESTMENT

Institute for Policy Studies Newsletter   *Business, Consumer*

Publishing Co: Institute for Policy Studies, 1601 Connecticut Ave. NW., Ste. 500, Washington, DC 20009 Tel # (202) 234-9382 Fax # (202) 387-7915
Editorial Description: Revealing and hard-hitting stories behind political news
General Info: (Formerly Counterpunch), Bi-weekly, 4 pages
Subscriptions: Indv. $40

Insurance Regulation/State Capitals
See: INSURANCE

Intellectual Activist

Publishing Co: Intellectual Activist, Inc., PO Box 262, Lincroft, NJ 07738-0262; Title Tel # (908) 842-6610
Personnel: Editor-Linda Reardon
Editorial Description: Covers newly developing political/economic issues from a pro-individual rights perspective.
General Info: Yr. Est. 1979, Bi-monthly, Trim Size-5½ x 8½, Sheetfed press, 16 pages, ISSN: 0730-2355, No Color, Newsprint
Subscriptions: $4/copy

Interdependent Voice

Publishing Co: U.S. Naturalized Citizen Assn., 399 Pendleton St., Alexandria, VA 22314-2049; Title Tel # (703) 549-2962

Interfaith Impact & Preparedness
See: RELIGIOUS & THEOLOGICAL

International Association of Educators for World Peace, Circulation Newsletter
Association

Publishing Co: World Peace Press, Mastin Lake St., Box 3282, Huntsville, AL 35810-0282; Title Tel # (205) 534-5501 Title Fax # (205) 536-1018
Personnel: Publisher, Editor-Charles Mercieca, Production Mgr.-Marrel Dingli Attard, Circ. Mgr., Adv. Dir.-Hortense Dodo, Mktg. Dir.-Mario Tabone, Promotion Dir.-Marcel Dingli Attard
Editorial Description: Discusses activities in human relations and world peace carried by IAEWP members.
General Info: Yr. Est. 1969, Bi-monthly, Trim Size-8½ x 11, Mimeo press, 2 pages, No Color
Subscriptions: Indv. $35
Circulation: (30% controlled), Total-10,000, Subscriptions-2,000, International-5,000, Readership-300,000
Advertising: Inquire for rates.

International Observer
See: INTERNATIONAL AFFAIRS

International Terrorism Newsletter
See: INTERNATIONAL AFFAIRS

Into the Night

Publishing Co: Into the Night, 1980 65th St Apt 3d, Brooklyn, NY 11204-3844
Personnel: Publisher, Editor-D. Stokes
Editorial Description: Contains information about political prisoners held in the U.S.
General Info: Yr. Est. 1987, Monthly, Trim Size-8½ x 11, Sheetfed press, 12 pages, Saddle-stitched
Subscriptions: Indv. $25, Inst. $25, Can. $15, For. $18, $3/copy
Acquistions: Publication Bought
Circulation: Total-800

Issues & Strategy Bulletin *Consumer*

Publishing Co: PAI, 9520 Bent Creek Ln, Vienna, VA 22182-1407 Tel # (703) 893-2777; Title Tel # (703) 759-3975 Title Fax # (703) 281-4108
Personnel: Editor-Howard Phillips, Circ. Mgr.-Mark Weaver
Editorial Description: Geopolitics, tax policy, social policy, crime & justice, foreign aid, defense & national security, Southern Africa, Central America, congressional reform, arms control, government expeditures.
General Info: Yr. Est. 1983, Semi-monthly
Subscriptions: Indv. $100, $5/copy
Circulation: Total-2,000
Advertising: Accepts Inserts.
List Rental: Rents Lists

JEI Report
See: INTERNATIONAL TRADE

Jack Anderson Confidential

Publishing Co: Target Publishing, Inc., PO Box 887, Springville, UT 84663-0887; Title Tel # (415) 463-2200 Title Fax # (415) 463-0173
Personnel: Publisher-Howard Ruff, Editor-Tom Walton, Production Mgr.-Michael Binstein
Editorial Description: Washington politics, international events, and business implications.
General Info: (Formerly Jack Anderson's Washington Letter), Yr. Est. 1984, Web press, 8 pages
Subscriptions: Indv. $89, $8/copy
Circulation: Total-8,000
List Rental: Actives: 6,952, $125/M

Jack Kemp's American Entrepreneur
See: BUSINESS & INDUSTRY

Jag *Consumer*

Publishing Co: Jag, Inc., 101 Hillside Dr W, Oelwein, IA 50662-2640; Title Tel # (319) 283-3491
Personnel: Publisher, Editor-Dr. R.S. Jaggard
Editorial Description: Avoid use of force, love neighbors, free enterprise. Libertarian.
General Info: Yr. Est. 1962, 7x/yr., Trim Size-8½ x 14, Mimeo press, 1 pages, ISSN: 0021-390X, No Color
Circulation: Total-1,000

Japan Economic Survey
See: INTERNATIONAL AFFAIRS

Japan Policy and Politics

Publishing Co: Kyodo News Intl., 50 Rockefeller Plaza #803, New York, NY 10020-1605; Title Tel # (212) 397-3723 Title Fax # (212) 397-3721
Editorial Description: Issues in Japan affecting Japanese politics.
General Info: Yr. Est. 1989, Weekly

Japan Weekly
See: INTERNATIONAL TRADE

Jewish Labor Committee Review
See: LABOR

Jewish Radical *Consumer*

Publishing Co: Jewish Radical Education Project, 1 Union Sq W Ste 302, New York, NY 10003-3303; Title Tel # (212) 675-9788
Personnel: Publisher-Robert Wolfe
Editorial Description: For those who support pro-Jewish/pro-radical beliefs.
General Info: Yr. Est. 1993, Monthly
Subscriptions: Indv. $10, $1/copy
Circulation: Total-500

Journal Update *Scholarly*

Publishing Co: Harvard Univ., JFK School of Government, 79 John F Kennedy St, Cambridge, MA 02138-5800; Title Tel # (617) 495-1311 Title Fax # (617) 496-9027
Personnel: Co-Editor-Mark Fassold, Co-Editor-Claudia Jasin
Editorial Description: Supplements the Harvard Journal of Hispanic Policy.
General Info: Monthly, Trim Size-8½ x 11, 4 pages, No Color, Matte

LAWS Quarterly

Publishing Co: Lawyers Alliance for Nuclear Arms Control, 1601 Connecticut Avenue, NW, Washington, DC 20009-1035; Title Tel # (202) 296-6054 Title Fax # (202) 296-6049
Personnel: Circ. Mgr.-Morgan Gale, Editor, Production Mgr., Art Dir.-Laura McGough
Editorial Description: Updates on organizational activities, progress on arms control treaties, movements & laws. Also reports on the rule of law in international relations.
General Info: (Formerly LANAC Newsletter), Yr. Est. 1981, Quarterly, Sheetfed press, 16 pages, 2 Color, Matte, Saddle-stitched
Subscriptions: Indv. $30
Advertising: Inquire for rates.

LFL Reports:
See: CIVIL RIGHTS

La Nueva Bandera (The New Flag) *Scholarly*

Publishing Co: New Flag, The, 30-08 Broadway, Suite #159, Queens, NY 11106 Fax # (401) 334-4703; Title Tel # (401) 334-4296
Personnel: Editor-Luis Quispe
Editorial Description: We are a group of intellectuals who work to educate Americans on the developments of the civil war in Peru. English Edion.
General Info: Yr. Est. 1993, Bi-monthly, Trim Size-8 x 11, 50 pages, 2 Color, Newsprint, Perfect bound
Subscriptions: Free To Qualified Recipient
Advertising: Accepts Inserts.

La Taupe Rouge

Publishing Co: Groupe Marxiste Revolutionnaire, 342 est, rue Ontario, Montreal, PQ Canada
Personnel: Editor-Michel Mill
General Info: Yr. Est. 1972, 8x/yr., 15 pages
Subscriptions: Indv. $3
Circulation: Total-2,000

Lambda Update
See: CIVIL RIGHTS

Latino
See: ETHNIC

Left Business Observer
See: BUSINESS & INDUSTRY

Left Out *Consumer, Association*

Publishing Co: Socialist Party/Solidarity, PO Box 41510, Santa Barbara, CA 93140-1510 Tel # (805) 965-4817
Personnel: Co-Editor-Jack Ceder, Co-Editor-Tom Garrison, Co-Editor-Debby Looker
Editorial Description: A compilation of analyses, opinions, and a calendar of events that are compatible with a democratic socialist, non-sectarian viewpoint.
General Info: Yr. Est. 1987, Bi-monthly, Trim Size-8½ x 11, Desktop press, 8 pages
Subscriptions: Indv. $10, Inst. $10, $1/copy
Circulation: Total-300
Advertising: Inquire for rates. Accepts Inserts.

Legalizing Freedom *Consumer*

Publishing Co: Tolerant Majority, PO Box 22930, Santa Barbara, CA 93121-2930; Title Tel # (805) 965-2741 Title Fax # (805) 965-2741
Editorial Description: Socially conscience newsletter about need for less society laws.
General Info: Annually
Circulation: Total-810

Legislative Alert *Business, Association*

Publishing Co: Sponsor-Women Strike for Peace, Women Strike for Peace, 110 Maryland Ave. NE, Suite 302, Washington, DC 20002; Title Tel # (202) 543-2660 Title Fax # (202) 546-0900
Personnel: Editor-Edith Villastrigo
Editorial Description: Informs & alerts people about issues of major concern such as nuclear disarmament, human rights & Third World intervention, & suggests legislative action.
General Info: Yr. Est. 1975, Monthly, Trim Size-8½ x 14, Mimeo press, 4 pages, No Color, Matte
Subscriptions: Indv. $15
Circulation: Total-3,500

Legislative Update

Publishing Co: Evangelical Lutheran Church in America, Office for Govt. Affairs, 122 C St., NW Ste. 300, Washington, DC 20001-2172; Title Tel # (202) 783-7507 Title Fax # (202) 783-7502
Personnel: Editor-John Lillie, Circ. Mgr.-Jackie Madden, Production Mgr.-Robert Kraay
Editorial Description: Publication highlights the public policy advocacy work of the Evangelical Lutheran Church in America.
General Info: Yr. Est. 1988
Circulation: Total-2,750

Letter to Friends Around the World
Consumer, Association

Publishing Co: Fourth World Movement, 7600 Willow Hill Dr, Landover, MD 20785-4658; Title Tel # (301) 336-9489 Title Fax # (301) 336-0092
Personnel: Publisher-Susan Devins
Editorial Description: To exchange experiences on extreme poverty & to think together, to support & influence development in order to ensure that no one is excluded. Published in France, distributed in the US by Fourth World Movement.
General Info: Yr. Est. 1981, Trim Size-8$\frac{1}{2}$ x 11, 8 pages, No Color, Coated
Subscriptions: Indv. $4

Liberalink

Publishing Co: Nova Scotia Liberal Assn., Box 723, Halifax, NS B3J 2T3 Canada; Title Tel # (902) 423-6128
Personnel: Editor-Carolyn Drysdale
General Info: (Formerly Nova Scotia Liberal), Yr. Est. 1986, Quarterly, Offset press, 4 pages, 2 Color
Circulation: Total-26,000
Printing Co: Cumberland Publishing Ltd., 10 Lawrence St., Amherst, NS B4H 3Z2 Canada Tel # (902) 667-5102

Libertarian Bulletin

Publishing Co: Ontario Libertarian Party, 1 St Johns Rd, Toronto, ON M4S 2A3 Canada; Title Tel # (416) 769-3223 Title Fax # (416) 763-7463
Personnel: Editor-George Dance, Adv. Dir., Promotion Dir.-Daniel Hunt
Editorial Description: News of the Ontario Libertarian Party.
General Info: (Formerly Libertarian Newsletter), Yr. Est. 1975, Quarterly, Trim Size-8$\frac{1}{2}$ x 11, 8 pages, 1% ads
Circulation: Total-1,200
Advertising: Inquire for rates.

Libertarian Volunteer, The   *Association*

Publishing Co: Libertarian National Committee, Inc., 2600 Virginia Ave. NW, Ste. 100, Washington, DC 20037; Title Tel # (202) 333-0008 Title Fax # (202) 333-0072
Editorial Description: Political strategy and tactics advice for Libertarian Party officers, activists, and canidates.
General Info: Yr. Est. 1993, Bi-monthly, Trim Size-8$\frac{1}{2}$ x 11, Sheetfed press, 16 pages, No Color, Matte, Saddle-stitched
Subscriptions: Free In Designated Area
Circulation: (100% controlled), Total-1,500
Printing Co: B & B Duplicators, 818 18th St., NW, Washington, DC 30006 Tel # (202) 293-1252

Lifelines

Publishing Co: Coalition to Free Soviet Jews, 711 3rd Ave Fl 12, New York, NY 10017-4014; Title Tel # (212) 354-1316
Editorial Description: Covers Coalition activities, issues regarding Soviet Jewry, general interest news for the Jewish community.
General Info: Yr. Est. 1981, Monthly
Circulation: Total-8,000

Limbaugh Letter   *Consumer*

Publishing Co: EFM Media Managment, 366 Madison Ave., 7th Floor, New York, NY 10017-3122 Fax # (212) 661-7945; Title Tel # (212) 661-7500 Title Fax # (212) 563-9166
Personnel: Editor in Chief-Rush Limbaugh, Mng. Editor-Diana Schneider
Editorial Description: Commentary from broadcaster Rush Limbaugh.
General Info: Yr. Est. 1993, Monthly, ISSN: 1065-0377
Subscriptions: Indv. $30
Circulation: Total-280,000
List Rental: List Management Co.: Conrad Direct, Inc., 300 Knickerbocker Road, Creskill, NJ 07626 Tel # (201) 567-3200, Fax # (201) 567-4959, Actives: 251,740, $125/M

Live and Let Live   *Consumer*

Publishing Co: Live and Let Live, PO Box 613, Redwood Valley, CA 95470-0613
Personnel: Publisher-James Dawson
Editorial Description: Defends and explores animal and fetal rights from libertarian-individualist perspective.
General Info: Irregular, Trim Size-5$\frac{1}{2}$ x 8$\frac{1}{2}$, 20 pages, No Color, Matte
Subscriptions: Indv. $3, $1/copy
Circulation: Total-200
Advertising: Inquire for rates.

Lottery, Paramutual & Casino Regulations/State Capitals
See: GAMBLING

MCPL Education Fund, Food and Population Newsletter   *Association*

Publishing Co: Members of Congress for Arms Control & Foreign Policy Caucus, 2700 Virginia Ave., N.W. #807, Washington, DC 20037-1908; Title Tel # (202) 226-3440
Personnel: Editor-Edith B. Wilke
Editorial Description: Encourages complete disarmament under enforceable world law.
General Info: Yr. Est. 1977, 9x/yr., Trim Size-8$\frac{1}{2}$ x 14
Circulation: Total-750

MSRRT Newsletter
See: LIBRARY

Majority Rules
See: WOMEN'S

Managing the Human Climate
See: MEDIA & COMMUNICATIONS

MediaWatch
See: MEDIA & COMMUNICATIONS

Mennonite Central Committee-Washington Memo

Publishing Co: Mennonite Central Committee-Peace Section, 110 Maryland Ave. NE, Washington, DC 20002-5681; Title Tel # (202) 544-6564
Personnel: Editor-Delton Franz
Editorial Description: Interprets national policy reflecting biblical concerns for justice and peace.
General Info: Yr. Est. 1969, Bi-monthly, 12 pages, No Color
Subscriptions: Indv. $10
Circulation: Total-6,000

Metro Justice News

Publishing Co: Metro Act, 36 St. Paul St., Rm. 112, Rochester, NY 14604; Title Tel # (716) 325-2560
Personnel: Editor-Jack Bradigane-Spula
General Info: (Formerly Peace & Justice Education Center Newsletter), 11x/yr., Trim Size-7 x 8$\frac{1}{2}$, 28 pages
Subscriptions: Indv. $5

Mexico Report, The
See: INTERNATIONAL AFFAIRS

Midwest Political Consultant   *Business, Consumer*

Publishing Co: Christian Schock & Associates, 361 S Commonwealth Ave, Elgin, IL 60123-7357; Title Tel # (708) 741-1753
Personnel: Publisher, Editor-Christian Schock
Editorial Description: Covers politics and campaigning in the Midwest.
General Info: Yr. Est. 1987, Monthly, Offset press, 8 pages, No Color, Newsprint
Subscriptions: Indv. $50
Circulation: (20% controlled), Total-1,000
Printing Co: Alpha Plus Instant Print, 1520 Larkin Ave, Elgin, IL 60123-5178 Tel # (708) 888-3433

Millennial Prophecy Report
See: RELIGIOUS & THEOLOGICAL

Mindszenty Report

Publishing Co: Mindszenty Report, PO Box 11321, Saint Louis, MO 63105-0121; Title Tel # (314) 991-2939 Title Fax # (314) 991-5128
Personnel: Publisher-Eleanor Schlafly, Editor-John Bolandi
Editorial Description: Information in defense of freedom and threats to it.
General Info: Yr. Est. 1958, Monthly, 4 pages
Subscriptions: Indv. $12
Circulation: Total-10,000

Minnesota International Center
See: INTERNATIONAL AFFAIRS

Monday: a weekly newsletter on refugee and immigration issues
See: ETHNIC

Monitor!

Publishing Co: Union of Councils for Soviet Jews, 1819 H St NW Ste 230, Washington, DC 20006-3603; Title Tel # (202) 775-9770 Title Fax # (202) 775-9776
Personnel: Editor-Stacy Burdett
General Info: Yr. Est. 1990, Weekly
Subscriptions: Indv. $60

More than a Paycheck · *Association*

Publishing Co: Natl. War Tax Resistance Coordinating Committee, PO Box 774, Monroe, ME 04951-0774; Title Tel # (207) 525-7774
Personnel: Editor-Karen Marysdaughter
Editorial Description: Supports conscientious objection to taxation for militarization & war.
General Info: (Formerly Network News), Yr. Est. 1982, Bi-monthly, Trim Size-8½ x 11, Desktop press, 8 pages, No Color
Subscriptions: Indv. $10
Circulation: Total-550
Printing Co: Lakeside Press, 1334 Williamson St, Madison, WI 53703-3757 Tel # (608) 255-1800

Motor Vehicle Regulation/State Capitals
See: AUTOMOTIVE

NAAWP News · *Association*

Publishing Co: Natl. Assn. for Advancement of White People, PO Box 10625, New Orleans, LA 70181-0625; Title Tel # (504) 831-6986
Personnel: Editor-David Duke, Circ. Mgr.-Glen Udell, Art Dir.-Bart Udell, Promotion Dir.-Tom Wilson
Editorial Description: News important to the rights and survivial of white people.
General Info: Yr. Est. 1979, Monthly, Web press, 16 pages, 2 Color
Subscriptions: Indv. $10, $1/copy
Circulation: Total-24,000

NCBA Reports
See: LAW

NYPIRG Agenda
See: CONSUMER INTERESTS

National Policy Watch · *Business*

Publishing Co: Natl. Center for Public Policy Research, 300 Eye St. NE, #3, Washington, DC 20002 Fax # (202) 543-1286; Title Tel # (202) 543-1286 Title Fax # (202) 543-4779
Personnel: Publisher-Burton Pines, Editor-Amy Moritz
Editorial Description: Covers U.S. foreign & domestic policy and activities of organization.
General Info: Yr. Est. 1984, Monthly, Sheetfed press, 8 pages, 4 Color, Newsprint
Subscriptions: Indv. $15
Circulation: Total-15,000

Nationalist

Publishing Co: Natl. Democratic Front, PO Box 30505, Knoxville, TN 37930-0505
Editorial Description: White nationalist ideology against capitalism & communism.
General Info: Yr. Est. 1985, Monthly, 8 pages

Natural Rights · *Consumer*

Publishing Co: Natural Rights Center, PO Box 90, Summertown, TN 38483-0090; Title Tel # (615) 964-3992 Title Fax # (615) 964-2200
Personnel: Editor-Albert Bates
General Info: Quarterly
Subscriptions: Free With Membership

Never Again

Publishing Co: Jewish Defense Organization, Youth Movement, 134 W 32nd St Ste 602, New York, NY 10001-3201; Title Tel # (212) 239-0447
Editorial Description: Explores current news and issues of special importance to the Jewish community. Covers Defense Organization activities.

New American View
See: GOVERNMENT

New Creation News
See: RELIGIOUS & THEOLOGICAL

New Democrat · *Consumer, Association*

Publishing Co: Nova Scotia New Democratic Party, 1657 Barrington St., Ste. 533, Halifax, NS B3J 2A1 Canada Fax # (902) 423-9618; Title Tel # (902) 423-9217
Personnel: Editor-Ross Fisher
General Info: Quarterly

New Forces
See: GOVERNMENT

New Outlook · *Consumer, Association*

Publishing Co: American Committee on US-Soviet Relations, PO Box 15334, Washington, DC 20003-0334; Title Tel # (202) 546-1700 Title Fax # (202) 543-3146
Personnel: Editor-Dr. Robert Burrows
Editorial Description: New Outlook is the official journal of the American Committee on U.S.-Soviet Relations.
General Info: Yr. Est. 1974, Quarterly, 8 pages
Subscriptions: Indv. $25
Circulation: Total-2,000

New Party · *Association*

Publishing Co: Sponsor-Sophia Circle, New Party, 8319 Fulham Ct, Richmond, VA 23227-1712; Title Tel # (804) 266-7400
Personnel: Editor-J. Gorman
Editorial Description: Activist, nonviolent publication. Resists death penalty, conscription, war patriarchy. Promotes goal of developing a new political party.
General Info: Yr. Est. 1978, Trim Size-8½ x 11, Letrpr. press, 3 pages, No Color

New Race Newsletter · *Consumer, Association*

Publishing Co: Phillip Genealogical Heritage House, 605 Benton Ave., Missoula, MT 59801-8633; Title Tel # (406) 543-3495
Editorial Description: The great mixture of European & Indian races over 400 years of time.
General Info: Annually
Subscriptions: Inst. $8, $10/copy
Acquistions: Publication Sold
Advertising: Accepts Inserts.
List Rental: Rents Lists
Printing Co: Phillip Heritage Genealogy House., 605 Benton Ave, Missoula, MT 59801-8633 Tel # (406) 543-3495

News From ICS · *Association*

Publishing Co: Institute for Contemporary Studies, 720 Market St., San Francisco, CA 94102; Title Tel # (415) 981-5353 Title Fax # (415) 981-5353
Personnel: Publisher-Robert Hawkins, Jr., Editor-Tracy Glagette, Production Mgr.-Debbie Rice, Mktg. Dir.-Kevin Heverin
Editorial Description: Issues and innovations in economics and public policy.
General Info: (Formerly Letter), Yr. Est. 1974, Bi-monthly, Trim Size-8.5 x 11, Sheetfed press, 16 pages, 2 Color, Newsprint, Saddle-stitched
Subscriptions: Free
Circulation: Total-6,000, Readership-25,000
Advertising: Accepts Inserts.
List Rental: Actives: 15,000, $125/M

News-N-Notes

Publishing Co: Sponsor-Atlanta Clergy and Laity Concerned, Atlanta CALC, 92 Piedmont Ave., N.E., Atlanta, GA 30303-2528; Title Tel # (404) 688-7407
Personnel: Editor-Sandra Mershon
Editorial Description: Disarmament, economic justice, racial justice and human rights.
General Info: (Formerly Georgia Peace & Justice Report), Yr. Est. 1977, Monthly, Trim Size-8½ x 14, Web press, 2 pages, 2% ads, Newsprint
Subscriptions: Indv. $8, Inst. $12
Circulation: Total-3,000
Advertising: Inquire for rates.

News from People for the American Way

Publishing Co: People for the American Way, 2000 M St. NW, Ste. 400, Washington, DC 20036-3307; Title Tel # (202) 467-4999 Title Fax # (202) 293-2672
General Info: Monthly
List Rental: Actives: $65/M, Expires: 50,000, $50/M

NewsNotes

Publishing Co: Maryknoll Fathers & Brothers Justice & Peace Office, 3700 Oakview Ter NE, Washington, DC 20017-2521; Title Tel # (202) 832-1780 Title Fax # (202) 832-5195
Personnel: Circ. Dir.-Linda K. Stewart
Editorial Description: Justice and peace issues around the world.
General Info: Bi-monthly
Subscriptions: Indv. $10
Circulation: Total-1,500

North American Indian

Publishing Co: North American Indian, 22720 Plymouth Rd, Detroit, MI 48239-1327 Tel # (313) 535-2966
Personnel: Editor-John Rochford
Editorial Description: Covers issues and current developments impacting upon Native American interests.
General Info: Yr. Est. 1980, Quarterly
Circulation: Total-1,200

North Star Compass
See: INTERNATIONAL AFFAIRS

Northern Lights Glimmer

Publishing Co: Patriots in Action, PO Box 140853, Anchorage, AK 99514-0853
Editorial Description: Revive American values.
General Info: Yr. Est. 1980, Trim Size-8½ x 11, 4 pages, 2 Color, Perfect bound
Subscriptions: Indv. $25
Acquistions: Publication Bought

Nuclear Resister · *Consumer, Association*

Publishing Co: Natl. No-Nukes Prison Support Collec., PO Box 43383, Tucson, AZ 85733-3383; Title Tel # (520) 323-8697
Personnel: Publisher, Editor-Felice Cohen-Joppa, Production Mgr.-Jack Cohen-Joppa
Editorial Description: Support tabloid for imprisoned anti-nuke activists; chronicles anti-nuclear civil disobedience.
General Info: (Formerly Newsletter of NNNPSC), Yr. Est. 1980, 8x/yr., Trim Size-11½ x 17, Web press, 8 pages, ISSN: 0883-9875, No Color, Newsprint
Subscriptions: Indv. $18, Can. $21, For. $28, Free
Circulation: (10% controlled), Total-1,000, Subscriptions-800, International-75
Printing Co: Territorial Publishers, 1 W Orange Grove Rd, Tucson, AZ 85704-5512

Oleary Report · *Business*

Publishing Co: O'Leary Kamber Report, 3050 K St NW Ste 105, Washington, DC 20007-5108 Fax # (202) 933-4560; Title Tel # (202) 944-4550 Title Fax # (202) 944-4560
Personnel: Mktg. Dir.-Susan M. Schultz
General Info: (Formerly O'Leary Kamber Report), Semi-annually, Offset press, 8 pages, 2 Color
Subscriptions: Free

©1996, Oxbridge Communications, Inc.

Olive Branch
Scholarly, Association

Publishing Co: American Friends Service Committee, Pasadena, 980 N Fair Oaks Ave, Pasadena, CA 91103-3009; Title Tel # (818) 791-1978 Title Fax # (818) 791-2205
Personnel: Publisher-Linda Lotz
Editorial Description: Calendar of events in LA & relating to the Middle East.
General Info: Yr. Est. 1987, Bi-monthly, Trim Size-8½ x 11, Desktop press, 6 pages, No Color
Subscriptions: Free In Designated Area
Circulation: Total-1,300

Open Doors News Brief
See: INTERNATIONAL AFFAIRS

Organizer
Association

Publishing Co: Natl. Alliance Against Racist & Political Repression, 11 John St Rm 702, New York, NY 10038-4009; Title Tel # (212) 406-3330 Title Fax # (212) 406-3542
Editorial Description: Chronicals struggle to defend and extend democratic rights in this country.
General Info: Yr. Est. 1973, Quarterly, Trim Size-8½ x 11, Sheetfed press, 8 pages, No Color
Subscriptions: Indv. $12, Inst. $50, $3/copy
Circulation: Total-10,000

Other Side, The

Publishing Co: The Michael Harrington Center, City Univ. of New York, Room 323, Flushing, NY 11367-1597
Personnel: Editor-Arthur Lipow, Production Dir.-Kathleen Donovan
Editorial Description: For democratic views and social change.
General Info: Trim Size-8½ x 11, 16 pages, No Color

Our Struggle/Nuestra Lucha

Publishing Co: Democratic Socialists of America, 2827 Catania Way, Sacramento, CA 95826-2228; Title Tel # (916) 361-9072
Personnel: Editor-Dwayen Campbell
General Info: Yr. Est. 1983, Quarterly, 12 pages
Subscriptions: Indv. $15, Inst. $30

Outfront

Publishing Co: Mayor's Office for Lesbian & Gay Community, 52 Chambers St., #311, New York, NY 10007-1222; Title Tel # (212) 788-2706 Title Fax # (212) 788-3160
Personnel: Editor-Jan Carl Park
General Info: Quarterly

Outlook/State Capitals, The
See: GOVERNMENT

PAIS International News
See: LIBRARY

PS: Intelligent Guide to Jewish Affairs
Consumer

Publishing Co: PS Reports, PO Box 48, Mineola, NY 11501-0048; Title Tel # (516) 248-1389 Title Fax # (516) 829-1248
Personnel: Publisher-Ben Levitman, Editor-Murray Polner, Editor-Adam Simms
Editorial Description: Liberal commentary on Jewish affairs.
General Info: Yr. Est. 1993, Bi-weekly, Trim Size-8½ x 11, Offset press, 4 pages, ISSN: 1081-1095, No Color, Matte
Subscriptions: Indv. $40, Can. $55, For. $70, $2/copy
Circulation: Total-1,200

PSR Reports
See: ENVIRONMENT & ECOLOGY

Patriot Cannon

Publishing Co: National Association of Independent Patriot Club, PO Box 2368, Anderson, SC 29622-2368; Title Tel # (803) 225-3061
Personnel: Publisher-Robert Clarkson
Editorial Description: Patriotic - libertarian & anti-statist.
General Info: Yr. Est. 1978, Bi-monthly, 8 pages, No Color
Subscriptions: Indv. $25, $3/copy
Circulation: Total-1,000

Peace & Democracy News

Publishing Co: Campaign for Peace & Democracy, Box 1640, Cathedral Station, New York, NY 10025-1560; Title Tel # (212) 666-5924 Title Fax # (212) 662-5892
Personnel: Publisher-Joanne Landy, Editor-Gail Daneker, Production Mgr.-Ed Hedermann
Editorial Description: Peace & Democracy News is the bulletin of the Campaign for Peace & Democracy, which brings together peace activists, environmentalists, trade unionists, feminists and minority rights activists with democratic movements East, West and South, inthe conviction that dialogue and common action from below are essential to world peace.
General Info: Yr. Est. 1984, Semi-annually, Trim Size-8½ x 10¾, Web press, 48 pages, ISSN: 0749-5900, Ind/Abs/Online: Alternative Press Index, Left Index, Color-cover, Matte, Saddle-stitched
Subscriptions: Indv. $7, Inst. $10, For. $10, $3/copy
Circulation: Total-6,000
Advertising: Inquire for rates. Accepts Inserts.
Printing Co: Boyd Printing Co., Inc., 49 Sheridan Ave, Albany, NY 12210-2735 Tel # (518) 436-9686, Fax # (518) 436-7433

Peace & Disarmament News

Publishing Co: Natl. Lawyer's Guild-P&D Subcommittee, 1205 Smith Tower, Seattle, WA 98104; Title Tel # (206) 622-5144
General Info: Bi-monthly
Subscriptions: Indv. $12

Peace & Justice News

Publishing Co: Peace & Justice Center, 1935 Lewiston Dr, Louisville, KY 40216-2523 Tel # (502) 448-8581; Title Tel # (502) 451-5451
Personnel: Editor-Myles McCabe
General Info: Bi-monthly, 6 pages

Peace Chronical
See: EDUCATION

Peace Conversion Times

Publishing Co: Alliance for Survival, 200 W. Main St., #M-2, Santa Ana, CA 92701-4851; Title Tel # (714) 547-6282 Title Fax # (714) 547-6322
Personnel: Editor-Jennifer Kops
Editorial Description: Pro-disarmament and peace related reporting and environmental issues.
General Info: (Formerly Survival), Yr. Est. 1983, Bi-monthly, Trim Size-8 x 10½, 8 pages
Subscriptions: Indv. $25
Circulation: Total-6,000
Advertising: Inquire for rates.

Peace Currents
Consumer, Association

Publishing Co: Sacramento Peace Ctr., 414 T St, Sacramento, CA 95814-6914 Tel # (916) 446-1092; Title Tel # (916) 446-0787
Personnel: Editor-Dale Crandall-Bare
Editorial Description: Issues and action regarding peace, nonviolence, social concerns, feminism.
General Info: Yr. Est. 1962, Bi-monthly, Trim Size-8½ x 11, Offset press, 10 pages, Color
Subscriptions: Indv. $10, Free
Circulation: Total-1,200

Peace Education Center Monthly
Consumer, Association

Publishing Co: Peace Education Center, 1118 S Harrison Rd, East Lansing, MI 48823-5201; Title Tel # (517) 351-4648
Personnel: Editor-Mary Wright
General Info: (Formerly Peace Education Center Newsletter), 11x/yr., Trim Size-7 x 8½, 20 pages
Subscriptions: Indv. $5
Circulation: Total-800

Peace Gazette
Association, Consumer

Publishing Co: Mount Diablo Peace Center, 65 Eckley Ln, Walnut Creek, CA 94596-6798; Title Tel # (415) 933-7850
Personnel: Editor-Arne Westerback, Production Mgr.-C. Haynes, Promotion Dir.-Chuck Goodmacher
Editorial Description: Covers peace and justice issues in society.
General Info: Monthly, Trim Size-8½ x 11, 14 pages, No Color
Subscriptions: Indv. $15, Inst. $25, Can. $20, For. $25, $1/copy

Peace Letter

Publishing Co: Washington Peace Ctr., 2111 Florida Ave NW, Washington, DC 20008-1912; Title Tel # (202) 234-2000
Personnel: Publisher-Lisa Fithian
Editorial Description: Peace & disarmament programs & actions in DC area.
General Info: Yr. Est. 1963, Monthly, Trim Size-12 x 16, Web press, 8 pages, 1% ads, No Color, Newsprint
Subscriptions: $1/copy
Circulation: Total-5,000
Advertising: Inquire for rates.

Peace Newsletter
Association

Publishing Co: Syracuse Peace Council, 924 Burnet Ave, Syracuse, NY 13203-3291; Title Tel # (315) 472-5478
Editorial Description: Collectively published, the PNL provides news, background and radical analysis of important issues, locally, nationally and internationally.
General Info: Yr. Est. 1936, Monthly, Trim Size-8½ x 11¼, Web press, 24 pages, ISSN: 0735-4134, 2 Color, Newsprint
Subscriptions: Indv. $10, $1/copy
Acquistions: Publication Bought
Circulation: (76% controlled)
Advertising: Inquire for rates.
Printing Co: Scotsman Press, Inc., PO Box 4970, 250 Bear St. West, Syracuse, NY 13221-4970 Tel # (315) 472-7825

Peace Office Newsletter
Consumer, Association

Publishing Co: Mennonite Central Committee, PO Box 500, 21 South 12th St., Akron, PA 17501-0500 Tel # (717) 859-1151 Fax # (717) 859-2171
Personnel: Editor-Gwenn Groff
Editorial Description: Features issues addressed by the MCC Peace Office.
General Info: Yr. Est. 1972, Quarterly, Trim Size-8½ x 11, Offset press, 12 pages, 2 Color, Matte, Saddle-stitched
Subscriptions: Indv. $10
Circulation: Total-4,000

Peace Press   *Consumer*

Publishing Co: Sonoma County Center for Peace & Justice, 540 Pacific Ave, Santa Rosa, CA 95404-2852; Title Tel # (707) 575-8902 Title Fax # (707) 575-8902
Editorial Description: Monthly publication covering issues of peace, justice & environment, particularly in Sonoma County, CA.
General Info: (Formerly Sonoma County Center for Peace & Justice), 10x/yr., Trim Size-8½ x 11, Ind/Abs/Online: Peace Net, Color
Subscriptions: Free With Membership
Circulation: Total-2,500
Advertising: Inquire for rates. Accepts Inserts.

Peace Research

Publishing Co: Brandon Univ., Brandon Campus, Brandon, MB R7A 6A9 Canada Tel # (204) 728-9520; Title Tel # (204) 729-9010
Personnel: Publisher, Editor-M.V. Naidu, Circ. Mgr., Production Mgr.-Thora Sowiak
Editorial Description: The Journal publishes scientific & scholarly work on world peace focussing on the problem of violence, war armament, international organization, liberty, human development, peace education, a better world order.
General Info: Yr. Est. 1969, Quarterly, Sheetfed press, 100 pages, Saddle-stitched
Subscriptions: Indv. $27, Inst. $39, Can. $24, For. $45, $10/copy
Circulation: Total-1,000
Advertising: Inquire for rates.
List Rental: Rents Lists
Printing Co: Star Printers, 835 Stickney Ave., Brandon, MB R7A 0E1 Canada Tel # (204) 727-1564

PeaceNotes   *Association*

Publishing Co: Lutheran Peace Fellowship, 1710 11th Ave, Seattle, WA 98122-2420
Personnel: Editor-Bonnie Block
General Info: Quarterly, Trim Size-17 x 11, 3 pages, No Color, Recycled
Circulation: Total-2,200

Peacework

Publishing Co: American Friends Service Committee, Cambridge, 2161 Massachusetts Ave., Cambridge, MA 02140-1299; Title Tel # (617) 661-6130
Editorial Description: New England peace & social justice newsletter, covering grassroots politics of a wide variety of groups in six-state region.
General Info: Yr. Est. 1972, Monthly, Trim Size-8½ x 11, Sheetfed press, 16 pages, ISSN: 0748-0725, No Color, Newsprint
Subscriptions: Indv. $10, $1/copy
Circulation: Total-2,500
Printing Co: Saltus Press, 31 Jolma Rd, Worcester, MA 01604-2009 Tel # (508) 752-1969

Penny Resistance   *Association*

Publishing Co: Penny Resistance, 8319 Fulham Ct, Richmond, VA 23227-1712; Title Tel # (804) 266-7400
Personnel: Editor-Jerome Gorman
Editorial Description: Works for the abolition of the death penalty by promoting economic and tax resistance to capital punishment. 90
General Info: Yr. Est. 1984, Semi-annually, Trim Size-8½ x 11, Letrpr. press, 8 pages, No Color
Circulation: Total-250

People United to Save Humanity P.U.S.H/ Operation Push

Publishing Co: People United to Save Humanity P.U.S.H/Operation Push, PO Box 5432, Chicago, IL 60680-5432 Tel # (312) 373-3366
Personnel: Editor-Jesse Jackson
General Info: Yr. Est. 1970, Monthly
Advertising: Inquire for rates.

Performing & Fine Arts for World Peace Newsletter

Publishing Co: Performing & Fine Arts for World Peace, General Delivery, Volcano, HI 96785-9999; Title Tel # (808) 245-7262
Personnel: Editor-Howard Shapiro
General Info: Yr. Est. 1986, Quarterly

Perot Periodical   *Consumer*

Publishing Co: The Perot Peerodical, PO Box 435, Riverdale, NY 10471; Title Tel # (718) 548-4360
Personnel: Publisher, Editor-Micah Sifry
Editorial Description: Covers and exposes the trail and events of Perot's activities.
General Info: Yr. Est. 1993, Quarterly, Trim Size-8½ x 11, 16 pages
Subscriptions: Indv. $15

Perryman Texas Letter, The
See: ECONOMICS

Perspectives on Contemporary Ukraine
See: INTERNATIONAL AFFAIRS

Planet Walker

Publishing Co: Planet Walk, Inc., PO Box 701, Inverness, CA 94937-0701
Editorial Description: Provides commentay on environmental & peace issues.
General Info: Yr. Est. 1983, Quarterly, 20 pages
Circulation: Total-1,000

Plenty Bulletin

Publishing Co: Plenty USA, PO Box 394, Summertown, TN 38483-0394; Title Tel # (916) 753-0731
Personnel: Editor-Peter Schweitzer
General Info: Yr. Est. 1974, Quarterly
Subscriptions: Indv. $10

Plowshare News

Publishing Co: Plowshare Peace Center, PO Box 1623, Roanoke, VA 24008-1623; Title Tel # (703) 985-0808 Title Fax # (703) 985-0808
Personnel: Production Mgr.-Pat Pratali, Editor, Art Dir.-Polly Branch
General Info: Yr. Est. 1978, Monthly, Mimeo press, 12 pages, No Color, Matte
Subscriptions: Indv. $10, Inst. $15, Free
Circulation: Total-700, Readership-800
Advertising: Inquire for rates.

Point

Publishing Co: Veterans for Peace, Butler Brigade, PO Box 1314, Jamaica Plain, MA 02130-0011; Title Tel # (617) 524-7207
Personnel: Editor-Barry Brodsky
Editorial Description: Massachusetts chapter of Veterans for Peace. Nationally recognized as leaders in the veteran anti-war movement.
General Info: Yr. Est. 1986, Quarterly
Subscriptions: Indv. $5

Political Analysis Newsletter

Publishing Co: Council for Canadian Unity, 2055 Peel St., Ste. 475, Montreal, PQ H3A 1V4 Canada
General Info: Yr. Est. 1984, 10x/yr.
Subscriptions: Indv. $25
Circulation: Total-4,500

Political Corruption

Publishing Co: Loan Broker, 917 S Park St, Owosso, MI 48867-4422

Political Finance & Lobby Reporter   *Business, Association*

Publishing Co: Amward Publications, Inc., 2030 Clarendon Blvd., Ste. 401, Arlington, VA 22201-2911; Title Tel # (703) 525-7227 Title Fax # (703) 525-3536
Personnel: Publisher, Editor-Edward Zuckerman
Editorial Description: Developments affecting political campaign financing and lobbying practices.
General Info: (Formerly PACs & Lobbies), Yr. Est. 1980, Semi-monthly, Trim Size-8½ x 11, Sheetfed press, 10 pages, ISSN: 0270-353X, Ind/Abs/Online: NewsNet, Lexis, Nexis, No Color
Subscriptions: Indv. $327, Can. $347, For. $347
List Rental: List Management Co.: Carol Hess & Associates, 252 Apple Tree Point, Burlington, VT 05406-4278 Tel # (802) 660-2869, Fax # (802) 864-9502, Actives: 1,500, $100/M

Political Pulse   *Business, Association*

Publishing Co: Political Pulse, 926 J St., Ste. 1218, Sacramento, CA 95814-2708; Title Tel # (916) 446-2048 Title Fax # (916) 446-5302
Personnel: Publisher, Editor-Bud Lembke
Editorial Description: Newsletter of California politics & government.
General Info: Yr. Est. 1985, Semi-monthly, Letrpr. press, 6 pages, ISSN: 8756-9248, No Color
Subscriptions: Indv. $125
Circulation: Total-200
Printing Co: Alphagraphics, 530 I St, Sacramento, CA 95814-2334 Tel # (916) 925-5140

Political Risk Letter
See: INTERNATIONAL TRADE

Political Stethoscope

Publishing Co: American Medical Association, 515 N. State St., Chicago, IL 60610 Tel # (312) 464-4512 Fax # (312) 464-5834; Title Tel # (312) 645-5000
Editorial Description: Reports on AMPAC political activities.
General Info: Quarterly
Subscriptions: Free

Political Woman Hotline   *Consumer*

Publishing Co: Political Woman, 276 Chatterton Pky., White Plains, NY 10606-2012; Title Tel # (914) 285-9761 Title Fax # (914) 285-9763
Personnel: Publisher-Robert Fertik, Publisher-Antonia Stolper
Editorial Description: Covering U.S. government and political from a feminist perspective. Directed to office holders, activists, and others interested in the growth of the women's political movement and the impact of women officeholders.
General Info: Yr. Est. 1992, Bi-weekly, ISSN: 1069-6652
Subscriptions: Indv. $45, $5/copy
Circulation: Total-5,000
List Rental: Rents Lists

Politics   *Business, Association*

Publishing Co: Business Industry Political Action Committee, 888 16th St., NW, Washington, DC 20006; Title Tel # (202) 833-1880 Title Fax # (202) 833-2338
Personnel: Editor-Carol Farquhar
Editorial Description: Covers trends & developments in politics, of interest to the business community.
General Info: Yr. Est. 1964, Quarterly, Trim Size-8½ x 11, Web press, 6 pages, 4 Color, Matte
Subscriptions: $8/copy
Circulation: Total-30,000

Politics in Minnesota

Publishing Co: Political Communications, Inc., 26 Exchange St. E., St. Paul, MN 55101-2264; Title Tel # (612) 293-3911
Editorial Description: Covers the political scene in Minnesota.
General Info: Yr. Est. 1976, 22x/yr.
Subscriptions: Indv. $48

Polling Report
Business, Association

Publishing Co: Polling Report, Inc., PO Box 42580, Washington, DC 20015-2580; Title Tel # (202) 237-2000 Title Fax # (202) 237-2001
Personnel: Publisher, Editor-Thomas Silver
Editorial Description: A compilation of the latest national & state opinion polls on politics & public affairs. Data from major survey organizations, such as Gallup, Harris & Roper, etc. Analytical articles by leading experts. Complete coverage of election polls from cong ressional and statewide races.
General Info: Yr. Est. 1985, Semi-monthly, ISSN: 0887-171X
Subscriptions: Indv. $195, $10/copy

Popline
See: ENVIRONMENT & ECOLOGY

Positive Alternatives
Consumer

Publishing Co: Center for Economic Conversion, 222 View St Ste C, Mountain View, CA 94041-1344; Title Tel # (415) 968-8798 Title Fax # (415) 968-1126
Personnel: Editor-Bruce Allen
General Info: (Formerly Plowshare Press), Yr. Est. 1975, Quarterly, 16 pages, ISSN: 1067-0075
Subscriptions: $3/copy
Circulation: Total-6,000

Positive Economist Bulletin
See: ECONOMICS

Program and Legislative Action
Association

Publishing Co: Women's International League for Peace and Freedom, 1213 Race St., Philadelphia, PA 19107-1691 Fax # (512) 563-5527; Title Tel # (215) 563-7110 Title Fax # (215) 563-5527
Personnel: Editor-Wendy Roserfield, Production Mgr.-Pamela Jones-Burnley
Editorial Description: Carries legislative articles and actions relevant to WILPF's goal of a world free of violence, racism, sexism and oppression.
General Info: (Formerly Legislative Alerts/Program & Action Bulletin), Bi-monthly, Trim Size-8½ x 11, Sheetfed press, 10 pages, No Color, Matte, Other
Subscriptions: Indv. $12, Inst. $12, Can. $12, For. $12, $3/copy
Circulation: Total-1,000

Progressive Conservative Association of Alberta Progress Bulletin

Publishing Co: Progressive Conservative Assn. of Alberta, 9912-106th St., Edmonton, AB T5K 1C5 Canada Tel # (403) 423-1624
General Info: 5x/yr.

Progressive Review
Business

Publishing Co: Progressive Review, 1739 Connecticut Ave NW, Washington, DC 20009-1126; Title Tel # (202) 232-5544 Title Fax # (202) 234-6222
Personnel: Editor-Sam Smith
Editorial Description: Progressive and transformational politics and articles on national alternatives.
General Info: (Formerly DC Gazette, Capitol East Gazette), Yr. Est. 1966, 10x/yr., Trim Size-7¼ x 10, Sheetfed press, 10 pages, ISSN: 0889-2202, No Color
Subscriptions: Indv. $17, Can. $27, For. $27, $2/copy
Circulation: Total-1,500

Psychologists for Social Responsibility Newsletter
Association

Publishing Co: Psychologists for Social Responsibility, 2607 Connecticut Ave NW, Washington, DC 20008-1522; Title Tel # (202) 745-7084 Title Fax # (202) 745-0051
Personnel: Publisher, Editor-Anne Anderson
Editorial Description: Discussion & review of contributions psychologists are making to the prevention of war & the building of a durable peace. Includes international comment, research news, lists of suggested activities & resources, and reports from PSYSR Task Forces.
General Info: Yr. Est. 1982, Quarterly, 8 pages
Subscriptions: Indv. $40, $2/copy
Circulation: Total-1,500

Public Affairs Report

Publishing Co: Institute of Governmental Studies, University of California, 102 Moses Hall, Berkeley, CA 94720-0001; Title Tel # (510) 642-6723 Title Fax # (510) 642-3020
Personnel: Editor-Maria Wolf, Promotion Dir.-Catherine West
Editorial Description: Summaries of research reports in the field of public affairs; news about public policy seminars at the Institute.
General Info: Yr. Est. 1960, Bi-monthly, Web press, 12 pages, ISSN: 0033-3417, Ind/Abs/Online: PAIS, SAGE, No Color
Subscriptions: Free
Circulation: Total-5,000
Printing Co: Apollo, 702 Harrison St, Berkeley, CA 94710-1314 Tel # (415) 528-1211

Public Eye
Association

Publishing Co: Political Research Associates, 120 Beacon St., Somerville, MA 02143-4304; Title Tel # (617) 661-9313 Title Fax # (617) 661-0059
Personnel: Editor-Jean Hardisty, Editor-Margaret Quigley
Editorial Description: Articles on politics and social issues.
General Info: Yr. Est. 1992, Quarterly, Trim Size-8½ x 11, 12 pages, ISSN: 0275-9322, 2 Color, Matte, Saddle-stitched
Subscriptions: Indv. $39, Inst. $29
Printing Co: Red Sun Press, 94 Green St, Jamaica Plain, MA 02130-2298 Tel # (617) 524-6822

Public Health/State Capitals
See: HEALTH

Public Interest Report
See: SCIENCE

Public Justice Report
Consumer, Association

Publishing Co: Center for Public Justice, PO Box 48368, Washington, DC 20002-0368; Title Tel # (410) 263-5909 Title Fax # (410) 263-3857
Personnel: Editor-James Skillen
Editorial Description: Analysis of current public policy issues, both domestic & international, from a Christian perspective.
General Info: (Formerly Public Justice Newsletter), Yr. Est. 1977, Bi-monthly, ISSN: 0742-5325, 2 Color
Subscriptions: Indv. $12, Inst. $12, For. $12
Circulation: Total-1,500

Public Sector

Publishing Co: Southam Business Communications, Inc., 1450 Don Mills Rd., Don Mills, ON M3B 2X7 Canada; Title Tel # (416) 445-6641 Title Fax # (416) 442-2200
Personnel: Publisher-Bob Douglas, Editor-T. Rasmussen, Circ. Mgr.-Lori Walker
Editorial Description: Govt. news-provincial & federal legislation, & intentions. Legislative summary-progress & amendments of bills.
General Info: Yr. Est. 1977, Weekly, Trim Size-8½ x 11, Sheetfed press, 8 pages, ISSN: 0700-2092, No Color, Newsprint
Subscriptions: Indv. $497, $12/copy
Acquistions: Publication Bought
Circulation: Total-500
List Rental: List Management Co.: Cornerstone List Mgrs., 2300 Yonge St., Ste. 2005, Box 2465, Toronto, ON M4P 1E4 Canada Tel # (416) 932-9555, Fax # (416) 932-9566

Quagmire
See: HUMOR & SATIRE

Quarterly Review of Doublespeak
See: EDUCATION

Questionable Cartoons

Publishing Co: Vanity Press, 160 6th Ave, New York, NY 10013-1674; Title Tel # (212) 925-3823
Personnel: Editor-Tuli Kupferberg
General Info: Yr. Est. 1986, Semi-annually

Quorum Report
See: GOVERNMENT

Red Menace

Publishing Co: Libertarian Socialist Collective, Box 171, Station D, Toronto, ON M6P 3J8 Canada
Personnel: Editor-Ulli Diemer
Editorial Description: An occasional publication dealing with issues of socialism and freedom.
General Info: Yr. Est. 1975, Semi-annually, Web press, 35 pages, No Color
Subscriptions: Indv. $10, $3/copy
Circulation: Total-800

Refugee Reports
Consumer, Association

Publishing Co: World Council of Churches, 475 Riverside Dr., Ste 915, New York, NY 10115-0122 Fax # (212) 870-2528; Title Tel # (212) 870-3340

Refugee Reports
See: INTERNATIONAL AFFAIRS

Religious Socialism
Association

Publishing Co: Sponsor-Institute for Democratic Socialism, Religion, 1 Maolis Rd, Nahant, MA 01908-1212; Title Tel # (617) 427-7953
Personnel: Publisher, Editor-John Cort
Editorial Description: Promotion of religious socialism & the Democratic Socialists of America.
General Info: Yr. Est. 1977, Quarterly, Trim Size-8½ x 11, 14 pages
Subscriptions: Indv. $5, $1/copy
Circulation: Total-800
Printing Co: Excelsior Press, 28 Damrell St, South Boston, MA 02127-2737 Tel # (617) 268-4220

Remedy

Publishing Co: Washington Physicians for Social Responsibility, 4554 12th Ave. NE, Seattle, WA 98105-4524; Title Tel # (206) 547-2630
Personnel: Editor-Bill Donnelly, Art Dir.-Richard Wilhelm
Editorial Description: Dedicated to education on the medical & health consequences of the continuing arms race.
General Info: Yr. Est. 1982, Quarterly, Desktop press, 16 pages, Color, Newsprint
Subscriptions: Indv. $15, $1/copy
Circulation: Total-3,000
Printing Co: Consolidated Press, 600 S. Spokane St., Seattle, WA 98134-2229 Tel # (206) 441-1844, Fax # (206) 441-2915

Renter's Rag
See: LEASING & RENTING

Reports

Publishing Co: Council for a Livable World, 110 Maryland Ave. NE, Suite 409, Washington, DC 20002 Tel # (202) 543-4100 Fax # (202) 543-6297; Title Tel # (617) 542-2282
General Info: Bi-monthly
List Rental: Actives: $65/M

Republican Liberty *Consumer*

Publishing Co: Republican Liberty Caucus, 1717 Apalachee Parkway, Ste. 434, Tallahassee, FL 32301 Tel # (904) 878-4464
Personnel: Publisher-Roger MacBride, Editor-Eric Rittberg, Sr. Ed.-Mike Holmes
Editorial Description: News and commentary of libertarian Republicans.
General Info: Bi-monthly, Trim Size-8½ x 11, 12 pages, Ind/Abs/Online: Usenet, CompuServe, No Color, Matte
Subscriptions: Indv. $15

Republican Quotes

Publishing Co: Republican Natl. Committee, Publications, 310 First St SE, Washington, DC 20003-1801; Title Tel # (202) 863-8500
General Info: Monthly

Republican Wire

Publishing Co: Republican Natl. Committee, Publications, 310 First St SE, Washington, DC 20003-1801; Title Tel # (202) 863-8500
General Info: Monthly

Resist

Publishing Co: Resist, 1 Summer St, Somerville, MA 02143-1704; Title Tel # (617) 623-5110
Personnel: Editor-Tatiana Schreiber, Circ. Mgr.-Nancy Wechsler
Editorial Description: Monthly peace & social justice newsletter, with comprehensive articles on natl. & intl. movements for social change.
General Info: Yr. Est. 1967, 10x/yr., Sheetfed press, 8 pages, No Color
Subscriptions: Indv. $10, Inst. $15, Can. $15, For. $25, $1/copy
List Management Co.: Manager: Nancy Wechsler; Names in the News-California, 1 Bush St Bsmt 3, San Francisco, CA 94104-4425 Tel # (415) 989-3350, Fax # (415) 433-7796, Actives: $60/M, Expires: $55/M
Printing Co: Red Sun Press, 94 Green St, Jamaica Plain, MA 02130-2298 Tel # (617) 524-6822

Rezo
See: SOCIOLOGY

Ron Paul Survival Report
See: INVESTMENT

Rothenberg Political Report

Publishing Co: Stuart Rothenberg, Publisher, 13305 Morning Field Way, Potomac, MD 20854; Title Tel # (202) 546-2822
Personnel: Publisher, Editor-Stuart Rothenberg
Editorial Description: Newsletter covering House & Senate Campaigns & Elections.
General Info: (Formerly Political Report), Yr. Est. 1978, Weekly, 8 pages, ISSN: 1051-4287
Subscriptions: Indv. $197
Circulation: Total-400

SANE World/Freeze Focus

Publishing Co: Sane/Freeze: Campaign for Global Security, 1819 H St NW Ste 1000, Washington, DC 20006-3603; Title Tel # (202) 862-9740 Title Fax # (202) 862-9762
Editorial Description: News opinion of activities to abolish nuclear weapons, reduce military budget, and create a peaceful foreign policy.
General Info: Yr. Est. 1957, Quarterly
List Rental: Actives: $60/M, Expires: 76,000, $55/M

Samisdat Publishers

Publishing Co: Samisdat Publishers, Box 791, Main P.O., Niagara Falls, NY 14302-0791; Title Tel # (416) 922-9850
Personnel: Publisher-Ernst Zundel
Editorial Description: Alternative or dissident viewpoint on art, history and modern politics.
General Info: Yr. Est. 1978, Monthly, Offset press, 2 Color, Newsprint

Science for Democratic Action

Publishing Co: Inst. for Energy and Environmental Research, 6935 Laurel Ave., Takoma Park, MD 20912 Tel # (301) 270-5500 Fax # (301) 270-3029
Personnel: Mng. Editor-Ellen Kennedy
General Info: Quarterly
Subscriptions: Indv. $10, Can. $20, For. $20, Free To Qualified Recipient

Science and Government Report
See: SCIENCE

Security Intelligence Report

Publishing Co: Interests Ltd., 8512 Cedar St, Silver Spring, MD 20910-4347 Fax # (301) 588-2009; Title Tel # (301) 588-7916 Title Fax # (301) 588-2085
Personnel: Publisher-Frank McGuire, Editor-Frank Mcguire
Editorial Description: Intelligence report on terrorism defense.
General Info: (Formerly Counter Terrorism & Security Intelligence), Yr. Est. 1984, Bi-weekly, 10 pages, ISSN: 1063-4105, Ind/Abs/Online: NewsNet
Subscriptions: Indv. $350

Select Hostile Actions Against Civil Aviation
See: LAW ENFORCEMENT & PENOLOGY

Shalom-Jewish Peace Newsletter
See: RELIGIOUS & THEOLOGICAL

Sleepy Foot

Publishing Co: Nike Thain, 1636 E. Main St #202, Kent, OH 44240
Editorial Description: A mixture of politics with thoughts about the human condition and spiritual awareness.
General Info: Quarterly, Trim Size-5 x 7, 18 pages
Subscriptions: Indv. $1

Smelly Hampster

Publishing Co: Ted Rosen, P.O. Box 4257, Bellingham, WA 98227
Editorial Description: A wonderful zine about revolutionary politics and the joys of human experience.
General Info: Trim Size-8.5 x 11, 28 pages
Subscriptions: Indv. $2

Socialist Action

Publishing Co: Socialist Action Publishing Assn., 3435 Army St Ste 308, San Francisco, CA 94110-4543
Personnel: Editor-Alan Benjamin
General Info: Annually, ISSN: 0747-4237
Subscriptions: $1/copy

South Asia Forum Quarterly
See: ETHNIC

Southeast Asia Program Series: Monographs, Translations, Bibliographies
See: INTERNATIONAL AFFAIRS

Southern Political Report *Business*

Publishing Co: Southern Political Report, PO Box 15507, Washington, DC 20003-0507; Title Tel # (202) 547-8098
Personnel: Publisher, Editor-Hastings Wyman, Jr.
Editorial Description: Covers the politics and politicians of the twelve southern states.
General Info: Yr. Est. 1978, Bi-weekly, Trim Size-8½ x 11, Offset press, 4 pages, ISSN: 0739-3938, No Color
Subscriptions: Indv. $157, $5/copy
Circulation: Total-750
Advertising: Accepts Inserts.
List Rental: List Management Co.: Information Marketing Services, 8130 Boone Blvd., Ste 310, Vienna, VA 22182-2640 Tel # (703) 821-8130, Fax # (703) 821-8243, Actives: 4,629, $85/M
Printing Co: Lettercomm, Inc., 310 Swann Ave, Alexandria, VA 22301-1042 Tel # (703) 683-3105

Springfield Scene, The
See: BUSINESS & INDUSTRY

Stanislaus Connections
See: SOCIAL SERVICES & WELFARE

Star News

Publishing Co: North Star Mission, 1414 S. Independence, Chicago, IL 60623; Title Tel # (312) 522-7610
Editorial Description: News commentary of Rev. Henry Mitchell of North Star Mission.

Straight Shooter
See: ECONOMICS

Straight Talk

Publishing Co: American Way Features, 128 Lighthouse Dr, Jupiter, FL 33469-3511; Title Tel # (407) 746-7815
General Info: Yr. Est. 1967, Weekly
Subscriptions: Indv. $67

Strategic Investment
  See: INVESTMENT

TV & Politics Watch
  See: TELEVISION & VIDEO

Tallahassee Peace Coalition

Publishing Co: Tallahassee Peace Coalition, PO Box 431, Tallahassee, FL 32302-0431; Title Tel # (904) 222-5845
Personnel: Publisher-Elaine Roberts
Editorial Description: Public education & citizen's legislative action on the nuclear arms race.
General Info: Yr. Est. 1980, Monthly
Subscriptions: Indv. $8
Circulation: Total-585

Tax Fax

Publishing Co: Independent American, PO BOX 621228, Littleton, CO 80162-1228 Tel # (303) 932-2663

Taxation and Revenue Policies/State Capitals
  See: TAXES

Tennessee Journal
  See: LAW

Texas Weekly   *Business*

Publishing Co: Printing Productions Systems, PO Box 5306, Austin, TX 78763-5306; Title Tel # (512) 322-9332
Personnel: Editor-George Kinch, Jr.
Editorial Description: Covers state political scene.
General Info: Yr. Est. 1983, Weekly
Subscriptions: Indv. $150
List Rental: List Management Co.: Political Resources, Inc., List Managment Division, Box 3177, Burlington, VT 05401 Tel # (802) 660-2869, Fax # (802) 864-9502, Actives: 3,138

Thinkpeace

Publishing Co: San Francisco Study Group for Peace, 2406 Larkin St, San Francisco, CA 94109-1726; Title Tel # (415) 673-7422
Personnel: Editor-A. Vanini
General Info: Bi-monthly, 8 pages
Subscriptions: Indv. $10

Tranet   *Consumer*

Publishing Co: Tranet, PO Box 567, Rangeley, ME 04970-0567; Title Tel # (207) 864-2252
Personnel: Editor-Bill Ellis
Editorial Description: A newsletter-directory of, by and for people who are changing the world by changing their lives.
General Info: Yr. Est. 1976, Bi-monthly, Sheetfed press, 16 pages, ISSN: 0739-0971
Subscriptions: Indv. $30, $5/copy
Circulation: (40% controlled), Total-1,500, Subscriptions-900, International-600
Printing Co: Heritage Press, PO Box 792, Farmington, ME 04938-0792 Tel # (207) 778-3581

Transitions
  See: MEN'S

Translation Series
  See: INTERNATIONAL AFFAIRS

UNITE!
  See: INTERNATIONAL AFFAIRS

Ultimate Issues
  See: LIFESTYLE

Underground Conservative

Publishing Co: Underground Conservative, PO Box 104, Sandy Spring, MD 20860-0104; Title Tel # (301) 593-1686
Personnel: Publisher, Editor-Abraham Kalish
Editorial Description: Practical solutions to modern problems.
General Info: Yr. Est. 1983, Bi-monthly, 10 pages
Subscriptions: Indv. $25
Circulation: Total-1,000

Understanding Defense
  See: MILITARY & NAVAL

Unipax

Publishing Co: Unitarian Universalist Peace Fellowship, 172 Pleasant St, Laconia, NH 03246-3030; Title Tel # (603) 524-6488
Personnel: Editor-Helen Dick
General Info: Yr. Est. 1984

Unitarian-Universalists in Support of Sanctuary Newsletter

Publishing Co: Unitarian-Universalist Church of Tucson, 4831 E 22nd St, Tucson, AZ 85711-4903; Title Tel # (602) 748-1551
Personnel: Editor-David Johnson
General Info: Yr. Est. 1986, Quarterly
Subscriptions: Indv. $10

U.S. English-Update

Publishing Co: U.S. English, 818 Conn. Ave. NW, #200, Washington, DC 20006; Title Tel # (202) 833-0100 Title Fax # (202) 833-0108
Personnel: Editor-Katita Carroll
Editorial Description: Newsletter for movement to make English the official language of the United States.
General Info: Yr. Est. 1983, Bi-monthly, Trim Size-8½ x 11, Web press, 8 pages, 2 Color, Other
Circulation: Total-200,000

United States Pacifist Party Report

Publishing Co: United States Pacifist Party, 5759 S Dorchester Ave, Chicago, IL 60637-1726; Title Tel # (312) 324-0654
Personnel: Editor-Bradford Lyttle
General Info: 8 pages

United We Stand America   *Consumer*

Publishing Co: United We Stand America, PO Box 6, Dallas, TX 75221
Editorial Description: Ross Perot's newsletter on government reform.
General Info: Monthly, Trim Size-10½ x 14, 8 pages, No Color, Newsprint

Update
  See: INTERNATIONAL AFFAIRS

Upright Ostrich

Publishing Co: Order of the Upright Ostrich, 2824 N Stowell Ave, Milwaukee, WI 53211-3774
Personnel: Editor-Peggy Poor, Adv. Dir.-Carl Forster, Art Dir.- Goot
General Info: Yr. Est. 1980, 10x/yr., Web press, 24 pages, 4 Color
Subscriptions: Indv. $25
Advertising: Inquire for rates.

Utopus Discovered   *Association, Consumer*

Publishing Co: University of Alaska, Anchorage, 3211 Providence Dr, Anchorage, AK 99508-4614
Personnel: Editor-Lyman Tower Sargent
Editorial Description: Newsletter of the Society for Utopian Studies.
General Info: Yr. Est. 1990, Quarterly
Subscriptions: Indv. $25

Valley Voice
  See: GENERAL INTEREST

Valley Women's Voice
  See: WOMEN'S

Vietnam Journal

Publishing Co: Indochina Human Rights Group, PO Box 1163, Burlingame, CA 94011-1163; Title Tel # (415) 343-4875
Personnel: Publisher-Diem Ngo, Editor-Stephen Denney, Adv. Dir.-Dam Dinh Bui
Editorial Description: News, documents, analytical articles, commentary, etc. To educate the public about human rights in Vietnam and among the refugees.
General Info: (Formerly Indochina Journal), Yr. Est. 1992, 3x/yr., Trim Size-8½ x 11, 20 pages
Subscriptions: Indv. $6, Can. $6, For. $10
Circulation: Total-350
List Rental: Rents Lists

Voluntaryist, The   *Consumer, Association*

Publishing Co: Voluntaryists, PO Box 1275, Gramling, SC 29348-0275; Title Tel # (803) 472-2750
Personnel: Editor, Circ. Mgr.-Carl Watner
Editorial Description: Information on, and activities of the Voluntaryist movement which advocates non-political strategies to achieve a free society.
General Info: Yr. Est. 1982, Bi-monthly, 8 pages
Subscriptions: Indv. $18, For. $23, $4/copy
Advertising: Accepts Inserts.
List Rental: Rents Lists

W5YI Report

Publishing Co: Fred Maia, P.O. Box 565101, Dallas, TX 75356-5101
Editorial Description: Nation's oldest ham radio newsletter, a twice-monthly ham radio newsletter featuring newbites, licensing, statistics, and regulation updates.
General Info: Trim Size-8.5 x 11, 10 pages
Subscriptions: Indv. $2

WAND Bulletin
  See: WOMEN'S

WESPAC Newsletter

Publishing Co: Westchester Peoples Action Coalition (WESPAC), 255 Grove St, White Plains, NY 10601-4103; Title Tel # (914) 682-0488
Personnel: Editor-Charles Scheiner
Editorial Description: Draws connections between local & natl. political issues.
General Info: Yr. Est. 1976, Quarterly, Trim Size-8½ x 11, Offset press, 16 pages
Subscriptions: Indv. $30
Circulation: Total-4,000
Advertising: Inquire for rates.

WNDC News

Publishing Co: Woman's National Democratic Club, 1526 New Hampshire Ave NW, Washington, DC 20036-1204; Title Tel # (202) 232-7363 Title Fax # (202) 986-2791
General Info: 3x/yr.

Wall Street Underground
See: INVESTMENT

Washington Memo
See: HEALTH

Washington Memo - MCC

Publishing Co: MCC Peace Section Washington Office, 110 Maryland Ave. NE, #502, Washington, DC 20002-5681; Title Tel # (202) 544-6564
Personnel: Editor-Deltan Franz
Editorial Description: Information on U.S. Governmen public policy issues. Includes discussions on peacemaking & justice in domestic & intl. affairs.
General Info: Yr. Est. 1968, Bi-monthly, Sheetfed press, 2 Color
Subscriptions: Indv. $10
Circulation: Total-6,376

Washington Pacific Report , The
See: INTERNATIONAL AFFAIRS

Washington Report

Publishing Co: Editors Release Service, PO Box 10309, Saint Petersburg, FL 33733-0309; Title Tel # (813) 866-1598 Title Fax # (813) 866-1598
Personnel: Publisher-P. Willie, Editor-William Leavell
Editorial Description: Non-partisan political, strong, biting, disrespectful but the truth.
General Info: Yr. Est. 1979, Monthly, Offset press, 4 pages, No Color
Subscriptions: Indv. $25, $2/copy
Circulation: Total-17,000

Washington Spectator   *Consumer*

Publishing Co: Public Concern Foundation, PO Box 20065, London Terrace Station, New York, NY 10011-0008; Title Tel # (212) 741-2365
Personnel: Publisher-Phillip Frazer, Editor-Ben A. Franklin
Editorial Description: Watchdog on capitol hill-excerpts from press, leadership, analyst sources.
General Info: Semi-monthly, Trim Size-8½ x 11, Sheetfed press, 4 pages, ISSN: 0145-160X, No Color, Matte
Subscriptions: Indv. $10, Inst. $10, Can. $24, For. $32, $1/copy
Circulation: Total-60,000
List Rental: List Management Co.: Names in the News-California, 1 Bush St Bsmt 3, San Francisco, CA 94104-4425 Tel # (415) 989-3350, Fax # (415) 433-7796, Actives: 51,716, $65/M, Hotline: 15,072, $75/M, Expires: 16,010, $55/M

Washington State Voter   *Association*

Publishing Co: League of Women Voters of Washington, 1406 18th Ave, Seattle, WA 98122-4126; Title Tel # (206) 622-8961

Week in Germany, The
See: INTERNATIONAL AFFAIRS

Weekly Terrorism Profile
See: SECURITY & SURVEILLANCE

West Coast Libertarian   *Consumer, Association*

Publishing Co: Greater Vancouver Libertarian Assn., 922 Cloverley St., North Vancouver, BC V7L 1N3 Canada; Title Tel # (604) 980-7370
Personnel: Editor-Kerry Pearson, Circ. Mgr.-Bill Tomlinson
Editorial Description: Newsletter containing original articles & letters of interest to libertarians. Reproduction permitted with acknowledgement to W.C.L.
General Info: Yr. Est. 1978, Bi-monthly, Trim Size-8½ x 11, 12 pages, No Color
Subscriptions: Indv. $15, Can. $15
Circulation: Total-400
Advertising: Inquire for rates.

What Is to Be Read
See: BOOKS & BOOK TRADE

Witness for Peace Newsletter
See: INTERNATIONAL AFFAIRS

Women for Peace
Newsletter, East Bay   *Association*

Publishing Co: East Bay Women for Peace, 2302 Ellsworth St, Berkeley, CA 94704-1522 Tel # (510) 525-7849; Title Tel # (510) 849-3020
Personnel: Editor-June Naboisek
Editorial Description: Items relating to peace & organizations activities.
General Info: Yr. Est. 1965, Monthly, 6 pages, Color
Subscriptions: Indv. $10, Inst. $10
Circulation: Total-500

Women's Political Times
See: WOMEN'S

Women's Recovery Network
See: WOMEN'S

Workers' Solidarity
See: LABOR

World Federalist News
See: INTERNATIONAL AFFAIRS

World Federalist
Newsletter   *Consumer*

Publishing Co: World Federalists Association, 418 7th St SE, Washington, DC 20003-2707; Title Tel # (202) 546-3950 Title Fax # (202) 546-3749
Personnel: Publisher-Walter Hoffman, Editor-Suzanne Picard, Circ. Mgr.-Irene Dargan, Adv. Dir.-Edward Rawson
Editorial Description: Progress toward world order (governmental institution based on law) world events of interest.
General Info: Yr. Est. 1975, Quarterly, Desktop press, 8 pages, No Color
Subscriptions: Indv. $5, $1/copy
Circulation: Total-9,000
List Rental: Rents Lists
Printing Co: Presstar Printing, 12201 Old Columbia Pike, Silver Spring, MD 20904-1968 Tel # (301) 622-5000, Fax # (301) 622-5403

World Freedom Bulletin
See: CIVIL RIGHTS

Young Republican News   *Association*

Publishing Co: Young Republican National Federation, 310 1st St SE, Washington, DC 20003-1801; Title Tel # (202) 662-1340
Personnel: Editor-Bill Goodwin
Editorial Description: Coverage of activities of Young Republicans around the country with special emphasis on the direction toward youth taken by the Republican Party and the Administration.
General Info: Yr. Est. 1967, Monthly, Trim Size-6 x 9, Offset press, 12 pages
Circulation: Total-16,000

POULTRY & POULTRY PRODUCTS

Arizona State Egg
Inspector, Report

Publishing Co: Arizona State Egg Inspection Board, 1688 W Adams St Ste 328, Phoenix, AZ 85007-2620; Title Tel # (602) 271-5741
General Info: Annually

Broadwater Market Letter
See: AGRICULTURE

Broiler Report

Publishing Co: Statistical Reporting Service, PO Box 1659, Richmond, VA 23213-1659; Title Tel # (804) 771-2493
Editorial Description: Table gives eggs set for broilers and broiler chicks, placed in Virginia. Main table gives chicks placed and eggs, set by state and week.
General Info: Weekly

Egg & Poultry National Weekly Review
See: AGRICULTURE

Egg Industry   *Business*   CPM$3600

Publishing Co: Watt Publishing Co., 122 S. Wesley Ave., Mt. Morris, IL 61054-1497; Title Tel # (815) 734-4171 Title Fax # (815) 734-4201
Personnel: Publisher-Charles Olentine, Jr., Editorial Dir.-David Amey, Editor-Virginia Lazar, Circ. Mgr.-Jim Kunger, Circ. Mgr.-Walter Stephens, Production Dir.-Jeffrey Swanson, Art Dir.-Sara Somers Matter, Sales Mgr.-Wesley Jones
Editorial Description: Edited for people commercially involved in producing, processing & marketing eggs.
General Info: Yr. Est. 1895, Monthly, Web press, 12 pages, ISSN: 0896-2804, 45% ads, 4 Color, Coated, Saddle-stitched
Subscriptions: Indv. $36, $8/copy
Circulation: Total-2,500
Advertising: $9,000.
List Rental: Rents Lists

Egg Market News *Business*

Publishing Co: Edison Market News Office, 103 Metroplex Dr, Edison, NJ 08817-2683;
Title Tel # (908) 985-8880 Title Fax # (908) 985-3732
Editorial Description: Developments in the egg market.
General Info: Semi-weekly
Subscriptions: Indv. $75

Egg Market News Report *Business*

Publishing Co: USDA Agricultural Marketing Service, Poultry Division, Market News, 800 Roosevelt
Rd., Bldg. A, Rm. 310, Glen Ellyn, IL 60137-5839; Title Tel # (708) 790-6910
Title Fax # (708) 790-6948
Editorial Description: Trading information & statistical data on eggs & egg products.
General Info: Semi-weekly, Trim Size-8½ x 14, Mimeo press, 2 pages, No Color
Subscriptions: Indv. $110, Can. $125, For. $160, $1/copy
Circulation: Total-110

Egg Producer *Business*

Publishing Co: Canadian Egg Marketing Agency, 320 Queen St., #1900, Ottawa, ON K1R 5A3
Canada; Title Tel # (613) 238-2514 Title Fax # (613) 238-1967
Personnel: Publisher, Editor, Production Mgr.-Kathryn Sauve
Editorial Description: Published in English & French. Articles of interest primarily to egg industry, as
well as those with an interest in agriculture. Contains 3 regular features: marketing update;
producer profile; & statistical information.
General Info: (Formerly Egg Scene), Yr. Est. 1982, Bi-monthly, Trim Size-8½ x 11, Sheetfed press, 6
pages, ISSN: 0821-4689, Matte
Circulation: (100% controlled), Total-3,000
Printing Co: Tri-Graphic Printing, 465 Industrial Ave., Ottawa, ON K1G 0Z1 Canada
Tel # (613) 731-7441

Fancy Feathers *Association*

Publishing Co: American Poultry Assn., 26363 S Tucker Rd, Estacada, OR 97023-9441;
Title Tel # (503) 630-6759
Personnel: Editor-Nona Shearer
General Info: (Formerly APA News & Views), Yr. Est. 1873, Quarterly, 20 pages

Federal Veterinarian
See: VETERINARY

Monthly Exports of Ducks & Geese *Business, Association*

Publishing Co: American Down Assn. (ADA), 3728 Canna Ct, Sacramento, CA 95821-3101;
Title Tel # (916) 971-1135
Personnel: Editor-Howard Winslow
Editorial Description: Statistical report covering exports of geese & ducks.
General Info: Monthly

Monthly Summary *Business*

Publishing Co: USDA Agricultural Marketing Service, Poultry Division, Market News, 800 Roosevelt
Rd., Bldg. A, Rm. 310, Glen Ellyn, IL 60137-5839; Title Tel # (708) 790-6910
Title Fax # (708) 790-6948
Editorial Description: Monthly cold storage & average prices of egg & poultry products.
General Info: Monthly, Trim Size-8½ x 11, Mimeo press, 20 pages, No Color
Subscriptions: Indv. $105, Can. $110, For. $130

National Broiler Council- Washington Report *Association*

Publishing Co: Natl. Broiler Council, 1155 15th St NW Ste 614, Washington, DC 20005-2706;
Title Tel # (202) 296-2622
Personnel: Editor-Margaret Ernst
Editorial Description: Reports on issues affecting poultry industry & activities of trade assn.
General Info: Weekly, 6 pages, 2 Color, Newsprint
Circulation: (100% controlled), Total-900

Perdue Newsletter
See: FOOD

Poultry & Egg Weekly Review *Business*

Publishing Co: USDA Agricultural Marketing Service, Poultry Division, Market News, 800 Roosevelt
Rd., Bldg. A, Rm. 310, Glen Ellyn, IL 60137-5839 Tel # (708) 790-6910 Fax # (708) 790-6948
General Info: Weekly
Subscriptions: Indv. $100, Can. $110, For. $115

Poultry and Egg Products, Ohio

Publishing Co: Federal-State Market News Service, 65 S. Front St., Columbus, OH 43215-4131
General Info: Semi-weekly

Poultry Market News Report *Business*

Publishing Co: Edison Market News Office, 103 Metroplex Dr, Edison, NJ 08817-2683
Tel # (908) 985-8880; Title Tel # (908) 985-3732
Personnel: Editor-Martin Lebowitz
Editorial Description: Trading information and statistical data on poultry & turkey products.
General Info: Trim Size-8½ x 14, Mimeo press, 4 pages, No Color
Subscriptions: Indv. $75, $1/copy
Circulation: Total-300

Poultry Market News Report *Business*

Publishing Co: USDA Agricultural Marketing Service, Poultry Division, Market News, 800 Roosevelt
Rd., Bldg. A, Rm. 310, Glen Ellyn, IL 60137-5839; Title Tel # (708) 790-6910
Title Fax # (708) 790-6948
Personnel: Publications Director-William S. Howath, Jr.
General Info: Semi-weekly
Subscriptions: Indv. $145, Can. $170, For. $290
Circulation: Total-194

Poultry Report *Business*

Publishing Co: U.S. Department of Agriculture, California Ag. Stat. Service, PO Box 1258,
Sacramento, CA 95812
Editorial Description: Chicken & turkey settings, hatchings, eggs produced, inventory, value, & cold
storage.
General Info: Monthly
Subscriptions: Indv. $15, For. $30

Poultry Stocks & Supplies *Association*

Publishing Co: Canadian Poultry & Egg Processors Council, 2 Gurdwara Rd. Ste. 406, Ottawa, ON
K2E 1A2 Canada Tel # (613) 224-0001 Fax # (613) 224-2023; Title Tel # (416) 622-8621
Personnel: Editor-R.W. McDannold
General Info: Yr. Est. 1970, Monthly, Trim Size-8½ x 11, Desktop press, 6 pages, Recycled, Other

Shaver Focus *Business*

Publishing Co: Shaver Poultry Breeding Farms Ltd., Box 400, Cambridge, ON N1R 5V9 Canada;
Title Tel # (519) 621-5191 Title Fax # (519) 621-9407
Personnel: Editor-Peter Hunton, Circ. Mgr.-Pat Attridge, Circ. Mgr.-Goretti Tomada
Editorial Description: Technical bulletin covering various aspects of poultry production
internationally.
General Info: Yr. Est. 1967, Semi-annually, Trim Size-8½ x 11, Sheetfed press, 4 pages, ISSN:
0315-6915, 2 Color, Newsprint
Circulation: (100% controlled), Total-6,000
Printing Co: Universal Printers, 50 Raglin Pl., Cambridge, ON N1R 5V9 Canada
Tel # (519) 621-5390, Fax # (519) 621-0682

Texas Poultry

Publishing Co: Texas Poultry, 7915 Braes Meadow Dr, Houston, TX 77071-1302
Personnel: Editor-Mrs. N.C. Garrison
Editorial Description: All phases of poultry industry in Texas and adjacent states.
General Info: Yr. Est. 1956, Monthly
Subscriptions: Indv. $1
Circulation: Total-5,500
Advertising: Inquire for rates.

Urner Barry's Price- Current *Business*

Publishing Co: Urner Barry Publications, Inc., PO Box 389, Toms River, NJ 08754-0389;
Title Tel # (908) 240-5330 Title Fax # (908) 341-0891
Personnel: Editor-Paul Brown, Sr., Production Mgr.-Bill Curro, Adv. Dir.-Lisa Sharkus, Promotion Dir.-
Sheila Deane
Editorial Description: Prices of poultry, eggs, dairy products and trends.
General Info: (Formerly Producers' Price-Current), Yr. Est. 1858, Daily, Trim Size-11 x 17, Sheetfed
press, 4 pages, ISSN: 0273-9992, Ind/Abs/Online: Comtell, Color, Newsprint
Subscriptions: Indv. $399, Can. $449, For. $574, $15/copy
Circulation: Total-3,000
Advertising: Inquire for rates.

Virginia Agriculture Commodity Newsletter
See: AGRICULTURE

Weekly Insiders Poultry Report *Business*

Publishing Co: Urner Barry Publications, Inc., PO Box 389, Toms River, NJ 08754-0389;
Title Tel # (908) 240-5330 Title Fax # (908) 341-0891
Personnel: Editor-Russell Whitman, Production Mgr.-Bill Curro, Adv. Dir.-Lisa Sharkus, Promotion
Dir.-Sheila Deane
Editorial Description: Statistical report on poultry. Basis for understanding market conditions.
General Info: Yr. Est. 1947, Weekly, Trim Size-8½ x 11, Sheetfed press, 4 pages, ISSN: 0160-4872,
No Color, Newsprint
Subscriptions: Indv. $164, Can. $174, For. $198, $15/copy

Weekly Insiders Turkey
Letter   *Business*

Publishing Co: Urner Barry Publications, Inc., PO Box 389, Toms River, NJ 08754-0389;
Title Tel # (908) 240-5330 Title Fax # (908) 341-0891
Personnel: Editor-Paul Brown, Sr., Production Mgr.-Bill Curro, Adv. Dir.-Lisa Sharkus, Promotion Dir.-Sheila Deane
Editorial Description: Statistical report on turkeys & their products.
General Info: Yr. Est. 1947, Weekly, Trim Size-8½ x 11, Sheetfed press, 4 pages, ISSN: 0160-4910, No Color, Newsprint
Subscriptions: Indv. $164, Can. $174, For. $198, $15/copy
Circulation: Total-230

Wyandotte Bantam Club
of America Newsletter   *Association*

Publishing Co: Wyandotte Bantam Club of America, PO Box 408, Cleburne, TX 76033-0408
Personnel: Editor, Circ. Mgr.-Pat Arnold
Editorial Description: Promotion of Wyandotte Bantam, rearing, breeding, housing, etc.
General Info: Yr. Est. 1940, Quarterly, Trim Size-6 x 8½, Offset press, 4 pages, 2 Color
Advertising: Inquire for rates.

POWER & POWER PLANTS

Air Pollution Monitoring & Sampling
See: ENVIRONMENT & ECOLOGY

All Source Digest   *Business, Association*   CPM: $100

Publishing Co: All Source Systems, PO Box 596, Morton, WA 98356-0596;
Title Tel # (206) 496-6262 Title Fax # (360) 496-6262
Personnel: Editor-Byron Peck
Editorial Description: Up to date news on R&D of over unity & other alternative power production technology.
General Info: Yr. Est. 1985, Monthly, Trim Size-8½ x 11, Offset press, 8 pages, No Color, Recycled
Subscriptions: Indv. $95, For. $120, $9/copy
Acquistions: Publication Bought
Circulation: (25% controlled), Total-400, Subscriptions-200, International-30, Source-IS
Advertising: $40. Accepts Inserts.
Printing Co: Creative Impressions, 206 2nd St., Morton, WA 98356

Alternative Energy Trends & Forecasts
See: ENERGY

Bechtel Briefs
See: ENGINEERING

Blue Bulletin   *Business, Association*

Publishing Co: National Association of Regulatory Utility Commissioners, PO Box 684, Washington, DC 20044-0684; Title Tel # (202) 898-2200 Title Fax # (202) 898-2213
Personnel: Editor-Paul Rodgers
Editorial Description: Reports regulatory agency & court decisions, Congressional legislative matters & other significant events affecting regulation of electric, gas, telephone, water & sewer utilities, CATV systems, air, motor & rail carriers.
General Info: Yr. Est. 1916, Weekly, Mimeo press, 26 pages, Color
Subscriptions: Indv. $110, $3/copy
Circulation: Total-2,000
List Rental: Rents Lists

Electric Utilities Industry - U.S. and Canada
See: PUBLIC UTILITIES

Electrostatic Precipitator
See: ENGINEERING

Exploratory Research Letter

Publishing Co: Electric Power Research Inst., PO Box 10412, Palo Alto, CA 94309-0412;
Title Tel # (415) 934-4212
Personnel: Editor-John Maulbetsch, Production Mgr.-Devi Mathieu
Editorial Description: The Exploratory Research Letter is distributed by the Electric Power Research Institute (EPRI), the research arm of the electric power industry. The Letter profiles exploratory research projects conducted by the Institute to help strengthen scientific kn wledge & innovative technology in areas affecting electric utilities.
General Info: Yr. Est. 1989, 6 pages
Circulation: (100% controlled), Total-2,200

FGD & DeNOx
See: ENVIRONMENT & ECOLOGY

Fabric Filter
See: ENVIRONMENT & ECOLOGY

Hydrowire

Publishing Co: HCI Publications, Inc., 410 Archibald St., Kansas City, MO 64111-3046;
Title Tel # (816) 931-1311 Title Fax # (816) 931-2015
Personnel: Publisher-Leslie Eden, Editor-John Braden, Circ. Mgr.-Sandy Sexton, Art Dir.-Sarah Bent, Promotion Dir.-Thomas Gilliams
Editorial Description: Covers the hydroelectric industry including such topics as business, finance, tax, project & environmental news, as it relates to the hydroelectric industry.
General Info: Bi-weekly, Letrpr. press, Ind/Abs/Online: NewsNet
Subscriptions: Indv. $295, Can. $402, $11/copy
Advertising: Accepts Inserts.

International Solar Energy Intelligence Report
See: ENERGY

Liquid Filtration
See: ENVIRONMENT & ECOLOGY

Louisiana Country

Publishing Co: Assn. of Louisiana Electric Cooperatives, 10725 Airline Hwy, Baton Rouge, LA 70816-4213; Title Tel # (504) 293-3450
Personnel: Editor-Whitney Belanger
Editorial Description: Association news and industry updates.
Circulation: Total-175,000

Nuclear Plant Maintenance
Newsletter   *Business*

Publishing Co: EQES, Inc., 799 Roosevelt Rd., Bldg #6, Suite 208, Glen Ellyn, IL 60137-5925;
Title Tel # (708) 858-6161 Title Fax # (708) 858-8787
Personnel: Publisher-Newal Agnihotri, Circ. Mgr.-Sue Agnihotri, Adv. Dir.-Anu Agnihotri
Editorial Description: Maintenance & qualification of electrical mechanical equipment in nuclear power plants.
General Info: (Formerly Equipment Qualification Newsletter), Yr. Est. 1981, Monthly, Trim Size-8½ x 11, Letrpr. press, 4 pages, ISSN: 1054-9447, No Color
Subscriptions: Indv. $220, Inst. $198, Can. $252, For. $252, $19/copy
Circulation: Total-200

Nuclear Remediation Week
See: NUCLEAR ENERGY

PV News
See: ENERGY

Power Quality Protection
PQP/FAX Report

Publishing Co: Darnell Group Inc., 4720 Crestview Dr, Norco, CA 91760-1623;
Title Tel # (909) 279-6684 Title Fax # (909) 273-9505
Personnel: Publisher-Jeff Shepard, Editor-David Tazza, Production Mgr.-Sharon Lancaster
Subscriptions: Indv. $159, For. $197

Power Source, The

Publishing Co: HCI Publications, Inc., 410 Archibald St., Kansas City, MO 64111-3046;
Title Tel # (816) 931-1311 Title Fax # (816) 931-2015
Personnel: Publisher-Leslie Eden, Editor-John Braden, Circ. Mgr.-Sandy Sexton, Art Dir.-Sarah Bent, Promotion Dir.-Thomas Gilliams
Editorial Description: Covers the cogeneration & independent power industry including such topics as business, finance, project, & tax news as it relates to the independent power industry.
General Info: (Formerly Purpa Lines), Yr. Est. 1984, Bi-weekly, Desktop press, Ind/Abs/Online: NewsNet
Subscriptions: Indv. $295, Can. $350, For. $375, $11/copy
Advertising: Accepts Inserts.

Power System News

Publishing Co: Los Angeles Dept. of Water, 111 N Hope St Rm 1509, Los Angeles, CA 90012-5701;
Title Tel # (213) 481-6414 Title Fax # (213) 580-0739
Personnel: Editor-Christine Geltz, Mng. Editor-Treva Miller
Editorial Description: Provides information on issues, events and projects impacting Los Angeles' electric operations, to Los Angeles Department of Water and Power employees.
General Info: Yr. Est. 1990, Bi-monthly
Circulation: Total-12,000

Radiological Inspection Reports
See: NUCLEAR ENERGY

Scrubber/Adsorber
See: ENVIRONMENT & ECOLOGY

Sedimentation & Centrifugation
See: ENVIRONMENT & ECOLOGY

Sermatech Review

Publishing Co: Sermatech International, Inc., 155 S Limerick Rd, Limerick, PA 19468-1603;
Title Tel # (215) 948-5100
Personnel: Editor-Bill McCune
Editorial Description: Technical information on coatings and repairs for power plants and related equipment.
General Info: Yr. Est. 1980, Quarterly, Sheetfed press, 8 pages, 2 Color, Coated
Circulation: (50% controlled), Total-40,000, Single Copy/Newsstand-7,500, International-3,500

Solid Waste Report
See: ENVIRONMENT & ECOLOGY

Switch Mode Power Conversion SMP/FAX Report
Business

Publishing Co: Darnell Group Inc., 4720 Crestview Dr, Norco, CA 91760-1623; Title Tel # (909) 279-6684 Title Fax # (909) 273-9505
Personnel: Publisher-Jeff Shepard, Editor-David Tazza, Circ. Mgr.-Sharon Lancaster
General Info: (Formerly Power Technology News), Yr. Est. 1991, Bi-weekly, 3 pages
Subscriptions: Indv. $159, For. $197
Circulation: Total-200

Technologies for Energy Management
Business

Publishing Co: Cutter Information Corp., 37 Broadway, Ste. 1, Arlington, MA 02174-5552 Tel # (617) 648-8700; Title Tel # (617) 641-5118 Title Fax # (617) 648-1950
Personnel: Publisher-Karen Coburn, Editor-Ira Krepchin, Circ. Mgr.-Carolyn Licata, Production Mgr.-Ellen McHale, Mktg. Dir.-Paul Bergeron
Editorial Description: Covers regulatory trends, case studies, research results, new products/services.
General Info: (Formerly Demand-Side Technology Report), Yr. Est. 1992, Monthly, Trim Size-8½ x 11, 16 pages, ISSN: 1076-3481
Subscriptions: Indv. $457, Can. $457, For. $517, $44/copy
Printing Co: Benjamin Franklin Smith Printers, 320 Stuart St, Boston, MA 02116-5242 Tel # (617) 426-1160

Utility Environment Report
Business

Publishing Co: McGraw-Hill, 1221 Ave. of the Americas, 36th Fl., New York, NY 10020-1095 Tel # (212) 512-2000 Fax # (212) 512-6590; Title Tel # (212) 512-6410
Editorial Description: Environmental issues for the utility and independent power industries.
General Info: Bi-weekly, ISSN: 1053-9379, Ind/Abs/Online: Dialog, Dow Jones, NewsNet, Nexis
Subscriptions: Indv. $745, Can. $795

Utility Reporter-Fuels, Energy & Power
See: ENERGY

WSEO Dispatch
See: ENERGY

PREMIUMS & INCENTIVES

Abstract of American Industrial Trend Analysis
See: BUSINESS & INDUSTRY

Creative Marketing Newsletter
See: ADVERTISING & MARKETING

Party Design Quarterly
See: ENTERTAINMENT

Publicity & Marketing Ideas
See: ADVERTISING & MARKETING

Team Marketing Report
See: SPORTS & SPORTING GOODS

PRINTING/GRAPHIC ARTS

APHA Newsletter
Association

Publishing Co: American Printing History Assn., Box 4922, Grand Central Station, New York, NY 10163-1005 Tel # (716) 475-2408; Title Tel # (212) 353-4250
Personnel: Publisher, Editor-Ed Colker
Editorial Description: Newsletter with essays & articles about printing history.
General Info: (Formerly APHA Letter), Yr. Est. 1974, Quarterly, 8 pages
Subscriptions: Indv. $30, Inst. $35
Circulation: (100% controlled), Total-1,000
List Rental: Actives: $100/M

APNY Newsletter
See: PHOTOGRAPHY

American Typecasting Fellowship Newsletter
Association

Publishing Co: American Typecasting Fellowship, PO Box 263, Terra Alta, WV 26764-0263; Title Tel # (304) 789-2455
Personnel: Editor-Richard Hopkins
Editorial Description: Devoted exclusively to preservation of hot metal type casting & letter design.
General Info: Yr. Est. 1978, Irregular, Trim Size-7 x 10, Letrpr. press, 20 pages, 1% ads, Saddle-stitched
Subscriptions: For. $4, $2/copy
Circulation: Total-300
Advertising: Inquire for rates.

Artistamp News
See: ART & SCULPTURE

Authentication News
See: PACKAGING

AutoGraph
See: COMPUTERS & AUTOMATION

BDA Update
Business, Association

Publishing Co: Broadcast Designers' Association, Inc., 2223 Shattuck Ave # 200, Berkeley, CA 94704-1415 Tel # (510) 540-1212 Fax # (510) 540-1218; Title Tel # (415) 788-2324
Personnel: Editor-Ron Lattin
General Info: Yr. Est. 1984, Monthly
Subscriptions: Free With Membership
Circulation: Total-700

BIN
See: BOOKS & BOOK TRADE

Board Report for Graphic Artists
Business, Consumer

Publishing Co: Board Report Publishing Co., Inc., Box 300789, Denver, CO 80203; Title Tel # (303) 839-9058 Title Fax # (303) 839-1272
Personnel: Publisher-Drew Allen Miller, Editor-Nancy Hobson
Editorial Description: Provides tools tips and techniques to help graphic artists and designers become more creative and professional. A complete graphic design service consisting of four different newsletters every month.
General Info: Yr. Est. 1978, Monthly, Trim Size-8½ x 11, 20 pages, ISSN: 1062-7774, Coated
Subscriptions: Indv. $107
Circulation: Total-5,000
List Rental: Actives: 3,000, $125/M, Expires: 2,000, $125/M

Book Marketing Update
See: BOOKS & BOOK TRADE

Business Indicator Report
Association

Publishing Co: National Association of Printers & Lithographers, 780 Palisade Ave., Teaneck, NJ 07666-3129; Title Tel # (201) 342-0707 Title Fax # (201) 692-0286
Personnel: Editor-Andrew Paparozzi, Production Mgr., Art Dir.-Catherine Vitale, Circ. Mgr., Adv. Dir., Promotion Dir.-Lynne Warshavsky
Editorial Description: Economic analysis of sales, profits, market trends for the graphic arts business.
General Info: (Formerly Quarterly Printing Industry Business Indicator Report), Yr. Est. 1979, Quarterly, Trim Size-8½ x 11, Web press, 12 pages, 2 Color, Coated, Saddle-stitched
Subscriptions: Indv. $150, $50/copy
Circulation: Total-4,000

CARD TALK
Business, Association

Publishing Co: American Business Card Club, PO Box 460297, Aurora, CO 80046-0297; Title Tel # (303) 690-6496
Personnel: Publisher-Avery Pitzak, Editor-Sue Pitzak
Editorial Description: Business card design news, articles, information & advertising, collecting.
General Info: Yr. Est. 1980, Quarterly, Trim Size-8½ x 11, Offset press, 9 pages, No Color, Matte
Subscriptions: Indv. $12, For. $12
Circulation: Total-1,200

CBFA Newsletter

Publishing Co: Canadian Printing Industries Assn., 75 Albert St., #906, Ottawa, ON K1P 5E7 Canada; Title Tel # (613) 236-7208
General Info: (Formerly Graphic Arts Industries Assn.), Yr. Est. 1958, Quarterly

CONCEPPTS Connections
Business

Publishing Co: National Association of Printers & Lithographers, 780 Palisade Ave., Teaneck, NJ 07666-3129
Personnel: Publications Director-Patrick Henry, Editor-Dawn Lospaluto, Editorial Dir.-Monica McCabe
Editorial Description: Reports on latest prepress developments featured at the prepublishing conference and exhibition.
General Info: Yr. Est. 1994, Annually
Subscriptions: $15/copy

Canadian Bookbinders & Book Artists Guild Newsletter
See: BOOKS & BOOK TRADE

Cheap Relief
See: ADVERTISING & MARKETING

Cole Papers, The
See: NEWSPAPER INDUSTRY

Collectible Newspapers
See: COLLECTIBLES

Color Businesss Report
See: COMPUTERS & AUTOMATION

Color Q Connection
See: ART & SCULPTURE

Converting Business Register
See: PACKAGING

DB Publisher
Business

Publishing Co: C.P. Gauger & Co., 8450 W Forest Home Ave, Milwaukee, WI 53228-3416
Tel # (414) 529-5555
Editorial Description: For managers who, produce catalogs and other data-intensive publications.
General Info: Yr. Est. 1994, Quarterly

DGEF Alumni Newsletter

Publishing Co: Sponsor-Dynamic Graphic Educational Fdtn., Dynamic Graphics, Inc., 6000 N Forest Park Dr, Peoria, IL 61614-3556 Tel # (309) 688-2300 Fax # (309) 688-3075;
Title Tel # (309) 688-8866
Personnel: Editor-Marlene Glick
Editorial Description: For alumni of dynamic graphics professional visual communication workshops.
General Info: Yr. Est. 1985, Quarterly, Trim Size-8½ x 11
Printing Co: C&H Printing, Inc., 1025 W Detweiller Dr, Peoria, IL 61615-2064 Tel # (309) 693-2363

Decisions
Business, Association

Publishing Co: Printing Industries of America, 100 Daingerfield Rd., Alexandria, VA 22314-2888;
Title Tel # (703) 519-8100 Title Fax # (703) 548-3227
Personnel: Publisher-Janet Bray, Editor-Colleen Scully, Editor-Cliff Weiss
Editorial Description: Technology management information for graphic arts companies.
General Info: Yr. Est. 1992, Quarterly, Trim Size-8.5 x 11, 4 pages, 4 Color
Subscriptions: Free With Membership
Circulation: Total-800
Advertising: Accepts Inserts.

Design Drafting News
See: ENGINEERING

Desktop for Profit
Business, Consumer

Publishing Co: National Association of Printers & Lithographers, 780 Palisade Ave., Teaneck, NJ 07666-3129
Editorial Description: Helps assist printers and separators to manage their desktop technologies.
General Info: Yr. Est. 1993, Monthly, Trim Size-8½ x 11, 6 pages, 2 Color, Coated
Subscriptions: Indv. $95

Discount & Wholesale Printing Newsletter
Business

Publishing Co: Prosperity & Profits Unlimited, PO Box 416, Denver, CO 80201-0416;
Title Tel # (303) 575-5676
Personnel: Publisher, Editor-A.C. Doyle
Editorial Description: Listings of printers whose prices are at discount or wholesale.
General Info: Yr. Est. 1990, Every two years, 8 pages, ISSN: 1053-3699, 2 Color
Subscriptions: Indv. $5, Inst. $5, Can. $7, For. $9, $5/copy

Dunn Report
Business

Publishing Co: Dunn Technology Inc., 1855 E Vista Way Ste 1, Vista, CA 92084-3399;
Title Tel # (619) 758-9460
Personnel: Publisher-Patrice Dunn, Editor-Thomas Dunn
Editorial Description: Market & technical information on electronic prepress, printing & corporate publishing.
General Info: Yr. Est. 1982, Monthly, 8 pages
Subscriptions: Indv. $295, Can. $310, For. $330, $25/copy

EPS Decisions
Association

Publishing Co: Printing Industries of America, 100 Daingerfield Rd., Alexandria, VA 22314-2888;
Title Tel # (703) 519-8100 Title Fax # (703) 548-3227
Personnel: Publisher-Scott W. Tilden
Editorial Description: Current news and applications on electronic composition & prepress technologies & issues.
General Info: Yr. Est. 1989, Monthly, Trim Size-8½ x 11, Offset press, 8 pages, Other, Other
Subscriptions: Free With Membership
Circulation: Total-1,100

Eco, The
Business

Publishing Co: Ecocenters Corporation, 31225 Bainbridge Rd, Solon, OH 44139-2230;
Title Tel # (216) 991-9000 Title Fax # (216) 752-8166
Personnel: Circ. Mgr.-Frank Piunno, Publisher, Editor, Production Mgr., Art Dir.-Michael Kovach
Editorial Description: Newsletter written by industry experts dealing with electronic printing, high volume typesetting, and data editing. For the publishing, association management, financial, direct mail and general business markets.
General Info: Yr. Est. 1988, Quarterly, Web press, 4 pages, Color-cover, Coated
Circulation: Total-5,000
Printing Co: Lorain Printing, 1310 Colorado Ave, Lorain, OH 44052-3385 Tel # (216) 288-6000

Ecology Notes
Business

Publishing Co: Banta Company, PO Box 60, Menasha, WI 54952-0060; Title Tel # (414) 722-7771
Editorial Description: Environmental issues facing the printing industry.
General Info: Irregular, Trim Size-7 x 10½, 2 pages, No Color

Editorial Eye
See: JOURNALISM

Editor's Workshop Newsletter
See: JOURNALISM

Ellipsis
See: COMPUTERS & AUTOMATION

Enviro Update
See: ENVIRONMENT & ECOLOGY

Environmental Advisor
Business, Association

Publishing Co: National Association of Printers & Lithographers, 780 Palisade Ave., Teaneck, NJ 07666-3129; Title Tel # (201) 342-0700 Title Fax # (201) 692-0286
Editorial Description: Environmental laws in the printing industry.
General Info: (Formerly Political Advisor), Quarterly
Subscriptions: Indv. $60

Flexible Packaging Assn. Update
See: PACKAGING

Footprints
Business

Publishing Co: Footprint Communications, 2400 Lemoine Ave., Ft. Lee, NJ 07024
Fax # (201) 461-5928; Title Tel # (201) 461-5252
Personnel: Editor-Richard Vinocur
Editorial Description: Production information and industry news for printers.
General Info: Yr. Est. 1987, Semi-monthly, Trim Size-8½ x 11, 4 pages
Subscriptions: Indv. $247

Free Focus
See: POETRY & CREATIVE WRITING

Freelancers' News

Publishing Co: Freelancer's News, Box 437, Murray Hill Sta., New York, NY 10156-0437;
Title Tel # (212) 353-1313
Personnel: Editor-Barbara Gordon
Editorial Description: Newsletter for artists, designers, photographers, & freelancers.
General Info: Yr. Est. 1988, 8x/yr.
Subscriptions: Indv. $25
Advertising: Accepts Inserts.
List Rental: Rents Lists

Function Key, The
See: COMPUTERS & AUTOMATION

Global Packaging & Brand Identity
See: PACKAGING

Graphic Communications World
Business

Publishing Co: Green Sheet Communications, Inc., PO Box 727, Hartsdale, NY 10530-0727;
Title Tel # (914) 472-3051 Title Fax # (914) 472-3880
Personnel: Publisher-John R. Werner, Editor-John Werner
Editorial Description: Management/technical report for printing and publishing industry executives.
General Info: (Formerly Tomorrow's Printer), Yr. Est. 1968, Bi-weekly, Trim Size-8½ x 11, Sheetfed press, 4 pages, ISSN: 0884-6901, No Color
Subscriptions: Indv. $297, Inst. $172, Can. $297, For. $322, $12/copy
Circulation: Total-3,500
Advertising: Accepts Inserts.

Graphic News
Association

Publishing Co: Printing Industry of Minnesota, Inc. (PIM), 450 N. Syndicate, Ste. 200, St. Paul, MN 55104-4127; Title Tel # (612) 646-4826 Title Fax # (612) 646-8673
Personnel: Publisher-Kelvin Johnson, Editor-Kathleen Conroy
Editorial Description: Monthly newsletter for printing and graphic arts industries, providing a variety of legal, management, sales and technical information. Sent to PIM members.
General Info: Yr. Est. 1985, Monthly, Trim Size-8½ x 11, Sheetfed press, 16 pages, Color-cover, Saddle-stitched
Subscriptions: Free With Membership
Circulation: Total-5,000
Printing Co: Challenge Printing, 7500 Golden Triangle Dr, Eden Prairie, MN 55344-3746
Tel # (612) 942-7086, Fax # (612) 942-0973

Gravure Environmental Reporter
Association

Publishing Co: Gravure Assn. of America, 1200A Scottsville Rd., Rochester, NY 14624-5703
Tel # (716) 436-2150 Fax # (716) 436-7689; Title Tel # (212) 255-0070 Title Fax # (212) 463-8935
Personnel: Publisher, Editor-David Smith
General Info: Yr. Est. 1947, Bi-monthly
Circulation: Total-1,200

Grids

Publishing Co: Society of Publication Designers, 60 E 42nd St Rm 721, New York, NY 10165-0799;
Title Tel # (212) 983-8585 Title Fax # (212) 983-6043
General Info: Bi-monthly
Acquistions: Publication Bought
Circulation: Total-500
List Rental: Actives: $150/M

Guild of Book Workers-Newsletter
Business

Publishing Co: Guild of Book Workers, Inc., 521 5th Ave Rm 1740, New York, NY 10175-0003; Title Tel # (212) 757-6454
Personnel: Editor-Margaret Johnson
Editorial Description: Newsletter providing information in book arts field.
General Info: Bi-monthly, 12 pages
Subscriptions: Indv. $40
Circulation: Total-650
Advertising: Inquire for rates.

Guild News
Association

Publishing Co: Graphic Artists Guild, 11 W. 20th St., Apt. 8, New York, NY 10011-3704; Title Tel # (212) 463-7730
Personnel: Editor-David Cavanagh
Editorial Description: Information on contracts, companies, legal matters, for artists.
General Info: (Formerly Graphic Artists Guild Newsletter), Yr. Est. 1980, Quarterly, Trim Size-11 x 17, Sheetfed press, 8 pages, 4% ads, No Color, Newsprint
Subscriptions: Free With Membership
Acquistions: Publication Bought
Circulation: (100% controlled), Total-5,000
List Rental: Actives: $100/M
Printing Co: B.D. Press, Box 138, Rt. #104A, Fairfax, VT 05454 Tel # (802) 893-4002

HESCA Feedback
See: HEALTH

Harvey's Cat
Business

Publishing Co: Andover Printing, 837 Industry Dr, Seattle, WA 98188-3411 Tel # (206) 575-4727 Fax # (206) 575-4502
Editorial Description: Information on printing from Andover Printing.
General Info: Quarterly

Hi-Tech Hi-Lites
Business

Publishing Co: Hi-Tech Color House, 5901 North Cicero Ave., Chicago, IL 60646; Title Tel # (312) 588-8200
Personnel: Editor-Albert Stevens
Editorial Description: Newsletter discussing Hi-Tech Color House's printing services.
General Info: Trim Size-8½ x 11, 4 pages, 2 Color, Matte, Saddle-stitched

Holography News
Business, Consumer

Publishing Co: Reconnaissance Holographics Ltd., 825 East Tufts Avenue, Cherry Hills, CO 80110; Title Tel # (303) 274-9874 Title Fax # (303) 274-4010
Personnel: Publisher-Lewis T. Kontnik, Editor-Ian M. Lancaster
Editorial Description: The international business newsletter reporting on the holography industry.
General Info: Yr. Est. 1984, Monthly, 12 pages, ISSN: 0895-9080, No Color
Subscriptions: Indv. $359
Circulation: Readership-2,000
Advertising: Accepts Inserts.
List Rental: Rents Lists

Hot Off the Press
Business

Publishing Co: Graham Communications, 40 Oval Rd, Quincy, MA 02170-3813 Tel # (617) 328-0069 Fax # (617) 471-1504; Title Tel # (617) 773-7606 Title Fax # (617) 471-8810
Personnel: Publisher-John Graham, Editor-Cindy Cantrell, Art Dir.-Bob Jankowski
Editorial Description: Newsletter for customers of the Ink Spot.
General Info: Yr. Est. 1988, 3x/yr., Sheetfed press, 4 pages, 2 Color, Saddle-stitched
Subscriptions: Free To Qualified Recipient
Circulation: Total-3,000, Readership-3,000
Printing Co: Ink Spot, The, 40 Oval Rd, Quincy, MA 02170-3813 Tel # (617) 273-7605, Fax # (617) 471-8810

INFOCUS
See: BUSINESS & INDUSTRY

Imagemaker
Business, Association

Publishing Co: Screen Printing Assn. Intl., 10015 Main St, Fairfax, VA 22031-3403; Title Tel # (703) 385-1335
Personnel: Editor-Bruce Joffe, Art Dir.-Michael Robertson
Editorial Description: Illustrates interesting applications of the second printing press.
General Info: Yr. Est. 1985, Quarterly, Sheetfed press, 2 pages, Color, Coated
Circulation: Total-3,500
Printing Co: Lake Lithograph, 9118 I Beam Ln, Manassas, VA 22110-5325 Tel # (703) 361-8030

Impressions
Business, Consumer

Publishing Co: S. Rosenthal & Co. Inc., 9933 Alliance Rd, Cincinnati, OH 45242-8959; Title Tel # (513) 984-0710 Title Fax # (513) 984-5643
Personnel: Publisher-Don Rahilly, Editor-Kathy Allard
Editorial Description: Printing information from and about S. Rosenthal and the industry in general.
General Info: Quarterly, Trim Size-8½ x 11, 8 pages, 2 Color, Coated, Saddle-stitched
Circulation: Total-3,000

In House Graphics
See: ADVERTISING & MARKETING

Ink on Paper
Business

Publishing Co: W. Caslon & Co., 100 Park Wood Ave., Rochester, NY 14620; Title Tel # (716) 346-2776 Title Fax # (716) 346-2276
Personnel: Circ. Mgr.-Donna Southworth, Co-Editor, Production Mgr.-Frank Cost, Co-Editor, Bk. Rev. Ed., Mktg. Dir.-Miles Southworth
Editorial Description: New imaging technologies and business strategies for graphic arts.
General Info: (Formerly Quality Control Scanner), Yr. Est. 1980, Monthly, Trim Size-8½ x 11, Sheetfed press, 8 pages, ISSN: 0739-6732, 2 Color, Newsprint, Saddle-stitched
Subscriptions: Indv. $175, Inst. $50, Can. $175, For. $190
Circulation: Total-500
Advertising: Accepts Inserts.
Printing Co: Eagle Graphics Inc., 1255 University Ave., Rochester, NY 14608 Tel # (716) 244-5006, Fax # (716) 244-5886

Inserts
Business

Publishing Co: Cambridge Automatic, 3 Huron Dr, Natick, MA 01760-1314 Tel # (508) 653-9002 Fax # (508) 651-3687
Editorial Description: Company information from this insert equipment manufacturer.
General Info: Semi-annually, Trim Size-8½ x 14, 2 pages, 2 Color, Matte

Intellectual, The
Business, Consumer

Publishing Co: Intelligencer Printing, 330 Eden Rd # 1768, Lancaster, PA 17601-4218; Title Tel # (717) 291-3100 Title Fax # (717) 569-2643
Personnel: Editor-Steve Brody
Editorial Description: News on Intelligencer Printing and the printing industry.
General Info: Quarterly, Trim Size-11 x 17, 4 pages, 4 Color, Coated, Saddle-stitched

Jay News
See: GENEALOGY

Lasertone News

Publishing Co: Spectrum, Inc., Spectrum Color Center, 6275 Joyce Drive, Golden, CO 80403; Title Tel # (303) 425-0400 Title Fax # (303) 425-0655
Personnel: Sales Mgr.-Lois Knight
Editorial Description: Valuable tips for desktop designers of catalogs.
General Info: Yr. Est. 1992, Quarterly

Mackazine
Business

Publishing Co: Mack Printing Co., 1991 Northampton St, Easton, PA 18042-3189; Title Tel # (215) 258-9111 Title Fax # (610) 250-7285
Editorial Description: Magazine of Mack color graphics from Mack Printing.
General Info: Irregular, Trim Size-8½ x 11, 14 pages, 4 Color, Coated, Saddle-stitched

Magnet Marketing
See: ADVERTISING & MARKETING

Management Portfolio
Association

Publishing Co: Printing Industries of America, 100 Daingerfield Rd., Alexandria, VA 22314-2888 Tel # (703) 519-8100; Title Tel # (703) 841-8100 Title Fax # (703) 548-3227
Personnel: Editor-Alex Graham
Editorial Description: News and industry developments devoted to managers of graphic arts businesses.
General Info: Yr. Est. 1980, Monthly, Trim Size-8½ x 11, Offset press, 20 pages, ISSN: 1050-2114, Color, Coated, Looseleaf
Subscriptions: $10/copy
Circulation: Total-13,300
Printing Co: AGS, 188 DeMarr Rd., White Plains, MD 20695 Tel # (301) 843-1800, Fax # (301) 843-6339

Michigan Association of Calligraphers-Newsletter
See: ART & SCULPTURE

Mini Lab Focus
See: PHOTOGRAPHY

NAQP News
Association

Publishing Co: Natl. Assn. of Quick Printers, 401 N. Michigan Ave., Chicago, IL 60611-4267; Title Tel # (312) 644-6610 Title Fax # (312) 321-6869
Personnel: Editor-Chris Martin, Adv. Dir.-Karen Watkins
Editorial Description: Owners and managers of duplicating shops who employ the photo direct printing process.
General Info: (Formerly NAQP Newsletter), Yr. Est. 1975, Monthly, Sheetfed press, 8 pages, No Color
Circulation: Total-3,800

Newsletter Trends
See: PERIODICAL INDUSTRY

Newsprint

Publishing Co: Print Club, 1614 Latimer St # 115, Philadelphia, PA 19103-6308; Title Tel # (215) 735-6090
Personnel: Art Dir.-Richard Frey
Editorial Description: News of printmaking & photography articles, reviews, opportunities for artists, exhibitions & activities of the Print Club.
General Info: (Formerly Counter Proof), Yr. Est. 1915, Quarterly
Subscriptions: Indv. $35, Can. $40, For. $50
Circulation: Total-2,000
List Rental: Rents Lists

Number 6 Bulletin
  See: LABOR UNION

Peerless Perspective   *Business*

Publishing Co: Peerless Engravers, 823 Main St, Little Rock, AR 72201-4691;
  Title Tel # (501) 375-8266
Editorial Description: Prepress information from Peerless Engravers.
General Info: Quarterly, Trim Size-8½ x 11, 4 Color, Coated
Subscriptions: Free

Personal Composition
  Report   *Business*

Publishing Co: Graphic Dimensions, 134 Caversham Woods, Pittsford, NY 14534-2834;
  Title Tel # (716) 381-3428
Personnel: Publisher, Editor-Michael Kleper, Circ. Mgr.-G. Schreiber
Editorial Description: Covers typographic communication, typesetting, desktop publishing, word/information processing, microcomputing information.
General Info: (Formerly Digest of Info. on Phototypesetting (DIPPY)), Yr. Est. 1978, 10x/yr., Trim Size-8½ x 11, 4 pages, ISSN: 0196-4127, 2 Color
Subscriptions: Indv. $100, For. $125, $10/copy

Photo Educators

Publishing Co: Eastman Kodak Co., 343 State St, Rochester, NY 14650-0001;
  Title Tel # (716) 724-4000
Personnel: Editor-Mary-Helen Magim
General Info: Yr. Est. 1976, Ind/Abs/Online: Charts.Illus.
Circulation: Total-10,000

Post Press Solutions   *Business*

Publishing Co: Bindagraphics, 2701 Wilmarco Ave, Baltimore, MD 21223-3352;
  Title Tel # (410) 362-7200
Editorial Description: Binding information for the publishing and printing industries.
General Info: Irregular, Trim Size-8½ x 11, 8 pages, 2 Color, Coated, Saddle-stitched

Prepress Business
  Observer   *Business*

Publishing Co: Prepress Business Observer, 234 Benjamin West Ave, Swarthmore, PA 19081-1421
  Tel # (610) 543-5194
Personnel: Editor-Steve Hannaford
Editorial Description: Covers issues and news that affect the prepress business industry.
General Info: Monthly
Subscriptions: Indv. $195

Prepress Market Watch   *Business*

Publishing Co: National Association of Printers & Lithographers, 780 Palisade Ave., Teaneck, NJ 07666-3129; Title Tel # (201) 342-0707 Title Fax # (201) 692-0286
Editorial Description: Surveys and tracks over 200 printers and trade shops.
General Info: Yr. Est. 1992, Quarterly
Subscriptions: Indv. $40

Press Check   *Business*

Publishing Co: C.J. Krehbiel Co., 3962 Virginia Ave., Cincinnati, OH 45227 Tel # (513) 271-6035;
  Title Fax # (513) 271-6082
Personnel: VP Sales-Rick Hastings
Editorial Description: Printing tips for customers of the C.J. Krehbiel printing company.
General Info: Yr. Est. 1995, Bi-monthly

Print Business
  Opportunities   *Business, Association*

Publishing Co: Synectics Network, Inc., 15050 NE 20th Ave., N. Miami, FL 33181-1123;
  Title Tel # (215) 884-5100
Personnel: Editor-Glenna McWilliams
Editorial Description: Prospective buyers & sellers of printing cos.
General Info: Bi-monthly, 5 pages

Print Business Register   *Business*

Publishing Co: Quoin Publishing, 800 W Huron St Ste 3n, Chicago, IL 60622-5973 Parent Co.-PTN Publishing Co., Melville; Title Tel # (312) 226-5600 Title Fax # (312) 226-4640
Personnel: Publisher, Editor-Rod Piechowski, Circ. Mgr.-Julie Schreiber
General Info: (Formerly Print Mergers & Acquisitions), Yr. Est. 1985, Bi-monthly, Trim Size-8½ x 11, 4 pages, No Color
Subscriptions: Indv. $297, Inst. $297, Can. $297, For. $349, $10/copy
Circulation: Total-425, Readership-425
Advertising: Accepts Inserts.
Printing Co: Ability Ad Co., 806 N. Peoria St., Chicago, IL 60622 Tel # (312) 226-5353, Fax # (312) 226-3821

Print Solutions   *Business*   CPM: $100

Publishing Co: Just in Time Publishing, 632 Trail Ave, Frederick, MD 21701-4934;
  Title Tel # (301) 663-5022 Title Fax # (301) 662-6202
Personnel: Publisher, Editor-R. Suzanne Carnes
Editorial Description: Technical and relationship techniques for print buyers and their suppliers.
General Info: Yr. Est. 1993, Bi-monthly, Trim Size-8½ x 11, 16 pages, 2 Color, Matte, Saddle-stitched
Subscriptions: Indv. $18
Circulation: Total-5,000
Advertising: $500.

Print/New Jersey
  Communicator   *Business, Association*

Publishing Co: Print/New Jersey, 75 Kearny Ave, Kearny, NJ 07032-2334;
  Title Tel # (201) 767-7333
Personnel: Editor-Sally Westphalen
Editorial Description: For the Print/New Jersey Graphic Arts Association.
General Info: Quarterly, Trim Size-8½ x 11, 4 pages, 2 Color, Coated
Advertising: Inquire for rates.

Printer's Apprentice   *Consumer*

Publishing Co: Cybernetics Design, 88 E. Main St., Ste. 457, Mendham, NJ 07945-1832
Personnel: Publisher, Editor-David Smith
Editorial Description: Information for those starting printing or self-publishing companies.
General Info: Semi-annually, Trim Size-8½ x 11, 8 pages, No Color, Matte
Subscriptions: Indv. $5

Printer's Ink   *Business*

Publishing Co: Thomson-Shore, 7300 W. Joy Rd., Dexter, MI 48130-9701;
  Title Tel # (313) 426-3939 Title Fax # (313) 426-6219
Editorial Description: Short run printing information.
General Info: Quarterly, Trim Size-8½ x 11, 6 pages, 2 Color, Matte
Printing Co: University Printing, 1330 S. Harrison Road, Michigan State University, E. Lansing, MI 48824-9455 Tel # (313) 426-3939, Fax # (313) 426-6219

Printers Shareware News   *Business*

Publishing Co: Printers Shareware News, 5019 W Lovers Ln # 5021, Dallas, TX 75209-3141;
  Title Tel # (214) 350-5353 Title Fax # (214) 350-2610
Personnel: Publisher-T. George Scott
Editorial Description: For printers to share computer and publishing news.
General Info: Yr. Est. 1986, Quarterly
Subscriptions: Indv. $29
Circulation: Total-9,600
List Rental: Actives: 8,400

Printing & Publishing Newsletter
  See: SAFETY

Printing Association of
  Florida Newsletter   *Association*

Publishing Co: Printing Association of Florida, PO Box 170010, Hialeah, FL 33017-0010
Editorial Description: Topics of interest to Florida printers.
General Info: Monthly, Trim Size-8½ x 11, 24 pages

Printing Business Report   *Business, Association*

Publishing Co: National Association of Printers & Lithographers, 780 Palisade Ave., Teaneck, NJ 07666-3129; Title Tel # (201) 342-0700
Editorial Description: Information and statistics on the printing industry.
General Info: Yr. Est. 1992, Quarterly, Trim Size-8½ x 11, 4 pages, 2 Color

Printing History   *Business, Association*   CPM: $250

Publishing Co: American Printing History Assn., Box 4922, Grand Central Station, New York, NY 10163-1005; Title Tel # (716) 475-2408
Personnel: Editor-David Pankow
Editorial Description: Scholarly journal dealing with cultural technical, research on printing history.
General Info: Semi-annually, Offset press, 40 pages, ISSN: 0192-9275, Ind/Abs/Online: LIB. LIT., 1% ads, No Color, Newsprint, Perfect bound
Subscriptions: Indv. $30, Inst. $35, Can. $35, For. $35, $15/copy
Circulation: Total-1,000
Advertising: $250.
List Rental: Actives: 850, $100/M
Printing Co: Stinehour Press, P.O Box 159, Lunenburg, VT 05906 Tel # (802) 328-2507

Printing Sales Index
  See: ECONOMICS

Printips   *Business*

Publishing Co: Printips Newsletter, P.O. Box 20610, Castro Valley, CA 94546 Tel # (510) 582-5366 Fax # (510) 581-1648
Personnel: Publisher-Dwight Perry, Assoc. Publ., Editor-Joyce Perry
Editorial Description: Camera-ready newsletter containing information about printing. Prepared for printers to distribute to customers.
General Info: Monthly
Subscriptions: Indv. $269

Quality Action Planner
  See: MANAGEMENT

Quality Improvement
Quarterly   *Business, Association*

Publishing Co: National Association of Printers & Lithographers, 780 Palisade Ave., Teaneck, NJ 07666-3129
Editorial Description: Information on how total quality management relates to printing operations. Contains articles on customer focus, management concepts, scientific approaches to quality improvement and teamwork theories, with actual case studies.
General Info: Yr. Est. 1994, Quarterly, Trim Size-8½ x 11, 6 pages
Subscriptions: Indv. $40, Free To Qualified Recipient

Quill

Publishing Co: Michigan Assn. of Calligraphers, PO Box 55, Royal Oak, MI 48068-0055; Title Tel # (313) 665-1386
Personnel: Editor-Susan Skarsgard
Editorial Description: Features artcles of calligraphic interest & photos of calligraphy.
General Info: Yr. Est. 1978, Semi-annually, Letrpr. press, 30 pages, No Color, Coated
Subscriptions: Indv. $10, $5/copy
Circulation: Total-300

Reproduction Bulletin   *Business*

Publishing Co: Andrews Paper & Chemical, 1 Channel Dr # 509, Port Washington, NY 11050-2216; Title Tel # (516) 767-2800
Personnel: Editor-Peter Muller
Editorial Description: News on reproduction processes particular emphasis on diazo and blueprint for engineering and office duplicating purposes.
General Info: Yr. Est. 1954, Quarterly, Trim Size-8½ x 11, Offset press, 1 pages, No Color
Circulation: Total-2,500

S&ME Forum   *Business*

Publishing Co: Printing Industries of America, 100 Daingerfield Rd., Alexandria, VA 22314-2888 Tel # (703) 519-8100; Title Tel # (703) 519-8137 Title Fax # (703) 548-3227
Personnel: Editor-Cliff Weiss
Editorial Description: Sales and marketing information for members.
General Info: Yr. Est. 1993, Quarterly, Trim Size-8½ x 11, 4 pages, 2 Color, Coated, Saddle-stitched

SPAN Connection
See: BOOKS & BOOK TRADE

SPEX: Small Publishers Exchange
See: BOOKS & BOOK TRADE

Self Publisher Newsletter
See: BOOKS & BOOK TRADE

Seybold Report on
Publishing Systems   *Business*

Publishing Co: Seybold Publications, Inc., 428 East Baltimore Pike, Media, PA 19063 Tel # (610) 565-2480; Title Tel # (215) 565-2480 Title Fax # (610) 565-4659
Personnel: Publisher-Jonathan Seybold, Editor-Stephen Edwards, Circ. Mgr.-Martha Morrison
Editorial Description: Analyzes text editing, typesetting and composition hardware and software and other front-end (pre-press) systems for newspaper, commercial and in-plant applications.
General Info: (Formerly Seybold Report, The), Yr. Est. 1971, Semi-monthly, Trim Size-8½ x 11, Offset press, 36 pages, Ind/Abs/Online: Newsnet, No Color, Newsprint, Saddle-stitched
Subscriptions: Indv. $288, Can. $300, For. $324

Sheet-fed Operations
Quarterly   *Business, Association*

Publishing Co: National Association of Printers & Lithographers, 780 Palisade Ave., Teaneck, NJ 07666-3129
Editorial Description: Designed to provide information for both NAPL and GATF members on trends and advancements in sheet-fed pressroom operations.
General Info: Yr. Est. 1994, Quarterly
Subscriptions: Free To Qualified Recipient

Shortruns   *Business*

Publishing Co: Marrakech Express, 500 Anclote Rd, Tarpon Springs, FL 34689-6701; Title Tel # (813) 942-2218 Title Fax # (813) 937-4758
Personnel: Publisher-Steen Sigmond, Editor-Shirley Copperman, Bk. Rev. Ed.-Lynn Coppenman, Art Dir.-Lou Tatalias
Editorial Description: To help publishers of books, journals, magazines, and newsletters with their printing & publishing.
General Info: Yr. Est. 1990, Quarterly, Trim Size-8½ x 11, Offset press, 8 pages, 2 Color, Matte, Saddle-stitched
Subscriptions: Free To Qualified Recipient
Circulation: Total-17,000
Printing Co: Account Manager: Sidney Kraff; Valley Web, 1299 Stowe Avenue, Medford, OR 97504 Tel # (503) 772-7039

Signature Service   *Business, Association*

Publishing Co: Society for Service Professionals in Printing, PO Box 25768, Alexandria, VA 22313-5768; Title Tel # (703) 684-5768 Title Fax # (703) 548-9137
Personnel: Editor-Marj Zager, Editor, Circulation-Debbie Ayres, Art Dir.-Pam Lipscomb
Editorial Description: For customer service reps in the printing industry.
General Info: (Formerly Service in Print), Yr. Est. 1993, Monthly, Trim Size-8½ x 11, 8 pages, ISSN: 1067-3245, 2 Color
Subscriptions: Indv. $89, Free With Membership
Circulation: Total-1,300
List Rental: Rents Lists
Printing Co: Newsletter Services, Inc., 9700 Philadelphia Court, Lanham, MD 20706 Tel # (301) 731-5200, Fax # (301) 731-5201

Specialty Lab Update
See: PHOTOGRAPHY

Stained Finger, The
See: COLLECTIBLES

Stamping Grounds   *Consumer*

Publishing Co: Stamping Grounds, PO Box 4065, Ogden, UT 84402; Title Tel # (801) 392-0115
Personnel: Publisher-Gracia Roemer
Editorial Description: For singles who enjoy plants and gardening.
General Info: Quarterly, Trim Size-8½ x 11, 8 pages
Subscriptions: Indv. $30
Circulation: Total-730

Step-By-Step Electronic Design
See: COMPUTERS & AUTOMATION

T & E Update   *Business*

Publishing Co: Technical & Education Center of the Graphic Arts- RIT, Frank E. Gannett Bldg., 66 Lomb Memorial Dr., Rochester, NY 14623-5604 Tel # (716) 475-5000
Personnel: Editor-Sandy Richolson, Design Ed.-Brenda Monahan
Editorial Description: Contains articles of interest to printers and graphic artists as well as information on courses.
General Info: (Formerly T & E News), Bi-monthly, Trim Size-8⅛ x 10½, Web press, 22 pages, ISSN: 0895-6537, 4 Color, Matte, Saddle-stitched
Subscriptions: Free

T-Shirt Business Info
Mapping Newsletter--How
To & Ideas Edition   *Business*

Publishing Co: Prosperity & Profits Unlimited, PO Box 416, Denver, CO 80201-0416; Title Tel # (303) 575-5676
Personnel: Publisher, Editor-A.C. Doyle
Editorial Description: Possibilities information sources, ideas on the T-shirt business.
General Info: Yr. Est. 1990, Every two years, Trim Size-8½ x 11, Letrpr. press, 6 pages, ISSN: 1053-6493, No Color
Subscriptions: Indv. $5, Inst. $5, Can. $7, For. $8, $5/copy

TAGA Newsletter   *Association*

Publishing Co: TAGA Newsletter, 68 Lomb Memorial Dr, Rochester, NY 14623-5604 Tel # (716) 475-7470; Title Tel # (716) 272-0557 Title Fax # (716) 475-2250
Personnel: Editor-Karen Lawrence
Editorial Description: Information on coming TAGA events, reports of meetings, and industry trends.
General Info: Yr. Est. 1949, Quarterly, Trim Size-8½ x 11, Offset press, 8 pages, 4 Color
Subscriptions: Indv. $85
Circulation: (100% controlled), Total-1,000

Tech Tips   *Business*

Publishing Co: Appollo Graphics, 1085 Industrial Blvd, Southampton, PA 18966-4056; Title Tel # (215) 953-0500 Title Fax # (215) 953-1144
Editorial Description: Technical printing and computer graphics information.
General Info: Quarterly, Trim Size-8½ x 11, 6 pages, 4 Color, Coated

Trends   *Business*

Publishing Co: Heidelberg USA, 1000 Gutenberg Drive, Kennesaw, GA 30144 Tel # (404) 419-6500; Title Tel # (718) 830-5993
Editorial Description: Heidelberg's magazine of printing information and trends.
General Info: Yr. Est. 1992, Quarterly, Trim Size-8¹²/ x 11, 42 pages, 4 Color, Coated, Saddle-stitched

Type   *Consumer*

Publishing Co: Garamond Press, 24667 Heather Ct, Hayward, CA 94545-2004; Title Tel # (415) 782-3674
Personnel: Editor-Fred Williams
Editorial Description: Devoted to Letterpress techniques, historical heritage of printing & works of private presses.
General Info: Yr. Est. 1974, Quarterly, Trim Size-7¼ x 10½, Letrpr. press, 8 pages, ISSN: 1042-105X, 2 Color, Matte, Saddle-stitched
Subscriptions: Indv. $4, Can. $3, For. $5, $1/copy
Circulation: Total-850
Advertising: Inquire for rates.

Umbrella
See: ART & SCULPTURE

Update, The
  See: LABOR UNION

Update   *Business*

Publishing Co: National Association of Printers & Lithographers, 780 Palisade Ave., Teaneck, NJ 07666-3129
Personnel: Mktg. Dir.-Rhona Bronson
General Info: Monthly, Trim Size-8½ x 11, 4 pages, 2 Color, Matte

Varityper Update   *Business*

Publishing Co: Varityper Inc., 11 Mount Pleasant Ave., East Hanover, NJ 07936-2601 Parent Co.-Tegra Inc., East Hanover; Title Tel # (201) 887-8000
Personnel: Sales & Mktg. Dir.-Lisa Geyette
Editorial Description: The latest on Varityper's prepress and imagesetting systems.
General Info: Yr. Est. 1992, Quarterly, Trim Size-8½ x 11, 4 pages, 2 Color, Coated

Weadon Printing Services-
  Newsletter

Publishing Co: Weadon Printing Services, Inc., 6430 General Green Way, Alexandria, VA 22312-2446; Title Tel # (703) 750-0800
Personnel: Editor-Jim Stevens
Editorial Description: Articles on printing & graphics techniques, marketing & Weadon Systems.
General Info: Yr. Est. 1983, Quarterly, Trim Size-8½ x 11, Sheetfed press, 4 pages, 2 Color, Coated
Circulation: Total-900

Weigand Report
  See: COMPUTERS & AUTOMATION

Worldwide Graphics
  See: INTERNATIONAL TRADE

PRODUCE

Alberta Agrologist
  See: AGRICULTURE

Apricot Quarterly Roundup   *Association*

Publishing Co: California Apricot Advisory Bd., 1280 Boulevard Way, Walnut Creek, CA 94595-1193; Title Tel # (415) 937-3660
Personnel: Editor-Gene Stokes
General Info: Yr. Est. 1971, Quarterly, Sheetfed press, 4 pages, 2 Color
Circulation: (100% controlled), Total-1,000

Atlanta Wholesale Fruit   *Business, Association*

Publishing Co: Federal-State Market News Service, 203 Administration Bldg., 1616 Forest Parkway, Forest Park, GA 30050; Title Tel # (404) 366-0575 Title Fax # (404) 363-2523
Editorial Description: Covers quality, condition, and prices of fresh fruits and vegetables.
General Info: Yr. Est. 1914, Weekly, Trim Size-8½ x 14, Mimeo press, 2 pages, No Color
List Rental: Rents Lists

Baltimore Wholesale Fruits
  and Vegetable Report

Publishing Co: AMS, F&V Division USDA, 7460 Conowingo Ave Ste 101, Jessup, MD 20794-9361; Title Tel # (301) 799-4840
Personnel: Publisher-Richard Hallinger
Editorial Description: Marketing and price information on fruits and vegetables.
General Info: Daily, Trim Size-8½ x 14, 2 pages
Subscriptions: Indv. $120

Benton Harbor Fruit &
  Vegetable Report

Publishing Co: AMS, F&V Division, USDA, PO Box 1204, Benton Harbor, MI 49023-1204; Title Tel # (616) 925-3270 Title Fax # (616) 925-3272
Subscriptions: Indv. $39

California Macadamia
  Society Yearbook   *Business, Association*

Publishing Co: California Macadamia Society, PO Box 1298, Fallbrook, CA 92088-1298; Title Tel # (619) 728-4532
Personnel: Editor-Jim Teeter
Editorial Description: Major source and information about macadamia nut trees-the industry, the propagation of new research, from contributors around the world.
General Info: Yr. Est. 1953, Quarterly, 150 pages, ISSN: 0068-5720, No Color
Subscriptions: Indv. $18, For. $26
Circulation: (100% controlled), Total-700
Advertising: Inquire for rates.

Dialogue   *Business, Association*

Publishing Co: The Lignin Institute, 5775 Peachtree Dunwoody Rd NE, Ste G500, Atlanta, GA 30342-1507 Tel # (404) 252-3663 Fax # (404) 252-0774
Editorial Description: Covers various uses of lignosulfonates.
General Info: Semi-annually

Direct Line
  See: CONFECTIONERY

F.C.M. Market Bulletin

Publishing Co: Florida Citrus Mutual, PO Box 89, Lakeland, FL 33802-0089
General Info: Quarterly

Florida Citrus Mutual
  Triangle

Publishing Co: Florida Citrus Mutual, PO Box 89, Lakeland, FL 33802-0089; Title Tel # (813) 682-1111
Personnel: Editor-Lynn Chase
Editorial Description: Provides information about citrus fruit marketing beneficial to member growers.
General Info: Yr. Est. 1948, Weekly, Trim Size-8½ x 11, Offset press, 6 pages, Color

Foreign Fruit and Nut
  Report

Publishing Co: Federal-State Market News Service, 1220 N Street, Sacramento, CA 95814-5621; Title Tel # (916) 445-5721
General Info: Weekly

Fraser's Potato
  Newsletter   *Business*   CPM: $545

Publishing Co: Harry Fraser, Publisher, R.R. 1, Charlottetown, PE C1A 7J6 Canada; Title Tel # (902) 569-2685 Title Fax # (902) 569-5589
Personnel: Publisher, Editor-Harry Fraser, Circ. Mgr.-Velma Jones, Art Dir.-Janet Fraser
Editorial Description: Covers all elements of the potato industry continent-wide.
General Info: Yr. Est. 1967, Weekly, Trim Size-8½ x 14, Sheetfed press, 4 pages, 2 Color
Subscriptions: Indv. $75
Circulation: Total-2,200
Advertising: $1,200. Accepts Inserts.

Fruit and Vegetable
  Division, Boston Daily
  Report

Publishing Co: Fruit and Vegetable Market News Service, 34 Market St Ste 10, Everett, MA 02149-5806; Title Tel # (617) 389-8090
General Info: Daily

Fruit and Vegetable
  Division, Detroit Daily
  Report

Publishing Co: Fruit and Vegetable Market News Service, 7201 W. Fort St., Detroit, MI 48209-2963; Title Tel # (313) 841-1111
General Info: Daily

Fruit and Vegetable
  Division, New Orleans
  Daily Report

Publishing Co: Federal-State Market News Service, New Fedl. Bldg. Rm. T-5031, New Orleans, LA 70113; Title Tel # (504) 568-7531
General Info: Annually

Fruit and Vegetable
  Division, New York Daily
  Report

Publishing Co: U.S. Department, of Agriculture, Consumer, Hunts Point Market, Rm. 4A, Bronx, NY 10474; Title Tel # (212) 542-2225 Title Fax # (212) 542-2572
General Info: Daily, 4 pages

Fruit and Vegetable Truck
  Rate Report   *Business, Association*

Publishing Co: USDA-AMS-F&V. Div., 630 Sansome St Ste 727, San Francisco, CA 94111-2215; Title Tel # (415) 705-1300 Title Fax # (415) 705-1301
Personnel: Editor-Fredrick Teensma
Editorial Description: Provides information on rates for shipping loads of selected produce items to various cities in the U.S. Also includes is a section on the volume of shipments in the U.S. compared to previous weeks and to last year. Once a month this publication includesa section called 'Tuck Cost Report' which detail truck operation costs.
General Info: Weekly, Trim Size-8½ x 14, 2 pages, No Color, Matte
Subscriptions: Indv. $120, Can. $120, For. $240

Great Lakes Fruit &
  Vegetable Report   *Business, Association*

Publishing Co: AMS, F&V Division, USDA, PO Box 1204, Benton Harbor, MI 49023-1204; Title Tel # (616) 925-3270 Title Fax # (616) 925-3272
Personnel: Publisher-Charles Hackensmith
Editorial Description: Marketing and price information on fruits and vegetables.
General Info: (Formerly Michigan Fruit and Vegetable Report), Daily, Trim Size-8½ x 14, 2 pages
Subscriptions: Indv. $220

Hints to Potato Growers

Publishing Co: New Jersey State Potato Assn., Dept. of Horticulture, Cook College, Box 231, New Brunswick, NJ 08903; Title Tel # (201) 932-9392
Personnel: Editor-Melvin Henninger
Editorial Description: To inform N.J.'s potato people on news briefs, crop conditions, and research data from or for N.J.
General Info: Yr. Est. 1919, Quarterly, Trim Size-8½ x 11, Mimeo press, 6 pages
Subscriptions: Indv. $10
Circulation: Total-200

Honey Report, Sacramento, California

Publishing Co: Federal-State Market News Service, 1220 N Street, Sacramento, CA 95814-5621
General Info: Semi-monthly

IAI Apple News   *Business, Association*

Publishing Co: International Apple Inst., PO Box 1137, Mc Lean, VA 22101-1137; Title Tel # (703) 442-8850 Title Fax # (703) 790-0845
Personnel: Publisher-Derl Derr, Editor-Bob Johnson, Promotion Dir.-Nadine Alemian
Editorial Description: Covers subject matter affecting Apple industry-i. e. crop & storage statistics, legislation, world trade, marketing, government regulations, etc.
General Info: (Formerly Special Letter), Bi-weekly, Trim Size-8½ x 11, 6 pages, 2 Color, Newsprint
Subscriptions: Indv. $300
Circulation: Total-850

Idaho Potato News   *Association*

Publishing Co: Idaho Potato Commission, PO Box 1068, Boise, ID 83701-1068; Title Tel # (208) 334-2350
Personnel: Editor-Don Odiorne
Editorial Description: To the growers, shippers and processors of Idaho-grown potatoes. Emphasis on production, improving quality, cultural practices, storage and marketing of the Idaho potato.
General Info: Quarterly, Trim Size-8½ x 11½, Roto. press, 8 pages, No Color
Subscriptions: Indv. $3
Circulation: Total-9,000

Illinois Soybean Farmer Leader Newsletter
See: AGRICULTURE

In a Nutshell   *Business, Association*

Publishing Co: National Pecan Shellers Assn., 5775 Peachtree Dunwoody Rd NE, Ste G500, Atlanta, GA 30342-1507 Tel # (404) 252-3663 Fax # (404) 252-0774
Editorial Description: Information and news for pecan processors.
General Info: Quarterly

Incider   *Business, Association*

Publishing Co: Processed Apples Institute, 5775 Peachtree Dunwoody Rd NE, Ste G500, Atlanta, GA 30342-1507 Tel # (404) 252-3663 Fax # (404) 252-0774
Editorial Description: Information for processors of apples and producers of apple products.
General Info: Quarterly

Le Producteur de Raisin d'Ontario, Ontario Grape Grower

Publishing Co: Ontario Grape Growers Marketing Bd., 215 Ontario St., St. Catharines, ON L2R 6Y3 Canada; Title Tel # (416) 688-0990 Title Fax # (905) 682-7481
Personnel: Circ. Mgr.-Gwen Hunt
General Info: 4 pages
Circulation: Total-8,500

Lemon Administrative Committee, Bulletin

Publishing Co: Lemon Administrative Committee, 2202 Monterey St., Ste. 102B, Fresno, CA 93721-3129; Title Tel # (805) 253-0495
Personnel: Editor-Mr. Bearers
General Info: Weekly
Subscriptions: Indv. $33
Circulation: Total-350

Lemon Administrative Committee, Report

Publishing Co: Lemon Administrative Committee, 2202 Monterey St., Ste. 102B, Fresno, CA 93721-3129 Tel # (805) 253-0495; Title Tel # (213) 624-3403
General Info: Annually

Marketing Great Lake Fruit

Publishing Co: AMS, F&V Division, USDA, PO Box 1204, Benton Harbor, MI 49023-1204; Title Tel # (616) 925-3270 Title Fax # (616) 925-3272
General Info: (Formerly Marketing Michigan Fruit), Annually
Subscriptions: Indv. $20

Newsletter Design
See: PERIODICAL INDUSTRY

Nut Kernel, The   *Association*   CPM: $161

Publishing Co: Pennsylvania Nut Growers Assn., 654 Beinhower Rd, Etters, PA 17319-9774; Title Tel # (717) 938-6090 Title Fax # (717) 938-6090
Personnel: Editor-Tucker Hill
Editorial Description: Covers culture, breeding, pest control, grafting and other topics related to nuts and nut trees.
General Info: Yr. Est. 1932, Quarterly, Trim Size-8½ x 11, Desktop press, 12 pages, No Color, Matte, Saddle-stitched
Subscriptions: Indv. $12
Circulation: Total-235, Readership-235
Advertising: $38. Accepts Inserts.
Printing Co: Penns Valley Printers, 1807 Market St, Camp Hill, PA 17011-4800 Tel # (717) 737-6769, Fax # (717) 737-1836

Olive Oil Report, Sacramento, California

Publishing Co: Federal-State Market News Service, 1220 N Street, Sacramento, CA 95814-5621
General Info: Weekly

Peach Fuzz   *Association*

Publishing Co: California Canning Peach Assn., PO Box 7001, Lafayette, CA 94549-7010; Title Tel # (415) 284-9171
Personnel: Editor-Ronald A. Schuler
Editorial Description: Covers marketing information for cling peach growers.
General Info: Yr. Est. 1954, Monthly, Trim Size-8½ x 14, Offset press, 2 pages, No Color
Subscriptions: Indv. $40
Circulation: Total-1,300
Advertising: Accepts Inserts.

Peanut Research   *Association*

Publishing Co: American Peanut Research & Education Society, 376 Ag. Hall Oklahoma State, Univ., Stillwater, OK 74078-0001 Tel # (405) 744-9634 Fax # (405) 744-5269
Personnel: Editor-C. Corley Holbrook
Editorial Description: Peanut research and education activities in America and worldwide. For members only.
General Info: Yr. Est. 1963, Quarterly, Trim Size-8½ x 11, Sheetfed press, 11 pages, No Color
Subscriptions: Indv. $8, Inst. $8, Can. $12, For. $16, $2/copy
Circulation: (100% controlled), Total-750

Polly Hale Newsletter   *Business, Consumer*

Publishing Co: Hale Indian River Groves, Indian River Plaza, Wabasso, FL 32970 Tel # (407) 388-5782 Fax # (407) 388-5782
Editorial Description: News and information about Hale Indian River Groves.
General Info: Monthly, Trim Size-8½ x 11, 4 pages, 4 Color, Coated

Potato and Onion Report, Daily

Publishing Co: Federal-State Market News Service, 1820 E 17th St Ste 130, Idaho Falls, ID 83404-6472; Title Tel # (208) 526-0747
General Info: Daily

Potato Report, Daily

Publishing Co: Federal-State Market News Service, PO Box 725, Presque Isle, ME 04769-0725; Title Tel # (207) 764-4470
General Info: Daily
Subscriptions: Inst. $78, Free In Designated Area

Prune Report, Daily

Publishing Co: Federal-State Market News Service, 1820 E 17th St Ste 130, Idaho Falls, ID 83404-6472
General Info: Daily

San Francisco Wholesale Fruit & Vegetable Report   *Business, Association*

Publishing Co: USDA-AMS-F&V. Div., 630 Sansome St Ste 727, San Francisco, CA 94111-2215; Title Tel # (415) 705-1300 Title Fax # (415) 705-1301
Personnel: Editor-Frederick Teensma
Editorial Description: Provides the latest prices on the produce markets in San Francisco and South San Francisco. It provides information on arrivals (in packages), of produce into the San Francisco-Oakland Bay area. Also included in this report is a shipping point summary for items available in the Western U.S.
General Info: Daily, Trim Size-8½ x 14, Mimeo press, 4 pages, No Color, Matte
Subscriptions: Indv. $240, Can. $240, For. $480
Circulation: Total-150

Strawberry Report   *Business*

Publishing Co: Federal State Market News, 630 Sansome St Ste 727, San Francisco, CA 94111-2215; Title Tel # (415) 556-5587
Personnel: Editor-F. Teensma
Editorial Description: Prices, supplies, & market conditions of U.S. strawberry markets, includes growing area & wholesale markets in major cities.
General Info: Weekly, Trim Size-8½ x 14, Mimeo press, 2 pages, No Color
Subscriptions: Indv. $120, Can. $120, For. $240

United Newswire   *Association*

Publishing Co: United Fresh Fruit & Vegetable Assn., 727 N Washington St, Alexandria, VA 22314-1924; Title Tel # (703) 836-3410
Personnel: Publisher-Roger Stroh, Editor-David Lewis
Editorial Description: Weekly newsletter for the produce industry.
General Info: (Formerly United Fresh Outlook), Yr. Est. 1943, Weekly, Sheetfed press, 4 pages, ISSN: 0194-763X, No Color, Newsprint
Subscriptions: Indv. $50, $2/copy
Circulation: Total-3,000
Printing Co: Plymouth Printing, 1200 Cushing Pl SE, Washington, DC 20003-3599 Tel # (202) 488-7777, Fax # (202) 863-1078

Vegetable Review

Publishing Co: U.S. Department of Agriculture, California Ag. Stat. Service, PO Box 1258, Sacramento, CA 95812
Editorial Description: Processing & fresh market vegetable, potato, berry acreage, production, & value.
General Info: Monthly
Subscriptions: Indv. $15, For. $30
Circulation: Total-12,900
Advertising: Inquire for rates.

Vegetarian Journal's Foodservice Update
See: FOOD

Virginia Fruit & Vegetable Bulletin
See: AGRICULTURE

PSYCHIATRY

Aid Bulletin - Addiction Intervention with the Disabled

Publishing Co: Kent State University Printing Service, Main & Lincoln Sts., Kent, OH 44242-0001; Title Tel # (216) 672-2440 Title Fax # (216) 672-2451
General Info: Yr. Est. 1981, Quarterly

American Psychoanalyst   *Association*

Publishing Co: Analytic Press, Inc., ATTN: Editoral, 101 West Street, Hillsdale, NJ 07642-1422 Fax # (201) 666-2394; Title Tel # (201) 358-9477 Title Fax # (201) 358-0621
Personnel: Publisher-Paul Stepansky, Editor-Arnold Richards, M.D., Circ. Mgr.-Nancy Seitz, Production Mgr.-Eleanor Starke Kobrin, Promotion Dir.-Joan Riegel
Editorial Description: A scholarly and clinical resources for analytic practitioners; historical essays, interviews and practice-related articles.
General Info: Yr. Est. 1967, Quarterly, Trim Size-8½ x 11, 28 pages, ISSN: 1052-7958
Subscriptions: Indv. $55, Inst. $140, Can. $28, For. $48, $8/copy
Circulation: (86% controlled), Total-3,800, Subscriptions-300
Advertising: Inquire for rates.

American Psychoanalyst, The   *Association*

Publishing Co: Sponsor-American Psychoanalytic Assn., Analxtic Press, Inc., The, 365 Broadway, Hillside, NJ 07642 Tel # (201) 358-9477 Fax # (201) 358-0621; Title Tel # (212) 752-0450 Title Fax # (212) 593-0571
Personnel: Editor-William Jeffrey, MD
Editorial Description: Current issues and developments in the Association and topics of concern to psychoanalysts.
General Info: (Formerly American Psychoanalytic Association Newsletter), Yr. Est. 1967, Quarterly, Trim Size-8½ x 11, 32 pages, ISSN: 1052-7958, 2 Color
Subscriptions: Indv. $28, Inst. $50
Circulation: Total-5,000
Advertising: Inquire for rates.

American Society of Adolescent Psychiatry Newsletter   *Association*   **CPM: $175**

Publishing Co: American Society for Adolescent Psychiatry, 4330 East-West Hwy. #1117, Bethesda, MD 20814; Title Tel # (301) 718-6502 Title Fax # (301) 656-0989
Personnel: Publisher-David Lewis, Editor-Leonard Henschel, Circ. Mgr., Adv. Dir.-Kristan Herrington
Editorial Description: Covers clinical developments & news relatign to adolescent psychiatry.
General Info: Yr. Est. 1967, Quarterly, Trim Size-8½ x 11, Desktop press, 20 pages, 10% ads, 2 Color, Coated, Saddle-stitched
Subscriptions: Indv. $10
Circulation: Total-2,000
Advertising: $350. Accepts Inserts.
List Rental: Actives: $100/M, Hotline: $100/M, Expires: $100/M

B.E.A.M. (Being Energetic About Multiplicity)
See: PSYCHOLOGY

Bell, The
See: PSYCHOLOGY

Biological Psychology Bulletin

Publishing Co: Univ. of Oklahoma, Dept. of Psychiatry, Health Science Center, 1100 N. Lindsay, Oklahoma City, OK 73104
Personnel: Editor-Van Tharp
General Info: Yr. Est. 1971, Ind/Abs/Online: Psychol. Abstr.
Subscriptions: Indv. $4
Circulation: Total-150

Clinical Pearl News   *Business, Consumer*

Publishing Co: ITS, 3301 Alta Arden Expy., Ste. 3, Sacramento, CA 95825-2121
Editorial Description: Covers clinical issues in psychiatry.
General Info: Monthly
Subscriptions: Indv. $46

Clinical Psychiatry Quarterly   *Business, Association*

Publishing Co: American Academy of Clinical Psychiatrists, PO Box 3212, San Diego, CA 92163-1212; Title Tel # (619) 298-0538
Personnel: Publisher, Editor, Production Mgr.-Rodrigo Munoz
Editorial Description: Contains original research & AACP news of interest to clinical psychiatrists.
General Info: (Formerly American Acadamy of Clinical Psychiatry Newsletter), Yr. Est. 1975, Quarterly, Trim Size-8½ x 11, Desktop press, 16 pages, 2 Color, Coated
Subscriptions: Free With Membership
Circulation: Total-15,000
Advertising: Accepts Inserts.
Printing Co: Medical Printing, 8870 La Mesa Blvd, La Mesa, CA 91941-5137 Tel # (619) 466-4105

Harvard Mental Health Letter
See: PSYCHOLOGY

ISSD News
See: PSYCHOLOGY

Interchange, The
See: PSYCHOLOGY

International Drug Therapy Newsletter

Publishing Co: Ayd Medical Communications, 1130 E. Cold Spring Ln., Baltimore, MD 21239-3931; Title Tel # (410) 433-9220 Title Fax # (410) 532-5419
Personnel: Editor-Frank Eyd, Jr., Circ. Mgr.-Ann Lovelace, Adv. Dir.-Bertram Morales, Production Mgr., Promotion Dir.-Mary Ann Ayd
Editorial Description: Up-to-date reports on all aspects of psychopharmacotherapy.
General Info: Yr. Est. 1966, Monthly, Offset press, 4 pages, ISSN: 0020-6571, 2 Color, Newsprint
Subscriptions: Indv. $42, $4/copy
Circulation: Total-20,000
Advertising: Accepts Inserts.

Journal Watch for Psychiatry   *Business*

Publishing Co: Massachusetts Medical Society-Publ. Dir, 1440 Main St., Waltham, MA 02154-1649 Tel # (617) 893-3800 Fax # (617) 893-8103
Personnel: Publisher-Bob Bovenschulte, Editor-Gary Tucker, MD, Circ. Mgr.-Jed Clifton, Production Mgr.-Alberta Fitzpatrick, Adv. Dir.-Art Wilschek
Editorial Description: Contains 10-12 abstracts per issue from major psychitric journals covering the latest research for practicing psychiatrists and psychologists.
General Info: Yr. Est. 1995, Monthly, Trim Size-8½ x 11, Web press, 8 pages, ISSN: 1081-5899, 2 Color, Matte, Saddle-stitched
Subscriptions: Indv. $79, Inst. $79, Can. $95, For. $95, $5/copy
List Rental: List Management Co.: Manager: Michelle Dinsmore; Response Media Products Inc., 2323 Perimeter Park Dr., Ste. 200, Atlanta, GA 30341-1335 Tel # (404) 451-5478, Fax # (404) 451-4929
Printing Co: Valley Web, 1299 Stowe Avenue, Medford, OR 97504 Tel # (503) 772-7039

Linkage
See: PSYCHOLOGY

Menninger Letter, The
See: PSYCHOLOGY

Mental Health Law Reporter
See: LAW

Mental Health News Alert
See: PHILANTHROPY

Mental Health Weekly
See: HEALTH

National Character Laboratory-Newsletter
See: MEDICINE

Newsletter of the American Academy of Psychiatry   *Association*

Publishing Co: American Academy of Psychiatry & the Law, PO Box 30, Bloomfield, CT 06002-0030; Title Tel # (860) 242-5450 Title Fax # (860) 286-0787
Personnel: Editor-Robert Miller, Circ. Mgr.-Jackie Coleman
Editorial Description: Published to provide the latest news & information in the areas in which mental health & legal issues overlap.
General Info: Yr. Est. 1976, Tri-annually, Offset press, 35 pages, No Color, Newsprint
Subscriptions: Indv. $25, $10/copy
Circulation: Total-1,700

PS: It Is News
See: PSYCHOLOGY

Psychiatric Topics

Publishing Co: Academy Professional Information Svcs. Inc., 116 W. 32nd St., New York, NY 10001-3212; Title Tel # (212) 736-6688 Title Fax # (212) 564-1763
Personnel: Editor-Olivia McFadden
Editorial Description: For psychiatrists: Europe and Canada only.
General Info: Yr. Est. 1980, Trim Size-11 x 17, 8 pages

Psychopharmacology Update
See: PSYCHOLOGY

Psychotherapy Letter, The
See: PSYCHOLOGY

Quality of Care
See: DISABILITY

Roche Report: Frontiers of Psychiatry

Publishing Co: Roche Labs., Div. of Hoffmann-La Roche, Inc, Nutley, NJ 07110; Title Tel # (201) 235-5000
General Info: Yr. Est. 1964

Saskatchewan Psychiatric Assn. Newsletter   *Association*

Publishing Co: Saskatchewan Psychiatric Assn., Saskatchewan Provincial Hosp., Box 39, N. Battleford, SK S9A 2X8 Canada Tel # (306) 446-6800
General Info: Monthly

Statewide Comprehensive Plan for Mental Health Services

Publishing Co: New York State Office of Mental Health, 44 Holland Avenue, Albany, NY 12229

PSYCHOLOGY

AACP Newsletter

Publishing Co: American Academy of Child Psychiatry, 3615 Wisconsin Ave., N.W., Washington, DC 20016-3007; Title Tel # (202) 966-7300
Editorial Description: Medical contributions to knowledge and treatment of psychiatic problems.
General Info: Yr. Est. 1973, Trim Size-8½ x 11, 16 pages, 2 Color, Newsprint
Circulation: Total-3,200
Advertising: Inquire for rates.

AAPT News   CPM: $249

Publishing Co: American Association of Psychiatric Technicians, 1789 N. Neltnor Blvd., Suite #260, West Chicago, IL 60185-2997; Title Tel # (602) 623-0522 Title Fax # (602) 748-0458
Personnel: Editor-George Blake
Editorial Description: News about mental health workers, psychiatric technicians, human services workers behavioral health aide, and para professional and whats happening in APPT.
General Info: Yr. Est. 1992, Quarterly, Letrpr. press, 6 pages, No Color, Matte
Subscriptions: Indv. $24, Inst. $150, $4/copy
Circulation: Total-2,000
Advertising: $498.

ABA Newsletter   *Association*

Publishing Co: Association for Behavior Analysis, 560 White Plains Road, Tarrytown, NY 10591-5112 Fax # (616) 387-4457; Title Tel # (616) 387-4494
Personnel: Editor-Stephen Graf, Circ. Mgr., Adv. Dir.-Shery Chamberlain
Editorial Description: Information about assn. activities, members & news of interest to behavior analysts.
General Info: Yr. Est. 1974, Quarterly, Trim Size-8½ x 11, Offset press, 28 pages, 3% ads, Color-cover, Recycled, Saddle-stitched
Subscriptions: Indv. $15, Inst. $15, $5/copy
Circulation: (100% controlled)
Advertising: Inquire for rates.
List Rental: Actives: $50/M, Expires: $50/M

ADHD Report   *Consumer, Scholarly*

Publishing Co: Guilford Publications, Inc., 72 Spring Street, New York, NY 10012 Tel # (212) 431-9800 Fax # (212) 966-6708
Personnel: Publisher-Robert Mahoff, Editor-Russell Barkley, Circ. Mgr.-David Mitchell, Production Mgr.-Katya Edwards, Mktg. Dir.-Marian Robinson
Editorial Description: Addresses clinical implications of important recent scientific reports dealing with attention deficit disorders.
General Info: Yr. Est. 1993, Bi-monthly, Trim Size-8½ x 11, 16 pages, ISSN: 1065-8025, 2 Color, Matte
Subscriptions: Indv. $65, Inst. $88
Circulation: Total-4,530
List Rental: Rents Lists

AFTA Newsletter   *Association*

Publishing Co: American Family Therapy Assn., 2020 Penn. Ave. NW, #273, Washington, DC 20006; Title Tel # (202) 994-2776 Title Fax # (202) 994-4812
Personnel: Adv. Dir.-Silas Flashman
Editorial Description: Clinical therapists specially trained to work with couples and their families.
General Info: Yr. Est. 1977, Quarterly, Trim Size-7½ x 9¾, 50 pages, 1% ads, No Color
Subscriptions: Indv. $16, $4/copy
Circulation: Total-1,100
Advertising: Inquire for rates.
List Rental: Actives: $100/M

AMHA Leader   *Association*

Publishing Co: Assn. of Mental Health Administrators, 60 Revere Dr Ste 500, Northbrook, IL 60062-1577; Title Tel # (708) 480-9626 Title Fax # (708) 480-9282
Personnel: Editor-James Rayhall
Editorial Description: Topical issues of interest to our membership.
General Info: (Formerly Association of Mental Health Administrators, Newsletter), Monthly, Trim Size-11 x 17, Web press, 6 pages, No Color
Advertising: Inquire for rates.
List Rental: Actives: $200/M

AMHCA News   *Association*

Publishing Co: American Mental Health Counselors Assn., 5999 Stevenson Ave., Alexandria, VA 22304-3302; Title Tel # (703) 823-9800
Personnel: Publisher-John Moracco, Editor-Carol Hacker, Adv. Dir.-Jean McGreey
General Info: Yr. Est. 1977, Bi-monthly, Web press, 16 pages, 1% ads, No Color, Coated
Subscriptions: Indv. $30, $5/copy
Circulation: (100% controlled), Total-10,000
Advertising: Inquire for rates.
Printing Co: Craftmaster, 902 Geneva St, Opelika, AL 36801-5813 Tel # (334) 749-5611, Fax # (205) 745-4653

APS Observer   *Scholarly, Association*   CPM: $109

Publishing Co: American Psychological Society, 1010 Vermont Ave., NW, Ste. 1100, Washington, DC 20005 Tel # (202) 783-2077 Fax # (202) 783-2083
Personnel: Publisher-K. Lee Herring, Adv. Dir.-Elizabeth Ruksznis
Editorial Description: Covers national and international events, current activities and policy relevant to the Society or psychology. Also includes noteworthy research, announcements, and employment listings.
General Info: Yr. Est. 1989, Bi-monthly, Trim Size-8½ x 11, Offset press, 54 pages, ISSN: 1050-4672, 2 Color, Matte, Saddle-stitched
Subscriptions: Indv. $35, Inst. $50, For. $65
Circulation: (BPA), Total-13,262, Readership-13,762
Advertising: $1,450.
List Rental: Actives: 15,500, $100/M, Expires: 1,500, $90/M
Printing Co: Corporate Press, 403 Brightseat Rd., Landover, MD 20785-4706 Tel # (301) 499-9200, Fax # (301) 499-5435

ATP Newsletter

Publishing Co: Association for Transpersonal Psychology, Box 3049, Stanford, CA 94309-3049; Title Tel # (415) 327-2066
Personnel: Editor-Miles Vich
Editorial Description: Articles, information & announcements about psychology & spiritual issues, including therapy, education, research. Non-sectarian, cross-cultural & multi-disciplinary.
General Info: Yr. Est. 1974, Quarterly, 24 pages, 2% ads
Circulation: Total-2,500
Advertising: Inquire for rates.
List Rental: Actives: $75/M, Expires: $75/M

AWP Newsletter
Association for Women in Psychology   *Association*   CPM: $125

Publishing Co: Association for Women in Psychology, c/o Lynn Collins, Eastern Connecticut State Univ, 83 Windham Street, Willimantic, CT 06226-2295; Title Tel # (203) 465-4546
Personnel: Editor-Maryka Biaggio
Editorial Description: For practitioners in field of counseling and psychology.
General Info: Yr. Est. 1969, Quarterly, Trim Size-8½ x 11, Letrpr. press, 16 pages, No Color
Subscriptions: Indv. $50, $3/copy
Circulation: (100% controlled), Total-2,400
Advertising: $300.

Abortion Research Notes

Publishing Co: Transnational Family Research Inst, 8307 Whitman Dr, Bethesda, MD 20817-6820; Title Tel # (301) 469-6313 Title Fax # (301) 469-0461
Personnel: Editor-Dr. Henry David
Editorial Description: Psychosocial aspects of fertility behavior, and the contraception/abortion relationship.
General Info: Yr. Est. 1972, Offset press, 6 pages, ISSN: 0361-1116, 2 Color
Subscriptions: Indv. $25, Can. $25, For. $25
Circulation: (100% controlled), Total-3,000
Advertising: Accepts Inserts.

Abstract of Marital Relationship Analysis   *Consumer, Association*

Publishing Co: Maxiplan Financial Club, Box 5255 Stn. C, 12687 52nd Ave., Montreal, PQ H1E 2H6 Canada Tel # (514) 648-2953
Editorial Description: Covers bride & bridegroom's psychologies; men's needs; women's values; romantic attitudes; lifestyle choices and more.
General Info: Yr. Est. 1980, Quarterly
Subscriptions: Indv. $25, $10/copy

Advance   *Association*

Publishing Co: Assn. for the Advancement of Psychology, PO Box 38129, Colorado Springs, CO 80937-8129; Title Tel # (619) 297-7174
Personnel: Editor-Stephen Pfeiffer
Editorial Description: Primarily a government liason operation. Advocates for federal support of mental health/behavioral research.
General Info: Yr. Est. 1974, Quarterly, Trim Size-8½ x 11, Sheetfed press, 12 pages, 2 Color, Newsprint, Saddle-stitched
Circulation: (100% controlled), Total-7,500

Aid Bulletin - Addiction Intervention with the Disabled
See: PSYCHIATRY

Alfred Adler Institute Newsletter

Publishing Co: Alfred Adler Institute, 250 W 57th Street, #527, New York, NY 10107-0001; Title Tel # (212) 923-5600
General Info: Monthly

American Art Therapy Assn. -Newsletter
See: ART & SCULPTURE

American Group Psychotherapy Association Newsletter   *Association*

Publishing Co: American Group Psychotherapy Assn., 25 E 21st St Fl 6, New York, NY 10010-6207; Title Tel # (212) 477-2677
Editorial Description: Chief means of communication to and between membership. Contains news items on association committees, members and affiliate societies.
General Info: Quarterly, Trim Size-8½ x 11, Offset press, 10 pages, No Color
Subscriptions: Free
Circulation: Total-3,500
Advertising: Inquire for rates.

American Psychoanalyst, The
See: PSYCHIATRY

Amplifier

Publishing Co: Assn. for Media Psychology, 1525 San Vicente Blvd, Santa Monica, CA 90402-2205 Tel # (213) 394-4546
General Info: Yr. Est. 1982, Quarterly, 8 pages
Circulation: Total-300

Analytical Psychology Club of New York, Bulletin   *Association*

Publishing Co: Analytical Psychology Club of New York, 28 E 39th St, New York, NY 10016-2555; Title Tel # (212) 697-7877
Personnel: Publisher-Carl Rieser
Editorial Description: Newsletter reporting the activities of a club devoted to analytical (Jungian) psychology.
General Info: Yr. Est. 1937, 8x/yr., Trim Size-7 x 8½, Offset press, 8 pages
Circulation: (100% controlled), Total-300

Association for Child Psychoanalysis Newsletter   *Association*

Publishing Co: Association for Child Psychoanalysis, 320 Glendale Dr, Chapel Hill, NC 27514-5914; Title Tel # (919) 967-5819
Personnel: Editor-Paul Brinich, PhD
Editorial Description: Publishes news relevant to members of the Association for Child Psychoanalysis.
General Info: Yr. Est. 1965, Tri-annually, Trim Size-8½ x 11, Desktop press, 24 pages, ISSN: 1077-0305, Color-cover, Matte, Saddle-stitched
Subscriptions: Indv. $20, Free With Membership
Circulation: Total-1,100

Association for Past-Life Research & Therapies   *Consumer, Association*   CPM: $250

Publishing Co: Assn. for Past Life Research & Therapies, Inc., 6825 D. Magnolia Avenue, Riverside, CA 92516-0151; Title Tel # (909) 784-1570 Title Fax # (909) 784-8440
Personnel: Editor-Terry Nash
Editorial Description: Concerned with techniques & research in the field of past-life therapy. Articles & news events.
General Info: (Formerly Newsletter of the Assn. for Past-Life Research & Therapies), Yr. Est. 1980, Quarterly, Trim Size-8½ x 11, Desktop press, 12 pages, ISSN: 1054-0792, 3% ads, Color, Matte
Subscriptions: Indv. $10, Can. $15, For. $18, $5/copy
Circulation: Total-1,000
Advertising: $250.
List Rental: Actives: $100/M
Printing Co: Postal Instant Print, 4023 Main St, Riverside, CA 92501-3701 Tel # (714) 682-2005

Association for Transpersonal Psychology, Newsletter   *Association*

Publishing Co: Transpersonal Institute, Box 3049, Stanford, CA 94309; Title Tel # (415) 327-2066
Editorial Description: News about Assn. for Transpersonal Psychology, & developemnts in transpersonal field.
General Info: Yr. Est. 1971, Quarterly, Trim Size-8½ x 11, Sheetfed press, 16 pages, No Color, Newsprint
Circulation: Total-2,600
Advertising: Inquire for rates.
List Rental: Actives: 14,000, $75/M

B.E.A.M. (Being Energetic About Multiplicity)   *Consumer*

Publishing Co: B.E.A.M., PO Box 20428, Louisville, KY 40250-0428; Title Fax # (502) 499-7796
Personnel: Publisher, Editor-Beth Hafling
General Info: Yr. Est. 1992, Bi-monthly, Trim Size-8½ x 11, Desktop press, 20 pages, ISSN: 1062-9750, No Color, Matte
Subscriptions: Inst. $20, Can. $25, For. $28, $3/copy
Acquistions: Publication Sold
Circulation: Total-6,150
Advertising: Accepts Inserts.

Bell, The   *Consumer, Association*

Publishing Co: National Mental Health Association, 1021 Prince St., Alexandria, VA 22314-2971; Title Tel # (703) 684-7722 Title Fax # (703) 684-5968
Personnel: Editor-Krista Hopkins
Editorial Description: Natl. mental health legislation, new developments in the field of prevention & treatment, & new mental health materials, upcoming mental health meetings.
General Info: (Formerly Focus), Yr. Est. 1995, Quarterly, Trim Size-11 x 17, Sheetfed press, 8 pages, 2 Color, Coated
Subscriptions: Indv. $18, $5/copy
Circulation: Total-1,500

Biological Therapies in Psychiatry Newsletter   *Association*

Publishing Co: Mosby, 11830 Westline Industrial Dr., St. Louis, MO 63146-3313 Parent Co.-Times Mirror Company, Los Angeles; Title Tel # (314) 872-8370 Title Fax # (314) 432-1380
Personnel: Editor-Alan J. Gelenberg, MD
Editorial Description: Examines uses of biological therapy methods in current psychiatric research & practice.
General Info: (Formerly Biological Therapies in Psychiatry), Yr. Est. 1977, Monthly, ISSN: 1044-422X
Subscriptions: Indv. $52, Inst. $70, Can. $63, For. $59, $8/copy
List Rental: Rents Lists

Bresler Center News
See: MEDICINE

Bridging The Gap
See: PHILOSOPHY

Brookridge Forum
See: HOSPITALS & NURSING HOMES

Bulletin of the Ontario Bd. of Examiners in Psychology   *Association*

Publishing Co: The College of Psychology of Ontario, 1246 Yonge Street, Suite 201, Toronto, ON M4T 1W5 Canada; Title Tel # (416) 961-8817
Personnel: Editor-Barbara Wand
Editorial Description: Articles of interest to the profession.
General Info: Yr. Est. 1960, Quarterly, Trim Size-8½ x 11, 4 pages, 2 Color
Subscriptions: $3/copy
Circulation: Total-1,900

CANCH-Gram
See: DISABILITY

CBASSE Newsletter
See: SOCIOLOGY

C.G. Jung Foundation
Newsletter

Publishing Co: C.G. Jung Foundation for Analytical Psychology, Inc., 28 E 39th St, New York, NY 10016-2555; Title Tel # (212) 697-6430
Personnel: Editor-Marci McGill

Cal Fam   *Consumer, Association*

Publishing Co: Phillips Graduate Institute, 5433 Laurel Canyon Blvd, North Hollywood, CA 91607-2193; Title Tel # (818) 509-5959
Editorial Description: News and information about the programs and people at the California Family Study Center.
General Info: Quarterly, Trim Size-8¹/₂ x 11, 20 pages, 2 Color, Matte, Saddle-stitched

Capitol Capsule
See: DISABILITY

Center for Creative Leadership
See: MANAGEMENT

Cheiron Newsletter   *Association*   **CPM: $750**

Publishing Co: Cheiron: The Intl. Soc. of the History of Behavioral and Soc, c/o Rare Bks. Countway Lib.Med, 10 Shattuck St., Boston, MA 02115; Title Tel # (617) 432-2147
Personnel: Editor-Eugene Taylor
Editorial Description: Interested in the history of the behavioral and social sciences.
General Info: Yr. Est. 1968, Semi-annually
Subscriptions: Indv. $10, Inst. $25
Circulation: Total-400
Advertising: $300.

Child and Adolescent Psychopharmacology News   *Consumer, Scholarly*   **CPM: $125**

Publishing Co: Guilford Publications, Inc., 72 Spring Street, New York, NY 10012 Tel # (212) 431-9800 Fax # (212) 966-6708
Personnel: Publisher-Robert Mattlott, Editor-Stanley Kutcher, Circ. Mgr.-David Mitchell
Editorial Description: Addresses issues relalted to psychopharmacology for children and addescents, such as with drugs work; drug interactions; treatment plans.
General Info: Yr. Est. 1996, Bi-monthly, Trim Size-8¹/₂ x 11, 12 pages, ISSN: 1085-0295
Subscriptions: Indv. $99, Inst. $125, $16/copy
Circulation: Total-2,000
Advertising: $250. Accepts Inserts.
List Rental: Rents Lists

Child Assessment News   *Scholarly, Association*   **CPM: $234**

Publishing Co: Guilford Publications, Inc., 72 Spring Street, New York, NY 10012 Tel # (212) 431-9800 Fax # (212) 966-6708
Personnel: Publisher-Robert Matloff, Editor-Randy Kamphaus, Circ. Mgr.-David Mitchell, Production Mgr.-Katya Edwards, Mktg. Dir.-Marian Robinson
Editorial Description: Devoted to the psychological and educational asssessment of children and adolescents. Presents new techniques, issues, and research findings emphasizing their implications for practice and further research.
General Info: Yr. Est. 1990, Bi-monthly, Trim Size-8¹/₂ x 11, 12 pages, ISSN: 1055-0518, 2 Color, Matte
Subscriptions: Indv. $70, Inst. $88, Can. $88
Circulation: Total-1,065
Advertising: $250. Accepts Inserts.
List Rental: Rents Lists

Children's Residential Treatment News

Publishing Co: American Association of Children's Residential Centers, 1021 Prince Street, Alexandria, VA 22314 Tel # (703) 838-7522 Fax # (703) 684-5968; Title Tel # (202) 638-1604 Title Fax # (202) 638-4004
Personnel: Publisher, Editor-Claudia Waller
Editorial Description: Contains news of politics, policy & practice in residential treatment.
General Info: (Formerly American Association of Children's Residential Centers), Yr. Est. 1957, Quarterly, Desktop press, 14 pages, 2 Color, Newsprint
Subscriptions: Free With Membership
Circulation: Total-375
Printing Co: Minuteman Press, 400 New Jersey Ave NW, Washington, DC 20001-2097

Clinician's Research Digest   *Association*

Publishing Co: American Psychological Association, 750 First St., NE, Washington, DC 20002-4242 Tel # (202) 336-5500 Fax # (202) 336-5568; Title Tel # (202) 336-5600
Personnel: Publisher-Susan Knapp, Editor-Douglas K. Snyder, Ph.D., Circ. Mgr.-Jaunita Brodie, Adv. Dir.-Jodi Ashcraft
Editorial Description: Selections from over 50 journals each month are highlighted in this 6-page monthly newsletter. Complete citations and the author's address accompany each summary.
General Info: Monthly, ISSN: 8756-3207
Subscriptions: Indv. $73, Inst. $97, For. $138
Circulation: Total-4,720
List Rental: Actives: 5,070, $110/M
Printing Co: Mt. Vernon Printing, 3229 Hubbard Rd, Landover, MD 20785-2008 Tel # (301) 341-5600, Fax # (301) 341-1359

Clio's Pscyhe   *Consumer, Scholarly*

Publishing Co: Psychohistory Forum, 627 Dakota Trail, Franklin Lakes, NJ 07417; Title Tel # (201) 891-6866 Title Fax # (201) 848-0454
Personnel: Editor-Paul Elovitz, Assoc. Ed.-Bob Lentz
Editorial Description: Examines the 'why' of history.
General Info: Yr. Est. 1994, Quarterly, Trim Size-8¹/₂ x 11, 16 pages, No Color, Matte
Subscriptions: Indv. $18, Can. $22

College of Psychologists of New Brunswick, Bulletin

Publishing Co: College of Psychologists of New Brunswick, Box 1194, Sta. A, Fredericton, NB E3B 5C8 Canada
General Info: Quarterly

Communique   *Association*

Publishing Co: Natl. Assn. of School Psychologists, 4340 East West Hwy., Ste. 402, Bethesda, MD 20814 Tel # (301) 567-0270; Title Tel # (301) 657-0270 Title Fax # (301) 657-0275
Personnel: Publisher, Editor-Alex Thomas
Editorial Description: Professional newsletter for National Association of School Psychologists; members free.
General Info: Yr. Est. 1969, 8x/yr., Sheetfed press, 28 pages, ISSN: 0164-775X, 3% ads, 2 Color
Subscriptions: Indv. $30, $4/copy
Circulation: (100% controlled), Total-11,000
Advertising: Inquire for rates.
List Rental: Rents Lists

Connection   *Business*

Publishing Co: Center for the Behavioral Sciences, 33 Kirkland St # 280, Cambridge, MA 02138-2044; Title Tel # (617) 495-3801
Personnel: Publisher, Editor-Dean Gallant, Production Mgr.-William Santoro
Editorial Description: Weekly newsletter, center for the behavioral sciences.
General Info: (Formerly L'Habitant), Yr. Est. 1965, Weekly, Mimeo press, 2 pages, No Color
Subscriptions: Indv. $5
Circulation: Total-300

Correctional Psychologist, The   *Association*

Publishing Co: American Assn. for Correctional Psychology, WV Graduate College, 100 Angus E. Peyton Drive, South Charleston, WV 25303-1600 Tel # (304) 746-1929; Title Tel # (304) 766-1929 Title Fax # (304) 766-1942
Personnel: Editor-Robt Smith
Editorial Description: Newsletter for the Amer. Assn. for Correctional Psychology. Reports on work by mental health/human services personnel employed in corrections & the academic community.
General Info: (Formerly Correctional Psychology), Yr. Est. 1953, Quarterly, Trim Size-8¹/₂ x 11, 14 pages
Subscriptions: Indv. $45
Circulation: Total-350
Advertising: Inquire for rates.

Cross-Cultural Psychology Bulletin   *Association*

Publishing Co: International Association for Cross-Cultural Psychology, 2765-5 Woodlake SW, Wyoming, MI 49509
Personnel: Editor-John Adamopoulos
General Info: Yr. Est. 1966, Quarterly
Subscriptions: Indv. $25

Culture & Psychology
See: CULTURE & HUMANITIES

Diplomate   *Association*

Publishing Co: American Board of Professional Psychology, 2100 E Broadway Ste 313, Columbia, MO 65201-6082; Title Tel # (573) 875-1267 Title Fax # (573) 443-1199
Personnel: Publisher-Nicholas Palo, Editor-Robert Goldberg
Editorial Description: A semi-annual newsletter of the board.
General Info: Yr. Est. 1980, Semi-annually, Offset press, 8 pages, Color, Newsprint, Saddle-stitched
Subscriptions: Free To Qualified Recipient
Circulation: Total-3,000

Dramascope   *Association*

Publishing Co: National Association for Drama Therapy, 44 Taylor Street, Branford, CT 06405 Tel # (203) 481-1161; Title Tel # (713) 538-1689
Personnel: Editor-Thelma McDaniel
General Info: Yr. Est. 1979, Semi-annually, 12 pages
Subscriptions: Free With Membership
Circulation: Total-500
Advertising: Inquire for rates.
List Rental: Rents Lists

EHE News
See: PARAPSYCHOLOGY

EcoPsychology Newsletter   *Business, Consumer*

Publishing Co: EcoPsychology Newsletter, PO Box 7487, Berkeley, CA 94707-0487
Editorial Description: Covers psychological issues related to environmental concerns,
General Info: Yr. Est. 1994, Tri-annually
Subscriptions: Indv. $10

Efficient Auditor
Business

Publishing Co: Audit/Watch, Inc., PO Box 1181, Annandale, VA 22003-9181; Title Tel # (703) 354-6834
Personnel: Publisher, Editor-Thomas Houck
Editorial Description: For improving then efficiency of the auditing process.
General Info: Yr. Est. 1994, Quarterly
Subscriptions: Indv. $29

Essence of Adolescence

Publishing Co: PeopleScience, 1015 S Park Ave, Highland Park, NJ 08904-2954; Title Tel # (908) 572-3120
Personnel: Publisher, Editor-Fred Streit
Editorial Description: A monthly abstract of current research about the adolescent.
General Info: Yr. Est. 1975, Monthly, Trim Size-8½ x 11, Offset press, 8 pages, 2 Color, Saddle-stitched
Subscriptions: Indv. $25, $3/copy
Circulation: Total-2,200

Express (l'Express)
Association

Publishing Co: Societe Quebecoise de l'Autisme/Quebec Society for Autism, 2300 Blvd. Rene Levesque Quest, Montreal, PQ H3H 2R5 Canada Fax # (514) 931-2397; Title Tel # (514) 931-2215
General Info: Quarterly, 28 pages
Circulation: Total-400

FMS Foundation
See: SOCIAL SERVICES & WELFARE

Florida Psychologist
Association **CPM: $138**

Publishing Co: Florida Psychological Assn., 408 Office Plz, Tallahassee, FL 32301-2757; Title Tel # (904) 656-2222 Title Fax # (904) 942-4586
Personnel: Editor-D. Michelle Morris
Editorial Description: News of interest to Florida Psychologists.
General Info: (Formerly FP), Yr. Est. 1950, Bi-monthly, 24 pages, 3% ads, No Color, Coated, Saddle-stitched
Subscriptions: Indv. $60
Circulation: Total-1,800
Advertising: $250. Accepts Inserts.
List Rental: Actives $100/M
Printing Co: Gandy Printers, 1800 S Monroe St, Tallahassee, FL 32301-5528 Tel # (904) 222-5847

GEI Newsletter

Publishing Co: Grief Education Institute, 4596 E Iliff Ave, Denver, CO 80222-6021; Title Tel # (303) 758-6048
Personnel: Editor-Holly Emrich
General Info: Quarterly
Subscriptions: Indv. $5

Geriatric Psychiatry News
Association

Publishing Co: American Association for Geriatric Psychiatry, 7910 Woodmont Ave., Ste. 700, Bethesda, MD 02814-3015; Title Tel # (301) 220-0952
Personnel: Editor-Jonathan D. Liess
Editorial Description: Promote better understanding and care of the mental health of the elderly.
General Info: (Formerly AAGP Newsletter), Yr. Est. 1978, Quarterly
Circulation: Readership-1,500

Group Circle
Association **CPM: $290**

Publishing Co: AGPA, 25 E. 21st St., 6th Fl., New York, NY 10010-6296; Title Tel # (212) 477-2677 Title Fax # (212) 979-9627
Personnel: Editor-Elizabeth Knight, MSW
Editorial Description: Covers issues relevant to field of group psychotherapy.
General Info: (Formerly AGPA Newsletter), Quarterly, Trim Size-11 x 15, Web press, 16 pages, 2 Color, Recycled, Saddle-stitched
Subscriptions: Free With Membership
Circulation: Total-4,300
Advertising: $1,250.
List Rental: Rents Lists
Printing Co: Cunningham Graphics, Inc., 629 Grove Street, Jersey City, NJ 07319 Tel # (201) 217-1990

Growing Together
See: CHILDREN

Growing Up
See: CHILDREN

Harvard Mental Health Letter
Business, Consumer

Publishing Co: Harvard Medical School Health Publications Group, 164 Longwood Ave, Fl. 1, Boston, MA 02115-5818 Tel # (617) 432-1802 Fax # (617) 432-1506; Title Tel # (617) 432-1485
Personnel: Publisher-Andrea Graham, Editor-Lester Grinspoon, MD, Production Mgr.-Timothy Evans
Editorial Description: Features information on mental health issues. Recently explored topics include child abuse, self help groups and false memory syndrome. Written for the professional and interested lay person by doctors at Harvard Medical School.
General Info: Yr. Est. 1984, Monthly, Trim Size-8½ x 11, 8 pages, ISSN: 0884-3783, 2 Color, Matte, Saddle-stitched
Subscriptions: Indv. $48
Circulation: Total-60,000
List Rental: List Management Co.: The Lake Group, 411 Theodore Freund Ave., Rye, NY 10580-1497 Tel # (914) 925-2400, Fax # (914) 925-2499, Actives: 52,363, $90/M, Hotline: $5/M

Highlights
Association

Publishing Co: Canadian Psychological Assn., 6 Vincent Rd., Old Chelsea, PQ J0X 1N0 Canada; Title Tel # (819) 827-3927
Personnel: Editor-Brenda Stoneham
Editorial Description: Association news, employment news, calendar of events.
General Info: Quarterly, Trim Size-10½ x 15, Web press, 24 pages, 1% ads, No Color
Subscriptions: Indv. $10
Circulation: Total-4,200
Advertising: Inquire for rates.

Hot Flash
Consumer, Association

Publishing Co: National Action Forum Midlife & Older Women, PO Box 816, Stony Brook, NY 11790-0816
Personnel: Editor-Jane Porcino, Circ. Mgr.-Judith Shivak
Editorial Description: Covers health & social issues for midlife & older women.
General Info: Yr. Est. 1981, Quarterly, 12 pages, No Color
Subscriptions: Indv. $25, Inst. $35, For. $30
Circulation: Total-1,800

Huna Work
See: RELIGIOUS & THEOLOGICAL

Hypnotherapy in Review
Association

Publishing Co: Academy of Scientific Hypnotherapy, PO Box 12041, San Diego, CA 92112-3041; Title Tel # (619) 427-6225 Title Fax # (619) 427-5650
Personnel: Editor-Sandy Pasqua
General Info: Yr. Est. 1977, Irregular, Sheetfed press, 4 pages, No Color, Newsprint
Subscriptions: Free To Qualified Recipient
Circulation: Total-2,000
Advertising: Accepts Inserts.

Hypnotherapy Today
See: HYPNOSIS

IPS Report
Association

Publishing Co: Illinois Psychiatric Society, 20 N. Michigan Ave., #700, Chicago, IL 60602-4811; Title Tel # (312) 263-7391 Title Fax # (312) 263-7391
Personnel: Editor-Richard Baer, Production Mgr.-Marty Wisler
Editorial Description: News and discussion of issues related to psychiatry in Illinois.
General Info: Bi-monthly, Trim Size-8½ x 11, Offset press, 4 pages, 2 Color, Newsprint
Circulation: (100% controlled), Total-1,500
Advertising: Accepts Inserts.

ISSD News
Association **CPM: $151**

Publishing Co: Intl. Soc. for Study of Multiple Personality & Dissociation, 4700 W. Lake Ave., Glenvieww, IL 60025; Title Tel # (847) 375-4718 Title Fax # (847) 375-4777
Personnel: Editor-Bennett G. Braun, M.D., Mng. Editor-Juliette Kurtz, Editorial Asst.-Carol Dikelsky, Adv. Dir.-Kathryn Checea, Production Mgr., Art Dir.-Dot Vartan, Natl. Sales Rep.-Michelle Ginocchio
Editorial Description: Newsletter for members of the International Society for the Study of Dissociation. It focuses on association news, educational topics, and areas of research in the field.
General Info: Yr. Est. 1982, Bi-monthly, 16 pages
Subscriptions: Free With Membership
Circulation: Total-2,600
Advertising: $395.
List Rental: Rents Lists
Printing Co: Sundance Press, 817 E 18th St, Tucson, AZ 85719-6614 Tel # (602) 622-5233, Fax # (602) 620-1593

Icarus File, The
See: HOSPITALS & NURSING HOMES

Idaho Guidance News

Publishing Co: Idaho Personnel, College of Education Univ., Moscow, ID 83843
Personnel: Editor-Thomas Fairchild
Circulation: Total-250

Imagery Today
Association

Publishing Co: International Imagery Association, PO Box 1046, Bronx, NY 10471-0618
Personnel: Editor-Akhter Ahsen, Ph.D.
General Info: Yr. Est. 1982, Semi-annually, Trim Size-8½ x 11, Sheetfed press, 4 pages, Other
Subscriptions: Indv. $10
Circulation: Total-3,314

Independent Thinking Review
See: EDUCATION

Interbehaviorist

Publishing Co: Univ. of Kansas Dept of Human Development, Univ. Of Kansas, Haworth Hall, Lawrence, KS 66045-0001; Title Tel # (913) 864-4840
Personnel: Publisher, Editor-Edward Morris
Editorial Description: News & articles on interbehavioral psychology; integrated field in perspective.
General Info: Yr. Est. 1970, Quarterly, Sheetfed press, 12 pages, ISSN: 8755-612X, 1% ads
Subscriptions: Indv. $6, Inst. $12, $2/copy
Advertising: Inquire for rates.
List Rental: Rents Lists
Printing Co: Univ. Of Kansas Printing Service, 2425 W 15th St, Lawrence, KS 66049-3903 Tel # (913) 864-4341

Interchange, The   *Business*

Publishing Co: Institute for Psychosocial Studies, Bldg. G, Executive Quarters, 2300 Computer Road, Willow Grove, PA 19090-9872
Editorial Description: Information for the mental health professional about industry issues and concerns.
General Info: Yr. Est. 1992, Monthly
Subscriptions: Indv. $39

International Psychologist   *Association*   CPM: $75

Publishing Co: Intl. Council of Psychologists, SW Texas State Univ., Psychology Dept., San Marcos, TX 78666-4601
Personnel: Publisher-Dr. Patricia Fontes, Editor-Dr. Carleton Shay
Editorial Description: Psychological developments of international interest; cross cultural research; calendar of international conferences. Contributions of psychology on international level.
General Info: Yr. Est. 1945, Quarterly, Trim Size-8½ x 11, Offset press, 24 pages, ISSN: 0047-116X, No Color
Subscriptions: Indv. $24, Free With Membership
Circulation: Total-2,000
Advertising: $150.

Jerome Riker Intl. Study of Organized Persecution of Children Newsletter
See: CHILDREN

Journal Watch for Psychiatry
See: PSYCHIATRY

Jung at Heart   *Consumer*

Publishing Co: Inner City Books, Box 1271, Station Q, Toronto, ON M4T 2P4 Canada; Title Tel # (416) 927-0355 Title Fax # (416) 924-1814
Personnel: Publisher, Editor-Daryl Sharp
Editorial Description: Written to promote understanding and practical application of Jung's work.
General Info: Yr. Est. 1981, Quarterly, Trim Size-8½ x 11, 4 pages, No Color, Matte
Subscriptions: Free To Qualified Recipient
Circulation: Total-25,000
List Rental: Actives: 12,000, $80/M

Linkage   *Consumer, Association*

Publishing Co: Maryland Dept. of Mental Health, 201 W Preston St, Ste.416A, Baltimore, MD 21201-2323; Title Tel # (410) 225-6611 Title Fax # (410) 335-5402
Personnel: Editor-Jean Smith
Editorial Description: Conveys news of activities in the mental health field for the Dept, in the State of Md from State facilities, Community Mental Health Programs, Advocacy groups and Private mental health facilities-general psychiatric hospitals.
General Info: (Formerly Maryland Mental Health, Newsletter), Yr. Est. 1976, Trim Size-8½ x 11, Web press, 6 pages, 2 Color, Coated
Subscriptions: Free
Circulation: (100% controlled), Total-1,100
Advertising: Accepts Inserts.
Printing Co: The Printery, 800 Snow Hill Rd, Salisbury, MD 21801-1938 Tel # (410) 749-2776

MAPS Newsletter   *Association*

Publishing Co: Multidisciplinary Association of Psychedelic Studies, 1801 Tippah Ave, Charlotte, NC 28205-3048 Tel # (704) 358-9830 Fax # (704) 358-1650
Editorial Description: News and information from the association on psyhcedelic research and studies.
General Info: Quarterly, Trim Size-8½ x 11, 4 pages, No Color, Matte

Massachusetts Psychological Center Employment Bulletin

Publishing Co: Massachusetts Psychological Center, Inc., 25 Huntington Ave Ste 300, Boston, MA 02116-5713; Title Tel # (619) 261-8585
General Info: Yr. Est. 1971, Bi-monthly
Subscriptions: Indv. $6, $1/copy

Mastering Life
See: SEX

Meditator's Newsletter
See: RELIGIOUS & THEOLOGICAL

Menninger Letter, The   *Consumer*

Publishing Co: Menninger Clinic, PO Box 829, Topeka, KS 66601-0829 Fax # (913) 273-8625; Title Tel # (913) 273-7500 Title Fax # (913) 273-9150
Personnel: Mng. Editor, Editorial Asst.-Mary Ann Clifft, MS, Clinical Ed.-Glen O. Gabbard, MD, Circ. Mgr.-Melba Ludvicek
Editorial Description: Your national resource for mental health.
General Info: Yr. Est. 1993, Monthly, Trim Size-8½ x 11, Desktop press, 8 pages, ISSN: 1066-937X, 2 Color, Matte
Subscriptions: Indv. $24, $4/copy
Circulation: Total-65,000
List Rental: List Management Co.: List Services Corp., 6 Trowbridge Dr., PO Box 516, Bethel, CT 06801-2858 Tel # (203) 743-2600, Fax # (203) 743-0589, Actives: 75,400, Expires: 50,000
Printing Co: Tempographics, 455 E North Ave, Carol Stream, IL 60188-2167 Tel # (708) 462-8200, Fax # (708) 462-0350

Mental Health Law Reporter
See: LAW

Mental Health Law Reporter   *Business*

Publishing Co: Business Publishers, Inc., 951 Pershing Dr., Silver Spring, MD 20910-4464 Tel # (301) 589-5103 Fax # (301) 589-8493; Title Tel # (301) 587-6300 Title Fax # (301) 587-1081
Personnel: Publisher-Eric Easton, Editor-Lisa Rabasca, Circ. Mgr.-Kathleen Harrow, Promotion Dir.-Pat Nussman
Editorial Description: Covers news and events in field and gives readers current strategies to receive funds from public and private sources.
General Info: (Formerly Mental Health Report), Yr. Est. 1976, Bi-weekly, Trim Size-8½ x 11, Desktop press, 8 pages, Ind/Abs/Online: Newsnet
Subscriptions: Indv. $325, Can. $325, For. $338
Advertising: Accepts Inserts.
List Rental: List Management Co.: Manager: Don Peterson; BPI Direct, 951 Pershing Dr., Silver Spring, MD 20910-4464 Tel # (301) 585-5976, Fax # (301) 587-4530

Mental Health News Alert
See: PHILANTHROPY

Mental Health Society Staten Island, News

Publishing Co: Mental Health Society, 657 Castleton Ave, Staten Island, NY 10301-2028
Personnel: Editor-Edward Nachison
Editorial Description: Covers community metal health.
General Info: Yr. Est. 1966, Quarterly
Subscriptions: Indv. $3

Mental Health Statistical Notes   *Association*

Publishing Co: Natl. Institute of Mental Health, 5600 Fischers Lane, Rockville, MD 20852-1750; Title Tel # (301) 443-3343
Editorial Description: Data collected from mental health facilities concerning their patients, staff and administrative data.
General Info: Yr. Est. 1969, Trim Size-7¾ x 10¼, Offset press, 25 pages, Ind/Abs/Online: IN. MED.
Circulation: (100% controlled), Total-4,000

Mental Health Weekly
See: HEALTH

Mental Medicine Update   *Consumer, Association*

Publishing Co: Center for Health Sciences, The, PO Box 176, Los Altos, CA 94023-0176
Personnel: Co-Editor-Robert Ornstein, Co-Editor-David Sobel, Circ. Mgr.-Jill Barnes, Production Mgr.-Maryann Cammarota
Editorial Description: Covers the new science of mood medicine for health professionals and laypersons.
General Info: Yr. Est. 1993, Tri-annually, Trim Size-8½ x 11, 8 pages, 2 Color, Matte
Subscriptions: Indv. $10
Circulation: Total-10,000
List Rental: List Management Co.: Pacific Lists, 100 Tamal Plaza Ste 50, Corte Madera, CA 94925 Tel # (415) 945-9450, Fax # (415) 945-9451

Mental Research Institute Newsletter

Publishing Co: Mental Research Institute, 555 Middlefield Rd, Palo Alto, CA 94301-2124; Title Tel # (415) 321-3055
Editorial Description: Information in the field of family therapy and MRI news.
General Info: Yr. Est. 1960, Annually, 4 pages, 2 Color
Circulation: Total-14,000

Mid Life Woman
See: WOMEN'S

Mind Science Foundation News

Publishing Co: Mind Science Foundation, 7979 Broadway St Ste 100, San Antonio, TX 78209-2657; Title Tel # (512) 821-6094
General Info: Yr. Est. 1977, Quarterly
Subscriptions: Indv. $25
Circulation: Total-550

Mind/Body Medicine Newsletter, The
See: HEALTH

Mini Examiner Newsletter   *Business, Consumer*

Publishing Co: Mini Examiner, Box 3893-SPD, Chatsworth, CA 91313-3893; Title Tel # (818) 347-6949
Personnel: Publisher-Irene Stephenson, Editor-Irene Hamlen Stephenson
Editorial Description: Biorhythm character and compatibility analysis of the famous and ordinary.
General Info: (Formerly Truth, The), Yr. Est. 1979, Semi-monthly, Mimeo press, 4 pages, No Color
Subscriptions: Indv. $17, $1/copy
Circulation: Total-1,100
List Rental: Rents Lists

Multiple Linear Regression
Viewpoints

Publishing Co: Behavioral Studies Dept., Univ. of Missouri, St. Louis, MO 63121-4499; Title Tel # (314) 553-5785 Title Fax # (314) 553-5227
Editorial Description: Articles dealing with the theory and application of multiple linear regression.
General Info: Trim Size-7 x 8½, Desktop press, 100 pages, Recycled, Case bound
Subscriptions: Indv. $10, Inst. $18

NAAP News   *Business, Association*

Publishing Co: National Association for the Advancement of Psychoanalysis, 80 Eighth Avenue, Suite 1501, New York, NY 10011; Title Tel # (212) 741-0515
Editorial Description: Association and psychoanalysis industry news.
General Info: Quarterly, Trim Size-11 x 17, 6 pages, No Color, Matte
Advertising: $600.

NMHA Prevention Update   *Scholarly, Association*

Publishing Co: National Mental Health Association, 1021 Prince St., Alexandria, VA 22314-2971 Tel # (703) 684-7722; Title Tel # (703) 838-7511 Title Fax # (703) 684-5968
Personnel: Editor-Krista Hopkins
Editorial Description: Prevention advocacy news, research updates, program information, general prevention resource.
General Info: Yr. Est. 1989, Quarterly, Trim Size-8½ x 11, Sheetfed press, 16 pages, 2 Color, Coated, Saddle-stitched
Subscriptions: Indv. $85, Inst. $125
Circulation: Total-1,000, Readership-1,000
Advertising: Inquire for rates.

N.P.A.P. News & Reviews   *Association*

Publishing Co: National Psychological Assn. for Psychoanalysis, 43 5th Ave, New York, NY 10003-4368
Personnel: Editor-Harvey Kaplan, Mng. Editor-Carl Jacobs
Editorial Description: News for and about members of the Natl. Psychological Assn. for Psychoanalysis.
General Info: Quarterly, Trim Size-8½ x 11, 8 pages, Matte
Subscriptions: Free With Membership

National Character Laboratory-Newsletter
See: MEDICINE

New Sense Bulletin
See: SOCIOLOGY

New York State
Psychologists   *Association*   CPM: $171

Publishing Co: Foundation of NYS Psychological Assn., Executive Park East, Albany, NY 12203-3513; Title Tel # (518) 456-7735 Title Fax # (518) 456-7823
Personnel: Editor-Diane Kermani, Staff Writer-R.K. Stevens, Adv. Dir.-Tammy St. Louis
Editorial Description: Yearly round-up of all activities & programs involving psychology for NYS psychologists.
General Info: Yr. Est. 1989, Quarterly, Trim Size-8½ x 11, Web press, 60 pages, ISSN: 0028-7687, 20% ads, Color-cover, Newsprint, Saddle-stitched
Subscriptions: Indv. $75, $1/copy
Circulation: Total-3,500
Advertising: $600.
List Rental: Rents Lists

Newsletter from Dick B on The Spiritual Roots of AA
See: HEALTH

Newsletter of the
Freudian Field

Publishing Co: Univ. of Florida English Dept., 4008 Turlington, Gainesville, FL 32611; Title Tel # (904) 377-7026
Personnel: Publisher, Editor-Ellie Ragland-Sulliva, Circ. Mgr., Adv. Dir.-Craig Saper, Art Dir.-Cheryl Kirkland
General Info: Yr. Est. 1987, Semi-annually, Web press, 96 pages, ISSN: 0894-1750, Color-cover
Subscriptions: Indv. $10, Inst. $12
Circulation: Total-1,000
Advertising: Inquire for rates.
List Rental: Actives: $500/M
Printing Co: Boyd Brothers, 425 E 15th St, Panama City, FL 32405-5498 Tel # (904) 763-1471, Fax # (904) 769-6526

Newslink

Publishing Co: American Association of Suicidology, 2459 S Ash St, Denver, CO 80222-6006; Title Tel # (303) 692-0985 Title Fax # (303) 756-3299
Personnel: Editor-Julie Perlman
Editorial Description: AAS networking newsletter.
General Info: Quarterly, 8 pages, 1% ads

Noetic Sciences Bulletin
See: PHILOSOPHY

North American Society
of Adlerian Psychology,
Newsletter   *Association*

Publishing Co: North American Society of Adlerian Psychology, 65 E Wacker Pl Ste 400, Chicago, IL 60601-7203; Title Tel # (312) 629-8801 Title Fax # (312) 201-5917
Personnel: Editor, News Ed.-Jerianne Garber
Editorial Description: Events, newsnotes, and articles of general interest to NASAP membership.
General Info: (Formerly American Society of Adlerian Psychology Newsletter), Yr. Est. 1967, Bi-monthly, Trim Size-8½ x 11, 7 pages, ISSN: 0889-9428, 2 Color, Newsprint
Subscriptions: Indv. $10, Can. $10, Free
Circulation: Total-1,100, Readership-1,100
Advertising: Inquire for rates.
Printing Co: Reinhardt-LaShore Press, 1104 S. Wabash Ave., Chicago, IL 60605 Tel # (312) 427-7377, Fax # (312) 427-0970

On Location

Publishing Co: Staten Island Mental Health Society, Inc., 669 Castleton Ave, Staten Island, NY 10301-2028; Title Tel # (718) 442-2225 Title Fax # (718) 442-2289
Personnel: Editor-Susan Avery-Hermidaz
Editorial Description: Informs readers of programs & events which are operated by the Staten Island Mental Health Society.
General Info: Yr. Est. 1966, Quarterly, Letrpr. press, 4 pages, 2 Color, Coated, Saddle-stitched
Circulation: (17% controlled)
Advertising: Inquire for rates.
Printing Co: Royal Press, 1973 Forest Ave, Staten Island, NY 10303-2199 Tel # (718) 447-2358

One Spirit
See: PHILOSOPHY

Open Minds, the
Behavioral Health
Industry Analyst   *Consumer*

Publishing Co: Behavioral Health Industry News, Inc., 44 S. Franklin Street, Gettysburg, PA 17325; Title Tel # (717) 334-1329 Title Fax # (717) 334-0538
Personnel: Editor-Monica Oss, Circ. Dir.-Dianne Foust, Production Mgr.-Claudia Winters, Art Dir.-Trev Stair
Editorial Description: Focuses on developments and trends in the behavioral health industry.
General Info: Yr. Est. 1988, Monthly, Trim Size-8½ x 11, Web press, 12 pages, ISSN: 1043-3880, 2 Color, Matte, Saddle-stitched
Subscriptions: Indv. $185, $20/copy
Circulation: Total-7,000
List Rental: Rents Lists
Printing Co: Caskey Printing, 850 Vogelsong Rd., York, PA 17404 Tel # (717) 632-4500, Fax # (717) 632-2472

Operant Subjectivity   *Consumer*

Publishing Co: Alumni Association, Williamson Alumni Center, Kent, OH 44242-0001 Tel # (216) 672-2586 Fax # (216) 672-4880; Title Tel # (216) 672-2060
Personnel: Editor-Dr. Steven Barr Brown
Editorial Description: Theory underlying and applications of Q technique and its methodology.
General Info: Yr. Est. 1977, Quarterly, Trim Size-5⅜ x 8⅜, Offset press, 36 pages, ISSN: 0193-2713, Ind/Abs/Online: Psych.Abstr., No Color, Saddle-stitched
Subscriptions: Indv. $5, Inst. $7

Organizations & Change
See: MANAGEMENT

Ortho Newsletter
See: HEALTH

P. M. Newsletter of the
Anxiety & Phobia Clinic   *Association*

Publishing Co: White Plains Hospital Center, Davis Ave. at post rd., White Plains, NY 10601; Title Tel # (914) 681-1038 Title Fax # (914) 681-2284
Personnel: Bk. Rev. Ed.-Judy Chessa
Editorial Description: Articles for & about anxiety & phobias & their treatment. Regular features: discuss treatment plans; recovery techniques; book reviews; physicians Q&A column; highlights of anxiety conferences; and letters to the editor.
General Info: Yr. Est. 1972, Bi-monthly, Trim Size-8½ x 11, Mimeo press, 10 pages, No Color
Subscriptions: Indv. $15, Can. $20, For. $20, $1/copy
Circulation: Total-900

PS: It Is News   *Business, Association*

Publishing Co: Psychology Society, 100 Beekman St., New York, NY 10038-1810; Title Tel # (212) 285-1872
Personnel: Editor-Pierre C. Haber
Editorial Description: Disseminates new developments and research in psychology as well as news about our meetings and members.
General Info: (Formerly Psychology Society-Newsletter), Yr. Est. 1960, Monthly, Letrpr. press, 16 pages
Subscriptions: Indv. $25, Inst. $25, Can. $30, For. $30
Circulation: Total-5,000

Pediatric Mental Health — *Business, Consumer*

Publishing Co: Pediatric Projects, Inc., PO Box 571555, Tarzana, CA 91357-1555; Title Tel # (818) 705-3660 Title Fax # (818) 705-3660
Personnel: Editor-Pat Azarnoff, Circ. Mgr.-Ann Reed, Production Mgr.-Virginia Lewis
Editorial Description: Carries news, research, and interviews about psychological preparation, play, and parenting of disabled or hospitalized children.
General Info: Yr. Est. 1982, Bi-monthly, Trim Size-8½ x 11, Offset press, 8 pages, ISSN: 0278-4998, Color
Subscriptions: Indv. $36, Inst. $36, Can. $40, For. $40, $5/copy
Circulation: Total-2,025
List Rental: List Management Co.: Manager: Ann Reed; Wilson Marketing Group, 11924 W Washington Blvd, Los Angeles, CA 90066-5880 Tel # (213) 398-2754, Actives: $90/M

People First

Publishing Co: Dept. of Health & Welfare, Office of Mental Health, Room 502, Harrisburg, PA 17120; Title Tel # (717) 787-6443
General Info: (Formerly Mental Health News)

Positive Economist Bulletin Supplement for Objectivists
See: PHILOSOPHY

Primal Institute Newsletter

Publishing Co: Primal Institute, 10379 W. Pico Blvd., Los Angeles, CA 90064-2608; Title Tel # (310) 785-9456
Personnel: Publisher-Vivian Janov, Editor-Nicholas Barton, Production Mgr.-Barry Bernfeld
Editorial Description: All information relating to primal therapy, psychology & research findings.
General Info: Yr. Est. 1978, Quarterly, 4 pages, ISSN: 0164-5056, No Color
Subscriptions: Indv. $11, Can. $11, For. $15
Circulation: Total-1,600

Professional Christian Counselor
See: RELIGIOUS & THEOLOGICAL

Progress Notes

Publishing Co: Society of Pediatric Psychology, College of Medicine, Univ. of Iowa, Iowa City, MA 02135; Title Tel # (617) 254-3800
Personnel: Editor-Mary Cerreto
Editorial Description: Issues and events relevant to psychologists who work in a wide variety of children's health care settings.
General Info: (Formerly Newsletter), Yr. Est. 1975, 24 pages, 1% ads, Saddle-stitched
Acquistions: Publication Bought
Circulation: Total-700
Advertising: Inquire for rates. Accepts Inserts.
List Rental: Rents Lists

Psi Chi Newsletter — *Association*

Publishing Co: Psi Chi, the National Honor Society in Psychology, 407 E 5th St # B, Chattanooga, TN 37403-1823; Title Tel # (615) 756-2044 Title Fax # (615) 265-1529
Personnel: Editor-Kay Wilson
Editorial Description: To stimulate and encourage scholarship. Record of society activities for national and international recognition of research by psychology students.
General Info: Yr. Est. 1929, Quarterly, Trim Size-8½ x 11, Offset press, 35 pages, ISSN: 0033-2569
Subscriptions: For. $9, $6/copy
Circulation: Total-21,000

PsycINFO — *Association*

Publishing Co: American Psychological Association, 750 First St., NE, Washington, DC 20002-4242 Tel # (202) 336-5500 Fax # (202) 336-5568; Title Tel # (202) 336-5650 Title Fax # (202) 336-5633
Personnel: Editor-William C. Hayward
Editorial Description: Information on psychology literature in print and on electronic media.
General Info: Quarterly, Trim Size-8½ x 11, 6 pages, 2 Color, Matte

Psych Discourse — *Consumer, Association* — CPM: $260

Publishing Co: Assn. of Black Psychologists, PO Box 55999, Washington, DC 20040-5999; Title Tel # (202) 722-0808 Title Fax # (202) 722-5941
Personnel: Editor-Halford Fairchild
Editorial Description: Publishes original articles in Black psychology and news of the association.
General Info: (Formerly Assn. of Black Psychologists Newsletter), Yr. Est. 1968, Monthly, Trim Size-8½ x 11, 44 pages, 50% ads, Matte
Subscriptions: Indv. $95, Inst. $110, Free With Membership
Circulation: Total-2,500, Readership-2,500
Advertising: $650.
List Rental: Rents Lists

Psychiatry Drug Alerts
See: DRUGS & PHARMACEUTICALS

Psychologists for Social Responsibility Newsletter
See: POLITICS

Psychopharmacology
Update — *Business*

Publishing Co: Manisses Communications Group, Inc., PO Box 3357, Providence, RI 02906-0757; Title Tel # (401) 831-6020 Title Fax # (401) 861-6370
Personnel: Publisher-Fraser Lang, Editor-Frank Tornatore, Ph.D., Circ. Mgr.-Deb Zajas, Mktg. Dir.-Betty Lang
Editorial Description: Advisory for mental health professionals.
General Info: Yr. Est. 1993, Monthly, ISSN: 1068-5308
Subscriptions: Indv. $96, Inst. $96, Can. $106, For. $126
Circulation: Total-1,500
List Rental: List Management Co.: Conrad Direct, Inc., 300 Knickerbocker Road, Creskill, NJ 07626 Tel # (201) 567-3200, Fax # (201) 567-4959, Actives: 1,500, Expires: 500

Psychotherapy Finances
See: MANAGEMENT

Psychotherapy Letter, The — *Business*

Publishing Co: Manisses Communications Group, Inc., PO Box 3357, Providence, RI 02906-0757; Title Tel # (401) 831-6020 Title Fax # (401) 861-6370
Personnel: Publisher-Fraser Lang, Editor-Linda Watts Jackim, Circ. Mgr.-Deb Zajas, Mktg. Dir.-Betty Lang
Editorial Description: A resource exchange for psychotherapy professionals.
General Info: (Formerly Psychotherapy Today), Yr. Est. 1992, Monthly, Offset press, 8 pages, ISSN: 1047-9848
Subscriptions: Indv. $97, Inst. $127, Can. $137, For. $147, $10/copy
Circulation: Total-2,000
List Rental: List Management Co.: Conrad Direct, Inc., 300 Knickerbocker Road, Creskill, NJ 07626 Tel # (201) 567-3200, Fax # (201) 567-4959, Actives: 6,000, $100/M, Expires: 6,000, $90/M
Printing Co: Newsletter Press, 76 Valley St, East Providence, RI 02914-4424 Tel # (401) 438-5352

RPNAM Update — *Association*

Publishing Co: Sponsor-Registered Psychiatric Nurses Assn. of Manitoba (R.P.N.A.M.), Registered Psychiatric Nurses Assn. of Manitoba (R.P.N.A.M.), 1854 Portage Ave., Winnipeg, MB R3J 0G9 Canada; Title Tel # (204) 888-4841 Title Fax # (204) 888-8638
Personnel: Editor-A.D. Osted
General Info: (Formerly RPNAM Prism), Yr. Est. 1971, Semi-annually, 24 pages, ISSN: 0080-2442
Circulation: Total-1,200

Reference Guide to Addiction Counseling
See: HEALTH

Reference Guide to Counseling Children & Adolescents
See: CHILDREN

Round Table Review — *Consumer*

Publishing Co: Round Table Press, PO Box 475, Southeastern, PA 19399-0475; Title Tel # (215) 647-4235
Personnel: Editor-Delores Elise Brien
Editorial Description: Reviews books covering Jungian psychology.
General Info: 5x/yr., Trim Size-8½ x 11, 16 pages, ISSN: 1069-8817, No Color, Matte, Saddle-stitched
Subscriptions: Indv. $22, For. $26

SGCA Newsletter
See: SOCIAL SERVICES & WELFARE

Saskatchewan Society for Autistic Children Newsletter — *Association*

Publishing Co: Saskatchewan Society for Autistic Children, 3510 25th Ave., Regina, SK S4S 1L8 Canada
General Info: Quarterly

Self Help Reporter Newsletter — *Consumer*

Publishing Co: National Self Help Clearinghouse, 25 W. 43rd Street, New York, NY 10036; Title Tel # (212) 354-8525 Title Fax # (212) 642-1956
Personnel: Editor-Audrey Gartner
Editorial Description: Covers self-help mutual support activities, research, & theory.
General Info: Yr. Est. 1976, Quarterly, Trim Size-8½ x 11, Offset press, 8 pages
Subscriptions: Indv. $10

Signa

Publishing Co: New Jersey State Dept. of Mental Health, Publications, Trenton, NJ 08608; Title Tel # (609) 777-0700
General Info: Bi-monthly

Societe Quebecoise de l'Autisme
Business, Association

Publishing Co: Societe Quebecoise de l'Autisme/Quebec Society for Autism, 2300 Blvd. Rene Levesque Quest, Montreal, PQ H3H 2R5 Canada; Title Tel # (514) 931-2215 Title Fax # (514) 931-2397
Personnel: Editor-Manon Carle Dagenais
General Info: (Formerly l'Express), Yr. Est. 1984, Quarterly, ISSN: 0834-129X, No Color
Subscriptions: Indv. $25, Inst. $35, Can. $35, Free With Membership
Circulation: Total-900
Advertising: Inquire for rates.

Society for the Psychological Study of Social Issues Newsletter
Association

Publishing Co: Society for the Psychological Study of Social Issues, PO Box 1248, Ann Arbor, MI 48106-1248; Title Tel # (313) 662-9130
Personnel: Editor-Linda Silka, Product Mgr.-Michelle Noelle
Editorial Description: House organ-activities of interest to SPSSI members.
General Info: Yr. Est. 1936, Tri-annually, Trim Size-8.5 x 11, Offset press, 24 pages, 2 Color, Other, Saddle-stitched
Subscriptions: Free With Membership
Circulation: Total-3,500
Advertising: Inquire for rates.
List Rental: Rents Lists

Soundings
Association

Publishing Co: Echoes Network Counseling Center, Inc., 12624 NE Halsey St, Portland, OR 97230-1931; Title Tel # (503) 287-2753
Personnel: Editor-Wendy Ann Wood, Adv. Dir.-Leslie Hatton, Mktg. Dir.-Mary Hatfield, Promotion Dir.-Janice Dennison
Editorial Description: Newsletter for and by adult survivors of childhood sexual abuse. Publishes writings on the subject of sexual abuse, ritualistic abuse, multiple personality disorder, spiritual recovery, male survivors, and therapists' viewpoints.
General Info: Yr. Est. 1983, Quarterly, Desktop press, 8 pages, No Color
Subscriptions: Indv. $14, Can. $18, For. $20, $4/copy
Circulation: Total-1,900
Advertising: Inquire for rates. Accepts Inserts.

Spiritual Frontiers Fellowship International Newsletter
See: PARAPSYCHOLOGY

Sport Psychology Training Bulletin
See: SPORTS & SPORTING GOODS

Statewide Comprehensive Plan for Mental Health Services
See: PSYCHIATRY

Substance Abuse Funding News
See: PHILANTHROPY

Surviving Suicide
Association

Publishing Co: American Association of Suicidology, 2459 S Ash St, Denver, CO 80222-6006; Title Tel # (303) 692-0985 Title Fax # (303) 756-3299
Editorial Description: Articles for people who have lost a loved one to suicide and for those who want to help the bereaved.
General Info: Yr. Est. 1988, Quarterly

Survivor Activist, The
Consumer

Publishing Co: Survivor Connections, Inc., 52 Lyndon Rd, Cranston, RI 02905-1121; Title Tel # (401) 941-2548 Title Fax # (401) 941-2335
Personnel: Publisher-Frank L. Fitzpatrick, Editor-Sara J. Fitzpatrick
Editorial Description: Directed towards survivors of sexual assault and their supportive relatives. Contains 'how-to' articles, legislation info, news items, events listings, resources, and reviews.
General Info: Yr. Est. 1993, Quarterly, Trim Size-8½ x 11, Desktop press, 16 pages, ISSN: 1073-3051, No Color, Matte
Subscriptions: Indv. $25, Free To Qualified Recipient
Circulation: Readership-3,000

TRIMS Therapy Notes

Publishing Co: Texas Research Institute of Mental Sciences, 1300 Moursund St, Houston, TX 77030-3406; Title Tel # (713) 797-1976
Personnel: Editor-Lore Feldman
General Info: Yr. Est. 1980, Monthly, 2 pages
Circulation: Total-2,500

Teachers In Touch
See: EDUCATION

Terrap News
Consumer, Association

Publishing Co: TSC Corp/Terra Programs, 932 Evelyn St, Menlo Park, CA 94025-4710; Title Tel # (415) 327-1804
Personnel: Editor-A.B. Hardy
Editorial Description: Articles on phobias such as agoraphobia and anxiety disorders.
General Info: (Formerly Terrap Times), Yr. Est. 1967, Bi-monthly, Trim Size-8½ x 11, Offset press, 7 pages
Subscriptions: Indv. $18
Circulation: Total-3,000
Advertising: Inquire for rates. Accepts Inserts.

Transender

Publishing Co: Live and Learn, PO Box 6061, Sherman Oaks, CA 91413-6061; Title Tel # (818) 995-7121
Personnel: Editor-Rich Monosson
General Info: 8x/yr., Trim Size-8½ x 14, 2 pages
Advertising: Inquire for rates.

Type Reporter
Consumer

Publishing Co: Type Reporter, 11314 Chapel Rd, Fairfax, VA 22039-1523; Title Tel # (703) 823-3730 Title Fax # (703) 823-2209
Personnel: Editor-Susan Scanlon, Circ. Mgr.-Anne Henderson
General Info: Yr. Est. 1984, 8x/yr., Web press, 20 pages, ISSN: 8756-4963, 2 Color
Subscriptions: Indv. $16, Can. $16, For. $23, $2/copy
Circulation: Total-3,000
List Rental: Rents Lists
Printing Co: Hundley Lithograph, Inc., 6503 Chillum Pl NW, Washington, DC 20012-2189 Tel # (202) 829-7800

Understanding People

Publishing Co: Cromwell-Sloan Pub. Co., 63 Vine Rd, Stamford, CT 06905-2012; Title Tel # (203) 323-6839
Personnel: Publisher-Marlene Cromwell, Editor-Paul Sloan, Ph. D.
Editorial Description: Psychotherapy topics (depression, phobias, separation, relationship problems, anxiety, substance abuse).
General Info: Yr. Est. 1984, Monthly, Trim Size-8½ x 11, 4 pages, 2 Color
Subscriptions: Indv. $37
Acquistions: Publication Bought

VHL News
See: GENETICS

WAW Newsletter
Association

Publishing Co: William Alanson White Institute, 20 W 74th St, New York, NY 10023-2401; Title Tel # (212) 873-0725
Personnel: Editor-Ira Moses, Ph.D.
Editorial Description: Psychiatry, psychology, psychoanalysis.
General Info: Trim Size-8½ x 11, Offset press, 12 pages, Color, Saddle-stitched
Circulation: Total-5,500
List Rental: Rents Lists

WarChild Monitor International
See: CHILDREN

Women and Recovery
See: WOMEN'S

Women's Recovery Network
See: WOMEN'S

World Federation for Mental Health Newsletter
Association

Publishing Co: World Federation for Mental Health, 1021 Prince St., Alexandria, VA 22314-2971; Title Tel # (703) 838-7543 Title Fax # (703) 684-5968
Personnel: Editor-Eugene Brody, M.D., Mng. Editor-Elena L. Berger
Editorial Description: Reports on improving the care of the mentally ill and and promoting mental health.
General Info: Yr. Est. 1948, 4x/yr., Trim Size-8¼ x 10¾, 8 pages, No Color
Subscriptions: Indv. $30, Inst. $25, Can. $30, For. $30, Free With Membership
Circulation: (100% controlled), Total-4,000

York University Institute for Social Research Newsletter
See: SOCIOLOGY

PUBLIC MANAGEMENT & PLANNING

AABPA Newsletter
Association

Publishing Co: American Assn. for Budget & Program Analysis, PO Box 1157, Falls Church, VA 22041-0157; Title Tel # (703) 941-4300 Title Fax # (703) 941-1535
Personnel: Editor-Judy Stubbs Ochs
General Info: Yr. Est. 1976, Monthly
Subscriptions: Indv. $30, Inst. $150, Free With Membership
Circulation: Total-615

AIDS & Society: International Research Policy Bulletin
See: MEDICINE

AIDS Clinical Care Newsletter
See: MEDICINE

A.S.I.F (Americans Seeking International Franchises)
See: INTERNATIONAL TRADE

Agenda Newsletter, The
See: REGIONAL INTEREST

Alternatives
Consumer, Association

Publishing Co: Center for Policy Alternatives, 1875 Connecticut Ave NW Ste, 710, Washington, DC 20009-5728 Tel # (202) 387-6030 Fax # (202) 986-2539
Personnel: Editor-Bill Rice, Exec. Ed.-Jeffrey Tryens
Editorial Description: Focuses on policy and economic development in each of the states in the the U.S.
General Info: Yr. Est. 1993, Monthly, ISSN: 0293-7416

Animal Sheltering Magazine
See: ANIMALS

Applied Demography
Association

Publishing Co: Population Assn. of America, 1722 N. Street, NW, Washington, DC 20036; Title Tel # (202) 429-0891
Personnel: Editor-Rena Cheskis
Editorial Description: Focuses on the uses of demographic information.
General Info: Yr. Est. 1985, Tri-annually
Subscriptions: Indv. $10
List Rental: Rents Lists

ArtsUSA UpDate
See: CULTURE & HUMANITIES

Association for Convention Operations Management Newsletter
See: HOTEL INDUSTRY

Blue Chip Job Growth Update: Ranking the States and MSAs
See: ECONOMICS

Bronx Report, The
Consumer

Publishing Co: Office of Borough President, The Bronx County Building, 851 Grand Concourse, Bronx, NY 10451
Personnel: Publications Director-Paulette Fineman, Editor-Clint Roswell
General Info: Quarterly, Trim Size-8$\frac{1}{2}$ x 14, 4 pages, 2 Color, Matte
Subscriptions: Free To Qualified Recipient

CUPA News
See: SCHOOL ADMINISTRATION

CUPReport
Association

Publishing Co: Center for Urban Policy Research, Rutgers University, Box 489, Piscataway, NJ 08855-0489
Personnel: Editor-Arlene Pashman
General Info: Quarterly, ISSN: 1062-1563

California Neighborhoods
Consumer

Publishing Co: California Dept. of Housing & Community Development, Box 951050, Sacramento, CA 94252-2050 Tel # (916) 324-8659; Title Tel # (916) 445-4775
Personnel: Publisher-Timothy L. Coyle
Editorial Description: Covers activities of the Department of Housing and Community Development and other related housing issues.
General Info: (Formerly California Communities), Quarterly
Subscriptions: Free

California Planning & Development Report
Business

Publishing Co: California Planning & Development Report, 1275 Sunnycrest Ave, Ventura, CA 93003-1212; Title Tel # (805) 642-7838
Personnel: Publisher-Bill Fulton
Editorial Description: On land use and environmental planning in California.
General Info: Yr. Est. 1986, Monthly, ISSN: 0891-382X, Ind/Abs/Online: Newsnet
Subscriptions: Indv. $179, Can. $199
Circulation: Total-1,000
List Rental: Actives: 600, $60/M

California Public Finance
See: BANKING & FINANCE

Canadian Assn. of Municipal Administrators, CAMA Bulletin

Publishing Co: Canadian Assn. of Municipal Administrators, 24 Clarence St., Ottawa, ON K1N 5P3 Canada; Title Tel # (613) 563-2590
Personnel: Editor-Helen Thomas
Editorial Description: News, views, issues of immediate importance to municipal administrators complimenting more thoughtful bi-monthly magazine.
General Info: Monthly, Desktop press, 6 pages, No Color
Circulation: Total-350
Advertising: Inquire for rates. Accepts Inserts.
Printing Co: Print 2,000, 185 Somebet St., W., Ottawa, ON K2P 0J1 Canada Tel # (613) 234-0030

Capsules

Publishing Co: Southern Rural Development Center, PO Box 5446, Mississippi State, MS 39762-5446; Title Tel # (601) 325-3207
Personnel: Editor-Jacque Tisdale
Editorial Description: Highlights new achievements and critical issues in community development.
General Info: Yr. Est. 1981, Monthly, Trim Size-7 x 8$\frac{1}{2}$, Offset press, 8 pages, No Color, Newsprint
Circulation: Total-2,000

Caveat Emptor
See: PURCHASING

Central Park Good Times
See: REGIONAL INTEREST

Chicago Department of Development and Planning and Progress

Publishing Co: Chicago Dept. of Development, 121 N. LaSalle, Chicago, IL 60602-1202 Tel # (312) 744-4190

Chicago Reporter

Publishing Co: Community Renewal Society, 332 S. Michigan Ave., Siute #500, Chicago, IL 60604-9863; Title Tel # (312) 427-4830 Title Fax # (312) 427-6130
Personnel: Publisher, Editor-Laura Washington, News Ed.-Thomas A. Corfman, Circ. Mgr.-MarvLun Reed
Editorial Description: Information service on urban affairs and racial issues in metropolitan Chicago.
General Info: Yr. Est. 1972, Monthly, Trim Size-8$\frac{1}{2}$ x 11, Sheetfed press, 12 pages, ISSN: 0300-6921, 2 Color, Newsprint
Subscriptions: Indv. $38, $3/copy
Circulation: Total-5,000
List Rental: Actives: 2,575, $200/M
Printing Co: Glenhard Graphics, 400 E Fullerton Ave, Carol Stream, IL 60188-5201 Tel # (708) 653-4550

Citizens Business
Association

Publishing Co: Pennsylvania Economy League, Inc., 1211 Chestnut St Ste 600, Philadelphia, PA 19107-4116; Title Tel # (215) 864-9562 Title Fax # (215) 864-9921
Editorial Description: Public issues in Philadelphia or in a county in SMSA.
General Info: Yr. Est. 1908, Trim Size-8$\frac{1}{2}$ x 11, 2 pages, Color-cover, Matte
Subscriptions: Indv. $4
Circulation: Total-3,000

Citizens Report

Publishing Co: Citizens Committee for New York City, 305 7th Avenue, New York, NY 10001; Title Tel # (212) 989-0909 Title Fax # (212) 989-0983
Personnel: Editor-Tim Wall
Editorial Description: Concerned for New York City neighborhoods.
General Info: Yr. Est. 1977, Quarterly, Trim Size-8$\frac{1}{2}$ x 11, Offset press, 8 pages, 2 Color, Matte, Saddle-stitched
Subscriptions: Indv. $5, Inst. $8, Free To Qualified Recipient

City Leaders Institute Briefings
See: GOVERNMENT

City Trees
Association　　CPM: $480

Publishing Co: Society of Municipal Arborists, Box 364, Wellesley Hills, MA 02181; Title Tel # (617) 235-7600 Title Fax # (617) 431-7569
Personnel: Editor-Leonard Phillips
Editorial Description: Contains technical articles on species of trees, pest control, conservation planning, design & equipment.
General Info: Yr. Est. 1964, Bi-monthly, Trim Size-8$\frac{1}{2}$ x 11, Offset press, 28 pages, 25% ads, 2 Color, Coated, Saddle-stitched
Subscriptions: Indv. $20, Free With Membership
Circulation: Total-250, Readership-800
Advertising: $120. Accepts Inserts.
List Rental: Rents Lists
Printing Co: Clinton Offset Printers, 472 High Street, Clinton, MA 01510 Tel # (508) 365-4396

Commonwealth

Publishing Co: Commonwealth Club of California, 595 Market St., San Francisco, CA 94105-2885; Title Tel # (415) 597-6700 Title Fax # (415) 597-6729
Personnel: Editor-Gail Burns-Wax
General Info: Yr. Est. 1903, Weekly, Trim Size-8$\frac{1}{2}$ x 11, Desktop press, 10 pages, ISSN: 0010-3349, No Color, Newsprint
Subscriptions: Indv. $17
Acquistions: Publication Sold
Circulation: Total-20,000

Community
Consumer, Association

Publishing Co: Social Planning Council of Hamilton, 255 West Ave., N, Hamilton, ON L8L 5C8 Canada; Title Tel # (905) 522-1148
Personnel: Editor-Michael Pennock
Editorial Description: Describes social planning and research council projects, emphasis on community development and citizen participation.
General Info: (Formerly Focus), Yr. Est. 1986, Quarterly, Mimeo press, 4 pages, No Color
Subscriptions: Indv. $5, Inst. $10
Circulation: Total-400

Community Advocate

Publishing Co: Southern Brooklyn Community Organization, 4520 18th Ave, Brooklyn, NY 11204-1204; Title Tel # (718) 435-1300
Editorial Description: Neighborhood rehabilitation through community involvement.

Community Development Services, Inc. *Business*

Publishing Co: CD Publications, 8204 Fenton St., Silver Spring, MD 20910-4571; Title Tel # (301) 588-6380 Title Fax # (301) 588-6385
Personnel: Publisher-Mike Gerecht, Editor-Wayne Welch, Circ. Mgr.-Kurt Eisentraut, Mktg. Dir.-Joyce Meals
Editorial Description: Natl. report on CD block grants & federal community development programs.
General Info: Yr. Est. 1965, Semi-monthly, Trim Size-8½ x 11, Sheetfed press, 16 pages, ISSN: 0094-2324, No Color, Matte, Other
Subscriptions: Indv. $339, Can. $409, For. $439, $15/copy
List Rental: List Management Co.: Manager: Amy Seyler; Washington Advertising Service, 8204 Fenton St., Silver Spring, MD 20910 Tel # (301) 588-7920, Fax # (301) 588-6385, Actives: 5,555, $150/M, Expires: 3,081, $150/M

Community Development Status Reports

Publishing Co: Community Development Status Reports, 1 Centre St., New york, NY 10007-1602

Community Economics
See: ECONOMICS

Community Living of Florida
See: CONSTRUCTION & BUILDING

Community Planning Association of Canada. Saskatchewan Division Newsletter *Association*

Publishing Co: Community Planning Assn. of Canada. SK Div. Newsletter, 2837 Dewdney Ave., Regina, SK S4T 0X8 Canada; Title Tel # (306) 569-1611 Title Fax # (306) 569-1611
Personnel: Editor-R.K. Leibel
Editorial Description: All facets of planning, physical & social.
General Info: Yr. Est. 1949, Quarterly, Trim Size-8½ x 11, Letrpr. press, 10 pages, No Color
Subscriptions: Indv. $20, Can. $20
Circulation: (100% controlled), Total-275

Community Service Newsletter
See: SOCIOLOGY

Composting News
See: ENVIRONMENT & ECOLOGY

County News
See: GOVERNMENT

Dallas Institute Newsletter, The *Association*

Publishing Co: Dallas Institute of Humanities and Culture, 2719 Routh St, Dallas, TX 75201-1975 Tel # (214) 721-5342
Personnel: Publications Director-Joanne Stroud, PhD
Editorial Description: Dedicated to awakening a sense of the sacred in the world through studies in literature, art, spirituality, spychology, architecture, city planning and economics.
General Info: Yr. Est. 1980, Tri-annually

Deficit Letter, The
See: U.S. (& CANADIAN) FED. GOV'T.

Downtown Idea Exchange *Business, Association*

Publishing Co: Alexander Research & Communications, Inc., 215 Park Ave S., Ste. 1301, New York, NY 10003-1603; Title Tel # (212) 228-0246 Title Fax # (212) 228-0376
Personnel: Publisher-Shirley B. Alexander, Editor-Laurence A. Alexander, Circ. Mgr.-Mary Pagliaroli, Promotion Dir.-Margaret DeWitt
Editorial Description: Downtown revitalization for downtown leaders & officials in local & state govenment. A basic source of data on downtown revitalization, implementation methods, funding sources, downtown planning, parking, zoning concepts, effective downtown organization,improvent districts, preservation, economic development, urban design, traffic, transit, infrastructure, safety-crime & retailing.
General Info: Yr. Est. 1954, Semi-monthly, Trim Size-8½ x 11, 8 pages, ISSN: 0012-5822
Subscriptions: Indv. $143, Can. $143, For. $167, $6/copy
List Rental: Rents Lists

Downtown Promotion Reporter
See: ADVERTISING & MARKETING

ETDD Newsletter *Association*

Publishing Co: East Tennessee Development District, 5616 Kingston Pike, Box 19806, Knoxville, TN 37919-6325; Title Tel # (615) 584-8553 Title Fax # (615) 584-5169
Personnel: Editor-Trudy Garrett
General Info: (Formerly E T D D District Report), Yr. Est. 1967, Quarterly, Trim Size-8½ x 11, 8 pages, No Color
Circulation: Total-1,724
Printing Co: J & R Quick Print, 5710 Kingston Pike, Knoxville, TN 37919 Tel # (615) 584-6920

Economic Development/State Capitals
See: BUSINESS & INDUSTRY

Electronic Public Information Newsletter *Business, Association*

Publishing Co: EPIN Publishing, PO Box 21001, Washington, DC 20009-0501; Title Tel # (301) 365-3621 Title Fax # (301) 365-3621
Personnel: Publisher-James McDonough
Editorial Description: Reports on transition of public information into electronic format.
General Info: Yr. Est. 1991, Bi-weekly, Trim Size-8½ x 11, Desktop press, 8 pages, ISSN: 1057-834X, Ind/Abs/Online: Internet, Color-cover, Recycled
Subscriptions: Indv. $249, Inst. $130, Can. $249

Emergency Management Today
See: GOVERNMENT

Employment & the Economy: Atlantic Coastal Region
See: EMPLOYMENT

Employment & the Economy: Northern Region
See: EMPLOYMENT

Employment & the Economy: Southern Region
See: EMPLOYMENT

Environmental Bulletin
See: ENVIRONMENT & ECOLOGY

Environmental Newsletter, The
See: ENVIRONMENT & ECOLOGY

Federal Assistance Monitor
See: PHILANTHROPY

Financing Local Government *Association*

Publishing Co: Government Information Services, Inc., 4301 Fairfax Dr., Ste. 875, Arlington, VA 22203-1627 Fax # (703) 528-6060; Title Tel # (703) 528-1000
Personnel: Publisher-Shirley Alexander, Editor-Laurence Alexander, Circ. Mgr.-Mary Pagliaroli, Lit. Ed., Mktg. Dir.-Margaret DeWitt
Editorial Description: Newsletter for professionals concerned with meeting the unique challenges of today's urban areas. Typical issues focus on: planning and land use, energy & environment, urban technology, infrastructure, health, economic development, demographics & lifestyles, taxes & finance, education, housing, grants & funding, crime & security and more.
General Info: (Formerly Cost Cutting Digest; Urban Futures Idea Exchange; Urban Outl), Yr. Est. 1977, Semi-monthly, 8 pages, ISSN: 0732-8265
Subscriptions: Indv. $157, Can. $157, For. $187, $7/copy
Acquistions: Publication Bought, Publication Sold
Advertising: Accepts Inserts.
List Rental: Rents Lists

Florida Administrative Law Reports
See: LAW

Funding Law Enforcement Hotline
See: LAW ENFORCEMENT & PENOLOGY

GFOA Newsletter *Business, Association*

Publishing Co: Govt. Finance Officers Assn. of the U.S. and Canada, 180 N Michigan Ave Ste 806, Chicago, IL 60601-7401; Title Tel # (312) 977-9700 Title Fax # (312) 977-4806
Personnel: Publisher-Jeffrey Esser, Editor-Karen Utterback
General Info: (Formerly Municipal Finance Newsletter), Yr. Est. 1974, Semi-monthly, Trim Size-8½ x 11, 6 pages, Ind/Abs/Online: Ed.Bd.Tr.Lit.
Circulation: Total-13,000

GRA Reporter *Association*

Publishing Co: Sponsor-Governmental Research Assn., Samford University, 315 Samford Hall, Birmingham, AL 35229-0001; Title Tel # (205) 870-2482
Personnel: Editor-Robert Norwood
General Info: Quarterly, ISSN: 0016-3619
Subscriptions: Indv. $40
Circulation: Total-200

Gildea Resource Newsletter
See: ENVIRONMENT & ECOLOGY

Government Microcomputer Letter (GML)
See: GOVERNMENT

Government Union Critique
See: LABOR UNION

Grants for Cities and Towns
Biweekly Hotline *Business*

Publishing Co: Quinlan Publishing, 23 Drydock Ave, Boston, MA 02210-2387 Tel # (617) 542-0048 Fax # (617) 345-9646
Editorial Description: Grants available for town development and improvement from crime prevention programs to historical preservation.
General Info: Bi-weekly
Subscriptions: Indv. $129

HAC News

Publishing Co: Housing Assistance Council, Inc., 1025 Vermont Ave NW Ste 606, Washington, DC 20005-3516; Title Tel # (202) 842-8600
Personnel: Editor-Tarah Phoenix
Editorial Description: Reports on legislative issues affecting rural housing, as well as pertinent research findings.
General Info: Yr. Est. 1971, Bi-weekly, Desktop press, 2 pages, 2 Color, Recycled
Circulation: Total-3,500

HDA World

Publishing Co: New York Housing Authority, 250 Broadway, #917, New York, NY 10007-2516 Tel # (212) 306-3000; Title Tel # (212) 566-4440
Personnel: Editor-David M. Glauberman
General Info: (Formerly Housing World), Yr. Est. 1967

Heritage Today

Publishing Co: Heritage Foundation, 214 Massachusetts Ave NE, Washington, DC 20002-4999; Title Tel # (202) 546-4400 Title Fax # (202) 546-8328
Personnel: Editor-John Retzer
Editorial Description: Newsletter containing information on activities & pubs. of the Foundation.
General Info: Bi-monthly, 12 pages
Circulation: Total-7,500

Highway Financing & Construction/State Capitals
See: ROADS & STREETS

Horizons *Association*

Publishing Co: Mid-Ohio Regional Planning Commission, 285 E Main St, Columbus, OH 43215-5222; Title Tel # (614) 228-2663 Title Fax # (614) 621-2401
Personnel: Editor-David Sweet, Art Dir.-Dan Landbo
Editorial Description: Describes the agency's work and developments in the planning field.
General Info: (Formerly Mid-Ohio Review), Yr. Est. 1969, Quarterly, Trim Size-8½ x 11, Sheetfed press, 4 pages, 2 Color, Coated
Circulation: (100% controlled), Total-4,800
Printing Co: Spencer Walker Press, 107 W Main St, Newark, OH 43055-5007 Tel # (614) 345-3465

Housing & Development Reporter
See: CONSTRUCTION & BUILDING

Housing Law Bulletin

Publishing Co: National Housing Law Project, Inc., 2201 Broadway Ste 815, Oakland, CA 94612-3024 Fax # (415) 548-7217; Title Tel # (415) 548-9400
Personnel: Editor-Katherine Castro
Editorial Description: Reports on low-& moderate-income housing issues nationwide, focusing on legislative & administrative activity & litigation concerning public, subsidized, & private housing & community development, including displacement & homelessness.
General Info: (Formerly Housing Law Project Bulletin), Yr. Est. 1971, Bi-monthly, Trim Size-8½ x 11, 20 pages, ISSN: 0277-8491, No Color
Subscriptions: Indv. $50, $5/copy
Circulation: Total-1,500
Printing Co: Copy Rite, 2154 University Ave, Berkeley, CA 94704-1026 Tel # (415) 540-6900

ICMA Newsletter *Association*

Publishing Co: International City/County Management Assn., 777 N Capitol St NE Ste 500, Washington, DC 20002-4201 Tel # (202) 289-4262; Title Tel # (202) 962-3624 Title Fax # (202) 962-3500
Personnel: Editor-Kathy Karas
Editorial Description: News about members and the association, developments in the profession, position vacancies and capsule descriptions of local government programs.
General Info: Yr. Est. 1926, Bi-weekly, Trim Size-8½ x 11, Desktop press, 12 pages, ISSN: 0047-0651, 2 Color
Subscriptions: Indv. $145, Inst. $145
Circulation: Total-8,500

IFCO News *Association*

Publishing Co: Interreligious Foundation for Community Organization, 402 W. 145th St., New York, NY 10031-5202; Title Tel # (212) 926-5757 Title Fax # (212) 926-5842
Personnel: Editor-Gail Walker
Editorial Description: A quarterly publication that highlights community development efforts nationally and internationally.
General Info: Yr. Est. 1970, Quarterly, Trim Size-8¼ x 10¾, Desktop press, 16 pages, 2 Color, Newsprint, Other
Subscriptions: Indv. $15, Inst. $20
Circulation: Total-10,000
Advertising: Inquire for rates.
List Rental: Rents Lists
Printing Co: Vanguard Offset Printers, 470 Mundet Place, Hillside, NJ 07205-1115 Tel # (908) 851-2222

Incentive Taxation
See: TAXES

Indiana Public Safety
Letter *Business, Association* CPM: $355

Publishing Co: Emergency Management Group, 1508 E 86th St., Ste 315, Indianapolis, IN 46240-1986 Tel # (317) 475-9572; Title Tel # (317) 475-9063 Title Fax # (317) 475-9403
Personnel: Editor-C.A. Heller, Circ. Dir.-A.J. Strong, Publisher, Adv. Dir.-Douglas Crichlow
Editorial Description: Covers fire, rescue, emergency medical, search/rescue and police services in Indiana. Special emphasis on incidents, public policy, new technology, and management.
General Info: Yr. Est. 1991, Bi-weekly, Trim Size-8½ x 11, Offset press, 8 pages, 2 Color, Matte, Saddle-stitched
Subscriptions: Indv. $24, Inst. $48
Circulation: Total-602
Advertising: $214.

Infotech Report *Business, Association*

Publishing Co: International City/County Management Assn., 777 N Capitol St NE Ste 500, Washington, DC 20002-4201 Tel # (202) 289-4262; Title Tel # (202) 962-3596 Title Fax # (202) 962-3500
Personnel: Editor-Christine Ulrich, Production Mgr.-Dawn Leland, Promotion Dir.-Phyllis Erickson
Editorial Description: Newsletter devoted exclusively to microcomputer applications in local governments and public agencies. Highlights software programs. Includes case studies that explain how local governments are using computers to improve services and increase productivity. Software reviews, new products and resources also.
General Info: (Formerly MicroSoftware News), Yr. Est. 1984, Monthly, Sheetfed press, 8 pages, No Color, Matte, Saddle-stitched
Subscriptions: Indv. $130, Can. $130, For. $130
Circulation: Total-300
List Rental: Rents Lists
Printing Co: CLB Publishers & Lithographers, 10580 Metropolitan Ave, Kensington, MD 20895-2606 Tel # (301) 933-5220, Fax # (301) 933-2498

Interaction
See: ENVIRONMENT & ECOLOGY

International Visitor
See: TRAVEL

Issue Brief *Association*

Publishing Co: Metropolitan Planning Council, 220 S State St Ste 1800, Chicago, IL 60604-2001; Title Tel # (312) 922-5616 Title Fax # (312) 922-5619
Personnel: Editor-Carrie Anne Ebers
Editorial Description: Housing, planning, regional & urban development, transportation, lakefront issues in Metropolitan Chicago.
General Info: (Formerly Issues and Positions), Yr. Est. 1968, Monthly, Trim Size-8½ x 11, Offset press, 6 pages, No Color
Subscriptions: Free
Circulation: Total-1,650

JPC Newsletter *Business, Association*

Publishing Co: Lehigh-Northampton Counties Joint Planning Comm., 961 Marcon Blvd #310, Allentown, PA 18103-9397; Title Tel # (610) 264-4544
Personnel: Editor-Frederick Brock
General Info: Yr. Est. 1971, Bi-monthly, Trim Size-8½ x 11, 10 pages, No Color
Circulation: (100% controlled), Total-1,600

KAB System Network

Publishing Co: Keep America Beautiful, Inc., 9 W. Broad St., Stamford, CT 06902-3734; Title Tel # (203) 323-8987
Personnel: Editor-John Kazzi
Editorial Description: Natl. report & case studies on program innovations in cities certified in KAB System., the behavioral approach to waste handling.
General Info: (Formerly CCS Bulletin), Yr. Est. 1975, Monthly, Trim Size-8½ x 11, Desktop press, 4 pages, No Color, Recycled
Subscriptions: Free
Circulation: Total-600

Local Government Law
See: LAW

MSHDA Review *Business, Association*

Publishing Co: Sponsor-Michigan State Housing Development Authority, MSHDA, PO Box 30044, Lansing, MI 48909-7544; Title Tel # (517) 373-8370
Personnel: Editor-Kathleen Fagan
Editorial Description: Actions of the Michigan State Housing Dev. Authority and other housing-related news.
General Info: Yr. Est. 1978, Bi-monthly, 5 pages, Coated
Circulation: Total-30,000
Printing Co: Craft Printers, 3024 Turner Rd, Lansing, MI 48906-3175 Tel # (517) 484-6900

MTCMA Newsletter *Business*

Publishing Co: Univ. of Maine, 25 N. Stevens, Orono, ME 04469-0001; Title Tel # (207) 581-4136
Personnel: Editor-Khi Thai
General Info: Yr. Est. 1971, Monthly
Subscriptions: Indv. $15
Circulation: Total-225

Maine on the Grow

Publishing Co: Maine State Dept. of Economic Development, Augusta, ME 04330; Title Tel # (207) 626-2336
General Info: Monthly

Making Cities Livable
Newsletter

Publishing Co: Center for Urban Well-Being, PO Box 7586, Carmel, CA 93921-7586
Editorial Description: New developments, guidelines, strategies and methods to protect the quality of life in the city and create successful urban spaces. For architects, city administrators, planners, urban designers, landscape architects, social scientists, developers and others committed to making cities livable.
General Info: Yr. Est. 1987, Quarterly, ISSN: 0891-8821
Subscriptions: Indv. $85, Inst. $95

Metro Planner

Publishing Co: Sponsor-Metropolitan Chapter of the American Planning Assn., Abeles Phillips Preiss & Shapiro, 434 6th Ave., New York, NY 10011-8411
General Info: Monthly

Michigan Resource Bulletin

Publishing Co: Michigan State University, Dept. of Resource Development, Publications, East Lansing, MI 48823; Title Tel # (517) 355-3421

Missouri Official

Publishing Co: Bush Pubs., 1006 W Harmony St, Neosho, MO 64850-1631
Editorial Description: For elected officials of the state, with subordinate emphasis on officials at the township, city and state level and superintendents of schools.
General Info: Bi-monthly
Subscriptions: Indv. $2, $1/copy
Circulation: Total-3,000
Advertising: Inquire for rates.

Montana League of Cities   *Association*

Publishing Co: Montana League of Cities, PO Box 1704, Helena, MT 59624-1704; Title Tel # (406) 442-8768
Personnel: Editor-Alec Hansen
Editorial Description: Local government operation, association activities, workshops available, assistance available to local governments, legal opinions and legislation affecting local government.
General Info: Yr. Est. 1966, 4 pages, No Color
Circulation: Total-1,200
Advertising: Inquire for rates.

Municipal Attorney   *Association*

Publishing Co: Natl. Institute of Municipal Law Officers, 1000 Connecticut Ave NW Ste, 902, Washington, DC 20036-5302; Title Tel # (202) 466-5424 Title Fax # (202) 785-0152
Personnel: Editor-Benjamin Brown
Editorial Description: Digest of recent court decisions concerning municipal law.
General Info: (Formerly Municipal Law Court Decisions), Bi-monthly, 8 pages
Circulation: Total-2,500

Municipal Law Docket   *Association*

Publishing Co: Natl. Institute of Municipal Law Officers, 1000 Connecticut Ave NW Ste, 902, Washington, DC 20036-5302; Title Tel # (202) 466-5424 Title Fax # (202) 785-0152
Personnel: Editor-Benjamin Brown
Editorial Description: Items of interest to municipal attorneys.
General Info: Bi-monthly, 8 pages

N.A.C.A.S. Newsletter   *Association*

Publishing Co: National Assn. of College Auxiliary Services, PO Box 870, Staunton, VA 24402-0870; Title Tel # (703) 885-8826
Editorial Description: Listing of new members and subscribers; job opening annoucements.
General Info: Monthly, 8 pages
Circulation: Total-1,025

NAHRO Monitor   *Association*

Publishing Co: National Association of Housing and Redevelopment Officials, 630 Eye St. NW, Washington, DC 20001-3736; Title Tel # (202) 289-3500 Title Fax # (202) 289-8181
Personnel: Editor-Joseph Haas, Production Mgr.-Francis Hart
Editorial Description: Summary of Lousina and community development news published as a service for NAHRO members.
General Info: (Formerly NAHRO Letter), Yr. Est. 1968, Semi-monthly, Trim Size-8½ x 11, Sheetfed press, 16 pages, 2 Color, Saddle-stitched
Subscriptions: Free With Membership
Circulation: Total-9,000
List Rental: Rents Lists
Printing Co: Atlantic Research Co., 5501 Backlick Rd, Springfield, VA 22151-3938 Tel # (703) 914-8400

NAN Bulletin   *Association*

Publishing Co: National Association of Neighborhoods, 1651 Fuller St., N.W., Washington, DC 20009-5622; Title Tel # (202) 332-7766 Title Fax # (202) 332-2314
Personnel: Editor, Circ. Mgr.-Althea Jackson, Art Dir.-Deborah Crain
Editorial Description: Description of models of neighborhood organizations.
General Info: Yr. Est. 1975, Quarterly, Trim Size-8½ x 11, Sheetfed press, 18 pages, 2 Color
Subscriptions: Indv. $25
Acquistions: Publication Bought
Circulation: (100% controlled), Total-10,000
Advertising: Inquire for rates.

NATAT Washington
Report   *Association*   **CPM: $75**

Publishing Co: National Assn. of Towns & Townships, 1522 K St. NW, Ste. 600, Washington, DC 20005-1202; Title Tel # (202) 737-5200 Title Fax # (202) 289-7996
Personnel: Circ. Dir.-Bruce Rosenthal, Adv. Dir.-Beverly Nykwest, Editor, Art Dir.-Ronnie Kweller
Editorial Description: Local government infrastructure management, hazardous materials management, economic development. News for local elected officials in small towns and rural areas on federal laws and regulations, especially in the environmental field. Examples of successful local programs in small towns in areas such as infrastructure management, economic development, etc.
General Info: (Formerly NATAT's Reporter, Natl. Community Reporter), Yr. Est. 1976, Bi-monthly, Trim Size-10 x 11, Web press, 12 pages, ISSN: 0735-9691, 2 Color, Recycled
Subscriptions: Indv. $36, Free With Membership
Circulation: Total-13,800
Advertising: $1,035. Accepts Inserts.
List Rental: List Management Co.: Manager: Bruce Rosenthal; Infocus Communications, 341 Victory Dr, Herndon, VA 22070-5217 Tel # (703) 834-0100, Fax # (703) 834-0110, Actives: $85/M
Printing Co: Record Printing, PO Box 7429, Silver Spring, MD 20907-7429 Tel # (301) 589-6400, Fax # (301) 589-7906

NCCEM Bulletin   *Association*

Publishing Co: National Coordinating Council on Emergency Management, 7297 Lee Hwy Ste N, Falls Church, VA 22042-1707; Title Tel # (703) 533-7672 Title Fax # (703) 241-5603
Personnel: Editor-Shari Coffin
Editorial Description: Addresses current issues of interest to local emergency managers.
General Info: Yr. Est. 1983, Monthly, 6 pages, ISSN: 1063-9918, No Color
Subscriptions: Indv. $85, Free With Membership
Circulation: Total-1,400
List Rental: Actives: 1,400

NCRWA News

Publishing Co: Community Resources Workshop Assn., Miami Univ., 205 McGuffey Hall, Oxford, OH 45056; Title Tel # (513) 529-6318

NIGP Technical Bulletin
See: PURCHASING

NOACA News   *Business, Association*

Publishing Co: Northeast Ohio Areawide Coordinating Agency, 668 Euclid Ave., Atrium Office Plz., Cleveland, OH 44114-3000; Title Tel # (216) 241-2414
Editorial Description: Informs readers of NOACA's plans, programs, and data base.
General Info: Yr. Est. 1970, Quarterly, Trim Size-25½ x 11, Web press, 6 pages, 2 Color, Newsprint
Subscriptions: Free
Acquistions: Publication Bought
Circulation: Total-2,500
Advertising: Accepts Inserts.
Printing Co: Erie Reproduction, 17827 Roseland Rd, Cleveland, OH 44112-1283 Tel # (216) 486-3434

NYLA Bulletin
See: LIBRARY

Neighborhood Caretaker

Publishing Co: Neighborhood Caretaker, 1522 Grand Ave Apt 4c, Saint Paul, MN 55105-2228; Title Tel # (612) 698-0349
Personnel: Circ. Mgr.-B. Dyson, Editor, Art Dir.-Elizabeth Dyson
Editorial Description: We choose stories from readers & abstract articles from journals that reflect interdisciplinary collaboration & new thought patterns needed for healthy urban neighborhoods in the 21st century.
General Info: Yr. Est. 1978, 10x/yr., Trim Size-8½ x 11, Desktop press, 16 pages, No Color
Subscriptions: Indv. $25
Circulation: Total-300
Advertising: Accepts Inserts.

Nevada Government
Today

Publishing Co: Nevada League of Cities, PO Box 2307, Carson City, NV 89702-2307 Tel # (702) 882-2121 Fax # (702) 882-2813
General Info: Yr. Est. 1973, Quarterly
Subscriptions: Indv. $6
Circulation: Total-2,000
Advertising: Inquire for rates.

Nevada Planner   *Association*

Publishing Co: State Planning Coordinators Office, Capital Bldg., Room 306, Carson City, NV 89701
General Info: Yr. Est. 1969, Quarterly
Circulation: Total-700

New England City & Town   *Business*

Publishing Co: New England City & Town, 19 Joslin St., Providence, RI 02909-2599 Tel # (401) 751-6217 Parent Co.-Fire-Medic Services, Providence
Personnel: Publisher, Editor-Thomas J. Lopatosky
Editorial Description: News and ideas for municipal leaders
General Info: Yr. Est. 1994, Semi-monthly, Trim Size-8½ x 11, 10 pages
Subscriptions: Indv. $40, Inst. $40, $3/copy

New Hampshire Journal of Economic Development
See: REGIONAL INTEREST

New Mexico Municipal League, Municipal Reporter
Association, Consumer

Publishing Co: New Mexico Municipal League, 1229 Paseo De Peralta # 846, Santa Fe, NM 87501-2758
Personnel: Editor-Donald C. Rider
General Info: Yr. Est. 1959, Monthly, ISSN: 0028-6257
Subscriptions: Indv. $20
Circulation: Total-1,700

OKI Topics Newsletter   *Association*

Publishing Co: Ohio, Kentucky, Indiana Regional Council of Governments, 801B W. 8th St., #400, Cincinnati, OH 45203-1607 Fax # (513) 621-9325; Title Tel # (513) 621-7060
Personnel: Editor-Louis Ethridge
Editorial Description: Covers news for and about governing bodies in the states of Ohio, Kentucky, and Indiana.
General Info: Monthly, 2 pages
Circulation: Total-2,500

Organizations & Change
See: MANAGEMENT

PBC Housing Briefs
See: CONSTRUCTION & BUILDING

Pacific Mountain Network News   *Association*

Publishing Co: Rural Community Assistance Corp., 2125 19th St., Ste. 203, Sacramento, CA 95818-1663 Fax # (916) 447-2878; Title Tel # (916) 447-2854 Title Fax # (416) 447-2878
Personnel: Publisher-William French, Editor-Richard Dreher, Technology Ed.-Kay Mulligan, Production Mgr.-Nicole Ryan
Editorial Description: Timely news for the rural development field. Special focus on housing, water, wastewater, agency management, & resource issues.
General Info: (Formerly Pacific Mountain Times), Yr. Est. 1983, 8x/yr., Trim Size-8$\frac{1}{2}$ x 11, Offset press, 16 pages, ISSN: 0738-1867, 2 Color, Matte, Saddle-stitched
Subscriptions: Free To Qualified Recipient
Circulation: Total-3,500
List Rental: Rents Lists
Printing Co: KP Graphics, 220 Riverside Ave, Roseville, CA 95678-3146 Tel # (916) 969-5748, Fax # (916) 784-0374

Planners' Network Newsletter   *Association*

Publishing Co: Planners Network, 379 DeKalb Avenue, Brooklyn, NY 11205; Title Tel # (718) 636-3486
Personnel: Publisher, Editor-Thomas Angotti, Circ. Mgr.-Jill Hamberg
Editorial Description: For progressive urban/rural planners.
General Info: Yr. Est. 1975, Bi-monthly, Offset press, 10 pages, No Color
Subscriptions: Free With Membership
Circulation: Total-800

Planning & Zoning News

Publishing Co: Planning & Zoning Center, Inc., 302 S. Waverly Rd., Lansing, MI 48917-3631; Title Tel # (517) 886-0555
Personnel: Publisher, Editor-Mark Wyckoff, Circ. Mgr.-Carolyn Freebury
Editorial Description: Contemporary analysis of lawful land use planning & regulatory techniques.
General Info: Yr. Est. 1982, Monthly, Trim Size-8$\frac{1}{2}$ x 11, Sheetfed press, 20 pages, ISSN: 0738-114X, 2 Color, Recycled, Saddle-stitched
Subscriptions: Indv. $140
Circulation: Total-2,700
Advertising: Inquire for rates.
Printing Co: Lansing Printing Co., 619 E Hazel St, Lansing, MI 48912-1091 Tel # (517) 487-8338

Planning Bulletin
See: TRAFFIC & TRANSPORTATION

Planning News   *Association*   **CPM: $26**

Publishing Co: New York Planning Federation, 488 Broadway #313, Albany, NY 12207-2911; Title Tel # (518) 432-4094
Personnel: Publisher, Editor-David Church
Editorial Description: Educational & informational newsletter dedicated to better planning.
General Info: Yr. Est. 1937, Quarterly, Letrpr. press, 8 pages, 3% ads, 2 Color, Coated
Subscriptions: Indv. $25, Inst. $60
Circulation: Total-9,300
Advertising: $250.
Printing Co: Whitehurst Press, 555 River St, Troy, NY 12180-2216 Tel # (518) 274-1616

Planning in Northeastern Illinois   *Consumer*

Publishing Co: Northeastern Illinois Planning Commission, 222 S. Riverside Plaza, Ste. 1800, Chicago, IL 60606-6001; Title Tel # (312) 454-0400
Personnel: Editor-Lawrence Christmas
Editorial Description: Includes reports on local governmental activities, Commission activities, and activities in areas such as water and air resource management, transportation, flooding.
General Info: Yr. Est. 1963, Quarterly, Offset press, 8 pages, ISSN: 0048-4318, 2 Color, Coated, Looseleaf
Circulation: Total-9,800

Planning Progress   *Association*

Publishing Co: Bucks County Planning Commission, Neshaminy Ctr., Alms House, Doylestown, PA 18901 Tel # (215) 345-3400; Title Tel # (215) 345-3402 Title Fax # (215) 345-3886
Personnel: Publisher, Editor-Robert Moore, Circ. Mgr.-Margaret Creeden, Production Mgr.-Art Dir.-Roberta Wilburn
Editorial Description: Presentation of contemporary land use planning issues for local government particularly in Bucks County, PA.
General Info: Yr. Est. 1957, Quarterly, Trim Size-8$\frac{1}{2}$ x 11, Sheetfed press, 8 pages, 2 Color, Matte
Subscriptions: Free

Planning Times

Publishing Co: Maryland State Dept. of Planning, 301 W. Preston St., State Offi, Baltimore, MD 21201-2305; Title Tel # (410) 225-4500
Personnel: Editor-Richard Gucker
Editorial Description: Land use, planning & management.
General Info: (Formerly Planning in Maryland), Bi-monthly, Trim Size-8$\frac{1}{2}$ x 11, 4 pages, No Color
Circulation: (100% controlled), Total-1,000

Policy Currents

Publishing Co: Institute for Policy Studies, Shriver Hall, Complex A, John Hopkins Univ., Baltimore, MD 21218 Tel # (410) 516-7174 Fax # (410) 516-8233; Title Tel # (301) 338-7174 Title Fax # (301) 338-8233
Personnel: Editor-Robert Seidel
Editorial Description: Policy currents is the newsletter of the Johns Hopkins Institute for policy studies, which through research, public education & citizenship training, works with government, business, & the nonprofit sector to analyze & formulate solution to problems of p blic concern in the Baltimore region, in the nation at large, & internationally.
General Info: Yr. Est. 1987, Semi-annually, Trim Size-8$\frac{1}{2}$ x 11, 20 pages, 2 Color, Coated
Subscriptions: Free
Circulation: Total-2,500
Printing Co: Duvall Printing, 2604 Sisson St., Baltimore, MD 21211 Tel # (301) 243-9300

Prince Edward Island Public Service Assn. News

Publishing Co: Prince Edward Island Public Service Assn., Box 1116, 51 Univ. Ave., Charlottetown, PE C1A 7M8 Canada Tel # (902) 368-0444
General Info: Yr. Est. 1961, Bi-monthly, Trim Size-11 x 15, 4 pages

Privatization Watch
See: GOVERNMENT

Problem Solving Information for State & Local Governments
See: BIBLIOGRAPHY

Professional Public Service   *Business*

Publishing Co: Professional Institute of the Public Service of Canada, 53 Auriga Dr., Nepean, ON K2E 8C3 Canada Tel # (613) 228-6310
Personnel: Editor-A. J. Mitchell
Editorial Description: For professional employees of Canadian Public Service.
General Info: Yr. Est. 1920, Monthly
Subscriptions: Indv. $3
Circulation: Total-11,500
Advertising: Inquire for rates.

Public Affairs Analyst

Publishing Co: Univ. of Kentucky Public Affairs Dept., Publications, Lexington, KY 40506-0001

Public Employee Dismissals Bulletin   *Business*

Publishing Co: Quinlan Publishing, 23 Drydock Ave, Boston, MA 02210-2387 Tel # (617) 542-0048 Fax # (617) 345-9646
Editorial Description: Review of case summaries of municipal personnel decisions.
General Info: Yr. Est. 1975, Monthly
Subscriptions: Indv. $69

Public Employment Law Notes
See: LAW

Public Innovation Abroad   *Business*

Publishing Co: Academy for State & Local Government, 444 N Capitol St NW Ste 345, Washington, DC 20001-1512; Title Tel # (202) 434-4850
Editorial Description: Provides state and local leaders with innovative new ideas.
General Info: Monthly
Subscriptions: Indv. $46

Public Investment   *Association*

Publishing Co: American Planning Association, 1313 E 60th St, Chicago, IL 60637-2891 Fax # (312) 955-8312; Title Tel # (312) 955-9100
Personnel: Publisher-Israel Stollman, Editor-David Bergman, Promotion Dir.-Ken East
Editorial Description: News concerning innovations in public financing of infrastructure, & economic development.
General Info: Yr. Est. 1984, Quarterly, Trim Size-8$\frac{1}{2}$ x 11, Web press, 4 pages, No Color
Circulation: (100% controlled), Total-1,700
List Rental: Rents Lists

Public Lands News

Publishing Co: Resources Publ. Co., 1010 Vermont Ave NW Ste 708, Washington, DC 20005-4995; Title Tel # (202) 638-7529 Title Fax # (202) 393-2075
Personnel: Publisher, Editor-James Coffin, Circ. Mgr.-Chris Crandell
Editorial Description: Reports on legislation & regulations from Washington on public lands.
General Info: Yr. Est. 1976, Bi-weekly, Trim Size-8½ x 11, Offset press, 10 pages, No Color
Subscriptions: Indv. $217
List Rental: Rents Lists

Public Sector Job Bulletin
See: EMPLOYMENT

Public Sector Management/ Management et Secteur Public
Consumer, Scholarly

Publishing Co: Institute of Public Administration, 150 Eglinton Ave. East, Suite #305, Toronto, ON M4P 1E8 Canada; Title Tel # (416) 932-3666 Title Fax # (416) 932-3667
Personnel: Circ. Mgr.-Marie Fortier, Adv. Dir.-Joseph Alimberti, Promotion Dir.-Donald Leniban
General Info: (Formerly Bulletin), Yr. Est. 1958, Quarterly, Trim Size-8¼ x 10¾, Desktop press, 31 pages, ISSN: 1183-1081, 1% ads, No Color, Coated, Saddle-stitched
Subscriptions: Indv. $20, $5/copy
Circulation: Total-3,800, Readership-3,900
Advertising: Inquire for rates.
Printing Co: Imperial Press Ltd., 385 Brunel Rd., Mississauga, ON L4Z 1Z5 Canada Tel # (905) 890-1083, Fax # (905) 890-7144

Public Works News
Business

Publishing Co: Reynolds Publishing Co. Inc., PO Box 578, Glen Echo, MD 20812-0578; Title Tel # (301) 229-2930
Personnel: Publisher, Editor, Adv. Dir.-William F. Reynolds
Editorial Description: Report on public works affairs in Congress, White House and Federal Government agencies.
General Info: Yr. Est. 1969, Weekly, Trim Size-6 x 8½, Letrpr. press, 8 pages, ISSN: 0176-5473
Subscriptions: $10/copy

Region News
Association

Publishing Co: Ohio-KY-Indiana Regional Council of Governments, 801B W. 8th St., Ste. 400, Cincinnati, OH 45203-1601 Fax # (513) 621-9325; Title Tel # (513) 621-7060
Personnel: Editor-Claudia Harrod
Editorial Description: Summary of planning and governmental activities, particularly in the areas of transportation, environment, land use and housing, for the nine county OKI region.
General Info: (Formerly OKI Annual Report), Bi-monthly, Trim Size-8½ x 11, Offset press, 6 pages, 2 Color
Circulation: (100% controlled), Total-3,000

Regional View
See: REGIONAL INTEREST

Regionews
See: REGIONAL INTEREST

The Regulatory Times
See: ENERGY

Rhode Island Monthly Progress Report
Business, Association

Publishing Co: State of RI & Providence Plantations, Div. of Planning, 265 Melrose St Rm 203, Providence, RI 02907-2102; Title Tel # (401) 277-2656
Personnel: Editor-Carol Ciotola
Editorial Description: Summary of state planning activities, publications, meetings of state planning council and committees.
General Info: Yr. Est. 1965, Monthly, Trim Size-8½ x 11, Offset press, 20 pages, ISSN: 0300-6468
Circulation: (100% controlled), Total-250

Right-To-Know Planning Guide
Business

Publishing Co: Bureau of National Affairs, Inc., 1231 25th St. NW, Bldg. N-200, Washington, DC 20037-1157; Title Tel # (202) 452-4200 Title Fax # (202) 822-8092
Personnel: Publisher-William A. Beltz, Editor-Eileen Joseph, Mng. Editor-Karen Walker, Circ. Mgr.-Gary C. Seltzer
Editorial Description: Provides information on new community right-to-know & community emergency response programs.
General Info: (Formerly Right-To-Know Planning Report), Yr. Est. 1987, Bi-weekly, Trim Size-8½ x 11, Web press, 4 pages, Ind/Abs/Online: HRIN
Subscriptions: Indv. $567

Riskwatch
See: INSURANCE

Rockefeller Institute Bulletin
See: GOVERNMENT

SEWRPC Newsletter
Association, Business

Publishing Co: Southeastern Wisconsin Regional Planning Commission, 916 N East Ave # 1607, Waukesha, WI 53186-4808; Title Tel # (414) 547-6721 Title Fax # (414) 547-1103
Personnel: Publisher, Editor-Kurt Bauer, Art Dir.-Leland Kreblin
Editorial Description: Summarizes SEWRPC work; articles on related subjects, conference/meeting announcements.
General Info: Yr. Est. 1960, Bi-monthly, Trim Size-7 x 8½, Sheetfed press, 40 pages, 2 Color
Subscriptions: Indv. $2
Circulation: (100% controlled), Total-1,750

SRA News

Publishing Co: Society of Research Administrators, 1200 19th Stree NW, Washington, DC 20036-2412; Title Tel # (202) 857-1141 Title Fax # (202) 223-4579
Personnel: Editor-Claudette Boyer
General Info: Bi-monthly

San Diego County Dept. of Planning and Land Use Population and Housing Estimates.

Publishing Co: San Diego County Dept. of Planning & Land Use, 5201 Ruffin Rd., Ste. B-5, San Diego, CA 92123-4310; Title Tel # (619) 565-3025
Personnel: Editor-Joey Perry
Editorial Description: Population and housing estimates by city and subregional area.
General Info: Yr. Est. 1965, Annually, Trim Size-8½ x 11, 10 pages, 2 Color
Subscriptions: Indv. $5
Circulation: Total-250

Signal
See: TRAFFIC & TRANSPORTATION

State Action Memorandum

Publishing Co: Housing Assistance Council, Inc., 1025 Vermont Ave NW Ste 606, Washington, DC 20005-3516; Title Tel # (202) 842-8600
Personnel: Editor-Tarah Phoenix
Editorial Description: Informs state agencies, legislators, & organizations about activity in other states to promote rural housing for low income persons.
General Info: Yr. Est. 1971, Bi-monthly, 6 pages, No Color
Circulation: Total-500

Statehouse Observer
Business, Association

Publishing Co: State Personnel Dept., PO Box 94905, Lincoln, NE 68509-4905
Personnel: Editor-C. Sorenson
General Info: Yr. Est. 1972, Monthly
Circulation: Total-18,000

Stateline
Business, Association

Publishing Co: New York State Dept. of Civil Service, State Office Building C/O, Public Relations Office, Albany, NY 12239-0001; Title Tel # (518) 457-9375 Title Fax # (518) 457-9377
Personnel: Editor-G. Modele Clarke
Editorial Description: Aimed at state agency heads & personnel offices, stateline focuses on managing the New York State work force.
General Info: (Formerly State Personnel News), Yr. Est. 1986, Monthly, Trim Size-8½ x 11, Offset press, 4 pages, 2 Color, Coated
Circulation: Total-25,000
Printing Co: Whitehurst Press, 555 River St, Troy, NY 12180-2216 Tel # (518) 274-1616

Surplus Property News Bulletin
Business, Association

Publishing Co: State of Michigan, Dept. of Management & Budgeting, 3369 N. Logan Property Secti, Fedl. Surplus Propert, Lansing, MI 48913-0001; Title Tel # (517) 335-9105

Times (Bethlehem)
See: ARCHITECTURE

UAA Communication
Association

Publishing Co: Urban Affairs Assn., Univ. of Delaware, Newark, DE 19711-4688; Title Tel # (302) 451-2394
Personnel: Editor-M.H. Callahan
General Info: (Formerly CUIUA Communiction), Yr. Est. 1970, Bi-monthly, Sheetfed press, 8 pages, Color, Newsprint
Subscriptions: Indv. $30
Circulation: (66% controlled), Total-1,500, Subscriptions-500
List Rental: Actives: $100/M

U.B.C Planning Papers

Publishing Co: School of Community & Regional Planning, Univ. of B.C., 6333 Memorial Rd., Vancouver, BC V6T 1W5 Canada

U.S. R & D

Publishing Co: Government Data Publications, 1155 Connecticut Avenue NW, Washington, DC 20036; Title Tel # (212) 627-0819
Personnel: Publisher-Siegfried Lobel, Editor-Siegfried Cobell
Editorial Description: Research events and developments.
General Info: Yr. Est. 1963, Monthly, Web press, 85 pages, No Color
Subscriptions: Indv. $96
Acquistions: Publication Bought

Urban & Regional Technology & Development   *Business*

Publishing Co: National Technical Information Service U.S., 5285 Port Royal Rd., Springfield, VA 22161-0001 Fax # (703) 487-4630; Title Tel # (703) 487-4630
Editorial Description: Bibliographic announcements of documents, subscriptions, computer searches, software available NTIS.
General Info: (Formerly Weekly Governmental Abstracts, Urban Technology), Weekly, Trim Size-8$\frac{1}{2}$ x 11, Offset press, 8 pages, ISSN: 0163-1535, No Color, Saddle-stitched
Subscriptions: Indv. $105, Can. $145
Circulation: Total-150

Urban Conservation Report

Publishing Co: Preservation Reports, Inc., PO Box 569, Fairfax, VA 22030-0569; Title Tel # (202) 466-4234
Personnel: Publisher-Frank Frantz, Editor-Constance Beaumont
Editorial Description: Current information on events affecting preservation and rehabilitation of older buildings and urban neighborhoods.
General Info: (Formerly Neighborhood Conservation and Reinvestment), Yr. Est. 1977, Semi-monthly, Trim Size-8$\frac{1}{2}$ x 11, Sheetfed press, 8 pages, ISSN: 0731-4205, No Color
Subscriptions: Indv. $117, $6/copy

WRC Notebook   *Business, Association*

Publishing Co: Washington Research Council, 1301 5th Ave Ste 2810, Seattle, WA 98101-2603; Title Tel # (360) 357-6643
Personnel: Editor-John Archer
Editorial Description: Contains facts, comments & analysis of state & local government in Washington state, with an emphasis on fiscal issues. Periodically includes an invert competitive strategies , and on market approaches to public policy.
General Info: (Formerly WRC Report), Yr. Est. 1932, Monthly, Trim Size-8$\frac{1}{2}$ x 11, Offset press, 8 pages, 2 Color
Subscriptions: Indv. $50, Free With Membership
Circulation: Total-2,500

Washington Health Week   *Business*

Publishing Co: Atlantic Information Svcs., Inc., 1100 17th St. NW, Ste. 300, Washington, DC 20036-5503; Title Tel # (202) 775-9008 Title Fax # (202) 331-9542
Personnel: Publisher-Richard Biehl, Circ. Mgr.-Gwen Arnold, Mktg. Dir.-Donna Lawton, Mktg. Mgr.-Christine Burdell
Editorial Description: Timely federal news of medical, medical, health care coverage and payment policy.
General Info: (Formerly Inside Health Care Reform), Yr. Est. 1993, Bi-weekly
Subscriptions: Indv. $393
List Rental: List Management Co.: Tony Murray & Assoc., P.O. Box 2409, Fairfax, VA 22031-3739 Tel # (703) 425-5356, Fax # (703) 425-4537

Washington Policy Choices   *Business, Association*

Publishing Co: Univ. of Washington Inst. for Public Policy, 324 Parrington Hall, Dc-14, Seattle, WA 98195-0001; Title Tel # (206) 543-0190 Title Fax # (206) 543-1096
Personnel: Editor-Lynne B. Iglitzin
Editorial Description: Essays related to various issues of public policy and public administration.
General Info: (Formerly Washington Public Policy Notes), Yr. Est. 1973, Quarterly, Trim Size-8$\frac{1}{2}$ x 11, Desktop press, 2 Color
Circulation: Total-2,500

Ways & Means
See: GOVERNMENT

Westchester Planning

Publishing Co: Westchester County Dept. of Planning, 432 County Office Bldg., White Plains, NY 10601; Title Tel # (914) 682-2564
Personnel: Editor-Mary Carlson
Editorial Description: Planning, statistics, and development activities in Westchester County, N.Y.
General Info: Yr. Est. 1966, Quarterly, Trim Size-11 x 17, Web press, 8 pages, 2 Color
Subscriptions: Indv. $15
Circulation: Total-2,000
Printing Co: Gazette Press, Inc., 16 School St., Yonkers, NY 10701 Tel # (914) 963-8300, Fax # (914) 476-1052

Your Region   *Association*

Publishing Co: North Central Texas Council of Governments, Drawer COG, Arlington, TX 76011
Personnel: Editor-Alexia Griffin
General Info: (Formerly Your Region in Action), Yr. Est. 1967, Monthly
Circulation: Total-5,000

ZPG Reporter, The
See: ENVIRONMENT & ECOLOGY

Zoning and Land Use Control

Publishing Co: Matthew Bender & Co., 11 Penn Plaza, New York, NY 10001-2006
Fax # (212) 244-3188; Title Tel # (212) 967-7707
Personnel: Editor-R. Lopatin
Editorial Description: The definitive treatise on zoning, land use & environmental law on the federal, state & local levels.
General Info: Yr. Est. 1977, Looseleaf
Subscriptions: $485/copy

Zoning News   *Business, Association*

Publishing Co: American Planning Association, 1313 E 60th St, Chicago, IL 60637-2891
Fax # (312) 955-8312; Title Tel # (312) 955-9100
Personnel: Publisher-Israel Stollman, Editor-Jim Schwab
Editorial Description: News of zoning issues, including court decisions & local land use plans.
General Info: Yr. Est. 1984, Monthly, Trim Size-8$\frac{1}{2}$ x 11, Sheetfed press, 4 pages, 2 Color
Subscriptions: Indv. $45, Can. $54, For. $54
Circulation: Total-4,000

PUBLIC UTILITIES

Accounting for Public Utilities
See: ACCOUNTING

Alert

Publishing Co: Three Mile Island Alert Inc., 315 Peffer St, Harrisburg, PA 17102-1834; Title Tel # (717) 233-7897
Personnel: Editor-Bill Cologie, Publisher, Production Mgr., Promotion Dir.-Kay Pickering
Editorial Description: News of Three Mile Island reactor, the TMIA organization, & nuclear powering general.
General Info: Yr. Est. 1977, Bi-monthly, Trim Size-8$\frac{1}{2}$ x 14, 8 pages
Subscriptions: Indv. $15
Circulation: Total-450, Readership-450
Advertising: Inquire for rates.

Association for Convention Operations Management Newsletter
See: HOTEL INDUSTRY

Blue Bulletin
See: POWER & POWER PLANTS

Bulletin   *Business, Consumer*

Publishing Co: Sponsor-Pennsylvania Electric Co., Pennsylvania Electric Co., 1001 Broad St, Johnstown, PA 15907-2437; Title Tel # (814) 533-8846
Personnel: Editor-Larry O'Reilly
Editorial Description: Weekly newssheet.
General Info: Yr. Est. 1983, Weekly, Trim Size-8$\frac{1}{2}$ x 11, 1 pages, 2 Color
Circulation: Total-300

Canada Petroleum Industry
See: PETROLEUM & NATURAL GAS

Central Hudson Newsletter
See: HOUSE ORGANS

Chronicle
See: ENERGY

Coastlines   *Consumer*

Publishing Co: Central Lincoln People's Utility Dist., 2129 N Coast Hwy # 1126, Newport, OR 97365-1705; Title Tel # (503) 265-3211
Personnel: Editor-G. Cockrum, K. Birkela
Editorial Description: Utility news; energy efficiency tips.
General Info: Yr. Est. 1966, Monthly, Trim Size-5$\frac{1}{2}$ x 8$\frac{1}{2}$, Offset press, 4 pages, Color
Circulation: Total-26,000

Daily Index

Publishing Co: Edison Electric Institute, 701 Pennsylvania Ave., NW, Washington, DC 20004-2696
Tel # (202) 508-5595 Fax # (202) 508-5759; Title Tel # (202) 778-6483
Personnel: Editor-N. Burkey Musselman
Editorial Description: Congressional & Federal register.
General Info: Daily, Trim Size-8$\frac{1}{2}$ x 11, 4 pages, 2 Color

Dialogue
See: ELECTRIC & ELECTRONIC EQUIPMENT

EEI Washington Letter

Publishing Co: Edison Electric Institute, 701 Pennsylvania Ave., NW, Washington, DC 20004-2696
Tel # (202) 508-5595 Fax # (202) 508-5759; Title Tel # (202) 778-6483
Personnel: Editor-N. Burkey Musselman
Editorial Description: Electricity, energy, general politics.
General Info: Yr. Est. 1945, Weekly, Trim Size-8$\frac{1}{2}$ x 11, 16 pages, ISSN: 0737-349X, 2 Color
Subscriptions: Indv. $75

East River Electric Power
Guardian

Publishing Co: East River Electric Power Co-Op, PO Box E, Madison, SD 57042-0227
Personnel: Editor-Gene Hexom
Editorial Description: Informs the rural consumers on current developments in all phases of electricity.
General Info: Yr. Est. 1962, Monthly
Subscriptions: Indv. $1

Electric Utilities Industry -
U.S. and Canada   *Business*

Publishing Co: Midwest Register Inc., 1120 E. 4th St., Tulsa, OK 74120-3220;
  Title Tel # (918) 582-2000 Title Fax # (918) 587-9349
Personnel: Publisher/President/Advisor-Will L. Hammack
General Info: (Formerly Electric Utilities - U.S. and Canada), Yr. Est. 1945, Annually, 950 pages
Subscriptions: Can. $75, For. $75, $75/copy
Advertising: Inquire for rates.
List Rental: Rents Lists

Electric Utility Rankings

Publishing Co: Argus Research Corp., 17 Battery Pl., New York, NY 10004-1101;
  Title Tel # (212) 425-7500 Title Fax # (212) 509-5408
Personnel: Editor-John Eade
Editorial Description: Analyzes specific public electric utility companies.
General Info: Yr. Est. 1975, Monthly
Subscriptions: Indv. $225, $35/copy
Printing Co: Argus Printing & Mailing, 226 New York Ave, Huntington, NY 11743-2748
  Tel # (516) 423-7710

Electric Utility Spotlight

Publishing Co: Argus Research Corp., 17 Battery Pl., New York, NY 10004-1101;
  Title Tel # (212) 425-7500 Title Fax # (212) 509-5408
Editorial Description: Focuses on utility trends.
General Info: Monthly
Subscriptions: Indv. $225, $35/copy

Electric Utility Week   *Business*

Publishing Co: McGraw-Hill, 1221 Ave. of the Americas, 36th Fl., New York, NY 10020-1095
  Tel # (212) 512-2000 Fax # (212) 512-6590; Title Tel # (212) 512-6410 Title Fax # (212) 512-2723
Personnel: Publisher-John Slater, Editor in Chief-Daniel Tanz, Circ. Mgr.-Georgia Safos, Promotion Dir.-Suzanne Goodman
Editorial Description: Emphasis is on financial management legislation, regulation, rates, environmental and commercial matters affecting electric utilites.
General Info: (Formerly Electrical Week), Yr. Est. 1970, Weekly, Trim Size-8$\frac{1}{2}$ x 11, 10 pages, ISSN: 0046-1695, Ind/Abs/Online: DIALOG, Dow Jones, NewsNet, Nexis
Subscriptions: Indv. $1,225, For. $1,245, $25/copy

Electric Utility Week's
Demand-Side Report   *Business*

Publishing Co: McGraw-Hill, 1221 Ave. of the Americas, 36th Fl., New York, NY 10020-1095
  Tel # (212) 512-2000 Fax # (212) 512-6590; Title Tel # (212) 512-6410 Title Fax # (212) 512-2723
Editorial Description: Tracks the growth of Demand-Side Management at utilities across the U.S. and Canada and reports on the regulation and politics that shape the programs .
General Info: Yr. Est. 1992, Bi-weekly, Ind/Abs/Online: Dialog, Dow Jones, NewsNet
Subscriptions: Indv. $445

Energy Design Update
See: CONSUMER INTERESTS

Energy Line   *Business, Association*

Publishing Co: Fitchburg Gas & Electric Light Co., 216 Epping Rd., Exeter, NH 03833-4571;
  Title Tel # (603) 772-0775
Personnel: Editor-Thomas Conry
Editorial Description: Newsletter for employees and retirees on company energy and personnel related matters.
General Info: (Formerly Dispatch), Bi-monthly, Trim Size-8$\frac{1}{2}$ x 11, Offset press, 8 pages, 2 Color, Newsprint, Saddle-stitched
Circulation: Total-300
Printing Co: Travers Printing Co., 32 Mission St, Gardner, MA 01440-2196

Energy News Exchange
See: APPLIANCES

Energy Services Marketing
Letter   *Business, Association*

Publishing Co: Synergic Resources Corporation, 111 Presidential Blvd., Bala Cynwyd, PA 19004
  Fax # (215) 667-5593; Title Tel # (215) 667-2160 Title Fax # (610) 667-5593
Personnel: Editor-Richard Smithers, Exec. Ed.-John Maxwell
Editorial Description: Customer energy service in the electric (primarily) & gas (occasionally) utility industries. Program descriptions & results, regulatory development, marketing approaches, new technologies, relevant conferences & information sources.
General Info: (Formerly DSM Letter; Electric Letter, The), Yr. Est. 1977, Bi-weekly, Trim Size-8$\frac{1}{2}$ x 11, Offset press, 6 pages, 2 Color, Recycled
Subscriptions: Indv. $245, For. $245
Circulation: Total-300
Printing Co: Southwest Graphics, Ridley Park, PA Tel # (215) 521-9500

Environmental Manager
See: ENVIRONMENT & ECOLOGY

Foster Electric Report   *Business, Association*

Publishing Co: Foster Associates, Inc., 1015 15th St NW Ste 1100, Washington, DC 20005-2605;
  Title Tel # (202) 408-7710
General Info: Yr. Est. 1993, Bi-weekly
Circulation: Total-350

Foster Natural Gas Report
See: PETROLEUM & NATURAL GAS

Gas Utilities Industry -
Worldwide   *Business*

Publishing Co: Midwest Register Inc., 1120 E. 4th St., Tulsa, OK 74120-3220;
  Title Tel # (918) 582-2000 Title Fax # (918) 587-9349
Personnel: Publisher/President/Advisor-Will L. Hammack
General Info: (Formerly Gas Utilities Worldwide), Yr. Est. 1945, Annually, 900 pages
Subscriptions: Can. $75, For. $75, $75/copy
Advertising: Inquire for rates.
List Rental: Rents Lists

IE News: Utilities   *Association*

Publishing Co: Institute of Industrial Engineers, 25 Technology Park/Atlanta, Norcross, GA 30092-2988 Tel # (770) 449-0461; Title Tel # (404) 449-0460 Title Fax # (770) 263-8532
Personnel: Production Mgr.-Dona Brown
Editorial Description: Newsletter for IIE Utilities Division.
General Info: Quarterly, Trim Size-8$\frac{1}{2}$ x 11, Sheetfed press, 4 pages, 2 Color, Matte, Saddle-stitched
Circulation: (100% controlled)
Advertising: $475. Accepts Inserts.
List Rental: Rents Lists

Income Advisor
See: INVESTMENT

Indoor Air Quality Update
See: ENVIRONMENT & ECOLOGY

Interchange

Publishing Co: Nebraska Public Power District, PO Box 499, Columbus, NE 68602-0499
  Tel # (402) 563-5823 Fax # (402) 563-5166; Title Tel # (402) 563-5971 Title Fax # (402) 563-5551
Personnel: Editor-Jill Novicki, Art Dir.-Dave Harrington
Editorial Description: Written for wholesale customer audience about district activities affecting customer needs and interests. Distributed to district employees to keep them informed of wholesale customer activities.
General Info: Yr. Est. 1990, Monthly, Sheetfed press, 4 pages, Recycled
Subscriptions: Free
Circulation: Total-4,600

International Solar Energy Intelligence Report
See: ENERGY

KMU Monthly Report   *Business*

Publishing Co: Kansas Municipal Utilities, Inc., Box 1225, McPherson, KS 67460-1225;
  Title Tel # (316) 241-1423 Title Fax # (316) 241-7829
Personnel: Editor, Adv. Dir.-Louis Stroup, Jr.
Editorial Description: Operation and activities of municipal electric, water and gas utilities in Kansas.
General Info: Yr. Est. 1930, Semi-monthly, Trim Size-8$\frac{1}{2}$ x 11, 8 pages, Color
Subscriptions: Indv. $175, $5/copy
Circulation: Total-750
Advertising: Inquire for rates.

Long Island Almanac

Publishing Co: Long Island Lighting Co., 175 E Old Country Rd, Hicksville, NY 11801-4257;
  Title Tel # (516) 933-4590

Louisiana Country
See: POWER & POWER PLANTS

Mid-Continent States Petroleum Industry
See: PETROLEUM & NATURAL GAS

Monthly Bulletin of Utility
Gas Sales   *Association*

Publishing Co: American Gas Association, 1515 Wilson Blvd., Arlington, VA 22209-2469
  Tel # (703) 841-8400 Fax # (703) 841-8406; Title Tel # (703) 841-8503
Personnel: Editor-Vanessa Chu
Editorial Description: Statistical tabulation of gas utility monthly sales, & compilation of data regarding residential appliance shipments, economic indicators, heating season degree days, spot prices, & transportation volumes.
General Info: Yr. Est. 1929, Monthly, Trim Size-8$\frac{1}{2}$ x 11, 2 pages, No Color
Subscriptions: Indv. $16
Circulation: Total-1,600

Northeast States Petroleum Industry
See: PETROLEUM & NATURAL GAS

OR ServiceLine   *Consumer*

Publishing Co: OR Orange and Rockland Utilities, 1 Blue Hill Plz, Pearl River, NY 10965-3104
Editorial Description: Various electricity and power info for customers of Orange and Rockland Utilities.
General Info: Quarterly

PULSE

Publishing Co: Salt River Project, PO Box 52025, Phoenix, AZ 85072-2025; Title Tel # (602) 236-8288 Title Fax # (602) 236-8221
Personnel: Editor-D. RaMar Orgeron, Art Dir.-Larry MacLean
Editorial Description: PULSE is produced for employees & retirees of SRP & is designed to provide a service, inform & educate, & to convey management approved messages to target audiences.
General Info: (Formerly Project PULSE), Yr. Est. 1967, Bi-weekly, Trim Size-8½ x 11, Web press, 8 pages, 1% ads, No Color, Saddle-stitched
Circulation: (100% controlled), Total-7,032
Advertising: Inquire for rates.

P.U.R. Utility Weekly   *Business*

Publishing Co: Public Utilities Reports, Inc., 8229 Boone Blvd., Suite #401, Vienna, VA 22182 Tel # (703) 847-7720 Fax # (703) 847-0683; Title Tel # (703) 243-7000 Title Fax # (703) 527-5829
Personnel: Publisher-Susan Johnson, Editor-Lori Burkhart, Mktg. Dir.-Carol Bray
Editorial Description: News of federal and state government actions affecting utility companies. Covers state commission fulings and federal regulatory issues.
General Info: (Formerly PUR Letter), Yr. Est. 1934, Weekly, Trim Size-8½ x 11, Sheetfed press, 4 pages, 2 Color, Matte
Subscriptions: Indv. $459, Can. $459, For. $489
Circulation: Total-500
List Rental: List Management Co.: W.I. Mail Marketing, 470 Main St. #317, Ridgefield, CT 06877-4516 Tel # (203) 438-6822, Fax # (203) 438-7756, Actives: 500, $350/M
Printing Co: Newsletter Services, Inc., 9700 Philadelphia Court, Lanham, MD 20706 Tel # (301) 731-5200, Fax # (301) 731-5201

PV News
See: ENERGY

Pipeline - Worldwide
See: PETROLEUM & NATURAL GAS

Power Markets Weekly   *Business*

Publishing Co: McGraw-Hill, 1221 Ave. of the Americas, 36th Fl., New York, NY 10020-1095 Tel # (212) 512-2000 Fax # (212) 512-6590
Editorial Description: Covers electricity and other power markets for investors.
General Info: Weekly

Power System News
See: POWER & POWER PLANTS

Procedures Review
See: NUCLEAR ENERGY

Public Power Weekly Newsletter   *Association*

Publishing Co: American Public Power Assn., 2301 M St NW, Washington, DC 20037-1484; Title Tel # (202) 467-2947
Personnel: Publisher-Jeanne LaBella, Mng. Editor-Jeannine Anderson, Circ. Mgr.-Susan Lynch, Adv. Rep.-Stacey Hubart
Editorial Description: Contains news affecting local publicly owned electric utilities.
General Info: Yr. Est. 1942, Weekly, Trim Size-8½ x 11½, Sheetfed press, 8 pages, 2 Color
Subscriptions: Indv. $400
Circulation: Total-10,000
Printing Co: Shakopee Valley Printing, 5101 Valley Industrial Blvd S, Shakopee, MN 55379-1821 Tel # (612) 445-8260, Fax # (612) 496-0007

Public Utilities/State Capitals   *Business, Consumer*

Publishing Co: Wakeman/Walworth, 300 N. Washington St., Alexandria, VA 22314-2530; Title Tel # (703) 549-8606 Title Fax # (703) 549-1372
Personnel: Publisher-Keyes Walworth
Editorial Description: Covers all forms of utilities with information on new rate structures, allowable profit margins, special taxes, consumer relations, environmental legislation and more.
General Info: (Formerly Public Utilities from the State Capitals), Yr. Est. 1946, Weekly, Trim Size-8½ x 11, Offset press, 5 pages, ISSN: 0016-1888, No Color
Subscriptions: Indv. $265, Inst. $212, Can. $235, For. $255

Quad Report, The
See: ENERGY

Quad Special Reports, The
See: ENERGY

The Regulatory Times
See: ENERGY

Risk Management Report   *Business*

Publishing Co: Tennessee Valley Public Power Assn., 1201 Chestnut St, Chattanooga, TN 37402-5021; Title Tel # (615) 756-6511
Personnel: Publisher-Jerry Campbell, Editor-Dennis Yocom
General Info: Quarterly, 4 pages
Circulation: Total-300

Solid Waste Report
See: ENVIRONMENT & ECOLOGY

Southeast Power Report
See: ENERGY

Southeast States Petroleum Industry
See: PETROLEUM & NATURAL GAS

TELCO Competition Report
See: TELECOMMUNICATIONS

Technologies for Energy Management
See: POWER & POWER PLANTS

Transmissions Newsletter   *Association*

Publishing Co: Power Transmission Distributors Assn., 6400 Schafer Ct., Rosemont, IL 60018-4909; Title Tel # (847) 825-2000 Title Fax # (847) 825-0953
Personnel: Editor-Beate Halligan
General Info: Monthly
Subscriptions: Free With Membership

Update
See: ENGINEERING

Utilities Law Reports   *Business*

Publishing Co: CCH, Inc., 2700 Lake Cook Rd., Riverwoods, IL 60015 Parent Co.-Kluwer Law & Taxation Publishers, Cambridge; Title Tel # (847) 267-7000 Title Fax # (800) 224-8299
Editorial Description: Federal and state public utilities laws, regulations, court decisions and Federal Regulatory Commission rulings and regulations, plus state commission decisions.
General Info: Yr. Est. 1928, Weekly, Trim Size-6 x 9, Web press, 125 pages, No Color, Looseleaf
Subscriptions: Indv. $2,408

Utility Reporter-Fuels, Energy & Power
See: ENERGY

ValleyLine   *Association*

Publishing Co: Tennessee Valley Public Power Assn., 1201 Chestnut St, Chattanooga, TN 37402-5021; Title Tel # (615) 756-6511
Personnel: Publisher-Jerry Campbell, Editor-Kent Lopez
Editorial Description: Public power management newsletter.
General Info: Yr. Est. 1979, Monthly, Trim Size-8½ x 11, Desktop press, 6 pages, No Color, Newsprint
Circulation: Total-2,180

WSEO Dispatch
See: ENERGY

Waste Recovery Report
See: ENVIRONMENT & ECOLOGY

Waterline

Publishing Co: East Bay Municipal Utility Dist., 2130 Adeline St # 24055, Oakland, CA 94607-2335; Title Tel # (415) 835-3000
Personnel: Editor-Ida McClendon
Editorial Description: District operations & related.
General Info: (Formerly Splashes), Yr. Est. 1917, Quarterly, Trim Size-8½ x 11, Offset press, 12 pages, No Color, Saddle-stitched
Circulation: (100% controlled), Total-2,500

Western States Petroleum Industry
See: PETROLEUM & NATURAL GAS

Whitfields Utility Letter
See: INVESTMENT

PURCHASING

Affiliated Warehouse Companies Newsletter
See: TRUCKING

Arizona Purchaser

Publishing Co: Purchasing Management Assn of Arizona, PO Box 40157, Mesa, AZ 85274-0157; Title Tel # (602) 253-6453
Personnel: Editor-Burton Barnett
General Info: Yr. Est. 1969, Monthly
Subscriptions: Indv. $6
Circulation: Total-1,196

Buying Strategy Forecast   *Business*

Publishing Co: Cahners Publishing Co., 275 Washington St., Newton, MA 02158-1630
Fax # (617) 558-4470 Parent Co.-Reed Elsevier, New York; Title Tel # (617) 964-3030
Personnel: Publisher-Jack O'Connor, Editor-Thomas Stundza, Promotion Mgr.-Kim Dempsey
Editorial Description: For purchasing managers. Forecasts of prices, leadtimes, I/S ratios, and
capacity utilization rates as well as general business outlook.
General Info: Yr. Est. 1971, Semi-monthly, Trim Size-8½ x 11, Offset press, 8 pages, No Color,
Newsprint
Subscriptions: Indv. $238, Can. $310, For. $310, $9/copy
Circulation: Total-450
List Rental: Rents Lists

Caveat Emptor   *Business, Association*

Publishing Co: Ontario Public Buyers Assn., Box 608, Maple, ON L6A 1S5 Canada;
Title Tel # (905) 682-3788 Title Fax # (905) 682-3788
Personnel: Editor-C. Bott, Editorial Page Ed.-M. Knight
Editorial Description: Furthering excellence in, and promoting awareness of, the public procurement
profession.
General Info: Yr. Est. 1981, 5x/yr., Trim Size-8½ x 11, Desktop press, 12 pages, Recycled
Subscriptions: Can. $25, $5/copy
Circulation: Total-450, Readership-450
List Rental: Actives: 350, $50/M

Common Sense Negotiations
See: MANAGEMENT

Government Contracts
Service   *Business*

Publishing Co: Procurement Associates, Inc., 733 N Dodsworth Ave, Covina, CA 91724-2408;
Title Tel # (818) 966-4576 Title Fax # (818) 915-1709
Personnel: Publisher-P.R. McDonald, Sr., Editor-Paul McDonald, Jr., Circ. Mgr.-Toni Casas, Adv.
Dir.-Marie Sirney
Editorial Description: A reference library and information system for personnel involved in marketing,
pricing, management and administration of Government contracts and sub-contracts.
General Info: Yr. Est. 1964, Bi-weekly, Trim Size-8½ x 11½, Offset press, 175 pages, No Color,
Looseleaf
Subscriptions: Indv. $525

Government Microcomputer Letter (GML)
See: GOVERNMENT

Hospital Materials Management
See: HOSPITALS & NURSING HOMES

Innovative Products   *Business, Association*   CPM$2351

Publishing Co: The Innovation Groups, PO Box 16645, Tampa, FL 33687-6645;
Title Tel # (813) 622-8484 Title Fax # (813) 664-0051
Personnel: Publisher-J. Robert Havlick, Editor-David Sieg, Technology Ed., Circ. Mgr., Adv. Dir., Art
Dir.-Liz Diaz
Editorial Description: Features new products from the private sector for local govts. & when possible
local govts. experiences with the products; also products developed by local govts.
General Info: Yr. Est. 1988, Quarterly, Trim Size-8½ x 11, Sheetfed press, 8 pages, ISSN: 1085-
8523, 25% ads, 2 Color, Other
Subscriptions: Indv. $19, Can. $24, For. $24, Free With Membership
Acquistions: Publication Bought
Circulation: Total-3,500, Readership-4,500
Advertising: $8,230. Accepts Inserts.
List Rental: Rents Lists

NAEB Bulletin   *Association*

Publishing Co: NAEB, 450 Wireless Blvd., Hauppauge, NY 11788-3934; Title Tel # (516) 273-2600
Title Fax # (516) 273-2305
Personnel: Editor-Neil Markee
Editorial Description: For purchasing professionals from higher education & nonprofit health care.
General Info: Monthly, 16 pages, Coated, Saddle-stitched
Subscriptions: Indv. $40
Circulation: (100% controlled), Total-2,290
List Rental: Rents Lists
Printing Co: Colahan-Saunders Corp., 160 Varick St., New York, NY 10013 Tel # (212) 675-1515

NIGP Technical Bulletin   *Business, Association*

Publishing Co: Natl. Institute of Governmental Purchasing, 11800 Sunrise Valley Dr., Ste. 1050,
Reston, VA 22091-5302; Title Tel # (703) 715-9400 Title Fax # (703) 715-9897
Personnel: Publisher-J.E. Brinkman, Editor-D'Arcy Roper, III, Production Mgr.-Jane Benton
Editorial Description: Information on standards, specifications, procurement methodology & other
technical issues. Also information on cooperative purchasing, technological solutions to purchasing
issues.
General Info: Yr. Est. 1976, Bi-monthly, Trim Size-8½ x 11, Offset press, 8 pages, 2 Color,
Newsprint, Saddle-stitched
Subscriptions: Indv. $50, $1/copy
Acquistions: Publication Bought
Circulation: Total-13,000
List Rental: Rents Lists
Printing Co: Discount Newsletter Printing, 1487 Persisterce Dr., PO Box 1487, Woodbridge, VA
22193-0487 Tel # (703) 690-1788, Fax # (703) 491-2563

New England Purchaser   *Business*

Publishing Co: Purchasing Management Assn of Boston, Inc., 200 Baker Ave Ste 306, Concord, MA
01742-2125; Title Tel # (508) 371-2522
Personnel: Publisher-Christiane Loup
Editorial Description: Articles and news items pertaining to industrial purchasing and materials
management.
General Info: (Formerly Connecticut Purchaser), Yr. Est. 1921, Quarterly, Trim Size-8⅛ x 10⅞,
Offset press, 8 pages, ISSN: 0028-4858, 4 Color
Circulation: (100% controlled), Total-2,000

Off the Shelf   *Business*

Publishing Co: Coalition for Government Procurement, 1990 M St NW Ste 400, Washington, DC
20036-3404; Title Tel # (202) 331-0975 Title Fax # (202) 659-5754
Personnel: Editor-Kathleen Cramer
Editorial Description: Reports on federal commercial product procurement issues.
General Info: Yr. Est. 1980, Monthly, Trim Size-8½ x 11, Desktop press, 8 pages, No Color, Matte
Subscriptions: Indv. $195
Acquistions: Publication Bought
Circulation: Total-200

Parametric World
See: ECONOMICS

Professional Purchasing   *Business, Association*

Publishing Co: American Purchasing Society, 11910 Oak Trail Way, Port Richey, FL 34668-1037;
Title Tel # (813) 862-7998 Title Fax # (813) 862-8199
Personnel: Publisher, Editor-Harry Hough
Editorial Description: How to buy for and manage purchasing departments; news about benefits of
membership; discounts on books; positions available.
General Info: Yr. Est. 1970, Monthly, Trim Size-8½ x 11, Desktop press, 6 pages, 2 Color, Matte
Subscriptions: Indv. $89, Inst. $99, Free With Membership
Acquistions: Publication Bought
Circulation: Total-3,400, Readership-5,000
Advertising: Inquire for rates.
List Rental: Actives: 40,000, $95/M

Progressive Purchasing   *Business, Association*

Publishing Co: Purchasing Management Assn of Canada, 2 Carlton St., #1414, Toronto, ON M5B
1J3 Canada; Title Tel # (416) 977-7111 Title Fax # (416) 977-8886
Personnel: Editor-Maureen Huntley
Editorial Description: Purchasing matters, association news. Text in English and French.
General Info: (Formerly PMAC News), Bi-monthly, Trim Size-8½ x 11, Web press, 4 pages, 2 Color
Circulation: (100% controlled), Total-7,000
Advertising: Accepts Inserts.

Project Equality-Update
See: CIVIL RIGHTS

Purchaser's Legal Adviser   *Business*

Publishing Co: Business Laws, Inc., 11630 Chillicothe Rd., Chesterland, OH 44026-1928;
Title Tel # (216) 729-7996 Title Fax # (216) 729-0645
Personnel: Editor-William Hancock
General Info: Yr. Est. 1978, Monthly, 16 pages, ISSN: 0898-994X
Subscriptions: Indv. $167, $20/copy

Purchasing Executive's
Bulletin   *Business*

Publishing Co: Bureau of Business Practice, 24 Rope Ferry Rd, Waterford, CT 06386-0001
Tel # (806) 442-4365 Fax # (860) 434-3341 Parent Co.-Prentice Hall, Waterford;
Title Tel # (860) 442-4365
Personnel: Publisher-Martin E. Kenney, Jr., Editor-Wayne Muller
Editorial Description: Identifies trends and developments that are making efficient purchasing
essential to success in the industry. Gives readers detailed techniques used by the most successful
purchasing organizations.
General Info: Yr. Est. 1969, Semi-monthly, 4 pages
Subscriptions: Indv. $119
Circulation: Total-3,000

Purchasing Professional
Newsletter   *Business*   CPM: $214

Publishing Co: J & B Publishing Co., 24 Hardwood Hill Rd, Pittsford, NY 14534-4544;
Title Tel # (716) 248-2486
Personnel: Publisher, Editor-John Bruno, Production Mgr.-Joan Mallett, Adv. Dir.-Gregg Wood, Art
Dir.-Seth Hagstrom
Editorial Description: Information and opinion for purchasing executives and agents and for buyers.
General Info: (Formerly Genesee Valley Buyer), Yr. Est. 1989, 5x/yr., Trim Size-8½ x 11, Sheetfed
press, 24 pages, ISSN: 0192-9607, 4% ads, 4 Color, Saddle-stitched
Subscriptions: Indv. $15, $2/copy
Circulation: (100% controlled), Total-2,500
Advertising: $535.
List Rental: Rents Lists
Printing Co: D & D Printing, 1728 Clinton St, Buffalo, NY 14206-3190 Tel # (716) 822-1422

Smart Buying
Business

Publishing Co: Economics Press, Inc., 12 Daniel Rd., Fairfield, NJ 07004-2565; Title Tel # (201) 227-1224 Title Fax # (201) 227-9742
Personnel: Editor-Robert Guder, Promotion Dir.-Diane Cody
Editorial Description: Each issue explain one fundamental purchasing technique and illustrates it with examples from real companies.
General Info: Yr. Est. 1986, Bi-weekly
Subscriptions: Indv. $35
Circulation: Total-2,000
List Rental: List Management Co.: Manager: Michael Korman; Names in the News, 411 Theodore Fremd Ave., Rye, NY 10580 Tel # (914) 925-2400
Printing Co: Beckley Press, 2 Sperry Rd, Fairfield, NJ 07004-2056 Tel # (201) 227-6350

Transport (De)Regulation Report
See: TRAFFIC & TRANSPORTATION

WorldWide Business Exchange
See: BUSINESS & INDUSTRY

RAILROADS

Advanced Transportation Technology News
See: TRAFFIC & TRANSPORTATION

Along the Track
See: HOUSE ORGANS

CN Lines
Consumer, Association

Publishing Co: CN Lines Special Interest Group, 2488 Paige Janette Dr, Harvey, LA 70058-2137 Tel # (504) 347-0503 Parent Co.-Natl. Model Railroad Assn., Chattanooga
Personnel: Publisher, Editor-Michael J. Christian, Circ. Dir.-Alf Goodall, Art Dir.-Dick Dermody, Promotion Dir.-Eric Potter
Editorial Description: Covers railway history of Canadian National Railways, US subsidiaries, and how to model them.
General Info: Quarterly, Trim Size-8½ x 11, Letrpr. press, 32 pages, ISSN: 1061-9739, No Color, Coated, Saddle-stitched
Subscriptions: Indv. $16, Inst. $24, Can. $20, For. $24, $5/copy
Circulation: Total-400
List Rental: Rents Lists
Printing Co: Account Manager: Dino Merusi; Beacon Printing, 18 S Main St, Randolph, VT 05060-1366

Canadian Railway Club Newsletter
Association

Publishing Co: Canadian Railway Club, Box 162, Montreal, PQ H3C 1C5 Canada; Title Tel # (514) 634-4515
Editorial Description: Railway club activities, industry news, personnel profiles.
General Info: Yr. Est. 1903, Trim Size-8½ x 11, Sheetfed press, 8 pages, ISSN: 0226-157X, 3% ads, 2 Color
Circulation: Total-2,000
Advertising: Inquire for rates.

FELA Reporter and Railroad Liability Monitor
Business

Publishing Co: Lewis L. Laska, 901 Church St, Nashville, TN 37203-3411; Title Tel # (615) 255-6288 Title Fax # (615) 255-6289
Personnel: Publisher, Editor-Lewis Laska, Editorial Asst.-Lorenda Sue Patterson, J.D.
Editorial Description: Independent news journal of railroad litigation.
General Info: Yr. Est. 1988, Monthly, Trim Size-8½ x 11, Sheetfed press, 24 pages
Subscriptions: Indv. $385
Acquistions: Publication Bought

Grain Shipments
See: AGRICULTURE

HazMat Transport News
See: TRUCKING

Headlights

Publishing Co: Electric Railroaders' Assn., Box 6588, G.C.Sta., New York, NY 10163-6588; Title Tel # (212) 986-4482
Personnel: Editor-Arthur Lonto
Editorial Description: Devoted to the history and development of all types of electric railways. Covers main line electrification and expanding field of rail transit.
General Info: Yr. Est. 1934, Monthly, Trim Size-8½ x 11, Offset press, 8 pages
Subscriptions: Indv. $12, $1/copy
Circulation: Total-1,700

High Speed Transport News
Business

Publishing Co: Waters Information Services, PO Box 2248, Binghamton, NY 13902-2248; Title Tel # (607) 770-4075 Title Fax # (607) 770-9435
Personnel: Circ. Dir.-Allan Nixon
Editorial Description: Devoted to the global Magnetic Levitation and High Speed Rail industry.
General Info: (Formerly Maglev News), Yr. Est. 1992, Bi-weekly
Subscriptions: Indv. $495

Inside DOT and Transportation Week
See: TRAFFIC & TRANSPORTATION

International Railway Traveler
See: TRAVEL

LINEUP
Association

Publishing Co: Motorcar Operators West, PO Box 50908, Palo Alto, CA 94303-0673 Fax # (415) 917-1241; Title Tel # (415) 917-1224
Personnel: Editor-Michael Raposa
Editorial Description: Aimed at individuals interested in railroad motorcar restoration and operation.
General Info: Yr. Est. 1992, Bi-monthly, Trim Size-8½ x 11, 20 pages, No Color
Subscriptions: Indv. $24
Circulation: Total-225
Advertising: Accepts Inserts.
List Rental: Rents Lists

Manual for Railway Engineering
Association

Publishing Co: American Railway Engineering Association, 50 F St. N.W., Washington, DC 20001-1530; Title Tel # (202) 639-2190 Title Fax # (202) 639-2183
Personnel: Editor, Production Mgr.-Stefanie Streever, Circ. Mgr., Adv. Dir.-Wendy Tayman
Editorial Description: Specifications, rules, plans, & instructions developed by technical committees and adapted by the area as recommended practice.
General Info: (Formerly Manual for Railway Engineering and Maintenance of Way), Yr. Est. 1905, Annually, Sheetfed press, No Color, Looseleaf
Subscriptions: Indv. $376
Printing Co: Reproductions, Inc., 7621 Rickenbacker Dr, Gaithersburg, MD 20879 Tel # (301) 840-5400, Fax # (301) 590-1065

Marklin Club
See: HOBBY

Marklin Digital Club
See: HOBBY

Nailer News
See: COLLECTIBLES

New England States Limited

Publishing Co: New England Rail Service, PO Box 249, Newbury, VT 05051-0249
General Info: Quarterly
Subscriptions: Indv. $11
Circulation: Total-2,500

Newsline
See: TRAFFIC & TRANSPORTATION

Pacific Southwest Railway Museum Assn. -Report

Publishing Co: Pacific Southwest Railway Museum Assn., 4695 Nebo Dr, La Mesa, CA 91941-5259; Title Tel # (619) 595-3030
Personnel: Editor-Harry Joerring
General Info: Yr. Est. 1960, Bi-monthly, Sheetfed press, 12 pages, Coated
Circulation: Total-1,100

Rail Business
Business, Association

Publishing Co: Fieldston Co., 1920 N Street, N.W., Ste. 210, Washington, DC 20036; Title Tel # (202) 775-0240 Title Fax # (202) 872-8045
Personnel: Publications Director-Jay Kumar, Editor-Kurt Hoffman, Assoc. Ed.-John Gallagher, Mktg. Dir.-Laura Dowe
Editorial Description: Transportation news and information service.
General Info: Yr. Est. 1995, Bi-weekly, Trim Size-8½ x 11, 8 pages
Subscriptions: Indv. $415
Printing Co: Plymouth Printing, 1200 Cushing Pl SE, Washington, DC 20003-3599 Tel # (202) 488-7777, Fax # (202) 863-1078

Rail Carrier Digest Service
Business

Publishing Co: Hawkins Publishing Co., Inc., 1207 B Central Avenue, Box 480, Mayo, MD 21106; Title Tel # (410) 798-1677 Title Fax # (410) 798-1098
Personnel: Publisher, Editor-C.R. Eyler
Editorial Description: A loose-leaf indexed-analysis of reports of the Interstate Commerce Commission, the Federal and U.S. Supreme Courts relating to the Interstate Commerce Act in 10 volumes supplemented monthly.
General Info: Yr. Est. 1927, Monthly, Trim Size-8 x 10¾, Sheetfed press, No Color, Matte, Looseleaf
Subscriptions: Indv. $370
Circulation: Total-600

Rail Indiana
Business, Consumer

Publishing Co: Emergency Management Group, 1508 E 86th St., Ste 315, Indianapolis, IN 46240-1986 Tel # (317) 475-9572; Title Tel # (317) 475-9063 Title Fax # (317) 475-9403
Personnel: Publisher-D.L. Crichlow, Editor-S.A. Katt, Circ. Mgr.-A.J. Strong
Editorial Description: News of rail industry in Great Lakes region. Covers freight, passenger, excursion services as well as historical aspects of rail industry.
General Info: Yr. Est. 1991, Bi-weekly, Trim Size-8½ x 11, Offset press, 6 pages, No Color, Matte, Saddle-stitched
Subscriptions: Indv. $30, Inst. $52, Can. $42
Circulation: Total-1,841
Advertising: Accepts Inserts.

Rail Mart, The
Business   CPM: $320

Publishing Co: Rail Mart, 502 River Bluff Dr, Carpentersville, IL 60110-2825; Title Tel # (847) 428-5899 Title Fax # (847) 428-5991
Personnel: Publisher-Conrad Tannhauser
Editorial Description: Listing of different companies with railroad equipment for sale-lease or wanted. Including rolling stock locomotives, & maintenance of way equipment.
General Info: Yr. Est. 1986, Monthly, Offset press, 8 pages, ISSN: 1070-7751, 8% ads, 2 Color, Matte
Subscriptions: Indv. $20, Can. $25, For. $45
Circulation: Total-2,500
Advertising: $800. Accepts Inserts.
List Rental: Actives: 6,500, $110/M

Railroad Capital
Association

Publishing Co: Railroad Club of Chicago, PO Box 8292, Chicago, IL 60680-8292; Title Tel # (708) 251-2262
General Info: Yr. Est. 1951, Semi-monthly
Subscriptions: Free With Membership
Acquistions: Publication Bought, Publication Sold
Advertising: Accepts Inserts.

Railroad Evangelist
See: RELIGIOUS & THEOLOGICAL

Railroad History
Business

Publishing Co: Railway & Locomotive Historical Society, 1 Dept. Of History Univ. Of, Akron, Akron, OH 44325-1902; Title Tel # (216) 972-6199
Personnel: Editor-H. Roger Grant
Editorial Description: Primarily historical about railroads.
General Info: Yr. Est. 1921, Semi-annually, Trim Size-6 x 9, Offset press, 80 pages, ISSN: 0090-7847, Color
Subscriptions: Indv. $18, Inst. $35, $7/copy
Circulation: Total-4,100
Advertising: Inquire for rates.

Speedev
Association   CPM: $226

Publishing Co: Motor Car Collectors of America, Inc., 5 Bay View Hills, Wever, IA 52658; Title Tel # (319) 372-4866
Personnel: Editor-Mark D. Mayfield, Technology Ed.-Bill Kaminsky, Contrib. Ed.-Bill Pollard, Circ. Mgr.-Susan Mayfield, Feature Ed., Art Dir.-Jeffery Dobek
General Info: Yr. Est. 1986, Quarterly, Trim Size-8½ x 11, Offset press, 32 pages, 10% ads, No Color, Matte, Other
Subscriptions: For. $15, $3/copy
Circulation: Total-825, Readership-1,200
Advertising: $187. Accepts Inserts.

Table Top Train News
See: HOBBY

Train It
Business

Publishing Co: Assn. of American Railroads, 50 F St NW, Washington, DC 20001-1564; Title Tel # (202) 639-2556 Title Fax # (202) 639-2558
Personnel: Editor-Thomas White
Editorial Description: News affecting the railroad industry-legislative actions, government agencies actions, technological advancements, industry actions.
General Info: (Formerly Rail News Update), Yr. Est. 1933, Bi-weekly, Trim Size-8½ x 11, Offset press, 4 pages, No Color, Newsprint
Circulation: Total-2,000

Transfer, The
See: HISTORY

Union Pacific Bulletin

Publishing Co: Union Pacific Railroad Co., 1415 Dodge St, Omaha, NE 68102-1602; Title Tel # (402) 271-5000
Editorial Description: Railroad industry news and features.
General Info: Quarterly
Circulation: Total-75,000

U.S. Rail News
Business

Publishing Co: Business Publishers, Inc., 951 Pershing Dr., Silver Spring, MD 20910-4464 Tel # (301) 589-5103 Fax # (301) 589-8493; Title Tel # (301) 587-6300 Title Fax # (301) 587-1081
Personnel: Publisher-Eric Easton, Editor-Steve Lash, Circ. Mgr.-Allison Inglesby
Editorial Description: Technical, regulatory & economic developments affecting America's rail lines and operators.
General Info: Yr. Est. 1978, Bi-weekly, Trim Size-8½ x 11, Desktop press, 8 pages, ISSN: 0275-3758, Ind/Abs/Online: Newsnet and Predicasts, No Color, Recycled
Subscriptions: Indv. $429, Can. $429, For. $442
Advertising: Accepts Inserts.
List Rental: List Management Co.: Manager: Donald Peterson; BPI Direct, 951 Pershing Dr., Silver Spring, MD 20910-4464 Tel # (301) 585-5976, Fax # (301) 587-4530

Urban Transport News
See: TRAFFIC & TRANSPORTATION

Views and News
Association

Publishing Co: American Short Line Railroad Assn., 1120 G St NW Ste 520, Washington, DC 20005-3801; Title Tel # (202) 785-2250 Title Fax # (202) 887-0275
Personnel: Editor-T. Dorsey
Editorial Description: Transportation topics, personnel.
General Info: Yr. Est. 1933, Weekly, Trim Size-8½ x 11, Offset press, 5 pages, No Color
Circulation: (100% controlled), Total-1,400

WG&L Human Resources Forms with Commentary
See: INDUSTRIAL RELATIONS/PERSONNEL

Waybill, The
Association   CPM: $45

Publishing Co: Mystic Valley Railway Society, PO Box 486, Hyde Park, MA 02136-0005; Title Tel # (617) 361-4445 Title Fax # (617) 361-4445
Personnel: Editor-W. Russell Rylko, Adv. Dir.-Richard Eaton, Promotion Dir.-Fannie Chung
Editorial Description: Schedules of events and unique activities relating to railroading.
General Info: Yr. Est. 1970, Quarterly, Trim Size-11 x 17, Web press, 8 pages, ISSN: 0897-7577, 25% ads, No Color, Newsprint
Subscriptions: Indv. $4
Acquistions: Publication Bought
Circulation: Total-14,000
Advertising: $640.
Printing Co: Bradford Printers, 20 Winthrop Street, Mansfield, MA 02048 Tel # (508) 337-6415

West Coast Railway Assn. Newsletter
Association

Publishing Co: West Coast Railway Assn., Box 2790, Vancouver, BC V6B 3X2 Canada; Title Tel # (604) 524-1011 Title Fax # (604) 522-1293
Personnel: Editor-Don Evans
Editorial Description: News of West Coast Railway Assn. museum & activities, current railway new from western Canada, rail tours.
General Info: Yr. Est. 1961, Monthly, 20 pages, ISSN: 1204-072x, No Color
Subscriptions: Indv. $30, $2/copy
Circulation: Total-450

REAL ESTATE

AOMA Newsletter
Business, Association

Publishing Co: Apt. Owners & Managers Assn. of America, PO Box 238, Watertown, CT 06795-0238; Title Tel # (203) 274-2589 Title Fax # (203) 274-2580
Personnel: Editor-Robert McGough
Editorial Description: Practical information for the builder/developer/owner of multi-family housing.
General Info: Yr. Est. 1967, Monthly, Trim Size-8½ x 11, Offset press, 4 pages, Ind/Abs/Online: Charts.Illus., Newsprint, Saddle-stitched
Subscriptions: Indv. $125, Free With Membership
Circulation: (100% controlled), Total-5,200
Advertising: Inquire for rates. Accepts Inserts.
List Rental: Actives: $75/M

Agency Law Quarterly Real Estate Intelligence Report
Business

Publishing Co: Agency Law Quarterly, PO Box 5702, Portsmouth, NH 03802-5702; Title Tel # (603) 433-2650 Title Fax # (603) 436-5202
Personnel: Publisher-Frank Cook, Editor-Pat Remick
Editorial Description: News regarding real estate , trends, issues, technology & legal cases.
General Info: (Formerly Agency Law Quarterly), Yr. Est. 1989, Monthly, Trim Size-8½ x 11, 16 pages, 2 Color
Subscriptions: Indv. $157

Alliance
Association

Publishing Co: American Rental Association, 1900 19th St., Moline, IL 61265-4198 Fax # (309) 764-1533; Title Tel # (309) 764-2475
Personnel: Editor-Michael Moore
Editorial Description: Updates on local & state assn. activities of the American Rental Assn.
General Info: (Formerly State Lines), Yr. Est. 1990, Monthly, Sheetfed press, No Color, Newsprint
Circulation: Total-450
Printing Co: Fuller's Printery, 835 5th Ave, Moline, IL 61265-1237 Tel # (309) 762-5811

American Chapter News — *Association*

Publishing Co: American Chapter, Int'l Real Estate Fed., 777 14th St NW, Washington, DC 20005-3201; Title Tel # (202) 383-1032
Personnel: Editor-Teresa Salmon, Adv. Dir.-Evie Eisenstein
General Info: Quarterly, 8 pages, 2 Color
Subscriptions: Indv. $110
Circulation: (100% controlled), Total-1,200

Apartment Management Newsletter — *Business*

Publishing Co: AMN Publishing Inc., 380 Lexington Ave. #1700, New York, NY 10168-0002; Title Tel # (212) 551-1166
Personnel: Publisher, Editor-Helene Mandelbaum, Circ. Mgr.-Vera West
Editorial Description: News & information for apartment owners & managers, including tips & techniques for marketing, maintenance, personnel & compliance with national laws & requirements.
General Info: Yr. Est. 1975, Monthly, Trim Size-8½ x 11, Offset press, 8 pages, ISSN: 0744-9143, 2 Color, Matte
Subscriptions: Indv. $95, Can. $95, $6/copy
Advertising: Accepts Inserts.
List Rental: List Management Co.: Walter Karl Business Lists, One American Lane, Greenwich, CT 06831 Tel # (203) 552-6700, Fax # (203) 552-6799, Actives: 29,488, $75/M

Apartment Management Report — *Business, Association*

Publishing Co: Apt. Owners & Managers Assn. of America, PO Box 238, Watertown, CT 06795-0238 Fax # (203) 274-2580; Title Tel # (203) 274-2589
Personnel: Editor-Robert McGough, Circ. Mgr., Adv. Dir.-Robt. McGough
Editorial Description: For managers/rental agents of apartments and condominiums.
General Info: Yr. Est. 1967, Monthly, Offset press, 4 pages
Subscriptions: Indv. $72, $6/copy
Circulation: Total-6,850
Advertising: Inquire for rates. Accepts Inserts.

Appraisal Institute Digest — *Business*

Publishing Co: Appraisal Inst. of Canada, 1111 Porpege Ave., Winnipeg, MB R3G OS8 Canada Tel # (204) 783-3224 Fax # (204) 783-5575; Title Tel # (204) 782-2224
Personnel: Publisher, Editor-Erin Foulkes
Editorial Description: Information on appraisal institute services & programs.
General Info: Yr. Est. 1968, Quarterly, Trim Size-8½ x 11, 4 pages, ISSN: 0003-7079, 2 Color
Acquistions: Publication Bought
Circulation: (100% controlled), Total-8,400
List Rental: Rents Lists

Appraisal Management & Marketing — *Business*

Publishing Co: Real Estate Communications Resources, 1815 Clement Ave. #7, Alameda, CA 94501-1313; Title Tel # (510) 865-8041 Title Fax # (510) 523-1138
Personnel: Publisher, Editor-Ann O'Rourke
Editorial Description: For owners of real estate appraisal businesses.
General Info: Yr. Est. 1992, Monthly, Trim Size-8½ x 11, Web press, 12 pages, ISSN: 1066-5900, 2 Color, Matte
Subscriptions: Indv. $250
Circulation: Total-700
List Rental: Rents Lists

Appraiser Gram — *Business, Association*

Publishing Co: National Association of Independent Fee Appraisers, 7501 Murdoch Ave., St. Louis, MO 63119-2810; Title Tel # (314) 781-6688 Title Fax # (314) 781-2872
Personnel: Editor-Donna Walter
Editorial Description: Assoication news as well as others news that affects real-estate appraisers.
General Info: Yr. Est. 1962, Monthly
Subscriptions: Indv. $10, For. $20
Circulation: Total-5,300
Advertising: Inquire for rates.

Appraiser News — *Association*

Publishing Co: Appraisal Institute, 875 N. Michigan Ave., Suite 2400, Chicago, IL 60611-1980; Title Tel # (312) 335-4100 Title Fax # (312) 335-4400
Personnel: Editor-Grace Hayek, Assoc. Ed.-Donna O'Loughlin
Editorial Description: News bulletin covering current events and trends in real estate appraisal. Regular features include regulatory and legislative issues, job listings, and national economic and real estate related data.
General Info: (Formerly The Appraiser), Yr. Est. 1991, Monthly, Trim Size-8½ x 11, Sheetfed press, 20 pages, ISSN: 1054-5999, 2 Color, Matte, Saddle-stitched
Subscriptions: Indv. $20, For. $25, $2/copy
Circulation: Total-38,500

Assisted Housing Management Insider — *Business*

Publishing Co: Brownstone Publishers, Inc., 149 5th Ave., 16th Floor, New York, NY 10010-6801; Title Tel # (212) 473-8200 Title Fax # (212) 473-8786
Personnel: Publisher-John Striker, Editor-David B. Klein, Circ. Dir.-Cassie Feng, Production Dir.-Mary Lopez, Promotion Dir.-James Bell
Editorial Description: Explains HUD regulatory requirements for federally-assisted housing and gives advice and tips. Includes sample copies of model lease clauses, letters, eviction notices, authorization forms, checklists, and signs.
General Info: (Formerly Commercial Property Law Digests), Yr. Est. 1992, Monthly, Trim Size-8½ x 11, Sheetfed press, 8 pages, ISSN: 1072-009X, 2 Color
Subscriptions: Indv. $245, $20/copy
List Rental: Rents Lists
Printing Co: Globe Mail Agency, Inc., 541 W 25th St, New York, NY 10001-5501 Tel # (212) 675-4600

BNA's Environmental Due Diligence Guide
See: ENVIRONMENT & ECOLOGY

Board Briefs
See: MANAGEMENT

British Columbia Real Estate Law Guide — *Business*

Publishing Co: CCH Canadian Ltd., 6 Garamond Ct., North York, ON M3C 1Z5 Canada Fax # (416) 444-8011 Parent Co.-CCH, Inc., Riverwoods; Title Tel # (416) 441-2992 Title Fax # (416) 444-9011
Personnel: Editor-Chris Probert
Editorial Description: Coverage of the law governing real estate transactions in B.C. Text of more than 50 consolidated statutes and regulations.
General Info: Monthly, Trim Size-6 x 9, Web press, No Color, Looseleaf
Subscriptions: Can. $490

Building Environment Report
See: CONSTRUCTION & BUILDING

Bulletin — *Association*

Publishing Co: Property Management Assn., 8811 Colesville Rd Apt G106, Silver Spring, MD 20910-4343; Title Tel # (301) 587-6543
Personnel: Publisher-J. Bachner, Editor-T. Cohn, Circ. Mgr.-Annie Vasquez, Production Mgr.-J. Ferguson, Adv. Dir.-MaryLou Schenkel
Editorial Description: News about industry & assoc. events & developments.
General Info: Yr. Est. 1952, Monthly, Trim Size-8½ x 11, Offset press, 24 pages, No Color, Newsprint
Subscriptions: Indv. $100
Circulation: Total-1,000
Advertising: Inquire for rates.

CAAS News — *Association*

Publishing Co: Sponsor-IAAO, International Association of Assessing Officers, 130 E. Randolph, Suite 850, Chicago, IL 60601-6217 Tel # (312) 819-6100; Title Tel # (312) 947-2060 Title Fax # (312) 819-6149
Personnel: Editor-Roberta Hilleman
Editorial Description: Deals with computer-assisted property appraisal techniques.
General Info: (Formerly EDP News), Yr. Est. 1984, Quarterly, Trim Size-8½ x 11, Offset press, 8 pages, ISSN: 8755-3732, 2 Color, Newsprint, Saddle-stitched
Circulation: (100% controlled), Total-800

CD-Housing Register — *Business*

Publishing Co: CD Publications, 8204 Fenton St., Silver Spring, MD 20910-4571; Title Tel # (301) 588-6380 Title Fax # (301) 588-6385
Personnel: Publisher-Mike Gerecht, Circ. Mgr.-Kurt Eisentraut, Mktg. Dir.-Joyce Meals
Editorial Description: Reprints material from the Federal Register, saving research time.
General Info: Yr. Est. 1983, Semi-monthly, Trim Size-8½ x 11, Sheetfed press, 24 pages, ISSN: 1050-3811, No Color, Matte, Looseleaf
Subscriptions: Indv. $399, $15/copy
Acquistions: Publication Bought, Publication Sold
List Rental: List Management Co.: Manager: Amy Seyler; Washington Advertising Service, 8204 Fenton St., Silver Spring, MD 20910 Tel # (301) 588-7920, Fax # (301) 588-6385, Actives: 1,971, $150/M, Expires: $150/M

CPM Aspects — *Association*

Publishing Co: Institute of Real Estate Management, 430 N. Michigan Ave., Chicago, IL 60611-4090 Tel # (312) 329-6000; Title Tel # (312) 329-6055 Title Fax # (312) 661-0217
Personnel: VP Pubs.-Joyce Travis Copess, Exec. VP/Group Publisher-Ronald Vuka, Editor-Pam Chwedyk, Editorial Dir.-Martha McGregor, Circ. Mgr.-Carole Hansen, Production-J. Stephen Reed, Production Mgr., Art Dir.-Thom Olson, Graphic Designer-Mark Gettner, Adv. Dir., Mktg. Dir.-Patricia Hoffman
Editorial Description: Membership newsletter for certified property manager CPM members of IREM and CPM Candidates. Includes news and features on industry trends; IREM policies and programs; legislation affecting real estate management; members' achievements; jobs bulletin.
General Info: Yr. Est. 1968, Bi-monthly, Trim Size-8½ x 11, 20 pages, ISSN: 0199-7653, No Color, Matte, Saddle-stitched
Subscriptions: Free With Membership
Circulation: (2% controlled), Subscriptions-12,276
List Rental: List Management Co.: Direct Media, Inc., 200 Pemberwick Rd., PO Box 4565, Greenwich, CT 06830 Tel # (203) 532-3713, Fax # (203) 531-1452, Actives: $100/M
Printing Co: Account Manager: Ian Scarlett; Chicago Press, 1112 N Homan Ave, Chicago, IL 60651-4007 Tel # (312) 276-1500, Fax # (312) 276-4595

CRA/HMDA Update
See: BANKING & FINANCE

California News Etc. *Business*

Publishing Co: California News Etc., 215 Beach St., Santa Cruz, CA 95060
Editorial Description: Covers real estate matters including legislation, in California.

California Real Estate Law and Practice *Business*

Publishing Co: Matthew Bender & Co., 11 Penn Plaza, New York, NY 10001-2006 Fax # (212) 244-3188; Title Tel # (212) 967-7707
Personnel: Editor-B. Ryan
Editorial Description: Treatise on California real estate law and practice.
General Info: Yr. Est. 1973, Irregular, Looseleaf
Subscriptions: $750/copy

California Real Estate Reporter *Business*

Publishing Co: Matthew Bender & Co., 11 Penn Plaza, New York, NY 10001-2006 Tel # (212) 967-7707 Fax # (212) 244-3188
Personnel: Editor-David W. Walters
Editorial Description: A monthly digest of all California real estate cases and newly enacted legislation, and regulations.
General Info: Yr. Est. 1986, Monthly, Looseleaf

Canadian Commercial Law Guide
See: LAW

Canadian Real Estate Income Tax Guide
See: TAXES

Capital Sources in Real Estate *Business*

Publishing Co: Warren, Gorham & Lamont, 31 Saint James Ave., Boston, MA 02116-4112 Parent Co.-Thomson Professional Publications, Stamford; Title Tel # (617) 423-2020 Title Fax # (617) 423-1914
Personnel: Publisher-Larry Selby, Mktg. Dir.-Sandra Fox
General Info: Yr. Est. 1994, Monthly
Subscriptions: Indv. $145
List Rental: List Management Co.: Manager: Seena Benedek; WG & L List Management, 1 Penn Plz Fl 42, New York, NY 10119-0002 Tel # (212) 971-5000

Caretaker Gazette, The
See: EMPLOYMENT

Carlson Report for Shopping Center Management *Business*

Publishing Co: Report Communications, 9595 Whitley Dr Ste 100, Indianapolis, IN 46240-1308; Title Tel # (317) 844-9024 Title Fax # (317) 848-6953
Personnel: Publisher, Editor-William Wilburn, Circ. Mgr.-Patty Williams, Production Mgr.-Bridget Gurtowsky, Adv. Dir.-Marsha Davis
Editorial Description: For shopping center managers.
General Info: Yr. Est. 1982, Monthly, Trim Size-8½ x 11, Offset press, 16 pages, ISSN: 0889-2288, 2 Color, Saddle-stitched
Subscriptions: Indv. $125, Can. $145, $18/copy
Acquistions: Publication Bought, Publication Sold
Circulation: Total-1,520
Advertising: Inquire for rates. Accepts Inserts.
List Rental: List Management Co.: Manager: Marsha Davis; Twin Peaks Press, PO Box 129, Vancouver, WA 98666-0129 Tel # (206) 694-2462, Fax # (206) 696-3210, Actives: $125/M

Clipboard

Publishing Co: American Assn. of Certified Appraisers, 800 Compton Rd # 10, Cincinnati, OH 45231-3847; Title Tel # (513) 729-1400 Title Fax # (513) 729-1401
Personnel: Editor-Tom Sherman
General Info: Yr. Est. 1977, 4 pages
Subscriptions: Free With Membership
Circulation: Total-2,000
Advertising: Accepts Inserts.

Collier Real Estate Transactions and the Bankruptcy Code *Business*

Publishing Co: Matthew Bender & Co., 11 Penn Plaza, New York, NY 10001-2006 Tel # (212) 967-7707 Fax # (212) 244-3188
Personnel: Editor in Chief-Lawrence P. King
Editorial Description: A practice-oriented guide to the impact of bankruptcy on real estate transactions. Examines the entire Bankruptcy Code with emphasis on provisions directly realted to real estate. Also provided are sample clauses & helpful drafting considerations for thereal estate transactions discussed.
General Info: Yr. Est. 1984, Irregular, Looseleaf

Commercial Lease Law Insider *Business*

Publishing Co: Brownstone Publishers, Inc., 149 5th Ave., 16th Floor, New York, NY 10010-6801; Title Tel # (212) 473-8200 Title Fax # (212) 473-8786
Personnel: Publisher-John Striker, Editor in Chief-Andrew Shapiro, Editor-Nicole Lefton, Circ. Mgr.-Cassie Feng, Production Mgr.-Mary Lopez, Promotion Dir.-Jim Bell
Editorial Description: Presents tested commercial leasing strategies techniques, and insights. Features include model lease causes and checklists, as well as coverage of new court decisions affecting commercial leases.
General Info: Yr. Est. 1982, Monthly, Trim Size-8½ x 11, Sheetfed press, 10 pages, ISSN: 0736-0517, 2 Color, Recycled
Subscriptions: Indv. $236, $19/copy
Acquistions: Publication Bought
List Rental: Actives: $110/M, Expires: $90/M
Printing Co: Globe Mail Agency, Inc., 541 W 25th St, New York, NY 10001-5501 Tel # (212) 675-4600

Commercial Mortgage Alert
See: BANKING & FINANCE

Commercial Real Estate Digest *Business*

Publishing Co: Vestal Communications, 334 Humphrey Dr, Evergreen, CO 80439-9655 Tel # (303) 674-0501; Title Tel # (800) 776-4515
Personnel: Publisher-Robert Vestal
Editorial Description: Ready-to-print newsletter for keeping in contact with clients available to real estate agents, etc.
General Info: Yr. Est. 1986, Quarterly
Subscriptions: Indv. $495
List Rental: Rents Lists

CommonWealth Letters
See: INVESTMENT

Community Association Law Reporter *Association*

Publishing Co: Sponsor-Community Ass. Institute, Community Associations Institute, 1630 Duke Street, Alexandria, VA 22314 Tel # (703) 548-8600; Title Tel # (708) 548-8600 Title Fax # (703) 684-1581
Personnel: Exec. VP/Group Publisher-Barbara Byrd-Lawler, Editor-Wayne Hyatt, Mng. Editor-Amanda Tirpak
Editorial Description: A review of recent court findings in Community Association Law for attorneys & community.
General Info: Yr. Est. 1974, Monthly, Sheetfed press, 8 pages, ISSN: 0190-1192, 2 Color, Other
Subscriptions: Indv. $150, $8/copy
Circulation: Total-3,800
Printing Co: Ameriprint, 300 Mill St NE, Vienna, VA 22180-4524 Tel # (703) 281-7800

Community Economics
See: ECONOMICS

Condo Sales Report *Business*

Publishing Co: Yale Robbins Inc., 31 E. 28th St., New York, NY 10016-7959; Title Tel # (212) 683-5700
Personnel: Publisher, Editor-Yale Robbins, Circ. Mgr.-Henry Robbins
Editorial Description: An analysis of condo sales in Manhattan, building by building, apt. by apt.
General Info: Monthly, Offset press, Newsprint

Coop/Condo Conversion Digest *Business*

Publishing Co: Yale Robbins Inc., 31 E. 28th St., New York, NY 10016-7959; Title Tel # (212) 683-5700
Personnel: Publisher, Editor-Yale Robbins, Circ. Mgr.-Henry Robbins
Editorial Description: Abstract of offering plans for the conversion of existing rental apartments to coop/condo for Manhattan, Bronx, Brooklyn, and Queens.
General Info: Yr. Est. 1978, Monthly, Offset press, No Color, Looseleaf

Cooperative Housing Bulletin CPM: $40

Publishing Co: National Association of Housing Cooperatives, 1614 King St, Alexandria, VA 22314-2719; Title Tel # (703) 549-5201 Title Fax # (703) 549-5204
Personnel: Editor-Herbert Levy, Circ. Mgr.-Michelle Soplop, Production Mgr., Adv. Dir.-Kate Law
Editorial Description: Report of national, congressional, state & local cooperative housing activities & court cases. Articles of interest to co-op housing community
General Info: Yr. Est. 1950, Bi-monthly, Trim Size-8½ x 11, Letrpr. press, 20 pages, ISSN: 0097-9759, 37% ads, 2 Color, Matte, Saddle-stitched
Subscriptions: Indv. $50, Inst. $50, Can. $55, For. $60, Free With Membership
Circulation: (40% controlled), Total-2,500
Advertising: $100.
Printing Co: Chelsea Printing Co., 1605 King St., Alexandria, VA 22314 Tel # (703) 684-1998

Cornerstone *Association*

Publishing Co: Natl. Realty Committee, 1420 New York Ave NW Ste 1100, Washington, DC 20005-2122; Title Tel # (202) 785-0808 Title Fax # (202) 223-3857
Personnel: Editor-Cary Brazeman
Editorial Description: Covers public policy issues affecting the real estate industry national level.
General Info: Yr. Est. 1982, Bi-monthly
Circulation: (100% controlled), Total-2,000

Cornerstone Landmark Newsletter
Consumer, Association

Publishing Co: The Landmark Society, 133 Fitzhugh St S, Rochester, NY 14608-2204; Title Tel # (716) 546-7029
Editorial Description: Information on historical landmarks.
General Info: (Formerly Landmark Newsletter), Bi-monthly

Council of New York Cooperatives Newsletter
Business, Association

Publishing Co: Council of New York Cooperatives, 2112 Broadway Rm 202, New York, NY 10023-2142; Title Tel # (212) 496-7400 Title Fax # (212) 580-7801
Personnel: Editor-Mary Ann Rothman
Editorial Description: For members of the CNYC giving association and cooperative industry information.
General Info: Semi-annually, Trim Size-8½ x 11, 22 pages, No Color, Matte

Country Bound Connection
Consumer

Publishing Co: Communication Creativity, 425 Cedar St., Box 909-OX, Buena Vista, CO 81211 Fax # (719) 395-8374; Title Tel # (719) 395-8659
Personnel: Publisher-Tom Ross, Editor-Marilyn Ross, Production Mgr.-Michelle Allen, Promotion Dir.-Ann Markham
Editorial Description: A clearinghouse of information for those who want to relocate from urban to rural areas. Our objective is to help people make successful moves and discover how they can earn a good living in 'Small Town America.'
General Info: Yr. Est. 1992, Quarterly, Sheetfed press, 8 pages, ISSN: 1065-4771
Subscriptions: Indv. $49
Advertising: Accepts Inserts.

Cricket Letter
Business

Publishing Co: Cricket Communications, Inc., PO Box 527, Ardmore, PA 19003-0527; Title Tel # (215) 747-6684 Title Fax # (215) 747-7082
Personnel: Publisher, Editor-Mark E. Battersby
Editorial Description: The newsletter for international investment in the U.S.
General Info: Yr. Est. 1971, Monthly, Trim Size-8½ x 11, Sheetfed press, 12 pages, No Color, Newsprint
Subscriptions: Indv. $315
Acquistions: Publication Bought
Circulation: Total-2,681

Crittenden Real Estate Buyers

Publishing Co: Crittenden Research, Inc., PO Box 1150, Novato, CA 94948 Fax # (619) 437-4204; Title Tel # (415) 382-2400
Personnel: Publisher-Bob Fink, Editor-John Goodwin, Circ. Mgr.-Bob Bonebrake
General Info: Yr. Est. 1984, Weekly, ISSN: 0888-9139
Subscriptions: Indv. $395

Crittenden Report Real Estate Financing

Publishing Co: Crittenden Research, Inc., PO Box 1150, Novato, CA 94948 Tel # (415) 382-2400 Fax # (619) 437-4204; Title Tel # (415) 382-2477
General Info: Weekly, ISSN: 0736-0339
Subscriptions: Indv. $395

DC Line
Business

Publishing Co: Washington D.C. Assn. Realtors, 777 14th St. , N. W. 2nd fl., Washington, DC 20005-3201; Title Tel # (202) 628-4646
Personnel: Editor-Virginia Kitzmiller
Editorial Description: Info. on Washington DC real estate industry, market activity, & legislation.
General Info: (Formerly Realtor), Yr. Est. 1956, Monthly, Sheetfed press, 12 pages, No Color, Coated
Circulation: (100% controlled), Total-4,000
Advertising: Inquire for rates. Accepts Inserts.
List Rental: Actives: $150/M
Printing Co: Corporate Press, 403 Brightseat Rd., Landover, MD 20785-4706 Tel # (301) 499-9200, Fax # (301) 499-5435

Dealmakers
See: CONSTRUCTION & BUILDING

Delogram

Publishing Co: Del Property Management, Inc., 4800 Dufferin St., Downsview, ON M3H 5S9 Canada Tel # (416) 661-3640 Fax # (416) 661-8653
Personnel: Editor-Patricia MacKellar
Editorial Description: Information for Del Property Management customers.

Developers and Chains

Publishing Co: Wayne Patterson, PO Box 130, Grimsby, ON L5M 4G3 Canada; Title Tel # (905) 945-8365
Personnel: Editor-Wayne Paterson, Circ. Mgr.-Diana Yeo
Editorial Description: Weekly information for shopping mall developers & retail chains.
General Info: Yr. Est. 1981, Weekly, Sheetfed press, 8 pages
Subscriptions: Indv. $289
Acquistions: Publication Sold
List Rental: Rents Lists

Digest of State Land Sales Regulations
Business

Publishing Co: Land Development Law Reporter, 1401 16th St NW, Washington, DC 20036-2201; Title Tel # (202) 232-2144 Title Fax # (202) 232-4757
Personnel: Publisher-Stuart Marshall Bloch, Editor-Steve Sullivan, Circ. Mgr.-Pat Hunter
Editorial Description: Summarizes state laws on land sales timesharing, resorts, & condominiums.
General Info: Yr. Est. 1975, Quarterly, Trim Size-8½ x 11, 24 pages, ISSN: 0739-6368, Matte, Looseleaf
Subscriptions: Indv. $220
Circulation: (100% controlled), Total-400

Directions in Commercial Real Estate
Business

Publishing Co: Vestal Communications, 334 Humphrey Dr, Evergreen, CO 80439-9655 Tel # (303) 674-0501; Title Tel # (800) 776-4515
Personnel: Publisher-Robert Vestal
Editorial Description: Ready-to-print newsletter for keeping in contact with clients.
General Info: Yr. Est. 1988, Quarterly
Subscriptions: Indv. $199
List Rental: Rents Lists

Distressed Property Investor's Monthly
Business

Publishing Co: Real Estate Publications, Inc., 322 W. Rid Vista Ct., Tampa, FL 33604-6941; Title Tel # (813) 237-0484
Personnel: Publisher-Thomas j. Lucier, Editor-Thomas J. Lucier, Production Mgr.-Barbara V. Lucier
Editorial Description: A do-it-yourself guide on how to make money from distressed properties such as foreclosures, probates, tax deed sales, IRS seized property sales, etc. Aimed at individual investors
General Info: (Formerly Diamonds in the Rough), Yr. Est. 1988, Monthly, Trim Size-8½ x 11, 4 pages, ISSN: 1048-2938
Subscriptions: Indv. $70, $6/copy
Circulation: Total-2,000

District of Columbia Real Estate Reporter
Business, Association

Publishing Co: Land Development Law Reporter, 1401 16th St NW, Washington, DC 20036-2201; Title Tel # (202) 232-2144 Title Fax # (202) 232-4757
Personnel: Publisher-William Ingersoll, Editor-Steve Sullivan, Circ. Mgr.-Pat Hunter
Editorial Description: Covering legal & regulatory developments in the D. C. real estate industry.
General Info: Yr. Est. 1979, Monthly, Trim Size-8½ x 11, Offset press, 8 pages, No Color
Subscriptions: Indv. $225
Circulation: Total-250

FMRA News
See: AGRICULTURE

Federal Income Taxation of Real Estate
Business

Publishing Co: Warren, Gorham & Lamont, 31 Saint James Ave., Boston, MA 02116-4112 Parent Co.-Thomson Professional Publications, Stamford; Title Tel # (617) 423-2020 Title Fax # (617) 423-1914
Personnel: Publisher-Wayne Barr, Production Mgr.-Mavra Kiey, Mktg. Dir.-Jim Spillane
Editorial Description: Explains problem areas and tax savings opportunities that exist in real estate.
General Info: Yr. Est. 1988, Irregular, Looseleaf
Subscriptions: Indv. $115
List Rental: List Management Co.: WG & L List Management, 1 Penn Plz Fl 42, New York, NY 10119-0002 Tel # (212) 971-5000

Federal Income Taxation of Real Estate: Forms & Analysis

Publishing Co: Warren, Gorham & Lamont, 31 Saint James Ave., Boston, MA 02116-4112 Parent Co.-Thomson Professional Publications, Stamford; Title Tel # (617) 423-2020 Title Fax # (617) 423-1914
Personnel: Publisher-William Barr, Production Mgr.-Mavra Kiey, Mktg. Dir.-Jim Spillane
Editorial Description: Collection of practice-tested forms covering purchase and sale, leases, partnerships, and exchanges in residential, commercial and investment property.
General Info: Yr. Est. 1989, Irregular, Looseleaf
Subscriptions: Indv. $110
List Rental: List Management Co.: WG & L List Management, 1 Penn Plz Fl 42, New York, NY 10119-0002 Tel # (212) 971-5000

Financial Services Daily Fax
See: BANKING & FINANCE

Flight Lines

Publishing Co: Real Estate Aviation Chapter, 5440 St. Charles Rd., Berkeley, IL 60163-1231; Title Tel # (708) 547-7100

Florida Real Estate & Development *Business*

Publishing Co: Boerner Communications, P.O. Box L, Manhasset, NY 11030;
Title Tel # (516) 741-8887 Title Fax # (516) 741-3131
Personnel: Editor-Henry Boerner
Editorial Description: Covers real estate development & land use in Florida.
General Info: Yr. Est. 1986, Monthly, 12 pages
Subscriptions: Indv. $200
Circulation: Total-2,000
Advertising: Accepts Inserts.

Florida Real Estate Transactions *Business*

Publishing Co: Matthew Bender & Co., 11 Penn Plaza, New York, NY 10001-2006
Fax # (212) 244-3188; Title Tel # (212) 967-7707
Editorial Description: Treatise on Florida Real Property Law.
General Info: Yr. Est. 1959, Irregular, Looseleaf
Subscriptions: $400/copy

Focus
See: COLLEGE STUDENT

Focus on Canadian Municipal Assessment & Taxation *Business, Association*

Publishing Co: CCH Canadian Ltd., 6 Garamond Ct., North York, ON M3C 1Z5 Canada
Fax # (416) 444-8011 Parent Co.-CCH, Inc., Riverwoods; Title Tel # (416) 441-2992
Title Fax # (416) 444-9011
Personnel: Editor-Steven Allan
Editorial Description: Surveys all aspects of real property appraisals & assessments in Canada.
General Info: Monthly, ISSN: 0833-0123
Subscriptions: Can. $185

Forecaster Moneyletter, The
See: ECONOMICS

Forum

Publishing Co: Arizona State University, Publications, Tempe, AZ 85287; Title Tel # (602) 965-5440
Title Fax # (602) 965-5458
Personnel: Publisher-Jay Butler, Editor-Nan Beams
Editorial Description: To examine all aspects of the various issues which are relevant to the Real Estate industry in Arizona.
General Info: Yr. Est. 1988, Quarterly, Trim Size-8½ x 11, Sheetfed press, 12 pages, ISSN: 1042-6817, 2 Color, Newsprint, Saddle-stitched
Circulation: (100% controlled), Total-2,500

Georgia Real Estate Law Letter
See: LAW

Gordon Office Market Report *Business*

Publishing Co: Edward S. Gordon Co., 200 Park Ave, New York, NY 10166-0106
Tel # (212) 984-8000 Fax # (212) 984-8207
Personnel: Editor-Kathleen McKee
General Info: Yr. Est. 1987, Semi-annually

Guide to Construction Activity in Manhattan *Business*

Publishing Co: Yale Robbins Inc., 31 E. 28th St., New York, NY 10016-7959;
Title Tel # (212) 683-5700
Personnel: Publisher, Editor-Yale Robbins, Circ. Mgr.-Henry Robbins
Editorial Description: 2 1/2 year forecast of construction activity in Manhattan, residential and commercial.
General Info: Annually, Offset press, No Color, Coated, Looseleaf

Housing Affairs Letter *Business*

Publishing Co: CD Publications, 8204 Fenton St., Silver Spring, MD 20910-4571;
Title Tel # (301) 588-6380 Title Fax # (301) 588-6385
Personnel: Publisher-Mike Gerecht, Editor-Bob Duke, Circ. Mgr.-Kurt Eisentraut, Mktg. Dir.-Joyce Meals
Editorial Description: Covers natl. housing legislation, regulations, mortgage, markets & local news.
General Info: Yr. Est. 1961, Weekly, Trim Size-8½ x 11, Sheetfed press, 8 pages, ISSN: 0018-6554, No Color, Matte, Other
Subscriptions: Indv. $384, Can. $394, For. $424, $15/copy
List Rental: List Management Co.: Manager: Amy Seyler; Washington Advertising Service, 8204 Fenton St., Silver Spring, MD 20910 Tel # (301) 588-7920, Fax # (301) 588-6385, Actives: 6,775, $150/M, Expires: 4,677, $150/M

Housing and Development Reporter/ Current Developments *Business*

Publishing Co: Warren, Gorham & Lamont, 31 Saint James Ave., Boston, MA 02116-4112 Parent Co.-Thomson Professional Publications, Stamford; Title Tel # (617) 423-2020
Title Fax # (617) 423-1914
Personnel: Publisher-Larry Selby, Mktg. Dir.-Sandra Fox
Editorial Description: Ongoing coverage and practical guidance on current activities in the housing development industry.
General Info: Yr. Est. 1986, Bi-weekly
Subscriptions: Indv. $575
List Rental: List Management Co.: Manager: Seena Benedek; WG & L List Management, 1 Penn Plz Fl 42, New York, NY 10119-0002 Tel # (212) 971-5000

Housing Market Report
See: CONSTRUCTION & BUILDING

Incentive Taxation
See: TAXES

Income Advisor
See: INVESTMENT

Information Returns Guide
See: TAXES

Inn Side Issues
See: HOTEL INDUSTRY

Inside Mortgage Finance
See: BANKING & FINANCE

Inside Mortgage Securities
See: BANKING & FINANCE

International Property Bulletin

Publishing Co: Landauer Assocs., 666 5th Ave., 25th Fl., New York, NY 10103-0001;
Title Tel # (212) 687-2323
Personnel: Editor-H. Parker
General Info: Yr. Est. 1985, Annually
Circulation: Total-1,600

International Real Estate Newsletter *Business, Association*

Publishing Co: International Real Estate Institute, 8383 E Evans Rd, Scottsdale, AZ 85260-3614;
Title Tel # (602) 998-8267 Title Fax # (602) 998-8022
Personnel: Editor, Adv. Dir.-Todd Johnson, Art Dir.-Stephen Schneck
Editorial Description: Area of real estate valuation, finance investment and development.
General Info: Yr. Est. 1975, Bi-monthly, Trim Size-11 x 17, Sheetfed press, 4 pages, 4 Color
Subscriptions: Indv. $24, $2/copy
Circulation: Total-14,000
Advertising: Inquire for rates.

Island Properties Report *Consumer*

Publishing Co: Island Properties Report Inc., 4061 Bonita Beach Rd Ste 201, Bonita Springs, FL 33923-4073 Tel # (813) 495-1604 Fax # (813) 495-1738; Title Tel # (813) 263-1222
Title Fax # (813) 263-3087
Personnel: Publisher-Glenn Thornhill, Editor-Joan Plate, Circ. Mgr., Production Mgr.-Joan Uscinski
Editorial Description: For private investors interested in residential or business properties in the Caribbean or Bahamas.
General Info: Yr. Est. 1983, Monthly, Trim Size-8½ x 11, Sheetfed press, 8 pages, ISSN: 0882-1879, 2 Color
Subscriptions: Indv. $44, $6/copy
Circulation: Total-10,699
List Rental: List Management Co.: Alan Drey Co., 333 N. Michigan Avenue, Chicago, IL 60601 Tel # (312) 236-8508, Fax # (312) 346-5834, Actives: 29,110, $75/M
Printing Co: Elm Tree Press, PO Box 209, Woodstock, VT 05091-0209 Tel # (802) 457-1440

John T. Reed's Real Estate Investor's Monthly *Business*

Publishing Co: John T. Reed Publishing, 342 Bryan Dr, Danville, CA 94526-1258;
Title Tel # (510) 820-6292 Title Fax # (510) 820-1259
Personnel: Publisher, Editor-John Reed
Editorial Description: Strategies and news for individual real estate investors.
General Info: Yr. Est. 1986, Monthly, Trim Size-8½ x 11, Web press, 8 pages, ISSN: 0887-1922, 2 Color, Matte
Subscriptions: Indv. $125, $9/copy
Acquistions: Publication Bought
Circulation: Total-700, Readership-700
List Rental: List Management Co.: Mail Marketing, Inc., 171 Terrace St., Haworth, NJ 07641-1899 Tel # (201) 387-1023, Fax # (201) 387-2976, Actives: 17,500, $90/M
Printing Co: Newsletter Services, Inc., 9700 Philadelphia Court, Lanham, MD 20706 Tel # (301) 731-5200, Fax # (301) 731-5201

JonesReport
See: ADVERTISING & MARKETING

L.A. Co-Ops & the Shared Housing Networker

Publishing Co: Cooperative Resources & Services Project, 3551 White House Pl, Los Angeles, CA 90004-5944; Title Tel # (213) 738-1254
Personnel: Editor-Louis Arkin
Editorial Description: Calendar & resources, listings & brief articles on co-ops of all kinds, shared housing & intl. communities.
General Info: Yr. Est. 1980, Bi-monthly, Desktop press, 16 pages, No Color, Newsprint
Subscriptions: Indv. $10
Advertising: Inquire for rates.
Printing Co: Glendale Rotary Offset Printing, 112 S Maryland Ave # 696, Glendale, CA 91205-1027 Tel # (213) 245-1825

Land Development Law Reporter/Land Trends

Publishing Co: Land Development Law Reporter, 1401 16th St NW, Washington, DC 20036-2201; Title Tel # (202) 232-2144 Title Fax # (202) 347-4469
Personnel: Publisher-Stuart Bloch, Editor-Steve Sullivan, Circ. Mgr.-Pat Hunter
Editorial Description: Covers land regulation, cases, state, local & federal administration policy.
General Info: Yr. Est. 1972, Monthly, ISSN: 0739-6376
Subscriptions: Indv. $395
Circulation: Total-350
List Rental: Rents Lists

Land Owner

Publishing Co: Oster Communications, Inc., 219 Parkade, PO Box 6, Cedar Falls, IA 50613 Tel # (319) 277-1278; Title Tel # (319) 277-1276 Title Fax # (319) 277-7982
Personnel: Publisher-Merrill Oster, Editor-Jerry Carlson
Editorial Description: News pertinent to buying, selling, & owning farmland.
General Info: Yr. Est. 1979, Bi-weekly, 4 pages, 2 Color, Coated, Saddle-stitched
Subscriptions: Indv. $79
Circulation: Total-6,000
List Rental: List Management Co.: Venture Communications, 60 Madison Avenue, 3rd fl., New York, NY 10010 Tel # (212) 684-4800, Fax # (212) 545-1680
Printing Co: Congdon Printing Co., 115 E 2nd St, Cedar Falls, IA 50613-3357 Tel # (319) 266-7578

Landlord Tenant Law Bulletin *Business*

Publishing Co: Quinlan Publishing, 23 Drydock Ave, Boston, MA 02210-2387 Fax # (617) 345-9646; Title Tel # (617) 542-0048
Editorial Description: Laws and cases for property managers.
General Info: Monthly
Subscriptions: Indv. $60
List Rental: List Management Co.: Stevens-Knox List Management, 304 Park Ave S., New York, NY 10010-5312 Tel # (212) 388-8800, Fax # (212) 388-8890

Law of Real Estate Financing *Business*

Publishing Co: Warren, Gorham & Lamont, 31 Saint James Ave., Boston, MA 02116-4112 Parent Co.-Thomson Professional Publications, Stamford; Title Tel # (617) 423-2020 Title Fax # (617) 423-1914
Personnel: Publisher-Larry Selby, Mktg. Dir.-Sandra Fox
Editorial Description: Deals with related legal, tax and business problems as they arise within specific real estate transactions.
General Info: Yr. Est. 1981, Semi-annually, Looseleaf
Subscriptions: Indv. $160
List Rental: List Management Co.: Manager: Seena Benedek; WG & L List Management, 1 Penn Plz Fl 42, New York, NY 10119-0002 Tel # (212) 971-5000

Lease Purchase Times *Business*

Publishing Co: Diamond Consulting, 539 Telegraph Canyon Rd Ste, 145, Chula Vista, CA 91910-6436
Personnel: Publisher-Claude Diamond
Editorial Description: Leasing strategies and tips for real estate professionals.
General Info: Quarterly
Subscriptions: Free

Ledger Quarterly *Association*

Publishing Co: Community Associations Institute, 1630 Duke Street, Alexandria, VA 22314; Title Tel # (703) 548-8600 Title Fax # (703) 684-1581
Personnel: Exec. VP/Group Publisher-Barbara Byrd-Lawler, Editor-Gary Porter, Mng. Editor-Amanda Tirpak
Editorial Description: A financial review for community association practioners.
General Info: Yr. Est. 1989, Quarterly, Sheetfed press, 8 pages, ISSN: 1058-7101, 2 Color, Other
Subscriptions: Indv. $40
Circulation: Total-2,650
Printing Co: Ameriprint, 300 Mill St NE, Vienna, VA 22180-4524 Tel # (703) 281-7800

Liquidation Alert *Business* CPM$1214

Publishing Co: Harrison Scott Publications, One Riverfront Plaza, Suite 1480, Newark, NJ 07102-5495; Title Tel # (201) 596-1300 Title Fax # (201) 596-0148
Personnel: Editor-Andrew Albert, Production Mgr.-Daniel Cowles
Editorial Description: Contains information for real estate and financial professionals looking for opportunities to buy or manage assets.
General Info: Yr. Est. 1989, Weekly, 8 pages, Ind/Abs/Online: Nexis, NewsNet, Predicasts, DataStar, DIALOG
Subscriptions: Indv. $837, Inst. $837, Can. $837, For. $877
Circulation: Total-700
Advertising: $850.
List Rental: Rents Lists
Printing Co: Account Manager: Sherri Winter; Sir Speedy, 40 Commerce St, Newark, NJ 07102-4003 Tel # (201) 242-4040

Mac News

Publishing Co: Mid-Atlantic Council of Shopping Cntr. Mgrs., 22560 Glenn Dr Ste 118, Sterling, VA 20164-4440; Title Tel # (301) 588-8668
Personnel: Publisher-Tom Cohn, Editor-John Bachner, Circ. Mgr., Production Mgr.-Bonnie Aubin, Adv. Dir.-Mary Lou Schenkel
Editorial Description: News of the Council; Information concerning events & developments in the industry.
General Info: Yr. Est. 1986, Quarterly, Trim Size-8½ x 11, Letrpr. press, 20 pages, 1% ads, No Color, Saddle-stitched
Subscriptions: Indv. $100
Circulation: Total-200
List Rental: Rents Lists

Managing Housing Letter
See: LEASING & RENTING

Market Cycles *Business, Association*

Publishing Co: Center for Real Estate Studies, 50-B Peninsula Center Dr., Rolling Hills, CA 90274-3604 Tel # (800) 955-3135; Title Tel # (310) 544-1156 Title Fax # (310) 544-3587
Editorial Description: Gives analysis of over 150 metropolitan areas as they pertain to apartment investing.
General Info: Yr. Est. 1986, Quarterly, Trim Size-8½ x 11, 8 pages, 2 Color, Matte, Saddle-stitched
Subscriptions: Indv. $95
Circulation: Total-5,110
List Rental: Rents Lists

Mealey's Litigation Report: Lead
See: LAW

Minfax

Publishing Co: Marketing Information Network, 15000 Gulf Blvd Apt 307, Saint Petersburg, FL 33708-2030; Title Tel # (813) 392-7536
Personnel: Publisher, Editor-Edward Birkner
General Info: Yr. Est. 1965, Monthly, 12 pages
Subscriptions: Indv. $125
Circulation: Total-450
Printing Co: Legal Systems, 345 Hudson St, New York, NY 10014-4583 Tel # (212) 691-2460

Mobilehome Parks Report
See: MOBILE HOMES

Modern Real Estate & Mortgage Forms: Checklists

Publishing Co: Warren, Gorham & Lamont, 31 Saint James Ave., Boston, MA 02116-4112 Parent Co.-Thomson Professional Publications, Stamford; Title Tel # (617) 423-2020 Title Fax # (617) 423-1914
Personnel: Publisher-Larry Selby, Mktg. Dir.-Sandra Fox
Editorial Description: Checklists selected from files of leading industry professionals and institutions to help determine the best way to proceed in real estate transactions.
General Info: Yr. Est. 1986, Annually, Looseleaf
Subscriptions: Indv. $130
List Rental: List Management Co.: Manager: Seena Benedek; WG & L List Management, 1 Penn Plz Fl 42, New York, NY 10119-0002 Tel # (212) 971-5000

Modern Real Estate Acquisition & Disposition Forms

Publishing Co: Warren, Gorham & Lamont, 31 Saint James Ave., Boston, MA 02116-4112 Parent Co.-Thomson Professional Publications, Stamford; Title Tel # (617) 423-2020 Title Fax # (617) 423-1914
Personnel: Publisher-Larry Selby, Mktg. Dir.-Sandra Fox
Editorial Description: Complete forms and specimen clauses from the files of leading law firms and institutions. Commentary on legal and federal tax considerations.
General Info: Yr. Est. 1981, Annually, Looseleaf
Subscriptions: Indv. $130
List Rental: List Management Co.: Manager: Seena Benedek; WG & L List Management, 1 Penn Plz Fl 42, New York, NY 10119-0002 Tel # (212) 971-5000

Money Maker Report

Publishing Co: Money Maker Report, PO Box F, Chipley, FL 32428-5005; Title Tel # (904) 638-0005
Personnel: Publisher, Editor-Jimmy Napier
General Info: Yr. Est. 1978, Monthly
Circulation: Total-18,000

Mortgage Bank Weekly
See: BANKING & FINANCE

Mortgage and Real Estate
Executives Report   *Business*

Publishing Co: Warren, Gorham & Lamont, 31 Saint James Ave., Boston, MA 02116-4112 Parent Co.-Thomson Professional Publications, Stamford; Title Tel # (617) 423-2020 Title Fax # (617) 423-1914
Personnel: Publisher-Larry Selby, Mktg. Dir.-Sandra Fox
Editorial Description: Professional information and guidance for real estate lending and investment executives. Constant source of news.
General Info: Yr. Est. 1967, Bi-weekly, Trim Size-8½ x 11, Offset press, 8 pages, ISSN: 0047-813X, 2 Color
Subscriptions: Indv. $155
List Rental: List Management Co.: Manager: Seena Benedek; WG & L List Management, 1 Penn Plz Fl 42, New York, NY 10119-0002 Tel # (212) 971-5000

Mr. Landlord   *Business, Association*

Publishing Co: Home Rental Publishing, PO Box 64442, Virginia Beach, VA 23467-4442 Tel # (804) 495-5809; Title Tel # (804) 424-7997 Title Fax # (804) 467-1427
Personnel: Publisher, Editor-Jeffrey Taylor, Circ. Mgr.-Dorothy Taylor, Production Mgr.-Bob Garrett
Editorial Description: The survival newsletter for do-it-yourself landlords, incl. real estate landlording, rental property management. Filled monthly with numerous recommendations to increase your cash flow.
General Info: Yr. Est. 1985, Monthly, 8 pages, 2 Color, Newsprint
Subscriptions: Indv. $69, Can. $69, For. $79, $6/copy
Acquistions: Publication Bought, Publication Sold
Circulation: Total-50,000
Advertising: Accepts Inserts.
List Rental: Actives: $150/M

NAREB Report

Publishing Co: Natl. Assn. of Real Estate Brokers, 1629 K St. NW, Ste. 602, Washington, DC 20006; Title Tel # (202) 638-1280
General Info: Monthly

NY Apartment Law Insider *Business*

Publishing Co: Brownstone Publishers, Inc., 149 5th Ave., 16th Floor, New York, NY 10010-6801; Title Tel # (212) 473-8200 Title Fax # (212) 473-8786
Personnel: Publisher-John Striker, Editor in Chief-Andrew Shapiro, Editor-Susan R. Lipp, Circ. Mgr.-Cassie Feng, Production Mgr.-Mary Lopez, Mktg. Dir., Promotion Dir.-James Bell
Editorial Description: Covers both current and new local, state, and federal rules and regulations governing New York City rent-stabilized and rent-controlled apartments, with instruction and advice on how to successfully deal with NYC housing bureaucracy.
General Info: Yr. Est. 1979, Monthly, Trim Size-8½ x 11, Sheetfed press, 8 pages, ISSN: 0898-2961, 2 Color, Recycled
Subscriptions: Indv. $159, $13/copy
List Rental: Actives: $110/M, Expires: $110/M
Printing Co: Globe Mail Agency, Inc., 541 W 25th St, New York, NY 10001-5501 Tel # (212) 675-4600

National Property Law Digests
See: LAW

New York Landlord Vs.
Tenant   *Business*

Publishing Co: Brownstone Publishers, Inc., 149 5th Ave., 16th Floor, New York, NY 10010-6801; Title Tel # (212) 473-8200 Title Fax # (212) 473-8786
Personnel: Publisher-John Striker, Editor in Chief-Andrew Shapiro, Editor-Susan R. Lipp, Circ. Mgr.-Cassie Feng, Production Mgr.-Mary Lopez, Promotion Dir.-James Bell
Editorial Description: Tracks and summarizes court judgements in landlord/tenant disputes in the New York City metropolitan area. Includes DHCR rulings and opinion letters, ECB administrative appeals decisions, and Housing Court cases.
General Info: Yr. Est. 1985, Monthly, Trim Size-8½ x 11, Sheetfed press, 16 pages, ISSN: 0883-0746, 2 Color, Matte, Saddle-stitched
Subscriptions: Indv. $349, $28/copy
Acquistions: Publication Bought
List Rental: Actives: $110/M, Expires: $110/M
Printing Co: Globe Mail Agency, Inc., 541 W 25th St, New York, NY 10001-5501 Tel # (212) 675-4600

New York Practice Guide:
Real Estate   *Business*

Publishing Co: Matthew Bender & Co., 11 Penn Plaza, New York, NY 10001-2006 Tel # (212) 967-7707 Fax # (212) 244-3188
Personnel: Editor in Chief-Eugene J. Morris
Editorial Description: 'How-to' guidance for handling real estate transactions and proceedings in New York State.
General Info: Yr. Est. 1986, Irregular, Looseleaf

New York Real Estate Law
Reporter   *Business, Consumer*

Publishing Co: Leader Publications, Inc., 345 Park Avenue South, New York, NY 10010 Parent Co.-New York Law Publishing Co., New York; Title Tel # (212) 545-6170 Title Fax # (212) 696-1848
Personnel: Publisher-Stuart M. Wise, Editor-Stewart Sterk, Circ. Mgr.-Kerry Kyle, Mktg. Dir.-RoseAnn Morangelei
Editorial Description: New York real estate legal questions, cases and ⊂sues.
General Info: Yr. Est. 1986, Monthly, Trim Size-8½ x 11, Offset press, 8 pages, Color
Subscriptions: Indv. $195, $16/copy
Printing Co: Columbus Bookbinding, 1343 Belfast Ave, Columbus, OH 31904 Tel # (206) 323-9313, Fax # (206) 323-2987

Newsline   *Association*

Publishing Co: American Society of Appraisers, Box 17265, Washington, DC 20041-0265; Title Tel # (703) 478-2228 Title Fax # (703) 742-8471
Personnel: Editor-Rebecca Downs, Production Mgr.-Amy Starliper
Editorial Description: News and events pertaining to the appraisal profession.
General Info: Yr. Est. 1952, Monthly, Trim Size-8½ x 11, Sheetfed press, 16 pages, 2 Color, Other, Saddle-stitched
Subscriptions: Free With Membership
Circulation: Total-6,500, Readership-6,500

Nichols on Eminent Domain *Business*

Publishing Co: Matthew Bender & Co., 11 Penn Plaza, New York, NY 10001-2006 Fax # (212) 244-3188; Title Tel # (212) 967-7707
Editorial Description: The only combined treatise and practice guide encompassing all topics in the field of eminent domain for all jurisdictions.
General Info: Irregular, Looseleaf
Subscriptions: $950/copy

Ontario Real Estate Law
Guide   *Business*

Publishing Co: CCH Canadian Ltd., 6 Garamond Ct., North York, ON M3C 1Z5 Canada Fax # (416) 444-8011 Parent Co.-CCH, Inc., Riverwoods; Title Tel # (416) 441-2992 Title Fax # (416) 444-9011
Editorial Description: Coverage of Ontario's laws governing real estate transactions in Ontario. Over 40 statutes and regulations. Extensive array of forms and precedents.
General Info: Yr. Est. 1945, Monthly, Trim Size-6 x 9, Web press, No Color, Looseleaf
Subscriptions: Can. $475

Ontra Update   *Business*

Publishing Co: Ontra, Inc., 816 Congress Ave., Austin, TX 78701; Title Tel # (512) 478-9455
Personnel: Editor-Gloria Souhami
Editorial Description: Covers Texas housing market (sales.) Also includes information about national banking and real estate trends.
General Info: Yr. Est. 1983, Monthly, Web press, 4 pages, No Color, Coated
Subscriptions: Free
Circulation: Total-5,000
List Rental: Actives: $500/M
Printing Co: JW Graphics, PO Box 2479, Austin, TX 78768-2479 Tel # (512) 474-9890

Open House

Publishing Co: State of Nevada-Real Estate Div., 201 S Fall St, Carson City, NV 89701-4765; Title Tel # (702) 885-4280
Personnel: Editor-Janet Windsor, Production Mgr.-Brenda Briscoe
Editorial Description: Real estate law, regulations and industry developments in Nevada.
General Info: Yr. Est. 1975, Quarterly, Trim Size-8½ x 11, Offset press, 6 pages, 2 Color
Circulation: (100% controlled), Total-13,000
List Rental: Actives: $120/M

Pasadena Realtor

Publishing Co: Pasadena Board of Realtors, 656 N Los Robles Ave, Pasadena, CA 91101-1098
Personnel: Editor-Helen Neve
General Info: Yr. Est. 1926, Monthly
Subscriptions: Indv. $1
Circulation: Total-600
Advertising: Inquire for rates.

Pocket Change Investor, The
See: CONSUMER INTERESTS

Professional Apartment
Management   *Business*

Publishing Co: Brownstone Publishers, Inc., 149 5th Ave., 16th Floor, New York, NY 10010-6801; Title Tel # (212) 473-8200 Title Fax # (212) 473-8786
Personnel: Publisher-John Striker, Editor in Chief-Andrew Shapiro, Editor-Marc Handelman, Circ. Mgr.-Cassie Feng, Production Mgr.-Mary Lopez, Promotion Dir.-James Bell
Editorial Description: Strategies, techniques, and tested methods for attracting and retaining tenants. Includes model lease language and sample ads, forms, and letters, and covers legal issues and recent court decisions.
General Info: (Formerly Professional Apartment Marketing), Yr. Est. 1986, Monthly, Trim Size-8½ x 11, Sheetfed press, 16 pages, ISSN: 0883-0746, 2 Color, Newsprint, Saddle-stitched
Subscriptions: Indv. $168, $14/copy
Acquistions: Publication Bought
List Rental: Actives: $110/M, Expires: $90/M
Printing Co: Rolland Graphics, 299 Edison Ave, West Babylon, NY 11704-1022 Tel # (516) 249-9660

Quarterly Byte, The — *Business, Association*

Publishing Co: Appraisal Institute, 875 N. Michigan Ave., Suite 2400, Chicago, IL 60611-1980; Title Tel # (312) 335-4100 Title Fax # (312) 335-4400
Personnel: Editor-Mary Dum, Mng. Editor-Grace Hayek
Editorial Description: Articles on computer use for real estate appraisers. Includes computer software reviews.
General Info: Yr. Est. 1985, Quarterly, Trim Size-8½ x 11, Sheetfed press, 20 pages, ISSN: 1052-5521, 2 Color, Coated, Saddle-stitched
Subscriptions: Indv. $30, $10/copy
Circulation: Total-2,670

REEAction — *Business, Association*

Publishing Co: Real Estate Educators Assn., 11 S. LaSalle St., Ste. 1400, Chicago, IL 60603-1210 Tel # (312) 201-0101 Fax # (312) 201-0214
Personnel: Editor, Production Mgr.-Terry Hayes, Circ. Mgr., Promotion Dir.-Cindy Clark
General Info: Yr. Est. 1981, Monthly, Trim Size-8½ x 11, Offset press, 8 pages, No Color, Newsprint, Saddle-stitched
Subscriptions: Free With Membership
Circulation: Total-1,300, Readership-1,300
Advertising: Inquire for rates.
List Rental: Actives: 1,300, $100/M

REIT Report — *Association*

Publishing Co: National Association of Real Estate Investment Trusts, Inc., 1129 20th St NW Ste 305, Washington, DC 20036-3403; Title Tel # (202) 785-8717 Title Fax # (202) 785-8723
Editorial Description: Articles on issues, trends, developments, legislation pending Congress and statistical data.
General Info: Quarterly, Trim Size-8½ x 11, Desktop press, 24 pages, 2 Color, Matte, Saddle-stitched
Advertising: $1,000.
Printing Co: Corporate Press II, 8900 Lee Hwy, Fairfax, VA 22031-1423 Tel # (703) 641-0900

RERC Real Estate Report — *Business*

Publishing Co: Real Estate Research Corp., 2 N La Salle St Ste 400, Chicago, IL 60602-3703; Title Tel # (312) 346-5885 Title Fax # (312) 726-7291
Personnel: Publisher-Richard Kateley, Editor-Marilyn Robson, Circ. Mgr.-Geri Ciancanelli, Art Dir.-Joel Spears, Promotion Dir.-Marion Buckley
Editorial Description: Trends in real estate investment, development, financing, appraisal, planning, and marketing.
General Info: (Formerly Real Estate Report), Yr. Est. 1975, Bi-monthly, Sheetfed press, 8 pages, 2 Color, Newsprint
Subscriptions: Indv. $150, $25/copy
Acquistions: Publication Bought
Circulation: (50% controlled), Total-3,000
Printing Co: Marquardt Printing, 7830 47th St, Lyons, IL 60534-1852 Tel # (708) 887-8500

RLS Home Marketing Letter — *Consumer*

Publishing Co: Robert L. Siegel & Associates, Inc., 26 Trianon Drive, Kohner, LA 70065 Tel # (504) 471-0300 Fax # (504) 471-0526
Editorial Description: All about real estate issues.
General Info: Yr. Est. 1983, Monthly
Subscriptions: Indv. $99

RTC Property Disposition Report

Publishing Co: DataTrends Pubs., Inc., 895 B Harrison Street SE, PO Box 4460, Leesburg, VA 22075 Tel # (703) 779-0574 Fax # (703) 760-9365
Editorial Description: Reports on the RTC's actions that affect the real estate industry.
General Info: Yr. Est. 1991, Bi-weekly

Radon News Digest
See: ENVIRONMENT & ECOLOGY

Real Estate
See: COMPUTERS & AUTOMATION

Real Estate Appraisal Newsletter — *Association*

Publishing Co: National Association of Real Estate Appraisers, 8383 E Evans Rd, Scottsdale, AZ 85260-3614; Title Tel # (602) 948-8000 Title Fax # (602) 998-8022
Personnel: Editor-E.K. Twichell
Editorial Description: Appraisal updates for members of Natl. Assn. of Real Estate Appraisers.
General Info: Yr. Est. 1966, Quarterly, Sheetfed press, 10 pages, 2 Color, Coated
Subscriptions: Indv. $35
Circulation: Total-35,000
List Rental: Actives: $300/M

Real Estate Computer Review — *Business*

Publishing Co: Real Estate Computer Review, 1564 A Fitzgerald Dr., #404, Pinole, CA 94565; Title Tel # (415) 928-8121
General Info: Monthly
Subscriptions: Indv. $48

Real Estate Coordinator — *Business*

Publishing Co: Research Institute of America, 117 E Stevens Ave, Valhalla, NY 10595-1264; Title Tel # (212) 645-4800
Personnel: Publisher-Robert Chapman, Editor-JAmes Cheeks
Editorial Description: Eight-volume service provides strategies to structure real estate transactions.
General Info: Yr. Est. 1985, Bi-weekly, Looseleaf
Subscriptions: Indv. $552
List Rental: List Management Co.: WG & L List Management, 1 Penn Plz Fl 42, New York, NY 10119-0002 Tel # (212) 971-5000

Real Estate Digest — *Business*

Publishing Co: InfoCom Group, 1250 45th St., Ste 200, Emeryville, CA 94608-2924 Tel # (510) 596-9300 Fax # (510) 596-9331; Title Tel # (415) 549-4300
Personnel: Publisher-Jim Sinkinson, Editor- DaveDiegelman, Production Mgr.-Stacey Ravel, Art Dir.-Cynthia Levitas, Promotion Dir.-Steve Gordon
Editorial Description: Real Estate taxes, law, finance, markers.
General Info: Yr. Est. 1978, Monthly, 4 pages
Circulation: Total-50,000

Real Estate Entrepreneur, The — *Business, Consumer*

Publishing Co: Real Estate Entrepreneur, PO Box 13246, Reading, PA 19612-3246; Title Tel # (215) 371-9977
Personnel: Publisher, Editor-Bryan Wittenmyer
Editorial Description: Specializing in helping self-employed real estate investors earn more income; property management, buying and selling huses, and money management. The letter is geared for small investors and business people.
General Info: Yr. Est. 1992, Monthly, Trim Size-8½ x 11, 4 pages, ISSN: 1070-5171
Subscriptions: Indv. $45, For. $55, $4/copy
Circulation: Total-150
Advertising: Accepts Inserts.

Real Estate Finance & Investment — *Business*

Publishing Co: Capital Cities/ABC, 488 Madison Ave., 16th Floor, New York, NY 10022-5751 Fax # (212) 224-3353 Parent Co.-Capital Cities/ABC, Inc., New York; Title Tel # (212) 224-3233 Title Fax # (212) 224-3111
General Info: Weekly, Trim Size-8½ x 11, Sheetfed press, 10 pages, 2 Color, Newsprint
Advertising: Inquire for rates.

Real Estate Insider — *Business*

Publishing Co: Alexander Research & Communications, Inc., 215 Park Ave S., Ste. 1301, New York, NY 10003-1603 Tel # (212) 228-0246 Fax # (212) 228-0376
Personnel: Publisher-Shirley Alexander
Editorial Description: Newsletter for real estate firm owners, managers and brokers.
General Info: Yr. Est. 1968, Bi-weekly, Trim Size-8½ x 11, Sheetfed press, 8 pages, ISSN: 0034-0715, Coated
Subscriptions: Indv. $225, Can. $225, For. $260, $10/copy
Circulation: Total-1,000
List Rental: List Management Co.: George Mann & Associates, 569 Abbington Dr., PO Box 930, Hightstown, NJ 08520-9990 Tel # (609) 443-1330, Fax # (609) 443-0397, Actives: $85/M, Expires: $75/M

Real Estate Investment Ideas — *Business*

Publishing Co: Research Institute of America, 90 5th Avenue, New York, NY 10011-7629 Tel # (212) 645-4800; Title Tel # (800) 562-0245 Title Fax # (201) 816-3484
Editorial Description: New developments and promising opportunities in the entire field of real estate. Covers financing ideas, tax strategies, property analysis and more.
General Info: Semi-monthly, Trim Size-8½ x 11, 8 pages
Subscriptions: Indv. $82
List Rental: List Management Co.: WG & L List Management, 1 Penn Plz Fl 42, New York, NY 10119-0002 Tel # (212) 971-5000

Real Estate Investment, Trends & Opportunities — *Business*

Publishing Co: Jarvis Investment Corp., PO Box 1031, Kent, WA 98035-1031; Title Tel # (206) 852-3910
Personnel: Editor-Ronald Jarvis
General Info: Yr. Est. 1977, Monthly, 4 pages
Subscriptions: Indv. $24
Circulation: Total-800

Real Estate Investors Classified
See: CONSTRUCTION & BUILDING

Real Estate Investor's Monthly — *Business, Consumer*

Publishing Co: InfoCom Group, 1250 45th St., Ste 200, Emeryville, CA 94608-2924 Tel # (510) 596-9300 Fax # (510) 596-9331
Personnel: Editor-John Reed
General Info: Yr. Est. 1981, Monthly, Trim Size-8½ x 11, Sheetfed press, 8 pages, ISSN: 0887-1922
Subscriptions: Indv. $125, $11/copy
Circulation: Total-1,000

Real Estate Law Report
See: LAW

Real Estate Leasing Practice Manual

Publishing Co: Warren, Gorham & Lamont, 31 Saint James Ave., Boston, MA 02116-4112 Parent Co.-Thomson Professional Publications, Stamford; Title Tel # (617) 423-2020 Title Fax # (617) 423-1914
Personnel: Publisher-Larry Selby, Mktg. Dir.-Sandra Fox
Editorial Description: Complete set of leasing forms accompanied by commentary explaining legal and tax consequences of leasing transactions; also individual specimen clauses for tailoring leases to individual needs.
General Info: (Formerly Modern Real Estate Leasing Forms), Yr. Est. 1980, Irregular, Looseleaf
Subscriptions: Indv. $185
List Rental: List Management Co.: Manager: Seena Benedek; WG & L List Management, 1 Penn Plz Fl 42, New York, NY 10119-0002 Tel # (212) 971-5000

Real Estate Manitoba

Publishing Co: Manitoba Real Estate Assn., 1240 Portage Ave., 2nd fl., Winnipeg, MB R3G 0T6 Canada; Title Tel # (204) 772-0405 Title Fax # (204) 783-9447
Personnel: Editor-Tom Lewicki
Editorial Description: Provides members of the Assn. with information about Assn. services & activities; presents information of value to realtors on a variety of topics; raises the Assns. profile with members, potential members & selected groups & organizations.
General Info: (Formerly Manitoba Memos), Yr. Est. 1984, Quarterly, Trim Size-8½ x 11, Sheetfed press, 8 pages, 1% ads, 2 Color, Matte, Saddle-stitched
Circulation: Total-2,300
Advertising: Inquire for rates.

Real Estate Marketing Letter
Business

Publishing Co: Ashland Equities, Inc., 1127 Mill Rd., Hatfield, PA 19440-1036; Title Tel # (215) 822-8099 Title Fax # (215) 997-7661
Personnel: Publisher-Derek D'Angiolini
Editorial Description: Covers current marketing ideas on investing in real estate and mortagage origination.
General Info: Yr. Est. 1992, 10x/yr.
Subscriptions: Indv. $99, $5/copy

Real Estate Marketing Management Alert
Business

Publishing Co: Damarka Enterprises, Inc., 6271-24 St. Augustine Rd. #234, Jacksonville, FL 32217; Title Tel # (904) 733-0881 Title Fax # (904) 636-5448
Personnel: Publisher-Robert H. Bosson, Editor-Naomie Trager, Circ. Mgr.-Allison Adams
Editorial Description: Marketing and management ideas to increase productivity of real estate brokers, sales managers, and agents.
General Info: Yr. Est. 1983, 10x/yr., Trim Size-8½ x 11, 6 pages
Subscriptions: Indv. $70, Inst. $59

Real Estate News

Publishing Co: State of Washington, Dept. of Licensing, Box 9012, Olympia, WA 98504-0001; Title Tel # (206) 753-0775
Personnel: Editor-Vianca Nigro
Editorial Description: Contains information on disciplinary action & changes in law & education dept. regarding Real Estate.
General Info: Yr. Est. 1953, Quarterly, Trim Size-8½ x 11, Sheetfed press, 12 pages, Color, Newsprint
Circulation: Total-53,000

Real Estate Newsline

Publishing Co: Kenneth Leventhal & Co., 2049 Century Park, #2300, Los Angeles, CA 90067-3125; Title Tel # (310) 277-0880 Title Fax # (310) 284-7970
Personnel: Editor-Stan Ross, Circ. Mgr.-Janice S. Jackson
Editorial Description: News and analysis of investment, management, and development of real estate.
General Info: Yr. Est. 1984, Monthly, Trim Size-8½ x 11, Web press, 8 pages, ISSN: 0749-8640, 4 Color, Matte, Saddle-stitched
Subscriptions: Free To Qualified Recipient
Circulation: (92% controlled), Total-26,000, International-2,000

Real Estate Reports
Business, Consumer

Publishing Co: Univ. of Connecticut Ctr. Real Estate, Center Real Estate/Urban Econ, U-41 RE, Rm 426, 368 Fairfield, Storrs, CT 06269; Title Tel # (203) 486-3227
General Info: Irregular
Circulation: Total-500

Real Estate Tax Digest
Business

Publishing Co: Matthew Bender & Co., 2101 Webster St., Oakland, CA 94612-3027; Title Tel # (415) 446-7100
Personnel: Editor-Robert Schindewatt
General Info: Yr. Est. 1979, 13x/yr.
Subscriptions: Indv. $170

Real Estate Tax Ideas
Business

Publishing Co: Warren, Gorham & Lamont, 31 Saint James Ave., Boston, MA 02116-4112 Parent Co.-Thomson Professional Publications, Stamford; Title Tel # (617) 423-2020 Title Fax # (617) 423-1914
Personnel: Publisher-Wdyne Barr, Production Mgr.-Mavra Kiey, Mktg. Dir.-Sandra Fox, Mktg. Dir.-Jim Spillane
Editorial Description: An alerting service for real estate professionals, their consultants, and advisors on developments and trends in tax treatment of real estate on federal, state, and local levels.
General Info: Yr. Est. 1973, Monthly, Trim Size-7½ x 10, Offset press, 6 pages, ISSN: 0162-7538, 2 Color
Subscriptions: Indv. $105
List Rental: List Management Co.: WG & L List Management, 1 Penn Plz Fl 42, New York, NY 10119-0002 Tel # (212) 971-5000

Real Estate Tax Letter
See: TAXES

Real Estate Technical Letter

Publishing Co: Sorel Investments, 1728 Union St Ste 311, San Francisco, CA 94123-4428; Title Tel # (415) 441-4499
Personnel: Publisher-Arthur Bruzzone
General Info: Yr. Est. 1987, Bi-monthly, Desktop press, 8 pages, No Color
Acquistions: Publication Bought

Real Estate Transaction Series
Business

Publishing Co: Matthew Bender & Co., 11 Penn Plaza, New York, NY 10001-2006 Fax # (212) 244-3188; Title Tel # (212) 967-7707
Personnel: Editor-M. Heend
Editorial Description: These volumes provide through coverage of the real estate subjects most important to the practicing attorney, with illustrative, difficult-to-obtain documents and forms, and procedural checklists.
General Info: Looseleaf
Subscriptions: $2,279/copy

Real Estate Transactions

Publishing Co: Warren, Gorham & Lamont, 31 Saint James Ave., Boston, MA 02116-4112 Parent Co.-Thomson Professional Publications, Stamford; Title Tel # (617) 423-2020 Title Fax # (617) 423-1914
Personnel: Publisher-Larry Selby, Mktg. Dir.-Sandra Fox
Editorial Description: Step-by-step guidance for negotiating and documenting profit-making real estate deals.
General Info: Yr. Est. 1990, Irregular, Looseleaf
Subscriptions: Indv. $78
List Rental: List Management Co.: Manager: Seena Benedek; WG & L List Management, 1 Penn Plz Fl 42, New York, NY 10119-0002 Tel # (212) 971-5000

Real Estate Workouts Report
See: LAW

Real Estate/Environmental Liability News
See: LAW

Real Estatement
Business

Publishing Co: Idaho Real Estate Commission, 633 N. 4th, Boise, ID 83720-0001; Title Tel # (208) 334-3285
Personnel: Editor-Jeri Pyeatt
Editorial Description: An educational service and information source for all Idaho Real Estate licensees.
General Info: Yr. Est. 1977, Semi-annually, Web press, 24 pages, No Color, Newsprint
Circulation: (100% controlled), Total-9,000
Advertising: Accepts Inserts.
Printing Co: Graphic Arts Publishing, Inc., 5325 Kendall St, Boise, ID 83706-1250 Tel # (208) 375-1010

Realtor(R) Voice, The
Business, Association

Publishing Co: Metropolitan Indianapolis Board of Realtors(R), Inc., 1912 N Meridian St, Indianapolis, IN 46202-1304; Title Tel # (317) 926-1912 Title Fax # (317) 921-3295
Editorial Description: News of MIBOR sponsored programs, events and educational opportunities; legislation affecting the industry; general real estate news and statistics on the residential real estate market in central Indiana.
General Info: (Formerly Metropolitan Indianapolis Realtor), Monthly, ISSN: 1057-4808
Subscriptions: Indv. $15

Relocation Report
Business

Publishing Co: Runzheimer Intl., Runzheimer Park, Rochester, WI 53167 Tel # (414) 767-2200 Fax # (414) 767-2254; Title Tel # (708) 291-9011 Title Fax # (708) 291-9581
Personnel: Publisher-Bradford Burris, Editor-Ken Groh
Editorial Description: News & information on corporate relocation for real estate personnel.
General Info: Yr. Est. 1979, Semi-monthly, ISSN: 0275-7613
Subscriptions: Indv. $79, $5/copy
Acquistions: Publication Bought, Publication Sold
List Rental: List Management Co.: Edith Roman Associates, Inc., 253 W 35th St Fl 16th, New York, NY 10001-1907 Tel # (212) 695-3836, Actives: 13,000, $100/M

Relocator
Association

Publishing Co: RELO/Inter City Relocation Service, 111 E. Wacker Drive, #220, Chicago, IL 60601;
Title Tel # (312) 616-0400
Personnel: Publisher-George Otto, Editor-Tom Watts
Editorial Description: Keep RELO members, their sales associates & customers informed of the activities of RELO offices throughout the world.
General Info: Trim Size-11 x 15, 6 pages

Resort Reports
Association

Publishing Co: Resort Property Owners Assn., PO Box 2395, Northbrook, IL 60065-2395;
Title Tel # (708) 291-0710 Title Fax # (708) 291-0766
Personnel: Publisher-Clinton Burr
General Info: Bi-monthly
Subscriptions: Indv. $20

Rhodes Real Estate Review
See: LAW

Robert Bruss Real Estate Newsletter
Business

Publishing Co: Tribune Media Services, 435 N. Michigan Avenue, Chicago, IL 60611-4008
Tel # (312) 222-4444 Fax # (312) 222-4328; Title Tel # (415) 344-2600
Personnel: Publisher-Keith Williams, Editor-Robert Bruss
Editorial Description: Reports recent real estate court decisions & new real estate laws.
General Info: Yr. Est. 1987, Monthly, Trim Size-8½ x 11, 8 pages, No Color
Subscriptions: Indv. $35, For. $68
List Rental: Rents Lists

Runzheimer Reports on Relocation
See: MANAGEMENT

Rural Property Investor
Business, Consumer

Publishing Co: Greener Pastures Institute, PO Box 2190, Pahrump, NV 89041-2190;
Title Tel # (702) 382-4847
Personnel: Art Dir.-Laurel Gillesse, Publisher, Editor, Circ. Mgr., Adv. Mgr., Mktg. Dir., Promotion Dir.-Bill Seavey
Editorial Description: To assist disenchanted urbanites in rediscovering and relocating to smaller cities and towns in rural areas throughout the US.
General Info: (Formerly Greener Pastures Gazatte), Yr. Est. 1985, Quarterly, Trim Size-8½ x 11, Offset press, 6 pages, 5% ads, Color
Subscriptions: Indv. $25, Inst. $19, Can. $35, For. $40, $6/copy
Circulation: Readership-500
Advertising: Inquire for rates.

SNL REIT Weekly
Business

Publishing Co: SNL Securities, 410 E. Main St., P.O. Box 2124, Charlottesville, VA 22902;
Title Tel # (804) 977-1600 Title Fax # (804) 977-4466
Personnel: Publisher-Reid Nagle, Editor-Jenn Nagaj, Circ. Mgr.-Pat Labua, Product Mgr.-Doug Spamer, Mktg. Dir.-Judy Lewis
Editorial Description: Provides weekly news and market information on the Reit industry.
General Info: Weekly, Trim Size-8½ x 11, Desktop press, No Color, Other
Subscriptions: Indv. $299
Advertising: Inquire for rates.

Sales & Marketing Magic
Business   **CPM: $142**

Publishing Co: Sales & Marketing Magic, 36473 Us Highway 19 N, Palm Harbor, FL 34684-1329
Fax # (813) 784-7978; Title Tel # (813) 784-9469
Personnel: Publisher, Editor-Tami Siewruk
Editorial Description: For owners, property managers and executives, covering the marketing and leasing of apartment communities.
General Info: Yr. Est. 1987, Bi-monthly, Trim Size-8½ x 11, 28 pages, 2 Color
Subscriptions: Indv. $98
Circulation: Total-7,000
Advertising: $1,000.
List Rental: Rents Lists

San Diego Regulatory Alert

Publishing Co: San Diego Regulatory Alert, PO Box 126301, San Diego, CA 92112-6301;
Title Tel # (619) 238-8160
Personnel: Editor-Matthew Potter
General Info: Yr. Est. 1986

Sea Island Real Estate Newsletter
Consumer

Publishing Co: Sea Island Properties, Sea Island, GA 31561; Title Tel # (912) 638-5161

Self Storage Legal Review
See: LAW

Seller/Servicer Update
See: BANKING & FINANCE

Shopping Center Digest
See: DEPARTMENT STORE & RETAIL

Sound Advice

Publishing Co: Sound Advice, 370 Diablo Rd Ste 201, Danville, CA 94526-3438;
Title Tel # (510) 838-8100 Title Fax # (510) 838-6253
Personnel: Publisher, Editor-Gray Cardiff, Circ. Dir.-Kooper Frame
Editorial Description: Real estate & tax advisory letter.
General Info: Yr. Est. 1979, Monthly, Trim Size-8½ x 11, Offset press, 16 pages, Newsprint, Saddle-stitched
Subscriptions: Indv. $89
Circulation: Total-12,000
List Rental: List Management Co.: InfoMat, 1815 W 213th St Ste 210, Torrance, CA 90501-2839 Tel # (310) 212-5944, Fax # (310) 212-5773, Actives: 11,897, $155/M, Expires: 3,988, $100/M

Spotlight
See: ARCHITECTURE

Steinman's Bergerman and Roth, New York Real Property Forms Annotated
Business

Publishing Co: Matthew Bender & Co., 11 Penn Plaza, New York, NY 10001-2006
Fax # (212) 244-3188; Title Tel # (212) 967-7707
Editorial Description: Over 4,000 pages of annotated forms, with statutory and case citations giving substantive and procedural background.
General Info: Yr. Est. 1931, Irregular, Looseleaf
Subscriptions: $495/copy

TAREI Times
Business, Association

Publishing Co: Texas Assn. of Real Estate Inspectors, 1601 Rio Grande St Ste 440, Austin, TX 78701-1149; Title Tel # (512) 479-0425
Personnel: Editor-Lisa Fry
Editorial Description: Official publication of the Texas Association of Real Estate Inspectors.
General Info: Quarterly, Trim Size-8½ x 11, Offset press, 12 pages, 10% ads, No Color, Matte
Subscriptions: Free With Membership
Advertising: $140.
Printing Co: Austex Printing Co., 501 W 3rd St, Austin, TX 78701-3807 Tel # (512) 476-7581

Tax Credit Advisor
Business

Publishing Co: Business Communication Services, Inc., 220 Montgomery St., Ste. 260, San Francisco, CA 94104-3524; Title Tel # (415) 546-7255 Title Fax # (415) 546-0954
Personnel: Publisher-Peter Bell, Editor-Andre Shashaty, Circ. Mgr.-Sheeba Bruning
Editorial Description: Covers management and development of low-income housing.
General Info: Yr. Est. 1990, Monthly, Trim Size-8½ x 11, 12 pages, No Color, Matte, Saddle-stitched
Subscriptions: Indv. $249
Circulation: Total-525

Tax Hotline
See: TAXES

Tax Management Real Estate
See: TAXES

Taxes-Property/State Capitals
See: TAXES

Title Management Today
See: LAW

TransitPulse
See: TRAFFIC & TRANSPORTATION

Trends in the Hotel Industry New York City
See: HOTEL INDUSTRY

Vermont Real Estate Newsletter
Business, Association

Publishing Co: Vermont Real Estate Commission, 7 E State St, Montpelier, VT 05602-3008;
Title Tel # (802) 828-3228
General Info: Quarterly
Circulation: Total-4,500

Warren's Weed New York Real Property
Business

Publishing Co: Matthew Bender & Co., 11 Penn Plaza, New York, NY 10001-2006
Fax # (212) 244-3188; Title Tel # (212) 967-7707
Personnel: Editor-M. Heend
Editorial Description: Encyclopedic treatment of real estate law, with over 250 articles, alphabetically arranged.
General Info: Yr. Est. 1920, Annually, Looseleaf
Subscriptions: $925/copy

Washington
Business

Publishing Co: Real Estate Div., Box 247, Olympia, WA 98504-0001; Title Tel # (206) 753-2700
Personnel: Editor, Art Dir.-Sharon Kinder
Editorial Description: Information news, education and comment on the real estate industry.
General Info: Yr. Est. 1953, Quarterly, Trim Size-8½ x 11, Web press, 8 pages, 2 Color, Newsprint, Saddle-stitched
Circulation: Total-60,000

Watersider

Publishing Co: Dwelling Managers, Inc., 30 Waterside Plz., New York, NY 10010-2693; Title Tel # (212) 725-5374
Personnel: Editor-Shelley Hainer
General Info: Monthly, Trim Size-8½ x 11, 10 pages
Circulation: Total-1,480

REGIONAL INTEREST

Tuscaloosa, Alabama

ASDC News   *Business, Consumer*

Publishing Co: University of Alabama, CBER/Box 870221, Tuscaloosa, AL 35487 Tel # (205) 348-6191 Fax # (205) 348-2951
Personnel: Publisher, Editor-Annette Watters, Circ. Mgr.-Deborah Hamilton, Art Dir.-Sherry O'Brien
Editorial Description: Articles on the demography of Alabama and related topics.
General Info: Yr. Est. 1983, Quarterly, Trim Size-8½ x 11, 4 pages, Matte
Subscriptions: Free In Designated Area
Circulation: Total-2,500

Anchorage, Alaska

AFN Newsletter
  See: ETHNIC

Apache Junction, Arizona

Superstition Mountain Historical Society-Newsletter
  See: HISTORY

Phoenix, Arizona

What's New in Arizona   *Business*

Publishing Co: Phoenix Publishing, Inc., 5555 N. 7th Avenue #B200, Phoenix, AZ 85013-1755; Title Tel # (602) 248-8900
Personnel: Publisher-Kenneth A. Welch, Editor-Rebecca Mong, Circ. Mgr.-Kristine Coryell
General Info: Yr. Est. 1975, Weekly
Subscriptions: Indv. $65
Circulation: Total-20,000

Tempe, Arizona

Arizona Blue Chip Economic Forecast
  See: ECONOMICS

Western Blue Chip Economic Forecast
  See: ECONOMICS

Fayetteville, Arkansas

Arkansas Biography
  Newsletter   *Consumer*

Publishing Co: University of Arkansas Press, 201 Ozark Ave, Fayetteville, AR 72701-4041
Editorial Description: Discusses those who have added to Arkansas' culture and talent.
General Info: Yr. Est. 1993, Semi-annually

Newport Beach, California

Martin Brower's Orange County Report
  See: BUSINESS & INDUSTRY

Oakland, California

Oakland Artscape   *Consumer*

Publishing Co: Cultural Arts Division, 475 14th Street, 11th Floor, Oakland, CA 94612; Title Tel # (510) 238-2103
Personnel: Editor-Adrienne Warren, Production Dir.-Suki O'Kane
Editorial Description: Info on cultural arts of Oakland.
General Info: Quarterly, Trim Size-8½ x 11, 8 pages, 2 Color, Coated, Saddle-stitched

Sacramento, California

C.J. Weekly
  See: POLITICS

Pacific Mountain Network News
  See: PUBLIC MANAGEMENT & PLANNING

WACA News
  See: AGRICULTURE

Tustin, California

Eye on Santa Ana   *Consumer*   CPM: $50

Publishing Co: Eye on Santa Ana, 14561 Livingston Ave, Tustin, CA 92680-2618; Title Tel # (714) 759-2116
Personnel: Publisher, Editor-Guy D. Ball
General Info: Yr. Est. 1989, Quarterly, Trim Size-11 x 17, Sheetfed press, 12 pages, Matte
Subscriptions: Free
Circulation: Total-10,000
Advertising: $500.

Woodland Hills, California

Freak Man Freak

Publishing Co: Eric Gamonal, 22415 Del Valle St, Woodland Hills, CA 91364
Editorial Description: A strange new zine from the publisher of McZine. Two essays on prayer and oration, along with comparing the recent election to elections from the past.
General Info: Trim Size-8.5 x 11, 2 pages
Subscriptions: Indv. $4

Colorado Springs, Colorado

Regionews

Publishing Co: Pikes Peak Area Council of Governments, 15 S 7th St, Colorado Springs, CO 80905-1501; Title Tel # (719) 471-7080
Personnel: Editor-Patrick Caldwell
General Info: (Formerly Pikes Peak Area Council of Governments), Yr. Est. 1971, Quarterly, Trim Size-8½ x 11, Sheetfed press, 8 pages, No Color
Circulation: Total-800

Washington, District of Columbia

Kiplinger Florida Letter
  See: BUSINESS & INDUSTRY

Peace Letter
  See: POLITICS

Melbourne, Florida

Roesch House Report
  See: HISTORY

Miami Beach, Florida

Gold Coast News   *Consumer*

Publishing Co: Charles Hesser, Box 3637, Miami Beach, FL 33140-3637; Title Tel # (305) 674-9746 Title Fax # (305) 674-1939
Personnel: Publisher, Editor-Charles Hesser, Entertainment Ed.-John Bowman, Travel Ed.-Carol Cohen, Food Editor-Ed Geiger, Feature Ed.-Ed Hayden, Sports Ed.-J.M. March, News Ed.-C.R. Roberts, Society Ed.-Dede Stroud, Calendar Ed.-Miriam Riggins, Circ. Mgr.-Bernie Orminski, Production Mgr.-John Kozak, Art Dir.-Art Wells, Mktg. Dir.-Bob Golden, Promotion Dir.-Albert Andux
Editorial Description: Describes events happening in the area from Palm Beach to Key West (Florida's Gold Coast), South East Florida.
General Info: Yr. Est. 1983, Monthly, Trim Size-8½ x 14, Sheetfed press, 12 pages, No Color, Matte, Perfect bound
Subscriptions: Indv. $20, $5/copy
Circulation: (9% controlled), Total-110,000, Subscriptions-100,000, Readership-150,000, Source-I
Printing Co: Tree Pine Press, 2445 Pinetree Dr., Miami Beach, FL 33140-4611

Marietta, Georgia

East Cobber   *Consumer*   CPM: $20

Publishing Co: CMR Communications, PO Box 672121, Marietta, GA 30067-0036; Title Tel # (404) 908-3973
Personnel: Publisher-Cynthia Rozzo
Editorial Description: Local interest publication for East Cobb County.
General Info: Monthly, Trim Size-8½ x 11, 2 Color, Newsprint
Subscriptions: Indv. $12
Circulation: Total-40,000
Advertising: $800.

Keaau, Hawaii

Wahine Wireless
  See: WOMEN'S

Chicago, Illinois

Chicago Reporter
  See: PUBLIC MANAGEMENT & PLANNING

Loves Park, Illinois

Reflections
See: RELIGIOUS & THEOLOGICAL

Palatine, Illinois

Art Lover's Art and Craft Fair Bulletin
See: ART & SCULPTURE

Sycamore, Illinois

Cornsilk from DeKalb County, IL
See: GENEALOGY

Berea, Kentucky

Appalachian Center-
Newsletter   *Scholarly*

Publishing Co: Appalachian Center-Berea College, College Box 2336, Berea, KY 40404-0001; Title Tel # (606) 986-9341
Personnel: Editor-Loyal Jones
General Info: Yr. Est. 1971, Quarterly
Subscriptions: Indv. $3
Circulation: Total-2,000

Frankfort, Kentucky

Circuit Rider
See: HISTORY

Castine, Maine

Wilson Museum Bulletin
See: MUSEUM PUBLICATIONS

Montgomery Village, Maryland

Montgomery Village News

Publishing Co: Montgomery Village Foundation, Inc., Box 2130, Montgomery Village, MD 20886 Tel # (301) 948-0110; Title Tel # (301) 948-6306
Personnel: Editor-Fay Jacobs
General Info: Yr. Est. 1967, Semi-monthly
Subscriptions: Indv. $10
Circulation: Total-7,300

Ann Arbor, Michigan

Great Lakes Newsletter
See: ENVIRONMENT & ECOLOGY

Sodus, Michigan

Sodus News, The   *Consumer*

Publishing Co: Sodus News, The, 3503 Edwards Rd., Sodus, MI 49126; Title Tel # (616) 944-5719 Title Fax # (616) 944-5719
Personnel: Publisher, Editor-Virginia Handy
Editorial Description: Events biographies, and local history of people in Sodus Township in rural Berien Country, South western, Michigan.
General Info: Yr. Est. 1995, Quarterly, Desktop press, 4 pages, ISSN: 1084-8452, No Color
Subscriptions: Indv. $5, Inst. $5
Advertising: Inquire for rates.

Burnsville, Minnesota

Cottage Connections

Publishing Co: Cottage Connections, 11113 Radisson Ct, Burnsville, MN 55337-1117
Personnel: Editor, Adv. Dir.-Mary Bevis
Editorial Description: Taking homemakers, their concerns, arts & gifts, seriously. Upbuilding - encouragement. Essays, family issues, activism & advocacy. Reader friendly, 90% written by subscriber/homemakers. Christian slant, pro-life, Habakkuk 2: 2.
General Info: (Formerly Cottage Cheese), Yr. Est. 1981, Monthly, Trim Size-8½ x 11, Sheetfed press, 10 pages, No Color
Subscriptions: Indv. $10, Can. $12, For. $17, $3/copy
Circulation: Total-1,000
Advertising: Inquire for rates.

St. Paul, Minnesota

Member News, Minnesota Historical Society
See: HISTORY

University, Mississippi

Southern Register
See: CULTURE & HUMANITIES

St. Louis, Missouri

News Brief
See: MUSEUM PUBLICATIONS

Regional Archivist
See: HISTORY

Omaha, Nebraska

What's Happening
See: GOVERNMENT

Concord, New Hampshire

Agenda Newsletter, The   *Business*

Publishing Co: NH Department of Resources and Economic Development, PO Box 1856, Concord, NH 03302-1856; Title Tel # (603) 271-2341 Title Fax # (603) 271-2629
Personnel: Editor-Margaret M. Joyce
Editorial Description: A monthly publication for New Hampshire's business & economic development community. Provides useful & timely info. on business & industrial development, intl. commerce & travel & tourism so that businesses can make maximum use of state programs in order to continue contributing to the economic development & well being of the state.
General Info: (Formerly NH Journal of Economic Development), Yr. Est. 1987, Monthly, Trim Size-8½ x 11, Sheetfed press, 8 pages, 2 Color, Newsprint
Subscriptions: Free
Circulation: (100% controlled), Total-7,000
Printing Co: Evans Printing Co., 276 North State Street, PO Box 49, Concord, NH 03302 Tel # (603) 225-5529, Fax # (603) 224-6926

New Hampshire Journal of
Economic Development

Publishing Co: New Hampshire State, Dept. of Resources & Economic Developme, PO Box 856, Concord, NH 03302-0856; Title Tel # (603) 271-2591 Title Fax # (603) 271-2629
Personnel: Editor-William Herman
Editorial Description: Bi-monthly publication outlining economic development activities and events in New Hampshire.
General Info: Yr. Est. 1987, Quarterly, Trim Size-8½ x 11, Offset press, 6 pages, 2 Color, Newsprint
Circulation: (100% controlled), Total-5,500
Printing Co: Wenday, PO Box 395, Concord, NH 03302-0395 Tel # (603) 225-5966

Salem, New Hampshire

Trivia Dispatch

Publishing Co: MRM Assocs., PO Box 763, Salem, NH 03079-0763
General Info: Monthly
Subscriptions: Indv. $12
Circulation: Total-11,500

Atlantic City, New Jersey

Atlantic City Report   *Consumer*

Publishing Co: Atlantic City Department of Planning & Development, City Hall, Rm. 504, Atlantic City, NJ 08401; Title Tel # (609) 347-5404
Personnel: Co-Editor-Gary Baker, Co-Editor-Ken Platt
Editorial Description: Information from City Hall for residents and visitors about programs aned events.
General Info: Yr. Est. 1994, Irregular

Rochelle Park, New Jersey

Multicultural Messenger   *Business*

Publishing Co: International Education Association, PO Box 70, Rochelle Park, NJ 07662-0070; Title Tel # (201) 712-0090
Personnel: Editor-Mary Jo Neuberger
Editorial Description: For elementary and secondary school superintendents, principals, board members and curriculum developers involved in multicultural education.
General Info: Yr. Est. 1993, Monthly

Albany, New York

NYS Environment
See: ENVIRONMENT & ECOLOGY

Arkville, New York

Catskills News Quarterly   *Association*

Publishing Co: The Catskill Center, Arkville, NY 12406-1010; Title Tel # (914) 586-2611
Title Fax # (914) 586-3044
Editorial Description: Information on the Catskill Center for Conservation and Development's field trips and cultural programs in the Catskills.
General Info: Quarterly

Auburn, New York

Cayuga County Connection   *Consumer*

Publishing Co: Cayuga County Extension Service Association, 248 Grant Ave, Auburn, NY 13021-1495; Title Tel # (315) 255-1183
Editorial Description: Family matters, gardening, etc.
General Info: Yr. Est. 1914, Monthly, Trim Size-8½ x 11, Sheetfed press, 20 pages, Newsprint
Subscriptions: Indv. $5
Circulation: Total-1,025
Advertising: Inquire for rates.

Bronx, New York

Bronx Report, The
    See: PUBLIC MANAGEMENT & PLANNING

Brooklyn, New York

Community Advocate
    See: PUBLIC MANAGEMENT & PLANNING

East Aurora, New York

Christ the King Seminary News
    See: COLLEGE ALUMNI

Ithaca, New York

Translation Series
    See: INTERNATIONAL AFFAIRS

New York, New York

BOMI Newsletter: Annual Conference Edition   *Association*

Publishing Co: Box Office Management International, 250 W. 37th Street, Suite 722, New York, NY 10107; Title Tel # (212) 581-0600 Title Fax # (212) 581-0885
Personnel: Publisher, Editor-Patricia Spira
Editorial Description: Publication targeted to ticket industry with articles about systems, technological advances, employment practices.
General Info: Yr. Est. 1981, Annually, Trim Size-11 x 17, Sheetfed press, 2 Color, Newsprint
Circulation: (80% controlled), Total-1,500, International-300
Advertising: Inquire for rates.
List Rental: Rents Lists
Printing Co: Pickwick Press, 125 Georges Rd # 36, New Brunswick, NJ 08901-3105
Tel # (908) 246-2151

California Public Finance
    See: BANKING & FINANCE

Central Park Good Times   *Consumer*

Publishing Co: Central Park Conservancy, The Arsenal, Central Park, New York, NY 10021
Tel # (212) 315-0385
Personnel: Editor-Deborah Kirschner
Editorial Description: News and information about Central Park in New York City and the activities there.
General Info: Quarterly, Trim Size-8½ x 11, 8 pages, 2 Color, Matte, Saddle-stitched
Subscriptions: Free To Qualified Recipient

Gramercy   *Consumer*

Publishing Co: Gramercy Neighborhood Assoc., Inc., Box 678, Madison Sq. Sta., New York, NY 10159-0808; Title Tel # (212) 673-2388
Personnel: Editor-Joan Lappin
Editorial Description: Neighborhood events, urban environmentalism, historic preservation.
General Info: (Formerly Gramercy Neighborhood News), Irregular, Trim Size-8½ x 11, 8 pages, No Color, Matte

Inside Manhattan

Publishing Co: Manhattan Borough Pres., One Centre St., 19th Fl., New York, NY 10007
Tel # (212) 669-3129 Fax # (212) 669-3380
General Info: Quarterly

Manhattan Borough Watch

Publishing Co: Manhattan Borough Pres., One Centre St., 19th Fl., New York, NY 10007;
Title Tel # (212) 669-3129 Title Fax # (212) 669-3380
General Info: (Formerly Dateline: Manhattan), Yr. Est. 1990

Manhattan Forum

Publishing Co: Office of the Borough Pres. of Manhattan, Municipal Bldg., New York, NY 10007
General Info: Yr. Est. 1989, Bi-monthly

Murray Hill News   *Consumer*

Publishing Co: Murray Hill News Publ. Co., 237 Madison Ave, New York, NY 10016-2818;
Title Tel # (212) 684-6728
Personnel: Publisher-Dorothy Frooks, Editor-Schuyler Vanderbilt
General Info: Yr. Est. 1942, Monthly, Trim Size-11 x 17, Letrpr. press, 8 pages
Subscriptions: Indv. $10, $1/copy
Circulation: Total-15,000

New Manhattan Project Newsletter
    See: NUCLEAR ENERGY

Tarrytown, New York

Hudson Highlights

Publishing Co: Historic Hudson Valley, 150 White Plains Rd, Tarrytown, NY 10591-5591;
Title Tel # (914) 631-8200
Personnel: Publisher-Thomas Lesser, Editor-Constance Collins, Circ. Mgr.-Joan Chandler, Production Mgr.-Carol Haber
Editorial Description: Covers the historic, cultural, scenic & environmental news of the region.
Subscriptions: Indv. $30

Charlotte, North Carolina

Robeson County Register

Publishing Co: Dr. Morris Britt, Doctors Bldg., 1012 S Kings Dr Ste 901, Charlotte, NC 28283-0001;
Title Tel # (704) 333-1443
Personnel: Editor-Morris Britt
General Info: Yr. Est. 1986, Quarterly, Offset press, 40 pages, ISSN: 0888-3807
Subscriptions: Indv. $25, Inst. $25, Can. $25, $7/copy
Circulation: Total-200
Advertising: Inquire for rates. Accepts Inserts.
Printing Co: IBS Graphics, PO Box 410404, Charlotte, NC 28241-0404 Tel # (704) 588-5008

Lebanon, Ohio

Historicalog
    See: HISTORY

Lima, Ohio

Ohio's Historical Detective
    See: HISTORY

Lawton, Oklahoma

Museum of the Great Plains Newsletter
    See: MUSEUM PUBLICATIONS

Oklahoma City, Oklahoma

Mistletoe Leaves
    See: HISTORY

Astoria, Oregon

Quarterdeck, The
    See: MUSEUM PUBLICATIONS

Salem, Oregon

Oregon Pharmacist
    See: DRUGS & PHARMACEUTICALS

Bryn Mawr, Pennsylvania

Valley Voice
    See: GENERAL INTEREST

Pittsburgh, Pennsylvania

LASA Forum
Association

Publishing Co: Latin American Studies Assn., William Pitt Union, #946, Univ. of Pittsburgh, Pittsburgh, PA 15260-0001; Title Tel # (412) 648-7929 Title Fax # (412) 624-7145
Personnel: Editor-Reid Reading
Editorial Description: The LASA Forum publishes news & reports of the Latin American Studies Assn. as well as brief research-based articles & other items of interest to members. Provides information on employment, grant opportunities, & conferences with Latin American themes.
General Info: (Formerly LASA Newsletter), Yr. Est. 1970, Quarterly, Trim Size-8½ x 11, Desktop press, 48 pages, ISSN: 0890-7218, Color-cover, Matte
Subscriptions: Indv. $22, $6/copy
Circulation: Total-3,800
Advertising: Inquire for rates.
List Rental: Actives: $50/M

Pennsylvania Ethnic Heritage Newsletter
See: ETHNIC

Plymouth Meeting, Pennsylvania

Small Business Chronicle
See: BUSINESS & INDUSTRY

State College, Pennsylvania

Mansion Notes
See: MUSEUM PUBLICATIONS

Charleston, South Carolina

Preservation Progress
See: ARCHITECTURE

Brookings, South Dakota

SDSU Census Data Center Newsletter

Publishing Co: SDSU Census Data Center, PO Box 504, Brookings, SD 57006-0504; Title Tel # (605) 688-4132
Personnel: Editor-Dr. James Satterlee, Circ. Mgr.-Don Atwood, Production Mgr.-Pat Joffer
General Info: Yr. Est. 1986, Quarterly, Trim Size-8½ x 11, Letrpr. press, 4 pages, Color, Newsprint
Circulation: Total-1,500

Knoxville, Tennessee

CORAspondent
See: RELIGIOUS & THEOLOGICAL

Austin, Texas

Texas Business Review
See: BUSINESS & INDUSTRY

Texas Industrial Expansion
Business

Publishing Co: Bureau of Business Research, University of Texas, 21st St. & Speedway, Austin, TX 78712-1104 Tel # (512) 471-1616; Title Tel # (512) 471-5179 Title Fax # (512) 471-1063
Personnel: Editor-Elaine Pinckard
Editorial Description: Reports on expansions of manufacturing plants in Texas, & establishment of new plants. Supplement to Directory of Texas Manufacturers.
General Info: Yr. Est. 1951, Monthly, Trim Size-8½ x 14, Sheetfed press, 8 pages, 2 Color
Subscriptions: Indv. $50, Inst. $50
Circulation: Total-3,200

San Antonio, Texas

AACOG Region
Association

Publishing Co: Alamo Area Council of Governments, 118 Broadway St Ste 400, San Antonio, TX 78205-1999; Title Tel # (512) 225-5201 Title Fax # (512) 225-5937
Personnel: Editor-Nancy Roth-Roffy
General Info: Monthly, 8 pages
Circulation: Total-3,500

Colchester, Vermont

Vermont ETV Program Guide
See: TELEVISION & VIDEO

Wallingford, Vermont

Vermont Foodnews Paper
See: FOOD

Alexandria, Virginia

Hayfield Citizens Association Newsletter
Consumer, Association

Publishing Co: Hayfield Citizens Association, 5807 Ashfield Rd., co Robin Moyer, Alexandria, VA 22310; Title Tel # (703) 922-1877
Personnel: Editor-Robin Moyer
Editorial Description: Community activities, events, and information for those in Hayfield Township Northern Virginia.
General Info: 10x/yr., Trim Size-8½ x 11, 30 pages, No Color, Matte
Circulation: Total-750
Advertising: Inquire for rates.

Sleeper News
Consumer

Publishing Co: Sleeper Co., The, PO Box 10570, Alexandria, VA 22310-0570
Editorial Description: A quarterly newsletter on Washington County, New York.
General Info: Quarterly

Norfolk, Virginia

Norfolk Foundation
Business, Association

Publishing Co: Norfolk Foundation, 1410 NationsBank Center, Norfolk, VA 23510-2113; Title Tel # (804) 622-7951
Personnel: Editor-Sally Kirby Hartman
Editorial Description: Newsletter of the Norfolk Foundation that seekd to gain donations for community improvement.
General Info: Quarterly, Trim Size-8½ x 11, No Color

Richmond, Virginia

Rural Virginia Voice
Association

Publishing Co: Rural Virginia, Inc., PO Box 105, Richmond, VA 23201-0105
Personnel: Publisher-Rick Cagan
Editorial Description: A voice for progressive, rural community development issues in Virginia.
General Info: Yr. Est. 1982, Quarterly, Trim Size-8½ x 11, Mimeo press, 20 pages, ISSN: 1059-6305, No Color
Subscriptions: Indv. $20
Circulation: Total-800
Advertising: Inquire for rates.
List Rental: Rents Lists

This Week in Richmond
See: TRAVEL

Roanoke, Virginia

Ski Tripper
See: SKIING & SNOWMOBILING

Olympia, Washington

Hanford Update Newsletter
See: WATER SUPPLY, POWER & WASTE

WSEO Dispatch
See: ENERGY

Seattle, Washington

Municipal News
Association

Publishing Co: Municipal League Foundation, 810 3rd Ave., Seattle, WA 98104; Title Tel # (206) 622-8333
Personnel: Publisher-Lyn Lamber, Circ. Mgr., Production Mgr.-HeatherLynn Holmes, Art Dir.-Clarice Keegan, Editor, Promotion Dir.-Liz Smith
Editorial Description: Looks in depth regional issues in King County. Incorporates The Municipal News.
General Info: (Formerly Municipal News), Yr. Est. 1990, Monthly, Letrpr. press, 12 pages, 2 Color, Coated
Subscriptions: Indv. $50, $4/copy
Circulation: Total-2,500
Printing Co: Frayne Printing, 2518 Western Ave, Seattle, WA 98121-1308 Tel # (206) 441-4222

Regional View
Association

Publishing Co: Puget Sound Regional Council, 1011 Western Avenue, #500, Seattle, WA 98104-1035 Tel # (206) 464-7090 Fax # (206) 587-4825
Personnel: Editor-Richard Milne
Editorial Description: Presents information about association of local governments in the Puget Sound region.
General Info: Yr. Est. 1992, Monthly
Subscriptions: Free

Morgantown, West Virginia

West Virginia & Regional History Collection-Newsletter
See: HISTORY

Black River Falls, Wisconsin

Monroe County of Wisconsin Historical Society Time Capsules
See: HISTORY

Milwaukee, Wisconsin

The Father, The Son
See: DRUGS & PHARMACEUTICALS

Sparta, Wisconsin

Historical Time Capsules of Monroe County
See: HISTORY

CANADA

Edmonton, Alberta

Edmonton Native News *Consumer, Association*
Publishing Co: Canadian Native Friendship Centre, 11205 101 Street, Edmonton, AB T5G 2A4 Canada; Title Tel # (403) 479-1999
General Info: Yr. Est. 1963, Monthly

Lelgary, Alberta

Archivists Society of Alberta Newsletter
See: CULTURE & HUMANITIES

Scarborough, Ontario

Ontario Taxation Service
See: TAXES

Simcoe, Ontario

Long Point Genealogist, The
See: GENEALOGY

Toronto, Ontario

Canadian Scene
Publishing Co: Canadian Scene, 73 Simcoe St., 3rd Fl., Toronto, ON M5J 1W9 Canada; Title Tel # (416) 593-0439 Title Fax # (416) 593-0448
Personnel: Editor-Ben Viccari
Editorial Description: For immigrants and new Canadians, government legislation, history, etc.
General Info: Yr. Est. 1951, Bi-weekly, Trim Size-8½ x 14, Mimeo press, 8 pages
Subscriptions: Indv. $65, Can. $45

Canadian Society of Environmental Biologists Newsletter
See: ENVIRONMENT & ECOLOGY

Impact!
See: THEATRE

Quebec, Quebec

Monthly Bulletin (Quebec)
Publishing Co: Dir Des Entreprise, C.P. 1153, Quebec, PQ G1K 7C3 Canada Tel # (514) 873-5324; Title Tel # (514) 288-6104
Personnel: Publisher-A. Martineau
Editorial Description: Collective labor agreement settlements.
General Info: Monthly

Whitehorse, Yukon Territory

Yukon Historical & Museums Association Newsletter
See: HISTORY

RELIGIOUS & THEOLOGICAL

GENERAL RELIGIOUS PERIODICALS-
(For specific religions, look under the name of the specific religious group)

475
Publishing Co: Interchurch Center, 475 Riverside Dr Ste 253, New York, NY 10115-0253; Title Tel # (212) 870-2932 Title Fax # (212) 870-2440
Personnel: Editor-Mark Isabel
Editorial Description: House organ for religious headquarters bldg.
General Info: Yr. Est. 1960, Monthly, Trim Size-8½ x 11, Offset press, 4 pages
Circulation: Total-2,000
Printing Co: Natl. Council of Churches, 475 Riverside Dr Ste 552, New York, NY 10115-0122

AACS Newsletter
See: EDUCATION

ACWR News
See: LIBRARY

ADRIS Newsletter
See: COMPUTERS & AUTOMATION

ALERTA
See: INTERNATIONAL TRADE

Accrediting Association of Bible Colleges Newsletter
See: EDUCATION

Action Line
See: SOCIAL SERVICES & WELFARE

Advocate
See: POLITICS

Alerte au Quebec
Publishing Co: Pubs. Alerte, 25 av. Royale, Ste-Petronille, PQ G0A 4C0 Canada
General Info: Yr. Est. 1975, Monthly
Subscriptions: Indv. $5

Alternative Models Newsletter *Association*
Publishing Co: Catechetical Renewal Network, PO Box 7550634, Dayton, OH 45475-0634 Tel # (513) 885-3921
Personnel: Publisher, Editor-Robert Humphrey, Bk. Rev. Ed.-Daniel Thomas
Editorial Description: Designed to facilitate communication among religious educators interested in developing and implementing alternative models of religious education.
General Info: Yr. Est. 1989, Quarterly, Trim Size-8½ x 11, Desktop press, 10 pages, 2 Color, Coated
Subscriptions: Indv. $10, Inst. $50, $3/copy
Circulation: Total-950

America Today
Publishing Co: America Today, PO Box 188, Houston, MO 65483-0188; Title Tel # (417) 967-3600
Personnel: Editor-Everett Sileven
Editorial Description: Events from a Christian perspective.
General Info: Monthly

American Association of Pastoral Counselors Newsletter *Association*
Publishing Co: American Assn. of Pastoral Counselors, 9504 A Lee Hwy., Fairfax, VA 22031-2303 Tel # (703) 358-6967; Title Tel # (703) 385-6967 Title Fax # (703) 352-7725
General Info: Quarterly, 2 Color, Saddle-stitched
Subscriptions: Indv. $15, For. $15, Free With Membership
Advertising: Inquire for rates.
Printing Co: Allen-Wayne, Ltd., 5404a Port Royal Rd, Springfield, VA 22151-2301 Tel # (703) 321-7414, Fax # (703) 321-8179

American Gay & Lesbian Atheist
See: GAY & LESBIAN INTEREST

American Society for the Study of Religion Newsletter *Association*
Publishing Co: American Society for the Study of Religion, Smu Dept. Of Religious Studies, Dallas, TX 75275-0001; Title Tel # (214) 692-2095
Personnel: Editor-Frederick Streng
Editorial Description: A group of scholars in a comparative study of religion.
General Info: Yr. Est. 1956

American Theological Library Association Newsletter
See: LIBRARY

Ancient Controversy

Publishing Co: Spencers Intl. Enterprises, PO Box 43822, Los Angeles, CA 90043-0822; Title Tel # (213) 937-3099
Personnel: Publisher-G.S. Lewis
General Info: Yr. Est. 1987, Monthly, 8 pages, ISSN: 1042-2471
Subscriptions: Indv. $96
Circulation: Total-2,500

AngelWatch   *Association, Consumer*

Publishing Co: AngelWatch, PO Box 1362, Mountainside, NJ 07092-0362; Title Tel # (908) 232-5240 Title Fax # (908) 233-1339
Personnel: Editor-Eileen Freeman
Editorial Description: Search for angels in everyday life.
General Info: Bi-monthly, Trim Size-8½ x 11, 16 pages, ISSN: 1063-8962
Subscriptions: Indv. $16

Assn. of Professors & Researchers in Religious Education Newsletter   *Association*

Publishing Co: Assn. of Professors & Researchers in Religious Education, 1100 E 55th St, Chicago, IL 60615-5112; Title Tel # (312) 271-0751
Personnel: Editor-Donald Williams
Editorial Description: Profs. & reschrs. in rel. ed in institutions of higher learning,denominatl & ecumenical organizations. 1.
General Info: Yr. Est. 1970, Semi-annually, Trim Size-8½ x 11, 15 pages, No Color, Newsprint
Subscriptions: Inst. $5
Circulation: Total-425

Association of Theological Schools in the U.S. and Canada Bulletin   *Association*

Publishing Co: Association of Theological Schools in the U.S. & Canada, 10 Summit Park Dr, Pittsburgh, PA 15275-1110 Tel # (412) 788-6505; Title Tel # (513) 898-4654
Personnel: Editor-Leon Pacala
Editorial Description: Information about the association, requirements for membership, constitutional structure and policy statements.
General Info: Yr. Est. 1937, Every two years, Trim Size-6 x 9, ISSN: 0362-1472
Subscriptions: $11/copy
Circulation: Total-800

At-One-Ment   *Association*

Publishing Co: Graymoor Ecumenical Inst., Route 9, PO Box 300, Garrison, NY 10524-0306; Title Tel # (914) 424-3458 Title Fax # (914) 424-3473
Personnel: Publisher-Emil Tomaskovic, Editor-Jim Gardiner
Editorial Description: Newsletter about ecumenical events.
General Info: Yr. Est. 1974, Bi-monthly, Trim Size-8½ x 11, 6 pages, 2 Color
Acquistions: Publication Bought
Circulation: Total-6,459

Augsburg Fortress Book Newsletter
See: BOOKS & BOOK TRADE

Baptist Voice   *Consumer, Association*

Publishing Co: American Baptist Society, 2843 Washington Ave., St. Louis, MO 63103 Fax # (314) 533-6084; Title Tel # (314) 533-0747
Personnel: Mng. Editor-Renee Fagan, Exec. Ed.-Ronald B. Packnett
General Info: Monthly

Bethphage Messenger   *Association*

Publishing Co: Bethphage Mission Inc., 13057 W. Center Rd., Ste. 20, Omaha, NE 68144-3723; Title Tel # (402) 592-7192
Editorial Description: News and human interest articles pertaining to the work of the Mission.
General Info: Yr. Est. 1913, Monthly, Trim Size-8½ x 11, Offset press, 12 pages, 2 Color
Circulation: Total-31,000

Between the Lines
See: LIBRARY

Beyond   *Association*

Publishing Co: JAARS Inc., 7405 JAARS Rd., PO Box 248, Waxhaw, NC 28173-0248 Tel # (704) 843-6095; Title Tel # (704) 843-6000 Title Fax # (704) 843-6355
Personnel: Editor-Robert Griffin, Art Dir.-Dempster Evans
Editorial Description: Information on the needs & missions of JAARS.
General Info: Yr. Est. 1973, Bi-monthly, Trim Size-4.5 x 11, Sheetfed press, 2 Color, Coated
Circulation: Total-30,000

Bondings

Publishing Co: New Ways Ministry, 4012 29th St, Mount Rainier, MD 20712-1800; Title Tel # (301) 277-5674 Title Fax # (301) 864-6948
Personnel: Publisher-Regina Miller, Editor-John Gallagher, Circ. Mgr.-Greg Link
Editorial Description: Gay/lesbian positive educational & religious approach.
General Info: Yr. Est. 1977, Quarterly, Roto. press, 12 pages, No Color, Newsprint
Subscriptions: Indv. $5, Can. $10, For. $15
Circulation: Total-5,000
Printing Co: Diamond Press, 1819 E Preston St, Baltimore, MD 21213-3190 Tel # (301) 327-5600

Brethren Peace Fellowship Newsletter   *Consumer, Association*

Publishing Co: Brethren Peace Fellowship, PO Box 455, New Windsor, MD 21776-0455; Title Tel # (410) 775-2254
Personnel: Editor-Dale Aukerman
General Info: Yr. Est. 1968, Bi-monthly, 4 pages
Subscriptions: Free With Membership
Circulation: Total-700

Bridging Peoples

Publishing Co: Emerging Missions-Overseas Crusades, PO Box 36900, Colorado Springs, CO 80936-3690; Title Tel # (408) 263-1101
Personnel: Publisher-Dr. Lawrence Keyes, Editor-Dr. Larry Pate, Circ. Mgr.-Bonnie Bagley
Editorial Description: A newsletter of information & encouragement for the leaders of non-western missionary organizations.
General Info: Yr. Est. 1983, Quarterly, Sheetfed press, 2 pages, 2 Color
Subscriptions: Indv. $5, $2/copy
Circulation: Total-2,500

Briefly
See: LAW

Broken Shackles

Publishing Co: Christian Chaplain Services, Inc., Box 4009, Los Angeles, CA 90086-0307; Title Tel # (213) 624-3945
Editorial Description: Newsletter for ministry supporters.
General Info: Bi-monthly
Circulation: Total-2,500

Bulletin General Theological Ctr. of Maine   *Consumer, Association*

Publishing Co: General Theological Library, 159 State St, Portland, ME 04101-3701; Title Tel # (207) 874-2214
Editorial Description: New accessions, book reviews, periodical list, information on General Theological Library services, list of officers.
General Info: Yr. Est. 1860, Quarterly, Trim Size-6 x 9, Offset press, 16 pages, ISSN: 1052-8202, No Color
Subscriptions: Indv. $10, $3/copy
Circulation: Total-1,200

CALC Report
See: POLITICS

CORAspondent   *Consumer, Association*

Publishing Co: Commission on Religion in Appalachia (CORA), PO Box 52910, Knoxville, TN 37950-2910 Tel # (423) 584-6133 Fax # (423) 584-8114; Title Tel # (615) 584-6133 Title Fax # (615) 584-8114
Personnel: Editor-Jamie Harris
Editorial Description: Covers Appalachian issues & work by churches in region.
General Info: Yr. Est. 1981, Quarterly, Trim Size-8½ x 11, Desktop press, 8 pages, No Color, Matte, Other
Circulation: Total-7,000

Canadian Bible Society News Letter   *Association*

Publishing Co: Canadian Bible Society, 10 Carnforth Rd., Toronto, ON M4A 2S4 Canada; Title Tel # (416) 757-4171 Title Fax # (416) 757-3376
Personnel: Publisher-Rev. Floyd Babcock, Editor-Michele Owens, Circ. Mgr.-Barbara Walkden, Art Dir.-Nelly Safari
Editorial Description: For the promotion of the work of the Canadian Bible Society in Canada and throughout the world.
General Info: Yr. Est. 1960, Tri-annually, Trim Size-5½ x 8½, Web press, 24 pages, 2 Color, Coated
Subscriptions: Free
Circulation: Total-150,000

Canadian Religious Conference. CRC Bulletin   *Association*

Publishing Co: Canadian Religious Conference, 324 Laurier Ave. E., Ottawa, ON K1N 6P6 Canada; Title Tel # (613) 236-0824
Personnel: Editor-Sr. Rita
General Info: Yr. Est. 1955, Quarterly, 8 pages, ISSN: 0316-8751, No Color
Circulation: Total-6,000

Celebration News
See: PHILOSOPHY

Center Focus
See: EDUCATION

Center for Plain Living Newsletter
See: LIFESTYLE

Center for Women and Religion - Newsletter
See: WOMEN'S

Choirboy Notes
See: MUSIC & MUSIC TRADES

Christian New Age
Quarterly   *Consumer*

Publishing Co: Bethsheva's Concern, PO Box 276, Clifton, NJ 07011-0276
Personnel: Publisher, Editor-Catherine Groves, Bk. Rev. Ed.-Stephen Mathis, Art Dir.-Judith Landaiche
Editorial Description: A forum for dialogue between Christians and New Agers.
General Info: Yr. Est. 1989, Quarterly, Trim Size-7 x 8½, 24 pages, ISSN: 0899-7292, Matte
Subscriptions: Indv. $13, Inst. $13, Can. $13, For. $19, $4/copy
Advertising: $45.

Church & Synagogue Computer
See: COMPUTERS & AUTOMATION

Church Council on
Justice & Corrections,
Update

Publishing Co: Church Council on Justice & Corrections, 507 Bank St., 2nd Fl., Ottawa, ON K2P 1Z5 Canada; Title Tel # (613) 563-1688 Title Fax # (613) 237-6129
General Info: Yr. Est. 1981, Semi-annually, Trim Size-8½ x 11
Circulation: Total-5,000

Church Growth Resource
News

Publishing Co: Institute for American Church Growth, PO Box 541, Monrovia, CA 91017-0541
Personnel: Editor-Dr. Win Arn
General Info: Semi-annually
List Rental: List Management Co.: Bernice Bush Co./Springdale Lists, 15052 Springdale St., Huntington Beach, CA 92649-1178 Tel # (714) 891-3344, Fax # (714) 897-0650, Actives: 32,000, $85/M

Church Law & Tax Report
See: LAW

Church Secretary's Communique
See: OFFICE METHODS & EQUIPMENT

Church and Synagogue Libraries
See: LIBRARY

Church Treasurer Alert
See: TAXES

Church Women Act

Publishing Co: Church Women United, 110 Maryland Ave., NE, Washington, DC 20002-5626 Fax # (202) 543-1297; Title Tel # (202) 544-8747
Personnel: Editor-Sally Timmel
General Info: Yr. Est. 1985

Common Lot

Publishing Co: Coordinating Center for Women in Church & Society, 700 Prospect Ave E, Cleveland, OH 44115-1131; Title Tel # (212) 683-5656
Personnel: Editor-Patricia Miller
General Info: Yr. Est. 1974, Quarterly, Trim Size-8½ x 11, Sheetfed press, 16 pages, No Color, Newsprint
Subscriptions: Indv. $12
Circulation: Total-25,000
Printing Co: Kutztown Publishing Co., 15076 Kutztown Rd, Kutztown, PA 19530-9275 Tel # (215) 683-7341

Community of Joy
See: INTERNATIONAL AFFAIRS

Compassion Today
See: CHILDREN

Contact
See: MEDICINE

Context   *Association*

Publishing Co: Claretian Publications, 205 W. Monroe St., Chicago, IL 60606-5033; Title Tel # (312) 236-7782 Title Fax # (312) 236-8207
Personnel: Editor-Martin Marty, Mktg. Dir.-Michelle Merten
Editorial Description: Interaction of religion and culture, surveys religious, political, social scene from an ecumenical viewpoint analyzing new trends in theology and new developments in church-state relations.
General Info: Yr. Est. 1969, 22x/yr., Trim Size-8½ x 11, Offset press, 6 pages, ISSN: 0361-8854, Color
Subscriptions: Indv. $30, For. $34, $1/copy
Circulation: Total-2,771
Advertising: Accepts Inserts.
List Rental: Actives: 5,575, $75/M, Expires: 3,300

Cornell Modern Indonesia Project:
See: INTERNATIONAL AFFAIRS

Council of Societies for
the Study of Religion
Bulletin   *Association*

Publishing Co: Council of Societies for the Study of Religion, Mercer Univ., Macon, GA 31207-0001; Title Tel # (912) 752-2376
Personnel: Publisher-Watson Mills, Editor-Rick Busse, Circ. Mgr., Adv. Dir., Art Dir.-Irene Palmer
Editorial Description: Articles on religious studies and reports on societies, calendar of upcoming meetings.
General Info: (Formerly Council on the Study of Religion Bulletin), Yr. Est. 1969, Quarterly, Trim Size-8½ x 11, Web press, 24 pages, ISSN: 0002-7170, 3% ads, No Color, Saddle-stitched
Subscriptions: Indv. $18, Inst. $24, Can. $24, For. $30, $9/copy
Acquistions: Publication Bought
Circulation: Total-6,500
Advertising: Inquire for rates. Accepts Inserts.
List Rental: Rents Lists

Counselor   *Association*

Publishing Co: Religious Public Relations Council, PO Box 296, Wernersville, PA 19565-0296; Title Tel # (610) 373-1067
Personnel: Editor-Londia Granger
General Info: Yr. Est. 1950, Quarterly, Offset press, 8 pages, No Color
Subscriptions: Indv. $1
Circulation: Total-1,000

Current Dialogue   *Association*

Publishing Co: World Council of Churches, 475 Riverside Dr., Ste 915, New York, NY 10115-0122 Fax # (212) 870-2528; Title Tel # (212) 870-3340
Editorial Description: Dialogue with people putting their faith into daily practice.
General Info: 3x/yr.

Dallas Institute Newsletter, The
See: PUBLIC MANAGEMENT & PLANNING

Deep Spring Newsletter   *Consumer, Association*

Publishing Co: Deep Spring Center For Meditation and Spiritual Inquiry, 3455 Charing Cross Rd, Ann Arbor, MI 48108-1911 Parent Co.-Deep Spring Center For Meditation and Spiritual Inquiry, Ann Arbor; Title Tel # (313) 971-3455
Personnel: Assoc. Ed.-Celeste Zygmont, Bk. Rev. Ed.-Barbara Brdsky, Editor, Feature Ed., Calendar Ed.-Barbara Brodsky
General Info: Yr. Est. 1989, Tri-annually, Trim Size-8½ x 11, Desktop press, 10 pages
Subscriptions: Free
Circulation: Total-1,000, Readership-1,500
Advertising: Inquire for rates.

Destiny

Publishing Co: Destiny Publishers, 43 Grove St, Merrimac, MA 01860-1807; Title Tel # (508) 346-9311
Editorial Description: Religious-Educational.
General Info: Yr. Est. 1928, Monthly
Subscriptions: Indv. $5, $1/copy
Circulation: Total-9,000

Dialogue on Campus
See: COLLEGE STUDENT

Discoveries
See: CHILDREN

Distant Drums
See: PHILOSOPHY

Divinity School News &
Notes

Publishing Co: Duke Univ. Divinity School, Publications, Durham, NC 27706-7706 Tel # (919) 660-3412 Fax # (919) 660-3473
Personnel: Editor-Carter Askden
Editorial Description: Update from Duke University School of Divinity.
General Info: (Formerly News & Notes), Yr. Est. 1985, Semi-annually, Trim Size-8½ x 13, Sheetfed press, 23 pages, 2 Color, Matte, Saddle-stitched

Dovetail: A Newsletter By
and For Jewish-
Christian Families   *Consumer*

Publishing Co: Dovetail Publishing, PO Box 19945, Kalamazoo, MI 49019; Title Tel # (616) 342-2900 Title Fax # (616) 342-1012
Personnel: Publisher, Editor-Joan Hawxhurst, Mktg. Dir.-Alison Siragusa
Editorial Description: Newsletter for Jewish-Christian Families.
General Info: Yr. Est. 1992, Bi-monthly, Trim Size-8½ x 11, Offset press, 16 pages, ISSN: 1062-7359, 5% ads, Color-cover, Matte, Saddle-stitched
Subscriptions: Indv. $25, For. $35, $5/copy
Circulation: Total-1,000
Advertising: Inquire for rates.

Drama Ministry
Consumer

Publishing Co: Communication Resources Inc., 4150 Belden Village St., NW, Suite 400, Canton, OH 44718-2553; Title Tel # (216) 493-7880 Title Fax # (216) 493-7897
Personnel: Publisher-Jennifer Fisher, Editor-Dave Mc. Clellan
Editorial Description: Information for church leaders using dramatic performance in worship services.
General Info: Yr. Est. 1995, Bi-monthly, Trim Size-8½ x 11, Sheetfed press, 18 pages, ISSN: 1084-5917, 2 Color, Matte, Other
Subscriptions: Indv. $80
List Rental: Rents Lists

EHE News
See: PARAPSYCHOLOGY

Echoes
Association

Publishing Co: World Council of Churches, 475 Riverside Dr., Ste 915, New York, NY 10115-0122
Fax # (212) 870-2528; Title Tel # (212) 870-3340
General Info: (Formerly Youth Newsletter; Women in a Changing World), Irregular

Ecu-Link
Association

Publishing Co: National Council of Churches, 475 Riverside Dr, New York, NY 10115-0122;
Title Tel # (212) 870-2227 Title Fax # (212) 870-2030
Personnel: Editor-Martin Bailey
Editorial Description: News about and of interest to NCC member churches to foster community among the members.
General Info: Yr. Est. 1986, Quarterly, 6 pages
Subscriptions: Indv. $6
Circulation: Total-5,000

Ecumenical Chartings

Publishing Co: New York State Council of Churches, 362 State St., Albany, NY 12210-1202;
Title Tel # (518) 436-9319 Title Fax # (518) 427-6705
Personnel: Editor-Arleon Kelley, Circ. Dir.-Sylvenia Cochran
Editorial Description: Sent to church leaders of 23 Protestant denominations, 43 ecumenical councils, & individuals interested in ecumenical affairs in New York State.
General Info: Yr. Est. 1988, Quarterly, Trim Size-8½ x 11, Offset press, 8 pages, 2 Color, Matte
Subscriptions: Free In Designated Area
Circulation: Total-8,600, Readership-8,600
Printing Co: Center Printing, 3049 E. Genesee St., Syracuse, NY 13224 Tel # (315) 446-6126, Fax # (518) 446-5789

Ecumenical Courier
Association

Publishing Co: World Council of Churches, 475 Riverside Dr., Ste 915, New York, NY 10115-0122;
Title Tel # (212) 870-3340 Title Fax # (212) 870-2528
Personnel: Editor-Andrea Rivera-Cano
Editorial Description: Aims to inform its readers of trends, opinions and events within the ecumenical movement.
General Info: Yr. Est. 1941, 3x/yr., 8 pages, No Color
Subscriptions: Indv. $15, $3/copy
Circulation: Total-10,000
Printing Co: Kutztown Publishing Co., 15076 Kutztown Rd, Kutztown, PA 19530-9275
Tel # (215) 683-7341

Education Newsletter
Consumer, Association

Publishing Co: World Council of Churches, 475 Riverside Dr., Ste 915, New York, NY 10115-0122
Fax # (212) 870-2528; Title Tel # (212) 870-3340
Editorial Description: Information from WCC's Office of Education. Text in English, Spanish & Korean.
General Info: 3x/yr.

Elisabeth Elliot Newsletter
Consumer

Publishing Co: Servant Publications, Ann Arbor, MI 48107-7711; Title Tel # (313) 761-8505
Personnel: Editor-Stephanie Giba, Circ. Mgr.-Louise Pare
Editorial Description: Articles, questions & answers, and personal news from Elisabeth Elliot.
General Info: Yr. Est. 1982, Bi-monthly, Trim Size-11 x 17, 4 pages, ISSN: 8756-1336, 2 Color
Subscriptions: Indv. $7
Circulation: Total-10,000

Emergency Services Chaplain

Publishing Co: Fire-Medic Services, 19 Joslin St., Providence, RI 02909-2599;
Title Tel # (401) 751-6217
Personnel: Publisher, Editor-Thomas Lopatosky
Editorial Description: Nondenominational publication providing ideas and information for chaplains of fire departments and other emergency service organizations.
General Info: Yr. Est. 1991, Bi-monthly, Sheetfed press, 8 pages, No Color, Matte
Subscriptions: Indv. $9, $2/copy

Emerging Trends
Consumer, Association

Publishing Co: Princeton Religion Research Co., Inc., P.O. Box 389, Princeton, NJ 08542;
Title Tel # (609) 921-8112
Personnel: Publisher, Editor-George Gallup, Circ. Mgr., Production Mgr.-Marie Swirsky
Editorial Description: Survey data from Gallup Poll on religion.
General Info: Yr. Est. 1979, 10x/yr., 6 pages
Subscriptions: Indv. $35, $3/copy
Circulation: Total-1,700

Entre Nous
Association

Publishing Co: Canadian Council of Churches, 40 St. Clair Avenue E., Toronto, ON M4T 1M9 Canada; Title Tel # (416) 921-4152 Title Fax # (416) 921-7478
Editorial Description: News of activities of the Canadian Council of Churches.
General Info: (Formerly Council Communicator & Bulletin), Yr. Est. 1970, Semi-annually, Trim Size-8½ x 11, Offset press, 6 pages, ISSN: 1184-0447, No Color, Recycled, Saddle-stitched
Subscriptions: Free
Circulation: Total-3,000

Ethics & Perspectives
See: PHILOSOPHY

Ethics & Public Policy Center Newsletter

Publishing Co: Ethics & Public Policy Center, 1015 15th St. NW, Ste. 900, Washington, DC 20005;
Title Tel # (202) 682-1200
Personnel: Editor-Carol Griffith, Circ. Mgr.-Timothy Kunes
General Info: Yr. Est. 1982, Quarterly, 6 pages
List Rental: Actives: $50/M

Ethics and Policy
See: PHILOSOPHY

Father Flood Lectionary Series
Association

Publishing Co: Liturgical Pubs., Inc., 2875 S James Dr, New Berlin, WI 53151-3662;
Title Tel # (414) 785-1188 Title Fax # (414) 785-9567
Editorial Description: Cartoon for every sunday of the month starting with advent 1995. Cartoons are based on sunday readings from the catholic lectionary.
General Info: Yr. Est. 1995, Quarterly, Looseleaf
Subscriptions: Indv. $130

Freedom Writer
See: CIVIL RIGHTS

Ganymedia

Publishing Co: David Lochman, PO Box 2516, Chicago, IL 60690-2516; Title Tel # (201) 686-2485
Personnel: Editor-David Lochman
General Info: Yr. Est. 1975, 12 pages
Circulation: Total-1,000

Gateways

Publishing Co: Gateways, 415 Summit Rd, Watsonville, CA 95076-9781; Title Tel # (408) 847-0406
General Info: Monthly, Trim Size-7 x 8½, 16 pages
Subscriptions: Indv. $5

Good News
Association

Publishing Co: Liturgical Pubs., Inc., 2875 S James Dr, New Berlin, WI 53151-3662;
Title Tel # (414) 785-1188 Title Fax # (414) 785-9567
Personnel: Editor-Joseph Nolan, Circ. Mgr.-Ruth Cooke
Editorial Description: Homily service scriptural comments; 52 Sundays all holy days and special occasions.
General Info: Yr. Est. 1972, Monthly, Trim Size-8½ x 11, Web press, 36 pages, Color-cover, Looseleaf
Subscriptions: Indv. $59, Can. $77, For. $104
Circulation: Total-2,700

Good News Letter

Publishing Co: God's Love We Deliver, Inc., 895 Amsterdam Ave, New York, NY 10025-4403
Tel # (212) 865-4900; Title Tel # (202) 529-0001
Personnel: Editor-John Burke
Editorial Description: Promoting sound biblical preaching & bible sharing to enable others to claim the strength of the scriptures.
General Info: Yr. Est. 1972, Quarterly, Web press
Circulation: Total-15,000
Printing Co: Suburban Record/Record Printing Co., 7676 Fenton St, Silver Spring, MD 20910-4903

IFRAA Quarterly
Consumer, Association

Publishing Co: Interfaith Forum/on Religion, Art & Architecture, 1735 New York Avenue NW, Washington, DC 20006-5209; Title Tel # (202) 387-8333
General Info: Quarterly

Idea Source
Consumer

Publishing Co: Communication Resources Inc., 4150 Belden Village St., NW, Suite 400, Canton, OH 44718-2553 Fax # (216) 493-7897; Title Tel # (216) 493-7880 Title Fax # (216) 493-7880
Personnel: Publisher-Robert Fisher, Editor-Anetta Brown
General Info: Yr. Est. 1994, Bi-monthly, Trim Size-8½ x 11, Sheetfed press, 12 pages, 2 Color, Matte, Other
Subscriptions: Indv. $30
List Rental: Rents Lists

In Action
See: HEALTH

In Contact
Association

Publishing Co: Pioneer Clubs, PO Box 788, Wheaton, IL 60189-0788; Title Tel # (708) 293-1600 Title Fax # (708) 293-3053
Personnel: Publisher-Virginia Patterson, Editor-Judy Gillispie, Production Mgr., Art Dir.-Linda Delaney
Editorial Description: Newsletter for updating donors on the ministry of Pioneer Clubs & Camp Cherith camps in the U.S.
General Info: Yr. Est. 1965, Quarterly, Trim Size-8½ x 11, Offset press, 4 pages, 2 Color
Circulation: Total-8,000

Inner Growth Newsletter

Publishing Co: Inner Growth Seminar, 216 Mirada Ave., San Rafael, CA 94903-3931 Tel # (415) 479-4673; Title Tel # (415) 328-8552
Personnel: Editor-Gloria Wilcox
General Info: 4 pages

Inside Information
Association

Publishing Co: Alban Institute, 4550 Montgomery Ave., Suite 433 North, Bethesda, MD 20814-3341 Tel # (301) 718-4407
Personnel: Editor-Celia Allison Hahn, Production Mgr.-Carol McKenzie
Editorial Description: Update on research & staff news of the Institute, which is involved in providing clergy & laity training, education, & publications to enhance the effectiveness of congregations.
General Info: Yr. Est. 1983, Quarterly, Trim Size-8½ x 11, Web press, 4 pages, 2 Color, Other, Saddle-stitched
Subscriptions: Free With Membership
Circulation: Total-8,700
List Rental: Actives: $75/M, Expires: $60/M

Interdependence

Publishing Co: International Association for Religious Freedom, 755 Massachusetts Ave., 221 Dean St, Woodstock, IL 60098
Personnel: Editor-Rev. Charles Eddis
General Info: Yr. Est. 1972, Semi-annually
Subscriptions: Indv. $10
Circulation: Total-400

Interfaith Impact & Preparedness

Publishing Co: Interfaith Impact for Justice & Peace, 110 Maryland Ave NE Ste 63, Washington, DC 20002-5622 Fax # (202) 547-8107; Title Tel # (202) 543-2800
Editorial Description: Works to advance the cause of justice and peace. It magnifies the voices of individuals and individual demnominations to speak in concert on social issues.
General Info: (Formerly Interfaith Action), Yr. Est. 1984, Quarterly, Trim Size-8½ x 11, Offset press, 16 pages, ISSN: 8755-9404, 2 Color, Recycled, Saddle-stitched
Subscriptions: Indv. $30, Inst. $150, Can. $30
Circulation: Total-5,300

International Assn. for Religious Freedom Newsletter

Publishing Co: International Association for Religious Freedom, 755 Massachusetts Ave., 221 Dean St, Woodstock, IL 60098; Title Tel # (617) 862-3805

John Kurluk Zine

Publishing Co: John Kurluk, 6212 Holabird Ave 'F', Baltimore, MD 21224
Editorial Description: A much thicker issue wich focus on the religious and the unusual.
General Info: Trim Size-8.5 x 11, 8 pages

Kashrus Faxletter
See: FOOD

Krotonian
See: PHILOSOPHY

LNBA Newsletter
Association

Publishing Co: Laymen's Natl. Bible Assn., 1865 Broadway #12, New York, NY 10023-7503; Title Tel # (212) 408-1390 Title Fax # (212) 408-1448
Personnel: Publisher-Thomas May, Editor-J.E. Winslow
Editorial Description: News related to the Bible, & the LNBA organization.
General Info: Yr. Est. 1941, Quarterly, Trim Size-8½ x 11½, Offset press, 4 pages, No Color
Circulation: (100% controlled), Total-9,500

La Vie Oecumenique
Consumer, Association

Publishing Co: World Council of Churches, 475 Riverside Dr., Ste 915, New York, NY 10115-0122 Fax # (212) 870-2528; Title Tel # (212) 870-3340
Editorial Description: News of the ecumenical movement. Text in French.
General Info: Semi-annually

Lay & Study Centres Newsletter
Consumer, Association

Publishing Co: World Council of Churches, 475 Riverside Dr., Ste 915, New York, NY 10115-0122 Fax # (212) 870-2528; Title Tel # (212) 870-3340
General Info: Quarterly

Library Lines
See: LIBRARY

Light Work
Consumer

Publishing Co: Visions Unlimited, PO Box 712167, Santee, CA 92072-2167; Title Tel # (619) 338-4248
Editorial Description: Religious teachings and inspirations.
General Info: (Formerly Master of Light), Yr. Est. 1994, Bi-monthly, Trim Size-8½ x 11, 12 pages, 2 Color, Matte, Saddle-stitched
Subscriptions: Indv. $30, Can. $50
Advertising: $50.

Locus Classicus
Association

Publishing Co: Saratoga Press, PO Box 8, Platteville, CO 80651-0008
General Info: Monthly
Subscriptions: Indv. $25
List Rental: List Management Co.: Response Unlimited, c/o The Old Plantation, Rte. 5, Box 251, Waynesboro, VA 22980-9111 Tel # (703) 943-6721, Fax # (703) 943-0841, Actives: 13,877, $70/M

Longyear Museum Quarterly News
See: MUSEUM PUBLICATIONS

Maryknoll News
Consumer, Association

Publishing Co: Maryknoll Fathers & Brothers, Box 305, Maryknoll, NY 10545-0305 Tel # (914) 941-7590
Editorial Description: Internal news for the community.
General Info: Bi-monthly, 22 pages
Subscriptions: Indv. $10

Mastering Life
See: SEX

Medical-Moral Newsletter
See: MEDICINE

Meditator's Newsletter
Consumer

Publishing Co: Sacred Orchard Corporation, Po Box 298, Harriman, NY 10926-0298; Title Tel # (914) 783-8154
Personnel: Editor-Daryl Bailin, Editor-George Bailin
Editorial Description: Articles and essays for spiritual seekers and meditators.
General Info: Yr. Est. 1994, Monthly, ISSN: 1075-9727
Subscriptions: Indv. $10, $1/copy

Mercury
See: CLUBS

Metro Ministry News

Publishing Co: Institute on the Church in Urban Industrial Society, 4750 N Sheridan, Chicago, IL 60640-5078; Title Tel # (312) 271-7070
Personnel: Editor-John Montgomery
Editorial Description: An ecumenical interdenominational newsletter focusing on models, issues & strategies of urban mission.
General Info: Yr. Est. 1985, Quarterly, Letrpr. press, 8 pages, Matte
Subscriptions: Indv. $8, $2/copy
Circulation: (50% controlled), Total-2,000, Subscriptions-1,000
Printing Co: Salsedo Press, 320 N Damen Ave, Chicago, IL 60612-2489 Tel # (312) 666-1674

Migration Today
Association

Publishing Co: World Council of Churches, 475 Riverside Dr., Ste 915, New York, NY 10115-0122 Fax # (212) 870-2528; Title Tel # (212) 870-3340
Editorial Description: Covers movements of the world's immigrants.
General Info: 3x/yr.

Millennial Prophecy Report
Business, Consumer

Publishing Co: Millennium Watch Institute, PO Box 34021, Philadelphia, PA 19101-4021 Tel # (215) 662-5677 Fax # (215) 386-6306; Title Tel # (215) 622-5677 Title Fax # (610) 356-6306
Personnel: Assoc. Publ.-Carol Daniels, Publisher, Editor-Ted Daniels
Editorial Description: Circulated to journalists and the general public, it covers secular and religious ideas of world transformation.
General Info: (Formerly Millennial Times/Millennial News), Yr. Est. 1992, Quarterly, Trim Size-8½ x 11, Offset press, 20 pages, ISSN: 1083-4761, No Color, Coated
Subscriptions: Indv. $90, Inst. $90, Can. $90, For. $90, $25/copy
Circulation: Total-200, Readership-200
Printing Co: Jade Press, 4420 Walnut St, Philadelphia, PA 19104-2947 Tel # (215) 556-0691, Fax # (215) 385-9495

Ministerial Formation
Association

Publishing Co: World Council of Churches, 475 Riverside Dr., Ste 915, New York, NY 10115-0122 Fax # (212) 870-2528; Title Tel # (212) 870-3340
Editorial Description: Education and development of ministers.
General Info: Quarterly

Modern Agnostic Journal, The
Consumer

Publishing Co: GNP Publications, PO Box 8642, Spokane, WA 99203-8642;
Title Tel # (509) 534-9525 Title Fax # (509) 536-1975
Personnel: Publisher, Editor-Aaron Caldwell, Circ. Mgr.-Kurt Wilcox, Adv. Dir., Mktg. Dir.-Dan Clausen
Editorial Description: Voice of the modern agnostic believer. Uses contemporary agnostic and religious values to better people's lives. Believes in the existence of G-d as mankind didn't create himself and the universe.
General Info: Yr. Est. 1994, Monthly, Trim Size-8$\frac{1}{2}$ x 11, 2 Color, Matte, Saddle-stitched
Subscriptions: Indv. $25, $3/copy
Advertising: Inquire for rates.

NCSE Reports
See: EDUCATION

NEWSLETTER Newsletter, The

Publishing Co: Communication Resources Inc., 4150 Belden Village St., NW, Suite 400, Canton, OH 44718-2553; Title Tel # (216) 493-7880 Title Fax # (216) 493-7897
Personnel: Publisher-Robert Fisher, Editor-Jennifer Ferrand
General Info: Yr. Est. 1979, Monthly, Trim Size-8$\frac{1}{2}$ x 11, Sheetfed press, 12 pages, ISSN: 0885-6966, 2 Color, Coated, Other
Subscriptions: Indv. $40
List Rental: Rents Lists

National Bulletin
See: GOVERNMENT

National Conference of Christians and Jews Newsletter
Association

Publishing Co: National Conference of Christians & Jews, 71 5th Ave., #1100, New York, NY 10003-3004; Title Tel # (212) 206-0006
Personnel: Editor-Harry Robinson
Editorial Description: News to keep its national constituencies abreast of program developments and other interesting activities of the NCCJ.
General Info: Yr. Est. 1928, Semi-annually, Trim Size-8$\frac{1}{2}$ x 11, Sheetfed press, 10 pages, Color, Newsprint
Acquistions: Publication Bought
Circulation: (100% controlled), Total-200,000
Printing Co: Paul Art Press, 424 W. 33rd, New York, NY 10001

National Conference on Ministry to the Armed Forces Newsletter

Publishing Co: Natl. Conference on Ministry to the Armed Forces, 4141 N Henderson Rd Ste 13, Arlington, VA 22203-2452; Title Tel # (703) 276-7905
Personnel: Editor-Clifford Weathers
General Info: Yr. Est. 1982, Quarterly, 20 pages
Circulation: Total-200

New Beginnings
Consumer

Publishing Co: New Beginnings, Inc., PO Box 228, Waynesville, NC 28786-2628
Tel # (704) 456-3628
Editorial Description: Non-denominational religious articles and information about books and audiotapes available.
General Info: Monthly, Trim Size-8$\frac{1}{2}$ x 11, 16 pages, 2 Color, Matte, Saddle-stitched

New Creation News
Consumer

Publishing Co: Mayan Crafts, 1035 N Edgewood St, Arlington, VA 22201-2119;
Title Tel # (703) 528-1446
Personnel: Editor-Marie Grosso, Adv. Dir.-Margaret Schellenberg, Promotion Dir.-Joan Urbanczyk
Editorial Description: Comprehensive social analysis, theological reflection, personal experience on critical social justice issues.
General Info: Yr. Est. 1979, Bi-monthly, 10 pages, Color, Newsprint
Subscriptions: Indv. $10
Circulation: Total-1,100
Printing Co: Charbray Printers, Rt. 1, Lovettsville, VA 22180 Tel # (703) 478-1109

New Horizons
Association

Publishing Co: United Board for Christian Higher Education in Asia, 475 Riverside Dr., New York, NY 10115-0109; Title Tel # (212) 870-2610 Title Fax # (212) 870-2322
Personnel: Editor-Michelle Gelber
Editorial Description: Information on Christian Universities related to the United Board in Asia.
General Info: (Formerly China Colleges, The), Yr. Est. 1952, Quarterly, Trim Size-8$\frac{1}{2}$ x 11, Letrpr. press, 4 pages, 2 Color, Coated
Circulation: Total-11,000
Printing Co: Mennonite Press, PO Box 867, Newton, KS 67114-0867 Tel # (316) 283-4680

News from the Congregational Christian Historical Society
Scholarly, Association

Publishing Co: Congregational Christian Historical Society, 14 Beacon St., Boston, MA 02108-37b Title Tel # (617) 523-0470 Title Fax # (617) 523-0491
Personnel: Editor-Harold Worthley
Editorial Description: Board & public meetings of the Society described; resources listed.
General Info: Yr. Est. 1969, Semi-annually, Trim Size-8$\frac{1}{2}$ x 11, Sheetfed press, 10 pages, ISSN: 0362-1510, No Color
Subscriptions: Free With Membership
Circulation: Total-1,058

News-N-Notes
See: POLITICS

Newsletter of the Afro-American Religious History Group
Association

Publishing Co: W.E.B. DuBois Institute, 12 Kane's Crossing, Worcester, MA 01609-1506 Fax # (617) 496-2871; Title Tel # (617) 495-4965 Title Fax # (617) 496-8547
Personnel: Editor-Randall Burkett
Editorial Description: Research for American Academy of Religion Working Group.
General Info: Yr. Est. 1976, Semi-annually, Trim Size-8$\frac{1}{2}$ x 11, Desktop press, 12 pages, No Color
Subscriptions: Indv. $10
Circulation: Total-400
Advertising: Inquire for rates.
List Rental: Actives: $50/M

Newsletter from Dick B on The Spiritual Roots of AA
See: HEALTH

Newsletter for Ugaritic Studies

Publishing Co: Programme in Religious Studies, Univ. of Calgary, Calgary, AB T2N 1N4 Canada;
Title Tel # (403) 284-5045
Personnel: Editor-P. Craigie
Editorial Description: Archaeological research at Ugarit in Syria, and its relevance to the Bible.
General Info: Yr. Est. 1972, Semi-annually, Trim Size-8 x 11, 14 pages, ISSN: 0702-8245, No Color
Circulation: (100% controlled), Total-500

Newslog
See: NEWSPAPER INDUSTRY

Northern Lights Glimmer
See: POLITICS

One Spirit
See: PHILOSOPHY

Open Doors News Brief
See: INTERNATIONAL AFFAIRS

Outreach
See: COLLEGE STUDENT

PCR Information
See: CIVIL RIGHTS

Panorama
Association

Publishing Co: Pittsburgh Theological Seminary, 616 N Highland Ave, Pittsburgh, PA 15206-2525;
Title Tel # (412) 362-5610 Title Fax # (412) 363-3260
Personnel: Publisher-Dr. C. Calian, Editor-Lisa Foster
Editorial Description: General information regarding activities of the school, its faculty & alumnilae.
General Info: 5x/yr., Trim Size-8$\frac{1}{2}$ x 11, Sheetfed press, 8 pages, ISSN: 8755-0954, No Color
Subscriptions: Free To Qualified Recipient
Circulation: Total-28,000

Pantheist Vision
See: PHILOSOPHY

Parables, Etc.
Association

Publishing Co: Saratoga Press, PO Box 8, Platteville, CO 80651-0008
Editorial Description: Selections for use by pastors, teachers and speakers.
General Info: Monthly
List Rental: List Management Co.: Response Unlimited, c/o The Old Plantation, Rte. 5, Box 251, Waynesboro, VA 22980-9111 Tel # (703) 943-6721, Fax # (703) 943-0841, Actives: 13,877, $70/M

Pastor's Story File
Association

Publishing Co: Saratoga Press, PO Box 8, Platteville, CO 80651-0008
General Info: Monthly
Subscriptions: Indv. $25
List Rental: List Management Co.: Response Unlimited, c/o The Old Plantation, Rte. 5, Box 251, Waynesboro, VA 22980-9111 Tel # (703) 943-6721, Fax # (703) 943-0841, Actives: 13,877, $70/M

Pastor's Tax & Money   *Consumer*

Publishing Co: Daniel D. Busby, PO Box 50188, Indianapolis, IN 46250-0188 Tel # (317) 576-8151;
Title Tel # (317) 576-8150 Title Fax # (317) 594-8311
Personnel: Publisher-Daniel D. Busby, Editor-Daniel Busby
Editorial Description: Up-to-date information for pastors & churches on income tax, compensation
planning, insurance, computers, financing church construction & related matters.
General Info: Yr. Est. 1990, Quarterly, Trim Size-8½ x 11, Sheetfed press, 8 pages, 2 Color, Coated
Subscriptions: Indv. $60
Circulation: (100% controlled), Total-6,000
Printing Co: Wesley Press, PO Box 50434, Indianapolis, IN 46250-0434 Tel # (317) 842-4230

Peace Chronical
See: EDUCATION

PeaceNotes
See: POLITICS

Perspective
See: COLLEGE ALUMNI

Perspective
See: EDUCATION

Phoenix Institute Newsletter

Publishing Co: Phoenix Institute Newsletter, PO Box 1690, Sedona, AZ 86339-1690;
Title Tel # (602) 282-1316
Personnel: Editor-Patricia Diegel
General Info: Bi-monthly, 6 pages

Pioneer
See: COLLEGE STUDENT

Prayer Letter

Publishing Co: Sports Ambassador, OC International, Box 36900, Colorado Springs, CO 80936-6900
General Info: Monthly

Prayers for Worship   *Association*

Publishing Co: Liturgical Pubs., Inc., 2875 S James Dr, New Berlin, WI 53151-3662;
Title Tel # (414) 785-1188 Title Fax # (414) 785-9567
Personnel: Editor-Leroy Koopman, Circ. Mgr.-Ruth Cooke
Editorial Description: Complete prayers for Sundays & special days.
General Info: Yr. Est. 1972, Quarterly, Trim Size-8½ x 11, Web press, 15 pages, No Color,
Looseleaf
Subscriptions: Indv. $25, Can. $31, For. $40
Circulation: Total-1,484

Priority
See: EDUCATION

Prophetic Newsletter   *Consumer*

Publishing Co: World Prophetic Ministry, Inc., PO Box 907, Colton, CA 92324-0907;
Title Tel # (714) 875-2767
Personnel: Publisher-Gordon Petersen, Editor-Dave Breese
General Info: Yr. Est. 1950, Monthly, Sheetfed press, 4 pages, 2 Color, Matte
Subscriptions: Indv. $8
Circulation: Total-15,000

Prosperous Living   *Business, Association*

Publishing Co: Golden Key Ministry, 6327 East Paradise Lane, Scottsdale, AZ 85234-1305;
Title Tel # (602) 996-9948 Title Fax # (602) 996-9948
Personnel: Publisher, Editor, Circ. Mgr.-John W. Adams
Editorial Description: For prosperity, success, and positive attitude. Positive ideas for abundance,
goal-setting & achieving of ideas and suggestions for healthful & prosperous living.
General Info: (Formerly Good News!), Yr. Est. 1974, Monthly, Trim Size-8½ x 11, Offset press, 4
pages, Color, Newsprint
Circulation: Total-450
Printing Co: Positive Impressions, 540 W. Iron Ave., Mesa, AZ 85202 Tel # (602) 898-9706

Qualelibet
See: LITERATURE & LINGUISTICS

REACH   *Association*

Publishing Co: Religious Education Association, 409 Prospect St, New Haven, CT 06511-2177;
Title Tel # (203) 865-6141 Title Fax # (203) 865-6142
Personnel: Editor-Barbara Ryan
Editorial Description: News of interest to religious educators & upcoming interfaith meetings.
General Info: (Formerly Religious Educator), Quarterly, Trim Size-8½ x 11, 10 pages, No Color
Subscriptions: Free With Membership
Circulation: Total-2,500
Advertising: Inquire for rates.
List Rental: Actives: $60/M

REC News Exchange   *Association*

Publishing Co: Reformed Ecumenical Council, 2017 Eastern Ave SE Ste 201, Grand Rapids, MI
49507; Title Tel # (616) 241-4424 Title Fax # (616) 241-4424
Personnel: Editor-Richard Van Houten
Editorial Description: News items of interest to the international Reformed community.
General Info: Yr. Est. 1964, Monthly, Trim Size-8½ x 11, Offset press, 8 pages, ISSN: 0033-6904,
No Color
Subscriptions: Indv. $7, Can. $7, For. $7, $1/copy
Circulation: Total-2,400

RIAL News

Publishing Co: Religion in American Life, 2 Queenston Pl., #200, Princeton, NY 08540-3820;
Title Tel # (609) 921-3639
Personnel: Editor-Nicholas Van Dyck, Production Mgr.-Lois Anderson
General Info: 14x/yr.

RNA Newsletter
See: JOURNALISM

RNS Daily News Reports   *Consumer, Association*

Publishing Co: Religion News Service, 1101 Connecticut Ave NW Ste, 350, Washington, DC
20036-4303 Tel # (202) 463-8777 Fax # (202) 463-0033
Personnel: Publisher-Dale Hanson Bourke, Editor-Joan Connell, News Ed.-Thomas Bizzitteri, Assoc.
Ed.-David Anderson, Assoc. Ed.-Ira Rifkin
General Info: Daily, 12 pages

R.T.C.A. Winner's Circle   *Consumer, Association*

Publishing Co: Race Track Chaplaincy of America, Box 1924, Galloway, OH 43119-0924;
Title Tel # (614) 878-0123
General Info: Yr. Est. 1987, Quarterly
Subscriptions: Free

Radical Islamic
Fundamentalism Update   *Association, Consumer*

Publishing Co: American Jewish Congress, 15 E. 84th St., New York, NY 10028-0458
Tel # (212) 879-4500
Personnel: Editor-Will Maslow, Production Mgr.-Ron Kaplan
Editorial Description: Reporting and analyzing current developments in the widespread effort of
radical Islamic fundamentalists to establish societies governed exclusively by the Koran and using
violence and terror as their indispensable tools.
General Info: (Formerly Boycott Report), Yr. Est. 1995, Bi-monthly
Subscriptions: Indv. $20

Reclaiming Newsletter

Publishing Co: Reclaiming Newsletter, PO Box 14404, San Francisco, CA 94114-0404;
Title Tel # (415) 849-0877
Personnel: Editor-Roy King
General Info: Quarterly, Trim Size-7 x 9, 40 pages
Subscriptions: Indv. $4
Advertising: Inquire for rates.

Reflections   *Association*

Publishing Co: Friends of Wayfarers Chapel, 5755 Palos Verdes Dr., S., Palos Verdes, CA
90274-5950; Title Tel # (213) 377-2692
Personnel: Editor-Therese Nagy, Production Mgr.-Sandra Thomson
Editorial Description: Wayfarers Chapel and FOWC happenings; history of Chapel architecture,
construction.
General Info: Yr. Est. 1981, Trim Size-8½ x 11, Offset press, 8 pages, 2 Color
Subscriptions: Indv. $5, $2/copy
Circulation: Total-1,500

Refugee Reports
See: POLITICS

Religion & Society Report   *Consumer*

Publishing Co: Rockford Institute, 934 N Main St, Rockford, IL 61103-7061 Tel # (815) 964-5053
Fax # (815) 965-1826; Title Tel # (815) 964-5813
Personnel: Publisher-Allan Carlson, Editor-Harold Brown, Circ. Mgr.-Rochelle Frank
Editorial Description: Analysis and reviews covering issues concerning the relationship between
religion and society.
General Info: Yr. Est. 1984, Monthly, Trim Size-8½ x 11, 8 pages, ISSN: 0742-6984, 2 Color, Matte
Subscriptions: Indv. $24
List Rental: List Management Co.: Main Street Agency, 934 N Main St, Rockford, IL 61103-7061
Tel # (815) 964-5811, Actives: 2,453, $110/M

Religion in America   *Consumer, Association*

Publishing Co: Princeton Religion Research Co., Inc., P.O. Box 389, Princeton, NJ 08542;
Title Tel # (609) 924-9600
Personnel: Publisher-George Gallup, Jr., Editor-Coleen McMurray, Circ. Mgr.-Marie Swirsky,
Production Mgr.-Coleen MacMurray
Editorial Description: Report covering such religious trends as church attendance, membership
preference & the impact of religion on American life.
General Info: Yr. Est. 1976, Irregular, Trim Size-8½ x 11, Offset press, 100 pages, No Color,
Newsprint, Saddle-stitched
Subscriptions: $25/copy
Circulation: Total-3,000
Printing Co: Trenton Printing Co., 1200 Southard St, Trenton, NJ 08638-5006

Religion and Life Letters

Publishing Co: Sponsor-Spiritual Studies Center, Spiritual Studies Center, PO Box 1104, Rockville, MD 20849-1104; Title Tel # (301) 963-9243
Personnel: Editor-Millard Nachtwey
Editorial Description: Discussion of effect of religion on individual life.
General Info: Yr. Est. 1981, Bi-weekly, Trim Size-8½ x 11, Offset press, 4 pages, ISSN: 0730-2363, No Color
Circulation: Total-37,000

Religion for Peace   *Association*

Publishing Co: World Conference on Religion, 777 United Nations Plaza, New York, NY 10017-3521; Title Tel # (212) 687-2163 Title Fax # (212) 983-0566
Personnel: Editor-William Vendley, Circ. Mgr.-Melissa Chase
General Info: (Formerly WCRP Report), Yr. Est. 1970, Quarterly, Trim Size-8½ x 11, 4 pages
Subscriptions: Indv. $25
Circulation: Total-1,000
Printing Co: Vintage Lithographers, 601 W. 26th St., New York, NY 10001 Tel # (212) 691-8443

Religious Coalition for Reproductive Choice Newsletter
See: WOMEN'S

Religious Education
Newsletter   *Association*

Publishing Co: American Ethical Union, 2 W 64th St, New York, NY 10023-7104; Title Tel # (212) 873-6500
Personnel: Editor-Pat Hortdorfer
General Info: Bi-monthly

Religious Socialism
See: POLITICS

Religious Studies News   *Association*

Publishing Co: Sponsor-American Academy of Religion, c/o James Wiggins, Scholars Press, PO Box 15399, Atlanta, GA 30333-0399; Title Tel # (404) 727-2320 Title Fax # (404) 727-2348
Personnel: Editor-Beth Mackie
Editorial Description: Newsletter for the American Academy of Religion & the Society of Biblical Literature.
General Info: Yr. Est. 1985, 5x/yr., Trim Size-11¼ x 16, Web press, 20 pages, ISSN: 0885-0372, 2 Color, Other
Subscriptions: Indv. $20, Free With Membership
Circulation: Total-14,000
Advertising: Inquire for rates.
List Rental: Rents Lists
Printing Co: Walton Press, Inc., 402 Mayfield Dr., P.O. Box 1047, Monroe, GA 30655-1706 Tel # (404) 267-2596

SCP Newsletter

Publishing Co: Spiritual Counterfeits Project, Inc., PO Box 4308, Berkeley, CA 94704-0308; Title Tel # (510) 540-0300
Personnel: Editor-Joseph Busey
General Info: Yr. Est. 1975, Semi-monthly, 12 pages
Subscriptions: Indv. $10, Inst. $10, Can. $20, For. $20, $2/copy

SSAP Newsletter
See: ENVIRONMENT & ECOLOGY

Sacred Music News & Review
See: MUSIC & MUSIC TRADES

St. George Association
Newsletter

Publishing Co: St. George Assn. of the U.S.A., 83 Christopher St, New York, NY 10014-4248
General Info: Quarterly

Secular Humanist Bulletin
See: PHILOSOPHY

Seminary News   *Association*

Publishing Co: General Theological Seminary, 175 9th Ave, New York, NY 10011-4977; Title Tel # (212) 243-5150 Title Fax # (212) 727-3907
Personnel: Editor-Herb Thomas
Editorial Description: Information pertinent to alumni and friends of this institution.
General Info: Yr. Est. 1975, Quarterly, Trim Size-8½ x 11, Offset press, 8 pages, No Color, Newsprint, Saddle-stitched
Circulation: Total-7,500

Serenity Sentinel

Publishing Co: Serenity Spirtualist Assn., 322 Upper Rd, San Rafael, CA 94903-3041
General Info: Monthly
Subscriptions: Indv. $11

Serran

Publishing Co: Serra Intl., 65 E Wacker Pl Ste 1210, Chicago, IL 60601-7203
Personnel: Editor-John A. Donahue
General Info: Monthly
Subscriptions: Indv. $2

Servant Life   *Consumer*

Publishing Co: Media Management, PO Box 21433, Roanoke, VA 24018-0145 Tel # (703) 989-1330 Fax # (709) 989-5890; Title Tel # (703) 989-1300 Title Fax # (703) 989-5890
Personnel: Publisher-Stephen M. Wike, Editor-Cheryl Hoffman, Sr. Ed.-Lawrence Pierce, Asst. Ed.-Stephen Little, Circ. Mgr.-Holly Beasley, Production Mgr.-Kathly Keoughan
Editorial Description: Topics includes: managing time, people and priorities; enriching marriages; improving relationships; mastering money; expending outreach; and sharpening personal skills.
General Info: Yr. Est. 1994, Monthly, Trim Size-8½ x 11, Offset press, 8 pages, ISSN: 1076-6987, 2 Color
Subscriptions: Indv. $30
Circulation: (8% controlled), Total-2,950, Subscriptions-2,700
List Rental: List Management Co.: Response Unlimited, c/o The Old Plantation, Rte. 5, Box 251, Waynesboro, VA 22980-9111 Tel # (703) 943-6721, Fax # (703) 943-0841, Actives: 2,288, $95/M

Service Committee News   *Consumer, Association*

Publishing Co: Unitarian Universalist Service Committee, 130 Prospect St., Cambridge, MA 02139-1813; Title Tel # (617) 868-6600 Title Fax # (617) 868-7102
Personnel: Publisher, Editor, Production Mgr., Art Dir.-Anne Le Royer
Editorial Description: Published for the members of the Unitarian Universalist Service Committee, devoted to affirming personal worth, the interdependence of all people and the individual's right to peace, justice, and freedom.
General Info: Tri-annually, Trim Size-11 x 17, Offset press, 8 pages, 2 Color, Recycled
Subscriptions: Free With Membership
Circulation: Total-74,000
List Rental: List Management Co.: Robert Hohler Assocs., 6 Faneuil Market, 4th Floor, Boston, MA 02109 Tel # (617) 742-5277

Service Illustrated
See: SOCIAL SERVICES & WELFARE

Showers of Blessings

Publishing Co: Quest for Knowledge, 5289 Preston St., Clarksburg, WV 26301-3748; Title Tel # (304) 622-6184
Personnel: Publisher, Editor-Joyce White
Editorial Description: Spiritually uplifting messages
General Info: Yr. Est. 1991, 3x/yr., Trim Size-8½ x 11, 6 pages, Color-cover
Subscriptions: Indv. $10, Inst. $8, Can. $12, $3/copy
Advertising: Inquire for rates.

Singles & Leaders
Newsletter   *Consumer, Association*

Publishing Co: Singles Support Services, PO Box 842, Norman, OK 73070-0842; Title Tel # (405) 364-4733 Title Fax # (405) 321-2087
Personnel: Editor-Hazel Bell
Editorial Description: To provide news & resources information relative to single adult ministry.
General Info: (Formerly Single Adult Ministry Information), Yr. Est. 1973, Monthly, Trim Size-8½ x 11, 4 pages, ISSN: 1077-0887
Subscriptions: Indv. $15, Can. $18, For. $21, $2/copy
Acquistions: Publication Bought
List Rental: Actives: $90/M

Spiritual Advisory Council-Newsletter
See: PARAPSYCHOLOGY

Spiritual Frontiers Fellowship International Newsletter
See: PARAPSYCHOLOGY

Spiritual Sciences Institute Newsletter
See: PARAPSYCHOLOGY

TRACE Newsletter   *Association*

Publishing Co: Teachers of Religion & Christian Ethics, Box 1108, Saskatoon, SK S7K 3N3 Canada Parent Co.-Saskatchewan Teachers' Federation, Saskatoon, Canada
Personnel: Editor-Miles Meyers
General Info: Irregular, ISSN: 0704-6421
Subscriptions: Indv. $15, Can. $10

Teamwork
See: LIBRARY

Theolog   *Association*

Publishing Co: School of Theology at Claremont, 1325 North College Ave., Public Relations Office, Claremont, CA 91711-3199; Title Tel # (714) 626-3521
Personnel: Editor-Juanita Hallett
Editorial Description: Student publication.
General Info: Weekly, 8 pages
Circulation: Total-200

Theology & Culture
Newsletter

Publishing Co: Theology & Culture Newsletter, Andover Newton Theol. School, Newton Centre, MA 02159; Title Tel # (617) 964-1100
Personnel: Editor-Dr. Gabriel Fackre
Editorial Description: Updates on issues of theology & culture for former students, present colleague & friends.
General Info: Yr. Est. 1967, Semi-annually, Mimeo press, 8 pages
Circulation: Total-2,500

Tie, The — *Association* — CPM: $71

Publishing Co: College of Chaplains, 1701 E Woodfield Rd Ste 311, Schaumburg, IL 60173-5191
Tel # (708) 240-1014; Title Tel # (708) 240-1010 Title Fax # (708) 240-1015
Personnel: Editor-Dr. Jessen, Production Mgr.-Mary Ann Browning
General Info: Yr. Est. 1968, Bi-monthly, Trim Size-8½ x 11, Desktop press, 12 pages, ISSN: 1077-8403, 2 Color, Matte, Saddle-stitched
Subscriptions: Free With Membership
Circulation: Total-2,800
Advertising: $200.
Printing Co: Plum Grove Printers, 2160 Stonington Ave, Hoffman Estates, IL 60195-5204
Tel # (708) 882-4020

Torch — *Association*

Publishing Co: National CGIT Association, 40 St. Clair Ave., Rm. 200, Toronto, ON M4T 1M9
Canada; Title Tel # (416) 961-2036
Personnel: Publications Director-Ruth Dobrensky
Editorial Description: Religious, leadership development.
General Info: Yr. Est. 1924, Annually, Trim Size-5½ x 8½, 32 pages, 2 Color, Looseleaf
Subscriptions: Indv. $3, $2/copy
Circulation: Total-3,000

ULC News

Publishing Co: Universal Life Church, 601 3rd St, Modesto, CA 95351-3395;
Title Tel # (209) 527-8111 Title Fax # (209) 527-8116
Personnel: Editor-Kirby Hensley
General Info: Bi-monthly, 32 pages
Subscriptions: Indv. $5
Advertising: Inquire for rates.

UWM World Scan — *Association*

Publishing Co: United World Mission, PO Box 250, Union Mills, NC 28167-0250;
Title Tel # (704) 287-8996 Title Fax # (704) 287-0580
Personnel: Editor-Jan Kuhn
Editorial Description: Aims to inform its readers of current events & trends on the 12 foreign fields where UWM has missionaries.
General Info: (Formerly United World Mission Reports), Yr. Est. 1964, Quarterly, Trim Size-8½ x 11, Offset press, 6 pages, ISSN: 0892-6050, 2 Color, Coated
Subscriptions: Free
Circulation: Total-30,000

Ultimate Issues
See: LIFESTYLE

Uniquest

Publishing Co: First Unitarian Church of Berkeley, 1 Lawson Rd, Berkeley, CA 94707-1015
Personnel: Editor-Joseph Fabry
Editorial Description: The search for meaning.
General Info: Yr. Est. 1976, Semi-annually, ISSN: 0360-8182

Unitarian-Universalists in Support of Sanctuary Newsletter
See: POLITICS

WICC Newsletter — *Consumer*

Publishing Co: Women's Inter-Church Council of Canada, 815 Danforth Ave., Suite 402, Toronto, ON M4J 1L2 Canada; Title Tel # (416) 462-2528 Title Fax # (416) 462-3915
Personnel: Editor-Marta Condolo
Editorial Description: An ecumenical women's newsletter with a focus on spiritual development & human rights issues in Canada & internationally. The World Day of Prayer & Fellowship of the Least Coin, two international prayer movements are regularly highlighted.
General Info: Yr. Est. 1972, Quarterly, 8 pages, ISSN: 0822-2061, No Color
Subscriptions: Indv. $10, Can. $5
Circulation: Total-12,500

Washington Reports — *Association*

Publishing Co: American Ethical Union, 2 W 64th St, New York, NY 10023-7104;
Title Tel # (212) 873-6500
Personnel: Editor-Herbert Blinder
Editorial Description: Watchdog report covering government actions from the Ethical Movement viewpoint.
General Info: Yr. Est. 1976, 10x/yr.
Subscriptions: Indv. $8

Waterwheel
See: WOMEN'S

Whittemore Newsletter — *Association*

Publishing Co: Sarah Lawrence College, Publications, 1 Meadway, Bronxville, NY 10708-5999;
Title Tel # (914) 337-0700
Personnel: Publisher, Editor-A. Sadler
Editorial Description: Study of Christian and comparative mysticism.
General Info: Yr. Est. 1982, Trim Size-8½ x 11, Offset press, 15 pages, Color
Subscriptions: Indv. $5, $2/copy
Circulation: Total-220

Witness for Peace Newsletter
See: INTERNATIONAL AFFAIRS

Women & Religion Newsletter
See: WOMEN'S

Word & Witness — *Association*

Publishing Co: Liturgical Pubs., Inc., 2875 S James Dr, New Berlin, WI 53151-3662;
Title Tel # (414) 785-1188 Title Fax # (414) 785-9567
Personnel: Editor-Paul Wilson, Circ. Mgr.-Ruth Cooke
Editorial Description: Sermon resource service for preaching, teaching follows common lectionary.
General Info: Yr. Est. 1976, Bi-monthly, Trim Size-8½ x 11, Web press, 44 pages, No Color, Looseleaf
Subscriptions: Indv. $49, Can. $61, For. $79
Circulation: Total-1,988

Working Together
See: SOCIAL SERVICES & WELFARE

World Missionary Press News — *Consumer*

Publishing Co: World Missionary Press, Inc., PO Box 120, New Paris, IN 46553-0120;
Title Tel # (219) 831-2111
General Info: Bi-monthly

Worldorama — *Consumer*

Publishing Co: Life Springs Resources, PO Box 12609, Oklahoma City, OK 73157-2609;
Title Tel # (405) 787-7110
Personnel: Editor-Harold Dalton, Exec. Ed.-J.D. Simmons
Editorial Description: Promotes world missions program.
General Info: Monthly, 6 pages, 2 Color, Coated
Subscriptions: Free
Circulation: Total-41,000
Printing Co: Life Springs Resources, 312 W. Main, Franklin Springs, GA 30639-0009
Tel # (404) 245-7272

Writers Information Network
See: POETRY & CREATIVE WRITING

Year One

Publishing Co: Jonah House, 1933 Park Ave, Baltimore, MD 21217-4895; Title Tel # (301) 669-6265
Personnel: Editor-Elizabeth McAlister
General Info: Yr. Est. 1975, Quarterly, Offset press, 16 pages
Circulation: Total-2,000

Young People and Cults — *Consumer, Association*

Publishing Co: American Family Foundation, PO Box 2265, Bonita Springs, FL 33959-2265;
Title Tel # (212) 249-7693
Personnel: Editor-Marcia Rudin
Editorial Description: Included with subscription to Cult Observer.
General Info: Yr. Est. 1987, Semi-annually, 4 pages
Subscriptions: Indv. $15
Circulation: Total-1,600

Youth Worker Update
See: YOUTH

Anglican

Anglican Church Women, News Bulletin

Publishing Co: Anglican Church of Canada, Diocese of Ottawa, 71 Bronson Ave., Ottawa, ON K1R 6O6 Canada
Personnel: Editor-Mrs. D. E. Long
General Info: 10x/yr., 4 pages
Subscriptions: Indv. $1

Arctic News — *Association*

Publishing Co: Anglican Church of Canada, Diocese of the Arctic, 1055 Avenue Road, Toronto, ON M5N 2C8 Canada; Title Tel # (416) 481-2263 Title Fax # (416) 487-4948
Personnel: Editor-Mary Crowe
Editorial Description: Missionary publication about the Church's work in the Diocese of the Arctic (Canada).
General Info: Yr. Est. 1933, Semi-annually, Trim Size-6½ x 9¾, Offset press, 16 pages
Subscriptions: Free
Circulation: Total-2,500

Bahai

Bahai News

Publishing Co: National Spiritual Assembly of the Bahai's of the US, 536 Sheridan Rd, Wilmette, IL 60091-2849; Title Tel # (708) 869-9039
Personnel: Editor-John Bowers
General Info: Yr. Est. 1976, Monthly
Subscriptions: Indv. $12

Hearts of the Handmaidens
See: WOMEN'S

Baptist

Adult Bible Study *Association*

Publishing Co: Baptist Sunday School Board, 127 9th Ave N, Nashville, TN 37234-0002; Title Tel # (800) 458-2772 Title Fax # (615) 251-5933
General Info: Quarterly, ISSN: 0162-4156
Subscriptions: Indv. $5

Advanced Bible Study *Association*

Publishing Co: Baptist Sunday School Board, 127 9th Ave N, Nashville, TN 37234-0002; Title Tel # (800) 458-2772 Title Fax # (615) 251-5933
General Info: Quarterly, ISSN: 0162-4148
Subscriptions: Indv. $6

Adventure *Association*

Publishing Co: Baptist Sunday School Board, 127 9th Ave N, Nashville, TN 37234-0002; Title Tel # (800) 458-2772 Title Fax # (615) 251-5933
Editorial Description: Story pages for ages 8-11, grades 3-6.
General Info: Monthly, ISSN: 0001-8783
Subscriptions: Indv. $10

BWA News *Association*

Publishing Co: Baptist World Alliance, 6733 Curran St, Mc Lean, VA 22101-6005; Title Tel # (703) 790-8980 Title Fax # (703) 893-5160
Personnel: Editor, Production Mgr.-Wendy Ryan
Editorial Description: News & information service of the Baptist World Alliance.
General Info: Monthly, 4 pages
Circulation: Total-1,400

Baptist Evangel

Publishing Co: Baptist Evangel, PO Box 59, Union, SC 29379-0059

Baptist Heritage Update *Association*

Publishing Co: Historical Commission, Southern Baptist Conv., 901 Commerce St., Nashville, TN 37203-3630; Title Tel # (615) 244-0344
Personnel: Editor-Charles Deweese, Production Mgr.-Kim Alley
Editorial Description: A newsletter relating to the history interests of Southern Baptists.
General Info: Yr. Est. 1985, Quarterly, Trim Size-8½ x 11, 6 pages, 2 Color, Coated
Subscriptions: Indv. $15, For. $22
Circulation: Total-7,500
Printing Co: Vaughan Printing Co., 411 Cowan St, Nashville, TN 37207-5686 Tel # (615) 256-2244, Fax # (615) 259-4676

Baptist Young Adults *Association*

Publishing Co: Baptist Sunday School Board, 127 9th Ave N, Nashville, TN 37234-0002 Fax # (615) 251-5933; Title Tel # (800) 458-2772
General Info: Quarterly
Subscriptions: Indv. $6

Baptist Youth *Association*

Publishing Co: Baptist Sunday School Board, 127 9th Ave N, Nashville, TN 37234-0002; Title Tel # (800) 458-2772 Title Fax # (615) 251-5933
Editorial Description: Ages 12-17, grades 7-12, leaders kit available.
General Info: Quarterly, ISSN: 0162-4199
Subscriptions: Indv. $6

Echoes
See: COLLEGE STUDENT

Encounter! *Association*

Publishing Co: Baptist Sunday School Board, 127 9th Ave N, Nashville, TN 37234-0002; Title Tel # (800) 458-2772 Title Fax # (615) 251-5933
Editorial Description: Youth daily devotion.
General Info: Quarterly, ISSN: 0162-4547
Subscriptions: Indv. $5

Exploring 1 *Association*

Publishing Co: Baptist Sunday School Board, 127 9th Ave N, Nashville, TN 37234-0002; Title Tel # (800) 458-2772 Title Fax # (615) 251-5933
Editorial Description: Ages 6-8, grades 1-3, leaders kit available.
General Info: Quarterly
Subscriptions: Indv. $5

Exploring 2 *Association*

Publishing Co: Baptist Sunday School Board, 127 9th Ave N, Nashville, TN 37234-0002; Title Tel # (800) 458-2772 Title Fax # (615) 251-5933
Editorial Description: Ages 9-11, grades 4-6, leaders kit available.
General Info: Quarterly
Subscriptions: Indv. $25

Harvest

Publishing Co: Baptist Mid-Missions, PO Box 308011, Cleveland, OH 44130-8011; Title Tel # (216) 826-3930 Title Fax # (216) 826-4457
Personnel: Editor-Bernice Piazza
Editorial Description: Information as to Baptist Mid-Missions. Mission activities worldwide.
General Info: (Formerly Mid-African Bulletin Harvest Report), Yr. Est. 1921, Quarterly, Trim Size-8½ x 11, 8 pages, 2 Color, Newsprint
Circulation: Total-90,000

Kristiga Baiss

Publishing Co: Union of Latvian Baptists in America, 832 Gettysburg Dr, Lansdale, PA 19446-3104
Editorial Description: Religious and ethnic news targeted at the Latvian Baptist community.
General Info: Yr. Est. 1980, Monthly

Mision a las Americas Hoy *Association*

Publishing Co: Conservative Baptist Home Mission Society, PO Box 828, Wheaton, IL 60189-0828; Title Tel # (708) 260-3800 Title Fax # (708) 653-4936
Personnel: Editor-Jack Estep, Production Mgr.-Sally Heerwagen
Editorial Description: Published for missionaries serving with the Conservative Baptist Home Mission Society in North and Central America. Text in Spanish.
General Info: (Formerly CBHMS Hoy), Yr. Est. 1994, Bi-monthly, Trim Size-5½ x 8½, 2 pages
Subscriptions: Free
Circulation: Total-10,000
Printing Co: CB International, PO Box 5, Wheaton, IL 60189-0005 Tel # (708) 260-3800

Music Time *Association*

Publishing Co: Baptist Sunday School Board, 127 9th Ave N, Nashville, TN 37234-0002 Fax # (615) 251-5933; Title Tel # (800) 458-2772
Editorial Description: Music and features for preschoolers.
General Info: Quarterly
Subscriptions: Indv. $7

New Jersey Baptist Bulletin

Publishing Co: ABC of New Jersey, 161 Freeway Dr E, East Orange, NJ 07018-4042
Personnel: Editor-George Younger
Editorial Description: Editorials and happenings of churches in the state.
General Info: Yr. Est. 1871, Monthly
Subscriptions: Indv. $1
Circulation: Total-15,000

News Deacons

Publishing Co: Natl. Baptist Deacons Convention of America, 179 Hollywood Ave, East Orange, NJ 07018-3941; Title Tel # (201) 674-2174
General Info: Quarterly

Outlook *Association*

Publishing Co: Southeastern Baptist Theological Seminary, PO Box 1889, Wake Forest, NC 27588-1889; Title Tel # (919) 556-3101
Personnel: Publisher, Editor-Rodney Byard
Editorial Description: News of seminary family, professors, administrators, alumni campus events, announcements and development plans.
General Info: Yr. Est. 1951, Bi-monthly, Trim Size-8½ x 11, Offset press, 8 pages, ISSN: 0030-7238, Color
Circulation: Total-15,000

Report from the Capital *Consumer, Association*

Publishing Co: Baptist Joint Committee on Public Affairs, 200 Maryland Ave., NE, Washington, DC 20002-5797; Title Tel # (202) 544-4226 Title Fax # (202) 544-2094
Personnel: Publisher-James Dunn, Editor-Larry Chesser, Assoc. Ed.-Pam Parry, Bk. Rev. Ed.-J. Brent Walker
Editorial Description: Covers church-state issues, public affairs, news; purpose is consciousness raising and information.
General Info: Yr. Est. 1946 Bi-weekly, Web press, 4 pages, ISSN: 0346-0661, No Color
Subscriptions: Indv. $10
Circulation: Total-9,500
Printing Co: McDonald & Eudy Printers, Inc., 4509 Beech Rd, Temple Hills, MD 20748-6705

Southwestern News
See: COLLEGE ALUMNI

Spectrum *Association*

Publishing Co: Conservative Baptist Association of America, PO Box 66, Wheaton, IL 60189-0066; Title Tel # (708) 653-5350 Title Fax # (708) 653-5387
Editorial Description: Information for and about our associated churches.
General Info: (Formerly CB Update), Yr. Est. 1992, Bi-monthly, Trim Size-8½ x 11, 8 pages
Subscriptions: Indv. $5, Free With Membership

Spires

Publishing Co: American Baptist Churches of Maine, 107 Winthrop St # 667, Augusta, ME 04330-5030; Title Tel # (207) 622-6291
Personnel: Editor-Calvin Moon
Editorial Description: Information of interest to Maine Baptist church parishioners.
General Info: 5x/yr., 6 pages, No Color

Tie   *Association*

Publishing Co: Southern Baptist Theological Seminary, 2825 Lexington Rd, Louisville, KY 40280-0001 Tel # (502) 897-4011; Title Tel # (502) 897-4141
Personnel: Editor-David Wilkinson, Mng. Editor-Patrick Cole, Production Mgr.-John Bailey
Editorial Description: Alumni publication.
General Info: Yr. Est. 1936, Bi-monthly, Trim Size-8½ x 11, Web press, 16 pages, ISSN: 0040-7232, 4 Color, Coated
Circulation: (100% controlled), Total-36,000
Printing Co: Gateway Press Co., 4500 Robards Ln, Louisville, KY 40218-4547 Tel # (502) 454-0431, Fax # (502) 459-7930

Years Ahead   *Association*

Publishing Co: Annuity Board/Southern Baptist Convention, PO Box 2190, Dallas, TX 75221-2190; Title Tel # (214) 720-0511
Personnel: Editor-Tim Tune, Art Dir.-G. Davis
Editorial Description: Newsletter which reports information on retirement, disability, geriatrics, aging and other related fields for readers who are ministers in the Southern Baptist Convention.
General Info: Yr. Est. 1956, Quarterly, Trim Size-8½ x 11, Offset press, 6 pages, 2 Color
Circulation: Total-60,000

Youth Disciple   *Association*

Publishing Co: Baptist Sunday School Board, 127 9th Ave N, Nashville, TN 37234-0002 Fax # (615) 251-5933; Title Tel # (800) 458-2772
Editorial Description: Ages 15-17, grades 10-12, leaders kit available.
General Info: Quarterly
Subscriptions: Indv. $6

Buddhist

American Buddhist

Publishing Co: American Buddhist Movement, 301 W. 45th St., New York, NY 10036; Title Tel # (212) 489-1075
Personnel: Editor-Kevin O'Neil
General Info: Yr. Est. 1981
Subscriptions: Indv. $15

Buddha World   *Association*

Publishing Co: American Zen College, Inc., 16815 Germantown Rd, Germantown, MD 20874-3014; Title Tel # (301) 428-0665
Personnel: Publisher-Dr. Gosung Shin, Editor, Production Mgr., Art Dir.-Barbara Abrams
Editorial Description: Zen Buddhist philosophy, history, theory & stories.
General Info: Yr. Est. 1970, Quarterly, Trim Size-5½ x 8½, Offset press, 16 pages, No Color, Newsprint, Saddle-stitched
Subscriptions: Indv. $12, $2/copy
Circulation: Total-850

Buddhist Study Center
Newsletter

Publishing Co: Honpa Hongwanji Mission of Hawaii, Buddhist Study Center, 1436 University Ave., Honolulu, HI 96822
General Info: Monthly, 6 pages

Karma Triyana Dharmachakra Monastery Newsletter   *Association*

Publishing Co: Karma Triyana Dharmachakra Monastery, 352 Meads Mtn Rd, Woodstock, NY 12498-1024; Title Tel # (914) 679-5906
Personnel: Publisher-Ayalwa Karmapa, Circ. Mgr.-John Cox, Adv. Dir.-Julie Case, Editor, Production Mgr., Art Dir., Promotion Dir.-Naomi Schmidt
Editorial Description: Presenting information on the Karma Kagyu school of Tibetan Buddhism.
General Info: Quarterly, Trim Size-8½ x 11, Sheetfed press, 24 pages, 1% ads, Coated
Subscriptions: Indv. $10, $2/copy
Circulation: Total-1,500
Printing Co: Hamilton Reproductions, 70 W Cedar St, Poughkeepsie, NY 12601-1334 Tel # (914) 471-3110

Kirpal Light Satsang International Newsletter   *Association*

Publishing Co: Kirpal Light Satsang, Inc., Rr 1 Box 125, Kinderhook, NY 12106-9720; Title Tel # (518) 758-1906
Personnel: Publisher, Editor-Joanie Solomon, Circ. Mgr.-Gail Young, Production Mgr.-Kurt Young, Art Dir.-Petra Nicol
General Info: Yr. Est. 1987, Bi-monthly, Offset press, 10 pages
Circulation: Total-3,000

Kwan Um School of Zen Newsletter   *Consumer, Association*

Publishing Co: Kwan Um of Zen, 528 Pound Rd, Cumberland, RI 02864-2712 Fax # (401) 658-1188; Title Tel # (401) 658-1476
Personnel: Editor-Richard Streitfeld, Production Mgr.-J.W. Harrington
Editorial Description: Buddhist teaching and news of Zen Master Seung Sahn Providence Zen Center, and its eleven branches, and ten affiliates.
General Info: (Formerly Newsletter of the Providence Zen Newsletter), Yr. Est. 1972, Monthly, Trim Size-8½ x 11, Sheetfed press, 4 pages, No Color, Recycled
Subscriptions: Indv. $6, $2/copy
Circulation: Total-850
Printing Co: American Speedy, 859 Diamond Hill Rd, Woonsocket, RI 02895-1455 Tel # (401) 765-7051, Fax # (401) 765-7052

Metta   M   *Scholarly, Association*

Publishing Co: Honpa Hongwanji Mission of Hawaii, Buddhist Study Center, 1436 University Ave., Honolulu, HI 96822; Title Tel # (808) 522-9200 Title Fax # (808) 522-9209
Personnel: Editor-Yoshiaki Fujitani, Circ. Mgr., Production Mgr.-Reynold Fujikawa
Editorial Description: Original scholarly and lay writings focusing primarily on Jodoshinshu Buddhism.
General Info: Yr. Est. 1972, Monthly, Trim Size-8½ x 11, Web press, 8 pages, No Color, Matte, Other
Circulation: Total-1,250
Printing Co: Letter Shop, 1218 S Beretania St, Honolulu, HI 96814-1513 Tel # (808) 537-2316

Monthly Guide   *Association*

Publishing Co: International Buddhist Center, 924 S New Hampshire Ave, Los Angeles, CA 90006-1623; Title Tel # (213) 384-0850 Title Fax # (213) 386-6643
Personnel: Editor-Venisarika Dharma
Editorial Description: Provide buddhist services to western born Americans.
General Info: Yr. Est. 1970, Monthly, Trim Size-8½ x 14, Desktop press, 1 pages, No Color, Newsprint
Subscriptions: Indv. $20, Free
Circulation: (43% controlled), Total-800
List Rental: Rents Lists

Seattle Betsuin

Publishing Co: Seattle Buddhist Church, 1427 S Main St, Seattle, WA 98144-2034
Editorial Description: English/Japanese text-news of the church and other religious news.
General Info: Monthly

Snow Lion Newsletter & Catalog   *Association, Consumer*

Publishing Co: Snow Lion Publishing, PO Box 6483, Ithaca, NY 14851-6483; Title Tel # (607) 273-8519 Title Fax # (607) 273-8508
Editorial Description: Covers Tibet's religious and philosophical traditions. Also a catalog of books and reading materials about Tibet.
General Info: Quarterly, Trim Size-11¼ x 16¾, 60 pages, ISSN: 1059-3691, No Color, Newsprint

Tantric Buddhism Black Sect

Publishing Co: Yun Lin Temple News, 2959 Russell Street, Berkeley, CA 94705

Washington Buddhist   *Association*

Publishing Co: Buddhist Vihara Society, 5017 16th St NW, Washington, DC 20011-3841; Title Tel # (202) 723-0773
Personnel: Editor-Bhante Gunaratana, Art Dir.-Dave ARnold
Editorial Description: A newsletter containing articles on Theravada Buddhism. Buddhist news and stories.
General Info: Yr. Est. 1973, Quarterly, Trim Size-7 x 8½, Web press, 24 pages, Color-cover
Subscriptions: Indv. $6, $2/copy
Circulation: Total-550

Zen Notes

Publishing Co: First Zen Institute of America, 113 E 30th St, New York, NY 10016-7302
Personnel: Editor-Mary Farkas
Editorial Description: Lives and teachings of Zen Masters, ancient and modern; book reviews, art, photos, news, translations of Zen texts, reports on American Buddhist activities.
General Info: Yr. Est. 1954, Monthly, Trim Size-7 x 8½, Offset press, 8 pages
Subscriptions: Indv. $5, $1/copy

Carpatho-Russian

SVS News   *Consumer*

Publishing Co: St. Vladimir's Orthodox Theological Seminary, 575 Scarsdale Rd., Crestwood, NY 10707-1199; Title Tel # (914) 961-8313 Title Fax # (914) 961-4507
Editorial Description: News of St. Vladimir's Orthodox Seminary.
General Info: Quarterly, 8 pages
Subscriptions: Free To Qualified Recipient

Catholic

American Catholic Studies
Newsletter   *Consumer, Association*

Publishing Co: Cushwa Center for the Study of American Catholicism, 614 Hesburgh Library, Notre Dame, IN 46556-5629; Title Tel # (219) 631-5441 Title Fax # (219) 631-8471
Personnel: Editor-Jaime Vidal
Editorial Description: Reports on research, publications, dissertations & archives related to American Catholic studies; personal notices; activities of the Center.
General Info: Yr. Est. 1975, Semi-annually, Trim Size-8½ x 11, 16 pages, No Color, Newsprint
Subscriptions: Indv. $3

The American Monastic
Newsletter

Publishing Co: Sponsor-American Benedictine Academy, Sacred Heart Monastry, PO Box 364, Richardton, ND 58652 Tel # (701) 974-3315; Title Tel # (701) 225-4220
Personnel: Editor-Judith Sutera, Circ. Mgr., Production Mgr.-Renee Branigan
Editorial Description: Covers current events and essays of interest to those who are interested in spirituality, Monasticism, Rule of Benedict, etc.
General Info: (Formerly ABA Newsletter), Yr. Est. 1987, 3x/yr., Trim Size-8¾ x 11¼, Sheetfed press, 8 pages, No Color, Newsprint
Subscriptions: Indv. $5, Free With Membership
Circulation: Total-875
Printing Co: Assumption Abbey, PO Box A, Richardton, ND 58652-0901 Tel # (701) 974-3315

Apostolate of the Little
Flower

Publishing Co: Apostolate of the Little Flower, 906 Kentucky Ave, San Antonio, TX 78201-6016
Editorial Description: Catholic publication.

Awareness

Publishing Co: Confraternity of Christian Doctrine, 153 Ush St., Manchester, NH 03101
Personnel: Editor-Sister M. Bendicta
Editorial Description: Covers Catholic education and changes in the Church.
General Info: Yr. Est. 1961, Quarterly
Subscriptions: Indv. $1
Circulation: Total-4,900

Aylesford Carmelite
Newsletter   *Association*

Publishing Co: Lay Carmelite Order of Our Lady of Mt. Carmel, 8501 Bailey Rd, Darien, IL 60561-8418; Title Tel # (708) 969-5050 Title Fax # (708) 969-5536
Personnel: Editor-Aloysius Sieracki
Editorial Description: Articles & information for those interested in Carmelite spirituality & its expression in our world today.
General Info: Yr. Est. 1985, Quarterly, 4 pages, 2 Color
Subscriptions: Indv. $4
Circulation: Total-13,000
Printing Co: Abbey Press, Hill Dr., St. Meinrad, IN 47577 Tel # (817) 357-8011

Benedicine Witness, The   *Association*

Publishing Co: Sponsor-American Benedictine Academy, Sacred Heart Monastry, PO Box 364, Richardton, ND 58652 Tel # (701) 974-3315; Title Tel # (701) 974-2121
Editorial Description: Reflections on spiritual life; news about Benedictine Sisters.
General Info: Yr. Est. 1979, 3x/yr., Trim Size-8¾ x 11¼, 4 pages, 2 Color
Subscriptions: Free
Circulation: Total-3,500

Bringing Religion Home   *Consumer*

Publishing Co: Claretian Publications, 205 W. Monroe St., Chicago, IL 60606-5033; Title Tel # (312) 236-7782 Title Fax # (312) 236-8207
Personnel: Publisher-Father Mark Brummel, Editor-Tom McGroth, Mktg. Dir.-Michelle Merten
Editorial Description: Helps parents pass on religious values to their children.
General Info: Yr. Est. 1976, 10x/yr., Trim Size-8½ x 11, 4 pages, No Color
Subscriptions: Indv. $12, For. $15, $1/copy
Circulation: Total-44,602
List Rental: Actives: 1,575

CHAS Communique
See: HEALTH

CUSAN   *Association*

Publishing Co: Catholics United for Spiritual Action, 176 W 8th St, Bayonne, NJ 07002-1227; Title Tel # (201) 437-0412
Personnel: Editor-Lawrence Jagfeld
Editorial Description: News about members; spiritually oriented features written primarily by members. Also articles regarding disability, and humor written by members.
General Info: (Formerly Cusa Newsletter), Yr. Est. 1947, Semi-annually, Trim Size-5½ x 8¼, Offset press, 40 pages, 2 Color
Circulation: (100% controlled)

Call Board   *Association*

Publishing Co: Catholic Actors Guild, 1501 Broadway Ste 518, New York, NY 10036-5501; Title Tel # (212) 398-1868 Title Fax # (212) 398-1868
Personnel: Publisher, Editor, Adv. Dir.-Martin Kiffel
Editorial Description: Articles relative to members, entertainment industry, religions.
General Info: Yr. Est. 1935, Monthly, Trim Size-8½ x 11, Offset press, 6 pages, No Color, Coated
Acquistions: Publication Bought
Circulation: Total-600
Printing Co: RCH Services, 6101 Broadway, Woodside, NY 11377-2199 Tel # (718) 899-6320

Canadian Catholic
Organization for
Development & Peace
Newsletter

Publishing Co: Canadian Catholic Organization for Development & Peace, 3028 Danforth Ave., Toronto, ON M4C 1N2 Canada
General Info: Monthly

Canadian Jesuit Missions   *Consumer*

Publishing Co: Canadian Jesuit Mission, 1190 Danforth Ave., Toronto, ON M4J 1M6 Canada; Title Tel # (416) 465-1824
Personnel: Editor-Rev. J. P. Horrigan
General Info: 5x/yr.

Canon Law Society of
America Newsletter   *Association*

Publishing Co: Canon Law Society of America, Catholic University 431, Caldwell Hall, Washington, DC 20064-0001; Title Tel # (202) 269-3491
Personnel: Editor-Rev. Edward Pfnausch
Editorial Description: Application of church law interacting with general law.
General Info: Yr. Est. 1964, 12 pages
Circulation: Total-2,000

Caring Community

Publishing Co: National Catholic Reporter Publishing Co., 115 E. Armour Blvd., Kansas City, MO 64111-1203 Fax # (816) 968-2280; Title Tel # (816) 531-0538 Title Fax # (816) 931-5082
Personnel: Publisher-William McSweeney, Editor-Carolyn Hoff, Circ. Mgr.-Ed Stankard, Production Mgr.-Vicki Breashears, Adv. Dir.-Anna Fantasma, Promotion Dir.-Dan Grippo
Editorial Description: Large-print newsletter designed for shut-ins. Includes scripture text, prayer-starters, & more.
General Info: Yr. Est. 1985, Monthly, Web press, 4 pages, 2 Color, Newsprint
Circulation: Total-36,000
List Rental: Actives: $100/M
Printing Co: McCann Printing, 529 N Prince Ln, Springfield, MO 65802-2552

Casa Cry
See: SOCIAL SERVICES & WELFARE

Catechists Connection

Publishing Co: National Catholic Reporter Publishing Co., 115 E. Armour Blvd., Kansas City, MO 64111-1203 Fax # (816) 968-2280; Title Tel # (816) 531-0538 Title Fax # (816) 931-5082
Personnel: Publisher-William McSweeney, Editor-Jean Marie Hiesberger, Circ. Mgr.-Ed Stankard, Production Mgr.-Vicki Breashears, Adv. Dir.-Anna Fantasma, Promotion Dir.-Dan Grippo
Editorial Description: Full-size newsletter that offers enrichment & encouragement for parish catechists.
General Info: Yr. Est. 1985, Monthly, 4 pages, Newsprint
Circulation: Total-40,000
List Rental: Actives: $150/M
Printing Co: McCann Printing, 529 N Prince Ln, Springfield, MO 65802-2552

Catholic Archives Newsletter
See: LIBRARY

Catholic Eye

Publishing Co: Natl. Committee of Catholic Laymen, 150 E 35th St Rm 840, New York, NY 10016-4178; Title Tel # (212) 685-6666 Title Fax # (212) 725-9793
Personnel: Editor-Jim McFadden
General Info: Bi-weekly, 4 pages, 2 Color
Subscriptions: Indv. $35
Circulation: Total-10,000

Catholic Lithuania Update
See: INTERNATIONAL AFFAIRS

Catholic Maritime News

Publishing Co: Natl. Catholic Conference for Seafarers, PO Box 8307, Savannah, GA 31412-8307; Title Tel # (912) 234-5890
General Info: Monthly
Circulation: Total-500

Catholic Peace Fellowship
Bulletin   *Association*

Publishing Co: Catholic Peace Fellowship, 339 Lafayette St, New York, NY 10012-2725;
   Title Tel # (212) 673-8990
Personnel: Publisher-Tom Cornell, Editor-Bill Ofenloch
Editorial Description: Christian nonviolence applied to disarmament, direct action, conscientious
   objection, the draft & Central America.
General Info: Yr. Est. 1965, Semi-annually, Trim Size-8½ x 11, Sheetfed press, 8 pages, ISSN:
   0008-8277, No Color
Circulation: Total-6,000

Catholic Study Council Bulletin
See: POLITICS

Catholic Update   *Association*

Publishing Co: St. Anthony Messenger Press, 1615 Republic St, Cincinnati, OH 45210-1219
   Fax # (513) 241-0399; Title Tel # (513) 241-5615
Personnel: Publisher-Jeremy Harrington, Editor-Jack Wintz, Art Dir.-Julie Lonneman, Circ. Mgr.,
   Promotion Dir.-Tom Bruce
Editorial Description: Illustrated articles covering religious education topics.
General Info: Yr. Est. 1973, Monthly, Trim Size-8½ x 11, Sheetfed press, 4 pages, 2 Color
Subscriptions: Indv. $9, Can. $12, For. $12
Acquistions: Publication Sold
Circulation: Total-300,000

Catholic Woman   *Association*

Publishing Co: Natl. Council of Catholic Women, 1275 K St NW Ste 975, Washington, DC
   20005-4006; Title Tel # (202) 682-0334
Personnel: Editor-Sheila Betite
Editorial Description: Church, family, community, international affairs and organization development.
General Info: Yr. Est. 1975, Bi-monthly, Trim Size-8½ x 11, Offset press, 16 pages, ISSN: 0270-
   3610, 2 Color
Subscriptions: Indv. $10, $2/copy
Circulation: Total-11,500

Centre News

Publishing Co: Catholic Information Center, 830 Bathurst St., Toronto, ON M5R 3G1 Canada
   Tel # (416) 534-2326
Personnel: Editor-Paul A. Lannan, C.S.P.
General Info: Quarterly
Circulation: Total-2,200

Chips
See: CLUBS

Christian Communications

Publishing Co: Saint Paul Society, 223 Main St., Ottawa, ON K1S 1C4 Canada
General Info: Quarterly
Subscriptions: Indv. $2
Circulation: Total-2,000

Christopher News Notes   *Consumer*

Publishing Co: Christophers, The Inc., 12 E 48th St, New York, NY 10017-1008;
   Title Tel # (212) 759-4050 Title Fax # (212) 838-5073
Personnel: Editor in Chief-Stephanie Raha, Assoc. Ed.-Margaret O'Connell, Production Mgr.-Anna
   Marie Tripodi
Editorial Description: The Christophers are a multi-media organization, dedicated to spreading two
   basic ideas; there's nobody like you and you can make a difference. The Christopher message is
   based on the Judeo-Christian concept of service to God and all humanity. Each issuedeals with
   single theme intended to offer encouragement & information. Themes deal with family spirituality,
   and personal life values.
General Info: Yr. Est. 1945, 10x/yr., Trim Size-3⅛ x 8¼
Subscriptions: Free
Circulation: Total-750,000

Claretian Newsletter

Publishing Co: Claretian Publications, 205 W. Monroe St., Chicago, IL 60606-5033;
   Title Tel # (312) 236-7782 Title Fax # (312) 236-8207
Personnel: Editor-Father Mark Brummel
General Info: Yr. Est. 1964, Quarterly
Subscriptions: Indv. $1
Circulation: Total-35,000

Claretian Profile

Publishing Co: Claretian Profile, 18127 S Alameda St, Compton, CA 90220-5708
Editorial Description: Catholic publication.

Conference Religieuse
Canadienne, Bulletin

Publishing Co: Conference Religieuse Canadienne, 324 E. Laurier Ave., Ottawa, ON K1N 6P6
   Canada Fax # (613) 236-0825; Title Tel # (613) 236-0824
Personnel: Editor-Marjory Gallagher
General Info: Yr. Est. 1955, 8x/yr., 8 pages
Circulation: Total-4,500

Connections

Publishing Co: National Federation for Cath. Youth Ministry, 3900a Harewood Rd NE, Washington,
   DC 20017-1505; Title Tel # (202) 636-3825 Title Fax # (202) 526-7544
Personnel: Editor-Dolores Brinkel
Editorial Description: Resource review, thematic essays, youth ministry ideas, calendar of events.
General Info: (Formerly Emmaus Letter), Yr. Est. 1989, Quarterly, Trim Size-8½ x 11, Web press, 8
   pages, 2% ads, 2 Color
Circulation: Total-350
Advertising: Inquire for rates.

Crux of the News   *Consumer*

Publishing Co: Clarity Publishing Inc., 3 Enterprise Dr, Albany, NY 12204-2520;
   Title Tel # (518) 465-4591 Title Fax # (518) 465-4333
Personnel: Publisher-Thomas Clemente, Editor-Richard Dowd
Editorial Description: Covers the most significant programs, plans, policies and happenings in the
   Church.
General Info: Yr. Est. 1965, Weekly, Trim Size-8½ x 11, Offset press, 6 pages
Subscriptions: Indv. $60
Circulation: Total-5,300

Der Deutsche Katholik in
Kanada

Publishing Co: St. Patrick's German Congregation, 131 McCarl St., Toronto, ON M5T 1W3 Canada;
   Title Tel # (416) 598-4835
Personnel: Editor-Karl Schindler
Editorial Description: German language publication.
General Info: Yr. Est. 1964, Monthly, 32 pages
Subscriptions: Indv. $2, $2/copy

Dimensions
See: PHILANTHROPY

Dominican Mission Impact

Publishing Co: Dominican Mission Impact, 411 E 68th St, New York, NY 10021-6340
Editorial Description: Catholic publication.

Echo z Afryki

Publishing Co: Society of St. Peter Claver, 265 Century Ave. S., St. Mary's Mission House, St. Paul,
   MN 55119-5206; Title Tel # (612) 824-9768
Personnel: Editor-Sr. Maria Moryl
Editorial Description: News relating to the Missionary Sisters of St. Peter Claver. Text is in Polish.
General Info: Yr. Est. 1892
Circulation: Total-8,000

Entretiens d'oraison:
Message Spirituel   *Association*

Publishing Co: Entretiens d'oraison: Message Spirituel, 4120, ave. de Verdome, Montreal, PQ H4A
   3N1 Canada; Title Tel # (514) 481-7018
Personnel: Publisher, Editor, Art Dir.-Fernande Charbonneau
Editorial Description: Spiritual message on interior life and the way to live in presence of God.
General Info: Yr. Est. 1974, Tri-annually
Subscriptions: Indv. $5, $1/copy
Circulation: (100% controlled), Total-900

Ethics and Medics
See: MEDICINE

Eucharistic Minister

Publishing Co: National Catholic Reporter Publishing Co., 115 E. Armour Blvd., Kansas City, MO
   64111-1203 Fax # (816) 968-2280; Title Tel # (816) 531-0538 Title Fax # (816) 931-5082
Personnel: Publisher-William McSweeney, Editor-Carolyn Hoff, Circ. Mgr.-Ed Stankard, Production
   Mgr.-Vicki Breashears, Adv. Dir.-Anna Fantasma, Promotion Dir.-Dan Grippo
Editorial Description: Helps ministry leaders inform, inspire & sustain their eucharistic ministers.
General Info: Yr. Est. 1984, Monthly, Web press, 4 pages, ISSN: 0743-524X, 2 Color, Newsprint
Circulation: Total-66,000
Printing Co: McCann Printing, 529 N Prince Ln, Springfield, MO 65802-2552

Father Solanus Guild News   *Consumer, Association*

Publishing Co: Father Solanus Guild, 1780 Mount Elliott St, Detroit, MI 48207-3496;
   Title Tel # (313) 579-2100
Editorial Description: Celebrates life and death of Father Solanus Casey.
General Info: Quarterly, Trim Size-8½ x 11, 8 pages, No Color, Coated

Fatima Findings   *Association*

Publishing Co: Reparation Society of the Immaculate Heart of Mary, Inc., 100 E 20th St, Baltimore,
   MD 21218-6037; Title Tel # (301) 685-7403
Personnel: Editor-John Ryan
Editorial Description: Propagates knowledge of the Fatima apparitions and devotion to the
   Immaculate Heart of Mary. Contains a monthly First Saturday meditation, true stories and editorial
   comments.
General Info: Yr. Est. 1946, Monthly, 8 pages, ISSN: 0014-8830, No Color
Subscriptions: Indv. $5, $1/copy
Circulation: Total-2,500

Federation of C.P.T.A.s of Ontario Newsletter
See: EDUCATION

Flashpoint
Consumer

Publishing Co: Living Truth Ministries, 1708 Patterson Rd, Austin, TX 78733-6507
Tel # (512) 263-9780
Editorial Description: living truth of the Living Truth Ministries.
General Info: Irregular, Trim Size-8½ x 11, 6 pages, 2 Color, Matte

Focus
Association

Publishing Co: Franciscan Communications Center, 1229 Santee St, Los Angeles, CA 90015-2566; Title Tel # (213) 746-2916
Personnel: Editor-Ken Martinet, Circ. Mgr.-Pat Bravo, Art Dir.-Maryam Gossling FSPA
Editorial Description: Information regarding products and plans of Franciscan Communications in its media ministry.
General Info: (Formerly News of Our Work), Yr. Est. 1975, Quarterly, Trim Size-8½ x 11, Offset press, 4 pages, No Color
Circulation: Total-4,500

Fund Raising Forum
See: PHILANTHROPY

Generation
Consumer, Association

Publishing Co: Claretian Publications, 205 W. Monroe St., Chicago, IL 60606-5033; Title Tel # (312) 236-7782 Title Fax # (312) 236-8207
Personnel: Publisher-Mark Brummel
Editorial Description: Spiritual enrichment for Christians, aged 55 & older by the Claretians, an order of Roman Catholic Priests. Written by Gerald Costello.
General Info: Yr. Est. 1980, Monthly, 4 pages
Subscriptions: Indv. $12, For. $15, $1/copy
Circulation: Total-11,635
List Rental: Actives: 737, $150/M

Gifts

Publishing Co: Natl. Conference of Catholic Bishops, 3211 4th St NE, Washington, DC 20017-1106; Title Tel # (202) 541-3000
Personnel: Editor-Sheila Garcia
General Info: Yr. Est. 1979, Quarterly, 8 pages
Subscriptions: Indv. $6
Circulation: Total-1,300

Grain and Fire

Publishing Co: Brothers of the Holy Eucharist, PO Box 25, Plaucheville, LA 71362-0025
General Info: Yr. Est. 1961, Quarterly, ISSN: 0017-3045

Heraut de Saint Paul

Publishing Co: St-Paul Herald, C.P. 339, Saint Paul, AB T0A 3A0 Canada
Editorial Description: Publication ecclesiatique. Text French and English.
General Info: Yr. Est. 1972, 10x/yr.

Homeless Child and Messenger of St. Joseph's Union

Publishing Co: Homeless Child, 108 Bedell St, Staten Island, NY 10309-3302; Title Tel # (718) 984-9296
Editorial Description: Catholic publication.
General Info: Yr. Est. 1877

Homily Helps
Association

Publishing Co: St. Anthony Messenger Press, 1615 Republic St, Cincinnati, OH 45210-1219; Title Tel # (513) 241-5615 Title Fax # (513) 241-0399
Personnel: Publisher-Jeremy Harrington, Editor-Hilarion Kistner, Circ. Mgr.-Tom Bruce
Editorial Description: Sunday sermon service for clergy, providing Scriptural background, homily outlines.
General Info: Yr. Est. 1971, Monthly, Trim Size-8½ x 11, Sheetfed press, 1 pages, 2 Color, Looseleaf
Subscriptions: Indv. $30
Circulation: Total-8,100

Hope, A Salvatorian Newsletter

Publishing Co: Sponsor-Society of The Devine Savor - American Province, Society of the Divine Savior, Salvatorian Center, New Holstein, WI 53062-0001; Title Tel # (414) 898-4201 Title Fax # (414) 898-4736
Personnel: Editor-Gregory Coulthard, S.D.S.
Editorial Description: Covers the apostolic work of the society.
General Info: (Formerly Salvatorian Newsletter), Yr. Est. 1974, Bi-monthly, Trim Size-8 x 10½, Offset press, 8 pages, 2 Color, Other
Subscriptions: Free
Circulation: Total-40,000

Il Messaggero

Publishing Co: Italian Mission, The, PO Box 30300, Kansas City, MO 64112-3300
Personnel: Editor-J. Bisceglia
Editorial Description: Text Italian & Eng. Religious & educational.
General Info: Yr. Est. 1925, Monthly
Circulation: Total-800

In The Meantime
Association

Publishing Co: Tabor Publishing, 200 East Bethany Drive, Allen, TX 75002 Tel # (214) 390-6300
Personnel: Publisher-Todd Brennan, Editor-John Sprague, Editor-Dick Westley
Editorial Description: Newsletter to encourage reflection and dialogue on the changing reality of the church in the United States.
General Info: Yr. Est. 1993, 10x/yr., Trim Size-8½ x 11, Offset press, 8 pages, 2 Color
Subscriptions: Indv. $28, $5/copy
Circulation: Total-1,200

Initiatives
Association

Publishing Co: Natl. Center for the Laity, 10 E Pearson St Ste 101, Chicago, IL 60611-2002; Title Tel # (312) 787-7525
Personnel: Publisher, Editor-William Droel
Editorial Description: Highlights initiatives lay people take to link faith & work.
General Info: Yr. Est. 1978, Bi-monthly, 6 pages
Subscriptions: Indv. $15, $2/copy
Circulation: Total-6,000

It's Our World
Association

Publishing Co: Holy Childhood Assn., 1720 Massachusetts Ave NW, Washington, DC 20036-1968; Title Tel # (202) 775-8637 Title Fax # (202) 429-2987
Personnel: Editor-Mary M. Connors, Art Dir.-Ellen Pattisail
Editorial Description: Mission news from the Holy Childhood Assn. in 2 editions: Grades K-4 and 5-8 plus a teacher's guide. Promotes global awareness & mission education.
General Info: (Formerly Annals of the Holy Childhood), Yr. Est. 1974, Quarterly, Trim Size-11 x 17, Web press, 4 pages, 4 Color
Subscriptions: Indv. $1, $1/copy
Acquistions: Publication Bought
Circulation: Total-366,500

Jesus & Mary Are Calling You

Publishing Co: Christian Family Renewal, PO Box 73, Clovis, CA 93613-0073; Title Tel # (209) 297-7818
Personnel: Publisher-Stephen Norris, Editor-Murray Norris, Circ. Mgr.-Hagop Karamanlian, Circ. Mgr.-Agnes Mulligan
Editorial Description: All articles in our pubs. are cleared through diocesan censors of the Diocese of Fresno to make sure they contain nothing against Faith & Morals.
General Info: Yr. Est. 1987, Quarterly, Web press, 6 pages, 2 Color, Newsprint
Subscriptions: Indv. $2, $1/copy
Circulation: Total-300,000
Advertising: Accepts Inserts.
Printing Co: JPAX Communications, PO Box 36, Sanger, CA 93657-0036 Tel # (209) 875-6585

K.J.Z.T. News

Publishing Co: Catholic Women's Fraternal of Texas-The K.J.Z.T., PO Box 1884, Austin, TX 78767-1884
Personnel: Editor-Benita Pavlu
Editorial Description: Text occasionally in Czech.
General Info: Yr. Est. 1955, Monthly

Knight of St. John

Publishing Co: Knights of St. John, 6517 Charles Ave, Parma, OH 44129-3712; Title Tel # (216) 845-0570
Personnel: Editor-Salvatore LaBianca
General Info: Yr. Est. 1898, Quarterly, 16 pages
Circulation: Total-7,200
Advertising: Inquire for rates.

L'Ami du Frere Andre/The Friend of Brother Andre
Association

Publishing Co: Oratoire St. Joseph du Mont-Royal, 3800 Queen Mary Rd., Montreal, PQ H3V 1H6 Canada Fax # (514) 733-9735; Title Tel # (514) 733-8211
Personnel: Publications Director-Zianney St. Michel, Editor-Jean-Guy Debuc
Editorial Description: Events, developments and projects at St. Joseph's Oratory.
General Info: Yr. Est. 1956, Quarterly, Trim Size-8½ x 10½, Offset press, 4 pages, No Color, Newsprint
Subscriptions: Indv. $1, Free
Circulation: Total-150,000

Le Feuillet Paroissial

Publishing Co: Imprimerie Drovin Inc., 815, rue Beaumont, Montreal, PQ H2N 1W1 Canada
Personnel: Editor-Mariel Dubois
Editorial Description: Fr/Eng Text.
General Info: Yr. Est. 1952, Weekly
Subscriptions: Indv. $5
Circulation: Total-600

Lily of the Mohawks

Publishing Co: Blessed Kateri Takakwitha League, Auriesville, NY 12016; Title Tel # (518) 853-3153
Personnel: Editor-John Paret, S.J.
Editorial Description: Promotes interest in and devotion to Blessed Kateri Tekakwitha, a Mohawk Indian and the only Native American blessed in the Catholic Church.
General Info: Quarterly, Trim Size-8½ x 11, 8 pages
Subscriptions: Indv. $3, Can. $5, For. $5

Lousavorich   *Association*

Publishing Co: St. Gregory Illuminator Church of Armenia, 630 2nd Ave, New York, NY 10016-4806; Title Tel # (212) 679-1728
Personnel: Editor-Joyce Sulahian
Editorial Description: Parish news.
General Info: Yr. Est. 1938, Bi-weekly, Trim Size-5¾ x 8¾, 2 pages, No Color
Subscriptions: Free
Circulation: Total-1,020

MIC Mission News   *Association*

Publishing Co: Missionary Sisters of the Immaculate Conception, 100 Place J. Desnoyers, Laval, PQ H7G 1A4 Canada; Title Tel # (514) 663-6460
Personnel: Editor-Maria Anthea Raso, Circ. Mgr.-Lucille LaSalle
Editorial Description: Information on the work of members in mission.
General Info: (Formerly The Precursor), Yr. Est. 1923, Bi-monthly, Trim Size-5½ x 8½, Letrpr. press, 16 pages, ISSN: 0315-9655, 4 Color, Matte, Saddle-stitched
Subscriptions: Indv. $5, Can. $5, For. $5
Acquisitions: Publication Bought
Circulation: (25% controlled), Total-4,000, Subscriptions-3,000

Markings   *Association*

Publishing Co: Thomas More Association, 205 West Monroe, Sixth Floor, Chicago, IL 60606-5097; Title Tel # (312) 609-8880 Title Fax # (312) 609-8891
Personnel: Publisher-Todd Brennan, Editor-John Sprague
Editorial Description: Homily preparation service for priests, deacons, and homilists.
General Info: Yr. Est. 1970, 11x/yr., Offset press, 20 pages, 2 Color
Subscriptions: Indv. $38
Circulation: Total-3,500

Master Thoughts

Publishing Co: Dominion Press, PO Box 4608, Salem, OR 97302-8608 Tel # (503) 362-9634; Title Tel # (619) 746-9430
Personnel: Publisher-A.S. Otto, Editor-Friend Stuart
Editorial Description: Verse by verse interpretive commentaries on scriptural words of Jesus Christ.
General Info: Yr. Est. 1972, Quarterly, Trim Size-5½ x 8½, Offset press, 16 pages, No Color, Other, Looseleaf
Subscriptions: Indv. $15
Circulation: Total-150

Medical Mission Sisters News
See: HEALTH

Messenger

Publishing Co: Messenger, 16010 Detroit Ave, Lakewood, OH 44107-3713
General Info: Monthly
Circulation: Total-11,000

Messenger of the Holy Family   *Consumer, Association*

Publishing Co: Holy Family Seminary, 3014 Oregon Ave, St. Louis, MO 63118-1412
Editorial Description: Catholic publication.
General Info: Quarterly

Messenger of St. Joseph's Union   *Association*

Publishing Co: St. Joseph's Union Staten Island, Inc., 108 Bedell St, Staten Island, NY 10309-3302; Title Tel # (718) 984-9296
General Info: (Formerly Homeless Child), Yr. Est. 1877, Annually
Circulation: Total-7,000

Mission News

Publishing Co: Missionary Assn. of Mary Immaculate, PO Box 96, San Antonio, TX 78291-0096
General Info: Quarterly, 4 pages

Mission Update   *Consumer, Association*

Publishing Co: U.S. Catholic Mission Association, 3029 4th St NE, Washington, DC 20017-1102; Title Tel # (202) 832-3112 Title Fax # (202) 832-3688
Personnel: Editor-M.E. Loftus
Editorial Description: Mission and Missions. Global issues.
General Info: (Formerly Mission Intercom), Yr. Est. 1970, Bi-monthly, Trim Size-8½ x 11, Offset press, 8 pages, Matte
Subscriptions: Indv. $25, Free With Membership
Circulation: Total-1,500

Missionaries Together

Publishing Co: Centre Missionnaire Ste-Therese, 4387 Esplanade, Montreal, PQ H2W 1T3 Canada; Title Tel # (514) 842-6875
Personnel: Editor-Clifford Cogger, Production Mgr.-Rolland Roy
Editorial Description: Missionary promotion.
General Info: (Formerly Capuchin Missions), Yr. Est. 1966, Quarterly, Trim Size-5½ x 8½, Web press, 16 pages, 4 Color, Newsprint
Circulation: Total-200,000

Missions-Etrangeres

Publishing Co: Quebec Canada Foreign Mission Society, 160 Plage Juge-Desnoyers, C.P. 69, L.D.R., Laval, PQ H7G 1A5 Canada; Title Tel # (514) 667-4190
Personnel: Editor-Hubert Laurin
Editorial Description: Information on Latin America, Japan and Philippines; special themes about mission of the Church in world today. Text in French.
General Info: Yr. Est. 1941, Bi-monthly, Trim Size-8⅜ x 10⅞, 32 pages, Color
Subscriptions: Indv. $5, For. $10
Circulation: Total-42,000
Printing Co: Interweb, Inc., 1603 Boul. Montarville, Boucherville, PQ J4B 5Y2 Canada Tel # (514) 655-2801, Fax # (514) 641-3650

Missions d' Afrique

Publishing Co: Les Peres Blancs D' Afrique, 180 Chemin Ste-foy, Quebec, PQ G1R 4R2 Canada
Personnel: Editor-Adrian Fontaine
General Info: Yr. Est. 1904, Bi-monthly
Subscriptions: Indv. $2

Mother Cabrini Messenger

Publishing Co: Mother Cabrini League, 2520 N Lakeview Ave, Chicago, IL 60614-1804; Title Tel # (312) 883-7300
Personnel: Editor-Sister Arlene
General Info: Yr. Est. 1938, Bi-monthly
Circulation: Total-65,000

Mount Angel Letter   *Association*

Publishing Co: Mount Angel Abbey, Publications Dept., St. Benedict, OR 97373-9999; Title Tel # (503) 845-3030 Title Fax # (503) 845-3594
Editorial Description: Letter from Superior, news stories about abbey, in-house advertising.
General Info: Yr. Est. 1949, Bi-monthly, Trim Size-8½ x 11¼, Sheetfed press, 8 pages, No Color, Newsprint
Circulation: (98% controlled), Total-40,000, International-500
Printing Co: Benedictine Press, 1 Abey Drive, St. Benedict, OR 97373 Tel # (503) 845-3313, Fax # (503) 845-3456

Mount Savior Chronicle   *Association*

Publishing Co: Mount Saviour Monastery, Pine City, NY 14871; Title Tel # (607) 734-1688
Personnel: Editor-Father Martin Boler
Editorial Description: Community news-spiritual messages for holidays-book lists.
General Info: 4 pages
Circulation: Total-9,000

NCBA Newsletter
See: MUSIC & MUSIC TRADES

NCEA Notes   *Association*

Publishing Co: Natl. Catholic Educational Assn., 1077 30th St. NW, Ste. 100, Washington, DC 20007-3852 Tel # (202) 337-6232 Fax # (202) 333-6706
Personnel: Editor-Rev. Steve O'Brien, Art Dir.-Chris LaMarca
Editorial Description: Items of interest to all educators; current trends,and abstracts of some publications, education news, and NCEA news.
General Info: Yr. Est. 1970, 5x/yr., Trim Size-8½ x 11, Offset press, 12 pages, 2 Color
Circulation: Total-17,850

National Catholic Committee on Scouting Newsletter
See: CLUBS

National Federation of Catholic Physicians Guilds Newsletter
See: MEDICINE

NewsNotes
See: POLITICS

Newsletter (Oblate School of Theology) OST News
See: COLLEGE ALUMNI

Nova Voice of Ministry   *Association*

Publishing Co: Liturgical Pubs., Inc., 2875 S James Dr, New Berlin, WI 53151-3662; Title Tel # (414) 785-1188 Title Fax # (414) 785-9567
Personnel: Editor-Albert Nevins, MM, Circ. Mgr.-Ruth Cooke
Editorial Description: Homily service following Roman Lectionary. Contains homily, instructions in the faith, worship aids, quotes and anecdotes, scriptural comments, special occasion supplements.
General Info: (Formerly Nova et Vetera), Yr. Est. 1972, Bi-monthly, Trim Size-8½ x 11, Web press, 65 pages, No Color, Looseleaf
Subscriptions: Indv. $56, Can. $68, For. $86
Circulation: Total-1,543

Nuestra Parroquia   *Consumer, Association*

Publishing Co: Claretian Publications, 205 W. Monroe St., Chicago, IL 60606-5033; Title Tel # (312) 236-7782 Title Fax # (312) 236-8207
Personnel: Mktg. Dir.-Michelle Merten
Editorial Description: Spanish-language newsletter for parish leaders to help them improve their parishes and the lives of their parishioners.
General Info: Monthly
Subscriptions: Indv. $18
Circulation: Total-1,476

Origins, CNS Documentary Service

Publishing Co: Catholic News Service, 3211 4th St NE, Washington, DC 20017-1100; Title Tel # (202) 541-3265 Title Fax # (202) 541-3255
Personnel: Editor-David Gibson
General Info: Yr. Est. 1971, Weekly, Ind/Abs/Online: NewsNet /compuserve
Subscriptions: Indv. $97

Our Lady's Missionary

Publishing Co: Natl. Shrine of Our Lady of LaSalette, Ipswich, MA 01938; Title Tel # (617) 356-3266
Personnel: Editor-Rev. Rene J. Butler, M.S.
Editorial Description: Catholic publication.
General Info: (Formerly Bulletin of the Missionaries of la Salette), Yr. Est. 1910, 10x/yr., Trim Size-4 x 6, 24 pages, Color
Subscriptions: Indv. $2
Circulation: Total-50,000

Overview: A Continuing Survey of Issues Affecting Catholics   *Association*

Publishing Co: Thomas More Association, 205 West Monroe, Sixth Floor, Chicago, IL 60606-5097; Title Tel # (312) 609-8880 Title Fax # (312) 609-8891
Personnel: Publisher-Todd Brennan, Editor-Sara Miller
Editorial Description: Focuses on trends, personalities, thinkers, news, opinions and events that comprise contemporary Catholic life around the world.
General Info: Yr. Est. 1966, 11x/yr., Trim Size-8$\frac{1}{2}$ x 11, Offset press, 6 pages, 2 Color
Subscriptions: Indv. $18
Circulation: Total-4,500

Ozanam News   *Association*

Publishing Co: Council of the U.S., Society of St. Vincent de Paul, 58 Progress Pkwy, St. Louis, MO 63043-3706; Title Tel # (314) 371-4980
Personnel: Publisher-Rita Porter, Editor-Gene Horn, Circ. Mgr.-Laura Zysk
Editorial Description: Natl., regional, local, society lectures-reports, information, etc.
General Info: Yr. Est. 1917, Quarterly, 40 pages
Circulation: Total-56,000

Parish Coordinator/Director of Religious Education   *Association*

Publishing Co: Natl. Catholic Educational Assn., 1077 30th St. NW, Ste. 100, Washington, DC 20007-3852 Tel # (202) 337-6232 Fax # (202) 333-6706; Title Tel # (202) 293-5954
Personnel: Publisher, Editor-Wayne Smith, Circ. Mgr.-Marlene Sanchez, Art Dir.-Mary Beth Brewer
Editorial Description: Letter from dir. of dept. of rel. educ./NCEA; news from around the country from directors of religious education; workshops/institutes of interest to coordinators/DREs.
General Info: (Formerly Parish Coordinator of Religious Education), Yr. Est. 1975, Quarterly, Trim Size-8$\frac{1}{2}$ x 11, Offset press, 6 pages, 2 Color
Circulation: (100% controlled), Total-2,800

Parish Teacher   *Association*

Publishing Co: Augsburg Fortress Publishers, PO Box 1209, 426 S. Fifth St., Minneapolis, MN 55440-1209 Fax # (612) 330-3215; Title Tel # (612) 330-3300
Personnel: Editor-Rebecca Grothe, Circ. Mgr.-Julianne Alstad
Editorial Description: Information ideas, and insights for volunteer teachers of Sunday church schools.
General Info: Yr. Est. 1976, Monthly, Trim Size-8$\frac{1}{2}$ x 11, Offset press, 16 pages, ISSN: 0738-7962, 2 Color
Subscriptions: Indv. $5, Inst. $5, Can. $5, For. $9
Circulation: Total-52,085

Patchquilt

Publishing Co: Catholic Committee of Appalachia, PO Box 662, Webster Springs, WV 26288-0662; Title Tel # (606) 633-8440
Personnel: Editor-Maura Ubinger
General Info: Yr. Est. 1973, Bi-monthly
Subscriptions: Indv. $12, Inst. $30
Circulation: Total-600

Pax   *Association*

Publishing Co: St. Paul's Abbey, PO Box 7, Newton, NJ 07860-0007; Title Tel # (201) 383-2470
Personnel: Editor-Joel Macul
Editorial Description: Newsletter for the friends & benefactors & retreatants of St. Paul's Abbey.
General Info: Quarterly, 4 pages
Subscriptions: Indv. $1
Circulation: Total-8,000

Philippines   *Association*

Publishing Co: Sponsor-Sacred Heart Brothers, Le Centre Cor Jesu d'Ottawa, 328 rue Chapel, Ottawa, ON K1N 7Z3 Canada; Title Tel # (613) 234-0724
Personnel: Editor-Gerard Lefevre
Editorial Description: Mission: Sacred Heart Brothers, Philippines. French & English text.
General Info: Yr. Est. 1963, Quarterly, Trim Size-8$\frac{1}{2}$ x 11, Offset press, 4 pages, No Color
Subscriptions: Indv. $1
Circulation: (100% controlled)
Printing Co: Imprimerie Brisson Inc., 524 rue Notre Dame, Gatineau, PQ S8P 1M5 Canada Tel # (819) 663-4981

Pilgrim   *Association*

Publishing Co: Shrine of Our Lady of Martyrs, Noeltener Road, Auriesville, NY 12016; Title Tel # (518) 853-3033
Personnel: Editor-John Paret, S.J.
Editorial Description: Produced to promote interest in the seventeenth century Jesuit missionaries and martyrs of New York State.
General Info: Yr. Est. 1885, Quarterly, Trim Size-7$\frac{1}{2}$ x 8$\frac{1}{2}$, Offset press, 6 pages, Color, Matte
Subscriptions: Indv. $1
Circulation: Total-23,000

Pope John Paul II Center Newsletter   *Association*

Publishing Co: Sponsor-The Orchard Lake Schools, Pope John Paul II Center, Orchard Lake Schools, Orchard Lake, MI 48033; Title Tel # (313) 682-1885
Personnel: Publisher-Stanley Milewski, Circ. Mgr.-Dorothea Jantz, Editor, Production Mgr.-Alfred Jantz
Editorial Description: Spreading knowledge of words and deeds of Pope John Paul II and work of the Center.
General Info: Yr. Est. 1979, Bi-monthly, Trim Size-8$\frac{1}{2}$ x 11, Letrpr. press, 8 pages, No Color, Newsprint
Subscriptions: Indv. $5, $1/copy
Circulation: Total-500
Printing Co: Pontiac Letter Shop, Inc., 145 E Pike St, Pontiac, MI 48342-2634 Tel # (313) 332-3611

Quote. . . Unquote

Publishing Co: Catholic Traditionalist Movement, Inc., 210 Maple Ave, Westbury, NY 11590-3117 Tel # (516) 333-6471; Title Tel # (516) 333-6470 Title Fax # (516) 333-7535
Personnel: Publisher-Gommar De Pauw
Editorial Description: Quotes regarding current religious events affecting the Catholic Church.
General Info: Yr. Est. 1980, Monthly, 4 pages, ISSN: 1044-0518
Subscriptions: Free To Qualified Recipient
Acquistions: Publication Bought

Radar
See: DEAF

Reign of the Sacred Heart   *Association*

Publishing Co: Priests of the Sacred Heart, Hales Corners, WI 53130; Title Tel # (414) 425-3383
Personnel: Editor-Father Brian, Circ. Mgr.-Dr. John Cain
Editorial Description: Activities & work of the priests of the Sacred Heart.
General Info: (Formerly Reign), Yr. Est. 1934, Bi-monthly, Web press, 32 pages, 2 Color

Religious Life   *Consumer, Association*

Publishing Co: Institute on Religious Life, PO Box 41007, Chicago, IL 60641-0007; Title Tel # (312) 267-1195 Title Fax # (312) 267-2044
Personnel: Circ. Dir.-Kevin Banet
Editorial Description: Promotes teaching of R.C. Church for Religious Life--i. e., those who have made vows of poverty, chastity & obedience.
General Info: Yr. Est. 1977, 10x/yr., Trim Size-8$\frac{1}{2}$ x 11, Offset press, 12 pages, ISSN: 0279-0459, 2 Color
Subscriptions: Indv. $10, Can. $13, For. $15, $1/copy
Circulation: Total-4,700
Printing Co: R.M. Nielsen Printing Co., 5825 W Irving Park Rd, Chicago, IL 60634-2609 Tel # (312) 523-4300

Rural Landscapes
See: SOCIAL SERVICES & WELFARE

St. Mary's Seminary and University Bulletin   *Association*

Publishing Co: St. Mary's Seminary, 5400 Roland Ave, Baltimore, MD 21210-1994; Title Tel # (410) 323-3200
Personnel: Editor, Circ. Mgr., Art Dir.-Rudi Ruckmann
Editorial Description: Reports and alumni seminary news.
General Info: Yr. Est. 1970, Quarterly, Trim Size-8$\frac{1}{2}$ x 11, Offset press, 24 pages, 2 Color
Circulation: Total-8,900

Scapular

Publishing Co: Carmelite Fathers, Inc., 339 E 28th St, New York, NY 10016-8602; Title Tel # (212) 532-2232
Personnel: Editor-Fr. Pius M. Gagnon, O. Carm.
Editorial Description: Marian magazine written in view of Vatican II.
General Info: Yr. Est. 1941, Bi-monthly
Subscriptions: Indv. $2
Circulation: Total-12,000

Scripture from Scratch   *Consumer*

Publishing Co: St. Anthony Messenger Press, 1615 Republic St, Cincinnati, OH 45210-1219 Fax # (513) 241-0399; Title Tel # (513) 241-5615
Personnel: Publisher-Jeremy Harrington, Editor-Diane Houdek
Editorial Description: Resource for adult Catholics seeking a better understanding of the Bible.
General Info: Yr. Est. 1994, Monthly, Trim Size-8$\frac{1}{2}$ x 11, 4 pages, 2 Color, Matte
Subscriptions: Indv. $11
Circulation: Total-40,000

Semeuse de Joie
Consumer, Association

Publishing Co: Missionnaire Oblats de Marie Immaculee, 460-1ere rue, Richelieu, PQ J3L 4B5 Canada
General Info: Yr. Est. 1944, Quarterly, Trim Size-3¾ x 5½, Sheetfed press, 16 pages, ISSN: 0704-1810, No Color, Newsprint
Subscriptions: Indv. $1
Circulation: Total-1,700

Shrine Bulletin
Consumer

Publishing Co: Sponsor-World Apostolate of Fatima, Blue Army USA Inc., The, Mountain View Rd., P.O. Box 976, Washington, NJ 07882; Title Tel # (908) 689-1700 Title Fax # (908) 689-6279
Personnel: Editor-Rev. Gerald Wright, OMV, Asst. Ed.-Peggy Sincock
Editorial Description: A listing of all reigious celebrations and events held at the National Blue Army Shrine of the Immaculate Heart of Mary in Washington, NJ. (Warren County)
General Info: Yr. Est. 1979, 3x/yr., Trim Size-8½ x 11, Sheetfed press, 4 pages, 2 Color, Newsprint
Subscriptions: Indv. $1
Circulation: Total-10,000
Printing Co: A.M.I. Press, Mountain View Rd., Box 976, Washington, NJ 07882-0976 Tel # (908) 689-1700, Fax # (908) 689-6279

Slowo I Liturgia

Publishing Co: Polish-American Liturgical Center, Orchard Lake Schools, Box 240492, Orchard Lake, MI 48324 Tel # (313) 683-0409; Title Tel # (810) 683-0409
Personnel: Editor-Jan Jagodzinski
Editorial Description: Text: Polish. Sermon-preparing aid for priests who preach in Rom. Cath. Church in Polish, but are not fluent in the language.
General Info: Yr. Est. 1970, Quarterly, Sheetfed press, 50 pages, No Color, Newsprint, Looseleaf
Subscriptions: Indv. $25, $7/copy
Circulation: Total-119

Sons

Publishing Co: Sons of Mary, Health of the Sick, Inc., 567 Salem End Rd, Framingham, MA 01701-5513; Title Tel # (617) 879-6711
Personnel: Editor-John Coss, F. M. S. I
Editorial Description: Promotes the missionary work of this Roman Catholic medical missionary group (Sons of Mary).
General Info: (Formerly Happiness), Yr. Est. 1952, Quarterly, Trim Size-8½ x 11, Offset press, 2 pages, No Color
Circulation: (100% controlled), Total-3,000

Texas Catholic Historical Society Newsletter
See: HISTORY

Touchstone
Association

Publishing Co: Sponsor-Natl. Federation of Priests', National Federation of Priests' Councils, 1337 W Ohio St Fl 3, Chicago, IL 60622-6430; Title Tel # (312) 226-3334 Title Fax # (312) 829-8915
Personnel: Publisher-Barnard Stratman, Editor-Jay O'Connor
Editorial Description: News & articles of interest to priests in U. S.
General Info: Yr. Est. 1985, Quarterly, Trim Size-7¾ x 11, Web press, 6 pages, No Color, Newsprint
Subscriptions: Indv. $8
Circulation: (100% controlled), Total-27,000
Printing Co: Abbey Press, Hill Dr., St. Meinrad, IN 47577 Tel # (817) 357-8011

U.S. Parish - the Newsletter to Make Good Parishes Better
Association

Publishing Co: Claretian Publications, 205 W. Monroe St., Chicago, IL 60606-5033; Title Tel # (312) 236-7782 Title Fax # (312) 236-8207
Personnel: Publisher-Mark Brummel, Mktg. Dir.-Michelle Merten
Editorial Description: Provides helpful practical information to help make good parishes better.
General Info: Yr. Est. 1983, Monthly, Sheetfed press, 6 pages, 2 Color, Matte, Other
Subscriptions: Indv. $25, For. $28
Circulation: Total-1,305
List Rental: Actives: 1,569, $150/M

Vatican Voices

Publishing Co: Truth, Inc., 10100 W. Blue Mound Rd., Wauwatosa, WI 53226; Title Tel # (414) 258-2665
Personnel: Editor-Rev. Cletus Healy, S.J.
Editorial Description: Excerpted entirely from Vatican's l'Osservatore Romano. Best of the best.
General Info: Yr. Est. 1979, Weekly, Trim Size-8½ x 11, Letrpr. press, 4 pages, No Color, Newsprint, Other
Subscriptions: Indv. $20, $1/copy
Circulation: Total-125
Printing Co: Copy Boy, 105 Bluemound Road, Wavwatosa 53226

Victorian
See: SOCIAL SERVICES & WELFARE

Weekday Homily Helps
Association

Publishing Co: St. Anthony Messenger Press, 1615 Republic St, Cincinnati, OH 45210-1219; Title Tel # (513) 241-5615 Title Fax # (513) 241-0399
Personnel: Publisher-Jeremy Harrington, Editor-Carol Luebering, Promotion Dir.-Tom Bruce
Editorial Description: Scripture commentary, homily suggestion for all weekdays.
General Info: Yr. Est. 1980, Monthly, Trim Size-8½ x 11, Sheetfed press, Ind/Abs/Online: GPAI, 2 Color, Looseleaf
Subscriptions: Indv. $55
Circulation: Total-4,000

Western Catholic Union Record
Association

Publishing Co: Western Catholic Union, 510 Maine St., P.O. Box 410, Quincy, IL 62306-0410; Title Tel # (217) 223-9721 Title Fax # (217) 223-9726
Personnel: Editor-Al Kath
Editorial Description: News primarily pertaining to events and activities of the Society.
General Info: Yr. Est. 1905, Quarterly, Trim Size-8½ x 11, Offset press, 8 pages, 2 Color, Other, Other
Circulation: Total-10,000, Readership-13,000
Printing Co: Royal Printing Co., 514 Jersey St., Quincy, IL 62301 Tel # (217) 222-0617

Word One

Publishing Co: Claretian Publications, 205 W. Monroe St., Chicago, IL 60606-5033; Title Tel # (312) 236-7782 Title Fax # (312) 236-8207
Personnel: Editor-Mark Brummel
Editorial Description: Short notes on religion and social action.
General Info: Yr. Est. 1972, Quarterly, Trim Size-4⅜ x 10⅞, Sheetfed press, 8 pages
Subscriptions: Free To Qualified Recipient
Circulation: Total-18,512

Work of Infinite Love of Sacred Heart Newsletter
Consumer

Publishing Co: Work of Infinite Love of Sacred Heart, 511 Durie St., Toronto, ON M6S 3G8 Canada; Title Tel # (416) 766-3095
Personnel: Editor-F. Isber
Editorial Description: Clear abbreviated edition of Roman Catholic teaching.
General Info: Yr. Est. 1965, Monthly
Circulation: Total-1,000

Xaverian Missions Newsletter
Consumer, Association

Publishing Co: Xaverian Missionary Fathers, 101 Summer St # 5857, Holliston, MA 01746-2207; Title Tel # (508) 429-2144
Personnel: Editor-Dominic Calarco, S.X., Circ. Mgr.-Francis Signorelli, Art Dir.-Shoshanna Szuch
Editorial Description: Sharing news, view, and experiences of Catholic Missionaries with friends and supporters.
General Info: (Formerly Xaverian Missions), Yr. Est. 1951, Bi-monthly, Trim Size-8½ x 11, Offset press, 6 pages, 2 Color
Subscriptions: Indv. $5
Circulation: Total-30,000
Printing Co: Metrowest Graphics, Inc., 9 Whitney St, Holliston, MA 01746-2010 Tel # (508) 429-3877, Fax # (508) 469-3874

Youth Mission for the Immaculata National Newsletter
Association

Publishing Co: Fr. Kolbe Missionaries, 531 E. Merced Ave., West Covina, CA 91790-5025; Title Tel # (818) 917-0040 Title Fax # (818) 917-0900
Personnel: Publisher, Editor-Ann O'Donnell
Editorial Description: National newsletter regarding calendar and report on events for member of YMI (Catholic movement for youth & young adults) and alumni news.
General Info: (Formerly YMI Intl. Newsletter; YMI Newsletter), Yr. Est. 1975, Semi-annually, Trim Size-8½ x 11, 4 pages, 2 Color, Newsprint, Saddle-stitched
Subscriptions: Free To Qualified Recipient
Circulation: Readership-5,000
Advertising: Inquire for rates.

Youth Update
Association

Publishing Co: St. Anthony Messenger Press, 1615 Republic St, Cincinnati, OH 45210-1219 Fax # (513) 241-0399; Title Tel # (513) 241-5615
Personnel: Publisher-Jeremy Harrington, Editor-Carol Ann Morrow, Production Mgr.-Art Runnels, Art Dir.-Julie Lonneman, Promotion Dir.-Tom Bruce
Editorial Description: Challenges teenager through addressing life questions in faith context.
General Info: Yr. Est. 1982, Monthly, Sheetfed press, 4 pages, 2 Color, Newsprint
Subscriptions: Indv. $6
Circulation: Total-45,000

Zorniska (Morning Star)
Consumer, Association

Publishing Co: Ladies Pennsylvania Slovak Catholic Union, Northeastern Bank Bldg. , #922, Wilkes Barre, PA 18701-2598; Title Tel # (717) 944-0461
Personnel: Editor-Nancy Knoche
Editorial Description: Organization news.
General Info: Monthly, Trim Size-8½ x 11, 8 pages, No Color
Circulation: Total-4,150
Printing Co: Jednota Printery, Rosedale Ave., Box 150, Middletown, PA 17057 Tel # (717) 944-0461

Christian Denominations

AIM International *Association*

Publishing Co: Africa Inland Mission, PO Box 178, Pearl River, NY 10965-0178;
Title Tel # (914) 735-4014 Title Fax # (914) 735-1814
Personnel: Editor-Ted Barnett, Production Mgr.-Andy Hornberter
Editorial Description: Activities of the Africa inland mission, current mission issues, church growth, development, evangelism and personnel matters.
General Info: Yr. Est. 1910, Quarterly, Trim Size-8¼ x 11, Web press, 8 pages, ISSN: 0020-1464, Color-cover, Coated, Saddle-stitched
Subscriptions: Free
Circulation: Total-20,000
Advertising: Inquire for rates.
Printing Co: Greenfield Printing & Publishing, 1025 N. Washington St., Greenfield, OH 45123-9719
Tel # (513) 981-2161, Fax # (513) 981-3078

AMBS Bulletin
See: COLLEGE STUDENT

AMOS Realm

Publishing Co: Ancient Mystic Order of Samaritans, 974 Willey St, Morgantown, WV 26505-5149;
Title Tel # (304) 292-9635
Personnel: Editor-Harold Swindler
General Info: Quarterly

Accrediting Association of Bible Colleges Newsletter *Association*

Publishing Co: Accrediting Assn. of Bible Colleges, PO Box 1523, Fayetteville, AR 72702-1523;
Title Tel # (501) 521-8164 Title Fax # (501) 521-9202
Personnel: Editor-Randall Bell, Editor, Circ. Mgr., Production Mgr.-J. Mondragon
Editorial Description: Articles, employment opportunities related to member colleges & Christian higher education.
General Info: Yr. Est. 1947, Tri-annually, Trim Size-8½ x 11, Sheetfed press, 16 pages, ISSN: 0094-260X, Color-cover, Matte, Saddle-stitched
Subscriptions: Indv. $6
Circulation: Total-1,118
List Rental: Rents Lists
Printing Co: Just-Us Printers, 555 N Old Missouri Rd, Springdale, AR 72764-3637
Tel # (501) 751-0385

Acts & Facts *Consumer, Association*

Publishing Co: Institute for Creation Research, 10946 Woodside Ave N, Santee, CA 92071-2833
Tel # (619) 448-0900; Title Tel # (619) 448-9000 Title Fax # (619) 448-3469
Personnel: Editor-John Morris, Mng. Editor-Donald Rohrer, Asst. Ed.-Marjorie Appelquist
Editorial Description: Disseminates articles and information of current interest dealing with creation, evolution and related topics from the creationist point of view.
General Info: Monthly, Trim Size-5½ x 8½, 8 pages, 2 Color, Coated, Saddle-stitched
Subscriptions: Free

Adult Study Guide

Publishing Co: Sponsor-Pentecostal Church of God, Messenger Publishing House, 4901 Pennsylvania Ave # 850, Joplin, MO 64804-4947 Fax # (417) 624-7102; Title Tel # (417) 624-7050
Personnel: Editor-Billie Blevins
Editorial Description: Sunday School lessons based on Evangelical Curriculum Commission Lesson outlines.
General Info: Quarterly, 2 Color
Subscriptions: $2/copy
Circulation: Total-3,500

Alternative Health Therapies Newsletter
See: HEALTH

American Protestant Correctional Chaplains Association Newsletter

Publishing Co: American Protestant Correctional Chaplains Assn., 5325 Green Point Dr., Stone Mountain, GA 30088
Editorial Description: Works to improve the ministry of Protestant clergy in correctional institutions.
General Info: Yr. Est. 1935, Quarterly

Billboards for Jesus

Publishing Co: United Christians, Inc., Box 1833-SPD, Santa Ana, CA 92702-1840
Personnel: Publisher-Lewis Whitehead, Editor, Circ. Mgr.-Rosemarie Avila, Art Dir.-Tom Moraitis
Editorial Description: Evangelism and social comment through outdoor advertising of various types.
General Info: Yr. Est. 1983, Trim Size-8½ x 11, Sheetfed press, 4 pages, 2 Color, Newsprint
Subscriptions: Free
Circulation: Total-2,000
Printing Co: Christian Printing Service, 579 S State College Blvd, Fullerton, CA 92631-5113
Tel # (714) 871-5200

Bright Side
See: HOUSE ORGANS

Bulletin of the Armenian Evangelical Church of NY *Association*

Publishing Co: Armenian Evangelical Church, 152 E 34th St, New York, NY 10016-4750;
Title Tel # (212) 685-3177 Title Fax # (212) 889-8338
Personnel: Editor-Dr. Leon Tavitian
Editorial Description: Text: Armenian & Eng.
General Info: (Formerly Amsatertig), Yr. Est. 1912, Monthly, Letrpr. press, 12 pages
Subscriptions: Indv. $5
Circulation: Total-1,000

CB *Association*

Publishing Co: Christian Businessmen's Committee of USA, 1800 Mccallie Ave # 3308, Chattanooga, TN 37404-3025; Title Tel # (423) 698-4444 Title Fax # (423) 629-4434
Personnel: Publisher-Phil Downer, Editor-Robert Tamasy, Asst. Ed.-Neil Magnusen, Art Dir.-Shannon Swann
Editorial Description: Newsletter of information and articles relevant to the ministry of CBMC of USA.
General Info: (Formerly Christian Businessman), Yr. Est. 1974, Quarterly, Trim Size-8.5 x 11, Offset press, 16 pages, 2 Color, Matte, Saddle-stitched
Subscriptions: Indv. $10, $3/copy
Circulation: Total-16,000
Printing Co: Chattanooga Printing Co., 110 Somerville Ave, Chattanooga, TN 37405-3266
Tel # (615) 266-6166

CSI Newsletter

Publishing Co: Christian Solidarity Intl., 1101 17th St. NW, Suite 607, Washington, DC 20036-4601
Tel # (202) 785-5266 Fax # (202) 785-5276; Title Tel # (301) 989-0298 Title Fax # (301) 989-0398
Personnel: Editor-Darren Jones
General Info: (Formerly Mission to the Persecuted), Yr. Est. 1995, Monthly, Trim Size-8½ x 11, Offset press, 4 pages, 2 Color, Coated
Subscriptions: Free

Canada Armenian Press Newsletter *Association*

Publishing Co: Armenian Evangelical Church, 34 Glenforest Rd., Toronto, ON M4N 1Z8 Canada;
Title Tel # (416) 489-3188
Personnel: Editor-Rev. Y. Sarmazian
Editorial Description: Religious, Armenian heritage, community news. Donations list, report church activities, text in Armenian and English.
General Info: Yr. Est. 1963, Quarterly, 36 pages, No Color
Subscriptions: $2/copy
Circulation: Total-450

Canadian Unitarian *Association*

Publishing Co: Canadian Unitarian Council, 188 Eglinton Ave. E. #706, Toronto, ON M4P 2X7 Canada; Title Tel # (416) 489-4121 Title Fax # (416) 489-9010
Personnel: Circ. Mgr.-Carol Dahlquistt, Editor, Art Dir.-Liz Kind
Editorial Description: Dissemination of news of interest to Canadian Unitarian universalist societies; information on social issues.
General Info: Yr. Est. 1957, Quarterly, Trim Size-8⅜ x 11, Offset press, 4 pages, ISSN: 0527-9860, No Color
Circulation: Total-5,060

Catalyst
See: SOCIAL SERVICES & WELFARE

Chalcedon Report

Publishing Co: Sponsor-Chalcedon Inc., Chalcedon Foundation, PO Box 158, Vallecito, CA 95251-0158; Title Tel # (209) 736-4365
Personnel: Circ. Mgr.-Mark Rushdoony, Editor, Production Mgr.-Garry Moes
Editorial Description: Essays addressing the Christian reconstruction of life, throught, and culture.
General Info: Yr. Est. 1965, Monthly, Trim Size-8½ x 11, Web press, 4 pages, No Color, Newsprint
Circulation: Total-11,500
Printing Co: Calaveras Press, PO Box 338, Angels Camp, CA 95222-0338 Tel # (209) 736-4332

Challenger *Association*

Publishing Co: Chinese Christian Mission, PO Box 750759, Petaluma, CA 94975-0759;
Title Tel # (707) 762-1314 Title Fax # (707) 762-1713
Personnel: Editor-Cecilia Yau, Circ. Mgr.-James Wong, Art Dir.-Loren Chin, Promotion Dir.-Daniel Wong
Editorial Description: To facilitate Christian communication and evangelism.
General Info: Yr. Est. 1961, Monthly, Trim Size-8 x 11, Sheetfed press, 6 pages, Color, Newsprint
Circulation: (100% controlled), Total-12,000
Printing Co: O'dell Printing Co. Inc., 5460 State Farm Dr Ste 11, Rohnert Park, CA 94928-1625
Tel # (707) 585-2718

Christian Aid Ministries Newsletter
See: SOCIAL SERVICES & WELFARE

Christian Anti-Communism Crusade Newsletter *Association*

Publishing Co: Christian Anti-Communism Crusade, PO Box 890, Long Beach, CA 90801-0890;
Title Tel # (310) 437-0941
Personnel: Editor-Fred Schwarz
Editorial Description: Contains up-to-date, accurate, documented information concerning Communist doctrines, organizations, activities & objectives as revealed by the statements & publications of the Communists.
General Info: Yr. Est. 1956, Annually, Offset press, 8 pages, Color
Circulation: Total-50,000

Christian Chiropractor & CCA Bulletin   *Association*

Publishing Co: Christian Chiropractors Assn., PO Box 9715, Fort Collins, CO 80525-0500; Title Tel # (303) 482-1404

Personnel: Editor-Ronald Murphy, Circ. Mgr.-Starla Manewal, Art Dir.-Debbie Messick, Promotion Dir.-Glenn Hultgren

Editorial Description: The propogation of the Gospel of Jesus Christ at home & abroad, to our patients, professional colleagues, & fellow students of chiropractic. The mutual, practical support & spiritual fellowship of Christian Chiropractors & Chiropratic students.

General Info: Yr. Est. 1955, Bi-monthly, Trim Size-8½ x 11, Offset press, 40 pages, 2 Color

Subscriptions: Indv. $7

Circulation: (100% controlled), Total-1,000

Christian Civic League Record   *Association*

Publishing Co: Christian Civic League of ME, Inc., PO Box 5459, Augusta, ME 04332-5459; Title Tel # (207) 622-7634 Title Fax # (207) 622-7635

Personnel: Editor-Jasper Wyman, Production Mgr.-Michael Heath

Editorial Description: Church, public service, and political action.

General Info: Yr. Est. 1900, Monthly, Trim Size-8½ x 11, Sheetfed press, 8 pages, Color, Perfect bound

Subscriptions: Indv. $10, $1/copy

Circulation: Total-5,500

Printing Co: Camera Ready Printing, Rte. 17, Augusta, ME 04330 Tel # (207) 622-4459

Christian Communicator   *Consumer*

Publishing Co: Joy Publishing, PO Box 827, San Juan Capistrano, CA 92693-0827; Title Tel # (714) 545-4321 Title Fax # (714) 493-6552

Personnel: Editor-Susan Titus-Osborn

Editorial Description: Information and book reviews for Christian writers.

General Info: Monthly

Subscriptions: Indv. $20

Circulation: Total-3,000

List Rental: List Management Co.: Response Unlimited, c/o The Old Plantation, Rte. 5, Box 251, Waynesboro, VA 22980-9111 Tel # (703) 943-6721, Fax # (703) 943-0841, Actives: 3,000

Christian Community News   *Association*

Publishing Co: Intl. Council of Community Churches, 197 15th South LaGrang, Mokena, IL 60448 Tel # (708) 479-8400; Title Tel # (815) 464-5690

Personnel: Editor-J. Ralph Shotwell

Editorial Description: Devoted to ideas of the Free Church and promotional methods, book reviews; and articles and news of community churches.

General Info: Yr. Est. 1948, 9x/yr.

Subscriptions: Indv. $3

Circulation: Total-1,200

Advertising: Inquire for rates.

Christian Horizons Newsletter
See: DISABILITY

Christian MoneyLetter, The
See: INVESTMENT

Christian Reform World Relief Committee of Canada, Newsletter

Publishing Co: Christian Reformed World Relief Committee of Canada, 2850 Kalamazoo, SE Box 5070, Grand Rapids, MI 49560-0001

Personnel: Editor-Jacob Kramer

Editorial Description: Informs constituency on development of programs taking place in 26 countries in Latin Americ, Africa and Asia.

General Info: Yr. Est. 1962, Quarterly

Circulation: (100% controlled), Total-40,000

Christian School Comment

Publishing Co: Association of Christian Schools International, P.O. Box 35097, Colorado, CO 80935; Title Tel # (719) 528-6906

Editorial Description: Privately funded schools with a religious orientation emphazing a

General Info: Yr. Est. 1978, Monthly

Circulation: Total-140,000

Christian Vanguard

Publishing Co: New Christian Crusade Church, PO Box 426, Metairie, LA 70004-0426; Title Tel # (504) 279-5940

Personnel: Editor-R. Craig DeMott

General Info: Yr. Est. 1971, Monthly

Subscriptions: Indv. $25

ChristianWeek   *Consumer*   **CPM: $79**

Publishing Co: Sponsor-Fellowship for Print Witness Inc., Fellowship for Print Witness Inc., 300-228 Nortre Dame Avenue, Winnipeg, MB R3B 1N7 Canada; Title Tel # (204) 943-1147 Title Fax # (204) 947-5632

Personnel: Mng. Editor-Doug Koop, Assoc. Ed.-Debra Fieguth, Publisher, Circ. Mgr.-Harold Jantz, Adv. Dir.-Bryan Rempel, Art Dir.-Ray Dirks

Editorial Description: An evangically oriented tabloid of news and comment providing a window on christian faith and life in Canada.

General Info: Yr. Est. 1987, Bi-weekly, Trim Size-10 x 15, 20 pages, ISSN: 0835-412X, Newsprint

Subscriptions: Indv. $28, Can. $25, For. $28, $1/copy

Circulation: Total-11,300

Advertising: $900.

List Rental: List Management Co.: Bernice Bush Co./Springdale Lists, 15052 Springdale St., Huntington Beach, CA 92649-1178 Tel # (714) 891-3344, Fax # (714) 897-0650, Actives: 6,000, $90/M

Printing Co: Derksen Printers Ltd., 377 Main St., Steinbach, MB R0A 2A0 Canada Tel # (204) 475-0494, Fax # (204) 326-4860

Christians in Crisis

Publishing Co: Christian Forum Research Foundation, 1111 Fairgrounds Rd, Grand Rapids, MN 55744-2457; Title Tel # (218) 326-2688

Personnel: Editor-Sidney Reiners

Editorial Description: News of religious liberty problems in America & abroad. Information on steps readers can take to influence outcome of situations.

General Info: Yr. Est. 1984, Bi-monthly, Sheetfed press, 4 pages, ISSN: 1044-5846, No Color, Coated

Subscriptions: Free

Circulation: Total-1,700

Church Around the World   *Consumer*

Publishing Co: Tyndale Publications, 351 Executive Dr, Carol Stream, IL 60188-2420 Tel # (708) 668-8300

Editorial Description: Information for Catholic Church attendees.

General Info: Monthly

List Rental: List Management Co.: Bernice Bush Co./Springdale Lists, 15052 Springdale St., Huntington Beach, CA 92649-1178 Tel # (714) 891-3344, Fax # (714) 897-0650, Actives: $80/M

Comboni

Publishing Co: Comboni Missionaries, 8108 Beechmont Ave, Cincinnati, OH 45255-3120; Title Tel # (513) 474-4997 Title Fax # (513) 474-0382

Personnel: Publisher-Brian Quigley, Editor-Jose Marques

Editorial Description: Covers the activities of the Comboni Missionaries, especially in the United States and Canada.

General Info: Yr. Est. 1983, Web press, Newsprint

Circulation: Total-22,000

Concerned Women for America   *Association*

Publishing Co: Concerned Women for America, 370 l'Enfant Promenade SW, Suite 800, Washington, DC 20035; Title Tel # (202) 488-7000 Title Fax # (202) 488-0806

Personnel: Publisher-Beverly LaHaye, Editor-Elaine Lussier, Circ. Mgr.-Lee LaHaye, Production Mgr.-Michael Jameson

Editorial Description: News and educational items on issues related to Christian women.

General Info: Yr. Est. 1979, Monthly, Trim Size-8½ x 11, Web press, 26 pages, 4 Color, Coated

Subscriptions: Indv. $15

Circulation: (100% controlled), Total-180,000

Advertising: Inquire for rates.

Printing Co: Johnson & Hardin Co., 3600 Red Bank Rd, Cincinnati, OH 45227-4113 Tel # (513) 271-8834, Fax # (513) 527-2170

Courage in the Struggle for Justice & Peace
See: INTERNATIONAL AFFAIRS

Covenant Discipleship Quarterly   *Consumer, Association*

Publishing Co: General Board of Discipleship of the United Methodist Church, PO Box 840, Nashville, TN 37202-0840 Tel # (615) 340-7200; Title Tel # (615) 340-7010 Title Fax # (615) 340-7006

Personnel: Circ. Mgr.-Metral Smith, Editor, Art Dir.-Ellen Bourne, Production Mgr., Promotion Dir.-Marigene Chamberlain

Editorial Description: A journal/newsletter dealing with the theme of Christian discipleship. Primarily, but not exclusively, geared towards members of Covenant Discipleship groups around the world. Articles include writings from the Christian tradition contemporary discipleship, Covenent Discipleship groups, & general interests.

General Info: Yr. Est. 1985, Quarterly, Trim Size-8½ x 11, Sheetfed press, 12 pages, ISSN: 1052-3790, 2 Color, Matte, Saddle-stitched

Subscriptions: Indv. $10, Inst. $10, Can. $10, For. $10, $3/copy

Circulation: Total-903, Readership-1,041

Advertising: Inquire for rates.

Printing Co: Pollock Printing, 928 6th Ave S, Nashville, TN 37203-4679 Tel # (615) 255-0526

Cropwalker, The
See: SOCIAL SERVICES & WELFARE

Cross & Quill, the Christian Writers Newsletter
See: EDUCATION

Daily Blessing

Publishing Co: Oral Roberts Evangelistic Association, Box 2187, Tulsa, OK 74171-0001;
Title Tel # (918) 495-6161
Personnel: Editor-Wayne A. Robinson
General Info: Yr. Est. 1959, 2x/yr.
Subscriptions: Indv. $5
Circulation: Total-137,357

Daily Word in Large Type

Publishing Co: Unity School of Christianity, 1901 NW Blue Parkway, Unity Village, MO 64065-0001;
Title Tel # (816) 524-3550 Title Fax # (816) 251-3550
Personnel: Editor-Colleen Zuck, Circ. Mgr.-Lois Cheatham
Editorial Description: Includes daily meditations, inspirational articles, and poetry 18' Type.
General Info: Yr. Est. 1975, Trim Size-5½ x 8⅝, 48 pages, ISSN: 0011-5525, 2 Color
Subscriptions: Indv. $7, $1/copy
Circulation: Total-36,000
Printing Co: Vile Goller/Fine Arts, 101 Greystone Ct., Kansas City, MO 66150 Tel # (913) 342-1393, Fax # (913) 621-4856

Diakoneo   *Consumer, Association*

Publishing Co: N. American Assn. for the Diaconate, Centre for the Diaconate, 271 N. Main St., Providence, RI 02903; Title Tel # (401) 455-0521 Title Fax # (401) 331-9430
Personnel: Editor-Ormonde Plater
General Info: Yr. Est. 1978, Bi-monthly, Trim Size-8½ x 11, 16 pages
Subscriptions: Indv. $25, Inst. $25
Circulation: Total-2,500

Donor's Newsletter

Publishing Co: World Missions Fellowship, PO Box 5148, Oregon City, OR 97045-8148;
Title Tel # (503) 479-3731
General Info: Monthly

Drumbeat
See: SOCIAL SERVICES & WELFARE

Eastern Challenge   *Consumer, Association*

Publishing Co: International Missions, Inc., PO Box 14866, Reading, PA 19612-4866;
Title Tel # (610) 375-0300 Title Fax # (610) 375-6862
Personnel: Editor-Osborne Buchanan, Jr., Editorial Asst.-Nancy Maurer, Art Dir.-Byron Barnshaw
Editorial Description: Reports on Christian missionary activities in unreached Asian communities worldwide.
General Info: Yr. Est. 1960, Quarterly, Trim Size-8 x 10¼, Sheetfed press, 8 pages, ISSN: 0893-9346, 2 Color, Coated
Subscriptions: Free
Acquistions: Publication Bought
Circulation: (100% controlled), Total-24,000

Europe Today   *Association*

Publishing Co: Greater Europe Mission Assn., 18950 Base Camp Rd, Monument, CO 80132-8009 Tel # (719) 488-8008 Fax # (719) 488-8019
Personnel: Editor-Devere K. Curtiss, Production Mgr.-Lora Riley, Design Director-Beverly Seefeldt
Editorial Description: Reports the spiritual need of Europe and the ministries of GEM there.
General Info: (Formerly Greater Europe Report; Europe Report), Yr. Est. 1971, Quarterly, Trim Size-8½ x 11, Web press, 5 pages, ISSN: 1084-3914, 2 Color, Newsprint
Subscriptions: Free To Qualified Recipient
Circulation: Total-40,000
Printing Co: Park Press, 930 E 162nd St, South Holland, IL 60473-2442 Tel # (708) 331-6352, Fax # (708) 596-9688

Evangelical and Reformed Historical Society Newsletter   *Association*

Publishing Co: Evangelical, 555 West James St., Lancaster Theol. Sem., Lancaster, PA 17603-2812; Title Tel # (717) 393-0654
Personnel: Editor-John Payne
Editorial Description: News of the activities of the society and articles of historical interest to the United Church of Christ.
General Info: Semi-annually, Trim Size-8½ x 11, Mimeo press, 10 pages

Every Home   *Association*

Publishing Co: Every Home for Christ, PO Box 35970, Colorado Springs, CO 80935-3597;
Title Tel # (818) 341-7870 Title Fax # (818) 709-5118
Personnel: Editor-Dick Eastman, Production Mgr.-Charlie Segura, Publisher, Art Dir.-Andy Lay
Editorial Description: To report news of what God has done overseas through the prayers and gifts of Christians in the U.S.A., Canada, Australia, New Zealand, & Great Britian.
General Info: (Formerly Everybody), Monthly, Trim Size-8½ x 11, Sheetfed press, 6 pages, 2 Color, Newsprint
Circulation: Total-150,000

Faithful Steward
See: INVESTMENT

Focus on Missions

Publishing Co: Fellowship of Missions, PO Box 136, Middletown, DE 19709-0136;
Title Tel # (302) 378-1525
Personnel: Editor-Henry Heijermans
General Info: Yr. Est. 1970, Irregular, Trim Size-8½ x 11, Letrpr. press, 2 pages, No Color, Matte
Subscriptions: Free
Circulation: Total-26,000
Printing Co: Biblical Ministries Worldwide, Box 464-250, Lawrenceville, GA 30246 Tel # (404) 339-3500

Forum Focus   *Association*

Publishing Co: Canadian Churches Forum for Global Ministries, 11 Madison Ave., Toronto, ON M5R 2S2 Canada; Title Tel # (416) 924-9351 Title Fax # (416) 924-5356
Personnel: Editor-Robert Faris
Editorial Description: Third world church on social issues, also Christian perspective on Canadian social issues.
General Info: (Formerly Fish Eye Lens), Yr. Est. 1974, Semi-annually, Trim Size-8½ x 11, Offset press, 8 pages, ISSN: 1201-558X, 2 Color, Saddle-stitched
Subscriptions: Indv. $15, Can. $15, $5/copy
Circulation: Total-500
Printing Co: Reliable Printing, 1149 Bellamy Rd., Unit 6, Scarborough, ON M1H 1H2 Canada Tel # (416) 438-6294

Frontline Report

Publishing Co: Society of African Missions, 23 Bliss Ave, Tenafly, NJ 07670-3000;
Title Tel # (201) 567-0450
General Info: Bi-monthly
Circulation: Total-1,230

Fundamental News Service

Publishing Co: American Council of Christian Churches, PO Box 19, Valling Ford, PA 19086;
Title Tel # (610) 566-8154 Title Fax # (610) 892-0992
Personnel: Editor-Donald McKnight, Production Mgr.-Debra Racz
Editorial Description: Issues facing and affecting fundamental churches nationally & internationally.
General Info: (Formerly Accent), Yr. Est. 1941, Bi-monthly, Trim Size-11 x 17, Sheetfed press, ISSN: 0896-5749, 2 Color, Newsprint
Subscriptions: Indv. $15
Acquistions: Publication Bought
Circulation: Total-12,000
Printing Co: Baker Printing, State St., Media, PA 19063 Tel # (215) 566-0691

Global Missions
See: SOCIAL SERVICES & WELFARE

Gospel Truth

Publishing Co: Southwest Radio Church, PO Box 1144, Oklahoma City, OK 73101-1144
Personnel: Editor-Rev. David F. Webber
General Info: Yr. Est. 1938, Monthly
Circulation: Total-6,000

Have a Good Day   *Consumer*

Publishing Co: Tyndale Publications, 351 Executive Dr, Carol Stream, IL 60188-2420 Tel # (708) 668-8300
General Info: Monthly
List Rental: List Management Co.: Bernice Bush Co./Springdale Lists, 15052 Springdale St., Huntington Beach, CA 92649-1178 Tel # (714) 891-3344, Fax # (714) 897-0650, Actives: $80/M

Home Work
See: BUSINESS & INDUSTRY

Homily Service   *Consumer*

Publishing Co: Liturgical Conference, 8750 Georgia Ave Ste 123, Silver Spring, MD 20910-3621;
Title Tel # (202) 898-0885
Personnel: Editor-Rachel Reeder, Circ. Mgr.-Andrew Wall
Editorial Description: Material designed to help preachers and lay persons prepare for the Sunday assembly, especially through study of the scriptures.
General Info: Yr. Est. 1970, Monthly, Offset press, 48 pages, ISSN: 0732-1872, 2 Color
Subscriptions: Indv. $55, $5/copy
Circulation: Total-4,500
Advertising: Inquire for rates.

Hume Lake News

Publishing Co: Hume Lake Christian Camps, 256 N Maple Ave, Fresno, CA 93702-2465;
Title Tel # (209) 251-6043
Personnel: Editor-Fred Dellard
Editorial Description: News of upcoming camps & conferences.
General Info: Bi-monthly
Circulation: Total-30,000

ICYE-US Newsletter   *Association*

Publishing Co: International Christian Youth Exchange, 134 W. 26th St., New York, NY 10001-6803;
Title Tel # (212) 206-7307
Personnel: Editor-Ed Gragert
Editorial Description: Activities of our exchanges around the U.S. as well as topics of interest to an internationally minded audience of young people ages 16 to 35 & American host families.
General Info: Yr. Est. 1957, 8 pages, No Color
Circulation: Total-10,000

Impact
Association

Publishing Co: Christian Missionary Fellowship, PO Box 501020, Indianapolis, IN 46250-6020; Title Tel # (317) 578-2700 Title Fax # (317) 578-2827
Personnel: Editor-Naomi Kouns
Editorial Description: A periodical reporting on the life and work of Christian Missionary Fellowship.
General Info: (Formerly Missionary Fellowship), Yr. Est. 1949, Irregular, Trim Size-8½ x 11, Sheetfed press, 16 pages, No Color, Coated
Acquistions: Publication Bought
Circulation: (100% controlled), Total-65,000
Printing Co: Benham Press, 1160 W. 16th St., Indianapolis, IN 46202-2162 Tel # (317) 266-1111

InterVarsity
Association

Publishing Co: InterVarsity Christian Fellowship, PO Box 7895, Madison, WI 53707-7895; Title Tel # (608) 274-9001 Title Fax # (608) 274-7882
Personnel: Publisher-Steve Hayner, Editor-Neal Kunde
Editorial Description: Information piece for those who support InterVarsity's work with college & univ. students.
General Info: Yr. Est. 1982, Quarterly, Trim Size-8½ x 11, Web press, 24 pages, 2 Color, Saddle-stitched
Circulation: Total-50,000
List Rental: List Management Co.: Bernice Bush Co./Springdale Lists, 15052 Springdale St., Huntington Beach, CA 92649-1178 Tel # (714) 891-3344, Fax # (714) 897-0650, Actives: 13,600, $85/M
Printing Co: Straus Printing, 1028 E Washington Ave, Madison, WI 53703-2992 Tel # (608) 251-3222

Intercessor
Association

Publishing Co: Inter-Varsity Christian Fellowship of Canada, Unit 17, 40 Vogell Rd., Richmond Hill, ON L4B 3N6 Canada; Title Tel # (905) 884-6880 Title Fax # (905) 884-6550
Personnel: Publisher-James Berney, Editor-Mary Bellows
Editorial Description: Prayer letter. Text in English.
General Info: Yr. Est. 1930, Bi-monthly, Trim Size-8½ x 18, Web press, 8 pages, No Color, Coated
Circulation: Total-3,000
Printing Co: Inkspot Printing, Inc., 5210 Finch Ave. E., #20, Agincourt, ON M1S 4Z8 Canada Tel # (416) 291-8653

International Christian Studies Association Newsletter (ICSA Newsletter)
Scholarly, Association   **CPM: $208**

Publishing Co: Institute for Interdisciplinary Research, 2828 3rd St Suite 11, Santa Monica, CA 90405-4150; Title Tel # (310) 396-0517
Personnel: Publisher, Editor-Oskar Gruenwald
Editorial Description: Official newsletter of the International Christian Studies Association. Co-sponsored & published by the Institute for Interdisciplinary Research.
General Info: Yr. Est. 1983, Annually, Trim Size-8½ x 11, Desktop press, 12 pages, ISSN: 1051-2772, 2% ads, Color, Saddle-stitched
Subscriptions: Free
Circulation: Total-1,200
Advertising: $250. Accepts Inserts.
List Rental: Actives: $100/M

Japan North American Commission on Cooperative Mission Bulletin

Publishing Co: Japan North American Commission on Cooperative Mission, 475 Riverside, New York, NY 10115-0122; Title Tel # (212) 870-2021

Jews for Jesus Newsletter
Association

Publishing Co: Jews for Jesus, PO Box 424885, San Francisco, CA 94142-4885; Title Tel # (415) 864-2600 Title Fax # (415) 552-8325
Personnel: Editor-Ceil Rosen, Production Mgr.-Milan Steffel
Editorial Description: Educational & inspirational articles for Jews interested in Christian related topics.
General Info: Yr. Est. 1973, Monthly, Trim Size-8½ x 11, Web press, 8 pages, ISSN: 0740-5901, 2 Color, Newsprint
Circulation: Total-300,000

Jottings
See: BLIND

Joyful Noiseletter

Publishing Co: Fellowship of Merry Christians, Inc., PO Box 895, Portage, MI 49081-0895; Title Tel # (616) 324-0990 Title Fax # (616) 324-3984
Personnel: Editor-Cal Samra, Assoc. Ed.-Rose McBride Samra
Editorial Description: Cartoons and anecdotes for use in church bulletins, services, etc.
General Info: Yr. Est. 1986, 10x/yr., ISSN: 1066-243X
Subscriptions: Indv. $22

Jubilee

Publishing Co: Prison Fellowship Ministries, Box 17500, Washington, DC 20041-0500; Title Tel # (703) 478-0100 Title Fax # (703) 318-0235
Personnel: Editor-Megs Singer, Mng. Editor-Becky Beane
Editorial Description: News about Prison Fellowship's ministry through local churches and volunteers.
General Info: Yr. Est. 1977, Monthly, Trim Size-8½ x 11, Sheetfed press, 8 pages, ISSN: 0893-1607, 2 Color, Newsprint
Circulation: Total-200,000

KEY Newsletter

Publishing Co: Great Lakes Christian College, 6211 W. Willow Hwy., Lansing, MI 48917-1299
General Info: Quarterly, Trim Size-8½ x 11, 8 pages
Subscriptions: Free To Qualified Recipient
Circulation: Total-13,000

Law & Justice
Business

Publishing Co: Canadian Centre for Law and Justice, PO Box 36038, 1318 Wellington St., Ottawa, ON K1Y 3A0 Canada; Title Tel # (613) 778-7718 Title Fax # (613) 778-3443
Editorial Description: A monthly briefing from the Canadian Center for law and justice. Dedicated to the promotion of freedom, life and pro-family issues.
General Info: Monthly, Trim Size-8½ x 11, 4 pages, No Color, Matte, Other

Letter from Plymouth Rock

Publishing Co: Plymouth Rock Foundation, Inc., P.O. Box 577, Marlborough, NH 03455; Title Tel # (603) 876-4685
Personnel: Publisher, Editor-Rus Walton, Circ. Mgr., Promotion Dir.-Jack Caulfield
Editorial Description: Bible-based analysis & commentary on contemporary issues. Reviews of books important to Christians.
General Info: Yr. Est. 1979, Monthly, Trim Size-8½ x 11, Sheetfed press, 4 pages
Subscriptions: Indv. $25

Liberation
Association

Publishing Co: Ken Campbell Evangelistic Assn., Box 100, Milton, ON L9T 2Y3 Canada Tel # (416) 878-8461
Editorial Description: Deals with grass-roots evangelism in North America, particularly Canada.
General Info: (Formerly Encounter), Yr. Est. 1972, Quarterly
List Rental: List Management Co.: Response Unlimited, c/o The Old Plantation, Rte. 5, Box 251, Waynesboro, VA 22980-9111 Tel # (703) 943-6721, Fax # (703) 943-0841, Actives: 29,483, $90/M

Looys
Consumer, Association

Publishing Co: St. James Armenian Apostolic Church, 465 Mount Auburn St, Watertown, MA 02172-4117; Title Tel # (617) 923-8860
Editorial Description: Text in Armenian and English.
General Info: Yr. Est. 1953, 10x/yr., Trim Size-7¾ x 10¾, Offset press, 12 pages
Subscriptions: Free To Qualified Recipient
Circulation: Total-1,750

Lutheran Braille Evangelism Bulletin
See: BLIND

MARC Newsletter

Publishing Co: Missions Advanced Research & Communication Ctr., 919 W Huntington Dr, Monrovia, CA 91016-3111; Title Tel # (818) 303-8811
Personnel: Publisher-Bryant Myers, Editor-Mitali Perkins, Production Mgr.-Mitaii Perkins
General Info: Yr. Est. 1967, Quarterly, Desktop press, 8 pages, 2 Color, Newsprint
Circulation: (100% controlled)

Mission Newsletter

Publishing Co: Prison Mission Assn., PO Box 1587, Port Orchard, WA 98366-0146; Title Tel # (714) 686-2613
Personnel: Publisher-Joe Mason
Editorial Description: Promotes Bible study and correspondence.
General Info: (Formerly Prison Echoes), Yr. Est. 1955, Quarterly
Circulation: Total-200

Missions Update

Publishing Co: InterVarsity Christian Fellowship, PO Box 7895, Madison, WI 53707-7895 Tel # (608) 274-9001 Fax # (608) 274-7882
Personnel: Publisher-Stephen Hayner, Editor-Bob Bondurant, Art Dir.-Bill Redinger
Editorial Description: Missions Update provides supporters & friends of Intervarsity Missions & the Urbana student missions convention with news about our ministry of mobilizing student involvement in the world mission of Jesus Christ.
General Info: Yr. Est. 1986, Quarterly
Circulation: Total-10,000

Moneychanger, The
See: INVESTMENT

Monthly Letter About Evangelism
Consumer, Association

Publishing Co: World Council of Churches, 475 Riverside Dr., Ste 915, New York, NY 10115-0122 Fax # (212) 870-2528; Title Tel # (212) 870-3340
Editorial Description: Discusses the evangelical movement.
General Info: 10x/yr.

Mortarboard
See: COLLEGE STUDENT LIFESTYLE

National & International
Religion Report *Consumer, Scholarly*

Publishing Co: Religion Today, PO Box 21505, Roanoke, VA 24018-0560 Tel # (703) 989-7500 Fax # (703) 989-0189
Personnel: Publisher-Stephen Wike, Editor-Cheryl Hoffman, Sr. Ed.-Lawrence Pierce
Editorial Description: Keeps church leaders up-to-date on events and trends that effect their ministry.
General Info: Bi-weekly, Trim Size-8½ x 11, 8 pages, No Color, Matte
Subscriptions: Indv. $49, Can. $49, For. $78
List Rental: List Management Co.: Response Unlimited, c/o The Old Plantation, Rte. 5, Box 251, Waynesboro, VA 22980-9111 Tel # (703) 943-6721, Fax # (703) 943-0841, Actives: 6,635, $95/M, Expires: 11,110, $65/M

National Retreat Center
Newsletter

Publishing Co: Foundation of the Twelve Apostles, PO Box 1231, Cheyenne, WY 82003-1231; Title Tel # (307) 638-3322
Personnel: Publisher-Barbara Griffin Moss, Editor-Barbara Moss
General Info: Bi-monthly, 4 pages, No Color
Printing Co: Pioneer Printing Co., 514 W 19th St, Cheyenne, WY 82001-4336 Tel # (307) 635-4114

National Spiritualist-Summit *Association*

Publishing Co: National Spiritualist Assn. of Churches, 3521 W Topeka Dr, Glendale, AZ 85308-2325; Title Tel # (602) 274-3161
Personnel: Editor-Sandra Pfortmiller
General Info: Yr. Est. 1919, Monthly, Trim Size-8½ x 11, 36 pages
Subscriptions: Indv. $18, Can. $24, For. $24, $2/copy

Net Results *Consumer, Association*

Publishing Co: Net Results, 5001 Ave N, Lubbock, TX 79412-2993; Title Tel # (806) 762-8094 Title Fax # (806) 762-8873
Editorial Description: Promotes evangelism in the Cristian churches.
General Info: Yr. Est. 1980, Monthly, Trim Size-8½ x 11, Offset press, 32 pages, ISSN: 0270-4900, 2 Color, Saddle-stitched
Subscriptions: Indv. $30
Circulation: Total-15,000
List Rental: List Management Co.: Doug Ross Communications, 3225 S Hardy Dr Ste 101, Tempe, AZ 85282-3329 Tel # (602) 966-1744

New Aurora

Publishing Co: Association of Evangelicals for Italian Missions, 13th & Tasker Sts., Philadelphia, PA 19148; Title Tel # (215) 334-1282
Personnel: Editor-Dr. Anthony Jasquez, Circ. Mgr.-Esther Bovo, Adv. Dir.-Evelyn Barkovich
Editorial Description: Features items of religion and of the evangelical faith. In Italian and English.
General Info: Yr. Est. 1903, Bi-monthly, Trim Size-8½ x 11½, Sheetfed press, 4 pages
Subscriptions: Indv. $3
Advertising: Inquire for rates.
Printing Co: Complete Graphic Svc., 374 N. Cooper Rd., Marlton, NJ 08053 Tel # (609) 768-7676

News, The
See: EDUCATION

News Notes *Association*

Publishing Co: Disciples Peace Fellowship, PO Box 1986, Indianapolis, IN 46206-1986; Title Tel # (317) 353-1491
Personnel: Editor-A. Garnett Day
Editorial Description: To keep church members sensitized to peace issues.
General Info: Yr. Est. 1935, Bi-monthly, 10 pages
Circulation: Total-2,000

Outreach Legislative Alert

Publishing Co: Unitarian Universalist Assn. of Churches in North America, 100 Maryland Ave NE, Washington, DC 20002-5625; Title Tel # (202) 547-0254
Personnel: Editor-Robert Alpern
General Info: (Formerly Outreach), Yr. Est. 1976, 4 pages
Circulation: Total-1,350

Pilgrim State News

Publishing Co: United Church of Christ, Massachusetts Conference, 14 Beacon St., Boston, MA 02108-3763
Personnel: Editor-Darrell Holland
General Info: Yr. Est. 1974, Monthly

Prayer & Share Newsletter

Publishing Co: Christ for the Nations, 3404 Conway St, Dallas, TX 75224-4092; Title Tel # (214) 376-1711
General Info: Monthly

Prayer Fellowship Bulletin *Consumer, Association*

Publishing Co: RBMU Intl., 1431 Stuckert Rd., Warrington, PA 18976-1526; Title Tel # (215) 491-4900 Title Fax # (215) 491-4910
Personnel: Editor-Ginny Crapser
Editorial Description: A daily prayer calender.
General Info: Yr. Est. 1966, Monthly, 2 pages
Circulation: Total-1,400

Prayer Letter
See: AGRICULTURE

Professional Christian
Counselor

Publishing Co: United Assn. of Christian Counselors Intl., 41 Short St, Harrisburg, PA 17109-3731; Title Tel # (717) 652-7688
Personnel: Editor-Art Sprunger, Adv. Dir.-Laura Marshall
Editorial Description: Christian professional counseling forum for all fields of counseling, directed at the membership of United Assn. of Christian Counselors Intl.
General Info: (Formerly Paracletic), Yr. Est. 1982, Quarterly, Trim Size-5½ x 8½, Sheetfed press, 14 pages, 1% ads, No Color, Newsprint
Subscriptions: Indv. $20, $5/copy
Circulation: Total-1,000
Advertising: Inquire for rates.

Profile *Association*

Publishing Co: Evangelical Training Association, 110 Bridge St # 327, Wheaton, IL 60187-4841; Title Tel # (708) 668-6400 Title Fax # (708) 668-8437
Personnel: Publisher, Editor-Jonathan Thigpen, Circ. Mgr., Production Mgr.-Linda Sorenson
Editorial Description: Informative articles pertaining to the preparation of lay leadership for church ministries.
General Info: Yr. Est. 1967, Quarterly, Trim Size-8½ x 11, Offset press, 6 pages, 2 Color
Subscriptions: Free To Qualified Recipient
Circulation: Total-15,000
List Rental: List Management Co.: Tri-Media, 5200 Main St Ste 205, Skokie, IL 60077-2158 Tel # (708) 673-4440, Fax # (708) 673-4469

Progress
See: EDUCATION

Projections
See: BLIND

Protestant Teachers
Association Newsletter *Association*

Publishing Co: Protestant Teachers Assn., 71 W 23rd St, New York, NY 10010-4156; Title Tel # (212) 255-0254
General Info: Annually

Public Justice Report
See: POLITICS

Pulse *Consumer*

Publishing Co: Evangelical Missions Information Service, PO Box 794, Wheaton, IL 60189-0794 Tel # (708) 653-2188; Title Tel # (708) 653-2158 Title Fax # (708) 653-0520
Personnel: Publisher, Editor-James Reapsome, News Ed.-Stan Guthrie, Circ. Mgr.-Karen Rummel, Adv. Dir.-Jean Warren, Production Mgr., Promotion Mgr.-Dona Diehl
Editorial Description: In-depth reports of significant events, trends, developments and issues reflecting missions concerns around the world.
General Info: Yr. Est. 1966, Semi-monthly, Trim Size-8½ x 11, Offset press, 8 pages, ISSN: 0747-8631, No Color, Newsprint
Subscriptions: Indv. $25, Can. $30, $2/copy
Circulation: Total-5,500
Printing Co: DuPage Dupliprint, 262 Commonwealth Dr, Carol Stream, IL 60188-2449 Tel # (708) 665-4320

Reach

Publishing Co: Christian Reformed World Relief Committee of Canada, 2850 Kalamazoo, SE Box 5070, Grand Rapids, MI 49560-0001; Title Tel # (616) 246-0767
Personnel: Editor-Donald J. McCrory
General Info: Yr. Est. 1975, Bi-monthly, 2 pages
Subscriptions: Indv. $4, Can. $5

Reflections *Association*

Publishing Co: Slavic Gospel Association, 6151 Commonwealth Dr., Loves Park, IL 61111 Tel # (815) 282-8900 Fax # (815) 282-8901; Title Tel # (708) 690-8900 Title Fax # (708) 690-9524
Personnel: Publisher, Editor, Assoc. Ed.-Paul Kamps
Editorial Description: Religious news of the Commonwealth of Independent States.
General Info: (Formerly NewsWire), Yr. Est. 1984, Bi-monthly, Trim Size-8½ x 11, Offset press, 4 pages, No Color, Coated
Circulation: Total-43,000

Report to Donors
See: PHILANTHROPY

Shalom *Association*

Publishing Co: Christian Ministry Among Jewish People, PO Box 500307, Atlanta, GA 31150-0307
Personnel: Editor-Simcha Newton
Editorial Description: CMJ/USA's purpose is to encourage Jewish people to recognize Jesus as their Messiah, & to educate Christians, especially Episcopalians, as to the Jewish origins of our Faith.
General Info: Yr. Est. 1982, Quarterly, Trim Size-8½ x 11, 6 pages, 2 Color, Matte, Saddle-stitched
Circulation: Total-6,000

Sharing Times

Publishing Co: Christ Truth Ministries, PO Box 610, Upland, CA 91785-0610;
Title Tel # (714) 981-2838
Personnel: Editor-Dr. Carl F. Davis, Jr.
General Info: Monthly

Sing! Jr.
See: MUSIC & MUSIC TRADES

Spreading the Fame of
Christ

Publishing Co: Fellowship of Assocs. of Medical Evangelism, PO Box 688, Columbus, IN
47202-0688; Title Tel # (812) 379-4351 Title Fax # (812) 379-1105
Editorial Description: Covers current issues relative to medical missions & the biblical base of
medical missions.
General Info: Quarterly

Temple Times

Publishing Co: Calvary Temple, 200 S University Blvd, Denver, CO 80209-3299;
Title Tel # (303) 744-7213
Personnel: Editor-Judy Stonecipher
Editorial Description: Promotes Calvary Temple Church activities.
General Info: Bi-weekly, 4 pages
Circulation: Total-3,200

Theologia 21

Publishing Co: Dominion Press, PO Box 4608, Salem, OR 97302-8608; Title Tel # (503) 362-9634
Personnel: Publisher, Editor-A.S. Otto
Editorial Description: Articles on Christian metaphysics; alternative approach to many traditional
theological concepts.
General Info: (Formerly The Immortality Newsletter), Yr. Est. 1970, Semi-annually, Offset press, 10
pages, ISSN: 0362-0085, No Color, Other, Looseleaf
Subscriptions: Indv. $15

Trim Tab   *Association*

Publishing Co: Fellowship of Christian Airline Personnel, 136 Providence Rd, Fayetteville, GA
30214-2844; Title Tel # (404) 461-9320
Personnel: Editor-Penny Myers, Circ. Dir.-Jim Morissey
Editorial Description: Articles challenge and encourage Christians within the airline industry;
evangelism.
General Info: Yr. Est. 1972, Bi-monthly, Trim Size-8½ x 11, Offset press, 6 pages, 2 Color, Matte
Subscriptions: Free
Circulation: Total-10,000

UME Letter   *Association*

Publishing Co: United Ministries in Education, C/o Rev. Turecky, 14214 Edgecrest Dr., Dallas, TX
75240; Title Tel # (214) 233-3101
Personnel: Publisher-Carol Kelly, Editor-Betsy Alden Turecky
Editorial Description: News of ministry in public and higher education.
General Info: Yr. Est. 1980, Quarterly, Trim Size-8½ x 11, Sheetfed press, 6 pages, No Color
Circulation: Total-4,000

United Evangelical Action   *Consumer, Association*   **CPM: $64**

Publishing Co: Natl. Assn. of Evangelicals, PO Box 28, Wheaton, IL 60189-0028;
Title Tel # (708) 665-0500 Title Fax # (708) 665-8575
Personnel: Publisher-Don Argue, Editor-Donald Brown, Circ. Mgr.-Esther Laughlin, Adv. Mgr.-Maxine
Hummel, Design Director-Dwight Walles
Editorial Description: Confronts issues of concern to evangelical Christian
General Info: Yr. Est. 1942, Bi-monthly, Trim Size-8½ x 11, Offset press, 8 pages, ISSN: 0041-7270,
2 Color, Matte, Saddle-stitched
Subscriptions: Indv. $12, $2/copy
Circulation: Total-7,804
Advertising: $500.

Unity Village News   *Association*

Publishing Co: Unity School of Christianity, 1901 NW Blue Parkway, Unity Village, MO 64065-0001
Fax # (816) 251-3550; Title Tel # (816) 524-3550
Editorial Description: Covers activities of personnel and friends, Unity events and announcements.
General Info: Yr. Est. 1935, Monthly, Trim Size-8½ x 11½, Offset press, 4 pages, No Color
Circulation: Total-1,000

Voice of Liberty   *Association*

Publishing Co: Voice of Liberty Assn., 692 Sunnybrook Dr., Decatur, GA 30033-5509;
Title Tel # (404) 633-3634
Personnel: Publisher, Editor, Adv. Dir.-Martha Andrews
Editorial Description: Analysis of current events in light of Bible prophecy; conservative.
General Info: Yr. Est. 1961, Semi-annually, Trim Size-8½ x 11, Mimeo press, 14 pages, No Color,
Matte
Circulation: Total-2,500, Readership-3,500

Walk Away

Publishing Co: Institute for First Amendment Studies, Inc., PO Box 589, Great Barrington, MA
01230-0589; Title Tel # (413) 274-3786 Title Fax # (413) 274-0245
Personnel: Publisher, Editor-Skipp Porteous, Editor-Barbara Simon
Editorial Description: A forum which offers support for former Fundamentalist, Pentecostal &
Charismatic Christians & other bible-based religious groups.
General Info: Yr. Est. 1989, Quarterly, Trim Size-8½ x 11, Sheetfed press, 4 pages, 90% ads, No
Color, Matte
Subscriptions: Indv. $12, $2/copy
Circulation: (71% controlled), Total-3,500
Advertising: Inquire for rates.

Waves
See: GAY & LESBIAN INTEREST

Western Tract News   *Association*

Publishing Co: Western Tract Mission Inc., 401-33rd St. W., Saskatoon, SK S7L 0V5 Canada;
Title Tel # (306) 244-0446
Personnel: Editor-Mel Anhorn
Editorial Description: A Christian publication designed to communicate the use of Gospel tracts, and
Bible correspondence lessons (the Mailbox Club).
General Info: Yr. Est. 1943, Bi-monthly, Trim Size-5½ x 8½, Offset press, 16 pages, ISSN: 0700-
642X, 2 Color, Newsprint
Circulation: (100% controlled), Total-2,000

Whole Earth Newsletter   *Consumer, Association*

Publishing Co: United Church Board for World Ministries, 700 Prospect Ave., Cleveland, OH
44115-1100; Title Tel # (216) 736-3206 Title Fax # (216) 736-3259
Personnel: Editor-Sandra Rooney
Editorial Description: Current work & issues of United Church Board for World Ministires.
General Info: (Formerly Missionary Herald), Yr. Est. 1805, Tri-annually, Trim Size-8½ x 11, 12
pages, ISSN: 0361-1930, No Color, Newsprint, Saddle-stitched
Subscriptions: Indv. $2
Circulation: Total-12,000
Printing Co: Kutztown Publishing Co., 15076 Kutztown Rd, Kutztown, PA 19530-9275
Tel # (215) 683-7341

World CWF News   *Association*

Publishing Co: World Christian Women's Fellowship, 130 E Washington Street, Indianapolis, IN
46206; Title Tel # (317) 635-3100 Title Fax # (317) 635-4426
Personnel: Editor-Janice Newborn
General Info: (Formerly World Christian Women's Fellowship-Newsletter), Yr. Est. 1954, Semi-
annually, 18 pages
Circulation: Total-5,800
List Rental: Rents Lists

World for Christ Crusader   *Consumer*

Publishing Co: World for Christ Crusader, Inc., 1005 Union Valley Rd, West Milford, NJ 07480-1220;
Title Tel # (201) 728-3267 Title Fax # (201) 728-3351
Personnel: Editor-Rev. William Stelpstra
General Info: Yr. Est. 1960, 3x/yr., Letrpr. press, 8 pages
Acquistions: Publication Bought

Worldwide Evangelist   *Association*

Publishing Co: Concordia Tract Mission, PO Box 201, Saint Louis, MO 63166-0201;
Title Tel # (314) 268-1362
Editorial Description: Promotes evangelism throughout the world.
General Info: Yr. Est. 1949, Quarterly, Trim Size-11⅜ x 15½, 8 pages, No Color
Subscriptions: Indv. $2
Circulation: (100% controlled), Total-17,000

Worldwide Thrust   *Association*

Publishing Co: Worldwide Evangelization Crusade, 709 Pennsylvania Ave # A, Fort Washington, PA
19034-2910
Personnel: Editor-M. McDermid, Circ. Mgr.-Helen Ramel, Art Dir.-Nancy Keene
Editorial Description: Emphasis on foreign fields of our mission.
General Info: Yr. Est. 1964, Monthly, Trim Size-5¼ x 8, Offset press, 20 pages, 4 Color, Newsprint
Circulation: (100% controlled), Total-8,500

Eastern Orthodox

Copts Newsletter   *Association*

Publishing Co: Sponsor-American Coptic Assn., Copts Newsletter, Box 9119 GIS, Jersey City, NJ
07309-9119; Title Tel # (201) 451-0972
Personnel: Editor-Dr. Monir Dawond, Circ. Mgr.-Rogaai Hanna, Production Mgr.-Foylz Khella, Art
Dir.-Fouod Saamaan
General Info: Yr. Est. 1974, Monthly, Trim Size-8½ x 11, Sheetfed press, 4 pages, No Color
Circulation: Total-4,000

Shoghagat

Publishing Co: St. Gregory Armenian Apostolic Church of Pasadena, 2215 E Colorado Blvd,
Pasadena, CA 91107-3642
Personnel: Editor-Michael Matosian
Editorial Description: Text: Armenian & Eng. Arm. history & religion, church & community news.
General Info: Yr. Est. 1950, Monthly
Circulation: Total-500

Eastern Religions

Aka Cord *Association*

Publishing Co: Huna Research, Inc., 1760 Anna St., Cape Girardeau, MO 63701-4504; Title Tel # (314) 334-3478 Title Fax # (314) 334-3478
Personnel: Publisher-E. Otha Wingo, Editor-Vinson Wingo
Editorial Description: News of Huna activities through the world.
General Info: Yr. Est. 1987, 8x/yr., Trim Size-8½ x 11, Offset press, 4 pages, No Color, Saddle-stitched
Circulation: Total-1,500
Printing Co: Concord Printing Services, 430 Broadway St, Cape Girardeau, MO 63701-5622 Tel # (314) 334-7100

Collaboration

Publishing Co: Sri Avrobindo Association, 2288 Fulton St., Beverley, CA 94704 Fax # (510) 848-8531; Title Tel # (510) 848-1841
Personnel: Editor-Jeanne Korstange, Circ. Mgr.-Julian Lines
Editorial Description: Dedicated to the spiritual vision of a transformed humanity.
General Info: Yr. Est. 1974, Semi-annually, 24 pages, ISSN: 0164-1522, No Color, Newsprint
Subscriptions: Indv. $15, $3/copy
Circulation: Total-750

Huna Work *Consumer, Association*

Publishing Co: Huna Research, Inc., 1760 Anna St., Cape Girardeau, MO 63701-4504; Title Tel # (314) 334-3478 Title Fax # (314) 334-3478
Personnel: Publisher, Editor-Dr. E. Otha Wingo
Editorial Description: Practical methods of personal achievement using Huna techniques. Articles about the philosophy of Huna.
General Info: (Formerly Huna Vistas), Yr. Est. 1948, Quarterly, Trim Size-8½ x 11, Sheetfed press, 24 pages, No Color, Saddle-stitched
Subscriptions: Indv. $25, $5/copy
Circulation: (100% controlled), Total-1,500
Printing Co: Concord Printing Services, 430 Broadway St, Cape Girardeau, MO 63701-5622 Tel # (314) 334-7100

Nexus *Association*

Publishing Co: Sri Avrobindo Association, 2288 Fulton St., Beverley, CA 94704 Fax # (510) 848-8531; Title Tel # (510) 848-1841
General Info: Yr. Est. 1992, Bi-monthly
Subscriptions: Indv. $15
Circulation: Total-750

Vedanta Society of Greater Washington Bulletin

Publishing Co: Vedanta Society of Greater Washington, 7430 Tower St, Falls Church, VA 22046-1935
General Info: Monthly

Way Fourth *Consumer, Association*

Publishing Co: Sponsor-Tayu Order,Inc., Tayu Center, PO Box 11554, Santa Rosa, CA 95406-1554; Title Tel # (707) 829-9579
Personnel: Editor-Stuart Goodnick
Editorial Description: Newsletter for Tayu Center-A Fourth Way spiritual school.
General Info: (Formerly Ganymede), Yr. Est. 1979, Quarterly, Trim Size-7 x 8½, Sheetfed press, 8 pages, Newsprint
Subscriptions: Indv. $13
Circulation: Total-400, Readership-400
Advertising: Inquire for rates.

Episcopal

Cathedral *Association*

Publishing Co: Cathedral of St. John the Divine, 1047 Amsterdam Ave, New York, NY 10025-1702; Title Tel # (212) 316-7400
Editorial Description: Reports on cultural, social, religious, and educational topics that involve the Cathedral of St. John the Divine.
General Info: Yr. Est. 1980, Quarterly, Trim Size-11¾ x 17½, Web press, 12 pages, 2 Color
Subscriptions: Free
Circulation: Total-8,300

Clergy

Publishing Co: Episcopal Conference of the Deaf, PO Box 27459, Philadelphia, PA 19118-0459; Title Tel # (215) 247-1059
Personnel: Editor-Roger Pickering
Editorial Description: Informational for Episcopal clergy involved with ministry to the deaf.
General Info: Bi-monthly, Mimeo press, 4 pages, No Color, Newsprint
Circulation: Total-170
List Rental: List Management Co.: Bernice Bush Co./Springdale Lists, 15052 Springdale St., Huntington Beach, CA 92649-1178 Tel # (714) 891-3344, Fax # (714) 897-0650, Actives: 8,800, $80/M

Deaf Episcopalian, The *Consumer*

Publishing Co: Episcopal Conference of the Deaf, PO Box 27459, Philadelphia, PA 19118-0459; Title Tel # (215) 247-1059
Personnel: Publisher, Editor-Hortense Auerbach, Circ. Mgr.-Arthur Steidemann, Art Dir.-Eugene Orr
Editorial Description: Church newsletter for deaf missions and peopple in Episcpal church.
General Info: Yr. Est. 1927, Bi-monthly, Trim Size-8½ x 11, Sheetfed press, 8 pages
Subscriptions: Indv. $5
Circulation: (100% controlled)
Printing Co: Newsletter Services, Inc., 9700 Philadelphia Court, Lanham, MD 20706 Tel # (301) 731-5200, Fax # (301) 731-5201

Episcopal Expressions

Publishing Co: Sponsor-Episcopal Marriage Encounter, St. Paul's Episcopal Church, 411 Washington St, Pekin, IL 61554-4288; Title Tel # (309) 353-7415
Personnel: Publisher-Lloyd Johnson, Editor, Circ. Mgr.-Jane Johnson
Editorial Description: Contains news of activities of Episcopal Marriage Encounter. Also contains sharings of couples whoe have made Marriage Encounter weekends.
General Info: Quarterly, Sheetfed press, 16 pages, No Color
Circulation: Total-3,400
Printing Co: Creative Laser Print, 511 Court St, Pekin, IL 61554-3347 Tel # (309) 347-7468

Episcopal Peace Fellowship Newsletter *Association*

Publishing Co: Episcopal Peace Fellowship, PO Box 28156, Washington, DC 20038-8156; Title Tel # (202) 543-7168
Personnel: Editor-Patricia M. Scharf, Editor-John Michael Sophos
Editorial Description: Church-oriented peace & justice news.
General Info: Yr. Est. 1939, Quarterly, Trim Size-8½ x 11, Desktop press, 8 pages, 2 Color
Subscriptions: Free With Membership
Circulation: Total-3,000

NOEL News

Publishing Co: National Organization of Episcopolians for Life, 10523 Main St., Fairfax, VA 22030-3310; Title Tel # (703) 591-6635 Title Fax # (703) 385-0415
Personnel: Editor-Kelly O. Young
General Info: Yr. Est. 1983, Bi-monthly, Web press, 16 pages, 2 Color, Newsprint
Subscriptions: Indv. $5, $1/copy
Circulation: Total-23,000
Printing Co: United Lithographic Services, 2818 Fallfax Dr., Falls Church, VA 22042-2804 Tel # (703) 560-5700, Fax # (703) 280-2678

Views & News
See: EDUCATION

Greek Orthodox

Ascension Bulletin

Publishing Co: Greek Orthodox Church of the Ascension, 4700 Lincoln Ave, Oakland, CA 94602-2535; Title Tel # (510) 531-3400
Editorial Description: News and social items pertaining to the church and its members.
General Info: Yr. Est. 1983, Monthly

Desert Voice *Consumer, Association* CPM: $333

Publishing Co: St. Anthony the Great Orthodox Pubs., 3044 N 27th St, Phoenix, AZ 85016-7926; Title Tel # (602) 957-3054
Personnel: Publisher, Editor-Fr. Bessarion, Asst. Ed.-Alex Lester, Circ. Mgr.-Anthony Morse, Production Mgr.-Sean O'Brien, Art Dir.-Eleni Venetos
Editorial Description: A traditional orthodox Christian periodical. Providing articles in Hagiography, Byzantine studies, history, & theology.
General Info: (Formerly Orthodox Southwest), Yr. Est. 1983, Monthly, Trim Size-11 x 17, Web press, 36 pages, 2% ads, 4 Color, Newsprint
Subscriptions: $1/copy
Circulation: (90% controlled), Total-3,000
Advertising: $1,000.

Huguenot

Huguenot Trails *Association*

Publishing Co: The Huguenot Society of Canada, 10 Adelaide St. E., Toronto, ON M5C 1J3 Canada; Title Tel # (416) 361-1685
Personnel: Publisher-Michael Harrison, Editor-M.A. Harrison
Editorial Description: Articles & book reviews concerning Huguenots. Histories of families of Huguenot descent.
General Info: Yr. Est. 1968, Quarterly, Trim Size-7 x 10, Offset press, 16 pages, ISSN: 0441-6910, No Color, Newsprint, Saddle-stitched
Subscriptions: Indv. $20, $5/copy
Circulation: Total-350
Printing Co: McNulty Printing Co., 12 Stewart, Collingwood, ON L9Y 4K1 Canada Tel # (705) 445-5024

Jewish

ADL on the Frontline *Association*

Publishing Co: Anti-Defamation League of B'nai B'rith, 823 U.N. Plaza, New York, NY 10017 Tel # (212) 490-2525 Fax # (212) 867-0779
Personnel: Editor-Jane R. Ornauer
General Info: Yr. Est. 1991, 10x/yr.
Subscriptions: Indv. $12

Action Memo

Publishing Co: Synagogue Council of America, 252 Soundview Ave., White Plains, NY 10606-3800; Title Tel # (212) 686-8670
General Info: Bi-monthly

Agenda in Brief   *Association*

Publishing Co: New Jewish Agenda, PO Box 198, New York, NY 10116-0198; Title Tel # (212) 227-5885
Personnel: Editor-Shelly Weiss
Editorial Description: Reports on New Jewish Agenda activities around the U.S.
General Info: (Formerly Agenda Newsletter), Yr. Est. 1979, Bi-monthly, Trim Size-8½ x 11, Web press, 6 pages, No Color
Subscriptions: Indv. $18

Ammi   *Consumer, Association*

Publishing Co: World Union for Progressive Judaism, 838 5th Ave, New York, NY 10021-7012; Title Tel # (212) 249-0100
Personnel: Publisher-Martin Strelzer, Editor-Alayne Zatulove
Editorial Description: Items concerning Jewish issues & Jewish concerns. Items of the nature to promote, debate & discussion.
General Info: Quarterly, Letrpr. press, 24 pages, 2 Color, Coated

Amudim   *Consumer*

Publishing Co: Univ. of Florida Jewish Studies Ctr., 441 Little Hall, PO Box 118165, Gainesville, FL 32611; Title Tel # (904) 392-9247 Title Fax # (904) 392-5378
Personnel: Publisher-Warren Bargad, Editor-Michael Cohen
Editorial Description: Covers Jewish studies programs & course offerings at Univ. of Florida.
General Info: Yr. Est. 1986, Annually, Letrpr. press, 8 pages
Subscriptions: Free
Circulation: Total-6,500
Printing Co: Storter-Childs Printing, 1540 NE Waldo Rd, Gainesville, FL 32641-4629 Tel # (904) 376-2658

Ani V'atah   *Association*

Publishing Co: North American Federation of Temple Youth, 838 5th Ave, New York, NY 10021-7012; Title Tel # (212) 249-0100
Personnel: Publisher-Allan Smith, Editor, Circ. Mgr.-Rabbi Ramie Arian, Art Dir.-Rayleen Buys
Editorial Description: North American Reform Synagogue youth programming and organizational news.
General Info: (Formerly Visions), Yr. Est. 1982, 3x/yr., Trim Size-8½ x 11, Offset press, 12 pages, 2 Color
Subscriptions: Indv. $1
Circulation: (100% controlled), Total-28,000

Artifacts
See: MUSEUM PUBLICATIONS

Batnua
See: INTERNATIONAL AFFAIRS

Bulletin   *Consumer*

Publishing Co: Susan & David Wilstein Inst. of Jewish Policy, University of Judaism, 15600 Mulholland Dr., Los Angeles, CA 90077; Title Tel # (213) 879-4114 Title Fax # (213) 476-9777
Personnel: Publisher-David M. Gordis, Assoc. Publ.-Yoav Ben-Horin, Publications Director-Dorit Gary

CMJS Centerpieces   *Consumer, Association*

Publishing Co: Center for Modern Jewish Studies, South Street, Waltham, MA 02254-9110; Title Tel # (617) 736-2060
Personnel: Editor-Sylvia Fishman, Publisher, Circ. Mgr., Production Mgr.-L. Sternberg
Editorial Description: Annual newsletter covering recent research in contemporary American Jewish life.
General Info: Annually, Trim Size-8½ x 11, 8 pages, ISSN: 0887-1639, 2 Color, Newsprint
Circulation: (100% controlled)

Canadian Jewish Congress, Intercom, Newsletter

Publishing Co: Canadian Jewish Congress, 1590 Ave. Dr. Penfield, Montreal, PQ H3G 1C5 Canada Tel # (514) 931-7531 Fax # (514) 931-0548; Title Tel # (514) 391-7531 Title Fax # (514) 391-0548
General Info: Quarterly
Circulation: (100% controlled), Total-1,500

Canadian Zionist
See: POLITICS

Cantorial - Congregational Relationships

Publishing Co: American Conference of Cantors, 170 W. 74th St., New York, NY 10023-2350 Fax # (212) 874-3527; Title Tel # (212) 874-4762
General Info: Yr. Est. 1990
Subscriptions: $10/copy

Cantors Voice

Publishing Co: Cantors Assembly of America, 3080 Broadway Rm 613, New York, NY 10027-4650; Title Tel # (212) 678-8834
General Info: Bi-monthly

Chai/Impact Newsletter

Publishing Co: Religious Action Ctr. -Union of American Hebrew Congregation, 2027 Massachusetts Ave., NW, Washington, DC 20036-1029; Title Tel # (202) 387-2800 Title Fax # (202) 667-9070
General Info: 30x/yr.
Subscriptions: Indv. $40

Community Advocate
See: PUBLIC MANAGEMENT & PLANNING

Confrontation
See: LAW

Daily News Bulletin

Publishing Co: Jewish Telegraphic Agency, Inc., 330 7th Ave., 11th Fl., New York, NY 10001-5010; Title Tel # (212) 643-1890 Title Fax # (212) 643-8498
Personnel: Publisher-Mark Seal, Editor in Chief-Philip Sanderson, Editor-David Mulcahy
Editorial Description: Covers Jewish news throughout the world.
General Info: Yr. Est. 1917, Daily, Trim Size-8½ x 14, Sheetfed press, 4 pages, No Color, Newsprint
Subscriptions: Indv. $295, Inst. $750, Can. $325, For. $455
Circulation: Total-2,500

Dallas Memorial Center for Holocaust Studies Newsletter
See: HISTORY

Dateline   *Consumer*

Publishing Co: World Jewish Congress, 501 Madison Ave Fl 17, New York, NY 10022-5602 Tel # (212) 753-5770; Title Tel # (212) 755-5770
General Info: Monthly

Dorot
See: GENEALOGY

Gesher

Publishing Co: Yeshiva University Student Organization, 185th St. & Amsterdam Ave., New York, NY 10033
Editorial Description: Text in English and Hebrew.
General Info: Annually

G'vanim   *Consumer, Association*

Publishing Co: Betj Chayim Chadashim, 6000 W Pico Blvd, Los Angeles, CA 90035-2625; Title Tel # (213) 931-7023
Personnel: Editor-Janet Marder
Editorial Description: Published by temple serving gay & lesbian Jewish community.
General Info: Monthly

Ha-Yonah

Publishing Co: Congregation Ahavat Shalom, PO Box 14392, San Francisco, CA 94114-0392; Title Tel # (415) 621-1020
General Info: Monthly

Hadassah Update
See: SOCIAL SERVICES & WELFARE

Hamizrachi

Publishing Co: Religious Zionists of America, 25 W. 26th St., New York, NY 10010-1077

Hatsofe
See: CLUBS

Herzl Institute Bulletin   *Association*

Publishing Co: Theodor Herzl Foundation, 110 E. 59Th. St., New York, NY 10022 Tel # (212) 339-6020; Title Tel # (212) 339-6000
Personnel: Editor-Ida Reich, Circ. Mgr.-Sidney Rosenfeld, Art Dir.-Philip Gutride
Editorial Description: Comtemporary Jewish scene, Jewish Zionists heritage.
General Info: Yr. Est. 1964, Bi-weekly, Trim Size-7 x 10, Offset press, 8 pages, Color
Subscriptions: Indv. $8
Circulation: Total-3,500

Highlights

Publishing Co: Synagogue Council of America, 252 Soundview Ave., White Plains, NY 10606-3800; Title Tel # (212) 686-8670
General Info: Bi-monthly

Highlights
See: CLUBS

Hillel Gate

Publishing Co: B'nai B'rith Hillel Foundation At Brooklyn College, 2901 Campus Rd, Brooklyn, NY 11210-2153; Title Tel # (718) 859-1151
Personnel: Editor-Paul Appelbaum
General Info: Yr. Est. 1969, Monthly, ISSN: 0018-1862
Subscriptions: Indv. $2
Circulation: Total-5,000
Advertising: Inquire for rates.

Holocaust Project/1990
See: HISTORY

In Brief

Publishing Co: American Jewish Congress Task Force on Nuclear Disarmament, 1 Lincoln Plz., #310, Boston, MA 02111-2671; Title Tel # (617) 330-9630
Personnel: Editor-Sheila Decter
General Info: Yr. Est. 1982, Bi-monthly
Subscriptions: Indv. $6

JDC World
See: SOCIAL SERVICES & WELFARE

JTA Community News
Reporter

Publishing Co: Jewish Telegraphic Agency, Inc., 330 7th Ave., 11th Fl., New York, NY 10001-5010 Fax # (212) 643-8498; Title Tel # (212) 643-1890
General Info: Weekly, Sheetfed press
Subscriptions: Indv. $100, Can. $115, For. $130
Circulation: Total-3,200

JTA Weekly News Digest
See: INTERNATIONAL AFFAIRS

JWB Personnel Reporter
See: EMPLOYMENT

J.W.V.A. Bulletin
See: VETERANS

Jewish Civic Press

Publishing Co: Jewish Civic Press, 924 Valmont St, New Orleans, LA 70115-3000; Title Tel # (504) 895-8784 Title Fax # (504) 895-8785
Personnel: Publisher, Editor-Abner Tritt, Adv. Dir.-Jim Klug, Production Mgr., Art Dir.-Sandra Alciatore
Editorial Description: Jewish content. Articles about and that interest jewish readers.
General Info: Yr. Est. 1965, Bi-weekly, Trim Size-11½ x 14, Web press, 48 pages, 40% ads
Subscriptions: Indv. $10, $1/copy
Circulation: (100% controlled), Total-32,470
Advertising: Inquire for rates. Accepts Inserts.
Printing Co: Roberson Adv., 3010 Lausat St, Metairie, LA 70001-5924 Tel # (504) 832-1481

Jewish Cultural News *Association*

Publishing Co: Natl. Foundation for Jewish Culture, 330 Seventh Ave., 21st Fl., New York, NY 10001-5010 Fax # (212) 629-0508; Title Tel # (212) 629-0500
Personnel: Editor-Abraham Atik, Art Dir.-Stewart Kampel
Editorial Description: Items of Jewish cultural content.
General Info: Yr. Est. 1974, Quarterly, 6 pages, 2 Color
Circulation: (100% controlled), Total-12,000

Jewish Educators Assembly
Yearbook *Scholarly, Association*

Publishing Co: Jewish Educators Assembly, 10606 Queens Blvd, Flushing, NY 11375-4248; Title Tel # (718) 268-9452 Title Fax # (718) 520-4369
Personnel: Publisher-Marr Silk, Editor-Edward Frankel
Editorial Description: Proceedings of convention and articles of interest to Jewish educators.
General Info: Yr. Est. 1962, Annually, Trim Size-6 x 9, 120 pages, No Color
Subscriptions: Free With Membership
Circulation: Total-1,000

Jewish Gaily Forward, The

Publishing Co: Sponsor-Union of American Hebrew Congregation, Congregation Shaar Zahav, 220 Danvers at Caselli, San Francisco, CA 94114; Title Tel # (415) 861-6932 Title Fax # (415) 861-6081
Personnel: Editorial Coord.-Batya Kalis
Editorial Description: News pretaining to the progress synagogue with outreach to lesbian & gay community.
General Info: Yr. Est. 1977, 11x/yr., Trim Size-8½ x 11, Offset press, 14 pages
Subscriptions: Indv. $18, Inst. $18, Free With Membership
Circulation: Total-900, Readership-900
Advertising: Accepts Inserts.
Printing Co: Genesis Printing & Graphics, 650 Fifth St., Suite 503, San Francisco, CA 94107 Tel # (415) 543-6586, Fax # (415) 543-2131

Jewish Labor Committee Review
See: LABOR

Jewish Radical
See: POLITICS

Jewish Ties

Publishing Co: Lewis & Clark Research, 6040 A. Six Forks Rd., Suite 112, Raleigh, NC 27609; Title Tel # (919) 676-2036 Title Fax # (919) 846-3652
Personnel: Editor-Doreen Clark
General Info: Yr. Est. 1989, Bi-monthly
Subscriptions: Indv. $19

Jewish Vegetarians
Newsletter *Consumer, Association*

Publishing Co: Jewish Vegetarians of N. America, 6938 Reliance Rd, Federalsburg, MD 21632-2722; Title Tel # (410) 754-5550
Personnel: Editor, Food Editor-Eva Mossman, Circ. Mgr., Art Dir.-Israel Mossman
Editorial Description: All aspects of vegetarianism within the Jewish tradition including ecology, health, world hunger, & recipes & animal rights.
General Info: Yr. Est. 1983, Quarterly, Trim Size-8½ x 11, Desktop press, 16 pages, ISSN: 0883-1904, No Color, Saddle-stitched
Subscriptions: Indv. $12, Can. $14, For. $14, Free To Qualified Recipient
Circulation: Total-1,000
Advertising: Accepts Inserts.
List Rental: Actives: $60/M

Kesher *Association*

Publishing Co: Association of Jewish Center Professionals, 15 E 26th St Ste 1430, New York, NY 10010-1505; Title Tel # (216) 382-4000
Personnel: Editor-Mary Ellen Saltzman
General Info: Yr. Est. 1975, 5x/yr., Trim Size-8½ x 11, Offset press, 8 pages
Circulation: (100% controlled), Total-1,000

Kol Bana'Yikh
See: EDUCATION

Koleinv

Publishing Co: American Conference of Cantors, 170 W. 74th St., New York, NY 10023-2350 Fax # (212) 874-3527; Title Tel # (212) 874-4762
General Info: Quarterly

Lifeline *Business, Consumer*

Publishing Co: North American Confernece on Ethiopian Jewry, 165 E 56th St, New York, NY 10022-2709; Title Tel # (212) 752-6340 Title Fax # (212) 980-5294
Editorial Description: Covers news on Ethiopian Jewry.
General Info: Quarterly

Lifelines
See: POLITICS

Lubavitch International

Publishing Co: Lubavitch News Svce., 770 Eastern Pky, Brooklyn, NY 11213-3409
Personnel: Editor-Baila Olidort
General Info: Quarterly

Maimonides Society Bulletin *Association*

Publishing Co: Center for Judiac Studies, Univ. of Denver, Denver, CO 80223-1900; Title Tel # (303) 871-3020
Personnel: Editor-Dr. Michael B. Allen
General Info: Semi-annually, 6 pages

Menorah *Association*

Publishing Co: Virginia Commonwealth Univ. Judaic Studies, Judaic Studies Program, Richmond, VA 23284; Title Tel # (804) 358-6757
Personnel: Editor-Jack Spiro
Editorial Description: Review essays on Judaica & original poetry on Jewish themes.
General Info: Yr. Est. 1984, Letrpr. press, 8 pages, 2 Color, Newsprint
Circulation: Total-4,800
List Rental: Rents Lists

Menorah: Sparks of
Jewish Renewal *Consumer*

Publishing Co: Public Resource Center, 1747 Connecticut Ave NW, Washington, DC 20009-1142; Title Tel # (202) 483-7902
Personnel: Editor-Arthur Waskow, Circ. Mgr.-Harry Hochman
Editorial Description: Handbook of vital Jewish life-practice including holidays. Political and personal issues, energy, food, family life, friendship, etc.
General Info: Yr. Est. 1979, Monthly, Trim Size-8 x 11, Web press, 6 pages, No Color
Subscriptions: Indv. $24, $1/copy
Circulation: Total-4,000
Advertising: Inquire for rates.

Mishpochah Message *Association*

Publishing Co: Jews for Jesus, PO Box 424885, San Francisco, CA 94142-4885; Title Tel # (415) 864-2600
Personnel: Editor-Ruth Rosen
Editorial Description: Affirms the faith and heritage of Jewish people who believe in Jesus with articles highlighting subjects of interest.
General Info: Yr. Est. 1983, Quarterly, Trim Size-8½ x 11, 7 pages, 2 Color, Newsprint
Circulation: Total-25,000

Morim Bulletin
See: EDUCATION

NAAM Letter

Publishing Co: North America Aliya Movement, 110 E 59th St Frnt 3, New York, NY 10022-1304; Title Tel # (212) 752-0600
General Info: Quarterly

NATE News
Business

Publishing Co: Natl. Assn. of Temple Educators, 707 Summerly Dr, Nashville, TN 37209-4218; Title Tel # (615) 352-0322 Title Fax # (615) 356-9285

Personnel: Editor-Richard Morin

Editorial Description: Jewish educational information plus conference news for professional Reform educators.

General Info: Yr. Est. 1957, Bi-monthly, Desktop press, 10 pages, No Color, Coated, Saddle-stitched

Acquistions: Publication Bought

Circulation: Total-900

Advertising: Inquire for rates.

National Archives Newsletter

Publishing Co: Canadian Jewish Congress, 1590 Ave. Dr. Penfield, Montreal, PQ H3G 1C5 Canada; Title Tel # (514) 931-7531 Title Fax # (514) 931-0548

Personnel: Editor-Janice Rosen

Editorial Description: Information on activities & materials in CJC Archives.

General Info: Yr. Est. 1984, Semi-annually, Trim Size-8½ x 11, 7 pages, ISSN: 0824-8907, No Color, Perfect bound

Subscriptions: Free

Circulation: Total-800

National Conference on Soviet Jewry-Newsbreak
See: INTERNATIONAL AFFAIRS

National Jewish Arts Newsletter
See: ART & SCULPTURE

Neshama

Publishing Co: Kfari Center, Inc., RFD 1, Box 256, Cabot, VT 05647-9801

General Info: Quarterly

Never Again
See: POLITICS

New Horizons in Community Services
See: WOMEN'S

NewMenorah

Publishing Co: P'Nai Or Religious Fellowship, 7318 Germantown Ave., Philadelphia, PA 19119-1793 Tel # (215) 242-1074; Title Tel # (215) 242-4074

Personnel: Publisher-Jeff Roth, Editor-Shana Margolin, Circ. Mgr., Production Mgr., Promotion Dir.-Floyd Platton

Editorial Description: Journal of Jewish Renewal.

General Info: (Formerly Menorah), Yr. Est. 1979, Quarterly, Trim Size-8½ x 11, Desktop press, 16 pages, ISSN: 0883-0215, No Color, Newsprint

Subscriptions: Indv. $18, $5/copy

Acquistions: Publication Bought

Circulation: Total-2,700

List Rental: Actives: $50/M

Printing Co: R'Mae Inc., 127 Pike Cir, Huntingdon Valley, PA 19006-1614 Tel # (215) 322-9788

Newsletter
Business, Association

Publishing Co: America-Israel Cultural Foundation, 41 E 42nd St Rm 608, New York, NY 10017-5201; Title Tel # (212) 557-1600 Title Fax # (212) 557-1611

Personnel: Editor-Kathleen Hat

Editorial Description: Focuses on activities in the U.S. and Israel of the Foundation.

General Info: (Formerly Hadashot), Quarterly, Trim Size-6½ x 10½, 12 pages

Subscriptions: Free With Membership

Circulation: Total-4,000

Newsletter

Publishing Co: American Jewish Committee, 165 E 56th St, New York, NY 10022-2709 Tel # (212) 571-4000; Title Tel # (212) 751-4000 Title Fax # (212) 750-0326

Editorial Description: News and developments of interest to American Jews.

General Info: Semi-annually

Subscriptions: Indv. $10

Newsletter of the Association for Social Scientific Study of Jewry
See: SOCIOLOGY

Notes for Now
See: WOMEN'S

ORT Bulletin
See: SOCIAL SERVICES & WELFARE

On Campus
Association

Publishing Co: Hillel: the Foundation for Jewish Campus Life, 1640 Rhode Island Ave NW, Washington, DC 20036 Title # (202) 857-6560 Fax # (202) 296-6693; Title Tel # (202) 857-6556 Title Fax # (202) 857-6693

Personnel: Editor-Ruth Fredman Cernea, PhD

Editorial Description: News and events of Jewish campus life throughout the world for Hillel professional staff, Jewish campus professionals and lay leaders.

General Info: (Formerly Igeret Newsletter), 4x/yr., Trim Size-8½ x 11, Desktop press, 12 pages, 2 Color

Subscriptions: Free To Qualified Recipient

Circulation: (66% controlled), Total-1,500

List Rental: Rents Lists

Options, The Jewish Resources Newsletter
Association

Publishing Co: Options Publishing Co., PO Box 311, Wayne, NJ 07474-0311; Title Tel # (201) 694-2327

Personnel: Publisher, Editor, Adv. Dir.-Betty J. Singer

Editorial Description: A clearinghouse of resources, organizations, and opportunities within the American Jewish community.

General Info: (Formerly Options: The Jewish Resources Letter), Yr. Est. 1974, Monthly, Offset press, 4 pages, ISSN: 0362-2770, No Color

Subscriptions: Indv. $21, Can. $23, For. $24, $2/copy

Ottawa Jewish Bulletin
Scholarly

Publishing Co: Jewish Community Council of Ottawa, 151 Chapel St., Ottawa, ON K1N 7Y2 Canada; Title Tel # (613) 789-7306 Title Fax # (613) 789-4593

Personnel: Editor-Myra Aronson, Product Mgr.-Brenda Vanvliet, Adv. Dir.-Alyce Baker

General Info: (Formerly Ottawa Jewish Bulletin and Review), Yr. Est. 1974, Bi-weekly, Trim Size-9.75 x 14.75, Web press, 28 pages, Color, Newsprint, Other

Subscriptions: Indv. $4, Can. $25, For. $32

Circulation: Total-4,000

Printing Co: Performance Printing, 65 Lorne Street, Smith Falls, ON K7A4TI Canada Tel # (613) 236-1121, Fax # (613) 283-7480

Our Way - NCSY
See: DEAF

PS: Intelligent Guide to Jewish Affairs
See: POLITICS

Perspective

Publishing Co: Rabbinical Alliance of America, 3 W. 16th St. 4th Fl., New York, NY 10011-6363; Title Tel # (212) 242-6420

General Info: Semi-annually

Philip and Muriel Berman Center for Jewish Studies Newsletter

Publishing Co: Philip and Muriel Berman Center for Jewish Studies, Lehigh Univ., Maginnes Hall #9, Bethlehem, PA 18015; Title Tel # (215) 758-3000

Personnel: Editor-Lawrence Filberstein

General Info: (Formerly Lehigh Valley Center for Jewish Studies Newsletter)

Post-Soviet Jewry Report
See: INTERNATIONAL AFFAIRS

Pumbedissa
Consumer

Publishing Co: Pumbedissa, PO Box 117, Seneca Rocks, WV 26884-0117

Editorial Description: Information and teachings of and for Rabbis.

General Info: Bi-monthly, Trim Size-8½ x 11, 12 pages, No Color

Recent Additions to the Library
See: LIBRARY

Research Notes from CUJS

Publishing Co: Center for Modern Jewish Studies, South Street, Waltham, MA 02254-9110; Title Tel # (617) 736-2060 Title Fax # (617) 736-2070

Personnel: Editor-Syliva Barack Fishman, Publisher, Circ. Mgr., Production Mgr.-L. Sternberg

Editorial Description: Individual research topics in contemporary American Jewish life.

General Info: Bi-monthly, ISSN: 0892-4104

Response
See: PHILOSOPHY

Sephardic Highlights

Publishing Co: American Sephardic Federation, 305 7th Ave., 11th Fl., New York, NY 10001; Title Tel # (212) 308-3455

Personnel: Editor-Devora Lang Mitrany

Editorial Description: Official publication of the american Sephardi Federation, with articles of interest to American Sephardic Jews and Judaic scholars. Listings of events, book and tapes.

General Info: Monthly, Trim Size-8½ x 11, Sheetfed press, 6 pages, No Color, Matte

Subscriptions: Inst. $500

Circulation: Total-14,000

Advertising: Inquire for rates. Accepts Inserts.

Printing Co: Express Printing, 627 Greenwich St, New York, NY 10014-3386 Tel # (212) 633-2828

Shalom — *Consumer*

Publishing Co: Shoresh USA/Inc., P.O. Box 551593, Jacksonville, FL 32255-1593
Tel # (904) 730-9751 Fax # (904) 730-3197
Editorial Description: A newsletter which seeks to awaken the worldwide church to its jewish roots through Israel study tours and teaching programs, and to enable the church to proclaim the gospel to the Jews first and also to the Gentiles.
General Info: Quarterly, Trim Size-8.5 x 11, Other press, 6 pages, 2 Color, Newsprint, Other

Shalom-Jewish Peace Newsletter — *Association*

Publishing Co: Jewish Peace Fellowship, PO Box 271, Nyack, NY 10960-0271;
Title Tel # (914) 358-4601 Title Fax # (914) 358-4924
Personnel: Editor-Murray Polner
Editorial Description: Judaism and peace, disarmament, Middle East.
General Info: (Formerly Shalom), Yr. Est. 1967, Quarterly, Trim Size-8½ x 11, Offset press, 8 pages, No Color
Subscriptions: Indv. $5
Circulation: Total-3,500

Shem Tov
See: GENEALOGY

Shema Newsletter

Publishing Co: Sponsor-Assn. of Jewish Parents of the Deaf, Natl. Conference of Synagogue Youth, 333 7th Ave, 18th Floor, New York, NY 10001-5004; Title Tel # (212) 244-2011
Personnel: Editor-Triona Bin Nun
Editorial Description: Newsletter for Jewish parents of hearing impaired children.
General Info: Quarterly, Mimeo press, 16 pages, 3% ads, 2 Color
Subscriptions: Indv. $5
Circulation: Total-400

Society for the Advancement of Judaism Bulletin

Publishing Co: Society for the Advancement of Judaism, 15 W 86th St, New York, NY 10024-3601; Title Tel # (212) 724-7146
Editorial Description: A Conservative & Reconstructionist Synagogue founded by Rabbi Mordecai M. Kaplan which blends traditional & modern. The SAJ offers a unique afternoon religious school for children from kindergarten through high school & a complet adult education program.
General Info: Yr. Est. 1922, Monthly

Special Interest Report — *Association*

Publishing Co: American Council for Judaism, PO Box 9009, Alexandria, VA 22304-0009; Title Tel # (703) 836-2546
Personnel: Editor-Alan Brownfeld
Editorial Description: Digest of news for U.S. Jews consonant with religious and democratic ideals.
General Info: Yr. Est. 1968, Monthly, Trim Size-8½ x 14, 2 pages

Straightalk — *Association*

Publishing Co: Foundation for Jewish Studies, 1531 S Negley Ave, Pittsburgh, PA 15217-1419
Tel # (412) 521-1959 Fax # (412) 521-2903
Personnel: Publisher, Editor-Ronald Brauner, Editorial Asst.-Darcy Silvers
Editorial Description: Classical and current topics of interest in Jewish ethics, history, religion.
General Info: Yr. Est. 1990, Quarterly, 8 pages, ISSN: 1061-2858
Subscriptions: Indv. $18, $5/copy
Circulation: Total-5,000, Readership-5,000
List Rental: List Management Co.: R.C. Direct, Inc., 200 S Water St, Milwaukee, WI 53204-1450
Tel # (414) 271-4244, Actives: 10,000, $75/M

Synagogue Council of America Analysis

Publishing Co: Synagogue Council of America, 252 Soundview Ave., White Plains, NY 10606-3800; Title Tel # (212) 686-8670
General Info: Semi-monthly

Synagogue School

Publishing Co: United Synagogue of Conservative Judaism, 155 5th Ave, New York, NY 10010-6811
Fax # (212) 353-9439; Title Tel # (212) 533-7800

Tarbuth Tidings

Publishing Co: Tarbuth Foundation, 129 W 67th St, New York, NY 10023-5917;
Title Tel # (212) 874-7837
Personnel: Editor-Leonard Fink
General Info: Quarterly

Textures

Publishing Co: Hadassah, 50 W 58th St, New York, NY 10019-2590; Title Tel # (212) 355-7900
Personnel: Editor-Carol Diament
Editorial Description: A discovery of Jewish thought, daily life in Israel; discusses Hebrew and Biblical texts, women's issues.
General Info: Yr. Est. 1982, Semi-annually, 8 pages
Subscriptions: Indv. $3
Circulation: Total-4,500

Torah Aura Newsletter — *Consumer*

Publishing Co: Torah Aura Productions, 4423 Fruitland Ave, Los Angeles, CA 90058-3238
Editorial Description: Issues and ideas for education of Jewish principles.
General Info: Quarterly, Trim Size-8½ x 11, No Color

Torchlight

Publishing Co: Federation of Jewish Men's Clubs, 475 Riverside Dr., New York, NY 10115-0122;
Title Tel # (212) 749-8100
Personnel: Circ. Mgr.-Al Kaufman
Editorial Description: Activities report.
General Info: (Formerly Torch), Quarterly, 12 pages, 2 Color
Circulation: Total-35,000

Trends

Publishing Co: Jewish Education Service of N. Amer., Inc., 730 Braoday, 2nd Fl., New York, NY 10003-9511; Title Tel # (212) 529-2000
General Info: Quarterly

UCSJ Quarterly Report

Publishing Co: Union of Councils for Soviet Jews, 1819 H St NW Ste 230, Washington, DC 20006-3603; Title Tel # (202) 775-9770
General Info: Quarterly
Circulation: Total-65,000

U.S. Holocaust Memorial Museum Campaign News
See: CIVIL RIGHTS

Viewpoints
See: SOCIAL SERVICES & WELFARE

Voice

Publishing Co: Jewish Fed. Camden County, 2395 Marlton Pike W, Cherry Hill, NJ 08002-3422
Personnel: Editor-Bernard Dubin
General Info: Yr. Est. 1941, Semi-monthly

WJC Report — *Consumer*

Publishing Co: World Jewish Congress, 501 Madison Ave Fl 17, New York, NY 10022-5602
Tel # (212) 753-5770; Title Tel # (212) 755-5770 Title Fax # (212) 755-5883
General Info: Bi-monthly
List Rental: Actives: $65/M

Washington Newsletter
See: GOVERNMENT

YIVO News — *Consumer, Association*

Publishing Co: YIVO Institute for Jewish Research, 555 W. 57th St., Ste. 1100, New York, NY 10019-2925; Title Tel # (212) 246-6080 Title Fax # (212) 292-1892
Personnel: Editor-Andrea Sherman
Editorial Description: Yiddish-English newsletter of YIVO's activities.
General Info: (Formerly News of the YIVO), Yr. Est. 1943, 2x/yr., ISSN: 0028-9302
Subscriptions: Indv. $50
Circulation: Total-9,000

Yiddish of Greater Washington Newsletter
See: LITERATURE & LINGUISTICS

Lutheran

Advance
See: COLLEGE ALUMNI

Beacon

Publishing Co: Lutheran Collegiate Bible Inst, Box 459, Outlook, SK S0L 2N0 Canada;
Title Tel # (306) 867-8971
Personnel: Editor-Kyle Doig
Editorial Description: Christian education especially as related to private church-owned schools.
General Info: Yr. Est. 1953, Bi-monthly, Offset press, 4 pages, No Color
Circulation: Total-4,000

Concord

Publishing Co: Lutherans Concerned/N. America, 12602 Park St, Cerritos, CA 90703-1142

Deaf Lutheran — *Consumer, Association*

Publishing Co: Intl. Lutheran Deaf Assn., 1004 Cherrywood Dr, Cedar Falls, IA 50613-1614
General Info: Yr. Est. 1909, Bi-monthly, 8 pages
Subscriptions: Indv. $6
Circulation: Total-12,000

Diaconalogue   *Association*

Publishing Co: Lutheran Deaconess Association, Center for Diaconal Ministry, 1304 Laporte Ave., Valparaiso, IN 46383; Title Tel # (219) 464-0909
Personnel: Editor-Diane Greve
Editorial Description: Supports daily diaconal ministry of the laity.
General Info: Yr. Est. 1984, Quarterly, 4 pages
Subscriptions: Indv. $5
Circulation: Total-1,000

Draudzes Vestis   *Association*

Publishing Co: Peace Latvian Lutheran Church, 83 Main St., Ottawa, ON K1S 1B5 Canada; Title Tel # (613) 230-4085
Editorial Description: Church life, Latvian community life.
General Info: Yr. Est. 1952, Bi-monthly, Trim Size-7 x 8½, Desktop press, 20 pages, No Color
Subscriptions: Indv. $15, $2/copy
Circulation: Total-200
Advertising: Inquire for rates.

Faith and Fellowship   *Association*

Publishing Co: Lutheran Brethren Publ Co., 704 W Vernon Ave # 655, Fergus Falls, MN 56537-2633; Title Tel # (218) 736-7357
Personnel: Editor-Rev. David Rinden, Circ. Mgr.-Mel Frank
Editorial Description: Official organ of the church of the Lutheran Bretheren.
General Info: Yr. Est. 1933, Bi-weekly, Trim Size-8¹/₁₆ x 10⅜, Sheetfed press, 16 pages, 2 Color, Newsprint
Subscriptions: Indv. $10, Can. $11, For. $11, $1/copy
Circulation: Total-5,300

Forum Letter   *Consumer*

Publishing Co: American Lutheran Publicity Bureau, PO Box 327, Delhi, NY 13753-0327; Title Tel # (607) 746-7511
Personnel: Editor-Russell Saltzman, Circ. Mgr.-Donna Roche, Adv. Dir.-Martin Christianson
General Info: Yr. Est. 1972, Monthly, Trim Size-8½ x 11, 8 pages, ISSN: 0046-4732, No Color
Subscriptions: Indv. $23, Inst. $25, Can. $26, For. $30, $2/copy
Circulation: Total-3,500
Advertising: Accepts Inserts.
List Rental: Actives: 3,500, $100/M, Expires: 2,200, $75/M
Printing Co: Stoyles Graphic Publishing Co., 204 N. 2nd Ave. W., Lake Mills, IA 50450-1223 Tel # (515) 424-4341

Gettysburg Seminary Bulletin
See: COLLEGE STUDENT

Historical Footnotes   *Association*

Publishing Co: Concordia Historical Institute, 801 De Mun Ave., St. Louis, MO 63105-3168 Fax # (314) 721-5902 Parent Co.-Lutheran Church Missouri Synod, Saint Louis; Title Tel # (314) 721-5934
Personnel: Editor-Marvin A. Huggins
Editorial Description: News, staff notes, announcements, meeting information. Institute meetings, history nuggets.
General Info: Yr. Est. 1955, Quarterly, Trim Size-8½ x 11, Mimeo press, 4 pages, ISSN: 0360-9030, No Color, Other
Subscriptions: Free With Membership
Circulation: Total-1,600

Kirkebaldet Church
Newsletter   *Consumer, Association*

Publishing Co: Danish Lutheran Church, 6010 Kincaid St., Burnaby, BC V5G 4N3 Canada; Title Tel # (604) 298-6112
Personnel: Editor-Kai Glud, Adv. Dir.-Anne Pagh
Editorial Description: Spiritual and practical magazine for danes settled in British Columbia.
General Info: Yr. Est. 1935, Monthly, Offset press, 16 pages, No Color
Subscriptions: Indv. $10, $1/copy
Circulation: Total-1,300
Advertising: Inquire for rates.

LYF Lines

Publishing Co: Lutheran Church Missouri Synod, Bd for Youth Services, 1333 S Kirkwood Rd, Saint Louis, MO 63122-7226; Title Tel # (314) 965-9000
Personnel: Publisher, Editor, Circ. Mgr., Production Mgr., Art Dir.-Terry Dittmer
Editorial Description: Resource material for Luteran Youth Groups.
General Info: (Formerly Supports/LYF Supports), Yr. Est. 1979, Trim Size-8½ x 11, Desktop press, 8 pages, Color, Newsprint, Saddle-stitched
Circulation: Total-6,000
Printing Co: LCMS Printshop, 1333 S Kirkwood Rd, Saint Louis, MO 63122-7226 Tel # (314) 965-9000

Lifedate
See: SOCIAL SERVICES & WELFARE

Lutheran Braille Workers
Newsletter

Publishing Co: Lutheran Braille Workers, Inc., PO Box 5000, Yucaipa, CA 92399-1450; Title Tel # (714) 795-8977
Personnel: Editor-LeRoy Delafosse
Editorial Description: Produces Braille in 40 languages, large print in 15 languages. All religious material given free upon request.
General Info: Yr. Est. 1954, Quarterly, Trim Size-8½ x 11, 2 pages
Circulation: Total-32,000

Lutheran Deaconess
Association Newsletter   *Association*

Publishing Co: Lutheran Deaconess Association, Center for Diaconal Ministry, 1304 Laporte Ave., Valparaiso, IN 46383; Title Tel # (219) 464-0909
Personnel: Editor-E. Louise Williams
General Info: Yr. Est. 1919, Semi-annually, 4 pages, No Color, Newsprint
Circulation: Total-20,000
Printing Co: Home Mountain Publishing, 558 Locust St, Valparaiso, IN 46383-6433 Tel # (219) 462-6601

Lutheran Vanguard   *Consumer, Association*

Publishing Co: Lutheran Vanguard, Inc., 5225 N 20th St, Phoenix, AZ 85016-3319; Title Tel # (602) 957-2922
Personnel: Mng. Editor-Marion R. Winkler
General Info: Yr. Est. 1991, Monthly, Trim Size-8½ x 11, Offset press, 4 pages
Subscriptions: Indv. $10
Circulation: Total-4,000

On the Edge   *Association*

Publishing Co: Lutheran Social Services, 27 Park Pl., New York, NY 10007-2502; Title Tel # (212) 406-9110
Personnel: Editor-Lloyd Berg
Editorial Description: News and notes on Christian Social Mission from Lutheran Social Services.
General Info: Yr. Est. 1978, Quarterly, Trim Size-8½ x 11, Web press, 4 pages, No Color
Subscriptions: Free
Circulation: Total-16,000
Printing Co: Hessey Printing, Inc., 424 Lafayette St # 100226, Nashville, TN 37203-4255 Tel # (615) 244-7180, Fax # (615) 255-6911

Regional Archivist
See: HISTORY

Reporter

Publishing Co: Concordia Publishing House, 3558 S. Jefferson Ave., St. Louis, MO 63118-3968 Tel # (314) 268-1091 Fax # (314) 268-1329; Title Tel # (314) 965-9000
Personnel: Publisher-Paul Devantier, Editor-David Mahsman
Editorial Description: To provide information and resources for lay and professional leaders of congregations belonging to the Lutheran Church-Missouri Synod.
General Info: (Formerly Advance), Yr. Est. 1954, Monthly, Trim Size-8⅛ x 10¾, Sheetfed press, 8 pages, ISSN: 0360-7119, No Color
Subscriptions: Indv. $10
Circulation: (100% controlled), Total-66,000

SPC Newsletter

Publishing Co: Lutheran Church Missouri Synod, 1333 S Kirkwood Rd, Saint Louis, MO 63122-7295; Title Tel # (314) 965-9917
Personnel: Editor-Richard Tetzloff, Art Dir.-Rosemary Defiglio
Editorial Description: Reports news related to Lutherans in specialized pastoral care.
General Info: (Formerly SPC), Yr. Est. 1978, 16 pages
Circulation: Total-1,200

Svetrita Zvani

Publishing Co: Latvian Evangelical Lutheran Church, 3152 17th Ave S, Minneapolis, MN 55407-1821; Title Tel # (612) 722-4622
Editorial Description: Religious and ethnic news relating to the Latvian Evangelical Lutheran Church.
General Info: Yr. Est. 1954, Monthly

Te Deum

Publishing Co: Trinity Lutheran Seminary, 2199 E Main St, Columbus, OH 43209-2334; Title Tel # (614) 235-4136
Personnel: Editor-Ann Russell
Editorial Description: Newsletter of Trinity Lutheran Seminary- Events at seminary; new programs; alumni, faculty/staff news.
General Info: Quarterly, Web press, 8 pages, 2 Color, Matte
Subscriptions: Free To Qualified Recipient
Acquistions: Publication Bought
Circulation: Total-8,000
Printing Co: Herald Printing, Inc., P.O. Box 367, New Washington, OH 44854-9769 Tel # (419) 492-2133, Fax # (419) 492-2128

Mennonite

Mennonite Central Committee-Washington Memo
See: POLITICS

Mirror
See: MUSEUM PUBLICATIONS

Peace Office Newsletter
See: POLITICS

Methodist

Action Memo

Publishing Co: General Commission on Archives & History, of the United Methodist Church, Box 127, Madison, NJ 07940; Title Tel # (201) 822-2787 Title Fax # (201) 408-3909
Personnel: Editor-Charles Yrigoyen, Jr.
Circulation: Total-550

American Waldensian Society Newsletter

Publishing Co: American Waldensian Society, 475 Riverside Dr Ste 1850, New York, NY 10115-0122; Title Tel # (212) 870-2671 Title Fax # (212) 870-2499
Personnel: Editor-Frank Gibson, Jr.
Editorial Description: Promotes solidarity among U.S. churches & Waldensian. Methodist ministries in Italy, & Argentina, Uruguay.
General Info: Yr. Est. 1906, Semi-annually, Trim Size-8½ x 11, Offset press, 16 pages, ISSN: 0894-9999, No Color, Matte, Saddle-stitched
Circulation: Total-2,500

Asian American News   *Consumer, Association*

Publishing Co: National Federation of Asian American United Metho, 330 Ellis St Ste 508, San Francisco, CA 94102-2735; Title Tel # (415) 776-7747 Title Fax # (415) 776-1154
Personnel: Publisher-Peter Sun, Editor-Douglas Franks
Editorial Description: News about resources for Asian Americans, especially those in the United Methodist Church.
General Info: Yr. Est. 1977, Monthly, Trim Size-8½ x 11, Offset press, 4 pages, No Color, Other
Subscriptions: Indv. $30, Free With Membership
Circulation: Total-1,700
Printing Co: United Printing, 573 Ofarrell St, San Francisco, CA 94102-1931 Tel # (415) 776-5799

Bush-Meeting Dutch
See: GENEALOGY

Facts for Action
See: POLITICS

Flyer   *Association*

Publishing Co: General Commission on the Status & Role of Women, in the United Methodist Church, 1200 Davis St., Evanston, IL 60201-4142; Title Tel # (708) 869-7330
Personnel: Editor-Bonnie Roth
Editorial Description: Addresses women's concerns, status, role in the United Methodist Church.
General Info: Yr. Est. 1978, 5x/yr., 8 pages, No Color
Subscriptions: Indv. $5
Circulation: Total-20,000

Foundations

Publishing Co: Wesley Foundation, Univ. of North Carolina, Rev. Robt. Johns, 214 Pittsboro St, Chapel Hill, NC 27516-2738
General Info: Quarterly

Historian's Digest

Publishing Co: Historical Society of the United Methodist Church, PO Box 127, Madison, NJ 07940-0127; Title Tel # (201) 822-2787
Personnel: Editor-Arthur Swarthout
General Info: Yr. Est. 1960, Quarterly, 4 pages, No Color
Subscriptions: For. $18
Circulation: Total-1,200
List Rental: Rents Lists

Historical Bulletin   *Consumer*

Publishing Co: World Methodist Historical Society, PO Box 127, Madison, NJ 07940-0127; Title Tel # (201) 822-2787 Title Fax # (201) 408-3909
Personnel: Publisher-Charles Yrigoyen, Jr., Editor-Theodore Agnew
Editorial Description: Historical publication dealing with the World Methodist Council & its constituent religious denominations.
General Info: (Formerly News Bulletin), Yr. Est. 1971, Quarterly, Trim Size-8½ x 11, Offset press, 8 pages, No Color, Newsprint
Subscriptions: Indv. $5
Circulation: Total-175

Maine United Methodist   *Association*

Publishing Co: Council on Ministries, ME Annual Conference, PO Box 277, Winthrop, ME 04364-0277; Title Tel # (207) 377-2912
Personnel: Editor-Beverly Abbott
Editorial Description: Church news for UMC in Maine.
General Info: (Formerly Maine Methodist), Yr. Est. 1961, Bi-monthly, Trim Size-8½ x 11, 6 pages, ISSN: 0745-0273, No Color
Circulation: Total-5,100
Advertising: Accepts Inserts.
Printing Co: Hallowell Printing Co., 145 Water St, Hallowell, ME 04347-1317 Tel # (207) 623-1161

Newscope   *Association*

Publishing Co: United Methodist Publishing House, 201 Eighth Avenue South, Nashville, TN 37203-0801 Tel # (615) 749-6292 Fax # (615) 749-6512; Title Tel # (615) 749-6334
Personnel: Publisher-Robert Feaster, Editor-J.P. Peck, Circ. Mgr.-Joyce Wolf, Promotion Dir.-Cindy Solomon
Editorial Description: Newsletter for United Methodist leaders.
General Info: Yr. Est. 1973, Weekly, Trim Size-8½ x 11, Offset press, 4 pages, No Color, Newsprint
Subscriptions: Indv. $18
Circulation: Total-10,000

Railroad Evangelist   *Association*

Publishing Co: Free Methodist Pub. House, 502 E Winona Ave, Warsaw, IN 46580-4444; Title Tel # (317) 844-3176
Personnel: Editor-Herman Rose, Publisher, Circ. Mgr.-Wilmer Bartel, Adv. Dir., Art Dir.-Esther Peterson
Editorial Description: Extended arm of churches reaching out to help unsaved & unchurched railroad employees.
General Info: Yr. Est. 1941, Bi-monthly, Trim Size-8½ x 11, Sheetfed press, 16 pages, No Color, Coated, Saddle-stitched
Subscriptions: Indv. $6, $1/copy
Circulation: (100% controlled)
List Rental: Rents Lists
Printing Co: Bartel Printing Co., 502 E Winona Ave, Warsaw, IN 46580-4496 Tel # (219) 267-7421

Social Questions Bulletin   *Association*

Publishing Co: Methodist Fed. for Social Action, 76 Clinton Ave, Staten Island, NY 10301-1107; Title Tel # (718) 273-6372
Personnel: Editor-George McClain
Editorial Description: Social, political, economic analysis, and theological perspective for Methodist social activists.
General Info: (Formerly Social Service Bulletin), Yr. Est. 1911, Bi-monthly, Trim Size-8½ x 11, Offset press, 4 pages, ISSN: 0731-0234, No Color
Subscriptions: Indv. $12, Inst. $15, $2/copy

UMCOR Update

Publishing Co: United Methodist Committee on Relief, 475 Riverside Dr Ste 350, New York, NY 10115-0122 Tel # (212) 870-3774; Title Tel # (212) 870-3814 Title Fax # (212) 749-2641
Personnel: Art Dir.-Roger Sadler
Editorial Description: News & interpretations of relief & rehabilitation agency.
General Info: (Formerly Inasmuch), Yr. Est. 1949, Semi-annually, Sheetfed press, 4 pages, 2 Color, Newsprint
Circulation: (100% controlled), Total-30,000

UMCommunity
See: HOUSE ORGANS

United Methodist Newscope

Publishing Co: United Methodist Publishing House, 201 Eighth Avenue South, Nashville, TN 37203-0801 Tel # (615) 749-6292 Fax # (615) 749-6512; Title Tel # (615) 749-6488 Title Fax # (615) 749-6079
Personnel: Publisher-Robert Feaster, Editor-Richard Peck, Circ. Mgr.-Paul Castavinski
General Info: Yr. Est. 1973, Weekly
Subscriptions: Indv. $25

World Parish   *Association*

Publishing Co: World Methodist Council, PO Box 518, Lake Junaluska, NC 28745-0518; Title Tel # (704) 456-9432 Title Fax # (704) 456-9433
Personnel: Publisher-Dr. Joe Hale
Editorial Description: Official organ of The World Methodist Council. It contains news of Methodism and ecumenical developments throughout the world.
General Info: Yr. Est. 1948, Bi-monthly, Trim Size-8½ x 11, Offset press, 8 pages, ISSN: 0043-8839, 2 Color
Subscriptions: Free
Circulation: Total-18,000

Mormon

Eastern Canada Church News

Publishing Co: Church of Jesus Christ of Latter Day Saints, 888 Byron Avenue, Ottawa, ON K2A 0J1 Canada; Title Tel # (613) 722-8436
General Info: Yr. Est. 1970, Monthly, 4 pages

Song of Zion
See: MUSIC & MUSIC TRADES

Muslim

Invitation, The   *Association*

Publishing Co: Islamic Info. Ctr. of America, PO Box 4052, Des Plaines, IL 60016-8052; Title Tel # (708) 541-8141 Title Fax # (708) 824-8436
Personnel: Publisher, Editor-Musa Qutub, Adv. Dir.-Vazir Ali, Promotion Dir.-Nancy Ali
Editorial Description: Application of Islam to societal problems, research topics.
General Info: Yr. Est. 1984, Quarterly, Trim Size-8½ x 11, Letrpr. press, 4 pages, 5% ads, 2 Color
Subscriptions: Indv. $10, For. $15
Circulation: Total-15,000
Advertising: Inquire for rates.

Islamic Center Bulletin

Publishing Co: Islamic Center, 2551 Massachusetts Ave NW, Washington, DC 20008-2866;
Title Tel # (202) 332-3451

Submitters Perspective

Publishing Co: Masjid Tucson, 739 E 6th St, Tucson, AZ 85719-5003; Title Tel # (602) 791-3989
Personnel: Editor-Rashad Khalifa
Editorial Description: Advocates worshipping God alone.
General Info: (Formerly Muslim Perspective), Yr. Est. 1985, Monthly, 4 pages
Subscriptions: Indv. $12, Inst. $12, Can. $12, For. $19

Pentecostal

At Ease   *Association*

Publishing Co: Assemblies of God, Inc., 1445 N Boonville Ave, Springfield, MO 65802-1894
Fax # (417) 863-7276; Title Tel # (417) 862-2781
Personnel: Editor-Lemuel McElyea, Mng. Editor-Traci L. Countryman
Editorial Description: A religious publication geared towards military personnel.
General Info: Bi-monthly, Trim Size-12$\frac{1}{8}$ x 18, ISSN: 0190-4280, 2 Color
Subscriptions: Free
Circulation: Total-26,000

Presbyterian

Briefly   *Association*

Publishing Co: Presbyterian Peace Fellowships, PO Box 271, Nyack, NY 10960-0271;
Title Tel # (914) 358-4601
Personnel: Editor-Nancy Head
Editorial Description: Informal report to Peace Fellowship members; issues concerning peace and relation of Presbyterian denomination to other peace groups. Made available to Commissioners to General Assemblies.
General Info: Yr. Est. 1944, Trim Size-8$\frac{1}{2}$ x 11$\frac{1}{2}$, Mimeo press, 8 pages, Color
Circulation: Total-2,250

More Light Update
See: GAY & LESBIAN INTEREST

Network

Publishing Co: Mission to the World, 1852 Century Pl NE Ste 201, Atlanta, GA 30345-4305;
Title Tel # (404) 320-3373
Personnel: Editor-Mary Lou Bohnsack
Editorial Description: Presbyterian Church in America missions news.
General Info: (Formerly WPM Newsletter), Yr. Est. 1957, Quarterly, Trim Size-7 x 10, Offset press, 8 pages, 2 Color, Coated
Circulation: (100% controlled), Total-75,000
Printing Co: Walker Printing, 2501 E 5th St, Montgomery, AL 36107-3105 Tel # (205) 832-4975

PANdemic   *Association*

Publishing Co: Presbyterian AIDS Network, c/o Peg Atkins, 747 N. Taylor, Kirkwood, MO 63122
Personnel: Editor-Peg Atkins
Editorial Description: Information and support for AIDS patients and those involved with them.
General Info: Bi-monthly

Presbyterian Comment

Publishing Co: Presbyterian Comment, P3-120 Edinburgh Rd., S., Guelph, ON N1H 5P7 Canada
General Info: Yr. Est. 1960, Bi-monthly

Washington Report to Presbyterians

Publishing Co: Presbyterian Church (USA), 110 Maryland Ave. NE, #104, Washington, DC 20002-5626; Title Tel # (202) 543-1126 Title Fax # (202) 543-7755
Personnel: Editor-Barbara Green
General Info: Yr. Est. 1979, Bi-monthly
Subscriptions: Indv. $5
Circulation: Total-1,300

Russian Orthodox

Fr. Seraphim Rose Foundation Newsletter   *Association*

Publishing Co: Fr. Seraphim Rose Foundation, PO Box 1656, Forestville, CA 95436-1656
Editorial Description: Dedicated to preserving Fr. Seraphim's original writings and teachings.
General Info: Yr. Est. 1993

InSight   *Association*

Publishing Co: Slavic Gospel Association, 6151 Commonwealth Dr., Loves Park, IL 61111;
Title Tel # (815) 282-8900 Title Fax # (815) 282-8901
Personnel: Publisher, Editor, Assoc. Ed.-Paul Kamps
Editorial Description: Informs spiritual needs of Russian-Slavic people.
General Info: (Formerly Breakthrough), Yr. Est. 1971, Bi-monthly, Trim Size-8$\frac{1}{2}$ x 11, Offset press, 8 pages, 2 Color, Coated
Circulation: (93% controlled), Total-43,000

Orthodox Herald   *Consumer*

Publishing Co: Orthodox Herald, Rr 3 Box A15, Hunlock Creek, PA 18621-9547;
Title Tel # (717) 256-7232
Personnel: Editor-Nina Stroyen, Editor-W. B. Stroyen
Editorial Description: The Eastern Orthodox faith in today's world. Also explores ethnic traditions of the Russian and Carpathoi-Russian peoples.
General Info: Yr. Est. 1952, Monthly, Trim Size-8$\frac{1}{2}$ x 10$\frac{1}{2}$, Letrpr. press, 6 pages
Subscriptions: Indv. $5
Circulation: Total-5,000

Society of Friends/Quaker

FLGC Newsletter
See: GAY & LESBIAN INTEREST

Gleamings

Publishing Co: University Friends Meeting, 4001 9th Ave NE, Seattle, WA 98105-6410;
Title Tel # (206) 549-6449
Personnel: Editor-Pablo Stanfield
General Info: Yr. Est. 1950, Monthly, Trim Size-8$\frac{1}{2}$ x 14, 4 pages, No Color
Subscriptions: Indv. $5
Circulation: Total-600

Unitarian

Ethics & Action

Publishing Co: Unitarian Universalist Assn. of Churches in North America, 100 Maryland Ave NE, Washington, DC 20002-5625; Title Tel # (202) 547-0254
General Info: Quarterly

Good News   *Association*

Publishing Co: Unitarian Universalist Christian Fellowship, 110 Arlington St, Boston, MA 02116-5320;
Title Tel # (508) 365-2427 Title Fax # (508) 368-1616
Personnel: Publisher-Thomas Wintle, Editor-Pamela Barz
Editorial Description: Provides news and a forum for Unitarian Universalist Christians.
General Info: Yr. Est. 1944, Bi-monthly, Trim Size-8$\frac{1}{2}$ x 11, Sheetfed press, 8 pages, ISSN: 0890-4375, 2 Color, Matte, Saddle-stitched
Subscriptions: Indv. $30, For. $40
Circulation: Total-1,100

Wiccan, Pagan

Our Pagan Times   *Consumer, Association*

Publishing Co: New Moon, Box 1471, Madison Square Station, New York, NY 10159;
Title Tel # (718) 522-1260
Editorial Description: Association and information for Pagans.
General Info: Monthly
Subscriptions: Indv. $15

Pagan Spirit Alliance Newsletter

Publishing Co: Circle, PO Box 219, Mount Horeb, WI 53572-0219; Title Tel # (608) 924-2216
Personnel: Editor-Dennis Carpenter
General Info: Quarterly, 16 pages
Subscriptions: Indv. $15

Themoporia

Publishing Co: Covenant of the Goddess, PO Box 11363, Oakland, CA 94611-0363;
Title Tel # (415) 452-0995
Personnel: Editor-J. Roslund
General Info: (Formerly Themis), Yr. Est. 1979, 8x/yr., 4 pages
Subscriptions: Indv. $13
Circulation: Total-1,500

Thunderbow II   *Consumer, Association*

Publishing Co: Church of Seven Arrows, Box 185, Wheatridge, CO 80034-0185;
Title Tel # (303) 232-5873
Personnel: Editor-George Dew
Editorial Description: Earth-Religionist news, dialogs, reviews, opinions.
General Info: (Formerly Thunderbow), Yr. Est. 1978, Monthly, Trim Size-5$\frac{1}{2}$ x 8$\frac{1}{2}$, 6 pages
Circulation: Total-200
Advertising: Inquire for rates.
Printing Co: Alameda Press & Copyquick, 1295 S Jason St, Denver, CO 80223-3114
Tel # (303) 733-8362

Witches International Craft Associates WICA Newsletter
Association

Publishing Co: Hero Press, 153 W 80th St Apt 1b, New York, NY 10024-7108
Personnel: Publisher, Editor-Dr. Leo Martello
Editorial Description: Pre-Judeo-Christian Paganism, defined in Dr. Martello's Witchcraft: The Old Religion.
General Info: Yr. Est. 1970, Monthly, Sheetfed press, 4 pages, No Color
Subscriptions: Indv. $4, $1/copy
Circulation: Total-3,500
Advertising: Inquire for rates.

RESTAURANTS & CATERING

American Wine & Food
See: FOOD

Biscuits & Gravy Quarterly

Publishing Co: Jack Lamb, P.O. Box 4290, Carlsbad, CA 92018
Editorial Description: An issue which features notes on restaurants whith detailed review sof the biscuits and gravy they serve. They're in California and Arizona, and include addresses and interviews with different people.
General Info: Trim Size-8.5 x 11, 12 pages
Subscriptions: Indv. $1

Bread Pudding Update
See: FOOD

CQSS Reporter
See: MANAGEMENT

California Chef
Business

Publishing Co: Paul Gillette Enterprises, 3284 Barham Blvd Apt 201, Los Angeles, CA 90068-1454; Title Tel # (213) 876-7590 Title Fax # (213) 876-4090
Personnel: Publisher-Paul Gillette, Editor-Dan Fendel, Adv. Dir.-Roger Zeidman
Editorial Description: News for chefs and senior executives in hotels and restaurants.
General Info: Yr. Est. 1994
Subscriptions: Indv. $60, Inst. $60, Can. $72, For. $84, $5/copy

Cameron's Foodservice Marketing Reporter
Business

Publishing Co: Cameron's Publications, 5325 Sheridan Dr., PO Box 1160, Williamsville, NY 14231-1160 Tel # (716) 634-2668; Title Tel # (716) 833-4369 Title Fax # (716) 834-4159
Personnel: Publisher-Bob McClelland, Editor-Nina Cameron, Circ. Mgr.-Peggy Kelly
Editorial Description: Successful marketing & advertising case histories from the restaurant & hotel industry.
General Info: (Formerly Cameron's Food Service Promotions Reporter), Yr. Est. 1983, Semi-monthly, Trim Size-8½ x 11, Sheetfed press, 8 pages, ISSN: 0735-5548, 2 Color, Newsprint
Subscriptions: Indv. $197, Can. $211, For. $227, $10/copy
Circulation: Total-10,000
List Rental: Actives: $125/M

Catering Service Idea Newsletter
See: BUSINESS & INDUSTRY

Child Nutrition Today
Association

Publishing Co: NYS Education Dept., Central Svces. #3 Rm. 546 Eb, Education Bldg.washin, Albany, NY 12234-0001; Title Tel # (518) 473-1525 Title Fax # (518) 473-0018
Personnel: Editor-Frank Rinaldi
Editorial Description: Covers child nutrition and nutrition programs.
General Info: (Formerly News & Notes), Yr. Est. 1950, Bi-monthly, 4 pages, Color

Customer Service Report
See: MANAGEMENT

Dining with Heart
See: MEDICINE

FIAE Association Spotlight
Association

Publishing Co: Food Industry Assn. Executives, c/o George R. Staton, P.O. Box 219, Las Cruces, NM 88004; Title Tel # (505) 523-1992
Editorial Description: Food industry information.
General Info: Trim Size-8½ x 11, 2 pages

Fine Wine Folio
See: BEVERAGES - BREWING

Food Industry Report
See: FOOD

Foodservice Planning

Publishing Co: Foodservice Planning Institute, PO Box 1169, Santa Barbara, CA 93102-1169; Title Tel # (805) 963-9808
Personnel: Publisher-James Degen
General Info: Yr. Est. 1987, Bi-monthly, Trim Size-8½ x 14, 4 pages, 2 Color
Subscriptions: Indv. $79
Circulation: Total-200
Printing Co: Automated Mailing Service, 132 Santa Barbara St, Santa Barbara, CA 93101-1876 Tel # (805) 963-9353

Fried Rice Times

Publishing Co: China Moon Cafe, 639 Post St, San Francisco, CA 94109-8215; Title Tel # (415) 775-4789
Personnel: Editor-Barbara Tropp
General Info: Yr. Est. 1989, Quarterly

Gift Basket Idea Newsletter
See: GIFTS, GAMES, TOYS

Gloria Pitzer's Secret Recipes Publications
See: FOOD

Gold Coast News
See: REGIONAL INTEREST

HRI Buyers Guide
See: HOTEL INDUSTRY

HRI Meat Price Report
See: MEAT & MEAT PROVISIONS

Hoosier Chef

Publishing Co: Indiana Restaurant Assn., Inc., 115 W. Washington St. #1165-S, Indianapolis, IN 46204-3407
Personnel: Editor-Leslie Green
General Info: Monthly
Subscriptions: Indv. $1
Circulation: Total-3,000
Advertising: Inquire for rates.

Illinois Restaurant Assn. Newsbulletin

Publishing Co: Illinois Restaurant Assn., 350 W Ontario St Ste 7, Chicago, IL 60610-4040; Title Tel # (312) 787-4000
General Info: Trim Size-8¼ x 11¼
Circulation: Total-4,500

Karas Executive Report

Publishing Co: Restaurant Business, Inc., 355 Park Ave S Fl 3, New York, NY 10010-1706; Title Tel # (212) 986-4800
Personnel: Publisher-Don Karas, Editor-Norma Vavolizza
Editorial Description: Focuses on developments in the restaurant/hotel industry.
General Info: Yr. Est. 1973, 50x/yr.

Make it Tasty with No/Low Salt--How To & Receipe Blends Edition
See: FOOD

Make it Tasty Spice Co. Blends Food Business Newsletter
See: FOOD

Meat Price Report

Publishing Co: National Provisioner, Inc., 15 W Huron St, Chicago, IL 60610-3812; Title Tel # (312) 944-3380 Title Fax # (312) 944-3632
Personnel: Publisher-Jeffrey Jankowak, Editor-Anne Sullivan, Editor-Carl Witta, Circ. Mgr.-Ruby Jones, Production Mgr.-Rob Leone, Promotion Dir.-Betsy Leyerle
Editorial Description: Meat & poultry price information as recorded in the hotel, reataurant & institutional procurement industries.
General Info: Yr. Est. 1967, Weekly
Subscriptions: Indv. $150
Acquistions: Publication Bought
Advertising: Inquire for rates. Accepts Inserts.

Mimi Sheraton's Taste

Publishing Co: Taste Guides, Inc., Box 1396, Old Chelsea Sta., New York, NY 10011; Title Tel # (212) 484-2494
Personnel: Editor-Mimi Sheraton
Editorial Description: Cooking and food related articles and information.
General Info: Yr. Est. 1987, 10x/yr.
Subscriptions: Indv. $48

Mobile and Industrial Catering *Business*

Publishing Co: Mobile Industrial Caterer's Assn. Internatl., 1240 N. Jefferson St., Ste. G, Anaheim, CA 92807; Title Tel # (714) 632-6800
Personnel: Publisher-Harold Fertig, Editor-Cathryn O'Conner
Editorial Description: Industrial catering and mobile food service in U.S. and Canada.
General Info: Yr. Est. 1958, Monthly, Trim Size-11 x 17, Offset press, 14 pages, 4 Color, Newsprint
Subscriptions: Indv. $10
Circulation: Total-15,000
Advertising: Inquire for rates.
Printing Co: Rio Hondo Valley Publishing, 11919 Burke St, Santa Fe Springs, CA 90670-2507 Tel # (213) 693-2781

National Hospitality News *Business, Association*

Publishing Co: Canadian Restaurant & Foodservices Assn., 316 Bloor St., W., Toronto, ON M5S 1W5 Canada; Title Tel # (416) 923-8416
Personnel: Editor-Douglas Needham
General Info: Monthly
Circulation: (100% controlled), Total-9,000

Nona Morelli's Press Release

Publishing Co: OTC Communications, 1040 Great Plain Avenue, Needham, MA 02192 Tel # (617) 444-6100 Fax # (617) 444-6101; Title Tel # (714) 833-2094 Title Fax # (714) 833-7854
Editorial Description: NONA MORELLI'S is an international leisure and entertainment holding company with four subsidiaries, one of which- NuOasis Graming, INc. is also publicly traded
General Info: Yr. Est. 1986, Bi-monthly, Trim Size-8.5 x 11, 4 pages, 2 Color

Oklahoma Surrey *Business*

Publishing Co: Oklahoma School Food Service Assn., 215 E 12th Ave, Stillwater, OK 74074-4613; Title Tel # (405) 372-0178
Personnel: Publisher, Editor-Vici Grimes
Editorial Description: Provides a means for distributing OSFSA information to members and foodservice vendors.
General Info: Yr. Est. 1962, Trim Size-8$\frac{1}{2}$ x 11, Letrpr. press, 24 pages, 2 Color
Subscriptions: $1/copy
Circulation: Total-2,000
Advertising: Inquire for rates.

Practical Gourmet See: TRAVEL

Pro-Motion *Business*

Publishing Co: National Restaurant Association, 1200 17th St., NW, Washington, DC 20036-3097; Title Tel # (202) 331-5900 Title Fax # (202) 331-2429
Personnel: Publisher-Jeff Prince, Editor-David Belman, Circ. Mgr.-Patricia Byrd, Production Mgr.-Ronda Bowers, Art Dir.-Mira Hudson
Editorial Description: A marketing and promotion guide for restaurant owners and operators, full of new ideas and practical promotions.
General Info: Yr. Est. 1980, Bi-monthly, Trim Size-11 x 17, Sheetfed press, 4 pages, 2 Color, Coated
Subscriptions: Indv. $25
Circulation: Total-2,000
Printing Co: Balmar Printing, 16780 Oakmont Ave, Gaithersburg, MD 20877-4188 Tel # (301) 258-0700

Report on Institutional Foodservice See: FOOD

Restaurant & Foodservices Assn. of British Columbia Newsletter

Publishing Co: Restaurant & Foodservices Assn. of B.C., 4190 Lougheed Hwy., #204, Burnaby, BC V5C 6A8 Canada; Title Tel # (604) 298-5956
General Info: Monthly

Restaurant, Caterer & Tavern Statistics *Business, Association*

Publishing Co: Statistics Canada, Holland Ave/RH Coats, Holland Ave/Tunney's Pasture, Ottawa, ON K1A O26 Canada Tel # (613) 951-8116 Fax # (613) 951-0581; Title Tel # (613) 990-8116
Editorial Description: Text in English & French. Estimates for chains and independents. 63-011.
General Info: Yr. Est. 1967, Monthly, 4 pages, ISSN: 0226-2320
Subscriptions: Indv. $7, Can. $6, For. $9, $7/copy

Restaurant Management Insider *Business*

Publishing Co: Restaurant Management Institute, 211 Freyer Drive, Marietta, GA 30060-1401 Tel # (770) 424-4444
Editorial Description: Restaurant management oriented news and information.
General Info: Yr. Est. 1981, Weekly
Subscriptions: Indv. $225

Restaurant Publicity News *Business*

Publishing Co: Gordon-Bay Group, Ltd., 770 N Halsted St Ste 205, Chicago, IL 60622-5972; Title Tel # (312) 421-2900 Title Fax # (312) 733-5616
Personnel: Editor-Alisa Gordon, Contrib. Ed.-Stefani Bay, Contrib. Ed.-Andrea Brook, Contrib. Ed.-Chris Gilroy
Editorial Description: Successful PR and promotion ideas for restaurant owners and managers.
General Info: Yr. Est. 1994, Monthly, Trim Size-8$\frac{1}{2}$ x 11, 8 pages, 2 Color, Coated
Subscriptions: Indv. $120, Can. $150, $10/copy
Circulation: Total-5,000
Advertising: Accepts Inserts.

School Food Services Bulletin

Publishing Co: Commonwealth of Pennsylvania, Dept. of Public Instruction, Education Bldg., Harrisburg, PA 17120-0001; Title Tel # (717) 783-6788
Personnel: Editor-Allison Munn
General Info: Monthly
Circulation: Total-6,000

School Lunch Administrative Newsletter

Publishing Co: Ohio State Dept. of Education, 270 E State St, Columbus, OH 43215-4312

Service that Sells! See: MANAGEMENT

Serving America

Publishing Co: Culinary Alliance, 515 Cabrillo Park Dr Ste 205, Santa Ana, CA 92701-5016
Personnel: Editor-James Stevens
Editorial Description: Hotel bar restaurant news.

Slice of Pizza

Publishing Co: N. American Pizza Assn., 23 N Washington St Ste 20, Ypsilanti, MI 48197-2617
Personnel: Editor-Lynda Boone
General Info: Yr. Est. 1968, Bi-monthly
Subscriptions: Indv. $15
Circulation: Total-24,300

Smith Restaurant Supply *Business*

Publishing Co: Smith Restaurant Supply Co., 500 Erie Blvd E, Syracuse, NY 13202-1109; Title Tel # (315) 474-8731 Title Fax # (315) 478-7004
Editorial Description: News and information relating to the Smith Restaurant Supply Co. and the industry in general.
General Info: Quarterly, Trim Size-11$\frac{1}{2}$ x 16$\frac{3}{4}$, 8 pages, 2 Color, Newsprint

Taste! *Business, Consumer*

Publishing Co: Paul Gillette Enterprises, 3284 Barham Blvd Apt 201, Los Angeles, CA 90068-1454; Title Tel # (213) 876-7590 Title Fax # (213) 876-4090
Personnel: Publisher-Pual Gillette, Editor-J.D. Kronman, Adv. Dir.-Roger Zeidman
Editorial Description: News and reviews of California restaurants.
General Info: Yr. Est. 1984, Bi-monthly
Subscriptions: Inst. $30, $5/copy
Advertising: Accepts Inserts.

Technomic Foodservice Digest See: FOOD

Technomic's Restaurant Information Svcs. *Business*

Publishing Co: TRA Information Svcs., Division of Technomic, Inc., 300 S Riverside Plz Ste 1940, Chicago, IL 60606-6613; Title Tel # (312) 876-0004 Title Fax # (312) 876-1158
Personnel: Publisher-Ronald Paul, Editor-Jan Sneesby
Editorial Description: Provides business profiles of over 275 restaurant chains.
General Info: Yr. Est. 1913, Quarterly
Subscriptions: Indv. $800, $400/copy

Travel Food & Wine See: TRAVEL

Travel Publicity Leads See: TRAVEL

Trend/Wire See: FOOD

Vegetarian Journal's Foodservice Update See: FOOD

Vendorscope See: BLIND

Vermont Foodnews Paper See: FOOD

Zip City
See: BEVERAGES - BREWING

ROADS & STREETS

ARTBA Newsletter   *Association*

Publishing Co: American Road & Transportation Builders Assn., 1010 Massachusetts Ave. NW, Washington, DC 20001; Title Tel # (202) 289-4434 Title Fax # (202) 488-3631
Personnel: Publisher-T.P. Ruane, Editor-John Yago
Editorial Description: Covers legislative/regulatory affairs involving transportation industry.
General Info: Yr. Est. 1956, Bi-weekly, Trim Size-8$\frac{1}{2}$ x 11, Desktop press, 6 pages, No Color, Other
Circulation: Total-4,600
Advertising: Inquire for rates.
Printing Co: CLB Publishers & Lithographers, 10580 Metropolitan Ave, Kensington, MD 20895-2606 Tel # (301) 933-5220, Fax # (301) 933-2498

Environmental Bulletin
See: ENVIRONMENT & ECOLOGY

Highway & Vehicle Safety Report
See: SAFETY

Highway Digest

Publishing Co: Salt Institute, 700 N Fairfax St Ste 600, Alexandria, VA 22314-2040; Title Tel # (703) 549-4648
Editorial Description: Use of salt for highway deicing; methods, application, judicious use to protect environment, improve efficiency, avoid waste of manpower & materials.
General Info: (Formerly Salt Digest), Semi-annually, Trim Size-8$\frac{1}{2}$ x 11, Sheetfed press, 4 pages, ISSN: 0732-0841, 2 Color
Subscriptions: Free
Circulation: Total-6,500

Highway Financing & Construction/State Capitals   *Business, Consumer*

Publishing Co: Wakeman/Walworth, 300 N. Washington St., Alexandria, VA 22314-2530 Fax # (703) 549-1372; Title Tel # (703) 549-8606
Personnel: Publisher-Keyes Walworth
Editorial Description: Covers state & local allocations for highway & bridge construction renovation, truck weight limits, toll roads, highway privatization, and other revenue sources.
General Info: (Formerly Highway Financing & Contruction from the State Capitals), Yr. Est. 1946, Weekly, 4 pages, ISSN: 0016-1705
Subscriptions: Indv. $365, Inst. $293, Can. $325, For. $345

Highway Safety Directions
See: SAFETY

Inside IVHS: Intelligent Vehicle/Highway Systems Update
See: TRAFFIC & TRANSPORTATION

Inside KDOT/Translines

Publishing Co: Kansas Dept. of Transportation, Public Info., Docking St. Office Bldg., Topeka, KS 66612
Personnel: Editor-Patrice Pomeroy
Editorial Description: Internal employee pubs. including news articles, employee profiles & items of interest which are highway & transportation related.
General Info: (Formerly Highway Highlights), Yr. Est. 1988, Bi-weekly, Trim Size-8$\frac{1}{2}$ x 11, Web press, 16 pages, Color-cover, Coated, Saddle-stitched
Circulation: Total-3,500

Intelligent Highway, The
See: TRAFFIC & TRANSPORTATION

Making Cities Livable Newsletter
See: PUBLIC MANAGEMENT & PLANNING

Municipal Routes   *Consumer, Association*

Publishing Co: Ontario Good Roads Assn., 530 Otto Rd., Unit 2, Mississauga, ON L5T 2L5 Canada; Title Tel # (905) 795-2555 Title Fax # (905) 795-2660
Editorial Description: Covers municipal transportation related topics of Ontario.
General Info: (Formerly Road Runner), Yr. Est. 1992, Monthly
Subscriptions: Free To Qualified Recipient
Circulation: Total-7,000

Northeastern Limousine Operators Association Nor'Easter Newsletter
See: TRAFFIC & TRANSPORTATION

Ontario Traffic

Publishing Co: Ontario Traffic Conference, 20 Carlton St., Ste. 121, Toronto, ON M5B 2H5 Canada
Personnel: Editor-J.S. Trew
General Info: (Formerly Ontario Traffic Conference Newsletter), Yr. Est. 1950, Bi-monthly, 24 pages
Circulation: Total-950
Advertising: Inquire for rates.

Planning Bulletin
See: TRAFFIC & TRANSPORTATION

Public Sector Job Bulletin
See: EMPLOYMENT

Reporter   *Business, Association*

Publishing Co: New Jersey Highway Authority, PO Box 5050, Woodbridge, NJ 07095-5050; Title Tel # (908) 442-8600 Title Fax # (908) 442-1480
Personnel: Editor-Ann McKee, Production Mgr.-Ray Stelnack, Art Dir.-Felicia Layne
Editorial Description: Employee Newsletter of the N.J.H.A., which operates the Garden State Parkway and the Garden State Arts Center.
General Info: Yr. Est. 1954, Bi-monthly, Trim Size-11$\frac{1}{2}$ x 14, Offset press, 8 pages, Color, Coated
Subscriptions: Free
Circulation: (100% controlled), Total-1,600

Transporation News   *Business*

Publishing Co: Colorado Transportation Dept., 4201 E Arkansas Ave, Denver, CO 80222-3406; Title Tel # (303) 757-9228 Title Fax # (303) 757-9153
Personnel: Editor-Carl Sorrentino
Editorial Description: News releases for bids on highways under construction, and other transportation activities.
General Info: (Formerly Highway News), Yr. Est. 1946, Weekly, Trim Size-8$\frac{1}{2}$ x 11, 2 pages, No Color
Circulation: (100% controlled), Total-1,400

Transportation Topics   *Association*

Publishing Co: Wyoming Transportation Dept., PO Box 1708, Cheyenne, WY 82003-1708 Tel # (307) 777-4437 Fax # (307) 777-4289; Title Tel # (307) 777-4375
Personnel: Editor-Keith Rounds
Editorial Description: Timely information about transportation.
General Info: (Formerly Road Construction News), Monthly, Offset press, 4 pages, 2 Color
Circulation: Total-2,000

Urban Transport News
See: TRAFFIC & TRANSPORTATION

W.H.I. Newsletter   *Association*

Publishing Co: Western Highway Inst., 1200 Bayhill Dr., San Bruno, CA 94066-3086; Title Tel # (415) 952-4900
Personnel: Publisher-Nancy Buchta, Editor-Byron Gevy
Editorial Description: Articles for members, on truck taxes, sizes, weights and on-going research.
General Info: Monthly, 2 pages
Circulation: Total-500

Zenith 12000

Publishing Co: California Div. of Highways, 2555 1st Ave, Sacramento, CA 95818-2608; Title Tel # (916) 445-1564

ROMANCE

Heartland Critiques   *Business, Consumer*

Publishing Co: Heartland Critiques, 125 E Linden Ave, Independence, MO 64050-4407; Title Tel # (816) 254-1868
Personnel: Publisher-Julie Meisinger, Editor-Bea Owens
Editorial Description: Critiques of approximately 130 Romance Novels a month. We critique both contemporary & Historicals as well as fiction & Regency Romances.
General Info: (Formerly Barbra Critiques), Yr. Est. 1980, Monthly, Sheetfed press, 35 pages, ISSN: 1063-1186
Subscriptions: Indv. $50
Circulation: Total-250

International True Story Group

Publishing Co: Macfadden Holdings Publishing, 233 Park Ave. South, New York, NY 10003-1663 Tel # (212) 979-4860 Fax # (212) 979-7431; Title Tel # (212) 983-5600
Editorial Description: Published in Spanish for Mexico (W); French (W); Swedish (W); German for Switzerland (M); Dutch (M).

Quicktrips Travel Letter
See: TRAVEL

RoMANtic, The

Publishing Co: Sterling Publications, 2291 Avent Ferry Rd., Suite #215, Raleigh, NC 27606
Personnel: Exec. Ed.-Michael Webb
Editorial Description: A newsletter created to help men be more romantic is being snapped up-mainly by women.
General Info: Bi-monthly, Trim Size-8$\frac{1}{2}$ x 11, 8 pages, 2 Color, Matte, Perfect bound
Subscriptions: Indv. $12
Circulation: Total-5,000

Romantic Notions   *Consumer*

Publishing Co: Romantic Notions, PO Box 705, Salem, OR 97308-0705; Title Tel # (503) 390-9027
Personnel: Editor-Michelle Marr
Editorial Description: Reviews contemporary romance novels.
General Info: Yr. Est. 1992, Quarterly, Trim Size-8½ x 11, Offset press, 8 pages
Subscriptions: Indv. $8, $2/copy
Circulation: Total-200

Satin Sheets   *Consumer*

Publishing Co: Satin Sheets, PO Box 427, Whitehall, PA 18052-0427; Title Tel # (610) 821-1324
Personnel: Editor-Amanda Maxwell
Editorial Description: Covers romantic reading and living.
General Info: Bi-monthly

RUBBER

Akron Daily Digest
See: HOUSE ORGANS

Braintree Express
See: HOUSE ORGANS

Inter-Action

Publishing Co: Dunlop Tire, PO Box 1109, Buffalo, NY 14240-1109; Title Tel # (716) 879-8228
Personnel: Editor-Norm Senf
Editorial Description: In-house newsletter.
General Info: (Formerly Interaction), Yr. Est. 1973, Bi-monthly, Trim Size-9½ x 14, Offset press, 8 pages, 2 Color, Coated
Acquistions: Publication Bought
Circulation: Total-2,500
Printing Co: Cox Graphics, 1057 Kensington Ave, Buffalo, NY 14215-2737 Tel # (716) 832-2578

PetroChemical News
See: CHEMISTRY & CHEMICALS

Retiree Roundup
See: HOUSE ORGANS

SAFETY

ABYC News
See: BOATS & BOATING

APC Currents
See: ELECTRIC & ELECTRONIC EQUIPMENT

Accident Facts Up-to-Date   *Business, Consumer*

Publishing Co: National Safety Council, 1121 Spring Lake Dr., Itasca, IL 60143-3201
Tel # (708) 285-1121 Fax # (708) 775-2285
Personnel: Editor-Alan Hoskin, Circ. Mgr.-Linda Liming
Editorial Description: Current estimates of accidental deaths, injuries, and costs. Special articles on safety and health topics.
General Info: Yr. Est. 1993, Monthly, Trim Size-8½ x 11, 4 pages, 2 Color
Subscriptions: Indv. $25
Circulation: Total-200

Accident Prevention Bi-Monthly   *Association*

Publishing Co: Industrial Accident Prevention Assn., 250 Yonge Street, Suite 2800, Toronto, ON M5B 2N4 Canada; Title Tel # (416) 506-8888
Personnel: Editor-Susan Stanton
Editorial Description: Matters relating to safety in industry and the retail trades.
General Info: Yr. Est. 1953, Bi-monthly, Sheetfed press, 24 pages, 2 Color, Coated, Saddle-stitched
Subscriptions: Indv. $40, For. $55
Circulation: (100% controlled), Total-60,000

Accident Prevention Bulletin

Publishing Co: Flight Safety Foundation, 2200 Wilson Blvd Ste 500, Arlington, VA 22201-3369; Title Tel # (703) 522-8300 Title Fax # (703) 525-6047
Personnel: Publications Director-Roger Rozelle, Feature Ed.-Russell Lawton, Art Dir.-Karen Bostick, Promotion Dir.-Ed Peery
Editorial Description: Newsletter presents an in-depth examination of a single commercial or corporate aircraft accident, based on official investigation reports each month.
General Info: Yr. Est. 1943, Monthly, Trim Size-8½ x 10, Letrpr. press, 6 pages, ISSN: 0898-5774, Color-cover, Matte, Other
Subscriptions: Indv. $80, Inst. $80, Can. $80, For. $90, $10/copy
Circulation: Total-2,200
Printing Co: Master Print, Inc., 8401-A Terminal Rd., Box 1467, Newington, VA 22122 Tel # (703) 550-9555

Advanced Transportation Technology News
See: TRAFFIC & TRANSPORTATION

Aerospace Newsletter   *Association*

Publishing Co: National Safety Council, 1121 Spring Lake Dr., Itasca, IL 60143-3201
Tel # (708) 285-1121 Fax # (708) 775-2285; Title Tel # (312) 527-4800
Editorial Description: Occupational safety and health specifically related to industries as noted in title.
General Info: Bi-monthly, Trim Size-8½ x 11, 4 pages
Circulation: Total-472

Air Safety Week   *Business, Association*

Publishing Co: Phillips Business Information, Inc., 1201 Seven Locks Rd., Ste 300, Potomac, MD 20854-2958 Tel # (301) 340-1520 Fax # (301) 424-4297; Title Tel # (703) 522-8333 Title Fax # (703) 522-3334
Personnel: Publisher-Thomas Phillias, Editor-Dan Cooc, Assoc. Ed.-Kim Brown, Mktg. Dir.-Margaret Cemski
General Info: (Formerly Air Safety Law and Technology), Yr. Est. 1987, Weekly, Trim Size-8½ x 11, Sheetfed press, 10 pages, ISSN: 0893-1003, 2 Color, Newsprint
Subscriptions: Indv. $795, For. $860
Acquistions: Publication Bought, Publication Sold
List Rental: Rents Lists

Air Transport Newsletter   *Association*

Publishing Co: National Safety Council, 1121 Spring Lake Dr., Itasca, IL 60143-3201
Tel # (708) 285-1121 Fax # (708) 775-2285; Title Tel # (312) 527-4800
Editorial Description: Occupational safety and health specifically related to industries as noted in title.
General Info: Bi-monthly, Trim Size-8½ x 11, 4 pages
Circulation: Total-324

Airport Operation Bulletin
See: AERONAUTICS/ASTRONAUTICS

Amerisure Companies Safety News   *Business*

Publishing Co: Michigan Mutual Insurance Co., 28 W. Adams Ave., Detroit, MI 48226; Title Tel # (313) 965-8600 Title Fax # (313) 965-7787
Personnel: Editor-Amy Stevens, Adv. Dir.-Judy Willis
Editorial Description: Safety in the home, at work, and on the road.
General Info: (Formerly Michigan Mutual Safety News), Yr. Est. 1918, Quarterly, Trim Size-11 x 17, Letrpr. press, 6 pages, Color, Coated
Subscriptions: Free To Qualified Recipient
Acquistions: Publication Bought
Circulation: Total-14,000

Art Hazards Newsletter   *Business, Consumer*

Publishing Co: Center for Safety in the Arts, 5 Beekman St Rm 820, New York, NY 10038-2206; Title Tel # (212) 227-6220 Title Fax # (212) 233-3846
Personnel: Editor-Michael McCann
Editorial Description: Health hazards in art, craft, theater materials, precautions, legislation, calendar of events.
General Info: Yr. Est. 1977, 10x/yr., Offset press, 4 pages, ISSN: 0197-7903, No Color
Subscriptions: Indv. $24, Can. $25, For. $30, $2/copy
Circulation: Total-4,500

Asbestos & Lead Abatement Report
See: ENVIRONMENT & ECOLOGY

Aviation Disaster Management
See: AERONAUTICS/ASTRONAUTICS

Aviation Mechanics Bulletin
See: AERONAUTICS/ASTRONAUTICS

Aviation Monthly
See: AERONAUTICS/ASTRONAUTICS

BNA's Health Care Facilities Guide
See: HEALTH

BNA's State Environment & Safety Regulatory Monitoring
See: ENVIRONMENT & ECOLOGY

Bertrage   *Association*

Publishing Co: Mountain Rescue Council, PO Box 67, Seattle, WA 98111-0067; Title Tel # (206) 488-8580
Personnel: Editor-George Sainsbury
Editorial Description: Mountain rescue and mountaineering safety.
General Info: Yr. Est. 1955, Quarterly, Trim Size-8½ x 11, Offset press, 10 pages, No Color
Circulation: Total-650

CTD News
See: HEALTH

Cal-OSHA Reporter

Publishing Co: Sten-O-Press, 1862 23rd St. #36, San Pablo, CA 94806-4838 Tel # (510) 233-1880 Parent Co.-Commanon Corp., Grass Valley; Title Tel # (415) 233-1880 Title Fax # (415) 233-1249
Personnel: Publisher-J. Dale Debber, Publisher-John McCaun, Editor-Anne Bell, Editor-Ellen Demmead, Circ. Mgr.-Kathy McCaun
Editorial Description: Practical advice, legal & legislative updates, for occupational safety & health professionals.
General Info: Yr. Est. 1973, Weekly, Trim Size-8½ x 11, Offset press, 10 pages, ISSN: 1054-1209
Subscriptions: Indv. $227
Acquistions: Publication Bought, Publication Sold
Circulation: Total-1,790

Campus Crime
See: LAW ENFORCEMENT & PENOLOGY

Campus Safety Newsletter   *Association*

Publishing Co: National Safety Council, 1121 Spring Lake Dr., Itasca, IL 60143-3201 Tel # (708) 285-1121 Fax # (708) 775-2285; Title Tel # (312) 527-4800
Personnel: Production Ed.-Diane Ghazarian, Assoc. Ed.-Marty Shaub, Staff Writer-Eve Brouwer
General Info: Yr. Est. 1965, Quarterly, Trim Size-8½ x 11, 6 pages, No Color
Subscriptions: Indv. $4
Circulation: (100% controlled), Total-1,500

Canadian Employment
Safety and Health Guide   *Business*

Publishing Co: CCH Canadian Ltd., 6 Garamond Ct., North York, ON M3C 1Z5 Canada Fax # (416) 444-8011 Parent Co.-CCH, Inc., Riverwoods; Title Tel # (416) 441-2992 Title Fax # (416) 444-9011
Personnel: Editor-Theodora Opie
Editorial Description: Federal and provincial law and regulations on employment safety and health, case law, and editorial commentary.
General Info: Monthly, Trim Size-6 x 9, Web press, No Color, Looseleaf
Subscriptions: Can. $590

Canadian Occupational
Health & Safety News

Publishing Co: Southam Business Communications, Inc., 1450 Don Mills Rd., Don Mills, ON M3B 2X7 Canada; Title Tel # (416) 445-6641 Title Fax # (416) 442-2200
Personnel: Publisher-Mary Mancini, Mng. Editor-Angela Stelmakowich, Circulation-Gwen Harris
Editorial Description: Occupational health & safety: legislation, interpretation of legal & economic implications, relevant news, technology, new equipment & products to detect measure & control.
General Info: Yr. Est. 1978, Weekly, Trim Size-8½ x 11, Sheetfed press, 6 pages, ISSN: 0709-6252, No Color, Newsprint
Subscriptions: Indv. $273
Circulation: Total-1,050
List Rental: List Management Co.: Cornerstone List Mgrs., 2300 Yonge St., Ste. 2005, Box 2465, Toronto, ON M4P 1E4 Canada Tel # (416) 932-9555, Fax # (416) 932-9566

Canadian Occupational
Safety & Health Law
Monthly Report   *Business*

Publishing Co: Southam Business Communications, Inc., 1450 Don Mills Rd., Don Mills, ON M3B 2X7 Canada; Title Tel # (416) 445-6641 Title Fax # (416) 442-2200
Personnel: Publisher-Mary Mancini, Sr. Ed.-Mark Sabourin, Circ. Mgr.-Jennepher Hunter, Promotion Dir.-Saundra Dobroski
Editorial Description: Legislative, regulatory & judicial developments in Canadian Occupational Health & Safety & Worker's Compensation. Full text of relevant legislation & regulations.
General Info: Yr. Est. 1983, Monthly, Trim Size-8½ x 11, Sheetfed press, 6 pages, ISSN: 0825-608X, No Color, Newsprint
Subscriptions: Can. $869, For. $969
List Rental: List Management Co.: Cornerstone List Mgrs., 2300 Yonge St., Ste. 2005, Box 2465, Toronto, ON M4P 1E4 Canada Tel # (416) 932-9555, Fax # (416) 932-9566

ChemEcology
See: CHEMISTRY & CHEMICALS

Chemical Newsletter   *Association*

Publishing Co: National Safety Council, 1121 Spring Lake Dr., Itasca, IL 60143-3201 Tel # (708) 285-1121 Fax # (708) 775-2285; Title Tel # (312) 527-4800
Editorial Description: Occupation safety and health specifically related to the industry as noted in title.
General Info: Bi-monthly, Trim Size-8½ x 11, Offset press, 4 pages
Subscriptions: Indv. $7
Circulation: Total-4,448

Citizens for Safe Cycling Newsletter
See: CYCLING-BICYCLE & MOTOR

Civil Penalty Case Digest Service
See: AERONAUTICS/ASTRONAUTICS

Code Authority, The   *Business*

Publishing Co: Underwriters Laboratories, Inc., 333 Pfingsten Rd, Northbrook, IL 60062-2096 Tel # (708) 272-8800 Fax # (708) 272-8129
Personnel: Editor-Carole Feil
Editorial Description: Targeted to building inspectors and code authorities relating UL news and standards.
General Info: Yr. Est. 1992, Irregular, Trim Size-8½ x 11, Sheetfed press, 6 pages, 2 Color, Matte
Subscriptions: Free To Qualified Recipient
Circulation: Total-32,000
Printing Co: Columbia Graphics, 2640 N Paulina St, Chicago, IL 60614-1069 Tel # (312) 477-5800, Fax # (312) 477-9525

Compliance Audits: OSHA,
EPA, DOT Manual   *Business*

Publishing Co: J.J. Keller & Assoc., Inc., PO Box 368, Neenah, WI 54957-0368; Title Tel # (414) 722-2848 Title Fax # (414) 727-7516
Personnel: Editor-Webb Shaw, Adv. Dir.-David Szczeparik
General Info: Yr. Est. 1992, Semi-annually, 400 pages, Looseleaf
Subscriptions: $79/copy
Circulation: Total-3,700

Construction Newsletter

Publishing Co: National Safety Council, 1121 Spring Lake Dr., Itasca, IL 60143-3201 Tel # (708) 285-1121 Fax # (708) 775-2285; Title Tel # (312) 527-4800
General Info: Bi-monthly, Trim Size-8½ x 11
Circulation: Total-2,894

Crane Safety Report, The   *Business, Association*

Publishing Co: First Saety, Inc., 1015 Semoran Blvd., #1476, Casselberry, FL 23707; Title Tel # (407) 875-1809 Title Fax # (407) 696-0909
Personnel: Publisher, Editor-Graham Brent, Circ. Mgr.-Pauline Katz, Art Dir.-Helen Crantston
Editorial Description: Safety information and advice on the latest developments in the safe, correct, and legal use of lifting equipment.
General Info: (Formerly Crane Report, The), Yr. Est. 1995, Monthly, Trim Size-8½ x 11, Web press, 12 pages, 2 Color, Matte, Saddle-stitched
Subscriptions: Indv. $65, Inst. $65, Can. $65, For. $75, $15/copy

Dispatch   *Business*   **CPM: $53**

Publishing Co: Emergency Film Group, 225 Water St., Plymouth, MA 02360 Fax # (508) 746-5220; Title Tel # (508) 746-0466
Personnel: Publisher-Gordon Massingham, Editor-Shirley Ayers
Editorial Description: Aimed at the emergency response community, including fire departments, government agencies, and training facilities. Content includes case studies of recent incidents and articles of interest to emergency responders.
General Info: Yr. Est. 1989, Quarterly, Trim Size-11.5 x 17, Other press, 12 pages, 2 Color, Newsprint, Other
Subscriptions: Free To Qualified Recipient
Circulation: Total-30,000
Advertising: $1,600.
List Rental: List Management Co.: Detrick Lawrence Corp, 225 Water Street, Plymouth, MA 02360 Tel # (508) 746-0466, Fax # (508) 746-5220, Actives: 10,000, $85/M
Printing Co: Charles River Publishing, 440 Rutherford Ave, Charlestown, MA 02129-1644 Tel # (617) 241-5100, Fax # (617) 241-5111

Driver Trainer Newsletter

Publishing Co: National Safety Council, 1121 Spring Lake Dr., Itasca, IL 60143-3201 Tel # (708) 285-1121 Fax # (708) 775-2285; Title Tel # (312) 527-4800
General Info: Bi-monthly, Trim Size-8½ x 11, 4 pages
Circulation: Total-17,000

Emergency Management Today
See: GOVERNMENT

Emergency Preparedness
News   *Business*

Publishing Co: Business Publishers, Inc., 951 Pershing Dr., Silver Spring, MD 20910-4464 Tel # (301) 589-5103 Fax # (301) 589-8493; Title Tel # (301) 587-6300 Title Fax # (301) 585-9075
Personnel: Publisher-Leonard A. Eiserer, Editor-Frances Raslan, Mktg. Dir.-Fay S. Gold
Editorial Description: Independent newsletter dedicated to disaster and crisis management worldwide.
General Info: Yr. Est. 1977, Bi-weekly, Trim Size-8½ x 11, Desktop press, 8 pages, ISSN: 0275-3782, Ind/Abs/Online: NewsNet and Predicasts, No Color, Recycled
Subscriptions: Indv. $314, Inst. $314, Can. $314, For. $327
Advertising: Accepts Inserts.
List Rental: List Management Co.: Manager: Jim Hauschild; BPI Direct, 951 Pershing Dr., Silver Spring, MD 20910-4464 Tel # (301) 585-5976, Fax # (301) 587-4530

Employment Safety and
Health Guide   *Business*

Publishing Co: CCH, Inc., 2700 Lake Cook Rd., Riverwoods, IL 60015 Parent Co.-Kluwer Law & Taxation Publishers, Cambridge; Title Tel # (847) 267-7000 Title Fax # (800) 224-8299
Editorial Description: All aspects of OSHA & MSHA Regulation, full text of Standards, administrative & Judicial Rulings, Standard-by-Standard explanation of the law, full text of agency directives & announcements, new developments reporting, federal & state coverage.
General Info: Yr. Est. 1971, Weekly, Trim Size-6 x 9, Web press, 120 pages, Color, Looseleaf
Subscriptions: Indv. $945

Fertilizer and Agricultural Chemical Newsletter *Association*

Publishing Co: National Safety Council, 1121 Spring Lake Dr., Itasca, IL 60143-3201
Tel # (708) 285-1121 Fax # (708) 775-2285; Title Tel # (312) 527-4800
Editorial Description: Occupational health and safety specifically related to industry as noted in title.
General Info: Bi-monthly, Trim Size-8½ x 11, Offset press, 4 pages
Subscriptions: Indv. $7
Circulation: Total-383

Field Reports
See: BUSINESS & INDUSTRY

Fire & Emergency World
See: FIRE PROTECTION

Fleet Safety Newsletter-Motor Transportation
See: TRAFFIC & TRANSPORTATION

Food & Beverage Newsletter *Association*

Publishing Co: National Safety Council, 1121 Spring Lake Dr., Itasca, IL 60143-3201
Tel # (708) 285-1121 Fax # (708) 775-2285; Title Tel # (312) 527-4800
Editorial Description: Occupational health and safety specifically related to the food and beverage industry.
General Info: (Formerly Safety Newsletter: Food & Beverage Section), Bi-monthly, Trim Size-8½ x 11, 4 pages
Subscriptions: Indv. $7
Circulation: Total-1,880

Forest Industries Newsletter *Association*

Publishing Co: National Safety Council, 1121 Spring Lake Dr., Itasca, IL 60143-3201
Tel # (708) 285-1121 Fax # (708) 775-2285; Title Tel # (312) 527-4800
Editorial Description: Occupational safety and health as specifically related to industries as noted in title.
General Info: (Formerly Wood Products Newsletter and Pulp and Paper Newsletter), Bi-monthly, Trim Size-8½ x 11
Circulation: Total-2,427

Hawkins Chief Counsel's Interpretations
See: AERONAUTICS/ASTRONAUTICS

Hazard Control Manager *Business*

Publishing Co: Academy of Hazard Control Management, 80009 Carita Ct., Bethesda, MD 20817;
Title Tel # (301) 984-8969
Editorial Description: Standards for professionals in government, industry and education concerned with occupational & environmental health.
General Info: Yr. Est. 1981, Semi-annually

Hazardous Materials Newsletter *Business* CPM: $247

Publishing Co: Hazardous Materials Newsletter, PO Box 204, Barre, VT 05641-0204;
Title Tel # (802) 479-2307
Personnel: Publisher, Editor-John Cashman
Editorial Description: Covers public safety: response to hazardous materials emergencies, leak/fire/spill control.
General Info: Yr. Est. 1980, Bi-monthly, Trim Size-8½ x 11, Desktop press, 12 pages, ISSN: 0889-3454, 1% ads, No Color, Matte
Subscriptions: Indv. $47, Inst. $47, Can. $47, For. $55
Acquistions: Publication Bought
Circulation: Total-647
Advertising: $160. Accepts Inserts.

Hazmat News
See: ENVIRONMENT & ECOLOGY

Health Care Newsletter *Association*

Publishing Co: National Safety Council, 1121 Spring Lake Dr., Itasca, IL 60143-3201
Tel # (708) 285-1121 Fax # (708) 775-2285; Title Tel # (312) 527-4800
Editorial Description: Occupational Health and safety specifically related to hospital industry.
General Info: Bi-monthly, Trim Size-8½ x 11, 4 pages
Circulation: Total-957

Health and Safety Resource
See: FORESTRY

Health in the Workplace
See: HEALTH

Highway & Vehicle Safety Report *Business, Association*

Publishing Co: Stamler Publishing Co., 178 Thimble Islands Rd., P.O. Box 3367, Branford, CT 06405-1967 Fax # (213) 488-3129; Title Tel # (203) 488-9808 Title Fax # (203) 488-3129
Personnel: Publisher, Editor in Chief-S. Paul Stamler, Assoc. Ed.-Pamela D. Boynton, Assoc. Ed.-Julie E. Marsh, Asst. Ed., Circ. Mgr.-Kathy-Leigh Russo
Editorial Description: New developments in highway and vehicle safety: Congress; Dot; State projects, programs and enforcement; research; new publications, new reports.
General Info: Yr. Est. 1974, Bi-weekly, Trim Size-11 x 17, Offset press, 8 pages, ISSN: 0161-0325, 2 Color
Subscriptions: Indv. $347, Inst. $347, Can. $347, For. $372, $15/copy
Printing Co: Nova Printing Service, 85 Hood Ter, West Haven, CT 06516-4107

Highway Loss Reduction States Report

Publishing Co: Highway Lost Data Institute, 1005 N Glebe Rd Ste 800, Arlington, VA 22201-4751;
Title Tel # (703) 247-1500 Title Fax # (703) 247-1678
Personnel: Editor-James Mooney
Editorial Description: News & analysis of highway & vehicle safety issues.
General Info: (Formerly IIHS Report), Yr. Est. 1984, 20x/yr., Trim Size-8½ x 11, 8 pages, ISSN: 0018-988X, No Color
Subscriptions: Free
Circulation: (100% controlled), Total-15,000

Highway Safety Directions *Association*

Publishing Co: Univ. of North Carolina, Highway Safety Research Center, 134 1/2 E. Franklin St. Cb, #3430, Chapel Hill, NC 27599-0001; Title Tel # (919) 962-2202 Title Fax # (919) 962-8710
Personnel: Editor, Art Dir.-Jeffrey Lowrance
Editorial Description: Research activities at HSRC including new projects & descriptions of recently completed technical reports, plus safety information for the general motoring public.
General Info: (Formerly Highway Safety Highlights), Yr. Est. 1986, Quarterly, Trim Size-8½ x 11, Offset press, 8 pages, 2 Color, Saddle-stitched
Subscriptions: Free
Acquistions: Publication Bought
Circulation: Total-3,700
Printing Co: University of North Carolina Printing, CB 1110 Bennett Bldg., Chapel Hll, NC 27514
Tel # (919) 962-5566

Hospital Safety Information Service *Consumer*

Publishing Co: Scientific Enterprises, Inc., 5104 Randolph Road, North Little Rock, AR 72116-7541;
Title Tel # (501) 771-1775 Title Fax # (501) 771-1775
Personnel: Editor-James Wear
Editorial Description: Hospital safety for the patient, employee, & visitor. Topics such as JCAHO & OSHA information, FDA recalls, hazards, questions & answers, off-the-job safety , & special features are in each issue.
General Info: Yr. Est. 1979, Bi-monthly, Trim Size-8½ x 11, Sheetfed press, 32 pages, ISSN: 0276-2323, No Color, Other, Other
Subscriptions: Indv. $98, Can. $110, For. $130, $20/copy

Hot Flashes
See: FIRE PROTECTION

Human Factors & Ergonomics Society Bulletin
See: ENVIRONMENT & ECOLOGY

Human Resources Management OSHA Compliance
See: MANAGEMENT

Impact

Publishing Co: Sponsor-Health & Welfare Canada, Traffic Injury Research Foundation, 171 Nepean St., 6th Fl., Ottawa, ON K2P 0B4 Canada; Title Tel # (613) 238-5235 Title Fax # (613) 238-5292
Personnel: Editor-D. Beirness
Editorial Description: News about steps to stop impaired driving.
General Info: (Formerly Crossroads: National Newsletter on Drinking & Driving), Yr. Est. 1987, Quarterly, Trim Size-8½ x 11, Web press, 8 pages, ISSN: 0835-4235, 2 Color, Newsprint, Saddle-stitched
Subscriptions: Free
Circulation: (100% controlled), Total-6,000
Printing Co: M.O.M. Printing, 300 Parkdale Ave., Ottawa, ON K1Y 1G2 Canada
Tel # (613) 729-4303

Impact: A Journal of Safety Litigation and News
See: AUTOMOTIVE

Indiana Public Safety Letter
See: PUBLIC MANAGEMENT & PLANNING

Indoor Air Bulletin
See: ENVIRONMENT & ECOLOGY

Industrial Health & Hazards
Update
Business

Publishing Co: Infoteam, Inc., PO Box 15640, Plantation, FL 33318-5640 Fax # (954) 472-0544; Title Tel # (954) 473-9560 Title Fax # (954) 473-0544
Personnel: Publisher, Editor-Merton Allen
Editorial Description: Occupational health, safety, illness, hazards, risks, regulations, toxicity, environmental, etc. From business, university, governmental, & private sources. Full-text reprints available of reviewed reports.
General Info: Yr. Est. 1984, Monthly, Trim Size-8½ x 11, Offset press, 20 pages, ISSN: 0890-3018, Ind/Abs/Online: NewsNet, Data-Star, DIALOG, HRIN
Subscriptions: Indv. $269, Can. $309, For. $379, $25/copy

Interconnect
Association

Publishing Co: Intl. Municipal Signal Assn., PO Box 539, 165 E. Union Street, Newark, NY 14513; Title Tel # (315) 331-2182 Title Fax # (315) 331-8205
Editorial Description: Membership info, tips, and other traffic/public safety items.
General Info: Bi-monthly
Subscriptions: Free With Membership

International Product Safety
News
Business, Consumer

Publishing Co: Product Safety International, Box 1561-OX, Middletown, CT 06457-8061; Title Tel # (203) 344-1651 Title Fax # (203) 346-9066
General Info: Yr. Est. 1988, Bi-monthly, ISSN: 1040-7529
Subscriptions: Indv. $87, Can. $87, For. $93, $20/copy

International Quality
See: MANAGEMENT

Job Safety Consultant
Business

Publishing Co: BRP Publications, Inc., 65 Bleecker Street, 5th Floor, New York, NY 10012-2420 Tel # (212) 673-4700 Parent Co.-BRP (Washington DC), Washington; Title Tel # (212) 673-6700 Title Fax # (212) 475-1790
Personnel: Publisher-John Roche, Editor-Marcia Wagshol, Circ. Mgr.-Loretta Netzer, Production Mgr.-Diane Cramer
Editorial Description: Covers occupational industrial safety & health, OSHA, safety incentives & equipment.
General Info: (Formerly OSHA Report), Yr. Est. 1972, Monthly, Trim Size-8½ x 11, Sheetfed press, 6 pages
Subscriptions: Indv. $225
List Rental: List Management Co.: Affinity Marketing Group Inc., P.O. Box 2409, Fairfax, VA 22031 Tel # (703) 978-4927, Fax # (703) 425-4537, Actives: 700, $95/M, Expires: 400, $95/M
Printing Co: Globe Mail Agency, Inc., 541 W 25th St, New York, NY 10001-5501 Tel # (212) 675-4600

Job Safety Consultant
Business

Publishing Co: Ransom & Benjamin Publishers LLC, P.O. Box 606, Old Greenwich, CT 06870-0417 Tel # (203) 637-0221 Fax # (203) 637-3594
Editorial Description: Safety programming ideas - accident reduction; workers' compensation cost reduction; OSHA compliance
General Info: Yr. Est. 1972, Monthly, Trim Size-8.5 x 11, 8 pages
Subscriptions: Indv. $119
List Rental: List Management Co.: Direct Media, Inc., 200 Pemberwick Rd., PO Box 4565, Greenwich, CT 06830 Tel # (203) 532-3713, Fax # (203) 531-1452

Job Safety and Health
Business

Publishing Co: Bureau of National Affairs, Inc., 1231 25th St. NW, Bldg. N-200, Washington, DC 20037-1157; Title Tel # (202) 452-4200 Title Fax # (202) 822-8092
Personnel: Publisher-William A. Beltz, Mng. Editor-Stanley S. Pond, Circ. Mgr.-Gary C. Seltzer
Editorial Description: A biweekly review of workplace safety and health regulations, policies, practices and trends.
General Info: Yr. Est. 1977, Bi-weekly, Trim Size-8½ x 11, Web press, 4 pages, ISSN: 0149-7510, Ind/Abs/Online: HRIN
Subscriptions: Indv. $680
Circulation: Total-4,373

Kaufman Letter, The
Business, Association   **CPM$1000**

Publishing Co: Kaufman & Assoc., 162 Worester Road, Natick, MA 01760-2252; Title Tel # (508) 640-0900 Title Fax # (508) 640-0062
Personnel: Editor-James A. Kaufman, Adv. Dir.-Nancy Irving
Editorial Description: Lab safety letter newsletter with information on regulatory compliance, accident reports, resources, and more.
General Info: Yr. Est. 1990, Quarterly, Trim Size-8½ x 11, 24 pages
Subscriptions: Indv. $25, Can. $30, For. $35
Circulation: Total-1,000
Advertising: $1,000. Accepts Inserts.
List Rental: Actives: 10,000, $200/M

Keller Regulatory Update
Business

Publishing Co: J.J. Keller & Assoc., Inc., PO Box 368, Neenah, WI 54957-0368; Title Tel # (414) 722-2848 Title Fax # (414) 727-7516
Personnel: Editor-Webb Shaw, Adv. Dir.-David Szczeparik, Mktg. Dir.-Ed Sieracki
General Info: Yr. Est. 1992, Semi-monthly, 8 pages
Subscriptions: $149/copy
Circulation: Total-3,900

Keller's Industrial Safety
Report
Business

Publishing Co: J.J. Keller & Assoc., Inc., PO Box 368, Neenah, WI 54957-0368; Title Tel # (414) 722-2848 Title Fax # (414) 727-7516
Personnel: Editor-Webb Shaw, Adv. Dir.-David Szczeparik, Mktg. Dir.-Ed Sieracki
General Info: Yr. Est. 1992, Monthly, 8 pages
Subscriptions: $90/copy
Circulation: Total-8,500

Keller's OSHA Safety
Training Newsletter
Business

Publishing Co: J.J. Keller & Assoc., Inc., PO Box 368, Neenah, WI 54957-0368; Title Tel # (414) 722-2848 Title Fax # (414) 727-7516
Personnel: Editor-Webb Shaw, Adv. Dir.-David Szczeparik
General Info: Yr. Est. 1994, Monthly, 8 pages
Subscriptions: $90/copy
Circulation: Total-5,500

Labor Safety Newsletter
Association

Publishing Co: National Safety Council, 1121 Spring Lake Dr., Itasca, IL 60143-3201 Tel # (708) 285-1121 Fax # (708) 775-2285; Title Tel # (312) 527-4800
Personnel: Editor-Patti Beese
Editorial Description: Occupational safety and health as specifically related to labor in industry.
General Info: Bi-monthly, Trim Size-8 x 11, Offset press, 4 pages
Subscriptions: Indv. $6

Lemon Times
See: AUTOMOTIVE

Lifelines
See: HEALTH

Marine Newsletter
Association

Publishing Co: National Safety Council, 1121 Spring Lake Dr., Itasca, IL 60143-3201 Tel # (708) 285-1121 Fax # (708) 775-2285; Title Tel # (312) 527-4800
Editorial Description: Occupational safety and health specifically related to industry as noted in title.
General Info: Bi-monthly, Trim Size-8½ x 11, 4 pages
Circulation: Total-719

Marine Safety Report
Business, Association

Publishing Co: Stamler Publishing Co., 178 Thimble Islands Rd., P.O. Box 3367, Branford, CT 06405-1967 Fax # (213) 488-3129; Title Tel # (203) 488-9808 Title Fax # (203) 488-3129
Personnel: Publisher, Editor-S. Paul Stamler, Mag. Ed.-Pamela D. Boyntan, Circ. Mgr.-Kathy-Leigh Russo
Editorial Description: New developments in marine and boating safety; congress; cost guard; stete projects, programs and enfarcement; research; new publications; new reports.
General Info: Yr. Est. 1993, Bi-weekly, Trim Size-11 x 17, Offset press, 4 pages, ISSN: 1067-0734, 2 Color
Subscriptions: Indv. $197, Inst. $197, Can. $197, For. $222, $10/copy
Printing Co: Nova Printing Service, 85 Hood Ter, West Haven, CT 06516-4107

Maryland State Police
Highway Safety Bulletin
Consumer, Association

Publishing Co: Maryland State Police, Pikesville, MD 21208
General Info: Monthly

Med News
See: HEALTH

Metals Newsletter
Association

Publishing Co: National Safety Council, 1121 Spring Lake Dr., Itasca, IL 60143-3201 Tel # (708) 285-1121 Fax # (708) 775-2285; Title Tel # (312) 527-4800
Editorial Description: Occupational safety and health specifically related to industries as noted in title.
General Info: Bi-monthly, Trim Size-8½ x 11, 4 pages
Circulation: Total-2,310

Michigan Traffic Accident
Facts
Business

Publishing Co: Michigan State Police, 714 S Harrison Rd, East Lansing, MI 48823-5143; Title Tel # (517) 322-1974
Editorial Description: Presents facts on accident types and severity; mileage and death rates; special accident summa ry information; alcohol involvement and restraint usage.
General Info: Yr. Est. 1952, Annually, Trim Size-6 x 9, 60 pages, 2 Color
Subscriptions: Free
Circulation: Total-3,500

Microwave News
See: HEALTH

Mine Safety and Health News
See: MINING & MINERALS

Mining Newsletter *Association*

Publishing Co: National Safety Council, 1121 Spring Lake Dr., Itasca, IL 60143-3201
Tel # (708) 285-1121 Fax # (708) 775-2285; Title Tel # (312) 527-4800
Editorial Description: Occupational safety and health specifically related to the industry as noted in title.
General Info: Bi-monthly, Trim Size-8½ x 11
Subscriptions: Indv. $7
Circulation: Total-852

Model Mugging News *Consumer*

Publishing Co: Resources for Personal Empowerment, Box 20316, New York, NY 10028-0052;
Title Tel # (212) 650-9546
Editorial Description: Newsletter by graduates of Model Mugging self-defense classes programs.

Modern Job Safety & Health

Publishing Co: Research Institute of America, 90 5th Avenue, New York, NY 10011-7629
Tel # (212) 645-4800; Title Tel # (800) 562-0245 Title Fax # (800) 562-0245
Personnel: Publisher-Lisa Galjanic, Editor-Michael O'Toole, Promotion Dir.-Claudia Levine
Editorial Description: This service shows you how to manage the safety function & how to set up good training programs, & informs you of safety developments concerning such critical issues as VDT hazards, hazard communications, ergonomics, & right-to-know laws. Discount pricin on multiple product purchases available.
General Info: Monthly, Trim Size-8½ x 11, Web press, Looseleaf
Subscriptions: Indv. $201
List Rental: List Management Co.: WG & L List Management, 1 Penn Plz Fl 42, New York, NY 10119-0002 Tel # (212) 971-5000

Motor Carrier Safety Report *Business*

Publishing Co: J.J. Keller & Assoc., Inc., PO Box 368, Neenah, WI 54957-0368;
Title Tel # (414) 722-2848 Title Fax # (414) 727-7516
Personnel: Publisher-J.J. Keller, Editor-Webb Shaw, Adv. Dir.-David Szczeparik, Mktg. Dir.-Ed Sieracki
Editorial Description: News of significant changes in the motor carrier safety field.
General Info: Yr. Est. 1973, Monthly, Trim Size-8 x 10¾, Offset press, 24 pages, No Color
Subscriptions: $90/copy
Circulation: Total-1,200
Printing Co: J.J. Keller & Assoc., 3003 Breezewood Ln, Neenah, WI 54956-9611
Tel # (414) 722-2848, Fax # (414) 727-7516

Motor Fleet Safety Supervision *Business, Association*

Publishing Co: Michigan State Univ., A364 Engineering Building, E. Lansing, MI 48824-0001;
Title Tel # (517) 353-1790
Editorial Description: Only book of its kind; for motor fleet safety personnel.
General Info: Yr. Est. 1972, Sheetfed press, 6 pages, 2 Color
Subscriptions: Indv. $25, $20/copy
Acquistions: Publication Bought, Publication Sold
Circulation: Total-1,000

NCOSH
See: INDUSTRIAL RELATIONS/PERSONNEL

NCRP News *Association*

Publishing Co: National Council on Radiation Protection, 7910 Woodmont Ave., Ste. 800, Bethesda, MD 20814-3015; Title Tel # (301) 657-2652 Title Fax # (301) 907-8768
Personnel: Editor-W. Roger Ney
Editorial Description: Announces new NCRP reports and subjects of interest regarding the Council's activities.
General Info: Yr. Est. 1964, Irregular, Trim Size-8½ x 11, Offset press, 6 pages, 2 Color
Subscriptions: Free
Circulation: Total-20,000

NEA Notes
See: LABOR

NEISS Data Highlights

Publishing Co: Consumer Product Safety Commission, 5401 Westbard Ave # 625, Washington, DC 20207-0001; Title Tel # (301) 492-6424
Editorial Description: Tabulates consumer product-related injuries treated in hospital emergency departments.
General Info: (Formerly NEISS News), Yr. Est. 1973, Annually, Trim Size-8½ x 11, 5 pages, Ind/Abs/Online: Charts Ind., No Color
Circulation: Total-1,500

NOx Report
See: CHEMISTRY & CHEMICALS

NTSB Reporter
See: AERONAUTICS/ASTRONAUTICS

National Transportation Safety Board Digest Service
See: AERONAUTICS/ASTRONAUTICS

New England Harbormaster
See: GOVERNMENT

OSHA Compliance Encyclopedia & Newsletter *Business*

Publishing Co: Business & Legal Reports, Inc., 39 Academy St., PO Box 1513, Madison, CT 06443-2646; Title Tel # (860) 245-7448 Title Fax # (860) 245-2559
Editorial Description: Full text explanation of every OSHA Part 1910 Rule, Subpart, and regulation backed up by expert analysis and recommendations to ensure compliance.
General Info: Yr. Est. 1989, Semi-monthly, Looseleaf
Subscriptions: Indv. $460

OSHA Compliance Manual *Business*

Publishing Co: J.J. Keller & Assoc., Inc., PO Box 368, Neenah, WI 54957-0368;
Title Tel # (414) 722-2848 Title Fax # (414) 727-7516
Personnel: Editor-Webb Shaw, Adv. Dir.-David Szczeparik, Mktg. Dir.-Ed Sieracki
General Info: Yr. Est. 1993, Semi-annually, 500 pages, Looseleaf
Subscriptions: $79/copy
Circulation: Total-11,452

OSHA Guide for Health Care Facilities
See: HOSPITALS & NURSING HOMES

OSHA News/OSHA Reference Manual *Business*

Publishing Co: Merritt Professional Publishing, 1661 9th St, Santa Monica, CA 90404-3703;
Title Tel # (310) 450-7234 Title Fax # (310) 396-4563
Personnel: Editor-John Hartnett
Editorial Description: OSHA News is a biweekly newsletter providing inside secrets and advance information on what the Occupational Safety and Health Administration is doing. Subscription includes the 2 volumes OSHA Reference Manual which takes the federal OSHA general industry regulations and translates them into plain English.
General Info: Yr. Est. 1972, Bi-weekly, Trim Size-8½ x 11, Web press, 4 pages, ISSN: 0740-1418, Newsprint
Subscriptions: Indv. $397
Circulation: Total-3,000

OSHA Regulations Part 1910 Guide *Business*

Publishing Co: J.J. Keller & Assoc., Inc., PO Box 368, Neenah, WI 54957-0368;
Title Tel # (414) 722-2848 Title Fax # (414) 727-7516
Personnel: Editor-Webb Shaw, Adv. Dir.-David Szczeparik, Mktg. Dir.-Ed Sieracki
General Info: Yr. Est. 1993, Semi-annually, 800 pages, Looseleaf
Subscriptions: $129/copy
Circulation: Total-11,452

OSHA Up to Date Newsletter *Association*

Publishing Co: National Safety Council, 1121 Spring Lake Dr., Itasca, IL 60143-3201
Tel # (708) 285-1121 Fax # (708) 775-2285; Title Tel # (312) 527-4800
Editorial Description: Latest information pertaining to the Occupational Safety and Health Administration (OSHA).
General Info: Monthly, Trim Size-8½ x 11, 4 pages
Subscriptions: Indv. $7

OSHA Week
See: INDUSTRIAL RELATIONS/PERSONNEL

Occupational Health & Safety Letter *Business*

Publishing Co: Business Publishers, Inc., 951 Pershing Dr., Silver Spring, MD 20910-4464;
Title Tel # (301) 589-5103 Title Fax # (301) 589-8493
Personnel: Publisher-Eric Easton, Editor-Erich Shea, Circ. Mgr.-Brenda Davenport, Mktg. Mgr.-Keith Payne, Promotion Dir.-Adam Goldstein
Editorial Description: Worker safety & health...developments in regulation, legislation and litigation.
General Info: Yr. Est. 1970, 26x/yr., Trim Size-8½ x 11, Offset press, 8 pages, ISSN: 0148-4079, Ind/Abs/Online: Information Access Company, 2 Color, Matte
Subscriptions: Indv. $286, Can. $286, For. $299
List Rental: List Management Co.: BPI Direct, 951 Pershing Dr., Silver Spring, MD 20910-4464 Tel # (301) 585-5976, Fax # (301) 587-4530
Printing Co: Business Publishers In-House Print Shop, 951 Pershing Drive, Silver Spring, MD 20910-4454 Tel # (301) 589-8493

Occupational Health & Safety News
See: CONSTRUCTION & BUILDING

Occupational Health Nursing Newsletter *Association*

Publishing Co: National Safety Council, 1121 Spring Lake Dr., Itasca, IL 60143-3201
Tel # (708) 285-1121 Fax # (708) 775-2285; Title Tel # (312) 527-4800
Editorial Description: Editorial material devoted to the field of Occupational Health Nursing.
General Info: (Formerly Safety Newsletter, Occupation), Yr. Est. 1916, Bi-monthly, Trim Size-8½ x 11, Offset press, 4 pages, No Color
Circulation: Total-1,082

Occupational Health and Safety Law   *Business*

Publishing Co: Business Law Reporting Service, Box 1762, Kingston, ON K7L 5J6 Canada; Title Tel # (613) 546-9163
Editorial Description: Compiled information & laws, regulations with updates & newsletter. Three binder service with monthly updates.
General Info: Yr. Est. 1977, Monthly, Trim Size-8½ x 11
Subscriptions: Can. $340

Occupational Safety & Health Reporter   *Business*

Publishing Co: Bureau of National Affairs, Inc., 1231 25th St. NW, Bldg. N-200, Washington, DC 20037-1157; Title Tel # (202) 452-4200 Title Fax # (202) 822-8092
Personnel: Publisher-William A. Beltz, Editor-Mary Worobec, Mng. Editor-Stanley S. Pond, Circ. Mgr.-Gary C. Seltzer.
Editorial Description: A weekly notification & reference service which provides information on federal & state regulation of occupational safety & health, standards, & legislation, enforcement activities, research & legal decisions.
General Info: Yr. Est. 1971, Weekly, Trim Size-8½ x 11, Web press, 30 pages, ISSN: 0095-3237, Ind/Abs/Online: HRIN, Dialog, Nexis, Lexis
Subscriptions: Indv. $1,082

Occupational Safety and Health Act   *Business*

Publishing Co: Matthew Bender & Co., 11 Penn Plaza, New York, NY 10001-2006 Fax # (212) 244-3188; Title Tel # (212) 967-7707
Personnel: Editor-R. Kaye
Editorial Description: Indispensable coverage for anyone responsible for the health and safety of employees, and those who represent injured employees.
General Info: Yr. Est. 1977, Annually, Looseleaf
Subscriptions: $210/copy

Petroleum Newsletter   *Association*

Publishing Co: National Safety Council, 1121 Spring Lake Dr., Itasca, IL 60143-3201 Tel # (708) 285-1121 Fax # (708) 775-2285; Title Tel # (312) 527-4800
Editorial Description: Occupational safety and health specifically related to industries as noted in title.
General Info: Bi-monthly, Trim Size-8½ x 11, 4 pages
Circulation: Total-3,744

Power Press & Forging   *Association*

Publishing Co: National Safety Council, 1121 Spring Lake Dr., Itasca, IL 60143-3201 Tel # (708) 285-1121 Fax # (708) 775-2285; Title Tel # (312) 527-4800
Editorial Description: Occupational safety and health as specifically related to industries as noted in title.
General Info: Bi-monthly, Trim Size-8½ x 11
Circulation: Total-891

Printing & Publishing Newsletter   *Association*

Publishing Co: National Safety Council, 1121 Spring Lake Dr., Itasca, IL 60143-3201 Tel # (708) 285-1121 Fax # (708) 775-2285; Title Tel # (312) 527-4800
Editorial Description: Occupational safety and health specifically related to industries as noted in title.
General Info: (Formerly Safety Newsletter, Printing & Publishing Section), Bi-monthly, Trim Size-8½ x 11, 4 pages
Subscriptions: Indv. $7
Circulation: Total-612

Proactive Risk Management
See: HOSPITALS & NURSING HOMES

Product Safety Letter   *Business, Consumer*

Publishing Co: Washington Business Information, Inc., 1117 19th St N Ste 200, Arlington, VA 22209-1708; Title Tel # (703) 247-3423 Title Fax # (703) 247-3421
Personnel: Publisher-David Swit, Editor-Dave Kramer, Circ. Mgr.-Chris Rogers, Production Mgr.-Jennea Myrick
Editorial Description: Monitors the Consumer Product Safety Commission, other agencies, & industry developments affecting production & sale of products ranging from TVs to toys & cleansers to clothing.
General Info: Yr. Est. 1972, Weekly, Trim Size-8½ x 11, Sheetfed press, 6 pages, ISSN: 0098-7530, Ind/Abs/Online: Newsnet, No Color, Matte
Subscriptions: Indv. $827, Inst. $827, Can. $827, For. $912
Acquistions: Publication Bought
List Rental: Actives: $110/M

Product Safety News   *Association*

Publishing Co: Institute for Product Safety, PO Box 1931, Durham, NC 27702-1931; Title Tel # (919) 489-2357 Title Fax # (919) 490-4954
Personnel: Editor-Verne L. Roberts, Circ. Mgr.-Angel Wagner
Editorial Description: Abstracts from the technical literature relating to product & transportation safety.
General Info: Yr. Est. 1973, Monthly, Trim Size-8½ x 11, Offset press, 10 pages, ISSN: 0009-1162, No Color, Looseleaf
Subscriptions: Indv. $120
Circulation: Total-350

Product Safety Up to Date   *Association*

Publishing Co: National Safety Council, 1121 Spring Lake Dr., Itasca, IL 60143-3201 Tel # (708) 285-1121 Fax # (708) 775-2285; Title Tel # (312) 527-4800
Editorial Description: All current information of interest pertaining to the area of product safety.
General Info: Yr. Est. 1972, Bi-monthly, Trim Size-8½ x 11, 4 pages, No Color
Circulation: Total-4,500

Prometheus Report: Journal of Firesafety
See: FIRE PROTECTION

Public Employee Newsletter   *Association*

Publishing Co: National Safety Council, 1121 Spring Lake Dr., Itasca, IL 60143-3201 Tel # (708) 285-1121 Fax # (708) 775-2285; Title Tel # (312) 527-4800
Editorial Description: Occupational safety & health specifically related to industries as noted in title.
General Info: Bi-monthly, Trim Size-8½ x 11, 4 pages
Circulation: Total-1,411

Public Safety   *Consumer, Association*

Publishing Co: New Jersey State Dept. of Motor Vehicles, Trenton, NJ 08666-0001; Title Tel # (609) 588-2424
General Info: Monthly

Public Safety and Justice Policies/State Capitals
See: LAW ENFORCEMENT & PENOLOGY

Public Sector Job Bulletin
See: EMPLOYMENT

Public Utilities Newsletter   *Association*

Publishing Co: National Safety Council, 1121 Spring Lake Dr., Itasca, IL 60143-3201 Tel # (708) 285-1121 Fax # (708) 775-2285; Title Tel # (312) 527-4800
Personnel: Publisher-Gordon Bieberle, Editor, Production Mgr.-Carrie Smith
Editorial Description: Occupational health and safety specifically related to industry as noted in title.
General Info: Bi-monthly, Trim Size-8½ x 11, 4 pages
Subscriptions: Indv. $9
Circulation: Total-3,700

RID-USA National Newsletter
See: LAW

Railroad Newsletter   *Association*

Publishing Co: National Safety Council, 1121 Spring Lake Dr., Itasca, IL 60143-3201 Tel # (708) 285-1121 Fax # (708) 775-2285; Title Tel # (312) 527-4800
Editorial Description: Occupational health and safety specifically related to industry as noted in title.
General Info: Bi-monthly, Trim Size-8½ x 11, 4 pages
Circulation: Total-393

Regulatory Watchdog Service
See: CONSUMER INTERESTS

Research & Development   *Association*

Publishing Co: National Safety Council, 1121 Spring Lake Dr., Itasca, IL 60143-3201 Tel # (708) 285-1121 Fax # (708) 775-2285; Title Tel # (312) 527-4800
Editorial Description: Occupational health and safety specifically related to industry as noted in title.
General Info: Bi-monthly, Trim Size-8½ x 11, 4 pages
Circulation: Total-1,585
List Rental: List Management Co.: Cahners Direct Marketing Services, 1350 E. Touhy Ave., Des Plaines, IL 60017-5080 Tel # (708) 390-2361, Fax # (708) 390-2779

Rhode Island Traffic Safety Reporter   *Consumer*

Publishing Co: Rhode Island Division of Motor Vehicles, 286 Main St, Pawtucket, RI 02860-2908; Title Tel # (401) 351-2790
Personnel: Editor-Richard H. Bishop
Editorial Description: Includes general highway safety features, articles on motor vehicle law, on seat belts, motorcycle safety, pedestrian safety, etc.
General Info: Yr. Est. 1964, Quarterly
Circulation: Total-500

Right-to-Know Compliance Manual   *Business*

Publishing Co: J.J. Keller & Assoc., Inc., PO Box 368, Neenah, WI 54957-0368; Title Tel # (414) 722-2848 Title Fax # (414) 727-7516
Personnel: Editor-Webb Shaw, Adv. Dir.-David Szczeparik
Editorial Description: Complete regulatory information pertaining to OSHA Right-to-know regulations.
General Info: Yr. Est. 1987, Semi-annually, 400 pages, Looseleaf
Subscriptions: $79/copy
Circulation: Total-3,790

Riskwatch
See: INSURANCE

Rubber & Plastics

Publishing Co: National Safety Council, 1121 Spring Lake Dr., Itasca, IL 60143-3201 Tel # (708) 285-1121 Fax # (708) 775-2285; Title Tel # (312) 527-4800
General Info: (Formerly Rubber Newsletter), Bi-monthly, Trim Size-8½ x 11
Circulation: Total-922

SIA Circuit
See: MANUFACTURING

Safety & Health Bulletin
See: WATER SUPPLY, POWER & WASTE

Safety & Security for Supervisors *Business*

Publishing Co: BRP Publications, Inc., 65 Bleecker Street, 5th Floor, New York, NY 10012-2420 Parent Co.-BRP (Washington DC), Washington; Title Tel # (212) 673-4700 Title Fax # (212) 475-1790
Personnel: Publisher-John Roche, Editor-Marcia Wagshol, Circ. Mgr.-Loretta Netzer, Production Mgr.-Diane Cramer
Editorial Description: Pocket-size calendar & memory jogger with a safety or security tip for each day of the week.
General Info: Monthly, Trim Size-3⅜ x 6⅜, Sheetfed press, 40 pages, ISSN: 1040-4236, No Color, Newsprint
Subscriptions: Indv. $28
List Rental: List Management Co.: Affinity Marketing Group Inc., P.O. Box 2409, Fairfax, VA 22031 Tel # (703) 978-4927, Fax # (703) 425-4537, Actives: 1,800, $95/M, Expires: 1,100, $95/M
Printing Co: Port City Press, 1323 Greenwood Rd, Pikesville, MD 21208-3611 Tel # (410) 486-3000, Fax # (410) 486-0706

Safety Activist

Publishing Co: Intl. Institute for Safety in Transportation, PO Box 63, Franklin Square, NY 11010-0063; Title Tel # (516) 485-0050
Circulation: Total-150

Safety Briefs *Association*

Publishing Co: New Jersey State Safety Council, 6 Commerce Dr., Cranford, NJ 07016-3509; Title Tel # (908) 272-7712 Title Fax # (908) 276-6622
Personnel: Editor-Carol Ann Dillon
Editorial Description: Safety education - highway - occupational - recreational - home.
General Info: Yr. Est. 1938, Quarterly, Trim Size-8½ x 11, Offset press, 8 pages, 2 Color, Matte
Circulation: Total-18,000

Safety Bulletin

Publishing Co: National Automobile Transporters Assn., 902 Buhl Bldg., Detroit, MI 48226; Title Tel # (313) 557-8855

Safety Compliance Alert *Business*

Publishing Co: Progressive Business Publications, 370 Technology Dr., #3019, Malverne, PA 19355-9863 Parent Co.-American Future Systems, Inc., Bryn Mawr; Title Tel # (610) 695-8600 Title Fax # (610) 647-8089
Personnel: Publisher-Edward M. Satell, Editorial Dir.-Stephen Meyer, Editor-Pieter VanBennekom
Editorial Description: Helps safety professionals avoid accidents and comply with OSHA regulations through real world examples.
General Info: Yr. Est. 1994, Bi-weekly, 8 pages
Subscriptions: Indv. $299
List Rental: List Management Co.: Mail Marketing, Inc., 171 Terrace St., Haworth, NJ 07641-1899 Tel # (201) 387-1023, Fax # (201) 387-2976

Safety Compliance Letter with OSHA Highlights *Business*

Publishing Co: Bureau of Business Practice, 24 Rope Ferry Rd, Waterford, CT 06386-0001 Tel # (806) 442-4365 Parent Co.-Prentice Hall, Waterford; Title Tel # (860) 442-4365 Title Fax # (860) 434-3341
Personnel: Publisher-James O'Shea, Editor-Michele Rubin
Editorial Description: Provide compliance information for safety professionals to implement in their companies to reduce accidents, injuird and related costs.
General Info: (Formerly OSHA Compliance Letter), Yr. Est. 1972, Semi-monthly, Trim Size-8½ x 11, 4 pages, ISSN: 1069-2037, 4 Color
Subscriptions: Indv. $180
Circulation: Total-8,000

Safety First *Business, Association*

Publishing Co: B.C. Safety Council, 8589 Baxter Place, Burnaby, BC V5A 4V7 Canada; Title Tel # (604) 420-4110 Title Fax # (604) 420-9043
Personnel: Publisher-Bryan Lowes
Editorial Description: Keeps community aware of safety issues.
General Info: (Formerly B.C. Safety Council Newsletter), Quarterly, 8 pages, 2 Color
Circulation: Total-6,500

Safety Information

Publishing Co: Royal-Globe Insurance Cos., 1 Chase Manhattan Plz., 38th Fl., New York, NY 10005-1401 Tel # (212) 553-3000; Title Tel # (212) 732-8400
Personnel: Editor-James P. Licata
General Info: Bi-monthly

Safety Insight *Association*

Publishing Co: MEMA-Motor & Equipment Manufacturers Assn., PO Box 13966, Rtp, NC 27709-3966 Tel # (919) 549-4800 Fax # (919) 549-4824
Personnel: Publisher-J. J. Conner
Editorial Description: Automotive safety developments with emphasis on federal motor vehicle safety standards, of interest to automotive and truck product suppliers and manufacturers.
General Info: Trim Size-8½ x 11, Sheetfed press, Color

Safety Is Elementary *Business, Association*

Publishing Co: Laboratory Safety Workshop, 101 Oak Street, Wellesley, MA 02181; Title Tel # (617) 237-1335 Title Fax # (617) 239-1457
Personnel: Editor-James A. Kaufman, Circ. Mgr.-Mary T. Bagley
Editorial Description: Newsletter devoted to the science safety concerns of teachers of elementary science.
General Info: Yr. Est. 1991, Tri-annually, Trim Size-8½ x 11, 20 pages
Subscriptions: Indv. $10, Can. $15, For. $25
Circulation: Total-500
List Rental: Rents Lists

Safety Management *Business*

Publishing Co: Bureau of Business Practice, 24 Rope Ferry Rd, Waterford, CT 06386-0001 Tel # (806) 442-4365 Parent Co.-Prentice Hall, Waterford; Title Tel # (860) 442-4365 Title Fax # (860) 434-3341
Personnel: Publisher-James O'Shea, Editor-Heather Vaughn
Editorial Description: For personnel in charge of safety & health in companies. Discusses pertinent legal issues in an easy-to-understand format. Describes successful safety programs. Subscription includes Safety Compliance Letter with OSHA Highlights.
General Info: Yr. Est. 1971, Monthly, Trim Size-8½ x 11, 8 pages, ISSN: 1069-2118, 2 Color
Subscriptions: Indv. $180
Circulation: Total-7,868

Safety Meeting Repro's *Business*

Publishing Co: Business & Legal Reports, Inc., 39 Academy St., PO Box 1513, Madison, CT 06443-2646; Title Tel # (860) 245-7448 Title Fax # (860) 245-2559
Editorial Description: Includes over 50 lesson plans on critical safety topics with illustrated employee handouts. all materials are reproducible so you can hand them out to workers. This all-inclusive program ensures efficient and effective meetings every time.
General Info: Yr. Est. 1995, Quarterly, Looseleaf
Subscriptions: Indv. $295
List Rental: List Management Co.: Marketing List Professionals, 39 Academy St # 1513, Madison, CT 06443-2646 Tel # (860) 245-2076, Fax # (860) 245-2559, Actives: $80/M, Hotline: $85/M

Safety News

Publishing Co: South Carolina Industrial Commission, PO Box 1715, Columbia, SC 29202-1715; Title Tel # (803) 737-5700
Personnel: Editor-Fred Derrick, Jr.
Editorial Description: Contains announcements of safety projects and activities as well as articles on safety.
General Info: Yr. Est. 1950, Monthly
Circulation: Total-2,200

Safety Signals

Publishing Co: Industrial Safety Equipment Assn., 1901 N. Moore St., Arlington, VA 22209-1706; Title Tel # (703) 525-1695 Title Fax # (703) 528-2148
Personnel: Editor-Bruce R. Clash
Editorial Description: Safety Signals is published six times per year by the industrial safety equipment association. It contains information about the safety equipment industry, member companies, association activities and upcoming methods and events.
General Info: Bi-monthly, 8 pages, 3% ads, Coated, Saddle-stitched
Circulation: Total-450
Advertising: Inquire for rates.

Safety Talks *Business*

Publishing Co: Business & Legal Reports, Inc., 39 Academy St., PO Box 1513, Madison, CT 06443-2646; Title Tel # (860) 245-7448 Title Fax # (860) 245-2559
Editorial Description: A dynamic program of short, prewritten 'talks' created to promote safety and reduce accidents.
General Info: Yr. Est. 1994, Quarterly, Looseleaf
Subscriptions: Indv. $200
List Rental: List Management Co.: Marketing List Professionals, 39 Academy St # 1513, Madison, CT 06443-2646 Tel # (860) 245-2076, Fax # (860) 245-2559, Actives: $80/M, Hotline: $85/M

Safety Works *Business*

Publishing Co: Business & Legal Reports, Inc., 39 Academy St., PO Box 1513, Madison, CT 06443-2646 Fax # (860) 245-2559; Title Tel # (860) 245-7448 Title Fax # (860) 245-1513
Personnel: Editor-John Brady, Art Dir.-John Kallio
Editorial Description: Facts and guidance supervisors need to reduce liabilities, meet right-to-know & Hazmat requirements, and maintain safety and health.
General Info: (Formerly OSHA Training Bulletin for Supervisors), Yr. Est. 1982, Monthly, Trim Size-11 x 17, Web press, 8 pages, ISSN: 0887-9125, 2 Color, Newsprint
Subscriptions: Indv. $99
Circulation: Total-3,000
List Rental: List Management Co.: Marketing List Professionals, 39 Academy St # 1513, Madison, CT 06443-2646 Tel # (860) 245-2076, Fax # (860) 245-2559, Actives: $80/M, Hotline: $85/M

St. John News
See: HEALTH

Saskatchewan Safety
Council Link
Business, Association

Publishing Co: Saskatchewan Safety Council, 445 Hoffer Drive, Regina, SK S4N 6E2 Canada; Title Tel # (306) 757-3197 Title Fax # (306) 569-1907
Personnel: Editor-Linda Saliken
General Info: (Formerly Safety Saskatchewan), Quarterly, Trim Size-11 x 17, Offset press, 2 pages, Color-cover, Newsprint
Subscriptions: Indv. $8, Free With Membership
Circulation: Total-600
Advertising: Inquire for rates. Accepts Inserts.
List Rental: Actives: $40/M

School Emergencies
See: SCHOOL ADMINISTRATION

School Safety World

Publishing Co: National Safety Council, 1121 Spring Lake Dr., Itasca, IL 60143-3201 Tel # (708) 285-1121 Fax # (708) 775-2285; Title Tel # (312) 527-4800
General Info: Quarterly, Trim Size-8½ x 11, 4 pages

Scientific Automobile Accident Reconstruction
See: LAW

Society Update
Association

Publishing Co: American Society of Safety Engineers, 1800 E. Oakton St., Des Plaines, IL 60018-2112; Title Tel # (708) 692-4121 Title Fax # (708) 296-3769
Personnel: Editor-Tricia Gadsby
Editorial Description: Membership newsletter.
General Info: Yr. Est. 1964, Monthly, Trim Size-8¼ x 11¼, Sheetfed press, 4 pages, 2 Color, Saddle-stitched
Circulation: (BPA), Total-29,000
List Rental: Actives: 29,000
Printing Co: IPC, 2180 Maiden Lane, St. Joseph, MI 49085 Tel # (616) 983-7105, Fax # (616) 983-5736

Speaking Out
Consumer

Publishing Co: Concerned Citizens Speak, Inc., Box 1108, Madison Square Station, New York, NY 10159-1108
Personnel: Editor-Milton Finkelman
Editorial Description: Society of concerned citizens for safety on New York streets.
General Info: Quarterly, Trim Size-8½ x 11, 6 pages, No Color, Matte
Subscriptions: Indv. $15

Speaking of Safety
Association, Business

Publishing Co: Laboratory Safety Workshop, 101 Oak Street, Wellesley, MA 02181; Title Tel # (617) 237-1335 Title Fax # (617) 239-1457
Personnel: Publisher-James A. Kaufman, Circ. Mgr.-Mary T. Bagley
Editorial Description: Laboratory safety workshop newsletter.
General Info: Yr. Est. 1987, Tri-annually, Trim Size-8½ x 11, Offset press, 16 pages, Matte
Subscriptions: Indv. $13, Can. $15, For. $25
Circulation: Total-2,200
List Rental: Rents Lists

Standards & Recommended Practices for Small Craft
See: BOATS & BOATING

Supervisor's Safety Meeting
Handbook
Business

Publishing Co: Business & Legal Reports, Inc., 39 Academy St., PO Box 1513, Madison, CT 06443-2646; Title Tel # (860) 245-7448 Title Fax # (860) 245-2559
Editorial Description: Over 70 ready to use safety meeting outlines, actual lesson plans, training outlines, and hand outs.
General Info: Yr. Est. 1989, Quarterly, Looseleaf
Subscriptions: Indv. $200

Surveillant

Publishing Co: La Ligue de Securite du Quebec, 2536 rue La Pierre, La Salle, PQ H8N 2W9 Canada; Title Tel # (514) 595-9110
Personnel: Editor-Robert Plunkett
General Info: Yr. Est. 1976, 4 pages
Subscriptions: $2/copy
Circulation: Total-700

Synopsis of Boiler &
Pressure Vessel Laws,
Rules & Regulations
Association

Publishing Co: Uniform Boiler & Pressure Vessel Laws Society, 308 N. Evergreen, Louisville, KY 40243; Title Tel # (502) 339-8162 Title Fax # (502) 425-7458
Personnel: Publisher-Raymond Swanson
Editorial Description: Summary of boiler and pressure vessel laws, rules and regulations.
General Info: Yr. Est. 1969, Trim Size-8½ x 11, Offset press, 100 pages, No Color, Looseleaf
Subscriptions: Indv. $87
Circulation: Total-2,400

Textile Newsletter
Association

Publishing Co: National Safety Council, 1121 Spring Lake Dr., Itasca, IL 60143-3201 Tel # (708) 285-1121 Fax # (708) 775-2285; Title Tel # (312) 527-4800
Editorial Description: Occupational safety and health specifically related to industries as noted in title.
General Info: Bi-monthly, Trim Size-8½ x 11, 4 pages
Circulation: Total-631

Trades & Services
Newsletter
Association

Publishing Co: National Safety Council, 1121 Spring Lake Dr., Itasca, IL 60143-3201 Fax # (708) 775-2285; Title Tel # (708) 285-1121
Editorial Description: Occupational safety and health specifically related to industries noted in title.
General Info: (Formerly Safety Newsletter, Trades & Services Section), Bi-monthly, Trim Size-8½ x 11, 4 pages
Subscriptions: Indv. $7
Circulation: Total-1,007

Transafety Reporter
Business

Publishing Co: Transafety, Inc., PO Box 3100, Sequim, WA 98382-5006 Tel # (360) 239-2122 Fax # (360) 683-6719
Personnel: Publisher, Editor-Roy Anderson, Promotion Dir.-Michelle Stuart
Editorial Description: News/analysis on highway safety litigation for attorneys & engineers.
General Info: Yr. Est. 1983, Monthly, Sheetfed press, 8 pages, ISSN: 0884-612X, No Color, Newsprint
Subscriptions: Indv. $196, Can. $196, $17/copy
Printing Co: Newsletter Services, Inc., 9700 Philadelphia Court, Lanham, MD 20706 Tel # (301) 731-5200, Fax # (301) 731-5201

Traumagram Newsletter
See: HEALTH

Volunteers Voice for
Community Safety

Publishing Co: National Safety Council, 1121 Spring Lake Dr., Itasca, IL 60143-3201 Tel # (708) 285-1121 Fax # (708) 775-2285; Title Tel # (312) 527-4800
General Info: Bi-monthly, Trim Size-8½ x 11, No Color

West Coast Lifeliner
See: HEALTH

Wire Talk
Business

Publishing Co: Underwriters Laboratories, Inc., 333 Pfingsten Rd, Northbrook, IL 60062-2096 Tel # (708) 272-8800 Fax # (708) 272-8129
Personnel: Editor-Michael Nissen
Editorial Description: Covers certification issues for the wire and cable industry.
General Info: Yr. Est. 1991, Quarterly, Trim Size-8½ x 11, Sheetfed press, 4 pages, 2 Color, Matte
Subscriptions: Free To Qualified Recipient
Circulation: (100% controlled), Total-3,800

Wisconsin Safety &
Health
Business

Publishing Co: WMC Service Corp., 501 E Washington Ave # 352, Madison, WI 53703-2914; Title Tel # (608) 258-3400 Title Fax # (608) 258-3413
Personnel: Editor, Production Mgr.-Kathleen Johnson
Editorial Description: Monthly newsletter devoted entirely to safety & health subjects.
General Info: (Formerly Wisconsin Safety News), Yr. Est. 1968, Bi-monthly, Trim Size-8½ x 11, Sheetfed press, 6 pages, 2 Color, Newsprint
Subscriptions: Indv. $25, Free With Membership
Circulation: (100% controlled), Total-5,000
Advertising: Inquire for rates.
Printing Co: Kramer Printing, 831 E Washington Ave, Madison, WI 53703-2991 Tel # (608) 256-1984

Your Safety
Consumer, Association

Publishing Co: North Carolina State Dept. of Safety, Raleigh, NC 27611; Title Tel # (919) 733-7166
General Info: Monthly

Your Safety News
Business

Publishing Co: A.M. Best Co., Inc., Ambest Rd., Oldwick, NJ 08858-0700 Tel # (908) 439-2200 Fax # (908) 439-3296
Personnel: Publisher-Arthur Snyder, Editor-Robin Chandler
Editorial Description: Reinforces safety programs by increasing employee awareness.
General Info: Monthly

SALESMANSHIP & SELLING

Advanced Selling Power
Business

Publishing Co: Thompson Group, 3371 Brunswick Plke, Ste. 302-174, Lawrenceville, NJ 08648; Title Tel # (609) 584-1939 Title Fax # (609) 890-9286
Personnel: Publisher-Terry E. Thompson, Editor-Valerie A. Canaday, Circ. Dir.-Karen N. Smith, Art Dir.-Victoria C. Flores
Editorial Description: Provides sales tactis, strategies, and ideas to sales professionls and entrepreneurs. Each issue helps salespeople learn how to put together presentations, develop openings that keep customers interested, use testimonials correctly, and more.
General Info: Yr. Est. 1993, 10x/yr., Trim Size-8½ x 11, Sheetfed press, 8 pages, 2 Color, Matte, Saddle-stitched
Subscriptions: Indv. $97, Can. $107, $10/copy
Circulation: Total-1,000
Printing Co: Graphic Data, inc., 528 Fellowship Rd, Mount Laurel, NJ 08054-3405 Tel # (609) 778-1560, Fax # (609) 778-9264

Advertising Via Telemarketing Script Presentations Newsletter
See: BUSINESS & INDUSTRY

Alert
See: BUSINESS & INDUSTRY

Art of Self Promotion, The
See: ADVERTISING & MARKETING

At Home with Consumers
See: CONSUMER INTERESTS

Blueprints
See: ADVERTISING & MARKETING

Business Review
See: BUSINESS & INDUSTRY

CARD TALK
See: PRINTING/GRAPHIC ARTS

Competitive Advantage
Business

Publishing Co: Competitive Advantage, PO Box 10091, Portland, OR 97210-0091; Title Tel # (503) 274-2953 Title Fax # (503) 274-4349
Personnel: Publisher, Editor-Jim Moran, Circ. Mgr.-Julie Erlandsen, Promotion Dir.-Tonya Shrives
Editorial Description: Provides sales, marketing & management tools to make careers & companies more prosperous.
General Info: Yr. Est. 1986, Monthly, Trim Size-8½ x 11, Web press, 8 pages, ISSN: 0886-1994, 2 Color, Matte, Saddle-stitched
Subscriptions: Indv. $99, Can. $111, For. $144
Acquistions: Publication Bought
Circulation: Total-12,000
List Rental: List Management Co.: Manager: Tonya Shrives; Target Marketing, PO Box 10091, Portland, OR 97210-0091 Tel # (503) 274-2953, Actives: 11,000, $95/M, Expires: 5,000, $85/M

Contact
Business, Association

Publishing Co: Canadian Professional Sales Association, 145 Wellington St. W., #310, Toronto, ON M5J 1H8 Canada; Title Tel # (416) 408-2685 Title Fax # (416) 408-2684
Personnel: Editor-Corinne James, Art Dir.-Christian Clare
Editorial Description: This newsletter provides members of the Canadian Professional Sales Association with up-to-date information on travel benefits offered by the association as well as professional development information including articles on selling techniques, industry trends and government relations.
General Info: (Formerly Canadian Salesman (Le Voyageur)), 5x/yr., Trim Size-8½ x 11, Letrpr. press, 20 pages, ISSN: 1193-7513, 2 Color, Matte, Saddle-stitched
Subscriptions: Free With Membership
Circulation: Total-31,000

Creative Selling
Business

Publishing Co: Creative Selling, 120 Walton St Ste 201, Syracuse, NY 13202-1211; Title Fax # (315) 422-3837
Personnel: Publisher-Bob Popyk, Editor-Virginia Yaruss, Mktg. Dir.-Bob Tringali
Editorial Description: Contains training material for sales managers and sales training managers.
General Info: (Formerly Hot Buttoneer), Yr. Est. 1983, Monthly, Trim Size-8½ x 11, Offset press, 8 pages, Color, Coated, Saddle-stitched
Subscriptions: Indv. $79, $7/copy
Circulation: Total-6,500

Culpepper Letter: Software Intelligence for Growth and Profits
See: COMPUTERS & AUTOMATION

Customer Service Report
See: MANAGEMENT

Customers First
Business

Publishing Co: Dartnell Corp., 4660 N. Ravenswood Ave., Chicago, IL 60640-4510 Tel # (312) 561-4000; Title Fax # (312) 561-3801
Personnel: Publisher-Clark Fetridge, Editor-Kim Andersen, Production Mgr.-Megan Mullingas, Art Dir.-Andrew Epstein, Mktg. Dir.-George Economos
Editorial Description: A practical periodical that provides employees with an organized plan of action for building & improving customer relations. Provides your team with innovative customer relations techniques & regular reinforcement of the overriding importance of good customer relations.
General Info: (Formerly Customers), Yr. Est. 1987, Bi-weekly, Trim Size-8½ x 11, 2 Color, Matte
Subscriptions: Indv. $59, $62/copy
List Rental: List Management Co.: Manager: Sue McDorman; Leland Company, 1801 W. Leland Ave., Chicago, IL 60640-4363 Tel # (312) 561-4005, Fax # (312) 561-4099, Actives: 40,937

Cyberspace PR Newsletter
See: ADVERTISING & MARKETING

Direct Selling Association International Bulletin
Business, Association

Publishing Co: World Federation of Direct Selling Association, 1666 K St. NW, Ste. 1010, Washington, DC 20006; Title Tel # (202) 293-5760 Title Fax # (202) 463-4569
Personnel: Editor-Neil Offen
Editorial Description: Association activities; legislation affecting direct selling; trends.
General Info: Quarterly, Offset press, Newsprint, Saddle-stitched
Circulation: (100% controlled), Total-1,200

Dynamic Selling
Business

Publishing Co: Economics Press, Inc., 12 Daniel Rd., Fairfield, NJ 07004-2565 Tel # (201) 227-1224; Title Fax # (201) 227-9742
Editorial Description: Covers sales issues and ways to improve sales.
General Info: Yr. Est. 1993, Bi-weekly, Trim Size-8½ x 11, 4 pages, Color
Subscriptions: Indv. $40

Early Warning Report
See: ELECTRIC & ELECTRONIC EQUIPMENT

Effective Telephone Techniques
Business

Publishing Co: Dartnell Corp., 4660 N. Ravenswood Ave., Chicago, IL 60640-4510; Title Tel # (312) 561-4000 Title Fax # (312) 561-3801
Personnel: Publisher-Clark Fetridge, Editor-Kim Anderson, Product Mgr.-Megan Mulligas, Production Mgr.-Megan Mulligan, Art Dir.-Andrew Epstein, Mktg. Dir.-George Economos
Editorial Description: This bi-weekly training bulletin will help your team build profitable customer relations with every call. Specially designed features encourage employees to make the most of their telephone contacts-in sales, telemarketing, customer service & other important areas of your business.
General Info: (Formerly Telephone Techniques), Yr. Est. 1989, Bi-weekly, Trim Size-8½ x 11, 4 pages, 2 Color, Matte
Subscriptions: Indv. $59, $62/copy
List Rental: List Management Co.: Manager: Sue McDorman; Leland Company, 1801 W. Leland Ave., Chicago, IL 60640-4363 Tel # (312) 561-4005, Fax # (312) 561-4099, Actives: 70,785, $90/M, Hotline: $125/M

Electrical Sales Builder
Business

Publishing Co: Business Marketing & Publishing, Inc., PO Box 7457, Wilton, CT 06897-7457; Title Tel # (203) 834-9959
Personnel: Publisher, Editor-George Young
Editorial Description: News and information about electrical supplies, manufacturers, sales aids, advertising, merchandising, and promotions.
General Info: Yr. Est. 1987, Quarterly
Subscriptions: Indv. $20, $5/copy
Advertising: $825. Accepts Inserts.
List Rental: Rents Lists

Exhibit Mexico
See: ADVERTISING & MARKETING

Flotation News

Publishing Co: Natl. Waterbed Retailers Assn., 36 S State St Ste 1506, Chicago, IL 60603-2606; Title Tel # (312) 236-6662

Front and Center
See: ADVERTISING & MARKETING

George Whalin's Retail Management Letter
See: ADVERTISING & MARKETING

Home Business Idea Possibility Newsletter
See: BUSINESS & INDUSTRY

In Control
See: ADVERTISING & MARKETING

Information Solutions: A newsletter of ideas & techniques on how to profit from info.
See: MANAGEMENT

Ink! Ink! Ink!
See: BUSINESS & INDUSTRY

Interaction
See: CHAMBER OF COMMERCE

Interactive Public Relations
See: ADVERTISING & MARKETING

LifeLine / Vitalite
See: INSURANCE

Limited Edition
See: ART & SCULPTURE

MIC/INFO
See: COMPUTERS & AUTOMATION

Management Portfolio
See: PRINTING/GRAPHIC ARTS

Master Salesmanship *Business*

Publishing Co: Clement Communications, Inc., Concord Industrial Park, Concordville, PA 19331-9987 Tel # (610) 459-1700; Title Tel # (215) 459-4200 Title Fax # (610) 459-5092
Personnel: Publisher-G.Y. Clement, Editor-Homer Smith, Exec. Ed.-Wendy Kaplan Ampolsk, Mng. Editor-Laurie Lo Sasso-Casey
Editorial Description: The newsletter for professional salespeople.
General Info: Bi-weekly, Trim Size-$8\frac{1}{2}$ x 11, Offset press, 4 pages, 4 Color, Coated
Subscriptions: Indv. $99, $2/copy
List Rental: Actives: $70/M

Mini Lab Focus
See: PHOTOGRAPHY

New Account Selling

Publishing Co: Dartnell Corp., 4660 N. Ravenswood Ave., Chicago, IL 60640-4510; Title Tel # (312) 561-4000 Title Fax # (312) 561-3801
Personnel: Publisher-Clark Fetridge, Editor-Terry Breen, Production Mgr.-Megan Mulligan, Art Dir.-Andrew Epstein, Mktg. Dir.-George Economos
Editorial Description: New account selling is jam-packed with timely & effective techniques for building sales & improving profits. This instructive series is ideal for training new sales people & for increasing the productivity of your sales veterans.
General Info: Yr. Est. 1991, Bi-weekly, Mimeo press, 4 pages, 2 Color
Subscriptions: Indv. $59, $62/copy
List Rental: List Management Co.: Manager: Sue McDorman; Leland Company, 1801 W. Leland Ave., Chicago, IL 60640-4363 Tel # (312) 561-4005, Fax # (312) 561-4099, Actives: 70,785, $90/M, Hotline: $125/M

PBC National Auctions and Sales News *Business, Consumer*

Publishing Co: Publishing & Business Consultants, 101 W. 64th St. Unit #3, Inglewood, CA 90302-1255 Tel # (213) 732-3477 Fax # (213) 732-3477
General Info: Quarterly, ISSN: 1059-1451
Subscriptions: Indv. $180
Advertising: Inquire for rates.

Perspective
See: ADVERTISING & MARKETING

Plastics Brief Newsletter
See: PLASTICS

Professional Selling *Business*

Publishing Co: Simon & Schuster, 24 Rope Ferry Rd, Waterford, CT 06386-0001 Fax # (860) 434-3341 Parent Co.-Viacom, New York; Title Tel # (860) 442-4365 Title Fax # (860) 434-3078
Personnel: Publisher-James E. Bradle, Editor-Paulette Kitchens, Mng. Editor-Wayne Muller, Art Dir.-Ellie Barber
Editorial Description: Written for professionals who sell equipment, products, & services out in the field. The pub. reports on the selling techniques, strategies, & skills vital in today's complex & competitive marketplace. Also addresses areas of special concern & nterestto salespeople in high-tech industries--consultative selling, market trends, account penetration & development, & the bidding, proposal,
General Info: Semi-weekly, Trim Size-$8\frac{1}{2}$ x 11, 8 pages, ISSN: 1077-436X, 4 Color, Matte
Subscriptions: Indv. $150, $6/copy
Circulation: Total-5,500

Publisher's Report
See: BOOKS & BOOK TRADE

Quality 1st.
See: INDUSTRIAL RELATIONS/PERSONNEL

Radio Promotion Bulletin
See: BROADCASTING

Real Estate Marketing Management Alert
See: REAL ESTATE

SHOWFAX
See: ADVERTISING & MARKETING

Sale$Maker$ *Business*

Publishing Co: Economics Press, Inc., 12 Daniel Rd., Fairfield, NJ 07004-2565; Title Tel # (201) 227-1224 Title Fax # (201) 227-9742
Personnel: Editor-Robert Guder, Circ. Mgr.-Anne Lanahan
Editorial Description: Helps salespeople hone selling skills using practical strategies.
General Info: Yr. Est. 1977, Bi-weekly, Trim Size-$3\frac{3}{4}$ x $7\frac{3}{8}$, 8 pages
Circulation: Total-5,878
List Rental: List Management Co.: Names in the News, 411 Theodore Fremd Ave., Rye, NY 10580 Tel # (914) 925-2400
Printing Co: Beckley Press, 2 Sperry Rd, Fairfield, NJ 07004-2056 Tel # (201) 227-6350

Sales & Marketing Executive Report
See: MANAGEMENT

Sales Automation Success *Business*

Publishing Co: Denali Group, Inc., 2815 NW Pine Cone Dr # 100, Issaquah, WA 98027-8698; Title Tel # (206) 392-3514 Title Fax # (206) 391-7982
Personnel: Publisher-Richard Bohn, Editor-Steven Pokin
Editorial Description: How to increase your sales and marketing efforts through effective use of technology.
General Info: Yr. Est. 1985, Monthly, Trim Size-$8\frac{1}{2}$ x 11, Web press, 8 pages, ISSN: 8756-8780, 2 Color
Subscriptions: Indv. $97, Can. $97, For. $117
Circulation: Total-5,000, Readership-20,000
Printing Co: Kaye Smith, Renton, WA 98057

Sales Bullet, A *Business*

Publishing Co: Economics Press, Inc., 12 Daniel Rd., Fairfield, NJ 07004-2565; Title Tel # (201) 227-1224 Title Fax # (201) 227-9742
Personnel: Editor-Robert Guder, Promotion Dir.-Diane Cody
Editorial Description: Covers the fundamental and subtleties of professional selling with methods, principles and ideas all salepeople will find useful.
General Info: Yr. Est. 1959, Bi-weekly
Subscriptions: Indv. $62
Circulation: Total-9,000
List Rental: List Management Co.: Manager: Michael Korman; Names in the News, 411 Theodore Fremd Ave., Rye, NY 10580 Tel # (914) 925-2400, Actives: $85/M
Printing Co: Beckley Press, 2 Sperry Rd, Fairfield, NJ 07004-2056 Tel # (201) 227-6350

Sales Leads *Business*

Publishing Co: Sales Leads Publishing Co., 705 Park Ave., Lake Park, FL 33403-2503; Title Tel # (407) 845-0133 Title Fax # (407) 848-2799
Personnel: Publisher-Johh B. Beecher, Editor-Michael Beecher
Editorial Description: Sales Leads consists of brief, 1-paragraph reports on industrial companies planning to build, expand or relocate plants, factories, or distribution facilities.
General Info: Yr. Est. 1959, Bi-weekly, Trim Size-$8\frac{1}{2}$ x 14, 1 pages, ISSN: 0889-4779, 2 Color, Other, Other
Subscriptions: Indv. $995, Can. $260
Circulation: Total-1,980
List Rental: Rents Lists

Sales Manager's Bulletin *Business*

Publishing Co: Bureau of Business Practice, 24 Rope Ferry Rd, Waterford, CT 06386-0001 Tel # (806) 442-4365 Fax # (860) 434-3341 Parent Co.-Prentice Hall, Waterford; Title Tel # (860) 442-4365 Title Fax # (860) 434-3078
Personnel: Publisher-James E. Bradler, Editor-Paulette Kitchens, Art Dir.-Ellie Barber
Editorial Description: For front-line sales management. Focus on sales hiring, training, managing, motivation, results. Reports what people in sales management field are doing to produce measurable sales profits.
General Info: Semi-monthly, Trim Size-$8\frac{1}{2}$ x 11, 8 pages, ISSN: 0036-3421, 4 Color, Matte
Subscriptions: Indv. $204, $9/copy
Circulation: Total-4,290

Sales Managers Idea Letter *Business*

Publishing Co: West, Adams, Christopher & Associates, 1000 W. McNab Rd., Suite 158, Pompano, FL 33069-9871 Fax # (305) 578-4200; Title Tel # (305) 384-8500 Title Fax # (305) 384-9700
Editorial Description: Ideas for sales and prospecting for sales managers.
General Info: Weekly

Sales Pro, The *Business*

Publishing Co: West, Adams, Christopher & Associates, 1000 W. McNab Rd., Suite 158, Pompano, FL 33069-9871 Fax # (305) 578-4200; Title Tel # (305) 384-8500 Title Fax # (305) 384-9700
Editorial Description: Covers technologies for sales professionals along with sales strategies and methods.
General Info: Weekly

Sales Productivity Review, The *Business*

Publishing Co: Penoyer Communications, PO Box 2509, Santa Clara, CA 95055-2509; Title Tel # (408) 296-6880 Title Fax # (408) 296-6917
Editorial Description: Edited for sales management (with emphasis on high tech products) with an editorial focus that will assist in improving sales productivity and effectiveness.
General Info: Yr. Est. 1992, Monthly, 4 pages, ISSN: 1063-6587, No Color, Matte
Subscriptions: Indv. $36, Inst. $36, $5/copy

Sales Professional   *Business*

Publishing Co: Research Institute of America, 117 E Stevens Ave, Valhalla, NY 10595-1264; Title Tel # (212) 645-4800
Personnel: Editor-Toni Apgar, Promotion Dir.-Rob Garber
Editorial Description: Bi-weekly reports & special studies to improve & enlarge basic selling skills-prospecting, presentations, etc.
General Info: (Formerly Salesman's Service), Yr. Est. 1953, Bi-weekly, 8 pages, Color, Looseleaf
Subscriptions: Indv. $120
List Rental: List Management Co.: WG & L List Management, 1 Penn Plz Fl 42, New York, NY 10119-0002 Tel # (212) 971-5000

Sales Rep's Advisor, The   *Business*

Publishing Co: Alexander Research & Communications, Inc., 215 Park Ave S., Ste. 1301, New York, NY 10003-1603; Title Tel # (212) 228-0246 Title Fax # (212) 228-0376
Personnel: Publisher-Shirley Alexander, Editor-Laurence Alexander, Mng. Editor-Paul Braus, Circ. Mgr.-Mary Pagliaroli, Mktg. Dir.-Margaret DeWitt
Editorial Description: For independent manufacturers sales representatives. Filled with concise advice & ideas for reducing costs & increasing profits. Provides valuable information on such topics as crises with power buyers, tax information & strategies, business management, partnering with principals, sales management, legal issues, changing laws & regulations and more.
General Info: Yr. Est. 1981, Semi-monthly, Trim Size-8½ x 11, 6 pages, ISSN: 0278-5048
Subscriptions: Indv. $123, Can. $123, For. $153, $6/copy
Acquistions: Publication Bought, Publication Sold
List Rental: Rents Lists

SalesCoach
See: DEPARTMENT STORE & RETAIL

Sales/Marketing Today

Publishing Co: Sales, 446 Statler Office Tower, Cleveland, OH 44115
Personnel: Editor-J. Bradley Robertson
General Info: Annually
Subscriptions: Indv. $1

Salesmanship   *Business*

Publishing Co: Dartnell Corp., 4660 N. Ravenswood Ave., Chicago, IL 60640-4510; Title Tel # (312) 561-4000 Title Fax # (312) 561-3801
Personnel: Publisher-Clark Fetridge, Editor-Terry Breen, Production Mgr.-Megan Mulligan, Art Dir.-Andrew Epstein, Mktg. Dir.-George Economos
Editorial Description: This biweekly bulletin enhances your training program with engaging & instructive reminders & shape-up tips that pay off in greater gains from your sales force. Salesmanship includes 'How to Sell Better' feature; checklist to help your salespeople evaluate their performance & quarterly 'Special Reports' throughout the year.
General Info: Yr. Est. 1974, Bi-weekly, Trim Size-8½ x 11, Offset press, 4 pages, 2 Color
Subscriptions: Indv. $59, $62/copy
Acquistions: Publication Bought
List Rental: List Management Co.: Manager: Sue McDorman; Leland Company, 1801 W. Leland Ave., Chicago, IL 60640-4363 Tel # (312) 561-4005, Fax # (312) 561-4099, Actives: 70,785, $90/M, Hotline: $125/M

Self Employment Update - Business Idea Letters Edition
See: BUSINESS & INDUSTRY

Selling Advantage   *Business*

Publishing Co: Progressive Business Publications, 370 Technology Dr., #3019, Malverne, PA 19355-9863 Tel # (610) 695-8600 Parent Co.-American Future Systems, Inc., Bryn Mawr; Title Fax # (610) 647-8089
Personnel: Publisher-Edward Satell, Editor-Philip Ahr, Editorial Dir.-Steve Meyer, Mktg. Dir.-Ed Moore
Editorial Description: Business-to-business sales advice to assist sales staff and sales managers.
General Info: Yr. Est. 1989, Bi-weekly, Trim Size-8½ x 11, 4 pages, ISSN: 1046-9036, 2 Color, Recycled
Subscriptions: Indv. $96
List Rental: List Management Co.: Mail Marketing, Inc., 171 Terrace St., Haworth, NJ 07641-1899 Tel # (201) 387-1023, Fax # (201) 387-2976, Actives: 42,451, $110/M

Small Market Radio Newsletter
See: BROADCASTING

Society of Manufacturers Agents, Newsletter

Publishing Co: Society of Manufacturers Agents, 42072 Queen Anne Ct., Northville, MI 48167-1903; Title Tel # (313) 473-2002
Personnel: Editor-Carol Kettenbeil
Editorial Description: Includes items of interest to the society, names of companies seeking manufacturer's agents and salesmen who are looking for employment.
General Info: Yr. Est. 1953, Monthly
Circulation: (100% controlled), Total-450

Soundview Executive Book Summaries
See: BUSINESS & INDUSTRY

Spare on Sales and Marketing
See: ADVERTISING & MARKETING

Success Orientation
See: MANAGEMENT

Successful Closing Techniques   *Business*

Publishing Co: Dartnell Corp., 4660 N. Ravenswood Ave., Chicago, IL 60640-4510; Title Tel # (312) 561-4000 Title Fax # (312) 561-3801
Personnel: Publisher-Clark Fetridge, Editor-Terry Breen, Circ. Mgr.-Jim Sherman, Production Mgr.-Megan Mulligan, Adv. Dir.-Diane Martino, Art Dir.-Andrew Epstein, Mktg. Dir.-George Economos
Editorial Description: Each issue of successful closing techniques gives fail-safe techniques for acquiring bigger sales and more frequent closings. Includes 4 special reports issued quarterly which address specific selling issues in depth.
General Info: Yr. Est. 1984, Semi-weekly, Trim Size-88½ x 11, 4 pages, 2 Color, Matte
Subscriptions: $62/copy
List Rental: List Management Co.: Manager: Sue Mcdorman; Leland Company, 1801 W. Leland Ave., Chicago, IL 60640-4363 Tel # (312) 561-4005, Fax # (312) 561-4099, Actives: 70,785, $90/M, Hotline: $125/M

Successful Telephone Selling   *Business*

Publishing Co: Economics Press, Inc., 12 Daniel Rd., Fairfield, NJ 07004-2565; Title Tel # (201) 227-1224 Title Fax # (201) 227-9742
Personnel: Publisher-John Beckley, Editor-Robert Guder, Circ. Mgr.-Anne Lanahan, Production Mgr.-Matt Farley, Art Dir.-Charles Palminteri, Promotion Dir.-Diane Cody
Editorial Description: Techniques to sharpen the skills of telephone salespeople.
General Info: (Formerly Better Telemarketing), Yr. Est. 1984, Bi-weekly, Trim Size-5½ x 8½, Sheetfed press, 4 pages, 2 Color, Coated
Subscriptions: Indv. $35, $1/copy
Circulation: Total-6,000
List Rental: List Management Co.: Manager: Michael Korman; Names in the News, 411 Theodore Fremd Ave., Rye, NY 10580 Tel # (914) 925-2400, Actives: $80/M
Printing Co: Beckley Press, 2 Sperry Rd, Fairfield, NJ 07004-2056 Tel # (201) 227-6350

Successtrax
See: LIFESTYLE

TSSA Report   *Association*

Publishing Co: Tackle/Shooting Sports Association, 1250 S Grove Ave Ste 300, Barrington, IL 60010-5066 Fax # (708) 381-9518; Title Tel # (708) 381-3032
Personnel: Editor-Nancy Lems, Circ. Mgr., Production Mgr.-Dee McIntyre
Editorial Description: For members only.
General Info: (Formerly Tackle Reps Association International), Yr. Est. 1953, Quarterly, Mimeo press, 4 pages, 2 Color
Subscriptions: Free With Membership
Circulation: (100% controlled), Total-380

Team Marketing Report
See: SPORTS & SPORTING GOODS

Telemarketing Tips, Tactics & Techniques   *Business*

Publishing Co: West, Adams, Christopher & Associates, 1000 W. McNab Rd., Suite 158, Pompano, FL 33069-9871 Fax # (305) 578-4200; Title Tel # (305) 384-8500 Title Fax # (305) 384-9700
Editorial Description: Ideas and methods for developing telemarketing teams and sales.
General Info: Yr. Est. 1994, Weekly

Telemarketing Update-Answering Service Business Script Presentations
See: ADVERTISING & MARKETING

Telemarketing Update-Catering Service Business Script Presentations
See: ADVERTISING & MARKETING

Telemarketing Update-Copier Service Business Script Presentations
See: ADVERTISING & MARKETING

Telemarketing Update-Secretarial Business Script Presentations
See: ADVERTISING & MARKETING

Telephone Selling Report
See: ADVERTISING & MARKETING

Time for R & R   *Business*

Publishing Co: Ross & Ross International, 1493 Beack Park Blvd., Suite 311, Foster City, CA 94404 Tel # (415) 572-0102
Editorial Description: Publication about travel and dining for sales and marketing professionals.
General Info: Yr. Est. 1991, Bi-monthly
Subscriptions: Indv. $59

Vendorscope
See: BLIND

Venture Views & News

Publishing Co: Venture Communications, 60 Madison Avenue, New York, NY 10010; Title Tel # (212) 684-4800 Title Fax # (212) 576-1129
Personnel: Editor-Rachel Krasny
Editorial Description: News and practical advice in the field of direct response marketing.
General Info: Yr. Est. 1990, Quarterly, 4 pages, 2 Color, Matte

What's Working in Sales Management *Business*

Publishing Co: Progressive Business Publications, 370 Technology Dr., #3019, Malverne, PA 19355-9863 Parent Co.-American Future Systems, Inc., Bryn Mawr; Title Tel # (610) 695-8600 Title Fax # (610) 647-8089
Personnel: Publisher-Edward M. Satell, Editor-Richard Kern, Editorial Dir.-Stephen Meyer, Mktg. Dir.-Ed Moor
Editorial Description: Sales management news and issues.
General Info: Yr. Est. 1992, Bi-weekly, 8 pages
Subscriptions: Indv. $264
List Rental: List Management Co.: Mail Marketing, Inc., 171 Terrace St., Haworth, NJ 07641-1899 Tel # (201) 387-1023, Fax # (201) 387-2976, Actives: 40,000, $115/M

SANITATION

ISSA Today *Business*

Publishing Co: International Sanitary Supply Association, 7373 N Lincoln Ave, Lincolnwood, IL 60646-1704; Title Tel # (708) 982-0800
Editorial Description: Industry & member co. news & developments.
General Info: Monthly, Offset press, 18 pages, 4 Color
Circulation: Total-3,500

MSW Solutions *Association*

Publishing Co: Solid Waste Association of North America, 1100 Wayne Ave., Suite #700, Silver Spring, MD 20910; Title Tel # (301) 585-2898 Title Fax # (301) 589-7068
Personnel: Publisher-H. Lanier Hickman, Jr., Editor-Michele Nebel Peake
Editorial Description: Features news on association chapter activities and services as well as industry profession updates.
General Info: (Formerly Municipal Solid Waste News), Monthly, Trim Size-8½ x 11, 12 pages, ISSN: 1062-8967, 2 Color, Matte, Saddle-stitched
Subscriptions: Indv. $50
Circulation: Total-6,000
Advertising: Inquire for rates.
Printing Co: Ecoprint, 9335 Fraser Ave, Silver Spring, MD 20910 Tel # (301) 585-7077, Fax # (301) 585-4899

Pest Control Letter *Business*

Publishing Co: Research Endeavors Co., 525 Walnut St. , Box 1381, San Carlos, CA 94070-2335; Title Tel # (415) 591-9311 Title Fax # (415) 591-1606
Personnel: Publisher, Editor-Billy Gillespie
Editorial Description: Authoritative, confidential news & advisory report on key developments affecting pest control industry.
General Info: Yr. Est. 1974, Monthly, Trim Size-8½ x 11, Offset press, 4 pages, No Color
Subscriptions: Indv. $76

Portable Sanitation Quarterly

Publishing Co: Satellite Industries Inc., 2530 Xenium Ln N, Minneapolis, MN 55441-3695

Supermarket Sanitation

Publishing Co: Dennis Thayer Assocs., 515 E Grant Rd Ste 361, Tucson, AZ 85705-5770; Title Tel # (602) 620-9099
Editorial Description: Features on supermarket sanitation and related topics.
General Info: Yr. Est. 1988, Bi-monthly
Subscriptions: Indv. $30

Waste Recovery Report
See: ENVIRONMENT & ECOLOGY

Waste Treatment Technology News *Business*

Publishing Co: Business Communications Co., 25 Van Zant St., Ste.13, Norwalk, CT 06855-1781; Title Tel # (203) 853-4266 Title Fax # (203) 853-0348
Personnel: Publisher-Louis Naturman, Editor-Donald Saxman, Mktg. Dir.-Robert Butler
Editorial Description: Reports on acid rain, toxic/hazardous material, solid waste, contaminated water.
General Info: Yr. Est. 1985, Monthly, Trim Size-8½ x 11, 10 pages, ISSN: 0885-0003, Ind/Abs/Online: DIALOG, No Color, Matte
Subscriptions: Indv. $325, Can. $375, For. $375, $26/copy
Advertising: Inquire for rates.
List Rental: List Management Co.: W.I. Mail Marketing, 470 Main St. #317, Ridgefield, CT 06877-4516 Tel # (203) 438-6822, Fax # (203) 438-7756, Actives: 8,590, $120/M

SCHOOL ADMINISTRATION

AFSA News *Association*

Publishing Co: American Federation of School Administrators, 1729 21st St. NW, Washington, DC 20009-1101; Title Tel # (202) 986-4209 Title Fax # (202) 986-4211
Editorial Description: School administrators and supervisors organizing committee.
General Info: Yr. Est. 1971, Monthly, Trim Size-8½ x 11, Web press, 8 pages, 2 Color, Newsprint
Subscriptions: $1/copy
Acquisitions: Publication Bought
Circulation: Total-18,000
Printing Co: Faculty Press, 75 Varick St Frnt 5, New York, NY 10013-1917 Tel # (212) 941-0702, Fax # (212) 941-0708

AP Special

Publishing Co: National Association of Secondary School Principals, 1904 Association Dr., Reston, VA 22091-1537; Title Tel # (703) 860-0200 Title Fax # (703) 476-5432
Personnel: Editor-Thomas Koerner
Editorial Description: Focuses on current research & issues of particular interest to assistant principals.
General Info: Yr. Est. 1985, Quarterly, Trim Size-8½ x 11, Sheetfed press, 8 pages, 2 Color, Coated
Subscriptions: $2/copy
Circulation: Total-10,000

ASBSD Bulletin *Association*

Publishing Co: Associated School Boards of South Dakota, PO Box 1211, Pierre, SD 57501-1211 Fax # (602) 224-6294; Title Tel # (605) 224-6293 Title Fax # (605) 224-6294
Personnel: Editor-Gene Enck, Adv. Dir.-Katie Mitchell-Boe
Editorial Description: Deals with policy-making, financing, and innovation in public education and seeks to promote reorganization and adequate financing.
General Info: Yr. Est. 1952, Semi-monthly, Trim Size-11½ x 16, Offset press, 4 pages, Color-cover
Subscriptions: Indv. $25, Free With Membership
Circulation: Total-2,600
Advertising: Inquire for rates.

ASSC Newsletter
See: EDUCATION

About Our Schools *Association*

Publishing Co: Master Teacher, Inc., Leadership La., Box 1207, Manhattan, KS 66502 Tel # (913) 539-0555 Fax # (913) 539-7739
Personnel: Publisher-Robert DeBruyn, Editor-Robert Debruyn, Circ. Mgr.-Lori Hanson, Production Mgr.-Brad Roberts, Art Dir.-Barry Anderson
Editorial Description: Covers public relations techniques for administrators.
General Info: Yr. Est. 1981, Monthly, Sheetfed press, 9 pages, 2 Color, Matte
Subscriptions: Indv. $64, Inst. $46, Can. $64, For. $64
Circulation: (100% controlled), Total-1,500
Printing Co: Educational Publishers, 3201 Marlatt Ave, Manhattan, KS 66502-8143 Tel # (913) 539-2469

Administrative Focus *Consumer*

Publishing Co: Oklahoma State Dept. of Education, Oliver Hodge Bldg., 2500 N. Lincoln, Oklahoma City, OK 73105-4599 Tel # (405) 521-3301 Fax # (405) 521-6205; Title Tel # (405) 521-3331 Title Fax # (405) 512-6205
Personnel: Publisher-Jon Dahlander, Editor-Wendy Pratt, Production Mgr.-Mike Brake, Art Dir.-David Barrow
Editorial Description: Provides current information on State Dept. of Ed. policy to school superintendents, principals, members, and others.
General Info: (Formerly Superintendent's Newsletter), Yr. Est. 1959, Semi-monthly, Trim Size-8½ x 11, Sheetfed press, 4 pages, ISSN: 0149-2322, 2 Color, Matte
Subscriptions: Free To Qualified Recipient
Circulation: Total-3,850

Administrator: The Source for Practical Ideas and Key Issues in Higher Education *Scholarly, Association*

Publishing Co: Magna Publications, Inc., 611 N Sherman Ave, Madison, WI 53704-4410 Tel # (608) 246-3580; Title Tel # (608) 249-0355 Title Fax # (608) 246-3597
Personnel: Publisher-Richard C. Perkins, Editorial Dir., Editor-Mary Lou Santovec, Circ. Mgr.-Tom Crawford, Art Dir.-Tami Cook, Promotion Dir.-Lisa Collios
Editorial Description: Management newsletter for higher education.
General Info: Yr. Est. 1982, Monthly, Trim Size-8½ x 11, Offset press, 8 pages, ISSN: 0744-7078, 2 Color
Subscriptions: Indv. $95, $4/copy
Circulation: Total-1,350
Advertising: Inquire for rates. Accepts Inserts.
List Rental: Actives: 2,200, $90/M

Aid for Education Report
See: EDUCATION

Arbitration in the Schools
See: LAW

Assessment Update   *Association*

Publishing Co: Jossey-Bass Publishers, Inc., 350 Sansome St., Fifth Fl., San Francisco, CA 94104-1310; Title Tel # (415) 433-1740 Title Fax # (415) 433-0499
Personnel: Editor-Trudy Banta, Circ. Mgr.-Paula Stacey, Production Mgr.-Jeff Wymeker, Promotion Dir.-Brian Bouldrey
Editorial Description: Covers the latest developments in higher education assessment. Contains practical advice on conducting assessments in a range of areas, including student learning & outcomes, faculty instruction, academic programs & curricula, student services & more.
General Info: Yr. Est. 1989, Bi-monthly, 16 pages, ISSN: 1041-6099, No Color, Matte, Saddle-stitched
Subscriptions: Indv. $57, Inst. $65, $21/copy
Acquistions: Publication Bought
Circulation: Total-1,250

Board & Administrator (Superintendent Edition)   *Business*

Publishing Co: Aspen Publishers, Inc., 200 Orchard Ridge Dr., Ste 200, Gaithersburg, MD 20878-5440 Parent Co.-Wolters Kluwer US Corporation, New York; Title Tel # (301) 417-7500 Title Fax # (301) 417-7655
Personnel: Editor-Chuck Elliot
Editorial Description: Keeps superintendents in touch with the successful strategies other superintendents and school administrators use to build strong relationships wiyh their boards.
General Info: Yr. Est. 1987, Monthly
Subscriptions: Indv. $144, For. $173, $16/copy
List Rental: List Management Co.: Stevens-Knox List Management, 304 Park Ave S., New York, NY 10010-5312 Tel # (212) 388-8800, Fax # (212) 388-8890

Bulletin   *Association*

Publishing Co: Michigan Assn. of Secondary School Principals, Univ. of Michigan, 2339 School of Educ. Bldg., Ann Arbor, MI 48109-0001; Title Tel # (313) 763-9850
Personnel: Editor-Maria Tolot
Editorial Description: Education, practices and innovations.
General Info: Monthly, Trim Size-8½ x 11, Offset press, 9 pages, 2 Color
Subscriptions: Indv. $285
Circulation: Total-2,500

COTH (Council of Teaching Hospitals) Report
See: MEDICINE

CSBA News   *Association*

Publishing Co: California School Boards Assn., 3100 Beacon Blvd, West Sacramento, CA 95691-3483; Title Tel # (916) 371-4691 Title Fax # (916) 371-3407
Personnel: Circ. Mgr.-Cindy Warfe, Editor, Production Mgr.-Cathryn Reynolds, Art Dir.-Lisa Lehrer
Editorial Description: CSBA news, upcoming events, government decision for California school board members. Board member and district profiles. Association leader columns. Education news.
General Info: Yr. Est. 1934, Monthly, Trim Size-11 x 17, 8 pages, No Color, Coated
Subscriptions: Indv. $15
Acquistions: Publication Bought
Circulation: Total-6,500
Printing Co: Citadel Press, Inc., 3300 Business Dr, Sacramento, CA 95820-2171 Tel # (916) 732-2070, Fax # (916) 732-2070

CUPA News   *Association*

Publishing Co: College & Univ. Personnel Assn., 1233 20th St. NW, Ste. 301, Washington, DC 20036-2304; Title Tel # (202) 429-0311 Title Fax # (202) 429-0149
Personnel: Publisher-Stephanie Jones, Publications Director-C. David Hopkins, Editor-Melinda Spray, Asst. Ed.-Erin Sweeney
Editorial Description: Human resource management: legal, legislative, association news; current trends, publications, programs.
General Info: (Formerly Personnelite), Yr. Est. 1973, Semi-monthly, Trim Size-8½ x 11, Web press, 8 pages, ISSN: 0892-7855, 2 Color, Matte, Other
Subscriptions: Indv. $150, Free With Membership
Circulation: Total-6,000
Advertising: Inquire for rates. Accepts Inserts.
List Rental: Actives: 6,000
Printing Co: Weadon Printing, 6430 General Green Way, Alexandria, VA 22312-2413 Tel # (703) 750-0800, Fax # (703) 750-0807

California School Law Digest
See: EDUCATION

Campus Crime
See: LAW ENFORCEMENT & PENOLOGY

Catalyst: Voices of Chicago School Reform
See: EDUCATION

Chiefline   *Association*

Publishing Co: Council of Chief State School Officers, 1 Massachusetts Ave NW Ste 700, Washington, DC 20001-1401; Title Tel # (202) 408-5505 Title Fax # (202) 408-8072
Personnel: Editor-Paula L. Delo
Editorial Description: E-Mail newsletter for our members
General Info: Yr. Est. 1928, Semi-weekly

Commission des Ecoles Catholiques de Quebec Bulletin

Publishing Co: Commission des Ecoles Catholiques de Montreal, 3737 Sherbrooke St., E., Montreal, PQ Canada
General Info: 8x/yr., 4 pages
Circulation: Total-900

Communicator   *Association*

Publishing Co: National Association of Elementary School Principals, 1615 Duke St, Alexandria, VA 22314-3406; Title Tel # (703) 684-3345
Personnel: Editor-Betsy Berlin
Editorial Description: For members who are elementary & middle school principals. Includes association news, education news, information for principals as managers, resources.
General Info: 9x/yr., Sheetfed press, 8 pages, ISSN: 0745-2233, 2 Color, Matte, Saddle-stitched
Subscriptions: Indv. $155, Inst. $95, $2/copy
Circulation: Total-26,000

Council on Postsecondary Accreditation-Presidents Bulletin   *Association*

Publishing Co: Commission on Recognition of Postsecondary Accreditation, 1 Dupont Cir. NW, Ste. 305, Washington, DC 20036-1110 Fax # (202) 331-9571; Title Tel # (202) 452-1433
Personnel: Editor-Janet D. Froom
Editorial Description: Membership activities newsletter. Special Features: Association news; employment opportunities; legislative news; list of new publications; news of position changes.
General Info: Irregular

Covering the Education Beat   *Business, Association*

Publishing Co: Education Writers Association, 1331 H St. NW, Ste. 307, Washington, DC 20005-4706 Tel # (202) 637-9700 Fax # (202) 637-9707; Title Tel # (202) 429-9700 Title Fax # (202) 637-9702
Personnel: Publisher, Editor-Lisa Walker
Editorial Description: Guidebook to current issues in education.
General Info: Yr. Est. 1981, Irregular, Looseleaf
Subscriptions: Indv. $50, $50/copy

Cubprints
See: HEARING & SPEECH

Day Care Guide
See: CHILDREN

Department Chair   *Business, Consumer*

Publishing Co: Anker Publishing Co., 176 Ballville Rd # 249, Bolton, MA 01740-1255; Title Tel # (508) 779-6190 Title Fax # (508) 779-6366
Personnel: Publisher-James Anker
Editorial Description: Practical information for developing high-level education.
General Info: Yr. Est. 1990, Quarterly, Trim Size-8½ x 11, Desktop press, 24 pages, ISSN: 1049-3255, 2 Color, Matte
Subscriptions: Indv. $69
Circulation: Total-4,000
Advertising: Inquire for rates.
List Rental: Actives: 1,000, $80/M

ERIC/CEM Information   *Association*

Publishing Co: ERIC Clearinghouse on Educational Management, Univ. of Oregon, 5207 Agate St., Eugene, OR 97403-5207; Title Tel # (541) 346-5043 Title Fax # (541) 346-2334
Personnel: Editor-Stuart Smith
Editorial Description: Newsletter announcing CH products & services.
General Info: Semi-annually, Trim Size-8½ x 11, 4 pages
Circulation: Total-5,500
List Rental: Actives: 5,600, $100/M

ERS Bulletin   *Association*

Publishing Co: Educational Research Service, 2000 Clarendon Blvd., Arlington, VA 22201-2900; Title Tel # (703) 243-2100 Title Fax # (703) 243-1985
Personnel: Editor-Deborah Gough
Editorial Description: Summary of available research studies, data, and information on school management and education.
General Info: Yr. Est. 1973, Monthly, 12 pages, No Color, Newsprint
Circulation: (100% controlled), Total-2,700
Printing Co: Sauls Lithograph, 2424 Evarts St NE, Washington, DC 20018-2120 Tel # (202) 529-9100

Education Daily
See: EDUCATION

Education Personnel Notes
See: EDUCATION

Education Technology News
See: EDUCATION

Education U.S.A.
See: EDUCATION

Educator
Association

Publishing Co: Clark County Board of Education, 1115 N Limestone St, Springfield, OH 45503-3675; Title Tel # (513) 325-7671
Personnel: Editor-Larry Zeakle, Circ. Mgr.-Helen Marcum, Publisher, Art Dir.-J. Karen Boysel
Editorial Description: Educational newsletter.
General Info: (Formerly Schooletter), Yr. Est. 1976, Quarterly, Trim Size-8½ x 11, Sheetfed press, 4 pages, 2 Color
Acquistions: Publication Bought
Circulation: Total-1,500

Educator's Guide to Controlling Sexual Harassment
See: LAW

Fair Labor Standards Handbook
See: GOVERNMENT

Federal Auditing Information Service for Higher Education
See: ACCOUNTING

Federal Legislative Bulletin
Association

Publishing Co: New York State School Boards Association, Inc., 119 Washington Ave., Albany, NY 12210-2284; Title Tel # (518) 465-3474
Personnel: Editor-Daniel Kinley
General Info: Yr. Est. 1985, Bi-weekly, 2 pages, 2 Color
Subscriptions: Indv. $60
Circulation: (100% controlled), Total-8,000

Fortnighter
Association

Publishing Co: Michigan Assn. of School Administrators, 421 W Kalamazoo St, Lansing, MI 48933-2006; Title Tel # (517) 371-5250
Personnel: Editor-David Kahn
General Info: Yr. Est. 1971, Bi-weekly
Circulation: Total-2,200

Funding Private Schools
Business

Publishing Co: Quinlan Publishing, 23 Drydock Ave, Boston, MA 02210-2387 Tel # (617) 542-0048 Fax # (617) 345-9646
Editorial Description: Articles, tips and foundation profiels geared toward the funding needs of individual private schools.
General Info: Monthly
Subscriptions: Indv. $99

Granite State School Leader
Association

Publishing Co: New Hampshire School Boards Assn., Morrill Hall, Univ. of NH, Durham, NH 03824; Title Tel # (603) 862-1384
Personnel: Publisher-Richard Goodman, Editor-Elinor Fox
Editorial Description: Public School concerns and interests.
General Info: (Formerly New Hampshire School Boards Assn.), Yr. Est. 1955, Monthly, Trim Size-8½ x 11, Letrpr. press, 12 pages, No Color
Subscriptions: Indv. $50, $5/copy
Acquistions: Publication Bought
Circulation: (100% controlled), Total-1,500
Advertising: Inquire for rates.

Grants for School Districts Biweekly Hotline
Business

Publishing Co: Quinlan Publishing, 23 Drydock Ave, Boston, MA 02210-2387 Tel # (617) 542-0048 Fax # (617) 345-9646
Editorial Description: Up-to-date listings of available grants, foundations, school programs, and business partnerships around the nation.
General Info: Bi-weekly
Subscriptions: Indv. $129

Health Professions Report
See: EDUCATION

Horace
Scholarly

Publishing Co: Coalition of Essential Schools/Brown Unv., PO Box 1969, Providence, RI 02912; Title Tel # (401) 863-3384 Title Fax # (401) 863-2045
Personnel: Publisher-Susan C. Fisher, Asst. Pub.-Linda Tammaro
Editorial Description: Essential school reform.
General Info: Yr. Est. 1988, 5x/yr.

Indiana Association of School Principals
Association

Publishing Co: Indiana Secondary School Administrators, PO Box 503250, Indianapolis, IN 46250-8250; Title Tel # (317) 576-5400 Title Fax # (317) 576-5408
Personnel: Editor-Edward Wall
Editorial Description: Update on current practices, association activities, PR for inservices, workshops, etc.
General Info: (Formerly Indiana Secondary School Administrators, Newsletter), Yr. Est. 1970, Monthly, Trim Size-8½ x 11, Mimeo press, 15 pages, 2 Color
Subscriptions: Free With Membership
Circulation: (39% controlled), Total-2,300
Advertising: Inquire for rates.

Inquiry & Analysis
Business

Publishing Co: National School Boards Assn., 1680 Duke St., Alexandria, VA 22314-3493; Title Tel # (703) 838-6722
Personnel: Editor-Thomas Shannon
Editorial Description: For attorneys representing public schools.
General Info: Yr. Est. 1973, Bi-monthly, 20 pages
Subscriptions: Indv. $60
Circulation: Total-3,000

Inside APPA
Association CPM: $187

Publishing Co: APPA: The Assn. of Higher Education Facilities Officers, 1446 Duke St, Alexandria, VA 22314-3492; Title Tel # (703) 684-1446 Title Fax # (703) 549-2772
Personnel: Publisher-Steve Glazner, Circ. Mgr.-Cotrenia Aytch, Editor, Production Mgr.-Medea Ranck, Adv. Dir., Promotion Dir.-Stephanie Gretchen
Editorial Description: Articles on APPA activities, technical/management information for facilities managers at colleges and universities.
General Info: (Formerly APPA Newsletter), Yr. Est. 1914, 8x/yr., Trim Size-8½ x 11, Sheetfed press, 2 pages, ISSN: 0736-7252, 2 Color, Other, Saddle-stitched
Subscriptions: Indv. $48, Can. $60, For. $60, Free With Membership
Circulation: Total-4,300
Advertising: $805.
Printing Co: Goetz Printing Co., 7939 Angus Ct., Springfield, VA 22153-2844 Tel # (703) 569-8232, Fax # (703) 569-9364

Kentucky Standard
See: HEARING & SPEECH

MASC Bulletin
Association

Publishing Co: Massachusetts Assn. of School Committees, Inc., 1 McKinley Square #2, Boston, MA 02109; Title Tel # (617) 542-3225
Personnel: Publisher, Editor-Jenifer Handy, Production Mgr.-Marcia Levin
General Info: Bi-monthly, Trim Size-8½ x 11, Web press, 8 pages, No Color, Newsprint
Circulation: Total-2,700

MN Educational Resource Guide
See: EDUCATION

MSMA Labor Relations Newsletter
Association

Publishing Co: Maine School Management Assn., 49 Community Dr., Augusta, ME 04330; Title Tel # (207) 622-4971
Personnel: Editor-Keith Kolodgie
Editorial Description: Review of current bargaining decisions pertaining to public schools.
General Info: Yr. Est. 1972, Monthly, Offset press, 4 pages, No Color
Circulation: Total-2,300

MUSENET
See: COLLEGE STUDENT

Maine Schools
Consumer, Association

Publishing Co: Maine State Dept. of Education, State House, Augusta, ME 04330; Title Tel # (207) 289-5800

Management Memo

Publishing Co: San Bernardino City Unified School District, 777 N F St, San Bernardino, CA 92410-3017; Title Tel # (714) 381-1250
Personnel: Editor-Barbara Spears-Kidd
Editorial Description: A resume of local management activities as well as review of established management skills and techniques.
General Info: Yr. Est. 1984, Quarterly, Trim Size-8½ x 11, Sheetfed press, 12 pages, 2 Color, Saddle-stitched
Circulation: Total-300

Middle School Companion, The
See: EDUCATION

Monday Memo
See: EDUCATION

NAEB Bulletin
See: PURCHASING

NAEIR Advantage
See: EDUCATION

NAEN Bulletin
Association

Publishing Co: North American Assn., Educational Negotiators, PO Box 4342, Springfield, IL 62708-4342 Tel # (217) 947-2727; Title Tel # (217) 529-7902 Title Fax # (217) 947-2334
Personnel: Publisher, Editor-Ron Booth, Circ. Mgr., Art Dir.-Laura Huck
Editorial Description: Labor relations and negotiations in public school systems. Directed to school administrators, chief negotiators & teams to improve mgmt. neg'ns.
General Info: Yr. Est. 1961, Monthly, Letrpr. press, 8 pages, 2 Color, Saddle-stitched
Subscriptions: Indv. $55, Inst. $125, $1/copy
Circulation: (66% controlled), Total-750

NASSP Curriculum Report   *Association*

Publishing Co: National Association of Secondary School Principals, 1904 Association Dr., Reston, VA 22091-1537; Title Tel # (703) 860-0200 Title Fax # (703) 476-5432
Personnel: Editor-James Theisen
Editorial Description: Describes current practices & evolving trends in secondary school curriculum & instruction.
General Info: Yr. Est. 1964, Bi-monthly, Trim Size-8.5 x 11, Sheetfed press, 8 pages, ISSN: 0547-4205, 2 Color, Newsprint
Subscriptions: $2/copy
Circulation: (100% controlled), Total-40,000
Printing Co: Cardinal Printing Co., 8425 Hillto Rd, Box 656, Merrifield, VA 22116 Tel # (705) 560-3312, Fax # (703) 560-1763

NASSP Legal Memorandum   *Association*

Publishing Co: National Association of Secondary School Principals, 1904 Association Dr., Reston, VA 22091-1537; Title Tel # (703) 860-0200 Title Fax # (703) 476-5432
Personnel: Editor-James Theisen
Editorial Description: Covers legal subjects of interest to educators, especially school administrators.
General Info: Yr. Est. 1969, Quarterly, Trim Size-8½ x 11, Offset press, 8 pages, ISSN: 0192-6152, No Color
Subscriptions: Indv. $85, Inst. $110, $1/copy
Circulation: Total-40,000
Printing Co: Cardinal Printing Co., 8425 Hillto Rd, Box 656, Merrifield, VA 22116 Tel # (705) 560-3312, Fax # (703) 560-1763

NASSP NewsLeader   *Association*

Publishing Co: National Association of Secondary School Principals, 1904 Association Dr., Reston, VA 22091-1537; Title Tel # (703) 860-0200 Title Fax # (703) 476-5432
Personnel: Editor-Thomas Koerner
Editorial Description: The assn. house organ, with news & photos of members & staff activities.
General Info: Yr. Est. 1953, Monthly, Offset press, 8 pages, ISSN: 0278-0569, 2 Color
Subscriptions: Indv. $4
Circulation: Total-40,000

NSPRA Network   *Association*

Publishing Co: National School Public Relations Assn., 1501 Lee Hwy Ste 201, Arlington, VA 22209-1109 Fax # (703) 528-7017; Title Tel # (703) 528-5840
Personnel: Publisher-Joseph Scherer, Editor-Beth Hakola
Editorial Description: Reports activities of the National School Public Relations Association, its chapters, and individual professional members.
General Info: (Formerly Paragraphs), Yr. Est. 1959, Monthly, Trim Size-8½ x 11, 8 pages, No Color, Newsprint
Circulation: Total-2,700

NSSBA Newsletter   *Association*   **CPM: $156**

Publishing Co: Nova Scotia School Boards Association, Box 605 Station M, Halifax, NS B3J 2R7 Canada; Title Tel # (902) 420-9191 Title Fax # (902) 429-7405
Personnel: Editor-Sharon Findlay
Editorial Description: For association members & interested individuals. Education articles of provincial, national, and international interest.
General Info: Yr. Est. 1970, 10x/yr., Trim Size-8½ x 11, Desktop press, 6 pages, ISSN: 0702-9292, 2 Color, Other
Subscriptions: Indv. $10, $1/copy
Circulation: Total-800
Advertising: $125.

New Jersey Education Law Report
See: EDUCATION

New Jersey Elementary School Principals Association, Bulletin

Publishing Co: New Jersey Elementary School Principals Assn., 180 W State St, Trenton, NJ 08608-1104
Personnel: Editor-Donald J. Schmidt
General Info: Yr. Est. 1970, Quarterly

New York Education Law Report
See: EDUCATION

New York Supervisor

Publishing Co: New York City Elementary School Principals Assn., Public School 48, 6015 18th Ave., Brooklyn, NY 11204
Personnel: Editor-Thomas J. Hiler, Adv. Dir.-Dr. George Hoffman
Editorial Description: Deals with the curriculum and the supervisor's specific problems. For administrators and supervisors on the elementary school level.
General Info: Yr. Est. 1945, Semi-annually
Subscriptions: Indv. $1
Circulation: Total-2,200
Advertising: Inquire for rates.

News   *Association*

Publishing Co: Ontario Public School Teachers' Federation, 5160 Orbitor Drive, Mississauga, ON L4W 5H2 Canada Fax # (416) 928-0179; Title Tel # (905) 238-0200 Title Fax # (905) 238-0201
Personnel: Publisher-David Lennox, Circ. Mgr.-Jackie Campbell, Editor, Art Dir.-Charlotte Morgan
General Info: Bi-weekly, Trim Size-8½ x 14, Letrpr. press, 36 pages
Subscriptions: Free With Membership
Circulation: Total-300,000

Newsletter   *Association*

Publishing Co: Ferguson-Florissant School District R-2, 1005 Waterford Dr, Florissant, MO 63033-3649; Title Tel # (314) 595-2114
Editorial Description: News bulletin for all school district employees.
General Info: (Formerly R-2 Review), Yr. Est. 1968, Weekly, Trim Size-8½ x 11, Offset press, 2 pages, No Color
Circulation: Total-2,000

Oakland Unified School District

Publishing Co: Oakland Unified School District, 1025 2nd Ave, Oakland, CA 94606-2212; Title Tel # (415) 836-2622
Personnel: Editor-Marjorie Henders
Editorial Description: Innovative policies and programs, items about what teachers and the administration are doing.
General Info: Monthly, Trim Size-6 x 9, Offset press, 6 pages

On Board   *Association*

Publishing Co: West Virginia School Boards Assn., PO Box 1008, Charleston, WV 25324-1008; Title Tel # (304) 346-0571
Personnel: Editor-Howard M. O'Cull
Editorial Description: Details state or national educator-related information of interest to county boards of education and supts.
General Info: (Formerly WVSBA Communicator), Yr. Est. 1959, Quarterly, Mimeo press, 8 pages, No Color
Circulation: (100% controlled), Total-330

Ontario Council for Leadership in Educational Admin.

Publishing Co: Ontario Council for Leadership in Eucational Admin., Ste. 12-115, Toronto, ON M5S 1V5 Canada Tel # (416) 944-2652
Personnel: Editor-H. Joyce
General Info: Yr. Est. 1974, Quarterly, 16 pages, Ind/Abs/Online: Can.Ed.In.
Circulation: Total-10,000

Ontario Federation of Home & School Association Bulletin

Publishing Co: Ontario Federation of Home & School Association, 252 Bloor St. West, Suite 12-200, Toronto, ON M5S 1V5 Canada Tel # (416) 924-7491
General Info: Quarterly, 4 pages
Circulation: Total-25,000

Oregon Independent College Foundation, Inc. Report   *Association*

Publishing Co: Oregon/Independent College Foundation, Inc., 121 S Salmon, Portland, OR 97204-2901; Title Tel # (503) 227-7568
Personnel: Publisher-George Henderson
Editorial Description: News items about our 8 independent colleges, officers, directors and fund raising information and results.
General Info: (Formerly Oregon Colleges Foundation), Yr. Est. 1952, Trim Size-8½ x 11, Web press, 4 pages, 2 Color, Coated
Circulation: Total-3,000
Printing Co: Oregonian Publishing Co., Portland, OR 97208

PEB Exchange
See: EDUCATION

P.S.B.G.M. Communique

Publishing Co: Protestant School Bd of Greater Montreal, 6000 Fielding Ave., Montreal, PQ H3X 1T4 Canada; Title Tel # (514) 483-7243
Personnel: Editor-N. Koshedub
Editorial Description: Public school board newspaper distributed to parents of 28,500 students.
General Info: Yr. Est. 1979, Trim Size-11½ x 17½, Roto. press, 8 pages, No Color
Circulation: (100% controlled), Total-40,000

Paideia   *Business*

Publishing Co: Hegeler Institute, The, 315 5th St, Peru, IL 61354-2859 Tel # (815) 223-2520; Title Tel # (815) 223-1500 Title Fax # (815) 223-4486
Personnel: Publisher, Editor-R.J. Willmot
Editorial Description: Reprint articles of interest to college & univ. presidents.
General Info: Yr. Est. 1970, Irregular, Trim Size-8½ x 11, Sheetfed press, 6 pages, 2 Color, Newsprint
Subscriptions: Free To Qualified Recipient
Circulation: (100% controlled), Total-2,500

Pennsylvania School Boards Association, Information Legislative Service
Association

Publishing Co: Pennsylvania School Boards Assn., Inc., 774 Limekiln Rd., New Cumberland, PA 17070-2398; Title Tel # (717) 774-2331 Title Fax # (717) 774-0718
Personnel: Editor-Lynn Mannion, Circ. Mgr.-Billie Demmy
Editorial Description: News of interest to Pennsylvania School Boards, including news about pending legislation at all levels of government; new trends in schools and school management.
General Info: Yr. Est. 1970, Weekly, Trim Size-5½ x 8½, Sheetfed press, 20 pages, 2 Color, Newsprint, Saddle-stitched
Subscriptions: Indv. $150, $3/copy
Circulation: Total-11,800

Personnel News for School Systems

Publishing Co: Robbins Assocs. Management Service, Inc., 21 Bowman Ct, Greenfield, IN 46140-2508 Tel # (317) 462-6011
General Info: Monthly
Subscriptions: Indv. $70

Perspective
See: LAW

Perspective
Association   **CPM: $222**

Publishing Co: Pennsylvania Assn. of Elementary School Principals, 801 N. Second St., Harrisburg, PA 17102; Title Tel # (717) 233-3001 Title Fax # (717) 232-7098
Personnel: Publisher-Terri Houck, Editor-Sharon Whittle
Editorial Description: Focuses on effective programs in elementary & middle schools as well as association news.
General Info: Yr. Est. 1970, 5x/yr., Trim Size-8½ x 11, Offset press, 8 pages, 2% ads, Color, Matte, Saddle-stitched
Subscriptions: $2/copy
Circulation: Total-1,800
Advertising: $400. Accepts Inserts.
List Rental: Actives: 1, $50/M
Printing Co: Abel Printers, 5223 E. Simpson Ferry Rd., Mechanicsburg, PA 17055 Tel # (717) 766-1533

Perspectives for Policymakers
See: EDUCATION

Practitioner
Association

Publishing Co: National Association of Secondary School Principals, 1904 Association Dr., Reston, VA 22091-1537; Title Tel # (703) 860-0200 Title Fax # (703) 476-5432
Personnel: Editor-James Theisen
Editorial Description: Quarterly newsletter for the on-line administrator, focusing on better school management.
General Info: Yr. Est. 1975, Quarterly, Trim Size-8½ x 11, Sheetfed press, 8 pages, ISSN: 0192-6160, 2 Color, Newsprint
Subscriptions: Inst. $110, $2/copy
Circulation: Total-40,000
Printing Co: Cardinal Printing Co., 8425 Hillto Rd, Box 656, Merrifield, VA 22116 Tel # (705) 560-3312, Fax # (703) 560-1763

Prince Edward Island Teachers' Federation Newsletter

Publishing Co: Prince Edward Island Teachers' Federation, 24 Glen Stewart Drive, PO Box 6000, Charlottetown, PE C1A 8B4 Canada; Title Tel # (902) 569-4157 Title Fax # (902) 569-3682
Personnel: Editor-Bob MacRae
General Info: Quarterly, 8 pages, ISSN: 0383-199X
Circulation: Total-2,000

Pro Principal
Business

Publishing Co: Aspen Publishers, Inc., 200 Orchard Ridge Dr., Ste 200, Gaithersburg, MD 20878-5440 Tel # (301) 417-7500 Fax # (301) 417-7655 Parent Co.-Wolters Kluwer US Corporation, New York; Title Tel # (410) 417-7500 Title Fax # (410) 417-7655
Personnel: Editor-Jeff Stratton
Editorial Description: Problems faced every day on the job are addressed in Pro Principal -and then solutions used successfully by other principals are described.
General Info: Yr. Est. 1988, Monthly
Subscriptions: Indv. $96, For. $115, $9/copy
List Rental: List Management Co.: Stevens-Knox List Management, 304 Park Ave S., New York, NY 10010-5312 Tel # (212) 388-8800, Fax # (212) 388-8890

Public School

Publishing Co: Montreal Catholic School Commission, 3737 Sherbrooke St. E., Montreal, PQ H1X 3B3 Canada; Title Tel # (514) 596-6000
Personnel: Editor-Andre Cloutier
General Info: Yr. Est. 1969, Bi-monthly, 8 pages
Circulation: Total-45,000

Query
Consumer, Association

Publishing Co: Syllabus Press, 1307 S. Mary Ave. #211, Box 2716, Sunnyvale, CA 94087 Parent Co.-Publix Information Products, Inc., Sunnyvale; Title Tel # (408) 773-0670 Title Fax # (408) 746-2711
Personnel: Publisher, Editor-John P. Noon, Assoc. Ed.-Mary Brush
Editorial Description: Query covers the integration of computer technology into higher education administration environments. Each issue has feature articles, news, resources, and in-depth looks at how campuses can better accomodate their computing needs.
General Info: Yr. Est. 1991, Quarterly, Trim Size-8½ x 11, Web press, 24 pages, ISSN: 1065-206X, 2 Color, Matte, Saddle-stitched
Subscriptions: Indv. $100, Inst. $48, Can. $130, For. $200, $200/copy
Circulation: Total-1,000
Advertising: Inquire for rates.
List Rental: List Management Co.: Twin Peaks Press, PO Box 129, Vancouver, WA 98666-0129 Tel # (206) 694-2462, Fax # (206) 696-3210, Actives: 50,000, $100/M
Printing Co: IPC Publishing Service, 501 Colonial Dr., Saint Joseph, MI 49085-2432 Tel # (616) 983-7105, Fax # (616) 983-5736

Re: Quest
See: EDUCATION

Region Six Sentinel

Publishing Co: Region Six Michigan Education Assn., 5460 Arden Ave, Warren, MI 48092-1190; Title Tel # (313) 987-8668
Personnel: Editor-R.M. Wirth
General Info: Yr. Est. 1960, Monthly
Subscriptions: Indv. $1
Circulation: Total-6,000
Advertising: Inquire for rates.

Report to the Board
See: EDUCATION

Report on Education of the Disadvantaged
See: EDUCATION

Report on Education Research
See: EDUCATION

Report on Preschool Programs
See: EDUCATION

SKOLE: The Journal of Alternative Education
See: EDUCATION

SSBA Newsletter
Association

Publishing Co: Saskatchewan Teachers' Federation, Box 1108, Saskatoon, SK S7K 3N3 Canada
Personnel: Editor-Alan W. Phillips
Editorial Description: News and information for Association members.
General Info: Yr. Est. 1994, Irregular
Subscriptions: Indv. $30

SSTA Newsletter
Association

Publishing Co: Saskatchewan School Trustees Assn., 400-2222-13th Ave., Regina, SK S4P 3M7 Canada; Title Tel # (306) 569-0750
Personnel: Publisher, Editor-G. Vizzutti, Circ. Mgr.-Lyle Thorson
Editorial Description: Informs trustees of Association business, planned events, etc.
General Info: Yr. Est. 1964, Monthly, Trim Size-8½ x 11, Offset press, 3 pages, No Color
Circulation: (100% controlled), Total-1,100

Safety Is Elementary
See: SAFETY

San Diego County Superintendent's Bulletin
Consumer, Association

Publishing Co: San Diego Dept. of Education, 6401 Linda Vista Rd, San Diego, CA 92111-7319

School Age Notes
Business

Publishing Co: School Age Notes, PO Box 40205, Nashville, TN 37204-0205; Title Tel # (615) 242-8464
Personnel: Editor-Richard Scofield
Editorial Description: For child care workers and administrators caring for school-age children.
General Info: Yr. Est. 1980, Monthly, Desktop press, 8 pages, ISSN: 0278-3126, 1% ads, 2 Color
Subscriptions: Indv. $23
Circulation: Total-5,500
List Rental: Actives: $80/M
Printing Co: Vaughan Printing Co., 411 Cowan St, Nashville, TN 37207-5686 Tel # (615) 256-2244, Fax # (615) 259-4676

School Board News

Publishing Co: National School Boards Assn., 1680 Duke St., Alexandria, VA 22314-3493; Title Tel # (703) 838-6722
Personnel: Editor-Ellie Ashford, Circ. Mgr.-Alvin Brockway, Adv. Dir.-Mike DiSanto
General Info: Yr. Est. 1981, Bi-weekly
Subscriptions: Indv. $36
Circulation: Total-20,000

School Board Notes   *Association*

Publishing Co: New Jersey School Boards Assn., 413 W State St # 909, Trenton, NJ 08618-5617
  Fax # (609) 695-0413; Title Tel # (609) 695-7600
Personnel: Editor-Peg Lawler
Editorial Description: Devoted to public education in New Jersey, particularly the interests of school
  boards. Attention is also given to national education news affecting all school boards.
General Info: Yr. Est. 1954, Weekly, Trim Size-8½ x 11, Offset press, 6 pages, No Color
Subscriptions: Indv. $55
Circulation: Total-8,000
Printing Co: Hermitage Press Inc., 1595 Fifth Ave., Ewing, NJ 08638 Tel # (609) 882-3600,
  Fax # (609) 882-1137

School Emergencies   *Business, Consumer*

Publishing Co: Emergency Management Group, 1508 E 86th St., Ste 315, Indianapolis, IN
  46240-1986 Tel # (317) 475-9572; Title Tel # (317) 475-9063 Title Fax # (317) 475-9403
Personnel: Publisher-Douglas Crichlow, Editor-Susan Mottis Crichlow, RN, Circ. Mgr.-A.J. Strong, Art
  Dir.-Jenny Crichlow
Editorial Description: Covers strategies and tactics in preparing for, responding to and lessening the
  effects of disasters and major emergencies in schools.
General Info: Yr. Est. 1990, Monthly, Trim Size-8½ x 11, Sheetfed press, 8 pages, 2 Color, Matte
Subscriptions: Indv. $210, Inst. $210, Can. $342
Circulation: Total-2,444

School Law News
See: EDUCATION

Signal   *Association*

Publishing Co: Washington State School Directors' Assn., 221 College St NE, Olympia, WA
  98516-5313; Title Tel # (206) 493-9231
Personnel: Editor-Sue Kerber
Editorial Description: House organ for school boards association.
General Info: Yr. Est. 1948, Monthly, Trim Size-8½ x 11, Sheetfed press, 8 pages, Recycled
Subscriptions: Indv. $12
Circulation: Total-4,500

Software and Networks for Learning
See: EDUCATION

Special Education Report
See: EDUCATION

Spectrum   *Business, Association*   **CPM: $162**

Publishing Co: Alberta School Boards Assn., 12310 105 Ave., Edmonton, AB T5N 0Y4 Canada;
  Title Tel # (403) 482-7311 Title Fax # (403) 482-5659
Personnel: Publisher-W. Frank Tuck, Editor-Ann M. Machin
Editorial Description: Published for school trustees, superintendents, and others who serve on
  Alberta school boards, and to other educational organizations.
General Info: 10x/yr., Trim Size-8½ x 11, 6 pages
Circulation: Total-2,000
Advertising: $324. Accepts Inserts.

Student Aid News
See: EDUCATION

Superannuated Teachers of
Ontario Newsletter

Publishing Co: Superannuated Teachers of Ontario, 1260 Bay St., Toronto, ON M5R 2B5 Canada
Personnel: Editor-Tom McGuffin
General Info: 8 pages
Circulation: Total-20,000

Superintendent's Digest

Publishing Co: Superintendent's Digest, 3433 Meadowbrook Ct, Napa, CA 94558-5239;
  Title Tel # (707) 255-1830
Personnel: Publisher-Robert S. Alvarez, Editor-Nancy Wallace
Editorial Description: Reprinted data & articles from other publications of interest to the school
  administrator.
General Info: Yr. Est. 1977, 10x/yr., Trim Size-8½ x 11, 8 pages, 2 Color

Superintendents Only   *Association*

Publishing Co: Master Teacher, Inc., Leadership La., Box 1207, Manhattan, KS 66502;
  Title Tel # (913) 539-0555 Title Fax # (913) 539-7739
Personnel: Publisher, Editor-Robert DeBrayn, Circ. Mgr.-Lori Hanson, Product Mgr.-Brad Roberts, Art
  Dir.-Barry Anderson
Editorial Description: Source of new ideas and information for superintendents.
General Info: Yr. Est. 1993, Monthly, Trim Size-8½ x 11, 8 pages, Other
Subscriptions: Indv. $45, Can. $45, For. $45
Circulation: (100% controlled), Total-2,000
Printing Co: Educational Publishers, 3201 Marlatt Ave, Manhattan, KS 66502-8143
  Tel # (913) 539-2469

TQM in Higher Education   *Scholarly, Association*

Publishing Co: Magna Publications, Inc., 611 N Sherman Ave, Madison, WI 53704-4410;
  Title Tel # (608) 246-3580 Title Fax # (608) 246-3597
Personnel: Publisher-Richard C. Perkins, Editorial Dir., Editor, Asst. Ed.-Mary Lou Santovec, Circ.
  Mgr.-Tom Crawford, Art Dir.-Tami Cook, Mktg. Dir.-Lisa Collins
Editorial Description: Case studies of institutional applications of TQM in colleges & universities.
General Info: Yr. Est. 1993, Monthly, Trim Size-8½ x 11, 8 pages, ISSN: 1065-6774, 2 Color
Subscriptions: Indv. $138
Circulation: Total-1,700
Advertising: Inquire for rates. Accepts Inserts.
List Rental: Actives: $90/M

Teacher's Guide to Classroom Management
See: EDUCATION

Teachers In Touch
See: EDUCATION

Technology Applications Quarterly
See: EDUCATION

Technology Pathfinder for Administrators
See: COMPUTERS & AUTOMATION

Tips for Principals   *Association*

Publishing Co: National Association of Secondary School Principals, 1904 Association Dr., Reston,
  VA 22091-1537; Title Tel # (703) 860-0200 Title Fax # (703) 476-5432
Personnel: Editor-James Theisen
Editorial Description: Provides helpful hints about common concerns, problems, and special
  situations.
General Info: Yr. Est. 1983, Monthly, Trim Size-8.5 x 11, Sheetfed press, 2 pages, 2 Color, Coated
Subscriptions: $2/copy
Circulation: Total-40,000
Printing Co: Cardinal Printing Co., 8425 Hillto Rd, Box 656, Merrifield, VA 22116
  Tel # (705) 560-3312, Fax # (703) 560-1763

Uqaqta
See: EDUCATION

Virginia School Boards
Association Newsletter

Publishing Co: Virginia School Boards Assn., Peabody Hall, Univ. of Va., Charlottesville, VA 22903
General Info: 10x/yr.
Circulation: Total-1,500

Vocational Training News
See: EDUCATION

WYO Network
See: EDUCATION

SCIENCE

AAB Bulletin   *Association*

Publishing Co: American Association of Bioanalysts, 818 Olive St., Ste. 918, St. Louis, MO
  63101-1544; Title Tel # (314) 241-1445
Personnel: Editor-Mark Birenbaum, Ph.D.
Editorial Description: For directors, owners, administrators, managers, & supervisors of clinical labs
  concerned in improving testing & procedures.
General Info: Yr. Est. 1956, Bi-monthly, Trim Size-8½ x 11, Offset press, 6 pages, 2 Color, Other,
  Other
Subscriptions: Free With Membership
Printing Co: Modern Litho-Print, 411 Madison St, Jefferson City, MO 65101-3190
  Tel # (314) 635-6119, Fax # (314) 636-2655

AI Trends Newsletter
See: COMPUTERS & AUTOMATION

AISES Newsletter

Publishing Co: American Indian Science & Engineering Society, 1630, 30th Sreet, Ste 301, Boulder,
  CO 80301-1014; Title Tel # (303) 939-0023
General Info: Yr. Est. 1978, Quarterly, 6 pages
Circulation: Total-1,000
Advertising: Inquire for rates.

ANR Educator
See: EDUCATION

ASTC Newsletter *Association*

Publishing Co: Association of Science-Technology Centers, 1025 Vermont Ave NW, Ste 500, Washington, DC 20005-3516 Fax # (202) 783-7207; Title Tel # (202) 783-7200 Title Fax # (202) 283-7207
Personnel: Publications Director, Production Mgr., Art Dir.-Chris Raymond
Editorial Description: Offers international coverage of science museum news; ASTC activities and events; exhibits, educational programs, and conferences; and topics of related interest, including topics in informal science education.
General Info: Yr. Est. 1975, Bi-monthly, Trim Size-$8\frac{1}{2}$ x 11, Desktop press, 24 pages, ISSN: 0895-7371, 2 Color, Matte, Saddle-stitched
Subscriptions: Indv. $30, For. $40
Circulation: Total-3,725
Printing Co: Van Cortlandt Press, 10123 Senate Dr, Lanham, MD 20706-4808 Tel # (301) 577-7377, Fax # (301) 459-7768

ASTI Newsletter *Association*

Publishing Co: Association for Science, Technology & Innovation, PO Box 1242, Arlington, VA 22210-0542 Fax # (703) 241-2850; Title Tel # (703) 241-2850 Title Fax # (703) 241-2850
Personnel: Editor-Robert Adams
General Info: Yr. Est. 1978, Bi-monthly, Trim Size-$8\frac{1}{2}$ x 11, Desktop press, 10 pages, Color-cover, Matte, Other
Subscriptions: Free With Membership

Academy Newsletter
See: MUSEUM PUBLICATIONS

Accelerator Newsletter
See: EDUCATION

Advanced Composites Bulletin
See: MANUFACTURING

Advanced Materials
See: MANUFACTURING

Alternative Energy Trends & Forecasts
See: ENERGY

Anomalistics: The CSAR Bulletin
See: SOCIOLOGY

Antarctica Project Newsletter, The
See: ENVIRONMENT & ECOLOGY

Applied Orgonometry
See: CULTURE & HUMANITIES

Aquaphyte *Scholarly*

Publishing Co: Aquatic Plant Information Retrieval System, 7922 NW 71st St, Gainesville, FL 32653-3071 Fax # (652) 392-3462 Parent Co.-Univ of Florida Sea Grant College, Gainesville; Title Tel # (352) 392-1799 Title Fax # (352) 392-3462
Personnel: Editor-Karen Brown, Editor-Victor Ramey
Editorial Description: Aquatic plant biology, ecology, utilization, and management research. Includes listings of literature, meetings, books.
General Info: Yr. Est. 1981, Semi-annually, Trim Size-$8\frac{1}{2}$ x 11, Web press, 16 pages, ISSN: 0893-7702, No Color, Coated, Saddle-stitched
Subscriptions: Free
Circulation: Total-5,000
Printing Co: Marsh Printing, 2140 NE 2nd St, Gainesville, FL 32609-3725 Tel # (904) 373-6761

Atlantic Science *Consumer, Association*

Publishing Co: Atlantic Provinces Council on the Sciences, Memorial Univ. of NF, Box 4200, St. John's, NF A1C 5S7 Canada; Title Tel # (709) 737-8918
Editorial Description: Covers APICS events and related scientific articles and notices.
General Info: (Formerly A.P.I.C.S. Newsletter), Yr. Est. 1962, Bi-monthly, 4 pages, No Color
Circulation: Total-2,000

B.C. Science Teacher
See: EDUCATION

BCS Science & Engineering
See: COMPUTERS & AUTOMATION

Battelle Today *Business*

Publishing Co: Battelle Memorial Institute, 505 King Ave., Columbus, OH 43201-2693; Title Tel # (614) 424-7818 Title Fax # (614) 424-3889
Personnel: Publisher, Editor-Harry Templeton, Mng. Editor-Harriet Craig, Circ. Mgr.-Nancy Hall, Art Dir.-Dean Kette
Editorial Description: Technology development, technology commercialization, and technical & management services.
General Info: Yr. Est. 1976, Quarterly, Trim Size-$8\frac{1}{2}$ x 11, Letrpr. press, 12 pages, ISSN: 0145-8477, 2 Color, Matte, Saddle-stitched
Subscriptions: Free To Qualified Recipient
Circulation: (100% controlled), Total-40,000
Printing Co: Watkins Printing Co., 1401 E. 17th Ave., Columbus, OH 43211-2863 Tel # (614) 297-8270, Fax # (614) 291-1961

Beta Kappa Chi Bulletin *Association*

Publishing Co: Beta Kappa Chi Scientific Honor Society, Hampton Univ. , Box 6409, Hampton, VA 23668; Title Tel # (804) 727-5278
Personnel: Editor-Vernon Clark
Editorial Description: News of member chapters, research articles and other materials of interest to members and scientists in general. Also, business matters requiring the attention of members and interested persons.
General Info: Yr. Est. 1943, Semi-annually
Subscriptions: Indv. $10, $5/copy
Circulation: Total-2,500
Advertising: Inquire for rates.

Biotechnology News *Business*

Publishing Co: CTB International Publishing, Inc., P.O. Box 218, Maplewood, NJ 07040-0218 Fax # (201) 379-1158; Title Tel # (201) 379-7749 Title Fax # (203) 379-1158
Personnel: Publisher-Oykue Brogna, Editor in Chief-Christopher Brogna, Editor-Tim Baker, Circ. Mgr.-William Robinson, Mktg. Mgr., Promotion Dir.-Ann Light
Editorial Description: Covers business, technology & regulatory news in the field of biotechnology & genetic engineering, enzyme technology, fermentation technology, diagnostics technology, as it relates to agricultural, pharmaceutical & veterinary industries.
General Info: Yr. Est. 1981, 30x/yr., Trim Size-$8\frac{1}{2}$ x 11, Offset press, 12 pages, ISSN: 0273-3226, No Color, Newsprint, Saddle-stitched
Subscriptions: Indv. $538, Can. $538, For. $561, $27/copy
Acquistions: Publication Bought
List Rental: Rents Lists

Brain Mind Bulletin

Publishing Co: Interface Press, 4717 N Figueroa St # 42211, Los Angeles, CA 90042-4406; Title Tel # (213) 223-2500 Title Fax # (213) 223-2519
General Info: (Formerly New Sense), Yr. Est. 1975, Monthly
Subscriptions: Indv. $35
List Rental: List Management Co.: Pacific Lists, 100 Tamal Plaza Ste 50, Corte Madera, CA 94925 Tel # (415) 945-9450, Fax # (415) 945-9451, Actives: 4,500, $75/M

Bulletin of Law Science and Technology
See: LAW

CESSE Quill
See: ENGINEERING

COSSA Washington Update
See: POLITICS

CRREL Benchnotes *Consumer*

Publishing Co: U.S. Army Cold Regions Research & Engineering Laboratory, 72 Lyme Rd, Hanover, NH 03755-1290; Title Tel # (603) 646-4100
Personnel: Editor-Edmund Wright
Editorial Description: Reviews ongoing research; includes abstracts of published CRREL research reports.
General Info: Yr. Est. 1976, Trim Size-$8\frac{1}{2}$ x 11, Web press, 8 pages, 2 Color, Newsprint
Circulation: (100% controlled)
Printing Co: U.S. Government Printing Office, JFK Bldg., Govt. Ctr., Boston, MA 02203 Tel # (617) 720-3680

Canadian Society of Laboratory Technologists, Bulletin *Association* CPM: $61

Publishing Co: Canadian Society of Laboratory Technologists, Box 2830, LCD 1, Hamilton, ON L8N 3N8 Canada; Title Tel # (905) 528-8642 Title Fax # (905) 528-4968
Personnel: Editor, Adv. Dir.-Kurt Davis
Editorial Description: Monthly newsletter of professional organization.
General Info: Yr. Est. 1951, Monthly, Trim Size-$8\frac{1}{8}$ x $10\frac{7}{8}$, Web press, 16 pages, ISSN: 0381-5838, 3% ads, 2 Color, Coated, Saddle-stitched
Subscriptions: Free With Membership
Circulation: (100% controlled), Total-19,500, Readership-23,500
Advertising: $1,200.
Printing Co: Web Offset Publications, 1800 Ironstone Manor, Pickering, ON L1W 3J9 Canada Tel # (905) 831-3000, Fax # (905) 831-3260

Cancer Letter, The
See: MEDICINE

Cancer Research News
See: MEDICINE

Career Services Bulletin
See: MEDICINE

Catalyst
See: EDUCATION

Champ Channels

Publishing Co: Lake Champlain Phenomena Investigations, Box 2134, Wilton, NY 12866-0999; Title Tel # (518) 587-7638
General Info: Yr. Est. 1983, Quarterly
Subscriptions: Indv. $9

Chemical Design Automation News
See: CHEMISTRY & CHEMICALS

Chercheurs: Bulletin des Activites de Recherche de l'Universite de Montreal

Publishing Co: Universite de Montreal, Box 6128, Station A, Montreal, PQ H3C 3J7 Canada
Tel # (514) 343-6111
General Info: Yr. Est. 1974, Monthly, 16 pages
Circulation: Total-3,500

Chihuahuan Desert
Discovery   *Consumer*

Publishing Co: Chihuahuan Desert Research Institute, PO Box 1334, Alpine, TX 79831-1334;
Title Tel # (915) 837-8370
Personnel: Editor-Alan Brenner
General Info: Yr. Est. 1975, Semi-annually, 16 pages, 2 Color, Coated
Subscriptions: $2/copy
Circulation: Total-2,000

Climatic Summaries for Nebraska

Publishing Co: Univ. of Nebraska Dept. of Agricultural Metereology, LW Chase Hall, Lincoln, NE 68553-0728; Title Tel # (402) 472-6709
Personnel: Editor-Mathew Werner
Editorial Description: Monthly summary of temperature & precipitation accross Nebraska.
General Info: Yr. Est. 1958, Monthly, 6 pages, No Color

Clinical Investigator News
See: DRUGS & PHARMACEUTICALS

Clinical Trials Monitor
See: DRUGS & PHARMACEUTICALS

Coastal Research

Publishing Co: Florida State University Geology Dept., Department of Geology, Tallahassee, FL 32306-3026; Title Tel # (904) 644-3208
Personnel: Publisher, Editor-W.F. Tanner
Editorial Description: Aspects of geology, biology, geography, meteorology, archeology, engineering, law, etc.
General Info: (Formerly Coastal Research Notes), Yr. Est. 1962, Trim Size-8½ x 11, Offset press, 12 pages, ISSN: 0271-5376, No Color
Subscriptions: Indv. $6, Inst. $6, For. $7, $2/copy
Circulation: Total-300

Cold Facts   *Association*   CPM: $304

Publishing Co: Sponsor-Cryogenic Society of America, Inc., Cryogenic Society of America, 1033 South Blvd., Ste. 13, Oak Park, IL 60302-2823; Title Tel # (708) 383-6220
Title Fax # (708) 383-9337
Personnel: Editor-Laurie Huget, Adv. Dir.-Michael Samec
Editorial Description: Covers developments in the engineering and science of low temperatures.
General Info: Yr. Est. 1984, Quarterly, Trim Size-8.5 x 11, Offset press, 220 pages, ISSN: 1085-5262, No Color, Other, Saddle-stitched
Subscriptions: Indv. $50, Can. $65, For. $65, $65/copy
Circulation: Total-3,000
Advertising: $913.
List Rental: Actives: $600/M

Collections
See: MUSEUM PUBLICATIONS

Committee on Data for Science and Technology Newsletter   *Consumer*

Publishing Co: CODATA, Univ. of Michigan, Dept. of Chemistry, Ann Arbor, MI 48109-0001; Title Tel # (313) 764-7357 Title Fax # (313) 747-4865
Personnel: Publisher, Editor-E. Westrum, Jr., Circ. Mgr.-Phyllis Glaeser
Editorial Description: Importance of scientific data to science and technology.
General Info: Yr. Est. 1972, Quarterly, Trim Size-8¼ x 11½, Offset press, 8 pages, 2 Color, Coated
Subscriptions: Free To Qualified Recipient
Circulation: (100% controlled), Total-6,000
Advertising: Inquire for rates.
Printing Co: University of Michigan Printing Services, 1919 Green Rd, Ann Arbor, MI 48105-2554
Tel # (313) 764-4392, Fax # (313) 763-5147

Connect
See: EDUCATION

Creation/Evolution   *Association*

Publishing Co: National Center for Science Education, 925 Kearney St., El Cerrito, CA 94530-2810; Title Tel # (510) 526-1674 Title Fax # (510) 526-1675
Personnel: Editor-John R. Cole, Circ. Mgr.-Erik Whecton, Promotion Dir.-E.C. Scott
Editorial Description: The answers creationist arguments and covers science and education.
General Info: Yr. Est. 1980, Bi-monthly, Trim Size-5½ x 8½, Sheetfed press, 50 pages, ISSN: 0738-6001, No Color, Newsprint
Subscriptions: Indv. $25, $6/copy
Circulation: Total-3,000
Advertising: Inquire for rates.
List Rental: Rents Lists

Currents

Publishing Co: Institute of Marine Sciences, Univ. of California, Santa Cruz, CA 95064;
Title Tel # (408) 429-2464
Editorial Description: Summary of activities in the Santa Cruz program. Intended for IMS faculty, staff, & students & financial supporters of the Marine program.
General Info: Quarterly, 4 pages

Diagnostics Intelligence
See: DRUGS & PHARMACEUTICALS

Diamond Industry Week   *Business*

Publishing Co: Superconductivity Publications, Inc., 828 Livingston Ave., North Brunswick, NJ 08902-2356; Title Tel # (908) 846-2002 Title Fax # (908) 846-2050
Personnel: Publisher, Editor in Chief-C. Jim Russell, Circ. Mgr., Mktg. Dir.-Kathy Kleppin
Editorial Description: Dedicated to the rapid coverage of diamond and related materials including CBN, PCD, CPBN, Wideband gap and competitive materials.
General Info: Yr. Est. 1994, 48x/yr., Trim Size-8½ x 11, 12 pages, ISSN: 1073-7316
Subscriptions: Indv. $377, For. $377, $8/copy
Advertising: Accepts Inserts.
List Rental: Hotline: 8,000, $125/M

Drosophila

Publishing Co: Indiana University, Publications, Bloomington, IN 47405-6801;
Title Tel # (812) 855-5782 Title Fax # (812) 855-2577
Personnel: Publisher-Kathleen Matthews, Editor-Carl Thummel
Editorial Description: Announcements, technical, genetic and computing notes relevant to the Drosophila community.
General Info: Yr. Est. 1990, Quarterly
Circulation: Total-436

ECCOMAS Newsletter   *Business, Association*   CPM: $26

Publishing Co: John Wiley & Sons, Inc., 605 Third Avenue, New York, NY 10158-0012
Tel # (212) 850-6000 Fax # (212) 850-6088
Personnel: Editor in Chief-J.A. Desideri, Editor-Jan de Landtsheer, Production Ed.-Simon Hall, Mktg. Mgr.-Caroline Sims
Editorial Description: Provides information to scientists & engineers on forthcoming European Community on Computational Methods in Applied Sciences (ECCOMAS) Conferences and also on a broad range of research activities & technological issues in the above fields which are first priorites for Europe.
General Info: Quarterly, Trim Size-8¼ x 11¾
Circulation: Total-28,000
Advertising: $755.

ENC Update
See: MATHEMATICS

Electronic Chemicals News
See: CHEMISTRY & CHEMICALS

Emerging Pharmaceuticals
See: DRUGS & PHARMACEUTICALS

Empire State Geogram-Research Issue
See: GEOLOGY

Environmental Laboratory Washington Report
See: LAW

Exploratory Research Letter
See: POWER & POWER PLANTS

Filter

Publishing Co: Lambda Delta Lambda, c/o Patricia Van Englehoven, Kansas State Teachers College, 1200 Commercial, Emporia, KS 66801

Flat Earth News   *Association*

Publishing Co: Flat Earth Research Soc. Int'l., PO Box 2533, Lancaster, CA 93539-2533;
Title Tel # (805) 727-1635
Personnel: Publisher, Editor-C.K. Johnson
Editorial Description: Tries to prove that the earth is flat and that the entire accepted scientific system is a hoax.
General Info: Yr. Est. 1971, Quarterly, Trim Size-11 x 17, Web press, 8 pages, ISSN: 8756-0313, No Color
Subscriptions: Indv. $25, $5/copy
Circulation: (57% controlled), Total-3,500

Forefront
See: AGRICULTURE

Foreign Technology   *Business*

Publishing Co: National Technical Information Service U.S., 5285 Port Royal Rd., Springfield, VA 22161-0001 Tel # (703) 487-4630 Fax # (703) 487-4630; Title Tel # (703) 487-4650
Editorial Description: Features news on current developments in foreign technology. Designed to keep US firms in touch with overseas developments.
General Info: Yr. Est. 1983, Weekly, Trim Size-8½ x 11, Offset press, 28 pages
Subscriptions: Indv. $165, Can. $165, For. $225

Frontiers in Immunoassay & Biotechnology

Publishing Co: DUWEST Research/Scientific Newsletters, Rr 4 Box 7, Middletown, NY 10940-9685; Title Tel # (714) 240-3579
Personnel: Editor-John Zack
General Info: Yr. Est. 1980, 10x/yr.
Subscriptions: Indv. $85

Future Technology Intelligence Report

Publishing Co: Future Technology Intelligence Report, Inc., PO Box 423652, San Francisco, CA 94142-3652; Title Tel # (415) 359-3757
Personnel: Editor-Antony Sutton, Production Mgr.-Nicale Peters
Editorial Description: Reports & predicts future technology from a global source network. Specializes in material not reported elsewhere (i.e. zero point energy, etheric weather engineering, space energy, radionics, and energy medicine).
General Info: Yr. Est. 1990, Monthly, Trim Size-$8\frac{1}{2}$ x 11, Letrpr. press, 8 pages, No Color, Coated
Subscriptions: Indv. $150, Inst. $150, Can. $150, For. $200, $15/copy
Circulation: Total-500

Futuretech — *Business*

Publishing Co: Technical Insights, Inc., PO Box 1304, Fort Lee, NJ 07024-9967; Title Tel # (201) 568-4744 Title Fax # (201) 568-8247
Personnel: Publisher-Kenneth A. Kovaly, Editorial Dir.-Peter R. Savage, Circ. Mgr.-Barbara Chaffee, Mktg. Dir.-Lyn Schmidt
Editorial Description: Each briefing analyzes the critical technology, its impact to the market, its potential for growth, its availability for joint venturing.
General Info: (Formerly Futuretech Strategic Markets), Yr. Est. 1986, Monthly, Sheetfed press, 18 pages, ISSN: 1056-8107, 2 Color, Matte, Other
Subscriptions: Indv. $1,500, For. $1,560
List Rental: Actives: $180/M, Expires: $235/M

Gene Therapy Newsletter
See: GENETICS

Geo-Monitor
See: GEOLOGY

Grant Advisor
See: EDUCATION

HESCA Feedback
See: HEALTH

HLB Newsletter
See: MEDICINE

Hawkhill Science Newsletter — *Consumer*

Publishing Co: Hawkhill Assocs., Inc., 125 E. Gilman St., PO Box 1029, Madison, WI 53701-1029
Personnel: Editor-Bill Stonebarger
Editorial Description: Entertaining and useful science tips and information.
General Info: Irregular, Trim Size-$8\frac{1}{2}$ x 11, 4 pages, No Color

High Performance Plastics
See: PLASTICS

High Tech Separations News — *Business*

Publishing Co: Business Communications Co., 25 Van Zant St., Ste.13, Norwalk, CT 06855-1781; Title Tel # (203) 853-4266 Title Fax # (203) 853-0348
Personnel: Publisher-Louis Naturman, Editor-Anna Crull, Editor-Dick Hilton, Mktg. Dir.-Robert Butler
Editorial Description: Covers the fast growing field of high technology organic and molecular separations, from classical techniques like electrophoresis to important news methods using super critical fluids.
General Info: Yr. Est. 1988, Monthly, Trim Size-$8\frac{1}{2}$ x 11, 14 pages, Ind/Abs/Online: DIALOG, Predicasts, No Color, Matte
Subscriptions: Indv. $365, Can. $415, For. $415, $35/copy
List Rental: List Management Co.: W.I. Mail Marketing, 470 Main St. #317, Ridgefield, CT 06877-4516 Tel # (203) 438-6822, Fax # (203) 438-7756, Actives: $120/M

History of Science Society-Newsletter
See: HISTORY

Huntsman Marine Science News
See: FISH & FISHERIES

IACM Bulletin — *Business, Association* — CPM: $503

Publishing Co: John Wiley & Sons, Inc., 605 Third Avenue, New York, NY 10158-0012 Tel # (212) 850-6000 Fax # (212) 850-6088
Personnel: Publisher-Jan de Landtsheer, Editor-N.P. Weatherill, Production Ed.-Simon Hall, Circ. Mgr.-Margaret Radbourne, Mktg. Mgr.-Tony Carwardine
Editorial Description: Newsletter of the International Association of Computational Mechanics that links engineers and scientists of different countries.
General Info: Yr. Est. 1985, Quarterly, Trim Size-$8\frac{1}{4}$ x $11\frac{3}{4}$, Sheetfed press, 4 Color
Circulation: Total-1,500, Readership-10,500
Advertising: $755. Accepts Inserts.
List Rental: Actives: $415/M

IEEE Professional Communication Society Newsletter
See: LITERATURE & LINGUISTICS

IMS Bulletin — *Consumer, Association*

Publishing Co: Univ. of Connecticut Inst. Materials Science, Publications, Storrs, CT 06268; Title Tel # (203) 486-4623
Personnel: Editor-Dr. Thomas Saxton
Editorial Description: Materials research from biomedical to metallurgy and crystallography.
General Info: Yr. Est. 1966, Semi-annually, Offset press, 4 pages, No Color
Circulation: Total-3,500
Printing Co: Univ. of Connecticut Publications, PR Office, 1266 Storrs Rd., Storrs, CT 06269-5144 Tel # (203) 486-4015

ISCLT Newsletter — *Association*

Publishing Co: International Society for Clinical Lab Technology, 818 Olive St Ste 918, Saint Louis, MO 63101-1544; Title Tel # (314) 241-1445
Personnel: Editor-Mark Birenbaum, Ph.D.
Editorial Description: Newsletter for clinical laboratory technologists, technicians, & physicians' office laboratory technicians providing education, technical data, meetings, conventions, & state activites.
General Info: Yr. Est. 1962, Bi-monthly, Trim Size-$8\frac{1}{2}$ x 11, Sheetfed press, 6 pages, 2 Color, Newsprint
Subscriptions: Free With Membership
Circulation: (100% controlled), Total-5,500
Printing Co: Modern Litho-Print, 411 Madison St, Jefferson City, MO 65101-3190 Tel # (314) 635-6119, Fax # (314) 636-2655

Index to Chemical Regulations
See: CHEMISTRY & CHEMICALS

Info
See: BIBLIOGRAPHY

Information North — *Association*

Publishing Co: Arctic Institute of North America, 2500 University Dr. N.W., Calgary, AB T2N 1N4 Canada; Title Tel # (403) 220-7515 Title Fax # (403) 282-4609
Personnel: Editor-Karen McCullough, Production Ed.-Ona Stonkus, Circ. Mgr.-Anne Nail
Editorial Description: Essays on current northern issues.
General Info: Yr. Est. 1973, Quarterly, Trim Size-$8\frac{1}{2}$ x 11, Desktop press, 8 pages, ISSN: 0315-2561, Ind/Abs/Online: CPI, Color-cover, Recycled, Saddle-stitched
Subscriptions: Free With Membership
Circulation: Total-2,500
Printing Co: Apache Superior Printing, Bay H, 6812 - 6 St., SE, Calgary, AB T2H 2G7 Canada Tel # (403) 253-7626

Information Report — *Business*

Publishing Co: Washington Researchers, Ltd., PO Box 19005, Washington, DC 20036-9005 Tel # (202) 333-3499; Title Tel # (202) 333-3533 Title Fax # (202) 625-0656
Personnel: Editor-Penny Hill Press, Promotion Dir.-Ellen O'Kane
Editorial Description: Filled with fact finding tips describing free or inexpensive publications/services.
General Info: Yr. Est. 1974, Monthly, Trim Size-$8\frac{1}{2}$ x 11, 8 pages, ISSN: 0773-8961, Ind/Abs/Online: Newsnet, 2 Color
Subscriptions: Indv. $160
Circulation: Total-2,000

Innovator's Digest
See: MANAGEMENT

Inventors News — *Association*

Publishing Co: Sponsor-Inventors Clubs of America, Inc., Inventors Clubs of America, Inc., PO Box 450261, Atlanta, GA 31145-0261 Fax # (404) 355-8889; Title Tel # (404) 938-5089
Personnel: Publisher, Editor-Alexande Marinaccio, Circ. Mgr.-Gail Morrell, Adv. Dir.-Tom Yoder
Editorial Description: New technology news.
General Info: Yr. Est. 1935, Bi-monthly, 8 pages
Subscriptions: Indv. $50
Circulation: Total-6,000
Advertising: Inquire for rates.

Japan Science Scan

Publishing Co: Kyodo News Intl., 50 Rockefeller Plaza #803, New York, NY 10020-1605; Title Tel # (212) 397-3723 Title Fax # (212) 397-3721
Editorial Description: Important findings from the Japanese science community.
General Info: Yr. Est. 1988, Weekly

Johns Hopkins University Undergraduate Science Bulletin

Publishing Co: Johns Hopkins University, Office of Student Affairs, 3400 N Charles St, Baltimore, MD 21218-2608; Title Tel # (301) 338-7501
Personnel: Editor-Lawrence Durban
General Info: Yr. Est. 1971, Semi-annually
Circulation: Total-3,000
Advertising: Inquire for rates.

Journal of the Mississippi Academy of Sciences   *Association*

Publishing Co: Mississippi Academy of Sciences, 405 Briarwood Dr Ste 107e, Jackson, MS 39206-3032; Title Tel # (601) 977-0627
Personnel: Editor-John Tiftickjian, Circ. Mgr.-Arlene Adams
Editorial Description: Contains abstracts and full papers as well as annual proceedings of the academy which includes roster of membership, resolutions, program, and minutes, etc.
General Info: Yr. Est. 1939, 4x/yr., Trim Size-8½ x 11, 150 pages, ISSN: 0076-9436, No Color
Subscriptions: Indv. $25
Acquistions: Publication Bought
Circulation: Total-1,500
Advertising: Inquire for rates.
Printing Co: Evergreen/Lakeland Press, 4262 Lakeland Dr, Jackson, MS 39208-9551

Kaufman Letter, The
See: SAFETY

Laboratory Computer Letter   *Business*

Publishing Co: Information Research, 24885 Corbit Pl, Yorba Linda, CA 92687
Tel # (714) 692-0227; Title Tel # (714) 846-7183
Personnel: Publisher, Editor-Phillip Good, Circ. Mgr.-Linda Bennett
Editorial Description: Provides management with up-to-date information on data acquisition & data analysis using microcomputers, plus free hotline access & bonus pubs.
General Info: Yr. Est. 1981, Monthly, Sheetfed press, 8 pages, ISSN: 0738-8772, No Color
Subscriptions: Indv. $124, $15/copy
Circulation: Total-500
List Rental: Rents Lists

Langer Report Newsletter

Publishing Co: Langer Assocs., Inc., 19 W 44th St Ste 601, New York, NY 10036-5902;
Title Tel # (212) 391-0350
Personnel: Editor-Judith Langer
Editorial Description: Changing values & lifestyle trends identified through qualitative research.
General Info: Yr. Est. 1986, Quarterly, Trim Size-8½ x 11, Mimeo press, 6 pages, No Color
Subscriptions: Indv. $45, $12/copy

Littoral Drift
See: ENVIRONMENT & ECOLOGY

Lunar & Planetary Information Bulletin

Publishing Co: Lunar & Planetary Institute, 3600 Bay Area Blvd, Houston, TX 77058-1113;
Title Tel # (713) 486-2175 Title Fax # (713) 486-2162
Personnel: Editor-P.B. Thompson
General Info: (Formerly Lunar Science Info Bulletin), Yr. Est. 1974, Quarterly, Trim Size-8½ x 11, Offset press, 20 pages, No Color, Matte, Saddle-stitched

MIRA Newsletter
See: ASTRONOMY

Manitoba Science Teacher

Publishing Co: Science Teachers' Assn. of Manitoba, 295 Sutton Ave., Winnipeg, MB R2G 0T1 Canada
Personnel: Editor-Brian Dentry
Editorial Description: An educational publication for science teachers at all levels. Contains both pedagogical info as well as teaching activities.
General Info: Yr. Est. 1960, Quarterly, Trim Size-8½ x 11, 42 pages
Subscriptions: Can. $15
Acquistions: Publication Bought
Circulation: Total-800
Advertising: Inquire for rates. Accepts Inserts.
Printing Co: M.T.S., 191 Harcourt St., Winnipeg, MB R3J 3H2 Canada Tel # (204) 888-7961

Materials and Processing Report

Publishing Co: MIT Press, 77 Massachusetts Ave Rm 36-709, Cambridge, MA 02139-4307;
Title Tel # (617) 253-2866
General Info: Monthly
Subscriptions: Indv. $395

Medical Abstracts Newsletter
See: HEALTH

Mercury Messenger

Publishing Co: Lunar & Planetary Institute, 3600 Bay Area Blvd, Houston, TX 77058-1113
Tel # (713) 486-2175 Fax # (713) 486-2162; Title Tel # (713) 486-2143
Personnel: Editor-Pamela Clark
Editorial Description: A pub. which provides the means for exchanging data & ideas, for planning collaborative activity, & for increasing awareness of ongoing Mercury work.
General Info: Yr. Est. 1987, Semi-annually, 4 pages, No Color, Newsprint
Circulation: Total-550

Meteor News

Publishing Co: Wanda Simmons, Box 1062, Rte. 3, Callahan, FL 32011-1062;
Title Tel # (904) 879-2646
Personnel: Publisher-Wanda Simmons, Editor-Karl Simmons
Editorial Description: News on meteor showers and meteorite finds.
General Info: Yr. Est. 1970, Quarterly, Trim Size-8½ x 11, Sheetfed press, 10 pages, ISSN: 0146-9959, 1% ads, No Color
Subscriptions: Indv. $6, Can. $9, For. $12, $2/copy
Circulation: Total-400
Advertising: Inquire for rates. Accepts Inserts.

Metric Reporter   *Association*

Publishing Co: American Natl. Metric Council, 4330 East West Hwy Ste 1117, Bethesda, MD 20814-4408; Title Tel # (301) 718-6508 Title Fax # (301) 656-0989
Personnel: Editor-Ruth Thaler-Carter
Editorial Description: Metric conversion activities in business and industry, government, and education.
General Info: Yr. Est. 1973, Monthly, Trim Size-8½ x 11, Desktop press, 4 pages, 2 Color, Coated
Subscriptions: $1/copy
Circulation: (100% controlled), Total-1,700

Microscopial Society of Canada. Bulletin
See: OPTICAL

Microwave News
See: HEALTH

Museletter   *Consumer*

Publishing Co: Museletter, 1433 Olivet Rd, Santa Rosa, CA 95401-3810
Personnel: Publisher-Richard Heinberg
Editorial Description: Covers the history of science to dicuss myth, spirituality and culture.
General Info: Monthly
Subscriptions: Indv. $15

NAACLS News
See: EDUCATION

NAOSMM Newsline

Publishing Co: Natl. Assn. of Scientific Materials Managers, Univ. Of New Orleans Chemistry, Dept., New Orleans, LA 70148-0001; Title Tel # (504) 286-6324
Personnel: Editor-Irene Hamilton
General Info: Yr. Est. 1978, Quarterly, Trim Size-8½ x 11, 10 pages, No Color, Saddle-stitched
Circulation: Total-250

NCSE Reports
See: EDUCATION

NSF Bulletin   *Association*

Publishing Co: Natl. Science Foundation, 4201 Wilson Boulevard, Arlington, VA 22230
Personnel: Editor-Mary Wilson
Editorial Description: Program announcements & deadlines, publications availability, personnel changes.
General Info: Yr. Est. 1974, 10x/yr., 6 pages
Acquistions: Publication Bought
Circulation: (100% controlled), Total-20,000

Nano Week   *Business*

Publishing Co: Superconductivity Publications, Inc., 828 Livingston Ave., North Brunswick, NJ 08902-2356; Title Tel # (908) 846-2002 Title Fax # (908) 846-2050
Personnel: Publisher, Editor-C. Jim Russell, Circ. Mgr., Mktg. Dir.-Kathy Kleppin
Editorial Description: Offers timely insights into nanotechnology, including nanostructured materials, nanofabrication techniques, nanobiology, etc. with brief descriptions of applicable US patents.
General Info: Yr. Est. 1996, 24x/yr., Trim Size-8½ x 11, 6 pages, ISSN: 1073-7308
Subscriptions: Indv. $277, For. $277, $12/copy

NanoNews   *Business*

Publishing Co: Superconductivity Publications, Inc., 828 Livingston Ave., North Brunswick, NJ 08902-2356; Title Tel # (908) 846-2002 Title Fax # (908) 846-2050
Personnel: Publisher, Editor-C. Jim Russell, Circ. Mgr., Adv. Dir., Mktg. Dir.-Kathy Kleppin
Editorial Description: Provides comprehensive insights into the world or nanotechnology and existing products such as zeolites, catalysts membranes as well as aplicable US patents.
General Info: Yr. Est. 1996, Bi-monthly, Trim Size-8½ x 11, 16 pages, ISSN: 1051-7294
Subscriptions: Indv. $97, Can. $97, For. $117, $16/copy
Advertising: $500.

National Character Laboratory-Newsletter
See: MEDICINE

National Conference of Standards Laboratories Newsletter
Business, Association

Publishing Co: Natl. Conference of Standards Laboratories, 1800 30th St Ste 305b, Boulder, CO 80301-1026; Title Tel # (303) 440-3339
Personnel: Editor-John Minck
Editorial Description: Association news, board minutes, annual conference paper reprints, articles of interest to metrology community.
General Info: Yr. Est. 1961, Bi-monthly, Trim Size-8½ x 11, Offset press, 60 pages, ISSN: 0194-5149, No Color
Subscriptions: Indv. $15, $5/copy
Circulation: Total-1,342

National Weather Assn. Newsletter
See: METEOROLOGY

Network Security
Business

Publishing Co: Elsevier Science Inc., 655 Avenue of the Americas, New York, NY 10010-5107
Tel # (212) 633-3916 Fax # (212) 633-3913 Parent Co.-Reed Elsevier, New York
Personnel: Publisher-Andrew Fletcher, Editor-John Meyer, Mktg. Dir.-Jeremy Whittingham
General Info: Monthly, ISSN: 1353-4858
Subscriptions: $454/copy

New Technology Week
Business, Association

Publishing Co: King Communications Group, 627 National Press Building, Washington, DC 20045-1601 Fax # (202) 662-9719; Title Tel # (202) 638-4260 Title Fax # (202) 662-9744
Personnel: Publisher-Llewellyn King, Editor-Ken Jacobson, Circ. Mgr.-Dawn Miles, Production Mgr.-Tony Russell, Art Dir.-Tony Campana, Mktg. Dir.-Julie Lee
Editorial Description: Provides comprehensive coverage of advanced and emerging technologies. Reports on business opportunities and strategies, federal policy, and technology transfer. Weekly publication features R&D, coverage of the national labs, budgets, legislative iniatives and the competitiveness issue.
General Info: Yr. Est. 1987, Weekly, Trim Size-8½ x 11, Sheetfed press, 12 pages, ISSN: 0894-0789, Ind/Abs/Online: NewsNet, DIALOG, Predicasts, 2 Color, Newsprint, Saddle-stitched
Subscriptions: Indv. $799, $18/copy
Acquistions: Publication Bought
List Rental: Rents Lists

News from Mote

Publishing Co: Mote Marine Laboratory, 1600 Ken Thompson Pky, Sarasota, FL 34236-1004 Fax # (818) 388-4312; Title Tel # (813) 388-4441 Title Fax # (813) 388-2383
Personnel: Editor-Honey Rand
Editorial Description: Recent activities of Mote Marine Laboratory & Mote Marine Aquarium, including current research projects & special events.
General Info: (Formerly Cape Haze Marine Laboratory Quarterly Newsletter), Yr. Est. 1955, Quarterly, 12 pages, Color-cover, Coated
Circulation: Total-10,000
Printing Co: J & G Printing, 3511 Clark Rd, Sarasota, FL 34231-8499 Tel # (813) 921-5508

News Report
Scholarly, Association

Publishing Co: National Research Council, 2101 Constitution Ave., NW, Washington, DC 20418; Title Tel # (202) 334-2138
Personnel: Editor-Pepper Leeper, Production Mgr.-Patricia Worns
Editorial Description: Reports both national and international activities of the National Academy of Sciences, National Research Council, National Academy of Engineering, and the Institute of Medicine.
General Info: Yr. Est. 1950, 3x/yr., Trim Size-8 x 10, Offset press, 20 pages, ISSN: 0027-8432, Color-cover, Coated, Saddle-stitched
Subscriptions: Indv. $10, For. $12, $1/copy
Circulation: Total-20,000
Printing Co: Hennage Creative Printers, 500 N Henry St, Alexandria, VA 22314-2233 Tel # (703) 683-8282

Occultation Newsletter
See: ASTRONOMY

Ontario Industrial Arts Bulletin
See: BUSINESS & INDUSTRY

PBC Science Briefs
Business, Consumer

Publishing Co: Publishing & Business Consultants, 101 W. 64th St. Unit #3, Inglewood, CA 90302-1255 Tel # (213) 732-3477 Fax # (213) 732-3477
Personnel: Publisher, Editor-Andeson Atia
General Info: Quarterly, 60 pages, ISSN: 1059-1990
Subscriptions: Indv. $180, Can. $198
Advertising: Inquire for rates.

PIASA Bulletin, The
See: INTERNATIONAL AFFAIRS

Pacific Science Association Information Bulletin
Association

Publishing Co: Pacific Science Association, PO Box 17801, Honolulu, HI 96817-0801
Tel # (808) 848-4139 Fax # (808) 841-8968; Title Tel # (808) 847-4139 Title Fax # (808) 847-8252
Personnel: Editor-L.G. Eldredge
Editorial Description: News of Association activities and Pacific biological & social science; original articles, notice of meetings & workshops; book reviews & publications rated; and other pertinent news.
General Info: Yr. Est. 1949, Semi-annually, Trim Size-5¾ x 8¾, Offset press, 40 pages, ISSN: 0030-8889, Ind/Abs/Online: Bibl., No Color
Subscriptions: Indv. $30, Inst. $50
Acquistions: Publication Bought
Circulation: Total-2,000
Printing Co: Edward Enterprises, PO Box 30468, 641 Waiakamilo Rd., Honolulu, HI 96820-0468 Tel # (808) 841-4231

Perinatal Addiction Research & Education Update
See: MEDICINE

Phi Lambda Upsilon Register
Consumer, Association

Publishing Co: Phi Lambda Upsilon, Wabash College, Dept. of Chemistry, Crawfordsville, IN 47933; Title Tel # (703) 961-5997
Personnel: Editor-Jack Graybeal
Editorial Description: News of society-features articles on chemistry and engineering.
General Info: Yr. Est. 1914, Semi-annually, Trim Size-6 x 9, Offset press, 24 pages, No Color
Subscriptions: Indv. $3, $2/copy
Circulation: Total-3,100

Priorities
See: HEALTH

Probe Newsletter
Business, Consumer

Publishing Co: Probe Newsletter, Inc., 139 W 13th St., Apt 6, New York, NY 10011-7856; Title Tel # (212) 647-0200 Title Fax # (212) 924-4121
Personnel: Publisher-David Zimmerman
Editorial Description: Reports on science, media, and policies with analytical depth.
General Info: Yr. Est. 1991, Monthly, ISSN: 1062-4155
Subscriptions: Indv. $60, Can. $60, For. $77, $5/copy

Professional Ethics Report

Publishing Co: American Assn. for the Advancement of Science, 1333 H St. NW, Washington, DC 20005-4707; Title Tel # (202) 326-6798 Title Fax # (202) 289-4950
Personnel: Editor-Mark Frankel, Contrib. Ed.-Alexander Fowler, Production Mgr.-Amy Crumpton
Editorial Description: Info on professional ethics in science, engineering & health care.
General Info: Yr. Est. 1988, Quarterly, Desktop press, 8 pages, 2 Color, Recycled
Subscriptions: Free
Circulation: Total-1,900
List Rental: Rents Lists
Printing Co: Tyler Business Service, 2121 Wisconsin Ave NW, Washington, DC 20007-2290 Tel # (202) 333-6599

Prometheus Report: Journal of Firesafety
See: FIRE PROTECTION

Public Interest Report

Publishing Co: Fed. of American Scientists, 307 Massachusetts Ave NE, Washington, DC 20002-5793; Title Tel # (202) 546-3300
Personnel: Editor-Jeremy Stone
General Info: Yr. Est. 1946, Monthly
Subscriptions: Indv. $13, $1/copy

Quantum Advantage Investment & Technology Report

Publishing Co: Agora, Inc., 105 W. Monoment St., Baltimore, MD 21202-4702 Tel # (410) 783-2647 Fax # (410) 223-2662; Title Tel # (410) 234-0515 Title Fax # (410) 837-3879
Personnel: Publisher-William Bonner, Editor-Laura Bernstein, Circ. Dir.-Daryl Berver, Production Mgr.-Alex Nosevitch
Editorial Description: Covers emerging technologies, new products, hi-tech investments and entrepreneurship opportunities.
General Info: Yr. Est. 1991, Monthly, Trim Size-8½ x 11, 8 pages
Subscriptions: Indv. $329
List Rental: List Management Co.: Name Bank, 14 W. Monument St., Baltimore, MD 21201 Tel # (410) 783-8463, Fax # (410) 783-8464

RIC Insight
Business

Publishing Co: Rare-Earth Information Ctr., 254 Spedding Hall, AMES LAboratory ISU, Ames, IA 50011-3020 Fax # (515) 294-3707; Title Tel # (515) 294-2272 Title Fax # (515) 294-3709
Personnel: Editor-Karl Gschneidner, Jr.
Editorial Description: Late breaking news that is of a commercial or potentially commercial nature and how it affects the rare earth industry.
General Info: Yr. Est. 1988, Monthly, Trim Size-8½ x 11, Letrpr. press, 2 pages, 2 Color, Matte, Other
Subscriptions: Indv. $300, $25/copy
Circulation: Total-180
List Rental: Rents Lists

RIC News
Business, Consumer

Publishing Co: Rare-Earth Information Ctr., 254 Spedding Hall, AMES LAboratory ISU, Ames, IA 50011-3020 Fax # (515) 294-3707; Title Tel # (515) 294-2272 Title Fax # (515) 294-3709
Personnel: Editor-Karl Gschneidner, Jr., Production Mgr.-Joel Calhoun
Editorial Description: Items of current interest concerning the science and technology of the rare earths.
General Info: Yr. Est. 1966, Quarterly, Trim Size-8½ x 11, Offset press, 8 pages, 2 Color, Recycled
Subscriptions: Free
Circulation: (93% controlled), Total-12,900, International-7,200
List Rental: Actives: $150/M

Reflector
Association

Publishing Co: Astronomical League, 2112 Kingfisher Lane, E., Rolling Meadows, IL 60008 Tel # (708) 398-0562; Title Tel # (847) 398-0562
Personnel: Editor-Edward Fafpoehler
Editorial Description: For amateur astronomers who belong to the Astronomical League.
General Info: Quarterly, 12 pages, ISSN: 0034-2963, No Color, Newsprint
Subscriptions: Indv. $4
Circulation: Total-12,000
Advertising: Inquire for rates.
List Rental: Rents Lists

Rensselaerville Newsletter
Consumer, Association

Publishing Co: Rensselaerville Inst., Pond Hill Rd., Rensselaerville, NY 12147; Title Tel # (518) 797-3783
Editorial Description: Report and review of projects and programs conducted by The Institute during the previous year.
General Info: Yr. Est. 1973, Quarterly, Trim Size-8½ x 11, Offset press, 6 pages, No Color
Circulation: Total-4,000

Report on Science and Human Rights
See: INTERNATIONAL AFFAIRS

Research News

Publishing Co: Catholic Univ. of America, 620 Michigan Ave NE, Washington, DC 20017-1556
Personnel: Publisher-Ann Smith, Editor-John Abbot
Editorial Description: Quarterly newsletter describing research projects at the unviersity.

Research Profiles

Publishing Co: Center for Gerontogical Studies, Univ. of Florida, 3357 Turlington Hall, Gainsville, FL 32611-2036; Title Tel # (904) 392-2116
Personnel: Editor-Dr. Otto von Mering
Editorial Description: Reviews Center Assocs. work in the field of aging.
General Info: Yr. Est. 1987, Semi-annually, 2 Color, Newsprint
Circulation: Total-2,000

Resonance
See: BIOPHYSICS

Resource
Consumer

Publishing Co: Canadian Council on Animal Care, 350 Albert St., Ste. 315, Ottawa, ON K1R 1B1 Canada; Title Tel # (613) 238-4031
Personnel: Editor-Gillian Griffin
Editorial Description: Articles on care and use of experimental animals in Canada.
General Info: Yr. Est. 1976, Semi-annually, Trim Size-8½ x 11, Offset press, 4 pages, 2 Color, Newsprint
Circulation: (100% controlled), Total-7,000

Robot Explorer
See: COMPUTERS & AUTOMATION

SCWIST News
See: WOMEN'S

SIPIscope

Publishing Co: Scientists' Institute for Public Information, 1328 Broadway #300, New York, NY 10001-2121; Title Tel # (212) 661-9110
Personnel: Publisher-Jay Letto, Editor-Barbara Allen
Editorial Description: Focuses on science & technology & health reporting by the media.
General Info: (Formerly Scientist and Citizen), Yr. Est. 1972, Quarterly, Trim Size-8½ x 11
Circulation: (50% controlled), Total-16,000, Subscriptions-8,000

SSI Update
See: AERONAUTICS/ASTRONAUTICS

STP Newsletter
Consumer

Publishing Co: WDC-A for STP, 325 Broadway, Boulder, CO 80303-3328; Title Tel # (303) 497-6323
Personnel: Publisher-J.H. Allen, Editor-Prof. C. H. Liu
Editorial Description: News about solar-terrestrial physics programs worldwide.
General Info: Yr. Est. 1976, Annually, Trim Size-8½ x 11, 20 pages, Saddle-stitched
Circulation: Total-3,600

Safety Is Elementary
See: SAFETY

San Bernardino County Museum Association Newsletter
See: MUSEUM PUBLICATIONS

School Science and Mathematics
See: EDUCATION

Science for Democratic Action
See: POLITICS

Science Education News

Publishing Co: American Assn. for the Advancement of Science, 1333 H St. NW, Washington, DC 20005-4707; Title Tel # (202) 326-6620
Personnel: Publisher-Richard Nicholson, Editor, Production Mgr.-Barbara Walthall
Editorial Description: News items brought together to inform people concerning science, mathematics, & technology education at the school level.
General Info: Yr. Est. 1959, Monthly, Trim Size-8½ x 11, Sheetfed press, 4 pages
Circulation: Total-5,500
Printing Co: Tyler Business Service, 2121 Wisconsin Ave NW, Washington, DC 20007-2290 Tel # (202) 333-6599

Science Frontiers
Consumer

Publishing Co: Sourcebook Project, PO Box 107, Glen Arm, MD 21057-0107; Title Tel # (410) 668-6047
Personnel: Publisher, Editor-William Corliss
Editorial Description: Scientific anomalies reported in the current literature.
General Info: Yr. Est. 1977, Bi-monthly, Trim Size-8½ x 11, Sheetfed press, 4 pages
Subscriptions: Indv. $7
Circulation: Total-1,200

Science and Government Report
Business

Publishing Co: Science & Government Report, Inc., 3736 Kanawha St NW, Washington, DC 20015-1810; Title Tel # (202) 244-4135 Title Fax # (202) 362-2790
Personnel: Publisher, Editor-Daniel Greenberg, Circ. Mgr.-Wanda Reif
Editorial Description: Policy in government affecting science & technology research & funding.
General Info: Yr. Est. 1971, 20x/yr., Trim Size-8½ x 11, Letrpr. press, 8 pages, ISSN: 0048-9581, No Color, Matte, Other
Subscriptions: Indv. $455, Inst. $425, $20/copy
Circulation: Total-1,300
List Rental: Actives: 1,500, $175/M, Expires: 1,000

Science Marketing Newsletter
See: ADVERTISING & MARKETING

Science Museum News
See: MUSEUM PUBLICATIONS

Science Periodical on Research & Technology in Sport
See: SPORTS & SPORTING GOODS

Science Watch
Business

Publishing Co: Institute for Scientific Information, 3501 Market St., Philadelphia, PA 19104-3302 Fax # (215) 386-2911; Title Tel # (215) 386-0100 Title Fax # (215) 387-1266
Personnel: Editor-Chris King, Editor-David Pendlebury
Editorial Description: Analyzes trends in scientific research using quantitative techniques. Examines performance of countries, universities and other research sponsoring entities.
General Info: Yr. Est. 1990, 10x/yr.
Subscriptions: Indv. $325, Inst. $325
Circulation: Total-500

Scientists Center for Animal Welfare's Newsletter
See: ANIMALS

Sealing Technology
Business

Publishing Co: Elsevier Science Inc., 655 Avenue of the Americas, New York, NY 10010-5107 Tel # (212) 633-3916 Fax # (212) 633-3913 Parent Co.-Reed Elsevier, New York; Title Tel # (212) 633-3750 Title Fax # (212) 633-3764
Personnel: Publisher-Guy Kitteringham, Editor-Mark Punis, Production Mgr.-Chidine Chemarey
General Info: Monthly, ISSN: 1350-4789
Subscriptions: Indv. $433

Seiche, The
See: ENVIRONMENT & ECOLOGY

Sky Calendar
See: EDUCATION

Smithsonian Institution Research Reports
Association

Publishing Co: Smithsonian Institution, 900 Jefferson Dr., S.W., Washington, DC 20560-0001 Tel # (202) 357-2888; Title Tel # (202) 357-2627 Title Fax # (202) 786-2377
Personnel: Editor-Jo Ann Webb
Editorial Description: Smithsonian research activities in astronomy, life sciences, marine biology, ecology and tropical ecology, geology, archaeology, radiation biology, art and history research.
General Info: Yr. Est. 1972, Quarterly, Offset press, 8 pages, No Color
Circulation: Total-80,000
List Rental: Actives: $85/M

Society of Vertebrate Paleontology News Bulletin *Association*

Publishing Co: Society of Vertebrate Paleontology, W. 436 Nebraska Hall, Box 880542, Univ. of Nebraska, Lincoln, NE 68588-0542; Title Tel # (402) 472-4604 Title Fax # (402) 472-8949
Personnel: Editor-Dave Berman, Mng. Editor-M. Schmidt
Editorial Description: Features society official business, news from worldwide members, calendar of events, obituaries, miscellaneous information.
General Info: Yr. Est. 1941, 3x/yr., Trim Size-5$\frac{1}{2}$ x 8$\frac{1}{2}$, Offset press, 64 pages, No Color, Newsprint, Saddle-stitched
Subscriptions: Indv. $25, Inst. $25, For. $25, $8/copy
Circulation: Total-1,500

Software Technology Transfer
See: ENGINEERING

Speaking of Safety
See: SAFETY

Spectra: the Newsletter of the Carnegie Institution of Washington *Consumer*

Publishing Co: Carnegie Institution of Washington, 1530 P St NW, Washington, DC 20005-1910; Title Tel # (202) 387-6411
Personnel: Editor-Ray Bowers, Production Mgr.-Patricia Parratt Craig
Editorial Description: Activities of Carnegie Institution scientists and employees.
General Info: (Formerly Carnegie Institution of Washington Newsletter), Yr. Est. 1970, Quarterly, Trim Size-8$\frac{1}{2}$ x 11, Sheetfed press, 12 pages, 2 Color
Circulation: (87% controlled), Total-4,000, International-500, Readership-4,000

Storage Technology Monitor

Publishing Co: Technology News of America Co., 110 Greene St Apt 1101, New York, NY 10012-3824; Title Tel # (212) 334-9750
General Info: Yr. Est. 1985, Weekly
Subscriptions: Indv. $845

Superconductivity News *Business* CPM$1250

Publishing Co: Superconductivity Publications, Inc., 828 Livingston Ave., North Brunswick, NJ 08902-2356; Title Tel # (908) 846-2002 Title Fax # (908) 846-2050
Personnel: Publisher, Editor-C. James Russell, Circ. Mgr., Adv. Dir., Mktg. Dir.-Kathy Kleppin
Editorial Description: A newsletter on superconductivity research and business; providing engineering and technical coverage of worldwide developments in the field of superconductivity.
General Info: Yr. Est. 1987, 64x/yr., Trim Size-8$\frac{1}{2}$ x 11, Sheetfed press, 24 pages, ISSN: 0897-2427, 5% ads, No Color, Matte, Saddle-stitched
Subscriptions: Indv. $297, Inst. $237, Can. $297, For. $347
Acquistions: Publication Bought
Circulation: Total-400
Advertising: $500. Accepts Inserts.
List Rental: Actives: 9,000, $50/M, Hotline: 1,000, $100/M

Superconductor Week *Business*

Publishing Co: Atlantic Information Svcs., Inc., 1100 17th St. NW, Ste. 300, Washington, DC 20036-5503; Title Tel # (202) 775-9008 Title Fax # (202) 331-9542
Personnel: Publisher-Richard Biehl, Editor-C. David Chaffee, Circ. Mgr.-Gwen Arnold, Production Dir.-Gary Peterson, Mktg. Mgr.-Christine Bundell
Editorial Description: News of superconductor applications, markets, products and business.
General Info: Yr. Est. 1987, Weekly, Ind/Abs/Online: DIALOG
Subscriptions: Indv. $427

TRANET *Consumer, Association*

Publishing Co: Transnational Network for Appropriate/Alternative TEchnologi, Box 567, Pond St., Rangeley, ME 04970-0567; Title Tel # (207) 864-2252
Personnel: Publisher-William N. Ellis, Editor-William Ellis
Editorial Description: Directory of appropriate/alternative technology centers, worldwide.
General Info: Yr. Est. 1976, Bi-monthly, Offset press, 20 pages, ISSN: 0739-0971, No Color
Subscriptions: Indv. $30, Inst. $150, $5/copy
Circulation: Total-2,500
Printing Co: Heritage Press, PO Box 792, Farmington, ME 04938-0792 Tel # (207) 778-3581

Technology Access Report *Business*

Publishing Co: Technology Access, 16 Digital Drive, #250, Novato, CA 94949-5760 Tel # (415) 883-7600 Fax # (415) 883-6421
Personnel: Publisher-Michael Odza, Editor-Michael Kloess, Art Dir.-Jeffrey Norman, Circ. Dir., Mktg. Dir.-Lauren Andersen
Editorial Description: Covers technology transfer, commercialization, deployment and management. Includes universities, medical centers, govt. & independent labs in all industries and fields.
General Info: Yr. Est. 1987, Monthly, Trim Size-8$\frac{1}{2}$ x 11, Sheetfed press, 24 pages, ISSN: 1050-043X, Ind/Abs/Online: Newsnet, Predicast, knowledge express data systems, Color-cover, Newsprint, Saddle-stitched
Subscriptions: Indv. $497, Inst. $497, Can. $497, For. $587, $65/copy
Advertising: $1,160. Accepts Inserts.
List Rental: List Management Co.: Media Management Group, 666 Plainsboro Rd Ste 340, Plainsboro, NJ 08536-3026 Tel # (609) 275-0050, Fax # (609) 275-6606, Hotline: 24,500, $150/M
Printing Co: Publications Ink, 2115 4th St, Berkeley, CA 94710-2239 Tel # (510) 549-4300, Fax # (510) 549-4342

Technology Forecasts & Technology Surveys *Business*

Publishing Co: Technology Forecasts, 205 S Beverly Dr Ste 208, Beverly Hills, CA 90212-3873; Title Tel # (310) 273-3486 Title Fax # (310) 858-8272
Personnel: Publisher-Willard Wilks, Editor-Irwin Stambler, Circ. Mgr.-A. White
Editorial Description: Science & technology--advances, forecasts of future trends forecasting methodology.
General Info: Yr. Est. 1969, Monthly, ISSN: 0886-0890
Subscriptions: Indv. $160, Can. $164, For. $172, $20/copy
Printing Co: IGA Printing, 1910 S Archibald Ave Ste G, Ontario, CA 91761-8503 Tel # (714) 947-0447

Technology Strategies Newsletter *Business*

Publishing Co: Strategic Direction Publishers, 5352 Ashley Rd., Fairfax, VA 22030; Title Tel # (703) 830-5507 Title Fax # (703) 830-5506
General Info: Monthly
Subscriptions: Indv. $485

Technotrends Newsletter *Business, Association*

Publishing Co: Burrus Research Assoc., Inc., PO Box 26413, Milwaukee, WI 53226-0413 Fax # (414) 774-3022; Title Tel # (414) 786-2308 Title Fax # (414) 786-3022
Personnel: Publisher-Daniel Burrus, Editor-Patti Thomsen, Mktg. Dir.-Rosey Queisser
Editorial Description: Updated reports on innovations in technology from around the world.
General Info: (Formerly Technology Futures Newsletter), Yr. Est. 1985, Monthly, Trim Size-8$\frac{1}{2}$ x 11, Offset press, 4 pages, 4 Color, Coated, Other
Subscriptions: Indv. $50, Can. $55, For. $62, $5/copy
Circulation: Total-900

Thermogram *Business*

Publishing Co: E.I. du Pont de Nemours, 10007 Market Street, Wilmington, DE 19898-0001 Tel # (302) 774-1000
Editorial Description: Happenings in the field of thermal analysis.
General Info: Yr. Est. 1965, Quarterly

Today's Science on File *Consumer*

Publishing Co: Facts on File, Inc., 11 Penn Plaza, New York, NY 10001-2006 Tel # (212) 967-8800 Parent Co.-Infobase Holdings Inc., New York; Title Tel # (212) 683-2244 Title Fax # (212) 683-3633
Personnel: Publisher-Remmel Nunn, Editor-William Allstetter, Circ. Mgr.-Steve Orlofsky
Editorial Description: Indexed newsmagazine of science for students.
General Info: Yr. Est. 1992, Monthly, Trim Size-8$\frac{1}{2}$ x 11, Sheetfed press, 24 pages, ISSN: 1058-8124, No Color, Matte, Saddle-stitched
Subscriptions: Indv. $190, Inst. $190, Can. $241
Circulation: Total-3,200
List Rental: Rents Lists
Printing Co: Science Press, 300 W Chestnut St, Ephrata, PA 17522-2002 Tel # (717) 738-9300, Fax # (717) 738-9413

Total Eclipse
See: HISTORY

Trade & Licensing Hot List *Business*

Publishing Co: Freiberg Publishing Co., PO Box 7, Cedar Falls, IA 50613-0007 Tel # (319) 277-3599 Fax # (319) 277-3783
Editorial Description: Lists international product & patent licenses available and university technology transfer opportunites.
General Info: Yr. Est. 1993

Tripolitan

Publishing Co: Tripoli Rocketry Association, PO Box 339, Kenner, LA 70063-0339; Title Tel # (412) 882-4594
Personnel: Editor-Thomas Blazarin
General Info: Yr. Est. 1968, Bi-monthly
Subscriptions: Indv. $15
Circulation: Total-400

Twins Letter *Consumer, Association*

Publishing Co: Twins Foundation, PO Box 6043, Providence, RI 02940-6043; Title Tel # (401) 729-1000
Personnel: Publisher-John Mack Carter, Editor-Kay Cassill, Bk. Rev. Ed.-Betty Simons, Production Mgr., Art Dir.-Anne Richards
Editorial Description: Covers all matters related to twins & other multiples as well as twin research.
General Info: Yr. Est. 1984, Quarterly, Trim Size-8$\frac{1}{2}$ x 11, 12 pages, ISSN: 0743-748X, 2 Color, Newsprint
Subscriptions: Indv. $25, Inst. $25, $6/copy
Circulation: Total-10,000
Printing Co: DES Offset, 55 Johnson St, Providence, RI 02905-4518 Tel # (401) 461-6560

Underground Storage Tank News
See: PETROLEUM & NATURAL GAS

Upwellings
See: ENVIRONMENT & ECOLOGY

Washington Federal Science Newsletter
Business, Association

Publishing Co: Murray Felsher, 1057-B Natl. Press Bldg., Washington, DC 20045; Title Tel # (202) 393-3640 Title Fax # (202) 393-3640
Personnel: Publisher, Editor-Murray Felsher
Editorial Description: News & reports of U.S. Federal Agency activities in science & technology.
General Info: Yr. Est. 1989, Semi-monthly, Sheetfed press, 8 pages, ISSN: 0740-0535, 2 Color, Newsprint
Subscriptions: Indv. $410, Inst. $410, Can. $410, For. $500

Water Current
Business, Association

Publishing Co: Water Center Environmental Programs, 103 Natural Resources Hall UNL, Lincoln, NE 68583-0844; Title Tel # (402) 472-3305
Personnel: Editor-Bettina Heinz
Editorial Description: Topics on water issues.
General Info: Yr. Est. 1970, Bi-monthly, Trim Size-8$\frac{1}{2}$ x 11, Offset press, 8 pages, 2 Color, Other, Saddle-stitched
Circulation: Total-4,000, Readership-4,000

SCIENCE FICTION & FANTASY

Academy of Science Fiction, Fantasy & Horror Films-Newsletter

Publishing Co: Academy of Science Fiction, Fantasy & Horror Films, 334 W 54th St, Los Angeles, CA 90037-3806; Title Tel # (213) 752-5811 Title Fax # (213) 752-5811
Personnel: Editor-Dr. Donald Reed
General Info: Yr. Est. 1972, Quarterly
Circulation: Total-3,500

Actuary of the Abstract
Consumer, Association **CPM: $145**

Publishing Co: Sponsor-Nomads of the Time Stream, Nomads of the Time Stream, PO Box 451048, Atlanta, GA 31145-9048; Title Tel # (404) 634-3609
Personnel: Publisher-Edward Kramer, Editor, Staff Writer-Paul W. Cashman
Editorial Description: Information about the British author Michael Moorcock, his works, and related topics.
General Info: (Formerly Megaflow Manifesto), Yr. Est. 1988, Quarterly, Desktop press, 4 pages, 10% ads
Subscriptions: Indv. $20, For. $30, $3/copy
Circulation: Total-275
Advertising: $40.

Afraid
See: MYSTERY & HORROR

DOE
Consumer

Publishing Co: Luna Ventures, Box 398, Suisun, CA 94585-0398; Title Tel # (707) 425-1869
Personnel: Publisher-Paul Doerr, Editor-Paul Doer
Editorial Description: Science-Fiction, fantasy, horror, space, convention stories and art, especially for the novice writer/artist.
General Info: (Formerly Scifant), Monthly, Trim Size-8$\frac{1}{2}$ x 11, Offset press, 24 pages, ISSN: 0882-1348, No Color
Subscriptions: Indv. $24, Inst. $18, Can. $26, For. $28, $4/copy
Advertising: $40. Accepts Inserts.
Printing Co: First Image

Dark Shadows Announcement
See: FAN MAGAZINES-MOVIE, RADIO, TV

Deanna Gram
See: TELEVISION & VIDEO

Emerald City Mirror
See: CHILDREN

Final Frontier, The
Consumer

Publishing Co: Brooklyn College Science Fiction Society, Central Depository/Boylan Hall, Bedford Avenue and Avenue H, Brooklyn, NY 11210
Editorial Description: The official newsletter of the Brooklyn College Science Fiction Society.
General Info: Yr. Est. 1987, Quarterly, Trim Size-8$\frac{1}{2}$ x 11, 20 pages, No Color
Advertising: Inquire for rates.

Friends of Doctor Who Newsletter
Consumer **CPM: $205**

Publishing Co: DHI, Inc., PO Box 14111, Reading, PA 19612-4111; Title Tel # (215) 478-9200 Title Fax # (610) 374-5570
Personnel: Publisher-David Blaise, Editor-Tom Beck
Editorial Description: Largest Doctor Who fan organization in the United States. Latest news from England. Contains interviews, convention coverage, local club interaction, full merchandise section, games, puzzles, letters from members and more.
General Info: Yr. Est. 1988, Quarterly, Trim Size-11 x 15, Web press, 20 pages, 2 Color, Matte
Subscriptions: Indv. $10, Can. $15, For. $10, $3/copy
Circulation: Total-5,700
Advertising: $1,170.

Genre Press Digest
Consumer

Publishing Co: Small-Press Genre Association, 2131 S. 227th Dr., Buckeye, AZ 85326-3872
Editorial Description: This is the newsletter for the Small-Press Genre Assn., whose members are into the genre markets. Stories & art in the SF, Horror, & fantasy genres.
General Info: Irregular, 48 pages
Subscriptions: $4/copy

Jews in Space: Newsletter of the Jewish Science Fiction Community
Consumer

Publishing Co: Jewish Science Fiction Society, 470 W. End Ave., New York, NY 10024-4933
Editorial Description: The zine is for those involved in both Judism and science fiction, and recent science fiction interest.
General Info: Monthly, 2 pages
Subscriptions: Indv. $5

L. Ron Hubbard's Writers and Illustrators of the Future Contests
Consumer

Publishing Co: L. Ron Hubbard Writers & Illustrators of the Future Contests, PO Box 1630-OC, Los Angeles, CA 90078-1630
Editorial Description: Contests for new and budding writers and artists. Cash prizes and swift judjing by professionals. Science fiction, fantasy and horror genres.

Munsters & the Addams Family Reunion
See: FAN MAGAZINES-MOVIE, RADIO, TV

Mythprint
See: LITERARY REVIEWS

Newsletter at the End of the Universe
Consumer, Association

Publishing Co: Boston Star Trek Association, PO Box 1108, Boston, MA 02103-1108; Title Tel # (617) 894-2782
Personnel: Publisher-Ira Perlow, Editor-Carol Jean Zelman
General Info: (Formerly Warped Mind; Son of Warped Mind), Yr. Est. 1973, Bi-monthly
Subscriptions: Indv. $15, Free With Membership
Circulation: Total-150

Outlines, Synopses, Proposals that Sold
See: BOOKS & BOOK TRADE

Phantom of the Movies' VideoScope, The
See: TELEVISION & VIDEO

Promises, Pro-Mss
Business, Association

Publishing Co: Science Fiction & Fantasy Workshop, 1193 S 1900 E, Salt Lake City, UT 84108-1855; Title Tel # (801) 582-2090
Personnel: Publisher-Kathleen Woodbury, Editor-Cathy Hicks, Art Dir.-Lester Hixon
Editorial Description: One short story & three critiques of that story by professional authors.
General Info: Yr. Est. 1985, Tri-annually, Trim Size-5$\frac{1}{2}$ x 8$\frac{1}{2}$, Offset press, 5 pages, No Color
Subscriptions: Indv. $8, $1/copy
Circulation: Total-150

Rising Star
Business **CPM: $233**

Publishing Co: Star & Sword Pubs., 47 Byledge Rd, Manchester, NH 03104-2101; Title Tel # (603) 623-9796
Personnel: Publisher, Editor-Scott Green, Art Dir.-P.S. Green
Editorial Description: Covers markets for science fiction/fantasy/horror writers & artists.
General Info: Yr. Est. 1982, Semi-monthly, Trim Size-8$\frac{1}{2}$ x 11, Mimeo press, 6 pages, 2% ads, No Color
Subscriptions: Indv. $8, Can. $8, $2/copy
Circulation: Total-150
Advertising: $35.
List Rental: Rents Lists

Robot Explorer
See: COMPUTERS & AUTOMATION

SFRA Newsletter

Publishing Co: Science Fiction Research Assn., 1265 S Clay St, Denver, CO 80219-4144
Personnel: Editor-Richard Miller
Editorial Description: Association news and information relating to the study of science fiction.
General Info: Yr. Est. 1971, 10x/yr.
Subscriptions: Indv. $35
Circulation: Total-450

Scavenger's Newsletter
Business, Consumer

Publishing Co: Scavenger's Newsletter, 519 Ellinwood St., Osage City, KS 66523-1329; Title Tel # (913) 528-3538
Personnel: Publisher, Editor-Janet Fox
Editorial Description: A market newsletter for science fiction, fantasy, horror & mystery writers & artists with an interest in the small press.
General Info: Yr. Est. 1984, Monthly, Desktop press, 30 pages, ISSN: 0894-2617, No Color, Saddle-stitched
Subscriptions: Indv. $16, Can. $19, For. $25, $2/copy
Circulation: Total-1,000
Advertising: Inquire for rates. Accepts Inserts.
List Rental: Rents Lists
Printing Co: Printgraphix, 1010 Commercial St, Emporia, KS 66801-2919 Tel # (316) 342-0250

Workshop
Association

Publishing Co: Science Fiction & Fantasy Workshop, 1193 S 1900 E, Salt Lake City, UT 84108-1855; Title Tel # (801) 582-2090
Personnel: Publisher, Editor, Circ. Mgr., Art Dir.-Kathleen Woodbury
Editorial Description: Newsletter for aspiring science fiction, fantasy and horror writers.
General Info: Yr. Est. 1980, Monthly, Trim Size-8$\frac{1}{2}$ x 11, Offset press, 10 pages
Subscriptions: Indv. $10, $1/copy
Circulation: Total-400
Advertising: Inquire for rates.

SECURITY & SURVEILLANCE

ABA Bank Security & Fraud Prevention
See: BANKING & FINANCE

ASIS Dynamics
See: BUSINESS & INDUSTRY

Assets Protection
See: ACCOUNTING

Authentication News
See: PACKAGING

Bank Security Report
Business

Publishing Co: Warren, Gorham & Lamont, 31 Saint James Ave., Boston, MA 02116-4112 Parent Co.-Thomson Professional Publications, Stamford; Title Tel # (617) 423-2020 Title Fax # (617) 423-1914
Personnel: Publisher-Larry Selby, Mktg. Mgr.-Sandra Fox
Editorial Description: Practical & general interest pub. for bank security officers.
General Info: Yr. Est. 1973, Monthly, Trim Size-8$\frac{1}{2}$ x 11, Offset press, 8 pages, ISSN: 0162-7457, No Color
Subscriptions: Indv. $149
List Rental: List Management Co.: Manager: Seena Benedek; WG & L List Management, 1 Penn Plz Fl 42, New York, NY 10119-0002 Tel # (212) 971-5000

CKC Report, The Hotel Technology Newsletter
See: HOTEL INDUSTRY

CM Bulletin
Association

Publishing Co: Natl. Classification Management Society, 6116 Roseland Dr, Rockville, MD 20852-3649; Title Tel # (301) 231-9191 Title Fax # (301) 231-6345
Personnel: Editor-Eugene Suto
Editorial Description: Govt. security classification & info. security.
General Info: Yr. Est. 1967, Bi-monthly, Trim Size-8$\frac{1}{2}$ x 11, Offset press, 8 pages, Color
Subscriptions: Indv. $25, $5/copy
Circulation: Total-2,500

COM-AND, Computer Audit News & Developments
See: COMPUTERS & AUTOMATION

CSAA Dispatch

Publishing Co: Central Station Alarm Assn., 7101 Wisconsin Ave., Ste. 1390, Bethesda, MD 20814-4805 Tel # (301) 907-0045 Fax # (301) 907-2930; Title Tel # (301) 907-3202 Title Fax # (301) 907-7897
Personnel: Publisher, Editor-Frank McNeirney
Editorial Description: Publication for members of the CSAA - a trade association for UL - listed central station burglar and fire alarms companies.
General Info: Yr. Est. 1950, Quarterly, Trim Size-8$\frac{1}{2}$ x 11, Web press, 16 pages, 3% ads, 2 Color, Coated, Saddle-stitched
Circulation: (94% controlled)
Advertising: $670. Accepts Inserts.

Computer Fraud & Security Bulletin
Business

Publishing Co: Elsevier Science Inc., 655 Avenue of the Americas, New York, NY 10010-5107 Tel # (212) 633-3916 Fax # (212) 633-3913 Parent Co.-Reed Elsevier, New York
Personnel: Publisher-A. Fletcher, Editor-John Meyer, Circ. Mgr.-Karen Richardson, Production Mgr.-J. Whittingham
Editorial Description: Covers security risks to computer-based systems & suitable counter measures.
General Info: Yr. Est. 1978, Monthly, Trim Size-8$\frac{1}{4}$ x 11$\frac{3}{4}$, 16 pages, ISSN: 0142-0496, Ind/Abs/Online: DIALOG, Predicasts
Subscriptions: Indv. $417

Computer Security Digest
Business

Publishing Co: Computer Protection Systems, Inc., 150 N Main St, Plymouth, MI 48170-1236; Title Tel # (313) 459-8787 Title Fax # (313) 459-2720
Personnel: Publisher, Editor-Jack Bologna, Circ. Mgr.-Barb Davis
Editorial Description: Covers computer crime and security incidents and protection measures.
General Info: Yr. Est. 1983, Monthly, Letrpr. press, 10 pages, ISSN: 0882-1453, No Color, Newsprint
Subscriptions: Indv. $125
Circulation: Total-300

Computers and Security
Business

Publishing Co: Elsevier Science Inc., 655 Avenue of the Americas, New York, NY 10010-5107 Tel # (212) 633-3916 Fax # (212) 633-3913 Parent Co.-Reed Elsevier, New York
Personnel: Publisher-Andrew Fletcher, Editor-John Meyer, Production Mgr.-J. Whittinghem
Editorial Description: The leading international newsletter for the management of computer and information security. Each issue draws together the most significant news from Europe, the ISA and the rest of the world. Over 30 consultants and advisors from business, finance, insurance, the law, police authorities and prestigious security consultancies worldwide ensure you receive the information you need in the right format at
General Info: 8x/yr., ISSN: 0167-4048
Subscriptions: Indv. $398

Computing & Communications: Law & Protection Report
See: COMPUTERS & AUTOMATION

Confidential Air Letter
See: AERONAUTICS/ASTRONAUTICS

Corporate Compliance: Internal Reviews, Audits, and Investigations
See: BUSINESS & INDUSTRY

Corporate Security
Business

Publishing Co: BRP Publications, Inc., 65 Bleecker Street, 5th Floor, New York, NY 10012-2420 Tel # (212) 673-4700 Parent Co.-BRP (Washington DC), Washington; Title Tel # (202) 842-0520 Title Fax # (212) 475-1790
Personnel: Publisher-John Roche, Editor-Susan Sonnesyn-Brooks, Circ. Mgr.-Ellen Hartman, Production Mgr.-Amy Ryan
Editorial Description: Policies, practices, procedures for securing plants, offices, facilities, personnel. SInside infor found nowhere else.
General Info: (Formerly Corporate Security's Technology Alert; Security Tech. News), Yr. Est. 1971, Bi-weekly, Trim Size-8$\frac{1}{2}$ x 11, Sheetfed press, 8 pages, 2 Color
Subscriptions: Indv. $295
Acquistions: Publication Bought
List Rental: List Management Co.: Taybi Direct East, Inc., 13321 New Hampshire Ave., Ste. 202, Silver Spring, MD 20904-3450 Tel # (301) 680-3633, Fax # (301) 680-3635
Printing Co: Jim Buckley Offsetting, 1101 Pennsylvania Ave SE, Washington, DC 20003-2229 Tel # (202) 546-0501

Data Security Letter
See: COMPUTERS & AUTOMATION

Data Security Management
See: COMPUTERS & AUTOMATION

Employee Security Connection
Business

Publishing Co: National Security Institute, 57 East Main Street, Suite 217, Westborough, MA 01581-1464; Title Tel # (508) 366-5800 Title Fax # (508) 858-0132
Personnel: Publisher-Brian Oyson, Editor-David Marston
Editorial Description: Security awareness newsletter for defense contractors.
General Info: Yr. Est. 1987, Quarterly, Trim Size-8$\frac{1}{2}$ x 11, 8 pages, ISSN: 0894-2080
Subscriptions: Indv. $595

Forensic Accounting Review

Publishing Co: Computer Protection Systems, Inc., 150 N Main St, Plymouth, MI 48170-1236; Title Tel # (313) 459-8787 Title Fax # (313) 459-2720
Personnel: Publisher, Editor-Jack Bologna, Circ. Mgr.-Barb Davis
Editorial Description: Reports on celebrated corporate frauds, fraud auditing and investigative accounting.
General Info: (Formerly Corporate Fraud Digest), Yr. Est. 1982, Monthly, Letrpr. press, 8 pages, ISSN: 8756-8888, No Color
Subscriptions: Indv. $125
Circulation: Total-300

Information Privacy
Business

Publishing Co: Reed Business Publishing Company, 475 Park Ave S, Front 2, New York, NY 10016-6901 Tel # (212) 679-8888 Parent Co.-Reed Elsevier, New York
General Info: Quarterly, ISSN: 0141-3406

International Counterterrorism & Security Report
Business　　　**CPM: $71**

Publishing Co: International Assn Counterterrorism & Security Professionals, PO Box 10265, Arlington, VA 22210-1265; Title Tel # (703) 243-0993 Title Fax # (703) 243-1197
Personnel: Publisher-Steven Fustero, Editor in Chief-Dale Andrade, Adv. Dir.-Phil Friedman, Art Dir.-Kurt Mulholland
Editorial Description: For diplomats, law enforcement officers, security professionals, international travelers and others with a vested interest in protection against terrorist activity. Covers terrorist activities worldwide.
General Info: (Formerly Counterterrorism & Security), Yr. Est. 1990, Bi-monthly, Trim Size-8¼ x 10⅞, Desktop press, 48 pages, ISSN: 1047-8779, 10% ads, 4 Color, Coated, Saddle-stitched
Subscriptions: Indv. $65, Can. $65, For. $85, $6/copy
Acquistions: Publication Bought
Circulation: Total-19,000, Readership-30,000, Source-I
Advertising: $1,350. Accepts Inserts.
Printing Co: American Press, One American Place, Gordonsville, VA 22942 Tel # (703) 832-2253, Fax # (703) 832-7253

Journal of the New York Institute of Legal Research
See: LAW

Kingalarm Review

Publishing Co: King Alarm Distributors, Inc., 35 Green St, Hackensack, NJ 07601-4003; Title Tel # (201) 488-4990
Personnel: Editor-Glenn Fischer

Lone Star Transmitter
Business, Association　　　**CPM: $136**

Publishing Co: Texas Burglar & Fire Alarm Assn., 1601 Rio Grande St Ste 440, Austin, TX 78701-1149; Title Tel # (512) 479-0425
Personnel: Editor-Lisa Fry
Editorial Description: Official publication of the Texas Burglar & Fire Alarm Assn., professionals in the security industry.
General Info: Quarterly, Trim Size-8½ x 11, Offset press, 40% ads, No Color, Recycled
Circulation: Total-2,200
Advertising: $300.

Loss Prevention Letter for Supermarket Executives
Business

Publishing Co: Food Marketing Institute, 800 Connecticut Ave., N.W., Washington, DC 20006-2701; Title Tel # (202) 452-8444
Personnel: Editor-Mary Ann House, Editor-Chuck Miller
General Info: Monthly
Subscriptions: Indv. $50, Inst. $50

Low Profile
See: BANKING & FINANCE

NSI Advisory
Business

Publishing Co: National Security Institute, 57 East Main Street, Suite 217, Westborough, MA 01581-1464; Title Tel # (508) 366-5800 Title Fax # (508) 858-0132
Personnel: Publisher-David Marston, Editor-Joseph Barcello
Editorial Description: Newsd and analysis on issues of concern to defense and intelligence communities..
General Info: Yr. Est. 1985, Monthly, Trim Size-8½ x 11, 12 pages, 2 Color
Subscriptions: Indv. $325
List Rental: Rents Lists

National Newsline
Business, Association　　　**CPM: $207**

Publishing Co: National Burglar & Fire Alarm Association, 7101 Wisconsin Ave Ste 1390, Bethesda, MD 20814-4805; Title Tel # (301) 907-3202 Title Fax # (301) 907-7897
Personnel: Publisher-Linda Gimbel, Promotion Dir.-Jay Velgos
Editorial Description: Covers the alarm industry: fire & burglar alarms, security personnel, installation, legislation, management, marketing, and customer service tips.
General Info: (Formerly News & Views), Yr. Est. 1968, Bi-monthly, Trim Size-8⅜ x 10⅞, Sheetfed press, 24 pages, ISSN: 0199-6835, 3% ads, 2 Color, Coated, Saddle-stitched
Subscriptions: Indv. $25, Can. $45, For. $45, Free With Membership
Circulation: Total-4,000
Advertising: $830. Accepts Inserts.
List Rental: Actives: $100/M

National Security Law Report
Association

Publishing Co: Sponsor-ABA Standing Committee on Law and National Security, Standing Committee on Law & Natl. Security, ABA, 1501 Trombone Ct, Vienna, VA 22182-1646; Title Tel # (703) 242-0629
Personnel: Publisher-James Miller, Editor-John Shenefield
Editorial Description: Court cases, articles, legislation, regulations concerning law and national security.
General Info: (Formerly Intelligence Report), Yr. Est. 1979, Monthly, Trim Size-8½ x 11, Sheetfed press, 8 pages, ISSN: 0736-2773, 2 Color, Newsprint
Circulation: Total-2,600
Printing Co: Charter Printing Co., 4202 Wheeler Ave, Alexandria, VA 22304-6413 Tel # (703) 370-1010, Fax # (703) 370-2009

Personal Identification News (PIN)
Business

Publishing Co: Warfel & Miller, Inc., 11619 Danville Dr, Rockville, MD 20852-3715 Fax # (301) 881-2554; Title Tel # (301) 881-6668
Personnel: Publisher, Editor-Benjamin Miller, Circ. Mgr.-Carolyn Connor, Production Mgr.-Deb Brailsford
Editorial Description: Covers Smart Cards, Biometrics & other advanced technology for security & identification. Subscription includes 2-104 page industry directories.
General Info: Yr. Est. 1985, Monthly, Trim Size-8½ x 11, Web press, 8 pages, ISSN: 0883-5608, 2 Color, Newsprint
Subscriptions: Indv. $345, Can. $345, For. $370, $30/copy
Acquistions: Publication Sold
List Rental: Actives $145/M

Privacy Law and Practice
See: LAW

Privacy Newsletter
See: CONSUMER INTERESTS

Private Security Case Law Reporter
Business

Publishing Co: Strafford Pubs., Inc., 590 Dutch Valley Rd., N.E., Postal Drawer 13729, Atlanta, GA 30324-0729; Title Tel # (404) 881-1141 Title Fax # (404) 881-0074
Personnel: Publisher-Richard Ossoff, Mng. Editor-Jennifer Vaughan, Circ. Mgr., Mktg. Mgr.-Marianne Mueller, Mktg. Mgr.-Maria Rawls Hill
Editorial Description: Monthly digest of judicial decisions on litigation involving private security operations; includes insights and trend analysis by nation's leading security expert.
General Info: Yr. Est. 1982, 10x/yr., Trim Size-8½ x 11, Sheetfed press, 12 pages, ISSN: 0738-6958, No Color, Newsprint
Subscriptions: Indv. $292, Can. $322, For. $347, $25/copy
Acquistions: Publication Bought, Publication Sold
List Rental: Actives: 16,512, $107/M

Protection of Assets Bulletin/Protection of Assets Manual
Business

Publishing Co: Merritt Professional Publishing, 1661 9th St, Santa Monica, CA 90404-3703 Tel # (310) 450-7234 Fax # (310) 396-4563; Title Tel # (310) 450-7238 Title Fax # (310) 391-4563
Personnel: Editor-Timothy J. Walsh
Editorial Description: News and developments into field ofsecurity management are featured in this monthly newsletter. The manual is a four-volume comprehensive 'bible' of security management.
General Info: Monthly, Trim Size-8½ x 11, 12 pages, ISSN: 0740-137X, No Color, Newsprint
Subscriptions: Indv. $397
Circulation: Total-2,800

Revelations of Awareness
See: NEW AGE

Safety & Security for Supervisors
See: SAFETY

Security Directors' Digest
Business

Publishing Co: Washington Crime News Services, 3918 Prosperity Ave Ste 318, Fairfax, VA 22031-3333; Title Tel # (703) 573-1600 Title Fax # (703) 573-1604
Personnel: Publisher-R. J. O'Connell, Editor-Betty Bosarge, Circ. Mgr.-Nancy Van Wyen
Editorial Description: A complete news service for the security professional.
General Info: (Formerly Security Systems Digest; Corporate Security Digest), Yr. Est. 1969, Weekly, Trim Size-8½ x 11, Sheetfed press, 10 pages
Subscriptions: Indv. $345, Can. $351, For. $395

Security Law Newsletter
Business

Publishing Co: Crime Control Research Corp., 1063 Thomas Jefferson St NW, Washington, DC 20007-5248; Title Tel # (202) 337-2700 Title Fax # (202) 337-8324
Personnel: Publisher-Ann Miler, Editor-Eva Sherman
Editorial Description: A national newsletter reporting the latest developments in private security litigation and providing expert analysis of security liability issues.
General Info: Yr. Est. 1981, Monthly, Trim Size-8½ x 11, 12 pages, 2 Color, Matte
Subscriptions: Indv. $297, $25/copy
Printing Co: Beacon Printing, Waldorf, MD Tel # (301) 843-1995

Security Letter
Business

Publishing Co: Security Letter, 166 E 96th St, New York, NY 10128-2565; Title Tel # (212) 348-1553 Title Fax # (212) 534-2957
Personnel: Publisher, Editor-Robert McCrie, Circ. Mgr.-Fulvia Madia, Production Mgr.-Luis Javier, Art Dir.-Ed Vollmer
Editorial Description: Largest privately circulated newsletter on protection of assets from loss. Includes Security Business section with general and financial news on the industry.
General Info: Yr. Est. 1970, Semi-monthly, Trim Size-8½ x 11, Sheetfed press, 8 pages, ISSN: 0363-4922, Ind/Abs/Online: Univ.Microfilm; ASIS Net, No Color
Subscriptions: Indv. $187, Inst. $187, Can. $187, For. $232, $10/copy

Security Management Bulletin: Protecting People, Property & Assets
Business

Publishing Co: Bureau of Business Practice, 24 Rope Ferry Rd, Waterford, CT 06386-0001 Tel # (806) 442-4365 Fax # (860) 434-3341 Parent Co.-Prentice Hall, Waterford; Title Tel # (860) 442-4365
Personnel: Editor-Alex Vaughn
Editorial Description: Gives security directors tips, techniques, and methods they can use every day.
General Info: Yr. Est. 1972, Semi-monthly, ISSN: 1062-1628
Subscriptions: Indv. $138

Security and Special Police Legal Update
Association

Publishing Co: AELE, 5519 N Cumberland Ave Ste 1008, Chicago, IL 60656-1480; Title Tel # (312) 763-2800
Personnel: Publisher-Wayne Schmidt, Editor-Bernard Farber
Editorial Description: Recent court cases involving security and special police personnel.
General Info: (Formerly Security Legal Update), Yr. Est. 1984, Monthly, Trim Size-8½ x 11, Offset press, 16 pages, ISSN: 0741-4824, Color-cover
Subscriptions: Indv. $168, Inst. $168
Circulation: Total-500

Security Technology News
Business

Publishing Co: Phillips Business Information, Inc., 1201 Seven Locks Rd., Ste 300, Potomac, MD 20854-2958 Tel # (301) 340-1520 Fax # (301) 424-4297; Title Tel # (301) 340-2100
Editorial Description: Technologies, regulations, etc. for the information security of corporate America.
General Info: Yr. Est. 1993, Bi-weekly
Subscriptions: Indv. $495

Select Hostile Actions Against Civil Aviation
See: LAW ENFORCEMENT & PENOLOGY

Surveillant: Acquisitions for Security & Intelligence Professionals
Scholarly   **CPM: $222**

Publishing Co: National Intelligence Book Center, 2020 Pennsylvania Ave. NW, Suite #165, Washington, DC 20006-1846; Title Tel # (202) 797-1234 Title Fax # (202) 331-7456
Personnel: Mng. Editor-Elizabeth Bancroft, Feature Ed.-Sam Halpern, Assign. Ed.-Samuel Harper, Bk. Rev. Ed.-Keith Melton, Production Mgr.-Eileen Elsen, Adv. Dir.-Bagley Fordyce, Mktg. Dir.-Jerry Goodwin
General Info: Yr. Est. 1990, Bi-monthly, Trim Size-8½ x 11, Sheetfed press, 40 pages, ISSN: 1051-0923, 2% ads, No Color, Matte, Saddle-stitched
Subscriptions: Indv. $110, Can. $120, For. $140, $20/copy
Circulation: Total-2,700
Advertising: $600.
List Rental: Actives: 2,700, $200/M, Expires: $200/M

Telecommunications Security
Business

Publishing Co: Quinlan Publishing, 23 Drydock Ave, Boston, MA 02210-2387 Tel # (617) 542-0048 Fax # (617) 345-9646
Editorial Description: Articles and reports on the latest ways to protect company information.
General Info: Monthly
Subscriptions: Indv. $129

Teller Vision
See: BANKING & FINANCE

Travel Security Intelligencer
See: TRAVEL

Weekly Terrorism Profile
Business

Publishing Co: V.A. Biro and Associates, 92 Beverley Street, Toronto, ON M5T 1Y1 Canada; Title Tel # (416) 595-1142 Title Fax # (416) 595-5827
Personnel: Editor-Victor Biro
Editorial Description: Weekly newsletter dealing with issues surrounding terrorism, counterterrorism and international crime.
General Info: Yr. Est. 1995, Weekly, ISSN: 1201-9895, Ind/Abs/Online: 'The Counter-Terrorism Page' - http://www.interlog.com/vabiro/
Subscriptions: Indv. $130, Inst. $130, Can. $130, For. $250, $3/copy

SENIOR CITIZENS

50 Plus -the Benefits Bulletin
Business

Publishing Co: Readers' Digest Publications, 28 W. 23rd, New York, NY 10010-5204 Tel # (212) 366-8853 Parent Co.-Reader's Digest Assn., Pleasantville; Title Tel # (212) 366-8850 Title Fax # (212) 366-8899
Personnel: Publisher-Betty J. Dais, Editor-MaryAnn Brinley
Editorial Description: Directed toward benefits managers involved in pre-retirement planning for large corporations.
General Info: (Formerly 50 Plus-Retirement Planning Newsletter), Yr. Est. 1975, Quarterly, Trim Size-8¼ x 11, 4 pages
Subscriptions: Indv. $25

A Friend Indeed
See: WOMEN'S

AARP Bulletin
Association

Publishing Co: American Association of Retired Persons, 601 E St NW, Washington, DC 20049-0001 Tel # (202) 434-3341
Personnel: Publisher-Charles W. Allen, Editor-Elliot Carlson, Production-Beth Martin, Adv. Dir.-Ina Josephson
Editorial Description: News & feature coverage of items of interest to older Americans.
General Info: (Formerly AARP News Bulletin), Yr. Est. 1959, Monthly, Trim Size-11 x 14, Offset press, 16 pages, No Color, Newsprint, Other
Subscriptions: Indv. $8
Circulation: (ABC), Total-33,000,000
Advertising: Inquire for rates.
Printing Co: R.R. Donnelley & Sons, 1600 N. Main St., Pontiac, IL 61764-1060 Tel # (815) 844-5181, Fax # (708) 390-2618

AGHE Exchange
Association   **CPM: $83**

Publishing Co: Association for Gerontology in Higher Education, 1001 Connecticut Ave NW Ste, 410, Washington, DC 20036-5504; Title Tel # (202) 429-9277
Personnel: Editor-Leslie Morgan, Circ. Mgr., Adv. Dir.-Joy Lobenstine
Editorial Description: Focuses on development & improvement of programs of gerontological education & training. Includes information on programs, resources, public policy, research, & assn. news.
General Info: Yr. Est. 1974, Quarterly, Trim Size-8½ x 11, Offset press, 14 pages, ISSN: 0890-278X, 2 Color, Saddle-stitched
Subscriptions: Indv. $25, Inst. $25, Can. $30, For. $30, $5/copy
Circulation: Total-3,600
Advertising: $300.
List Rental: Actives: 3,200, $325/M

Activity Director's Guide
Business

Publishing Co: Eymann Publications, Inc., PO Box 3577, Reno, NV 89505-3577 Fax # (702) 323-2770; Title Tel # (702) 333-6651
Personnel: Publisher, Editor-Ken Eymann, Mng. Editor-Laurie Hall, Circ. Mgr.-K. Pace
Editorial Description: Activity program ideas for people who work with the elderly.
General Info: Yr. Est. 1974, Monthly, Offset press, 8 pages, No Color
Subscriptions: Indv. $24
Circulation: Total-6,000

Adult Day Care Letter
See: HOSPITALS & NURSING HOMES

Aging America Resources
CPM: $346

Publishing Co: Demko Publishing, 21946 Pine Trace, Boca Raton, FL 33428-3057; Title Tel # (407) 482-6271
Personnel: Editor-David Demko
Editorial Description: The nation's desk reference to new products, services, media, and trends.
General Info: (Formerly Resources in Aging), Yr. Est. 1987, Monthly, Trim Size-8 x 10, 4 pages, ISSN: 0892-0818, No Color, Matte
Subscriptions: Indv. $50, $5/copy
Circulation: Total-3,468
Advertising: $1,200. Accepts Inserts.

Aging Digest
Consumer

Publishing Co: Texas Dept. on Aging, Box 12786, Capitol Station, Austin, TX 78711-2786; Title Tel # (512) 444-2727 Title Fax # (512) 440-5290
Personnel: Publisher, Editor-James Grabbs, Circ. Mgr.-Georgie Edmonds, Production Mgr.-Beverly Scott, Art Dir.-Russell Smith
Editorial Description: Reports activities of the Texas Dept. of Aging and regional activities of its affiliated area agencies on aging. Includes general information relating to aging.
General Info: Yr. Est. 1982, Quarterly, Web press, 12 pages, 2 Color, Matte, Saddle-stitched
Circulation: Total-2,700
Printing Co: Futura Communications, 3019 Alvin Devane Blvd Ste 500, Austin, TX 78741-7419 Tel # (512) 389-1500

Aging and the Human Spirit
Newsletter
Consumer, Scholarly

Publishing Co: Univ. of Texas, Medical Branch, 301 University Blvd., Galveston, TX 77555-1311; Title Tel # (409) 772-2376 Title Fax # (409) 772-5640
Personnel: Editor-Thomas R. Cole, Editor-Marry R. Moody, Editor-Carter C. Williams, Mag. Ed.-Diane Pfeil
Editorial Description: Life satisfaction & lifelong development.
General Info: (Formerly Human Values & Aging Newsletter), Yr. Est. 1991, Semi-annually, Offset press, 12 pages
Subscriptions: Free
Circulation: Total-1,500

Aging News
Consumer

Publishing Co: Office for the Aging, 2 Empire State Plz, Albany, NY 12223-1200; Title Tel # (518) 474-5731
Personnel: Editor-Richard Wendover
Editorial Description: Issues and programs devoted to aging and those concerned with aging.
General Info: (Formerly New York Office for the Aging Newsletter), Yr. Est. 1975, Quarterly, Trim Size-11 x 12, Offset press, 8 pages, 2 Color, Matte
Subscriptions: Free
Circulation: Total-35,000

Aging News Alert
Business

Publishing Co: CD Publications, 8204 Fenton St., Silver Spring, MD 20910-4571; Title Tel # (301) 588-6380 Title Fax # (301) 588-6385
Personnel: Publisher-Mike Gerecht, Editor-Ken Silverstone, Circ. Mgr.-Kurt Eisentraut, Mktg. Dir.-Joyce Meals
Editorial Description: Reports on developments in the aging field.
General Info: (Formerly Aging Action Alert), Yr. Est. 1984, Semi-monthly, Trim Size-8½ x 11, Sheetfed press, 16 pages, ISSN: 1050-3196, No Color, Matte, Other
Subscriptions: Indv. $227, Can. $237, For. $267, $15/copy
List Rental: List Management Co.: Manager: Amy Seyler; Washington Advertising Service, 8204 Fenton St., Silver Spring, MD 20910 Tel # (301) 588-7920, Fax # (301) 588-6385, Actives: 6,138, $150/M, Expires: 2,530, $150/M

Aging Research & Training News
Business, Association

Publishing Co: Business Publishers, Inc., 951 Pershing Dr., Silver Spring, MD 20910-4464 Tel # (301) 589-5103 Fax # (301) 589-8493; Title Tel # (301) 587-6300 Title Fax # (301) 587-1081
Personnel: Publisher-Leonard A. Eiserer, Editor-Nancy Aldrich, Circ. Mgr.-Brenda Davenport, Promotion Mgr.-Kathleen Jacob
Editorial Description: Covers federal grants & contracts dealing with aging research and training, plus private foundation funding.
General Info: Yr. Est. 1978, Semi-monthly, Trim Size-8½ x 11, Desktop press, 8 pages, ISSN: 0197-4017, Ind/Abs/Online: Newsnet, No Color
Subscriptions: Indv. $240, Inst. $240, Can. $240, For. $253
Advertising: Accepts Inserts.
List Rental: List Management Co.: BPI Direct, 951 Pershing Dr., Silver Spring, MD 20910-4464 Tel # (301) 585-5976, Fax # (301) 587-4530

American Geriatrics Society-Newsletter
Association

Publishing Co: American Geriatrics Society, 770 Lexington Ave Rm 300, New York, NY 10021-8165 Tel # (212) 308-1414
Personnel: Editor-Patricia Miller
Editorial Description: Society news, CME listings, award, meetings & grant announcements.
General Info: Yr. Est. 1972, Bi-monthly, 8 pages, 1% ads
Circulation: Total-11,500
Advertising: Inquire for rates.
Printing Co: Sheridan Press, 450 Fame Avenue, Hanover, PA 17331-9581 Tel # (717) 632-3535, Fax # (717) 633-8900

Between Classes/Elderhostel Catalog
See: EDUCATION

Bifocal
See: LAW

Bottom Line/Tomorrow
See: CONSUMER INTERESTS

Briefings on Assisted Living
See: HEALTH

Brown University Geriatric Research Application Digest, The
See: HEALTH

Brown University Long Term Care Quality Letter, The
See: HEALTH

CAG Newsletter
Association

Publishing Co: Canadian Assn. Gerontology/Assn.Canadienne de Gerontologie, 1306 Wellington, #500, Ottawa, ON K1Y 3B2 Canada Tel # (613) 728-8913 Fax # (613) 728-9347
Editorial Description: Contains up-to-date information on provincial, national, and international news, resources, events, and other items of interest to the Candian gerontological community.
General Info: Quarterly, ISSN: 0712-676X
Subscriptions: Indv. $95

California Medi-Cal Guide

Publishing Co: CCH, Inc., 2700 Lake Cook Rd., Riverwoods, IL 60015 Parent Co.-Kluwer Law & Taxation Publishers, Cambridge; Title Tel # (847) 267-7000 Title Fax # (800) 224-8299
Editorial Description: Contains all-explanatory, nontechnical information on the California Medicaid program. Also includes full texts of relevant state law and the Department of Health Services regulations that implement the program, plus a list of Contract Drugs.
General Info: Monthly, Looseleaf
Subscriptions: Indv. $462

Canadian Pensioners Concerned Alberta Div. Newsletter

Publishing Co: Canadian Pensioners Concerned-Alberta Div., 11113 113th St., Edmonton, AB T5G 2V1 Canada; Title Tel # (403) 452-9704
Personnel: Editor-Holger Larsen
General Info: Yr. Est. 1976, Quarterly, Mimeo press, 12 pages, Color
Circulation: Total-450
Printing Co: A-1 Reproductions Photocopies, 123 118th Ave., Edmonton, AB T6G 1V3 Canada Tel # (403) 455-0992

Center for the Study of Pre-Retirement & Aging Newsletter

Publishing Co: Center for the Study of Pre-Retirement & Aging, St. John's Hall Catholic Univ., Of America, Washington, DC 20064-0001; Title Tel # (202) 319-5483
Personnel: Editor-Sr. Mary Bush
General Info: Quarterly

Choices
See: HEALTH

Currents
Association

Publishing Co: American Association of Homes and Services for the Aging, 901 E St., N.W. #500, Washington, DC 20004-2037 Fax # (202) 783-2255; Title Tel # (202) 783-2242
Personnel: Editor-Jean Van Ryzin, Production Mgr.-Jennifer Cooney
Editorial Description: Reports issues concerning homes, housing, and services for the aging.
General Info: (Formerly Nonprofit Provider News; AAHA Provider News), Yr. Est. 1983, Monthly, 12 pages, 2 Color, Recycled, Saddle-stitched
Circulation: (85% controlled), Total-6,000
List Rental: Rents Lists
Printing Co: Charter Printing Co., 4202 Wheeler Ave, Alexandria, VA 22304-6413 Tel # (703) 370-1010, Fax # (703) 370-2009

Debt-Free & Prosperous Living
See: CONSUMER INTERESTS

Elder Voices
Association

Publishing Co: Natl. Indian Council on Aging, 6400 Uptown Blvd NE Ste 510w, Albuquerque, NM 87110-4203 Tel # (505) 888-3302 Fax # (505) 888-3276; Title Tel # (505) 242-9505 Title Fax # (505) 243-2536
Personnel: Production Mgr.-Renee Paisano
General Info: (Formerly NICOA News), Yr. Est. 1976
Subscriptions: Free With Membership
Acquistions: Publication Bought, Publication Sold
Circulation: Total-3,000

Eldercare
Business

Publishing Co: Shepard's/McGraw-Hill, Inc., 555 Middle Creek Pky, Colorado Springs, CO 80921-3622 Tel # (719) 488-3000; Title Fax # (719) 481-7448
Editorial Description: Legal advice and information regarding the elderly.
General Info: Yr. Est. 1991, Monthly
Subscriptions: Indv. $99

Finance Over Fifty
See: INVESTMENT

Generation
See: RELIGIOUS & THEOLOGICAL

Geri-Source

Publishing Co: Jefferson House Gerontology Resource Center, 1 John Stewart Dr, Newington, CT 06111-3126; Title Tel # (203) 667-4453
Personnel: Editor-Virginia Corcoran
General Info: Yr. Est. 1982, 2 pages
Circulation: Total-800

Geriatric Care
See: NURSING

Geriatric Care News
See: HEALTH

Geriatric Psychiatry News
See: PSYCHOLOGY

Gerofiles

Publishing Co: Center for Gerontogical Studies, Univ. of Florida, 3357 Turlington Hall, Gainsville, FL 32611-2036; Title Tel # (904) 392-2116
Personnel: Editor-Dr. Otto von Mering
Editorial Description: Reports on research & other activities of the gerontology ctr., its assocs. & its student organization.
General Info: Yr. Est. 1977, 8 pages, No Color, Coated
Circulation: Total-2,000

Gerontology News
See: MEDICINE

Gold Pages, The
See: SOCIAL SERVICES & WELFARE

Grandparent Times   *Consumer*

Publishing Co: Caring Grandparents of America, PO Box 96444, Washington, DC 20090-6444 Tel # (202) 783-0950
Editorial Description: Activities, news and information for senior citizens.
General Info: Yr. Est. 1994, Monthly, Trim Size-8½ x 11, 8 pages, 2 Color, Matte
Subscriptions: Indv. $10
Circulation: Total-75,000
List Rental: List Management Co.: List Services Corp., 6 Trowbridge Dr., PO Box 516, Bethel, CT 06801-2858 Tel # (203) 743-2600, Fax # (203) 743-0589

HealthPlus55 Calendar
See: HOSPITALS & NURSING HOMES

Housing the Elderly Report
See: HOSPITALS & NURSING HOMES

Integrated Senior Care: Assisted Living and Long-Term Care Newsletter   *Business*

Publishing Co: Thompson Publishing Group, 747 Third Ave., New York, NY 10017 Tel # (212) 888-7220 Fax # (212) 486-3400; Title Tel # (212) 888-1245 Title Fax # (800) 949-2320
Personnel: Publisher-Kenneth R. Gesser, Editor-Judy Pokras, Production Mgr.-R.D. Whitney, Mktg. Dir.-Kevin Mahon
Editorial Description: The latest developments in the assisted living field: planning, development, acquisition, marketing, operation, regulatory and legal advice. Subscription includes updates and monthly newsletter.
General Info: Monthly, 8 pages, 2 Color
Subscriptions: Indv. $315

International Senior Citizen News

Publishing Co: International Senior Citizen Assn., 255 S. Hill St., Suite 409, Los Angeles, CA 90012; Title Tel # (213) 625-5008
Personnel: Editor-Ted Ellsworth
General Info: Yr. Est. 1963, 8 pages
Subscriptions: Indv. $6, Inst. $30
Circulation: Total-1,000

Kiplinger's Retirement Report   *Consumer*

Publishing Co: Kiplinger Washington Editors, Inc., 1729 H Street N.W., Washington, DC 20006-3924 Tel # (202) 887-6400
Personnel: Editor-Tony Cappasso
Editorial Description: Wide variety of information for retired and soon-to-be-retired persons.
General Info: Yr. Est. 1994, Monthly, Trim Size-8½ x 11, 12 pages
Subscriptions: Indv. $60

Locke Report

Publishing Co: Locke Report, 594 Front St, Marion, MA 02738-1415
Personnel: Publisher, Editor-Edward M. Cooney
General Info: Bi-monthly
Subscriptions: Indv. $6

Long-Term Care Administrator
See: HOSPITALS & NURSING HOMES

Long Term Care Monitor
See: HEALTH

Maine State Retirement System Newsletter   *Association*

Publishing Co: Maine State Retirement System, State House, Sta. #46, Augusta, ME 04333-0001; Title Tel # (207) 289-3461
Personnel: Editor-Susan Cottle
Subscriptions: Free With Membership
Circulation: Total-70,000

Managing Senior Care
See: HOSPITALS & NURSING HOMES

Mature Market Report   *Business, Association*

Publishing Co: Lifestyle Change Communications, 5885 Glenridge Dr., Atlanta, GA 30328 Tel # (404) 252-0554 Fax # (404) 250-4295; Title Tel # (404) 252-3774 Title Fax # (404) 252-4295
Personnel: Publisher-Robert Perlstein, Editor-Catherine Hagin, Circ. Mgr.-Becky Pennington, Production Mgr.-Kimberly Merritt, Promotion Dir.-Diane Sparks
Editorial Description: Serves the 50+ markets with case studies, how-to articles, investigative reports, etc. Regular departments on media, healthcare, insurance, retirement, housing, travel and much more.
General Info: Yr. Est. 1987, Monthly, Trim Size-8½ x 11, 8 pages, ISSN: 0894-2609, 2 Color, Coated
Subscriptions: Indv. $175, Can. $200
Circulation: Total-300
Printing Co: Doss Printing Services, PO Box 1332, Canton, GA 30114-1332

Mature Traveler
See: TRAVEL

Mexico Retirement and Travel Assistance
See: TRAVEL

Mid-America Senior Tennis
See: TENNIS

Misuse of Medications   *Consumer*

Publishing Co: Parker Geriatric Institute, 27111 76th Ave, New Hyde Park, NY 11040-1423; Title Tel # (516) 437-0090

NAFC Quarterly Newsletter
See: HEALTH

NCOA Networks   *Association*   CPM: $282

Publishing Co: Natl. Council on the Aging, Inc., 409 Third St. SW, Washington, DC 20024; Title Tel # (202) 479-1200 Title Fax # (202) 479-0735
Personnel: Publications Director-Louise Cleveland, Editor-Paul Girolami
Editorial Description: News of senior centers, adult day care, voluntary agencies, older worker services, rural aging, community-based long-term care, senior housing, health promotion, & family caregiving, plus latest legislative news on aging.
General Info: Yr. Est. 1989, 9x/yr., Trim Size-11 x 17, Web press, 16 pages, ISSN: 1045-9073, 9% ads, 2 Color
Subscriptions: $5/copy
Circulation: Total-7,795
Advertising: $2,200.
List Rental: Actives: 15,000, $85/M

NSCLC Washington Weekly

Publishing Co: Natl. Senior Citizens Law Center, 1815 H St. NW, Suite #700, Washington, DC 20006-3604 Fax # (202) 785-6792; Title Tel # (202) 887-5280
Personnel: Editor-Brendan McTaggart
Editorial Description: Complete coverage of current events in the field of aging.
General Info: Yr. Est. 1974, Weekly, 4 pages, ISSN: 0277-7460, No Color
Subscriptions: $275/copy
Circulation: Total-1,700
List Rental: Actives: $250/M
Printing Co: Newsletter Services, Inc., 9700 Philadelphia Court, Lanham, MD 20706 Tel # (301) 731-5200, Fax # (301) 731-5201

National Indian Council on Aging News

Publishing Co: Natl. Indian Council on Aging, 6400 Uptown Blvd NE Ste 510w, Albuquerque, NM 87110-4203 Tel # (505) 888-3302 Fax # (505) 888-3276; Title Tel # (505) 766-2276
Personnel: Editor-Larry Curley
Editorial Description: Published for elderly American Indians.
General Info: Quarterly

Newsletter of the Brookdale Center on Aging   *Association*

Publishing Co: Brookdale Center on Aging, 425 E 25th St, New York, NY 10010-2547; Title Tel # (212) 481-4426
Editorial Description: Contains information on the Brookdale Ctr. and news of its activities as well as general information on aging in America.
General Info: Yr. Est. 1975, Quarterly
Subscriptions: Free To Qualified Recipient
Circulation: Total-5,000

North American Association of Jewish Home & Housing for the Aged-Perspectives

Publishing Co: North American Assn. of Jewish Homes & Housing for the Aged, 2525 Centerville Rd, Dallas, TX 75228-2634; Title Tel # (214) 327-4503
Personnel: Editor-Dr. Herbert Shore
Editorial Description: Info on services for the aged.
General Info: Yr. Est. 1960, Quarterly, 25 pages
Circulation: Total-500

Nursing Home Law Letter

Publishing Co: Natl. Senior Citizens Law Center, 1815 H St. NW, Suite #700, Washington, DC 20006-3604 Fax # (202) 785-6792; Title Tel # (202) 887-5280
Personnel: Editor-Toby Edelman
Editorial Description: Monitors law & legislation affecting nursing homes.
General Info: Monthly
Subscriptions: Indv. $100, Inst. $100

Old Marblehead Cod   *Association*

Publishing Co: Town of Marblehead Council on Aging, Widger Rd., Mary Alley Hosp., Marblehead, MA 01945; Title Tel # (617) 631-6225
Editorial Description: Council news, legal and health clinic information and an activities calendar.
General Info: Yr. Est. 1979, Monthly, Trim Size-8½ x 11, 8 pages, Color
Circulation: Total-1,750
Advertising: Inquire for rates.

Older Adult Centres Assn. of Ontario Newsletter   *Association*

Publishing Co: Older Adult Centres Assn. of Ontario, 1220 Sheppard Ave., E. 350, Ste. 409A, Willowdale, ON M2K 2X1 Canada; Title Tel # (416) 426-7038
Personnel: Editor-Anita Machin
Editorial Description: Info for members of the Older Adult Association of Ontario.
General Info: Yr. Est. 1976, Quarterly, Trim Size-11 x 17, Sheetfed press, 12 pages, Color-cover, Matte
Subscriptions: Indv. $5
Circulation: Total-300
Advertising: Inquire for rates. Accepts Inserts.

Older Americans Report   *Business*

Publishing Co: Business Publishers, Inc., 951 Pershing Dr., Silver Spring, MD 20910-4464 Tel # (301) 589-5103 Fax # (301) 589-8493; Title Tel # (301) 587-6300 Title Fax # (301) 587-1081
Personnel: Publisher-Leonard A. Eiserer, Editor-Nancy Aldrich, Circ. Mgr.-Brenda Davenport, Production Mgr.-Kathleen Jacob
Editorial Description: Tracks Older Americans Act programs, long-term care issues, Medcare, Medicaid, Social Security & SSI, nursing home regulation, retirement/pension issues, all block grants for the aged and key assistance programs such as housing, energy, nutrition, employment, and training.
General Info: (Formerly Aging Services News), Yr. Est. 1976, Weekly, Trim Size-8½ x 11, Desktop press, 10 pages, ISSN: 0146-3640, Ind/Abs/Online: Newsnet and Predicasts, No Color, Recycled
Subscriptions: Indv. $345, Can. $345, For. $370
Advertising: Accepts Inserts.
List Rental: List Management Co.: BPI Direct, 951 Pershing Dr., Silver Spring, MD 20910-4464 Tel # (301) 585-5976, Fax # (301) 587-4530

Options

Publishing Co: New York City Dept. for the Aging, 2 Lafayette St., New York, NY 10007-1307; Title Tel # (212) 577-0846
Personnel: Editor-Virginia Starke
Editorial Description: Brings information of services & entitlements to older people in New York City.
General Info: Yr. Est. 1974, Quarterly, Trim Size-11 x 17, Web press, 8 pages, No Color
Circulation: Total-35,000

PBC Senior Newsletter   *Consumer*

Publishing Co: Publishing & Business Consultants, 101 W. 64th St. Unit #3, Inglewood, CA 90302-1255 Tel # (213) 732-3477 Fax # (213) 732-3477
Personnel: Publisher, Editor-Andeson Atia
General Info: Quarterly, ISSN: 1059-1982
Circulation: Total-50,000
Advertising: Inquire for rates.

Parent Care Advisor   *Consumer*

Publishing Co: LRP Publications, 747 Dresher Rd., P.O. Box 980, Horsham, PA 19044-0980 Tel # (215) 784-0910 Fax # (215) 784-0317
Editorial Description: Legal, financial and medical information for those caring for elderly loved ones.
General Info: Monthly
Subscriptions: Indv. $95
Acquistions: Publication Sold
Circulation: Total-2,000

Parsley, Sage & Time

Publishing Co: Pike Market Senior Center, 1931 1st Ave, Seattle, WA 98101-1092; Title Tel # (206) 728-2773
Personnel: Editor-Constance Pedersen
Editorial Description: Senior citizens.
General Info: Yr. Est. 1980, Monthly

Partners for Travel
See: TRAVEL

Pension Actuary, The
See: INSURANCE

Pension Plan Fix-It Handbook   *Consumer*

Publishing Co: Thompson Publishing Group, 1725 K Street, NW, Washington, DC 20006 Tel # (202) 872-4000
Editorial Description: Guide to avoiding and solving pension problems. Subscription includes monthly updates.
General Info: Monthly, Looseleaf
Subscriptions: Indv. $329

Pension Tax Reports
See: TAXES

Pipeline to Seniors

Publishing Co: New Jersey Natural Gas Co., PO Box 1464, Wall, NJ 07719-1464; Title Tel # (908) 938-1223
Personnel: Editor-Glenn Philips
Editorial Description: Designed to enlighten seniors about company policies as well as general information.
General Info: Yr. Est. 1982, Semi-annually, Trim Size-11½ x 17½, 4 pages, 2 Color
Circulation: Total-13,000

Prime of Life

Publishing Co: Kelly Communications, Rr 13 Box 28, Charlottesville, VA 22901-7927; Title Tel # (804) 296-5676 Title Fax # (804) 296-3972
Personnel: Publisher-Joseph Kelly, Editor-Jim Travisano, Circ. Mgr.-Lundi Palmer, Production Mgr.-Paxson MacDonald, Art Dir.-Steven Black
Editorial Description: Prime of life is a full-color magazine-quality newsletter that speaks as a trusted friend & health adviser to men & women over the age of 55.
General Info: Yr. Est. 1988, Bi-monthly, Trim Size-8½ x 11, 12 pages, 4 Color, Coated, Saddle-stitched

Public Assistance & Welfare Trends/State Capitals
See: SOCIAL SERVICES & WELFARE

Quality Care Advocate
See: HEALTH

Report on Institutional Foodservice
See: FOOD

Retirement Facility Guide   *Business*

Publishing Co: Retirement Facility Guide, PO Box 11885, Reno, NV 89510-1885; Title Tel # (702) 333-6651
Personnel: Publisher, Editor-Mary Pat Eymann
Editorial Description: Activities and programs for retirement centers.
General Info: Yr. Est. 1992, Monthly, Offset press, 4 pages, 2 Color
Subscriptions: $25/copy

Retirement Letter   *Consumer*

Publishing Co: Phillips Publishing, Inc., 7811 Montrose Rd., Potomac, MD 20854-3394 Fax # (301) 294-1307 Parent Co.-Phillips Business Information, Inc., Potomac; Title Tel # (301) 340-2100 Title Fax # (301) 424-7034
Personnel: Publisher-Thomas Phillips, Editor-Peter Dickinson, Mktg. Dir.-Nancy Cathey
Editorial Description: Creating a richer, longer retirement experience through making and saving money in and approaching retirement.
General Info: Yr. Est. 1973, Monthly, Trim Size-8½ x 11, Offset press, 8 pages, ISSN: 0093-5352, 2 Color, Newsprint
Subscriptions: Indv. $50, $6/copy
Acquistions: Publication Bought, Publication Sold
List Rental: Actives: 84,312, $195/M, Expires: 175,934, $95/M

Retirement Planning Advisor   *Business*

Publishing Co: Hearst Business Communications, RAI Division, 645 Stewart Ave., Garden City, NY 11530-4709; Title Tel # (516) 227-1300 Title Fax # (516) 229-3636
Personnel: Publisher-W. Boyd Griffin, Assoc. Publ.-Susan Barbey, Editor-Elaine Laramee
Editorial Description: Company sponsored pre-retirement planning newsletter.
General Info: Yr. Est. 1974, Quarterly, Trim Size-8½ x 11, Offset press, 6 pages

Retirement Planning Advisory

Publishing Co: WPI Communications, Inc., 55 Morris Ave, Springfield, NJ 07081-1496; Title Tel # (201) 467-8700 Title Fax # (201) 467-0368
Personnel: Editor-Ken Berry
General Info: Bi-weekly
List Rental: Rents Lists

Retirement Plans Bulletin   *Business, Consumer*

Publishing Co: Universal Pensions Inc., PO Box 979, Brainerd, MN 56401-0979; Title Tel # (218) 829-4781 Title Fax # (218) 829-2106
Personnel: Mng. Editor-Jennifer Norquist
Editorial Description: Coveres IRA & retirement plan issues for financial organizations.
General Info: (Formerly IRA Bulletin), Yr. Est. 1993, Monthly, Trim Size-8.5 x 11, Sheetfed press, 10 pages, Matte, Other
Subscriptions: Indv. $89

Selling to Seniors
See: ADVERTISING & MARKETING

Senior Citizens Post

Publishing Co: Coordinating Council for Senior Citizens, 807 S. Duke St., Durham, NC 27701-3701; Title Tel # (919) 688-8247 Title Fax # (919) 683-3406
General Info: Yr. Est. 1971, Quarterly
Subscriptions: Indv. $2

Senior Dynamics

Publishing Co: Lewis County Senior Svcs., PO Box 297, Chehalis, WA 98532-0297; Title Tel # (206) 748-9121
Personnel: Editor-Cherylyn Reed, Adv. Dir.-Patricia Sabin
Editorial Description: Senior citizens.
General Info: Yr. Est. 1975, Monthly, Trim Size-10 x 12½, Web press, 48 pages, 3% ads, 4 Color, Newsprint
Subscriptions: Indv. $5
Circulation: (100% controlled)
Advertising: Inquire for rates.
Printing Co: Longview Publishing Co., 11th at Douglas, Longview, WA 98632 Tel # (206) 577-2500

Senior Golf
See: GOLF

Senior Guardian   *Consumer*

Publishing Co: Sponsor-Natl. Alliance of Senior Citizens, National Alliance of Senior Citizens, 1700 18th St NW # 401, Washington, DC 20009-2508; Title Tel # (202) 986-0117 Title Fax # (202) 986-2974
Personnel: Publisher-Peter Luciano
Editorial Description: Senior citizen membership publication.
General Info: Yr. Est. 1974, Bi-monthly, Trim Size-8½ x 11, 4 pages, ISSN: 0730-577X, 2 Color, Newsprint
Subscriptions: Indv. $10
Circulation: Total-60,000
Advertising: Accepts Inserts.

Senior Housing: Assisted Living & Long-term Care Manual   *Business*

Publishing Co: Thompson Publishing Group, 747 Third Ave., New York, NY 10017; Title Tel # (212) 888-7220 Title Fax # (212) 486-3400
Personnel: Editor-David Rusch, Production Mgr.-Mauro Vaisman, Mktg. Dir.-James Kavanage
General Info: Yr. Est. 1994, Monthly, Looseleaf
Subscriptions: Indv. $295

Senior Sports News   *Association*

Publishing Co: Natl. Senior Sports Assn., PO Box 882, Fairfax, VA 22030-0882; Title Tel # (703) 385-7540
Personnel: Publisher, Editor-Lloyd Wright, Adv. Dir.-Bobbi Beck
Editorial Description: Sports events for mature sportsmen.
General Info: Yr. Est. 1979, Monthly, Trim Size-8½ x 11, Offset press, 8 pages, ISSN: 0196-6243, 2 Color
Circulation: Total-6,000

Senior Sun   *Consumer*

Publishing Co: New York State Electric & Gas Corp., 4500 Vestal Parkway, Box 3607, Binghamton, NY 13902-3607; Title Tel # (607) 762-4827
Personnel: Editor-Pamela Hatchett-Rogers
Editorial Description: Addresses consumer & energy issues relative to older customers of New York State Electric & Gas Corp.
General Info: Yr. Est. 1981, Trim Size-11½ x 17, Web press, 8 pages, 2 Color
Circulation: (100% controlled), Total-35,000

Seniornet Online Newsletter *Association*

Publishing Co: Seniornet, 1 Kearny St., 3rd Floor, San Francisco, CA 94108-5501; Title Tel # (415) 352-1210
Editorial Description: For seniors who use the electronic mail service Seniornet - a part of the Americ Online service.
General Info: Quarterly

Seniors in Sacramento   *Consumer*

Publishing Co: CRLA Foundation, 2424 K St., 1st Fl., Sacramento, CA 95816-5002; Title Tel # (916) 446-7904 Title Fax # (916) 446-3057
Personnel: Editor-Shelley Rouillard
Editorial Description: Legislative newsletter on issues affecting the elderly, poor, & disabled in California.
General Info: Yr. Est. 1972, Monthly, Offset press, 6 pages
Subscriptions: Indv. $20, Inst. $125
Circulation: Total-950

Silver Times   *Consumer*

Publishing Co: Little/Silver Times, The, 100 6th Ave., 7th Fl., New York, NY 10013-1605; Title Tel # (212) 765-3301 Title Fax # (212) 765-3630
Personnel: Editor in Chief-Lori Bernstein
Editorial Description: Information and articles for senior citizens and elder care.
General Info: Yr. Est. 1993, Quarterly, Trim Size-8½ x 11, 8 pages, No Color, Matte, Saddle-stitched
Circulation: Total-10,000
Advertising: Inquire for rates.

Social Security/SSI Informational Mailing   *Business, Consumer*

Publishing Co: Natl. Senior Citizens Law Center, 1815 H St. NW, Suite #700, Washington, DC 20006-3604; Title Tel # (202) 887-5280 Title Fax # (202) 785-6792
Personnel: Editor-Ethel Zelenske, Circ. Mgr.-Gloria Crawford
Editorial Description: Compilation and analyses of legislative, administrative and litigation developments in the social security and SSI Programs.
General Info: Yr. Est. 1982, Monthly, 200 pages
Subscriptions: Indv. $200, Inst. $200
Circulation: Total-200, Readership-2,000

Steelworkers Oldtimer   *Association, Consumer*

Publishing Co: United Steelworkers of America, PO Box 112730, Pittsburgh, PA 15241-0330; Title Tel # (412) 833-4761
Personnel: Editor-Raymond Pasnick
Editorial Description: Devoted to news, information, & entertainment for those in retirement.
General Info: (Formerly The Oldtimer), Yr. Est. 1978, Quarterly, Trim Size-8½ x 11, Letrpr. press, 16 pages, 2 Color, Coated
Circulation: Total-385,075
Printing Co: Interform, P.O. Box 8, Pittsfield, PA 16340 Tel # (412) 221-3300

Sylvia Porter's Active Retirement Newsletter   *Consumer*

Publishing Co: Sylvia Porter Organization, Inc., 15 Columbus Circle, 23rd fl., New York, NY 10023; Title Tel # (212) 373-7745
General Info: Yr. Est. 1988, Monthly
Subscriptions: Indv. $50

Tax, Estate and Financial Planning for the Elderly
See: BANKING & FINANCE

Times of Your Life

Publishing Co: FPL Corporate Communications, PO Box 029100, Miami, FL 33102-9100
Personnel: Editor-Dave Wolverton
Editorial Description: Issues & information.
General Info: Yr. Est. 1984, Quarterly, 8 pages, No Color, Coated

Tipsheet
See: EDUCATION

Travel Companions
See: TRAVEL

Travel Scoop Consumer Newsletter
See: TRAVEL

Une Veritable Amie
See: WOMEN'S

Voice of United Senior Citizens of Ontario Inc. *Consumer, Association*   CPM: $15

Publishing Co: United Senior Citizens of Ontario Inc., 3033 Lakeshore Blvd., W., Toronto, ON M8V 1K5 Canada Tel # (416) 252-2021 Fax # (416) 252-5770
Personnel: Publisher-Allan Smith, Editor-Barbara Skelton, Adv. Dir.-Mary Lamb
General Info: Yr. Est. 1970, 10x/yr., Offset press, 40 pages, No Color, Newsprint
Subscriptions: Can. $15
Circulation: Total-3,500
Advertising: $55.

Wise Ideas   *Consumer, Association*

Publishing Co: Better Directions, PO Box 752, Melbourne, FL 32902-0752; Title Tel # (407) 724-5553 Title Fax # (407) 724-5767
Personnel: Publisher, Editor-Kathy Laurenhue
Editorial Description: Written for family members, professionals and private caregivers of those with Alzheimer's disease and related dementias.
General Info: (Formerly Wiser Now), Yr. Est. 1992, Monthly, Trim Size-8½ x 11, 4 pages, ISSN: 1071-2275, 2 Color
Subscriptions: Indv. $25, Inst. $25, Can. $27, For. $29

Workamper News
See: TRAVEL

Working Age

Publishing Co: American Association of Retired Persons, 3200 Carson St, Lakewood, CA 90712-4038 Tel # (310) 496-2277 Fax # (310) 496-1397 Parent Co.-American Association of Retired Persons, Washington; Title Tel # (202) 434-2045
Personnel: Editor-Ronald Allen
Editorial Description: Covers employment trends & issues affecting middle-age & older persons.
General Info: (Formerly AARP Action), Yr. Est. 1985, Bi-monthly, 8 pages, Color, Newsprint, Saddle-stitched
Circulation: (100% controlled), Total-30,000

World of A.S.P.
See: LIFESTYLE

Years Ahead
See: RELIGIOUS & THEOLOGICAL

Your Retirement Advisor
See: INDUSTRIAL RELATIONS/PERSONNEL

SEX

Alternative Health Therapies Newsletter
See: HEALTH

Bi Women Newsletter
See: GAY & LESBIAN INTEREST

Canadian Society of Environmental Biologists Newsletter
See: ENVIRONMENT & ECOLOGY

Celebrate the Self   *Consumer*

Publishing Co: Factor Press, PO Box 8888, Mobile, AL 36689
Editorial Description: A newsletter about enjoying you life and your body. Compiling reader tips, health questions, product reviews, and essays on life. It's directed primarily to men with a spirit that embraces both gay and straight mentalities.
General Info: Bi-monthly, 20 pages
Subscriptions: Indv. $17, $4/copy

Contemporary Sexuality   *Consumer, Association*   **CPM: $161**

Publishing Co: American Assn. of Sex Educators, Counselors, and Therapists, 435 N. Michigan Ave., #1917, Chicago, IL 60611-4008; Title Tel # (312) 644-0828 Title Fax # (312) 644-8557
Personnel: Editor-Mary Ann Williams
General Info: Yr. Est. 1967, Monthly, Trim Size-8½ x 11, 12 pages, 2 Color
Subscriptions: Indv. $65, Inst. $95
Circulation: Total-3,100
Advertising: $500.
List Rental: Actives: $225/M
Printing Co: Original Smith Printing, 2200 E. Devon, Des Plaines, IL 60018 Tel # (708) 296-4080

Emerge Playcouple
See: LIFESTYLE

Ethics and Medics
See: MEDICINE

Garden Views
See: WOMEN'S

Genuine Article, The
See: MEN'S

Greenery: For Women and Men Exploring Female Domination   *Consumer*

Publishing Co: Lady Green, 3739 Balboa Ave. #195, San Francisco, CA 94121
Editorial Description: A truly wonderful newsletter directed toward women but may be useful for men or couples. Full of honest advice about female domination and other related topics.
General Info: Quarterly, 4 pages
Subscriptions: Indv. $8

It's Okay   *Consumer*

Publishing Co: Phoenix Counsel Inc., 1 Springbank Dr., St. Catharines, ON L2S 2K1 Canada
Editorial Description: Providing information about sex and sexuality for people with disabilities.
General Info: Quarterly, 36 pages

Lesbian and Gay Archivist
See: GAY & LESBIAN INTEREST

Masquerade Erotic Newsletter, The   *Consumer*

Publishing Co: Masquerade Books, Inc., 801 Second Avenue, New York, NY 10017; Title Tel # (212) 661-7878 Title Fax # (212) 986-7355
Personnel: Publisher-Richard Kasak, Editor-Jennifer Reut, Art Dir.-Dayna Navaro
Editorial Description: Featuring some of the best articles on erotica, fetishes, sex clubs, and the politics of porn.
General Info: Yr. Est. 1989, Bi-monthly, 32 pages, ISSN: 1-878320
Subscriptions: Indv. $30, $5/copy
Circulation: Total-4,000
Advertising: Inquire for rates. Accepts Inserts.

Mastering Life   *Consumer*

Publishing Co: Mastering Life Ministries, P.O. box 110072, Nashville, TN 37222 Tel # (615) 831-0675
Personnel: Editor-David K. Foster
Editorial Description: Mastering life is a newsletter that contains articles, inerviews and news about our ministry to sexually broken people. We discuss and teach on every major area of sexual addiction and dysfunction from a biblical, christian perspective-showing people howto get set free and healed.
General Info: Yr. Est. 1988, Quarterly, Trim Size-8½ x 11, Sheetfed press, 8 pages, No Color
Circulation: Total-1,500
Printing Co: Beyer Printing, 315 Wilhages Rd., Nashville, TN 37217 Tel # (615) 366-0301, Fax # (615) 366-0220

Military & Police Uniform Association Newsletter
See: CLUBS

NASCA Inside Report   *Association*

Publishing Co: Sponsor-NASCA, Inc. (North American Swing Club Assn.), Lifestyles Press, 2641 W La Palma Ave # A, Anaheim, CA 92801-2602; Title Tel # (715) 821-9953 Title Fax # (714) 821-1465
Personnel: Editor-Robert McGinley, Ph D, Calendar Ed.-Frank Lomas
Editorial Description: News & educational articles on swinging, relationships, sexuality & NASCA news.
General Info: (Formerly Emerge Newsletter), Yr. Est. 1980, Bi-monthly, Trim Size-8½ x 11, 4 pages
Subscriptions: Indv. $15, Free With Membership
Acquistions: Publication Sold
Circulation: Total-1,500

Newsletter of the National Task Force on Sexuality and Disability.

Publishing Co: Michigan Univ. Hospital, Dept. of Physical Medicine, c/o Nathan D. Zasler,MD, 11654 Rutgers Drive, Richmond, VA 73233
General Info: Annually
Subscriptions: Indv. $10

Prosecution and Defense of Sex Crimes   *Business*

Publishing Co: Matthew Bender & Co., 11 Penn Plaza, New York, NY 10001-2006 Fax # (212) 244-3188; Title Tel # (212) 967-7707
Editorial Description: Full coverage of legal problems involved in both forcible and non-forcible sex crimes including sexual and physical abuse of children and spouses, and prostitution.
General Info: Yr. Est. 1976, Annually, Looseleaf
Subscriptions: $90/copy

SIECUS Report

Publishing Co: Sponsor-Sex Information & Education Council of the U.S., SIECUS (Sex Information & Education Council of the U.S.), New York, NY 10003; Title Tel # (212) 673-3850
Personnel: Editor-Janet Jamar
Editorial Description: Covers all aspects of human sexuality, including AIDS, & related resources. Includes articles by experts, book & audio visual reviews, news items, seminar/conference calendars, & recommended resources.
General Info: (Formerly SIECUS Newsletter), Yr. Est. 1972, Bi-monthly, Trim Size-8½ x 11, 28 pages, ISSN: 0091-3995, 2 Color, Newsprint
Subscriptions: Indv. $75, Inst. $100, $8/copy
Circulation: Total-31,000

Sex Over Forty   *Consumer*

Publishing Co: DKT International, PO Box 1600, Chapel Hill, NC 27515-1600; Title Tel # (919) 644-1616 Title Fax # (919) 644-8150
Personnel: Publisher-E. Douglas Whitehead, Editor-Shirley Zussman, Circ. Dir.-Betsey Gross
Editorial Description: For enhancing intimacy in older adults. Edited by medical experts.
General Info: Yr. Est. 1982, Monthly, 8 pages, 2 Color
Subscriptions: Indv. $36
Circulation: Readership-35,000
List Rental: List Management Co.: Mail Marketing, Inc., 171 Terrace St., Haworth, NJ 07641-1899 Tel # (201) 387-1023, Fax # (201) 387-2976, Actives: 98,944, $90/M

Slur
See: MUSIC & MUSIC TRADES

Smoke Signals: A Monthly Newsletter Devoted to the Smoking Fetish   *Consumer*

Publishing Co: Smoke Signals, 500 Waterman Ave., Ste. 193, East Providence, RI 02914
Editorial Description: It's a zine for people who get turned on by women who smoke. It provides information on which videos (Hollywood, porn, and cigarette fetish) offer the best smoking scenes, letters from readers, discussions, personal ads, and fiction.
General Info: Monthly, 12 pages
Subscriptions: Indv. $40, $5/copy

Society for the Scientific Study of Sex-Society Newsletter

Publishing Co: Society for the Scientific Study of Sex, PO Box 208, Mount Vernon, IA 52314-0208; Title Tel # (215) 782-1430 Title Fax # (319) 895-6203
Personnel: Editor-Andrew Behrendt
General Info: Yr. Est. 1958, Quarterly, 6 pages
Subscriptions: Indv. $20
Circulation: Total-1,200
List Rental: Rents Lists

Survivor Activist, The
See: PSYCHOLOGY

Trying Times
See: HEALTH

SHIPS & SHIPPING

Advanced Transportation Technology News
See: TRAFFIC & TRANSPORTATION

American Marine Engineer
Publishing Co: Natl. Marine Engineers' Beneficial Assn., AFL-CIO, 444 N Capitol St NW Ste 800, Washington, DC 20001-1512; Title Tel # (202) 347-8585
Personnel: Editor-Robert S. Burns
General Info: Yr. Est. 1966, Monthly
Advertising: Inquire for rates.

Ameriport Sailing Schedule
Publishing Co: Delaware River Port Authority, Box 1949, Camden, NJ 08101-1949; Title Tel # (215) 925-8780
Editorial Description: Scheduled sailing to world ports.
General Info: Yr. Est. 1950, Bi-monthly, Offset press, 12 pages, Looseleaf
Circulation: Total-3,900

Arbitrator
Publishing Co: Society of Maritime Arbitrators, Inc., 61 Broadway Rm 1650, New York, NY 10006-2701 Fax # (212) 480-3320; Title Tel # (212) 483-0616
Editorial Description: Maritime reviews of current arbitration awards & society maritime arbitrator's activities.
General Info: Yr. Est. 1963, Quarterly, Offset press, 6 pages
Circulation: Total-1,000

Association of Ship Brokers and Agents Newsletter   *Association*
Publishing Co: ASBA, PO Box 738, Millburn, NJ 07041-0738; Title Tel # (212) 385-4060
Personnel: Publisher, Editor-Virginia Redstone
Editorial Description: Information on the activities of ship brokers.
General Info: Quarterly, 4 pages
Circulation: Total-200

Benedict on Admiralty
See: LAW

CIB Daily Maritime Newsletter   *Business*
Publishing Co: Congressional Information Bureau, Inc., 3030 Clarendon Blvd., Ste. 202, Arlington, VA 22201-2845 Tel # (703) 516-4801 Fax # (703) 516-4804; Title Tel # (202) 347-2275 Title Fax # (202) 347-2278
General Info: Yr. Est. 1897, Daily
Subscriptions: Indv. $1,260, Inst. $1,260, $35/copy

CIB Newsletter   *Association*
Publishing Co: Congressional Information Bureau, Inc., 3030 Clarendon Blvd., Ste. 202, Arlington, VA 22201-2845 Tel # (703) 516-4801 Fax # (703) 516-4804
Personnel: Publisher-R.P. Cazalas, Editor-Robert Cazales
Editorial Description: Daily maritime newsletters, federal agencies and their reports on the industry.
General Info: Yr. Est. 1897, Daily, Trim Size-11½ x 14, Sheetfed press, 25 pages, No Color
Subscriptions: Indv. $1,080
Circulation: (CCAB)

Claim Digest
Publishing Co: Shippers Natl. Freight Claim Council, Inc., 120 Main St # Z, Huntington, NY 11743-6906; Title Tel # (516) 549-8984
Personnel: Editor-William Augello
General Info: Yr. Est. 1973, Monthly, 20 pages, No Color
Subscriptions: Indv. $295
Circulation: Total-800
List Rental: Actives: $50/M

Connections
Publishing Co: Toledo-Lucas County Port Authority, 1 Maritime Plaza, Toledo, OH 43604-1866; Title Tel # (419) 243-8251 Title Fax # (419) 243-1835
Personnel: Editor-Mark Sweeney
Editorial Description: Activities involving the port of Toledo aviation in Toledo, & economic development.
General Info: (Formerly Port of Toledo News), Yr. Est. 1959, Quarterly, Trim Size-11 x 17, Sheetfed press, 4 pages, No Color, Coated
Circulation: (100% controlled), Total-10,000

Cruise & Freighter Travel Letter
See: TRAVEL

Deepwater
Publishing Co: Greater Baton Rouge Port Commission, PO Box 380, Port Allen, LA 70767-0380; Title Tel # (504) 342-1660 Title Fax # (504) 342-1666
Personnel: Publisher-Karen K. St. Cyr
Editorial Description: Newsletter, highlights port activity and items of interest to the local maritime community.
General Info: Quarterly, Trim Size-8½ x 11, 6 pages
Subscriptions: Free
Circulation: Total-1,100, Readership-1,100
Advertising: Accepts Inserts.

FACS Forum
Publishing Co: Federation of American Controlled Shipping, 50 Broadway Rm 3400, New York, NY 10004-1607; Title Tel # (212) 344-1483
Editorial Description: Represents the interests of U.S. companies operating under the Liberian and Panamanian flags.
General Info: Yr. Est. 1958, Monthly

Federal Maritime Commission Digest Service   *Business*
Publishing Co: Hawkins Publishing Co., Inc., 1207 B Central Avenue, Box 480, Mayo, MD 21106; Title Tel # (410) 798-1677 Title Fax # (410) 798-1098
Personnel: Publisher, Editor-C.R. Eyler
Editorial Description: Reports of the Federal Maritime Commission, and Federal and U.S. Supreme Courts relating to the Shipping and Merchant Marine Acts.
General Info: Yr. Est. 1970, Irregular, Trim Size-8½ x 11, Sheetfed press, No Color, Matte, Looseleaf
Subscriptions: Indv. $320

Great Lakes Navigation   *Business*
Publishing Co: Canadian Marine Publications, Ltd., 1434 St. Catherine W., Ste 512, 5th Fl., Montreal, PQ H3G 1R4 Canada; Title Tel # (514) 861-6715 Title Fax # (514) 861-0966
Personnel: Publisher-J. W. McManus, Editor-M.D. Perkins, Circ. Mgr.-Megan Perkins, Adv. Dir.-Marilyn Belanger
Editorial Description: Shipping, ports and related multi-modal activities on Great Lakes and St. Lawrence Seaway.
General Info: Yr. Est. 1917, Annually, Trim Size-7 x 10, Offset press, 116 pages, Color
Subscriptions: $30/copy
Circulation: Total-3,090
Advertising: Inquire for rates.

HazMat Transport News
See: TRUCKING

Inside DOT and Transportation Week
See: TRAFFIC & TRANSPORTATION

Marine Management Letter   *Business*
Publishing Co: Fleet Data Service, 1218 Portola Ave # B, Torrance, CA 90501-2611; Title Tel # (409) 569-0375
Personnel: Publisher-J.O. Covington, Editor-J. O. Covington
Editorial Description: Current news of the offshore petroleum service vessel market. Focus on industry trends & statistics.
General Info: Yr. Est. 1976, 10x/yr., Trim Size-8½ x 11, Offset press, 4 pages, ISSN: 0197-1077, No Color, Newsprint
Subscriptions: $10/copy
Circulation: Total-300

Marine Safety Report
See: SAFETY

Maritime Newsletter
Publishing Co: Maritime Assn., Port of New York/New Jersey, 17 Battery Pl Rm 1115, New York, NY 10004-1101; Title Tel # (212) 425-5704 Title Fax # (212) 635-9498
Personnel: Editor-Patrick Purcell, Editor-Mary-Pat Volino
Editorial Description: Trade newsletter consisting of news around the New York/NewJersey/Connecticut port areas, membership news, legislation look-out and other maritime related information and activities.
General Info: (Formerly Maritime Exchange Bulletin), Yr. Est. 1973, Monthly, 12 pages, 1% ads, Coated
Circulation: Total-1,500
Advertising: Inquire for rates.
Printing Co: Westchester Lithographers, 34 Weyman Ave, New Rochelle, NY 10805-1496 Tel # (914) 636-7787

Maritime Research Charter Newsletter   *Business*
Publishing Co: Maritime Research, Inc., 499 Ernston Rd., Box 805, Parlin, NJ 08859-1406; Title Tel # (908) 727-8040 Title Fax # (908) 727-0243
Personnel: Editor-Jay Lillianthal
Editorial Description: Complete listing of all ship charters reported throughout the world. Graphical representation of dry cargo charter fixture rates.
General Info: Yr. Est. 1952, Weekly, Trim Size-8½ x 11½, Offset press, 4 pages, No Color
Subscriptions: Indv. $260, Can. $280, For. $280
Circulation: Total-2,000
Advertising: Inquire for rates.

NMU Government Operations News

Publishing Co: District #4 - MEBA/NMU, 30 Montgomery Street, New Jersey, NJ 07302-3821; Title Tel # (201) 332-7070
Personnel: Editor-Kenn Palinkas
General Info: Quarterly

National Reporter
See: LAW

Newsletter

Publishing Co: Permanent Intl. Assn. of Navigation Congresses, Water Resources Ctr., Ft. Belvoir, VA 22060-5586

Offshore International Newsletter
See: PETROLEUM & NATURAL GAS

Offshore Rig Locator International
See: ENERGY

Offshore Rig Newsletter
See: ENERGY

On Scene   *Business*

Publishing Co: U.S. Coast Guard, 2100 2nd St SW, Washington, DC 20593-0001; Title Tel # (202) 426-2631
General Info: Yr. Est. 1969, Quarterly, Offset press, 36 pages
Circulation: Total-7,500

Port O Call   *Business*

Publishing Co: South Jersey Port Corp, 2500 Broadway, Camden, NJ 08104-2409; Title Tel # (609) 541-8500
Personnel: Editor, Production Mgr., Promotion Dir.-Robert Banks
Editorial Description: International trade, ships and commodities, port activities, commerce, industries located at the port.
General Info: Yr. Est. 1972, Quarterly, Trim Size-8½ x 11, Offset press, 4 pages, Color
Subscriptions: $1,500/copy
Circulation: Total-1,500

Port Progress   *Business*

Publishing Co: Port of Oakland, P.O. Box 2064, Oakland, CA 94604-2064; Title Tel # (510) 272-1188 Title Fax # (510) 839-1766
Editorial Description: Port of Oakland activities, including maritime, aviation and real estate.
General Info: Yr. Est. 1964, Bi-monthly, Trim Size-8½ x 11, Web press, 8 pages, 4 Color, Coated, Saddle-stitched
Circulation: (100% controlled), Total-15,000

Proceedings of the American Merchant Marine Conference

Publishing Co: Propeller Club of the U. S., 3927 Old Lee Hwy Ste 101a, Fairfax, VA 22030-2422; Title Tel # (703) 691-2777 Title Fax # (703) 691-4173
General Info: Annually

Quarterdeck, The
See: MUSEUM PUBLICATIONS

Sail Assistance News

Publishing Co: Sail Assistance Intl. Liason Associates, 1553 Bayville St, Norfolk, VA 23503-1060; Title Tel # (804) 588-6022
General Info: Yr. Est. 1981, Quarterly
Subscriptions: Indv. $25

Salute   *Business*

Publishing Co: U.S. Navy, Code 165.4, Puget Sound Naval Shipyard, Bremerton, WA 98314-0001; Title Tel # (206) 476-2544
Personnel: Editor-Deborah Franz-Anderson
Editorial Description: U.S. Navy shipyard house organ.
General Info: Yr. Est. 1941, Bi-weekly, Trim Size-8½ x 11, Sheetfed press, 16 pages, 2 Color, Coated, Saddle-stitched
Acquistions: Publication Bought
Circulation: Total-12,000
Printing Co: Bremerton Printing Co., 245 4th St., Bremerton, WA 98310 Tel # (206) 373-1454

Seaposter
See: PHILATELY & POSTAL AFFAIRS

Shipboard Cruiser, The
See: TRAVEL

Ships & Shipwrecks: The Newsletter of Nautical History & Discovery
See: ARCHAEOLOGY

Shipyard Chronicle   *Association*

Publishing Co: Shipbuilders Council of America, 4301 N. Fairfax Drive, Arlington, VA 22203-1627; Title Tel # (703) 276-1700 Title Fax # (703) 276-1707
Personnel: Editor-W. Patrick Morris
Editorial Description: Developments affecting U.S. shipyard industry either directly or indirectly.
General Info: (Formerly Shipyard Weekly), Yr. Est. 1957, Bi-weekly, 4 pages, ISSN: 0737-7428, No Color
Subscriptions: Indv. $125, For. $175, Free To Qualified Recipient
Circulation: (100% controlled), Total-3,000

Stockton's Port Soundings

Publishing Co: Port of Stockton, PO Box 2089, Stockton, CA 95201-2089 Tel # (209) 946-0246
General Info: Monthly
Subscriptions: Indv. $12

Traffic Blotter

Publishing Co: McAvoy Representation, 3820 Nostrand Ave # 102, Brooklyn, NY 11235-2013; Title Tel # (212) 964-3373
Personnel: Editor-John A. McAvoy
Editorial Description: Articles on shipping, foreign trade, personnel announcements, etc.
General Info: Yr. Est. 1953, Weekly
Subscriptions: Indv. $5
Circulation: Total-3,400
Advertising: Inquire for rates.

USS Henrico APA-45 Newsletter
See: MILITARY & NAVAL

USS Reports
See: SOCIAL SERVICES & WELFARE

USS St. Louis Hubble-Bubble   *Association*

Publishing Co: USS St. Louis CL 49 Assn., Hubble Bubble Office, 28561 Hardiman Rd., Madison, AL 35758-2904 Tel # (205) 772-7127; Title Tel # (205) 772-7172
Personnel: Editor-Harry Price
Editorial Description: News and information for former shipmates on the USS St. Louis.
General Info: Irregular, Trim Size-8½ x 11, 12 pages, No Color, Matte, Other
Subscriptions: Free With Membership

U.S. Merchant Marine Data Sheet   *Business, Association*

Publishing Co: U.S. Dept. of Transportation, 400 7th St SW, Washington, DC 20590-0001; Title Tel # (202) 426-5807
Editorial Description: Reports statistical information concerning the active privately owned U.S. merchant fleet (vessels of 1,000 gross tons and over), shipboard jobs, and construction.
General Info: Yr. Est. 1951, Monthly, Trim Size-8½ x 11, Offset press, 8 pages, No Color
Circulation: Total-1,000

World Shipping Laws and Fact Finding Tools
See: LAW

SKIING & SNOWMOBILING

ASF Washington Letter   *Business, Association*

Publishing Co: American Ski Federation, 207 Constitution Ave NE, Washington, DC 20002-7307; Title Tel # (202) 543-1595
Personnel: Editor-Joe Prendergast
Editorial Description: Represents the interests of the American skiing industry.
General Info: Yr. Est. 1979, Monthly, 4 pages
Subscriptions: Indv. $25, Inst. $100

Avalanche Echoes

Publishing Co: Alpine Club of Canada, 1815 St. Denis Rd., West Vancouver, BC V7V 3W4 Canada; Title Tel # (604) 926-5359
Personnel: Editor-Lem Legg
General Info: Monthly, 8 pages, No Color
Circulation: (100% controlled), Total-518

Iron Dog Tracks   *Association*

Publishing Co: Antique Snowmobile Club of America, 217 W Alta Loma Cir, Thiensville, WI 53092-1719; Title Tel # (715) 762-2678
Editorial Description: Events and association news.
General Info: Bi-monthly
Circulation: Total-300

NSRA Newsletter *Association*

Publishing Co: National Ski Retailers Association, 1699 Wall St., Mt. Prospect, IL 60056-5762; Title Tel # (708) 439-4293 Title Fax # (708) 439-0111
Personnel: Publisher, Editor-Thomas Doyle
Editorial Description: For members (ski shops, ski area shops & sporting goods stores with ski depts.) News & articles on ski equipment standards, shop practices & industry marketing programs.
General Info: Yr. Est. 1988, Quarterly, Trim Size-8½ x 11, 2 Color, Matte
Subscriptions: Free With Membership
Circulation: Total-500
List Rental: Rents Lists

Nordic Network *Association* CPM: $214

Publishing Co: Cross Country Ski Areas Association, 259 Bolton Rd, Winchester, NH 03470-2603; Title Tel # (603) 239-4341 Title Fax # (603) 239-6387
Personnel: Publisher, Editor, Adv. Dir.-Chris Frado
Editorial Description: Industry news relevant to owners & operators of cross country ski areas & related businesses. Includes advertising.
General Info: Yr. Est. 1976, Quarterly, Trim Size-8½ x 11, Offset press, 16 pages, 2% ads, Matte, Saddle-stitched
Subscriptions: Indv. $25, $30/copy
Circulation: Total-350
Advertising: $75. Accepts Inserts.
List Rental: Actives: 1,000, $55/M
Printing Co: Hinsdale Press, 9 Main St., Hinsdale, NH 03451 Tel # (603) 336-7253

Photogear *Consumer*

Publishing Co: Viewpoint Networks, Inc, 403 Darwin Drive, Amherst, NY 14226; Title Tel # (716) 833-0929 Title Fax # (716) 833-0930
Personnel: Publisher, Editor-John Horan
Editorial Description: Candid reviews of all photography equipment and related products without the taint of advertising pressures.
General Info: Yr. Est. 1995, Bi-monthly, Trim Size-8½ x 11, 16 pages, Matte, Saddle-stitched
Subscriptions: Indv. $24, Can. $24, For. $24, $6/copy
Circulation: Total-900, Readership-1,200

Ski for Light Bulletin
See: HEALTH

Ski Nautique News *Consumer, Association*

Publishing Co: Canadian Water Ski Assn., 1600 James Naismith Dr., Gloucester, ON K1B 5N4 Canada Tel # (613) 748-5683 Fax # (613) 748-5867
General Info: (Formerly Ski Canada Nautique), Trim Size-8½ x 11, 24 pages, 2 Color, Matte, Saddle-stitched
Subscriptions: Indv. $6, $3/copy
Circulation: Total-3,500
Advertising: Inquire for rates. Accepts Inserts.

Ski Tripper *Consumer* CPM: $833

Publishing Co: Ski Tripper, PO Box 20305, Roanoke, VA 24018-0031 Tel # (540) 773-7644; Title Tel # (540) 772-7644
Personnel: Publisher, Editor-Tom Gibson, Mktg. Dir.-Jamie Hendry
Editorial Description: For the downhill skier in the Mid-Atlantic and southeast region. Covers resorts from, Alabama to Southern PA.
General Info: Yr. Est. 1993, 5x/yr., Trim Size-8½ x 11, 8 pages, No Color, Matte
Subscriptions: Indv. $18
Circulation: Total-300
Advertising: $250.

Skiland/Mid America Skier

Publishing Co: U.S. Ski Assn., Central Div., PO Box 117, Charlevoix, MI 49720-0117
Personnel: Editor-Martin P. Harney
Editorial Description: Area and general news of interest to skiers.
General Info: Yr. Est. 1955, 9x/yr.
Subscriptions: Indv. $1
Circulation: Total-16,210

Sybarite Review

Publishing Co: Amherst College, Publications, Rtes. 9 and 116 S., Amherst, MA 01002-5000
Personnel: Editor-Jody Brockway
General Info: Yr. Est. 1969, Monthly
Subscriptions: Indv. $3
Advertising: Inquire for rates.

U.S. Ski Writers Association, Newsletter *Association*

Publishing Co: U.S. Ski Writers Assn., 1207 Valley Rd, Fairfield, CT 06432-1663; Title Tel # (503) 253-8524
Personnel: Publisher, Editor-Ken Maloney
Editorial Description: Information of the USSWA, its members and the skiing and wintersports industry.
General Info: Yr. Est. 1963, Quarterly, Trim Size-8½ x 11, Sheetfed press, 4 pages, No Color, Newsprint
Subscriptions: Free
Circulation: (100% controlled)
Advertising: Inquire for rates.

SOCIAL SERVICES & WELFARE

A.H.R.C. Chronicle *Association*

Publishing Co: Assn. for the Help of Retarded Children, 200 Park Ave., S., New York, NY 10003-1503; Title Tel # (212) 254-8203
Personnel: Publisher-Walter Kaner, Editor-Shirley Berenstein
Editorial Description: News and features relating to the Association's programs for the retarded.
General Info: Trim Size-8⅛ x 10⅜, 10 pages
Circulation: Total-10,000

AIDS & Society: International Research Policy Bulletin
See: MEDICINE

AIDS/STD News Report
See: PHILANTHROPY

AJL Newsline *Association*

Publishing Co: Association of Junior Leagues, Inc., 660 1st Ave, New York, NY 10016-3295; Title Tel # (212) 683-1515
Personnel: Editor-Betsey Steeger
General Info: Trim Size-8½ x 10⅞, Web press, 8 pages, 2 Color
Subscriptions: Indv. $8, Inst. $10
Circulation: Total-182,000

ARNOVA News *Association*

Publishing Co: ARNOVA, Washington State University, Rt 2, Box 696 - Barbara Long, Pullman, WA 99163
Editorial Description: Association for Research on Nonprofit Organizationa and Voluntary Action memebership letter.
General Info: (Formerly AVAS), Quarterly

Accent on DD

Publishing Co: Maryland State Planning Council on Developmental Disabilitie, 1 Market Ctr. Box 10, 300 W. Lexington St., Baltimore, MD 21201; Title Tel # (301) 333-3688
Editorial Description: Information on developmental disabilities issues in Maryland.
General Info: (Formerly MD State Planning Council on Developmental Disabilities), Yr. Est. 1977, Bi-monthly, Trim Size-8½ x 11, 8 pages, No Color, Newsprint
Circulation: Total-2,000

Action Line

Publishing Co: Sponsor-Christian Action Council, Christian Action Council, 109 Carpenter Dr., Ste. 100, Sterling, VA 20164-4467; Title Tel # (703) 237-2100
Personnel: Editor-Dr. Scott
Editorial Description: Monthly newsletter of political and legislative developments re abortion, infanticide and euthanasia.
General Info: Yr. Est. 1975, Monthly, Trim Size-8½ x 11, Offset press, 4 pages, 2 Color, Newsprint
Subscriptions: Indv. $25
Circulation: Total-35,000

Adolescent Medicine
See: MEDICINE

Adoptalk *Association*

Publishing Co: North American Council on Adoptable Children, 970 Raymond Ave Ste 106, Saint Paul, MN 55114-1146; Title Tel # (612) 644-3036 Title Fax # (612) 644-9848
Editorial Description: Areas of adoption and children in temporary care; permanency for all children; advocacy for waiting children.
General Info: Yr. Est. 1974, Quarterly, Trim Size-11 x 17, Offset press, 8 pages, No Color
Subscriptions: Indv. $30
Circulation: Total-5,000

Adventures in Movement *Business, Consumer*

Publishing Co: Adventures in Movement for Handicapped Children, 945 Danbury Rd, Dayton, OH 45420-1606; Title Tel # (513) 294-4611 Title Fax # (513) 294-3783
Personnel: Editor-Belinda Long
General Info: Yr. Est. 1958, Quarterly, Trim Size-8½ x 11, Desktop press, 10 pages, 2 Color
Subscriptions: Free
Circulation: Total-10,000
Advertising: Inquire for rates. Accepts Inserts.

Advocate, The

Publishing Co: Alberta Assn. of Social Workers, #52, 9912 106th Street, Edmonton, AB T5K 1C5 Canada; Title Tel # (403) 421-1167 Title Fax # (403) 421-1168
Personnel: Editor-Hazel Sangster
General Info: Yr. Est. 1975, Bi-monthly, Trim Size-8½ x 11, 16 pages, ISSN: 0847-2890
Subscriptions: Indv. $20

Aging Digest
See: SENIOR CITIZENS

Aging News Alert
See: SENIOR CITIZENS

Al-Anon in Institutions — *Consumer, Association*

Publishing Co: Al-Anon Family Group Headquarters, Inc., 1600 Corporate Landing Pkwy., Virginia Beach, VA 23456 Tel # (804) 563-1600; Title Tel # (212) 302-7240 Title Fax # (212) 869-3757
Personnel: Editor-Claire Ricewasser
Editorial Description: Experiences of Al-Anon and Alateen members in institutions; includes suggestions for forming groups, and using Al-Anon literature.
General Info: Yr. Est. 1974, Offset press, 4 pages, ISSN: 1054-142X
Subscriptions: Indv. $2, Free To Qualified Recipient
Circulation: (50% controlled), Total-4,000, Subscriptions-2,000

Al-Anon Speaks Out — *Consumer, Association*

Publishing Co: Al-Anon Family Group Headquarters, Inc., 1600 Corporate Landing Pkwy., Virginia Beach, VA 23456 Tel # (804) 563-1600; Title Tel # (212) 302-7240 Title Fax # (212) 869-3757
Personnel: Editor-Ellen Duffy
Editorial Description: Al-Anon Speaks Out provides an explanation of the Al-Anon/Alateen program & how it works; reports on developments & items of interest in the fellowship & explains how members cooperate with the professional community.
General Info: Yr. Est. 1978, Semi-annually, 2 pages, ISSN: 1054-1446, 2 Color, Coated
Subscriptions: Free
Circulation: Total-6,000

Alateen Talk — *Consumer, Association*

Publishing Co: Al-Anon Family Group Headquarters, Inc., 1600 Corporate Landing Pkwy., Virginia Beach, VA 23456 Tel # (804) 563-1600; Title Tel # (212) 302-7240 Title Fax # (212) 869-3757
Personnel: Editor-Bonnie Cummings
Editorial Description: A newsletter for teens whose lives have been affected by someone else's drinking. The Alateen members share their experience, strength & hope through written words & drawings. Alateen is a part of Al-Anon's self-help Twelve Step program.
General Info: Yr. Est. 1961, Quarterly, Trim Size-$8\frac{1}{2}$ x 11, Web press, 4 pages, ISSN: 1054-1411, 2 Color, Coated
Subscriptions: Indv. $3, Inst. $8, $1/copy
Circulation: Total-5,000
Printing Co: Spanish American Printing, 231 W 18th St, New York, NY 10011-4582 Tel # (212) 243-7952

Altrusa Accent

Publishing Co: Altrusa Intl., Inc., 332 S. Michigan Ave., Chicago, IL 60604-4301; Title Tel # (312) 427-4410
Personnel: Editor-Mimi Stewart, Circ. Mgr., Promotion Dir.-Susan Day
Editorial Description: Official newsletter of Altrusa Intl., an intl. organization of locally-based clubs providing service to the community.
General Info: Yr. Est. 1985, Quarterly, Sheetfed press, 12 pages, No Color, Newsprint
Subscriptions: Indv. $8, $2/copy
Circulation: Total-18,000

Americans with Disabilities Newsletter
See: DISABILITY

America's Spirit — *Consumer*

Publishing Co: United Service Organizations, Inc., Washington Navy Yard, 901 M Street SE Building 198, Washington, DC 20374-5096 Tel # (202) 610-5700 Fax # (202) 610-5701; Title Tel # (202) 783-8121 Title Fax # (202) 638-4716
Personnel: Editor-Amy Adler
Editorial Description: Describes the activities & events sponsored by USO World Headquarters & USO locations around the world.
General Info: Yr. Est. 1965, Quarterly, 4 pages, ISSN: 0886-1996, 2 Color, Newsprint
Acquistions: Publication Bought
Circulation: Total-100,000

Archives Sharing Bulletin
See: HEALTH

Arson Prevention Idea File
See: FIRE PROTECTION

Assembly Lines Newsletter — *Association*

Publishing Co: Sponsor-The National Collaboration for Youth, National Collaboration for Youth, 1319 F St., NW, Ste. 601, Washington, DC 20004 Fax # (202) 393-4517; Title Tel # (202) 347-2080
Personnel: Editor-Kim Helfgott
Editorial Description: Youth development agencies including the Scouts, 4-H, Big Brothers/Big Sisters of America, Boys & Girls Clubs, and others collaborate to increase publica awareness of youth needs and improve services for youth.
General Info: (Formerly NCY Today), Yr. Est. 1984, Semi-annually, Offset press, 4 pages, Color
Circulation: Total-2,000

Association, The — *Association*

Publishing Co: National Indian Social Workers Association, PO Box 45, Valentine, AZ 86437-0045
Circulation: Total-200

Birthright Life-Guardian

Publishing Co: Birthright Intl., 777 Coxwell Ave., Toronto, ON M4C 3C6 Canada; Title Tel # (416) 469-4789 Title Fax # (416) 469-1772
Personnel: Editor-Mary Berney, Product Mgr.-Elizabeth Burman
General Info: Yr. Est. 1970, Bi-monthly, Trim Size-8.5 x 11, Other press, 8 pages, Other, Saddle-stitched
Subscriptions: Indv. $10, Can. $10, Free With Membership
Circulation: Total-1,500
Printing Co: The Printing House, 16 Cumberland St., Toronto, ON M4W 1J5 Canada Tel # (416) 924-1416

Black Child Advocate
See: CHILDREN

Board Fund Raising Strategies — *Business*

Publishing Co: Aspen Publishers, Inc., 200 Orchard Ridge Dr., Ste 200, Gaithersburg, MD 20878-5440 Parent Co.-Wolters Kluwer US Corporation, New York; Title Tel # (301) 417-7500 Title Fax # (301) 417-7655
Personnel: Editor-Sheri Campbell
Editorial Description: A four-page section for the administrator where peers share practical strategies they've used successfully to motivate their board members to generate sources of revenue.
General Info: Yr. Est. 1981, Monthly
Subscriptions: Indv. $129, For. $155, $13/copy
List Rental: List Management Co.: Stevens-Knox List Management, 304 Park Ave S., New York, NY 10010-5312 Tel # (212) 388-8800, Fax # (212) 388-8890

Box Project-Newsletter

Publishing Co: Box Project, PO Box 435, Plainville, CT 06062-0435; Title Tel # (203) 747-8182
Personnel: Editor-Nancy Normen
General Info: Yr. Est. 1962, 5x/yr.
Circulation: Total-4,500

Bread for the World Newsletter — *Association*

Publishing Co: Bread for the World Inst., 1100 Wayne Ave Ste 1000, Silver Spring, MD 20910-5603; Title Tel # (301) 608-2400 Title Fax # (301) 608-2401
Personnel: Editor-Carol Zimmerman
Editorial Description: Newsletter of Bread for the World, a Christian citizen's lobby on hunger issues.
General Info: Yr. Est. 1974, 8x/yr., Trim Size-$8\frac{1}{4}$ x $10\frac{1}{2}$, 12 pages, ISSN: 1045-1005, 2 Color, Saddle-stitched
Subscriptions: Indv. $25
Circulation: Total-42,000

Brother

Publishing Co: Natl. Org. for Men Against Sexism, 1812 Arctic Blvd, Anchorage, AK 99503-1812; Title Tel # (907) 277-7293
Personnel: Editor-Robert Heasley
General Info: Yr. Est. 1982, Quarterly, 8 pages
Circulation: Total-1,000

CALM Newsletter

Publishing Co: Child Abuse Listening Mediation, Inc., PO Box 90754, Santa Barbara, CA 93190-0754; Title Tel # (805) 965-2376
Personnel: Editor-Linda Rae
General Info: Quarterly, 4 pages

CAN Do

Publishing Co: Community Action Network, 211 E 43rd St Rm 1400, New York, NY 10017-4707; Title Tel # (212) 818-1360
Personnel: Publisher-Norman Glenn, Editor-Jim Mann
Editorial Description: Ideas for the solution of critical social problems.
General Info: Yr. Est. 1988, Sheetfed press, 4 pages

CARE World Report — *Association*

Publishing Co: CARE, 151 Ellis Street, Atlanta, GA 30303 Fax # (404) 577-6271; Title Tel # (404) 681-2552
Personnel: Editor-Matthew De Galan
Editorial Description: Interesting overseas stories & domestic fundraising events.
General Info: Yr. Est. 1972, Quarterly, Trim Size-8.5 x 11, Sheetfed press, 8 pages, 2 Color, Newsprint, Other
Circulation: Total-500,000
List Rental: Actives: $55/M

CD-Housing Register
See: REAL ESTATE

CFLE Network — *Association* — CPM: $230

Publishing Co: Natl. Council on Family Relations, 3989 Central Ave. NE, Ste. 550, Minneapolis, MN 55421-3972 Tel # (612) 781-9331 Fax # (612) 781-9348
Editorial Description: Cover family life education issues as well as matters related to the certification program.
General Info: Quarterly, Trim Size-8.5 x 11
Circulation: Total-650
Advertising: $150.
List Rental: Rents Lists

CHF Newsbriefs
See: INTERNATIONAL AFFAIRS

Cal Fam
See: PSYCHOLOGY

California Department of Social Welfare, Circular Letter

Publishing Co: California State Department of Social Welfare, 744 P St., Sacramento, CA 95814-6413 Tel # (916) 657-3661; Title Tel # (916) 322-2400

California Department of Social Welfare, Department Bulletin

Publishing Co: California State Department of Social Welfare, 744 P St., Sacramento, CA 95814-6413 Tel # (916) 657-3661

Canadaid: A News Report to Sponsors and Friends   *Association*

Publishing Co: Christian Children's Fund of Canada, 1027 McNicoll Ave. E., Scarborough, ON M1W 3X2 Canada; Title Tel # (416) 495-1174 Title Fax # (416) 495-9395
Personnel: Editor-Mary-Lynne Stewart, Contrib. Ed.-Graham Knope, Production Mgr., Art Dir.-Julie Nurse
Editorial Description: Administration of person-to-person sponsorship of 35,000 Third World children, & integrated community development projects.
General Info: Yr. Est. 1969, Quarterly, Trim Size-11 x 8½, Sheetfed press, 6 pages, 4 Color, Newsprint
Circulation: (100% controlled), Total-65,000
Printing Co: Cober Printing, 844 Courtland Ave., E., Kitchener, ON N2C 1K3 Canada Tel # (519) 745-7136

Canadian Red Cross Society News and Views   *Association*

Publishing Co: Canadian Red Cross Society, Manitoba Div., 226 Osborne St. N., Winnipeg, MB R3C 1V4 Canada; Title Tel # (204) 772-2551
Personnel: Editor-Kay Beggs, Publisher, Circ. Mgr.-Terry Hind
Editorial Description: Red Cross services and programs in Manitoba, fund raising needs.
General Info: Yr. Est. 1971, Quarterly, Trim Size-11 x 15, Offset press, 8 pages, ISSN: 0770-9828, 2 Color
Circulation: (100% controlled), Total-6,500

Capsule   *Consumer*

Publishing Co: Children of Aging Parents, 1609 Woodbourne Rd., Woodbourne Office Campus #302A, Levittown, PA 19057-1506; Title Tel # (215) 945-6900
Personnel: Editor-LOuise Fradkin, Art Dir.-Leon Fradkin
Editorial Description: Information on issues relating to care giving of the elderly and to support groups.
General Info: Yr. Est. 1983, Bi-monthly, Trim Size-8½ x 11, Offset press, 4 pages, No Color, Newsprint
Subscriptions: Indv. $20, Inst. $100, For. $40
Circulation: Total-2,000

Caring Connection   *Association*

Publishing Co: Handicap News, 3060 E Bridge St Lot 342, Brighton, CO 80601-2724; Title Tel # (303) 659-4463
Personnel: Publisher, Editor-Phyllis Burns
Editorial Description: News on rights, medical research, and other topics of interest to caregivers of the ill, frail and disabled.
General Info: (Formerly Handicap News), Yr. Est. 1984, Monthly, Offset press, 3 pages
Subscriptions: Indv. $14, Can. $30, For. $42, $2/copy
Acquistions: Publication Bought
Circulation: Total-500

Carolina Justice Policy Center News
See: LAW ENFORCEMENT & PENOLOGY

Casa Cry

Publishing Co: Casa Maria Catholic Worker, 1131 N 21st St # 5206, Milwaukee, WI 53233-1110; Title Tel # (414) 344-5745
Personnel: Publisher, Editor-Don Timmerman
Editorial Description: Contains local, nationals & international worlds in context of Christian living.
General Info: (Formerly Catholic Radical), Yr. Est. 1973, Monthly
Printing Co: Kinkos Copies, 1634 W Wisconsin Ave, Milwaukee, WI 53233-2112 Tel # (414) 344-3506

Catalyst   CPM: $250

Publishing Co: North American Association of Christians in Social Work, PO Box 7090, Saint Davids, PA 19087-7090 Tel # (610) 687-5777; Title Tel # (215) 687-5777 Title Fax # (215) 321-1460
Personnel: Publisher, Editor-Edward Kuhlmann, Circ. Mgr.-Jean Claude Cerin
Editorial Description: Informs members about the programs of NACSW.
General Info: Yr. Est. 1958, Bi-monthly, Desktop press, 4 pages
Subscriptions: Free With Membership
Circulation: Total-1,000
Advertising: $250.
List Rental: Actives: $120/M

Catalyst Newsletter
See: LAW ENFORCEMENT & PENOLOGY

Center on Social Welfare Policy and Law Library Bulletin
See: LIBRARY

Center for the Study of Human Rights Newsletter

Publishing Co: Center for the Study of Human Rights, Columbia Univ., 420 W. 118th St., New York, NY 10027-2399; Title Tel # (212) 854-2479
Personnel: Editor-Judith Shampanier
General Info: Quarterly, 4 pages, Matte
Circulation: Total-800

Chain of Life   *Consumer*

Publishing Co: Chain of Life, PO Box 8081, Berkeley, CA 94707-8081

Chalice   *Association*

Publishing Co: Calix Society, 7601 Wayzata Blvd., Minneapolis, MN 55426-1626; Title Tel # (612) 546-0544
Personnel: Editor-R. Dickinson
Editorial Description: News about society and articles on alcoholism and spiritual recovery.
General Info: Yr. Est. 1947, Bi-monthly, 6 pages, No Color
Subscriptions: Indv. $15
Circulation: Total-1,500

Changemakers

Publishing Co: Ashoka: Innovators for the Public, 1700 N. Moore St., Suite 1920, Arlington, VA 22209-3644; Title Tel # (703) 527-8300 Title Fax # (703) 527-8383
Personnel: Publisher-Sushmita Ghosh, Editor-Manisha Gupta
Editorial Description: Quarterly magazine published for the Ashoka fellowship which highlights the work of social entrepreneurs in developing countries.
General Info: Yr. Est. 1991, Quarterly, Desktop press, 40 pages, Coated, Saddle-stitched
Subscriptions: Indv. $25, $7/copy
Circulation: Total-1,000
Advertising: Inquire for rates.

Cherokee Boys Club-Newsletter & Cherokee Voice
See: ETHNIC

Child Development Research News

Publishing Co: Child Development Research, 30 Soundview Ln, Sands Point, NY 11050-1341; Title Tel # (516) 883-7135
General Info: Semi-annually
Subscriptions: Indv. $35

Child Protection Report
See: CHILDREN

Child Welfare Report (CWR)   *Business*   CPM$1099

Publishing Co: Jones Publishing Inc., N7450 Aanstad Rd., PO Box 5000, Iola, WI 54945-5000; Title Tel # (715) 445-5000 Title Fax # (715) 445-4053
Personnel: Publisher-Scott Kolpien, Asst. Pub.-Gregory Bayer, Editor-Carol Woodmansee, Circ. Mgr., Adv. Dir.-Barb Beyersdorf, Art Dir.-Julie King
Editorial Description: Provides practical solutions for administrators of foster care agencies.
General Info: Yr. Est. 1993, Monthly, Trim Size-8½ x 11, Sheetfed press, 13 pages, ISSN: 1073-5666, 2 Color, Matte
Subscriptions: Indv. $149, Can. $159, For. $159
Circulation: Total-221
Advertising: $243. Accepts Inserts.
List Rental: Actives: 221, $150/M, Expires: 889, $125/M

Children & Youth Funding Report
See: PHILANTHROPY

Christian Aid Ministries Newsletter

Publishing Co: Christian Aid for Romania, PO Box 360, Berlin, OH 44610-0360; Title Tel # (216) 893-2428 Title Fax # (330) 893-2305
Personnel: Editor-David Toyer
General Info: (Formerly Through the Iron Curtain with Love), Monthly

Clinic News

Publishing Co: Center for Population Options, 1025 Vermont Ave NW Ste 210, Washington, DC 20005-3516; Title Tel # (202) 347-5700 Title Fax # (202) 347-2263
General Info: Yr. Est. 1984, Quarterly, Trim Size-8½ x 11, 8 pages, Coated
Subscriptions: Indv. $15, Can. $25
Circulation: Total-500
List Rental: Rents Lists

Common Ground   *Business, Association*

Publishing Co: United Way of Summit County, 90 N Prospect St #1260, Akron, OH 44304-1273; Title Tel # (216) 762-7601 Title Fax # (216) 762-0317
Personnel: Publisher-Gerard Cerny, Editor-Lisa Millovich, Mktg. Dir.-Lisa Swan
Editorial Description: A quarterly publication distributed to volunteers, non-profit agencies, companies and contributors affiliated with United Way of Summit County.
General Info: (Formerly Insights), Yr. Est. 1992, Quarterly, Trim Size-17 x 11, Desktop press, 4 pages, Matte, Other
Subscriptions: Free
Circulation: Total-4,300
Printing Co: The Printing System, Main St., Akron, OH 44308 Tel # (216) 375-9128

Communique

Publishing Co: Children's Aid Society of Ottawa-Carleton, 1602 Telesat Ct., Gloucester, ON K1B
1B1 Canada; Title Tel # (613) 748-0670
Personnel: Editor-C. Johnson
Editorial Description: Covers programs, needs of agency and special events.
General Info: (Formerly CAS Record), Yr. Est. 1965, Letrpr. press, 8 pages, Color
Circulation: (100% controlled), Total-3,500

Communique
See: DISABILITY

Community
See: PUBLIC MANAGEMENT & PLANNING

Community Change
See: GOVERNMENT

Community Health Funding Report
See: PHILANTHROPY

Compassion Today
See: CHILDREN

Concern News   *Association*

Publishing Co: Project Concern Intl., 3550 Afton Rd, San Diego, CA 92123-2165;
Title Tel # (619) 279-9690
Personnel: Co-Editor-C. Goldberg, Editor, Circ. Mgr., Art Dir.-V. Blackwell
Editorial Description: Healthcare training & development organization serving needy people in
America & abroad.
General Info: Yr. Est. 1961, Quarterly, Trim Size-8½ x 11, Offset press, 4 pages, 2 Color
Circulation: (100% controlled), Total-7,000

Conciliation Quarterly   *Consumer, Association*

Publishing Co: Mennonite Central Committee, PO Box 500, 21 South 12th St., Akron, PA
17501-0500 Tel # (717) 859-1151 Fax # (717) 859-2171
Personnel: Editor-Alice Price, Co-Editor-Carolyn Schrock Shenk, Co-Editor-Jim Stutzman
Editorial Description: Presents techniques & information in the field of dispute resolution.
General Info: (Formerly Occasional Quarterly), Yr. Est. 1982, Quarterly, Trim Size-8½ x 11, Offset
press, 12 pages, 2 Color, Matte, Saddle-stitched
Subscriptions: Indv. $12
Circulation: Total-2,000
Printing Co: MCC, PO Box 500, Akron, PA 17501-0500

Connections   *Association*

Publishing Co: Washington State Dept. of Social & Health, Mail Stop Ob-46, Olympia, WA
98504-0001; Title Tel # (206) 753-1165
Personnel: Editor-Kathy Davis
General Info: (Formerly Overview), Quarterly, Trim Size-8½ x 11, 20 pages, 2 Color

Connector   *Consumer, Association*

Publishing Co: Minnesota State Council on Disability, 121 7th Pl E Ste 107, Saint Paul, MN
55101-2114; Title Tel # (612) 296-6785 Title Fax # (612) 296-5935
Editorial Description: Articles on programs and services concerning disabled persons.
General Info: (Formerly Handicaptions), Yr. Est. 1975, Bi-monthly, Trim Size-8½ x 11½, Offset
press, 4 pages, No Color
Circulation: Total-8,500

Correspondent

Publishing Co: Big Brothers/Big Sisters of America, 230 N 13th St, Philadelphia, PA 19107-1538;
Title Tel # (215) 567-7000
Personnel: Editor-George Beiswinger
Editorial Description: Affiliated agency newsletter.
General Info: (Formerly Communicator), Sheetfed press, 8 pages
Circulation: (100% controlled), Total-10,000
Advertising: Inquire for rates.

Crime & Drug Report
See: LAW ENFORCEMENT & PENOLOGY

Crime Prevention News
See: LAW ENFORCEMENT & PENOLOGY

Crimes Eye Newsletter

Publishing Co: Natl. Assn. for Crime Victims Rights, PO Box 16161, Portland, OR 97216-0161;
Title Tel # (503) 252-9012
Editorial Description: Concerned with the rights of crime victims.
General Info: Bi-monthly
Circulation: Total-2,100

Cropwalker, The   *Association*

Publishing Co: Church World Service, 28606 Phillips St, Elkhart, IN 46514-1239;
Title Tel # (219) 264-3102 Title Fax # (219) 262-0966
Personnel: Editor-Frances Jones
Editorial Description: Provides news relating to overseas need and response for volunteer leaders
of CEFR, the Community Hunger Appeal of Church World Service, and of the Church World
Service Clothing Appeal.
General Info: (Formerly Service News/Harvest), Yr. Est. 1947, 2x/yr., Trim Size-11½ x 15, Web
press, 8 pages, Color, Coated
Subscriptions: Free
Circulation: Total-140,000

Crossroads   *Association*

Publishing Co: American Red Cross, 1900 25th Ave S, Seattle, WA 98144-4708;
Title Tel # (206) 323-2345
Personnel: Editor-Chris Ramos, Art Dir.-Don Smith
Editorial Description: Provides coverage of the Seattle-Kings County chapter of the American Red
Cross in terms of disastor relief, community involvement, the continuous development of new
programs & volunteerism.
General Info: (Formerly Red Cross News), Quarterly, Trim Size-8½ x 11, Web press, 8 pages, 2
Color, Coated
Subscriptions: Free
Circulation: Total-20,000

Cryer, The

Publishing Co: California Children's Lobby, PO Box 448, Sacramento, CA 95812-0448;
Title Tel # (916) 444-7477
Personnel: Editor-Katan Kinder
Editorial Description: Objective, non-partisan class advocacy for children.
General Info: Yr. Est. 1970, 9x/yr., Trim Size-8½ x 11, Desktop press, 4 pages
Subscriptions: Indv. $30
Acquistions: Publication Bought, Publication Sold
Circulation: Total-1,800

DLD Times
See: EDUCATION

DRC Mississippi
Newsletter

Publishing Co: Delta Resources Committee, Inc., PO Box 584, Greenville, MS 38702-0584;
Title Tel # (601) 335-3121
Personnel: Editor-Rev. Roger Smith
Editorial Description: A pub. by an ecumenical church related organization for the dual purpose of
disseminating information on church & society & raising funds for a wholistic ministry.
General Info: Yr. Est. 1972, Quarterly, Trim Size-8½ x 14, Offset press, 2 pages, Color
Circulation: (100% controlled), Total-1,500
Advertising: Accepts Inserts.
Printing Co: Office Supply Co., 640 Washington Ave, Greenville, MS 38701-3621

DSS Newsletter

Publishing Co: Baltimore City Dept. of Social Services, 1500 Greenmount Ave, Baltimore, MD
21202-3926; Title Tel # (301) 361-2002 Title Fax # (301) 361-3150
Personnel: Publisher-Shirley Marcus, Editor, Circ. Mgr., Adv. Dir., Art Dir.-Sue Fitzsimmons
Editorial Description: Events within the agency & of interest to employees.
General Info: Yr. Est. 1975, Monthly, Trim Size-8½ x 11, Mimeo press, 15 pages, No Color
Acquistions: Publication Bought
Circulation: (100% controlled), Total-3,000

Daffodil News

Publishing Co: Canadian Cancer Society-Ontario Div., 1639 Yonge St., Toronto, ON M4T 2W6
Canada; Title Tel # (416) 488-5400
Personnel: Circ. Mgr.-L. Boreland
Editorial Description: Recognition, information, & motivational articles for Ontario Division
volunteers.
General Info: (Formerly Canadian Cancer Society Ontario Division), Monthly, Trim Size-11 x 17, Web
press, 4 pages, 2 Color, Newsprint
Circulation: (100% controlled), Total-7,500

Disability Funding News
See: PHILANTHROPY

Domestic Abuse Is Not An
Indian Tradition

Publishing Co: Ne-Naiah-Kaha-Kok, PO Box 1055, Keshena, WI 54135-1055;
Title Tel # (715) 799-4398
General Info: Yr. Est. 1975, 225 pages, Looseleaf
Subscriptions: $25/copy
Circulation: (CAC)

Dovetail: A Newsletter By and For Jewish-Christian Families
See: RELIGIOUS & THEOLOGICAL

Drug Policy Report
See: LAW ENFORCEMENT & PENOLOGY

Drumbeat · *Association*

Publishing Co: Salvation Army Carolinas Division, PO Box 241808, Charlotte, NC 28224-1808; Title Tel # (704) 375-9881
Personnel: Editor-John Edwards
Editorial Description: Salvation Army activities, news/perspectives.
General Info: Yr. Est. 1981, Quarterly, Trim Size-8½ x 11, Sheetfed press, 6 pages, 2 Color, Newsprint
Subscriptions: Free
Acquistions: Publication Bought
Circulation: (100% controlled), Total-82,000

E.M.S. Officer's Notebook
See: MEDICINE

Economic Opportunity Report · *Business*

Publishing Co: Business Publishers, Inc., 951 Pershing Dr., Silver Spring, MD 20910-4464 Tel # (301) 589-5103 Fax # (301) 589-8493; Title Tel # (301) 587-6300 Title Fax # (301) 587-1081
Personnel: Publisher-Eric Easton, Editor-Jay Fletcher, Circ. Mgr.-Kathleen Harrow, Promotion Dir.-Connie Arnold
Editorial Description: Weekly roundup of news on antipoverty programs, including nutrition, health, housing, education, homeless assistance, job training, Congressional and White House initiatives, and more.
General Info: Yr. Est. 1965, 50x/yr., Trim Size-8½ x 11, Desktop press, 8 pages, ISSN: 0013-0206, Ind/Abs/Online: Newsnet and Predicasts, No Color, Recycled, Other
Subscriptions: Indv. $365, Can. $365, For. $390
Advertising: Accepts Inserts.
List Rental: List Management Co.: Manager: Don Peterson; BPI Direct, 951 Pershing Dr., Silver Spring, MD 20910-4464 Tel # (301) 585-5976, Fax # (301) 587-4530
Printing Co: Business Publishers In-House Print Shop, 951 Pershing Drive, Silver Spring, MD 20910-4454 Tel # (301) 589-8493

FMS Foundation

Publishing Co: FMS Foundation, 3401 Market Street, Suite #130, Philadelphia, PA 19104; Title Tel # (215) 387-1865 Title Fax # (215) 387-1917
General Info: 10x/yr., Trim Size-8½ x 10½, 20 pages, ISSN: 1069-0484, No Color, Matte, Saddle-stitched
Subscriptions: Indv. $30, Can. $35, For. $40, $3/copy

Families in Crisis Funding Report
See: FAMILY

Federal Assistance Monitor
See: PHILANTHROPY

Feeding the Hungry · *Consumer*

Publishing Co: Food for the Hungry, 7729 E Greenway Rd, Scottsdale, AZ 85260-1795; Title Tel # (602) 998-3100 Title Fax # (612) 998-4806
Personnel: Publisher-Ted Yamamri, Editor-Karen Randau, Production Mgr.-Kirk Calkins, Art Dir.-Lisa Leff
Editorial Description: World hunger perspectives.
General Info: (Formerly Food for the Hungry), Yr. Est. 1982, Monthly, Trim Size-7 x 10, Web press, 16 pages, 2 Color, Saddle-stitched
Circulation: Total-50,000
List Rental: List Management Co.: Bernice Bush Co./Springdale Lists, 15052 Springdale St., Huntington Beach, CA 92649-1178 Tel # (714) 891-3344, Fax # (714) 897-0650

Food First Books
See: FOOD

Food First News & Views · *Consumer, Association*

Publishing Co: Institute for Food & Development, 398 60th St, Oakland, CA 94618-1212; Title Tel # (510) 654-4400 Title Fax # (510) 654-4551
Personnel: Editor-Walden Bello, Circ. Mgr.-Marilyn Borchardt
General Info: (Formerly Food First), Yr. Est. 1975, Quarterly, Trim Size-8½ x 11, Offset press, 8 pages, No Color, Recycled
Subscriptions: Indv. $30, Inst. $100, Can. $35, For. $35
Circulation: Total-20,000
List Rental: List Management Co.: Names in the News-California, 1 Bush St Bsmt 3, San Francisco, CA 94104-4425 Tel # (415) 989-3350, Fax # (415) 433-7796, Actives: 11,000, $60/M

Global Link

Publishing Co: Canadian Hunger Foundation., 323 Chapel St., Ottawa, ON K1N 7Z2 Canada; Title Tel # (613) 237-0180
Personnel: Editor-Bruce Moore
Editorial Description: Text in English.
General Info: (Formerly Thought for Food), Yr. Est. 1979, Quarterly, 8 pages, ISSN: 0715-7320, Ind/Abs/Online: Bk. Rev.
Circulation: Total-10,000

Global Missions · *Consumer, Association*

Publishing Co: International Christian Leprosy Mission, Inc., PO Box 23353, Portland, OR 97281-3353; Title Tel # (503) 244-5935 Title Fax # (503) 244-5935
Personnel: Editor-June Pillers
General Info: Yr. Est. 1943, 4 pages
Circulation: Total-2,000

Gold Pages, The

Publishing Co: Seniors Inc. of Centerville/Washington Twp., 8100 Clyo Rd, Centerville, OH 45458-2720; Title Tel # (513) 435-2415
Editorial Description: Senior citizen center newsletter.
General Info: Yr. Est. 1982, Monthly
Circulation: Total-450
Advertising: Inquire for rates.

Goodwill Dimensions

Publishing Co: Goodwill Industries of Toronto, 234 Adelaide St., E., Toronto, ON M5A 1M9 Canada; Title Tel # (416) 362-4711 Title Fax # (416) 362-0720
Personnel: Editor-Mary Lou Frazer
Editorial Description: Covers Goodwill's various services & depts.
General Info: (Formerly Good News), Yr. Est. 1988, Semi-annually, Trim Size-11 x 17, Web press, 4 pages, 2 Color, Newsprint
Subscriptions: Free
Circulation: Total-25,000

Goodwill News
See: DISABILITY

Grapevine, The (Genesee Valley)
See: ETHNIC

HAI News · *Consumer, Association*

Publishing Co: Hospital Audiences, Inc. (HAI), 220 West 42 Street, New York, NY 10036 Tel # (212) 575-7676 Fax # (212) 575-7669
Editorial Description: Information on the programs and activities of HAI, which provides art and cultural experiences for the disabled.
General Info: Irregular, Trim Size-11 x 14, 12 pages, No Color, Coated, Saddle-stitched

HIV - Drug Exposure & Foster Care: Network Bulletin · *Association, Consumer*

Publishing Co: Leake & Watts, 487 S Broadway Ste 201, Yonkers, NY 10705-3252; Title Tel # (914) 376-4415
Personnel: Editor-Michele Erazo
Editorial Description: Information on HIV and prenatal drug exposure for foster care professionals.
General Info: (Formerly Pediatric AIDS Foster Care Network Bulletin), Yr. Est. 1989, 3x/yr., Trim Size-8½ x 11, Offset press, 12 pages, 2 Color, Matte
Circulation: Total-2,500

HIV Connect
See: HEALTH

Hadassah Update

Publishing Co: Hadassah, 50 W 58th St, New York, NY 10019-2590; Title Tel # (212) 355-7900
Personnel: Editor-Marc Brandress
General Info: Bi-weekly

Happenings
See: CHILDREN

Hazelden Voice · *Business, Association*

Publishing Co: Hazelden Foundation, 15251 Pleasant Valley Rd., PO Box 11, Center City, MN 55012-0011; Title Tel # (612) 213-4455
Personnel: Editor-Marty Duda
Editorial Description: Chemical dependency prevention & treatment.
General Info: (Formerly Hazelden News and Professional Update), Yr. Est. 1983, Semi-annually, Trim Size-8½ x 11, Sheetfed press, 8 pages, 2 Color, Newsprint
Circulation: Total-90,000

Highlander Reports · *Consumer, Association*

Publishing Co: Highlander Research & Education Center, Inc., 1959 Highlander Way, New Market, TN 37820; Title Tel # (423) 933-3443 Title Fax # (423) 933-3424
Editorial Description: Covers programs and activities of the Center
General Info: (Formerly Report from Highlander), Yr. Est. 1955, Quarterly, 4 pages
Circulation: Total-8,000

Homecare Administrative Horizons
See: HEALTH

Homecare Direction
See: HEALTH

IAAOC Report
See: LAW ENFORCEMENT & PENOLOGY

ICPA Quarterly Bulletin · *Association*

Publishing Co: Narcotics Education, Inc., 12501 Old Columbia Pike, Silver Spring, MD 20904-6601; Title Tel # (301) 680-6719 Title Fax # (301) 680-6090
Personnel: Editor-Thomas Neslund
Editorial Description: Presents activities of ICPA in its world wide prevention program.
General Info: Yr. Est. 1955, Quarterly, 8 pages, No Color
Subscriptions: Indv. $4, Can. $5
Circulation: Total-6,000

IFCO Newsletter *Association*

Publishing Co: Interreligious Foundation for Community Organization, 402 W. 145th St., New York, NY 10031-5202 Fax # (212) 926-5842; Title Tel # (212) 926-5757
Personnel: Editor-Gail Walker
General Info: Yr. Est. 1970, Bi-monthly

IPJ Newsletter

Publishing Co: Institute for Peace & Justice, 4144 Lindell Blvd Ste 122, Saint Louis, MO 63108-2931; Title Tel # (314) 533-4445
Personnel: Editor-Jim Ford
Editorial Description: Supports IPJ in its mission of peace & justice education, public awareness, & response.
General Info: Yr. Est. 1979, Trim Size-8½ x 11, Sheetfed press, 6 pages, No Color
Subscriptions: Indv. $3
Circulation: Total-1,300
Printing Co: Peace Institute Printing, 4436 Olive St, Saint Louis, MO 63108-1808

ISS Newsletter *Association*

Publishing Co: International Social Service, 390 Park Ave S Fl 7, New York, NY 10016-8803; Title Tel # (212) 532-5858
Personnel: Editor-Marie Mercer
General Info: Yr. Est. 1957, Quarterly

I.V.U.N. News
See: HEALTH

Infolines
See: HEALTH

Inside Al-Anon
See: HEALTH

Interfaith Impact & Preparedness
See: RELIGIOUS & THEOLOGICAL

JACS Volunteer
See: EMPLOYMENT

JDC World

Publishing Co: American Jewish Joint Distribution Committee, 711 3rd Ave., New York, NY 10017-4039; Title Tel # (212) 687-6200 Title Fax # (212) 370-5467
Personnel: Production Mgr.-Miriam Feldman
Editorial Description: Reports on global humanitarian work of JDC.
General Info: Yr. Est. 1976, Semi-annually, Trim Size-8½ x 11, Sheetfed press, 12 pages, Color-cover, Coated, Saddle-stitched
Acquistions: Publication Bought
Circulation: Total-30,000

Juvenile Law Reports
See: LAW

Keeping the Trust *Business*

Publishing Co: Cleveland Foundation, 1400 Hanna Bldg., 1422 Euclid Ave., Cleveland, OH 44115-2001; Title Tel # (216) 861-3810 Title Fax # (216) 861-1729
Personnel: Editor-Lynne E. Woodman
General Info: Yr. Est. 1986, Quarterly, Trim Size-8½ x 11½, 6 pages, 2 Color, Matte
Subscriptions: Free
Circulation: Total-5,000

Kesher
See: RELIGIOUS & THEOLOGICAL

Latino
See: ETHNIC

Latinogram
See: ETHNIC

Leadership Times
See: EDUCATION

Learning Disabilities Assn. of California *Association*

Publishing Co: Learning Disabilities Assn. LDA-CA, 655 Lewelling Blvd # 355, San Leandro, CA 94579-1851; Title Tel # (415) 343-1411 Title Fax # (415) 343-1854
Personnel: Editor-Rob Schiemenz
Editorial Description: Learning Disabilities Assn. of California is a non-profit organization whose purpose is to support the education & general welfare of the learning disabled population.
General Info: (Formerly CANHC-Gram), Yr. Est. 1968, Quarterly, Trim Size-8½ x 11, 16 pages, Matte, Saddle-stitched
Subscriptions: Indv. $10
Acquistions: Publication Bought
Circulation: Total-3,000
Advertising: Inquire for rates.

Legislative Bulletin *Business*

Publishing Co: Michigan League for Human Services, 300 Washington Sq N Ste 401, Lansing, MI 48933-1223; Title Tel # (517) 487-5436
Personnel: Editor-Beverly McDonald
Editorial Description: Includes human service legislation: health, mental health, children and youth, utilities.
General Info: Quarterly, Trim Size-8½ x 11, Offset press, 18 pages, No Color

Liaison
See: ADVERTISING & MARKETING

Lifedate *Association*

Publishing Co: Lutherans for Life, PO Box 819, Benton, AR 72018-0819 Tel # (501) 794-2212 Fax # (501) 794-1437; Title Tel # (612) 645-5444
Personnel: Editor-Ed Fehskens
Editorial Description: A pro-life, religious educational newsletter (abortion, euthanasia, infanticide & family issues). A publication of Lutherans for Life.
General Info: Yr. Est. 1979, Quarterly, Sheetfed press, 4 pages, 2 Color, Newsprint

Link to Link

Publishing Co: Links, Inc., 1200 Massachusetts Ave NW, Washington, DC 20005-4501; Title Tel # (202) 842-8686
Personnel: Editor-Yvone Jefferson
General Info: Quarterly
Circulation: Total-6,100

Linkages
See: FAMILY

Louisiana Cancer Reporter *Association*

Publishing Co: American Cancer Soc. Louisiana Div., 837 Gravier St Ste 700, New Orleans, LA 70112-1509; Title Tel # (504) 522-6823
Personnel: Editor-John DiCarla
Editorial Description: Informative newsletter of the activities of the Louisiana Division, American Cancer Society.
General Info: Yr. Est. 1974, Quarterly, Trim Size-8½ x 11, Letrpr. press, 4 pages, Color
Circulation: (100% controlled), Total-3,000

MRC Relay

Publishing Co: Multi Resource Centers, Inc., 1900 Chicago Ave, Minneapolis, MN 55404-1903; Title Tel # (612) 871-2402
Personnel: Editor-Gary Stern
General Info: Yr. Est. 1983, Quarterly, 8 pages
Circulation: Total-5,000

Making Contact *Association*

Publishing Co: United Way Services, 1331 Euclid Ave., Cleveland, OH 44115; Title Tel # (216) 436-2100 Title Fax # (216) 436-2257
Personnel: Editor-Sharon Artruc
Editorial Description: Human services in the Greater Cleveland area.
General Info: (Formerly United Way Leader; Torchtalk), Quarterly, Trim Size-8½ x 11, Offset press, 8 pages, 2 Color
Circulation: Total-6,000

Meals for Millions/Freedom from Hunger Foundation Newsbriefs

Publishing Co: Meals for Millions/Freedom from Hunger Foundation, PO Box 2000, Davis, CA 95617-2000; Title Tel # (916) 758-6200
Personnel: Editor-Harlan Hobgood
General Info: (Formerly American Freedom from Hunger Foundation-Bulletin)

Medicare and Medicaid Guide *Business*

Publishing Co: CCH, Inc., 2700 Lake Cook Rd., Riverwoods, IL 60015 Parent Co.-Kluwer Law & Taxation Publishers, Cambridge; Title Tel # (847) 267-7000 Title Fax # (800) 224-8299
Editorial Description: Provides complex reimbursement, eligibility and coverage rules for health services plus CCH Specials on key federal bills and Committee Reports.
General Info: (Formerly Medicare), Yr. Est. 1969, Weekly, Trim Size-6 x 9, Web press, 250 pages, No Color, Looseleaf
Subscriptions: Indv. $1,320

Medina Connection *Association*

Publishing Co: Medina Children's Services, 123 16th Ave, Seattle, WA 98122-5684 Tel # (206) 461-4520 Fax # (206) 461-8372
Personnel: Publisher-Dini Duclos
General Info: Yr. Est. 1982, Semi-annually, Trim Size-8½ x 11, 6 pages, No Color, Newsprint
Circulation: Total-2,500

Mennonite Disaster Service-Newsletter

Publishing Co: Mennonite Central Committee, PO Box 500, 21 South 12th St., Akron, PA 17501-0500 Tel # (717) 859-1151 Fax # (717) 859-2171
Personnel: Editor-Lowell Detweiler
General Info: Yr. Est. 1971, Quarterly
Circulation: Total-2,300

Mental Health News Alert
See: PHILANTHROPY

Mentor
See: GENERAL INTEREST

Minority Funding Report *Business*

Publishing Co: Government Information Services, Inc., 4301 Fairfax Dr., Ste. 875, Arlington, VA 22203-1627; Title Tel # (703) 528-1000 Title Fax # (703) 528-6060
Personnel: Publisher-James J. Marshall, Publications Director-Don Hoffman, Editor-David Lytle, Circ. Mgr.-Joyce Gulizia, Mktg. Dir.-Richard Orb
Editorial Description: Covers public and private programs that aid those in need.
General Info: Yr. Est. 1989, Monthly, Trim Size-8½ x 11, 12 pages, ISSN: 1047-3300
Subscriptions: Indv. $128
Printing Co: Newsletter Press, 76 Valley St, East Providence, RI 02914-4424 Tel # (401) 438-5352

Mom's Apple Pie
See: GAY & LESBIAN INTEREST

Mountain Women's Exchange-Newsletter

Publishing Co: Mountain Women's Exchange, 205 5th St, Jellico, TN 37762-2107; Title Tel # (615) 784-8780
Personnel: Editor-Barbara Greene
General Info: Yr. Est. 1979, Bi-monthly
Circulation: Total-200

NAN Bulletin
See: PUBLIC MANAGEMENT & PLANNING

NAPO News

Publishing Co: Natl. Anti-Poverty Org., 256 King Edward Ave., 3rd Fl., Ottawa, ON K1N 7M1 Canada; Title Tel # (613) 789-0096 Title Fax # (613) 789-0141
General Info: Yr. Est. 1983, Quarterly, Sheetfed press, 4 pages, ISSN: 0820-7364, No Color
Subscriptions: Indv. $10
Circulation: Total-1,000

NASW News *Association* **CPM: $17**

Publishing Co: National Association of Social Workers, 750 1st St NE Ste 700, Washington, DC 20002-4241 Fax # (202) 336-8312; Title Tel # (202) 408-8600 Title Fax # (301) 336-8312
Personnel: Editor-Susan Landers, Exec. Ed.-Linda Beebe, Mng. Editor-Scott Moss, Adv. Dir.-Lyn Carter, Mktg. Dir.-Amy Eades, Mktg. Dir.-Peggy O'Hare
Editorial Description: Activities and programs as well as public issues facing social work.
General Info: Yr. Est. 1955, 10x/yr., Trim Size-11½ x 16¼, Web press, 32 pages, 50% ads, 2 Color, Newsprint
Subscriptions: Indv. $25, $3/copy
Circulation: Total-150,000
Advertising: $2,590.

NASWHP Information and Exchange Service

Publishing Co: Natl. Assn. of Sheltered Workshops, Box 17675, Washington, DC 20041-0675; Title Tel # (301) 654-5882
Editorial Description: Publication for exchange of ideas and articles of interest to the national workshop movement.
General Info: Yr. Est. 1967, Monthly
Subscriptions: Indv. $3
Circulation: Total-800
Advertising: Inquire for rates.

NCOA Networks
See: SENIOR CITIZENS

NFADB Newsletter
See: DEAF

NLADA Cornerstone
See: LAW

NRA Newsletter *Association*

Publishing Co: Natl. Rehabilitation Assn., 633 S Washington St, Alexandria, VA 22314-4109; Title Tel # (703) 836-0850
Personnel: Editor-Dr. Paul Leung
Editorial Description: General NRA house organ.
General Info: 8x/yr., Trim Size-8½ x 11, 12 pages
Circulation: Total-17,000
Advertising: Inquire for rates.

Narcotics and Youth

Publishing Co: Natl. Family Council on Drug Addiction, 40 Westminister Dr, Pearl River, NY 10965-2840; Title Tel # (212) 787-7202

National Assistance League Letter

Publishing Co: Natl. Assistance League Letter, 5627 Fernwood Ave., Hollywood, CA 90028-8590; Title Tel # (213) 469-5897

National Center for Children in Poverty News & Issues
See: CHILDREN

National Coalition for the Homeless-Safety Network

Publishing Co: National Coalition for the Homeless, PO Box 2410, Merrifield, VA 22116-2410; Title Tel # (202) 265-2371 Title Fax # (202) 265-2615
Personnel: Editor-Joan Alker
Editorial Description: Reports on natl. & local policies affecting homeless people. Provides information to & on advocacy efforts on behalf of homeless Americans.
General Info: Yr. Est. 1982, Monthly, Sheetfed press, 4 pages
Circulation: Total-15,000
Printing Co: Northern Virginia Sun, 2710-C Prosperity Ave., Fairfax, VA 22031 Tel # (703) 204-2800

National Directory of Private Social Agencies

Publishing Co: Croner Publications, Inc., 34 Jericho Tpke, Jericho, NY 11753-1042; Title Tel # (516) 333-9085 Title Fax # (516) 338-4986
Personnel: Publisher-Ron Guggenheimer, Editor-Carol Sixt, Circ. Mgr.-Regina Friel
Editorial Description: A directory of private social agencies listing agencies by field of service.
General Info: Yr. Est. 1964, Monthly, Trim Size-7½ x 9½, Offset press, Looseleaf
Subscriptions: Indv. $80

National Humanitarian *Association*

Publishing Co: United Humanitarians, PO Box 14587, Philadelphia, PA 19115-0587; Title Tel # (215) 750-0171
Personnel: Editor-Adele Hudson
Editorial Description: Membership news, views, comments on legislation.
General Info: Quarterly, 4 pages, 2 Color, Newsprint
Subscriptions: Indv. $4
Acquistions: Publication Bought
Printing Co: Tursacks Printing, Rt. #23 at 100 Rd. 2, Pottstown, PA 19464 Tel # (215) 469-0260

National Institute of Diaper Services Newsletter *Business*

Publishing Co: Natl. Institute of Diaper Services, 2017 Walnut St, Philadelphia, PA 19103-4403; Title Tel # (215) 569-3650
General Info: Bi-monthly, Trim Size-8½ x 11
Circulation: (100% controlled), Total-250

National Organization for Victim Assistance-Newsletter *Consumer, Association*

Publishing Co: Natl. Organization for Victim Assistance, 1757 Park Rd NW, Washington, DC 20010-2101; Title Tel # (202) 232-6682 Title Fax # (202) 462-2255
Personnel: Editor-John Stein
Editorial Description: A newsletter for the victim's movement. Covers training & technical assistance & state natl. news.
General Info: Yr. Est. 1976, Monthly, 8 pages, No Color, Newsprint
Subscriptions: Indv. $30, Inst. $100, Can. $50, For. $50, $3/copy
Circulation: Total-4,000
List Rental: Rents Lists
Printing Co: Linemark Printing, Inc., 1220 Caraway Ct., Landover, MD 20785 Tel # (301) 925-9000

Native Child Advocate
See: CHILDREN

Neighborhood Caretaker
See: PUBLIC MANAGEMENT & PLANNING

Network News (Runaway Youths) *Association*

Publishing Co: Natl. Network of Runaway & Youth Services, 1319 F St NW Ste 401, Washington, DC 20004-1106 Tel # (202) 783-7949; Title Tel # (202) 682-4114
Personnel: Editor-Twylia Fannin
Editorial Description: Membership oriented newsletter.
General Info: Yr. Est. 1974, Quarterly, Trim Size-8½ x 11, 16 pages, 2 Color
Subscriptions: Indv. $25, $5/copy
Circulation: Total-1,200

New Horizons *Business, Consumer*

Publishing Co: South Carolina Vocational Rehabilitation Dept., PO Box 15, West Columbia, SC 29171-0015; Title Tel # (803) 896-6830 Title Fax # (803) 896-6525
Personnel: Editor-Mary Beth Smith
Editorial Description: Stories deal with programs available for citizens with disabilities & other activities, etc. of dept.
General Info: Quarterly, Trim Size-8½ x 11, Sheetfed press, 8 pages, 2 Color, Matte, Saddle-stitched
Subscriptions: Free
Circulation: Total-5,200
Printing Co: Wentworth Printing Corp., PO Box 4660, West Columbia, SC 29171 Tel # (803) 796-9990, Fax # (803) 739-0556

New York City Coalition for the Homeless-Safety Network
Consumer, Association

Publishing Co: NY City Coalition for the Homeless, 89 Chambers St Apt 3, New York, NY 10007-1811 Tel # (212) 695-8700; Title Tel # (212) 460-8110
Personnel: Editor-Margaret Knox
Editorial Description: Newsletter addresses issues dealing with homelessness & low-income housing.
General Info: Yr. Est. 1982, Monthly, 2 pages
Circulation: Total-4,000

News & Notes
Association

Publishing Co: American Assn. on Mental Retardation, 444 N. Capitol Street NW, #ST846, Washington, DC 20001-1512; Title Tel # (202) 387-1968 Title Fax # (202) 387-2193
Personnel: Publisher-Doreen Croser, Editor-Margaret Seiter, Circ. Mgr.-Ana Montoulieu, Production Mgr., Adv. Dir.-Stephen Stidinger
Editorial Description: Natl. news in developmental idsabilities & associate AAMR news.
General Info: Yr. Est. 1987, Bi-monthly, Trim Size-11 x 17, Sheetfed press, 8 pages, ISSN: 0895-8033, 2% ads, No Color, Newsprint
Subscriptions: Indv. $40, Inst. $40, Can. $46, For. $55, $5/copy
Circulation: (72% controlled), Total-10,500
Advertising: Inquire for rates.
List Rental: Actives: $80/M
Printing Co: Suburban Printing Service, 5380a Eisenhower Ave, Alexandria, VA 22304-4856 Tel # (703) 370-5800, Fax # (703) 751-8637

News from Bailey House
Consumer

Publishing Co: AIDS Resource Center, Inc., 275 7th Ave Fl 12, New York, NY 10001-6708; Title Tel # (212) 633-2500 Title Fax # (212) 633-2932
Editorial Description: Contains news about volunteers and their efforts to provide permanent housing and support services to homeless men, women and families with AIDS and HIV illness.
General Info: (Formerly News from the AIDS Resource Center, Inc.), Quarterly, Trim Size-8½ x 11, 6 pages, 2 Color, Matte
Subscriptions: Indv. $10
Circulation: Total-10,000
List Rental: Rents Lists

Newsletter of the Brookdale Center on Aging
See: SENIOR CITIZENS

Ngoma: The Talking Drum
Association

Publishing Co: Canadian Organization for Development through Education, 321 Chapel St., Ottawa, ON K1N 7Z2 Canada Tel # (613) 232-3569 Fax # (613) 232-7435
Editorial Description: Covers programs and projects aimed at creating a sustainable and literate environment.
General Info: Semi-annually

ORT Bulletin

Publishing Co: American ORT, 817 Broadway Fl 10, New York, NY 10003-4709; Title Tel # (212) 677-4400 Title Fax # (212) 979-9545
Personnel: Editor-Avi Feinglass
Editorial Description: Current news and information relating to ORT activities.
General Info: Quarterly
Circulation: Total-18,000

On the Edge
See: RELIGIOUS & THEOLOGICAL

One World
Association

Publishing Co: Plan International Canada, 95 St. Clair Ave. W., Suite 1001, Toronto, ON M4V 3B5 Canada; Title Tel # (416) 920-1654 Title Fax # (416) 920-9942
Personnel: Editor-Kimberly Campbell
General Info: Yr. Est. 1990, Quarterly, Trim Size-8½ x 11, Web press, 8 pages, 2 Color, Matte, Saddle-stitched
Circulation: Total-1,500

Ontario Division Bulletin

Publishing Co: Canadian Red Cross, Ontario Div., 5700 Cancross Ct., Mississauga, ON L5R 3E9 Canada; Title Tel # (905) 890-1000 Title Fax # (905) 890-1008
Personnel: Editor-Lynn Badger
Editorial Description: Bulletin on all services and programs offered by the Red Cross in Ontario. Each edition is themed by programme (ie: June edition deals with the water safety programme).
General Info: (Formerly Newsbulletin), Yr. Est. 1944, Quarterly, Roto. press, 8 pages, ISSN: 0715-366x, 2 Color, Matte
Subscriptions: Free With Membership
Circulation: Total-15,000, Readership-15,000
Printing Co: Thistle Printing, 14 Coldwater Rd., Don Mills, ON M3B 1Y7 Canada Tel # (416) 447-6421

Open Doors for the Handicapped Newsletter

Publishing Co: Open Doors for the Handicapped, 601 Pressley st., Pittsburgh, PA 15212-5654; Title Tel # (412) 321-4646
Personnel: Editor-Robert Hull
Editorial Description: Information about economic, cultural and recreational opportunities for the handicapped and news of the association.
General Info: Monthly
Subscriptions: Indv. $2
Circulation: Total-500

Options

Publishing Co: Center for Population Options, 1025 Vermont Ave NW Ste 210, Washington, DC 20005-3516; Title Tel # (202) 347-5700 Title Fax # (202) 347-2263
Personnel: Editor-Robin Lewis
Editorial Description: Focuses on issues relating to adolescent pregnancy and prevention of sexually transmitted diseases.
General Info: (Formerly Issues & Action), Yr. Est. 1980, Quarterly, Trim Size-8½ x 11, Sheetfed press, 8 pages, Matte
Acquistions: Publication Bought
List Rental: Rents Lists

Ortho Newsletter
See: HEALTH

P & L Connections

Publishing Co: Paul & Lisa, Inc., PO Box 348, Westbrook, CT 06498-0348; Title Tel # (203) 388-5067
Personnel: Editor-Carol Pytel
General Info: Yr. Est. 1981
Circulation: Total-2,000

PBC Comprehensive Health Briefs
See: HEALTH

PBC Immigration Briefs
See: LAW

PUN, The

Publishing Co: Parents United, Inc., 615 15th St, Modesto, CA 95354-2510 Tel # (408) 453-7616; Title Tel # (408) 280-5055
Personnel: Editor-Peggy Stoddard
General Info: Bi-monthly

Pacific Mountain Network News
See: PUBLIC MANAGEMENT & PLANNING

Passages

Publishing Co: Center for Population Options, 1025 Vermont Ave NW Ste 210, Washington, DC 20005-3516; Title Tel # (202) 347-5700 Title Fax # (202) 347-2263
Personnel: Editor-Gary Barker
Editorial Description: Robin Lewis
General Info: (Formerly Information Summary), Yr. Est. 1980, Quarterly, Trim Size-8½ x 11, Sheetfed press, Matte
Subscriptions: Indv. $15
List Rental: Rents Lists

Pen-Point

Publishing Co: Checks Anonymous, PO Box 2500, Lincoln, NE 68542-0500; Title Tel # (402) 477-3957
General Info: Annually

Penn Notes

Publishing Co: William Penn House, 515 E Capitol St SE, Washington, DC 20003-1142; Title Tel # (202) 543-5560
General Info: Quarterly

Pension Benefits
Business

Publishing Co: Aspen Publishers, Inc., 200 Orchard Ridge Dr., Ste 200, Gaithersburg, MD 20878-5440 Fax # (301) 417-7655 Parent Co.-Wolters Kluwer US Corporation, New York; Title Tel # (301) 417-7500 Title Fax # (301) 417-7550
Personnel: Editor-Bruce Carveth
Editorial Description: Monthly pension industry review.
General Info: Yr. Est. 1992, Monthly, ISSN: 1063-2476
Subscriptions: Indv. $164, For. $197
List Rental: List Management Co.: Stevens-Knox List Management, 304 Park Ave S., New York, NY 10010-5312 Tel # (212) 388-8800, Fax # (212) 388-8890

People

Publishing Co: New York City Human Resources Administration, 220 Church St., Rm. 657, New York, NY 10013-3843
Personnel: Editor-Ronald P. Smolin
General Info: Yr. Est. 1970, 8x/yr.
Circulation: Total-30,000

People Concerned for the Unborn Child-Newsletter
Association

Publishing Co: People Concerned for the Unborn Child, 3050 Pioneer Ave, Pittsburgh, PA 15226-1739; Title Tel # (412) 531-9272 Title Fax # (412) 531-5885
Personnel: Editor-Helen Cindrich
Editorial Description: Information, direction, opportunities for pro-lifers, both locally & nationally.
General Info: Yr. Est. 1970, Bi-monthly, Trim Size-8½ x 11, Offset press, 6 pages, No Color, Matte
Subscriptions: Indv. $15, Free With Membership
Acquistions: Publication Bought
Circulation: Total-4,500
Printing Co: Slavia Printing Co., 157 Mcneilly Rd, Pittsburgh, PA 15226-2624 Tel # (412) 343-4444

Perinatal Addiction Research & Education Update
See: MEDICINE

Peyron Tax Letter & Social Security Report
See: TAXES

Philanthropic Digest
See: PHILANTHROPY

Philanthropic Trends Digest

Publishing Co: Douglas M. Lawson Associates, 545 Madison Ave., New York, NY 10022; Title Tel # (212) 759-5660 Title Fax # (212) 759-1893
General Info: Bi-weekly
Subscriptions: Indv. $48

Planning and Action   *Association*

Publishing Co: Federation for Community Planning, 614 W Superior Ave Ste 300, Cleveland, OH 44113-1306; Title Tel # (216) 781-2944 Title Fax # (216) 781-2988
Editorial Description: Newsletter of the FCP to keep community informed of FCP activities & activity in human services field.
General Info: (Formerly Federation Forum), Yr. Est. 1948, Quarterly, Trim Size-8½ x 11, Web press, 4 pages, No Color, Newsprint
Subscriptions: Free
Circulation: Total-3,800

Polish Assistance Bulletin
See: ETHNIC

Population

Publishing Co: United Nations Population Fund, 220 E. 42nd St., New York, NY 10017-5880; Title Tel # (212) 850-5846
Personnel: Editor-Alex Marshall, Circ. Mgr.-Mirey Chaljub
Editorial Description: Concerned with population & its ramifications.
General Info: Yr. Est. 1974, Monthly, Trim Size-11½ x 15¾, 4 pages
Printing Co: Tabard Press, 75 Varick St Fl 9, New York, NY 10013-1917 Tel # (212) 925-0303

Poverty & Race Newsletter
See: SOCIOLOGY

Pro-Life Action League-
Action News

Publishing Co: Pro-Life Action League, Inc., 6160 N. Cicero Ave., Chicago, IL 60646-4308; Title Tel # (312) 777-2900
Personnel: Editor-Joseph Scheidler
Editorial Description: A vehicle to report on the activities of the Pro-life Action League & other activist pro-life groups around the country & internationally.
General Info: 8 pages

Professional Placement Newsnotes
See: HOSPITALS & NURSING HOMES

Projects Communique   *Consumer, Association*

Publishing Co: UNICEF Canada, 443 Mt. Pleasant Rd., Toronto, ON M4S 2L8 Canada Tel # (416) 482-4444 Fax # (416) 482-8035
Editorial Description: Provides information on the projects undertaken by UNICEF Canada over the past year.
General Info: Annually, 8 pages
Circulation: Total-10,000

Public Assistance &
Welfare Trends/State
Capitals   *Consumer*

Publishing Co: Wakeman/Walworth, 300 N. Washington St., Alexandria, VA 22314-2530; Title Tel # (703) 549-8606 Title Fax # (703) 549-1372
Personnel: Publisher-Keyes Walworth
Editorial Description: Summarizes trends and developments concerning state welfare programs, including AFDC & Medicaid, AIDS legislation, services for the elderly and disabled and more.
General Info: (Formerly Public Assistance & Welfare Trends from the State Capitals), Yr. Est. 1946, Weekly, Trim Size-8½ x 11, Offset press, ISSN: 0734-1601, No Color
Subscriptions: Indv. $265, Inst. $212, Can. $235, For. $255

Quaker Concern   *Association*

Publishing Co: Canadian Friends Service Committee, 60 Lowther Ave., Toronto, ON M5R 1C7 Canada; Title Tel # (416) 920-5213
Editorial Description: Peace education & action, Quaker relief & development projects, native issues & justice concerns.
General Info: (Formerly Quaker Service Report), Yr. Est. 1971, Quarterly, Trim Size-8½ x 11, Web press, 8 pages, ISSN: 0229-1916, No Color
Circulation: (100% controlled), Total-3,500

Recruiting & Retention Idea File
See: FIRE PROTECTION

Reference Guide to Counseling Children & Adolescents
See: CHILDREN

Rehab Review

Publishing Co: California State Dept. of Rehabilitation, 830 K St Rm 320, Sacramento, CA 95814-3510; Title Tel # (916) 445-8638
Personnel: Editor-Russ Enyart
General Info: (Formerly What's Happening), Yr. Est. 1981, Bi-monthly
Circulation: Total-2,000

Rehab Tab
See: DISABILITY

Rehabilitation Gazette

Publishing Co: Gazette International Networking Institute, 4207 Lindell Boulevard, #110, St. Louis, MO 63108; Title Tel # (314) 534-0475 Title Fax # (314) 534-5070
Personnel: Publisher, Editor-Joan Headley
Editorial Description: An annual international newsletter written by individuals with a disability for individuals with a disability.
General Info: Yr. Est. 1958, Semi-annually, Trim Size-8½ x 11, Offset press, 16 pages, ISSN: 0361-4166, No Color, Newsprint, Saddle-stitched
Subscriptions: Indv. $12, Inst. $20, Can. $14, For. $16
Circulation: Total-3,000

Rehabilitation Review   *Association*

Publishing Co: Natl. Assn. of Rehabilitation Facilities, 1910 Association Dr Fl 2, Reston, VA 22091-1502; Title Tel # (703) 556-8848
Personnel: Publisher-John Doyle
Editorial Description: Weekly analysis of legislation, regulation and appropriations affecting rehabilitation.
General Info: Yr. Est. 1980, Weekly, Web press, 8 pages, No Color
Subscriptions: Indv. $160
Circulation: (100% controlled), Total-1,000

Rehabilitation Technology
Newsletter

Publishing Co: Natl. Institute for Rehabilitation Engineering, PO Box T, Hewitt, NJ 07421-1020; Title Tel # (201) 853-6585
General Info: (Formerly Rehabilition Engineering Newsletter), Quarterly
Subscriptions: Indv. $35, Inst. $75, $4/copy
Circulation: Total-600

Renter's Rag
See: LEASING & RENTING

Report from the Hill   *Business, Consumer*

Publishing Co: League of Women Voters of the U.S., 1730 M St., N.W., Ste. 1000, Washington, DC 20036-4587; Title Tel # (202) 429-1965 Title Fax # (202) 429-0854
Personnel: Editor-Ellen Weir
Editorial Description: Natl. legislative issues. Focus on the environment, social policy & arms control.
General Info: Bi-monthly, 8 pages, ISSN: 0893-0708, 2 Color
Subscriptions: Indv. $10, $3/copy
Circulation: Total-5,500

Rescue Officer's Notebook
See: FIRE PROTECTION

Retarded Infants Services
News

Publishing Co: Retarded Infants Services, 386 Park Ave., S., New York, NY 10016-8804; Title Tel # (212) 889-5464
General Info: Quarterly

Rural Landscapes   *Consumer*

Publishing Co: Natl. Catholic Rural Life Conference, 4625 Beaver Ave, Des Moines, IA 50310-2145 Tel # (515) 272-2634; Title Tel # (515) 270-2634 Title Fax # (515) 272-9447
Personnel: Editor-Sandra LaBlanc
Editorial Description: Interprets issues of land, water, energy, family life and food in light of Catholic social teaching.
General Info: (Formerly Common Ground), Yr. Est. 1981, Monthly, Trim Size-8½ x 11, Offset press, 4 pages, 2 Color, Matte
Subscriptions: Indv. $25, Inst. $100, For. $35, Free With Membership
Circulation: Total-3,000
Printing Co: Town Crier, 810 East First St., Pella, IA 50219-1585 Tel # (515) 628-1130, Fax # (515) 628-2826

Ruth Dykeman Center
Community Report   *Association*

Publishing Co: Ruth Dykeman Center, 1033 SW 152nd St, Seattle, WA 98166-1845; Title Tel # (206) 242-1698
Personnel: Editor-Guy Tobin
General Info: Quarterly, Trim Size-8½ x 11, 6 pages, No Color

SGCA Newsletter   *Association*

Publishing Co: Saskatchewan Guidance & Counselling Assn., Box 1108, Saskatoon, SK S7K 3N3 Canada Parent Co.-Saskatchewan Teachers' Federation, Saskatoon, Canada
Personnel: Editor-Janice Solem
General Info: 2x/yr.
Subscriptions: Indv. $50, Inst. $100
Advertising: Inquire for rates.

Safety Network

Publishing Co: National Coalition for the Homeless, PO Box 2410, Merrifield, VA 22116-2410
Tel # (202) 265-2371 Fax # (202) 265-2615; Title Tel # (202) 659-2371
Personnel: Editor-John Alker
General Info: Monthly
Circulation: Total-10,000

Saskatchewan Society for Autistic Children Newsletter
See: PSYCHOLOGY

Sassafras — *Association, Consumer*

Publishing Co: Peoples Music Network for Songs of Freedom & Struggle, 1539 Pine St, Philadelphia, PA 19102-4623
Personnel: Publisher-Jane Treet
Editorial Description: News and events for singers and songwriters interested in political and social expression.
General Info: Semi-annually
Circulation: Total-800

Service — *Association*

Publishing Co: Canadian Red Cross, Ontario Div., 5700 Cancross Ct., Mississauga, ON L5R 3E9 Canada; Title Tel # (613) 739-2264
Editorial Description: Covers Canadian Red Cross programme & service activities.
General Info: (Formerly Despatch), Yr. Est. 1940, Quarterly, Trim Size-7 x 10¾, Web press, 8 pages, ISSN: 0277-034X, 2 Color
Circulation: Total-45,000

Service Illustrated — *Association*

Publishing Co: Church World Service, 28606 Phillips St, Elkhart, IN 46514-1239; Title Tel # (219) 264-3102 Title Fax # (219) 262-0966
Editorial Description: Provides news relating to overseas and domestic programs of Church World Service, with a particular emphasis on the CWS blanket, kit and layette programs.
General Info: Yr. Est. 1995, 2x/yr., Trim Size-25½ x 11, Sheetfed press, 6 pages, Color, Newsprint, Other
Subscriptions: Free
Circulation: Total-107,000

Sharing Life

Publishing Co: Heifer Project International, 1015 Louisiana St, Little Rock, AR 72202-3851; Title Tel # (501) 376-6836
Personnel: Editor-Julie Moncrief
Editorial Description: Quarterly newsletter highlighting HPI's work around the world & in the U.S. Features with photos illustrate HPI's program by showing aspects of long term development projects.
General Info: Quarterly, Trim Size-8½ x 11, Web press, 12 pages, 2 Color, Recycled, Saddle-stitched
Circulation: Total-80,000
Printing Co: Democrat Printing & Lithographing Co., 6401 Lindsey Rd, Little Rock, AR 72206-3823 Tel # (501) 490-1575, Fax # (501) 490-2568

Social Legislation Information Bulletin

Publishing Co: Child Welfare League of America, Inc., 440 1st St. NW, Washington, DC 20001; Title Tel # (202) 638-2952
Personnel: Publisher-Susan Brite, Editor-Marjorie Kopp
Editorial Description: Reports impartially on federal social legislation & activities of federal agencies affecting children, elderly, handicapped, delinquents, health, education, welfare, housing, employment & other social welfare positions.
General Info: Yr. Est. 1944, Bi-weekly, ISSN: 0149-2578, No Color
Subscriptions: Indv. $65
List Rental: Actives: $65/M, Hotline: $70/M

Social Science News Letter
See: SOCIOLOGY

Social Service Jobs

Publishing Co: ELSS, 10 Angelica Dr, Framingham, MA 01701-3618; Title Tel # (508) 626-8644 Title Fax # (508) 626-9389
Personnel: Publisher, Editor-M. Sack
Editorial Description: Available jobs throughout the U.S. for human service professionals, including social workers, psychologist, & counsellors.
General Info: Yr. Est. 1975, Bi-weekly, Trim Size-6 x 9, Offset press, 16 pages, 9% ads, No Color
Subscriptions: Indv. $118
Advertising: Inquire for rates.

Social Work Practice

Publishing Co: Columbia University Press, 562 W 113th St, New York, NY 10025-8099; Title Tel # (212) 688-8885
General Info: Yr. Est. 1962, Annually

Special Delivery — *Consumer, Association*

Publishing Co: NY State Dept. of Social Services, Div. Of Family & Children Serv, 40 N. Pearl Street, Albany, NY 12243-0001
Editorial Description: Foster care placement info for NY professionals.
General Info: Monthly, Trim Size-8½ x 11, 12 pages, ISSN: 1053-9085, 2 Color, Matte

Special Libraries Assn., Social Science Division Bulletin
See: LIBRARY

Spectrum — *Consumer, Association*

Publishing Co: Parsons Child/Family Center, 60 Academy Rd, Albany, NY 12208-3103; Title Tel # (518) 426-2600
Personnel: Editor-Bonser Unser, Design Ed.-Liz Roemer
Editorial Description: Articles on mental health, social services oriented towards families & communities.
General Info: Yr. Est. 1978, Quarterly, Trim Size-8½ x 11, Letrpr. press, 6 pages, 2 Color, Matte
Acquistions: Publication Bought
Circulation: Total-25,000

Spotlight

Publishing Co: Greater Toledo Area American Red Cross, 2275 Collingwood Blvd, Toledo, OH 43620-1148; Title Tel # (419) 248-3331
Personnel: Editor-Leslie Swigart
Editorial Description: Keep volunteers informed and involved in Red Cross activities; all Red Cross subjects featured.
General Info: Yr. Est. 1952, Quarterly, Trim Size-11 x 17, Offset press, 4 pages, Color
Circulation: Total-5,000

Stanislaus Connections

Publishing Co: Modesto Peace/Life Center, PO Box 134, Modesto, CA 95353-0134; Title Tel # (209) 529-5750
Personnel: Editor-Fred Herman, Circ. Mgr.-Jim Costello, Production Mgr.-Dan Onorato, Adv. Dir.-Jann Spallina
Editorial Description: Nuclear free zones, grassroots organizing. Peace, social justice, sustainable environment, housing, energy efficiency alternatives, peace education, non-violent action.
General Info: (Formerly Modesto Peace/Life Center Newsletter), Yr. Est. 1970, Monthly, Web press, 12 pages, 1% ads, No Color, Newsprint
Subscriptions: Free
Circulation: (2% controlled), Total-5,000, Single Copy/Newsstand-1,700
Advertising: Inquire for rates. Accepts Inserts.

Substance Abuse Funding News
See: PHILANTHROPY

Supported Employment InfoLines
See: EMPLOYMENT

Supreme Herald — *Association*

Publishing Co: Supreme Shrine-Order of the White Shrine of Jerusalem, 107 E New Haven Ave, Melbourne, FL 32901-4572 Tel # (407) 952-5323 Fax # (407) 728-0011; Title Tel # (305) 727-1125
Personnel: Publisher, Editor-Helen Piechulis
Editorial Description: Reports on activities of the Shrine--a charitable organization of women relatives of Master Masons giving aid for artificial limbs, wheel chairs, hearing aids, eye glasses & seeing & hearing dogs. Available to members only.
General Info: Yr. Est. 1978, Quarterly, Trim Size-8½ x 11, Sheetfed press, 32 pages, Color-cover
Subscriptions: Indv. $3
Circulation: Total-12,000
Printing Co: Minuteman Printery, Inc., 107 E New Haven Ave, Melbourne, FL 32901-4594

Survivor Activist, The
See: PSYCHOLOGY

Tapestry

Publishing Co: U.S. Peace Corps, 1990 K St NW, Washington, DC 20526-0001; Title Tel # (202) 606-3086 Title Fax # (202) 606-3024
Personnel: Editor-Judith G. Benjamin, Editor-Christopher Broadway
Editorial Description: Covers project ideas, technical information, development for issues & program directions for Peace Corps volunteers & others working at a grassroots level in developing countries.
General Info: (Formerly Program), Yr. Est. 1973, Quarterly, Trim Size-11 x 14, Web press, 8 pages, No Color
Circulation: Total-21,000

Tax, Estate and Financial Planning for the Elderly
See: BANKING & FINANCE

Tennessee Hunger Coalition News

Publishing Co: Tennessee Hunger Coalition, PO Box 120961, Nashville, TN 37212-0961; Title Tel # (615) 298-3888
Personnel: Editor-Callie Hutchison
General Info: Yr. Est. 1980, Quarterly, 16 pages, No Color
Subscriptions: Indv. $5, Inst. $10, $2/copy
Circulation: Total-16,000

Texas Alliance for Human Needs, The — *Association*

Publishing Co: The Texas Alliance for Human Needs, 2520 Longview St Apt 311, Austin, TX 78705-4235; Title Tel # (512) 474-5019 Title Fax # (512) 476-0130
Personnel: Editor-Jude Filler
Editorial Description: Concerned with issues affecting low and moderate income people in Texas.
General Info: Yr. Est. 1984, 10x/yr., Trim Size-8½ x 11, Offset press, 6 pages, 2 Color, Matte
Subscriptions: Indv. $25, Free With Membership
Circulation: Total-8,000

This Is WICS · *Association*

Publishing Co: Women in Community Service, Inc., 1900 N Beauregard St Ste 103, Alexandria, VA 22311-1716; Title Tel # (703) 671-0500
Personnel: Editor-Angie Isidro
Editorial Description: For volunteers interested in helping at-risk women in the USA.
General Info: Yr. Est. 1965, Quarterly, Web press, 10 pages, 2 Color, Newsprint
Subscriptions: Free
Circulation: Total-10,000

This Week in Washington · *Business, Association*

Publishing Co: American Public Welfare Assn., 810 1st St. NE, Ste. 500, Washington, DC 20002-4267 Fax # (202) 289-6555; Title Tel # (202) 682-0100
Personnel: Editor-Susan Kellam, Circ. Mgr.-Brenda Jones, Production Mgr.-Amy Plotmik
Editorial Description: Update of congressional legislation week-by-week in social services.
General Info: Yr. Est. 1980, Weekly, Trim Size-8½ x 11, Desktop press, 2 pages, ISSN: 0743-2437, No Color, Matte
Subscriptions: Indv. $95, For. $105
Circulation: Total-500
List Rental: Actives: $50/M

Tidings/Gros Plan · *Association*

Publishing Co: Plan International Canada, 95 St. Clair Ave. W., Suite 1001, Toronto, ON M4V 3B5 Canada; Title Tel # (416) 920-1654 Title Fax # (416) 920-9942
Personnel: Editor-Debra Schutt
Editorial Description: To advise foster parents of developments in Plan programs overseas and to create inter-cultural understanding.
General Info: (Formerly Plan Canada News), Yr. Est. 1974, Quarterly, Trim Size-8½ x 11, Web press, 12 pages, 2 Color, Matte, Saddle-stitched
Acquistions: Publication Bought
Circulation: Total-100,000

Today Child

Publishing Co: Children's Home Society of Minnesota, 1605 Ustin Street, St. Paul, MN 55108; Title Tel # (612) 646-7771 Title Fax # (612) 646-8676
Personnel: Editor-Mary Ann Nord
Editorial Description: Articles on child welfare issues and on Children's Home Society programs and activities.
General Info: (Formerly Minnesota Children's Home Finder/Children's Home News), Yr. Est. 1889, Quarterly, Sheetfed press, 16 pages, 2 Color
Subscriptions: Indv. $2
Circulation: Total-27,000

TrainingScope · *Business, Association*

Publishing Co: Center for Development of Human Services, SUNY College at Buffalo, 1300 Elmwood Ave., Letchworth, Buffalo, NY 14222-1095; Title Tel # (716) 881-2800
Personnel: Editor-Ramona Pando Whitaker
Editorial Description: Helps assist community human services agencies improve their service qualities.
General Info: Monthly, Trim Size-8½ x 11, 18 pages, 2 Color, Matte, Saddle-stitched

Transition: The Newsletter About Reforming Economies
See: INTERNATIONAL AFFAIRS

Transition Summary
See: DISABILITY

UNH News

Publishing Co: United Neighborhood Houses of New York, 475 Park Ave S Fl 6, New York, NY 10016-6901; Title Tel # (212) 481-5570 Title Fax # (212) 481-5582
Personnel: Publisher-Emily Menlo Marks
General Info: Yr. Est. 1959, Quarterly, 2 Color
Circulation: Total-2,000
Printing Co: Gutenberg Printing, 37 W. 65th St., New York, NY 10023 Tel # (212) 362-8638

UNICEF Communique · *Consumer, Association*

Publishing Co: UNICEF Canada, 443 Mt. Pleasant Rd., Toronto, ON M4S 2L8 Canada Tel # (416) 482-4444 Fax # (416) 482-8035
Editorial Description: Covers the activities of UNICEF in Canada.
General Info: Yr. Est. 1979, Semi-annually, 8 pages
Subscriptions: Free With Membership
Circulation: Total-6,000

USO: America's Spirit · *Association*

Publishing Co: USO World Headquarters, Washington Navy Yard, 901 M St., SE, Bldg. 198, Washington, DC 20374-5096; Title Tel # (202) 610-5700 Title Fax # (202) 610-5701
Personnel: Editor-A. Adler
Editorial Description: Staff, administrative and program developments of interest to USO professionals, volunteers, and contributors.
General Info: (Formerly USO Newsletter), Quarterly, Trim Size-11 x 17, Roto. press, 6 pages, 2 Color
Subscriptions: Free
Circulation: Total-50,000

USS Reports · *Consumer, Association*

Publishing Co: American Merchant Marine Library Assn., 1 World Trade Ctr Ste 2161, New York, NY 10048-0202 Tel # (212) 775-1038; Title Tel # (212) 775-1033 Title Fax # (212) 432-5492
Personnel: Publisher-Roger T. Korner, Editor-Elizabeth Leach
Editorial Description: Reports on the activities and related happenings of the United Seamen's Service and it's affiliate the American Merchant Marine Library Association.
General Info: Irregular, Trim Size-8½ x 11, Web press, 12 pages, Coated, Saddle-stitched
Subscriptions: Free
Circulation: Total-3,000

Unemployment Insurance Reports with Social Security-Federal & All States

Publishing Co: CCH, Inc., 2700 Lake Cook Rd., Riverwoods, IL 60015 Parent Co.-Kluwer Law & Taxation Publishers, Cambridge; Title Tel # (847) 267-7000 Title Fax # (800) 224-8299
Editorial Description: Social security taxes, old age survivors and disability benefits, supplemental security income, into to medicine, unemployment insurance, explanations, tables, laws, and court cases.
General Info: 50x/yr., Looseleaf
Subscriptions: Indv. $2,470

University of Washington Forum · *Scholarly, Association*

Publishing Co: University of Washington, School of Social Work, 4101 15th Ave. NE, Seattle, WA 98185-6299 Tel # (206) 543-5640 Fax # (206) 543-1228; Title Tel # (206) 685-1693
Personnel: Editor-Vicki O'Keef
General Info: Yr. Est. 1980, Quarterly, Trim Size-8½ x 11, Sheetfed press, 6 pages, 2 Color
Circulation: (100% controlled), Total-7,000

Update

Publishing Co: Easter Seal Society, 250 Ferrand Dr., Ste. 200, Don Mills, ON M3C 3P2 Canada; Title Tel # (416) 421-8377
Personnel: Editor-Pamela Hampson, Art Dir.-gina Grant
Editorial Description: Features Easter Seal Society activities and developments.
General Info: Yr. Est. 1988, Quarterly, ISSN: 0845-1338
Circulation: Total-10,000

Update on Quality · *Consumer*

Publishing Co: Accreditation Council on Svcs. for People with Disabilities, 100 West Rd., Ste. 406, Towson, MD 21204; Title Tel # (410) 583-0060
Personnel: Editor-Sylvia Nudler
Editorial Description: Current news in quality enhancement in human services.
General Info: (Formerly Accreditation Update), Yr. Est. 1979, Quarterly, Trim Size-17 x 11, Desktop press, 6 pages, No Color
Acquistions: Publication Bought
Circulation: Total-8,000
Advertising: Inquire for rates.

Us · CPM: $910

Publishing Co: Human Resources Administration, City of New York, 250 Church St, New York, NY 10013-3430; Title Tel # (212) 274-2414 Title Fax # (212) 966-0740
Personnel: Editor-Daniel Jacobson, Art Dir.-Michael Lavin
Editorial Description: Employee newsletter for the staff of the Human Resources Administration, the agency that administers all social services and welfare payments for the City of New York. Goes to all staff and to list of government officials and private agencies.
General Info: Yr. Est. 1982, Web press, 8 pages, No Color, Coated, Saddle-stitched
Circulation: (100% controlled), Total-32,000
Advertising: $29,140.

Victorian

Publishing Co: Our Lady of Victory Homes of Charity, Ridge Rd., Lackawanna, NY 14218
Personnel: Editor-William J. Lang
Editorial Description: Information on the activities of Our Lady of Victory Homes.
General Info: Yr. Est. 1915, Quarterly
Subscriptions: Indv. $1
Circulation: Total-26,000

Viewpoints

Publishing Co: Association of Jewish Center Professionals, 15 E 26th St Ste 1430, New York, NY 10010-1505; Title Tel # (212) 532-4949
General Info: Semi-annually

Vis-A-Vis · *Consumer, Association*

Publishing Co: Canadian Council on Social Development, 55 Parkdale Avenue, PO Box 3505, Station C, Ottawa, ON K1Y 4G1 Canada; Title Tel # (613) 728-1865 Title Fax # (613) 728-9387
Personnel: Editor-Tom Uradenburg
Editorial Description: National newsletter on family violence.
General Info: Yr. Est. 1985, Quarterly, ISSN: 0823-0404
Circulation: (100% controlled), Total-15,500
Printing Co: Love Printing Services Ltd., 5972 Hazeldean Rd., Stittsville, ON K2S 1B9 Canada Tel # (613) 831-5683

Volunteering — *Business, Association*

Publishing Co: Points of Light Foundation, 1737 H Street SW, Washington, DC 20006; Title Tel # (703) 276-0542
Personnel: Editor-Brenda Hanlon, Circ. Mgr.-Kathy Wallace
Editorial Description: Legislative matters, corp. initiatives, & activities of voluntary action centers.
General Info: Yr. Est. 1981, Bi-monthly, 6 pages, 2 Color, Newsprint
Acquistions: Publication Bought
Circulation: Total-3,000

Wesleyan Witness

Publishing Co: Methodist Peace Fellowship, 206 W Main St, Crisfield, MD 21817-1327; Title Tel # (302) 368-7449
General Info: Quarterly
Circulation: Total-1,500

Women and Recovery
See: WOMEN'S

Working Together — *Consumer, Association*

Publishing Co: Center for the Prevention of Sexual & Domestic Violence, 936 N. 34th St. #200, Seattle, WA 98103-8869; Title Tel # (206) 634-1903
Personnel: Publisher-Marie Fortune, Editor-Frances Wood
Editorial Description: Journal addressing issues relevant to sexual and domestic violence and particularly a clinical and pastoral response.
General Info: Yr. Est. 1979, Quarterly, Trim Size-8½ x 11, Offset press, 6 pages, No Color
Subscriptions: Indv. $12
Circulation: Total-2,900
Printing Co: Arctic Printing, 501 2nd Ave W, Seattle, WA 98119-3927 Tel # (206) 281-7600

Workplace in the Community
See: EMPLOYMENT

SOCIETY

ALERTA
See: INTERNATIONAL TRADE

Aging America Resources
See: SENIOR CITIZENS

Alumeto
See: LITERATURE & LINGUISTICS

Communique
See: CULTURE & HUMANITIES

Gallup Poll, The
See: POLITICS

Horizons Newsletter
See: CIVIL RIGHTS

Impact!
See: THEATRE

International Christian Studies Association Newsletter (ICSA Newsletter)
See: RELIGIOUS & THEOLOGICAL

Interracial Club of Buffalo Newsletter
See: ETHNIC

Limbaugh Letter
See: POLITICS

Manuscript Society News
See: HOBBY

Mentor
See: GENERAL INTEREST

Millennial Prophecy Report
See: RELIGIOUS & THEOLOGICAL

Monthly Product Announcement
See: BUSINESS & INDUSTRY

News From ICS
See: POLITICS

North Star Compass
See: INTERNATIONAL AFFAIRS

PS: Intelligent Guide to Jewish Affairs
See: POLITICS

Pacific Science Association Information Bulletin
See: SCIENCE

Philanthropic Digest
See: PHILANTHROPY

Rampant Lion
See: ETHNIC

SSAP Newsletter
See: ENVIRONMENT & ECOLOGY

Society for the Psychological Study of Social Issues Newsletter
See: PSYCHOLOGY

Waves
See: GAY & LESBIAN INTEREST

SOCIOLOGY

AAHE Newsletter
See: ARCHITECTURE

AGHE Exchange
See: SENIOR CITIZENS

AIDS & Society: International Research Policy Bulletin
See: MEDICINE

AIDS Literature & Law Review
See: LAW

Anomalistics: The CSAR Bulletin — *Association*

Publishing Co: Center for Scientific Anomalies Research, Eastern Michigan Univ., Dept. of Sociology, Ypsilanti, MI 48197; Title Tel # (517) 522-3551 Title Fax # (517) 522-3555
Personnel: Editor-Marcello Truzzi
Editorial Description: News, opinion, & bibliography re scientific anomalies research, available to members of CSAR only.
General Info: (Formerly CSAR Bulletin), Yr. Est. 1985, Irregular, Trim Size-8½ x 11, 8 pages, No Color
Subscriptions: Free With Membership

Bare Texan

Publishing Co: Sponsor-Live Oak Resort, Inc., KIB Communications, PO Box 1676, Humble, TX 77347-1676; Title Tel # (713) 590-1139
Personnel: Publisher, Editor, Adv. Dir.-Veal Johnson
Editorial Description: Club regional, natl. & intl. news regarding the nudist lifestyle & social family nudism.
General Info: Yr. Est. 1981, Bi-monthly, Trim Size-8½ x 11, Mimeo press, 30 pages, No Color, Newsprint
Subscriptions: Indv. $70
Circulation: Total-1,400

Behavior & Society — *Business*

Publishing Co: National Technical Information Service U.S., 5285 Port Royal Rd., Springfield, VA 22161-0001 Fax # (703) 487-4630; Title Tel # (703) 487-4630
Editorial Description: Bibliographic announcements produced weekly from NTIS scientific/technical database.
General Info: (Formerly Weekly Government Abstracts, Behavior and Society), Weekly, Trim Size-8½ x 11, Offset press, ISSN: 0145-0034, No Color
Subscriptions: Indv. $105, Can. $105, For. $155

Bioethics Literature Review
See: MEDICINE

Brown University Child and Adolescent Behavior Letter, The
See: CHILDREN

Bulletin
See: RELIGIOUS & THEOLOGICAL

CBASSE Newsletter

Publishing Co: Commission on Behavioral & Social Sciences & Education, Natl. Research Council 2101, Constitution Ave., Washington, DC 20418-0001; Title Tel # (202) 334-2300
Personnel: Editor-Christine McShane
Editorial Description: Reports activities of the Commission.
General Info: (Formerly ABASS Newsletter), Yr. Est. 1976, Irregular, Trim Size-8½ x 11, 12 pages, ISSN: 0734-5119, No Color, Newsprint
Circulation: Total-2,500

CIS Backgrounder

Publishing Co: Center for Immigration Studies, 1815 H St NW Ste 1010, Washington, DC 20006-3604 Tel # (202) 466-8185 Fax # (202) 466-8076; Title Tel # (202) 328-7228
Personnel: Editor-Dave Simcox
General Info: Yr. Est. 1987, Irregular, 6 pages

CORAspondent
See: RELIGIOUS & THEOLOGICAL

COSSA Washington Update
See: POLITICS

Canadian Ethnic Studies Association Bulletin
See: ETHNIC

Center for Creative Leadership
See: MANAGEMENT

Center for Migration Studies
Newsletter   *Association*

Publishing Co: Center for Migration Studies of New York, Inc., 209 Flagg Pl, Staten Island, NY 10304-1199 Fax # (718) 667-4598; Title Tel # (718) 351-8800 Title Fax # (418) 667-4598
Personnel: Editor-Lydio Tomasi, Circ. Mgr.-Ann Munafo, Adv. Dir.-Carolyn Durante, Art Dir.-Ezio Marchetto
Editorial Description: Reports on the conferences, publications, documentation, research, and archive activities of the Center for Migration Studies.
General Info: Yr. Est. 1964, Semi-annually, Trim Size-8½ x 11, Letrpr. press, 8 pages, ISSN: 8756-4467, Coated, Saddle-stitched
Subscriptions: Free
Circulation: Total-2,000
Printing Co: F & D Printing, 610 Midland Ave, Staten Island, NY 10306-6017 Tel # (718) 979-4441

Clinical Sociology
Newsletter

Publishing Co: Clinical Sociology Assn., Dept. of Sociology, Box 13408, N. Texas State Univ., Denton, TX 76203-3408
General Info: Yr. Est. 1978, Quarterly, ISSN: 0731-194X
Circulation: Total-700

Community Service
Newsletter

Publishing Co: Community Service, Inc., 114 E Whiteman St # 243, Yellow Springs, OH 45387-1826; Title Tel # (513) 767-2161
Personnel: Production Mgr., Art Dir.-Angela Carmichael, Publisher, Editor, Promotion Dir.-Jane Morgan
Editorial Description: Promotes awareness of importance of small communities as the basis & substance of society. Helps small communities become better places to live.
General Info: (Formerly Community Comments), Yr. Est. 1943, Quarterly, Trim Size-7 x 8½, Offset press, 16 pages, ISSN: 0277-6189, 1% ads, No Color
Subscriptions: Indv. $25, Can. $30, For. $30, $2/copy
Circulation: Total-400
Printing Co: Van Pelt Press, 4742 Peacock Rd, Springfield, OH 45502-8713 Tel # (513) 325-2861

Connection
See: PSYCHOLOGY

Constructive Citizen
Participation

Publishing Co: Development Press, 5096 Catalina Terrace, Victoria, BC V8Y 2A5 Canada; Title Tel # (604) 658-1323 Title Fax # (604) 658-8110
Editorial Description: Improving the practice of Public Construction.
General Info: Yr. Est. 1968, Trim Size-8½ x 11, 8 pages, ISSN: 0219-2385, No Color, Recycled, Saddle-stitched

CrossCurrents
See: ETHNIC

Crosscurrents
See: MUSIC & MUSIC TRADES

Emerging Trends
See: RELIGIOUS & THEOLOGICAL

Ethics & International Affairs Newsletter
See: INTERNATIONAL AFFAIRS

Ethics and Policy
See: PHILOSOPHY

European Studies Newsletter
See: HISTORY

Facts for Action
See: POLITICS

Fernand Braudel Center-
Newsletter

Publishing Co: Fernand Braudel Center, Binghamton University, Box 6000, Binghamton, NY 13902-6000; Title Tel # (607) 777-4924
Personnel: Editor-Immanuel Wallerstein
General Info: Yr. Est. 1977, Annually, Ind/Abs/Online: CC, HisA
Subscriptions: Free
Circulation: Total-2,500

Footnotes   CPM: $108

Publishing Co: American Sociological Association, 1722 N St., N.W., Washington, DC 20036-2981; Title Tel # (202) 833-3410 Title Fax # (202) 785-0146
Personnel: Editor-Carla Howery, Production Mgr.-Karen Edwards, Adv. Dir.-Michele Walczak
Editorial Description: A newsletter containing feature stories, calls for papers, meeting calendar, funding and other notices, obituaries, developments on the Wsahington scene, and the Asa official reports and proceedings.
General Info: 10x/yr., Trim Size-11 x 17, Offset press, 16 pages, ISSN: 0749-6931, No Color, Newsprint
Subscriptions: Indv. $23, Inst. $23, Can. $29, For. $29, $3/copy
Circulation: Total-13,500
Advertising: $1,470.
List Rental: Rents Lists
Printing Co: Boyd Printing Co., Inc., 49 Sheridan Ave, Albany, NY 12210-2735 Tel # (518) 436-9686, Fax # (518) 436-7433

Future Watch
See: POLITICS

Gallup Poll, The
See: POLITICS

Gypsy Lore Society Newsletter
See: ANTHROPOLOGY

Human Survival

Publishing Co: Negative Population Growth, Inc., 210 The Plz, P.O Box 1206, Teaneck, NJ 07666-5161; Title Tel # (201) 837-3555
Personnel: Publisher, Editor-Donald Mann
General Info: Yr. Est. 1972, Semi-annually, Trim Size-8½ x 11, 6 pages
Subscriptions: Indv. $25
Circulation: Total-20,000
List Rental: Actives: 28,000, $65/M

ISR Newsletter   *Association*

Publishing Co: Univ. of Michigan Institute for Social Research, PO Box 1248, Ann Arbor, MI 48106-1248 Tel # (313) 764-1817; Title Tel # (313) 764-8363
Personnel: Publisher-Robert Zajone
Editorial Description: Urban/environmental studies, economic behavior, organization research, political behavior, survey methodology computer methodology, major social issues.
General Info: Yr. Est. 1950, Quarterly, Trim Size-8½ x 11, Offset press, 8 pages, ISSN: 0020-2622, No Color
Circulation: Total-13,000

Itza Voice
See: ETHNIC

Japan Folio   *Business, Association*

Publishing Co: Japan Info Ctr., Consulate Gen. of Japan At Chicago, Olympia Center, Ste. 1000, 737 N. Michigan Ave., Chicago, IL 60611 Tel # (312) 280-0431 Fax # (312) 280-6883; Title Tel # (312) 280-0400
Personnel: Editor-Takeshi Nakamora
Editorial Description: General newsletter about Japan and local events relating to Japan in the six state jurisdiction of the Consulate General of Japan in Chicago.
General Info: (Formerly News for the Midwest), Yr. Est. 1978, Quarterly, Offset press, 8 pages, 2 Color, Coated
Subscriptions: Free In Designated Area
Circulation: Total-1,000
Printing Co: Willard Graphics, 1144 W Washington Blvd, Chicago, IL 60607-2078 Tel # (312) 666-1104

Latin American Jewish Studies
See: ETHNIC

Legal-eyes
See: DRUGS & PHARMACEUTICALS

Long Waves Newsletter

Publishing Co: Fernand Braudel Center, Binghamton University, Box 6000, Binghamton, NY 13902-6000; Title Tel # (607) 777-4924
Personnel: Editor-Immanuel Wallerstein
General Info: Yr. Est. 1984, Irregular, 15 pages
Subscriptions: Free
Circulation: Total-300

Making Cities Livable Newsletter
See: PUBLIC MANAGEMENT & PLANNING

Midwest Sociologist — *Association*
Publishing Co: Midwest Sociological Society, Dept. Of Sociology Creighton, Univ., Omaha, NE 68178-0001; Title Tel # (515) 271-3623
Personnel: Editor-Barbara Keating
Editorial Description: News of the Midwest Sociological society and regional Sociology Department news: Society, its annual meeting program, and regional sociology depts.
General Info: (Formerly Newsletter of the Midwest Sociological Society), Yr. Est. 1962, Trim Size-8½ x 11, Sheetfed press, 30 pages, No Color, Newsprint, Saddle-stitched
Subscriptions: Free With Membership
Circulation: Total-1,450

Modern Divorce
See: LIFESTYLE

Monthly Product Announcement
See: BUSINESS & INDUSTRY

NNC Information Report — *Association*
Publishing Co: National Neighborhood Coalition, 1875 Connecticut Ave. NW, Ste. 710, Washington, DC 20009-5728; Title Tel # (202) 986-2096 Title Fax # (202) 986-2539
General Info: (Formerly National Neighbors), Yr. Est. 1971, Bi-monthly
Subscriptions: Indv. $25

National Opinion Research Center, Newsletter — *Association*
Publishing Co: Natl. Opinion Research Center, 1155 E. 60ht St., Chicago, IL 60637-2799; Title Tel # (312) 753-7500
Personnel: Editor-Jeff Hackett
Editorial Description: Reports on current studies being conducted by N.O.R.C. and lists new publications and news about the center.
General Info: Yr. Est. 1967, Quarterly, Trim Size-8½ x 11, Offset press, 4 pages, No Color
Subscriptions: Free
Circulation: Total-1,000

Native American Policy Network
Publishing Co: Barry Univ., 11300 N.E. 2nd Ave., Miami Shores, FL 33161-6695; Title Tel # (305) 899-3473 Title Fax # (305) 899-3279
Personnel: Editor-Michael Melody
Editorial Description: Native American policy issues.
General Info: Yr. Est. 1980, Quarterly, Trim Size-8½ x 11, Offset press, 5 pages, No Color
Subscriptions: Indv. $5
Acquistions: Publication Bought
Circulation: (100% controlled)
Advertising: Accepts Inserts.
List Rental: Rents Lists

New Environment Bulletin
See: ENVIRONMENT & ECOLOGY

New Sense Bulletin — *Consumer*
Publishing Co: Interface Press, 4717 N Figueroa St # 42211, Los Angeles, CA 90042-4406; Title Tel # (213) 223-2500
Personnel: VP & Exec. Ed.-Paul Coubet, Publisher, Exec. Ed.-Marilyn Ferguson, Contrib. Ed.-Eric Ferguson, Research Editor-Greg Wright
Editorial Description: Discusses psychology, consciousness, human potential, early learning, drugs, hypnosis, parapsychology & similar subjects. Recurring features include editorials, commentaries, news of research, a calendar of events, book reviews, & lists of resources.
General Info: (Formerly Brain/Mind Bulletin), Yr. Est. 1975, Monthly, Trim Size-8½ x 11, Offset press, 8 pages, ISSN: 1057-0705, No Color, Newsprint
Subscriptions: Indv. $45, Can. $55, For. $55, $3/copy
Circulation: Total-7,500
List Rental: Actives: $75/M
Printing Co: Crown Litho, 1011 Venice Blvd, Los Angeles, CA 90015-3231 Tel # (213) 386-3566

News and Announcements — *Association*
Publishing Co: Assn. for the Sociology of Religion, Marist Hall Room 108 Cua, Washington, DC 20064-0001; Title Tel # (717) 867-6336
Personnel: Publisher-Barbara Denison
Editorial Description: News-letter for the members of the ass'n for the Sociology of Religion.
General Info: Quarterly, Offset press, 6 pages, No Color
Circulation: Total-600
List Rental: Rents Lists

NewsNotes
See: POLITICS

Newsletter of the Association for Social Scientific Study of Jewry — *Association*
Publishing Co: Assn. for the Sociological Study of Jewry, Brooklyn College Dept. of Soco, Bedford Ave. & Ave H, Brooklyn, NY 11210-2889; Title Tel # (718) 780-5314
Personnel: Publisher-David Varady, Editor-Egan Mayer
Editorial Description: News items social research on Jewish communities.
General Info: Yr. Est. 1979, Mimeo press, 12 pages
Subscriptions: Indv. $18

Note Us
Publishing Co: Sociological Abstracts, Inc., 7428 Trade St., San Diego, CA 92121-2410; Title Tel # (619) 695-8803 Title Fax # (619) 695-0416
Personnel: Editor-Miriam Chall
Editorial Description: A medium describing the activities (workshops, pub., content, etc.) of Sociological Abstracts, Inc., which publishes and maintains in online and CD-ROM format three databases.
General Info: Yr. Est. 1983, Quarterly, Sheetfed press, 4 pages, Color
Subscriptions: Free
Circulation: Total-6,700
Advertising: Inquire for rates.

Open Adoption Birthparent
See: FAMILY

PAIS International News
See: LIBRARY

PRL in Summary — *Business, Association*
Publishing Co: Population Research Laboratory, U. of Alberta-Sociology, 1-62 HM Tory Bldg., Edmonton, AB T6G 2H4 Canada; Title Tel # (403) 492-4659 Title Fax # (403) 492-2589
Personnel: Editor, Circ. Mgr.-Ilze Hobin
Editorial Description: Newsletter on events, research & pubs. of the Population Research Laboratory.
General Info: Yr. Est. 1979, 3x/yr., Trim Size-8½ x 11, Desktop press, 2 pages, ISSN: 0228-2518, Color, Newsprint
Subscriptions: Free
Circulation: Total-600
Printing Co: Quality Color Press, 4-28 Mech. Eng. Building, University of Alberta, Edmonton, AB T6G 2H1 Canada Tel # (403) 492-9491

Peace Press
See: POLITICS

Policy Currents
See: PUBLIC MANAGEMENT & PLANNING

Polling Report
See: POLITICS

Poppin' Zits! — *Consumer* — **CPM: $200**
Publishing Co: Jerod Pore, 1800 Market St Ste 141, San Francisco, CA 94102-6227; Title Tel # (415) 477-9779
Personnel: Publisher, Editor-Jerod Pore, Production Mgr.-Ida Libido
Editorial Description: Biological/computer interface; total chaos on demand; use of tribal model to study corporate social structures; obscure data; manifesto of the Artificial Life Liberation Front; experimental and anecdotal data from Japan; fringe religions.
General Info: Yr. Est. 1987, Irregular, 40 pages, Color, Recycled
Subscriptions: $3/copy
Circulation: Total-500
Advertising: $100.

Population Today — *Association*
Publishing Co: Population Reference Bureau, Inc., 1875 Connecticut Ave. NW, Ste. 520, Washington, DC 20009-5728; Title Tel # (202) 483-1100 Title Fax # (202) 328-3937
Personnel: Editor-Susan Kalish, Circ. Mgr.-Jacki Majewski, Asst. Ed., Production Mgr.-Sharon Hershey, Asst. Prod. Mgr.-Jaqueline Guenther
Editorial Description: Worldwide trends and activities in population and family planning, features on the impact of population change on resources, environment, food supply, quality of life, reviews of relevant books.
General Info: Yr. Est. 1973, Monthly, Trim Size-8½ x 11, Offset press, 8 pages, ISSN: 0749-2448, 2 Color, Matte
Subscriptions: $2/copy
Circulation: Total-4,000

Positive Economist Bulletin Supplement for Objectivists
See: PHILOSOPHY

Poverty & Race Newsletter — *Association*
Publishing Co: Poverty & Race Research Action Council, 1711 Connecticut Ave NW Ste, 207, Washington, DC 20009-1139; Title Tel # (202) 387-9887 Title Fax # (202) 387-0764
Personnel: Publisher, Editor-Chester Hartman, Production Mgr.-Catherine Dorn
Editorial Description: Links social science research and advocacy work in order to successfully address problems at the intersection of race and poverty.
General Info: Yr. Est. 1992, Bi-monthly, Trim Size-8½ x 11, 24 pages, 2 Color, Saddle-stitched
Subscriptions: Indv. $10, Inst. $25
List Rental: Actives: 5,800, $50/M

Public Pulse, The — *Business*
Publishing Co: Roper Organization, 205 E. 42nd St., New York, NY 10017-5706; Title Tel # (212) 599-0700 Title Fax # (212) 867-7008
Personnel: Editor-Thomas Miller, Circ. Mgr.-Margaret Curbey
Editorial Description: Analyses, forecasts of public opinion trends affecting business & government.
General Info: Yr. Est. 1986, Monthly, 8 pages
Subscriptions: Indv. $247
List Rental: Actives: 1,500, $400/M, Expires: 1,748, $200/M

Religion & Society Report
See: RELIGIOUS & THEOLOGICAL

Rezo

Publishing Co: Regroupement Quebecois des Sciences Sociales, INRS, 3465 Durocher, Montreal, PQ H2X 2C6 Canada
Editorial Description: Covers social science research in and about Quebec.
General Info: Yr. Est. 1989, 7x/yr.
Circulation: Total-370

Russia and Her Neighbors, Facts & Views on Daily Life
See: INTERNATIONAL AFFAIRS

SINET (Social Indicators Network News) *Consumer*

Publishing Co: Sponsor-International Society for Quality of Life Studies, SINET, Duke University, PO Box 90088, Durham, NC 27708-0088; Title Tel # (919) 660-5615 Title Fax # (919) 660-5623
Personnel: Publisher, Editor-Abbott Ferriss
Editorial Description: Information on Social Indicators development and uses, quality of life studies, social reports, methodological developments, etc.
General Info: (Formerly Social Indicators), Yr. Est. 1984, Quarterly, Trim Size-8½ x 11, Sheetfed press, 12 pages, ISSN: 0885-6729, No Color, Newsprint
Subscriptions: Indv. $16, Inst. $24, Can. $16, For. $18, $4/copy
Circulation: Total-400
List Rental: Actives: $50/M

SSAP Newsletter
See: ENVIRONMENT & ECOLOGY

SWS Network *Association*

Publishing Co: Mandle, PO Box 157, Hamilton, NY 13346-0157
Personnel: Editor-Janet Hunt, Circ. Mgr.-Marcia Segal, Adv. Dir.-Judith Hammond
Editorial Description: News, commentary of interest to social scientists commited to change in position of women in professions and society.
General Info: (Formerly Sociologists for Women in Society Newsletter), Yr. Est. 1971, 20 pages, No Color
Subscriptions: Indv. $15
Circulation: Total-1,400
Advertising: Inquire for rates.

Social Science News Letter *Association*

Publishing Co: Inst. for Research in Social Science, Univ. of NC Cb# 3355, Manning Hall, Chapel Hill, NC 27599-0001 Tel # (919) 962-3062; Title Tel # (919) 962-3061 Title Fax # (919) 962-4777
Personnel: Publisher-Angell Beza, Editor-Jennifer O'Lear
Editorial Description: Provides statewide social science news collected from social science faculty and researchers. Distributed only to state social scientists, government agencies, the media, libraries and universities.
General Info: (Formerly Univ of NC Newsletter), Yr. Est. 1914, 7x/yr., Trim Size-8½ x 11, Desktop press, 4 pages, ISSN: 0743-8974, No Color, Matte, Perfect bound
Acquistions: Publication Bought
Circulation: Total-1,500

Social Science Reporter and Public Relations Research Review

Publishing Co: Social Science Reporter, 850 Webster St Apt 600, Palo Alto, CA 94301-2837
Personnel: Editor-Rex F. Harlow
General Info: Yr. Est. 1953, Monthly
Subscriptions: Indv. $30

Sociation

Publishing Co: N.C. Sociological Assn., NCSA/UNC Charlotte, Charlotte, NC 28223; Title Tel # (919) 342-4261
Personnel: Editor-Lee Dodson
Editorial Description: Sociation is the bulletin of the N.C. Sociological Assn.
General Info: Yr. Est. 1970, 6 pages, No Color
Circulation: Total-450

Society for the Psychological Study of Social Issues Newsletter
See: PSYCHOLOGY

South Asia Forum Quarterly
See: ETHNIC

Southern Demographic News

Publishing Co: Sponsor-Southern Regional Demographic Group, Southern Demographic Assn., PO Box 70192, Louisville, KY 40270-0192; Title Tel # (502) 569-5161
Personnel: Editor-Isaac Eberstein
Editorial Description: Newsletter on demographic research in the south.
General Info: Yr. Est. 1971, Quarterly, Offset press, 4 pages, No Color, Newsprint
Subscriptions: Indv. $10
Circulation: Total-350

Southern Sociologist, The *Association*

Publishing Co: Sponsor-Southern Sociological Society, Southern Sociological Society, P.O. Box 6245, Mississippi State, MS 39762 Tel # (601) 325-2495 Fax # (601) 325-4564; Title Tel # (601) 325-8602
Personnel: Co-Editor-James D. Jones, Co-Editor-George S. Rent
Editorial Description: Society affairs, articles of professional sociological interest, regarding research, teaching, service, news of academic departments and of individual sociologists.
General Info: Yr. Est. 1969, Tri-annually, Trim Size-8½ x 11, Offset press, 26 pages, Color, Newsprint
Subscriptions: Indv. $15, Can. $20, For. $20, $5/copy
Advertising: Inquire for rates. Accepts Inserts.
List Rental: Rents Lists
Printing Co: EBSCO Media, 801 5th Ave. S., Birmingham, AL 35233-1102 Tel # (205) 323-1508, Fax # (205) 226-8400

Special Libraries Assn., Social Science Division Bulletin
See: LIBRARY

Subterranean Sociology Newsletter *Association*

Publishing Co: Subterranean Sociology Assn., Dept. of Sociology, Eastern Michigan Univ., Ypsilanti, MI 48197; Title Tel # (313) 487-4246
Personnel: Editor-Marcello Truzzi
Editorial Description: Socological satire, ethnography, bibliography & book reviews.
General Info: Yr. Est. 1967, Trim Size-5½ x 8½, 20 pages, No Color, Newsprint
Subscriptions: Indv. $3
Circulation: Total-250

Survey Research *Scholarly*

Publishing Co: Survey Research Laboratory, 909 W Oregon St Ste 300, Urbana, IL 61801-3327 Parent Co.-University of Illinois at Urbana-Champaign, Urbana; Title Tel # (217) 333-7109 Title Fax # (217) 244-4408
Personnel: Editor-Diane O'Rourke, Circ. Mgr., Production Mgr.-Marya Ryan
Editorial Description: Summaries of current & completed studies & of personnel & other news at academic & other survey research organizations worldwide.
General Info: Yr. Est. 1969, Quarterly, Trim Size-8½ x 11, Offset press, 20 pages, No Color, Other, Saddle-stitched
Subscriptions: Indv. $10, Inst. $50
Circulation: Total-1,300
Printing Co: Univ. of Illinois at Urbana-Champaign Printing Division, 542 E. Gregory Dr., Champaign, IL 61820 Tel # (217) 333-0428, Fax # (217) 244-7277

Tranet
See: POLITICS

Transitions
See: MEN'S

Urban Research Review

Publishing Co: Howard Univ., Inst. for Urban Affairs/Res., 2900 Van Ness St NW, Washington, DC 20008-1106; Title Tel # (202) 806-8770
Personnel: Editor-Lula Beatty
Editorial Description: Publishes research findings related to physical & mental health, violence & criminal justice, human resource development, community services, religion, & education, focusing primarily on Blacks.
General Info: Yr. Est. 1974, Semi-annually, 12 pages, ISSN: 0732-7277, No Color, Saddle-stitched
Acquistions: Publication Bought
Circulation: Total-3,500

Washington Social Legislation Bulletin
See: LAW

What Is to Be Read
See: BOOKS & BOOK TRADE

Women's Research Network News
See: WOMEN'S

York University Institute for Social Research Newsletter *Business, Association*

Publishing Co: York University Institute for Social Research, 4700 Keele St., North York, ON M3J 1P3 Canada; Title Tel # (416) 736-5061 Title Fax # (416) 736-5749
Personnel: Editor-John Pollard
Editorial Description: Survey projects, research reports, courses in statistical analysis and research methods, conference information, ISR publications, methodological research.
General Info: Yr. Est. 1967, 3x/yr., Trim Size-8½ x 11, Desktop press, 4 pages, ISSN: 0834-1729, 2 Color, Recycled
Subscriptions: Free
Circulation: Total-3,000

SOUND ENGINEERING

ARSC Newsletter   *Association*   CPM: $90

Publishing Co: Association for Recorded Sound Collections, Inc., PO Box 543, Annapolis, MD 21404-0543; Title Tel # (410) 757-0488 Title Fax # (410) 349-0175
Personnel: Publisher-Ted Sheldon, Editor-Mike Devecka, Record Reviews-Gary Galo, Bk. Rev. Ed.-Michaul Gray, Adv. Dir.-Ricki Kushner
Editorial Description: Coverage of Association activities, information on sound collections, etc., research projects, book & record reviews.
General Info: Yr. Est. 1977, Quarterly, Offset press, 8 pages, Matte
Subscriptions: Indv. $30, Inst. $30, Can. $40, For. $40, Free With Membership
Circulation: Total-1,100
Advertising: $100. Accepts Inserts.
List Rental: Actives: $75/M

Alumni Update

Publishing Co: National Council of Accoustical Consultants, 66 Morris Ave., Suite 1A, Springfield, NJ 07081-1409 Tel # (201) 564-5859 Fax # (201) 564-7480; Title Tel # (201) 379-1100
General Info: Quarterly, Trim Size-11½ x 17, 8 pages
Circulation: Total-22,000

B.A.S. Speaker

Publishing Co: Boston Audio Society, PO Box 211, Mattapan, MA 02126-0002; Title Tel # (617) 282-8335
Personnel: Editor-Mark Fishman
General Info: Yr. Est. 1972, Bi-monthly
Subscriptions: Indv. $22
Circulation: Total-1,500

Disc Collector   *Consumer*

Publishing Co: Disc Collectors Newsletter, PO Box 315, Cheswold, DE 19936-0315
Editorial Description: Research, record reviews. book reviews of old time country/ bluegrass music.
General Info: Yr. Est. 1950, 10x/yr., Trim Size-4¼ x 5½, Sheetfed press, 20 pages, No Color, Newsprint
Subscriptions: Indv. $5, $1/copy
Circulation: Total-1,000
Printing Co: Henry Birtle Co., 1143 E Colorado St, Glendale, CA 91205-1308 Tel # (818) 241-1598

Film Technology News
See: FILM

Parascope   *Association*

Publishing Co: Professional Audio Video Retailers Assn., 10 E 22nd St Ste 310, Lombard, IL 60148-6191; Title Tel # (708) 268-1500 Title Fax # (708) 953-8957
Personnel: Editor-Melinda Miller
Editorial Description: News of association and audio speciality industry.
General Info: Yr. Est. 1979, Bi-monthly, Offset press, 8 pages
Printing Co: State Line Printer, 9140 Ward Pkwy., Kansas City, MO 64114 Tel # (816) 444-3536, Fax # (816) 444-0330

Syn-Aud-Con Newsletter

Publishing Co: Synergetic Audio Concepts, Rr 1 Box 267, Norman, IN 47264-9777; Title Tel # (812) 995-8212
Personnel: Editor-Don Lewis
Subscriptions: Indv. $32, For. $38

Technical Brief
See: THEATRE

Trebas Track

Publishing Co: Trebas Institute of Recording Arts, 6464 Sunset Blvd., Penthouse, Hollywood, CA 90028-8001; Title Tel # (213) 467-6800 Title Fax # (213) 467-0946
Personnel: Publisher-David Leonard, Editor-Joe Csida
General Info: Yr. Est. 1989, Quarterly, 8 pages, 2 Color, Coated
Circulation: (100% controlled), Total-5,000

Voice Coil Newsletter   *Business*   CPM: $333

Publishing Co: Audio Amateur Publications, Inc., 305 Union St., PO Box 576, Peterborough, NH 03458-0576; Title Tel # (603) 924-9464 Title Fax # (603) 924-9467
Personnel: Publisher-Edward Dell, Jr., Editor-Vance Dickason, Mng. Editor-Dennis Brisson, Circ. Dir.-Laurel Humphrey, Adv. Dir.-Martha L. Povey
Editorial Description: Newsletter for the loudspeaker industry featuring industry news and product reports, software and driver reviews.
General Info: Yr. Est. 1987, Monthly, Trim Size-8 x 10½, Offset press, 16 pages, 4 Color, Coated, Saddle-stitched
Subscriptions: Indv. $98, Inst. $118, Can. $98, For. $98, Free To Qualified Recipient
Circulation: (83% controlled), Total-3,000, Subscriptions-300, International-500, Readership-3,000
Advertising: $1,000. Accepts Inserts.
List Rental: Rents Lists

SPORTS & SPORTING GOODS

4 for 20   *Consumer, Association*

Publishing Co: Ontario Assn. of Archers, 1220 Sheppard Ave., E., Willowdale, ON M2K 2X1 Canada; Title Tel # (416) 426-7179
Personnel: Editor-Doug Warrick
General Info: Bi-monthly, 30 pages
Circulation: Total-600
Advertising: Inquire for rates.

5th Down
See: FOOTBALL

20/20   *Association*

Publishing Co: Canadian Table Tennis Association, 1600 James Naismith Dr., Gloucester, ON K1B 5N4 Canada Fax # (613) 748-5705; Title Tel # (613) 748-5675
Personnel: Editor, Production Mgr.-Tim Gautreau
Editorial Description: Natl. Team Bulletin-Articles are usually personal points of view/story like format/experiences at intl.
General Info: (Formerly Top Ping), Yr. Est. 1986, Bi-monthly, Trim Size-8½ x 11, 10 pages
Subscriptions: Indv. $20, Can. $20, For. $25

AAAD Bulletin   *Association*

Publishing Co: American Assn. of the Deaf, Inc., 814 Thayer Ave Ste 3, Silver Spring, MD 20910-4500; Title Tel # (301) 588-6545 Title Fax # (801) 393-2263
Personnel: Editor-Jack Levesque, Circ. Mgr.-Shirley Platt
General Info: Yr. Est. 1945, Quarterly, Mimeo press, 26 pages, No Color, Newsprint
Subscriptions: Indv. $4
List Rental: Rents Lists

AAKF Newsletter

Publishing Co: American Amateur Karate Fed., 1930 Wilshire Blvd Ste 1208, Los Angeles, CA 90057-3622; Title Tel # (213) 483-8261
Personnel: Publisher, Editor-Hidetaka Nishiyama
Editorial Description: Concerned with improving the physical & mental health of the public through the practice of Karate.
General Info: Monthly
Circulation: Total-238

ABYC News
See: BOATS & BOATING

ASF Washington Letter
See: SKIING & SNOWMOBILING

Academy-USSA News   *Association*

Publishing Co: United States Sports Academy, 1 Academy Dr # 8650, Daphne, AL 36526-7055; Title Tel # (334) 626-3303 Title Fax # (334) 626-3874
Personnel: Publisher-Thomas Rosandich, Editor-Keith Cannon
Editorial Description: Sport professionals in such things as management, fitness, coaching, medicine.
General Info: Yr. Est. 1975, Quarterly, Trim Size-8½ x 11, Web press, 12 pages, 2 Color, Saddle-stitched
Circulation: (100% controlled), Total-7,500
Advertising: Inquire for rates.
Printing Co: Quad Graphics, Inc., W224 N3322 Duplainville Rd., Pewaukee, WI 53072 Tel # (414) 691-9200

Acrosports News   *Consumer, Association*

Publishing Co: U.S. Sports Acrobatics Fed., PO Box 8158, Riverside, CA 92515-8158 Fax # (909) 785-2291; Title Tel # (909) 785-2293 Title Fax # (909) 783-2291
Personnel: Publisher-Roger McFarland, Editor-Julie Neves
Editorial Description: General information about the sport of sports acrobatics, a recognized sport of the U.S. Olympic Committee.
General Info: Yr. Est. 1981, Bi-monthly, Trim Size-8½ x 11, Roto. press, 8 pages, 3% ads, No Color, Newsprint
Subscriptions: Indv. $20, Inst. $20, Can. $20, For. $20
Circulation: Total-1,500
Advertising: Inquire for rates. Accepts Inserts.
List Rental: Actives: $30/M

Affiliate & Instructor News
See: BOATS & BOATING

Aggressive Hockey Report   *Consumer*

Publishing Co: Edgemere Enterprises, 429 Merrick Rd, Lynbrook, NY 11563-2433
Personnel: Publisher-Mark Topaz, Editor-Dennis Ehrlich
Editorial Description: For U.S. and Canadian fans of aggressive, rough hockey play and players.
General Info: Yr. Est. 1991, 7x/yr., Trim Size-5½ x 8½, 32 pages, No Color, Matte, Saddle-stitched
Subscriptions: Indv. $20
Circulation: Total-400

Alberta Gymnast   *Association*

Publishing Co: Alberta Gymnastics Fed., #207, 5800 2nd Street SW, Calgary, AB T2H 0H2 Canada; Title Tel # (403) 259-5500 Title Fax # (403) 259-5588
General Info: (Formerly AGF Newsletter), Yr. Est. 1986, 5x/yr.
Circulation: Total-2,000
Advertising: Inquire for rates.

American Boat Builders & Repairers Assn. -Newsletter
See: BOATS & BOATING

America's Cup Report
See: BOATS & BOATING

America's Fan

Publishing Co: Tom Rottkamp, America's Fan, 54 Flamingo Rd, Levittown, NY 11756
Editorial Description: A very spirited zine about prosports.
General Info: Trim Size-8.5 x 11, 12 pages
Subscriptions: Indv. $2

Annual Ringette Review   *Association*

Publishing Co: Sponsor-Ringette Canada, Ringette Canada Publications, 1600 James Nassmith Dr., Gloucester, ON K1B 5N4 Canada Fax # (617) 748-5860; Title Tel # (613) 748-5655 Title Fax # (613) 748-5860
Personnel: Publisher-Carolyne Hudson, Editor-Laura Webb, Promotion Dir.-Deb Marek
Editorial Description: Ringette Review is the national newsletter of Ringette Canada. Articles include current issues, event and meeting reporting, training tips, association progress, and upcoming events.
General Info: (Formerly Ringette Review), Yr. Est. 1979, Annually, Trim Size-8½ x 11, Sheetfed press, 36 pages, Ind/Abs/Online: SIRC, 1% ads, Color, Coated
Subscriptions: Indv. $2, Can. $2, $3/copy
Acquistions: Publication Bought, Publication Sold
Circulation: Total-30,000
Advertising: Inquire for rates. Accepts Inserts.
List Rental: Rents Lists

Ash Breeze
See: BOATS & BOATING

Atlantic Inflight
See: HOBBY

Avalanche Echoes
See: SKIING & SNOWMOBILING

BBIA Flashes   *Consumer, Association*

Publishing Co: Billiard & Bowling Institute, 200 Castlewood Dr, North Palm Beach, FL 33408-5604; Title Tel # (407) 842-4100
Personnel: Publisher-Sebastian Di Casoli
Editorial Description: News of interest to billiard & bowling trade: new products, legislation, personnel, economics.
General Info: Yr. Est. 1934, Bi-monthly, Trim Size-8½ x 11, Mimeo press, 1 pages
Subscriptions: Free
Circulation: Total-500

BOAT/U.S. Reports
See: BOATS & BOATING

BSR On Tap   CPM: $500

Publishing Co: Bay Sports Review, P.O. Box 4520, Berkeley, CA 94704; Title Tel # (510) 633-9096 Title Fax # (510) 635-2981
Personnel: Publisher-Christopher Weills, Editor-Diane Lind
Editorial Description: Nesletters sent to the owners and managers of over 800 bars, restaurants, beverage distributors, business owners and media representatives in the San Farnacisco Bay Area. This unique vehicle allows people in the beverage industry to communicate their message to industry decision-makers with the authority to purchase products for their business.
General Info: Yr. Est. 1995, Monthly, Trim Size-8½ x 11, Sheetfed press, 6 pages, No Color
Subscriptions: Free
Circulation: Total-1,000
Advertising: $500.

Badminton Today   CPM: $212

Publishing Co: Ontario Badminton Assn., 1220 Sheppard Ave., E., Willowdale, ON M2K 2X1 Canada; Title Tel # (416) 426-7195 Title Fax # (416) 495-4310
Personnel: Editor-Sterling Ivany
General Info: (Formerly Ontario Badminton), Yr. Est. 1977, Bi-monthly, 16 pages, ISSN: 0841-6036
Subscriptions: Indv. $15
Circulation: Total-2,000
Advertising: $425.

Baseball Forecaster
See: BASEBALL

Baseball Insight
See: BASEBALL

Baseball News
See: BASEBALL

Better Boat
See: BOATS & BOATING

Between the Lines
See: BASEBALL

Bicycle Nova Scotia Newsletter

Publishing Co: Bicycle Nova Scotia, Box 3010 S., Halifax, NS B3J 3G6 Canada; Title Tel # (902) 425-5450
Personnel: Editor-C. Kerr
General Info: Bi-monthly, 20 pages
Circulation: Total-350
Advertising: Inquire for rates.

Bicycle Wholesale Distributors Assn. Newsletter
See: CYCLING-BICYCLE & MOTOR

Bicycling: BC
See: CYCLING-BICYCLE & MOTOR

Bill Nelson Newsletter
See: COLLECTIBLES

Bird Hunting Report, The
See: HUNTING & FISHING

Blind Bowler, The
See: BLIND

Boast

Publishing Co: Barents, 17187 Wildemere St, Detroit, MI 48221-2720; Title Tel # (313) 863-7321 Title Fax # (313) 861-6565
Personnel: Editor-Herb Barents
General Info: Yr. Est. 1971, 17x/yr., Mimeo press, 8 pages, No Color
Subscriptions: Indv. $12, $1/copy

Boating Safety Circular
See: BOATS & BOATING

Bob Larson's Tennis Newswire
See: TENNIS

Borgward-Owners' Club-Newsletter
See: AUTOMOTIVE

Boston Cyclist
See: CYCLING-BICYCLE & MOTOR

Bowling-Golfing News   *Consumer*   CPM: $4

Publishing Co: Townsend Pubs., 131 Winthrop Ave. Ext., Liberty, NY 12754-1219 Fax # (914) 292-9114; Title Tel # (914) 292-9114
Personnel: Publisher, Editor-E. Townsend
Editorial Description: Bowling and golfing news.
General Info: (Formerly Bowling Highlights News), Yr. Est. 1975, Weekly, Trim Size-8½ x 11, Desktop press, 12 pages, 50% ads, Color-cover, Newsprint, Other
Subscriptions: Indv. $5, Free
Circulation: (100% controlled), Total-125,000
Advertising: $500. Accepts Inserts.
Printing Co: Townsend Publications, 131 Winthrop Ave. Ext., Liberty, NY 12754-1219 Tel # (914) 383-9114, Fax # (914) 292-9114

Break, The   *Association*

Publishing Co: Billiard Congress of America, 1700 S 1st Ave Ste 25a, Iowa City, IA 52240-6036; Title Tel # (319) 351-2112 Title Fax # (319) 351-7767
Personnel: Editor-Kirstin Pires
Editorial Description: Official newsletter of the billiard congress of America. Industry news, events, new products and services, business tips and more.
General Info: Yr. Est. 1968, Quarterly, 24 pages, Ind/Abs/Online: Charts,Illus.
Subscriptions: Free With Membership
Circulation: Total-100,000
Advertising: Inquire for rates.

Brooklyn Sports Foundation Newsletter   *Association, Consumer*   CPM: $200

Publishing Co: Brooklyn Sports Foundation, 7 Metrotech Ctr., Ste. 2000, Brooklyn, NY 11201-3841; Title Tel # (718) 875-7000 Title Fax # (718) 237-4274
Personnel: Editor-Bud Perone, Adv. Dir.-Andy Deitel
Editorial Description: Information on the Brooklyn Sports Foundation's activities.
General Info: Quarterly, Trim Size-8½ x 11, 8 pages, No Color, Matte, Saddle-stitched
Subscriptions: Free
Circulation: Total-5,000
Advertising: $1,000. Accepts Inserts.
Printing Co: Select Mail, 25 Flatbush Ave., Brooklyn, NY 11217 Tel # (718) 624-2696

Business of Pleasure Boats
See: BANKING & FINANCE

Butterflyer, The
See: BOATS & BOATING

CAHPERD Journal/Times
See: HEALTH

CBA News
Business, Association

Publishing Co: Continental Basketball Association, 701 Market Street, Suite 140, St. Louis, MO 63101; Title Tel # (314) 621-7222 Title Fax # (314) 621-1202
Personnel: Editor-Brett Meister
Editorial Description: Weekly newsletter of the professional minor basketball league.
General Info: (Formerly CBA Update), Yr. Est. 1946, Weekly, Trim Size-8½ x 11, Offset press, 12 pages, 2 Color, Newsprint
Subscriptions: Indv. $40, For. $60, $2/copy
Circulation: (100% controlled), Total-1,500
Advertising: Inquire for rates.
List Rental: Actives: $35/M

Canadian Amateur Boxing News

Publishing Co: Canadian Amateur Boxing News, 1600 James Naismith Dr., Gloucester, ON K1B 5N4 Canada; Title Tel # (613) 748-5611
Personnel: Editor-Gordon Anderson
Editorial Description: Eng./Fr. text.
General Info: Yr. Est. 1972, 10x/yr.
Subscriptions: Indv. $5
Circulation: Total-700
Advertising: Inquire for rates.

Canadian Archer

Publishing Co: Fed. of Canadian Archers, Inc., 1600 James Naismith Dr., Gloucester, ON K1B 5N4 Canada; Title Tel # (613) 748-5604 Title Fax # (613) 748-5785
Personnel: Editor-Jude Hooey
Editorial Description: The official voice of all archers in Canada who are members of the Fed. of Canadian Archers.
General Info: (Formerly Official Newsletter), Yr. Est. 1951, Bi-monthly, Trim Size-8½ x 11, Web press, 20 pages, ISSN: 0319-2571, Color-cover, Matte, Saddle-stitched
Subscriptions: Indv. $35, Inst. $25, Can. $25, For. $50
Acquistions: Publication Bought
Circulation: Total-1,000
Advertising: Inquire for rates. Accepts Inserts.
List Rental: Rents Lists
Printing Co: Federation of Canadian Archers, 1600 James Naismith Dr., Gloucester, ON K1B 5N4 Canada Tel # (613) 748-5604

Canadian Professional Golfers' Assn., Bulletin
See: GOLF

Canadian Special Olympics, Bulletin

Publishing Co: Canadian Special Olympics, 40 St. Clair Ave. W., #209, Toronto, ON M4V 1M2 Canada; Title Tel # (416) 927-9050
Personnel: Editor-Wendy Woodside
General Info: Semi-annually

Canews
See: BOATS & BOATING

Career Services Bulletin
See: MEDICINE

Cartel: A Newsletter of Toreo in Mexico

Publishing Co: Cartel: A Newsletter of Toreo in Mexico, PO Box 318, Cortaro, AZ 85652-0318; Title Tel # (602) 744-3634 Title Fax # (602) 297-5160
Personnel: Publisher-H. David Tuggle, Editor-David Tuggle
Editorial Description: Monthly summary of bullfighting activity in Mexico.
General Info: Yr. Est. 1986, Monthly, Trim Size-8½ x 11, Letrpr. press, 4 pages
Subscriptions: Indv. $15
Circulation: Total-400

Cheval de Fer
See: CYCLING-BICYCLE & MOTOR

Cheval d'Alliage
See: CYCLING-BICYCLE & MOTOR

Chicago Sportscene

Publishing Co: Mountain Media, Box 880524, 1360 Skyview Terrace, Steamboat Springs, CO 80488; Title Tel # (303) 879-7860
General Info: Yr. Est. 1989, Monthly
Subscriptions: Indv. $24

ChokeHold

Publishing Co: Lance LeVine, 507 W. 43rd Place Chicago, IL 60609
Editorial Description: Lace LeVine is trying to get things going again, writing columns about wrestling, also trying to start up a radio program
General Info: Trim Size-8.5 x 11, 10 pages
Subscriptions: Indv. $2

Circle

Publishing Co: Figure Skating Coaches of Canada, Box 93, Agincourt, ON M1S 3B4 Canada Tel # (613) 748-5635
General Info: Bi-monthly
Subscriptions: Indv. $5

Club News
Consumer, Association

Publishing Co: U.S. Team Handball Federation, 1750 E Boulder St, Colorado Springs, CO 80909-5724; Title Tel # (719) 578-4582 Title Fax # (719) 475-1240
Editorial Description: Updates on local club activities, national and international competitions, election results, and other special events.
General Info: Quarterly
Subscriptions: Free With Membership
Circulation: Total-120

College Sports Information Directors Digest
Association

Publishing Co: College Sports Information Directors of America, Texas A&I Univ., Box 114, Kingsville, TX 78363; Title Tel # (512) 595-3908
Personnel: Editor-Fred Nuesch
Editorial Description: Pub. for members of College Sports Information Directors of America.
General Info: Yr. Est. 1957, Monthly, Trim Size-8½ x 11, Offset press, 24 pages, 1% ads, 4 Color, Newsprint, Saddle-stitched
Subscriptions: Indv. $25
Circulation: (100% controlled), Total-1,400
Printing Co: Printers Unlimited, 112 Tarlton St, Corpus Christi, TX 78415-4328 Tel # (512) 883-1724

Court Awareness
Consumer   **CPM:** $40

Publishing Co: Jaw Travers Publishing, 2177 Carol Drive, Harrisburg, PA 17110; Title Tel # (717) 545-7429
Personnel: Publisher-Jan Travers
Editorial Description: Covers many different aspects of women's basketball, inciding interviews, product reviews, recruiting issues.
General Info: Yr. Est. 1995, Quarterly, Trim Size-8½ x 11, Offset press, 12 pages, ISSN: 1084-2675, 20% ads, 2 Color, Matte, Saddle-stitched
Subscriptions: Indv. $12, Can. $15, For. $15, $3/copy
Circulation: Total-5,000
Advertising: $200.

Crossbow Chit Chat, The

Publishing Co: National Crossbowmen of the U.S., 203 Washington Grove Lane, Washington Grove, MD 20880; Title Tel # (610) 388-6413 Title Fax # (610) 388-2051
Personnel: Publisher, Editor-Charles L. Sacco, Mktg. Dir., Promotion Dir.-Bill Pimm
Editorial Description: Target Crossbow shooting oriented, plans for making a crossbow available.
General Info: Yr. Est. 1959, Trim Size-8½ x 11, Sheetfed press, 20 pages, No Color, Matte
Subscriptions: Indv. $10, Can. $10, For. $10, Free With Membership
Circulation: Total-300
Advertising: Inquire for rates.

Cruisabout
See: BOATS & BOATING

Current
See: BOATS & BOATING

Cycle Ontario
See: CYCLING-BICYCLE & MOTOR

Devilirium
See: COLLEGE STUDENT

Discus
Association

Publishing Co: Lake Shore Club, 850 N Lake Shore Dr, Chicago, IL 60611-2428

Dive
Association

Publishing Co: Canadian Amateur Diving Assn., 1600 James Naismith, 10th Fl., Gloucester, ON K1B 5N4 Canada; Title Tel # (613) 748-5631 Title Fax # (613) 748-5766
Personnel: Editor, Circ. Mgr.-Benoit Seguin
Editorial Description: Edited primarily for members of C.A.D.A. and active diving enthusiasts.
General Info: Yr. Est. 1980, Quarterly, Trim Size-8½ x 11, Offset press, 12 pages, 1% ads, No Color, Saddle-stitched
Subscriptions: Indv. $15
Circulation: Total-5,000
Advertising: Inquire for rates.

Double Eagle Newsletter
Association   **CPM:** $6

Publishing Co: ADO Inc.-American Darts Organization, 7603 Firestone Blvd Ste E-6, Downey, CA 90241-4205 Fax # (310) 806-3909; Title Tel # (310) 806-8319 Title Fax # (310) 806-3907
Personnel: Editor, Circ. Mgr., Adv. Dir.-Della Fleetwood
Editorial Description: Tournament info & results; player rankings & achievements; league highlights & intl. darts information.
General Info: Yr. Est. 1977, Quarterly, Trim Size-8 x 10, Web press, 44 pages, 5% ads, 2 Color, Newsprint
Subscriptions: Indv. $20
Circulation: Total-90,000
Advertising: $625. Accepts Inserts.

Eighth Inning *Consumer*

Publishing Co: Softball Saskatchewan, 2205 Victoria Ave., Regina, SK S4P 0S4 Canada
Tel # (306) 780-9235
Personnel: Editor-Guy Jacobson
General Info: Yr. Est. 1983, Bi-monthly
Subscriptions: Indv. $10
Circulation: Total-1,300
Advertising: Inquire for rates.

European TV Sports
See: TELEVISION & VIDEO

Exsports *Business, Association*

Publishing Co: Sporting Goods Manufacturers Association, 200 Castlewood Dr, North Palm Beach, FL 33408-5604 Tel # (407) 842-4100; Title Tel # (407) 840-1150 Title Fax # (407) 863-8984
Personnel: Publisher-John Riddle, Editor-Maria Stefan
General Info: (Formerly IMIS Council Newsletter), Yr. Est. 1983, Irregular, 5 pages
Subscriptions: Free To Qualified Recipient
Acquistions: Publication Sold
Circulation: Total-1,500

FANS of Women's Sports *Consumer*

Publishing Co: FANS of Women's Sports, PO Box 49648, Austin, TX 78765-9648; Title Tel # (512) 458-3267
Personnel: Editor-Winifred Simon
Editorial Description: Dedicated to supporting women's sports.
General Info: Bi-monthly, Trim Size-8½ x 11, 8 pages
Subscriptions: Indv. $13

Fast Break *Consumer*

Publishing Co: Youth Basketball of America, PO Box 3067, Orlando, FL 32802-3067 Tel # (407) 363-9262 Fax # (407) 363-0599; Title Tel # (919) 784-4926
Personnel: Editor, Adv. Dir.-Jack Hutslar
General Info: Yr. Est. 1989, Quarterly
Subscriptions: Indv. $15, Inst. $45
Advertising: Inquire for rates.

Fast Break Alert *Business*

Publishing Co: Women's Basketball Coaches Assn., 4646 Highway 29 NW #B, Lilburn, GA 30247-3620; Title Tel # (770) 279-8027
Personnel: Publisher-Betty Jaynes, Editor-Pam Glattes
Editorial Description: Newsletter to women's basketball coaches that focuses on NCAA legislation.
General Info: Monthly
Circulation: Total-3,800, Readership-3,800

Fishing Hot Spots 'Newsline'
See: HUNTING & FISHING

Fishtail West
See: CYCLING-BICYCLE & MOTOR

Flying Lizards Newsletter
See: TRACK & FIELD

For the Record
See: LAW

For the Record EXTRA *Business, Association*

Publishing Co: National Sports Law Institute, Marquette Univ. Law School, P.O Box 1881, Milwaukee, WI 53201-1881; Title Tel # (414) 288-5815 Title Fax # (414) 288-5818
Personnel: Publisher-James Gray, Editor-Don Watz
Editorial Description: Articles address sports law, sports business, and sports ethics.
General Info: Yr. Est. 1989, Monthly, Trim Size-8½ x 11, 8 pages, 2 Color
Circulation: Total-500
Advertising: Inquire for rates.
List Rental: Rents Lists

G&W Recruiting Service
See: FOOTBALL

Girls' Rodeo Association News
See: HORSES

Glove Collector Newsletter, The
See: HOBBY

Gold Sheet
See: FOOTBALL

Golf Clubmaker
See: GOLF

Golf Collectors Society Bulletin
See: GOLF

Golf Update Newsletter
See: GOLF

Golf Writers Association of America Newsletter
See: JOURNALISM

Goren Bridge Letter
See: HOBBY

HAC Techline
See: AERONAUTICS/ASTRONAUTICS

Harley Hummer
See: CYCLING-BICYCLE & MOTOR

Here's the Pitch
See: BASEBALL

Historical Roller Skating Overview
See: HISTORY

Hoosier Auto Racing Fans-Newsletter

Publishing Co: Hoosier Auto Racing Fans, 616 S Fuller Dr, Indianapolis, IN 46241-2232; Title Tel # (317) 243-7728
Personnel: Editor-Rita Crafton
Editorial Description: Coverage of motor sports within state of Indiana.
General Info: Yr. Est. 1951, Bi-monthly, Trim Size-8½ x 14, 2 pages, No Color, Newsprint
Subscriptions: Indv. $10
Circulation: Total-1,000
Printing Co: Whitt Photo Service, 4863 W. 106th St., Indianapolis, IN 46290 Tel # (317) 873-5507

IDEA Fitness Manager *Business, Consumer*

Publishing Co: Assn. for Fitness Professionals (IDEA), 6190 Cornerstone Ct E Ste 204, San Diego, CA 92121-4701 Tel # (619) 535-8979
Personnel: Publisher-Peter Davis
Editorial Description: Helps fitness managers build their businesses and maintain their staffs.
General Info: 10x/yr.
Circulation: Total-3,000

ISIA Newsletter *Association* CPM: $78

Publishing Co: ISIA Newsletter, 355 W. Dundee Rd., Buffalo Grove, IL 60089-3500; Title Tel # (708) 808-7528 Title Fax # (708) 808-8329
Personnel: Editor-Justine Smith, Mag. Ed.-Lara D. Lowery, Adv. Dir.-Karen Schell
Editorial Description: Features information on the ice skating industry and ISIA services, including rink management, inmstructor information, education, programs and marketing.
General Info: Yr. Est. 1961, Bi-monthly, Trim Size-8¼ x 10½, Web press, 32 pages, 40% ads, No Color, Other, Saddle-stitched
Subscriptions: Indv. $36, For. $50, $7/copy
Circulation: Total-3,500, Readership-11,000
Advertising: $275. Accepts Inserts.
Printing Co: Hi-Liter Graphics, Inc., 280 E Chestnut St, Burlington, WI 53105-1455 Tel # (414) 344-4441

Ice Skating Institute of America Newsletter
See: PARKS & RECREATION AREAS

Indoor Score

Publishing Co: JL Sports Enterprises, c/o Luchowski, 4549 South Blvd. N.W. #20, Canton, OH 44718-2025; Title Tel # (216) 321-5502
Personnel: Editor-Paul Luchowski
General Info: Yr. Est. 1988, Bi-monthly, 6 pages
Subscriptions: Indv. $50

Insider, The
See: FOOTBALL

Insider

Publishing Co: Stratford American Sports Careers, 2408 E Arizona Biltmore Cir, Phoenix, AZ 85016-2103; Title Tel # (602) 954-8106 Title Fax # (602) 955-3441
General Info: (Formerly Sports Careers Newsletter), Yr. Est. 1989, Monthly
Subscriptions: Indv. $125

Insight Newsletter
See: BLIND

Inter-Port
See: BOATS & BOATING

International Association of Physical Ed.

Publishing Co: International Association of Physical Ed., Dept. Of Physical Education, U, College Park, MD 20742-0001; Title Tel # (301) 454-2928
General Info: Semi-annually

International Soccer Update   *Consumer*

Publishing Co: International Soccer Update, 4455 Torrance Blvd # 202, Torrance, CA 90503-4335; Title Tel # (310) 375-3811 Title Fax # (310) 373-9330
Personnel: Publisher-Tony McGuiness
Editorial Description: Covers international soccer news for fans.
General Info: Yr. Est. 1994, Monthly
Subscriptions: Indv. $39

International University Collegiate Sports Report   *Consumer, Association*

Publishing Co: International University, The, 1301 S Noland Rd, Independence, MO 64055-1390; Title Tel # (816) 461-3633
Personnel: Publisher-John Johnston, Editor-John Johnston, Circ. Mgr.-Ian Johnston, Production Mgr.-Josef Walker, Art Dir.-Israel Abundis, Promotion Dir.-Cecil Johnston
Editorial Description: Major sports interest developments relative to international higher education.
General Info: Yr. Est. 1973, Quarterly, Trim Size-8½ x 11, Sheetfed press, 18 pages, ISSN: 0748-9668, No Color, Newsprint, Saddle-stitched
Subscriptions: Indv. $300, Inst. $300, $75/copy
Circulation: (100% controlled), Total-2,000

Iron Dog Tracks
See: SKIING & SNOWMOBILING

The Iron Lung

Publishing Co: Molly Stamos, 7621 Aurora Averue, North Seattle, WA 98103
Editorial Description: Bicycle messenger zine from the high-adrenaline couriers of Seatle.
General Info: Trim Size-8.5 x 11., 24 pages
Subscriptions: Indv. $1

JEG Sponsorship Report
See: ADVERTISING & MARKETING

JSI
See: MUSIC & MUSIC TRADES

Joe Henderson's Running Commentary
See: TRACK & FIELD

Keeper's Line

Publishing Co: Dan Gaspar, 161 Main St, Wethersfield, CT 06109-2339; Title Tel # (203) 563-6263
Personnel: Publisher-Tony DiCicco, Editor-Dan Woog
Editorial Description: The newsletter
General Info: Yr. Est. 1985, Monthly
Subscriptions: Indv. $20
Circulation: Total-500
List Rental: Rents Lists

Keeping in Touch with Manitoba Gymnastic Assn.   *Association*

Publishing Co: Manitoba Gymnastic Assn., Inc., 200 Main Street, Winnipeg, MB R3C 4M2 Canada; Title Tel # (204) 985-4152
Personnel: Editor-Donna Tesarowski, Circ. Mgr.-Donna Tesawski, Art Dir.-Mo Tipples
Editorial Description: Relays information on news throughout association.
General Info: Yr. Est. 1970, Quarterly, Trim Size-3½ x 11, Sheetfed press, 20 pages, No Color
Subscriptions: Indv. $7
Circulation: Total-900
Advertising: Inquire for rates.

Keynotes   *Business, Association*

Publishing Co: Natl. Employee Services & Recreation Assn., 2211 York Rd., Ste. 207, Oak Brook, IL 60521-2371; Title Tel # (708) 368-1280 Title Fax # (708) 368-1286
Personnel: Publisher-Patrick Stinson, Editor-Karen Beagley
Editorial Description: Exploring news, legislative issues, survey findings, management tips and programming ideas affecting employee services and recreation managers.
General Info: Yr. Est. 1941, Monthly, Trim Size-8½ x 11, 4 pages, 2 Color, Newsprint
Subscriptions: Free With Membership
Circulation: Total-4,000
Printing Co: K.C. Printing, PO Box 68176, Schaumburg, IL 60168 Tel # (708) 734-0090

MIAA Newsletter   *Association*

Publishing Co: M.I.A.A.-Massachusetts Interscholastic Athletic Assn., 83 Cedar St, Milford, MA 01757-1165; Title Tel # (508) 478-5641 Title Fax # (508) 634-3044
Personnel: Publisher, Editor-Richard Neal
Editorial Description: Articles relative to assn. meetings, legislative rules and regulations, dates of athletic events.
General Info: 10x/yr., 8 pages
Circulation: Total-1,900

MJF Baseball Card Advisory
See: HOBBY

Mainsheet
See: BOATS & BOATING

Man Underwater   *Association*   **CPM: $100**

Publishing Co: Manitoba Underwater Council Inc., Box 711, Winnipeg, MB R3C 2K3 Canada; Title Tel # (204) 985-4210
Personnel: Editor-Leah Carlson
Editorial Description: Local and national scuba diving events; general information on safe diving practices.
General Info: Yr. Est. 1964, Bi-monthly, 15 pages, No Color
Subscriptions: Indv. $12, $15/copy
Circulation: Total-1,000
Advertising: $100.

Manhattan Chess Club News

Publishing Co: Manhattan Chess Club, 353 W 46th St, New York, NY 10036-3810; Title Tel # (212) 333-5888
Personnel: Editor-Russ Garber
General Info: Quarterly, Trim Size-8½ x 11, Newsprint
Subscriptions: Indv. $10, Inst. $10
Circulation: Total-500
Advertising: Inquire for rates. Accepts Inserts.

Many Happy Returns - U.S. Boomerang Assn. Newsletter   *Consumer, Association*

Publishing Co: U.S. Boomerang Assn., PO Box 182, Delaware, OH 43015-0182; Title Tel # (614) 363-8332 Title Fax # (614) 363-8332
Personnel: Editor, Adv. Dir.-Gregg Snouffer, Publisher, Circ. Mgr., Promotion Dir.-Chet Snouffer
Editorial Description: Promotes all aspects of the sport and science of boomerangs and related flying objects.
General Info: Yr. Est. 1981, Quarterly, Trim Size-8½ x 11, Offset press, 20 pages, 1% ads, Color-cover, Coated, Saddle-stitched
Subscriptions: Indv. $10, For. $20
Circulation: (70% controlled), Total-500, International-150
Advertising: Inquire for rates. Accepts Inserts.
List Rental: Rents Lists

Marble Mania
See: HOBBY

Marina Management/Marketing
See: BOATS & BOATING

Med News
See: HEALTH

Media Sports Business
See: MEDIA & COMMUNICATIONS

Mid-America Senior Tennis
See: TENNIS

Mighty Mopars
See: AUTOMOTIVE

Milestones and Memories
See: BASEBALL

Motorsports Marketing Sponsorship News
See: ADVERTISING & MARKETING

N.A.I.R. News   *Business, Association*

Publishing Co: National Association of Independent Resurfacers, 5806 W 127th St, Alsip, IL 60658-3521 Tel # (708) 371-8237; Title Tel # (312) 371-6384
Personnel: Editor-Nancy Surprenant
Editorial Description: Newsletter for bowling lane resurfacing trade.
General Info: Yr. Est. 1975, Quarterly

NARHA News   *Association*

Publishing Co: North American Riding for the Handicapped Assn., Inc., PO Box 33150, Denver, CO 80233-0150 Fax # (303) 252-4610; Title Tel # (303) 452-1212 Title Fax # (303) 525-4610
Personnel: Editor-William Scebbi, Production Mgr.-Derek Woodbury
Editorial Description: Membership newsletter concerning information about therapeutic horseback riding programs.
General Info: Yr. Est. 1969, 8x/yr., Trim Size-8½ x 11, Offset press, 2 pages, ISSN: 1067-5876, 2 Color, Coated, Saddle-stitched
Subscriptions: Free With Membership
Acquisitions: Publication Bought
Circulation: Total-3,000
Advertising: Inquire for rates.
Printing Co: Dilley Graphics, 1124 S Kalamath St, Denver, CO 80223-3117 Tel # (303) 744-7800

NASCAR News *Association*

Publishing Co: National Association for Stock Car Auto Racing, Inc., 1801 Intl. Speedway Blvd., Daytona Beach, FL 32114 Tel # (904) 253-0311; Title Tel # (904) 253-0611 Title Fax # (904) 239-8615
Personnel: Publisher-Bill France, Jr., Editor-Paul Schaefer, Adv. Dir.-Bill Seaborn, Jr.
Editorial Description: News & information on all types of NASCAR racing.
General Info: (Formerly NASCAR Newsletter), Yr. Est. 1949, Bi-weekly, Trim Size-11½ x 13, Web press, 16 pages, ISSN: 0027-5999, 2 Color, Newsprint
Subscriptions: Indv. $25
Circulation: (100% controlled), Total-30,000
Advertising: Inquire for rates.

NFLCC Gazette
See: CLUBS

NSCA Bulletin
See: HEALTH

NSRA Newsletter
See: SKIING & SNOWMOBILING

Naismith Memorial Basketball Hall of Fame Newsletter *Consumer*

Publishing Co: Naismith Memorial Basketball Hall of Fame, 1150 W Columbus Ave # 179, Springfield, MA 01105-2532; Title Tel # (413) 781-6500 Title Fax # (413) 781-1939
General Info: Quarterly
Subscriptions: Free With Membership

National Mah Jongg League Newsbulletin

Publishing Co: Natl. Mah Jongg League, 250 W 57th St, New York, NY 10107-0054; Title Tel # (212) 246-3052
General Info: Annually

National Qualifier

Publishing Co: U.S. Swimming, Inc., 1750 E Boulder St, Colorado Springs, CO 80909-5724; Title Tel # (303) 578-4578
General Info: Irregular
Subscriptions: Free To Qualified Recipient

National Softball Hall of Fame Newsletter *Association*

Publishing Co: Natl. Softball Hall of Fame, 2801 NE 50th St, Oklahoma City, OK 73111-7203; Title Tel # (405) 424-5266 Title Fax # (405) 424-3855
Personnel: Editor-Bill Plummer Plummer
Editorial Description: Highlights the National Softball Hall of Fame and its displays.
General Info: Yr. Est. 1979, Quarterly, Trim Size-8½ x 11, 4 pages, No Color, Coated, Saddle-stitched
Circulation: (100% controlled), Total-500

National Team News & Digest

Publishing Co: U.S.A. Gymnastics Federations, 201 S Capitol Ave Ste 300, Indianapolis, IN 46225-1066; Title Tel # (317) 638-8743
Personnel: Editor-Mike Botkin
General Info: Yr. Est. 1984, Semi-annually, 4 pages
Circulation: Total-300

National Wheelchair Basketball Assn. Newsletter *Association*

Publishing Co: National Wheelchair Basketball Assn., 110 Seaton Bldg.,Univ. Of Ky., Lexington, KY 40506-0001; Title Tel # (606) 257-1623
General Info: Semi-weekly

Net Friends News
See: TENNIS

Net News *Consumer, Association*

Publishing Co: Youth Basketball of America, PO Box 3067, Orlando, FL 32802-3067 Tel # (407) 363-9262 Fax # (407) 363-0599; Title Tel # (910) 784-4926
Personnel: Editor, Adv. Dir.-Jack Hutslar
General Info: Yr. Est. 1989, Quarterly
Subscriptions: Indv. $15, Inst. $45
Advertising: Inquire for rates.

New York Division of State Athletic Commission, Bulletin

Publishing Co: New York Div. of State Athletic Commission, 270 Broadway, New York, NY 10007-2357; Title Tel # (212) 417-5700
General Info: Monthly, Mimeo press

Newsletter of Water Polo Canada

Publishing Co: Canadian Water Polo Assn., 1600 James Naismith Dr., Gloucester, ON K1B 5N4 Canada; Title Tel # (613) 748-5682
Personnel: Editor-Brian Lane
Editorial Description: Purpose to inform interested persons of the on-going programs, policies & activities of the Assn.
General Info: Yr. Est. 1986, Bi-monthly, Trim Size-8½ x 11, 10 pages, 1% ads, No Color
Subscriptions: Indv. $10, $2/copy
Circulation: (90% controlled), Total-1,000
Advertising: Accepts Inserts.

Newsline
See: GOLF

Newswheel

Publishing Co: Canadian Wheelchair Sports Assn., 1200 Hornby St., #224, 1367 W. Broadway, Vancouver, BC V6H 4A9 Canada
Personnel: Editor-Kathy Newman
General Info: Yr. Est. 1980, Quarterly
Circulation: Total-600

Nordic Network
See: SKIING & SNOWMOBILING

North American Curling News

Publishing Co: U.S. Curling Assn., C/O Elgie Noble, Box 428, Poynette, WI 53955; Title Tel # (608) 635-2464
General Info: Bi-monthly

North American Society for Sports History Newsletter *Association*

Publishing Co: North American Society for Sports History, 101 White Bldg., Penn State University, University Park, PA 16802-3903; Title Tel # (814) 865-2416
Personnel: Publisher, Editor, Circ. Mgr.-Ronald Smith
Editorial Description: Contains convention program & society news.
General Info: Yr. Est. 1973, Semi-annually, Trim Size-8 x 11, Letrpr. press, 8 pages, ISSN: 0093-6235, No Color
Subscriptions: Indv. $40, Inst. $50, Can. $40, For. $45, $10/copy
Circulation: Total-1,000
List Rental: Actives: $135/M
Printing Co: Commercial Printing, 1224 N Atherton St, State College, PA 16803-2928 Tel # (814) 238-3025

Notice to Mariners
See: BOATS & BOATING

Nova Scotia Special Olympics Newsletter

Publishing Co: Nova Scotia Special Olympics, Box 3010 South, Halifax, NS B3J 3G6 Canada
General Info: Quarterly, 10 pages

Nutmeg Notes
See: FISH & FISHERIES

Odyssey *Business, Consumer* CPM: $85

Publishing Co: Central Calif. Council of Diving Clubs, PO Box 779, Daly City, CA 94017-0779; Title Tel # (415) 583-8492 Title Fax # (415) 583-0614
Personnel: Editor-Mary Ann Williamson, Publisher, Circ. Mgr.-Carol Rose
Editorial Description: Organized recreational skin/scuba diving education, conservation, safety & underwater sports-state wide.
General Info: Yr. Est. 1977, Bi-monthly, Trim Size-8½ x 11, Offset press, 12 pages, ISSN: 1084-8347, No Color, Newsprint, Saddle-stitched
Subscriptions: Indv. $15, Can. $20, For. $20, Free With Membership
Circulation: Total-1,400, Readership-2,000
Advertising: $120. Accepts Inserts.
Printing Co: KSM Printing, 140 C Linden Ave., So. San Francisco, CA 94080 Tel # (415) 952-2403

On One Wheel
See: CYCLING-BICYCLE & MOTOR

Ontario Judoka

Publishing Co: Judo Ontario, 1185 Eglinton Ave. East, North Nork, ON M3C 3C6 Canada; Title Tel # (416) 426-7006
Personnel: Editor-Kevin Casey
Editorial Description: Judo news and special feature articles in Ontario.
General Info: Yr. Est. 1975, Bi-monthly, Trim Size-8½ x 11, Offset press, 25 pages, ISSN: 0823-9134, No Color
Subscriptions: Indv. $10, $2/copy
Circulation: Total-1,000
Advertising: Inquire for rates.

Ontario Wrestler   *Association*

Publishing Co: Ontario Amateur Wrestling Assn., 1185 Eglington Ave. East, N. York, ON M3C 3C6 Canada; Title Tel # (416) 426-7274 Title Fax # (416) 426-7343
Personnel: Editor-Sean Norris
Editorial Description: Information, schedules, articles, and advertising
General Info: Yr. Est. 1979, Quarterly, 30 pages, ISSN: 0226-1561
Subscriptions: Indv. $20
Circulation: Total-3,000
Advertising: Inquire for rates.

Outside View

Publishing Co: Outsiders Association, 3934 Bryce Ave, Fort Worth, TX 76107-4419;
Title Tel # (817) 737-7555
Personnel: Editor-Rig Perry
General Info: Yr. Est. 1984, Bi-monthly
Subscriptions: Indv. $38

PGA Tour News
See: GOLF

Pennant Fever

Publishing Co: D.A.T.A. Enterprises, Box 28954, Chapel Hill, NC 27515-2895;
Title Tel # (404) 631-4804
Personnel: Editor-Douglas Decatur
Editorial Description: Statistical analysis articles, comments, information, contests concerning computer & board game. Baseball & basketball manufactured by the Pursue the Pennant game co.
General Info: (Formerly PTP Club), Yr. Est. 1989 Monthly
Subscriptions: Indv. $24
Advertising: Inquire for rates. Accepts Inserts.

People to People Sports Newsletter

Publishing Co: People-To-People Sports Committee, Inc., 80 Cutter Mill Rd., Great Neck, NY 11021-3108; Title Tel # (516) 482-5158 Title Fax # (516) 482-3239
Personnel: Editor-Rand Milton
General Info: Yr. Est. 1956, Quarterly, Trim Size-8½ x 11, Letrpr. press, 48 pages, Color-cover, Coated, Saddle-stitched
Acquistions: Publication Bought

Play Book

Publishing Co: Major Indoor Soccer League Players Assn., 2021 L St NW Ste 407, Washington, DC 20036-4909; Title Tel # (202) 463-2200
Personnel: Editor-Frank Woschitz
General Info: Bi-weekly, Mimeo press, 2 pages, No Color
Circulation: Total-240

Poop Sheet   *Consumer*

Publishing Co: Sports Letter, Inc., PO Box 4323, Chapel Hill, NC 27515-4323;
Title Tel # (919) 967-7789
Personnel: Publisher-Dennis Wuycik, Editor-Thad Mumau
General Info: Yr. Est. 1977, Bi-weekly
Subscriptions: Indv. $33
Circulation: Total-10,000

Power Hotline   *Consumer*

Publishing Co: Powerlifting USA, PO Box 467, Camarillo, CA 93011-0467;
Title Tel # (805) 482-2378 Title Fax # (805) 997-4275
Personnel: Publisher, Editor-Mike Lambert
Editorial Description: Quick coverage of major powerlifting news and events.
General Info: Yr. Est. 1981, Semi-monthly, Trim Size-7 x 8½, No Color
Subscriptions: Indv. $28
Circulation: Total-300

President's Newsletter   *Association*

Publishing Co: Little League Baseball, PO Box 3485, Williamsport, PA 17701-0485;
Title Tel # (717) 326-1921 Title Fax # (717) 326-1074
General Info: Quarterly
Subscriptions: Free To Qualified Recipient

Pro Bike News
See: CYCLING-BICYCLE & MOTOR

Professional Air Racing   *Association*

Publishing Co: National Air Racing Group, 1313 Los Arboles Ave, Sunnyvale, CA 94087-4409;
Title Tel # (408) 733-7967
Personnel: Editor-Sylvia Sweeney
General Info: (Formerly NAG Rag), Yr. Est. 1974, 10x/yr.
Circulation: Total-1,400

Propwash   *Association*

Publishing Co: NAMBA Intl., 1815 Halley St., San Diego, CA 92154; Title Tel # (619) 424-6380
Personnel: Editor-Myrtle Coad
General Info: Yr. Est. 1948, Monthly, 8 pages
Subscriptions: Indv. $10
Circulation: Total-800
Printing Co: Sullivan Printing, 2395 C Ogulin Canyon, Box 1778, Clear Lake, CA 95422
Tel # (707) 994-2913

RBI Newsletter
See: BASEBALL

Racing Pigeon Bulletin   *Consumer*

Publishing Co: Racing Pigeon Bulletin, 34 E Franklin St, Bellbrook, OH 45305-2098;
Title Tel # (513) 848-4972 Title Fax # (513) 848-3012
Personnel: Publisher-Wayne Reinke, Editor-Mike Reinke
General Info: Weekly, Trim Size-8½ x 11, 28 pages, 4 Color, Matte, Saddle-stitched
Subscriptions: Indv. $30, $2/copy
Circulation: Total-6,000

Recreation Executive Report   *Business*

Publishing Co: Leisure Industry/Recreation News, PO Box 43563, Washington, DC 20010-9563;
Title Tel # (202) 232-7107
Personnel: Publisher-Marj Jensen
Editorial Description: Provides information on sports participation; state, local, and federal park use for business and recreation professionals.
General Info: Yr. Est. 1972, 10x/yr., ISSN: 0890-2194
Subscriptions: Indv. $65

Replay   *Association*

Publishing Co: National Retired Basketball Player's Association, 1 International Place, Boston, MA 02110-2624; Title Tel # (617) 951-7286
Personnel: Publisher-Dennis Coleman, Editor-Carolyn Parello
Editorial Description: News and information for the retired basketball player.
General Info: Quarterly, Trim Size-11 x 17, 6 pages, 2 Color, Coated, Saddle-stitched
Circulation: Total-1,000

Ride On
See: CYCLING-BICYCLE & MOTOR

Ring Rhetoric

Publishing Co: American Assn. for the Improvement of Boxing, 86 Fletcher Ave, Mount Vernon, NY 10552-3319; Title Tel # (914) 664-4571
Personnel: Editor-Steven Hacento
Circulation: Total-250

Ringontario   *Association*

Publishing Co: Ringontario, 1220 Shepard Ave E, Willowdale, ON M0K 2X1 Canada;
Title Tel # (416) 426-7204
Personnel: Editor-Mike Nowosad
Editorial Description: An information magazine for ringette enthusiasts.
General Info: (Formerly ORA Newsletter), Yr. Est. 1983, Trim Size-5½ x 8½, Offset press, 24 pages, 2 Color
Subscriptions: Indv. $3
Circulation: (100% controlled), Total-10,000
Advertising: Inquire for rates.

Road Race Management   *Business, Association*

Publishing Co: Road Race Management, 4904 Glen Cove Pky, Bethesda, MD 20816-3006
Tel # (301) 320-6865
Personnel: Publisher-Phil Stewart, Circ. Mgr.-Stephanie Tetu
General Info: Yr. Est. 1982, Monthly, Trim Size-8½ x 11, 8 pages
Subscriptions: Indv. $97, For. $112, $10/copy
Circulation: Total-334
Advertising: Accepts Inserts.

Roller Sports Report

Publishing Co: Fred Argoff, 1204 Avenue U #1290, Brooklyn, NY 11229
Editorial Description: About the history of sports and skater bios, photos, and reprints.
General Info: Trim Size-5 x 7, 20 pages
Subscriptions: Indv. $3

Rusty Rudder
See: BOATS & BOATING

SBA Newsletter   *Consumer, Association*

Publishing Co: Saskatchewan Badminton Assn., 2205 Victoria Ave., Reginia, SK S4P 0S4 Canada
General Info: Quarterly, 30 pages
Circulation: Total-500
Advertising: Inquire for rates.

SPEA Newsletter   *Association*

Publishing Co: Saskatchewan Assn. of Teachers of German, Dept. of German & Slavic Langs, University of Regina, Regina, SK S4S 0A2 Canada Parent Co.-Saskatchewan Teachers' Federation, Saskatoon, Canada; Title Tel # (306) 373-1660
Editorial Description: For persons interested in physical education.
General Info: (Formerly Leisure & Movement), Yr. Est. 1971, Trim Size-8½ x 11, Offset press, No Color
Subscriptions: $10/copy
Circulation: (100% controlled), Total-150

Sailrite Newsletter
See: BOATS & BOATING

Sasiac

Publishing Co: Sasiac Unlimited, 153 E Beech St, Long Beach, NY 11561-4119
General Info: Bi-monthly
Subscriptions: Indv. $5

Saskatchewan Special Olympics Society Newsletter

Publishing Co: Saskatchewan Special Olympics Society, 1870 Lorne St., Regina, SK S4P 2L7 Canada
General Info: Quarterly

Science Periodical on Research & Technology in Sport   *Association*

Publishing Co: Coaching Assn. of Canada, 1600 James Naismith Dr., Gloucester, ON K1B 5N4 Canada; Title Tel # (613) 748-5624 Title Fax # (613) 748-5707
Personnel: Editor-M. Gelinas, Circ. Mgr.-S. Guy, Production Mgr.-J. Salton
Editorial Description: SPORTS (Science Periodical on Research & Technology in Sport) provides the latest information on sport science & coaching theory for coaches, athletic directors, sports administrators, therapists & scientists.
General Info: Yr. Est. 1980, 8x/yr., Trim Size-8½ x 11, 8 pages, Ind/Abs/Online: SIRC, No Color, Saddle-stitched
Subscriptions: Indv. $24, Inst. $20, $3/copy
Circulation: Total-1,500

Scoop   *Association*

Publishing Co: Saskatchewan Volleyball Assn., 1870 Lorne St., Regina, SK S4P 2L7 Canada; Title Tel # (306) 780-9250 Title Fax # (306) 780-9288
General Info: Quarterly
Subscriptions: Free With Membership
Advertising: Inquire for rates.

Score Board   *Business*

Publishing Co: Athletic Equipment Managers Assn., 723 Keil Ct, Bowling Green, OH 43402-2235; Title Tel # (419) 352-1207
General Info: Yr. Est. 1974, Quarterly

Senior Golf
See: GOLF

Senior Sports News
See: SENIOR CITIZENS

Shuttle (Regina, CN)   *Association*

Publishing Co: Saskatchewan Badminton Assn., 2205 Victoria Ave., Reginia, SK S4P 0S4 Canada; Title Tel # (306) 522-3651
Editorial Description: Technical, coaching & information specific to badminton and coaching.
General Info: (Formerly SBA Newsletter), Yr. Est. 1975, Quarterly, Trim Size-8½ x 11, Offset press, 40 pages, No Color

Skaters Edge

Publishing Co: Canadian Figure Skating Assn. Alberta Sect., 11759 Groat Rd., Edmonton, AB T5M 3K6 Canada; Title Tel # (403) 453-8505
General Info: (Formerly Big A), Yr. Est. 1986, Quarterly
Subscriptions: $2/copy
Circulation: Total-1,500
Advertising: Inquire for rates.

Ski Focus

Publishing Co: Canadian Ski Council, 7035 Fir Tee Dr., Mississauga, ON L5S 1V6 Canada; Title Tel # (905) 677-0020 Title Fax # (905) 677-2055
General Info: Quarterly
Subscriptions: Free
Circulation: Total-2,000

Ski for Light Bulletin
See: HEALTH

Ski Nautique News
See: SKIING & SNOWMOBILING

Ski Tripper
See: SKIING & SNOWMOBILING

Skiland/Mid America Skier
See: SKIING & SNOWMOBILING

Softball America

Publishing Co: GDE Publications, PO Box 304, Lima, OH 45802-0304; Title Tel # (419) 229-6338
General Info: Yr. Est. 1978, Bi-monthly
Subscriptions: Indv. $20

Softball Prince Edward Island Newsletter

Publishing Co: Softball Prince Edward Island, Bonshaw, PE C0A 1C0 Canada; Title Tel # (902) 675-2210
General Info: Yr. Est. 1940, Bi-monthly, Offset press, 8 pages, 2% ads, No Color
Acquistions: Publication Bought, Publication Sold
Advertising: Inquire for rates.
List Rental: Rents Lists

Solo
See: BOATS & BOATING

Southpaw Activities
See: GOLF

Sport Performance Report

Publishing Co: Sports Performance Institute, 6392 1st Ave N, Saint Petersburg, FL 33710-8400; Title Tel # (813) 367-6675 Title Fax # (813) 367-6545
General Info: Yr. Est. 1988, Monthly
Subscriptions: Indv. $95

Sport Psychology Training Bulletin   *Business*

Publishing Co: Sport Psychology Training Bulletin, 1023 Hunters Pointe Dr, Statesboro, GA 30458-6467
General Info: Bi-monthly
Subscriptions: Indv. $18

Sport Scene   *Consumer*

Publishing Co: North American Youth Sport Institute, 4985 Oak Garden Drive, Kernersville, NC 27284-9520; Title Tel # (910) 784-4926
Personnel: Publisher, Editor, Adv. Dir.-Jack Hutslar, Ph.D.
Editorial Description: Provides current information about tots, children, teens & sports, recreation, education, fitness & health. Sports Scene contains articles to help leaders & parents become more effective teachers & coaches; increase participation, decrease drop outs & injuries; & show how sports can be made more fun for all kids-the players.
General Info: Yr. Est. 1979, Irregular, Trim Size-8½ x 11, Sheetfed press, 16 pages, ISSN: 0270-1812, No Color, Saddle-stitched
Subscriptions: Indv. $16, Inst. $24, Can. $16, For. $25, $1/copy
Advertising: Inquire for rates. Accepts Inserts.
List Rental: Actives: 2,000, $200/M

Sporting Goods Intelligence   *Business*

Publishing Co: Sports Management News, Inc., 442 Featherbed Ln., Glen Mills, PA 19342-1512; Title Tel # (610) 558-1601 Title Fax # (610) 558-1650
Personnel: Publisher, Editor-John Horan, Circ. Mgr.-Katee Yorke, Adv. Dir.-Jon Bogert
Editorial Description: Designed for management of sports industry.
General Info: Yr. Est. 1984, 50x/yr., 6 pages
Subscriptions: Indv. $395, Can. $435, For. $435
Circulation: Total-1,300
List Rental: Rents Lists
Printing Co: Stover Printing, 1460 Garnet Mine Rd, Boothwyn, PA 19061-2112 Tel # (610) 459-2851

Sports Book File
See: BOOKS & BOOK TRADE

Sports Business

Publishing Co: Center for Sports Sponsorship, PO Box 280, Plainsboro, NJ 08536-0280; Title Tel # (609) 924-0319
General Info: Monthly

Sports Fact Sheet   *Consumer*

Publishing Co: Vegas Visitor, 2711 Sandalwood Ave, Henderson, NV 89014-1224
Personnel: Publisher, Editor-Keith Glantz, Adv. Dir.-Russ Culver
Editorial Description: Home and away team stats for all sports.
General Info: Yr. Est. 1979, Weekly, Offset press, 12 pages, 2 Color, Newsprint
Subscriptions: Indv. $190, $5/copy
Circulation: Total-1,000

Sports Industry News

Publishing Co: Game Point Publishing, PO Box 946, Camden, ME 04843-0946; Title Tel # (207) 236-8346
Personnel: Editor-Ray Swan
General Info: Yr. Est. 1983, Weekly
Subscriptions: Indv. $244

Sports Licensing International   *Business*

Publishing Co: Times-Mirror Magazines, Inc., 2 Park Avenue, New York, NY 10016-5675 Tel # (212) 779-5000 Fax # (212) 779-5465 Parent Co.-Times Mirror Company, Los Angeles; Title Tel # (212) 779-5556
Personnel: Editor in Chief-Michael Jacobsen, Circ. Mgr.-Margaret Morin, Art Dir.-Ron Gabriel
Editorial Description: Covers sports licensing issues and news.
General Info: Yr. Est. 1992, Bi-weekly, Trim Size-8½ x 11, 8 pages, 2 Color
Subscriptions: Indv. $275

Sports Medicine Bulletin
See: MEDICINE

Sports Medicine Digest

Publishing Co: PM Inc., 1185 Ave of The Americas, New York, NY 10036-2601;
Title Tel # (213) 873-4399 Title Fax # (818) 997-1316
Personnel: Publisher-Mervyn Oakner, Editor-James Puffer, Circ. Mgr.-H. Oakner, Production Mgr.-John Pearce
Editorial Description: Prevention & treatment of injuries associated with sports & recreational activities.
General Info: Yr. Est. 1979, Monthly, Letrpr. press, 8 pages, ISSN: 0731-9770, Ind/Abs/Online: indexed
Subscriptions: Indv. $49, Can. $49, For. $75, $4/copy
Acquistions: Publication Bought, Publication Sold
Circulation: Total-2,500
List Rental: Actives: $150/M

Sports Medicine Digest
See: MEDICINE

Sports Medicine in Primary Care
See: MEDICINE

Sports Supplement   *Association*

Publishing Co: United States Sports Academy, 1 Academy Dr # 8650, Daphne, AL 36526-7055;
Title Tel # (334) 626-3303 Title Fax # (334) 626-3874
Editorial Description: For those with an interest in the academy's activities.
General Info: Quarterly
Circulation: Total-7,000

Sports Weekly Newsletter-Baseball
See: BASEBALL

Sports Weekly Newsletter-Basketball   *Consumer*

Publishing Co: R.W. Livingston, Publishing, PO Box 60008, North Charleston, SC 29419-0008;
Title Tel # (803) 797-6173
Personnel: Editor-R. W. Livingston
General Info: Weekly, Trim Size-8½ x 14, Offset press, 2 pages
Circulation: Total-500

Sports Weekly Newsletter-Football
See: FOOTBALL

Sportsbriefs

Publishing Co: Media Marketing Svcs., PO Box 642, Saint Charles, IL 60174-0642;
Title Tel # (708) 584-4486
Personnel: Publisher, Editor-Fred Rosenthal, Production Mgr.-Seth Rosenthal
Editorial Description: Co-op source book for programs & camera-ready ad layouts.
General Info: Yr. Est. 1989, Weekly, Trim Size-8½ x 11, Offset press, 120 pages, No Color
Subscriptions: $1/copy
Circulation: Total-25,000

Spotlight on Youth Sports
See: EDUCATION

Standards & Recommended Practices for Small Craft
See: BOATS & BOATING

Starlights
See: BOATS & BOATING

Stern Words

Publishing Co: Saskatchewan Canoe Assn., Box 6064, Saskatoon, SK S7K 4E5 Canada
Personnel: Editor-Doreen Chapman
General Info: Yr. Est. 1981, Quarterly, 12 pages
Circulation: Total-350

Stringer's Assistant
See: TENNIS

Stringer's Digest   *Association*   CPM: $375

Publishing Co: U.S. Racquet Stringer's Assn., PO Box 40, Del Mar, CA 92014-0040;
Title Tel # (619) 481-3545 Title Fax # (619) 481-6024
Personnel: Publisher-Jill Workman, Editor-David Workman
Editorial Description: Manual providing stringing instructions for all racquets.
General Info: Yr. Est. 1975, Annually, Trim Size-8¾ x 11, Sheetfed press, 200 pages, 4 Color, Coated, Perfect bound, Looseleaf
Subscriptions: Indv. $54, Can. $66, For. $86
Circulation: Total-8,000
Advertising: $3,000. Accepts Inserts.
List Rental: Actives: $750/M

Surf Report   *Consumer*

Publishing Co: Surfer Publishing Group, PO Box 1028, Dana Point, CA 92629-5028;
Title Tel # (714) 496-5922 Title Fax # (714) 496-7849
Personnel: Editor-Donna Oakley
Editorial Description: Contains summaries & forecasts of worldwide surf conditions.
General Info: Yr. Est. 1980, Monthly, 12 pages, ISSN: 0270-2630
Subscriptions: Indv. $35
Circulation: Total-1,100

Surflines

Publishing Co: Natl. Scholastic Surfing Assn., Box 495, Huntington, CA 92648-0495;
Title Tel # (714) 841-3254
Personnel: Editor-Janice Aragon
Editorial Description: Provides student surfers with the opportunity to participate in Natl. surfing competitions.
General Info: Monthly
Circulation: Total-4,000

Sybarite Review
See: SKIING & SNOWMOBILING

Tanzer Talk Newsletter
See: BOATS & BOATING

Team Lineup   *Business, Association*

Publishing Co: National Sporting Goods Assn., 1699 Wall St., Mount Prospect, IL 60056-5780;
Title Tel # (708) 439-4000 Title Fax # (708) 439-0111
Personnel: Publisher-James Faltinek, Editor-Thomas B. Doyle
Editorial Description: Intended for members who specialize in supplying sports equipment to high schools, colleges & organized teams. Monitors athletic rule-making bodies & carries articles on sport safety & equipment & product liability in sports.
General Info: Yr. Est. 1967, Quarterly, Trim Size-8.5 x 11, Offset press, 2 Color, Matte
Subscriptions: Free With Membership
Circulation: Total-2,000
List Rental: Rents Lists

Team Marketing Report   *Business*

Publishing Co: Full Court Press, 660 W Grand Ave Ste 100e, Chicago, IL 60610-3906;
Title Tel # (312) 829-7060 Title Fax # (312) 733-4071
Personnel: Publisher, Editor-Alan Friedman, Assoc. Ed.-George Doig
Editorial Description: Reports revenue-generating sports marketing and promotion ideas for professional & college sports teams, corporate sponsors & sports marketing agencies.
General Info: Yr. Est. 1988, Monthly, Desktop press, 10 pages, 2 Color, Coated
Subscriptions: Indv. $159, Can. $169, For. $189
Acquistions: Publication Bought
Circulation: Total-4,000

Tell Tale

Publishing Co: Squash Nova Scotia, Box 3010 South, Halifax, NS B3J 3G6 Canada
Personnel: Editor-Bill Johns
General Info: 20 pages
Circulation: Total-500
Advertising: Inquire for rates.

Tempest, The
See: BOATS & BOATING

Thoroughbred, Quarterly Journal
See: BOATS & BOATING

Tidings
See: BOATS & BOATING

Time Out   *Association*

Publishing Co: Natl. Basketball Players Assn., 1775 Broadway Ste 2401, New York, NY 10019-1903;
Title Tel # (212) 333-7510 Title Fax # (212) 956-5687
Personnel: Publisher-Charles Grantham, Editor-Carolyn Parello
Editorial Description: Membership activities newsletter.
General Info: Monthly, Trim Size-8 x 11, Offset press, 16 pages, 2 Color, Matte, Saddle-stitched
Subscriptions: Free To Qualified Recipient
Circulation: Total-1,700

Topside

Publishing Co: All-American Soap Box Derby, PO Box 7233, Akron, OH 44306-0233;
Title Tel # (216) 733-8723
Personnel: Editor-Bob Troyer
Editorial Description: Devoted to the personalities supporting & participating in the Soap Box Derby program.
General Info: Yr. Est. 1974, Annually, 4 pages
Circulation: Total-5,000
Printing Co: Crawford Printing Co., 553 Carroll St, Akron, OH 44304-1948 Tel # (216) 535-6107

Torch Bearer
See: EDUCATION

Touchline
Consumer, Association

Publishing Co: Soccer Assn. for Youth, 4903 Vine St. #1, Cincinnati, OH 45217-1252;
Title Tel # (513) 242-4263 Title Fax # (513) 482-7162
Editorial Description: Promotes soccer among children ages 6-18.
General Info: Quarterly
Subscriptions: Free With Membership
Circulation: Total-100,000
List Rental: List Management Co.: Amity Unlimited, 531 N Wayne Ave, Cincinnati, OH 45215-2800
Tel # (513) 554-4500

Tournament News
See: BASEBALL

Track Newsletter
See: TRACK & FIELD

Trade Fax
Business

Publishing Co: Krause Publications, Inc., 700 E. State St., Iola, WI 54990-0001;
Title Tel # (715) 445-2214 Title Fax # (715) 445-4087
Personnel: Publisher-Hugh McAloon, Editor-Kevin Isaacson
Editorial Description: A must-read for industry insiders, Trade Fax is 'the source' for news in the sports collectible business. Offers breaking news from all facets of the industry. It includes updates on new products, personnel changes, & an analysis of new product performance in the marketplace.
General Info: Yr. Est. 1995, Semi-weekly, Trim Size-8$\frac{1}{2}$ x 11, 2 pages
Subscriptions: Indv. $300
Circulation: Total-175
List Rental: List Management Co.: Aggressive List Management, 18-2 E Dundee Rd Ste 101, Barrington, IL 60010-5273 Tel # (708) 304-4030, Fax # (708) 304-4032

Transmedia News
See: FOOD

Twitter
See: CYCLING-BICYCLE & MOTOR

USA Rugby Fives Assn. - News Letter
Association

Publishing Co: USA Rugby Fives Assn. -St. Mark's School, Southborough, MA 01772;
Title Tel # (617) 485-0050
Personnel: Editor-John Carey
Editorial Description: Association news and developments. promotes the game of fives.
General Info: Yr. Est. 1979, Irregular, Desktop press, 10 pages
Circulation: Total-140

USAC News

Publishing Co: U.S. Auto Club, 4910 W 16th St, Indianapolis, IN 46224-5703;
Title Tel # (317) 247-5151
Personnel: Editor, Adv. Dir.-Dick Jordan
Editorial Description: Contains schedules, results, and point standings from USAC's five divisions.
General Info: Yr. Est. 1956, Bi-weekly, Trim Size-8$\frac{1}{2}$ x 14$\frac{1}{2}$, Offset press, 4 pages, Color
Circulation: Total-7,500
Advertising: Inquire for rates.

USDF Participating Member Newsletter
Association

Publishing Co: U.S. Dressage Federation, Inc., PO Box 6669, 7700 'A' St., Lincoln, NE 68506-0669
Tel # (402) 939-8550; Title Tel # (402) 434-8550 Title Fax # (402) 434-8570
Personnel: Publisher-Robin Urmanic
Editorial Description: News relating to the equestrian sport of dressage (at all levels).
General Info: Yr. Est. 1973, Quarterly
Subscriptions: Indv. $9,000

USFA National Newsletter
Consumer, Association

Publishing Co: U.S. Fencing Assn., 1 Olympic Plaza, Colorado Springs, CO 80909-5774
Tel # (719) 578-4511 Fax # (518) 632-5737
Personnel: Editor-Ann McBain Ezzell
Editorial Description: Newsletter of the U.S. Fencing Association.
General Info: Yr. Est. 1993, Quarterly, Trim Size-8$\frac{1}{2}$ x 11, 12 pages, ISSN: 1074-9314, No Color, Coated
Subscriptions: Indv. $12, For. $18, Free With Membership
Circulation: (PSS, 100% controlled As of 12/16/95), Total-10,238
List Rental: Rents Lists

Undercurrent
See: TRAVEL

U.S. Committee Sports for Israel-Newsletter

Publishing Co: U.S. Committee Sports for Israel, Inc., 1926 Arch St Ste 3f, Philadelphia, PA 19103-1444; Title Tel # (215) 561-6900 Title Fax # (215) 561-5470
Personnel: Editor-Joy Gordon
General Info: Yr. Est. 1950, Quarterly
Circulation: Total-25,000

U.S. Handgunner
See: GUNS & FIREARMS

U.S. Roller Skating

Publishing Co: U.S. Amateur Roller Skating, PO Box 6579, Lincoln, NE 68506-0579;
Title Tel # (402) 483-7551 Title Fax # (402) 483-1465
Personnel: Publisher-George Pickard, Editor-Dwain Hebda, Production Mgr.-Patty Shorney
Editorial Description: News magazine of American competitive roller skating. Features, results, calendar, commentary, sports medicine.
General Info: Yr. Est. 1973, 11x/yr., Trim Size-8$\frac{1}{2}$ x 11, Web press, 24 pages, 4% ads, 2 Color, Newsprint, Saddle-stitched
Subscriptions: Indv. $8, Can. $14, For. $14, $2/copy
Acquistions: Publication Bought
Circulation: Total-4,200
Advertising: Inquire for rates.

U.S. Ski Writers Association, Newsletter
See: SKIING & SNOWMOBILING

Update
See: EDUCATION

Visibility
Business, Association   **CPM: $40**

Publishing Co: Underwater Society of America, PO Box 628, Daly City, CA 94017-0628
Fax # (408) 294-3496; Title Tel # (415) 583-8492 Title Fax # (415) 583-0614
Personnel: Editor, Circ. Mgr., Production Mgr.-Carol Rose
Editorial Description: Natl. organization focusing on skin/scuba diving-education, safety, conservation & underwater sports.
General Info: Yr. Est. 1983, Bi-monthly, Trim Size-8$\frac{1}{2}$ x 11, Offset press, 12 pages, 25% ads, No Color, Newsprint, Saddle-stitched
Subscriptions: Indv. $20, Inst. $50, Can. $25, For. $25, Free With Membership
Circulation: (100% controlled), Total-3,000
Advertising: $120. Accepts Inserts.
Printing Co: KSM Printing, 140 C Linden Ave., So. San Francisco, CA 94080 Tel # (415) 952-2403

Walker's World Newsletter
Consumer

Publishing Co: Rodale Press, 33 East Minor St., Emmaus, PA 18098-0001 Tel # (610) 967-5171
Fax # (610) 967-8963
Editorial Description: Newsletter featuring information and motivation for members of the Prevention Magazine walking club to start an effective walking program.
General Info: Monthly
List Rental: List Management Co.: Direct Media, Inc., 200 Pemberwick Rd., PO Box 4565, Greenwich, CT 06830 Tel # (203) 532-3713, Fax # (203) 531-1452. Actives: 57,555, $75/M

Winning Points

Publishing Co: Winpoint Corp., 438 W. 37th St., New York, NY 10018-4001
Personnel: Publisher-Jim Bradley, Editor-Lindsat Hamilton, Adv. Dir.-James Owen
General Info: Yr. Est. 1972, 19x/yr.
Subscriptions: Indv. $129, $5/copy
Circulation: Total-20,000

World of A.S.P.
See: LIFESTYLE

World Aquatic News & Travel
CPM: $150

Publishing Co: 1117 Publishing Co., 3519 E. Colorado Blvd., PO Box 1415, Duarte, CA 91009-4415;
Title Tel # (818) 793-2582 Title Fax # (818) 792-7947
Personnel: Publisher, Production Mgr.-P.M. Samson, Editor, Circ. Mgr., Adv. Dir.-Margaret Samson, Art Dir., Promotion Dir.-Tina Turcotte
Editorial Description: News from around the world, Intl. Calendar & Intl. Directory-swimming, diving, synchronized swimming, long distance swimming, water polo & travel to promote aims of Masters Swimming, fitness, friendship & understanding through swimming.
General Info: (Formerly M.S.I. News), Yr. Est. 1982, Quarterly, Trim Size-5$\frac{1}{2}$ x 8$\frac{1}{2}$, Desktop press, 32 pages, ISSN: 1063-3448, No Color, Saddle-stitched
Subscriptions: Indv. $8, For. $10, $3/copy
Circulation: Total-1,000
Advertising: $150. Accepts Inserts.

World Softball

Publishing Co: International Softball Federation, 2801 NE 50th St., Oklahoma, OK 73111-7203;
Title Tel # (405) 424-6714 Title Fax # (405) 427-5700
Personnel: Editor-Larry Floyd
Editorial Description: Focuses on international amateur softball.
General Info: Quarterly, Sheetfed press, 4 pages, 2 Color
Circulation: Total-1,000
Printing Co: Transcript Press, 222 E Eufaula St, Norman, OK 73069-6019 Tel # (405) 360-7999

Wrestlin Perspective

Publishing Co: Paul McArthur, P.O. Box 401, Camillus, NY 13031
Editorial Description: One of the more thoughtful prowrestling mags.
General Info: Trim Size-8.5 x 11, 12 pages
Subscriptions: Indv. $2

Wrestling Observer Newsletter — *Consumer*

Publishing Co: Wrestling Observer Newsletter, PO Box 1228, Campbell, CA 95009-1228; Title Tel # (408) 379-8067
Personnel: Publisher, Editor-Dave Meltzer
Editorial Description: Covers pro wrestling news and issues from an inside viewpoint.
General Info: Yr. Est. 1982, Weekly, 10 pages, No Color
Subscriptions: Indv. $65
Circulation: Total-3,700

YABA Framework — *Association*

Publishing Co: Young American Bowling Alliance, 5301 S 76th St, Greendale, WI 53129-1192 Fax # (414) 421-1301; Title Tel # (414) 421-4700
Personnel: Editor-Laura Plizka
Editorial Description: The youth bowling information guide; gives high scores, national tournament results, and the most current YABA information.
General Info: (Formerly Junior Bowler; YABA World), Yr. Est. 1946, Bi-monthly, Trim Size-11 x 14, Web press, 12 pages, 2 Color, Coated, Saddle-stitched
Subscriptions: Indv. $10, Free To Qualified Recipient
Circulation: Total-25,000

YMCA, Weekly News — *Association*

Publishing Co: Y.M.C.A., 955 Burrard St., Vancouver, BC V6Z 1Y2 Canada; Title Tel # (604) 681-0221
Personnel: Editor-Terry Connolly
Editorial Description: Health & fitness education, program promotion competition results, helpful hints, human interest studies.
General Info: Yr. Est. 1959, Weekly, Trim Size-8½ x 14, Mimeo press, 2 pages, 2 Color
Subscriptions: Indv. $10, Free
Circulation: Total-1,200

Your Season Ticket
See: BASEBALL

Youth Soccer Letter — *Consumer*

Publishing Co: Sponsor-Soccer America, Soccer America, 301 Post Rd., Westport, CT 06880; Title Tel # (203) 227-1755 Title Fax # (203) 226-6087
Personnel: Publisher-Clay Berling, Editor-Dan Woog, Circ. Mgr.-Phil Semler, Adv. Dir., Promotion Dir.-Lynn Berling-Manuel
Editorial Description: News, features & profiles for coaches, referees, & administrators working in youth soccer.
General Info: Yr. Est. 1982, Monthly, 4 pages, No Color
Subscriptions: Indv. $49, $2/copy
Circulation: Total-70,000

SUGAR

Molasses Market News — *Business, Association*

Publishing Co: U.S.D.A., 711 O St, Greeley, CO 80631-9540; Title Tel # (303) 353-9750 Title Fax # (303) 353-9790
General Info: Weekly, Trim Size-8½ x 11, ISSN: 0145-0662
Subscriptions: Indv. $40, Can. $45, For. $75

On Your Mark — *Consumer, Association*

Publishing Co: Sugar Association Inc., 1101 15th St NW Ste 600, Washington, DC 20005-5002; Title Tel # (202) 785-1122 Title Fax # (202) 785-5019
Personnel: Editor-Michelle Sutton
Editorial Description: Focuses on health, nutrition, fitness and how sugar plays a role in these areas.
General Info: Yr. Est. 1976, Quarterly, Trim Size-8.5 x 11, Sheetfed press, 4 pages, ISSN: 1083-5024, 2 Color, Coated
Subscriptions: Free
Circulation: Total-10,000

Sugar Notes and News — *Business, Association*

Publishing Co: Sugar Association Inc., 1101 15th St NW Ste 600, Washington, DC 20005-5002; Title Tel # (202) 785-1122
Personnel: Editor-Michelle Sutton
General Info: Yr. Est. 1987, Quarterly, Trim Size-8.5 x 11, Sheetfed press, 4 pages, ISSN: 1083-5016, 2 Color, Matte
Subscriptions: Free
Circulation: Total-5,000

Sugar World
See: LABOR

SURVIVAL, WEAPONS

Civil Defense Perspectives — *Consumer*

Publishing Co: Civil Defense Perspectives, 1601 N Tucson Blvd Ste 9, Tucson, AZ 85716-3405; Title Tel # (602) 325-2680
Editorial Description: Covers topics related to homeland defense including risk assessment, protective technology, and arms control.

Directions — *Association*

Publishing Co: Live Free, Inc., PO Box 1743, Harvey, IL 60426-7743; Title Tel # (708) 928-5830
Personnel: Publisher-James Jones, Editor-Duncan Long, Adv. Dir.-Marie Jones
Editorial Description: Information on emergency survival, outdoor survival, self-reliance, self-defense & personal freedom.
General Info: Yr. Est. 1977, Monthly, Trim Size-8½ x 11, Sheetfed press, 12 pages, 3% ads, No Color, Matte
Subscriptions: Indv. $20, Can. $20, For. $30, $2/copy
Advertising: Inquire for rates.

Emergency Planning Bulletin

Publishing Co: Office of Civil Defense, 310 Turner Rd., Richmond, VA 23225-6400; Title Tel # (804) 272-1441
General Info: Monthly

Five Star Review

Publishing Co: 704th Tank Destroyer Battalion Assn., 71 Route 25A, Smithtown, NY 11787-1403; Title Tel # (516) 265-2560
Personnel: Editor-Richard Bowman
Circulation: Total-300

Florida Emergency Preparedness Assn. - Newsletter

Publishing Co: Florida Emergency Preparedness Assn., 110 N. Apopka Ave., Inverness, FL 32650-4245; Title Tel # (904) 726-8500
Personnel: Editor-George Allen
General Info: Yr. Est. 1964, Monthly
Circulation: Total-125

Grey Geese Flyer

Publishing Co: 11th Bombardment Group Assn., PO Box 637, Seffner, FL 33584-0637; Title Tel # (813) 681-3544
Personnel: Editor-Robert May
General Info: Yr. Est. 1961, Trim Size-8½ x 11, 12 pages, 2 Color
Circulation: Total-1,500

Hammerterz Forum
See: HISTORY

Hood's Texas Brigade Association-Newsletter

Publishing Co: Hood's Texas Brigade Association, PO Box 619, Hillsboro, TX 76645-0619; Title Tel # (817) 582-2555
Personnel: Editor-B.D. Patterson
General Info: Yr. Est. 1966, Semi-annually
Subscriptions: Free With Membership
Circulation: Total-1,000

Missouri State Emergency Management Agency Newsletter — *Business*

Publishing Co: Missouri State Emergency Management Agency, PO Box 116, Jefferson City, MO 65102-0116; Title Tel # (314) 526-9136 Title Fax # (314) 634-7966
Personnel: Editor-Susie Stonner
Editorial Description: For local Civil preparedness coordinators. Includes state & natl. policies which affect local coordinators.
General Info: Quarterly, Trim Size-8½ x 11, Sheetfed press, 12 pages, ISSN: 0197-6672, Color
Subscriptions: Free
Circulation: Total-1,400

Our Green Emerald
See: GENERAL INTEREST

PSR Reports
See: ENVIRONMENT & ECOLOGY

Privacy Newsletter
See: CONSUMER INTERESTS

Rakkasan, The — *Association*

Publishing Co: 187th Airborne Regimental Combat Team Assn., c/o Frank Schock, 10501 Cook Lake Ct., Leesburg, FL 34788; Title Tel # (201) 752-1342
General Info: Quarterly
Circulation: Total-1,600

Self-Reliant Living

Publishing Co: Survival Tomorrow, Inc., PO Box 910, Merlin, OR 97532-0910; Title Tel # (503) 479-6699
Editorial Description: Devoted to enthusiasts of survivalism and self-reliant living.
General Info: Yr. Est. 1977, Monthly
Subscriptions: Indv. $72

Sproutletter
See: NUTRITION

TACDA Alert, The   *Consumer, Association*

Publishing Co: American Civil Defense Assn., PO Box 1057, Starke, FL 32091-1057;
Title Tel # (904) 964-5397 Title Fax # (904) 964-9641
Personnel: Editor-Helen Baker
General Info: 8x/yr., Trim Size-8½ x 14, 2 pages, ISSN: 0740-0179, Matte

Talking Leaves Newsletter
See: OUTDOORS

**Washington Emergency
Management News**   *Business*

Publishing Co: Washington State Dept. of Emergency Mgt., 4220 E. Martin Way, Olympia, WA
98504-0001; Title Tel # (206) 753-5255
Personnel: Editor-Mark Stewart
General Info: Bi-monthly, 8 pages
Circulation: Total-600

TAXES

**ADASPO Sales and Use
Tax Survey**   *Business*

Publishing Co: Information Technology Association of America, 1616 Fort Myer Dr Ste 1300,
Arlington, VA 22209-3103; Title Tel # (703) 522-5055
Personnel: Editor-Mitchell Gorsen, Circ. Mgr.-Shelly Eckenroth
Editorial Description: State sales taxation of computer software & services, updates available.
General Info: Yr. Est. 1961, Semi-annually, Looseleaf
Subscriptions: Indv. $150

AICPA Professional Standards
See: ACCOUNTING

Abapa Freer
See: LIFESTYLE

Accounting Articles
See: ACCOUNTING

**Agricultural Estate, Tax &
Business Planning**   *Business*

Publishing Co: Matthew Bender & Co., 11 Penn Plaza, New York, NY 10001-2006
Tel # (212) 967-7707 Fax # (212) 244-3188
Editorial Description: A practical guide detailing the effect of federal taxes on farmers, and offering
estate planning models to meet their specific goals.
General Info: Tri-annually, Looseleaf

**Alberta, N.W.T. and Yukon
Tax Reports**   *Business, Association*

Publishing Co: CCH Canadian Ltd., 6 Garamond Ct., North York, ON M3C 1Z5 Canada
Fax # (416) 444-8011 Parent Co.-CCH, Inc., Riverwoods; Title Tel # (416) 441-2992
Title Fax # (416) 444-9011
Personnel: Editor-Joe Weisberg
Editorial Description: Covers every aspect of taxation for Alberta Yukon and N.W.T. Indentical
arrangement of contents makes for easy cross reference between tax reports of different provinces.
General Info: (Formerly Prairies Tax Reports), Yr. Est. 1950, Monthly, Trim Size-6 x 9, Web press,
No Color, Looseleaf
Subscriptions: Can. $310

All States Tax Guide   *Business*

Publishing Co: Research Institute of America, 90 5th Avenue, New York, NY 10011-7629
Tel # (212) 645-4800; Title Tel # (800) 562-0245
Personnel: Publisher-Jeff Gattesfeld, Product Mgr.-Alan Kellett
Editorial Description: Authoritative reference guide to taxes imposed by every state including latest
tax developments, weekly updates, & compliance requirements.
General Info: (Formerly State and Local Taxes), Yr. Est. 1960, Weekly, Trim Size-6 x 9¼, Offset
press, Looseleaf
Subscriptions: Indv. $550
List Rental: List Management Co.: Manager: Phyllis Ball; WG & L List Management, 1 Penn Plz Fl
42, New York, NY 10119-0002 Tel # (212) 971-5000

**American Federal Tax
Reports**   *Business*

Publishing Co: Research Institute of America, 90 5th Avenue, New York, NY 10011-7629
Tel # (212) 645-4800
Editorial Description: All decisions handed down by courts on federal tax cases. Each volume
covers six months.
General Info: Semi-annually, Trim Size-6 x 9¼, Offset press, Looseleaf
List Rental: List Management Co.: WG & L List Management, 1 Penn Plz Fl 42, New York, NY
10119-0002 Tel # (212) 971-5000

Annotated Tax Forms   *Business*

Publishing Co: Research Institute of America, 90 5th Avenue, New York, NY 10011-7629
Tel # (212) 645-4800; Title Tel # (800) 562-0245
Personnel: Publisher-Deborah Launer, Product Mgr.-Alan Kellett
General Info: Yr. Est. 1969, Bi-monthly, Trim Size-8½ x 11, Offset press, Looseleaf
Subscriptions: Indv. $397
Circulation: Total-650
List Rental: List Management Co.: WG & L List Management, 1 Penn Plz Fl 42, New York, NY
10119-0002 Tel # (212) 971-5000

**Australian Federal Tax
Reports**

Publishing Co: CCH, Inc., 2700 Lake Cook Rd., Riverwoods, IL 60015 Parent Co.-Kluwer Law &
Taxation Publishers, Cambridge; Title Tel # (847) 267-7000 Title Fax # (800) 224-8299
Editorial Description: Provides explanations of the Income Tax Assessment Act & the Fringe Benefit
Tax Assessment Act. Each section is followed by detailed commentary, providing practical
examples, case references & Commissioner's rulings.
General Info: Weekly, Looseleaf
Subscriptions: Indv. $1,425

**Australian Income Tax
Guide**

Publishing Co: CCH, Inc., 2700 Lake Cook Rd., Riverwoods, IL 60015 Parent Co.-Kluwer Law &
Taxation Publishers, Cambridge; Title Tel # (847) 267-7000 Title Fax # (800) 224-8299
Editorial Description: A concise tax service for the non-specialist, the Australian Income Tax Guide
provides a practical up-to-date understanding of income tax and how the changing rules affect
business in Australia.
General Info: Bi-weekly, Looseleaf
Subscriptions: Indv. $555

Baldwin's Ohio Tax Service

Publishing Co: Banks-Baldwin Law Publishing Co., PO Box 318063, Cleveland, OH 44131-8063;
Title Tel # (216) 721-7373 Title Fax # (216) 721-8055
Personnel: Publisher-P.J. Lucier, Editor-Maryann Gall, Promotion Dir.-Larry Tomsick
Editorial Description: This quarterly reporter delivers commentary on current developments; the full
text of new tax laws, with selected analysis; & digests of court decisions, Board of Tax Appeals
decisions, & Attorney General Opinions.
General Info: Yr. Est. 1978, Quarterly, ISSN: 0739-1234, Looseleaf
Subscriptions: Indv. $150

Bender's Federal Tax Week   *Business*

Publishing Co: Matthew Bender & Co., 11 Penn Plaza, New York, NY 10001-2006
Fax # (212) 244-3188; Title Tel # (212) 967-7707
Editorial Description: Rapid reporting service of significant decisions.
General Info: (Formerly U.S. Tax Week), Yr. Est. 1951, Weekly, 32 pages, Looseleaf
Subscriptions: $235/copy

Bender's Payroll Tax Guide   *Business*

Publishing Co: Matthew Bender & Co., 11 Penn Plaza, New York, NY 10001-2006
Fax # (212) 244-3188; Title Tel # (212) 967-7707
Editorial Description: A time- and money-saving guide to payroll tax planning. Procedures, forms
and examples to help you design and run a payroll system that is both economical and efficient.
General Info: Yr. Est. 1982, Irregular, Looseleaf

Bookkeeping & Accounting Service Profit/Growth
See: ACCOUNTING

Bowman's Accounting Report
See: ACCOUNTING

**British Columbia Tax
Reports**   *Business*

Publishing Co: CCH Canadian Ltd., 6 Garamond Ct., North York, ON M3C 1Z5 Canada
Fax # (416) 444-8011 Parent Co.-CCH, Inc., Riverwoods; Title Tel # (416) 441-2992
Title Fax # (416) 444-9011
Personnel: Editor-Rebecca Strachan
Editorial Description: Covers every aspect of taxation for British Columbia. Indentical arrangement
of contents makes for easy cross reference between Tax Reports of differnet provinces.
General Info: Yr. Est. 1945, Monthly, Trim Size-6 x 9, Web press, No Color, Looseleaf
Subscriptions: Can. $310

**British Columbia Taxation
Service**   *Business*

Publishing Co: Carswell, 2075 Kennedy Road, One Corporate Plaza, Scarborough, ON M1T 3V4
Canada; Title Tel # (416) 609-8000 Title Fax # (416) 298-5094
Personnel: Publisher-Barry Garnet, Editor-Colin Braithwaite, Adv. Dir.-Sandra Kay
Editorial Description: Continuously updated tax service for the business/legal professions.
General Info: Monthly, Trim Size-6½ x 9, 64 pages, No Color, Looseleaf
Subscriptions: Indv. $215, Can. $215
Circulation: Total-400

British Company Law and Practice, with Legislation

Publishing Co: CCH, Inc., 2700 Lake Cook Rd., Riverwoods, IL 60015 Parent Co.-Kluwer Law & Taxation Publishers, Cambridge; Title Tel # (847) 267-7000 Title Fax # (800) 224-8299
Editorial Description: Features topically-arranged commentaries & case reports & explains British law affecting companies. Provides provisions of Companies Acts from 1948 to date plus pertinent rules, regulations & orders.
General Info: Monthly, Looseleaf
Subscriptions: Indv. $765

British Tax Cases

Publishing Co: CCH, Inc., 2700 Lake Cook Rd., Riverwoods, IL 60015 Parent Co.-Kluwer Law & Taxation Publishers, Cambridge; Title Tel # (847) 267-7000 Title Fax # (800) 224-8299
Editorial Description: Provides headnoted texts of tax judgments.
General Info: Irregular, Looseleaf
Subscriptions: Indv. $395

British Tax Guide

Publishing Co: CCH, Inc., 2700 Lake Cook Rd., Riverwoods, IL 60015 Parent Co.-Kluwer Law & Taxation Publishers, Cambridge; Title Tel # (847) 267-7000 Title Fax # (800) 224-8299
Editorial Description: Explanatory treatment of British taxes by topic.
General Info: Monthly, Looseleaf
Subscriptions: Indv. $530

British Tax Reports and Legislation   *Business*

Publishing Co: CCH, Inc., 2700 Lake Cook Rd., Riverwoods, IL 60015 Parent Co.-Kluwer Law & Taxation Publishers, Cambridge; Title Tel # (847) 267-7000 Title Fax # (800) 224-8299
Editorial Description: Detailed information on United Kingdom income tax, surtax and profits tax with the full texts of pertinent laws and regulations.
General Info: (Formerly British Tax Guide), Yr. Est. 1963, Weekly, Trim Size-6 x 9, Web press, 140 pages, No Color, Looseleaf
Subscriptions: Indv. $1,360

Business Accounting for Lawyers Newsletter
See: ACCOUNTING

Business Strategies
See: BUSINESS & INDUSTRY

CAAS News
See: REAL ESTATE

CCH Family Law Tax Guide

Publishing Co: CCH, Inc., 2700 Lake Cook Rd., Riverwoods, IL 60015 Tel # (847) 267-7000 Parent Co.-Kluwer Law & Taxation Publishers, Cambridge; Title Tel # (847) 267-7003 Title Fax # (800) 224-8299
Editorial Description: Combines, in one volume, the tax law, rules and regulations as they apply to the family- united, separated or divorced.
General Info: Monthly, Looseleaf
Subscriptions: Indv. $538

CCH Federal Tax: Internal Revenue Bulletin
See: U.S. (& CANADIAN) FED. GOV'T.

CCH Federal Tax Service

Publishing Co: CCH, Inc., 2700 Lake Cook Rd., Riverwoods, IL 60015 Parent Co.-Kluwer Law & Taxation Publishers, Cambridge; Title Tel # (847) 267-7000 Title Fax # (800) 224-8299
General Info: Weekly
Subscriptions: Indv. $1,110
List Rental: Rents Lists

CCH Federal Tax Service Analysis Only
See: U.S. (& CANADIAN) FED. GOV'T.

CCH Fringe Benefits Tax Guide

Publishing Co: CCH, Inc., 2700 Lake Cook Rd., Riverwoods, IL 60015 Parent Co.-Kluwer Law & Taxation Publishers, Cambridge; Title Tel # (847) 267-7000 Title Fax # (800) 224-8299
Editorial Description: The one volume guide provides a concise, yet thorough, explanation of an array of alphabetically arranged fringe benefits including cafeteria plans, ESOPs, 401(K) plans, moving expenses, & travel. Selected portions of the Internal Revenue Code & Regulations are also reproduced.
General Info: Monthly, Looseleaf
Subscriptions: Indv. $461

CCH Tax Day Report   *Business, Association*

Publishing Co: CCH, Inc., 2700 Lake Cook Rd., Riverwoods, IL 60015 Parent Co.-Kluwer Law & Taxation Publishers, Cambridge; Title Tel # (847) 267-7000 Title Fax # (800) 224-8299
Editorial Description: Gathers important tax news from Washington, D.C., and across the country for print and electronic availability every business day.
General Info: Yr. Est. 1983, Daily, Trim Size-8½ x 11, 18 pages, 2 Color, Looseleaf
Subscriptions: Indv. $1,390, Inst. $925

Cal-Tax News   *Association*

Publishing Co: California Taxpayers' Assn, 921 11th St Ste 800, Sacramento, CA 95814-2821; Title Tel # (916) 441-0490 Title Fax # (916) 441-1619
Personnel: Editor-Ron Roach
Editorial Description: All items relating to efficiency and economy in government and to issues affecting taxes.
General Info: Yr. Est. 1960, Bi-weekly, Trim Size-8½ x 11, Offset press, 12 pages, No Color
Subscriptions: Indv. $59, $4/copy
Circulation: (100% controlled), Total-5,000

California Employer Newsletter   *Business*

Publishing Co: California Employment Development Department, 800 Capitol Mall, MIC 84, Sacramento, CA 95814-4807; Title Tel # (916) 645-7079 Title Fax # (916) 654-5843
Personnel: Editor-Kevin Callori
Editorial Description: News and notes for California employers from the California State Employment Development Department.
General Info: (Formerly California State Employment Development Department), Yr. Est. 1937, Quarterly
Subscriptions: Free
Circulation: Total-800,000

California Family Tax Planning   *Business*

Publishing Co: Matthew Bender & Co., 11 Penn Plaza, New York, NY 10001-2006 Fax # (212) 244-3188; Title Tel # (212) 967-7707
Editorial Description: Provides plans, methods, procedures and sample forms for optimum family tax saving under California and federal income, estate and gift tax law.
General Info: Yr. Est. 1959, Annually, Looseleaf
Subscriptions: $160/copy

California Tax Analysis   *Business, Association*

Publishing Co: CCH, Inc., 2700 Lake Cook Rd., Riverwoods, IL 60015 Parent Co.-Kluwer Law & Taxation Publishers, Cambridge; Title Tel # (847) 267-7000 Title Fax # (800) 224-8299
Editorial Description: California tax analysis is an analytical & reporting service with 4 volumes (over 4,000 pages) of explanatory text & primary source material covering California personal income bank & corporate, sales & use property & estate taxes. Text chapters written by & directed to tax experts & practioners new to field.
General Info: (Formerly California Taxation), Monthly, Looseleaf
Subscriptions: Indv. $529
List Rental: Rents Lists

California Tax Guide   *Business*

Publishing Co: CCH, Inc., 2700 Lake Cook Rd., Riverwoods, IL 60015 Parent Co.-Kluwer Law & Taxation Publishers, Cambridge; Title Tel # (847) 267-7000 Title Fax # (800) 224-8299
Editorial Description: Provides concise reporting of what the California, personal income, corporate income, & sales & use tax laws say, how they relate to federal law, & the procedures necessary for full compliance. Also includes California personal & corporate income tax return forms, withholding forms, & sales & use forms.
General Info: Monthly, Looseleaf
Subscriptions: Indv. $384

California Taxation   *Business*

Publishing Co: Matthew Bender & Co., 11 Penn Plaza, New York, NY 10001-2006 Tel # (212) 967-7707 Fax # (212) 244-3188
Editorial Description: Complete expert coverage of California tax law, with in-depth treatment of: Personal Income Tax, Bank and Corporation Tax, Sales and Use Tax, Property Tax and Estate and Gift Tax.
General Info: Monthly, Looseleaf

Canada Income Tax Guide   *Business*

Publishing Co: CCH Canadian Ltd., 6 Garamond Ct., North York, ON M3C 1Z5 Canada Fax # (416) 444-8011 Parent Co.-CCH, Inc., Riverwoods; Title Tel # (416) 441-2992 Title Fax # (416) 444-9011
Personnel: Editor-Danielle Trepanier
Editorial Description: Explanations, laws, rulings and regulations of the Canadian federal income tax.
General Info: Yr. Est. 1952, 18x/yr., Trim Size-6 x 9, Offset press, No Color, Looseleaf
Subscriptions: Can. $325

Canadian Current Income Tax Proposals   *Business*

Publishing Co: CCH Canadian Ltd., 6 Garamond Ct., North York, ON M3C 1Z5 Canada Fax # (416) 444-8011 Parent Co.-CCH, Inc., Riverwoods; Title Tel # (416) 441-2992 Title Fax # (416) 444-9011
Editorial Description: Reproduces all proposed amendments to the federal income Tax Act and Regulations including Notices of Ways and Means Motion, Draft Legislation, Bills, Draft Regulations and etc.
General Info: Irregular, Looseleaf
Subscriptions: Can. $165

Canadian Current Tax

Publishing Co: Butterworths, 75 Clegg Rd., Markham, ON L6G 1A1 Canada Tel # (905) 479-2665 Fax # (905) 479-2826; Title Tel # (416) 479-2665
Personnel: Editor-Vern Krishna
General Info: Yr. Est. 1980, Monthly, 2 Color, Newsprint, Saddle-stitched
Subscriptions: Indv. $175

Canadian Estate Planning & Administration Reporter
See: LAW

Canadian Goods & Services Tax Reporter   *Business*

Publishing Co: CCH Canadian Ltd., 6 Garamond Ct., North York, ON M3C 1Z5 Canada Fax # (416) 444-8011 Parent Co.-CCH, Inc., Riverwoods; Title Tel # (416) 441-2992 Title Fax # (416) 444-9011
Editorial Description: Provides up-to-date developments concerning the GST. Provides detailed commentary on and analysis of the GST.
General Info: Monthly, Looseleaf
Subscriptions: Can. $320

Canadian Income Tax Act, Regulations & Rulings   *Business*

Publishing Co: CCH Canadian Ltd., 6 Garamond Ct., North York, ON M3C 1Z5 Canada Fax # (416) 444-8011 Parent Co.-CCH, Inc., Riverwoods; Title Tel # (416) 441-2992 Title Fax # (416) 444-9011
Personnel: Editor-Danielle Trepanier
Editorial Description: Consolidated texts of Income Tax Act and Income Tax Regulations, with historical notes, references to related sections and summaries of Amendments.
General Info: Yr. Est. 1945, Monthly, Trim Size-6 x 9, Offset press, No Color, Looseleaf
Subscriptions: Can. $325

Canadian Income Tax Research Index   *Business*

Publishing Co: CCH Canadian Ltd., 6 Garamond Ct., North York, ON M3C 1Z5 Canada Fax # (416) 444-8011 Parent Co.-CCH, Inc., Riverwoods; Title Tel # (416) 441-2992 Title Fax # (416) 444-9011
Editorial Description: Contains some 700 pages with thousands of references which direct the subscriber to specific tax articles or publications.
General Info: Yr. Est. 1981, Quarterly, Trim Size-6 x 9, Web press, No Color, Looseleaf
Subscriptions: Can. $310

Canadian Real Estate Income Tax Guide   *Business*

Publishing Co: CCH Canadian Ltd., 6 Garamond Ct., North York, ON M3C 1Z5 Canada Fax # (416) 444-8011 Parent Co.-CCH, Inc., Riverwoods; Title Tel # (416) 441-2992 Title Fax # (416) 444-9011
Personnel: Co-Editor-Peter Clark, Co-Editor-Jan MacInnis
Editorial Description: Provides a comprehensive analysis & explanation of the tax implications of buying, owning, developing, leasing & selling Canadian Real Estate.
General Info: Yr. Est. 1990, Quarterly, Looseleaf
Subscriptions: Can. $220

Canadian Sales Tax Reporter   *Business*

Publishing Co: CCH Canadian Ltd., 6 Garamond Ct., North York, ON M3C 1Z5 Canada Fax # (416) 444-8011 Parent Co.-CCH, Inc., Riverwoods; Title Tel # (416) 441-2992 Title Fax # (416) 444-9011
Personnel: Editor-Vida Vukadinovic
Editorial Description: Reports on federal sales and excise taxes statutes, regulations, court decisions, departmental rulings.
General Info: Yr. Est. 1945, Monthly, Trim Size-6 x 9, Web press, No Color, Looseleaf
Subscriptions: Can. $380

Canadian Small Business Financing and Tax Planning Guide   *Business*

Publishing Co: CCH Canadian Ltd., 6 Garamond Ct., North York, ON M3C 1Z5 Canada Fax # (416) 444-8011 Parent Co.-CCH, Inc., Riverwoods; Title Tel # (416) 441-2992 Title Fax # (416) 444-9011
Personnel: Editor-Donald Schrank
Editorial Description: Useful to the financial management of a small business and their financial tax advisors.
General Info: Yr. Est. 1984, Monthly, Trim Size-6 x 9, Web press, No Color, Looseleaf
Subscriptions: Can. $380

Canadian Tax Forms   *Business*

Publishing Co: CCH Canadian Ltd., 6 Garamond Ct., North York, ON M3C 1Z5 Canada Fax # (416) 444-8011 Parent Co.-CCH, Inc., Riverwoods; Title Tel # (416) 441-2992 Title Fax # (416) 444-9011
Editorial Description: One stop source of all federal individual and corporate income tax forms subscribers will be rushed any new forms as they are released by the government.
General Info: Looseleaf
Subscriptions: Can. $210

Canadian Tax Highlights   *Business, Association*

Publishing Co: Canadian Tax Foundation, One Queen St. E., Suite 1800, Toronto, ON M5C 2Y2 Canada; Title Tel # (416) 863-9784 Title Fax # (416) 863-9585
Personnel: Editor-Laurel Amalia, Law Ed.-Vivien Morgan
Editorial Description: Provides brief analyses on current tax issues for tax practitioners, small business and corporate tax executives.
General Info: Yr. Est. 1993, Monthly, Trim Size-8½ x 11, Sheetfed press, 8 pages, ISSN: 1192-2672, 2 Color, Matte, Saddle-stitched
Subscriptions: Can. $150, Free With Membership
Circulation: (96% controlled), Total-8,800
Printing Co: The Press Run, Don Mills, ON

Canadian Tax News

Publishing Co: Carswell, 2075 Kennedy Road, One Corporate Plaza, Scarborough, ON M1T 3V4 Canada Tel # (416) 609-8000; Title Tel # (416) 609-3800 Title Fax # (416) 298-5094
Personnel: Publisher-Colin Braithwaite
General Info: Yr. Est. 1969, 8x/yr.

Canadian Tax Objection & Appeal Procedures   *Business*

Publishing Co: CCH Canadian Ltd., 6 Garamond Ct., North York, ON M3C 1Z5 Canada Fax # (416) 444-8011 Parent Co.-CCH, Inc., Riverwoods; Title Tel # (416) 441-2992 Title Fax # (416) 444-9011
Personnel: Editor-Fraiser,Beatty Barristers, Solicitors
Editorial Description: Explains the new rules of procedure in Tax Court. Covers GST and other federal taxes.
General Info: Yr. Est. 1991, Quarterly, Looseleaf
Subscriptions: Can. $205

Canadian Tax Planner's Newsletter   *Business*

Publishing Co: Canadian Tax Planners Ltd., Box 6489, London, ON N5W 3S5 Canada; Title Tel # (519) 472-2799
Personnel: Editor-D. Pollock
Editorial Description: Comprehensive analysis of the Canadian income tax scene.
General Info: Yr. Est. 1980, Bi-monthly, Trim Size-8½ x 11, Web press, 8 pages, No Color
Subscriptions: Indv. $75

Canadian Tax Reporter   *Business*

Publishing Co: CCH Canadian Ltd., 6 Garamond Ct., North York, ON M3C 1Z5 Canada Fax # (416) 444-8011 Parent Co.-CCH, Inc., Riverwoods; Title Tel # (416) 441-2992 Title Fax # (416) 444-9011
Personnel: Editor-Robin Mackie
Editorial Description: Reporting on federal, corporate and personal income tax laws, regulations, rulings. All federal taxing act and regulations in full text including bulletins, circulars and advance rulings.
General Info: Yr. Est. 1939, Weekly, Trim Size-6 x 9, Web press, No Color, Looseleaf
Subscriptions: Can. $1,150

Canadian Taxpayer, The   *Business*

Publishing Co: Carswell, 2075 Kennedy Road, One Corporate Plaza, Scarborough, ON M1T 3V4 Canada Tel # (416) 609-8000 Fax # (416) 298-5094; Title Tel # (416) 445-4940 Title Fax # (416) 445-5352
Personnel: Publisher-Barry Garnet, Editor-Arthur Drache, Adv. Dir.-Melanie Causton
General Info: Yr. Est. 1979, Semi-monthly, Trim Size-8½ x 11, ISSN: 0225-0608
Subscriptions: Indv. $240

Capital Adjustments   *Business*

Publishing Co: Research Institute of America, 90 5th Avenue, New York, NY 10011-7629 Tel # (212) 645-4800; Title Tel # (800) 562-0245 Title Fax # (201) 816-3484
Editorial Description: Reference that traces complex basis of more than 25,000 securities through takeovers, mergers, spinoffs, reorganizations & liquidations.
General Info: Yr. Est. 1940, Weekly, Trim Size-6 x 9¼, Offset press, No Color, Looseleaf
Subscriptions: Indv. $655
List Rental: List Management Co.: WG & L List Management, 1 Penn Plz Fl 42, New York, NY 10119-0002 Tel # (212) 971-5000

Capital Changes Reports   *Business*

Publishing Co: CCH, Inc., 2700 Lake Cook Rd., Riverwoods, IL 60015 Parent Co.-Kluwer Law & Taxation Publishers, Cambridge; Title Tel # (847) 267-7000 Title Fax # (800) 224-8299
Editorial Description: Changes in the capital structures of corporations affecting the investment and federal income status of investors reported.
General Info: Yr. Est. 1928, Weekly, Trim Size-6 x 9, Web press, 40 pages, ISSN: 0196-237X, No Color, Looseleaf
Subscriptions: Indv. $1,199
Circulation: Total-3,950

Charitable Giving & Solicitation

Publishing Co: Research Institute of America, 90 5th Avenue, New York, NY 10011-7629 Tel # (212) 645-4800; Title Tel # (800) 562-0245 Title Fax # (201) 816-3484
Editorial Description: Reference to the laws governing charitable giving & solicitation with numerous tips & proven fund raising ideas each month by experts in the field.
General Info: Yr. Est. 1981, Monthly, Looseleaf
Subscriptions: Indv. $362
List Rental: List Management Co.: WG & L List Management, 1 Penn Plz Fl 42, New York, NY 10119-0002 Tel # (212) 971-5000

Charitable Giving Tax Service
See: PHILANTHROPY

Church Law & Tax Report
See: LAW

Church Treasurer Alert   *Business*

Publishing Co: Christian Ministry Resources, 617 Greenbrook Pky, Matthews, NC 28105-7745; Title Tel # (704) 841-8066 Title Fax # (704) 846-5923
Editorial Description: Review of tax and financial developments affecting churches.
General Info: Yr. Est. 1993, Monthly, Trim Size-8½ x 11, 4 pages, 2 Color
Subscriptions: Indv. $30
Circulation: Total-16,000
List Rental: List Management Co.: Bernice Bush Co./Springdale Lists, 15052 Springdale St., Huntington Beach, CA 92649-1178 Tel # (714) 891-3344, Fax # (714) 897-0650

Code and Regulations
See: LAW

Collier, Sarner & Associates Doctors Newsletter
See: BANKING & FINANCE

Commodity Tax Series   *Business*

Publishing Co: Canadian Institute of Chartered Accountants, 277 Wellington Street West, Toronto, ON M5V 3H2 Canada Tel # (416) 977-3222 Fax # (414) 204-3416; Title Tel # (416) 927-2322
Personnel: Editor-Peter Wood
Editorial Description: Commodity Tax Series consists of: Provinced Sales Tax Handbook, Goods and Services Tax Handbook, Customs Handbook.
General Info: Yr. Est. 1985, Irregular, Offset press, No Color, Looseleaf
Subscriptions: Indv. $200

CommonWealth Letters
See: INVESTMENT

Connecticut Public Expenditure Council-News & Views   *Association*

Publishing Co: Connecticut Public Expenditure Council, 21 Lewis St, Hartford, CT 06103-2506; Title Tel # (203) 527-8177
Personnel: Publisher-L.J. DeNardis, Editor-Natalie Bancroft
Editorial Description: Reports on news and research of interest to Connecticut taxpayers.
General Info: (Formerly CPEC News & Views), Yr. Est. 1944, Trim Size-8½ x 11, Offset press, 4 pages, 2 Color
Subscriptions: Indv. $25
Circulation: (100% controlled), Total-2,500

Conscience and Military Tax Campaign   *Consumer*

Publishing Co: Conscience and Military Tax Campaign, 4554 12th Ave. NE, Seattle, WA 98105-4524; Title Tel # (206) 547-0952 Title Fax # (206) 547-2723
Personnel: Editor-Vivien Sharples
Editorial Description: For war tax resisters.
General Info: Quarterly, Trim Size-8½ x 11, 2 Color, Matte, Saddle-stitched

Consolidated Finding Lists   *Business*

Publishing Co: CCH Canadian Ltd., 6 Garamonc Ct., North York, ON M3C 1Z5 Canada Fax # (416) 444-8011 Parent Co.-CCH, Inc., Riverwoods; Title Tel # (416) 441-2992 Title Fax # (416) 444-9011
Personnel: Editor-Michael Dyet, Mktg. Dir.-Rick Humphrey
General Info: Annually, Looseleaf
Subscriptions: Can. $130

Cumulative Changes   *Business*

Publishing Co: Research Institute of America, 90 5th Avenue, New York, NY 10011-7629 Tel # (212) 645-4800; Title Tel # (800) 562-0245
Editorial Description: Reports each section of the regulations that has been amended after enactment of Tax Reform Act of 1986. Contains charts relating to income, estate & gift taxes, withholding, procedure & administration, & more.
General Info: Yr. Est. 1986, Quarterly, Offset press, Looseleaf
Subscriptions: Indv. $396
List Rental: List Management Co.: WG & L List Management, 1 Penn Plz Fl 42, New York, NY 10119-0002 Tel # (212) 971-5000

Current Legal Forms with Tax Analysis
See: LAW

Daily Report for Executives
See: ECONOMICS

Daily Tax Report   *Business*

Publishing Co: Bureau of National Affairs, Inc., 1231 25th St. NW, Bldg. N-200, Washington, DC 20037-1157; Title Tel # (202) 452-4200 Title Fax # (202) 822-8092
Personnel: Publisher-William A. Beltz, Mng. Editor-Rebecca McCracken, Circ. Mgr.-Gary C. Seltzer
Editorial Description: A daily tax notification service that covers legislative, regulatory, judicial, & policy developments on a national basis, designed to give tax professionals rapid notification & comprehensive coverage of those developments.
General Info: Yr. Est. 1954, Daily, Trim Size-8½ x 11, Web press, 25 pages, ISSN: 0092-6884, Ind/Abs/Online: BNA, Mead Data Central, WESTLAW, Lexis, Dialcom, Tax News Network
Subscriptions: Indv. $2,003

Daily TaxFax

Publishing Co: Tax Analysts, 6830 N. Fairfax Dr., Arlington, VA 22213-1098 Fax # (703) 533-4444; Title Tel # (703) 533-4400 Title Fax # (703) 533-4440
Personnel: Publisher-Thomas Field, Mktg. Dir.-Barbara Halberstam
Editorial Description: Provides each days tax news developments, from court decisions to congressional hearings to IRS announcements, classified by Internal Revenue Code section, state and country.
General Info: Yr. Est. 1989, Daily
Subscriptions: Indv. $1,999
List Rental: Rents Lists

Debt-Free & Prosperous Living
See: CONSUMER INTERESTS

Depreciation & Capital Planning
See: BANKING & FINANCE

Dictionary of 1040 Deductions   *Business*

Publishing Co: Matthew Bender & Co., 11 Penn Plaza, New York, NY 10001-2006 Fax # (212) 244-3188; Title Tel # (212) 967-7707
Editorial Description: Guidance on claiming deductions on individual income tax.
General Info: Annually, Looseleaf
Subscriptions: $39/copy

Divorce Taxation

Publishing Co: Research Institute of America, 90 5th Avenue, New York, NY 10011-7629 Tel # (212) 645-4800; Title Tel # (800) 562-0245 Title Fax # (201) 816-3484
Editorial Description: Explains tax consequences of spousal & child support payments, property rights & interests, special marital assets, as well as highlights provisions of new legislations.
General Info: Yr. Est. 1981, Monthly, Looseleaf
Subscriptions: Indv. $375
List Rental: List Management Co.: WG & L List Management, 1 Penn Plz Fl 42, New York, NY 10119-0002 Tel # (212) 971-5000, Actives: $85/M, Expires: $85/M

Doctor's Tax Report   *Business*

Publishing Co: Research Institute of America, 90 5th Avenue, New York, NY 10011-7629 Tel # (212) 645-4800; Title Tel # (201) 767-5059
Editorial Description: Shows physician and dentist how to maximize savings.
General Info: Bi-weekly, 8 pages
Subscriptions: Indv. $191
List Rental: List Management Co.: WG & L List Management, 1 Penn Plz Fl 42, New York, NY 10119-0002 Tel # (212) 971-5000

Doing Business in Eastern Europe
See: BUSINESS & INDUSTRY

Dollars & Sense / Capital Ideas   *Consumer, Association*

Publishing Co: National Taxpayers Union/NTU Foundation, 108 N. Alfred St., Alexandria, VA 22314 Tel # (703) 683-5700 Fax # (703) 683-5722; Title Tel # (202) 543-1300 Title Fax # (202) 546-2086
Personnel: Editor in Chief-Peter Sepp, Design Ed.-Steve Hansberg
Editorial Description: Membership newsletter providing policy analyses and action alerts for taxpayers.
General Info: Yr. Est. 1969, Bi-monthly, Trim Size-8½ x 11, 8 pages, ISSN: 0745-9092
Subscriptions: Indv. $15, $2/copy
Circulation: Total-100,000
List Rental: List Management Co.: Conrad Direct, Inc., 300 Knickerbocker Road, Creskill, NJ 07626 Tel # (201) 567-3200, Fax # (201) 567-4959

Dominion Tax Cases   *Business*

Publishing Co: CCH Canadian Ltd., 6 Garamond Ct., North York, ON M3C 1Z5 Canada Fax # (416) 444-8011 Parent Co.-CCH, Inc., Riverwoods; Title Tel # (416) 441-2992 Title Fax # (416) 444-9011
Personnel: Editor-David Gordon
Editorial Description: Full texts and digests of all Court and Tax Review Board decisions on federal tax questions. Case Table, Citator and Topical Index.
General Info: Yr. Est. 1949, Bi-weekly, Trim Size-6 x 9, Offset press, No Color, Looseleaf
Subscriptions: Can. $505

EAlert   *Business, Association*

Publishing Co: National Association of Enrolled Agents, 200 Orchard Ridge Dr Ste 302, Gaithersburg, MD 20878-1978 Tel # (301) 212-9608 Fax # (301) 990-1611; Title Tel # (301) 984-6232 Title Fax # (301) 231-8961
Personnel: Publisher-Joe T. Davis, Editor, Circ. Mgr.-Deborah Vieder
Editorial Description: Contains timely briefs on taxation, government relations updates, affiliate society & local chapter news, articles on association activities & our NAEA and NAEAEF education calendars.
General Info: Yr. Est. 1986, Monthly, 20 pages, ISSN: 0891-592X, No Color, Matte, Saddle-stitched
Subscriptions: Indv. $12, $1/copy
Circulation: Total-7,500
Printing Co: Hagerstown Bookbinding & Printing, 952 Frederick St, Hagerstown, MD 21740-6821 Tel # (301) 733-2000, Fax # (301) 733-6586

E.F.T.A., A Service Mark
See: ACCOUNTING

Electronic Filer's Report   *Business*

Publishing Co: Professional Newsletters, Inc, State Taxation Institute, PO Box 81143, Atlanta, GA 30366-1143; Title Tel # (770) 457-1000
Personnel: Publisher-Robert Palmer
Editorial Description: New developments and 'how-to' help for those in the business of filing tax returns electronically.
General Info: Yr. Est. 1993, Monthly
Subscriptions: Indv. $57

Empire Valuation News   *Business*

Publishing Co: Empire Valuation Consultants, Inc., 350 5th Ave Ste 5713, New York, NY 10118-0110; Title Tel # (212) 714-0122 Title Fax # (212) 714-0124

Employer's Handbook: Complying with IRS Employee Benefits Rules   *Business*

Publishing Co: Thompson Publishing Group, 1725 K Street, NW, Washington, DC 20006 Tel # (202) 872-4000
Editorial Description: Answers tough compliance questions, untangling the complex web of IRS employee benefit rules. Subscription includes monthly supplements and bulletins.
General Info: Annually, Looseleaf
Subscriptions: Indv. $262

Employment Tax Forms

Publishing Co: CCH, Inc., 2700 Lake Cook Rd., Riverwoods, IL 60015 Parent Co.-Kluwer Law & Taxation Publishers, Cambridge; Title Tel # (847) 267-7000 Title Fax # (800) 224-8299
Editorial Description: Reproduces federal and state employment tax forms, including information returns.
General Info: Yr. Est. 1991, Irregular, Looseleaf
Subscriptions: Indv. $255

Ernst & Young's Oil and Gas Tax Reporter
See: PETROLEUM & NATURAL GAS

Estate Planners Alert   *Business*

Publishing Co: Research Institute of America, 117 E Stevens Ave, Valhalla, NY 10595-1264; Title Tel # (212) 645-4800
Personnel: Editor-James Cheeks
Editorial Description: Latest developments on estate planning from tax and legal viewpoints.
General Info: Monthly, 8 pages
List Rental: List Management Co.: WG & L List Management, 1 Penn Plz Fl 42, New York, NY 10119-0002 Tel # (212) 971-5000, Actives: 10,415, $60/M

Estate Planning Review   *Consumer*

Publishing Co: CCH, Inc., 2700 Lake Cook Rd., Riverwoods, IL 60015 Parent Co.-Kluwer Law & Taxation Publishers, Cambridge; Title Tel # (847) 267-7000 Title Fax # (800) 224-8299
Editorial Description: Covers new developments and cases to aid sound estate and financial planning.
General Info: Yr. Est. 1975, Monthly, Trim Size-6 x 9, Web press, 15 pages, No Color
Subscriptions: Indv. $186

Estate and Tax Bulletin
See: LAW

Estate Tax Freeze: Tools and Techniques
See: LAW

Estate Tax Techniques
See: LAW

Estates, Powers, & Trusts Law

Publishing Co: Gould Publications, Inc, 1333 N US Highway 17-92, Longwood, FL 32750-3724 Tel # (407) 695-9500 Fax # (407) 695-2906; Title Tel # (607) 724-3000
Editorial Description: Complete text NY statues.
General Info: Annually, Trim Size-5$\frac{1}{2}$ x 8$\frac{1}{2}$, Sheetfed press, 175 pages, No Color, Looseleaf
Subscriptions: $10/copy

Excise Taxes   *Business*

Publishing Co: Research Institute of America, 90 5th Avenue, New York, NY 10011-7629 Tel # (212) 645-4800; Title Tel # (800) 562-0245
Editorial Description: All new laws, regulations decisions and rulings.
General Info: Monthly, Trim Size-6 x 9$\frac{1}{4}$, Offset press, Looseleaf
Subscriptions: Indv. $228
List Rental: List Management Co.: WG & L List Management, 1 Penn Plz Fl 42, New York, NY 10119-0002 Tel # (212) 971-5000

Executive Compensation   *Business*

Publishing Co: Research Institute of America, 117 E Stevens Ave, Valhalla, NY 10595-1264; Title Tel # (212) 645-4800
Editorial Description: Three-volume service providing guidance on the tax consequences of compensation packages for executives at every level of responsibility in every major industry.
General Info: No Color, Looseleaf
List Rental: List Management Co.: WG & L List Management, 1 Penn Plz Fl 42, New York, NY 10119-0002 Tel # (212) 971-5000, Actives: $95/M, Expires: $60/M

Executive Compensation Alert   *Business*

Publishing Co: Research Institute of America, 117 E Stevens Ave, Valhalla, NY 10595-1264; Title Tel # (212) 645-4800
General Info: Monthly
List Rental: List Management Co.: WG & L List Management, 1 Penn Plz Fl 42, New York, NY 10119-0002 Tel # (212) 971-5000, Actives: $95/M, Expires: $60/M

Executives Tax Report

Publishing Co: Research Institute of America, 90 5th Avenue, New York, NY 10011-7629 Tel # (212) 645-4800; Title Tel # (201) 767-5059
Editorial Description: Concentrates on the newest most profitable tax savings ideas.
General Info: Weekly
Subscriptions: Indv. $167
Circulation: Total-20,000
List Rental: List Management Co.: WG & L List Management, 1 Penn Plz Fl 42, New York, NY 10119-0002 Tel # (212) 971-5000

Exempt Organizations Report   *Association, Business*

Publishing Co: CCH, Inc., 2700 Lake Cook Rd., Riverwoods, IL 60015 Parent Co.-Kluwer Law & Taxation Publishers, Cambridge; Title Tel # (847) 267-7000 Title Fax # (800) 224-8299
Editorial Description: Sets out & explains federal tax & state organizational & operational rules governing tax-exempt organizations, contributors & managers. Emphasizes rules for tax exempt status, investment income, state charitable trust laws, etc. & detials & describes current developments, IRS activity & areas of special interest.
General Info: (Formerly Private Foundations Reports), Yr. Est. 1971, Bi-weekly, Trim Size-6 x 9, Web press, 150 pages, No Color, Looseleaf
Subscriptions: Indv. $846
Advertising: Accepts Inserts.

Family Tax Planning   *Business*

Publishing Co: Matthew Bender & Co., 11 Penn Plaza, New York, NY 10001-2006 Fax # (212) 244-3188; Title Tel # (212) 967-7707
Personnel: Editor-R. Ross
Editorial Description: Complete planning & procedural guidance for combining tax savings under federal income, estate & gift tax with the financial goals & needs of the family unit.
General Info: Yr. Est. 1960, Irregular, Looseleaf
Subscriptions: $190/copy

Farm and Ranch Tax Letter
See: AGRICULTURE

Farm Tax Saver
See: AGRICULTURE

Farmers Federal Tax Alert

Publishing Co: Research Institute of America, 117 E Stevens Ave, Valhalla, NY 10595-1264; Title Tel # (212) 645-4800
General Info: Monthly
List Rental: List Management Co.: WG & L List Management, 1 Penn Plz Fl 42, New York, NY 10119-0002 Tel # (212) 971-5000, Actives: $95/M, Expires: $60/M

Federal Estate & Gift Taxes

Publishing Co: Research Institute of America, 90 5th Avenue, New York, NY 10011-7629 Tel # (212) 645-4800
Editorial Description: Comprehensive reference for every aspect of estate planning including the impact of related transfer, taxes; simplifies complex estate planning decisions.
General Info: Yr. Est. 1926, Bi-weekly
Subscriptions: Indv. $327
List Rental: List Management Co.: WG & L List Management, 1 Penn Plz Fl 42, New York, NY 10119-0002 Tel # (212) 971-5000

Federal Estate and Gift Tax Reports   *Business, Scholarly*

Publishing Co: CCH, Inc., 2700 Lake Cook Rd., Riverwoods, IL 60015 Parent Co.-Kluwer Law & Taxation Publishers, Cambridge; Title Tel # (847) 267-7000 Title Fax # (800) 224-8299
Editorial Description: Internal Revenue Code provisions, regulations, explanations, decisions, rulings relating to federal estate, gift and generation-skipping transfer taxes.
General Info: Yr. Est. 1913, Weekly, No Color, Looseleaf
Subscriptions: Indv. $494

Federal Excise Tax

Publishing Co: Research Institute of America, 90 5th Avenue, New York, NY 10011-7629 Tel # (212) 645-4800; Title Tel # (800) 562-0245
Editorial Description: Explains & clarifies the rulings, laws & decisions shaping this tax area, as well as provides monthly bulletins which outline regulatory changes & other developments.
General Info: Yr. Est. 1956, Monthly, Ind/Abs/Online: Prentice-Hall Info. Network
Subscriptions: Indv. $228
List Rental: List Management Co.: WG & L List Management, 1 Penn Plz Fl 42, New York, NY 10119-0002 Tel # (212) 971-5000

Federal Excise Tax Reports   *Business, Consumer*

Publishing Co: CCH, Inc., 2700 Lake Cook Rd., Riverwoods, IL 60015 Parent Co.-Kluwer Law & Taxation Publishers, Cambridge; Title Tel # (847) 267-7000 Title Fax # (800) 224-8299
Editorial Description: Sets out federal excise tax laws, regulations, decisions, rulings and explanation.
General Info: Yr. Est. 1958, Monthly, Trim Size-6 x 9, Web press, 50 pages, No Color, Looseleaf
Subscriptions: Indv. $362

Federal Income, Gift and Estate Taxation
See: LAW

Federal Income Tax Regulations

Publishing Co: Research Institute of America, 90 5th Avenue, New York, NY 10011-7629 Tel # (212) 645-4800
Editorial Description: Presents the full text of income tax regulations & details regulatory activity following tax reform legislation. It includes compliance requirements, transitional rules, & other provisions affecting your practice.
General Info: Monthly
Subscriptions: Indv. $270
List Rental: List Management Co.: WG & L List Management, 1 Penn Plz Fl 42, New York, NY 10119-0002 Tel # (212) 971-5000

Federal Income Taxation of Banks and Financial Institutions   *Business*

Publishing Co: Warren, Gorham & Lamont, 31 Saint James Ave., Boston, MA 02116-4112 Parent Co.-Thomson Professional Publications, Stamford; Title Tel # (617) 423-2020 Title Fax # (617) 423-1914
Personnel: Publisher-Wayne Barr, Production Mgr.-Mavra Kiey, Mktg. Dir.-Jim Spillane
Editorial Description: Helps plan a bank's tax position from a legal and accounting point of view.
General Info: Looseleaf
Subscriptions: Indv. $215
List Rental: List Management Co.: WG & L List Management, 1 Penn Plz Fl 42, New York, NY 10119-0002 Tel # (212) 971-5000

Federal Income Taxation of Corporations Filing Consolidated Returns   *Business*

Publishing Co: Matthew Bender & Co., 11 Penn Plaza, New York, NY 10001-2006 Fax # (212) 244-3188; Title Tel # (212) 967-7707
Editorial Description: A manual that meets the demand of substantial analysis of this domain of tax law.
General Info: Yr. Est. 1975, Irregular, No Color, Looseleaf
Subscriptions: $310/copy

Federal Income Taxation of Corporations and Shareholders   *Business*

Publishing Co: Warren, Gorham & Lamont, 31 Saint James Ave., Boston, MA 02116-4112 Parent Co.-Thomson Professional Publications, Stamford; Title Tel # (617) 423-2020 Title Fax # (617) 423-1914
Personnel: Publisher-Wayne Barr, Production Mgr.-Mavra Kiey, Mktg. Dir.-Jim Spillane
Editorial Description: Covers all types of corporation tax situations.
General Info: Yr. Est. 1971, Looseleaf
Subscriptions: Indv. $185
List Rental: List Management Co.: WG & L List Management, 1 Penn Plz Fl 42, New York, NY 10119-0002 Tel # (212) 971-5000

Federal Income Taxation of Inventories   *Business*

Publishing Co: Matthew Bender & Co., 11 Penn Plaza, New York, NY 10001-2006 Fax # (212) 244-3188; Title Tel # (212) 967-7707
Personnel: Editor-A. Sarakin
Editorial Description: Detailed analysis of al general inventory requirements, with clear explanations of the complex tax & accounting problems involved in the area.
General Info: Yr. Est. 1979, Irregular, Looseleaf
Subscriptions: $295/copy

Federal Income Taxation of Real Estate
See: REAL ESTATE

Federal Income Taxation of Real Estate: Forms & Analysis
See: REAL ESTATE

Federal Revenue Forms

Publishing Co: Research Institute of America, 90 5th Avenue, New York, NY 10011-7629 Tel # (212) 645-4800; Title Tel # (800) 562-0245
Personnel: Publisher-Deborah Launer, Product Mgr.-Alan Kellet
Editorial Description: Provides quick access to current IRS forms & official instructions, with this reference, you confind forms quickly by form number, subject matter, key word.
General Info: Yr. Est. 1974, Monthly
Circulation: Total-3,600
List Rental: List Management Co.: WG & L List Management, 1 Penn Plz Fl 42, New York, NY 10119-0002 Tel # (212) 971-5000

Federal Tax Articles   *Business*

Publishing Co: CCH, Inc., 2700 Lake Cook Rd., Riverwoods, IL 60015 Parent Co.-Kluwer Law & Taxation Publishers, Cambridge; Title Tel # (847) 267-7000 Title Fax # (800) 224-8299
Editorial Description: Describes federal tax articles published in tax, law, accounting, business and other journals, and tells where to get the full story.
General Info: Yr. Est. 1962, Monthly, Trim Size-6 x 9, Web press, 50 pages, Color, Looseleaf
Subscriptions: Indv. $516

Federal Tax Coordinator 2d

Publishing Co: Research Institute of America, 117 E Stevens Ave, Valhalla, NY 10595-1264; Title Tel # (212) 645-4800
General Info: Quarterly
List Rental: List Management Co.: WG & L List Management, 1 Penn Plz Fl 42, New York, NY 10119-0002 Tel # (212) 971-5000, Actives: $95/M, Expires: $60/M

Federal Tax Expeditor

Publishing Co: Research Institute of America, 90 5th Avenue, New York, NY 10011-7629 Tel # (212) 645-4800
Editorial Description: Time-saving topical locator of tax coverage in major reporters; provides concise details on tax ramifications of a transaction.
General Info: Yr. Est. 1987, Monthly
Subscriptions: Indv. $225
List Rental: List Management Co.: WG & L List Management, 1 Penn Plz Fl 42, New York, NY 10119-0002 Tel # (212) 971-5000

Federal Tax Forms   *Business*

Publishing Co: CCH, Inc., 2700 Lake Cook Rd., Riverwoods, IL 60015 Parent Co.-Kluwer Law & Taxation Publishers, Cambridge; Title Tel # (847) 267-7000 Title Fax # (800) 224-8299
Editorial Description: Reproduces virtually every federal income, estate and gift, excise and employment tax form and schedule with official instructions.
General Info: Yr. Est. 1973, Irregular, Trim Size-8$\frac{1}{2}$ x 11, Web press, 200 pages, No Color, Looseleaf
Subscriptions: Indv. $350

Federal Tax Guide   *Business*

Publishing Co: Research Institute of America, 90 5th Avenue, New York, NY 10011-7629 Tel # (212) 645-4800; Title Tel # (800) 562-0245
Personnel: Publisher-Deborah Launer, Product Mgr.-Alan Kellett
Editorial Description: Analyzes the entire body of federal tax law & provides a wealth of practical how-to aids & tips; efficiently organized for fast access to answers; weekly newsletters report on current developments.
General Info: Yr. Est. 1931, Weekly, Trim Size-6 x 9$\frac{1}{4}$, Offset press, Looseleaf
Subscriptions: Indv. $315
Circulation: Total-8,300
List Rental: List Management Co.: WG & L List Management, 1 Penn Plz Fl 42, New York, NY 10119-0002 Tel # (212) 971-5000

Federal Tax Guide Reports   *Consumer*

Publishing Co: CCH, Inc., 2700 Lake Cook Rd., Riverwoods, IL 60015 Parent Co.-Kluwer Law & Taxation Publishers, Cambridge; Title Tel # (847) 267-7000 Title Fax # (800) 224-8299
Editorial Description: All-explanatory treatment of federal income, estate and gift taxes and tax-saving methods.
General Info: Yr. Est. 1958, Weekly, Trim Size-6 x 9, Web press, No Color, Looseleaf
Subscriptions: Indv. $802

Federal Tax Manual With Monthly Reports
See: U.S. (& CANADIAN) FED. GOV'T.

Federal Taxation of Life Insurance Companies   *Business*

Publishing Co: Matthew Bender & Co., 11 Penn Plaza, New York, NY 10001-2006 Fax # (212) 244-3188; Title Tel # (212) 967-7707
Personnel: Editor-A. Sarakin
Editorial Description: Analysis of life insurance company taxation.
General Info: Yr. Est. 1965, Looseleaf
Subscriptions: $290/copy

Federal Taxation of Oil and Gas Transactions
See: PETROLEUM & NATURAL GAS

Federal Taxation of Partnerships and Partners   *Business*

Publishing Co: Warren, Gorham & Lamont, 31 Saint James Ave., Boston, MA 02116-4112 Fax # (617) 423-1914 Parent Co.-Thomson Professional Publications, Stamford; Title Tel # (617) 423-2020
Personnel: Publisher-Wayne Barr, Production Mgr.-Mavra Kiey, Mktg. Dir.-Jim Spillane
Editorial Description: Guide to every type of partnership problem.
General Info: Quarterly, Looseleaf
Subscriptions: Indv. $215
List Rental: List Management Co.: American List Counsel, 88 Orchard Cir # Cn-5219, Princeton, NJ 08540-3026 Tel # (908) 874-4300, Fax # (908) 874-4433

Federal Taxation of Trusts, Grantors and Beneficiaries
See: LAW

Federal Taxes — *Business, Consumer*

Publishing Co: Research Institute of America, 90 5th Avenue, New York, NY 10011-7629
Tel # (212) 645-4800
Personnel: Publisher-James Cheeks, Editorial Dir.-Jonathan E. Koschei, Mng. Editor-Edward Titano
Editorial Description: Complete explanation of federal taxes with analysis & all the official material in one authoritative source-laws, regulations, decisions, rulings plus a weekly newsletter covering current tax developments.
General Info: Yr. Est. 1919, Weekly
Subscriptions: Indv. $1,350
List Rental: List Management Co.: WG & L List Management, 1 Penn Plz Fl 42, New York, NY 10119-0002 Tel # (212) 971-5000

Federal Taxes Citator — *Business*

Publishing Co: Research Institute of America, 90 5th Avenue, New York, NY 10011-7629
Tel # (212) 645-4800; Title Tel # (800) 562-0245
Editorial Description: Reliable research guide to the strengths & weaknesses of court cases & tax rulings. Provides complete judicial history for cases/rulings & evaluation of how case stood up in courts.
General Info: Yr. Est. 1933, Monthly, Trim Size-6 x 9¼, Offset press, Ind/Abs/Online: Prentice-Hall Info. Network, Looseleaf
Subscriptions: Indv. $550
List Rental: List Management Co.: WG & L List Management, 1 Penn Plz Fl 42, New York, NY 10119-0002 Tel # (212) 971-5000

Fiduciary Duties in Canada

Publishing Co: Carswell, 2075 Kennedy Road, One Corporate Plaza, Scarborough, ON M1T 3V4 Canada; Title Tel # (416) 609-8000 Title Fax # (416) 298-5094
Personnel: Publisher-Barry Garnet, Editor-Mark Ellis, Adv. Dir.-Melanie Causton
Editorial Description: A comprehensive, up-to-date case law analysis of fiduciary responsibility. Provides a basis to assess when a fiduciary duty exists, what is required to fulfill that duty, resulting remedies if that duty is not satisfied.
General Info: Annually, Looseleaf
Subscriptions: Indv. $165

Fiduciary Tax Guide

Publishing Co: CCH, Inc., 2700 Lake Cook Rd., Riverwoods, IL 60015 Parent Co.-Kluwer Law & Taxation Publishers, Cambridge; Title Tel # (847) 267-7000 Title Fax # (800) 224-8299
Editorial Description: Provides thorough coverage of federal income taxation of estates, trusts, their beneficiaries & decedents, federal estate, gift & generation-skipping taxation, & state estate, gift & generation-skipping law summaries, plus the reponsibilities of fiduciaries.
General Info: Monthly, Looseleaf
Subscriptions: Indv. $417

Financial & Estate Planning — *Business*

Publishing Co: CCH, Inc., 2700 Lake Cook Rd., Riverwoods, IL 60015 Parent Co.-Kluwer Law & Taxation Publishers, Cambridge; Title Tel # (847) 267-7000 Title Fax # (800) 224-8299
Editorial Description: Professional planning aids for capital accumulation, wealth preservation, and transfer at death.
General Info: Yr. Est. 1980, Semi-monthly, Looseleaf
Subscriptions: Indv. $802

Financial Advantage, The
See: MANAGEMENT

Financial Observer - Canadian Financial Industry Digest, The
See: BUSINESS & INDUSTRY

Financial Privacy Report
See: INVESTMENT

Fiscalite Quebecoise — *Business*

Publishing Co: CCH Canadian Ltd., 6 Garamond Ct., North York, ON M3C 1Z5 Canada
Fax # (416) 444-8011 Parent Co.-CCH, Inc., Riverwoods; Title Tel # (416) 441-2992
Title Fax # (416) 444-9011
Editorial Description: Covers all aspects of provincial taxation in Quebec.
General Info: Bi-monthly, Trim Size-6 x 9, Web press, No Color, Looseleaf
Subscriptions: Can. $645

Florida Estates Practice Guide
See: LAW

Florida Taxation

Publishing Co: Research Institute of America, 117 E Stevens Ave, Valhalla, NY 10595-1264; Title Tel # (212) 645-4800
Personnel: Publisher-Robert Chapman, Editor-James Cheeks
Editorial Description: Five volumes encompass entire body of Florida tax law.
General Info: Yr. Est. 1984, Quarterly, Looseleaf
Subscriptions: Indv. $275
List Rental: List Management Co.: WG & L List Management, 1 Penn Plz Fl 42, New York, NY 10119-0002 Tel # (212) 971-5000, Actives: $95/M, Expires: $60/M

Focus on Canadian Municipal Assessment & Taxation
See: REAL ESTATE

Foreign Investment in Canada
See: BANKING & FINANCE

Foreign Tax Law Bi-Weekly Bulletin
See: LAW

Foreign Tax and Trade Briefs

Publishing Co: Matthew Bender & Co., 11 Penn Plaza, New York, NY 10001-2006
Fax # (212) 244-3188; Title Tel # (212) 967-7707
Personnel: Editor-T. Kennelty
Editorial Description: Designed to provide a general overall picture of taxation and trading laws in over 100 foreign countires where American capital is most frequently invested.
General Info: Yr. Est. 1951, Monthly, Trim Size-6 x 9, Looseleaf
Subscriptions: $275/copy

Free Enterprise Society News

Publishing Co: Free Enterprise Society, 300 W. Shaw Ave., #205, Clovis, CA 93612-3680;
Title Tel # (209) 294-0665
Editorial Description: Taxes and law.
General Info: Monthly

GST & Commodity Tax — *Business, Consumer*

Publishing Co: Carswell, 2075 Kennedy Road, One Corporate Plaza, Scarborough, ON M1T 3V4 Canada Tel # (416) 609-8000 Fax # (416) 298-5094; Title Tel # (416) 445-4940
Title Fax # (416) 445-5352
Personnel: Publisher-Barry Garnet, Editor-Allan Taitz, Adv. Dir.-Melanie Causton
Editorial Description: Provides business professionals with news & expert commentary on the goods & services tax. Provincial sales tax, customs & excise tax, as well as other sales & commodity tax issues are also discussed. Subscribers are kept apprised of actual & potential areas of concern with emphasis on tax planning & compliance.
General Info: Yr. Est. 1989, Bi-monthly, Trim Size-7⅛ x 9¼, 8 pages, ISSN: 0847-3528, Other, Other
Subscriptions: Indv. $185
Printing Co: Sunview Press, 636 Howden Road, Scarborough, ON M1R 3C7 Canada
Tel # (416) 752-9293

German Tax & Business Law Guide

Publishing Co: CCH, Inc., 2700 Lake Cook Rd., Riverwoods, IL 60015 Parent Co.-Kluwer Law & Taxation Publishers, Cambridge; Title Tel # (847) 267-7000 Title Fax # (800) 224-8299
Editorial Description: Reports on German tax and business law, including new bills and laws, regulations, rulings, decisions, and official forms.
General Info: Monthly, Looseleaf
Subscriptions: Indv. $555

Good News
See: INVESTMENT

Government Accounting and Auditing Update
See: ACCOUNTING

Guide to Early Retirement
See: INVESTMENT

Guide to the Form 5500 Series — *Business*

Publishing Co: Thompson Publishing Group, 1725 K Street, NW, Washington, DC 20006
Tel # (202) 872-4000
Editorial Description: Practical guidance for filling out Form 5500 and related IRS forms.
General Info: Annually, Looseleaf
Subscriptions: Indv. $239

Guide to Unrelated Business Income Tax — *Business*

Publishing Co: Thompson Publishing Group, 1725 K Street, NW, Washington, DC 20006
Tel # (202) 872-4000
Editorial Description: Guide to taxation of nonprofit organizations' unrelated business income.
General Info: Semi-monthly
Subscriptions: Indv. $327

Highlights & Documents — *Business, Consumer*

Publishing Co: Tax Analysts, 6830 N. Fairfax Dr., Arlington, VA 22213-1098 Fax # (703) 533-4444; Title Tel # (703) 533-4400 Title Fax # (703) 533-4440
Personnel: Publisher-Thomas Field, Editor-Herman Ayayo, Mktg. Dir.-Barbara Halberstam
Editorial Description: Provides comprehensive , daily coverage of IRS, congressional, judicial, state and international tax news together with critical full text documents released within the previous 24-48 hours.
General Info: Yr. Est. 1985, Daily, ISSN: 0889-3055
Subscriptions: Indv. $1,999
List Rental: Rents Lists

Hong Kong Revenue Law — *Business*

Publishing Co: Matthew Bender & Co., 11 Penn Plaza, New York, NY 10001-2006
Tel # (212) 967-7707 Fax # (212) 244-3188
Editorial Description: A comprehensive source of the intricacies of Hong Kong revenue & tax laws. Coverage includes an overview of the law, complete annotations of legislation, official practice guides & forms, & proposed tax reforms.
General Info: Yr. Est. 1981, Irregular, Looseleaf

How to Save Time and Taxes with Federal Partnership Return *Business*

Publishing Co: Matthew Bender & Co., 11 Penn Plaza, New York, NY 10001-2006 Fax # (212) 244-3188; Title Tel # (212) 967-7707
Personnel: Editor-R. Ross
Editorial Description: Provides complete guidance on preparing Form 1065.
General Info: Yr. Est. 1964, Irregular, Looseleaf
Subscriptions: $100/copy

How to Save Time and Taxes in Handling Estates *Business*

Publishing Co: Matthew Bender & Co., 11 Penn Plaza, New York, NY 10001-2006 Fax # (212) 244-3188; Title Tel # (212) 967-7707
Editorial Description: Comprehensive guide to the federal estate tax.
General Info: Yr. Est. 1964, Irregular, Looseleaf
Subscriptions: Indv. $50, $90/copy

How to Save Time and Taxes Preparing Fiduciary Income Tax Returns-Federal and State *Business*

Publishing Co: Matthew Bender & Co., 11 Penn Plaza, New York, NY 10001-2006 Fax # (212) 244-3188; Title Tel # (212) 967-7707
Editorial Description: Comprehensive coverage of the federal income taxation of trusts & estates item-by-item, line-by-line preparation guide to Federal Form 1041. Provides background necessary for effective tax planning.
General Info: Yr. Est. 1969, Irregular, Looseleaf
Subscriptions: Indv. $45, $90/copy

IRS Letter Rulings Reports *Consumer*

Publishing Co: CCH, Inc., 2700 Lake Cook Rd., Riverwoods, IL 60015 Parent Co.-Kluwer Law & Taxation Publishers, Cambridge; Title Tel # (847) 267-7000 Title Fax # (800) 224-8299
Editorial Description: Weekly reports providing thousands of private letter rulings in full text, applying IRS thinking to specific taxpayer situations.
General Info: Yr. Est. 1977, Weekly, Trim Size-6 x 9, Web press, 300 pages, No Color, Looseleaf
Subscriptions: Indv. $1,308

IRS Positions Reports

Publishing Co: CCH, Inc., 2700 Lake Cook Rd., Riverwoods, IL 60015 Parent Co.-Kluwer Law & Taxation Publishers, Cambridge; Title Tel # (847) 267-7000 Title Fax # (800) 224-8299
Editorial Description: Reflects the legal reasoning the IRS uses in General Counsel's Memoranda (GCMs) for Revenue Rulings, Private Letter Rulings & Technical Advice Memoranda. New industry program papers & market segment specialization program audit guides are also included.
General Info: Irregular, Trim Size-6 x 9, 100 pages, Looseleaf
Subscriptions: Indv. $571

IRS Practice and Procedures

Publishing Co: Mark A. Stevens Ltd., 10018 Colesville Rd, Silver Spring, MD 20901-2306; Title Tel # (301) 593-0443
Personnel: Editor-Lavaughn Davis
General Info: Yr. Est. 1977, Monthly
Subscriptions: Indv. $77

IRS Publications *Business*

Publishing Co: CCH, Inc., 2700 Lake Cook Rd., Riverwoods, IL 60015 Parent Co.-Kluwer Law & Taxation Publishers, Cambridge; Title Tel # (847) 267-7000 Title Fax # (800) 224-8299
Editorial Description: Reproduces public-use publications reflecting pertinent IRS positions when applying the rules on income, estate and gift, excise & employment tax areas. Publications also aid in the completion & filing of tax returns.
General Info: Yr. Est. 1977, Irregular, Trim Size-8½ x 11, Web press, 200 pages, No Color, Looseleaf
Subscriptions: Indv. $307

Illinois Tax Service *Business*

Publishing Co: Matthew Bender & Co., 11 Penn Plaza, New York, NY 10001-2006 Tel # (212) 967-7707 Fax # (212) 244-3188
Editorial Description: A complete tax service for Illinois accountants, tax practitiners, & attorneys involved in state & local tax matters.
General Info: Yr. Est. 1985, Monthly, Looseleaf

Incentive Taxation

Publishing Co: Henry George Foundation of America, 2000 Century Plaza, #238, Columbia, MD 21044; Title Tel # (410) 740-1177 Title Fax # (410) 740-3279
Personnel: Publisher, Editor-Steven Cord, Circ. Mgr.-Joshva Vincent
Editorial Description: Land-only property tax reform exempting buildings from taxation.
General Info: Yr. Est. 1974, Bi-monthly, Trim Size-8½ x 11, Offset press, 4 pages, No Color, Matte
Subscriptions: Indv. $15, $1/copy
Circulation: Total-7,000
List Rental: Actives: $45/M
Printing Co: American Institute for Economic Research, Olvision Street, Great Barrington, MA 01230-1000

Income Taxation in Canada *Business*

Publishing Co: Prentice-Hall Canada, 1870 Birchmont Rd., Scarborough, ON M1P 2T1 Canada Tel # (416) 293-3621 Fax # (416) 299-2529 Parent Co.-Simon & Schuster, Waterford; Title Tel # (800) 562-0245 Title Fax # (201) 816-3484
Personnel: Publisher-Yolanda DeRooy, Circ. Mgr.-Joanne Zinck, Production Dir.-Anita Boyle, Mktg. Dir.-Jerry Smith
Editorial Description: Provides explanation & full text of Canadian tax structure-explains the statutes, regulations, treaties, rulings, forms, & more.
General Info: Yr. Est. 1977, Weekly, Trim Size-5½ x 8½, Offset press, 60 pages, No Color, Coated, Looseleaf
Subscriptions: Can. $942
Circulation: Total-363
List Rental: Rents Lists

Income Taxation of Foreign Related Transactions *Business*

Publishing Co: Matthew Bender & Co., 11 Penn Plaza, New York, NY 10001-2006 Fax # (212) 244-3188; Title Tel # (212) 967-7707
Personnel: Editor-T. Kennelly
Editorial Description: The recognized basic text on all aspects of U.S. taxation of Americans doing business abroad & foreigners investing in the U.S. Annotated texts of all U.S. income tax treaties & how to work with them. In addition, includes selected U.S. estate tax treaties.
General Info: Yr. Est. 1971, Semi-monthly, Looseleaf
Subscriptions: $510/copy

Income Taxation of Natural Resources

Publishing Co: Research Institute of America, 90 5th Avenue, New York, NY 10011-7629 Tel # (212) 645-4800; Title Tel # (800) 562-0245 Title Fax # (201) 816-3484
Editorial Description: Offers complete tax coverage of oil, gas, solid minerals and timber in the U.S. and Canada. Provides all the provisions, restrictions and rules that govern the taxation of natural resources.
General Info: Yr. Est. 1954, Monthly
List Rental: List Management Co.: WG & L List Management, 1 Penn Plz Fl 42, New York, NY 10119-0002 Tel # (212) 971-5000

Individual Retirement Plans Guide-IRA, SEP, Keogh See: U.S. (& CANADIAN) FED. GOV'T.

Individual Tax Return Guide

Publishing Co: Research Institute of America, 117 E Stevens Ave, Valhalla, NY 10595-1264; Title Tel # (212) 645-4800
Personnel: Publisher-Robert Chapman, Editor-James Cheeks
Editorial Description: Complete with filled-in schedules & detailed line-by-line explanations.
General Info: Annually, Looseleaf
Subscriptions: $5/copy
List Rental: List Management Co.: WG & L List Management, 1 Penn Plz Fl 42, New York, NY 10119-0002 Tel # (212) 971-5000, Actives: $95/M, Expires: $60/M

Information Returns Guide *Business*

Publishing Co: CCH, Inc., 2700 Lake Cook Rd., Riverwoods, IL 60015 Parent Co.-Kluwer Law & Taxation Publishers, Cambridge; Title Tel # (847) 267-7000 Title Fax # (800) 224-8299
Editorial Description: Sets out federal information reporting no rules for non-wage income & is directed at the person who must do the reporting. Topics include (1) interest dividend & original issue discount, (2) pensions & IRA, (3) real estate & property, (4) broker & (5) miscellaneous reporting.
General Info: Monthly, Looseleaf
Subscriptions: Indv. $296

Inheritance, Estate and Gift Tax Reports Fed-All States *Consumer*

Publishing Co: CCH, Inc., 2700 Lake Cook Rd., Riverwoods, IL 60015 Parent Co.-Kluwer Law & Taxation Publishers, Cambridge; Title Tel # (847) 267-7000 Title Fax # (800) 224-8299
Editorial Description: Covers state inheritance, federal and estate, and gift tax, statutes, regulations, decisions, rulings, and explanations.
General Info: Yr. Est. 1928, Weekly, Trim Size-6 x 9, Web press, 150 pages, No Color, Looseleaf
Subscriptions: Indv. $1,231

Inheritance Estate and Gift Tax Reports, Home State *Business, Scholarly*

Publishing Co: CCH, Inc., 2700 Lake Cook Rd., Riverwoods, IL 60015 Parent Co.-Kluwer Law & Taxation Publishers, Cambridge; Title Tel # (847) 267-7000 Title Fax # (800) 224-8299
Editorial Description: State inheritance, estate & gift tax laws, regulations and court decisions.
General Info: Monthly, Looseleaf
Subscriptions: Indv. $428

Insurance Tax Review *Business*

Publishing Co: Tax Analysts, 6830 N. Fairfax Dr., Arlington, VA 22213-1098 Fax # (703) 533-4444; Title Tel # (703) 533-4400 Title Fax # (703) 533-4440
Personnel: Publisher-Thomas Field, Editor-Meegan Reilly, Mktg. Dir.-Barbara Halberstam
Editorial Description: Covers news, federal and state taxation of insurance companies, insurance products and policyholders with full text documentation and in depth commentary.
General Info: Yr. Est. 1986, Monthly, ISSN: 0890-9164, Ind/Abs/Online: Lexis
Subscriptions: Indv. $599
List Rental: Rents Lists

Internal Memoranda of the IRS

Publishing Co: Research Institute of America, 90 5th Avenue, New York, NY 10011-7629
Tel # (212) 645-4800
Editorial Description: Provides immediate access to thinking behind decisions of IRS-General Counsel memoranda, actions on decisions, technical memoranda, new memoranda is reproduced verbatim each week.
General Info: Yr. Est. 1982, Weekly
Subscriptions: Indv. $390
List Rental: List Management Co.: WG & L List Management, 1 Penn Plz Fl 42, New York, NY 10119-0002 Tel # (212) 971-5000

Internal Revenue Manual- Audit and Administration *Business*

Publishing Co: CCH, Inc., 2700 Lake Cook Rd., Riverwoods, IL 60015 Parent Co.-Kluwer Law & Taxation Publishers, Cambridge; Title Tel # (847) 267-7000 Title Fax # (800) 224-8299
Editorial Description: Important, hot-topic IRS tax audit provisions and procedures.
General Info: Yr. Est. 1977, Irregular, Trim Size-6 x 9, Web press, 200 pages, No Color, Looseleaf
Subscriptions: Indv. $1,187

International Business Planning: Law and Taxation (United State)
See: INTERNATIONAL TRADE

International Offshore Financial Centres

Publishing Co: CCH, Inc., 2700 Lake Cook Rd., Riverwoods, IL 60015 Parent Co.-Kluwer Law & Taxation Publishers, Cambridge; Title Tel # (847) 267-7000 Title Fax # (800) 224-8299
Editorial Description: Provides basic principles of the tax strategies and profitability of offshore locales, along with tax and business laws and analysis of 14 countries .
General Info: Irregular, Looseleaf
Subscriptions: Indv. $510

International Tax Planners Alert

Publishing Co: Research Institute of America, 117 E Stevens Ave, Valhalla, NY 10595-1264; Title Tel # (212) 645-4800
Personnel: Publisher-Robert Chapman, Editor-James Cheeks
General Info: Monthly
Subscriptions: Indv. $150
List Rental: List Management Co.: WG & L List Management, 1 Penn Plz Fl 42, New York, NY 10119-0002 Tel # (212) 971-5000, Actives: $95/M, Expires: $60/M

International Tax Planning- Expatriates & Migrants

Publishing Co: CCH, Inc., 2700 Lake Cook Rd., Riverwoods, IL 60015 Parent Co.-Kluwer Law & Taxation Publishers, Cambridge; Title Tel # (847) 267-7000 Title Fax # (800) 224-8299
Editorial Description: Prepared for transferred executives and business migrants to enable them to optimize their tax planning when leaving their home country and relocating to another.
General Info: Quarterly, Looseleaf
Subscriptions: Indv. $510

International Tax Planning Manual-Corporations

Publishing Co: CCH, Inc., 2700 Lake Cook Rd., Riverwoods, IL 60015 Parent Co.-Kluwer Law & Taxation Publishers, Cambridge; Title Tel # (847) 267-7000 Title Fax # (800) 224-8299
Editorial Description: Explains the Basic tax laws and provides the planning strategies for doing business in 42 major trading countries.
General Info: Quarterly, Looseleaf
Subscriptions: Indv. $875

International Tax Report

Publishing Co: International Business Communications, 290 Eliot St # 91004, Ashland, MA 01721-2376; Title Tel # (508) 881-2800 Title Fax # (508) 881-0982
Personnel: Publisher-Tony Powell, Editor-Richard Casna, Promotion Dir.-Bernice Rubenstien
Editorial Description: IBC tax publication published by its IBC Publishing subsidiary (London). Discusses practical strategies for personal and business tax planning.
General Info: Yr. Est. 1972, Monthly, ISSN: 0300-1628
Subscriptions: Indv. $630
Advertising: Accepts Inserts.
List Rental: List Management Co.: PRS List Management, 222 Teal Ave., POB 6482, Syracuse, NY 13217-6482 Tel # (315) 472-1224, Fax # (315) 472-1235, Actives: $250/M

International Taxation Series *Business*

Publishing Co: Barrows Co., Inc., 116 E 66th St, New York, NY 10021-6547; Title Tel # (212) 772-1199 Title Fax # (212) 288-7242
Personnel: Publisher, Editor-Gordon Barrows, Circ. Mgr.-L.M. Guerra, Production Mgr.-Kenneth Hussman, Adv. Dir., Art Dir.-Dominique Jeune
Editorial Description: International Taxation Series is designed to give an immediate overview of the taxation of oil and gas, with a summary and analysis for every country. Kept to date by regular supplements.
General Info: Quarterly, Trim Size-8½ x 11, Offset press, 98 pages, No Color, Perfect bound, Looseleaf
Subscriptions: Indv. $4,000
Circulation: Total-10,000
Printing Co: Barrows Co. Wyoming, 700 Main St., Ralston, WY 82440 Tel # (307) 745-3759

International Withholding Tax Treaty Guide *Business*

Publishing Co: Matthew Bender & Co., 11 Penn Plaza, New York, NY 10001-2006
Tel # (212) 967-7707 Fax # (212) 244-3188
Editorial Description: Gives you the withholding tax rates for interest paid on: foreign loans, dividends, royalties, film royalties, rentals, bank deposits, technical fees, and shipping and aircraft income.
General Info: Yr. Est. 1974, Irregular, Looseleaf

J.K. Lasser Monthly Tax Letter *Business, Consumer*

Publishing Co: J.K. Lasser Tax Institute, PO Box 493, Mount Morris, IL 61054-0493; Title Tel # (815) 734-1104 Title Fax # (815) 734-1223
Personnel: Publisher-L. Wolff, Editor-Elliot Eiss, Circ. Mgr.-M. Grossman
Editorial Description: Provides up-to-the- minute tax law changes.
General Info: (Formerly J.K. Lasser Tax Service), Monthly, Trim Size-8½ x 11, Sheetfed press, 6 pages, ISSN: 0895-3147, Color
Subscriptions: Indv. $24, $2/copy
Acquistions: Publication Bought
Circulation: Total-43,000
List Rental: List Management Co.: Kleid Company, Inc., 530 5th Ave., 17 Floor, New York, NY 10036-5101 Tel # (212) 819-3406, Fax # (212) 719-9788, Actives: $75/M
Printing Co: Direct Graphics, 829 S Vandemark Rd, Sidney, OH 45365-8984 Tel # (513) 498-2194, Fax # (513) 492-1100

Jacobs Report on Asset Protection Strategies
See: INVESTMENT

Japanese International Taxation *Business*

Publishing Co: Matthew Bender & Co., 11 Penn Plaza, New York, NY 10001-2006
Tel # (212) 967-7707 Fax # (212) 244-3188
Editorial Description: Examines the tax laws affecting all foreign entities earning income in Japan & covers: classes of taxpayers, tax nexus, permanent establishment & fixed base, sources of foreigners' income, transfer pricing, tax avoidance, United States tax treaty.
General Info: Yr. Est. 1983, Irregular, Looseleaf

Kiplinger Tax Letter *Business*

Publishing Co: Kiplinger Washington Editors, Inc., 1729 H Street N.W., Washington, DC 20006-3924; Title Tel # (202) 887-6400
Personnel: Publisher-Austin H. Kiplinger, Editor-Steven Ivins
Editorial Description: A service devoted exclusively to domestic tax matters. Written from the business and personal rather than the technical point of view.
General Info: Yr. Est. 1925, Bi-weekly, Trim Size-8½ x 11, 4 pages, ISSN: 0023-1762
Subscriptions: Indv. $48
Circulation: Total-125,000
List Rental: List Management Co.: Kleid Company, Inc., 530 5th Ave., 17 Floor, New York, NY 10036-5101 Tel # (212) 819-3406, Fax # (212) 719-9788, Actives: 114,508, $90/M, Hotline: $100/M

LLC Advisor *Business*

Publishing Co: CCH, Inc., 2700 Lake Cook Rd., Riverwoods, IL 60015 Parent Co.-Kluwer Law & Taxation Publishers, Cambridge; Title Tel # (847) 267-7000 Title Fax # (800) 224-8299
Editorial Description: Monthly newsletter provides Fed Tax, State Tax & business news & developments impacting limited liability companies.
General Info: Yr. Est. 1994, Monthly
Subscriptions: Indv. $186

Lawyers Tax Alert
See: LAW

Lawyer's Weekly Report *Business*

Publishing Co: Research Institute of America, 90 5th Avenue, New York, NY 10011-7629
Tel # (212) 645-4800; Title Tel # (201) 767-5059
Editorial Description: Covers taxation and government regulations of business.
General Info: Yr. Est. 1945, Weekly
Subscriptions: Indv. $180
List Rental: List Management Co.: WG & L List Management, 1 Penn Plz Fl 42, New York, NY 10119-0002 Tel # (212) 971-5000

Leader's Equipment Leasing Newsletter
See: LAW

Letter Ruling Index-Digest Bulletins *Business, Consumer*

Publishing Co: Tax Analysts, 6830 N. Fairfax Dr., Arlington, VA 22213-1098 Fax # (703) 533-4444; Title Tel # (703) 533-4400 Title Fax # (703) 533-4440
Personnel: Publisher-Thomas Field, Editor-Susan Weiss, Mktg. Dir.-Barbara Halberstam
Editorial Description: Each index entry is accompanied by a summary , describing the content of each ruling. Entries are also indexed by Internal Revenue Code Section, subject matter and ruling number.
General Info: Yr. Est. 1977, Semi-annually, ISSN: 0730-9287
Subscriptions: Indv. $199
List Rental: Rents Lists

Letter Ruling Review   *Business, Consumer*

Publishing Co: Tax Analysts, 6830 N. Fairfax Dr., Arlington, VA 22213-1098 Fax # (703) 533-4444; Title Tel # (703) 533-4400 Title Fax # (703) 533-4440
Personnel: Publisher-Thomas Field, Editor-Michael Moriaty, Mktg. Dir.-Barbara Halberstam
Editorial Description: Tax experts pinpoint key rulings and discuss them in depth.
General Info: Yr. Est. 1988, Monthly, 10 pages, ISSN: 1047-1596, No Color
Subscriptions: Indv. $199
Circulation: Total-600
List Rental: Rents Lists

Letter Ruling Service   *Business, Consumer*

Publishing Co: Tax Analysts, 6830 N. Fairfax Dr., Arlington, VA 22213-1098 Fax # (703) 533-4444; Title Tel # (703) 533-4400 Title Fax # (703) 533-4440
Personnel: Publisher-Thomas Field, Editor-Shari Garrett, Mktg. Dir.-Barbara Halberstam
Editorial Description: Contains the full texts of all IRS letter rulings and technical advice memorandums issued each week , together with copyrighted summaries and indexes.
General Info: (Formerly IRS Letter Rulings, Full Text), Yr. Est. 1985, Weekly, ISSN: 1066-6303
Subscriptions: Indv. $1,249
List Rental: Rents Lists

Limited Liability Company
Guide   *Business*

Publishing Co: CCH, Inc., 2700 Lake Cook Rd., Riverwoods, IL 60015 Parent Co.-Kluwer Law & Taxation Publishers, Cambridge; Title Tel # (847) 267-7000 Title Fax # (800) 224-8299
Editorial Description: Includes explanations, practice aids, state & federal official text & other practice - based tools for conducting research in Limited Liability Companies.
General Info: Trim Size-6 x 9
Subscriptions: Indv. $406

Liquor Control Law Reports
See: BEVERAGES - BREWING

Lottery, Paramutual & Casino Regulations/State Capitals
See: GAMBLING

Major Tax Planning-Univ. of
Southern California Law
Ctr. Annual Inst. on Fed.
Taxatation   *Business*

Publishing Co: Matthew Bender & Co., 11 Penn Plaza, New York, NY 10001-2006 Fax # (212) 244-3188; Title Tel # (212) 967-7707
Editorial Description: The latest professional tax planning strategies directly from the experts who formulate them.
General Info: (Formerly Major Tax Planning U.S.C.), Yr. Est. 1950, Annually, Looseleaf
Subscriptions: $185/copy

Malaysian Tax Reports

Publishing Co: CCH, Inc., 2700 Lake Cook Rd., Riverwoods, IL 60015 Parent Co.-Kluwer Law & Taxation Publishers, Cambridge; Title Tel # (847) 267-7000 Title Fax # (800) 224-8299
Editorial Description: Contains authoritative, detailed commentary on Malaysian income tax and property gains tax.
General Info: Irregular, Looseleaf
Subscriptions: Indv. $670

Managing Your Future
See: INVESTMENT

Manitoba and
Saskatchewan Tax
Reports   *Business, Association*

Publishing Co: CCH Canadian Ltd., 6 Garamond Ct., North York, ON M3C 1Z5 Canada Fax # (416) 444-8011 Parent Co.-CCH, Inc., Riverwoods; Title Tel # (416) 441-2992 Title Fax # (416) 444-9011
Editorial Description: Covers every aspect of taxation for Manitoba and Saskatchewan. Identical arrangement of contents makes for easy cross reference between Tax Reports of different provinces.
General Info: Yr. Est. 1950, Monthly, Trim Size-6 x 9, Web press, No Color, Looseleaf
Subscriptions: Can. $310

Maritimes Tax Reports   *Business*

Publishing Co: CCH Canadian Ltd., 6 Garamond Ct., North York, ON M3C 1Z5 Canada Fax # (416) 444-8011 Parent Co.-CCH, Inc., Riverwoods; Title Tel # (416) 441-2992 Title Fax # (416) 444-9011
Editorial Description: Covers every aspect of taxation for the Maritime provinces. Identical arrangement of contents makes for easy cross reference between Tax Reports of different provinces.
General Info: Yr. Est. 1950, Monthly, Trim Size-6 x 9, Offset press, No Color, Looseleaf
Subscriptions: Indv. $210, Can. $260

Maryland Tax Court Service   *Business*

Publishing Co: Hawkins Publishing Co., Inc., 1207 B Central Avenue, Box 480, Mayo, MD 21106 Fax # (410) 798-1098; Title Tel # (410) 798-1677
Personnel: Publisher, Editor-Carl Eyler
Editorial Description: A loose-leaf indexed-anlaysis of reports the Maryland Tax Court, MD special court & MD court of appeals & includes complete text of tax court decisions since Dec. 1970.
General Info: Yr. Est. 1990, Irregular, Trim Size-8 1/2 x 11, Sheetfed press, No Color, Matte, Looseleaf
Subscriptions: Indv. $385

Massachusetts Corporation Law with Federal Tax Analysis
See: LAW

Miami Institute on Estate Planning
See: LAW

Michigan Corporation Law with Federal Tax Analysis
See: LAW

More than a Paycheck
See: POLITICS

Multistate Corporate
Income Tax Guide

Publishing Co: CCH, Inc., 2700 Lake Cook Rd., Riverwoods, IL 60015 Parent Co.-Kluwer Law & Taxation Publishers, Cambridge; Title Tel # (847) 267-7000 Title Fax # (800) 224-8299
Editorial Description: The guide includes state by state explanations, summaries of legislation, digests of court opinions, filled-in forms, comparison charts and thorough indexing.
General Info: Monthly, Looseleaf
Subscriptions: Indv. $709

Multistate Sales Tax Guide   *Business*

Publishing Co: CCH, Inc., 2700 Lake Cook Rd., Riverwoods, IL 60015 Parent Co.-Kluwer Law & Taxation Publishers, Cambridge; Title Tel # (847) 267-7000 Title Fax # (800) 224-8299
Editorial Description: Sales & use tax explanations, laws, rulings, regulations, digests of Board & Court decisions.
General Info: Yr. Est. 1940, Weekly, Trim Size-6 x 9, Web press, 75 pages, No Color, Looseleaf
Subscriptions: Indv. $1,286

NAEIR Advantage
See: EDUCATION

NCBA Reports
See: LAW

National Association of Tax
Consultors Newsletter   *Business, Association*

Publishing Co: Natl. Assn. of Tax Consultors Inc., 454 N 13th St, San Jose, CA 95112-1719; Title Tel # (408) 298-1458
Personnel: Publisher, Editor-Les Berlemann, Adv. Dir., Art Dir.-Ken Valentine
Editorial Description: Tax planning ideas suitable for tax preparers, accountants & business people.
General Info: Yr. Est. 1970, Quarterly, 48 pages, ISSN: 0271-9150
Subscriptions: Indv. $60
Circulation: Total-2,500

National Campaign for A
Peace Tax Fund
Newsletter   *Association*

Publishing Co: Natl. Campaign for A Peace Tax Fund, 2121 Decatur Pl NW, Washington, DC 20008-1923; Title Tel # (202) 483-3751 Title Fax # (202) 986-0667
Editorial Description: Seeks legislation establishing conscientious objection to taxes for military purposes.
General Info: Yr. Est. 1972, 3x/yr., Trim Size-8 1/2 x 11, Offset press, 16 pages, No Color, Recycled, Saddle-stitched
Circulation: Total-5,000

National Consultor   *Business*

Publishing Co: Natl. Assn. of Tax Consultors Inc., 454 N 13th St, San Jose, CA 95112-1719; Title Tel # (408) 298-1458
Personnel: Publisher-Michael R. Savage, Editor-Richard M. Savage, Adv. Dir.-Les Berlemann, Art Dir.-Lloyd Dixon
Editorial Description: Tax planning ideas suitable for tax preparers, accountants and business people.
General Info: Yr. Est. 1970, Quarterly, 48 pages, ISSN: 0271-9150, No Color
Subscriptions: Indv. $60
Circulation: Total-2,000

National Property Tax
Manual   *Business*

Publishing Co: Vertex Systems, Inc., 1041 Old Cassatt Rd., Berwyn, PA 19312-1151; Title Tel # (215) 640-4200
Personnel: Editor, Production Mgr.-Edward Laurente
Editorial Description: 4-volume reference for property tax compliance, tax rates, local assessors, reporting requirements.
General Info: Yr. Est. 1987, Monthly, Trim Size-8 1/2 x 11, Mimeo press, 300 pages, No Color, Newsprint, Looseleaf
Subscriptions: Indv. $960
Circulation: Total-200

National Sales Tax Manual   *Business*

Publishing Co: Vertex Systems, Inc., 1041 Old Cassatt Rd., Berwyn, PA 19312-1151; Title Tel # (215) 640-4200
Personnel: Editor, Production Mgr.-Edward Laurente
Editorial Description: 7-volume reference for sales tax compliance, taxable items/services, reporting requirements.
General Info: Yr. Est. 1987, Monthly, Trim Size-8½ x 11, Mimeo press, 300 pages, No Color, Newsprint, Looseleaf
Subscriptions: Indv. $858
Circulation: Total-425

National Sales Tax Rate
Directory   *Business*

Publishing Co: Vertex Systems, Inc., 1041 Old Cassatt Rd., Berwyn, PA 19312-1151; Title Tel # (215) 640-4200
Personnel: Editor, Production Mgr.-Edward Laurente
Editorial Description: Single source reference for all U.S./Canadian sales/use/rental tax rates.
General Info: Yr. Est. 1974, Monthly, Trim Size-8½ x 11, Mimeo press, 250 pages, No Color, Newsprint, Looseleaf
Subscriptions: Indv. $530
Circulation: Total-2,600

New Jersey Department of the Treasury, Local Property and Public Utility Branch News   *Business, Association*

Publishing Co: NJ Dept. of the Treasury, Division of Taxation, 50 Barrack St., Trenton, NJ 08608-2006 Tel # (609) 625-2359; Title Tel # (609) 984-3276
Personnel: Publisher, Editor-Gary Dal Corso
Editorial Description: Articles of instruction and information concerning local property tax administration in New Jersey, court decision reviews, new property tax laws in New Jersey, statutory date reminders.
General Info: (Formerly Local Property & Public Utility Branch News), Yr. Est. 1953, Bi-monthly, Trim Size-8½ x 11, Letrpr. press, 2 pages, No Color, Newsprint
Circulation: (100% controlled), Total-2,300
Printing Co: Treasury Print Shop, 420 E State St # Cn211, Trenton, NJ 08608-1502

New Jersey State Tax
News   *Business, Association*

Publishing Co: N.J. Div. of Taxation, 50 Barrack St., CN 281, Trenton, NJ 08646-0001; Title Tel # (609) 633-8426 Title Fax # (609) 777-4319
Personnel: Editor-Linda B. Hickey
Editorial Description: A newsletter of tax items of general interest; also features amendments to New Jersey tax laws, regulations, and division policies.
General Info: Yr. Est. 1972, Quarterly, Trim Size-8½ x 11, Offset press, 24 pages, No Color
Subscriptions: Free
Circulation: Total-18,600

New Jersey Tax Service   *Business*

Publishing Co: Matthew Bender & Co., 11 Penn Plaza, New York, NY 10001-2006 Tel # (212) 967-7707 Fax # (212) 244-3188
Editorial Description: Written by experts on state & local taxation, this comprehensive service for accountants, tax practitioners, & attorneys involved in tax matters in New Jersey.
General Info: Yr. Est. 1986, Monthly, Looseleaf

New York Tax Service   *Business*

Publishing Co: Matthew Bender & Co., 11 Penn Plaza, New York, NY 10001-2006 Tel # (212) 967-7707 Fax # (212) 244-3188
Personnel: Editor-Paul Comeau, Editor-Robert Helm, Editor-Joseph H. Murphy
Editorial Description: A comprehensive, easy-to-use tax service for practitioners in New York.
General Info: Yr. Est. 1985, Monthly, Looseleaf

New Zealand Income Tax
Law and Practice

Publishing Co: CCH, Inc., 2700 Lake Cook Rd., Riverwoods, IL 60015 Parent Co.-Kluwer Law & Taxation Publishers, Cambridge; Title Tel # (847) 267-7000 Title Fax # (800) 224-8299
Editorial Description: Comprehensive coverage of income tax law and practice in New Zealand.
General Info: Monthly, Looseleaf
Subscriptions: Indv. $1,685

Non-Profit Legal & Tax
Letter   *Association*

Publishing Co: Organization Management Inc., 13231 Pleasantview Ln, Fairfax, VA 22033-3015; Title Tel # (703) 968-7039 Title Fax # (703) 818-0259
Personnel: Publisher-Ellis Meredith, Editor-George Webster, Circ. Mgr.-Shirley Hess
Editorial Description: Keeps non-profits and advisors updated on happenings in tax-exempt area.
General Info: (Formerly Non-Profit Organization Tax Letter), Yr. Est. 1962, 18x/yr., Trim Size-8½ x 11, Web press, 8 pages, ISSN: 1066-1018, Color, Matte
Subscriptions: Indv. $235, Inst. $235, Can. $235, For. $235, $12/copy
Acquistions: Publication Bought
Printing Co: Plymouth Printing, 1200 Cushing Pl SE, Washington, DC 20003-3599 Tel # (202) 488-7777, Fax # (202) 863-1078

NonProfit Insights   *Business*

Publishing Co: Whitaker Newsletters, 313 South Ave., Box 340, Fanwood, NJ 07023-1350; Title Tel # (908) 889-6336 Title Fax # (908) 889-6339
Personnel: Publisher-Joel Whitaker, Editor-Fred Rossi, Circ. Mgr.-Sandra Smith
General Info: (Formerly Tax Exempt News), Yr. Est. 1980, Bi-weekly, Trim Size-8½ x 11, Desktop press, 8 pages, ISSN: 1056-4594, No Color
Subscriptions: Indv. $250, Inst. $249, Can. $300, For. $300, $15/copy
Acquistions: Publication Bought, Publication Sold
List Rental: List Management Co.: The Lake Group, 411 Theodore Freund Ave., Rye, NY 10580-1497 Tel # (914) 925-2400, Fax # (914) 925-2499, Actives: 29,196, $70/M

Nonprofit Report: Accounting, Taxation, & Management
See: ACCOUNTING

Ohio Corporation Law with Federal Tax Analysis
See: LAW

Ohio State Taxation   *Business*

Publishing Co: Matthew Bender & Co., 11 Penn Plaza, New York, NY 10001-2006 Tel # (212) 967-7707 Fax # (212) 244-3188
Editorial Description: Prepared by a team of expert authors and consultants, this treatise provides complete coverage of Ohio state tax law.
General Info: Yr. Est. 1985, Monthly, Looseleaf

Ohio Tax Alert   *Business*

Publishing Co: Professional Newsletters, Inc, State Taxation Institute, PO Box 81143, Atlanta, GA 30366-1143; Title Tel # (770) 457-1000
Personnel: Publisher-Robert Palmer
Editorial Description: New developments in Ohio taxes: income, franchise, sales & property.
General Info: Yr. Est. 1993, Monthly
Subscriptions: Indv. $189

Oil and Gas Tax Quarterly
See: PETROLEUM & NATURAL GAS

Ontario Tax Reports   *Business*

Publishing Co: CCH Canadian Ltd., 6 Garamond Ct., North York, ON M3C 1Z5 Canada Fax # (416) 444-8011 Parent Co.-CCH, Inc., Riverwoods; Title Tel # (416) 441-2992 Title Fax # (416) 444-9011
Personnel: Editor-Steven Allen
Editorial Description: Covers every aspect of taxation for Ontario identical arrangement of contents makes for easy cross reference between Tax Reports of different provinces.
General Info: Yr. Est. 1950, Monthly, Trim Size-6 x 9, Offset press, No Color, Looseleaf
Subscriptions: Can. $270

Ontario Taxation Service   *Business*

Publishing Co: Carswell, 2075 Kennedy Road, One Corporate Plaza, Scarborough, ON M1T 3V4 Canada Fax # (416) 298-5094; Title Tel # (416) 609-8000 Title Fax # (416) 298-5063
Personnel: Publisher-Barry Garnet, Editor-Colin Braithwaite, Adv. Dir.-Sandra Kay
Editorial Description: Continously updated tax service for the business and legal professions in Ontario.
General Info: Monthly, Trim Size-6½ x 9, 100 pages, No Color, Looseleaf
Subscriptions: Indv. $215
Circulation: Total-450

Outlook/State Capitals, The
See: GOVERNMENT

P-H Dentist's Tax Report

Publishing Co: Research Institute of America, 90 5th Avenue, New York, NY 10011-7629 Tel # (212) 645-4800
General Info: Yr. Est. 1960, Bi-weekly
Subscriptions: Indv. $36
List Rental: List Management Co.: WG & L List Management, 1 Penn Plz Fl 42, New York, NY 10119-0002 Tel # (212) 971-5000

P-H Doctor's Tax Report

Publishing Co: Research Institute of America, 90 5th Avenue, New York, NY 10011-7629 Tel # (212) 645-4800
General Info: Yr. Est. 1960, Bi-weekly
Subscriptions: Indv. $36
List Rental: List Management Co.: WG & L List Management, 1 Penn Plz Fl 42, New York, NY 10119-0002 Tel # (212) 971-5000

P-H Federal Tax Course   *Business*

Publishing Co: Research Institute of America, 90 5th Avenue, New York, NY 10011-7629 Tel # (212) 645-4800; Title Tel # (201) 767-5059
Editorial Description: Current data on the latest tax setup.
General Info: Annually, Looseleaf
Subscriptions: $73/copy
List Rental: List Management Co.: WG & L List Management, 1 Penn Plz Fl 42, New York, NY 10119-0002 Tel # (212) 971-5000

P-H Federal Taxes   *Business*

Publishing Co: Research Institute of America, 90 5th Avenue, New York, NY 10011-7629 Tel # (212) 645-4800; Title Tel # (800) 562-0245 Title Fax # (201) 816-3484
Editorial Description: Complete information plus changes in law and current Federal Court decisions.
General Info: Weekly, Trim Size-6 x 9¼, Offset press, Looseleaf
Subscriptions: Indv. $1,197
List Rental: List Management Co.: WG & L List Management, 1 Penn Plz Fl 42, New York, NY 10119-0002 Tel # (212) 971-5000

PBC Tax Briefs   *Business, Consumer*

Publishing Co: Publishing & Business Consultants, 101 W. 64th St. Unit #3, Inglewood, CA 90302-1255 Tel # (213) 732-3477 Fax # (213) 732-3477
Personnel: Publisher, Editor-Andeson Atia
General Info: Quarterly, ISSN: 1059-1974
Subscriptions: Indv. $180
Advertising: Inquire for rates.

Partnership Tax Planning & Practice   *Business*

Publishing Co: CCH, Inc., 2700 Lake Cook Rd, Riverwoods, IL 60015 Parent Co.-Kluwer Law & Taxation Publishers, Cambridge; Title Tel # (847) 267-7000 Title Fax # (800) 224-8299
Editorial Description: Provides explanations, practice aids, applicable Code & Regulator text, & appropriate new developments (i.e., cases, rulings, procedures, etc.).
General Info: (Formerly Partnership Tax Reporter), Monthly, Trim Size-6 x 9, 72 pages, Looseleaf
Subscriptions: Indv. $417

Pastor's Tax & Money
See: RELIGIOUS & THEOLOGICAL

Patriot Cannon
See: POLITICS

Patriots for Liberty

Publishing Co: Patriots for Liberty, PO Box 334, Rochester, IN 46975-0334; Title Tel # (219) 223-2566
Personnel: Publisher, Editor-Bob Minarik
Editorial Description: Internal revenue & legal help. Individual rights orientated.
General Info: Yr. Est. 1985
Acquistions: Publication Bought

Payroll Administration Guide
See: INDUSTRIAL RELATIONS/PERSONNEL

Payroll Management Guide
See: INDUSTRIAL RELATIONS/PERSONNEL

Payroll Management Journal
See: INDUSTRIAL RELATIONS/PERSONNEL

Pennsylvania Tax Service   *Business*

Publishing Co: Matthew Bender & Co., 11 Penn Plaza, New York, NY 10001-2006 Tel # (212) 967-7707 Fax # (212) 244-3188
Editorial Description: Complete coverage of Pennsylvania state & local taxes, plus pertient federal tax provisions.
General Info: Yr. Est. 1987, Monthly, Looseleaf

Pension Actuary, The
See: INSURANCE

Pension Tax Reports   *Consumer*

Publishing Co: Hybrid Press Ltd., Box 589, Orleans, ON K1C 1S9 Canada; Title Tel # (613) 824-8988 Title Fax # (613) 824-1732
Personnel: Editor-Marcel Theroux
General Info: Yr. Est. 1990, Bi-weekly

Peyron Tax Accountants Communique   *Business, Association*

Publishing Co: Peyron Associates, Inc., PO Box 175, Sellersburg, IN 47172-0175; Title Tel # (502) 637-7483 Title Fax # (812) 282-4057
Personnel: Publisher, Editor-Dan Peyron
Editorial Description: Tax saving tips for accountants & tax practitioners who prepare tax returns for middle income individuals and small businesses. Also tips on how to increase tax and accounting business volume.
General Info: Yr. Est. 1967, Monthly, Offset press, 4 pages
Subscriptions: Indv. $44
Circulation: Total-1,000, Readership-2,500
Printing Co: Budget Printing Co., 711 Building, Hwy. 131, Clarksville, IN 47129 Tel # (812) 282-6660, Fax # (812) 282-4057

Peyron Tax Letter & Social Security Report   *Consumer*

Publishing Co: Peyron Associates, Inc., PO Box 175, Sellersburg, IN 47172-0175; Title Tel # (502) 637-7483 Title Fax # (812) 282-4057
Personnel: Publisher, Editor-Dan Peyron
Editorial Description: Income Tax & Social Security Tax saving tips for average middle income people. Plus updates on SS Benefits & Medicare. Also tips on ways to increase S.S. benefits.
General Info: Yr. Est. 1981, Monthly, Letrpr. press, 4 pages, Color
Subscriptions: Indv. $44
Circulation: Total-1,000, Readership-2,500
Printing Co: Budget Printing Co., 711 Building, Hwy. 131, Clarksville, IN 47129 Tel # (812) 282-6660, Fax # (812) 282-4057

Practitioners Provincial Tax Service - Quebec   *Business*

Publishing Co: Carswell, 2075 Kennedy Road, One Corporate Plaza, Scarborough, ON M1T 3V4 Canada; Title Tel # (416) 609-8000 Title Fax # (416) 298-5094
Personnel: Publisher-Barry Garnet, Adv. Dir.-Melanie Causton
Editorial Description: Continuously updated tax service for the business/legal professions.
General Info: Monthly, 64 pages, No Color, Looseleaf
Subscriptions: Indv. $205

Private Letter Rulings

Publishing Co: Research Institute of America, 90 5th Avenue, New York, NY 10011-7629 Tel # (212) 645-4800
Editorial Description: Provides latest IRS opinions on specific situations-official interpretation on new & amended provisions to the Tax Code.
General Info: Yr. Est. 1976, Weekly
List Rental: List Management Co.: WG & L List Management, 1 Penn Plz Fl 42, New York, NY 10119-0002 Tel # (212) 971-5000

Property Tax Alert   *Business*

Publishing Co: Professional Newsletters, Inc, State Taxation Institute, PO Box 81143, Atlanta, GA 30366-1143 Tel # (770) 457-1000; Title Tel # (771) 457-1000
Personnel: Publisher-Robert Palmer
Editorial Description: Coverage of business property tax matters in all 50 states.
General Info: Yr. Est. 1995, Monthly
Subscriptions: Indv. $197
List Rental: Rents Lists

Property Taxes

Publishing Co: Research Institute of America, 90 5th Avenue, New York, NY 10011-7629 Tel # (212) 645-4800
Editorial Description: Specialized tax information on property taxes statewide.
General Info: Yr. Est. 1925, Weekly
Subscriptions: Indv. $1,197
List Rental: List Management Co.: WG & L List Management, 1 Penn Plz Fl 42, New York, NY 10119-0002 Tel # (212) 971-5000

Provincial Tax Reorts

Publishing Co: CCH, Inc., 2700 Lake Cook Rd., Riverwoods, IL 60015 Parent Co.-Kluwer Law & Taxation Publishers, Cambridge; Title Tel # (847) 267-7000 Title Fax # (800) 224-8299
Editorial Description: Covers provincial taxes in separate units, including editorial comment and case law annotations.
General Info: Monthly, Looseleaf
Subscriptions: Indv. $1,390

Public Employer's Guide to Payroll Administration   *Business*

Publishing Co: Thompson Publishing Group, 1725 K Street, NW, Washington, DC 20006 Tel # (202) 872-4000
Editorial Description: A practical guide for payroll administrators.
General Info: Monthly

Pubs. of the IRS   *Business*

Publishing Co: Research Institute of America, 90 5th Avenue, New York, NY 10011-7629 Tel # (212) 645-4800; Title Tel # (800) 562-0245
Personnel: Publisher-Deborah Launer, Product Mgr.-Alan Kellett
Editorial Description: Provides essential information on the IRS position on compliance issues-collection of over 140 tax pubs. designed to clarify new laws.
General Info: Yr. Est. 1979, Monthly, Trim Size-8½ x 11, Looseleaf
Subscriptions: Indv. $249
Circulation: Total-4,000
List Rental: List Management Co.: Manager: Phyllis Ball; WG & L List Management, 1 Penn Plz Fl 42, New York, NY 10119-0002 Tel # (212) 971-5000

Puerto Rico Tax Reports   *Business*

Publishing Co: CCH, Inc., 2700 Lake Cook Rd., Riverwoods, IL 60015 Parent Co.-Kluwer Law & Taxation Publishers, Cambridge; Title Tel # (847) 267-7000 Title Fax # (800) 224-8299
Editorial Description: Explanation of Puerto Rico taxes. English translation of tax slaws, digests of cases and agency releases, summaries of recent legislation, thorough indexing.
General Info: Yr. Est. 1964, Monthly, Trim Size-6 x 9, Web press, 55 pages, No Color, Looseleaf
Subscriptions: Indv. $489

Puerto Rico Taxes

Publishing Co: Research Institute of America, 90 5th Avenue, New York, NY 10011-7629
Tel # (212) 645-4800; Title Tel # (800) 562-0245
Personnel: Publisher-Jeff Gottesfeld, Product Mgr.-Alan Kelett
Editorial Description: Shows how to capitalize on tax breaks available to manufacturing cos. & certain service operations in Puerto Rico, explains clearly the laws & regulations & provides how-to information for forms.
General Info: Yr. Est. 1983, Monthly, Looseleaf
Subscriptions: Indv. $331
Circulation: Total-850
List Rental: List Management Co.: Manager: Phyllis Ball; WG & L List Management, 1 Penn Plz Fl 42, New York, NY 10119-0002 Tel # (212) 971-5000

Quebec Tax Reports   *Business, Association*

Publishing Co: CCH Canadian Ltd., 6 Garamond Ct., North York, ON M3C 1Z5 Canada
Fax # (416) 444-8011 Parent Co.-CCH, Inc., Riverwoods; Title Tel # (416) 441-2992
Title Fax # (416) 444-9011
Personnel: Editor-Steven Allen
Editorial Description: Covers every aspect of taxation for Quebec. Identical arrangement of contents makes for easy cross reference between Tax Reports of different provinces.
General Info: Yr. Est. 1950, Monthly, Trim Size-6 x 9, Offset press, No Color, Looseleaf
Subscriptions: Can. $320

RIA Tax Guide Developments

Publishing Co: Research Institute of America, 117 E Stevens Ave, Valhalla, NY 10595-1264;
Title Tel # (800) 431-9025
Editorial Description: Charts and statistics.
General Info: Yr. Est. 1974, Bi-weekly
List Rental: List Management Co.: WG & L List Management, 1 Penn Plz Fl 42, New York, NY 10119-0002 Tel # (212) 971-5000, Actives: $95/M, Expires: $60/M

RIA's Special Studies

Publishing Co: Research Institute of America, 117 E Stevens Ave, Valhalla, NY 10595-1264;
Title Tel # (212) 645-4800
General Info: Monthly
Subscriptions: Indv. $48
List Rental: List Management Co.: WG & L List Management, 1 Penn Plz Fl 42, New York, NY 10119-0002 Tel # (212) 971-5000, Actives: $95/M, Expires: $60/M

Rabkin and Johnson's Federal Income Gift and Estate Taxation
See: LAW

Real Estate Tax Letter

Publishing Co: John Clark Financial Development, 505 E 1st St Ste H, Tustin, CA 92680-3305;
Title Tel # (714) 832-6246
Personnel: Editor-John Clark
General Info: Yr. Est. 1986, Monthly
Subscriptions: Indv. $42

Reasonable Action   *Business*

Publishing Co: Save-A-Patriot Fellowship, PO Box 91, Westminster, MD 21158-0991;
Title Tel # (301) 876-6342 Title Fax # (301) 857-5249
Editorial Description: Taxes and law.
General Info: Bi-monthly
Subscriptions: Indv. $35

Research Recommendations
See: BUSINESS & INDUSTRY

Revenue Canada, Excise/ Cest News   *Business*

Publishing Co: Excise/Cest News, 9th Floor, Place Vanier 'C', 25 McArthur Avenue, Ottawa, ON K1A 0L5 Canada; Title Tel # (613) 954-0005 Title Fax # (613) 952-0681
Editorial Description: Text in English & French Canadian - on sales/excise taxes.
General Info: (Formerly Federal Sales Tax News), Yr. Est. 1991, Quarterly, Trim Size-8½ x 11, 4 pages, ISSN: 1183-689X, No Color, Newsprint
Circulation: Total-1,800,000

Ruxton Report

Publishing Co: Ruxton Company, PO Box 20090, Santa Barbara, CA 93120-0090;
Title Tel # (805) 962-7030 Title Fax # (805) 963-7643
Personnel: Editor-Jack Kennedy, Sr.
General Info: Yr. Est. 1982, Monthly
Subscriptions: Indv. $72

S Corporations Guide   *Business*

Publishing Co: CCH, Inc., 2700 Lake Cook Rd., Riverwoods, IL 60015 Parent Co.-Kluwer Law & Taxation Publishers, Cambridge; Title Tel # (847) 267-7000 Title Fax # (800) 224-8299
Editorial Description: Comprehensive coverage of the rules for attaining and maintaining S Corporation status.
General Info: Yr. Est. 1983, Monthly, 64 pages, No Color, Looseleaf
Subscriptions: Indv. $472

SBANE Enterprise
See: BUSINESS & INDUSTRY

SEC Accounting Report
See: ACCOUNTING

Sales & Use Tax Alert   *Business*

Publishing Co: Professional Newsletters, Inc, State Taxation Institute, PO Box 81143, Atlanta, GA 30366-1143; Title Tel # (770) 457-1000
Personnel: Publisher-Robert Palmer
Editorial Description: Covers developments in the sales and use tax areas.
General Info: Yr. Est. 1991, Monthly
Subscriptions: Indv. $189

Sales Taxes

Publishing Co: Research Institute of America, 90 5th Avenue, New York, NY 10011-7629
Tel # (212) 645-4800
Editorial Description: Provides complete information regarding sales use, receipts & related taxes for states, cities, counties imposing such laws. Full text of laws & regulations with details, extensive annotations including decisions, interpretations & rulings.
General Info: Yr. Est. 1925, Weekly, Trim Size-6 x 9½, Offset press
Subscriptions: Indv. $798
List Rental: List Management Co.: WG & L List Management, 1 Penn Plz Fl 42, New York, NY 10119-0002 Tel # (212) 971-5000

Section of Taxation Newsletter   *Association*

Publishing Co: American Bar Association, 740 15th St. NW, Washington, DC 20005-1009
Tel # (202) 662-1016 Fax # (202) 662-1032
Personnel: Publisher-Della Nesbitt
Editorial Description: Short scholary , timely topics regarding taxation.
General Info: Yr. Est. 1981, Quarterly, Trim Size-8½ x 11, Sheetfed press, 20 pages, 2 Color
Subscriptions: Indv. $14, $4/copy
Circulation: Total-30,000
Printing Co: Hundley Lithograph, Inc., 6503 Chillum Pl NW, Washington, DC 20012-2189
Tel # (202) 829-7800

Singapore Revenue Legislation

Publishing Co: CCH, Inc., 2700 Lake Cook Rd., Riverwoods, IL 60015 Parent Co.-Kluwer Law & Taxation Publishers, Cambridge; Title Tel # (847) 267-7000 Title Fax # (800) 224-8299
Editorial Description: A complete and authoritative collection of all the relevant Singapore tax laws, reproduced in full text.
General Info: Quarterly, Looseleaf
Subscriptions: Indv. $320

The Small Business Advisor
See: BUSINESS & INDUSTRY

Small Business Tax Control
See: BUSINESS & INDUSTRY

Small Business Tax Planner

Publishing Co: Research Institute of America, 117 E Stevens Ave, Valhalla, NY 10595-1264;
Title Tel # (212) 645-4800
General Info: Monthly, Looseleaf
List Rental: List Management Co.: WG & L List Management, 1 Penn Plz Fl 42, New York, NY 10119-0002 Tel # (212) 971-5000, Actives: $95/M, Expires: $60/M

Small Business Tax Reporter   *Business*

Publishing Co: Small Business Council of America, 1000 Elm St., Box 3701, Manchester, NH 03105-3701; Title Tel # (603) 627-8149
Personnel: Editor-Alan Cleveland
General Info: Yr. Est. 1984, Monthly
Circulation: Total-1,000

Small Business Tax Review   *Business*

Publishing Co: A/N Group, PO Box 895, Melville, NY 11747-0895; Title Tel # (516) 549-4090
Personnel: Publisher, Editor-Steven Hopfenmuller
Editorial Description: Analysis of tax law changes, court cases & IRS ruling and articles on small business.
General Info: Yr. Est. 1980, Monthly, Trim Size-8½ x 11, Offset press, 10 pages, ISSN: 0276-5322, Ind/Abs/Online: NewsNet, No Color, Matte
Subscriptions: Indv. $84
Acquistions: Publication Bought
Printing Co: Printing Factory, 802 Cedar Ln, Teaneck, NJ 07666-1706 Tel # (201) 928-0139

Small Business Tax Saver   *Business*

Publishing Co: Enterprise Publishing Co Inc, 107 West 2nd Street, Flandreau, SD 57028;
Title Tel # (605) 997-3725
General Info: Yr. Est. 1980, Monthly
Subscriptions: Indv. $72

Small Corporation Update
See: BUSINESS & INDUSTRY

Society Page
See: INSURANCE

Software Taxation Letter
See: LAW

Sound Advice
See: REAL ESTATE

Southeastern Tax Alert *Business*

Publishing Co: Professional Newsletters, Inc, State Taxation Institute, PO Box 81143, Atlanta, GA 30366-1143; Title Tel # (770) 457-1000
Personnel: Publisher-Robert Palmer
Editorial Description: Covers state tax developments in Alabama, Florida and Georgia.
General Info: Yr. Est. 1992, Monthly
Subscriptions: Indv. $189

Spencer's Compliance Guide for Health & Benefit Plans

Publishing Co: Charles D. Spencer & Assocs., Inc., 250 S. Wacker Dr., Ste. 600, Chicago, IL 60606-5834; Title Tel # (312) 993-7900 Title Fax # (312) 993-7910
Personnel: Publisher-Charles D. Spencer, Editor-Stephen Huth, Mktg. Dir.-Art Cohen
Editorial Description: Information on Federal Legislation affecting employee benefit health plans.
General Info: Yr. Est. 1988, Monthly, Desktop press, Looseleaf
Subscriptions: Indv. $450
Circulation: Total-2,500

Spencer's Research Reports on Employee Benefits
See: INDUSTRIAL RELATIONS/PERSONNEL

Spencer's Retirement Plan Service
See: INDUSTRIAL RELATIONS/PERSONNEL

Spidell's California TAXFAX *Business*

Publishing Co: Spidell Publishing Inc., 1110 N Gilbert St, Anaheim, CA 92801-1401
Tel # (714) 776-7850 Fax # (714) 776-9906
Editorial Description: Weekly summary of new California tax developments.
General Info: Yr. Est. 1994, Weekly

Spidell's California Taxletter *Business*

Publishing Co: Spidell Publishing Inc., 1110 N Gilbert St, Anaheim, CA 92801-1401;
Title Tel # (714) 776-7850 Title Fax # (714) 776-9906
Personnel: Publisher, Editor-Bob Spidell, Production Mgr.-Bill Clardy
Editorial Description: California tax law changes, legislation, court cases and ballot propositions.
General Info: Yr. Est. 1979, Monthly, Trim Size-8 1/2 x 11, Web press, 6 pages, 2 Color, Matte
Subscriptions: Indv. $89
Circulation: (100% controlled), Total-7,500

Standard Federal Tax Reports *Business*

Publishing Co: CCH, Inc., 2700 Lake Cook Rd., Riverwoods, IL 60015 Parent Co.-Kluwer Law & Taxation Publishers, Cambridge; Title Tel # (847) 267-7000 Title Fax # (800) 224-8299
Editorial Description: Weekly issues on the federal income tax, with laws, regulations, court decisions. Tax Court case digests, rulings, and tax planning current comments.
General Info: Yr. Est. 1913, Weekly, Trim Size-6 x 9, Web press, 200 pages, ISSN: 0162-3494, No Color, Looseleaf
Subscriptions: Indv. $1,869

State Income Tax Alert *Business*

Publishing Co: Professional Newsletters, Inc, State Taxation Institute, PO Box 81143, Atlanta, GA 30366-1143; Title Tel # (770) 457-1000
Personnel: Publisher-Robert Palmer
Editorial Description: State income tax information for companies with multi-state operations.
General Info: Yr. Est. 1992, Semi-monthly
Subscriptions: Indv. $247

State Income Taxes *Business*

Publishing Co: Research Institute of America, 90 5th Avenue, New York, NY 10011-7629
Tel # (212) 645-4800; Title Tel # (800) 562-0245
Personnel: Publisher-Jeff Gottesfeld, Product Mgr.-Alan Kellett
Editorial Description: Complex income (& franchise) tax requirements are outlined & explained in detail to address state specific tax issues with authority.
General Info: Yr. Est. 1925, Weekly, Trim Size-6 x 9 1/4, Offset press, ISSN: 0194-6692, Looseleaf
Subscriptions: Indv. $1,274
Circulation: Total-300
List Rental: List Management Co.: Manager: Phyllis Ball; WG & L List Management, 1 Penn Plz Fl 42, New York, NY 10119-0002 Tel # (212) 971-5000

State Inheritance Taxes

Publishing Co: Research Institute of America, 90 5th Avenue, New York, NY 10011-7629
Tel # (212) 645-4800
Editorial Description: Complete, state-by-state details on every aspect of estate planning. Outlines varying death & gift taxes imposed by all the states, Puerto Rico, & the District of Columbia.
General Info: Yr. Est. 1925, Bi-weekly, Ind/Abs/Online: Prentice-Hall Info Network
List Rental: List Management Co.: WG & L List Management, 1 Penn Plz Fl 42, New York, NY 10119-0002 Tel # (212) 971-5000

State and Local Taxes *Business*

Publishing Co: Research Institute of America, 90 5th Avenue, New York, NY 10011-7629
Tel # (212) 645-4800; Title Tel # (800) 562-0245
Personnel: Publisher-Jeff Gottesfeld, Product Mgr.-Alan Kellett
Editorial Description: Thorough coverage of aspects of state & local governments including full text of statutes, official regulations, court decisions, rulings & interpretations.
General Info: Yr. Est. 1925, Monthly, Trim Size-6 x 9 1/4, Offset press, Ind/Abs/Online: Prentice-Hall Info Network, Looseleaf
List Rental: List Management Co.: Manager: Phyllis Ball; WG & L List Management, 1 Penn Plz Fl 42, New York, NY 10119-0002 Tel # (212) 971-5000

State Tax Action Coodinator

Publishing Co: Research Institute of America, 117 E Stevens Ave, Valhalla, NY 10595-1264;
Title Tel # (212) 645-4800
General Info: Monthly, Looseleaf
List Rental: List Management Co.: WG & L List Management, 1 Penn Plz Fl 42, New York, NY 10119-0002 Tel # (212) 971-5000, Actives: $95/M, Expires: $60/M

State Tax Cases Reports *Business*

Publishing Co: CCH, Inc., 2700 Lake Cook Rd., Riverwoods, IL 60015 Parent Co.-Kluwer Law & Taxation Publishers, Cambridge; Title Tel # (847) 267-7000 Title Fax # (800) 224-8299
Editorial Description: Genral principles developed from controlling case law of state and local taxation.
General Info: Yr. Est. 1948, Monthly, Trim Size-6 x 9, Web press, 75 pages, Color, Looseleaf
Subscriptions: Indv. $450

State Tax Guide *Business*

Publishing Co: CCH, Inc., 2700 Lake Cook Rd., Riverwoods, IL 60015 Parent Co.-Kluwer Law & Taxation Publishers, Cambridge; Title Tel # (847) 267-7000 Title Fax # (800) 224-8299
Editorial Description: Fast facts about the taxes of all states.
General Info: Yr. Est. 1937, Bi-weekly, Trim Size-6 x 9, Web press, 250 pages, No Color, Looseleaf
Subscriptions: Indv. $923

State Tax Reports All-States *Consumer*

Publishing Co: CCH, Inc., 2700 Lake Cook Rd., Riverwoods, IL 60015 Parent Co.-Kluwer Law & Taxation Publishers, Cambridge; Title Tel # (847) 267-7000 Title Fax # (800) 224-8299
Editorial Description: Separate reporters for each state & D.C. provide an authoritative guide to all state taxes, including sale & use, corporate income, personal income, property, administration & many more.
General Info: Yr. Est. 1917, Monthly, Trim Size-6 x 9, Web press, No Color, Looseleaf
Advertising: Inquire for rates.

State Tax Review *Business, Consumer*

Publishing Co: CCH, Inc., 2700 Lake Cook Rd., Riverwoods, IL 60015 Parent Co.-Kluwer Law & Taxation Publishers, Cambridge; Title Tel # (847) 267-7000 Title Fax # (800) 224-8299
Editorial Description: Highlights of new state tax developments from all states, including new laws, decisions, regulations, administrative releases, etc.
General Info: Weekly, Ind/Abs/Online: NewsNet
Subscriptions: Indv. $89

TMA Tobacco Taxes Guide
See: TOBACCO

Tax Accounting *Business*

Publishing Co: Matthew Bender & Co., 11 Penn Plaza, New York, NY 10001-2006
Tel # (212) 967-7707 Fax # (212) 244-3188
Editorial Description: Comprehensive analysis of the accounting methods & periods available for tax purposes, with in-depth explanation of their tax advantages & disadvantages. Details the requirements for electing, using, or changing a method to ensure effective tax planning.
General Info: Yr. Est. 1982, Irregular, Looseleaf

Tax Action Coordinator *Association*

Publishing Co: Research Institute of America, 117 E Stevens Ave, Valhalla, NY 10595-1264;
Title Tel # (212) 645-4800
Editorial Description: Six-volume service designed to expedite your tax answers by providing all federal tax forms and agreements needed for reference and reproduction.
General Info: Quarterly, Looseleaf
Subscriptions: Indv. $342
List Rental: List Management Co.: WG & L List Management, 1 Penn Plz Fl 42, New York, NY 10119-0002 Tel # (212) 971-5000, Actives: $95/M, Expires: $60/M

Tax Administrators News *Association*

Publishing Co: Federation of Tax Administrators, 444 N Capitol St NW Ste 348, Washington, DC 20001-1512; Title Tel # (202) 624-5890
Personnel: Editor-Audrey Maynard, Circ. Mgr.-Dot Menard
Editorial Description: Recent developments relating to state tax administration, state legislation, federal legislation, court litigation, and other.
General Info: Yr. Est. 1937, Monthly, 12 pages, No Color, Saddle-stitched
Subscriptions: Indv. $35, $3/copy
Circulation: Total-1,800

Tax Alert for Management

Publishing Co: Research Institute of America, 117 E Stevens Ave, Valhalla, NY 10595-1264;
Title Tel # (212) 645-4800
General Info: Weekly, ISSN: 0196-8882
List Rental: List Management Co.: WG & L List Management, 1 Penn Plz Fl 42, New York, NY 10119-0002 Tel # (212) 971-5000, Actives: $95/M, Expires: $60/M

Tax Back Talk
Association

Publishing Co: California Tax Reform Assn., 926 J St Ste 710, Sacramento, CA 95814-2707
Fax # (916) 444-6611; Title Tel # (916) 446-4300
Personnel: Publisher, Editor-Lenny Goldberg
Editorial Description: Reports on progressive tax reform legislation.
General Info: Yr. Est. 1974, Tri-annually, Trim Size-8$\frac{1}{2}$ x 14, Sheetfed press, 6 pages, No Color
Subscriptions: Indv. $15
Circulation: Total-3,500

Tax Coordinator

Publishing Co: Research Institute of America, 117 E Stevens Ave, Valhalla, NY 10595-1264;
Title Tel # (800) 431-9025
General Info: Yr. Est. 1965, Weekly
Subscriptions: Indv. $243
List Rental: List Management Co.: WG & L List Management, 1 Penn Plz Fl 42, New York, NY
10119-0002 Tel # (212) 971-5000, Actives: $95/M, Expires: $60/M

Tax Court Decisions
Business

Publishing Co: CCH, Inc., 2700 Lake Cook Rd., Riverwoods, IL 60015 Parent Co.-Kluwer Law &
Taxation Publishers, Cambridge; Title Tel # (847) 267-7000 Title Fax # (800) 224-8299
Editorial Description: Provides full-text regular and memo decisions only, for those not needing
more complete court coverage.
General Info: Yr. Est. 1924, Weekly, Trim Size-6 x 9, Web press, 50 pages, No Color, Looseleaf
Subscriptions: Indv. $714

Tax Court Reports
Business

Publishing Co: CCH, Inc., 2700 Lake Cook Rd., Riverwoods, IL 60015 Parent Co.-Kluwer Law &
Taxation Publishers, Cambridge; Title Tel # (847) 267-7000 Title Fax # (800) 224-8299
Editorial Description: Details on new Tax Court petitions, full text decisions, with analysis of key
current petitions.
General Info: Yr. Est. 1924, Weekly, Trim Size-6 x 9, Web press, 80 pages, No Color, Looseleaf
Subscriptions: Indv. $967

Tax Credit Advisor
See: REAL ESTATE

Tax, Estate and Financial Planning for the Elderly
See: BANKING & FINANCE

Tax-Exempt
Organizations
Business

Publishing Co: Research Institute of America, 117 E Stevens Ave, Valhalla, NY 10595-1264;
Title Fax # (401) 816-3484
Editorial Description: Explains the effect of tax reform on tax-exempt enterprises, & shows how to
remain tax & penalty free. Helps organizations to maintain tax exempt status & avoid penalties.
General Info: Yr. Est. 1971, Monthly, Looseleaf
Subscriptions: Indv. $590
List Rental: List Management Co.: WG & L List Management, 1 Penn Plz Fl 42, New York, NY
10119-0002 Tel # (212) 971-5000

Tax Features

Publishing Co: Tax Foundation, 1250 H St NW Ste 750, Washington, DC 20005-3952;
Title Tel # (202) 488-8200 Title Fax # (202) 488-8282
General Info: 11x/yr.
Subscriptions: Indv. $50

Tax Fraud and Evasion
Business

Publishing Co: Warren, Gorham & Lamont, 31 Saint James Ave., Boston, MA 02116-4112
Fax # (617) 423-1914 Parent Co.-Thomson Professional Publications, Stamford;
Title Tel # (617) 423-2020
Personnel: Publisher-Wayne Barr, Production Mgr.-Mavra Kiey, Mktg. Dir.-Jim Spillane
Editorial Description: Treatise on the legal and practical ramifications of tax fraud and evasion
litigation.
General Info: Yr. Est. 1963, Semi-annually, Looseleaf
Subscriptions: Indv. $150
List Rental: List Management Co.: American List Counsel, 88 Orchard Cir # Cn-5219, Princeton, NJ
08540-3026 Tel # (908) 874-4300, Fax # (908) 874-4433

Tax Free Trade Zones of the World

Publishing Co: Matthew Bender & Co., 11 Penn Plaza, New York, NY 10001-2006
Fax # (212) 244-3188; Title Tel # (212) 967-7707
Personnel: Editor-T. Kennelty
Editorial Description: Details nearly 400 tax-free zones, free ports and similarly designated areas of
the world, including more than 60 such zone in the U.S. alone.
General Info: Yr. Est. 1977, Irregular, Looseleaf
Subscriptions: $275/copy

Tax Havens of the World
Business

Publishing Co: Matthew Bender & Co., 11 Penn Plaza, New York, NY 10001-2006
Fax # (212) 244-3188; Title Tel # (212) 967-7707
Personnel: Editor-T. Kennelty
Editorial Description: Examines tax havens in 50 areas around the world and rates each on the
basis of 30 vital features. Tax reform pitfalls are also analyzed.
General Info: Yr. Est. 1974, Quarterly, Looseleaf
Subscriptions: $275/copy

Tax Hotline
Business, Consumer

Publishing Co: Boardroom Publishing, PO Box 2614, 55 Railroad Ave., Greenwich, CT 06836-6378;
Title Tel # (203) 625-5216 Title Fax # (203) 861-7442
Personnel: Publisher-Martin Edelston, Editor-David Ellis, Circ. Mgr.-Michael Weil, Production Mgr.-
Kathleen Boehme, Art Dir.-Ray Holland, Promotion Dir.-Brian Kurtz
Editorial Description: To alert taxpayers the opportunities & traps in the broad range of tax laws,
rules & regulations that affect business operations & business decisions. To bring tax knowledge &
ideas from the tax experts who create them to the individuals who use them.
General Info: Yr. Est. 1980, Monthly
Subscriptions: Indv. $59, For. $74, $5/copy
Circulation: Total-130,000
List Rental: Actives: $85/M, Hotline: $95/M, Expires: $60/M

Tax Ideas
Business

Publishing Co: Research Institute of America, 90 5th Avenue, New York, NY 10011-7629
Tel # (212) 645-4800; Title Tel # (800) 562-0245
Editorial Description: Provides in-depth analysis of tax-saving devices, with special emphasis on the
changes brought by tax reforms. Offers creative solutions to specific federal tax problems.
General Info: Yr. Est. 1958, Semi-monthly, Trim Size-6 x 9$\frac{1}{4}$, Offset press, Looseleaf
Subscriptions: Indv. $420
List Rental: List Management Co.: WG & L List Management, 1 Penn Plz Fl 42, New York, NY
10119-0002 Tel # (212) 971-5000

Tax Laws of the World
See: LAW

Tax Letter Europe
Business

Publishing Co: Matthew Bender & Co., 11 Penn Plaza, New York, NY 10001-2006
Tel # (212) 967-7707 Fax # (212) 244-3188
Editorial Description: With editorial input from tax experts all over Europe, this importnat biweekly
newsletter reports on the latest events taking place in Burssels, the EC member states & their trade
partners.
General Info: Yr. Est. 1990, Bi-weekly

Tax Management Estates, Gifts & Trusts
Business

Publishing Co: Bureau of National Affairs, Inc., 1231 25th St. NW, Bldg. N-200, Washington, DC
20037-1157 Fax # (202) 822-8092; Title Tel # (202) 452-4200 Title Fax # (202) 833-7297
Personnel: Publisher-William A. Beltz, Mng. Editor-Glenn B. Davis, Circ. Mgr.-Gary C. Seltzer
Editorial Description: A portfolio & bi-monthly journal service covering specific areas of estate
planning & administration.
General Info: Yr. Est. 1967, Bi-monthly, Trim Size-8$\frac{1}{2}$ x 11, Offset press, 31 pages, Ind/Abs/Online:
Lexis, Westlaw, Dialog, Looseleaf
Subscriptions: Indv. $859

Tax Management Estates, Gifts & Trusts Reference File
Business

Publishing Co: Bureau of National Affairs, Inc., 1231 25th St. NW, Bldg. N-200, Washington, DC
20037-1157 Fax # (202) 822-8092; Title Tel # (202) 452-4200 Title Fax # (202) 833-7297
Personnel: Publisher-William A. Beltz, Mng. Editor-Glenn B. Davis, Circ. Mgr.-Gary C. Seltzer
Editorial Description: A three volume compilation of basic textual material (including the IRS code,
regulations, & rulings) relating to estates, gifts, & trusts, with bi-weekly supplements.
General Info: Yr. Est. 1984, Bi-weekly, Trim Size-8$\frac{1}{2}$ x 11, Offset press, Looseleaf
Subscriptions: Indv. $612

Tax Management-Foreign Income Portfolios

Publishing Co: Bureau of National Affairs, Inc., 1231 25th St. NW, Bldg. N-200, Washington, DC
20037-1157 Fax # (202) 822-8092; Title Tel # (202) 452-4200 Title Fax # (202) 833-7297
Personnel: Publisher-William A. Beltz, Mng. Editor-Glenn B. Davis, Circ. Mgr.-Gary C. Seltzer, Adv.
Dir.-Donald Broadous
Editorial Description: Problems arising from foreign taxation of U.S. companies abroad, U.S.
taxation of foreign operations, & the conduct of business in selected countries around the world.
General Info: (Formerly Tax Management-Foreign Income), Yr. Est. 1964, Bi-monthly, Trim Size-8$\frac{1}{2}$
x 11, Web press, Ind/Abs/Online: Lexis,Westlaw, No Color, Looseleaf
Subscriptions: Indv. $1,215, $75/copy

Tax Management IRS Forms
Business

Publishing Co: Bureau of National Affairs, Inc., 1231 25th St. NW, Bldg. N-200, Washington, DC
20037-1157 Fax # (202) 822-8092; Title Tel # (202) 452-4200 Title Fax # (202) 452-4096
Personnel: Publisher-William A. Beltz, Mng. Editor-Glenn B. Davis, Circ. Mgr.-Gary C. Seltzer
Editorial Description: Four-binder service providing tax practitioners with copies of IRS forms.
Periodical supplements.
General Info: Yr. Est. 1988, Irregular, Trim Size-8$\frac{1}{2}$ x 11, Offset press, Looseleaf
Subscriptions: Indv. $330

Tax Management IRS Practice & Policy
Business

Publishing Co: Bureau of National Affairs, Inc., 1231 25th St. NW, Bldg. N-200, Washington, DC
20037-1157; Title Tel # (202) 452-4200 Title Fax # (202) 822-8092
Personnel: Publisher-William A. Beltz, Mng. Editor-Glenn B. Davis, Circ. Mgr.-Gary C. Seltzer
Editorial Description: Seven-volume reference service providing a comprehensive discussion of IRS
practice from audits through collections. Includes practice documents, IRS directories, industry
specific bandbooks & excerpts from the Internal Revenue Manual.
General Info: Yr. Est. 1990, Monthly, Trim Size-8$\frac{1}{2}$ x 11, Offset press, 16 pages, Looseleaf
Subscriptions: Indv. $827

Tax Management
International Forum *Business*

Publishing Co: Bureau of National Affairs, Inc., 1231 25th St. NW, Bldg. N-200, Washington, DC 20037-1157 Fax # (202) 822-8092; Title Tel # (202) 452-4200 Title Fax # (800) 473-9284
Personnel: Publisher-William A. Beltz, Editor-Sondra Beecroft, Mng. Editor-Virginia A. Jackson, Circ. Mgr.-Gaina Hadley
Editorial Description: A quarterly comparative discussion of intl. tax law problems by distinguished practitioners in major industrial countries.
General Info: Yr. Est. 1980, Quarterly, Trim Size-8¼ x 11¾, Offset press, 32 pages, ISSN: 0143-7941, Looseleaf
Subscriptions: Indv. $350

Tax Management
International Portfolios *Business, Consumer*

Publishing Co: Bureau of National Affairs, Inc., 1231 25th St. NW, Bldg. N-200, Washington, DC 20037-1157 Fax # (202) 822-8092; Title Tel # (202) 452-4200 Title Fax # (202) 833-7297
Personnel: Publisher-William A. Beltz, Mng. Editor-Glenn B. Davis, Circ. Mgr.-Richard Whelan
Editorial Description: A portfolio service, each covering an individual country, with complete tax planning guidance on conducting successful business operations in that country.
General Info: Yr. Est. 1972, Irregular, Trim Size-8½ x 11, Offset press, Looseleaf
Subscriptions: Indv. $998

Tax Management Primary
Sources Series V *Business*

Publishing Co: Bureau of National Affairs, Inc., 1231 25th St. NW, Bldg. N-200, Washington, DC 20037-1157 Fax # (202) 822-8092; Title Tel # (202) 452-4200 Title Fax # (202) 833-7297
Personnel: Publisher-William B. Beltz, Mng. Editor-Glenn B. Davis, Circ. Mgr.-Gary C. Seltzer
Editorial Description: On-going legislative history of the Tax Reform Act of 1986 & subsequent legislation.
General Info: (Formerly Tax Management Primary Source IV), Yr. Est. 1987, Monthly, Trim Size-8½ x 11, Web press, ISSN: 0738-5285, Looseleaf
Subscriptions: Indv. $1,060

Tax Management Primary
Sources Washington Tax
Review

Publishing Co: Bureau of National Affairs, Inc., 1231 25th St. NW, Bldg. N-200, Washington, DC 20037-1157 Tel # (202) 452-4200 Fax # (202) 822-8092; Title Tel # (202) 452-4556 Title Fax # (202) 452-4096
Personnel: Publisher-William A. Beltz, Mng. Editor-Glenn B. Davis, Circ. Mgr.-Gary C. Seltzer
Editorial Description: A monthly analysis of tax legislative developments: including BNA's Advisory Board Outlook, summaries of recent tax legislation & analyses by tax practitioners of current issues.
General Info: Yr. Est. 1979, Monthly, Trim Size-3½ x 11, Offset press, 24 pages, ISSN: 0738-5285, Looseleaf
Subscriptions: Indv. $183

Tax Management Real
Estate *Business*

Publishing Co: Bureau of National Affairs, Inc., 1231 25th St. NW, Bldg. N-200, Washington, DC 20037-1157 Tel # (202) 452-4200 Fax # (202) 822-8092; Title Tel # (202) 452-4556 Title Fax # (202) 833-7297
Personnel: Publisher-William A. Beltz, Mng. Editor-Glenn B. Davis, Circ. Mgr.-Gary C. Seltzer
Editorial Description: A real estate tax reference service consisting of a series of portfolios, each written by an experienced tax practitioner, & a journal which covers new developments in the field.
General Info: Yr. Est. 1984, Monthly, Trim Size-8½ x 11, Web press, 24 pages, Ind/Abs/Online: Westlaw, Lexis, Looseleaf
Subscriptions: Indv. $822

Tax Management U.S.
Income *Business, Consumer*

Publishing Co: Bureau of National Affairs, Inc., 1231 25th St. NW, Bldg. N-200, Washington, DC 20037-1157 Tel # (202) 452-4200 Fax # (202) 822-8092; Title Tel # (202) 452-4556 Title Fax # (202) 833-7297
Personnel: Publisher-William A. Beltz, Mng. Editor-Glenn B. Davis, Circ. Mgr.-Gary C. Seltzer
Editorial Description: A portfolio service covering tax planning problems related to federal taxation of domestic income. Includes a subscription to the Tax Management Revenue Forms Service.
General Info: Yr. Est. 1959, Bi-weekly, Trim Size-8½ x 11, Offset press, Ind/Abs/Online: Westlaw, Lexis, Looseleaf
Subscriptions: Indv. $1,778

Tax Notes International *Business, Consumer*

Publishing Co: Tax Analysts, 6830 N. Fairfax Dr., Arlington, VA 22213-1098 Fax # (703) 533-4444; Title Tel # (703) 533-4400 Title Fax # (703) 533-4440
Personnel: Publisher-Thomas Field, Editor-Susan Lyons, Mktg. Dir.-Barbara Halberstam
Editorial Description: Provides international tax news and commentary from a world wide reporting staff, along with summaries of statutes, regulations, rulings, court decisions and tax treaties.
General Info: Yr. Est. 1980, Weekly, ISSN: 1058-3971, Ind/Abs/Online: Lexis and Dialog
Subscriptions: Indv. $899
List Rental: Rents Lists

Tax Planning *Business*

Publishing Co: Research Institute of America, 90 5th Avenue, New York, NY 10011-7629 Tel # (212) 645-4800; Title Tel # (800) 562-0245
Personnel: Publisher-Robert Martin, Editor-Burton DeFren, Adv. Dir.-Dorothy Ripin
Editorial Description: Reference tool for the tax simplification of business, personal and family affairs. Defines typical problems, shows alternative solutions, compares results.
General Info: Monthly, Trim Size-8½ x 11, Offset press, Looseleaf
Subscriptions: Indv. $312
Advertising: Inquire for rates.
List Rental: List Management Co.: WG & L List Management, 1 Penn Plz Fl 42, New York, NY 10119-0002 Tel # (212) 971-5000

Tax Planning for
Corporations and
Shareholders *Business*

Publishing Co: Matthew Bender & Co., 11 Penn Plaza, New York, NY 10001-2006 Fax # (212) 244-3188; Title Tel # (212) 967-7707
Personnel: Editor-R. Ross
Editorial Description: Offers advice in this field.
General Info: Yr. Est. 1974, Looseleaf
Subscriptions: $150/copy

Tax Planning Ideas *Business*

Publishing Co: Research Institute of America, 90 5th Avenue, New York, NY 10011-7629 Tel # (212) 645-4800; Title Tel # (201) 592-2040
Personnel: Publisher-Robert Martin, Editor-Burton DeFren, Adv. Dir.-Dorothy G. Ripin
Editorial Description: Highlights important new tax developments and analyzes their implications. Explores new taxsaving angles and shows when and how to apply new decisions and interpretations.
General Info: Yr. Est. 1954, Semi-monthly, Trim Size-8½ x 11, Offset press, 8 pages, Color
Subscriptions: Indv. $48
Advertising: Inquire for rates.
List Rental: List Management Co.: WG & L List Management, 1 Penn Plz Fl 42, New York, NY 10119-0002 Tel # (212) 971-5000

Tax Preparers Liability
Service *Association*

Publishing Co: Research Institute of America, 117 E Stevens Ave, Valhalla, NY 10595-1264; Title Tel # (212) 645-4800
General Info: Quarterly
List Rental: List Management Co.: WG & L List Management, 1 Penn Plz Fl 42, New York, NY 10119-0002 Tel # (212) 971-5000, Actives: $95/M, Expires: $60/M

Tax Profile *Business*

Publishing Co: CCH Canadian Ltd., 6 Garamond Ct., North York, ON M3C 1Z5 Canada Fax # (416) 444-8011 Parent Co.-CCH, Inc., Riverwoods; Title Tel # (416) 441-2992 Title Fax # (416) 441-3418
Personnel: Editor-Don Schrank
Editorial Description: Comments on items of interest regarding federal income tax & other federal & provincial taxes.
General Info: Yr. Est. 1984, Monthly, Trim Size-8½ x 11, Web press, ISSN: 0827-3677, No Color
Subscriptions: Can. $125

Tax Quarterly Alert

Publishing Co: WPI Communications, Inc., 55 Morris Ave, Springfield, NJ 07081-1496; Title Tel # (201) 467-8700 Title Fax # (201) 467-0368
General Info: Quarterly

Tax Report *Business, Consumer*

Publishing Co: Newkirk Products, Inc., 15 Corporate Cir, Albany, NY 12203-5154 Tel # (518) 452-1000
Editorial Description: Custom publication for distribution by tax attorneys, consultants or others. Available monthly or quarterly.
General Info: Monthly

Tax Savings Report *Business, Consumer*

Publishing Co: National Taxpayers Union/NTU Foundation, 108 N. Alfred St., Alexandria, VA 22314; Title Tel # (703) 683-5700 Title Fax # (703) 683-5722
Personnel: Editor-Ellen Katz
Editorial Description: Tax information for consumers.
General Info: Yr. Est. 1982, 10x/yr., Trim Size-8¼ x 10¾, 8 pages, 2 Color, Matte
Subscriptions: Indv. $29
Circulation: Total-35,000
List Rental: List Management Co.: Conrad Direct, Inc., 300 Knickerbocker Road, Creskill, NJ 07626 Tel # (201) 567-3200, Fax # (201) 567-4959, Actives: 18,300, $125/M, Expires: 13,845, $75/M

Tax Treaties *Business*

Publishing Co: CCH, Inc., 2700 Lake Cook Rd., Riverwoods, IL 60015 Parent Co.-Kluwer Law & Taxation Publishers, Cambridge; Title Tel # (847) 267-7000 Title Fax # (800) 224-8299
Editorial Description: Treaties between the U.S. and foreign countries on income and estate taxes, with U.S. regulations and withholding provisions.
General Info: Yr. Est. 1952, Monthly, Trim Size-6 x 9, Web press, 30 pages, No Color, Looseleaf
Subscriptions: Indv. $538

Tax Treaties

Publishing Co: Research Institute of America, 90 5th Avenue, New York, NY 10011-7629
Tel # (212) 645-4800; Title Tel # (800) 562-0245 Title Fax # (201) 816-3484
Editorial Description: Up-to-date analysis of intl. tax agreements. Includes full official text of every treaty, & protocol relating to income taxes, gift taxes & estate taxes.
General Info: Yr. Est. 1969, Monthly, Looseleaf
Subscriptions: Indv. $325
List Rental: List Management Co.: WG & L List Management, 1 Penn Plz Fl 42, New York, NY 10119-0002 Tel # (212) 971-5000

Tax Update for Business Owners
See: BUSINESS & INDUSTRY

Tax Watch   *Business*

Publishing Co: Research Institute of America, 1340 Braddock Pl., Ste. 400, Alexandria, VA 22314-1651; Title Tel # (703) 706-8260 Title Fax # (703) 683-4824
Editorial Description: Helps companies deal with and understand tax law changes,
General Info: Yr. Est. 1993, Weekly
Subscriptions: Indv. $576

Tax Wise Money   *Consumer*

Publishing Co: Agora, Inc., 105 W. Monoment St., Baltimore, MD 21202-4702 Tel # (410) 783-2647 Fax # (410) 223-2662; Title Tel # (410) 234-0515 Title Fax # (410) 539-7348
Personnel: Publisher-Bill Bonner, Editor-Robert Carlson, Mag. Ed.-Christoph Amberger, Circ. Mgr.-Cynthia Rott, Mktg. Dir.-Deeba Jafri
Editorial Description: Advice and tips on how to save on taxes in accordance with new laws.
General Info: Monthly, ISSN: 0733-2254
Subscriptions: Indv. $39
Circulation: Total-42,000

TaxLetter, The   *Consumer*

Publishing Co: Hume Publishing Company Ltd., Suite 515, 4100 Yonge St., Willowdale, ON M2P 2B9 Canada; Title Tel # (416) 221-4596 Title Fax # (416) 221-4968
Personnel: Publisher-A. Micheal Keerma, Editorial Dir.-A. Michael Keerma, Editor-David Louis, Circ. Mgr.-Robin Young, Mktg. Dir.-Barbara Ritchie
Editorial Description: Canada's leading advisory on tax-saving strategies for both professional and nonprofessional readers.
General Info: Yr. Est. 1982, Monthly, Trim Size-8½ x 11, 8 pages, ISSN: 0703-7613, 2 Color, Matte, Other
Subscriptions: Indv. $89, $10/copy
List Rental: List Management Co.: Herbert A. Watts, 455 Horner Ave., Toronto, ON M8W 4W9 Canada Tel # (416) 252-7741

TaxPractice   *Business, Consumer*

Publishing Co: Tax Analysts, 6830 N. Fairfax Dr., Arlington, VA 22213-1098 Fax # (703) 533-4444; Title Tel # (703) 533-4400 Title Fax # (703) 533-4440
Personnel: Publisher-Thoams Field, Editor-Charles Davenport, Editor-Robert Manning, Mktg. Dir.-Barbara Halberstam
Editorial Description: A comprehensive weekly guide to tax developments, including IRS rulings and regulations, tax developments in Congress, and tax decisions from the courts.
General Info: (Formerly Tax-Related Administrative Documents), Yr. Est. 1985, Weekly, Mimeo press, 32 pages, ISSN: 1074-5858, 2 Color, Saddle-stitched
Subscriptions: Indv. $199
List Rental: Rents Lists

Taxation of Corporate Liquidations   *Business, Association*

Publishing Co: Research Institute of America, 90 5th Avenue, New York, NY 10011-7629
Tel # (212) 645-4800; Title Tel # (800) 562-0245 Title Fax # (201) 816-3484
Editorial Description: Practical guide to maximizing benefits-forms, provided.
General Info: Yr. Est. 1987, Semi-annually, Trim Size-7 x 9, Looseleaf
Subscriptions: Indv. $125
List Rental: List Management Co.: WG & L List Management, 1 Penn Plz Fl 42, New York, NY 10119-0002 Tel # (212) 971-5000

Taxation of Mining Operations   *Business*

Publishing Co: Matthew Bender & Co., 11 Penn Plaza, New York, NY 10001-2006
Tel # (212) 967-7707 Fax # (212) 244-3188
Editorial Description: Thorough, in-depth treatment, expert analysis & relevant cases covering federal income taxation of operations involving minerals other than oil & gas.
General Info: Yr. Est. 1981, Irregular, Looseleaf

Taxation and Revenue Policies/State Capitals   *Business*

Publishing Co: Wakeman/Walworth, 300 N. Washington St., Alexandria, VA 22314-2530;
Title Tel # (703) 549-8606 Title Fax # (703) 549-1372
Personnel: Publisher-Keyes Walworth
Editorial Description: Covers state revenue-raising programs other than property taxes. Reports on income-raising programs such as sales taxes, excise taxes, business, occupation, inheritance, gasoline, capital gains taxes and lotteries.
General Info: (Formerly Taxation and Revenue Policies from the State Capitals), Yr. Est. 1946, Weekly, Trim Size-8½ x 11, Offset press, 5 pages, ISSN: 0749-2820, No Color
Subscriptions: Indv. $365, Inst. $293, Can. $325, For. $345

Taxation of Securities Transactions   *Business*

Publishing Co: Matthew Bender & Co., 11 Penn Plaza, New York, NY 10001-2006
Fax # (212) 244-3188; Title Tel # (212) 967-7707
Editorial Description: 1 vol. with annual updates. How to save substantial tax dollars in securities transactions.
General Info: Yr. Est. 1971, Looseleaf
Subscriptions: $110/copy

Taxes Interpreted   *Business*

Publishing Co: MJM Publishing Co., 575 Lexington Ave Rm 2700, New York, NY 10022-6102; Title Tel # (212) 752-9700
Personnel: Editor-Michael Savage
Editorial Description: News and advice for professional tax practitioners.
General Info: Yr. Est. 1961, Bi-weekly, Trim Size-8½ x 11, 8 pages, ISSN: 0040-0203, No Color
Subscriptions: Indv. $147, $15/copy

Taxes on Parade   *Business, Consumer*

Publishing Co: CCH, Inc., 2700 Lake Cook Rd., Riverwoods, IL 60015 Parent Co.-Kluwer Law & Taxation Publishers, Cambridge; Title Tel # (847) 267-7000 Title Fax # (800) 224-8299
Personnel: Editor-James Rooney, Adv. Dir.-Joan Goode
Editorial Description: Review of week's Federal income tax developments.
General Info: Weekly, Trim Size-8½ x 11, 8 pages
Subscriptions: Indv. $97

Taxes-Property/State Capitals   *Business*

Publishing Co: Wakeman/Walworth, 300 N. Washington St., Alexandria, VA 22314-2530;
Title Tel # (703) 549-8606 Title Fax # (703) 549-1372
Personnel: Publisher-Keyes Walworth
Editorial Description: Follows trends in property tax laws and regulations. Special emphasis on school financing including state aid formulas, alternative school financing and budgetary issues.
General Info: (Formerly Taxes-Property from the State Capitals), Yr. Est. 1946, Weekly, Trim Size-8½ x 11, Offset press, 5 pages, ISSN: 0734-1121, No Color
Subscriptions: Indv. $365, Inst. $293, Can. $325, For. $345

Tennessee Tax Quarterly   *Business, Association*

Publishing Co: State of Tennessee Department of Revenue, 500 Deaderick St, Nashville, TN 37242-0001; Title Tel # (615) 741-2461 Title Fax # (615) 532-2285
Personnel: Editor-Kelly Johnson, Art Dir.-Mike Rock
General Info: Quarterly, Trim Size-8½ x 11, 6 pages, 2 Color
Subscriptions: Free
Circulation: Total-4,000

Texas Tax Service   *Business*

Publishing Co: Matthew Bender & Co., 11 Penn Plaza, New York, NY 10001-2006
Tel # (212) 967-7707 Fax # (212) 244-3188
Editorial Description: A comprehensive tax service offering up-to-the-minute treatment of administrative procedures and judicial remedies available to Texas taxpayers.
General Info: Yr. Est. 1985, Monthly, Looseleaf

Trust Administration and Taxation
See: LAW

Tulane Tax Institute

Publishing Co: Tulane Tax Institute, Tulane Univ., New Orleans, LA 70118-6397
Tel # (504) 865-5000
General Info: Yr. Est. 1951, Annually, ISSN: 0564-4402
Subscriptions: $30/copy

U.S.C. Law Center Tax Institute-Major Tax Planning

Publishing Co: Matthew Bender & Co., 11 Penn Plaza, New York, NY 10001-2006
Fax # (212) 244-3188; Title Tel # (212) 967-7707
General Info: (Formerly Univ. of Southern Cal. Law Center, Tax Institute), Annually, Looseleaf
Subscriptions: $85/copy

Understanding Income Tax   *Business*

Publishing Co: Carswell, 2075 Kennedy Road, One Corporate Plaza, Scarborough, ON M1T 3V4 Canada; Title Tel # (416) 609-8000 Title Fax # (416) 298-5094
Personnel: Publisher-Barry Garnet, Editor-Rene Huot, Adv. Dir.-Sandra Kay
Editorial Description: A comprehensive system for all levels of tax instruction. The author takes a logical approach to the complexities of the Income Tax Act. The system is flexible & can be readily adapted to specific course requirements.
General Info: Annually, Looseleaf

Unemployment Insurance Reports with Social Security-Federal & All States
See: SOCIAL SERVICES & WELFARE

U.S. International
Practice & Procedure   *Business*

Publishing Co: Warren, Gorham & Lamont, 31 Saint James Ave., Boston, MA 02116-4112 Parent
Co.-Thomson Professional Publications, Stamford; Title Tel # (617) 423-2020
Title Fax # (617) 423-1914
Personnel: Publisher-Wayne Barr, Production Mgr.-Maura Kiey, Mktg. Dir.-Jim Spillane
General Info: Yr. Est. 1994, Bi-monthly
Subscriptions: Indv. $195
List Rental: List Management Co.: Manager: Jim Spillane; WG & L List Management, 1 Penn Plz Fl
42, New York, NY 10119-0002 Tel # (212) 971-5000

U.S. Taxation of Intl.
Operations

Publishing Co: Research Institute of America, 90 5th Avenue, New York, NY 10011-7629
Tel # (212) 645-4800; Title Tel # (800) 562-0245 Title Fax # (201) 816-3484
Editorial Description: Examines special concerns of U.S. Corps. & American citizens operating &/or
investing abroad; also provides tax-saving techniques & ideas tailored to businesses that operate
abroad.
General Info: Yr. Est. 1973, Semi-monthly, Looseleaf
Subscriptions: Indv. $419
List Rental: List Management Co.: WG & L List Management, 1 Penn Plz Fl 42, New York, NY
10119-0002 Tel # (212) 971-5000

WRC Notebook
See: PUBLIC MANAGEMENT & PLANNING

WTA Newsletter   *Business, Association*

Publishing Co: Wyoming Taxpayers Association, 2410 Pioneer Ave., Cheyenne, WY 82001-3021;
Title Tel # (307) 635-8761
Personnel: Publisher-Michael Walden-Newman, Editor-John Allen, Circ. Mgr.-Jean Aschmar
General Info: Yr. Est. 1937, Monthly, Trim Size-8½ x 11, 5 pages, Color
Subscriptions: Indv. $50, $5/copy
Circulation: (100% controlled), Total-1,400

Weekly Alert   *Business*

Publishing Co: Research Institute of America, 117 E Stevens Ave, Valhalla, NY 10595-1264;
Title Tel # (212) 645-4800
Personnel: Editor-Frank Gruber
Editorial Description: Business intelligence & guidance for closely held businesses.
General Info: Weekly, Web press, 8 pages
List Rental: List Management Co.: WG & L List Management, 1 Penn Plz Fl 42, New York, NY
10119-0002 Tel # (212) 971-5000, Actives: $95/M, Expires: $60/M

Wills Estates and Trusts
See: LAW

Window on Canadian Tax   *Business*

Publishing Co: CCH Canadian Ltd., 6 Garamond Ct., North York, ON M3C 1Z5 Canada
Fax # (416) 444-8011 Parent Co.-CCH, Inc., Riverwoods; Title Tel # (416) 441-2992
Title Fax # (416) 444-9011
Personnel: Editor-Thorstein,s Sons Legal Firm, Adv. Dir.-Michael Dyet, Mktg. Dir.-Rick Humphrey
Editorial Description: Commentary on and an analysis of the most important Revenue Canada
income tax documents obtained under the Access to Information Act.
General Info: Yr. Est. 1991, Monthly, Looseleaf
Subscriptions: Can. $235

Wisconsin Taxpayer   *Association*

Publishing Co: Wisconsin Taxpayers Alliance, 335 W Wilson St, Madison, WI 53703-3612;
Title Tel # (608) 255-4581
Personnel: Editor-James R. Morgan
Editorial Description: Articles on Wisconsin state and local government and taxation.
General Info: Yr. Est. 1933, Monthly, Trim Size-6 x 9, Offset press, 9 pages, No Color, Newsprint,
Saddle-stitched
Subscriptions: Indv. $7, $1/copy
Circulation: Total-9,700

TELECOMMUNICATIONS

A-E-C Automation Newsletter
See: COMPUTERS & AUTOMATION

ACUTA News   *Association*

Publishing Co: Assn. of College & Univ. Telecommunication Administrators, 152 W Zandale Dr Ste
200, Lexington, KY 40503-2486; Title Tel # (606) 278-3338 Title Fax # (606) 278-3268
Personnel: Editor-Pat Scott
Editorial Description: Concerns telecommunication applications in educational institutions & industry.
General Info: Yr. Est. 1973, Monthly, Trim Size-8½ x 11, 12 pages, Other, Saddle-stitched
Subscriptions: Indv. $45, Inst. $45, Free With Membership
Circulation: Total-2,100

ADRIS Newsletter
See: COMPUTERS & AUTOMATION

AM Journal
See: BROADCASTING

ASR News
See: COMPUTERS & AUTOMATION

Advanced Intelligent Network News
See: COMPUTERS & AUTOMATION

Advanced Wireless
Communications   *Business*

Publishing Co: Capitol Publications, Inc., 1101 King St., Ste. 444, Alexandria, VA 22314-2968
Fax # (703) 739-6501; Title Tel # (703) 683-4100 Title Fax # (703) 739-6490
Personnel: Publisher-Paul Rubin, Editor-Elizabeth Soper, Production Mgr.-
John P. Fallon, Mktg. Dir.-Marc O'Brien
Editorial Description: Business opportunities in next generation wireless communications.
General Info: Yr. Est. 1990, Bi-weekly, Trim Size-8½ x 11, Offset press, 12 pages, Ind/Abs/Online:
NewsNet, Information Access, FT Profile, Newsprint
Subscriptions: Indv. $492, For. $470
List Rental: Actives: $185/M

Alumeto
See: LITERATURE & LINGUISTICS

Audiotex News   *Business, Consumer*

Publishing Co: Audiotex News, Inc., 2362 Hempstead Tpke Fl 2, East Meadow, NY 11554-2030;
Title Tel # (516) 735-3398 Title Fax # (516) 735-3682
Personnel: Publisher, Editor-Carol Morse Ginsburg, Circ. Mgr.-Debra Velsmid, Production Mgr.-
Virginia Hagherty
Editorial Description: To give the Audiotex industry access to the information it needs; quickly,
accurately, efficiently & to select & generate that information free from the influence of advertising.
General Info: Yr. Est. 1989, Monthly, Trim Size-8½ x 11, Sheetfed press, 8 pages, ISSN: 1063-1348,
2 Color, Matte
Subscriptions: Indv. $249, Can. $249, For. $249, $20/copy
Acquisitions: Publication Sold
Circulation: Total-1,000
Advertising: Accepts Inserts.
List Rental: Rents Lists
Printing Co: Press, The, 3000 Hempstead Tpke., Levittown, NY 11756 Tel # (516) 731-4892,
Fax # (516) 731-4602

Bandwidth Report   *Business*

Publishing Co: Probe Research, Inc., 3 Wing Dr Ste 240, Cedar Knolls, NJ 07927-1006
Fax # (201) 285-1519 Parent Co.-Phillips Business Information, Inc., Potomac;
Title Tel # (201) 285-1500
Personnel: Publisher-Victor Schnee, Editor-Jeffrey Berger, Circ. Mgr.-Donna Keller
Editorial Description: The global source on ISDN equpment, services, and applications. Covers
narrowband and broadband ISDN, frame relay, FDDI, SMDS, SONET, ATM and more.
General Info: (Formerly ISDN Report), Yr. Est. 1986, Bi-weekly, 8 pages
Subscriptions: Indv. $497, Can. $497, For. $527, $20/copy

Bellcore Exchange

Publishing Co: Bellcore, Room 1B101 - Box 486, 290 W. Mount Pleasant Ave., Livingstone, NJ
07093-0486
Personnel: Editor-Joel Schwartz
Editorial Description: Articles and information on telecommunications technology and strategies.
General Info: Bi-monthly, Trim Size-8½ x 11, 30 pages, ISSN: 0891-4877, 4 Color, Coated, Saddle-
stitched
Subscriptions: Indv. $35
Printing Co: Intelligencer Printing Co., 330 Eden Rd #1768, Lancaster, PA 17601-4218
Tel # (717) 291-3100, Fax # (717) 569-2643

Bulletin

Publishing Co: Maritime Telegraph & Telephone, Public Affairs Dept., PO Box Box 880, Halifax, NS
B3J 2W3 Canada; Title Tel # (902) 421-4959
Personnel: Editor-Pearleen Mofford
Editorial Description: Company and industry news for MT&T employees, pensioners and their
families.
General Info: Yr. Est. 1908, Monthly, Trim Size-8½ x 11, Sheetfed press, 6 pages, 2 Color, Recycled
Circulation: Total-5,200

CKC Report, The Hotel Technology Newsletter
See: HOTEL INDUSTRY

Cable Optics   *Business*

Publishing Co: Information Gatekeepers, Inc., 214 Harvard Ave., Boston, MA 02134-4651;
Title Tel # (617) 232-3111 Title Fax # (617) 782-8562
Personnel: Publisher, Editor-Paul Polishuk, Circ. Mgr.-Brendan Monroe, Art Dir.-Diana Towers
Editorial Description: Provides information on the lastest news and analysis on the markets and
applications of fiber optics for CATV and local distribution. CATV is one of the fast growing markets
for fiber optics and advanced multimedia applicatons.
General Info: Yr. Est. 1990, Monthly, Letrpr. press, ISSN: 1051-1938, 2 Color
Subscriptions: Indv. $575, Can. $575, For. $625, $50/copy
Advertising: Accepts Inserts.
List Rental: Rents Lists
Printing Co: Eagle Graphics, 30 Lancaster St, Boston, MA 02114-1779 Tel # (617) 742-7575

Cable TV and New Media
Law & Finance *Business, Association*

Publishing Co: Leader Publications, Inc., 345 Park Avenue South, New York, NY 10010 Parent Co.-New York Law Publishing Co., New York; Title Tel # (212) 545-6170 Title Fax # (212) 696-1848
Personnel: Publisher-Stuart M. Wise, Editor in Chief-Michael Botein, Editor in Chief-David M. Rice, Mag. Ed.-Mark Hopkins, Circ. Mgr.-Kerry Kyle, Promotion Dir.-Rose-Ann Morangelli
Editorial Description: Legal & regulatroy issues facing the cable industry.
General Info: (Formerly Cable TV Law & Finance), Yr. Est. 1983, Monthly, Trim Size-8½ x 11, Offset press, 8 pages, ISSN: 0736-489X, Color
Subscriptions: Indv. $225, $19/copy
Printing Co: Columbus Bookbinding, 1343 Belfast Ave, Columbus, OH 31904 Tel # (206) 323-9313, Fax # (206) 323-2987

Cable Telco Report, The
See: TELEVISION & VIDEO

Cabling News *Business*

Publishing Co: PennWell Publishing Company, Ten Tara Blvd., 5th Floor, Nashua, NH 03062-2801 Tel # (603) 891-9174 Fax # (603) 891-0574 Parent Co.-PennWell Publishing Co., Tulsa
Editorial Description: Provides accurate, timely news for the cabling industry; covers business and technological developments. Subscription includes either access via e-mail or Cabling Installation & Maintenance Buyers Guide.
General Info: Yr. Est. 1995, Semi-monthly
Subscriptions: Indv. $350, For. $375, $15/copy

Campus Computing and Communications
See: COMPUTERS & AUTOMATION

Canadian
Communications
Network Letter *Business*

Publishing Co: Evert Communications Ltd., 1296 Carling Ave., Ottawa, ON K1Z 7K8 Canada; Title Tel # (613) 728-4621 Title Fax # (613) 728-0385
Personnel: Publisher-Gordon Hutchison, Editor-Brant Scott, Assoc. Ed.-Debbie Lawes, Asst. Ed.-Jason Rodham, Circ. Mgr.-Carole Jeffrey
Editorial Description: Regulation and policy at both the federal and provincial levels, and reports on operating telecommunications companies, other carriers and new entries into Canadian telecommunications.
General Info: Yr. Est. 1980, 40x/yr., Trim Size-8½ x 11, Sheetfed press, 6 pages, ISSN: 0825-3021, No Color, Matte
Subscriptions: Inst. $775, Can. $775, For. $775
List Rental: Actives: $850/M
Printing Co: Bradda Printing Services, 130 Slater Street, Ottawa, ON K1P 6E2 Canada Tel # (613) 238-5433

Cellular Networking
Perspectives *Business*

Publishing Co: Cellular Neetworking Perspectives, 2636 Toronto Crown, Calgary, AB T2N 3WI Canada; Title Tel # (403) 289-6658 Title Fax # (403) 289-6659
Personnel: Publisher-David R. Crowe
Editorial Description: Focuses on industry standards for networking cell sites to create cellular telephone systems. Monitors activities of TIA standards committee, FCC, and Bellcore.
General Info: Yr. Est. 1992, Monthly, Trim Size-8.5 x 11, 5 pages
Subscriptions: Indv. $250, Can. $250, For. $300

Cellular Sales & Marketing
Newsletter *Business*

Publishing Co: Creative Communications, Inc., Box 1519-OX, Herndon, VA 22070-1524; Title Tel # (703) 742-9696
Personnel: Publisher, Editor-Stuart Crump, Jr., Circ. Mgr.-Margaret Peto
Editorial Description: Provides news & information on cellular telecommunications technology, products, & marketing.
General Info: Yr. Est. 1987, Monthly, Trim Size-8½ x 11, Other press, 8 pages, ISSN: 0892-2683, Ind/Abs/Online: NewsNet, No Color, Matte
Subscriptions: Indv. $347
Acquistions: Publication Sold

Cellular
Telecommunications *Business*

Publishing Co: Information Gatekeepers, Inc., 214 Harvard Ave., Boston, MA 02134-4651; Title Tel # (617) 232-3111 Title Fax # (617) 782-8562
Personnel: Publisher-Paul Polishuk, Circ. Mgr.-Brendan Monroe
General Info: (Formerly Wireless Cellular), Monthly, Letrpr. press, ISSN: 1058-6717, 2 Color
Subscriptions: Indv. $575, Can. $575, For. $625, $50/copy
Advertising: Accepts Inserts.
List Rental: Rents Lists
Printing Co: Eagle Graphics, 30 Lancaster St, Boston, MA 02114-1779 Tel # (617) 742-7575

Channel
See: LIBRARY

China Telecom *Business*

Publishing Co: Information Gatekeepers, Inc., 214 Harvard Ave., Boston, MA 02134-4651 Fax # (617) 782-8562; Title Tel # (617) 232-3111 Title Fax # (617) 734-8562
Editorial Description: Devoted to tracking the latest developments in the China telecommunications market. It is intended for busy executives who need up-to-date information on the markets, competitors, changing business conditions, tenders, RFPs and most importantly information on 'How to' get your share of this explosive market.
General Info: Monthly, ISSN: 1078-2214
Subscriptions: Indv. $575, Can. $575, For. $625, $50/copy
Advertising: Accepts Inserts.

Closer to the Customer
See: CONSUMER INTERESTS

Communication *Business*

Publishing Co: National Technical Information Service U.S., 5285 Port Royal Rd., Springfield, VA 22161-0001 Fax # (703) 487-4630; Title Tel # (703) 487-4630
Editorial Description: Covers common carrier & satellite communications, information theory, graphics, policies, regulations, studies, radio, & television.
General Info: Weekly, Trim Size-8½ x 11, ISSN: 0364-4944
Subscriptions: Indv. $135, Can. $135, For. $195

Communication
Booknotes *Business*

Publishing Co: Center for Advanced Study in Telecommunications, Ohio State Unv., 210 Baker, 1971 Neil Ave., Columbus, OH 43210; Title Tel # (614) 292-8444 Title Fax # (614) 292-7852
Personnel: Editor-Christopher Sterling, Circ. Mgr., Circ. Mgr.-Susan Brown, Art Dir.-Christopher Pacione, Promotion Dir.-Thomas McCain
Editorial Description: Descriptive reviews of new pubs. in telecommunications, media & information.
General Info: (Formerly Mass Media Booknotes), Yr. Est. 1969, Bi-monthly, Trim Size-8⁵⁄₁₆ x 8⁵⁄₁₆, Sheetfed press, 32 pages, ISSN: 0045-3188, 2 Color, Saddle-stitched
Subscriptions: Indv. $45, Inst. $95, For. $100
Circulation: Total-700
List Rental: Actives: $100/M

Communication Standards News
See: MEDIA & COMMUNICATIONS

Communications Business & Finance
See: BROADCASTING

Communications Daily *Business*

Publishing Co: Warren Publishing, Inc., 2115 Ward Ct. NW, Washington, DC 20037-1213; Title Tel # (202) 872-9200 Title Fax # (202) 293-3435
Personnel: Publisher-Albert Warren, Editor-Daniel Warren, Circ. Mgr.-Betty Alvine, Mktg. Dir.-Gary Madderom
Editorial Description: Daily pub. covering entire telecommunications industry.
General Info: Yr. Est. 1980, Daily, Trim Size-8½ x 11, 10 pages, ISSN: 0277-0679, Ind/Abs/Online: NewsNet, DIALOG, Mead Data Central, Nexis, Predicasts, 2 Color, Newsprint
Subscriptions: Indv. $2,899, For. $2,899
Acquistions: Publication Bought, Publication Sold
Advertising: $1.

Communications InfoDisk *Business*

Publishing Co: Faulkner Technical Reports, Inc., 7905 Browning Road, 114 Cooper Center, Pennsauken, NJ 08109; Title Tel # (609) 662-2070 Title Fax # (609) 662-3380
Editorial Description: CD-ROM updated reference service, covers product comparisons, technology overviews of communications products and services.
General Info: Yr. Est. 1992, Monthly, Looseleaf
Subscriptions: Indv. $2,087

Communications Report *Business*

Publishing Co: Warren Publishing, Inc., 2115 Ward Ct. NW, Washington, DC 20037-1213; Title Tel # (202) 872-9200 Title Fax # (202) 293-3435
Personnel: Publisher-Albert Warren, Editor-Michael French, Circ. Mgr.-Betty Alvine, Mktg. Dir.-Gary Madderom
Editorial Description: Authoritative report on aeronautical, maritime, & land satellites and radiodetermination.
General Info: (Formerly Mobile Satellite Reports), Yr. Est. 1987, Bi-weekly, Trim Size-8½ x 11, 10 pages, ISSN: 0146-6061, Ind/Abs/Online: Newsnet; Predicasts
Subscriptions: Indv. $514, For. $537
Acquistions: Publication Bought
List Rental: Rents Lists

Communications Today *Business*

Publishing Co: Phillips Business Information, Inc., 1201 Seven Locks Rd., Ste 300, Potomac, MD 20854-2958 Tel # (301) 340-1520 Fax # (301) 424-4297
General Info: Yr. Est. 1995, Daily, ISSN: 1079-669X
Subscriptions: Indv. $1,495

Communique-United
Telephone *Association*

Publishing Co: United Telephone System-Midwest Group, 6666 W 110th St, Overland Park, KS 66211-1501; Title Tel # (913) 791-4687
Personnel: Editor-Brian Newby
Editorial Description: Telephone co. employee newsletter.
General Info: Yr. Est. 1981, Bi-weekly, 4 pages
Circulation: Total-800

Computer & Communications Library
  See: COMPUTERS & AUTOMATION

Computing & Communications: Law & Protection Report
  See: COMPUTERS & AUTOMATION

Consumer Information - Appliances   *Consumer*

Publishing Co: Jupiter Communications, 627 Broadway, 2nd Fl., New York, NY 10012-2612
  Tel # (212) 780-6060 Fax # (212) 780-6075; Title Tel # (212) 941-9252 Title Fax # (212) 941-7376
Personnel: Circ. Mgr.-Harry R. Larson, Mktg. Dir.-David Schwartz
Editorial Description: Consumer electronics, computing, telecommunications, home shopping, etc.
General Info: Yr. Est. 1987, Monthly
Subscriptions: Indv. $475, Can. $475, For. $515
Advertising: Inquire for rates.
List Rental: List Management Co.: List Technology Systems Group, Inc., 1001 Ave. of the Americas, New York, NY 10018 Tel # (212) 719-3850, Fax # (212) 719-1878, Actives: 34,000, $150/M

Convergence   *Business*

Publishing Co: Information Gatekeepers, Inc., 214 Harvard Ave., Boston, MA 02134-4651;
  Title Tel # (617) 232-3111 Title Fax # (617) 782-8562
Editorial Description: Covering the convergence of telecommunications, computers, broadcasting, publishing, graphic design, ect. Highlights what might seem unrelated developments but could become significant.
General Info: 11x/yr.
Subscriptions: Indv. $265, Can. $265, For. $265, $50/copy

Cybernautics Digest
  See: MEDIA & COMMUNICATIONS

DOT. Com
  See: COMPUTERS & AUTOMATION

Data Channels
  See: COMPUTERS & AUTOMATION

Data Communications Management

Publishing Co: Auerbach Publishers, One Penn Plz., 42nd Floor, New York, NY 10119-0002
  Fax # (212) 971-5024 Parent Co.-Warren, Gorham & Lamont, Boston; Title Tel # (212) 971-5000 Title Fax # (212) 971-5025
Personnel: Publisher-Tom Kelly, Editor-Paul Berk, Production Mgr.-Geoff Braine, Promotion Dir.-Ed Novack
Editorial Description: Technical and management information for communications systems managers. Provides solid information and advice to accurately evaluate, design, and expand communications networks. Subscription includes main volume and 6 monthly updates.
General Info: Bi-monthly, Trim Size-6½ x 9, ISSN: 0735-9992, No Color, Saddle-stitched, Looseleaf
Subscriptions: Indv. $395, Can. $395, For. $514
Acquistions: Publication Bought
Circulation: Total-500
List Rental: Rents Lists

Data Entry Awareness Report
  See: COMPUTERS & AUTOMATION

Data Security Letter
  See: COMPUTERS & AUTOMATION

DataWorld
  See: COMPUTERS & AUTOMATION

Dealing with Technology
  See: BUSINESS & INDUSTRY

EDP Weekly
  See: COMPUTERS & AUTOMATION

East European Kranz Report
  See: COMPUTERS & AUTOMATION

Electronic Business Forecast
  See: ADVERTISING & MARKETING

Electronic Information Report
  See: MEDIA & COMMUNICATIONS

Electronic Mail & Micro Systems   *Business, Association*

Publishing Co: BRP (Washington DC), 1333 H St., NW, Suite 1100, West Tower, Washington, DC 20005-4707 Tel # (202) 842-3006 Fax # (202) 842-3047; Title Tel # (202) 842-3022 Title Fax # (202) 842-1875
Personnel: Publisher-Andrew Jacobson, Editor-Eric Arnum
Editorial Description: All aspects of electronic mail, including computer-based electronic-mail, telex, paging, facsimile, EDI, modems, multiplexers, etc.
General Info: (Formerly Telecam Eye-Bee-Em, Netline, Advanced Office Technologies), Yr. Est. 1977, Bi-weekly, Trim Size-8½ x 11, Offset press, 20 pages, ISSN: 8756-2537, 2 Color, Newsprint
Subscriptions: Indv. $595, Inst. $595, Can. $595, For. $655, $35/copy
Acquistions: Publication Bought, Publication Sold
Printing Co: Jim Buckley Offsetting, 1101 Pennsylvania Ave SE, Washington, DC 20003-2229 Tel # (202) 546-0501

Electronic Marketplace Report   *Association, Business*

Publishing Co: Simba Information, Inc., 213 Danbury Rd. PO Box 7430, Wilton, CT 06897-7430
  Fax # (203) 834-1771 Parent Co.-Cowles Business Media, New York; Title Tel # (203) 834-0033 Title Fax # (203) 834-0729
Personnel: Publisher-Chris Elwell, Mng. Editor-Elizabeth Estroff, Circ. Mgr.-Cara Paul, Circulation-Hillary Veeder, Mktg. Dir.-Michael Genaro
Editorial Description: Provides news, analysis & opinion for the emerging business of electronic marketing, electronic classified and yellow pages, online shopping malls & transectional services, the role of the Internet & CD Rom catalogs.
General Info: (Formerly Electronic Directory & Classified Report), Yr. Est. 1986, Bi-weekly, ISSN: 1071-247X
Subscriptions: Indv. $449, For. $499
Printing Co: Success Printing, 10 Pearl Street, Norwalk, CT 06850 Tel # (203) 847-1112, Fax # (203) 846-2770

Electronic Messaging News   *Business*

Publishing Co: Phillips Business Information, Inc., 1201 Seven Locks Rd., Ste 300, Potomac, MD 20854-2958 Tel # (301) 340-1520; Title Tel # (301) 340-2100 Title Fax # (301) 424-4297
Personnel: Publisher-Chris Scotton, Editor-Lana Sansur, Production Mgr.-Sherry Mitchell, Circ. Mgr., Promotion Dir.-Ruth Zellers
Editorial Description: An executive report on electronic messaging/E-mail strategies & applications. Each issue provides insightful case studies, updates on legal and security issues, helpful product comparison charts, and international news.
General Info: Yr. Est. 1989, Bi-weekly, Trim Size-8½ x 11, 8 pages, ISSN: 1044-9892, Ind/Abs/Online: NewsNet; Predicasts
Subscriptions: Indv. $597, Inst. $597, Can. $597, For. $630
Advertising: Inquire for rates. Accepts Inserts.
List Rental: Rents Lists

Electronic Public Information Newsletter
  See: PUBLIC MANAGEMENT & PLANNING

Enterprise Networking
  See: COMPUTERS & AUTOMATION

European Telecommunications   *Business*

Publishing Co: Probe Research, Inc., 3 Wing Dr Ste 240, Cedar Knolls, NJ 07927-1006 Parent Co.-Phillips Business Information, Inc., Potomac; Title Tel # (201) 285-1500 Title Fax # (201) 285-1519
Personnel: Publisher-Victor Schnee, Editor-Paul Broadhead, Circ. Mgr.-Donna Keller
Editorial Description: Comprehensive compilation of news and commentary on European telecommunications developments.
General Info: (Formerly Euro-East Telecommunications), Yr. Est. 1982, Bi-weekly, Mimeo press, 8 pages, ISSN: 8754-4459, Color
Subscriptions: Indv. $497, Can. $497, For. $527, $20/copy

Exchange: The Communications News Weekly   *Business*

Publishing Co: Information Gatekeepers, Inc., 214 Harvard Ave., Boston, MA 02134-4651;
  Title Tel # (617) 232-3111 Title Fax # (617) 782-8562
Editorial Description: Covers developments in telecommunications in Australia and New Zealand.
General Info: 48x/yr.
Subscriptions: Indv. $695

FCC Report   *Business*

Publishing Co: Telecom Publishing Group, 1101 King St Ste 444, Alexandria, VA 22314-2944 Parent Co.-Capitol Publications, Inc., Alexandria; Title Tel # (703) 683-4100 Title Fax # (703) 739-6490
Personnel: Publisher-Chris Vestal, Circ. Mgr.-Elizabeth Soper, Promotion Dir.-Betty Lehnus
Editorial Description: Off-the-record analysis of telecommunications regulation and federal policy.
General Info: (Formerly FCC Week), Yr. Est. 1981, Bi-weekly, Trim Size-8½ x 11, Offset press, 12 pages, ISSN: 0748-5714, Ind/Abs/Online: NewsNet, Information Access, FT Profile, Newsprint
Subscriptions: Indv. $579, For. $627
Acquistions: Publication Bought

Fax Reporter   *Business*

Publishing Co: Buyer's Laboratory, Inc., 20 Railroad Ave, Hackensack, NJ 07601-3309;
  Title Tel # (201) 488-0404 Title Fax # (201) 488-0461
Personnel: Editor-Peter Davidson
General Info: Yr. Est. 1987, Monthly
Subscriptions: Indv. $365
Circulation: Total-1,600
List Rental: Rents Lists

Faxfacts

Publishing Co: PM Company, 24 Triangle Park Dr, Cincinnati, OH 45246-3411;
Title Tel # (513) 772-5057 Title Fax # (513) 772-5098

Fiber Datacom   *Business*

Publishing Co: Information Gatekeepers, Inc., 214 Harvard Ave., Boston, MA 02134-4651
Fax # (617) 782-8562; Title Tel # (617) 232-3111 Title Fax # (617) 734-8562
Personnel: Editor-Paul Polishuk, Circ. Mgr.-Brendan Monroe, Art Dir.-Diana Towers
Editorial Description: Contains the latest news & analysis on the markets, technology, & applications of fiber optics for data communications, process control, building & campus wiring, high speed data links such as Fiber Channels, ESCON, HIPPI, & plastic optical fiber.
General Info: Yr. Est. 1987, Monthly, Letrpr. press, ISSN: 1051-1954, 2 Color
Subscriptions: Indv. $575, Can. $575, For. $625, $50/copy
Advertising: Accepts Inserts.
List Rental: Rents Lists
Printing Co: Eagle Graphics, 30 Lancaster St, Boston, MA 02114-1779 Tel # (617) 742-7575

Fiber in the Loop   *Business*

Publishing Co: Information Gatekeepers, Inc., 214 Harvard Ave., Boston, MA 02134-4651
Fax # (617) 782-8562; Title Tel # (617) 232-3111 Title Fax # (617) 782-8877
Personnel: Publisher, Editor-Paul Polishuk, Circ. Mgr.-Brendan Monroe, Art Dir.-Diana Towers
Editorial Description: Keeps you informed of the latest news & analysis on the markets, technology & applications of fiber in the local loop. Major developments on video dialtone, video-on-demand, fiber hybrid coax, & passive optical networks are also covered.
General Info: Yr. Est. 1989, Bi-monthly, Letrpr. press, ISSN: 1051-192X, 2 Color
Subscriptions: Indv. $575, Can. $575, For. $625, $50/copy
Advertising: Accepts Inserts.
List Rental: Rents Lists
Printing Co: Eagle Graphics, 30 Lancaster St, Boston, MA 02114-1779 Tel # (617) 742-7575

Fiber Optics Business   *Business*

Publishing Co: Information Gatekeepers, Inc., 214 Harvard Ave., Boston, MA 02134-4651
Fax # (617) 782-8562; Title Tel # (617) 232-3111 Title Fax # (617) 734-8562
Personnel: Publisher-Paul Polishuk, Circ. Mgr.-Brendan Monroe, Art Dir.-Diana Towers
Editorial Description: Gives the lasted news and analysis on markets, procurements, technology, and applications of fiber optics in government and military. Worldwide developments, plans, industry, RFP, contact awards, and competitive assessment.
General Info: (Formerly Military Fiber Optic Communications), Yr. Est. 1987, Bi-weekly, Letrpr. press, ISSN: 1057-5375, 2 Color
Subscriptions: Indv. $575, Can. $575, For. $625, $50/copy
Circulation: Total-500
Advertising: Accepts Inserts.
List Rental: Rents Lists
Printing Co: Eagle Graphics, 30 Lancaster St, Boston, MA 02114-1779 Tel # (617) 742-7575

Fiber Optics and Communications   *Business*

Publishing Co: Information Gatekeepers, Inc., 214 Harvard Ave., Boston, MA 02134-4651
Fax # (617) 782-8562; Title Tel # (617) 232-3111 Title Fax # (617) 734-8562
Personnel: Publisher, Editor-Paul Polishuk, Circ. Mgr.-Brendan Monroe, Art Dir.-Diana Towers
Editorial Description: Provides comprehensive and timely information that keeps you in touch with new opportunities, technology, applications, products, & market trends in fiber optics worldwide. Fiber optics continues to be the major drive for telecommunications growth.
General Info: Yr. Est. 1983, Monthly, Trim Size-8½ x 11, Letrpr. press, 20 pages, ISSN: 0275-0457, 2 Color
Subscriptions: Indv. $575, Can. $575, For. $625, $50/copy
Circulation: Total-400
Advertising: Accepts Inserts.
List Rental: Rents Lists
Printing Co: Eagle Graphics, 30 Lancaster St, Boston, MA 02114-1779 Tel # (617) 742-7575

Fiber Optics News   *Business*

Publishing Co: Phillips Business Information, Inc., 1201 Seven Locks Rd., Ste 300, Potomac, MD 20854-2958 Tel # (301) 340-1520; Title Tel # (301) 340-2100 Title Fax # (301) 424-4297
Personnel: Publisher-Ellen Hamm, Editor-Mark Mikolas, Circ. Mgr.-Vanessa Henderson, Production Mgr.-William Wynne, Promotion Dir.-Mark Ziebarth
Editorial Description: Fiber optics in telecommunications, local area networks & cable covered.
General Info: (Formerly Fiber/Laser News; Military & Commerical Fiber Business), Yr. Est. 1980, Weekly, Trim Size-8½ x 11, Sheetfed press, 8 pages, ISSN: 8756-2049, Ind/Abs/Online: NewsNet, DIALOG, Predicasts, No Color
Subscriptions: Indv. $697, For. $760, $37/copy
Acquistions: Publication Bought, Publication Sold
List Rental: Rents Lists

Fiber Optics Sensors & Systems (FOS2)
See: COMPUTERS & AUTOMATION

Fiber Optics Weekly Update   *Business, Consumer*

Publishing Co: Information Gatekeepers, Inc., 214 Harvard Ave., Boston, MA 02134-4651
Fax # (617) 782-8562; Title Tel # (617) 232-3111 Title Fax # (617) 734-8562
Personnel: Publisher, Editor-Paul Polishuk, Circ. Mgr.-Brendan Monroe, Art Dir.-Diana Towers
Editorial Description: Provides dependable and timely informatin that keeps you in touch with new opportunitities, technology, applications, products, and market trends. This publication is for those that need to keep up-to-date on a weekly basis.
General Info: (Formerly Fiber Optics Weekly News Service), Yr. Est. 1981, Weekly, Trim Size-8½ x 11, Letrpr. press, 8 pages, ISSN: 1051-189X, 2 Color
Subscriptions: Indv. $575, Can. $575, For. $625, $20/copy
Advertising: Accepts Inserts.
List Rental: Rents Lists
Printing Co: Eagle Graphics, 30 Lancaster St, Boston, MA 02114-1779 Tel # (617) 742-7575

Friday Memo   *Association*

Publishing Co: Information Industry Assn., 555 New Jersey Ave. NW, #800, Washington, DC 20001-2082; Title Tel # (202) 544-1969
Personnel: Editor-Lisa Isenman, Production Mgr.-Leslie Chase
Editorial Description: Includes articles on industry concerns; legislation and association-sponsored events.
General Info: Yr. Est. 1977, Weekly, Trim Size-8½ x 11, 2 pages, Ind/Abs/Online: NewsNet, No Color
Circulation: (100% controlled), Total-1,963

G-Map, the Geographic Information, Mapping & Publishing Newsletter
See: GEOGRAPHY

GA-SK Newsletter
See: DEAF

GTE Telenet Packet

Publishing Co: GTE Telenet, 12490 Sunrise Valley Dr, Reston, VA 22091-3470;
Title Tel # (703) 689-6000
Personnel: Editor-Tim Wilson
General Info: (Formerly The Packet), Yr. Est. 1975, Bi-monthly, 12 pages
Circulation: Total-2,000

Global Vision Investor Newletter Monthly
See: INVESTMENT

HDTV Report
See: TELEVISION & VIDEO

High Performance Computing & Communications Week
See: COMPUTERS & AUTOMATION

IQ Quarterly
See: COMPUTERS & AUTOMATION

ISA Update   *Business, Association*

Publishing Co: Interactive Services Association, 8403 Colesville Rd Ste 865, Silver Spring, MD 20910-3368; Title Tel # (301) 495-4955 Title Fax # (301) 495-4959
Personnel: Editor-Suzanne Nicolas
Editorial Description: Written as a membership service for businesses that deliver interactive telecommunications
General Info: (Formerly VIA Update), Yr. Est. 1981, Monthly, Trim Size-8½ x 11, Web press, 29 pages, 2 Color, Saddle-stitched
Subscriptions: Free With Membership
Circulation: Total-500
List Rental: Rents Lists
Printing Co: Network

ISDN News
See: COMPUTERS & AUTOMATION

ISDN User Newsletter   *Business*

Publishing Co: Information Gatekeepers, Inc., 214 Harvard Ave., Boston, MA 02134-4651
Fax # (617) 782-8562; Title Tel # (617) 232-3111 Title Fax # (617) 734-8562
Personnel: Publisher-Paul Polishuk, Editor-Scott Cherenma, Mng. Editor-Kent Kelly, Circ. Mgr.-Brendan Monroe, Art Dir.-Diana Towers
Editorial Description: Focuses on applications of ISDN for medium to large enterprises. The need for total solutions of business problems are stressed. The economies of ISDN applications are presented to allow users to make cost benefit analysis.
General Info: Yr. Est. 1987, Bi-monthly, Trim Size-8½ x 11, Web press, 36 pages, ISSN: 1078-1005, 4 Color, Coated, Saddle-stitched
Subscriptions: Indv. $80, Can. $80, For. $95
Advertising: $1,600.
List Rental: Rents Lists
Printing Co: Western Services, PO Box 1184, Sioux Falls, SD 57101-1184 Tel # (605) 339-2383

Industry Pulse   *Business, Association*

Publishing Co: Telecommunications Industry Association, 2500 Wilson Blvd., Ste. 300, Arlington, VA 22201-3834 Tel # (703) 907-7700 Fax # (703) 907-7727; Title Tel # (703) 907-7721
Editorial Description: Includes regular features such as 'Standards Action,' which provides standards proposals and new documents available; 'Business Connections,' which promotes opportunities, seminars, conference, and publications; a variety of feature articles, and more.
General Info: Yr. Est. 1979, 10x/yr., Trim Size-8½ x 11, 8 pages
Subscriptions: Indv. $65, Free With Membership
Circulation: Total-5,000
Printing Co: Reinhardt-LaShore Press, 1104 S. Wabash Ave., Chicago, IL 60605 Tel # (312) 427-7377, Fax # (312) 427-0970

Information Superhighways   *Business*

Publishing Co: Information Gatekeepers, Inc., 214 Harvard Ave., Boston, MA 02134-4651
Fax # (617) 782-8562; Title Tel # (617) 232-3111 Title Fax # (617) 734-8562
Editorial Description: Covers major policy, regulation, technical, marketing and user aspects of the subject worldwide.
General Info: Monthly, ISSN: 1078-6589
Subscriptions: Indv. $575, Can. $575, For. $625, $50/copy
Advertising: Accepts Inserts.
List Rental: Rents Lists

Inside CUE
See: EDUCATION

Integrated Services Digital Network (ISDN)
See: COMPUTERS & AUTOMATION

Interactions   *Business*

Publishing Co: Sponsor-New England Telephone, Marblehead Communications, Inc., 376 Boylston St., Boston, MA 02116-3812 Tel # (617) 424-7700 Fax # (617) 424-8905
Editorial Description: Published for telecommunications and MIS managers at companies that are major telephone service users.
General Info: Quarterly

Interactive TV Strategies   *Business*

Publishing Co: Capitol Publications, Inc., 1101 King St., Ste. 444, Alexandria, VA 22314-2968 Fax # (703) 739-6501; Title Tel # (703) 683-4100 Title Fax # (703) 739-6490
Personnel: Publisher-Chris Vestal, Editor-Michael Cavsey, Circ. Mgr.-Elizabeth Soper, Production Mgr.-John P. Fallon, Mktg. Dir.-Marc O'Brien
Editorial Description: Interactive Video & Data Networks.
General Info: (Formerly Imaging News; Enhanced Services Outlook/Information Networks), Yr. Est. 1988, Bi-weekly, Trim Size-8½ x 10½, Offset press, 12 pages, ISSN: 0897-2915, Ind/Abs/Online: NewsNet, Info Access, FT Profile, Newsprint
Subscriptions: Indv. $397, For. $409
Acquistions: Publication Bought

Interactive Television Report
See: TELEVISION & VIDEO

Interactive Video News   *Business*

Publishing Co: Phillips Business Information, Inc., 1201 Seven Locks Rd., Ste 300, Potomac, MD 20854-2958 Tel # (301) 340-1520 Fax # (301) 424-4297
Editorial Description: For professionals dealing with multimedia, video on demand, pay-per-view, home shopping and cable tv, online and software development.
General Info: (Formerly Video Marketing News; Pay-per-View Event Update), Yr. Est. 1994, Bi-weekly, ISSN: 1067-3849
Subscriptions: Indv. $597, For. $630

International Cellular   *Business*

Publishing Co: Kagan World Media Inc., 126 Clock Tower Pl., Carmel, CA 93923-8734 Parent Co.-Paul Kagan Associates Inc., Carmel; Title Tel # (408) 624-1536 Title Fax # (408) 625-3225
Personnel: Publisher-Paul Kagan, Circ. Mgr.-Judy Pinney, Adv. Mgr.-Johanne Hardy
Editorial Description: Facts and figures on cellular's rapid growth...and the countries and companies that lead the way.
General Info: (Formerly European Cellular), Yr. Est. 1989, Monthly, Trim Size-7¼ x 10, Other press, 12 pages, No Color, Other, Saddle-stitched
Subscriptions: Indv. $595
Advertising: $1,560.

Jamieson & Assocs. - Trends

Publishing Co: Jamieson & Assocs., Inc., 4133 W 45th St, Minneapolis, MN 55424-1040; Title Tel # (612) 920-3770
Personnel: Editor-Marjorie Jamieson
General Info: Yr. Est. 1983, Semi-annually, Trim Size-8½ x 11, 6 pages, 2 Color, Coated
Circulation: Total-2,500

Japan Computer Industry Scan   *Business*

Publishing Co: Kyodo News Intl., 50 Rockefeller Plaza #803, New York, NY 10020-1605; Title Tel # (212) 397-3723 Title Fax # (212) 397-3721
Personnel: Mktg. Dir.-Toshi Mitsudome
Editorial Description: General survey of Japanese computer industry with breakthroughs, marketing & licensing rights.
General Info: Yr. Est. 1984, Weekly, Ind/Abs/Online: NewsNet, DIALOG

LAN Product News
See: COMPUTERS & AUTOMATION

Land Mobile Radio News   *Business*

Publishing Co: Phillips Business Information, Inc., 1201 Seven Locks Rd., Ste 300, Potomac, MD 20854-2958 Tel # (301) 340-1520; Title Tel # (301) 340-2100 Title Fax # (301) 424-4297
Personnel: Publisher-Ellen Hamm, Publisher-Ellen Stuhlmann, Editor-Sharpe Smith, Circ. Mgr.-Vanessa Henderson, Production Mgr.-William Wynne, Mktg. Dir.-Kismet Gould, Promotion Dir.-Mark Ziebarth
Editorial Description: Private radio & cellular telephone business & regulation coverage.
General Info: (Formerly Industrial Communications), Yr. Est. 1946, Weekly, Trim Size-8½ x 11, Mimeo press, 16 pages, ISSN: 1070-6593, Ind/Abs/Online: NewsNet, DIALOG, Predicasts, No Color
Subscriptions: Indv. $597, For. $660, $37/copy
Acquistions: Publication Bought, Publication Sold
List Rental: Rents Lists

Local Telecom Competition News   *Business*

Publishing Co: Phillips Business Information, Inc., 1201 Seven Locks Rd., Ste 300, Potomac, MD 20854-2958 Tel # (301) 340-1520 Fax # (301) 424-4297
General Info: (Formerly US Telecommunications), Yr. Est. 1992, Bi-weekly, ISSN: 1067-6333
Subscriptions: Indv. $597, For. $630

Manufacturing Market Insider
See: MANUFACTURING

Metropolitan Area Networks (MAN)
See: COMPUTERS & AUTOMATION

Mexico Telecom   *Business*

Publishing Co: Information Gatekeepers, Inc., 214 Harvard Ave., Boston, MA 02134-4651 Fax # (617) 782-8562; Title Tel # (617) 232-3111 Title Fax # (617) 782-4651
Editorial Description: Covering all aspects of telecommunications in Mexico. Mexico is one of the largest & fastest growing telecommunications markets in Central & South America. Major markets have just started to develop & as the economy grows opportunities will expand.
General Info: Monthly
Subscriptions: Indv. $575, Can. $575, For. $675, $50/copy

MicroCell News   *Business*

Publishing Co: Probe Research, Inc., 3 Wing Dr Ste 240, Cedar Knolls, NJ 07927-1006 Parent Co.-Phillips Business Information, Inc., Potomac; Title Tel # (201) 285-1500 Title Fax # (201) 285-1519
Personnel: Publisher-Victor Schnee, Editor-David Toll, Circ. Mgr.-Donna Keller
Editorial Description: International source on cordless telephony, personal communications networks, microcellular technologies and the wireless office.
General Info: Yr. Est. 1989, Bi-weekly
Subscriptions: Indv. $497, Can. $497, For. $527

Microwave News
See: HEALTH

Mobile Phone News   *Business*

Publishing Co: Phillips Business Information, Inc., 1201 Seven Locks Rd., Ste 300, Potomac, MD 20854-2958 Tel # (301) 340-1520; Title Tel # (301) 340-2100 Title Fax # (301) 424-4297
Personnel: Publisher-Ellen Hamm, Editor-Andrea Knotts Bona, Circ. Mgr.-Vanessa Henderson, Production Mgr.-William Wynne, Mktg. Dir.-Kismet Gould, Promotion Dir.-Mark Ziebarth
Editorial Description: Cellular mobile telephone & paging industries marketing strategy covered.
General Info: Yr. Est. 1983, Weekly, Trim Size-8½ x 11, Sheetfed press, 10 pages, ISSN: 0737-5077, Ind/Abs/Online: NewsNet, Predicasts, No Color, Newsprint
Subscriptions: Indv. $697, For. $760, $37/copy
Acquistions: Publication Bought, Publication Sold

Mobile Satellite News   *Business, Consumer*

Publishing Co: Phillips Business Information, Inc., 1201 Seven Locks Rd., Ste 300, Potomac, MD 20854-2958 Tel # (301) 340-1520; Title Tel # (301) 340-2100 Title Fax # (301) 424-4297
Personnel: Publisher-Ellen Hamm, Editor-Kevin Dennehy, Production Mgr.-Sherry Mitchell, Circ. Mgr., Mktg. Dir., Promotion Dir.-Kismet Gould
Editorial Description: Executive report on voice processing, recognition & applications.
General Info: Yr. Est. 1989, Bi-weekly, 12 pages, ISSN: 1046-5286, Ind/Abs/Online: Newsnet, No Color
Subscriptions: Indv. $597, For. $630
Acquistions: Publication Bought, Publication Sold
Advertising: Accepts Inserts.
List Rental: Actives: $95/M

Modem User News
See: COMPUTERS & AUTOMATION

Multimedia Daily
See: COMPUTERS & AUTOMATION

Multimedia Monitor
See: COMPUTERS & AUTOMATION

Multimedia Telecommunication News   *Business*

Publishing Co: Stoneridge Technical Services, PO Box 1891, Rockville, MD 20849-1891 Tel # (301) 424-0114; Title Tel # (301) 424-0014 Title Fax # (301) 424-8971
Personnel: Publisher, Editor-William W. Creitz
Editorial Description: Concerned with multimedia telecommunications technology combining text, graphics, images, data, voice, and/or video.
General Info: (Formerly Integrated Messaging News), Yr. Est. 1991, Monthly, Trim Size-8½ x 11, Offset press, 10 pages, Newsprint
Subscriptions: Indv. $240, Can. $240, For. $270, $20/copy

NATAS News
See: TELEVISION & VIDEO

NYLA Bulletin
See: LIBRARY

National Consumers League Bulletin
See: CONSUMER INTERESTS

National Telephone Cooperative Association-Washington Report *Association*

Publishing Co: National Telephone Cooperative Association, 2626 Pennsylvania Ave., N.W., Washington, DC 20037-1695; Title Tel # (202) 298-2300 Title Fax # (202) 298-2320
Personnel: Publisher-Chris Lehner, Editor-Lisa Westbrook, Production Mgr.-Heidi Lyons
Editorial Description: Legislative & regulatory developments in telecommunications.
General Info: Yr. Est. 1968, Weekly, Trim Size-8½ x 11, Sheetfed press, 2 pages, No Color, Matte
Subscriptions: Indv. $100, Inst. $100
Circulation: Total-2,800
Printing Co: Lettercomm, Inc., 310 Swann Ave, Alexandria, VA 22301-1042 Tel # (703) 683-3105

Network Consultant Quarterly *Business, Consumer*

Publishing Co: Telematics International, 1201 W Cypress Creek Rd, Fort Lauderdale, FL 33309-1912
Editorial Description: For the telecommunications industry.
General Info: Quarterly

New Era: Japan *Business*

Publishing Co: Kyodo News Intl., 50 Rockefeller Plaza #803, New York, NY 10020-1605; Title Tel # (212) 397-3723 Title Fax # (212) 397-3721
Personnel: Publisher-Joji Tashiro, Circ. Mgr.-Toshiaki Mitsudome
Editorial Description: Covering developments in the newly deregulated Japanese telecommunications industry.
General Info: Semi-monthly, Ind/Abs/Online: Newsnet

NewsNet Action Letter *Business*

Publishing Co: NewsNet, Inc., 945 Haverford Rd., Bryn Mawr, PA 19010-3814; Title Tel # (215) 527-8030 Title Fax # (610) 527-0338
Personnel: Publisher-Andrew Elston, Editor-Ellen Keech
Editorial Description: News about online business information hardware and software for telecommunications-as it relates to the newsnet database
General Info: Yr. Est. 1982, Monthly, Trim Size-8½ x 11, Web press, 8 pages, Ind/Abs/Online: Newsnet, Color, Newsprint
Subscriptions: Indv. $20, $2/copy
Circulation: Total-10,000
List Rental: Actives: 39,620, $75/M
Printing Co: Kingswood Inc., Cricket Terrace Center, Ardmore, PA 19003 Tel # (215) 896-9260

Online Hotline News Service on CD-ROM *Business*

Publishing Co: Information Intelligence, Inc., PO Box 31098, Phoenix, AZ 85046-1098; Title Tel # (602) 996-2283
Personnel: Editor-Richard Huleatt
Editorial Description: Covers all news articles for all newsletters published by III from January 1980 to June 1989 covering online, CD-ROM, & library automation fields.
General Info: Yr. Est. 1980, Irregular, ISSN: 1040-6646, Ind/Abs/Online: CD-ROM
Subscriptions: Indv. $10

Online Newsletter *Business*

Publishing Co: Information Intelligence, Inc., PO Box 31098, Phoenix, AZ 85046-1098; Title Tel # (602) 996-2283
Personnel: Publisher, Editor-Richard Huleatt
Editorial Description: Covers all on-line services, suppliers, vendors, CD-ROM data bases, microcomputers & associated equipment, (Subscribers in over 70 countries).
General Info: (Formerly Information Intelligence Online Newsletter), Yr. Est. 1980, Monthly, Trim Size-8½ x 11, Sheetfed press, 14 pages, ISSN: 0194-0694, Ind/Abs/Online: NewsNet, DataStar, DIALOG, CARL,essa-irs,datatimes,stninternational, 1% ads, No Color
Subscriptions: Indv. $63, Inst. $63, For. $88, $6/copy
Advertising: Inquire for rates.

Open Systems Communications *Business*

Publishing Co: Phillips Business Information, Inc., 1201 Seven Locks Rd., Ste 300, Potomac, MD 20854-2958 Tel # (301) 340-1520; Title Tel # (301) 340-2100 Title Fax # (301) 424-4297
Personnel: Publisher-Christopher Scotton, Editor-Patricia Brown, Adv. Dir., Mktg. Dir.-Ruth Zellers, Promotion Mgr.-Sherry Mitchell
Editorial Description: Provides up-to-date coverage on Open Systems Interconnection (OSI) including, MHS, ISDN, ODA, EDI & related technologies by reporting on international, North American & European standards; general interest & user groups.
General Info: (Formerly OSI Communication; OpenSystems Report), Yr. Est. 1982, Bi-weekly, Trim Size-8½ x 11, Sheetfed press, 10 pages, ISSN: 1052-701X, 2 Color, Newsprint
Subscriptions: Indv. $497, Inst. $497, Can. $497, For. $530, $25/copy
Advertising: Inquire for rates. Accepts Inserts.
List Rental: Rents Lists

Orbiter

Publishing Co: Society of Satellite Professionals, 2200 Wilson Blvd., No. 102-258, Arlington, VA 22201; Title Tel # (703) 243-8948
Personnel: Editor-Scott Chase
Editorial Description: Highlights Society & chapter news & major satellite communication industry events.
General Info: Yr. Est. 1984, Bi-monthly
Circulation: Total-800

PBX Systems Guide *Business, Consumer*

Publishing Co: Telecommunications Product Review & CPE Strategies, 5643C Harpers Farm Rd., Columbia, MD 21044; Title Tel # (301) 840-0800 Title Fax # (301) 840-0809
Personnel: Publisher-Edward Garner, Editor-Byron Battles
Editorial Description: Communications systems product analysis annual service with quarterly updates and inquiry service.
General Info: Yr. Est. 1972, Quarterly, Offset press, 450 pages, ISSN: 0092-8828, No Color, Looseleaf
Subscriptions: Indv. $695, $399/copy
Circulation: Total-1,300

Pacific Rim Telecommunications *Business*

Publishing Co: Probe Research, Inc., 3 Wing Dr Ste 240, Cedar Knolls, NJ 07927-1006 Parent Co.-Phillips Business Information, Inc., Potomac; Title Tel # (201) 285-1500 Title Fax # (201) 285-1519
Editorial Description: Written by telecommunications experts in Japan, Hong Kong, and Australia. Covers public network services, private networks, cellular, ISDN, and CATV. Contains timely information on profit potential in the region.
General Info: Yr. Est. 1993, Monthly
Subscriptions: Indv. $389, Can. $389, For. $422

Program on Information Resources Policy-Review

Publishing Co: Program on Info Resources Policy, Harvard Univ., 200 Aiken, Cambridge, MA 02138; Title Tel # (617) 495-4114
Editorial Description: Provides info on the Program, which works to

R & D Innovator *Business, Association*

Publishing Co: Winston J. Brill & Associates, 4134 Cherokee Dr., Madison, WI 53711-3031 Fax # (608) 231-6766; Title Tel # (608) 231-6766 Title Fax # (608) 231-6794
Personnel: Publisher-Winston Brill, Editor-David Tenenbaum
Editorial Description: Articles by top industrial and academic researchers, creativity experts, management specialists, and technology historians.
General Info: Yr. Est. 1992, Monthly, Trim Size-8½ x 11, 12 pages, ISSN: 1061-1894, 2 Color, Recycled
Subscriptions: Indv. $144, Can. $144, For. $168, $12/copy
List Rental: Rents Lists

RBOC Update *Business*

Publishing Co: Worldwide Videotex Co., PO Box 3273, Boynton Beach, FL 33424-3273 Tel # (407) 738-2276 Fax # (407) 738-2276
Editorial Description: Information on Regional Bell Operating Companies, including marketing and operations news.
General Info: Yr. Est. 1990, Monthly, Ind/Abs/Online: DIALOG
Subscriptions: Indv. $150, Inst. $150, Can. $150, For. $165

RLE Currents
See: ENGINEERING, ELECTRICAL

RTCM Newsletter

Publishing Co: Radio Tech. Commission for Maritime Svcs. ; RTCM, PO Box 19087, Washington, DC 20036-0087; Title Tel # (202) 639-4006
Editorial Description: Monitors developments in maritime telecommunications, including radio communications, radar & radio navigation.
General Info: Yr. Est. 1982, Monthly, 8 pages
Circulation: Total-400

Report on AT&T *Business*

Publishing Co: Telecom Publishing Group, 1101 King St Ste 444, Alexandria, VA 22314-2944 Parent Co.-Capitol Publications, Inc., Alexandria; Title Tel # (703) 683-4100 Title Fax # (703) 739-6490
Personnel: Publisher-Chris Vestal, Editor-J. Michael Causey, Circ. Mgr.-Elizabeth Soper, Promotion Dir.-Betty Lehnus
Editorial Description: Reports exclusively on all activities of AT&T.
General Info: Yr. Est. 1983, Bi-weekly, Trim Size-8½ x 11, Offset press, 12 pages, ISSN: 0741-8361, Ind/Abs/Online: NewsNet, Information Access FT Profile, Predicasts, No Color, Newsprint
Subscriptions: Indv. $697, For. $747
Acquistions: Publication Bought

STC Lines *Business, Association*

Publishing Co: Society of Telecommunications Consultants, 13766 Center Street #212, Carmel Valley, CA 93924-9693
Editorial Description: Information on society events, consulting tips & practices.
General Info: Yr. Est. 1980, Quarterly, Offset press, 16 pages, No Color, Newsprint, Saddle-stitched
Subscriptions: Free
Circulation: (100% controlled), Total-325
List Rental: Actives: $150/M

SWL
See: HOBBY

Satellite Business News
See: TELEVISION & VIDEO

Satellite News
See: BROADCASTING

Satellite Week   *Business*

Publishing Co: Warren Publishing, Inc., 2115 Ward Ct. NW, Washington, DC 20037-1213;
Title Tel # (202) 872-9200 Title Fax # (202) 293-3435
Personnel: Publisher-Albert Warren, Editor-Michael French, Circ. Mgr.-Betty Alvine, Mktg. Dir.-Gary Madderom
Editorial Description: Authoritative newsletter for satellite communications and related fields.
General Info: Yr. Est. 1979, Weekly, Trim Size-8½ x 11, 12 pages, ISSN: 0193-2861, Ind/Abs/Online: NewsNet, DIALOG, 2 Color, Newsprint
Subscriptions: Indv. $903, For. $949
Acquistions: Publication Bought, Publication Sold

Service Level Newsletter
See: MANAGEMENT

Shosteck Cellular
Strategies   *Business*

Publishing Co: Sponsor-Herschel Shosteck Assoc., Ltd., Church Street Publishing, Inc., 10 Church St, Woburn, MA 01801-3025 Tel # (617) 938-7115; Title Tel # (617) 938-7184
Personnel: Publisher-Richard Luhr, Editor-Herschel Shosteck
Editorial Description: Cellular telephone business, marketing, and technology.
General Info: (Formerly Shotsteck Report, The), Yr. Est. 1994, Bi-monthly, Trim Size-8½ x 11, Offset press, 8 pages, ISSN: 1079-0594, 2 Color, Matte, Saddle-stitched
Subscriptions: Indv. $347, Inst. $347, $50/copy
Printing Co: Miano Printing, 21r Olympia Ave, Woburn, MA 01801-6307 Tel # (617) 935-2830

Signal   *Consumer*

Publishing Co: Washington Telephone Fedl. Credit Union, 3015 University Blvd W, Kensington, MD 20895-1936; Title Tel # (301) 933-9100
Personnel: Editor-Janis Forostiak
General Info: (Formerly WTFCU News), Quarterly, 4 pages
Subscriptions: Free
Circulation: (100% controlled), Total-25,000

Signature
See: EDUCATION

Solar Space-Letter

Publishing Co: Blue Rose Ministry, PO Box 332, Cornville, AZ 86325-0332;
Title Tel # (602) 634-6269
Editorial Description: Periodical directed towards UFO's & allied subjects.
General Info: Yr. Est. 1959, Bi-monthly, Mimeo press, 4 pages, 5% ads, No Color
Circulation: Total-2,000
Advertising: Inquire for rates.

Spargo

Publishing Co: Teleglobe Canada, 680 Sherbrooke St., W., Montreal, PQ H3A 2S4 Canada;
Title Tel # (514) 289-7478
Personnel: Editor-Ginette Boucher
Editorial Description: In-house employee pub.
General Info: Yr. Est. 1963, 10x/yr., 16 pages, 2 Color, Newsprint
Circulation: Total-1,200
Printing Co: Trandek Printing, 4980 Buchan, Montreal, PQ H4P 1S8 Canada

State Telephone
Regulation Report   *Business*

Publishing Co: Telecom Publishing Group, 1101 King St Ste 444, Alexandria, VA 22314-2944 Parent Co.-Capitol Publications, Inc., Alexandria; Title Tel # (703) 683-4100 Title Fax # (703) 739-6490
Personnel: Publisher-Chris Vestal, Editor-Herb Kirchhoff, Circ. Mgr.-Elizabeth Soper, Promotion Dir.-Betty Lehnus
Editorial Description: State regulation of tele-communications industry.
General Info: Yr. Est. 1983, Bi-weekly, Trim Size-8½ x 11, Web press, 12 pages, ISSN: 0741-8388, Ind/Abs/Online: NewsNet, Information Access, FT Profile, No Color, Newsprint
Subscriptions: Indv. $487, For. $511
Acquistions: Publication Bought
List Rental: Rents Lists

Stay in Touch

Publishing Co: AT&T Communications, 295 N Maple Ave Rm 5418a3, Basking Ridge, NJ 07920-1002 Tel # (908) 221-2000; Title Tel # (201) 221-2816
Editorial Description: Offers info on AT&T long distance rates, billing procedures, services for AT&T customers.
General Info: Monthly

Submarine Fiber Optic
Communications
Systems (SFOCS)   *Business*

Publishing Co: Information Gatekeepers, Inc., 214 Harvard Ave., Boston, MA 02134-4651;
Title Tel # (617) 232-3111 Title Fax # (617) 782-8562
Editorial Description: Devoted to developments of Fiber Optics to Submarine Communication Systems. Each issue will contain a worldwide review of recent developments affecting submarine fiber optics markets, technology, and applications. Major new markets include unrepreated submarine systems using optical amplifiers.
General Info: Monthly, ISSN: 1070-096X
Subscriptions: Indv. $575, Can. $575, For. $625, $50/copy

Successful Telephone Selling
See: SALESMANSHIP & SELLING

Syndication News
See: TELEVISION & VIDEO

TELCO Competition Report   *Business*

Publishing Co: BRP (Washington DC), 1333 H St., NW, Suite 1100, West Tower, Washington, DC 20005-4707; Title Tel # (202) 842-3006 Title Fax # (202) 842-3047
Personnel: Publisher-Andrew Jacobson, Editor-Victoria Mason, Circ. Dir.-Nigel Sonariwo, Mktg. Dir.-Adam Goldstein
Editorial Description: Tracks events stemming from FCC and state decisions opening local telephone markets to competition.
General Info: Yr. Est. 1992, Bi-weekly, Trim Size-8½ x 11, 16 pages, Ind/Abs/Online: Newsnet
Subscriptions: Indv. $459, Inst. $499, Can. $499, For. $535

TR Wireless News   *Business*

Publishing Co: BRP (Washington DC), 1333 H St., NW, Suite 1100, West Tower, Washington, DC 20005-4707; Title Tel # (202) 842-3006 Title Fax # (202) 842-3047
Personnel: Publisher-Andrew Jacobson, Editor in Chief-Victoria Mason, Editor-Jennifer Walsh, Circ. Dir.-Nigel Sonariwo, Mktg. Dir.-Adam Goldstein
Editorial Description: News on regulatory, technological, and market developments in the wireless telecommunications industry.
General Info: (Formerly Microcell Report), Yr. Est. 1991, Bi-weekly, Trim Size-8½ x 11, 18 pages, Ind/Abs/Online: NewsNet
Subscriptions: Indv. $497, Inst. $497, For. $533

Technology Applications Quarterly
See: EDUCATION

Technology Industry Growth Forecaster
See: EMPLOYMENT

Telco Business Report   *Business*

Publishing Co: Capitol Publications, Inc., 1101 King St., Ste. 444, Alexandria, VA 22314-2968 Fax # (703) 739-6501; Title Tel # (703) 683-4100 Title Fax # (703) 739-6490
Personnel: Publisher-Chris Vestal, Editor-Michael Cavsey, Editor-CR Stirba, Circ. Mgr.-Elizabeth Soper, Production Mgr.-John Fallon, Mktg. Dir.-Marc O'Brien
Editorial Description: Exclusive reporting on BOCs and independent telcos.
General Info: (Formerly Telephone Week), Yr. Est. 1992, Bi-weekly, Trim Size-8½ x 11, Offset press, 12 pages, Ind/Abs/Online: Newsnet, Information Access, FT Profile, Newsprint
Subscriptions: Indv. $632, For. $667
List Rental: Actives: $185/M

Tele-Service News   *Business*

Publishing Co: Worldwide Videotex Co., PO Box 3273, Boynton Beach, FL 33424-3273 Tel # (407) 738-2276 Fax # (407) 738-2276
Editorial Description: Product and service news of the telecommunications industry.
General Info: Yr. Est. 1990, Monthly
Subscriptions: Indv. $150, Inst. $150, Can. $150, For. $165

TeleNews Asia   *Business*

Publishing Co: Information Gatekeepers, Inc., 214 Harvard Ave., Boston, MA 02134-4651;
Title Tel # (617) 232-3111 Title Fax # (617) 782-8562
Editorial Description: Covers all aspects of the telecommunications market in S.E. Asia and the Pacific Rim.
General Info: Bi-weekly
Subscriptions: Indv. $750, Can. $750, For. $800

TelePuting Hotline and
Field Computing Source
Letter   *Business*

Publishing Co: The TelePuting Hotline and Field Computing Source Letter, 215 Winter Ave NE, Atlanta, GA 30317-1425 Fax # (404) 378-0794; Title Tel # (404) 373-7634 Title Fax # (404) 373-7634
Personnel: Editor-Dana Blankenhorn, Editor-Masayuki Miyazawa, European Ed.-Steve Gold, Sales Mgr.-Hiro Miyazawa
General Info: Bi-month y

Telecom Advertising Report   *Business*

Publishing Co: Cowles Magazine, Inc., 4 High Ridge Park, Stamford, CT 06905 Tel # (203) 322-2900 Fax # (203) 322-1966; Title Tel # (914) 833-0600 Title Fax # (914) 833-0558
Personnel: Editor-D. McCarthy
General Info: 22x/yr.
Subscriptions: Indv. $468

Telecom Calendar   *Business, Consumer*

Publishing Co: Information Gatekeepers, Inc., 214 Harvard Ave., Boston, MA 02134-4651 Fax # (617) 782-8562; Title Tel # (617) 232-3111 Title Fax # (617) 734-8502
Editorial Description: Contians a 10 year listing of worldwide conferences & expostions in the telecommunications, fiber optics, optoelectronics, computer, & applied fields. This is a valuable resource for market planners, researchers, & convention planners.
General Info: Quarterly ISSN: 1057-6002
Subscriptions: Indv. $275, Can. $275, For. $315, $75/copy
Advertising: Accepts Inserts.
List Rental: Rents Lists

Telecom Data Report — *Business, Association*

Publishing Co: BRP (Washington DC), 1333 H St., NW, Suite 1100, West Tower, Washington, DC 20005-4707; Title Tel # (202) 842-3006 Title Fax # (202) 842-3047
Personnel: Publisher-Andrew Jacobson, Editor-Ted Leventhal, Circ. Mgr.-Nigel Sonarino, Mktg. Dir.-Adam Goldstein
Editorial Description: Covers data networking and service activities of the telephone companies, long distance carriers, competitive access providers, long-haul fiber carriers, value added carriers, and international carriers.
General Info: Yr. Est. 1992, Bi-weekly
Subscriptions: Indv. $498, Inst. $498, Can. $498, For. $533
Printing Co: Jim Buckley Offsetting, 1101 Pennsylvania Ave SE, Washington, DC 20003-2229 Tel # (202) 546-0501

Telecom Market Letter — *Business*

Publishing Co: Northern Business Information/Datapro, 1221 Ave. of the Americas #37, New York, NY 10020-1001
Personnel: Publisher-Michael Miller, Editor-Karen Nielsen, Circ. Mgr.-Louise Thayer, Production Mgr.-Michael O'Brien, Promotion Dir.-Kathy Bonifacio
Editorial Description: Market share data & analysis of the telecommunications market.
General Info: Yr. Est. 1980, Bi-weekly, Sheetfed press, 8 pages, ISSN: 0712-3663
Subscriptions: Indv. $595

Telecom Newsflash, The — *Business, Scholarly*

Publishing Co: Auditel, 213 Stage road, Hapstead, NH 03841; Title Tel # (603) 329-5000 Title Fax # (603) 329-5511
Personnel: Publisher-Bob Klemme, Editor-Joe Scotti, Circ. Mgr.-Mary Hodgdon
Editorial Description: 'Telecommunications Solutions' is the Auditel.
General Info: Yr. Est. 1992, Quarterly, Trim Size-8½ x 11, 5 pages, No Color
Subscriptions: Free To Qualified Recipient
Circulation: Total-500

Telecom Standards Newsletter — *Business*

Publishing Co: Information Gatekeepers, Inc., 214 Harvard Ave., Boston, MA 02134-4651; Title Tel # (617) 232-3111 Title Fax # (617) 782-8562
Editorial Description: Covering telecommunications standards activities worldwide. Contains important information on status, availability of standards, and how to obtain standards.
General Info: Monthly, ISSN: 1064-1076
Subscriptions: Indv. $575, Can. $575, For. $625, $50/copy

Telecom Strategy Letter — *Business*

Publishing Co: Northern Business Information/Datapro, 1221 Ave. of the Americas #37, New York, NY 10020-1001; Title Tel # (212) 732-0775 Title Fax # (212) 233-6233
Personnel: Publisher, Editor-Suzanne Brennan, Circ. Mgr.-Louise Thayer, Production Mgr.-Michael O'Brien, Promotion Dir.-Kathy Bonifacio
Editorial Description: In-depth analyses of telecommunications cos. & market strategies.
General Info: Yr. Est. 1982, Monthly, ISSN: 0739-683X
Subscriptions: Indv. $995
List Rental: Rents Lists

Telecommunications Alert — *Business*

Publishing Co: United Communications Group, 11300 Rockville Pike, Ste. 1100, Rockville, MD 20852-3030 Tel # (301) 816-8950 Fax # (301) 816-8945; Title Tel # (301) 961-8700
Personnel: Publisher-Doug O'Boyle, Editor-Samuel Reifler, Circ. Mgr.-Sharon Welch
Editorial Description: Reports on the telecommunications industry, digests, magazines and other newsletters.
General Info: Yr. Est. 1983, Monthly, 16 pages, ISSN: 0742-5384, Ind/Abs/Online: NewsNet, DIALOG, 2 Color, Newsprint, Saddle-stitched
Circulation: Total-3,600
List Rental: Rents Lists

Telecommunications Product Review and CPE Strategies — *Business*

Publishing Co: Telecommunications Product Review & CPE Strategies, 5643C Harpers Farm Rd., Columbia, MD 21044; Title Tel # (410) 997-8059 Title Fax # (410) 997-8059
Personnel: Publisher-Edward Garner, Editor-Sue Rubinstein
Editorial Description: Review and analysis of new telecommunications products and services.
General Info: Yr. Est. 1974, Monthly, Offset press, 4 pages, ISSN: 0736-4156, No Color
Subscriptions: Indv. $199, $17/copy
Circulation: Total-750

Telecommunications Reports — *Business*

Publishing Co: BRP (Washington DC), 1333 H St., NW, Suite 1100, West Tower, Washington, DC 20005-4707; Title Tel # (202) 842-3006 Title Fax # (202) 842-3047
Personnel: Publisher-Andrew Jacobson, Editor-Victoria Mason, Circ. Mgr.-Nigel Sonariwo, Production Dir.-Chris Taniguchi, Mktg. Dir.-Adam Goldstein
Editorial Description: News coverage of legislative, regulatory, technological, and business developments affecting the domestic and international telecommunications industry.
General Info: Yr. Est. 1934, Weekly, Trim Size-8½ x 11, Sheetfed press, 48 pages, Ind/Abs/Online: Newsnet, No Color
Subscriptions: Indv. $995, Inst. $995, Can. $995, For. $1,070
Printing Co: Jim Buckley Offsetting, 1101 Pennsylvania Ave SE, Washington, DC 20003-2229 Tel # (202) 546-0501

Telecommunications Reports International — *Business*

Publishing Co: BRP (Washington DC), 1333 H St., NW, Suite 1100, West Tower, Washington, DC 20005-4707; Title Tel # (202) 842-3006 Title Fax # (202) 842-3047
Personnel: Publisher-Andrew Jacobson, Editor in Chief-Victoria Mason, Editor-George Brandon, Circ. Mgr.-Nigel Sonariwo, Mktg. Dir.-Adam Goldstein
Editorial Description: International telecom policy and trade issues, global services, satellites, tariffs and financial developments.
General Info: Yr. Est. 1990, Bi-weekly, Trim Size-8½ x 11, Web press, 24 pages, Ind/Abs/Online: NewsNet, No Color, Matte, Saddle-stitched
Subscriptions: Indv. $997, Inst. $997, Can. $997, For. $1,047
Printing Co: Jim Buckley Offsetting, 1101 Pennsylvania Ave SE, Washington, DC 20003-2229 Tel # (202) 546-0501

Telecommunications Security
See: SECURITY & SURVEILLANCE

Telecommunications Week — *Business*

Publishing Co: BRP (Washington DC), 1333 H St., NW, Suite 1100, West Tower, Washington, DC 20005-4707; Title Tel # (202) 842-3006 Title Fax # (202) 842-3047
Personnel: Publisher-Andrew Jacobson, Editor in Chief-Victoria Mason, Editor-Karen Kinard, Circ. Mgr.-Nigel Sonariwo, Mktg. Dir.-Adam Goldstein
Editorial Description: Covers domestic telecommunications news centering on regulatory, legislative & judicial fronts.
General Info: Yr. Est. 1982, Weekly, Trim Size-8½ x 11, 8 pages, Ind/Abs/Online: NewsNet, No Color
Subscriptions: Indv. $395, Inst. $395, Can. $395
List Rental: Rents Lists
Printing Co: Jim Buckley Offsetting, 1101 Pennsylvania Ave SE, Washington, DC 20003-2229 Tel # (202) 546-0501

Telecommunicator — *Business*

Publishing Co: Assn. of Telemessaging Services Intl., 1200 19th St. NW, Washington, DC 20036-2412; Title Tel # (703) 684-0016 Title Fax # (703) 684-3415
Personnel: Editor-Denise Nebb
Editorial Description: News concerning telephone rates, legislative & governmental actions, assn. activities & equipment.
General Info: Yr. Est. 1950, Monthly, Trim Size-8½ x 11, Web press, 4 pages, Color-cover
Subscriptions: Indv. $20
Circulation: Total-1,200

Teleforum — *Consumer*

Publishing Co: NYNEX Teleforum, 1095 Ave. of the Americas, Room 3440, New York, NY 10036
Personnel: Editor in Chief-Pamela Puckett
Editorial Description: News and information about NYNEX and telecommunications.
General Info: Monthly

Telemanagement

Publishing Co: Angus Telemanagement Group, Inc., 8 Old Kingston Road, Ajax, ON L1T 2Z7 Canada Tel # (416) 686-5050 Fax # (416) 686-2655; Title Tel # (416) 420-5050 Title Fax # (905) 420-2344
Personnel: Publisher-Ian Angus, Editor-Elisabeth Angus, Circ. Mgr.-Rosita Fox
Editorial Description: Telecommunications industry news & management analysis.
General Info: (Formerly Telemanagement Report), Yr. Est. 1983, Monthly, Desktop press, 24 pages, ISSN: 0840-5476, No Color, Newsprint
Subscriptions: Indv. $247, $35/copy

Telemarketing Update-Answering Service Business Script Presentations
See: ADVERTISING & MARKETING

Telemedium
See: MEDIA & COMMUNICATIONS

Telephone Angles
See: OFFICE METHODS & EQUIPMENT

Telephone IP News — *Business*

Publishing Co: Worldwide Videotex Co., PO Box 3273, Boynton Beach, FL 33424-3273 Tel # (407) 738-2276 Fax # (407) 738-2276
Editorial Description: News and information on the telephone services industries.
General Info: Yr. Est. 1991, Monthly, Ind/Abs/Online: DIALOG
Subscriptions: Indv. $150, Inst. $150, Can. $150, For. $165

Telephone Statistics

Publishing Co: Statistics Canada, Holland Ave/RH Coats, Holland Ave/Tunney's Pasture, Ottawa, ON K1A O26 Canada Fax # (613) 951-0581; Title Tel # (613) 951-8116
Editorial Description: Operating revenue, expenses, salaries, number of toll messages, employees & telephones. Catalog #56-002.
General Info: Yr. Est. 1977, Monthly, 4 pages, ISSN: 0707-9753
Subscriptions: Indv. $10, Can. $8, For. $12, $10/copy

Telespan Newsletter — *Business*

Publishing Co: Telespan Publishing, 50 W Palm St, Altadena, CA 91001-4337;
Title Tel # (818) 797-5482 Title Fax # (818) 797-2035
Personnel: Publisher-Elliot Gold, Editor-Shirley Singletary
Editorial Description: Essays amd news items on teleconferencing: equipment, applications, events calendar.
General Info: Yr. Est. 1981, 40x/yr., Trim Size-8½ x 11, Offset press, 4 pages, ISSN: 0743-2283, 2 Color, Matte
Subscriptions: Indv. $357, Can. $367, For. $397, $11/copy

TidBITS
See: COMPUTERS & AUTOMATION

Trends in Communications Policy — *Business*

Publishing Co: Economics & Technology, Inc., 1 Washington Mall, Boston, MA 02108-2603
Tel # (617) 227-0900; Title Tel # (617) 423-3780 Title Fax # (617) 423-0708
Personnel: Editor-Paul Keller, Circ. Mgr.-Christine Gregorio, Production Mgr.-Joseph Carlino
Editorial Description: Trends in Communications Policy offers an authoritative analysis of major events in the telecommunications industry.
General Info: (Formerly Trends in Communications Regulation), Yr. Est. 1975, Monthly, 12 pages
Subscriptions: Indv. $195

Two Way Transmissions
See: LUMBER & WOOD

U.S. Telecom Digest — *Business*

Publishing Co: Telecom Publishing Group, 1101 King St Ste 444, Alexandria, VA 22314-2944 Parent Co.-Capitol Publications, Inc., Alexandria; Title Tel # (703) 683-4100 Title Fax # (703) 739-6490
Subscriptions: Indv. $192

Utilities Telecommunications News — *Business*

Publishing Co: Information Gatekeepers, Inc., 214 Harvard Ave., Boston, MA 02134-4651;
Fax # (617) 782-8562; Title Tel # (617) 232-3111 Title Fax # (617) 734-8562
Editorial Description: Covers all aspects of utility communications technology, regulatory and legislative proceedings, new projects, applications and government policies affectng utilities' advance on the information highway.
General Info: Monthly
Subscriptions: Indv. $575, Can. $575, For. $625, $50/copy
Advertising: Accepts Inserts.

Video Technology Newsletter
See: TELEVISION & VIDEO

Voice Processing Newsletter — *Business*

Publishing Co: Probe Research, Inc., 3 Wing Dr Ste 240, Cedar Knolls, NJ 07927-1006 Parent Co.-Phillips Business Information, Inc., Potomac; Title Tel # (201) 285-1500 Title Fax # (201) 285-1519
Personnel: Publisher-Victor Schnee, Editor-Jennifer Walsh, Circ. Mgr.-Donna Weller
Editorial Description: Strategic newsletter providing information & analysis on the voice (messaging, response, synthesis, and recognition) industries.
General Info: (Formerly Voice Technology & Services News; Facsimile & Voice Services), Yr. Est. 1981, Bi-weekly, 8 pages, ISSN: 0884-6685
Subscriptions: Indv. $497, Can. $497, For. $527, $20/copy

VoiceNews — *Business*

Publishing Co: Stoneridge Technical Services, PO Box 1891, Rockville, MD 20849-1891;
Title Tel # (301) 424-0114 Title Fax # (301) 424-8971
Personnel: Publisher, Editor-William Creitz
Editorial Description: Covers voice technology for telecommunications & office automation: voice messaging, voice response, speech recognition, speech synthesis.
General Info: Yr. Est. 1981, Monthly, Trim Size-8½ x 11, Offset press, 10 pages, ISSN: 0886-2087, No Color, Newsprint
Subscriptions: Indv. $297, Can. $297, For. $327, $25/copy

WEB IMPRESSIONS

Publishing Co: Web Offset Association/PIA, 100 Daingerfield Road, Alexandria, VA 22314
Tel # (703) 519-8156; Title Tel # (708) 519-8142 Title Fax # (703) 548-3227
Editorial Description: Information on the latest technical advances, potential changes, plus current operations and procedures.
General Info: Bi-monthly, Trim Size-8.5 x 11, 4 pages, 4 Color
Advertising: Inquire for rates.

WaferNews Confidential
See: ELECTRIC & ELECTRONIC EQUIPMENT

Warren's Telecom Regulation Monitor — *Business*

Publishing Co: Warren Publishing, Inc., 2115 Ward Ct. NW, Washington, DC 20037-1213;
Title Tel # (202) 872-9200 Title Fax # (202) 293-3435
Personnel: Publisher-Albert Warren, Editor-Edith Herman, Circ. Mgr.-Betty Alvine, Mktg. Dir.-Gary Madderom
Editorial Description: Covers the telecommunications industry.
General Info: (Formerly Commoon Carrier Week), Yr. Est. 1984, Weekly, Trim Size-8½ x 11, 12 pages, ISSN: 0743-4812, Ind/Abs/Online: NewsNet, DIALOG, Predicasts, 2 Color, Newsprint
Subscriptions: Indv. $724, For. $770
Acquistions: Publication Bought

Washington Bulletin

Publishing Co: C.L. Pace Associates, 36 Henry Austin Dr., Wilton, CT 06897-3210
Fax # (203) 834-0207; Title Tel # (203) 834-0533
Personnel: Publisher, Editor-Charles Pace
General Info: Yr. Est. 1984, Monthly
Subscriptions: Indv. $50

Washington Telecom News — *Business*

Publishing Co: Phillips Business Information, Inc., 1201 Seven Locks Rd., Ste 300, Potomac, MD 20854-2958 Tel # (301) 340-1520 Fax # (301) 424-4297
Personnel: Sales Mgr.-Susan Incarnato
Editorial Description: Issues on the global allocation of frequencies.
General Info: (Formerly Spectrum Rpt; Telephone News; Telecommunications Regulatory), Yr. Est. 1991, Weekly, ISSN: 1069-7500
Subscriptions: Indv. $597, For. $660
List Rental: Rents Lists

Washington Update — *Association*

Publishing Co: North American Telecommunications Assn., 2000 M St NW Ste 550, Washington, DC 20036-3307
Personnel: Publisher-Sue Graves, Editor-Adam Kernan-Shloss
Editorial Description: Digest of public issues in competitive telecommunications.
General Info: Yr. Est. 1981, Semi-monthly, Mimeo press, 1 pages, No Color
Circulation: Total-2,100

Washington Weekly Report — *Association*

Publishing Co: Organization for Protection&Advancement/Small Telephone Cos., 21 Dupont Cir NW Ste 700, Washington, DC 20036-1109; Title Tel # (202) 659-5990 Title Fax # (202) 659-4619
Personnel: Editor-Rachel Brown
Editorial Description: Monitors legislative & regulatory issues & actions affecting telecommunications in rural areas.
General Info: (Formerly OPASTCO Network), Yr. Est. 1966, Weekly, Trim Size-8½ x 11, 2 pages, No Color
Circulation: Total-2,200

Westlink Report — *Business*

Publishing Co: Poco Press, 28221 Stanley Ct, Canyon Country, CA 91351-3818;
Title Tel # (805) 251-5558
Personnel: Editor-Bill Pastenak
General Info: Yr. Est. 1982, Bi-weekly
Subscriptions: Indv. $24

Wire Talk
See: SAFETY

Wireless Business & Finance — *Business*

Publishing Co: Phillips Business Information, Inc., 1201 Seven Locks Rd., Ste 300, Potomac, MD 20854-2958 Tel # (301) 340-1520 Fax # (301) 424-4297
General Info: (Formerly Global Telecom Report), Bi-weekly, ISSN: 1059-4485
Subscriptions: Indv. $697, For. $730

Wireless Cellular Telecommunications — *Business*

Publishing Co: Information Gatekeepers, Inc., 214 Harvard Ave., Boston, MA 02134-4651;
Title Tel # (617) 232-3111 Title Fax # (617) 782-8562
Editorial Description: Keeps you up to date on world wide developments from a business perspective. New technologies, standards and government policies applied to this market are covered.
General Info: Monthly, ISSN: 1058-6717
Subscriptions: Indv. $575, Can. $575, For. $625, $50/copy

Wireless Data News — *Business*

Publishing Co: Phillips Business Information, Inc., 1201 Seven Locks Rd., Ste 300, Potomac, MD 20854-2958 Tel # (301) 340-1520 Fax # (301) 424-4297
General Info: (Formerly Personal Devices Report), Bi-weekly, ISSN: 1069-3416
Subscriptions: Indv. $597, For. $630
List Rental: Rents Lists

Wireless Media & Messaging
Business

Publishing Co: Probe Research, Inc., 3 Wing Dr Ste 240, Cedar Knolls, NJ 07927-1006 Parent Co.-Phillips Business Information, Inc., Potomac; Title Tel # (201) 285-1500 Title Fax # (201) 285-1519
Editorial Description: Complete authoritative coverage of devices, networks, and applications in the areas of peronal communications, integration of voice, data, facsimile, video, WLANs, CPE, modems, and software. Covers major players and market potential.
General Info: Yr. Est. 1993, Monthly
Subscriptions: Indv. $347, Can. $347, For. $367

Wireless PCN

Publishing Co: Information Gatekeepers, Inc., 214 Harvard Ave., Boston, MA 02134-4651
Fax # (617) 782-8562; Title Tel # (617) 232-3111 Title Fax # (617) 734-8562
Personnel: Publisher-Paul Polishuk, Circ. Mgr.-Brendan Monroe, Art Dir.-Diana Towers
Editorial Description: Covers world wide developments in the 'Personal Communications Services.' This is one of the hottest markets for products & services in the telecommunications field today. A key element is how countries will allocate spectrum for PCS services.
General Info: (Formerly PCN Newsletter), Yr. Est. 1991, Monthly, Letrpr. press, ISSN: 1058-6725, 2 Color
Subscriptions: Indv. $575, Can. $575, For. $625, $50/copy
Advertising: Accepts Inserts.
List Rental: Rents Lists
Printing Co: Eagle Graphics, 30 Lancaster St, Boston, MA 02114-1779 Tel # (617) 742-7575

Wireless Satellite & Broadcasting
Business

Publishing Co: Information Gatekeepers, Inc., 214 Harvard Ave., Boston, MA 02134-4651;
Title Tel # (617) 232-3111 Title Fax # (617) 782-8562
Editorial Description: Covering worldwide developments in the sataellite & broadcasting telecommunications industry. Wireless Statellite & Broadcasting will keep you current on international developments in technology, regulation and applications.
General Info: Monthly, ISSN: 1058-6695
Subscriptions: Indv. $545, Can. $575, For. $625, $50/copy

Wireless Spectrum Management Telecommunications
Business

Publishing Co: Information Gatekeepers, Inc., 214 Harvard Ave., Boston, MA 02134-4651
Fax # (617) 782-8562; Title Tel # (617) 232-3111 Title Fax # (617) 734-8562
Personnel: Publisher-Paul Polishuk, Circ. Mgr.-Brendan Monroe
Editorial Description: A monthly newsletter covering worldwide developments inthe spectrum management industry.
General Info: (Formerly Wireless Spectrum Management), Monthly, Letrpr. press, ISSN: 1058-6709, 2 Color
Subscriptions: Indv. $575, Can. $575, For. $625, $50/copy
List Rental: Rents Lists
Printing Co: Eagle Graphics, 30 Lancaster St, Boston, MA 02114-1779 Tel # (617) 742-7575

Wireless Telecom Investor
Business

Publishing Co: Paul Kagan Associates Inc., 126 Clock Tower Pl., Carmel, CA 93923-8746
Tel # (408) 624-1536; Title Tel # (404) 624-1536 Title Fax # (408) 625-3225
Personnel: Publisher, Editor-Paul Kagan, Circ. Mgr.-Judith Pinney, Adv. Mgr.-Johanne Hardy
Editorial Description: Exclusive analysis of private & public values of wireless telecommunications companies.
General Info: (Formerly Cellular Investor), Yr. Est. 1988, Monthly, Trim Size-7$\frac{1}{4}$ x 10, Other press, 16 pages, 1% ads, No Color, Other, Saddle-stitched
Subscriptions: Indv. $745
Advertising: Inquire for rates.

Wireless Telecommunications

Publishing Co: Information Gatekeepers, Inc., 214 Harvard Ave., Boston, MA 02134-4651
Fax # (617) 782-8562; Title Tel # (617) 232-3111 Title Fax # (617) 734-8562
Editorial Description: Provides worldwide coverage of wireless LANs, LAN interconnection, wireless in-building & major applications such as point-of-sales, portable computer interconnections, & remote data collection. Also included are infrared techniques.
General Info: Monthly, Letrpr. press, ISSN: 1057-5391, 2 Color
Subscriptions: Indv. $575, Can. $575, For. $625, $50/copy
Advertising: Accepts Inserts.
List Rental: Rents Lists
Printing Co: Eagle Graphics, 30 Lancaster St, Boston, MA 02114-1779 Tel # (617) 742-7575

Wireless Week
Business

Publishing Co: Four Pines Publishing, PO Box 3209, Boulder, CO 80307-3209;
Title Tel # (303) 494-6522 Title Fax # (303) 494-4977
Personnel: Publisher, Editor-Tammy Parker
Editorial Description: Covers the wireless telecommunications industry.
General Info: (Formerly Inside Wireless), Yr. Est. 1993, Semi-monthly, Trim Size-8$\frac{1}{2}$ x 11, Desktop press, 8 pages, ISSN: 1073-7707, 2 Color, Case bound
Subscriptions: Indv. $499
Circulation: Total-113
Advertising: Inquire for rates. Accepts Inserts.

World Press Watch
Business, Consumer

Publishing Co: World Press Watch Press, PO Box 4177, Lantana, FL 33465-4177
Personnel: Editor-Walter Brooks
General Info: Yr. Est. 1980, 50x/yr.

Worldwide Telecom
Business

Publishing Co: Worldwide Videotex Co., PO Box 3273, Boynton Beach, FL 33424-3273
Fax # (407) 738-2276; Title Tel # (407) 738-2276 Title Fax # (407) 738-2275
Personnel: Editor-Mark Wright
Editorial Description: Covers the latest news on international & telecommunication's products, services, companies land marketing strategies.
General Info: Yr. Est. 1989, Monthly, Ind/Abs/Online: NewsNet, DIALOG
Subscriptions: Indv. $150, Can. $150, For. $165, $13/copy

Yellow Pages & Directory Report
Business

Publishing Co: Simba Information, Inc., 213 Danbury Rd. PO Box 7430, Wilton, CT 06897-7430
Tel # (203) 834-0033 Fax # (203) 834-1771 Parent Co.-Cowles Business Media, New York
Personnel: Publisher-Chris Elwell, Editor-Tom Maguire, Mng. Editor-Natalie Schwartz, Circ. Mgr.-Joyce Brigish, Production Mgr.-Michael Genaro, Promotion Dir.-Michele Wolff
Editorial Description: Presents timely news and information on the yellow pages industry. Covers the activities of utility and independent yellow pages publishers, suppliers, certified marketing representatives, sales agents and yellow pages associations. Subscription price includes Directory World Magazine.
General Info: Yr. Est. 1985, Bi-weekly, Trim Size-8.5 x 11
Subscriptions: Indv. $549, Can. $599, For. $599
List Rental: Rents Lists

Your Telephone Personality
Business

Publishing Co: Economics Press, Inc., 12 Daniel Rd., Fairfield, NJ 07004-2565;
Title Tel # (201) 227-1224 Title Fax # (201) 227-9742
Personnel: Editor-Robert Guder, Circ. Mgr.-Ann Lanahan
Editorial Description: Each issue deals with a single topic related to the skillful handling of phone calls, both inbound and outgoing.
General Info: Yr. Est. 1972, Bi-weekly, Trim Size-5$\frac{1}{4}$ x 6$\frac{1}{2}$, 8 pages
Subscriptions: Indv. $77
Circulation: Total-29,390
List Rental: List Management Co.: Names in the News, 411 Theodore Fremd Ave., Rye, NY 10580 Tel # (914) 925-2400
Printing Co: Beckley Press, 2 Sperry Rd, Fairfield, NJ 07004-2056 Tel # (201) 227-6350

TELEVISION & VIDEO

AM Journal
See: BROADCASTING

AMIA Newsletter (Assn. of Moving Image Archivists)
See: LIBRARY

Art on Screen
See: ART & SCULPTURE

Broadcast & Cable Financial Management Assn. -Topical Reference Papers
Association

Publishing Co: Broadcast Cable Financial Management Association, 701 Lee St Ste 1010, Des Plaines, IL 60016-4555; Title Tel # (708) 296-0200
Editorial Description: Provides reprints of articles from Broadcast Cable Financial Journal.
General Info: Looseleaf

Broadcasting & Cable's TV International
See: BROADCASTING

Brooklyn Community Access Newsletter
Consumer

Publishing Co: Fund for the Borough of Brooklyn, The, 30 Flatbush Ave, Brooklyn, NY 11217-1121
Tel # (718) 855-7882 Fax # (718) 802-9095
Editorial Description: BCAT offers the residents of Brooklyn a broad range of services and support programs that will enable the creation, production, and cablecasting of programs to Brooklynites. BCAT promotes and develops public awareness, use and involvement in public access cable television. BCAT creates an environment for Brooklyn's communities to preserve, enhance and share the Borough's diversity of thought and cultur
General Info: Yr. Est. 1991, Quarterly, Trim Size-8$\frac{1}{2}$ x 11, 4 pages, No Color
Subscriptions: Indv. $25, Inst. $75, Free With Membership
Advertising: Accepts Inserts.

Bullet
See: FAN MAGAZINES-MOVIE, RADIO, TV

Bullet, The
Consumer, Association

Publishing Co: The Andy Griffith Show Rerun Watchers Club, 9 Music Sq S Ste 146, Nashville, TN 37203-3203
Personnel: Publisher, Editor-Jim Clark
Editorial Description: All about 'The Andy Griffith Show'
General Info: Yr. Est. 1982, Quarterly, Trim Size-8$\frac{1}{2}$ x 11, 16 pages
Subscriptions: Indv. $10, Inst. $10, Can. $10, For. $10

Cable Re-Regulation Handbook — *Business*

Publishing Co: Thompson Publishing Group, 1725 K Street, NW, Washington, DC 20006 Tel # (202) 872-4000
Editorial Description: Provides information for operators, franchising authorities, and broadcasters on how the law affects their operations. Subscription includes monthly bulletin and frequent updates.
General Info: Annually, Looseleaf
Subscriptions: Indv. $295

Cable System Manager — *Business*

Publishing Co: Cowles Magazine, Inc., 4 High Ridge Park, Stamford, CT 06905 Tel # (203) 322-2900 Fax # (203) 322-1966
Editorial Description: For managers of local cable television networks.
General Info: Monthly, Trim Size-8½ x 11
Acquistions: Publication Sold

Cable TV Advertising — *Business*

Publishing Co: Paul Kagan Associates Inc., 126 Clock Tower Pl., Carmel, CA 93923-8746; Title Tel # (408) 624-1536 Title Fax # (408) 625-3225
Personnel: Publisher-Paul Kagan, Circ. Mgr.-Judith Pinney, Adv. Dir.-Johanne Hardy
Editorial Description: Sales of commercial time by cable TV systems & networks.
General Info: Yr. Est. 1980, Monthly, Trim Size-7¼ x 10, Other press, 10 pages, ISSN: 0270-855X, No Color, Other, Saddle-stitched
Subscriptions: Indv. $695
Advertising: $1,560.

Cable TV Finance — *Business*

Publishing Co: Paul Kagan Associates Inc., 126 Clock Tower Pl., Carmel, CA 93923-8746; Title Tel # (408) 624-1536 Title Fax # (408) 625-3225
Personnel: Publisher-Paul Kagan, Circ. Mgr.-Judith Pinney, Adv. Dir.-Johanne Hardy
Editorial Description: Newsletter on banking, insurance and commercial loans to cable operators, selling and buying of cable systems.
General Info: (Formerly Cable TV Banker/Broker), Yr. Est. 1982, Monthly, Trim Size-7¼ x 10, Other press, 12 pages, ISSN: 0893-2131, 1% ads, Other, Saddle-stitched
Subscriptions: Indv. $745
Advertising: $1,560.

Cable TV Investor — *Business*

Publishing Co: Paul Kagan Associates Inc., 126 Clock Tower Pl., Carmel, CA 93923-8746; Title Tel # (408) 624-1536 Title Fax # (408) 625-3225
Personnel: Publisher, Editor-Paul Kagan, Circ. Mgr.-Judith Pinney, Adv. Dir.-Johanne Hardy
Editorial Description: Financial and business analysis of cable TV industry.
General Info: (Formerly Cablecast), Yr. Est. 1969, Monthly, Trim Size-7¼ x 10, Other press, 12 pages, ISSN: 0731-0250, 1% ads, No Color, Other, Saddle-stitched
Subscriptions: Indv. $895
Advertising: Inquire for rates.

Cable TV Marketing Letter
See: ADVERTISING & MARKETING

Cable TV and New Media Law & Finance
See: TELECOMMUNICATIONS

Cable TV Programming — *Business*

Publishing Co: Paul Kagan Associates Inc., 126 Clock Tower Pl., Carmel, CA 93923-8746; Title Tel # (408) 624-1536 Title Fax # (408) 625-3225
Personnel: Publisher-Paul Kagan, Circ. Mgr.-Judith Pinney, Adv. Dir.-Johanne Hardy
Editorial Description: Economics of basic cable & pay TV program networks, line-ups.
General Info: Yr. Est. 1981, Monthly, Trim Size-7¼ x 10, Other press, 15 pages, ISSN: 0278-503X, No Color, Other, Saddle-stitched
Subscriptions: Indv. $745
Advertising: $1,560.

Cable TV Regulation — *Business*

Publishing Co: Paul Kagan Associates Inc., 126 Clock Tower Pl., Carmel, CA 93923-8746; Title Tel # (408) 624-1536 Title Fax # (408) 625-3225
Personnel: Publisher-Paul Kagan, Circ. Mgr.-Judith Pinney
Editorial Description: Covers federal, state and local regulation, rate increases, franchise applications.
General Info: (Formerly Cable TV Franchising), Yr. Est. 1975, Monthly, Trim Size-7¼ x 10, Other press, 10 pages, ISSN: 0731-0269, No Color, Other, Saddle-stitched
Subscriptions: Indv. $675
Advertising: $1,560.

Cable TV Technology — *Business*

Publishing Co: Paul Kagan Associates Inc., 126 Clock Tower Pl., Carmel, CA 93923-8746; Title Tel # (408) 624-1536 Title Fax # (408) 625-3225
Personnel: Publisher-Paul Kagan, Circ. Mgr.-Judith Pinney, Adv. Mgr.-Johanne Hardy
Editorial Description: Technical advances, construction of new systems.
General Info: Yr. Est. 1981, Monthly, Trim Size-7¼ x 10, Other press, 12 pages, ISSN: 0276-5713, 1% ads, No Color, Other, Saddle-stitched
Subscriptions: Indv. $695
Advertising: $1,560.

Cable Telco Report, The — *Business*

Publishing Co: BRP (Washington DC), 1333 H St., NW, Suite 1100, West Tower, Washington, DC 20005-4707; Title Tel # (202) 842-3006 Title Fax # (202) 842-3047
Personnel: Publisher-Andrew Jacobson, Editor-Victoria Mason
Editorial Description: Reports on cable TV and telco strategies in the video service marketplace.
General Info: Bi-weekly, Trim Size-8½ x 11, 18 pages, Ind/Abs/Online: Newsnet
Subscriptions: Indv. $549, Inst. $549, Can. $549, For. $582

CableFAX — *Business*

Publishing Co: Phillips Business Information, Inc., 1201 Seven Locks Rd., Ste 300, Potomac, MD 20854-2958 Tel # (301) 340-1520 Fax # (301) 424-4297; Title Fax # (301) 309-9473
Personnel: Editor-Paul Maxwell
Editorial Description: Daily newsfax newsletter for the cable television industry.
General Info: Daily, ISSN: 1069-6644
Subscriptions: Indv. $495
List Rental: Rents Lists

California Cable Letter — *Business*

Publishing Co: Thomas Karwin, 121 Easterby Ave,PO Box 7600, Santa Cruz, CA 95061-7600; Title Tel # (408) 426-5981
Personnel: Publisher, Editor-Thomas Karwin, Circ. Mgr.-Janette Karwin, Art Dir.-Linda Hoeger Thompson
Editorial Description: Current community perspectives & directions of cable communications in California.
General Info: Yr. Est. 1984, Monthly, Trim Size-8½ x 11, Sheetfed press, 8 pages, ISSN: 0740-0527, Color-cover, Matte
Subscriptions: Indv. $48, $4/copy
Printing Co: Community Printers, 1827 Soquel Ave, Santa Cruz, CA 95062-1385 Tel # (408) 426-4682

Call Board
See: RELIGIOUS & THEOLOGICAL

Canadian Communications Reports — *Business*

Publishing Co: Evert Communications Ltd., 1296 Carling Ave., Ottawa, ON K1Z 7K8 Canada; Title Tel # (613) 728-4621 Title Fax # (613) 728-0385
Personnel: Publisher-Gordon Hutchison, Editor-Debbie Lawes, Circ. Mgr.-Carole Jeffrey
Editorial Description: Applications of communications technology and related public policy issues.
General Info: Semi-monthly, ISSN: 0316-3083
Subscriptions: Inst. $395, Can. $395, For. $395
List Rental: Actives: $850/M
Printing Co: Bradda Printing Services, 130 Slater Street, Ottawa, ON K1P 6E2 Canada Tel # (613) 238-5433

Children's Video Review Newsletter
See: CHILDREN

Clearing the Air

Publishing Co: East Bay Media Center, 2054 University Ave Ste 203, Berkeley, CA 94704-1059; Title Tel # (415) 843-3699
Personnel: Editor-Melvin Vapour
General Info: Quarterly, 4 pages
Subscriptions: Indv. $8

Clips — *Consumer, Association*

Publishing Co: Videazimut, 3680 rue Jeanne Mance #430, Montreal, PQ H2X 2K5 Canada; Title Tel # (514) 982-6660 Title Fax # (514) 982-6122
Editorial Description: Promotes international alternative and independent video and television.
General Info: Yr. Est. 1992, Trim Size-8½ x 11, 12 pages, 2 Color, Matte, Saddle-stitched
Subscriptions: Indv. $10, Can. $10, For. $10, Free With Membership
Circulation: Total-2,000

Communications Business & Finance
See: BROADCASTING

Communications Law
See: LAW

Consumer Multimedia Report — *Business*

Publishing Co: Warren Publishing, Inc., 2115 Ward Ct. NW, Washington, DC 20037-1213; Title Tel # (202) 872-9200 Title Fax # (202) 293-3435
Personnel: Publisher-Albert Warren, Circ. Mgr.-Betty Alvine, Mktg. Dir.-Garry Madderom
Editorial Description: The authoritative news service covering the emerging interactive video and audio industries.
General Info: (Formerly Smart Media Business), Yr. Est. 1992, Bi-weekly, Trim Size-8½ x 11, 8 pages
Subscriptions: Indv. $453, For. $476
List Rental: Rents Lists

Converge-The Multimedia Developer's Resources
See: COMPUTERS & AUTOMATION

Dark Shadows Announcement
See: FAN MAGAZINES-MOVIE, RADIO, TV

Deanna Gram   *Consumer*

Publishing Co: Friends of Deanna Lund, 545 Howard Dr, Salem, VA 24153-2167
Editorial Description: Newsletter about science-fiction actress Deanna Lund.
General Info: Quarterly, Trim Size-8½ x 11, 10 pages, Color-cover, Matte
Subscriptions: Indv. $15

Digest of the Univ. Film & Video Assn.
See: FILM

Directory of Advertising & Public Relations   *Business*

Publishing Co: Newscast/Nielsen Media Research, Nielsen Plaza, Northbrook, IL 60062;
    Title Tel # (708) 498-6300
Personnel: Publisher, Editor-Lawrence Frerk
Editorial Description: Information & news concerning Nielsen audience research services.
General Info: (Formerly Newscast), Yr. Est. 1960, Quarterly, Trim Size-5½ x 8½, 20 pages, 2 Color, Coated
Circulation: (100% controlled), Total-10,000

ETV Newsletter

Publishing Co: S. Tepfer Publishing Co., Inc., PO Box 597, Ridgefield, CT 06877-0597;
    Title Tel # (203) 454-2618 Title Fax # (203) 454-2618
Personnel: Publisher, Editor-Charles Tepfer, Circ. Mgr.-Sandra Abrams
Editorial Description: A news service devoted exclusively to educational, instructional and training television. Includes bid requests and software programming news, frequent market report supplements.
General Info: Yr. Est. 1966, Bi-weekly, Trim Size-8½ x 11, 8 pages, No Color, Newsprint
Subscriptions: Indv. $195, Can. $195, For. $220, $10/copy
Acquistions: Publication Sold
Advertising: Inquire for rates.

Early Warning Report
See: ELECTRIC & ELECTRONIC EQUIPMENT

Emerging Media Report
See: MEDIA & COMMUNICATIONS

Euro Cable TV Programming   *Business*

Publishing Co: Kagan World Media Inc., 126 Clock Tower Pl., Carmel, CA 93923-8734 Parent Co.-Paul Kagan Associates Inc., Carmel; Title Tel # (408) 624-1536 Title Fax # (408) 625-3225
Personnel: Publisher-Paul Kagan, Circ. Mgr.-Judy Pinney, Adv. Mgr.-Johanne Hardy
Editorial Description: Programming economics, network values, viewer shares and the financial impact of changes in Europe's cable/DBS industries.
General Info: Monthly, Trim Size-7¼ x 10, Other press, 16 pages, No Color, Other, Saddle-stitched
Subscriptions: Indv. $595
Advertising: $1,560.

European Cable/Pay TV   *Business*

Publishing Co: Kagan World Media Inc., 126 Clock Tower Pl., Carmel, CA 93923-8734 Parent Co.-Paul Kagan Associates Inc., Carmel; Title Tel # (408) 624-1536 Title Fax # (408) 625-3225
Personnel: Publisher-Paul Kagan, Publisher-Pual Kagan, Circ. Mgr.-Judith Pinney, Circ. Mgr.-Judy Pinney, Adv. Mgr.-Johanne Hardy
Editorial Description: Tracking European emerging TV technologies, cable, pay TV, DBS, satellite transmitted, etc. with reporting on programming, financing, building & equipment, valuations of European media companies.
General Info: Yr. Est. 1988, Monthly, Trim Size-7¼ x 10, Other press, 16 pages, ISSN: 1041-3014, No Color, Other, Saddle-stitched
Subscriptions: Indv. $695
Advertising: $1,560.

European Home Video   *Business*

Publishing Co: Kagan World Media Inc., 126 Clock Tower Pl., Carmel, CA 93923-8734 Parent Co.-Paul Kagan Associates Inc., Carmel; Title Tel # (408) 624-1536 Title Fax # (408) 625-3225
Personnel: Publisher-Paul Kagan, Circ. Mgr.-Judy Pinney
Editorial Description: Analysis of the economics of the business, hardware growth, software distribution, etc.
General Info: Yr. Est. 1990, Monthly, Trim Size-7¼ x 10, Other press, 12 pages, No Color, Other, Saddle-stitched
Subscriptions: Indv. $595
Advertising: $1,560.

European TV Sports   *Business*

Publishing Co: Kagan World Media Inc., 126 Clock Tower Pl., Carmel, CA 93923-8734 Parent Co.-Paul Kagan Associates Inc., Carmel; Title Tel # (408) 624-1536 Title Fax # (408) 625-3225
Personnel: Publisher-Paul Kagan, Circ. Mgr.-Judy Pinney, Adv. Dir.-Johanne Hardy
Editorial Description: Covers the business aspects of TV sports broadcasting in Europe.
General Info: Yr. Est. 1989, Monthly, Trim Size-7¼ x 10, Other press, 12 pages, No Color, Other, Saddle-stitched
Subscriptions: Indv. $595
Advertising: $1,560.

European Television   *Business*

Publishing Co: Kagan World Media Inc., 126 Clock Tower Pl., Carmel, CA 93923-8734 Parent Co.-Paul Kagan Associates Inc., Carmel; Title Tel # (408) 624-1536 Title Fax # (408) 625-3225
Personnel: Publisher-Paul Kagan, Circ. Mgr.-Judith Pinney, Adv. Mgr.-Johanne Hardy
Editorial Description: Development of European commercial TV markets, valuations of programming, ad sales, networks & companies.
General Info: (Formerly Euro TV Investor), Yr. Est. 1989, Monthly, Trim Size-7¼ x 10, Other press, 10 pages, ISSN: 1043-9420, No Color, Other, Other
Subscriptions: Indv. $625
Advertising: $1,560.

Film Analyst, The
See: FILM

Film Technology News
See: FILM

Get Ready Sheet   *Business*

Publishing Co: Mid-York Library System, 1600 Lincoln Ave, Utica, NY 13502-5340;
    Title Tel # (315) 735-8328
Personnel: Editor-Susan Wawrzaszek, Circ. Dir.-Nancy Hotaling
Editorial Description: Book reviews on TV talk shows, TV and movie tie-ins to books; special features.
General Info: Yr. Est. 1977, Bi-weekly, Trim Size-8½ x 11, Offset press, 8 pages, ISSN: 0148-7566, No Color
Subscriptions: Indv. $23
Circulation: Total-1,350
Advertising: Inquire for rates.

Gilligan's Island News
See: CLUBS

HDTV Report   *Business, Association*

Publishing Co: Phillips Business Information, Inc., 1201 Seven Locks Rd., Ste 300, Potomac, MD 20854-2958 Tel # (301) 340-1520; Title Tel # (301) 340-2100 Title Fax # (301) 424-4297
Personnel: Publisher-Ellen Stuhlmann, Editor-Chris McConnell
Editorial Description: Covers the widely expanding technology developments in the high-definition television industry.
General Info: Yr. Est. 1991, Bi-weekly, 8 pages, ISSN: 1055-9280, Ind/Abs/Online: NewsNet, Predicasts
Subscriptions: Indv. $497, For. $530, $37/copy
Advertising: Accepts Inserts.
List Rental: Rents Lists

High Speed Networking Newsletter
See: COMPUTERS & AUTOMATION

INTV Capitol Newsletter

Publishing Co: Assn. of Independent Television Stations, 1320 19th St. NW, Washington, DC 20036;
    Title Tel # (202) 887-1970 Title Fax # (202) 887-0950
Personnel: Publisher-James Hedlund, Editor-Lawrence Laurent
Editorial Description: Public policy & marketign information for the 339 TV stations in the U.S. not affiliated with the ABC, CBS or NBC networks.
General Info: (Formerly INN Newsletter; Assn. of Independent TV Stations Newsletter), Yr. Est. 1972, Bi-weekly, Mimeo press, 8 pages, No Color

ISA Update
See: TELECOMMUNICATIONS

ITVA News   *Association*   CPM: $130

Publishing Co: International Television Assn., 6311 N. O'Connor Rd., Ste. 230, Irving, TX 75039-3511; Title Tel # (214) 869-1112 Title Fax # (214) 869-2980
Personnel: Publisher-Fred Wehrli, Editor, Adv. Dir.-Deborah Moore
Editorial Description: Industry and natl. membership news for the non-broadcast video industry and institutional markets..
General Info: (Formerly Industrial Television News; International Television News), Yr. Est. 1968, Bi-monthly, Trim Size-8½ x 11, Web press, 20 pages, 30% ads, 2 Color, Coated, Saddle-stitched
Subscriptions: Indv. $150, Free With Membership
Circulation: (100% controlled), Total-8,000, Readership-8,000
Advertising: $1,040. Accepts Inserts.
Printing Co: Baltimore Gas & Electric, Printing Svcs. Dept., 523 Monument St. 2nd Floor, Baltimore, MD 21202 Tel # (410) 291-3416, Fax # (410) 291-3523

Imedia Impact

Publishing Co: Media Network, 39 W 14th St Ste 403, New York, NY 10011-7489;
    Title Tel # (212) 929-2663
General Info: Quarterly

Infocus
See: FILM

Infomercial Marketing Report
See: ADVERTISING & MARKETING

Interactive Television Report
Business

Publishing Co: Simba Information, Inc., 213 Danbury Rd. PO Box 7430, Wilton, CT 06897-7430 Tel # (203) 834-0033 Fax # (203) 834-1771 Parent Co.-Cowles Business Media, New York; Title Tel # (714) 557-8800 Title Fax # (714) 557-5445
Personnel: Publisher-Chris Elwell, Editor-Erik Elward, Mng. Editor-Rob Agee, Circ. Mgr.-Joyce Brigish, Mktg. Dir.-Michael Genaro
Editorial Description: Timely news and analysis with often exclusive information. Covers issues which challenge the industry and provides solutions to key business decisions.
General Info: Yr. Est. 1992, Bi-weekly, ISSN: 1081-8278
Subscriptions: Indv. $595, Can. $595, For. $645
List Rental: Rents Lists

Interactivity Report
Business

Publishing Co: Arlen Communications, Inc., 7315 Wisconsin Ave., Ste. 600E, Bethesda, MD 20814-3203; Title Tel # (301) 656-7940 Title Fax # (301) 656-3204
Personnel: Publisher, Editor-Gary Arlen
Editorial Description: Covers interactive networked multimedia.
General Info: (Formerly Intl. Videotex Teletext News), Yr. Est. 1980, Monthly, Trim Size-8½ x 11, Sheetfed press, 12 pages, ISSN: 0197-677X, No Color, Newsprint, Saddle-stitched, Looseleaf
Subscriptions: Indv. $500, For. $408, $20/copy
Acquistions: Publication Bought

International Co-Productions
Business

Publishing Co: Kagan World Media Inc., 126 Clock Tower Pl., Carmel, CA 93923-8734 Parent Co.-Paul Kagan Associates Inc., Carmel; Title Tel # (408) 624-1536 Title Fax # (408) 625-3225
Personnel: Publisher-Paul Kagan, Circ. Mgr.-Judy Pinney, Adv. Dir.-Johanne Hardy
Editorial Description: Analysis of the deals, money, and people involved in worldwide program development.
General Info: Yr. Est. 1990, Monthly, Trim Size-7¼ x 10, Other press, 10 pages, No Color, Other, Saddle-stitched
Subscriptions: Indv. $595
Advertising: Inquire for rates.

Internet Content Report, The
Business

Publishing Co: Publications Resource Group, P.O. Box 765, N. Adams, MA 01247 Tel # (413) 664-6185 Fax # (413) 664-9343
Editorial Description: Covers developments and trends in video on demand and broadband technology for the home.
General Info: (Formerly Residential Interactive Digest), Yr. Est. 1995, Monthly
Subscriptions: Indv. $495, Can. $495, For. $545

Jamieson & Assocs. -Trends
See: TELECOMMUNICATIONS

Kagan Media Index
Business

Publishing Co: Paul Kagan Associates Inc., 126 Clock Tower Pl., Carmel, CA 93923-8746; Title Tel # (408) 624-1536 Title Fax # (408) 625-3225
Personnel: Publisher-Paul Kagan, Circ. Mgr.-Judith Pinney, Adv. Dir.-Johanne Hardy
Editorial Description: Current estimates of industries growth for a dozen different media businesses, shown on a 145 line spreadsheet, projected forward & updated monthly.
General Info: Yr. Est. 1987, Monthly, Trim Size-7¼ x 10, Other press, 16 pages, ISSN: 0734-5399, No Color, Other, Saddle-stitched
Subscriptions: Indv. $625
Advertising: $1,560.

Kids Club News
See: CHILDREN

Laser Disc Newsletter, The
See: HOME & HOME ENTERTAINMENT

Leased Access Report - Audience
Business

Publishing Co: Videomaker, Inc., 920 Main Street, Chico, CA 95928; Title Tel # (916) 891-8410 Title Fax # (916) 891-8443
Personnel: Publisher-Matthew York, Editor-Stephen Muratore, Production Mgr.-Rhonda Swanson
Editorial Description: Guides interested developers through the process of getting programs on the air, keeps you up to date on related regulatory activity, and will even show you how to launch your own network.
General Info: Yr. Est. 1994, Monthly, Trim Size-8½ x 11, Sheetfed press, 8 pages, No Color, Matte
Subscriptions: Indv. $79, $8/copy
Circulation: Total-2,500
Printing Co: Graphic Fox, The, 313 Walnut Street, Chico, CA 95928 Tel # (916) 895-1359, Fax # (916) 895-3604

Lewis Letter on Cable Marketing
Business

Publishing Co: Lewis Assocs., Inc., PO Box 567, Housatonic, MA 01236-0567; Title Tel # (413) 274-6100 Title Fax # (413) 528-1753
Personnel: Publisher-John Mooney, Editor, Circ. Mgr.-Eileen Willner
Editorial Description: Information on marketing, communication, community & media-relations techniques that work for cable television systems.
General Info: Yr. Est. 1976, Monthly, Web press, 6 pages, No Color, Newsprint
Subscriptions: Indv. $95, $8/copy
Acquistions: Publication Bought

Local Government Newsnet

Publishing Co: The Innovation Groups, PO Box 16645, Tampa, FL 33687-6645 Tel # (813) 622-8484 Fax # (813) 664-0051
Personnel: Publisher-Robert Havlick, Editor-Liz Diaz
Editorial Description: Features examples showing how city and county governments are using electronic communication services to improve the quality of service to and communication with citizens. It highlights what is happening with the information superhighway at all levels ofgovernment and what the implications are for local governments.
General Info: Bi-monthly, Trim Size-8½ x 11, 4 pages, Newsprint
Subscriptions: Indv. $19, Free With Membership
Advertising: Inquire for rates. Accepts Inserts.
List Rental: Rents Lists

Lyon Lamb Newsletter
See: FILM

Marketing New Media
Business

Publishing Co: Cable World Associates, 1905 Sherman St Ste 1000, Denver, CO 80203-1149 Tel # (303) 837-0900; Title Tel # (203) 837-0900
Personnel: Publisher-Paul Kagan, Editor-Larry Gerbrandt, Circ. Mgr.-Judith Pinney
Editorial Description: Sales, promotion of cable, pay-cable, SMATV, MDS, DBS, STV. Marketing New Media runs as an insert in Cable World.
General Info: Yr. Est. 1984, Monthly, Trim Size-8½ x 11, 10 pages, ISSN: 0743-2178
Subscriptions: Indv. $425

Media Business News
See: MEDIA & COMMUNICATIONS

Media Matters
See: MEDIA & COMMUNICATIONS

Multimedia Monitor
See: COMPUTERS & AUTOMATION

Munsters & the Addams Family Reunion
See: FAN MAGAZINES-MOVIE, RADIO, TV

NATAS News
Association

Publishing Co: National Academy of Television Arts & Sciences, 111 W. 57th St., Ste. 1020, New York, NY 10019-2211; Title Tel # (212) 586-8424 Title Fax # (212) 246-8129
Personnel: Editor-Bob Blake, Circ. Mgr.-Ed Eberling
Editorial Description: The newsletter of the National Acadamy of Television Arts and Sciences.
General Info: Quarterly, 4 pages, ISSN: 1062-9637, No Color
Subscriptions: Indv. $25, For. $30
Circulation: Total-12,000

NCTV News
Association

Publishing Co: National Coalition on Television Violence, PO Box 2157, Champaign, IL 61825-2157; Title Tel # (810) 489-3177
Personnel: Publisher-Carole Liberman, Editor-Carole Lieberman
Editorial Description: News opposing violence on TV & violence in all forms of entertainment including videogames, toys, sports, music, etc.
General Info: Yr. Est. 1980, Bi-monthly, Trim Size-8½ x 11, Offset press, 12 pages, No Color, Newsprint
Subscriptions: Indv. $25
Circulation: Total-11,000
Printing Co: Broadside Press, PO Box 1001, Champaign, IL 61824-1001 Tel # (217) 356-7034

NVR Reports
Business

Publishing Co: National Video Resources, 73 Spring St Rm 606, New York, NY 10012-5802; Title Tel # (212) 274-8080 Title Fax # (212) 274-8081
Editorial Description: For increasing publis awareness of quality independent films and videos.
General Info: Yr. Est. 1990, Irregular, Trim Size-8½ x 11, 6 pages, No Color

National Friends of Public Broadcasting Newsletter
See: BROADCASTING

Newsletter at the End of the Universe
See: SCIENCE FICTION & FANTASY

PBS Video News
Consumer

Publishing Co: PBS Video, 1320 Braddock Pl., Alexandria, VA 22314-1698; Title Tel # (703) 739-5380
General Info: Bi-monthly

PRC News
Business CPM: $750

Publishing Co: Corbell Publishing Co., 4676 Admiralty Way, Ste. 300, Marina Del Rey, CA 90292; Title Tel # (310) 574-5337 Title Fax # (310) 574-5383
Personnel: Publisher-Maureen Healy, Editor-Deborah Rolfe
Editorial Description: Pre-recorded cassette news. News briefs for the video industry.
General Info: Yr. Est. 1988, Weekly, Trim Size-8 x 11, Desktop press, 6 pages, ISSN: 0898-302X, No Color, Matte
Subscriptions: Indv. $477, For. $75
Circulation: Total-2,000
Advertising: $1,500. Accepts Inserts.
List Rental: Actives: $150/M

Parental Discretion
See: FAMILY

Pay TV Newsletter
Business

Publishing Co: Paul Kagan Associates Inc., 126 Clock Tower Pl., Carmel, CA 93923-8746; Title Tel # (408) 624-1536 Title Fax # (408) 625-3225
Personnel: Publisher-Paul Kagan, Circ. Mgr.-Judith Pinney, Adv. Dir.-Johanne Hardy
Editorial Description: News and analysis of the pay TV industry.
General Info: Yr. Est. 1973, Monthly, Trim Size-7¼ x 10, Other press, 16 pages, ISSN: 0146-0072, No Color, Other, Saddle-stitched
Subscriptions: Indv. $745
Advertising: $1,560.

Phantom of the Movies' VideoScope, The
Consumer

Publishing Co: PhanMedia, PO Box 216, Ocean Grove, NJ 07756-0216 Tel # (908) 988-6264 Fax # (908) 988-9180; Title Fax # (908) 739-2834
Personnel: Publisher, Editor-Joe Kane, Adv. Dir.-Nancy Naglin
Editorial Description: Rates all the latest video releases in the horror, science fiction, fantasy, and action genres.
General Info: Yr. Est. 1993, Quarterly, Trim Size-8¼ x 10¼, Web press, 68 pages, 2 Color, Newsprint, Saddle-stitched
Subscriptions: Indv. $15, Can. $20, For. $30, $3/copy
Advertising: $200.
List Rental: Rents Lists

Primate Library Report: Audio-Visual Acquisitions
See: ZOOLOGY

Public Broadcasting Report
Business

Publishing Co: Warren Publishing, Inc., 2115 Ward Ct. NW, Washington, DC 20037-1213; Title Tel # (202) 872-9200 Title Fax # (202) 293-3435
Personnel: Publisher-Albert Warren, Editor-Elena Lucini, Circ. Mgr.-Betty Alive, Mktg. Dir.-Gary Madderom
Editorial Description: Independent newsletter for public broadcasting & allied fields.
General Info: Yr. Est. 1978, Bi-weekly, Trim Size-8½ x 11, 12 pages, ISSN: 0193-3663, Ind/Abs/Online: NewsNet, DIALOG, Predicasts, 2 Color, Newsprint
Subscriptions: Indv. $434, For. $457
Acquistions: Publication Bought, Publication Sold

RTS Video Gazette

Publishing Co: RTS, PO Box 93897, Las Vegas, NV 89193-3897; Title Tel # (702) 896-1300
Personnel: Publisher-R. Saeda, Editor-J. Nii
Editorial Description: Video rentals and industry news.
General Info: Yr. Est. 1983, Monthly, Trim Size-8 x 10¾, Sheetfed press, 24 pages, No Color, Newsprint, Saddle-stitched
Subscriptions: Indv. $15, Inst. $5, Can. $15, For. $25, $1/copy
Circulation: Total-24,000
Advertising: Inquire for rates.
List Rental: Actives: 2,000, $100/M
Printing Co: San Dieguito Publishing, 1910 Diamond St, San Marcos, CA 92069-5120 Tel # (619) 744-0910

SBCA Report
Business, Association

Publishing Co: Satellite Broadcasting & Communications Assn., 225 Reinekers Ln Ste 500, Alexandria, VA 22314-2875; Title Tel # (703) 549-6990
Personnel: Editor-Christine Gliozzo, Publisher, Editor, Circ. Mgr.-Margaret Parone
Editorial Description: Information for industry members as well as association members.
General Info: (Formerly SatVision), Yr. Est. 1993, Monthly, Looseleaf
Subscriptions: Indv. $65
Circulation: Total-3,000
Advertising: Inquire for rates.

Satellite Business News
Business

Publishing Co: Satellite Business News Inc., 1730 Rhode Island Ave. NW, Ste. 600, Washington, DC 20036; Title Tel # (202) 785-0505 Title Fax # (202) 785-9291
Personnel: Publisher, Editor-Bob Scherman
General Info: Bi-weekly, 30 pages, ISSN: 1043-0865
Circulation: Total-9,000
Advertising: Inquire for rates.
List Rental: Rents Lists

Satellite News
See: BROADCASTING

Satellite Television Newsletter
Business

Publishing Co: Richard Scherer & Assocs., PO Box 201676, Austin, TX 78720-1676; Title Tel # (512) 258-1230
Personnel: Publisher-Richard Scherer
General Info: Yr. Est. 1983, Monthly
Subscriptions: Indv. $99

Subway Entertainment Guide
See: MUSIC & MUSIC TRADES

Syndication News
Business

Publishing Co: Copley Entertainment Inc., 3006 Fairfield Ave, Bridgeport, CT 06605-3216; Title Tel # (203) 333-6633 Title Fax # (203) 333-8844
Personnel: Publisher-Paul R. Kurmins, Research Mgr.-Bill Miller, Mktg. Dir.-Lisa Lombardo
General Info: Yr. Est. 1990, 25x/yr., Trim Size-8.5 x 11, Offset press, 4 pages, ISSN: 1092-4290, 2 Color
Subscriptions: Indv. $195, Can. $245, For. $245

TV & Politics Watch
Business, Consumer

Publishing Co: TV & Politics Watch, 17 E University Ave Apt 630, Champaign, IL 61820-4036 Fax # (217) 355-0444; Title Tel # (217) 355-0444
Personnel: Publisher, Editor-Peter Donhowe
Editorial Description: For descriminating tv viewers. Covers television's handling of political issues.
General Info: Yr. Est. 1992, Monthly, Trim Size-8½ x 11, 4 pages, No Color
Subscriptions: Indv. $20

TV Pro-Log
Business, Consumer

Publishing Co: Television Index, Inc., 4029 27th St Fl 2, Long Island City, NY 11101-3814; Title Tel # (718) 937-3990 Title Fax # (718) 937-5432
Personnel: Publisher, Editor-Timothy Hunter
Editorial Description: Television programs and production news. Concerning network and Syndication.
General Info: Yr. Est. 1972, Weekly, Trim Size-8½ x 11, Offset press, 2 pages, ISSN: 0739-5574, No Color, Matte
Subscriptions: Indv. $100

TV Satellite Videoworld

Publishing Co: Harris Publications, Inc., 1115 Broadway, 8th Fl., New York, NY 10010-2803 Tel # (212) 807-7100 Fax # (212) 627-4678
Personnel: Editor-David Elrich
General Info: Monthly
Subscriptions: $3/copy

Techline
Association

Publishing Co: Nat'l. Cable Television Assn., 1724 Massachusetts Ave. NW, Washington, DC 20036-1905; Title Tel # (202) 775-3550
Personnel: Editor-Katherine Rutkowski, Production Mgr.-Robert Thorpe
Editorial Description: Cable television industry coverage engineering emphasis.
General Info: Yr. Est. 1980, 10x/yr., Trim Size-8½ x 11, Sheetfed press, 8 pages, No Color, Newsprint
Subscriptions: Free With Membership
Circulation: (100% controlled), Total-3,600

Television & Cable Action Update
Business

Publishing Co: Warren Publishing, Inc., 2115 Ward Ct. NW, Washington, DC 20037-1213; Title Tel # (202) 872-9200 Title Fax # (202) 293-3435
Personnel: Publisher-Albert Warren, Editor-Susan Seiler, Circ. Mgr.-Betty Alvine, Adv. Dir.-Gene Edwards, Mktg. Dir.-Gary Madderom
Editorial Description: Weekly update for those who wish to follow new applications, permits, sales franchises, grants and regulatory changes.
General Info: Yr. Est. 1964, Weekly, ISSN: 1061-5741
Subscriptions: Indv. $446, For. $556
List Rental: Rents Lists

Television & Radio Newsletter
See: BROADCASTING

Television Digest with Consumer Electronics
Business

Publishing Co: Warren Publishing, Inc., 2115 Ward Ct. NW, Washington, DC 20037-1213; Title Tel # (202) 872-9200 Title Fax # (202) 293-3435
Personnel: Publisher, Editor-Albert Warren, Circ. Mgr.-Betty Alvine, Mktg. Dir.-Gary Madderom
Editorial Description: Authoritative service for broadcasting, cable, consumer electronics & allied industries.
General Info: (Formerly Television Digest/Consumer Electronics), Yr. Est. 1945, Weekly, Trim Size-8½ x 11, 16 pages, ISSN: 0497-1515, Ind/Abs/Online: Newsnet, No Color, Newsprint
Subscriptions: Indv. $885, For. $995
Acquistions: Publication Bought, Publication Sold
List Rental: Actives: $75/M

Ten Thousand Words
See: MEDIA & COMMUNICATIONS

Trebas Track
See: SOUND ENGINEERING

Tyndall Report
See: JOURNALISM

Variety Deal Memo
See: FILM

Vermont ETV Program
Guide   *Consumer*

Publishing Co: Vermont ETV, 88 Ethan Allen Ave, Colchester, VT 05446-3335;
Title Tel # (802) 655-4800
Personnel: Publisher-Ann Curran, Editor-Virginia Simmon
Editorial Description: Contains program listings and articles about a local public television station in Vermont.
General Info: Yr. Est. 1967, Monthly, Trim Size-$8\frac{1}{2}$ x 11, Web press, 16 pages, 2 Color
Subscriptions: Indv. $35
Circulation: Total-40,000
Advertising: Inquire for rates. Accepts Inserts.
List Rental: Rents Lists

Video Industry Statistical
Report   *Business*   CPM: $750

Publishing Co: Corbell Publishing Co., 4676 Admiralty Way, Ste. 300, Marina Del Rey, CA 90292;
Title Tel # (310) 574-5337 Title Fax # (310) 574-5383
Personnel: Publisher-Maureen A. Healy, Editor-Deborah A. Rolfe
Editorial Description: Home video, software, and hardware statistical data in such areas are genre, demographics, international and more.
General Info: Yr. Est. 1989, Annually, Trim Size-8 x 11, Desktop press, 200 pages, Looseleaf
Subscriptions: For. $435, $365/copy
Circulation: Total-2,000
Advertising: $1,500. Accepts Inserts.
List Rental: Rents Lists

Video Inn/Mailer/
Newsletter

Publishing Co: Satellite Video Exchange Society, 1965 Main St., Vancouver, BC V5T 3C1 Canada
Tel # (604) 872-8449 Fax # (604) 876-1185
Personnel: Editor-Joe Sarahan, Circ. Mgr.-Crista Haukedal
Editorial Description: Published 5 times a year, to inform members of special screenings, workshops, call for submissions, etc.
General Info: Yr. Est. 1984, Bi-monthly, Desktop press
Subscriptions: Indv. $5, Can. $5, For. $5
Circulation: Total-800
Advertising: Accepts Inserts.

Video Investor   *Business*

Publishing Co: Paul Kagan Associates Inc., 126 Clock Tower Pl., Carmel, CA 93923-8746;
Title Tel # (408) 624-1536 Title Fax # (408) 625-3225
Personnel: Publisher-Paul Kagan, Circ. Mgr.-Judith Pinney, Adv. Dir.-Johanne Hardy
Editorial Description: Report on the business of renting & selling video cassettes exclusive estimates of retail & wholesale transactions & inventories.
General Info: (Formerly VCR Letter), Yr. Est. 1984, Monthly, Trim Size-$7\frac{1}{4}$ x 10, Other press, 10 pages, ISSN: 1042-7694, No Color, Other, Saddle-stitched
Subscriptions: Indv. $575
Advertising: $1,560.

Video Retailers Choice   *Business*   CPM: $183

Publishing Co: Connell Communications, Inc., 86 Elm St, Peterborough, NH 03458-1052;
Title Tel # (603) 924-7271 Title Fax # (603) 924-7013
Personnel: Editor-Melissa Stephenson
Editorial Description: Information for retailers in the video trade.
General Info: (Formerly Video Choice), Yr. Est. 1988, Monthly, Trim Size-8 x $10\frac{3}{4}$, Web press, 6 pages, 2 Color, Coated, Perfect bound
Subscriptions: Indv. $20
Circulation: Total-6,000
Advertising: $1,100.

Video Services News   *Business*

Publishing Co: Phillips Business Information, Inc., 1201 Seven Locks Rd., Ste 300, Potomac, MD 20854-2958 Tel # (301) 340-1520 Fax # (301) 424-4297
Editorial Description: Covers FCC rules, new technologies, and industry events.
General Info: Yr. Est. 1993, Bi-weekly
Subscriptions: Indv. $497

Video Specialist and New
Technology   *Business*   CPM$1900

Publishing Co: J. Lahm Consultants, Inc., 2630 N. Coronado Dr., Fullerton, CA 92635-2513
Fax # (714) 738-4860; Title Tel # (714) 738-8422 Title Fax # (714) 738-8460
Personnel: Editor-James Lahm
Editorial Description: Leading edge advisory publication for retailers and suppliers to the home entertainment industry.
General Info: (Formerly Video Specialist), Yr. Est. 1981, Monthly, Trim Size-$8\frac{1}{2}$ x 11, Offset press, 6 pages, No Color
Subscriptions: Indv. $144, For. $156, Free To Qualified Recipient
Circulation: Total-500, Readership-1,000
Advertising: $950.
List Rental: Rents Lists

Video Technology
Newsletter   *Business, Association*

Publishing Co: Phillips Business Information, Inc., 1201 Seven Locks Rd., Ste 300, Potomac, MD 20854-2958 Tel # (301) 340-1520 Fax # (301) 424-4297; Title Tel # (301) 340-2100
Title Fax # (301) 424-4247
Personnel: Publisher-Tim Baskerville, Editor-Kristopher Brown, Circ. Mgr., Promotion Dir.-Claudette Duran
Editorial Description: Covers new media: HDTV, pay per view, advanced displays, production, fiber optics.
General Info: (Formerly Futurehome Technology Newsletter; Home Media Technology News), Yr. Est. 1987, Bi-weekly, 8 pages, ISSN: 1040-2772, Ind/Abs/Online: NewsNet, DIALOG, Predicasts
Subscriptions: Indv. $497, For. $530
Acquistions: Publication Bought
Advertising: Accepts Inserts.
List Rental: Actives: $300/M

Video Week   *Business*

Publishing Co: Warren Publishing, Inc., 2115 Ward Ct. NW, Washington, DC 20037-1213;
Title Tel # (202) 872-9200 Title Fax # (202) 293-3435
Personnel: Publisher-Albert Warren, Editor-Cindy Spielvogel, Circ. Mgr.-Betty Alvine, Mktg. Dir.-Gary Madderom
Editorial Description: Weekly news service devoted to home video industry.
General Info: (Formerly Video Info Paper), Yr. Est. 1979, Weekly, Trim Size-$8\frac{1}{2}$ x 11, 10 pages, ISSN: 0196-5905, Ind/Abs/Online: NewsNet, DIALOG, Predicasts, 2 Color, Newsprint
Subscriptions: Indv. $850, For. $896
Acquistions: Publication Bought, Publication Sold

Viewer & Listener   *Consumer*

Publishing Co: King Communications Group, 627 National Press Building, Washington, DC 20045-1601 Tel # (202) 638-4260 Fax # (202) 662-9719
Personnel: Publisher-Llewellyn King
Editorial Description: Covers public television and radio.
General Info: Yr. Est. 1995, 24x/yr., 16 pages
Subscriptions: Indv. $50

Visual Literacy Review & Newsletter
See: EDUCATION

Warren's Cable
Regulation Monitor   *Business*

Publishing Co: Warren Publishing, Inc., 2115 Ward Ct. NW, Washington, DC 20037-1213;
Title Tel # (202) 872-9200 Title Fax # (202) 293-3435
Personnel: Publisher-Alberl Warren, Editor-Michael Grebb, Circ. Mgr.-Betty Alvine, Mktg. Dir.-Gary Madderom
Editorial Description: The authoritative weekly news service carering federal,state, and local cable activites and trends.
General Info: Yr. Est. 1993, Weekly, Trim Size-$8\frac{1}{2}$ x 11, 10 pages
Subscriptions: Indv. $557, For. $603
List Rental: Rents Lists

Women in Cable Newsletter   *Association*

Publishing Co: P.M. Haeger & Assoc., 500 N Michigan Ave Ste 1400, Chicago, IL 60611-3703;
Title Tel # (312) 661-1700 Title Fax # (312) 661-0769
Personnel: Publisher-P.M. Haeger, & Assoc., Editor-Christine Kane
Editorial Description: Focus on achievements and activities of members.
General Info: Yr. Est. 1979, Bi-monthly, Trim Size-$8\frac{1}{2}$ x 11, Offset press, 8 pages, 2 Color
Circulation: (100% controlled), Total-2,000

Worldwide Videotex Update
See: COMPUTERS & AUTOMATION

TENNIS

Bob Larson's Tennis
Newswire

Publishing Co: Bob Larson's Tennis, PO Box 24379, Edina, MN 55424-0379;
Title Tel # (612) 920-8947
Personnel: Publisher-Bob Larson, Editor-Ron Larson
Editorial Description: Tennis sports marketing newsletter covering the business side of tennis professional tour internationally manufacturing, & politics.
General Info: Yr. Est. 1983
Subscriptions: Indv. $79, Can. $99, For. $99
Circulation: Total-500

Mid-America Senior Tennis

Publishing Co: John W. Bartlett, PO Box 465, Aurora, IL 60507-0465; Title Tel # (708) 896-3143
Personnel: Editor-John Bartlett
General Info: (Formerly Western Senior Tennis), Yr. Est. 1983, Monthly, Trim Size-$8\frac{1}{2}$ x 11, 8 pages
Subscriptions: Indv. $28
Circulation: Total-125

Net Friends News — *Association*

Publishing Co: Tennis Foundation of North America, 200 Castlewood Dr, North Palm Beach, FL 33408-5604; Title Tel # (305) 848-1026
Personnel: Editor-Brad Patterson
Editorial Description: Information to those members of the association.
General Info: (Formerly Drop Shots), Bi-monthly, 8 pages, No Color, Coated
Circulation: Total-10,000
Printing Co: Star Publishing, 609 N Railroad Ave, Boynton Beach, FL 33435-3804
  Tel # (407) 732-6426

Stringer's Assistant — *Business*

Publishing Co: U.S. Racquet Stringer's Assn., PO Box 40, Del Mar, CA 92014-0040;
  Title Tel # (619) 481-3545 Title Fax # (619) 481-0624
Personnel: Publisher-Jill Workman, Editor-David Workman, Circ. Mgr.-Marie Moser
Editorial Description: Marketing information on racquet stringing; industry news; product info.
General Info: Yr. Est. 1974, Monthly, Trim Size-8½ x 11, Sheetfed press, 20 pages, 6% ads, 4 Color, Coated, Saddle-stitched
Subscriptions: Indv. $54
Acquistions: Publication Bought
Circulation: (43% controlled), Total-8,000
Advertising: Inquire for rates. Accepts Inserts.
List Rental: Actives: 8,000, $1,000/M

TEXTILES

ATHA Newsletter
  See: HOBBY

Advanced Materials
  See: MANUFACTURING

Advertised Retail Prices of Down & Down-&-Feather Filled Pillows

Publishing Co: American Down Assn. (ADA), 3728 Canna Ct, Sacramento, CA 95821-3101;
  Title Tel # (916) 971-1135
Personnel: Editor-Howard Winslow
Editorial Description: Statistical report covering prices of down & down-&-feather filled pillows.
General Info: Monthly

American Home Sewing and Craft Association — *Business, Association*

Publishing Co: American Home Sewing & Craft Assn., 1375 Broadway, New York, NY 11360;
  Title Tel # (212) 302-2150 Title Fax # (212) 391-8009
Personnel: Art Dir.-Tina Bliss, Publisher, Production Mgr., Promotion Dir.-Joan Katz
Editorial Description: Sewing industry newsletter for AHSCA members. Contains industry information as well as fashion and home decorating trends, Washington Update, market information and more.
General Info: Yr. Est. 1978, Bi-monthly, Trim Size-8½ x 11, Sheetfed press, 8 pages, 2 Color, Matte
Subscriptions: Free With Membership
Circulation: (100% controlled), Total-2,500

Braintree Express
  See: HOUSE ORGANS

CAUS News — *Business, Association*

Publishing Co: Color Association of the U.S., 409 W. 44th St., New York, NY 10036-4402;
  Title Tel # (212) 582-6884 Title Fax # (212) 757-4557
Personnel: Publisher-Manielle Bawcou, Editor-Margaret Walch
Editorial Description: Devoted to color/design issues for apparel and interior environmental colorations.
General Info: (Formerly CAUS Newsletter), Yr. Est. 1980, Monthly, Trim Size-8½ x 11, 4 pages, 2 Color, Coated
Subscriptions: Inst. $100, Free With Membership
Circulation: Total-6,000

Cotton: Review of the World Situation Update by Fax — *Business*

Publishing Co: International Cotton Advisory Committee, 1629 K St. NW, Ste. 702, Washington, DC 20006-1602; Title Tel # (202) 463-6660 Title Fax # (202) 463-6950
Editorial Description: A monthly 6-to-10 page fax provides information on the latest events affecting the world cotton market and presents up-to-date supply, demand and price projections.
General Info: Monthly
Subscriptions: Indv. $230

Cotton's Week

Publishing Co: National Cotton Council of America, PO Box 12285, Memphis, TN 38182-0285;
  Title Tel # (901) 274-9030
Personnel: Editor-Fred Middleton
Editorial Description: Covers legislation & regulatory developments related to the cotton industry.
General Info: Yr. Est. 1946, Weekly, Sheetfed press, 2 pages, No Color
Subscriptions: Indv. $250
Circulation: Total-7,800

Craft News
  See: GLASS, STONE & CLAY

EDI News
  See: BUSINESS & INDUSTRY

Embroidery News — *Business, Association*

Publishing Co: Schiffli Lace and Embroidery Manufacturers Assn., 8555 Tonnelle Ave, North Bergen, NJ 07047-4738; Title Tel # (201) 868-7200 Title Fax # (201) 868-9833
Personnel: Editor, Circ. Mgr., Adv. Dir., Art Dir.-Leonard Seiler
Editorial Description: Covers fashion and business news, industry information applicable to embroidery manufacturers and those servicing the embroidery industry.
General Info: (Formerly Schiffli News), Yr. Est. 1955, Bi-monthly, Trim Size-8½ x 11, Offset press, 12 pages, No Color, Coated
Subscriptions: Indv. $10, Inst. $10, Can. $15, For. $20, Free With Membership
Circulation: (100% controlled), Total-500
Advertising: Inquire for rates.
Printing Co: Gracis Inc, 608 New York Ave, Union City, NJ 07087 Tel # (201) 867-2424,
  Fax # (201) 867-4335

Flax Craft — *Business, Scholarly*

Publishing Co: Flax Craft, 3503 Edwards Rd, Sodus, MI 49126-9707; Title Tel # (616) 944-5719
  Title Fax # (616) 944-5719
Personnel: Publisher-Virginia Handy, Editor-Virgina Handy
Editorial Description: Flax culture, the growing of flax for fiber or oilseed; the use of the fiber for spinning, weaving and other crafts; the history of linen; news of flax and linen all over the world; craft ideas; book reviews,calenders of events.
General Info: Yr. Est. 1993, Quarterly, Trim Size-8½ x 11, Desktop press, 4 pages, ISSN: 1078-0335, No Color
Subscriptions: Indv. $8, Inst. $8, Can. $10, $2/copy
Circulation: Total-200

High Performance Textiles — *Business*

Publishing Co: Elsevier Science Inc., 655 Avenue of the Americas, New York, NY 10010-5107
  Tel # (212) 633-3916 Fax # (212) 633-3913 Parent Co.-Reed Elsevier, New York
Personnel: Publisher-Guy Kitteringham, Editor-A. Weawes
Editorial Description: Monthly up-date on latest developments in textile industry.
General Info: Monthly, 16 pages, ISSN: 0144-5871, Ind/Abs/Online: DIALOG
Subscriptions: Indv. $474

Inside Textiles Newsletter — *Business*

Publishing Co: Point Publishing Co., PO Box 1309, Point Pleasant, NJ 08742-1309;
  Title Tel # (908) 295-8258
Personnel: Editor-N.C. Heimbold
Editorial Description: Marketing, manufacturing of textiles and fibers.
General Info: Yr. Est. 1979, Bi-weekly, Sheetfed press, 8 pages, ISSN: 0733-8244, No Color
Subscriptions: Indv. $167, Can. $167, For. $197

Medical Textiles — *Business*

Publishing Co: Elsevier Science Inc., 655 Avenue of the Americas, New York, NY 10010-5107
  Tel # (212) 633-3916 Fax # (212) 633-3913 Parent Co.-Reed Elsevier, New York;
  Title Tel # (212) 633-3650
Personnel: Publisher-G. Kitteringham, Editor-Ananda Weawer
General Info: Yr. Est. 1983, Monthly, ISSN: 0266-2078, Ind/Abs/Online: DIALOG, Newsprint
Subscriptions: Indv. $474
List Rental: Rents Lists

Monthly Imports & Exports of Feathers & Down

Publishing Co: American Down Assn. (ADA), 3728 Canna Ct, Sacramento, CA 95821-3101;
  Title Tel # (916) 971-1135
Personnel: Editor-Howard Winslow
Editorial Description: Statistical report comparing imports & exports of feathers.
General Info: Monthly

Monthly Imports & Exports of Finished Products by Firm

Publishing Co: American Down Assn. (ADA), 3728 Canna Ct, Sacramento, CA 95821-3101;
  Title Tel # (916) 971-1135
Personnel: Editor-Howard Winslow
Editorial Description: Statistical report covering imports & exports of finished down products.
General Info: Monthly

Monthly Imports & Exports of Pillows & Comforters

Publishing Co: American Down Assn. (ADA), 3728 Canna Ct, Sacramento, CA 95821-3101;
  Title Tel # (916) 971-1135
Personnel: Editor-Howard Winslow
Editorial Description: Statistical report covering imports & exports of pillows & comforters.
General Info: Monthly

Monthly Imports & Exports
of Sleeping Bags

Publishing Co: American Down Assn. (ADA), 3728 Canna Ct, Sacramento, CA 95821-3101;
Title Tel # (916) 971-1135
Personnel: Editor-Howard Winslow
Editorial Description: Statistical report comparing imports & exports of down sleeping bags.
General Info: Monthly

National Textile Processors
Guild, Bulletins   *Association*

Publishing Co: Natl. Textile Processors Guild, 75 Livingston St., Brooklyn, NY 11201-5054;
Title Tel # (718) 875-2300

Nonwoven Markets   *Business*

Publishing Co: Miller Freeman Publications, 411 Borel Ave., Ste. 100, San Mateo, CA 94402
Tel # (415) 358-9500 Fax # (415) 358-8725; Title Tel # (415) 905-2250 Title Fax # (415) 905-2240
Personnel: Grp. Pub.-Peter Sutton, Assoc. Publ., Editor-Johanna Kleppe, Production Mgr.-Andrew Mickus
Editorial Description: News on markets, technology, finance, U.S. & worldwide.
General Info: Yr. Est. 1986, Bi-weekly
Subscriptions: Indv. $527, $35/copy

Performance Materials
See: AERONAUTICS/ASTRONAUTICS

Supima Association of America Newsletter
See: AGRICULTURE

TRI News & Research
Briefs

Publishing Co: Textile Research Institute, Box 625, Princeton, NJ 08540; Title Tel # (609) 924-3150
Personnel: Editor-Dr. Harriet Heilweil
Editorial Description: TRI News & Research Briefs, reporting activities of the research & administrative staff at Textile Research Institute, & summarizing selected TRI research achievements, is sent to supporters & interested persons.
General Info: Yr. Est. 1945, Semi-annually, Trim Size-8½ x 11, Offset press, 4 pages, No Color, Newsprint
Circulation: Total-2,000

Textile Museum Bulletin
See: MUSEUM PUBLICATIONS

USA Textiles/Apparel
Newsletter   *Association*

Publishing Co: Prent Thomas Textile Consultants, PO Box 7005, Columbus, GA 31908-7005;
Title Tel # (706) 568-1386
General Info: Semi-monthly, 4 pages
Subscriptions: Indv. $145

THEATRE

AATE Newsletter   *Association*

Publishing Co: American Alliance for Theatre & Education, Arizona State University, Theatre Department, Box 873411, Tempe, AZ 85287-3411; Title Tel # (602) 965-6064
Personnel: Editor-Jean Campbell
Editorial Description: Primary source of the news and information about the ongoing activities of the association & the field.
General Info: Yr. Est. 1987, Quarterly
Subscriptions: Free With Membership
List Rental: Rents Lists

ASTR Newsletter   *Association*

Publishing Co: American Society for Theatre Research, Southern Illinois Univ., Dept. of Theatre-6608, Carbondale, IL 62901; Title Tel # (618) 453-7593
Personnel: Editor-Sarah J. Blackstone
Editorial Description: News and information relating to the association and theatre research.
General Info: Yr. Est. 1957, Semi-annually, 12 pages, No Color
Circulation: (100% controlled), Total-600

Alternate Roots

Publishing Co: Regional Organization of Theatres South, 1083 Austin Ave NE, Atlanta, GA 30307-1940; Title Tel # (404) 577-1079
Personnel: Editor-Greg Carraway
General Info: Yr. Est. 1976, Semi-annually
Subscriptions: Free

American Ballroom Theater

Publishing Co: American Ballroom Theater, 129 W. 27th Street, Room 705, New York, NY 10001;
Title Tel # (212) 627-8337 Title Fax # (212) 627-8275

Art Hazards Newsletter
See: SAFETY

Arts Center News
See: MUSEUM PUBLICATIONS

Association of Theatrical
Press Agents and
Managers Highlights of
Bimonthly Meeting   *Association*

Publishing Co: Assn. of Theatrical Press Agents, 165 W. 46th St., New York, NY 10036-2501;
Title Tel # (212) 719-3666

Atlanta Opera News
See: MUSIC & MUSIC TRADES

Brief Chronicles

Publishing Co: Players, The, 16 Gramercy Park S, New York, NY 10003-1705;
Title Tel # (212) 475-6116
Personnel: Publisher-Robert Keefe, Editor-Tom Ferriter, Production Mgr.-Fred Weidner, Art Dir.-Robert Herald
Editorial Description: Members newsletter for & by Players, a private club of practitioners and enthusiasts of the creative arts, primarily the performing arts.
General Info: (Formerly Players Bulletin), Yr. Est. 1922, 8x/yr., Trim Size-8½ x 11, Web press, 8 pages
Circulation: Total-950
Printing Co: Fred Weidner & Son, 111 8th Ave., New York, NY 10011 Tel # (212) 989-1070

Broadside, the Newsletter
of the Theatre Library
Association   *Association*

Publishing Co: Theatre Library Association, 111 Amsterdam Ave, New York, NY 10023-7410;
Title Tel # (212) 870-1670
Personnel: Editor-Alan Pally
Editorial Description: Makes available information on many sources of theatre in all its forms.
General Info: Yr. Est. 1940, Quarterly, Trim Size-8½ x 11, Offset press, 4 pages, ISSN: 0068-2748, No Color, Coated, Saddle-stitched
Subscriptions: Indv. $20, Inst. $25, $2/copy
Circulation: (100% controlled), Total-500
List Rental: Actives: 500, $150/M

Call Board
See: RELIGIOUS & THEOLOGICAL

Canplay   *Association*

Publishing Co: Playwrights Union of Canada, 54 Wolseley Street, Second Floor, Toronto, ON M5T 1A5 Canada; Title Tel # (416) 947-0201 Title Fax # (416) 947-0159
Personnel: Publisher-Angela Rebeiro, Editor-Jodi Armstrong
General Info: (Formerly Playwrights Union of Canada, Newsletter), Yr. Est. 1984, Bi-monthly, Trim Size-8½ x 11, Desktop press, 32 pages, ISSN: 0829-3627, No Color, Coated
Subscriptions: Indv. $26
Circulation: Total-3,000
Advertising: Accepts Inserts.

Common Ground News   *Consumer*

Publishing Co: Common Ground Stage & Film Co., 332 Bleeker St., Ste. K114, New York, NY 10014; Title Tel # (212) 604-4222
Editorial Description: News and information about the Common Ground Stage & Film Co.
General Info: Monthly, Trim Size-8½ x 14, 1 pages, No Color, Matte

Council of Jewish Theatres
Newsletter   *Business*

Publishing Co: Natl. Foundation for Jewish Culture, 330 Seventh Ave., 21st Fl., New York, NY 10001-5010; Title Tel # (212) 629-0500 Title Fax # (212) 629-0508
Personnel: Editor-Laurie Wessely-Baldwin
Editorial Description: Dedicated to promoting the interest of non-profit theatres in North America whose primary mission is the development and production of plays relevant to Jewish life and values.
General Info: Quarterly

Critics Quarterly   *Association*

Publishing Co: American Theatre Critics Assn., 825 President Street, Apt 4, Brooklyn, NY 11212
Personnel: Editor-Harry Cherkinian, Exec. Ed.-Clara Hieronymous
Editorial Description: Association news and theatre criticism issues.
General Info: Yr. Est. 1988, Quarterly
Subscriptions: Indv. $25

Drama Ministry
See: RELIGIOUS & THEOLOGICAL

Dramatists Guild
Newsletter, The   *Association*

Publishing Co: Dramatists Guild, The, 234 W. 44th, 11th fl., New York, NY 10036-3986
    Fax # (212) 944-0420; Title Tel # (212) 398-9366
Personnel: Editor-Jeff Zadroga
Editorial Description: Items of interest to members. The Guild is the Professional Association of Playwrights, Composers & Lyricists. Publication is only available to members and Institutional subsidiaries of The Dramatists Guild.
General Info: Yr. Est. 1977, 8x/yr., Trim Size-8½ x 11, Offset press, 16 pages, No Color
Subscriptions: Inst. $100
Circulation: Total-7,000
Advertising: Inquire for rates.
List Rental: Actives: 6,000, $100/M

EDAM Review

Publishing Co: Sponsor-Medieval Institute, Medieval Institute Publications, Western Michigan Univ., Kalamazoo, MI 49008-3851; Title Tel # (616) 387-4153 Title Fax # (616) 387-4152
Personnel: Editor-Clifford Davidson, Circ. Mgr.-Thomas Seiler
Editorial Description: Interdisciplinary notes on medieval and renaissance drama and related areas.
General Info: (Formerly EDAM Newsletter), Yr. Est. 1978, Semi-annually, Trim Size-5½ x 8¼, Offset press, 45 pages, ISSN: 0148-9401, Ind/Abs/Online: RILM, MLA, IBT, No Color
Subscriptions: Indv. $6, Inst. $8, Can. $6, For. $6, $4/copy
Circulation: Total-175

Fanfares   *Association*

Publishing Co: Stratford Shakespearean Festival Foundation of Canada, Box 520, Stratford, ON N5A 6V2 Canada; Title Tel # (519) 271-4040 Title Fax # (519) 271-2734
Personnel: Editor-Keith Courtney, Art Dir.-Andy Foster
Editorial Description: Members quarterly newsletter.
General Info: Yr. Est. 1967, Quarterly, Trim Size-8½ x 11, Sheetfed press, 12 pages, 4 Color, Coated
Subscriptions: Free
Circulation: (100% controlled), Total-20,000

Forum   *Association*   CPM: $833

Publishing Co: ISPAA International Society, 2920 Fuller Ave. NE, Ste. 205, Grand Rapids, MI 49505-3458; Title Tel # (616) 874-6200 Title Fax # (616) 874-5723
Personnel: Editor-Michael Hardy, Adv. Dir.-Peggy Klus
Editorial Description: News & information relevant to the concerns & interests of performing arts administrators.
General Info: (Formerly Bulletin), Yr. Est. 1948, 10x/yr., Trim Size-8½ x 11, Offset press, 10 pages, ISSN: 0739-1161, 20% ads, No Color, Coated
Subscriptions: Indv. $25, $4/copy
Acquistions: Publication Bought
Circulation: Total-600
Advertising: $500.
List Rental: Rents Lists
Printing Co: Commercial Printing Co., 90 Market Ave SW, Grand Rapids, MI 49503-4082 Tel # (616) 454-9334

Impact!   *Consumer, Association*

Publishing Co: Professional Assn. of Canadian Theatres, Communications Centre, 64 Charles St. E., 2nd fl., Toronto, ON M4Y 1T1 Canada Tel # (416) 968-3033 Fax # (416) 968-3035
Personnel: Editor-Beverly Sweeting, Feature Ed.-Rick Sherman
Editorial Description: Chronicles the activities and news from professional theatres across Canada.
General Info: Yr. Est. 1976, Quarterly, Trim Size-8½ x 11, Desktop press, 20 pages, ISSN: 0848-1482, Newsprint, Perfect bound
Subscriptions: Indv. $25, Can. $25, Free With Membership

Jester   *Association*

Publishing Co: Masquers, 11110 Victory Blvd, North Hollywood, CA 91606-3702;
    Title Tel # (818) 760-9367
Editorial Description: Information of interest to members of Masquers Club: entertainment industry developments and membership news.
General Info: (Formerly Jester), Monthly, Mimeo press, 2 pages, Color
Circulation: (100% controlled), Total-400

Julliard Journal
See: MUSIC & MUSIC TRADES

Kurt Weill Newsletter
See: MUSIC & MUSIC TRADES

LHAT Bulletin

Publishing Co: League of Historic American Theatres, 1511 K St NW Ste 923, Washington, DC 20005-1401; Title Tel # (202) 783-6966 Title Fax # (202) 393-2141
Personnel: Editor-Grey Hautaluoma
Editorial Description: General & technical information relevant to restoring & operating historic theatres.
General Info: Yr. Est. 1976, Bi-monthly, Trim Size-8½ x 11, Desktop press, 12 pages, 8% ads, No Color, Coated, Saddle-stitched
Subscriptions: Indv. $50, Inst. $195, Can. $55, For. $55, Free With Membership
Circulation: Total-600
Advertising: Inquire for rates.
List Rental: Actives: 560, $75/M
Printing Co: Park Press, 1518 K St., NW, Washington, DC 20005

Mime Times

Publishing Co: Montanaro Mime Theatre, 116 Carlyle Rd, Portland, ME 04103-3485;
    Title Tel # (207) 743-8452
Personnel: Editor-Kim Ingels
Editorial Description: Mime and related theatre arts.
General Info: Yr. Est. 1977, Quarterly, Letrpr. press, 8 pages, No Color
Subscriptions: Indv. $5, $1/copy
Circulation: Total-3,000

Musical Show

Publishing Co: Tams-Witmark Music Library, Inc., 560 Lexington Ave., New York, NY 10022-6873;
    Title Tel # (212) 688-2525
Personnel: Editor-Robert A. Hut
General Info: Yr. Est. 1962, Quarterly, Sheetfed press, Color, Coated
Circulation: Total-200,000

NETC News   *Business, Association*

Publishing Co: New England Theatre Conference, c/o Dept. of Theatre, Northeastern University, 360 Huntington Ave., Boston, MA 02115 Fax # (617) 424-9275; Title Tel # (617) 424-9275 Title Fax # (612) 429-9275
Personnel: Editor-Dorene Carey, Adv. Dir.-Sally Monroe
Editorial Description: NETC Program/Project Info; New Play Contests & Productions; Theatre Pubs; Job Openings/Auditions/Fellowships; Other regional & national Conferences/Festivals/Workshops; Grants & Awards; New England state Arts Councils info; genl. news items of theatre activity in New England region.
General Info: Yr. Est. 1952, 5x/yr., Trim Size-8½ x 11, Offset press, 8 pages, No Color, Other, Saddle-stitched
Circulation: Total-1,850
Advertising: Inquire for rates.
List Rental: Rents Lists
Printing Co: Adidas Printing, Melford, MA

NTD Newsletter

Publishing Co: National Theatre of the Deaf, 5 W Main St # 659, Chester, CT 06412-1302;
    Title Tel # (203) 526-4971 Title Fax # (203) 526-9732
Personnel: Editor-Laurie Beth Roberts
Editorial Description: Mailed annually to the National Theatre of the Deaf's contributors, this newsletter offers info on the current season - the national tour and Connecticut events at the NTD headquarters.
General Info: Annually
Circulation: Total-5,000

New York Puppet Times   *Association*

Publishing Co: Puppetry Guild of Greater NY, PO Box 117, New York, NY 10116-0117;
    Title Tel # (212) 929-1568
Personnel: Publisher, Editor-Susan Wall
Editorial Description: Adult regional news of puppet art and puppet theatre - professional level.
General Info: (Formerly Involvement), Yr. Est. 1962, Bi-monthly, Trim Size-8½ x 11, Desktop press, 8 pages, No Color, Newsprint
Subscriptions: Indv. $20, $2/copy
Circulation: (100% controlled), Total-200

News & Views   *Association*

Publishing Co: National Association of Theatre Owners, 4605 Lankershim Blvd Ste 340, North Hollywood, CA 91602-1818; Title Tel # (818) 506-1778 Title Fax # (818) 506-0269
Personnel: Publisher-Mary Ann Grasso, Editor-Jim Kozak, Circ. Mgr.-Lisa Levinson
General Info: Yr. Est. 1969, Monthly, Trim Size-8½ x 11, Web press, 25 pages, ISSN: 0279-120X, Coated
Subscriptions: Indv. $50, For. $65, Free With Membership
Circulation: Total-3,000
Advertising: Inquire for rates.
Printing Co: Cummings Printing Co., 4 Peters Brook Dr., P.O. Box 16495, Hooksett, NH 03106 Tel # (603) 625-6901, Fax # (603) 623-5132

Newsletter of I.T.I.U.S.   *Association*

Publishing Co: International Theatre Institute of the US, Inc., 47 Great Jones St., New York, NY 10012-1114; Title Tel # (212) 944-1490 Title Fax # (212) 944-1506
Personnel: Editor-Louis Rachow
Editorial Description: Reports on activities, programs, and services of the ITI.
General Info: Yr. Est. 1970, Quarterly, Trim Size-8½ x 11, Letrpr. press, 8 pages, No Color
Subscriptions: Free With Membership
Acquistions: Publication Bought
Circulation: Total-2,000

O'Neill, The

Publishing Co: Eugene O'Neill Memorial Theater Center, 305 Great Neck Rd, Waterford, CT 06385-3825; Title Tel # (203) 443-5378
Personnel: Editor-Phyllis Kaye
General Info: Quarterly
Circulation: Total-1,000

Oakland Artscape
See: REGIONAL INTEREST

Ontario Puppetry
Association Letter   *Association*

Publishing Co: Ontario Puppetry Assn., Box 180, 65 Front St. W., Suite 0116, Toronto, ON M2J 1E6 Canada Tel # (416) 861-0202; Title Tel # (416) 494-7011
Editorial Description: News of Canadian puppetry events, book reviews, articles on puppetry technique, philosophy and criticism.
General Info: Yr. Est. 1962, Bi-monthly, Trim Size-7 x 8½, Web press, 10 pages, ISSN: 0030-3062, No Color
Circulation: Total-250

Opera America Newsline
See: MUSIC & MUSIC TRADES

Opera Today   *Consumer, Association*

Publishing Co: Center for Contemporary Opera, Gracie Station, Box 1350, New York, NY 10028-0010; Title Tel # (212) 308-6728 Title Fax # (212) 308-6744
Personnel: Publisher-Richard Marshall, Editor-Antonio Ramirez
Editorial Description: From the Center for Contemporary Opera.
General Info: Yr. Est. 1984, Quarterly
Circulation: Total-17,000
Advertising: Inquire for rates.

Parental Discretion
See: FAMILY

Passing Show   *Scholarly, Association*

Publishing Co: Shubert Archive, 149 W. 45th St., New York, NY 10036-4004 Parent Co.-Shubert Foundation, New York; Title Tel # (212) 944-3895 Title Fax # (212) 944-4139
Personnel: Editor-Mark Swartz
Editorial Description: Publishes articles concerning the history of theatrical productions on Broadway and, in particular, of the Shubert Organization's producing activities throughout the U.S.
General Info: Yr. Est. 1977, Semi-annually, Trim Size-8½ x 11, Desktop press, 20 pages, ISSN: 1061-8112, No Color, Coated, Saddle-stitched
Subscriptions: Free To Qualified Recipient
Circulation: Total-2,500
Printing Co: Pickwick Press, PO Box 7634, Princeton, NJ 08543 Tel # (908) 246-2151, Fax # (609) 655-2525

Play in Chelsea   *Consumer*

Publishing Co: Chelsea Arts Consortium, 120 W. 28th St., 2nd Fl., New York, NY 10001
Personnel: Editor-Martha Bowden
Editorial Description: Theatre arts activities in the Chelsea area in New York City.
General Info: Quarterly, Trim Size-11½ x 15½, 8 pages, 2 Color, Newsprint

Play View   *Consumer*

Publishing Co: Greenwich Street Theatre, 286 Spring St., Ste. 202B, New York, NY 10013
Editorial Description: Information about plays presented at the Greenwich Street Theatre.
General Info: Yr. Est. 1995, Quarterly, Trim Size-8½ x 11, 4 pages, No Color, Matte

Prologue   *Consumer*

Publishing Co: Balch Arena Theatre, Tufts University, Medford, MA 02155 Fax # (617) 627-3803; Title Tel # (617) 627-3493
Personnel: Editor-Peter Arnoff, Circ. Mgr., Art Dir.-Joanne Barnett
Editorial Description: Theater program for the Balch Arena Theater, including articles on all aspects of drama.
General Info: Yr. Est. 1945, 3x/yr., Trim Size-8 x 10, 4 pages, Color
Circulation: Total-5,250

Prologue   *Consumer*

Publishing Co: Milwaukee Repertory Theater, 108 E Wells St, Milwaukee, WI 53202-3525; Title Tel # (414) 224-1761
Personnel: Editor-Cindy Moran, Art Dir.-Jerry Haslbeck
Editorial Description: Content covers productions & programming for 3 stages at theater as well as special interest stories.
General Info: Bi-monthly, Trim Size-11 x 17, Sheetfed press, 8 pages, 2 Color, Newsprint
Circulation: (100% controlled), Total-15,000
Printing Co: Community Newspapers, 640 E. Ryan Rd., Waukesha, WI 53186 Tel # (414) 768-5800

Pshaw   *Consumer*

Publishing Co: Show Festival Theatre Foundation, Box 774, Niagara, ON L0S 1J0 Canada; Title Tel # (416) 468-2153 Title Fax # (416) 465-5438
Personnel: Editor-Jock Sutherland
General Info: Yr. Est. 1973, Quarterly, 4 pages
Circulation: Total-5,000

Readings

Publishing Co: New Dramatists, 424 W 44th St, New York, NY 10036-5298; Title Tel # (212) 757-6960
Personnel: Editor-Scott Stohler, Production Mgr.-Marl Lutwak, Art Dir.-Beth Nathason
General Info: 4 pages

Records of Early English Drama Newsletter
See: LITERATURE & LINGUISTICS

SDA Newsletter   *Association*

Publishing Co: Saskatchewan Drama Association, 2135 Albert St., #203, Regina, SK S4P 2V1 Canada Parent Co.-Saskatchewan Teachers' Federation, Saskatoon, Canada
Personnel: Editor-Catherine Anderson
Editorial Description: News and information for and about the Saskatchewan Drama Assn.
General Info: Semi-annually
Advertising: Inquire for rates.

Showboat Centennials
See: HISTORY

Spotlight Newsletter

Publishing Co: Cumberland County Playhouse, PO Box 484, Crossville, TN 38557-0484
General Info: Monthly, 4 pages

Super Trouper   *Association*

Publishing Co: Educational Theatre Association, 3368 Central Pky, Cincinnati, OH 45225-2307; Title Tel # (513) 559-1996
Personnel: Editor-Debbie Speed
Editorial Description: Association and theatre news, etc.
General Info: 3x/yr., Color
Circulation: Total-4,000

Technical Brief   *Business, Association*

Publishing Co: Yale School of Drama, 222 York St, New Haven, CT 06511-4804; Title Tel # (203) 432-9664 Title Fax # (203) 432-8336
Personnel: Publisher-Yale School of Drama, Editor-Don Harvey, Editor-Ben Sammler, Editor-Bronislau Sammler, Circ. Mgr.-Laraine Sammler
Editorial Description: Provides a dialogue between technical practicioners in the performing arts. Articles & drawings representing the best solutions to common technical problems.
General Info: Yr. Est. 1982, 3x/yr., Trim Size-8½ x 11, Offset press, 12 pages, ISSN: 1053-8860, No Color, Matte, Case bound
Subscriptions: Indv. $10, Inst. $14, Can. $13, For. $13, $5/copy
Acquistions: Publication Sold
Circulation: Total-600, Readership-1,000
Advertising: Inquire for rates.
List Rental: Actives: 600, $50/M
Printing Co: MSC, Yale University, New Haven, CT 06520 Tel # (203) 785-4675

Theatre Events Guide, Inc.   *Consumer*

Publishing Co: Theatre Events Guide, Inc., 180 West End Ave Apt 26d, New York, NY 10023-4925; Title Tel # (212) 799-5901
Personnel: Publisher, Editor-Peter Moumousis, Adv. Dir.-Adele Gold, Promotion Dir.-William Berkowitz
Editorial Description: Information for New York City visitors in entertainment and other events in the city such as music, dance, sports, art, sightseeing, etc.
General Info: Yr. Est. 1960, Monthly, Trim Size-3¾ x 6, Offset press, 40 pages
Subscriptions: Indv. $18, $1/copy
Circulation: Total-50,000

Theatre Information Bulletin   *Business, Consumer*

Publishing Co: Corporate Information Svces., Inc., PO Box 965, Midlothian, VA 23113-0965; Title Tel # (203) 656-3300 Title Fax # (203) 656-3382
Personnel: Publisher-Rod Conklin, Editor-Richmond Shepard
Editorial Description: Current/advance information of professional theatre-NY, Regional, tours, summer theatres. Published monthly with weekly updates.
General Info: Yr. Est. 1944, Monthly, Mimeo press
Subscriptions: $5/copy

Theatre Products Report

Publishing Co: San Diego State Univ. Drama Dept., Publications, San Diego, CA 92182; Title Tel # (619) 594-6220
Personnel: Editor-William Hektner, Circ. Mgr.-Ed Gordon
General Info: Yr. Est. 1984, Trim Size-8½ x 11, 16 pages
Subscriptions: Indv. $12, Inst. $20, $6/copy

U.S. Outdoor Drama   *Association*

Publishing Co: Institute of Outdoor Drama, CB 3240 National Bank Plaza, Univ. of North Carolina, Chapel Hill, NC 27599-3240; Title Tel # (919) 962-1328 Title Fax # (919) 962-4212
Personnel: Editor-Cindy Biles
Editorial Description: Information related to outdoor historical drama production.
General Info: Yr. Est. 1963, Quarterly, Trim Size-8½ x 11, Sheetfed press, 8 pages, No Color, Coated, Saddle-stitched
Subscriptions: Indv. $12
Circulation: Total-1,500, Readership-2,500

WRITE!
See: FILM

TOBACCO

Ashtray Journal   *Business, Consumer*   CPM: $150
Publishing Co: Ashtray Collectors' Club, PO Box 11652, Houston, TX 77293-1652;
  Title Tel # (713) 442-7200
Editorial Description: Lists names and newsletter addresses of buyers, sellers, traders, clubs, publications and more related to the use of tobacco in any form.
General Info: Yr. Est. 1993, Bi-monthly
Subscriptions: Can. $21, For. $25, $5/copy
Circulation: Total-500
Advertising: $75.

Brandstand
   See: HOBBY

Executive Summary   *Association*
Publishing Co: Tobacco Merchants Assn. of the U.S., PO Box 8019, Princeton, NJ 08543-8019;
  Title Tel # (609) 275-4900
Personnel: Editor-Nancy Publicover
Editorial Description: Top-line news on tobacco & related industries.
General Info: Yr. Est. 1984, Weekly, Offset press, 2 pages, Ind/Abs/Online: Newsnet, No Color
Circulation: (100% controlled), Total-833

Mealey's Litigation Report: Tobacco
   See: LAW

Production & Disposition of
   Tobacco Products   *Business, Association*
Publishing Co: Statistics Canada, Holland Ave/RH Coats, Holland Ave/Tunney's Pasture, Ottawa, ON K1A O26 Canada Tel # (613) 951-8116 Fax # (613) 951-0581; Title Tel # (613) 951-1581 Title Fax # (613) 951-1584
Editorial Description: Production, sales and inventory of cigarettes, cigars, cut tobacco, etc. 32-022.
General Info: Monthly, 3 pages, ISSN: 0708-336X
Subscriptions: Indv. $6, Can. $5, For. $7, $6/copy

TMA Issues Monitor   *Association*
Publishing Co: Tobacco Merchants Assn. of the U.S., PO Box 8019, Princeton, NJ 08543-8019;
  Title Tel # (609) 275-4900
Personnel: Editor-Farrell Delman
Editorial Description: Current issues and developments in the tobacco industry.
General Info: Yr. Est. 1980, Annually, Ind/Abs/Online: Newsnet
Circulation: (100% controlled), Total-500

TMA Leaf Bulletin   *Association*
Publishing Co: Tobacco Merchants Assn. of the U.S., PO Box 8019, Princeton, NJ 08543-8019;
  Title Tel # (609) 275-4900
Personnel: Editor-Thomas Slane
Editorial Description: Current developments affecting leaf tobacco markets in U.S. and abroad.
General Info: Yr. Est. 1950, Bi-weekly, Trim Size-8½ x 11, Offset press, 4 pages, Ind/Abs/Online: Newsnet, No Color
Circulation: (100% controlled), Total-300

TMA Tobacco Taxes Guide   *Association*
Publishing Co: Tobacco Merchants Assn. of the U.S., PO Box 8019, Princeton, NJ 08543-8019;
  Title Tel # (609) 275-4900
Personnel: Editor-James Vari
Editorial Description: Summaries of key provisions of the tobacco taxlaws, all tobacco products, all states.
General Info: Yr. Est. 1962, Quarterly, Trim Size-8½ x 11, Looseleaf
Circulation: Total-253

TMA Tobacco Weekly
Publishing Co: Tobacco Merchants Assn. of the U.S., PO Box 8019, Princeton, NJ 08543-8019;
  Title Tel # (609) 275-4900
Personnel: Editor-Nancy Publicover
Editorial Description: News on domestic tobacco and related industries.
General Info: (Formerly Executive Summary), Yr. Est. 1984, Weekly, 2 pages, Ind/Abs/Online: Newsnet
Circulation: (100% controlled), Total-833

TMA World Alert   *Association*
Publishing Co: Tobacco Merchants Assn. of the U.S., PO Box 8019, Princeton, NJ 08543-8019;
  Title Tel # (609) 275-4900
Personnel: Editor-Darryl Jayson
Editorial Description: News on international tobacco and related industries.
General Info: (Formerly International Executive Summary), Yr. Est. 1985, Weekly, 12 pages
Circulation: Total-500

Tobacco Barometer:
   Cigarettes Cigars   *Business, Association*
Publishing Co: Tobacco Merchants Assn. of the U.S., PO Box 8019, Princeton, NJ 08543-8019;
  Title Tel # (609) 275-4900
Personnel: Editor-Thomas Slane
Editorial Description: Taxable, tax-exempt removals, cigarettes, cigars, little cigars, chewing tobacco, pipes tobacco, statistics.
General Info: Yr. Est. 1923, Monthly, Trim Size-8½ x 11, Offset press, 4 pages, Ind/Abs/Online: Newsnet, No Color
Circulation: Total-350

Tobacco Barometer:
   Smoking, Chewing, Snuff   *Consumer, Association*
Publishing Co: Tobacco Merchants Assn. of the U.S., PO Box 8019, Princeton, NJ 08543-8019;
  Title Tel # (609) 275-4900
Personnel: Editor-Thomas Slane
Editorial Description: Sales of smoking tobacco, chewing tobacco, snuff.
General Info: Yr. Est. 1923, Quarterly, Trim Size-8½ x 11, Offset press, 4 pages, No Color
Circulation: Total-325

Tobacco Industry Litigation Reporter
   See: LAW

Tobacco Merchants Assn.
   of the U.S.-Legislative
   Bulletin
Publishing Co: Tobacco Merchants Assn. of the U.S., PO Box 8019, Princeton, NJ 08543-8019;
  Title Tel # (609) 275-4900
Personnel: Editor-James Vari
Editorial Description: Federal and state legislative activity on all issues affecting all tobacco products.
General Info: (Formerly Natl. Bulletin), Yr. Est. 1967, Bi-weekly, 8 pages, Ind/Abs/Online: Newsnet
Circulation: Total-425

Tobacco Products Litigation
   Reporter
Publishing Co: TPLR, Inc., Box 1162, Back Bay Annex, Boston, MA 02117-1162;
  Title Tel # (617) 424-0094 Title Fax # (617) 393-3672
Personnel: Editor-Richard Daynard, Production Mgr.-Susan Laws
Editorial Description: A resource for tobacco liability litigators. Hundreds of pages of material per year including updates of legal opinions.
General Info: Yr. Est. 1986, Monthly, 200 pages, Looseleaf
Subscriptions: Indv. $725

Tobacco Trade Barometer:
   Exports   *Association*
Publishing Co: Tobacco Merchants Assn. of the U.S., PO Box 8019, Princeton, NJ 08543-8019;
  Title Tel # (609) 275-4900
Personnel: Editor-Thomas Slane
Editorial Description: Exports tobacco leaf and products, monthly by country of destination.
General Info: Yr. Est. 1970, Monthly, Trim Size-8½ x 11, Offset press, 4 pages, Ind/Abs/Online: Newsnet, No Color
Circulation: Total-250

Tobacco Trade Barometer:
   Imports   *Association*
Publishing Co: Tobacco Merchants Assn. of the U.S., PO Box 8019, Princeton, NJ 08543-8019;
  Title Tel # (609) 275-4900
Personnel: Editor-Thomas Slane
Editorial Description: Imports tobacco leaf and products monthly, by country of origin.
General Info: Yr. Est. 1970, Monthly, Trim Size-8½ x 11, Offset press, 4 pages, Ind/Abs/Online: Newsnet, No Color
Subscriptions: Free
Circulation: Total-225

Tobacco on Trial
Publishing Co: TPLR, Inc., Box 1162, Back Bay Annex, Boston, MA 02117-1162;
  Title Tel # (617) 373-2026 Title Fax # (617) 373-3672
Personnel: Editor-Laurie Morin
Editorial Description: Summarizes developments in tobacco litigation and other developments in the battle against the tobacco industry.
General Info: Yr. Est. 1985, 10x/yr.
Subscriptions: Indv. $95

TRACK & FIELD

4 for 20
   See: SPORTS & SPORTING GOODS

Flying Lizards Newsletter *Consumer*

Publishing Co: Flying Lizards Athletic Club, 911 4th St, Jackson, MI 49203-3048; Title Tel # (517) 788-9261
Personnel: Publisher, Editor-Gary Pageau
Editorial Description: Designed for competitive runners and other active people.
General Info: Yr. Est. 1981, Bi-monthly, Trim Size-8½ x 11, 2 pages
Subscriptions: Free To Qualified Recipient

Joe Henderson's Running Commentary

Publishing Co: Rodale Press, 33 East Minor St., Emmaus, PA 18098-0001 Tel # (610) 967-5171 Fax # (610) 967-8963; Title Tel # (215) 967-5171
Personnel: Editor-Joe Henderson
Editorial Description: For participants in long-distance, marathon-type running; news, comment, practical advice.
General Info: Yr. Est. 1982, Monthly, Web press, 4 pages, No Color, Newsprint
Subscriptions: Indv. $36, Inst. $21, Can. $19, For. $21
Acquistions: Publication Sold
Circulation: Total-1,000
Printing Co: Eugene Copy Center, 224 E 11th Ave, Eugene, OR 97401-3247 Tel # (503) 344-4062

Track Newsletter *Consumer*

Publishing Co: Track & Field News, 2570 El Camino Real, #606, Mountain View, CA 94040-1300; Title Tel # (415) 948-8188 Title Fax # (415) 948-9445
Personnel: Editor-Garry Hill, Circ. Mgr-Erica Pahl
Editorial Description: Contains results and summaries of track meets.
General Info: Yr. Est. 1955, 42x/yr., Trim Size-8½ x 11, Offset press, 8 pages, No Color
Subscriptions: Indv. $49, Can. $49, For. $75
Circulation: Total-500

TRAFFIC & TRANSPORTATION

AAMVA Bulletin
See: AUTOMOTIVE

ABA Regulatory Digest *Association*

Publishing Co: American Bus Assn., 1100 New York Ave. NW, Suite 1050, Washington, DC 20005-3934; Title Tel # (202) 842-1645
Personnel: Editor-Charles Webb
General Info: Semi-weekly
Subscriptions: Free With Membership

ABF By-Lines
See: HOUSE ORGANS

ARTBA Newsletter
See: ROADS & STREETS

ASTRALOG Newsletter *Association*

Publishing Co: American Society of Transportation & Logistics, 216 E Church St, Lock Haven, PA 17745-2010; Title Tel # (502) 451-8150
Personnel: Circ. Mgr.-Eugene Knapp, Editor, Production Mgr., Promotion Dir.-Otis Amanda Dick
Editorial Description: Newsletter of society activities & member news.
General Info: Yr. Est. 1946, Bi-monthly, Trim Size-8½ x 11, Sheetfed press, 4 pages, No Color, Newsprint
Circulation: (100% controlled)
List Rental: Actives: $125/M
Printing Co: Commonwealth Printing Co., 2901 S 2nd St, Louisville, KY 40208-1405 Tel # (502) 636-1100

ATSSA Newsletter (Flash) *Business, Association*

Publishing Co: American Traffic Safety Services Assn., 5440 Jefferson Davis Hwy, Fredericksburg, VA 22407-2627; Title Fax # (703) 898-5510
Personnel: Publisher-Robert Garrett, Editor-Caroline Carver, Mktg. Dir.-Shawn Settle
Editorial Description: Information on current specifications; traffic control industry & members of assoc.
General Info: Monthly, Trim Size-8½ x 11, Desktop press, 12 pages, No Color
Subscriptions: Free With Membership
Circulation: (100% controlled), Total-980
Printing Co: Cardinal Press, 125 Industrial Dr, Fredericksburg, VA 22408-2409 Tel # (703) 898-4351

AWO Letter *Business, Association*

Publishing Co: American Waterways Operators, 1600 Wilson Blvd Ste 1000, Arlington, VA 22209-2597; Title Tel # (703) 841-9300 Title Fax # (703) 841-0389
Personnel: Editor-Tia Gibbs
Editorial Description: News, & analysis of domestic waterway transportation issues, safety, oil spills, trade, operations, locks & dams, legislatiton & environmental protection.
General Info: Yr. Est. 1944, Bi-weekly, Trim Size-8½ x 11, Sheetfed press, 8 pages, 2 Color, Newsprint
Subscriptions: Indv. $75
Circulation: Total-3,000
Advertising: Accepts Inserts.

Advanced Transportation Technology News *Business*

Publishing Co: Business Communications Co., 25 Van Zant St., Ste.13, Norwalk, CT 06855-1781; Title Tel # (203) 853-4266 Title Fax # (203) 853-0348
Personnel: Publisher-Louis Natvrman, Editor-Bob Katzoff, Mktg. Dir.-Robert Butler
Editorial Description: Brings you the latest technical and business related developments in the entire transportation sector, and the applications of related technologies to rail, ships, and aircraft as well.
General Info: Yr. Est. 1994, Monthly, Trim Size-8½ x 11, 14 pages, ISSN: 1077-6877
Subscriptions: Indv. $365, Can. $415, For. $415, $35/copy
Advertising: Inquire for rates.
List Rental: List Management Co.: W.I. Mail Marketing, 470 Main St. #317, Ridgefield, CT 06877-4516 Tel # (203) 438-6822, Fax # (203) 438-7756

Aviation Regulatory Digest Service *Business*

Publishing Co: Hawkins Publishing Co., Inc., 1207 B Central Avenue, Box 480, Mayo, MD 21106; Title Tel # (410) 798-1677 Title Fax # (410) 798-1098
Personnel: Publisher, Editor-C.R. Eyler
Editorial Description: A loose-leaf indexed-analysis of reports of the Dept. of Transportation, Civil Aeronautics Board, the Federal & U. S. Supreme Courts.
General Info: Yr. Est. 1965, Monthly, Trim Size-8½ x 11, Sheetfed press, No Color, Matte, Looseleaf
Subscriptions: Indv. $320

Bohman Traffic News Summary

Publishing Co: Bohman Industrial Traffic Consultants, Inc., 335 Broadway, Box 889, Gardner, MA 01440; Title Tel # (508) 632-1913 Title Fax # (508) 945-4815
General Info: Yr. Est. 1976, Monthly
Subscriptions: Indv. $30

British Columbia Motor Transport Assn., News & Views *Business, Association*

Publishing Co: British Columbia Trucking Assn., 1-1610 Kebet Way, Port Coquitlam, BC V3C 5W1 Canada Tel # (604) 942-3206 Fax # (604) 942-3191
Personnel: Editor-Rob Weston
General Info: Bi-weekly, Mimeo press, 15 pages, No Color
Circulation: Total-550

Buses Intl. Assn. Newsletter *Business, Association*

Publishing Co: Buses Intl. Assn., PO Box 1472, Spokane, WA 99210-1472; Title Tel # (509) 328-9181 Title Fax # (509) 325-5396
Personnel: Editor-William Luke
Editorial Description: Newsletter for members of the Buses Intl. Assn.
General Info: Yr. Est. 1981, Quarterly, Trim Size-8½ x 5½, Web press, 12 pages, Color-cover, Coated, Saddle-stitched
Subscriptions: Indv. $25

CRA Review
See: ECONOMICS

CTS Network

Publishing Co: Center for Transportation, Morgan State Univ., Box 924, Baltimore, MD 21239-4093; Title Tel # (301) 444-3394
Personnel: Editor-Vernessa Woods
Editorial Description: The CTS Network Newsletter is published in an effort to establish a communication link among Historically Black Colleges & Universities (HBCUs) to share information concerning education, research & career opportunities in transportation.
General Info: Yr. Est. 1984, Semi-annually, 4 pages
Acquistions: Publication Bought
Circulation: Total-1,500
Printing Co: Time Printers, Inc., 227 N Warwick Ave, Baltimore, MD 21223-1416

CUTA Forum *Association*

Publishing Co: Canadian Urban Transit Assn., 55 York St., Suite 901, Toronto, ON M5J 1R7 Canada; Title Tel # (416) 365-9800
Personnel: Editor-A. Cormier, Production Mgr., Adv. Dir.-David Onodera
Editorial Description: News of the urban transit industry, including equipment, personnel, technology, etc. Canadian focus.
General Info: (Formerly Transit Topics), Yr. Est. 1955, Monthly, Trim Size-8½ x 11, Sheetfed press, 22 pages, 2 Color, Coated, Saddle-stitched
Circulation: (100% controlled), Total-600
Advertising: Inquire for rates.

California Vehicle Code
See: LAW

Canadian Motorcycle Assn., The Link

Publishing Co: Canadian Motorcycle Assn., Inc., 500 James St. N., #201, Hamilton, ON L8L 1J3 Canada; Title Tel # (905) 522-5705 Title Fax # (905) 522-5716
Personnel: Editor-Marilyn Bastedo
General Info: Yr. Est. 1980, Bi-monthly
Subscriptions: Free With Membership
Circulation: Total-7,000
Advertising: Accepts Inserts.

Canadian Museum Of Flight And Transportation
See: AERONAUTICS/ASTRONAUTICS

Canadian Trade Law
Reporter   *Business*

Publishing Co: CCH Canadian Ltd., 6 Garamond Ct., North York, ON M3C 1Z5 Canada
Fax # (416) 444-8011 Parent Co.-CCH, Inc., Riverwoods; Title Tel # (416) 441-2992
Title Fax # (416) 444-4011
General Info: Monthly, Looseleaf
Subscriptions: Can. $380

Canadian Transportation
Law Reporter   *Business*

Publishing Co: CCH Canadian Ltd., 6 Garamond Ct., North York, ON M3C 1Z5 Canada
Fax # (416) 444-8011 Parent Co.-CCH, Inc., Riverwoods; Title Tel # (416) 441-2992
Title Fax # (416) 444-9011
Editorial Description: Provides authoritative, current & ongoing coverage of Federal & Provincial
laws & regulations governing transportation of goods by rail, road, water, air, and pipeline.
General Info: Yr. Est. 1990, Monthly, Looseleaf
Subscriptions: Can. $370

Confidential Air Letter
See: AERONAUTICS/ASTRONAUTICS

Distribution Center Management
See: BUSINESS & INDUSTRY

Distributor's & Wholesaler's Advisor, The
See: BUSINESS & INDUSTRY

Docket

Publishing Co: United Bus Owners of America, 1300 L St NW Ste 1050, Washington, DC
20005-4107; Title Tel # (202) 484-5623
General Info: Monthly
Circulation: Total-2,000

Driver Trainer Newsletter
See: SAFETY

Dual News

Publishing Co: Driving School Assn. of the Americas, 111 W Pomona Blvd, Monterey Park, CA
91754-7208; Title Tel # (213) 728-2100
Personnel: Publisher, Editor-George Hensel
Editorial Description: Deals with traffic safety, teaching techniques, legislation and operating
techniques of interest to driving schools throughout the United States and Canada.
General Info: Monthly, 8 pages, 3% ads
Subscriptions: Indv. $150
Circulation: (70% controlled)
Advertising: Inquire for rates. Accepts Inserts.

Electric Vehicle News   *Business, Consumer*

Publishing Co: Electric Vehicle News, PO Box 148, Arlington, VA 22210-0148
Personnel: Editor-Lewis Gulick
Editorial Description: Product and other news on developments in the electric vehicle industry.
General Info: 11x/yr.
Circulation: Total-600

Environmental Bulletin
See: ENVIRONMENT & ECOLOGY

European Travel Report
See: TRAVEL

Expediter
See: MILITARY & NAVAL

Federal Carriers Reports   *Business*

Publishing Co: CCH, Inc., 2700 Lake Cook Rd., Riverwoods, IL 60015 Parent Co.-Kluwer Law &
Taxation Publishers, Cambridge; Title Tel # (847) 267-7000 Title Fax # (800) 224-8299
Editorial Description: Federal controls over motor and water carriers, freight forwarders.
General Info: Yr. Est. 1937, Bi-weekly, Trim Size-6 x 9, Web press, No Color, Looseleaf
Subscriptions: Indv. $1,280

Federal Maritime Commission Digest Service
See: SHIPS & SHIPPING

Fleet Safety Newsletter-
Motor Transportation   *Association*

Publishing Co: National Safety Council, 1121 Spring Lake Dr., Itasca, IL 60143-3201
Tel # (708) 285-1121 Fax # (708) 775-2285; Title Tel # (312) 527-4800
General Info: Yr. Est. 1966, Bi-monthly, Trim Size-8½ x 11, 4 pages, 2 Color
Subscriptions: Indv. $7
Circulation: Total-13,000

Fleet Street   *Business*   CPM: $64

Publishing Co: Greenwich Consulting, 15821 Setlock Ave., Chino Hills, CA 91709;
Title Fax # (909) 393-9405
Personnel: Publisher-Richard Bathurst, Editor-James Holzer, Circ. Mgr.-Tony Vercillo, Production
Mgr.-Karen Edwards, Adv. Dir.-Bob Matheny, Mktg. Dir.-Leigh Fryant
Editorial Description: Consulting newsletter geared toward Distribution and Fleet Management
Executives - provides transportation managers with cost-cutting methodologies, expert techniques
and sound ideas to change the way they do business.
General Info: Yr. Est. 1993, Quarterly, Trim Size-8½ x 11, Web press, 16 pages, 2 Color, Matte,
Saddle-stitched
Subscriptions: Indv. $199, Inst. $199, Can. $199, For. $199
Circulation: Total-15,500
Advertising: $995.
List Rental: List Management Co.: Manager: Lisa Carole Gray; Greenwich Consulting, 15821 Fetlock
Ln, Chino Hills, CA 91709-5232, Actives: 15,000, $60/M
Printing Co: RC Graphics, 1715 Newport Cir, Santa Ana, CA 92705-5111 Tel # (714) 436-1501,
Fax # (714) 436-1503

Florida Motor Vehicle Laws
See: LAW

Freight Management Report   *Business*

Publishing Co: Transportation Research Assocs., 154 Pulaski Blvd, Toms River, NJ 08757-6426;
Title Tel # (201) 505-0970
Personnel: Publisher, Editor, Production Mgr.-Thomas Dillon, Circ. Mgr., Art Dir., Promotion Dir.-Ellen
Dillon
Editorial Description: Monthly report on freight transportation economics, and cost reduction
methods.
General Info: (Formerly Freight Marketing Report), Yr. Est. 1983, Monthly, Offset press, 8 pages,
ISSN: 0892-3566, No Color, Newsprint
Subscriptions: Indv. $135

G-Map, the Geographic Information, Mapping & Publishing Newsletter
See: GEOGRAPHY

Goods in Transit   *Business*

Publishing Co: Matthew Bender & Co., 11 Penn Plaza, New York, NY 10001-2006
Tel # (212) 967-7707 Fax # (212) 244-3188
Editorial Description: How to recover or avoid liability for lost, damaged or delayed goods shipped
by air, sea, rail or truck anywhere in the world. Practical coverage of the rights, obligations and
remedies for losses, demages and delays.
General Info: Yr. Est. 1976, Irregular, Looseleaf

HazMat Transport News
See: TRUCKING

Hazardous Materials
Transportation   *Business*

Publishing Co: Bureau of National Affairs, Inc., 1231 25th St. NW, Bldg. N-200, Washington, DC
20037-1157 Fax # (202) 822-8092; Title Tel # (202) 452-4200 Title Fax # (202) 452-4610
Personnel: Publisher-William A. Beltz, Mng. Editor-Bernard S. Chabel, Circ. Dir.-Gary C. Seltzer
Editorial Description: Contains rules & regulations governing shipment of hazardous materials by
rail, air, ship, highway & pipeline, including DOT's Hazardous Materials Tables & EPA's rule for its
hazardous waste tracking system.
General Info: Yr. Est. 1982, Monthly, Trim Size-8½ x 11, Offset press, ISSN: 0148-7973, Looseleaf
Subscriptions: Indv. $624

Hazardous Materials Transportation
See: ENVIRONMENT & ECOLOGY

Highway & Vehicle Safety Report
See: SAFETY

Highway Common Carrier News Letter
See: TRUCKING

Highway Financing & Construction/State Capitals
See: ROADS & STREETS

IE News:
Transportation &
Distribution   *Association*

Publishing Co: Institute of Industrial Engineers, 25 Technology Park/Atlanta, Norcross, GA
30092-2988 Tel # (770) 449-0461; Title Tel # (404) 449-0460 Title Fax # (770) 263-8532
Personnel: Production Mgr.-Dona Brown
Editorial Description: Newsletter for IIE Transportation & Distribution Division.
General Info: Quarterly, Trim Size-8½ x 11, Sheetfed press, 4 pages, 2 Color, Matte, Saddle-stitched
Circulation: (100% controlled), Total-1,600
Advertising: Inquire for rates. Accepts Inserts.
List Rental: Rents Lists

IEEE Vehicular Technology Society News
See: ENGINEERING

ITS Review
Business, Association

Publishing Co: Univ. of California Transportation Studies Inst., Inst. of Transport. Studies, 109 Mclaughlin Hall, Berkeley, CA 94720-0001; Title Tel # (510) 642-3585 Title Fax # (510) 642-1246
Personnel: Editor-Betsy Wing
Editorial Description: Articles on ITS research & education programs.
General Info: (Formerly Institute of Transportation), Yr. Est. 1977, Quarterly, Sheetfed press, 8 pages, ISSN: 0192-3994, 2 Color, Newsprint
Subscriptions: Free To Qualified Recipient
Circulation: Total-5,000
Printing Co: University of California Printing, 2120 Oxford St. Univ. Of, California, Berkeley, CA 94720-7340

Illinois Vehicle Code
See: LAW

Impact
See: SAFETY

Impact: A Journal of Safety Litigation and News
See: AUTOMOTIVE

Inside DOT and Transportation Week
Business, Association

Publishing Co: Business Publishers, Inc., 951 Pershing Dr., Silver Spring, MD 20910-4464 Tel # (301) 589-5103 Fax # (301) 589-8493
General Info: Yr. Est. 1990, Weekly, Sheetfed press, 2 Color, Newsprint, Saddle-stitched
Subscriptions: $15/copy

Inside IVHS: Intelligent Vehicle/Highway Systems Update
Business

Publishing Co: Waters Information Services, PO Box 2248, Binghamton, NY 13902-2248 Tel # (607) 770-4075 Fax # (607) 770-9435; Title Tel # (607) 770-9242 Title Fax # (607) 798-1692
Personnel: Publisher-Dennis Waters, Exec. Ed.-Philip Alling, Mng. Editor-Merrill Douglas, Adv. Dir.-George Divinell, Circ. Mgr., Mktg. Dir.-Allan Nixon
Editorial Description: Covers the intelligent vehicle/highway system industry in North America.
General Info: Yr. Est. 1991, Bi-weekly, 16 pages, ISSN: 1054-2647, Ind/Abs/Online: Newsnet, Predicasts
Subscriptions: Indv. $495, Can. $495, For. $645, $25/copy

Intelligent Highway, The
Business

Publishing Co: Waters Information Services, PO Box 2248, Binghamton, NY 13902-2248; Title Tel # (607) 770-4075 Title Fax # (607) 770-9435
Personnel: Circ. Dir.-Allan Nixon
Editorial Description: Reports on the Intelligent Vehicle/Highway Systems industry in Europe.
General Info: Bi-weekly
Subscriptions: Indv. $495

Intercom

Publishing Co: Washington Metropolitan Area Transit Authority, 600 5th St NW, Washington, DC 20001-2651; Title Tel # (202) 962-1056
Personnel: Publisher, Editor, Circ. Mgr., Art Dir.-Paul Willis
Editorial Description: Employee newspaper. News about Metro, features about employees.
General Info: Yr. Est. 1980, Monthly, Trim Size-8½ x 11, Sheetfed press, 16 pages, No Color, Newsprint
Circulation: Total-8,500

Interconnect
See: SAFETY

Intermodal Reporter
Business

Publishing Co: K-III Directory Corp., 10 Lake Dr., PO Box 4000, Hightstown, NJ 08520 Tel # (909) 371-7700; Title Tel # (202) 626-4510
Personnel: Publisher-D. Byrne, Editor-K. Hoffman, Circ. Mgr.-D. Heist, Production Mgr.-C. Lovelace
Editorial Description: News & analysis of the Intermodal industry.
General Info: Yr. Est. 1985, Bi-weekly, 8 pages, ISSN: 0882-8059
Subscriptions: Indv. $230, $3/copy
Circulation: Total-1,250
List Rental: List Management Co.: Venture Communications, 60 Madison Avenue, 3rd fl., New York, NY 10010 Tel # (212) 684-4800, Fax # (212) 545-1680, Actives: 1,345, $250/M

International Transportation Assn. Newsletter

Publishing Co: Intermodal Transportation Assn., 6410 Kenilworth Ave Ste 108, Riverdale, MD 20737-1202; Title Tel # (301) 864-2661
General Info: Yr. Est. 1981, Monthly

Japan Transportation Scan
See: AUTOMOTIVE

KUTC Newsletter

Publishing Co: University of Kansas Transportation Center, 2011 Learned Hall, Lawrence, KS 66045-2965; Title Tel # (913) 864-5658 Title Fax # (913) 864-3199
Personnel: Editor-Lisa Harris
General Info: (Formerly TRG Newsletter), Yr. Est. 1979, Quarterly, Trim Size-8½ x 11, Offset press, 20 pages, No Color, Matte, Saddle-stitched
Subscriptions: Free
Circulation: Total-5,600

Kansas Trans Reporter
Business, Consumer

Publishing Co: University of Kansas Transportation Center, 2011 Learned Hall, Lawrence, KS 66045-2965 Tel # (913) 864-5658 Fax # (913) 864-3199; Title Tel # (913) 869-5658
Personnel: Editor-Lisa Harris
Editorial Description: Published for rural and specialized transportation providers in Kansas.
General Info: Yr. Est. 1987, Quarterly, No Color, Matte, Saddle-stitched
Subscriptions: Free

LNG Express

Publishing Co: Zeus Development Corporation, P.O. Box 272505, Houston, TX 77277-2505; Title Tel # (713) 952-9500 Title Fax # (713) 782-9594
Editorial Description: Central information source for LNG's expanding use in transporation.
General Info: Yr. Est. 1991, Monthly
Subscriptions: Indv. $297

Lemon Times
See: AUTOMOTIVE

Lexington Quarterly

Publishing Co: Lexington Group in Transportation History, Dept. of History, St. Cloud St. U., St. Cloud, MN 56301; Title Tel # (612) 255-4906 Title Fax # (612) 654-5198
Personnel: Editor-Don Hofsommer
Editorial Description: Bibliographic data in transportation history.
General Info: (Formerly Lexington Newsletter), Yr. Est. 1942, Quarterly, Trim Size-8½ x 11, Sheetfed press, 14 pages, ISSN: 0888-7837, 1% ads, No Color
Subscriptions: Indv. $15
Circulation: Total-500
Advertising: Inquire for rates. Accepts Inserts.
List Rental: Rents Lists

Mass. Transit
Consumer, Association

Publishing Co: Assn. for Public Transportation, 100 Boylston St Ste 200, Boston, MA 02116-4610; Title Tel # (617) 482-0282 Title Fax # (617) 695-9805
Personnel: Editor-Charles Bahne
Editorial Description: Issues relating to public transit in greater Boston & Eastern Massachusetts.
General Info: Yr. Est. 1986, Quarterly, Trim Size-8½ x 11, Sheetfed press, 4 pages, No Color, Recycled
Subscriptions: Indv. $7
Circulation: Total-2,500
Printing Co: McAdams Industries, Broadway, Cambridge, MA Tel # (617) 354-3019

McTrans

Publishing Co: Center for Microcomputers in Transportation, 512 Weil Hall, Univ. of Fl., Gainesville, FL 32611-2083; Title Tel # (904) 392-0378
Personnel: Publisher-C.E. Wallace, Editor-William Sampson, Circ. Mgr.-Eric Roberson, Circ. Mgr.-Ruth Tower
Editorial Description: Information about microcomputer software & resources in transportation.
General Info: Yr. Est. 1986, Quarterly, Trim Size-8½ x 11, Web press, 32 pages, No Color, Newsprint
Circulation: Total-8,000
Advertising: Inquire for rates.
List Rental: Actives: $22/M

Messenger & Delivery Services Newsletter

Publishing Co: Messenger & Delivery Services Newsletter, 149 Dawson Ave, Clifton, NJ 07012-1131; Title Tel # (201) 779-3582
Personnel: Editor-Peter Abbate
General Info: Yr. Est. 1979, Bi-monthly
Subscriptions: Indv. $23

Michigan Motor Vehicle Laws
See: LAW

Mighty Mopars
See: AUTOMOTIVE

Motor Carrier-Freight Forwarder Service
Business

Publishing Co: Hawkins Publishing Co., Inc., 1207 B Central Avenue, Box 480, Mayo, MD 21106; Title Tel # (410) 798-1677 Title Fax # (410) 798-1098
Personnel: Publisher, Editor-C.R. Eyler
Editorial Description: A looseleaf indexed-anaylsis of reports of Interstate Commerce Commission, the Federal and US Supreme Courts relating to the Interstate Commerce Act in four volumes supplemented monthly.
General Info: Yr. Est. 1938, Monthly, Trim Size-8 x 10¾, Sheetfed press, No Color, Matte, Looseleaf
Subscriptions: $375/copy
Circulation: Total-600

Museum Newsletter
See: MUSEUM PUBLICATIONS

NAATS Bulletin

Publishing Co: Natl. Assn. of Air Traffic Specialists, 11303 Amherst Ave Ste 4, Silver Spring, MD 20902-4600; Title Tel # (301) 595-2012
Personnel: Editor-Joanne Bentz
Editorial Description: Labor union newsletters.
General Info: Bi-monthly

NOACA News
See: PUBLIC MANAGEMENT & PLANNING

NYC Traffic Rules & Regulations
See: LAW

National Automobile Transporters Association, Bulletin

Publishing Co: National Automobile Transporters Assn., 902 Buhl Bldg., Detroit, MI 48226; Title Tel # (313) 965-6533

National School Transportation Assn. - Newsletter

Publishing Co: Natl. School Transportation Assn., PO Box 2639, Springfield, VA 22152-0639; Title Tel # (703) 644-0700
Personnel: Editor-Karen Finkel
Editorial Description: Newsletter providing information on federal regulation affecting school busing.
General Info: Monthly
Circulation: Total-1,100

New Jersey Motor Vehicle & Traffic Laws
See: LAW

New York Streetcar News   *Business, Consumer*

Publishing Co: Committee for Better Transit, Inc., PO Box 3106, Long Island City, NY 11103-0106 Tel # (708) 728-0091; Title Tel # (718) 728-0091
Personnel: Publisher-Stephen Dobrow, Editor-Wayne Fields
Editorial Description: Covers the New York light rail transportation industry.
General Info: Yr. Est. 1994, Bi-monthly
Subscriptions: Indv. $12

New York Vehicle & Traffic Law

Publishing Co: Gould Publications, Inc, 1333 N US Highway 17-92, Longwood, FL 32750-3724 Tel # (407) 695-9500 Fax # (407) 695-2906; Title Tel # (607) 724-3000
Editorial Description: Text of vehicle & traffic law of N.Y. unannotated w/changes in text book.
General Info: (Formerly Vehicle & Traffic Laws of New York), Annually, Trim Size-5$\frac{1}{2}$ x 8$\frac{1}{2}$, Sheetfed press, 570 pages, No Color, Looseleaf
Subscriptions: $10/copy

Newsline

Publishing Co: Northwestern University's Transportation Center, 1936 Sheridan Rd, Evanston, IL 60208-0849; Title Tel # (847) 491-8350 Title Fax # (847) 491-3090
Personnel: Editor-Moira Toner
Editorial Description: News of research, education, and outreach activities of Northwestern University's Transportation Center.
General Info: Yr. Est. 1975, Semi-annually, Trim Size-8$\frac{1}{2}$ x 11, Web press, 40 pages, 2 Color, Matte, Saddle-stitched
Subscriptions: Free
Circulation: Total-12,000

Northeastern Limousine Operators Association Nor'Easter Newsletter   *Business, Association*

Publishing Co: Northeastern Limousine Operators Association, P.O. Box 2239-ESP, Albany, NY 12220-0239; Title Fax # (518) 356-7230
Personnel: Publisher, Editor, Editorial Page Ed., Feature Ed., Circ. Mgr., Production Mgr., Art Dir., Mktg. Dir., Promotion Dir.-K Irish
General Info: Yr. Est. 1986, Monthly, Trim Size-8$\frac{1}{2}$ x 11, Mimeo press, 10 pages, 2% ads, No Color
Subscriptions: Indv. $20, Inst. $15, Free With Membership
Acquistions: Publication Bought
Advertising: $88. Accepts Inserts.
List Rental: Rents Lists

Notes from Underground   *Association*

Publishing Co: Committee for Better Transit, Inc., PO Box 3106, Long Island City, NY 11103-0106 Tel # (708) 728-0091; Title Tel # (718) 728-0091
Personnel: Editor-Dr. Stephen B. Dobrow
Editorial Description: News and views on urban transportation and related subjects, with particular emphasis on New York-New Jersey metropolitan area.
General Info: (Formerly Better Transit Bulletin), Yr. Est. 1970, Irregular, Trim Size-8$\frac{1}{2}$ x 11, Offset press, 4 pages, ISSN: 0029-4039, No Color
Subscriptions: Indv. $16, Inst. $25, Can. $16
Circulation: Total-2,500
List Rental: Rents Lists

Ohio Motor Vehicle Laws
See: LAW

Orange Empire Railway Museum-Gazette

Publishing Co: Orange Empire Railway Museum, PO Box 548, Perris, CA 92572-0548; Title Tel # (714) 657-2605
Personnel: Editor-Jim Walker
General Info: Yr. Est. 1956, Monthly, Looseleaf

Paratranist News

Publishing Co: Paratransit, Inc., 2700 Stone Barn Ter, Lawrence, KS 66047-2845; Title Tel # (913) 749-0698
Personnel: Editor-Patricia Weaver
General Info: Yr. Est. 1985, 5x/yr., 6 pages

Passenger Shipping International
See: INTERNATIONAL TRADE

Planning Bulletin   *Association*

Publishing Co: American Assn. of State Highway Transportation Officials, 444 N Capitol St NW Ste 249, Washington, DC 20001-1512; Title Tel # (202) 624-5800
Personnel: Editor-David Clawson, Mktg. Dir.-Patty Kelley
Editorial Description: Information on highway and transportation planning.
General Info: Yr. Est. 1992, Irregular, Trim Size-8$\frac{1}{2}$ x 11, Mimeo press, 12 pages
Subscriptions: Inst. $100, Can. $100, For. $125

Portal

Publishing Co: Household Goods Forwarders Association of America, 2320 Mill Rd. #102, Alexandria, VA 22314-4691; Title Tel # (703) 293-1800
General Info: Monthly

Private Carrier
See: TRUCKING

Private Line
See: TRUCKING

Pro Bike News
See: CYCLING-BICYCLE & MOTOR

Pro-Development Letter/ Astra Log Newsletter   *Association*

Publishing Co: American Society of Transportation & Logistics, 216 E Church St, Lock Haven, PA 17745-2010; Title Tel # (502) 425-1780 Title Fax # (504) 425-1726
Personnel: Circ. Mgr.-Eugene Knapp, Editor, Production Mgr., Promotion Dir.-Otis Amanda Dick
Editorial Description: Newsletter for professional development in transportation & logistics.
General Info: Yr. Est. 1982, Bi-monthly, Trim Size-8$\frac{1}{2}$ x 11, Sheetfed press, 4 pages, No Color, Newsprint
Subscriptions: Indv. $25, $10/copy
List Rental: Actives: $125/M
Printing Co: Suburban Printing, 2152 Lancashire Ave, Louisville, KY 40205-2952 Tel # (502) 458-6574

Proclaim   *Association*

Publishing Co: Silesia Companies, Inc., 619 Broad Creek Dr, Fort Washington, MD 20744-5806 Tel # (301) 292-1970; Title Tel # (301) 292-1988 Title Fax # (301) 292-1787
Personnel: Editor-Dale Anderson
Editorial Description: Covers transportation freight claims & baggage losses.
General Info: Quarterly, Sheetfed press, 24 pages, Saddle-stitched
Subscriptions: Indv. $40
Circulation: Total-600
Advertising: Inquire for rates.
Printing Co: Silesia Companies, Inc., 619 Broad Creek Dr, Fort Washington, MD 20744-5806 Tel # (301) 292-2600

Professional Airways Systems Specialists- Dateline   *Business, Association*

Publishing Co: Professional Airways Systems Specialists, 1150 17th St NW,Ste 702, Washington, DC 20036-4603 Fax # (202) 293-7727; Title Tel # (202) 293-7277
General Info: Bi-monthly

Professional Airways Systems Specialists- Local Presidents Mailing

Publishing Co: Seaplane Pilots Assn., 421 Aviation Way, Frederick, MD 21701-4756 Fax # (301) 695-2375; Title Tel # (301) 695-2083

Profiles in PDM
See: MANAGEMENT

Quad Report, The
See: ENERGY

Quad Special Reports, The
See: ENERGY

Rail Business
See: RAILROADS

Rail Carrier Digest Service
See: RAILROADS

Rail Indiana
See: RAILROADS

Rail Mart, The
See: RAILROADS

Railway Progress News *Association*

Publishing Co: Railway Progress Institute, 700 N. Fairfax St., Suite 661, Alexandria, VA 22314-2098; Title Tel # (703) 836-2332 Title Fax # (703) 548-0058
Personnel: Editor-P.O. Hovey
General Info: (Formerly RPI Report), Irregular, 4 pages
Circulation: Total-1,500

Rider's Digest *Consumer*

Publishing Co: Sponsor-Metropolitan Atlanta Rapid Transit Authority, Marta, 2424 Piedmont Rd NE, Atlanta, GA 30324-3330; Title Tel # (404) 848-5157 Title Fax # (404) 848-5098
Personnel: Editor-Judith Weisberg
Editorial Description: Public transporation news, Atlanta events for the rapid transit rider.
General Info: (Formerly Two Bells), Yr. Est. 1921, Bi-weekly, Trim Size-8$\frac{1}{2}$ x 11, Sheetfed press, 2 pages, No Color, Newsprint
Acquistions: Publication Bought
Circulation: Total-155,000

Runzheimer Reports on Fleet Management *Business*

Publishing Co: Runzheimer Intl., Runzheimer Park, Rochester, WI 53167 Fax # (414) 767-2254; Title Tel # (414) 767-2200 Title Fax # (708) 291-9581
Personnel: Publisher-Bradford Burris, Editor-Robert Overend
Editorial Description: News & information for fleet managers.
General Info: Yr. Est. 1980, Monthly, Trim Size-8$\frac{1}{2}$ x 11, Sheetfed press, 14 pages, ISSN: 0730-8655, No Color, Newsprint
Subscriptions: Indv. $196, $20/copy
Acquistions: Publication Bought, Publication Sold
List Rental: List Management Co.: Edith Roman Associates, Inc., 253 W 35th St Fl 16th, New York, NY 10001-1907 Tel # (212) 695-3836

SC & RA Newsletter

Publishing Co: SC & RA Newsletter, 2750 Prospetity Ave., Suite #260, FairFax, VA 22031-4312; Title Tel # (703) 698-0291
Personnel: Editor-N. E. Brymer
General Info: (Formerly Weekly Notes), Yr. Est. 1945, Weekly, 4 pages
Circulation: Total-850

Safety & Compliance News
See: TRUCKING

Scan *Association*

Publishing Co: American Bus Assn., 1100 New York Ave. NW, Suite 1050, Washington, DC 20005-3934; Title Tel # (202) 842-1645
Personnel: Publisher-George Snyder, Jr., Editor-Ginger Grace
Editorial Description: Legislative & other news that affects the intercity bus industry & travel industry.
General Info: Monthly, Mimeo press, 10 pages, Color-cover, Newsprint
Subscriptions: Free With Membership
Circulation: Total-1,000

Sea-Tac Forum

Publishing Co: Port of Seattle, Aviation Communications, PO Box 68727, Seattle, WA 98168-0727 Tel # (206) 433-4645; Title Tel # (206) 433-4604 Title Fax # (206) 439-7725
Personnel: Co-Editor-Marlys St. Laurent, Co-Editor-Barbara Stewart
Editorial Description: Keeps airport neighbors informed about airport-related issues.
General Info: Yr. Est. 1985, Monthly, Trim Size-8$\frac{1}{2}$ x 11, Desktop press, 2 pages, 2 Color, Matte
Circulation: Total-27,000
Printing Co: Southgate Press, 15040 1st Ave., S., Seattle, WA 98148 Tel # (206) 248-1700, Fax # (206) 244-4740

Select Hostile Actions Against Civil Aviation
See: LAW ENFORCEMENT & PENOLOGY

Shore-Train Rider *Consumer, Association*

Publishing Co: Shore-Train Riders Club, 5503 Moreland Ct Apt 4, Mechanicsburg, PA 17055-5435
General Info: Quarterly

Signal *Association*

Publishing Co: American Traffic Safety Services Assn., 5440 Jefferson Davis Hwy, Fredericksburg, VA 22407-2627; Title Fax # (703) 898-5510
Personnel: Publisher-Bob Garrett, Editor-Caroline Carver, Mktg. Dir.-Shawn Settle
Editorial Description: Contains information on current regulations & specifications in the traffic control industry. Sent to municipal, state & city employees.
General Info: Quarterly, Trim Size-8$\frac{1}{2}$ x 11, Desktop press, 8 pages, 2 Color, Matte
Subscriptions: Free To Qualified Recipient
Circulation: Total-4,300
Advertising: Accepts Inserts.
Printing Co: Cardinal Press, 125 Industrial Dr, Fredericksburg, VA 22408-2409 Tel # (703) 898-4351

Southern Motor Carriers Bulletin

Publishing Co: Southern Motor Carriers Bulletin, 1307 Peachtree St NE, Atlanta, GA 30309-3503; Title Tel # (404) 892-2434

TAC News *Business, Association*

Publishing Co: Transportation Assn. of Canada, 2323 St. Laurent Blvd., Ottawa, ON K1G 4K6 Canada; Title Tel # (613) 736-1350 Title Fax # (613) 736-1395
Editorial Description: Covers TAC's activities & transportation in general.
General Info: (Formerly TAC Express), Yr. Est. 1975, Bi-monthly, Trim Size-8$\frac{1}{2}$ x 11, Sheetfed press, 8 pages, ISSN: 0317-1280, 1% ads, No Color
Subscriptions: Indv. $60
Circulation: Total-2,100
Advertising: Inquire for rates. Accepts Inserts.

TAC News/Nouvelles de L'ATC *Business, Association*

Publishing Co: Transportation Assn. of Canada, 2323 St. Laurent Blvd., Ottawa, ON K1G 4K6 Canada; Title Tel # (613) 736-1350 Title Fax # (613) 736-1395
Personnel: Editor-Harvey Chartrand
Editorial Description: French edition of Transportation Assn. of Canada newsletter--TAC News.
General Info: (Formerly Nouvelles de l'ATC/Express de l'ATC), Yr. Est. 1975, Bi-monthly, Trim Size-8$\frac{1}{2}$ x 11, Sheetfed press, 8 pages, ISSN: 0317-2422, No Color
Subscriptions: Indv. $60
Circulation: Total-250
Advertising: Accepts Inserts.

TD Access & Safety Report *Business*

Publishing Co: Serif Press, 1331 H St., N.W., Washington, DC 20005; Title Tel # (202) 737-4650 Title Fax # (202) 783-1931
Personnel: Publisher-Roseann Schwaderer, Editor-Marcela Kogan
Editorial Description: Information for transportation officials serving special-needs passengers.
General Info: (Formerly TD Safety Report), Yr. Est. 1993, Bi-weekly
Subscriptions: Indv. $145, Can. $171

TMTA Newsletter *Business, Association* CPM: $325

Publishing Co: Texas Motor Transportation Assn, PO Box 1669, Austin, TX 78767-1669 Fax # (512) 474-6494; Title Tel # (512) 478-2541
Personnel: Publisher-Deborah Swift, Editor-Debra Buss
Editorial Description: Features and news of interest to the Texas truck and bus industry.
General Info: (Formerly Steering Wheel), Yr. Est. 1936, 17x/yr., Trim Size-8$\frac{1}{2}$ x 11, Letrpr. press, 22 pages, 4 Color, Matte, Saddle-stitched
Subscriptions: Free With Membership
Circulation: Total-2,000
Advertising: $650.

Texas Transportation *Business*

Publishing Co: Report Publications, Inc., PO Box 12368, Austin, TX 78711-2368; Title Tel # (512) 478-5663
Personnel: Editor-Bill Kidd, Circ. Mgr.-Shirl Scott
Editorial Description: Detailed account of orders and action by the Texas Railroad Commission and other state agencies involved in the regulation of transportation or energy resources.
General Info: Yr. Est. 1969, Weekly, Trim Size-8$\frac{1}{2}$ x 14, Mimeo press, 3 pages, No Color
Subscriptions: $2/copy

Texas Transportation Researcher *Business*

Publishing Co: Texas Transportation Institute, 101 Tti/Ce Texas A&m, University System, College Station, TX 77843-0001 Tel # (409) 845-1734 Fax # (409) 845-9848; Title Tel # (409) 845-4726 Title Fax # (409) 845-7575
Personnel: Editor-Susan Lancaster, Mng. Editor-Bernie Fette
Editorial Description: Informs readers about TTI research, professional and service activities.
General Info: Yr. Est. 1965, Quarterly, Trim Size-8$\frac{1}{2}$ x 11, Offset press, 16 pages, 2 Color, Saddle-stitched
Subscriptions: Free In Designated Area
Circulation: Total-4,500

Tips and Topics *Business, Association*

Publishing Co: Atlantic Provinces Transportation Commission, #330 1133 St. George Blvd., Moncton, NB E1E 4E1 Canada; Title Tel # (506) 857-2820 Title Fax # (506) 857-2835
Personnel: Editor-Jack MacQuarrie
Editorial Description: Designed to provide awareness of transportation developments to the industries and producers in the Atlantic Provinces
General Info: Yr. Est. 1961, Monthly, 4 pages, ISSN: 0381-9345
Subscriptions: Free In Designated Area
Circulation: Total-3,000

Tollways
Business, Association

Publishing Co: International Bridge, Tunnel & Turnpike Assn., 2120 L St NW Ste 305, Washington, DC 20037-1527; Title Tel # (202) 659-4620 Title Fax # (202) 659-0500
Personnel: Editor-Janet Chalkin
Editorial Description: News items on members, the toll industry, highways and transportation in general.
General Info: Yr. Est. 1932, Monthly, Trim Size-8.5 x 11, Sheetfed press, 12 pages, 2 Color, Coated
Subscriptions: Indv. $35
Circulation: (100% controlled), Total-2,200
Printing Co: Corporate Press, 403 Brightseat Rd., Landover, MD 20785-4706 Tel # (301) 499-9200, Fax # (301) 499-5435

Tracks
See: HISTORY

Traffic Clubs International, News Bulletin

Publishing Co: Traffic Clubs Intl., 203 E 3rd St Ste 201, Sanford, FL 32771-1879; Title Tel # (407) 322-3364
General Info: Quarterly

Traffic Law Reports

Publishing Co: Knehans-Miller Publications, PO Box 88, Warrensburg, MO 64093-0088; Title Tel # (816) 429-1102
Personnel: Publisher-Jaclyn Miller, Editor-Dane Miller
Editorial Description: In-depth summaries, often with verbatim excerpts, and thorough subject/jurisdictional indexing of all federal and state appellate court descisions dealing with all aspects of traffic enforcement and administration.
General Info: Yr. Est. 1987, Monthly, Trim Size-8½ x 11, 20 pages, ISSN: 0893-3030, No Color, Looseleaf
Subscriptions: Indv. $120, Inst. $120, Can. $120, For. $155
Acquistions: Publication Bought

Train It
See: RAILROADS

Transit Record
Association

Publishing Co: New York City Transit Authority, 370 Jay St, Brooklyn, NY 11201-3814
General Info: Monthly

TransitPulse
Business

Publishing Co: Trans 21, Fields Corner Station, Box 249, Boston, MA 02122 Fax # (617) 482-7417; Title Tel # (617) 825-2318 Title Fax # (617) 487-7417
Personnel: Publisher, Editor-Lawrence Fabian
Editorial Description: Worldwide news of the emerging automated people mover industry.
General Info: Yr. Est. 1983, Bi-monthly, Trim Size-8½ x 11, Letrpr. press, 4 pages, ISSN: 0748-7347, No Color, Newsprint
Subscriptions: Indv. $75, Inst. $75, Can. $75, For. $90
Circulation: Total-1,000
Printing Co: Kendall Press, 36 Charles St, Cambridge, MA 02141-2150 Tel # (617) 354-2584

Transport (De)Regulation Report
Business

Publishing Co: Transportation Services, 960 Broadway, Hicksville, NY 11801-5028; Title Tel # (516) 822-1183 Title Fax # (516) 822-1126
Personnel: Publisher, Editor-Anthony Nuzio
Editorial Description: Monthly source of news, analysis and forecasts for transportation and distribution executives. Provides insight to changes in the freight transportation industry and the impact to shippers and carriers alike.
General Info: Yr. Est. 1981, Monthly, Trim Size-8½ x 11, 10 pages, 2 Color
Subscriptions: Indv. $167, Inst. $110, For. $181, $25/copy
List Rental: Rents Lists

Transport Info
Association

Publishing Co: Canadian Industrial Transportation League, 1090 Don Mills Road, #602, Toronto, ON M3C 3R6 Canada; Title Tel # (416) 447-7766 Title Fax # (416) 447-7312
Personnel: Editor-Stewart Wallace, Adv. Dir.-Patricia Mackle
Editorial Description: Happenings in the transportation and physical distribution field.
General Info: (Formerly Traffic Notes), Yr. Est. 1984, Bi-weekly, Desktop press, 10 pages, ISSN: 0826-8770
Subscriptions: Can. $300, Free With Membership
Circulation: (100% controlled), Total-1,100
Advertising: Inquire for rates.

Transportation
Business

Publishing Co: National Technical Information Service U.S., 5285 Port Royal Rd., Springfield, VA 22161-0001 Fax # (703) 487-4630; Title Tel # (703) 487-4630
Editorial Description: Covers air, pipeline, surface & subsurface transportation. Includes information on transportation safety & global navigation systems.
General Info: Weekly, Trim Size-8½ x 11, Offset press, 36 pages, ISSN: 0163-1529, No Color, Saddle-stitched
Subscriptions: Indv. $135, Can. $135, For. $195

Transportation Topics for Consumers
Consumer, Association

Publishing Co: U.S. Dept. of Transportation, 400 7th St SW, Washington, DC 20590-0001
General Info: Yr. Est. 1972, Quarterly
Circulation: Total-6,000

Travel Monthly
See: TRAVEL

Trolley Coach News
Association

Publishing Co: North American Trackless Trolly Assn., 455 S 4th Ave Ste 1077, Louisville, KY 40202-2511; Title Tel # (502) 459-5261
Personnel: Publisher, Editor-Harry R. Porter, Circ. Mgr.-T.G.J. Gascoigne
Editorial Description: Documenting current N.A. Trolleybus news with world Trolleybus headlines.
General Info: Yr. Est. 1969, Quarterly, Trim Size-8½ x 11, Offset press, 28 pages, 2 Color, Newsprint, Saddle-stitched
Subscriptions: Indv. $14, Inst. $39
Circulation: Total-450

Trolley Fare
Association

Publishing Co: Arden Trolley Museum, PO Box 832, Pittsburgh, PA 15230-0832; Title Tel # (412) 734-5780
Personnel: Publisher-M. McGrew, Editor-Harold M. Englund, Circ. Mgr.-Martha Ellis
Editorial Description: Detailed news from the Arden Trolley Museum. Reports on urban transportation systems world-wide.
General Info: Yr. Est. 1955, Bi-monthly, Trim Size-8½ x 11, Offset press, 8 pages, No Color
Subscriptions: Indv. $5, $1/copy
Circulation: Total-400

Trucking Activity Report
See: TRUCKING

Urban Transport News
Business

Publishing Co: Business Publishers, Inc., 951 Pershing Dr., Silver Spring, MD 20910-4464 Tel # (301) 589-5103 Fax # (301) 589-8493; Title Tel # (301) 587-6300 Title Fax # (301) 587-1081
Personnel: Publisher-Eric Easton, Editor-Tom Ramstack, Circ. Mgr.-Allison Inglesby
Editorial Description: Urban Transport News highlights news of importance to those involved in mass transit. Includes regulatory and legislative news as well as insights into what cities around North America are doing in urban transport.
General Info: (Formerly Public Transit Report), Yr. Est. 1973, Bi-weekly, Trim Size-8½ x 11, Desktop press, 8 pages, ISSN: 0148-4087, Ind/Abs/Online: NewsNet, Predicasts, DIALOG, No Color, Recycled
Subscriptions: Indv. $338, Can. $338, For. $351
Advertising: Accepts Inserts.
List Rental: List Management Co.: Manager: Donald Peterson; BPI Direct, 951 Pershing Dr., Silver Spring, MD 20910-4464 Tel # (301) 585-5976, Fax # (301) 587-4530

Warehouse Management and Control Systems
See: BUSINESS & INDUSTRY

Waybill, The
See: RAILROADS

World Diesel & Off-Highway News
Business

Publishing Co: Forecast International/DMS, Inc., 22 Commerce Rd., Newtown, CT 06470-1643 Fax # (203) 426-1964; Title Tel # (203) 426-0800 Title Fax # (203) 426-4262
General Info: Monthly
Subscriptions: Indv. $475

World ITS Market
Business

Publishing Co: Forecast International/DMS, Inc., 22 Commerce Rd., Newtown, CT 06470-1643 Fax # (203) 426-1964; Title Tel # (203) 426-0800 Title Fax # (203) 426-4262
General Info: Quarterly, Looseleaf
Subscriptions: Indv. $945

TRAVEL

ASTA Notes
Association

Publishing Co: American Assn. of Travel Agents, 1101 King St., Alexandria, VA 22314-2944; Title Tel # (703) 739-2782
Personnel: Editor-David Love
Editorial Description: News in the travel and tourism industry of importance to members.
General Info: Bi-weekly, Trim Size-8½ x 11, 8 pages, 2 Color
Circulation: (100% controlled), Total-16,500
List Rental: List Management Co.: Infocus Communications, 341 Victory Dr, Herndon, VA 22070-5217 Tel # (703) 834-0100, Fax # (703) 834-0110

Accessible Journeys
See: DISABILITY

Affordable Caribbean, The *Consumer*

Publishing Co: Caribbean Travel & Life, Inc., 8403 Colesville Rd., Ste. 830-M, Silver Spring, MD 20910-3368; Title Tel # (301) 588-2300 Title Fax # (301) 588-2256
Personnel: Publisher-Patricia Fox, Editor-Michael Harms, Adv. Mgr.-Lyn Savedge, Art Dir.-Lydia Scalletar
Editorial Description: An insider's guide to getting the very best buys/prices available in the Caribbean. Tips and advice on how to save money on your Caribbean vacation.
General Info: Yr. Est. 1992, Monthly, 8 pages, 2 Color, Saddle-stitched
Subscriptions: Indv. $49
Circulation: Total-3,500
List Rental: Rents Lists
Printing Co: Friendship Creative Printers, 1120m Benfield Blvd, Millersville, MD 21108-2540

African-American Traveler

Publishing Co: Universal Black Writer Press, Box 5, Radio City Station, New York, NY 10101-0005;
Title Tel # (718) 398-8941
General Info: Yr. Est. 1987, Quarterly
Subscriptions: Indv. $16

Alumeto
See: LITERATURE & LINGUISTICS

Andre Gayot's Tastes   *Business, Consumer*

Publishing Co: Gault Millau, Inc., 5900 Wilshire Blvd Ste 650, Los Angeles, CA 90036-5018;
Title Tel # (213) 965-3529 Title Fax # (213) 936-2883
Personnel: Publisher-Alain Gayot, Publisher, Editor-Andre Gayot, Circ. Mgr.-Pat Asher
Editorial Description: Focuses on fine foods and travel internationally.
General Info: Yr. Est. 1990, Bi-monthly, Trim Size-8$\frac{1}{2}$ x 11, Desktop press, 8 pages, ISSN: 1062-0184, 2 Color
Subscriptions: Indv. $20, For. $45, $5/copy
Circulation: Total-15,000
List Rental: Rents Lists

Andrew Harper's Hideaway
Report   *Business, Consumer*

Publishing Co: Harper Assocs., Inc., PO Box 50, Sun Valley, ID 83353-0050;
Title Tel # (208) 622-3183
Personnel: Publisher, Editor-Andrew Harper, Assoc. Publ., Circ. Mgr.-Richard Harper
Editorial Description: Reviews of selected vacation resorts for sophisticated travelers.
General Info: Yr. Est. 1979, Monthly, Trim Size-8$\frac{1}{2}$ x 11, 8 pages, 2 Color
Subscriptions: Indv. $100, Can. $110, For. $110, $8/copy
Circulation: Total-18,000

Angling Report, The
See: HUNTING & FISHING

Around the World with
Bonnie Kogos   *Consumer*

Publishing Co: Kogos Publications Co., 104 E. 37th St., New York, NY 10016-3016;
Title Tel # (212) 679-9438
Personnel: Editor-Bonnie Kogos
Editorial Description: Contains travel information & news.
General Info: Yr. Est. 1975, Quarterly
Subscriptions: Indv. $25, $5/copy
Circulation: Total-4,000
Advertising: Inquire for rates.

Ashington-Pickett Airlines
and Travel Report

Publishing Co: Ashington-Pickett Mid-Corp Inc., 550 N Bumby Ave Ste 110, Orlando, FL 32803-4927; Title Tel # (407) 898-9139 Title Fax # (407) 896-6585
General Info: Yr. Est. 1986, 8x/yr.
Subscriptions: Indv. $48

Asian Foodbookery
See: FOOD

Asian Pacific Travel Facts   *Business, Consumer*

Publishing Co: Asian Pacific Travel Facts, 6414 Kelly Elliott Rd, Arlington, TX 76017-5130;
Title Tel # (817) 483-2216 Title Fax # (817) 483-2216
Personnel: Publisher-Steve Coryell
Editorial Description: Quality travel info for readers.
General Info: Yr. Est. 1993, Monthly, Trim Size-8$\frac{1}{2}$ x 11, 8 pages, No Color
Subscriptions: Indv. $45
Advertising: Accepts Inserts.

Asian Travel & Nigthlife   *Business, Consumer*

Publishing Co: Transpacific Media Inc., 22761 Pacific Coast Hwy., Ste. 100, Malibu, CA 90265-5064
Tel # (310) 456-0790 Fax # (310) 456-3672; Title Tel # (213) 456-0790 Title Fax # (213) 456-3672
General Info: Monthly
Subscriptions: Indv. $59

Asian/Pacific Travel Facts   *Consumer*

Publishing Co: Asian/Pacific Travel Facts, 6414 Kelly Elliott Rd Ste 220, Arlington, TX 76017-5130
Editorial Description: Tips on money saving ideas on travel to Asia, Pacific Rim, and the South Pacific.
General Info: Yr. Est. 1993, Monthly
Subscriptions: Indv. $45

Association for Community
Travel Clubs Bulletin   *Association*

Publishing Co: Feature News Service, 9328 Sondra Avenue, St. Louis, MO 63144-1010;
Title Tel # (314) 961-2300 Title Fax # (314) 961-9828
Editorial Description: Covers Association news and events.
General Info: (Formerly Assn. of Transport Flying Clubs), Yr. Est. 1962, Monthly, Web press, 24 pages, 4 Color, Coated

Atterbury Letter   *Consumer*

Publishing Co: Atterbury Letter, PO Box 1359, Bethel Island, CA 94511-1197;
Title Tel # (415) 684-3142
Personnel: Editor-Kirby Atterbury
General Info: Yr. Est. 1976, Irregular, Trim Size-8$\frac{1}{2}$ x 11, Offset press, 8 pages, ISSN: 0739-3733, No Color, Coated
Circulation: Total-1,000
Advertising: Accepts Inserts.

Attractions America

Publishing Co: Travel Industry Association of America, 2 Lafayette Centre, 1133 21 St., NW, Washington, DC 20036; Title Tel # (202) 293-1433 Title Fax # (202) 293-3155
Personnel: Editor-Donnie Layne
Editorial Description: Newsletter of the National Council of Travel Attractions, an industry council of the Travel Industry Association of America.
General Info: Yr. Est. 1983, Quarterly, Trim Size-8$\frac{1}{2}$ x 11, Mimeo press, 6 pages
Subscriptions: Free With Membership
Circulation: (100% controlled), Total-160

Baltimore Banner   *Business, Association*

Publishing Co: Baltimore Area Convention & Visitors Assn., 100 Light Street #12, Baltimore, MD 21202-1014; Title Tel # (301) 659-7300 Title Fax # (301) 727-2308
Personnel: Editor-Gil Stotler
Editorial Description: Describes events, new developments, topics for tourists.
General Info: (Formerly Baltimore Clipper), Trim Size-8$\frac{1}{2}$ x 11, 6 pages, 2 Color, Newsprint
Circulation: (85% controlled), Total-7,000, International-1,000

Barbara's View: Paris   *Consumer*

Publishing Co: Barbara's View, PO Box 531006, Miami, FL 33153-1006; Title Tel # (305) 757-7638
Title Fax # (305) 756-5353
Personnel: Publisher, Editor-Barbara W. Levy
Editorial Description: Travel guide emphasizing shopping tours. Set of European guides for $40.
General Info: Yr. Est. 1976, Annually, Looseleaf
Subscriptions: For. $13, $8/copy

Belganews   *Business*

Publishing Co: Belgian Tourist Office, 780 3rd Ave Rm 1501, New York, NY 10017-2024
Fax # (212) 355-7675; Title Tel # (212) 758-8130
Editorial Description: Provides tourist information on Belgium to the press.
General Info: (Formerly Belgium Newsbreaks), Quarterly
Subscriptions: Free To Qualified Recipient

Bermuda Shorts   *Business*

Publishing Co: Bermuda Dept. of Tourism, 310 Madison Ave., Rm. 201, New York, NY 10017-6009;
Title Tel # (212) 818-9800 Title Fax # (212) 983-5289
Personnel: Publisher, Editor-Mario Almonte
Editorial Description: Up to date Bermuda news geared to US & Canada travel industry.
General Info: Yr. Est. 1971, Quarterly, Offset press
Subscriptions: Free To Qualified Recipient
Circulation: Total-4,000

Big Island Update

Publishing Co: Paradise Pubs., 8110 SW Wareham Cir, Portland, OR 97223-6992;
Title Tel # (503) 246-1555
General Info: Yr. Est. 1989, Quarterly
Subscriptions: Indv. $10, $3/copy

Bird Hunting Report, The
See: HUNTING & FISHING

Bridges
See: EDUCATION

Britainews   *Association, Business*

Publishing Co: British Tourist Authority, 551 5th Ave Rm 701, New York, NY 10176-0799;
Title Tel # (212) 986-2266
Personnel: Editor-Robin Prestage, Adv. Dir.-Charles Patricolo
Editorial Description: For U.S. Travel Agents who sell travel to Britain.
General Info: Bi-monthly, Web press, 20 pages, 4 Color, Coated
Subscriptions: Free To Qualified Recipient
Circulation: Total-8,000
Advertising: Inquire for rates. Accepts Inserts.
List Rental: Rents Lists

Business Flyer   *Business*

Publishing Co: Holcon, PO Box 276, Newton Center, MA 02159-0002; Title Tel # (203) 782-2155
Personnel: Editor-Jane Costello, Publisher, Promotion Dir.-John Holland
Editorial Description: Designed to keep the business traveler up to date on the monthly promotions and specials offere which save time and money.
General Info: Yr. Est. 1986, Monthly, 8 pages
Subscriptions: Indv. $50, Can. $60, For. $70, $5/copy
Acquistions: Publication Bought
Circulation: Total-70,000

CHAdvance
Association

Publishing Co: Sponsor-American Express, Caribbean Hotel Assn., 18 Marseilles St., Suite 2-B, Santurce, PR 00907 Fax # (809) 725-9108; Title Tel # (809) 725-9139 Title Fax # (809) 725-9166
Personnel: Editor-Beverley Telemague
Editorial Description: Membership newsletter sent by fax.
General Info: (Formerly Caribbean Reporter-Update), Yr. Est. 1994, Bi-monthly
Subscriptions: Indv. $50
Circulation: Total-2,300
Advertising: Inquire for rates.

CIEE

Publishing Co: CIEE, 729 Boylston St Ste 201, Boston, MA 02116-2639; Title Tel # (617) 266-4412

Canadian Institutes of Travel Counsellors, Update

Publishing Co: Canadian Institutes of Travel Counsellors, 55 Eglinton Ave. East, Suite #209, Toronto, ON M4P 1G8 Canada; Title Tel # (416) 484-4450
Personnel: Editor-Mary Notley
Editorial Description: Newsletter of interest to professional travel counsellors contains information on institutes activities & general items of interest.
General Info: Yr. Est. 1976, Quarterly, Trim Size-8$\frac{1}{2}$ x 11, Coated
Subscriptions: $1/copy
Circulation: (100% controlled), Total-5,000
List Rental: Rents Lists

Cartogram

Publishing Co: Travel Industry Association of America, 2 Lafayette Centre, 1133 21 St., NW, Washington, DC 20036; Title Tel # (202) 293-1433 Title Fax # (202) 293-3155
Personnel: Editor-Donnie Layne
Editorial Description: Newsletter of National Council of Area & Regional Travel Organizations, an industry council of the Travel Industry Association of America.
General Info: Yr. Est. 1982, Quarterly, Trim Size-8$\frac{1}{2}$ x 11, Mimeo press, 8 pages, No Color, Matte, Other
Subscriptions: Free With Membership
Circulation: Total-140

Cartomania
See: GEOGRAPHY

Consumer Reports Travel Letter
Consumer

Publishing Co: Consumer Union, 101 Truman Avenue, Yonkers, NY 10703-1057 Tel # (914) 378-2000; Title Tel # (914) 378-2562
Personnel: Publisher-James Davis, Editor-Ed Perkins, Circ. Mgr.-Asa Orsino, Promotion Dir.-Barbara Nelson
Editorial Description: Provides consumer-oriented unbiased travel guidance & money-saving advice.
General Info: Yr. Est. 1985, Monthly, Trim Size-8$\frac{1}{2}$ x 11, 24 pages, Ind/Abs/Online: DIALOG, AOL, 2 Color, Newsprint, Saddle-stitched
Subscriptions: Indv. $39, Can. $42, $5/copy
Circulation: Total-100,000
Printing Co: Offset House Printers, 89 Sand Hill Rd., Essex, VT 05451

Contact
See: SALESMANSHIP & SELLING

Costa Vida Vallarta Newsletter

Publishing Co: Trading Places, 145 Columbia Ste 210, Aliso Viejo, CA 92656-1490; Title Tel # (714) 362-1048
Personnel: Editor-Cindy Barry
General Info: Quarterly

Country Inns Gazette
Consumer

Publishing Co: Housatonic Press Inc., Box 6976, FDR Station, New York, NY 10150; Title Tel # (212) 752-6039
General Info: Yr. Est. 1987, Monthly
Subscriptions: Indv. $60

Cruise & Freighter Travel Letter
Consumer

Publishing Co: Klevens Publications, Inc., 7600 E Avenue V, Littlerock, CA 93543-3203; Title Tel # (805) 944-4111 Title Fax # (805) 944-1800
Personnel: Publisher-Gilbert Klevens, Editor-Herbert Schwartz, Circ. Mgr.-Gregg Herbert
Editorial Description: Reports on new sailings, ships, & places thruout world.
General Info: Yr. Est. 1969, 12x/yr., Trim Size-8$\frac{1}{2}$ x 11, Sheetfed press, 12 pages, No Color, Newsprint
Subscriptions: Indv. $39
Circulation: Total-5,500

Cruise Industry News
Business

Publishing Co: Nissen-Lie Communications, 441 Lexington Ave Rm 1209a, New York, NY 10017-3910; Title Tel # (212) 986-1025 Title Fax # (212) 986-1033
Personnel: Publisher, Editor-Oivind Mathisen, Adv. Dir.-Karin Masbrouck
Editorial Description: Covers all industry news related to cruise shipping & travel.
General Info: Yr. Est. 1985, Bi-weekly, Offset press, 6 pages, ISSN: 0893-1240, 2 Color, Newsprint
Subscriptions: Indv. $495, $25/copy
Acquistions: Publication Bought
Circulation: Total-2,500

Cruise News

Publishing Co: Nissen-Lie Communications, 441 Lexington Ave Rm 1209a, New York, NY 10017-3910; Title Tel # (212) 986-1025 Title Fax # (212) 986-1033
General Info: Yr. Est. 1987, Monthly
Subscriptions: Indv. $120

Cruiseletter

Publishing Co: Seaspray Publishing, RD 2 Box 736, Sussex, NJ 07461; Title Tel # (201) 827-1435
Personnel: Publisher, Editor-Janet Gregory
Editorial Description: Written by and for those who love cruising.
General Info: Yr. Est. 1993, Monthly, 6 pages
Subscriptions: Indv. $24

Culturgrams
See: CULTURE & HUMANITIES

Diabetic Traveler
Consumer

Publishing Co: Diabetic Traveler, Box 8223 RW, Stamford, CT 06905-8223; Title Tel # (203) 327-5832
Personnel: Publisher-Maury Rosenbaum
Editorial Description: Assists diabetics in planning safe travel. Medical advisory panel reviews info, writes articles, and repsonds to readers' questions.
General Info: Yr. Est. 1986, Quarterly, Trim Size-8$\frac{1}{2}$ x 11, Sheetfed press, 6 pages, ISSN: 0899-2398, 2 Color, Matte
Subscriptions: Indv. $19, Inst. $19, Can. $19, For. $22, $3/copy
Acquistions: Publication Bought
Circulation: Total-3,000
Advertising: Accepts Inserts.
List Rental: List Management Co.: Manager: M. Rosenbaum; Mercury Marketing, PO Box 8223, Stamford, CT 06905-8223 Tel # (203) 327-5832, Actives: $125/M, Hotline: $125/M, Expires: $115/M
Printing Co: Woodway Print, 48 Union Street, Stamford, CT 06906 Tel # (203) 323-6423

Directions
Business

Publishing Co: Phillip Camp Assocs., Cox Rd., Woodstock, VT 05091; Title Tel # (802) 457-3282
Personnel: Publisher, Editor-Phillip Camp
Editorial Description: Information about U.S. resort and travel activities-for media people.
General Info: (Formerly NE Wire Svc.), Yr. Est. 1970, Bi-weekly, Trim Size-8$\frac{1}{2}$ x 11, Offset press, 8 pages, No Color, Newsprint
Circulation: Total-7,100
List Rental: Rents Lists

Discerning Traveler
Consumer

Publishing Co: Lida Ltd., 504 W Mermaid Ln, Philadelphia, PA 19118-4206; Title Tel # (215) 247-5578
Personnel: Editor, Circ. Mgr.-Linda Glickstein, Publisher, Production Mgr.-David Glickstein
Editorial Description: Covers weekend travel in the East, from Maine to Florida. Includes lodging, dining, shopping, driving tours, budgets, maps, recipes, book reviews. The newsletter usually focuses on one area or town in each issue.
General Info: Yr. Est. 1987, Bi-monthly, Trim Size-8$\frac{1}{2}$ x 11, Sheetfed press, 16 pages, No Color, Matte, Saddle-stitched
Subscriptions: Indv. $50, Inst. $50, Can. $60, For. $65, $8/copy
Printing Co: Sun Printing, 4811 Stenton Ave, Philadelphia, PA 19144-3091 Tel # (215) 842-1800

DogGone
Consumer

Publishing Co: DogGone, PO Box 651155, Vero Beach, FL 32965-1155; Title Tel # (407) 569-8434
Personnel: Publisher-Wendy Ballard
Editorial Description: Vacation spots and travel tips for dog owners. Creative activities for dogs and owners to enjoy together, at home as well away.
General Info: Yr. Est. 1993, Bi-monthly, Trim Size-8$\frac{1}{2}$ x 11, 12 pages, 2 Color, Matte
Subscriptions: Indv. $24, $5/copy
Circulation: Total-3,000

DreamTrips!
Consumer

Publishing Co: DreamTrips!, PO Box 670466, Dallas, TX 75367-0466; Title Tel # (214) 692-1085 Title Fax # (214) 692-0105
Personnel: Publisher-Jack Plunkett, Art Dir.-Mary Lee Plunkett
Editorial Description: In depth reports on top qquality resorts distributed by travel agencies/travel providers to their clients.
General Info: Yr. Est. 1988, Quarterly, Trim Size-8$\frac{1}{2}$ x 11, Sheetfed press, 4 pages, 3% ads, 2 Color, Newsprint
Acquistions: Publication Bought
Circulation: Total-125,000
Advertising: Inquire for rates.

Educated Traveler, The   *Business, Consumer*

Publishing Co: Educated Traveler, Inc., The, PO Box 220822, Chantilly, VA 22022-6822; Title Tel # (703) 471-1063 Title Fax # (703) 471-4807
Personnel: Publisher, Editor-Ann H. Waigand, Circ. Mgr.-Robin Smith, Asst. Ed., Adv. Dir.-Deborah Vichr
Editorial Description: Newsletter on international specialty travel: cultural tourism, educational travel, special interest tours, ecotourism, museum travel, activity holidays, intercultural and socially responsible tourism. Subscription includes annual directory of museum sponsored tours.
General Info: Yr. Est. 1990, Bi-monthly, Trim Size-8½ x 11, Sheetfed press, 12 pages, ISSN: 1052-0597, 2 Color, Matte, Saddle-stitched
Subscriptions: Indv. $45, Can. $45, For. $54, $8/copy
Circulation: Total-2,000
Advertising: Inquire for rates.
List Rental: List Management Co.: Manager: Brandy Carpenter; InfoMat, 1815 W 213th St Ste 210, Torrance, CA 90501-2839 Tel # (310) 212-5944, Fax # (310) 212-5773, Actives: 9,000, $95/M

Entertainment and Travel Mode
See: ENTERTAINMENT

Entree Travel Newsletter   *Business, Consumer*

Publishing Co: Entree Travel, 695 Olive Rd., Santa Barbara, CA 93108-1442; Title Tel # (805) 969-5848 Title Fax # (805) 966-7095
Personnel: Assoc. Publ.-Edward L. Stephenson, Publisher, Editor-William Tomicki, Women's Editor-Barbara Daugherty
Editorial Description: Uncompromising assessments of hotels, cruises, spas, restaurants, tours, shops around the world, plus wine and book reviews.
General Info: Yr. Est. 1981, Monthly, Trim Size-8½ x 11, Letrpr. press, 6 pages, 2 Color, Matte
Subscriptions: Indv. $59, Can. $71, For. $71, $5/copy
Circulation: Total-7,000
Advertising: Accepts Inserts.

Erie Motorist   *Association*

Publishing Co: Erie County Motor Club, 420 W 6th St, Erie, PA 16507-1295

Europe Through the Back Door Travel Newsletter   *Consumer*

Publishing Co: Europe Through the Back Door, 109 4th Ave N # 2009, Edmonds, WA 98020-3115 Tel # (206) 771-8303
Personnel: Mag. Ed.-Rich Sorensen
Editorial Description: A free travel newsletter filled with tips, stories, advice and more from 'Back Door' travel guru Rick Steves.
General Info: Quarterly
Subscriptions: Free
Circulation: Total-25,000

European Travel Report

Publishing Co: Travel to Europe, 49 Waltham St., Box 439, Lexington, MA 02173-5411; Title Tel # (617) 863-0125
Personnel: Publisher, Editor-Caroline Nijenberg
Editorial Description: For the travel professional reporting on the European travel market.
General Info: Yr. Est. 1985, 8x/yr., Trim Size-8½ x 11, Offset press, 12 pages, 2 Color, Saddle-stitched
Subscriptions: Indv. $18, $2/copy
Circulation: Total-5,000

Exploring Ireland   *Business, Consumer*

Publishing Co: CATSTONE Inc., 318 Pershing Ave, Roselle Park, NJ 07204-2166; Title Tel # (908) 298-0315 Title Fax # (908) 298-0315
Personnel: Co-Editor-Charlene Romar Storey, Co-Editor-G.D. Storey
Editorial Description: Travel newsletter for Americans interested in touring Ireland.
General Info: Yr. Est. 1990, Bi-monthly, ISSN: 1066-5358
Subscriptions: Indv. $39, $7/copy
Circulation: Total-900

Fairfax Newsletter
See: AERONAUTICS/ASTRONAUTICS

Family Travel Times   *Business, Consumer*

Publishing Co: Dorthy Jordon & Assoc./TWYCH, Travel with Your Children, 40 5th Ave., New York, NY 10011-8843; Title Tel # (212) 206-0688 Title Fax # (212) 645-5942
Personnel: Publisher-Dorothy Jordon, Editor-Joy Anderson
Editorial Description: Dedicated to planning fun & successful family vacations--across the country or around the globe. Custom travel advice available for subscribers.
General Info: Yr. Est. 1984, 10x/yr., Trim Size-8½ x 11, Sheetfed press, 8 pages, 2 Color, Coated
Subscriptions: Indv. $55, Inst. $50, Can. $59, For. $68
List Rental: Actives: $95/M
Printing Co: Newsletter Services, Inc., 9700 Philadelphia Court, Lanham, MD 20706 Tel # (301) 731-5200, Fax # (301) 731-5201

Fast Tracks   *Consumer*

Publishing Co: Forsyth Travel Library, 9154 W. 57th St., P.O. Box 2975, Shawnee Mission, KS 66201-1375; Title Tel # (913) 384-3440
Editorial Description: News and information about traveling.
General Info: Irregular, Trim Size-8½ x 13¾, 2 pages, 4 Color, Coated

Foghorn   *Association*

Publishing Co: Passenger Vessel Association, 1600 Wilson Blvd., Ste. 1000-A, Arlington, VA 22209; Title Tel # (703) 807-0100 Title Fax # (703) 807-0103
Personnel: Publisher-Eric Scharf, Editor-Mark Wright, Adv. Dir.-Juana Hopkins
Editorial Description: Provides information to the members of the association.
General Info: Yr. Est. 1988, Monthly, Trim Size-8½ x 11, Letrpr. press, 28 pages, Coated, Saddle-stitched
Subscriptions: Indv. $275, Free With Membership
Circulation: Total-950
Advertising: Inquire for rates.
Printing Co: Lettercomm, Inc., 310 Swann Ave, Alexandria, VA 22301-1042 Tel # (703) 683-3105

Freighter Travel News   *Consumer, Association*

Publishing Co: Freighter Travel Club of America, 3524 Harts Lake Rd., Roy, WA 98580-9125; Title Tel # (206) 458-4178
Personnel: Publisher, Editor-Leland Pledger
Editorial Description: Information on all aspects of freighter travel.
General Info: Yr. Est. 1958, Monthly, Trim Size-8½ x 11, Letrpr. press, 8 pages, ISSN: 0016-089X, No Color, Coated
Subscriptions: Indv. $20, Can. $24, For. $27, $2/copy
Circulation: Total-3,000
Advertising: Inquire for rates.

Frommer's Travel Book Club Tips & Travel   *Association, Consumer*

Publishing Co: Viacom, 15 Columbus Cir, New York, NY 10023-7780 Tel # (212) 258-6000; Title Tel # (815) 734-1104
Personnel: Editor in Chief-Marilyn Wood
Editorial Description: Travel information and list of Frommers travel guides to purchase.
General Info: Quarterly, Trim Size-8½ x 11, 16 pages, 2 Color, Matte, Saddle-stitched

Gay Airline & Travel Club Newsletter, The   *Consumer, Association*   **CPM: $40**

Publishing Co: Fan Club Publishing Co. / Louis Wendruck, Box 69A04-Dept. OX, West Hollywood, CA 90069-0066; Title Tel # (213) 650-5112
Personnel: Publisher, Editor-Louis Wendruck
Editorial Description: Published for gay men who work for airlines, the travel industry, who collect airline memorabilia or who enjoy traveling and are looking for travel partners and friends.
General Info: (Formerly Gay Airline Club Newsletter), Yr. Est. 1992, Quarterly, Trim Size-8½ x 11, Offset press, 24 pages
Subscriptions: Indv. $29, Can. $39, For. $39, $8/copy
Circulation: Total-20,000
Advertising: $800. Accepts Inserts.
List Rental: Rents Lists

Globe Corner Bookstore   *Consumer*

Publishing Co: Globe Corner Bookstore, 1 School St, Boston, MA 02108-4305; Title Fax # (617) 227-2771
Editorial Description: Selected books and maps on travel and interviews with travel writers.
General Info: Quarterly, Trim Size-8½ x 11, 12 pages, 2 Color, Matte

Going Solo

Publishing Co: Doerfer Communications, Box 1035, Cambridge, MA 02138; Title Tel # (617) 876-2764
General Info: Yr. Est. 1989, 8x/yr.
Subscriptions: Indv. $39

Gold Coast News
See: REGIONAL INTEREST

Golden Gateway   *Consumer*

Publishing Co: Golden Companions Club, PO Box 754, Pullman, WA 99163-0754; Title Tel # (208) 858-2183
Personnel: Editor-Joanne Buteau
Editorial Description: Lists discounts and tours for people age 50 and over.
General Info: (Formerly Golden Traveler), Yr. Est. 1987, Bi-monthly
Subscriptions: Indv. $85, $2/copy
Circulation: Total-1,500
Advertising: Inquire for rates. Accepts Inserts.

Golf Travel: The Guide for Discriminating Golfers
See: GOLF

Hagstrom Map & Travel Center Newsletter   *Business, Consumer*

Publishing Co: Hagstrom Map & Travel Center, 57 W 43rd St, New York, NY 10036-7407; Title Tel # (212) 398-1222
Personnel: Editor-Douglas Rose
Editorial Description: Information about new maps, updated maps, rare maps.
General Info: Yr. Est. 1986, Quarterly

Hawaii, the Big Island Update

Publishing Co: Paradise Pubs., 8110 SW Wareham Cir, Portland, OR 97223-6992; Title Tel # (503) 246-1555
Personnel: Publisher-Christie Stilson, Editor-Greg Stilson, Art Dir.-Susie O'Day
Editorial Description: A quarterly newsletter featuring current travel information for Hawaii.
General Info: (Formerly Big Island Update), Yr. Est. 1989, Quarterly, Letrpr. press, 4 pages, ISSN: 1042-8046, Matte
Subscriptions: Indv. $10, Can. $10, $3/copy

Hawaii Traveler

Publishing Co: Hawaii Traveler, Honolulu, HI 96839-1162; Title Tel # (808) 988-3484
General Info: Yr. Est. 1987, Monthly
Subscriptions: Indv. $39

Hazardous Materials Transportation
See: ENVIRONMENT & ECOLOGY

Hideaway Report   *Consumer*

Publishing Co: Harper Assocs., Inc., PO Box 50, Sun Valley, ID 83353-0050; Title Tel # (208) 622-3183
Personnel: Publisher, Editor-Andrew Harper, Circ. Mgr.-Richard Harper
Editorial Description: Reports on small, secluded resorts and executive retreats around the world.
General Info: Yr. Est. 1979, Monthly, Trim Size-8½ x 11, Sheetfed press, 8 pages, ISSN: 0884-7622, 2 Color
Subscriptions: Indv. $90, Can. $100, For. $100, $8/copy
Circulation: Total-16,500

Hotel, Resort, Cruise Ship and Spa Report   *Consumer*

Publishing Co: Enterprises Unlimited, 400 E 59th St., Apt 9F, New York, NY 10022-2344 Tel # (212) 755-4363
Personnel: Publisher-Tom Weston, Editor-John Edwards
Editorial Description: Reviews various hotels, spas, cruises and resorts.
General Info: Yr. Est. 1993, Monthly, Trim Size-8½ x 10½, 4 pages, No Color, Looseleaf
Subscriptions: Indv. $50
Circulation: Total-1,000

ICTA Update   *Association*

Publishing Co: Inst. of Certified Travel Agents, 148 Linden St., Box 812059, Wellesley, MA 02181-0012; Title Tel # (617) 237-0280 Title Fax # (617) 237-3860
Personnel: Editor-Dawn Ringel
Editorial Description: Information on educational programs for travel industry members; marketing and management tios; listings of new Certified Travel Couselors (CTCs); members' achievements.
General Info: (Formerly ICTA News), Yr. Est. 1967, Bi-monthly, Trim Size-8½ x 11, Sheetfed press, 8 pages, 2 Color, Coated, Saddle-stitched
Circulation: Total-25,000

IVIS Newsletter

Publishing Co: International Visitors Information Service, 1623 Belmont St NW, Washington, DC 20009-4010; Title Tel # (202) 939-5566 Title Fax # (202) 232-9783
Personnel: Editor-Marianne H. Cruze
Editorial Description: Projects and programs handled by volunteers, Board of Directors, Staff to assist international visitors in Washington, DC.
General Info: Yr. Est. 1964, Semi-annually, Trim Size-8½ x 11, Letrpr. press, 6 pages, 2 Color, Newsprint
Subscriptions: Free
Circulation: (100% controlled), Total-1,200

Inn Marketing   *Consumer*

Publishing Co: Inn Marketing, 105 E Court St, P.O. Box 1789, Kankakee, IL 60901-3823; Title Tel # (815) 939-3509 Title Fax # (815) 939-7996
Personnel: Publisher-Norman Strasma, Editor-Anne Miller
Editorial Description: News of people, places, events of the Inn World. Includes annual Directory/Catalog of information sources about the Industry.
General Info: (Formerly Inn Business Review), Yr. Est. 1982, 10x/yr., Desktop press, 12 pages, ISSN: 0748-8408, No Color
Subscriptions: Indv. $49, Can. $55, For. $60, $5/copy
Advertising: Inquire for rates.
List Rental: Actives: 15,000, $90/M

Inside Flyer
See: AERONAUTICS/ASTRONAUTICS

Inside Tourism

Publishing Co: North Dakota Dept. of Economic Development and Finance, 1833 E Bismarck Expy, Bismarck, ND 58504-6708 Tel # (701) 328-2374; Title Tel # (701) 244-2526
Personnel: Publisher-Jim Fuglie, Editor-Tracy Potter
Editorial Description: North Dakota tourism promotion news and information.
General Info: Yr. Est. 1980, Quarterly, 4 pages, 2 Color
Circulation: Total-2,300

Inside Travel News   *Consumer*

Publishing Co: Inside Travel News, 6229 Bristol Pky, Culver City, CA 90230-6903; Title Tel # (213) 649-3401 Title Fax # (213) 649-3191
Personnel: Editor-Loretta Slaton
General Info: Yr. Est. 1971, Monthly
Subscriptions: Indv. $9

Insideflyer   *Business, Consumer*

Publishing Co: Frequent Publications, 4715c Town Center Dr, Colorado Springs, CO 80916-4701; Title Tel # (719) 597-8889 Title Fax # (719) 597-6855
Personnel: Publisher, Editor-Randy Petersen, Circ. Mgr.-Ken Heldt
Editorial Description: Considered the leading publication of information about & for frequent flyer programs and their members. Provides the latest information regarding bonuses and earning & using free awards.
General Info: (Formerly Frequent), Yr. Est. 1986, Monthly, Trim Size-7 x 10.87, Web press, 36 pages, ISSN: 0889-7646, 1% ads, 4 Color, Coated, Saddle-stitched
Subscriptions: Indv. $33, Can. $33, For. $38
Acquistions: Publication Bought, Publication Sold
Circulation: Total-108,000
Advertising: Inquire for rates. Accepts Inserts.
List Rental: List Management Co.: Thulin Communications, 5511 Laurel Canyon Blvd, North Hollywood, CA 91607-2116 Tel # (213) 930-1919, Actives: $90/M, Expires: $65/M

Insider's Guide to First Class Travel   *Consumer*

Publishing Co: Insider's Guide, 3419 Via Lido Ste 620, Newport Beach, CA 92663-3908
Personnel: Publisher-John Niven
General Info: Yr. Est. 1993, Monthly, 16 pages
Subscriptions: Indv. $49, For. $59, $10/copy

Interactive Travel Report   *Business*

Publishing Co: Garrett Communications, 210 North Adams Street, Suite 1000, Rockville, MD 20850; Title Tel # (301) 738-7927 Title Fax # (301) 738-7896
Personnel: Publisher-Thomas Woodall, Editor-David Kirby, Production Mgr.-Hanta Ralay, Mktg. Dir.-Robin Woodall
Editorial Description: Information on electronic travel sales and interactive distribution channels.
General Info: Yr. Est. 1995, Bi-weekly
Subscriptions: Indv. $447, For. $487, $20/copy
Advertising: Inquire for rates. Accepts Inserts.
List Rental: Rents Lists

Interlocken Globe
See: YOUTH

International Airline Review
See: AERONAUTICS/ASTRONAUTICS

International Bicycle Touring Society Newsletter   *Association*

Publishing Co: International Bicycle Touring Society, PO Box 6979, San Diego, CA 92166-0979 Tel # (619) 226-8687; Title Tel # (619) 454-6428 Title Fax # (619) 459-0243
Personnel: Publisher-Clifford Graves, Editor-Catharina Graves
Editorial Description: Announcements and reports of bicycle tours.
General Info: Yr. Est. 1964, Quarterly, Trim Size-8½ x 11, Offset press, 10 pages, No Color
Subscriptions: Indv. $25
Circulation: Total-1,000

International Golfer
See: GOLF

International Living
See: LIFESTYLE

International Railway Traveler   *Consumer*   CPM: $261

Publishing Co: Hardy Publishing Co., 1810 Sils Ave # 306b, Louisville, KY 40205-2161; Title Tel # (502) 454-0277 Title Fax # (502) 454-0277
Personnel: Publisher-Owen Hardy, Editor-Gena Holle, Adv. Dir.-Richard Vaughan, Art Dir.-Steve Sebree
Editorial Description: For the railroad travel enthusiast.
General Info: Yr. Est. 1983, Bi-monthly, Trim Size-8½ x 11, 16 pages, ISSN: 0891-7655, 2 Color, Coated, Saddle-stitched
Subscriptions: Indv. $40, Can. $41, For. $46, $7/copy
Circulation: Total-4,200, Readership-8,500
Advertising: $1,100.
List Rental: List Management Co.: Publishing Management Associates, 129 Phelps Ave Ste 312, Rockford, IL 61108-2447 Tel # (815) 398-8569, Fax # (815) 398-8579, Actives: 3,000, $100/M
Printing Co: Commonwealth Printing Co., 2901 S 2nd St, Louisville, KY 40208-1405 Tel # (502) 636-1100

International Visitor

Publishing Co: Walter Mathews Assoc, 799 Broasway, Ste 309, New York, NY 10003; Title Tel # (212) 533-9405 Title Fax # (212) 533-9295
Personnel: Publisher-Walter Mathews, Editor-Scott Wagendorf
Editorial Description: Published for U.S. travel executive who want to attract more inbound business & learn how to take better care of them when they get here.
General Info: Yr. Est. 1991, 10x/yr., Trim Size-11 x 17, Offset press, 4 pages, ISSN: 1058-5575, 2 Color, Matte
Subscriptions: Indv. $78, Can. $85, For. $95
Circulation: (95% controlled), Total-10,000, Subscriptions-500, International-100, Readership-12,500
Advertising: Accepts Inserts.

Islands Escapes
Consumer

Publishing Co: Islands Publishing Co., 3886 State St, Santa Barbara, CA 93105-3112;
Title Tel # (805) 682-7177 Title Fax # (805) 569-0349
Personnel: Publisher-William Kasch, Editor-Tony Gibbs, Circ. Dir.-Barry Service, Product Mgr.-Brenda Black, Art Dir.-Albert Chang
Editorial Description: The traveler's newsletter from the editors of Islands Magazine, brings unmatched experience to evaluating island getaways for the demanding traveler. Our experts are choosy, independent and uncompromising in their ratings of where to go, how to get there, where to stay, where to eat and what to do.
General Info: Yr. Est. 1991, Monthly, Trim Size-8½ x 11, 8 pages, ISSN: 1056-392X
Subscriptions: Indv. $39, Can. $45, For. $45, $5/copy
Circulation: Total-3,000

Italian Traveler, The
Business, Consumer

Publishing Co: Cognoscenti Publications, Inc., PO Box 32-M, Livingston, NJ 07039-0032
Fax # (201) 994-3847; Title Tel # (201) 535-6572 Title Fax # (201) 994-3844
Personnel: Publisher, Editor-Howard Isaacs, Assoc. Ed.-Nadia Rigoni, Art Dir.-Donna Isaacs
Editorial Description: Travel tips for visitors to Italy.
General Info: 11x/yr., Trim Size-8½ x 11, 8 pages, No Color, Matte
Subscriptions: Indv. $59, For. $69, $10/copy

JULUKA Newsletter
See: ETHNIC

Journal n' Footnotes
See: WOMEN'S

Kauai Update

Publishing Co: Paradise Pubs., 8110 SW Wareham Cir, Portland, OR 97223-6992;
Title Tel # (503) 246-1555
Personnel: Publisher-Greg Stilson, Editor-Christie Stilson, Production Mgr.-Judy Estes, Art Dir.-Susie O'Day
Editorial Description: A quarterly newsletter featuring current travel information for Kauai. A companion pub. to travel guide, A Paradise Guide'.'
General Info: Yr. Est. 1986, Quarterly, Trim Size-8½ x 11, Desktop press, 4 pages, ISSN: 0898-1418, 1% ads, Newsprint
Subscriptions: Indv. $10, Can. $10, $3/copy
Circulation: (50% controlled), Total-2,000
Advertising: Inquire for rates.

Kerrville Tours Newsletter
Consumer

Publishing Co: Kerrville Tours, PO Box 79, Shreveport, LA 71161-0079
Editorial Description: Information for and about Kerrville Tours and travellers.
General Info: Quarterly, Trim Size-8½ x 11, 8 pages, Matte

La Belle France
Consumer

Publishing Co: Travel Guide Inc., PO Box 3485, Charlottesville, VA 22903-0485;
Title Tel # (804) 295-1200 Title Fax # (804) 296-0948
Personnel: Publisher-Terence Sieg, Editor-W. Carter Hoerr, Art Dir.-Barbara Sieg
Editorial Description: Consumer guide to French travel.
General Info: Yr. Est. 1984, Monthly, 8 pages, ISSN: 8750-9180
Subscriptions: Indv. $67, $10/copy
Acquistions: Publication Bought, Publication Sold
Circulation: Total-8,000

La Vista de Mexico
Consumer

Publishing Co: Deyo Communications, 218 Tree Summit Pky, Duluth, GA 30136-6398;
Title Tel # (404) 923-1926 Title Fax # (770) 717-1584
Personnel: Publisher, Editor-Steve Deyo, Circ. Mgr.-Chela Deyo
Editorial Description: The only publication that delivers independent reporting on hotels, restaurants, pricing, current conditions, as well as insightful suggestions for the traveling American.
General Info: Yr. Est. 1988, Bi-monthly, 8 pages, ISSN: 0895-6464, 2 Color
Subscriptions: Indv. $30, Can. $36, For. $36, $5/copy
Circulation: Total-7,500
Advertising: Accepts Inserts.

Lancaster Motorist
Association, Consumer

Publishing Co: Lancaster Automobile Club, 34 N Prince St, Lancaster, PA 17603-3866
General Info: Yr. Est. 1920, Monthly
Subscriptions: Indv. $1
Circulation: Total-35,000

Las Vegas Advisor
Consumer

Publishing Co: Huntington Press, PO Box 28041, Las Vegas, NV 89126-2041;
Title Tel # (702) 871-4363
Personnel: Publisher-Anthony Curtis, Editor-Deke Castleman, Prod. Coord.-Sharon Liggio, Mktg. Dir.-Bethany Coffey
Editorial Description: Newsletter for Las Vegas visitors.
General Info: Yr. Est. 1983, Monthly, Trim Size-8½ x 11, Offset press, 12 pages, ISSN: 1064-167X, Color-cover, Coated, Saddle-stitched
Subscriptions: Indv. $45, Can. $50, For. $50, $5/copy
Circulation: Total-7,200

Las Vegas Insider
Business, Association

Publishing Co: Good 'N' Lucky Promotions, PO Box 29274, Las Vegas, NV 89126-3274;
Title Tel # (602) 636-1649 Title Fax # (602) 636-1649
Editorial Description: Travel-Money saving-Gaming Info.
General Info: Yr. Est. Monthly
Subscriptions: Indv. $42, Can. $42, $4/copy
Advertising: Accepts Inserts.

Le Soleil Francais
Consumer

Publishing Co: Le Soleil Francais, 1633 Monument Avenue, Richmond, VA 23220-2906
Editorial Description: Travel and culture of southern France and the French Caribbean.
General Info: Monthly

Le Traveller

Publishing Co: Fundy Group Pubs., Box 128, 2 Second St., Yarmouth, NS B5A 4B1 Canada;
Title Tel # (902) 742-7111
Personnel: Editor-John Prince
General Info: Monthly, Offset press
Subscriptions: Indv. $5
Circulation: Total-10,000
Advertising: Inquire for rates.

Leonard Moss
See: DANCE

Lonely Planet Newsletter
Consumer

Publishing Co: Lonely Planet Pubs., 155 Filbert St., Ste 251, Oakland, CA 94607-2531;
Title Tel # (510) 893-8555 Title Fax # (510) 893-8563
Personnel: Circ. Mgr.-Hugh D'Andrade, Mag. Ed., Adv. Dir.-Eric Kettunen, Promotion Dir.-Carolyn Miller
Editorial Description: Travel information culled form letters written by readers of Lonely Planet Guides and from the guide authors.
General Info: (Formerly Lonely Planet Update), Yr. Est. 1981, Quarterly, Trim Size-8½ x 11, 8 pages, 2 Color, Recycled, Saddle-stitched
Subscriptions: Free
Circulation: Total-10,000

Long Trail News, The
See: OUTDOORS

Mature Traveler
Consumer   **CPM: $80**

Publishing Co: GEM Publishing Group, PO Box 50820, Reno, NV 89513-0820;
Title Tel # (702) 786-7419
Personnel: Publisher, Editor-Gene Malott
Editorial Description: Vacation plans for older Americans. Deals, trips and travel tips for 49ers-plus. Destinations of interest to seniors.
General Info: Yr. Est. 1984, Monthly, Desktop press, 12 pages, No Color, Newsprint
Subscriptions: Indv. $30, Can. $38, For. $38, $5/copy
Acquistions: Publication Bought
Circulation: Total-2,500
Advertising: $200. Accepts Inserts.
List Rental: Actives: $100/M, Hotline: 6,000, $100/M, Expires: 12,000, $100/M

Maui Update

Publishing Co: Paradise Pubs., 8110 SW Wareham Cir, Portland, OR 97223-6992;
Title Tel # (503) 246-1555
Personnel: Publisher-Greg Stilson, Editor-Christie Stilson, Production Mgr.-Judy Estes, Art Dir.-Susie O'Day
Editorial Description: A quarterly newsletter featuring current travel information for Maui.
General Info: Yr. Est. 1986, Quarterly, Trim Size-8½ x 11, Desktop press, 6 pages, ISSN: 0895-9390, 1% ads, No Color, Newsprint
Subscriptions: Indv. $10, $3/copy
Circulation: (50% controlled), Total-2,000
Advertising: Inquire for rates.
List Rental: Rents Lists

Mexico Retirement and Travel Assistance

Publishing Co: Mexico Retirement and Travel Assistance, 436 Scenic Dr # 2190, Henderson, NV 89015-8356
Personnel: Editor-John Bryant
General Info: Yr. Est. 1990, Quarterly
Subscriptions: Indv. $17

Mexico West
Consumer

Publishing Co: Mexico West Travel Club, Inc., PO Box 1646, Bonita, CA 91908-1646;
Title Tel # (619) 585-3033 Title Fax # (619) 420-8133
Personnel: Editor, Circ. Mgr.-Shirley Miller
Editorial Description: Baja California travel information & saving.
General Info: Yr. Est. 1975, Monthly, Trim Size-8½ x 11, Web press, 8 pages, ISSN: 0889-7107, 1% ads, No Color, Newsprint
Subscriptions: Indv. $35, $3/copy
Circulation: Total-7,000
Advertising: Inquire for rates.
List Rental: Rents Lists
Printing Co: B-Z Printing, McFadden, Santa Ana, CA 92648 Tel # (714) 546-0866

Mileposts

Publishing Co: MTA Metro-North Railroad/Corporate Communications, 345 Madison Avenue, New York, NY 10017-3706; Title Tel # (212) 340-2512 Title Fax # (212) 340-3280
Editorial Description: Railroad information published for Metro-North Commuters - operations, capital projects, promotions, features.
General Info: Monthly, 4 pages, No Color
Subscriptions: Free
Circulation: Total-60,000

Nationwide Intelligence Strategic Information for US Travel
Business, Consumer

Publishing Co: Nationwide Intelligence, PO Box 1922, Saginaw, MI 48605-1922; Title Tel # (517) 752-6123 Title Fax # (517) 752-1605
Personnel: Publisher-David Oppermann
Editorial Description: Updates on major cities, airports, and airlines for the corporate traveler. Information also includes an extensive guidelines and reference section which includes glossary of terms used in the airline industry, and airline & airport codes.
General Info: Yr. Est. 1987, Monthly, Trim Size-8$\frac{1}{2}$ x 11, Sheetfed press, 2 pages, Color, Looseleaf
Subscriptions: Indv. $350

Nationwide Intelligence Travel Alert Bulletin
Business, Consumer

Publishing Co: Nationwide Intelligence, PO Box 1922, Saginaw, MI 48605-1922; Title Tel # (517) 752-6123 Title Fax # (517) 752-1605
Personnel: Publisher, Editor-David Oppermann, Circ. Mgr.-Debra Podany
Editorial Description: For the corporate traveler or travel planner. Alerts on potential problems with airlines, airports, & cities.
General Info: (Formerly Strategic Information for U.S. Air Travel), Yr. Est. 1987, Semi-monthly, Trim Size-8$\frac{1}{2}$ x 11, Offset press, 4 pages, Color
Subscriptions: Indv. $95
Acquistions: Publication Bought, Publication Sold

Newsletter-International Academy for the Study of Tourism
Scholarly, Association

Publishing Co: University of Minnesota, Tourism Center, 116 COB, St Paul, MN 55108; Title Tel # (612) 624-4947 Title Fax # (612) 624-4264
Editorial Description: Covers Academy news & studies as well as topics relating to travel & tourism in general.
General Info: Yr. Est. 1988, Tri-annually, Trim Size-8$\frac{1}{2}$ x 11, 12 pages, ISSN: 1012-8042
Subscriptions: Indv. $60, Free With Membership

North Carolina Travel Report
Association

Publishing Co: N.C. Div. of Travel, 430 N Salisbury St, Raleigh, NC 27603-5926; Title Tel # (919) 733-4171
Personnel: Editor-Hope Tyndall
Editorial Description: Articles relating to recent activities of the travel and tourism division with regard to promotions of the travel industry in North Carolina.
General Info: Quarterly, Sheetfed press, 8 pages, 2 Color, Saddle-stitched
Circulation: Total-6,800

North Star
See: ENVIRONMENT & ECOLOGY

Northeastern Limousine Operators Association Nor'Easter Newsletter
See: TRAFFIC & TRANSPORTATION

Ocean & Cruise News
Association

Publishing Co: World Ocean & Cruise Liner Society, PO Box 92, Stamford, CT 06904-0092; Title Tel # (203) 329-2787 Title Fax # (203) 329-2787
Personnel: Publisher, Editor-George Devol
Editorial Description: Complete news on cruises, new ships and itineraries. Special features on cruise ships with ratings. Annual ship classification guide and survey.
General Info: Yr. Est. 1980, Monthly, Offset press, 16 pages, No Color
Subscriptions: Indv. $28, Can. $32, For. $32, $3/copy
Circulation: Total-6,500
List Rental: Expires: $75/M

Odyssey
Consumer

Publishing Co: Summerhill, 2780 State St., Santa Barbara, CA 93105-5518
Personnel: Publisher-Syd Summerhill, Editor-Priscilla Sesma
Editorial Description: Travel newsletter for the private pilot.
General Info: Yr. Est. 1988, Quarterly
Subscriptions: Indv. $45, $11/copy
Circulation: Total-2,000
Printing Co: Rapid Print, 5880 Hollister Ave., Goleta, CA 93117 Tel # (805) 964-6498

Ontario Vacation Farms

Publishing Co: Ontario Vacation Farms Association, c/o S. Putzel, RR #2, Alma, ON N0B 1A0 Canada; Title Tel # (519) 846-9378
Personnel: Editor-Sharon Grose
General Info: Yr. Est. 1967, Annually, 40 pages, 2 Color, Matte, Saddle-stitched
Acquistions: Publication Bought
Circulation: Total-100,000
Advertising: Inquire for rates.

Out and About
Consumer

Publishing Co: Out and About, 542 Chapel St., New Haven, CT 06511 Tel # (203) 789-8518 Fax # (203) 789-8759
Personnel: Publisher-David Alport, Editor-Billy Kolber
Editorial Description: Travel information for gay readers.
General Info: Yr. Est. 1992, 10x/yr., Trim Size-8$\frac{1}{2}$ x 11, Letrpr. press, 16 pages, ISSN: 1066-7776, 2 Color, Matte, Saddle-stitched
Subscriptions: Indv. $49, Can. $59, For. $69, $5/copy
Circulation: Total-6,500
List Rental: List Management Co.: Triangle Marketing Services, Inc., 80 8 Ave. Suite #305, New York, NY 10011 Tel # (212) 242-4040, Fax # (212) 242-1344, Actives: 8,000, $125/M, Expires: 3,000, $115/M
Printing Co: Phoenix Press, 15 James St, New Haven, CT 06513-4253 Tel # (203) 865-5555

Over the Rainbow
Consumer

Publishing Co: Mobility Intl. USA, PO Box 10767, Eugene, OR 97440-2767; Title Tel # (503) 343-1284 Title Fax # (503) 343-6812
Personnel: Editor-Sharon Brown
Editorial Description: Educational exchanges and travel-referral services for the diabled.
General Info: Yr. Est. 1982, Quarterly, 8 pages, 2% ads, No Color
Subscriptions: Indv. $10
Circulation: Total-1,000
Advertising: Inquire for rates.
Printing Co: MIUSA, Box 3551, Eugene, OR 97403 Tel # (503) 343-1284

PBC Travel Newsletter
Consumer

Publishing Co: Publishing & Business Consultants, 101 W. 64th St. Unit #3, Inglewood, CA 90302-1255 Tel # (213) 732-3477 Fax # (213) 732-3477
Personnel: Publisher, Editor-Andeson Atia
General Info: Quarterly, ISSN: 1059-1966
Advertising: Inquire for rates.

Partners for Travel
Consumer

Publishing Co: Partners for Travel, Inc., PO Box 560337, Miami, FL 33256-0337
Personnel: Publisher, Editor-Clarice MacGarvey
Editorial Description: Travel tips, money-saving ideas and updates on travel opportunities worldwide for single travelers. Focus on items and destinations of interest to single men and women over 35.
General Info: Yr. Est. 1992, Monthly, Trim Size-8$\frac{1}{2}$ x 11, Letrpr. press, 8 pages, Matte
Subscriptions: Indv. $36, $3/copy
Circulation: (40% controlled), Total-1,000, Subscriptions-600
Advertising: Inquire for rates.
Printing Co: Valley Web, 1299 Stowe Avenue, Medford, OR 97504 Tel # (503) 772-7039

Passport Newsletter
Consumer

Publishing Co: Remy Publishing Co., 350 W Hubbard St # 440, Chicago, IL 60610-4011; Title Tel # (312) 464-0300 Title Fax # (312) 464-0166
Editorial Description: The world's premier luxury travel newsletter.
General Info: Yr. Est. 1965, Monthly, 8 pages
Subscriptions: Indv. $75, Inst. $75, Can. $75, For. $100

Pepper Bird Pathways
Consumer

Publishing Co: Pepper Bird Publications, P.O. Box 1071, Williamsburg, VA 23187-5604 Tel # (804) 258-4403 Fax # (804) 258-5604
Personnel: Publisher-Joanne F. Limric, Editor-Rosanne Smith
Editorial Description: African American events and cultural attractions in Virginia.
General Info: Annually

Personal Travel Report
Business, Consumer

Publishing Co: Nationwide Intelligence, PO Box 1922, Saginaw, MI 48605-1922; Title Tel # (517) 752-6123 Title Fax # (517) 752-1605
Personnel: Publisher-David Oppermann
Editorial Description: Helps the individual business or leisure traveler get the best value while avoiding the rip-offs and over rated products and services. Includes our respected travel alerts, comprehensive city reports, recommended best buys, cruise buys of the month, our favorite resorts and city hotels, airline critiques, and what others are recommending.
General Info: Yr. Est. 1992, Monthly, Trim Size-8$\frac{1}{2}$ x 11, Desktop press, 4 pages
Subscriptions: Indv. $25

Pinkerton World Status Map
Business

Publishing Co: Pinkerton Risk Assessment Services, 1600 Wilson Blvd Ste 901, Arlington, VA 22209-2505 Tel # (703) 525-6111; Title Tel # (703) 564-8473 Title Fax # (703) 525-2454
Editorial Description: Danger/medical warnings for intl. travelers in colorful map form.
General Info: (Formerly World Status Map), Yr. Est. 1983, Bi-monthly, Trim Size-11 x 17, Sheetfed press, 4 pages, ISSN: 0887-9559, Color, Coated
Subscriptions: Indv. $70, $13/copy
Circulation: Total-1,500

Portable Practitioner: Opportunities in the Healing Arts
See: HEALTH

Portugal Update
Consumer

Publishing Co: Portuguese National Tourist Office, 590 Fifth Avenue, 4th Floor, New York, NY 10036-4704 Fax # (212) 764-6137; Title Tel # (212) 354-4403
Personnel: Editor-Evelyn Heyward
Editorial Description: Travel and hotel information on Portuagal.
General Info: Quarterly, Trim Size-8½ x 11, 4 pages, 4 Color, Coated
Subscriptions: Free

Practical Gourmet
Consumer

Publishing Co: L.K. Publishing Co., 7 Putter La. P.O Box 102, Gourmet Bldg. 102, Middle Island, NY 11953-0102 Tel # (516) 924-3888 Fax # (516) 924-3890; Title Tel # (516) 924-8555
Personnel: Publisher, Editor-Gaylen Andrews, Circ. Mgr.-Roger Dextor, Adv. Dir.-Andrew Linick, Ph.D, Production Mgr., Art Dir.-Marsha Huckeba, Promotion Dir.-Robert Kaplan
Editorial Description: Written for the North American and international gourmet traveler. Focuses on wine tasting, food festivals, healthy cooking, national and international travel destinations, fine restaurants, luxury cruises, four to five star hotels, spas, resorts and allinclusive properties. Emphasis on leisure lifestyles of the over 40 age group.
General Info: Yr. Est. 1981, Monthly, Trim Size-8½ x 11, Web press, 24 pages, ISSN: 0732-8710, 4 Color, Matte, Saddle-stitched
Subscriptions: Indv. $48, Can. $60, For. $75, $5/copy
Acquistions: Publication Bought
Circulation: Total-215,000, Readership-500,000
Advertising: Accepts Inserts.
List Rental: List Management Co.: Manager: Shane Clarke; L.K. Lists, P.O Box 102, Middle Island, NY 11953 Tel # (516) 924-3888, Actives: $75/M, Hotline: $90/M, Expires: $60/M
Printing Co: L.K. Litho Div., The Linick Group, Inc., Communications Tower, P.O Box 102, Middle Island, NY 11953-0102 Tel # (516) 924-3888

Presidents' Journal
See: HISTORY

Questing
Consumer

Publishing Co: Questing Adventure Society, 24720 Calle Altamira, Calabasas, CA 91302-3004; Title Tel # (818) 591-9554 Title Fax # (818) 591-8595
Personnel: Publisher-Laura Greenburg
Editorial Description: Out of the ordinary vacation information center. Bicycling, trekking, kayaking, ballooning, etc.
General Info: Yr. Est. 1989, Monthly, Trim Size-8½ x 11, Desktop press, 16 pages

Quicktrips Travel Letter
Business, Consumer

Publishing Co: Colbert's Corner, PO Box 266, Churchville, MD 21028-0266; Title Tel # (410) 836-0297 Title Fax # (410) 836-7409
Personnel: Publisher-Fran Severn
Editorial Description: Monthly subscription newsletter featuring 3-4-5 day getaways.
General Info: Yr. Est. 1990, Monthly, Trim Size-8½ x 11, Offset press, 8 pages, ISSN: 1064-0339, Matte
Subscriptions: Indv. $45, $5/copy
Circulation: Total-500
Printing Co: Bel Air Copy & Print, 110 South Main Street, Bel Air, MD 21014 Tel # (410) 879-0577, Fax # (410) 879-0594

RV Park & Campground Report
See: PARKS & RECREATION AREAS

Recreation Advisor
See: MOBILE HOMES

Resort Reports
See: REAL ESTATE

RestQuest Compass
Consumer

Publishing Co: RestQuest Corporation, 72 Spring Street, New York, NY 10012; Title Tel # (212) 334-5100 Title Fax # (212) 334-2285
Personnel: Publisher-Steven Spiegel, Editor-Lisa Silberlicht
Editorial Description: Rest and recreation guide for the Northeast.
General Info: Yr. Est. 1993, Bi-monthly, Trim Size-9¼ x 12¼, 2 Color
Subscriptions: Indv. $12

Romantic Hideaways
Consumer

Publishing Co: Barbara Brass Communications, Inc., PO Box 659, East Hampton, NY 11937-0501; Title Tel # (212) 969-8682
Personnel: Publisher, Editor-Barbara Brass
Editorial Description: Dedicated to the discovery of Romantic places for the sophisticated & discriminating traveler. Each issue covers, in detail, a romantic hideaway in an le locations.
General Info: Yr. Est. 1986, Monthly, ISSN: 1042-7422
Subscriptions: Indv. $75, $8/copy
Circulation: Total-15,423
Advertising: Accepts Inserts.

Rudder Flutter
See: AERONAUTICS/ASTRONAUTICS

Runzheimer Reports on Travel Management
Business

Publishing Co: Runzheimer Intl., Runzheimer Park, Rochester, WI 53167; Title Tel # (414) 767-2200 Title Fax # (414) 767-2254
Personnel: Editor-Jackie Trimble
General Info: Yr. Est. 1981, Monthly, Trim Size-8½ x 11, Sheetfed press, 14 pages, No Color, Newsprint
Subscriptions: Indv. $295, $30/copy
Acquistions: Publication Bought, Publication Sold
List Rental: Rents Lists

Rural Property Investor
See: REAL ESTATE

Russia & China Travel Newsletter
Business, Consumer

Publishing Co: Printing Consultants, Federal Sq., Box 636, Newark, NJ 07101; Title Tel # (908) 682-2382
Personnel: Editor-John Felber
Editorial Description: Travel, transportation and other information about Russia and Eastern Europe.Land trade, marketing.
General Info: (Formerly Russia & East Travel Newsletter), Yr. Est. 1988, Weekly, Trim Size-8½ x 11, 4 pages, ISSN: 1059-4957
Subscriptions: Indv. $62

Sailaway
Consumer

Publishing Co: Travel Agents International, PO Box 42008, St. Petersburg, FL 42008
Personnel: Editor-Bill Beckler
Editorial Description: For those interested in cruises.
General Info: Monthly, Trim Size-8½ x 11, 6 pages

Shipboard Cruiser, The
Consumer

Publishing Co: Shipboard Cruiser, The, PO Box 533737, Orlando, FL 32853-3737; Title Tel # (407) 422-6095 Title Fax # (407) 422-3608
Personnel: Publisher, Editor-Phil Beach
Editorial Description: Information about shipboard vacation cruising.
General Info: Yr. Est. 1993, Monthly, Trim Size-8½ x 11, 12 pages, ISSN: 1066-9981, No Color
Subscriptions: Indv. $49, For. $59, $5/copy

Shoestring Traveler, The
Consumer   **CPM: $52**

Publishing Co: International Features, Inc., 8 South J St., Ste. 3, Box 1349, Lake Worth, FL 33460-3742; Title Tel # (407) 582-8320 Title Fax # (407) 582-8320
Personnel: Publisher-William Bates, Editor-Byron Lutz, Travel Ed., Feature Ed.-Ken Roon, Adv. Dir.-Lachelle Granholm
Editorial Description: World-wide travel tips for adventurous individuals who want to see the world on a shoestring. Columns include air courier travel, budget getaways, discount ticketing, etc.
General Info: Yr. Est. 1991, Bi-monthly, Trim Size-8½ x 11, Offset press, 16 pages, 2 Color, Matte, Saddle-stitched
Subscriptions: Indv. $29, Inst. $29
Circulation: Total-10,550
Advertising: $550.
Printing Co: Lake Worth Herald, South H St., Lake Worth, FL 33460

Side Streets of the World
Business, Consumer

Publishing Co: Holland & Edwards Publishing, Inc., 250 Mercer St., Apt. A-203, New York, NY 10012-1144; Title Tel # (212) 431-1652 Title Fax # (212) 966-1203
Personnel: Publisher-Edward Holland, Editor-Christopher Holland, Circ. Mgr., Production Mgr.-Gina Dililo, Art Dir.-Karen Holland
Editorial Description: A very literate travel guide with color photos.
General Info: Yr. Est. 1984, Monthly, Web press, 12 pages, ISSN: 0741-7624, 4 Color, Coated
Subscriptions: Indv. $37, Can. $40, For. $45
Circulation: (100% controlled), Total-160,000
Printing Co: Strathmore Printing, 200 Gary Lane, Geneva, IL 60134 Tel # (708) 232-9677, Fax # (708) 232-0198

Ski Tripper
See: SKIING & SNOWMOBILING

Smithsonian 'Traveler'
Association

Publishing Co: Smithsonian Institution, 900 Jefferson Dr., S.W., Washington, DC 20560-0001 Tel # (202) 357-2888; Title Fax # (212) 642-0309
Editorial Description: Published for well-educated, affluent and active individuals with a keen interest in natural science, history, art, and air & space who enjoy traveling and are members of the Smithsonian Institution.
General Info: Monthly
List Rental: List Management Co.: Coolidge List Marketing, 25 W. 43rd St., New York, NY 10036-7491 Tel # (212) 274-0630, Fax # (212) 274-0650, Actives: 128,000, $80/M

Sodus News, The
See: REGIONAL INTEREST

Sound of Giants

Publishing Co: Greater Independent Assn. of Natl. Travel Services, 2 Park Ave Rm 2205, New York, NY 10016-9301; Title Tel # (212) 505-5665
Personnel: Editor-Janice Wilk
General Info: Bi-monthly, Trim Size-8½ x 11, 4 pages

Source I
Consumer

Publishing Co: RKS Marketing, Box 7985, Northridge, CA 91327-7985; Title Tel # (818) 886-7940
Personnel: Publisher-Ron Silver, Editor-Judy Ewing, Circ. Mgr.-Mark Silver
Editorial Description: News items & features for vacation travel news letters.
General Info: Yr. Est. 1981, Bi-monthly, Trim Size-8½ x 11, Mimeo press, 6 pages, ISSN: 0278-4378
Subscriptions: Indv. $60, Can. $65, For. $75
Acquistions: Publication Bought
Circulation: Total-550
Advertising: Accepts Inserts.
Printing Co: Kinkos Copies, 9132 Reseda Blvd, Northridge, CA 91324-3030 Tel # (818) 701-0362

Source II
Business   **CPM: $250**

Publishing Co: RKS Marketing, Box 7985, Northridge, CA 91327-7985; Title Tel # (818) 886-7940
Personnel: Publisher-Ronald Silver, Editor-Judy Ewing, Circ. Mgr.-Mark Silver
Editorial Description: News items and features for business travel newsletters.
General Info: Yr. Est. 1981, Bi-monthly, Trim Size-8½ x 11, Mimeo press, 6 pages, ISSN: 0278-4378, Ind/Abs/Online: SagePub.Admin.Abstr.
Subscriptions: Indv. $60, Can. $65, For. $70
Acquistions: Publication Bought
Circulation: Total-400
Advertising: $100. Accepts Inserts.
Printing Co: Kinkos Copies, 9132 Reseda Blvd, Northridge, CA 91324-3030 Tel # (818) 701-0362

Speedev
See: RAILROADS

Star Service
Consumer

Publishing Co: Reed Travel Group, 500 Plaza Dr., 4th Floor, Secaucus, NJ 07094-3626
Fax # (201) 902-7989; Title Tel # (201) 902-2000
Personnel: Publisher, Editor-Steven Gordon
Editorial Description: Critiques of hotels & cruise ships worldwide.
General Info: (Formerly Sloan Travel Agency Reports; ABC Star Service), Yr. Est. 1960, Quarterly, Trim Size-8½ x 11, Sheetfed press, 200 pages, No Color, Newsprint, Looseleaf
Subscriptions: Indv. $210
Printing Co: Vicks Lithography, Commercial Dr., Yorkville, NY 13495 Tel # (315) 736-9344, Fax # (315) 736-1901

StateSide

Publishing Co: Travel Industry Association of America, 2 Lafayette Centre, 1133 21 St., NW, Washington, DC 20036; Title Tel # (202) 293-1433 Title Fax # (202) 293-3155
Personnel: Editor-Donnie Layne
Editorial Description: Newsletter of the National Council of State Travel Directors, an industry council of the Travel Industry Association of America.
General Info: Yr. Est. 1983, Quarterly, Trim Size-8½ x 11, Mimeo press, 6 pages
Subscriptions: Free With Membership

TAISSA Letter

Publishing Co: Victims's Service Agency, 2 Lafayette St, New York, NY 10007-1380; Title Tel # (212) 679-0200
Personnel: Editor-Maureen O'Brien
General Info: (Formerly ISS Letter), Yr. Est. 1940, Bi-monthly
Circulation: Total-5,200

This Week in Richmond

Publishing Co: This Week in Richmond, 117 Matoaka Rd, Richmond, VA 23226-2214
Personnel: Editor-Chena Allison
General Info: Yr. Est. 1969, Weekly
Subscriptions: Indv. $10
Circulation: Total-7,000
Advertising: Inquire for rates.

Thrifty Traveler
Consumer

Publishing Co: Thrifty Traveler, Inc., PO Box 5126, Clearwater, FL 34618-5126; Title Tel # (813) 791-1945 Title Fax # (813) 797-6790
Personnel: Publisher, Editor-Mary Van Meer, Production Mgr.-LeAnn Lane, Promotion Dir.-Maury Rosenbaum
Editorial Description: Show travelers how to stretch their travel dollars and how to travel in a safe and hassle-free manner.
General Info: Yr. Est. 1993, Monthly, Trim Size-8½ x 11, Offset press, 8 pages, ISSN: 1076-9099, 2 Color, Matte
Subscriptions: Indv. $26, Can. $30, For. $41, $3/copy
Circulation: Total-12,000

Top Drawer
Association

Publishing Co: Maine Publicity Bureau, 97 Winthrop St, Hallowell, ME 04347-1238; Title Tel # (207) 289-2423
Personnel: Editor-Jane Thompson
Editorial Description: Tourism and news about the publicity bureau.
General Info: Quarterly, Trim Size-8½ x 11, Offset press, 16 pages
Circulation: Total-4,000

Topics
Business, Association

Publishing Co: Assn. of Group Travel Executives, 424 Madison Ave Rm 706, New York, NY 10017-1106; Title Tel # (212) 486-4300
Editorial Description: Information for members of this executive travel association.
General Info: Yr. Est. 1965, Semi-annually

TopoZine

Publishing Co: Fred Argoff, 1204 Avenue U, # 1290, Brooklyn, NY 11229
Editorial Description: A zine is devoted to maps with discussions about old maps and examples of some new ones.
General Info: Trim Size-5 x 7, 8 pages
Subscriptions: Indv. $5

Tourism Update

Publishing Co: Tourism Industry Assn. of Manitoba, 375 York Ave., Ste. 232, Winnipeg, MB R3C 3J3 Canada
Personnel: Editor-Adele Stevens
General Info: Yr. Est. 1984, Quarterly, Offset press, 8 pages, 2 Color
Circulation: Total-5,000
Advertising: Inquire for rates.

Tourist Office of Spain
Travel Notes
Consumer

Publishing Co: Tourist Office of Spain, 665 Fifth Avenue, New York, NY 10022
Fax # (212) 980-1053; Title Tel # (212) 759-8822
Editorial Description: Covers scheduled flight information, transportation within Spain, accommodations and gastronomy.
General Info: Irregular, Trim Size-8½ x 11, 4 pages, 2 Color, Coated

Tourist Outfitter
See: APPAREL & ACCESSORIES

Tracks RV News
See: MOBILE HOMES

Trail Less Traveled
Consumer

Publishing Co: Winsor Publishing Company, 1919 14th St Ste 300, Boulder, CO 80302-5321; Title Tel # (303) 444-6879 Title Fax # (303) 443-1842
Personnel: Publisher-Tom Winsor, Editor-Ty Wyant, Circ. Mgr.-Lisa Newell
Editorial Description: Natural resistance-free training for horses a how to guide.
General Info: Yr. Est. 1994, Monthly, Trim Size-8½ x 11, 2 Color
Subscriptions: Indv. $38, For. $60, $4/copy

Trail Riders of the Canadian Rockies Newsletter
Consumer

Publishing Co: Trail Riders of the Canadian Rockies Newsletter, P.O. Box 6742, Postal St. D, Calgary, AB T2P 2E6 Canada Tel # (403) 251-3077; Title Tel # (403) 264-8656 Title Fax # (403) 264-8657
Personnel: Publisher, Editor-Marlene Lea
Editorial Description: Tourist information on trail riding in the Canadian Rocky Mountains.
General Info: (Formerly Trail Chatter), Yr. Est. 1923, Quarterly, Trim Size-8½ x 11, Mimeo press, 7 pages, 1% ads, No Color
Subscriptions: $2/copy
Circulation: Total-450
Advertising: Inquire for rates.

Travel & Tourism Executive Report
Business, Association   **CPM: $500**

Publishing Co: Leisure Industry/Recreation News, PO Box 43563, Washington, DC 20010-9563; Title Tel # (202) 232-7107
Personnel: Publisher-Marj Jensen
Editorial Description: Travel and tourism marketing and demographics for industry executives in all travel segments: destinations, lodging, cruise, air lines, etc.
General Info: Yr. Est. 1981, 10x/yr., Trim Size-8½ x 11, Desktop press, 8 pages, ISSN: 1070-8855
Subscriptions: Indv. $65, For. $75, Free With Membership
Circulation: Total-2,000
Advertising: $1,000.
List Rental: Actives: 4,000, $125/M

Travel Books Worldwide
Business, Consumer

Publishing Co: Travel Keys Books, PO Box 162266, Sacramento, CA 95816-2266; Title Tel # (916) 452-5200
Personnel: Publisher-P. Mansion, Editor-R.C. Bynum
Editorial Description: Reviews travel books for world travelers, booksellers, librarians, and editors.
General Info: Yr. Est. 1990, 10x/yr., Trim Size-8½ x 11, Desktop press, 20 pages, ISSN: 1058-7098
Subscriptions: Indv. $36, Can. $48, For. $72
Circulation: Total-1,600

Travel Companions
Consumer

Publishing Co: Travel Companion Exchange, Inc., PO Box 833, Amityville, NY 11701-0833; Title Tel # (516) 454-0880
Personnel: Publisher, Editor-Jens Jurgen
Editorial Description: North America's newsletter for travel minded singles in all age groups. Gives money saving travel tips; reviews books helpful to singles. Contains hundreds of listings from singles seeking travel companions & partners.
General Info: Yr. Est. 1982, Bi-monthly, Trim Size-8½ x 11, Sheetfed press, 46 pages, ISSN: 1076-5719, 2 Color, Saddle-stitched
Subscriptions: Indv. $48, Can. $7, For. $68, $5/copy
Acquistions: Publication Bought, Publication Sold
Circulation: Total-5,800

Travel Confidential — *Business, Consumer*

Publishing Co: Lowell Communications, 88 Bleeker St., New York, NY 10012; Title Tel # (212) 254-1069 Title Fax # (212) 260-5920
Personnel: Editor-Paul Edwards
Editorial Description: Travel discounts and hints for frequent fliers.
General Info: (Formerly Travel Smarter), Yr. Est. 1991, Monthly, ISSN: 1056-0025
Subscriptions: Indv. $95

Travel Distribution Report — *Business*

Publishing Co: Garrett Communications, 210 North Adams Street, Suite 1000, Rockville, MD 20850; Title Tel # (301) 738-7927 Title Fax # (301) 738-7896
Personnel: Publisher-Thomas Woodall, Editor-Patricia Coates, Production Mgr.-Hanta Ralay, Mktg. Dir.-Robin Woodall
Editorial Description: Information on travel reservations, ticketing and distribution.
General Info: (Formerly CRS Update), Yr. Est. 1993, Bi-weekly, ISSN: 1074-1615
Subscriptions: Indv. $437, For. $477, $20/copy
Advertising: Inquire for rates. Accepts Inserts.
List Rental: Rents Lists

Travel Expense Management — *Business*

Publishing Co: Health Resource Publishing, 3100 Hwy. 138, PO Box 1442, Wall Township, NJ 07719-1442; Title Tel # (908) 681-1133 Title Fax # (908) 681-0490
Personnel: Publisher-Robert Jenkins, Editor-Melanie Jenkins
Editorial Description: Information on: how to save money on corporate travel; how to prepare for successful meetings; locations where airfare and hotel savings can still be found; how to reclaim value-added taxes and the latest news from Washington, DC.
General Info: Yr. Est. 1979, 24x/yr., Trim Size-8½ x 11, Offset press, 6 pages, ISSN: 0272-569X, 1% ads, No Color, Newsprint
Subscriptions: Indv. $397, $10/copy
Circulation: Total-1,500
Advertising: Inquire for rates. Accepts Inserts.
List Rental: Actives: $95/M
Printing Co: ACN Graphics, 1602 Birchwood Ln, Neptune, NJ 07753-6910 Tel # (908) 681-6083

Travel Food & Wine — *Consumer*

Publishing Co: Punch in Syndicate, 400 E. 59th St., Apt. 9F, New York, NY 10022-2344; Title Tel # (212) 755-4363 Title Fax # (212) 755-4365
Personnel: Publisher-J. Walman, Editor-Nancy Pretster
Editorial Description: Features, articles, reviews of topics related to travel, foods & wines including restaurants, hotels, airlines, cruise ships, resorts, spas, entertainment, art, videos, and computer products.
General Info: Yr. Est. 1980, Monthly, Desktop press, Ind/Abs/Online: Enterprise Network
Subscriptions: $25/copy
Circulation: Total-40,000
Advertising: Accepts Inserts.

Travel For Less — *Consumer*

Publishing Co: Bellwoods Publications, 31878 Del Obispo #330, San Juan Capistrano, CA 92675 Fax # (714) 491-0936; Title Tel # (714) 496-0347 Title Fax # (719) 149-0936
Personnel: Publisher, Editor-Eric Bollmann
Editorial Description: Article and reports would not spend less on Lodging, Cruises and any other means of travel.
General Info: (Formerly Bellwoods Publications), Yr. Est. 1992, Monthly, Trim Size-17 x 11, Desktop press, 4 pages
Subscriptions: Indv. $12, Can. $15, $2/copy
Circulation: Total-300

Travel Management Newsletter — *Business*

Publishing Co: Official Airline Guides, Inc., 500 Plaza Drive, 6th Floor, Secaucus, NJ 07096 Parent Co.-Official Airline Guides, Inc., Oak Brook; Title Tel # (201) 902-1775
Personnel: Publisher-Martin Deutsch, Editor-Jim Glab, Promotion Dir.-Rudy Pins
Editorial Description: Travel industry newsletter for management personnel.
General Info: Yr. Est. 1964, Semi-weekly, Trim Size-8½ x 11, Offset press, 4 pages, No Color
Subscriptions: Indv. $325

Travel Marketing and Agency Management Guidelines

Publishing Co: RKS Marketing, Box 7985, Northridge, CA 91327-7985; Title Tel # (818) 886-7940
Personnel: Publisher-Ronald Silver, Editor-Judy Ewing, Circ. Mgr.-Mark Silver
Editorial Description: Leading advisory newsletter for the travel agency industry.
General Info: Yr. Est. 1973, Bi-monthly, Trim Size-8½ x 11, Offset press, 8 pages, ISSN: 0275-3545, No Color
Subscriptions: Indv. $49, Can. $59, For. $64
Advertising: $300. Accepts Inserts.
Printing Co: Kinkos Copies, 9132 Reseda Blvd, Northridge, CA 91324-3030 Tel # (818) 701-0362

Travel Marketing Trends

Publishing Co: Newsletter Factory, 1000 Parkwood Cir. NW, Suite #823, Atlanta, GA 30339-2139; Title Tel # (770) 664-1175
Personnel: Publisher-T. Hartman, Editor-Dianne Breen
General Info: Yr. Est. 1987, Monthly
Subscriptions: Indv. $235

Travel Minute — *Consumer, Association*

Publishing Co: Minnesota Office of Tourism, 375 Jackson St Ste 250, Saint Paul, MN 55101-1810; Title Tel # (612) 297-3291
Personnel: Editor-Chuck Lennon
Editorial Description: Events, plans, research studies, and personnel changes of interest to the MN travel industry.
General Info: (Formerly Minnesota Tourist Travel Notes), Yr. Est. 1986, 17x/yr., Trim Size-8½ x 11, Offset press, 8 pages, 2 Color
Subscriptions: Indv. $3
Circulation: (100% controlled), Total-5,982

Travel Monthly — *Consumer*

Publishing Co: Father & Son Publishing, 1959 Loiza St., #912, Santurce, PR 00911-1850; Title Tel # (809) 728-6393
Personnel: Publisher-Pedro Rodriguez Goycoolea, Adv. Dir.-Juan M. Rodriguez, Editor, Production Mgr., Promotion Dir.-Pedro Rodriguez-Palou
Editorial Description: Travel industry in Puerto Rico.
General Info: (Formerly Parati Industira de Viajes; Travel Source), Yr. Est. 1988, Monthly, Trim Size-7½ x 10, Sheetfed press, 24 pages, 2 Color, Newsprint, Saddle-stitched
Subscriptions: Indv. $15, Free To Qualified Recipient
Circulation: Total-3,000
Advertising: Inquire for rates. Accepts Inserts.

Travel Printout — *Business*

Publishing Co: U.S. Travel Data Center, 1100 New York Ave., NW, Ste. 450, Washington, DC 20005 Tel # (202) 408-1832 Fax # (202) 408-1255; Title Tel # (202) 293-1040
Personnel: Editor-Ida Simmons
Editorial Description: Reports on results of Data Center projects, trends and research in the travel industry.
General Info: Yr. Est. 1973, Monthly, Sheetfed press, 5 pages, ISSN: 0744-6233, Color, Coated
Subscriptions: Indv. $70, $6/copy
Printing Co: Todd-Allan Printing Co., Inc., 6011 Blair Rd NW, Washington, DC 20011-1463

Travel Publicity Leads — *Business*

Publishing Co: Scott American Corp., Box 88, West Redding, CT 06896-0088; Title Tel # (203) 938-2955 Title Fax # (203) 938-2955
Personnel: Publisher, Editor-Frank Scott
Editorial Description: Summarizes what travel writers and broadcasters, from around the world, will be writing about. Provides travel editorial placement opportunities for worldwide subscribers such as the PR professionals at resorts, hotels, cruise lines, airlines, tour operators, destination attraction, CVBs, city/regional/national tourism promotion organizations, and public relations firms with travel industry clients.
General Info: Yr. Est. 1988, Semi-monthly, Trim Size-8½ x 11, 2 pages, ISSN: 1059-8251, 4 Color
Subscriptions: Indv. $157, Inst. $157, Can. $157, For. $157

Travel Review — *Business*

Publishing Co: Sunset Publishing Corp., 80 Willow Rd, Menlo Park, CA 94025-3661 Tel # (415) 321-3600 Fax # (415) 328-6215 Parent Co.-Time Inc. Ventures, New York; Title Tel # (213) 380-9680 Title Fax # (213) 380-4217
Personnel: Editor-Lorelli Embry
Editorial Description: Distributed to travel agents in the 13 western states.
General Info: 8x/yr.
Subscriptions: Free To Qualified Recipient
Circulation: (100% controlled), Total-7,750

Travel Safety Alert
See: AERONAUTICS/ASTRONAUTICS

Travel Sales & Marketing Newsletter — *Business*

Publishing Co: Nissen-Lie Communications, 441 Lexington Ave Rm 1209a, New York, NY 10017-3910; Title Tel # (212) 986-1025 Title Fax # (212) 986-1033
Personnel: Publisher-Angela Reale, Editor-Oivind Mathisen
General Info: Yr. Est. 1987, Monthly
Subscriptions: Indv. $130, For. $150

Travel Scoop Consumer Newsletter — *Business, Consumer*

Publishing Co: Travel Scoop, 1110 Yonge St., Suite 200, Toronto, ON M4V 2L6 Canada; Title Tel # (416) 926-0111 Title Fax # (416) 926-0222
Personnel: Editor-Ann Wallace, Circ. Dir.-Matt Oliver, Publisher, Adv. Dir., Promotion Dir.-Nigel Raincock
Editorial Description: Canada's only consumer travel newsletter focusing on budget & value travel in N. America and around the world.
General Info: Yr. Est. 1983, 10x/yr., Trim Size-8¼ x 10½, Sheetfed press, 24 pages, ISSN: 0822-9228, 4% ads, 2 Color, Recycled, Saddle-stitched
Subscriptions: Indv. $44, Inst. $44, Can. $44, For. $44
Circulation: Total-12,000, Readership-24,000
Advertising: Accepts Inserts.
List Rental: List Management Co.: Cornerstone List Mgrs., 2300 Yonge St., Ste. 2005, Box 2465, Toronto, ON M4P 1E4 Canada Tel # (416) 932-9555, Fax # (416) 932-9566, Actives: 12,100, $120/M

Travel Security Intelligencer — *Business, Consumer*

Publishing Co: Travel Security Intelligencer, 437 Grosvenor, Suite 12, Westmount, PQ H3Y 2S5 Canada; Title Tel # (514) 933-6314 Title Fax # (514) 933-6314
Personnel: Publisher-Tod Hoffman
Editorial Description: Devoted exclusively to the dissemination of intelligence on travel related issues.
General Info: Monthly, Perfect bound
Subscriptions: Indv. $80, Can. $80

Travel Smart
Consumer

Publishing Co: Communications House, Inc., 40 Beechdale Rd, Dobbs Ferry, NY 10522-3021;
Title Tel # (914) 693-8300
Personnel: Publisher, Editor-Herbert Teison, Mng. Editor-Nancy Dunnan
Editorial Description: Information on current travel picture. Contains promos, etc. to allow reader to travel better for less. Discounts on travel for subscribers.
General Info: Yr. Est. 1976, Monthly, Offset press, 12 pages, ISSN: 0741-5826
Subscriptions: Indv. $44, $5/copy
Circulation: Total-13,000
List Rental: List Management Co.: Media Marketplace, 140 Terry Drive, P.O. Box 500, Newtown, PA 18940-0500 Tel # (215) 968-5020, Fax # (215) 968-9410, Actives: 43,000, $80/M, Expires: 21,000, $65/M
Printing Co: King Lithographers, 245 S 4th Ave, Mount Vernon, NY 10550-3804
Tel # (914) 667-4200

Travel Smart for Business

Publishing Co: Runzheimer Intl., Runzheimer Park, Rochester, WI 53167 Tel # (414) 767-2200
Fax # (414) 767-2254
Editorial Description: Designed to help frequent business travelers travel get the most out of their travel dollar.
General Info: Monthly
List Rental: List Management Co.: Direct Media, Inc., 200 Pemberwick Rd., PO Box 4565, Greenwich, CT 06830 Tel # (203) 532-3713, Fax # (203) 531-1452

Travel Writer
Association

Publishing Co: Society of American Travel Writers, 4101 Lake Boone Trail, Ste. 201, Raleigh, NC 27607; Title Tel # (919) 787-5181 Title Fax # (919) 787-4916
Personnel: Editor-Cathy Young
Editorial Description: Society news and travel industry news.
General Info: 10x/yr., 8 pages, 2 Color
Circulation: Total-800

Travelin' Talk
Association

Publishing Co: Travelin' Talk Network, PO Box 3534, Clarksville, TN 37043-3534;
Title Tel # (615) 552-6670 Title Fax # (615) 552-1182
Editorial Description: Members write in to share information.
General Info: Quarterly, ISSN: 1052-1615
Subscriptions: Indv. $15
Circulation: Total-5,000
Printing Co: Mediaworks, 538 Madison St, Clarksville, TN 37040-3620

Travelin' Woman
Consumer

Publishing Co: Nancy Mills Communications, 855 Moraga Dr. Apt 14, Los Angeles, CA 90049-1641;
Title Tel # (310) 472-6318 Title Fax # (310) 476-8389
Personnel: Publisher, Editor-Nancy Mills
Editorial Description: Travel information, tips and advice for women.
General Info: Yr. Est. 1994, Monthly, Trim Size-8½ x 11, Offset press, 10 pages, No Color, Coated, Other
Subscriptions: Indv. $48, For. $58, $4/copy
Circulation: Total-600
Advertising: Inquire for rates. Accepts Inserts.
List Rental: Actives: 2,000, $100/M
Printing Co: B.J's Printers, 200 E. Broadway, Glendale, CA 91205 Tel # (818) 551-7840

Traveling Healthy Newsletter
Business, Consumer

Publishing Co: Traveling Healthy, Inc., 108-48 70th Rd., Forest Hills, NY 11375-3961;
Title Tel # (718) 268-7290
Personnel: Publisher, Editor-Karl Neumann, Production Mgr., Promotion Dir.-Maury Rosenbaum
Editorial Description: Provides info on many aspects of travel & health, advice on immunizations, health alerts. For individuals interested in safe, healthy & comfortable travel.
General Info: Yr. Est. 1988, Bi-monthly, 8 pages, ISSN: 0899-2169
Subscriptions: Indv. $32, Can. $38, For. $38
Circulation: Total-1,200
List Rental: Rents Lists

Travelore Report
Business, Consumer

Publishing Co: T.R. Report, 1512 Spruce St., Philadelphia, PA 19102-4524;
Title Tel # (215) 735-3838 Title Fax # (215) 545-7976
Personnel: Publisher, Editor-T. Barkus, Circ. Mgr.-Allen Barkus
Editorial Description: News letter candidly appraising cities, resorts, hotels, restaurants, carriers for best values for travelers, vacationers and group travel planners.
General Info: Yr. Est. 1971, Monthly, Trim Size-8½ x 11, Offset press, 8 pages, ISSN: 0270-2398, No Color, Coated, Saddle-stitched
Subscriptions: Indv. $24, Can. $30, For. $38, $3/copy

Travelwriter Marketletter
See: JOURNALISM

Travltips
Association, Consumer

Publishing Co: Travltips Cruise & Freighter Travel Association, 163-07 Depot Rd, Flushing, NY 11358-2043; Title Tel # (212) 239-2400 Title Fax # (718) 939-2400
Editorial Description: First hand info of cruises taken by members of the association.
General Info: Yr. Est. 1967, Bi-monthly, ISSN: 0162-9816
Subscriptions: Indv. $20, Can. $27
Circulation: Total-25,000
List Rental: List Management Co.: Listworks, 1 Campus Dr., Pleasantville, NY 10570-1602
Tel # (914) 769-7100, Fax # (914) 769-8070

Trends in the Hotel Industry New York City
See: HOTEL INDUSTRY

Tropical American Cruising
See: BOATS & BOATING

Tuesday
Association

Publishing Co: National Tour Marketing, 546 E Main St, Lexington, KY 40508-2342
Tel # (606) 226-4259 Fax # (606) 226-4424; Title Tel # (606) 226-4288 Title Fax # (606) 226-4321
Personnel: Editor-Loralyn Cecil
Editorial Description: The official newsletter of the Natl. Tour Assn. which focuses on Assn. news & travel industry issues.
General Info: Bi-weekly, Trim Size-8.52 x 11, Sheetfed press, 6 pages, ISSN: 0877-9931, No Color, Recycled, Other
Subscriptions: Indv. $18, Free With Membership
Circulation: Total-4,200
Advertising: Inquire for rates.
List Rental: Rents Lists

Umbrella Singles Ltd.
Consumer

Publishing Co: Stardust Dance Productions, Church St., Box 157, Woodburne, NY 12788
Tel # (914) 434-6871; Title Tel # (800) 537-2797 Title Fax # (914) 434-3532
Personnel: Editor-Ann Prince, Art Dir.-Tom Sutton, Publisher, Production Mgr., Promotion Dir.-Leonard Moss
Editorial Description: Devoted to North East Coast singles' lifestyle. Travel - getaway weekends.
General Info: Yr. Est. 1980, Bi-monthly, Trim Size-8½ x 11, Sheetfed press, Newsprint
Subscriptions: Free
Acquistions: Publication Bought
Circulation: Total-50,000
Advertising: Accepts Inserts.

Undercurrent
Consumer

Publishing Co: Insightful Newsletters, 175 Great Neck Rd Ste 307, Great Neck, NY 11021-3313;
Title Tel # (212) 873-5900 Title Fax # (212) 799-1728
Personnel: Publisher-Beverley Walker, Editor-Ben Davidson, Circ. Mgr.-Pamela Ortiz, Production Mgr.-Eladia Orellana, Art Dir.-Romeo Cloma, Promotion Dir.-Charles Antin
Editorial Description: A monthly newsletter for serious scuba divers featuring resort & equipment reviews, safety tips & ways to have fun underwater.
General Info: Yr. Est. 1975, Monthly, Trim Size-8½ x 11, Sheetfed press, 14 pages, ISSN: 0192-0871, Color, Newsprint
Subscriptions: Indv. $58, Can. $57, For. $82, $5/copy
Acquistions: Publication Bought
Circulation: Total-14,000
List Rental: Actives: $75/M, Hotline: $85/M

Unique & Exotic Travel Reporter
Business, Consumer

Publishing Co: Unique, 6716 Eastside Dr. N.E., Suite 12-M, Brown's Point, WA 98422-1114;
Title Tel # (206) 927-1688 Title Fax # (206) 927-1688
Personnel: Publisher-L.K. Chesebro, Editor-Pat Chesebro, Circ. Mgr.-Shelly Chesebro, Adv. Dir.-Art Evans
Editorial Description: Reports unusual or one time only travel to consumers.
General Info: Yr. Est. 1981, Monthly, Trim Size-8½ x 11, Desktop press, 8 pages, No Color, Newsprint
Subscriptions: Indv. $45, Can. $45, For. $57, $4/copy
Circulation: Total-10,000

Upscale Traveler
Consumer

Publishing Co: Upscale Traveler, 4521 Alla Road, Suite 3, Marina del Rey, CA 90292
Tel # (310) 823-2073
Personnel: Publisher-John Winston Whitmore
Editorial Description: Information about how to travel in style and comfort for less money.
General Info: Monthly
Subscriptions: Indv. $96

Voyager Intl.
Consumer   CPM: $29

Publishing Co: Argonaut Enterprises, PO Box 2777, Westport, CT 06880-0777
Fax # (203) 846-2796; Title Tel # (203) 226-1647 Title Fax # (203) 226-1938
Personnel: Publisher-Nigel Fisher, Editor-Jason Fisher, Adv. Dir.-Lois Anderson, Promotion Dir.-Stacy Styles
Editorial Description: Critical evaluation of travel destinations including hotels, restaurants, sights, theatre & events. Cultural, economic & social perspectives are also included.
General Info: Yr. Est. 1985, Bi-monthly, Trim Size-8½ x 11, Web press, 32 pages, ISSN: 1040-8541, 15% ads, No Color, Coated
Subscriptions: Indv. $38, Can. $45, For. $55, $5/copy
Acquistions: Publication Bought, Publication Sold
Circulation: Total-22,000
Advertising: $650.
List Rental: Actives: 10,000, $150/M
Printing Co: Option One, Fairfield, CT

Wanderlust
Consumer

Publishing Co: R & R Publication, 283 Columbine St., Dept. M, Denver, CO 80206;
Title Tel # (303) 926-2420
Personnel: Publisher-Chris Reynolds, Editor-Wendy Reynolds
Editorial Description: Information and recomendations for travelling to the world's most enchanting places.
General Info: Monthly, Trim Size-8½ x 11, 8 pages
Subscriptions: Indv. $100

Waybill, The
See: RAILROADS

West Coast Railway Assn. Newsletter
See: RAILROADS

Workamper News　　　　　*Business, Consumer*

Publishing Co: Workamper News, 201 Hiram Rd, Heber Springs, AR 72543-8747; Title Tel # (501) 362-2637 Title Fax # (501) 362-2637
Personnel: Publisher-Debbie Robus, Editor-Greg Robus
Editorial Description: Unique publication compiles employment & business opportunities for recreational vehicle travelers (RVers). Salaried & volunteer job vacancies in travel, tourism & park management fields are published at no charge to employers. Workamper News helps employers recruit mature, dependable employees & helps RVers find extra income & new adventures.
General Info: Yr. Est. 1987, Bi-monthly, Trim Size-8½ x 11, Web press, 40 pages, ISSN: 0895-3678, 2% ads, 2 Color, Newsprint
Subscriptions: Indv. $23, Can. $33, For. $43
Circulation: Total-10,000
Advertising: Inquire for rates.

TRUCKING

AMTA Newsletter

Publishing Co: Arizona Motor Transport Assn., 2111 W Mcdowell Rd, Phoenix, AZ 85009-3010; Title Tel # (602) 252-7559
Personnel: Editor-Jeanine Bleicher
General Info: (Formerly Friday Final)
Circulation: Total-350

Affiliated Warehouse Companies Newsletter　　*Association*

Publishing Co: Affiliated Warehouse Companies, Inc., PO Box 295, Hazlet, NJ 07730-0295; Title Tel # (908) 739-2323 Title Fax # (908) 739-4154
Personnel: Publisher, Editor-Jim McBride
Editorial Description: Assists public warehouse users by gathering rates, data and providing information on warehousing and distribution at no charge or obligation on behalf of 85 public warehouse clients in the United States, Canada and Mexico.
General Info: Yr. Est. 1953, Monthly, Trim Size-8½ x 14, Mimeo press, 3 pages, Color, Newsprint
Subscriptions: Free To Qualified Recipient
Circulation: Total-105
List Rental: Actives: 7,500

Alcohol & Drugs: Dot Compliance Manual　　　*Business*

Publishing Co: J.J. Keller & Assoc., Inc., PO Box 368, Neenah, WI 54957-0368; Title Tel # (414) 722-2848 Title Fax # (414) 727-7516
Personnel: Editor-Webb Shaw, Adv. Dir.-David Szczeparik, Mktg. Dir.-Ed Sieracki
General Info: Yr. Est. 1994, Semi-annually, Looseleaf
Subscriptions: $129/copy
Circulation: Total-6,500

Canadian Transportation Law Reporter
See: TRAFFIC & TRANSPORTATION

Current Economic Bulletin
See: ECONOMICS

Federal Excise Tax Guide　　　*Business*

Publishing Co: National Accounting & Finance Council, 2200 Mill Rd, Alexandria, VA 22314-4686; Title Tel # (703) 838-1915 Title Fax # (703) 838-6070
Editorial Description: Federal excise taxes relevant to the trucking industry.
General Info: Yr. Est. 1990, Semi-annually, 80 pages
Subscriptions: Indv. $150

Fleet Safety Compliance Manual　　　*Business*

Publishing Co: J.J. Keller & Assoc., Inc., PO Box 368, Neenah, WI 54957-0368; Title Tel # (414) 722-2848 Title Fax # (414) 727-7516
Personnel: Publisher-J.J. Keller, Editor-Webb Shaw, Adv. Dir.-David Ellis, Adv. Dir.-David Szczepanik, Mktg. Dir.-Ed Sierncki
Editorial Description: Federal regulatory data on fleet safety compliance methods, rules, etc.
General Info: Yr. Est. 1979, Semi-annually, Web press, 340 pages, Newsprint, Looseleaf
Subscriptions: $79/copy
Circulation: Total-27,732
Printing Co: J.J. Keller & Assoc., 3003 Breezewood Ln, Neenah, WI 54956-9611 Tel # (414) 722-2848, Fax # (414) 727-7516

Fleet Street
See: TRAFFIC & TRANSPORTATION

Fruit & Vegetable Truck Rate Report
See: AGRICULTURE

Government Tender Report　　*Business*

Publishing Co: American Trucking Assn., Inc., Statistics Dept., 2200 Mill Rd., Alexandria, VA 22314-4686 Tel # (703) 838-1799; Title Tel # (703) 838-1792 Title Fax # (703) 683-9751
Editorial Description: Daily summary of tenders submitted to the interstate commerce commission by motor carriers, rail carriers, water carriers, & freight forwarders.
General Info: Yr. Est. 1969, Weekly, 8 pages
Subscriptions: Indv. $350

Government Traffic Bulletin　　*Business*

Publishing Co: American Trucking Assn., Inc., Statistics Dept., 2200 Mill Rd., Alexandria, VA 22314-4686 Tel # (703) 838-1799; Title Tel # (703) 838-1792 Title Fax # (703) 683-9751
Personnel: Editor-Susan Stowell
Editorial Description: Bulletin reporting traffic requirements of the Dept. of Defense & other major U.S. govt. shippers. Report is intended to keep motor carriers up-to-date on changes in federal transportation policies & procedures.
General Info: Yr. Est. 1969, Weekly, 2 pages
Subscriptions: Indv. $150

Grain Shipments
See: AGRICULTURE

HazMat Transport News　　*Business*

Publishing Co: Business Publishers, Inc., 951 Pershing Dr., Silver Spring, MD 20910-4464; Title Tel # (301) 589-5103 Title Fax # (301) 589-8493
Personnel: Publisher-Leonard A. Eiserer, Editor-Steve Lash, Circ. Mgr.-Brenda Davenport, Mktg. Dir.-Keith Payne
Editorial Description: Federal regulation of hazardous materials transportation, highlighting new laws and compliance strategies.
General Info: (Formerly HazMatTranspt.Matls; ToxicMatls.Transpt; Asbestos Contrl Rpt), Yr. Est. 1980, Bi-weekly, Trim Size-8½ x 11, Desktop press, 8 pages, Ind/Abs/Online: Newsnet and Information Access Company, No Color, Recycled
Subscriptions: Indv. $457, Can. $457, For. $460
Advertising: Accepts Inserts.
List Rental: List Management Co.: BPI Direct, 951 Pershing Dr., Silver Spring, MD 20910-4464 Tel # (301) 585-5976, Fax # (301) 587-4530

Highway & Vehicle Safety Report
See: SAFETY

Highway Common Carrier News Letter　　　*Business*

Publishing Co: Regular Common Carrier Conference, 5205 Leesburg Pike Ste 1110, Falls Church, VA 22041-3802; Title Tel # (703) 824-8775 Title Fax # (703) 824-8783
Personnel: Publisher-James Harkins, Editor-Kevin Williams
Editorial Description: Developments within transportation affecting the motor common carrier industry.
General Info: Yr. Est. 1948, Bi-weekly, Trim Size-8½ x 11, Sheetfed press, 4 pages, No Color
Subscriptions: Indv. $26
Circulation: Total-1,100

Hotline Newsletter　　　*Business*

Publishing Co: Newport Communications, 38 Executive Park, Ste. 300, Irvine, CA 92714-6755 Fax # (714) 261-1636; Title Tel # (714) 261-1636
Personnel: Publisher-George Jacovides, Editor-Doug Condra
General Info: Monthly, 4 pages, No Color
Subscriptions: Indv. $175
Circulation: Total-2,500

ITCC Truckload Carrier Report　　　*Business, Association*

Publishing Co: Interstate Truckload Carriers Conference, 2200 Mill Rd, Alexandria, VA 22314-4686; Title Tel # (703) 838-1950 Title Fax # (703) 838-6610
Editorial Description: Information for common & contract irregular route truckload motor carriers.
General Info: (Formerly CCCIR Weekly Bulletin; ITCC Newsletter), Yr. Est. 1942, Bi-weekly, Trim Size-8½ x 11, Offset press, 8 pages, 2 Color
Subscriptions: Free With Membership
Circulation: (100% controlled), Total-1,100

Inside DOT and Transportation Week
See: TRAFFIC & TRANSPORTATION

Interstate Commerce Guide　　*Business*

Publishing Co: J.J. Keller & Assoc., Inc., PO Box 368, Neenah, WI 54957-0368; Title Tel # (414) 722-2848 Title Fax # (414) 727-7516
Personnel: Editor-Webb Shaw, Adv. Dir.-David Szczepanik, Mktg. Dir.-Ed Sieracki
Editorial Description: Guide for managing freight movement in the era of deregulation.
General Info: Yr. Est. 1982, Semi-annually, Web press, 800 pages, Looseleaf
Subscriptions: $99/copy
Circulation: Total-1,402
Printing Co: J.J. Keller & Assoc., 3003 Breezewood Ln, Neenah, WI 54956-9611 Tel # (414) 722-2848, Fax # (414) 727-7516

Interstate Information
Report
Business

Publishing Co: American Trucking Assn., Inc., Statistics Dept., 2200 Mill Rd., Alexandria, VA 22314-4686 Tel # (703) 838-1799 Fax # (703) 683-9751; Title Tel # (703) 838-1779 Title Fax # (703) 838-1992
Personnel: Editor-Renee Griest
Editorial Description: Compilation of newly enacted state legislation regulations having direct impact on vehicle operations, fuel taxes, registration size & weight, & other areas of interest to the trucking industry.
General Info: Yr. Est. 1977, Monthly, Trim Size-11 x 17, 12 pages, ISSN: 0884-8394, Color
Subscriptions: Indv. $60

Maintenance: Managers

Publishing Co: American Trucking Assn., Inc., Statistics Dept., 2200 Mill Rd., Alexandria, VA 22314-4686 Tel # (703) 838-1799 Fax # (703) 683-9751; Title Tel # (800) 282-5463 Title Fax # (703) 684-5720
Personnel: Editor-Carl Kirk
Editorial Description: Focuses on current equipment management issues, new equipment & products & management training.
General Info: Yr. Est. 1986, Monthly, ISSN: 0890-1775
Subscriptions: Indv. $75

Monthly Truck Tonnage
Report

Publishing Co: American Trucking Assn., Inc., Statistics Dept., 2200 Mill Rd., Alexandria, VA 22314-4686 Tel # (703) 838-1799; Title Tel # (703) 838-1792 Title Fax # (703) 683-9751
Editorial Description: Tonnage indices of Class 1 & Class 11 general freight motor carriers. Includes weekly report. Comparison with other economic indicators.
General Info: Yr. Est. 1955, Monthly, Trim Size-8½ x 11, Sheetfed press, 2 pages, No Color
Subscriptions: Indv. $35

Nationalease News
Association

Publishing Co: National Truck Leasing System, 15450 Summit Ave., Suite 300, Villa Park, IL 60181-3976; Title Tel # (708) 571-2022
Personnel: Publisher, Editor-T.W.H. Miller, Circ. Mgr.-Anne Calek
Editorial Description: Reciprocal service stories; trends in the truck leasing industry, promotion material on meetings & seminars, membership news.
General Info: Yr. Est. 1944, Weekly, Mimeo press, 2 pages, No Color
Circulation: (100% controlled), Total-330

Newsline
See: TRAFFIC & TRANSPORTATION

Owner Operator News

Publishing Co: Owner Operators of America, PO Box 582, Orchard Park, NY 14127-0582; Title Tel # (716) 941-5582
Personnel: Editor-Charles DeVaul
General Info: Yr. Est. 1983
Circulation: Total-1,000
Advertising: Inquire for rates.

Private Carrier
Business, Association   CPM: $236

Publishing Co: National Private Truck Council, 66 Canal Center Plz., Ste. 600, Alexandria, VA 22314-1591; Title Tel # (703) 683-1300 Title Fax # (703) 683-1217
Personnel: Publisher-Gene Bergoffen, Editor-Jim Galligan, Circ. Mgr.-Elaine Rosenbaum
Editorial Description: News of developments in private truck field; interstate commerce commission, department of transportation, state regulations, congressional actions, federal court decisions. Also: case studies, management advisories, personnel issues.
General Info: Yr. Est. 1962, Monthly, Trim Size-8¼ x 10⅞, 44 pages, ISSN: 0032-8871
Subscriptions: Indv. $60, Can. $77, $6/copy
Circulation: (BPA, 78% controlled), Total-12,000, Readership-64,000, Source-I
Advertising: $2,842.
List Rental: Actives: $125/M
Printing Co: United Lithographic Services, 2818 Fallfax Dr., Falls Church, VA 22042-2804 Tel # (703) 560-5700, Fax # (703) 280-2678

Private Line
Business, Association

Publishing Co: National Private Truck Council, 66 Canal Center Plz., Ste. 600, Alexandria, VA 22314-1591; Title Tel # (703) 683-1300 Title Fax # (703) 683-1217
Personnel: Publisher-Gene Bergoffen, Editor-Jim Galligan
General Info: Yr. Est. 1966, Monthly, Sheetfed press, 2 Color, Coated, Saddle-stitched
Subscriptions: Free With Membership
Circulation: Total-2,500
List Rental: Rents Lists

Runzheimer Reports on
Fleet Maintenance &
Safety

Publishing Co: Runzheimer Intl., Runzheimer Park, Rochester, WI 53167 Fax # (414) 767-2254; Title Tel # (414) 767-2200
Personnel: Publisher-Bradford Burris, Editor-Philip Lazar
General Info: Yr. Est. 1986, Monthly, Trim Size-8½ x 11, Sheetfed press, ISSN: 0894-492X, No Color, Newsprint
Subscriptions: Indv. $156, $20/copy
Acquistions: Publication Bought, Publication Sold

Safety & Compliance
News
Association

Publishing Co: National Private Truck Council, 66 Canal Center Plz., Ste. 600, Alexandria, VA 22314-1591; Title Tel # (703) 683-1300 Title Fax # (703) 683-1217
Personnel: Editor-James Galligan
General Info: Yr. Est. 1993, 9x/yr., 2 Color, Coated, Saddle-stitched
Subscriptions: Free With Membership
Circulation: Total-2,500
Advertising: Inquire for rates.

Sales Tax Service

Publishing Co: National Accounting & Finance Council, 2200 Mill Rd, Alexandria, VA 22314-4686; Title Tel # (703) 838-1915
Editorial Description: Sales tax law, regulation and court cases on state sales and use taxes.
General Info: Quarterly, 100 pages, Looseleaf
Subscriptions: Indv. $125

ShopTalk
See: AUTOMOTIVE

Tax Information Service
Business

Publishing Co: National Accounting & Finance Council, 2200 Mill Rd, Alexandria, VA 22314-4686; Title Tel # (703) 838-1915
Personnel: Editor-Chamain O'Mahony
Editorial Description: Federal & state tax changes affecting motor carrier industry.
General Info: Monthly, 25 pages, No Color, Newsprint
Subscriptions: Indv. $125

Towing News
Association, Business

Publishing Co: Towing & Recovery Association of America, 2200 Mill Rd, Alexandria, VA 22314-4686; Title Tel # (703) 838-1897 Title Fax # (703) 684-6720
Personnel: Publisher-Anne Grant
Editorial Description: Covers current information on legislative issues affecting industry.
General Info: (Formerly National Towing News), Yr. Est. 1979, Monthly
Subscriptions: Indv. $24
Circulation: Total-2,000
Advertising: Inquire for rates.

Transport (De)Regulation Report
See: TRAFFIC & TRANSPORTATION

Trucking Activity Report
Business

Publishing Co: American Trucking Assn., Inc., Statistics Dept., 2200 Mill Rd., Alexandria, VA 22314-4686 Tel # (703) 838-1799; Title Tel # (703) 838-1792 Title Fax # (703) 683-9751
Editorial Description: Provides detailed information on fleet operations, including: Traffic levels, fuel costs, expenses, equipment utilization, and driver turn over for different segments of the industry.
General Info: Monthly, 8 pages, 2 Color, Saddle-stitched

Trucking Permit & Tax
Bulletin
Business

Publishing Co: J.J. Keller & Assoc., Inc., PO Box 368, Neenah, WI 54957-0368; Title Tel # (414) 722-2848 Title Fax # (414) 727-7516
Personnel: Publisher-J.J. Keller, Editor-Webb Shaw, Adv. Dir.-David Suzepanik, Mktg. Dir.-Ed Sieracki
Editorial Description: Changes in legal and regulatory requirements concerning taxation and permitting of the motor carrier industry.
General Info: (Formerly Trucking Permit), Yr. Est. 1968, Monthly, Trim Size-8 x 10¾, Offset press, 22 pages, No Color
Subscriptions: Indv. $90
Circulation: Total-2,490
Printing Co: J.J. Keller & Assoc., 3003 Breezewood Ln, Neenah, WI 54956-9611 Tel # (414) 722-2848, Fax # (414) 727-7516

Trucking Permit Guide
Business

Publishing Co: J.J. Keller & Assoc., Inc., PO Box 368, Neenah, WI 54957-0368; Title Tel # (414) 722-2848 Title Fax # (414) 727-7516
Personnel: Editor-Webb Shaw, Adv. Dir.-David Suzepanik, Mktg. Dir.-Ed Sieracki
Editorial Description: Provides complete vehicle license, permit, & third structure tax information.
General Info: Yr. Est. 1974, Quarterly, Web press, 800 pages, 2 Color, Newsprint, Looseleaf
Subscriptions: $129/copy
Circulation: Total-4,144
Printing Co: J.J. Keller & Assoc., 3003 Breezewood Ln, Neenah, WI 54956-9611 Tel # (414) 722-2848, Fax # (414) 727-7516

Trucking Safety Guide
Business

Publishing Co: J.J. Keller & Assoc., Inc., PO Box 368, Neenah, WI 54957-0368; Title Tel # (414) 722-2848 Title Fax # (414) 727-7516
Personnel: Editor-Webb Shaw, Adv. Dir.-David Szczepaink, Mktg. Dir.-Ed Sieracki
Editorial Description: Publication of Federal & State motor carrier operational safety requirements.
General Info: Quarterly, Web press, 900 pages, Looseleaf
Subscriptions: $129/copy
Circulation: Total-3,460
Printing Co: J.J. Keller & Assoc., 3003 Breezewood Ln, Neenah, WI 54956-9611 Tel # (414) 722-2848, Fax # (414) 727-7516

Truxfax Bulletin   *Association*

Publishing Co: Alberta Trucking Association, Box 5520, Station A, Calgary, AB T2H 1X9 Canada;
   Title Tel # (403) 253-8401 Title Fax # (403) 255-2724
Personnel: Editor-Jim Bradbury
Editorial Description: Regulations, trends, laws and association affairs concerning truck
   transportation.
General Info: (Formerly Truxpress), Yr. Est. 1978, 10x/yr., Sheetfed press, 8 pages, No Color,
   Newsprint
Circulation: (100% controlled), Total-600
Advertising: Inquire for rates.
Printing Co: Miller Printing, 332 40th Ave., N.E., Calgary, AB T2E 2M7 Canada Tel # (403) 276-3361

Vehicle Sizes & Weights
Manual   *Business*

Publishing Co: J.J. Keller & Assoc., Inc., PO Box 368, Neenah, WI 54957-0368;
   Title Tel # (414) 722-2848 Title Fax # (414) 727-7516
Personnel: Editor-Webb Shaw, Adv. Dir.-David Szczepanik, Mktg. Dir.-Ed Sieracki
Editorial Description: Offers complete overdimensional permit information for Federal and all states.
General Info: Yr. Est. 1973, Semi-annually, Web press, 400 pages, Newsprint, Looseleaf
Subscriptions: $109/copy
Circulation: Total-1,344
Printing Co: J.J. Keller & Assoc., 3003 Breezewood Ln, Neenah, WI 54956-9611
   Tel # (414) 722-2848, Fax # (414) 727-7516

Wisconsin Motor Carrier   *Association*

Publishing Co: Wisconsin Motor Carriers Assn., PO Box 44849, Madison, WI 53744-4849;
   Title Tel # (608) 255-6789
Personnel: Publisher, Editor-Thomas Howells
Editorial Description: News and technical coverage of truck transportation.
General Info: Yr. Est. 1938, Monthly, Trim Size-8¼ x 11, Offset press, 4 Color
Advertising: Inquire for rates.

U.S. (& CANADIAN) FED. GOV'T.

**14-Point Program to Reform and Restructure the U.N.
System**
   See: GOVERNMENT

ABA Washington Letter
   See: LAW

ABA Washington Summary   *Association*

Publishing Co: American Bar Association, 740 15th St. NW, Washington, DC 20005-1009;
   Title Tel # (202) 662-1016 Title Fax # (202) 662-1032
Personnel: Editor-Elizabeth Rogers
Editorial Description: Federal legislative & regulatory tracking service.
General Info: Yr. Est. 1972, Bi-weekly, Trim Size-8½ x 11, Offset press, 8 pages, No Color,
   Newsprint, Saddle-stitched
Subscriptions: Indv. $50
Circulation: Total-1,400
Printing Co: Reprint Co., 1733 I St., NW, Washington, DC 20006 Tel # (202) 783-4477,
   Fax # (202) 783-0346

ACTION
   See: MANAGEMENT

APDU Newsletter   *Business, Association*

Publishing Co: Assn. of Public Data Users, 87 Prospect Ave, Princeton, NJ 08544-2007;
   Title Tel # (609) 258-6025 Title Fax # (609) 258-3943
Editorial Description: To create and continue dialogue between public data users, producers and
   distributors concerned with the collection dissemination and interpretation of public data.
General Info: Yr. Est. 1976, 10x/yr., Trim Size-8½ x 11, Letrpr. press, 12 pages, No Color, Matte
Subscriptions: Indv. $175, Free With Membership
Circulation: (100% controlled), Total-600

Access Reports /Canada
Newsletter   *Business*

Publishing Co: Access Reports, Inc., 1624 Dogwood Lane, Lynchburg, VA 24503;
   Title Tel # (804) 384-5334 Title Fax # (804) 384-8272
Personnel: Publisher, Editor-Harry Hammitt, Promotion Dir.-Kathy Morland
Editorial Description: Focuses on recent court rulings and legislative regulatory developments in
   Canada , both federal and provincial.
General Info: Monthly
Subscriptions: Indv. $200, Can. $250, $200/copy
Printing Co: Serif Press, Inc., 1331 H St. NW, #110LL, Washington, DC 20005 Tel # (202) 737-4650

Access Reports/Freedom of
Information - U.S
Newsletter

Publishing Co: Access Reports, Inc., 1624 Dogwood Lane, Lynchburg, VA 24503;
   Title Tel # (804) 384-5334 Title Fax # (804) 384-8272
Personnel: Publisher, Editor-Harry Hammitt, Promotion Dir.-Kathy Morland
Editorial Description: Focuses on recent court rulings and legislative and regulatory developments,
   on federal and state levels.
General Info: Yr. Est. 1975, Bi-weekly, Trim Size-8½ x 11, Sheetfed press, 16 pages, ISSN: 0364-
   7625, Ind/Abs/Online: Newsnet, 2 Color
Subscriptions: Indv. $325, Can. $325, For. $375
Circulation: Total-450
Printing Co: Serif Press, Inc., 1331 H St. NW, #110LL, Washington, DC 20005 Tel # (202) 737-4650

Aging News Alert
   See: SENIOR CITIZENS

Air/Water Pollution Report's Environment Week
   See: ENVIRONMENT & ECOLOGY

Alert
   See: BUSINESS & INDUSTRY

American Banker's Washington Watch
   See: BANKING & FINANCE

ArtsUSA UpDate
   See: CULTURE & HUMANITIES

CCH Federal Tax: Internal
Revenue Bulletin   *Business*

Publishing Co: CCH, Inc., 2700 Lake Cook Rd., Riverwoods, IL 60015 Parent Co.-Kluwer Law &
   Taxation Publishers, Cambridge; Title Tel # (847) 267-7000 Title Fax # (800) 224-8299
Editorial Description: Provides subscribers with all Revenue Rulings, Revenue Procedures and
   other official Internal Revenue Service information.
General Info: Weekly, Trim Size-7 x 9½, 40 pages, Looseleaf
Subscriptions: Indv. $110
List Rental: Rents Lists

CCH Federal Tax Service
   See: TAXES

CCH Federal Tax Service
Analysis Only

Publishing Co: CCH, Inc., 2700 Lake Cook Rd., Riverwoods, IL 60015 Parent Co.-Kluwer Law &
   Taxation Publishers, Cambridge; Title Tel # (847) 267-7000 Title Fax # (800) 224-8299
General Info: Weekly
Subscriptions: Indv. $758
List Rental: Rents Lists

CD-Housing Register
   See: REAL ESTATE

C.L. Pace Report   *Business*

Publishing Co: C.L. Pace Associates, 36 Henry Austin Dr., Wilton, CT 06897-3210;
   Title Tel # (203) 834-0533 Title Fax # (203) 834-0207
Personnel: Publisher, Editor-Charles Pace
Editorial Description: Contains news coverage of Washington.
General Info: Yr. Est. 1984, Monthly, Trim Size-8½ x 11, 12 pages, No Color, Matte
Subscriptions: Indv. $100
Circulation: Total-300

COHA's Washington Report on the Hemisphere
   See: INTERNATIONAL AFFAIRS

California Statesman's Legislative Survey
   See: LAW

Canada Corporations Law Reporter
   See: LAW

Canadian Energy Program Reporter
   See: ENERGY

Canadian FOIA Reference
File   *Association, Business*

Publishing Co: Access Reports, Inc., 1624 Dogwood Lane, Lynchburg, VA 24503;
   Title Tel # (804) 384-5334 Title Fax # (804) 384-8272
Personnel: Publisher, Editor-Harry Hammitt, Promotion Dir.-Kathy Morland
Editorial Description: Full Text of federal agency FDIA regulations, legislative history, agency
   guidance, list of cases in Canada both federal and provincial
General Info: Annually, Trim Size-8½ x 11, 16 pages, 2 Color, Looseleaf
Subscriptions: Indv. $250, Can. $275, $250/copy
Printing Co: Serif Press, Inc., 1331 H St. NW, #110LL, Washington, DC 20005 Tel # (202) 737-4650

Canadian Government Programs & Services   *Business*

Publishing Co: CCH Canadian Ltd., 6 Garamond Ct., North York, ON M3C 1Z5 Canada
Fax # (416) 444-8011 Parent Co.-CCH, Inc., Riverwoods; Title Tel # (416) 441-2992
Title Fax # (416) 444-9011
Personnel: Editor-Joe Weisberg
Editorial Description: Guide to federal government organization information on all departments; their structure, chief officers, jurisdiction, responsibilities, budgets, etc.
General Info: Yr. Est. 1971, Monthly, Trim Size-6 x 9, Web press, No Color, Looseleaf
Subscriptions: Can. $280

Canadian Occupational Safety & Health Law Monthly Report
See: SAFETY

Canadian Securities Law Reporter
See: INVESTMENT

Canadian Studies Update
See: EDUCATION

Canadian Tax Objection & Appeal Procedures
See: TAXES

Children & Youth Funding Report
See: PHILANTHROPY

Civil Rights Monitor
See: CIVIL RIGHTS

Community Development Services, Inc.
See: PUBLIC MANAGEMENT & PLANNING

Community Health Funding Report
See: PHILANTHROPY

Congress Daily   *Business, Association*

Publishing Co: National Journal, Inc., 1501 M. St. NW, Ste. 300, Washington, DC 20005-1700
Tel # (202) 739-8500 Fax # (202) 296-8651
Editorial Description: Electronic service covering events in Congress.
General Info: Daily

Congress Daily/PM   *Business, Association*

Publishing Co: National Journal, Inc., 1501 M. St. NW, Ste. 300, Washington, DC 20005-1700
Tel # (202) 739-8500 Fax # (202) 296-8651
Editorial Description: Covers Congressional events occurring after 3PM each day.
General Info: Yr. Est. 1993, Daily

Congress in Print   *Business, Association*

Publishing Co: Congressional Quarterly, Inc., 1414 22nd St. NW, Washington, DC 20037-1096
Tel # (202) 887-8500 Fax # (202) 728-1863; Title Tel # (202) 887-8515 Title Fax # (202) 728-1862
Personnel: Publisher-Neil Skene, Editor-Brian Nutting, Production Mgr.-I. D. Fuller
Editorial Description: Just-released committee hearings, prints, reports and staff studies.
General Info: Yr. Est. 1977, Weekly, Trim Size-8½ x 11, Offset press, 4 pages, Ind/Abs/Online: Washington Alert, No Color
Subscriptions: Indv. $198
Acquistions: Publication Bought
List Rental: Rents Lists

Congressional Activities   *Association*

Publishing Co: Oliphant Washington News Service, PO Box 9808, Washington, DC 20016-8808;
Title Tel # (202) 298-7226 Title Fax # (202) 333-5006
Personnel: Editor-John Oliphant
Editorial Description: Congressional schedules, background, bills, reports, laws & articles.
General Info: Yr. Est. 1930, Weekly, Trim Size-8½ x 11, Sheetfed press, 10 pages, ISSN: 0733-0227, Ind/Abs/Online: Newsnet, No Color
Subscriptions: Indv. $300

Congressional Index   *Business*

Publishing Co: CCH, Inc., 2700 Lake Cook Rd., Riverwoods, IL 60015 Parent Co.-Kluwer Law & Taxation Publishers, Cambridge; Title Tel # (847) 267-7000 Title Fax # (800) 224-8299
Editorial Description: Reports action of all Public Bills and Resolutions from introduction to final disposition.
General Info: Yr. Est. 1937, Weekly, Trim Size-6 x 9, Web press, 100 pages, No Color, Looseleaf
Subscriptions: Indv. $1,042

Congressional Monitor   *Business, Association*

Publishing Co: Congressional Quarterly, Inc., 1414 22nd St. NW, Washington, DC 20037-1096
Fax # (202) 728-1863; Title Tel # (202) 887-8500
Personnel: Publisher-Neil Skene, Editor-Larry Liebert, Mng. Editor-Brian Nutting, Production Mgr.-I. D. Fuller, Adv. Dir.-Bob Wallace
Editorial Description: Daily listing of all scheduled congressional committee hearings, with witnesses.
General Info: Yr. Est. 1965, Daily, ISSN: 0010-5902, Ind/Abs/Online: Washington Alert
Subscriptions: Indv. $1,399
Acquistions: Publication Bought
List Rental: Rents Lists

Congressional Record Abstracts-Energy

Publishing Co: ETSI, 1200 Quince Orchard Blvd, Gaithersburg, MD 20878-4103 Parent Co.-Information Handling Services, Englewood
General Info: Looseleaf

Congressional Record Abstracts-Foreign Affairs Edition

Publishing Co: ETSI, 1200 Quince Orchard Blvd, Gaithersburg, MD 20878-4103 Parent Co.-Information Handling Services, Englewood
General Info: Daily, 4 pages, Looseleaf

Congressional Record Abstracts-Master Edition   *Business*

Publishing Co: ETSI, 1200 Quince Orchard Blvd, Gaithersburg, MD 20878-4103 Parent Co.-Information Handling Services, Englewood
Editorial Description: Abstracts entire Congressional Record by subject.
General Info: Yr. Est. 1977, Daily, Mimeo press, 8 pages, No Color, Looseleaf

Congressional Record Abstracts-Natl. Defense Edition

Publishing Co: ETSI, 1200 Quince Orchard Blvd, Gaithersburg, MD 20878-4103 Parent Co.-Information Handling Services, Englewood
General Info: Daily, 2 pages, Looseleaf

Congressional Record Abstracts-Natl. Oceanic & Atmospheric Admin Edition

Publishing Co: ETSI, 1200 Quince Orchard Blvd, Gaithersburg, MD 20878-4103 Parent Co.-Information Handling Services, Englewood
Personnel: Editor-Mattana Gilbert, Circ. Mgr.-Albert Coia
General Info: Daily, 2 pages, Looseleaf
Subscriptions: Indv. $495

Congressional Record Report   *Business*

Publishing Co: ETSI, 1200 Quince Orchard Blvd, Gaithersburg, MD 20878-4103 Parent Co.-Information Handling Services, Englewood
Editorial Description: SDI profiles covering the Congressional Record.
General Info: Yr. Est. 1976, Daily, 4 pages, No Color, Looseleaf

Congressional Record Scanner   *Business, Association*

Publishing Co: Congressional Quarterly, Inc., 1414 22nd St. NW, Washington, DC 20037-1096
Tel # (202) 887-8500 Fax # (202) 728-1863; Title Tel # (202) 887-6279 Title Fax # (202) 728-1862
Personnel: Publisher-Neil Skene, Mng. Editor-Evelyn Russell, Fulflmnt. Mgr.-Judy Stachnik, Production Mgr.-I. D. Fuller
Editorial Description: Edited index of each issue of Congressional Record.
General Info: Yr. Est. 1973, Daily, Trim Size-8½ x 11, Offset press, 4 pages, Ind/Abs/Online: Washington Alert, No Color
Subscriptions: Indv. $395
Acquistions: Publication Bought
List Rental: Rents Lists

Congressional Staff Club Bulletin   *Association*

Publishing Co: Congressional Staff Club, Box 2000, LHOB, Longworth House Off. Bldg., Washington, DC 20013-2000; Title Tel # (202) 226-3250
General Info: Monthly, Trim Size-8½ x 11, 4 pages, No Color
Circulation: Total-2,000
Advertising: Inquire for rates.
Printing Co: Majority & Minority Printers, U.S. House of Representatives, Washington, DC

Counterpoint NewsNotes
See: COMPUTERS & AUTOMATION

Crime Prevention News
See: LAW ENFORCEMENT & PENOLOGY

Daily, The   *Business*

Publishing Co: Statistics Canada, Holland Ave/RH Coats, Holland Ave/Tunney's Pasture, Ottawa, ON K1A O26 Canada Tel # (613) 951-8116 Fax # (613) 951-0581
Editorial Description: Canadian statistical report. (#11-001E)
General Info: Daily

Daily Congressional Monitor *Business, Association*

Publishing Co: Congressional Quarterly, Inc., 1414 22nd St. NW, Washington, DC 20037-1096
Tel # (202) 887-8500 Fax # (202) 728-1863; Title Tel # (202) 887-8690
Personnel: Publisher-Neil Skene, Editor-Brian Nutting, Circ. Mgr.-Bob Smith, Adv. Dir.-James Bullard, Art Dir.-Donna Colona
Editorial Description: Listing of daily & future committee actions, hearings, markups, & other meetings. News for Congress.
General Info: Yr. Est. 1965, Daily, Trim Size-8½ x 11, Offset press, 25 pages, No Color
Subscriptions: Indv. $1,258
Circulation: Total-1,600

Defense Week
See: MILITARY & NAVAL

Deficit Letter, The *Consumer*

Publishing Co: Wright Publishing Co., 1800 Diagonal Rd Ste 600, Alexandria, VA 22314-2840; Title Tel # (703) 684-4470
Personnel: Publisher-Christopher Wright
Editorial Description: Criticizes the national debt, open-ended social spending, and useless government programs. Discusses ways of elimnating or reducing spending.
General Info: Yr. Est. 1994, Monthly, Ind/Abs/Online: Compuserve
Subscriptions: Indv. $29

Devices & Diagnostics Letter
See: HEALTH

Drug GMP Report
See: DRUGS & PHARMACEUTICALS

Eco/Log Canadian Pollution Legislation
See: LAW

Economic Issues
See: ECONOMICS

Employment Tax Forms
See: TAXES

Environmental Compliance Report, The
See: ENVIRONMENT & ECOLOGY

Environmental Health Letter
See: ENVIRONMENT & ECOLOGY

Executive News Service *Association*

Publishing Co: American Group Practice Association, 1422 Duke St., Alexandria, VA 22314-3430; Title Tel # (703) 838-0033 Title Fax # (703) 548-1890
Personnel: Publisher-Donald Fisher, Editor-Brent Miller
Editorial Description: Covers federal health policy, primarily Medicaid/Medicare physician reimbursement, medical liability, health law.
General Info: Yr. Est. 1980, Bi-weekly, 4 pages, Matte, Saddle-stitched
Circulation: (PSS), Total-2,100
List Rental: Rents Lists
Printing Co: Global Printing, Inc., 4116 Wheeler Ave, Alexandria, VA 22304-6411
Tel # (703) 751-3611

FCNL Washington Newsletter *Association*

Publishing Co: Friends Committee on Natl. Legislation, 245 2nd St NE, Washington, DC 20002-5719; Title Tel # (202) 547-6000
Editorial Description: Educational materials on Congressional legislation; international relations, war and peace, militarism, U.N., budget, civil rights, basic human needs, American Indians.
General Info: Yr. Est. 1943, Monthly, Trim Size-8½ x 11½, Offset press, 6 pages, No Color
Subscriptions: Indv. $20
Circulation: Total-10,000

FDA Advertising and Promotion Manual
See: LAW

FDA Enforcement Manual
See: LAW

Fair Employment Report
See: EMPLOYMENT

Families in Crisis Funding Report
See: FAMILY

Family and Medical Leave Handbook
See: LAW

Fed/Direct
See: ADVERTISING & MARKETING

Federal Action Affecting the States/State Capitals *Business, Consumer*

Publishing Co: Wakeman/Walworth, 300 N. Washington St., Alexandria, VA 22314-2530; Title Tel # (703) 549-8606 Title Fax # (703) 549-1372
Personnel: Publisher-Keyes Walworth
Editorial Description: Review of federal funding, & legislation affecting state programs. Gives a state perspective on Federal court rulings and programs that involve both the state and federal government.
General Info: (Formerly Federal Acation Affecting the States from the State Capitals), Yr. Est. 1946, Weekly, 8 pages, ISSN: 0734-1202
Subscriptions: Indv. $265, Inst. $212, Can. $235, For. $255

Federal Contract Disputes
See: LAW

Federal Employees News Digest *Consumer*

Publishing Co: Federal Employees' News Digest, Inc., 1850 Centennial Park Dr Ste, 520, Reston, VA 22091-1517; Title Tel # (703) 533-3031
Personnel: Publisher-Stephen E. Young, Editor-Don Mace, Promotion Dir.-Kim Bright
Editorial Description: News on legislation, court decisions, administrative actions on government and postal employment and benefits.
General Info: (Formerly Weekly Federal Employees News Digest), Yr. Est. 1951, Weekly, Trim Size-8½ x 11, Web press, 4 pages, ISSN: 1065-0970, Color
Subscriptions: Indv. $49, $2/copy
Acquistions: Publication Bought
Circulation: Total-35,000
Advertising: Inquire for rates.
List Rental: Actives: 124,200, $95/M, Hotline: 4,000, $100/M, Expires: 12,000, $95/M

Federal Grants Management Handbook *Business*

Publishing Co: Thompson Publishing Group, 1725 K Street, NW, Washington, DC 20006
Tel # (202) 872-4000; Title Tel # (202) 872-1766
Personnel: Publisher-Richard Thompson, Editor-Susan Lauscher, Circ. Mgr.-Judy Ellingsworth, Promotion Dir.-Cathy Schilling
Editorial Description: Describes developments in federal grants management. Subscription includes monthly updates and newsletters.
General Info: Yr. Est. 1978, Monthly, Trim Size-8½ x 11, Offset press, 28 pages, ISSN: 0195-2617, No Color, Newsprint, Looseleaf
Subscriptions: Indv. $246

Federal Human Resources Week
See: INDUSTRIAL RELATIONS/PERSONNEL

Federal Labor-Management & Employee Relations Consultant *Business, Association*

Publishing Co: U.S. Office of Personnel Management, Office Of Workforce Info., 1900 E. St. NW #7494, Washington, DC 20415-0001 Tel # (202) 606-2684 Fax # (202) 606-1719; Title Tel # (202) 606-2898 Title Fax # (202) 606-2613
Personnel: Editor-Mary Hennessy
Editorial Description: Order from Supt. of Doc., GPO, Wash. DC 20402. Using List ID FLMC
General Info: (Formerly Federal Labor-Management Consultant), Yr. Est. 1971, Bi-weekly, Trim Size-8½ x 11, Sheetfed press, 4 pages, ISSN: 0046-3418, 2 Color, Newsprint
Subscriptions: Indv. $38, For. $48
Circulation: Total-9,000

Federal Register Abstracts-Business Edition

Publishing Co: ETSI, 1200 Quince Orchard Blvd, Gaithersburg, MD 20878-4103 Parent Co.-Information Handling Services, Englewood
Personnel: Editor-Mattana Gilbert, Circ. Mgr.-Albert Coia
General Info: Daily, 2 pages, Looseleaf

Federal Register Abstracts-Master Edition *Business*

Publishing Co: ETSI, 1200 Quince Orchard Blvd, Gaithersburg, MD 20878-4103 Parent Co.-Information Handling Services, Englewood
Personnel: Editor-Mattana Gilbert, Circ. Mgr.-Albert Coia
Editorial Description: Abstracts entire Federal Register by subject.
General Info: Yr. Est. 1977, Daily, Mimeo press, 4 pages, No Color, Looseleaf

Federal Register Report *Business*

Publishing Co: ETSI, 1200 Quince Orchard Blvd, Gaithersburg, MD 20878-4103 Parent Co.-Information Handling Services, Englewood
Personnel: Editor-Mattana Gilbert, Circ. Mgr.-Albert Coia
Editorial Description: SDI profiles covering the Federal Register.
General Info: Yr. Est. 1977, Daily, 2 pages, No Color, Looseleaf
Subscriptions: Indv. $400

Federal Tax Forms
See: TAXES

**Federal Tax Manual With
  Monthly Reports**

Publishing Co: CCH, Inc., 2700 Lake Cook Rd., Riverwoods, IL 60015 Parent Co.-Kluwer Law & Taxation Publishers, Cambridge; Title Tel # (847) 267-7000 Title Fax # (800) 224-8299
Editorial Description: More than 2,000 fact-filled pages and scores of filled-in forms and practical examples simplify tax return preparation.
General Info: Monthly, Looseleaf
Subscriptions: Indv. $299

Federal Tort Claims Act News
  See: LAW

Fourth Circuit Review
  See: LAW

Franklin Pierce Times
  See: HISTORY

Free Trade Law Reporter
  See: INTERNATIONAL TRADE

Futures International Law Letter
  See: LAW

Global Statesmanship Ratings of the U.S. House
  See: GOVERNMENT

Global Statesmanship Ratings of the U.S. Senate
  See: INTERNATIONAL AFFAIRS

**Government Contracts
  Reports**   *Business*

Publishing Co: CCH, Inc., 2700 Lake Cook Rd., Riverwoods, IL 60015 Parent Co.-Kluwer Law & Taxation Publishers, Cambridge; Title Tel # (847) 267-7000 Title Fax # (800) 224-8299
Editorial Description: Bids, awards, forms, amortization, termination, renegotiations, adjustments, industrial security, regulations.
General Info: Weekly, Web press, No Color, Looseleaf
Subscriptions: Indv. $2,120

**Government Prime
  Contracts Monthly**

Publishing Co: Government Data Publications, 1155 Connecticut Avenue NW, Washington, DC 20036
Personnel: Editor-Siegfried Cobell
Editorial Description: Firms which received prime contracts for production of goods from federal govn't agencies during preceding months.
General Info: Yr. Est. 1976, Monthly, Web press, 110 pages, No Color, Newsprint
Subscriptions: Indv. $96
Acquistions: Publication Bought
List Rental: Actives: $40/M

Harris Survey

Publishing Co: Louis Harris, 630 Fifth Ave., New York, NY 10111-0124; Title Tel # (212) 698-9600
Personnel: Publisher, Editor-Louis Harris, Circ. Mgr.-Barbara Winokur
Editorial Description: Public opinion surveys on current topics.
General Info: (Formerly ABC News/Harris Survey), Yr. Est. 1963, Semi-weekly, Trim Size-$8\frac{1}{2}$ x 11, Offset press, 3 pages, ISSN: 0273-1037, No Color
Subscriptions: Indv. $450
Circulation: Total-200

Housing Affairs Letter
  See: REAL ESTATE

Immigration Law Report   *Business*

Publishing Co: Clark Boardman Callaghan, 375 Hudson St, New York, NY 10014-3685 Fax # (212) 807-6209; Title Tel # (212) 929-7500 Title Fax # (212) 924-0460
Personnel: Publisher-David Doughty, Art Dir.-William Rushford, Promotion Dir.-Robert Arkin
Editorial Description: Newsletter providing analysis and practical application of immigration developments.
General Info: Yr. Est. 1981, 11x/yr., Trim Size-$8\frac{1}{2}$ x 11, Sheetfed press, 8 pages, ISSN: 0731-5767, No Color
Subscriptions: Indv. $295
List Rental: Rents Lists
Printing Co: Port City Press, 1323 Greenwood Rd, Pikesville, MD 21208-3611 Tel # (410) 486-3000, Fax # (410) 486-0706

Immigration Policy & Law
  See: LAW

Indian Report

Publishing Co: Friends Committee on Natl. Legislation, 245 2nd St NE, Washington, DC 20002-5719; Title Tel # (202) 547-6000
Personnel: Editor-Cindy Darcy
General Info: Yr. Est. 1977, Quarterly, 8 pages
Circulation: Total-2,400

**Individual Retirement Plans
  Guide-IRA, SEP, Keogh**   *Business*

Publishing Co: CCH, Inc., 2700 Lake Cook Rd., Riverwoods, IL 60015 Parent Co.-Kluwer Law & Taxation Publishers, Cambridge; Title Tel # (847) 267-7000 Title Fax # (800) 224-8299
Editorial Description: Subscribers informed on changes in the tax, contribution, reporting & disclosure, qualification, prohibited transactions, distribution, rollover & other rules that apply to these plans.
General Info: Monthly, Looseleaf
Subscriptions: Indv. $286

Indoor Pollution News
  See: CHEMISTRY & CHEMICALS

Inside the PTO
  See: PATENTS/COPYRIGHTS/TRADE MARKS

International Securities Regulation Report
  See: INVESTMENT

International Solar Energy Intelligence Report
  See: ENERGY

MDR Watch
  See: HEALTH

**McGraw-Hill's Tech
  Transfer Report**   *Business, Association*

Publishing Co: McGraw-Hill, 1221 Ave. of the Americas, 36th Fl., New York, NY 10020-1095 Tel # (212) 512-2000 Fax # (212) 512-6590; Title Tel # (202) 463-1662 Title Fax # (202) 463-1611
Personnel: Publisher-John Slater, Editor-William E. Loveless, Circ. Dir.-Georgia Safos
Editorial Description: Monthly update on commercial opportunities at federal laboratories.
General Info: Yr. Est. 1989, Monthly, ISSN: 1042-9158, Ind/Abs/Online: Dialog; Dow-Jones News Retrieval
Subscriptions: Indv. $395, Can. $395, For. $410

Medical Waste News
  See: ENVIRONMENT & ECOLOGY

Mental Health News Alert
  See: PHILANTHROPY

Metric Today
  See: CONSUMER INTERESTS

Minorities in Business Insider
  See: BUSINESS & INDUSTRY

NCUA Watch
  See: BANKING & FINANCE

NIGP Technical Bulletin
  See: PURCHASING

NIMLO Congressional News
  See: GOVERNMENT

National Information Infrastructure News
  See: COMPUTERS & AUTOMATION

New Democrat
  See: POLITICS

News From ICS
  See: POLITICS

Newsletter   *Association*

Publishing Co: President's Council on Physical Fitness & Sports, 701 Pennsylvania Ave NW Ste, 250, Washington, DC 20004-2608 Tel # (202) 272-3430
Personnel: Editor-Diana d'Avino
Editorial Description: This publication carries information regarding the functions, goals & programs of the Presidential Council on physical fitness & sports.
General Info: Bi-monthly, Trim Size-$8\frac{1}{2}$ x 11, Offset press, 8 pages, ISSN: 0364-8079
Acquistions: Publication Bought
Circulation: Total-13,000

Noise Regulation Report
  See: HEARING & SPEECH

ORSANCO Quality Monitor
  See: WATER SUPPLY, POWER & WASTE

Oil Spill Planning Manual, The
  See: ENVIRONMENT & ECOLOGY

Ottawa Update
Business, Association

Publishing Co: Canadian Chamber of Commerce, 55 Metcalfe St. #1160, Ottawa, ON K1P 6N4 Canada; Title Tel # (613) 238-4000
Personnel: Editor-Margaret Crook
Editorial Description: Update of federal govt. legislation and Parliamentary activities.
General Info: Yr. Est. 1984, 8x/yr., Offset press, 12 pages, No Color, Saddle-stitched
Subscriptions: Indv. $15
Circulation: (100% controlled), Total-8,500

Ottawa Weekly Update
Business, Association

Publishing Co: Informetrica Limited, Box 828, Station B, Ottawa, ON K1P 5P9 Canada
Fax # (613) 230-7698; Title Tel # (613) 238-4831 Title Fax # (613) 238-7698
Personnel: Editor-Steve Hall, Production Mgr.-Kelly Themal
Editorial Description: Briefings on the House of Commons and the Senate activities and legislation status.
General Info: Yr. Est. 1986, Weekly, Trim Size-8½ x 11, 50 pages, ISSN: 0840-9196, No Color
Subscriptions: Can. $700
List Rental: Rents Lists

Personnel Management Guideposts for Federal Supervisors
See: INDUSTRIAL RELATIONS/PERSONNEL

Political Finance & Lobby Reporter
See: POLITICS

Product Safety Letter
See: SAFETY

Real Estate/Environmental Liability News
See: LAW

Reference File U.S
Business

Publishing Co: Access Reports, Inc., 1624 Dogwood Lane, Lynchburg, VA 24503; Title Tel # (804) 384-5334 Title Fax # (804) 384-8272
Personnel: Publisher, Editor-Harry Hammitt, Promotion Dir.-Kathy Morland
Editorial Description: Full texts of federal agency FOIA regulations. Legislative history, agency guidance, list of cases for U.S.
General Info: Yr. Est. 1975, Quarterly, Trim Size-8½ x 11, 16 pages, 2 Color, Looseleaf
Subscriptions: Indv. $450, Can. $450, For. $500
Printing Co: Serif Press, Inc., 1331 H St. NW, #110LL, Washington, DC 20005 Tel # (202) 737-4650

The Regulatory Times
See: ENERGY

Regulatory Watchdog Service
See: CONSUMER INTERESTS

Senate History
Consumer

Publishing Co: Senate Historical Office, Sec'y Of The Senate The, Capitol, Rm. Sh 201, Washington, DC 20510-0001; Title Tel # (202) 224-6900

Sixth Circuit Review
See: LAW

Small Business Preferential Subcontracts Opportunities Monthly
Business

Publishing Co: Government Data Publications, 1155 Connecticut Avenue NW, Washington, DC 20036
Personnel: Publisher-Siegfried Lobel, Editor-Siegfried Cobell
Editorial Description: Lists and describes government contracts exceeding $500,000, $1,000,000 in construction.
General Info: Yr. Est. 1981, Monthly, Web press, 36 pages, No Color
Subscriptions: Indv. $84
Acquistions: Publication Bought

Social Security Alert

Publishing Co: Research Institute of America, 117 E Stevens Ave, Valhalla, NY 10595-1264; Title Tel # (212) 645-4800
Personnel: Publisher-Robert Chapman, Editor-James Cheeks
Editorial Description: Significant social security developments from SSA, federal courts, congress.
General Info: Yr. Est. 1984, Monthly, ISSN: 0196-8882
List Rental: List Management Co.: WG & L List Management, 1 Penn Plz Fl 42, New York, NY 10119-0002 Tel # (212) 971-5000, Actives: $95/M

Social Security Coordinator

Publishing Co: Research Institute of America, 117 E Stevens Ave, Valhalla, NY 10595-1264; Title Tel # (212) 645-4800
Personnel: Publisher-Robert Chapman, Editor-James Cheeks
Editorial Description: Eight volumes provide strategies for handling social security cases.
General Info: Yr. Est. 1983, Monthly, ISSN: 0196-8882, Looseleaf
Subscriptions: Indv. $550
List Rental: List Management Co.: WG & L List Management, 1 Penn Plz Fl 42, New York, NY 10119-0002 Tel # (212) 971-5000, Actives: $95/M

State Advocate, The
Association

Publishing Co: Natl. Conference of State Legislatures, 1560 Broadway, Ste. 700, Denver, CO 80202-5140; Title Tel # (303) 830-2200 Title Fax # (303) 863-8003
Personnel: Editor-Susan Selandones, Circ. Mgr.-Gail Loos
Editorial Description: Covers national legislation affecting the states.
General Info: (Formerly NCSL Federal Update; Capitol to Capitol), Yr. Est. 1975, Irregular, Trim Size-8½ x 11, Mimeo press, 4 pages, ISSN: 0898-4298, 2 Color, Newsprint
Subscriptions: Indv. $35, Can. $38, $2/copy
Circulation: Total-13,500

Target Washington
Business

Publishing Co: EPIN Publishing, PO Box 21001, Washington, DC 20009-0501 Tel # (301) 365-3621 Fax # (301) 365-3621
Editorial Description: Reports on policy and practices of the federal government as it relates to Puerto Rico and companies doing business in Puerto Rico.
General Info: Bi-weekly, Trim Size-8½ x 11, Desktop press, 6 pages, Recycled
Subscriptions: Indv. $175, Inst. $175

Technology Access Report
See: SCIENCE

Third Circuit Digest
See: LAW

U.S. Rail News
See: RAILROADS

United States Space Law: Natl. & Intl. Regulation
See: LAW

Washington Drug Letter
See: DRUGS & PHARMACEUTICALS

Washington Report
See: POLITICS

Washington Social Legislation Bulletin
See: LAW

Water Regulation Watch
See: WATER SUPPLY, POWER & WASTE

Weekly Congressional Monitor
Business, Association

Publishing Co: Congressional Quarterly, Inc., 1414 22nd St. NW, Washington, DC 20037-1096 Fax # (202) 728-1863; Title Tel # (202) 887-8500
Personnel: Publisher-Neil Skene, Editor-Larry Liebert, Mng. Editor-Brian Nutting, Fulflmnt. Mgr.-Judy Stachnik, Production Mgr.-I. D. Fuller, Adv. Dir.-Bob Wallace, Mktg. Dir.-Edward Hauck, Promotion Dir.-Bob Smith
Editorial Description: Weekly listing of congressional committee hearings, with witnesses.
General Info: Yr. Est. 1972, Weekly, Trim Size-8½ x 11, Offset press, 10 pages, Ind/Abs/Online: Washington Alert, No Color
Subscriptions: Indv. $498
Acquistions: Publication Bought
List Rental: Rents Lists

UNIDENTIFIED FLYING OBJECTS

AFSCA Information Sheets
Association

Publishing Co: Amalgamated Flying Saucer Clubs of America, PO Box 39, Yucca Valley, CA 92286-0039; Title Tel # (619) 365-1141
Personnel: Editor-Gabriel Green
General Info: 10 pages

Awakening

Publishing Co: Awakening, 948 Almshouse Rd., Ivyland, PA 18974-1202; Title Tel # (215) 357-2909
Personnel: Publisher, Editor-Anthony Volpe, Circ. Mgr.-Lynn Volpe
Editorial Description: Dedicated to universal love & interplanetary brotherhood.
General Info: (Formerly Del Val UFO Newsletter), Yr. Est. 1972, 10x/yr., Trim Size-5½ x 8½, Offset press, 14 pages
Subscriptions: Indv. $9, $1/copy
Circulation: Total-300

Continuum
See: PARAPSYCHOLOGY

Cricket Letter
See: REAL ESTATE

Fair Witness Focus *Consumer*

Publishing Co: Fair Witness Project, 4219 W Olive Ave # 247, Burbank, CA 91505-4215; Title Tel # (818) 980-8758
Personnel: Publisher-W.L. Moore, Editor-Jimmy Ward, Circ. Mgr.-Richard Stingel, Adv. Dir.-B.H. Shaffer
Editorial Description: Well researched articles on UFOs & similar para-normal events.
General Info: Yr. Est. 1984, Quarterly, Trim Size-8½ x 11, Sheetfed press, 20 pages, ISSN: 1054-4208, No Color, Coated
Subscriptions: Indv. $20, Can. $24, For. $25, $4/copy
Circulation: Total-500
Advertising: Inquire for rates.
List Rental: Actives: $60/M

Interspacelink Confidential Newsletter *Consumer*

Publishing Co: Sponsor-Nicufo, Natl. Investigations Committee on Unidentified Flying Object, 14617 Victory Blvd., Ste. 4, Van Nuys, CA 91411-1675; Title Tel # (818) 989-5942 Title Fax # (818) 989-5942
Personnel: Editor, Circ. Mgr.-Dr. F.E. Stranges, Production Mgr.-Terry Dezur, Adv. Dir.-Grehville Johnson
Editorial Description: UFO updates, space and science info; personal spirtual growth.
General Info: Yr. Est. 1983, Monthly, Desktop press, 5 pages, No Color
Subscriptions: Indv. $75, For. $100, $10/copy
Circulation: (41% controlled), Total-1,200, Subscriptions-500, International-100

Iridis
See: PARAPSYCHOLOGY

Revelations of Awareness
See: NEW AGE

Star Beacon *Consumer* CPM: $120

Publishing Co: Earth Star Publications, PO Box 117, Paonia, CO 81428-0117; Title Tel # (970) 527-3257
Personnel: Publisher, Editor-Ann Ulrich, Art Dir.-Ethan Miller, Adv. Dir., Mktg. Dir.-Kari Schumacher
Editorial Description: Covers issues relating to UFO phenomena, metaphysical questions and spiritual awareness & growth.
General Info: Yr. Est. 1987, Monthly, Trim Size-8½ x 11, Offset press, 8 pages, ISSN: 1081-5171
Subscriptions: Indv. $17, Can. $17, For. $24, $2/copy
Circulation: Total-500
Advertising: $60.
Printing Co: High Country Printing, P.O. Box 236, Paonia, CO 81428 Tel # (970) 527-4567

UFO Newsclipping Service

Publishing Co: Lucius Farish, # 2 Caney Valley Drive, Plumerville, AR 72127-8725; Title Tel # (501) 354-2558
Personnel: Publisher, Editor-Lucius Farish
Editorial Description: Reprints of newspaper reports on UFOs and unexplained phenomena.
General Info: Yr. Est. 1969, Monthly, Sheetfed press, 20 pages, No Color
Subscriptions: Indv. $55, Can. $70, For. $80, $5/copy
Circulation: Total-550, Readership-600

USPA Newsletter
See: PARAPSYCHOLOGY

VENDING MACHINES

AMOA Location
See: ENTERTAINMENT

Access
See: COMPUTERS & AUTOMATION

Bulletin
See: HOUSE ORGANS

Chronicle
See: ENERGY

Coin Machine Trader *Business, Consumer*

Publishing Co: Salveson Co., PO Box 602, Huron, SD 57350-0602 Tel # (605) 352-3870 Fax # (605) 352-7590
General Info: Yr. Est. 1976, Monthly, 25 pages
Subscriptions: Indv. $20, Can. $30, For. $40, $4/copy
Advertising: Inquire for rates.
List Rental: Actives: 5,000, $100/M

Communications Product Reports
See: COMPUTERS & AUTOMATION

Pointe of View

Publishing Co: Fujitsu Business Communications, 3190 E Miraloma Ave, Anaheim, CA 92806-1906; Title Tel # (602) 921-5900 Title Fax # (602) 921-4800
Personnel: Publisher-Barbie Wingle, Editor-Darrell Richardson, Production Mgr.-Carolina Hunt, Promotion Dir.-Marisa Negrete
Editorial Description: Editorial material: Product info on FBCS' integrated telecomm. Sys., customer application stories, subsidiary product information, consultant program updates.
General Info: (Formerly Omni News), Yr. Est. 1989, Quarterly
Circulation: Total-2,300

Video Specialist and New Technology
See: TELEVISION & VIDEO

VETERANS

American Veterans of Israel Newsletter

Publishing Co: American Veterans of Israel, 136 E 39th St, New York, NY 10016-0914; Title Tel # (516) 431-8316
Personnel: Editor-Samuel Alexander
General Info: Quarterly

Citizen Soldier
See: MILITARY & NAVAL

Commonwealth of Massachusetts of Veteran's Services, Bulletin *Association*

Publishing Co: Commonwealth of Massachusetts Dept. of Veteran's Services, 100 Cambridge St Rm 1002, Boston, MA 02202-0044; Title Tel # (617) 727-3578 Title Fax # (617) 727-5903
Editorial Description: Newsletter to communicate current issues that concern the Commonwealth veterans. Apprise veterans of current activities, legislation, events, etc.
General Info: 4x/yr.

J.W.V.A. Bulletin *Association*

Publishing Co: Jewish War Veterans of the U.S., 1811 R St NW, Washington, DC 20009-1603; Title Tel # (202) 265-6280
Personnel: Editor-Caren Kaplan
Editorial Description: News of national events & issues, guest writers, features, letters.
General Info: Yr. Est. 1968, Quarterly, Trim Size-8½ x 11, 12 pages, ISSN: 0021-3799, No Color
Subscriptions: Indv. $1
Circulation: Total-20,000

Texas Veterans Affairs Commission, Bulletin

Publishing Co: Texas Veterans Affairs Commission, Austin, TX 78711

Vets' News Letter

Publishing Co: Oregon Department of Veterans' Affairs, 700 Summer St NE, Salem, OR 97310-1351 Tel # (503) 373-2386 Fax # (503) 373-2362; Title Tel # (503) 373-2385 Title Fax # (503) 323-2362
Personnel: Editor-Sharon Robertson
Editorial Description: Information on veterans' benefits, both State and Federal. Also state loan holders news. (State G.I. Loan Program).
General Info: Yr. Est. 1945, Bi-monthly, Trim Size-8½ x 11, Offset press, 8 pages, No Color, Newsprint, Saddle-stitched
Subscriptions: Free
Circulation: Total-46,000
Printing Co: Oregon State Printing Division, 500 Airport Rd SE, Salem, OR 97310-1300 Tel # (503) 378-3560

Vietnam Veterans of New Mexico Newsletter

Publishing Co: Vietnam Veterans of New Mexico, Bataan Memorial Bldg., Galisteo St., Box 2324, Santa Fe, NM 87503-0001; Title Tel # (505) 827-6300
Personnel: Publisher, Editor-Al Sanchez, Promotion Dir.-Gil Jacquez
General Info: Yr. Est. 1982, Monthly, Trim Size-8½ x 11, Offset press, 6 pages, 3% ads, 2 Color
Circulation: Total-2,500
Advertising: Inquire for rates.

Vietnam Veterans Newsletter

Publishing Co: Ranger Regimental Assn., PO Box 29965, Atlanta, GA 30359-0965; Title Tel # (404) 296-0800
General Info: Quarterly

West Virginia Legionnaire *Association*

Publishing Co: West Virginia Legionnaire, PO Box 3191, Charleston, WV 25332-3191; Title Tel # (304) 343-7591
Personnel: Editor-Robert Vass, Sr.
Editorial Description: Veterans affairs and National American Legion programs.
General Info: Yr. Est. 1925, Bi-monthly, Trim Size-11½ x 15, Offset press, 12 pages, Color
Subscriptions: Indv. $4
Circulation: Total-30,000

VETERINARY

AAEP Report
  See: HORSES

AASRP Newsletter   *Association*

Publishing Co: Sponsor-Amer. Assn. of Small Ruminant Practitioners, American Association of Small Ruminant Practitioners, 1675 Ellis Hollow Rd, Ithaca, NY 14850-9689; Title Tel # (607) 539-6181 Title Fax # (607) 539-6181
Personnel: Editor-Mary Smith
Editorial Description: Contains news of meetings, conferences, and publications. Includes abstracts of scientific papers on sheep goats, llamas, deer, and other small ruminants.
General Info: (Formerly Wool & Wattles; AASGP Newsletter), Yr. Est. 1969, Quarterly, Sheetfed press, 19 pages, Other
Subscriptions: Indv. $25, Can. $30, For. $30, Free With Membership
Circulation: Total-1,310

AHI Quarterly

Publishing Co: Animal Health Institute, Box 1417, #D50, Alexandria, VA 22313-1480; Title Tel # (703) 684-0011 Title Fax # (703) 684-0125
Personnel: Editor-Patrick McCabe
Editorial Description: Covers current issues involving animal health products used in livestock.
General Info: (Formerly Animal Health Letter), Yr. Est. 1941, Quarterly, Offset press, 6 pages, No Color, Coated
Circulation: Total-3,100

AMC CenterScope   *Consumer*

Publishing Co: Animal Medical Center, 510 E 62nd St, New York, NY 10021-8383; Title Tel # (212) 838-8100
Personnel: Editor-Joan Foster
Editorial Description: Newsletter of the animal medical center.
General Info: Quarterly, 2 Color
Subscriptions: Free In Designated Area
Circulation: Total-15,000

AV Magazine, The   *Association*

Publishing Co: American Anti-Vivisection Society, 801 Old York Rd., Suite #204, Jenkintown, PA 19046-1685; Title Tel # (215) 887-0816 Title Fax # (215) 887-2088
Personnel: Editor-W.G. Kelly
Editorial Description: To educate regarding the cruelty, immorality and waste of vivisection.
General Info: Yr. Est. 1883, 6x/yr., Trim Size-7⅜ x 10½, Letrpr. press, 20 pages, ISSN: 0001-2831, No Color
Subscriptions: Indv. $15
Circulation: (100% controlled), Total-15,000

AVEA Newsletter   *Business, Association*

Publishing Co: American Veterinary Exhibitors Assn., PO Box 6842, Santa Barbara, CA 93160-6842; Title Tel # (805) 683-0489
Editorial Description: Information for and about exhibitors at veterinary conventions.
General Info: Quarterly
Subscriptions: Free With Membership

AWV Bulletin   *Association*

Publishing Co: Association for Women Veterinarians, 16706 Rolling Rock Dr, Tampa, FL 33618-1133; Title Tel # (303) 795-0130
Personnel: Editor-Deborah Mitchell, DVM, Asst. Ed.-Nil Wilkins, DVM, Adv. Dir.-Cari Schafer, DVM
Editorial Description: Women's issues in veterinary medical profession.
General Info: (Formerly WVMA), Yr. Est. 1947, Quarterly, Trim Size-8½ x 11, Offset press, 20 pages, 2% ads, No Color, Newsprint, Saddle-stitched
Subscriptions: Indv. $10
Circulation: Total-10,000
Advertising: Inquire for rates.

Advances in Small Animal Medicine and Surgery

Publishing Co: W.B. Saunders Co., Curtis Ctr., Independence Square West, Philadelphia, PA 19106 Tel # (215) 238-7800 Fax # (215) 238-6445 Parent Co.-Harcourt Brace Professional Publishing, Orlando
Personnel: Editor-Rhea V. Morgan, DVM
Editorial Description: Features abstracts of material from recent publication and presntations, followed by comments from specialists in the field.
General Info: Monthly, ISSN: 1041-7826
Subscriptions: Indv. $57, Inst. $75, For. $73, $10/copy

American Association of Veterinary Anatomists Newsletter

Publishing Co: American Assn. of Veterinary Anatomists, 1900 Coffey Rd # A100, Columbus, OH 43210-1006; Title Tel # (614) 292-1171
General Info: Semi-annually

American College of Veterinary Pathologists-Newsletter

Publishing Co: Am. College of Veterinary Pathologists, 875 Kings Highway, STe. 200, W. Deptford, NJ 08096-3168; Title Tel # (609) 848-7784 Title Fax # (609) 853-0411
Personnel: Editor-Dr. Helen Acland
General Info: Yr. Est. 1951, Bi-monthly
Circulation: Total-800

Animal News   *Consumer, Association*

Publishing Co: Morris Animal Foundation, 45 Inverness Dr E, Englewood, CO 80112-5480; Title Tel # (303) 790-2345 Title Fax # (303) 790-4066
Personnel: Editor-Janice Rooney
Editorial Description: Studies on animal health and wildlife.
General Info: (Formerly Companion Animal News), Trim Size-10 x 12, Web press, 8 pages, 2 Color
Circulation: Total-141,000

Animal Pharm World Animal Health & Nutrition News   *Business, Association*

Publishing Co: Pharmabooks, 1775 Broadway Ste 511, New York, NY 10019-1903; Title Tel # (212) 262-8230 Title Fax # (212) 262-8234
Personnel: Publisher-Philip Brown, Editor-Jeanette Marchant, Adv. Dir.-Peter Coltart
General Info: Bi-weekly, Trim Size-209mm x 296mm, Offset press, 28 pages, 2 Color, Newsprint, Saddle-stitched
Subscriptions: Indv. $530
Circulation: (PSS), Total-1,143
Advertising: Inquire for rates.

Animal Welfare Information Center Newsletter
  See: ANIMALS

Arizona Veterinary Medical Assn. Newsletter   *Association*

Publishing Co: Arizona Veterinary Medical Assn., 5502 N 19th Ave, Phoenix, AZ 85015-2401; Title Tel # (602) 242-7936
Personnel: Editor-Dr. Bob Koch, Production Mgr.-Judy Grana
General Info: Monthly, 8 pages, Color, Newsprint
Subscriptions: Indv. $35
Circulation: Total-550
Advertising: Inquire for rates.
List Rental: Rents Lists

Arkansas Animal Morbidity Report   *Association*

Publishing Co: Arkansas Dept. of Health, 4815 W Markham St, Little Rock, AR 72205-3866; Title Tel # (501) 661-2264
Personnel: Editor-Thomas McChesney, DVM, Circ. Mgr., Art Dir.-Marquerite Edelmann
Editorial Description: Animal diseases in Ark.
General Info: Yr. Est. 1956, Quarterly, Trim Size-8½ x 11½, Offset press, 23 pages, No Color
Circulation: (100% controlled), Total-600

Beastly News
  See: DOGS

Black Sheep Newsletter
  See: LIVESTOCK

CATsumer Report
  See: CATS

Cat Industry Newsletter
  See: CATS

Catnip
  See: CATS

Commercial Cattle Issue
  See: LIVESTOCK

Comparative Pathology Bulletin
  See: MEDICINE

Cornell Animal Health Newsletter   *Business, Consumer*

Publishing Co: Cornell Veterinarian, Inc., Publications, Ithaca, NY 14853-6401 Tel # (607) 253-3336
Personnel: Publisher-Deborah White, Editor-Katherine Houpt, DVM
Editorial Description: Information for animal lovers and owners.
General Info: Monthly
Subscriptions: Indv. $28

Crest
Business, Association

Publishing Co: Ontario Veterinary College, Univ. of Guelph, Dean's Office, Guelph, ON N1G 2W1 Canada; Title Tel # (519) 823-8800 Title Fax # (519) 837-3230
Personnel: Editor-Martha Leibbrandt
Editorial Description: Published for the Ontario veterinary profession, includes reports on events programs and people at the college.
General Info: Quarterly, Trim Size-8½ x 11, Desktop press, 8 pages, 2 Color, Matte, Saddle-stitched
Circulation: Total-4,000

Digest of Veterinary Matters

Publishing Co: Oregon State Dept. of Agriculture, 635 Capitol St NE, Salem, OR 97310-1315 Tel # (503) 986-4558 Fax # (503) 986-4747; Title Tel # (503) 378-4710
Personnel: Publisher, Editor-Rosalie Pedroso
Editorial Description: Newsletter for Oregon veterinarians.
General Info: Yr. Est. 1986, Mimeo press, 4 pages, No Color, Newsprint
Circulation: Total-460

Dog Industry Newsletter
See: DOGS

Equine Veterinary Data

Publishing Co: Veterinary Data, PO Box 1209, Wildomar, CA 92595-1209; Title Tel # (714) 678-1889 Title Fax # (714) 678-1885
Personnel: Publisher, Editor-William Jones, DVM, Ph. D, Circ. Mgr.-Callie Roe
Editorial Description: Equine veterinary update & report.
General Info: Yr. Est. 1980, Monthly, 12 pages, ISSN: 0739-9065
Subscriptions: Indv. $95, Inst. $120, Can. $105, For. $120, $6/copy
Circulation: Total-1,500

Federal Veterinarian
Association

Publishing Co: National Association of Federal Veterinarians, 1101 Vermont Ave NW Ste 710, Washington, DC 20005-3521; Title Tel # (202) 289-6334
Personnel: Publisher, Editor-Edward Menning
Editorial Description: Developments in federal veterinary medicine and personnel policy affecting veterinarians.
General Info: Yr. Est. 1920, Monthly, Trim Size-8½ x 11, Offset press, 12 pages, ISSN: 0164-6257, No Color
Subscriptions: Indv. $35, Can. $35, For. $50, $4/copy
Circulation: Total-1,800
Advertising: Inquire for rates.

Feline Health Topics

Publishing Co: Cornell Feline Health Center, College of Veterinary Medicine, Cornell University, Ithaca, NY 14853; Title Tel # (607) 253-3414 Title Fax # (607) 253-3419
Personnel: Editor-June Tuttle
Editorial Description: Focuses on diseases of cats.
General Info: (Formerly Cornell Feline Health Center News), Yr. Est. 1979, Quarterly, Sheetfed press, 8 pages, 2 Color, Recycled, Saddle-stitched
Subscriptions: Indv. $25, Can. $30, For. $30, Free To Qualified Recipient
Circulation: Total-26,000
Printing Co: Cayuga Press, 1650 Hanshaw Rd, Ithaca, NY 14850-9102 Tel # (607) 257-2811

Georgia Extension Veterinary News
Association

Publishing Co: Univ. of Georgia Cooperative Extension, Cooperative Extension Service, Athens, GA 30602; Title Tel # (404) 542-2875
Editorial Description: Animal health-all species.
General Info: Yr. Est. 1960, Monthly
Circulation: (100% controlled), Total-2,000

Horse!
See: HORSES

Horse Report, The
See: HORSES

IAAAM News

Publishing Co: International Association for Aquatic Animal Medicine, School of Public Health, Univ. of CA, Berkeley, CA 94709-1399; Title Tel # (415) 522-6715
General Info: Yr. Est. 1970, 6 pages

Journal of Equine Veterinary Science

Publishing Co: Veterinary Data, PO Box 1209, Wildomar, CA 92595-1209; Title Tel # (714) 678-1889 Title Fax # (714) 678-1885
Personnel: Publisher, Editor-William Jones
Editorial Description: New developments in the field of equine sportsmedicine.
General Info: (Formerly Equine Sportsmedicine News), Yr. Est. 1983, Monthly
Subscriptions: Indv. $48

Large Animal Veterinary Report

Publishing Co: Veterinary Data, PO Box 1209, Wildomar, CA 92595-1209; Title Tel # (714) 678-1889 Title Fax # (714) 678-1885
Personnel: Editor-William Jones DVM, Circ. Mgr.-Callie Roe
Editorial Description: Large animal veterinary practice update.
General Info: Monthly
Subscriptions: Inst. $75, Can. $60, For. $75
Circulation: Total-600

MSU Veterinarian

Publishing Co: American Veterinary Medical Assn., Michigan Chapter, East Lansing, MI 48823; Title Tel # (517) 332-2913
Editorial Description: Articles are slanted to a select group of graduate veterinarians, composed both of practitioners and educators. Circulation is approximmately 75% domestic and the remainder foreign.
General Info: Yr. Est. 1931
Subscriptions: Indv. $2
Circulation: Total-1,700

Manitoba Veterinary Medical Assn. Newsletter

Publishing Co: Manitoba Veterinary Medical Assn., 2989 Pembina Highway #203, Winnipeg, MB R3T 2H5 Canada; Title Tel # (204) 269-0625
Personnel: Editor-Dr. Kevin Millar
General Info: Bi-monthly
Subscriptions: Indv. $20
Circulation: Total-250
Advertising: Inquire for rates.

NAVS Bulletin
Association

Publishing Co: Natl. Anti-Vivisection Society, 53 W Jackson Blvd Ste 1550, Chicago, IL 60604-3703; Title Tel # (312) 427-6065
Personnel: Editor-Bobbi Morrison
Editorial Description: Quarterly news magazine covering the animal advocacy movement. Contains articles on a wide array of related topics.
General Info: Bi-monthly, 32 pages
Subscriptions: Indv. $15

New Methods: The Journal of Animal Health Technology
Business, Association   **CPM: $32**

Publishing Co: New Methods Co., PO Box 22605, San Francisco, CA 94122-0605; Title Tel # (415) 664-3469
Personnel: Production Mgr.-Larry Rosenberg, Publisher, Editor, Editorial Page Ed., Feature Ed., Bk. Rev. Ed., Circ. Mgr., Production Dir., Adv. Dir., Art Dir., Mktg. Dir., Promotion Dir.-Ronald S. Lippert
Editorial Description: Animal health technician's direct news network covering national & state associations & schools.
General Info: (Formerly Methods), Yr. Est. 1981, Monthly, Trim Size-8½ x 11, Sheetfed press, 6 pages, ISSN: 0277-3015, Color, Coated, Saddle-stitched
Subscriptions: Indv. $29, Inst. $29, Can. $29, For. $29, $3/copy
Circulation: (43% controlled), Total-8,843, Subscriptions-4,900, International-1,000
Advertising: $290. Accepts Inserts.
List Rental: Actives: 5,600, $290/M

North American Bull Buyers Guide
See: LIVESTOCK

Ohio Veterinary Medical Association Newsletter
Association

Publishing Co: Ohio Veterinary Medical Assn., 3168 Riverside Dr, Columbus, OH 43221-2540; Title Tel # (614) 486-7253 Title Fax # (614) 486-1325
Personnel: Editor-George Kukor
General Info: (Formerly Ohio Veterinarian), Yr. Est. 1970, Monthly, 8 pages
Subscriptions: Indv. $2
Circulation: Total-1,823
Advertising: Inquire for rates.
Printing Co: Vincent Graphics, PO Box 386, Dublin, OH 43017-0386 Tel # (614) 889-2559

PVMA Newsletter
Association

Publishing Co: Pennsylvania Veterinary Medical Assoc., PO Box 403, Harrisburg, PA 17108-0403; Title Tel # (717) 233-7720
Personnel: Editor-Ray Thompson
Editorial Description: Research and educational material around which the veterinary profession revolves.
General Info: Yr. Est. 1959, Bi-monthly, Trim Size-8½ x 11, Offset press, 24 pages, No Color
Circulation: Total-1,900

Pet News
See: ANIMALS

Pigletter
See: LIVESTOCK

Primate Library Report: Audio-Visual Acquisitions
See: ZOOLOGY

Scientists Center for Animal Welfare's Newsletter
See: ANIMALS

TechAgra News
See: AGRICULTURE

Update   *Association*

Publishing Co: College of Veterinarians of Ontario, 2106 Gordon St., Guelph, ON N1L 1G6 Canada; Title Tel # (519) 824-5600 Title Fax # (519) 824-6497
Personnel: Editor-D. Lowe
Editorial Description: Professional: matters concerning licensing & regulation of veterinarians in Ontario.
General Info: Yr. Est. 1978, Bi-monthly, Trim Size-8½ x 11, Offset press, 16 pages, ISSN: 0821-6320, Color, Newsprint
Subscriptions: Indv. $35
Circulation: (90% controlled), Total-3,300

Veterinary Advisory Report

Publishing Co: Chubb Communications, 222 Milwaukee St Ste 408, Denver, CO 80206-5012; Title Tel # (303) 321-8966
Personnel: Editor-Dr. David Chubb
Editorial Description: Information on managing a veterinary practice.
General Info: (Formerly Vet. Marketing), Yr. Est. 1986, Bi-monthly, 12 pages, 2% ads
Subscriptions: Indv. $139

Veterinary Industry Newsletter   *Business*

Publishing Co: Good Communications, Inc., PO Box 10069, Austin, TX 78766; Title Tel # (512) 454-6090 Title Fax # (512) 454-3420
Personnel: Publisher, Editor-Ross Becker, Mng. Editor-Judi Sklar
Editorial Description: A monthly newsletter for Senior Executives at veterinary products pharmaceuticals, pet product and pet food companies. Provides sensitive information about new products, strategies and promotions to the veterinary market.
General Info: Yr. Est. 1993, Monthly, Trim Size-8½ x 11, 9 pages, ISSN: 1074-7796
Subscriptions: Indv. $295

Your Dog
See: DOGS

WATER SUPPLY, POWER & WASTE

American Rivers
See: ENVIRONMENT & ECOLOGY

Appalachian Alternatives
See: CONSUMER INTERESTS

Aquatic Plant Control Research Program Newsletter
See: ENVIRONMENT & ECOLOGY

Arroyo

Publishing Co: Sponsor-Univ. of Arizona, Water Resources Research Center, Univ. of Arizona, Tucson, AZ 85721-0001; Title Tel # (520) 792-9591 Title Fax # (520) 792-8518
Personnel: Editor-Joe Gelt
Editorial Description: Covers water issues affecting Arizona and the West.
General Info: Yr. Est. 1987, Quarterly, Trim Size-8½ x 11, Roto. press, 8 pages, No Color, Newsprint
Acquistions: Publication Bought, Publication Sold
Circulation: Total-2,500
Printing Co: Owl Printing Co., 933 N. Stone Ave., Tucson, AZ 85706-0001 Tel # (520) 622-7311

Bottle/Can Recycling Update
See: ENVIRONMENT & ECOLOGY

CTWA Newsletter

Publishing Co: Council of Trade Waste Assns., Inc., Box 70-1380, Trainsmeadow Sta., Flushing, NY 11370; Title Tel # (718) 335-0303 Title Fax # (718) 335-0399
Personnel: Editor-M. McAleer
General Info: Monthly

California Water Law & Policy Reporter
See: LAW

Colorado Stream Lines   *Association*

Publishing Co: Colorado Division of Water Resources, 1313 Sherman St Ste 818, Denver, CO 80203-2238; Title Tel # (303) 861-3581
Personnel: Editor-George Van Slyke, Circ. Mgr.-Paula Lacey
Editorial Description: Water administration, water studies, dams, legislation, wells.
General Info: (Formerly Colorado Water News), Yr. Est. 1988, Quarterly, Trim Size-8½ x 11, Offset press, 5 pages, Color, Newsprint
Subscriptions: Indv. $10
Circulation: (100% controlled), Total-510
Printing Co: State of Colorado, 1313 Sherman, Denver, CO 80203 Tel # (303) 297-1192

Composting News
See: ENVIRONMENT & ECOLOGY

ConnTAP Quarterly
See: ENVIRONMENT & ECOLOGY

Cycle/the Waste Paper
See: ENVIRONMENT & ECOLOGY

Divining Rod
See: ENVIRONMENT & ECOLOGY

Effluent   *Business*

Publishing Co: Association Quebecoise des Techniques de l'Eau, 407 St-Laurent, Bureau 500, Montreal, PQ H2Y 2Y5 Canada; Title Tel # (514) 874-3700 Title Fax # (514) 866-4020
Personnel: Editor-Irene Langis, Adv. Dir.-Francine Perrault
General Info: Yr. Est. 1976, Monthly, Web press, 12 pages, 1% ads, No Color, Saddle-stitched
Circulation: Total-1,800
Advertising: Accepts Inserts.
Printing Co: CNT-CANGRAFT, 5731 Ferrier St., Montreal, PQ H4P 1N3 Canada Tel # (514) 731-7460

Electric Power   *Business*

Publishing Co: Hart Publications, 7811 Montrose Rd., Potomac, MD 20854 Tel # (301) 340-2100 Parent Co.-Phillips Business Information, Inc., Potomac
Editorial Description: Covers all aspects of the electric power industry worldwide.
General Info: Yr. Est. 1995, Quarterly

Electric Power Alert
See: ENERGY

Electric Utility Week
See: PUBLIC UTILITIES

Electric Utility Week's Demand-Side Report
See: PUBLIC UTILITIES

Energy
See: ENERGY

Environmental Health & Safety CFR Update
See: ENVIRONMENT & ECOLOGY

Environmental Pollution & Control
See: ENVIRONMENT & ECOLOGY

Environmental Regulation/State Capitals
See: ENVIRONMENT & ECOLOGY

Everglades Reporter
See: ENVIRONMENT & ECOLOGY

Faucet Facts

Publishing Co: Town of Hempstead Office of Communication & Public Affairs, 1 Washington St, Hempstead, NY 11550-4921; Title Tel # (516) 489-5000
Personnel: Editor-Alexandra Trias
Editorial Description: Town of Hempstead Water Department publication for its water customers, describing water conservation measures, educational materials, and use of classroom visits with school children to familiarize them with water problems.
General Info: Semi-annually
Circulation: Total-37,000

Federation Highlights
See: ENVIRONMENT & ECOLOGY

Foster Electric Report
See: PUBLIC UTILITIES

GEM Notes   *Consumer*

Publishing Co: Michigan State University Inst. of Water Res., 334 Natural Res. Bldg., East Lansing, MI 48824-0001; Title Tel # (517) 353-3742 Title Fax # (517) 353-3742
Personnel: Editor-W. Helstowski
Editorial Description: Features highlights of the Groundwater Education in Michigan Programs supported by the W.K. Kellogg Foundation. Federal, state & local issues related to groundwater protection are also examined.
General Info: Yr. Est. 1986, Bi-monthly, Web press, 4 pages, No Color

Groundwater Management Districts Assn. Newsletter   *Business, Association*

Publishing Co: Groundwater Management Districts Assn., PO Box 795, Dumas, TX 79029-0795; Title Tel # (913) 462-3915
Editorial Description: Management and conservation of water resources.
General Info: Yr. Est. 1975, Quarterly, 4 pages

Groundwater Newsletter, The
Business, Consumer

Publishing Co: Water Information Center, Inc., 1099 18th St., Ste 2150, Denver, CO 80202-1921
Fax # (303) 294-1239 Parent Co.-Geraghty & Miller, Inc., Danver; Title Tel # (303) 391-8799
Title Fax # (810) 294-1239
Personnel: Publisher-Fred Troise, Editor-Judith Schoeck, Mng. Editor-Fred L. Troise, Bk. Rev. Ed.-Dee Farrell, Circ. Mgr.-Michelle Hankins
Editorial Description: Covers the latest technologies, studies, and legislation for protecting groundwater rescources and remediating hazardous wastes. Includes upcoming meetings, new publications, and references for further information.
General Info: Yr. Est. 1971, Semi-weekly, Trim Size-8 x 10, Offset press, 6 pages, ISSN: 0090-5070, 2 Color, Matte
Subscriptions: Indv. $347, Can. $347, For. $377, $14/copy

H2O Quality Newsletter
Association **CPM: $980**

Publishing Co: Texas Water Quality Assn., 1601 Rio Grande St Ste 440, Austin, TX 78701-1149; Title Tel # (512) 419-0425
Personnel: Editor-Lisa Fry
Editorial Description: Offical publication of the Texas Water Quality Assn., professionals in the water conditioning industry.
General Info: Quarterly, Trim Size-8½ x 11, Offset press, 12 pages, 10% ads, No Color, Coated, Saddle-stitched
Subscriptions: Free With Membership
Circulation: Total-250
Advertising: $245.

H2Observer
Business, Consumer

Publishing Co: New Jersey Department of Environmental Protection, Water Supply Element, CN 426, Bureau of Safe Drinking Water, Trenton, NJ 08625-0426
Editorial Description: Covers the quality of water issues facing Jersey water supplies.
General Info: Quarterly, Trim Size-8½ x 11, 4 pages

Hanford Update Newsletter
Business, Association

Publishing Co: Nuclear Waste Program, P.O Box 47600, Olympia, WA 98504-7600
Tel # (360) 407-7126; Title Tel # (360) 407-7121 Title Fax # (360) 407-7151
Personnel: Editor-Mark Wallace
Editorial Description: A quarterly newsletter covering issues related to cleanup of the Hanford site in Washington state.
General Info: Quarterly, Trim Size-8½ x 11, 6 pages, Color
Subscriptions: Free
Circulation: Total-4,000, Readership-4,000

Hazardous Substances & Public Health
Consumer

Publishing Co: U.S. Dept. of Health & Human Services, Toxic Substances/Disease Reg., 1600 Clifton Rd. N.E., E-33, Atlanta, GA 30333; Title Tel # (404) 639-6206 Title Fax # (404) 639-6208
Personnel: Editor-Lynn Storck
Editorial Description: Explores issues relating to hazardous waste and its effect on human health.
General Info: Yr. Est. 1990, Bi-monthly, Trim Size-8½ x 11, 16 pages, 2 Color, Matte, Saddle-stitched

Hazardous Waste Business
Business

Publishing Co: McGraw-Hill, 1221 Ave. of the Americas, 36th Fl., New York, NY 10020-1095
Tel # (212) 512-2000 Fax # (212) 512-6590; Title Tel # (212) 512-6410
Personnel: Publisher-John Slater, Editor in Chief-Kevin Hamilton, Mng. Editor-Steven Lang
Editorial Description: Covers news and develops relating to hazardous waste, disposal, etc.
General Info: Yr. Est. 1985, Bi-weekly, ISSN: 0897-2699, Ind/Abs/Online: Dialog, Dow Jones, NewsNet, Nexis
Subscriptions: Indv. $540

Hydata News and Views
Association

Publishing Co: American Water Resources Assn., 950 Herndon Pky., Ste. 300, Herndon, VA 22070-5528 Fax # (703) 904-1228; Title Tel # (703) 904-1225 Title Fax # (903) 904-1228
Personnel: Publisher-Kenneth Reid, Editor-Earl Spangenberg, Circ. Mgr.-Christopher Byrne, Production Mgr.-Charlene Young
Editorial Description: Disseminates information relating to water resources science & monitors news affecting the water resources profession.
General Info: Yr. Est. 1964, Bi-monthly, Trim Size-8½ x 11, Sheetfed press, 20 pages, 1% ads, No Color, Newsprint, Saddle-stitched
Subscriptions: Indv. $20, $5/copy
Circulation: Total-3,800
Advertising: Inquire for rates.
List Rental: Actives: $100/M

Independent Power Markets Quarterly
See: ENERGY

Independent Power Report
See: LAW

Industrial Bioprocessing
See: BIOCHEMISTRY

Integrated Waste Management
See: ENERGY

Intra
Business

Publishing Co: Trinity River Authority, 5300 S Collins St, Arlington, TX 76018-1710; Title Tel # (817) 467-4343 Title Fax # (817) 465-0970
Personnel: Editor-Cami McKillop
Editorial Description: Articles about and relating to TRA projects and employees.
General Info: Yr. Est. 1975, Bi-monthly, Trim Size-11 x 17, Sheetfed press, 8 pages, 2 Color, Coated, Other
Subscriptions: Free To Qualified Recipient
Circulation: Total-850
Printing Co: Torrant Printing, 3228 W. Euless Blvd, Suite 15, Euless, TX 76039-2306
Tel # (817) 571-9960, Fax # (817) 545-9069

Jet News
Association

Publishing Co: Water Jet Technology Association, 818 Olive St Ste 918, Saint Louis, MO 63101-1544; Title Tel # (314) 241-1445 Title Fax # (314) 241-1449
Personnel: Editor-George Savanick, Ph.D
Editorial Description: Includes research findings, new applications for water jet technology, & member activities.
General Info: Yr. Est. 1983, Bi-monthly, Trim Size-8½ x 11, Offset press, 6 pages, No Color
Subscriptions: Free With Membership
Circulation: Total-750

Job Bank, The
See: EMPLOYMENT

Lakes Letter
Consumer, Association

Publishing Co: International Assn. for Great Lakes Research, 2200 Bonisteel Dr, Ann Arbor, MI 48109-2099
Personnel: Editor-Thomas Murphy
Editorial Description: Association newsletter.
General Info: Yr. Est. 1975, Semi-annually, Trim Size-8½ x 11, 12 pages, ISSN: 0380-1330, No Color
Circulation: Total-1,000

Liquid Filtration
See: ENVIRONMENT & ECOLOGY

Missouri River Report
Business, Association

Publishing Co: Missouri Basin States Assn., Inc., PO Box 301, Lewistown, MT 59457-0301; Title Tel # (406) 542-6272 Title Fax # (406) 542-7585
Editorial Description: Water related news from the Missouri River Basin.
General Info: (Formerly MBSA Basin Bulletin), Yr. Est. 1990, Quarterly, Trim Size-8½ x 11, Desktop press, 10 pages, ISSN: 0733-8112, Other
Subscriptions: Free With Membership
Circulation: Total-1,800
Printing Co: Artcraft Printers, Missoula, MT 59802

Mono Lake Newsletter
Consumer, Association

Publishing Co: Mono Lake Committee, Inc., P.O Box 29, Lee Vining, CA 93541
Tel # (619) 647-6595 Fax # (619) 647-6377; Title Tel # (818) 972-2025 Title Fax # (818) 972-2720
Personnel: Publisher, Editor-Geoff McQuilkin
Editorial Description: Developments affecting Mono Lake's future, articles on natural and human history at Mono and Great Basin Lakes.
General Info: (Formerly Mono Lake Committee Newsletter), Yr. Est. 1978, Quarterly, Trim Size-8 x 10, Web press, 24 pages, ISSN: 0275-6633, No Color, Newsprint
Subscriptions: Indv. $25
Circulation: Total-20,000
List Rental: Actives: $65/M

NAWDEX Newsletter

Publishing Co: Natl. Water Data Exchange Program Office, Us Geological Survey 421 Natl., Ctr., 12201 Sunrise, Reston, VA 22092-0001; Title Tel # (703) 648-6848
General Info: Yr. Est. 1976, Semi-annually, Trim Size-8½ x 11, Offset press, 2 pages, Color
Subscriptions: Free
Circulation: Total-3,000

National Water Line
Business, Consumer

Publishing Co: Natl. Water Resources Assn., 3800 Fairfax Dr, Ste 4, Arlington, VA 22203-1703; Title Tel # (703) 524-1544 Title Fax # (703) 524-1548
General Info: (Formerly Natl. Waterlife Or Reclamation News & Water Life), Yr. Est. 1949, Monthly, Letrpr. press, 6 pages, No Color, Coated
Subscriptions: Indv. $150
Circulation: (100% controlled), Total-5,000
List Rental: Rents Lists

National Wetlands Newsletter

Publishing Co: Environmental Law Institute, 1616 P St NW Ste 200, Washington, DC 20036-1493; Title Tel # (202) 328-5150 Title Fax # (202) 328-5002
Personnel: Publisher-J. William Futrell, Editor-Steve Mattox, Circ. Mgr.-Linda Stefkovic, Promotion Dir.-Anne Phelan
Editorial Description: Federal and state programs related to wetland and floodplain management and coastal water resources.
General Info: Yr. Est. 1979, Bi-monthly, Trim Size-8½ x 11, Sheetfed press, 20 pages, ISSN: 0164-0712, No Color, Recycled
Subscriptions: Indv. $48
Circulation: Total-2,000

News & Views (Fluid Controls) *Consumer, Association*

Publishing Co: Fluid Controls Institute, 1300 Sumner Ct., Cleveland, OH 44115-2851; Title Tel # (201) 829-0990
Personnel: Publisher, Editor-Edward Rutter
General Info: Yr. Est. 1921, Quarterly, 6 pages
Circulation: Total-450

Newsletter *Consumer, Association*

Publishing Co: Water Resources Assn. of the Delaware River Basin, Box 867, Davis Rd., Valley Forge, PA 19482-0867; Title Tel # (610) 783-0634 Title Fax # (610) 783-0635
Personnel: Editor-W.H. Palmer
Editorial Description: Timely newsletter regarding current water resources issues in Del. R. Basin.
General Info: Yr. Est. 1959, Quarterly, Web press, 5 pages, Color-cover, Newsprint
Subscriptions: Indv. $25
Circulation: (100% controlled), Total-1,500
Printing Co: Sir Speedy, 150 Allandale Rd., King of Prussia, PA 19406 Tel # (215) 337-7468

Northeast Power Report
See: ENERGY

Northwater *Consumer*

Publishing Co: Inst. of Northern Engineering, Univ. of Alaska, Fairbanks, AK 99775-0001; Title Tel # (907) 474-6113 Title Fax # (907) 474-6087
Personnel: Editor-S. Faussett
Editorial Description: Reviews Arctic research on water resources, alternative energy, environment, engineering & biotechnology.
General Info: Yr. Est. 1975, Semi-annually, Sheetfed press, 4 pages, 2 Color, Matte
Circulation: Total-2,200

ORSANCO Quality Monitor

Publishing Co: Ohio River Valley Water Sanitation Commission, 5735 Kellogg Ave, Cincinnati, OH 45228-1112; Title Tel # (513) 231-7719 Title Fax # (513) 231-7761
Editorial Description: Features information on water pollution in the Ohio River Valley and related subjects.
General Info: Semi-annually, Trim Size-12 x 9, 20 pages, No Color, Matte, Saddle-stitched
Subscriptions: Free

On the Watch
See: ENERGY

Paper Stock Report:News and Trends of the Paper recycling Markets
See: ENVIRONMENT & ECOLOGY

Pipeline

Publishing Co: Allied Corp., Water Treatment Chem. Dept., Box 1139R, Morristown, NJ 07960
General Info: 8 pages

Plastics Recycling Update
See: ENVIRONMENT & ECOLOGY

RCRA Land Disposal Restrictions-A Guide to Compliance
See: CHEMISTRY & CHEMICALS

Reuse/Recycle
See: ENVIRONMENT & ECOLOGY

SARA Title III: Regulations & Keyword Index
See: CHEMISTRY & CHEMICALS

Safety & Health Bulletin *Business, Association*

Publishing Co: Water Environment Federation, 601 Wythe St, Alexandria, VA 22314-1994; Title Tel # (703) 684-2400 Title Fax # (703) 684-2492
Personnel: Publisher-Berinda Ross, Editor-Jerry Wright, Production Mgr.-Jennifer Darnell, Mktg. Dir.-Matthew Rowan, Promotion Dir.-Joan Martin
General Info: Yr. Est. 1975, Quarterly, Trim Size-8½ x 11, Offset press, 6 pages, Saddle-stitched
Subscriptions: Indv. $15, For. $20
List Rental: Rents Lists

Schlumberger Sonde Off

Publishing Co: Schlumberger Well Services, PO Box 2175, Houston, TX 77252-2175; Title Tel # (713) 928-4000
Personnel: Editor-Sandra Fleming
General Info: Yr. Est. 1949, Monthly
Circulation: Total-4,000

Sedimentation & Centrifugation
See: ENVIRONMENT & ECOLOGY

Sludge Newsletter
See: ENVIRONMENT & ECOLOGY

Snow Survey Bulletin *Association*

Publishing Co: British Columbia, Ministry of Environment, Lands and Parks, 810 Blanshard, 1st Fl., Victoria, BC V8V 1X4 Canada Tel # (604) 387-9422; Title Tel # (604) 387-1111
Editorial Description: A review of current snow-pack conditions, from which an outlook for runoff conditions is made.
General Info: Yr. Est. 1940, Bi-monthly, Trim Size-8½ x 11, Offset press, 30 pages
Circulation: Total-1,100

Southwestern Ice Association Newsletter
See: MANUFACTURING

Surview
See: GEOLOGY

Texas Water Report *Business*

Publishing Co: Report Publications, Inc., PO Box 12368, Austin, TX 78711-2368; Title Tel # (512) 478-5663
Personnel: Editor-Bill Kidd, Circ. Mgr.-Shirl Scott
Editorial Description: A weekly summary of action taken by Texas water agencies with particular emphasis on water development.
General Info: Yr. Est. 1954, Weekly, Trim Size-7 x 9, Offset press, 4 pages, No Color
Subscriptions: Indv. $45, $2/copy
Circulation: Total-200

USCOLD Newsletter *Business, Association*

Publishing Co: U.S. Committee on Large Dams, 1616 17th St Ste 483, Denver, CO 80202-1277; Title Tel # (303) 628-5430 Title Fax # (303) 628-5431
Personnel: Editor-Larry Stephens
Editorial Description: News items and technical articles on water resources, especially dams, reservoirs, and hydropower.
General Info: Tri-annually, Trim Size-8½ x 11, Desktop press, 20 pages, No Color, Saddle-stitched
Subscriptions: Indv. $50, Inst. $450, Free With Membership
Advertising: Inquire for rates.

Update
See: ENGINEERING

Utility Environment Report
See: POWER & POWER PLANTS

WOTS/Water Operations Technical Support
See: ENVIRONMENT & ECOLOGY

Waste Management News *Business*

Publishing Co: Stevens Publishing Corp., 3630 J.H. Kultgen Frwy., Waco, TX 76706 Tel # (817) 662-1134; Title Tel # (817) 776-9000 Title Fax # (817) 662-7075
Editorial Description: Designed to provide accurate and authoritative information in regard to the subject matter of waste management.
General Info: Semi-monthly, ISSN: 1062-7529

Waste Management: Western Europe *Business*

Publishing Co: Cutter Information Corp., 37 Broadway, Ste. 1, Arlington, MA 02174-5552 Tel # (617) 648-8700 Fax # (617) 648-1950
General Info: Semi-monthly
Subscriptions: Indv. $357, For. $417

Waste Minimization & Recycling Report
See: ENVIRONMENT & ECOLOGY

Waste Recovery Report
See: ENVIRONMENT & ECOLOGY

Wastewater Works News *Business, Association*

Publishing Co: Michigan Water Environment Association, PO Box 82410, Rochester, MI 48308-2410
Editorial Description: Water quality issues for Michigan.
General Info: Yr. Est. 1964, Quarterly, ISSN: 0043-1028
Circulation: Total-1,200

Water Current
See: SCIENCE

Water Desalination Report *Business*

Publishing Co: Maria Smith, PO Box 10, Tracys Landing, MD 20779-0010; Title Tel # (301) 261-5010 Title Fax # (301) 261-5010
Personnel: Publisher, Editor-Maria Smith
Editorial Description: Covers international and domestic desalination industry.
General Info: Yr. Est. 1965, Weekly, Trim Size-8½ x 11, Mimeo press, 4 pages, ISSN: 0043-1206, Color, Newsprint
Subscriptions: Indv. $300, For. $325
Acquistions: Publication Sold
Advertising: Accepts Inserts.

Water Environment Lab
Solutions
Business, Association

Publishing Co: Water Environment Federation, 601 Wythe St, Alexandria, VA 22314-1994; Title Tel # (703) 684-2400 Title Fax # (703) 684-2492
Personnel: Editor-Laura Conrad, Production Mgr.-Jennifer Darnell, Publisher, Mktg. Dir.-Matthew Rowan, Promotion Dir.-Jean Martin
Editorial Description: Only natl. pub. specifically serving water quality laboratory analysts.
General Info: (Formerly Bench Sheet), Yr. Est. 1979, 9x/yr., Trim Size-8½ x 11, Sheetfed press, 12 pages, ISSN: 0737-4186, 3% ads, 2 Color, Matte, Saddle-stitched
Subscriptions: Indv. $79, For. $99, $8/copy
Circulation: Total-1,800
Advertising: Inquire for rates.
List Rental: Rents Lists
Printing Co: Colortone Press, 2400 17th St NW, Washington, DC 20009-2799 Tel # (202) 387-6800

Water Highlights
See: ENVIRONMENT & ECOLOGY

Water Investment
Newsletter
Business

Publishing Co: U.S. Water News, Inc., 230 Main St, Halstead, KS 67056-1913; Title Tel # (316) 835-2222 Title Fax # (316) 835-2223
Personnel: Publisher-Thomas Bell, Editor-Steven Seibel
Editorial Description: Follows publicly held companies in the water industry.
General Info: Yr. Est. 1987, Monthly, Trim Size-8½ x 11, Sheetfed press, 8 pages, ISSN: 1049-443X, 2 Color, Matte, Other
Subscriptions: Indv. $49

Water Law Newsletter
See: LAW

Water Newsletter/Research and Development News
See: ENVIRONMENT & ECOLOGY

Water Pollution Control
See: ENVIRONMENT & ECOLOGY

Water Quality Newsletter
Association

Publishing Co: Water Quality Research Council, 4151 Naperville Rd., Lisle, IL 60532-3696; Title Tel # (708) 505-0160 Title Fax # (708) 505-9637
Personnel: Editor-Maribeth Robb, Assign. Ed.-Keith Reid
Editorial Description: Concerned with the improvement of water quality.
General Info: Bi-monthly, 12 pages, 2 Color, Coated
Acquistions: Publication Bought
Circulation: (100% controlled), Total-2,600
Printing Co: Republic Printing, 701 E North St, Elburn, IL 60119-9052 Tel # (708) 365-5588

Water Regulation Watch
Business, Association

Publishing Co: Water Environment Federation, 601 Wythe St, Alexandria, VA 22314-1994 Tel # (703) 684-2400 Fax # (703) 684-2492
Personnel: Publisher-John Thorner, Editor-Steve Bagwell, Production Mgr.-Jennifer Darnell, Mktg. Dir.-Matthew Rowan, Promotion Dir.-Joan Martin
Editorial Description: Extensive coverage of US legislative and regulatory actions affecting water quality and water pollution control.
General Info: (Formerly Washington Bulletin), Yr. Est. 1975, Monthly, Trim Size-8½ x 11, Sheetfed press, 6 pages, 2 Color, Recycled
Subscriptions: Indv. $79, For. $99, $5/copy
Advertising: Inquire for rates.
List Rental: Rents Lists

Water Resources Center News
See: ENVIRONMENT & ECOLOGY

Water Resources Research Institute News
See: ENVIRONMENT & ECOLOGY

Water Review
Consumer, Association

Publishing Co: Water Quality Research Council, 4151 Naperville Rd., Lisle, IL 60532-3696; Title Tel # (708) 505-0160 Title Fax # (708) 505-9637
Personnel: Editor-Maribeth Robb
Editorial Description: Contains information pertaining to research & applications of point of use & point of entry water quality improvement products & issues for technical & consumer audiences.
General Info: (Formerly Point-Of-Use Report), Yr. Est. 1984, Quarterly, Sheetfed press, 6 pages, 2 Color, Coated
Subscriptions: Indv. $18
Circulation: (100% controlled), Total-16,500
Printing Co: Republic Printing, 701 E North St, Elburn, IL 60119-9052 Tel # (708) 365-5588

Water Supply Outlook for
Utah
Association

Publishing Co: U.S. Dept. of Agriculture, Soil Conservation Service, 125 S State St Ste 4012, Salt Lake City, UT 84138-1102; Title Tel # (801) 524-5213
Personnel: Editor-Jon Werner
Editorial Description: Snow survey data in Utah mountains and forecasts of water supply particularly for irrigation.
General Info: Yr. Est. 1920, Monthly, Trim Size-8½ x 11, Offset press, 20 pages, ISSN: 0364-4995, 2 Color, Matte
Circulation: Total-600

Water Tap

Publishing Co: Water Supply & Waste Section, Mail Stop Ld-11, Olympia, WA 98504-0001; Title Tel # (206) 753-3466
Editorial Description: Washington's drinking water news.
General Info: Yr. Est. 1985

Water Works News
Association

Publishing Co: American Water Works Assn., Michigan Section, 3423 N. Logan, Box 30195, Lansing, MI 48906-2934; Title Tel # (517) 335-8316
Personnel: Editor-Sheryl Topliff
Editorial Description: Timely information relating to the water supply industry in Michigan.
General Info: Yr. Est. 1964, Quarterly, Desktop press, 12 pages, 2 Color
Circulation: Total-3,000

Well Log, The
See: ENVIRONMENT & ECOLOGY

Western Canada Water
See: INDUSTRIAL RELATIONS/PERSONNEL

Western States Water
See: ENVIRONMENT & ECOLOGY

WELDING

Compressions
See: CHEMISTRY & CHEMICALS

Modern Blacksmith
See: METALS & METALWORKING

NTL News

Publishing Co: International Brotherhood of Boilermakers, Iron Shipbuilders, 753 State Ave., Ste. 570, Kansas City, KS 66101-2511 Fax # (913) 281-8104; Title Tel # (913) 371-2640
Personnel: Editor-George Rogers
Editorial Description: Membership activities newsletter.
General Info: Yr. Est. 1985, Quarterly
Circulation: Total-5,000

Reports of Progress
Association

Publishing Co: Welding Research Council, 345 E 47th St Rm 1301, New York, NY 10017-2330; Title Tel # (212) 705-7956
Personnel: Editor-Dr. Martin Prager
Editorial Description: Reports from projects sponsored by the council, papers before engineering societies, etc.
General Info: Yr. Est. 1936, Monthly, Offset press, No Color
Subscriptions: Indv. $300

Stabilizer

Publishing Co: Lincoln Electric Co., 22801 Saint Clair Ave, Cleveland, OH 44117-1199; Title Tel # (216) 481-8100
Personnel: Editor-Robert Mattoon, Production Mgr.-Randy Glassburn
Editorial Description: Articles & correspondence regarding arc welding projects & practices.
General Info: Yr. Est. 1926, Quarterly, Trim Size-8½ x 11, Web press, 16 pages, 2 Color, Newsprint, Saddle-stitched
Subscriptions: Free
Circulation: Total-80,000

Welding Research Abroad
Business, Association

Publishing Co: Welding Research Council, 345 E 47th St Rm 1301, New York, NY 10017-2330; Title Tel # (212) 705-7956
Personnel: Editor-Dr. Martin Prager
Editorial Description: Includes activities of International Institute of Welding.
General Info: Yr. Est. 1954, 10x/yr.
Subscriptions: Indv. $175

WOMEN'S

9 to 5 Newsletter
Association

Publishing Co: 9 to 5 Natl. Assn. of Working Women, 238 W Wisconsin Ave Ste 700, Milwaukee, WI 53203-2308; Title Tel # (414) 274-0925 Title Fax # (414) 272-2870
Personnel: Editor-Sherri Jones
Editorial Description: Prime source of information for and about office workers from how to get a raise to health & safety. For office workers, researchers, & employers.
General Info: Yr. Est. 1978, 5x/yr., Trim Size-8½ x 11, 4 pages, 2 Color
Subscriptions: Indv. $25, Inst. $40, $2/copy
Circulation: Total-15,000
Advertising: Inquire for rates. Accepts Inserts.

A Friend Indeed   *Consumer*

Publishing Co: A Friend Indeed Publications, Inc., 3575 Boul. Saint-Laurent, Ste. 402, Montreal, PQ H2X 2T7 Canada; Title Tel # (514) 843-5730 Title Fax # (514) 843-4917
Personnel: Publisher, Editor-Janine O'Leary Cobb, Production Mgr.-Maria Araujo
Editorial Description: Information (medical & self-help) for menopausal or midlife women.
General Info: Yr. Est. 1984, Monthly, Trim Size-8½ x 11, Sheetfed press, 8 pages, ISSN: 0824-1961, 2 Color, Recycled
Subscriptions: Indv. $30, Inst. $30, Can. $32
Printing Co: Maurice Seguin Inc., 3939 Bannatyne Ave., Montreal, PQ H4G 1C2 Canada Tel # (514) 768-2320, Fax # (514) 768-2684

ACOG Newsletter   *Association*

Publishing Co: American College of Obstetricians & Gynecologists, 409 12th St., SW, Washington, DC 20024; Title Tel # (202) 638-5577 Title Fax # (202) 479-6826
Personnel: Publisher-Rebecca Rinehart, Editor-Patrick Tucker, Production Mgr.-Thomas Dineen, Art Dir.-Rick Johnston
Editorial Description: Legislation, trends, information affecting women's health care. Fellowship news.
General Info: Yr. Est. 1952, Monthly, Trim Size-9 x 12, Offset press, 12 pages, ISSN: 0400-048X, No Color, Matte, Other
Circulation: (70% controlled), Total-37,000
Printing Co: Corporate Press, 403 Brightseat Rd., Landover, MD 20785-4706 Tel # (301) 499-9200, Fax # (301) 499-5435

ACTION   *Association*

Publishing Co: Manitoba Action Committee on the Status of Women, 702-70 Arthur St., Winnipeg, MB R3B 1G7 Canada; Title Tel # (204) 946-5049
General Info: Yr. Est. 1971, Bi-monthly
Subscriptions: Indv. $25

ALF News   *Association*

Publishing Co: Association of Libertarian Feminists, Box 20252, London Terrace, New York, NY 10011
Personnel: Publisher, Editor-Joan Kennedy Taylor, Production Dir.-, Art Dir.-Jon Carriel
Editorial Description: Articles, book reviews, issues and activities of interest to libertarian feminists.
General Info: Yr. Est. 1975, Quarterly
Subscriptions: Indv. $10
Circulation: Total-300

APLIC International Communicator
See: LIBRARY

AVSC News
See: HEALTH

AWNY Matters
See: ADVERTISING & MARKETING

AWNY Roster
See: ADVERTISING & MARKETING

AWRC Newsletter

Publishing Co: Alaska Women's Resource Center, 111 W 9th Ave, Anchorage, AK 99501-3650; Title Tel # (907) 276-0528
Personnel: Editor-Mary Day
General Info: (Formerly Sourceline), Yr. Est. 1975, Monthly
Subscriptions: Indv. $6
Circulation: Total-500
Advertising: Inquire for rates.

AWV Bulletin
See: VETERINARY

Abortion Report
See: POLITICS

Abortion Research Notes
See: PSYCHOLOGY

About Marketing to Women
See: ADVERTISING & MARKETING

About Women on Campus
See: COLLEGE STUDENT

Act Now

Publishing Co: Comite Canadien d'Action sur le Statut de la Femme, 234 Eglinton Ave. E., Ste. 203, Toronto, ON M4P 1K5 Canada Tel # (416) 759-5252; Title Tel # (416) 932-1718 Title Fax # (416) 932-0646
Personnel: Editor-Madeleine Parent, Circ. Mgr.-Jeri Stubbings, Circ. Mgr., Production Mgr.-M. Hermolin
Editorial Description: News on matters of interest to Canadian women.
General Info: (Formerly Feminist Action (Action Feministe); NAC Memo), Yr. Est. 1985, 8x/yr., 16 pages, ISSN: 0831-3377
Subscriptions: $5/copy
Circulation: (57% controlled), Total-3,500, Subscriptions-1,500

Action   *Association*

Publishing Co: Manitoba Action Committee on the Status of Women, 702-70 Arthur St., Winnipeg, MB R3B 1G7 Canada; Title Tel # (204) 453-3879
Editorial Description: News, events, issues of importance to members.
General Info: Yr. Est. 1972, 10x/yr., Sheetfed press, 16 pages, Matte, Saddle-stitched
Subscriptions: Indv. $25, Inst. $50
Circulation: Total-600

Action Agenda
See: MEDIA & COMMUNICATIONS

Action News
See: CONSUMER INTERESTS

Alert   *Association*

Publishing Co: Fed. of Organizations for Professional Women, 1825 I St. N.W., Ste.400, Washington, DC 20006-5403; Title Tel # (202) 328-1415
Editorial Description: Promotes equal status for women in all education levels and career fields.
General Info: Yr. Est. 1972, Bi-monthly, Offset press, 4 pages
Subscriptions: $2/copy
Circulation: (100% controlled), Total-1,200
Advertising: Inquire for rates.

American Association of Women Dentists Chronicle
See: DENTAL

American CattleWoman
See: LIVESTOCK

Ample Information

Publishing Co: Ample Opportunity, PO Box 40621, Portland, OR 97240-0621; Title Tel # (503) 645-0497
General Info: Monthly, 8 pages

Association for Women in Mathematics, Newsletter   *Association*

Publishing Co: Women's Research Center, Box 178, Wellesley College, Wellesley, MA 02194-0910; Title Tel # (617) 235-0320
Editorial Description: Articles by & about women in mathematics; position advertisements.
General Info: Yr. Est. 1971, Bi-monthly, Trim Size-8½ x 11, 25 pages, 3% ads, No Color
Subscriptions: Inst. $35
Circulation: Total-2,000

Atalanta: Newsletter of the Atlanta Lesbian Feminist Alliance   *Association*

Publishing Co: ALFA, PO Box 5502, Atlanta, GA 30307-0502
General Info: Yr. Est. 1973, Monthly, Trim Size-8½ x 11, Mimeo press, 12 pages
Subscriptions: Indv. $15, Inst. $25
Circulation: Total-300
Advertising: Inquire for rates.

Awed in Business
See: BUSINESS & INDUSTRY

Backfence Quarterly   *Consumer*

Publishing Co: Backfence Quarterly, PO Box 76, Berwick, ME 03908
Editorial Description: Addresses health, career and relationship info for women,
General Info: Quarterly, Trim Size-8½ x 11, 16 pages
Subscriptions: Free

Bi Women Newsletter
See: GAY & LESBIAN INTEREST

Birthright Life-Guardian
See: SOCIAL SERVICES & WELFARE

Bookwoman
See: BOOKS & BOOK TRADE

Bread Pudding Update
See: FOOD

Breast Implant Litigation Reporter
See: LAW

Bulletin Match
See: INTERNATIONAL AFFAIRS

Bulletin of the NPA
See: BABY

Busy Woman's Newsletter   *Consumer*

Publishing Co: Busy Woman's Newsletter, PO Box 757, Cordova, TN 38088-0757
Editorial Description: For women balancing careers, families and social demands.
General Info: Bi-monthly

CARAL Newsletter   *Association*

Publishing Co: California Abortion Rights Action League, 330 Townsend St., Ste. 204, San Francisco, CA 94107-1630; Title Tel # (415) 546-7211
Personnel: Editor-Karen Booth
General Info: Quarterly, 6 pages, Color
Subscriptions: Indv. $30, $1/copy
Circulation: Total-7,000

CAWP News & Notes
See: POLITICS

CCWHP Newsletter

Publishing Co: Coordinating Committee on Women in Historical Profession, 1737 Vaughn Dr, Manhattan, KS 66502-2623
Personnel: Editor-Ruth Willard
General Info: Yr. Est. 1970, Quarterly
Circulation: Total-750

CLUW News
See: LABOR UNION

CRIAW ICREF Newsletter

Publishing Co: Canadian Research Institute for the Advancement of Women, 151 Slater St., #408, Ottawa, ON K1P 5H3 Canada; Title Tel # (613) 563-0681
Personnel: Editor-Linda Clippindale, Promotion Dir.-Linda O'Neil
General Info: Yr. Est. 1982, Quarterly, Mimeo press, 36 pages, ISSN: 0229-7256, Saddle-stitched

CWAS Newsletter

Publishing Co: Sponsor-Committee on Women in Asian Studies (CWAS), Assn. for Asian Studies, Committee on Women in Asian Studies, Ctr. for Intl. Studies, 170 Uris Hall, Cornell Univ., Ithaca, NY 14853-6501 Tel # (607) 255-4370; Title Tel # (517) 353-5040
Personnel: Editor-Barbara Diane Miller
General Info: Yr. Est. 1982, ISSN: 0738-3207
Subscriptions: Indv. $7
Circulation: Total-200

CWC Communicator   *Association*

Publishing Co: California Women's Caucus, 2900 Amby Place, Hermosa Beach, CA 90254-2216; Title Tel # (310) 376-7378 Title Fax # (310) 374-1360
Personnel: Editor-Pat Nellor Wickwire
Editorial Description: Current information about women and girls.
General Info: Yr. Est. 1993, Quarterly, Trim Size-8½ x 11, Desktop press, 2 pages
Subscriptions: Indv. $10, Free With Membership
Circulation: Total-200, Readership-200
List Rental: Rents Lists

California NOW Activist   *Consumer, Association*

Publishing Co: California National Organization for Women, Inc., 926 J St Ste 523, Sacramento, CA 95814-2706; Title Tel # (916) 442-3414
Personnel: State Ed.-Elizabeth Toleda
Editorial Description: Legislative information of interest to NOW,
General Info: Monthly, Trim Size-8½ x 11, 4 pages
Subscriptions: Indv. $18
Circulation: Total-1,000

California NOW News   *Association*

Publishing Co: California National Organization for Women, Inc., 926 J St Ste 523, Sacramento, CA 95814-2706
Editorial Description: News about NOW events and info.
General Info: Monthly, 12 pages
Subscriptions: Free With Membership
Circulation: Total-52,000
Advertising: Inquire for rates.

Canadian Research Institute for the Advancement of Women, Papers

Publishing Co: Canadian Research Institute for the Advancement of Women, 151 Slater St., #408, Ottawa, ON K1P 5H3 Canada; Title Tel # (613) 563-0681
Personnel: Editor-Linda Clippindale
General Info: Yr. Est. 1981
Subscriptions: Indv. $3

Career Opportunities News
See: EMPLOYMENT

Center Focus
See: EDUCATION

Center for the Study of Women & Society- Newsletter

Publishing Co: Graduate School & Univ. Ctr. of CUNY, Ctr. Study of Women & Society, 33 W. 42nd St., Box 135-192, New York, NY 10036; Title Tel # (212) 642-2954
Personnel: Editor-Sue Zalk
General Info: Yr. Est. 1972, Semi-annually, 10 pages
Subscriptions: Free To Qualified Recipient
Circulation: Total-1,000

Center for Women and Religion - Newsletter   *Association*

Publishing Co: Graduate Theological Union, 2400 Ridge Rd, Berkeley, CA 94709-1212; Title Tel # (415) 649-2490

Chain of Life
See: SOCIAL SERVICES & WELFARE

Changemakers
See: SOCIAL SERVICES & WELFARE

Circumference
See: EDUCATION

Citywomen   *Business, Consumer*

Publishing Co: Sullivan Publishing, 10310 Detrick Ave, Kensington, MD 20895-3911 Tel # (301) 942-2332
Personnel: Publisher-Lydia Sullivan
Editorial Description: Written for women in the Washington D.C. area. Emphasis is placed on feminist ideals.
General Info: Yr. Est. 1993, 11x/yr.

Clothing for Less Newsletter
See: CONSUMER INTERESTS

Club Natural
See: BARBER & BEAUTICIAN

Committee on South Asian Women Bulletin
See: ETHNIC

Concerned Women for America
See: RELIGIOUS & THEOLOGICAL

Conference Religieuse Canadienne, Bulletin
See: RELIGIOUS & THEOLOGICAL

Cooperative News Intl.
See: AGRICULTURE

Cornerstone
See: EDUCATION

Cottage Connections
See: REGIONAL INTEREST

Country Cottage Penpals   *Consumer*

Publishing Co: FT Marketing, 224 Cherry Creek Rd, Marquette, MI 49855-8909; Title Tel # (906) 249-9157
Personnel: Publisher-Bev Qualheim
Editorial Description: To promote friendship through penpals, reader shared recipies & country crafts, info about home businesses and places to volunteer help to others.
General Info: (Formerly Families Together), Yr. Est. 1988, Bi-monthly, Trim Size-5½ x 8½, Mimeo press, 20 pages, Color-cover
Subscriptions: Indv. $6, Can. $12, For. $17, $2/copy
Circulation: Readership-125
Advertising: Inquire for rates.

Coupon Treasure Hunt Newsletter
See: HOME ECONOMICS

Court Awareness
See: SPORTS & SPORTING GOODS

Creative Escapes
See: HEALTH

DES Action Voice
See: HEALTH

Delta Kappa Gamma News
See: CLUBS

Dinah
See: GAY & LESBIAN INTEREST

Directory of Resources for Women

Publishing Co: Resources for Women, Inc., 5210 E Pima St Ste 130, Tucson, AZ 85712-3656; Title Tel # (602) 881-4506 Title Fax # (602) 795-9493
Personnel: Editor-Donna Reed
Editorial Description: Lists RFW members; contains biographical descriptions; business listings and Speakers' Bureau information.
General Info: Yr. Est. 1984, Semi-annually, Trim Size-5½ x 8½, Sheetfed press, 200 pages, No Color, Coated
Subscriptions: $27/copy
Circulation: Total-500
Advertising: Inquire for rates.
Printing Co: Isbell Printing Co., 2535 N Jackrabbit Ave, Tucson, AZ 85745-1206

Displaced Homemakers Network News

Publishing Co: Displaced Homemakers Network, 1625 K St NW Ste 300, Washington, DC 20006-1604; Title Tel # (202) 628-6767
Personnel: Publisher-Howard Reed
Editorial Description: Covers displaced homemaker issues.
General Info: (Formerly Advertising World), Yr. Est. 1979, Quarterly, Trim Size-8½ x 11, 12 pages, ISSN: 0885-3363, 4 Color
Subscriptions: Inst. $50, $6/copy
Circulation: (ABC), Total-4,000

Doris Lessing Newsletter
See: LITERATURE & LINGUISTICS

EDK Forecast: Women Consumers   *Business, Consumer*

Publishing Co: EDK Associates, 235 W 48th St Apt 35j, New York, NY 10036-1432; Title Tel # (212) 582-4504 Title Fax # (212) 265-9348
Personnel: Publisher-Ethel D. Klein, Editor-Mary T. Brouder
Editorial Description: What motivates women to buy. Original market-relevant data from our continuous polling of American women consumers.
General Info: (Formerly EDK), Monthly
Subscriptions: Indv. $341, $50/copy

Ecos Nacionales
See: ETHNIC

ElderCare Forum   *Consumer*

Publishing Co: ElderCare Financial Management Inc., 170 Elaine Dr., Rosewell, CA 30075; Title Tel # (770) 518-2767
Personnel: Publisher, Editor-Laura Beller
Editorial Description: Provides information, helpful tips and advice on aging issues and caring for an aging parent. Topics covered and legal, financial, housing, insurance, health, etc.
General Info: Yr. Est. 1993, Quarterly, Trim Size-8½ x 11, Desktop press, 6 pages, No Color, Newsprint
Subscriptions: Indv. $12
Circulation: Total-15,000

Endometriosis Assn. International Newsletter
See: HEALTH

Equity for the Education of Women & Girls

Publishing Co: Sponsor-Marymount Institute for the Education of Women & Girls, Marymount College, 100 Marymount Ave, Tarrytown, NY 10591-3796 Tel # (914) 332-3200; Title Tel # (914) 332-4917 Title Fax # (914) 631-8586
Personnel: Publisher-Ellen Silber, Editor-Robin Gongh
Editorial Description: Equity is a newsletter about what is looking to make classrooms gender fair from kindergarden through college. It is designed to connect all concerned about educational equity for girls & women by publishing news briefs & information ,new research publications, individuals making a difference,a resource clearinghouse & reports on current legislation.
General Info: Yr. Est. 1995, Tri-annually, Trim Size-8½ x 11, 12 pages
Subscriptions: Indv. $21, Inst. $35, $7/copy
Advertising: Accepts Inserts.

FANS of Women's Sports
See: SPORTS & SPORTING GOODS

Family Relations/State Capitals
See: LAW

Fare Share-The Food Letter
See: FOOD

Federated News   *Association*

Publishing Co: Federated Women's Institutes of Canada, 251 Bank St. #606, Ottawa, ON K2P 1X3 Canada; Title Tel # (613) 234-1090 Title Fax # (613) 234-1090
Personnel: Editor-Arlene Strugnell
Editorial Description: Focuses on personal development, family and community action.
General Info: Yr. Est. 1942, Tri-annually, Trim Size-8½ x 11, 12 pages, ISSN: 0046-3485, Saddle-stitched
Subscriptions: Indv. $4, Can. $4
Circulation: Total-3,500

Fed. of Medical Women of Canada, Newsletter
See: MEDICINE

Federation of Organizations for Professional Women-Newsletter   *Business, Association*

Publishing Co: Fed. of Organizations for Professional Women, 1825 I St. N.W., Ste.400, Washington, DC 20006-5403; Title Tel # (202) 328-1415
Editorial Description: Promotes equal status for women in all educational levels & career fields.
General Info: Yr. Est. 1972, Bi-monthly, Trim Size-8 x 11, Mimeo press, 4 pages, No Color
Circulation: Total-1,200

Feminists for Animal Rights   *Business, Consumer*

Publishing Co: Feminists for Animal Rights, Box 694 Cathedral Station, New York, NY 10025; Title Tel # (212) 866-6422
General Info: Yr. Est. 1985, Semi-annually
Subscriptions: Indv. $15, Inst. $25, Free With Membership

Figure and Face

Publishing Co: Figure and Face, 24 Bellair St., Toronto, ON M5R 2C7 Canada; Title Tel # (416) 960-6200
Personnel: Publisher-Carola Barczak, Editor-Anne Dranitsaris
General Info: Yr. Est. 1982, Quarterly
Circulation: Total-5,000
List Rental: Rents Lists

Financial Woman Today   *Business, Association*   CPM: $125

Publishing Co: Financial Women International, 200 N. Glebe Rd., Ste. 814, Arlington, VA 22203-3728; Title Tel # (703) 807-2007 Title Fax # (703) 807-0111
Personnel: Editor-Megan Eisel, Mng. Editor-Valette Piper
Editorial Description: For women in the financial services industry. Conveys cutting edge workplace issues to female executives within the financial service industry.
General Info: (Formerly FWI Quarterly), Yr. Est. 1921, 7x/yr., Trim Size-8½ x 11, Web press, 14 pages, ISSN: 1059-3950, Color-cover, Coated, Saddle-stitched
Subscriptions: Indv. $24, Free With Membership
Circulation: Total-8,000
Advertising: $1,000.
Printing Co: Reproductions, Inc., 7621 Rickenbacker Dr, Gaithersburg, MD 20879 Tel # (301) 840-5400, Fax # (301) 590-1065

Flashsheet & Newsletter   *Association*

Publishing Co: Natl. Council of Women of Canada, Room 20, 270 MacLaren St., Ottawa, ON K2P 0M3 Canada; Title Tel # (613) 233-4953
Personnel: Editor-Pearl Dobson
Editorial Description: Local council news from across Canada, brief summaries of special events and activities.
General Info: 25 pages
Subscriptions: Indv. $5, $2/copy

Free Focus
See: POETRY & CREATIVE WRITING

Gaea
See: GEOLOGY

Garden Views   *Consumer*

Publishing Co: Eve's Garden, 119 W 57th St., Ste 420, New York, NY 10019-2383
Editorial Description: Information for women on sexual health and enlightenment.
General Info: Yr. Est. 1973, Quarterly, Trim Size-8½ x 11

Genuine Article, The
See: MEN'S

Girl Groups ('60's Rock N' Roll) Gazette
See: FAN MAGAZINES-MOVIE, RADIO, TV

Girls' Rodeo Association News
See: HORSES

Guide

Publishing Co: Christian Labour Assn. of Canada, 5920 Atlantic Dr., Mississauga, ON L4W 1N6 Canada; Title Tel # (416) 670-7383 Title Fax # (516) 997-0839
Personnel: Publisher-Georganne Fiumara, Editor-Dan der Kloet
Editorial Description: Provides help and information for mothers who choose to work at home.
General Info: (Formerly Christian Labour Assn. of Canada, Bulletin), Yr. Est. 1952, 9x/yr., 16 pages, ISSN: 0533-5051
Subscriptions: Indv. $10, $3/copy
Circulation: Total-10,000
List Rental: Actives: $90/M

Hadassah Update
See: SOCIAL SERVICES & WELFARE

Harvard Women's Health Watch
See: HEALTH

Healing Woman, The   *Consumer*

Publishing Co: Healing Woman, PO Box 3038, Moss Beach, CA 94038-3038;
Title Tel # (415) 728-0339 Title Fax # (415) 728-1324
Personnel: Editor-Rhiannon Paine, Publisher, Editor-Margot Silk Forrest
Editorial Description: For women who have survived childhood sexual abuse.
General Info: Yr. Est. 1992, Monthly, Trim Size-8½ x 11, 12 pages, ISSN: 1065-8289
Subscriptions: Indv. $25, Can. $31, For. $41, $3/copy
Acquistions: Publication Sold
Circulation: Total-5,000

Health Wisdom for Women   *Consumer*

Publishing Co: Phillips Publishing, Inc., 7811 Montrose Rd., Potomac, MD 20854-3394 Parent Co.-Phillips Business Information, Inc., Potomac; Title Tel # (301) 340-2100 Title Fax # (301) 294-1307
Personnel: Publisher-Thomas L. Phillips, Editor-Christiane Northrup, Mktg. Dir.-Laurie Hoffman
Editorial Description: Women's health information edited by a female physician.
General Info: Yr. Est. 1994, Monthly
Subscriptions: Indv. $40
List Rental: List Management Co.: Manager: John Baldwin; Phillips Publishing List Marketing, 7811 Montrose Rd., Potomac, MD 20854-3394 Tel # (301) 340-2100, Fax # (301) 294-1307, Actives: 35,604, $125/M

Health Words for Women
See: HEALTH

Healthletters
See: HEALTH

Hearts of the Handmaidens   *Consumer*

Publishing Co: Media Management Assoc., PO Box 303, Carlsbad, CA 92018-0303;
Title Tel # (206) 776-4844
Personnel: Editor-Judy Maddox, Art Dir.-Richard Maddox
Editorial Description: Readers share their views on being a woman and/or being a Baha'i.
General Info: Yr. Est. 1989, Bi-monthly, Trim Size-8½ x 11, Desktop press, 4 pages, No Color, Matte
Subscriptions: Indv. $10, Can. $12, For. $12, $3/copy
Circulation: Total-1,000
Printing Co: Kinkos Copies, 2530 Vista Way, Oceanside, CA 92057 Tel # (619) 433-5112

Home & Country   *Consumer, Association*

Publishing Co: New Brunswick Women's Institute, 65 Brunswick St., #251, Fredericton, NB E3B 1G5 Canada; Title Tel # (506) 454-0798
Personnel: Editor-Sandra Thomas
General Info: Yr. Est. 1945, Bi-monthly, Trim Size-5½ x 8½, Desktop press, 12 pages, 2 Color, Coated
Subscriptions: Indv. $5
Circulation: Total-2,200

House of Ruth Newsletter   *Consumer*

Publishing Co: House of Ruth, 5 Thomas Circle, NW, Washington, DC 20005;
Title Tel # (202) 667-7001 Title Fax # (202) 667-7047
Personnel: Circ. Asst.-Monica Ault
General Info: (Formerly Friends of Ruth), Semi-annually, 4 pages
List Rental: Rents Lists

IDRA Newsletter
See: EDUCATION

Institute for Research on Women & Gender-Newsletter

Publishing Co: Institute for Research on Women & Gender, Serra House, Stanford University, Stanford, CA 94305-8640; Title Tel # (415) 723-1994 Title Fax # (415) 725-0374
Personnel: Editor-Sherri Matteo
General Info: Yr. Est. 1974, Quarterly, 6 pages
Subscriptions: Indv. $12, $3/copy
Circulation: Total-1,200

International Guild of Professional Electrologists-Newsletter
See: MEDICINE

Iowa Woman   *Consumer*   CPM: $125

Publishing Co: Iowa Woman, PO Box 680, Iowa City, IA 52244-0680; Title Tel # (319) 987-2879
Personnel: Editor-Marianne Abel
Editorial Description: Fiction, poetry, essays, feature articles, interviews, history, book reviews, graphics, & photography by women everywhere. Subscription includes quarterly newsletter.
General Info: Yr. Est. 1979, Quarterly, Trim Size-8½ x 10⅞, Desktop press, 48 pages, ISSN: 0271-8227, 2 Color, Coated, Saddle-stitched
Subscriptions: Indv. $18, Inst. $18, Can. $23, For. $30, $6/copy
Circulation: Total-2,400
Advertising: $300.
Printing Co: Woolverton Printing Co., 115 E 4th St, Cedar Falls, IA 50613-2825 Tel # (319) 277-2616, Fax # (319) 277-8136

Journal n' Footnotes   *Association, Consumer*

Publishing Co: Wander Women, 136 N Grand Ave # 237, West Covina, CA 91791-1728
Editorial Description: Covers travel ideas for women along with being a forum for women to share their travel experiences.
General Info: Quarterly, Trim Size-8½ x 11, 12 pages
Subscriptions: Indv. $29

Kennedy's Career Strategist
See: EMPLOYMENT

LEAF Lines
See: LAW

LFL Reports:
See: CIVIL RIGHTS

Legal Action for Women

Publishing Co: Litigation Project, Inc., 1145 Candlewood Cir, Pensacola, FL 32514-1604
Personnel: Publisher-Michael Conroy
Editorial Description: Explore the physical and emotional damage caused bu abortion. Includes clinic investigation, showing criminal activities of operators, and unsanitary conditions that actually threaten women's lives and health.
General Info: Yr. Est. 1987, Quarterly, Trim Size-8½ x 11, Sheetfed press, 6 pages
Subscriptions: Indv. $10
Acquistions: Publication Bought
Circulation: Total-1,000

Listen Real Loud: News of Women's Liberation Worldwide   *Consumer*

Publishing Co: American Friends Service Comm (AFSC)-International Division, 1501 Cherry St, Philadelphia, PA 19102-1429 Tel # (215) 241-7168; Title Tel # (215) 241-7181 Title Fax # (215) 864-0104
Personnel: Editor-Sara Lee Hamilton, Production Mgr.-Sandra Smith
Editorial Description: News of Women's Liberation Worldwide is intended to promote regional, national, & overseas staff and committee members as well as movements with whom AFSC engages.
General Info: (Formerly AFSC Women's Newsletter), Yr. Est. 1979, Quarterly, Trim Size-8½ x 11, Desktop press, 16 pages, ISSN: 0893-8083
Subscriptions: Indv. $20, Inst. $20, Can. $20, For. $20, $3/copy
Circulation: Total-4,000

Majority Rules   *Business, Consumer*

Publishing Co: Jenkins Hill Publishing Co., 12340 B Minsummer Lane #302, Lake Ridge, VA 22192; Title Tel # (703) 799-1324 Title Fax # (703) 799-8766
Personnel: Publisher-Myron Struck, Circ. Mgr.-Mike Fediw, Adv. Dir.-Hilda Schmid, Editor, Mktg. Dir.-Mary Struck
Editorial Description: Newsletter for and about women in politics.
General Info: Bi-weekly, Trim Size-8½ x 11, 24 pages, 10% ads, 2 Color, Saddle-stitched
Subscriptions: Indv. $68
Advertising: $300. Accepts Inserts.
List Rental: List Management Co.: Rich List Company, 4 East 81st St., New York, NY 10028 Tel # (212) 737-8917, Fax # (212) 861-5384
Printing Co: Discount Newsletter Printing, 1487 Persisterce Dr., PO Box 1487, Woodbridge, VA 22193-0487 Tel # (703) 690-1788, Fax # (703) 491-2563

Mamaroots   *Consumer, Association*

Publishing Co: Asungi Productions, 3661 N Campbell Ave Ste 108, Tucson, AZ 85719-1527; Title Tel # (602) 327-0987
Editorial Description: Spiritual and cultural network for women of African heritage
Subscriptions: Free With Membership

Media Report to Women   *Business*

Publishing Co: Communication Research Assocs., Inc., 10606 Mantz Rd, Silver Spring, MD 20903-1247 Tel # (301) 445-3231; Title Tel # (301) 445-3230
Personnel: Publisher-Ray Hiebert, Editor-Sheila Gibbons, Circ. Mgr.-Betty Russo
Editorial Description: The nation's oldest & most authoritative newsletter covering women in the media.
General Info: Yr. Est. 1972, Quarterly, 12 pages, ISSN: 0145-9651, 8% ads
Subscriptions: Indv. $30, Inst. $50, $10/copy
Advertising: Inquire for rates.

Medical Mission Sisters News
See: HEALTH

Mid Life Woman   *Consumer, Scholarly*

Publishing Co: Mid-Life Women's Network, 5129 Logan Ave S, Minneapolis, MN 55419-1000 Tel # (512) 925-0020; Title Tel # (612) 925-0020 Title Fax # (612) 925-5430
Personnel: Publisher-Sharon Slettehaugh, Editor-Sharon Roe
Editorial Description: In depth look at topics of concern to women 35-60: health and wellness as well as social roles, careers, etc. Contains book reviews, letters from readers, and research updates.
General Info: Yr. Est. 1992, Bi-monthly, Trim Size-8½ x 11, 12 pages, ISSN: 1061-348X
Subscriptions: Indv. $25, Inst. $50, Can. $30, For. $35, $6/copy
Circulation: Total-3,000
List Rental: Actives: 15,000, $115/M

Mom to Mom   *Consumer*

Publishing Co: Mom to Mom, PO Box 36160, Cincinnati, OH 45236-0160; Title Tel # (513) 891-6244
Personnel: Publisher-Chris Klein
Editorial Description: Newsletter written for stay-at-home mothers of young children.
General Info: Yr. Est. 1993, Monthly, Trim Size-8½ x 11, 8 pages
Subscriptions: Indv. $15
Circulation: Total-1,000
Advertising: Inquire for rates. Accepts Inserts.
List Rental: Actives: 1,000, $100/M, Hotline: 3,000, $100/M

Mom's Apple Pie
See: GAY & LESBIAN INTEREST

MoneyWorks for Women   *Business, Consumer*

Publishing Co: K2 Communications, 217 East 85th Street, Box 144, New York, NY 10028-0144;
Title Tel # (212) 288-5271
Personnel: Editor in Chief-Mary Rowland
Editorial Description: Personal financial advice for women in business.
General Info: Yr. Est. 1993, Monthly, Trim Size-8½ x 11, 12 pages, No Color, Matte, Saddle-stitched
Subscriptions: Indv. $59

Mother & Co.   *Consumer*

Publishing Co: National Information Corp., 1101 King Street, Alexandria, VA 22314;
Title Tel # (703) 548-2400 Title Fax # (703) 683-6974
Personnel: Publisher-Anne Hunt Cheevers, Editor-Roberta Weiner
Editorial Description: The woman's guide to balanced living.
General Info: Yr. Est. 1993, Bi-weekly
Subscriptions: Indv. $39

Mother-To-Mother
See: FAMILY

NAFC Quarterly Newsletter
See: HEALTH

NAFE Member News   *Business, Association*

Publishing Co: National Association for Female Executives, Inc., 30 Irving Pl., 5th Floor, New York, NY 10003-2303 Tel # (212) 477-2200 Fax # (212) 477-8215
Editorial Description: News of programs and meetings in the tri-state area of New York, New Jersey, and Connecticut.

NAWBO Time

Publishing Co: National Assn. of Women Business Owners, 1100 Wayne Ave., Ste. 830, Silver Spring, MD 20910; Title Tel # (301) 608-2590

NAWJ Counterbalance
See: LAW

NOW Newsletter, San Francisco

Publishing Co: Natl. Organization for Women, PO Box 1267, San Francisco, CA 94161-1267;
Title Tel # (415) 861-8880
Personnel: Editor-Lisa Cutler
Editorial Description: Also called
General Info: Bi-monthly, Trim Size-8½ x 11, 4 pages, No Color
Circulation: Total-1,500
Advertising: Inquire for rates.

NOW San Diego News   *Association*

Publishing Co: Natl. Organization for Women, PO Box 80292, San Diego, CA 92138-0292;
Title Tel # (619) 238-1824
Personnel: Editor-Ellen Goodwin
General Info: Yr. Est. 1971, Monthly, 6 pages
Subscriptions: Indv. $8
Circulation: (100% controlled), Total-1,200
Advertising: Inquire for rates.

NPA Bulletin
See: BABY

National Association of Women Artists Newsletter
See: ART & SCULPTURE

National ClearingHouse on Marital and Date Rape
See: LAW

National Council of Women of the United States Bulletin
See: CLUBS

National Lawyers Wives Newsletter
See: LAW

National Women's Health Report
See: HEALTH

Network   *Business, Association*

Publishing Co: International Women's Writing Guild, Box 810 Gracie Sta., New York, NY 10028-0082; Title Tel # (212) 737-7536 Title Fax # (212) 737-9469
Personnel: Publisher-Hannelore Hahn
Editorial Description: Member news, publishing/employment opportunities, round-robins, cluster meetings, correspondence corner, conference/workshop opportunities, literary agent referrals, women writer's supportive network.
General Info: Yr. Est. 1976, Bi-monthly, Trim Size-8 x 10, Desktop press, 32 pages, No Color, Newsprint
Subscriptions: For. $45, Free With Membership
Circulation: Total-4,000

Network News   *Consumer, Association*

Publishing Co: National Women's Health Network, 1325 G St NW, Washington, DC 20005-3189;
Title Tel # (202) 347-1140
Editorial Description: Answers to women's health questions.
General Info: Bi-monthly, ISSN: 8755-867X
Subscriptions: Free With Membership
Circulation: Total-15,000
Advertising: Inquire for rates.
List Rental: Actives: $65/M

Network of Saskatchewan Women   *Association*   **CPM: $125**

Publishing Co: Saskatchewan Action Committee, 2343 Cornwall St., Regina, SK S4P 2L4 Canada;
Title Tel # (306) 525-8329 Title Fax # (306) 757-4548
Editorial Description: Feminist analysis of economic and political world.
General Info: Yr. Est. 1971, Quarterly, Trim Size-8 x 11, Desktop press, 24 pages, Coated, Saddle-stitched
Subscriptions: Indv. $10, Inst. $25, $2/copy
Acquistions: Publication Sold
Circulation: Total-800
Advertising: $100. Accepts Inserts.

New Horizons in Community Services

Publishing Co: Natl. Council of Jewish Women, 53 W. 23rd St., New York, NY 10010-4299
Tel # (212) 645-4040; Title Tel # (212) 532-1740

New Moon Network
See: FAMILY

Newfoundland and Labrador Women's Institute Newsletter   *Association*

Publishing Co: Newfoundland & Labrador Women's Inst., Box 1854, St. John's, NF A1C 5P9 Canada; Title Tel # (709) 753-8780
Personnel: Editor-Sylvia Manning
Editorial Description: Rural women's information--Branch news; cultural, economic, legal, health issues.
General Info: Quarterly, Trim Size-8½ x 11, 15 pages, No Color
Subscriptions: Indv. $5, $1/copy
Circulation: Total-750

Newfoundland Status of Women Council Newsletter

Publishing Co: Sponsor-St. John's Status of Women Council, Newfoundland Status of Women Council, Box 6072, St. John's, NF A1C 5X8 Canada
Personnel: Editor-Roberta Buchanan
General Info: Yr. Est. 1974, Monthly, Mimeo press, 20 pages, No Color
Circulation: Total-200

News on Women in Government   *Consumer, Association*

Publishing Co: Center for Women in Government, 135 Western Ave., Albany, NY 12222
Tel # (518) 442-3900; Title Tel # (518) 442-3896
Personnel: Publisher-Judith Saidel, Editor, Production Mgr.-Audrey Seidman
Editorial Description: News on women and minorities in public sector.
General Info: Yr. Est. 1978, Semi-annually, Trim Size-8½ x 11, Sheetfed press, 5 pages, 2 Color, Matte
Circulation: (100% controlled), Total-25,000

Newsletter of the International Women's Brass Conference
See: MUSIC & MUSIC TRADES

North Pacific Women Writers Retreat   *Consumer, Association*

Publishing Co: North Pacific Women Writers Association, 3091 West 15th Avenue, Vancouver, BC V6K 3A5 Canada; Title Tel # (604) 734-9816
General Info: Annually

Notes & News
Consumer, Association

Publishing Co: Prince Edward Island Women's Institute, P.E.I. Dept. of Agriculture, Fisheries & Forestry, POB 2000, Charlottetown, PE C1A 7N8 Canada; Title Tel # (902) 368-4860
Personnel: Editor-Karen Craig
Editorial Description: Current news and information about the Prince Edward Island Women's Inst.
General Info: Monthly

Notes for Now
Association

Publishing Co: Women of Reform Judaism, 838 5th Ave, New York, NY 10021-7012 Fax # (212) 650-4059; Title Tel # (212) 650-4050
Personnel: Editor-Eve Roshevsky
Editorial Description: Information for the leaders of the Reform Jewish Sisterhoods.
General Info: (Formerly Current Copy), Semi-annually, Trim Size-8½ x 11, 4 pages, 4 Color
Subscriptions: Free With Membership
Circulation: Total-1,200

On the Record
Business, Association

Publishing Co: Sponsor-Women in Government Relations, Inc., Women in Government Relations, Inc., 1029 Vermont Ave NW Ste 510, Washington, DC 20005-3517 Fax # (202) 347-5434; Title Tel # (202) 347-5432
Personnel: Editor-Nancy McCabe
Editorial Description: Reports on the activities of WGR.
General Info: Yr. Est. 1976, Bi-monthly, Trim Size-8½ x 11, Web press, 8 pages, 2 Color, Coated
Subscriptions: Indv. $35
Circulation: Total-1,000
List Rental: Rents Lists

Ontario Vacation Farms
See: TRAVEL

Ozark Feminist Review
Consumer CPM: $500

Publishing Co: Ozark Feminist Review, PO Box 1662, Fayetteville, AR 72702-1662; Title Tel # (501) 443-3184
Personnel: Editor-Karin Wiggins
Editorial Description: Feminist newsletter for women in the Ozark regions.
General Info: Yr. Est. 1991, Bi-monthly, Desktop press, 16 pages, 15% ads
Subscriptions: Indv. $15
Circulation: Total-200
Advertising: $100. Accepts Inserts.
List Rental: Rents Lists

Parent & Preschooler
See: EDUCATION

Peace Press
See: POLITICS

Pennsylvania Nurse
See: NURSING

Perspective
See: BUSINESS & INDUSTRY

Philanthropic Digest
See: PHILANTHROPY

Political Woman Hotline
See: POLITICS

Pro-Choice News

Publishing Co: Canadian Abortion Right Action League, 344 Bloor St., Ste. 306, Toronto, ON M5S 3A7 Canada; Title Tel # (416) 961-1507 Title Fax # (416) 961-5771
Editorial Description: Focuses on pro-choice issues.
General Info: Yr. Est. 1985, Quarterly, 16 pages, ISSN: 0836-7221
Subscriptions: Indv. $10, Can. $10

Professional Directory of Indy Women

Publishing Co: Shepard Poorman Communications Corp., 7301 N. Woodland Dr., Box 68110, Washington, DC 46268; Title Tel # (317) 293-1500
Personnel: Editor-Ginger Schmidt, Production Mgr.-Jayne Bennett, Adv. Dir.-Greg Huff
Editorial Description: Comprehensive annual directory of women business owners & other business women.
General Info: (Formerly Indywomen), Yr. Est. 1984, Annually, Trim Size-8⅜ x 10¹³/₁₆, Sheetfed press, 100 pages, 2% ads, Color, Newsprint, Perfect bound
Subscriptions: Indv. $67, $5/copy
Circulation: Total-5,000

Program and Legislative Action
See: POLITICS

Quicktrips Travel Letter
See: TRAVEL

RTW Review
See: APPAREL & ACCESSORIES

Recipe Greetings Update
See: POETRY & CREATIVE WRITING

Refunding Update - Introduction to Refunding
See: CONSUMER INTERESTS

Religious Coalition for Reproductive Choice Newsletter

Publishing Co: Religious Coalition for Reproductive Choice, 1025 Vermont Ave. NW, Suite #1130, Washington, DC 20005-3516; Title Tel # (202) 628-7700
Personnel: Editor-Ann Thompson Cook
Editorial Description: Newsletter supporting women's rights to an abortion. Covers legislative, regulatory, and religious efforts to stop funding of state financed abortions.
General Info: (Formerly Religious Coalition for Abortion Rights-Options), Yr. Est. 1973, Irregular
Circulation: Total-50,000
List Rental: Rents Lists

Responsibility

Publishing Co: Natl. Assn. of Negro Business & Professional Women's Clubs, 1806 New Hampshire Ave. NW, Washington, DC 20009; Title Tel # (202) 483-4206
General Info: (Formerly Natl. Assn. of Negro Business and Professional Women's Club)

SCWIST News

Publishing Co: Society for Canadian Women in Science & Technology, 140-515 W. Hastings St., Vancouver, BC V6B 5K3 Canada Fax # (604) 291-5236; Title Tel # (604) 291-5163 Title Fax # (604) 291-5112
Editorial Description: Membership newsletter.
General Info: Yr. Est. 1983, Quarterly, Mimeo press, 4 pages, 2 Color
Subscriptions: Indv. $25, Can. $25
Circulation: (100% controlled), Total-150

SIROW Newsletter

Publishing Co: Southwest Institute for Research on Women, Douglass Bldg., #102 Univ. Of, Arizona, Tucson, AZ 85721-0001; Title Tel # (602) 621-7338 Title Fax # (602) 621-9424
Personnel: Editor-Janice Monk
Editorial Description: A newsletter about feminist scholarship and women's studies in the southwest.
General Info: Yr. Est. 1979, Trim Size-8½ x 11, Sheetfed press, 12 pages, 2 Color
Circulation: Total-3,300
Printing Co: Owl Printing Co., 933 N. Stone Ave., Tucson, AZ 85706-0001 Tel # (520) 622-7311

Shenabe Quai (Indian Women)

Publishing Co: Ne-Naiah-Kaha-Kok, PO Box 1055, Keshena, WI 54135-1055; Title Tel # (715) 799-4398
Editorial Description: Domestic abuse prevention, alcohol & drug intervention information, any Womens' issues.
General Info: Yr. Est. 1975, Quarterly, 10 pages
Subscriptions: Indv. $15
Acquistions: Publication Bought
Circulation: (CAC), Total-1,500

SingleMOTHER
See: FAMILY

Sisterhood Newsletter

Publishing Co: Sisterhood of Black Single Mothers, 1504 Bedford Ave, Brooklyn, NY 11216-4116; Title Tel # (718) 638-0413
Personnel: Editor-Daphne Busby
General Info: Quarterly, 14 pages
Subscriptions: Indv. $10, $3/copy
Circulation: Total-400
Advertising: Inquire for rates.

Sobering Thoughts
Association

Publishing Co: Women for Sobriety, Inc., PO Box 618, Quakertown, PA 18951-0618; Title Tel # (215) 536-8026 Title Fax # (215) 536-8026
Personnel: Editor-Dr. Jean Kirkpatrick, Production Mgr.-Rebecca Fenner
Editorial Description: Newsletter for women alcoholics & persons interested in alcoholism.
General Info: Yr. Est. 1975, Monthly, Trim Size-8½ x 11, Sheetfed press, 16 pages, 2 Color, Matte
Subscriptions: Indv. $18, Can. $25, For. $30, $2/copy
Circulation: Total-2,000

Sonoma County Women's Voices
Consumer, Association CPM: $95

Publishing Co: Women's Support Network, PO Box 4448, Santa Rosa, CA 95402-4448; Title Tel # (707) 575-5654
Editorial Description: Local news, calendar of events, reviews, opinion written by & for women.
General Info: Yr. Est. 1980, 10x/yr., Trim Size-11 x 17, Web press, 16 pages, Newsprint
Subscriptions: Indv. $13, $2/copy
Circulation: Total-4,500, Readership-7,000
Advertising: $430.
Printing Co: Sonoma Valley Publishing, 117 West Napa, Sonoma, CA 95476 Tel # (707) 938-0637

Soundings
See: PSYCHOLOGY

Stateswoman

Publishing Co: Sponsor-Wisconsin Women's Network, Wisconsin Women's Network, 122 State St Ste 406, Madison, WI 53703-2500; Title Tel # (608) 255-9809
Personnel: Editor-Melissa Keyes
Editorial Description: Dedicated to alleviating discrimination against women.
General Info: Yr. Est. 1979, Quarterly, Sheetfed press, 8 pages, 2 Color, Newsprint
Subscriptions: Indv. $25, Inst. $100
Circulation: (100% controlled), Total-1,200
Printing Co: Royal Publishing Co., 1301 Williamson St, Madison, WI 53703-3756 Tel # (608) 251-6636

Status Report   *Consumer*

Publishing Co: New York City Commission on the Status of Women, 1 Cenre Street., #2358, New York, NY 10007-1222; Title Tel # (212) 788-2738 Title Fax # (212) 788-3298
Personnel: Publisher, Editor-Karen Arthur
General Info: Yr. Est. 1978, Quarterly, Trim Size-8½ x 11, Matte, Perfect bound
Circulation: Total-9,500
List Rental: Actives: $30/M

Survivor Activist, The
See: PSYCHOLOGY

Textures
See: RELIGIOUS & THEOLOGICAL

This Is WICS
See: SOCIAL SERVICES & WELFARE

Tipsheet
See: EDUCATION

Trade Trax   *Business*

Publishing Co: Tradeswomen, Inc., PO Box 2622, Berkeley, CA 94702-0622; Title Tel # (510) 649-6260 Title Fax # (510) 649-6277
Personnel: Publisher, Editor, Production Mgr.-C.J. Thompson-White
Editorial Description: Focuses on non-traditional, blue collar women in Northern California, and other parts of the U.S.A. Is included with membership subscription to Tradeswomen Magazine.
General Info: Yr. Est. 1980, Bi-monthly, Trim Size-8½ x 14, Letrpr. press, 4 pages, 5% ads, No Color, Newsprint
Circulation: Total-1,000
Advertising: Inquire for rates.

Travel Companions
See: TRAVEL

Travelin' Woman
See: TRAVEL

Tribuna   *Association*

Publishing Co: International Women's Tribune Centre, 777 United Nations Plaza, New York, NY 10017-3551; Title Tel # (212) 687-8633 Title Fax # (212) 661-2704
Personnel: Editor-Anne Walker
Editorial Description: Covers development issues relevant to women around the world. Spanish edition of Tribune.
General Info: (Formerly International Women's Tribune Center Newsletter), Yr. Est. 1977, Quarterly
Subscriptions: Indv. $12, $3/copy
Circulation: Total-10,000

Tribune   *Consumer, Association*

Publishing Co: International Women's Tribune Centre, 777 United Nations Plaza, New York, NY 10017-3551; Title Tel # (212) 687-8633 Title Fax # (212) 661-2704
Personnel: Publisher-Dr. Anne Walker
Editorial Description: Development issues of relevance to women in Asia, Africa, Latin America, Middle East, the South Pacific and Caribbean. Distributed free in those areas. Available in English, Spanish, and French.
General Info: (Formerly IWY/TP Newsletter), Yr. Est. 1976, Quarterly, Trim Size-8½ x 11, Web press, 40 pages, ISSN: 0738-9779, Newsprint, Perfect bound
Subscriptions: Indv. $12, Can. $12, For. $16, $3/copy
Circulation: Total-17,000
Printing Co: John S. Swift Co., Rt. 46, Teterboro, NJ 07608 Tel # (201) 288-2050

Twin Services Reporter
See: BABY

Une Veritable Amie   *Consumer*

Publishing Co: A Friend Indeed Publications, Inc., 3575 Boul. Saint-Laurent, Ste. 402, Montreal, PQ H2X 2T7 Canada Fax # (514) 843-4917; Title Tel # (514) 843-5730 Title Fax # (514) 843-5681
Personnel: Publisher-Janine O'Leary Cobb, Editor-Lucette Proulx-Sammut, Production Mgr.-Maria Araujo
Editorial Description: Information (medical & self-help) on menopause & midlife. Text in French.
General Info: Yr. Est. 1985, Monthly, Trim Size-8½ x 11, Sheetfed press, 12 pages, ISSN: 0831-0866, 2 Color, Recycled
Subscriptions: Indv. $30, Inst. $30, Can. $32, For. $40, $4/copy
Circulation: Total-850
Printing Co: Maurice Seguin Inc., 3939 Bannatyne Ave., Montreal, PQ H4G 1C2 Canada Tel # (514) 768-2320, Fax # (514) 768-2684

Valley Women's Voice   *Consumer*   **CPM: $102**

Publishing Co: Sponsor-Univ. of Massachusetts, Turley Publications, Inc., 24 Water St, Palmer, MA 01069-1840 Tel # (413) 283-8393; Title Tel # (413) 545-2436
Personnel: Production Mgr.-Wendy Beck, Circ. Mgr., Art Dir.-Nancy O'Neill, Adv. Dir., Mktg. Dir.-Aisha Gabriel, Promotion Dir.-Michelle DePesa
Editorial Description: Free feminist paper that includes a survivor's page, listing of area events, global women's news & local women's news.
General Info: Yr. Est. 1979, Monthly, Desktop press, 10 pages, 100% ads, Newsprint
Subscriptions: Indv. $9, $1/copy
Circulation: Total-5,000
Advertising: $512.
Printing Co: Turley Publications, 24 Water St, Palmer, MA 01069-1840 Tel # (413) 283-8393

Voices   *Consumer, Association*

Publishing Co: Canadian Voice of Women for Peace, 736 Bathurst St., Ste. 215, Toronto, ON M5S 2R4 Canada; Title Tel # (416) 537-9343 Title Fax # (416) 531-6214
Personnel: Production Mgr.-Carolyn Langdon
Editorial Description: Peace, disarmament, environmental & social justice issues from a feminist perspective.
General Info: (Formerly Voice of Women Newsletter), Yr. Est. 1960, Tri-annually, Web press, Newsprint
Subscriptions: Inst. $40, Can. $40, For. $40
Printing Co: K-T Printing, 146 Hallam St., Toronto, ON M6H 1X2 Canada Tel # (416) 533-1116

WAND Bulletin   *Consumer, Association*

Publishing Co: Women's Action for Nuclear Disarmament, 360 Hilldale Drive, Ann Arbor, MI 48105; Title Tel # (313) 662-2475
Personnel: Editor-Margaret Covert
Editorial Description: Women's newsletter on disarmament.
General Info: (Formerly Women's Peace Party), Yr. Est. 1982, Quarterly, Trim Size-8½ x 11, Sheetfed press, 8 pages, 2 Color, Newsprint
Subscriptions: Indv. $30
Circulation: (100% controlled), Total-10,000
Printing Co: Champagne Offset Co., 210 Needham St, Newton, MA 02164-1508 Tel # (617) 969-1703

WI News   *Consumer, Association*

Publishing Co: Prince Edward Island Women's Institute, P.E.I. Dept. of Agriculture, Fisheries & Forestry, POB 2000, Charlottetown, PE C1A 7N8 Canada
Personnel: Editor-Anne Boswell
General Info: (Formerly Prince Edward Island Women's Institute News), Yr. Est. 1928, Quarterly, Trim Size-11 x 15, 8 pages

WICC Newsletter
See: RELIGIOUS & THEOLOGICAL

WID Bulletin

Publishing Co: Assn. for Asian Studies, Committee on Women in Asian Studies, Ctr. for Intl. Studies, 170 Uris Hall, Cornell Univ., Ithaca, NY 14853-6501 Tel # (607) 255-4370; Title Tel # (517) 353-5040 Title Fax # (517) 353-7254
Personnel: Editor-Rita Gallin, Circ. Mgr.-Tracey Wolf, Production Mgr.-Laura Carantza
Editorial Description: For women involved in intl. development.
General Info: 22 pages
Subscriptions: Indv. $9, $3/copy
Acquistions: Publication Bought, Publication Sold
Advertising: Accepts Inserts.

WLDF News   *Association*

Publishing Co: Women's Legal Defense Fund, 1875 Connecticut Ave NW Ste 71, Washington, DC 20009-5728; Title Tel # (202) 986-2600 Title Fax # (202) 986-2539
Personnel: Editor-Virginia Sassamon
Editorial Description: Reports on women's legal rights and WLDF activities.
General Info: Yr. Est. 1971, 3x/yr., Trim Size-8½ x 11, Offset press, 12 pages, ISSN: 0736-9433, 2 Color, Newsprint
Subscriptions: Indv. $10, Inst. $15
Circulation: (100% controlled), Total-2,500

Wahine Wireless   *Consumer*

Publishing Co: Rainbow Bridge Consultants, PO Box 599, Keaau, HI 96749-0599 Tel # (808) 982-7862 Fax # (808) 982-7862; Title Tel # (808) 966-8511
Personnel: Publisher, Editor, Adv. Dir.-Paula Harris-White
Editorial Description: A newsletter for women in Hawaii, about women in Hawaii.
General Info: Yr. Est. 1990, Quarterly, Trim Size-8½ x 11, Letrpr. press, 8 pages, 25% ads
Subscriptions: Indv. $15, Inst. $15, Can. $15, For. $18, $2/copy
Advertising: $150. Accepts Inserts.
List Rental: Actives: 1,500, $250/M

Walnut Avenue Women's Center Newsletter

Publishing Co: Walnut Avenue Women's Center, 303 Walnut Ave., Santa Cruz, CA 95060-3659; Title Tel # (408) 426-3062
General Info: Irregular, 8 pages
List Rental: List Management Co.: Fred Woolf List Co., Inc., 110 Corporate Park Dr., White Plains, NY 10604-3800 Tel # (914) 694-4466, Fax # (914) 694-1710, Actives: $45/M

Washington Memo
See: HEALTH

Waterwheel
Consumer, Association

Publishing Co: WATER Women's Alliance for Theology, Ethics, & Ritual, 8035 13th St, Silver Spring, MD 20910-4803; Title Tel # (301) 589-2509 Title Fax # (301) 589-3150
Personnel: Co-Editor-Mary E. Hunt, Co-Editor-Diann L. Neu, Copy Editor-Carol Murdak Scinto
Editorial Description: Promotes religious education with a feminist and liberation perspective.
General Info: Yr. Est. 1987, Quarterly, Trim Size-8½ x 11, Desktop press, 8 pages, ISSN: 0898-6606, No Color, Other
Subscriptions: Indv. $35, For. $50, $5/copy
Circulation: (40% controlled), Subscriptions-3,000
List Rental: Rents Lists
Printing Co: EU Services, 649 N Horners Ln, Rockville, MD 20850-1299 Tel # (301) 424-3300

Webb Report, The
See: BUSINESS & INDUSTRY

Woman Alive

Publishing Co: Man Watchers Inc., Box 1616, Canal St. Station, New York, NY 10013; Title Tel # (213) 458-5989
General Info: Yr. Est. 1974, Quarterly
Subscriptions: Indv. $20

Woman Oughta Know
Association

Publishing Co: Woman's Marketplace, The, Box 161775, Cupertino, CA 95016
Editorial Description: Newsletter of the Women's Marketplace for those women that would rather buy from woman owned businesses.
General Info: Monthly

Woman's Day Helpful Hints Newsletter
Consumer

Publishing Co: Hachette Filipacchi Magazines, Inc., 1633 Broadway, New York, NY 10019-6741 Tel # (212) 767-6000 Fax # (212) 489-4577
Editorial Description: Household tips and timesavers.
General Info: Monthly
Subscriptions: Indv. $10
Circulation: Total-91,000
List Rental: List Management Co.: Direct Media, Inc., 200 Pemberwick Rd., PO Box 4565, Greenwich, CT 06830 Tel # (203) 532-3713, Fax # (203) 531-1452, Actives: 48,562, $60/M

Woman's Work
Business, Consumer

Publishing Co: Woman's Work, P.O. Box 480311, Kansas City, MO 64148-9982
Editorial Description: Information covering both the business and personal needs of working women.
General Info: Monthly, Trim Size-8½ x 11, 4 pages, Matte
Subscriptions: Indv. $25

Women & Religion Newsletter

Publishing Co: Center for Women & Religion, 2400 Ridge Rd, Berkeley, CA 94709-1212; Title Tel # (415) 649-2490 Title Fax # (415) 649-1417
Personnel: Editor-Amy Teichman, Publisher, Production Mgr.-Pamela Cooper-White
Editorial Description: Lead articles on feminist theology/spirituality and ethics, plus book reviews, job listings, events, and scholarship notices.
General Info: Yr. Est. 1970, Monthly
Subscriptions: Indv. $35, Inst. $50, $1/copy
Circulation: Total-750

Women Against Pornography Newsreport

Publishing Co: Women Against Pornography, 321 West 47th Street, New York, NY 10036-2400; Title Tel # (212) 307-5055
General Info: Yr. Est. 1979, 25 pages
Circulation: Total-10,000

Women in the Arts Bulletin
See: CULTURE & HUMANITIES

Women At Work

Publishing Co: Wider Opportunities for Women, 1325 G St. N. W. , LL, Washington, DC 20005-3189; Title Tel # (202) 638-3143
Editorial Description: Follows employment & training issues, related legislation & economic developments that affect women.
General Info: Quarterly, 18 pages
Subscriptions: Indv. $40, For. $50
Circulation: Total-8,000

Women in Libraries
See: LIBRARY

Women and Money
Business, Consumer

Publishing Co: F.J. Mclaughlin Newsletter Network, 1346 Joan Dr, Southampton, PA 18966-4341; Title Tel # (215) 322-1346
Personnel: Publisher, Editor-Flo McLaughlin
Editorial Description: The common sense guide for practical money management; how to make, save, and spend money wisely.
General Info: Yr. Est. 1991, Bi-monthly, Trim Size-8½ x 11, Desktop press, 8 pages
Subscriptions: Indv. $18, Can. $18, For. $19, $3/copy
Circulation: Total-1,000
List Rental: Rents Lists

Women for Peace Newsletter, East Bay
See: POLITICS

Women and Recovery
Consumer

Publishing Co: Women to Women Communications, P.O. Box 161775, Ste. 111, Cupertino, CA 95016
Editorial Description: Positive and action-oriented publication.
General Info: Monthly
Subscriptions: Indv. $18, $1/copy

Women with Wheels
Consumer

Publishing Co: Women with Wheels, 1718 A. Northfield Square, Northfield, IL 60093; Title Tel # (708) 501-3519
Personnel: Publisher, Editor-Susan Frissell, PhD, Circ. Mgr.-Patricia L. Stringer
Editorial Description: Car maintenance information for women.
General Info: Yr. Est. 1989, Quarterly, Trim Size-8½ x 11, Desktop press, 12 pages, ISSN: 1043-979X, No Color, Matte, Other
Subscriptions: Indv. $20, Inst. $20
Advertising: $250.
List Rental: Actives: $250/M, Expires: $250/M

Women Who Write

Publishing Co: The Eleanor Press, 16216 Freyman Rd, Cygnet, OH 43413-9766

Women around New York
Business, Consumer

Publishing Co: New York State Div. for Women, Exec. Chamber, 2 World Trade Center, 57th fl., New York, NY 10047 Tel # (212) 417-2100; Title Tel # (518) 474-3612
Personnel: Editor-Jackie McGinnis
Editorial Description: Advocacy activities.
General Info: (Formerly New York Women), Quarterly, Trim Size-8½ x 11, 12 pages, 2 Color, Matte, Saddle-stitched
Circulation: Total-5,000

Women as Managers
See: MANAGEMENT

Women's Business Exclusive
Business, Consumer

Publishing Co: Minority Business Entrepreneur, 3528 Torrance Blvd., Ste. 101, Torrance, CA 90503-4803; Title Tel # (310) 540-9398 Title Fax # (310) 792-8263
Personnel: Publisher-Ginger Conrad, Editor-Jeanie Barnett
Editorial Description: Newsletter for and about women business owners and the issues affecting them.
General Info: Yr. Est. 1993, 10x/yr., Trim Size-8½ x 11, 8 pages, ISSN: 1068-9087, No Color, Matte, Saddle-stitched
Subscriptions: Indv. $39
Circulation: Readership-2,000
List Rental: Rents Lists

Women's Classical Caucus Newsletter

Publishing Co: Women's Classical Caucus, Iowa State University, Ames, IA 50011
General Info: 2x/yr.
Subscriptions: Indv. $12

Women's Health Center Management
See: HEALTH

Women's Health Issues

Publishing Co: Elsevier Science Inc., 655 Avenue of the Americas, New York, NY 10010-5107 Tel # (212) 633-3916 Fax # (212) 633-3913 Parent Co.-Reed Elsevier, New York; Title Tel # (212) 989-5800 Title Fax # (212) 633-3990
Editorial Description: Devoted to health issues of particular concern to women.
General Info: Yr. Est. 1990, Quarterly, ISSN: 1049-3867
Subscriptions: Inst. $72

Women's Health Letter
Consumer

Publishing Co: Soundview Publications, 7100 Peachtree Dunwoody Rd., Suite #100, Atlanta, GA 30328-4134 Tel # (770) 668-0432 Fax # (770) 668-0692; Title Tel # (770) 399-5617 Title Fax # (770) 399-0815
Personnel: Publisher-Wallis W. Wood, Mng. Editor-Kerri Bodmer, Art Dir.-Elizabeth Bame
Editorial Description: Health issues and information for women from leading experts.
General Info: Yr. Est. 1992, Monthly, Trim Size-8½ x 11, 8 pages, ISSN: 1062-4163, 2 Color, Matte
Subscriptions: Indv. $39
Circulation: Total-5,000
List Rental: List Management Co.: Names in the News-California, 1 Bush St Bsmt 3, San Francisco, CA 94104-4425 Tel # (415) 989-3350, Fax # (415) 433-7796, Actives: 8,000, $70/M, Expires: 3,264, $50/M

Women's Health Matters
See: HEALTH

Women's International League for Peace and Freedom
Consumer

Publishing Co: Women's International League for Peace and Freedom, 339 Lafayette St, New York, NY 10012-2725 Tel # (212) 533-2125; Title Tel # (212) 563-7110 Title Fax # (215) 864-2022
Editorial Description: Multi-issue, multi-racial bimonthly newsletter dealing with international, national and local issues of peace, freedom and justice.
General Info: Monthly

Women's Investment Newsletter
See: INVESTMENT

Women's Market Share
Consumer

Publishing Co: Women's Market Share, PO Box 512, Stillwater, MN 55082-0512; Title Tel # (612) 439-1161
Personnel: Publisher, Editor-Colleen Callahan
Editorial Description: Financial and monetary choices and ideas for women.
General Info: Yr. Est. 1994, Monthly
Subscriptions: Indv. $29

Women's Political Times
Association

Publishing Co: National Women's Political Caucus, 1211 Connecticut Ave NW Ste, 425, Washington, DC 20036-2701; Title Tel # (202) 898-1100
Personnel: Editor-Pat Reilly
Editorial Description: News and features on women in politics. Lively, sophisticated.
General Info: Yr. Est. 1976, Quarterly, Trim Size-9¾ x 14, Sheetfed press, 12 pages, 8% ads, No Color
Subscriptions: Free With Membership
Circulation: Total-40,000
List Rental: Actives: $60/M, Expires: 30,000, $50/M

Women's Recovery Network
Consumer

Publishing Co: WebWords Press Inc., PO Box 1145, New Albany, IN 47151-1145
Editorial Description: A grassroots feminist forum for women who have known abuse and/or addiction, and who now seek political and spiritual solutions.
General Info: Yr. Est. 1991, Bi-monthly, Trim Size-8½ x 11, 16 pages, ISSN: 1052-1763
Subscriptions: Indv. $27, Can. $37, For. $42, $4/copy

Women's Research Network News

Publishing Co: Natl. Council for Research on Women, 530 Broadway, 10th Floor, New York, NY 10012 Tel # (212) 274-0730
Personnel: Editor-Debra L. Schultz
General Info: Quarterly

Women's Studies Newsletter
Consumer, Association

Publishing Co: Center for Women's Studies At OSU, 286 University Hall, 230 N. Oval Mall, Columbus, OH 43210; Title Tel # (614) 292-1021
Personnel: Editor-Sue Green
Editorial Description: Our goal is to celebrate the varieties of feminist expression and to continue the tradition of connecting the Center for Women's Studies to Women's Communities through its publication.
General Info: (Formerly Feminisms), Yr. Est. 1988, Bi-monthly, Trim Size-8½ x 11, Sheetfed press, 24 pages, ISSN: 1041-1801, No Color
Subscriptions: Indv. $8, Can. $10, For. $11
Circulation: Total-500

Women's Watch
Association, Consumer

Publishing Co: IWRAW/WPPD, Humphrey Inst of Public Affair, Univ. Minn., 301-19th Ave. S., Minneapolis, MN 55455
Editorial Description: Helping to eliminate discrimination against women internationally.
General Info: Monthly
Subscriptions: Indv. $20

WomensWord
Business, Association

Publishing Co: Fort Wayne Women's Bureau, Inc., 303 E Washington Blvd, Fort Wayne, IN 46802-3123; Title Tel # (219) 424-7977
Personnel: Editor-Beth Goegein
Editorial Description: Fort Wayne women's bureau newsletter. Covers agency news, women's issues.
General Info: Yr. Est. 1976, Bi-monthly, Trim Size-5½ x 8½, 16 pages, No Color
Subscriptions: Indv. $20
Circulation: Total-1,400
Advertising: Inquire for rates.

Working at Home
See: EMPLOYMENT

World of A.S.P.
See: LIFESTYLE

World CWF News
See: RELIGIOUS & THEOLOGICAL

World Goodwill Commentary
See: INTERNATIONAL AFFAIRS

ZPG Reporter, The
See: ENVIRONMENT & ECOLOGY

Zorniska (Morning Star)
See: RELIGIOUS & THEOLOGICAL

YOUTH

ADHD Report
See: PSYCHOLOGY

APLIC International Communicator
See: LIBRARY

Acrosports News
See: SPORTS & SPORTING GOODS

Ani V'atah
See: RELIGIOUS & THEOLOGICAL

Assembly Lines Newsletter
See: SOCIAL SERVICES & WELFARE

Astro News
See: AERONAUTICS/ASTRONAUTICS

Boys' and Girls' Clubs of Greater Vancouver, Bulletin
Association

Publishing Co: Boys' & Girls' Clubs of Greater Vancouver, 2875 St. George St., Vancouver, BC V5T 3R8 Canada; Title Tel # (604) 879-6554 Title Fax # (604) 321-0747
Personnel: Publisher-Rick Ryan
Editorial Description: Promote the work of the organization to its adult and corporate members.
General Info: Yr. Est. 1938, Quarterly, Trim Size-10¾ x 17, Offset press, 4 pages, 2 Color, Newsprint
Circulation: (40% controlled), Total-5,000

CVC Bulletin
Association

Publishing Co: City Volunteer Corps., 838 Broadway Fl 4, New York, NY 10003-4812; Title Tel # (212) 475-6444
Personnel: Publisher-Harry Hernandez, Editor-Diana Eccevarria, Circ. Mgr.-Art Dir.-Anthony Effinger
Editorial Description: Covers NYC Natl. Youth Service demonstration program & other programs nationally.
General Info: (Formerly CVC Newsletter), Yr. Est. 1985, Quarterly, 8 pages
Circulation: Total-2,000
Printing Co: Lehmann Printing Co., 48 W 25th St, New York, NY 10010-2761 Tel # (212) 929-2395

Camps Canada
See: PARKS & RECREATION AREAS

Careers Bridge Newsletter
See: EDUCATION

Catalyst Newsletter
See: LAW ENFORCEMENT & PENOLOGY

Cherokee Boys Club-Newsletter & Cherokee Voice
See: ETHNIC

Child and Adolescent Psychopharmacology News
See: PSYCHOLOGY

Child Assessment News
See: PSYCHOLOGY

Child Labor Monitor
See: CONSUMER INTERESTS

Children & Youth Funding Report
See: PHILANTHROPY

Choirboy Notes
See: MUSIC & MUSIC TRADES

Connections
See: RELIGIOUS & THEOLOGICAL

Covering the Education Beat
See: SCHOOL ADMINISTRATION

Day Care Guide
See: CHILDREN

Dept. of Education Reports
See: EDUCATION

Encounter!
See: RELIGIOUS & THEOLOGICAL

FFA Update
See: AGRICULTURE

Fast Break
See: SPORTS & SPORTING GOODS

Focus
See: EDUCATION

Forum
See: EDUCATION

Friends of Youth Newsletter   *Association*
Publishing Co: Friends of Youth, Inc., 16225 NE 87th St Ste A6, Redmond, WA 98052-3536; Title Tel # (206) 869-6940 Title Fax # (216) 869-6666
Personnel: Editor-Pamela Telkamp
Editorial Description: Agency, client & volunteer activities; program information.
General Info: Yr. Est. 1954, Quarterly, Trim Size-8$\frac{1}{2}$ x 11, Sheetfed press, 6 pages, Color, Newsprint, Saddle-stitched
Circulation: Total-2,500

Hotline
Publishing Co: Children's Rights of NY, 15 Arbutus Ln, Stony Brook, NY 11790-1408; Title Tel # (516) 751-7840
Personnel: Editor-John Gill
General Info: Quarterly

ICYE-US Newsletter
See: RELIGIOUS & THEOLOGICAL

In Focus - NAVH   *Consumer*
Publishing Co: National Association for Visually Handicapped, 22 W. 21st St., New York, NY 10010-6904; Title Tel # (212) 889-3141 Title Fax # (212) 727-2931
Personnel: Editor-Lorraine Marchi
Editorial Description: Provides partially seeing youth, their families, friends & professionals who serve them update on services, technological advances, large print sources; also accepts for publication original essays, short fiction, poetry & drawings by and for partially seeing youth.
General Info: Yr. Est. 1975, Annually
Subscriptions: Free
Circulation: Total-10,000

Inclusion Times
See: DISABILITY

Interlocken Globe   *Consumer*
Publishing Co: Interlocken Center for Experiential Learning, Rr 2 Box 165, Hillsboro, NH 03244-9506; Title Tel # (603) 478-3166
Personnel: Editor-Judi Wisch
Editorial Description: Information for and about camp and travel programs for young people.
General Info: Yr. Est. 1961, Monthly, Trim Size-11$\frac{1}{4}$ x 17, 16 pages, 2 Color, Matte
Subscriptions: Free To Qualified Recipient

JACS Volunteer
See: EMPLOYMENT

Junior Citizen
Publishing Co: Connecticut Junior Republic, Inc., The, Box 161, Goshen Rd., Litchfield, CT 06759-0161; Title Tel # (203) 567-9423
Personnel: Publisher-Carl Hooper, Editor-Kevin Canawan
Editorial Description: Newsletter describing activities, goals of CJR, a residential center for emotionally troubled youth.
General Info: Yr. Est. 1921, Trim Size-11$\frac{1}{4}$ x 16$\frac{1}{2}$, Letrpr. press, 4 pages, No Color
Circulation: Total-11,000

Juvenile Miscellany   *Consumer, Association*
Publishing Co: Univ. of Southern Mississippi Library, McCain Library, Box 5148, Children's Lit. Research, Hattiesburg, MS 39406-5148; Title Tel # (601) 266-4349
Personnel: Editor-Dee Jones
Editorial Description: Lena Y. deGrummond Children's Literature Research collection. News about contributions, accessions to the Collection, etc.
General Info: Yr. Est. 1970, Trim Size-8$\frac{1}{2}$ x 11, 8 pages, No Color
Circulation: Total-1,400

Kids Club News
See: CHILDREN

Learning Edge
See: EDUCATION

Link
Publishing Co: Roman Catholic School Bd., 140 Cumberland, Ottawa, ON K1N 7G9 Canada; Title Tel # (613) 224-2222
General Info: Yr. Est. 1974, 13x/yr.
Circulation: Total-1,400

Magyar Cserke'sz
See: CLUBS

Maloda Ukraina
See: ETHNIC

NJDA News
See: LAW ENFORCEMENT & PENOLOGY

National Catholic Committee on Scouting Newsletter
See: CLUBS

National Coalition News
See: EDUCATION

National Service Newsletter
Publishing Co: Natl. Service Secretariat-Augsburg Co., 4905 Del Ray Ave., Bethesda, MD 20814-2527; Title Tel # (202) 244-5828
Personnel: Publisher, Editor-Donald Eberly
Editorial Description: Educational, manpower, military, and youth topics linked to national service.
General Info: Yr. Est. 1966, Semi-annually, Trim Size-8$\frac{1}{2}$ x 11, Offset press, 4 pages

Net News
See: SPORTS & SPORTING GOODS

News Digest
See: DISABILITY

Ontario Vacation Farms
See: TRAVEL

Order of the Arrow Bulletin
Publishing Co: Boy Scouts of America, 1325 W Walnut Hill Ln, Irving, TX 75038-3096 Tel # (214) 580-2350; Title Tel # (214) 580-2000
Personnel: Editor-W.F. Downs
Editorial Description: Information for members of the Order of the Arrow.
General Info: Bi-monthly, Trim Size-8$\frac{1}{2}$ x 11, Web press, 4 pages, Color
Subscriptions: Indv. $2
Circulation: Total-13,000

Provincial Notes   *Association*
Publishing Co: Boy Scouts of Canada, Toronto, 9 Jackes Ave., Toronto, ON M4T 1E2 Canada; Title Tel # (416) 923-2461
Personnel: Editor, Circ. Mgr., Art Dir.-Barry Hardaker
Editorial Description: House organ.
General Info: 5x/yr., Trim Size-8$\frac{1}{2}$ x 11, Offset press, 8 pages, 2 Color
Circulation: (100% controlled), Total-10,500

Reading Programs with Stories that Educate, Inform, Entertain and Rhyme
See: CHILDREN

Real Talk   *Association*
Publishing Co: Boces Geneseo Migrant Center, 210 Holcomb Bldg., Geneseo, NY 14454; Title Tel # (716) 245-5681 Title Fax # (716) 245-5680
Personnel: Editor-Mary Fink
Editorial Description: Communication vehicle with youth, 13-21 who travel the migrant farmworks streams to harvest crops & who have dropped out of school before high school graduation.
General Info: Yr. Est. 1977, Monthly, Trim Size-8$\frac{1}{2}$ x 11, Sheetfed press, 4 pages, No Color
Subscriptions: Indv. $12
Circulation: Total-10,000
Printing Co: Conolly Printing, 1940 Lisle Ave., Rochester, NY 14606 Tel # (716) 254-0150

Reference Guide to Counseling Children & Adolescents
See: CHILDREN

Scouter's Digest   *Consumer, Association*
Publishing Co: Scouter's Digest, PO Box 1052, Marinette, WI 54143-6052; Title Tel # (906) 863-3863 Title Fax # (906) 863-3863
Personnel: Publisher, Editor-Paul Ferris
Editorial Description: Condensed scouting news for busy Boy Scout leaders.
General Info: Yr. Est. 1986, Bi-monthly, Trim Size-8$\frac{1}{2}$ x 11, Desktop press, 4 pages, ISSN: 0890-8206, 2 Color, Matte
Subscriptions: Indv. $18, Can. $25, For. $25, $4/copy
Advertising: Accepts Inserts.
List Rental: List Management Co.: Paul Ferris & Associates, PO Box 1052, Marinette, WI 54143-6052 Tel # (906) 863-3863, Fax # (906) 863-3863, Actives: 44,500, $60/M, Hotline: $70/M, Expires: $60/M
Printing Co: Bandar Printing, 717 10th Ave, Menominee, MI 49858-3012 Tel # (906) 863-8136, Fax # (906) 863-7793

Scouting Bulletin of the National Catholic Committee on Scouting

Publishing Co: Boy Scouts of America, 1325 W Walnut Hill Ln, Irving, TX 75038-3096
Tel # (214) 580-2350; Title Tel # (214) 580-2000
Personnel: Editor-Joseph P. Kessler
Editorial Description: News stories of coming events and other related information pertinent to the Boy Scouts of America and the National Catholic Committee on Scouting.
General Info: Quarterly
Circulation: Total-8,000

Scouting News　　　*Consumer, Association*

Publishing Co: New Brunswick Provincial Council Boy Scouts of Canada, 55 Rothesay Ave., St. John, NB E2J 2B2 Canada; Title Tel # (506) 634-1566
Personnel: Publisher, Editor-B. Hallett, Art Dir.-Joyce Doucette
Editorial Description: Boy Scout newsletter.
General Info: Yr. Est. 1950, Bi-monthly, Trim Size-8½ x 11, 6 pages, 4 Color
Subscriptions: $1/copy
Circulation: (100% controlled), Total-2,000
Advertising: Inquire for rates.

SimAntics
See: GIFTS, GAMES, TOYS

Spotlight on Youth Sports
See: EDUCATION

Squires Newsletter　　　*Association*

Publishing Co: Knights of Columbus Supreme Council, One Columbus Plaza, New Haven, CT 06510-3326; Title Tel # (203) 772-2130 Title Fax # (203) 772-1923
Personnel: Editor-Ronald J. Tracz
General Info: Yr. Est. 1929, Monthly, Offset press
Subscriptions: Indv. $1
Circulation: Total-37,000

Story Rhyme Reproducible Newsletter
See: EDUCATION

Teacher Education Reports
See: EDUCATION

Teacher's PET Term Paper
See: EDUCATION

This Is WICS
See: SOCIAL SERVICES & WELFARE

Transition Summary
See: DISABILITY

Trumpet, The

Publishing Co: Girl Guides of Canada, 1939 deMaisonneuve Blvd. West, Montreal, PQ H3H 1K3 Canada; Title Tel # (514) 933-5839 Title Fax # (514) 933-7591
General Info: 3x/yr., 44 pages
Subscriptions: Free With Membership
Circulation: Readership-1,200

USBBY
See: BOOKS & BOOK TRADE

World Goodwill Commentary
See: INTERNATIONAL AFFAIRS

Y-Canada　　　*Association*

Publishing Co: Natl. Council of YMCA's of Canada, 2160 Yonge St., Toronto, ON M4S 2A9 Canada; Title Tel # (416) 485-9447
Personnel: Editor-Don McCuaige
Editorial Description: Eng. & Fr. text.
General Info: Yr. Est. 1971, Semi-annually, 12 pages, ISSN: 0315-095X
Circulation: Total-2,400

YABA Framework
See: SPORTS & SPORTING GOODS

Young Adult/Teen Market Report
See: ADVERTISING & MARKETING

Your Child's Wellness
See: BABY

Youth Bureau News

Publishing Co: New York Youth Bureau, 44 Court St., Brooklyn, NY 11201-4463; Title Tel # (718) 403-5310
Personnel: Editor-Alvin E. White, Circ. Mgr.-Peter Haley
General Info: Yr. Est. 1965

Youth Law News
See: LAW

Youth Mission for the Immaculata National Newsletter
See: RELIGIOUS & THEOLOGICAL

Youth Record　　　*Consumer*

Publishing Co: Youth Policy Institute, 1221 Massachusetts Ave NW Ste, B, Washington, DC 20005-5302; Title Tel # (202) 638-2144
Personnel: Editor-Donna Power, Circ. Dir.-Brian Shively, Art Dir.-Valentin Padron
Editorial Description: Reports on federal youth-related policy.
General Info: Semi-monthly, ISSN: 1047-7144
Subscriptions: Indv. $127

Youth Worker Update　　　*Business*

Publishing Co: Youth Specialties, 1224 Greenfield Dr, El Cajon, CA 92021-3399
Fax # (619) 440-4939; Title Tel # (619) 440-2333
Editorial Description: Practical newsletter designed to keep the busy youth worker abreast of the latest new youth ministry resources.
General Info: Monthly
List Rental: List Management Co.: Bernice Bush Co./Springdale Lists, 15052 Springdale St., Huntington Beach, CA 92649-1178 Tel # (714) 891-3344, Fax # (714) 897-0650, Actives: 6,500, $75/M, Expires: 4,700, $75/M

ZOOLOGY

Animal Welfare Information Center Newsletter
See: ANIMALS

Ascidian News　　　*Consumer*

Publishing Co: California State Univ. at Fullerton Biology Dept., Publications, Fullerton, CA 92634; Title Tel # (714) 773-3481
Personnel: Production Mgr.-Gretchen Lambert, Editor, Adv. Dir.-Charles Lambert
Editorial Description: Biology of lower chordates including cephalochordata urochordata and hemichordata.
General Info: Yr. Est. 1966, Semi-annually, Trim Size-8½ x 11, Offset press, 12 pages, ISSN: 0066-8222, No Color, Newsprint
Subscriptions: Free
Circulation: Total-200

Breeder's Registry Newsletter
See: ANIMALS

Canadian Society of Environmental Biologists Newsletter
See: ENVIRONMENT & ECOLOGY

Fish & Wildlife Reference Service Newsletter
See: ENVIRONMENT & ECOLOGY

Fur-Bearers Newsletter

Publishing Co: Association for the Protection of Fur-Bearing Animals, 2235 Commercial Dr., Vancouver, BC V5N 4B6 Canada
Personnel: Editor-Bunty Clements
General Info: Yr. Est. 1973, Quarterly, 8 pages
Subscriptions: Free With Membership
Circulation: Total-7,000

Hawaiian Shell News
See: NATURAL HISTORY

Herpetological Review　　　*Association*

Publishing Co: Society for the Study of Amphibians & Reptiles, PO Box 626, Hays, KS 67601-0626; Title Tel # (216) 368-3558
Personnel: Editor-Martin Rosenberg, Adv. Dir.-Raymond Stein
Editorial Description: Distribution, husbandry, techniques, legislation, photographs, regional societies, and current research on amphibians and reptiles.
General Info: Yr. Est. 1967, Quarterly, Trim Size-8½ x 11, Sheetfed press, 40 pages, ISSN: 0018-084X, Ind/Abs/Online: Zoo.Rec.,Bio.Abs., No Color
Subscriptions: Indv. $25, For. $25
Circulation: Total-2,200
Printing Co: Meseraull Printing, Inc., Rr 6 Box 1, Lawrence, KS 66046-8901

Humane News
See: ANIMALS

The ISC Newsletter　　　*Association*

Publishing Co: International Society of Cryptozoology, PO Box 43070, Tucson, AZ 85733-3070
Tel # (652) 088-8369; Title Tel # (520) 884-8369 Title Fax # (520) 884-8369
Personnel: Editor-J.Richard Greenwell
Editorial Description: News on all matters related to cryptozoology.
General Info: Yr. Est. 1982, Quarterly, Trim Size-8½ x 11, Offset press, 12 pages, ISSN: 0741-5362, No Color
Subscriptions: Indv. $32, Inst. $45, $4/copy
Circulation: Total-1,000
Printing Co: Digitgraph, P.O Box 5907, Tucson, AZ 85703 Tel # (520) 622-1006

Indianapolis Zoo — *Association*

Publishing Co: Indianapolis Zoological Society, Inc., 1200 W Washington St, Indianapolis, IN 46222-4552; Title Tel # (317) 630-2001
Editorial Description: Contains information relating to Indianapolis Zoo, its animals, staff and functions.
General Info: (Formerly Zoosletter), Yr. Est. 1961, Bi-monthly, Letrpr. press, 8 pages, ISSN: 0044-5304, No Color, Saddle-stitched
Subscriptions: Indv. $20, $3/copy
Circulation: Total-6,000

International Bear News — *Consumer, Association*

Publishing Co: Sponsor-Intl. Assn./Bear Research & Management, c/o Sterling Miller, International Bear News, 10907 NW Copeland St., Portland, OR 97229-6145 Fax # (503) 643-4072; Title Tel # (503) 643-4008 Title Fax # (503) 226-0074
Personnel: Editor-Teresa De Lorenzo
Editorial Description: For those dedicated to the conservation of all bear species.
General Info: Yr. Est. 1992, Quarterly, Trim Size-8½ x 11, Offset press, 24 pages, ISSN: 1064-1564, No Color, Matte, Saddle-stitched
Subscriptions: Indv. $20
Circulation: Total-700
Advertising: Inquire for rates. Accepts Inserts.

International Wild Waterfowl Association Newsletter — *Association*

Publishing Co: International Wild Waterfowl Assn., 7 James Farm Rd, Durham, NH 03824-6529; Title Tel # (912) 924-9297
Personnel: Publisher, Editor-Ray Gwynes
Editorial Description: Member oriented: ads, meetings; research activities, conservation, tips & questions, veterinary helps on propagating wild water fowl in captivity.
General Info: Yr. Est. 1958, Quarterly, Trim Size-5½ x 8½, 30 pages, No Color, Newsprint
Subscriptions: Indv. $25, For. $30
Circulation: Total-600

Koala Club News
See: CHILDREN

NYTTS NewsNotes — *Consumer, Association* CPM: $60

Publishing Co: New York Turtle & Tortoise Society, 163 Amsterdam Ave. #365, New York, NY 10023-5001 Fax # (212) 275-3307; Title Tel # (212) 459-4803
Personnel: Publisher, Editor-Jim Van Abbema
Editorial Description: Carries articles on turtle behavior, diet, habitat conservation, legislation, medical care & other useful information.
General Info: (Formerly Plastron Papers), Yr. Est. 1970, Quarterly, Web press, 24 pages
Subscriptions: Indv. $20
Circulation: (24% controlled), Total-2,500, Subscriptions-500
Advertising: $150.

Nature Views
See: NATURAL HISTORY

Pacific Seabird Group Bulletin
See: ORNITHOLOGY

Plastron Papers — *Association*

Publishing Co: New York Turtle & Tortoise Society, 163 Amsterdam Ave. #365, New York, NY 10023-5001; Title Tel # (212) 459-4803 Title Fax # (212) 275-3307
Personnel: Editor-Jim Van Abbema
Editorial Description: Articles on turtle conservation and husbandry.
General Info: Yr. Est. 1970, Semi-annually
Subscriptions: Indv. $20
Circulation: Total-2,500, Readership-5,000
Advertising: Inquire for rates. Accepts Inserts.
List Rental: Rents Lists

Primate Library Report: Audio-Visual Acquisitions — *Association*

Publishing Co: Wisconsin Regional Primate Research Center, 1220 Capitol Ct, Madison, WI 53715-1237; Title Tel # (608) 263-3512 Title Fax # (608) 263-4031
Personnel: Editor, Circ. Mgr.-Raymond Hamel, Production Mgr.-Lawrence Jacobsen
Editorial Description: Inform subscribers about recent audiovisual acquisitions of the Wisconsin Regional Primate Research Center Library.
General Info: Yr. Est. 1982, Semi-annually, Trim Size-8½ x 11, Desktop press, 14 pages, Ind/Abs/Online: primate info net, No Color
Subscriptions: Free
Circulation: Total-836

Scales and Tales — *Consumer*

Publishing Co: Centre for Endangered Reptiles, 347 Rue Bourget, Granby, PQ J2G 1E8 Canada; Title Tel # (514) 372-9113
Personnel: Editor, Circ. Mgr.-Geoff Gaherty
Editorial Description: Short articles & updates on the work of the Center for Endangered Reptiles.
General Info: Yr. Est. 1986, Quarterly, 4 pages, ISSN: 0832-5693
Subscriptions: Indv. $20, Can. $25
Circulation: Total-2,600

Scientists Center for Animal Welfare's Newsletter
See: ANIMALS

Spyhopper
See: ENVIRONMENT & ECOLOGY

Trumpeter Swan Society Newsletter
See: ORNITHOLOGY

Vancouver Aquascene Aquarium Newsletter
See: NATURAL HISTORY

Winging It
See: ORNITHOLOGY

Wolf Park News
See: ANIMALS

Zoolog — *Association*

Publishing Co: Zoological Society of Manitoba, Box 21059 Charleswood P.O., Winnipeg, MB R3R 3R2 Canada; Title Tel # (204) 896-0296 Title Fax # (204) 896-3927
Personnel: Publisher, Editor-Denise Debets
General Info: (Formerly Manitoba Nature), Bi-monthly, 8 pages
Circulation: Total-390

Multi-Publisher Index

- Features publishers of more than one title in alphabetical order. Includes addresses, list of titles and page numbers.

A

AELE
5519 N Cumberland Ave Ste 1008, Chicago, IL, 60656-1480
Jail & Prisoner Law Bulletin, 787
Law Enforcement Liability Reporter, 787
Security and Special Police Legal Update, 1,105
A Friend Indeed Publications, Inc.
3575 Boul. Saint-Laurent, Ste. 402, Montreal, PQ, H2X 2T7, Canada
A Friend Indeed, 1,206
Une Veritable Amie, 1,212
AHA Stroke Connections
7272 Greenville Ave, Dallas, TX, 75231-5129
Courage News, 503
Meeting Ground, 278
Stroke Connection, 529
AIDS Project Los Angeles
6721 Romaine St, Los Angeles, CA, 90038-2417
APLA Update, 496
Optimist, 522
Positive Living, 525
A.M. Best Co., Inc.
Ambest Rd., Oldwick, NJ, 08858-0700
BestWeek Life/Health Edition, 618
BestWeek, Property/Casualty Edition, 618
Best's Casualty Loss Reserve Development Series, 618
Best's Experience By State, 618
Best's Intelligencer, 618
Best's Loss Control Engineering Manual, 618
Best's Underwriting Guide, 618
Your Safety News, 1,085
AMS, F&V Division, USDA
PO Box 1204, Benton Harbor, MI, 49023-1204
Benton Harbor Fruit & Vegetable Report, 1,008
Great Lakes Fruit & Vegetable Report, 1,008
Marketing Great Lake Fruit, 1,009
A.S. Pratt & Sons
1911 Fort Myer Dr., Ste 308, Arlington, VA, 22209-1603
Bank Wage-Hour & Personnel Report, 341
Federal Banking Law Service of A.S. Pratt, 736
Pratt's Letter, 97
Abbott & Hast Publications, Inc.
761 Lighthouse Ave., Ste. A, Monterey, CA, 93940-1033
Funeral Monitor, 437
Mortuary Science Monitor, 437
Access Reports, Inc.
1624 Dogwood Lane, Lynchburg, VA, 24503
Access Reports /Canada Newsletter, 1,194
Access Reports/Freedom of Information - U.S Newsletter, 1,194
Canadian FOIA Reference File, 1,194
Reference File U.S, 1,198
Accrediting Assn. of Bible Colleges
PO Box 1523, Fayetteville, AR, 72702-1523
Accrediting Association of Bible Colleges Newsletter, 299
Accrediting Association of Bible Colleges Newsletter, 1,061
Action Kit for Hospital Law
4614 Fifth Ave., Pittsburgh, PA, 15213-3663
Action Kit for Hospital Law, 561
Action Kit for Hospital Trustees, 561
Medical Staff Law Manual, 568
Patient Care Law, 570
Administrator's Digest, Inc.
PO Box 993, South San Francisco, CA, 94083-0993
Business Information from Your Public Library, 794
Library Administrator's Digest, 801
Advertising Specialty Institute
1120 Wheeler Way, Langhorne, PA, 19047-1785
Briefings, 11
Market, 17
Profile Briefings, 21
Advertising Women of New York
153 E 57th St Fl 3a, New York, NY, 10022-2121
AWNY Matters, 9
AWNY Roster, 9
Aeltus Managing, Inc.
242 Trumbull St., Hartford, CT, 06156
Aeltus Weekly, 617
Aetna-Izer, 576
AetnaSphere, 576
Good Word, 584
In the News, 586
Ag Executive, Inc.
115 E. Twyman, PO Box 180, Bushnell, IL, 61422
Ag Executive, 36
Farm and Ranch Tax Letter, 40
Agora, Inc.
105 W. Monoment St., Baltimore, MD, 21202-4702
Adrian Day's Investment Analyst, 654
Crisis Investing, 661
Czeschin Mutual Funds, 661
Health & Longevity, 509
Health Revelations, 510
Home Inc., 140
Insiders' Health Letter, 514
International Living, 814
Predictions, 682
Quantum Advantage Investment & Technology Report, 1,099
Scientific Investment, 685
Strategic Investment, 687
Taipan, 688
Tax Avoidance Digest, 688
Tax Wise Money, 1,155
What Doctors Don't Tell You, 889
World Investor, 692
World Money Analyst, 692
Agricultural Marketing Service
U.S. Dept. of Agriculture, South Bldg., Rm. 2613, Washington, DC, 20090-6456
Grain & Feed Market News, 41
Livestock, Meat, and Wool Market News, 828

Air-Conditioning & Refrigeration Institute (ARI)
4301 Fairfax Dr Ste 425, Arlington, VA, 22203-1627
Koldfax, 535
Minuteman, 535
Air-Conditioning & Refrigeration Wholesalers
10251 W Sample Rd # B, Coral Springs, FL, 33065-3939
ARW Supplier News, 534
Counterline, 534
Obsolete & Excess Inventory Program, 56
Wholesaler News, 156
Air Daily Ltd.
4418 MacArthur Blvd. NW, Ste. 202, Washington, DC, 20007-2563
AirDaily, 371
Air Quality Week, 371
Air Incident Research
PO Box 4745, East Lansing, MI, 48826-4745
Confidential Air Letter, 28
Select Hostile Actions Against Civil Aviation, 790
Al-Anon Family Group Headquarters, Inc.
1600 Corporate Landing Pkwy., Virginia Beach, VA, 23456
Al-Anon in Institutions, 1,114
Al-Anon Speaks Out, 1,114
Alateen Talk, 1,114
Archives Sharing Bulletin, 498
Inside Al-Anon, 514
Alabama Public Library Service
6030 Monticello Dr., Montgomery, AL, 36130-0001
Cottonball, 796
What's Line, 813
Alan B. Lancz & Assocs., Inc.
2400 N Reynolds Rd, Toledo, OH, 43615-2818
Lancz Letter, 674
Sound Investing Basics, 686
Alberta Environmental Protection
Resource Planning Branch, 9820 106th St., 9th Fl., Edmonton, AB, T5K 2J5, Canada
LRIS Newsletter, 386
Planning in Progress, 391
Steward, The, 394
Alberta Genealogical Society
Box 12015, Edmonton, AB, T5J 3L2, Canada
Alberta Genealogical Society Newsletter, 446
Clandigger, 450
Alberta Teachers' Association
11010-142 St., Edmonton, AB, T5N 2R1, Canada
Alberta Counselletter, 299
Alberta Teachers' Association-Learning Resources Council-Newsletter, 299
Council on School Administration Newsletter, 306
Courier Alberta Teachers' Association, Modern and Classical Languages Council, Newsletter, 306
FACTA Newsletter, 309
Home Ec News, 558
News & Notes, 322
Voices, 335
Albuquerque Archaeological Society
PO Box 4029, Albuquerque, NM, 87196-4029
Albuquerque Archaeological Society-Newsletter, 57
Pottery Southwest, 58
Alert Publications Inc.
401 W Fullerton Pky Apt 1403, Chicago, IL, 60614-2805
Business Information Alert:Sources,Strategies & Signposts for Information Professionals, 794
Legal Information Alert: What's New in Legal Publications, 750
Research Advisor : Information Solutions for Today's Legal Professionals, 773
Alexander Hamilton Inst.
70 Hilltop Rd, Ramsey, NJ, 07446-1119
Manager's Legal Bulletin, 841
Personnel Legal Alert, 148
Alexander Research & Communications, Inc.
215 Park Ave S., Ste. 1301, New York, NY, 10003-1603
Customer Communicator, The, 836
Customer Service Newsletter, 135
Distribution Center Management, 136
Distributor's & Wholesaler's Advisor, The, 136
Downtown Idea Exchange, 1,020
Downtown Promotion Reporter, 13
Electric Vehicle Progress, 72
Executive Report on Customer Satisfaction, 137
Real Estate Insider, 1,037
Sales Rep's Advisor, The, 1,088
Warehouse Management and Control Systems, 156
Ambit International, Inc.
665 3rd St Ste 508, San Francisco, CA, 94107-1923
Ambit International, 212
Tag's Channel Compass, 240
AmeriTrust Co.
900 Euclid Ave, Cleveland, OH, 44115-1461
Bank Notes, 577
Mid American Outlook, 145
American Academy of Actuaries
1100 17th St. NW, 7th Fl., Washington, DC, 20036
Actuarial Update, 617
Enrolled Actuaries Report, 620
American Academy of Esthetic Dentistry
500 N. Michigan Ave., Ste 1920, Chicago, IL, 60611-3703
American Academy of Esthetic Dentistry Newsletter, 267
Esthetics, 269
American Accounting Assn
5717 Bessie Dr, Sarasota, FL, 34233-2399
Accounting Education News, 1
American Accounting Assn. Newsletter, 2
American Advertising Federation
1101 Vermont Ave NW Ste 500, Washington, DC, 20005-3521
Communicator, 12
Government Report, 15
American Alliance for Health, Physical Education, Recreation
1900 Association Dr, Reston, VA, 22091-1599
Spotlight on Dance, 331
Update, 335

American Anthropological Assn.
4350 N. Fairfax Drive, Suite 640, Arlington, VA, 22203-1621
Anthropology Newsletter, 51
Communicator, 51
American Apparel Manufacturers Assn.
2500 Wilson Blvd Ste 301, Arlington, VA, 22201-3834
AAMA Washington Newsletter, 712
American Apparel Manufacturers Association Newsletter, 54
Apparel Research Notes, 54
American Arbitration Assn.
140 W. 51 St., New York, NY, 10020-1203
Arbitration in the Schools, 698
Claims Forum, 724
Labor Arbitration in Government, 708
Lawyers' Arbitration Letter, 750
New York No-Fault Arbitration Reports, 623
Punch List, 249
Study Time, 705
Summary of Labor Arbitration Awards, 705
American Assn. for the Advancement of Science
1333 H St. NW, Washington, DC, 20005-4707
Professional Ethics Report, 1,099
Report on Science and Human Rights, 637
Science Education News, 1,100
American Assn. for Career Education
2900 Amby Pl, Hermosa Beach, CA, 90254-2216
AACE Bonus Briefs, 297
AACE Careers Update, 297
American Assn. for Clinical Chemistry, Inc.
2101 L St., NW, Ste. 202, Washington, DC, 20037-1526
Endocrinology and Metabolism, 164
Therapeutic Drug Monitoring & Toxicology, 288
American Assn. of Engineering Societies
1111 19th St. NW, Ste. 608, Washington, DC, 20036-3603
Engineers, 360
Engineers-Quarterly bulletin, 360
American Assn. of State Highway Transportation Officials
444 N Capitol St NW Ste 249, Washington, DC, 20001-1512
Environmental Bulletin, 379
Planning Bulletin, 1,179
American Association of Suicidology
2459 S Ash St, Denver, CO, 80222-6006
Newslink, 1,016
Surviving Suicide, 1,018
American Association of Variable Star Observers
25 Birch St, Cambridge, MA, 02138-1205
AAVSO Bulletin, 68
AAVSO Circular, 68
Solar Bulletin, 69
American Banker Newsletters
One State Plaza, New York, NY, 10004-1505
American Banker's Washington Watch, 80
Asset Sales Report, 80
Banking Attorney, 82
California Public Finance, 84
Credit Union Accountant, 86
High Yield Report, 668
Insurance Accountant, 620
Insurance Regulator, 621
International Banking Regulator, 92
LDC Debt Report, 93
Mortgage Marketplace, 95
NCUA Watch, 95
Private Placement Reporter, 683
Regulatory Compliance Watch, 97
American Bankers Association
1120 Connecticut Ave NW, Washington, DC, 20036-3902
ABA Bank Security & Fraud Prevention, 79
ABA Trust Letter, 79
American Institute of Banking Leaders Letter, 80
Bank Operations Bulletin, 82
Bank Personnel News, 82
Retail Banking Digest, 98
American Bar Association
740 15th St. NW, Washington, DC, 20005-1009
ABA Washington Letter, 712
ABA Washington Summary, 1,194
Dispute Resolution, 732
Environmental Law, 735
International Law News, 746
Section of Taxation Newsletter, 1,151
State Legislative Report, 777
American Bar Association
750 N. Lake Shore Dr., Chicago, IL, 60611-4497
Administrative Law News, 713
Bulletin of Law Science and Technology, 720
Communications Lawyer, 726
Compleat Lawyer, 726
Entertainment and Sports Lawyer, 734
LRE Report, 315
Labor and Employment Law News, 748
Lawyer Referral Network, 750
Litigation News, 752
PTC Newsletter, 951
Passport To Legal Understanding, 325
Preview of U.S. Supreme Court Cases, 770
Public Contract Law News, 771
Urban, State & Local Law News, 493
American Boat and Yacht Council
3069 Solomons Island Rd, Edgewater, MD, 21037-1416
ABYC News, 112
Standards & Recommended Practices for Small Craft, 114
American Bus Assn.
1100 New York Ave. NW, Suite 1050, Washington, DC, 20005-3934
ABA Regulatory Digest, 1,176
Scan, 1,180
American Chemical Society
1155 16th St. NW, Washington, DC, 20036-4899
Chemical Bond, 163
Del-Chem Bulletin, 164
Minnesota Chemist, 165

MULTI-PUBLISHER INDEX

American Civil Liberties Union - National Prison Project
American Traffic Safety Services Assn.

Government Bus. Worldwide Rpts.
Huttlinger's Energy Reports

MULTI-PUBLISHER INDEX

Intl. Events Group
215 W. Institute Pl., Ste. 303, Chicago, IL, 60610-3125
JEG Sponsorship Report, 16
Special Events Report, 22

Intl. Executive Reports
717 D St. NW, Ste. 300, Washington, DC, 20004-2807
East Asian Business Intelligence, 645
Middle East Business Intelligence, 145

International Features, Inc.
8 South J St., Ste. 3, Box 1349, Lake Worth, FL, 33460-3742
Bates International Trade Update, 641
Publicity & Marketing Ideas, 21
Shoestring Traveler, The, 1,188

International Federation of Accountants (IFAC)
114 West 47th St., Ste. 2410, New York, NY, 10036-1510
Guidelines on Auditing, Education, Ethics, & Management Accounting, 5
International Federation of Accountants-Newsletter, 6

International Foundation of Employee Benefit Plans
18700 W Bluemound Rd #69, P O Box 69, Brookfield, WI, 53008-0069
Employee Benefits Basics, 609
Employee Benefits Digest, 609
Employee Benefits Practices, 610
Legal-Legislative Reporter, 750

International Health Awareness Ctr.
350 E Michigan Ave Ste 301, Kalamazoo, MI, 49007-3854
Hope Health Letter, 513
Looking Forward, 516

International Insight, Inc.
1200 18th St NW Ste 305, Washington, DC, 20036-2506
Executive International Insight, 630
Middle East Insight, 634

Intl. Institute of Municipal Clerks
1206 N San Dimas Canyon Rd., San Dimas, CA, 91773-1223
International Institute of Municipal Clerks Directory, 487
News Digest, 489

International Risk Management Institute
12222 Merit Dr Ste 1660, Dallas, TX, 75251-3207
Commercial Liability Insurance- Executive Briefings, 619
Construction Risk Management, 619
Professional Liability Insurance, 623
Risk Report, 624

International Sign Association
801 N Fairfax St Ste 205, Alexandria, VA, 22314-1757
Perspectives, 339
Signals, 340

International Society for Individual Liberty
1800 Market St, San Francisco, CA, 94102-6227
Freedom Network News, 990
World Freedom Bulletin, 176

International Society for Technology in Education
1787 Agate St, Eugene, OR, 97403-1923
ISTE Update, 312
Microsoft Works in Education, 230

International Trademark Association
1133 Avenue of the Americas, New York, NY, 10036-6710
Remarks: Trademark News for Business, 952
Trademark Checklist, 952

International Union of Petroleum & Industrial Workers
8131 E. Rosecrans Ave., Paramount, CA, 90723-2798
IUPIWI - Views, 708
International Union of Petroleum Workers Views, 708

International University, The
1301 S Noland Rd, Independence, MO, 64055-1390
International University Collegiate Sports Report, 1,132
International University Newsletter, 202

International Women's Tribune Centre
777 United Nations Plaza, New York, NY, 10017-3551
Tribuna, 1,212
Tribune, 1,212

Interreligious Foundation for Community Organization
402 W. 145th St., New York, NY, 10031-5202
IFCO News, 1,021
IFCO Newsletter, 1,118

Intertec Publishing Corporation
9800 Metcalf Ave., PO Box 12901, Overland Park, KS, 66212-2215
Electrical Marketing Newsletter, 338
Postal Watch, 972

Interwood Publications
3 Interwood Pl., Box 20241, Cincinnati, OH, 45220-1821
Health Labor Relations Reports, 611
Mental Health Law News, 518

InvesTech Research
2472 Birch Glen Rd, Whitefish, MT, 59937-3349
InvesTech Market Analyst, 671
InvesTech Mutual Fund Advisor, 671

Investment Information Services, Inc.
680 North Lake Shore Drive, Ste. #2038, Chicago, IL, 60611-4402
Investment Horizons, 671
Mutual Fund Letter, 678

Investment Rarities, Inc.
7850 Metro Pky Ste 106, Minneapolis, MN, 55425-1521
Currencies & Credit Markets, 135
Jim Cook's Market Update & Other Essays, 673

Investment Research Institute, Inc.
1259 Kemper Meadows Dr. #100, Cincinnati, OH, 45240
Daily Trader, 661
Fund Profit Alert, 665
Option Advisor, The, 681

Investor Responsibility Research Ctr.
1350 Connecticut Ave. N.W., Suite 700, Washington, DC, 20036-1701
Corporate Governance Bulletin, 134
News for Investors, 680
South Africa Review Service Reporter, 686

Investor's Hotline, Inc.
10616 Beaver Dam Rd., Hunt Valley, MD, 21030-2232
Investor's Hotline, 672
ValuTalk, 690

Iowa Agricultural Statistics
833 Federal Bldg., 210 Walnut St., Des Moines, IA, 50309-2195
Agri-News, 36

Iowa Crop Report, 42
Iowa Crops & Weather, 42
Iowa Livestock Report, 828

Issue Action Pubs. Inc.
207 Loudoun St. SE, Leesburg, VA, 22075-3115
Corporate Public Issues and Their Management, 134
International Barometer, 142

J

J.B. Speed Art Museum
PO Box 2600, Louisville, KY, 40201-2600
Insight, 904
J.B. Speed Art Museum Bulletin, 905

J.D. Power & Assocs.
30401 Agoura Rd., Agoura Hills, CA, 91301-2084
Magazine, 74
Power Report on Automotive Marketing, 75

JFO Enterprises
PO Box 818, Palm Springs, CA, 92263-0818
MUSENET, 197
Voice in the Wilderness, 262

J.J. Keller & Assoc., Inc.
PO Box 368, Neenah, WI, 54957-0368
Alcohol & Drugs: Dot Compliance Manual, 1,192
Compliance Audits: OSHA, EPA, DOT Manual, 1,079
Environmental Regulatory Advisor, 164
Fleet Safety Compliance Manual, 1,192
Hazardous Regulation Guide, 164
Hazardous Waste Guide, 164
Hazardous Waste Regulatory Guide, 165
Interstate Commerce Guide, 1,192
Keller Regulatory Update, 1,081
Keller's Industrial Safety Report, 1,081
Keller's OSHA Safety Training Newsletter, 1,081
Motor Carrier Safety Report, 1,082
OSHA Compliance Manual, 1,082
OSHA Regulations Part 1910 Guide, 1,082
Right-to-Know Compliance Manual, 1,083
Trucking Permit Guide, 1,193
Trucking Permit & Tax Bulletin, 1,193
Trucking Safety Guide, 1,193
Vehicle Sizes & Weights Manual, 1,194

JK Publishing Inc.
PO Box 71020, Milwaukee, WI, 53211-7120
Business Publisher, 854
Legal Publisher, The, 751

J.R. O'Dwyer Company, Inc.
271 Madison Ave Ste 600, New York, NY, 10016-1001
Jack O'Dwyer's Newsletter, 858
O'Dwyer PR Marketplace, 347
O'Dwyer's Washington Report, 19

J.R. Publishing, Inc.
PO Box 6654, Mc Lean, VA, 22106-6654
Federal & State Insurance Week, 620
Liability Week, 621

Jacobsen Publishing Co.
300 W Adams St Ste 835, Chicago, IL, 60606-5109
Feed Bulletin, 418
Hide and Leather Bulletin, 791

James Whitaker & Associates
1 Waters Park Dr., Ste. 104, San Mateo, CA, 94403-1137
Smart's California Worker's Comp Bulletin, 624
Smart's Insurance Bulletin, 624
Smart's National Comp & Health Bulletin, 624

Jamestown Area Labor Management Committee
PO Box 819, Jamestown, NY, 14702-0819
HR Fact Finder, 611
Managing Diversity, 612

Japan Economic Institute of America
1000 Connecticut Ave., N.W., Washington, DC, 20036-5347
JEI Report, 649
Japan Economic Survey, 633
Japan-U.S. Business Report, 649

Japan External Trade Organization
1221 Ave. of the Americas, New York, NY, 10020-1001
China Newsletter, 628
Inside/Outside Japan, 647

Jay Mitchell Associates
Rte. 2, Box 1285, Fairfield, IA, 52556-1285
Small Market Radio Newsletter, 125
Sound Thinking, 845

Jefferson County Public Schools
PO Box 34020, Louisville, KY, 40232-4020
Monday Memo, 318
Pinnacle, 326

Jefferson Davis State Junior College
Brewton, AL, 36426
Beauvoir, 195
Tarter, 195

Jefferson State Junior College
2601 Carson Rd, Birmingham, AL, 35215-3007
Jefferson State News, 195
Pioneer, 195

Jewish Labor Committee
25 E. 21st St., 2nd Fl., New York, NY, 10010-6297
Alumni Newsletter, 299
Jewish Labor Committee Review, 701

Jewish Telegraphic Agency, Inc.
330 7th Ave., 11th Fl., New York, NY, 10001-5010
Daily News Bulletin, 1,068
JTA Community News Reporter, 1,069
JTA Weekly News Digest, 633

Jewish War Veterans of the U.S.
1811 R St NW, Washington, DC, 20009-1603
J.W.V.A. Bulletin, 1,199
Routes to Roots, 898

Jews for Jesus
PO Box 424885, San Francisco, CA, 94142-4885
Jews for Jesus Newsletter, 1,064
Mishpochah Message, 1,069

Joe Williams Communications
PO Box 924, Bartlesville, OK, 74005-0924
Community Relations Report, 835
Williams Report, 847

John C. Calhoun State Community College
PO Box 2216, Decatur, AL, 35602-2216
Graffiti, 195
Talon, 195

John Skipper
707 6th St. SE, Mason City, IA, 50401-4155
Batter Up!, 101
Write Direction, 826

John W. Bartlett
PO Box 465, Aurora, IL, 60507-0465
Bartlett Letters, 655
Mid-America Senior Tennis, 1,170

John Wiley & Sons, Inc.
605 Third Avenue, New York, NY, 10158-0012
Banks in Insurance Report, 618
Cell & Tissue Culture: Laboratory Procedures, 107
ECCOMAS Newsletter, 1,096
EEO Review, 609
Environmental Manager, 380
Fun-Raising Regulation Report, 968
IACM Bulletin, 1,097
Letters of Credit Report, 93
Librarian's Newsletter, 801
Management Report for Nonunion Organizations, 703
Nonprofit Counsel, 969
Spang Robinson Report on Artificial Intelligence, 239
Spang Robinson Report on Supercomputing & Parallel Processing, 239
Wiley Librarians' Newsletter, The, 120
Wiley Static SIMS Library, The, 167

Johns Hopkins Univ.
Milton S. Eisenhower Library, Baltimore, MD, 21218
Ex Libris, 797
Level Talk, 801

Johns Hopkins University Press
2715 N Charles St, Baltimore, MD, 21218-4363
Decodings, 820
Imagine, 201

Johnson & Higgins
125 Broad St, New York, NY, 10004-2424
Benenet Bulletin, 577
J & H Infaline, 587

Joint Council of Allergy & Immunology
PO Box 4620, Arlington Heights, IL, 60006-4620
President's Newsletter, 885
Reports, 886

Jones Publishing Inc.
N7450 Aanstad Rd., PO Box 5000, Iola, WI, 54945-5000
Child Welfare Report (CWR), 1,115
Job Training and Placement Report, 278

Jossey-Bass Publishers, Inc.
350 Sansome St., Fifth Fl., San Francisco, CA, 94104-1310
Assessment Update, 1,090
Healthy Companies: Leadership for the New Workplace, 140

Julian Associates
6831 Spencer Hwy. Suite 203, Pasadena, TX, 77505-1772
Night Owl's Newsletter, 983
Our Write Mind, 983

Jupiter Communications
627 Broadway, 2nd Fl., New York, NY, 10012-2612
Consumer Information - Appliances, 1,158
Digital Kids Report, The, 220
Interactive Content, 226
Online Marketplace, 233

Justex Systems
PO Box 6224, Huntsville, TX, 77342-6224
Fire Service Labor Monthly, 421
Police Labor Monthly, 789

K

KCI Communications, Inc.
1101 King St., Ste. 400, Alexandria, VA, 22314-2980
Big Picture, The, 655
Personal Finance, 682

K.D. Information Notes, Inc.
PO Box 14430, Minneapolis, MN, 55414-0430
Hard Hat Times, 857
K.D. Investment Notes, 673

Kagan World Media Inc.
126 Clock Tower Pl., Carmel, CA, 93923-8734
Euro Cable TV Programming, 1,167
Euromedia Acquisitions & Finance, 137
Euromedia Regulation, 856
European Cable/Pay TV, 1,167
European Home Video, 1,167
European Radio, 124
European TV Sports, 1,167
European Television, 1,167
International Cellular, 1,160
International Co-Productions, 1,168

Kansas City Life Insurance Co.
PO Box 419139, Kansas City, MO, 64141-6139
Lifetime, 588
Tempo, 600

Kelly Communications
Rr 13 Box 28, Charlottesville, VA, 22901-7927
HealthAction, 511
HealthSense, 511
Prime of Life, 1,108

Kennedy Publications
Templeton Rd., Fitzwilliam, NH, 03447
Consultants News, 835
Executive Recruiter News, 610

Kent Feeds, Inc.
1600 Oregon St, Muscatine, IA, 52761-1404
Beef Producer News, 827
Dairy Producer News, 264

MULTI-PUBLISHER INDEX

Moody's Investors Service, Inc.
Natl. Council of Teachers of English

Q

QEC & S
4057 North Drake, Chicago, IL, 60618-2219
Food, the Newsletter!, 429
Quick, Easy, Cheap and Simple..the Newsletter, 558
QW Communications, Co.
PO Box 6591, Concord, NH, 03303-6591
Disaster Trends Update, 856
Remote Sensing Update, 861
Space Trends Update, 33
Queen's Medical Center
1301 Punchbowl St., Honolulu, Oahu, HI, 96813-2499
Queen's Connection, 571
Queen's Vision, 571
Quest Publishing Co.
1351 Titan Way, Brea, CA, 92621-3787
Biomedical Safety & Standards, 868
Biomedical Technology Information Service, 868
Clinical Lab Letter, 871
Nutrition & the M.D., 934
Radiology & Imaging Letter, 885
Quinlan Publishing
23 Drydock Ave, Boston, MA, 02210-2387
Arrest Law Bulletin, 716
Building Permits Law Bulletin, 244
Commish, 420
Employee Terminations Law Bulletin, 699
Firehouse Lawyer Monthly, 738
Funding Law Enforcement Hotline, 786
Funding Private Schools, 1,091
Grants for Cities and Towns Biweekly Hotline, 1,021
Grants for School Districts Biweekly Hotline, 1,091
Grants for School Districts Monthly Hotline, 311
Hiring Compliance Update, 700
Labor Contract Law Bulletin, 701
Landlord Tenant Law Bulletin, 1,035
Municipal Law Bulletin, 758
Narcotics Law Bulletin, 759
National Bulletin on Police Misconduct, 788
National Report on Employee Termination Bulletin, 760
Police Department Disciplinary Bulletin, 789
Police Officer Grievances Bulletin, 789
Public Employee Dismissals Bulletin, 1,023
School Law Bulletin, 329
Search & Seizure Bulletin, 774
Telecommunications Security, 1,105
Unfair Labor Practices Law Bulletin, 705
Workers' Compensation Biweekly Bulletin, 783
Workers' Compensation Cost Control, 783
Worker's Compensation Law Bulletin, 783
Zoning Bulletin, 250
Quoin Publishing
800 W Huron St Ste 3n, Chicago, IL, 60622-5973
Converting Business Register, 945
Print Business Register, 1,006

R

RAM Research Corporation
Box 1700, College Estates, Frederick, MD, 21702-0700
Bankcard Update, 257
Cardtrak, 257
R. C. Publications
10221 North 32nd Street, Suite J-1, Phoenix, AZ, 85028-3849
Rate Controls, 571
Universal Healthcare Almanac, 573
RESNA Technical Assistance Project
1700 N. Moore St., Ste. 1540, Arlington, VA, 22209
A.T. Quarterly, 126
RESNA News, 526
RJM Communications
PO Box 6645, Lubbock, TX, 79493-6645
Land Rig Newsletter, The, 959
Well Service Market Report, 966
RKS Marketing
Box 7985, Northridge, CA, 91327-7985
Source I, 1,189
Source II, 1,189
Travel Marketing and Agency Management Guidelines, 1,190
R.S. Means Co., Inc.
100 Construction Plaza, Kingston, MA, 02364-0100
Change Notice, The, 245
Construction Market Intelligence: Russia, 246
RTS
PO Box 93897, Las Vegas, NV, 89193-3897
RTS Music Gazette, 916
RTS Video Gazette, 1,169
R.W. Livingston, Publishing
PO Box 60008, North Charleston, SC, 29419-0008
Sports Weekly Newsletter-Baseball, 101
Sports Weekly Newsletter-Basketball, 1,136
Sports Weekly Newsletter-Football, 434
R. W. Mansfield Co
2973 John F. Kennedy Blvd., Jersey City, NJ, 07306-3884
Mansfield Stock Chart Service, 675
Stock Chart Service, 687
RX-Data-Pac Service
PO Box 42020, Cincinnati, OH, 45242-0020
Drug & Device Recall Bulletin, 282
Hospital Pharmacy Director's Monthly Management Series, 284
Instant Up-Date, 284
Pharmacy Health-Line, 287
Vital Signs Pharmacy-Nursing Newsletter, 288
Rachel P.R. Services
1650 S. Pacific Coast Hwy., Suite #200-C, Redondo Beach, CA, 90277
PR Marcom Jobs East, 347
PR Marcom Jobs Mid-America, 347
PR Marcom Jobs West-No. Calif./Pacific Nothwest, 347
PR Marcom Jobs West-So. Calif., 347

Random Lengths Publications, Inc.
PO Box 867, Eugene, OR, 97440-0867
Random Lengths Export Report, 831
Random Lengths Locator, 831
Random Lengths Market Report, 831
Random Lengths Midweek Market Report, 831
Random Lengths Yardstick, 831
Ransom & Benjamin Publishers LLC
P.O. Box 606, Old Greenwich, CT, 06870-0417
Job Safety Consultant, 1,081
Product: H R Manager's Legal Reporter, 843
Rare-Earth Information Ctr.
254 Spedding Hall, AMES LAboratory ISU, Ames, IA, 50011-3020
RIC Insight, 1,099
RIC News, 1,100
Readmore
22 Cortlandt St., New York, NY, 10007-3194
Readmore Newsletter, 808
Readmore Reporter, 808
Reconnaissance Holographics Ltd.
825 East Tufts Avenue, Cherry Hills, CO, 80110
Authentication News, 945
Holography News, 1,005
Reinhardt College
7300 Reinhardt College Pkwy., Waleska, GA, 30183-0128
On Campus, 199
Reinhardt Report, 188
Remy Publishing Co.
350 W Hubbard St # 440, Chicago, IL, 60610-4011
Human Resource Management News, 611
Investor Relations Newsletter, 93
Passport Newsletter, 1,187
Recruiting Trends, 348
What's Ahead in Human Resources, 616
Report Communications
9595 Whitley Dr Ste 100, Indianapolis, IN, 46240-1308
Carlson Report for Shopping Center Management, 1,032
JonesReport, 16
SalesCoach, 273
Report Publications, Inc.
PO Box 12368, Austin, TX, 78711-2368
Austin Insurance Report, 618
Austin Report, 986
Texas Finance Report, 99
Texas Pollution Report, 395
Texas Transportation, 1,180
Texas Water Report, 1,204
Republican Natl. Committee
Publications, 310 First St SE, Washington, DC, 20003-1801
Commonsense, 988
Republican Quotes, 998
Republican Wire, 998
Research Done Write!
8726 South Sepulveda Blvd., #B261-OX, Los Angeles, CA, 90045-4082
Bootstrappin' Entrepreneur, 128
Bootstrappin' Entrepreneur Bulletin, 128
Research Institute of America
90 5th Avenue, New York, NY, 10011-7629
All States Tax Guide, 1,139
American Federal Tax Reports, 1,139
Annotated Tax Forms, 1,139
Capital Adjustments, 1,141
Charitable Giving & Solicitation, 1,141
Communications, 855
Corporate Acquisitions, Mergers & Divestiture's, 660
Corporation Forms, 729
Cumulative Changes, 1,142
Depreciation & Capital Planning, 87
Divorce Taxation, 1,142
Doctor's Tax Report, 1,142
EEO Compliance, 609
Equal Employment Opportunity Compliance, 610
Excise Taxes, 1,143
Executives Tax Report, 1,143
Federal Estate & Gift Taxes, 1,143
Federal Excise Tax, 1,143
Federal Income Tax Regulations, 1,144
Federal Revenue Forms, 1,144
Federal Tax Expeditor, 1,144
Federal Tax Guide, 1,144
Federal Taxes, 1,145
Federal Taxes Citator, 1,145
Foreign Investment in Canada, 90
Guide to Employment Law and Regulation, 611
Human Resources Policies & Practices, 612
IRA Compliance Manual, 612
Income Taxation of Natural Resources, 1,146
Internal Memoranda of the IRS, 1,147
Lawyer's Weekly Report, 1,147
Managing Employee Benefits, 612
Modern Job Safety & Health, 1,082
Over-55 Financial Management Letter, 681
P-H Dentist's Tax Report, 1,149
P-H Doctor's Tax Report, 1,149
P-H Federal Tax Course, 1,149
P-H Federal Taxes, 1,150
Pension and Profit Sharing, 614
Phorum, 594
Plan Administrators Compliance Manual, 710
Practicing Attorney's Letter, 770
Private Letter Rulings, 1,150
Profit-Sharing and Pension Forms, 614
Property Taxes, 1,150
Pubs. of the IRS, 1,150
Puerto Rico Taxes, 1,151
Real Estate Investment Ideas, 1,037
SEC Compliance, 98
Sales Taxes, 1,151
Securities Regulations, 845
State Income Taxes, 1,152
State Inheritance Taxes, 1,152
State and Local Taxes, 1,152

Strategy & Management, 615
Tax Ideas, 1,153
Tax Planning, 1,154
Tax Planning Ideas, 1,154
Tax Treaties, 1,155
Taxation of Corporate Liquidations, 1,155
U.S. Taxation of Intl. Operations, 1,156
Wills-Estate Planning Forms, 782
Wills Estates and Trusts, 783
Research Institute of America
117 E Stevens Ave, Valhalla, NY, 10595-1264
Employee Benefits Alert, 609
Employment Alert, 343
Estate & Financial Planners Alert, 88
Estate Planners Alert, 1,143
Estate Planning, 735
Executive Compensation, 1,143
Executive Compensation Alert, 1,143
Farmers Federal Tax Alert, 1,143
Federal Tax Coordinator 2d, 1,144
Florida Taxation, 1,145
Individual Tax Return Guide, 1,146
International Tax Planners Alert, 1,147
Lawyers Tax Alert, 750
RIA Tax Guide Developments, 1,151
RIA's Special Studies, 1,151
Real Estate Coordinator, 1,037
Sales Professional, 1,088
Small Business Tax Planner, 1,151
Social Security Alert, 1,198
Social Security Coordinator, 1,198
State Tax Action Coodinator, 1,152
Tax Action Coordinator, 1,152
Tax Alert for Management, 1,152
Tax Coordinator, 1,153
Tax-Exempt Organizations, 1,153
Tax Preparers Liability Service, 1,154
Weekly Alert, 1,156
Research Institute of America
1340 Braddock Pl., Ste. 400, Alexandria, VA, 22314-1651
Drugs in the Workplace, 283
Employee Relations in Action, 707
Inside Labor Relations, 708
Labor Trends, 709
Management Policies & Personnel Law, 841
Substance Abuse Report, 529
Tax Watch, 1,155
Research Press Inc.
4500 W 72nd Ter, Prairie Village, KS, 66208-2824
Financial News Online, 664
Jacobs Report on Asset Protection Strategies, 673
Retirement & Tax Planning with 1-2-3, 7
Reserve Research Ltd.
Box 4135, Stn. A, Portland, ME, 04101-0335
Powell Gold Industry Guide and International Mining Analyst, 901
Powell Monetary Analyst, 682
Resource Central
6339 W. 110th St. #11250, Overland Park, KS, 66211-1509
A2-Central, 211
Script-Central, 237
Studio City for the IIGS, 239
TimeOut-Central, 241
Resource Recycling, Inc.
PO Box 10540, Portland, OR, 97210-0540
Bottle/Can Recycling Update, 373
Plastics Recycling Update, 391
Resources For Educators
1717 Commonwealth Drive, Front Royal, VA, 22630
Home & School Connection, 312
Kindergarten Connection, 315
Resources Publ. Co.
1010 Vermont Ave NW Ste 708, Washington, DC, 20005-4995
Federal Parks and Recreation, 950
Public Lands News, 1,024
Retail Reporting Corp.
302 5th Ave Fl 11, New York, NY, 10001-3604
Costume Jewelry Review, 693
Fashion Jewelry Review, 693
Men's Art Service, 19
Retail News Fashion Merchandising Report, 55
Store Planning Service, 273
Rice Journal Enterprises, Inc.
Box 14260, Ben Franklin Sta., Washington, DC, 20044-4260
Rice Price Advisory, 45
Washington Aquafarm Letter, 47
Risk Communications
33 Lindall St., Laguna Niguel, CA, 92677-4738
Auto Insurance Report, 618
Property Insurance Report, 771
Risk Management Society Publishing, Inc.
655 Third Ave., 2nd Floor, New York, NY, 10017
Governmental Risk Mgmt. Manual, 620
RIMScope, 623
Roanoke Valley Chamber of Commerce
212 S. Jefferson, Roanoke, VA, 24011
Roanoke Valley Chamber of Commerce-Business & Professional Directory, 150
Valley Commerce, 162
Robert L. Siegel & Associates, Inc.
26 Trianon Drive, Kohner, LA, 70065
RLS Home Marketing Letter, 1,037
Robert L. Siegel Letter, 150
Robert Miko
PO Box 1312, New York, NY, 10018-0727
Communicator's Notebook, 855
Pacific Dialogue, 860
Robert Stanger & Co.
1129 Broad St., Box 7490, Shrewsbury, NJ, 07702-4314
Stanger Report: A Guide to Partnership Investing, The, 687
Stanger Review: Partnership Sales, 687
Robin & Russ Handweavers
533 N Adams St, McMinnville, OR, 97128-5513
Draft & Design, 256

Shaklee Corp.
444 Market St, San Francisco, CA, 94111-5378
Shaklee Spirit, 598
Shaklee Survey, 598
Shannon Publications, Inc.
9441 L.B.J. Fwy, Ste. #510 Box #2, Dallas, TX, 75243-4541
Medicare Advisor, 569
Medicare Manager, 880
Medicare Review, 880
Shelby Publishing Corp
155 Federal Street, Boston, MA, 02110-1727
Insurance Marketing Insider, 621
John Liner Letter, 621
Personal Lines Letter, 623
Policies in Review, 623
Shell Oil Co.
PO Box 60193, New Orleans, LA, 70160-0193
New Oiler, 591
Record, 596
Shell Record, 598
Shell Oil Company, Shell Chemical Co.
50 W 50th St, New York, NY, 10112-1507
Scan, 964
Shell Manhattan, 598
Shepard's/McGraw-Hill, Inc.
555 Middle Creek Pky, Colorado Springs, CO, 80921-3622
California Construction Law Reporter, 721
California Insurance Law & Regulation Report, 721
California Tort Reporter, 722
California Water Law & Policy Reporter, 722
Construction Litigation Reporter, 728
Eldercare, 1,106
Environmental Liability Enforcement & Penalties Report, 735
Federal Litigator, 737
Insurance Litigation Reporter, 745
Lawyer's PC, 750
Medical Liability Reporter, 755
New Jersey Insurance Law and Regulation Reporter, 761
Perfect Lawyer, 769
Probate Practice Reporter, 770
Professional Liability Reporter, 771
Shepard's Expert & Scientific Evidence Quarterly, 775
Verdicts & Settlements, 781
Siefer Consultants, Inc.
525 Cayuga St., PO Box 1384, Storm Lake, IA, 50588
Community Bank President, The, 85
Consumer Lending News, 86
Cost Control News, 86
Cost Control Strategies for Health Care Providers, 86
Cost Controller, The, 135
Cross Sales Report, 87
Deposit Growth Strategies, 87
Fee Income Report, 89
Quality Customer Service, 97
Technology News and Trends, 99
The Silver Institute
1112 16th St NW Ste 240, Washington, DC, 20036-4823
Gold News/Nouvelles de l'Or, 891
Silver Institute Letter, 892
Simba Information, Inc.
213 Danbury Rd. PO Box 7430, Wilton, CT, 06897-7430
Book Publishing Report, 116
Computer Publishing & Advertising Report, 953
Cowles/SIMBA Media Daily, 953
Educational Marketer, 14
Electronic Education Report, 309
Electronic Information Report, 856
Electronic Marketplace Report, 1,158
Interactive Television Report, 1,168
Media and the Law, 124
Multimedia Business Report, 231
NewsInc., 924
Online Tactics, 233
SIMBA Report on Directory Publishing, 954
Telecommunications Advertising Report, 862
Yellow Pages & Directory Report, 1,165
Sixteenth Century Publishers
NMSU LB 115, Kirksville, MO, 63501
Editing History, 540
Scholars of Early Modern Studies, 548
Skin Cancer Foundation
245 Fifth Ave., Ste. 2402, New York, NY, 10016
Melanoma Letter, 880
Sun & Skin News, 529
Slavic Gospel Association
6151 Commonwealth Dr., Loves Park, IL, 61111
InSight, 1,074
Reflections, 1,065
Smithsonian Institution
900 Jefferson Dr., S.W., Washington, DC, 20560-0001
Cooper-Hewitt Newsletter, 903
Smithsonian Institution Research Reports, 1,100
Smithsonian Runner, 548
Smithsonian 'Traveler', 1,188
Societe Quebecoise de l'Autisme/Quebec Society for Autism
2300 Blvd. Rene Levesque Quest, Montreal, PQ, H3H 2R5, Canada
Express (l'Express), 1,014
Societe Quebecoise de l'Autisme, 1,018
Society of Actuaries/Casualty Acturial Society
475 N. Martingale Rd.,, Suite 800, Schaumburg, IL, 60173-2226
Actuary, 617
Future Actuary, The, 199
Society of American Archivists
600 S. Federal St., Ste. 504, Chicago, IL, 60605-1898
Archival Outlook, 536
Newsletter of the Congressional Archives Roundtable, 806
SAA Employment Bulletin, 548
Society of American Archivists
New York State Archives C.E.C., Empire State Plaza, Albany, NY, 12230-0001
Descriptive Notes, 796
Government Records News, 798

Society of Manufacturing Engineers
One SME Dr., Box 930, Dearborn, MI, 48121
SME News, 363
Vision, 851
Society of Toxicology of Canada
Box 517, Beaconsfield, PQ, H9W 5V1, Canada
Society of Toxicology of Canada Newsletter, 887
Society of Toxicology of Canada, Proceedings, 887
Soundview Publications
7100 Peachtree Dunwoody Rd., Suite #100, Atlanta, GA, 30328-4134
Eco-Profiteer, The, 662
Gold Stock Alert, 666
Insider's Alert, 670
Second Opinion, 528
Women's Health Letter, 1,213
South Carolina State Library
1500 Senate St. #11469, Columbia, SC, 29211-3815
News About Library Services for the Blind, 112
News for South Carolina Libraries, 806
Southam Business Communications, Inc.
1450 Don Mills Rd., Don Mills, ON, M3B 2X7, Canada
Canadian Occupational Health & Safety News, 1,079
Canadian Occupational Safety & Health Law Monthly Report, 1,079
Eco/Log Canadian Pollution Legislation, 733
Eco/Log Week, 378
Energy Pricing News, 353
Environmental Compliance Report, The, 379
Public Sector, 997
Southam Building Reports, 250
Southam Information & Technology Group
999 8th St. SW, #300, Calgary, AB, T2R 1N7, Canada
Energy Analects, 352
The Regulatory Times, 358
Southeast Asia Program- Cornell Univ.
640 Stewart Ave., Ithaca, NY, 14850
Cornell Modern Indonesia Project:, 629
Southeast Asia Program Series: Monographs, Translations, Bibliographies, 638
Translation Series, 638
The Southern Company
270 Peachtree St NW, Suite 2100, Atlanta, GA, 30303
Inside, 586
Southern Highlights, 599
Southern Forest Products Assn
PO Box 641700, Kenner, LA, 70064-1700
SF Newsletter, 831
Southern Pine Lumber Mill Activity Summary, 831
Southern Regional Education Bd
592 10th St NW, Atlanta, GA, 30318-5776
Issues in Higher Education, 314
Regional Spotlight, 327
Southern States Cooperative
PO Box 26234, Richmond, VA, 23260-6234
Pacesetter, 594
Southern Statesman, 599
Southwest Texas Methodist Hospital
7700 Floyd Curl Dr, San Antonio, TX, 78229-3902
Alpha, 561
Reflections, 596
Space Age Publishing Company
75-5751 Kuakini Hwy., Ste. 209, Kailua-Kona, HI, 96740-1705
Space Calendar, 33
Space Fax Daily, 33
Sparks Companies Inc.
6708 Whittier Ave, Mc Lean, VA, 22101-4529
Food and Drink Weekly, 428
Food & Fiber Letter, 40
SCI Policy Report, 684
Special Libraries Assn.
1700 18th St NW, Washington, DC, 20009-2508
Business & Finance Division-Bulletin, 794
Chapter News, 795
Food for Thought-SLA, 798
SpeciaList, 810
Spidell Publishing Inc.
1110 N Gilbert St, Anaheim, CA, 92801-1401
Spidell's California TAXFAX, 1,152
Spidell's California Taxletter, 1,152
Spiritual Studies Center
PO Box 1104, Rockville, MD, 20849-1104
Religion and Life Letters, 1,051
SSC Booknews, 120
Springer-Verlag Inc.
175 5th Ave., New York, NY, 10010-7858
Bibliography of Plant Protection, 121
Plant Cell Reports, 122
Urologe, 888
Sri Avrobindo Association
2288 Fulton St., Beverley, CA, 94704
Collaboration, 1,067
Nexus, 1,067
Staffing Industry Analysts
2235 Grant Rd # 3, Los Altos, CA, 94024-6954
Home Health Business Report, 513
Staffing Industry Report, 349
Stamats Communications, Inc.
427 6th Ave. SE, Cedar Rapids, IA, 52401-1931
Access, 298
Re: Quest, 327
Stamler Publishing Co.
178 Thimble Islands Rd., P.O. Box 3367, Branford, CT, 06405-1967
Highway & Vehicle Safety Report, 1,080
Marine Safety Report, 1,081
Standard Oil Co. of California
225 Bush St., San Francisco, CA, 94104-4207
Bulletin, 955
Standard Oil Co. of California, Bulletin, 599
Standard & Poor's Corp.
25 Broadway, New York, NY, 10004
American Stock Exchange Reports, 654
Blue List, 656
Called Bond Record, 657

Commercial Paper Ratings Guide, 659
Corporate Registered Bond Interest Record, 660
Corporation Records, 660
Corporation Records with Daily News Supplement, 660
Credit Review, 290
Dividend Record-Daily, 662
Dividend Record-Quarterly, 662
Industry Group Market Values, 669
Industry Surveys, 669
Nasdaq and Regiora Exchange Stock Reports, 679
New York Stock Exchange Reports, 680
Outlook, 96
S&P 500 Information Bulletin, 685
S&P MidCap 400 Information Bulletin, 685
Standard & Poor's CreditWeek International, 687
Standard & Poor's Emerging & Special Situations, 687
Standard & Poor's Insurance Ratings, 625
Standard & Poor's The Outlook, 687
Standard & Poor's Review of Securities & Commodities Regulation, 776
Standard & Poor's Semi-Weekly Called Bond Record, 99
Standard & Poor's Stock Guide, 687
Standard & Poor's Trendline Daily Action Stock Charts, 687
Statistical Service, 687
Stock Price & Ratio Indexes, 687
Trends & Projections, 296
Stardust Dance Productions
Church St., Box 157, Woodburne, NY, 12788
Leonard Moss, 266
Umbrella Singles Ltd., 1,191
Stark Research, Inc.
141 S Whitehall Ct # 591, Palatine, IL, 60067-5836
Norwood Index Report, 680
Stark Research CTA Report, 687
State Bar of Texas
PO Box 12487 Capitol Station, Austin, TX, 78711-2487
Environmental Law Journal, 735
Texas Lawyer's Weekly Letter, 779
State Farm Mutual Auto Insurance Co.
1500 W. Highway 36, Saint Paul, MN, 55161-0001
Bellringer, 577
Pine-Aire, 595
State Historical Society of Wisconsin
816 State St., Madison, WI, 53706-1488
Columns, 538
Wisconsin Preservation, 550
State Policy Research, Inc.
182 W. Royal Forest Blvd., Columbus, OH, 43214-2029
State Budget & Tax News, 493
State Policy Reports, 493
Statistical Indicator Assocs.
PO Box 187, North Egremont, MA, 01252-0187
Inside the Economy, 92
S.I. Reports, 98
Statistics Canada
Holland Ave/RH Coats, Holland Ave/Tunney's Pasture, Ottawa, ON, K1A O26, Canada
Capacity Utilization Rates in Canadian Manufacturing, 848
Coal and Coke Statistics, 899
Consumption of Containers and Other Packaging Supplies by the Manufacturing Industries, 848
Daily, The, 1,195
Factory Sales of Electric Storage Batteries, 338
Family Incomes, 291
Field Crop Reporting Series, 40
Fur Production, 437
Gypsum Products, 900
Infomat, 106
Logging, 830
Oils and Fats, 940
Other Converted Paper Products Industries Including Asphalt Roofing Industry, 946
Production & Disposition of Tobacco Products, 1,175
Production and Shipments of Steel Pipe, Tubings and Fittings, 892
Products Shipped by Canadian Manufacturers, 850
Restaurant, Caterer & Tavern Statistics, 1,076
Specified Domestic Electrical Appliances, 56
System of National Accounts, Financial Flow Accounts, 296
System of National Accounts-Financial Flow Accounts: Preliminary Data, 296
System of National Accounts, National Income and Expenditure Accounts, 296
Telephone Statistics, 1,163
Wholesale Trade, 273
Sterling Communications
1920 Ellesmere Road, Suite 104, Scarborough, ON, M1H 2WY, Canada
Fanfare, 453
Newsletter Trends, 954
Stevens Publishing Corp.
3630 J.H. Kultgen Frwy., Waco, TX, 76706
Environmental Protection News, 381
Hazmat News, 384
OSHA Week, 613
Occupational Health & Safety News, 249
Waste Management News, 1,204
Stoneridge Technical Services
PO Box 1891, Rockville, MD, 20849-1891
Multimedia Telecommunication News, 1,160
VoiceNews, 1,164
Story Time Stories that Rhyme
PO Box 416, Denver, CO, 80201-0416
Reading Programs with Stories that Educate, Inform, Entertain and Rhyme, 170
Stories that Rhyme, Every Time Kids Pages, 170
Story Rhyme Reproducible Newsletter, 331
Story Rhyme Word Mapping, 258
Story Time Stories That Rhyme, 170
Strafford Pubs., Inc.
590 Dutch Valley Rd., N.E., Postal Drawer 13729, Atlanta, GA, 30324-0729
Auditor-Trak, 654
CPA Managing Partner Report, 721

Town of Hempstead Office of Communication & Public Affairs
Univ. Corp. for Atmospheric Research

MULTI-PUBLISHER INDEX

Index to Publishers by State

- Lists publishers by state in alphabetical order. Includes address, title produced and page number.

Alabama

AGS Depository Hdqtrs.
Samford Univ. Lib. 800, Lakeshore Dr., Birmingham, AL, 35229-0001
Alabama Genealogical Society Newsletter, 446

Academy of Ambulatory Foot Surgery
PO Box 2730, Tuscaloosa, AL, 35403-2730
Academy of Ambulatory Foot Surgery, 865

Al Owen's Newsletter Digest
2201 Big Cove Rd SE, Huntsville, AL, 35801-1349
Al Owen's Newsletter Digest, 654

Alabama A & M Univ.
Publications, Normal, AL, 35762
SGA Newsletter, 195

Alabama Archaeological Society
Moundville Archaeological Park, Moundville, AL, 35474
Stones and Bones Newsletter, 58

Alabama Consortium of Legal Services Programs
500 Bell Bldg., 207 Montgomery St., Montgomery, AL, 36104-3304
Legal Services Bulletin, 751

Alabama Council American Institute of Architects
1521 Mulberry St, Montgomery, AL, 36106-1519
Eagle, 59

Alabama Development Office
State Capital 401 Adams Ave., Montgomery, AL, 36130-0001
Alabama Development News, 126

Alabama Power Co.
PO Box 2641, Birmingham, AL, 35291
Powergrams, 595

Alabama Prison Project
410 S Perry St, Montgomery, AL, 36104-4236
Alabama Prison Project Newsletter, 784

•Alabama Public Library Service
6030 Monticello Dr., Montgomery, AL, 36130-0001

Alabama State Dept. of Industrial Relations
3440 3rd Ave S, Birmingham, AL, 35222-1712
Labor Market News, Birmingham Area, 702

Alabama State Nurses Assn.
360 N Hull St, Montgomery, AL, 36104-3644
ASNA Reporter, 928

American College of Heraldry, Inc.
PO Box Cg, Tuscaloosa, AL, 35486-2870
Armiger's News, 447

American Fertility Society for Reproductive Medicine
1209 Montgomery Hwy., Birmingham, AL, 35216-2809
Fertility News, 874

Assn. of Administrative Law Judges
117 Gemini Cir # 407, Birmingham, AL, 35209-5840
AALJ Newsletter, 712

Auburn University
Ludwig von Mises Institute, Auburn, AL, 36849
Free Market, 292

Auburn University Alumni Assoc.
317 S. College St., Auburn, AL, 36849-5150
Plainsman, 194

Autrey Family Assn., AFA-199
Rt. I, Box 106-B, Thomasville, AL, 36784
Autrey, Autry, Autery Bulletin, 447

Business Council of Alabama
PO Box 76, Montgomery, AL, 36101-0076
Alabama Today, 127

Calhoun County Chamber of Commerce
PO Box 1087, Anniston, AL, 36202-1087
Chamber Forum, 158

Capstone Intl. Program Center
Univ. of Alabama, Box 870254, Tuscaloosa, AL, 35487
International Notes, 314

Center for Labor Education
Univ. Station, Univ. Of A, Birmingham, AL, 35294-0001
Clear Report, 699

•Chi Chapter, Phi Delta Chi Frat
School of Pharmacy, Auburn University, Auburn, AL, 36849

Craig Rhodes
133 Montclair Loop, Daphne, AL, 36526-8151
Rhodes Crossroads Newsletter, 465

Ductile Iron Pipe Research Assn.
245 Riverchase Pky E Ste O, Birmingham, AL, 35244-1856
Ductile Iron Pipe News, 891

EBSCO Subscription Services
PO Box 1431, Birmingham, AL, 35201-1431
At Your Service, 793

Factor Press
PO Box 8888, Mobile, AL, 36689
Celebrate the Self, 1,110

Falconer Facets
2431 Crestwood Dr SW, Huntsville, AL, 35805-3150
Falconer Facets, 453

•Federation of Southern Cooperatives
PO Box 95, Epes, AL, 35460-0095

Gadsden State Junior College
PO Box 227, Gadsden, AL, 35902-0227
Coosada, 195

Genealogical Researcher
c/o Lynda S. Eller, Box 249, Lanett, AL, 36863
Heard Heritage, 456

Gulfcoast Pulpwood Assn
PO Box 100, Forest Home, AL, 36030-0100
Gulf Coast Pulpwood News, 830

Hoverclub of America
PO Box 908, Foley, AL, 36536-0908
Hovernews, 30

Huntingdon College
Student Life Office, 1500 E. Fairview Ave., Montgomery, AL, 36106-2148
Bells, 195

Inside Alabama Politics
PO Box 66200, Mobile, AL, 36660-1200
Inside Alabama Politics, 991

Jefferson County Medical Society
901 18th St. S., Birmingham, AL, 35205-3733
Pulse, 885

•Jefferson Davis State Junior College
Brewton, AL, 36426

•Jefferson State Junior College
2601 Carson Rd, Birmingham, AL, 35215-3007

•John C. Calhoun State Community College
PO Box 2216, Decatur, AL, 35602-2216

Kelli Fannon
1317 Lovette Lane, Daphne, AL, 36526
Circumspect, 694

Klanwatch Project Southern Poverty Law Center
400 Washington St # 548, Montgomery, AL, 36104-4344
Klanwatch Intelligence Report, 173

•Lusa R. Franklin
4604 Virginia Loop Rd., Apt. 3156-G, Montgomery, AL, 36116-4739

Mansanto Fibers
PO Box 2204, Decatur, AL, 35602-2204
Pipeline, 595

Marion Military Institute
Alumni Office, Marion, AL, 36756
Alumni Bulletin, 186

•Miles College
Box 3800, Birmingham, AL, 35208

Mises Institute
Auburn Univ., Auburn, AL, 36849
Austrian Economics Newsletter, 289

Mobile Area Chamber of Commerce
PO Box 2187, Mobile, AL, 36652-2187
View, The, 162

•Mobile Public Library
700 Government St, Mobile, AL, 36602-1499

Nat'l. Assn. of Lively Families
Rte. 1, Box 36904, Butler, AL, 36904-9801
Lively Newsletter, 459

Natl. Weather Assn.
6704 Wolke Ct, Montgomery, AL, 36116-2134
National Weather Assn. Newsletter, 893

Negro Airmen International, Inc.
PO Box 1340, Tuskegee Institute, AL, 36087-1340
Negro Airmen International Newsletter, 31

Newsletter Digest
2201 Big Cove Rd SE, Huntsville, AL, 35801-1349
Newsletter Digest, 680

Patrick Henry Junior College
PO Box 2000, Monroeville, AL, 36461-2000
Orator, 195

Peanut Pals
PO Box 4465, Huntsville, AL, 35815-4465
Peanut Papers, 185

Redstone Arsenal
U.S. Army Missle Command, Publ, Redstone, AL, 35898-0001
Redstone Rocket, 898

Reynolds Historical Library
1700 University Blvd, Birmingham, AL, 35233-1816
Treasures, 549

S.D. Bishop State Junior College
351 N Broad St, Mobile, AL, 36603-5833
Newsline, 195

•Samford University
800 Lakeshore Dr. ROBH 305D, Birmingham, AL, 35229-0001

Security Objective Services
Rr 4 Box 403, Bay Minette, AL, 36507-9314
Wall Street S.O.S. Options Alert, 691

Society of Alabama Archivists
Alabama Dept. Of Archives 624, Washington Ave., Montgomery, AL, 36130-0001
ACCESS, 791

Society for the History of Technology
Auburn University, Dept of History, Auburn, AL, 36849-5207
SHOT Newsletter, 548

Southern Junior College of Business
115 Office Park Dr, Birmingham, AL, 35223-2401
Grapevine, 195

Southern Natural Resources Inc.
PO Box 2563, Birmingham, AL, 35202-2563
Southern Natural Resources, 599

Southern Union State Junior College
Publications, Wadley, AL, 36276
SUC News, 195

Stillman College
PO Box 1430, Tuscaloosa, AL, 35403-1430
Stillman Bulletin, 186

Talladega County Historical Assn.
106 Broome St, Talladega, AL, 35160-2167
Newsletter (Talladega County Historical Assn.), 545

Tennessee Valley Historical Society
Univ. of N. Alabama, Dept. of History, Florence, AL, 35630-0001
Journal of Muscle Shoals History, 542

Tom Davies & Assocs.
3608 Linden Ln, Mobile, AL, 36608-1410
HVAC ProfitMaker, 140

Troy State Univ. Dothan
500 University Dr., Box 8368, Dothan, AL, 36304
Logos, 209

Troy State Univ. in Montgomery
PO Box 4419, Montgomery, AL, 36103-4419
Troy State Montgomery Newsletter, 195

Tuskegee Institute
Public Relations Office, Tuskegee, AL, 36083
News of Tuskegee Institute, 195

USS St. Louis CL 49 Assn.
Hubble Bubble Office, 28561 Hardiman Rd., Madison, AL, 35758-2904
USS St. Louis Hubble-Bubble, 1,112

U.S. Pipe and Foundry Co.
PO Box 10406, Birmingham, AL, 35202-0406
U.S. Piper, 893

•United States Sports Academy
1 Academy Dr # 8650, Daphne, AL, 36526-7055

•University of Alabama
Box 870252, Tuscaloosa, AL, 35403-1609

University of Alabama School of Communication
Publications, Tuscaloosa, AL, 35487-0172
International Communication Bulletin, 858

University of Alabama, Univ. Ctr.
1400 University Blvd., Ste. 135, Birmingham, AL, 35294-1150
Dr. Free's Radio Remedies, 195

University Aviation Association
3410 Skyway Dr, Opelika, AL, 36801-7123
UAA Newsletter, 334

Univ. of South Alabama
The Vanguard Box U-25100, P.O. Drawer U-25100, Mobile, AL, 36688-0001
Vanguard , The, 186

Vocational Evaluation & Work Adj. Assn.
1234 Haley Ctr,, Auburn University, AL, 36849
VEWAA Newsletter, 335

Walker College
Publications, Jasper, AL, 35501
Arcana, 195

World Peace Press
Mastin Lake St., Box 3282, Huntsville, AL, 35810-0282
International Association of Educators for World Peace, Circulation Newsletter, 992

Yuchi Pines Institute
PO Box 319, Fort Mitchell, AL, 36856-0319
Science/Health Abstracts, 528

• See ***MULTI-PUBLISHER INDEX*** for list of publications.

Alaska

Alaska Dept. of Natural Resources
Div./Geol. & Geophys. Surveys, 794 University Ave., Ste. 200, Fairbanks, AK, 99709-3645
Alaska Geology, 899

Alaska Federation of Natives
1577 C St. #201, Anchorage, AK, 99501-5138
AFN Newsletter, 405

Alaska Information & Research
3037 South Circle, Anchorage, AK, 99507-3956
Alaska Legislative Digest, 985

Alaska Library Assn.
PO Box 81084, Fairbanks, AK, 99708-1084
Newspoke, 806

Alaska Loggers Assn. Inc.
111 Stedman St Ste 200, Ketchikan, AK, 99901-6549
Alaska Forest Perspective, 576

Alaska Metaphysical Newsletter
3701 Eureka St Lot 21c, Anchorage, AK, 99503-5838
Alaska Metaphysical Council Newsletter, 973

Alaska Nurses Association
237 E. 3rd, Anchorage, AK, 99501-2532
Alaska Nurse, 928

Alaska State Council on the Arts
411 W. 4th Ave., #1E, Ste. 220, Anchorage, AK, 99501-2302
Alaska State Council on the Arts Bulletin, 62

Alaska State Data Center
Alaska Dept. of Labor, Box 25504, Juneau, AK, 99802-5504
AKCENS, 480

Alaska State Library
PO Box 110571, Juneau, AK, 99811-0571
Polar Libraries Bulletin, 807

Alaska Women's Resource Center
111 W 9th Ave, Anchorage, AK, 99501-3650
AWRC Newsletter, 1,206

Aleut Corp. The
4000 Old Seward Hwy Ste 300, Anchorage, AK, 99503-6068
Aleutian Current, 576

American Assn. of Stratigraphic Palynologists
Arco Alaska Inc., 700 G St., Anchorage, AK, 99501
American Assn. of Stratigraphic Palynologists-Newsletter, 475

•**Inst. of Northern Engineering**
Univ. of Alaska, Fairbanks, AK, 99775-0001

Natl. Org. for Men Against Sexism
1812 Arctic Blvd, Anchorage, AK, 99503-1812
Brother, 1,114

Ovulation Method Teachers Assn.
Box 10-1780, Anchorage, AK, 99510-1780
Ovulation Method Newsletter, 523

Patriots in Action
PO Box 140853, Anchorage, AK, 99514-0853
Northern Lights Glimmer, 994

Transmart Company
3581 Kachemak Cir, Anchorage, AK, 99515-2337
Joint Venture News, 649

University of Alaska Alumni Association
Publications Dept., Fairbanks, AK, 99775-0001
UAF Alumni Assn. Newsletter, 186

University of Alaska, Anchorage
3211 Providence Dr, Anchorage, AK, 99508-4614
Utopus Discovered, 999

•**University of Alaska, Cooperative Extension**
193 Arctic Health Bldg., Fairbanks, AK, 99775-6180

Arizona

3-D Data
C/O M.D. Chamberlain, 13650 No. Frontage Rd. #334, Yuma, AZ, 85367
3-D Data, 446

AG Communication Systems
PO Box 52179, Phoenix, AZ, 85072-2179
CS News, 579

AMS, F&V Division, USDA-Market News Dept.
522 N Central Ave Ste 245, Phoenix, AZ, 85004-2168
Western Melon and Vegetable Report, 47

A.R.E. Clinic
4017 N 40th St, Phoenix, AZ, 85018-5204
Pathways to Health, 523

American Academy of Dental Group Practice
5110 N 40th St Ste 250, Phoenix, AZ, 85018-2151
American Academy of Dental Group Practice Newsletter, 267

American Alliance for Theatre & Education
Arizona State University, Theatre Department, Box 873411, Tempe, AZ, 85287-3411
AATE Newsletter, 1,172

American Pointer Club
5430 N. Camino Escuela, Tucson, AZ, 85718-5021
Pointer Points, 50

•**Applied Computer Research**
PO Box 82266, Phoenix, AZ, 85071-2266

Arizona Bank
PO Box 2511, Phoenix, AZ, 85002-2511
Courier, 86

Arizona Dept. of Economic Security, Research Administration
Box 6123, SC-733A, Phoenix, AZ, 85005-6123
Arizona Economic Trends, 340

Arizona Dept. of Education
1535 W Jefferson St, Phoenix, AZ, 85007-3280
Ed.WORD, 308

•**Arizona Dept. of Environmental Quality, OCSEA Section**
3033 N. Central Ave, Phoenix, AZ, 85012

Arizona Geological Survey
416 W Congress St., #100, Tucson, AZ, 85701-1315
Arizona Geology, 475

Arizona Motor Transport Assn.
2111 W Mcdowell Rd, Phoenix, AZ, 85009-3010
AMTA Newsletter, 1,192

Arizona Nurses' Assn.
1850 E Southern Ave # 1, Tempe, AZ, 85282-5832
Arizona Nurse, 928

Arizona State Egg Inspection Board
1688 W Adams St Ste 328, Phoenix, AZ, 85007-2620
Arizona State Egg Inspector, Report, 1,000

Arizona State Library Assn.
14449 N. 73rd. St., Scottsdale, AZ, 85260-3133
AZLA Newsletter, 792

•**Arizona State University**
Research Publications, P.O Box 878206, Tempe, AZ, 85287-8206

Arizona State University, Center for Business Research
PO Box 874406, Tempe, AZ, 85287-4406
Arizona Business, 127

Arizona State University, Department of Anthropology
Publications, Tempe, AZ, 85281
Advances in Computer Archaeology, 57

•**Arizona State University, Economic Outlook Center**
PO Box 874406, Tempe, AZ, 85287-4406

Arizona Veterinary Medical Assn.
5502 N 19th Ave, Phoenix, AZ, 85015-2401
Arizona Veterinary Medical Assn. Newsletter, 1,200

Art Baron Management Corp.
PO Box 5365, Scottsdale, AZ, 85261-5365
World Fine Art, 54

Associated Church Press
PO Box 30215, Phoenix, AZ, 85046-0215
Newslog, 924

•**Assn. of American Physicians and Surgeons**
1601 N Tucson Blvd Ste 9, Tucson, AZ, 85716-3405

Assn. for Americans Seeking Intl. Franchises
2765 N. Scottsdale Rd., Ste. 104-D, Scottsdale, AZ, 85257
A.S.I.F (Americans Seeking International Franchises), 641

Association of New Gay & Lesbian Entrepreneurs (A.N.G.L.E.)
2765 N. Scottsdale Rd., Ste. 104-D, Scottsdale, AZ, 85257
Association of New Gay & Lesbian Entrepreneurs, 444

Asungi Productions
3661 N Campbell Ave Ste 108, Tucson, AZ, 85719-1527
Mamaroots, 1,209

Atlatl
2303 N Central Ave Ste 104, Phoenix, AZ, 85004-1323
Native Arts Update, 66

The Authors Resource Center
4725 E Sunrise Dr # 219, Tucson, AZ, 85718-4534
TARC Writers Report, 120

Big Cat Sculpture Assn.
2765 N. Scottsdale Rd., Ste. 104-D, Scottsdale, AZ, 85257
Big Cat Sculpture Association, 157

Blue Rose Ministry
PO Box 332, Cornville, AZ, 86325-0332
Solar Space-Letter, 1,162

C/S Communications, Inc.
PO Box 23899, Tempe, AZ, 85285-3899
Southwest Technology Report, 367

•**Carefree Communications**
PO Box 5268, Carefree, AZ, 85377-5268

Cartel: A Newsletter of Toreo in Mexico
PO Box 318, Cortaro, AZ, 85652-0318
Cartel: A Newsletter of Toreo in Mexico, 1,130

Cement Squeeze
P.O. Box 2112, Tempe, AZ, 85280
Cement Squeeze, 988

Certified Mint
3550 N Central Ave Ste 705, Phoenix, AZ, 85012-2109
Monetary Digest, 677

Children's Resource Center
P.O Box 8697, Scootsdale, AZ, 85257
Mind Garden Newsletter, The, 413

Civil Defense Perspectives
1601 N Tucson Blvd Ste 9, Tucson, AZ, 85716-3405
Civil Defense Perspectives, 1,138

Classified Communiucation, Inc.
PO Box 4242, Prescott, AZ, 86302-4242
Classified Communication Newsletter, 12

The Cogent Communicator
9571 E Caldwell Dr, Tucson, AZ, 85747-9218
Cogent Communicator, The, 133

•**Composite Market Reports**
1345 E. Main St., Suite 100, Mesa, AZ, 85203-8950

The Contingency Crier
P.O. Box 16875, Phoenix, AZ, 85011
The Contingency Crier, 342

Crawford Perspectives
655 N. Canyon Crest, # 19101, Tuscan, AZ, 85715
Crawford Perspectives, 660

DM Data, Inc.
10170 E Jenan Dr, Scottsdale, AZ, 85260-5921
Semiconductor Reliability News, 339

DNA-People's Legal Services, Inc.
PO Box 306, Window Rock, AZ, 86515-0306
DNA Newsletter, 730

Daniel Rosenthal & Assoc.
PO Box 84905, Phoenix, AZ, 85071-4905
Aden Analysis, 654

Dennis Thayer Assocs.
515 E Grant Rd Ste 361, Tucson, AZ, 85705-5770
Supermarket Sanitation, 1,089

Doctors for Disaster Preparedness
2509 N Campbell Ave # 272, Tucson, AZ, 85719-3304
Doctors for Disaster Preparedness, 504

Editors Only
PO Box 17108, Fountain Hills, AZ, 85269-7108
Editors Only, 953

Empire Communications
5818 N 7th St Ste 103, Phoenix, AZ, 85014-5810
Nobis Marketing Letter, 19

Environmental Assessment Association
8383 E. Evans Rd., Scottsdale, AZ, 85260-3614
Environmental Times, The, 381

Financial Foresight
8020 E Tuckey Ln, Scottsdale, AZ, 85250-5652
Financial Foresight, 664

First Natl. Bank of Arizona, Western Bancorporation
100 W. Washington, Phoenix, AZ, 85003-1805
First Nat'l. Bank's Arizona Times, 583

Five Star Publications
4696 West Tyson St., Chandler, AZ, 85226-2903
Kosher Kettle, 404

Food Conspiracy, Inc.
412 N 4th Ave, Tucson, AZ, 85705-8443
Food Conspiracy Newsletter, 428

Food for the Hungry
7729 E Greenway Rd, Scottsdale, AZ, 85260-1795
Feeding the Hungry, 1,117

General Motors Corp.
Box 10100, GM Desert Proving Ground, Mesa, AZ, 85216-0100
Roadrunner, 75

Gentlestrength
234 W University Dr, Tempe, AZ, 85281-3689
Gentlestrength Times, 260

Golden Key Ministry
6327 East Paradise Lane, Scottsdale, AZ, 85234-1305
Prosperous Living, 1,050

Good Samaritan Hospital
Public Relations, 1111 E. McDowell, Phoenix, AZ, 85203
Good Samaritan Today, 563

* See **MULTI-PUBLISHER INDEX** for list of publications.

Gunsite Press
PO Box 401, Paulden, AZ, 86334-0401
Gunsite Gossip, 553

Hampton Intl. Comm, Inc.
4520 E. Grant Rd., Tucson, AZ, 85712-2617
Chocolate News, 243

•Harness Tracks of America
4640 E. Sunrise Srive, Suite 200, Tucson, AZ, 85718-4576

Histree
803 S 5th Ave, Yuma, AZ, 85364-3842
Journal of American Indian Research Monthly Newsletter, 458

Information Central
PO Box 3900, Prescott, AZ, 86302-3900
Report on Institutional Foodservice, 432

•Information Intelligence, Inc.
PO Box 31098, Phoenix, AZ, 85046-1098

Integrated Circuit Engineering Corp.
15022 N 75th St, Scottsdale, AZ, 85260-2425
ICECAP Report, 366

International Real Estate Institute
8383 E Evans Rd, Scottsdale, AZ, 85260-3614
International Real Estate Newsletter, 1,034

International Seal, Label & Cigar Band Society
8915 E Bellevue St, Tucson, AZ, 85715-5618
Intl. Seal, Label & Cigar Band Society, News Bulletin, 554

International Society of Cryptozoology
PO Box 43070, Tucson, AZ, 85733-3070
The ISC Newsletter, 1,216

International Virtual Reality Assn.
2765 N. Scottsdale Rd., Ste. 104-D, Scottsdale, AZ, 85257
International Virtual Reality Association, 369

Ken Lange Inc.
7112 N 15th Pl # 1, Phoenix, AZ, 85020-5416
Monthly Report for Hairstylists & Salon Owners, 100

Key Collectors Intl.
PO Box 9397, Phoenix, AZ, 85068-9397
Chain Gang, 552

Leasing Professional
PO Box 5675, Scottsdale, AZ, 85261-5675
Leasing Professional, 791

Luce Press Clippings
42 S Center, Mesa, AZ, 85210-1306
Luce Media Report, 17

Lutheran Vanguard, Inc.
5225 N 20th St, Phoenix, AZ, 85016-3319
Lutheran Vanguard, 1,072

Market Timing Report
PO Box 225, Tucson, AZ, 85702-0225
Market Timing Report, 676

Market Vision
2625 S. Roosevelt, Ste. 101, Tempe, AZ, 85282
Market Vision, 676

Marketing Timing Report
PO Box 225, Tucson, AZ, 85702-0225
Marketing Timing Report, 676

Masjid Tucson
739 E 6th St, Tucson, AZ, 85719-5003
Submitters Perspective, 1,074

McMurry Publishing Inc.
8805 N 23rd Ave Ste 11, Phoenix, AZ, 85021-4171
Heart Direct, 512

Mexican American Studies & Research Center
University Of Arizona Douglas, Bldg., Rm. 315, Tucson, AZ, 85721-0001
MASRC Newsletter, 405

Mini Co., Inc.
2531 W. Dunlap Ave., #201, Phoenix, AZ, 85021-2715
Mini Manager, 841

Mining Club of the Southwest
PO Box 42317, Tucson, AZ, 85733-2317
Concentrates, 900

Moraga & Associates
1915 E Glencove St, Mesa, AZ, 85203-4520
Latinogram, 402

•Nancy L. Childress Svces.
3709 W Gardenia Ave., Phoenix, AZ, 85051-8266

Narcissus Press
P.O. Box 2430, Chandler, AZ, 85244-2430
Mitzymitzy Ennui, 471

Natl. Assn. for Ethnic Studies
Dept. of English, Arizona State U. Box 870302, Tempe, AZ, 85287-0302
Ethnic Reporter, 398

National Association of Real Estate Appraisers
8383 E Evans Rd, Scottsdale, AZ, 85260-3614
Real Estate Appraisal Newsletter, 1,037

National Environmental Training Assn.
2930 E Camelback Rd Ste 185, Phoenix, AZ, 85016-4412
NETA Newsletter, 388

National Indian Social Workers Association
PO Box 45, Valentine, AZ, 86437-0045
Association, The, 1,114

Natl. No-Nukes Prison Support Collec.
PO Box 43383, Tucson, AZ, 85733-3383
Nuclear Resister, 994

National Spiritualist Assn. of Churches
3521 W Topeka Dr, Glendale, AZ, 85308-2325
National Spiritualist-Summit, 1,065

Native Seeds/SEARCH
2509 N Campbell Ave # 325, Tucson, AZ, 85719-3304
Seedhead News, 46

Nelson Newsletter Publishing Corp.
PO Box 41630, Tucson, AZ, 85717-1630
Bill Nelson Newsletter, 183

•Northern Arizona Univ.
News & Publications Box 6000, Flagstaff, AZ, 86011-0001

Northern Arizona University, School of Forestry
Publications, Flagstaff, AZ, 86011-0001
Arizona Forestry Notes, 435

Office of Climatology
Arizona State Univ., Box 871508, Tempe, AZ, 85287-1508
Arizona Climate Summary, 893

On-Line Audiovisual Catalogers
Catalog Dept., Univ. of Arizona Library, Tuscon, AZ, 85721-0001
O L A C Newsletter, 806

Oryx Press, The
4041 N. Central Ave., Ste. 700, Indian School Rd., Phoenix, AZ, 85012-3397
AgriBioScan, 35

Parnell Publishing Co.
PO Box 16432, Phoenix, AZ, 85011-6432
Self Publisher Newsletter, 120

Pendleton Shop
PO Box 233, Sedona, AZ, 86339-0233
Looming Arts, The, 554

Phoenix Institute Newsletter
PO Box 1690, Sedona, AZ, 86339-1690
Phoenix Institute Newsletter, 1,050

Phoenix Publishing, Inc.
5555 N. 7th Avenue #B200, Phoenix, AZ, 85013-1755
What's New in Arizona, 1,040

Post-Tensioning Institute
1717 W Northern Ave Ste 114, Phoenix, AZ, 85021-5470
Post-Tensioning Institute-Newsletter, 249

Prescott College
220 Grove Ave, Prescott, AZ, 86301-2990
Transitions, 196

•Publishers Management Co.
PO Box 84900, Phoenix, AZ, 85071-4900

Purchasing Management Assn of Arizona
PO Box 40157, Mesa, AZ, 85274-0157
Arizona Purchaser, 1,027

•R. C. Publications
10221 North 32nd Street, Suite J-1, Phoenix, AZ, 85028-3849

Remember That Song
5623 N 64th Ave, Glendale, AZ, 85301-5610
Remember That Song, 917

Resources for Women, Inc.
5210 E Pima St Ste 130, Tucson, AZ, 85712-3656
Directory of Resources for Women, 1,208

SYZGY: The Journal of Contemporary Mentalism
2901 North 55th Avenue, Phoenix, AZ, 85031
SYZGY: The Journal of Contemporary Mentalism, 923

St. Anthony the Great Orthodox Pubs.
3044 N 27th St, Phoenix, AZ, 85016-7926
Desert Voice, 1,067

St. Joseph's Hospital
350 W Thomas Rd, Phoenix, AZ, 85013-4496
Vision, 573

Salt River Project
PO Box 52025, Phoenix, AZ, 85072-2025
PULSE, 1,027

Sedona Institute
4501 N 22nd St Ste 100, Phoenix, AZ, 85016-4625
Release, 526

Self-Publisher's Business Letter
PO Box 5234, Apache Junction, AZ, 85278-5234
Self-Publisher's Business Letter, 120

Small-Press Genre Association
2131 S. 227th Dr., Buckeye, AZ, 85326-3872
Genre Press Digest, 1,102

Southwest Institute for Research on Women
Douglass Bldg., #102 Univ. O, Arizona, Tucson, AZ, 85721-0001
SIROW Newsletter, 1,211

Southwestern Mission Research Center
Arizona State Museum Univ. Of, Arizona, Tucson, AZ, 85721-0001
SMRC Newsletter, 52

Stratford American Sports Careers
2408 E Arizona Biltmore Cir, Phoenix, AZ, 85016-2103
Insider, 1,131

Superstition Mountain Historical Society, Inc.
PO Box 3845, Apache Junction, AZ, 85217-3845
Superstition Mountain Historical Society-Newsletter, 549

Supima Assn. of America
4141 E. Broadway Rd., Phoenix, AZ, 85040-8803
Supima Association of America Newsletter, 46

T R C Publishing
2765 N. Scottsdale Rd, Suite 104-D, Scottsdale, AZ, 85257
Franchise Wise (Quarterly newsletter of the intl gay & lesbian franchise assoc.), 444

•Techno-Fundamental Investments, Inc.
PO Box 14111, Scottsdale, AZ, 85267-4111

Timing Financial Services, Ltd.
3219 W Mescal St, Phoenix, AZ, 85029-4123
Timing, 689

Touchpoint
P.O. Box 408, Chloride, AZ, 86431
Touchpoint, 816

Tucson Education Assn.
4625 E 2nd St, Tucson, AZ, 85711-1198
TEA Newsletter, 332

Unitarian-Universalist Church of Tucson
4831 E 22nd St, Tucson, AZ, 85711-4903
Unitarian-Universalists in Support of Sanctuary Newsletter, 999

University of Arizona
1052 North Highland Ave., Tucson, AZ, 85721-0001
Arizona's Economy, 127

Univ. of Arizona
Douglass Bldg., #102, Tucson, AZ, 85721-0001
NewsNotes: Teaching Women's Studies from An Intl. Perspective, 323

Univ. of Arizona, College of Business & Public Admin.
Mcclelland Hall 204a, Tucson, AZ, 85721-0001
Arizona Economic Indicators Chartbook, 289

Univ. of Arizona, College of Pharmacy
Publications, Tucson, AZ, 85721-0001
Arizona Poison Control System Newsletter, 281

•University of Arizona Computer Science Dept.
Gould-Simpson Building, Tucson, AZ, 85721-0001

VME, Inc.
2618 S Shannon Dr, Tempe, AZ, 85282-2936
VMEnews, 242

Virtual Fusion
5160 Calla Bonita, Sierra Vista, AZ, 85635
Virtual Inc., 242

Volume Reversal Survey
PO Box 1451, Sedona, AZ, 86339-1451
Volume Reversal Survey, 691

Volunteer Committees of Art Museums
6121 N 22nd St, Phoenix, AZ, 85016-2033
Volunteer Committees of Art Museums-Newsletter, 67

Water Resources Research Center
Univ. of Arizona, Tucson, AZ, 85721-0001
Arroyo, 1,202

Weldon Publishing
202 Cactus Dr., #20, PO Box 4146, Prescott, AZ, 86302
Electrical Sensitivity News, 378

Western International University
9215 N Black Canyon Hwy, Phoenix, AZ, 85021-2718
Pinstripes, 196

WordPerfect Special Interest Group, The
P.O. Box 39742, Tucson, AZ, 85751-0742
Function Key, The, 223

World University Roundtable
PO Box 2470, Benson, AZ, 85602-2470
Liftoff, 316

• See **MULTI-PUBLISHER INDEX** for list of publications.

Arkansas

ABF Freight System, Inc.
PO Box 48, Ft. Smith, AR, 72902-0048
ABF By-Lines, 575

AR Genealogical Society Inc.
PO Box 908, Hot Springs, AR, 71902-0908
Arkansas Family Historian, 447

•Accrediting Assn. of Bible Colleges
PO Box 1523, Fayetteville, AR, 72702-1523

American Agricultural Law Association
Univ. of Arkansas, Leflar Law Center, Fayetteville, AR, 72701
Agricultural Law Update, 714

American Indian & Alaska Native Newspapers & Periodicals Res
2801 S. University, 3301 S. University, Little Rock, AR, 72204-1000
American Native Press, 952

Amnesty Intl. USA's Natl. Steering Committee on Human Rights
1603 Honeysuckle Ln, Jonesboro, AR, 72401-5104
Human Rights Education: The Fourth R, 631

Arkansas Archeological Society
PO Box 1222, Fayetteville, AR, 72702-1222
Field Notes, Newsletter of the Arkansas Archeological Society, 57

Arkansas Country Dance Society
52 Ridge Dr, Greenbrier, AR, 72058-9646
Arkansas Country Dancer, 265

Arkansas Dept. of Health
4815 W Markham St, Little Rock, AR, 72205-3866
Arkansas Animal Morbidity Report, 1,200

Arkansas Game & Fish Commission
2 Natural Resources Dr., Little Rock, AR, 72205-1501
Arkansas Outdoors, 943

Arkansas School Study Council
234 Graduate Education Bldg., Univ. of Arkansas, Fayetteville, AR, 72701
ASSC Newsletter, 298

Boone County Historical & Railroad Society, Inc.
PO Box 1094, Harrison, AR, 72602-1094
Boone County Historian, 448

Campaign Consultants
PO Box 7281, Little Rock, AR, 72217-7281
Grass Roots Campaigning, 990

Center on War & the Child
PO Box 487, Eureka Springs, AR, 72632-0487
WarChild Monitor International, 171

Civil War Round Table Assoc.
PO Box 7388, Little Rock, AR, 72217-7388
Civil War Round Table Digest, 538

Confederate Historical Institute
PO Box 7388, Little Rock, AR, 72217-7388
CHI Dispatch, 537

Crescent Park Press
PO Box 448, Eureka Springs, AR, 72632-0448
Six Months to Six Years, 330

Detroit Concert Band, Inc.
7443 E. Butherus St., Ste. 100, Scottsdale, AR, 85260-2423
Band Fan, 910

Donrey Media Group (Pine Bluff Commercial)
300 S Beech St, Pine Bluff, AR, 71601-4039
UAPB Campus Weekly, 196

Forestry, Conservation Communications Assn. News
3821 Roosevelt Road, West Little Rock, AR, 72204-6369
Forestry, Conservation Communications Association News and Views, 435

Good Earth Assn., Inc.
Living Farm of the Ozarks, 202 E. Church St. at N. Bettis, Pocahontas, AR, 72455-2899
Good Earth Times, 904

Heifer Project International
1015 Louisiana St, Little Rock, AR, 72202-3851
Sharing Life, 1,122

Herbal Healer Academy
HC 32 Box 97B, Mt. View, AR, 72560-9106
Herbal Healer Academy Newsletter, 512

Historic Preservation Alliance of Arkansas
PO Box 305, Little Rock, AR, 72203-0305
Arkansas Preservation Digest, 536

Houp Houpe Houpt Haupt Family Assn.
PO Box 608, Alma, AR, 72921-0608
Houp Houpe Houpt Haupt Family Historian Quarterly, 456

Jayhill's
PO Box 5362, Little Rock, AR, 72215-5362
Bookkeeping & Accounting Service Profit/Growth, 2

Jonna Baker
PO Box 217, Omaha, AR, 72662-0217
East Wind, 452

Judicial Dept., Administrative Office of the Courts
Justice Bldg., 625 Marshall, Little Rock, AR, 72201
Friends of the Court, 740

KFFA AM/1360
PO Box 430, Helena, AR, 72342-0430
King Biscuit Times, 913

LCHS
PO Box 14, Lonoke, AR, 72086-0014
Lonoke County Historical Society Newsletter, 460

Lucius Farish
2 Caney Valley Drive, Plumerville, AR, 72127-8725
UFO Newsclipping Service, 1,199

Lutherans for Life
PO Box 819, Benton, AR, 72018-0819
Lifedate, 1,118

Northwest Arkansas Archaeological Society, Inc.
PO Box 1154, Fayetteville, AR, 72702-1154
Arkansas Amateur, 57

O-C Genealogical Society
PO Box 2092, Camden, AR, 71701-2092
Researchin' Ouachita-Calhoun Counties AR, 465

Order of the Indian Wars
PO Box 7401, Little Rock, AR, 72217-7401
OIW Communique, 546

Orphan Train Heritage Society of America
4912 Trout Farm Rd, Springdale, AR, 72762-8834
Crossroads, 539

Ozark Feminist Review
PO Box 1662, Fayetteville, AR, 72702-1662
Ozark Feminist Review, 1,211

Ozark Society
PO Box 2914, Little Rock, AR, 72203-2914
Pack & Paddle, 390

Peerless Engravers
823 Main St, Little Rock, AR, 72201-4691
Peerless Perspective, 1,006

Scientific Enterprises, Inc.
5104 Randolph Road, North Little Rock, AR, 72116-7541
Hospital Safety Information Service, 1,080

Southern Arkansas Univ.
SAU Box 1400, Magnolia, AR, 71753
SAU Stater, 186

State Board of Education, Vocational Div.
Education Building West-303D, Little Rock, AR, 72201
Arkansas Vocational Visitor, 300

Stone County Historical Society
PO Box 284, Mountain View, AR, 72560-0284
Heritage of Stone, 456

Survival Food Storage Newsletter
PO Box 362, Calico Rock, AR, 72519-0362
Survival Food Storage Newsletter, 433

Texarkana Genealogical Soc.
2404a Briar Rose Dr, Texarkana, AR, 75502-3304
Texarkana U.S.A. Quarterly, 468

Towne Family Association
145 Oriole, Batesville, AR, 72501-6500
About Towne, 446

Tri-County Genealogical Society
PO Box 580, Marvell, AR, 72366-0580
Tri-County Genealogy, 468

Union County Genealogical Society C/O Barton Library
200 E 5th St, El Dorado, AR, 71730-3824
Tracks & Traces, 468

Univ. of Arkansas, College of Business Administration
Bureau of Business & Ec. Res., Fayetteville, AR, 72701
Arkansas Business Bulletin, 127

University of Arkansas Press
201 Ozark Ave, Fayetteville, AR, 72701-4041
Arkansas Biography Newsletter, 1,040

Univ. of Arkansas at Little Rock
2801 S University Ave, Little Rock, AR, 72204
UALR Alumnus, 186

Wallace Assn.
PO Box 1836, Little Rock, AR, 72203-1836
Arkansas Report, 481

Wayne Vandal Masterson
PO Box 193, Bull Shoals, AR, 72619-0193
Vandal Newsletter, 469

Workamper News
201 Hiram Rd, Heber Springs, AR, 72543-8747
Workamper News, 1,192

California

1117 Publishing Co.
3519 E. Colorado Blvd., PO Box 1415, Duarte, CA, 91009-4415
World Aquatic News & Travel, 1,137

ACLU of Northern California
1663 Mission St., San Francisco, CA, 94103-2449
ACLU News, 171

ACS Publications
PO Box 34487, San Diego, CA, 92163-4487
Astroflash, 68

ADO Inc.-American Darts Organization
7603 Firestone Blvd Ste E-6, Downey, CA, 90241-4205
Double Eagle Newsletter, 1,130

AD-PR Agency Report
Box 715, San Rafael, CA, 94914-0715
AD-PR Agency Report, 8

A.G Media
P.O Box 2626, Almeda, CA, 06836
American Gunsmith, 495

•AIDS Project Los Angeles
6721 Romaine St, Los Angeles, CA, 90038-2417

ALS & Neuromuscular Research Foundation
California Pacific Med Center, 2351 Clay St., #419, San Francisco, CA, 94115
Support Group Newsletter, 888

ATN Publications
PO Box 411256, San Francisco, CA, 94141-1256
AIDS Treatment News, 864

ATUNC
PO Box 16427, San Francisco, CA, 94116-0427
ATUNC Newsletter, 211

AWAIR (Arab World Islamic Resources & School Services)
1865 Euclid Ave Apt 4, Berkeley, CA, 94709-1301
AWAIR News, 399

•Abbott & Hast Publications, Inc.
761 Lighthouse Ave., Ste. A, Monterey, CA, 93940-1033

Academic Press, Inc.
525 B St., Ste 1900, San Diego, CA, 92101-4495
Atomic Data and Nuclear Data Tables, 925

Academy of Country Music
6255 Sunset Blvd., #923, Hollywood, CA, 90028-7410
Academy of Country Music Newsletter, 909

Academy of Family Films & Family Television
334 W 54th St, Los Angeles, CA, 90037-3806
Academy of Family Films & Family Television Newsletter, 410

Academy of Science Fiction, Fantasy & Horror Films
334 W 54th St, Los Angeles, CA, 90037-3806
Academy of Science Fiction, Fantasy & Horror Films-Newsletter, 1,102

Academy of Scientific Hypnotherapy
PO Box 12041, San Diego, CA, 92112-3041
Hypnotherapy in Review, 1,014

Acquisition Resource Corp.
49 Main St, Tiburon, CA, 94920-2507
National Review of Corporate Acquisitions, 146

Activists for Protective Animal Legislation
PO Box 11743, Costa Mesa, CA, 92627-0743
Political Watchdog, 280

Acu Press
1533 Shattuck Ave, Berkeley, CA, 94709-1516
Acupressure Workshop, 497

AdVantage Point Press
17 Paul Dr, San Rafael, CA, 94903-2043
AdVantage Point, 9

•Administrator's Digest, Inc.
PO Box 993, South San Francisco, CA, 94083-0993

Adventures for Kids
3457 Telegraph Rd, Ventura, CA, 93003-3314
Adventures for Kids-Newsletter, 167

Aetherius Society
6202 Afton Place, Hollywood, CA, 90028-8298
Cosmic Voice, 922

Afraid
857 N Oxford Ave # 4, Los Angeles, CA, 90029-3758
Afraid, 919

African Studies Center, Univ. of California, Los Angeles
405 Hilgard Ave, Los Angeles, CA, 90024-1301
ASC Newsletter, 626

Al Frank Asset Management, Inc.
PO Box 1767, Santa Monica, CA, 90406-1767
Prudent Speculator, The, 683

** See **MULTI-PUBLISHER INDEX** for list of publications.*

Alldata
9412 Big Horn Blvd., Elk Grove, CA, 95758
Alldata News, 212

Alliance for Survival
200 W. Main St., #M-2, Santa Ana, CA, 92701-4851
Peace Conversion Times, 995

Alpha Beta Acme Markets, Inc., Acme Markets Inc.
777 S Harbor Blvd, La Habra, CA, 90631-6839
Vanguard, 602

Alva Svoboda
P.O. Box 10604, Oaland, CA, 94610, ; '''
Solitary Pleasures, 472

Amalgamated Flying Saucer Clubs of America
PO Box 39, Yucca Valley, CA, 92286-0039
AFSCA Information Sheets, 1,198

•Ambit International, Inc.
665 3rd St Ste 508, San Francisco, CA, 94107-1923

American Academy of Clinical Psychiatrists
PO Box 3212, San Diego, CA, 92163-1212
Clinical Psychiatry Quarterly, 1,010

American Academy of Ophthalmology
655 Beach St, San Francisco, CA, 94109-1336
Refractive Surgery Outlook, 886

American Amateur Karate Fed.
1930 Wilshire Blvd Ste 1208, Los Angeles, CA, 90057-3622
AAKF Newsletter, 1,128

American Ambulance Assn.
3800 Auburn Blvd Ste C, Sacramento, CA, 95821-2102
Ambulance Industry Digest, 498

American Assn. of Attorney CPA's
24196 Alicia Pky., Ste. K, Mission Viejo, CA, 92691-3926
Attorney-CPA, 716

•American Assn. for Career Education
2900 Amby Pl, Hermosa Beach, CA, 90254-2216

American Association for Fuel Cells
50 San Miguel Ave, Daly City, CA, 94015-3950
American Association for Fuel Cells Newsletter, 350

American Association of Retired Persons
3200 Carson St, Lakewood, CA, 90712-4038
Working Age, 1,109

American Cetacean Society
PO Box 1391, San Pedro, CA, 90733-1391
Spyhopper, 394

American Deli-Bakery News
PO Box 194130, San Francisco, CA, 94119-4130
American Deli-Bakery News, 79

•American Down Assn. (ADA)
3728 Canna Ct, Sacramento, CA, 95821-3101

American Dreams
11875 Dublin Blvd., #D-272, Dublin, CA, 94568
American Dreams, 470

American Electronics Assn.
5201 Great America Pkwy., Ste. 520, Santa Clara, CA, 95054-1133
Impact, 338

American Endodontic Society
1440 N Harbor Blvd Ste 719, Fullerton, CA, 92635-4120
AES Newsletter, 267

•American Environmental Institute
45 Belden St., 3rd Fl., San Francisco, CA, 94104-2808

American Friends Service Committee, Pasadena
980 N Fair Oaks Ave, Pasadena, CA, 91103-3009
Olive Branch, 995

•American Grand Jury Foundation
PO Box 1690, Modesto, CA, 95353-1690

American Herb Association
PO Box 1673, Nevada City, CA, 95959-1673
American Herb Association -Quarterly Newsletter, 440

American Honda Motor Co. Inc.
Employee Relations, 1919 Torrance Blvd., Torrance, CA, 90501-2746
Momentum, 590

American Inst. for International Steel
Pacific Chapter, 3808 W. Riverside Dr. Ste. 600, Burbank, CA, 91505-4360
Pacific Chapter Update, 892

American Institute of Wine & Food
1550 Bryant St., San Francisco, CA, 94103-4832
American Wine & Food, 426

American Longevity Assn.
1000 W Carson St, Torrance, CA, 90502-2004
Longevity Letter, 516

American Lupus Society
3914 Del Amo Blvd Ste 922, Torrance, CA, 90503-2159
Lupus Today, 878

American Mustang Assn.
PO Box 338, Yucaipa, CA, 92399-0338
American Mustang World, 559

American Physicians Art Association
1130 N Cabrillo Ave, San Pedro, CA, 90731-1316
American Physicians Art Association Newsletter, 62

American Romanian Academy
3328 Monte Vista Ave, Davis, CA, 95616-4929
ARA Journal, 985

American Sailing Association
13922 Marquesas Way, Marina Del Rey, CA, 90292-6000
Affiliate & Instructor News, 112

American Shore & Beach Preservation Assn.
1724 Indian Way, Oakland, CA, 94611-1221
American Shore & Beach Preservation Assn. - Newsletter, 372

American Shortwave Listeners Club
16182 Ballad Ln, Huntington Beach, CA, 92649-2272
SWL, 556

American Society for Aesthetic Plastic Surgery
3922 Atlantic Ave, Long Beach, CA, 90807-3502
Aesthetic Surgery, 865

American Society of Bookplate Collectors & Designers
605 N Stoneman Ave Apt F, Alhambra, CA, 91801-1406
Bookplates in the News, 116

American Veterinary Exhibitors Assn.
PO Box 6842, Santa Barbara, CA, 93160-6842
AVEA Newsletter, 1,200

American Yankee Association
PO Box 1531, Cameron Park, CA, 95682-1531
American Star, 26

Americans for Nonsmokers' Rights
2530 San Pablo Ave.,Ste. #J, Berkeley, CA, 94702-2000
Americans for Nonsmokers' Rights Update, 498

Animal Legal Defense Fund
1363 Lincoln Ave Ste 7, San Rafael, CA, 94901-2124
Animals' Advocate, 48

Anza-Borrego Desert Natural History Assn.
PO Box 311, Borrego Springs, CA, 92004-0311
Sand Paper, 950

Apple Computer, Inc.
4 Infinite Loop, Cupertino, CA, 95014-2083
Apple Library Users Group Newsletter, 212

Arachne Publishing
PO Box 4100, Mountain View, CA, 94040-0100
Cartoons by Bulbul, 210

Arcana Workshops
PO Box 506, Manhattan Beach, CA, 90267-0506
Thoughtline, 975

•Ariel Owners Motorcycle Club
PO Box 1256, Topanga, CA, 90290

Armed Forces Broadcasters Assn.
10888 La Tuna Canyon Rd #, Carnes, Sun Valley, CA, 91352-2009
AFBA Transmitter, 122

•Art Network
18757 Wildflower Dr., P.O. Box 1268, Penn Valley, CA, 95946-9717

Artists in Print, Inc.
665 Third St., #530, San Francisco, CA, 94107-1901
In Brief, 64

Asbestos Victims of America (AVA)
PO Box 559, Capitola, CA, 95010-0559
AVA Advisor, 243

Asia Foundation
Box 3223, San Francisco, CA, 94119
Asia Foundation News, 259

•Asia Letter Group
PO Box 88189, Los Angeles, CA, 90009-8189

Asian American Certified Public Accountants
1 Embarcadero Ctr., #610, San Francisco, CA, 94111-3671
Asian American Certified Public Accountants-Newsletter, 2

Asian American Studies Center
405 Hilgard Ave., University of California, Los Angeles, CA, 90095-1546
CrossCurrents, 400

Association of Asian/Pacific American Artists
10153 1/2 Riverside Dr #, Toluca Lake, CA, 91602-2533
Inside Moves, 369

Association of Computer Users
1250 45th St Ste 200, Emeryville, CA, 94608-2924
Executive Computing Newsletter, 222

Assn. for Fitness Professionals (IDEA)
6190 Cornerstone Ct E Ste 204, San Diego, CA, 92121-4701
IDEA Fitness Manager, 1,131

Assn. of Insolvency Accountants
31332 Via Colinas Ste 112, Westlake Village, CA, 91362-3910
Association of Insolvency Accountants Newsletter, 2

Assn. for Media Psychology
1525 San Vicente Blvd, Santa Monica, CA, 90402-2205
Amplifier, 1,012

Assn. for Past Life Research & Therapies, Inc.
6825 D. Magnolia Avenue, Riverside, CA, 92516-0151
Association for Past-Life Research & Therapies, 1,012

Assn. of Pediatric Oncology Nurses
Box 7999, Pacific Med.Ctr., San Francisco, CA, 94120-7999
Association of Pediatric Oncology Nurses, 929

Association of Private Postal Systems
5580 Power Inn Rd Ste F, Sacramento, CA, 95820-6748
Association of Private Postal Systems Update, 970

Association for Transpersonal Psychology
Box 3049, Stanford, CA, 94309-3049
ATP Newsletter, 1,011

Astro Analytics Productions
PO Box 16927, Encino, CA, 91416-6927
Astro-Analytics, 68

Astronomical Society of the Pacific
390 Ashton Ave, San Francisco, CA, 94112-1722
Universe in the Classroom, 334

Atlantis
4016 3rd Ave, San Diego, CA, 92103-2102
Atlantis, The Imagery Newsletter, 868

Atterbury Letter
PO Box 1359, Bethel Island, CA, 94511-1197
Atterbury Letter, 1,182

Audubon Society, Santa Barbara Chapter
5679 Hollister Ave., 5B, Goleta, CA, 93117
El Tecolote, 941

Augustan Society, Inc.
PO Box P, Torrance, CA, 90508-0210
Augustaeum, 447

Automated Office Resources
812 Via Tornasol, Aptos, CA, 95003-5624
AOR Observer, 937

Automatic Transmission Rebuilders Assn.
2472 Eastman Ave Ste 23, Ventura, CA, 93003-5776
Good Guys, The, 73

Automobile Club of Southern California
2601 S. Figueroa St., 3rd Fl., Los Angeles, CA, 90007-3289
Shoptalk, 598

BMW Vintage Club of America, Inc.
PO Box S, San Rafael, CA, 94913-4358
BMW Vintage/Classic Bulletin, 70

Backspace Ink
1131 Galvez Dr, Pacifica, CA, 94044-4210
Backboard, 470

Baking with the American Harvest
1341 Ocean Ave., #526, Santa Monica, CA, 90401
Baking with the American Harvest, 79

Bank of America NT & SA
555 California St., San Francisco, CA, 94104-1590
Economic & Business Outlook, 88

Bank Lease Consultants
2590 Merced St, San Leandro, CA, 94577-4213
Auto Financing Update, 80

Bar Assn. of San Francisco
685 Market St # 700, San Francisco, CA, 94105-4200
In Re, 744

•Barclays Law Publishers
400 Oyster Point Blvd., S. San Francisco, CA, 94080

Barger & Walen
530 W. 6th St., 9th Fl., Los Angeles, CA, 90014-1203
Barger & Walen Newsletter, 718

Barnes Assocs., Inc.
735 Sunrise Ave., Suite #155, Roseville, CA, 95661
National Fund Raiser, 969

Baseball Perspective
PO Box 12212, La Jolla, CA, 92039-2212
Baseball Perspective, 101

•Baskerville Communications
2455 Teller Rd, Newbury Park, CA, 91320-2218

Baskin-Robbins Inc.
1201 S Victory Blvd, Burbank, CA, 91502-2552
Scoops, 597

* See ***MULTI-PUBLISHER INDEX*** *for list of publications.*

Bay Area Air Quality Management District
939 Ellis St, San Francisco, CA, 94109-7714
Air Currents, 371

Bay Area CISPES
3382 26th St., San Francisco, CA, 94110
Bay Area CISPES, 627

•**Bay Sports Review**
P.O. Box 4520, Berkeley, CA, 94704

Bechtel Corp.
50 Beale St, San Francisco, CA, 94105-1895
Bechtel Briefs, 359

Being Alive, People with HIV/AIDS Coalition
3626 W Sunset Blvd, Los Angeles, CA, 90026-1059
Being Alive, 868

Bellwoods Publications
31878 Del Obispo #330, San Juan Capistrano, CA, 92675
Travel For Less, 1,190

Berkeley-Leon Sister City Assn.
PO Box 1004, Berkeley, CA, 94701-1004
Berkeley-Leon Sister City Newsletter, 627

Betj Chayim Chadashim
6000 W Pico Blvd, Los Angeles, CA, 90035-2625
G'vanim, 1,068

Big Brothers of Grtr Los Angeles Inc.
1486 Colorado Blvd, Los Angeles, CA, 90041-2340
Image, 586

•**Bio Engineering News**
109 Minna St # 304, San Francisco, CA, 94105-3728

Bio-Rad Laboratories
1200 Alfred Nobel Dr., Hercules, CA, 94547
Bio-Rad, 108

•**BioVenture Publishing**
32 W. 25th Ave., Ste. 203, San Mateo, CA, 94403-2236

Biomedical Engineering Soc.
PO Box 2399, Culver City, CA, 90231-2399
BMES Bulletin, 359

•**Biomedical Market Newsletter, Inc.**
3237 Idaho Pl, Costa Mesa, CA, 92626-2207

Blue Mountain Center of Meditation
PO Box 256, Tomales, CA, 94971-0256
Blue Mountain, 813

Bollinger Capital Management, Inc.
PO Box 3358, Manhattan Beach, CA, 90266-1358
John Bollinger's Capital Growth Letter, 673

Bonsai by the Bay
PO Box 1246, Trinidad, CA, 95570-1246
Bonsai Bark, 440

BookLine Publishing Company
PO Box 150119, San Rafael, CA, 94915
Mystery Collectors' Bookline, 920

Book Passage Book Store
51 Tamal Vista Blvd, Corte Madera, CA, 94925-1145
Book Passage, 820

Botanical Dimensions
PO Box 807, Occidental, CA, 95465-0807
PlantWise, 442

•**Braille Institute of America**
741 N Vermont Ave, Los Angeles, CA, 90029-3514

Breeder's Registry
PO Box 255373, Sacramento, CA, 95865-5373
Breeder's Registry Newsletter, 49

Bresler Center, Inc.
115 S. Topanga Cyn. Blvd #15, Topanga, CA, 90272-0967
Bresler Center News, 869

BrikaBrak
438 Pennsylvania Avenue, Santa Cruz, CA, 95026
BrixaBrak, 694

Broadcast Designers' Association, Inc.
2223 Shattuck Ave # 200, Berkeley, CA, 94704-1415
BDA Update, 1,003

Brookridge Institute
1209 Palm Ave, San Mateo, CA, 94402-2437
Brookridge Forum, 562

Bruce Babcock, Jr.
1731 Howe Ave # 149, Sacramento, CA, 95825-2210
Commodity Traders Consumer Report, 659

Bruce, Dean & Company
116 New Montgomery St., Suite 914, San Francisco, CA, 94105-3607
Bruce Report, The, 274

•**Bureau of Criminal Statistics**
4949 Broadway Rm E231, Sacramento, CA, 95820-1528

Business Communication Services, Inc.
220 Montgomery St., Ste. 260, San Francisco, CA, 94104-3524
Tax Credit Advisor, 1,039

Business Intelligence Program-SRI Intl.
333 Ravenswood Ave, Menlo Park, CA, 94025-3453
Datalog, 836

Business Research
537 Newport Center Dr Ste 355, Newport Beach, CA, 92660-6937
Business Trends Report, 130

•**Butane-Propane News, Inc.**
338 E Foothill Blvd # 660698, Arcadia, CA, 91006-2542

Butte County Historical Society
PO Box 2195, Oroville, CA, 95965-2195
Slickens, 548

Butte-Sierra District Dental Society
951 Live Oak Blvd Ste 30, Yuba City, CA, 95991-3447
Newsletter, 270

•**CAD/CAM Publishing, Inc.**
1010 Turquoise St., Ste. 320, San Diego, CA, 92109-1159

CDS Associates
926 Coachella Ave, Sunnyvale, CA, 94086-3435
TrainMaster, 615

•**CIP Communications**
6585 Commerce Blvd., Suite 292, Rohnert Park, CA, 94928-2407

CJA
17852 17th St Ste 209, Tustin, CA, 92680-2143
CJA Forum, 131

•**COMPU-CHART**
363 S. Park Victoria Dr., Milpitas, CA, 95035-5708

•**COR Healthcare Resources**
PO Box 40959, Santa Barbara, CA, 93140-0959

CRLA Foundation
2424 K St., 1st Fl., Sacramento, CA, 95816-5002
Seniors in Sacramento, 1,109

•**CSI03COM**
3165 Kifer Rd # Csi03com, Santa Clara, CA, 95051-0804

CTSL Publishing Partners
PO Box 308, Half Moon Bay, CA, 94019-0308
California Technology Stock Letter, 657

Calif. Wool Growers Assn.
1225 H St # 101, Sacramento, CA, 95814-1910
California Wool Growers Newsletter, 827

California Abortion Rights Action League
330 Townsend St., Ste. 204, San Francisco, CA, 94107-1630
CARAL Newsletter, 1,207

California Academy of Sciences
Golden Gate Park, San Francisco, CA, 94118-4599
Academy Newsletter, 902

California Against Waste
PO Box 289, Sacramento, CA, 95812-0289
Waste Watch, 396

California Apricot Advisory Bd.
1280 Boulevard Way, Walnut Creek, CA, 94595-1193
Apricot Quarterly Roundup, 1,008

California Art Education Assn.
1836 Walnut Ave, Carmichael, CA, 95608-5417
Painted Monkey, 66

California Association of AIDS Agencies
926 J St Ste 803, Sacramento, CA, 95814-2707
CAAA Reports, 500

California Assn. for Health, Phys. Ed., Recreation & Dance
1501 El Camino Ave Ste 3, Sacramento, CA, 95815-2748
CAHPERD Journal/Times, 500

California Assn. of Life Underwriters
70 Washington St. #325, Oakland, CA, 94607-3737
CALUnderwriter, 619

California Association of Medical Product Suppliers
1 Capitol Mall, Ste. 320, Sacramento, CA, 95814
CAMPS Newsletter, 869

California Assn. for Newly Handicapped Children
17583 Daves Ave, Monte Sereno, CA, 95030-3214
CANCH-Gram, 276

California Board of Registered Nursing
PO Box 944210, Sacramento, CA, 94244-2100
BRN Report, 929

California Canning Peach Assn.
PO Box 7001, Lafayette, CA, 94549-7010
Peach Fuzz, 1,009

California Center for Equine Health and Performance
University of California, Davis, CA, 95616-8589
Horse Report, The, 559

California Chamber of Commerce
1201 K St Ste 1200, Sacramento, CA, 95814-3923
Alert, 127

California Children's Lobby
PO Box 448, Sacramento, CA, 95812-0448
Cryer, The, 1,116

California Clearinghouse on Library Instruction
UCLA College Library, Los Angeles, CA, 90024-1450
CCLI Newsletter, 795

California College for Health Sciences
222 W 24th St, National City, CA, 91950-6605
Pneumo Pneus, 196

California Confederation of the Arts
704 O St Fl 2, Sacramento, CA, 95814-5506
California Arts Advocate, 259

California Continuation Education Assn.
6501 Balboa Blvd., Van Nuys, CA, 91406-5526
Continuation Education, 305

California Credit Union League
2322 S Garey Ave, Pomona, CA, 91766-5805
Credit Union Digest, 257

California Dental Association
1201 K St. Mall, Sacramento, CA, 95814-3906
CDA Update, 268

•**California Dept. of Food & Agriculture**
Communications Dept., 1220 N St. Rm. 100, Sacramento, CA, 95814

California Dept. of Housing & Community Development
Box 951050, Sacramento, CA, 94252-2050
California Neighborhoods, 1,019

California Div. of Highways
2555 1st Ave, Sacramento, CA, 95818-2608
Zenith 12000, 1,077

California Employer Alert, Inc.
98 Main Street, Suite 700, Tiburon, CA, 94920
California Employer Advisor, 341

California Employment Development Department
800 Capitol Mall, MIC 84, Sacramento, CA, 95814-4807
California Employer Newsletter, 1,140

California Environmental Insider
PO Box 10106, San Rafael, CA, 94912-0106
California Environmental Insider, 374

California Genealogical Society
PO Box 77105, San Francisco, CA, 94107-0105
California Genealogical Society Newsletter, 450

California Grapevine
PO Box 22152, San Diego, CA, 92192-2152
California Grapevine, 102

•**California League of Conservation Voters**
10951 W Pico Blvd Ste 201, Los Angeles, CA, 90064-2126

California League of Savings Institutions
1960 E. Grand Ave., Ste. 1000, El Segundo, CA, 90245
Hotline, 91

•**California Library Assn.**
717 K St Ste 300, Sacramento, CA, 95814-3406

California Macadamia Society
PO Box 1298, Fallbrook, CA, 92088-1298
California Macadamia Society Yearbook, 1,008

California Monitor of Education
PO Box 402, Alamo, CA, 94507-0402
National Monitor of Education, 321

California Municipal Bond Advisor
1037 S. Palm Canyon Dr., Palm Springs, CA, 92264-8378
California Municipal Bond Advisor, 657

•**California National Organization for Women, Inc.**
926 J St Ste 523, Sacramento, CA, 95814-2706

California News Etc.
215 Beach St., Santa Cruz, CA, 95060
California News Etc., 1,032

California Numismatic Investments, Inc.
525 W Manchester Blvd, Inglewood, CA, 90301-1627
Investors' Update, 928

California Park & Recreation Society, Inc.
3031 F St Ste 202, Sacramento, CA, 95816-3809
Leisure Lines, 950

California Planning & Development Report
1275 Sunnycrest Ave, Ventura, CA, 93003-1212
California Planning & Development Report, 1,019

California Political Week, Inc.
PO Box 1468, Beverly Hills, CA, 90213-1468
California Political Week, 987

California Prune Board
5990 Stoneridge Dr Ste 101, Pleasanton, CA, 94588-3234
California Prune News, 426

California Public Interest Research Group
15 Shattuck Sq., Ste 210, Berkeley, CA, 94704
CALPIRG News, 251

California Redwood Association
405 Enfrente Rd # 200, Novato, CA, 94949-7206
Redwood News, 61

• See **MULTI-PUBLISHER INDEX** for list of publications.

California School Boards Assn.
3100 Beacon Blvd, West Sacramento, CA, 95691-3483
CSBA News, 1,090

California School for the Deaf
3044 Horace St, Riverside, CA, 92506-4420
Cubprints, 533

California Society of Anesthesiologists, Inc.
1065 E. Hillsdale Blvd., Ste. 806, Foster City, CA, 94404-1613
California Society of Anesthesiologists, INC Bulletin, 869

California Soc. of Pathologists
1 Capitol Mall, Ste. 320, Sacramento, CA, 95814
CSP Bulletin, 869

California Society for Psychical Study
PO Box 844, Berkeley, CA, 94701-0844
Iridis, 948

California State Dept. of Rehabilitation
830 K St Rm 320, Sacramento, CA, 95814-3510
Rehab Review, 1,121

•**California State Department of Social Welfare**
744 P St., Sacramento, CA, 95814-6413

•**California State Employment Development Dept.**
800 Capitol Mall, Sacramento, CA, 95814-4807

California State Fire Marshal
7171 Bowling Dr Ste 600, Sacramento, CA, 95823-2034
SFM, 422

California State Library
914 Capitol Mall, Box 942837, Sacramento, CA, 94237-0001
California State Library Newsletter, 795

California State Prison
State Prison, San Quentin, CA, 94964
San Quentin News, 790

California State Univ. Biology Dept.
School of Natural Sciences, Biology Dept., San Bernardino, CA, 92407
Tribolium Information Bulletin, 371

California State Univ. Dept. of Geography
Publications, Northridge, CA, 91330-0001
Historical Geography, 475

California State Univ. at Fullerton Biology Dept.
Publications, Fullerton, CA, 92634
Ascidian News, 1,216

California Tax Reform Assn.
926 J St Ste 710, Sacramento, CA, 95814-2707
Tax Back Talk, 1,153

California Taxpayers' Assn
921 11th St Ste 800, Sacramento, CA, 95814-2821
Cal-Tax News, 1,140

Cal-i Tomorrow
Ft. Mason Ctr. Bldg. B, #345, San Francisco, CA, 94123-1380
California Tomorrow, 303

California Wine Club
2175 Goodyear Ave Ste 114, Ventura, CA, 93003-7761
Uncorked, 105

California Women's Caucus
2900 Amby Place, Hermosa Beach, CA, 90254-2216
CWC Communicator, 1,207

Californians Against Waste
PO Box 289, Sacramento, CA, 95812-0289
Recycling Advocate, The, 392

Camping Women
7623 Southbreeze Dr, Sacramento, CA, 95828-5107
Camping Women Trails, 943

Can-Do
6737 Morella Ave, North Hollywood, CA, 91606-1618
Can-Do, 276

Cantu's Comedy Newsletter
PO Box 590634, San Francisco, CA, 94159-0634
Cantu's Newsletter, 854

Capital Growth Letter
PO Box 3358, Manhattan Beach, CA, 90266-1358
Capital Growth Letter, 657

Career Planning & Adult Development Network
4965 Sierra Rd., San Jose, CA, 95132-3414
Career Planning & Adult Development Network Newsletter, 699

Casa Nuestra Vineyards
3473 Silverado Trl N, Saint Helena, CA, 94574-9662
Casa Nuestra Journal, 103

Cascade Seaview Corp.
PO Box 1336, Mill Valley, CA, 94942-1336
Guerrilla Marketing, 15

Celebration Decor
410 Plateau Ave, Santa Cruz, CA, 95060-6353
Party Design Quarterly, 369

Center for Applied Ethics
Santa Clara University, Santa Clara, CA, 95053-0001
Issues in Ethics, 974

Center for Applied Intuition
333 Ruth Ave, Mountain View, CA, 94043-4114
New Eyes, 949

Center for Economic Conversion
222 View St Ste C, Mountain View, CA, 94041-1344
Positive Alternatives, 997

Center for Ethics & Social Policy
Graduate Theological Union, 2400 Ridge Rd., Berkeley, CA, 94709
Ethics and Policy, 973

Center for Health Sciences, The
PO Box 176, Los Altos, CA, 94023-0176
Mental Medicine Update, 1,015

Center for Law in the Public Interest
5750 Wilshire Blvd Ste 561, Los Angeles, CA, 90036-3697
Public Interest Briefs, 772

Center for Magnetic Recording Research
Univ. of California-San Diego, La Jolla, CA, 92093-0002
CMRR Report, 214

Center for Performing Arts Resources
9582 Hamilton Avenue, Huntington Beach, CA, 92646
Information Quarterly, 912

Center for Process Studies
1325 N College Ave, Claremont, CA, 91711-3154
Newsletter of Center for Process Studies, 974

Center for Real Estate Studies
50-B Peninsula Center Dr., Rolling Hills, CA, 90274-3604
Market Cycles, 1,035

Center for Socialist History
2633 Etna St, Berkeley, CA, 94704-3408
Center for Socialist History Interbulletin, 538

Center for Study of the Americas
2288 Fulton St # 103, Berkeley, CA, 94704-1449
CENSA's Strategic Report, 627

Center for Technology and Democracy
PO Box 460516, San Francisco, CA, 94146-0516
Post Industrial Issues, 491

Center for Urban Well-Being
PO Box 7586, Carmel, CA, 93921-7586
Making Cities Livable Newsletter, 1,022

Center for Women & Religion
2400 Ridge Rd, Berkeley, CA, 94709-1212
Women & Religion Newsletter, 1,213

Central Calif. Council of Diving Clubs
PO Box 779, Daly City, CA, 94017-0779
Odyssey, 1,133

Central Committee for Conscientious Objectors
655 Sutter Street, Suite 514, San Francisco, CA, 94102-1034
CCCO News Notes, 987

•**Certified Grocers of Calif., Ltd.**
2601 S Eastern Ave, Los Angeles, CA, 90040-1401

Chain of Life
PO Box 8081, Berkeley, CA, 94707-8081
Chain of Life, 1,115

Chalcedon Foundation
PO Box 158, Vallecito, CA, 95251-0158
Chalcedon Report, 1,061

•**Charitable Gift Planning News**
41 Sutter St Ste 1129, San Francisco, CA, 94104-4903

Chartist
PO Box 758, Seal Beach, CA, 90740-0758
Chartist, 658

•**Chasen & Luck**
410 N Bronson Ave, Los Angeles, CA, 90004-1504

Cheapskate Monthly
PO Box 2135, Paramount, CA, 90723-8135
Cheapskate Monthly, 84

Chek-Chart, H. M. Gousha Co.
320 Soquel Way, Sunnyvale, CA, 94086-4101
Chek-Chart Service Bulletin, 71

Child Abuse Listening Mediation, Inc.
PO Box 90754, Santa Barbara, CA, 93190-0754
CALM Newsletter, 1,114

Children's Hospital of Orange County
Box5700, Orange, CA, 92613
CHOC Talk, 562

Children's Video Review Newsletter
16765 Lena Ct., Grass Valley, CA, 95949-7369
Children's Video Review Newsletter, 168

China Agribusiness Report
PO Box 92619, Los Angeles, CA, 90009-2619
China Agribusiness Report, 628

China Forum
PO Box 13781, Berkeley, CA, 94712-4781
China Forum Newsletter, 628

China Moon Cafe
639 Post St, San Francisco, CA, 94109-8215
Fried Rice Times, 1,075

Chinese for Affirmative Action
17 Walter U Lum Pl, San Francisco, CA, 94108-1890
CAA Newsletter, 171

Chinese Christian Mission
PO Box 750759, Petaluma, CA, 94975-0759
Challenger, 1,061

Chinese Historical Society of America
650 Commercial St, San Francisco, CA, 94111-2504
Chinese Historical Society of America Bulletin, 538

Chips off the Writer's Block
PO Box 83371, Los Angeles, CA, 90083-0371
Chips off the Writer's Block, 694

Christ Truth Ministries
PO Box 610, Upland, CA, 91785-0610
Sharing Times, 1,066

Christian Anti-Communism Crusade
PO Box 890, Long Beach, CA, 90801-0890
Christian Anti-Communism Crusade Newsletter, 1,061

Christian Chaplain Services, Inc.
Box 4009, Los Angeles, CA, 90086-0307
Broken Shackles, 1,045

Christian Family Renewal
PO Box 73, Clovis, CA, 93613-0073
Jesus & Mary Are Calling You, 1,057

Christic Institute
PO Box 845, Malibu, CA, 90265-0845
Convergence, 988

Circus Report
525 Oak St, El Cerrito, CA, 94530-3699
Circus Report, 368

Circus Week
PO Box 3952, San Bernardino, CA, 92413-3952
Circus Week, 368

Clan McClellan in America, Inc.
8636 Don Carol Dr, El Cerrito, CA, 94530-2733
Think On, 468

Clara Felix, Publisher
PO Box 7094, Berkeley, CA, 94707-0094
Felix Letter, 933

Claremont McKenna College
400 E. 9th, Claremont, CA, 91711
ASCMC Newsletter, 186

Claretian Profile
18127 S Alameda St, Compton, CA, 90220-5708
Claretian Profile, 1,056

•**Classic Philatelics**
PO Box 5637, Huntington Beach, CA, 92615-5637

Clothespin Fever Press
10393 Spur Ct, La Mesa, CA, 91941
Lesbianline, 445

CoHousing Newsletter
2169 E. San Francisco Blvd., Ste. E, San Rafael, CA, 94901
CoHousing Newsletter, 375

Coalition for Free & Open Elections
POB 470296 St., San Francisco, CA, 94147-0296
Ballot Access News, 986

•**Coin Dealer Newsletter**
PO Box 7939, Torrance, CA, 90504-9339

Cole Group, The
2590 Greenwich St., Ste. 9, San Francisco, CA, 94123-3333
Cole Papers, The, 923

Columbia Pacific Univ.
1415 3rd St, San Rafael, CA, 94901-2860
Columbia Pacific University Alumni Newsletter, 187

Commanon Corp.
PO Box 1100, Grass Valley, CA, 95945-1100
Workers' Comp Executive, 625

Committee Opposed to Militarism and the Draft
PO Box 15195, San Diego, CA, 92175-5195
Draft Notices, 989

Commonwealth Club of California
595 Market St., San Francisco, CA, 94105-2885
Commonwealth, 1,019

Community Alliance with Family Farmers
PO Box 464, Davis, CA, 95617-0464
Agrarian Advocate, 371

Community Environmental Council
930 Miramonte Dr, Santa Barbara, CA, 93109-1384
Gildea Resource Newsletter, 382

* See **MULTI-PUBLISHER INDEX** for list of publications.

Community Memory Project
1442a Walnut St # 411, Berkeley, CA, 94709-1405
Community Memory Network, 215

Composites Worldwide Inc.
991 Lomas Santa Fe Dr # C469, Solana Beach, CA, 92075-2125
Composites News: Infrastructure, 980

•**Computer Economics, Inc.**
5841 Edison Pl., Carlsbad, CA, 92008-6519

Computer Entertainer
12115 Magnolia Blvd # 189, North Hollywood, CA, 91601
Computer Entertainer, 216

Computer Information Exchange
PO Box 159, San Luis Rey, CA, 92068-0159
S-Eighty, 235

•**Computer Sciences Corp.**
650 N Sepulveda Blvd, El Segundo, CA, 90245-3419

Congregation Ahavat Shalom
PO Box 14392, San Francisco, CA, 94114-0392
Ha-Yonah, 1,068

Congregation Shaar Zahav
220 Danvers at Caselli, San Francisco, CA, 94114
Jewish Gaily Forward, The, 1,069

Connoisseurs' Guide to California Wine
PO Box V, Alameda, CA, 94501-0265
Connoisseurs' Guide to California Wine, 103

•**Conomikes Reports, Inc.**
6033 W. Century Blvd. #990, Los Angeles, CA, 90045-5309

Constitutional Rights Foundation
601 S Kingsley Dr, Los Angeles, CA, 90005-2319
Bill of Rights Newsletter, 171

Construction Market Data
2625 Manhattan Beach Blvd., #110, Redondo Beach, CA, 90278-1604
Construction Market Data, 246

Consumer Action
116 New Montgomery St., San Francisco, CA, 94105-3607
Consumer ActioNews, 252

Continental Features/Continental News Service
341 W Broadway # 265, San Diego, CA, 92101-3802
Inkslinger's Review, 953

Contra Costa College
2600 Mission Bell Dr, San Pablo, CA, 94806-3195
Advocate, 197

Cooks Corner
PO Box 50116, Irvine, CA, 92619-0116
Cooks Corner, The, 427

Cooperative Resources & Services Project
3551 White House Pl, Los Angeles, CA, 90004-5944
L.A. Co-Ops & the Shared Housing Networker, 1,035

•**Corbell Publishing Co.**
4676 Admiraity Way, Ste. 300, Marina Del Rey, CA, 90292

•**Correctional Education Assn. Region VII**
L.A. County Office of Ed., 9300 E. Imperial Hwy., Downey, CA, 90242

Coryell Newsletter
PO Box 662, Santa Barbara, CA, 93102-0662
Coryell Newsletter, 451

Cossman International, Inc.
PO Box 4480, Palm Springs, CA, 92263
Think Yourself Rich, 154

•**Council on Education in Management**
321 Lennon Lane, Walnut Creek, CA, 94598

Council of Film Organizations
334 W 54th St, Los Angeles, CA, 90037-3806
Film Councilor, 419

Covenant of the Goddess
PO Box 11363, Oakland, CA, 94611-0363
Themoporia, 1,074

Crawdaddy!
PO Box 231155, Encinitas, CA, 92023-1155
Crawdaddy!, 911

Creative Direct Marketing
1815 W 213th St Ste 210, Torrance, CA, 90501-2839
Direct Response, 274

CreeYadio Services
PO Box 9787, Fresno, CA, 93794-9787
One to One, the Journal of Creative Broadcasting, 124

•**Crittenden Research, Inc.**
PO Box 1150, Novato, CA, 94948

Culinary Alliance
515 Cabrillo Park Dr Ste 205, Santa Ana, CA, 92701-5016
Serving America, 1,076

Cultural Arts Division
475 14th Street, 11th Floor, Oakland, CA, 94612
Oakland Artscape, 1,040

The Curmudgeon's Home Companion
PO Box 3312, Yountville, CA, 94599-3312
Curmudgeon's Home Companion, The, 427

Cyberedge Information Services
#1 Gate Six Rd., Ste. G, Sausalito, CA, 94965
CyberEdge Journal, 218

Cycad Society
c/o David S. Mayo, 1161 Phyllis Ct., Mountain View, CA, 94040
Cycad Newsletter, 109

Cypress College
9200 Valley View St, Cypress, CA, 90630-5897
Charge, 196

DES Action USA
1615 Broadway, Ste. 510, Oakland, CA, 94612-2125
DES Action Voice, 503

•**Daily Graphs, Inc.**
12655 Beatrice St, Los Angeles, CA, 90066-7300

Dal Investment Co.
235 Montgomery St., Ste. 662, San Francisco, CA, 94104-2994
No Load Fund X, 680

Dance Bay Area
2403 16th St, San Francisco, CA, 94103-4210
In Dance, 266

•**Darnell Group Inc.**
4720 Crestview Dr, Norco, CA, 91760-1623

Darrells Graphic & Print
8554 Loretto Ave, Cotati, CA, 94931-4471
Meeting Planners Alert, 575

DataBase Associates
PO Box 215, Morgan Hill, CA, 95038-0215
Database Review, 219

Data Processing Digest, Inc.
PO Box 1249, Los Angeles, CA, 90078-1249
Data Processing Digest, 219

•**Dataquest Div. Dun & Bradstreet Corp.**
1290 Ridder Park Dr, San Jose, CA, 95131-2304

Dateline: Mexico Today
9297 Siempre Viva Rd # 5-144, San Diego, CA, 92173-3628
Dateline: Mexico Today, 629

David H. Menashe & Co.
PO Box 663, Woodland Hills, CA, 91365-0663
Fundline, 665

David Hall's Rare Coins & Collectibles
1936e E Deere Ave # 102, Santa Ana, CA, 92705-5723
David Hall's Inside View, 661

De Anza College
21250 Stevens Creek Blvd, Cupertino, CA, 95014-5797
Grapevine, 196

Delco Systems Operations
6767 Hollister Ave, Goleta, CA, 93117-3086
Highlights, 585

Democratic Socialists of America
2827 Catania Way, Sacramento, CA, 95826-2228
Our Struggle/Nuestra Lucha, 995

Dialog Information Services, Inc.
3460 Hillview Ave, Palo Alto, CA, 94304-1338
Searching Dialogue: A Complete Guide, 22

Diamond Consulting
539 Telegraph Canyon Rd Ste, 145, Chula Vista, CA, 91910-6436
Lease Purchase Times, 1,035

Dicks of America
PO Box 600782, San Diego, CA, 92160-0782
Dickin' Around, 177

Document Center
1504 industrial Way, Unit 9, Belmont, CA, 94002
Document Center Update, 797

Dominican School of Philosophy & Theology
Graduate Theological Union, 2401 Ridge Road, Berkeley, CA, 94709
Cross Currents, 196

Don Chaddock
Chaddock Productions, 216 Brimmer Road, 216 brimmer Road, CA, 95340
Sorcerer's Scroll, 370

Dow Theory Letters, Inc.
PO Box 1759, La Jolla, CA, 92038-1759
Dow Theory Letters, 662

Driving School Assn. of the Americas
111 W Pomona Blvd, Monterey Park, CA, 91754-7208
Dual News, 1,177

Dunn Technology Inc.
1855 E Vista Way Ste 1, Vista, CA, 92084-3399
Dunn Report, 1,004

Dynamic Investor
8010 S Highway 101, Ukiah, CA, 95482-9342
Dynamic Investor, The, 662

•**ECCE Clampsus Vitos**
Drawer 2247, Menlo Park, CA, 94026-2247

EMS Network International
858 Longview Rd, Burlingame, CA, 94010-6974
Competitive Concepts, 133

ETS Research
80 Narcissa Dr # 700-32, Rancho Palos Verdes, CA, 90275-5910
Monitor, We the People & Our Two Cents Worth, 471

Early Typewriter Collectors Assn.
2591 Military Ave, Los Angeles, CA, 90064-1933
ETCetera, 53

East Bay Media Center
2054 University Ave Ste 203, Berkeley, CA, 94704-1059
Clearing the Air, 1,166

East Bay Municipal Utility Dist.
2130 Adeline St # 24055, Oakland, CA, 94607-2335
Waterline, 1,027

East Bay Women for Peace
2302 Ellsworth St, Berkeley, CA, 94704-1522
Women for Peace Newsletter, East Bay, 1,000

Eco-Home Network
4344 Russell Ave, Los Angeles, CA, 90027-4508
Ecolution: The Eco-Home Newsletter, 378

EcoPsychology Newsletter
PO Box 7487, Berkeley, CA, 94707-0487
EcoPsychology Newsletter, 1,013

Eden Ranch
PO Box 370, Topanga, CA, 90290-0370
Organic Consumer Report, 522

Educational Communications
Environmental Res. Library, Box 351419, Los Angeles, CA, 90035-9119
Compendium Newsletter 'Your Guide to the Worlds Environmental Crises', 376

Edward Howell Family Assn.
22723 Rio Gusto Ct, Valencia, CA, 91354-2355
Edward Howell Family Assn. -Newsletter, 452

ElderCare Financial Management Inc.
170 Elaine Dr., Rosewell, CA, 30075
ElderCare Forum, 1,208

Electric Power Research Inst.
PO Box 10412, Palo Alto, CA, 94309-0412
Exploratory Research Letter, 1,002

Eli Grad
22 Haven Rd., Wellesley Hills, CA, 02181-2405
Grad Family Newsletter, 455

•**Elk Horn Publishing**
25420 Via Cincindela, Carmel, CA, 93923-8412

Elvis Now Fan Club
PO Box 6581, San Jose, CA, 95150-6581
Elvis Now Fan Club Newsletter, 417

•**Elysium Institute**
814 Robinson Rd, Topanga, CA, 90290-3627

Employment Development Dept.
1350 Front St Ste 3010, San Diego, CA, 92101-3610
San Diego Labor Market Bulletin, 705

End Violence Against the Next Generation, Inc.
977 Keeler Ave, Berkeley, CA, 94708-1440
Last Resort, 169

Energy Modeling Forum
Stanford Univ., Terman Engineering Ctr., Stanford, CA, 94305-1901
EMF Update, 352

Entree Travel
695 Olive Rd., Santa Barbara, CA, 93108-1442
Entree Travel Newsletter, 1,184

Environmental Business International, Inc.
PO Box 371769, San Diego, CA, 92137-1769
Environmental Business Journal, 379

Environmental Law Society
U.C. Davis School of Law, Davis, CA, 95616
Environs, 381

Epiphyllum Society of America
PO Box 1395, Monrovia, CA, 91017-1395
Epiphyllum Society of America Bulletin, 440

Equal Relationships Institute
PO Box 731, Pacific Palisades, CA, 90272-0731
New Relationships, 815

Equestrian Trails, Inc.
13741 Foothill Blvd., 2201, Sylmar, CA, 91342-3133
Equestrian Trails, 559

* See ***MULTI-PUBLISHER INDEX*** for list of publications.

Eric Gamonal
22415 Del Valle St, Woodland Hills, CA, 91364
Freak Man Freak, 1,040

Ernest Bloch Society
34844 Old Stage Rd., Gualala, CA, 95445
Ernest Bloch Society Bulletin, 912

Esperanto League for North America
PO Box 1129, El Cerrito, CA, 94530-1129
Esperanto U.S.A., 821

Evento Pubs.
PO Box 77291, San Francisco, CA, 94107-0291
California Wine Merchant's Gazette, 102

•Executive Press, Inc.
PO Box 21639, Concord, CA, 94521

Eye on Santa Ana
14561 Livingston Ave, Tustin, CA, 92680-2618
Eye on Santa Ana, 1,040

Fabian Investment Resources
2100 Main Street, Ste. 300, Huntington Beach, CA, 92648
Fabian Domestic Investment Resource, 663

Fair Witness Project
4219 W Olive Ave # 247, Burbank, CA, 91505-4215
Fair Witness Focus, 1,199

Falcon Pubs.
8432 Steller Dr, Culver City, CA, 90232-2425
Key, 369

•Family Connection
730 Grand Ave, Pomona, CA, 91765-4462

Family Services Program
PO Box 1296, Bishop, CA, 93515-1296
Toiyable Indian Health Project, Inc., 416

Family University
PO Box 270616, San Diego, CA, 92198-2616
Smart Dads, 416

•Fan Club Publishing Co. / Louis Wendruck
Box 69A04-Dept. OX, West Hollywood, CA, 90069-0066

Fancy Publications, Inc.
P.O. Box 6050, Irvine, CA, 92718
Motorcycle Consumer News, 263

Fandango
1613 Escalero Rd, Santa Rosa, CA, 95409-3909
Czech Republic Business & Investment News, 644

Farmers Insurance Group
4680 Wilshire Blvd, Los Angeles, CA, 90010-3807
Emblem Flashes, 583

•Fedl. Reserve Bank of San Francisco
Box 7702, Public Information Department, San Francisco, CA, 94120-7702

•Federal State Market News
1220 N St. #216, Box 942871, Sacramento, CA, 94271-0001

•Federal-State Market News Service
1220 N Street, Sacramento, CA, 95814-5621

Felton Enterprises
501 Palmetto Dr # 100, Pasadena, CA, 91105-1608
Personal Moneyplan, 682

Fenstermaker Newsnotes
4223 Hackett Ave, Lakewood, CA, 90713-3207
Fenstermaker Newsnotes, 453

Ferrell
13800 Biola Ave Ste 1488, La Mirada, CA, 90639-0002
Construction Management World, 246

Ferris Networks
353 Sacramento Street, #600, San Francisco, CA, 94111
Ferris E-Mail Analyzer, 222

The Fielding Institute
2112 Santa Barbara St, Santa Barbara, CA, 93105-3538
Fielding Networker, The, 197

Fields Family Findings
4740 Roosevelt Ave., Sacramento, CA, 95820-4522
Fields Family Findings, 453

Film Analyst
2404 Narbonne Way, Costa Mesa, CA, 92627-1424
Film Analyst, The, 419

Film Technology Co.
726 Cole Ave, Los Angeles, CA, 90038-3606
Film Technology News, 419

Finnish-American Soc. of Santa Clara Cnty.
878 Hummingbird Dr, San Jose, CA, 95125-2918
Finnish-American Soc. of Santa Clara Cnty. Newsletter, 401

First Air Commandos Assn.
PO Box 466, Broderick, CA, 95605-0466
Basha Blabber, 27

First Interstate Bank of California
633 W. 5th St., Los Angeles, CA, 90071-2005
Q, 596

First Unitarian Church of Berkeley
1 Lawson Rd, Berkeley, CA, 94707-1015
Uniquest, 1,052

Fitness Motivation, Institute of America
36 Harold Ave, San Jose, CA, 95117-1026
Fitfax Journal, 506

Flat Earth Research Soc. Int'l.
PO Box 2533, Lancaster, CA, 93539-2533
Flat Earth News, 1,096

Fleet Data Service
1218 Portola Ave # B, Torrance, CA, 90501-2611
Marine Management Letter, 1,111

Floatation Tank Assn.
PO Box 1396, Grass Valley, CA, 95945-1396
Floating, 506

Flower Essence Society
PO Box 459, Nevada City, CA, 95959-0459
Flower Essence Society Newsletter, 506

Floyd Oydegard
114 Trenethan Ave., Box 2201, Santa Cruz, CA, 95062-1312
Viking Kinfolk, 469

Flush Rush Quarterly
PO Box 270525, San Diego, CA, 92198-2525
Flush Rush Quarterly, 990

Foodservice Planning Institute
PO Box 1169, Santa Barbara, CA, 93102-1169
Foodservice Planning, 1,075

Foodtalk
Box 6543, San Francisco, CA, 94101-0120
Foodtalk, 429

•Ford Investor Services
11722 Sorrento Valley Rd., Suite 1, San Diego, CA, 92121-1099

Forecaster Publishing Co.
19623 Ventura Blvd., Tarzana, CA, 91356-2918
Forecaster Moneyletter, The, 292

Forensic Drug Abuse Advisor
PO Box 5139, Berkeley, CA, 94705-0139
Forensic Drug Abuse Advisor, 284

Forest Landowners of California
3807 Pasadena Ave Ste 100, Sacramento, CA, 95821-2863
Forest Land Owner, 435

Forest Lawn Memorial Parks
1712 S Glendale Ave, Glendale, CA, 91205-3320
Grapevine, 585

Forum for Health Care Planning
314 Vista De Valle, Mill Valley, CA, 94941-4017
Forum News, 563

Foundation for Homeopathic Education and Research
2124 Kittredge St., Berkeley, CA, 94704-1436
Homeopathic Research Reports, 875

Foundation for San Francisco's Architectural Heritage
2007 Franklin St, San Francisco, CA, 94109-2909
Heritage Newsletter, 60

Four Winds Publishing
4729 Amelia Dr, Fair Oaks, CA, 95628-5517
Connections to Mail Order/World Trade and Homebased Business Info., 12

Fr. Kolbe Missionaries
531 E. Merced Ave., West Covina, CA, 91790-5025
Youth Mission for the Immaculata National Newsletter, 1,060

Fr. Seraphim Rose Foundation
PO Box 1656, Forestville, CA, 95436-1656
Fr. Seraphim Rose Foundation Newsletter, 1,074

Frances Nelson
4041 Pedley Rd Spc 18, Riverside, CA, 92509-2822
Russell Register, 466

Franciscan Communications Center
1229 Santee St, Los Angeles, CA, 90015-2566
Focus, 1,057

Frank Maga & Assocs.
Box 6805, Pine Mountain Club, CA, 93222
Newsletter of Engineering Analysis Software, 362

Fred DeRuvo
1141 Holly Avenue, Clovis, CA, 93611
The Modeler's Resource, 554

Free Enterprise Society
300 W. Shaw Ave., #205, Clovis, CA, 93612-3680
Free Enterprise Society News, 1,145

FreeNetwork
PO Box 224, Long Beach, CA, 90801-0224
Freeperson Network News, 630

Freeland Family Assn.
220 4th St, Del Mar, CA, 92014-3254
Freeland, 454

Fresno County Public Library
2420 Mariposa St, Fresno, CA, 93721-2204
Impulse, 799

Fresno Teachers Assn
5334 N Fresno St # A, Fresno, CA, 93710-6828
Chalk Talk, 304

Frick Winery
23072 Walling Rd., Geyserville, CA, 95441-9676
Frick Winery Information Letter, 103

Friends of the Bancroft Library, Inc., The
Univ. Of Calif., Berkeley, CA, 94720-6000
Bancroftiana, 536

Friends Committee on Legislation of California
926 J St Ste 707, Sacramento, CA, 95814-2707
FCL Newsletter, 173

Friends of Photography
250 4th St, San Francisco, CA, 94103-3117
Re:view, 978

Friends of the River
Bldg. C, Ft. Mason Ctr., San Francisco, CA, 94123-1380
Headwaters, 384

Friends of Wayfarers Chapel
5755 Palos Verdes Dr., S., Palos Verdes, CA, 90274-5950
Reflections, 1,050

Friends of the Western Philatelic Library Inc.
PO Box 2219, Sunnyvale, CA, 94087-0219
Bay Phil, 970

Frost Family Assn.
2665 Orchard St, Soquel, CA, 95073-2625
Frost on the Vine, 454

Fujitsu Business Communications
3190 E Miraloma Ave, Anaheim, CA, 92806-1906
Pointe of View, 1,199

Fun Seekers
3455 Euclid Ave, Concord, CA, 94519-2320
Fun Seekers, 369

Future Scan
2118 Wilshire Blvd # 826, Santa Monica, CA, 90403-5704
FutureScan, 15

Future Technology Intelligence Report, Inc.
PO Box 423652, San Francisco, CA, 94142-3652
Future Technology Intelligence Report, 1,097

G & B Records
PO Box 10150, Terra Bella, CA, 93270-0150
Sales Letter, 21

Gambling Times, Inc.
16140 Valerio St. #B, Van Nuys, CA, 91406-2916
Experts Blackjack Newsletter, 438

Garamond Press
24667 Heather Ct, Hayward, CA, 94545-2004
Type, 1,007

Garside
5200 Irvine Blvd Spc 370, Irvine, CA, 92720-2060
Garside Forecast, 666

Gateways
415 Summit Rd, Watsonville, CA, 95076-9781
Gateways, 1,047

Gault Millau, Inc.
5900 Wilshire Blvd Ste 650, Los Angeles, CA, 90036-5018
Andre Gayot's Tastes, 1,182

Gay & Lesbian Historical Soc. of Northern California
2940 16th Street, San Francisco, CA, 94103
OurStories, 445

Gay & Lesbian Press Assn.
PO Box 8185, Universal City, CA, 91608-0185
Media Reporter, 445

Gene Lees Jazzletter
PO Box 240, Ojai, CA, 93024-0240
Gene Lees Jazzletter, 912

•Gene Perret's Round Table & Comedy Svces.
2135 Huntington Drive, San Marino, CA, 91108-2045

General Motors Corp., GM Assembly Div.
8000 Van Nuys Blvd, Van Nuys, CA, 91402-6025
Auto-Gram, 576

•Genesis Publishing, Inc.
10455 Sorrento Valley Rd Ste, 103, San Diego, CA, 92121-1621

Geo-Monitor
65 Washington St # 400, Santa Clara, CA, 95050-6138
Geo-Monitor, 476

Georgian Church
1908 Verde St, Bakersfield, CA, 93304-2841
Georgian Newsletter, 948

• See **MULTI-PUBLISHER INDEX** for list of publications.

German Genealogical Society of America
PO Box 291818, Los Angeles, CA, 90029-8818
Newsletter of the German Genealogical Society of America, 462

Gerson Institute
PO Box 430, Bonita, CA, 91908-0430
Healing Newsletter, 508

Getty Conservation Institute
4503 Glencoe Ave, Marina Del Rey, CA, 90292-6372
Conservation: The Getty Conservation Institute Newsletter, 903

Geyser, Inc., The
PO Box 1738, Santa Monica, CA, 90406-1738
Geyser Geothermal Energy Newsletter, 354

Gileland/Gilliland Newsletter
1400 Glenwood Rd Apt 201, Glendale, CA, 91201-1919
Gileland/Gilliland Newsletter, 454

•**Glaucoma Research Fondation**
490 Post St Ste 830, San Francisco, CA, 94102-1409

Global Business Technology Report
5100-1B, Suite 170, Concord, CA, 94521
Global Business Technology Report, 139

Goethe Society of N. America
German Dept., Univ of California, Irvine, Irvine, CA, 92717-3150
Goethe News & Notes, 821

Gold Mining Stock Report
PO Box 1217, Lafayette, CA, 94549-1217
Gold Mining Stock Report, 666

Golden Apple Pubs.
15208 Carnell St, Whittier, CA, 90603-2205
Uncommon Cook, 433

Golden State Mutual Life Ins. Co.
1999 W Adams Blvd, Los Angeles, CA, 90018-3514
Golden Pen, 584

Gomberg Fredrikson & Assocs.
703 Market St., Ste. 2101, San Francisco, CA, 94103-2131
Gomberg-Fredrikson Report, 103

Goodkin Group
501 Pine Needles Dr, Del Mar, CA, 92014-3333
Goodkin Report, 990

Graduate Management Admission Council
2400 Broadway St Ste 230, Santa Monica, CA, 90404-3064
Inside GMAC, 313

•**Graduate Theological Union**
2400 Ridge Rd, Berkeley, CA, 94709-1212

Graham-Rea Investment Analysis
10966 Chalon Rd, Los Angeles, CA, 90077-3208
Graham-Rea Investment Analysis, 667

Grateful Dead Mercantile Co.
PO Box X, Novato, CA, 94948-1210
Grateful Dead Almanac, 417

Grayson Associates, Inc.
108 Loma Media Rd, Santa Barbara, CA, 93103-2178
Grayson Report, 15

•**Greater Stockton Chamber of Commerce**
445 W Weber Ave Ste 220, Stockton, CA, 95203-3148

Greek Orthodox Church of the Ascension
4700 Lincoln Ave, Oakland, CA, 94602-2535
Ascension Bulletin, 1,067

Green City Project
P.O. Box 31251, San Francisco, CA, 94131
Green City Calendar, 814

Greenwich Consulting
15821 Setlock Ave., Chino Hills, CA, 91709
Fleet Street, 1,177

Grossmont District Hospital
PO Box 158, La Mesa, CA, 91944-0158
Capsule, 579

Growing Native Research Institute
PO Box 489, Berkeley, CA, 94701-0489
Growing Native Newsletter, 441

Guatemala News & Information Bureau
PO Box 28594, Oakland, CA, 94604-8594
Report on Guatemala, 637

Guide Dogs for the Blind, Inc
PO Box 151200, San Rafael, CA, 94915-1200
Guide Dog News, 111

The Guide to Early Retirement
PO Box 6824, Laguna Niguel, CA, 92607-6824
Guide to Early Retirement, 667

Guidelines
PO Box 456, Orinda, CA, 94563-0456
Guidelines Letter, 60

Gullwing Group Intl.
2229 Via Cerritos, Palos Verdes, CA, 90274-2141
300 Star Letter, 69

H.C. Williams
P.O. Box 423653, San Francisco, CA, 94142
Beem, 813

H.M. Gousha, Simon & Schuster, Inc.
320 Soquel Way, Sunnyvale, CA, 94086-4101
Chek-Chart Tractor Digest, 35

HSN Consultants, Inc.
300 Esplanade, Suite 1790, Oxnard, CA, 93030
Nilson Report, 96

HTE Research, Inc.
400 Oyster Pt. Blvd., Ste. 220, S. San Francisco, CA, 94080-1918
SIBS Newsletter, 339

Hamersky & Allied Families Newsletter
PO Box 1334, San Diego, CA, 92112-1334
Hamersky & Allied Families Newsletter, 455

Harlynne Geisler
5361 Javier St, San Diego, CA, 92117-3215
Story Bag: A National Storytelling Newsletter, 331

Harris Publishing
1563 Solan Avenue, Suite 201, Berkeley, CA, 94707-2116
Garlic Times, 933

Harrison Fisher Society, The
PO Box 8188, Redlands, CA, 92375-1388
Harrison Fisher Society Newsletter, 53

Hataye
43 Deerwood, Aliso Viejo, CA, 92656-2105
Japan Robotics, 227

Hawthorne Community Hospital
11711 Grevillea Ave, Hawthorne, CA, 90250-2222
Responses, 572

Healing Woman
PO Box 3038, Moss Beach, CA, 94038-3038
Healing Woman, The, 1,209

Health Alert
PO Box 22620, Carmel, CA, 93922
Health Alert, 509

Health Media of America
3309 4th Ave., San Diego, CA, 92103-5703
Nutrition Report, 934

Healthline
830 Menlo Ave., Ste. 100, Menlo Park, CA, 90425
Healthline, 511

Heese & Assocs.
15957 Alta Vista Dr., #4, La Mirada, CA, 90638-3244
Investment Forecast, 671

Henderson Ventures
101 1st St Ste 444, Los Altos, CA, 94022-2706
Henderson Electronic Market Forecast, 338

Hennessey's Wines & Spirits
3600 16th, San Francisco, CA, 94114-1566
Hennessey's Wines & Spirits, 103

Henry-Madison Research
PO Box 1616-xo, Rocklin, CA, 95677-7616
U.S. & World Early Warning Report for Investors, 690

Herst Corp., The
PO Box 3373, Thousand Oaks, CA, 91359-0373
Elvis Intl. Forum, 912

•**High-Tech Hot Sheet**
114 Sansome St., Ste. 1224, San Francisco, CA, 94104-3823

Highgate Road Social Science Research Station
32 Highgate Rd, Berkeley, CA, 94707-1141
Russia and Her Neighbors, Facts & Views on Daily Life, 637

Hispanic Business, Inc.
360 S. Hope Ave., Ste. 300C, Santa Barbara, CA, 93105-4017
Se Habla Espanol Newsletter, 861

Holistic Health/Academy
218 Avenue B, Redondo Beach, CA, 90277-4706
Holistic, 512

Hollywood Radio & Television Society
13701 Riverside Dr Ste 205, Sherman Oaks, CA, 91423-2447
Ollie, The, 124

Hollywood Scriptwriter
1626 N. Wilcox, #385, Hollywood, CA, 90028-6273
Hollywood Scriptwriter, 982

Hospital Council of Southern California
201 N. Figueroa St., 4th Fl., Los Angeles, CA, 90012-2623
Newswatch, 521

Hospital & Service Employees Union
1247 W 7th St, Los Angeles, CA, 90017-2309
Voice of Local 399, 711

House Ear Institute
2100 W. 3rd, Los Angeles, CA, 90057-2115
Review, The, 886

Houston Fearless 76 Corp.
203 W Artesia Blvd, Compton, CA, 90220-5550
HF News, 585

Hughes Aircraft Co.
Box 45066, Bldg. C1/C114, Los Angeles, CA, 90045-0066
Hughesnews, 585

Human Factors and Ergonomics Society
PO Box 1369, Santa Monica, CA, 90406-1369
Human Factors & Ergonomics Society Bulletin, 384

HumanWare, Inc.
6245 King Rd., Loomis, CA, 95650-8801
HumanAwareness and Low Vision Perspectives, 277

Hume Lake Christian Camps
256 N Maple Ave, Fresno, CA, 93702-2465
Hume Lake News, 1,063

Humor Defense Publ.
PO Box 10944, Pleasanton, CA, 94588-0944
Humor Defense, 604

Humphreys College
6650 Inglewood Ave, Stockton, CA, 95207-3896
Humphreys College Quarterly News Bulletin, 187

Huntington Library Press
1151 Oxford Rd, San Marino, CA, 91108-1299
Huntington Calendar, 904

Hydro-Aire, Crane
3000 Winona Ave, Burbank, CA, 91504-2540
Hy-Lites, 585

•**IMR, INC-Industry Market Reports**
960, N. San Antonio Rd., Suite 130, Los Altos, CA, 94022-1322

I.Q. Trends
7440 Girard Ave Ste 4, La Jolla, CA, 92037-5157
Investment Quality Trends, 672

I S G A
2205 Dixon St., Chico, CA, 95926-2179
Kiwifruit Growers of California-Newsletter, 43

•**ITOM Intl. Co.**
PO Box 1450, Los Altos, CA, 94023-1450

ITS
3301 Alta Arden Expy., Ste. 3, Sacramento, CA, 95825-2121
Clinical Pearl News, 1,010

Immigrant Genealogical Society
PO Box 7369, Burbank, CA, 91510-7369
Immigrant Genealogical Society Newsletter, 457

Imperial Beach Times, Inc.
PO Box 1208, Imperial Beach, CA, 91933-1208
Imperial Beach Times, 982

In ONE EAR Publications
29481 Manzanita Dr, Campo, CA, 91906-1128
Bueno, 820

Income Investment Advisory
P.O Box 882002, San Diego, CA, 92168
Income Advisor, 669

Independent Scholars of Asia, Inc.
2321 Russell St Apt 3a, Berkeley, CA, 94705-1959
Independent Scholars of Asia Newsletter, 632

Indochina Human Rights Group
PO Box 1163, Burlingame, CA, 94011-1163
Vietnam Journal, 999

Indoor Air Information Service
PO Box 8446, Santa Cruz, CA, 95061-8446
Indoor Air Bulletin, 385

Industry Publishing Company
155 Bovet Rd., Ste. 800, San Mateo, CA, 94402
P.C. Letter, 233

•**InfoCom Group**
1250 45th St., Ste 200, Emeryville, CA, 94608-2924

Infomercial Marketing Report
11533 Thurston Cir, Los Angeles, CA, 90049-2426
Infomercial Marketing Report, 16

Information Access Co.
362 Lakeside Dr, Foster City, CA, 94404-1146
Online News, 233

Info to Go
P.O. Box 272, Garden Grove, CA, 92642-0272
Info to Go, 225

Information for Public Affairs, Inc.
State Net, 2101 K Street, Sacramento, CA, 95816-4920
C.J. Weekly, 987

* See ***MULTI-PUBLISHER INDEX*** for list of publications.

Information Research
24885 Corbit Pl, Yorba Linda, CA, 92687
Laboratory Computer Letter, 1,098

Information Services on Latin America
464 19th St, Oakland, CA, 94612-2297
ISLA, 632

Informtech Int'l Inc.
10734 Jefferson Blvd. #516, Culver City, CA, 90230-4969
In Touch, 225

Inglewood Public Library
101 W Manchester Blvd, Inglewood, CA, 90301-1753
Inglewood Public Library Quarterly Report, 800

Initiative Resource Center
235 Douglass St, San Francisco, CA, 94114-2424
Initiative & Referendum: The Power of the People!, 991

Inner Growth Seminar
216 Mirada Ave., San Rafael, CA, 94903-3931
Inner Growth Newsletter, 1,048

Innovative Thinking Network
1324 State Street J-153, Santa Barbara, CA, 93101-2620
Mind Play, 145

Inside Report on New Media
901 Mariner's Blvd., San Mateo, CA, 94404
Inside Report on New Media, 858

Inside Travel News
6229 Bristol Pky, Culver City, CA, 90230-6903
Inside Travel News, 1,185

Insider's Guide
3419 Via Lido Ste 620, Newport Beach, CA, 92663-3908
Insider's Guide to First Class Travel, 1,185

Institute for American Church Growth
PO Box 541, Monrovia, CA, 91017-0541
Church Growth Resource News, 1,046

Institute for Civil Justice-Rand Corp.
1700 Main St # 2138, Santa Monica, CA, 90401-3208
Civil Justice Roundtable, 724

Institute for Contemporary Studies
720 Market St., San Francisco, CA, 94102
News From ICS, 994

Institute for Creation Research
10946 Woodside Ave N, Santee, CA, 92071-2833
Acts & Facts, 1,061

Institute of Electrical & Electronics Engineers, Inc.,
1515 West 190th Street, Suite 530, Gardena, CA, 90248-4323
IEEE Bulletin, 366

•**Institute for Food & Development**
398 60th St, Oakland, CA, 94618-1212

Institute for the Future
2740 Sand Hill Rd, Menlo Park, CA, 94025-7020
IFTF Perspectives, 471

Institute of Governmental Studies, University of California
102 Moses Hall, Berkeley, CA, 94720-0001
Public Affairs Report, 997

Institute of Human Origins
2700 Bancroft Way, Berkeley, CA, 94704-1719
Institute of Human Origins, 51

Institute for Interdisciplinary Research
2828 3rd St Suite 11, Santa Monica, CA, 90405-4150
International Christian Studies Association Newsletter (ICSA Newsletter), 1,064

Institute of Marine Sciences
Univ. of California, Santa Cruz, CA, 95064
Currents, 1,096

Institute of Metal Repair
1558 S Redwood St, Escondido, CA, 92025-5643
Repairing Metalware, 892

Institute of Metaphysics
PO Box 640, Yucca Valley, CA, 92286-0640
Light of the Logos, 974

Institute of Modern Culture
Univ. Of Southern California, Mc 4353, Los Angeles, CA, 90089-0001
Institute of Modern Russian Culture Newsletter, 408

Institute of Noetic Sciences
475 Gate 5 Rd Ste 300, Sausalito, CA, 94965-2835
Noetic Sciences Bulletin, 974

Institute for Research on Women & Gender
Serra House, Stanford University, Stanford, CA, 94305-8640
Institute for Research on Women & Gender-Newsletter, 1,209

Institute for the Study of Human Knowledge
Center for Health Sciences, PO Box 176, Los Altos, CA, 94023
Mind/Body Medicine Newsletter, The, 518

Insurance Marketing & Management Services
12424 Wilshire Blvd., Ste. 600, Santa Monica, CA, 90025-1040
IMMS Weekly Marketeer, 620

Inter-Tribal Council of California
2755 Cottage Way, Ste. 14, Sacramento, CA, 95825-1221
Tribal Spokesman, 406

Interactive Marketing Newsletter
2200 Pacific Coast Hwy Ste 318, Hermosa Beach, CA, 90254-2702
Interactive Marketing Newsletter, 16

•**Interface Press**
4717 N Figueroa St # 42211, Los Angeles, CA, 90042-4406

Interfaith Hunger Coalition of Southern California
2449 Hyperion Ave Apt 100, Los Angeles, CA, 90027-4760
Bread & Justice, 171

Interior Concerns Publications
PO Box 2386, Mill Valley, CA, 94942-2386
Interior Concerns Newsletter, 386

International Academy Holistic Health/Medicine
218 Avenue B, Redondo Beach, CA, 90277-4706
Holistic & Preventive Update, 512

International Academy of Trial Lawyers
4 N 2nd St Ste 175, San Jose, CA, 95113-1306
International Academy of Trial Lawyers Bulletin, 745

International Association for Aquatic Animal Medicine
School of Public Health, Univ. of CA, Berkeley, CA, 94709-1399
IAAAM News, 1,201

International Association of Calculator Co.
14561 Livingston Ave, Tustin, CA, 92680-2618
International Calculator Collector, 554

International Banana Club
2524 El Molino Ave, Altadena, CA, 91001-2318
Woddis Newsletter, 606

International Bicycle Touring Society
PO Box 6979, San Diego, CA, 92166-0979
International Bicycle Touring Society Newsletter, 1,185

International Buddhist Center
924 S New Hampshire Ave, Los Angeles, CA, 90006-1623
Monthly Guide, 1,054

International Business Information Service
First St. , Box 3271, Tustin, CA, 92681-3271
IBIS International Traders Newsletter, 647

International Career Association Network
2900 Amby Pl, Hermosa Beach, CA, 90254-2216
Career Connections, 304

International Center for Dance Ortho.
7922 Oceanus Dr., Hollywood, CA, 90046-2045
Dance Medicine-Health Newsletter, 265

Intl. Ecosystems Univ.
310 Oak Vue Rd, Pleasant Hill, CA, 94523-3618
Ecosphere Magazine/Newsletter, 378

International Fancy Guppy Assn. (IFGA)
20935 Golden Springs Rd., Walnut, CA, 91789
Official Rules and Judging Standards, 50

International Fluidized Bed Institute
4440 Mountain View Ave, Oakland, CA, 94605-1210
International Fluidized Bed Review, 355

Intl. Food, Wine & Travel Writers Assn.
1556 Plateau Ave, Los Altos, CA, 94024-5320
Hospitality World, 574

Intl. Indian Treaty Council Info. Office
54 Mint St., Ste. 400, San Francisco, CA, 94103-1823
Treaty Council News, 493

•**Intl. Institute of Municipal Clerks**
1206 N San Dimas Canyon Rd., San Dimas, CA, 91773-1223

International Jack Benny Fan Club
3190 Oak Rd., Apt. 303, Walnut Creek, CA, 94596-7736
Jack Benny Times, 417

Intl. Light Tackle Tournament Assn.
2044 Fedl. Ave., Costa Mesa, CA, 92627-4132
International Light Tackle Tournament Association, Bulletin, 606

Intl. MIDI Assn.
5316 W 57th St, Los Angeles, CA, 90056-1339
IMA Bulletin, The, 224

Intl. Macrobiotic Shiatsu Society
1122 M St, Eureka, CA, 95501-2442
Healthways, 933

Intl. Radio Club of America
6059 Essex St, Riverside, CA, 92504-1544
DX Monitor, 123

International Reference Organization in Forensic Medicine
1877 Claudia Ave., Simi Valley, CA, 93065-3642
Inform Quarterly Newsletter, 876

International Report
PO Box 4882, Irvine, CA, 92716-4882
International Report, 632

International Rivers Network
1847 Berkeley Way, Berkeley, CA, 94703-1576
World Rivers Review, 398

International Senior Citizen Assn.
255 S. Hill St., Suite 409, Los Angeles, CA, 90012
International Senior Citizen News, 1,107

International Soccer Update
4455 Torrance Blvd # 202, Torrance, CA, 90503-4335
International Soccer Update, 1,132

•**International Society for Individual Liberty**
1800 Market St, San Francisco, CA, 94102-6227

International Spa and Tub Institute
240 S Feldner Rd, Orange, CA, 92668-2716
ISTI Newswire, 849

•**International Union of Petroleum & Industrial Workers**
8131 E. Rosecrans Ave., Paramount, CA, 90723-2798

Intertec International, Inc.
2472 Eastman Ave., Bldg. 33-34, Ventura, CA, 93003
Sales Prospector, 151

Inventor's Workshop Intl.
7332 Mason Ave, Canoga Park, CA, 91306-2822
Lightbulb Journal for Inventors, 951

Investment Quality Trends
7440 Girard Ave Ste 4, La Jolla, CA, 92037-5157
IQ Trends, 668

Investment Reporter
4600 Campus Dr., Ste. 205, Newport Beach, CA, 92660-1801
Investment Reporter, 672

Investor Alert
PO Box 1160, Pacifica, CA, 94044-6160
Investor Alert, 672

Irvine Valley College
5500 Irvine Center Dr, Irvine, CA, 92720-4399
Issues, Irvine Valley College, 186

Isla Vista Food Co-Op
6575 Seville Rd, Isla Vista, CA, 93117-5073
Natural Selections, 432

Islands Publishing Co.
3886 State St, Santa Barbara, CA, 93105-3112
Islands Escapes, 1,186

Israel Foreign Affairs
PO Box 19580, Sacramento, CA, 95819-0580
Israel Foreign Affairs, 633

Ivan Levison & Associates
14 Los Cerros Dr, Greenbrae, CA, 94904-1157
Levison Letter, 17

JAX Mobile Auto Service
1308 Walnut Ave., Manhattan Beach, CA, 90266-5051
Auto Mi$er, 70

JB & ME Publishing
Manhattan Beach, CA, 90266
Selling Space, 22

•**J.D. Power & Assocs.**
30401 Agoura Rd., Agoura Hills, CA, 91301-2084

JEMS Communications Inc.
PO Box 2789, Carlsbad, CA, 92018-2789
EMS Insider, 873

•**JFO Enterprises**
PO Box 818, Palm Springs, CA, 92263-0818

J. Lahm Consultants, Inc.
2630 N. Coronado Dr., Fullerton, CA, 92635-2513
Video Specialist and New Technology, 1,170

J. Taylor Block
P.O. Box 1055, Suisun City, CA, 94585
Total Eclipse, 549

Jack Lamb
P.O. Box 4290, Carlsbad, CA, 92018
Biscuits & Gravy Quarterly, 1,075

James Dines & Co.
PO Box 22, Belvedere, CA, 94920-0022
Dines Letter, 662

•**James Whitaker & Associates**
1 Waters Park Dr., Ste. 104, San Mateo, CA, 94403-1137

Japan Publications Inc.
41 Sutter St. #1112, San Francisco, CA, 94104-4903
Japan Medical Review, 877

* See **MULTI-PUBLISHER INDEX** for list of publications.

Jay Family Assn. West
4406 Moffett Rd, Ceres, CA, 95307-9427
Jay News, 457

Jerod Pore
1800 Market St Ste 141, San Francisco, CA, 94102-6227
Poppin' Zits!, 1,126

Jerry Baly
P.O. Box 505, Claremont, CA, 91711
The Prairie Rambler, 547

Jet Products
5656 Buffalo Ave, Van Nuys, CA, 91401-4505
Desktop Direct Marketing News, 274

•**Jews for Jesus**
PO Box 424885, San Francisco, CA, 94142-4885

Jin Shin Do Foundation Newsletter
P O Box 1097, Felton, CA, 95018
Jin Shin Do Acupressure Newsletter, 515

Joe Sullivan
300 E Arbor St Spc 57, Long Beach, CA, 90805-6855
Mobile Home Living, 902

John Clark Financial Development
505 E 1st St Ste H, Tustin, CA, 92680-3305
Real Estate Tax Letter, 1,151

John T. Reed Publishing
342 Bryan Dr, Danville, CA, 94526-1258
John T. Reed's Real Estate Investor's Monthly, 1,034

Jon S. Strebler's Investment Outlook
229 Citrus Ave, Imperial Beach, CA, 91932-1012
Jon Strebler's Investment Outlook, 673

Joseph Conrad Society of America
C/O Prof. David R. Smith, California Inst. Of Techn, Pasadena, CA, 91125-0001
Joseph Conrad Today, 822

Josh Zander Consulting Services
4286 Redwood Hwy., Ste. 376, San Rafael, CA, 94903
Russian Business News Update, 651

•**Jossey-Bass Publishers, Inc.**
350 Sansome St., Fifth Fl., San Francisco, CA, 94104-1310

Journal of Hospital Occupational Health
PO Box 5241, Concord, CA, 94524-0241
Journal of Hospital Occupational Health, 877

Journalism Assn. of Community Colleges
Los Angeles Pierce College, 6201 Winnetka Ave., Woodland Hills, CA, 91371
Journalism Association of Community Colleges, Newsletter, 696

Joy Publishing
PO Box 827, San Juan Capistrano, CA, 92693-0827
Christian Communicator, 1,062

Judah Magnes Museum
2911 Russell St, Berkeley, CA, 94705-2333
Magnes News, 905

Just Compensation
PO Box 5133, Sherman Oaks, CA, 91413-5133
Just Compensation, 747

•**Kagan World Media Inc.**
126 Clock Tower Pl., Carmel, CA, 93923-8734

Kaslow & Associates
2203 Los Angeles Ave, Berkeley, CA, 94707-2619
Smart's Health and Safety Newsletter, 528

Ken Weisbrod Productions
PO Box 5359, Chatsworth, CA, 91313-5359
Katherine's of Broadway Market, 431

Kenneth Leventhal & Co.
2049 Century Park, #2300, Los Angeles, CA, 90067-3125
Real Estate Newsline, 1,038

Kern County Dental Society
1701 Westwind Drive, Bakersfield, CA, 93301
Kern County Dental Society Newsletter, 270

Kinsman & Assocs.
1901 Sobre Vista Rd, Sonoma, CA, 95476-3237
Telephone Growth Income Service, 689

Klevens Publications, Inc.
7600 E Avenue V, Littlerock, CA, 93543-3203
Cruise & Freighter Travel Letter, 1,183

Kobrin Letter, The
732 Greer Rd, Palo Alto, CA, 94303-3022
Kobrin Letter, The, 169

Korean Research Council
1565 Miramar Ave., Seaside, CA, 93955-3326
Korean Research Bulletin, 633

Kranz Research International
1979 Catrina Ct., San Jose, CA, 95124-5500
East European Kranz Report, 221

Krotona Institute of Theosophy
Ojai, CA, 93023
Krotonian, 974

L/G Research Inc.
4 Orinda Way Ste 230d, Orinda, CA, 94563-2522
No-Load Fund Analyst, 680

L. Ron Hubbard Writers & Illustrators of the Future Contests
PO Box 1630-OC, Los Angeles, CA, 90078-1630
L. Ron Hubbard's Writers and Illustrators of the Future Contests, 1,102

La Fierra University
4700 Pierce St., Riverside, CA, 92515-8247
SDA Dentist, 271

Labor Committee on the Middle East
PO Box 421546, San Francisco, CA, 94142-1546
Middle East Labor Bulletin, 634

Lady Green
3739 Balboa Ave. #195, San Francisco, CA, 94121
Greenery: For Women and Men Exploring Female Domination, 1,110

Latham Foundation
Latham Plaza Bldg., 1826 Clement Ave., Alameda, CA, 94501
Latham Letter, 49

Laucks Foundation
PO Box 5012, Santa Barbara, CA, 93150-5012
Reprint Mailing, 328

Laughter Prescription Newsletter
3011 Quebrada Circle, Carlsbad, CA, 92009-8338
Laughter Prescription Newsletter, 605

Laughter Works Seminars
PO Box 1076, Fair Oaks, CA, 95628-1076
Laughter Works, 605

League to Save Lake Tahoe
989 Tahoe Keys Blvd Ste 6, South Lake Tahoe, CA, 96150-7133
Keep Tahoe Blue, 386

Leahy Newsletter
PO Box 467, Tustin, CA, 92681-0467
Leahy Newsletter, 228

Learning Disabilities Assn. LDA-CA
655 Lewelling Blvd # 355, San Leandro, CA, 94579-1851
Learning Disabilities Assn. of California, 1,118

Leathercraft Guild
PO Box 734, Artesia, CA, 90702-0734
Leathercraft Newsletter, 791

Legionarios del Trabajo en America
2154 S San Joaquin St, Stockton, CA, 95206-3254
Grand Lodge, 178

•**Lemon Administrative Committee**
2202 Monterey St., Ste. 102B, Fresno, CA, 93721-3129

Lepidopterists Society
1900 John St., Manhattan Beach, CA, 90266-2608
Lepidopterists' Society News, 371

Lepp & Assocs.
PO Box 6240, Los Osos, CA, 93412-6240
Natural Image, 977

Lesher Families in America
18310 Florwood Ave., Torrance, CA, 90504
Lesher Families in America, 459

Lewis, D'Amato, Brisbois & Bisgaard
221 N Figueroa St Ste 1200, Los Angeles, CA, 90012-2601
Transnational Bulletin, The, 780

Libertarians for Gay & Lesbian Concerns
1800 Market St # 210, San Francisco, CA, 94102-6227
Civil Libertarian, 988

Liberty Amendment Committee of the USA
PO Box 2386, El Cajon, CA, 92021-0386
Yes on 23/Liberty Amendment News, 494

•**Lifestyles Press**
2641 W La Palma Ave # A, Anaheim, CA, 92801-2602

Light Aircraft Manufacturers Assn.
22 Deer Oaks Ct, Pleasanton, CA, 94588-8233
Light Aircraft Manufacturers Assn. -Newsletter, 30

Lilliputian Bottle Club
5626 S Corning Ave, Los Angeles, CA, 90056-1305
Gulliver's Gazette, 553

Limerick Special Interest Group
Box 365, Moffet, CA, 94035-0365
Pentatette, 605

•**Links Genealogy Publications**
7677 Abaline Way, Sacramento, CA, 95823-4224

Linus Pauling Institute of Science & Medicine
440 Page Mill Rd, Palo Alto, CA, 94306-2025
LPI Newsletter, 877

Litton Industries, Data Systems Div.
29851 Agoura Rd, Agoura Hills, CA, 91301-2511
Data Systems News, 582

Litton Systems Inc. -G/CS Div.
5500 Canoga Ave, Woodland Hills, CA, 91367-6621
Link, 589

Live and Learn
PO Box 6061, Sherman Oaks, CA, 91413-6061
Transender, 1,018

Live and Let Live
PO Box 613, Redwood Valley, CA, 95470-0613
Live and Let Live, 993

•**Lockheed Aircraft Svc. Co.**
PO Box 33, Ontario, CA, 91761-0033

Lonely Planet Pubs.
155 Filbert St., Ste 251, Oakland, CA, 94607-2531
Lonely Planet Newsletter, 1,186

Los Angeles City College
855 N Vermont Ave, Los Angeles, CA, 90029-3588
El Machete Mecha, 982

Los Angeles College of Chiropractic
16200 Amber Valley Dr # B116, Whittier, CA, 90604-4051
News and Alumni Report, 187

Los Angeles County Fed. of Labor, AFL-CIO
2130 W 9th St, Los Angeles, CA, 90006-2202
Los Angeles Citizen, 709

Los Angeles Dental Society
3660 Wilshire Blvd Ste 1152, Los Angeles, CA, 90010-2717
Los Angeles Dental Society, Bulletin, 270

Los Angeles Dept. of Water
111 N Hope St Rm 1509, Los Angeles, CA, 90012-5701
Power System News, 1,002

Los Angeles Health Services
313 N Figueroa St, Los Angeles, CA, 90012-2659
Public Health Letter, 525

Los Angeles Jr. Chamber of Commerce
404 S Bixel St, Los Angeles, CA, 90017-1420
Profile, 161

Los Angeles Music Network
PO Box 8934, Universal City, CA, 91608-0934
Network News, 915

Los Angeles Stamp Collector
Box 1387, Hollywood, CA, 90078
Mitchell Report, The, 677

Los Ninos
9765 Marconi Dr Ste 105, San Ysidro, CA, 92173-3264
Border Connections, 301

Love Letters
1300 Arbolita Dr., La Habra, CA, 90631-3206
Love Letters, 460

Lowen Publishing
2464 Rue Le Charlene, Rancho Palos Verdes, CA, 90275-6361
Office Newsletter, 939

Luciano Curuchet
532 W. Olive ST #8, Inglewood, CA, 90301
Chautauqua, 470

Luna Ventures
Box 398, Suisun, CA, 94585-0398
DOE, 1,102

Lupin Naturalist Club
PO Box 1274, Los Gatos, CA, 95031-1274
California Naturalist, 920

Lutheran Braille Workers, Inc.
PO Box 5000, Yucaipa, CA, 92399-1450
Lutheran Braille Workers Newsletter, 1,072

Lutherans Concerned/N. America
12602 Park St, Cerritos, CA, 90703-1142
Concord, 1,071

Luz Bilingual Publishing, Inc.
PO Box 571062, Tarzana, CA, 91357-1062
Boletin Informativo Newsletter, 115

Lynx Software
PO Box 3510, Los Angeles, CA, 90078-3510
First Edition, 222

Lyon Lamb
4531 W Empire Ave, Burbank, CA, 91505-1143
Lyon Lamb Newsletter, 420

M.AmM.M.A,Co.
P.O. Box 92334, Long Beach, CA, 90809
California Record Collector, 183

MFE Collectors' Bookline
PO Box 150119, San Rafael, CA, 94915-0119
MFE Collectors' Bookline, 118

•**Madent Publishing Inc.**
1280 Coast Village Cir Ste C, Santa Barbara, CA, 93108-2738

Magic Bread Letter
P.O. Box 337-KA, Moss Beach, CA, 94038-0337
Magic Bread Letter, 79

* See **MULTI-PUBLISHER INDEX** for list of publications.

• See **MULTI-PUBLISHER INDEX** for list of publications.

National Association of Home & Workshop Writers
PO Box 10, Palomar Mountain, CA, 92060-0010
NAHWW Newsletter, 557

National Association of Music Merchants
5140 Avenida Encinas, Carlsbad, CA, 92008-4372
National Association of Music Merchants News, 915

•**Natl. Assn. of Tax Consultants Inc.**
454 N 13th St, San Jose, CA, 95112-1719

National Association of Theatre Owners
4605 Lankershim Blvd Ste 340, North Hollywood, CA, 91602-1818
News & Views, 1,173

Natl. Bicycle Dealers Assn.
2240 University Dr # 100, Newport Beach, CA, 92660-3319
Outspokin', 263

Natl. Center for Employee Ownership
2201 Broadway Ste 807, Oakland, CA, 94612-3024
Employee Ownership Report, 137

Natl. Center for Film & Video Preservation
The American Film Institute, 2021 N. Western Ave., Los Angeles, CA, 90027
AMIA Newsletter (Assn. of Moving Image Archivists), 792

National Center for Financial Education
PO Box 34070, San Diego, CA, 92163-4070
NCFE Motivator, 254

•**National Center for Science Education**
925 Kearney St., El Cerrito, CA, 94530-2810

Natl. Congress of Jewish Deaf
13580 Osborne St, Arleta, CA, 91331-5524
National Congress of Jewish Deaf Quarterly, 267

National Council Against Health Fraud
PO Box 1276, Loma Linda, CA, 92354-1276
National Council Against Health Fraud Newsletter, 520

Natl. Ctr. for Youth Law
114 Sansome St., #950, San Francisco, CA, 94104-3820
Youth Law News, 784

National Datsun 510 Club
PO Box 150, Pacific Grove, CA, 93950-0150
510 Again Newsletter, 69

National Federation of Asian American United Metho
330 Ellis St Ste 508, San Francisco, CA, 94102-2735
Asian American News, 1,073

National Forest Recreation Assn.
PO Box 409, Mammoth Lakes, CA, 93546-0409
N.F.R.A. Newsletter, 950

National Health Law Program
2639 S. La Cienega Blvd., Los Angeles, CA, 90034-2675
Health Advocate, 741

National Hobo Association
World Way Center, Box 90430, Los Angeles, CA, 90009-0430
Hobo Times, 814

National Housing Law Project, Inc.
2201 Broadway Ste 815, Oakland, CA, 94612-3024
Housing Law Bulletin, 1,021

Natl. Investigations Committee on Unidentified Flying Object
14617 Victory Blvd., Ste. 4, Van Nuys, CA, 91411-1675
Interspacelink Confidential Newsletter, 1,199

Natl. Lawyers Guild-Santa Clara
131 George St, San Jose, CA, 95110-2116
Anti-Sexism Newsletter, 171

National Marine Fisheries Service
501 W Ocean Blvd Ste 4200, Long Beach, CA, 90802-4221
Foreign Fishery Information Release, 423

Natl. Maritime Museum Assn.
PO Box 470 0310, San Francisco, CA, 94147-0310
Sea Letter, 898

Natl. Motel Brokers
3 37th Ave Ste 5, San Mateo, CA, 94403-4457
Motel News, 575

National Notary Association
8236 Remmet Ave, Canoga Park, CA, 91309-7184
Notary Bulletin, 765

Natl. Nutritional Foods Assn.
150 Paularino Ave Ste 285, Costa Mesa, CA, 92626-3302
NNFA Today, 934

Natl. Org. of Circumcision Info. Res. Ctrs.
PO Box 2512, San Anselmo, CA, 94979-2512
NOCIRC Newsletter, 519

•**Natl. Organization for Women**
PO Box 1267, San Francisco, CA, 94161-1267

National Packing News
403 Main St # 1349, Murphys, CA, 95247-9628
National Packing News, 431

Natl. Scholastic Surfing Assn.
Box 495, Huntington, CA, 92648-0495
Surflines, 1,136

Natl. Second Mortgage Assn.
3833 Schaefer Ave #K, Chino, CA, 91710
NHEMA Legislative Report, 95

Natl. Sheet Music Society, Inc.
1597 Fair Park Ave, Los Angeles, CA, 90041-2255
Song Sheet, The, 917

Nat'l United Front for the Liberation of Vietnam
PO Box 7826, San Jose, CA, 95150
Vietnam Insight, 494

National University
4141 Camino Del Rio S, San Diego, CA, 92108-4193
National University Weekly, 197

National Valentine Collectors Association
PO Box 1404, Santa Ana, CA, 92702-1404
National Valentine Collectors Bulletin, 555

Natl. Women's History Project
7738 Bell Rd, Windsor, CA, 95492-8518
Women's History Network News, 336

Naval Energy & Environmental Support Activities
1001 Lyons St Ste 1, Port Hueneme, CA, 93043-4339
Energy & Environmental News, 352

New Insights
303 Vallejo St., Crockett, CA, 94525
SMT Trends, 851

New Methods Co.
PO Box 22605, San Francisco, CA, 94122-0605
New Methods: The Journal of Animal Health Technology, 1,201

New Orleans Jazz Club of Southern California
PO Box 15212, Long Beach, CA, 90815-0212
Intermission, 912

New Ways to Work
785 Market St Ste 950, San Francisco, CA, 94103-2016
Work Times, 616

New Zealand Consulate
12400 Wilshire Blvd Ste 1150, Los Angeles, CA, 90025-1030
New Zealand Economic Bulletin, 635

Newport Communications
38 Executive Park, Ste. 300, Irvine, CA, 92714-6755
Hotline Newsletter, 1,192

Next Generation Swing Dance Club
236 W Portal Ave Ste 329, San Francisco, CA, 94127-1423
Next Generation Newsletter, 266

Nicaragua Interfaith Committee for Action
942 Market St Ste 411, San Francisco, CA, 94102-4008
Nicaragua Update, 635

Nissan Motor Corp. in USA
PO Box 191, Gardena, CA, 90248-0191
Nissan People, 592

Northcoast Arcata Fortuna Cooperative
977 9th St, Arcata, CA, 95521-6112
Co-Op Newsletter, The, 133

Northern California Academy of General Dentistry
5396 Briar Ridge Dr, Castro Valley, CA, 94552-1710
Northern California Academy of General Dentistry Newsletter, 271

Northern California Association of Law Libraries
Santa Clara University, Santa Clara, CA, 95053-0001
NOCALL Newsletter, 805

Northern California Transplant Bank
Box 7999, San Francisco, CA, 94120-7999
Transplant, 888

Northrop Corp., Aircraft Div.
1 Northrop Ave, Hawthorne, CA, 90250-3277
Northrop News, 593

Nursing Educators MicroWorld
1600 Saratoga Ave., Ste. 403, San Jose, CA, 95129-5108
Nursing Educators MicroWorld, 931

Nurturing Press
975 York Street, JW Mahan, San Francisco, CA, 94110-2812
Nurturing News, 414

O-Hayo Sensei
1032 Irving St. Ste# 508, San Francisco, CA, 94122
O-Hayo Sensei, 347

Oakland Unified School District
1025 2nd Ave, Oakland, CA, 94606-2212
Oakland Unified School District, 1,092

Obedinenie Pervopokhodnikov
1315 Chelten Way, South Pasadena, CA, 91030-3911
Pervopokhodnik, 408

Occidental College
1600 Campus Rd, Los Angeles, CA, 90041-3376
Robinson Jeffers Newsletter, 824

Office of the Americas
8124 W 3rd St Ste 201, Los Angeles, CA, 90048-4328
Focus-Off. of Americas, 990

One Institute
PO Box 69679, West Hollywood, CA, 90069
One-IGLA Bulletin, 445

Open Chain Publishing, Inc.
PO Box 2634, Menlo Park, CA, 94026-2634
Creative Machine Newsletter, 552

Open Doors with Brother Andrew
PO Box 27001, Santa Ana, CA, 92799-7001
Open Doors News Brief, 635

Opportunities in Options
PO Box 2126, Malibu, CA, 90265-7126
Opportunities in Options, 681

Oral-B
1 Lagoon Dr., Redwood City, CA, 94065-1562
Brush Up, 578

Orange County Dental Society
295 S Flower St, Orange, CA, 92668-3466
Impressions, 270

Orange County Report
180 Newport Center Dr., Ste. 180, Newport Beach, CA, 92660-6915
Martin Brower's Orange County Report, 144

Orange Empire Railway Museum
PO Box 548, Perris, CA, 92572-0548
Orange Empire Railway Museum-Gazette, 1,179

Over 30 Parenting
PO Box 57046, Sherman Oaks, CA, 91413-2046
Over 30 Parenting, 415

•**Owens-Illinois Inc.**
3600 Alameda Ave, Oakland, CA, 94601-3329

PAF Associates
8080 Dagger Street, San Diego, CA, 92071-2326
Tucker Topics, 77

P.A.I.I.
PO Box 90710, Santa Barbara, CA, 93190-0710
Innkeeping, 574

PC World Communication, Inc.
501 Second Street, San Francisco, CA, 94107
PC World, 233

•**PEN/LENS Press**
142 N Milpitas Blvd #280, Milpitas, CA, 95035-4401

Pacific Bakers News
180 Mendell St., San Francisco, CA, 94124-1740
Pacific Bakers News, 79

Pacific Book Auction Galleries
139 Townsend St Ste 305, San Francisco, CA, 94107-1922
Pacific Currents, 119

Pacific Christian College
2500 E Nutwood Ave, Fullerton, CA, 92631-3199
Alum News, 186

Pacific Coast Archaeological Society, Inc.
PO Box 10926, Costa Mesa, CA, 92627-0926
PCAS Newsletter, 58

Pacific Coast Stock Exchange
115 Sansome St., San Francisco, CA, 94104-3601
PSE Highlights, 681

Pacific Health Resources
1423 S Grand Ave, Los Angeles, CA, 90015-3073
Messenger, 590

Pacific Southwest Railway Museum Assn.
4695 Nebo Dr, La Mesa, CA, 91941-5259
Pacific Southwest Railway Museum Assn. -Report, 1,029

Pacific Studies Center
222b View St, Mountain View, CA, 94041-1344
Global Electronics, 338

Pacific Telephone
1010 Wilshire Blvd Rm 501, Los Angeles, CA, 90017-5601
Weekly Update, 603

Pacific Valves, Inc.
3201 Walnut Ave, Long Beach, CA, 90807-5225
Globe, 584

Palo Alto Jaycees
325a Forest Ave, Palo Alto, CA, 94301-2515
Palo Alto Jaycee Connection, 181

Palo Verde College
811 W. Chanslorway, Blythe, CA, 92225-1118
Pirate Log, 196

* See **MULTI-PUBLISHER INDEX** for list of publications.

• See **MULTI-PUBLISHER INDEX** for list of publications.

Richard Russell's Dow Theory Letters
PO Box 1759, La Jolla, CA, 92038-1759
Richard Russell's Dow Theory Letters, 684

Richland Co.
7865 E Roseland Dr, La Jolla, CA, 92037-4016
Richland Report, 684

•**Risk Communications**
33 Lindall St., Laguna Niguel, CA, 92677-4738

Rita Bee
6960 Abel Stearns Ave., Riverside, CA, 92509
Florence Collector's Club, 184

Robert Kahn & Associates
PO Box 249, Lafayette, CA, 94549-0249
Retailing Today, 273

Rock & Rap Confidential
PO Box 341305, Los Angeles, CA, 90034
Rock & Rap Confidential, 917

Rock & Roll Confidential
PO Box 341305, Los Angeles, CA, 90034-9305
Rock & Roll Confidential, 917

Rodent Publications
2531 Sawtelle Blvd # 30, Los Angeles, CA, 90064-3163
Rodent, The, 773

Rollmag
PO Box 5001, Mill Valley, CA, 94942-5001
Rollmag, 984

Ron Jackson Co.
22 Yankee Hill, Oakland, CA, 94618-2332
Finance Over Fifty, 664

Rose Family Assn.
1474 Montelegre Dr., San Jose, CA, 95120-4831
Rose Family Newsletter, 466

Ross & Ross International
1493 Beack Park Blvd., Suite 311, Foster City, CA, 94404
Time for R & R, 1,088

Rosten Publishing Co.
1009 W. Balboa Blvd., #B, Balboa, CA, 92661-1003
Rosten Intl. Commodities Report, 684

Round Table Assocs./SAB Inc.
PO Box 90776, Los Angeles, CA, 90009-0776
Computer Business, 216

Rule/Howard
7770 El Camino Rd., Carlsbad, CA, 92009
Rule/Howard Oil and Gas Analyst, 684

Rural Community Assistance Corp.
2125 19th St., Ste. 203, Sacramento, CA, 95818-1663
Pacific Mountain Network News, 1,023

Rusty Sabre
434 Daisy Ave, Imperial Beach, CA, 91932-2006
Details Omitted for Clarity, 820

Ruxton Company
PO Box 20090, Santa Barbara, CA, 93120-0090
Ruxton Report, 1,151

Ryal Investment report
16372 Chippewa Rd, Apple Valley, CA, 92307-1512
Ryals Investment Report, 684

SAGE Publication, Inc.
2455 Teller Rd., Thousand Oaks, CA, 91320-2218
Culture & Psychology, 260

S.F.C.S
P.O. Box 426392, San Francisco, CA, 94142
Rough Draft, 816

•**SRI Intl. -Chemical Bus. Research Division**
333 Ravenswood Ave., Menlo Park, CA, 94025-3453

Sacramento Peace Ctr.
414 T St, Sacramento, CA, 95814-6914
Peace Currents, 995

St. Gregory Armenian Apostolic Church of Pasadena
2215 E Colorado Blvd, Pasadena, CA, 91107-3642
Shoghagat, 1,066

•**St. Joseph Medical Center**
Mktg. & Public Relations, 501 S. Buena Vista St., Burbank, CA, 91505

St. Mary Armenian Apostolic Church
PO Box 367, Yettem, CA, 93670-0367
Yettem, 400

•**San Bernardino City Unified School District**
777 N F St, San Bernardino, CA, 92410-3017

San Bernardino County Library
104 W. 4th St., San Bernardino, CA, 92415-0001
San Bernardino County Library Newsletter, 809

San Bernardino County Museum Assn.
2024 Orange Tree Ln, Redlands, CA, 92374-2850
San Bernardino County Museum Association Newsletter, 908

San Diego County Dental Society
1275 W Morena Blvd # B, San Diego, CA, 92110-3837
San Diego County Dental Society, Facets, 271

San Diego County Dept. of Planning & Land Use
5201 Ruffin Rd., Ste. B-5, San Diego, CA, 92123-4310
San Diego County Dept. of Planning and Land Use Population and Housing Estimates., 1,024

San Diego Dept. of Education
6401 Linda Vista Rd, San Diego, CA, 92111-7319
San Diego County Superintendent's Bulletin, 1,093

San Diego Gas
101 Ash St, San Diego, CA, 92101-3017
UpDate, 602

San Diego Historical Society
PO Box 81825, San Diego, CA, 92138-1825
San Diego Historical Society Times, 548

San Diego Regulatory Alert
PO Box 126301, San Diego, CA, 92112-6301
San Diego Regulatory Alert, 1,039

San Diego State Univ. Drama Dept.
Publications, San Diego, CA, 92182
Theatre Products Report, 1,174

San Fernando Valley Dental Assistants Society
10626 Gothic Ave, Granada Hills, CA, 91344-6826
Bridging the Gap, 268

San Francisco Advertising Club
150 Post St Ste 325, San Francisco, CA, 94108-4707
Prisoners of Advertising, 20

San Francisco Anti-Apartheid Committee
916 Laguna St, San Francisco, CA, 94115-4815
Anti-Apartheid Alert, 986

San Francisco Study Group for Peace
2406 Larkin St, San Francisco, CA, 94109-1726
Thinkpeace, 999

San Gabriel Valley Dental Society
312 E Las Tunas Dr, San Gabriel, CA, 91776-1502
San Gabriel Valley Dental Society, Bulletin, 271

San Gorgonio Pass Gen. Soc.
PO Box 3261, Beaumont, CA, 92223-1204
Pass Genealogical Reporter, 464

San Jose Bible College
PO Box 1090, San Jose, CA, 95108-1090
Broadcaster, 197

San Jose Teachers Assn.
2476-A Almaden expwy., San Jose, CA, 95125-2901
SJTA News, 328

Sandia Labs Computer Applications Div.
Livermore, CA, 94550
GCS Users' Group Newsletter, 223

Sanford Resources, Inc.
PO Box 20324, San Jose, CA, 95160-0324
Electronic Display World, 365

Santa Barbara Museum of Natural History
2559 Puesta Del Sol, Santa Barbara, CA, 93105-2936
Santa Barbara Museum of Natural History Museum Bulletin, 908

Santa Barbara Research Center, Subs Hughes Aircraft Co.
75 Coromar Dr, Goleta, CA, 93117-3088
SBRC News, 597

Santa Clara Valley TIPC Users Group
55 Temescal Ter, San Francisco, CA, 94118-4324
TImes, The, 240

Save-The-Redwoods League
114 Sansome St Ste 605, San Francisco, CA, 94104-3814
Save-The-Redwoods League Bulletin, 393

Saving & Preserving Arts & Cultural Environments
1804 N Van Ness Ave, Los Angeles, CA, 90028-5615
SPACES; Notes on America's Folk Art Environments, 66

Savory Times (The)
P.O. Box 9115, Stockton, CA, 95212
Savory Thymes, 432

Saybrook Institute
450 Pacific Avenue #300, San Francisco, CA, 94133-4640
Forum, 197

Scaffold Industry Association
14039 Sherman Way Ste 100, Van Nuys, CA, 91405-2599
Scaffold Industry Association Newsletter, 250

Scandinavian Philatelic Library of Southern California, Inc.
PO Box 310, Claremont, CA, 91711-0310
Luren, 971

School for the Deaf
393 50 Gallaudet Dr., Fremont, CA, 94538
School for the Deaf, Report, 267

•**School of Theology at Claremont**
1325 North College Ave., Public Relations Office, Claremont, CA, 91711-3199

Science of Mind Church Counseling & Healing Ctr.
PO Box 1439, La Jolla, CA, 92038-1439
Alternative Health Therapies Newsletter, 498

•**Scripps Memorial Hospital**
9888 Genesee Ave # 28, La Jolla, CA, 92037-1200

Sea Wind Press
PO Box 222964, Carmel, CA, 93922-2964
Sea Wind Letter, 975

•**Search Group, Inc.**
7311 Greenhaven Dr Ste 145, Sacramento, CA, 95831-3572

Sector Fund Connection
8949 La Riviera Dr, Sacramento, CA, 95826-2159
Sector Fund Connection, 685

Sector Funds Newsletter
PO Box 270048, San Diego, CA, 92198-2048
Sector Funds Newsletter, 685

Security Pacific Corp.
333 S Hope St, Los Angeles, CA, 90071-2701
Market Advantage, 675

Security Pacific National Bank
Research Dept. H8-3, Box 2097, Los Angeles, CA, 90051-0097
Security News, 598

•**Select Press**
PO Box 37, Corte Madera, CA, 94976-0037

Selectrend Research, Inc.
4641 Don Zarembo Dr, Los Angeles, CA, 90008-4122
Selectrend, 685

Self Storage Legal Review
2203 Los Angeles Ave, Berkeley, CA, 94707-2619
Self Storage Legal Review, 775

Semiconductor Currents
930 Brookgrove Ln, Cupertino, CA, 95014-4668
Semiconductor Currents, 339

•**Semiconductor Equipment & Materials Intl.**
805 E Middlefield Rd, Mountain View, CA, 94043-4025

Semiconductor Industry Assn.
181 Metro Dr., Ste. 450, San Jose, CA, 95110-1346
SIA Circuit, 851

Seniornet
1 Kearny St., 3rd Floor, San Francisco, CA, 94108-5501
Seniornet Online Newsletter, 1,109

•**Seraphim Press**
4805 Courageous Ln, Carlsbad, CA, 92008-3783

Serenity Spirtualist Assn.
322 Upper Rd, San Rafael, CA, 94903-3041
Serenity Sentinel, 1,051

•**Shaklee Corp.**
444 Market St, San Francisco, CA, 94111-5378

Shamakami
PO Box 460456, San Francisco, CA, 94146-0456
Shamakami, 446

Sherwin-Williams Co.
754 Kevin Ct, Oakland, CA, 94621-4040
Where the Action Is!, 603

Shrewbury Publishing
PO Box 3894, Santa Barbara, CA, 93130-3894
Software and Networks for Learning, 330

•**Sierra Club**
923 12th St Ste 200, Sacramento, CA, 95814-2923

Sierra Club Legal Defense Fund
180 Montgomery St., Ste. 1400, San Francisco, CA, 94104-4209
In Brief, 385

Silicon Systems, Inc.
14351 Myford Rd, Tustin, CA, 92680-7039
SSignals, 237

Silky Terrier Club of America
PO Box 1132, Alameda, CA, 94501-0116
Silky Terrier Club of America Newsletter, 280

Silver Dollars Collector Club, Ltd.
1760 S Escondido Blvd, Escondido, CA, 92025-6520
Value Advisor, 928

Simon Wiesenthal Center
9760 W Pico Blvd, Los Angeles, CA, 90035-4792
Response, 975

Single Lifestyle
PO Box 11692, Santa Ana, CA, 92711-1692
Single Lifestyle, 816

Sino-Judaic Institute
232 Lexington Dr, Menlo Park, CA, 94025-2910
Points East, 637

•**Smart Basics, Inc.**
1626 Union Street, San Francisco, CA, 94123
Smart Basics, 925

* See ***MULTI-PUBLISHER INDEX*** for list of publications.

Smart Products, Inc.
870 Market St Ste 1262, San Francisco, CA, 94102-2907
Intelli-Scope, 284

Smith's Report
PO Box 3267, Visalia, CA, 93278-3267
Smith's Report, 697

Social Science Reporter
850 Webster St Apt 600, Palo Alto, CA, 94301-2837
Social Science Reporter and Public Relations Research Review, 1,127

Socialist Action Publishing Assn.
3435 Army St Ste 308, San Francisco, CA, 94110-4543
Socialist Action, 998

Socialist Party/Solidarity
PO Box 41510, Santa Barbara, CA, 93140-1510
Left Out, 992

Society for the Advancement of Good English
4501 Riverside Ave # 30, Anderson, CA, 96007-2759
Counterforce, 306

Society of California Archivists
Honnold-Mudd Library, Claremont Coll., 800 Dartmouth, Claremont, CA, 91711
Society of California Archivists Newsletter, 810

Society of California Pioneers
PO Box 191850, San Francisco, CA, 94119-1850
Society of California Pioneers Newsletter, 182

Society for Citizen Education in World Affairs
2038 Freda Laney #G-106, Cardiff by the Sea, CA, 92007-1419
Public Affairs Newsletter, 637

Society for the Conservation of Bighorn Sheep
2106 Mesita Ave, West Covina, CA, 91791-2720
Sheepherder, The, 394

Society for Creative Anachronism
1277 Fallen Leaf Dr, Milpitas, CA, 95035-6216
Page, 181

Society of Flight Test Engineers
PO Box 4047, Lancaster, CA, 93539-4047
Flight Test News, 29

Soc. of Genealogy of Durkee
Bernice Gunderson, 3753 E. 15th St., Long Beach, CA, 90804-2943
Durkee Family Newsletter, 452

Society of Insurance Trainers & Educators
2120 Market Street, Suite 108, San Francisco, CA, 94114
In-SITE, 620

Society for the Preservation of Birds of Prey
PO Box 66070, Los Angeles, CA, 90066-0070
Raptor Report, The, 942

Society for the Preservation of Film Music
2930 El Caminito St, La Crescenta, CA, 91214-2005
Cue Sheet, The, 911

Society to Preserve & Encourage Radio Drama/ Variety/Comedy
Box 1587, Hollywood, CA, 90078
SPERDVAC Radiogram, 125

Society of Telecommunications Consultants
13766 Center Street #212, Carmel Valley, CA, 93924-9693
STC Lines, 1,161

Sociological Abstracts, Inc.
7428 Trade St., San Diego, CA, 92121-2410
Note Us, 1,126

Solano County Genealogical Society, Inc.
PO Box 2494, Fairfield, CA, 94533-0249
Root Digger Newsletter, 466

Sonoma County Center for Peace & Justice
540 Pacific Ave, Santa Rosa, CA, 95404-2852
Peace Press, 996

Sonoma State Univ. English Dept.
1801 E Cotati Ave, Rohnert Park, CA, 94928-3613
Virginia Woolf Miscellany, 825

Sorel Investments
1728 Union St Ste 311, San Francisco, CA, 94123-4428
Real Estate Technical Letter, 1,038

Sound Advice
370 Diablo Rd Ste 201, Danville, CA, 94526-3438
Sound Advice, 1,039

Southeast Asia Community Resource Center
Folsom Cordova Unified Schools, 2460 Cordova Lane, Rancho Cordova, CA, 95670
Context: Southeast Asians in California, 259

Southern California Cooperating Warehouse
3547 White House Pl, Los Angeles, CA, 90004-5944
Raisin Consciousness, 432

Southern California DX Club
12567 Brooklake St., Box 56292, Mar Vista, CA, 90066-1809
Southern California DX Club Bulletin, 182

Southern California Dental Laboratory Association
3333 Glendale Blvd Ste 4, Los Angeles, CA, 90039-1840
Southern California Dental Laboratory Association, Bulletin, 271

Southern California Ecumenical Center
1340 S Bonnie Brae St, Los Angeles, CA, 90006-5416
El Rescate, 630

Southern California Gas Co.
555 W. 5th St., Los Angeles, CA, 90013-1011
Memo to Management, 590

Southern California Gas Co., Pacific Lighting System
800 S. Flower St., Los Angeles, CA, 90017-4608
SO CAL Gas News, 597

Southern California Library for Social Studies & Research
6120 S Vermont Ave, Los Angeles, CA, 90044-3718
Heritage, 799

Southern California Water Co.
630 E Foothill Blvd, San Dimas, CA, 91773-1207
Southern California Water Co. Bulletin, 599

Southwest Marine Education Assn.
Monterey Bay Aquarium, 886 Cannery Row, Monterey, CA, 93940-1085
Southwest Marine Educators Assn. Newsletter, 330

Spa Specs International
21548 Hyde Rd, Sonoma, CA, 95476-9732
Spa Specs, 528

Spectrum Concepts
2117 Foothill blvd., Ste. 138, La Verne, CA, 91750
Spectrum Tidbits, 473

Spencers Intl. Enterprises
PO Box 43822, Los Angeles, CA, 90043-0822
Ancient Controversy, 1,045

•**Spidell Publishing Inc.**
1110 N Gilbert St, Anaheim, CA, 92801-1401

Spiritual Counterfeits Project, Inc.
PO Box 4308, Berkeley, CA, 94704-0308
SCP Newsletter, 1,051

Spiritual Sciences Institute Newsletter
PO Box 22714, Santa Barbara, CA, 93121-2714
Spiritual Sciences Institute Newsletter, 949

Spread Scope, Inc.
Box 5841, Mission Hills, CA, 91395-0841
Spread Letter, 686

•**Sri Avrobindo Association**
2288 Fulton St., Beverley, CA, 94704

•**Staffing Industry Analysts**
2235 Grant Rd # 3, Los Altos, CA, 94024-6954

•**Standard Oil Co. of California**
225 Bush St., San Francisco, CA, 94104-4207

Stanford Univ. History Dept.
Publications, Stanford, CA, 94305
Stanford Historian, 549

Stanford University Libraries
Green Library, Stanford, CA, 94305
SUL News Notes, 809

Stanford University, School of Medicine
Dept. of Dermatology, Stanford, CA, 94305
International Psoriasis Bulletin, 270

State of California Dept. of Health Services
2151 Berkeley Way, Berkeley, CA, 94704-1011
California Morbidity, 501

Steinbeck Research Center
San Jose State Univ., San Jose, CA, 95192-0001
Steinbeck Newsletter, The, 825

Sten-O-Press
1862 23rd St. #36, San Pablo, CA, 94806-4838
Cal-OSHA Reporter, 1,079

Sterling Software Marketing
11050 White Rock Rd # 100, Rancho Cordova, CA, 95670-6001
Software Times, 239

Sterling & Stone, Inc.
1668 Lombard St., San Francisco, CA, 94123
New Leaders, The, 146

Stewart Associates
12625 Frederick St., #I-5, Ste. 243, Moreno Valley, CA, 92553-5216
Success Today, 153

Stockmarket Cycles
PO Box 6873, Santa Rosa, CA, 95406-0873
Stockmarket Cycles, 687

Stone/Scott
2222 Foothill Blvd. #E344, La Canada, CA, 91011
Followup File, 857

Stratton Press
PO Box 96, San Ramon, CA, 94583-0096
Bad Faith Law Report, 717

Strongest Stocks
PO Box 565, Sausalito, CA, 94966-0565
Strongest Stocks, 688

Successful Investing Co.
256 S Robertson Blvd # 711, Beverly Hills, CA, 90211-2898
Successful Investing, 688

Summerhill
2780 State St., Santa Barbara, CA, 93105-5518
Odyssey, 1,187

Sunbeam Alpine Club
1752 Oswald Pl, Santa Clara, CA, 95051-3026
Sunbeam Tiger Owners Association -Newsletter, 76

Sunkist Growers, Inc.
PO Box 7888, Van Nuys, CA, 91409-7888
Slices, 598

•**Sunset Publishing Corp.**
80 Willow Rd, Menlo Park, CA, 94025-3661

Superintendent's Digest
3433 Meadowbrook Ct, Napa, CA, 94558-5239
Superintendent's Digest, 1,094

Surfer Publishing Group
PO Box 1028, Dana Point, CA, 92629-5028
Surf Report, 1,136

Surveyors Historical Society
31457 Hugh Way, Hayward, CA, 94544-7741
Backsights, 359

Survival News Service
PO Box 41834, Los Angeles, CA, 90041-0834
Talking Leaves Newsletter, 944

Susan & David Wilstein Inst. of Jewish Policy
University of Judaism, 15600 Mulholland Dr., Los Angeles, CA, 90077
Bulletin, 1,068

Syllabus Press
1307 S. Mary Ave. #211, Box 2716, Sunnyvale, CA, 94087
Query, 1,093

Syntex Labs. Inc.
3401 Hillview Ave, Palo Alto, CA, 94304-1320
Syntex Reporter, 600

T/C Press
PO Box 36006, Los Angeles, CA, 90036-0006
Composites & Adhesives Newsletter, 360

THEOS Software Corporation
1777 Botelho Drive, Walnut Creek, CA, 94596-5022
THEOS Times, 240

TPG Communications
555 Hamilton Ave., Palo Alto, CA, 94301-2015
Tom Peters: On Achieving Excellence, 846

TSC Corp/Terra Programs
932 Evelyn St, Menlo Park, CA, 94025-4710
Terrap News, 1,018

TV Game Show
PO Box 157, Agoura Hills, CA, 91376-0157
TV Game Show: Newsletter for Game Show Fans, 417

Tabloid Tattler
P.O. Box 93944, Hollywood, CA, 90093
Tabloid Tattler, 473

Talisman
719 Swift, Santa Cruz, CA, 95060-5853
Talisman, 984

•**Tax Institute**
PO Box 191091, San Francisco, CA, 94119-1091

Tayu Center
PO Box 11554, Santa Rosa, CA, 95406-1554
Way Fourth, 1,067

Technology Access
16 Digital Drive, #250, Novato, CA, 94949-5760
Technology Access Report, 1,101

•**Technology Forecasts**
205 S Beverly Dr Ste 208, Beverly Hills, CA, 90212-3873

•**Tele-Drop Inc.**
PO Box 3996, North Hollywood, CA, 91609-0996

TeleSensory Corporation
455 Bernardo Ave, Mountain View, CA, 94043-5237
Infocus, 338

•**Telespan Publishing**
50 W Palm St, Altadena, CA, 91001-4337

Therapeutic Research Center
PO Box 8190, Stockton, CA, 95208-0190
Prescriber's Letter, 287

•**Third World Resources**
DataCenter, 464 19th St., Oakland, CA, 94612-2297

Thomas Aquinas College
10000 Ojai Rd, Santa Paula, CA, 93060-9622
Thomas Aquinas College Newsletter, 197

* See **MULTI-PUBLISHER INDEX** for list of publications.

Thomas F. Burola & Assoc.
6477 Telephone Rd Ste 7r, Ventura, CA, 93003-4459
United Nations Jobs Newsletter, 349

Thomas J. Keany
520 N Brookhurst St Ste 230, Anaheim, CA, 92801-5207
Money Talks, 94

Thomas Jefferson Research Center
2700 E. Foothill Blvd., #302, Pasadena, CA, 91107-3443
Jefferson Research Letter, 314

Thomas Karwin
121 Easterby Ave,PO Box 7600, Santa Cruz, CA, 95061-7600
California Cable Letter, 1,166

Thomson Publications
1118 W Stuart Ave, Fresno, CA, 93711-2039
Agricultural Chemical Newsletter, 36

Tin Can Collectors Association
11326 Ventura Blvd, Studio City, CA, 91604-3137
Kanvention Xtra, 554

Tolerant Majority
PO Box 22930, Santa Barbara, CA, 93121-2930
Legalizing Freedom, 992

Tonatiuh-Quinto Sol Intl., Inc.
PO Box 9275, Berkeley, CA, 94709-0275
TQS News, 825

Topor & Assocs.
655 Castro Street, Suite 8, Mountain View, CA, 94041
Marketing Higher Education, 317

Torah Aura Productions
4423 Fruitland Ave, Los Angeles, CA, 90058-3238
Torah Aura Newsletter, 1,071

Touch for Health Foundation
11194 Spruce Ave, Bloomington, CA, 92316-3226
In Touch for Health, 514

Track & Field News
2570 El Camino Real, #606, Mountain View, CA, 94040-1300
Track Newsletter, 1,176

•**Trade Service Publications, Inc.**
10996 Torreyana Rd, San Diego, CA, 92121-1105

Tradeswomen, Inc.
PO Box 2622, Berkeley, CA, 94702-0622
Trade Trax, 1,212

Trading Places
145 Columbia Ste 210, Aliso Viejo, CA, 92656-1490
Costa Vida Vallarta Newsletter, 1,183

Trager Institute
21 Locust Ave., Mill Valley, CA, 94941-2806
Trager Newsletter, 530

•**Transamerica Life Co.**
1150 S Olive St, Los Angeles, CA, 90015-2271

Transpacific Media Inc.
22761 Pacific Coast Hwy., Ste. 100, Malibu, CA, 90265-5064
Asian Travel & Nigthlife, 1,182

Transpersonal Institute
Box 3049, Stanford, CA, 94309
Association for Transpersonal Psychology, Newsletter, 1,012

Transpharma, Inc.
13072 Camino Del Valle, Poway, CA, 92064-1917
Pharmascope, 287

Travel Keys Books
PO Box 162266, Sacramento, CA, 95816-2266
Travel Books Worldwide, 1,189

Trebas Institute of Recording Arts
6464 Sunset Blvd., Penthouse, Hollywood, CA, 90028-8001
Trebas Track, 1,128

Treepeople
12601 Mulholland Dr, Beverly Hills, CA, 90210-1364
Seedling News, 393

Triton Museum of Art
1505 Warburton Ave, Santa Clara, CA, 95050-3712
Members Bulletin, 905

Twin Creeks Entertainment
PO Box 410867, San Francisco, CA, 94141-0867
Consumer Electronics Edge, 337

Twinline
PO Box 10066, Berkeley, CA, 94709-5066
Twin Services Reporter, 78

•**Tyjak, Inc.**
4731 El Camino Ave, Carmichael, CA, 95608-4938

The Typhooner
23311 Country Road 88, Winters, CA, 95694
The Typhooner, 115

UCLA Center for Health Sciences
Univ. of California-LA, 10-247 Louis Factor Bldg., Los Angeles, CA, 90024
UCLA Cancer Center Bulletin, 888

UCLA Institute of Archaeology
A222 Fowler, 405 Hilgard, Los Angeles, CA, 90024-1510
Backdirt, 57

UNESCO Assn. /USA
5815 Lawton Ave, Oakland, CA, 94618-1510
UNESCO Assn. /USA-Newsletter, 639

•**USDA-AMS-F&V. Div.**
630 Sansome St Ste 727, San Francisco, CA, 94111-2215

Ukrainian Culture Center
4315 Melrose Ave, Los Angeles, CA, 90029-3510
Ukrainian Times, 410

Ultimate Issues
10573 W Pico Blvd Ste 167, Los Angeles, CA, 90064-2348
Ultimate Issues, 816

Umbrella Assocs.
Box 3692, Pasadena, CA, 91114
Umbrella, 67

Underground Contractors Assn.
7041 Koll Center Pky Bldg 130, Pleasanton, CA, 94566-3128
DIGGER Reporter, 364

Underwater Society of America
PO Box 628, Daly City, CA, 94017-0628
Visibility, 1,137

Union of American Physicians & Dentists
1330 Broadway Ste 730, Oakland, CA, 94612-2506
UAPD Report, 705

Union Bank
445 S Figueroa St, Los Angeles, CA, 90071-1655
Money Engineer, 591

Union for Democratic Communications
1016 61st St, Oakland, CA, 94608-2355
Democratic Communique, 856

Union for Radical Political Economics
Univ. of CA Dept. of Economics, Riverside, CA, 92521-0001
URPE Newsletter, 296

•**United Assn. of Manufacturers Representatives**
34071 La Plaza, PO Box 986, Dana Point, CA, 92629

United Christians, Inc.
Box 1833-SPD, Santa Ana, CA, 92702-1840
Billboards for Jesus, 1,061

United Farm Workers Organizing Committee, AFL-CIO
PO Box 62, Keene, CA, 93531
Malcriado/Voice of the Farm Worker, 709

United Prospectors Inc.
166 W H St, Benicia, CA, 94510-3127
Locating Gold, Gems and Minerals, 900

United Scleroderma Foundation, Inc.
PO Box 399, Watsonville, CA, 95077-0399
Scleroderma Spectrum, 887

•**U.S. Department of Agriculture**
California Ag. Stat. Service, PO Box 1258, Sacramento, CA, 95812

U.S. Import-Export Publications Co.
PO Box 428, Bellflower, CA, 90707-0428

U.S. Metric Association, Inc.
10245 Andasol Ave, Northridge, CA, 91325-1504
Metric Today, 254

U.S. Navy
S.F. Bay Naval Shipyard, Vallejo, CA, 94590
SFBNS Tie Line, 597

•**U.S. Racquet Stringer's Assn.**
PO Box 40, Del Mar, CA, 92014-0040

U.S. Research, Inc.
PO Box 7242, Burbank, CA, 91510-7242
Hefley Psychic Report, 948

U.S. Sports Acrobatics Fed.
PO Box 8158, Riverside, CA, 92515-8158
Acrosports News, 1,128

Universal Fellowship of Metropolitan Community Churches
5300 Santa Monica Blvd Ste 304, Los Angeles, CA, 90029-1131
Alert, 498

Universal Life Church
601 3rd St, Modesto, CA, 95351-3395
ULC News, 1,052

Universal Pantheist Society
PO Box 265, Big Pine, CA, 93513-0265
Pantheist Vision, 974

Univ. of California/Archive for New Poetry
Central Univ. Library, C-075-S, La Jolla, CA, 92093
Archive Newsletter, 817

Univ. of California At Los Angeles, Library
Los Angeles, CA, 90024
UCLA Librarian, 811

Univ. of California At Riverside, Lib. Admin.
Box 5900, Riverside, CA, 92517
UCR Library News, 811

Univ. of California At San Francisco
Box 0622, 3rd Ave. & Parnassus, San Francisco, CA, 94143-0001
Pharmacy & Therapeutics Forum, 287

University of California, CASFS
1156 High St., Santa Cruz, CA, 95064-1077
Cultivar: Newsletter of the UCSC Center for Agroecology & Sustainable Food Systems, 39

•**Univ. California-Davis Dept. Wildlife and Fisheries Biology**
Univ. of California-Davis, Davis, CA, 95616-8751

Univ. of California Earth Sciences Dept.
Rm. 475, Earth Sci Bldg., Berkeley, CA, 94720-0001
Bulletin of the Seismographic Stations, 477

Univ. of California History Dept.
Santa Barbara, Dept. of Hist., Santa Barbara, CA, 93106
New Directions in Middle East Studies Newsletter, 635

Univ. of California Library
La Jolla, CA, 92093
University of California Library, Friends Newsletter, 812

Univ. of California-Los Angeles
Wm Andrews Clark Mem. Library, 2520 Cimarron St., Los Angeles, CA, 90018
Clark & Center Newsletter, The, 796

University of California, Office of the President
Division of Library Automation, 300 Lakeside Drive, 8th Floor, Oakland, CA, 94612-3550
DLA Bulletin, 796

Univ. of California Transportation Studies Inst.
Inst. of Transport. Studies, 109 Mclaughlin Hall, Berkeley, CA, 94720-0001
ITS Review, 1,178

University of California at Berkeley
215 Evans Hall, Berkeley, CA, 94720-0001
Computing Services Newsletter, 217

Univ. of California at Berkeley, Dept. of Electrical Eng.
203 Cory Hall, Berkeley, CA, 94720-1770
EECS/ERL News, 365

University of California at Berkeley Earthquake Engineering
Research Center, 1301 South 46th Street, Richmond, CA, 94804-4698
EERC News, 365

Univ. of California at Los Angeles
405 Hilgard Ave., 3121 Campbell Hall, Los Angeles, CA, 90024-1301
Noticias de Aztlan, 983

University for Humanistic Studies
380 Stevens Ave., Ste. 210, Solana Beach, CA, 92075-2068
University for Humanistic Studies Quarterly Newsletter, 975

Univ. of the Pacific, Publishing Bd.
3601 Pacific Ave. Hand Hall,, 3rd Fl., Stockton, CA, 95211-0001
Naranjado, 197

Univ. of Southern California, School of Pharmacy
Univ. Park, Los Angeles, CA, 90007
Pharmacy USC, 287

University of West Los Angeles
1155 W Arbor Vitae St, Inglewood, CA, 90301-2902
Brief, The, 196

Upscale Traveler
4521 Alla Road, Suite 3, Marina del Rey, CA, 90292
Upscale Traveler, 1,191

Valley Presbyterian Hospital
15107 Vanowen St, Van Nuys, CA, 91405-4597
Valley Pres, 602

Vegan Action
P.O. Box 4353, Berkeley, CA, 94704
Vegan News, The, 396

Velocette Owners Club of North America
C/O Phil Swartz, 10623 Darby Ave., Northridge, CA, 91326
Fishtail West, 263

Ventura County Historical Society
100 E Main St, Ventura, CA, 93001-2698
Heritage and History, 541

* See **MULTI-PUBLISHER INDEX** for list of publications.

* See **MULTI-PUBLISHER INDEX** for list of publications.

Center for Judiac Studies
Univ. of Denver, Denver, CO, 80223-1900
Maimonides Society Bulletin, 1,069

Children's Book Insider
PO Box 1030, Fairplay, CO, 80440-1030
Children's Book Insider, 117

Christian Chiropractors Assn.
PO Box 9715, Fort Collins, CO, 80525-0500
Christian Chiropractor & CCA Bulletin, 1,062

Chubb Communications
222 Milwaukee St Ste 408, Denver, CO, 80206-5012
Veterinary Advisory Report, 1,202

Church of Seven Arrows
Box 185, Wheatridge, CO, 80034-0185
Thunderbow II, 1,074

Citicorp Diners Club-Carte Blanche
183 Inverness Dr W, Englewood, CO, 80112-5203
Living in Style, 438

Citizens for Health
PO Box 2260, Boulder, CO, 80306-2260
Citizens for Health, 502

City of Boulder Div. of Research
PO Box 791, Boulder, CO, 80306-0791
Research Perspectives, 492

Color Q Inc., Art Education Division
2651 S Kearney St, Denver, CO, 80222-6327
Color Q Connection, 64

Colorado Archivist
Colorado State Univ. Libraries, Fort Collins, CO, 80523-0001
Colorado Archivist, 796

Colorado College History Dept.
Publications, Colorado Springs, CO, 80903
CCP Research Newsletter, 987

Colorado Dept. of Education/Colo.St. Lib. & Adult Educ. Off.
201 E. Colfax, Denver, CO, 80203-1704
Centennial State Libraries, 795

Colorado Division of Water Resources
1313 Sherman St Ste 818, Denver, CO, 80203-2238
Colorado Stream Lines, 1,202

Colorado Historical Society
1300 Broadway, Denver, CO, 80203-2104
Colorado History News, 538

Colorado Nurses Assn.
5453 E. Evans Pl., Denver, CO, 80222-5206
Colorado Nurse, 929

Colorado Public Interest Research Group
1530 Blake St., #220, Denver, CO, 80202-1336
COPIRG Outlook, 374

Colorado Society of Certified Public Accountants
7979 East Tufts Avenue, Suite 500, Denver, CO, 80237-2845
NewsAccount, 7

Colorado Springs Fine Arts Center
30 W Dale St, Colorado Springs, CO, 80903-3210
Artsfocus, 902

Colorado Transporation Dept.
4201 E Arkansas Ave, Denver, CO, 80222-3406
Transporation News, 1,077

Columbia Savings
1740 Broadway, Denver, CO, 80274-0001
Columbia Hi-Lites, 580

Communication Creativity
425 Cedar St., Box 909-OX, Buena Vista, CO, 81211
Country Bound Connection, 1,033

Country Press
PO Box 5024, Durango, CO, 81301-6813
Creative Outlets, 52

Country Press, Inc.
PO Box 5880, Snowmass Village, CO, 81615-5880
Nutshell, 347

DCD Management Resources
3773 Cherry Creek N. Dr., Ste. 575, Denver, CO, 80209
Financial Advantage, The, 838

Danish Brotherhood in America
Po Box 266000, Highlands Ranch, CO, 80163-6000
Harbor Highlights, 178

Denver Museum of Natural History
2001 Colorado Blvd, Denver, CO, 80205-5798
Museum Monthly, 906

Digit Fund
45 Inverness Dr., E., Englewood, CO, 80112-5411
Digit Fund, 376

•Dream It, Inc.
1255 Cedar Ridge Ln, Colorado Springs, CO, 80919-1403

Dredging Contract News
PO Box 1487, Fort Collins, CO, 80522-1487
Dredging Contract News, 360

Earth Star Publications
PO Box 117, Paonia, CO, 81428-0117
Star Beacon, 1,199

Emerging Missions-Overseas Crusades
PO Box 36900, Colorado Springs, CO, 80936-3690
Bridging Peoples, 1,045

En Garde
1660 Lincoln St Ste 2525, Denver, CO, 80264-2501
En Garde, 734

Every Home for Christ
PO Box 35970, Colorado Springs, CO, 80935-3597
Every Home, 1,063

Family Research Institute, Inc.
PO Box 62640, Colorado Springs, CO, 80962
Family Research Report, 412

First American Monetary & Economic Review
3500 JFK Pkwy., Ft. Collins, CO, 80525
Monetary & Economic Review, 677

Forensic Sciences Foundation, Inc.
PO Box 669, Colorado Springs, CO, 80901-0669
Forensic Serology News, 739

Four Pines Publishing
PO Box 3209, Boulder, CO, 80307-3209
Wireless Week, 1,165

Frequent Flyer Services
4715C Town Center Dr., Colorado Springs, CO, 80916-4701
Inside Flyer, 30

Greater Europe Mission Assn.
18950 Base Camp Rd, Monument, CO, 80132-8009
Europe Today, 1,063

Grief Education Institute
4596 E Iliff Ave, Denver, CO, 80222-6021
GEI Newsletter, 1,014

•Handicap News
3060 E Bridge St Lot 342, Brighton, CO, 80601-2724

Hart Publications, Inc.
1900 Grant St., Ste. 720, Denver, CO, 80203
Oil & Gas Interest Newsletter, 961

Henry A. Pohs, Ed.
4537 Quitman St, Denver, CO, 80212-2535
Underground Lamp Post, 54

•IRT Environment, Inc./Results Center, The
PO Box 2239, Basalt, CO, 81612

Iliff School of Theology
2201 S University Blvd, Denver, CO, 80210-4798
Iliff Reporter, 197

Independent American
PO BOX 621228, Littleton, CO, 80162-1228
Tax Fax, 999

Intermountain Referral Service
311 14th St, Glenwood Springs, CO, 81601-3949
Rocky Mountain Employment Newsletter, 349

Intl. Fantasy Gaming Society
PO Box 3577, Boulder, CO, 80307-3577
Chainmail, 552

Intl. Society for Prevention of Child Abuse and Neglect
1205 Oneida St, Denver, CO, 80220-2944
Link, The, 169

International Texas Longhorn
P.O. Box 1609, Monument, CO, 80132-1609
Texas Longhorn Journal, 829

J.L. Walker
PO Box 5024, Durango, CO, 81301-6813
Country Press, The, 552

Jeff McFadden
R.E. Foods, 820 Struthers, Grand Junction, CO, 81501
The Zealot, 434

Jobs in Higher Education
PO Box 10100, Colorado Springs, CO, 80932-1100
Jobs in Higher Education, 314

Junior Achievement, Inc.
National Headquarters, One Education Way, Colorado Springs, CO, 80906-4477
Partners, 294

Kellogg Corp.
1801 Broadway #1000, Denver, CO, 80202-3828
KC News, 247

•Laughing Bear Press
PO Box 36159, Denver, CO, 80236-0159

Leman Publications, Inc.
P.o. Box 4101, Golden, CO, 80401-0101
Quilter's Newsletter Magazine, 555

Lierle Public Relations
PO Box 440745, Aurora, CO, 80044-0745
U.S. Lease Price Report, 358

Maher Studios
PO Box 420, Littleton, CO, 80160-0420
Newsy Vents, 555

Masonry Society, The
3970 Broadway, Suite 201D, Boulder, CO, 80302-3808
Masonry Society-Journal, 248

Media Business Corp.
607 10th St Ste 103, Golden, CO, 80401-1053
Media Business News, 859

•Medical Group Management Association
104 Inverness Terrace E., Englewood, CO, 80112-5306

Mizel Museum of Judaica
560 S Monaco Pky, Denver, CO, 80224-1227
Artifacts, 902

Morris Animal Foundation
45 Inverness Dr E, Englewood, CO, 80112-5480
Animal News, 1,200

Mountain Bell
PO Box 960, Denver, CO, 80201-0960
Management Newsletter, 590

Mountain Media
Box 880524, 1360 Skyview Terrace, Steamboat Springs, CO, 80488
Chicago Sportscene, 1,130

Mountain States Legal Foundation
1660 Lincoln St Ste 2300, Denver, CO, 80264-2301
Freedom Forum, 485

Natl. Assn. of Counsel for Children
1205 Oneida St, Denver, CO, 80220-2944
Guardian, The, 741

National Assn. of Private Non-Traditional Schools and Colleg
182 Thompson Rd., Grand Junction, CO, 81503-2246
NAPNSC Newsletter: Current Events & Comments, 319

National Cattlemen's Beef Assn.
5420 S. Quebec St., PO Box 3469, Englewood, CO, 80155-3469
Beef Business Bulletin, 827

Natl. Commodity & Barter Assn.
PO Box 2255, Longmont, CO, 80502-2255
NCBA Reports, 758

Natl. Conference of Standards Laboratories
1800 30th St Ste 305b, Boulder, CO, 80301-1026
National Conference of Standards Laboratories Newsletter, 1,099

•Natl. Conference of State Legislatures
1560 Broadway, Ste. 700, Denver, CO, 80202-5140

National Farmers Union
12025 E. 45th Ave., Denver, CO, 80251-0001
National Farmers Union Washington Newsletter, 43

National Indian Health Board
1385 S. Colorado Blvd., #A-708, Denver, CO, 80222-3304
NIHB Health Reporter, 519

•Natl. Jewish Ctr. for Immunology and Respiratory Medicine
1400 Jackson St, Denver, CO, 80206-2761

Natl. Potato Council
5690 DTC Blvd., Ste. 230-E, Englewood, CO, 80111-3200
Spudletter, 46

Natl. Potato Promotion Board
7555 E Hampden Ave Ste 412, Denver, CO, 80231-4835
Tater News, 46

National Rural Education Assoc.
Education Bldg., Rm. 230, Colorado State University, Fort Collins, CO, 80523-1588
NREA News, 321

Natl. Strength & Conditioning Assn.
PO Box 38909, Colorado Springs, CO, 80937-8909
NSCA Bulletin, 520

•Natl. Writers Assn./Associated Business Writers of America
1450 S. Havana, Ste. 424, Aurora, CO, 80012

Native American Rights Fund
1506 Broadway, Boulder, CO, 80302-6296
NARF Legal Review, 758

•Natural Hazards Information Center
Box 482, Univ. of Colorado, Boulder, CO, 80309-0001

•Nelson R. Crow Pubs.
650 S Lipan St, Denver, CO, 80223-2307

Newman Family Society c/o Shirley Ann Sheets
1675 S Steele St, Denver, CO, 80210-2939
Newman News, 462

* See **MULTI-PUBLISHER INDEX** for list of publications.

North American Riding for the Handicapped Assn., Inc.
PO Box 33150, Denver, CO, 80233-0150
NARHA News, 1,132

Nuclear Arsenal Project
2216 Race St, Denver, CO, 80205-5640
Nuclear Arsenal Handbook, 898

OR Manager
PO Box 17487, Boulder, CO, 80308-0487
OR Manager, 522

Occidental Society of Metempiric Analysis
PO Box 308, Simla, CO, 80835-0308
OSMA Beacon, 949

Oil, Chemical & Atomic Workers
PO Box 281200, Lakewood, CO, 80228-8200
Lifelines, 516

Otero Junior College
Publications, La Junta, CO, 81050
Rattler News, 197

ParaNet Information Services, Inc.
PO Box 172, Denver, CO, 80034-0172
Continuum, 948

Pencom Inc.
511 16th St., Ste. 400, Denver, CO, 80202
Service that Sells!, 845

Penny Fortune Newsletter
1837 South Navara, Colorado Spring, CO, 80906
Penny Fortune Newsletter, 681

•**Petroleum Information Corp.**
PO Box 2612, Denver, CO, 80201-2612

Phoenix Communications Group Ltd.
1837 S Nevada Ave # 223, Colorado Springs, CO, 80906-2516
Women's Investment Newsletter, 692

Pikes Peak Area Council of Governments
15 S 7th St, Colorado Springs, CO, 80905-1501
Regionews, 1,040

Porter Memorial Hospital
2525 S Downing St, Denver, CO, 80210-5876
Portercare, 570

Project Salvador Crafts
P.O. Box 300105, Denver, CO, 80218
Project Salvador Crafts, 256

•**Prosperity & Profits Unlimited**
PO Box 416, Denver, CO, 80201-0416

Provenant Health Partners
4231 W 16th Ave, Denver, CO, 80204-1374
Teamwork, 572

R & R Publication
283 Columbine St., Dept. M, Denver, CO, 80206
Wanderlust, 1,191

•**Reconnaissance Holographics Ltd.**
825 East Tufts Avenue, Cherry Hills, CO, 80110

Renaissance Educational Assocs.
4817 N. County Rd., #29, Loveland, CO, 80538-9515
Renaissance Educator, 327

Rocky Mountain CoHousing
1705 14th St # 317, Boulder, CO, 80302-6321
Rocky Mountain CoHousing Quarterly, The, 393

•**Rocky Mountain Mineral Law Foundation**
7039 E 18th Ave, Denver, CO, 80220-1826

Roofing Industry Educational Institute
14 Inverness Dr., E., Bldg. H, #110, Englewood, CO, 80112-5625
RIEI Information Letter, 249

S.A. Toney & Assoc.
3750 W Union Ave, Denver, CO, 80236-3631
Contest News Wire, 438

•**Saratoga Press**
PO Box 8, Platteville, CO, 80651-0008

Science Fiction Research Assn.
1265 S Clay St, Denver, CO, 80219-4144
SFRA Newsletter, 1,102

•**Shepard's/McGraw-Hill, Inc.**
555 Middle Creek Pky, Colorado Springs, CO, 80921-3622

Small Publishers Association of North America
P.O. Box 1306, Buena Vista, CO, 81211
SPAN Connection, 119

Society for Photographic Education
Campus Box Univ. Colo. #318, Boulder, CO, 80309-0001
SPE Newsletter, 978

Sparks Publishing & Reporting Corp.
PO Box 260558, Littleton, CO, 80163
Continental Franchise Review, 134

Spectrum, Inc.
Spectrum Color Center, 6275 Joyce Drive, Golden, CO, 80403
Lasertone News, 1,005

Sports Ambassador
OC International, Box 36900, Colorado Springs, CO, 80936-6900
Prayer Letter, 1,050

Stock Fund Management, Inc.
1125 17th St Ste 1700, Denver, CO, 80202-2032
Zenith Financial Report, 692

•**Story Time Stories that Rhyme**
PO Box 416, Denver, CO, 80201-0416

Tattered Cover Book Store
1628 16th Street, Denver, CO, 80202
Tattered Cover, 120

Technologies Tomorrow
85 W. Stirrup Trail, Monument, CO, 80132-8730
Technologies Tomorrow, 240

Technology Automation Services
PO Box 3593, Englewood, CO, 80155-3593
Engineering Automation Report, 360

Titanium Development Association
4141 Arapahoe Ave Ste 100, Boulder, CO, 80303-1032
Titanium, 892

U.S.D.A.
711 O St, Greeley, CO, 80631-9540
Molasses Market News, 1,138

U.S. Assn. for Blind Athletes
33 N Institute St, Colorado Springs, CO, 80903-3508
Insight Newsletter, 111

U.S. Committee on Irrigation & Drainage
1616 17th St Ste 483, Denver, CO, 80202-1277
USCID Newsletter, 395

U.S. Committee on Large Dams
1616 17th St Ste 483, Denver, CO, 80202-1277
USCOLD Newsletter, 1,204

•**U.S. Dept. of Agriculture**
711 O St., Greeley, CO, 80631-9540

U.S. Fencing Assn.
1 Olympic Plaza, Colorado Springs, CO, 80909-5774
USFA National Newsletter, 1,137

U.S. Space Foundation
2860 S Circle Dr Ste 2301, Colorado Springs, CO, 80906-4184
Spacewatch, 33

U.S. Swimming, Inc.
1750 E Boulder St, Colorado Springs, CO, 80909-5724
National Qualifier, 1,133

U.S. Team Handball Federation
1750 E Boulder St, Colorado Springs, CO, 80909-5724
Club News, 1,130

Univ. of Colorado Computing & Network Services
Campus Box 455, Boulder, CO, 80309-0001
DIGIT, 209

Univ. of Colorado, Graduate School of Business Admin.
Campus Box 420, Boulder, CO, 80309-0001
Colorado City Retail Sales by SIC, 133

•**Univ. Corp. for Atmospheric Research**
Box 3000, Boulder, CO, 80307-3000

Univ. of Southern Colorado
2200 Bonforte Blvd, Pueblo, CO, 81001-4901
USC Alumni Newsletter, 187

Up with People
1 International Ct, Broomfield, CO, 80021-3482
Up with People News, 334

•**Update Publicare Co**
P O Box 416, Denver, CO, 80201

•**Vestal Communications**
334 Humphrey Dr, Evergreen, CO, 80439-9655

WDC-A for STP
325 Broadway, Boulder, CO, 80303-3328
STP Newsletter, 1,100

Wary Canary Press
PO Box 2204, Ft. Collins, CO, 80522-2204
Wary Canary, 396

•**Water Information Center, Inc.**
1099 18th St., Ste 2150, Denver, CO, 80202-1921

Wheat Ridge Regional Ctr.
10285 Ridge Rd, Wheat Ridge, CO, 80033-2399
Ridge News, 526

Whole Health Institute
4817 N County Road 29, Loveland, CO, 80538-9515
Healing Currents, 508

Wilsearch Investments Management Corp.
620 S 42nd St, Boulder, CO, 80303-5909
Wilsearch Investment Letter, 692

Windstar Foundation
2317 Snowmass Creek Rd, Snowmass, CO, 81654-9198
Windstar Newsletter/Products Catalog, 397

•**Winsor Publishing Company**
1919 14th St Ste 300, Boulder, CO, 80302-5321

Connecticut

•**Aeltus Managing, Inc.**
242 Trumbull St., Hartford, CT, 06156

American Academy of Psychiatry & the Law
PO Box 30, Bloomfield, CT, 06002-0030
Newsletter of the American Academy of Psychiatry, 1,011

American Boat Builders & Repairers Assn.
PO Box 1236, Stamford, CT, 06904-1236
American Boat Builders & Repairers Assn. - Newsletter, 112

American Electrology Assn.
106 Oakridge Rd, Trumbull, CT, 06611-5213
Electrolysis World, 164

American Indian Archaeological Institute
PO Box 1260, Curtis Road, Washington, CT, 06793-0260
NETOP, The, 58

American Institute of Building Design
991 Post Road East, Westport, CT, 06880
Design Line, 59

American Position
115 Lords Hwy, Weston, CT, 06883-1715
From the Right, 990

Americana Unit-American Topical Assn.
PO Box 127, New Britain, CT, 06050-0127
Americana Philatelic News, 970

Ancillary Profits
PO Box 301, Rowayton, CT, 06853-0301
Ancillary Profits, 853

Annhurst College
Publishing, Woodstock, CT, 06281
Canto, 198

•**Apt. Owners & Managers Assn. of America**
PO Box 238, Watertown, CT, 06795-0238

Aquaculture Newsletter International
3 Pinefield, Weston, CT, 06883
Aquaculture Newsletter International, 422

Archaeological Society of Connecticut
C/O Joseph Parkos, 60 Bashan Rd., East Haddam, CT, 06423
Connecticut News, 57

Argonaut Enterprises
PO Box 2777, Westport, CT, 06880-0777
Voyager Intl., 1,191

•**Arnold Bakers Inc.**
Hamilton Ave., Greenwich, CT, 06830

Association of Bridal Consultants
200 Chestnut Land Rd, New Milford, CT, 06776-2521
ABC Dialogue, 122

Association of College & Research Libraries
100 Riverview Ctr., Middletown, CT, 06457-3445
RBMS Newsletter, 808

Assn. of Collegiate Licensing Administrators
638 Prospect Ave., Hartford, CT, 06105-4298
Alert, 209

Association for Women in Psychology, c/o Lynn Collins
Eastern Connecticut State Univ, 83 Windham Street, Willimantic, CT, 06226-2295
AWP Newsletter Association for Women in Psychology, 1,011

Automatic Printing & Mailing Inc.
300 Shaw Rd, North Branford, CT, 06471-1055
Connecticut Libraries, 796

BI Research
PO Box 133, Redding, CT, 06875-1133
BI Research, 655

•**Bankers Research Inc.**
34 Imperial Ave # 431, Westport, CT, 06880-4304

Baxter Co.
1030 E. Putnam Ave., Greenwich, CT, 06836
Baxter Newsletter, 83

•**Belvoir Pubs.**
75 Holly Hill Lane, Greenwich, CT, 06836

Beverage Digest
PO Box 238, Old Greenwich, CT, 06870-0238
Jesse Meyers' Beverage Digest, 104

Blumenfeld and Associates
397 Post Road, Ste. 202, Darien, CT, 06820
Expedition News, 943

* See ***MULTI-PUBLISHER INDEX*** for list of publications.

•Boardroom Publishing
PO Box 2614, 55 Railroad Ave., Greenwich, CT, 06836-6378

Botsford Family Historical Assn.
c/o Mrs. Janet Elton, 80 E. Main St., Plymouth, CT, 06782
Band of Botsford Bulletin, 447

Box Project
PO Box 435, Plainville, CT, 06062-0435
Box Project-Newsletter, 1,114

Bridge Group
345 Woodcreek Rd, Bethlehem, CT, 06751-1014
Green MarketAlert, 139

Bridgeport Engineering Institute
785 Unquowa Rd., Fairfield, CT, 06430-5002
Night Hawk, 197

Bridgeport Hospital
267 Grant St, Bridgeport, CT, 06610-2870
Capsule, 562

•Bureau of Business Practice
24 Rope Ferry Rd, Waterford, CT, 06386-0001

•Business Communications Co.
25 Van Zant St., Ste.13, Norwalk, CT, 06855-1781

Business Journals, Inc.
50 Day St. #5550, S. Norwalk, CT, 06854-3127
Turbomachinery Maintenance Newsletter, 832

•Business & Legal Reports, Inc.
39 Academy St., PO Box 1513, Madison, CT, 06443-2646

•Business Marketing & Publishing, Inc.
PO Box 7457, Wilton, CT, 06897-7457

Butterbrooke Farm
78 Barry Rd, Oxford, CT, 06478-1529
Germinations, 441

•C.L. Pace Associates
36 Henry Austin Dr., Wilton, CT, 06897-3210

•CM Alliance
140 Garden St, Hartford, CT, 06154-0001

Camarro Research
345 Carroll Rd # 691, Fairfield, CT, 06430-3071
Authorized OA Dealer Report, 937

Central Connecticut State University
1615 Stanley St # 101, New Britain, CT, 06053-2439
Central Courier, 197

Champion International Corp.
1 Champion Plz, Stamford, CT, 06921-6001
Printing Salesman's Herald, 595

Charting the Economy
PO Box 829, New Haven, CT, 06504-0829
Charting the Economy, 290

Children's Writer
95 Long Ridge Rd., West Redding, CT, 06896-1124
Children's Writer, 117

Clowns of America
210 Glen Haven Rd., New Haven, CT, 06513-1145
Calliage, 368

Commission on Official Legal Publications
111 Phoenix Ave., Office of Prod. & Distr., Enfield, CT, 06082-4453
Connecticut Law Journal, 727

Community Health Center
635 Main St, Middletown, CT, 06457-2730
Quarterly Community Health Center News, 525

Connecticut Audubon Society
2325 Burr St, Fairfield, CT, 06430-1806
Connecticut Warbler, 920

Connecticut Broadcasters Assn.
101 Tall Timbers Ln, Glastonbury, CT, 06033-3339
Connecticut Broadcasters Association Newsletter, 123

Connecticut Dental Assn.
62 Russ St, Hartford, CT, 06106-1522
Communicator, 268

Connecticut Dept. of Agriculture
165 Capitol Ave., #263, State Office Bldg., Hartford, CT, 06106-1630
Connecticut Weekly Agricultural Report, 39

Connecticut Educational Media Assoc.
25 Elmwood Ave, Trumbull, CT, 06611-3503
CEMA Update, 302

Connecticut Hospice, Inc.
61 Burban Dr, Branford, CT, 06405-4003
Connecticut Hospice Newsletter, 411

Connecticut Humane Society
701 Russell Rd, Newington, CT, 06111-1527
Connecticut Humane Bulletin, 49

Connecticut Joint Council on Economic Education
Univ. of Connecticut, U-55, One Bishop Circle, Storrs, CT, 06269-4055
CJCEE Newsletter, 302

Connecticut Joint Federation
2600 Dixwell Ave., Hamden, CT, 06514-1833
Connecticut Engineers, 360

Connecticut Junior Republic, Inc., The
Box 161, Goshen Rd., Litchfield, CT, 06759-0161
Junior Citizen, 1,215

•Connecticut Labor Dept.
Business Management, 200 Folly Brook Blvd., Wethersfield, CT, 06109-1114

Connecticut Nurses Assn.
377 Research Pky Ste 2d, Meriden, CT, 06450-7155
Connecticut Nursing News, 929

Connecticut Public Expenditure Council
21 Lewis St, Hartford, CT, 06103-2506
Connecticut Public Expenditure Council-News & Views, 1,142

Connecticut State Labor Department, Office o fResearch
Office of Research, 111 High Ridge Rd., 3rd Fl., Stamford, CT, 06905
Stamford Labor Market Review, 705

Connecticut Technical Assistance Program
50 Columbus Blvd Ste 4, Hartford, CT, 06106-1910
ConnTAP Quarterly, 376

Copley Entertainment Inc.
3006 Fairfield Ave, Bridgeport, CT, 06605-3216
Syndication News, 1,169

Cornelia de Lange Syndrome Foundation
60 Dyer Ave, Collinsville, CT, 06022-1201
Reaching Out, 279

•Cowles Magazine, Inc.
4 High Ridge Park, Stamford, CT, 06905

•Cromwell-Sloan Pub. Co.
63 Vine Rd, Stamford, CT, 06905-2012

Dan Gaspar
161 Main St, Wethersfield, CT, 06109-2339
Keeper's Line, 1,132

Department of Mental Retardation
Region #3, 670 Main Street, Willimantic, CT, 06226
Mansfield Weekly, 787

Diabetic Traveler
Box 8223 RW, Stamford, CT, 06905-8223
Diabetic Traveler, 1,183

Diamond Analytics
PO Box 7302, Wilton, CT, 06897-7302
Benson's Baseball Monthly, 101

•Dictaphone Corp.
3191 Broadbridge Ave, Stratford, CT, 06497-2566

•Digital Information Group
PO Box 110235, Stamford, CT, 06911-0235

Direct Marketing Day in New York, Inc.
65 Commerce Rd., Stamford, CT, 06902-4549
Day Break, 274

Direct Media
200 Pemberwick Rd, P.O. Box 4565, Greenwich, CT, 06830-4273
Computer Monitor Quarterly, 274

Directosip Inc.
8 Sound Shore Dr Ste 254, Greenwich, CT, 06830-7242
Directorship, 136

•Dun & Bradstreet
PO Box 870, Wilton, CT, 06897

Earth Matters
6 Patriot Ln, Newington, CT, 06111-4421
Earth Patrol, 377

Edina
PO Box 5065, New haven, CT, 06525
Grassroots Economic Organizing (GEO), 253

Electronic Banking Economics Society
56 Roberts Rd, Marlborough, CT, 06447-1454
Electronic Banking Economics Society Newsletter, 88

Energy Investment Research, Inc.
Box 73, Glenville Sta., Greenwich, CT, 06831-0773
Israeli Investor Network, 356

Entertainment Art Co., The
1200 High Ridge Road, Stamford, CT, 06905-1202
Classic Chevrolet Memories, 71

Eugene O'Neill Memorial Theater Center
305 Great Neck Rd, Waterford, CT, 06385-3825
O'Neill, The, 1,173

Exec-u-Net
25 Van Zant St., Ste. 15-3, Norwalk, CT, 06855
Exec-u-Net, 344

F.M. Future Music
P.O. Box 4073, Hamden, CT, 06514
Subway Entertainment Guide, 918

Factory Outlet Newsletter
11 Tory Lane Rt. 3, Newtown, CT, 06470-1531
Factory Outlet Newsletter, 253

Fairfield University
Greek and Roman Studies, c/o Vincent Rosivach, Fairfield, CT, 06430
New England Classical Newsletter & Journal, 823

Filigree Inc.
25 Diaz St, Stamford, CT, 06902-5608
Petroleum Outlook, 963

•Food & Nutrition Press Inc.
2 Corporate Drive, Box 374, Trumbull, CT, 06611-1338

•Foreign Military Markets Latin American
22 Commerce Rd., Newtown, CT, 06470-1643

•Forecast International/DMS, Inc.
22 Commerce Rd., Newtown, CT, 06470-1643

•Forecast International/DMS, Inc.
22 Commerce Rd., Newtown, CT, 06470-1643

Foundation for Community Encouragement
109 Danbury Rd Ste 8, Ridgefield, CT, 06877-4109
Communique, 259

Fraser Paper, Ltd.
9 West Broad St., Box 10055, Stamford, CT, 06904
Fraser Voyageur, 584

French-Canadian Genealogical Society of Connecticut, Inc.
PO Box 45, Tolland, CT, 06084-0045
Connecticut Maple Leaf, 451

Friends in Art of ACB
166 Little Deer Rd, Bridgeport, CT, 06606-1750
Log of the Bridgetender, 111

GE
1285 Boston Ave, Bridgeport, CT, 06610-2612
GE News, 584

G.H. Brooks Associates Inc.
221 West Ave, Darien, CT, 06820-4202
Whisper On Wall Street, 692

Gallery Press
One River Road, Essex, CT, 06426-1071
Folk Art Finder, 64

Gartner Group
56 Top Gallant Rd, Stamford, CT, 06902-7700
Yardstick, 242

General Motors Corp.
780 James P Casey Rd, Bristol, CT, 06010-2200
Newsletter, 592

Gluten Free Pantry
PO Box 881, Glastonbury, CT, 06033-0881
Gluten Free Pantry, 430

Governmental Accounting Standards Board
401 Merritt 7, PO Box 5116, Norwalk, CT, 06856-5116
Governmental Accounting Standards Board-Action Report, 5

Greater New Haven Chamber of Commerce
195 Church St Ste 15, New Haven, CT, 06510-2009
Profit-The Bottom Line in Greater New Haven Business, 161

Greater New Haven State Technical College
88 Bassett Rd, North Haven, CT, 06473-1901
SAC, 198

•Greenfield Press
PO Box 176, Southport, CT, 06490-0176

•Greenwood Publishing Group, Inc.
88 Post Rd. W., PO Box 5007, Westport, CT, 06881-5007

Hard Core Marketing
239 Ethan Allen Highway, Ridgefield, CT, 06877
Bellmark Times, The, 910

Hartford Dental Society
230 Scarborough St, Hartford, CT, 06105-1100
Hartford Dental Society Newsletter, 270

Hartford Graduate Center
275 Windsor St, Hartford, CT, 06120-2910
Newsletter, 197

Home Builders Association of Hartford County
Connecticut Home Show, 1310 Silas Deane Highway, Weathersfield, CT, 06109-4303
Connecticut Builder, 245

Hunt-Scanlon Publishing Co., Inc.
Two Pickwick Plaza, Greenwich, CT, 06830
Executive Search Review, 344

Image Publishing
PO Box 3149, Westport, CT, 06880-8149
Imaging Service Bureau News, 225

Institute of Public Service
Univ. of Conn., Box U14, Storrs, CT, 06268
IPS, Local Government Newsletter, 486

---

* See **MULTI-PUBLISHER INDEX** for list of publications.

Intellectual Properties Council
Four High Ridge Park, Stamford, CT, 06905
Subrights Letter, 120

International Amateur Radio Union
Box AAA, Newington, CT, 06107-0901
Calendar, 123

International Information Systems
PO Box 3127, Westport, CT, 06880-8127
Ukrainian Business Digest, 155

International Philatelic Press Club
PO Box 127, New Britain, CT, 06050
Report to Members, 972

International Sand Collectors Society
43 Highview Ave, Old Greenwich, CT, 06870-1703
Sand Paper, The, 556

Irving Levin Associates, Inc.
72 Park Street, New Canaan, CT, 06840
Healthcare Investor, 667

Jameson Newsletter
112 Belaire Cir, Windsor Locks, CT, 06096-2809
Jameson Newsletter, 457

Jay Hickerson
PO Box 4321, Hamden, CT, 06514-0321
Hello Again, 417

Jefferson House Gerontology Resource Center
1 John Stewart Dr, Newington, CT, 06111-3126
Geri-Source, 1,106

Just Books
19 E Putnam Ave, Greenwich, CT, 06830-5443
Just Books, 822

Keep America Beautiful, Inc.
9 W. Broad St., Stamford, CT, 06902-3734
KAB System Network, 1,021

Knights of Columbus Supreme Council
One Columbus Plaza, New Haven, CT, 06510-3326
Squires Newsletter, 1,216

Legal Assistant Management Association
638 Prospect Ave., Hartford, CT, 06105-4250
LAMA Manager, 840

•**MBA Track, Inc.**
10 Bay St Ste 104, Westport, CT, 06880-4324

MJF Publications
PO Box 3056, Stamford, CT, 06905-0056
MJF Baseball Card Advisory, 554

Magny Families Association
PO Box 684, Windsor, CT, 06095-0684
Magny Families Association Newsletter, 460

Marble Collectors' Society of America
PO Box 222, Trumbull, CT, 06611-0222
Marble Mania, 554

Mark Twain Memorial Newsletter
351 Farmington Ave., Hartford, CT, 06105-4401
Mark Twain Memorial Newsletter, 905

McMahon Publishing Co.
83 Peaceable St., W. Reading, CT, 06896-3198
Intravenous Therapy News, 877

Meca Software Ltd.
55 Walls Drive, Fairfield, CT, 06430-0912
Managing Your Money Better, 675

Media Notes
PO Box E, Avon, CT, 06001-0305
Media Notes, 804

Medical Practice Letter
227 Everit St, New Haven, CT, 06511-1335
Medical Practice Letter, 879

•**Middletown Bulletin, Inc.**
PO Box 906, Middletown, CT, 06457-0906

Modern Greek Studies Association
Box 1826, New Haven, CT, 06508
Modern Greek Studies Association Bulletin, 544

National Association for Drama Therapy
44 Taylor Street, Branford, CT, 06405
Dramascope, 1,013

National Association of Police Community Relations Officers
125 Columbus Blvd., New Britain Police Dept., New Britain, CT, 06051
News Update, 788

National Milk Glass Collectors Society
80 Crestview Dr, Newington, CT, 06111-2405
Opaque News, 53

Natl. Schools Committee for Economic Education, Inc.
PO Box 295, Cos Cob, CT, 06807-0295
Freedom & Enterprise, 310

National Theatre of the Deaf
5 W Main St # 659, Chester, CT, 06412-1302
NTD Newsletter, 1,173

Northeastern Forest Fire Protection Commission
66 Buckley Hwy, Stafford Springs, CT, 06076-4406
Northeastern Forest Fire Protection Commission Compact News, 422

Northwestern Connecticut Community-Technical College
Rm. 110, Green Woods Hall, Student Activities Office, Winsted, CT, 06098
Jabberwocky, 198

Nutmeg Chapter, Trout Unlimited
PO Box 1594, Fairfield, CT, 06430-1594
Nutmeg Notes, 423

Oceanic Society LI Chapter & the Long Island Sound Study
185 Magee Ave., Stamford Marine Ctr., Stamford, CT, 06902-5906
Long Island Sound Study Update, 936

Online, Inc.
462 Danbury Rd., Wilton, CT, 06897-2125
CD-ROM News Extra, 214

Open Book Publishing, Inc.
PO Box 2288, 90 Holmes Avenue, Darien, CT, 06820
Subtext, 120

Orphan Disease Update
PO Box 8923, New Fairfield, CT, 06812-8923
Orphan Disease Update, 286

Otis Elevator Co.
1 Farm Springs Rd, Farmington, CT, 06032-2500
Otis Bulletin, 594

Out and About
542 Chapel St., New Haven, CT, 06511
Out and About, 1,187

Owenoak International
3 Parklands Dr., Darien, CT, 06830
International Golfer, 480

Paul & Lisa, Inc.
PO Box 348, Westbrook, CT, 06498-0348
P & L Connections, 1,120

Penny Saver
PO Box 628, Old Saybrook, CT, 06475-0628
Penny Saver, 24

•**Perkin-Elmer Corp.**
761 Main Ave., Norwalk, CT, 06859-0105

Pfizer Inc.
Eastern Pt. Rd., Groton, CT, 06340
Capsule, 579

Phenix Society
PO Box 351, Cheshire, CT, 06410-0351
Mind-Expander, 974

Photography Assocs.
PO Box A, Old Greenwich, CT, 06870-0601
Photography, 978

Posy Collection
PO Box 394, Simsbury, CT, 06070-0394
Home Work, 140

Potes & Poets Press
181 Edgemont Ave., Elmwood, CT, 06110-1005
ABACUS, 981

Pratt
400 Main St, East Hartford, CT, 06118-1873
Power Plant, 595

Product Safety International
Box 1561-OX, Middletown, CT, 06457-8061
International Product Safety News, 1,081

•**Productivity Inc.**
101 Merritt 7, Norwalk, CT, 06851-1059

Publishing Dynamics, Inc.
15 Bank St., Ste. 101, Stamford, CT, 06901-3008
Interior Fashion News, 438

Quinebaug Valley Community-Technical College
742 Upper Maple St., Danielson, CT, 06239-1440
Crazy River Press, 197

R & C
1 Commercial Plz, Hartford, CT, 06103-3512
Law & the Land, 748

R.J. Julia
768 Boston Post Rd, Madison, CT, 06443-3047
R.J. Julia Booksellers, 824

•**Ransom & Benjamin Publishers LLC**
P.O. Box 606, Old Greenwich, CT, 06870-0417

Religious Education Association
409 Prospect St, New Haven, CT, 06511-2177
REACH, 1,050

Rockville Reminder
130 Old Town Rd., Box 27, Vernon, CT, 06066-2362
Rockville Reminder, 24

S. Tepfer Publishing Co., Inc.
PO Box 597, Ridgefield, CT, 06877-0597
ETV Newsletter, 1,167

School Market Research Institute
1721 Saybrook Rd., P.O. Box 10, Haddam, CT, 06438-1324
School Marketing Newsletter, 22

Schreff
9 Frontier Rd, Cos Cob, CT, 06807-1208
Cable Theft Newsletter, 123

Scott American Corp.
Box 88, West Redding, CT, 06896-0088
Travel Publicity Leads, 1,190

Seidman News Bulletin
51 Pine Mountain Rd., West Redding, CT, 06896-2717
Seidman News Bulletin, 56

Select Fiction
P.O. Box 1041, Sharon, CT, 06069
Select Fiction, 818

Sierra Club, Connecticut Chapter
118 Oak St, Hartford, CT, 06106-1514
Quinnehtukqut, 391

•**Simba Information, Inc.**
213 Danbury Rd. PO Box 7430, Wilton, CT, 06897-7430

Simon & Schuster
24 Rope Ferry Rd, Waterford, CT, 06386-0001
Professional Selling, 1,087

Soccer America
301 Post Rd., Westport, CT, 06880
Youth Soccer Letter, 1,138

Society Farsarotul
PO Box 753, Trumbull, CT, 06611-0753
Newsletter of the Society Farsarotul, 401

Society for Hungarian Philately
Box 1162, Samp-Mortar Station, Fairfield, CT, 06430-1162
News of Hungarian Philately, 971

Source Publications
PO Box 654, Monroe, CT, 06468-0654
Genuine Article, The, 890

Sperry Remington Co.
Sperry Rand Corp., 60 Main St., Bridgeport, CT, 06611
Sperry Remington News, 599

Stamford Historical Society
1508 High Ridge Rd, Stamford, CT, 06903-4107
Stamford Historical Society Newsletter, 548

Stamford Teachers Federal Credit Union
PO Box 2269, Stamford, CT, 06906-0269
Credit Line, 257

•**Stamler Publishing Co.**
178 Thimble Islands Rd., P.O. Box 3367, Branford, CT, 06405-1967

State of CT Commission on Fire Prevention
PO Box 3383, Windsor Locks, CT, 06096-3383
Hot Flashes, 421

Stonington Historical Soc.
PO Box 103, Stonington, CT, 06378-0103
Historical Footnotes, 541

Stowe-Day Foundation
77 Forest St., Hartford, CT, 06105-3243
Harriet Beecher Stowe House & Library, 540

Suburban Reminder
130 Old Town Rd., Box 27, Vernon, CT, 06066-2322
Suburban Reminder, 24

Sunglass Association of America
49 East Ave., Norwalk, CT, 06851
Sunglass Association of America-Newsletter, 56

Survey Sampling, Inc.
1 Post Rd., Fairfield, CT, 06430-6215
Frame, The, 14

Technical Trends
PO Box 792, Wilton, CT, 06897-0792
Technical Trends, 688

Teikyo Post University
800 Country Club Rd, Waterbury, CT, 06708-3200
Postcripts Newsletter, 187

Textron Lycoming
550 S Main St, Stratford, CT, 06497-7572
Radian, 596

Theta Corp.
8 Old Indian Trl, Middlefield, CT, 06455-1200
Changing Medical Markets, 870

Timer Digest, Inc.
PO Box 1688, Greenwich, CT, 06836-1688
Timer Digest, 689

Trade Dimensions
263 Tresser Blvd., Stamford, CT, 06901
Insider, 790

---

* See **MULTI-PUBLISHER INDEX** for list of publications.

Traditional Small Craft Assn.
PO Box 350, Mystic, CT, 06355-0350
Ash Breeze, 113

Transamerica Media Corp.
PO Box 2626, Greenwich, CT, 06836-2626
Insider's Chronicle, 670

Travelers Corp.
1 Tower Sq, Hartford, CT, 06115-1501
Tips & Trends, 625

Trinity College Library
Publications, Hartford, CT, 06106
Trinity College Library Newsletter, 811

Turkish Sephardi Federation
46 Benson Pl., Fairfield, CT, 06430-6904
Erensia Sefardi, 407

Two Ems, Inc.
786 Boston Post Rd, Madison, CT, 06443-3047
In Business, 141

Union Trust Co.
Public Relations, 300 Main Street, Stamford, CT, 06904
Union Trust Topics, 601

Uniroyal Inc.
PO Box 846, Middlebury, CT, 06762-0846
Uniroyal World, 601

U.S. Ski Writers Assn.
1207 Valley Rd, Fairfield, CT, 06432-1663
U.S. Ski Writers Association, Newsletter, 1,113

•**Univ. of Connecticut**
32 Hillside Ave, Waterbury, CT, 06710-2217

University of Connecticut
U-67, 1376 Storrs Rd., Storrs, CT, 06269-4067
Connecticut Greenhouse Newsletter, 424

Univ. of Connecticut, Ctr. for Instruct. Media
Box U-1, #3, 249 Glen Brook Rd., Storrs, CT, 06269
Interface, 858

Univ. of Connecticut Ctr. Real Estate
Center Real Estate/Urban Econ, U-41 RE, Rm 426, 368 Fairfield, Storrs, CT, 06269
Real Estate Reports, 1,038

Univ. of Connecticut-Groton
Publications, Groton, CT, 06340
Student News, 197

Univ. of Connecticut Inst. Materials Science
Publications, Storrs, CT, 06268
IMS Bulletin, 1,097

Univ. of Hartford/Hartt School of Music
200 Bloomfield Ave., W. Hartford, CT, 06117-1500
Kodaly Musical Training Institute, 913

University of New Haven
300 Orange Ave, West Haven, CT, 06516-1916
University of New Haven Insight, 198

University of New Haven Public Relations Office
300 Orange Ave, West Haven, CT, 06516-1916
Insight, 187

Vegetable Factory, Inc.
495 Post Road East, WestPort, CT, 06880-4400
Grow Letter, 441

Vietnam Market Resources
1616 Post Rd Ste 1106, Fairfield, CT, 06430-5912
Vietnam Market Watch, 652

Vietnam War Newsletter
PO Box 469, Collinsville, CT, 06022-0469
Vietnam War Newsletter, 899

Virus Bulletin
590 Danbury Rd., Ridgefield, CT, 06877-2722
Virus Bulletin, 242

WHA Enterprises, Inc.
P.O. Box 164, East Glastonbury, CT, 06025-0164
Winsor Report, The, 156

Weigand
356 Salem Tpke, Bozrah, CT, 06334-1518
Weigand Report, 242

Wild Geese, The
6 N Water St, Greenwich, CT, 06830-5817
Gander, The, 403

•**Wildwood Assocs.**
66 Shelter Rock Rd, Stamford, CT, 06903-3529

William Baxter
1030 E. Putnam Ave., Box 2200, Greenwich, CT, 06836
Baxter World Economic Service, 655

World Ocean & Cruise Liner Society
PO Box 92, Stamford, CT, 06904-0092
Ocean & Cruise News, 1,187

Wright Investors' Service
1000 Lafayette Blvd, Bridgeport, CT, 06604-4720
Wright Investment Advice and Analysis, 100

Writers in Exile Center
42 Derby Ave, Orange, CT, 06477-1433
International Pen Club-Newsletter, 982

Yale School of Drama
222 York St, New Haven, CT, 06511-4804
Technical Brief, 1,174

Yale University, School of Medicine
333 Cedar St, New Haven, CT, 06510-3206
Yale Children's Health Letter, 532

Delaware

American Philosophical Association
University of Delaware, Newark, DE, 19716
APA Newsletters, The, 973

Bank of Delaware
222 Delaware Ave, Wilmington, DE, 19801-1600
Teller, 600

•**Blue Cross, Blue Shield of Delaware**
One Brandywine Gateway,, Box 1991, Wilmington, DE, 19899

Bonsai & Orchid Association
26 Pine St., Dover, DE, 19901-4452
Green World News, 441

Bureau of Disease Control
Div. of Public Health, Dover, DE, 19901
Delaware Biweekly Morbidity Report, 503

Catalysis Soc. of North America
C/O Dupont Experimental Sta., Bldg. 402, C/O Linn, Wilmington, DE, 19898-0001
Catalysis Society Newsletter, 163

Chesapeake Bay Girl Scout Council
501 S College Ave, Newark, DE, 19713-1301
Newsletter, 180

Delaware Nurses Assn.
2634 Capitol TRL #C, Newark, DE, 19711-7263
Delaware Nurses' Association Reporter, 929

Delaware State Museum
Court & Federal, Dover, DE, 19901
Delaware State Museum, News, 903

Delaware Today, Inc.
PO Box 2087, Wilmington, DE, 19899-2087
Delaware Today Aware, 135

Disc Collectors Newsletter
PO Box 315, Cheswold, DE, 19936-0315
Disc Collector, 1,128

•**E.I. du Pont de Nemours**
10007 Market Street, Wilmington, DE, 19898-0001

Fellowship of Missions
PO Box 136, Middletown, DE, 19709-0136
Focus on Missions, 1,063

General Motors Corp.
Boxwood & Dodson Rds., Wilmington, DE, 19899
Newsletter, 75

Hagley Museum & Library
PO Box 3630, Wilmington, DE, 19807-0630
Business History Bulletin, 129

Happy Hobbies Pubs.
PO Box 70, Claymont, DE, 19703-0070
Happy Hobbies, 553

Haratio
P.O. Box 5092, Wilmington, DE, 19808
The Realm of Out-There, 417

ICI Pharmaceuticals
PO Box 751, Wilmington, DE, 19897-0001
Wellspring Services, 289

IRA
PO Box 8139, Newark, DE, 19714-8139
USBBY, 120

ISM Independent School Management, Inc.
1316 N. Union St., Wilmington, DE, 19806-2534
Teachers In Touch, 332

Integrated Automotive Resources
4 Polly Drummond Hill Rd, Newark, DE, 19711-5703
Fast Track News - Automotive Sales & Production, 72

Newark Historical Society
PO Box 711, Newark, DE, 19715-0711
Newark Historical Society Newsletter, 545

Society of Rheology, c/o Dr. Arthur Metzner
Chemical Engineering, Univ. of Delaware, Newark, DE, 19716
Rheology Bulletin, 979

State Board of Ed., Planning, Research & Evaluation Div.
PO Box 1402, Dover, DE, 19903-1402
Statwise; Statistical and Research Newsletter, 331

TCI Marketing Inc.
1011 Centre Rd., Ste. 403, Wilmington, DE, 19805-1266
Directions, 582

Univ. of Delaware Water Resource Ctr.
133 Townsend Hall, Newark, DE, 19717-1303
Water Resources Center News, 397

Urban Affairs Assn.
Univ. of Delaware, Newark, DE, 19711-4688
UAA Communication, 1,024

Widener Univ. -Delaware Law School
PO Box 7474, Wilmington, DE, 19803-0474
Delaware Law Forum, 198

Wilmington Trust Co.
Rodney Sq., N., Wilmington, DE, 19801-1284
Bank Notes, 577

District of Columbia

ADC Research Institute
4201 Connecticut Ave NW Ste, 500, Washington, DC, 20008-1158
ADC Times, 399

AFL-CIO
815 16th St NW, Washington, DC, 20006-4145
Bulletin, 707

AFL-CIO Department of Education
815 16th St. NW, Ste. 407, Washington, DC, 20006-4104
Education Update, 309

AFL-CIO Public Employee Dept.
816 16th St. NW, PED Ste. 308, Washington, DC, 20006-4102
PED Forum, 710

AGC Natl. Newsletter
1957 East St., N.W., Washington, DC, 20006
AGC National Newsletter, 243

AIA Press
1735 New York Ave. NW, Washington, DC, 20006-5292
AIAS News, 59

A.T.I.
1828 L Street, Ste 1000, Washington, DC, 20036-4706
Catalyst - ATI's Technical Bulletin, 628

Academia, Inc.
4455 Connecticut Ave NW Ste, 330, Washington, DC, 20008-2328
AIM Report, 694

Academy for State & Local Government
444 N Capitol St NW Ste 345, Washington, DC, 20001-1512
Public Innovation Abroad, 1,023

Accountants for the Public Interest
1012 14th St. NW, Ste. 906, Washington, DC, 20005-3406
API Account, 1

Action for Corporate Accountability
910 17th St. NW, Ste. 413, Washington, DC, 20006-2601
Action News, 251

Action on Smoking and Health
2013 H St. NW, Washington, DC, 20006-4207
ASH Smoking & Health Review, 497

Adolescent Medicine
821 Delaware Ave SW, Washington, DC, 20024-4207
Adolescent Medicine, 865

Advanced Intl. Studies Institute
1740 Massachusetts Ave NW, Washington, DC, 20036-1984
Soviet World Outlook, 638

Advisory Board Company
600 New Hampshire Ave., N.W., Washington, DC, 20037
Financial Reading Review, 90

Advisory Newsletter Group, Inc.
PO Box 90833, Washington, DC, 20090-0833
Ryan Advisory for Health, Facilities Governing Boards, 527

Aerospace Industries Assn of America
1250 Eye St., NW, #1100, Washington, DC, 20005-3922
Aerospace Industries Assn. Newsletter, 25

African-American Labor Center
1925 K St NW Ste 300, Washington, DC, 20006-1105
AALC Reporter, 706

African Insider
Box 53398, Temple Heights Station, Washington, DC, 20009
African Insider, 626

Agency for International Development
320 21 St. N.W., Ste 4889, Washington, DC, 20523-0001
USAID Developments, 639

Agricultural Cooperative Development Intl.
50 F St NW Ste 900, Washington, DC, 20001-1530
Cooperative News Intl., 39

* See ***MULTI-PUBLISHER INDEX*** for list of publications.

* See **MULTI-PUBLISHER INDEX** for list of publications.

American Road & Transportation Builders Assn.
1010 Massachusetts Ave. NW, Washington, DC, 20001
ARTBA Newsletter, 1,077

American Short Line Railroad Assn.
1120 G St NW Ste 520, Washington, DC, 20005-3801
Views and News, 1,030

American Ski Federation
207 Constitution Ave NE, Washington, DC, 20002-7307
ASF Washington Letter, 1,112

American Society of Appraisers
Box 17265, Washington, DC, 20041-0265
Newsline, 1,036

•**American Society of Association Executives**
1575 'I' St., N.W., 11th Fl., Washington, DC, 20005-1168

American Society of Internal Medicine
2011 Pennsylvania Ave NW Ste, 800, Washington, DC, 20006-1813
Internist's Intercom, 877

American Society of International Law
2223 Massachusetts Ave. NW, Washington, DC, 20008-2864
American Society of International Law Newsletter, 714

American Society of Landscape Architects
4401 Connecticut Ave. NW, Washington, DC, 20008
LAND: Landscape Architectural News Digest, 60

American Society for Psychoprophylaxis in Obstetrics
1200 19th St NW Ste 300, Washington, DC, 20036-2412
Genesis, 507

American Sociological Association
1722 N St., N.W., Washington, DC, 20036-2981
Footnotes, 1,125

American Studies Assn.
1120 19th Street NW, Suite 301, Washington, DC, 20036
American Studies Assn. Newsletter, 258

American Symphony Orchestra League
777 14th St NW Ste 500, Washington, DC, 20005-3201
Upbeat: Youth Orchestra Newsletter, 919

American Trails
1400 16th St NW Ste 300, Washington, DC, 20036-2217
Trail Tracks-American Trails Newsletter, 950

Amer. Unit of ATA
PO Box 179, Washington, DC, 20044-0179
American Philatelic News, 970

American Wholesale Marketers Assn.
1128 16th St. NW, Washington, DC, 20036-4808
Quick Topics, 243

•**American Wind Energy Assn.**
122 C St. NW, Washington, DC, 20001

•**Americans for Democratic Action**
1625 K St NW Ste 210, Washington, DC, 20006-1604

•**America's Community Bankers**
900 19th St. NW, Ste. 400, Washington, DC, 20006-2105

Amersham Associates
1209 G St NE, Washington, DC, 20002-4423
International High Technology Report, 142

Animal Welfare Institute
PO Box 3650, Washington, DC, 20007-0150
Animal Welfare Institute Quarterly, 372

•**Antarctica & Southern Ocean Coalition**
424 C St NE, Washington, DC, 20002-5818

Artists Equity Fund, Inc.
Box 28068, Central Sta., Washington, DC, 20038-8068
Artists Equity Fund-Newsletter, 63

Asphalt Rubber Producers Group
312 Massachusetts Ave NE, Washington, DC, 20002-5702
Rebounder, 964

Associated Accounting Firms Intl.
1000 Connecticut Ave NW Ste, 1006, Washington, DC, 20036-5302
Associated Accounting Firms International, 2

Associated Air Balance Council
1518 K St NW Ste 503, Washington, DC, 20005-1203
AABC Newsletter, 359

Associated Press Broadcast Services
1825 K St NW Ste 615, Washington, DC, 20006-1202
Associated Press Broadcasters Association News, 122

Association of American Colleges and Univ.
1818 R St NW, Washington, DC, 20009-1604
On Campus with Women, 324

•**Association of American Geographers**
1710 16th St NW, Washington, DC, 20009-3104

•**Association of American Law Schools**
1201 Conn. Ave. NW, #800, Washington, DC, 20036-2605

•**Association of American Medical Colleges**
2450 N Street, N.W., Washington, DC, 20037-1167

Assn. of American Railroads
50 F St NW, Washington, DC, 20001-1564
Train It, 1,030

•**Association for Biomedical Research**
818 Connecticut Ave NW Ste 303, Washington, DC, 20006-2702

Association of Biotechnology Companies
1625 K St NW Ste 1100, Washington, DC, 20006-1604
Details, 110

Assn. of Black Psychologists
PO Box 55999, Washington, DC, 20040-5999
Psych Discourse, 1,017

Association for Canadian Studies in the U.S.
1 Dupont Cir. NW, Ste. 620, Washington, DC, 20036-1182
Canadian Studies Update, 303

Association of Catholic Colleges/Universities
1 Dupont Cir NW Ste 650, Washington, DC, 20036-1110
Update, 334

Association of Collegiate Schools of Architecture, Inc.
1735 New York Ave., Washington, DC, 20006-5209
ACSA News, 59

Assn. for Community Based Education
1806 Vernon St NW, Washington, DC, 20009-1217
CBE Report, 302

Assn. of Community College Trustees
1740 N Street, N.W., Washington, DC, 20036-2907
Advisor, 299

Association for Gerontology in Higher Education
1001 Connecticut Ave NW Ste, 410, Washington, DC, 20036-5504
AGHE Exchange, 1,105

Assn. for Hospital Med. Education
1101 Connecticut Ave NW Ste, 700, Washington, DC, 20036-4303
AHME News, 561

Assn. of Independent Television Stations
1320 19th St. NW, Washington, DC, 20036
INTV Capitol Newsletter, 1,167

Association of Jesuit Colleges and Universities
1 Dupont Cir NW Ste 405, Washington, DC, 20036-1110
ACJU Higher Education Report, 297

Assn. of Local Air Pollution Control Officials
444 N Capitol St NW Ste 306, Washington, DC, 20001-1512
Washington Update, 396

Assn. of Program Directors in Internal Medicine
700 13th St NW Ste 250, Washington, DC, 20005-3960
Careers in Internal Medicine, 870

Association of Research Libraries
21 Dupont Cir NW Ste 800, Washington, DC, 20036-1109
ARL Newsletter, 792

Association of Science-Technology Centers
1025 Vermont Ave NW, Ste. 500, Washington, DC, 20005-3516
ASTC Newsletter, 1,095

Assn. for the Sociology of Religion
Marist Hall Room 108 Cua, Washington, DC, 20064-0001
News and Announcements, 1,126

Assn. of Systematics Collections
730 11th St. NW 2nd Fl., Washington, DC, 20001-4521
Association of Systematics Collections Newsletter, 108

Assn. of Telemessaging Services Intl.
1200 19th St. NW, Washington, DC, 20036-2412
Telecommunicator, 1,163

Association of Trial Lawyers of America
1050 31st St., NW, Washington, DC, 20007-4409
ATLA Advocate, 713

Association to Unite the Democracies
1506 Pennsylvania Ave SE, Washington, DC, 20003-3116
UNITE!, 639

•**Atlantic Information Svcs., Inc.**
1100 17th St. NW, Ste. 300, Washington, DC, 20036-5503

Austin Grill
2404 Wisconsin Ave NW, Washington, DC, 20007-1845
Grilled News, 430

Aviation Consumer Action Project
PO Box 19029, Washington, DC, 20036-9029
News from ACAP, 31

Azadegan Foundation
PO Box 40152, Washington, DC, 20016-0152
Focus on Iran, 630

•**BRP (Washington DC)**
1333 H St., NW, Suite 1100, West Tower, Washington, DC, 20005-4707

Bank Marketing Assn.
1120 Connecticut Ave NW Ste, 300, Washington, DC, 20036-3902
Marketing Update, 94

Baptist Joint Committee on Public Affairs
200 Maryland Ave., NE, Washington, DC, 20002-5797
Report from the Capital, 1,053

•**Beard Group, Inc.**
PO Box 9867, Washington, DC, 20016-8867

Bicycle Institute of America
1506 21st St NW # 200, Washington, DC, 20036-1006
Pro Bike News, 263

Biometric Society
808 17th St. NW, Washington, DC, 20006-3910
Biometric Bulletin, 108

•**Black Child Development Inst**
1023 15th Street NW, Suite 600, Washington, DC, 20005

Board of Governors of the Fedl. Reserve System
Pub. Svcs. #m5138, Washington, DC, 20551-0001
Federal Reserve Bulletin, 89

Bookbuilders of Washington
PO Box 23805, Washington, DC, 20026-3805
Bookbuilders of Washington, 116

British Trading Co.
821 Delaware Ave SW, Washington, DC, 20024-4207
HLB Newsletter, 875

Buddhist Vihara Society
5017 16th St NW, Washington, DC, 20011-3841
Washington Buddhist, 1,054

Building & Construction Trades Dept. AFL-CIO
815 16th St., N.W., Washington, DC, 20006-4189
Builder, The, 707

Building Research Board, Natl. Research Council
2101 Constitution Ave NW, Washington, DC, 20037-2955
BRB Research Briefs, 244

Bureau of Alchohol, Tobacco, & Firearms
1200 Penn. Ave. NW Ste. #724, Washington, DC, 20226-0001
FFL Newsletter, 736

Bureau of the Census
Data User Services Div., Washington Plaza, Wp-1-317, Washington, DC, 20233-0001
Census & You, 215

Bureau of Mines
810 7th St NW, Washington, DC, 20241-0002
Technology Transfer, 901

•**Bureau of National Affairs, Inc.**
1231 25th St. NW, Bldg. N-200, Washington, DC, 20037-1157

Business Executives for National Security
601 Pennsylvania Ave NW Apt, 700, Washington, DC, 20004-2611
BENS Trendline, 127

Business Industry Political Action Committee
888 16th St., NW, Washington, DC, 20006
Politics, 996

CATO Institute
1000 Massachusetts Ave. NW, #6, Washington, DC, 20001-5403
CATO Policy Report, 986

CCH Washington Service Bureau, Inc.
655 15th St NW Ste 275, Washington, DC, 20005-5701

•**CEO Job Opportunities Update - ARA**
325 7th St. NW, Ste. 1000, Washington, DC, 20004-2801

•**CRC Press Inc.**
1101 Pennsylvania Ave SE, Washington, DC, 20003-2229

•**CRMA Commercial Refrigerator Manufacturers Assn.**
1101 Connecticut Ave NW Ste, 700, Washington, DC, 20036-4303

Callahan & Assocs., Inc.
1001 Connecticut Ave NW Ste, 1022, Washington, DC, 20036-5504
Callahan's Credit Union Report, 84

•**Campaign for U.N. Reform**
713 D St SE, Washington, DC, 20003-2153

•**Can Manufacturers Institute**
1625 Massachussetts Ave., NW, Washington, DC, 20036-2289

•**The Cancer Letter Inc.**
PO Box 15189, Washington, DC, 20003-0189

Cane Collector's Chronicle
15 2nd St NE, Washington, DC, 20002-7301
Cane Collector's Chronicle, 183

* See **MULTI-PUBLISHER INDEX** for list of publications.

Canon Law Society of America
Catholic University 431, Caldwell Hall, Washington, DC, 20064-0001
Canon Law Society of America Newsletter, 1,055

•Caribbean Dateline Pubs.
L'Enfant Plz., Box 23276, Washington, DC, 20026

Caring Grandparents of America
PO Box 96444, Washington, DC, 20090-6444
Grandparent Times, 1,107

Carnegie Institution of Washington
1530 P St NW, Washington, DC, 20005-1910
Spectra: the Newsletter of the Carnegie Institution of Washington, 1,101

Carrying Capacity Network
2000 P St. NW, Ste.240, Washington, DC, 20036-5915
Carrying Capacity Network Network Clearinghouse Bulletin, 374

Case Publications
11 Dupont Cir NW Ste 400, Washington, DC, 20036-1207
Matching Gift Notes, 144

Catholic News Service
3211 4th St NE, Washington, DC, 20017-1100
Origins, CNS Documentary Service, 1,059

•Catholic Univ. of America
Marist Hill, Washington, DC, 20064-0001

•Center for Auto Safety
2001 S St NW Ste 410, Washington, DC, 20009-1160

Center for Community Change
1000 Wisconsin Ave NW, Washington, DC, 20007-3651
Community Change, 483

Center of Concern
3700 13th St NE, Washington, DC, 20017-2592
Center Focus, 304

Center for Immigration Studies
1815 H St NW Ste 1010, Washington, DC, 20006-3604
CIS Backgrounder, 1,125

Center for Marine Conservation
1725 Desales St NW Ste 500, Washington, DC, 20036-4408
Marine Conservation News, 387

Center for Media & Public Affairs
2100 L St NW Ste 300, Washington, DC, 20037-1525
Media Monitor, 859

Center for National Security Studies
122 Maryland Ave NE, Washington, DC, 20002-5610
First Principles: National Security and Civil Liberties, 173

•Center for Policy Alternatives
1875 Connecticut Ave NW Ste, 710, Washington, DC, 20009-5728

•Center for Population Options
1025 Vermont Ave NW Ste 210, Washington, DC, 20005-3516

Center for Public Justice
PO Box 48368, Washington, DC, 20002-0368
Public Justice Report, 997

Center for Science in the Public Interest
1875 Connecticut Ave NW, Ste. 300, Washington, DC, 20009-5728
Nutrition Action Healthletter, 934

Center for Strategic and International Studies(CSIS)
1800 K St NW-Ste 400, Washington, DC, 20006
Post-Soviet Prospects, 637

Center for the Study of Pre-Retirement & Aging
St. John's Hall Catholic Univ., Of America, Washington, DC, 20064-0001
Center for the Study of Pre-Retirement & Aging Newsletter, 1,106

Central American Refugee Ctr.
3112 Mount Pleasant St NW, Washington, DC, 20010-2710
CARECEN Speaks, 627

Centre for Development & Population Activities
1717 Massachusetts Ave NW Lowr, 202, Washington, DC, 20036-2001
World Wide, 641

Chem. Waste Lit. Rep. Inc.
1519 Connecticut Ave., Ste. 20, 0, Washington, DC, 20036-1115
Chemical Waste Litigation Reporter, 723

Chemical Specialties Manufacturers Assn.
1913 Eye St., NW, Washington, DC, 20006-5103
CSMA Executive Newswatch, 163

Child Welfare League of America, Inc.
440 1st St. NW, Washington, DC, 20001
Social Legislation Information Bulletin, 1,122

Children's Bureau
330 Independence Ave., S.w., Washington, DC, 20201-0001
Research Reports, 170

Children's Defense Fund
25 E St NW, Washington, DC, 20001-1591
CDF Reports, 167

Children's Foundation
725 15th St NW Ste 505, Washington, DC, 20005-2109
CF Child Care Bulletin, 411

Children's Hospice Intl.
1850 M. St. NW, Ste. 900, Washington, DC, 20036-5803
Children's Hospice International Newsletter, 168

Christian College Coalition
329 8th St., NE, Washington, DC, 20002-6158
News, The, 322

Christian Solidarity Intl.
1101 17th St. NW, Suite 607, Washington, DC, 20036-4601
CSI Newsletter, 1,061

Church Women United
110 Maryland Ave., NE, Washington, DC, 20002-5626
Church Women Act, 1,046

Citizens Against Goverment Waste
Suite 400, 1301 Conneticut Ave., NW, Washington, DC, 20036
Government WasteWatch, 486

Clean Air Report
Box 7167, Ben Franklin Station, Washington, DC, 20044-7167
Inside EPA's Clean Air Report, 385

Clearinghouse on the Handicapped
330 C St. SW Switzer Bldg.,, Rm. 3132, Washington, DC, 20202-0001
OSERS News in Print, 522

Coalition for Government Procurement
1990 M St NW Ste 400, Washington, DC, 20036-3404
Off the Shelf, 1,028

Coalition to Stop Gun Violence
100 Maryland Ave NE # 402, Washington, DC, 20002-5625
Banner, 986

Coin-Op Newsletter
909 26th St NW, Washington, DC, 20037-2029
Coin-Op Newsletter, 52

College Republican Natl. Committee, The
440 1st St SE, Suite #303, Washington, DC, 20001
College Republican, 209

College & Univ. Personnel Assn.
1233 20th St. NW, Ste. 301, Washington, DC, 20036-2304
CUPA News, 1,090

Commissariat of the Holy Land
1400 Quincy St NE, Washington, DC, 20017-3041
Crusader's Almanac, 48

Commission on Behavioral & Social Sciences & Education
Natl. Research Council 2101, Constitution Ave., Washington, DC, 20418-0001
CBASSE Newsletter, 1,124

Commission on Preservation & Access
1400 16th St NW Ste 740, Washington, DC, 20036-2217
Commission on Preservation & Access Newsletter, 796

Commission on Recognition of Postsecondary Accreditation
1 Dupont Cir. NW, Ste. 305, Washington, DC, 20036-1110
Council on Postsecondary Accreditation-Presidents Bulletin, 1,090

Community Nutrition Institute
2001 S St NW Ste 530, Washington, DC, 20009-1125
Nutrition Week, 935

Co-Op America
1612 K St NW Ste 600, Washington, DC, 20006
Boycott Action News, 251

Computer Law Reporter
1519 Connecticut Ave., NW, Suite 200, Washington, DC, 20036-1111
Computer Law Reporter, 217

Computer Leasing & Remarketing Association
1200 19th St. NW, Ste. 300, Washington, DC, 20036-2412
CDLA Printout, 214

•Computer Society Press
1730 Massachusetts Ave NW, Washington, DC, 20036-1903

Concerned Women for America
370 l'Enfant Promenade SW, Suite 800, Washington, DC, 20035
Concerned Women for America, 1,062

Conference of State Bank Supervisors
1015 18th St. NW #1100, Washington, DC, 20036-5275
CSBS Examiner, 84

•Congressional Quarterly, Inc.
1414 22nd St. NW, Washington, DC, 20037-1096

Congressional Staff Club
Box 2000, LHOB, Longworth House Off. Bldg., Washington, DC, 20013-2000
Congressional Staff Club Bulletin, 1,195

Conservation Foundation
2828 Pennsylvania Ave., NW, Ste.402, Washington, DC, 20007
Resolve, 392

Conservation Intl.
1015 18th St. NW, #1002, Washington, DC, 20036-5203
Tropicus, 395

Consortium of Social Science Assocs.
1522 K St NW Ste 836, Washington, DC, 20005-1202
COSSA Washington Update, 987

Consumer Affairs Letter
PO Box 65313, Washington, DC, 20035-5313
Consumer Affairs Letter, The, 252

Consumer Alert
1735 I St. NW, Ste. 603, Washington, DC, 20006-2402
Consumer Alert Comments, 252

•Consumer Energy Council of America Research Foundation
2000 L St., NW, Ste. 802, Washington, DC, 20036-4907

Consumer Fed. of America
1424 16th St NW Ste 604, Washington, DC, 20036-2211
CFAnews, 251

Consumer Product Safety Commission
5401 Westbard Ave # 625, Washington, DC, 20207-0001
NEISS Data Highlights, 1,082

Consumers for World Trade
2000 L St NW Ste 200, Washington, DC, 20036-4907
Consumers for World Trade Newsletter, 644

Cooperative Economics News Service
1736 Columbia Rd NW Apt 202, Washington, DC, 20009-2846
What Is to Be Read, 120

Cooperative Housing Foundation
PO Box 91280, Washington, DC, 20090-1280
CHF Newsbriefs, 627

Corporate Crime Reporter
PO Box 18384, Washington, DC, 20036-8384
Corporate Crime Reporter, 134

Council for American Private Educ.
1726 M St NW Ste 1102, Washington, DC, 20036-4502
CAPE Outlook, 302

Council of the Americas
1310 G St. NW, Ste. 690, Washington, DC, 20005-3000
Washington Report, 640

Council of Chief State School Officers
1 Massachusetts Ave NW Ste 700, Washington, DC, 20001-1401
Chiefline, 1,090

Council of Community Blood Centers
725 15th St NW Ste 700, Washington, DC, 20005-2109
CCBC Newsletter, 869

Council of Engineering
C/o AGU, 2000 Florida Ave., NW, Washington, DC, 20009
CESSE Quill, 359

Council on Foundations, Inc.
1828 L St NW Ste 300, Washington, DC, 20036-5104
Council Columns, 967

Council on Hemispheric Affairs
724 9th St., NW, Washington, DC, 20001-4505
COHA's Washington Report on the Hemisphere, 627

Council of Independent Colleges
1 Dupont Cir. NW, Ste. 320, Washington, DC, 20036-1110
CIC Independent, The, 209

Council on Library Resources, Inc.
1400 16th St NW Ste 510, Washington, DC, 20036-2217
CLR Reports, 795

•Council for a Livable World
110 Maryland Ave. NE, Suite 409, Washington, DC, 20002

Crafts Center
1001 Connecticut Ave NW Ste, 1138, Washington, DC, 20036-5504
Crafts News, 64

---

* See **MULTI-PUBLISHER INDEX** for list of publications.

Crime Control Research Corp.
1063 Thomas Jefferson St NW, Washington, DC, 20007-5248
Security Law Newsletter, 1,104

Criminal Justice Statistics Assn.
444 N Capitol St NW Ste 606, Washington, DC, 20001-1512
CJSA Forum, 720

Cuba Business
PO Box 15020, Washington, DC, 20003-0020
Cuba Business, 644

Cuban-American Committee, Inc.
1601 Connecticut Ave NW Ste, 500, Washington, DC, 20009-1035
U.S. Cuba Bulletin, 493

Cuban American Natl. Foundation
1000 Thomas Jefferson St NW, Ste 503, Washington, DC, 20007-3835
Cuban in Brief, 629

DC Water Resources Research Ctr.
Univ. of Dist. of Columbia, 4200 Connecticut Ave., Washington, DC, 20008
Water Highlights, 396

Daily Treasury Statement
G.P.O., Washington, DC, 20402-0001
Daily Treasury Statement, 87

DataNet Security Holding Inc.
1825 I Street N.W., Suite #400, Washington, DC, 20006
Network Security Observations, 232

Deafpride
1350 Potomac Ave SE, Washington, DC, 20003-4412
Deafpride Advocate Quarterly, 267

Defense Credit Union
805 15th St NW Ste 300, Washington, DC, 20005-2207
ALERT, 894

Department of the Army
Hqda (dape-Zxf), Washington, DC, 20310-0001
Army Families, 894

Dept. of Employment Services
500 C St NW, Washington, DC, 20001-2110
Metropolitan Washington D.C. Area Labor Summary, 703

Diplomatic and Consular Officers, retired
1801 F St. NW, Washington, DC, 20006-4497
DACOR Bulletin, 629

Direct Selling Education Foundation
1666 K St., NW, Ste. 1010, Washington, DC, 20006-2387
At Home with Consumers, 251

Displaced Homemakers Network
1625 K St NW Ste 300, Washington, DC, 20006-1604
Displaced Homemakers Network News, 1,208

Drug Policy Foundation
4455 Connecticut Ave. NW, Ste. B-500, Washington, DC, 20008-2328
Drug Policy Letter, 283

EDUCOM
1112 16th St NW Ste 600, Washington, DC, 20036-4823
EDUCOM Update, 307

EKA Publications, Inc.
1050 Connecticut Avenue, NW, Suite 1250, Washington, DC, 20036
One Step Ahead, 278

•**EPIN Publishing**
PO Box 21001, Washington, DC, 20009-0501

ESOP Association, The
1726 M St NW Ste 501, Washington, DC, 20036-4502
ESOP Profile, 699

•**Eagle Publishing, Inc.**
422 First Street SE, Suite 300, Washington, DC, 20003

•**Edison Electric Institute**
701 Pennsylvania Ave., NW, Washington, DC, 20004-2696

•**Editorial Resources, Inc.**
PO Box 21129, Washington, DC, 20009-0629

•**Education Writers Association**
1331 H St. NW, Ste. 307, Washington, DC, 20005-4706

Embassy of Chile, Press Office
1736 Mass. Ave. NW, Washington, DC, 20036
Chile: Summary of Recent Events, 628

Embassy of the Czech Republic
3900 Spring of Freedom St., NW, Washington, DC, 20008
Czech News, 629

Embassy of Fedl. Republic of Germany
4645 Reservoir Rd NW, Washington, DC, 20007-1918
German Press Review, 695

Embassy of Guatemala
2220 R St NW, Washington, DC, 20008-4081
Voice of Guatemala, 640

Embassy of New Zealand
37 Observatory Cir NW, Washington, DC, 20008-3686
New Zealand Update, 635

Embassy of the Republic of Iraq
1801 P St NW, Washington, DC, 20036-1201
Republic of Iraq, Bulletin of The, 637

Embassy of the Republic of the Philippines
1617 Massachusetts Ave NW, Washington, DC, 20036-2209
Republic of the Phillipines Newsletter, 637

Embassy of the Republic of Uganda
5909 16th St NW, Washington, DC, 20011-2816
Uganda Newsletter, 639

Embassy of Sri Lanka
2148 Wyoming Ave NW, Washington, DC, 20008-3906
Embassy of Sri Lanka Newsletter, 630

Embassy of Switzerland
2900 Cathedral Ave NW, Washington, DC, 20008-3499
Embassy of Switzerland Bulletin, 630

•**Employee Benefit Research Institute**
2121 K St NW Ste 600, Washington, DC, 20037-1801

•**Environmental Law Institute**
1616 P St NW Ste 200, Washington, DC, 20036-1493

Episcopal Peace Fellowship
PO Box 28156, Washington, DC, 20038-8156
Episcopal Peace Fellowship Newsletter, 1,067

Ernst & Young
1225 Connecticut Ave. NW, Washington, DC, 20036
Ernst & Young Financial Planning Reporter, 663

Esperanto Studies Foundation
3900 Northampton St., Washington, DC, 20015
Esperantic Studies, 814

Ethics & Public Policy Center
1015 15th St. NW, Ste. 900, Washington, DC, 20005
Ethics & Public Policy Center Newsletter, 1,047

Evangelical Lutheran Church in America
Office for Govt. Affairs, 122 C St., NW Ste. 300, Washington, DC, 20001-2172
Legislative Update, 993

Exchange Monitor Publications
PO Box 5757, Washington, DC, 20016
Radioactive Exchange, 927

Eye Bank Assn. of America
1001 Connecticut Ave NW Ste, 601, Washington, DC, 20036-5504
Insight, 876

FAIR
1666 Connecticut Ave., N.W., Suite 400, Washington, DC, 20009
Immigration Report, 487

FALJC
800 K St NW Ste 400, Washington, DC, 20001-8000
Federal Administrative Law Judges Conference Newsletter, 736

•**Family Research Council**
700 13th St NW Ste 500, Washington, DC, 20005-3960

•**Fannie Mae Foundation**
4000 Wisconsin Ave NW, Washington, DC, 20016-2892

Farm Credit Council
50 F St NW Ste 900, Washington, DC, 20001-1530
Insider, The, 92

•**Faulkner & Gray Healthcare Information Center**
1133 15th St NW, Ste. 450, Washington, DC, 20005-2710

Federal Bar Association
1815 H St. NW, Ste. 408, Washington, DC, 20006-3697
Lawyers Job Bulletin Board, 346

Federal Deposit Insurance Corp.
Division of Bank Supervision, 550 17th St. NW, Washington, DC, 20429
FDIC Consumer News, 88

•**Federal Library & Information Center Committee**
Library Of Congress, Washington, DC, 20540-5100

Federal Programs Advisory Service
1725 K St NW Ste 200, Washington, DC, 20006-1401
Gas Transportation Marketing Service, 957

•**Federal Pubs., Inc.**
1120 20th St., NW, Fifth Floor, South Building, Washington, DC, 20036-3484

Federation of American Hospitals
1111 19th St NW Ste 402, Washington, DC, 20036-3603
Federation of American Health Systems Hotline, 874

•**Federation for American Immigration Reform**
1666 Connecticut Ave NW, Ste. 400, Washington, DC, 20009-1039

•**Fed. of American Scientists**
307 Massachusetts Ave NE, Washington, DC, 20002-5793

Federation of Nurses and Health Professionals
555 New Jersey Ave., NW, Washington, DC, 20001-2029
Healthwire, 708

•**Fed. of Organizations for Professional Women**
1825 I St. N.W., Ste.400, Washington, DC, 20006-5403

Federation of Tax Administrators
444 N Capitol St NW Ste 348, Washington, DC, 20001-1512
Tax Administrators News, 1,152

•**Feistritzer Pubs.**
4401a Connecticut Ave NW # 2, Washington, DC, 20008-2325

•**Fieldston Co.**
1920 N Street, N.W., Ste. 210, Washington, DC, 20036

Flexible Packaging Assn.
1090 Vermont Ave NW, Suite 500, Washington, DC, 20005-4960
Flexible Packaging Assn. Update, 945

Folklore Society of Greater Washington
P.O. Box 5693, Washington, DC, 20016-5693
Folklore Society of Greater Washington Newsletter, 425

•**Food Chemical News**
1101 Pennsylvania Ave SE, Washington, DC, 20003-2229

•**Food Marketing Institute**
800 Connecticut Ave., N.W., Washington, DC, 20006-2701

Footwear Industries of America
1420 K St. NW, Ste. 600, Washington, DC, 20005-2505
FIA Executive Digest, 55

Foreign Student Service Council
2337 18th St NW, Washington, DC, 20009-1814
Foreign Student Service Council Newsletter, 310

Forum for American-Iranian Relations
2000 L St NW Ste 200, Washington, DC, 20036-4907
U.S.-Iran Review, 639

•**Foster Associates, Inc.**
1015 15th St NW Ste 1100, Washington, DC, 20005-2605

Foundation for Biomedical Research
818 Connecticut Ave NW Ste 303, Washington, DC, 20006-2702
Foundation for Biomedical Research-Newsletter, 874

•**Friends Committee on Natl. Legislation**
245 2nd St NE, Washington, DC, 20002-5719

Friends of the FBI
1001 Connecticut Ave NW, Ste. 1135, Washington, DC, 20036
Friends of the FBI Natl. Newsletter, 786

Friends of the Superior Court
500 Indiana Ave. NW, Room 1146, Washington, DC, 20001-2131
Newsletter, 764

Fulbright Alumni Assn.
1130 17th St NW Ste 310, Washington, DC, 20036-4604
Fulbrighters' Newsletter, 311

Galileo
1110 21st St NW, Washington, DC, 20036-3303
Il Cuoco, 430

Gallaudet University Outreach Services
800 Florida Ave., NE - KS#6, Washington, DC, 20002-3695
Gallaudet Alumni Newsletter, 187

General Grand Chapter
1618 New Hampshire Ave NW, Washington, DC, 20009-2549
Proceedings of the General Grand Chapter, 181

•**General Services Admin.**
18th and F Streets, Washington, DC, 20406-0001

•**George Washington University Medical Center**
2300 I St NW, Washington, DC, 20037-2337

•**Georgetown Publishing House**
1101 30th St., NW, Washington, DC, 20007

Georgetown University, Center for Personalized Instruction
Loyola Hall, Georgetown Univer., Washington, DC, 20057-0001
PSI Newsletter, 324

Georgetown Univ. Dept. of History
Georgetown Univ., Washington, DC, 20057-0001
British Studies Intelligencer, 537

German American Business Council
1413 K St NW Ste 800, Washington, DC, 20005-3405
German American Business Council, 646

German Marshall Fund of the U.S.
11 Dupont Circle, NW, Washington, DC, 20036-1207
Transatlantic Perspectives, 638

* See **MULTI-PUBLISHER INDEX** for list of publications.

Gerontological Society of America, The
1275 K St NW Ste 350, Washington, DC, 20005-4006
Gerontology News, 874

•**Gilston Communications Group**
PO Box 467, Washington, DC, 20044-0467

Gina Young
Box 22, 5863 Chevy Chase Pkwy NW, Washington,
DC, 20015
Teen Star Zine, 170

Global Network, Inc.
1101 30th Street, NW, Suite 130, Washington, DC, 20007
John Naisbitt's Trend Letter, 293

Global Tomorrow Coalition
1325 G St NW Ste 1010, Washington, DC, 20005-3104
Interaction, 385

Global Volcanism Network
Natl. Museum Of Nat. History, Mail Stop 129, Washington,
DC, 20560-0001
Bulletin of the Global Volcanism Network, 477

•**Government Bus. Worldwide Rpts.**
PO Box 5997, Washington, DC, 20016-1597

•**Government Data Publications**
1155 Connecticut Avenue NW, Washington, DC, 20036

Greenpeace
1436 U St. NW, Washington, DC, 20009-3994
Greenpeace, 383

•**Group Health Assn. of America, Inc.**
1129 20th St NW, Ste. 600, Washington, DC, 20036-3403

•**Guatemala Human Rights Commission**
3321 12th St NE, Washington, DC, 20017

**H.W. 'Bud' Kerr, Dir. of Office for Small Scale
Argriculture**
Ag Box 2244, Washington, DC, 20250-2244
Small Scale Agriculture Today, 46

Health Education Foundation
600 N.H. Ave. NW, #452, Washington, DC, 20037
HEF News, 508

•**Heritage Foundation**
214 Massachusetts Ave NE, Washington, DC, 20002-4999

•**Hillel: the Foundation for Jewish Campus Life**
1640 Rhode Island Ave NW, Washington, DC, 20036

Hispanic Foundation
1377 K St NW Ste 611, Washington, DC, 20005-3303
National Hispanic Reporter, 402

Hispanic Link News Service
1420 N St., NW, Washington, DC, 20005
Hispanic Link Weekly Report, 857

Holy Childhood Assn.
1720 Massachusetts Ave NW, Washington, DC,
20036-1968
It's Our World, 1,057

Home Automation Association
808 17th St NW Ste 200, Washington, DC, 20006-3910
Home Automation News, 338

Hospice Association of America
519 C St., N.E., Stanton Park, Washington, DC,
20002-5809
Hospice Forum, 513

House of Ruth
5 Thomas Circle, NW, Washington, DC, 20005
House of Ruth Newsletter, 1,209

•**Housing Assistance Council, Inc.**
1025 Vermont Ave NW Ste 606, Washington, DC,
20005-3516

Howard Univ., Inst. for Urban Affairs/Res.
2900 Van Ness St NW, Washington, DC, 20008-1106
Urban Research Review, 1,127

Human Rights Compaign Fund
PO Box 1396, Washington, DC, 20013
Momentum, 445

Humane Society of the United States
2100 L St., NW, Washington, DC, 20037-1525
Animal Sheltering Magazine, 48

**IFLA PAC Core Programme, Natl. Preservation
Program Office**
Library Of Congress, Washington, DC, 20540-0001
International Preservation News, 800

Independent Action
645 Pennsylvania Ave. SE, Ste. 2, Washington, DC,
20003-4317
Independent Action News, 991

Independent Bakers Assn.
PO Box 3731, Washington, DC, 20007-0231
Independent, 79

Independent Bankers Assn. of America
1 Thomas Cir NW Ste 950, Washington, DC, 20005-5802
Washington Weekly Report, 100

Independent Liquid Terminals Association
1133 15th St NW Ste 650, Washington, DC, 20005-2710
Independent Liquid Terminals Assn. -Newsletter, 165

Independent Sector
1828 L St NW, Washington, DC, 20036-5107
Dimensions of the Independent Sector, 290

Industrial Newsletters
1545 New York Ave NE, Washington, DC, 20002-1765
Our Washington Newsletter, 294

Industrial Union Dept., AFL-CIO
815 16th St NW Ste 301, Washington, DC, 20006-4104
IUD Action, 708

Information Industry Assn.
555 New Jersey Ave. NW, #800, Washington, DC,
20001-2082
Friday Memo, 1,159

Information Service of India, Embassy of India
2107 Massachusetts Ave NW, Washington, DC,
20008-2811
India News, 632

•**Inside Mortgage Finance Publications**
Box 42387, Washington, DC, 20015

Inside NAFTA
PO Box 7167, Ben Franklin Station, Washington, DC,
20044
Inside NAFTA, 647

•**Inside Washington Publishers**
P.O. Box 7167, Ben Franklin Station, Washington, DC,
20044

Inst. of Clean Air Companies
1707 L St NW Ste 570, Washington, DC, 20036-4201
Clean Air Technology News, 375

Institute for Policy Studies
1601 Connecticut Ave. NW., Ste. 500, Washington,
DC, 20009
Institute for Policy Studies Newsletter, 991

Institute of Scrap Recycling Industries
1325 G St., NW, Ste. 1000, Washington, DC, 20005-3104
ISRI Report, 891

•**Intelligence Press**
PO Box 70587, Washington, DC, 20024-0587

•**Inter-American Bar Association**
1211 Connecticut Ave., NW, Ste. 202, Washington,
DC, 20036

Inter-American Development Bank
1300 New York Ave NW, Washington, DC, 20577-0006
IDB, 631

Interfaith Forum/on Religion, Art & Architecture
1735 New York Avenue NW, Washington, DC, 20006-5209
IFRAA Quarterly, 1,047

Interfaith Impact for Justice & Peace
110 Maryland Ave NE Ste 63, Washington, DC, 20002-5622
Interfaith Impact & Preparedness, 1,048

Intergovernmental Health Policy Project
2021 K St NW Ste 800, Washington, DC, 20006-1003
State Health Notes, 529

International Academy of Oral Pathology
3900 Reservoir Rd NW, Washington, DC, 20007-2187
International Academy of Oral Pathology, Bulletin, 270

International Airline Passenger Association
5335 Wisconsin Ave NW Ste 440, Washington, DC,
20015-2030
Travel Safety Alert, 33

International Association for Continuing Education
1200 19th St NW Ste 300, Washington, DC, 20036-2412
IACET Reporter, 312

**International Association of Fish and Wildlife
Agencies**
444 N. Capitol St. NW, Suite 544, Washington, DC,
20001-1512
I.A.F.W.A. Newsletter, 384

International Bridge, Tunnel & Turnpike Assn.
2120 L St NW Ste 305, Washington, DC, 20037-1527
Tollways, 1,181

**International Brotherhood of Teamsters, Chauffers,
Warehouse**
25 Louisiana Ave NW, Washington, DC, 20001-2130
Retiree Newsletter, 710

International Business Govt. Counsellors
818 Conn Ave. NW, 2nd Fl., Washington, DC, 20006
Washington International Business Report, 652

**International Centre for the Settlement of
Investment Disput**
1818 H St NW, Washington, DC, 20433-0001
News from ICSID, 680

•**International City/County Management Assn.**
777 N Capitol St NE Ste 500, Washington, DC, 20002-4201

International Cotton Advisory Committee
1629 K St. NW, Ste. 702, Washington, DC, 20006-1602
*Cotton: Review of the World Situation Update by
Fax, 1,171*

Intl. Downtown Assn.
915 15th St NW Ste 900, Washington, DC, 20005-2375
IDA: Center City Report, 247

•**Intl. Executive Reports**
717 D St. NW, Ste. 300, Washington, DC, 20004-2807

Intl. Food Policy Research Institute
1200 Seventeenth St., N.W., Washington, DC, 20036
IFPRI Report, 631

Intl. Human Rights Law Group
1601 Connecticut Ave NW Ste, 700, Washington, DC,
20009-1035
Law Group Docket, 174

•**International Insight, Inc.**
1200 18th St NW Ste 305, Washington, DC, 20036-2506

Intl. Law Students Assn.
2223 Massachusetts Ave., N.W., Tillar House,
Washington, DC, 20008
ILSA Newsletter, 743

International Monetary Fund
700 19th St NW Ste 10-540, Washington, DC, 20431-0001
IMF Survey, 292

Intl. Society for Performance & Instruction
1300 L St. NW., Ste. 1250, Washington, DC, 20005-4107
News & Notes, 613

International Union of Bricklayers
815 Fifteenth St., N.W., Washington, DC, 20005-2201
Chalkline, 245

International Visitors Information Service
1623 Belmont St NW, Washington, DC, 20009-4010
IVIS Newsletter, 1,185

Internews Media Services
1060-C National Press Bldg.NW, Washington, DC,
20045-0001
Internewsletter, 632

Interstate Natural Gas Assn. of America
555 13th St NW Ste 300w, Washington, DC, 20004-1109
INGAA Washington Report, 957

Investment Company Institute
1401 H St. NW, Ste. 1200, Washington, DC, 20005-2148
*Monthly Statistics/Open-End Investment Companies
Trends, 678*

•**Investor Responsibility Research Ctr.**
1350 Connecticut Ave. N.W., Suite 700, Washington, DC,
20036-1701

Iraqi Press Office
1801 P St NW, Washington, DC, 20036-1201
Iraq Views & News, 633

Islamic Center
2551 Massachusetts Ave NW, Washington, DC,
20008-2866
Islamic Center Bulletin, 1,074

Japan-America Society of Washington, Inc.
1020 19th Street NW, #LL, Washington, DC, 20036-6101
Japan-America Society Bulletin, 404

•**Japan Economic Institute of America**
1000 Connecticut Ave., N.W., Washington, DC, 20036-5347

Jean Lawrence
3217 Connecticut Ave NW Apt 78, Washington, DC,
20008-2504
Cheap Relief, 11

•**Jewish War Veterans of the U.S.**
1811 R St NW, Washington, DC, 20009-1603

Joint Action in Community Service
5225 Wisconsin Ave NW Ste 404, Washington, DC,
20015-2014
JACS Volunteer, 345

Joint Center for Political Studies
1090 Vermont Ave. NW Ste. 1100, Washington, DC,
20005-4905
Focus, 990

•**King Communications Group**
627 National Press Building, Washington, DC, 20045-1601

•**Kiplinger Washington Editors, Inc.**
1729 H Street N.W., Washington, DC, 20006-3924

L & B Ltd.
19 Rock Creek Church Rd NW, Washington, DC,
20011-6005
Military Robotics, 897

* See **MULTI-PUBLISHER INDEX** for list of publications.

Labor Heritage Foundation
815 16th St NW Ste 301, Washington, DC, 20006-4104
Art Works, 62

•**Land Development Law Reporter**
1401 16th St NW, Washington, DC, 20036-2201

Latin American Management Assn.
419 New Jersey Ave SE, Washington, DC, 20003-4007
LAMA's Watch on Washington, 143

Lawyers Alliance for Nuclear Arms Control
1601 Connecticut Avenue, NW, Washington, DC, 20009-1035
LAWS Quarterly, 992

Lawyers' Committee for Civil Rights Under Law
1450 G St NW Ste 400, Washington, DC, 20005-2001
Committee Report, 726

Leadership Conference Education Fund
1629 K St NW Ste 1010, Washington, DC, 20006-1602
Civil Rights Monitor, 172

League of Historic American Theatres
1511 K St NW Ste 923, Washington, DC, 20005-1401
LHAT Bulletin, 1,173

League of United Latin American Citizens
2100 M St. NW, Ste. 602, Washington, DC, 20037-1207
LULAC News, 402

League of Women Voters of the U.S.
1730 M St., N.W., Ste. 1000, Washington, DC, 20036-4587
Report from the Hill, 1,121

The Lebanese Center for Policy Studies
1700 17th St NW Apt 306, Washington, DC, 20009-2419
Lebanon Report, The, 633

Legal Research International, Inc.
3701 Connecticut Ave., NW, Ste. 200, Washington, DC, 20008-4501
Mexico Report, The, 634

Legi-Slate, Inc., Washington Post Co.
777 N Capitol St NE Ste 900, Washington, DC, 20002-4239
Legi-Slate Letter, 488

•**Leisure Industry/Recreation News**
PO Box 43563, Washington, DC, 20010-9563

Len Mor Pubs.
PO Box 75035, Washington, DC, 20013-0035
Black Congressional Monitor, 481

Libertarian National Committee, Inc.
2600 Virginia Ave. NW, Ste. 100, Washington, DC, 20037
Libertarian Volunteer, The, 993

Library, The
1771 N St. , N. W., Washington, DC, 20036-2898
Broadcast Pioneers Library Reports, 123

Library of Congress
Cataloging Distribution Svc., Washington, DC, 20541-0001
CDS Connection, 795

Linguistic Society of America
1325 18th St. NW, Ste 211, Washington, DC, 20036-6505
LSA Bulletin, 822

Links, Inc.
1200 Massachusetts Ave NW, Washington, DC, 20005-4501
Link to Link, 1,118

MCC Peace Section Washington Office
110 Maryland Ave. NE, #502, Washington, DC, 20002-5681
Washington Memo - MCC, 1,000

MCI
1111 19th Street, Washington, DC, 20036
MCI Connections Gold, 143

•**MII Publications, Inc.**
1211 Conn. Ave. NW, #705, Washington, DC, 20036-2701

Magazine Publisher's Assn.
1211 Connecticut Ave NW Ste, 406, Washington, DC, 20036-2701
MPA Washington Newsletter, 954

Major Indoor Soccer League Players Assn.
2021 L St NW Ste 407, Washington, DC, 20036-4909
Play Book, 1,134

Maritime Trades Dept.
215 16th St. NW, Ste. 310, Washington, DC, 20006
Maritime Newsletter, 709

Marriott International
Marriott Dr., Dept. 935.27, Washington, DC, 20058
Marriott World, 590

Marvelous Market
5016 Connecticut Ave NW, Washington, DC, 20008-2023
Marvelous Market, 431

Maryknoll Fathers & Brothers Justice & Peace Office
3700 Oakview Ter NE, Washington, DC, 20017-2521
NewsNotes, 994

Mathematical Association of America
1529 18th St NW, Washington, DC, 20036-1358
Focus, The, 852

•**McGraw-Hill**
1200 G St NW Ste 1100, Washington, DC, 20005-3814

•**McGraw-Hill Aviation Group**
1200 G St NW Ste 200, Washington, DC, 20005-3814

Members of Congress for Arms Control & Foreign Policy Caucus
2700 Virginia Ave., N.W. #80, Washington, DC, 20037-1908
MCPL Education Fund, Food and Population Newsletter, 993

Mennonite Central Committee-Peace Section
110 Maryland Ave. NE, Washington, DC, 20002-5681
Mennonite Central Committee-Washington Memo, 993

Menswear Retailers of America
325 7th St. NW, Ste. 1000, Washington, DC, 20004-2801
Business Newsletter, 55

Middle East Policy Group, Inc.
3405 Rodman St NW, Washington, DC, 20008-3116
Middle East Policy Survey, 634

Moorland-Spingarn Research Center
Howard University, Washington, DC, 20059-0001
African-American and Third World Archivists Roundtable Newsletter, 792

•**Mortgage Bankers Assn. of America**
1125 15th St., NW, Washington, DC, 20005-2766

•**Murray Felsher**
1057-B Natl. Press Bldg., Washington, DC, 20045

NAFSA Association of International Educators
1875 Connecticut Ave., NW, Washington, DC, 20009-5728
NAFSA Newsletter, 319

NOAA/USDA Joint Agricultural Weather Facility
Usda S. Bldg., Rm. 5844, Washington, DC, 20250-0001
Weekly Weather & Crop Bulletin, 47

NOWLDEF/Peer
1333 H St. NW, 14th Fl., Washington, DC, 20005-4707
Equal Education Alert, 309

National Abortion Federation
1436 U St NW Ste 103, Washington, DC, 20009-3997
NAF Update, 519

National Abortion Rights Action League
Communications Office, 1156 15th St. NW, Ste. 700, Washington, DC, 20005-1704
NARAL News, 519

Natl. Agricultural Chemicals Assn.
1156 15th St NW Ste 400, Washington, DC, 20005-1704
National Agricultural Chemicals Association News, 165

Natl. Agricultural Library
Agriculture Dept., Washington, DC, 20250-0001
Food for Thought, 933

•**Natl. Alliance of Business**
1201 New York Ave NW Ste 700, Washington, DC, 20005-3917

National Alliance of Senior Citizens
1700 18th St NW # 401, Washington, DC, 20009-2508
Senior Guardian, 1,109

Natl. Aquarium Society
Dept. Of Commerce Bldg. Rm., B-037, Washington, DC, 20230-0001
Fish Lines, 422

National Association of Activity Professionals
1225 Eye St. NW, #300, Washington, DC, 20005
NAAP News, 569

Natl. Assn. of Alcoholic Beverage Importers
1025 Vermont Ave., N.W., Suite, Washington, DC, 20005-3516
National Association of Alcoholic Beverage Importers Bulletin, 104

•**National Association of Attorneys General**
444 N Capitol St NW Ste 339, Washington, DC, 20001-1512

•**Natl. Assn. of Beverage Importers, Inc.**
1025 Vermont Ave NW Ste 1205, Washington, DC, 20005-3516

Natl. Assn. for Bilingual Education
1220 L St NW Ste 605, Washington, DC, 20005-4018
NABE News, 319

•**National Association of Business Economists**
1233 20th St., NW, Suite 505, Washington, DC, 20036-2304

Natl. Assn. of Chemical Recyclers
1200 G St NW Ste 800, Washington, DC, 20005-3814
Flashpoint, 382

National Association of College Women
1501 11th St NW, Washington, DC, 20001-3215
National Association of College Women Bulletin, 180

National Association of Conservation Districts
509 Capitol Ct NE, Washington, DC, 20002-4937
Tuesday Letter, 395

National Association of Corporate Directors
1707 L St NW Ste 560, Washington, DC, 20036-4201
Director's Monthly, 836

Nat'l Assn. of Counties
440 1st St NW, 8th Fl., Washington, DC, 20001-2080
County News, 483

Natl. Assn. of Credit Unions
PO Box 3769, Washington, DC, 20007-0269
National Association of Federal Credit Unions - Update, 95

Natl. Assn. of Criminal Defense Lawyers
1627 K Street NW, Suite 1200, Washington, DC, 20006
Champion, 723

Natl. Assn. of Development Organizations
444 N Capitol St NW Ste 630, Washington, DC, 20001-1512
NADO News, 248

Natl. Assn. of Federal Credit Unions
PO Box 3769, Washington, DC, 20007-0269
Cuso Network, 87

National Association of Federal Veterinarians
1101 Vermont Ave NW Ste 710, Washington, DC, 20005-3521
Federal Veterinarian, 1,201

•**National Association of Home Builders**
1201 15th St NW, Washington, DC, 20005-2842

National Association for Home Care
519 C St NE, Washington, DC, 20002-5809
N.A.H.C. Report, 519

National Association of Housing and Redevelopment Officials
630 Eye St. NW, Washington, DC, 20001-3736
NAHRO Monitor, 1,022

Natl. Assn. of Investment Companies
1111 14th St NW Ste 700, Washington, DC, 20005-5603
Perspective, 148

National Association for Law Placement
1666 Connecticut Ave NW Ste, 325, Washington, DC, 20009-1039
NALP Bulletin, 346

•**Natl. Assn. of Manufacturers**
1331 Pennsylvania Ave., NW, N. Lobby, Ste. 1500, Washington, DC, 20004-1703

Natl. Assn. of Negro Business & Professional Women's Clubs
1806 New Hampshire Ave. NW, Washington, DC, 20009
Responsibility, 1,211

National Association of Neighborhoods
1651 Fuller St., N.W., Washington, DC, 20009-5622
NAN Bulletin, 1,022

National Association of People with AIDS (NAPWA)
1413 K Street NW, Washington, DC, 20005
Medical Alert, 517

Natl. Assn. of Private Schools for Exceptional Children
1522 K St NW Ste 1032, Washington, DC, 20005
NAPSEC News, 319

Natl. Assn. for Public Interest Law
1118 22nd Street NW, Washington, DC, 20009
Justice Report, 747

Natl. Assn. of Real Estate Brokers
1629 K St. NW, Ste. 602, Washington, DC, 20006
NAREB Report, 1,036

National Association of Real Estate Investment Trusts, Inc.
1129 20th St NW Ste 305, Washington, DC, 20036-3403
REIT Report, 1,037

National Association of Regulatory Utility Commissioners
PO Box 684, Washington, DC, 20044-0684
Blue Bulletin, 1,002

•**Natl. Assn. of Securities Dealers, Inc.**
1735 K St., N.W., Washington, DC, 20006-1500

Natl. Assn. of Sheltered Workshops
Box 17675, Washington, DC, 20041-0675
NASWHP Information and Exchange Service, 1,119

National Association of Social Workers
750 1st St NE Ste 700, Washington, DC, 20002-4241
NASW News, 1,119

---

* See **MULTI-PUBLISHER INDEX** for list of publications.

National Association of State Alcohol & Drug Abuse Directors
444 N Capitol St NW Ste 642, Washington, DC, 20001-1512
Public Policy Quarterly, 287

•**Natl. Assn. of Student Financial Aid Administrators**
1920 L St. NW, #200, #100, Washington, DC, 20036-5020

National Association of Student Personnel Administration
1875 Connecticut Ave NW Ste, 418, Washington, DC, 20009-5728
NASPA Forum, 319

Natl. Assn. of Surety Bond Producers
5301 Wisconsin Ave NW Ste 450, Washington, DC, 20015-2015
Producers Pipeline, 623

National Assn. of Towns & Townships
1522 K St. NW, Ste. 600, Washington, DC, 20005-1202
NATAT Washington Report, 1,022

•**National Association of Wholesaler-Distributors**
1725 K St. NW, Washington, DC, 20006-1401

National Association for Women in Education
1325 18th St. NW, Ste. 210, Washington, DC, 20036-6511
About Women on Campus, 198

National Bankers Association, Inc.
1802 T St NW, Washington, DC, 20009-7126
NBA Today, 95

Natl. Bar Assn.
1225 11th St NW, Washington, DC, 20001-4217
National Bar Bulletin, 759

Natl. Beauty Culturists' League
25 Logan Cir NW, Washington, DC, 20005-3725
Forecast, 100

Natl. Broiler Council
1155 15th St NW Ste 614, Washington, DC, 20005-2706
National Broiler Council-Washington Report, 1,001

•**National Business Aircraft Association**
1200 18th St. NW, Ste. 400, Washington, DC, 20036-2506

•**National Business Aviation Assn.**
1200 18th St., NW, Washington, DC, 20036-2506

Nat'l. Cable Television Assn.
1724 Massachusetts Ave. NW, Washington, DC, 20036-1905
Techline, 1,169

Natl. Campaign for A Peace Tax Fund
2121 Decatur Pl NW, Washington, DC, 20008-1923
National Campaign for A Peace Tax Fund Newsletter, 1,148

Natl. Catholic Conference for Interracial Justice
3033 4th St NE, Washington, DC, 20017-1102
Commitment, 172

•**Natl. Catholic Educational Assn.**
1077 30th St. NW, Ste. 100, Washington, DC, 20007-3852

National Center for Early Childhood Workforce
733 15th St NW Ste 800, Washington, DC, 20005-2112
Child Care Employee News, 411

•**Natl. Center for Public Policy Research**
300 Eye St. NE, #3, Washington, DC, 20002

Natl. Center for Small Communities
1522 K St NW Ste 600, Washington, DC, 20005-1202
Town Crier, 493

Natl. Chamber Litigation Center, Inc.
1615 H St NW, Washington, DC, 20006-4975
Business Counsel, 720

Natl. Child Support Enforcement Reference Ctr.
330 C St SW # 2094, Washington, DC, 20201-0001
Techniques for Effective Management of Program Operations, 790

National Citizens' Coalition for Nursing Home Reform
1424 16th St. NW, Ste 202, Washington, DC, 20036
Quality Care Advocate, 525

National Coalition Against the Misuse of Pesticides
701 E St. S.E., Ste. 200, Washington, DC, 20003-2841
NCAMP's Technical Report, 388

National Coalition on Black Voter Participation
1629 K St NW Ste 801, Washington, DC, 20006-1602
Operation Big Vote Newsletter, 490

National Coalition of Hispanic Health & Human Services Orgs
1501 16th St NW, Washington, DC, 20036-1401
COSSMHO Reporter, The, 501

National Collaboration for Youth
1319 F St., NW, Ste. 601, Washington, DC, 20004
Assembly Lines Newsletter, 1,114

National Commission for Full Employment
815 16th St NW Ste 301, Washington, DC, 20006-4104
Jobs Impact Bulletin, 345

National Committee Against Repressive Legislation
3321 12th St NE, Washington, DC, 20017-4008
Right to Know & the Freedom to Act, The, 175

National Committee for Responsive Philanthropy
2001 S. St. N.W., Suite 620, Washington, DC, 20009-1125
Responsive Philanthropy, 969

Natl. Conference of Catholic Bishops
3211 4th St NE, Washington, DC, 20017-1106
Gifts, 1,057

Natl. Conference of Puerto Rican Women
5 Thomas Cir., NW, Washington, DC, 20005-4153
Ecos Nacionales, 407

•**National Consumers League**
1701 K St. NW, Ste. 1200, Washington, DC, 20006

•**Natl. Corrugated Steep Pipe Assn.**
1255 23rd St NW Ste 850, Washington, DC, 20037-1125

National Council for Accreditation of Teacher Education
2010 Massachusetts Ave NW, Ste #500, Washington, DC, 20036-1023
Quality Teaching, 326

•**Natl. Council for Adoption, Inc.**
1930 17th St NW, Washington, DC, 20009-6235

Natl. Council on the Aging, Inc.
409 Third St. SW, Washington, DC, 20024
NCOA Networks, 1,107

Natl. Council of Agricultural Employers (NCAE)
1735 I St. NW, Ste. 704, Washington, DC, 20006-2402
NCAE Newsletter, 43

•**Natl. Council of Architectural Registration Boards**
1735 NY Ave., NW, Ste. 700, Washington, DC, 20006

Natl. Council of Catholic Women
1275 K St NW Ste 975, Washington, DC, 20005-4006
Catholic Woman, 1,056

Natl. Council for Children's Rights
220 Eye Street N.W., Ste. 230, Washington, DC, 20002-4307
Speak Out for Children, 416

National Council of Laraza
1111 19th St. NW, Washington, DC, 20036-3603
Agenda, 171

National Council for Urban Economic Development
1730 K St NW Ste 915, Washington, DC, 20006-3868
Economic Developments, 291

Natl. Crime Prevention Council
1700 K St NW 2nd Floor, Washington, DC, 20006-3817
Catalyst Newsletter, 785

Natl. Dome Council
15th & Main Sts. NW, Washington, DC, 20005
Dome Home Mortgage White Paper, 246

•**National Education Association**
1201 16th St., NW, Washington, DC, 20036

Natl. Energy Information Center
Forrestal Bldg., Washington, DC, 20585-0001
Energy Information Administration New Releases, 353

Natl. Family Planning & Reproductive Health Assn.
122 C St NW Ste 380, Washington, DC, 20001-2109
NFPRHA News, 519

National Federation for Cath. Youth Ministry
3900a Harewood Rd NE, Washington, DC, 20017-1505
Connections, 1,056

National Federation of Community Broadcasting
666 11th St NW Ste 805, Washington, DC, 20001-4542
Community Radio News, 123

Natl. Federation of Independent Business Education Fndn.
600 Maryland Ave. SW, Suite 770, Washington, DC, 20024-2520
Small Business Economic Trends, 152

•**National Federation of Republican Women**
310 1st St SE, Washington, DC, 20003-1801

•**National Food Processors Assn.**
1401 New York Ave. NW, Washington, DC, 20005-2154

Natl. Gay & Lesbian Task Force
1734 14th St NW, Washington, DC, 20009-4309
Task Force Report, 446

National Geographic Society
1145 17th St NW, Washington, DC, 20036-4701
Geography Education Program UPDATE, 475

Natl. Governors' Assn.
444 N Capitol St NW Ste 267, Washington, DC, 20001-1512
Governors' Bulletin, 486

National Grange
1616 H St NW, Washington, DC, 20006-4999
National Grange-Newsletter, 180

•**Natl. Health Lawyers Assn.**
1120 Connecticut Ave NW Ste, 950, Washington, DC, 20036-3902

National Historical Publications and Records Commission
National Archives Bldg., Washington, DC, 20408-0001
Annotation, 536

National Home Study Council
1601-18th St., N.W., Washington, DC, 20009
NHSC Report, 320

National Housing Rehabilitation Association
1726 18th St NW, Washington, DC, 20009-2525
National Housing Rehabilitation Association Newsletter, 248

•**National Information Center for Children with Disabilities**
PO Box 1492, Washington, DC, 20013-1492

National Institute for the Conservation of Cultural Property
NIC Exchange, 3299 K Street NW, Washington, DC, 20007
NIC Exchange, 261

•**Natl. Institute of Municipal Law Officers**
1000 Connecticut Ave NW Ste, 902, Washington, DC, 20036-5302

Natl. Institute of Oilseed Products
412 1st St. SE, #100, Washington, DC, 20003-1804
Washington Correspondence, 940

National Intelligence Book Center
2020 Pennsylvania Ave. NW, Suite #165, Washington, DC, 20006-1846
Surveillant: Acquisitions for Security & Intelligence Professionals, 1,105

Natl. Intelligence Study Center
1800 K St NW Ste 1102, Washington, DC, 20006-2202
Foreign Intelligence Literary Scene (FILS), 990

Natl. Italian American Foundation
1860 19th St. NW, Washington, DC, 20009-5501
NIAF News, The, 403

National Job Corps Alumni Association
607 14th St. NW, Ste. 610, Washington, DC, 20005-2000
NJCAA Proof Sheet, 346

•**National Journal, Inc.**
1501 M. St. NW, Ste. 300, Washington, DC, 20005-1700

Natl. Landscape Assn.
1250 Eye St. NW, #500, Washington, DC, 20004-1901
NLA Landscape News, 442

National League of Families of American Prisoners
1001 Connecticut Ave NW Ste, 919, Washington, DC, 20036-5504
National League of POW/MIA Families, 634

Natl. Legal Aid & Defender Assn.
1625 K St NW Ste 8, Washington, DC, 20006-1604
NLADA Cornerstone, 758

•**Natl. Library Service for the Blind & Physically Handicapped**
1291 Taylor St NW, Washington, DC, 20542-0001

Natl. Marine Engineers' Beneficial Assn., AFL-CIO
444 N Capitol St NW Ste 800, Washington, DC, 20001-1512
American Marine Engineer, 1,111

•**National Mining Association**
1130 17th St., N.W., Washington, DC, 20036-4677

•**National Neighborhood Coalition**
1875 Connecticut Ave. NW, Ste. 710, Washington, DC, 20009-5728

Natl. Network of Runaway & Youth Services
1319 F St NW Ste 401, Washington, DC, 20004-1106
Network News (Runaway Youths), 1,119

Natl. Organization for Competency Assurance
1200 19th St NW Ste 300, Washington, DC, 20036-2412
Professional Regulation News, 525

Natl. Organization for Victim Assistance
1757 Park Rd NW, Washington, DC, 20010-2101
National Organization for Victim Assistance-Newsletter, 1,119

National Peace Foundation
1835 K St NW Ste 610, Washington, DC, 20006-1203
Peace Reporter, 636

Natl. Preservation Program Office
Library of Congress, Lm G07, Washington, DC, 20540-0001
National Preservation News, 805

* See **MULTI-PUBLISHER INDEX** for list of publications.

Natl. Press Club
Natl. Press Bldg., 529 14th St. NW, Washington, DC, 20045-0001
National Press Club Record, 696

National Press Foundation
1282 National Press Building, Washington, DC, 20045-2200
National Press Foundation Update, 696

National Rainbow Coalition Labor Network
PO Box 27385, Washington, DC, 20038-7385
Labor Network News, 261

Natl. Realty Committee
1420 New York Ave NW Ste 1100, Washington, DC, 20005-2122
Cornerstone, 1,032

National Research Council
2101 Constitution Ave., NW, Washington, DC, 20418
News Report, 1,099

National Restaurant Association
1200 17th St., NW, Washington, DC, 20036-3097
Pro-Motion, 1,076

National Retail Federation Enterprises, Inc.
325 7th St. NW, Ste. 1000, Washington, DC, 20004-2802
Retail Operations News Bulletin, 255

Natl. Security Industrial Assn.
1025 Connecticut Ave NW Ste, 300, Washington, DC, 20036-5405
NSIA Newsletter, 897

•**Natl. Senior Citizens Law Center**
1815 H St. NW, Suite #700, Washington, DC, 20006-3604

National Small Business United
1155 15th St NW Ste 710, Washington, DC, 20005-2706
Small Business-USA, 152

National Society of Professional Resident Managers
1518 K St NW Ste 503, Washington, DC, 20005-1203
National Society of Professional Resident Managers-Newsletter, 842

Natl. Society, U.S. Daughters of 1812
1461 Rhode Island Ave NW, Washington, DC, 20005-5402
National Society, United States Daughters of 1812 News-Letter, 180

Natl. Soft Drink Assn.
1101 16th St NW, Washington, DC, 20036-4877
NSDA Dateline, 104

Natl. Star Route Mail Carriers Assn
324 E Capitol St SE, Washington, DC, 20003-3809
Star Carrier, 972

National Telephone Cooperative Association
2626 Pennsylvania Ave., N.W., Washington, DC, 20037-1695
National Telephone Cooperative Association-Washington Report, 1,161

•**National Tire Dealers and Retreaders Assn.**
1250 I St NW Ste 400, Washington, DC, 20005-3922

National Treasury Employees Union
901 E. St., N.W. Ste.600, Washington, DC, 20004
NTEU Bulletin, 709

•**National Trust for Historic Preservation**
1785 Massachusetts Ave., NW, Washington, DC, 20036-2117

Natl. University Continuing Education Assn.
1 Dupont Cir NW Ste 615, Washington, DC, 20036-1110
NUCEA News, 321

Nat'l. Wildlife Federation Corporate Conservation Council
1400 16th Street NW, Washington, DC, 20036-2266
Operation Wildlife News, 414

National Women's Health Network
1325 G St NW, Washington, DC, 20005-3189
Network News, 1,210

National Women's Health Resource Center
2440 M St NW Ste 325, Washington, DC, 20037-1404
National Women's Health Report, 520

National Women's Political Caucus
1211 Connecticut Ave NW Ste, 425, Washington, DC, 20036-2701
Women's Political Times, 1,214

•**Nautilus Press, Inc.**
1054 National Press Building, Washington, DC, 20045-2001

Naval Historical Center
Bldg. 157-1 WNY, Washington, DC, 20374-0001
Pull Together, 898

Near East Report, Inc.
440 1st St NW Ste 307, Washington, DC, 20001-2028
Near East Report, 634

Nicaragua Network
1247 E St., S.E., Washington, DC, 20003-2221
Nicaragua Network News, 635

North American Telecommunications Assn.
2000 M St NW Ste 550, Washington, DC, 20036-3307
Washington Update, 1,164

Northeast-Midwest Institute
218 D St., SE, Washington, DC, 20003-1900
Northeast-Midwest Economic Review, 294

Nuclear Information & Resource Service
1424 16th St NW Ste 601, Washington, DC, 20036-2211
Nuclear Monitor, 926

•**Nutrition Legislation Services**
PO Box 75035, Washington, DC, 20013-0035

O'Leary Kamber Report
3050 K St NW Ste 105, Washington, DC, 20007-5108
Oleary Report, 994

OMB Watch/Focus Project
1731 Connecticut Ave., N.W., Washington, DC, 20009-1146
OMB Watcher, 490

Office of Child Support Enforcement
370 L'enfant Promenade S.W., 4th Floor, Washington, DC, 20447-0001
Child Support Report, 168

Office of Governmental Relations-Natl. PTA
2000 L St NW Ste 600, Washington, DC, 20036-4907
What's Happening in Washington, 336

Oil Daily Co.
1401 New York Ave. NW, Ste. 500, Washington, DC, 20005-2102
Natural Gas Week, 960

•**Oliphant Washington News Service**
PO Box 9808, Washington, DC, 20016-8808

Opera America
1156 15th St. NW, Siute #810, Washington, DC, 20005-1704
Opera America Newsline, 915

•**Orbis Publications, L.L.C.**
3201 New Mexico Ave., NW, Ste. 249, Washington, DC, 20016

•**Organization of American States**
19th Constitution Ave. N W, Suite #300, Washington, DC, 20006

Organization of Chinese Americans, Inc.
1001 Connecticut Ave NW Ste, 707, Washington, DC, 20036-5504
OCA Image, 400

•**Organization for Economic Cooperation & Development**
2001 L St NW Ste 650, Washington, DC, 20036-4910

Organization of Professional Employees of the U.S. Dept. of
Usda South Bldg. , Rm. 1414, Washington, DC, 20250-0001
Organization of Professional Employees of the U.S. Dept. of Agriculture Newsletter, 710

Organization for Protection&Advancement/Small Telephone Cos.
21 Dupont Cir NW Ste 700, Washington, DC, 20036-1109
Washington Weekly Report, 1,164

The Oxford Club
2020 Pennsylvania Ave. NW, Suite 654, Washington, DC, 20006
Agora, Inc., 80

P.C.A.O.
18th & C St., NW Ms-3152-Mib, Washington, DC, 20240-0001
President's Commission on Americans Outdoors, 944

Pan American Development Foundation
1889 F St., N.W., Washington, DC, 20006-4499
PADF News, 636

Partners of the Americas
1424 K St NW Ste 700, Washington, DC, 20005-2410
Partners, 636

Peace Links
747 8th St SE, Washington, DC, 20003-2802
Connection, 988

Peace Pac
110 Maryland Ave., NE, Washington, DC, 20002-5626
Peace Pac Newsletter, 898

People for the American Way
2000 M St. NW, Ste. 400, Washington, DC, 20036-3307
News from People for the American Way, 994

People for the Ethical Treatment of Animals
PO Box 42516, Washington, DC, 20015-0516
PETA News, 390

•**Pharmaceutical Manufacturers Assn.**
1100 15th St NW Ste 900, Washington, DC, 20005-1707

Phi Beta Kappa Society
1811 Q St NW, Washington, DC, 20009-1613
Key Reporter, 179

Physicians for Social Responsibility
1101 14th St NW Ste 700, Washington, DC, 20005-5601
PSR Reports, 390

Pigafetta Press
PO Box 39244, Washington, DC, 20016-9244
Multinational PR Report, 19

Points of Light Foundation
1737 H Street SW, Washington, DC, 20006
Volunteering, 1,124

Political Report
717 2nd St., N.E., Washington, DC, 20002
Family, Law and Democracy Report, 484

Polling Report, Inc.
PO Box 42580, Washington, DC, 20015-2580
Polling Report, 997

•**Population Assn. of America**
1722 N. Street, NW, Washington, DC, 20036

Population Institute
110 Maryland Ave. NE, Washington, DC, 20002-5626
Popline, 391

Population Reference Bureau, Inc.
1875 Connecticut Ave. NW, Ste. 520, Washington, DC, 20009-5728
Population Today, 1,126

Poverty & Race Research Action Council
1711 Connecticut Ave NW Ste, 207, Washington, DC, 20009-1139
Poverty & Race Newsletter, 1,126

Presbyterian Church (USA)
110 Maryland Ave. NE, #104, Washington, DC, 20002-5626
Washington Report to Presbyterians, 1,074

President's Council on Physical Fitness & Sports
701 Pennsylvania Ave NW Ste, 250, Washington, DC, 20004-2608
Newsletter, 1,197

Prison Fellowship Ministries
Box 17500, Washington, DC, 20041-0500
Jubilee, 1,064

Privacy Times, Inc.
PO Box 21501, Washington, DC, 20009-9501
Privacy Times, 770

Professional Airways Systems Specialists
1150 17th St NW,Ste 702, Washington, DC, 20036-4603
Professional Airways Systems Specialists-Dateline, 1,179

Progressive Review
1739 Connecticut Ave NW, Washington, DC, 20009-1126
Progressive Review, 997

Psychologists for Social Responsibility
2607 Connecticut Ave NW, Washington, DC, 20008-1522
Psychologists for Social Responsibility Newsletter, 997

Public Affairs Council
1019 19th St NW Ste 200, Washington, DC, 20036-5105
Impact, 857

Public Citizen
2000 P St., NW, #610, Washington, DC, 20036
Public Citizen Health Letter, 525

Public Citizen's Critical Mass Energy Project
215 Pennsylvania Ave., SE, Washington, DC, 20003-1155
Critical Mass Energy Bulletin, 351

Public Lands Council
1301 Penn Ave. NW, #300, Washington, DC, 20004
Public Lands Council-Washington Highlight Report, 391

Public Resource Center
1747 Connecticut Ave NW, Washington, DC, 20009-1142
Menorah: Sparks of Jewish Renewal, 1,069

Public Technology, Inc.
1301 Pennsylvania Ave NW, Washington, DC, 20004-1793
PTI Prism, 491

Public Voice for Food & Health Policy
1001 Connecticut Ave NW Ste, 522, Washington, DC, 20036-5504
Advocacy Update, 251

RFE/RL Research Institute
1201 Connecticut Ave NW Ste, 410, Washington, DC, 20036-2605
RFE/RL Research Report, 637

Radio Tech. Commission for Maritime Svcs. ; RTCM
PO Box 19087, Washington, DC, 20036-0087
RTCM Newsletter, 1,161

* See **MULTI-PUBLISHER INDEX** for list of publications.

Radio Television News Directors Assn.
1000 Connecticut Ave NW Ste, 615, Washington, DC, 20036-5302
RTNDA Weekly, 125

Rails to Trails Conservancy
1400 16th St., NW, Ste. 300, Washington, DC, 20036-2217
Trailblazer, 493

Reading is Fundemental, Inc.
600 Maryland Avenue SW Room, Suite #600, Washington, DC, 20024-2569
RIF Newsletter, 327

Refugee Service Center
Center for Applied Linguistics, 1118 22nd St. NW, Washington, DC, 20037
In America, 400

Registry of Comparative Pathology
Armed Forces Inst. Of Pathol., Washington, DC, 20306-0001
Comparative Pathology Bulletin, 871

Religion News Service
1101 Connecticut Ave NW Ste, 350, Washington, DC, 20036-4303
RNS Daily News Reports, 1,050

Religious Action Ctr. -Union of American Hebrew Congregation
2027 Massachusetts Ave., NW, Washington, DC, 20036-1029
Chai/Impact Newsletter, 1,068

Religious Coalition for Reproductive Choice
1025 Vermont Ave. NW, Suite #1130, Washington, DC, 20005-3516
Religious Coalition for Reproductive Choice Newsletter, 1,211

Renew America
1400 16th St NW Ste 710, Washington, DC, 20036-2217
Environmental Success Index, 353

•**Republican Natl. Committee**
Publications, 310 First St SE, Washington, DC, 20003-1801

Resource Recovery Report
5313 38th St NW, Washington, DC, 20015-1831
Resource Recovery Report, 392

Resources for the Future, Inc.
1616 P St NW, Washington, DC, 20036-1400
Resources, 393

•**Resources Publ. Co.**
1010 Vermont Ave NW Ste 708, Washington, DC, 20005-4995

Rhythm & Blues Foundation
14th & Constitution Ave, NW, Rm. 4603, Mrc 657, Washington, DC, 20560-0001
Rhythm & Blues Foundation News, 917

•**Rice Journal Enterprises, Inc.**
Box 14260, Ben Franklin Sta., Washington, DC, 20044-4260

Robert McKay Clan Newsletter
5319 Manning Pl NW, Washington, DC, 20016-5311
Robert McKay Clan Newsletter, 466

Rotornews
1333 H St NW Ste 410, Washington, DC, 20005-4707
Rotornews, 32

Rowan & Bleuitt
1000 Vermont Ave, N.W., Washington, DC, 20005
Corporate Governance Update, 836

Royal Norwegian Embassy
2720-34th St., NW, Washington, DC, 20008
News of Norway, 635

Sabrina I. Pacifici
1722 Eye St. NW, Washington, DC, 20006
PLL Perspectives, 807

Sacha Millstone
1720 Eye St., N.W., Washington, DC, 22006
Concerned Investor, The, 660

Sane/Freeze: Campaign for Global Security
1819 H St NW Ste 1000, Washington, DC, 20006-3603
SANE World/Freeze Focus, 998

Satellite Business News Inc.
1730 Rhode Island Ave. NW, Ste. 600, Washington, DC, 20036
Satellite Business News, 1,169

Savings Bonds Division
Treasury Dept, Washington, DC, 20226-0001
Bond Teller, 656

•**Savings & Community Bankers of America**
900 19th St. NW, Ste. 400, Washington, DC, 20006-2105

Science & Government Report, Inc.
3736 Kanawha St NW, Washington, DC, 20015-1810
Science and Government Report, 1,100

Senate Historical Office
Sec'y Of The Senate The, Capitol, Rm. Sh 201, Washington, DC, 20510-0001
Senate History, 1,198

Senior Executives Association
PO Box 7610, Washington, DC, 20044-7610
ACTION, 833

Serif Press
1331 H St., N.W., Washington, DC, 20005
TD Access & Safety Report, 1,180

Service Employees Intl. Union
1313 L St. , N. W., Washington, DC, 20005-4100
Building Service Division Update, 707

Shepard Poorman Communications Corp.
7301 N. Woodland Dr., Box 68110, Washington, DC, 46268
Professional Directory of Indy Women, 1,211

•**The Silver Institute**
1112 16th St NW Ste 240, Washington, DC, 20036-4823

Small Business Development Ctr. -Howard Univ.
2600 Sixth St. N.w., Rm. 125, Washington, DC, 20059-0001
Profits, 149

•**Smithsonian Institution**
900 Jefferson Dr., S.W., Washington, DC, 20560-0001

Smithsonian Institution-Folklife Programs & Cultural Studies
955 L'Enfant Plaza, SW, Ste. 2600, MRC 914, Washington, DC, 20560
Smithsonian Talk Story, 425

Snow Biz
PO Box 53262, Washington, DC, 20009-9262
Snow Biz, 54

Social Legislation Information Service
440 1st St NW Ste 310, Washington, DC, 20001-2085
Washington Social Legislation Bulletin, 782

Society for American Archaeology
900 2nd St NE Ste 12, Washington, DC, 20002-3557
Society for American Archaeology Bulletin, 58

Society for Intl. Dev., Washington Chapter
1875 Connecticut Ave. NW, Ste. 900, Washington, DC, 20009-5728
Development Connections, 629

Society of Physics Students
1825 Connecticut Ave NW Ste, 213, Washington, DC, 20009-5708
SPS Newsletter, 979

Society of Research Administrators
1200 19th Stree NW, Washington, DC, 20036-2412
SRA News, 1,024

Society for Values in Higher Education
Georgetown Univ., PO Box 571205, Washington, DC, 20057-0001
Society for Values in Higher Education-Newsletter, 330

Southern Political Report
PO Box 15507, Washington, DC, 20003-0507
Southern Political Report, 998

•**Special Libraries Assn.**
1700 18th St NW, Washington, DC, 20009-2508

Spina Bifida Association of America
4590 Macarthur Blvd NW Ste 250, Washington, DC, 20007-4226
Spina Bifida Insights, 887

State CDBG Update
444 N Capitol St NW Ste 224, Washington, DC, 20001-1512
State CDBG Update, 493

Statistics on Banking
550 17th St NW, Washington, DC, 20429-0001
Statistics on Banking, 99

Student American Pharmaceutical Assn.
2215 Constitution Ave NW, Washington, DC, 20037-2975
Pharmacy Student, 287

Student National Education Association
1201 16th St NW, Washington, DC, 20036-3207
SNEA Impact: The Student Voice of the United Teaching Profession, 328

•**Sugar Association Inc.**
1101 15th St NW Ste 600, Washington, DC, 20005-5002

Synthetic Organic Chemical Manufacturers Assn., Inc.
1100 New York Ave. NW, Suite 1090, Washington, DC, 20005-3934
SOCMA Newsletter, 166

TCI, Inc.
2126 Connecticut Ave NW # 52, Washington, DC, 20008-1729
Linkages, 413

Task Force Against Nuclear Pollution
PO Box 1817, Washington, DC, 20013-1817
Progress Report, 927

Tax Foundation
1250 H St NW Ste 750, Washington, DC, 20005-3952
Tax Features, 1,153

•**Telecommunications Reports**
1333 H St. NW, 2nd Fl., West Tower, Washington, DC, 20005

Textile Museum
2320 S Street N.W., Washington, DC, 20008-4088
Textile Museum Bulletin, 908

•**Thompson Publishing Group**
1725 K Street, NW, Washington, DC, 20006

Tilden Press, Inc.
1519 Connecticut Ave NW, Washington, DC, 20036
Green Business Letter, The, 139

Trade Communications, Inc.
733 15th St NW Ste 1100, Washington, DC, 20005-2112
Export Update, 646

•**Trade Reports International Group**
2104 National Press Bldg., Washington, DC, 20045

•**Travel Industry Association of America**
2 Lafayette Centre, 1133 21 St., NW, Washington, DC, 20036

Trends Publishing, Inc.
1079 Natl. Press Bldg., Washington, DC, 20045-0001
Energy Today, 353

Tucker's Letter
1840 Vermont Ave NW, Washington, DC, 20001-5006
Tucker's Letter, 689

Tufty Communications, Inc.
2107 National Press Building, Washington, DC, 20045
Value Engineering & Management Digest, 364

Turf Grass Trends
1775 T Street NW, Washington, DC, 20009
TurfGrass Trends, 443

USCEA
1776 I St NW Ste 400, Washington, DC, 20006-3700
INFO Newsletter, 926

USDA Radio & TV Div.
Off. Of Public Affairs #410-, Washington, DC, 20250-0001
Farm Broadcasters Letter, 40

•**US/ICOMOS**
1600 H St NW, Washington, DC, 20006-4907

USO World Headquarters
Washington Navy Yard, 901 M St., SE, Bldg. 198, Washington, DC, 20374-5096
USO: America's Spirit, 1,123

USS Callaway Assn.
c/o Wallace Shipp, 5319 Manning Pl., NW, Washington, DC, 20016-5311
Now Hear This, 897

•**Union of Councils for Soviet Jews**
1819 H St NW Ste 230, Washington, DC, 20006-3603

Union Label & Services Trades
815 16th St., N.W., Rm. 607, Washington, DC, 20006
Label Letter, 708

•**Unitarian Universalist Assn. of Churches in North America**
100 Maryland Ave NE, Washington, DC, 20002-5625

United Automobile Workers
1757 N St NW, Washington, DC, 20036-2884
UAW Washington Report, 711

United Bus Owners of America
1300 L St NW Ste 1050, Washington, DC, 20005-4107
Docket, 1,177

United Church of Christ Office for Church & Society
110 Maryland Ave., N.E., Suite #207, Washington, DC, 20002
Courage in the Struggle for Justice & Peace, 629

United Service Organizations, Inc.
Washington Navy Yard, 901 M Street SE Building 198, Washington, DC, 20374-5096
America's Spirit, 1,114

U.S. Air Force, Chief of Security Police
Washington, DC, 20314-0001
Security Police Digest, 790

•**U.S. Bureau of the Census - Dept. of Commerce**
Data User Services Division, Customer Services, Washington, DC, 20233-1900

U.S. Business & Industrial Council
122 C Street NW, Suite #815, Washington, DC, 20001-2109
Bulletin-U.S. Business & Indust. Council, 129

U.S. Catholic Mission Association
3029 4th St NE, Washington, DC, 20017-1102
Mission Update, 1,058

• See **MULTI-PUBLISHER INDEX** for list of publications.

•**U.S. Chamber of Commerce**
1615 H St NW, Washington, DC, 20062-0002

U.S. Civil Aeronautics Board, Bureau of Operating Rights
1825 Connecticut Ave NW, Washington, DC, 20428-0001
Integrated Voice/Data PBXs, 226

•**U.S. Coast Guard**
2100 2nd St SW, Washington, DC, 20593-0001

U.S. Committee for Refugees
1717 Massachusetts Ave. NW, Suite 701, Washington, DC, 20036-2001
Refugee Reports, 637

U.S. Conference of Local Health Officers
1620 Eye St. , N. W., Washington, DC, 20006
Local Health Officers News, 488

U.S. Conference of Mayors
1620 I St NW, Washington, DC, 20006-4073
AIDS Information Exchange, 496

United States Council for Energy Awareness
17761 I Street NW, Suite 400, Washington, DC, 20006-3708
Nuclear Energy Info, 926

U.S. Dept. of Ag-FSIS
Rm. 1165, S. Bldg. 12th &, Independence, Washington, DC, 20250-0001
Food News for Consumers, 429

U.S. Dept. of the Air Force
Hq Usaf/Rdcx, Washington, DC, 20330-0001
Contracting and Acquisition Newsletter, 895

U.S. Dept. Justice, Drug Enforcement Administration
1405 Eye Street, N.w., Washington, DC, 20537-0001
Drug Enforcement, 732

•**U.S. Dept. of Transportation**
400 7th St SW, Washington, DC, 20590-0001

US EPA
Office Of Solid Waste 401 M, Street SW, Washington, DC, 20460-0001
EPA Reusable News, 377

U.S. English
818 Conn. Ave. NW, #200, Washington, DC, 20006
U.S. English-Update, 999

U.S. Environmental Protection Agency
401 M St., S.w., A-107, Washington, DC, 20460-0001
EPA Bulletin, 377

U.S. Federal Election Commission
999 E St NW, Washington, DC, 20463-0002
Federal Election Commission Record, 989

U.S. Government Energy Regulatory Commission
826 N Capitol St NE, Washington, DC, 20002-4233
Chronicle, 351

•**U.S. Gov't Printing Office**
2100 2nd St. S.W., Washington, DC, 20593-0001

U.S. Hispanic Chamber of Commerce
1030 15th St NW Ste 206, Washington, DC, 20005-1503
Networking-Newsletter, 146

U.S. Holocaust Memorial Council
100 Raoul Wallenberg Pl SW, Washington, DC, 20024-2126
U.S. Holocaust Memorial Museum Campaign News, 176

U.S.-Kazakhstan Council
2000 L St NW, Ste 200, Washington, DC, 20036-4907
U.S.-Kazakhstan Monitor, 639

U.S. Library of Congress, Cataloging Distribution Services
Washington, DC, 20541-0001
MARC Formats for Bibliographic Data, 803

U.S. Library of Congress Professional Association
Library Of Congress, Washington, DC, 20540-0001
Insights: Library of Congress Professional Assn. Newsletter, 800

U.S. MAB Secretariat
OES/ETC/MAB, Department of State, Washington, DC, 20522-4401
U.S. MAB Bulletin, 395

U.S. Natl. Park Service
Interior Bldg., Washington, DC, 20240-0001
Parks, 950

•**U.S. Office of Personnel Management**
Office Of Workforce Info., 1900 E. St. NW #7494, Washington, DC, 20415-0001

U.S. Peace Corps
1990 K St NW, Washington, DC, 20526-0001
Tapestry, 1,122

U.S. Postal Service
475 L'Enfant Plz SW, Rm 10541, Washington, DC, 20260-0004
Memo to Mailers, 19

United States Students Assn.
1612 K St. NW, Ste. 510, Washington, DC, 20006
Legislative Update, 316

U.S. Travel Data Center
1100 New York Ave., NW, Ste. 450, Washington, DC, 20005
Travel Printout, 1,190

U.S. Wheat Assocs.
1620 Eye St., NW, #801, Washington, DC, 20006
U.S. Wheatletter, 419

United Way of the Natl. Capital Area
95 M St SW, Washington, DC, 20024-3622
United Way Newsletter, 602

The Urban Age
Room S10-108, The World Bank, 1818 H Street NW, Washington, DC, 20433-0001
The Urban Age, 639

•**Urban and Regional Information Systems Association (URISA)**
900 Second Street, NE, Suite 304, Washington, DC, 20002

Valve Manufacturers Assn. of America
1050 17th St NW Ste 701, Washington, DC, 20036-5503
Valve World, 851

Vegetarian Society of the District of Columbia
PO Box 4921, Washington, DC, 20008-0121
VSDC News, 433

Volunteer - The National Center
736 Jackson Pl NW, Washington, DC, 20503-0007
Workplace in the Community, 350

•**Warren Publishing, Inc.**
2115 Ward Ct. NW, Washington, DC, 20037-1213

Washington Area Bicyclist Assn.
1819 H St NW Ste 640, Washington, DC, 20006-3603
Ride On, 263

Washington Center for Central American Studies
PO Box 29355, Washington, DC, 20017-0355
El Salvador On Line, 630

Washington D.C. Assn. Realtors
777 14th St. , N. W. 2nd fl., Washington, DC, 20005-3201
DC Line, 1,033

•**Washington G-2 Reports**
1111 14th St NW Ste 711, Washington, DC, 20005-5603

Washington Independent Writers
733 15th St NW Ste 220, Washington, DC, 20005-2112
Independent Writer, 696

Washington Metropolitan Area Transit Authority
600 5th St NW, Washington, DC, 20001-2651
Intercom, 1,178

Washington Office on Africa
110 Maryland Ave NE, Washington, DC, 20002-5699
Washington Notes on Africa, 640

•**Washington Office on Latin America**
110 Maryland Avenue, NE, Suite 404, Washington, DC, 20002

Washington Peace Ctr.
2111 Florida Ave NW, Washington, DC, 20008-1912
Peace Letter, 995

Washington Performing Arts Society
2000 L St NW Ste 810, Washington, DC, 20036-4907
W.P.A.S. Museletter, 262

•**Washington Researchers, Ltd.**
PO Box 19005, Washington, DC, 20036-9005

Waterfront Center
1536 44th St NW, Washington, DC, 20007-2066
Spotlight, 61

•**Welt Publishing Co.**
1413 K St. NW, Ste. 800, Washington, DC, 20005-3405

Wider Opportunities for Women
1325 G St. N. W. , LL, Washington, DC, 20005-3189
Women At Work, 1,213

Wildlife Management Institute
1101 14th St NW Ste 801, Washington, DC, 20005-5601
Outdoor News Bulletin, 390

William Penn House
515 E Capitol St SE, Washington, DC, 20003-1142
Penn Notes, 1,120

•**Wine Industry News Inc.**
PO Box 19502, Washington, DC, 20036-0502

Wine & Spirits Wholesalers of America, Inc.
1023 15th St NW Ste 4, Washington, DC, 20005-2602
Upfront, 105

Witness for Peace
110 Maryland Ave. NE #311, Washington, DC, 20002-5626
Witness for Peace Newsletter, 640

Woman's National Democratic Club
1526 New Hampshire Ave NW, Washington, DC, 20036-1204
WNDC News, 1,000

Women in Government Relations, Inc.
1029 Vermont Ave NW Ste 510, Washington, DC, 20005-3517
On the Record, 1,211

Women Strike for Peace
110 Maryland Ave. NE, Suite 302, Washington, DC, 20002
Legislative Alert, 992

Women's Association of Alcohol Beverage Industries
1250 Eye Street NW, Suite 900, Washington, DC, 20005
Industry World, 103

Women's Legal Defense Fund
1875 Connecticut Ave NW Ste 71, Washington, DC, 20009-5728
WLDF News, 1,212

Woodrow Wilson International Center for Scholars
100 Jefferson Dr., S.w., Washington, DC, 20560-0001
Cold War International History Project Bulletin, 988

•**World Bank**
1818 H St., NW N-9023, Washington, DC, 20433-0001

World Federalists Association
418 7th St SE, Washington, DC, 20003-2707
World Federalist Newsletter, 1,000

World Federation of Direct Selling Association
1666 K St. NW, Ste. 1010, Washington, DC, 20006
Direct Selling Association International Bulletin, 1,086

•**World Peace Through Law Center**
1000 Connecticut Ave., N.W., Washington, DC, 20036-5302

•**World Wildlife Fund-U.S.**
1250 24th St NW Ste 400, Washington, DC, 20037-1175

Worldpost Services
United States Postal Service, PO Box 23793, Washington, DC, 20026-3793
Passport, 971

Young Astronaut Council
1308 19th St NW, Washington, DC, 20036-1602
Astro News, 26

Young Republican National Federation
310 1st St SE, Washington, DC, 20003-1801
Young Republican News, 1,000

Youth Policy Institute
1221 Massachusetts Ave NW Ste, B, Washington, DC, 20005-5302
Youth Record, 1,216

•**Zero Population Growth Inc.**
1400 16th St NW Ste 320, Washington, DC, 20036-2290

Florida

11th Bombardment Group Assn.
PO Box 637, Seffner, FL, 33584-0637
Grey Geese Flyer, 1,138

187th Airborne Regimental Combat Team Assn.
c/o Frank Schock, 10501 Cook Lake Ct., Leesburg, FL, 34788
Rakkasan, The, 1,138

After the Fact
4100 N 58th Ave Apt 210, Hollywood, FL, 33021-1532
After the Fact, 340

•**Air-Conditioning & Refrigeration Wholesalers**
10251 W Sample Rd # B, Coral Springs, FL, 33065-3939

Alert Publications Partners
1401 Brickell Ave, Ste 570, Miami, FL, 33131-3503
Money Laundering Alert, 757

Aloes International Inc.
2421 Curry Ford Rd, Orlando, FL, 32806-2503
Catherine's Aloe Journal, 501

•**American Accounting Assn**
5717 Bessie Dr, Sarasota, FL, 34233-2399

American Bartenders' Assn.
PO Box D, Plant City, FL, 33564-9004
Mixin', 104

American Civil Defense Assn.
PO Box 1057, Starke, FL, 32091-1057
TACDA Alert, The, 1,139

American Consultants League
1290 N Palm Ave # 112, Sarasota, FL, 34236-5604
Consulting Intelligence, 133

American Family Foundation
PO Box 2265, Bonita Springs, FL, 33959-2265
Young People and Cults, 1,052

* See **MULTI-PUBLISHER INDEX** for list of publications.

INDEX TO PUBLISHERS BY STATE

American Film & Video Assn.
760 Plantation Rd, Merritt Island, FL, 32952-4039
AFVA Bulletin, 419

American Institute of Constructors
466 94th Ave. N., Saint Petersburg, FL, 33702-2522
American Institute of Constructors Newsletter, 243

American Institute of Polish Culture
1440 79th St. Causeway, Miami, FL, 33141
Good News, 631

American Nudist Research Library
4425 S. Pleasant Hill Rd., Kissimmee, FL, 34746-2703
American Nudist Research Library, 813

•**American Purchasing Society**
11910 Oak Trail Way, Port Richey, FL, 34668-1037

American Small Business & Investors Association
375 Douglas Ave., Ste 1012, Altamonte Springs, FL, 32714-3315
Under $5 Stock Survey, 690

American Society of Notaries
PO Box 7663, Tallahassee, FL, 32314-7663
American Notary, 714

American Standard Chinchilla Rabbit Assn.
1607 9th St W, Palmetto, FL, 34221-4465
American Standard Chinchilla Rabbit Assn. News, 48

American Subacute Care Association
1440 Kennedy Crossway, Suite 421, North Bay Village, FL, 33141
ASCA Quarterly, 497

American Way Features
128 Lighthouse Dr, Jupiter, FL, 33469-3511
Straight Talk, 998

Applied Benefits Research
34125 U.S. Highway 19N, Palm Harbor, FL, 34684
Benefits Watch, 128

Aquatic Exercise Assoc.
PO Box 1609, Nokomis, FL, 34274
Akwa Letter, 497

Aquatic Plant Information Retrieval System
7922 NW 71st St, Gainesville, FL, 32653-3071
Aquaphyte, 1,095

Art Deco Society of the Palm Beaches
325 SW 29th Ave., Delray Beach, FL, 33445-4409
Streamline, 625

Art Institute of Ft. Lauderdale
1799 SE 17th St, Fort Lauderdale, FL, 33316-3013
Buzz, 198

Ashington-Pickett Mid-Corp Inc.
550 N Bumby Ave Ste 110, Orlando, FL, 32803-4927
Ashington-Pickett Airlines and Travel Report, 1,182

Assn. of Birth Defect Children
827 Irma Ave, Orlando, FL, 32803-3806
ABDC Newsletter, 496

Association for Women Veterinarians
16706 Rolling Rock Dr, Tampa, FL, 33618-1133
AWV Bulletin, 1,200

Aviation News from South Florida
1711 N Anhinga Ln, Homestead, FL, 33035-1001
Aviation News of South Florida, 27

•**Bank Rate Monitor, Inc.**
PO Box 88888, North Palm Beach, FL, 33408-8888

•**Barbara's View**
PO Box 531006, Miami, FL, 33153-1006

•**Barrow Investment Management, Inc.**
3800 W Bay To Bay Blvd Ste 21, Tampa, FL, 33629-6844

Barry Univ.
11300 N.E. 2nd Ave., Miami Shores, FL, 33161-6695
Native American Policy Network, 1,126

Barter News Report
511 Royal Oak Rd, Webster, FL, 33597-9560
Commodity Market Exchange, 659

•**Bauer Communications, Inc.**
PO Drawer 145510, 2655 LeJeune Rd PH1, Coral Gables, FL, 33114-5510

Better Directions
PO Box 752, Melbourne, FL, 32902-0752
Wise Ideas, 1,109

Billiard & Bowling Institute
200 Castlewood Dr, North Palm Beach, FL, 33408-5604
BBIA Flashes, 1,129

Broadcasting and the Law Inc.
1 SE 3rd Ave Ste 1450, Miami, FL, 33131-1715
Broadcasting and the Law, 123

Bull & Bear Financial Newspaper
PO Box 917179, Longwood, FL, 32791-7179
Monetary Digest, 94

Bureau of Economic & Business Research
University of Florida, 221 Matherly Hall, Box 117145, Gainesville, FL, 32611-7145
Florida Population Studies, 292

BusinessGram Inc.
PO Box 273390, Tampa, FL, 33688-3390
BusinessGram, 130

CSG Information Services
3922 Coconut Palm Drive, Tampa, FL, 33619-8321
Fashion Retail Intelligence Newsletter, 55

Campus Communications, Inc.
PO Box 115500, Gainesville, FL, 32611-5500
Graduate School Review, 187

Campus Crusade for Christ
100 Sunport Ln., Ste 1600, Orlando, FL, 32809-7871
Bright Side, 578

Capital Pubs.
Box 2132, Hollywood, FL, 33022
Final Edition Newsletter, 664

Casino Chronicle Inc.
10880 Crescendo Circle, Boca Raton, FL, 33498
Casino Chronicle, 368

Caucus on Social Theory & Art Education
Florida State Univ., 123 Carothers Hall, B-171, Tallahassee, FL, 32306-3014
Bulletin of the Caucus on Social Theory & Art Education, 63

•**Center for Gerontogical Studies**
Univ. of Florida, 3357 Turlington Hall, Gainsville, FL, 32611-2036

Center for Microcomputers in Transportation
512 Weil Hall, Univ. of Fl., Gainesville, FL, 32611-2083
McTrans, 1,178

Central District Dental Hygiene Society
1842 Wind Drift Rd, Orlando, FL, 32809-6842
Central Incisor, 268

Charles Hesser
Box 3637, Miami Beach, FL, 33140-3637
Gold Coast News, 1,040

Charles R. Appler
10417 New Bedford Ct SE, Lehigh Acres, FL, 33936-7253
Appler Family Newsletter, 447

Cheryl Pryor
5304 Kingswood Dr., Orlando, FL, 32810
Priority, 326

Children & Adults With Attention Deficit Disorders
499 Northwest 70th Ave., Suite 308, Plantation, FL, 33317
C.H.A.D.D.ER Box, 276

Clearwater Christian College
3400 Gulf To Bay Blvd, Clearwater, FL, 34619-4514
Report, 198

Coin Previewer
PO Box 770396, Coral Springs, FL, 33077-0396
Coin Previewer, 927

Commodity Trend Service
PO Box 32309, Palm Beach Gardens, FL, 33420-2309
Future Charts, 665

•**Corporate Relations Group/Gulf Atlanti Publishing**
1801 Lee Rd Ste 301, Winter Park, FL, 32789-2165

Cota & Assocs., Inc.
PO Box 14070, Sarasota, FL, 34278-4070
Automation Equipment Marketing Report, 212

Crane Flock Newsletter
Poinsettia Drive #21, Ft. Myers, FL, 33905-4343
Crane Flock Newsletter, 451

Crowley Publishing Co., Inc.
5100 NW 33rd Ave Ste 155, Fort Lauderdale, FL, 33309-6399
Money Pro 'The Steve Crowley Report', 94

Cuba Newsletter Inc.
501 Brickell Key Dr Ste 200, Miami, FL, 33131-2608
Cuba Report, The, 644

Cycle Research Institute of Florida, Inc.
PO Box 5220, Deltona, FL, 32728-5220
Astro-Cycle Forecaster, 654

Damarka Enterprises, Inc.
6271-24 St. Augustine Rd. #2, Jacksonville, FL, 32217
Real Estate Marketing Management Alert, 1,038

•**Deadfromtheneckup Inc.**
PO Box 8306, St. Petersburg, FL, 33738

Demko Publishing
21946 Pine Trace, Boca Raton, FL, 33428-3057
Aging America Resources, 1,105

•**Dick Davis Publishing**
1080 SE 3rd Ave., Fort Lauderdale, FL, 33316-1108

DogGone
PO Box 651155, Vero Beach, FL, 32965-1155
DogGone, 1,183

Don Bell Reports
544 Ferguson Lane, Palm Beach, FL, 33415-3527
Don Bell Reports, 989

Eckerd College
Letters Collegium, 4200 54th Avenue South, St. Petersburg, FL, 33711
Eckerd College Thimblerig, 198

Economic Advice
3910 NE 26th Ave, Lighthouse Point, FL, 33064-8044
Penny Stock Future, 681

Editors Release Service
PO Box 10309, Saint Petersburg, FL, 33733-0309
Washington Report, 1,000

Edna Hibel Society
PO Box 9721, Coral Springs, FL, 33075-9721
Edna Hibel Society Newsletter, 64

Electric Boat Association of the Americas
PO Box 4151, Deerfield Beach, FL, 33442
Current, 113

Electrical Generating Systems Association
10251 W Sample Rd # Sv-B, Coral Springs, FL, 33065-3939
Powerline, 339

Emphysema Anonymous, Inc.
726 N. Highland Ave., Clearwater, FL, 34615-5463
Batting the Breeze, 499

Employment Relations Bulletin
Florida State University, Tallahassee, FL, 32306-1096
Employment Relations Bulletin, 610

Environmental Healthcare, Inc.
PO Box 2286, Delray Beach, FL, 33447-2286
Environmental File, The, 380

Environmental Info Ctr.
1251b Miller Ave, Winter Park, FL, 32789-4827
ENFO, 377

Environmental Opportunities
PO Box 547158, Surfside, FL, 33154
Environmental Opportunities, 344

Epicurean Revue
PO Box 35128, Sarasota, FL, 34242-5128
Epicurean Revue, 428

FALR, Inc.
PO Box 2309, Gainesville, FL, 32602-2309
Florida Administrative Law Reports, 738

FPL Corporate Communications
PO Box 029100, Miami, FL, 33102-9100
Times of Your Life, 1,109

Fedl. Home Life Ins. Co.
6277 Sea Harbor Dr, Orlando, FL, 32887-0001
Spectrum, 599

Financial News Corp.
10 N. Newman St., P.O. Box 176, Jacksonville, FL, 32202-3322
Financial News, 90

Financial Planning Newsletter
7665 Sun Island Dr S Apt 101, Saint Petersburg, FL, 33707-4433
Financial Planning Newsletter, 90

First Saety, Inc.
1015 Semoran Blvd., #1476, Casselberry, FL, 23707
Crane Safety Report, The, 1,079

Florida Archivist
4191 Bradfordville Rd, Tallahassee, FL, 32308-6401
Florida Archivist, 797

Florida Baptist Theological College
5400 College Dr., P.O. Box 1306, Graceville, FL, 32440-3306
Echoes, 198

Florida Christian College
1011 Bill Beck Blvd, Kissimmee, FL, 34744-5301
Sonlife, 198

•**Florida Citrus Mutual**
PO Box 89, Lakeland, FL, 33802-0089

Florida Communications Network, Inc.
PO Box 2099, Gainesville, FL, 32602-2099
Florida Insight, 485

•**Florida Department of Agriculture & Consumer Services**
PO Box 147100 m, Gainesville, FL, 32614-7100

Florida Dept. of Corrections
2601 Blairstone Rd, Tallahassee, FL, 32399-2500
Correctional Compass, 785

Florida Department of Insurance
The Capitol; LL-25, Tallahassee, FL, 32301
Facts, 620

Florida Education Association
118 N Monroe St, Tallahassee, FL, 32301-1531
Focus, 310

• See **MULTI-PUBLISHER INDEX** for list of publications.

Florida Emergency Preparedness Assn.
110 N. Apopka Ave., Inverness, FL, 32650-4245
Florida Emergency Preparedness Assn. -Newsletter, 1,138

Florida Folklore Society
4011 State Rd., 52, Dade City, FL, 33525-8240
Florida Folklore Society Newsletter, 425

Florida Historical Society
1320 Highland Ave., Melbourne, FL, 32935
Roesch House Report, 548

Florida Junior Chamber of Commerce
PO Box 90125, Lakeland, FL, 33804-0125
Florida Jaycee News, 159

Florida Keys Community College
5901 W. Jr. College Rd., Key West, FL, 33040-4397
Voices, 198

Florida Legal Periodicals, Inc.
PO Box 3730, Tallahassee, FL, 32315-3730
Florida Jury Verdict Reporter, 739

Florida Magazine Association
1133 W Morse Blvd Ste 201, Winter Park, FL, 32789-3743
Blue Pencil, 952

Florida Nurses Assn.
PO Box 536985, Orlando, FL, 32853-6985
Florida Nurse, 929

Florida Psychological Assn.
408 Office Plz, Tallahassee, FL, 32301-2757
Florida Psychologist, 1,014

Florida Public Interest Research Group
420 E. Call St., Tallahassee, FL, 32301-7612
Florida PIRG Citizen Agenda, 382

Florida Public Relations Assn.
PO Box 7511, Winter Haven, FL, 33883-7511
Proof, 861

Florida School for the Deaf & the Blind
207 San Marco Ave., St. Augustine, FL, 32084-2762
Florida School Herald, 533

Florida Solar Energy Ctr.
1679 Clearlake Rd., Cocoa, FL, 32922-5703
Solar Collector, 358

Florida Southern College
111 Lake Hollingsworth Dr, Lakeland, FL, 33801-5607
Southernnews, 187

Florida State Library
R.A. Gray Bldg., Tallahassee, FL, 32399-0250
Orange Seed Technical Bulletin, 807

Florida State Poetry Soc., Inc.
1110 N Venetian Dr, Miami Beach, FL, 33139-1019
N.P.D.C. Newsletter, 983

Florida State University Geology Dept.
Department of Geology, Tallahassee, FL, 32306-3026
Coastal Research, 1,096

Florida State Univ. Library School
School/Library & Info Studies, Tallahassee, FL, 32306-2048
Alumni Newsletter, School of Library & Info Studies, 187

Florida Trail Assn.
PO Box 13708, Gainesville, FL, 32604-1708
Footprint, The, 943

Florida Wildlife Federation
PO Box 6870, Tallahassee, FL, 32314-6870
Florida Fish & Wildlife News, 382

Flying Engineers Intl.
507 NW 60th St Ste C, Gainesville, FL, 32607-2055
Flying Engineers Newsletter, 29

•**Foreign Tax Law Publishers, Inc.**
PO Box 2189, Ormond Beach, FL, 32175-2189

Foundations of Education
College of Education, Univ. of Florida, Gainesville, FL, 32611
Foundations Monthly Newsletter, 310

Friends of the Everglades
101 Westward Dr Ste 2, Miami Springs, FL, 33166-5211
Everglades Reporter, 381

Gage Family Newsletter
29 Seminole Ct. NE, Winter Haven, FL, 33881-9451
Gage Family Newsletter, 454

Gary Galyean's Golf Letter
PO Box 3899, Vero Beach, FL, 32964
Gary Galyean's Golf Letter, 480

Gary Halbert Letter
820 Ocean Dr. #308, Miami Beach, FL, 33139-5809
Gary Halbert Letter, 15

Gazette Publishing
1309 N Halifax Ave, Daytona Beach, FL, 32118-3658
Pet Gazette, 50

Genealogical Society of Okeechobee
PO Box 371, Okeechobee, FL, 34973-0371
Genealogical Society of Okeechobee Newsletter, 454

Geraventure Corp.
PO Box 2131, Melbourne, FL, 32902-2131
Living Off the Land, Subtropic Newsletter, 43

Gerosota Publications
3530 Pine Valley Dr, Sarasota, FL, 34239-4335
Conferee, 855

Global Vision
375 Douglas Ave., Ste. 1012, Altamonte Springs, FL, 32714
Global Vision Investor Newletter Monthly, 666

Golden Horse Culture Business Development
PO Box 772161, Coral Springs, FL, 33077-2161
China Information, 628

Gopher Tortoise Council
Florida Museum of Natural Hist, ory, Univ. of Florida, Gainesville, FL, 32611
Tortoise Burrow Bulletin, 395

Gospel Assn. for the Blind, Inc.
PO Box 62, Delray Beach, FL, 33447-0062
Jottings, 111

•**Gould Publications, Inc**
1333 N US Highway 17-92, Longwood, FL, 32750-3724

HWUP!
PO Box 12743, Tallahassee, FL, 32317-3743
Hwup!: The Wordshop For Poets, 982

Hale Indian River Groves
Indian River Plaza, Wabasso, FL, 32970
Polly Hale Newsletter, 1,009

Hanson
2149 14th Ave SW, Largo, FL, 34640-4750
TI PPC Notes, 240

•**Harcourt Brace Professional Publishing**
6277 Sea Harbor Dr, Orlando, FL, 32887-0001

Hatton Heritage Assn.
1451 Sandy Ln, Clearwater, FL, 34615-2044
Hatton Family Newsletter, 456

Healthtrac, Inc.
PO Box 13552, Tallahassee, FL, 32317-3552
Healthtrac Tallahassee Report on Health Care Issues, 512

Hialeah Hospital
651 E 25th St, Hialeah, FL, 33013-3878
Horizons, 565

Hippocrates Health Institute
1443 Palmdale Ct, West Palm Beach, FL, 33411-3388
Hippocrates Health Institute-Newsletter, 512

Historical Society of Fort Lauderdale
PO Box 14043, Fort Lauderdale, FL, 33302-4043
New River News, 545

•**Hotline Publishing**
PO Box 161132, Altamonte Springs, FL, 32716-1132

Humanities Exchange Inc.
PO Box 1608, Largo, FL, 34649-1608
Travelling Exhibition Information Service Newsletter, 67

•**Hunting Report Inc.**
9300 S Dadeland Blvd Ste 605, Miami, FL, 33156-2721

IBA
PO Box 1447, Boynton Beach, FL, 33425-1447
Institute of Business Appraiser's Newsletter, 142

In House Personal Publishing
PO Box 1047, Winter Park, FL, 32790-1047
Frump Update, 369

•**Infoteam, Inc.**
PO Box 15640, Plantation, FL, 33318-5640

Innisbrook Resort
PO Box 1088, Tarpon Springs, FL, 34688-1088
Innisbrook Conference Review, 839

•**The Innovation Groups**
PO Box 16645, Tampa, FL, 33687-6645

Inside Edge
10151 University Blvd., Orlando, FL, 32817
Inside Edge, 669

Inside Wall Street
PO Box 940245, Maitland, FL, 32794-0245
Inside Wall Street, 669

Institute for Advanced Study of the Communication Processes
Dauer Hall 63, ASB-63, Gainesville, FL, 32611
IASCP Bulletin, 533

Institute of Diving
17314 Panama City Beach Pkwy, Panama City Beach, FL, 32413-2020
Institute of Diving Newsletter, 936

•**Institute for Econometric Research**
3471 N. Federal Hwy., Ft. Lauderdale, FL, 33306-1019

Institute of Internal Auditors, Inc.
249 Maitland Ave., Altamonte Springs, FL, 32701-4201
IIA Today, 5

Institute of Wall Street Studies
5301 N. Federal Highway, Boca Raton, FL, 33434
Wall Street Money Letter, 691

Inter American Press Association
Press Freedom Program, 2911 NW 39th Street, Miami, FL, 33142-5148
IAPA News, 696

International Affiliation of Independent Accounting Firms
9200 S Dadeland Blvd Ste 510, Miami, FL, 33156-2713
International Affiliation of Independent Accounting Firms-Update, 6

International Assn. of Industrial Accident Boards & Comm.
1575 Aviation Center Pky Ste, 509, Daytona Beach, FL, 32114-3863
IAIABC Newsletter, 701

•**International Features, Inc.**
8 South J St., Ste. 3, Box 1349, Lake Worth, FL, 33460-3742

International Game Fish Assn.
1301 East Atlantic Blvd., Pompano Beach,, FL, 33060
International Angler, 606

Investors Alliance
219 Commercial Blvd., PO Box 11209, Fort Lauderdale, FL, 33339-1209
Investor News, 672

Iron Overload Diseases Association, Inc.
433 Westwind Dr, North Palm Beach, FL, 33408-5123
Ironic Blood, 877

Island Properties Report Inc.
4061 Bonita Beach Rd Ste 201, Bonita Springs, FL, 33923-4073
Island Properties Report, 1,034

Jacksonville Community Council
21 W. Church Street, Jacksonville, FL, 32202-3155
Briefing, 481

Jacksonville Univ.
2800 University Blvd N, P.O. Box 281-014, Jacksonville, FL, 32211-2294
Lamplighter, 187

Jewish Librarians Caucus c/o Sylvia Eisen
1118 N Lombardo Ave, Lecanto, FL, 34461-9505
Jewish Librarians Caucus Newsletter, 800

Job Svc. of Florida
236 W Garden St # 1393, Pensacola, FL, 32501-5729
Pensacola Labor Market Trends, 704

Judy Wall
684 County Rd. #535, Sumterville, FL, 33585
Resonance, 110

Kimball Assocs.
4640 Rummell Rd, Saint Cloud, FL, 34771-1708
Kimball Letter, 673

L.D. Pankey Institute
240 Crandon Blvd., Ste. 302, Dupont Pl. Ctr., Key Biscayne, FL, 33149-1543
Pankey-Gram, 271

Learning Publications, Inc.
Safe School Coalition, P.O.Box 1338, Holmes Bch., FL, 34218
School Microcomputing Bulletin, 237

Leesburg Printing Co.
1100 North Blvd. East, Leesburg, FL, 34748
Soilless Grower, 46

Libertarian Info. Services
PO Box 817802, Hollywood, FL, 33081-1802
Common Sense, 988

Litigation Project, Inc.
1145 Candlewood Cir, Pensacola, FL, 32514-1604
Legal Action for Women, 1,209

Litton Laser Systems
PO Box 547300, Orlando, FL, 32854-7300
Laserline, 979

Lowell Dunahay
4513 Lake Haven Blvd, Sebring, FL, 33872-5227
Dunahay, 452

Lowenthal & Miller
25601 SW 137th Ave, Princeton, FL, 33032-6726
Bonsai Business, 440

Luther Family Association
2531 Lakeview St, Lakeland, FL, 33801-2556
Luther Family Newsletter, 460

* See **MULTI-PUBLISHER INDEX** for list of publications.

M. Bryce & Associates
777 Alderman Rd, Palm Harbor, FL, 34683-2604
OS/2 Connect, 232

MD Resources, Inc.
9360 Sunset Dr Ste 250, Miami, FL, 33173-3273
Vital Signs, 889

Market Metrics
5048 Brywill Cir., Sarasota, FL, 34234-3727
Wall Street Generalist, 691

Marketimer Investment Letter
2023 N. Atlantic Avenue, Suite 301, Cocoa Beach, FL, 32931
Bob Brinker's Marketimer, 656

•**Marketing Information Network**
15000 Gulf Blvd Apt 307, Saint Petersburg, FL, 33708-2030

Marrakech Express
500 Anclote Rd, Tarpon Springs, FL, 34689-6701
Shortruns, 1,007

Martin Marietta Eagle Electronics & Missiles Group
Box 5837, Orlando, FL, 32855
Eagle, 582

Master Indicator of the Stock Market
11371 Torchwood Ct, West Palm Beach, FL, 33414-6040
Master Indicator of the Stock Market, 676

Measurements & Data Corporation
100 Wallace Ave., Ste. 100, Sarasota, FL, 34237
Healthy & Natural Journal, Part 1 - Health & Natural News, 512

Metal Treating Institute
302 3rd St Ste 1, Neptune Beach, FL, 32266-5138
Around the Open Hearth, 890

Metropolitan Dade County Transit Agency
6601 NW 72nd Ave, Miami, FL, 33166-3029
M News, 589

Miami-Dade Community College-Medical Ctr. Campus
950 NW 20th St, Miami, FL, 33127-4622
Antidote, 198

Miami Herald Publ. Co
1 Herald Plz, Miami, FL, 33132-1609
Cuba News, 661

•**Miami Medical Letter, Inc.**
9700 SW 67th Ave, Miami, FL, 33156-3272

Miami Univ. School of Medicine
1600 NW 10th Ave Rm 1149a, Miami, FL, 33136-1015
Miami University School of Medicine Bulletin, 880

Microbiological Applications, Inc.
132 San Remo Dr, Islamorada, FL, 33036-3307
Microbiological Update, 894

Milgo Electric Corp.
Box 407044, Sunrise, FL, 33340-7044
Count-Down, 581

Minsk Business News
1000 West McNab, Road Pompano Beach, FL, 33069
Minsk Business News, 634

Money Maker Report
PO Box F, Chipley, FL, 32428-5005
Money Maker Report, 1,035

Mote Marine Laboratory
1600 Ken Thompson Pky, Sarasota, FL, 34236-1004
News from Mote, 1,099

Museum of Fine Arts
255 Beach Dr. NE, St. Petersburg, FL, 33701-3498
Mosaic-News from the Museum of Fine Arts, 906

N.E. Regional Data Ctr. of the State Univ. System of Florida
112 SSRB-Univ. of Florida, Box 112050, Gainesville, FL, 32611-2050
Update, 242

National Association of Independent Publishers
PO Box 430, Highland City, FL, 33846-0430
Publisher's Report, 119

National Association of Professional Baseball Leagues
PO Box A, Saint Petersburg, FL, 33731-1950
Baseball News, 101

National Association for Stock Car Auto Racing, Inc.
1801 Intl. Speedway Blvd., Daytona Beach, FL, 32114
NASCAR News, 1,133

Natl. Assn. of Store Fixture Manufacturers
1776 N. Pine Island Road, #1, Plantation, FL, 33322
NASFM NEWs, 850

National Capital Corp.
PO Box 21172, Tampa, FL, 33622-1172
CommonWealth Letters, 660

National Farm Workers Minority Newsletter
1109 Cass St, Deland, FL, 32720-6510
National Farm Workers Minority Newsletter, 43

National Hay Association, Inc.
102 Treasure Island Causeway, St. Petersburg, FL, 33706-4716
Hay There!, 42

National Parkinson Foundation, Inc.
1501 NW 9th Ave, Miami, FL, 33136-1407
Parkinson Report, 883

National Payment Corporation
100 W Kennedy Blvd Ste 260, Tampa, FL, 33602-5116
Electronic Payment Journal, 221

National Perinatal Assn.
3500 E. Flecher Ave. #209, Tampa, FL, 33613-4712
Bulletin of the NPA, 78

Ned Davis Research
PO Box 1287, Nokomis, FL, 34274-1287
Ned Davis Research - Stock Market Strategy, 679

Needlepoint, Inc.
PO Box 13165, North Palm Beach, FL, 33408-7165
Needlepoint Bulletin, 922

Newfound Harbor Marine Institute
Rt. 3, Box 170, Big Pine Key, FL, 33043
Seacamp Association News, 937

Nicholas Direct
PO Box 877, Indian Rocks Beach, FL, 34635-0877
Direct Marketing Success Letter, 274

No Load Mutual Fund Consensus
143 Seminole Ave., Palm Beach, FL, 33480-3732
No Load Mutual Fund Consensus, 680

North Florida Astrology Assn.
PO Box 1741, Jacksonville, FL, 32201-1741
North Florida Astrology Assn. Newsletter, 68

O Globo/Multimedia Inc.
7061 Grand National Dr., Ste. 127, Orlando, FL, 32819-8377
GloboFax, 400

Orange County Library System
101 E Central Blvd, Orlando, FL, 32801-2462
Friends of the Orlando County Library System, 798

Order of St. Benedict of Florida
St. Leo Abbey, St. Leo, FL, 33574-9999
Benedictine Monks of Florida, 577

Orrell Family Genealogical Assn.
PO Box 4828, South Daytona, FL, 32121-4828
Orrell Family Genealogical Assn. Newsletter, 463

Osmundsen & Rains
PO Box 321450, Cocoa Beach, FL, 32932-1450
Studio Link, 67

PGA Tour
112 TPC Blvd., Ponte Vedra Beach, FL, 32082
PGA Tour News, 480

PRI Group
PO Box 9433, Panama City Beach, FL, 32417-9433
Recruiting & Search Report, 348

Panos Communications Ltd.
R.R. 5, Box 867, Big Pine, FL, 33043-9404
Yours For Health, 532

Parsons Holder Lifestyle Institute
PO Box 10979, Daytona Beach, FL, 32120-1979
Environmental Life Newsletter, 380

Partners for Travel, Inc.
PO Box 560337, Miami, FL, 33256-0337
Partners for Travel, 1,187

Pearson Investment Letter
1628 White Arrow Dr, Dover, FL, 33527-5741
Pearson Investment Letter, 681

Pet Project
3748 Sunray Dr, Holiday, FL, 34691-3239
Antique Comb Collector, 52

Pete Silver Assn.
PO Box 432152, Miami, FL, 33243-2152
Marketing Communications Report, 17

Phi Theta Pi
2103 Cortez Rd, Jacksonville, FL, 32246-2313
Symbol, 182

•**Photofinishing News, Inc.**
10915 Bonita Beach Rd Ste 1091, Bonita Springs, FL, 33923-9049

Pinellas County Government
Personnel Dept., 400 S. St. Harrison Ave., Clearwater, FL, 33516-5113
Pinellas Pen, 595

Pinson & Assoc.
13575 58th St N, Clearwater, FL, 34620-3704
Investment Digest, 671

Poor Man's Pubs.
7000 20th St Lot 930, Vero Beach, FL, 32966-8878
Poor Man's Sawdust Plansletter, 555

Printing Association of Florida
PO Box 170010, Hialeah, FL, 33017-0010
Printing Association of Florida Newsletter, 1,006

Professional Golf Club Repairmen's Assn.
2295 Dan Hogan Dr., Dunedin, FL, 34698-2612
Golf Clubmaker, 480

RLT Resource Group
PO Box 520, Gonzalez, FL, 32560-0520
Recreation Advisor, 902

Radcap Inc.
Box 2407, Hollywood, FL, 33022-2407
Professional Tape Reader, 683

Radiance Technique Association International, Inc.
PO Box 40570, Saint Petersburg, FL, 33743-0570
Radiance Technique Newsletter, The, 526

Ram Financial Consultants
PO Box 770190, Ocala, FL, 34477-0190
International Investor, 671

Real Estate Publications, Inc.
322 W. Rid Vista Ct., Tampa, FL, 33604-6941
Distressed Property Investor's Monthly, 1,033

Redgate Communications Corp.
660 Beachland Blvd., Vero Beach, FL, 32963
Macintosh Multimedia & Product Registry, 228

Republican Liberty Caucus
1717 Apalachee Parkway, Ste. 434, Tallahassee, FL, 32301
Republican Liberty, 998

Ridgewood Financial Inst., Inc.
1016 Clemmons St Ste 407, Jupiter, FL, 33477-3303
Psychotherapy Finances, 844

Ringling Museum of Art
5401 Bay Shore Rd, Sarasota, FL, 34243-2161
John & Mable Ringling Museum of Art-Newsletter, 905

Rollin' Rock Club
15 Kennington Dr., Warrington, FL, 32507-1026
Rollin' Rock Club-News Letter, 556

SEP Publishing
PO Box 144, Gotha, FL, 34734
Get Organized! News, The, 471

St. Augustine Historical Society
271 Charlotte St, Saint Augustine, FL, 32084-5033
East-Florida Gazette, 539

Sales Leads Publishing Co.
705 Park Ave., Lake Park, FL, 33403-2503
Sales Leads, 1,087

Sales & Marketing Magic
36473 Us Highway 19 N, Palm Harbor, FL, 34684-1329
Sales & Marketing Magic, 1,039

Samuel Beckett Society
Dept. of English, Florida State Univ., Talahassee, FL, 32306
Beckett Circle, 819

Sears Roebuck
901 N. Fedl. Hwy., Fort Lauderdale, FL, 33304-2787
Gold Coaster, 584

Sewing & Crafts Wholesale Hotline
PO Box 402091, Miami Beach, FL, 33140
Sewing & Crafts Hotline, 256

Shipboard Cruiser, The
PO Box 533737, Orlando, FL, 32853-3737
Shipboard Cruiser, The, 1,188

Shoresh USA/Inc.
P.O. Box 551593, Jacksonville, FL, 32255-1593
Shalom, 1,071

Skinflint News
1460 Noell Blvd, Palm Harbor, FL, 34683-5637
Skinflint News, 472

Slovak Garden, Inc.
3110 Howell Branch Rd., Ste. 5075, Winter Park, FL, 32792-6006
Floridsky Slovak, 409

Society of Nematologists
3012 Skyview Dr, Lakeland, FL, 33801-7072
Nematology Newsletter, 110

Southeastern University of the Health Sciences
Sentinel, 1750 N.E. 167th Street, N. Miami Beach, FL, 33152-3017
Sentinel, 198

Special Libraries Assn., Florida & Caribbean Chapter
Blue Cross Blue Shield of FL, Corp. Library, 532 Riverside, Jacksonville, FL, 32231
Bulletin, Florida & Caribbean Chapter Special Libraries Assn., 794

• See ***MULTI-PUBLISHER INDEX*** for list of publications.

* See ***MULTI-PUBLISHER INDEX*** for list of publications.

Center for Inventory Management
900 Secret Cove Dr, Sugar Hill, GA, 30518-5366
Inventory Management Newsletter, 849

Christian Financial Concepts
601 Broad St E, Gainesville, GA, 30501-3729
How to Manage Your Money, 253

Christian Ministry Among Jewish People
PO Box 500307, Atlanta, GA, 31150-0307
Shalom, 1,065

Clan Anderson Society Ltd.
1947 Kensington High St SW, Lilburn, GA, 30247-2523
Stand Sure, 467

College Band Directors Natl. Assn.
Georgia State Univ., Atlanta, GA, 30304
College Band Directors National Association Newsletter, 911

Colonial Pipeline Co.
PO Box 18855, Atlanta, GA, 31126-0855
Mainline Newsletter, 589

Columbus College
101 Richard Hall, Columbus, GA, 31907-5645
Columbus College Focus, 187

Construction Market Data
4126 Pleasantdale Rd, Atlanta, GA, 30340-3516
Construction Market Data, 59

Conway Data Inc.
40 Technology Park, Norcross, GA, 30092-9990
New Plant Report, 248

Council on Battered Women
PO Box 54383, Atlanta, GA, 30308-0383
Council on Battered Women Newsletter, 172

Council of Societies for the Study of Religion
Mercer Univ., Macon, GA, 31207-0001
Council of Societies for the Study of Religion Bulletin, 1,046

Counselors Writing Services
PO Box 190, Lawrenceville, GA, 30246
Counselor's Dispatch, 729

Coweta County Genealogical Society
PO Box 1014, Newnan, GA, 30264-1014
Coweta County Genealogical Society Magazine, 451

Culpepper & Assocs.
7000 Peachtree Dunwoody Rd, NE #10, Atlanta, GA, 30328-1615
Culpepper Letter: Software Intelligence for Growth and Profits, 218

Daily Report Co.
190 Pryor St SW, Atlanta, GA, 30303-3607
Fulton County Daily Report, 740

Day Researcher
319 N Houston Lake Blvd, Centerville, GA, 31028-1117
Day Researcher, 452

DeKalb College
2101 Womack Rd, Dunwoody, GA, 30338-4435
James Dickey Newsletter, 817

DeKalb Musicians Supply Co.
115 Clairemont Ave., Decatur, GA, 30030-2502
Viol., 919

Decision Sciences Institute
University Plaza, Atlanta, GA, 30303
Decision Line, 307

Deyo Communications
218 Tree Summit Pky, Duluth, GA, 30136-6398
La Vista de Mexico, 1,186

E. U.
P.O. Box 23687, Atlanta, GA, 30322
Melrose Valhalla, 696

•**Elliott Wave International**
PO Box 1618, Gainesville, GA, 30503-1618

Energy Engineering
700 Indian Trail Rd NW, Lilburn, GA, 30247-3724
Cogeneration Letter, 351

Epidemiology Monitor
2560 Whisper Wind Ct., Roswell, GA, 30076-3664
New Epidemiology Monitor, The, 521

•**Equifax Inc.**
1600 Peachtree St. NW, Atlanta, GA, 30309

Erik S. Nelson, Inc.
PO Box 672223, Marietta, GA, 30067
Investment Update Newsletter, 672

•**Federal Reserve Bank of Atlanta**
104 Marietta St NW, Atlanta, GA, 30303-2713

Federal-State Market News Service
203 Administration Bldg., 1616 Forest Parkway, Forest Park, GA, 30050
Atlanta Wholesale Fruit, 1,008

Fellowship of Christian Airline Personnel
136 Providence Rd, Fayetteville, GA, 30214-2844
Trim Tab, 1,066

Fire Mark Circle of the Americas (FMCA)
2859 Marlin Dr., Chamblee, GA, 30341-5119
FMCA Newsletter, 620

Freelance Studios
139 Old South River Rd., Jackson, GA, 30233
Portfolio, 983

Friends of the State Botanical Garden of Georgia, Inc.
University of Georgia, 2450 S. Milledge, Athens, GA, 30605-1624
Garden Newsletter, 441

General Motors Corp.
281 Mount Lion Rd. SW, Atlanta, GA, 30354
Newsletter, 592

Georgia Dept. of Revenue
270 Washington St SW #424 E, Atlanta, GA, 30334-9009
ReveNews, 596

Georgia Historical Society
501 Whitaker St, Savannah, GA, 31401-4889
G.H.S. Foot-Notes, 540

Georgia Institute of Technology
Student Services Building, Atlanta, GA, 30332-0290
Research Horizons, 363

Georgia International Life Insurance Co.
PO Box 7325, Atlanta, GA, 30357-0325
Tempo, 600

Georgia Military College
201 E. Green St., Milledgeville, GA, 31061-3398
Cadence, The, 188

•**Georgia State Dept. of Labor**
148 International Blvd NE, Atlanta, GA, 30303-1751

Goody Press
PO Box 33515, Decatur, GA, 30033-0515
Anglofile, 368

Gwinnett Historical Society, Inc.
PO Box 261, Lawrenceville, GA, 30246-0261
Heritage, The, 541

Habitat for Humanity Int'l., Inc.
121 Habitat St., Americus, GA, 31709-3423
Mortarboard, 209

Haverty Furniture Cos. Inc.
866 West Peachtree St NW, Atlanta, GA, 30308-1123
Haverty's Half Hour, 438

Heidelberg USA
1000 Gutenberg Drive, Kennesaw, GA, 30144
Trends, 1,007

Hudson Sawyer Professional Services Marketing
950 E Paces Ferry Rd NE, Ste. 2425, Atlanta, GA, 30326-9868
Bowman's Accounting Report, 2

•**The Hume Group**
PO Box 105627, Atlanta, GA, 30348-5627

Institute of the Black World
1275 Capitol Ave SW, Atlanta, GA, 30315-2707
IBW Monthly Report, 34

Institute of Higher Education
Univ. of Georgia, Candler Hall, Athens, GA, 30602
IHE Newsletter, 312

•**Institute of Industrial Engineers**
25 Technology Park/Atlanta, Norcross, GA, 30092-2988

Institute of Paper Science & Technology
500 Tenth St. NW, Atlanta, GA, 30318
Abstract Bulletin of the Institute of Paper Science & Technology, 946

Institute of Paper Science & Technology, Inc.
500 10th St NW, Atlanta, GA, 30318-5794
IPC-Reporter, 946

International Association for Learning Laboratories
304C Moore College Bldg., UGA Language Labs, Athens, GA, 30602
National Association of Language Laboratory Directors Newsletter, 321

Intl. Jelly & Preserve Assn.
5775 Peachtree Dunwoody Rd NE, Ste G500, Atlanta, GA, 30342-1507
Direct Line, 243

International Society of Weighing & Measurement
2299 Brockett Rd, Tucker, GA, 30084-4400
ISWM News, 312

Inventors Clubs of America, Inc.
PO Box 450261, Atlanta, GA, 31145-0261
Inventors News, 1,097

Kappa Epsilon Fraternity
PO Box 870393, Stone Mountain, GA, 30087-0010
Bond, 177

Kinder Family
PO Box 264, Acworth, GA, 30101-0264
Kinder Family, 458

•**Lifestyle Change Communications**
5885 Glenridge Dr., Atlanta, GA, 30328

The Lignin Institute
5775 Peachtree Dunwoody Rd NE, Ste G500, Atlanta, GA, 30342-1507
Dialogue, 1,008

•**Lionheart Publishing Inc.**
2555 Cumberland Pkwy. #299, Atlanta, GA, 30339-3908

Luther Rice Seminary
3038 Evans Mill Rd, Lithonia, GA, 30038-2454
Pioneer, 199

•**Marta**
2424 Piedmont Rd NE, Atlanta, GA, 30324-3330

Mission to the World
1852 Century Pl NE Ste 201, Atlanta, GA, 30345-4305
Network, 1,074

Morehouse College
317 Gloster Hall, 830 Westview Dr., SW, Atlanta, GA, 30314
Morehouse Update, 199

Mrs. H.C. McGarity
PO Box 200504, Cartersville, GA, 30120-9009
Working at Home, 350

National Automotive Parts Assn.
2999 Circle 75 Pky. NW, Atlanta, GA, 30339-3050
NAPA News, 74

Natl. Catholic Conference for Seafarers
PO Box 8307, Savannah, GA, 31412-8307
Catholic Maritime News, 1,055

National Down Syndrome Congress
1605 Chantilly Dr. NE, #250, Atlanta, GA, 30324-3269
Down Syndrome News, 473

Natl. Faculty of the Humanities, Arts & Sciences
57 Forsythe St., Ste. 600, Atlanta, GA, 30303
National Faculty Forum, 371

Natl. Fed. of Housing Counselors
PO Box 5607, Savannah, GA, 31414-5607
Housing Pipeline, 384

National Health Information, L.L.C.
4671 E Forest Peak, Marietta, GA, 30066-1763
Capitation Management Report, 501

National Hydrocephalus Foundation
1670 Green Oak Circle, Lawrenceville, GA, 30243
Hydrocephalus News & Notes, 876

National Pecan Shellers Assn.
5775 Peachtree Dunwoody Rd NE, Ste G500, Atlanta, GA, 30342-1507
In a Nutshell, 1,009

•**Newsletter Factory**
1000 Parkwood Cir. NW, Suite #823, Atlanta, GA, 30339-2139

Newsletters Plus
100 Crescent Center Pky Ste, 1,200, Tucker, GA, 30084-7039
Headlines, 857

Nomads of the Time Stream
PO Box 451048, Atlanta, GA, 31145-9048
Actuary of the Abstract, 1,102

Omega Psi Phi Fraternity, Inc.
3951 Snapfinger Pky., Decatur, GA, 30035-3203
Oracle, 180

P & A Communications, Inc.
PO Box 464731, Lawrenceville, GA, 30246-4731
Georgia Contrarian, The, 666

Parapsychological Services Institute
5575 B. Chamblee Dunwoody Rd., Atlanta, GA, 30338
Insider, The, 948

Phi Delta Chi
PO Box 6565, Athens, GA, 30604
Communicator, 282

Physical Education Fitness Ltd
235 Mountainview Street, Decatur, GA, 30030
Sports Medicine in Primary Care, 887

Pierre Chastain Family Assn.
1903 Forest Green Dr NE, Atlanta, GA, 30329-2604
Chestnut Tree, 450

Premier Allergy
100 Crestent Center Park, Suite 1200, Tucker, GA, 30084
Allergy Edge, 866

•**Prent Thomas Textile Consultants**
PO Box 7005, Columbus, GA, 31908-7005

Pricing Advisor
3277 Roswell Rd NE Ste 620, Atlanta, GA, 30305-1840
Pricing Advisor, The, 20

• See **MULTI-PUBLISHER INDEX** for list of publications.

Processed Apples Institute
5775 Peachtree Dunwoody Rd NE, Ste G500, Atlanta, GA, 30342-1507
Incider, 1,009

•**Professional Newsletters, Inc**
State Taxation Institute, PO Box 81143, Atlanta, GA, 30366-1143

Professional Solutions, Inc.
660 Village Trce Ste 203, Marietta, GA, 30067-4081
Real World Software & Computer Newsletter, 235

Progressive Publishing Co.
2678 Henry St, Augusta, GA, 30904-4656
Progressive Teacher, The, 326

R. H. Macy
180 Peachtree St. NW, Atlanta, GA, 30303-1725
Macy-Go-Round, 589

Ranger Regimental Assn.
PO Box 29965, Atlanta, GA, 30359-0965
Vietnam Veterans Newsletter, 1,199

Real Entrepreneur
PO Box 1, Varnell, GA, 30756-0001
The Real Entrepreneur, 149

Regional Organization of Theatres South
1083 Austin Ave NE, Atlanta, GA, 30307-1940
Alternate Roots, 1,172

•**Reinhardt College**
7300 Reinhardt College Pkwy., Waleska, GA, 30183-0128

Reproductive Technology Update
67 Peachtree Park Dr NE, Atlanta, GA, 30309-1303
Reproductive Technology Update, 886

Restaurant Management Institute
211 Freyer Drive, Marietta, GA, 30060-1401
Restaurant Management Insider, 1,076

Richard Siedlecki Marketing & Management
4767 Lake Forrest Drive, NE, Atlanta, GA, 30342-2539
Siedlecki on Business, 22

Robert W. Woodruff Arts Center
1280 Peachtree St NE, Atlanta, GA, 30309-3502
Arts Center News, 902

Savannah State College
PO Box 20482, Savannah, GA, 31404-9716
Alumni Granule, 188

Sayers Publishing Co.
P.O. Box 3323, Marietta, GA, 30061
Direct Marketing Savings Report, 274

•**Scholars Press**
PO Box 15399, Atlanta, GA, 30333-0399

Scientific-Atlanta Inc.
3845 Pleasantdale Rd, Atlanta, GA, 30340-4266
Scientific-Atlanta World, 597

Sea Island Properties
Sea Island, GA, 31561
Sea Island Real Estate Newsletter, 1,039

Simple Living News
PO Box 1884, Jonesboro, GA, 30237
Simple Living News, 255

Society of Georgia Archivists
Box 80631, University of Georgia, Athens, GA, 30608
SGA Newsletter, 809

Soil and Plant Analysis Council
Univ. Sta., Box 2007, Athens, GA, 30612-0007
Soil-Plant Analyst, 122

•**Soundview Publications**
7100 Peachtree Dunwoody Rd., Suite #100, Atlanta, GA, 30328-4134

Southern Assn. of Colleges
1866 Southern Ln, Decatur, GA, 30033-4033
Proceedings, 326

•**The Southern Company**
270 Peachtree St NW, Suite 2100, Atlanta, GA, 30303

Southern Motor Carriers Bulletin
1307 Peachtree St NE, Atlanta, GA, 30309-3503
Southern Motor Carriers Bulletin, 1,180

•**Southern Regional Education Bd**
592 10th St NW, Atlanta, GA, 30318-5776

Southern Wholesalers Assn.
3522 Habersham At Northlake, Tucker, GA, 30084-4009
Southern Wholesalers Assn. -News & Views, 153

Sport Psychology Training Bulletin
1023 Hunters Pointe Dr, Statesboro, GA, 30458-6467
Sport Psychology Training Bulletin, 1,135

•**Strafford Pubs., Inc.**
590 Dutch Valley Rd., N.E., Postal Drawer 13729, Atlanta, GA, 30324-0729

Success Publications Inc.
PO Box 487, Roswell, GA, 30077-0487
Success Orientation, 846

Szabo Assocs., Inc.
3355 Lenox Rd NE Ste 945, Atlanta, GA, 30326-1332
Szabo Collective Wisdom, 258

•**TAPPI**
Box 105113, Tech Park/ATL, Atlanta, GA, 30348-5113

Tara Collectors Club
10698 Sandpiper Rd, Jonesboro, GA, 30236-6696
Jonesboro Wind, 554

Technology Publications, Inc.
5920 Roswell Rd., B107336, Atlanta, GA, 30328-4922
A-E-C Automation Newsletter, 210

The TelePuting Hotline and Field Computing Source Letter
215 Winter Ave NE, Atlanta, GA, 30317-1425
TelePuting Hotline and Field Computing Source Letter, 1,162

Trust Co. of Georgia
25 Park Pl. NE, Atlanta, GA, 30303-2900
Pony Express, 595

U.S.A. Finn Assn.
C/O John McIntosh, Jr., 208 Salisbury Road, Savannah, GA, 31410-3920
Solo, 114

United Parcel Service Corp. Office
55 Glendale Parkway, Atlanta, GA, 30328
Inside UPS, 587

U.S. Dept. of Health & Human Services
Toxic Substances/Disease Reg., 1600 Clifton Rd. N.E., E-33, Atlanta, GA, 30333
Hazardous Substances & Public Health, 1,203

Univ. of Georgia Cooperative Extension
Cooperative Extension Service, Athens, GA, 30602
Georgia Extension Veterinary News, 1,201

Valdosta State College Dept. Political Science
Publications, Valdosta, GA, 31698-0001
Czechoslovak History Newsletter, 401

Vinegar Institute
5775 Peachtree Dunwoody Rd NE, Ste G500, Atlanta, GA, 30342-1507
Vinegar Views, 434

Voice of Liberty Assn.
692 Sunnybrook Dr., Decatur, GA, 30033-5509
Voice of Liberty, 1,066

Women's Basketball Coaches Assn.
4646 Highway 29 NW #B, Lilburn, GA, 30247-3620
Fast Break Alert, 1,131

Word Merchants, Inc.
PO Box 440755, Kennesaw, GA, 30144-9513
Bill Shipp's Georgia, 481

World Development Council
40 Technology Park, Norcross, GA, 30092-9934
Super Projects, 638

Yankee Permaculture
PO Box 672, Dahlonega, GA, 30533-0672
Robin, 393

Guam

Marine Lab/Univ. of Guam
UOG Station, Mangilao, GU, 96923
Coral Reef Newsletter, 109

Hawaii

AAMA Intl.
1350 S King St., Ste 104, Honolulu, HI, 96814-2008
International Society of Islands, 632

Academy of International Business
Univ. of Hawaii Manoa-CBA, Honolulu, HI, 96822
AIB Newsletter, 641

American Friends Service Committee, Hawaii
2426 Oahu Ave, Honolulu, HI, 96822-1967
Asian & Pacific Newsletter, 986

Assn. of Pacific Systematists
PO Box 19000a, Honolulu, HI, 96817-0916
Assn. of Pacific Systematists Newsletter, 108

Bank of Hawaii, Economics Dept.
PO Box 2900, Honolulu, HI, 96846-0001
Business Trends, 130

•**Bishop Museum**
1525 Bernice St # 19000-A, Honolulu, HI, 96817-2704

C. Brewer
PO Box 1826, Honolulu, HI, 96805-1826
C. Brewer Today, 579

Chaminade University of Honolulu
3140 Waialae Ave, Honolulu, HI, 96816-1510
Alumni News & Notes, 188

East-West Center
1777 East-West Rd., Honolulu, HI, 96848-0001
AsiaPacific Briefing Paper, 626

Ewa Sugar Company, Inc.
Box O, Waipahu, HI, 96797
Ewa Hurri-Cane, 583

First Hawaiian Bank
PO Box 3200, Honolulu, HI, 96847-0001
First Hawaiian Bank Economic Indicators, 292

Good Book Publishing Company
2747 S. Kihei Road, Kihei, HI, 96753-9622
Newsletter from Dick B on The Spiritual Roots of AA, 521

Hawaii Agricultural Statistics Service
1428 S King St # 22159, Honolulu, HI, 96814-2512
Hawaii Weekly Weather, 41

Hawaii Library Association
PO Box 4441, Honolulu, HI, 96812-4441
Hawaii Library Association Newsletter, 799

•**Hawaii Loa College**
45-045 Kamehameha Hwy, Kaneohe, HI, 96744-5297

Hawaii Medical Services Assn.
PO Box 860, Honolulu, HI, 96808-0860
Blue Review, 562

Hawaii State Dept. of Health
Box 3378, Communication Office, Honolulu, HI, 96801-3378
Hawaii Health Messenger, 508

Hawaii State Health Planning
335 Merchant St Ste 214e, Honolulu, HI, 96813-2921
Hawaii Health Planning News, 354

Hawaii Traveler
Honolulu, HI, 96839-1162
Hawaii Traveler, 1,185

Hawaiian Malacological Society
PO Box 22130, Honolulu, HI, 96823-2130
Hawaiian Shell News, 921

Hilo Coast Processing Co.
PO Box 4190, Hilo, HI, 96720
Hilo Coast Processing News, 585

Honolulu Board of Water Supply
630 S Beretania St, Honolulu, HI, 96843-0002
Ka Waipuna, 588

Honolulu Office of Information
City Hall, Honolulu, HI, 96813
Honolulu Employee Journal, 486

•**Honpa Hongwanji Mission of Hawaii**
Buddhist Study Center, 1436 University Ave., Honolulu, HI, 96822

IBSNAT Project
2500 Dole St., Krauss Hall 23, Honolulu, HI, 96822-2332
Agrotechnology Transfer, 37

International Studies Assn.
Univ. Of Hawaii Soc. Sci., Dept, C/O F.w. Riggs, Honolulu, HI, 96844-0001
ISA Comparative Interdisciplinary Studies Section Bulletin, 631

International Tsunami Information Center
737 Bishop Street, Suite #2200, Honolulu, HI, 96813
Tsunami Newsletter, 937

Jamaican Style
4-771 Kuhio Hwy #7-C, Kapaa, HI, 96746
Dread Times, 814

Kaua'i Community College
3-1901 Kaumualii Hwy., Anthrop, Lihue, HI, 96766-9591
Archaeology on Kaua'i, 57

Maka'ainana Media
2252 Puna St, Honolulu, HI, 96817-1539
Philippine Labor Alert, 636

Meadow Gold Dairies
PO Box 1880, Honolulu, HI, 96805-1880
Under Our Roof, 601

The Neon News
PO Box 668, Volcano, HI, 96785-0668
Neon News, 817

Pacific Science Association
PO Box 17801, Honolulu, HI, 96817-0801
Pacific Science Association Information Bulletin, 1,099

Performing & Fine Arts for World Peace
General Delivery, Volcano, HI, 96785-9999
Performing & Fine Arts for World Peace Newsletter, 996

•**Queen's Medical Center**
1301 Punchbowl St., Honolulu, Oahu, HI, 96813-2499

Rainbow Bridge Consultants
PO Box 599, Keaau, HI, 96749-0599
Wahine Wireless, 1,212

* See **MULTI-PUBLISHER INDEX** for list of publications.

Selected Acquisitions
2425 Campus Rd, Honolulu, HI, 96822-2216
Selected Acquisitions, 810

•**Space Age Publishing Company**
75-5751 Kuakini Hwy., Ste. 209, Kailua-Kona, HI, 96740-1705

Tom Adams Productions
PO Box 10246, Honolulu, HI, 96816-0246
Comic Highlights, 604

Troubadour, Inc.
PO Box 1490, Hanalei, HI, 96714-1490
Goldstock Letter, 666

Univ. of Hawaii Animal Science Dept.
1800 E West Rd, Honolulu, HI, 96822-2318
Animal Sciences Newsletter, 827

Univ. of Hawaii, Computing Center
2565 The Mall, Keller Hall, Honolulu, HI, 96822-2233
University of Hawaii, Computing Center Newsletter, 241

•**Univ. of Hawaii Sea Grant Program**
Sea Grant College Program, 1000 Pope Rd., #213, Honolulu, HI, 96822

•**Univ. of Hawaii at Manoa**
1890 East-West Rd., Moore Hall, #416, Honolulu, HI, 96822

Univ. of Hawaii at Manoa Education Dept.
College of Education, 1776 Univ. Ave., Hall 132, Honolulu, HI, 96822
Science Education Newsletter, 329

Wellington Financial Corp.
Hawaii Kai Executive Plaza, 6700 Kalanianaole Hwy #218, Honolulu, HI, 96825-1299
Wellington Letter, 692

Yamamoto Forecast
PO Box 573, Kahului, HI, 96732-0573
Yamamoto Forecast, 692

Idaho

American Assn. of Presidents of Independent Colleges and Uni
Rick College, Rexburg, ID, 83460-0001
Private Higher Education, 326

American Information Newsletter
2308 N Cole Rd Ste G, Boise, ID, 83704-7361
American Information Newsletter, 470

Anne Long
Rr 2 Box 671, Grangeville, ID, 83530-9635
Cross Collections, 451

Assn. of Idaho Cities
3314 Grace St, Boise, ID, 83703-5836
Idaho Cities, 486

Bank Research Assocs.
PO Box 7812, Boise, ID, 83707-1812
Current Issues in Bank Auditing, 87

Blumenfeld Education Newsletter
PO Box 45161, Boise, ID, 83711-5161
Blumenfeld Education Newsletter, 301

Boise Bible College
8695 Marigold St, Boise, ID, 83714-1220
Outreach, 199

Boise Peace Quilt Project
1110 Warm Springs Ave, Boise, ID, 83712-7949
Peaceful Pieces, 636

City Leaders Institute, Inc.
3045 Thayen Pl, Boise, ID, 83709-3953
City Leaders Institute Briefings, 482

Creneau Inc.
1620 Northwest Blvd., Coeur d'Alene, ID, 83814
Creneau, 87

Division of Aeronautics
PO Box 7129, Boise, ID, 83707-1129
Rudder Flutter, 32

Emshock Letter
Box 411, Randall Flat Rd., Troy, ID, 83871-0411
Emshock Letter, 982

•**Federal-State Market News Service**
1820 E 17th St Ste 130, Idaho Falls, ID, 83404-6472

•**Harper Assocs., Inc.**
PO Box 50, Sun Valley, ID, 83353-0050

Home-Based Business Newsletter
PO Box 1232, Meridian, ID, 83680-1232
Home-Based Business Newsletter, 140

Home Publisher
PO Box 451, Coeur D Alene, ID, 83816-0451
Mylan Messenger, 461

Idaho Personnel
College of Education Univ., Moscow, ID, 83843
Idaho Guidance News, 1,014

Idaho Potato Commission
PO Box 1068, Boise, ID, 83701-1068
Idaho Potato News, 1,009

Idaho Real Estate Commission
633 N. 4th, Boise, ID, 83720-0001
Real Estatement, 1,038

Idaho State Dental Assn.
1220 W. Hays St., Boise, ID, 83702-5315
ISDA Newsletter, 270

Idaho State Dept. of Employment
317 Main St., Boise, ID, 83735-0001
Idaho Employment, 345

Idaho State Historical Society
210 Main St, Boise, ID, 83702-7264
Mountain Light, 544

Idaho State Nurses' Assn
200 N. 4th, #M-20, Boise, ID, 83702-6001
RN Idaho, 931

Idaho Trails Council, Inc.
PO Box 1629, Sun Valley, ID, 83353-1629
Trailhead, 944

Idaho Wool Growers Assn.
PO Box 2596, Boise, ID, 83701-2596
Idaho Wool Growers Association, 828

•**Impact Pubs.**
PO Box 3113, Ketchum, ID, 83340-3113

Latah Co. Genealogical Society
327 E 2nd St, Moscow, ID, 83843-2852
Latah County Genealogical Society Newsletter, 459

Lewis-Clark State College
8th Ave. & 6th St., Lewiston, ID, 83501
Blue Arrow, 199

Northwest Association of Schools & Colleges
1910 University Dr, Boise, ID, 83725-0001
Northwest Association of Schools & Colleges-Newsletter, 323

Peregrine Fund, Inc.
5666 W Flying Hawk Ln, Boise, ID, 83709-7289
Peregrine Fund Newsletter, 942

Pridemore/Pridmore/Prigmore Assn.
545 Jefferson St, Kimberly, ID, 83341-1825
Journal of the Predmore/Pridemore/Pridmore/Prigmore Assn., 458

Univ. of Idaho
Pubications, Moscow, ID, 83843
Spur, 199

Victor Vanek
5757 Boone, Boise, ID, 83705
Eaten Alive, 695

Illinois

AACC Secretariat
Northwestern Univ., Dept. EES, 2145 Sheridan Rd., Evanston, IL, 60208-0001
AACC Newsletter, 359

AARP Pharmacy Service
PO Box 883, Libertyville, IL, 60048-0883
HealthLetter, 284

•**AELE**
5519 N Cumberland Ave Ste 1008, Chicago, IL, 60656-1480

ARSI Group, The
19W068 Granville Road, Itasca, IL, 60143
Medical Business Letter, The, 517

ASA Communications,Inc.
222 Merchandise Mart #1360, Chicago, IL, 60654
ASA News, 626

ATO Fraternity
4001 W Kirby Ave, Champaign, IL, 61821-9725
ATO Leader, 176

Academy of the Street of Puerto Rican Congress
2315 W North Ave, Chicago, IL, 60647-5314
El Puertorrigueto, 260

Adhesives Manufacturers Assn.
401 N. Michigan Avenue, Chicago, IL, 60611-4267
Adhesive Trends, 847

•**Ag Executive, Inc.**
115 E. Twyman, PO Box 180, Bushnell, IL, 61422

•**Alert Publications Inc.**
401 W Fullerton Pky Apt 1403, Chicago, IL, 60614-2805

Alphabets, Inc.
P.O. Box 5448, Evanston, IL, 60204
Ellipsis, 222

Altrusa Intl., Inc.
332 S. Michigan Ave., Chicago, IL, 60604-4301
Altrusa Accent, 1,114

Alzheimer's Association
919 N Michigan Ave Ste 1000, Chicago, IL, 60611-1676
Alzheimer's Association Newsletter, 498

American Academy for Cerebral Palsy & Developmental Medicine
6300 N River Rd Ste 727, Rosemont, IL, 60018-4238
AACPDM News, 496

American Academy of Cosmetic Surgery
401 N. Michigan Ave., Chicago, IL, 60611-4212
American Academy of Cosmetic Surgery, 866

American Academy of Dental Practice Admin.
1063 S Whippoorwill Ln, Palatine, IL, 60067-7064
Communicator, 268

•**American Academy of Esthetic Dentistry**
500 N. Michigan Ave., Ste 1920, Chicago, IL, 60611-3703

American Academy of Matrimonial Lawyers
150 N Michigan Ave Ste 2040, Chicago, IL, 60601-7524
American Academy of Matrimonial Lawyers Newsletter, 714

American Academy of Orthopaedic Surgeons
6300 N River Rd Ste 300, Rosemont, IL, 60018-4232
AAOS Report, 863

American Academy of Periodontology
737 N Michigan Ave Ste 800, Chicago, IL, 60611-2615
AAP News, 267

American Academy of Physical Medicine and Rehabilitation
One IRM Plaza Suite #250, Chicago, IL, 60611-3604
Physiatrist, The, 884

American Architectural Manufacturers Association
1540 E Dundee Rd Ste 310, Palatine, IL, 60067-8321
AAMA Quarterly Review, 59

American Art Therapy Assn., Inc.
1202 Allanson Rd, Mundelein, IL, 60060-3808
American Art Therapy Assn. -Newsletter, 62

American Assn. of Agricultural Communicators of Tomorrow
67 Mumford Hall, 1301 W. Gregory, Urbana, IL, 61801
ACT Newsletter, 35

American Assn. of Dental Examiners
211 E Chicago Ave Ste 844, Chicago, IL, 60611-2616
Bulletin of the American Association of Dental Examiners, 268

American Assn. of Handwriting Analysts
820 W Maple St, Hinsdale, IL, 60521-3043
AAHA Newsletter, 981

American Association of Individual Investors
625 N. Michigan Ave. Ste. 1900, Chicago, IL, 60611-3109
Computerized Investing, 660

American Association of Law Libraries
53 W Jackson Blvd Ste 940, Chicago, IL, 60604-3612
Automatome, 793

American Association of Psychiatric Technicians
1789 N. Neltnor Blvd., Suite #260, West Chicago, IL, 60185-2997
AAPT News, 1,011

American Assn. of Senior Physicians
515 N. State St., Chicago, IL, 60610-4320
American Association of Senior Physicians-Newsletter, 866

American Assn. of Sex Educators, Counselors, and Therapists
435 N. Michigan Ave., #1917, Chicago, IL, 60611-4008
Contemporary Sexuality, 1,110

American Association of Teachers of French
57 E Armory Ave, Champaign, IL, 61820-6601
AATF National Bulletin, 297

American Association for Therapeutic Humor
2218 Crabtree Ln, Northbrook, IL, 60062-3520
Laugh It Up, 605

American Assn. of Women Dentists
401 N. Michigan Ave., Chicago, IL, 60611-4212
American Association of Women Dentists Chronicle, 268

•**American Bar Association**
750 N. Lake Shore Dr., Chicago, IL, 60611-4497

American Bar Assn. Sect. of Nat. Res., Energy, & Env. Law
750 N. Lake Shore Dr., Chicago, IL, 60611-4497
SONREEL News, 774

American Cancer Society, Illinois Div.
77 E Monroe St, Chicago, IL, 60603-5700
Illinois Cancer News, 876

• See **MULTI-PUBLISHER INDEX** for list of publications.

American College of Occupational and Environmental Medicine
55 W. Seegers Rd., Arlington Hts., IL, 60005-3922
MRO Update, 516

American Concrete Pavement Assn.
3800 N Wilke Rd Ste 490, Arlington Heights, IL, 60004-1268
American Concrete Pavement Assn. Newsletter, 243

American Dairy Products Institute
130 N Franklin St, Chicago, IL, 60606-1823
Tech News Quarterly, 265

American Dental Assn.
211 E. Chicago Ave., Chicago, IL, 60611-2678
Mouthpiece, 270

American Dialect Society
MacMurray Coll. English Dept., Jacksonville, IL, 62650
Newsletter of the American Dialect Society, 823

American Farm Bureau
225 Puhy Ave., Parker Ridge, IL, 60068
American Farm Bureau Official Newsletter, 37

American Hardware Mfgs. Assn.
801 N. Plaza Dr., Schaumburg, IL, 60173-4977
American Hardware Manufacturers Assn. Newsletter, 495

American Health Information Management Association
919 N Michigan Ave Fl 1400, Chicago, IL, 60611-1601
AOE Network, 865

American Hearing Research Found.
55 E Washington St., Ste. 2022, Chicago, IL, 60602-2202
Newsletter of American Hearing Research Foundation, 533

American Home Lighting Inst
435 N. Michigan Ave., #1770, Chicago, IL, 60611-4008
Lightrays, 339

•**American Hospital Publishing, Inc.**
737 N. Michigan Ave., Ste. 700, Chicago, IL, 60611-2431

American Interprofessional Foundation
601 Driftwood Ln, Northbrook, IL, 60062-5501
AIF/NERF News, 532

American Judicature Society
25 E Washington St 1600, Chicago, IL, 60602-1899
Judicial Conduct Reporter, 747

American Lawyers Auxilary
750 N. Lake Shore Dr., Chicago, IL, 60611-4497
National Lawyers Wives Newsletter, 760

American Library Assn./MAGERT
50 E. Huron St., Chicago, IL, 60611
Base Line, 793

•**American Library Association**
50 E Huron St, Chicago, IL, 60611-2795

•**American Medical Association**
515 N. State St., Chicago, IL, 60610

•**American Nuclear Society**
555 N. Kensington Ave., La Grange Park, IL, 60526

American Pain Society
5700 Old Orchard Rd., 1st fl., Skokie, IL, 60077-1057
APS Bulletin, 497

•**American Planning Association**
1313 E 60th St, Chicago, IL, 60637-2891

American Railway Bridge & Building Assn.
18154 Harwood Ave., Homewood, IL, 60430-2128
Bridge & Building News, 244

•**American Rental Association**
1900 19th St., Moline, IL, 61265-4198

American Society of Anesthesiologists
520 N Northwest Hwy, Park Ridge, IL, 60068-2538
American Society of Anesthesiologists Newsletter, 867

American Society of Artists, Inc.
PO Box 1326, Palatine, IL, 60078-1326
Art Lover's Art and Craft Fair Bulletin, 62

American Society of Business Press Editors
376 E. Saint Charles Road, Lombard, IL, 60148-2361
ASBPE National Newshound, 694

American Society of Clinical Hypnosis
2200 E Devon Ave Ste 291, Des Plaines, IL, 60018-4501
American Society of Clinical Hypnosis-Newsletter, 867

Amer. Soc. for Concrete Construction/E. Burr Bennett, Ltd.
2849 Dundee Rd. #138, Northbrook, IL, 60062-2501
American Society for Concrete Construction Membership Bulletin, 243

American Society of Dentistry for Children
875 N Michigan Ave Ste 4040, Chicago, IL, 60611-1901
ASDC Newsletter, 267

American Society for Hospital Marketing & Public Relations D
840 N. Lake Shore Dr., Chicago, IL, 60611-2497
Health Care Marketing and Public Relations, 564

American Soc. for Hospital Material Mgt.
840 N. Lake Shore Dr., Chicago, IL, 60611-2497
Hospital Materials Management News, 566

American Society of Safety Engineers
1800 E. Oakton St., Des Plaines, IL, 60018-2112
Society Update, 1,085

American Society for Theatre Research
Southern Illinois Univ., Dept. of Theatre-6608, Carbondale, IL, 62901
ASTR Newsletter, 1,172

American Supply Association
222 Merchandise Mart Plz., Ste. 1360, Chicago, IL, 60654-1016
ASA News, 534

American Theological Library Association
820 Church St., Suite 300, Evanston, IL, 60201-5613
American Theological Library Association Newsletter, 793

American Woman's Society of Certified Public Accountants
401 N. Michigan Ave., Chicago, IL, 60611-4212
AWSCPA Newsletter, 1

Amusement & Music Operators Assn.
401 N. Michigan Ave., Chicago, IL, 60611-4267
AMOA Location, 368

Andent, Inc.
1000 North Ave, Waukegan, IL, 60085-2938
Dental Computer Newsletter, 269

Antique Doorknob Collectors of America
PO Box 126, Eola, IL, 60519-0126
Doorknob Collector, The, 552

•**Appraisal Institute**
875 N. Michigan Ave., Suite 2400, Chicago, IL, 60611-1980

Architectural Aluminum Mfgrs. Assn.
1540 E Dundee Rd Ste 310, Palatine, IL, 60067-8321
AAMA Update, 59

Art Institute of Chicago
S. Michigan Ave. & Adams St., Chicago, IL, 60603
News & Events, 66

Assn. of Catholic Diocesan Archivists
Archdiocese of Chicago Archive, 5150 Northwest Hwy., Chicago, IL, 60630
ACDA Bulletin, 791

Assn. of College of Research Libraries
American Libr. Assn., 50 E. Huron St., Chicago, IL, 60611-2795
SEES Newsletter, 809

Assn. of Earth Science Editors
616 East Peabody Dr., C/O Susan Doenges, Champaign, IL, 61820
Blueline, 694

•**Assn. of Home Appliance Manufacturers (AHAM)**
20 N Wacker Dr Ste 1500, Chicago, IL, 60606-2903

Assn. of Mental Health Administrators
60 Revere Dr Ste 500, Northbrook, IL, 60062-1577
AMHA Leader, 1,011

Assn. of Professors & Researchers in Religious Education
1100 E 55th St, Chicago, IL, 60615-5112
Assn. of Professors & Researchers in Religious Education Newsletter, 1,045

Association of Rehabilitation Nurses
5700 Old Orchard Rd., 1st fl., Skokie, IL, 60077-1057
ARN News, 497

Assn. of Steel Distributors
401 N. Michigan, Chicago, IL, 60611-4212
News & Views, 892

Astronomical League
2112 Kingfisher Lane, E., Rolling Meadows, IL, 60008
Reflector, 1,100

•**Auburn-Cord-Duesenberg Club**
9n089 Corron Rd, Elgin, IL, 60123-8304

•**Audit Bureau of Circulations**
900 N. Meacham Rd., Schaumburg, IL, 60173-4968

Augustana Historical Society
Augustana College, Rock Island, IL, 61201-2296
Augustana Historian, 536

Automotive Booster Clubs International
1806 Johns Dr, Glenview, IL, 60025-1657
Booster News: Topics, 71

•**Automotive Engine Rebuilders Assn.**
330 Lexington Dr, Buffalo Grove, IL, 60089-6933

Auxiliary to the American Osteopathic Assn.
212 E Ohio St, Chicago, IL, 60611-3203
AAOA Record, 863

•**BGM Pubs.**
28635 W Old Hideway Rd, Cary, IL, 60013-9794

BPI Communications
The Merchandise Mart, Suite 936, Chicago, IL, 60654
New Product News, 495

•**Balzekas Museum of Lithuanian Culture**
6500 S Pulaski Rd, Chicago, IL, 60629-5136

•**Bank Administration Institute**
One N. Franklin St., Chicago, IL, 60606

•**Bankers Life**
4444 W Lawrence Ave, Chicago, IL, 60630-2546

Banking Law Briefs
521 W Main St Ste 200, Belleville, IL, 62220-1533
Banking Law Briefs, 718

Barbara Brabec Prod.
PO Box 2137, Naperville, IL, 60567-2137
Self-Employment Survival Letter, 151

Barber Greene World
3000 Barber Greene Rd, De Kalb, IL, 60115-9590
B-G World, 576

Barlist Publishing Company
Box 948, Northbrook, IL, 60065
Producer News, 623

Barry Urner Publications Inc
730 N Franklin Street, Chicago, IL, 60610
Daily Market & News Service, 853

•**Behavioral Images, Inc.**
302 Leland, Bloomington, IL, 61701-5646

Beltone Electronics Corp.
4201 W Victoria St, Chicago, IL, 60646-6700
Between Friends, 532

Bertrand Russell Society, Inc.
3802 N Kenneth Ave, Chicago, IL, 60641-2814
Bertrand Russell Society-Newsletter, 973

Bill of Rights Foundation
523 S Plymouth Ct Fl 800, Chicago, IL, 60605-1511
Campus Watch, 987

Binding Industries of America
70 E. Lake St., Chicago, IL, 60601-5907
Binders Bulletin, 115

Bond County Genealogical Society
C/o Nelda Anthony, Corr. Sec., 911 Killarney, Greenville, IL, 62246
B.C.G.S. News, 447

Bonnet-T-E's
314 Glenwood Rd, Lake Forest, IL, 60045-3020
Bonnet-T-E's and Kin, 448

Bradley University, Department of History
Publications, Peoria, IL, 61625-0001
Vincent of Beauvais Newsletter, 550

Broadcast Cable Financial Management Association
701 Lee St Ste 1010, Des Plaines, IL, 60016-4555
Broadcast & Cable Financial Management Assn. - Topical Reference Papers, 1,165

Building Officials & Code Administrators International, Inc.
4051 Flossmoor Rd, Country Club Hills, IL, 60478-5771
Building Officials and Code Administrators International Bulletin, 244

Bureau of Economic & Business Research
428 Commerce West, 120L S. Sixth St., Champaign, IL, 61820-6915
Illinois Business Review, 141

Bureau of Labor Statistics
230 S. Dearborn, Chicago, IL, 60604-1505
Consumer Price Index, 290

Business One Irwin
1333 Burr Ridge Pky, Burr Ridge, IL, 60521-6489
A.S.A.P., 833

Business & Professional People for the Public Interest
17 E. Monroe St., #212, Chicago, IL, 60603-5609
BPI Newsletter, 128

•**CCH, Inc.**
2700 Lake Cook Rd., Riverwoods, IL, 60015

•**CHRN**
PO Box 539, Medinah, IL, 60157-0539

CME
30 South Wacker, Chicago, IL, 60606-7402
Chicago Mercantile Exchange Newsletter, 658

Cahner's Publishing Co.
1350 E. Touhy Ave., Des Plaines, IL, 60018-3358
EP&P Nepcon East Show Daily, 365

* See **MULTI-PUBLISHER INDEX** for list of publications.

Cahokia Mounds Museum Society
PO Box 382, Collinsville, IL, 62234-0382
Cahokian, 57

•**Callaghan & Company**
155 Pfingsten Rd., Deerfield, IL, 60015-5293

Calumet Photographic, Inc.
890 Supreme Dr, Bensenville, IL, 60106-1181
Calumet View, 976

Camcar Screw Mfg. Co.
600 18th Ave, Rockford, IL, 61104-5159
Camcar Camera, 579

Cantwell-Conteville Family Assn.
3402 Fairlawn Dr, Glenview, IL, 60025-4520
Cantwell-Conteville Family Newsletter, 450

Career Strategies
1150 Wilmette Ave., Wilmette, IL, 60091-2603
Kennedy's Career Strategist, 345

Casket & Funeral Supply Assn. of America
708 Church St., Evanston, IL, 60201-3867
CFSA Newsletter, 437

•**Cast Metals Assn.**
455 State St Ste 201, Des Plaines, IL, 60016-2281

Catholic League for Religious Assistance to Poland
1200 N. Ashland Ave., Chicago, IL, 60622-2259
Liga, 407

Center for American Archaeology
PO Box 22, Kampsville, IL, 62053-0022
Prehistoric Times, 58

Center for Icarian Studies
Western Ill. Univ., 438 Morgan Hall, Macomb, IL, 61455-1396
Center for Icarian Studies-Newsletter, 973

Center for Latin American Studies
Univ of Chicago, 5848 S.University Ave., Chicago, IL, 60611-1798
Latin America/Chicago, 315

Center for Research Libraries
6050 S Kenwood Ave, Chicago, IL, 60637-2804
Focus on the Center for Research Libraries, 798

Central States Roller Canary Breeders Assn.
C/O Robert Wild, 305 Grosvenor Ct., Bolingbrook, IL, 60440
Vocal Roll, 942

Ceramic Tile Distributors Assn.
800 Roosevelt Rd Ste C20, Glen Ellyn, IL, 60137-5849
CTDA Tile News & Views, 245

•**Charles D. Spencer & Assocs., Inc.**
250 S. Wacker Dr., Ste. 600, Chicago, IL, 60606-5834

Chicago Assn. of Direct Marketing
200 N. Michigan Ave. #300, Chicago, IL, 60601-5909
AdMarks, 9

Chicago Astronomical Society
PO Box 30287, Chicago, IL, 60630-0287
Cosmic Quarterly, 68

Chicago Board Options Exchange
400 S La Salle St, Chicago, IL, 60605-1090
Options Update, 681

Chicago Dept. of Development
121 N. LaSalle, Chicago, IL, 60602-1202
Chicago Department of Development and Planning and Progress, 1,019

Chicago Local 458-3M GCIU
204 S Ashland Ave, Chicago, IL, 60607-5302
Craftsman, 707

Chicago Nurses Association
203 N. Wabash Ave., Ste. 818, Chicago, IL, 60601-2411
Chicago District, 929

Chicago Park District
425 E Mcfetridge Dr, Chicago, IL, 60605-2801
Park Notes, 594

Chicago Playing Card Collector, Inc.
1559 W. Pratt Blvd., Chicago, IL, 60626-4228
Chicago Playing Card Collectors, Membership Roster, 552

Chicago Teachers Union
222 Merchandise Mart Plaza, Chicago, IL, 60654-1005
Chicago Union Teacher, 707

China Judaic Studies Association
Oakton Community College, 1600 Goff Rd., Des Plaines, IL, 60016
China/Judaic Connection, 400

Christian Schock & Associates
361 S Commonwealth Ave, Elgin, IL, 60123-7357
Midwest Political Consultant, 993

Citation Corporation
3538 Willow Valley Rd., Long Grove, IL, 60047
Citation, 724

Citizens for A Better Environment
407 S Dearborn St Ste 1775, Chicago, IL, 60605-1198
CBE Environmental Review, 374

•**Claretian Publications**
205 W. Monroe St., Chicago, IL, 60606-5033

•**Clark Boardman Callaghan & Co.**
155 Pfingsten Rd., Deerfield, IL, 60015

Clark Consulting International, Inc.
14n921 Lac Du Beatrice, Dundee, IL, 60118-3115
TechAgra News, 46

Coin Laundry Association
1315 Butterfield Rd Ste 212, Downers Grove, IL, 60515-5602
Management Guidelines, 712

Cole County Genealogical Society
PO Box 225, Charleston, IL, 61920-0225
Among the Coles, 447

College of Chaplains
1701 E Woodfield Rd Ste 311, Schaumburg, IL, 60173-5191
Tie, The, 1,052

Columbia College Center for Black Music Research
600 S. Michigan Ave., Chicago, IL, 60605-1966
CBMR Digest, 910

•**Community Renewal Society**
332 S. Michigan Ave., Siute #500, Chicago, IL, 60604-9863

Compassionate Friends, Inc.
Box 3696, Oak Brook, IL, 60522-3696
Compassionate Friends Newsletter, 411

Computer Counsel, Inc.
641 W Lake St # 403, Chicago, IL, 60661-1012
Computer Counsel, 216

•**Concrete Reinforcing Steel Inst**
933 N Plum Grove Rd, Schaumburg, IL, 60173-4758

Conservative Baptist Association of America
PO Box 66, Wheaton, IL, 60189-0066
Spectrum, 1,053

Conservative Baptist Home Mission Society
PO Box 828, Wheaton, IL, 60189-0828
Mision a las Americas Hoy, 1,053

Consumer Bankruptcy Issues
PO Box 535, Princeton, IL, 61356-0535
Consumer Bankruptcy Issues, 85

Consumer Credit Insurance Assn.
542 S Dearborn St Ste 400, Chicago, IL, 60605-1522
Consumer Credit Insurance Association Newsletter, 619

Continental Bank
231 S. La Salle St., Chicago, IL, 60697-0001
Currency, 581

Continental Grain Co., Wayne Feed Div.
10 S. Riverside Plaza, Chicago, IL, 60606-3708
Innovator, 586

Coopers & Lybrand
203 N La Salle St, Chicago, IL, 60601-1296
Focus, the Business Continuity Planning Newsletter, 838

Corn Belt Library System
PO Box 1744, Bloomington, IL, 61702-1744
Corn Belt Library System, Sum and Substance, 796

Corn Item Collectors Assn., Inc.
613 N Long St, Shelbyville, IL, 62565-1544
Bang Board, The, 551

•**Cornucopia Press**
3 Golf Ctr Ste 221, Hoffman Estates, IL, 60195-3710

Cosmedent Inc.
5419 N. Sheridan Rd, Chicago, IL, 60640-1917
Forum of Esthetic Dentistry, 269

Council for Adult & Experiential Learning
243 S Wabash Ave # 800, Chicago, IL, 60604-2302
CAEL News, 301

Council of Biology Editors, Inc.
11 S. LaSalle St., Ste. 1400, Chicago, IL, 60603-1210
CBE Views, 108

Council of Communication Management
17W703/E Butterfield Rd., Oakbrook Terrace, IL, 60181-4280
CCM Communicator, 131

Council of Logistics Management
2803 Butterfield Rd., Suite #380, Oak Brook, IL, 60521-1156
Logistics Comment, 840

Council of Planning Libraries
1313 E 60th St, Chicago, IL, 60637-2897
CPL Newsletter, 795

Courtesy Graphics Inc.
940 N Milwaukee Ave, Libertyville, IL, 60048-1934
Matthews Revelations, 18

Courtney Chronicle
RR 1 Box 77A, Pawnee, IL, 62558-9710
Courtney Chronicle, 451

Crain Communications Inc
740 N. Rush St., Chicago, IL, 60611-2590
InfoAge Marketing, 16

Crosspoint Paper Corp.
Marketing Dept., Chicago, IL, 60680
Sales Association of the Paper Industry, Bulletin, 947

Cryogenic Society of America
1033 South Blvd., Ste. 13, Oak Park, IL, 60302-2823
Cold Facts, 1,096

Cult Awareness Network
2421 W Pratt Blvd # 1173, Chicago, IL, 60645-4621
CAN News, 172

•**Czechoslovak Nat'l Council of America**
2137 S Lombard Ave Rm 202, Cicero, IL, 60650-2037

D'Arcy McNickle Center for History of American Indian, the N
60 W Walton St, Chicago, IL, 60610-3305
Meeting Ground, 406

•**Dartnell Corp.**
4660 N. Ravenswood Ave., Chicago, IL, 60640-4510

David Koss
114 Dundee Ave., Barrington, IL, 60010-4202
Schale (Westfalen) Newsletter, 466

David Lochman
PO Box 2516, Chicago, IL, 60690-2516
Ganymedia, 1,047

DeKalb County Historical & Genealogical Society
PO Box 295, Sycamore, IL, 60178-0295
Cornsilk from DeKalb County, IL, 451

De Paul Univ.
1 E Jackson Blvd, Chicago, IL, 60604-2201
De Paul Newsline, 199

Deadelvis Fan Club
PO Box 1903, Evanston, IL, 60204-1903
Deadelvis Fan Club: 50,000,000 Elvis Fans Don't Have a Clue, 604

Dearborn Financial Publishing
520 N. Dearborn St., Chicago, IL, 60610-4354
Advanced Underwriting Service, 617

Del Mar Publications
1165 Elmwood Pl., Deerfield, IL, 60015-1209
Alcoholism Briefs, 498

•**Delta Communications, Inc.**
455 N. Cityfront Plaza Dr., Chicago, IL, 60611-5593

•**Delta Dental Plans Assn.**
1515 W. 22nd St. #1200, Oak Brook, IL, 60521-2007

Delta Mu Delta
PO Box 48028, Niles, IL, 60714-0028
Delta Mu Delta Newsletter, 177

Dermatology Foundation
1560 Sherman Ave., Evanston, IL, 60201-3698
Progress in Dermatology, 885

•**Doings Newspapers, Inc.**
118 W 1st St, Hinsdale, IL, 60521-4013

Douglas County Genealogical Society
PO Box 113, Tuscola, IL, 61953-0113
Douglas Trails & Traces, 452

Douglas Furniture Corp.
PO Box 97, Bedford Park, IL, 60499-0097
Douglas Top-CS, 582

Duraclean Intl.
Duraclean Bldg., Deerfield, IL, 60015
Duraclean Journal, 582

•**Dynamic Graphics, Inc.**
6000 N Forest Park Dr, Peoria, IL, 61614-3556

Dystonia Medical Research Found.
1 E Wacker Dr Ste 2900, Chicago, IL, 60601-2001
Dystonia Medical Research Foundation Newsletter, 505

E.J. Brach
4656 W Kinzie St, Chicago, IL, 60644-2041
Brach Family News, 578

EQES, Inc.
799 Roosevelt Rd., Bldg #6, Suite 208, Glen Ellyn, IL, 60137-5925
Nuclear Plant Maintenance Newsletter, 1,002

EQ/EW Intl. U.S.A.
1021 Gregory St, Normal, IL, 61761-4236
Bullet, 416

•**ERIC EECE, Univ. of Illinois**
805 W. PA Ave., Urbana, IL, 61801

• See **MULTI-PUBLISHER INDEX** for list of publications.

Eagle Forum
PO Box 618, Alton, IL, 62002-0618
Phyllis Schafly Report, 491

East Asian Library
Univ. of Southern California, Los Angeles, IL, 90089-0182
Intl. Assn. of Orientalist Libraries Bulletin, 800

Eastern Illinois University
Publications, Charleston, IL, 61920
Old Main Line, 188

Ecological Illness Law Report
PO Box 6099, Wilmette, IL, 60091-6099
Ecological Illness Law Reports, 733

Elco Industries, Inc.
1111 Samuelson Rd # 7009, Rockford, IL, 61109-3641
Elco Extra, 583

Electric-Motive Div.
9301 E 55th St, La Grange, IL, 60525-3214
Steamliner, 599

Electronic Representatives Assn.
20 E Huron St, Chicago, IL, 60611-2706
Representor, 339

Electronic Service Dealers Assn. of Illinois
4927 W Irving Park Rd, Chicago, IL, 60641-2620
The Word, 340

Employment Research Inst., Inc.
5009 W Windsor Ave, Chicago, IL, 60630-3926
Employment Health Law & Benefits, 610

Energy Resources Center
Univ. of Ill. at Chicago, 1919 W. Taylor Street, Chicago, IL, 60612-7246
Illinois Energy Newsletter, 355

•**Enesco Corp. The Memories of Yesterday Collector's Society**
PO Box 245, Elk Grove Village, IL, 60009-0245

Europa Study Unit
512 Church Rd., #4N, Bensenville, IL, 60106
Europa News, 971

Evangelical Missions Information Service
PO Box 794, Wheaton, IL, 60189-0794
Pulse, 1,065

Evangelical Training Association
110 Bridge St # 327, Wheaton, IL, 60187-4841
Profile, 1,065

FMC Corp., Agricultural Machinery Div.
103 E. Maple St., Hoopeston, IL, 60942-1627
Comments, 580

FS Original
3024 Sunnyside Dr, Rockford, IL, 61114-6025
Original Art Report, The (TOAR), 66

F.W. Robbins & Co.
1416 W. Fletcher, Chicago, IL, 60657
On Buying or Selling a Business, 147

Fabricators & Manufacturers Assn., Intl.
833 Featherstone Rd, Rockford, IL, 61107-6301
FMA News, 848

Family Resource Coalition
200 S Michigan Ave Ste 1520, Chicago, IL, 60604-2404
Family Resource Coalition Report, 412

Farm Progress Publications
191 S Gary Ave, Carol Stream, IL, 60188-2095
Farm Tax Saver, 40

Faulkner & Gray, Inc.
300 S. Wacker Dr., 18th Fl., Chicago, IL, 60606
Automated Medical Payments News, 618

•**Fedl. Reserve Bank of Chicago**
Public Information Center, Box 834, Chicago, IL, 60690

Federal State Market News Service
PO Box 19281, Springfield, IL, 62794-9281
Grain and Livestock Market News, 827

Federation of Prosthodontic Org.
211 E Chicago Ave Ste 948, Chicago, IL, 60611-2616
Federation of Prosthodontic Organizations, Newsletter, 269

Fellowship of Brethren Genealogists
518 Miller Dr, Elgin, IL, 60123-7256
Fellowship of Brethren Genealogists Newsletter, 453

Financial Instns. Mktg. Assn.
401 North Michigan Avenue, Suite 2200, Chicago, IL, 60611-4206
Financial Marketing Newsletter, 90

Financial Sourcebooks
PO Box 313, Naperville, IL, 60566-0313
Sourcebank, 152

Follet Corporation
1391 Corporate Dr., McHenry, IL, 60050
Follet Automation News, 798

Foundation of Funeral Services
2250 E Devon Ave Ste 250, Des Plaines, IL, 60018-4509
NFFS News, 437

Free Press Newspaper Group
Box 250 Western Ave., Crystal Lake, IL, 60039
Ink Spot, 586

Frugal Finances
PO Box 243, Grayslake, IL, 60030-0243
Frugal Finances, 253

Fruitful Yield Inc.
550 Mitchell Rd., Glendale Heights, IL, 60139-2581
Fruitful Yield Nutrition & Health Update, 507

Full Court Press
660 W Grand Ave Ste 100e, Chicago, IL, 60610-3906
Team Marketing Report, 1,136

Furnas Electric Co
1000 Mckee St, Batavia, IL, 60510-1682
Contact, 337

•**Furst-McNess Co.**
120 E Clark St, Freeport, IL, 61032-3300

G.D. Searle
4711 Golf Rd., Skokie, IL, 60076-1224
Searle Circlet, 598

GSB/CHAS
5627 S Drexel Ave, Chicago, IL, 60637-1417
Doctor - Patient Studies, 873

Gardner, Carton & Douglas
Quaker Twr., 321 N. Clark St., Chicago, IL, 60610
Clipnotes, 12

Gas Research Institute
8600 W. Bryn Mawr, Chicago, IL, 60631-3562
GRID, 354

Gay, Lesbian and Bisexual Task Force
American Library Assn., 50 E. Huron St., Chicago, IL, 60611-2795
GLTF Newsletter, 444

General Commission on the Status & Role of Women
in the United Methodist Church, 1200 Davis St., Evanston, IL, 60201-4142
Flyer, 1,073

Gerald Moriarty
8657 Golfview Drive, Orland Park, IL, 60462
Moriarty Clan, 461

Ghost Research Society
PO Box 205, Dept. OC, Oak Lawn, IL, 60454-0205
Ghost Trackers Newsletter, 948

Giltspur Inc.
500 Park Blvd., Itasca, IL, 60143-1267
Bottom Line Exhibit Marketing, 11

Girth & Mirth
PO Box 14384, Chicago, IL, 60614-0384
Girth Shaking News/Midwest, 178

Gordon-Bay Group, Ltd.
770 N Halsted St Ste 205, Chicago, IL, 60622-5972
Restaurant Publicity News, 1,076

Government Finance Officers Assn.
180 N Michigan Ave Ste 800, Chicago, IL, 60601-7401
Public Investor, 683

Govt. Finance Officers Assn. of the U.S. and Canada
180 N Michigan Ave Ste 806, Chicago, IL, 60601-7401
GFOA Newsletter, 1,020

Grant Thornton
One Prudential Plz., 130 E. Randolph Dr., Ste. 700, Chicago, IL, 60601
Tax & Business Adviser, 8

Great Central Insurance Co.
PO Box 807, Peoria, IL, 61652-0807
Great Centralizer, 585

Great Lakes Sport Fishing Council
PO Box 297, Elmhurst, IL, 60126-0297
Great Lakes Basin Report, 423

Greater O'Hare Assn.
PO Box 1516, Elk Grove Village, IL, 60009-1516
Interaction, 160

Green Party USA
PO Box 9693, Downers Grove, IL, 60515-9693
Green Party Newsletter, 990

Greenhome
3705 N Spaulding Ave, Chicago, IL, 60618-4411
GreenViews, 383

HMR Publishing Co.
Box 3073, Barrington Hill, IL, 60011-3073
Alexander Paris Report, 654

Hallicrafters Company, Northrop Corp.
600 Hicks Rd, Rolling Meadows, IL, 60008-1015
Communicator, 580

Harling Communications
18-4 E. Dunde Rd., Ste. 202, Barrington, IL, 60010
National Report on Subacute Care, 569

Harmony Intl., Inc.
901 S Ashland Ave Apt 218a, Chicago, IL, 60607-4054
Acadia Club, The, 813

Harris Bank
111 W. Monroe St., Chicago, IL, 60694-0001
Investor's Advisory Service, 672

Healthcare Financial Management Assn.
Two Westbrook Corp. Ctr., #7, Westchester, IL, 60154-5700
Patient Accounts, 570

Hegeler Institute, The
315 5th St, Peru, IL, 61354-2859
Paideia, 1,092

Hi-Tech Color House
5901 North Cicero Ave., Chicago, IL, 60646
Hi-Tech Hi-Lites, 1,005

History of Anthropology Newsletter, George W. Stocking
1126 E. 59th, Univ. of Chicago, Chicago, IL, 60637-1539
History of Anthropology Newsletter, 51

Home Ventilating Institute, Div. of AMCA
30 W. University Dr., Arlington Heights, IL, 60004-1806
Home Ventilating Guide, 534

Howe & Hutton, Attorneys at Law
20 N Wacker Dr Ste 3550, Chicago, IL, 60606-3102
Howe & Hutton Report, 742

Hyatt Intl. Corp.
200 W. Madison, Chicago, IL, 60606-3414
What You Didn't Know, 575

IADA
PO Box 1288, Elmhurst, IL, 60126-8288
Automotive Newsletter, 70

ISIA Newsletter
355 W. Dundee Rd., Buffalo Grove, IL, 60089-3500
ISIA Newsletter, 1,131

Ice Skating Institute of America
355 W. Dundee, Buffalo Grove, IL, 60089-3500
Ice Skating Institute of America Newsletter, 950

•**Illinois Bankers Association**
111 N. Canal St., Chicago, IL, 60606-7299

Illinois Bar Assn.
424 S 2nd St, Springfield, IL, 62701-1779
Illinois Courts Bulletin, 743

•**Illinois Bell Tel. Co.**
225 W Randolph St, Chicago, IL, 60606-1824

Illinois College
Dr. David Koss, Prof. of Religion, Jacksonville, IL, 62650
Bush-Meeting Dutch, 449

Illinois Council of the Blind
PO Box 1336, Springfield, IL, 62705-1336
Illinois Braille Messenger, 111

Illinois Criminal Justice Info. Authority
120 S Riverside Plz Fl 10, Chicago, IL, 60606-3913
Compiler, 785

Illinois Dental Hygienists Assn.
8051 S Wabash Ave, Chicago, IL, 60619-3516
Illinois Dental Hygienists' Association, Bulletin, 270

Illinois Department of Agriculture
State Fairgrounds, Springfield, IL, 62706-0001
Illinois Grain & Livestock Market News, 42

•**Illinois Dept. of Conservation**
524 S. Second, Springfield, IL, 62701

Illinois Dept. of Employment Security
401 S. State St. - 2 South, Chicago, IL, 60605-1225
Illinois Labor Market Review, 701

Illinois Dept. of Insurance
320 W. Washington, Springfield, IL, 62767-0001
Illinois Insurance, 620

Illinois Early Childhood Intervention Clearinghouse
840 S Spring St, Springfield, IL, 62704-2652
Early Intervention, 78

Illinois Farm Bureau
1701 N. Towanda Ave, Bloomington, IL, 61701-2051
Inside News, 587

Illinois League of Savings
220 E Adams St, Springfield, IL, 62701-1123
Illinois Reporter, 585

Illinois Library Assn.
33 W Grand Ave # 301, Chicago, IL, 60610-4306
ILA Reporter, 799

Illinois Natural History Survey
Natural Resources Bldg., 607 E. Peabody, Champaign, IL, 61820
Illinois Natural History Survey, Reports, 921

* See **MULTI-PUBLISHER INDEX** for list of publications.

Illinois Power Co.
500 S 27th St, Decatur, IL, 62521-2200
Hi-Lines, 585

Illinois Psychiatric Society
20 N. Michigan Ave. , #700, Chicago, IL, 60602-4811
IPS Report, 1,014

Illinois Restaurant Assn.
350 W Ontario St Ste 7, Chicago, IL, 60610-4040
Illinois Restaurant Assn. Newsbulletin, 1,075

Illinois South Project, Inc.
PO Box 648, Rochester, IL, 62563-0648
Notes from Illinois South, 389

Illinois Soybean Checkoff Board
2422 E. Washington, Bloomington, IL, 61704
Illinois Soybean Farmer Leader Newsletter, 42

Illinois State AFL-CIO
828 S 2nd St Ste 200, Springfield, IL, 62704-2638
Illinois State Federation of Labor, 701

•Illinois State Chamber of Commerce
215 E Adams St, Springfield, IL, 62701-1122

Illinois State Historical Society
Old State Capital, Springfield, IL, 62701
Dispatch/ News, 539

Illinois State Library- Communications
474 Hewlett Bldg., Springfield, IL, 62756-0001
Insight, 800

Illinois State Univ.
6123 English Language Inst., Normal, IL, 61790-0001
Illinois TESOL/BE Newsletter, 822

Illinois Writers, Inc.
ISU English Department, Normal, IL, 61701-6901
Illinois Writers Monthly, 822

Imperial Eastman Div.
6300 W. Howard St., Chicago, IL, 60648-3492
Imperial Clevite, Inc., 586

Independent Order of Svithiod
5518 W Lawrence Ave, Chicago, IL, 60630-3412
Svithiod Journal, 182

Ingersoll Milling Machine Co.
707 Fulton Ave, Rockford, IL, 61103-4092
Ingersolletter, 586

Inn Marketing
105 E Court St, P.O. Box 1789, Kankakee, IL, 60901-3823
Inn Marketing, 1,185

Institute for Certification of Computer Professionals
2200 E Devon Ave Ste 268, Des Plaines, IL, 60018-4501
I.C.C.P. Newsletter, 224

Institute on the Church in Urban Industrial Society
4750 N Sheridan, Chicago, IL, 60640-5078
Metro Ministry News, 1,048

•Institute of Gas Technology
1700 S. Mt. Prospect Road, Des Plaines, IL, 60018

Institute of Real Estate Management
430 N. Michigan Ave., Chicago, IL, 60611-4090
CPM Aspects, 1,031

Institute on Religious Life
PO Box 41007, Chicago, IL, 60641-0007
Religious Life, 1,059

Inter-Univ. Seminar on Armed Forces & Society
Univ. of Chicago, 1126 E. 59th St., Chicago, IL, 60611-1798
IUS Newsletter, 896

International Association of Agriculture Economists
1211 W. 22nd St., Oak Brook, IL, 60521-2109
International Association of Agriculture Economists-Proceedings of Conferences, 42

International Association of Assessing Officers
130 E. Randolph, Suite 850, Chicago, IL, 60601-6217
CAAS News, 1,031

Intl. Association of Correctional Officers
1333 S. Wabash Ave #53, Box 53, Chicago, IL, 60605-2504
Keepers' Voice, 787

International Association of Ethicists
117 W. Harrison Bldg., 6th Fl. #I-104, Chicago, IL, 60605-1709
Ethics & Perspectives, 973

International Association for Orthodontics
1100 Lake St Ste 240, Oak Park, IL, 60301-1035
IAO Straight Talk, 270

•International Association for Religious Freedom
755 Massachusetts Ave., 221 Dean St, Woodstock, IL, 60098

International Baseball Rundown
PO Box 608, Glen Ellyn, IL, 60138-0608
International Baseball Rundown, 101

International College of Surgeons
1516 N Lake Shore Dr, Chicago, IL, 60610-1607
News & Notes, 882

Intl. Council of Community Churches
197 15th South LaGrang, Mokena, IL, 60448
Christian Community News, 1,062

International Cultural Enterprises, Inc.
1241 Dartmouth Ln, Deerfield, IL, 60015-4072
Worldwide Business Practices Report, 653

Intl. Customer Service Assn.
401 N. Michigan Ave., Chicago, IL, 60611-4267
ICSA News, 15

•Intl. Events Group
215 W. Institute Pl., Ste. 303, Chicago, IL, 60610-3125

International Federation of Audit Bureau of Circulations
900 N. Meacham Road, Schaumburg, IL, 60173-4968
Audit Bureau of Circulations, 127

International Fire Equipment
22155 W. Hwy. 22, Box 141, Lake Zurich, IL, 60047
United Fire Equipment Service Association Information Bulletin, 422

Intl. Foodservice Mfrs. Assn.
180 N Stetson Ave Fl 4400, Chicago, IL, 60601-6710
IFMA World, 430

International Formalwear Association
401 N. Michigan Ave., Chicago, IL, 60611-4212
Formalworks, 55

International Meat Processors Association
1211 Gerry St, Woodstock, IL, 60098-3613
International Meat Processors Assn. Newsletter, 828

International Sanitary Supply Association
7373 N Lincoln Ave, Lincolnwood, IL, 60646-1704
ISSA Today, 1,089

International Society of Fine Arts Appraisers Ltd.
701 S. Euclid Ave., Oak Park, IL, 60304-1205
Evaluator, The, 53

Intl. Soc. for Study of Multiple Personality & Dissociation
4700 W. Lake AVe., Glenvieww, IL, 60025
ISSD News, 1,014

International Star Class Yacht Racing Assn.
1545 Waukegan Rd., Glenview, IL, 60025-2185
Starlights, 114

International Wizard of Oz Club, The
PO Box 95, Kinderhook, IL, 62345-0095
Oz Trading Post, 555

•Investment Information Services, Inc.
680 North Lake Shore Drive, Ste. #2038, Chicago, IL, 60611-4402

Iroquois County Historical Society
103 W Cherry St, Watseka, IL, 60970-1524
Iroquois County Historical Society Newsletter, 457

Islamic Info Ctr. of America
PO Box 4052, Des Plaines, IL, 60016-8052
Invitation, The, 1,073

Israel Council for Israeli-Palestinian Peace
4816 Cornell Ave, Downers Grove, IL, 60515-3323
Other Israel, The, 635

J-C Communications Co., Inc
176 W. Adams St., Ste. 1732, Chicago, IL, 60603
Stark's Off-Highway Ledger, 832

J & J Postcards
213 E Lilac St, Elburn, IL, 60119-8948
Stadium Newsletter, 101

J.K. Lasser Tax Institute
PO Box 493, Mount Morris, IL, 61054-0493
J.K. Lasser Monthly Tax Letter, 1,147

J.L. Clark Mfg. Co.
2300 S 6th St, Rockford, IL, 61104-7117
J-L-C News, 587

•Jacobsen Publishing Co.
300 W Adams St Ste 835, Chicago, IL, 60606-5109

Japan Info Ctr., Consulate Gen. of Japan At Chicago
Olympia Center, Ste. 1000, 737 N. Michigan Ave., Chicago, IL, 60611
Japan Folio, 1,125

Jesuit Fathers of Della Strada
5620 S Claremont Ave, Chicago, IL, 60636-1039
Musu Zinios, 404

Jewel Food Stores
1955 W North Ave, Melrose Park, IL, 60160-1181
Flashes, 584

•John W. Bartlett
PO Box 465, Aurora, IL, 60507-0465

•Joint Council of Allergy & Immunology
PO Box 4620, Arlington Heights, IL, 60006-4620

Just Good Food
1955 W Cornelia Ave, Chicago, IL, 60657-1021
Just Good Food, 430

Kamora Culinary Club
PO Box 11172, Chicago, IL, 60611-0172
Kamora Culinary Trends, 430

Kelly P. Reynolds & Assoc.
833 W Chicago Ave Ste 200, Chicago, IL, 60622-5406
Codes and Standards, 245

Kelly-Springfield Tire Co.
Rte. 20 E., Freeport, IL, 61032
Kelly-Springfield Today, 588

Kemper National Insurance Companies
Pub. Affairs & Commisions, F-3, 1 Kemper Dr., Long Grove, IL, 60049-0001
Kemper Insurance Magazine, 588

La Leche League International, Inc.
1400 N. Meacham Rd., Schaumburg, IL, 60173
New Beginnings, 78

Labor News
PO Box 1184, Quincy, IL, 62306-1184
Labor News, 709

Labor Record
724 Railroad St, Joliet, IL, 60436-9524
Labor Record, 702

Lake Shore Club
850 N Lake Shore Dr, Chicago, IL, 60611-2428
Discus, 1,130

Lance LeVine
507 W. 43rd Place, Chicago, IL, 60609
ChokeHold, 1,130

Latin America News Update
PO Box 257247, Chicago, IL, 60625-7247
Latin America News Update, 633

Latino Institute
228 S. Wabash, Ste. 600, Chicago, IL, 60604-2314
Latino, 402

Law Bulletin Publishing Co.
415 N. State St., Chicago, IL, 60610-4674
Illinois Courts Rule Book, 743

•Lawrence Ragan Communications, Inc.
212 W.Superior St,Ste 200, Chicago, IL, 60610-3533

Lawyers' Micro Users Group Newsletter
333 N Ontario St Apt 2102b, Chicago, IL, 60611-3033
Lawyers' Micro Users Group Newsletter, 228

Lay Carmelite Order of Our Lady of Mt. Carmel
8501 Bailey Rd, Darien, IL, 60561-8418
Aylesford Carmelite Newsletter, 1,055

League of Women Voters of Illinois
332 S Michigan Ave Ste 1142, Chicago, IL, 60604-4305
Illinois Voter, 991

Learning Exchange News
2940 N Lincoln Ave, Chicago, IL, 60657-4109
Learning Exchange News, 315

Lemont Area Historical Society
PO Box 126, Lemont, IL, 60439-0126
Cornerstone, The, 451

Liberian Philatelic Society
9027 S Oakley Ave, Chicago, IL, 60620-6131
Liberian Philatelic Society Journal, 971

Libertarian Party of Illinois
PO Box 313, Chicago, IL, 60690-0313
Illinois Libertarian, 991

Library Friends of the Univ. of Illinois at Urbana-Champaign
227 Library, 1408 W. Gregory, Urbana, IL, 61801
Friendscript, 798

Lincoln Library
326 S 7th St, Springfield, IL, 62701-1691
Lincoln Library Bulletin, 803

Lithuanian American Council, Inc.
6500 S Pulaski Rd, Chicago, IL, 60629-5136
Lithuanian-American Bulletin, 404

Live Free, Inc.
PO Box 1743, Harvey, IL, 60426-7743
Directions, 1,138

Lois Libbin
PO Box 710, Atwood, IL, 61913-0710
Bridge-Covered, 551

London House
9701 W Higgins Rd Ste 770, Rosemont, IL, 60018-4720
Management Journal, 841

Lutherans Education Assn.
7400 Augusta St, River Forest, IL, 60305-1402
LEA News, 315

• See *MULTI-PUBLISHER INDEX* for list of publications.

MBH Commodity Advisors, Inc.
Northbrook Pl., 60 Revere Dr., #888, Northbrook, IL, 60062
MBH Weekly Commodity Letter, 675

Machinery Outlook
1110 W Lake Cook Rd Ste 295, Buffalo Grove, IL, 60089-1968
Machinery Outlook, 832

Manufactured Housing Newsletter
598 Shorely Dr., Barrington, IL, 60010-3340
Manufactured Housing Newsletter, 248

Maritime Retailers Assn. of America
150 E Huron St Apt 802, Chicago, IL, 60611-2912
Bearings, 113

Marketing Agents for Food Service Industry
401 N. Michigan Ave., Chicago, IL, 60611-4212
MAFSI News, 17

Mathews & Associates, Inc.
2549 W Golf Rd # 350, Hoffman Estates, IL, 60194-1165
Cheap Investor, The, 658

•**Maxwell Sroge Publishing, Inc.**
522 Forest Ave, Evanston, IL, 60202-3005

•**McIlvaine Co., The**
2970 Maria Ave., Northbrook, IL, 60062-2024

McLean County Farm Bureau
402 N Hershey Rd, Bloomington, IL, 61704-3512
McLean County Farm Bureau News, 43

Meat Sheet, Inc.
PO Box 124, Westmont, IL, 60559-0124
Meat Sheet, 853

Media Marketing Svcs.
PO Box 642, Saint Charles, IL, 60174-0642
Sportsbriefs, 1,136

Medical Library Association
6 N Michigan Ave Ste 300, Chicago, IL, 60602-4805
MLA News, 803

Metropolitan Planning Council
220 S State St Ste 1800, Chicago, IL, 60604-2001
Issue Brief, 1,021

Micro Switch, A Div. of Honeywell
11 W. Spring St., Freeport, IL, 61032-4353
Micro Switch News, 590

Midwest Chesterton News
740 Spruce St, Barrington, IL, 60010-3142
Midwest Chesterton News, 818

Midwest Universities Energy Consortium
PO Box 5478, Chicago, IL, 60680-5478
Midwest Energy Newsletter, 356

Miniature Arms Society
4910 Kilburn Ave., Rockford, IL, 61101-1746
Shooting the Breeze, 556

Mobile Post Office Society
2434 W 103rd St, Chicago, IL, 60655-1002
Transit Postmark Collector, 972

Monterey Coal Co., Div. of Exxon
PO Box 496, Carlinville, IL, 62626-0496
Conveyor, 581

Montgomery Ward
1 Montgomery Ward Plz # 8-3, Chicago, IL, 60671-0001
Forward, 584

MoorMan's Inc.
1000 N 30th St, Quincy, IL, 61305-3115
Feed Facts, 827

•**Morningstar, Inc.**
225 W. Wacker Dr., Chicago, IL, 60604-3606

Mother Cabrini League
2520 N Lakeview Ave, Chicago, IL, 60614-1804
Mother Cabrini Messenger, 1,058

Motorola Inc.
1301 E. Algonquin Rd., Roselle, IL, 60196-1078
Voice of Motorola, 602

Moultrie County Historical & Genealogical Society
PO Box 588, Sullivan, IL, 61951-0588
Moultrie County Heritage, 544

Mozambique Support Network
PO Box 2284, Chicago, IL, 60690-2284
MSN Newsletter, 633

Myasthenia Gravis Foundation
222 S. Riverside Plaza, Ste. 1540, Chicago, IL, 60606
Myasthenia Gravis Foundation Newsletter, 880

Nabisco Inc.
7300 S Kedzie Ave, Chicago, IL, 60629-3534
Nabisco News, 591

Natl. Accrediting Agency for Clinical Lab. Sciences
8410 W. Bryn Mawr Ave., Ste. 670, Chicago, IL, 60631-3402
NAACLS News, 318

Natl. Amusement Park Historical Assn.
PO Box 83, Mount Prospect, IL, 60056-0083
National Amusement Park Historical News, 369

Natl. Anti-Vivisection Society
53 W Jackson Blvd Ste 1550, Chicago, IL, 60604-3703
NAVS Bulletin, 1,201

Natl. Assn. for Advancement of Black Americans in Vocation
Southern Ill. Univ., Edwardsville, IL, 62026-0001
National Association for the Advancement of Black Americans in Vocational Education-Newsle, 321

National Association of Anorexia Nervosa & Assoc. Disorder
PO Box 7, Highland Park, IL, 60035-0007
Working Together, 532

Natl. Assn. for Bank Cost & Management Accounting
PO Box 458, Northbrook, IL, 60065-0458
NABCA Bulletin, 6

•**Natl. Assn. of Boards of Pharmacy**
700 Busse Hwy, Park Ridge, IL, 60068-2402

Natl. Assn. of Concessionaires
35 E. Wacker Dr., Ste. 1545, Chicago, IL, 60601-2202
Concessionaire, The, 427

•**Natl. Assn. of Dealers in Antiques**
PO Box 421, Barrington, IL, 60011-0421

Natl. Assn. of Enrolled Fedl. Tax Accountants
6108 N Harding Ave, Chicago, IL, 60659-3108
E.F.T.A., A Service Mark, 5

Natl. Assn. of Evangelicals
PO Box 28, Wheaton, IL, 60189-0028
United Evangelical Action, 1,066

National Assn. for the Exchange of Industrial Resources
560 McClure St, Galesburg, IL, 61401-4286
NAEIR Advantage, 319

National Association of Fire Investigators
PO Box 957257, Hoffman Estates, IL, 60195-7257
NAFI Newsletter, 421

National Association General Merchandise Representatives
401 N. Michigan Ave., Chicago, IL, 60611-4212
Representative, 21

National Association of Independent Resurfacers
5806 W 127th St, Alsip, IL, 60658-3521
N.A.I.R. News, 1,132

National Association for Perinatal Addiction Research & Ed.
200 N. Michigan Avenue, # Fl., Chicago, IL, 60601-5909
Perinatal Addiction Research & Education Update, 883

•**Natl. Assn. of Quick Printers**
401 N. Michigan Ave., Chicago, IL, 60611-4267

Natl. Assn. of Service Managers
1030 W. Higgins Rd., Ste. 109, Hoffman Estates, IL, 60195-3248
Service Management, 851

National Cattlemen's Beef Association
444 N. Michigan Ave., Chicago, IL, 60611-3978
Food & Nutrition Newsletter, 933

Natl. Center for the Laity
10 E Pearson St Ste 101, Chicago, IL, 60611-2002
Initiatives, 1,057

National Clearinghouse for Legal Services
205 W Monroe St Unit 2, Chicago, IL, 60606-5013
CCAR Pool, 720

National Coalition on Police Accountability
59 E. Van Buren, #2418, Chicago, IL, 60605
Policing by Consent, 789

National Coalition on Television Violence
PO Box 2157, Champaign, IL, 61825-2157
NCTV News, 1,168

National College of Education
2840 Sheridan Rd, Evanston, IL, 60201-1730
President's Report, 199

Natl. Consortium for Computer-Based Music Instruction
School of Music, Univ. of Illinois, Urbana, IL, 61801
NCCBMI Newsletter, 231

•**Natl. Coun. of Teachers of English**
1111 W Kenyon Rd, Urbana, IL, 61801-1096

•**Natl. Council of Teachers of English**
1111 W Kenyon Rd, Urbana, IL, 61801-1010

•**National Dairy Council**
10255 W Higgins Rd Ste 900, Rosemont, IL, 60018-5616

Natl. Easter Seal Society
230 W. Monroe Street, 18th Floor, Chicago, IL, 60606-4703
Easter Seal Communicator, 177

Natl. Employee Services & Recreation Assn.
2211 York Rd., Ste. 207, Oak Brook, IL, 60521-2371
Keynotes, 1,132

National Farm Worker Ministry
1337 W Ohio St, Chicago, IL, 60622-6430
NFWM Newsletter, 703

National Federation of Priests' Councils
1337 W Ohio St Fl 3, Chicago, IL, 60622-6430
Touchstone, 1,060

National Housewares Manufacturers Assn.
6400 Shafer Ct Ste 650, Rosemont, IL, 60018-4929
NHMA Reports, 438

Natl. Independent Bank Equipment & Systems Assn.
1411 Peterson, Park Ridge, IL, 60068-5071
NIBESA News, 95

Natl. Marine Bankers Assn.
401 N Michigan Ave Ste 1150, Chicago, IL, 60611-4205
Business of Pleasure Boats, 83

Natl. Opinion Research Center
1155 E. 60ht St., Chicago, IL, 60637-2799
National Opinion Research Center, Newsletter, 1,126

Natl. Propane Gas Assn.
1600 Eisenhower Ln, Lisle, IL, 60532-2167
NPGA Reports, 356

National Provisioner, Inc.
15 W Huron St, Chicago, IL, 60610-3812
Meat Price Report, 1,075

•**National Research Bureau**
150 N. Wacher Drive, Chicago, IL, 60601

•**National Safety Council**
1121 Spring Lake Dr., Itasca, IL, 60143-3201

Natl. Sash & Door Jobbers Assn.
2400 E. Devan Ave., Des Plaines, IL, 60018
National Sash and Door Jobbers Association Newsletter, 248

National Selected Morticians
5 Revere Dr., Ste. 340, Northbrook, IL, 60062-8009
National Selected Morticians Bulletin, 437

National Ski Retailers Association
1699 Wall St., Mt. Prospect, IL, 60056-5762
NSRA Newsletter, 1,113

Natl. Society for the Prevention of Blindness
500 E. Remington Rd., Schaumburg, IL, 60173-4557
Prevent Blindness, 112

National Spiritual Assembly of the Bahai's of the US
536 Sheridan Rd, Wilmette, IL, 60091-2849
Bahai News, 1,052

National Sporting Goods Assn.
1699 Wall St., Mount Prospect, IL, 60056-5780
Team Lineup, 1,136

Natl. Steel Corp.
20th & State, Granite City, IL, 62040-4622
Mill, 590

Natl. Terrazo & Mosaic Association
3166 Des Plaines Ave., Suite 132, Des Plaines, IL, 60018-4204
Terrazzo Topics, 625

Natl. Toothpick Holder Collectors Society
PO Box 204, Eureka, IL, 61530-0204
Toothpick Bulletin, 556

National Truck Leasing System
15450 Summit Ave., Suite 300, Villa Park, IL, 60181-3976
Nationalease News, 1,193

Natl. Tumors Registrars Assn., Inc.
505 E. Hawley St., Mundelein, IL, 60060-2458
Abstract, 497

Natl. Waterbed Retailers Assn.
36 S State St Ste 1506, Chicago, IL, 60603-2606
Flotation News, 1,086

Native American Educational Services College
2838 W. Peterson, Chicago, IL, 60659
Native Child Advocate, 170

Nelson B. Heller & Associates
1910 1st St Ste 303, Highland Park, IL, 60035-3146
Internet Strategies for Education, 314

•**New Consumer Institute, Inc.**
PO Box 51, Wauconda, IL, 60084

•**Newberry Library**
Renaissance Center, 60 W. Walton St., Chicago, IL, 60610-3380

Newscast/Nielsen Media Research
Nielsen Plaza, Northbrook, IL, 60062
Directory of Advertising & Public Relations, 1,167

North American Assn., Educational Negotiators
PO Box 4342, Springfield, IL, 62708-4342
NAEN Bulletin, 1,091

* See ***MULTI-PUBLISHER INDEX*** for list of publications.

North American Building Material Distribution Association
401 N Michigan Ave Ste 2200, Chicago, IL, 60611-4206
Journal, The, 247

North American Society of Adlerian Psychology
65 E Wacker Pl Ste 400, Chicago, IL, 60601-7203
North American Society of Adlerian Psychology, Newsletter, 1,016

North Star Mission
1414 S. Independence, Chicago, IL, 60623
Star News, 998

North Suburban Genealogical Society
C/o Winnetka Public Library,, 768 Oak St., Winnetka, IL, 60093
Newsletter of the North Suburban Genealogical Society, 462

Northeastern Illinois Planning Commission
222 S. Riverside Plaza, Ste. 1800, Chicago, IL, 60606-6001
Planning in Northeastern Illinois, 1,023

•Northern Illinois University Education Dept.
Office of Public Affairs NIU, DeKalb, IL, 60115

•Northern Trust Co.
50 S. La Salle St., Chicago, IL, 60675-0001

Northwestern University Archives
Deering Library, Evanston, IL, 60201
Chicago Area Archivists Newsletter, 795

Northwestern University, Dental School
311 E Chicago Ave # 10-305, Chicago, IL, 60611-3008
Bridge, 268

Northwestern Univ. Library Council
1935 Sheridan Rd, Evanston, IL, 60208-0821
Footnotes, 798

Northwestern Univ. Library, Special Collections
1935 Sheridan Rd, Evanston, IL, 60201-2924
Women's Collection Newsletter, 813

Northwestern Univ. Library, Staff Association
1935 Sheridan Rd, Evanston, IL, 60201-2924
Lantern's Core, 801

Northwestern University's Transportation Center
1936 Sheridan Rd, Evanston, IL, 60208-0849
Newsline, 1,179

Norwood Securities
6134 N Milwaukee Ave, Chicago, IL, 60646-3894
Norwood Commodity Fund Index, 680

Numisco Rare Coins
1423 W Fullerton Ave, Chicago, IL, 60614-2011
Coin Quote, 927

Nutrition for Optimal Health Assn.
PO Box 380, Winnetka, IL, 60093-0380
NOHA News, 934

Oberweis Securities, Inc.
1 Constitution Dr., Aurora, IL, 60506
Oberweis Report, 681

•Office of International Criminal Justice
1333 S Wabash Ave # 53, Chicago, IL, 60605-2504

Ogle County Illinois Genealogical Soc.
PO Box 251, Oregon, IL, 61061-0251
Ogle County Links Newsletter, 463

Olney Central College
305 N West St, Olney, IL, 62450-1043
Knightline, 199

Optima Investment Research, Inc.
111 W. Jackson, 15th Fl., Chicago, IL, 60604
Financial & Economic Research, 664

Overground Railroad
722 Monroe St, Evanston, IL, 60202-2613
Overground Railroad: Telegraph News, 636

P.G. Springer
206 N Woods St, Urbana, IL, 61801-2620
Men & Wife Newsletter, 413

•PJS Publications, Inc.
2 News Plaza, PO Box 1790, Peoria, IL, 61656

•P.M. Haeger & Assoc.
500 N Michigan Ave Ste 1400, Chicago, IL, 60611-3703

PanAngling Ltd.
180 N. Michigan Ave., Chicago, IL, 60601-7480
PanAngler, 606

People United to Save Humanity P.U.S.H/Operation Push
PO Box 5432, Chicago, IL, 60680-5432
People United to Save Humanity P.U.S.H/Operation Push, 996

People's Alliance on Central America
284 Illinois Union, Univ. of ILL., 1401 W. Green, Urbana, IL, 61801-7321
PACA News, 636

Petersen Aluminum Corp.
965 Estes Ave, Elk Grove Village, IL, 60007-4905
Petersen Aluminum Corp. News, 892

Philip Lesly Co.
155 N Harbor Dr Apt 5311, Chicago, IL, 60601-7326
Managing the Human Climate, 859

Phycological Society of America
Dept. Biological Sciences, 1036 W. Belden - DePaul Univ., Chicago, IL, 60614
Phycological Newsletter, 121

Physician's & Scientists Publishing
PO Box 435, Glenview, IL, 60025-0435
New Developments in Medicine & Drug Therapy, 882

Pi Kappa Lamda Music Honor Society
Northwestern U. Music School, 711 Elgin Rd., Evanston, IL, 60208-0001
Pi Kappa Lambda Newsletter, 916

Piatt County Historical Society
Box 111, Monticello, IL, 61856-0111
Piatt County Historical Society, 464

Pioneer Clubs
PO Box 788, Wheaton, IL, 60189-0788
In Contact, 1,048

Plain Talk Investor, Inc.
1500 Skokie Blvd Ste 203, Northbrook, IL, 60062-4113
Plain Talk Investor, 682

The Planning Forum
435 N. Michigan Ave., Ste. 1700, Chicago, IL, 60611-4008
Network, 842

Polish Arts Club of Chicago
5378 N Lynch Ave, Chicago, IL, 60630-1443
Polish Arts Club Bulletin, 407

Polish Genealogical Society
984 N Milwaukee Ave, Chicago, IL, 60622-4101
Polish Genealogical Society Bulletin, 464

Power Transmission Distributors Assn.
6400 Schafer Ct., Rosemont, IL, 60018-4909
Transmissions Newsletter, 1,027

Presbyterian
1753 W Congress Pky, Chicago, IL, 60612-3809
Alumni Newsletter, Presbyterian, 866

Preservation Section, Soc. of American Archivists
2104 W Addison St, Chicago, IL, 60618-6124
Infinity, 799

Prestressed Concrete Institute
175 W Jackson Blvd Ste 1859, Chicago, IL, 60604-2801
Prestressed Concrete Institute, Bridge Bulletin, 249

Pro-Life Action League, Inc.
6160 N. Cicero Ave., Chicago, IL, 60646-4308
Pro-Life Action League-Action News, 1,121

Professional Audio Video Retailers Assn.
10 E 22nd St Ste 310, Lombard, IL, 60148-6191
Parascope, 1,128

Prospects Report
PO Box 6193, Evanston, IL, 60204-6193
Prospects Report, 101

Psychotronic Film Society
PO Box 14683, Chicago, IL, 60614-0683
It's Only A Movie, 369

Public Safety Employment Institute, Inc.
5519 N Cumberland Ave Ste 1008, Chicago, IL, 60656-1480
Corrections Legal Defense Quarterly, 785

Public Safety Personnel Research Institute, Inc.
5519 N Cumberland Ave Ste 1008, Chicago, IL, 60656-1480
Fire and Police Personnel Reporter, 700

Public Works Historical Society
1525 East 53rd Street, Chicago, IL, 60615-4530
Public Works History, 547

Publications Plus
655 Rockland Road, Suite 7, Lake Bluff, IL, 60044-1700
ReCareering Newsletter, 348

Pun American Newsletter
1165 Elmwood Pl, Deerfield, IL, 60015-1209
Pun American Newsletter, 605

•QEC & S
4057 North Drake, Chicago, IL, 60618-2219

Quill Corp.
100 Schelter Rd, Lincolnshire, IL, 60069-3621
The Quill Pen Pal, 472

•Quoin Publishing
800 W Huron St Ste 3n, Chicago, IL, 60622-5973

RELO/Inter City Relocation Service
111 E. Wacker Drive, #220, Chicago, IL, 60601
Relocator, 1,039

R&R Newkirk
8695 Archer Ave Ste 10, Willow Springs, IL, 60480-1260
Charitable Giving Tax Service, 966

Rail Mart
502 River Bluff Dr, Carpentersville, IL, 60110-2825
Rail Mart, The, 1,030

Railroad Club of Chicago
PO Box 8292, Chicago, IL, 60680-8292
Railroad Capital, 1,030

Real Estate Aviation Chapter
5440 St. Charles Rd., Berkeley, IL, 60163-1231
Flight Lines, 1,033

Real Estate Educators Assn.
11 S. LaSalle St., Ste. 1400, Chicago, IL, 60603-1210
REEAction, 1,037

Real Estate Research Corp.
2 N La Salle St Ste 400, Chicago, IL, 60602-3703
RERC Real Estate Report, 1,037

•Remy Publishing Co.
350 W Hubbard St # 440, Chicago, IL, 60610-4011

Resort Property Owners Assn.
PO Box 2395, Northbrook, IL, 60065-2395
Resort Reports, 1,039

Respiratory Nursing Society
4700 W. Lake Ave., Glenview, IL, 60025
Perspectives in Respiratory Nursing, 524

Robbins Trading Co.
222 S. Riverside Plz., Chicago, IL, 60606-5808
Futures Market Alert, 90

•Rockford Institute
934 N Main St, Rockford, IL, 61103-7061

Rockford Newspapers Inc.
99 E State St, Rockford, IL, 61104-1004
Byline, 579

Rosie Wells Enterprises
Rr 1 Box 255, Canton, IL, 61520-9730
Weekly Collectors' Gazette, 186

Rusty Iron Monthly
PO Box 342, Sandwich, IL, 60548-0342
Rusty Iron Monthly, 54

SPSS Inc.
444 N Michigan Ave, Chicago, IL, 60611-3962
Keywords, 227

Safety-Kleen Corporation
1000 North Randall Road, Elgin, IL, 60123
Total Compliance, 846

St. Paul's Episcopal Church
411 Washington St, Pekin, IL, 61554-4288
Episcopal Expressions, 1,067

Scranton Gillette Communications, Inc.
380 E. Northwest Hwy., Des Plaines, IL, 60016-2282
AV Guide Newsletter, 853

Screen Manufacturers Assn.
Fitzgerald Corp., 3950 Lake Shre Dr. #502-A, Chicago, IL, 60613-3431
Screening Industry, 851

Sealed Insulating Glass Manufacturers Assn.
401 N. Michigan Ave., Chicago, IL, 60611-4212
SIGMA Newsletter, 249

•Sears Roebuck
Sears Tower Dept. 703, Bsc, #40-09, Chicago, IL, 60684-0001

Serra Intl.
65 E Wacker Pl Ste 1210, Chicago, IL, 60601-7203
Serran, 1,051

Shelf Presence
740 Shady Grove Ln, Buffalo Grove, IL, 60089-1425
Shelf Presence, 946

Shopper
924 E 162nd St, South Holland, IL, 60473-2442
Shopper, 24

Showmen's League of America
300 W Randolph St, Chicago, IL, 60606-1705
Showmen's League News Flashes, 370

Siegel Trading Co, Inc.
118 N Clinton St Ste 200, Chicago, IL, 60661-2308
Siegel Weekly Newsletter, 686

Sigma Tau Delta
Northern IL Univ., English Dep, DeKalb, IL, 60115
Sigma Tau Delta Newsletter, 825

Skil Corp.
4300 W Peterson Ave, Chicago, IL, 60646-5928
Skil Extra, 598

Skysail, Inc.
5435 S. Ellis Avenue, Chicago, IL, 60615
Jack London Newsletter, 822

•Slavic Gospel Association
6151 Commonwealth Dr., Loves Park, IL, 61111

• See **MULTI-PUBLISHER INDEX** for list of publications.

* See **MULTI-PUBLISHER INDEX** for list of publications.

•**Ashby Newsletter**
1013 Illinois St, Bicknell, IN, 47512-3000

Asian/Pacific American Librarians Assn.
Ball State University Library, Muncie, IN, 47306-0001
Asian/Pacific American Librarians Assn. Newsletter, 793

Association of College Unions-International
400 E. 7th St., Bloomington, IN, 47405-3085
Union Wire, 334

Assn. of Fraternity Advisors , inc
3901 W 86th St Ste 390, Indianapolis, IN, 46268-1702
Perspectives, 209

Association for Living Historical Farms
Conner Prairie, 13400 Allisonville Rd., Fishers, IN, 46038
Bulletin-Association for Living Historical farms and Agricultural Museums, 903

Auto Craft
Rr 4 Box 116, Alexandria, IN, 46001-9413
CMI News (Complete Mercury Interest), 71

Babbitt & Associates
PO Box 7117, Evansville, IN, 47719-7117
Downscaling, 662

Berry Newsletter
1013 Illinois St, Bicknell, IN, 47512-3000
Berry Newsletter, 448

Bloomington Cooperative Services
PO Box 821, Bloomington, IN, 47402-0821
Blooming Foods, 426

Bonsib Agencies Inc.
PO Box 6152, Bloomington, IN, 47407-6152
Lobby Law Update, 488

Bowen Newsletter
1013 Illinois St, Bicknell, IN, 47512-3000
Bowen Newsletter, 449

CINDAS
2595 Yeager Rd, West Lafayette, IN, 47906-1398
Thermophysics and Electronics Newsletter, 979

Cast, Hursh & Assoc.
4601 N. Wash. Rd, Ft. Wayne, IN, 46804
Medical Business Review, 517

Center for Instructional Services
Purdue Univ., W. Lafayette, IN, 47907
C/S Newsletter, 303

Central Eurasian Studies
Indiana Univ., Bloomington, IN, 47405
Permanent International Altaistic Conference Newsletter, 824

Chas. Pfizer
PO Box 88, Terre Haute, IN, 47808-0088
Vigo View, 602

Choosing Home
PO Box 15868, Fort Wayne, IN, 46885-5868
Choosing Home, 411

Christian Missionary Fellowship
PO Box 501020, Indianapolis, IN, 46250-6020
Impact, 1,064

•**Church World Service**
28606 Phillips St, Elkhart, IN, 46514-1239

Clover Ann Hankins
5373 Sunset Ave, Indianapolis, IN, 46208-2538
Strange Branches & Twigs, 467

Communications Media Group, Inc.
Box 50188, Indianapolis, IN, 46250
Christian MoneyLetter, The, 659

Conner Prairie
13400 Allisonville Rd, Fishers, IN, 46038-3457
Alhfam Bulletin, 902

Cooking Contest Chronicle
Box 10792, Merrillville, IN, 46411-0792
Cooking Contest Chronicle, 427

Cottontail Pubs.
79 Drakes Ridge Rd., Bennington, IN, 47011-1802
Presidents' Journal, 547

Cranial Academy
3500 Depauw Blvd Ste 1080, Indianapolis, IN, 46268-1136
Cranial Letter, 503

Cuban American Legal Defense & Education Fund
2119 Webster St, Fort Wayne, IN, 46802-6433
Hispanic Newsletter, 742

Cushwa Center for the Study of American Catholicism
614 Hesburgh Library, Notre Dame, IN, 46556-5629
American Catholic Studies Newsletter, 1,055

DRIP Investor
7412 Calumet Ave, Hammond, IN, 46324-2622
DRIP Investor, 661

Daniel D. Busby
PO Box 50188, Indianapolis, IN, 46250-0188
Pastor's Tax & Money, 1,050

David Lantz, Government Affairs Consultant
7802 Cannonade Dr, Indianapolis, IN, 46217-4302
Indiana Issues, 487

Disciples of Christ
PO Box 1986, Indianapolis, IN, 46206-1986
Issues & Concerns, 173

•**Disciples Peace Fellowship**
PO Box 1986, Indianapolis, IN, 46206-1986

•**Dow Theory Forecasts, Inc.**
7412 Calumet Ave, Hammond, IN, 46324-2622

Dresser Industries, Inc.
900 W Mount St, Connersville, IN, 47331-1675
Blower Outlet, 578

•**Dunn & Hargitt**
22 N. 2nd St., Ste. 620, Lafayette, IN, 47902-0620

ERIC Clearinghouse for Social Studies/Social Science Educati
Univ. of Indiana, Bloomington, 2805 E. 10th St., Suite 120, Bloomington, IN, 47408
Keeping Up, 314

•**Elton Stephens Investments**
4016 S Michigan St, South Bend, IN, 46614-2544

•**Emergency Management Group**
1508 E 86th St., Ste 315, Indianapolis, IN, 46240-1986

Evansville Vanderburgh County Public Library
22 SE 5th St., Evansville, IN, 47708-1604
River City Library Times, 809

Evansville-Vanderburgh School Corp.
1 SE 9th St, Evansville, IN, 47708-1821
Kaleidoscope, 314

Fellowship of Assocs. of Medical Evangelism
PO Box 688, Columbus, IN, 47202-0688
Spreading the Fame of Christ, 1,066

Finnsheep Breeders Association
PO Box 512, Zionsville, IN, 46077-0512
Finnsheep Short Tales, 827

Fort Wayne Museum of Art
311 E Main St, Fort Wayne, IN, 46802-1997
Fort Wayne Museum of Art-Newsletter, 64

Fort Wayne State Developmental Center
4900 Saint Joe Rd, Fort Wayne, IN, 46835-3275
Centerpiece, 563

Fort Wayne Women's Bureau, Inc.
303 E Washington Blvd, Fort Wayne, IN, 46802-3123
WomensWord, 1,214

Free Methodist Pub. House
502 E Winona Ave, Warsaw, IN, 46580-4444
Railroad Evangelist, 1,073

Friends of the Third World, Inc.
611 W Wayne St, Fort Wayne, IN, 46802-2125
Alternative Trading News, 626

Frog Pond, The
PO Box 193, Beech Grove, IN, 46107-0193
Director, 552

Fulton County Historical Society, Inc.
37 E. 375 North, Rochester, IN, 46975-8384
Indian Awareness Center Newsletter, 542

Gingerbread House Pubs.
11216 N 500 E, Ossian, IN, 46777-9728
Cook's Notebook, 427

Goodwill Industries of Central Indiana
1635 W Michigan St, Indianapolis, IN, 46222-3852
Working Times, 603

Goshen Biblical Seminary
3003 Benham Ave, Elkhart, IN, 46517-1999
AMBS Bulletin, 199

Hanover College
Office of Public Relations, P.O. Box #108, Hanover, IN, 47243
Hill Thoughts, 200

Hardware Assn. of the Carolinas & Virginia
5822 W. 74th St., Indianapolis, IN, 46278-1756
HACV, 496

Harrington/Herrington Kin
1013 Illinois St, Bicknell, IN, 47512-3000
Harrington/Herrington Kin, 455

Henry County Historical Soc.
606 S 14th St, New Castle, IN, 47362-3339
Henry County Historicalog, 456

Hoosier Auto Racing Fans
616 S Fuller Dr, Indianapolis, IN, 46241-2232
Hoosier Auto Racing Fans-Newsletter, 1,131

Hoosier Environmental Pubs.
801 Congressional Blvd # 200, Carmel, IN, 46032-5650
Radon News Digest, 392

Hudson Institute
Herman Kahn Center, 5395 Emerson Way, Box 26-919, Indianapolis, IN, 46226
Hudson Institute Report, 991

ITT, Aerospace/Optical Div.
PO Box 3700, Fort Wayne, IN, 46801-3700
A/OD News, 575

Indiana Chapter Special Libraries Assn., C/o IU Sch. Med. Li
635 Barnhill, Indianapolis, IN, 46223-0001
Indiana Slant, 799

Indiana Farmers Mutual Ins.
10 W. 106th St., P.O. Box 527-, Indianapolis, IN, 46206-0527
Agents News, 576

Indiana Historical Bureau
140 N Senate Ave Rm 408, Indianapolis, IN, 46204-2207
Indiana History Bulletin, 542

Indiana Historical Society
315 W Ohio St, Indianapolis, IN, 46202-3210
Black History News & Notes, 536

Indiana Minority Business Report
8054 Harvest Ln, Indianapolis, IN, 46256-3401
Indiana Minority Business Report, 141

Indiana Restaurant Assn., Inc.
115 W. Washington St. #1165-, Indianapolis, IN, 46204-3407
Hoosier Chef, 1,075

Indiana Secondary School Administrators
PO Box 503250, Indianapolis, IN, 46250-8250
Indiana Association of School Principals, 1,091

Indiana State Bar Assn.
230 E. Ohio St., Indianapolis, IN, 46204-2199
Addendum, 713

Indiana State Nurses Assn.
2915 N High School Rd, Indianapolis, IN, 46224-2969
ISNA Bulletin, 929

Indiana Transportation Museum
Forest Park, Box 83, Noblesville, IN, 46060-0083
Tracks, 549

Indiana University
Publications, Bloomington, IN, 47405-6801
Drosophila, 1,096

Indiana Univ. Bloomington Libraries
Main Library, C-2, Bloomington, IN, 47405
Library Associate, 801

Indiana University, Chemistry Dept.
QCPE Creative Arts Bldg. #18, Bloomington, IN, 47405
Current Awareness Profile on Quantum Chemistry, 164

Indiana University Department of Afro-American Studies
Memorial Hall #32, Bloomington, IN, 47405
Black Camera, 419

Indiana Univ. Libraries
Lib Admin. Library C-Z, Bloomington, IN, 47405
Faculty Newsletter IUB Libraries, 797

Indiana University Northwest
3400 Broadway, Gary, IN, 46408-1101
By the Numbers, 852

Indiana Univ. School of Library and Information Science
Indiana Univ., Main Library, Bloomington, IN, 47405
Vibrations, 812

Indianapolis District Dental Society
3901 N Meridian St Ste 10, Indianapolis, IN, 46208-4026
IDDS Newsletter, 270

Indianapolis-Marion County Public Library
PO Box 211, Indianapolis, IN, 46206-0211
Reading in Indianapolis, 808

Indianapolis Zoological Society, Inc.
1200 W Washington St, Indianapolis, IN, 46222-4552
Indianapolis Zoo, 1,217

•**Insight Group**
PO Box 383, Noblesville, IN, 46060-0383

Insurance Forum, Inc.
PO Box 245, Ellettsville, IN, 47429-0245
Insurance Forum, 621

Intercollegiate Music Council, Inc.
Wabash College, Dept of Music, Crawfordsville, IN, 47933
Quodlibet, 916

International Carnival Glass Assn.
PO Box 306, Mentone, IN, 46539-0306
Town Pump, 557

Intl. Group of Agencies & Bureaus
6845 Parkdale Pl., Ste. A, Indianapolis, IN, 46254-5605
Bureau Talk, 854

* See **MULTI-PUBLISHER INDEX** for list of publications.

Irish Setter Club of American
12318 Hwy. 62, Charlestown, IN, 47111-1634
Irish Setter Club of American, Memo to Members, 280

Jafari Intl.
PO Box 192, Osceola, IN, 46561-0192
Hitch, 943

Jenny Wren Press
11 E. Main St., P.O. Box 505, Mooresville, IN, 46158
Children's Historical Newsletter, 538

Kappa Delta Pi
PO Box A, West Lafayette, IN, 47906-0576
Scroll & Stylus, 330

•**Kiwanis International**
3636 Woodview Trce, Indianapolis, IN, 46268-3196

Lafayette Instrument Co.
PO Box 5729, Lafayette, IN, 47903-5729
Polygraph Update, 175

Link-Belt Div., FMC Corp.
220 S Belmont Ave, Indianapolis, IN, 46222-4210
Link-Belt Today, 589

Listening Inc.
8716 Pine Ave, Gary, IN, 46403-1441
Stepfamilies & Beyond, 416

•**Lutheran Deaconess Association**
Center for Diaconal Ministry, 1304 Laporte Ave., Valparaiso, IN, 46383

ME
448 N Mitchner Ave, Indianapolis, IN, 46219-5116
Humor Digest and Conversation Piece - Chuckles & Grins, 604

Mary Rucker Snyder
1516 Elliott Ave, Jeffersonville, IN, 47130-4502
Rucker Ruckus, 466

Medical Education & Research Foundation
1100 Waterway Blvd, Indianapolis, IN, 46202-2156
Medical Update, 518

Metropolitan Indianapolis Board of Realtors(R), Inc.
1912 N Meridian St, Indianapolis, IN, 46202-1304
Realtor(R) Voice, The, 1,038

Miles Inc.
1127 Myrtle St # 40, Elkhart, IN, 46514-2201
Miles Alkalizer, 590

Milestone Car Society Inc.
PO Box 24612, Indianapolis, IN, 46224-0612
Mile Post, 554

Mongolia Society
322 Goodbody Hall, Indiana University, Bloomington, IN, 47405-2401
Mongolia Survey, 261

•**Mull Pubs.**
PO Box 11133, Indianapolis, IN, 46201-0133

•**Muncie Public Library**
301 E Jackson St, Muncie, IN, 47305-1878

Natl. Assn. of Canada Dry Franchise Bottlers
1535 Southbrook Dr, South Bend, IN, 46614-1549
Canada Dry Crown, 103

Natl. Birman Fanciers News
8507 N Illinois St, Indianapolis, IN, 46260-2321
National Birman Fanciers News, 157

Natl. Catholic Band Assn.
PO Box 1023, Notre Dame, IN, 46556-1023
NCBA Newsletter, 915

Natl. Council for Black Studies
Memorial Hall West 105, Indiana Univ., Bloomington, IN, 47405
Voices in Black Studies, 335

Natl. Farm-City Council, Inc.
3636 Woodview Trce, Indianapolis, IN, 46268-1168
Farm City Week Newsletter, 40

Natl. Fed. of State Poetry Societies
C/O Kinnaman, RR 3, Box 348, Alexandria, IN, 46001
Strophes, 984

Natl. Friends of Public Broadcasting
620 Folcroft Ct, Indianapolis, IN, 46234-2103
National Friends of Public Broadcasting Newsletter, 124

Natl. Interfraternity Foundation
3901 W 86th St Ste 380, Indianapolis, IN, 46268-1799
Interfraternity Bulletin, 313

National Precast Concrete Association
10333 N Meridian St Ste 272, Indianapolis, IN, 46290-1081
National Precaster, 248

Natl. Society of Insurance Premium Auditors
PO Box 68401, Indianapolis, IN, 46268-0401
National Auditor, The, 622

Noble County Historical Society
PO Box 152, Albion, IN, 46701-0152
Pioneer Echoes, 464

North American Wildlife Park Foundation Inc.
Wolf Park, Rt 1, Battle Ground, IN, 47920
Wolf Park News, 50

Northwest Indiana Dental Society
1205 W Lincoln Hwy Ste 7a, Merrillville, IN, 46410-5336
Northwest Indiana Dental Society Newsletter, 271

Notre Dame Alumni Assoc.
201 Main Bldg., Notre Dame, IN, 46556
Alumni, the Newsletter for Notre Dame Alumni, 188

Orange County Genealogical Society
PO Box 344, Paoli, IN, 47454-0344
Orange Peelings, 463

Organization of American Historians
112 N Bryan Ave, Bloomington, IN, 47408-4141
OAH Newsletter, 546

Orland Stanley
RR 2 Box 97, Sullivan, IN, 47882-9612
Joseph Lines, 458

Owen County Historical & Genealogical Society
110 E Market St, Spencer, IN, 47460-1867
Owen County History & Genealogy, 464

Parent Care, Inc.
9041 Colgate St, Indianapolis, IN, 46268-1210
Parent Care News Brief, 78

Patriots for Liberty
PO Box 334, Rochester, IN, 46975-0334
Patriots for Liberty, 1,150

•**Peyron Associates, Inc.**
PO Box 175, Sellersburg, IN, 47172-0175

Phi Delta Kappa, Inc.
8th & Union, Box 789, Bloomington, IN, 47402
News, Notes and Quotes, 180

Phi Lambda Upsilon
Wabash College, Dept. of Chemistry, Crawfordsville, IN, 47933
Phi Lambda Upsilon Register, 1,099

Priority Parenting Pubs.
830 S Union St, Warsaw, IN, 46580-4701
Priority Parenting, 415

Professional Ins. Comm. of America
C/O Natl. Assn. of Mutual Ins., 3601 Vincennes Rd. Box 68700, Indianapolis, IN, 46268-0700
Mutual Piper, The, 622

Purdue Musical Organizations
Edward Elliott Hall of Music, Purdue Univ., W. Lafayette, IN, 47906
P.M.O. Notes, 916

Purdue University Agriculture Dept.
Dept. Agricultural Engineering, 1146 Ag. Engineering Bldg., West Lafayette, IN, 47907
Breaking New Ground, 276

Purdue University Civil Engineering Dept.
Civil Engineering Bldg., W. Lafayette, IN, 47907
Environmental Engineering News, 380

Purdue University, Dept. of English
1356 Heavilon, W. Lafayette, IN, 47907-1356
Writing Lab Newsletter, 336

Purdue Univ. Pharmacy Library
Pharmacy Bldg., W. Lafayette, IN, 47907
Purdue University, Pharmacy, Nursing & Health Sciences Library Notes, 808

Quilt Peddler
PO Box 1485, Valparaiso, IN, 46384-1485
Quilt Peddler, 922

•**Report Communications**
9595 Whitley Dr Ste 100, Indianapolis, IN, 46240-1308

Robbins Assocs. Management Service, Inc.
21 Bowman Ct, Greenfield, IN, 46140-2508
Personnel News for School Systems, 1,093

Robert W. Golobish
64 King Dr., Indianapolis, IN, 46260
Future Watch, 990

•**Rough Notes Company, Inc.**
11690 Technology Dr., Carmel, IN, 46032-5600

•**Rutkowski & Associates, Inc.**
PO Box 15250, Evansville, IN, 47716-0250

Ryukyu Philatelic Specialty Society
C/O Howard Wallace, Box 653, South Bend, IN, 46624
Dragon's Digest, The, 971

Sailrite Enterprises
305 W Van Buren St, Columbia City, IN, 46725-2039
Sailrite Newsletter, 114

Saint Meinrad College
Publications, Saint Meinrad, IN, 47577
St. Meinrad Newsletter, 188

Slavic Dept.
Indiana Univ., Bloomington, IN, 47405
Slovak Studies Assn. Newsletter, 409

Society of Indiana Archivists
Univ. Archives Indiana State, Univ., Terre Haute, IN, 47809-0001
SIA Newsletter, 809

South Bend Genealogical Society
PO Box 1222, South Bend, IN, 46624-1222
South Bend Area Genealogical Society, 467

Southern Indiana Genealogical Soc.
PO Box 665, New Albany, IN, 47151-0665
Southern Indiana Genealogical Society Quarterly, 467

State Life Insurance Co
PO Box 406, Indianapolis, IN, 46206-0406
State Life Bulletin, 625

Sullivan County Historical Society
PO Box 326, Sullivan, IN, 47882-0326
Sullivan County Historical Society Newsletter, 468

Synergetic Audio Concepts
Rr 1 Box 267, Norman, IN, 47264-9777
Syn-Aud-Con Newsletter, 1,128

Taylor Univ.
500 W. Read AVe., Upland, IN, 46989
Profile, 188

U.S.A. Gymnastics Federations
201 S Capitol Ave Ste 300, Indianapolis, IN, 46225-1066
National Team News & Digest, 1,133

United Duroc Swine Registry
1769 Us Highway 52 W # 2347, West Lafayette, IN, 47906-5308
Duroc News, 827

U.S. Auto Club
4910 W 16th St, Indianapolis, IN, 46224-5703
USAC News, 1,137

U.S. Office
PO Box 90410, Indianapolis, IN, 46290-0410
Co-Operatively Speaking, 305

United Student Aid Funds, Inc.
PO Box 6180, Indianapolis, IN, 46206-6180
United Student Aid Funds Newsletter, 334

University & College Labor Education Association
Indiana Univ., Poplars 630, Div. of Labor Studies, Bloomington, IN, 47405
Labor Studies Forum, 702

Vigo County Public Library
Reference, 1 Library Sq., Terre Haute, IN, 47807
Vigo County Public Library Staff Bulletin, 812

Vincennes Univ.
1002 N 1st St, Vincennes, IN, 47591-1504
Views from VU, 188

WebWords Press Inc.
PO Box 1145, New Albany, IN, 47151-1145
Women's Recovery Network, 1,214

Wilderness Medical Society
PO Box 2463, Indianapolis, IN, 46206-2463
Wilderness Medicine Letter, 889

World Christian Women's Fellowship
130 E Washington Street, Indianapolis, IN, 46206
World CWF News, 1,066

World Council for Gifted & Talented Children
Purdue University, 1446 S. Campus Courts, Bldg. G, West Lafayette, IN, 47907
World Gifted, 336

World Missionary Press, Inc.
PO Box 120, New Paris, IN, 46553-0120
World Missionary Press News, 1,052

Yoder Newsletter
PO Box 594, Goshen, IN, 46527-0594
Yoder Newsletter, 470

Zane Grey's West Society
708 Warwick Ave, Fort Wayne, IN, 46825-5653
Zane Grey Review, The, 826

Zeta Beta Tau
3905 Vincennes Rd., Ste. 101, Indianapolis, IN, 46268-3025
Good and Welfare, 178

Iowa

Ad-Lib Publications
51 1/2 W. Adams, PO Box 1102, Fairfield, IA, 52556-1102
Book Promotion Hotline, 11

Ag/Innovator
PO Box 1, Linn Grove, IA, 51033-0001
Ag/Innovator, 36

---

* See **MULTI-PUBLISHER INDEX** for list of publications.

Air Power Museum Inc.
22001 Bluegrass Road, Ottumwa, IA, 52501-8569
Air Power Museum Bulletin, 902

Allied Group Insurance Svcs.
Box 974, 701 Fifth Ave., Des Moines, IA, 50304-0974
Communicaid, 580

American College Testing
2201 N. Dodge St., Iowa City, IA, 52243-0168
Activity, 299

American Society of Electroneurodiagnostic Technologists
204 W 7th St, Carroll, IA, 51401-2317
ASET Newsletter, 865

•**Arthur L. Davis Publishing Agency**
517 Washington Street, PO Box 216, Cedar Falls, IA, 50613

Benton City Electric Cooperative Assn.
1006 W 4th St # 488, Vinton, IA, 52349-1017
Kilowatt Komments, 588

Billiard Congress of America
1700 S 1st Ave Ste 25a, Iowa City, IA, 52240-6036
Break, The, 1,129

Blanden Memorial Art Museum
920 3rd Ave S, Fort Dodge, IA, 50501-4723
Blanden Memorial Art Museum-Bulletin, 903

Blue Cross-Blue Shield
636 Grand Ave, Des Moines, IA, 50309-2551
Link, 589

Boone County Genealogical Society
PO Box 453, Boone, IA, 50036-0453
Boone County Genealogical Society Newsletter, 448

Century Life of America
Heritage Way, Waverly, IA, 50677
In the LimeLite, 586

Charles H. MacNider Museum
303 2nd St SE, Mason City, IA, 50401-3925
Charles MacNider Museum-Newsletter, 903

Concerned United Birthparents
2000 Walker St., Des Moines, IA, 50317-5201
CUB Communicator, 411

Corn Belt Power Cooperative
PO Box 508, Humboldt, IA, 50548-0508
Watts Watt, 603

Council for Agricultural Science & Technology
4420 W. Lincoln Way, Ames, IA, 50014-3447
News from CAST, 44

Crosley Automobile Club
217 N Gilbert St, Iowa City, IA, 52245-2125
Crosley Automobile Club-Quarterly, 72

Customer Service Report
PO Box 1720, Dubuque, IA, 52004-1720
Customer Service Report, 836

Czech Heritage Foundation, Inc.
PO Box 761, Cedar Rapids, IA, 52406-0761
Nase Ceske Dedictvi, 401

Delta Sigma Chi
Palmer College of Chiropractic, 1000 Brady St., Davenport, IA, 52803-5214
Brotherhood, The, 188

Dubuque County Historical Society
PO Box 266, Dubuque, IA, 52004-0266
River Yarns- National Rivers Hall of Fame Newsletter, 547

Equitable Life Insurance Co. of Iowa
PO Box 1635, Des Moines, IA, 50306-1635
Dividend, 619

•**Ertl Co., The**
PO Box 500, Dyersville, IA, 52040-0500

Farm Equipment Wholesalers Assn. (FEWA)
611 Southgate Ave., Iowa City, IA, 52240-4443
TIPS, 35

Farmers Grain & Livestock Corp.
1400 50th St., #400, Box 65537, W. Des Moines, IA, 50265-0914
Farmers Grain & Livestock Corp. -Viewpoint, 40

Fed. of Genealogical Societies
2003 E 12th St, Davenport, IA, 52803-3917
FGS, 453

Fire Service Ext.
Iowa State Univ., Ames, IA, 50011-0001
Fire Service Information, 421

Foundation for Chiropractic Education and Research
66 Washington, Des Moines, IA, 50314
Staying Well Newsletter, 529

Freiberg Publishing Co.
PO Box 7, Cedar Falls, IA, 50613-0007
Trade & Licensing Hot List, 1,101

GTE Telephone Ops.
PO Box 330, Grinnell, IA, 50112-0330
Iowa Highlights, 587

Glenn Miller Birthplace Society
PO Box 61, Clarinda, IA, 51632-0061
Miller Notes, 914

Glenwood State Hospital-School
711 S Vine St, Glenwood, IA, 51534-1927
Hill Topic, 565

Greene Recorder
701 Park St, Greene, IA, 50636-9439
American Mother, 410

Grinnell College
PO Box 805, Grinnell, IA, 50112-0813
Newsletter, 200

•**Grinnell Mutual Reinsurance Co.**
Int. 80 at Hwy. 146, Grinnell, IA, 50112

Hakes Pubs.
PO Box 603, Storm Lake, IA, 50588-0603
Chamber Executive Network, 158

Healthy Exchanges
PO Box 124, Des Moines, IA, 50301-0124
Healthy Exchanges, 430

•**Heartland Communications Group**
1003 Central Ave., PO Box 1115, Fort Dodge, IA, 50501

Independent Small Business Employers
520 S. Pierce Ave., Ste. 224, Mason City, IA, 50401-2751
Smart Workplace Practices, 845

Integrity Communications
PO Box 1125, Ames, IA, 50014-1125
Home Business Express, 140

Intl. Lutheran Deaf Assn.
1004 Cherrywood Dr, Cedar Falls, IA, 50613-1614
Deaf Lutheran, 1,071

Interstate Power Co.
PO Box 769, Dubuque, IA, 52004-0769
Interstate News, 587

•**Iowa Agricultural Statistics**
833 Federal Bldg., 210 Walnut St., Des Moines, IA, 50309-2195

Iowa Archeological Society
IAS Office of Newsletter, Box 27, Highlandville, IA, 52149
Newsletter./Journal, 58

Iowa Beef Industry Council
PO Box 1730, Ames, IA, 50010-1730
Beef Update, 827

Iowa Civil Rights Commission
211 E. Maple St., 2nd Fl., Des Moines, IA, 50319-0001
Iowa Civil Rights Communicator, 173

Iowa Congress of Parents
610 Merle Hay Towers, Des Moines, IA, 50310-1327
Iowa PTA Bulletin, 314

Iowa Educational Media Assn.
4401 6th St SW, Cedar Rapids, IA, 52404-4432
Iowa Media Message, 858

Iowa Genealogical Society
PO Box 7735, Des Moines, IA, 50322-7735
Iowa Genealogical Society Newsletter, 457

Iowa Legislative News Service, Inc.
PO Box 8370, Des Moines, IA, 50301-8370
Iowa Legislative News Service Bulletin, 487

Iowa Power
823 Walnut St, Des Moines, IA, 50309-3604
Spectrum, 599

Iowa Public Health Association
PO Box 4772, Des Moines, IA, 50306-4772
IPHA Newsletter, 514

Iowa State Dept. of Soil Conservation
Wallace State Office Bldg., Des Moines, IA, 50319-0001
Resource Review, 392

Iowa State Dept. of Transportation
Air & Transit Div. State, Capitol, Des Moines, IA, 50319-0001
Iowa Aviation Bulletin, 30

Iowa State Scientist, Inc.
16c Hamilton Hall, Ames, IA, 50011-0001
Adult Students Newsletter, 200

Iowa State Univ.
137 Lynn, Ames, IA, 50010-7126
SBDC News, 150

Iowa Woman
PO Box 680, Iowa City, IA, 52244-0680
Iowa Woman, 1,209

Jag, Inc.
101 Hillside Dr W, Oelwein, IA, 50662-2640
Jag, 992

•**Jay Mitchell Associates**
Rte. 2, Box 1285, Fairfield, IA, 52556-1285

•**John Skipper**
707 6th St. SE, Mason City, IA, 50401-4155

•**Kent Feeds, Inc.**
1600 Oregon St, Muscatine, IA, 52761-1404

Kent Whealy
3076 N Winn Rd, Decorah, IA, 52101-7776
Seed Savers Exchange, 443

Lennox Industries
200 S. 12th Ave., Marshall, IA, 50158-3005
Echoes, 582

Linn County Rural Electric Cooperative Assn.
PO Box 69, Marion, IA, 52302-0069
News Lines on the Line, 592

Maharishi Intl. Univ.
301 S Court St, Fairfield, IA, 52556-3452
MIU Review, 200

Marian Health Center
801 5 th Street, Sioux City, IA, 51101-1399
Marian Newsletter, 568

Marsha Lockerby-Pilger
807 Madison Ave, Council Bluffs, IA, 51503-6735
Pilger News, 464

Maytag Co.
1 Dependability Sq, Newton, IA, 50208-9239
Maytag Commercial Merchandiser, 712

Meredith Corp.
1716 Locust St, Des Moines, IA, 50309-3023
In the Kitchen, 430

Motor Car Collectors of America, Inc.
5 Bay View Hills, Wever, IA, 52658
Speedev, 1,030

Mount St. Clare College
400 N Bluff Blvd, Clinton, IA, 52732-3910
Clarian, 200

Natl. Catholic Rural Life Conference
4625 Beaver Ave, Des Moines, IA, 50310-2145
Rural Landscapes, 1,121

Natl. Education Ctr.
1119 5th St, West Des Moines, IA, 50265-2608
Live Wire, 188

•**Natl. Travelers Life Co.**
820 Keosauqua Way, Des Moines, IA, 50309-1599

Norwegian American Museum Corp.
502 W Water St, Decorah, IA, 52101-1782
Vesterheim Rosemaling Letter, 443

Open Horizons
PO Box 205, Fairfield, IA, 52556-0205
Book Marketing Update, 115

•**Oster Communications, Inc.**
219 Parkade, PO Box 6, Cedar Falls, IA, 50613

Poweshiek County Historical & Genealogical Soc.
206 N. Mill St., Montezuma, IA, 50171
Poweshiek County Historical & Genealogical Society, 465

Preferred Risk Mutual Ins. Cos.
1111 Ashworth Rd, West Des Moines, IA, 50265-3544
Preferred Word, 595

Public Sector Job Bulletin
PO Box 1222, Newton, IA, 50208-1222
Public Sector Job Bulletin, 348

•**Rare-Earth Information Ctr.**
254 Spedding Hall, AMES LAboratory ISU, Ames, IA, 50011-3020

Ray Gillem
Rr 2 Box 210, Fort Atkinson, IA, 52144-9771
Ray's Adlet, 21

Rockwell Corp.
400 Collins Rd., Cedar Rapids, IA, 52498
Rockwell News, 597

Roto-Rooter Corp.
300 Ashworth Rd, West Des Moines, IA, 50265-3737
Roto Rooter Exchange, 597

•**St. Luke's Hospital**
1227 E Rusholme St, Davenport, IA, 52803-2498

Scott Community College
500 Belmont Rd, Bettendorf, IA, 52722-6804
Weekly Update, 200

•**Siefer Consultants, Inc.**
525 Cayuga St., PO Box 1384, Storm Lake, IA, 50588

Society for German American Studies
500 Belmont Rd, Bettendorf, IA, 52722-5649
Society for German-American Studies Newsletter, 825

Society for the Scientific Study of Sex
PO Box 208, Mount Vernon, IA, 52314-0208
Society for the Scientific Study of Sex-Society Newsletter, 1,110

* See **MULTI-PUBLISHER INDEX** for list of publications.

Stamats Communications, Inc.
427 6th Ave. SE, Cedar Rapids, IA, 52401-1931

Stanley Foundation
216 Sycamore St # 500, Muscatine, IA, 52761-3838
Courier, 629

State Library of Iowa
East 12 And Grand140-B, Des Moines, IA, 50319-0001
Footnotes, 798

Stevenson Consultants, Inc
417 Eton Court, PO Box 4528, Sioux City, IA, 51104
Successful Fund Raising, 23

Susan Boren
P.O. Box 569, Iowa City, IA, 52244
Whatever Works, 816

Thaddeus Computing, Inc.
PO Box 869, Fairfield, IA, 52556-0869

Thunderbirds of America
PO Box 2766, Cedar Rapids, IA, 52406-2766
Big Bird, 71

USDA, Market News Svc.
225 Livestock Exchange Bldg., Box 2437, Sioux City, IA, 51107
Hay Market News, 41

Univ. of Dubuque
2000 University Ave, Dubuque, IA, 52001-5050

Univ. of Iowa College of Dentistry
Publications, Iowa City, IA, 52240
Iowa Dental Bulletin, 270

University of Iowa College of Law
290 Boyd Law Building, Iowa City, IA, 52242-1113
Law Alumni Report, 188

Univ. of Iowa Libraries
Main Library, Iowa City, IA, 52242-1420
University of Iowa, Libraries, Newsletter, 812

University of Iowa Russian Lang. Dept.
Dept. of Russian, Phillips Hall 674, Iowa City, IA, 52242-1316
American Association of Teachers of Slavic & Eastern European Languages News, 819

Univ. of Iowa, School of Library & Info. Science
Publications, Iowa City, IA, 52242
School of Library and Information Science Newsletter, 810

Univ. of Iowa Univ. Hygienic Lab.
Oakdale Campus, Iowa City, IA, 52242-0001
Lab Hotline, 515

Univ. of Osteopathic Med.
3200 Grand Ave, Des Moines, IA, 50312-4198
Chronicle, 871

Vesterheim, the Norwegian-American Museum
502 W Water St, Decorah, IA, 52101-1734
Norwegian-American Museum Newsletter, 907

Wasendorf & Son Co.
802 Main St # 849, Cedar Falls, IA, 50613-2953
Futures and Options Factors, 666

White Park Cattle Association of America
419 N Water St, Madrid, IA, 50156-1057
Park Post, 829

Women's Classical Caucus
Iowa State University, Ames, IA, 50011
Women's Classical Caucus Newsletter, 1,213

Kansas

A Great Mother company
PO Box 4382, Overland Park, KS, 66204-0382
Mentor, 471

Agricultural & Industrial Mfgs. Representatives Assn. (AIMRA
5818 Reeds Rd, Mission, KS, 66202-2740
Representative, 35

Alpha Tau Delta
350 Bluemont Hall, Kansas St. Univ., Manhattan, KS, 66502-5724
Alpha Tau Delta President's Letter, 176

American Agri-Women
6835 Road Two, Kanorado, KS, 67741-9400
Voice of the American Agri-Woman, 47

American Alfalfa Processors Association
9948 Santa Fe Dr., SE, Overland Park, KS, 66212-4744
AAPA Bulletin, 35

•**American Institute of Baking**
1213 Bakers Way, Manhattan, KS, 66502-4576

Antin Marketing Group
9204 W. 71st Street, Merriam, KS, 66204
Antin Marketing Letter, 10

Barclay College
Box 288, 607 N. Kingman, Haviland, KS, 67059-0288
Progress, 326

Barton County Genealogical Society
PO Box 425, Great Bend, KS, 67530-0425
Quarterly, 465

•**Botanical Society of America**
University of Kansas, RL McGregor Herbarium, Lawrence, KS, 66047

Cardinal Club
1701 Saint Andrews Dr, Lawrence, KS, 66047-1703
Cardinal Club Newsletter, 28

Center for Historical Research
6425 SW 6th Street, Topeka, KS, 66615-1099
Kansas State Historical Society Mirror, 542

Chartrand Communications
130 N. Cherry St., #202, Olathe, KS, 66061-3460
Kansas City Insurance Report, 93

City of Wichita
455 N Main St, Wichita, KS, 67202-1603
Personnelly Speaking, 491

Clan Archibald in America
302 S Wilson St, Hillsboro, KS, 67063-1826
Archibald Clan Newsletter, 447

Coordinating Committee on Women in Historical Profession
1737 Vaughn Dr, Manhattan, KS, 66502-2623
CCWHP Newsletter, 1,207

Council for Learning Disabilities
PO Box 40303, Overland Park, KS, 66204-4303
L.D. Forum, 315

Credenza Company, The
6620 W. 93 rd Street, Overland Park, KS, 66212
Trend/Wire, 433

Donnelly College
608 N 18th St, Kansas City, KS, 66102-4298
Digest, 189

Douglas County Genealogical Soc.
PO Box 3664, Lawrence, KS, 66046-0664
Pioneer, The, 464

Emporia State Univ., School of Library & Info. Management
1200 Commerical St., Emporia, KS, 66801-5087
S.L.I.M. In-Focus, 188

Emprise Bank
20 W 2nd Ave, Hutchinson, KS, 67501-5246
Emprise Investment Newsletter, 663

Fairplain Publications
PO Box 3747, Lawrence, KS, 66046
Growing for Market, 41

Fisk(E) Family Assn.
2215 Anderson Ave, Manhattan, KS, 66502-3608
Fisk(E) Family Assn. Newsletter, 453

Flat Glass Marketing Assn.
3310 S.W. Harrison St., Topeka, KS, 66611-2252
Glass Reflections, 479

Forsyth Travel Library
9154 W. 57th St., P.O. Box 2975, Shawnee Mission, KS, 66201-1375
Fast Tracks, 1,184

Fungal Genetics Stock Center
U Of K Med. Ctr., Microbiology, Kansas City, KS, 66160-0001
Fungal Genetics Newsletter, 109

•**General Motors Corp.**
GM Assembly Div.-Fairfax GMC, Kansas City, KS, 66115

Goddard Assn. of America
118 S. Volustia, Wichita, KS, 67211-2038
Goddard Newsletter, 455

•**Golf Course Superintendents Assn. of America**
1421 Research Park Dr, Lawrence, KS, 66049-3858

Grassland Heritage Foundation
PO Box 394, Shawnee Mission, KS, 66201-0394
Prairie Center Newsletter, 391

Health Industry Rep. Assn.
5818 Reeds Rd, Mission, KS, 66202-2740
HIRA News, 564

Independent Medical Distributors Assn.
5818 Reeds Rd., Mission, KS, 66202-2740
Independent Medical Distributors Association Update, 338

International Brotherhood of Boilermakers, Iron Shipbuilders
753 State Ave., Ste. 570, Kansas City, KS, 66101-2511
NTL News, 1,205

Intl. Occultation Timing Assn.
2760 SW Jewell Ave, Topeka, KS, 66611-1614
Occultation Newsletter, 69

•**Intertec Publishing Corporation**
9800 Metcalf Ave., PO Box 12901, Overland Park, KS, 66212-2215

Journalism Education Association
Kansas State University, 103 Kedzie Hall, Manhattan, KS, 66506-1505
Newswire, 323

Kansas Anthropological Association
6425 SW 6th Ave, Topeka, KS, 66615-1099
Kansas Anthropological Association Newsletter, 51

Kansas Commission on Civil Rights
900 SW Jackson St Rm 851s, Topeka, KS, 66612-1220
Spectrum, 176

Kansas Crop Improvement Assn.
2000 Kimball Ave, Manhattan, KS, 66502-3354
Kansas Crop Improvement Assn. -News Letter, 441

Kansas Dept. of Human Resources
401 SW Topeka Blvd, Topeka, KS, 66603-3151
Kansas Monthly Employment Review, 345

Kansas Dept. of Transportation
Public Info., Docking St. Office Bldg., Topeka, KS, 66612
Inside KDOT/Translines, 1,077

Kansas Dietetic Assn.
Dept. HRIMD Justin Hall 103, Kansas State University, Manhattan, KS, 66506-1404
KDA Sunflower, 933

Kansas Gas & Electric Co.
PO Box 208, Wichita, KS, 67201-0208
Servicegraph, 598

Kansas Municipal Utilities, Inc.
Box 1225, McPherson, KS, 67460-1225
KMU Monthly Report, 1,026

Kansas Oil Marketeers Association
PO Box 8479, Topeka, KS, 66608-0479
Kansas Oil Marketer, 958

Kansas State Library
State Capital, 3rd Fl., Topeka, KS, 66612
Kansas Libraries, 801

Kansas State University Computing Center
Cardwell Hall, Manhattan, KS, 66506
Computing Newsletter, 217

Kansas State University English Dept.
122 Denison Hall, Manhattan, KS, 66506-0700
Spenser Newsletter, 984

Kansas Turfgrass Foundation Dept. of Horticulture
Waters Hall, Kansas State University, Manhattan, KS, 66506-4000
K.T.F. Newsletter, 441

Kaweah Indian Nation
PO Box 3121, Hutchinson, KS, 67504-3121
Itza Voice, 405

Lambda Delta Lambda, c/o Patricia Van Englehoven
Kansas State Teachers College, 1200 Commercial, Emporia, KS, 66801
Filter, 1,096

•**Learning Resources Network**
1550 Hayes Dr, Manhattan, KS, 66502-5068

•**Master Teacher, Inc.**
Leadership La., Box 1207, Manhattan, KS, 66502

Menninger Clinic
PO Box 829, Topeka, KS, 66601-0829
Menninger Letter, The, 1,015

Miss Jackie Music Co.
10001 El Monte, Overland Park, KS, 66207-3631
Ultimate Early Childhood Music Resource, 334

Natl. Assn. for Management
5920 E. Central Ave., #205, Wichita, KS, 67208-4241
Applied Management Newsletter, 833

National Board for Respiratory Care, Inc.
8310 Nieman Rd, Lenexa, KS, 66214-1562
NBRC Horizons, 881

•**Natl. Organization on Legal Problems of Education**
3601 SW 29th St., Ste. 223, Topeka, KS, 66614-2047

New Force Publishing
6505 E Central Ave # 176, Wichita, KS, 67206-1924
New Forces, 489

Old Fort Genealogical Society of SE Kansas
502 S National Ave, Fort Scott, KS, 66701-1327
Old Fort Log, 463

PSI
4820 W 15th St, Lawrence, KS, 66049-3846
On Board, 593

Paratransit, Inc.
2700 Stone Barn Ter, Lawrence, KS, 66047-2845
Paratranist News, 1,179

Pizza Hut Inc.
9111 E Douglas Ave, Wichita, KS, 67207-1296
Pizza Hut Today, 595

* See **MULTI-PUBLISHER INDEX** for list of publications.

* See ***MULTI-PUBLISHER INDEX*** for list of publications.

National Wheelchair Basketball Assn.
110 Seaton Bldg.,Univ. Of Ky., Lexington, KY, 40506-0001
National Wheelchair Basketball Assn. Newsletter, 1,133

Nelson County Genealogical Round Table
PO Box 409, Bardstown, KY, 40004-0409
Nelson County Genealogist, 462

Newsletter for Leonardisti
Western Kentucky Univ., Dept. of Art, Bowling Green, KY, 42101-3576
Newsletter for Leonardisti, 66

Nextstep Publications
475 Simpson Rd., Greensburg, KY, 42743-9460
Stepfamilies, 416

North American Assn. of Wardens
PO Box 128, Eddyville, KY, 42038-0128
Grapevine, 787

North American Trackless Trolly Assn.
455 S 4th Ave Ste 1077, Louisville, KY, 40202-2511
Trolley Coach News, 1,181

Omicron Delta Kappa Soc.
118 Bradley Hall, Lexington, KY, 40506
Circle, 177

Peace & Justice Center
1935 Lewiston Dr, Louisville, KY, 40216-2523
Peace & Justice News, 995

Personnel Policy Svc., Inc.
PO Box 7697, Louisville, KY, 40257-0715
Personnel Policy Manual, 842

Pikeville College
Sycamore St., Pikeville, KY, 41501
Echo, 200

Pryor & Associates
2337 Glen Eagle Dr, Louisville, KY, 40222-6435
Sound Mind Investing, 686

Racing Update Inc.
PO Box 11052, Lexington, KY, 40512-1052
Racing Update, 560

Ruth Lanphear
633 E 13th St, Bowling Green, KY, 42101-2531
Clark Clarion, 450

Sachs Co., The
1346 S 3rd St, Louisville, KY, 40208-2351
Trendway Advisory Service, 689

School for the Deaf
PO Box 27, S. Second St., Danville, KY, 40423-0027
Kentucky Standard, 533

South Central Kentucky Historical & Genealogical Society, In
PO Box 157, Glasgow, KY, 42142-0157
Traces, 468

Southern Baptist Theological Seminary
2825 Lexington Rd, Louisville, KY, 40280-0001
Tie, 1,054

Southern Demographic Assn.
PO Box 70192, Louisville, KY, 40270-0192
Southern Demographic News, 1,127

Sue Bennett College
West Fifth, London, KY, 40741-1915
Alumni Newsletter, 189

Taylor County Historical Society
PO Box 14, Campbellsville, KY, 42719-0014
Central Kentucky Researcher, 538

•**Texas Gas Transmission Corp.**
3800 Frederica St., Owensboro, KY, 42301-6900

Thomas More College
333 Thomas More Pkway., Crestview Hills, KY, 41017-3428
Utopian, 200

Tools of the Trade: Books for Communicators
PO Box 23556, Lexington, KY, 40523-3556
Tools of the Trade: Books for Communicators, 120

Uniform Boiler & Pressure Vessel Laws Society
308 N. Evergreen, Louisville, KY, 40243
Synopsis of Boiler & Pressure Vessel Laws, Rules & Regulations, 1,085

Union College
Box 841, College St., Barbourville, KY, 40906
Union College Alumnus, 189

Univ. of Kentucky Public Affairs Dept.
Publications, Lexington, KY, 40506-0001
Public Affairs Analyst, 1,023

•**University of Louisville Alumni Assn.**
2001 S. Brook St., Louisville, KY, 40292-0001

West Central Kentucky Family Research Assoc.
PO Box 1932, Owensboro, KY, 42302-1932
West Central Kentucky Family Research Assoc. Bulletin, 469

Louisiana

Advance Planning Letter
14 Audubon Pl, New Orleans, LA, 70118-5526
Advance Planning Letter, 654

Alton Moran
18435 S Mission Hills Ave, Baton Rouge, LA, 70810-7943
Green Family Quarterly, 455

American Cancer Soc. Louisiana Div.
837 Gravier St Ste 700, New Orleans, LA, 70112-1509
Louisiana Cancer Reporter, 1,118

American Mosquito Control Assn, Inc.
707 E Prien Lake Rd # 5416, Lake Charles, LA, 70601-8613
AMCA Newsletter, 370

American Recovery Assn., Inc.
PO Box 6788, New Orleans, LA, 70174-6788
American Recovery Association, Inc. News & Views, 80

Art & Crafts Catalyst
PO Box 159, Bogalusa, LA, 70429-0159
Art & Crafts Catalyst, 62

Assn. of Louisiana Electric Cooperatives
10725 Airline Hwy, Baton Rouge, LA, 70816-4213
Louisiana Country, 1,002

Bale Books
PO Box 2727, New Orleans, LA, 70176-2727
COINfidential Report, 927

•**Blanchard & Co.**
110 Veterans Blve. Suite #20, P.O. Box 61740, New Orleans, LA, 70161-1740

Brothers of the Holy Eucharist
PO Box 25, Plaucheville, LA, 71362-0025
Grain and Fire, 1,057

CN Lines Special Interest Group
2488 Paige Janette Dr, Harvey, LA, 70058-2137
CN Lines, 1,029

Charity-Delgado School of Nursing Alumni Assn.
450 S Claiborne Ave, New Orleans, LA, 70112-1310
White Cap, 189

Delgado Community College
615 City Park Ave, New Orleans, LA, 70119-4326
Communique, 200

•**Exxon Co. USA**
P.O. Box 551, Baton Rouge, LA, 70821

Federal-State Market News Service
New Fedl. Bldg. Rm. T-5031,, New Orleans, LA, 70113
Fruit and Vegetable Division, New Orleans Daily Report, 1,008

Florida Parishes Genealogical Newsletter
20011 Will Hughes Road, Livingston, LA, 70754-2642
Florida Parishes Genealogical Newsletter, 453

Greater Baton Rouge Port Commission
PO Box 380, Port Allen, LA, 70767-0380
Deepwater, 1,111

HEAL of Louisiana
8618 GSRI Ave., Baton Rouge, LA, 70810-6221
Heal Prints, 508

Hogan Jazz Archive
Tilton Memorial Library, New Orleans, LA, 70118
Jazz Archivist, 913

Home Builders Association of Greater New Orleans
2424 N Arnoult Rd, Metairie, LA, 70001-1813
Home Builders Assn. of Greater New Orleans-Newsletter, 247

Homosexual Information Center
115 Monroe St, Bossier City, LA, 71111-4539
HIC Newsletter, 444

Ingram Corp.
4100 One Shell Sq., New Orleans, LA, 70139
Ingram News, 586

Intl. Listening Assn.
McNeese State Univ., Comm., Box 9042, Lake Charles, LA, 70609-9998
Listening Post, 179

J & W Enterprises
PO Box 17706, Shreveport, LA, 71138-0706
Claiborne Parish Trails, 450

Jewish Civic Press
924 Valmont St, New Orleans, LA, 70115-3000
Jewish Civic Press, 1,069

Kaiser Aluminum
PO Box 1031, Baton Rouge, LA, 70821-1031
Aluminator, 576

Kemper/Leila Williams Foundation Historic New Orleans Collec
533 Royal St., New Orleans, LA, 70130-2113
Historic New Orleans Collection Quarterly, 541

Kerrville Tours
PO Box 79, Shreveport, LA, 71161-0079
Kerrville Tours Newsletter, 1,186

Legiscon Statehouse Report
703 N 7th St, Baton Rouge, LA, 70802-5327
Legiscon Statehouse Report, 488

Louisiana Archives and Manuscripts Association
PO Box 51213, New Orleans, LA, 70151-1213
Louisiana Archives & Manuscripts Association Newsletter, 803

Louisiana Bankers Assn.
PO Box 2871, Baton Rouge, LA, 70821-2871
Louisiana Banker, 94

•**Louisiana Dept. of Agriculture**
Office of Marketing, Box 3334, Baton Rouge, LA, 70821

•**Louisiana Dept. of Labor**
Box 94094, Baton Rouge, LA, 70804-9094

Louisiana Dept. of Veterans Affairs
Box 94095, Capitol Statio, Baton Rouge, LA, 70804-9095
Servo, 181

Louisiana Oil Marketers Assn.
PO Box 80357, Baton Rouge, LA, 70898-0357
LOMA Bulletin, 958

Louisiana Power
142 Delaronde St, New Orleans, LA, 70114-2326
Profit Builder, 595

Louisiana School Boards Assn.
7912 Summa Ave, Baton Rouge, LA, 70809-3416
LSBA Quarter Notes, 315

Louisiana State Univ., College of Engineering
3216 Ceba Bldg., Baton Rouge, LA, 70803-0001
LSU Engineering News, 200

Louisiana State Univ. Medical Center Lib.
Medical Center Library, 1542 Tulane Ave., New Orleans, LA, 70112-2274
LSU Medical Center Library Bulletin, 801

Louisiana State Univ., Sea Grant Legal Program
170 Law Ct., Baton Rouge, LA, 70803-0001
Louisiana Coastal Law, 752

Marina Management/Marketing
PO Box 24351, New Orleans, LA, 70184-4351
Marina Management/Marketing, 114

Natl. Assn. for Advancement of White People
PO Box 10625, New Orleans, LA, 70181-0625
NAAWP News, 994

Natl. Assn. of Scientific Materials Managers
Univ. Of New Orleans Chemistry, Dept., New Orleans, LA, 70148-0001
NAOSMM Newsline, 1,098

Natl. Marine Fisheries Service
1 Canal Place, Ste. 2340, 365 Canal St., New Orleans, LA, 70130
Fishery Market News Reports (New Orleans-Goldenrod Sheet), 423

New Christian Crusade Church
PO Box 426, Metairie, LA, 70004-0426
Christian Vanguard, 1,062

New Orleans Board of Trade
316 Board of Trade Pl, New Orleans, LA, 70130-2431
New Orleans Board of Trade Membership Bulletin, 146

Notarial Archives
421 Loyola Ave, New Orleans, LA, 70112-1195
Greater New Orleans Archivists Newsletter, 799

Orleans Parish Medical Society
1800 Canal St, New Orleans, LA, 70112-3014
New Orleans Physician, 882

The Orton Dyslexia Society
823 Cresswell Ln, Opelousas, LA, 70570-5881
LaBods Journal, 278

P.Q. Wall Forecast, Inc.
PO Box 15558, New Orleans, LA, 70175-5558
P.Q. Wall Forecast, 96

•**Public Affairs Research Council of Louisiana, Inc.**
4664 Jamestown Ave, #300, Baton Rouge, LA, 70808

Richard III Society, Inc.
c/o Word Catering, 4702 Dryades St., New Orleans, LA, 70115
Ricardian Register, 547

•**Robert L. Siegel & Associates, Inc.**
26 Trianon Drive, Kohner, LA, 70065

* See **MULTI-PUBLISHER INDEX** for list of publications.

Sears Roebuck
4400 Veterans Blvd., Metairie, LA, 70002
Serono Lagniappe, 598

•**Shell Oil Co.**
PO Box 60193, New Orleans, LA, 70160-0193

Shrimp World, Inc.
417 Eliza St, New Orleans, LA, 70114-2335
Shrimp Notes, 424

Sixth District Dental Assn.
6721 Government St., Baton Rouge, LA, 70806-6239
Sixth District Dental Assn. Newsletter, 271

Society for Louisiana Irises
Box 40175, USL, Lafayette, LA, 70504-0175
Society for Louisiana Irises Newsletter, 443

Society for the Study of Southern Literature
Box 50, New Orleans, LA, 70118
Society for the Study of Southern Literature Newsletter, 825

•**Southern Forest Products Assn**
PO Box 641700, Kenner, LA, 70064-1700

Southwestern Archivist
Howard-Tilton Library, Tulane Univ., New Orleans, LA, 70118-5682
Southwestern Archivist, 810

Stewardship Publishing Co.
PO Box 2628, Monroe, LA, 71207-2628
Faithful Steward, 664

Terrebone Genealogical Society
Sta. #2, Box 295, Houma, LA, 70360
Terrebonne Life Lines, 468

Tripoli Rocketry Association
PO Box 339, Kenner, LA, 70063-0339
Tripolitan, 1,101

Tulane Tax Institute
Tulane Univ., New Orleans, LA, 70118-6397
Tulane Tax Institute, 1,155

Univ. of New Orleans/Division of Business & Economic Res.
Lakefront, New Orleans, LA, 70148-0001
Louisiana Business Survey, 143

Maine

Albert Barnes
61 Woodville Rd, Falmouth, ME, 04105-1105
MPA Bulletin, 696

Albert Weymouth, Jr.
RR 1, Box 120, Belfast, ME, 04915-9704
Weymouth Surname Newsletter, 469

American Baptist Churches of Maine
107 Winthrop St # 667, Augusta, ME, 04330-5030
Spires, 1,053

•**American Game Collector's Association**
49 Brooks Ave., Lewiston, ME, 04240-5901

Atlantic Salmon Federation
PO Box 807, Calais, ME, 04619-0807
Salar Newsletter, 423

Backfence Quarterly
PO Box 76, Berwick, ME, 03908
Backfence Quarterly, 1,206

Bangor Theological Seminary
300 Union St, Bangor, ME, 04401-4642
Open Door, 189

Bethel Historical Society, Inc.
14 Broad St # 12, Bethel, ME, 04217-3802
Bethel Courier, 536

Boehmer & Boehmer
Box 365, Monhegan Island, ME, 04852-0365
Seafood Soundings, 255

Castine Research Corporation
PO Box 110, Castine, ME, 04421
Overcrowded Times, 789

Castine Scientific Society
Box 196, Perkins St., Castine, ME, 04421-0196
Wilson Museum Bulletin, 908

Central Maine Power Co.
Edison Drive, Augusta, ME, 04336-0001
Exciter, 583

Central Maine Vocational Technical Institute
1250 Turner St, Auburn, ME, 04210-6436
Weekly News Bulletin, 200

Christian Civic League of ME, Inc.
PO Box 5459, Augusta, ME, 04332-5459
Christian Civic League Record, 1,062

Conservatory of American Letters
PO Box 7, North Waterford, ME, 04267-0007
C.A.L. Newsletter, 981

Cook & Tell
Love's Cove, W. Southport, ME, 04576
Cook & Tell, 427

Council on Ministries, ME Annual Conference
PO Box 277, Winthrop, ME, 04364-0277
Maine United Methodist, 1,073

Down East Enterprise Inc.
PO Box 679, Camden, ME, 04843-0679
Fly-Tackle Dealer, 606

Federal-State Market News Service
PO Box 725, Presque Isle, ME, 04769-0725
Potato Report, Daily, 1,009

Food History News
HCR 81, Box 354A, Islesboro, ME, 04848
Food History News, 428

Friendship Letter, The
PO Box 278, Friendship, ME, 04547-0278
Friendship Letter, The, 471

Fuller Society
Hc 69 Box 675, Friendship, ME, 04547-9610
Fuller Society Newsletter, 454

Game Point Publishing
PO Box 946, Camden, ME, 04843-0946
Sports Industry News, 1,135

General Theological Library
159 State St, Portland, ME, 04101-3701
Bulletin General Theological Ctr. of Maine, 1,045

Greater Portland Chamber of Commerce
145 Middle St, Portland, ME, 04101-4121
Chamber, The, 158

Greater Portland Landmarks, Inc.
165 State St, Portland, ME, 04101-3701
Landmarks Observer, 543

Green Politics Network
Rr 2 Box 3292, Bowdoinham, ME, 04008-9606
Green Horizon, 383

Jackson Laboratory
600 Main St, Bar Harbor, ME, 04609-1500
Jax, 588

Maine Art Education Assn.
PO Box 10463, Portland, ME, 04104-0463
Mixed Media, 65

Maine Audubon Society
PO Box 6009, Falmouth, ME, 04105-6009
Maine Audubon Quarterly, 942

Maine Bureau of Forestry Station
State House Station 22, Augusta, ME, 04333-0001
Primary Processor Newsletter, 830

•**Maine Dept of Agriculture**
State House Station #28, Augusta, ME, 04333-0001

Maine Dept. of Human Services
Bureau Of Health 157 Capitol, Street, Augusta, ME, 04333-0001
EPI-Gram, 505

Maine Dept. of Labor
20 Union St, Augusta, ME, 04330-6826
Maine Labor Market Digest, 703

Maine Genealogical Society
PO Box 221, Farmington, ME, 04938-0221
Maine Genealogical Society Newsletter, 460

•**Maine Library Assn.**
Local Govt. Ctr., Community Dr, Augusta, ME, 04333-0001

Maine Lung Assn.
128 Sewall St, Augusta, ME, 04330-6822
Maine Events, 516

Maine Publicity Bureau
97 Winthrop St, Hallowell, ME, 04347-1238
Top Drawer, 1,189

Maine School Boards Assn.
49 Community Dr, Augusta, ME, 04330-9405
MSBA Update, 317

Maine School Management Assn.
49 Community Dr., Augusta, ME, 04330
MSMA Labor Relations Newsletter, 1,091

Maine State Dept. of Economic Development
Augusta, ME, 04330
Maine on the Grow, 1,021

Maine State Dept. of Education
State House, Augusta, ME, 04330
Maine Schools, 1,091

Maine State Nurses Assn.
PO Box 2240, Augusta, ME, 04338-2240
Maine Nurse, 930

Maine State Planning Office
Station 38, State House, Augusta, ME, 04333-0001
Turning the Tide, 395

Maine State Retirement System
State House, Sta. #46, Augusta, ME, 04333-0001
Maine State Retirement System Newsletter, 1,107

Montanaro Mime Theatre
116 Carlyle Rd, Portland, ME, 04103-3485
Mime Times, 1,173

Natl. War Tax Resistance Coordinating Committee
PO Box 774, Monroe, ME, 04951-0774
More than a Paycheck, 994

Natural Resources Council of Maine
271 State St, Augusta, ME, 04330-6912
Maine Environment, 387

Nature Conservancy, Maine Chapter
14 Maine St., Ste. 401, Brunswick, ME, 04011
Maine Legacy, 387

Norman, Hanson & DeTroy
PO Box 4600, Portland, ME, 04112-4600
Norman, Hanson & DeTroy Newsletter, 765

Northeastern Lumber Mfgs. Assn.
272 Tuttle Rd., Box 87A, Cumberland, ME, 04021-9321
Information Log, 830

Northern Maine Technical College
33 Edgemont Dr, Presque Isle, ME, 04769-2016
Toward Excellence, 201

Paper Industry Information Office
PO Box 5670, Augusta, ME, 04332-5670
Newspaper, 947

Pediatrics for Parents, Inc.
PO Box 1069, Bangor, ME, 04402-1069
Pediatrics for Parents, 415

•**Reserve Research Ltd.**
Box 4135, Stn. A, Portland, ME, 04101-0335

St. Croix Paper Co.
Woodland, ME, 04694
St. Croix Observer, 947

St. Helena
PO Box 1306, Greenville, ME, 04441-1306
St. Helena, 972

St. John-Aroostock-RC&D
PO Box 745, Presque Isle, ME, 04769-0745
St. John-Aroostock-RC&D Newsletter, 393

St. Regis Paper Co.
Box 1200, Bucksport, ME, 04416-1200
Seaboard Bulletin, 947

Sanford-Springvale Chamber of Commerce
261 Main St., P.O. Box 270, Sanford, ME, 04073-3545
Sanford-Springvale Chamber of Commerce, Monthly Report, 161

Simple Cooking
PO Box 88, Steuben, ME, 08680-0008
Simple Cooking, 432

Small Woodland Owners Association of Maine (SWOAM)
PO Box 926, Augusta, ME, 04332-0926
SWOAM News, 436

Society of Maine Archivists
The Edmund S. Muskie Archives, Baker College, 70 Campus Ave., Lewiston, ME, 04240-6018
Newsletter of the Society of Maine Archivists, 545

Soyatech, Inc.
318 Main St, P.O. Box 84, Bar Harbor, ME, 04609-1637
Bluebook Update Newsletter, 38

Special Library Group, Maine Lib. Assn.
Community Dr., Augusta, ME, 04333-0001
SLG News, 809

Stires Family Newsletter
Rr 2 Box 3249, Livermore Falls, ME, 04254-9549
Stires Family Newsletter, 467

Stony Hill Productions
Rr 1 Box 780, New Sharon, ME, 04955-9716
Small Press News, 818

Tightwad Gazette
RR 1 Box 3570, Leeds, ME, 04263-9710
Tightwad Gazette, 255

Tranet
PO Box 567, Rangeley, ME, 04970-0567
Tranet, 999

Transnational Network for Appropriate/Alternative TEchnologi
Box 567, Pond St., Rangeley, ME, 04970-0567
TRANET, 1,101

•**Unity College**
Quaker Hill Rd., HC 78, Box 1, Unity, ME, 04988-9502

•**Univ. of Maine**
265 Stevens Hall, Orono, ME, 04469-0001

Univ. of Maine Cooperative Ext. Serv.
103 Nutting Hall, Orono, ME, 04469-0001
Yankee Woodlot, 436

* See **MULTI-PUBLISHER INDEX** for list of publications.

Univ. of New England
11 Hills Beach Rd, Biddeford, ME, 04005-9526
News Flash, 201

Voight Industries, Inc.
PO Box 200, Lubec, ME, 04652-0200
Boot Cove Economic Forecast, 290

Maryland

AMS, F&V Division USDA
7460 Conowingo Ave Ste 101, Jessup, MD, 20794-9361
Baltimore Wholesale Fruits and Vegetable Report, 1,008

ASFE-Assn. of Professional Firms Practicing the Geosciences
8811 Colesville Rd Apt G106, Silver Spring, MD, 20910-4343
Newslog, 365

About Alfords
1403 Kingsford Dr., Florissant, MD, 63061
About Alfords, 446

Academy of Hazard Control Management
80009 Carita Ct., Bethesda, MD, 20817
Hazard Control Manager, 1,080

Accreditation Council on Svcs. for People with Disabilities
100 West Rd., Ste. 406, Towson, MD, 21204
Update on Quality, 1,123

Advertising Club of Metropolitan Washington, Inc., The
7200 Wisconsin Ave Ste 200, Bethesda, MD, 20814-4811
Ad Clubber, 9

•**Agora, Inc.**
105 W. Monoment St., Baltimore, MD, 21202-4702

Agricultural Research Institute
9650 Rockville Pike, Bethesda, MD, 20814-3998
ARI Newsletter, 36

Alban Institute
4550 Montgomery Ave., Suite 433 North, Bethesda, MD, 20814-3341
Inside Information, 1,048

Alice Borealis
2802 Parkview Terrace, Baltimore, MD, 21214
Prove it Pretzel Boy, 697

Amazon Times
Box 135, Owing Mills, MD, 21170-0135
Amazon Times, 443

American Academy of Otolaryngic Allergy
8455 Colesville Rd Ste 745, Silver Spring, MD, 20910-3318
AAOA News, 863

American Academy of Podiatric Sports Medicine
1729 Glastonberry Rd, Potomac, MD, 20854-2642
American Academy of Podiatric Sports Medicine Newsletter, 866

American Association of Blood Banks
8101 Glenbrook Rd., Bethesda, MD, 20814-2749
AABB Weekly Report, 862

American Assn. of Christian Schools
4500 Selsa Rd., Blue Springs, MD, 64015-2221
AACS Newsletter, 297

American Assn. of Colleges of Podiatric Medicine
1350 Piccard Dr Ste 322, Rockville, MD, 20850-4307
AACPM Newsletter, 862

American Assn. of the Deaf, Inc.
814 Thayer Ave Ste 3, Silver Spring, MD, 20910-4500
AAAD Bulletin, 1,128

American Assn. Electronic Voice Phenomena
816 Midship Ct, Annapolis, MD, 21401-7387
American Association-Electronic Voice Phenomena, 948

American Association for Geriatric Psychiatry
7910 Woodmont Ave., Ste. 700, Bethesda, MD, 02814-3015
Geriatric Psychiatry News, 1,014

American Association of Physics Teachers Publications
1 Physics Ellipse, College Park, MD, 20740
AAPT Announcer, 978

American Automobile Association of Maryland
1401 W Mt Royal Ave, Baltimore, MD, 21217-4245
Maryland Motorist, 74

•**American Boat and Yacht Council**
3069 Solomons Island Rd, Edgewater, MD, 21037-1416

•**American College of Cardiology**
9111 Old Georgetown Rd, Bethesda, MD, 20814-1699

American College Health Assn.
PO Box 28937, Baltimore, MD, 21240-8937
ACHA Action, 496

•**American College of Medical Quality**
9005 Congressional Ct, Potomac, MD, 20854-4608

American Correctional Association
4380 Forbes Blvd., Lanham, MD, 20706-4322
On the Line, 789

American Design Drafting Association
PO Box 799, Rockville, MD, 20848-0799
Design Drafting News, 360

American Federation of Home Health Agencies
1320 Fenwick Ln Ste 500, Silver Spring, MD, 20910-3514
Home Health Agency Gazette, 513

American Handel Society
Univ. Of Maryland Dept. Of, Music, College Park, MD, 20742-0001
Newsletter of the American Handel Society, 915

American Hungarian Educators Assn.
PO Box 4103, Silver Spring, MD, 20914-4103
American Hungarian Educator, 403

American Institute of Nutrition
9650 Rockville Pike, Bethesda, MD, 20814-3998
Nutrition Notes, 934

American Institute of Parliamentarians
10535 Metropolitan Ave, Kensington, MD, 20895-2627
Communicator, 580

•**American Institute of Physics**
One Physics Ellipse, College Park, MD, 20740-3843

American Institute of Professional Bookkeepers
6001 Montrose Rd., Ste. 207, Rockville, MD, 20852-4874
General Ledger, The, 5

American Latvian Association in the U.S.
PO Box 4578, Rockville, MD, 20849-4578
Latvian Dimensions, 404

American Medical Informatics Association
4915 Saint Elmo Ave Ste 302, Bethesda, MD, 20814-6052
AAMSI News, 863

American Natl. Metric Council
4330 East West Hwy Ste 1117, Bethesda, MD, 20814-4408
Metric Reporter, 1,098

•**American Occupational Therapy Assn.**
4720 Montgomery Lane,, PO Box 31220, Bethesda, MD, 20824-1220

American Physiological Society
9650 Rockville Pike, Bethesda, MD, 20814-3998
Physiologist, 980

•**American Political Research Corp.**
7316 Wisconsin Ave Ste 215, Bethesda, MD, 20814-2925

American Polygraph Association
PO Box 1061, Severna Park, MD, 21146-8061
APA Newsletter, 784

American Pulpwood Association
600 Jefferson Plaza, St 350, Rockville, MD, 20852
Pulpwood Highlights, 831

American Running & Fitness Association
4405 East West Hwy Ste 405, Bethesda, MD, 20814-4535
Running & FitNews, 526

American Society for Adolescent Psychiatry
4330 East-West Hwy. #1117, Bethesda, MD, 20814
American Society of Adolescent Psychiatry Newsletter, 1,010

American Society for Clinical Laboratory Science
7910 Woodmont Ave Ste 530, Bethesda, MD, 20814-3015
ASCLS Today, 865

American Society of Health System Pharmacists
7272 Wisconsin Ave., Bethesda, MD, 20814-3410
ASHP Newsletter, 281

American Society for Pharmacology
9650 Rockville Pike, Bethesda, MD, 20814-3998
Drug Metabolism Newsletter, 283

•**American Society of Plant Physiologists**
15501 Monona Dr., Rockville, MD, 20855-2768

American Society of Trial Consultants
Dept. of Speech & Mass Comm., Towson State Univ., Towson, MD, 21204
Court Call, 729

American Transit Collectors' Assn.
C/O Bruce Gilson, 601 Silver Springs Ave #4, Silver Springs, MD, 20910-4649
Collectors' Item, The, 552

American Trauma Society
8903 Presidential Pky Ste 512, Upper Marlboro, MD, 20772-2656
Traumagram Newsletter, 530

American Type Culture Collection
12301 Parklawn Dr, Rockville, MD, 20852-1749
American Type Culture Collection-Quarterly Newsletter, 108

American Zen College, Inc.
16815 Germantown Rd, Germantown, MD, 20874-3014
Buddha World, 1,054

Americans for Religious Liberty
PO Box 6656, Silver Spring, MD, 20916-6656
Voice of Reason Newsletter, 176

America's At Our Doorstep
PO Box 411, Churchton, MD, 20733-0411
America's At Our Doorstep, 604

Amtower & Co.
PO Box 339, Ashton, MD, 20861-0339
Fed/Direct, 14

Andreas Spiliadis
3019 Abell Ave, Baltimore, MD, 21218
Yous, 819

Animal Welfare Information Center
Nat. Agricultural Library, 10301 Baltimore Blvd., Beltsville, MD, 20705-2351
Animal Welfare Information Center Newsletter, 48

Anxiety Disorders Assn. of America
6000 Executive Blvd Ste 513, Rockville, MD, 20852-3803
ADAA Reporter, 863

Archives of the Peabody Institute
1 E Mt Vernon Pl, Baltimore, MD, 21202-2308
SAA Muse, 809

Archivists for Congregations of Women Religious
10319 K Malcolm Circle, Cockeysville, MD, 21030
ACWR News, 791

•**Arlen Communications, Inc.**
7315 Wisconsin Ave., Ste. 600E, Bethesda, MD, 20814-3203

•**Aspen Publishers, Inc.**
200 Orchard Ridge Dr., Ste 200, Gaithersburg, MD, 20878-5440

Asphalt Roofing Manufacturers Assn.
6000 Executive Blvd Ste 201, Rockville, MD, 20852-3803
Asphalt Roofing Manufacturers Assn.-Newsletter, 244

Association of African American Women Business Owners
PO Box 13933, Silver Spring, MD, 20911-0933
Chronicle of Minority Business, 132

Assn. of Pathology Chairmen
9650 Rockville Pike, Bethesda, MD, 20814-3998
Association of Pathology Chairmen Newsletter, 867

Association for Recorded Sound Collections, Inc.
PO Box 543, Annapolis, MD, 21404-0543
ARSC Newsletter, 1,128

Asthma Update
123 Monticello Ave, Annapolis, MD, 21401-3432
Asthma Update, 867

Automated Graphic Systems
4590 Graphics Dr., White Plains, MD, 20695
AutoGraph, 212

•**Automotive Parts and Accessories Assn.**
4600 E.W. Hwy., Ste. 300, Bethesda, MD, 20814

•**Ayd Medical Communications**
1130 E. Cold Spring Ln., Baltimore, MD, 21239-3931

Bader & Associates, Inc.
P.O. Box 2106, Rockville, MD, 20847-2106
Health Systems Leader, 838

Baltimore Area Convention & Visitors Assn.
100 Light Street #12, Baltimore, MD, 21202-1014
Baltimore Banner, 1,182

Baltimore City Dept. of Social Services
1500 Greenmount Ave, Baltimore, MD, 21202-3926
DSS Newsletter, 1,116

Baltimore County Dental Assn.
201 Pandonia Rd. W., #101, Timomiun, MD, 20193
Baltimore County Dental Assn. Newsletter, 268

Baltimore County Public Library
320 York Road, Towson, MD, 21204-5179
Branching Out, 794

Baltimore Museum of Art
Art Museum Drive, Baltimore, MD, 21218-3898
BMA Today, 903

•**Bancroft Information Group, Inc.**
PO Box 65360, Baltimore, MD, 21209-0560

Bar Assn. of Montgomery County
27 W. Jefferson St., Rockville, MD, 20850-4200
Newsletter of the Bar Association of Montgomery County, Md., 764

Baseball Cards Unlimited
106 Liberty Rd., Woodsboro, MD, 21798
Your Season Ticket, 102

* See **MULTI-PUBLISHER INDEX** for list of publications.

Bendix Field Engineering Corp.
1 Bendix Rd, Columbia, MD, 21045-1832
BFEC Update, 576

Bernan
46111 Assembly Dr, Lanham, MD, 20706-4370
Government Pubs. News, 486

Beyond the Byte Co.
2501 Laurel Brook Rd. #388, Fallston, MD, 21047-2336
Pro-Motion: A Quarterly Newsletter for the Media Escort Network, 861

Bindagraphics
2701 Wilmarco Ave, Baltimore, MD, 21223-3352
Post Press Solutions, 1,006

Blue Book of Mutual Fund Reports
1023 Glenvilla Dr, Glen Burnie, MD, 21061-4178
Blue Book of Mutual Fund Reports, 656

Borders Book Shop
11301 Rockville Pike, Kensington, MD, 20895-1021
Bibliofile, 115

Bowie State University
14000 Jericho Park Rd., Bowie, MD, 20715
Alumni Newsletter, 189

Bread for the World Inst.
1100 Wayne Ave Ste 1000, Silver Spring, MD, 20910-5603
Bread for the World Newsletter, 1,114

Brethren Peace Fellowship
PO Box 455, New Windsor, MD, 21776-0455
Brethren Peace Fellowship Newsletter, 1,045

Brewster Society
100 Severn Ave Apt 605, Annapolis, MD, 21403-2621
Brewster Society News Scope, 183

Bureau of Natl. Affairs, Inc. -Executive Telecom System
1200 Quince Orchard Blvd, Gaithersburg, MD, 20878-4103
HR Update, 383

•**Business Information Services**
12811 N Point Ln, Laurel, MD, 20708-2341

•**Business Publishers, Inc.**
951 Pershing Dr., Silver Spring, MD, 20910-4464

CAMFOR
PO Box 1423, Baltimore, MD, 21203-1423
Mutual Fund Performance and Review, 679

•**CDA Investment Technologies Inc.**
1355 Piccard Dr., Ste. 220, Rockville, MD, 20850-4315

•**CD Publications**
8204 Fenton St., Silver Spring, MD, 20910-4571

CEPA, Inc.
6408 Bells Mill Rd, Bethesda, MD, 20817-1634
CEPA Newsletter, 214

COSMOS Inc.
PO Box 30437, Bethesda, MD, 20824-0437
Romanian Business News, 637

•**CRU International**
7500 Greenway Center Dr., Suite 480, Greenbelt, MD, 20770-4430

Calvert County Genealogy Society
PO Box 9, Sunderland, MD, 20689-0009
Calvert County Genealogy Newsletter, 450

Capitol College
11301 Springfield Rd, Laurel, MD, 20708-9759
Short Circuit, 201

Capitol Comedy
8801 Jones Mill Rd, Chevy Chase, MD, 20815-4726
Capitol Comedy, 604

Caribbean Travel & Life, Inc.
8403 Colesville Rd., Ste. 830-M, Silver Spring, MD, 20910-3368
Affordable Caribbean, The, 1,181

Carmel McCaffrey
2542 Vance Dr, Mount Airy, MD, 21771-8814
Wild About Wilde Newsletter, 826

Catonsville Community College
800 S Rolling Rd, Baltimore, MD, 21228-5384
Archway, 189

Center for Archaeoastronomy
PO Box X, College Park, MD, 20741-3022
Archaeoastronomy & Ethnoastronomy News, 68

Center for Plant Conservation
Box 299, Saint Louis, MD, 83100-0200
Plant Conservation Newsletter, 391

Center for Transportation
Morgan State Univ., Box 924, Baltimore, MD, 21239-4093
CTS Network, 1,176

Central Station Alarm Assn.
7101 Wisconsin Ave., Ste. 1390, Bethesda, MD, 20814-4805
CSAA Dispatch, 1,103

Challenge Press, Inc.
5907 Key Ave., Baltimore, MD, 21215-3820
Review of Maryland Laws, The, 773

Chesapeake Bay Foundation
162 Prince George St, Annapolis, MD, 21401-1758
Chesapeake Bay Foundation News, 375

Chief Executives Organization
5430 Grosvenor Ln Ste 210, Bethesda, MD, 20814-2100
CEF News, 834

Chinese-English Translation Assistance Group
3910 Knowles Ave # 400, Kensington, MD, 20895-2427
CETA Bulletin, 820

Chris Olson & Associates
857 Twin Harbor Dr, Arnold, MD, 21012-1027
Marketing Treasures, 18

Chrysler Product Owners Club
5203 Edmonson Ave., Baltimore, MD, 21229-2305
Torsion Bar, 77

Clark Publishing
904 Merridale Blvd, Mount Airy, MD, 21771-5266
Prometheus Report: Journal of Firesafety, 422

Club Natural
P.O. Box 14088, Baltimore, MD, 21268
Club Natural, 100

Colbert's Corner
PO Box 266, Churchville, MD, 21028-0266
Quicktrips Travel Letter, 1,188

Communication Research Assocs., Inc.
10606 Mantz Rd, Silver Spring, MD, 20903-1247
Media Report to Women, 1,209

Consultants National Resource Center
PO Box 430, Clear Spring, MD, 21722-0430
Consulting Opportunities Journal, 133

Consulting Engineers Council of Metropolitan Washington
8811 Colesville Rd Apt G106, Silver Spring, MD, 20910-4343
Exchange, 361

Convenient Automotive Services Institute
PO Box 34595, Bethesda, MD, 20827-0595
CASI Lubricator, 71

Coppin State College
2500 W North Ave, Baltimore, MD, 21216-3698
Coppin-Hopkins Newsletter, 201

Costume Society of America
55 Edgewater Dr # 73, Earleville, MD, 21919-2226
CSA News, 55

Creative Business Communications
PO Box 476, Columbia, MD, 21045-0476
Computeriter, 217

Cystic Fibrosis Foundation
6931 Arlington Rd, Bethesda, MD, 20814-5200
Commitment, 502

Dennis W. Brezina
P.O. Box 683, Chesapeake, MD, 21915
Enough Is Enough: Simpler Living in the Complex, Post Modern World, 814

Dewitt Letter
11619 Gilsan St, Silver Spring, MD, 20902-3122
DeWitt Letter, The, 661

Diamond Duds
PO Box 10153, Silver Spring, MD, 20914-0153
Diamond Duds, 101

•**Direct Marketing Association**
PMDS Book Distribution Co., PO Box 391, Annapolis Junction, MD, 20701-0391

Directory Digest
1713 Cedar Park Rd., Annapolis, MD, 21401-3251
Directory Digest, 117

District of Columbia Library Assn.
7117 Poplar Ave, Takoma Park, MD, 20912-4671
Inter-Com: Washington Area Librarians, 800

Dr. Samuel A. Mudd Society
P.O. Box 1043, LaPlata, MD, 20646-1043
Dr. Samuel A. Mudd Society Newsletter, 539

•**ETSI**
1200 Quince Orchard Blvd, Gaithersburg, MD, 20878-4103

Editors' Service
P.O. Box 737, Glen Echo, MD, 20812
Internet Newsroom, The, 696

Electricians, Inspectors, Engineers & Interested Others
3419 41st Ave., Colmar Manor, MD, 20722-1904
Flexible Conduit, The, 246

Embassy of Vietnam
12719 Robindale Dr, Rockville, MD, 20853-3442
Vietnam Bulletin, 639

Enoch Pratt Free Library
400 Cathedral St, Baltimore, MD, 21201-4484
Enoch Pratt Free Library, 797

Entomological Society of America
9301 Annapolis Rd., Lanham, MD, 20706-3125
ESA Newsletter, 370

Environews, Inc.
408 Neale Ct, Silver Spring, MD, 20901-4436
Genetic Engineering Letter, 474

Environmental Research Foundation
PO Box 5036, Annapolis, MD, 21403-7036
Rachel's Environment & Health Weekly, 392

Exxon Co. USA
6301 Ivy Lane, # 7000, Greenbelt, MD, 20770-1402
Record, 596

•**F-D-C Reports, Inc.**
5550 Friendship Blvd, Chevy Chase, MD, 20815-7278

Family Line Pubs.
63 E Main St Rear, Westminster, MD, 21157-5026
Maryland & Delaware Genealogy, 461

Family Matters Press
PO Box 5674, Rockville, MD, 20855-0674
Radiological Inspection Reports, 927

Fed. of American Societies for Experimental Biology
9650 Rockville Pike, Bethesda, MD, 20814-3998
FASEB Newsletter, 109

Fish & Wildlife Reference Service Newsletter
5430 Grosvenor Ln Ste 110, Bethesda, MD, 20814-2142
Fish & Wildlife Reference Service Newsletter, 382

Food Distributor Research Society
PO Box 441110, Fort Washington, MD, 20749-1110
Food Distribution Research Society Newsletter, 428

•**Food & Drug Administration**
5600 Fishers La., Rockville, MD, 20852-1750

Foundation for Education About Eating Disorders
5238 Duvall Dr, Bethesda, MD, 20816-1876
Vitality, 531

Foundation Fighting Blindness, The
Executive Plaza, 11350 McCormick Rd., Ste. 800, Hunt Valley, MD, 21031
Fighting Blindness News, 874

•**Fourth World Movement**
7600 Willow Hill Dr, Landover, MD, 20785-4658

GOTACH Center for Health
7051 Poole Jones Rd # 606, Frederick, MD, 21702-2447
Living Health Bulletin, 516

•**Garrett Communications**
210 North Adams Street, Suite 1000, Rockville, MD, 20850

Garrett Park Press
PO Box 190, Garrett Park, MD, 20896-0190
Career Opportunities News, 342

General Motors Corp.
GM Assembly Div.-Baltimore Pla, Baltimore, MD, 21203
Weekly News Bulletin, 603

•**Genz Assoc. of America**
5821 Rowland Hill Rd., Cascade, MD, 21719-1939

Gold Horse Publishing/Theriault's
PO Box 151, Annapolis, MD, 21404-0151
Dollmasters, The, 53

Gold Standard Review
c/o Thomas, Box 1311, Germantown, MD, 20875-1311
Gold Standard Review, 91

•**Government Institutes, Inc.**
4 Research Pl Ste 200, Rockville, MD, 20850-3226

Governor William Bradford Compact
5204 Kenwood Ave, Chevy Chase, MD, 20815-6604
Bradford Compact Newsletter, 449

Group 1 Software
4200 Parliament Place, Suite 600, Lanham, MD, 20706
Group 1 Report, 274

•**Growth Stock Outlook, Inc.**
4405 East West Hwy Ste 305, Bethesda, MD, 20814-4534

Gypsy Lore Society
5607 Greenleaf Rd, Cheverly, MD, 20785-1110
Gypsy Lore Society Newsletter, 51

Hamilton National Genealogical Society, Inc.
215 SW 20th Terrace, Oak Grove, MD, 64075-9248
Connector, 451

• See **MULTI-PUBLISHER INDEX** for list of publications.

Hammerterz Verlag
PO Box 13448, Baltimore, MD, 21202
Hammerterz Forum, 540

Harley Hummer Club
4527 Chase Ave., Bethesda, MD, 20814
Harley Hummer, 263

•**Hart Publications**
7811 Montrose Rd., Potomac, MD, 20854

•**Hawkins Publishing Co., Inc.**
1207 B Central Avenue, Box 480, Mayo, MD, 21106

•**HazTECH Publications, Inc.**
14120 Huckleberry Ln, Silver Spring, MD, 20906-2012

Health Trends Inc.
4405 East-West Highway, Ste. 406, Bethesda, MD, 20814
Healthcare Trends Report, 511

Henry A. Wallace Institute for Alternative Agriculture, Inc.
9200 Edmonston Rd Ste 117, Greenbelt, MD, 20770-1506
Alternative Agriculture News, 37

Henry George Foundation of America
2000 Century Plaza, #238, Columbia, MD, 21044
Incentive Taxation, 1,146

Historical Society of Carroll County
210 E Main St, Westminster, MD, 21157-5225
Carroll County History Journal, 537

•**Huttlinger's Energy Reports**
PO Box 409, Poolesville, MD, 20837-0409

•**IAQ Publications Inc**
2 Wisconsin Cir., Ste. 430, Chevy Chase, MD, 20815-7003

Independent Scholar
8202 Kenfield Court, Bethesda, MD, 20817-3147
Independent Scholar, 313

Information USA, Inc.
PO Box E, Kensington, MD, 20895-0418
Lesko's Info-Power Newsletter, 143

Insight Communications
5870 Hubbard Dr, Rockville, MD, 20852-4818
Insight Washington; Insight Focus, 941

Insta Mod
P.O. Box 4626, Gaithersburg, MD, 20885
Insta Mod, 260

Inst. for Energy and Environmental Research
6935 Laurel Ave., Takoma Park, MD, 20912
Science for Democratic Action, 998

Institute for Philosophy & Public Policy
University Of Maryland Rm 3111, Van Munching Hall 31110, College Park, MD, 20742-0001
Report from the Institute for Philosophy & Public Policy, 975

Institute for Policy Studies
Shriver Hall, Complex A, John Hopkins Univ., Baltimore, MD, 21218
Policy Currents, 1,023

Interactive Services Association
8403 Colesville Rd Ste 865, Silver Spring, MD, 20910-3368
ISA Update, 1,159

•**Interests Ltd.**
8512 Cedar St, Silver Spring, MD, 20910-4347

Intermodal Transportation Assn.
6410 Kenilworth Ave Ste 108, Riverdale, MD, 20737-1202
International Transportation Assn. Newsletter, 1,178

International Association of Physical Ed.
Dept. Of Physical Education, U, College Park, MD, 20742-0001
International Association of Physical Ed., 1,131

•**International Business Affairs Corp.**
c/o Richard Barovick, 4938 Hampden Lane, Bethesda, MD, 20814-2914

•**International College of Dentists**
51 Monroe St Ste 1501, Rockville, MD, 20850-2408

Intl. Eye Foundation, Sibley Memorial Hospital
7801 Norfolk Ave., Bethesda, MD, 20814-6015
Eye to Eye, 940

International Montessori Society
912 Thayer Ave Ste 207, Silver Spring, MD, 20910-4570
Montessori Observer, 318

International Show Car Assn.
8667 Georgia Ave, Silver Spring, MD, 20910-3475
Show Stopper, 76

International Society for Neoplatonic Studies
Coppin State College, 2500 W. North Ave., Baltimore, MD, 21216-3698
International Society for Neoplatonic Studies-Newsletter, 974

International Society of Tropical Foresters
5400 Grosvenor Ln, Bethesda, MD, 20814-2161
ISTF News, 436

International Trade Services
PO Box 5950, Bethesda, MD, 20824-5950
Autoparts Reports, 70

Interstate Commission on the Potomac River Basin
6110 Executive Blvd Ste 300, Rockville, MD, 20852-3903
Potomac Basin Reporter, 391

Investing with Barry Ziskin
824 E. Baltimore St., Baltimore, MD, 21202
Investing with Barry Ziskin, 671

•**Investor's Hotline, Inc.**
10616 Beaver Dam Rd., Hunt Valley, MD, 21030-2232

JULUKA Corporation, The
PO Box 34095, Bethesda, MD, 20827-0095
JULUKA Newsletter, 399

Jewish Vegetarians of N. America
6938 Reliance Rd, Federalsburg, MD, 21632-2722
Jewish Vegetarians Newsletter, 1,069

John Kurluk
6212 Holabird Ave 'F', Baltimore, MD, 21224
John Kurluk Zine, 1,048

•**Johns Hopkins Univ.**
Milton S. Eisenhower Library, Baltimore, MD, 21218

Johns Hopkins University/Chemical Propulsion Info Agency
10630 Little Patuxent Pky Ste, 202, Columbia, MD, 21044-3204
CPIA Bulletin, 28

Johns Hopkins University, Office of Student Affairs
3400 N Charles St, Baltimore, MD, 21218-2608
Johns Hopkins University Undergraduate Science Bulletin, 1,097

•**Johns Hopkins University Press**
2715 N Charles St, Baltimore, MD, 21218-4363

Jonah House
1933 Park Ave, Baltimore, MD, 21217-4895
Year One, 1,052

Junior Nat'l. Assn. for the Deaf
814 Thayer Ave., Silver Springs, MD, 20910-4500
Junior NAD Newsletter, 533

Just in Time Publishing
632 Trail Ave, Frederick, MD, 21701-4934
Print Solutions, 1,006

Law Library Assoc. of Maryland
20 N Paca St, Baltimore, MD, 21201-1725
Law Library Assn. of Maryland News, 801

Libertarians for Life
13424 Hathaway Dr., #17, Wheaton, MD, 20906-3221
LFL Reports:, 173

•**Life Technologies, Inc.**
8717 Grovemont Circle, P.O. Box 6009, Gaithersburg, MD, 20884-9980

Liturgical Conference
8750 Georgia Ave Ste 123, Silver Spring, MD, 20910-3621
Homily Service, 1,063

Lomond Pubs., Inc.
PO Box 88, Mount Airy, MD, 21771-0088
Information Retrieval & Library Automation, 226

M.C. Horsey & Co., Inc.
PO Box H, Salisbury, MD, 21802-1130
Stock Picture, 687

Maria Smith
PO Box 10, Tracys Landing, MD, 20779-0010
Water Desalination Report, 1,204

Mark A. Stevens Ltd.
10018 Colesville Rd, Silver Spring, MD, 20901-2306
IRS Practice and Procedures, 1,146

MarketFax
1498M Reistertown Rd., Ste. 327, Baltimore, MD, 21208
Israel MarketFax, 673

Maryland Congress of Parents
3121 Saint Paul Street, Suite 25, Baltimore, MD, 21218-3857
Maryland PTA Bulletin, 317

Maryland-Delaware-D.C. Press Assn.
Univ. Of Maryland College Of, Journalism, College Park, MD, 20742-0001
Maryland-Delaware-D.C. Press News, 924

Maryland Dept. of Employment
1100 N Eutaw St, Baltimore, MD, 21201-2206
Employment Report for Maryland, 343

Maryland Dept. of Mental Health
201 W Preston St, Ste.416A, Baltimore, MD, 21201-2323
Linkage, 1,015

Maryland Dept. of State Planning
301 W Preston St Ste 1101, Baltimore, MD, 21201-2305
Maryland Tomorrow, 387

Maryland Division of State Documents
PO Box 2249, Annapolis, MD, 21404-2249
Code of Maryland Regulations, 482

Maryland Hall of Records
350 Rowe Blvd, Annapolis, MD, 21401-1685
Newsletter of the Maryland Archives, 545

Maryland Historical Society
201 W Monument St, Baltimore, MD, 21201-4674
Maryland Historical Society News and Notes, 544

Maryland Library Assn.
400 Cathedral St Fl 3, Baltimore, MD, 21201-4401
Crab, 796

Maryland Office of Planning
State Office Bldg., 301 W. Preston, Baltimore, MD, 21201
Maryland State Data Center Newsletter, 488

Maryland Plumbing Heating Cooling Contractors, Inc.
10176 Baltimore National Pike, Ste 205, Ellicott City, MD, 21042-3672
Maryland News and Views, 535

Maryland Society for Medical Research
522 W Lombard St, Baltimore, MD, 21201-1636
Maryland Society for Medical Research, Bulletin of The, 878

Maryland State Dental Assn.
Columbia Business Ctr., 6470 Dobbin Rd., Columbia, MD, 21045
Maryland State Dental Assn. Newsletter, 270

Maryland State Dept. of Agriculture
c/o S.C. Miller, Dept. of Agri, Annapolis, MD, 24101
National Association of Marketing Officials, Bulletin, 19

Maryland State Dept. of Planning
301 W. Preston St., State Offi, Baltimore, MD, 21201-2305
Planning Times, 1,023

Maryland State Planning Council on Developmental Disabilitie
1 Market Ctr. Box 10, 300 W. Lexington St., Baltimore, MD, 21201
Accent on DD, 1,113

Maryland State Police
Pikesville, MD, 21208
Maryland State Police Highway Safety Bulletin, 1,081

Masonic Service Association of the U.S.
8120 Fenton St., Silver Spring, MD, 20910
Short Talk Bulletin, 181

Mastiff Club of America
355 Jasontown Rd, Westminster, MD, 21158-3523
Mastiff Newsletter, 280

McVicker Assocs., Inc.
PO Box 6353, Silver Spring, MD, 20916-6353
Recall/Regulatory Analysis, 288

Mellowbriar Enterprises
Box 49, Jerico Springs, MD, 64756
K-9 Courier, 280

•**Methodist Peace Fellowship**
206 W Main St, Crisfield, MD, 21817-1327

Milestones and Memories
PO Box 679, Jessup, MD, 20794-0679
Milestones and Memories, 101

Mitchell Guide Pubs.
23997 Cliff Dr Ext, Worton, MD, 21678-1322
New Jersey Notes of Grants and Funding, 969

Montgomery Village Foundation, Inc.
Box 2130, Montgomery Village, MD, 20886
Montgomery Village News, 1,041

•**Moroney & Co.**
PO Box 720, Glen Echo, MD, 20812-0720

Mountain Club of Maryland
802 Kingston Rd, Baltimore, MD, 21212-1908
MCM Newsletter, 944

Mullac Co.
822 Bonaparte Ave, Baltimore, MD, 21218-6219
Kane Family News Notes, 458

Music Critics Assoc.
6201 Tuckerman Ln, Rockville, MD, 20852-3509
Music Critics Association Newsletter, 914

NAPNES
1400 Spring St Ste 310, Silver Spring, MD, 20910-2735
Forum, The, 929

NASA Center for AeroSpace Information
800 Elkridge Landing Road, Linthicum Heights, MD, 21090-2934
NASA STI Bulletin, 31

* See **MULTI-PUBLISHER INDEX** for list of publications.

Narcotics Education, Inc.
12501 Old Columbia Pike, Silver Spring, MD, 20904-6601
ICPA Quarterly Bulletin, 1,117

Natl. Amateur Baseball Fed.
12406 Keynote Ln, Bowie, MD, 20715-2739
Tournament News, 102

Natl. Assn. of Air Traffic Specialists
11303 Amherst Ave Ste 4, Silver Spring, MD, 20902-4600
NAATS Bulletin, 1,178

Natl. Assn. of the Deaf
814 Thayer Ave., Silver Spring, MD, 20910-4500
NAD Broadcaster, 533

National Association of Enrolled Agents
200 Orchard Ridge Dr Ste 302, Gaithersburg, MD, 20878-1978
EAlert, 1,142

National Association of Jewelry Appraisers
PO Box 6558, Annapolis, MD, 21401-0558
Jewelry Appraiser, The, 693

Natl. Assn. of Public Insurance Adjusters
300 Water St., Baltimore, MD, 21202
NAPIA Bulletin, 622

Natl. Assn. of School Psychologists
4340 East West Hwy., Ste. 402, Bethesda, MD, 20814
Communique, 1,013

National Assn. of Women Business Owners
1100 Wayne Ave., Ste. 830, Silver Spring, MD, 20910
NAWBO Time, 1,210

National Burglar & Fire Alarm Association
7101 Wisconsin Ave Ste 1390, Bethesda, MD, 20814-4805
National Newsline, 1,104

Natl. Capital Historical Museum of Transportation, Inc.
PO Box 4007, Silver Spring, MD, 20914-4007
Headway Recorder, 904

Natl. Catholic Office for the Deaf
814 Thayer Ave., Silver Spring, MD, 20910-4500
Radar, 267

•**National Center for Research Resources Information Ctr.**
Bldg. 31, Room 2B03, 9000 Rockville Pike, Bethesda, MD, 20892

Natl. Classification Management Society
6116 Roseland Dr, Rockville, MD, 20852-3649
CM Bulletin, 1,103

Natl. Clearinghouse for Commuter Programs
1195 Stamp Student Union Univ., University of Maryland, College Park, MD, 20742-0001
Commuter, The, 305

National Council for Geocosmic Research, Inc.
PO Box 1220, Dunkirk, MD, 20754-1220
Memberletter, 68

National Council on Radiation Protection
7910 Woodmont Ave., Ste. 800, Bethesda, MD, 20814-3015
NCRP News, 1,082

National Crossbowmen of the U.S.
203 Washington Grove Lane, Washington Grove, MD, 20880
Crossbow Chit Chat, The, 1,130

National Electrical Contractors Assn., Inc.
3 Bethesda Metro Ctr., Suite 1100, Bethesda, MD, 20814-5372
National Electrical Contractors Association, Newsletter, 339

National Federation of the Blind
1800 Johnson St., Baltimore, MD, 21230-4998
National Federation of the Blind, Legislative Bulletin, 760

Natl. Foundation for Infectious Diseases
4733 Bethesda Ave Ste 750, Bethesda, MD, 20814-5228
Double Helix, 873

National Gaucher Foundation
11140 Rockville Pike, #350, Rockville, MD, 20852-3106
Gaucher's Disease Registry Newsletter, 507

National Geodetic Information Center
Rockville, MD, 20852
NOAA Geodetic News, 936

National Information Standards Organization (NISO)
4733 Bethesda Ave, Suite 300, Bethesda, MD, 20814
Information Standards Quarterly, 106

Natl. Institute of Mental Health
5600 Fischers Lane, Rockville, MD, 20852-1750
Mental Health Statistical Notes, 1,015

National Institute of Packaging, Handling
6902 Lyle St, Lanham, MD, 20706-3454
PHL Bulletin, 946

Natl. Lawyer's Guild-Cuba Subcommittee
5513 Oakmont Ave, Bethesda, MD, 20817-3527
Cuba Subcommittee Newsletter, 629

The National Library of Poetry
11419-10 Cronridge Drive, P.O. Box 704, Owings Mills, MD, 21117
The National Library of Poetry, 983

National Liquor Stores Assn.
5101 River Rd Apt 108, Bethesda, MD, 20816-1560
National Liquor Stores Association News & Views, 104

National News
PO Box 37, Kensington, MD, 20895-0037
Alternative Delivery Today, 970

National One-Write Systems Association
PO Box 8187, Silver Spring, MD, 20907-8187
NOSA Newsletter, 6

Natl. Phlebotomy Assn.
5615 Landover Rd., Hyattsville, MD, 20784-1228
Tourniquet, The, 888

Natl. Service Secretariat-Augsburg Co.
4905 Del Ray Ave., Bethesda, MD, 20814-2527
National Service Newsletter, 1,215

National Shoe Retailers Assn.
9861 Broken Land Pky Ste 255, Columbia, MD, 21046-1170
Shoe Retailing Today, 791

Natl. Slag Assn.
900 Spring St, Silver Spring, MD, 20910-4015
Slag Runner, 479

Natl. Tooling & Machining Assn.
9300 Livingston Rd., Ft. Washington, MD, 20744-4905
NTMA Record, 892

Natl. Tuberous Sclerosis Assn., Inc.
8000 Corporate Dr Ste 120, Landover, MD, 20785-2239
NTSA Newsletter, 520

Natl. Wildlife Refuge Assn.
PO Box 60318, Potomac, MD, 20859-0318
Blue Goose Flyer, 373

Network City News
11415 Walpole Ct, Bowie, MD, 20720-3425
Network City News, 146

New Ways Ministry
4012 29th St, Mount Rainier, MD, 20712-1800
Bondings, 1,045

•**Newsletter Services, Inc.**
9700 Philadelphia Ct., Lanham, MD, 20706-4405

•**Newsletters, Inc.**
P.O. Box 342730, Bethesda, MD, 20827-2730

Nutz & Boltz
PO Box 123, Butler, MD, 21023-0123
Nutz & Boltz, 75

Organization for the Enforcement of Child Support
1712 Deer Park Rd, Finksburg, MD, 21048-2032
Pied Piper, The, 415

Orton Dyslexia Society
8600 LaSalle Rd., Chester Bldg., Suite 382, Baltimore, MD, 21286-2044
Perspectives on Dyslexia, 325

Parenteral Drug Association, Inc.
7500 Old Georgetown Rd., Suite 620, Bethesda, MD, 20814
PDA Letter, 286

Peanut Butter & Nut Processors Assn.
9005 Congressional Ct, Potomac, MD, 20854-4608
Peanut Butter & Nut Processors Assn. -Bulletin, 432

Penny Hill Press
6440 Wiscasset Rd, Bethesda, MD, 20816-2115
Congressional Research Report, 483

Perdue Farms
P.O. Box 2417 NCL, Salisbury, MD, 21802
Perdue Newsletter, 432

•**Phillips Business Information, Inc.**
1201 Seven Locks Rd., Ste 300, Potomac, MD, 20854-2958

Phillips Publishing
Phillips Business Information, 1201 Seven Locks Rd. Suite 300, Potomac, MD, 20854-2958
Document Imaging Report, 221

•**Phillips Publishing, Inc.**
7811 Montrose Rd., Potomac, MD, 20854-3394

•**Pike & Fischer Inc.**
4600 East-West Hwy., Ste. 200, Bethesda, MD, 20814-1438

Potomac Antique Tools & Industries Assn.
13004 Clarion Rd, Fort Washington, MD, 20744-2816
PATINAGRAM, 54

Prince George's County Genealogical Society
PO Box 819, Bowie, MD, 20718-0819
Prince George's County Genealogical Society Bulletin, 465

Property Management Assn.
8811 Colesville Rd Apt G106, Silver Spring, MD, 20910-4343
Bulletin, 1,031

•**RAM Research Corporation**
Box 1700, College Estates, Frederick, MD, 21702-0700

Registry of Interpreters for the Deaf
8719 Colesville Rd Ste 310, Silver Spring, MD, 20910-3919
Views, 534

Reparation Society of the Immaculate Heart of Mary, Inc.
100 E 20th St, Baltimore, MD, 21218-6037
Fatima Findings, 1,056

Retail Bakers of America
14239 Park Center Dr, Laurel, MD, 20707-5261
RBA Insight, 432

Reynolds Publishing Co. Inc.
PO Box 578, Glen Echo, MD, 20812-0578
Public Works News, 1,024

Riderwood Publishing Co.
5049 Smith Rd, Rohrersville, MD, 21779-1039
Ships & Shipwrecks: The Newsletter of Nautical History & Discovery, 58

Road Race Management
4904 Glen Cove Pky, Bethesda, MD, 20816-3006
Road Race Management, 1,134

SLN Inc.
PO Box 6523, Annapolis, MD, 21401-0523
Service Level Newsletter, 845

St. Agnes Hospital
900 S Caton Ave, Baltimore, MD, 21229-5299
St. Agnes News, 572

St. Mary's County Historical Society
PO Box 212, Leonardtown, MD, 20650-0212
Chronicles of St. Mary's, 538

St. Mary's Seminary
5400 Roland Ave, Baltimore, MD, 21210-1994
St. Mary's Seminary and University Bulletin, 1,059

Save-A-Patriot Fellowship
PO Box 91, Westminster, MD, 21158-0991
Reasonable Action, 1,151

Schabacker Investment Management
8945 Shady Grove Ct., Gaithersburg, MD, 20877-1308
Switch Fund Advisory, 688

Scientists Center for Animal Welfare
7833 Walker Dr Ste 340, Greenbelt, MD, 20770-3211
Scientists Center for Animal Welfare's Newsletter, 50

Seaplane Pilots Assn.
421 Aviation Way, Frederick, MD, 21701-4756
Professional Airways Systems Specialists-Local Presidents Mailing, 1,179

Silesia Companies, Inc.
619 Broad Creek Dr, Fort Washington, MD, 20744-5806
Proclaim, 1,179

Skye Terrier Club of America
Dale, 180 Marsh Creek Road, Gettysburg, MD, 17325-7121
Skye Terrier Club of America-Bulletin, 280

Society for Applied Spectroscopy
201 B Broadway St., Frederick, MD, 21701-6501
SAS Newsletter, 150

Society of Logistics Engineers
8100 Professional Pl Ste 211, Hyattsville, MD, 20785-2225
Soletter, 363

Solid Waste Association of North America
1100 Wayne Ave., Suite #700, Silver Spring, MD, 20910
MSW Solutionsr, 1,089

Sons of the American Revolution
233 Linden Ave., Towson, MD, 21204-5427
Baltimore County Muster, 176

Sourcebook Project
PO Box 107, Glen Arm, MD, 21057-0107
Science Frontiers, 1,100

South Asia Forum
4615 Morgan Dr, Chevy Chase, MD, 20815-5314
South Asia Forum Quarterly, 400

Southern Maryland Dental Society
4920 Niagara Rd Ste 306, College Park, MD, 20740-1110
Oracle, 271

•**Spiritual Studies Center**
PO Box 1104, Rockville, MD, 20849-1104

---

* See **MULTI-PUBLISHER INDEX** for list of publications.

Steger Family Newsletter
12717 Gores Mill Rd, Reisterstown, MD, 21136-5100
Steger Family Newsletter, 467

•**Stoneridge Technical Services**
PO Box 1891, Rockville, MD, 20849-1891

Street Voice Outreach
101 W. Read St. #421, Baltimore, MD, 21201
Street Voice, 331

Stuart Rothenberg, Publisher
13305 Morning Field Way, Potomac, MD, 20854
Rothenberg Political Report, 998

Sullivan Publishing
10310 Detrick Ave, Kensington, MD, 20895-3911
Citywomen, 1,207

TASH: The Assn. for Persons with Severe Handicaps
29 W. Susquehanna Ave., Ste. 210, Baltimore, MD, 21204-5201
TASH Newsletter, 279

Tate Andale Inc.
1941 Lansdowne Rd, Baltimore, MD, 21227-1707
Tate Andale Inc., 851

Telecommunications for the Deaf
8719 Colesville Rd Ste 300, Silver Spring, MD, 20910-3919
GA-SK Newsletter, 267

•**Telecommunications Product Review & CPE Strategies**
5643C Harpers Farm Rd., Columbia, MD, 21044

Training Media Distributors Assn.
198 Thomas Johnson Dr Ste 206, Frederick, MD, 21702-4317
Training Media Assn., 862

Transnational Family Research Inst
8307 Whitman Dr, Bethesda, MD, 20817-6820
Abortion Research Notes, 1,012

Transportation Communications International Union
3 Research Pl., Rockville, MD, 20850-3213
Telling It Like It Is, 711

Treasure Chest
400 E. Dover St., Apt. 308, Easton, MD, 21601-3605
Egger's Journal, 64

Trusted Information Systems
3060 Route 97, Glenwood, MD, 21738
Data Security Letter, 219

•**UNIPUB**
4611-F Assembly Dr, Lanham, MD, 20706-4370

Ubique
1420 N Charles St, Baltimore, MD, 21201-5720
Ubique, 201

Underground Conservative
PO Box 104, Sandy Spring, MD, 20860-0104
Underground Conservative, 999

Undersea & Hyperbaric Medical Society
10531 Metropolitan Ave., Kensington, MD, 20895-2627
Pressure, 885

•**United Communications Group**
11300 Rockville Pike, Ste. 1100, Rockville, MD, 20852-3030

U.S. Federal Aviation Adm./Dept. of Transportation Warehouse
Publications Dept., 3341Q 75th Ave., Landover, MD, 20785
Federal Air Surgeon's Medical Bulletin, 29

U.S. Food & Drug Administration
5600 Fishers Ln., Rm. 15A-07, Rockville, MD, 20852
Medical Bulletin, 285

U.S. Natl. Agricultural Library
10301 Baltimore Ave, Beltsville, MD, 20705-2351
Agricultural Libraries Information Notes, 792

U.S. National Library of Medicine
8600 Rockville Pike, Bethesda, MD, 20894-0001
U.S. National Library of Medicine News, 812

US Naval Academy Museum
118 Maryland Ave, Annapolis, MD, 21402-1316
Anchor Watch, 894

Univ. of Maryland College of Business & Management
University Of Maryland, College Park, MD, 20742-0001
Maryland Workplace, 703

Univ. of Maryland, Music Library
Hombake 3210, College Park, MD, 20742-0001
International Piano Archives At Maryland Newsletter, 913

•**University Publishing Group, Inc.**
12 South Market St., Suite 300, Frederick, MD, 21701-5441

Univ. Pubs. of America, Inc.
4520 East West Hwy Ste 800, Bethesda, MD, 20814-3319
Bioethics Reporter, 868

Varex Corp.
4000 Blackthorn La., Burtonsville, MD, 20866-1104
Varex Reports, 937

Vegetarian Resource Group
PO Box 1463, Baltimore, MD, 21203-8804
Vegetarian Journal's Foodservice Update, 433

•**Victor O. Schinnerer**
2 Wisconsin Cir., Chevy Chase, MD, 20815-7022

WATER Women's Alliance for Theology, Ethics, & Ritual
8035 13th St, Silver Spring, MD, 20910-4803
Waterwheel, 1,213

Warfel & Miller, Inc.
11619 Danville Dr, Rockville, MD, 20852-3715
Personal Identification News (PIN), 1,104

Washington Defense Reports, Inc.
PO Box 34312, Bethesda, MD, 20827-0312
C3I News, 894

•**Washington Information Source**
8901 Battery Pl, Bethesda, MD, 20814-2638

Washington Telephone Fedl. Credit Union
3015 University Blvd W, Kensington, MD, 20895-1936
Signal, 1,162

Wayne Pump Company, Symington Wayne Corp.
124 E College Ave, Salisbury, MD, 21801-6467
Pep Talk, 594

Wildlife Society
5410 Grosvenor Ln, Bethesda, MD, 20814-2197
Wildlifer, The, 397

Will Moss
15705 Presswick Ln, Mitchellville, MD, 20716-1714
Bright Ideas Dealer Newsletter, 970

•**Williams & Wilkins**
351 W. Camden St., Baltimore, MD, 21201-2436

Windstar Enterprises, Inc.
3603 Fry Road, Jefferson, MD, 21755
WindStar Wildlife Institute Journal, 945

Wine Advocate
PO Box 311, Monkton, MD, 21111-0311
Wine Advocate, 105

Yiddish of Greater Washington, Inc.
6125 Montrose Rd, Rockville, MD, 20852-4857
Yiddish of Greater Washington Newsletter, 826

Massachusetts

ABT Associates
55 Wheeler Street, Cambridge, MA, 02138
ABT INSIGHTS, 833

AIC Investment Advisors, Inc.
440 South St, Pittsfield, MA, 01201-8217
AIC Investment Bulletin, 653

AIDS Prevention Fund
PO Box 431, Wilbraham, MA, 01095-0431
AIDS World Newsletter, 864

ATX
P.O. Box 382507, Cambridge, MA, 02238
AOL, 817

About Women Inc.
33 Broad St., Boston, MA, 02109
About Marketing to Women, 9

Action for Post Soviet Jewry, Inc.
24 Crescent St., Ste. 306, Waltham, MA, 02154-4060
Post-Soviet Jewry Report, 637

Adams/Laux Publishing Co., Inc.
63 Great Road, Maynard, MA, 01754
Collected Letters in Surgery, 871

Addison Investment Management Co.
PO Box 402, Franklin, MA, 02038-0402
Addison Report, 654

Advertising Club of Greater Boston
38 Newbury St., #7, Boston, MA, 02116-3210
Ad Club Directory, 9

Agri-Mark, Inc.
Box 5800, Lawrence, MA, 01842-2813
Agri-Mark Monthly, 264

Albanian Orthodox Archdiocese in America
523 E Broadway, South Boston, MA, 02127-4415
Drita E Vertete/True Light, 399

Alliance of Massachusetts Asian Lesbians & Gay Men
Box 543, Boston, MA, 02199
AMALGM Newsletter, 443

Allmerica Financial
440 Lincoln St, Worcester, MA, 01653-0002
Sightings, 598

American Academy of the Arts and Sciences
Norton Woods, 136 Irving St., Cambridge, MA, 02138
Bulletin of the American Academy of Arts and Sciences, 259

American Antiquarian Society
185 Salisbury St, Worcester, MA, 01609-1636
Book, The: Newsletter of the Program in the History of the Book in American Culture, 116

American Assn. for Advancement of Slavic Studies
8 Story St., Cambridge, MA, 02138
AAASS Newsletter, 408

•**American Association of Variable Star Observers**
25 Birch St, Cambridge, MA, 02138-1205

American Engineering Model Soc.
1 Walnut St., Boston, MA, 02108-3616
American Engineering Model Society Newsletter, 359

American Friends Service Committee, Cambridge
2161 Massachusetts Ave., Cambridge, MA, 02140-1299
Peacework, 996

American Healthcare Radiology Administrators
111 Boston Post Rd. #215, PO Box 334, Sudbury, MA, 01776-2403
AHRA Link, 561

•**American Institute for Economic Research**
PO Box 1000, Great Barrington, MA, 01230-1000

American Investment Services, Inc.
PO Box 1000, Great Barrington, MA, 01230-1000
Investment Guide, 671

American Jewish Congress Task Force on Nuclear Disarmament
1 Lincoln Plz., #310, Boston, MA, 02111-2671
In Brief, 1,069

American Jewish Historical Society
2 Thornton Rd, Waltham, MA, 02154-7711
Heritage, 541

American Meteorological Society
45 Beacon St., Boston, MA, 02108-3693
AMS Newsletter, 893

American Philological Assn.
Holy Cross College, Dept. of Classics, Worcester, MA, 01610-2391
Newsletter, 823

American Physicians Fellowship, Inc. for Medicine in Israel
2001 Beacon St., Brookline, MA, 02146-4227
APF News, 865

American Vecturist Association
PO Box 1204, Boston, MA, 02104-1204
Fare Box, 927

Amherst College
Publications, Rtes. 9 and 116 S., Amherst, MA, 01002-5000
Sybarite Review, 1,113

Anker Publishing Co.
176 Ballville Rd # 249, Bolton, MA, 01740-1255
Department Chair, 1,090

Apriori Assoc.
278 Gorwin Dr, Holliston, MA, 01746-1535
On Principle, 490

Art Deco Society of Boston
1 Murdock Ter, Brighton, MA, 02135-2817
Motif, 53

Arthur D. Little
Acorn Park, Cambridge, MA, 02140-2390
Futurescope, 838

Association of Engineering Geologists
323 Boston Post Road, Suite 2D, Sudbury, MA, 01776-3022
AEG News, 475

Assn. for Gravestone Studies
30 Elm St, Worcester, MA, 01609-2504
AGS Quarterly: Bulletin of the Association for Gravestone Studies, 535

Assn. of Map Memorabilia
c/o Siegfried Feller, 8 Amherst Rd., Pelham, MA, 01002-9746
Cartomania, 474

Association of North American Directory Publishers
105 Summer St, Wrentham, MA, 02093-1875
Directory Journal, 953

Association of Population Libraries & Information Centers In
9 Galen St Ste 217, Watertown, MA, 02172-4521
APLIC International Communicator, 792

Assn. for Public Transportation
100 Boylston St Ste 200, Boston, MA, 02116-4610
Mass. Transit, 1,178

* See **MULTI-PUBLISHER INDEX** for list of publications.

Atex, Inc.
15 Crosby Dr, Bedford, MA, 01730-1401
Atex Times, 576

•**BIS Strategic Decisions**
1 Longwater Cir, Norwell, MA, 02061-1620

Babson-United
101 Prescott St, Wellesley Hills, MA, 02181-7528
United & Babson Inv. Report, 690

Balch Arena Theatre
Tufts University, Medford, MA, 02155
Prologue, 1,174

Baltic Ventures
1075 Washington St, West Newton, MA, 02165-2118
Baltic Business Report, 641

Bay State News Service
8 Whittier Place, (Suite 7A), Boston, MA, 02114-1437
Beacon Hill Roll Call, 481

Berkshire Life Insurance Co.
700 South St, Pittsfield, MA, 01201-8212
Berkshire Life Newsletter, 577

Bette Brengle-Poole
2203 Aquila's Delight, Faliston, MA, 21047-1035
Worthington Descendants, 470

Better Business Bureau of Eastern Massachusetts, Inc.
20 Park Plz Ste 820, Boston, MA, 02116-4303
BBB Member Exchange, 251

Birkhauser Boston, Inc.
675 Massachusetts Ave., Cambridge, MA, 02139
Maple Tech, 229

Blackstone Research Assoc.
PO Box 345, Uxbridge, MA, 01569-0345
Color Businesss Report, 215

•**Blackwell Publishers**
238 Main St., Cambridge, MA, 02142

•**Blue Dolphin Communications**
83 Boston Post Rd, Sudbury, MA, 01776-2438

•**Bohman Industrial Traffic Consultants, Inc.**
335 Broadway, Box 889, Gardner, MA, 01440

Boston Area Bicycle Coalition
Box 1015, Kendall Sq. Branch, Cambridge, MA, 02142-0008
Boston Cyclist, 263

Boston Audio Society
PO Box 211, Mattapan, MA, 02126-0002
B.A.S. Speaker, 1,128

Boston Bisexual Women' Network
C/O Bisexual Resource Center, PO Box 639, Cambridge, MA, 02140
Bi Women Newsletter, 444

Boston Computer Exchange
55 Temple Pl., Boston, MA, 02111-1305
Boston Computer Exchange Index, 213

•**Boston Computer Society, Inc.**
101 A First Ave. Suite #2, Waltham, MA, 02154

Boston Food Cooperative
449 Cambridge St, Allston, MA, 02134-2010
BFC Flyer, 426

Boston Mobilization for Survival
11 Garden St, Cambridge, MA, 02138-3617
Update, 639

Boston Mutual Life Ins. Co.
Royal St., Canton, MA, 02021
Telstar, 600

Boston Star Trek Association
PO Box 1108, Boston, MA, 02103-1108
Newsletter at the End of the Universe, 1,102

Boston Swing Dance Society
PO Box 1260, Boston, MA, 02134-0008
Boston Swing Dance Society Newsletter, 265

Boston University, Center for Defense Journalism
67 Bay State Rd, Boston, MA, 02215-1897
Defense Media Review, 695

Boston University Goldman School of Graduate Dentistry
100 East Newton St, Boston, MA, 02118-2392
Spectrum, 271

Boston University Library
771 Commonwealth Ave, Boston, MA, 02215-1401
Boston University Library Letter, 794

Boston University School of Law
765 Commonwealth Ave., Boston, MA, 02215-1401
Disability Advocates Bulletin, 277

Boston Visual Artists Union
Art Institute of Boston, 700 Beacon St., Boston, MA, 02215
BVAU News, 63

•**Brumberg Publications, Inc.**
124 Harvard St., Brookline, MA, 02146-6432

CIEE
729 Boylston St Ste 201, Boston, MA, 02116-2639
CIEE, 1,183

CLSI, Inc.
320 Nevada St, Newtonville, MA, 02160-1435
CLSI Newsletter of Library Automation, 795

COM/Energy Services Co.
PO Box 9150, Cambridge, MA, 02139-9150
Communicator, 580

CWC Software, Inc.
150 Grossman Dr Ste 201, Braintree, MA, 02184-4902
Quickfill Application Notes, 234

•**Cabot Heritage Corp.**
PO Box 3067, Cabot Farm, 176 North St., Salem, MA, 01970-6344

•**Cahners Publishing Co.**
275 Washington St., Newton, MA, 02158-1630

Cambridge Automatic
3 Huron Dr, Natick, MA, 01760-1314
Inserts, 1,005

Cambridge Commodities Corp.
55 Cambridge Parkway, Cambridge, MA, 02142
Cambridge Financial Manager, 657

Cape Ann Chamber of Cmrc.
33 Commercial St., Gloucester, MA, 01930-5040
Chamber Bulletin Soundings, 158

Capt. Robert Bennet Forbes House
215 Adams St, Milton, MA, 02186-4215
Forbes House Jottings, 904

Carney Marketing Resources, Inc.
12 Burnham Rd., Andover, MA, 01810-3104
Home Advantage, 15

Catholic Assn. of Foresters
347 Commonwealth Ave, Boston, MA, 02115-1999
Chips, 177

Center for the Behavioral Sciences
33 Kirkland St # 280, Cambridge, MA, 02138-2044
Connection, 1,013

Center for Corporate Community Relations at Boston College
36 College Rd., Chestnut Hill, MA, 02167-3800
Corporate Community Relations Letter, 134

•**Center for Modern Jewish Studies**
South Street, Waltham, MA, 02254-9110

Center for Parent Education
81 Wyman St., Wapham, MA, 02160
Center for Parent Education Newsletter, 304

Central Mass. Regional Library System
Worcester Public Library, Salem Sq., Worcester, MA, 01608-2074
Cracmer Cruhbs, 796

Cerebral Palsy of the South Shore Area, Inc.
105 Adams St, Quincy, MA, 02169-2004
South Shore Cerebral Palsy News, 528

Charles Oliver Co.
20 Oak Neck Rd., Hyanas, MA, 02601
Young Adult/Teen Market Report, 24

Charles River Associates, Inc.
200 Clarendon St., T-33, Boston, MA, 02116-5092
CRA Review, 290

Charles Singer & Co.
401 Edgewater Pl Ste 580, Wakefield, MA, 01880-6210
Singer Report on Managed Care Systems and Technology, The, 238

Cheiron: The Intl. Soc. of the History of Behavioral and Soc
c/o Rare Bks. Countway Lib.Med, 10 Shattuck St., Boston, MA, 02115
Cheiron Newsletter, 1,013

China Trade Corporation
267 Windsor St, Cambridge, MA, 02139-1512
China Trade, 643

Church Street Publishing, Inc.
10 Church St, Woburn, MA, 01801-3025
Shosteck Cellular Strategies, 1,162

Cigarette Pack Collectors Assn.
61 Searle St, Georgetown, MA, 01833-2213
Brandstand, 551

City of Boston, Office of Communications
1 City Hall Plaza, New City Ha, Boston, MA, 02201-0001
City Holler, 580

Commercial Union Assurance Cos.
One Beacon St., Boston, MA, 02108-3100
Aim, 617

•**Committee for Accuracy in Middle East Reporting in America**
Box 428, Boston, MA, 02258-0428

Committees of Correspondence, Inc.
57 Conant, #113, Danvers, MA, 01923-2952
Drug Abuse Newsletter, 282

Common Stocks Common Sense Newsletter
PO Box 224, Concord, MA, 01742-0224
Common Stocks Common Sense Newsletter, 659

Commonwealth of Massachusetts
State Bookstore, State House, Rm. 116, Boston, MA, 02133-1019
Goods & Services Bulletin, 139

Commonwealth of Massachusetts Dept. of Veteran's Services
100 Cambridge St Rm 1002, Boston, MA, 02202-0044
Commonwealth of Massachusetts of Veteran's Services, Bulletin, 1,199

Concepts in Healthcare
171 Main St # 102, Ashland, MA, 01721-1153
Material & Finance Strategy, 568

Concerned Educators Allied for A Safe Environment
17 Gerry St, Cambridge, MA, 02138-5745
CEASE News, 987

Conference of Consumer Organizations
Box 158, Newton Centre, MA, 02159-0001
COCO Intercom, 251

Congregational Christian Historical Society
14 Beacon St., Boston, MA, 02108-3782
News from the Congregational Christian Historical Society, 1,049

Consultant Compendium
125 High Street, Boston, MA, 02110-2704
Consultant Compendium, 660

The Cookbook Review
60 Kinnaird St, Cambridge, MA, 02139-3128
Cookbook Review, The, 117

CorpTech
12 Alfred St., Ste. 200, Woburn, MA, 01801-1915
Technology Industry Growth Forecaster, 349

Council for Responsible Genetics
5 Upland Rd # 3, Cambridge, MA, 02140-2717
GeneWATCH, 474

Counterpoint Publishing
84 Sherman St., Cambridge, MA, 02140
Counterpoint NewsNotes, 218

Country Dance & Song Society
17 New South St., Northampton, MA, 01060-1921
Country Dance & Song Society News, 259

Cranberry Experiment Station
Glen Charlie Rd., Box 569, E. Wareham, MA, 02538
Cranberry Station Newsletter, 427

•**Cutter Information Corp.**
37 Broadway, Ste. 1, Arlington, MA, 02174-5552

DML Associates, Inc.
367 W. Main St., PO Box 1130, Northboro, MA, 01532
Collected Letters in Obstetrics & Gynecology, 871

Data Base Research Group
1 State St., Ste. 1150, Boston, MA, 02109-3507
Data Base Newsletter, 218

Decision & Developments
260 Bear Hill Rd., Waltham, MA, 02154
Decisions & Developments, 730

Delphi Consulting Group
100 City Hall Plaza, Boston, MA, 02108-2106
Delphi Report, The, 836

Delphi and GVC
1030 Massachusetts Ave., Cambridge, MA, 02138-5302
Apple II Software Review, 212

Destiny Publishers
43 Grove St, Merrimac, MA, 01860-1807
Destiny, 1,046

Doerfer Communications
Box 1035, Cambridge, MA, 02138
Going Solo, 1,184

Dram Shop & Alcohol Reporter
PO Box 590, Falmouth, MA, 02541-0590
Dram Shop & Alcohol Reporter, 732

Duane Publishing
319 West St, Braintree, MA, 02185
Asbestos Removal, 244

•**EBSCO**
83 Pine Street, PO Box 2250, Peabody, MA, 01960-7250

ELSS
10 Angelica Dr, Framingham, MA, 01701-3618
Social Service Jobs, 1,122

• See **MULTI-PUBLISHER INDEX** for list of publications.

EPSCO-Educational Planning Services Corp.
PO Box 930, East Sandwich, MA, 02537-0930
Program Plans/Nursing Basic, 326

ERISA Newsletter
11 Pleasant St, Berlin, MA, 01503-1610
ERISA Newsletter, 88

Eastern Massachusetts Regional Library System
666 Boylston St, Boston, MA, 02116-0247
Eastern Region News, 797

Ecodex
584 Marrett Rd # 16-18, Lexington, MA, 02173-7606
Indoor Health, 385

Economics & Technology, Inc.
1 Washington Mall, Boston, MA, 02108-2603
Trends in Communications Policy, 1,164

Educators for Social Responsibility
23 Garden St, Cambridge, MA, 02138-3623
Forum, 310

Elderhostel, Inc.
75 Federal St., Boston, MA, 02110-1904
Between Classes/Elderhostel Catalog, 301

Emergency Film Group
225 Water St., Plymouth, MA, 02360
Dispatch, 1,079

Emerson College
100 Beacon St, Boston, MA, 02116-1596
ASCH Newsletter, 535

Endicott College
376 Hale St, Beverly, MA, 01915-2098
Endicotter, 201

Ezra Medical Pubs.
23 Manns Hill Rd, Sharon, MA, 02067-2271
Issues & Solutions, 840

Facing History and Ourselves National Foundation, Inc.
16 Hurd Rd, Brookline, MA, 02146-6919
Facing History & Ourselves News, 309

Faxon Co., Inc.
15 S.W. Park, Westwood, MA, 02090-1725
Faxletter, 797

•**Fedl. Reserve Bank of Boston**
PO Box 2076, Boston, MA, 02106-2076

Fiends of the Worcester Public Library
3 Salem Sq, Worcester, MA, 01608-2074
Your Library, 813

Financial Publishing Co.
82 Brookline Ave, Boston, MA, 02215-3905
Consumer Finance Newsletter, 86

Finnish American Club of Saima, Inc.
PO Box 30, Fitchburg, MA, 01420-0030
FACS Newsletter, 178

First Natl. Bank of Boston
100 Federal, Boston, MA, 02110-1898
About the First, 575

Fotec, Inc.
529 Main St., Box 246, Boston, MA, 02129-1101
Fotec Fiber Optic Testing News, 366

•**Franklin's Insight**
711 Atlantic Ave., 5th Fl., Boston, MA, 02111-2809

French Cultural Svcs.
126 Mount Auburn St, Cambridge, MA, 02138-5701
Le Calendrier, 815

Frugal Bugle
Box 60567, Dept. OC, Florence, MA, 01060-0567
Frugal Bugle, The, 90

Fruit and Vegetable Market News Service
34 Market St Ste 10, Everett, MA, 02149-5806
Fruit and Vegetable Division, Boston Daily Report, 1,008

•**Fund Family Shareholder Assn., Inc.**
42 Pleasant St, Watertown, MA, 02172-2316

G. Fox & Company
426 Washington St, Boston, MA, 02108-5219
Foxtales, 584

G&R Pubs., Inc.
185 Devonshire St., Boston, MA, 02110-1407
Lab Report, 877

Gems, Minerals & Jewelry Study Unit-American Topical Assn.
PO Box 632, Tewksbury, MA, 01876-0632
Philagems Intl., 971

Globe Corner Bookstore
1 School St, Boston, MA, 02108-4305
Globe Corner Bookstore, 1,184

•**Graham Communications**
40 Oval Rd, Quincy, MA, 02170-3813

* See **MULTI-PUBLISHER INDEX** for list of publications.

Greater Boston Diabetes Society
1330 Beacon St., Brookline, MA, 02146-3202
Diabetes Update, 504

Greystone Media Services, Inc.
PO Box 2947, Woburn, MA, 01888-1747
Muni Bond Fund Report, 678

Growth Stock Services
135 Massachusetts Ave, Boston, MA, 02115-2606
Growth Stock Services, 667

Hard Copy Observer
PO Box 304, Newton Highlands, MA, 02161-0004
Hard Copy Observer, 223

•**Harvard AIDS Institute**
8 Story St, Cambridge, MA, 02138-4925

Harvard Educational Review
35 Longfellow Hall / Gutman, 6 Appian Way, Ste. 349, Cambridge, MA, 02138
Harvard Education Letter, 311

•**Harvard Medical School Health Publications Group**
164 Longwood Ave, Fl. 1, Boston, MA, 02115-5818

Harvard Univ.
32 Quincy St., Cambridge, MA, 02138-3804
Harvard University Art Museums Review, 64

Harvard Univ., JFK School of Government
79 John F Kennedy St, Cambridge, MA, 02138-5800
Journal Update, 992

Harvard University Library
Wadsworth House, Cambridge, MA, 02138
Harvard Librarian, 799

Harvard University, Museum of Comparative Zoology
Cambridge, MA, 02138
MCZ Newsletter, 905

Harvard Univ. News Office for the Medical Area
25 Shattuck St, Boston, MA, 02115-6027
Focus, 874

Health Source Corporation, The
443 Western Ave, Boston, MA, 02135-1010
TopHealth, 530

Hellenic College
50 Goddard Ave, Brookline, MA, 02146-7496
Directions, 201

High Technology Growth Stocks
402 Border Rd, Concord, MA, 01742-4605
High Technology and Other Growth Stocks, 668

Historic Deerfield, Inc.
PO Box 321, Deerfield, MA, 01342-0321
Historic Deerfield Quarterly, 904

Holcon
PO Box 276, Newton Center, MA, 02159-0002
Business Flyer, 1,182

Howard Wilson & Co.
185 Marlborough St., Boston, MA, 02116-1827
Kitchen Times, 431

Huenefeld Company, The
41 North Rd., Ste. 201, Bedford, MA, 01730
Huenefeld Report, The, 118

•**IBC/Donoghue, Inc.**
290 Eliot St., PO Box 9104, Ashland, MA, 01721-9104

•**IDG Intl. Publishing Services**
31 Milk St., Ste. 210, Boston, MA, 02109-5104

•**IDG Newsletter Corporation**
77 Franklin St., Boston, MA, 02110

INFACT
256 Hanover St., Ste. 3, Boston, MA, 02113-2337
Infact News, 632

Independent Union of Plant Protection Employees
PO Box 2163, Pittsfield, MA, 01202-2163
Independent Union of Plant Protection Employees News, 708

Individual, Inc.
8 New England Executive Pk., Burlington, MA, 01803
HeadsUp, 925

Indochina Newsletter
2161 Massachusetts Ave., Cambridge, MA, 02140-1336
Indochina Newsletter, 632

Info Ctr. for Individuals with Disabilities
29 Stanhope St., Boston, MA, 02116-5111
Disabilities Issues, 277

•**Information Gatekeepers, Inc.**
214 Harvard Ave., Boston, MA, 02134-4651

Insight: The Advisory Letter for Concerned Investors
711 Atlantic Ave., 5th Fl., Boston, MA, 02111-2809
Insight: The Advisory Letter for Concerned Investors, 670

Inst. of Certified Travel Agents
148 Linden St., Box 812059, Wellesley, MA, 02181-0012
ICTA Update, 1,185

Institute for Community Economics
57 School St, Springfield, MA, 01105-1331
Community Economics, 290

Inst. for Defense & Disarmament Studies
675 Massachusetts Ave., Cambridge, MA, 02139-3309
Arms Control Reporter, 626

•**Institute for First Amendment Studies, Inc.**
PO Box 589, Great Barrington, MA, 01230-0589

Institute for Massachusetts Studies
Box 237, Westfield, MA, 01086
NEWSCOPE, 320

Interinvest Corp.
84 Stage St., 7th Fl., Boston, MA, 02109-2202
Interinvest Review and Outlook, 670

InternAmerica
105 Chestnut St., #34, Needham, MA, 02192
InternAmerica, 345

International Business Communications
290 Eliot St # 91004, Ashland, MA, 01721-2376
International Tax Report, 1,147

International Etchells Class Association
22 Sewall Street, Marblehead, MA, 01945
Etchells News, 113

Intl. Ford Retractable Club, Inc.
PO Box 389, Marlborough, MA, 01752-0389
International Ford Retractable Club, Inc., 73

International Management Services
363 East Central St., Franklin, MA, 02038-1300
Minicomputer/LAN Applications Analyzer, 230

International Physicians for the Prevention of Nuclear War
126 Rogers St, Cambridge, MA, 02142-1024
IPPNW Report, 991

International Wildlife Coalition
70 E Falmouth Hwy, East Falmouth, MA, 02536-5900
Whalewatch, 397

Investment Management Pubs.
1 Liberty Sq., 12th Fl., Boston, MA, 02109-4825
Investment Management Weekly, 672

Itek Corp.
10 Maguire Rd, Lexington, MA, 02173-3199
Item, 587

JBT Communications
PO Box 782, Needham Heights, MA, 02194-0006
Manufacturing Market Insider, 850

J.R. Campbell & Associates, Inc.
5 Militia Dr., Lexington, MA, 02173
CryoGas International, 164

Jacob's Meadow, Inc.
PO Box 67, Taunton, MA, 02780-0067
New England Farm Bulletin & Garden Gazette, 44

Jewish Genealogical Society of Greater Boston, Inc.
PO Box 366, Newton Highlands, MA, 02161-0003
Mass-Pocha, 461

John Hancock Financial Services, Inc.
John Hancock Pl., Box 111, Boston, MA, 02117
Working Capital, 100

John Hancock Mutual Life Ins. Co.
200 Berkeley St., Boston, MA, 02116-5023
BusinessLine, 578

Johnson/Johansson Family News
171 Clinton Rd, Brookline, MA, 02146-5815
Johnson/Johansson Family News, 457

Jokesmith, The
44 Queensview Rd, Marlborough, MA, 01752-1501
Jokesmith, The, 605

Kaufman & Assoc.
162 Worester Road, Natick, MA, 01760-2252
Kaufman Letter, The, 1,081

Kitchen Sink Press
320 Riverside, Northampton, MA, 01060-2717
Kitchen Sink Pipeline, 210

•**Laboratory Safety Workshop**
101 Oak Street, Wellesley, MA, 02181

Latin American Adoptive Families
23 Evangeline Rd, Falmouth, MA, 02540-2201
LAAF Quarterly, 413

Lawyers Weekly Publications
41 West St, Boston, MA, 02111-1233
Massachusetts Lawyers Weekly, 753

Learning for All Seasons, Inc.
6 Saddle Club Rd # 579x, Lexington, MA, 02173-2115
Non-Credit Learning News, 323

Legal Information Svcs.
PO Box 67, Newton Highlands, MA, 02161-0001
Law Librarian's Bulletin Board, 749

•**Legal-Medical Studies, Inc.**
Box 8219, JFK Sta., Boston, MA, 02114-0032

Lesley College
29 Everett St, Cambridge, MA, 02138-2790
Lesley News, 201

•**Lewis Assocs., Inc.**
PO Box 567, Housatonic, MA, 01236-0567

Lightning Technologies, Inc.
10 Downing Pkwy., Pittsfield, MA, 01201-3839
Lightning Flash, 386

Limmat Pubs. Inc.
PO Box 1718, Orleans, MA, 02653-1718
Dessauer's Journal of Financial Markets, 662

Locke Family Assn.
102 Crooked Spring Rd., Chelmsford, MA, 01863-2307
Locke Sickle & Sword, 459

Locke Report
594 Front St, Marion, MA, 02738-1415
Locke Report, 1,107

Longyear Historical Society
120 Seaver St, Brookline, MA, 02146-5719
Longyear Museum Quarterly News, 905

Lowell Technological Inst.
Publications, Lowell, MA, 01854
Delta Kappa Phi Bulletin, 201

METCO, Inc.
55 Dimock St, Boston, MA, 02119-1029
New Images, 322

M.I.A.A.-Massachusetts Interscholastic Athletic Assn.
83 Cedar St, Milford, MA, 01757-1165
MIAA Newsletter, 1,132

MIT Museum Shop, The
265 Massachusetts Ave, Cambridge, MA, 02139-4162
MIT Museum Newsletter, 905

MIT Press
77 Massachusetts Ave Rm 36-709, Cambridge, MA, 02139-4307
Materials and Processing Report, 1,098

MIT-Research Laboratory of Electronics
MIT Rm. 36-412, Cambridge, MA, 02139-4307
RLE Currents, 366

Management Advisory Services & Publications
57 Greylock Rd # 81151, Wellesley Hills, MA, 02181-1301
COM-AND, Computer Audit News & Developments, 214

Marble Collectors Unlimited
Box 206, Northboro, MA, 01532-0206
Marble Mart Newsletter, 185

Marblehead Communications, Inc.
376 Boylston St., Boston, MA, 02116-3812
Interactions, 1,160

Margo's Market Monitor
PO Box 642, Lexington, MA, 02173-0006
Margo's Market Monitor, 675

Marketing Science Inst
1000 Massachusetts Ave, Cambridge, MA, 02138-5379
Marketing Science Institute Newsletter, 18

Masonic Study Unit
59 Greenwood Rd, Andover, MA, 01810-3311
Philatelic Freemason, 971

Mass. Board of Library Commissioners
648 Beacon St, Boston, MA, 02215-2002
MBLC Notes, 803

Massachusetts Archaeological Society
PO Box 700, Middleboro, MA, 02346-0700
Newsletter of the Massachusetts Archaeological Society, Inc., 58

Massachusetts Assn. of School Committees, Inc.
1 McKinley Square #2, Boston, MA, 02109
MASC Bulletin, 1,091

Massachusetts Assn. of Teachers of English to Speakers of Ot
730 Commonwealth Ave., Boston Univ., Boston, MA, 02159-1133
MATSOL Newsletter, 316

Massachusetts Coalition for the Homeless
288 A St, Boston, MA, 02210-1600
Streetlife, 473

Massachusetts College of Pharmacy
179 Longwood Ave, Boston, MA, 02115-5896
Massachusetts College of Pharmacy, Bulletin, 285

Massachusetts Dental Society
83 Speen St., Natick, MA, 01760-4144
MDS News, 516

Massachusetts Div. of Employment Security
C.F. Hurley Bldg., Boston, MA, 02114
Massachusetts Employment Review, 703

Massachusetts General Hospital
32 Fruit St, Boston, MA, 02114-2620
MGH News, 568

Massachusetts Historical Society
1154 Boylston St, Boston, MA, 02215-3695
M.H.S. Miscellany, 543

Massachusetts Home Learning Assn.
23 Mountain St, Sharon, MA, 02067-2234
Massachusetts Home Learning Assn. Newsletter, 317

Massachusetts Housing Finance Agency
1 Beacon St., Ste. 26-28, Boston, MA, 02108-3106
MHFA Update, 94

•**Massachusetts Medical Society-Publ. Dir**
1440 Main St., Waltham, MA, 02154-1649

Massachusetts Postal Research Society
Box 202, N. Abington, MA, 02351-0202
Massachusetts Spy, 971

Massachusetts Psychological Center, Inc.
25 Huntington Ave Ste 300, Boston, MA, 02116-5713
Massachusetts Psychological Center Employment Bulletin, 1,015

Massachusetts Society of Certified Public Accountants Inc.
105 Chauncy St., 10th Floor, Boston, MA, 02111-1726
Sum Monthly News, 8

McLean Hospital, Dept. of Scientific Pubs.
115 Mill St, Belmont, MA, 02178-1048
McLean Bulletin, 590

Medlex Consulting, Inc.
PO Box 748, Marblehead, MA, 01945-0748
Physician's Malpractice Advisor, 884

Mercury Group Inc.
17 Main St, Watertown, MA, 02172-4491
Softletter, 238

Middle East Justice Network
PO Box 495, Boston, MA, 02112
Breaking the Siege, 627

Millenium Pop
173 Morrison Ave, Somerville, MA, 02144-2016
Millennium Pop, 914

Millipore Corp.
PO Box 255, Bedford, MA, 01730-0255
Millipore Process News, 362

Milton Bradley Co.
PO Box 3400, Springfield, MA, 01101-3400
Milton Bradley News, 590

Morgan Construction Co.
15 Belmont St, Worcester, MA, 01605-2665
Square and Crescent, 599

Mt. Holyoke College Art Museum
Mt. Holyoke College, South Hadley, MA, 01075
Mt. Holyoke College Art Museum-Newsletter, 906

Museum Insights
73 Juggler Meadow Rd, Amherst, MA, 01002-9521
Museum Insights, 906

Museum of Science
Science Park, Boston, MA, 02114
Museum of Science Magazine, 907

Music Business File
PO Box 266, Astor Station, Boston, MA, 02123-0266
Music Business Insight, 914

•**Music Library Assn.**
PO Box 487, Canton, MA, 02021-0487

Mutual Fund Investors Assn.
20 William Street, #310, Box 9135, Wellesley, MA, 02181-9135
Fidelity Insight, 664

Mystic Valley Railway Society
PO Box 486, Hyde Park, MA, 02136-0005
Waybill, The, 1,030

NEIWPCC
255 Ballardvale St, Wilmington, MA, 01887-1013
Water Connection, 396

•**NYNEX**
125 High St Ste 30, Boston, MA, 02110-2704

Naismith Memorial Basketball Hall of Fame
1150 W Columbus Ave # 179, Springfield, MA, 01105-2532
Naismith Memorial Basketball Hall of Fame Newsletter, 1,133

Natl. Assn. for Armenian Studies & Research, Inc.
395 Concord Ave, Belmont, MA, 02178-3036
NAASR Newsletter, 400

National Association of Government Employees
159 Burgin Parkway, Quincy, MA, 02169-4213
Fednews, 707

Natl. Assn. of Master Mechanics
117 Beaumont Ave, Newtonville, MA, 02160-2315
National Association of Master Mechanics, 710

National Bureau of Economic Research
1050 Massachusetts Ave., Cambridge, MA, 02138
NBER Digest, 294

Natl. Council on Public History
403 Richards Hall, Northeastern Univ., Boston, MA, 02115
Public History News, 547

Natl. Fire Protection Assn.
1 Batterymarch Park, Quincy, MA, 02169
Fire News, 421

National Retired Basketball Player's Association
1 International Place, Boston, MA, 02110-2624
Replay, 1,134

Natl. Scoliosis Foundation
72 Mt. Auburn St., Watertown, MA, 02172-3930
Spinal Connection, 887

•**National Security Institute**
57 East Main Street, Suite 217, Westborough, MA, 01581-1464

Natl. Shoe Traveler's Assn.
PO Box 456, Abington, MA, 02351-0456
National Shoe Traveler's Association News, 791

Natl. Shrine of Our Lady of LaSalette
Ipswich, MA, 01938
Our Lady's Missionary, 1,059

National Yiddish Book Center
PO Box 969, Amherst, MA, 01004-0969
Book Peddler/der Pakn-Treger, 116

Nebs Computer Forms Div.
500 Main St., Groton, MA, 01471-0001
CashFlow, 214

New England
501 Boylston St, Boston, MA, 02116-3706
Wheel, 603

New England Archivists
Massachusetts Archives, 220 Morrissey Blvd., Boston, MA, 02125
NEA Newsletter, 58

•**New England Assn. of Teachers of English**
PO Box 291, Chelmsford, MA, 01824-0291

New England Council, Inc.
580 Boylston St., 5th Fl., Boston, MA, 02199-8001
Council Reports, 135

New England Electric System
20 Turnpike Rd, Westborough, MA, 01581-3903
Neespaper, 591

New England Fisheries Development Foundation, Inc.
309 World Trade Center, Boston, MA, 02210-2001
Fish News, 423

•**New England Historic Genealogical Society**
101 Newbury St., Boston, MA, 02116-3007

New England Press Assn.
360 Huntington Ave, Boston, MA, 02115-5096
New England Press Association Bulletin, 697

New England Theatre Conference, c/o Dept. of Theatre
Northeastern University, 360 Huntington Ave., Boston, MA, 02115
NETC News, 1,173

New England Wild Flower Society
180 Hemenway Rd., Framingham, MA, 01701-2699
NEWFSletter, 121

•**New Generation Research, Inc.**
225 Friend St Ste 801, Boston, MA, 02114-1812

Newton-Needham Chamber of Commerce
PO Box 66028, Auburndale, MA, 02166-0986
Newton-Needham Business, 161

North Conway Institute, Inc.
14 Beacon St, Boston, MA, 02108-3746
NCI Catalyst, 519

North Shore Chamber of Commerce
5 Cherry Hill Dr Ste 100, Danvers, MA, 01923-2500
North Shore Business Journal, 161

Northfield Information Services, Inc.
184 High St., Boston, MA, 02110-3001
NIS Equity Research Service, 679

Nuclear Free America
325 E. 25th St., Baltimore, MA, 21218-5303
New Abolitionist, 389

Nurse Healers-Professional Assocs., Inc.
85 Hawthorne Rd, Williamstown, MA, 01267-2700
Cooperative Connection, 503

• See **MULTI-PUBLISHER INDEX** for list of publications.

INDEX TO PUBLISHERS BY STATE

Nye Lubricants, Inc.
PO Box 8927, New Bedford, MA, 02742-8927
Nye Lubeletter Newsletter, 850

Nynex
82 Brigham Street, Marlborough, MA, 01752-3137
StepAhead, 157

OEM Health Information
181 Elliott St Ste 814, Beverly, MA, 01915-3061
Occupational & Environmental Medicine Report, 882

OTC Communications
1040 Great Plain Avenue, Needham, MA, 02192
Nona Morelli's Press Release, 1,076

•OTC Research Corp.
1040 Great Plain Avenue, Needham, MA, 02192-2517

Oil Statistics Co.
PO Box 189, Whitman, MA, 02382-0189
Oil/Energy Statistics Bulletin, 962

Old Dartmouth Historical Soc.
18 Johnny Cake Hill, Whaling Museum, New Bedford, MA, 02740-6317
Bulletin from Johnny Cake Hill, 537

Omega Arts Network News
PO Box 1227, Jamaica Plain, MA, 02130-0011
Omega Arts Network News, 66

•Opus Communications, Inc.
Box 1168, 100 Hoods Lane, Marblehead, MA, 01945

Oxfam America
26 West St, Boston, MA, 02111-1206
Viewpoint, 640

•Pairpoint Cup Plate Collectors of America
Box A2058, New Bedford, MA, 02741-2058

Paper Mate Co.
Mini Pru Bldg. , 23rd Flr., C/O B. DeStefano, Boston, MA, 02199
Paper Mate Points, 594

Parexel Intl. Corp.
195 West St., Waltham, MA, 02154-1116
U.S. Regulatory Reporter, 288

Party Platter
229 Coolidge Ave. #304, Watertown, MA, 02172-1554
Party Platter, 266

•Patricia Seybold's Group
148 State St., 7th Fl., Boston, MA, 02109-2506

Pediatric Alert
PO Box 338, Newton Highlands, MA, 02161-0004
Pediatric Alert, 883

Pegasus Communications, Inc.
P.O. Box 120, Kendall Square, Cambridge, MA, 02142
Systems Thinker, The, 240

Pekingese Club of America
3 Carolyn Terrace, Southboro, MA, 01772
Pekingese Club of America, Bulletin, 280

Philanthropic Digest
PO Box 380252, Cambridge, MA, 02238-0252
Philanthropic Digest, 969

Photographic Resource Center
Boston University, 602 Commonwealth Ave., Boston, MA, 02215-1300
PRC Newsletter, 977

Plastics Connection
PO Box 814, Amherst, MA, 01004-0814
Plastics Focus, 981

Political Research Associates
120 Beacon St., Somerville, MA, 02143-4304
Public Eye, 997

Pope John XXIII Ctr.
186 Forbes Rd., Braintree, MA, 02184-2612
Ethics and Medics, 873

Practical Stock Picker
8 W Parish Ct, Haverhill, MA, 01832-1166
Practical Stock Picker, 682

•Practice Management Associates Ltd.
10 Midland Ave., Newton, MA, 02158-1021

Proceedings in Print, Inc.
PO Box 369, Halifax, MA, 02338-0369
Proceedings in Print, 107

•Productivity Development Group, Inc.
PO Box 488, Westford, MA, 01886-0013

Program on Info Resources Policy
Harvard Univ., 200 Aiken, Cambridge, MA, 02138
Program on Information Resources Policy-Review, 1,161

Protestant Guild for the Blind, Inc.
441 Waverley Oaks Rd, Waltham, MA, 02154-8405
Projections, 112

Psy-Ed Corp
209 Harvard St Ste 303, Brookline, MA, 02146-5005
Rehab Update, 886

•Publications Resource Group
P.O. Box 765, N. Adams, MA, 01247

Purchasing Management Assn of Boston, Inc.
200 Baker Ave Ste 306, Concord, MA, 01742-2125
New England Purchaser, 1,028

•Quinlan Publishing
23 Drydock Ave, Boston, MA, 02210-2387

•R.S. Means Co., Inc.
100 Construction Plaza, Kingston, MA, 02364-0100

Religion
1 Maolis Rd, Nahant, MA, 01908-1212
Religious Socialism, 997

Resist
1 Summer St, Somerville, MA, 02143-1704
Resist, 998

Resolve, Inc.
1310 Broadway, Somerville, MA, 02144-1779
Resolve National Newsletter, 415

Retail Systems Alert
P.O. Box 332, 77 Oak Street, Newton Upper Falls, MA, 02164-9806
Retail Systems Alert, 273

Rhodes 19 Class Assn.
c/o George Gail, 22 W. Shore Dr., Marblehead, MA, 01945
Mainsheet, 114

Ross Pubs., Inc.
PO Box 80, Boston, MA, 02113-0001
Hospital Technology Alerts, 567

The Rugging Room
10 Sawmill Dr # 824, Westford, MA, 01886-2236
Rugging Room Bulletin, 922

S.D. Warren
225 Franklin St., Boston, MA, 02110
Warren Standard, The, 948

SEAK, Inc.
13 Falmouth Heights, P.O. Box 590, Falmouth, MA, 02541-0590
Workers' Compensation Monthly, 706

S.I. Assocs.
PO Box 107, North Egremont, MA, 01252-0107
Statistical Indicator Reports, 687

St. James Armenian Apostolic Church
465 Mount Auburn St, Watertown, MA, 02172-4117
Looys, 1,064

Sea Grant College Program
Bldg. E38-320, Cambridge, MA, 02139
MIT Sea Grant Quarterly Report, 936

Sebell Publishing Co., Inc.
965 Concord St, Framingham, MA, 01701-4685
Winning Sweepstakes Newsletter, 557

Shannon Knows DEC
135 Leland Farm Road, Ashland, MA, 01721
Shannon Knows DEC, 238

•Shelby Publishing Corp
155 Federal Street, Boston, MA, 02110-1727

Sierra Club, New England Chapter
3 Joy St., Boston, MA, 02108
New England Sierran, 389

Simmons College, School of Library Science, Alumni Assn.
300 The Fenway, Boston, MA, 02115-5898
Simmons Librarian, 810

Small Business Service Bureau, Inc.
554 Main St # 1441, Worcester, MA, 01608-2014
Small Business Service Bureau, Inc. Bulletin, 152

Smaller Business Assn. of N.E.
204 Second Ave, Waltham, MA, 02154
SBANE Enterprise, 150

Social Investment Forum
PO Box 2234, Boston, MA, 02107
Forum, The, 665

Society of Harvard Engineers
Harvard Univ., Rm. G12B, Pierc, Cambridge, MA, 02138-3800
H.E.S. Bulletin, 361

Society for Italian Historical Studies
Boston College Historical Dept, Chestnut Hill, MA, 02167
Society for Italian Historical Studies-Newsletter, 548

Society of Municipal Arborists
Box 364, Wellesley Hills, MA, 02181
City Trees, 1,019

Society of Pediatric Psychology
College of Medicine, Univ. of Iowa, Iowa City, MA, 02135
Progress Notes, 1,017

Soc. for the Preservation of New England Antiquities
141 Cambridge St, Boston, MA, 02114-2702
SPNEA News, 61

Soft Letter
17 Main St, Watertown, MA, 02172-4491
Soft Letter, 238

Software Success
175 Highland Ave., Needham, MA, 02194-3034
Software Success, 239

Sons of Mary, Health of the Sick, Inc.
567 Salem End Rd, Framingham, MA, 01701-5513
Sons, 1,060

South Shore Chamber of Commerce
36 Miller Stile Rd, Quincy, MA, 02169-5400
WAVES, 162

State Street Boston Corp.
PO Box 351, Boston, MA, 02101-0351
Now, 593

•Statistical Indicator Assocs.
PO Box 187, North Egremont, MA, 01252-0187

Stockwell Family Association
Donald F. Stockwell, 10 Fruit St., Mansfield, MA, 02048
Stockwell Family Association Newsletter, 416

Strategy Gaming Society
87 Park Ave Apt 6, Worcester, MA, 01605-3929
Strategist, 478

•Suffolk Univ.
8 Ashburton Pl, Boston, MA, 02108-2701

Supreme Council of the Royal Arcanum
61 Batterymarch St., Boston, MA, 02110-3206
Royal Arcanum Bulletin, 624

Survey Research Consultants International, Inc.
PO Box 25, Williamstown, MA, 01267-0025
World Opinion Update, 640

•TPLR, Inc.
Box 1162, Back Bay Annex, Boston, MA, 02117-1162

TVC Enterprises
PO Box 1088, Easton, MA, 02334-1088
Promotional Programming, 124

Technical Data Intl.
11 Farnsworth St, Boston, MA, 02210-1250
Investext Advisor, 671

Technical Education Research Centers
2067 Massachusetts Ave., Cambridge, MA, 02140
Hands On!, 311

Theology & Culture Newsletter
Andover Newton Theol. School, Newton Centre, MA, 02159
Theology & Culture Newsletter, 1,051

Thimbletter
93 Walnut Hill Rd, Newton, MA, 02161-1836
Thimbletter, 185

Third Reich Study Group-Germany Philatelic Society
PO Box 283, Needham Heights, MA, 02194-0904
Third Reich Study Group-Bulletin, 972

Thomas Associates
335 Washington St # 154, Woburn, MA, 01801-2115
Thomas Report, The, 154

Town of Marblehead Council on Aging
Widger Rd., Mary Alley Hosp., Marblehead, MA, 01945
Old Marblehead Cod, 1,108

•Trans 21
Fields Corner Station, Box 249, Boston, MA, 02122

Travel to Europe
49 Waltham St., Box 439, Lexington, MA, 02173-5411
European Travel Report, 1,184

Tufts Kinsmen Assn.
PO Box 571, Dedham, MA, 02027-0571
Tufts Kinsmen, 469

Tufts Medical School
236 Harrison Ave, Boston, MA, 02111-1835
Tufts Medical Alumni Bulletin, 888

•Tufts Univ.
Communications & Publ. Rel., 419 Boston Ave., Medford, MA, 02155

•Tufts University School of Veterinary Medicine
200 Westboro Rd., North Grafton, MA, 01536

Turley Publications
24 Water St, Palmer, MA, 01069-1840
Valley Women's Voice, 1,212

Two/Ten International Footwear Foundation
56 Main St, Watertown, MA, 02172-4413
Two/Ten International Footwear Foundation-Two/Ten Today, 56

U.N. Univ., Cambridge Programme Office
MIT, Cambridge, MA, 02139-3594
Food & Nutrition Bulletin, 428

USA Rugby Fives Assn. -St. Mark's School
Southborough, MA, 01772
USA Rugby Fives Assn. -News Letter, 1,137

* See **MULTI-PUBLISHER INDEX** for list of publications.

©1996, Oxbridge Communications, Inc.

* See **MULTI-PUBLISHER INDEX** for list of publications.

Lapeer County Genealogical Society
921 W Nepessing St, Lapeer, MI, 48446-1872
Lapeer County Genealogical Society Newsletter, 459

Latin American Jewish Studies Assn.
2104 Georgetown Blvd., Ann Arbor, MI, 48105-1535
Latin American Jewish Studies, 404

Latin American Paper Money Society
3304 Milford Mill Rd., Baltimore, MI, 21244-2041
LANSA, 928

•**Law Reporter Co.**
209 Michigan Ave # 270, Crystal Falls, MI, 49920-1312

Lisle Fellowship
433 W Sterns Rd, Temperance, MI, 48182-9568
Lisle Interaction, 316

Loan Broker
917 S Park St, Owosso, MI, 48867-4422
Political Corruption, 996

MOPAR Scat Pack Club
PO Box 2303, Dearborn, MI, 48123-2303
Mighty Mopars, 74

MSHDA
PO Box 30044, Lansing, MI, 48909-7544
MSHDA Review, 1,021

Madonna University
36600 Schoolcraft Rd, Livonia, MI, 48150-1176
Madonna Now, 201

Marquette County Historical Society, Inc.
213 N Front St, Marquette, MI, 49855-4220
Harlow's Wooden Man, 540

Matrix Software
315 Marion Ave, Big Rapids, MI, 49307-1345
Astrotalk, 68

McKinstry Bros. Publishing Group, Inc.
PO Box 833, Petoskey, MI, 49770-0833
Old Tyme Baseball News, 101

Mead Publishing Paper Div.
PO Box 757, Escanaba, MI, 49829-0757
Report, 947

Mechanical Bank Collectors of America
PO Box 128, Allegan, MI, 49010-0128
Mechanical Banker, The, 53

Medical Manufacturing Tech Source
40 N Huron St, Ypsilanti, MI, 48197-2608
Pharmaceutical Production Tech Source, 287

Medieval Institute Publications
Western Michigan Univ., Kalamazoo, MI, 49008-3851
EDAM Review, 1,173

Merriman Market Analyst
PO Box 250012, West Bloomfield, MI, 48325-0012
MMA Cycles Report, 675

Metropolitan Detroit Convention & Visitors Bureau
100 Renaissance Center, Ste. 1900, Detroit, MI, 48243-1006
Conventionews, 134

Michigan Antique Phonograph Society
2609 Devonshire Ave., Lansing, MI, 48910-3671
In the Groove, 184

Michigan Archival Assn.
Walter Reuther Library, Wayne State Univ., 5401 Cass, Detroit, MI, 48202
Open Entry, 807

•**Michigan Assn. of Calligraphers**
PO Box 55, Royal Oak, MI, 48068-0055

Michigan Assn. of School Administrators
421 W Kalamazoo St, Lansing, MI, 48933-2006
Fortnighter, 1,091

Michigan Assn. of Secondary School Principals
Univ. of Michigan, 2339 School of Educ. Bldg., Ann Arbor, MI, 48109-0001
Bulletin, 1,090

Michigan Cattlemen's Assn.
2145 University Park Dr Ste, 300, Okemos, MI, 48864-3982
Michigan Beef Industry News, 828

Michigan Civil Rights Dept.
303 W. Kalamazoo 4th Floor, Lansing, MI, 48913-0001
Michigan Civil Rights Commission Newsletter, 174

Michigan Dept. of Agriculture
PO Box 30017, Lansing, MI, 48909-7517
AASCO Newsletter, 35

Michigan Dept. of Civil Service
320 S Walnut St # 30002, Lansing, MI, 48933-2014
Michigan Department of Civil Service, Newsletter, 346

Michigan Diabetes Research & Training Ctr.
Univ. of Michigan, 3700 Upjohn Ctr., Ann Arbor, MI, 48109-1189
Michigan Diabetes Research & Training Center-Newsletter, 880

•**Michigan Employment Security Commission**
7310 Woodward Ave, Detroit, MI, 48202-3152

Michigan Guild of Artists & Artisans
118 N 4th Ave, Ann Arbor, MI, 48104-1402
Limited Edition, 65

Michigan Horse Council
PO Box 22008, Lansing, MI, 48909-2008
Over the Fence, 560

Michigan Information & Research Service, Inc.
421 W Ionia St, Lansing, MI, 48933-1103
MIRS Legislative Report & Capitol Capsule, 488

Michigan League for Human Services
300 Washington Sq N Ste 401, Lansing, MI, 48933-1223
Legislative Bulletin, 1,118

Michigan Library Assn.
6810 S. Cedar St., Ste. 6, Lansing, MI, 48911-6909
Michigan Librarian, 804

Michigan Mutual Insurance Co.
28 W. Adams Ave., Detroit, MI, 48226
Amerisure Companies Safety News, 1,078

Michigan Nurses Assn.
2310 Jolly Oak Rd, Okemos, MI, 48864-4599
Michigan Nurse, 930

Michigan Reading Assn.
PO Box 7509, Grand Rapids, MI, 49510-7509
News & Views, 322

Michigan Sea Grant College Program
2200 Bonisteel Blvd., Ann Arbor, MI, 48109-2099
Upwellings, 395

Michigan State Police
714 S Harrison Rd, East Lansing, MI, 48823-5143
Michigan Traffic Accident Facts, 1,081

Michigan State Univ.
A364 Engineering Building, E. Lansing, MI, 48824-0001
Motor Fleet Safety Supervision, 1,082

Michigan State Univ., College of Social Science
South Kedzie Hall, East Lansing, MI, 48824-0001
School of Labor and Industrial Relations, Newsletter, 705

Michigan State Univ. Computer Laboratory
404f Computer Ctr, East Lansing, MI, 48824-1042
Acronyms, 211

Michigan State Univ., Dept. of Ag. & Ext. Ed.
409 Ag. Hall, East Lansing, MI, 48824-1039
ANR Educator, 298

Michigan State University, Dept. of Resource Development
Publications, East Lansing, MI, 48823
Michigan Resource Bulletin, 1,022

Michigan State University Inst. of Water Res.
334 Natural Res. Bldg., East Lansing, MI, 48824-0001
GEM Notes, 1,202

•**Michigan State University Libraries**
Publications, E. Lansing, MI, 48824-1048

Michigan State Univ., School of Labor & Industrial Relations
403 S Kedzie Hall, East Lansing, MI, 48824-1032
Michigan State University, School of Labor and Industrial Relations, Newsletter, 703

Michigan United Thoroughbred Breeders & Owners Assn.
PO Box 2752, Livonia, MI, 48151-0752
Michigan United Thoroughbred Breeders, 560

Michigan Water Environment Association
PO Box 82410, Rochester, MI, 48308-2410
Wastewater Works News, 1,204

Mick Family Newsletter
6555 Manson Dr, Waterford, MI, 48329-2736
Mick Family Newsletter, 461

Monica Gruler & Co.
PO Box 2095, Petoskey, MI, 49770-2095
Portable Practitioner: Opportunities in the Healing Arts, 525

Motor City Stamp & Cover Club
22608 Poplar Ct, Hazel Park, MI, 48030-1928
On Cover, 971

Mountainside Publishing, Inc.
321 S. Main St., Ste. 300, P.O. Box 8330, Ann Arbor, MI, 48107
Library Issues: Briefings for Faculty & Administrators, 802

Munson Medical Ctr.
1105 6th St, Traverse City, MI, 49684-2386
Intercom, 587

Muskegon Labor Council
490 W Western Ave, Muskegon, MI, 49440-1041
Western Michigan AFL-CIO News, 712

N. American Pizza Assn.
23 N Washington St Ste 20, Ypsilanti, MI, 48197-2617
Slice of Pizza, 1,076

Natl. Assn. of College Univ. Food Services
1405 S. Harrison, Manly Miles Bldg., Ste 304, E. Lansing, MI, 48824
NACUFS News Wave, 431

Natl. Assn. of Investors Corp.
PO Box 220, Royal Oak, MI, 48068-0220
NAIC Investor Advisory Service, 679

•**National Automobile Transporters Assn.**
902 Buhl Bldg., Detroit, MI, 48226

National Institute of Burn Medicine
909 E Ann St, Ann Arbor, MI, 48104-1613
NBIE Newsletter, 881

Natl. Librarians Assn.
PO Box 486, Alma, MI, 48801-0486
National Librarian: The NLA Newsletter, 805

National Renal Administrators Association
4046 Gratridt Ave., Pt. Huron, MI, 48060-1202
NRAA Journal, 569

National Service Robot Assn.
900 Victors Way Ste 220, Ann Arbor, MI, 48108-1779
NSRA News, 231

Natl. Steel Corp. - Great Lakes Division
1 Quality Dr., Ecorse, MI, 48229
Focus, 584

•**Nationwide Intelligence**
PO Box 1922, Saginaw, MI, 48605-1922

Navy Wives Clubs of America
225 Euclid St, Mount Clemens, MI, 48043-1723
Navy Wives News, 180

Newspaper Collectors Society of America
PO Box 19134, Lansing, MI, 48901-9134
Collectible Newspapers, 183

North American Indian
22720 Plymouth Rd, Detroit, MI, 48239-1327
North American Indian, 994

North American Rockwell Corp., Automotive Div.
2135 W Maple Rd, Troy, MI, 48084-7121
Rockwell-Standard News, 597

North American Students of Cooperation
530 S State St # 7715, Ann Arbor, MI, 48109-1349
NASCO Newsbriefs, 254

North Country Trail Assn.
3777 Sparks Drive, Suite 105, Grand Rapids, MI, 49546
North Star, 389

Noteworthy Communications
34518 Warren Road #315, Westland, MI, 48185
Choirboy Notes, 911

OMI Intl. Corp.
21441 Hoover Rd, Warren, MI, 48089-3161
World of Metal Finishing, 603

Oakland Co. Genealogical Soc.
PO Box 1094, Birmingham, MI, 48012-1094
Acorns to Oaks, 446

Oldsmobile Div., G.M.C.
Public Relations Dept., 920 Townsend St., Lansing, MI, 48921-0001
Oldsmobile Team, 593

Olivet College
S. Main, Olivet, MI, 49076
Olivet College Bulletin, 202

Omicron Nu Home Economics Honor Society
PO Box 247, Haslett, MI, 48840-0247
Home Economics Forum, 558

On the Garden Line
PO Box 6047, Wexon, MI, 48393
On the Garden Line, 442

PM Group
1109 Comerica Building, Battle Creek, MI, 49016
Professional Practice Today, 843

Pascit Publications
PO Box 1125, Traverse City, MI, 49685-1125
Making Ends Meet, 94

Pat Worden
1201 Glendale St, Midland, MI, 48642-5105
Wordens Past, 470

Peace Education Center
1118 S Harrison Rd, East Lansing, MI, 48823-5201
Peace Education Center Monthly, 995

Performance Resource Press, Inc.
1863 Technology Dr, Troy, MI, 48083-4244
Health Sentry, 510

•**Photo Marketing Association International**
3000 Picture Pl, Jackson, MI, 49201-8853

• See ***MULTI-PUBLISHER INDEX*** for list of publications.

Pierian Press
PO Box 1808, Ann Arbor, MI, 48106-1808
Library Hi Tech News, 802

Planning & Zoning Center, Inc.
302 S. Waverly Rd., Lansing, MI, 48917-3631
Planning & Zoning News, 1,023

Poetry Resource Center of Michigan
Wayne State Unv., Eng. Dept., 51 Warren, Detroit, MI, 48202
P.R.C. Newsletter and Calendar, 983

Polish-American Liturgical Center
Orchard Lake Schools, Box 240492, Orchard Lake, MI, 48324
Slowo I Liturgia, 1,060

Pope John Paul II Center
Orchard Lake Schools, Orchard Lake, MI, 48033
Pope John Paul II Center Newsletter, 1,059

Porsche Club of America, Western Michigan Region
1503 43rd St SW, Wyoming, MI, 49509-4342
Porsche Uber Alles, 75

•**Proteus Publishing**
P.O. Box 2940, Ann Arbor, MI, 48106

Public Interest Research Group on Michigan
338 1/2 S State St, Ann Arbor, MI, 48104-2412
PIRGIM Citizen Connection, 390

Public Relations Enterprises, Inc.
PO Box 12236, Lansing, MI, 48901-2236
Michigan Banker, 94

R-Squared Press
2113 Arborview Blvd., Ann Arbor, MI, 48103-3513
Open Adoption Birthparent, 414

Railtech, Inc.
PO Box 3280, Ann Arbor, MI, 48106-3280
Table Top Train News, 556

Reformed Ecumenical Council
2017 Eastern Ave SE Ste 201, Grand Rapids, MI, 49507
REC News Exchange, 1,050

Region Six Michigan Education Assn.
5460 Arden Ave, Warren, MI, 48092-1190
Region Six Sentinel, 1,093

Robotic Industries Assn.
900 Victors Way, P.O. Box 3724, Ann Arbor, MI, 48106
Robot Times, 235

•**Romanian American Heritage Ctr.**
2540 Grey Tower Rd, Jackson, MI, 49201-9120

•**St. John Hospital Inc.**
Marketing & Public Relations, 22101 Moross Rd., Detroit, MI, 48236-2148

Saul Bellow Society
6533 Post Oak Dr, West Bloomfield, MI, 48322-3831
Saul Bellow Society Newsletter, 824

Servant Publications
Ann Arbor, MI, 48107-7711
Elisabeth Elliot Newsletter, 1,047

Sid Cato Communications, Inc.
PO Box 19850, Kalamazoo, MI, 49019-0850
Sid Cato's Newsletter on Annual Reports, 151

Sierra Club, Mackinac Chapter
300 Washington Sq. N., Ste. 411, Lansing, MI, 48933-1223
Mackinac, 387

Smiths Industries
4141 Eastern Ave SE, Grand Rapids, MI, 49508-3469
Interface, 587

Society for Industrial Archeology
Houghton, MI, 49931
Society for Industrial Archeology Newsletter, 58

Society of Manufacturers Agents
42072 Queen Anne Ct., Northville, MI, 48167-1903
Society of Manufacturers Agents, Newsletter, 1,088

•**Society of Manufacturing Engineers**
One SME Dr., Box 930, Dearborn, MI, 48121

Society for the Psychological Study of Social Issues
PO Box 1248, Ann Arbor, MI, 48106-1248
Society for the Psychological Study of Social Issues Newsletter, 1,018

Society for the Study of Midwestern Literature
Michigan State University, Ernst Bessey Hall, East Lansing, MI, 48824
Society for the Study of Midwestern Literature Newsletter, 825

Sodus News, The
3503 Edwards Rd., Sodus, MI, 49126
Sodus News, The, 1,041

Spark Plug Collectors of America
PO Box 2229, Ann Arbor, MI, 48106-2229
Ignitor, 553

Spartan Stores, Inc.
850 76th St. , S. W., Grand Rapids, MI, 49508
Spartan News, 599

Spill Control Association of America
400 Renaissance Ctr, Detroit, MI, 48243
Spill Briefs, 394

State of Michigan, Dept. of Management & Budgeting
3369 N. Logan Property Secti, Fedl. Surplus Propert, Lansing, MI, 48913-0001
Surplus Property News Bulletin, 1,024

The Stearns Collection of Musical Instruments
School of Music, Univ. of Michigan, Ann Arbor, MI, 48109
Stearns Newsletter, The, 918

•**Strawberry Media, Inc.**
2460 Lexington, Owosso, MI, 48867-1015

Studium: N. American Study Center for Polish Affairs
1281 Rugby Cir, Bloomfield, MI, 48302-0945
Studium Papers, 638

Subterranean Sociology Assn.
Dept. of Sociology, Eastern Michigan Univ., Ypsilanti, MI, 48197
Subterranean Sociology Newsletter, 1,127

•**Taft Group**
835 Penobscot Bldg., Detroit, MI, 48226-4094

Thomson-Shore
7300 W. Joy Rd., Dexter, MI, 48130-9701
Printer's Ink, 1,006

Triangle Foundation
19641 W 7 Mile Rd, Detroit, MI, 48219-2721
Tripod, The, 446

Trust Dept.
Natl. Bank Of Woodward & Fo, Detroit, MI, 48278-0001
Estate and Tax Bulletin, 735

UMI
300 N Zeeb Rd, Ann Arbor, MI, 48103-1553
Serials Focus, 810

Unicycling Society of America, Inc.
PO Box 40534, Redford, MI, 48240-0534
On One Wheel, 263

U.S. Dept. of Agriculture, Milk Market Administrator
2684 11 Mile Rd, Berkley, MI, 48072-3050
Milk Market Bulletin, 264

U.S. Ski Assn., Central Div.
PO Box 117, Charlevoix, MI, 49720-0117
Skiland/Mid America Skier, 1,113

Univ. of Michigan
Dept. of the History of Art, Tappan Hall, Rm. 50, Ann Arbor, MI, 48109-1357
Newsletter East Asian Art & Archaeology, 66

•**Univ. of Michigan Assoc. in the Social Found. of Educ.**
4001 School of Educ. Bldg., Ann Arbor, MI, 48104

University of Michigan Fitness Research Center
401 Washtenaw Ave., Ann Arbor, MI, 48109-2214
Healthlines, 511

Univ. of Michigan Institute for Social Research
PO Box 1248, Ann Arbor, MI, 48106-1248
ISR Newsletter, 1,125

Univ. of Michigan, School of Dentistry
Univ. of Michigan, Ann Arbor, MI, 48109-1078
Dentalum, 189

Vintage Triumph Register Inc.
15218 W Warren Ave, Dearborn, MI, 48126-1356
English Channel, 72

Walrus Press, The
32 Trimountain Ave., Box 280, South Range, MI, 49963
BIN, 115

Walsh College of Accountancy and Business Administration
PO Box 7006, Troy, MI, 48007-7006
Campus Insight, 202

Walter Reuther Library
Wayne State University, 5401 Cass Ave., Detroit, MI, 48202-3613
Archives of Labor, 698

•**Ward's Communications,**
3000 Town Center, Ste. 2750, Southfield, MI, 48075-1212

Warner Vineyards
PO Box 269, Paw Paw, MI, 49079-0269
Warner, 105

Wayne State Univ. -Center
2319 Faculty/Admin. Bldg., Detroit, MI, 48202
Center for Peace & Conflict Studies Newsletter, 628

Wendy
P.O. Box 43036, Mt. Clements, MI, 48043
World Links, 817

Western Michigan University Alumni Relations
1201 Oliver St, Kalamazoo, MI, 49008-3804
Westerner, The, 189

Whirlpool Corp.
2000 N M 63, Benton Harbor, MI, 49022-2692
Whirlpool World, 603

Wolanchuk Report
28037 Gratiot Ave, Roseville, MI, 48066-4204
Wolanchuk Report, 692

Wolverine World Wide
N Main St., Rockford, MI, 49341
Wolverine News, 603

Women's Action for Nuclear Disarmament
360 Hilldale Drive, Ann Arbor, MI, 48105
WAND Bulletin, 1,212

World Medical Relief
11745 12th St., Detroit, MI, 48206-1270
World Medical Relief-Newsletter, 532

Wyandotte General Hospital
2333 Biddle St, Wyandotte, MI, 48192-4693
Capsule, 562

Yoder Distributors
1422 Wealthy St SE, Grand Rapids, MI, 49506-2717
Howe Research Newsletter, 457

Minnesota

Acu Trend
1830 W Saint Germain St # 34, Saint Cloud, MN, 56301-4015
Acu Trend, 654

Advanstar Communications
431 W 1st Street, Duluth, MN, 55802-2065
Africa Fund, 171

Al Hanson's Economic Newsletter
PO Box 9, Ottertail, MN, 56571-0009
Al Hanson's Economic Newsletter, 126

American Collectors Assn., Inc.
4040 W 70th St, Minneapolis, MN, 55435-4104
Cred-Alert, 86

American Commercial Collectors Assn.
4040 W 70th St, Minneapolis, MN, 55435-4104
Scope, 98

American Fraternal Union
111 S 4th Ave E, Ely, MN, 55731-1460
New Era/Nova Doba, 180

American Institute of Hydrology
2499 Race St. Ste. 135, St. Paul, MN, 55113
AIH Bulletin, 475

American Peony Society
250 Interlachen Rd, Hopkins, MN, 55343-8526
American Peony Society Bulletin, 440

•**American Phytopathological Society**
3340 Pilot Knob Rd, St. Paul, MN, 55121-2055

American Shire Horse Assn.
9251 Lansing Ave N, Stillwater, MN, 55082-8414
American Shire Horse Association -Newsletter, 559

American Sleep Disorders Association
1610 14th St NW Ste 300, Rochester, MN, 55901
ASDA News, 865

American Society of Brewing Chemists
3340 Pilot Knob Rd, Saint Paul, MN, 55121-2055
ASBC Newsletter, 102

American Swedish Institute
2600 Park Ave, Minneapolis, MN, 55407-1090
ASI Posten, 409

Antique Automobile Club of America, Minnesota Region
621 E. 61st St., Minneapolis, MN, 55417
Northern Lights (Minneapolis), 53

•**Architecture Technology Corp.**
PO Box 24344, Minneapolis, MN, 55424-0344

Armenian Cultural Organization of Minnesota
18275 Hummmingbird Rd., Deephaven, MN, 55391-3226
ACOM Newsletter, 399

Arts Criticism
2402 University Avenue West, Suite 208, Saint Paul, MN, 55110
Critical Angels, 814

Association for Women Geoscientists
4779 126th St. N., St. Paul, MN, 55110-5910
Gaea, 476

•**Augsburg Fortress Publishers**
PO Box 1209, 426 S. Fifth St., Minneapolis, MN, 55440-1209

•**Aviation/Space Writers Assn.**
6540 50th St. N, Oakdale, MN, 55128-1708

* See **MULTI-PUBLISHER INDEX** for list of publications.

Bakken Library & Museum of Electricity in Life
3537 Zenith Ave S, Minneapolis, MN, 55416-4623
Bakken, The, 793

Bering Communications
PO Box 19116, Minneapolis, MN, 55419
Reading Woman, 419

Bob Larson's Tennis
PO Box 24379, Edina, MN, 55424-0379
Bob Larson's Tennis Newswire, 1,170

Born Young
347 12th Ave. N, St. Paul, MN, 55075-1957
Born Young Newsletter, 448

Bunnie Timmons-Runman
PO Box 262, Montrose, MN, 55363-0262
Timmons Family Newsletter, 468

•Business Newsletter, Inc.
537 E Vine St, Owatonna, MN, 55060-2518

Calix Society
7601 Wayzata Blvd., Minneapolis, MN, 55426-1626
Chalice, 1,115

Carlson School of Management
Univ. of Minnesota, 271 19th Ave., S., Minneapolis, MN, 55455-0100
Minnesota Management Review, 145

Chatfield Brass Band Library
81 Library Lane, P.O Box 578, Chatfield, MN, 55923
Chatfield Brass Band-Newsletter, 911

Children's Home Society of Minnesota
1605 Ustin Street, St. Paul, MN, 55108
Today Child, 1,123

Christian Forum Research Foundation
1111 Fairgrounds Rd, Grand Rapids, MN, 55744-2457
Christians in Crisis, 1,062

Citizens' Scholarship Foundation of America
1505 Riverview Rd, Saint Peter, MN, 56082-1556
CSFA News, 303

College of St. Scholastica
1200 Kenwood Ave, Duluth, MN, 55811-4199
Inside Times, 189

Computers and the Media Center
515 Oak St. N., Cannon Falls, MN, 55009-1630
CMC News (Computers in the Media Center), 214

Concordia College
275 Syndicate St N, Saint Paul, MN, 55104-5494
Short Alert, 638

Cottage Connections
11113 Radisson Ct, Burnsville, MN, 55337-1117
Cottage Connections, 1,041

DOT Publications, Inc.
10600 University Ave. NW, Minneapolis, MN, 55448-6166
Dancing USA, 266

•Data Research, Inc.
4635 Nicols Rd Ste 100, Eagan, MN, 55122-3337

Electric Machinery Mfg. Co.
800 Central Ave NE, Minneapolis, MN, 55413-2403
E-M Diamond, 582

Environmental Conservation Library
300 Nicollet Mall, Minneapolis, MN, 55401-1925
ECOL News, 377

Exhibitor Publications, Inc.
206 S. Broadway, Ste. 745, Rochester, MN, 55904-6565
Exhibitor Extra, 138

FARMS Intl., Inc.
PO Box 270, Knife River, MN, 55609-0270
Prayer Letter, 45

FM Atlas Publishing
PO Box 336, Esko, MN, 55733-0336
FMedia!, 124

Federal Reserve Bank of Minneapolis
250 Marquette Ave, Minneapolis, MN, 55401-2117
Agricultural Credit Conditions Survey, 36

Fielder's Choice
PO Box 456, Waite Park, MN, 56387-0456
Fielder's Choice, 101

Financial Privacy Report
1129 Cliff Rd E, Burnsville, MN, 55337-1514
Financial Privacy Report, 664

Finnish-American Heritage Society, Inc.
1027 Rhode Island Ave N, Minneapolis, MN, 55427-4522
Finnish-American Heritage, 401

The Fire Fly
P.O. Box 133, Angle Inlet, MN, 56711
The Fire Fly, 990

Five Owls
2004 Sheridan Ave S, Minneapolis, MN, 55405-2354
Five Owls, 821

Freeborn County Genealogical Soc.
PO Box 403, Albert Lea, MN, 56007-0403
Freeborn County Tracer, 454

•Freshwater Foundation
2500 Shadywood Road, Navarre, MN, 55331

Friends of the Dard Hunter Paper Museum
4517 Penn Ave N, Minneapolis, MN, 55412-1132
Bull & Branch, 903

Grawunder Technical Services
13108 Penn Ave., Burnsville, MN, 55337-2015
Grawunder and Graffunder Connection, The, 455

Hazelden Foundation
15251 Pleasant Valley Rd., PO Box 11, Center City, MN, 55012-0011
Hazelden Voice, 1,117

Health Physics Society
Rte. 1, Box 139H, Elysian, MN, 56028
Health Physics Society Newsletter, 510

Historical Aircraft Corp.
536 Star Ln, South Saint Paul, MN, 55075-1511
HAC Techline, 29

Hubert H. Humphrey Institute of Public Affairs
301 19th Ave., Public Affairs, Univ. of Minnesota, Minneapolis, MN, 55455-0429
HHH Institute News, 990

ICEA
PO Box 20048, Minneapolis, MN, 55420-0048
ICEA Review, 78

IWRAW/WPPD
Humphrey Inst of Public Affair, Univ. Minn., 301-19th Ave. S., Minneapolis, MN, 55455
Women's Watch, 1,214

•Immunization Action Coalition
1573 Selby Ave Ste 229, St. Paul, MN, 55104-6328

Independent School District No. 709, Communications
Lake Ave. & Second St., Duluth, MN, 55802
School Bulletin, 329

Industrial Relations Service Bureau
2909 Wayz Blvd., Minneapolis, MN, 55405-2182
Public Sector Arbitration Awards, 710

International Childbirth Education Assn.
PO Box 20048, Minneapolis, MN, 55420-0048
ICEA Journal, 412

Intl. Ecology Society
1471 Barclay St, Saint Paul, MN, 55106-1405
Eco-Humane Letter, 378

International Society of Differentiation
Univ. of Minnesota, Biological Sciences Ctr., St. Paul, MN, 55108-1004
Intl. Society of Differentiation-Newsletter, 109

Investment Notes
PO Box 14430, Minneapolis, MN, 55414-0430
Investment Notes, 672

•Investment Rarities, Inc.
7850 Metro Pky Ste 106, Minneapolis, MN, 55425-1521

Irish American Culture Institute
2115 Summit Ave # 5026, Saint Paul, MN, 55105-1048
Ducas, 403

Irish Genealogical Society, Intl.
PO Box 16585, St. Paul, MN, 55116-0585
The Septs, 467

Irish Music & Dance Assn.
PO Box 65187, Saint Paul, MN, 55165-0187
Irish Music & Dance Assn. -Newsletter, 369

Iron Range Historical Society
Gilbert City Hall, Box 786, Gilbert, MN, 55741
Range History, 547

Jacqui Meadows
9304 Claremont NE, Albuquerque, MN, 87112
Captn' Nola, 694

Jamieson & Assocs., Inc.
4133 W 45th St, Minneapolis, MN, 55424-1040
Jamieson & Assocs. -Trends, 1,160

•K.D. Information Notes, Inc.
PO Box 14430, Minneapolis, MN, 55414-0430

Kristus Draudzes Vestis
4025 Chowen Ave S, Minneapolis, MN, 55410-1013
Kristus Draudzes Vestis, 404

•Lakewood Publications, Inc.
50 S. Ninth St., Minneapolis, MN, 55402-3165

Latvian Evangelical Lutheran Church
3152 17th Ave S, Minneapolis, MN, 55407-1821
Svetrita Zvani, 1,072

Latvian House, Inc.
PO Box 18491, Minneapolis, MN, 55418-0491
Latvian House, Inc. Bulletin, 404

Lexington Group in Transporation History
Dept. of History, St. Cloud St. U., St. Cloud, MN, 56301
Lexington Quarterly, 1,178

Linder Family Assn.
Hc 73 Box 989, Walker, MN, 56484-9531
Linder Quarterly, 459

Lutheran Braille Evangelism Association
1740 Eugene St, White Bear Lake, MN, 55110-3312
Lutheran Braille Evangelism Bulletin, 111

Lutheran Brethren Publ Co.
704 W Vernon Ave # 655, Fergus Falls, MN, 56537-2633
Faith and Fellowship, 1,072

MN Licensing Data Services
Market Communications, PO Box 16568, St. Paul, MN, 55116
MN Educational Resource Guide, 316

MN Speech-Language-Hearing Assn.
PO Box 26115, St. Louis Park, MN, 55426-0115
MN Speech-Language-Hearing Assn., 533

Mankato State Univ.
PO Box 109, Mankato, MN, 56002-0109
Microlink, 230

Mankato State Univ. Economics Dept.
MSU 14, P.O. Box 8400, Mankato, MN, 56002-8400
Mankato Area Business & Economic Indicators, 293

Mankato State University Human Economy Center
Box 14, Economics Dept., Mankato, MN, 56002-0014
Human Economy Newsletter, 292

•Mayo Foundation-Mayo Medical School
200 1st St SW, Rochester, MN, 55905-0001

Men's Defense Assn.
17854 Lyons St NE, Forest Lake, MN, 55025-8107
Liberator, The, 174

Mid-Life Women's Network
5129 Logan Ave S, Minneapolis, MN, 55419-1000
Mid Life Woman, 1,209

Miller Publishing Co.
12400 Whitewater Dr., Ste. 160, Minnetonka, MN, 55343-9466
Feed Additive Compendium, 418

Minneapolis Grain Exchange
130 Grain Exchange Bldg., 400 S. 4th St., Minneapolis, MN, 55415
Trading Trends, 689

Minnesota Apple Computer Users' Group, Inc.
PO Box 796, Hopkins, MN, 55343-0796
Mini' App'les, 230

Minnesota Arthritis Foundation
Arthritis Fndn. MN Chapter, 1730 Clifton Pl. #A1, Minneapolis, MN, 55403-3242
Tipsheet, 333

Minnesota Bible College
920 Mayowood Rd SW, Rochester, MN, 55902-2382
On The Move, 202

Minnesota Center for Book Arts
24 N 3rd St, Minneapolis, MN, 55401-1612
Minnesota Center for Book Arts, 118

Minnesota Chamber of Commerce
30 7th St E Ste 1700, Saint Paul, MN, 55101-4901
Minnesota Views, 160

Minnesota Composers Forum
332 Minnesota Street, #E145, St. Paul, MN, 55101-1314
Minnesota Composers Forum, 914

Minnesota Computer Industry Coalition
365 Summit Ave, Saint Paul, MN, 55102-2120
MCIC Publication, 228

•Minnesota Correctional Facility
PO Box B, Saint Cloud, MN, 56302-1000

Minnesota Council of Teachers of English
c/o Terrance Flaherty, Mankato State University, Mankato, MN, 56001
Minnesota English Newsletter, 318

Minnesota Dept. of Ag. Plant Protection Div.
90 Plato Blvd W, Saint Paul, MN, 55107-2004
Minnesota Pest Report, 43

Minnesota Department of Commerce
133 7th St E, Saint Paul, MN, 55101-2333
Commerce Contact, 482

Minnesota Dept. of Conservation
90 Plato Blvd W, Saint Paul, MN, 55107-2004
Minnesota Division of Game and Fish, Technical Bulletin, 387

Minnesota Dept. of Jobs & Training
390 Robert St N, Saint Paul, MN, 55101-1812
Minnesota Labor Market Review, 703

•Minnesota Extension Service
231 ClassRm. Office Bldg., 1994 Buford Avenue., St. Paul, MN, 55108-6040

* See **MULTI-PUBLISHER INDEX** for list of publications.

Minnesota Futurists
365 Summit Ave., Saint Paul, MN, 55102-2120
Future Trends, 471

Minnesota Genealogical Society
PO Box 16069, St. Paul, MN, 55116-0069
Minnesota Genealogical Society Newsletter, 461

Minnesota Government Report
PO Box 441, Willernie, MN, 55090-0441
Minnesota Government Report, 488

•**Minnesota Historical Society**
345 Kellogg Blvd W, St. Paul, MN, 55102-1906

Minnesota Ink, Inc.
P.O. Box 25376, St. Paul, MN, 55125-0376
Con$umer Wi$e, 252

Minnesota Institute on Black Chemical Abuse
2616 Nicollet Ave, Minneapolis, MN, 55408-1628
MIBCA Scope, 516

Minnesota International Center
711 E River Rd, Minneapolis, MN, 55455-0369
Minnesota International Center, 634

Minnesota Landscape Arboretum Foundation
3675 Arboretum Blvd # 39, Chanhassen, MN, 55317-9338
Minnesota Landscape Arboretum News, 442

Minnesota League for Nursing
PO Box 24713, Edina, MN, 55424-0713
MLN New Directions, 930

Minnesota Legal Register
PO Box 3645, Duluth, MN, 55803-3645
Minnesota Legal Register, 788

Minnesota Library Assn.
1315 Lowry Ave. N., Minneapolis, MN, 55411-1326
Minnesota Library Assn. Newsletter, 804

Minnesota Library Assn. Social Responsibilities Round Table
4645 Columbus Ave, Minneapolis, MN, 55407-3527
MSRRT Newsletter, 804

Minnesota Literature
1 Nord Circle Rd, Saint Paul, MN, 55127-6513
Minnesota Literature, 823

Minnesota Nurses Assn.
1295 Bandana Blvd. N., Ste. 140, St. Paul, MN, 55108-5115
Minnesota Nursing Accent, 930

Minnesota Occupational Information Coordinating Committee
Dept. of Economic Security, 390 N. Robert, St. Paul, MN, 55101
MOICC News - Net, 703

Minnesota Office of Tourism
375 Jackson St Ste 250, Saint Paul, MN, 55101-1810
Travel Minute, 1,190

Minnesota State Council on Disability
121 7th Pl E Ste 107, Saint Paul, MN, 55101-2114
Connector, 1,116

Minnesota State Services for the Blind
2200 University Ave., W., St. Paul, MN, 55114
Minnesota Bulletin, 111

•**Moneypower**
PO Box 2240, Minneapolis, MN, 55422

Moorhead State Univ.
Publications, Moorhead, MN, 56563-0001
Bulletin, 202

•**Multi Resource Centers, Inc.**
1900 Chicago Ave, Minneapolis, MN, 55404-1903

NWTC & FHC
PO Box 29397, Brooklyn Center, MN, 55429-0397
Cousins et Cousines, 451

Natl. Assn. of the 6th Infantry Div.
5649 39th Ave S, Minneapolis, MN, 55417-2917
Sightseer, 898

Natl. Assn. of Farm Broadcasters
26 Exchange St E Ste 307, Saint Paul, MN, 55101-2264
Chats, 123

Natl. Ataxia Foundation
15500 Wayzata Blvd Ste 750, Wayzata, MN, 55391-1490
Generations, 507

•**Natl. Council on Family Relations**
3989 Central Ave. NE, Ste. 550, Minneapolis, MN, 55421-3972

Natl. Foster Parent Assn.
4874 Bloom Ave, White Bear Lake, MN, 55110-2734
National Advocate, 414

•**National Mail Order Association**
2807 Polk St. NE., Minneapolis, MN, 55418-2954

Neighborhood Caretaker
1522 Grand Ave Apt 4c, Saint Paul, MN, 55105-2228
Neighborhood Caretaker, 1,022

New Moon Publishing
PO Box 3620, Duluth, MN, 55803-3620
New Moon Network, 414

North American Council on Adoptable Children
970 Raymond Ave Ste 106, Saint Paul, MN, 55114-1146
Adoptalk, 1,113

•**North Hennepin Community College**
7411 85th Ave N, Brooklyn Park, MN, 55445-2231

Northwestern Natl. Life Ins. Co.
20 Washington Ave S, Minneapolis, MN, 55401-1908
Columns, 580

Norwegian-American Historical Assn.
St. Olaf College, 1510 St. Olaf Ave., Northfield, MN, 55057-1097
Norwegian-American Historical Association Newsletter, 406

Norwegian Singers Assn. of America
Rr 2 Box 137, Kenyon, MN, 55946-9340
Sanger-Hilsen/Singers Greetings, 407

Norwest Corp. -Economics Dept.
Sixth & Marquette, Minneapolis, MN, 55479-0001
Economic Indicators, 291

Odegaard Printing Co.
2502 W 3rd St, Duluth, MN, 55806-1839
Twin Ports Financial Record, 100

•**Office of Library Development & Services**
440 Capital Square Bldg., 550 Cedar St., St. Paul, MN, 55101

Onan Corp.
1400 73rd Ave NE, Minneapolis, MN, 55432-3796
Onan News, 593

Order of St. Benedict, Inc.
St. John's Univ., Collegeville, MN, 56321-9999
Record, 181

Outdoor Amusement Business Assn.
4600 W. 77th St., Minneapolis, MN, 55435
OABA News, 950

Patricia Maynard
2745 Winnetka Ave N # 121, New Hope, MN, 55427-2830
Language Maintenance, 822

Pig World Inc.
204 N. Oak Ave., #312, Owatonna, MN, 55060
Pigletter, 829

Place in the Woods, The
3900 Glenwood Ave., Golden Valley, MN, 55422-5302
Read, America!, 327

Political Communications, Inc.
26 Exchange St. E., St. Paul, MN, 55101-2264
Politics in Minnesota, 997

Positive Employee Practice Institute
50 South Ninth Street, Minneapolis, MN, 55402
PEPI Update, 704

Power Systems Research, Inc.
1301 Corporate Center Dr Ste, 113, Saint Paul, MN, 55121-1259
Power Products Business, 843

Printing Industry of Minnesota, Inc. (PIM)
450 N. Syndicate, Ste. 200, St. Paul, MN, 55104-4127
Graphic News, 1,004

Rasmussen Business College
12450 Wayzata Blvd., Minnetonka, MN, 55343
Razz Ma Tazz, 202

Recipes Unlimited
12125 16th Ave S # 1271, Burnsville, MN, 55337-2982
Cooking Connection, The, 427

Ronald S. Miller
4106 Degardner Cir NW, Saint Francis, MN, 55070-9705
Distant Drums, 973

Saint Mary's University of Minnesota
700 Terrace Heights, Campus Box 36, Winona, MN, 55987-1399
Campus Notes, 202

St. Paul Area Chamber of Commerce
55 5th St E Ste 101, Saint Paul, MN, 55101-1718
Business Today, 158

St. Paul Dispatch
55 4th St E, Saint Paul, MN, 55101-1106
On the Scene, 593

Satellite Industries Inc.
2530 Xenium Ln N, Minneapolis, MN, 55441-3695
Portable Sanitation Quarterly, 1,089

Sea Grant, Univ. of Minnesota
2305 East 5th Street, Duluth, MN, 55812
Seiche, The, 394

Ski for Light
1455 W. Lake St., Minneapolis, MN, 55408-2648
Ski for Light Bulletin, 528

Society for Biomaterials
6518 Walker Street, Suite #150, Minneapolis, MN, 55426-4244
Biomaterials Forum, 868

Society of Inkwell Collectors
5136 Thomas Ave S, Minneapolis, MN, 55410-2241
Stained Finger, The, 184

Society of St. Peter Claver
265 Century Ave. S., St. Mary's Mission House, St. Paul, MN, 55119-5206
Echo z Afryki, 1,056

Southcentral Minnesota Inter-Library Exchange (SMILE)
PO Box 3031, Mankato, MN, 56002-3031
SMILEtter, 809

Southeastern Minnesota Forest Resource Ctr.
Rr 2 Box 156a, Lanesboro, MN, 55949-9648
Shiitake News, 432

Spinal Cord Society
Rr 5 Box 22a, Fergus Falls, MN, 56537-9205
Spinal Cord Society-Newsletter, 887

•**State Farm Mutual Auto Insurance Co.**
1500 W. Highway 36, Saint Paul, MN, 55161-0001

Stearns County Historical Society
C/O David Ebnet, 235 South 33rd Ave. Box 702, St. Cloud, MN, 56302-0702
Crossings, 539

TTSS
3800 County Road 24, Maple Plain, MN, 55359-9652
Trumpeter Swan Society Newsletter, 942

Teddy Tribune
254 Sidney St W, Saint Paul, MN, 55107-3494
Teddy Tribune, 556

Tennant Co.
701 Lilac Dr N, Minneapolis, MN, 55422-4687
Tennant Topics, 600

Thayer Corp Graphic International
PO Box 8465, Mankato, MN, 56002-8465
Thayer Advertising Co., 940

Twin Cities Archives Round Table
Minneapolis Public Library, 300 Nicollet Mall, Minneapolis, MN, 55401
TCART Newsletter, 811

•**United Hospitals**
333 Smith Ave N, St. Paul, MN, 55102-2389

•**Universal Pensions Inc.**
PO Box 979, Brainerd, MN, 56401-0979

Univ. of Minnesota
309 19th Ave S, Minneapolis, MN, 55455-0438
Library, 801

Univ. of Minnesota, Dept. of Agricultural Education
St. Paul Campus, St. Paul, MN, 55108
Visitor, 47

Univ. of Minnesota Dept. of Extension Classes
180 Westbrook Hall, 77 Pleasant St., SE, Minneapolis, MN, 55455
Info, 313

Univ. of Minnesota Immigration History Research Center
Immigration History Res. Ctr., 826 Berry St., St. Paul, MN, 55114-1076
IHRC News, 398

Univ. of Minnesota Map Library
S76 Wilson Library, Minneapolis, MN, 55455-0414
Northern Latitudes, 806

Univ. of Minnesota, Office of Intl. Education
Univ. Of Minnesota, 216 Pillsbury Drive, S.E., Minneapolis, MN, 55455
International Dateline, 314

Univ. of Minnesota Technical College-Crookston
Crookston, MN, 56716-5001
Trojan Shorts, 202

University of Minnesota, Tourism Center
116 COB, St Paul, MN, 55108
Newsletter-International Academy for the Study of Tourism, 1,187

Valspar Corp.
1101 S. 3rd St., Minneapolis, MN, 55415-1211
Scope, 597

Vidas & Arrett, P.A.
920 2nd Ave S Ste 1540, Minneapolis, MN, 55402-4014
Quarterly Counselor, 772

WE Unlimited
PO Box 120633, Saint Paul, MN, 55112-0021
WE: Walk-ins for Evolution/A Newsletter for Conscious Connection, 923

Wall Street Underground
1129 E. Cliff Rd, Burnsville, MN, 55337-1514
Wall Street Underground, 691

* See ***MULTI-PUBLISHER INDEX*** for list of publications.

•West Publishing
620 Opperman Dr., Eagan, MN, 55123-1340

Women's Market Share
PO Box 512, Stillwater, MN, 55082-0512
Women's Market Share, 1,214

World Pen Pals
1694 Como Ave, Saint Paul, MN, 55108-2710
Pen Pal Post, 555

Yugoslav-American Society
PO Box 23336, Minneapolis, MN, 55423-0336
Yugoslav-American Society Newsletter, 410

Mississippi

Alpha Epsilon Delta
Jones Junior College, Ellisville, MS, 39437
Scalpel, 887

Argus Agronomics
PO Box 1420, 14920 Highway 61N, Clarksdale, MS, 38614
Euro-Turf, 440

Blue Mountain College
PO Box 160, Blue Mountain, MS, 38610-0160
Bulletin, 190

Center for the Study of Southern Culture
University of Mississippi, University, MS, 38677
Southern Register, 262

Delta Catfish Processors, Inc.
Industrial Park, Box 850, Indianola, MS, 38751
Delta Pride News, 422

Delta Resources Committee, Inc.
PO Box 584, Greenville, MS, 38702-0584
DRC Mississippi Newsletter, 1,116

General Motors Corp.
PO Box 260, Clinton, MS, 39060-0260
Wiretapper, 77

Gulf Coast Research Lab.
PO Box 7000, Ocean Springs, MS, 39566-7000
Marine Briefs, 936

Huber Farm Management
PO Box 1616, Greenville, MS, 38702-1616
Land Letter, 35

Ingalls Shipbuilding Division, Litton
PO Box 149, Pascagoula, MS, 39568-0149
Ingalls News, 586

Jackson Chamber of Commerce
PO Box 849, Jackson, MS, 39205-0849
Jackson Commerce, 160

Lamar Life Insurance Co.
317 E Capitol St, Jackson, MS, 39201-3493
Tower Talk, 601

Meridian Community College
910 Highway 19 N, Meridian, MS, 39307-5890
MCC Today, 190

Mississippi Academy of Sciences
405 Briarwood Dr Ste 107e, Jackson, MS, 39206-3032
Journal of the Mississippi Academy of Sciences, 1,098

Mississippi-Alabama Sea Grant Legal Program
Univ. of Miss. Law Ctr., University, MS, 38677
Water Log, 782

Mississippi Baptist Medical Center
1225 N. State St., Jackson, MS, 39202-2002
Healthcaring, 565

Mississippi Library Commission
PO Box 10700, Jackson, MS, 39289-0700
Packet, 807

Mississippi Museum of Art
201 E. Pascagoula St., Jackson, MS, 39201-4199
Museum Matters, 906

Mississippi Power & Light Co. (MP&L)
PO Box 1640, Jackson, MS, 39215-1640
Insight, 587

Mississippi State Dept of Archives
PO Box 571, Jackson, MS, 39205-0571
Mississippi History Newsletter, 544

Mississippi State University
English Dept., Mississippi State, MS, 39762
Thackeray Newsletter, 825

North Mississippi Rural Legal Services
PO Box 767, Oxford, MS, 38655-0767
NMRLS Notes, 759

Northwest Mississippi Community College
Publications, Senatobia, MS, 38668
Northwest Now, 190

Oxford Publishing, Inc.
307 Jackson Ave W, Oxford, MS, 38655-2154
Oxford Modern Languages & Literature, 824

Ruth Land Hatten
86 Saint Andrews Dr, Jackson, MS, 39211-2467
Land Newsletter, 459

Shamrock Publishing
RR 3 Box 272-D, Ripley, MS, 38663-9803
Southern Rose Review, 984

Soc. of Mississippi Archivists
PO Box 1151, Jackson, MS, 39215-1151
Primary Source, 808

Southern Rural Development Center
PO Box 5446, Mississippi State, MS, 39762-5446
Capsules, 1,019

Southern Sociological Society
P.O. Box 6245, Mississippi State, MS, 39762
Southern Sociologist, The, 1,127

Southern States Communication Association
Speech Communication Dept., Box 5131, Hattiesburg, MS, 39406-5131
Connections, 855

Square Books
1126 Van Buren Ave, Oxford, MS, 38655-3998
Dear Reader, 820

Tougaloo College
Publications, Tougaloo, MS, 39174-9999
Tougaloo News, 202

Trustmark Natl. Bank
PO Box 539, Brookhaven, MS, 39601-0539
Vault Talk, 602

USAE Waterways Experiment Station
Attn: CEWES-CV-I, 3909 Halls Ferry Rd., Vicksburg, MS, 39180
Quarterly CERCular Information Bulletin, 937

•U.S. Army Engineer Waterways Experiment Station
3909 Halls Ferry Rd, Vicksburg, MS, 39180-6133

Univ. of Mississippi Pharmacy School
School of Pharmacy, University, MS, 38677
Bulletin of the Bureau of Pharmaceutical Services, 281

Univ. of Southern Mississippi
USM Box 5013, Hattiesburg, MS, 39406-5013
Southern News and Views, 190

Univ. of Southern Mississippi Library
McCain Library, Box 5148, Children's Lit. Research, Hattiesburg, MS, 39406-5148
Juvenile Miscellany, 1,215

Yoknapatawpha Press, Inc.
PO Box 248, Oxford, MS, 38655-0248
Faulkner Newsletter, 821

Missouri

AT&T Southwestern Region
1111 Woods Mill Rd, Ballwin, MO, 63011-2943
News/Views, 592

Alana Kumber
P.O. Box 4988, Springfield, MO, 65808-4988
Wild Rumpus, 77

Allen Arpadi
5846 Waterman Blvd, Saint Louis, MO, 63112-1516
Photographs: A Collector's Newsletter, 977

Allen Family Circle
4906 Ridgeway Ave, Kansas City, MO, 64133-2545
Allen Family Circle, 447

Allied-Signal, Inc., Kansas City Division
Box 1159, Kansas City, MO, 64141
Newsbreak, 592

America Today
PO Box 188, Houston, MO, 65483-0188
America Today, 1,044

American Assembly of Collegiate Schools of Business
600 Emerson Rd Ste 300, Saint Louis, MO, 63141-6762
AACSB Newsline, 297

American Association of Bioanalysts
818 Olive St., Ste. 918, St. Louis, MO, 63101-1544
AAB Bulletin, 1,094

American Assn. of Orthodontists
401 N Lindbergh Blvd, Saint Louis, MO, 63141-7816
American Association of Orthodontists Bulletin, 268

American Baptist Society
2843 Washington Ave., St. Louis, MO, 63103
Baptist Voice, 1,045

American Board of Professional Psychology
2100 E Broadway Ste 313, Columbia, MO, 65201-6082
Diplomate, 1,013

American Council on Consumer Interests
240 Stanley Hall University Of, Missouri, Columbia, MO, 65211-0001
Consumer News and Reviews, 252

American Dexter Cattle Assn.
RR I, Box 378, Concordia, MO, 64020-9233
American Dexter Cattle Association, Bulletins, 826

American Institute of Philanthropy
393 N. Euclid Ave., Ste. 236, St. Louis, MO, 63108
Charity Rating Guide & Watchdog Report, 966

American Murray Grey Assn.
PO Box 34590, North Kansas City, MO, 64116-0990
American Murray Grey News, 827

American Optometric Assn. (AOA)
243 N. Lindbergh Blvd., St. Louis, MO, 63141-7881
AOSA Foresight, 298

American Osteopathic College of Anesthesiologists
17201 E. U.S. Highway 40, Lees Summit, MO, 64055
American Osteopathic College of Anesthesiologists Newsletter, 867

American Osteopathic College of Radiology
1402 Cottage Lane Ave, Kirksville, MO, 63501-4512
Viewbox, 889

American Silkie Bantam Club
2221 Blue Ridge Blvd, Independence, MO, 64052-1658
American Silkie Bantam Club-Newsletter, 827

America's Future
7800 Bonhomme Ave., St. Louis, MO, 63105
America's Future, 986

Andrew Duba
6307 Alexander Drive, St. Louis, MO, 63105
The Neo-Geo Gamer, 478

Assemblies of God, Inc.
1445 N Boonville Ave, Springfield, MO, 65802-1894
At Ease, 1,074

Assn. of Diesel Specialists
9140 Ward Pkwy., Kansas City, MO, 64114-3313
Nozzle Chatter, 832

Automotive Warehouse Distributors Association
9140 Ward Pky Ste 200, Kansas City, MO, 64114-3313
Aftermarket Distribution, 69

B.A.S.H.
12161 Lackland Rd # 101, Saint Louis, MO, 63146-4003
B.A.S.H., Inc., 499

Behavioral Studies Dept.
Univ. of Missouri, St. Louis, MO, 63121-4499
Multiple Linear Regression Viewpoints, 1,016

Board of Curators of the Univ of Missouri
University Hall Missouri, University, Columbia, MO, 65211-0001
Maneater, The, 202

Board of Trustees of Missouri Botanical Garden
PO Box 299, Saint Louis, MO, 63166-0299
Bulletin, 121

Bonnie Culley
1416 Green Berry Rd, Jefferson City, MO, 65101-3620
Coffey Cousin's Clearinghouse, 451

Bouchard Family Newsletter
PO Box 13548, Saint Louis, MO, 63138-0548
Bouchard Family Newsletter, 448

Boy Scouts of America, St. Louis Area Council
4568 W Pine Blvd, Saint Louis, MO, 63108-2110
Duffel Bag, 582

Buckeye Pietenpol Association
6364 Franks Rd., Byrnes Mill, MO, 63051-1103
Buckeye Pietenpol Association Newsletter, 28

Bush Pubs.
1006 W Harmony St, Neosho, MO, 64850-1631
Missouri Official, 1,022

•Business Communications Group
3727 N Oak Trfy, Kansas City, MO, 64116-2778

Business Men's Assurance Co.
BMA Tower, Box 419458, Kansas City, MO, 64141
BMA Skylines, 576

•Business Technolgy Assn.
12411 Wornall Rd, Kansas City, MO, 64145-1119

Butler Mfg. Co.
7400 E 13th St, Kansas City, MO, 64126-2339
Butler Builder, 579

Cape Girardeau Chamber of Commerce
PO Box 98, Cape Girardeau, MO, 63702-0098
Action, 157

Catholic Health Assn. of the US
4455 Woodson Rd, Saint Louis, MO, 63134-3797
Law Reports, 749

Center for Reformation Research
6477 San Bonita Ave, St. Louis, MO, 63105-3117
Center for Reformation Research, Newsletter, 538

* See **MULTI-PUBLISHER INDEX** for list of publications.

Central Christian College of the Bible
The Sentinel, 911 Urbandale Drive East, Moberly, MO, 65270
Sentinel, The, 202

Central Missouri State University Public Relations
Administration 302, Warrensburg, MO, 64093
Central Missouri State University News, 304

Chemtech Industries, Inc.
PO Box 31000, Saint Louis, MO, 63131-1000
Chemscope, 580

Children's Ministries
6401 The Paseo, Kansas City, MO, 64131
Discoveries, 168

Cleveland Chiropractic College
6401 Rockhill Rd, Kansas City, MO, 64131-1181
Alumni News, 190

Communications Management, Inc.
13523 Barrett Parkway Dr., Suite 221, Ballwin, MO, 63021-3800
Yellow Sheet, The, 24

•**Concordia Historical Institute**
801 De Mun Ave, St. Louis, MO, 63105-3168

Concordia Publishing House
3558 S. Jefferson Ave., St. Louis, MO, 63118-3968
Reporter, 1,072

Concordia Tract Mission
PO Box 201, Saint Louis, MO, 63166-0201
Worldwide Evangelist, 1,066

Continental Basketball Association
701 Market Street, Suite 140, St. Louis, MO, 63101
CBA News, 1,130

Cookbook Collectors Club of America
PO Box 56, Saint James, MO, 65559-0056
Cookbook Gossip Newsletter, 427

Council of the U.S., Society of St. Vincent de Paul
58 Progress Pkwy, St. Louis, MO, 63043-3706
Ozanam News, 1,059

Crystal Jensen
118 Saw Mill Rd, Union, MO, 63084-4012
Baker Family Newsletter International, 447

Dameron-Damron Family Assn.
203 E Portland St, Springfield, MO, 65807-2036
Dameron-Damron Family Assn. Newsletter, 452

DeSoto Club of America
105 East 96, Kansas City, MO, 64114-1827
DeSoto Days, 72

Department of Health, Center for Health Statistics
PO Box 570, Jefferson City, MO, 65102-0570
Missouri Monthly Vital Statistics, 518

Derrick & Ida
P.O. Box 981, Columbia, MO, 65205
The Feat Sheet, 471

Diamond Council of America
9140 Ward Pky, Kansas City, MO, 64114-3336
Diamontologist, 693

•**Doane Agricultural Services Co.**
11701 Borman Dr., Ste. 100, St. Louis, MO, 63146-4199

Dog Museum, The
1721 S Mason Rd, Saint Louis, MO, 63131-1518
Sirius, 908

Electrical Apparatus Service Assn., Inc.
1331 Baur Blvd, Saint Louis, MO, 63132-1903
EASA Currents, 337

Ellsbury Records
PO Box 206, Chillicothe, MO, 64601-0206
Prather Bulletin, 465

•**Facts & Comparisons, Inc.**
111 West Port Plaza, Suite 300, St. Louis, MO, 63146-3098

Farm Equipment Mfrs. Assn.
243 N. Lindbergh, St. Louis, MO, 63141-7851
Shortliner, 35

•**Feature News Service**
9328 Sondra Avenue, St. Louis, MO, 63144-1010

Federal Reserve Bank of Kansas City
Public Affairs Dept. 925 Grand, Blvd, Kansas City, MO, 64198-0001
Fed Letter, 89

•**Ferguson-Florissant School District R-2**
1005 Waterford Dr, Florissant, MO, 63033-3649

Frank Ashley
Box 79, Spickard, MO, 64679-0079
Backpacking Newsletter, 943

•**Gazette International Networking Institute**
4207 Lindell Boulevard, #110, St. Louis, MO, 63108

General Motors Corp.
6817 Stadium Dr, Kansas City, MO, 64129-1815
Newsletter, 592

•**General Motors Corp., GM Assembly Div.**
1500 E. Route A, Wentzville, MO, 63385-3630

Governmental Affairs Newsletter
206 Professional Bldg. Univ., Of Missouri-Columbia, Columbia, MO, 65211-0001
Governmental Affairs Newsletter, 486

Granville Market Letter
PO Box 412006, Kansas City, MO, 64141-2006
Granville Market Letter, 667

Greater Kansas City Chamber of Commerce
2600 Commerce Tower,, 911 Main St., Kansas City, MO, 64105-2049
Kansas Citian, 160

Gunter Schmidt
7777 Bonhomme Ave Ste 1400, Saint Louis, MO, 63105-1911
Newsletter of the American Academy of Oral Medicine, 270

•**HCI Publications, Inc.**
410 Archibald St., Kansas City, MO, 64111-3046

Harry S. Truman Library Institute
U.S. Hwy. 24 & Delaware St., Independence, MO, 64050
Whistle Stop, 813

Hart Lines Newsletter
15875 Interurban Rd., Platte City, MO, 64079-9185
Hart Lines Newsletter, 455

Heart of America Genealogical Society
C/O K.C. Public Lib., 311 E 12th St., Kansas City, MO, 64106-2412
Heartlines, 456

Heartland Critiques
125 E Linden Ave, Independence, MO, 64050-4407
Heartland Critiques, 1,077

Heritage Programs & Museums
22807 Easdt Woods Chapel Road, Blue Springs, MO, 64015-9747
Heritage Programs & Museums Newsletter, 904

Historic Kansas City Found.
712 Broadway St Ste 404, Kansas City, MO, 64105-1537
Historic Kansas City Foundation Gazette, 541

Holy Family Seminary
3014 Oregon Ave, St. Louis, MO, 63118-1412
Messenger of the Holy Family, 1,058

Home Office Management Svces.
1151 NE Todd George Rd, Lees Summit, MO, 64086-5332
Homebased Business News Report, 141

Horizone
PO Box 67, Saint Charles, MO, 63302-0067
Covert Intelligence Letter, 895

Hotel & Motel Brokers of America
10220 N. Executive Hills Blvd., Ste. 610, Kansas City, MO, 64153-2327
Inn Side Issues, 574

Hubbell Family Historical Society
106 W. 14th St., 25th Fl., Kansas City, MO, 64105-1992
Hubbell Family Historical Society-Family Notes, 457

•**Huna Research, Inc.**
1760 Anna St., Cape Girardeau, MO, 63701-4504

Hussmann Refrigerator Co.
12999 Saint Charles Rock Rd, Bridgeton, MO, 63044-2419
Inside Bridgeton, 586

•**Institute for Peace & Justice**
4144 Lindell Blvd Ste 122, Saint Louis, MO, 63108-2931

International Association of Arson Investigators
300 S Broadway # 100, Saint Louis, MO, 63102-2800
Selected Articles for Arson Investigators, 422

International Association of Fairs & Expositions
3043 E Cairo St # 985, Springfield, MO, 65802-6204
Fairs & Expositions, 368

International Association of Panoramic Photographers
2725 Sutton Blvd, Saint Louis, MO, 63143-3007
International Association of Panoramic Photographers, 976

Intl. Credit Assn.
243 N. Lindbergh Blvd., PO Box 419057, St. Louis, MO, 63141-1757
Consumer Trends, 86

International Rose O'Neill Club
c/o L. Holman, 309 Walnut Lane, Branson, MO, 65616
Kewpiesta Kourier, 822

International Society for Clinical Lab Technology
818 Olive St Ste 918, Saint Louis, MO, 63101-1544
ISCLT Newsletter, 1,097

International Society of Parametic Analysts
PO Box 6402, Chesterfield, MO, 63006-6402
Parametric World, 294

International Steel Guitar Convention
9535 Midland Blvd, Saint Louis, MO, 63114-3314
Steel Guitar Intl. Newsletter, 918

•**International University, The**
1301 S Noland Rd, Independence, MO, 64055-1390

International Women's Brass Conference
540 S Geyer Rd, Saint Louis, MO, 63122-5933
Newsletter of the International Women's Brass Conference, 915

Irish Family Newsletter
PO Box 13548, Saint Louis, MO, 63138-0548
Irish Family Newsletter, 457

Italian Mission, The
PO Box 30300, Kansas City, MO, 64112-3300
Il Messaggero, 1,057

Julian Edison
16 Dromara Rd, Saint Louis, MO, 63124-1880
Miniature Book News, 118

Kansas City Area Archivists
Nazarene Archives, 6401 The Paseo, Kansas City, MO, 64131
Dusty Shelf, 797

Kansas City Art Institute
4415 Warwick Blvd, Kansas City, MO, 64111-1820
Alumni Hotline, 190

Kansas City Community Foundation
1055 Broadway St Ste 130, Kansas City, MO, 64105-1595
Greater Kansas City Community Foundation Newsletter, 667

•**Kansas City Life Insurance Co.**
PO Box 419139, Kansas City, MO, 64141-6139

Kappa Tau Alpha
School of Journalism, Univ. of Missouri, Columbia, MO, 65211
Kappa Tau Alpha Newsletter, 696

Kemper Military School & College
701 3rd St, Boonville, MO, 65233-1670
Adjutant, 202

•**Kimberly Organization**
PO Box 31011, Saint Louis, MO, 63131-0011

Kirksville College of Osteopathic Medicine
800 W Jefferson St, Kirksville, MO, 63501-1497
Tenaculum, 202

•**Knehans-Miller Publications**
PO Box 88, Warrensburg, MO, 64093-0088

Landmark Legal Foundation
1006 Grand, 8th Floor, Kansas City, MO, 64106-2300
Landmark Litigation Report, 748

Liberty Shopper News
12 N Main St, Liberty, MO, 64068-1698
Liberty Shopper News, 24

Lincoln Univ.
Young Hall, 802 Chestnut St., Rm.303, Jefferson City, MO, 65102
Alumni Line, 202

Livestock Marketing Assn.
7509 NW Tiffany Springs Pky, Kansas City, MO, 64153-1386
LMA Businessletter, 828

Lutheran Church Missouri Synod
1333 S Kirkwood Rd, Saint Louis, MO, 63122-7295
SPC Newsletter, 1,072

Lutheran Church Missouri Synod, Bd for Youth Services
1333 S Kirkwood Rd, Saint Louis, MO, 63122-7226
LYF Lines, 1,072

MLPGA, Inc.
4100 Country Club Dr, Jefferson City, MO, 65109-0302
MLPGA News, 959

Mark Twain Boyhood Home Assocs.
208 Hill St, Hannibal, MO, 63401-3316
Fence Painter, 821

Merchants' Exchange of Saint Louis
5100 Oakland Avenue, St. Louis, MO, 63110-1441
St. Louis Market Record, 418

Messenger Publishing Co.
PO Box 30300, Kansas City, MO, 64112-3300
Messaggero/Messenger, 403

Messenger Publishing House
4901 Pennsylvania Ave # 850, Joplin, MO, 64804-4947
Adult Study Guide, 1,061

Metro Publications
PO Box 28203, Kansas City, MO, 64188-0203
Metro Singles, 815

Metropolitan Medical Society of Greater Kansas City
3036 Gillham Rd, Kansas City, MO, 64108-3119
Medical Directory of Gtr. Kansas City, 879

* See **MULTI-PUBLISHER INDEX** for list of publications.

Midwest Center for the Literary Arts
The Writers Place, 3607 Pennsylvania, Kansas City, MO, 64111
Keep, The, 982

Midwest Museums Conference
PO Box 11940, St. Louis, MO, 63112-0040
News Brief, 907

Midwestern Enterprises
5412 Raytown Rd, Kansas City, MO, 64133-2744
Talley, Tally Researcher, 468

Mindszenty Report
PO Box 11321, Saint Louis, MO, 63105-0121
Mindszenty Report, 993

Missouri Archeological Society
PO Box 958, 101A Museum Support Center, Columbia, MO, 65205-0958
Missouri Archeological Society Quarterly, 57

Missouri Bar
326 Monroe, Box 119, Box 119, Jefferson City, MO, 65101-3106
Missouri Bar Bulletin, 757

Missouri Botanical Garden
PO Box 299, Saint Louis, MO, 63166-0299
Herbarium News, 121

Missouri Chamber of Commerce
PO Box 149, Jefferson City, MO, 65102-0149
Missouri Business, 160

Missouri Congress of Parents
324 S 11th St, Bowling Green, MO, 63334-1914
Missouri Parent-Teacher, 318

Missouri Department of Agriculture
PO Box 630, Jefferson City, MO, 65102-0630
Weekly Market Summary, 47

Missouri Dept. of Education
PO Box 480, Jefferson City, MO, 65102-0480
Missouri Schools, 318

Missouri Library Assn.
1806 Business 63 S. #B, Columbia, MO, 65201-8404
MO Library Info, 803

Missouri State Dept. of Economic Development
PO Box 1157, Jefferson City, MO, 65102-1157
Missouri Enterprise, 293

Missouri State Emergency Management Agency
PO Box 116, Jefferson City, MO, 65102-0116
Missouri State Emergency Management Agency Newsletter, 1,138

Missouri State Highway Patrol
1510 E. Elm St., PO Box 568, Jefferson City, MO, 65102-0568
Patrol News, 789

Missouri State Library
PO Box 387, Jefferson City, MO, 65102-0387
Missouri Libraries, 804

Moila Temple
701 N Noyes Blvd, St. Joseph, MO, 64506-2860
Moila Temple Bulletin, 179

Morgan Car Club of Washington DC, Inc.
616 Gist Ave., Silver Spring, MO, 20910-5232
Rough Rider, 76

•**Mosby**
11830 Westline Industrial Dr., St. Louis, MO, 63146-3313

National Association of Independent Fee Appraisers
7501 Murdoch Ave., St. Louis, MO, 63119-2810
Appraiser Gram, 1,031

•**National Association of Insurance Commissioners**
120 W. 12th St., Ste. 1100, Kansas City, MO, 64105-1925

Natl. Assn. of Parents
RR 1 Box 646, Marble Hill, MO, 63764-9725
NAPSAC News, 413

Natl. Assn. of Professional Surplus Line Offices
6405 N. Cosby Avenue #201, Kansas City, MO, 64151-3963
NAPSLO Newsletter, 622

•**National Catholic Reporter Publishing Co.**
115 E. Armour Blvd., Kansas City, MO, 64111-1203

•**National Decorating Products Assn., Inc.**
1050 N Lindbergh Blvd, Saint Louis, MO, 63132-2912

National Federation of Paralegal Associations
PO Box 33108, Kansas City, MO, 64114-0108
National Federation of Paralegal Associations, 788

Natl. Fed. of Parents for Drug Free Youth
11159b S Towne Sq, Saint Louis, MO, 63123-7814
NFP News, 286

National Fishing Lure Collector's Club
1418 E Portland St, Springfield, MO, 65804-1221
NFLCC Gazette, 180

•**Natl. Food & Energy Council, Inc.**
409 Vandiver W., Ste. 202, Bldg. 4, Columbia, MO, 65202-1587

News Division, SLA.
101 N. Fourth St., POB 798, Columbia, MO, 65205
News Library News, 924

North Central Missouri College
1301 Main St, Trenton, MO, 64683-1824
Newsletter, 203

Office Systems Research Assn.
S.W. Missouri State Univ., 901 South National Ave., Springfield, MO, 65804-0089
OSRA Newsletter, 232

Ophelia Wade
Rr 1 Box 26, Bragg City, MO, 63827-9705
Moore Family Register, 461

Ozark Genealogical Society
P.O. Box 3945, Springfield, MO, 65808-3945
Ozar'Kin, 464

People's Guide
5927 Dr. M.L. King Dr., St. Louis, MO, 63112
People's Guide, 399

Perfins Bulletin
PO Box 82, Grandview, MO, 64030-0082
Perfins Bulletin, 971

Polish-American Cultural Soc. /St. Louis
12205 Kollingsford Dr., Florissant, MO, 63033
Hejna, 407

Pony Express Historical Assn., Inc.
Box 1022, 12th & Penn, St. Joseph, MO, 64502-1022
Pony Express Mail, 546

Prader Willi Syndrome Assn.
2510 S Brentwood Blvd Ste 220, Saint Louis, MO, 63144-2326
Gathered View, The, 277

Presbyterian AIDS Network
c/o Peg Atkins, 747 N. Taylor, Kirkwood, MO, 63122
PANdemic, 1,074

Professional Aviation Maintenance Association
500 Northwest Plaza, Suite 1016, Saint Ann, MO, 63074-2225
PAMA News, 32

Project Equality
6301 Rockhill Rd Ste 315, Kansas City, MO, 64131-1117
Project Equality-Update, 175

Quality Medica Publishing, Inc
2086 Craigshire Rd, Saint Louis, MO, 63146-4010
Plastic Surgery Outlook, 884

Raleigh Clayton Muns
1178 Margaret Ln, Olivette, MO, 63132-2319
Fugitive Pope, 798

Ralston Purina Co.
Checkerboard Square, Saint Louis, MO, 63164-0001
Checkerlinks, 579

Randy H. Smith
89 Arundel Place, St. Louis, MO, 63105
Beyond Gaming, 368

Rannken Technical Institute
4431 Finney Ave, Saint Louis, MO, 63113-2811
Student Staff Newsletter, 203

Researcher
PO Box 206, Chillicothe, MO, 64601-0206
Researcher, 465

Ritenour School District
2420 Woodson Rd, Saint Louis, MO, 63114-5499
Ritenour Reporter, 596

S & S Bovine Images
PO Box 12315, North Kansas City, MO, 64116-0315
Beefalo Nickel, 853

•**SSM Health Care System**
477 N Lindbergh Blvd, Saint Louis, MO, 63141-7832

St. Louis Blues Society
PO Box 21652, St. Louis, MO, 63109-0652
Bluesletter, 910

St. Louis Community College at Florissant Valley
3400 Pershall Rd, St. Louis, MO, 63135-1408
Student Planner, 202

St. Louis Genealogical Society
9011 Manchester Rd Ste 3, St. Louis, MO, 63144-2643
St. Louis Genealogical Society, News and Notes, 466

St. Louis Public Schools
901 Locust St, St. Louis, MO, 63101-1401
Careers Bridge Newsletter, 304

Sink Full of Dirty Dishes
P.O. Box 160122, St. Louis, MO, 63116
Sinkfull Of Dishes, 472

•**Sixteenth Century Publishers**
NMSU LB 115, Kirksville, MO, 63501

Society of Commercial Seed Technologists
PO Box 1393, Saint Joseph, MO, 64502-1393
Seed Technologist News, 46

Society of Medical-Dental Management Consultants
6215 Larson, Kansas City, MO, 64133
Consultant's Newsletter, 836

Society of Teachers of Family Medicine
8880 Ward Pkwy., Box 8729, Kansas City, MO, 64114-2756
STFM Messenger, 886

Special Libraries Assn., Greater St. Louis Chapter
PO Box 7090, Saint Louis, MO, 63177-7090
Slate, 810

Springfield Public Schools
940 N Jefferson Ave, Springfield, MO, 65802-3718
Springfield Public Schools, News and Views, 331

Stove Furnace
2929 S Jefferson Ave, Saint Louis, MO, 63118-1510
Stove Furnace, 711

Sunset Hill School
400 W 51st St, Kansas City, MO, 64112-2316
Ecosources, 291

Theta Psi Fraternity
2305 York St, Kirksville, MO, 63501-2067
Signet of Theta Psi, 182

Traders' Horn
1903 Schoettler Valley Dr., Chesterfield, MO, 63017-5203
Traders' Horn, 478

Training Consultants, Inc.
PO Box 31052, Saint Louis, MO, 63131-0052
RAP Session, 348

Travelers Protective Association
3755 Lindell Blvd, Saint Louis, MO, 63108-3476
Travelers Protective Association of America, Bulletin, 625

Triological Society
10 S. Broadway, Ste. 1401, St. Louis, MO, 63102-1741
Triologistics, 888

Twentieth Century Services
PO Box 419200, Kansas City, MO, 64141-6200
Investor Advantage, 672

USS Henrico APA-45 Association
15875 Interurban Rd., Platte City, MO, 64079-9185
USS Henrico APA-45 Newsletter, 899

Union Electric Co.
PO Box 149, St. Louis, MO, 63166-0149
Union Electric News, 601

United Telephone Co. of Missouri
319 Madison St, Jefferson City, MO, 65101-3108
Mirror, 590

•**Unity School of Christianity**
1901 NW Blue Parkway, Unity Village, MO, 64065-0001

•**Univ. of Missouri**
P. R. Beuselinck, 207 Waters, Columbia, MO, 65211-0001

Univ. of Missouri Conservatory of Music
4949 Cherry, Ctr. for the Performing Arts, Kansas City, MO, 64110-2229
Music Notes, 202

University of Missouri-University Extension
822 Clark Hall, Columbia, MO, 65211-0001
Exclaimer, 39

•**Veterans of Foreign Wars of the U.S.**
406 W. 34th St., Kansas City, MO, 64111-2736

W.D. Gann Research, Inc.
PO Box 8508, Saint Louis, MO, 63126-0508
W.D. Gann Weekly Technical Stock & Commodity Letter, 691

W.L. Johnson
205 W 66th Ter, Kansas City, MO, 64113-1854
Here's the Pitch, 101

Washington University, School of Medicine Library
PO Box 8132, Saint Louis, MO, 63156-8132
Washington University School of Medicine Library, Library Newsletter, 812

Water Jet Technology Association
818 Olive St Ste 918, Saint Louis, MO, 63101-1544
Jet News, 1,203

Western Historical Manuscript Association
UM - St. Louis, 8001 Natural Bridge Rd., St. Louis, MO, 63121
MAC Newsletter, 803

William Woods College
200 W 12th St, Fulton, MO, 65251-1004
Echoes from the Woods, 190

Wolfe's Version
PO Box 99, Blue Springs, MO, 64013-0099
Wolfe's Version, 297

• See ***MULTI-PUBLISHER INDEX*** for list of publications.

Woman's Work
P.O. Box 480311, Kansas City, MO, 64148-9982
Woman's Work, 1,213

World Archaeological Society
120 Lakewood Dr, Hollister, MO, 65672-5176
W.A.S. Newsletter, 59

Worldwide Investment Notes
PO Box 16041, Saint Louis, MO, 63105-0741
Worldwide Investment Notes, 692

Montana

Aeronautics Div.
PO Box 5178, Helena, MT, 59604-5178
Montana and the Sky, 31

American Wildlands
40 E. Main St., Ste. 2, Bozeman, MT, 59715
American Wildlands, 372

Bits & Bytes Computer Resources
623 Iowa Ave, Whitefish, MT, 59937-2336
Bits & Bytes Review, 213

C. M. Russell Museum
400 13th St N, Great Falls, MT, 59401-1498
Latch String, The, 905

Confederated Salish
PO Box 278, Pablo, MT, 59855-0278
Char-Koosta, 405

•**Cox Pubs.**
PO Box 20316, Billings, MT, 59104-0316

Curran Productions
PO Box 3141, Missoula, MT, 59806-3141
Curran's Ginseng Farmer, 39

Flathead Valley Genealogical Soc.
PO Box 584, Kalispell, MT, 59903-0584
Trees & Trails, 468

Friends of the Assiniboines Foundation
623 Knapp St, Wolf Point, MT, 59201-1806
Nakodabi, The Assiniboine People, 406

Great Falls Genealogy Society
1400 1st Ave N, Great Falls, MT, 59401-3205
Treasure State Lines, 468

Information Advisory Services
300 Mcleod Ave, Missoula, MT, 59801-4302
Information Advisor, 799

•**InvesTech Research**
2472 Birch Glen Rd, Whitefish, MT, 59937-3349

Kalamazoo Valley Genealogical Society
Box 405, Comstock, MT, 49041
Kalamazoo Valley Heritage, 458

Kettle Care
710 Trap Road, Columbia Falls, MT, 59912
Kettle Care-Pure Herbal Body Care, 16

Missouri Basin States Assn., Inc.
PO Box 301, Lewistown, MT, 59457-0301
Missouri River Report, 1,203

Montana Congress of Parents
Cascade, MT, 59421
Montana Parent-Teacher, 318

Montana Education Assn.
1232 E 6th Ave, Helena, MT, 59601-3995
M.E.A. Today, 316

Montana Historical Society
225 N. Roberts St., P.O. Box 201201, Helena, MT, 59620-1201
Montana Post, 544

Montana League of Cities
PO Box 1704, Helena, MT, 59624-1704
Montana League of Cities, 1,022

Montana Legislative Services Division
P.O. Box 201706, Helena, MT, 59620-1706
Interim, 745

Montana Office of Public Instruction
State Capitol, Helena, MT, 59620-0001
Montana Schools, 318

Montana State Library
1515 E 6th Ave, Helena, MT, 59601-4542
Montana State Library News Update, 805

Montana State Univ. Alumni Assn.
1501 South 11, Foundation & Alumni Center, Bozeman, MT, 59717-0001
MSU Mathematics Letter, 852

Montana State Univ. Dept. of Mathematical Sciences
Publications, Bozeman, MT, 59717-0001
Montana State Univ. Mathematics Univ., 852

Natl. Assn. of Dumpster Driver & Urban Miners
PO Box 8040, Bigfork, MT, 59911-8040
Naddum News, 388

Northwest Archivists, Inc.
c/o Montana Historical Society, 225 N. Roberts St., Helena, MT, 59620-1201
Easy Access, 797

•**Phillip Genealogical Heritage House**
605 Benton Ave., Missoula, MT, 59801-8633

Professional Timing Service
PO Box 7483, Missoula, MT, 59807-7483
Professional Timing Service, 683

St. Patrick Hospital
500 W Broadway St, Missoula, MT, 59802-4008
Messenger, The, 569

•**Seven Buffaloes Press**
Box 249, Big Timber, MT, 59011-0249

Tekakwitha Conference Natl. Ctr.
PO Box 6768, Great Falls, MT, 59406-6768
Tekakwitha Conference Newsletter, 406

Nebraska

Alcoholic Beverage Executive's Newsletter
PO Box 3188, Omaha, NE, 68103-0188
Alcoholic Beverage Executive's Newsletter, 102

B.E. Gillett
1103 W. 1st St., McCook, NE, 69001-2504
Gillet, Gillette, Gillett Pride 'n' Joy, 455

Beatrice State Development Ctr.
3000 Lincoln Blvd, Beatrice, NE, 68310-3300
Sower, 528

Beta Alpha Psi
Dept. of Accounting, Univ. NE, Lincoln, NE, 68588-0001
Beta Alpha Psi Newsletter, 2

Bethphage Mission Inc.
13057 W. Center Rd., Ste. 20, Omaha, NE, 68144-3723
Bethphage Messenger, 1,045

Blue Cross
PO Box 3248, Omaha, NE, 68103-0248
Sound of the Blues, 598

•**Bryan Memorial Hospital**
1600 S 48th St, Lincoln, NE, 68506-1299

Bureau of Business Research - UNL
114 CBA, Lincoln, NE, 68588-0406
Nebraska County Profiles, 146

Business By Phone, Inc.
13254 Stevens St, Omaha, NE, 68137-1728
Telephone Selling Report, 23

CEGA Services
PO Box 81826, Lincoln, NE, 68501-1826
Written Word, 336

Center for Rural Affairs
101 South Taliman, Box 406, Walthill, NE, 68067-0406
Center for Rural Affairs Newsletter, 38

Checks Anonymous
PO Box 2500, Lincoln, NE, 68542-0500
Pen-Point, 1,120

Clarkson College
101 S 42nd St, Omaha, NE, 68131-2739
Clarkson College Connection, 203

Dana College
2848 College Dr, Blair, NE, 68008
Dana Review, 190

Division of Continuing Studies
University of Nebraska-Lincoln, Lincoln, NE, 68583-0001
DCS News, 306

Eastern Nebraska Genealogical Society
8686 N 204th St, Elkhorn, NE, 68022-3900
Roots & Leaves, 466

Greater Omaha Chamber of Commerce
1301 Harney St, Omaha, NE, 68102-1832
Omaha Profile, 161

Hartman Publishing Co.
Box 30367, Lincoln, NE, 68503-0367
Cartoon Tips, 368

Hastings College
PO Box 269, Hastings, NE, 68902-0269
Hastings College Today, 203

John G. Neihardt Foundation, Inc.
Attn: Publications, Bancroft, NE, 68004
Neihardt Foundation Newsletter, 818

Joslyn Art Museum
2200 Dodge St, Omaha, NE, 68102-1292
Joslyn News, 905

Mari Sandoz Heritage Society
c/o Chadron State College, Chadron, NE, 69337
Mari Sandoz Heritage, 823

Marketarian Inc.
PO Box 1283, Grand Island, NE, 68802-1283
Marketarian Letter, 676

Metropolitan Area Planning Agency
2222 Cuming St, Omaha, NE, 68102-4328
What's Happening, 494

Midwest Sociological Society
Dept. Of Sociology Creighton, Univ., Omaha, NE, 68178-0001
Midwest Sociologist, 1,126

National Arbor Day Foundation
100 Arbor Ave, Nebraska City, NE, 68410-1099
Arbor Day, 435

Natl. Assn. of Barber Styling Schools
304 S 11th St, Lincoln, NE, 68508-2102
NABS Weekly, 100

Natl. Assn. of Student Employment Administrators
PO Box 8214, Omaha, NE, 68108-0214
NASEA News, 703

Natl. Blacksmiths & Welders Assn.
PO Box 123, Arnold, NE, 69120-0123
Modern Blacksmith, 892

Natl. Museum of Roller Skating
4730 South St, Lincoln, NE, 68506-1256
Historical Roller Skating Overview, 541

Native American Public Broadcasting Consortium, Inc.
1800 N 33rd St # 83111, Lincoln, NE, 68503-1409
NAPBC Newsletter, 124

Nebraska Dental Assn.
3120 0 St., Ste. A, Lincoln, NE, 68510-1533
Nebraska Dental Assn. Newsletter, 270

Nebraska Department of Aeronautics
PO Box 82088, Lincoln, NE, 68501-2088
PIREPS, 32

Nebraska Dept. of Labor
550 S 16th St, Lincoln, NE, 68508-2601
Labor Lines, 346

Nebraska Farmers Union
1305 Plum St, Lincoln, NE, 68502-2343
Nebraska Union Farmer, 44

Nebraska Grain and Feed Association
1233 Lincoln Mall, Lincoln, NE, 68508-2847
Grain and Feed Merchants, The, 418

Nebraska Library Association
7500 Mercy Rd, Omaha, NE, 68124-2319
Nebraska Library Association Quarterly, 805

Nebraska Library Commission
1200 N St Ste 120, Lincoln, NE, 68508-2020
N-Compass, 805

Nebraska Natural Resources Comm.
301 Centennial Mall S # 9487, Lincoln, NE, 68508-2529
Nebraska Resources, 388

Nebraska Public Power District
PO Box 499, Columbus, NE, 68602-0499
Interchange, 1,026

Nebraska State Bar Assn.
PO Box 81809, Lincoln, NE, 68501-1809
NSBA Newsletter, 759

Nebraska State Dept. of Economic Development
PO Box 94666, Lincoln, NE, 68509-4666
Nebraska Development News, 294

Nebraska State Dept. of Health
301 Centennial Mall S # 9500, Lincoln, NE, 68508-2529
Better Health, 499

•**Nebraska State Genealogical Society**
704 Maple St, Kimball, NE, 69145-1814

•**Nebraska State Historical Society**
Box 82554, Lincoln, NE, 68501-2554

Nebraska State Pest Control Assn., Inc.
1111 Lincoln Mall, Ste. 308, Lincoln, NE, 68508-2882
Nebraska Pest Control Association Newsletter, 35

OKU Dental Honorary Society
40th & Holdrege, Lincoln, NE, 68583-0001
Omicron Kappa Upsilon Bulletin, 271

Ray's Surname Index File
Box 482, McCook, NE, 69001-0482
Ray Newsletter, 465

Richardson Heritage Society
944 S G St # 123, Broken Bow, NE, 68822-2444
Richardson Family Researcher and Historical News, 465

Richman Gordman Stores
12100 W. Center Rd., Omaha, NE, 68144-3998
Intercom, 587

Society of Vertebrate Paleontology
W. 436 Nebraska Hall, Box 880542, Univ. of Nebraska, Lincoln, NE, 68588-0542
Society of Vertebrate Paleontology News Bulletin, 1,101

* See **MULTI-PUBLISHER INDEX** for list of publications.

State Personnel Dept.
PO Box 94905, Lincoln, NE, 68509-4905
Statehouse Observer, 1,024

Union Pacific Railroad Co.
1415 Dodge St, Omaha, NE, 68102-1602
Union Pacific Bulletin, 1,030

U.S. Amateur Roller Skating
PO Box 6579, Lincoln, NE, 68506-0579
U.S. Roller Skating, 1,137

U.S. Dressage Federation, Inc.
PO Box 6669, 7700 'A' St., Lincoln, NE, 68506-0669
USDF Participating Member Newsletter, 1,137

University of Nebraska College of Dentistry Alumni Assn.
1520 R St, Lincoln, NE, 68508-1651
Univ. of Nebraska College of Dentistry Alumni Bulletin, 272

Univ. of Nebraska College of Medicine
600 S. 42nd St., PO Box 985200, Omaha, NE, 68198-5200
Alumni News, 190

Univ. of Nebraska Dept. of Agricultural Metereology
LW Chase Hall, Lincoln, NE, 68553-0728
Climatic Summaries for Nebraska, 1,096

Univ. of Nebraska-Lincoln, Library
Love Library, Lincoln, NE, 68588-0410
Link, 803

•**Univ. of Nebraska Medical Ctr.**
600 So. 42nd St., Omaha, NE, 68198-0001

Water Center Environmental Programs
103 Natural Resources Hall UNL, Lincoln, NE, 68583-0844
Water Current, 1,102

Wellness Councils of America
Community Health Plaza, #311, 7101 Newport Ave., Omaha, NE, 68152-2100
Worksite Wellness Works, 532

Willa Cather Pioneer Memorial
326 N Webster St, Red Cloud, NE, 68970-2550
Willa Cather Pioneer Memorial Newsletter, 336

Nevada

American Bashkir Curly Registry
PO Box 246, Ely, NV, 89301-0246
Curly Cues, 559

•**American Gem Society**
8881 W. Sahara Ave., Las Vegas, NV, 89117-5865

Basque Studies Program 322
Univ. Of Nevada Library, Reno, NV, 89557-0001
Basque Studies Program-Newsletter, 400

California Writers Report
3654 4th St., Sparks, NV, 89431-1230
California Writer's Report, 694

Citizen Alert
PO Box 5339, Reno, NV, 89513-5339
Citizen Alert Newsletter, 375

Day Care Guide
PO Box 11885, Reno, NV, 89510-1885
Day Care Guide, 168

Destiny Syndicate
PO Box 5637, Reno, NV, 89513-5637
Cupid's Destiny, 814

•**Eymann Publications, Inc.**
PO Box 3577, Reno, NV, 89505-3577

GEM Publishing Group
PO Box 50820, Reno, NV, 89513-0820
Mature Traveler, 1,186

Gambler's Book Club
630 S 11th St, Las Vegas, NV, 89101-7106
Overlay, The, 439

Geno Munari
3426 Biela Ave, Las Vegas, NV, 89120-2208
Gaming Confidential, 439

Good 'N' Lucky Promotions
PO Box 29274, Las Vegas, NV, 89126-3274
Las Vegas Insider, 1,186

Greener Pastures Institute
PO Box 2190, Pahrump, NV, 89041-2190
Rural Property Investor, 1,039

Huntington Press
PO Box 28041, Las Vegas, NV, 89126-2041
Las Vegas Advisor, 1,186

International Academy of Nutritional Consultants
2375 Tropicana, Ste. 270, Las Vegas, NV, 90109
Health Express, 933

Jobel Financial Co.
PO Box 2560, Carson City, NV, 89702-2560
Compleat Investor, 660

Mexico Retirement and Travel Assistance
436 Scenic Dr # 2190, Henderson, NV, 89015-8356
Mexico Retirement and Travel Assistance, 1,186

•**Natl. Judicial College**
Univ. Of Nevada, Reno, NV, 89557-0001

National Opera Association
Dept of Music Univ. of Nevada, 4505 Maryland Pky., Las Vegas, NV, 89154-5025
The Opera Journal, 915

Navellier & Assocs., Inc.
PO Box 10012, Incline Village, NV, 89450-1012
MPT Review, 675

Nevada Casino Journal
3100 W Sahara Ave Ste 205, Las Vegas, NV, 89102-6008
Casino Journal's National Gaming Summary, 438

Nevada Families Eagle Forum
PO Box 656, Sparks, NV, 89432-0656
Nevada Families, 489

Nevada League of Cities
PO Box 2307, Carson City, NV, 89702-2307
Nevada Government Today, 1,022

Nevada Nurses Association
3660 Baker Lane, Reno, NV, 89509-5409
Nevada RNformation, 930

•**RTS**
PO Box 93897, Las Vegas, NV, 89193-3897

Rapaport USA, Inc.
3557 S. Valley View Bldg. C, Los Vegas, NV, 89103
Rapaport Diamond Report, 693

Retirement Facility Guide
PO Box 11885, Reno, NV, 89510-1885
Retirement Facility Guide, 1,108

Reynolds Electrical
PO Box 14400, Las Vegas, NV, 89114-4400
NTS News, 591

Rolling Ventures
PO Box 2190, Henderson, NV, 89041-2190
Rolling Ventures, 902

Scotty Barclay Poker Products
220 East Flamingo Road, Suite 127, Las Vegas, NV, 89109
1H3PA Newsletter & Poker Tips, 367

State of Nevada-Real Estate Div.
201 S Fall St, Carson City, NV, 89701-4765
Open House, 1,036

State Planning Coordinators Office
Capital Bldg., Room 306, Carson City, NV, 89701
Nevada Planner, 1,022

Univ. of Nevada, Las Vegas
4505 S Maryland Pky, Las Vegas, NV, 89154-9900
R.N.R. Reports, 45

Vegas Visitor
2711 Sandalwood Ave, Henderson, NV, 89014-1224
Sports Fact Sheet, 1,135

New Hampshire

700 Elves Press
RR 2 Box 806, Warner, NH, 03278-9202
Color Wheel Review, 817

AC Bergin
P.O. Box 105, Amherst, NH, 03031
Illustratotor's Swap incl JW Anglund Collectors News, 169

Action for Franco-Americans
PO Box 504, Manchester, NH, 03105-0504
Informaction, 401

Ad Club of New Hampshire
PO Box 4448, Manchester, NH, 03108-4448
Ad News, 9

Advanced Circuit Technology
118 Northeastern Blvd, Nashua, NH, 03062-1919
Connection Ideas, 218

African-Caribbean Institute
4 W. Wheelock St., Hanover, NH, 03755
AIDS & Society: International Research Policy Bulletin, 864

Agency Law Quarterly
PO Box 5702, Portsmouth, NH, 03802-5702
Agency Law Quarterly Real Estate Intelligence Report, 1,030

Akro Agate Art Assn.
PO Box 1524, Salem, NH, 03079-1141
Akro Agate Gem, 478

Appropriate Solutions, Inc.
145 Grove St., P.O. Box 458, Peterborough, NH, 03458-0458
Robot Explorer, 235

Armstrong Graphics
PO Box 628, Windham, NH, 03087-0628
Supreme Court Reporter, 777

Audio Amateur Publications, Inc.
305 Union St., PO Box 576, Peterborough, NH, 03458-0576
Voice Coil Newsletter, 1,128

Auditel
213 Stage road, Hapstead, NH, 03841
Telecom Newsflash, The, 1,163

Audubon Society of New Hampshire
3 Silk Farm Rd., Concord, NH, 03301-8200
New Hampshire Audubon, 942

Bridal Collectors News
PO Box 105, Amherst, NH, 03031-0105
Bridal Collectors News, 122

•**Butterworth Legal Publishers**
8 Industrial Way # C, Salem, NH, 03079-2837

C. Everett Koop Foundation
P.O. Box 998, Hanover, NH, 03755
C. Everett Koop Foundation Health Letter, 500

CNW Publishing
PO Box A, North Stratford, NH, 03590-0167
Freelance Writer's Report, 695

Chalet Suisse Intl. Inc.
Chalet Dr., Rt. 101, Wilton, NH, 03086
Good Night News, 574

Chubb Life America
1 Granite Pl, Concord, NH, 03301-3258
Insight, 587

Confraternity of Christian Doctrine
153 Ush St., Manchester, NH, 03101
Awareness, 1,055

Connell Communications, Inc.
86 Elm St, Peterborough, NH, 03458-1052
Video Retailers Choice, 1,170

Cross Country Ski Areas Association
259 Bolton Rd, Winchester, NH, 03470-2603
Nordic Network, 1,113

Dartmouth College
38 North Main Street, Hanover, NH, 03755-3762
Dartmouth College Bulletin, 190

Datalex Corp.
402 Amherst St Ste 303, Nashua, NH, 03063-4228
Macintosh Update, 228

Delahaye Group, The
117 Bow Street, Portsmouth, NH, 03801
Gauge, The, 857

Elm Research Institute
J.P. Hansel, Harrisville, NH, 03450
Elm Research Institute Newsletter, 378

Fitchburg Gas & Electric Light Co.
216 Epping Rd., Exeter, NH, 03833-4571
Energy Line, 1,026

Folk Arts Quarterly
686 Old Homestead Hwy, Richmond, NH, 03470-5012
Folk Arts Quarterly, 64

Greater Manchester Chamber of Commerce
889 Elm St., Manchester, NH, 03101-2000
Chamber Report, 159

•**Hale Ridge Publishing**
PO Box 370, Windham, NH, 03087

IDG Communications
86 Elm St., Peterborough, NH, 03458-1052
InCider's AppleWatch, 225

Innovative Marketing, Inc.
PO Box 912, Meredith, NH, 03253-0912
Recreation News, 327

Interlocken Center for Experiential Learning
Rr 2 Box 165, Hillsboro, NH, 03244-9506
Interlocken Globe, 1,215

International Wild Waterfowl Assn.
7 James Farm Rd, Durham, NH, 03824-6529
International Wild Waterfowl Association Newsletter, 1,217

Joan Walsh Anglund Collector's News
PO Box 105, Amherst, NH, 03031-0105
Joan Walsh Anglund Collector's News, 169

•**Kennedy Publications**
Templeton Rd., Fitzwilliam, NH, 03447

Kirkpatrick & Co.
PO Box 1066, Exeter, NH, 03833-1066
Kirkpatrick's Market Strategist, 673

* See **MULTI-PUBLISHER INDEX** for list of publications.

MRM Assocs.
PO Box 763, Salem, NH, 03079-0763
Trivia Dispatch, 1,041

•**Management Resources. Inc.**
861 Lafayette Rd. #5, Hampton, NH, 03842-1232

Miniature Precision Bearings, Inc.
Precision Park, Keene, NH, 03431
Inside Bearings, 586

Mount Washington Observatory
P.O. Box 2310, Main Street, North Conway, NH, 03860
Windswept, 893

Music for People
7 Middletown Road, Roxbury, NH, 03431
Connections, 911

NH Department of Resources and Economic Development
PO Box 1856, Concord, NH, 03302-1856
Agenda Newsletter, The, 1,041

NH Fish & Game Dept.
2 Hazen Dr, Concord, NH, 03301-6507
Fish & Game Highlights, 943

N.H. State Council on the Arts
40 N Main St, Concord, NH, 03301-4912
NH Arts, 261

Nashua Corp.
44 Franklin St, Nashua, NH, 03060-2686
Communicator, 580

•**Natl. Arborist Assn. (NAA)**
Meeting Place Mall, PO Box 1094 Rt. 101, Amherst, NH, 03031-1094

Natl. Education Assn. -New Hampshire
103 N State St, Concord, NH, 03301-4334
New Hampshire Educator, 322

Nelson Designs
PO Box 422, Dublin, NH, 03444-0422
Scroll Saw News, 256

New Hampshire Assn. of Conservation Commissions
54 Portsmouth St, Concord, NH, 03301-5486
Conservation Commission News, 376

New Hampshire Council on World Affairs
11 Rosemary Ln, Durham, NH, 03824-2332
New Hampshire Council on World Affairs Bulletin, 635

New Hampshire Dental Society
Box 2229, 2 S. State St., Concord, NH, 03302-2229
New Hampshire Dental Society Newsletter, 270

New Hampshire Dept of Education
101 Pleasant St, Concord, NH, 03301-3860
Tiffin Topics Newsletter, 935

New Hampshire Historical Society
30 Park St, Concord, NH, 03301-6316
New Hampshire Historical Society Newsletter, 545

New Hampshire Pharmacy Assn.
2 Eagle Sq. 3400, Concord, NH, 03001
New Hampshire Pharmacy News, 286

New Hampshire School Boards Assn.
Morrill Hall, Univ. of NH, Durham, NH, 03824
Granite State School Leader, 1,091

New Hampshire Society for CPAs
3 Executive Park Dr., Bedford, NH, 03110-6918
Granite State CPA Newsletter, 5

New Hampshire Society of Genealogists, Inc.
PO Box 2316, Concord, NH, 03302-2316
NHSG Newsletter, 462

New Hampshire State, Dept. of Resources & Economic Developme
PO Box 856, Concord, NH, 03302-0856
New Hampshire Journal of Economic Development, 1,041

New Hampshire State Library
20 Park St, Concord, NH, 03301-6314
Granite State Libraries, 799

North East Heather Society
Box 101, Highland View, Alstead, NH, 03602-0101
Heather Notes, 121

Office of Alcohol & Drug Abuse Prevention
105 Pleasant St, Concord, NH, 03301-3852
Different Drummer, 504

PR Publishing Co., Inc.
PO Box 600, Exeter, NH, 03833-0600
Channels, 854

•**PennWell Publishing Company**
Ten Tara Blvd., 5th Floor, Nashua, NH, 03062-2801

Plymouth Rock Foundation, Inc.
P.O. Box 577, Marlborough, NH, 03455
Letter from Plymouth Rock, 1,064

•**QW Communications, Co.**
PO Box 6591, Concord, NH, 03303-6591

Rockingham Society of Genealogists
PO Box 81, Exeter, NH, 03833-0081
Kinship Kronicle, 458

SCA Student Conservation Assn.
PO Box 550, Charlestown, NH, 03603-0550
Student Conservation Association Newsletter, 394

•**Salvage Bids**
PO Box 5, Laconia, NH, 03247-0005

Small Business Council of America
1000 Elm St., Box 3701, Manchester, NH, 03105-3701
Small Business Tax Reporter, 1,151

Star & Sword Pubs.
47 Byledge Rd, Manchester, NH, 03104-2101
Rising Star, 1,102

Strawbery Banke Museum
PO Box 300, Portsmouth, NH, 03802-0300
Strawbery Banke Newsletter, 908

Tolkien Society of America
RFD 1, Box 63, Center Harbour, NH, 03226-9801
Green Dragon, 822

UNITIL Service Corp.
216 Epping Rd, Exeter, NH, 03833-4575
UNITIL News, 601

Unitarian Universalist Peace Fellowship
172 Pleasant St, Laconia, NH, 03246-3030
Unipax, 999

U.S. Army Cold Regions Research & Engineering Laboratory
72 Lyme Rd, Hanover, NH, 03755-1290
CRREL Benchnotes, 1,095

University of New Hampshire
Elliott Alumni Center, 9 Edgewood Road, Durham, NH, 03824
Alumni Companion, 190

Univ. of New Hampshire Agriculture Dept.
Agricultural Experiment Stn., Durham, NH, 03824
New Hampshire Agricultural Experiment Station Bulletin, 44

Univ. of New Hampshire Computer Service Dept.
Kinsbridge Hall, Durham, NH, 03824
On-Line, 233

University of New Hampshire Sea Grant Program
Kingman Farm, Durham, NH, 03824
Seafare, 393

Wisdom Conservancy at Merriam Hilll Education Ctr.
148 Merriam Hill Rd, Greenville, NH, 03048-3300
Wisdom Conservancy Newsletter, The, 976

New Jersey

21st Century Research
41 Tappan Rd., Norwood, NJ, 07648-1708
Interactive Multimedia Communications, 670

ABC of New Jersey
161 Freeway Dr E, East Orange, NJ, 07018-4042
New Jersey Baptist Bulletin, 1,053

•**A.M. Best Co., Inc.**
Ambest Rd., Oldwick, NJ, 08858-0700

APMI International
105 College Rd. E., Princeton, NJ, 08540-6692
P/M Technology Newsletter, 892

ARCA/NJ
66 Morris Ave., Springfield, NJ, 07081-1409
ARCA Update, 534

ASBA
PO Box 738, Millburn, NJ, 07041-0738
Association of Ship Brokers and Agents Newsletter, 1,111

AT&T Closer to the Customer Newsletter
PO Box 1060, Piscataway, NJ, 08855-1060
Closer to the Customer, 252

AT&T Communications
295 N Maple Ave Rm 5418a3, Basking Ridge, NJ, 07920-1002
Stay in Touch, 1,162

Accordion Teachers' Guild, Inc.
334 S Broadway, Pitman, NJ, 08071-2405
Accordion Teachers' Guild-Newsletter, 909

Ad-Com, Inc.
1259 Rte. 46, Bldg. #1, Parsippany, NJ, 07054-4909
Psychic Guide Psychic Fair Network News, 922

Adastra West, Inc.
PO Box 874, Mahwah, NJ, 07430-0874
Mawewi, 471

Advance Notice
PO Box 1223, Princeton, NJ, 08542-1223
Advance Notice, 446

Affiliated Warehouse Companies, Inc.
PO Box 295, Hazlet, NJ, 07730-0295
Affiliated Warehouse Companies Newsletter, 1,192

•**Alexander Hamilton Inst.**
70 Hilltop Rd, Ramsey, NJ, 07446-1119

Allied Corp.
Water Treatment Chem. Dept., Box 1139R, Morristown, NJ, 07960
Pipeline, 1,204

Am. College of Veterinary Pathologists
875 Kings Highway, STe. 200, W. Deptford, NJ, 08096-3168
American College of Veterinary Pathologists-Newsletter, 1,200

American Academy of Ambulatory Nursing
56 N Woodbury Rd # 56, Pitman, NJ, 08071-1252
Ambulatory Nursing Administration, 928

American Academy of Podiatry Administration
c/o John V. Cicero, 10 Meadow Lane, Bloomfield, NJ, 07003
American Academy of Podiatry Administration News-Letter, 866

American Association of Teachers of German
112 Haddontowne Ct Ste 104, Cherry Hill, NJ, 08034-3662
American Association of Teachers of German Newsletter, 819

American Cyanamid Co.
1 Cyanamid Plz, Wayne, NJ, 07470-2076
Waynews, 603

American Home Foods Division, American Home Products Corp.
5 Giralda Farms, Madison, NJ, 07940-1027
AHP Vista, 575

•**American Hungarian Foundation**
P.O. Box 1084, New Brunswick, NJ, 08901-2248

•**American Institute of CPA's**
Harborside Financial Center, 201 Plaza Three, Jersey City, NJ, 07311-3881

American List Counsel
88 Orchard Cir # CN-5219, Princeton, NJ, 08543
Preserving Family Lands, 391

American Littoral Society
Sandy Hook, Highlands, NJ, 07732
Coastal Reporter, 375

American Musicians Union
8 Tobin Ct, Dumont, NJ, 07628-3329
AMU Quarternote, 909

American Society of Media Photographers
14 Washington Rd Ste 502, Princeton Junction, NJ, 08550-1028
American Society of Media Photographers, Bulletin, 976

Analxtic Press, Inc., The
365 Broadway, Hillside, NJ, 07642
American Psychoanalyst, The, 1,010

Analytic Press, Inc.
ATTN: Editoral, 101 West Street, Hillsdale, NJ, 07642-1422
American Psychoanalyst, 1,010

AngelWatch
PO Box 1362, Mountainside, NJ, 07092-0362
AngelWatch, 1,045

Anthony Jannetti, Inc.
E. Holly Ave. Box 56, Pitman, NJ, 08071
DNA Focus, 929

Antique & Classic Boat Society, Inc.
234 Ridgedale Ave, Cedar Knolls, NJ, 07927-2103
Rusty Rudder, 114

Arab Voice
956 Main St., Paterson, NJ, 07503
Arab Voice, 258

•**Archeological Society of New Jersey**
Seton Hall Univ. Museum, South Orange, NJ, 07079

Arthritis Foundation - NJ Chapter
200 Middlesex Turnpike, Iselin, NJ, 08830
Newsletter, The, 521

Associated Humane Societies
124 Evergreen Ave, Newark, NJ, 07114-2133
Humane News, 49

Assn. for the Advancement of Baltic Studies,Inc
111 Knob Hill Rd, Hackettstown, NJ, 07840-4222
Baltic Studies Newsletter, 300

Assn. of Food Industries
5 Ravine Dr, Matawan, NJ, 07747-3106
AFI Newsletter, 426

Association of Lincoln Presenters
1143 River Rd., Neshanic, NJ, 08853
Lincarnations, 543

---

* See **MULTI-PUBLISHER INDEX** for list of publications.

Assn. of Public Data Users
87 Prospect Ave, Princeton, NJ, 08544-2007
APDU Newsletter, 1,194

Association of Retail Marketing Services
3 Caro Ct, Red Bank, NJ, 07701-2315
Creative Marketing Newsletter, 12

Atlantic City Action
PO Box 5059, Atlantic City, NJ, 08404-5059
Atlantic City Action, 573

Atlantic City Department of Planning & Development
City Hall, Rm. 504, Atlantic City, NJ, 08401
Atlantic City Report, 1,041

Atlantic County Historical Society
907 Shore Rd # 301, Somers Point, NJ, 08244-2335
Atlantic County Historical Society Newsletter, 447

Atlantic Highlands Historical Society
PO Box 108, Atlantic Highlands, NJ, 07716-0108
Portland Poynts, 547

Atlantic Scale Co.
136 Washington Ave, Nutley, NJ, 07110
Upscale Report, 602

Audit Investment Inc.
92 Kennedy Rd., Box 7, Tranquility, NJ, 07879-0007
Realty Stock Review, 683

Automatic Data Processing Inc.
ADP Employer Services MS#245, One ADP Blvd., Roseland, NJ, 07068
ADP Advisor, 80

Automotive Week Publishing
573 Valley Road, PO Box 3495, Wayne, NJ, 07470-3495
Automotive Week, 70

Barbara Nivison-Patton
1912 Powder Horn Rd, Toms River, NJ, 08755-1709
Patton Exchange Letter, 464

Barbara Silberstein
c/o W. Leslie Rogers Library, 5605 Crescent Blvd., Pennsauken, NJ, 08110
Pennsauken Library Newsletter, 807

Barnard Enterprises, Inc.
515 Mountain Avenue, #100, Berkeley, NJ, 07922-2500
Barnard's Retail Marketing Report, 272

Baseball Coach
76 N Maple Ave Ste 172, Ridgewood, NJ, 07450-3212
Baseball Coach, 100

Bellcore
Room 1B101 - Box 486, 290 W. Mount Pleasant Ave., Livingstone, NJ, 07093-0486
Bellcore Exchange, 1,156

Bergen County Dental Society
1060 Main St, River Edge, NJ, 07661-2013
BCDS-Newsletter, 268

Bethsheva's Concern
PO Box 276, Clifton, NJ, 07011-0276
Christian New Age Quarterly, 1,046

Blenheim
Ft. Lee Executive Park, One Executive Dr., Ft. Lee, NJ, 07024
Networld Netlink, 248

Bloomfield Chamber of Commerce
547 Bloomfield Ave, Bloomfield, NJ, 07003-3301
Chamber of Commerce Bulletin, 158

Bloomfield College
Publications, Bloomfield, NJ, 07003
On-The-Green, 203

Blue Army USA Inc., The
Mountain View Rd., P.O. Box 976, Washington, NJ, 07882
Shrine Bulletin, 1,060

Bookviews
9 Brookside Rd, Maplewood, NJ, 07040-1201
Bookviews, 116

Bowker Reed Reference Electronic Publishing
121 Chanlon Road, New Providence, NJ, 07974
PLUS EXTENSIONS, 234

Brown's Letters, Inc.
1167 Mcbride Ave, West Paterson, NJ, 07424-2539
Advanced Construction Information Service, 243

Budget Message of the Governor of New Jersey
Office of the Governor, Trenton, NJ, 08625
Budget Message of the Governor of New Jersey, 481

Bulletin of the Savitz Library
Glassboro State College, Glassboro, NJ, 08028-1702
Savitz Reports, 809

Bunker Family Assn.
Carole Bunker, 9 Sommerset Rd., Turnersville, NJ, 08012
Bunker Banner, 449

Burlington County Medical Society
PO Box 1023, Mount Laurel, NJ, 08054-7023
Burlington County Medical Society Newsletter, 869

Burrelle's Information Services
75 E. Northfield Rd., Livingston, NJ, 07039-4501
Your Clipping Analyst, 24

•**Buyer's Laboratory, Inc.**
20 Railroad Ave, Hackensack, NJ, 07601-3309

CATSTONE Inc.
318 Pershing Ave, Roselle Park, NJ, 07204-2166
Exploring Ireland, 1,184

CPA Associates
201 Rte. 17 N, 4th fl., Rutherford, NJ, 07070
Outlook (CPA), 7

CPC Intl. Inc.
Intl. Plaza, Englewood Cliffs, NJ, 07632
Best Foods Marketing News, 577

•**CTB International Publishing, Inc.**
P.O. Box 218, Maplewood, NJ, 07040-0218

Caldwell College
9 Ryerson Ave, Caldwell, NJ, 07006-6195
Consort, 203

•**Camden County Historical Society**
Park Blvd. & Euclid Ave., Camden, NJ, 08103

Campbell Soup Co.
375 Memorial Ave., Camden, NJ, 08103
Campbell's News, Front Page, 579

Captan Associates, Inc.
PO Box 504, 744 Durham Terrace, Brick, NJ, 08723-0504
Cureletter, 848

Caribbean Update
52 Maple Ave, Maplewood, NJ, 07040-2626
Caribbean Update, 643

Carriage Association of America, Inc.
177 Pointers Auburn Road, Salem, NJ, 08079-9742
New Hub, The, 560

Carson City Publications
PO Box 36, Midland Park, NJ, 07432-0036
Fortune-Teller, 665

Catholic Library Assn., Northern New Jersey Unit
Immaculate Conception H. S., 33 Cottage Pl., Montclair, NJ, 07042-3497
Northern New Jersey Unit Newsletter, 806

Catholics United for Spiritual Action
176 W 8th St, Bayonne, NJ, 07002-1227
CUSAN, 1,055

Center for the American Woman and Politics
Eagleton Institute of Politics, Rutgers University, New Brunswick, NJ, 08901
CAWP News & Notes, 987

Center for Social & Legal Research
Two University Plaza, Suite 414, Hackensack, NJ, 07601
Privacy & American Business, 148

Center for Sports Sponsorship
PO Box 280, Plainsboro, NJ, 08536-0280
Sports Business, 1,135

Center for Urban Policy Research
Rutgers University, Box 489, Piscataway, NJ, 08855-0489
CUPReport, 1,019

Charles B. Slack, Inc.
6900 Grove Rd, Thorofare, NJ, 08086-9447
Psychosocial Nursing & Mental Health Service, 931

Chinese American Medical Society
281 Edgewood Ave, Teaneck, NJ, 07666-3023
Chinese American Medical Society Newsletter, 870

Clan Stewart Society in America, Inc.
28 Harwich Rd, Morristown, NJ, 07960-2640
Fesse Cheguy, 408

Clifford Kirsch
10 Hopkins Dr, Lawrenceville, NJ, 08648-2018
Court Management & Administration Report, 729

Cognoscenti Publications, Inc.
PO Box 32-M, Livingston, NJ, 07039-0032
Italian Traveler, The, 1,186

Colby & Hyatt LLC
P.O Box 466, Dover, NJ, 07802
Procedures Review, 927

College of St. Elizabeth
Publications, Convent Station, NJ, 07961
Mortarboard, 318

Coming to Order
660 Fairmont Ave, Westfield, NJ, 07090-1361
Coming to Order, 215

•**Commodex (R) System**
7000 Blvd E., Guttenberg, NJ, 07093-4814

Concerned Persons for Adoption
PO Box 179, Whippany, NJ, 07981-0179
Adoption Today Newsletter, 410

Connaught Press Inc.
212 Hillside Ave, Hillside, NJ, 07205-1824
Modern Nutrition News, 934

Conrad Heinrichs, Dragoco, Inc.
King Road, Totowa, NJ, 07512
Dragoco Report, 100

Consulting Engineers Council of NJ
66 Morris Ave., Springfield, NJ, 07081-1409
Consultant, 360

Cook College, Rutgers Univ.
Nichol Ave., New Brunswick, NJ, 08901
Research, 45

Cook Network Consultants
431 Greenway Avenue, Ewing, NJ, 08618
Cook Report on Internet-NREN, 218

Copts Newsletter
Box 9119 GIS, Jersey City, NJ, 07309-9119
Copts Newsletter, 1,066

Creative Escapes
PO Box 1257, Piscataway, NJ, 08855-1257
Creative Escapes, 503

Creative Marketing & Management
303 Park Ave, Hoboken, NJ, 07030-3805
Art of Self Promotion, The, 10

Curly-Coated Retriever Club of America
C/O Mary Alice Hembree, 951 Brown Rd., Bridgewater, NJ, 08807
Curly Commentator, 279

Curriculum Innovations Group
3001 Cindel Dr., Delran, NJ, 08370
Your Health Report, 532

Custom Papers Group
P.O. Box 1140, Alpha, NJ, 08865-1140
Super Riegal Custom, 947

Cybernetics Design
88 E. Main St., Ste. 457, Mendham, NJ, 07945-1832
Printer's Apprentice, 1,006

Dan Newman Co.
1051 Bloomfield Ave., Clifton Lake, NJ, 07012-2120
Business Ideas, 129

•**Datapro Research Corp.**
600 Delran Pky, Delran, NJ, 08075-1255

Davcol Group
1660 Oak Tree Rd # 155, Edison, NJ, 08820-2805
Options Unlimited, 347

Deep Foundations Institute
120 Charlotte Pl., Englewood Cliffs, NJ, 07632-2607
Fulcrum, 247

Delaware River Port Authority
Box 1949, Camden, NJ, 08101-1949
Ameriport Sailing Schedule, 1,111

Dept of Corrections
PO Box 7387, Trenton, NJ, 08628-0387
New Jersey Correction News, 788

Direct Marketing Consultants, Inc.
705 Franklin Tpke, Allendale, NJ, 07401-1637
Direction, 274

District #4 - MEBA/NMU
30 Montgomery Street, New Jersey, NJ, 07302-3821
NMU Government Operations News, 1,112

Doughty Family Assn.
PO Box 203, Mays Landing, NJ, 08330-0203
Doughty Tree, 452

Douglass College
80 Clifton Ave, New Brunswick, NJ, 08901-1568
Douglass Alumnae Bulletin, 190

Dow Beaters, Inc.
PO Box 284, Ironia, NJ, 07845-0284
Dowbeaters, 662

Dow Jones Financial Publishing Corp.
179 Ave. at the Common, Shrewsbury, NJ, 07702
Selling Mutual Funds, 685

Dow Jones Newspaper Fund, Inc.
PO Box 300, Princeton, NJ, 08543-0300
Adviser Update, 832

Dowden Publishing Co.
110 Summit Ave., Montvale, NJ, 07645-1712
Health Words for Women, 511

Draft Insiders' Digest
PO Box 702, Red Bank, NJ, 07701-0702
Draft Insiders' Digest, 434

Dun & Bradstreet Corp.
3 Sylvan Way, Parsippany, NJ, 07054-3805
Dun's Dataline, 221

* See **MULTI-PUBLISHER INDEX** for list of publications.

Dun & Bradstreet Information Services
DATALINE, 3 Sylvan Way, Parsippany, NJ, 07054
DUN & BRADSTREET- DATALINE, 925

Dun's Marketing Services
3 Sylvan Way, Parsippany, NJ, 07054-3805
Reference Point, 808

E.I. du Pont de Nemours
Exploder Mag., Pompton Lakes, NJ, 07442
Exploder, 583

E.M. Enterprises
3 Hickory Rd, Denville, NJ, 07834-9315
Home Economist's Computer Newsletter, 223

•**E.R. Squibb**
Box 609, Princeton, NJ, 08543

•**Economics Press, Inc.**
12 Daniel Rd., Fairfield, NJ, 07004-2565

Ed Burnett/Database America
100 Paragon Dr, Montvale, NJ, 07645-1718
List Update, 275

•**Edison Market News Office**
103 Metroplex Dr, Edison, NJ, 08817-2683

Educational Press Association of America
Rowan College of New Jersey, 201 Mullica Hill Rd.,
Glassboro, NJ, 08028-1701
EdPress News, 308

Educational Testing Service
Rosedale Rd., Princeton, NJ, 08541-0001
ETS Developments, 307

Educators Against Racism and Apartheid
625 Linden Ave, Teaneck, NJ, 07666-2353
Educators Against Racism and Apartheid, 172

Elbeetian Legion
PO Box 9127, North Bergen, NJ, 07047-1327
Elbeetee, 177

Elizabeth Linington Society
1223 Glen Ter, Glassboro, NJ, 08028-1315
Linington Lineup, 818

Engineering Information, Inc.
1 Castle Point Terr, Hoboken, NJ, 07030-5996
Engineering Information Inc., 360

Entrepreneur's Guild
142 Morris Ave, Mountain Lakes, NJ, 07046-1127
Entrepreneur's Alert, 137

Essex County Medical Society
80 Compton Ave., Verona, NJ, 07044
Essex County Medical Society Bulletin, 873

Ethicon Inc.
Johnson & Johnson, Somerville, NJ, 08876
Ethicon News, 583

Executive Health Publications
383 Route 46 West, Fairfield, NJ, 07004-2402
Executive Health's Good Health Report, 506

FCIB - NACM Corp.
100 Wood Ave. South, Ishlin, NJ, 08830-2716
FCIB Intl. Bulletin, 88

F.E.A.R.
PO Box 5424, Somerset, NJ, 08875-5424
F.E.A.R. Chronicles, 173

Fairleigh Dickinson University
1000 River Rd, Teaneck, NJ, 07666-1996
FDU Alumni News, 190

•**Faulkner Technical Reports, Inc.**
7905 Browning Road, 114 Cooper Center, Pennsauken,
NJ, 08109

Federation of Workers Singing Socs. of USA
1729 Springfield Ave, Maplewood, NJ, 07040-2914
Saenger-Zeitung, 917

•**Fides-Vandame, Inc.**
105 N. Main St., Boonton, NJ, 07005-1257

Financial Executives Institute
10 Madison Ave., Box 1938, Morristown, NJ, 07960-6096
FEI Briefing, 88

Fluid Power Distributors Association
201 Barclay Pavilion W, Cherry Hill, NJ, 08034-2129
FPDA News, 848

The Food Institute
28-12 Broadway, Fair Lawn, NJ, 07410-3913
Food Institute Report, 429

Footprint Communications
2400 Lemoine Ave., Ft. Lee, NJ, 07024
Footprints, 1,004

Ford Dealers Alliance
Continental Plaza, 401 Hackensack Ave., Hackensack,
NJ, 07601
FDA Newsletter, 72

Frary Family Association
12 Lohmann Pl., Dumont, NJ, 07628-1521
Frary Family Newsletter, 454

Frederick Research Corp.
1441 Prospect Ave, Plainfield, NJ, 07060-3197
Cris Commentary, 660

Frohlinger's Marketing Report
7 Coppel Dr, Tenafly, NJ, 07670-2903
Frohlinger's Marketing Report, 14

Front Room Publ.
PO Box 1541, Clifton, NJ, 07015-1541
Craft Marketing News, 552

G2 Computer Intelligence
3 Maple Place, P.O. Box 7, Glen Head, NJ, 11545-9864
Client Server News, 215

GAF Corp.
1361 Alps Rd, Wayne, NJ, 07470-3700
World of GAF, 603

•**GAG Recap Publications**
12 Hedden Place, New Povidence, NJ, 07974

GTE-Sylvania
500 Frank W Burr Blvd., Teaneck, NJ, 07666-6802
Sylvania News, 56

Gak-Law Communications Media, Inc.
529A Central Ave, Jersey City, NJ, 07307-2538
German-American World, 311

Garden Sate Horror Writers
PO Box 696, Matawan, NJ, 07747
*New Jersey Graveline: Official Newsletter of the
Garden Sate Horror Writers, 920*

General Commission on Archives & History
of the United Methodist Church, Box 127, Madison, NJ,
07940
Action Memo, 1,073

General Dynamics/Electro Dynamics
150th Ave., Avenel, NJ, 07001
ED Newsletter, 582

•**General Motors Corp.**
1300 Raritan Rd, Clark, NJ, 07066-1102

General Motors Corp. Linden Assembly
1016 W Edgar Rd, Linden, NJ, 07036-6522
Lindens Lines, 73

Gianturco
301 N. Harrison Bldg., #229, Bldg. B, #229, Princeton,
NJ, 08540-3599
Princeton Portfolios, 682

Giftbeat
145 Woodland Ave., Westwood, NJ, 07675-3217
Giftbeat, 272

Giles Road Press
PO Box 212, Harrington Park, NJ, 07640-0212
Macintosh Tips & Tricks, 228

Gold Seal Co.
PO Box 941, Wayne, NJ, 07474-0941
Work, 603

Golden Retriever Club of America
3 Station Plaza, Ramsey, NJ, 07446-1805
Golden Retriever Club of America News, 280

Goodall Rubber Co.
Grovers Mill Rd. #203, Trenton, NJ, 08648-4708
Goodall News, 584

Greater Delaware Valley Kite Society
PO Box 888, Newfield, NJ, 08344-0888
Tight Lines, 556

Greystone Park Psychiatric Hospital
Greystone Park, NJ, 07950
Psychogram, 571

•**Harrison Scott Publications**
One Riverfront Plaza, Suite 1480, Newark, NJ, 07102-5495

•**Health Resource Publishing**
3100 Hwy. 138, PO Box 1442, Wall Township, NJ,
07719-1442

Herbert W. Davis & Co.
One Executive Dr., Ste. 280, Fort Lee, NJ, 07024-3311
Davis Database, 219

•**Hirsch Organization**
6 Deer Trl, Old Tappan, NJ, 07675-7125

Historical Society of Haddonfield
343 Kings Hwy E, Haddonfield, NJ, 08033-1214
Bulletin of the Historical Society of Haddonfield, 537

Historical Society of the United Methodist Church
PO Box 127, Madison, NJ, 07940-0127
Historian's Digest, 1,073

Hobby Industry Association
319 E. 54th St., Elmwood Park, NJ, 07407-2712
Size of Craft/Hobby Industry Survey, 256

Holistic Health Assn. of the Princeton Area
360 Nassau St, Princeton, NJ, 08540-4615
Holistic Living, 513

Holocaust Resource Center
Kean College - Dr. J. Preil, 1000 Morris Avenue, Union,
NJ, 07083-7131
Diversity 2000, 307

Home Income Quarterly
PO Box 424, Morganville, NJ, 07751-0424
Home Income Quarterly, 15

Hudson City Savings Bank
Marketing Dept., W. 80 Century Rd., Paramus, NJ, 07652
Hudson City Trends, 91

Hungarian Scouts Association
PO Box 68, Garfield, NJ, 07026-0068
Magyar Cserke'sz, 179

Hunterdon County Historical Society
114 Main St, Flemington, NJ, 08822-1415
Hunterdon Historical Newsletter, 542

Hypoglycemia Foundation, Inc.
Adrenal Metabolic Resrch Soc., 32 Sunrise Terrace,
Clifton Park, NJ, 12065-2327
Homeostasis Quarterly, 876

INSPEC
445 Hoes Ln., PO Box 1331, Piscataway, NJ, 08855-1331
Inspec Matters, 366

Inform
PO Box 489, Elizabeth, NJ, 07207-0489
Inform, 991

•**Information Today, Inc.**
143 Old Marlton Pike, Medford, NJ, 08055-8758

•**Infosources Publishing**
140 Norma Rd, Teaneck, NJ, 07666-4234

Inside Radio Inc.
1930 Marlton Pike E Ste S93, Cherry Hill, NJ, 08003-4208
Inside Radio, 124

•**Institute of Electrical & Electronics Engineers, Inc.**
445 Hoes Lane, PO Box 1331, Piscataway, NJ, 08855-
1331

Institute of Management Accountants
10 Paragon Dr., Montvale, NJ, 07645-1760
IMA Focus, 5

Intellectual Activist, Inc.
PO Box 262, Lincroft, NJ, 07738-0262
Intellectual Activist, 991

Interflo
PO Box 42, Maplewood, NJ, 07040-0042
*Interflo: Trade Monitor of the Former Soviet
Republics, 647*

International Documents Review
318 Edgewood Ave, Teaneck, NJ, 07666-3021
International Documents Review, 632

International Education Association
PO Box 70, Rochelle Park, NJ, 07662-0070
Multicultural Messenger, 1,041

International Intertrade Index
Box 636, Federal Square, Newark, NJ, 07101-0636
Foreign Trade Fairs New Products Newsletter, 646

International Schools Services
15 Roszel Rd., P.O. Box 5910, Princeton, NJ, 08543-5910
NewsLinks, 323

Investors Research Bureau Inc.
10 Mountainview Road, Upper Saddle River, NJ,
07458-1933
Securities Class Action Alert, 775

Italica
Rutgers Univ., New Brunswick, NJ, 08903
American Association of Teachers of Italian, 819

JLCom Publishing Co.
571 Passaic Ave., Nutley, NJ, 07110-1236
Advertising Compliance Service, 713

J.M. Kesslinger and Associates
2444 Morris Avenue, Union, NJ, 07083-5711
Back Talk, 576

Jack Rushing
PO Box 15, Liberty Corner, NJ, 07938-0015
Rushing Past, 466

James E. Mooney & Co.
262 Mountain Ave # 50, Springfield, NJ, 07081-2215
Risk Management News, 624

Jen
LPO 16261, P.O. Box 5064, New Brunswick, NJ,
08903-5064
Stardift, 984

Jersey Central Power & Light Co.
Public Relations, 300 Madison Avenue, Morristown, NJ,
07962-1911
Online, 593

Jersey Society of Parapsychology
PO Box 2071, Morristown, NJ, 07962-2071
Insights, 948

* See ***MULTI-PUBLISHER INDEX*** for list of publications.

Jewish Fed. Camden County
2395 Marlton Pike W, Cherry Hill, NJ, 08002-3422
Voice, 1,071

John Patrick Productions
P.O. Box 289, Short Hills, NJ, 07078-0289
So You Wanna Be a Gambler, 439

John Pugsley's Journal
23-00 Route 208, Fairlawn, NJ, 07410
John Pugsley's Journal, 93

Judaica Society International
16 Housman Ct, Maplewood, NJ, 07040-3006
Judaica Society International, 633

K-III Directory Corp.
10 Lake Dr., PO Box 4000, Hightstown, NJ, 08520
Intermodal Reporter, 1,178

King Alarm Distributors, Inc.
35 Green St, Hackensack, NJ, 07601-4003
Kingalarm Review, 1,104

Kross Publications & Research Services
PO Box 9, Franklin Park, NJ, 08823-0009
Eastern Genealogical PPQ, 452

Lambda Financial Advisor
PO Box 3569, Jersey City, NJ, 07303-3569
Lambda Financial Advisor, 673

Lawrence Erlbaum Associates, Inc.
10 Industrial Ave., Mahwah, NJ, 07430-2205
Teaching Thinking and Problem Solving, 473

Let's Be Human
454 Prospect Ave. #111, West Orange, NJ, 07052-4103
Let's Be Human, 702

Library Learning Resources
PO Box 87, Berkeley Heights, NJ, 07922-0087
School Librarian's Workshop, 810

Lincoln Owners Club
99 Drakestown Rd., Long Valley, NJ, 07853-3298
Lincoln Owners Club, Bulletin, 554

•**Lipper Analytical Svcs., Inc.**
47 Maple St., Suite 101, Summit, NJ, 07901-2571

Liquid Assets
169 Nassau St, Princeton, NJ, 08542-7007
Liquid Assets, 104

Louis-Ferdinand & Co., Inc.
206 Warren St, Harrison, NJ, 07029-1738
Pipelines, 651

Lovejoy Corporation
Box 1442, Palmer Sq., Princeton, NJ, 08542-1442
MarketBrief Ratings, 676

Lovejoy's College Guide, Inc.
Drawer Q, Red Bank, NJ, 07701-8039
Lovejoy's Guidance Digest, 316

Loving Brotherhood
PO Box 556, Sussex, NJ, 07461-0556
Loving Brotherhood Newsletter, 445

Lybarger Memorial Associates
PO Box 7792, West Trenton, NJ, 08628-0792
Lybarger Linkages, 460

MIC
1111 Marlkress Rd., P.O. Box 5062, Cherry Hill, NJ, 08013
MIC/INFO, 228

•**M.J. Powers**
374 Millburn Ave, Millburn, NJ, 07041-1361

Maghreb Report
PO Box 1593, Princeton, NJ, 08542-1593
Maghreb Report, 634

Mail Call
Dept. S, Box 5031, South Hackensack, NJ, 07606
Mail Call, 543

Maritime Research, Inc.
499 Ericsson Rd., Box 805, Parlin, NJ, 08859-1406
Maritime Research Charter Newsletter, 1,111

Masback, Inc.
2400 83rd St, North Bergen, NJ, 07047-1406
Mas-Back-Talk, 590

Mathews, Woodbridge & Collins
100 Thanet Cir Ste 306, Princeton, NJ, 08540-3674
M. W. & C. Newsletter, 752

Maxwell House Div., General Foods Corp.
1125 Hudson St, Hoboken, NJ, 07030-5305
Maxwell House Messenger, 590

McMillan Analysis Corp.
39 Meadowbrook Rd, Randolph, NJ, 07869-3808
Option Strategist, The, 681

Medical Horizons Publishers
240 Cedar Knolls Rd., #220, Cedar Knolls, NJ, 07927-1621
Cardiology Trends & Product News, 870

Mendham Technology Group
144 Talmadge Rd., Mendham, NJ, 07945
Windows Letter, 242

Messenger & Delivery Services Newsletter
149 Dawson Ave, Clifton, NJ, 07012-1131
Messenger & Delivery Services Newsletter, 1,178

Metro Scene
PO Box 911, Westwood, NJ, 07675-0911
Metro Scene, 185

Mexico Business Monthly
52 Maple Ave, Maplewood, NJ, 07040-2626
Mexico Business Monthly, 650

Middle Atlantic States Komondor Club, Inc.
102 Russell Rd, Princeton, NJ, 08540-6773
MASKC Komondor News, 280

Minolta Corp.
101 Williams Dr, Ramsey, NJ, 07446-1293
Minolta Contact Sheet, 977

Monetary Outlook
PO Box 476, Leonia, NJ, 07605-0476
Monetary Outlook, The, 677

Morfogen Assocs. Newsletter
Elm Rd., Box 324, Mountain Lakes, NJ, 07046
Morfogen Assocs. Newsletter, 145

Mutual Funds Scoreboard
6 Deer Trl, Old Tappan, NJ, 07675-7125
Mutual Funds Scoreboard, 679

•**N.J. Conservation Foundation**
300 Mendham Rd., Morristown, NJ, 07960-4806

NJDOT-Office of Aviation
1035 Parkway Ave., CN 610, Trenton, NJ, 08625-0610
New Jersey Aviation News, 31

N.J. Dept. of Environmental Protection
401 E. State St., CN 402, Trenton, NJ, 08608-1501
Environmental News, 381

NJ Dept. of the Treasury
Division of Taxation, 50 Barrack St., Trenton, NJ, 08608-2006
New Jersey Department of the Treasury, Local Property and Public Utility Branch News, 1,149

N.J. Div. of Taxation
50 Barrack St., CN 281, Trenton, NJ, 08646-0001
New Jersey State Tax News, 1,149

NJ Speech-Language-Hearing Assn.
2 Greentree Centre, Suite 225 / Box 955, Marlton, NJ, 08053
NJSHA Newsletter, 533

N.V. Business Publishers Corp.
43 Main St., Avon by the Sea, NJ, 07717
Board Converting News, 945

Nabisco Brands, Inc.
Nabisco Brands Plaza, Parsippany, NJ, 07054-4471
NBI Today, 591

Natl. Art Materials Trade Assn
178 Lakeview Ave, Clifton, NJ, 07011-4019
NAMTA News & Views, 65

National Association of Fleet Administrators, Inc
120 Wood Ave S Ste 615, Iselin, NJ, 08830-2709
NAFA Fleet Focus, 74

•**National Association of Printers & Lithographers**
780 Palisade Ave., Teaneck, NJ, 07666-3129

National Association of Recording Merchandisers
3 Eves Dr Ste 307, Marlton, NJ, 08053-3129
NARM Sounding Board, 915

Natl. Baptist Deacons Convention of America
179 Hollywood Ave, East Orange, NJ, 07018-3941
News Deacons, 1,053

•**National Council of Accoustical Consultants**
66 Morris Ave., Suite 1A, Springfield, NJ, 07081-1409

Natl. Disabled Law Officers Assoc.
75 New St, Nutley, NJ, 07110-1601
NDLOA Newsletter, 788

Natl. Forensic Center
17 Temple Ter, Lawrenceville, NJ, 08648-3254
Expert and the Law, 735

National Guild of Community Schools of the Arts
Box 8018, 40 N. Van Brunt St., Englewood, NJ, 07631
Employment Opportunities, 309

Natl. Institute for Rehabilitation Engineering
PO Box T, Hewitt, NJ, 07421-1020
Rehabilitation Technology Newsletter, 1,121

Natl. Kitchen & Bath Assn.
687 Willow Grove St., Hackettstown, NJ, 07840
Perspectives, 438

National Life Center, Inc.
686 N Broad St, Woodbury, NJ, 08096-1672
National Pulse, 414

Natl. Premium Sales Executives
1600 Rt. 22, Union, NJ, 07083-3478
AIM Newsletter, 9

National Prepared Frozen Food Assn.
1415 Queene Ann Rd #201, Teaneck, NJ, 07666-3521
NPFFA News, 431

•**Natl. Quotation Bureau, Inc.**
150 Commerce Rd., Cedar Grove, NJ, 07009-1208

Natl. Starch
PO Box 6500, Bridgewater, NJ, 08807-0500
NSC Today, 591

Natural Hygiene of New Jersey Inc.
PO Box 142, Pompton Plains, NJ, 07444-0142
Natural Hygiene Soc. of New Jersey Newsletter, 934

Negative Population Growth, Inc.
210 The Plz, P.O Box 1206, Teaneck, NJ, 07666-5161
Human Survival, 1,125

Nell Zink
81 Grand ST #4, Jersey City, NJ, 07302
Animal Review, 48

New Jersey Committee for the Humanities
28 W State St Ste 6, Trenton, NJ, 08608-1602
New Jersey Humanities, 261

New Jersey Department of Environmental Protection
Water Supply Element, CN 426, Bureau of Safe Drinking Water, Trenton, NJ, 08625-0426
H2Observer, 1,203

•**New Jersey Department of Labor**
Office of Research & Planning, CN 056, Trenton, NJ, 08625-0056

New Jersey Education Assn.
180 W State St, P.O. Box 1211, Trenton, NJ, 08608-1104
New Jersey Education Association, Research Bulletin, 322

New Jersey Elementary School Principals Assn.
180 W State St, Trenton, NJ, 08608-1104
New Jersey Elementary School Principals Association, Bulletin, 1,092

New Jersey Highway Authority
PO Box 5050, Woodbridge, NJ, 07095-5050
Reporter, 1,077

New Jersey Historical Commission
Cn305, Trenton, NJ, 08608-0305
New Jersey Historical Commission Newsletter, 545

•**New Jersey Historical Society**
230 Broadway, Newark, NJ, 07104-3926

New Jersey Music Educators Assn.
Morris Hills High School, Rockaway, NJ, 07866
Tempo, 918

•**New Jersey Natural Gas Co.**
PO Box 1464, Wall, NJ, 07719-1464

New Jersey Poetry Soc. Inc.
RTE 1, POB 720, Franklinville, NJ, 08322
Poetidings, 983

New Jersey Public Interest Research Group
11 N Willow St, Trenton, NJ, 08608-1203
NJPIRG, 388

•**New Jersey School Boards Assn.**
413 W State St # 909, Trenton, NJ, 08618-5617

New Jersey Self-Help Clearinghouse
St. Clare's Riverside Med. Ctr, Pocono Rd., Denville, NJ, 07834
New Jersey Self-Help Clearinghouse-Network, 815

New Jersey Shade Tree Federation
Box 231, Blake Hall, Cook College, New Brunswick, NJ, 08903-0231
Shade Tree, 443

New Jersey Shore Builders Assn.
190 Oberlin Ave N, Lakewood, NJ, 08701-4524
Bulletin Board, 244

New Jersey Society of Prof. Engineers
150 W. State St., Trenton, NJ, 08608
Perspectives in Engineering, 363

•**New Jersey State Bar Association**
New Jersey Law Center, 1 Constitution Sq., New Brunswick, NJ, 08901-1520

•**New Jersey State Dept. of Education**
Public Information Office, 225 W. State St., CN 500, Trenton, NJ, 08625-0500

New Jersey State Dept. of Mental Health
Publications, Trenton, NJ, 08608
Signa, 1,017

New Jersey State Dept. of Motor Vehicles
Trenton, NJ, 08666-0001
Public Safety, 1,083

New Jersey State Library
185 W. State St., CN 520, Trenton, NJ, 08625-0520
Impressions, 799

* See ***MULTI-PUBLISHER INDEX*** for list of publications.

New Jersey State Nurses Assn.
320 W State St, Trenton, NJ, 08618-5704
New Jersey Nurse, 930

New Jersey State Potato Assn., Dept. of Horticulture
Cook College, Box 231, New Brunswick, NJ, 08903
Hints to Potato Growers, 1,009

New Jersey State Safety Council
6 Commerce Dr., Cranford, NJ, 07016-3509
Safety Briefs, 1,084

New York C. S. Lewis Society
419 Springfield Ave, Westfield, NJ, 07090-1009
CSL Bulletin, 820

New York Opera Newsletter
PO Box 278, Maplewood, NJ, 07040-0278
New York Opera Newsletter, 369

Newark Museum, The
49 Washington St # 450, Newark, NJ, 07102-3109
Newark Museum Exhibitions & Events, 907

North American Vexillological Association
1977 N Olden Avenue Ext Ste, 225, Trenton, NJ, 08618-2193
NAVA News, 544

Official Airline Guides, Inc.
500 Plaza Drive, 6th Floor, Secaucus, NJ, 07096
Travel Management Newsletter, 1,190

Opticians Assn. of New Jersey
150 W. State St., Trenton, NJ, 08608
In Focus, 941

Options Publishing Co.
PO Box 311, Wayne, NJ, 07474-0311
Options, The Jewish Resources Newsletter, 1,070

Packard Automobile Classics
84 Hoy Ave, Fords, NJ, 08863-1938
Cormorant News Bulletin, 72

Passaic County Dental Society
999 Mcbride Ave. #2, W. Paterson, NJ, 07424-2534
Passaic County, Dental Society, Bulletin, 271

Passaic County Historical Society
Lambert Castle, 3 Valley Rd., Paterson, NJ, 07503
Castle Light, 537

Passaic County Medical Society
999 Mcbride Ave Suite B-202, West Paterson, NJ, 07424-2534
Passaic County Medical Society Newsnotes, 883

Paul Sniffen
PO Box 124, Red Bank, NJ, 07701-0124
Grapevine: Kniffin-Sniffen Family Newsletter, 455

Paznmes
67 Stevens Ave, Old Bridge, NJ, 08857-2244
Egg Cup Collectors Corner, 553

PeopleScience
1015 S Park Ave, Highland Park, NJ, 08904-2954
Essence of Adolescence, 1,014

Perrin & Treggett Booksellers
937 Jamestown Rd., Hightstown, NJ, 08520-5645
Perrin & Treggett's Review, 524

PhanMedia
PO Box 216, Ocean Grove, NJ, 07756-0216
Phantom of the Movies' VideoScope, The, 1,169

Pharmaeo-Medical Documentation, Inc.
205 Main St, Chatham, NJ, 07928-2408
Unlisted Drugs, 288

•**Phillips Decision Point Resources**
1111 Marlkress Road., P.O. Box 5062, Cherry Hill, NJ, 08063-5062

Point Publishing Co.
PO Box 1309, Point Pleasant, NJ, 08742-1309
Inside Textiles Newsletter, 1,171

Polish American Historical Assn.
Jersey City State College, Jersey City, NJ, 07305
PAHA Newsletter, 407

Premium Merchandising Club of America
1600 Rt. 22, Union, NJ, 07083-3410
PMC NY Newsletter, 20

Prentice-Hall Business and Professional Publishing
113 Sylvan Ave., Englewood Cliffs, NJ, 07632
Advertising Manager's Handbook, 25

Presbyterians for Lesbian & Gay Concerns
c/o James D. Anderson, Box 38, New Brunswick, NJ, 08903-0038
More Light Update, 445

Preservation New Jersey, Inc.
149 Kearny Ave., Perth Amboy, NJ, 08861-4700
Preservation Perspective, 61

Princeton Academic Press
3175 Princeton Pike., Princeton, NJ, 08648
Spiritual Frontiers Fellowship Journal, 949

Princeton China Initiative
PO Box 209, Princeton, NJ, 08542-0209
China Focus, 628

Princeton Economic Consultants, Inc.
PO Box 7227, Princeton, NJ, 08543-7227
Armstrong Report, 654

•**Princeton Religion Research Ctr., Inc.**
P.O. Box 389, Princeton, NJ, 08542

Princeton Univ., School of Engineering & Applied Science
C-218, E-Quad, Princeton, NJ, 08544-0001
E-Quad News, 190

Print/New Jersey
75 Kearny Ave, Kearny, NJ, 07032-2334
Print/New Jersey Communicator, 1,006

•**Printing Consultants**
Federal Sq., Box 636, Newark, NJ, 07101

•**Probe Research, Inc.**
3 Wing Dr Ste 240, Cedar Knolls, NJ, 07927-1006

Pro$perity Network
PO Box 1406, Hoboken, NJ, 07030-1301
Pro$perity Alert, 295

Prudential Insurance Co. of America
Prudential Plz, Newark, NJ, 07102-3777
Pru-Echo, 596

Psychohistory Forum
627 Dakota Trail, Franklin Lakes, NJ, 07417
Clio's Pscyhe, 1,013

Public Domain Report
PO Box 3102, Margate, NJ, 08402
Public Domain Report, 66

R.R. Bowker
121 Chanlon Rd, New Providence, NJ, 07974-1541
Cornerstone, The, 953

•**R. W. Mansfield Co**
2973 John F. Kennedy Blvd., Jersey City, NJ, 07306-3884

Reckitt & Colman Inc.
1655 Valley Rd # 943, Wayne, NJ, 07470-2044
Inside Reckitt & Colman Inc., 587

Recording for the Blind
20 Roszel Rd, Princeton, NJ, 08540-6294
RFB News, 278

Red Hot Publishing Co.
PO Box 7423, Trenton, NJ, 08628-0423
Home Income Reporter, 140

Reed & Carnick
257 Cornelison Ave., Jersey City, NJ, 07302-3198
Cardiogram, 870

Reed Travel Group
500 Plaza Dr., 4th Floor, Secaucus, NJ, 07094-3626
Star Service, 1,189

Rejoyce Ink
42 Melrose Pl, Montclair, NJ, 07042-2028
Sherlockin Tidbits, 824

•**Robert Stanger & Co.**
1129 Broad St., Box 7490, Shrewsbury, NJ, 07702-4314

Robert Weatherford
531 Majestic Ave, Bellmawr, NJ, 08031-1461
Weather - Watch, 469

Roche Labs.
Div. of Hoffmann-La Roche, Inc, Nutley, NJ, 07110
Roche Report: Frontiers of Psychiatry, 1,011

Roy W. Walter & Assoc.
744 Prescott Place, Paramus, NJ, 07652-3720
RWA Reporter, 596

Rutgers Univ.
Publications, New Brunswick, NJ, 08903
Rutgers University, Bureau of Conservation and Environmental Science, News, 393

Rutgers University
Suite 431, New Brunswick, NJ, 08903
Dickens Quarterly, 821

Rutgers University, College of Pharmacy
Publications, New Brunswick, NJ, 08903
Rutgers Pharmacy Newsletter, 288

Rutgers Univ. Computing Svces.
User Services, Box 879-Newsletter, Piscataway, NJ, 08855-0879
RUCS Newsletter, 234

Rutgers University, Graduate School of Education
Publications, New Brunswick, NJ, 08903
N.J.S.D.C. Research Bulletin, 320

S. Goldberg
20 E Broadway, Hackensack, NJ, 07601-6820
Goldberg Bulletin, 584

SMB Whole Health
PO Box 263, Little Falls, NJ, 07424-0263
Whole Person's Health Letter, 531

St. Paul's Abbey
PO Box 7, Newton, NJ, 07860-0007
Pax, 1,059

•**Scandinavian Airlines System, Inc.**
Public Relations, 9 Polito Ave., 10th Floor, Lyndhurst, NJ, 07071

Schiffli Lace and Embroidery Manufacturers Assn.
8555 Tonnelle Ave., North Bergen, NJ, 07047-4738
Embroidery News, 1,171

Science Associates/International, Inc.
6 Hastings Rd., Marlboro, NJ, 07746-1313
Information Hotline, 225

Seaspray Publishing
RD 2 Box 736, Sussex, NJ, 07461
Cruiseletter, 1,183

•**Securities Arbitration Commentator**
6 1/2 Highland Pl, PO Box 112, Maplewood, NJ, 07040-0112

Seeing Eye, Inc., The
PO Box 375, Morristown, NJ, 07963-0375
Seeing Eye Guide, The, 112

Selden Assn.
1223 Glen Ter, Glassboro, NJ, 08028-1315
Selden Millennium, 975

Sherwin-Williams Co.
Brown St. & Lister Ave., Newark, NJ, 07105
Newarker, 591

Sierra Club, New Jersey Chapter
57 Mountain Ave, Princeton, NJ, 08540-2611
Jersey Sierran, 386

Society of African Missions
23 Bliss Ave, Tenafly, NJ, 07670-3000
Frontline Report, 1,063

Society of American Archivists
Archives, Rutgers University, New Brunswick, NJ, 08903
Academic Archivist, 792

Society for the History of Authorship, Reading & Publishing
Drew University, History Department, Madison, NJ, 07940
SHARP News, 119

Soc. for the Preservation & Enhancement of the Recognition
of Millard Fillmore, 37 Hillside Rd., Stratford, NJ, 08084
Fillmore Bungle, 604

Songwriters Guild of America
1500 Harbor Blvd., Weehawken, NJ, 07087-6732
Songwriters Guild News, 918

South Jersey Port Corp
2500 Broadway, Camden, NJ, 08104-2409
Port O Call, 1,112

Space Studies Institute
PO Box 82, Princeton, NJ, 08542-0082
SSI Update, 32

Special Libraries Assn., Metals/Materials Div.
471 E. Mesa Ave., Teaneck, NJ, 07666
Sci-Tech News, 810

Straight Shooter
PO Box 1584, Ridgewood, NJ, 07451-1584
Straight Shooter, 296

Strategic Marketing Communications
550 N Maple Ave, Ridgewood, NJ, 07450-1632
Collegiate Trends, 12

Stumpwork Society
1315 Anderson Ave. #23, Fort Lee, NJ, 07024-1702
Stumpwork Society Chronicle, 54

Summit Impressions, Inc.
Hwy. 36, Airport Plz., Hazlet, NJ, 07730
SAYN, 409

•**Superconductivity Publications, Inc.**
828 Livingston Ave., North Brunswick, NJ, 08902-2356

Systems Literacy, Inc.
696 9th St, Secaucus, NJ, 07094-3029
Microcomputer Trainer, 230

•**TJFR Publishing**
545 N Maple Ave Fl 2, Ridgewood, NJ, 07450-1612

TKO Real Estate Group
100 Youngs Rd., Mercerville, NJ, 08619
Dealmakers, 246

Tappan Group, Inc.
PO Box 167, Harrington Park, NJ, 07640-0167
Netherlands News, 651

Tau Epsilon Rho Law Society
36 Kresson Rd Ste E, Cherry Hill, NJ, 08034-3227
Summons, 777

•**Technical Insights, Inc.**
PO Box 1304, Fort Lee, NJ, 07024-9967

* See **MULTI-PUBLISHER INDEX** for list of publications.

Textile Research Institute
Box 625, Princeton, NJ, 08540
TRI News & Research Briefs, 1,172

Thomas Edison State College
101 W. State St., Trenton, NJ, 08608-1176
Invention, 203

Thompson Group
3371 Brunswick Plke, Ste. 302-174, Lawrenceville, NJ, 08648
Advanced Selling Power, 1,086

•**Tobacco Merchants Assn. of the U.S.**
PO Box 8019, Princeton, NJ, 08543-8019

Tomato Club, The
114 E. Main St., Bogota, NJ, 07603
Tomato Club, The, 443

Trade Union News
20 Branford Pl, Newark, NJ, 07102-2725
Trade Union News, 711

Transportation Research Assocs.
154 Pulaski Blvd, Toms River, NJ, 08757-6426
Freight Management Report, 1,177

Tri-County Dental Society
110 Madison Ave, Morristown, NJ, 07960-6013
Tri-County Dental Society, Bulletin, 272

Truck-Frame & Axle Repair Association
P.O Box 122, Adelphia, NJ, 07710-0122
TARA News & Topics, 76

Unexpected Wildlife Refuge
PO Box 765, Newfield, NJ, 08344-0765
Beaver Defenders, 373

U.S. Equestrian Team, Inc.
Pottersville Rd., Gladstone, NJ, 07934
USET News, 560

University Publications of America
121 Chanlon Rd, New Providence, NJ, 07974-1541
BioLaw, 868

Unschoolers Network
2 Smith St, Farmingdale, NJ, 07727-1006
Unschoolers Network, 334

•**Urner Barry Publications, Inc.**
PO Box 389, Toms River, NJ, 08754-0389

VHL Foundation
PO Box 733, Toms River, NJ, 08754-0733
VHL News, 474

Varityper Inc.
11 Mount Pleasant Ave, East Hanover, NJ, 07936-2601
Varityper Update, 1,008

Village Press
27 Canfield St, Orange, NJ, 07050-3714
Alloy Digest, 890

Vitamin Shoppe
4700 Westside Ave., N. Bergen, NJ, 07047-9808
Healthy Talk, 512

The Vitaphone Project
5 Meade Court, Piscataway, NJ, 08854
Vitaphone News, 919

•**Vox Juris, Inc.**
P.O. Box 389, Pennington, NJ, 08534

•**WD&S Publishing**
20 Highland Ave, Metuchen, NJ, 08840-1949

•**WPI Communications, Inc.**
55 Morris Ave, Springfield, NJ, 07081-1496

Wacky Business
P.O. Box 373, Hohokus, NJ, 07423
Wacky Business Report, 155

•**Walden-Mott Corp.**
225 N. Franklin Trnpke., Ramsey, NJ, 07446-1600

•**Whitaker Newsletters**
313 South Ave., Box 340, Fanwood, NJ, 07023-1350

Wine Odyssey
PO Box 5157, Hoboken, NJ, 07030-1502
Wine Odyssey, 105

World for Christ Crusader, Inc.
1005 Union Valley Rd, West Milford, NJ, 07480-1220
World for Christ Crusader, 1,066

World Methodist Historical Society
PO Box 127, Madison, NJ, 07940-0127
Historical Bulletin, 1,073

New Mexico

•**Albuquerque Archaeological Society**
PO Box 4029, Albuquerque, NM, 87196-4029

Archaeological Conservancy
5301 Central Ave. N.E., Ste. 12181, Albuquerque, NM, 87108-1517
Archaeological Conservancy-Newsletter, 57

Beyond Words
1534 Wells Dr NE, Albuquerque, NM, 87112-6383
Beyond Words, 301

Capitol Government Reports Weekly
P.O. Box 602, Santa Fe, NM, 87504
Capitol Government Reports Weekly, 482

Center for Holistic Resource Management
PO Box 7128, Albuquerque, NM, 87194-7128
Holistic Resource Management Quarterly, 384

Computers Foodservice & You
1201 S. Second St., PO Box 338, Raton, NM, 87740
Computers Foodservice & You, 217

Council of Administrators of Special Education
615 16th St., NW, Albuquerque, NM, 87104
CASE Newsletter, 302

Deming-Luna County Chamber of Commerce
PO Box 8, Deming, NM, 88031
For Members Only, 159

Deul Co.
7208 Jefferson St NE, Albuquerque, NM, 87109-4309
D&A Hazardous Waste Hotline, 164

Eastern New Mexico University-Roswell Campus
PO Box 6000, Roswell, NM, 88202-6000
Eastern Clips, 190

Economic Outlook
1187 Laurel Loop NE, Albuquerque, NM, 87122-1108
Economic Outlook, 291

•**Ferdic, Inc.**
PO Box 367, Las Cruces, NM, 88004-0367

Food Industry Assn. Executives
c/o George R. Staton, P.O. Box 219, Las Cruces, NM, 88004
FIAE Association Spotlight, 1,075

Foundation for Indian Leadership
Hal Schultz, PO Box 5340, Santa Fe, NM, 87505
Newsletter, 406

Goodwin Family Organization
39 Lost Trail Rd, Roswell, NM, 88201-9509
Goodwin News, 455

Interhemispheric Resource Center
PO Box 4506, Albuquerque, NM, 87196-4506
Resource Center Bulletin, 637

International Water Resources Association
Economics Building, UNM, Albuquerque, NM, 87131
IWRA Update, 384

Investor's Analysis, Inc.
PO Box 460, Santa Fe, NM, 87504-0460
Bob Nurock's Advisory, 656

Juxtapedia Press
PO Box 25771, Albuquerque, NM, 87125-0771
Leak News Service and Room 101 Revisited, 369

Latin American Institute
University Of New Mexico 801, Yale N.e., Albuquerque, NM, 87131-0001
LAI Notes, 633

Millicent Rogers Museum
PO Box A, Taos, NM, 87571-0546
Las Palabras, 261

Mills Capitol Observer
PO Box 5141, Santa Fe, NM, 87502-5141
Ernie Mills' Legislative Report, 484

Natl. Association for Legal Support of Alternative Schools
PO Box 2823, Santa Fe, NM, 87504-2823
Tidbits, 333

National Coalition of Alternative Community Schools
PO Box 15036, Santa Fe, NM, 87506-5036
National Coalition News, 321

•**Natl. Indian Council on Aging**
6400 Uptown Blvd NE Ste 510w, Albuquerque, NM, 87110-4203

National Indian Youth Council
318 Elm St SE, Albuquerque, NM, 87102-3614
Americans Before Columbus, 405

New Mexico Book League
8632 Horacio Pl. NE, Albuquerque, NM, 87111-3218
Book Talk, 116

New Mexico Municipal League
1229 Paseo De Peralta # 846, Santa Fe, NM, 87501-2758
New Mexico Municipal League, Municipal Reporter, 1,023

New Mexico State Library
325 Don Gaspar, Santa Fe, NM, 87501-2777
Hitch Hiker, 799

New Mexico State Univ.
Box CC, University Park, NM, 88003
Swastika, 203

New Mexico State Univ. English Dept.
c/o Andrew Wiget, Las Cruces, NM, 88003
ASAIL Notes, 819

New Mexico Water Resources Research Institute
Box 30001, Dept. 3167, Las Cruces, NM, 88003-0001
Divining Rod, 377

Open Mind Book Store
119 Harverd SE, P.O. Box 4722, Albuquerque, NM, 87196
Vibrations, 975

•**Publications Company**
7015 Prospect Pl. NE, Albuquerque, NM, 87110-4311

•**SALALM Secretariat**
General Library University Of, New Mexico, Albuquerque, NM, 87131-0001

Santa Fe Health Education Project
PO Box 577, Santa Fe, NM, 87504-0577
Healthletters, 511

Securities Investment Management
1224 Vallecita Dr, Santa Fe, NM, 87501-8803
Buy Low - Sell High, 657

Silver Prescription Press Inc.
524 Camino Del Monte Sol, Santa Fe, NM, 87501-2828
Silver Prescription, 151

Soulmate News
PO Box 769, Ramah, NM, 87321-0769
Soulmate News, 923

State Bar of New Mexico
PO Box 25883, Albuquerque, NM, 87125-0883
Bar Bulletin, 718

Through the Flower Corp.
PO Box 5280, Santa Fe, NM, 87502-5280
Holocaust Project/1990, 542

Tyuonyi
PO Box 23266, Santa Fe, NM, 87502-3266
Innervisions, 64

U.S. Bur. of Indian Affairs
PO Box 1060, Gallup, NM, 87305-1060
Navajo Area Newsletter, 406

University of Albuquerque
St. Joseph's Pl., NW, Albuquerque, NM, 87140-0001
Dialogue, 203

Univ. of New Mexico
2701 Campus Blvd. , N. E., Albuquerque, NM, 87131-0001
CIRT Newsletter, 214

University of New Mexico-Gallup
200 College Rd, Gallup, NM, 87301-5603
Newsletter, 203

Univ. of New Mexico, Office of Research
102 Scholes Hall, Albuquerque, NM, 87131-0001
Univ. of New Mexico, Office of Research, Research Notes, 334

University of New Mexico Student Publications
Marron Hall, Rm. 131, Albuquerque, NM, 87131-0001
University of New Mexico, Computing Center Newsletter, 241

Vietnam Veterans of New Mexico
Bataan Memorial Bldg., Galisteo St., Box 2324, Santa Fe, NM, 87503-0001
Vietnam Veterans of New Mexico Newsletter, 1,199

New York

13D Research, Inc.
SE Executive Park, 100 Executive Drive, Brewster, NY, 10509
Street Smart Investing, 688

2000AD, Inc.
2 Grace Ct., Apt 2U, Brooklyn, NY, 11201-4156
Tick, Tick, Tick..., 241

704th Tank Destroyer Battalion Assn.
71 Route 25A, Smithtown, NY, 11787-1403
Five Star Review, 1,138

92nd St.-YM-YWHA
1395 Lexington Ave, New York, NY, 10128-1647
Jewish Storytelling Newsletter, 425

AAFRC Trust for Philanthropy
25 W 43rd St Fl 820, New York, NY, 10036-7406
Giving USA Update, 968

ADT Research
135 Rivington St., Rm.4, New York, NY, 10002
Tyndall Report, 697

AFS Intercultural Programs
220 East 42nd Street, Third Floor, New York, NY, 10017-5806
Bridges, 301

* See ***MULTI-PUBLISHER INDEX*** for list of publications.

AGEHR, Inc. The
99 Sunnybrook Cir, Highland, NY, 12528-1324
Twice Tolled Tales, 370

AG Editions
41 Union Sq W Ste 523, New York, NY, 10003-3208
Guilfoyle Report, 921

AGPA
25 E. 21st St., 6th Fl., New York, NY, 10010-6296
Group Circle, 1,014

AIDS Resource Center, Inc.
275 7th Ave Fl 12, New York, NY, 10001-6708
News from Bailey House, 1,120

AMN Publishing Inc.
380 Lexington Ave. #1700, New York, NY, 10168-0002
Apartment Management Newsletter, 1,031

AMR Publishing
122 E 42nd St Rm 1605, New York, NY, 10168-0002
Wrap Fee Advisor, 100

A/N Group
PO Box 895, Melville, NY, 11747-0895
Small Business Tax Review, 1,151

ARTnews Associates
48 W. 38th St., New York, NY, 10018-6238
ARTnewsletter, 61

AVSC International
79 Madison Ave., New York, NY, 10016-7802
AVSC News, 497

Abeles Phillips Preiss & Shapiro
434 6th Ave., New York, NY, 10011-8411
Metro Planner, 1,022

Academy of Hospital Public Relations
33 Irving Pl., New York, NY, 10003-2332
Academia, 9

Academy of Management
PO Box 3020, Briarcliff Manor, NY, 10510-8020
Academy of Management Newsletter, 833

Academy Professional Information Svcs. Inc.
116 W. 32nd St., New York, NY, 10001-3212
Psychiatric Topics, 1,011

Act-Action
417 Churchill Ave., Apt. 2306, Syracuse, NY, 13205-2123
Constructive Action Newsletter, 503

Actors' Equity Association
165 W. 46th St., New York, NY, 10036-2598
Equity News, 707

Ad Club, B.K. Hensey Assoc.
18 Stirrup Trl, Pawling, NY, 12564-2222
Ad Club of Greater Hartford Newsletter, 9

Adoptees Liberty Movement Assn.
Box 154 Washington Bridge Sta., New York, NY, 10033-0154
ALMA Searchlight, 171

Advertising Photographers of New York
27 W. 20th St., New York, NY, 10011-3707
APNY Newsletter, 976

Advertising Production Club of New York
60 E 42nd St Rm 721, New York, NY, 10165-0799
TDC Letterspace, 23

Advertising Research Foundation
641 Lexington Ave Fl 11, New York, NY, 10022-4503
ARF Quarterly Report, 9

•**Advertising Women of New York**
153 E 57th St Fl 3a, New York, NY, 10022-2121

Advocacy Communications
95 Brown Rd., Box 4716, Ithaca, NY, 14852
Nutrition Advocate, 934

Adweek, Inc.
1515 Broadway, New York, NY, 10036
Adweek Special Report, 10

Aesthetic Realism Foundation
141 Greene St., New York, NY, 10012
Right of Aesthetic Realism to Be Known, The, 472

Africa Inland Mission
PO Box 178, Pearl River, NY, 10965-0178
AIM International, 1,061

Africa Operations Research & Technical Assistance Project
Population Council, One Dag Hammarskjold Plaza, New York, NY, 10017-2291
African Alternatives, 497

Agorot Ltd.
1040 First Ave., Ste. 305, New York, NY, 10022-2902
Global Investing, 666

Akwe-Kon Press/Cornell University
300 Caldwell Hall, Cornel University, Ithaca, NY, 14853-8605
Web, The, 406

Akwesanse Library
St. Regis Mohawk Indian Res., RR 1, Box 14C, Hogansburg, NY, 13655-9705
Ka Ri Weh Ha Wi, 800

Alan Guttmacher Institute
120 Wall Street, New York, NY, 10005
Washington Memo, 531

Alan Lawrence Co.
279 E. 44th Street, New York, NY, 10017
2 Minute Break, 8

Albany County Historical Assn.
9 Ten Broeck Pl, Albany, NY, 12210-2524
Ten Broeck Newsletter, 549

Albert Einstein College of Medicine
1308 Belfer Building, Bronx, NY, 10461
Albert Einstein College of Medicine Faculty News, 866

Alcoholism Council of Greater NY
49 E 21st St Fl 3, New York, NY, 10010-6213
Healthy Information, 512

•**Alexander Research & Communications, Inc.**
215 Park Ave S., Ste. 1301, New York, NY, 10003-1603

Alfred Adler Institute
250 W 57th Street, #527, New York, NY, 10107-0001
Alfred Adler Institute Newsletter, 1,012

Allegany County Cooperative Extension
5435A County Road 48, Belmont, NY, 14813-9758
News & Views, 44

Allen Tech
PO Box 139, White Plains, NY, 10605-0139
WorldScan, 156

Alliance for Parental Involvement in Education, Inc.
PO Box 59, East Chatham, NY, 12060-0059
Options in Learning, 324

Alternative Education Resource Organization
417 Roslyn Rd, Roslyn Heights, NY, 11577-2620
Aero-Gramme, 299

Alternatives Federal Credit Union
301 West State Street, Ithaca, NY, 14850
Alternative Currents, 80

Amateur Astronomers Association
1010 Park Ave, New York, NY, 10028-0903
Eyepiece, 68

Amateur Chamber Music Players, Inc.
1123 Broadway Ste 304, New York, NY, 10010-2007
Amateur Chamber Music Players-Newsletter, 909

Amazon Network
339 Lafayette St # 8, New York, NY, 10012-2725
Amanaka'a, 372

Amcan Inc.
187 Vanderbilt Ave., Ste. 3, Brooklyn, NY, 11205-3305
Fiction Digest, 117

America-Israel Cultural Foundation
41 E 42nd St Rm 608, New York, NY, 10017-5201
Newsletter, 1,070

America Italy Society
3 E 48th St Fl 6, New York, NY, 10017-1027
America Italy Society Newsletter, 403

American Academy in Rome
7 E 60th St, New York, NY, 10022-1030
AmAcademy, 62

American Anorexia/Bulimia Assn., Inc.
293 Central Park W., Suite 12, New York, NY, 10024-3009
American Anorexia/Bulimia Assn. -Newsletter, 498

•**American Arbitration Assn.**
140 W. 51 St., New York, NY, 10020-1203

American Assn. of Exporters and Importers
11 W 42nd St Fl 30, New York, NY, 10036-8002
International Trade Alert, 648

American Assn. for the Improvement of Boxing
86 Fletcher Ave, Mount Vernon, NY, 10552-3319
Ring Rhetoric, 1,134

American Association for the Intl. Commission of Jurists
777 UN Plaza, 9th Fl., New York, NY, 10017
International Commission of Jurists Newsletter/Quarterly Report, 632

American Association of Small Ruminant Practitioners
1675 Ellis Hollow Rd, Ithaca, NY, 14850-9689
AASRP Newsletter, 1,200

American Ballroom Theater
129 W. 27th Street, Room 705, New York, NY, 10001
American Ballroom Theater, 1,172

American Bamboo Society
750 Krumkill Road, Albany, NY, 12203-5976
American Bamboo Society-Newsletter, 439

American Banker-Bond Buyer
1 State Street Plz, New York, NY, 10004-1549
Florida Public Finance, 90

•**American Banker Newsletters**
One State Plaza, New York, NY, 10004-1505

American Beefalo World Registry
116 Executive Pk., Louisville, NY, 40207-4201
Beefalo News, 852

American Booksellers Assn.
828 S Broadway, Tarrytown, NY, 10591-6600
ABA Newswire, 115

American Brass Chamber Music
30 Lincoln Plaza, Suite 3N, New York, NY, 10023
American Brass Quintet Newsletter, 909

American Buddhist Movement
301 W. 45th St., New York, NY, 10036
American Buddhist, 1,054

American Business Association
292 Madison Ave., New York, NY, 10017
Associations' Forum, 127

American Center for the Alexander Technique, Inc.
129 W 67th St, New York, NY, 10023-5917
ACAT News, 496

American Civil Liberties Union of New York
132 West 43 St., New York, NY, 10036-6599
Civil Liberties, 172

American Committee on Africa
17 John St Fl 12, New York, NY, 10038-4010
ACOA Action News, 626

American Committee on Italian Migration
352 W 44th St, New York, NY, 10036-5419
ACIM News, 403

•**American Conference of Cantors**
170 W. 74th St., New York, NY, 10023-2350

American Council for the Arts
1 E. 53rd St., New York, NY, 10022-4294
ArtsUSA UpDate, 259

American Council for Drug Education
136 E 64th St, New York, NY, 10021-7360
Drug Educator, 505

American Council of Learned Societies
228 E. 45th St., New York, NY, 10017-3398
ACLS Newsletter, 258

American Council on Science and Health
18th Floor, 1995 Broadway, New York, NY, 10023
Priorities, 525

•**American Crossword Federation**
PO Box 69, Massapequa Park, NY, 11762-0069

American Crystallographic Association
73 High St., Buffalo, NY, 14203-0096
ACA Newsletter, 162

American Dance Guild, Inc.
31 W. 21st St. 3 Fl., New York, NY, 10010-6806
American Dance, 265

American Demographics
PO Box 68, Ithaca, NY, 14851
Numbers News, 19

•**American Ethical Union**
2 W 64th St, New York, NY, 10023-7104

American Express Publishing Corp.
1120 Ave. of the Americas, 9th Floor, New York, NY, 10036-6770
Senior Membership Horizons, 258

American Federation of Arts
41 E 65th St, New York, NY, 10021-6508
Art: The Newsletter of the American Federation of Arts, 62

American Foreign Law Assn.
C/O Milton Schwartz, Pres., 645 Madison Ave,. 17th Floor, New York, NY, 10166-0005
American Foreign Law Association, Newsletter, 714

American Forum for Global Education
120 Wall St Ste 2600, New York, NY, 10005-4001
Access, 298

American Foundation for AIDS Research
733 3rd Ave Fl 12, New York, NY, 10017-3204
AMFAR Report, 496

American Foundation for the Blind
11 Penn Plz., Ste. 300, New York, NY, 10001-2018
AFB News, 110

American Friends Service Committee, NY City
15 Rutherford Pl, New York, NY, 10003-3705
New Manhattan Project Newsletter, 926

American Fund for Alternatives to Animal Research (AFAAR)
175 W 12th St Apt 16g, New York, NY, 10011-8220
News Abstracts, 389

* See **MULTI-PUBLISHER INDEX** for list of publications.

American Fur Industry (AFI)
101 W 30th St # 512, New York, NY, 10001-4001
Fashion Reports, 437

American Geriatrics Society
770 Lexington Ave Rm 300, New York, NY, 10021-8165
American Geriatrics Society-Newsletter, 1,106

American Group Psychotherapy Assn.
25 E 21st St Fl 6, New York, NY, 10010-6207
American Group Psychotherapy Association Newsletter, 1,012

American Guild of Musical Artists
1727 Broadway, New York, NY, 10019-5284
AGMA Newsletter, 909

American Guild of Variety Artists
184 5th Ave, New York, NY, 10010-5995
AGVA News, 368

American Home Sewing & Craft Assn.
1375 Broadway, New York, NY, 11360
American Home Sewing and Craft Association, 1,171

American Humanist Association
7 Harwood Dr, PO Box 1188, Amherst, NY, 14226-7188
Free Mind, 973

American Institute of Marine Underwriters
14 Wall St., New York, NY, 10005-2145
American Institute of Marine Underwriters, Bulletins, 617

American Institute of Stress, Inc.
124 Park Ave, Yonkers, NY, 10703-2904
Health and Stress: The News Letter of the American Institute of Stress, 875

American Institute for Verdi Studies
N.Y.U. Dept. of Music, 24 Waverly Pl., Rm. 268, New York, NY, 10003-6687
Verdi Newsletter, 919

American Italian Heritage Association
PO Box 419, Morrisville, NY, 13408-0419
American Italian Heritage Association Newsletter, 403

•**American Jewish Committee**
165 E 56th St, New York, NY, 10022-2709

American Jewish Congress
15 E. 84th St., New York, NY, 10028-0458
Radical Islamic Fundamentalism Update, 1,050

American Jewish Joint Distribution Committee
711 3rd Ave., New York, NY, 10017-4039
JDC World, 1,118

American Lawyer Media, L.P.
600 3rd Ave., New York, NY, 10016-1999
Corporate Control Alert, 86

American Liszt Society
c/o Fernando Laires, 210 Devonshire Dr., Rochester, NY, 14625
American Liszt Society, Inc., Newsletter, 909

American Lutheran Publicity Bureau
PO Box 327, Delhi, NY, 13753-0327
Forum Letter, 1,072

•**American Management Association**
135 West 50th Street, New York, NY, 10020-1201

American Medallic Sculpture Assn.
22 N. Main St. #356, New City, NY, 10956-3720
Members Exchange, 65

American Merchant Marine Library Assn.
1 World Trade Ctr Ste 2161, New York, NY, 10048-0202
USS Reports, 1,123

American Museum of Natural History
Museum Shop Catalog, Central Park West & 79th St., New York, NY, 10024
Rotunda, 907

American Music Center
30 W. 26th St., #1001, New York, NY, 10010-2011
News from the Center, 232

American Natl. Standards Inst
11 W 42nd Sreet, 13th Fl., New York, NY, 10036-8002
ANSI Reporter/Standards Action, 359

•**American Numismatic Society**
Broadway at 155th St., New York, NY, 10032

American ORT
817 Broadway Fl 10, New York, NY, 10003-4709
ORT Bulletin, 1,120

American Orthopsychiatric Assn.
330 7th Ave., 18th Floor, New York, NY, 10001-5010
Ortho Newsletter, 522

American Parkinson Disease Association
60 Bay St., Staten Island, NY, 10301-2500
American Parkinson Disease Association Newsletter, 867

American Photographic Historical Society
1150 6th Ave., New York, NY, 10036-2701
In Focus, 976

•**American Printing History Assn.**
Box 4922, Grand Central Station, New York, NY, 10163-1005

American Professional Practice Assn.
292 Madison Ave., New York, NY, 10017-6351
APPA Digest, 865

American Renaissance for the Twenty-first Century, Inc.
FDR Station, P.O. Box 8379, New York, NY, 10150
ART Ideas, 61

American Sanskrit Institute
73 Four Corners Rd., Warwick, NY, 10990
Sanskrit Today, 824

American-Scandinavian Foundation, The
725 Park Ave, New York, NY, 10021-5025
Scan, 408

American Scottish Foundation
Box 537, Lenox Hill Sta., New York, NY, 10021-0033
Calling All Scots, 408

American Sephardic Federation
305 7th Ave., 11th Fl., New York, NY, 10001
Sephardic Highlights, 1,070

American Society of Civil Engineers
345 E. 47th St., New York, NY, 10017-2398
Emerging Technology, 222

American Society of Journalists & Authors
1501 Broadway Ste 302, New York, NY, 10036-5501
ASJA Newsletter, 694

American Society for Psychical Research, Inc.
5 W 73rd St, New York, NY, 10023-3101
ASPR Newsletter, 948

American Stock Exchange
86 Trinity Place, New York, NY, 10006-1881
American Stock Exchange Weekly Bulletin, 654

American Theatre Critics Assn.
825 President Street, Apt 4, Brooklyn, NY, 11212
Critics Quarterly, 1,172

American Veterans of Israel
136 E 39th St, New York, NY, 10016-0914
American Veterans of Israel Newsletter, 1,199

American Wagner Assn.
32 W 82nd St Apt 6c, New York, NY, 10024-5622
American Wagner Assn. Newsletter, 910

American Waldensian Society
475 Riverside Dr Ste 1850, New York, NY, 10115-0122
American Waldensian Society Newsletter, 1,073

American Watercolor Society
47 5th Ave., New York, NY, 10003-4322
American Watercolor Society Newsletter, 62

American Woman's Economic Development Co.
71 Vanderbilt Ave Fl 3, New York, NY, 10169-0099
Awed in Business, 127

Americans for A Safe Israel
147 E. 76th St., New York, NY, 10021-2822
Outpost, 636

Amityville Historical Society
PO Box 764, Amityville, NY, 11701-0764
Dispatch, The, 539

Analytical Psychology Club of New York
28 E 39th St, New York, NY, 10016-2555
Analytical Psychology Club of New York, Bulletin, 1,012

Anchor Computer, Inc.
1900 New Hwy, Farmingdale, NY, 11735-1509
Anchor Line, 576

Andrews Paper & Chemical
1 Channel Dr # 509, Port Washington, NY, 11050-2216
Reproduction Bulletin, 1,007

Animal Medical Center
510 E 62nd St, New York, NY, 10021-8383
AMC CenterScope, 1,200

Anti-Defamation League of B'nai B'rith
823 U.N. Plaza, New York, NY, 10017
ADL on the Frontline, 1,067

Antiquarian Booksellers Assn. of America
50 Rockefeller Plaza, New York, NY, 10020
ABAA Newsletter, 52

Appearances
165 W. 26th St., New York, NY, 10001-6802
Appearances, 981

Appleton Services
P.O. Box 107, Larchmont, NY, 10538-0107
Metalworking Insiders' Report, 891

Appraisers Association of America
386 Park Avenue South, New York, NY, 10016-8804
Appraiser, The, 52

Arba Sicula
PO Box 040328, Brooklyn, NY, 11204-0328
Sicilia Parra, 404

Architects/Designers/Planners for Social Responsibility
175 Fifth Ave. Ste., #2210, New York, NY, 10010
ADPSR News, 985

Archive
132 Crosby St, New York, NY, 10012-3326
Archive of Contemporary Music, The, 910

•**Argus Research Corp.**
17 Battery Pl., New York, NY, 10004-1101

Arielle Greenberg
P.O. Box 8040, Long Island, NY, 11101-8040
William Wants A Doll, 698

Armenian Evangelical Church
152 E 34th St, New York, NY, 10016-4750
Bulletin of the Armenian Evangelical Church of NY, 1,061

Armenian Welfare Assn. of New York Inc.
137 45th Ave., Flushing, NY, 11355
Armenian Welfare Association of New York News, 399

Arnot Art Museum
235 Lake St, Elmira, NY, 14901-3191
Column, 903

The Art/Antiques Investment Report
99 Wall St., New York, NY, 10005-4301
Art/Antiques Investment Report, 62

Arthur Young
277 Park Ave., New York, NY, 10172-0269
Arthur Young Tax Guide, 2

Asahi Shimbun Publishing Company
757 3rd Ave., 3rd fl., New York, NY, 10017
Asahi Shimbun Satellite Edition, 641

Asia Pacific Communications, Inc.
60 Madison Ave Lbby 3, New York, NY, 10010-1600
Tokyo Insider, 638

Assist International
60 Madison Ave., 2nd Fl., New York, NY, 10010-1600
Global Glimpses, 646

Associated Business Publications Co., Ltd.
41 E. 42nd St., Ste. 921, New York, NY, 10017-5301
Russian Tech Briefs, 32

•**Assn. of American Publishers, Inc.**
71 Fifth Avenue, New York, NY, 10003-3004

•**Association of American University Presses, Inc.**
584 Broadway Rm 410, New York, NY, 10012-3264

•**Assn. for Asian Studies, Committee on Women in Asian Studies**
Ctr. for Intl. Studies, 170 Uris Hall, Cornell Univ., Ithaca, NY, 14853-6501

Association of Audio-Visual Technicians
PO Box 603, Farmingdale, NY, 11735-0603
Fast Foreward, 419

Association of the Bar of the City of New York
42 W 44th St, New York, NY, 10036-6686
Committee, 482

Association for Behavior Analysis
560 White Plains Road, Tarrytown, NY, 10591-5112
ABA Newsletter, 1,011

Association of College & Research Libraries - NY
PO Box 8331, New York, NY, 10116-8331
ACRL/NY, 791

•**Association for Computing Machinery**
1515 Broadway, 17th Fl., New York, NY, 10036-5701

Assn for the Coordination of Univ. Religious Affairs
c/o R.L. Johnson, Cornell Univ, Anabel Taylor Hall, Ithaca, NY, 14882
Dialogue on Campus, 204

Assn. of Episcopal Colleges
815 Second Ave., New York, NY, 10017-4559
Views & News, 335

Association of Graduates USMA
698 Mills Rd., Herbert Hall, West Point, NY, 10996
West Point Museum Bulletin, 908

Assn. of Group Travel Executives
424 Madison Ave Rm 706, New York, NY, 10017-1106
Topics, 1,189

Assn. for the Help of Retarded Children
200 Park Ave., S., New York, NY, 10003-1503
A.H.R.C. Chronicle, 1,113

Association of Hispanic Arts, Inc.
173 E 116th St Fl 2, New York, NY, 10029-1352
AHA! Hispanic Arts News, 61

Assn. of Internal Management Consultants
PO Box 304, East Bloomfield, NY, 14443-0304
AIMC Newsletter, 833

* See **MULTI-PUBLISHER INDEX** for list of publications.

•**Association of Jewish Center Professionals**
15 E 26th St Ste 1430, New York, NY, 10010-1505

Assn. of Jewish Libraries
15 East 26th Street, Room 1034, New York, NY, 10010-1579
AJL Newsletter, 791

Association of Junior Leagues, Inc.
660 1st Ave, New York, NY, 10016-3295
AJL Newsline, 1,113

Association of Libertarian Feminists
Box 20252, London Terrace, New York, NY, 10011
ALF News, 1,206

Assn. of Lithuanian Workers
26 N St., #42, Middletown, NY, 10940
Tiesa, 182

•**Assn. of Natl. Advertisers, Inc.**
155 E. 44th St., New York, NY, 10017-4201

Association of Productivity Specialists
521 Fifth Ave., New York, NY, 10175
APS Spokesman, 607

Assn. of Reform Zionists of America
838 5th Ave, New York, NY, 10021-7012
ARZA Report, 626

Assn. for Research of Childhood Cancer, Inc.
PO Box 251, Buffalo, NY, 14225-0251
AROCC Newsletter, 865

Assn. for the Sociological Study of Jewry
Brooklyn College Dept. of Soco, Bedford Ave. & Ave H, Brooklyn, NY, 11210-2889
Newsletter of the Association for Social Scientific Study of Jewry, 1,126

Assn. of Teachers of Latin American Studies
PO Box 620754, Flushing, NY, 11362-0754
Perspective, 325

Assn. of Theatrical Press Agents
165 W. 46th St., New York, NY, 10036-2501
Association of Theatrical Press Agents and Managers Highlights of Bimonthly Meeting, 1,172

Association of Water Transportation Accounting Officers
Box 53, Bowling Green Sta., New York, NY, 10004
AWTAO Bulletin, 126

Atcom, Inc.
140 Riverside Dr Ste 14h, New York, NY, 10024-2605
Car & Truck Rental / Leasing Insider, 71

Attica Brigade of Richmond College
Stuyvesant Pl., Staten Island, NY, 10301
Fight Back, 34

•**Aubrey G. Lanston**
1 Chase Manhattan Plaza, 53rd Fl., New York, NY, 10005

Audiotex News, Inc.
2362 Hempstead Tpke Fl 2, East Meadow, NY, 11554-2030
Audiotex News, 1,156

•**Auerbach Publishers**
One Penn Plz., 42nd Floor, New York, NY, 10119-0002

Aura Publishing Co.
441 Central Ave., Box 1367, Scarsdale, NY, 10583-9367
Aura Wealth Newsletter, 654

Australian Information Service
630 5th Ave., New York, NY, 10111-0110
Australian Business News, 127

Auto-Free New York Committee of Transportation Alternatives
92 St. Marks Place, New York, NY, 10009-5840
Auto Free Press, 70

Ayco Investment Report
PO Box 15073, Albany, NY, 12212-5073
Ayco Investment Report, 655

B & B Press Inc.
Box 801, Radio City Station, New York, NY, 10102-0001
Quality Executive, 844

BPA International
270 Madison Ave., New York, NY, 10016-0699
BPA International Forum, 952

•**BRP Publications, Inc.**
65 Bleecker Street, 5th Floor, New York, NY, 10012-2420

Bache
100 Gold St., New York, NY, 10038-1605
Action Advisory, 653

Baha'i International Community
866 United Nations Plaza, Suite 120, New York, NY, 10017
One Country, 635

Bandele Communications
P.O. Box 050410, Brooklyn, NY, 11205-0008
Overground, 55

Bank of New York
1 Wall St Fl 13, New York, NY, 10005-2501
Bank One, 577

Bank Street Bookstore
Broadway at 112th Street, New York, NY, 10025
Bank Street Bookstore Bookmark, 115

•**Bank Street College of Education**
610 W 112th St, New York, NY, 10025-1898

Bantam Doubleday Dell Publishing Group
1540 Broadway, New York, NY, 10036-4039
HBE Buyer, 494

Barbara Brass Communications, Inc.
PO Box 659, East Hampton, NY, 11937-0501
Romantic Hideaways, 1,188

Barre Coe
PO Box 476, Peck Slip Station, New York, NY, 10038
Music Connoisseur, The, 914

Barricade Books
150 Fifth Ave., Ste. 700, New York, NY, 10011-4311
Hot News, 118

•**Barrows Co., Inc.**
116 E 66th St, New York, NY, 10021-6547

Barry Mandell- Writing and Publishing
1069 Alexander Dr., Rotterdam Junction, NY, 12150-9708
Sports Book File, 120

Beauty Without Cruelty
175 W 12th St Apt 16g, New York, NY, 10011-8220
Compassionate Shopper, 376

Becky Thorp
12 Norcross St, Rockville Center, NY, 11570
Alone, 694

•**Beer Marketer's Insights, Inc.**
51 Virginia Ave., West Nyack, NY, 10994-2005

Belgian Tourist Office
780 3rd Ave Rm 1501, New York, NY, 10017-2024
Belganews, 1,182

Bellevue Hospital
First Ave. at 27th St., New York, NY, 10016
Bellevue Bulletin, 561

Benjamin Shimon
457 FDR Dr.(1604), New York, NY, 10002-5954
Esoteric Newsletter, 973

Bermuda Dept. of Tourism
310 Madison Ave., Rm. 201, New York, NY, 10017-6009
Bermuda Shorts, 1,182

Berthel Thorvaldsen Lodge No. 530, IOOF, Inc.
220 E 15th St, New York, NY, 10003-3901
Danish Odd Fellow Bulletin, 177

Best of Health
Box 40-1232, Brooklyn, NY, 11240-1232
Best of Health, 499

Best for Less, The
14 Washington Place, New York, NY, 10003-6609
Best for Less, The, 251

Bialystoker Center
228 E Broadway, New York, NY, 10002-5699
Bialystoker Stimme, 401

Bibliographic Retrieval Service, Inc.
5 Computer Dr S, Albany, NY, 12205-1608
BRS Bulletin, 853

Bide-A-Wee Home Assn.
410 E 38th St, New York, NY, 10016-2702
Bide-A-Wee News, 49

Black Veterans for Social Justice
680 Fulton St, Brooklyn, NY, 11217-1609
Black Vet, 894

Blessed Kateri Takakwitha League
Auriesville, NY, 12016
Lily of the Mohawks, 1,057

Bloch Publishing Co., Inc.
37 W 26th St Fl 9, New York, NY, 10010-1006
Bloch's Book Bulletin, 115

Bloom & Gelb
232 Madison Ave Rm 1106, New York, NY, 10016-2901
Test Patterns, 23

•**Bloomberg Financial Markets**
499 Park Ave, New York, NY, 10022

Blue Cross-Blue Shield of Greater New York
622 Third Ave., New York, NY, 10017-6794
Inside AHS-UMS, 586

B'nai B'rith Hillel Foundation At Brooklyn College
2901 Campus Rd, Brooklyn, NY, 11210-2153
Hillel Gate, 1,068

Boces Geneseo Migrant Center
210 Holcomb Bldg., Geneseo, NY, 14454
Real Talk, 1,215

•**Boerner Communications**
P.O. Box L, Manhasset, NY, 11030

Book-of-the-Month Club, Inc.
1271 Avenue of the Americas, Bsmt 3, New York, NY, 10020-1302
Book-of-the-Month Club News, 115

Books About Birds
Box 150106, Kew Gardens, Jamaica, NY, 11415-0106
Books About Birds, 116

•**Books of Wonder**
132 7th Avenue at 18th Street, New York, NY, 10011-1803

Boombah Herald
15 Park Blvd, Lancaster, NY, 14086-2510
Boombah Herald, 537

Boosey & Hawkes Inc.
24 E. 21st St., New York, NY, 10010-7200
Boosey and Hawkes Newsletter, 910

Borgward-Owners' Club
77 New Hampshire Ave, Bay Shore, NY, 11706-2520
Borgward-Owners' Club-Newsletter, 71

Bowbridge Press
PO Box 7415, New York, NY, 10116-7415
Free Focus, 982

•**Box Office Management International**
250 W. 37th Street, Suite 722, New York, NY, 10107

Bradford Creative
24 Fifth Ave., New York, NY, 10011-8817
Beauty Spot: News You Can Use, 854

Brazilian American Chamber of Commerce
22 W. 48th St., Ste. 404, New York, NY, 10036-1803
News Bulletin, 651

•**Bristol-Myers Company, Products Div.**
345 Park Ave Fl 9, New York, NY, 10154-0004

•**British-American Chamber of Commerce**
52 Vanderbilt Ave Fl 20, New York, NY, 10017-3808

British Tourist Authority
551 5th Ave Rm 701, New York, NY, 10176-0799
Britainews, 1,182

Brookdale Center on Aging
425 E 25th St, New York, NY, 10010-2547
Newsletter of the Brookdale Center on Aging, 1,107

Brookdale Hospital Medical Center
Linden Blvd at Brookdale Plaza, Brooklyn, NY, 11212-3198
Brookdale Hospital Medical Center News-Scope, 562

Brooklyn Academy of Music
30 Lafayette Ave, Brooklyn, NY, 11217-1486
Monthly Guide of Brooklyn Academy of Music, 914

Brooklyn Botanic Garden
1000 Washington Ave, Brooklyn, NY, 11225-1008
Plants & Gardens News, 442

Brooklyn College Hillel Society
2900 Bedford Ave, Brooklyn, NY, 11210-2814
Hillel Highlights, 209

Brooklyn College Science Fiction Society
Central Depository/Boylan Hall, Bedford Avenue and Avenue H, Brooklyn, NY, 11210
Final Frontier, The, 1,102

Brooklyn Economic Development Corp.
30 Flatbush Ave, Brooklyn, NY, 11217-1121
BEDC Update, 157

•**Brooklyn Historical Society**
128 Pierrepont St, Brooklyn, NY, 11201-2794

Brooklyn Public Library
Grand Army Plaza, Brooklyn, NY, 11238
Brooklyn Public Library Bulletin, 794

Brooklyn Sports Foundation
7 Metrotech Ctr., Ste. 2000, Brooklyn, NY, 11201-3841
Brooklyn Sports Foundation Newsletter, 1,129

Brooklyn Union
1 Metrotech Ctr, Brooklyn, NY, 11201-3850
Energy Exchange, 956

•**Brownstone Publishers, Inc.**
149 5th Ave., 16th Floor, New York, NY, 10010-6801

Brownstone Revival Committee
PO Box 577, New York, NY, 10113-0577
Brownstoner, 244

Buffalo & Erie County Public Library
Lafayette Square, Buffalo, NY, 14203
Buffalo & Erie County Public Library Bulletin, 794

Buffalo Society of Natural Sciences, Buffalo Museum of Scien
1020 Humboldt Pkwy., Buffalo, NY, 14211
Collections, 903

* See **MULTI-PUBLISHER INDEX** for list of publications.

Builders' Hardware Manufacturers Assn., Inc.
355 Lexington Ave Fl 17, New York, NY, 10017-6603
Builders' Hardware Manufacturers Association, Bulletin, 495

Building Series Study Group of the Germany Philatelic Soc.
107 Hoover Rd, Rochester, NY, 14617-3611
Spec Sheet, 972

Bunn Coffee Service
51 Alpha Plaza, Hicksville, NY, 11801
Take a Bunnbreak, 105

Burson-Marsteller
230 Park Ave S, New York, NY, 10003-1566
Connections, 855

Business Committee for the Arts, Inc.
1775 Broadway Ste 510, New York, NY, 10019-1903
BCA News, 63

•**Business Council of New York State**
152 Washington Ave, Albany, NY, 12210-2203

Business Council for the United Nations
60 E 42nd St Rm 2925, New York, NY, 10165-2999
BCUN Briefing, 986

C.F. Peters Corp.
373 Park Ave., S., New York, NY, 10016-8869
Peters Notes, 916

C.G. Jung Foundation for Analytical Psychology, Inc.
28 E 39th St, New York, NY, 10016-2555
C.G. Jung Foundation Newsletter, 1,013

C.H.E.A.R., Inc.
928 Mclean Ave, Yonkers, NY, 10704-4103
Hearing Research Developments, 533

CH II Publishing
200 W. 57th St., 15th Floor, New York, NY, 10019
Race Relations Newsletter, 399

C.H. Kaplan Research Assoc.
26 Broadway, #200, New York, NY, 10004-1703
Special Situations Newsletter, 686

CIBA Geigy Corp.
444 Saw Mill River Rd, Ardsley, NY, 10502-2600
On-Stream, 593

•**C.J. Lawrence/Deutsche Bank Securities**
1290 Ave. of the Americas, New York, NY, 10104-0051

CMP Publications, Inc.
600 Community Dr., Manhasset, NY, 11030-3875
Internet Business Report, 142

C.R.S., Inc.
PO Box 430, Fayetteville, NY, 13066-0430
Food Industry Futures-A Strategy Service, 429

CSM Communications Co., Inc.
195 Smithtown Blvd., Nesconset, NY, 11767-1869
Retail Performance Monitor, 273

CSP Advisor
PO Box 246, Forest Hills, NY, 11375-0246
Cumulative Stock Profits, 661

CUNY-College of Staten Island
130 Stuyvesant Pl, Staten Island, NY, 10301-1907
Alumnotes, 191

•**CUNY-Hunter College**
695 Park Ave., Library, New York, NY, 10021-5085

CUNY-Kingsborough Community College
2001 Oriental Blvd, Brooklyn, NY, 11235-2336
Odyssey, 203

•**Cahners Publishing Co.**
249 W. 17th St., New York, NY, 10011-5300

•**Calendar Planning Corporation**
237 Park Ave., Ste. 900, New York, NY, 10017

Cameron's Publications
5325 Sheridan Dr., PO Box 1160, Williamsville, NY, 14231-1160
Cameron's Foodservice Marketing Reporter, 1,075

Campaign for New York Hospital-Cornell Medical
525 E 68th St # 123, New York, NY, 10021-4873
New Horizons for Medicine, 882

Campaign for Peace & Democracy
Box 1640, Cathedral Station, New York, NY, 10025-1560
Peace & Democracy News, 995

Campana Printing Co.
3096 42nd St, Astoria, NY, 11103-3031
Campana, 402

Cantors Assembly of America
3080 Broadway Rm 613, New York, NY, 10027-4650
Cantors Voice, 1,068

Cap Communications
3520 Broadway, Astoria, NY, 11106-1114
Contacts: The Media Pipeline for P.R. People, 12

•**Capital Cities/ABC**
488 Madison Ave., 16th Floor, New York, NY, 10022-5751

Cardinal Star Corp.
Box A76, New York, NY, 10163-9506
Ostaro's Market Newsletter, 681

Carmelite Fathers, Inc.
339 E 28th St, New York, NY, 10016-8602
Scapular, 1,059

Carnegie Corp. of New York
437 Madison Avenue, New York, NY, 10022-7001
Carnegie Quarterly, 304

•**Carnegie Council on Ethics & Intl. Affairs**
170 E 64th St, New York, NY, 10021-7478

Cat Mews Pubs.
57 Whitehall Blvd # 7, Garden City, NY, 11530-4248
Cat Mews, 157

•**Catalyst**
250 Park Ave S Fl 5, New York, NY, 10003-1402

Cathedral of St. John the Divine
1047 Amsterdam Ave, New York, NY, 10025-1702
Cathedral, 1,067

Catholic Actors Guild
1501 Broadway Ste 518, New York, NY, 10036-5501
Call Board, 1,055

Catholic Medical Mission Bd.
Placement Desk, 10 W. 17th St., New York, NY, 10011-5701
Professional Placement Newsnotes, 571

Catholic Peace Fellowship
339 Lafayette St, New York, NY, 10012-2725
Catholic Peace Fellowship Bulletin, 1,056

Catholic Traditionalist Movement, Inc.
210 Maple Ave, Westbury, NY, 11590-3117
Quote. . . Unquote, 1,059

The Catskill Center
Arkville, NY, 12406-1010
Catskills News Quarterly, 1,042

Cayuga County Extension Service Association
248 Grant Ave, Auburn, NY, 13021-1495
Cayuga County Connection, 1,042

Cazenovia College
c/o Robin Reagan, Cazenovia, NY, 13035
Cazenovia College Bulletin, 203

•**Celebrity Service Intl.**
1780 Broadway Ste 300, New York, NY, 10019-1414

Celtic League, American Branch
Box 20153, Dag Hammarskjold Ctr., New York, NY, 10017
Six Nations, One Soul, 638

Center for Bead Research
4 Essex St, Lake Placid, NY, 12946-1236
Margaretologist, The, 693

Center for Book Arts
626 Broadway Fl 5, New York, NY, 10012-2601
Koob Stra, 118

Center for Constitutional Rights
666 Broadway Fl 7, New York, NY, 10012-2317
Movement Support Network News, 758

Center for Contemporary Opera
Gracie Station, Box 1350, New York, NY, 10028-0010
Opera Today, 1,174

Center for Cuban Studies
124 W. 23rd St., New York, NY, 10011-2400
Cuba Update Newsletter, 629

Center for Development of Human Services
SUNY College at Buffalo, 1300 Elmwood Ave., Letchworth, Buffalo, NY, 14222-1095
TrainingScope, 1,123

Center for Entrepreneurial Management
180 Varick Street, Penthouse, New York, NY, 10014-4606
Chief Executive Newsletter, 835

Center for Human Environments
33 W 42nd St, New York, NY, 10036-8003
Children's Environments Quarterly, 375

Center for Intl. Business Cycles Research
Columbia Univ., Business School, Uris Hall, New York, NY, 10027-2399
Recession-Recovery Watch, 295

Center for Lesbian and Gay Studies
CUNY Graduate Center, 33 W. 42nd St., Rm.404N, New York, NY, 10036-8099
CLAGS, 444

Center for Medical Consumers
237 Thompson St, New York, NY, 10012-1017
Health Facts, 510

Center for Medieval and Early Renaissance Studies
SUNY Binghamton, Box 6000, Binghamton, NY, 13902-6000
Old English Newsletter, 823

•**Center for Migration Studies of New York, Inc.**
209 Flagg Pl, Staten Island, NY, 10304-1199

Center for Safety in the Arts
5 Beekman St Rm 820, New York, NY, 10038-2206
Art Hazards Newsletter, 1,078

Center on Social Welfare Policy & Law
275 7th Ave Fl 6, New York, NY, 10001-6708
Center on Social Welfare Policy and Law Library Bulletin, 795

Center for the Study of Human Rights
Columbia Univ., 420 W. 118th St., New York, NY, 10027-2399
Center for the Study of Human Rights Newsletter, 1,115

Center for Thanatology Research
391 Atlantic Ave, Brooklyn, NY, 11217-1701
Thanatology Librarian, 530

•**Center for War, Peace & the News Media**
NYU, 10 Washington Pl. 4th Fl., New York, NY, 10003

Center for Women in Government
135 Western Ave., Albany, NY, 12222
News on Women in Government, 1,210

Central Hudson Gas & Electric Corp.
284 South Ave, Poughkeepsie, NY, 12601-4838
Central Hudson Newsletter, 579

Central Park Conservancy
The Arsenal, Central Park, New York, NY, 10021
Central Park Good Times, 1,042

Channel Media, Inc.
250 W. 57th Street, Suite 1527-89, New York, NY, 10107
Perfect Partner Network, 816

•**Chartcraft, Inc.**
30 Church St # 2046, New Rochelle, NY, 10801-6302

Chas. Pfizer
235 East 42nd Street, New York, NY, 10017-5703
Pfizer Scene, 594

Chase Communications Group Ltd.
25-35 Beechwood, Box 9001, Mt. Vernon, NY, 10552-9001
Cibgny Month, 619

Chautauqua County Geneological Society
PO Box 404, Fredonia, NY, 14063-0404
Chautauqua Genealogist, 450

Checker Car Club of America
469 Tremaine Ave, Kenmore, NY, 14217-2537
Checkerboard News, 71

Cheese Importers Assn.
460 Park Ave., New York, NY, 10022-1906
Cheese Importers Association of America Bulletin, 264

Chelsea Arts Consortium
120 W. 28th St., 2nd Fl., New York, NY, 10001
Play in Chelsea, 1,174

•**Chemical Bank**
270 Park Avenue, New York, NY, 10017

Chemical Monitor
PO Box 314, Lindenhurst, NY, 11757-0314
Chemical Monitor, 163

Chemists' Club Library
40 W 45th St, New York, NY, 10036-4202
Retort, 166

Chervenak, Keane & Co.
307 E. 44th St., New York, NY, 10017-4400
CKC Report, The Hotel Technology Newsletter, 574

Chevrolet-Pontiac-Canada Group
199 Beekman Ave, North Tarrytown, NY, 10591-2403
Beacon Bulletin, 577

Child Care Action Campaign
330 7th Ave., 17th fl., New York, NY, 10001
Child Care ActioNews, 167

•**Child Development Research**
30 Soundview Ln, Sands Point, NY, 11050-1341

Child Growth & Development Corp.
599 Broadway Fl 9, New York, NY, 10012-3235
Parent Hotline, 415

Children's Book Council, Inc.
568 Broadway Ste. 404, New York, NY, 10012-0000
CBC Features, 167

Children's Creative Response to Conflict
521 N. Broadway, P.O. Box 271, Nyack, NY, 10960-0271
Sharing Space, 330

Children's Rights of NY
15 Arbutus Ln, Stony Brook, NY, 11790-1408
Hotline, 1,215

China Institute in America
125 E 65th St, New York, NY, 10021-7088
China Institute in America Bulletin, 259

• See **MULTI-PUBLISHER INDEX** for list of publications.

Choice In Dying Inc.
200 Varick Street, New York, NY, 10014-4810
Choices, 502

Chorale
c/o Robert Schartoff, 30 Fifth Ave., Suite 15E, New York, NY, 10011
Chorale, 911

Christ the King Seminary
711 Knox Rd., P.O. Box 607, East Aurora, NY, 14052-9444
Christ the King Seminary News, 191

Christie's Publications Dept.
502 Park Avenue, New York, NY, 10022-1196
Auction News from Christie's, 63

Christophers, The Inc.
12 E 48th St, New York, NY, 10017-1008
Christopher News Notes, 1,056

Chronicle Guidance Publications, Inc.
PO Box 1190, Moravia, NY, 13118-1190
Washington Counseletter, 336

Church World Service
475 Riverside Dr Ste 656, New York, NY, 10115-0122
Monday: a weekly newsletter on refugee and immigration issues, 399

Churchill Livingstone, Inc.
650 Ave. of the Americas, New York, NY, 10011
Report on Pediatric Infectuous Diseases, 886

Citibank
Business & Professional Sort, 7836, One Court Squar, Long Island City, NY, 11120-0001
Gateway, 646

Citibank/GFNA
55 Water St., 43rd Floor, New York, NY, 10043-0001
Economic Week, 291

Citizen Exchange Council
12 W. 31st St., 4th Fl., Ste. 1004-1005, New York, NY, 10001-4415
Citizen Exchange Communique, 628

Citizen Soldier
175 5th Ave Ste 808, New York, NY, 10010-7703
Citizen Soldier, 895

Citizens Committee for New York City
305 7th Avenue, New York, NY, 10001
Citizens Report, 1,019

•Citizens Union of the City of New York
198 Broadway, New York, NY, 10038-2515

City College Library
138th Street and Convent Ave., New York, NY, 10031
CircumSpice, 796

City Volunteer Corps.
838 Broadway Fl 4, New York, NY, 10003-4812
CVC Bulletin, 1,214

Civil Service Retired Employees Assn.
267 Broadway, New York, NY, 10007-2387
Civil Service Sentinel, 580

Clairol, Inc., Bristol-Myers Squibb
345 Park Ave., New York, NY, 10154-0192
Clairol Highlights, 580

Clarity Publishing Inc.
3 Enterprise Dr, Albany, NY, 12204-2520
Crux of the News, 1,056

•Clark Boardman Callaghan
375 Hudson St, New York, NY, 10014-3685

Clearwater Navigator
112 Market St, Poughkeepsie, NY, 12601-4031
Clearwater Navigator, 375

Clinton County Historical Association
48 Court St, Plattsburgh, NY, 12901-2831
North County Notes, 545

•Clothing Manufacturers Assn. of the U.S.A.
730 Broadway, 9th Floor, New York, NY, 10003

Club of Channel Islands Collectors
PO Box 579, New York, NY, 10028-0019
Channel Islands Reporter, 970

Coalition to Free Soviet Jews
711 3rd Ave Fl 12, New York, NY, 10017-4014
Lifelines, 993

Coalition of Labor Union Women
15 Union Sq W, New York, NY, 10003-3308
CLUW News, 707

Coalition to Protect Animals in Parks & Refuges
PO Box 26, Slain, NY, 14884-0026
Civil Abolitionist, 502

Cochlear Implant Club International
PO Box 464, Buffalo, NY, 14223-0464
Contact, 533

Codesh Inc.
PO Box 664, Buffalo, NY, 14226-0664
Secular Humanist Bulletin, 975

•Coffee, Sugar & Cocoa Exchange, Inc.
Four World Trade Center, New York, NY, 10048-0896

Cold Spring Harbor Laboratory
1 Bungtown Rd, Cold Spring Harbor, NY, 11724-2209
Fill Transcript, 109

Colgate Rochester Divinity School
1100 Goodman St S, Rochester, NY, 14620-2530
Bulletin from the Hill, 191

College Art Assn.
275 7th Ave Frnt 5, New York, NY, 10001-6708
CAA News, 64

College of Arts & Sciences
Cornell University, Gold Smith Hall, Ithaca, NY, 14850-3201
Arts & Sciences Newsletter, 203

College of Mt. St. Vincent
6301 Riverdale Ave., Riverdale, NY, 10471
Campus Record, 204

College of New Rochelle
29 Castle Pl, New Rochelle, NY, 10805-2339
Quarterly, 191

Colombian American Assn.
150 Nassau St., New York, NY, 10038-1516
Colombian Newsletter, 628

Color Association of the U.S.
409 W. 44th St., New York, NY, 10036-4402
CAUS News, 1,171

Columbia Gay & Lesbian Alliance
Columbia Univ., 304 Earl Hall, New York, NY, 10027-2399
Pride of Lions, 445

Columbia Univ. American Culture Center
603 Lewisohn Hall, New York, NY, 10027
Dispatch, 260

Columbia Univ., Harriman Institute
420 W 118th St Fl 12, New York, NY, 10027-7213
The Harriman Review, 631

Columbia University Press
562 W 113th St, New York, NY, 10025-8099
Social Work Practice, 1,122

Columbia University -School of Law
435 W. 116th St. #D25, New York, NY, 10027-7201
Columbia Law Alumni Observer, 191

•Comedy Writers Assn.
PO Box 023304, Brooklyn, NY, 11202-3304

Comex Rista Co.
22 Juniper Rd, Port Washington, NY, 11050-1435
Retail Roundup, 273

•Committee for Better Transit, Inc.
PO Box 3106, Long Island City, NY, 11103-0106

Committee of Interns
386 Park Ave., S., New York, NY, 10016-8852
CIR News, 869

Committee/Scientific Investigation of Claims of Paranormal
PO Box 703, Amherst, NY, 14226-0703
Skeptical Briefs, 949

Commodities Law Press Associates
40 Broad St Fl 20, New York, NY, 10004-2315
Futures International Law Letter, 740

•Commodity Exchange, Inc.
4 World Trade Ctr Ste 7451, New York, NY, 10048-0204

•Commodity Research Bureau
75 Wall St., New York, NY, 10005

Common Ground Stage & Film Co.
332 Bleeker St., Ste. K114, New York, NY, 10014
Common Ground News, 1,172

Communications House, Inc.
40 Beechdale Rd, Dobbs Ferry, NY, 10522-3021
Travel Smart, 1,191

Community Action Network
211 E 43rd St Rm 1400, New York, NY, 10017-4707
CAN Do, 1,114

Community Capital Bank
111 Livingston St, Brooklyn, NY, 11201-8111
Community First, 85

Community Development Status Reports
1 Centre St., New york, NY, 10007-1602
Community Development Status Reports, 1,020

Community Prescription Service
349 W. 12th St., P.O. Box 1937, New York, NY, 10014
InfoPack, 284

Community Spirit
34-12 113th St., Apt. 12-E, Corona, NY, 11368
Community Spirit, 967

Co-Optics of America
Box 398, Box 393, Oneonta, NY, 13820-0398
Gift of Sight, 940

Composers' Forum, Inc.
260 W. Broadway, New York, NY, 10013-2259
Composers' Forum Network News, 911

Computer Merchants, Inc.
200 Brady Ave., Box 1006, Hawthorne, NY, 10532-1823
Computer Price Guide, 217

Computer People for Peace
291 Sterling Pl, Brooklyn, NY, 11238-4403
Interrupt, 227

•Concept Publishing
PO Box 500, York, NY, 14592-0500

Concerned Citizens Speak, Inc.
Box 1108, Madison Square Station, New York, NY, 10159-1108
Speaking Out, 1,085

•Conference Board, Inc.
845 3rd Ave., New York, NY, 10022-6679

Consolidated Marketing Services , inc
Box 1361, New York, NY, 10017
Drop Shipping News, 13

Consortium for Continental Reflection Profiling
Cornell Univ., Dept. of Geological Studies, Ithaca, NY, 14850-3995
Consortium for Continental Reflection Profiling-Newsletter, 477

•Consumer Union
101 Truman Avenue, Yonkers, NY, 10703-1057

Contel of New York
850 Harrison St. Ext., Johnstown, NY, 12095
New York Divisionnews, 591

Cook-Waite Labs Inc., Sterling Drug Inc.
90 Park Ave., New York, NY, 10016-1389
Local Topics, 589

Cooke Stock Newsletter
1345 Anchor Dr, Wantagh, NY, 11793-2323
Cooke Stock Newsletter, 660

Cooking on the Edge
175 Fifth Avenue, Suite 2117, New York, NY, 10010
Cooking on the Edge, 427

Cooperative Extension Association
21 S. Grove St., E. Aurora, NY, 14052-2398
Extension Line Lookout, 558

Cooperative Extension Assn. of Albany County, Agricultural D
Martin Rd., Voorheesville, NY, 12186
Extension News-Albany, Rensselaer, Saratoga, Washington Counties, 40

Cooperative Extension Assn. of Tioga County
56 Main Street, Owego, NY, 13827-1588
Dairy and Field Crops Digest, 264

Cooperative Extension of Schenectady County
620 State St, Schenectady, NY, 12305-2114
Schenectady County Cooperative Extension News, 46

Copy Editor
P.O. Box 604, Ansonia Station, New York, NY, 10023-0604
Copy Editor Newsletter, 695

Core Communications
98 Cuttermill Rd., Great Neck, NY, 11021
Next Wave Stocks, 232

Cornell Cooperative Extension/Clinton County
Clinton County, RFD 6, Box 16B, Plattsburgh, NY, 1290
4-H Child Care, 167

•Cornell Feline Health Center
College of Veterinary Medicine, Cornell University, Ithaca, NY, 14853

Cornell Univ. ILR
198 Ives Hall, Ithaca, NY, 14851-0952
ILR Alumni News, 701

Cornell Univ. Medical College
1300 York Ave # 61, New York, NY, 10021-4805
Histamine Club Bulletin, 284

Cornell Univ. Ornithology Lab
159 Sapsucker Woods Rd, Ithaca, NY, 14850-1923
Birdscope, 941

Cornell Veterinarian, Inc.
Publications, Ithaca, NY, 14853-6401
Cornell Animal Health Newsletter, 1,200

Corporacion de Fomento de la Produccion
1 World Trade Ctr Ste 5151, New York, NY, 10048-0202
Chile Economic Report, 643

•Cortland County Historical Society
25 Homer Ave, Cortland, NY, 13045-2018

* See **MULTI-PUBLISHER INDEX** for list of publications.

Cosmetic World, Inc.
530 5th Ave. 4th Fl., New York, NY, 10036-5101
Cosmetic World, 256

Council on Economic Priorities
30 Irving Pl., New York, NY, 10003-2303
CEP Research Report, 290

Council on the Environment of NYC
51 Chambers St Ste 228, New York, NY, 10007-1208
CENYC Environmental Bulletin, 374

Council for European Studies
808-809 International Aff.Bldg, Columbia Univ., New York, NY, 10027-0044
European Studies Newsletter, 540

Council of Jewish Federations
730 Broadway, 2nd Fl., New York, NY, 10003
CJF Endowment Review, 966

Council of Literary Magazines & Presses
154 Christopher St. #3C, New York, NY, 10014-2839
CLMPages, 953

Council of Nephrology Social Workers-Natl. Kidney Foundation
30 E. 33rd St., New York, NY, 10016-5337
CNSW Newsletter, 869

Council of New York Cooperatives
2112 Broadway Rm 202, New York, NY, 10023-2142
Council of New York Cooperatives Newsletter, 1,033

Council of New York Law Assocs.
99 Hudson St., New York, NY, 10013-2815
Council of New York Law Associates Newsletter, 729

Council of Trade Waste Assns., Inc.
Box 70-1380, Trainsmeadow Sta., Flushing, NY, 11370
CTWA Newsletter, 1,202

•**Crain Communications, Inc.**
220 E. 42nd St., New York, NY, 10017-5806

Creativa
305 8th Ave., Apt. B7, Brooklyn, NY, 11215-6618
Creativa, 922

Creative Education Foundation
1050 Union Rd., Buffalo, NY, 14224-3402
Creativity in Action, 814

Creative License
42 Hicks St., Suite 4N, Brooklyn, NY, 11201-6906
Freelance Success Newsletter, 695

Creative Selling
120 Walton St Ste 201, Syracuse, NY, 13202-1211
Creative Selling, 1,086

•**Croner Publications, Inc.**
34 Jericho Tpke., Jericho, NY, 11753-1042

Crowley Foods, Inc.
PO Box 549, Binghamton, NY, 13902-0549
Dairy Foods Group, 581

Customs & Intl. Trade Bar Assn.
c/o Andrew P. Vance, 475 Park Ave. S., New York, NY, 10016
Customs and International Trade Bar Association Newsletter, 730

D'Agostino Supermarkets
1385 Boston Post Rd, Larchmont, NY, 10538-3904
D'Agostino Consumer Newsletter, 427

•**DMA Catalog Council**
11 W 42nd St Fl 25, New York, NY, 10036-8002

DMD, Inc.
603 Bayville Rd # 402, Locust Valley, NY, 11560-1207
Dentists Medical Digest, 269

•**DUWEST Research/Scientific Newsletters**
Rr 4 Box 7, Middletown, NY, 10940-9685

Damon Runyon-Walter Winchell Cancer Research Fund
131 E 36th St, New York, NY, 10016-3404
Damon Runyon-Walter Winchell Cancer Research Fund Newsletter, 503

Dance Critics Assn.
Box 1882 Chelsea Stn., New York, NY, 10011
DCA News, 265

Dance Films Assn.
31 West 21st Street, 3rd Fl., New York, NY, 10010-6806
Dance on Camera News, 265

Dance Masters of America, Inc.
PO Box 610533, Bayside, NY, 11361-0533
Dance Masters of America-Bulletin, 265

Daniel Cole Society
PO Box 367, Mahopac Falls, NY, 10542-0367
Daniel Cole Society Newsletter, 452

•**Data Conversion Laboratory**
18413 Horace Harding Expy, Fresh Meadows, NY, 11365-2207

Data Direction Inc.
PO Box 1052, Port Washington, NY, 11050-0204
Florida Market UpDate, 139

Datasearch Group
14 Hadden Rd, Scarsdale, NY, 10583-3328
Information Searcher, 313

DeLay Letter
PO Box 58, Jamaica, NY, 11426-0058
DeLay Letter, 13

De Nieuwe Amsterdammer
54 W 39th St Fl 11, New York, NY, 10018-3808
De Nieuwe Amsterdammer, 401

Deadly Serious Press
PO Box 1045, Cooper Station, New York, NY, 10276-1045
Deadly Serious, 920

The Dealmakers
100 Youngs Road, Mercerville, NY, 08629
Real Estate Investors Classified, 249

Decorator's Insider
38 Grove Street, New York, NY, 10014
Decorator's Insider, 625

Delaney Report
149 Fifth Ave., Ste. 725, New York, NY, 10010-6801
Delaney Report, 13

Dental Lab. Assn. of the State of New York, Inc.
1 Barstow Rd., Ste. P20, Great Neck, NY, 11021-3501
D.L.A.N.Y. Newsletter, 269

Department of City Planning
22 Reade Street 4N, New York, NY, 10007
Proposed Consolidated Plan, 491

Dept. of Environmental Protection
59-17 Junction Blvd., #3FL, Flushing, NY, 11373-5107
Environs, 381

•**Dept. of General Services**
Manhattan Municipal Bldg., 1 Centre St., 17th Fl. S., New York, NY, 10007

Derivatives Strategy & Tactics
153 Waverly Place, New York, NY, 10014
Derivatives Tactics, 662

Descarga
328 Flatbush Ave Ste 180, Brooklyn, NY, 11238-4302
Descarga Newsletter, The, 912

Diamond Registry, The
580 5th Ave., Rm. 806, New York, NY, 10036-4701
Diamond Registry Bulletin, 693

Direct International
1501 Third Ave., New York, NY, 10028-2101
Publisher's Multinational Direct, 21

Directory Publishers' Forum Northeast
21 Greenhouse Ln, Poughkeepsie, NY, 12603-3634
Forum, 117

Disability Resources, Inc.
4 Glatter Ln, Centereach, NY, 11720-1032
Disability Resources Monthly, 277

Disarm Education Fund
36 E. 12th St., 6th Fl., New York, NY, 10003-4604
Plowshares Update, 326

Dominican Mission Impact
411 E 68th St, New York, NY, 10021-6340
Dominican Mission Impact, 1,056

Donald B. McShane
155 E. 55th St., New York, NY, 10022-4072
McShane Letter, 676

Donna Karan Company, The
550 Seventh Avenue, New York, NY, 10018
Woman to Woman, 56

•**Doran Pubs., Inc.**
PO Box 391, Clifton Park, NY, 12065-0391

Dorthy Jordon & Assoc./TWYCH, Travel with Your Children
40 5th Ave., New York, NY, 10011-8843
Family Travel Times, 1,184

Douglas M. Lawson Associates
545 Madison Ave., New York, NY, 10022
Philanthropic Trends Digest, 1,121

Down-To-Earth Books
72 Philip St, Albany, NY, 12202-1729
SKOLE: The Journal of Alternative Education, 328

Downstate Medical Center
450 Clarkson Ave, Brooklyn, NY, 11203-2012
Focus, 563

•**Dr. Edward H. Miles**
888 8th Ave., New York, NY, 10019-5704

Dracula Press
29 Washington Mews, New York, NY, 10003-6608
Dracula News Journal, 920

Dramatists Guild, The
234 W. 44th, 11th fl., New York, NY, 10036-3986
Dramatists Guild Newsletter, The, 1,173

Dreaded Broccoli
121 W. 92nd St., New York, NY, 10025
Dreaded Broccoli, 428

Drug, Chemical and Allied Trades Assn.
2 Roosevelt Ave., Syosset, NY, 11791-3012
DCAT Digest, 282

Drug & Market Development
2124 Broadway Ste 1200, New York, NY, 10023-1722
Drug & Market Development, 282

Duke University Metropolitan Area Alumni Association
PO Box 6740, FDR Station, New York, NY, 10150
Metropolitan, The, 191

Dunlop Tire
PO Box 1109, Buffalo, NY, 14240-1109
Inter-Action, 1,078

Dwelling Managers, Inc.
30 Waterside Plz., New York, NY, 10010-2693
Watersider, 1,040

EDK Associates
235 W 48th St Apt 35j, New York, NY, 10036-1432
EDK Forecast: Women Consumers, 1,208

EDventure Holdings, Inc.
104 Fifth Ave., 20th Floor, New York, NY, 10011-6987
Release 1.0 Esther Dysons Monthly Report, 235

EFM Media Managment
366 Madison Ave., 7th Floor, New York, NY, 10017-3122
Limbaugh Letter, 993

EKHE Advertising
PO Box 1, Brooklyn, NY, 11231-0001
Justice Weekly, 747

•**EPM Communications, Inc.**
160 Mercer St., 3rd Floor, New York, NY, 10012-3212

Early American Industries Association
P.O. Box 143, Delmar, NY, 12054
Shavings, 250

Eastman Kodak Co.
343 State St, Rochester, NY, 14650-0001
Photo Educators, 1,006

Economics America - Natl. Council on Economic Education
1140 Avenue of Americas, New York, NY, 10036-5803
Senior Economist, 296

Economics Group
Ways & Means Committee State, Capitol, Room 412, Albany, NY, 12248-0001
Economic Update, 484

•**Economist Intelligence Unit**
111 W. 57th St., New York, NY, 10019

Edgemere Enterprises
429 Merrick Rd, Lynbrook, NY, 11563-2433
Aggressive Hockey Report, 1,128

Editorial Freelancers Assn.
71 West 23rd St Ste 1504, New York, NY, 10159-2050
The Freelancer, 695

Edward S. Gordon Co.
200 Park Ave, New York, NY, 10166-0106
Gordon Office Market Report, 1,034

Eggleston Enterprize
PO Box 27, Milford, NY, 13807-0027
Contest/Sweepstakes Bulletin, 438

Electric Railroaders' Assn.
Box 6588, G.C.Sta., New York, NY, 10163-6588
Headlights, 1,029

Electronic Publishing Special Working Group
150 5th Ave Ste 302, New York, NY, 10011-4311
Electronic Publishing Forum, 953

•**Elsevier Science Inc.**
655 Avenue of the Americas, New York, NY, 10010-5107

Embassy of the Republic of Poland
Commercial Counsellor's Office, 100 Park Ave., 10th Fl., New York, NY, 10017-5516
Economic and Legal Information from Poland, 645

•**Empire State Development**
One Commerce Plaza, Albany, NY, 12245-0001

Empire Valuation Consultants, Inc.
350 5th Ave Ste 5713, New York, NY, 10118-0110
Empire Valuation News, 1,143

English-Speaking Union of the U.S.
16 E 69th St, New York, NY, 10021-4906
English Speaking E-SU News, 821

Enterprise Technology Corp.
305 Madison Ave., New York, NY, 10165-0006
Technology Trends, 240

• See **MULTI-PUBLISHER INDEX** for list of publications.

•**Enterprises Unlimited**
400 E 59th St., Apt 9F, New York, NY, 10022-2344

Environment Group, Inc., The
PO Box 1269, Wainscott, NY, 11975-1269
Environment Health & Safety Management, 379

Environmental Action Coalition
625 Broadway Fl 2, New York, NY, 10012-2611
Cycle/the Waste Paper, 376

•**Environmental Defense Fund**
257 Park Ave S Fl 16, New York, NY, 10010-7386

Environmental Nutrition, Inc.
52 Riverside Dr., Apt 15A, New York, NY, 10024-6558
Environmental Nutrition, 933

Ephemera Society of America, Inc.
PO Box 95, Cazenovia, NY, 13035
Ephemera News, 553

Epilepsy Institute
257 Park Avenue South, New York, NY, 10010
Understanding Epilepsy, 888

•**Equitable Life Assurance Society**
787 Seventh Avenue, New York, NY, 10019-1201

Eric Robison
33 Gaymor Lane, Commack, NY, 11725
Rational Enquirer, 472

•**Espirit de Corps**
11 Hanover Square, New York, NY, 10005

Essence Communications, Inc.
1500 Broadway, New York, NY, 10036
HomeWorking, 140

Euronomics, Inc.
PO Box 13683, Albany, NY, 12212-3683
Euronomics Review, 88

Events/USA Publishing Co.
136 E 57th St Ste 1001, New York, NY, 10022-2707
What's Ahead Report, 24

Everson Museum of Art of Syracuse
401 Harrison St, Syracuse, NY, 13202-3019
Everson Museum of Art Bulletin, 904

Eve's Garden
119 W 57th St., Ste 420, New York, NY, 10019-2383
Garden Views, 1,208

Executive Communications, Inc.
185 E 85th St Ste 11c, New York, NY, 10028-2148
Ad Business Report, 9

FCIA Management Co., Inc.
40 Rector St Fl 11, New York, NY, 10006-1705
FCIA News, 620

FIND/SVP, the Information Clearinghouse, Inc.
625 Avenue of Americas, New York, NY, 10011-2095
Ice Cream Reporter, 430

•**FI Publishing, Inc.**
153 E. 87th St., New York, NY, 10128

FXC Investors Corp.
6219 Cooper Ave, Glendale, NY, 11385-6138
FXC Investors Corp., 663

•**Facts on File, Inc.**
11 Penn Plaza, New York, NY, 10001-2006

Fakes and Forgeries Study Group
107 Hoover Rd, Rochester, NY, 14617-3611
Fakes and Forgeries, 971

Family Ties Genealogy
3950 60th St Apt 22a, Woodside, NY, 11377-3418
Origins, 463

Fanciful Feasting Caterers
486 Union Ave, Brooklyn, NY, 11211-3435
Feasting Fancies, 428

•**Faulkner & Gray, Inc.**
11 Penn Plz., 17th Floor, New York, NY, 10001-2006

Federal Law Enforcement Officers Assn.
106 Cedarhurst Ave, Selden, NY, 11784-2908
FLEOA Newsletter, 786

Federation of American Controlled Shipping
50 Broadway Rm 3400, New York, NY, 10004-1607
FACS Forum, 1,111

Fed. Home Loan Bank of New York
1 World Trade Ctr Fl 103, New York, NY, 10048-0202
Second District Member Activity Report, 98

Federation of Jewish Men's Clubs
475 Riverside Dr., New York, NY, 10115-0122
Torchlight, 1,071

Fed. of Ukrainian Student Organizations of America
2 E 79th St, New York, NY, 10021-0106
Federation of Ukrainian Student Organizations of America Newsletter, 410

Feminists for Animal Rights
Box 694 Cathedral Station, New York, NY, 10025
Feminists for Animal Rights, 1,208

•**Fernand Braudel Center**
Binghamton University, Box 6000, Binghamton, NY, 13902-6000

Fiberlux, Inc.
3010 Westchester Avenue, Purchase, NY, 10577-2524
Tips, 600

Financial Women's Association of N.Y.
215 Park Ave S Ste 2010, New York, NY, 10003-1603
FWANY/News, 89

Finger Lakes Library System
314 N Cayuga St, Ithaca, NY, 14850-4209
Finger Lakes Library System Newsletter, 797

Fire Bell Club of New York, Inc.
150 E. 23rd St., New York, NY, 10010-4501
Fire Bell Club News Notes, 421

FirstGroup
2013 Crompond Rd, Yorktown Heights, NY, 10598-4230
Laptopics, 228

First Trust
201 S Warren St, Syracuse, NY, 13202-1606
Key Bank Flashes, 588

First Zen Institute of America
113 E 30th St, New York, NY, 10016-7302
Zen Notes, 1,054

Flower Council of Holland
PO Box 749, Glenwood, NY, 11547-0749
Holland Flower, 424

Folkers & Powell
Rr 3 Box 56, Hudson, NY, 12534-9508
Traverso, 918

Forbes Publishing
60 5th Ave, New York, NY, 10011-8882
Forbes Special Situation Survey, 664

Ford Foundation, Office of Communications
320 E. 43rd St., New York, NY, 10017-4890
Ford Foundation Report, 260

Fordham Univ.
Box 707, 501 Philosophy Hall, Bronx, NY, 10458-0702
Teaching Language Through Literature, Newsletter, 825

Foreign Press Assn.
110 E 59th St Lbby 2, New York, NY, 10022-1304
Foreign Press News, 630

Fort Ticonderoga Museum
PO Box 390, Ticonderoga, NY, 12883-0390
Haversack, The, 904

Forte Communications
111 Broadway Rm 1900, New York, NY, 10006-1901
Today's Investor, 689

Fortune Society
39 W. 19th St., New York, NY, 10011-4225
Fortune News, 786

Forty Plus of New York
15 Park Row, New York, NY, 10038-2334
Forty Plus Newsletter, 344

Foundation for the Community of Artists
280 Broadway Ste 412, New York, NY, 10007-1809
Art & Artists, 62

Foundation for Economic Education, Inc.
30 S Broadway, Irvington, NY, 10533-1861
Notes from FEE, 294

Foundation of NYS Psychological Assn.
Executive Park East, Albany, NY, 12203-3513
New York State Psychologists, 1,016

Frank-Ly Speaking
1310 Surf Ave, Brooklyn, NY, 11224-2404
Frank-Ly Speaking, 584

Franklin Communications
92 S Highland Ave, Ossining, NY, 10562-5615
NASNewsletter, 930

Franklin Soc. Fed. Saving
1274 Ave. of Americas, New York, NY, 10020-1704
Inner Circle Newsletter, 586

•**Fred Argoff**
1204 Avenue U #1290, Brooklyn, NY, 11229

Freedom Guide Dogs
1210 Hardscrabble Rd, Cassville, NY, 13318-1304
Freedom Forum, 111

Freelancer's News
Box 437, Murray Hill Sta., New York, NY, 10156-0437
Freelancers' News, 1,004

French-American Chamber of Commerce in the US Inc.
1350 Ave. of the Americas, 6th Fl., New York, NY, 10019-4702
French-American News, 631

French Bulldog Club of America
86 Gold Rd, Wappingers Falls, NY, 12590-3534
French Bulldog Club of America Newsletter, 280

Friends of Clermont, The
One Clermont Avenue, Germantown, NY, 12526
Livingston Genealogical Register, 459

Friends for Jamaica Collective
PO Box 20392, New York, NY, 10025-1513
Caribbean Newsletter, 628

Friends for Lesbian & Gay Concerns
143 Campbell Avenue, Ithaca, NY, 14850-0222
FLGC Newsletter, 444

Fulfillment Management Assn, Hearst Magazines
250 W 55th St, New York, NY, 10019-5201
FMA Bulletin, 837

Fulton Newspapers, Inc.
Cor. 2nd & Oneida Sts., Fulton, NY, 13069
Fulton Patriot, The, 925

Fund for the Borough of Brooklyn, The
30 Flatbush Ave, Brooklyn, NY, 11217-1121
Brooklyn Community Access Newsletter, 1,165

G-2 Computer Intelligence
3 Maple Place,P.O. Box 7, Glen Head, NY, 11545-9864
Unigram X, 241

G-4 Productions
Box 615, Yonkers, NY, 10703-0615
International MIDI Users Group Newszine, 227

G.S. Schwartz & Co., Inc.
470 Park Ave S Fl 10, New York, NY, 10016-6819
Boomer Report, 83

G. Schirmer Inc. /Assn. Music Publishers, Inc.
257 Park Ave. S., New York, NY, 10011
Schirmer/News, 917

Gabriele Hueglin & Cashman
44 Wall St, New York, NY, 10005-2488
News & Offerings, 680

Garden Club of America
598 Madison Ave, New York, NY, 10022-1693
Garden Club of America Newsletter, 441

Garrison Publishing Co.
PO Box 1378, Pleasant Valley, NY, 12569-1378
Analyst, 654

The Gay & Lesbian Alliance Against Defamation, Inc.
150 W 26th St Rm 503, New York, NY, 10001-6813
GLAAD Newsletter, 444

Gay & Lesbian Community Center
208 W 13th St, New York, NY, 10011-7702
Center Voice, 444

Gay Men's Health Crisis
Medical Information, 129 W. 20th. St. 2nd Fl., New York, NY, 10011-3629
Treatment Issues, 888

Gay Officers Action League
Box 2038, Canal St. Stn., New York, NY
GOAL Gazette, 444

General Contractors Assn.
60 E 42nd St, New York, NY, 10165-3510
General Contractors Association, Bulletin of The, 365

•**General Foods Corp.**
250 North St, White Plains, NY, 10605-2236

General Mills Inc.
54 S Michigan Ave, Buffalo, NY, 14203-3086
Waterfront General, 602

General Motors Corp.
Roosevelt Hwy., P.O. Box 460, Massena, NY, 13662-0460
Newsletter, 592

General Theological Seminary
175 9th Ave, New York, NY, 10011-4977
Seminary News, 1,051

•**Genium Publishing Corp.**
1 Genium Plz, Schenectady, NY, 12304-4607

George Eastman House International Museum of Photography and
900 East Ave, Rochester, NY, 14607-2219
International Museum of Photography At George Eastman House Newsletter, 976

Georgeson
Wall St. Plaza, New York, NY, 10005
Georgeson Report, 139

German-American Chamber of Commerce
40 West 57th Street, New York, NY, 10019
German American Commerce, 159

German Information Center
950 3rd Ave., New York, NY, 10022-2781
Week in Germany, The, 640

* See **MULTI-PUBLISHER INDEX** for list of publications.

German Masonic Home Corp
220 E 15th St, New York, NY, 10003-3997
Ninth Manhattan Masonic News, 180

Gerstman+Meyers
111 W. 57th St., New York, NY, 10019-2211
Off the Shelf, 20

Glanville Publishers, Inc.
75 Main St, Dobbs Ferry, NY, 10522-1601
Legal Periodicals in English, 954

Global Community
214 West 92nd Street, New York, NY, 10025
Community of Joy, 628

Global Packaging & Brand Identity Report
1562 1st Ave Ste 344, New York, NY, 10028-4004
Global Packaging & Brand Identity, 945

God's Love We Deliver, Inc.
895 Amsterdam Ave, New York, NY, 10025-4403
Good News Letter, 1,047

Good Advice Press
PO Box 78, Elizaville, NY, 12523-0078
Pocket Change Investor, The, 254

Goulds Pumps Inc.
240 Fall St, Seneca Falls, NY, 13148-1590
Pumplines, 596

Graceway Publishing Co.
Box 670159, Flushing, NY, 11367-0159
Quarterly Domestic & Global Forecasts of Key Economic Indicators, 149

Graduate School & Univ. Ctr. of CUNY
Ctr. Study of Women & Society, 33 W. 42nd St., Box 135-192, New York, NY, 10036
Center for the Study of Women & Society-Newsletter, 1,207

Gramercy Neighborhood Assoc., Inc.
Box 678, Madison Sq. Sta., New York, NY, 10159-0808
Gramercy, 1,042

•**Graphic Artists Guild**
11 W. 20th St., Apt. 8, New York, NY, 10011-3704

Graphic Dimensions
134 Caversham Woods, Pittsford, NY, 14534-2834
Personal Composition Report, 1,006

Gravure Assn. of America
1200A Scottsville Rd., Rochester, NY, 14624-5703
Gravure Environmental Reporter, 1,004

Graymoor Ecumenical Inst.
Route 9, PO Box 300, Garrison, NY, 10524-0306
At-One-Ment, 1,045

Greater Independent Assn. of Natl. Travel Services
2 Park Ave Rm 2205, New York, NY, 10016-9301
Sound of Giants, 1,188

Greater New York Fund Inc., The
99 Park Ave., New York, NY, 10016-1503
Pledge, 595

Greater New York Hospital Assn
555 W. 57th St., New York, NY, 10019-2974
Skyline News, 572

Green Point Savings Bank
4160 Main St, Flushing, NY, 11355-3800
Pointer, 595

Green Sheet Communications, Inc.
PO Box 727, Hartsdale, NY, 10530-0727
Graphic Communications World, 1,004

Greene County Council on the Arts
398 Main Street, Catskill, NY, 12414
Artistic Opportunities, 300

Greenleaf Partners
110 W 40th St Rm 2404, New York, NY, 10018-3616
Insights & Trends, 670

Greenwich Street Theatre
286 Spring St., Ste. 202B, New York, NY, 10013
Play View, 1,174

•**Guardian Life Insurance Co. of America**
201 Park Ave. S., New York, NY, 10003-1699

Guild of Book Workers, Inc.
521 5th Ave Rm 1740, New York, NY, 10175-0003
Guild of Book Workers-Newsletter, 1,005

•**Guilford Publications, Inc.**
72 Spring Street, New York, NY, 10012

HIAS, Inc.
333 Seventh Avenue, New York, NY, 10001-5004
HIAS Headlines & Highlights, 631

Habonim Dror North America
27 W. 20th St., New York, NY, 10011-3707
Batnua, 627

•**Hachette Filipacchi Magazines, Inc.**
1633 Broadway, New York, NY, 10019-6741

•**Hadassah**
50 W 58th St, New York, NY, 10019-2590

Hagstrom Map & Travel Center
57 W 43rd St, New York, NY, 10036-7407
Hagstrom Map & Travel Center Newsletter, 1,184

Harmonic Research
650 5th Ave.,166fl., New York, NY, 10019-6142
Harmonic Research, 667

Harris Publications, Inc.
1115 Broadway, 8th Fl., New York, NY, 10010-2803
TV Satellite Videoworld, 1,169

Harvest Times
PO Box 27, Mount Tremper, NY, 12457-0027
Harvest Times, 383

Hastings Historial Society
41 Washington Ave, Hastings On Hudson, NY, 10706-2204
Hastings Historian, 541

•**Healtcare Assn. of N.Y. State**
74 N. Pearl St., Albany, NY, 12207-2788

Health Care Communications
11 Heritage Ln, Rye, NY, 10580-3713
Strategic Health Care Marketing, 529

Healthcare Computing Publications
462 2nd St, Brooklyn, NY, 11215-2503
Medical Software Reviews, 879

Healthletter Assocs.
632 Broadway, New York, NY, 10012-2614
University of California at Berkeley, Wellness Letter, 530

•**Hearst Business Communications, RAI Division**
645 Stewart Ave., Garden City, NY, 11530-4709

Hecht Rubber Corp.
Box 1550 Madison Sq. Sta., New York, NY, 10159-1550
Private Lives, 816

Helen Keller Intl.
90 Washington St Fl 15, New York, NY, 10006-2214
Insight, 111

•**Helen Keller Technical Assistance Center**
111 Middle Neck Rd, Sands Point, NY, 11050-1298

Hellenic-American Chamber of Commerce
960 6th Ave., #1204, New York, NY, 10001-2112
Hellenic-American Chamber of Commerce Newsletter, 160

Henry George School of Social Science
121 E 30th St, New York, NY, 10016-7302
Henry George News, 292

Heritage Roses Group
Box 228, RD 1, Clinton Corners, NY, 12514-0228
Rose Letter, 443

Hero Press
153 W 80th St Apt 1b, New York, NY, 10024-7108
Witches International Craft Associates WICA Newsletter, 1,075

Hi, Neighbour
PO Box 324, Cazenovia, NY, 13035-0324
Hi, Neighbour, 25

Hidden Child Foundation/ADL
823 United Nations Plaza, New York, NY, 10017
Hidden Child, The, 486

Historic Brass Society
148 W 23rd St Apt 2A, New York, NY, 10011-2447
Historic Brass Society Newsletter, 912

Historic House Trust of New York City
830 5th Ave, Room 203, New York, NY, 10021-7001
Historic House News, 541

Historic Hudson Valley
150 White Plains Rd, Tarrytown, NY, 10591-5591
Hudson Highlights, 1,042

Historical Society of Rockland County
20 Zukor Rd, New City, NY, 10956-4302
News, 545

•**Hofstra Univ.**
121 Hofstra University, Hempstead, NY, 11550-1090

•**Hoke Communications, Inc.**
224 Seventh St., Garden City, NY, 11530-5771

•**Holland & Edwards Publishing, Inc.**
250 Mercer St., Apt. A-203, New York, NY, 10012-1144

Homeless Child
108 Bedell St, Staten Island, NY, 10309-3302
Homeless Child and Messenger of St. Joseph's Union, 1,057

Hope Reports, Inc.
58 Carverdale Dr, Rochester, NY, 14618-4004
Hope Reports Industry Quarterly, 857

Horticultural Data Processors
PO Box 489, New York, NY, 10028-0005
Avant Gardener, 440

Hospital Audiences, Inc. (HAI)
220 West 42 Street, New York, NY, 10036
HAI News, 1,117

Hotel Roosevelt
45th St. -Madison Ave., New York, NY, 10017
Roosevelt Ramblings, 597

Housatonic Press Inc.
Box 6976, FDR Station, New York, NY, 10150
Country Inns Gazette, 1,183

•**Hudson Associates, Inc.**
44 W. Market St., PO Box 311, Rhinebeck, NY, 12572-1403

Human Resources Administration, City of New York
250 Church St, New York, NY, 10013-3430
Us, 1,123

Human Rights Watch
485 5th Ave., New York, NY, 10017-6104
News from Americas Watch, 174

Humane Society of New York
306 E 59th St, New York, NY, 10022-2006
Humane Society of New York News, 49

Hunt Personnel Ltd.
21 W. 38th St., New York, NY, 10018-5506
Profiles in PDM, 844

Hunter College English Dept.
English Dept., 695 Park Ave., New York, NY, 10021
Murder is Academic, 318

I/B/E/S International, Inc.
345 Hudson St., New York, NY, 10014-4511
I/B/E/S Monthly Comments, 91

IBIS International Direct
249 W. 17th St. 10th Fl., New York, NY, 10011-5300
MailShot, 275

IBM Corp.
P.O. Box 218, Yorktown Heights, NY, 10598-0218
IBM Technical Disclosure Bulletin, 223

IBM Workers United
PO Box 634, Johnson City, NY, 13790-0634
Resistor, 705

•**IDD Enterprises**
2 World Trade Ctr. 18th Fl., New York, NY, 10048-0203

IOMA
29 W. 35th St., 5th Fl., New York, NY, 10001-2299
Managing International Credit & Collections, 6

ISIS
21 Greenhouse Ln., Poughkeepsie, NY, 12603-3634
ISIS Forum, 118

ITT World Communications Inc.
380 Madison Avenue, New York, NY, 10017-2513
Via ITT, 602

Industry Analyst
50 Chestnut St, Rochester, NY, 14604-2318
Office Products Analyst, 939

Industry Forecast Inc.
223 N Greeley Ave # 26, Chappaqua, NY, 10514-3411
Industry Forecast, 293

InfoLink
P.O. Box 306, 31 Albany Post Rd, Montrose, NY, 10458
HealthInform, 511

Inform., Inc.
120 Wall Street, New York, NY, 10005-3904
Inform Reports, 385

Information Plus
14 Lafayette Square, Suite 2000, Buffalo, NY, 14203-1920
Information Solutions: A newsletter of ideas & techniques on how to profit from info., 839

Info Press, Inc.
PO Box 550, Lewiston, NY, 14092-0550
Info Franchise Newsletter, 141

Insightful Newsletters
175 Great Neck Rd Ste 307, Great Neck, NY, 11021-3313
Undercurrent, 1,191

Institute for Studies in American Music
Brooklyn College, Conservatory of Music, Brooklyn, NY, 11210
Newsletter, Institute for Studies in American Music, 915

Insurance Information Institute
110 William St, New York, NY, 10038-3970
I.I.I. Insurance Daily, 620

Insurance Services Office
7 World Trade Center, New York, NY, 10048
Inside ISO, 586

•**Intelligence**
PO Box 20008, New York, NY, 10025-1510

* See ***MULTI-PUBLISHER INDEX*** for list of publications.

Interchurch Center
475 Riverside Dr Ste 253, New York, NY, 10115-0253
475, 1,044

•**Interest Rate Publishing Corporation**
30 Wall St., New York, NY, 10005-2201

Interfaith Center on Corporate Responsibility
475 Riverside Dr Ste 566, New York, NY, 10115-0122
Corporate Examiner, 134

Intergalactic Enterprises
28 Brookhaven Blvd., Port Jefferson Sta., NY, 11776
Success Track, 861

International Advertising Association
521 5th Ave., Rm. 1807, New York, NY, 10175
IAA World News, 15

International Association for Study of Popular Music
SUNY/Dept. Of Music, Stony Brook, NY, 11794-0001
RPM: Review of Popular Music, 916

International Center for Creative Thinking/JMW Group
1385 Boston Post Rd, Larchmont, NY, 10538-3904
Letter to Thinkers, 858

International Christian Youth Exchange
134 W. 26th St., New York, NY, 10001-6803
ICYE-US Newsletter, 1,063

Intl. Data Services, Inc.
Box 222, Endwell, NY, 13760-0222
Dairy Products Newsletter, 264

•**International Federation of Accountants (IFAC)**
114 West 47th St., Ste. 2410, New York, NY, 10036-1510

Intl. Foundation for Art Research
46 E 70th St, New York, NY, 10021-4928
IFARreports, 53

International Imagery Association
PO Box 1046, Bronx, NY, 10471-0618
Imagery Today, 1,014

Intl. Institute of Rural Reconstruction
475 Riverside Dr Ste 1270, New York, NY, 10115-0122
IIRR Report, 631

Intl. Institute for Safety in Transportation
PO Box 63, Franklin Square, NY, 11010-0063
Safety Activist, 1,084

Intl. League for Human Rights
432 Park Ave S Ste 1103, New York, NY, 10016-8013
Human Rights Bulletin, 173

Intl. Longshoremen's Assn.
17 Battery Pl., Rm. 1530, New York, NY, 10004-1261
ILA Longshore News, 708

Intl. Municipal Signal Assn.
PO Box 539, 165 E. Union Street, Newark, NY, 14513
Interconnect, 1,081

International Publishers Co., Inc.
239 W 23rd St Fl 5, New York, NY, 10011-2302
Book Newsletter & Catalog, 116

International Radio & Television Society
420 Lexington Ave Rm 1714, New York, NY, 10170-1799
IRTS News, 124

International Research Service
345 Kear Street, Yorktown, NY, 10598
Insurance Research Letter, 621

International Social Service
390 Park Ave S Fl 7, New York, NY, 10016-8803
ISS Newsletter, 1,118

International Theatre Institute of the US, Inc.
47 Great Jones St., New York, NY, 10012-1114
Newsletter of I.T.I.U.S., 1,173

•**International Trademark Association**
1133 Avenue of the Americas, New York, NY, 10036-6710

International Wealth Success, Inc.
24 Canterbury Rd., Rockville Center, NY, 11570-1310
Money Watch Bulletin, 94

•**International Women's Tribune Centre**
777 United Nations Plaza, New York, NY, 10017-3551

International Women's Writing Guild
Box 810 Gracie Sta., New York, NY, 10028-0082
Network, 1,210

Interracial Club of Buffalo
7 Harwood Dr. #400, Buffalo, NY, 14226-4610
Interracial Club of Buffalo Newsletter, 398

•**Interreligious Foundation for Community Organization**
402 W. 145th St., New York, NY, 10031-5202

Interstitial Cystitis Assn., Inc.
Box 1553, Madison Sq. Sta., New York, NY, 10159-1553
ICA Update, 514

Into the Night
1980 65th St Apt 3d, Brooklyn, NY, 11204-3844
Into the Night, 992

Investment Media Inc.
909 3rd Ave., 6th Fl., New York, NY, 10022-4731
Global Investment Technology, 91

Investor U.S.A.
PO Box 370, Remsenburg, NY, 11960-0370
Investor, U.S.A., 672

Investors Intelligence
30 Church St, New Rochelle, NY, 10801-6302
Encyclopedia of Stock Market Techniques, 663

Iona College
Department of English, New Rochelle, NY, 10801-1890
Shakespeare Newsletter, 824

Israel Publications Inc.
47 Byron Pl, Scarsdale, NY, 10583-1901
Israel High-Tech Report, 649

Italian Charities of America
83-20 Queens Blvd., Queens, NY, 11373-4245
Italian Charities of America Bulletin, 968

Italian Trade Commission-Tile Center
499 Park Ave., New York, NY, 10022-1240
Tile News, 652

Italian Trade Commission-Wine Center
499 Park Avenue, New York, NY, 10022
Vinotizie, 105

J & B Publishing Co.
24 Hardwood Hill Rd, Pittsford, NY, 14534-4544
Purchasing Professional Newsletter, 1,028

J. Girl
P.O. Box 819, Peter Stuyvesant St, NY, 10019
Plotz, 261

•**J.R. O'Dwyer Company, Inc.**
271 Madison Ave Ste 600, New York, NY, 10016-1001

JWB Jewish Book Council
15 E. 26th St., New York, NY, 10010-1505
Jewish Book World, 118

Jackpotunities, Inc.
Box 393, Centuck Station, Yonkers, NY, 10710-0393
Jackpotunities, 439

James Fenimore Cooper Society
8 Lake Street, Cooperstown, NY, 13326
James Fenimore Cooper Society Newsletter, 822

Jamestown Area Chamber of Commerce
101 W 5th St, Jamestown, NY, 14701-5013
Jamestown Chamber of Commerce Newsletter, 160

•**Jamestown Area Labor Management Committee**
PO Box 819, Jamestown, NY, 14702-0819

Jamestown Community College
525 Falconer St, Jamestown, NY, 14701-1920
Communicator, 204

Japan Airlines
655 5th Ave, New York, NY, 10022-5347
JAL Newsletter, 30

•**Japan External Trade Organization**
1221 Ave. of the Americas, New York, NY, 10020-1001

Japan Market Research, Inc.
609 Columbus Ave., New York, NY, 10024
Japan Financial Market Report, 649

Japan North American Commission on Cooperative Mission
475 Riverside, New York, NY, 10115-0122
Japan North American Commission on Cooperative Mission Bulletin, 1,064

Japan Society, Inc.
333 E 47th St, New York, NY, 10017-2399
Japan Society Newsletter, 260

Jerusalem Foundation, Inc.
60 E 42nd St Rm 1936, New York, NY, 10165-1999
News from Jerusalem, 969

Jewelers of America
1185 6 Ave., 30th Fl., New York, NY, 10036
JA Report, 693

Jewish Civil Service Employees, Inc.
Box 688, G.P.O., New York, NY, 10121-0035
National Bulletin, 489

Jewish Community Centers Assn. of North America
15 E. 26 St., New York, NY, 10010-1579
JWB Personnel Reporter, 345

Jewish Defense Organization, Youth Movement
134 W 32nd St Ste 602, New York, NY, 10001-3201
Never Again, 994

Jewish Education Service of N. Amer., Inc.
730 Braoday, 2nd Fl., New York, NY, 10003-9511
Trends, 1,071

Jewish Educators Assembly
10606 Queens Blvd, Flushing, NY, 11375-4248
Jewish Educators Assembly Yearbook, 1,069

Jewish Genealogical Society, Inc.
PO Box 6398, New York, NY, 10128-0004
Dorot, 452

Jewish Guild for the Blind
15 W 65th St, New York, NY, 10023-6694
Jewish Guild for the Blind Newsletter, 111

•**Jewish Labor Committee**
25 E. 21st St., 2nd Fl., New York, NY, 10010-6297

Jewish Lawyers Guild
110 Wall St., New York, NY, 10005-3801
Confrontation, 727

Jewish Peace Fellowship
PO Box 271, Nyack, NY, 10960-0271
Shalom-Jewish Peace Newsletter, 1,071

Jewish Radical Education Project
1 Union Sq W Ste 302, New York, NY, 10003-3303
Jewish Radical, 992

Jewish Science Fiction Society
470 W. End Ave., New York, NY, 10024-4933
Jews in Space: Newsletter of the Jewish Science Fiction Community, 1,102

Jewish Teachers Assn.
45 E. 33rd St., New York, NY, 10016-5336
Morim Bulletin, 318

•**Jewish Telegraphic Agency, Inc.**
330 7th Ave., 11th Fl., New York, NY, 10001-5010

John Charles Mallon & Associates
305 Madison Avenue, Suite 1166, New York, NY, 10165
Security Investing, 685

John Jay College of Criminal Justice
899 10th Ave Rm 623, New York, NY, 10019-1029
ISG Newsletter, 743

•**John Wiley & Sons, Inc.**
605 Third Avenue, New York, NY, 10158-0012

Johnson & Hayward
516 W 19th St # 22, New York, NY, 10011-2807
Postal Link, 637

•**Johnson & Higgins**
125 Broad St, New York, NY, 10004-2424

Jomurpa Publishing Inc.
7 S Myrtle Ave # 1708, Spring Valley, NY, 10977-5543
Shopping Center Digest, 273

Joyce E. Francis, Publisher
450 Lexington Ave., Grand Central P.O., Box 2614, New York, NY, 10163-2614
Homebased, 140

Judicial Process Commission
121 Fitzhugh St N, Rochester, NY, 14614-1214
Justica, 747

Julliard School, The
60 Lincoln Center Plaza, New York, NY, 10023-7498
Julliard Journal, 913

•**Jupiter Communications**
627 Broadway, 2nd Fl., New York, NY, 10012-2612

K2 Communications
217 East 85th Street, Box 144, New York, NY, 10028-0144
MoneyWorks for Women, 1,210

KPMG Peat Marwick
767 Fifth Avenue, New York, NY, 10153
Management Controls, 840

KRC Letter
4 Gelber St., Larchmont, NY, 10536
KRC Letter, 314

Kappa Alpha
317 W State St, Ithaca, NY, 14850-5431
Kappa Alpha News, 178

Karma Triyana Dharmachakra Monastery
352 Meads Mtn Rd, Woodstock, NY, 12498-1024
Karma Triyana Dharmachakra Monastery Newsletter, 1,054

Kermit Development & Distribution
Columbia Academic Info Systems, 612 W. 115th St., New York, NY, 10025
Kermit News, 227

Key-Volume Strategies, Inc.
PO Box 407, White Plains, NY, 10602-0407
Key-Volume Strategies, 673

Keyboard Teachers Association International, Inc.
361 Pin Oak Ln, Westbury, NY, 11590-1941
Keyboard Teacher, 913

Kid News
PO Box 797, Forest Hills, NY, 11375-0797
Kid News, 55

KidTECH/BG Associates
PO Box 200, New York, NY, 10044-0204
KidTECH News, 315

* See **MULTI-PUBLISHER INDEX** for list of publications.

Kindred Spirits
PO Box 252, White Plains, NY, 10602-0252
Kindred Spirits, 542

Kirpal Light Satsang, Inc.
Rr 1 Box 125, Kinderhook, NY, 12106-9720
Kirpal Light Satsang International Newsletter, 1,054

Knight MediaCom International
780 Piermont Ave, Piermont, NY, 10968-1032
Emerging Media Report, 856

Kogos Publications Co.
104 E. 37th St., New York, NY, 10016-3016
Around the World with Bonnie Kogos, 1,182

Kon-Lin Research & Analysis Corp.
5 Water Rd, Rocky Point, NY, 11778-9331
Kon-Lin Letter, 673

Korean Church Coalition
475 Riverside Dr, New York, NY, 10115-0697
Korea Update, 633

Korean Traders Assn., Inc.
460 Park Ave., New York, NY, 10022-1906
Korean Trade News, 649

Kosciuszko Foundation
15 E 65th St, New York, NY, 10021-6595
Kosciuszko Foundation Newsletter, 407

Kurt Weill Foundation for Music
7 E. 20th St., New York, NY, 10003-1106
Kurt Weill Newsletter, 913

Kwartler Communications Inc.
79 Verbena Ave., Floral Park, NY, 11001-3014
MBA Newsletter, 316

•**Kyodo News Intl.**
50 Rockefeller Plaza #803, New York, NY, 10020-1605

LAMAR
96 Hillside Avenue, Rochester, NY, 14610
PopularLife, 472

L. Davis Press, Inc.
1125 Oxford Pl, Schenectady, NY, 12308-2913
News Letter of the Astronomical Society of NY, 69

LJK Wellness Corp.
130 W 30th St Fl 15, New York, NY, 10001-4004
Kidfit Newsletter, 169

L.K. Publishing Co.
7 Putter La. P.O Box 102, Gourmet Bldg. 102, Middle Island, NY, 11953-0102
Practical Gourmet, 1,188

LLP Maritime
611 Broadway Rm 308, New York, NY, 10012-2608
Lloyd's Aviation Law Newsletter, 752

•**LYDA Assocs., Inc.**
PO Box 700, Palisades, NY, 10964-0700

LaLoggia Letter
PO Box 167, Rochester, NY, 14601-0167
LaLoggia Letter, The, 673

Laban/Bartenieff Institute of Movement Studies, Inc.
11 E 4th St, New York, NY, 10003-6902
LIMS News, 877

•**Labor Research Assn.**
145 W 28th St Fl 6, New York, NY, 10001-6191

•**Lafferty Publications**
420 Lexington Ave., Ste. 1745, New York, NY, 10170

Lake Champlain Phenomena Investigations
Box 2134, Wilton, NY, 12866-0999
Champ Channels, 1,095

Lambda Legal Defense & Education Fund, Inc.
666 Broadway, Suite 1200, New York, NY, 10012-2317
Lambda Update, 174

Landauer Assocs.
666 5th Ave., 25th Fl., New York, NY, 10103-0001
International Property Bulletin, 1,034

The Landmark Society
133 Fitzhugh St S, Rochester, NY, 14608-2204
Cornerstone Landmark Newsletter, 1,033

Langer Assocs., Inc.
19 W 44th St Ste 601, New York, NY, 10036-5902
Langer Report Newsletter, 1,098

Laser Disc Newsletter, The
PO Box 420, East Rockaway, NY, 11518-0420
Laser Disc Newsletter, The, 557

•**Latin American Info Services**
159 W 53rd St # 28B, New York, NY, 10019-6050

Laurence Leamer
221 Torrance Ave, Vestal, NY, 13850-1328
Lehmer-Leamer-Lamer Newsletter, 459

Lawyers Committee for Human Rights
330 7th Ave., #10N, New York, NY, 10001-5010
Newsbriefs, 764

Lawyer's Committee on Nuclear Policy
666 Broadway Rm 610, New York, NY, 10012-2317
Lawyer's Committee on Nuclear Policy Newsletter, 750

Lawyers Co-Operative Publishing Co.
Aqueduct Bldg., Rochester, NY, 14694-0001
Bankruptcy Alert, 718

Laymen's Natl. Bible Assn.
1865 Broadway #12, New York, NY, 10023-7503
LNBA Newsletter, 1,048

Lead Belly Society
PO Box 6679, Ithaca, NY, 14851-6679
Lead Belly Letter, 913

•**Leader Publications, Inc.**
345 Park Avenue South, New York, NY, 10010

League of Arab States, Arab Information Center
747 3rd Ave., New York, NY, 10017-2803
Palestine Digest, 636

Leake & Watts
487 S Broadway Ste 201, Yonkers, NY, 10705-3252
HIV - Drug Exposure & Foster Care: Network Bulletin, 1,117

Lebhar-Friedman Inc.
425 Park Ave., New York, NY, 10022-3556
Inside Retailing, 272

Lee Lo's New York Jazz Newsletter
308 W 104th St Apt 2d, New York, NY, 10025-4134
Lee Lo's New York Jazz Newsletter, 913

Lee Marc Stein Ltd.
41 Executive Dr, Hauppauge, NY, 11788-2112
Direct Marketing Optimization Letter, 274

Left Business Observer
250 W. 85th St., New York, NY, 10024-3217
Left Business Observer, 143

Lehrfeld
55 Northern Blvd Ste 300, Great Neck, NY, 11021-4058
Airspeed, 853

•**Leo Baeck Institute, Inc.**
129 E. 73rd Street, New York, NY, 10021

Leonard Bernstein Society
25 Central Park W Apt 1y, New York, NY, 10023-7212
Prelude, Fugue & Riffs, 916

Lesbian & Gay Community Svcs. Ctr., Inc.
208 W 13th St, New York, NY, 10011-7702
Gay Center Voice, 444

Lesbian & Gay Law Association of Greater New York
799 Broadway #340, New York, NY, 10003-6811
Lesbian/Gay Law Notes, 445

Lesbian Herstory Educational Foundation, Inc.
PO Box 1258, New York, NY, 10116-1258
Lesbian Herstory Archives News, 445

Leukemia Society of America
600 3rd Ave Fl 4, New York, NY, 10016-1900
Newsline, 882

Levin Public Relations & Marketing
30 Glenn St., White Plains, NY, 10603-3213
Levin's Public Relations Report, 858

Library for AIDS/HIV Resources
NYC Dept. of Health, 125 Worth Street, Box A/1, New York, NY, 10013
HIV Connect, 508

Library, Jewish Theological Seminary of America
3080 Broadway, New York, NY, 10027-4650
Between the Lines, 794

Life Entitlements
4 World Trade Ctr., Ste. 5270, New York, NY, 10048-0204
Life Entitlements, 515

Lincoln First Bank of Rochester
PO Box 20472, Rochester, NY, 14602-0472
Link, 589

Linnaean Society of New York
15 W 77th St, New York, NY, 10024-5153
Linnean Newsletter, 942

Lion Publishing Company
Box 150-559 Van Brunt Station, Brooklyn, NY, 11215-0559
Entertainment and Travel Mode, 368

Lithuanian Catholic Religious Aid
351 Highland Blvd, Brooklyn, NY, 11207-1910
Catholic Lithuania Update, 628

•**Little/Silver Times, The**
100 6th Ave., 7th Fl., New York, NY, 10013-1605

Living Free, c/o Jim Stumm
Box 29, Hiler Branch, Buffalo, NY, 14223
Living Free, 815

•**Lloyd's of London Press**
611 Broadway Rm 308, New York, NY, 10012-2608

Local 1-2, Utility Workers Union of America, AFL-CIO
386 Park Avenue South, New York, NY, 10016-8846
Record, 710

Local 144, Hotel, Hospital, Nursing Home & Allied Services U
233 W 49th St, New York, NY, 10019-7404
Local 144 Courage, 709

Local 1814, Intl. Longshoremen's Assn.
70 20th St., Brooklyn, NY, 11232-1101
Brooklyn Longshoreman, 707

Long Island Archives Conference
History Dept. St. John's Univ., Jamaica, NY, 11439-0001
LIAC Newsletter, 801

Long Island Direct Marketing Assn.
17 Bettina Ct, Hampton Bays, NY, 11946-1229
LIDMA, 143

Long Island Lighting Co.
175 E Old Country Rd, Hicksville, NY, 11801-4257
Long Island Almanac, 1,026

Long Island Pick Society
c/o ComprehensiveComputerSvces, 555 Broadhollow Rd., Ste. 302, Melville, NY, 11747
LIPService, 227

Long Island Police News
PO Box 36, Copiague, NY, 11726-0036
Long Island Police News, 787

Long Island Rail Road
Jamaica Sta., Jamaica, NY, 11432-5597
Along the Track, 576

Lori Key
11-34 44th Dr. #7, Long Island City, NY, 11101
Fluff, 417

Louis Harris
630 Fifth Ave., New York, NY, 10111-0124
Harris Survey, 1,197

Lowell Communications
88 Bleeker St., New York, NY, 10012
Travel Confidential, 1,190

Lubavitch News Svce.
770 Eastern Pky, Brooklyn, NY, 11213-3409
Lubavitch International, 1,069

Lucis Publishing Co.
120 Wall Street 24th Floor, New York, NY, 10005
Triangles Bulletin, 182

Luggage & Leather Goods Manufacturers Assoc.
350 5th Ave., Ste. 2624, New York, NY, 10118-0058
LLGMA Association News, 791

Lutheran Social Services
27 Park Pl., New York, NY, 10007-2502
On the Edge, 1,072

Lynch-Bowes, Inc.
301 Main St., #206, Port Washington, NY, 11050-2705
Lynch International Investment Survey, 675

Lynch Municipal Bond Advisory
PO Box 20476, New York, NY, 10025
Lynch Municipal Bond Advisory, 675

MASTCA Publishing Corp.
PO Box 55, Loch Sheldrake, NY, 12759-0055
Middle/Fixed Income Letter, 677

MJM Publishing Co.
575 Lexington Ave Rm 2700, New York, NY, 10022-6102
Taxes Interpreted, 1,155

•**M. Shanken Communications, Inc.**
387 Park Ave S., 8th Floor, New York, NY, 10016-8810

MTA Metro-North Railroad/Corporate Communications
345 Madison Avenue, New York, NY, 10017-3706
Mileposts, 1,187

M & T Bank
1 M And T Plz, Buffalo, NY, 14203-2399
M&T Observer, 589

Macedonian Arts Council
PO Box 905, New York, NY, 10023-0905
Macedonia, Curiosum Mundi, 261

Macfadden Holdings Publishing
233 Park Ave. South, New York, NY, 10003-1663
International True Story Group, 1,077

•**Magazine Publishers of America**
919 3rd Avenue, 22nd Floor, New York, NY, 10022-3801

Man Computer Systems, Inc.
8413 168th St, Jamaica, NY, 11432-2027
Best Investor, 655

Man Watchers Inc.
Box 1616, Canal St. Station, New York, NY, 10013
Woman Alive, 1,213

•**Managed Account Reports**
220 Fifth Ave., New York, NY, 10001

* See *MULTI-PUBLISHER INDEX* for list of publications.

* See **MULTI-PUBLISHER INDEX** for list of publications.

Murray Hill News Publ. Co.
237 Madison Ave, New York, NY, 10016-2818
Murray Hill News, 1,042

Museum of the City of New York
1220 5th Ave, New York, NY, 10029-5287
Quarterly, 907

•**Museum of Modern Art**
11 W 53rd St, New York, NY, 10019-5498

Museum of Staten Island
75 Stuyvesant Pl, Staten Island, NY, 10301-1912
Museum of Staten Island News, 907

Music From China
170 Park Row Apt 12d, New York, NY, 10038-1100
Music From China, 914

Music Theatre Group
29 Bethune St, New York, NY, 10014-1724
Music-Theatre Group Newsletter, 591

Musical Engineering Group
1 Pheasant Ln, Ithaca, NY, 14850-6311
Electronotes, 912

Mutual of New York
1740 Broadway, New York, NY, 10019-4315
MONY Today, 589

Mycological Society of America
SUNY College at Oswego, Biology Dept., Oswego, NY, 13126
Mycological Society of America Newsletter, 110

Mystery Writers of America, Inc.
17 E. 47th St., 6th Fl., New York, NY, 10017-1920
Third Degree, 920

NAEB
450 Wireless Blvd., Hauppauge, NY, 11788-3934
NAEB Bulletin, 1,028

NAS Newsletter
92 S Highland Ave, Ossining, NY, 10562-5615
NAS Newsletter, 930

NCCP
154 Haven Ave, New York, NY, 10032-1180
National Center for Children in Poverty News & Issues, 170

NEA New York
217 Lark St, Albany, NY, 12210-1101
Advocate, The, 299

NTID at Rochester Inst. of Technology
LBJ 2264, Box 9887, Rochester, NY, 14623-0887
News n' Notes, 322

NYC Board of Ed.; Div. of Instruction & Professional Dev.
131 Livingston St Rm 410, Brooklyn, NY, 11201-5181
Arts Partners Newsletter, 63

N.Y.C. Central Labor Council AFL-CIO
386 Park Ave., S., New York, NY, 10016-8842
Labor News, 709

NYC Dept. of Records & Information Services
31 Chambers St Rm 305, New York, NY, 10007-1210
NOTES, 489

NY City Coalition for the Homeless
89 Chambers St Apt 3, New York, NY, 10007-1811
New York City Coalition for the Homeless-Safety Network, 1,120

N.Y. Food Letter
50 W 67th St # 6c, New York, NY, 10023-6227
N.Y. Food Letter, 431

NYNEX Teleforum
1095 Ave. of the Americas, Room 3440, New York, NY, 10036
Teleforum, 1,163

•**NYPER Publications**
PO Box 662, Latham, NY, 12110-0662

N.Y. Recorder Guild
145 W. 93rd St., New York, NY, 10025
Early Music Newsletter, 912

NYS Contract Reporter
PO Box 4452, Utica, NY, 13504-4452
New York State Contract Reporter, 489

NYSERNet, Inc.
200 Elwood Davis Rd, Liverpool, NY, 13088-6147
NYSERNet User, 231

NYS Education Dept.
Central Svces. #3 Rm. 546 Eb, Education Bldg.washin, Albany, NY, 12234-0001
Child Nutrition Today, 1,075

NY State Dept. of Social Services
Div. Of Family & Children Serv, 40 N. Pearl Street,, Albany, NY, 12243-0001
Special Delivery, 1,122

NYW Publishing Ltd.
210 5th Ave., New York, NY, 10010-2102
New York Wine Companion, 146

Nacion Taina
PO Box 883, New York, NY, 10025-0883
Nacion Taina, 407

Nassau Community College, State Univ. of New York
Education Drive, English Dept., Garden City, NY, 11530-5793
Evelyn Waugh Newsletter & Studies, 821

National Academy of Design
1083 5th Ave, New York, NY, 10128-0114
Academy Bulletin, 62

National Academy of Pop Music
885 2nd Ave Fl 26, New York, NY, 10017-2201
Words About Music, 919

National Academy of Television Arts & Sciences
111 W. 57th St., Ste. 1020, New York, NY, 10019-2211
NATAS News, 1,168

National Action Forum Midlife & Older Women
PO Box 816, Stony Brook, NY, 11790-0816
Hot Flash, 1,014

Natl. Alliance Against Racist & Political Repression
11 John St Rm 702, New York, NY, 10038-4009
Organizer, 995

•**The National Arts Club**
15 Gramercy Park S, New York, NY, 10003-1796

National Assoc. of Export Companies
PO Box 1330, Murray Hill Station, NY, 10156
Trade Lines, 652

National Association for the Advancement of Psychoanalysis
80 Eighth Avenue, Suite 1501, New York, NY, 10011
NAAP News, 1,016

Natl. Assn. of Black Accountants
New York, NY
News Plus, 7

Natl. Assn. on Drug Abuse Problems, Inc.
355 Lexington Ave., New York, NY, 10017-6603
NADAP News/Report, 346

•**National Association for Female Executives, Inc.**
30 Irving Pl., 5th Floor, New York, NY, 10003-2303

National Association of Hebrew Day School PTA's
160 Broadway, New York, NY, 10038-4201
PTA National Bulletin, 324

National Association for Industry - Education Cooperation
235 Hendricks Blvd., Buffalo, NY, 14226-3304
NAIEC Newsletter, 319

Natl. Assn. of Letter Carriers
NY Letter Carriers, Branch 36, 347 W. 41st St., New York, NY, 10036
New York Letter Carriers, 710

Natl. Assn. of Men's Sportswear Buyers, Inc.
500 5th Ave Fl 1425, New York, NY, 10110-0002
NAMSB News, 55

•**Natl. Assn. of Pharmaceutical Manufacturers**
320 Old Country Road, Suite #205, Garden City, NY, 11530-1743

National Association for Poetry Therapy
PO Box 551, Port Washington, NY, 11050-0105
Museletter, The, 519

Natl. Assn. of the Professions
292 Madison Ave., New York, NY, 10017-6307
NAP Forum, 145

•**Natl. Assn. for Regional Ballet**
140 W 79th St Apt 11d, New York, NY, 10024-6424

National Association of Residents & Interns
292 Madison Ave., New York, NY, 10017-6351
NARI Stethoscope, 880

Natl. Assn. of Science Writers, Inc.
PO Box 294, Greenlawn, NY, 11740-0294
Science Writers, 697

National Association of State Boards of Accountancy
380 Lexington Ave, New York, NY, 10168-0002
State Board Report, 8

Natl. Assn. of Uniform Manufacturers
1156 Ave. of Americas, New York, NY, 10036-2702
NAUMD Newsletter, 55

•**National Association for Visually Handicapped**
22 W. 21st St., New York, NY, 10010-6904

National Association of Women Artists
41 Union Square W, New York, NY, 10003-3208
National Association of Women Artists Newsletter, 65

Natl. Basketball Players Assn.
1775 Broadway Ste 2401, New York, NY, 10019-1903
Time Out, 1,136

National Braille Association, Inc.
3 Townline Cir, Rochester, NY, 14623-2513
National Braille Association Bulletin, 321

Natl. Cartoonists Society
PO Box 20267, New York, NY, 10023-1484
National Cartoonist Society Newsletter: 'The Cartoonist', 65

•**National Catholic Development Conference**
86 Front St, Hempstead, NY, 11550-3617

National Center for Collective Bargaining - Higher Ed.
Baruch College, 17 Lexington Ave., Box G-1050, New York, NY, 10010
Newsletter for the National Center for Collective Bargaining, 704

National Center for Wilderness Activities
PO Box 655, Pomona, NY, 10970-0655
NCWA Letter, 388

Natl. Charities Info Bureau, Inc.
19 Union Sq., W., New York, NY, 10003-3395
Wise Giving Guide, 970

National Coaliation Against Censorship
275 7th Ave Fl 20, New York, NY, 10001-6708
Censorship News, 172

National Coalition of Free Men
PO Box 129, Manhasset, NY, 11030-0129
Transitions, 890

National Coffee Association of U.S.A., Inc.
110 Wall St Fl 13, New York, NY, 10005-3801
National Coffee Association of U.S.A., Inc., Newsletter, 104

Natl. Committee on American Foreign Policy, Inc.
320 Park Ave., New York, NY, 10022
American Foreign Policy Entrance, 626

Natl. Committee of Catholic Laymen
150 E 35th St Rm 840, New York, NY, 10016-4178
Catholic Eye, 1,055

Natl. Committee for Independent Political Action
PO Box 170610, Brooklyn, NY, 11217-0610
Discussion Bulletin, 989

Natl. Committee on U.S.-China Relations
71 W. 23rd St., 19th Fl., New York, NY, 10010-4102
Notes from the National Committee, 635

National Conference of Black Lawyers
2 W. 125 St., New York, NY, 10027
NCBL Notes, 758

National Conference of Christians & Jews
71 5th Ave., #1100, New York, NY, 10003-3004
National Conference of Christians and Jews Newsletter, 1,049

Natl. Conference on Soviet Jewry
730 Broadway, 2nd Floor, New York, NY, 10003-9511
National Conference on Soviet Jewry-Newsbreak, 634

Natl. Conference of Synagogue Youth
333 7th Ave, 18th Floor, New York, NY, 10001-5004
Shema Newsletter, 1,071

•**National Council of Churches**
475 Riverside Dr, New York, NY, 10115-0122

•**Natl. Council of Jewish Women**
53 W. 23rd St., New York, NY, 10010-4299

Natl. Council for Research on Women
530 Broadway, 10th Floor, New York, NY, 10012
Women's Research Network News, 1,214

Natl. Council of States on Inservice Education
Syracuse Univ. 402 Huntington, Hall, Syracuse, NY, 13244-0001
NCSIE Inservice, 320

Natl. Council of Women of the U.S.
777 UN Plaza, New York, NY, 10017
National Council of Women of the United States Bulletin, 180

•**Natl. Employment Law Project**
36 W 44th St Ste 1415, New York, NY, 10036-8102

Natl. Family Council on Drug Addiction
40 Westminister Dr, Pearl River, NY, 10965-2840
Narcotics and Youth, 1,119

National Federation of Community Development Credit Unions
120 Wall St Fl 10, New York, NY, 10005-3902
CDCU Report, 657

•**Natl. Foundation for Jewish Culture**
330 Seventh Ave., 21st Fl., New York, NY, 10001-5010

Natl. Foundation for Jewish Genetic Diseases, Inc.
250 Park Ave Ste 1000, New York, NY, 10177-1099
Genetically Speaking, 474

•**Natl. Hemophilia Foundation**
110 Greene St Apt 303, New York, NY, 10012-3832

* See **MULTI-PUBLISHER INDEX** for list of publications.

National Kidney Foundation
30 East 33 Street, New York, NY, 10016
NKF Newsletter, 881

•**Natl. Lawyer's Guild**
55 6th Ave, New York, NY, 10013-1679

Natl. League of Masonic Clubs
1 North Dr, Plandome, NY, 11030-1416
National League of Masonic Clubs, League News, 180

Natl. Mah Jongg League
250 W 57th St, New York, NY, 10107-0054
National Mah Jongg League Newsbulletin, 1,133

Natl. Marfan Foundation
382 Main St., Pt. Washington, NY, 11050-3121
Connective Issues, 871

•**Natl. Marine Manufacturers Assn.**
600 Third Avenue, New York, NY, 10016-1901

Natl. Medical Fellowships
110 W 32st St, New York, NY, 10001
Connections, 871

•**National Neurofibromatosis Foundation, Inc.**
95 Pine St, New York, NY, 10005-1611

•**Natl. Professional Resources**
25 South Regent Street, P.O. Box 1479, Pt. Chester, NY, 10573

National Psychological Assn. for Psychoanalysis
43 5th Ave, New York, NY, 10003-4368
N.P.A.P. News & Reviews, 1,016

National Scrabble Association
PO Box 700, Greenport, NY, 11944-0700
Scrabble News, 478

Natl. Sculpture Society
1177 6th Avenue, 15 Floor, New York, NY, 10036-2705
National Sculpture Society Newsletter, 66

National Self Help Clearinghouse
25 W. 43rd Street, New York, NY, 10036
Self Help Reporter Newsletter, 1,017

National Temporal Bone, Hearing, & Balance Pathology Registry
Deafness Research Foundation, 15 W. 39th St., New York, NY, 10018-3806
Registry, The, 533

Natl. Textile Processors Guild
75 Livingston St., Brooklyn, NY, 11201-5054
National Textile Processors Guild, Bulletins, 1,172

National Video Resources
73 Spring St Rm 606, New York, NY, 10012-5802
NVR Reports, 1,168

Natural Resources Defense Council
40 W 20th St Fl 11, New York, NY, 10011-4211
NRDC Newsline, 388

Nelson A. Rockefeller Institute of Govt.
411 State St, Albany, NY, 12203-1003
Rockefeller Institute Bulletin, 492

Neptune World Wide Moving
55 Weyman Ave, New Rochelle, NY, 10805-1410
Neptune on the Move, 591

Netherlands Chamber of Commerce in the USA
1 Rockefeller Plz., 11th Fl., New York, NY, 10020-2002
International Marketing Intelligence News, 648

Netherlands Consulate General, Economic Information Service
One Rockefeller Plz., New York, NY, 10020-2094
Holland Info., 631

New Dramatists
424 W 44th St, New York, NY, 10036-5298
Readings, 1,174

New Environment Association
270 Fenway Dr, Syracuse, NY, 13224-1537
New Environment Bulletin, 389

New Flag, The
30-08 Broadway, Suite #159, Queens, NY, 11106
La Nueva Bandera (The New Flag), 992

New Jewish Agenda
PO Box 198, New York, NY, 10116-0198
Agenda in Brief, 1,068

New Moon
Box 1471, Madison Square Station, New York, NY, 10159
Our Pagan Times, 1,074

New Music Seminar
332 Bleecker St # G-29, New York, NY, 10014-2980
Update: New Music Seminar, 919

•**New York Academy of Medicine**
2 E 103rd St, New York, NY, 10029-5207

New York Advertising & Communications Network, Inc.
Box 149, 332 Bleecker St., New York, NY, 10014-2980
Newsbreaks, 445

New York African Studies Association
STL-G14 Suny, New Paltz, NY, 12561
New York African Studies Association Newsletter, 322

New York Board of Trade
PO Box 3020, New York, NY, 10185-3020
Business Speaks, 130

New York Brass Conference for Scholarships
315 W 53rd St, New York, NY, 10019-5701
Brass Player, 910

New York Business Group on Health
622 3rd Ave Fl 34, New York, NY, 10017-6707
New York Business Group on Health, 146

•**New York Chamber of Commerce & Industry**
1 Battery Park Plz, New York, NY, 10004-1491

New York Chapter Hadassah
250 West 57th Street, New York, NY, 10107-0230
Highlights, 178

New York City Audubon Society
71 W 23rd St Ste 1430, New York, NY, 10010-4102
Urban Audubon, 395

New York City Board of Elections
200 Varick St Fl 10, New York, NY, 10014-4810
Election Connection, 484

New York City Commission on Human Rights
40 Rector St Fl 10, New York, NY, 10006-1705
RightsLine, 175

New York City Commission on the Status of Women
1 Cenre Street., #2358, New York, NY, 10007-1222
Status Report, 1,212

New York City Dept. for the Aging
2 Lafayette St., New York, NY, 10007-1307
Options, 1,108

New York City Department of Health
125 Worth St., Box 44, New York, NY, 10013-4006
CHI (City Health Information) Newsletter, 500

New York City Dept. of Records & Info Services
31 Chambers St Rm 305, New York, NY, 10007-1210
Notes, 490

New York City Elementary School Principals Assn.
Public School 48, 6015 18th Ave., Brooklyn, NY, 11204
New York Supervisor, 1,092

New York City Homebrewers Guild
299 Prospect Pl # 3f, Brooklyn, NY, 11238-3909
Written Wort, 106

New York City Housing Patrolmen's Benevolent Assn., Inc.
4740 21st St, Long Island City, NY, 11101-5407
On the Beat, 788

New York City Human Resources Administration
220 Church St., Rm. 657, New York, NY, 10013-3843
People, 1,120

New York City Library
5th Ave. & 42nd St., New York, NY, 10018
Library Workers for Peace Newsletter, 803

New York City Office of Business Development
17 John St., New York, NY, 10038-1610
OBD News, 490

New York City Opera
New York State Theater, 20 Lincoln Center, New York, NY, 10023
Curtain Call, 911

New York City Transit Authority
370 Jay St, Brooklyn, NY, 11201-3814
Transit Record, 1,181

New York Civil Liberties Union
132 W. 43rd St., New York, NY, 10036-6599
N.Y. Civil Liberties, 174

New York Conference of Mayors
119 Washington Ave, Albany, NY, 12210-2291
Across the Table, 481

•**New York Cotton Exchange**
4 World Trade Ctr., S.E. Plz., New York, NY, 10048-0137

New York County Lawyers' Association
14 Vesey St, New York, NY, 10007-2906
N.Y. County Lawyer, 759

New York Div. of State Athletic Commission
270 Broadway, New York, NY, 10007-2357
New York Division of State Athletic Commission, Bulletin, 1,133

New York Family Law Institute, Inc.
32 S Monsey Rd, P.O. Box 774, Monsey, NY, 10952-0774
New York Family Law Update, 762

New York Genealogical & Biographical Society
122 E. 58th St., New York, NY, 10022-1939
NYG&B Newsletter, The, 462

New York Hospital-Cornell Medical Center
525 E 68th St, New York, NY, 10021-4873
Window, 573

New York Housing Authority
250 Broadway, #917, New York, NY, 10007-2516
HDA World, 1,021

New York Institute of Legal Research
PO Box 398, Yorktown Heights, NY, 10598-0398
Journal of the New York Institute of Legal Research, 746

•**New York Legislative Service**
299 Broadway, New York, NY, 10007-1978

New York Library Assn.
252 Hudson Ave, Albany, NY, 12210-1802
NYLA Bulletin, 805

New York Life Insurance Co.
51 Madison Ave., #152, New York, NY, 10010-1655
New York Life News, 591

•**New York Mercantile Exchange**
4 World Trade Center, New York, NY, 10048-0137

New York Metropolitan Reference
57 E 11th St Fl 4, New York, NY, 10003-4605
For Reference, 798

New York News, Inc.
450 W. 33rd St., 3rd Fl., New York, NY, 10001-2603
News Pix, 592

New York Parent-Teacher Quarterly
10 Plymouth St, New Hyde Park, NY, 11040-3143
New York Parent-Teacher Quarterly, 322

New York Planning Federation
488 Broadway #313, Albany, NY, 12207-2911
Planning News, 1,023

New York Public Interest Research Group, Inc.
9 Murray St., New York, NY, 10007-2223
NYPIRG Agenda, 254

New York Public Library
Fifth Avenue & 42nd St., New York, NY, 10018
New York Public Library News, 805

New York School of Interior Design
170 E. 70th St., New York, NY, 10021-5110
NY School of Interior Design, 204

New York Special Olympics
504 Balltown Rd., Schenectady, NY, 12304-2201
Torch Bearer, 333

New York State AFL-CIO
100 S Swan St, Albany, NY, 12210-1939
Unity, 711

New York State Assn. of Teachers of Mentally Retarded
1721 E 54th St, Brooklyn, NY, 11234-3921
Special Teacher, 331

New York State Bankers Assn.
485 Lexington Ave Fl 25, New York, NY, 10017-2630
New York State Banker, 96

New York State Bar Association
1 Elk St, Albany, NY, 12207-1002
New York State Law Digest, 764

New York State Business Group
180 E. Main St., Patchogue, NY, 11772
Member Advantage, 144

New York State Council of Churches
362 State St., Albany, NY, 12210-1202
Ecumenical Chartings, 1,047

New York State Council of Genealogical Organizations
PO Box 2593, Syracuse, NY, 13220-2593
Lifeline, 459

New York State Dept. of Agriculture
1 Winners Circle, Albany, NY, 12235-0001
Journal, 42

New York State Dept. of Civil Service
State Office Building C/O, Public Relations Office, Albany, NY, 12239-0001
Stateline, 1,024

New York State Dept. Div. of Substance Abuse Services
1450 Western Ave., Albany, NY, 12203- 352
OASAS Today, 522

•**New York State Department of Environmental Conservation**
Division of Water, 50 Wolf Rd., Albany, NY, 12233

New York State Dept. of Labor
State Campus, Pubs. Unit Bldg., 12 Room 511, Albany, NY, 12240-0001
Employment in New York State, 343

New York State Div. for Women
Exec. Chamber, 2 World Trade Center, 57th fl., New York, NY, 10047
Women around New York, 1,213

* See ***MULTI-PUBLISHER INDEX*** for list of publications.

New York State Electric & Gas Corp.
4500 Vestal Parkway, Box 3607, Binghamton, NY, 13902-3607
Senior Sun, 1,109

New York State Energy Office
Two Rockefeller Plaza, Albany, NY, 12223-0001
ENERCOM, 352

New York State Insurance Dept.
160 W Broadway, New York, NY, 10013-3393
Bulletin, 618

New York State Library
Gift & Exchange Section, Albany, NY, 12225
New York State Library Bibliography Bulletin, 107

New York State Museum
Cultural Education Center Rm., 3136, Albany, NY, 12230-0001
Empire State Geogram-Research Issue, 476

New York State Office of Mental Health
44 Holland Avenue, Albany, NY, 12229
Statewide Comprehensive Plan for Mental Health Services, 1,011

New York State Public Employees Federation, AFL-CIO
1168 Troy Schenectady Rd # 7, Latham, NY, 12110-1006
Communicator, The, 342

New York State School Boards Association, Inc.
119 Washington Ave., Albany, NY, 12210-2284
Federal Legislative Bulletin, 1,091

New York State Society of Anesthesiologists
41 E 42nd St Rm 1605, New York, NY, 10017-5301
NYSSA Sphere, 881

•New York Telephone Co.
140 West St, New York, NY, 10007-2174

New York Times Newspaper Guild
229 W 43rd St, New York, NY, 10036-3913
Guild Watch, 923

•New York Turtle & Tortoise Society
163 Amsterdam Ave. #365, New York, NY, 10023-5001

New York Typographical Union No. 6
817 Broadway, New York, NY, 10003-4709
Number 6 Bulletin, 710

New York University
537 East Bldg., 239 Greene St., New York, NY, 10003
New York University Education Quarterly, 322

New York Univ. Alumni Dept.
25 W 4th St, New York, NY, 10012-1119
Gallatin Today, 191

•New York Univ. Elmer Holmes Bobst Library
70 Washington Sq S, New York, NY, 10012-1019

•New York Univ. Graduate School of Arts and Science
25 W 4th St Fl 5, New York, NY, 10012-1119

New York Univ. Libraries
70 Washington Sq S, New York, NY, 10012-1019
Tamiment Library Bulletin, 811

•New York Univ. Medical Center
550 1st Ave, New York, NY, 10016-6481

New York University Public Affairs Office
7 E 12th St Fl 11, New York, NY, 10003-4475
Changing Scenes, 204

New York University, Society for the Libraries
70 Washington Sq S, New York, NY, 10012-1019
New York University, Society for the Libraries Bulletin, 805

New York Univ. Stern School of Business Graduate Div.
Public Relations, 40 W. 4th St., Rm. 537, New York, NY, 10012-7501
Stern Alumni News & Notes, 191

New York Youth Bureau
44 Court St., Brooklyn, NY, 11201-4463
Youth Bureau News, 1,216

New Yorkers for Companion Animals
1324 Lexington Ave. #2, New York, NY, 10128
NYCA News, 50

•Newkirk Products, Inc.
15 Corporate Cir, Albany, NY, 12203-5154

News
200 Park Ave. #6Fl-W, New York, NY, 10166-0005
News; New York League of Savings Institution, 96

Newsday
Electronic Publishing, 235 Pinelawn Rd., Melville, NY, 11747-4250
Newsday Connections, 924

•Newsweek, Inc.
251 W 57th St, New York, NY, 10019-1802

NexTech Systems Corp.
3671 Old Yorktown Rd., Shrub Oak, NY, 10588
NexTech Users Group Newsletter, 232

Niagara Falls Memorial Medical Ctr.
621 10th St., Niagara Falls, NY, 14301-1890
Healthbeat, 511

Nigerian Consulate General
828 2nd Ave, New York, NY, 10017-4301
Nigerian Students Union in the Americas Newsletter, 204

Nikkei Weekly
1325 Ave. of the Americas, New York, NY, 10019
Nikkei Weekly, 977

Nippon Club, Inc.
145 W 57th St., New York, NY, 10019
Nippon Club Dayori, 180

•Nissen-Lie Communications
441 Lexington Ave Rm 1209a, New York, NY, 10017-3910

No-Load Fund Investor, Inc.
Box 318, Irvington-on-Hudson, NY, 10533
No-Load Fund Investor, 680

Norma A. Lee Co.
220 E. 54th St., Apt. 4H, New York, NY, 10022-4839
P.R. Clock, 20

North America Aliya Movement
110 E 59th St Frnt 3, New York, NY, 10022-1304
NAAM Letter, 1,069

North American Conferncе on Ethiopian Jewry
165 E 56th St, New York, NY, 10022-2709
Lifeline, 1,069

North American Federation of Temple Youth
838 5th Ave, New York, NY, 10021-7012
Ani V'atah, 1,068

North Country Library System
Outer W. Main St., Box 99, Watertown, NY, 13601
North Country Library News, 806

North Country Reference Research
7 Commerce Ln, Canton, NY, 13617-9666
North Country Reference Research, 806

North Shore Agency
117 Cutter Mill Rd., Great Neck, NY, 11021
Credit Line, The, 257

Northeastern Limousine Operators Association
P.O. Box 2239-ESP, Albany, NY, 12220-0239
Northeastern Limousine Operators Association Nor'Easter Newsletter, 1,179

•Northern Business Information/Datapro
1221 Ave. of the Americas #3, New York, NY, 10020-1001

Notes from the Songwriters Showcase
PO Box 8098, 600 Franklin Ave., Garden City, NY, 11530
Notes from the Songwriters Showcase, 915

Nuclear Records Management Assn.
210 5th Ave., New York, NY, 10010-2102
NRMA Newsletter, 356

Numismatic Counseling Inc.
PO Box 38, Plainview, NY, 11803-0038
Rosen Numismatic Advisory, 928

Nurses Assn. of the Counties of Long Island
99 Tulip Ave # 404, Floral Park, NY, 11001-1959
Nursing News, 931

Nutrition Forum
7111 60th Ave., Maspeth, NY, 11378-2907
Nutrition Forum, 934

Nyando Roots Genealogical Club
PO Box 175, Massena, NY, 13662-0175
Nyando Roots, 463

O'Brien
4985 Meadowbrook Rd, Williamsville, NY, 14221-4215
National Faculty Placement Bureau Bulletin, 321

OCR
521 W. 23rd St., New York, NY, 10011
Routes, 370

OR Orange and Rockland Utilities
1 Blue Hill Plz, Pearl River, NY, 10965-3104
OR ServiceLine, 1,027

•Oceana Publications, Inc.
75 Main St, Dobbs Ferry, NY, 10522-1601

Office for the Aging
2 Empire State Plz, Albany, NY, 12223-1200
Aging News, 1,106

Office of the Borough Pres. of Manhattan
Municipal Bldg., New York, NY, 10007
Manhattan Forum, 1,042

Office of the Borough President
209 Joralemon St., Rm 320, Brooklyn, NY, 11201
Brooklyn Newsletter, 481

Office of Borough President
The Bronx County Building, 851 Grand Concourse, Bronx, NY, 10451
Bronx Report, The, 1,019

Office of Tibet
801 Second Ave., New York, NY, 10017
News-Tibet, 635

Oley Foundation for Home Parenteral & Enteral Nutrition
214 Hun Memorial, Albany Medical Ctr. A-23, Albany, NY, 12208-3478
LifelineLetter, 933

Omega Institute
260 Lake Dr, Rhinebeck, NY, 12572-3212
Friends of Omega, 922

The Omnipotent Nectarine
286 Croidin Place, #2E, Brooklyn, NY, 11235
The Omnipotent Nectarine, 472

Once Daily, Inc.
263 West End Ave Apt 2a, New York, NY, 10023-2613
Holistic Dental Digest Plus, 512

•Opera Index, Inc.
P.O. Box 492 Gracie Stn., New York, NY, 10028

Orange County Agricultural Co-Op Extension Service
Community Campus, Dillion Drive, Middletown, NY, 10940
Orange County Ag Focus, 44

Orange County Cooperative Extension, Agricultural Division
239 Wisner Ave, Middletown, NY, 10940-2400
Ag Focus, 36

Orientalia Journal
PO Box 94, Little Neck, NY, 11363-0094
Orientalia Journal, 635

Orthodox Union
333 7th Ave, New York, NY, 10001-5072
Our Way - NCSY, 267

Our Lady of Victory Homes of Charity
Ridge Rd., Lackawanna, NY, 14218
Victorian, 1,123

Our Voice
365 W 25th St Apt 13e, New York, NY, 10001-5816
Our Voice, 522

•Overseas Academic Opportunities
P.O. Box 768, Merrick, NY, 11566-0368

Overseas Press Club of America, Inc.
320 E. 42nd St., New York, NY, 10017-5900
Overseas Press Club Bulletin, 697

Owner Operators of America
PO Box 582, Orchard Park, NY, 14127-0582
Owner Operator News, 1,193

P.E.N. American Center
568 Broadway Rm 401, New York, NY, 10012-3225
PEN Newsletter, 824

PKF Consulting
420 Lexington Ave., Suite 2400, New York, NY, 10170
Trends in the Hotel Industry New York City, 575

•PM Inc.
1185 Ave of The Americas, New York, NY, 10036-2601

PSI, Inc.
75 Maiden Lane, 12th Fl., New York, NY, 10038-4810
India Business and Investment Report, 647

PS Reports
PO Box 48, Mineola, NY, 11501-0048
PS: Intelligent Guide to Jewish Affairs, 995

PTN Publishing Co.
445 Broad Hollow Rd., Ste. 21, Melville, NY, 11747-3601
TC-HW Reporter, 250

•Pace Publications
443 Park Ave. South, New York, NY, 10016

Paget's Disease Foundation, Inc.
200 Varick Street, # 1004, New York, NY, 10014-4810
PDF Update, 883

Palatines to America
Elpis Rd., RD #1, Box 128, Camden, NY, 13316
Yorker Palatine Newsletter, 470

Paleontological Research Institution
1259 Trumansburg Rd, Ithaca, NY, 14850-1313
American Paleontologist, 475

Palestine Liberation Organization
115 E 65th St, New York, NY, 10021-7006
Palestine Issue, 636

Pan Hellenic Society Inventors of Greece in U.S.A.
2053 Narwood Ave., South Merrick, NY, 11566-3927
Pan Hellenic Society Inventors of Greece in U.S.A. Newsletter, 951

* See **MULTI-PUBLISHER INDEX** for list of publications.

Paperweight Collectors' Assn.
47 Windsor Rd, Scarsdale, NY, 10583-4824
Paperweight Collectors' Association, Bulletin, 555

Paramount Pictures Corp.
Gulf & Western Bldg., New York, NY, 10023
Paramount World, 594

ParentAge
27 W 20th St Ste 305, New York, NY, 10011-3707
ParentAge, 415

Parent SIG
PO Box 2377, New York, NY, 10185-2377
Parent SIG, 415

Parenting Center Newsletter
92nd St. Y, 1395 Lexington, New York, NY, 10128
Parenting Center Newsletter, 415

Park Avenue South Publications
165 W. 46th St., New York, NY, 10036-2501
Park Avenue South, 20

Parker Geriatric Institute
27111 76th Ave, New Hyde Park, NY, 11040-1423
Misuse of Medications, 1,107

Parkinson's Disease Foundation
710 W 168th St, 10th FL., New York, NY, 10032-9982
Parkinson's Disease Foundation-Newsletter, 883

Parsons Child/Family Center
60 Academy Rd, Albany, NY, 12208-3103
Spectrum, 1,122

Partyline Publishing
35 Sutton Pl, New York, NY, 10022-2464
Partyline, Public Relations Media Newsletter, 20

Paul McArthur
P.O. Box 401, Camillus, NY, 13031
Wrestlin Perspective, 1,137

Pedal Steel Guitar Assn.
PO Box 248, Floral Park, NY, 11002-0248
Pedal Steel Newsletter, 916

Penny Pincher
PO Box 809, Kings Park, NY, 11754-0809
Penny Pincher, 415

People-To-People Sports Committee, Inc.
80 Cutter Mill Rd., Great Neck, NY, 11021-3108
People to People Sports Newsletter, 1,134

People With AIDS Coalition (N.Y.)
245 8th Ave # 316, New York, NY, 10011-1607
PWA Coalition Newsline, 523

People With AIDS (PWA) Health Group
150 W 26th St Rm 201, New York, NY, 10001-6813
Notes from the Underground, 521

Peoplenet
PO Box 897, Levittown, NY, 11756-0911
Peoplenet, 816

Peregrine Communications
160 E 48th St, New York, NY, 10017-1225
Beverage Alcohol Market Report, 102

The Perot Peerodical
PO Box 435, Riverdale, NY, 10471
Perot Periodical, 996

Pet Services Unlimited
1625 Emmons Ave., Brooklyn, NY, 11235-2758
Tatoo-A-Pet News, 50

•**Peter Berlin Retail Consulting Group, Inc.**
380 N Broadway Ste 206, Jericho, NY, 11753-2109

•**Peter Katz Productions**
PO Box 831, White Plains, NY, 10602-0831

•**Petroleum Intelligence Weekly, Inc.**
575 Broadway 4th Fl., New York, NY, 10012

•**Pharmabooks**
1775 Broadway Ste 511, New York, NY, 10019-1903

Phi Chi Chronicles
Central Office - Phi Chi, 1201 E. Spring St., New Albany, NY, 47150
Phi Chi Chronicles, 884

Phillip Morris, USA
800 Westchester Ave., Rye Brook, NY, 10573
Phillip Morris Globe, 594

Phillips Business Info.
305 Madison Ave., Ste. 4417, New York, NY, 10165-0006
MIN: Media Industry Newsletter, 858

Photocollect
740 West End Ave., New York, NY, 10025-6246
Photofolio, 977

Photographic Arts Center
163 Amsterdam Ave #201, New York, NY, 10023-5001
Photograph Collector, 977

Photographics Unlimited
17 W. 17th St.,, New York, NY, 10011-5510
PWP Newsletter, 977

Photography for Industry (PFI) Books
38 Rick Lane, W., RR4, Peekskill, NY, 10566-9804
Rotkin Review, 978

Pictorial Photographers of America
299 W. 12th St., New York, NY, 10014-1824
Light and Shade, 976

Picture Buyer
32 Union Square, New York, NY, 10003
Picture Buyer and F.P.G. Newsletter to Photographers, 978

Pierce-Arrow Society, Inc.
135 Edgerton St, Rochester, NY, 14607-2945
Pierce-Arrow Service Bulletin, 75

Pirquet Bulletin of Clinical Medicine
310 E 14th St, New York, NY, 10003-4200
Pirquet Bulletin of Clinical Medicine, 884

Planners Network
379 DeKalb Avenue, Brooklyn, NY, 11205
Planners' Network Newsletter, 1,023

Planning Bureau, Police Dept., City of New York
1 Police Plz, New York, NY, 10038-1403
Police Management Review, 789

Players, The
16 Gramercy Park S, New York, NY, 10003-1705
Brief Chronicles, 1,172

Poetry Society of America
15 Gramercy Park S, New York, NY, 10003-1705
Poetry Society of America Newsletter, 983

Polish Assistance, Inc.
15 E. 65th St., New York, NY, 10021-6501
Polish Assistance Bulletin, 407

Polish Institute of Arts
208 E 30th St, New York, NY, 10016-8202
PIASA Bulletin, The, 636

Polish Veterans of W.W. II
PO Box 179, New York, NY, 10116-0179
Kombatant W Ameryce, 179

•**Political Risk Services**
6320 Fly Road Suite #102, PO Box 248, East Syracuse, NY, 13057-0248

Political Woman
276 Chatterton Pky., White Plains, NY, 10606-2012
Political Woman Hotline, 996

Pollack Associates
140 E. 81st St., Apt 5E, New York, NY, 10028-1875
Supermarket Strategic Alert, 495

Poplar Ridge Vineyards
9782 Rt 414, Valois, NY, 14888
Case Club News, 103

Portuguese National Tourist Office
590 Fifth Avenue, 4th Floor, New York, NY, 10036-4704
Portugal Update, 1,188

Positive Workforce for America, Inc.
PO Box 365, Hillsdale, NY, 12529-0365
Americans with Disabilities Newsletter, 276

Postgraduate Center for Mental Health
124 E 28th St, New York, NY, 10016-8402
Postgraduate Center for Mental Health-News, 884

Practising Law Institute
810 7th Ave., New York, NY, 10019-5856
Business Accounting for Lawyers Newsletter, 2

Presbyterian Peace Fellowships
PO Box 271, Nyack, NY, 10960-0271
Briefly, 1,074

Preschool Pubs., Inc.
PO Box 1167, Cutchogue, NY, 11935-0888
Parent & Preschooler, 324

Preservation League of New York State
44 Central Ave, Albany, NY, 12206-3002
Preservation New York, 547

Price Waterhouse
1251 Ave. of Americas, New York, NY, 10020
Federal Budget Report, 484

Private Effort
90 Park Ave Fl 12, New York, NY, 10016-1301
WMF Newsletter, 155

Pro Israel/Yesha Heartland Campaign
17 East 45th Street, Suite 603, New York, NY, 10017
Yesha Report, The, 404

Probe Newsletter, Inc.
139 W 13th St., Apt 6, New York, NY, 10011-7856
Probe Newsletter, 1,099

Prodigy Services Co.
445 Hamilton Ave, White Plains, NY, 10601-1807
Prodigy Star, 234

Program for Art on Film
2875 Broadway, 2nd Fl., New York, NY, 10025-7805
Art on Screen, 62

Protestant Teachers Assn.
71 W 23rd St, New York, NY, 10010-4156
Protestant Teachers Association Newsletter, 1,065

Psychology Society
100 Beekman St., New York, NY, 10038-1810
PS: It Is News, 1,016

Public Affairs Information Service, Inc.
521 W 43rd St, 5th Floor, New York, NY, 10036-4396
PAIS International News, 807

Public Concern Foundation
PO Box 20065, London Terrace Station, New York, NY, 10011-0008
Washington Spectator, 1,000

Public Education Association
39 W. 32nd, New York, NY, 10001-3803
Public Education Alert, 326

Public Employment Relations Board
80 Wolf Rd Fl 5, Albany, NY, 12205-2604
PERB News, 704

Public Relations News
PO Box 1416, New York, NY, 10021-1416
Public Relations News, 861

Public Relations Society of America, Inc.
33 Irving Place, New York, NY, 10003-2376
Cyberspace PR Newsletter, 13

Publishers Information Bureau
919 Third Ave., 22nd Fl., New York, NY, 10022
Publishers Information Bureau-Reports, 21

Pubwatch
350 W. 85th Street, New York, NY, 10024
Pubwatch Update, 119

Punch in Syndicate
400 E. 59th St., Apt. 9F, New York, NY, 10022-2344
Travel Food & Wine, 1,190

Puppetry Guild of Greater NY
PO Box 117, New York, NY, 10116-0117
New York Puppet Times, 1,173

Q-M Consulting Group, Inc.
141 5th Ave 12th Fl, New York, NY, 10010-7105
PC Software & Hardware Evaluation Newsletter, 233

Quaker UN Office
777 UN Plaza, New York, NY, 10017
In & Around the United Nations, 632

Quality of Care for Mentally Disabled
99 Washington Ave Ste 1002, Albany, NY, 12210-2801
Quality of Care, 278

Queens Borough Public Library
8911 Merrick Blvd, Jamaica, NY, 11432-5200
Library Matters, 802

Queens Botanical Garden Society Inc.
4350 Main St, Flushing, NY, 11355-4742
Queens Botanical Garden News, 443

Queens County Bar Assn.
9035 148th St, Jamaica, NY, 11435-4097
Queens County Bar Association, Queens Bar Bulletin, 772

Quickel International Corp.
25 5th Ave Apt 4c, New York, NY, 10003-4308
U.S. Investment Report, 690

Quintcentennial Foundation of Istanbul
c/o GCI Group, 777 Third Avenue, 23rd Fl, New York, NY, 10017
Quintcentennial Quarterly, The, 409

RPCV Writers & Readers
4 Lodge Pole Rd, Pittsford, NY, 14534-4550
RPCV Writers & Readers, 824

Rabbinical Alliance of America
3 W. 16th St. 4th Fl., New York, NY, 10011-6363
Perspective, 1,070

Radio Advertising Bureau
304 Park Ave S, New York, NY, 10010-5312
RAB Instant Background, 125

Radius, Group, Inc.
408 West 57th Street, New York, NY, 10019-3053
Arts Management, 259

Rail Splitter, The
PO Box 275, New York, NY, 10044
Rail Splitter, The, 185

Rainforest Alliance
65 Bleeker Street, New York, NY, 10012-2187
Canopy, 374

Raisin Blowme
31 West Northrup Pl., Buffalo, NY, 14214-1162
Bufaloon Newsletter, 604

Random House
201 E. 50th St., New York, NY, 10022-7799
Both Angles, 116

* See **MULTI-PUBLISHER INDEX** for list of publications.

Readers' Digest Publications
28 W. 23rd, New York, NY, 10010-5204
50 Plus -the Benefits Bulletin, 1,105

•**Readmore**
22 Cortlandt St., New York, NY, 10007-3194

Record Research
65 Grand Ave, Brooklyn, NY, 11205-2593
Record Research, 917

Redstone Publishing
8 Thomas St., New York, NY, 10007-1197
Stock Shooter, 978

Reed Business Publishing Company
475 Park Ave S, Front 2, New York, NY, 10016-6901
Information Privacy, 1,103

Reed Organ Society, The
The Musical Museum, Deansboro, NY, 13328
ROS Bulletin, 907

Refundle Bundle
Box 141, Centuck Sta., Yonkers, NY, 10710-0141
Refundle Bundle, 255

Rehabilitation Intl.
25 E 21st St, New York, NY, 10010-6298
One-In-Ten, 882

Relay
Box 1670, Canal St. Station, New York, NY, 10013-1670
Who: The Relay, The, 919

Reliability Analysis Center
201 Mill St # 4700, Rome, NY, 13440-6916
RAC Journal, 363

Religion in American Life
2 Queenston Pl., #200, Princeton, NY, 08540-3820
RIAL News, 1,050

Religious Zionists of America
25 W. 26th St., New York, NY, 10010-1077
Hamizrachi, 1,068

Remove Intoxicated Drivers-USA, Inc.
PO Box 520, Schenectady, NY, 12301-0520
RID-USA National Newsletter, 772

Renee Phillips Assocs.
200 E 72nd St Apt 26l, New York, NY, 10021-4546
Success Now! for Artists, 67

Rensselaerville Inst.
Pond Hill Rd., Rensselaerville, NY, 12147
Rensselaerville Newsletter, 1,100

•**Research Institute of America**
90 5th Avenue, New York, NY, 10011-7629

Resources for Personal Empowerment
Box 20316, New York, NY, 10028-0052
Model Mugging News, 1,082

RestQuest Corporation
72 Spring Street, New York, NY, 10012
RestQuest Compass, 1,188

Restaurant Business, Inc.
355 Park Ave S Fl 3, New York, NY, 10010-1706
Karas Executive Report, 1,075

•**Retail Reporting Corp.**
302 5th Ave Fl 11, New York, NY, 10001-3604

Retarded Infants Services
386 Park Ave., S., New York, NY, 10016-8804
Retarded Infants Services News, 1,121

Rhodes Press
50 Broadway, Hawthorne, NY, 10532-1245
Rhodes Real Estate Review, 773

Richardson Boat Owners Association
C/O Chamber of Commerce, 20 Main St., Tonawanda, NY, 14150-2106
Cruisabout, 113

Risk Manaement Unit
100 Church Street, 20th Floor, New York, NY, 10007
Risky Business, 492

•**Risk Management Society Publishing, Inc.**
655 Third Ave., 2nd Floor, New York, NY, 10017

Robert J. Fabian Foundation
Box 1303, Old Chelsea Stn., New York, NY, 10011-1303
Chronic Pain Letter, 502

•**Robert Miko**
PO Box 1312, New York, NY, 10018-0727

Robin Hadley
P.O. Box 424, Sea Cliff, NY, 11579
Kestrel, 982

Rochester Engineering Society
1806 Lyell Ave, Rochester, NY, 14606-2396
Rochester Engineer, 363

Rochester Genealogical Society
PO Box 10501, Rochester, NY, 14610-0501
Hear Ye Hear Ye, 456

Rochester Institute of Technology Alumni Relations
Box 9887, Alumni Relations Dept., Rochester, NY, 14623-0887
Photo Scientist, 977

Rochester Savings Bank
40 Franklin St, Rochester, NY, 14604-1413
RSB Dollars, 596

•**Rockefeller Archive Center**
15 Dayton Ave., Pocantico Hills, North Tarrytown, NY, 10591-1598

Roditti Reports Corp.
954 Lexington Ave # 253, New York, NY, 10021-5013
Computer Law & Tax Report, 216

•**Roosevelt Hospital**
428 W 59th St, New York, NY, 10019-1192

Roosevelt Savings Bank
1122 Franklin Ave, Garden City, NY, 11530-1694
Roosevelt Review, 597

Roper Organization
205 E. 42nd St., New York, NY, 10017-5706
Public Pulse, The, 1,126

Roper Starch Worldwide
566 E Boston Post Rd, Mamaroneck, NY, 10543-3705
Starch Tested Copy, 22

Royal Club of Oz
Box 714, New York, NY, 10011
Emerald City Mirror, 168

•**Royal-Globe Insurance Cos.**
1 Chase Manhattan Plz., 38th Fl., New York, NY, 10005-1401

Royal Mail
152 Madison Ave., Ste. 304, New York, NY, 10157-1973
Royal Mail, The, 275

Royal Society of Medicine
150 E 58th St Fl 32, New York, NY, 10155-0002
AIDS Letter, 864

Ruder, Finn & Rotman
301 E. 57th St., New York, NY, 10022-2995
Japan Trade Center Information Service Monthly Economic Report, 633

S&B Report
108 East 38th Street, New York, NY, 10016
S&B Report, 56

SEIU, Local 32E
4234 Bronx Blvd, Bronx, NY, 10466-2611
32E Events, 706

SIECUS (Sex Information & Education Council of the U.S.)
New York, NY, 10003
SIECUS Report, 1,110

•**SIGS Publications Group**
71 W. 23rd Street, 3rd Floor, New York, NY, 10010-4102

S.J. Rundt Assocs.
130 E. 63rd St., New York, NY, 10021-7334
Rundt's Weekly Intelligence, 651

SKO/Brenner America
196 Merrick Rd, Oceanside, NY, 11572-1420
Executives' Digest, 837

•**SMR International**
Box 948, Murray Hill Station, New York, NY, 10156-0948

SUNY Maritime College
Ft. Schuyler, Bronx, NY, 10465
Maritime College at Fort Schuyler, 203

SUNY Maritime College Humanities Dept.
Publications, Bronx, NY, 10465
Journal of the William Morris Society in the United States, 818

SUNY-Upstate Medical Ctr.
766 Irving Ave, Syracuse, NY, 13210-1605
Library Bulletin, 802

SUNY at Stony Brook Dept. Philosophy
Publications, Stony Brook, NY, 11794-0001
IAPL Newsletter, 974

SYOL
Box 728 Westview Stn., Binghamton, NY, 13905-0728
Amethyst, 444

Sacred Orchard Corporation
Po Box 298, Harriman, NY, 10926-0298
Meditator's Newsletter, 1,048

St. Andrew Society of the State of N.Y.
71 W. 23rd St., New York, NY, 10010
Pibroch, 408

St. George Assn. of the U.S.A.
83 Christopher St, New York, NY, 10014-4248
St. George Association Newsletter, 1,051

St. Gregory Illuminator Church of Armenia
630 2nd Ave, New York, NY, 10016-4806
Lousavorich, 1,058

St. Joseph's College
245 Clinton Ave, Brooklyn, NY, 11205-3688
Footprints, 203

St. Joseph's Union Staten Island, Inc.
108 Bedell St, Staten Island, NY, 10309-3302
Messenger of St. Joseph's Union, 1,058

St. Lawrence County Historical Association
3 E Main St, P.O Box 8, Canton, NY, 13617-0008
Newsletter of St. Lawrence City Historical Association, 545

St. Vladimir's Orthodox Theological Seminary
575 Scarsdale Rd., Crestwood, NY, 10707-1199
SVS News, 1,054

Saks Fifth Avenue
611 5th Ave, New York, NY, 10022-6899
Saks Fifth Avenue News, 597

Salmagundi Club
47 5th Ave, New York, NY, 10003-4396
The Salmagundian, 66

Samisdat Publishers
Box 791, Main P.O., Niagara Falls, NY, 14302-0791
Samisdat Publishers, 998

Sandford Advertising, Inc.
363 7th Ave, New York, NY, 10001-3904
Sandy Parker Reports: Weekly Intl. Fur News, 437

Sanus Health Plan of Greater New York/New Jersey
75-20 Astoria Blvd., Jackson Heights, NY, 11370
Sanus Healthy Update, 527

Sarah Lawrence College
Publications, 1 Meadway, Bronxville, NY, 10708-5999
Whittemore Newsletter, 1,052

•**Saratoga County Historical Society**
Saratoga County Museum, 6 Charlton Street, Ballston Spa, NY, 12020-1707

Sasiac Unlimited
153 E Beech St, Long Beach, NY, 11561-4119
Sasiac, 1,135

Sawchuk, Brown Associates
41 State St., Ste. 500, Albany, NY, 12207-2833
Albany Report, 985

Scan Newsletter
11 Middle Neck Rd., Great Neck, NY, 11021-2301
Scan Newsletter, 237

Scenic Hudson
9 Vassar St, Poughkeepsie, NY, 12601-3091
Scenic Hudson News, 393

Schenectady County Community College
78 Washington Ave, Schenectady, NY, 12305-2215
Van Curler Newsletter, 204

Scherago Associates, Inc.
11 Penn Plz Rm 1003, New York, NY, 10001-2006
Science Marketing Newsletter, 22

Schnell Publishing Co., Inc.
80 Broad St Fl 23, New York, NY, 10004-2209
Chemical Profiles, 163

Scholastic Inc.
555 Broadway, New York, NY, 10012-3999
Bananas, 604

Schoonmaker Assocs.
PO Box 973, Coram, NY, 11727-0973
Mainly Marketing, 17

Science Support Center
Box 7507, FDR Station, NY, NY, 10150-7507
Medical Research Funding Bulletin, 968

•**Scientific American, Inc.**
415 Madison Ave., New York, NY, 10017-1179

•**Scientific Newsletters**
Rr 4 Box 7, Middletown, NY, 10940-9685

Scientists' Institute for Public Information
1328 Broadway #300, New York, NY, 10001-2121
SIPIscope, 1,100

Scovill, Paterson Inc.
141 Fifth Avenue, New York, NY, 10010
Student Aid Newsletter, 332

•**Seagram Distillers Co.**
375 Park Avenue, New York, NY, 10152-0152

Searchlight
Route #8, Carmel, NY, 10512-9808
Searchlight, 467

•**Securities Data Co.**
40 W 57th St Ste 802, New York, NY, 10019-4001

Securities Data Publishing, Inc.
40 W. 57th St., Ste. 802, New York, NY, 10019-4001
Venture Capital Journ., 690

•**Securities Industry Assn.**
120 Broadway, New York, NY, 10271-0080

* See **MULTI-PUBLISHER INDEX** for list of publications.

Security Letter
166 E 96th St, New York, NY, 10128-2565
Security Letter, 1,104

Seneca Nation of Indians
Box 231, Plummer Bldg., Salamanca, NY, 14779-0231
Oh Hi Yoh Noh, 406

•**Senior Action in A Gay Environment**
208 W 13th St, New York, NY, 10011-7702

Separation/Divorce Newsletter
18 Reade Pl., Poughkeepsie, NY, 12601-4507
Separation/Divorce Newsletter, 775

Shafer Books, Inc.
PO Box 40, Croton On Hudson, NY, 10520-0040
Software Legal Book, 424

Sharleen Leahey
P.O. Box 090-312, Brooklyn, NY, 11209-0006
Song's for Peace, 472

Shearson Lehman Bros.
1 Penn Plz, New York, NY, 10119-0082
Weekly Futures Research Report, 691

•**Shell Oil Company, Shell Chemical Co.**
50 W 50th St, New York, NY, 10112-1507

Shippers Natl. Freight Claim Council, Inc.
120 Main St # Z, Huntington, NY, 11743-6906
Claim Digest, 1,111

Shoals Marine Laboratory
Cornell Univ., G-14 Stimson Hall, Ithaca, NY, 14853-7101
Appledore Times, 935

Shrine of Our Lady of Martyrs
Noeltener Road, Auriesville, NY, 12016
Pilgrim, 1,059

Shubert Archive
149 W. 45th St., New York, NY, 10036-4004
Passing Show, 1,174

Sierra Club, Atlantic Chapter
353 Hamilton St, Albany, NY, 12210-1709
Sierra Atlantic, 394

Sierra Club-NYC Group
625 Broadway Fl 2, New York, NY, 10012-2611
City Sierran, 375

Signalert Corp.
150 Great Neck Rd Ste 204, Great Neck, NY, 11021-3309
Systems & Forecasts, 688

Simmons-Boardman Publishing Corp.
345 Hudson St., New York, NY, 10014-4590
Bank Directors Briefing, 81

Sisterhood of Black Single Mothers
1504 Bedford Ave, Brooklyn, NY, 11216-4116
Sisterhood Newsletter, 1,211

Sisters of Charity Hospital
2157 Main St, Buffalo, NY, 14214-2648
Horizons, 565

•**Skin Cancer Foundation**
245 Fifth Ave., Ste. 2402, New York, NY, 10016

Sleepy Hollow Restorations
150 White Plains Rd., Tarrytown, NY, 10591-5521
Friends Newsletter, 60

Slovak-American Cultural Center
20219 36th Ave, Bayside, NY, 11361-1157
Slovak Press Digest, 409

Small Business Advisors
PO Box 436, Woodmere, NY, 11598-0436
The Small Business Advisor, 152

Small Press Center
50 W. 44th St., New York, NY, 10036-6604
Small Press Center News, 120

Smith Restaurant Supply Co.
500 Erie Blvd E, Syracuse, NY, 13202-1109
Smith Restaurant Supply, 1,076

Snow Lion Publishing
PO Box 6483, Ithaca, NY, 14851-6483
Snow Lion Newsletter & Catalog, 1,054

Soap & Detergent Assn.
475 Park Ave S, New York, NY, 10016-6947
SDA Newsletter, 166

Society for the Advancement of Judaism
15 W 86th St, New York, NY, 10024-3601
Society for the Advancement of Judaism Bulletin, 1,071

•**Society of American Archivists**
New York State Archives C.E.C., Empire State Plaza, Albany, NY, 12230-0001

Society of Animal Artists
151 Carroll St # 24, Bronx, NY, 10464-1430
Society of Animal Artists Newsletter, 67

Society for the Anthropology of Visual Communication
Suny/Brockport, Anthrop. Dept., Brockport, NY, 14420
SAVICOM, 52

Society of Glass Decorators
207 Grant St, Port Jefferson, NY, 11777-1230
SGD Newsletter, 249

Society of Maritime Arbitrators, Inc.
61 Broadway Rm 1650, New York, NY, 10006-2701
Arbitrator, 1,111

Society of the New York Hospital
528 E 68th St, New York, NY, 10021-6342
New York Hospital News, 569

Society of Publication Designers
60 E 42nd St Rm 721, New York, NY, 10165-0799
Grids, 1,004

Society of Rosicrucians
Box 192-13, Preston Hollow, NY, 12469
Mercury, 179

Sommelier Society of America
205 E. 25th St., New York, NY, 10159
Sommelier Society of America-Newsletter, 105

Songwriters Club
C/O Robert Makinson, Box 023304, Brooklyn, NY, 11202-0066
Songwriters & Lyricist Club Newsletter, 918

Sotheby's
980 Madison Ave., New York, NY, 10021
Sotheby's Newsletter, 54

South Street Seaport Museum
207 Front St, New York, NY, 10038-2106
South Street Seaport Museum Development Beacon, 908

•**Southeast Asia Program- Cornell Univ.**
640 Stewart Ave., Ithaca, NY, 14850

Southern Brooklyn Community Organization
4520 18th Ave, Brooklyn, NY, 11204-1204
Community Advocate, 1,020

Southern Tier Library System
301 Civic Plaza, Corning, NY, 14830
Topics, 811

Space Philatelists Intl. Society
C/O Martin Michaelson, Box 771, West Nyack, NY, 10994
Rapid Notice News Service, 972

Space Settlement Studies Project
Niagara Univ., Sociology Dept., New York, NY, 14109
Extraterrestrial Society, 29

Spanish Benevolent Society
239 W 14th St, New York, NY, 10011-7144
Plus Ultra, 402

Special Libraries Assn., Upstate New York Chapter
Stuyvesant Plaza, C/O Kate Storms, Albany, NY, 12203-3790
Special Libraries Association, Upstate New York Chapter Bulletin, 810

Sperry Corp.
Mail Sta. 1W113, Marcus Ave., Great Neck, NY, 11020
Technology Report, 898

•**Springer-Verlag Inc.**
175 5th Ave., New York, NY, 10010-7858

Sri Lanka Association of New York, Inc.
19 Lake Ave, New Rochelle, NY, 10801-2311
Sri Lankan, 409

•**Standard & Poor's Corp.**
25 Broadway, New York, NY, 10004

•**Stardust Dance Productions**
Church St., Box 157, Woodburne, NY, 12788

State Univ. of New York
Publications, Syracuse, NY, 13210
Upstate Medical Center Library Bulletin, 812

Staten Island Historical Society
441 Clarke Ave, Staten Island, NY, 10306-1125
Historic Richmond Town, 541

Staten Island Inst. of Arts & Sciences
75 Stuyvesant Pl, Staten Island, NY, 10301-1912
S.I.I.A.S. News, 908

Staten Island Mental Health Society, Inc.
669 Castleton Ave, Staten Island, NY, 10301-2028
On Location, 1,016

Steel Industry Weekly Review Ltd.
2 Uxbridge Rd, Scarsdale, NY, 10583-2725
Steel Industry Weekly Review, 901

Steinway
Steinway Place, Long Island City, NY, 11105
Lyra, 914

Stellar-7 Communications
532 Lakeview Ave # 2, Jamestown, NY, 14701-3352
Eagle-Eye Communicator, 471

Stephen Wolf Publishers
247 Arlington Ave, Syracuse, NY, 13207-1603
Between the Lines, 101

Stephen Wright
Box 1341, F.D.R. Station, New York, NY, 10150-1341
Mystery Notebook, 920

Studio Museum
144 W. 125th St., New York, NY, 10027-4423
Education Program Calendar, 904

Sun Words
332 Furman St., Schenectady, NY, 12304-1118
RE News Digest, 357

Sunnyside Foundation
4518 Skiliman Ave, Sunnyside, NY, 11104-2117
Sunnyside Gardener, 394

Survey Publications
Box 20429, New York, NY, 10028
Bond Fund Survey, 656

Swaps Monitor
648 Broadway, Suite 705, New York, NY, 10012
Swaps Monitor, 688

Sweet's Group - McGraw Hill
1221 Avenue of the Americas, New York, NY, 10020
Building Products for Export, 642

Sylvia Porter Organization, Inc.
15 Columbus Circle, 23rd fl., New York, NY, 10023
Sylvia Porter's Active Retirement Newsletter, 1,109

Symphony for United Nations (SUN)
205 West End Ave Apt 21c, New York, NY, 10023-4813
Sunspots, 262

•**Synagogue Council of America**
252 Soundview Ave., White Plains, NY, 10606-3800

Syracuse China Corp.
2900 Court St, Syracuse, NY, 13208-3218
Syracuse China News, 600

Syracuse Community Radio
P.O. Box 6365, Syracuse, NY, 13217
Off The Air, 815

Syracuse Peace Council
924 Burnet Ave, Syracuse, NY, 13203-3291
Peace Newsletter, 995

Syracuse University
4-194 Cst, Syracuse, NY, 13244-0001
ERIC/IR Update, 307

Syracuse Univ. Library Assocs.
600 Bird Library, Syracuse, NY, 13244-2001
Library Connection, The, 802

Systems Strategies, Inc.
225 W 34th St, New York, NY, 10122-0598
DataComm Report, 219

TAGA Newsletter
68 Lomb Memorial Dr, Rochester, NY, 14623-5604
TAGA Newsletter, 1,007

TAWCO Inc.
200 Katonah Ave., Katonah, NY, 10536
Apparel Strategist, 54

TBR Communications, Ltd.
60 Gramercy Park North, New York, NY, 10010
Ballroom Review, The, 265

TGA, Inc.
PO Box 290014, Brooklyn, NY, 11229-0014
Generation After, 540

TODD Enterprises
31 Water Mill Lane, Great Neck, NY, 11021
TODDNews, 240

•**TPR Publishing Co., Inc.**
81 Montgomery St, Scarsdale, NY, 10583-5150

TRR Publishing Co., Inc.
81 Montgomery St, Scarsdale, NY, 10583-5150
Profit-Building Strategies for Business Owners, 149

Tams-Witmark Music Library, Inc.
560 Lexington Ave., New York, NY, 10022-6873
Musical Show, 1,173

Tanzer Business Communications, Inc.
Box 392, Prince Station, New York, NY, 10012
New York Wine Cellar, 104

Tarbuth Foundation
129 W 67th St, New York, NY, 10023-5917
Tarbuth Tidings, 1,071

Taste Guides, Inc.
Box 1396, Old Chelsea Sta., New York, NY, 10011
Mimi Sheraton's Taste, 1,075

Taurus Littrow Publishing
424 West End Ave 7th flr, New York, NY, 10024-5777
Sturza's Medical Investment Letter, 688

Taylor Hard Money Advisors, Inc.
3342 61st St # 871, Woodside, NY, 11377-2234
J. Taylor's Gold & Gold Stocks, 673

* See **MULTI-PUBLISHER INDEX** for list of publications.

Teachers College Dept. Communications in Education
Columbia University, Box 8, New York, NY, 10027-0008
Matrix Newsletter, 317

TechProse, Inc.
370 Central Park W., Apt 210, New York, NY, 10025-6517
Sarah Stambler's Marketing with Technology News, 22

Technical & Education Center of the Graphic Arts- RIT
Frank E. Gannett Bldg., 66 Lomb Memorial Dr., Rochester, NY, 14623-5604
T & E Update, 1,007

Technologic Partners
120 Wooster Street, New York, NY, 10012
Computer Letter, 217

Technology New York Report
1223 Peoples Ave., Troy, NY, 12181
Technology New York Report, 154

•Technology News of America Co.
110 Greene St Apt 1101, New York, NY, 10012-3824

Television Index, Inc.
4029 27th St Fl 2, Long Island City, NY, 11101-3814
TV Pro-Log, 1,169

Telluride Newsletter
217 West Ave, Ithaca, NY, 14850-3911
Telluride Newsletter, 333

Temper of the Times
1010 Mamaroneck Ave, Mamaroneck, NY, 10543-1632
Money Paper, The, 677

Thanks to Scandinavia
745 5th Ave., New York, NY, 10151-0002
Thanks to Scandinavia Newsletter, 333

Theatre Communications Group, Inc.
355 Lexington Ave., New York, NY, 10017-6695
Artsearch, 340

Theatre Equipment Assn.
244 W 49th St Ste 305, New York, NY, 10019-7411
TEA News, 420

Theatre Events Guide, Inc.
180 West End Ave Apt 26d, New York, NY, 10023-4925
Theatre Events Guide, Inc., 1,174

Theatre Library Association
111 Amsterdam Ave, New York, NY, 10023-7410
Broadside, the Newsletter of the Theatre Library Association, 1,172

Theodor Herzl Foundation
110 E. 59Th. St., New York, NY, 10022
Herzl Institute Bulletin, 1,068

Third Millenium
817 Broadway Fl 6, New York, NY, 10003-4709
Slacker, 472

Third Street Music School Settlement
235 E. 11th St., New York, NY, 10003-7398
Third Street Music School Settlement Bulletin, 918

•Thompson Publishing Group
747 Third Ave., New York, NY, 10017

Tim Wong, D.D.S.
85 4th Ave., New York, NY, 10003-5205
Eastern Dental Society Bulletin, 269

•Time Warner Publishing Inc.
1271 Ave. of the Americas, Rockefeller Center, New York, NY, 10020-1300

Times-Mirror Magazines, Inc.
2 Park Avenue, New York, NY, 10016-5675
Sports Licensing International, 1,135

Tolstoy Foundation, Inc.
104 Lake Rd., Valley Cottage, NY, 10989
TF Newsletter, 970

Tom Rottkamp
America's Fan, 54 Flamingo Rd, Levittown, NY, 11756
America's Fan, 1,129

Totally for Teachers
55 Larchwood Drive, Pittsford, NY, 14534-2458
Middle School Companion, The, 318

Tourette Syndrome Association
4240 Bell Blvd, Bayside, NY, 11361-2820
Tourette Syndrome Association Newsletter, 530

Tourist Office of Spain
665 Fifth Avenue, New York, NY, 10022
Tourist Office of Spain Travel Notes, 1,189

Towanda Printing
PO Box 149, Owego, NY, 13827-0149
Owego Pennysaver Press, 25

•Town of Hempstead Office of Communication & Public Affairs
1 Washington St, Hempstead, NY, 11550-4921

Town of Rochester Environmental Commission
PO Box 65, Accord, NY, 12404-0065
Environmental Newsletter, The, 381

Townsend Pubs.
131 Winthrop Ave. Ext., Liberty, NY, 12754-1219
Bowling-Golfing News, 1,129

•Translation Co. of America, Inc.
10 W 37th St, New York, NY, 10018-7491

Transportation Services
960 Broadway, Hicksville, NY, 11801-5028
Transport (De)Regulation Report, 1,181

Travel Companion Exchange, Inc.
PO Box 833, Amityville, NY, 11701-0833
Travel Companions, 1,189

Traveling Healthy, Inc.
108-48 70th Rd., Forest Hills, NY, 11375-3961
Traveling Healthy Newsletter, 1,191

Travelwriter Marketletter
Waldorf-Astoria, 301 Park Ave., Ste. 1850, New York, NY, 10022
Travelwriter Marketletter, 697

Travltips Cruise & Freighter Travel Association
163-07 Depot Rd, Flushing, NY, 11358-2043
Travltips, 1,191

Treadway Inns Corp.
23 Holcroft Rd W, Rochester, NY, 14612-5519
Treadway Co-Operator, 601

Tri-State Industrial Laundries, Inc.
1634 Lincoln Ave # 4145, Utica, NY, 13502-5312
Cover-All, 581

Trilateral Commission
345 E 46th St, New York, NY, 10017-3518
Trialogue, 638

Trotting Horse Museum
240 Main St, Goshen, NY, 10924-2157
Hall of Fame of the Trotter Newsletter, 559

Tryon Mercantile Inc.
790 Madison Avenue, New York, NY, 10021-6124
Diamond Insight, 693

Tube Council of North America
740 Broadway, New York, NY, 10003-9518
Tube Topics, 893

Tufts Graduate School of Nutrition
53 Park Pl., Fl. 8, New York, NY, 10007
Tufts University Diet and Nutrition Letter, 935

•Turkish-American Assn. for Cultural Exchange
1600 Broadway, New York, NY, 10019-7413

Turok's Choice
Box 202, Old Chelsea Station, New York, NY, 10113-0202
Turok's Choice, 919

Turtle Bay Assn.
224 E 47th St, New York, NY, 10017-2102
Turtle Bay News, 182

Twentieth Century Fund
41 E 70th St, New York, NY, 10021-4972
Twentieth Century Fund Newsletter, 639

Twin Laboratories, Inc.
2120 Smithtown Ave, Ronkonkoma, NY, 11779-7327
Nutrition Update, 935

USLA Justice Committee
535 W. 51st St. #4-0, New York, NY, 10019-5068
USLA Reporter, 639

USPS: Communications
J.A. Farley Bldg., New York, NY, 10199-9641
Focus: Eye on the Mailer, 584

USS Liberty Veterans Assn.
3 Burns Ave, Hicksville, NY, 11801-2601
USS Liberty Newsletter, 899

Ukrainian Academy of Arts
206 W 100th St, New York, NY, 10025-5018
Novyny z Akademii (UVAN), 410

Ulmer Brothers Research Institute
80 Maiden Lane, New York, NY, 10038
Japan M & A Reporter, 649

Ulsterites Fight Overflight Noise
PO Box 681, Stone Ridge, NY, 12484-0681
Overflights Newsletter, 254

Uncommon Desires Newsletter
PO Box 2377, New York, NY, 10185-2377
Uncommon Desires Newsletter, 176

Uniformed Fire Fighters Assn. of Greater NY
225 Broadway, New York, NY, 10007-3092
Fire Lines, 421

Uniformed Sanitationmen's Assn.
23 Cliff St # 25, New York, NY, 10038-2820
USA Record, 711

United Baltic Appeal
115 W 183rd St, Bronx, NY, 10453-1103
BATUN News, 401

United Board for Christian Higher Education in Asia
475 Riverside Dr., New York, NY, 10115-0109
New Horizons, 1,049

•United Cerebral Palsy Assn., Inc.
7 Penn Plz Ste 804, New York, NY, 10001-3900

United Federation of Teachers
260 Park Ave S, New York, NY, 10010-7272
United Teacher, 711

United Food
106 Memorial Pky, Utica, NY, 13501-4818
Voice of Local 1, 711

United Israel World Union
1123 Broadway, New York, NY, 10010-2007
United Israel Bulletin, 403

United Methodist Committee on Relief
475 Riverside Dr Ste 350, New York, NY, 10115-0122
UMCOR Update, 1,073

United Methodist Communications
475 Riverside Dr Ste 1370, New York, NY, 10115-0122
PEP Talk, 860

United Nations Dept. of Public Information
Centres Programme Section, Rm. S-1060, New York, NY, 10017
DPI Programme Update, 629

United Nations Population Fund
220 E. 42nd St., New York, NY, 10017-5880
Population, 1,121

•United Nations Publications
Two UN Plaza, Room DC2-853, New York, NY, 10017

United Neighborhood Houses of New York
475 Park Ave S Fl 6, New York, NY, 10016-6901
UNH News, 1,123

•United Parcel Service
643 W 43rd St, New York, NY, 10036-1917

•U.S. Council for International Business
1212 Ave of the Americas, New York, NY, 10036-1689

U.S. Department, of Agriculture, Consumer
Hunts Point Market, Rm. 4A, Bronx, NY, 10474
Fruit and Vegetable Division, New York Daily Report, 1,008

U.S. Dept. of Commerce
201 Varick St Rm 951, New York, NY, 10014-4811
Fishery Market News Reports (New York Green Sheet), 423

U.S. Harness Writer's Association
PO Box 10, Batavia, NY, 14021-0010
Newsletter (Harness Writers), 697

U.S. Japan Foundation
145 E. 32nd St., New York, NY, 10016-6002
Forum, 630

U.S.-Korea Economic Council
PO Box 174, Saint James, NY, 11780-0174
Economic Newsletter, 645

U.S. Mariners Class Assn.
C/O Raymond Gerber 56, Amityville, NY, 11701
Notice to Mariners, 114

United States Offshore Funds Directory
405 Park Ave Ste 500, New York, NY, 10022-4405
Hedge Fund News, 91

U.S. Plywood-Champion Papers Inc.
885 Conklin St, Farmingdale, NY, 11735-2400
Weldwood News, 603

U.S. Postal Service
Executive Offices, 8th Ave. and 33rd St., New York, NY, 10001
New York Metro Area Update, 591

United States Trust Co.
114 W. 47th St., New York, NY, 10036
Perspectives on Managing Personal Assets, 682

•United Synagogue of Conservative Judaism
155 5th Ave, New York, NY, 10010-6811

United Way of Tri-State
160 Water St., New York, NY, 10038-4922
Together, 600

Universal Black Writer Press
Box 5, Radio City Station, New York, NY, 10101-0005
African-American Traveler, 1,182

University Art Museum
SUNY at Binghamton, Binghamton, NY, 13901
Univ. Art Museum Newsletter, 908

Univ. of Rochester School of Medicine
601 Elmwood Ave, Rochester, NY, 14642-0001
Bulletin of the Edward G. Miner Library, 794

* See **MULTI-PUBLISHER INDEX** for list of publications.

University of the State of New York - State Education Dept.
Office Of Middle/Secondary Ed., Room 967 EBA, Albany, NY, 12234-0001
Technology Applications Quarterly, 333

Unlimited Positive Communications Inc.
11 N Chestnut St, New Paltz, NY, 12561-1706
Marketing Pulse, 859

VALB
799 Broadway Ste 227, New York, NY, 10003-6811
Volunteer, 899

•**Value Line, Inc.**
220 E 42nd St., 6th Fl., New York, NY, 10017-5891

Vampire Research Center
Box 252, Elmhurst, NY, 11373
VRC Newsletter, 920

Van Nostrand Reinhold Co., Inc.
115 5th Ave, New York, NY, 10003-1085
Hazchem Alert, 165

Vanity Press
160 6th Ave, New York, NY, 10013-1674
Questionable Cartoons, 997

•**Vassar College**
Publications, Poughkeepsie, NY, 12601

Vaughan Report
277 West End Ave., New York, NY, 10023-2604
Vaughan Report, 690

Venezuelan American Assn. of the U.S.
150 Nassau St., New York, NY, 10038-1516
Venezuela News Bulletin, 639

Venture Communications
60 Madison Avenue, New York, NY, 10010
Venture Views & News, 1,089

•**Veronis, Suhler & Associates, Inc.**
350 Park Avenue, New York, NY, 10022

Veterans of the Abraham Lincoln Brigade
799 Broadway Ste 227, New York, NY, 10003-6811
Volunteer of Liberty, 640

Viacom
15 Columbus Cir, New York, NY, 10023-7780
Frommer's Travel Book Club Tips & Travel, 1,184

•**Vickers Stock Research Corp.**
226 New York Ave, Huntington, NY, 11743-2748

Victims's Service Agency
2 Lafayette St, New York, NY, 10007-1380
TAISSA Letter, 1,189

Viewpoint Networks, Inc
403 Darwin Drive, Amherst, NY, 14226
Photogear, 1,113

Viola d'Amore Society of America
3923 47th St, Sunnyside, NY, 11104-1419
Viola d'Amore Society of America-Newsletter, 919

Visiting Nurse Assn. of B'klyn.
Public Relations Dept., 138 S. Oxford St., Brooklyn, NY, 11217
VNAB Newsletter, 932

Volvo Club of America
PO Box 16, Afton, NY, 13730-0016
Rolling, 75

Vos, Gruppo, Capell
60 E 42nd St Rm 3810, New York, NY, 10165-0006
Capell's Circulation Report, 11

Vulcan Society, Vulcan Hall
739 Eastern Pky, Brooklyn, NY, 11213-3410
Vulcan Newsletter, 422

W. Caslon & Co.
100 Park Wood Ave., Rochester, NY, 14620
Ink on Paper, 1,005

•**W.H. White Publications, Inc.**
53 Park Pl, New York, NY, 10007-2407

WNY Documentary Heritage Program
4455 Genesee Street, PO Box 400, Buffalo, NY, 14225-0400
Documentary Heritage Program Newsletter, 539

WOM'N
Box 1616, Canal St. Sta., New York, NY, 10013-0869
Woman of Mystery, 920

•**W-Two Publications**
202 The Commons, #401, Ithaca, NY, 14850-5578

WWWWW/Information Services, Inc.
PO Box 10046, Rochester, NY, 14610-0046
Buyerism Newsletter, 130

Wall Street On-Line Publishing
Box 6, Riverdale, NY, 10471-0006
Wall Street Micro Investor, 691

Wall Street Reports
99 Wall St., New York, NY, 10005-4393
Wall Street Reports, 691

Wall Street Transcript Corp.
99 Wall St., New York, NY, 10005-4393
Wall Street Transcript, 156

Walter Mathews Assoc
799 Broasway, Ste 309, New York, NY, 10003
International Visitor, 1,185

Walter Mathews Assocs., Inc.
799 Broadway, New York, NY, 10003
Briefing, 574

•**Waters Information Services**
PO Box 2248, Binghamton, NY, 13902-2248

•**Welding Research Council**
345 E 47th St Rm 1301, New York, NY, 10017-2330

Werner International Apparel Marketing
111 W. 40th St., New York, NY, 10018-2564
Apparel Sourcing Analysis, 54

Westchester Academy of Medicine
84 Purchase St, Purchase, NY, 10577-2612
Westchester Academy of Medicine Newsletter, 889

Westchester Business Partnership
427 Bedford Rd., Pleasantville, NY, 10570
Westchester Business Partnership, 296

Westchester Country Club News
Westchester Country Club, Rye, NY, 10580-1891
Westchester Country Club News, 183

Westchester County Dept. of Planning
432 County Office Bldg., White Plains, NY, 10601
Westchester Planning, 1,025

Westchester Library System
8 Westchester Plaza, Elmsford, NY, 10523-1604
Hot Off the Computer, 223

Westchester Peoples Action Coalition (WESPAC)
255 Grove St, White Plains, NY, 10601-4103
WESPAC Newsletter, 1,000

Western New York Browns Backers
106 Woodgate Terrace, Rochester, NY, 14625
Woof!, 434

Western New York Library Resources Council
4455 Genessee St., P.O. Box 400, Buffalo, NY, 14225-0400
For Your Information, 798

White Plains Hospital Center
Davis Ave. at post rd., White Plains, NY, 10601
P. M. Newsletter of the Anxiety & Phobia Clinic, 1,016

William Alanson White Institute
20 W 74th St, New York, NY, 10023-2401
WAW Newsletter, 1,018

William J. Miller Assoc., Inc.
45 Villa Rd., Pearl River, NY, 10965-1440
Dialogues in Pediatric Urology, 872

William Petschek Natl. Jewish Family Ctr. -American Jewish C
165 E 56th St, New York, NY, 10022-2709
William Petschek Natl. Jewish Family Center-Newsletter, 416

Windsor Systems Dev., Inc.
11 W 42nd St Fl 12, New York, NY, 10036-8002
Windsor Report, 862

Winpoint Corp.
438 W. 37th St., New York, NY, 10018-4001
Winning Points, 1,137

Wire Service Guild, Local 222
133 W 44th St, New York, NY, 10036-4012
Wireport, 712

Women Against Pornography
321 West 47th Street, New York, NY, 10036-2400
Women Against Pornography Newsreport, 1,213

Women in the Arts Foundation, Inc.
1175 York Ave Apt 2g, New York, NY, 10021-7170
Women in the Arts Bulletin, 262

Women of Reform Judaism
838 5th Ave, New York, NY, 10021-7012
Notes for Now, 1,211

Women's International League for Peace and Freedom
339 Lafayette St, New York, NY, 10012-2725
Women's International League for Peace and Freedom, 1,214

Women's National Book Association
160 Fifth Ave., New York, NY, 10010-7000
Bookwoman, 116

Woodlawn Cemetery
Webster Ave. & 233rd St., New York, NY, 10470
Woodlawn Cemetery News, 437

Work in America Institute
700 White Plains Road, Scarsdale, NY, 10583
Work in America, 706

•**Workers Solidarity Alliance**
339 Lafayette St Rm 202, New York, NY, 10012-2725

World Association of Estonians
243 E 34th St, New York, NY, 10016-4852
Free Estonian Word, 401

World Conference on Religion
777 United Nations Plaza, New York, NY, 10017-3521
Religion for Peace, 1,051

•**World Council of Churches**
475 Riverside Dr., Ste 915, New York, NY, 10115-0122

World Federalist Movement
777 UN Plaza, 12th Fl., New York, NY, 10017
World Federalist News, 640

•**World Goodwill**
Box 722, Cooper Station, New York, NY, 10276-0722

World Health Organization
United Nations, New York, NY, 10017-3582
Weekly Epidemiological Record, 531

•**World Jewish Congress**
501 Madison Ave Fl 17, New York, NY, 10022-5602

World Monument Funds
949 Park Ave., New York, NY, 10028-0307
World Monuments Fund, 61

World Pumpkin Confederation
14050 Rt. 62, Collins, NY, 14034-9704
Cucurbits, 440

•**World Reports Ltd.**
280 Madison Ave Rm 1209, New York, NY, 10016-0801

World Union for Progressive Judaism
838 5th Ave, New York, NY, 10021-7012
Ammi, 1,068

Writer Unlimited Agency, Inc.
PO Box 698, Centereach, NY, 11720-0698
Writers Ink Press, 819

The Writers Alliance
12 Skylark Ln, Stony Brook, NY, 11790-3121
The Street Irregular, 984

Writers Guild of America East
555 W 57th St, New York, NY, 10019-2967
Writers Guild of America East Newsletter, 712

Writers Studio
78 Charles St., New York, NY, 10014
Dis-Connections, 982

•**Xavier Society for the Blind**
154 E. 23rd St., New York, NY, 10010-4501

Xerox Corp.
Xerox Sq. 021, Rochester, NY, 14644-0001
Xerox World, 603

Xtreme
270 Lafayette St Ste 612, New York, NY, 10012-3327
Zandl/Slant, 24

YIVO Institute for Jewish Research
555 W. 57th St., Ste. 1100, New York, NY, 10019-2925
YIVO News, 1,071

•**Yale Robbins Inc.**
31 E. 28th St., New York, NY, 10016-7959

Yeshiva Birkas Reuven
PO Box 204, Brooklyn, NY, 11204-0204
Kashrus Faxletter, 430

Yeshiva University
500 W 185th St, New York, NY, 10033-3299
Yeshiva University Sephardic Bulletin, 409

Yeshiva University Student Organization
185th St. & Amsterdam Ave., New York, NY, 10033
Gesher, 1,068

York College
9420 Guy R Brewer Blvd, Jamaica, NY, 11433-1101
Pandora's Box, 204

Young Audiences, Inc.
115 E 92nd St, New York, NY, 10128-1688
Young Audiences Newsletter, 336

Your Child's Wellness
244 Madison Ave Apt 9h, New York, NY, 10016-2813
Your Child's Wellness, 78

Zip City Brewing Co.
3 West 18th Street, New York, NY, 10011
Zip City, 106

•**Zweig Securities Advisory Service, Inc.**
PO Box 2900, Wantagh, NY, 11793-0926

North Carolina

Alexander County Genealogical Soc. NC
PO Box 241, Hiddenite, NC, 28636-0241
Kinfolks & Connections, 458

* See *MULTI-PUBLISHER INDEX* for list of publications.

Alpha Alpha Chapter
PO Box 99308, Duke University, Durham, NC, 27708-9308
Alumni Newsletter - Alpha Alpha Chapter, 191

Ameribanc-First Union Natl. Bank
301 S. Tryon St., 2 First Union Ctr., 15th fl., Charlotte, NC, 28288-0570
First Union Network, 584

American Dairy Goat Assn.
PO Box 865, Spindale, NC, 28160-0865
ADGA News & Events, 826

American Matchcover Collecting Club
PO Box 18481, Asheville, NC, 28814-0481
Front Striker Bulletin, 184

•**American Social Health Assn.**
PO Box 13827, Research Triangle Pk, NC, 27709-3827

Americans for the Univ. of UNESCO
PO Box 18418, Asheville, NC, 28814-0418
Americans for the Univ. of UNESCO Newsletter, 626

Art Libraries Society of North America
4101 Lake Boone Trl Ste 201, Raleigh, NC, 27607-7506
ARLIS/NA Update, 792

Arthur Morgan School
1901 Hannah Branch Rd, Burnsville, NC, 28714-7582
Celo Education Notes, 304

Asheville Area Chamber of Commerce
PO Box 1010, Asheville, NC, 28802-1010
Asheville Report, 157

Assn. of American Editorial Cartoonists
4101 Lake Boone Trl Ste 201, Raleigh, NC, 27607-7506
Cartoonists Notebook, 923

Association for Child Psychoanalysis
320 Glendale Dr, Chapel Hill, NC, 27514-5914
Association for Child Psychoanalysis Newsletter, 1,012

Assn. for Humanistic Education & Development
404 W Warren St, Shelby, NC, 28150-5330
Infochange, 313

Bald Headed Men of America
102 Bald Dr, Morehead City, NC, 28557-2919
Chrome-Dome, 177

Bennett College
900 E Washington St, Greensboro, NC, 27401-3298
Belle Ringer, 470

Bolt Beranek & Newman
1000 Park Forty Plaza, Suite 300, Durham, NC, 27713
Computer Communication Review, 216

Botanical Garden Foundation
NC Botanical Garden UNC, CB, 3375 Totten Center, Chapel Hill, NC, 27599-3375
N.C. Botanical Garden Newsletter, 442

Branch Banking
PO Box 1847, Wilson, NC, 27894-1847
Insight, 587

Burroughs Wellcome
3030 Cornwallis Rd., Research Triangle, NC, 27709-2700
Wellcome News, 603

Carolina Biological Supply Co.
2700 York Rd, Burlington, NC, 27215-3398
Carolina Tips, 109

Carolina Justice Polce Center
PO Box 309, Durham, NC, 27702-0309
Carolina Justice Policy Center News, 785

•**Center for Creative Leadership**
One Leadership Place, PO Box 26300, Greensboro, NC, 27438-6300

Center for Professional Well Being
21 W Colony Pl Ste 150, Durham, NC, 27705-5589
Being Well, 499

Cherokee Boys Club
PO Box 507, Cherokee, NC, 28719-0507
Cherokee Boys Club-Newsletter & Cherokee Voice, 405

•**Christian Ministry Resources**
617 Greenbrook Pky, Matthews, NC, 28105-7745

Coordinating Council for Senior Citizens
807 S. Duke St., Durham, NC, 27701-3701
Senior Citizens Post, 1,109

Creative Services Inc.
PO Box 6008, High Point, NC, 27262-6008
Nido Qubein Letter, 19

D.A.T.A. Enterprises
Box 28954, Chapel Hill, NC, 27515-2895
Pennant Fever, 1,134

DKT International
PO Box 1600, Chapel Hill, NC, 27515-1600
Sex Over Forty, 1,110

DS Design
2440 SW Cary P'way, #210, Cary, NC, 27513-5318
Cut & Paste, 209

Dr. Morris Britt, Doctors Bldg.
1012 S Kings Dr Ste 901, Charlotte, NC, 28283-0001
Robeson County Register, 1,042

Duke University Career Development Center
PO Box 90950, Durham, NC, 27708-0950
DukeSource News, 191

Duke University Civil Eng. Dept.
Dept. Civil/Environmental Eng., Box 90287, Durham, NC, 27708-0287
Department of Civil and Environmental Engineering Newsletter, 365

Duke Univ. Divinity School
Publications, Durham, NC, 27706-7706
Divinity School News & Notes, 1,046

•**Duke Univ. History Dept.**
614 Chapel Dr, Durham, NC, 27706-2500

Duke Univ. Library
Publications, Durham, NC, 27706
Duke University Libraries, 797

Economic Issues
179 East Franklin Street, Post Office Box 989, Chapel Hill, NC, 27514-0989
Economic Issues, 291

Elizabeth City State Univ.
Box 841, Elizabeth City, NC, 27909
Campus Perspective, 303

Employment Management Association
4101 Lake Boone Trl Ste 201, Raleigh, NC, 27607-7506
EMA Reporter, 342

Evry Tanian Assn. of America
121 Greenwich Rd., Charlotte, NC, 28211-2343
Velouchi Bulletin, 402

Exceptional Human Experience Network, Inc.
414 Rockledge Road, New Bern, NC, 28562
EHE News, 948

•**Family Health International**
PO Box 13950, Rtp, NC, 27709-3950

Financial Training Group, The
300 East Blvd., Suite B-4, Charlotte, NC, 28203-4784
Bill Staton's Money Advisory, 128

First Flight Society
PO Box 1903, Kitty Hawk, NC, 27949-1903
Wright Flyer, 34

Forest History Society, Inc.
701 Vickers Ave, Durham, NC, 27701-3162
Forest History Cruiser, 540

•**Forum Intl. Group, Inc.**
PO Box 6415, High Point, NC, 27262-6415

Friends of the Filipino People
PO Box 2125, Durham, NC, 27702-2125
Friends of the Filipino People Bulletin, 631

G.I. Joe Collectors' Club
12513 Birchfall Dr., Raleigh, NC, 27614
G.I. Joe Collectors Club, 184

Gaston/Lincoln Genealogical Society
PO Box 584, Mount Holly, NC, 28120-0584
Footprints in Time, 453

Genealogical Soc. of Iredell Co.
PO Box 946, Statesville, NC, 28687-0946
Iredell County Tracks, 457

Genealogical Society of Watauga Co., NC
530 Forrest Hill Dr, Boone, NC, 28607-4428
Watauga Ancestry, 469

Grassroots Leadership
1300 Baxter St. 200, Box 36006, Charlotte, NC, 28204-3053
Grassroots, 990

Healthcare Publishing
200 McCleary Ct., Raleigh, NC, 27607
Managed Care & Health Care Marketing, 516

Human Kindness Foundation
Rt. 1, Box 201-N, Durham, NC, 27705-9801
Prison-Ashram Project Newsletter, 975

Institute of Outdoor Drama
CB 3240 National Bank Plaza, Univ. of North Carolina, Chapel Hill, NC, 27599-3240
U.S. Outdoor Drama, 1,174

Institute for Product Safety
PO Box 1931, Durham, NC, 27702-1931
Product Safety News, 1,083

Inst. for Research in Social Science
Univ. of NC Cb# 3355, Manning Hall, Chapel Hill, NC, 27599-0001
Social Science News Letter, 1,127

Insurance Accounting & Systems Assn.
PO Box 51340, Durham, NC, 27717-1340
Interpreter, 6

International Academy of Nutrition & Preventive Medicine
PO Box 18433, Asheville, NC, 28814-0433
Your Health, 889

Intl. Guild of Professional Electrologists
202 Boulevard St # B, High Point, NC, 27262-4302
International Guild of Professional Electrologists-Newsletter, 876

Intl. Lead Zinc Research Organization
PO Box 12036, Rtp, NC, 27709-2036
R & D Focus, 892

International Society of Financiers
PO Box 18508, Asheville, NC, 28814-0508
International Financier, 92

International Society of Industrial Fabric Manufacturers
PO Box 1369, Kings Mountain, NC, 28086-1369
American Textile Reporter, 127

Intersteel Technology, Inc.
8301 University Exec Park Dr, Ste 130, Charlotte, NC, 28262-3355
Steel Digest, 892

JAARS Inc.
7405 JAARS Rd., PO Box 248, Waxhaw, NC, 28173-0248
Beyond, 1,045

JW Hartman Center for Sales, Advertising and Mktg. History
Special Collections Library, Duke University, Durham, NC, 27708-0185
Front and Center, 14

James Willard Schultz Society
135 Wildwood Dr, New Bern, NC, 28562-9560
Piegan Storyteller, 824

Johnston County Genealogical Society
305 E Market St, Smithfield, NC, 27577-3919
Johnston County Genealogical Society Journal, 458

Kershner Family Association
1449 Fox Run Dr, Charlotte, NC, 28212-7125
Kershner Kinfolk, 458

Lance Inc.
PO Box 32368, Charlotte, NC, 28232-2368
VL-Voice of Lance, 602

Legion of Valor of the U.S. of America
92 Oak Leaf Ln, Chapel Hill, NC, 27516-9440
General Orders, 896

•**Lewis & Clark Research**
6040 A. Six Forks Rd., Suite 112, Raleigh, NC, 27609

Luptonian
P.O. Box 43, Bayboro, NC, 28515-0443
Luptonian, 460

•**MEMA-Motor & Equipment Manufacturers Assn.**
PO Box 13966, Rtp, NC, 27709-3966

•**Material Handling Industry of America**
8720 Red Oak Blvd Ste 201, Charlotte, NC, 28217-3990

McCrary
406 Jefferson Dr, Charlotte, NC, 28270-5344
McCrary, 461

Middle East Trade Letter
PO Box 472986, Charlotte, NC, 28247-2986
Middle East Trade Letter, 650

Moravian Music Foundation
20 Cascade Ave., Winston-Salem, NC, 27127-2904
Moravian Music Foundation Newsletter, 914

Multidisciplinary Association of Psychedelic Studies
1801 Tippah Ave, Charlotte, NC, 28205-3048
MAPS Newsletter, 1,015

Museum of the Cherokee Indian
PO Box 770a, Cherokee, NC, 28719-0770
NAIMA Museum News, 907

N.A. American Soc. for Oceanic History
Program in Maritime History, East Carolina University, Greenville, NC, 27858-4353
NASOH Newsletter, 897

N.C. Div. of Travel
430 N Salisbury St, Raleigh, NC, 27603-5926
North Carolina Travel Report, 1,187

NC Occupational Safety & Health Project
PO Box 2514, Durham, NC, 27715-2514
NCOSH, 613

N.C. Sociological Assn.
NCSA/UNC Charlotte, Charlotte, NC, 28223
Sociation, 1,127

N.U.T.R.A. Program
PO Box 1217, Cashiers, NC, 28717-1217
Nutritioning Parents, 935

* See **MULTI-PUBLISHER INDEX** for list of publications.

Nason & Associates
PO Box 8204, Asheville, NC, 28814-8204
Today's Hospital Gift Shop Business, 478

Natl. Assn. of American Business Clubs
PO Box 5127, High Point, NC, 27262-5127
AMBUC Leader, 176

•**National Climatic Data Center**
NOAA/NESDIS E/Ccx2, Federal Bldg. 151 Patton Ave,
Asheville, NC, 28801-5001

National Humanities Ctr. Newsletter
PO Box 12256, Rtp, NC, 27709-2256
National Humanities Center Newsletter, 261

Natl. Nurses Society on Addictions
4101 Lake Boone Trail, Ste. 201, Raleigh, NC, 27607
Perspectives on Addictions Nursing, 524

National Organization of Single Mothers
PO Box 68, Midland, NC, 28107-0068
SingleMOTHER, 416

National Sharecropper's Fund/Rual Advancement Fund
PO Box 18217, Charlotte, NC, 28218-0217
Sharecropper, 46

Natl. Sportscasters and Sportswriters Assn.
PO Box 559, Salisbury, NC, 28145-0559
NSSA News, 696

Natl. Wholesale Furniture Assn.
164 S. Main St., #404, Box 2482, High Point, NC,
27261-2482
Tips for Salesmen, 438

New Beginnings, Inc.
PO Box 228, Waynesville, NC, 28786-2628
New Beginnings, 1,049

•**Noble Publishing Co.**
PO Box 1509, Candler, NC, 28715-1509

North American Brass Band Assn.
PO Box 2438, Cullowhee, NC, 28723
Brass Band Bridge, 910

North American Youth Sport Institute
4985 Oak Garden Drive, Kernersville, NC, 27284-9520
Sport Scene, 1,135

North Carolina A&T State Univ.
F.d. Bluford Library, Greensboro, NC, 27411-0001
Bluford Notes and Quotes, 794

North Carolina Assn. of Educators
PO Box 27347, Raleigh, NC, 27611-7347
NCAE News Bulletin, 320

North Carolina Cooperative Extension Service
Box 8119, Ncsu, Raleigh, NC, 27695-0001
NC State Economist, 294

North Carolina Dept. of Environment
PO Box 27687, Raleigh, NC, 27611-7687
Epi Notes, 505

North Carolina Dept. of Public Instruction
Educational Media & Technica, Raleigh, NC, 27611
Media Matters, 804

North Carolina Division of Archives & History
109 E Jones St, Raleigh, NC, 27601-2806
Carolina Comments, 537

North Carolina Folklore Society
Appalachian State Univ. Dept., Of English, Boone, NC,
28608-0001
Newsletter of the North Carolina Folklore Soc., 425

North Carolina Foreign Language Ctr.
Cumberland County Pub. Lib., 300 Maiden La.,
Fayetteville, NC, 28301-5000
NCFLC Quarterly, 261

North Carolina Music Teachers Assn.
Univ. Of North Carolina, Dept., Chapel Hill, NC, 27599-
0001
North Carolina Music Teacher, 915

North Carolina Nurses Assn.
PO Box 12025, Raleigh, NC, 27605-2025
Tar Heel Nurse, 932

North Carolina Office of Intergovernmental Relations
116 W Jones St, Raleigh, NC, 27603-1300
North Carolina Environmental Bulletin, 389

North Carolina State Dept. of Public Instruction
Raleigh, NC, 27602
North Carolina Public School Bulletin, 323

North Carolina State Dept. of Safety
Raleigh, NC, 27611
Your Safety, 1,085

•**North Carolina State Employment Security Commission**
111 E 3rd Ave, Gastonia, NC, 28052-4362

North Carolina State Library
109 E Jones St, Raleigh, NC, 27601-2806
Tar Heel Libraries, 811

North Carolina State Univ.
Box 7318, Raleigh, NC, 27695-0001
Statelog, 191

North Carolina State Univ., Minerals Research Lab.
180 Coxe Ave., Asheville, NC, 28801-4041
Minerals Research Laboratory Newsletter, 901

OMGS
PO Box 32453, Charlotte, NC, 28232-2453
Olde Mecklenburg Genealogical Society Quarterly, 463

Office of State Budge & Mgmt.
116 W Jones St, Raleigh, NC, 27603-8005
NC State Data Center Newsletter, 489

Old Time Western Film Club
PO Box 142, Siler City, NC, 27344-0142
Old Time Western Film Club-Newsletter, 420

Organization for Tropical Studies
PO Box 90632, Durham, NC, 27708-0632
OTS Liana, 389

Overseas Orientation Service
PO Box 1611, Cullowhee, NC, 28723-1611
Overseas Living, 651

Phoenix-Hecht
68 T.W. Alexander Dr., Box 13628, Reseach Triangle
Pk., NC, 27709
Treasury Pro, 99

Roanoke-Chowan Technical Institute
Rr 2 Box 46a, Ahoskie, NC, 27910-9522
Student Activity Newsletter, 204

Royce Family Assn.
4033 Somerdale Ln, Charlotte, NC, 28205-4639
Royce Quarterly, 466

Rural Advancement Fund
2124 Commonwealth Ave, Charlotte, NC, 28205-5126
Rural Advance, 45

SINET
Duke University, PO Box 90088, Durham, NC, 27708-
0088
SINET (Social Indicators Network News), 1,127

Salisbury-Rowan County Chamber of Commerce
PO Box 559, Salisbury, NC, 28145-0559
Salisbury-Rowan County in Action, 161

Salvation Army Carolinas Division
PO Box 241808, Charlotte, NC, 28224-1808
Drumbeat, 1,117

Scottish Heritage USA, Inc.
PO Box 457, Pinehurst, NC, 28374-0457
Scottish Heritage U.S.A. Newsletter, 466

Scribes-The American Society of Writers on Legal Subjects
Box 7206, Winston-Salem, NC, 27109-7206
Scrivener, 697

Sentinel Communications, Inc.
15113 Steele Creek Rd, Charlotte, NC, 28273-6855
American Sentinel, 986

Shaw Univ.
118 E South St, Raleigh, NC, 27601-2341
Shaw University Bulletin, 191

Society of American Archivists
Special Collections Dept., Univ. of North Carolina Lib.,
Charlotte, NC, 28223
Acquisitions & Appraisal Section News, 792

Society of American Travel Writers
4101 Lake Boone Trail, Ste. 201, Raleigh, NC, 27607
Travel Writer, 1,191

Society of North Carolina Archivists
PO Box 20448, Raleigh, NC, 27619-0448
North Carolina Archivist, 806

Southeastern Baptist Theological Seminary
PO Box 1889, Wake Forest, NC, 27588-1889
Outlook, 1,053

Southeastern Historical Keyboard Society
PO Box 32022, Charlotte, NC, 28232-2022
*Southeastern Historical Keyboard Society
Newsletter, 918*

Southern Highland Handicraft Guild
PO Box 9545, Asheville, NC, 28815-0545
Highland Highlights, 553

Sports Letter, Inc.
PO Box 4323, Chapel Hill, NC, 27515-4323
Poop Sheet, 1,134

Sterling Publications
2291 Avent Ferry Rd., Suite #215, Raleigh, NC, 27606
RoMANtic, The, 1,077

Tanzer 16 Class Assn.
PO Box 26003, Raleigh, NC, 27611-6003
Tanzer Talk Newsletter, 114

•**Thoreau Society, Inc.**
c/o Bradley Dean, Rte. 2, Box 36, Ayden, NC, 28513-9502

UNC Dept. Envir. Sci. & Eng.
Sch. Of Public Health Cb#740, Chapel Hill, NC, 27599-
0001
ESE Notes, 377

USAir Frequent Traveler Program
Box 5, Winston-Salem, NC, 27102-0005
USAir Frequent Traveler Program News, 33

U.S. Intl. Tempest Assn.
111 Maple Dr NW, Lenoir, NC, 28645-5031
Tempest, The, 114

U.S. Natl. Climatic Data Ctr.
Federal Bldg., MC-02, Asheville, NC, 28801
Hourly Precipitation Data, 893

U.S. Police Canine Assn.
Rr 2 Box 221j, Angier, NC, 27501-9638
Canine Courier, 785

United World Mission
PO Box 250, Union Mills, NC, 28167-0250
UWM World Scan, 1,052

Univ. of North Carolina
Campus Box 7912, Raleigh, NC, 27695-0001
Water Resources Research Institute News, 397

Univ. of North Carolina, Highway Safety Research Center
134 1/2 E. Franklin St. Cb, #3430, Chapel Hill, NC,
27599-0001
Highway Safety Directions, 1,080

Univ. of North Carolina Library
Undergraduate Library Cb# 39, Chapel Hill, NC,
27599-0001
Library Notes, 802

Univ. of North Carolina at Asheville
Public Information Office, University Heights, Asheville,
NC, 28804-3251
UNCA Today, 191

Univ. of North Carolina at Chapel Hill, Alumni Assn.
School Of Info. & Library Sci., Chapel Hill, NC, 27599-
0001
News from Chapel Hill, 805

University North Carolina at Chapel Hill, Davis Library
Campus Box 3920, Chapel Hill, NC, 27599-0001
Windows, 813

Upholstered Furniture Action Council
PO Box 2436, High Point, NC, 27261-2436
UFAC Volunteer, 438

Vanguard Information Pubs.
PO Box 667, Chapel Hill, NC, 27514-0667
Employee Testing & the Law, 342

Village Publishing Co.
PO Box 2777, Chapel Hill, NC, 27515-2777
Village Advocate, 25

Virginia Carolina Peanut Promotions
PO Box 8, Nashville, NC, 27856-0008
P-Nutty News & Notes, 432

Virginia Mutual Benefits Life Ins. Co., Agency Dept.
PO Box 201, Durham, NC, 27702-0201
Weekly Bulletin, 603

Wake County Genealogical Society
5253 Vann St, Raleigh, NC, 27606-1579
Wake County Genealogical Society Newsletter, 469

Wake County Hospital System Inc.
PO Box 14465, Raleigh, NC, 27620-4465
Pulsebeat, 571

Wellington's Books
120 Kilmayne Dr, Cary, NC, 27511-4465
Reader's Review, 824

Wesley Foundation, Univ. of North Carolina, Rev. Robt. Johns
214 Pittsboro St, Chapel Hill, NC, 27516-2738
Foundations, 1,073

•**William F. Bland Co.**
111 Cloister Court, Suite 114, PO Box 16666, Chapel
Hill, NC, 27516-6666

Wix Corp.
PO Box 1967, Gastonia, NC, 28053-1967
Wix Folks and Facts, 603

Worden Brothers
PO Box 3458, Chapel Hill, NC, 27515-3458
Worden's Optioneer, 692

World Methodist Council
PO Box 518, Lake Junaluska, NC, 28745-0518
World Parish, 1,073

* See **MULTI-PUBLISHER INDEX** for list of publications.

North Dakota

Bismarck-Mandan Historical & Genealogical Soc.
PO Box 485, Bismarck, ND, 58502-0485
Dakota Homestead Historical Newsletter, 451

Council on Vocational Education; ND
PO Box 1373, Bismarck, ND, 58502-1373
ND Council on Vocational Education-Biennial Evaluation Report, 320

Dakota Resource Council
PO Box 1095, Dickinson, ND, 58602-1095
Dakota Counsel, 352

Foreign Language Assn. of the Red River
Dept. of Modern Languages, Fargo, ND, 58105
FLARR Foreign Language Assoc. of the Red River, 821

Geological Survey
Univ. Station, Grand Forks, ND, 58202
NDGS Newsletter, 476

North Dakota Dental Assn.
419 Dakota Ave, Wahpeton, ND, 58075-4413
North Dakota Dental Association Newsletter, 270

•**North Dakota Dept. of Economic Development and Finance**
1833 E Bismarck Expy, Bismarck, ND, 58504-6708

North Dakota League of Cities
PO Box 2235, Bismarck, ND, 58502-2235
Bulletin-N.D., 481

North Dakota Society for Medical Technology
2103 20th Ave S, Grand Forks, ND, 58201-6162
North Dakota Society for Clinical Laboratory Sciences Newsletter, 882

North Dakota State Library
Liberty Memorial Bldg., 604 E. Boulevard Ave., Bismarck, ND, 58505-0800
Flickertale Newsletter, 797

Northwood Deaconess Hospital
Northwood, ND, 58267
Northwood Ermissaeren, 569

•**Sacred Heart Monastry**
PO Box 364, Richardton, ND, 58652

State Historical Soc. of N.D.
North Dakota Heritage Ctr., Bismarck, ND, 58505-0830
Plains Talk: The Quarterly Newsletter of the State Historical Society of North Dakota, 546

Steiger Tractor Inc.
3101 1st Ave N, Fargo, ND, 58102-3005
Steiger Tr-Action News, 600

Ukrainian Cultural Institute
DSU Box 6, Dickinson, ND, 58601
Ukrainian Cultural Inst. Newsletter, 410

U.S. Durum Growers Assn.
824 Thompson St, Bottineau, ND, 58318-1726
Durum Kernels, 39

•**Univ. of North Dakota**
Box 9040, Univ. Sta., Grand Forks, ND, 58202-8237

University of North Dakota Printing Centre
Box 133, Grand Forks, ND, 58202
Good Stuff, 798

Ohio

AMS, F&V Division, USDA
Federal Building, 550 Main St., Rm. 9522, Cincinnati, OH, 45202-3222
Officer-In-Charge, 44

ASM International
Materials Information, 9639 Kinsman Rd., Materials Park, OH, 44073-0002
Casting Digest, 891

Advanstar Communications, Inc.
7500 Old Oak Blvd., Cleveland, OH, 44130-3369
Official Board Markets, 947

Adventures in Movement for Handicapped Children
945 Danbury Rd, Dayton, OH, 45420-1606
Adventures in Movement, 1,113

Aeronautical Navigator Assn.
640 Brumbaugh Dr, New Carlisle, OH, 45344-2523
Navigator Newsletter, 31

Akron City Hospital
525 E Market St, Akron, OH, 44304-1619
Pacemaker, 570

Akron-Summit County Public Library
55 S Main St, Akron, OH, 44326-0001
Insight, 800

•**Alan B. Lancz & Assocs., Inc.**
2400 N Reynolds Rd, Toledo, OH, 43615-2818

Alaskan Malamute Club of America
8565 Hill Rd S, Pickerington, OH, 43147-8536
Alaskan Malamute Club of America Newsletter, 279

All-American Soap Box Derby
PO Box 7233, Akron, OH, 44306-0233
Topside, 1,136

Allen County Historical Society
620 W Market St, Lima, OH, 45801-4604
Allen County Historical Society, Newsletter, 536

Alumni Association
Williamson Alumni Center, Kent, OH, 44242-0001
Operant Subjectivity, 1,016

•**AmeriTrust Co.**
900 Euclid Ave, Cleveland, OH, 44115-1461

American Assn. of Certified Appraisers
800 Compton Rd # 10, Cincinnati, OH, 45231-3847
Clipboard, 1,032

American Assn. of Veterinary Anatomists
1900 Coffey Rd # A100, Columbus, OH, 43210-1006
American Association of Veterinary Anatomists Newsletter, 1,200

American Carnival Glass Assn., Inc.
153 Douglas Dr, Rittman, OH, 44270-1329
American Carnival Glass News, 478

American Correctional Health Services Assn.
PO Box 2307, Dayton, OH, 45401-2307
Corhealth, 503

American Economic Foundation
1215 Terminal Tower, Cleveland, OH, 44113
American Economic Foundation Newsletter, 289

American Electric Power Customer Service Center
Box 400, Canton, OH, 44701
Ohio Power Review, 593

American Gourd Society
PO Box 274, Mount Gilead, OH, 43338-0274
Gourd, 441

•**American Institute of Plant Engineers**
8180 Corporate Park Dr., Suite 305, Cincinnati, OH, 45242-3309

American School Health Association
PO Box 708, 7263 State Rte. 43, Kent, OH, 44240-0708
Pulse, 525

American Self-Protection Assn.
825 Greengate Oval, Sagamore Hills, OH, 44067-2311
World of A.S.P., 817

American Society for Sanitary Engineering
PO Box 40326, Bay Village, OH, 44140-0326
American Society of Sanitary Engineering Newsletter, 364

Ameritech
PO Box 6250, Cleveland, OH, 44101-1250
News in Brief, 592

•**Anadem, Inc.**
3620 N High St Ste 310, Columbus, OH, 43214-3643

Aquarium Systems, Inc.
8141 Tyler Blvd., Mentor, OH, 44060
SeaScope, 50

Art Glass Supplies Association Intl.
1100 Brandywine Blvd. #H, PO Box 2188, Zanesville, OH, 43701-2188
AGSA Newsletter, 478

Ashtabula County Genealogical Society
Geneva Library, 117 West Main Street, Geneva, OH, 44041-1227
Ancestor Hunt, 447

Association of Crafts & Creative Industries
1100 H. Brandywine Blvd., P.O. Box 2188, Zanesville, OH, 43702-2188
ACCI Newsletter, 550

Association for Dev. of Computer-Based Instructional Systems
1601 W 5th Ave, Columbus, OH, 43212-2367
ADCIS Newsletter, 298

Assn. for the Gifted-Council for Exceptional Children
Kent State U, 401 White Hall, 729 21st St., Kent, OH, 44242-0001
Tag Update, 332

Assn. for Quality & Participation
801b W 8th St # 501, Cincinnati, OH, 45203-1601
AQP Report, 833

Athletic Equipment Managers Assn.
723 Keil Ct, Bowling Green, OH, 43402-2235
Score Board, 1,135

Aullwood Audubon Ctr. & Farm
1000 Aullwood Rd, Dayton, OH, 45414-1129
Aullwood, 373

Aviation Safety Institute
6797 N. High St., Worthington, OH, 43085-2533
Aviation Safety Monitor, 27

Baldwin Wallace College
120 E Grand St, Berea, OH, 44017-2012
Pursuit, 192

Bancohio Corp.
155 E. Broad St., Columbus, OH, 43251-0001
BancAccount, 576

•**Banks-Baldwin Law Publishing Co.**
PO Box 318063, Cleveland, OH, 44131-8063

Baptist Mid-Missions
PO Box 308011, Cleveland, OH, 44130-8011
Harvest, 1,053

Battelle Memorial Institute
505 King Ave., Columbus, OH, 43201-2693
Battelle Today, 1,095

Bean & Petrie, Inc.
1636 Club Trail Dr., Westerville, OH, 43081
Liaison, 17

Bethesda Hospital
Oak St. & Reading Rd., Cincinnati, OH, 45206
Bethes-Data, 561

Better Business Bureau Inc.
2217 E 9th St, Cleveland, OH, 44115-1299
Market Monitor, 144

Black Rose Communications
PO Box 464, Dublin, OH, 43017-0464
PEG Times, 363

Black Swamp Heritage
18620 W Moline Martin Rd, Martin, OH, 43445-9720
Black Swamp Heritage, 448

Blue Cross & Blue Shield of Ohio
2066 E 9th St, Cleveland, OH, 44115-1303
Journal, 588

Books & Co.
350a E Stroop Rd, Dayton, OH, 45429-2828
Up All Night, 825

Bowling Green State Univ.
Bowling Green State Campus, Bowling Green, OH, 43403-0001
Ohio Folklore, 425

Brimfield Memorial House Assn., Inc.
PO Box 1231, Kent, OH, 44240-0024
Kelso Courier, 542

Buchtel College of Arts and Sciences, Department of English
350 Blin Hall, Akron, OH, 44325-0001
D.H. Lawrence Society of N. America Newsletter, 820

•**Business Laws, Inc.**
11630 Chillicothe Rd., Chesterland, OH, 44026-1928

•**Business Network**
5420 Mayfield Rd., Lyndhurst, OH, 44124-2924

Byberry Walton Newsletter
6940 Southern Vista Dr, Enon, OH, 45323-1544
Byberry Walton Newsletter, 449

C.A.L./NX211 Collector's Society
727 Youn Kin Pky S, Columbus, OH, 43207-4788
CAL/NX211 Collectors Society Newsletter, 537

C.J. Krehbiel Co.
3962 Virginia Ave., Cincinnati, OH, 45227
Press Check, 1,006

Candlewick Publications
6534 South Ave., Holland, OH, 43528
Candlewick Collector Newsletter, The, 479

Carthage Mills Inc.
1821 Summit Rd., Cincinnati, OH, 45237-2868
Rug Raps, 597

Catechetical Renewal Network
PO Box 7550634, Dayton, OH, 45475-0634
Alternative Models Newsletter, 1,044

Center for Advanced Study in Telecommunications
Ohio State Unv., 210 Baker, 1971 Neil Ave., Columbus, OH, 43210
Communication Booknotes, 1,157

Center on Education & Training for Employment
1900 Kenny Rd, Columbus, OH, 43210-1016
Centergram, 304

Center for Medieval & Renaissance Studies
Ohio State Univ. Rm. 256 Cunz, 1841 Millikin Rd., Columbus, OH, 43210
Nouvelles Nouvelles, 545

Center for Plain Living
PO Box 100, Chesterhill, OH, 43728-0100
Center for Plain Living Newsletter, 813

• See ***MULTI-PUBLISHER INDEX*** for list of publications.

Center for Women's Studies At OSU
286 University Hall, 230 N. Oval Mall, Columbus, OH, 43210
Women's Studies Newsletter, 1,214

Certified Ballast Manufacturers Association
1422 Euclid Ave Ste 402, Cleveland, OH, 44115-1901
CBM News, 337

Cervantes Society of America
Dept. of Modern Languages, Denison University, Granville, OH, 43023
Newsletter of the Cervantes Society, 823

•**Children's Hospital Medical Center**
Elland & Bethesda Ave., Cincinnati, OH, 45229-2899

Christian Aid for Romania
PO Box 360, Berlin, OH, 44610-0360
Christian Aid Ministries Newsletter, 1,115

Christian Brotherhood Newsletter
127 Hazelwood Ave, Barberton, OH, 44203-1316
Christian Brotherhood Newsletter, 619

Cincinnati Bar Assn.
35 E 7th St, Cincinnati, OH, 45202-2492
CBA Report, 720

Cincinnati Enquirer, Inc.
312 Elm St, Cincinnati, OH, 45202-2739
RNA Newsletter, 697

Cincinnati Folk Life Organization
PO Box 9008, Cincinnati, OH, 45209-9998
Cincinnati Folk Life, 265

Cincinnati Gas
139 E 4th St, Cincinnati, OH, 45202-4003
O-K News, 593

•**Cincinnati Milacron**
4701 Marburg Ave, Cincinnati, OH, 45209-1025

City of Cincinnati
City Hall, 801 Plum St., #10, Cincinnati, OH, 45202
Insider, 487

Clark County Board of Education
1115 N Limestone St, Springfield, OH, 45503-3675
Educator, 1,091

Cleveland Engineering Society
3100 Chester Ave, Cleveland, OH, 44114-4683
Cleveland Engineering, 359

Cleveland Food Dealers Association, Inc.
5800 Grant Ave, Cleveland, OH, 44105
Cleveland Food Dealer, 494

Cleveland Foundation
1400 Hanna Bldg., 1422 Euclid Ave., Cleveland, OH, 44115-2001
Keeping the Trust, 1,118

Cleveland Institute of Art
11141 East Blvd, Cleveland, OH, 44106-1700
Newsletter, 205

Cleveland Institute of Music
11021 East Blvd, Cleveland, OH, 44106-1705
Notes, 205

Coleraine Historical Society
1442 Cedar Ave, Cincinnati, OH, 45224-3062
Coleraine Pageant, 451

College English Assn., Inc.
English Dept., Youngstown State Univ., Youngstown, OH, 44555-0001
CEA Forum, 302

College of Nursing Alumni Assn.
Ohio State Univ., 1585 Neil Ave., Columbus, OH, 43210-1289
Carenotes, 929

Collier, Sarner & Associates, Inc
30195 Chagrin Boulevard, #10, Cleveland, OH, 44124
Collier, Sarner & Associates Doctors Newsletter, 85

Columbia Sheep Breeders Assn. of America
PO Box 272, Upper Sandusky, OH, 43351-0272
Speaking of Columbias, 829

Columbus Foundation
1234 E Broad St, Columbus, OH, 43205-1453
Commentary, 967

Comboni Missionaries
8108 Beechmont Ave, Cincinnati, OH, 45255-3120
Comboni, 1,062

•**Communication Resources Inc.**
4150 Belden Village St., NW, Suite 400, Canton, OH, 44718-2553

Community Resources Workshop Assn.
Miami Univ., 205 McGuffey Hall, Oxford, OH, 45056
NCRWA News, 1,022

Community Service, Inc.
114 E Whiteman St # 243, Yellow Springs, OH, 45387-1826
Community Service Newsletter, 1,125

Concrete Sawing and Drilling Association
4900 Blazer Pky, Dublin, OH, 43017-3357
Concrete Openings Newsletter, 245

Convivium
PO Box 835, East Liverpool, OH, 43920-5835
Convivium, 427

Cooper Tire
Lima & Western Aves., Findlay, OH, 45840
Tire Tracks, 600

Coordinating Center for Women in Church & Society
700 Prospect Ave E, Cleveland, OH, 44115-1131
Common Lot, 1,046

Copperweld
Shelby Div., 132 W. Main St., Shelby, OH, 44875-1300
Outlook, 594

Coronary Club, Inc.
9500 Euclid Ave., #EE37, Cleveland, OH, 44195-0001
Heartline, 512

Council of Colleges of Arts & Sciences
186 University Hall, 230 N. Oval Mall, Columbus, OH, 43210-1319
CCAS Newsletter, 302

Cuyahoga Community College-Western Campus
11000 W. Pleasant Valley Rd, Parma, OH, 44130
Spectrum, 205

Darius Milhaud Society
15715 Chadbourne Rd, Cleveland, OH, 44120-3333
Darius Milhaud Society Newsletter, 911

Davey Tree Expert Co.
1500 N Mantua St, Kent, OH, 44240-2399
Davey Bulletin, 582

David M. Coffman
P.O. Box 75, Castilla, OH, 44824
Davey's Journal, 695

Dawes Arboretum
7770 Jacksontown Rd SE, Newark, OH, 43056-9358
Dawes Arboretum Newsletter, 440

Dayton
215 E 3rd St, Dayton, OH, 45402-2103
Spotlight on Your Library, 810

Dayton Chamber of Commerce
1 Chamber Plaza, Dayton, OH, 45402-2400
Business Leader, 158

Dayton Power
Courthouse Plaza S.W., Dayton, OH, 45402
DP&L News, 581

Dayton Progress Corp.
500 Progress Rd, Dayton, OH, 45449-2351
Punch Lines, 596

Deaconess Hospital
311 Straight St, Cincinnati, OH, 45219-1099
DH Pulse, 563

Degenhart Paperweight & Glass Museum
65323 Highland Hills Rd # 18, Cambridge, OH, 43725-9657
Heartbeat, 479

Delaware County Chapter OGS
PO Box 1126, Delaware, OH, 43015-8126
Delaware Genealogist, 452

Delco Products Division
2000 Forrer Blvd Stop 1042, Dayton, OH, 45420-1373
Delco Doings, 582

Designed Resources
PO Box 53798, Cincinnati, OH, 45253
TSM Reports, 615

Devilbiss Co.
1724 Indian Wood Circle, Maumee, OH, 43537-4005
Goodtimers Newsletter, 585

Diversity Water Technology, Inc.
7145 Pine St., Chagrin Falls, OH, 44022
Insight, 587

Dobie Clan of North America
20001 Ridge Rd, Cleveland, OH, 44133-6270
Dobie Connection, 452

Drackett Div., Bristol-Myers Co.
8600 Governors Hill Dr. #300, Cincinnati, OH, 45249-1388
Drackett Diamonds, 582

Dresser Industries-Marion Div.
617 W Center St, Marion, OH, 43302-3509
News & Review, 901

•**Ductile Iron Society**
28938 Lorain Rd Ste 202, North Olmsted, OH, 44070-4014

Dukeman Publications Company
4111 Yellowood Street, Lima, OH, 45806-1121
Ohio's Historical Detective, 546

Eaton Corp.
1111 Superior Ave., Eaton Ctr., Cleveland, OH, 44114-2584
Eaton Today, 582

Ecocenters Corporation
31225 Bainbridge Rd, Solon, OH, 44139-2230
Eco, The, 1,004

Educational Theatre Association
3368 Central Pky, Cincinnati, OH, 45225-2307
Super Trouper, 1,174

Effective Classrooms
14110 S Park Blvd, Cleveland, OH, 44120-1326
Effective Classrooms: Research Based Solutions to Improve Learning, 309

Eisenhower National Clearinghouse for Mathematics & Science
Ohio State University, 1929 Kenny Rd., Columbus, OH, 43210-1079
ENC Update, 852

The Eleanor Press
16216 Freyman Rd, Cygnet, OH, 43413-9766
Women Who Write, 1,213

Executive Speaker Co.
PO Box 292437, Dayton, OH, 45429-0437
Executive Speaker, 837

F.E. Myers
1101 Myers Pky, Ashland, OH, 44805-1969
On Target, 593

FFFFF
P.O. Box 39, Macedonia, OH, 44056
Frostbite Falls FAr Flung Flier, 817

•**F & W Publications**
1507 Dana Ave., Cincinnati, OH, 45207-1056

•**Federal Reserve Bank of Cleveland**
E. 6th & Superior, Cleveland, OH, 44114

Federal-State Market News Service
65 S. Front St., Columbus, OH, 43215-4131
Poultry and Egg Products, Ohio, 1,001

Federation for Community Planning
614 W Superior Ave Ste 300, Cleveland, OH, 44113-1306
Planning and Action, 1,121

Fiesta Collector's Quarterly
PO Box 471, Valley City, OH, 44280-0471
Fiesta Collector's Quarterly, 479

Fluid Controls Institute
1300 Sumner Ct., Cleveland, OH, 44115-2851
News & Views (Fluid Controls), 1,204

Forging Industry Educational & Research Foundation
LTV Bldg. 300/25 Prospect A, Cleveland, OH, 44115
FIERF Newsletter, 309

Fox Kids Club
6130 Sun Bay, Westerville, OH, 43081
Kids Club News, 169

Franklin County Genealogical Society
Box 3406, Columbus, OH, 43216-2406
Franklintonian, 454

Friends of Hopalong Cassidy
6310 Friendship Dr, New Concord, OH, 43762-9708
Hoppy Talk, 417

GDE Publications
PO Box 304, Lima, OH, 45802-0304
Softball America, 1,135

GIE Publishing, Inc. (Group Interest Enterprises)
4012 Bridge Ave., Cleveland, OH, 44113-3320
Fibre Market News, 946

Gamma Iota Sigma
1775 S College Rd, Columbus, OH, 43210-1309
Sextant, 624

General Motors Corp.
200 Georgesville Rd, Columbus, OH, 43228-2020
News Bulletin, 592

General Motors Corp., GM Assembly Div.
Lordstown Plant GMC, Lordstown, OH, 44482
Assembler, 576

General Motors Power Train
PO Box 909, Toledo, OH, 43697-0909
Intra Comm, 587

Gold Star Owners Club
C/O Ron Pallinger, 32450 Walker Rd., Avon Lake, OH, 44012
Twitter, 263

Goob, The
P.O Box 148056, Toledo, OH, 43614
Goob, The, 822

Good Samaritan Hospital
2222 Philadelphia Dr, Dayton, OH, 45406-1891
Profiles, 571

* See ***MULTI-PUBLISHER INDEX*** for list of publications.

•**Goodyear Tire & Rubber Co.**
1144 E. Market St., Akron, OH, 44316-0001

Great Lakes Historical Society
Inland Seas Maritime Museum, 480 Main St., Vermilion, OH, 44089-1015
Chadburn, 538

Greater Cleveland Growth Assn.
200 Tower City Ctr., 50 Public Square, Cleveland, OH, 44113-2291
Clevelander, 159

Greater Toledo Area American Red Cross
2275 Collingwood Blvd, Toledo, OH, 43620-1148
Spotlight, 1,122

Greene County Chapter, OGS
PO Box 706, Xenia, OH, 45385-0706
Leaves of Greene, 459

Greg Jarvela
P.O. Box 14, Vienna, OH, 44473
Enter Title Here, 695

Hall Collector's Club Newsletter
PO Box 360488, Cleveland, OH, 44136
Hall Collector's Club Newsletter, 479

Hamilton County Pharmaceutical Association
PO Box 19923, Cincinnati, OH, 45219-0923
HCPA Pharmacist, 284

Hancock County Chapter, OGS
PO Box 672, Findlay, OH, 45839-0672
Hancock Heritage, 455

Harden Newsletter
7041 Kilbourne Rd, Sunbury, OH, 43074-9567
Harden Newsletter, 455

Harvey Whitney Books Co.
PO Box 42696, Cincinnati, OH, 45242-0696
Clinical Abstracts/Current Therapeutic Findings, 282

Hobart Bros. Co.
701 Ridge Ave., Troy, OH, 45374-0001
Hobart Plant News, 585

Home Economists in Business
5008-16 Pine Creek Dr., Westerville, OH, 43081-4899
Corporate Consumer Forum Trendletter, 558

Hubecore Communications, Inc.
29100 Aurora Rd., Ste 200, Solon, OH, 44139-1855
Precision, 892

Huntington Bankshares, Inc.
17 S. High St., Columbus, OH, 43215-3456
Huntington Highlights, 585

Independent Oxygen Manufacturers Assn
PO Box 16248, Cleveland, OH, 44116-0248
IOMA Broadcaster, 165

Interlake Sailing Class Association
1341 Frank Dr., Monroe, OH, 48161-3483
Interlake Sailing Class Association Intercom, 113

International Association for Energy Economics
28790 Chagrin Blvd., Ste. 210, Cleveland, OH, 44122-4630
IAEE Newsletter, 355

International Association of Hygienic Physicians
204 Stambaugh Bldg., Youngstown, OH, 44503
IAHP Newsletter, 876

International Business Information, Inc.
PO Box 8312, Cincinnati, OH, 45208-0312
International Currency Report, 92

International Lightning Class Association
P O Box 586, Worthington, OH, 43085
Lightning Flashes, 113

International Precious Metals Institute
705 Robinwood Ave, Columbus, OH, 43213-1757
Precious Metals News & Review, 892

International Registry of Organization Dev. Professionals
11234 Walnut Ridge Rd, Chesterland, OH, 44026-1240
Organizations & Change, 842

•**Interwood Publications**
3 Interwood Pl., Box 20241, Cincinnati, OH, 45220-1821

•**Investment Research Institute, Inc.**
1259 Kemper Meadows Dr. #100, Cincinnati, OH, 45240

Iota Lambda Sigma
305 Teachers College, Univ. Of, Cincinnati, OH, 45221-0001
Grand Chapter News, 178

JI Case Collector's Association
4004 Coal Valley Rd, Vinton, OH, 45686-9109
Old Abe's News, 185

JL Sports Enterprises
c/o Luchowski, 4549 South Blvd. N.W. #20, Canton, OH, 44718-2025
Indoor Score, 1,131

Javelin Class Association
874 Beecher's Brook Rd., Mayfield Village, OH, 44143
Spearhead, The, 114

Jewish Genealogical Soc. of Cleveland
996 Eastlawn Dr, Highland Heights, OH, 44143-3126
Cleveland Kol, 450

Jewish Hospital of Cincinnati
3200 Burnet Ave, Cincinnati, OH, 45229-3099
JH News, 588

John B. Dempsey, II
1127 Euclid Ave Ste 375, Cleveland, OH, 44115-1601
Dempsey Canadian Letter, 135

Junior Classical League
Miami Univ., Oxford, OH, 45056
Torch; U.S., 334

Kappa Gamma Pi
2415 Hillcrest Dr, Stow, OH, 44224-4278
Kappa Gamma Pi News, 179

Karen Kerkhoff Gromada
Box 412, Dept. NP, Amelia, OH, 45102-0412
Double Talk, 412

Kennedy Society of America, Inc.
520 Harrison Ave., Cambridge, OH, 43725-1472
Kennedy Gazette, 458

Kent State University Printing Service
Main & Lincoln Sts., Kent, OH, 44242-0001
Aid Bulletin - Addiction Intervention with the Disabled, 1,010

Keystone Press
1440 S Byrne Rd, Toledo, OH, 43614-2363
American Flint, 698

Knights of St. John
6517 Charles Ave, Parma, OH, 44129-3712
Knight of St. John, 1,057

Kovels on Antiques and Collectibles
30799 Pinetree Rd., Pepper Pike, OH, 44124
Kovels on Antiques & Collectibles, 53

Kroger Co.
1014 Vine St, Cincinnati, OH, 45202-1100
Merry-Go-Round, 590

L. M. Berry
PO Box 6000, Dayton, OH, 45401-6000
Yellow Pages by Berry, 603

Larry Knarr
7657 Squirrel Creek Ln, Cincinnati, OH, 45247-3614
Newsletter of the Knarr-Knerr-Knorr Family, 462

Lesbian Activist Bureau, Inc.
PO Box 1485, Cincinnati, OH, 45201-1485
Dinah, 444

Library Benchmarking International
231 W 4th St Apt 505a, Cincinnati, OH, 45202-2679
Library Benchmarking Newsletter, 801

Licensed Practical Nurse Assn. of Ohio, Inc.
1310 Saint Paris Pike, Springfield, OH, 45504-1615
Ohio Licensed Practical Nurse, 593

Lincoln Electric Co.
22801 Saint Clair Ave, Cleveland, OH, 44117-1199
Stabilizer, 1,205

Lutheran Medical Ctr.
2609 Franklin Blvd., Cleveland, OH, 44113-2992
Connections, 581

MUNZ
9423 Montgomery Rd, Cincinnati, OH, 45242-7602
Hoosier Challenger, 817

Madden Family Newsletter
1101 Wilmington Ave Apt A, Dayton, OH, 45420-1681
Madden Family Newsletter, 460

Management Computer Systems
2790 Fisher Rd, Columbus, OH, 43204-3581
Today's Parts Manager, 76

Marion Area Genealogical Society
671 Vernon Heights Blvd, Marion, OH, 43302-5377
Marion Memories, 460

Maritime Postmark Society
141 Gordon Ave, Wadsworth, OH, 44281-2310
Seaposter, 972

•**Market Search, Inc.**
2727 N Holland Sylvania Rd Ste, A, Toledo, OH, 43615-1800

•**McEntee Media Corp.**
13727 Holland Rd., Cleveland, OH, 44142-3920

Median Iris Society
1440 N Fountain Blvd, Springfield, OH, 45504-1425
Medianite, 442

Meister Publishing Co.
37733 Euclid Ave., Willoughby, OH, 44094-5925
Cotton Grower, 39

Melton Center for Jewish Studies
399 Dulles Hall, 230 W. 17th Ave., Columbus, OH, 43210
Melton Center for Jewish Studies-Newsletter, 317

•**Meredith Graphics**
1231 E. 286th St., Euclid, OH, 44132-2194

Messenger
16010 Detroit Ave, Lakewood, OH, 44107-3713
Messenger, 1,058

Miami Valley Hospital
1 Wyoming St, Dayton, OH, 45409-2763
Insider (Miami Valley Hospital), 567

Mid-Ohio Regional Planning Commission
285 E Main St, Columbus, OH, 43215-5222
Horizons, 1,021

Milton Society Of America
Ohio University, 378 Ellis Hall, Athens, OH, 45701
Milton Society of America, Bulletin, 823

Miniatures Industry Assn. of America
1100h Brandywine Blvd # 2188, Zanesville, OH, 43702-2188
MIAA Industry News, 554

Mom to Mom
PO Box 36160, Cincinnati, OH, 45236-0160
Mom to Mom, 1,210

Monroe County Historical Society
PO Box 538, Woodsfield, OH, 43793-0538
Monroe County Heritage, 544

Montgomery County Medical Society
40 S. Perry St., Dayton, OH, 45402-1429
Medical Bulletin: Montgomery County Medical Society, 878

Morris Minor Registry of North America
318 Hampton Park, Westerville, OH, 43081-5723
Minor News, 74

Music Box, Inc.
3606 Edwin Ave, Cincinnati, OH, 45204-1234
Music Box, 914

NCR Corp.
1700 S. Patterson Blvd., Dayton, OH, 45479-0001
Insight, 587

NSU Enthusiasts USA
11192 Prouty Rd, Concord, OH, 44077-2318
Neckarsulm News, 75

Natl. Assn of Agricultural Journalists
312 Valley View Dr., Huron, OH, 44839
National Association of Agricultural Journalists Newsletter, 696

Natl. Assn. of Bank Services
5008-02 Pine Creek Dr., Westerville, OH, 43081-4899
NABS Newsletter, 95

Natl. Assn. of Chemical Dist.
C/O United Technologies, 5100 Springfield Pike, #412, Dayton, OH, 45431
Chemical Distributors, 163

Natl. Assn. of College Stores
500 E Lorain St, Oberlin, OH, 44074-1238
Campus Market Report, 11

Natl. Assn. for Core Curriculum
1100 E Summit St Ste 5, Kent, OH, 44240-4094
Core Teacher, 306

National Association for Health Care Recruitment
PO Box 5769, Akron, OH, 44372-5769
Recruitment Directions, 931

Natl. Assn. of the Physically Handicapped. Inc.
244 W. Sturbridge Dr., Medina, OH, 44256-3887
NAPH National Newsletter, 278

National Business Incubation Association
20 E. Circle Dr., Ste.190, Athens, OH, 45701-3751
NBIA Review, 146

Natl. Cambridge Collectors, Inc.
PO Box 416, Cambridge, OH, 43725-0416
Cambridge Crystal Ball, 478

Natl. City Bank of Cleveland
1900 E. 9th St., Cleveland, OH, 44114-3484
National City News, 591

Natl. Fed. of Flemish Giant Rabbit Breeders
233 Aultman Ave NW, Canton, OH, 44708-5524
National Federation of Flemish Giant Rabbit Breeders, Bulletin, 828

National Ground Water Association
2600 Ground Water, Columbus, OH, 43219
Well Log, The, 397

Natl. Homeschool Assn.
PO Box 157290, Cincinnati, OH, 45215-7290
National Homeschool Assn. Newsletter, 321

• See **MULTI-PUBLISHER INDEX** for list of publications.

Natl. Ice Cream & Yogurt Retailers Assn.
1429 King Ave # 210, Columbus, OH, 43212-2108
National Ice Cream & Yogurt Retailers Association Newsletter, 265

National Registry of Emergency Medical Technicians
PO Box 29233, Columbus, OH, 43229-0233
Registry, 526

National Reye's Syndrome Foundation
PO BOX 829, Bryan, OH, 43506-0829
National Reye's Syndrome Foundation-In the News, 520

Natl. Staff Development Council
PO Box 240, Oxford, OH, 45056-0240
Developer, The, 307

Network of Small Businesses
5420 Mayfield Rd # 205, Lyndhurst, OH, 44124-2924
Network News, 146

News of Cosca
4232 Poe Rd, Medina, OH, 44256-9740
News of Cosca, 560

News Notice
4758 Ridge Rd # 2633, Cleveland, OH, 44144-3327
News Notice, 472

Nickelby's Bookstore
1425 Grandview Ave, Columbus, OH, 43212-2853
Nickleby's Bookstore, 823

Nike Thain
1636 E. Main St #202, Kent, OH, 44240
Sleepy Foot, 998

North American Assn. for Environmental Education
PO Box 400, Troy, OH, 45373-0400
North American Association for Environmental Education, 389

North Central Ohio Dental Soc.
2355 W State Route 18, Tiffin, OH, 44883-8826
Articulator, 268

North Coast Advertising
1601 Cottage St, Ashland, OH, 44805-1235
Coffee Break, 580

Northeast Ohio Areawide Coordinating Agency
668 Euclid Ave., Atrium Office Plz., Cleveland, OH, 44114-3000
NOACA News, 1,022

OCLC Online Computer Library Ctr.
6565 Frantz Rd, Dublin, OH, 43017-5308
OCLC Newsletter, 806

O.M. Scott & Sons Co.
14111 Scottslawn Rd., Marysville, OH, 43041-0001
On Course, 480

Oberlin Other
285 E College St, Oberlin, OH, 44074-1354
Oberlin Other, 818

Ohio AFL-CIO
271 E State St, Columbus, OH, 43215-4370
Ohio AFL-CIO News and Views, 710

Ohio Arts Council
727 E Main St, Columbus, OH, 43205-1796
Artspace, 63

Ohio Bankers Assoc.
37 W. Broad St., Ste. 1001, Columbus, OH, 43215-4162
Ohio Banker, 96

Ohio Chamber of Commerce
P O Box 15159, Columbus, OH, 43215-0159
Network, 160

Ohio Connection
PO Box 14296, Dayton, OH, 45413-0296
Emerick Family Newsletter, 453

Ohio Credit Union League
1201 Dublin Rd, Columbus, OH, 43215-1044
High Spots, 91

Ohio Dept. of Health
246 N. High St., P.O. Box 118, Columbus, OH, 43215-2429
Progress in Public Health, 525

Ohio Educational Broadcasting Network Commission
2470 N Star Rd, Columbus, OH, 43221-3405
Ohio Network Notes, 124

•**Ohio Environmental Council**
OEC 400 Dublin Ave, Suite #120, Columbus, OH, 43215

Ohio Environmental Protection Agency
PO Box 163669, Columbus, OH, 43216-3669
Environment Ohio, 379

Ohio Florists' Assn.
2130 Stella Ct. #200, Columbus, OH, 43215-1033
Ohio Florists' Association Bulletin, 424

Ohio Genealogical Society
Ottawa County Chapter, Box 193, Port Clinton, OH, 43452
Marshland to Heartland, 460

Ohio Genealogical Soc.
6252 Spring St, Ravenna, OH, 44266-1338
Portage Path to Genealogy Portage Co. Chapter, 465

Ohio Genealogical Society
PO Box 414, Upper Sandusky, OH, 43351-0414
Wyandot Tracers, 470

Ohio Genealogical Society, Crawford County Chapter
PO Box 92, Galion, OH, 44833-0092
Tracking in Crawford County, 468

Ohio Genealogical Society Morgan County Chapter
Box 418, McConnelsville, OH, 43756-0418
Morgan Link, 461

Ohio Genealogical Society Summit County Chapter
PO Box 2232, Akron, OH, 44309-2232
Highpoint, 456

Ohio Health Letter
224 Pleasant St, Yellow Springs, OH, 45387-2015
Ohio Health Letter, 522

Ohio Historical Society
1982 Velma Ave, Columbus, OH, 43211-2497
Echoes, 539

•**Ohio-KY-Indiana Regional Council of Governments**
801B W. 8th St., Ste. 400, Cincinnati, OH, 45203-1601

Ohio, Kentucky, Indiana Regional Council of Governments
801B W. 8th St., #400, Cincinnati, OH, 45203-1607
OKI Topics Newsletter, 1,023

Ohio National Companies
PO Box 237, Cincinnati, OH, 45201-0237
ONLI Echoes, 593

Ohio Naturalist Newsletter, The
PO Box 429142, Cincinnati, OH, 45242-9142
Ohio Naturalist Newsletter, The, 389

Ohio River Valley Water Sanitation Commission
5735 Kellogg Ave, Cincinnati, OH, 45228-1112
ORSANCO Quality Monitor, 1,204

Ohio Rural Letter Carriers' Assn
S. Twp. Rd. 187, Attica, OH, 44807
Ohio Rural Carriers, 971

Ohio Society of Hospital Pharmacists
53 Haddam Pl W, Westerville, OH, 43081-1266
Bulletin, 281

Ohio State Dept. of Education
270 E State St, Columbus, OH, 43215-4312
School Lunch Administrative Newsletter, 1,076

Ohio State Univ.
2120 Fyffe Rd., Columbus, OH, 43210-1010
Outlook News, 828

Ohio State University, Center for Slavic Studies
303 Oxley Hall, Columbus, OH, 43210-1219
Ohio Slavic and East European Newsletter, 635

Ohio State University, College of Agriculture
204 Agriculture Admin. Bldg., 2120 Fyffe Rd., Columbus, OH, 43210
Agri-Naturalist, 36

Ohio Veterinary Medical Assn.
3168 Riverside Dr, Columbus, OH, 43221-2540
Ohio Veterinary Medical Association Newsletter, 1,201

Ohio Wesleyan Univ.
English Dept., Slocum Hall, Delaware, OH, 43015
Transcript, 205

Ohioana Library Assn.
65 S. Front St., Suite 1105, Columbus, OH, 43215
Ohioana Quarterly, 806

Osteopathic College of Ophthalmology & Otorhinolaryngology
405 W Grand Ave, Dayton, OH, 45405-4720
Osteopathic College of Ophthamology & Otorhinolaryngology-Newsletter, 883

Owens-Corning Fiberglas Corp.
Fiberglas Tower, #t21, Toledo, OH, 43659-0001
Toledo News Bulletin Board, 601

•**PBS-Professional Business Svces.**
450 Potter St, Wauseon, OH, 43567-1138

PM Company
24 Triangle Park Dr, Cincinnati, OH, 45246-3411
Faxfacts, 1,159

•**PRC Publishing, Inc.**
4418 Belden Village St NW, Canton, OH, 44718-2516

Packard Electric Div., GMC
PO Box 431, Warren, OH, 44486-0001
Direct Connection, 582

Palatines to America
Capital Univ., Box 101, Columbus, OH, 43209-2394
Palatine Patter, 464

Parents of Murdered Children
100 E. 8th St., #B-41, Cincinnati, OH, 45202-2129
Survivors, 529

Peter Dag Investment Letter
65 Lake Front Dr, Akron, OH, 44319-3660
Peter Dag Investment Letter, 682

Phantastic Phunnies
1450 Loop N. Rd., Kent, OH, 44240-4619
Phantastic Phunnies, 605

Phi Delta Theta Fraternity
2 S Campus Ave, Oxford, OH, 45056-1872
Scroll, The, 181

Philosophy Documentation Center
Bowling Green State Univ., Bowling Green, OH, 43403-0001
Phil Facts, 974

Pioneer Electronics
4800 E 131st St, Cleveland, OH, 44105-7132
Pen, The, 234

Pizazz Comics Unlimited
1840 Garden Ridge, Apt. #3, Toledo, OH, 43614
Pizazz Comics Unlimited: Newsletter of Pizazz Comics, 210

Polycrystalline Products Assn.
6089 Frantz Rd., Ste. 101, Dublin, OH, 43017
Poly Probe, 892

Popular Press
Bowling Green State Univ., Bowling Green, OH, 43403-0001
PCAN: Popular Culture Assn. Newsletter, 261

Portage County Historical Society Newsletter
6549 N Chestnut St, Ravenna, OH, 44266-3907
Portage County Historical Society Newsletter, 547

Public Library of Youngstown
305 Wick Ave, Youngstown, OH, 44503-1003
Biblio-Files, 794

Putnam County Historical Society
201 E. Main St., Box 264, Kalida, OH, 45853
Putnam County Heritage, 547

R.A.D.A.R.
4949 S. 25A, Tipp City, OH, 45371
RADAR, 75

•**RX-Data-Pac Service**
PO Box 42020, Cincinnati, OH, 45242-0020

Race Track Chaplaincy of America
Box 1924, Galloway, OH, 43119-0924
R.T.C.A. Winner's Circle, 1,050

Racing Pigeon Bulletin
34 E Franklin St, Bellbrook, OH, 45305-2098
Racing Pigeon Bulletin, 1,134

Railway & Locomotive Historical Society
1 Dept. Of History Univ. Of, Akron, Akron, OH, 44325-1902
Railroad History, 1,030

Richmond Heights General Hospital
27100 Chardon Rd, Richmond Heights, OH, 44143-1198
Vital Signs, 573

Roman Reports Pub.
12600 Rockside Rd Ste 107, Garfield Heights, OH, 44125-4525
Roman Reports, 275

•**Ross Labs.**
625 Cleveland Ave, Columbus, OH, 43215-1754

Roxane Laboratories, Inc.
PO Box 16532, Columbus, OH, 43216-6532
White Sheet, 289

Rubbermaid
1147 Akron Rd, Wooster, OH, 44691-2596
Rubbermaid Review, 597

S. Rosenthal & Co. Inc.
9933 Alliance Rd, Cincinnati, OH, 45242-8959
Impressions, 1,005

Saharan Peoples Support Committee
217 E Lehr Ave, Ada, OH, 45810-1431
SPSC Letter, 638

•**St. Alexis Hospital**
5163 Broadway Ave, Cleveland, OH, 44127-1532

•**St. Anthony Messenger Press**
1615 Republic St, Cincinnati, OH, 45210-1219

Sales
446 Statler Office Tower, Cleveland, OH, 44115
Sales/Marketing Today, 1,088

•**Scitec Services, Inc.**
5324 Sinclair Rd, Columbus, OH, 43229-5002

---

* See **MULTI-PUBLISHER INDEX** for list of publications.

Seneca County Genealogical Society
PO Box 157, Tiffin, OH, 44883-0157
Seneca Searchers, 467

Seniors Inc. of Centerville/Washington Twp.
8100 Clyo Rd, Centerville, OH, 45458-2720
Gold Pages, The, 1,117

Sherwin-Williams Co.
101 Prospect Ave., N.W., Cleveland, OH, 44115
Viewpoint, 602

Sherwin-Williams Co., Container Plant
Carolina & Myron Sts., Hubbard, OH, 44425
Can-A-Gram, 579

Showboat Centennials
76 Glen Dr, Worthington, OH, 43085-4010
Showboat Centennials, 548

Soccer Assn. for Youth
4903 Vine St. #1, Cincinnati, OH, 45217-1252
Touchline, 1,137

Societe pour l'Etude de la Numismatique Francaise
4304 Belden Village St NW, Canton, OH, 44718-2514
SAENT, 928

Society for American Baseball Research
PO Box 93183, Cleveland, OH, 44101-5183
Current Baseball Publications, 101

Society Corp.
127 Public Sq., Cleveland, OH, 44114-1216
Society Now, 598

Society of Ohio Archivists
2700 Kenny Road, Columbus, OH, 43210-1157
Ohio Archivist, 546

South Bend Football Recruiting News
281 Bruce Ct., Westerville, OH, 43081
South Bend Football Recruiting News, 434

Southwest General Hospital
18697 Bagley Rd, Middleburg Heights, OH, 44130-3497
News Capsule, 592

Southwestern Craft & Hobby Association
1100 H Brandywine Blvd., P.O. Box 2188, Zanesville, OH, 43702-2188
SWCHA Newsletter, 556

Specialty Papers Co.
PO Box 1031, Dayton, OH, 45401-1031
Showcase, 946

Staff Association, Public Library of Cincinnati
800 Vine St, Cincinnati, OH, 45202-2009
Staff Notes, 811

State Chemical Mfg. Co.
3100 Hamilton Ave., Cleveland, OH, 44114-3701
Communicator, 580

•**State Policy Research, Inc.**
182 W. Royal Forest Blvd., Columbus, OH, 43214-2029

Stereotypers
90 E 214th St, Cleveland, OH, 44123-1073
Stereotypers, 710

Strategy Group Inc., The
290 Beckley Ln, Dublin, OH, 43017-1346
People Trends, 614

Studerbaker Family Natl. Assn.
6555 S State Route 202, Tipp City, OH, 45371-9468
Studebaker Family, 467

Suspension Specialists Assn.
4015 Marks Rd., Ste. 2B, Median, OH, 44256
Leaf, The, 73

TW Cincinnati Enquirer
312 Elm Street, Cincinnati, OH, 45202
TW Cincinnati Enquirer, 925

Tait Tech, Inc.
500 Webster St, Dayton, OH, 45404-1525
Taitline, 600

Taylor-Winfield Corp.
1052 Mahoning Ave NW, Warren, OH, 44483-4622
T-W News, 600

Teague Publishing Group
PO Box 14689, Dayton, OH, 45413-0689
Direct Success Ideas, 274

Thomas Edison Program
Ohio Dept. Of Development Box, 1001, Columbus, OH, 43266-0001
Edison Entrepreneur, 484

Tiffin Glass Collectors Club
PO Box 554, Tiffin, OH, 44883-0554
Tiffin Glassmasters, 479

Tinnerman Prod. Inc.
PO Box 6688, Cleveland, OH, 44101-1688
Speed Notes, 599

Toledo Area Chamber of Commerce
Enterprise Suite 200, 300 Madison Ave., Toledo, OH, 43604-1575
Insider, The, 142

Toledo-Lucas County Port Authority
1 Maritime Plaza, Toledo, OH, 43604-1866
Connections, 1,111

Toledo Scale Company, Toledo Scale Div.
350 W Wilson Bridge Rd, Worthington, OH, 43085-2217
Toledo System, 601

Tremco News
10701 Shaker Blvd, Cleveland, OH, 44104-3752
Tremco News, 250

Trinity Lutheran Seminary
2199 E Main St, Columbus, OH, 43209-2334
Te Deum, 1,072

Trumbull County Chapter
PO Box 309, Warren, OH, 44482-0309
Ancestry Trails, 447

USBE
2969 W 25th St, Cleveland, OH, 44113-5332
USBE News: For Members Only, 811

Union
1367 W 65th St, Cleveland, OH, 44102-2109
Union, 408

Union Fork & Hoe Co.
500 Dublin Ave, Columbus, OH, 43215-2382
Union Forever, 601

United Church Board for World Ministries
700 Prospect Ave., Cleveland, OH, 44115-1100
Whole Earth Newsletter, 1,066

United Church Coalition for Lesbian/Gay Concerns
18 N College St, Athens, OH, 45701-2436
Waves, 446

United Fanzine Organization
7534 Kingsgate Way, West Chester, OH, 05069
Tetragammaton Fragments: Official Newsletter of the United Fanzine Organization, 418

U.S. Boomerang Assn.
PO Box 182, Delaware, OH, 43015-0182
Many Happy Returns - U.S. Boomerang Assn. Newsletter, 1,132

U.S. Highland Dancing Association
5135 Kneale Dr, Lyndhurst, OH, 44124-1226
Highland News, 408

U.S. Industrial Chemicals Co.
11500 Northlake Dr, Cincinnati, OH, 45249-1642
U.S.I. News, 166

United Telephone Co of Ohio
PO Box 3555, Mansfield, OH, 44907-0555
United of Ohio News, 602

United Way Inc. of the Dayton Area
PO Box 67, Dayton, OH, 45401-0067
Spirit, 599

United Way Services
1331 Euclid Ave., Cleveland, OH, 44115
Making Contact, 1,118

United Way of Summit County
90 N Prospect St #1260, Akron, OH, 44304-1273
Common Ground, 1,115

Univ. of Cincinnati.
Dept. of Classics, Cincinnati, OH, 45221-0226
Nestor, 823

Univ. of Cincinnati Computing Info. Tech. Svces.
45 Beecher Hall, Mail Loc. 88, Cincinnati, OH, 45221
Technical Update, 240

Univ. of Cincinnati, Ctr. for Information Technology Svce.
Academic Info. Technology Svce, 45 Beecher Hall, Mail Loc.0088, Cincinnati, OH, 45221-0001
Technical Update, 240

Univ. of Cincinnati Evening College
102 Hanna-Mcmicken Hall, Ml19, Cincinnati, OH, 45221-0001
University of Cincinnati Evening College Newsletter, 205

Univ. Circle Inc.
10831 Magnolia Dr, Cleveland, OH, 44106-1807
University Circle Bulletin, 262

Univ. of Toledo English Dept.
Dept. of English Lang & Lit, 2801 W. Bancroft St., Toledo, OH, 43606
Eudora Welty Newsletter, 821

Vita-Mix Corp.
8615 Usher Rd, Cleveland, OH, 44138-2103
Vita-Mix Health Digest, The, 531

Vortec Corp.
10125 Carver Rd, Cincinnati, OH, 45242-4798
Vortecnology News, 602

Warren County Hist. Society
PO Box 223, Lebanon, OH, 45036-0223
Historicalog, 541

Western Reserve Girl Scout Council
345 White Pond Dr, Akron, OH, 44320-1119
Trefoil, 601

Western Reserve Historical Society
10825 East Blvd., Cleveland, OH, 44106-1703
Western Reserve Historical Society Genealogical Committee Bulletin, 469

Western-Southern Life Insurance
Public Relations, 400 Broadway, Cincinnati, OH, 45202-3341
Newsletter, 592

Whirlpool Corp.
1300 Marion Agosta Rd., Marion, OH, 43302-9577
Conveyor, 581

Whiz Bang Graphics
43 Ankara Ave # 98, Brookville, OH, 45309-1207
Letters from Abraham Lincoln, 65

William Horstman & Associates
PO Box 784, Troy, OH, 45373-0784
On Target-For Individuals Running Small & Midsize Companies, 147

Williams County Genealogical Society
PO Box 293, Bryan, OH, 43506-0293
Ohio's Last Frontier, 463

Wood County Chapter Ohio Genealogical Society
PO Box 722, Bowling Green, OH, 43402-0722
Wood County Chapter Ohio Genealogical Society Newsletter, 470

•**Writer's Nook Press**
38114 3rd St Ste 181, Willoughby, OH, 44094-6140

•**Yellowstone Information Services**
RR 2 Box 42A, Bloomingdale, OH, 43910-9802

Oklahoma

American Peanut Research & Education Society
376 Ag. Hall Oklahoma State, Univ., Stillwater, OK, 74078-0001
Peanut Research, 1,009

Assn. of American Indian Physicians
1235 Sovereign Row Ste C7, Oklahoma City, OK, 73108-1833
Association of American Indian Physicians Newsletter, 867

Bank of Oklahoma
PO Box 2300, Tulsa, OK, 74192
Banknotes, 577

Bartlesville Wesleyan College
2201 Silverlake Rd, Bartlesville, OK, 74006-6299
Tower, 192

Broken Arrow Genealogical Society
PO Box 1244, Broken Arrow, OK, 74013-1244
Green Country Quarterly, 455

Bryan County Heritage Assn.
PO Box 153, Calera, OK, 74730-0153
Bryant County Heritage Quarterly, 449

COSEC Intl., Inc.
8141 E 44th St, Tulsa, OK, 74145-4846
Forum, 437

Commodity Information Systems, Inc.
210 Park Ave. Bldg 2970, Oklahoma City, OK, 73102-5604
Price Perceptions, 682

Cooper House Publishing, Inc.
PO Box 54947, Oklahoma City, OK, 73154-1947
Poets' Digest, 983

Council Courier
PO Box 26182, Oklahoma City, OK, 73126-0182
Council Courier, 559

Da Lee Newsletter
1810 Linwood Blvd, Oklahoma City, OK, 73106-2626
Da Lee Newsletter, 451

Digest of Attorney General
112 State Capitol Building, 2300 N. Lincoln Blvd., Oklahoma City, OK, 73105
Digest of Attorney General Opinions, 731

•**Dover Corp.**
Norris-O'Bannon Div., Box 2070, Tulsa, OK, 74101-2070

Energy Consumers and Producers Assn.
PO Box 1288, Muskogee, OK, 74402-1288
ECPA Newsline, 352

Fire Protection Pubs.
Ok State Univ., Stillwater, OK, 74078-0001
Speaking of Fire, 422

* See ***MULTI-PUBLISHER INDEX*** for list of publications.

Football Writers Association of America
PO Box 1022, Edmond, OK, 73083-1022
5th Down, 434

George E. Failing Co.
PO Box 872, Enid, OK, 73702-0872
Core Driller, 581

HTB Inc.
Box 1845, 1411 Classen Bl, Oklahoma City, OK, 73101-1845
HTB Happenings, 585

Hillsdale Free Will Baptist College
PO Box 7208, Moore, OK, 73153-1208
Insight, 205

Institute of the Great Plains
601 NW Ferris Ave., P.O. Box 68, Lawton, OK, 73502-0068
Museum of the Great Plains Newsletter, 906

International Porcelain Artists/Teachers
4125 NW 57th St, Oklahoma City, OK, 73112-1505
International Porcelain Artists/Teachers News, 65

International Softball Federation
2801 NE 50th St., Oklahoma, OK, 73111-7203
World Softball, 1,137

•**Joe Williams Communications**
PO Box 924, Bartlesville, OK, 74005-0924

Kappa Kappa Iota
1875 E 15th St, Tulsa, OK, 74104-4610
Kappa Profile, 179

Life Springs Resources
PO Box 12609, Oklahoma City, OK, 73157-2609
Worldorama, 1,052

Light of Christ Community Church
22 Summit Ridge Dr, Tahlequah, OK, 74464-9260
Sparrow Hawk Villager, 975

•**Midwest Register Inc.**
1120 E. 4th St., Tulsa, OK, 74120-3220

Mu Alpha Theta
University Of Oklahoma 601 Elm, Ave., Room 423, Norman, OK, 73019-0001
Mathematical Log, 852

Napoleonic Age Philatelists
7513 Clayton Dr., Oklahoma City, OK, 73132-5636
Campaign, 970

NatCom, Inc.
5300 City Plex Tower, 2448 E. 31st St., Tulsa, OK, 74137-4207
Winning!, 370

Natl. Society of Scabbard
205 Thatcher Hall, Okla State, Stillwater, OK, 74078-0001
National Society of Scabbard and Blade Newsletter, 180

Natl. Softball Hall of Fame
2801 NE 50th St, Oklahoma City, OK, 73111-7203
National Softball Hall of Fame Newsletter, 1,133

Neva Hill & Company
PO Box 6388, Oklahoma City, OK, 73153-0388
Hill Report, The, 990

New Breed
PO Box 50126, Tulsa, OK, 74150-0126
New Breed, 192

Ninety-Nines Inc., The
Box 965, Will Rogers Airport, Oklahoma City, OK, 73159-0008
International Women Pilots, 30

Oklahoma Anthropological Society
RR 1 Box 62B, Cheyenne, OK, 73628-9729
Oklahoma Anthropological Society, Newsletter, 51

Oklahoma Employment Security Commission
Research Division, 2401 N. Lincoln Blvd., Rm. 302, Oklahoma City, OK, 73105-4495
Oklahoma Labor Market Information, 704

Oklahoma Historical Society
2100 N Lincoln Blvd, Oklahoma City, OK, 73105-4997
Mistletoe Leaves, 544

Oklahoma Library Assn.
300 Hardy Dr, Edmond, OK, 73013-5101
Oklahoma Librarian, 806

Oklahoma Museum of Natural History
Univ. Of Oklahoma 1335 Asp, Ave., Norman, OK, 73019-0001
OMNH Newsletter, 907

Oklahoma School Food Service Assn.
215 E 12th Ave, Stillwater, OK, 74074-4613
Oklahoma Surrey, 1,076

Oklahoma State Dept. of Education
Oliver Hodge Bldg., 2500 N. Lincoln, Oklahoma City, OK, 73105-4599
Administrative Focus, 1,089

•**Oklahoma State Dept. of Health**
1000 NE 10th St, Oklahoma City, OK, 73117-1299

Oklahoma State Dept. of Industrial Development
2401 N Lincoln Blvd Dept 500, Oklahoma City, OK, 73105-4402
Oklahoma Rep!, 593

Oral Roberts Evangelistic Association
Box 2187, Tulsa, OK, 74171-0001
Daily Blessing, 1,063

Organization of Psychic Research Associates
PO Box 720366, Norman, OK, 73070
OPRA Newsletter, 949

Partners in Publishing
PO Box 50347, Tulsa, OK, 74150-0347
PIP College 'HELPS', 324

•**PennWell Publishing Co.**
1421 South Sheridan Rd., Tulsa, OK, 74112-6600

Percussive Arts Society, Inc.
701 NW Ferris Ave # 25, Lawton, OK, 73507-5442
Percussion News, 916

Petroleum Equipment Inst.
6514 E. 69th St., Tulsa, OK, 74133-1729
Tulsa Letter, 965

Phillips Univ.
Pillipian Dept., 100 South University Road, Enid, OK, 73701
Oklahoma English Bulletin, 324

Porsche Market Letter
PO Box 54679, Oklahoma City, OK, 73154-1679
Porsche Market Letter, 75

Rodeo Historical Society
1700 NE 63rd St, Oklahoma City, OK, 73111-7906
Ketch Pen, 560

Sadie's Chatter Newsletter
PO Box 2061, Tulsa, OK, 74101-2061
Sadie's Chatter Newsletter, 557

St. John Medical Center
1923 S Utica Ave, Tulsa, OK, 74104-6502
Pager, 570

ShoeBox Ford Enterprises
Box 30647, Midwest City, OK, 73140-3647
1949-50-51 Mercury Owners Newsletter, 69

Singles Support Services
PO Box 842, Norman, OK, 73070-0842
Singles & Leaders Newsletter, 1,051

Southwest Alliance for Latin America
1700 Asp Ave., Norman, OK, 73037-0001
Southwest Alliance for Latin America Bulletin, 402

Southwest Radio Church
PO Box 1144, Oklahoma City, OK, 73101-1144
Gospel Truth, 1,063

State Bureau of Investigation
2132 NE 36th St, Oklahoma City, OK, 73111-5306
Oklahoma Law Enforcement Bulletin, 788

Tulsa City- County Library System
400 Civic Ctr, Tulsa, OK, 74103-3830
Info, 106

University of Central Oklahoma
100 N University, Edmond, OK, 73034-5209
Alumni Newsletter, 192

Univ. of Oklahoma, Ctr. for Economics
307 W Brooks St Rm 4, Norman, OK, 73019-4000
Oklahoma Business Bulletin, 147

Univ. of Oklahoma, Dept. of Psychiatry
Health Science Center, 1100 N. Lindsay, Oklahoma City, OK, 73104
Biological Psychology Bulletin, 1,010

Univ. of Oklahoma School of Library & Information Studies
401 W Brooks St # 120, Norman, OK, 73069-8824
Tracings, 811

University of Tulsa
600 S College Ave, Tulsa, OK, 74104-3189
Conservation Administration News, 796

Warren Petroleum Corp., Gulf Oil Corp.
PO Box 1589, Tulsa, OK, 74102-1589
Expander, 583

Western Plains Library System
PO Box 1027, Clinton, OK, 73601-1027
Western Plains Library System Newsletter, 813

William Shaklee
14901 North Pennsylvania Ave., # 369, Oklahoma City, OK, 73134-6072
Descendants of Peter Shaklee (1756-1834), 452

Womans Professional Rodeo Association
Rr 5 Box 698, Blanchard, OK, 73010-9351
Girls' Rodeo Association News, 559

•**World Neighbors, Inc.**
4127 NW 122nd St, Oklahoma City, OK, 73120-8882

Oregon

Access to Energy
PO Box 1250, Cave Junction, OR, 97523
Access to Energy, 350

Alcyone Light Centre
910 Glendale Ave., Ashland, OR, 97520-2521
Alcyone Journal, 813

American Heart Assn., Oregon Affiliate, Inc.
1425 NE Irving St Ste 100, Portland, OR, 97232-4201
Oregon Heartline, 522

American Poultry Assn.
26363 S Tucker Rd, Estacada, OR, 97023-9441
Fancy Feathers, 1,001

Amer. Soc. of Corp. Secretaries
9275 SW Peyton Ln., Wilsonville, OR, 97070-9200
L.A. Group, A.S.C.S. Newsletter, 840

Ample Opportunity
PO Box 40621, Portland, OR, 97240-0621
Ample Information, 1,206

Armstrong Mfg. Co.
PO Box 3008, Portland, OR, 97208-3008
Armstrong Saw Engineer, 495

Associated Court
2014 NW 24th Ave, Portland, OR, 97210-2345
Associated Court and Commercial Newspapers, Bulletin, 923

Associated Oregon Industries
1149 Court St., NE, PO Box 12519, Salem, OR, 97309
AOI Business Viewpoint, 126

Belgian Researchers
62073 Fruitdale Ln., La Grande, OR, 97850-5312
Belgian Laces, 536

Biokinesiology Institute
5432 Highway 227, Trail, OR, 97541-9710
Creative Health Newsletter, 503

Birth to Three
3875 Kincaid St # 15, Eugene, OR, 97405-4554
Birth to Three, 78

Black Sheep Press
25455 NW Dixie Mountain Rd, Scappoose, OR, 97056-9500
Black Sheep Newsletter, 827

Bozarth Beacon
38518 Kickbush Ln, Springfield, OR, 97478-8667
Bozarth Beacon, 449

Brighton Academy, Foundation of Human Understanding
1121 NE 7th St, Grants Pass, OR, 97526-1421
Brighton Times, 301

Bureau of Governmental Research and Service, U. of Oregon
PO Box 3177, Eugene, OR, 97403-0177
Oregon Governmental Notes, 490

Business Forms Management Assn. Inc.
519 SW 3rd Ave Ste 712, Portland, OR, 97204-2519
INFOCUS, 141

Business Strategies
PO Box 19358, Portland, OR, 97280-0358
Ethical Management, 837

C.C. Crow Publications, Inc.
PO Box 25749, Portland, OR, 97225-0749
Crow's Weekly Market Report, 830

•**CD Kloek & Associates**
843 E Main St Ste 100, Medford, OR, 97504-7137

CPA Publishing
PO Box 905, Sandy, OR, 97055-0905
Patriot Review, 472

Central Lincoln People's Utility Dist.
2129 N Coast Hwy # 1126, Newport, OR, 97365-1705
Coastlines, 1,025

Church & Synagogue Library Association
PO Box 19357, Portland, OR, 97280-0357
Church and Synagogue Libraries, 796

•**Code of the West Publishing**
1633 Best Ln, Eugene, OR, 97401-5030

Columbia River Maritime Museum
1792 Marine Dr, Astoria, OR, 97103-3525
Quarterdeck, The, 907

Comp/Graphics Inc.
PO Box 1376, Eugene, OR, 97440-1376
Brown's Business Reporter, 129

Competitive Advantage
PO Box 10091, Portland, OR, 97210-0091
Competitive Advantage, 1,086

* See **MULTI-PUBLISHER INDEX** for list of publications.

Conscious Living Foundation
PO Box 9, Drain, OR, 97435-0009
Health Master, 510

Correspan
Box 759 - xbr, Veneta, OR, 97487-0759
Abapa Freer, 813

Culver Research Pubs.
840 Mesman Dr, Grants Pass, OR, 97527-6018
Nash Notations, 462

Dark Horse Comics, Inc.
10956 SE Main St, Milwaukie, OR, 97222-7644
Dark Horse Insider, 210

David Braynen
Oregon State, Dept. of Anthropology, Corvallis, OR, 97331
Anthropology Northwest, 51

DeClare Publishing
PO Box 1475, Clackamas, OR, 97015-1475
Network for Citizen Enlightenment, 472

Derek Humphry
24829 Norris Ln, Junction City, OR, 97448-9559
World Right-To-Die Newsletter, 532

Dogs for the Deaf, Inc.
10175 Wheeler Rd., Central Point, OR, 97502-9360
Canine Listener, 279

•**Dominion Press**
PO Box 4608, Salem, OR, 97302-8608

ERIC Clearinghouse on Educational Management
Univ. of Oregon, 5207 Agate St., Eugene, OR, 97403-5207
ERIC/CEM Information, 1,090

Echoes Network Counseling Center, Inc.
12624 NE Halsey St, Portland, OR, 97230-1931
Soundings, 1,018

Edu/Gram
Oregon Board Of Education 942, Salem, OR, 97310-0001
Edu/Gram, 583

Eller Family Assn.
914 James St, Independence, OR, 97351-9404
Eller Cronicles, 452

Finnish-American Historical Society of the West
PO Box 5522, Portland, OR, 97228-5522
Finnam Newsletter, 401

First Interstate Bank of OR
PO Box 3131, Portland, OR, 97208-3131
Statement, 599

Forest Industries Telecomm.
871 Country Club Rd # A, Eugene, OR, 97401-6009
Two Way Transmissions, 831

Frontier Genealogy Resources
PO Box 22026, Milwaukie, OR, 97269-2026
Old Oregon Country News, 463

Geological Society of Oregon Country
PO Box 907, Portland, OR, 97207-0907
Geological Newsletter, 476

Gunderson, Inc.
4350 NW Front Ave, Portland, OR, 97210-1499
Gunderson News, 849

Heim Investment Services
PO Box 19435, Portland, OR, 97280-0435
Heim Investment Letter, 667

Hemlock Society
1551 Pearl St., Eugene, OR, 97440-4030
Hemlock Timelines, 875

Heritage
35145 Balboa Pl SE, Albany, OR, 97321-9751
Heritage, 456

Home Treasures
1250 Clark Mill Rd., Sweet Home, OR, 97386-3014
Home Treasures Newsletter, 140

Howard Historian, Inc.
2904 SE 35th Ave., Portland, OR, 97202-1802
Howard Historian, The, 456

Howard L. Shenson
123 NW 2nd Ave. #403, Portland, OR, 97209-3927
Professional Consultant & Information Marketing Report, 843

IICS Executive Office
14657 SW Teal Blvd., Ste. 119, Beaverton, OR, 97007-6194
IQ Quarterly, 224

Intel Corp.
PO Box 10266, Portland, OR, 97210-0266
Smart Network Services, 238

International Bear News
10907 NW Copeland St., Portland, OR, 97229-6145
International Bear News, 1,217

International Christian Leprosy Mission, Inc.
PO Box 23353, Portland, OR, 97281-3353
Global Missions, 1,117

Intl. Guild of Candle Artisans
867 Browning Ave S, Salem, OR, 97302-6112
Candlelighter, 132

•**International Society for Technology in Education**
1787 Agate St, Eugene, OR, 97403-1923

Invest/O-Registered Investment Advisors
PO Box 5996, Bend, OR, 97708-5996
Risk Factor Method of Investing, 684

James McGraw
P.O. Box, Portland, OR, 97242
NOBODY YOU KNOW, 815

Jim Green, Horticulture Department, OSU
Corvallis, OR, 97331
Ornamentals Northwest, 442

Ken Keyes College
1620 Thompson Rd., Coos Bay, OR, 97420-2150
Ken Keyes College Newsletter, 314

Klamath County Chamber of Commerce
507 Main St., Klamath Falls, OR, 97601-6031
Klamath County Chamber of Commerce Newsletter, 160

Learning Information Network of Oregon
31960 SE Chin St, Boring, OR, 97009-9708
LUNO, 315

Learning Unlimited Network of Oregon
31960 SE Chin St, Boring, OR, 97009-9708
Learning Unlimited Network of Oregon, 316

Linden Agency
PO Box 1319, Ashland, OR, 97520-0044
Perspectives on Hard Assets, 682

Lookin' for Lockes
7650 Fairview Rd., Tillamook, OR, 97141-9009
Lookin' for Lockes, 460

Maestro Takatak
The Sonic Buffalo, P.O. Box 734, Mt Angel, OR, 97362
Ninety Three Point Five, 472

Mazamas
909 NW 19th Ave, Portland, OR, 97209-1496
Mazama, 179

Mobility Intl. USA
PO Box 10767, Eugene, OR, 97440-2767
Over the Rainbow, 1,187

Mount Angel Abbey
Publications Dept., St. Benedict, OR, 97373-9999
Mount Angel Letter, 1,058

Natl. Assn. for Crime Victims Rights
PO Box 16161, Portland, OR, 97216-0161
Crimes Eye Newsletter, 1,116

Natl. Extension Homemakers Council
835 W. 7th St., Loveland, OR, 80537-5360
NEHC Update, 558

•**National Psoriasis Foundation/USA**
6600 SW 92nd Ave. #300, Portland, OR, 97223-7195

Native American Connections
PO Box 414, Coos Bay, OR, 97420-0043
Native American Connection, 406

Northwest Power Planning Council
851 SW 6th Ave Ste 1100, Portland, OR, 97204-1348
Northwest Energy News, 356

Northwest Regional Educational Laboratory
101 SW Main, #500, Portland, OR, 97204-3213
Northwest Report, 323

Obsidians, Inc.
840 Martin St, Eugene, OR, 97405-4661
Obsidian, The, 944

Oregon Dept. of Forestry
2600 State St., Salem, OR, 97310-1336
Forest Log, 435

Oregon Department of Veterans' Affairs
700 Summer St NE, Salem, OR, 97310-1351
Vets' News Letter, 1,199

Oregon Electric Railway Historical Society, Inc.
1836 N Emerson St, Portland, OR, 97217-3855
Transfer, The, 549

•**Oregon Employment Division**
PO Box 751, Salem, OR, 97308-0751

Oregon Employment Div., Research
875 Union St NE, Salem, OR, 97311-0800
Local Labor Force Trends, McMinnville Office,, 703

Oregon Environmental Council
520 SW 6th Avenue, #940, Portland, OR, 97204-1535
Earthwatch Oregon, 377

Oregon Health Sciences University
3181 SW Sam Jackson Park Rd, Portland, OR, 97201-3011
Campus Gram, 205

Oregon Health Sciences University Foundation
1121 SW Salmon Street, Portland, OR, 97201-3098
Oregon Health Sciences University News, 522

Oregon/Independent College Foundation, Inc.
121 S Salmon, Portland, OR, 97204-2901
Oregon Independent College Foundation, Inc. Report, 1,092

Oregon Latvian Society
1245 Hallinan St, Lake Oswego, OR, 97034-4935
Oregonietis, 404

Oregon PTA Publ.
531 SE 14th Ave, Portland, OR, 97214-2427
Oregon PTA Bulletin, 324

Oregon Stamp Soc.
PO Box 18165, Portland, OR, 97218-0165
Album Page, 970

Oregon State Dept. of Agriculture
635 Capitol St NE, Salem, OR, 97310-1315
Digest of Veterinary Matters, 1,201

•**Oregon State Employment Service**
700 Union St., #105, The Dalles, OR, 97058-1893

Oregon State Fire Marshal
4760 Portland Rd NE # 534, Salem, OR, 97305-1760
Gated Wye, 421

Oregon State Pharmacists Assn.
1460 State St, Salem, OR, 97301-4247
Oregon Pharmacist, 286

Oregon State Univ. Intl. Plant Protection Ctr.
Publications, Corvallis, OR, 97331
Infoletter, 42

Oregon State University, School of Forestry
Publications, Corvallis, OR, 97331
Forestry Update, 435

Oregon Tilth, Inc.
PO Box 218, Tualatin, OR, 97062-0218
In Good Tilth, 42

PSI Research
300 N Valley Dr, Grants Pass, OR, 97526-8533
PSI Research Memo, 147

Pacific Northwest Grain
200 SW Market St Ste 1730, Portland, OR, 97201-5718
Pacific Northwest Grain and Feed Association Newsletter, 418

Pacific Power
920 SW 6th Ave, Portland, OR, 97204-1297
Bulletin, 578

Pacific States Marine Fisheries Commission
45 82nd Street Drive, #100, Gladstone, OR, 97027-2522
Pacific States Marine Fisheries Commission Newsletter, 423

•**Paradise Pubs.**
8110 SW Wareham Cir, Portland, OR, 97223-6992

Parrish Pubs.
PO Box 23205, Portland, OR, 97281-3205
Baseball Insight, 101

Pay Less Drug Stores N.W. Inc.
9275 SW Peyton Ln, Wilsonville, OR, 97070-9200
People to People, 594

Personal Survival Center Inc.
PO Box 1050, Rogue River, OR, 97537-1050
Survival Tomorrow, 688

Portable Dwelling Info Letter
PO Box 190, Philomath, OR, 97370-0190
Dwelling Portably, 943

Portland Art Museum
1219 SW Park Ave, Portland, OR, 97205-2486
Portland Art Museum Newsletter, 66

Portland State Univ.
Continuing Education Pr., Box 1491, Portland, OR, 97207
Italic Newsletter, 314

Power Transmission Products
2750 NW 31st Ave, Portland, OR, 97210-1718
In Gear, 586

Public Forestry Foundation
PO Box 371, Eugene, OR, 97440-0371
Citizen Forester, The; Western Forest Report, 435

Public Risk Insurance Services & Management, Inc.
411 E 3rd Ave, Eugene, OR, 97401-2403
PRISM, 623

•**Random Lengths Publications, Inc.**
PO Box 867, Eugene, OR, 97440-0867

•**Resource Recycling, Inc.**
PO Box 10540, Portland, OR, 97210-0540

* See **MULTI-PUBLISHER INDEX** for list of publications.

•**Robin & Russ Handweavers**
533 N Adams St, McMinnville, OR, 97128-5513

Romantic Notions
PO Box 705, Salem, OR, 97308-0705
Romantic Notions, 1,078

Roseburg Forest Products Co.
PO Box 1088, Roseburg, OR, 97470-0252
News & Views, 592

Rotary Club of Portland
111 SW 5th Ave., Portland, OR, 97204-3604
Spokes, 182

Shawn Swagerty
P.O. Box 433, Portland, OR, 97207
Storefront Bar-B-Q, 816

Solar Energy Assn. of Oregon
418 SW Washington Street, Suite 306, Portland, OR, 97204-2209
Energizer, The, 352

Sprouting Publications
PO Box 62, Ashland, OR, 97520-0070
Sproutletter, 935

State Accident Insurance Fund
Saif Bldg., Salem, OR, 97312-0001
Scope, 597

Steve Mandich
P.O. Box 10412, Portland, OR, 97210
Heinous, 814

Sugar Art Partners
1301 N Highway 99w # 298, Mcminnville, OR, 97128-2722
Sugar Art Sharing Confectionary Ideas, 243

Survival Tomorrow, Inc.
PO Box 910, Merlin, OR, 97532-0910
Self-Reliant Living, 1,138

Tiller Trails
PO Box 787, Winston, OR, 97496-0787
Tiller Trails, 468

Transoniq Hacker
1402 SW Upland Dr, Portland, OR, 97221-2649
Transoniq Hacker, 918

Understanding Defense
1574 Coburg Rd # 160, Eugene, OR, 97401-4802
Understanding Defense, 899

United Telecommunications Inc.
601 State St, Hood River, OR, 97031-1871
Intercom, 587

Valley Calligraphy Guild
2352 Van Ness St, Eugene, OR, 97403-1862
Valley Calligraphy Guild Newsletter, 67

Veitch Historical Society
6060 SW Coyote Ave, Redmond, OR, 97756-9536
Veitch Chronicle, 469

Veridian Press
4326 S.E. Woodstock Blvd., Suite #500, Portland, OR, 97206-6270
Practically Green, 254

Vestibular Disorders Association
PO Box 4467, Portland, OR, 97208-4467
On the Level, 522

Well Spring Publishing
P.O. Box 3594, Ashland, OR, 97520
Well Spring, 698

Western Forest Industries Assn.
1500 SW Taylor St, Portland, OR, 97205-1894
Out of the Woods, 436

•**Western Wood Products Assn.**
522 SW 5th Ave., Yeon Bldg., Portland, OR, 97204-2133

Willamette Publishing, Inc.
111 S.W. 5th Ave., #2150, Portland, OR, 97204-3624
Western Investor Newsletter, 692

Willamette Valley Genealogical Society
PO Box 2083, Salem, OR, 97308-2083
Beaver Briefs, 448

World Missions Fellowship
PO Box 5148, Oregon City, OR, 97045-8148
Donor's Newsletter, 1,063

World Peace University
400 2nd St # 77, Lake Oswego, OR, 97034-3127
Cutting Edge, 989

Worm Digst
P.O. Box 544, Eugene, OR, 97440
Worm Digest, 50

Yamhill County- Genealogical Society
PO Box 568, Mcminnville, OR, 97128-0568
Timber Trails, 468

Yeomen Genealogy Services
2330 SE Brookwood Ave Apt 108, Hillsboro, OR, 97123-8168
Quaker Yeomen, 465

Pennsylvania

401(k) Association
1 Summit Square, Doublewoods Rd. & Rte. 413, Langhorne, PA, 19047
401(k) Legislative News, 79

A. B. Murray Co. Inc.
58 Cabot Blvd E, Langhorne, PA, 19047-9101
Murray Tube Bulletin, 591

ACPA/Cleft Palate Foundation
1218 Grandview Ave, Pittsburgh, PA, 15211-1239
ACPA/CPF Newsletter, 863

ALS Association
1323 Forbes Ave., #200, Pittsburgh, PA, 15219
News & Views, 882

AUS Consultants
ICR Survey Research Group, 605 W. State St., Media, PA, 19063
On-Line, 20

Accessible Journeys
35 W Sellers Ave, Ridley Park, PA, 19078-2113
Accessible Journeys, 276

•**Action Kit for Hospital Law**
4614 Fifth Ave., Pittsburgh, PA, 15213-3663

Advertising Specialty Institute
1120 Wheeler Way, Langhorne, PA, 19047-1785

Agricultural Extension Service
Agriculture Adimistration Bldg., ., University Park, PA, 16802
Farm Economics, 40

Albert Einstein Medical Center
York and Tabor Roads, Philadelphia, PA, 19141
Einstein Health Update, 563

Allegheny County Bar Association
400 Koppers Bldg., Pittsburgh, PA, 15219
Allegheny Lawyer, 714

Allegheny County Pharmaceutical Assn.
2 Parkway Ctr Ste 111, Pittsburgh, PA, 15220-3501
Allegheny County Pharmacist, 281

Alles Knitting Publications, Inc.
1000 Jefferson Heights Rd, Pittsburgh, PA, 15235-4707
Alles' Around the World Knitting Machine News & Views, 551

Alternative Aquaculture Association
PO Box 109, Breinigsville, PA, 18031-0109
Alternative Aquaculture Network, 422

Altman Weil Pensa Publications Inc.
2 Campus Blvd., Newtown Square, PA, 19073
Report to Legal Management, 773

Altman & Weil Publications
PO Box 625, Newtown Square, PA, 19073-0625
Law Office Technology Review, 749

American Anti-Vivisection Society
801 Old York Rd., Suite #204, Jenkintown, PA, 19046-1685
AV Magazine, The, 1,200

American Association of Botanical Gardens and Arboreta
786 Church Rd, Wayne, PA, 19087-4713
AABGA Newsletter, 439

American Assn. of Meat Processors
1 Meating Pl # 269, Elizabethtown, PA, 17022-2883
AAMPlifier/Capitol Line-Up, 852

American Council of Christian Churches
PO Box 19, Valling Ford, PA, 19086
Fundamental News Service, 1,063

•**American Friends Service Comm (AFSC)- International Division**
1501 Cherry St, Philadelphia, PA, 19102-1429

American Hawkwatcher
629 W Green St, Allentown, PA, 18102-1601
American Hawkwatcher, 941

•**American Inst. for Chartered Property Casualty Underwriters**
720 Providence Road, PO Box 3016, Malvern, PA, 19355-0716

American Law Institute
4025 Chestnut St., Philadelphia, PA, 19104-3099
ALI Reporter, The, 713

American Musical Instrument Society
RD#3 Box 205-B, Franklin, PA, 16323-9804
American Musical Instrument Society Newsletter, 909

American Musicological Society
201 S 34th St Rm 201, Philadelphia, PA, 19104-6313
American Musicological Society Newsletter, 909

American Philatelic Society
PO Box 8000, State College, PA, 16803-8000
American Philatelic Society Chapter Activities Committee Newsletter, 970

American Society of CLU & CFC
270 S Bryn Mawr Ave, Bryn Mawr, PA, 19010-2105
Query, 623

•**American Society of CLU & ChFC**
270 S Bryn Mawr Ave # 59, Bryn Mawr, PA, 19010-2105

American Society of Marine Artists
PO Box 90, Ambler, PA, 19002-0090
ASMA News, 62

•**American Society of Transportation & Logistics**
216 E Church St, Lock Haven, PA, 17745-2010

American Swedish Historical Foundation
1900 Pattison Ave, Philadelphia, PA, 19145-5901
American Swedish Historical Foundation and Museum Newsletter, 409

•**Andrews Publications, Inc.**
1646 West Chester Pike, PO Box 1000, Westtown, PA, 19395

Anglers Art
PO Box 148n, Plainfield, PA, 17081-0148
Anglers Art, 606

Antique Truck Club of America, Inc.
PO Box 291, Hershey, PA, 17033-0291
Double Clutch, 72

Appollo Graphics
1085 Industrial Blvd, Southampton, PA, 18966-4056
Tech Tips, 1,007

Aquarian Research Foundation
5620 Morton St, Philadelphia, PA, 19144-1330
Aquarian Alternatives, 813

Arden Trolley Museum
PO Box 832, Pittsburgh, PA, 15230-0832
Trolley Fare, 1,181

•**Armstrong World Industries**
Employee Communications, Box 3001, Lancaster, PA, 17604

Ashland Equities, Inc.
1127 Mill Rd., Hatfield, PA, 19440-1036
Real Estate Marketing Letter, 1,038

Association of Directory Marketing
One Thorn Run Ctr., Ste. 202, 1187 Thorn Run Rd., Moon Township, PA, 15108-3198
ADM Flash, 8

Association of Evangelicals for Italian Missions
13th & Tasker Sts., Philadelphia, PA, 19148
New Aurora, 1,065

Assn. for the History of Chiropractic
207 S Grandview Dr, Pittsburgh, PA, 15215-1822
Association for the History of Chiropractic-Bulletin, 867

Assn. of North American Radio Clubs
2216 Burkey Drive, Wyomissing, PA, 19610-1553
ANARC Newsletter, 122

Association of Theological Schools in the U.S. & Canada
10 Summit Park Dr, Pittsburgh, PA, 15275-1110
Association of Theological Schools in the U.S. and Canada Bulletin, 1,045

Awakening
948 Almshouse Rd., Ivyland, PA, 18974-1202
Awakening, 1,198

Barbara Robb Kabel
421 Kemmerer Rd, State College, PA, 16801-6408
Robb Relatives, 466

Baseball's Active Leaders
1263 Paso Fino Dr, Warrington, PA, 18976-1928
Baseball's Active Leaders, 101

Bayberry Farm Peddlers
PO Box 447, Perkasie, PA, 18944
Bayberry Farm Peddlers, 183

Beastly News
718 Earp St, Philadelphia, PA, 19147-5723
Beastly News, 279

Behavioral Health Industry News, Inc.
44 S. Franklin Street, Gettysburg, PA, 17325
Open Minds, the Behavioral Health Industry Analyst, 1,016

•**Bell Telelphone Co. of PA**
One Parkway, 9th fl., Philadelphia, PA, 19102-1589

Berks Arts Council
The Pagoda, P.O. Box 854, Reading, PA, 19603
Berks Arts, 63

* See **MULTI-PUBLISHER INDEX** for list of publications.

Beta Phi Mu, School of Library
Univ. of Pittsburgh, Pittsburgh, PA, 15260-0001
Beta Phi Mu News Letter, 794

BiFocus
PO Box 30372, Philadelphia, PA, 19103-8372
BiFocus, 444

Bicycle Wholesale Distributors Assn.
1900 Arch St, Philadelphia, PA, 19103-1498
Bicycle Wholesale Distributors Assn. Newsletter, 263

Big Brothers/Big Sisters of America
230 N 13th St, Philadelphia, PA, 19107-1538
Correspondent, 1,116

Binney & Smith
1100 Church Ln, Easton, PA, 18040-6638
Rainbow Reporter, 596

Blair Corporation
220 Hickory St, Warren, PA, 16366-0001
Procession, 595

Bradley Communications Corp.
PO Box 1206, 135 East Plumstead, Lansdowne, PA, 19050-8206
Radio-TV Interview Report, 125

Brewers Assn. of America
PO Box 6296, Harrisburg, PA, 17112-0296
Brewers Association of America Bulletin, 102

Bryn Mawr College
Public Information Office, Bryn Mawr, PA, 19010-2899
Bryn Mawr Alumnae Bulletin, 192

Bucknell Computer & Communications Services
Bucknell Univ., Lewisburg, PA, 17837
In Sync, 225

Bucknell University
Lewisburg, PA, 17837
What's Happening, 205

Bucks County Genealogical Society
PO Box 1092, Doylestown, PA, 18901-0020
Bucks County Genealogical Society Newsletter, 449

Bucks County Planning Commission
Neshaminy Ctr., Alms House, Doylestown, PA, 18901
Planning Progress, 1,023

•**Bureau of Research and Statistics**
300 Capitol Associates Bld., Harrisburg, PA, 17120-0034

CAPTEK Custom Applied Technology
PO Box 888, Southeastern, PA, 19399-0888
CAPTALK, 276

Cadillac la Salle Club, Inc.
223 S. Fairfield Rd., Devon, PA, 19333-1630
Self-Starter, The, 76

Cancer Guidance Institute
1323 Forbes Ave., Pittsburgh, PA, 15219-4725
Cancer Challenge, The, 870

Carnegie Museum of Natural History
4400 Forbes Ave, Pittsburgh, PA, 15213-4007
Science Museum News, 908

Center for Metals Production-Mellon Institute
4400 5th Ave, Pittsburgh, PA, 15213-2683
CMP Newsletter, 890

Center for the Teaching of the Americas
Immaculata College, c/o Sister, Immaculata, PA, 19345-9999
Boletin, 301

Center for Workplace Health, The
410 Lancaster Ave., Ste. 15, PO Box 239, Haverford, PA, 19041-0239
CTD News, 501

Centre County Historical Society
1001 E College Ave, State College, PA, 16801-6806
Mansion Notes, 905

Century Boat Club
936 Jackman Ave, Pittsburgh, PA, 15202-2808
Thoroughbred, Quarterly Journal, 114

•**Charles Moore Associates, Inc.**
PO Box 6, Southampton, PA, 18966-0006

Chartered Property Casualty Underwriters Society
720 Providence Rd., PO Box 3009, Malvern, PA, 19355-0709
CPCU News, 619

Cheswick Historical Society
208 Allegheny Ave, Cheswick, PA, 15024-1604
Stamps, Old Letters & History, 972

Children of Aging Parents
1609 Woodbourne Rd., Woodbourne Office Campus #30, Levittown, PA, 19057-1506
Capsule, 1,115

Children's Hospital of Philadelphia
34th St. & Civic Ctr. Blvd., Philadelphia, PA, 19104
Children's Hospital Times, 563

Chilton Publications
One Chilton Way, Radnor, PA, 19089-0001
Iron Age Scrap Price Bulletin, 891

Chorus America
1811 Chestnut St., Ste 401, Philadelphia, PA, 19103-3721
Voice of Chorus America, The, 919

•**Christian Literacy Assocs.**
541 Perry Hwy, Pittsburgh, PA, 15229-1851

Civil War Library & Museum
1805 Pine St, Philadelphia, PA, 19103-6601
Civil War Library & Museum, 538

•**Clement Communications, Inc.**
Concord Industrial Park, Concordville, PA, 19331-9987

Clinical Laboratory Management Assoc.
9 Old Lincoln Highway, #201, Malvern, PA, 19355-2135
Management Briefs, 840

•**College Placement Council, Inc.**
62 Highland Ave., Bethlehem, PA, 18017-9481

Common Sense on Energy & Our Environment
PO Box 215, Morrisville, PA, 19067-0215
Common Sense on Energy & Our Envirnoment, 375

Commonwealth of Pennsylvania, Dept. of Public Instruction
Education Bldg., Harrisburg, PA, 17120-0001
School Food Services Bulletin, 1,076

Communications Counselors, Inc.
PO Box 427, Newtown Square, PA, 19073-0427
Cockshaw's Construction Labor News + Opinion, 699

Comquest Inc
112 Schubert Drive, Downingtown, PA, 19335
Communications Insights, 835

Concerned Citizens of the Delaware Valley
PO Box 47, Bryn Mawr, PA, 19010-0047
Valley Voice, 473

Conductors Guild Inc.
103 South High Street, Room 6, West Chester, PA, 19382-3262
Conductors' Guild Newsletter, 911

Constantian Society, The
123 Orr Rd, Pittsburgh, PA, 15241-2219
Constantian, The, 988

Copper & Brass Servicenter Assn.
251 W. DeKalb Pike, King of Prussia, PA, 19406-2433
CBSA Capsules, 890

Copperweld Corp.
4 Gateway Cemter, Suite 2200, Pittsburgh, PA, 15222
Across Copperweld, 575

Corporate Transfer Agents Assn.
600 Grant St Ste 611, Pittsburgh, PA, 15219-2703
Output, 96

Council on Tall Buildings & Urban Habitat
Lehigh University, 13 East Packer Avenue, Bethlehem, PA, 18015-3044
Times (Bethlehem), 61

Covato Research Corp.
Manor Oak II, Ste. 333, 1910 Cochran Rd., Pittsburgh, PA, 15220
Timing Analysis Projection, 689

Cowtree Collector
240 Wahl Ave, Evans City, PA, 16033-1053
MOOsletter, The, 264

•**Cricket Communications, Inc.**
PO Box 527, Ardmore, PA, 19003-0527

Cupola Productions
966 N Randolph St, Philadelphia, PA, 19123-1408
Rockingchair, 917

DHI, Inc.
PO Box 14111, Reading, PA, 19612-4111
Friends of Doctor Who Newsletter, 1,102

Dairy Society International
7185 Ruritan Dr, Chambersburg, PA, 17201-9242
DSI Bulletin, 264

Dana Corp.
PO Box 13445, Reading, PA, 19612-3445
Dana Reading Communicator, 582

•**David Bruce**
PO Box 7109, Mount Jewett, PA, 16740-7109

Decorative Arts Trust
106 Bainbridge St, Philadelphia, PA, 19147-2402
Decorative Arts Trust-Newsletter, 52

Delaware County Chamber of Commerce
602 E Baltimore Pike, Media, PA, 19063-1752
Delaware County Chamber of Commerce Newsletter, 159

Deltiologists of America
PO Box 8, Norwood, PA, 19074-0008
Postcard Classics, 185

Dentsply Intl. Inc.
570 W College Ave, York, PA, 17404-3886
Dimensions, 582

Dept. of Health & Welfare
Office of Mental Health, Room 502, Harrisburg, PA, 17120
People First, 1,017

Design House International
PO Box 14111, Reading, PA, 19612-4111
Bead and Button, 551

Direct Marketing Publishers
1304 University Dr, Yardley, PA, 19067-2829
Business Marketing Notepad, 11

•**Doctor's Press, The**
1866 Colonial Village Lane, Lancaster, PA, 17605-0488

Dollar Savings Bank
PO Box 987, Pittsburgh, PA, 15230-0987
Lion's Roar, 589

Doyle Research Group
PO Box 42753, Philadelphia, PA, 19101-2753
Shopper Report, 255

Drug Information Assn., Inc.
PO Box 3113, Maple Glen, PA, 19002-8113
Dia Newsletter, 282

•**ECRI**
5200 Butler Pike, Plymouth Meeting, PA, 19462-1298

E.S. Proteus
1657 The Fairway Ste 123, Jenkintown, PA, 19046-1423
MusiCopyright Intelligence, 914

Electric Vehicle Digest
301 Seola Road, Brookhaven, PA, 19015
Electric Vehicle Digest, 72

Elk County Historical Society
109 Center St # 361, Ridgway, PA, 15853-1701
Elk Horn, 540

Emily Jean Hetrick
4707 Delbrook Road, Mechanicsburg, PA, 17055-3042
Kat Barf, 814

Environmental Coalition on Nuclear Power
433 Orlando Ave, State College, PA, 16803-3477
News from ECNP, 356

Environmental Resources Research Institute
Pennsylvania State Univ., University Park, PA, 16802
Environmental Resources Research Institute, Newsletter, 381

•**Episcopal Conference of the Deaf**
PO Box 27459, Philadelphia, PA, 19118-0459

Erie County Motor Club
420 W 6th St, Erie, PA, 16507-1295
Erie Motorist, 1,184

Ernie Saxon Communications
1448 Hollywood Ave, Langhorne, PA, 19047-7417
Motorsports Marketing Sponsorship News, 19

Evangelical
555 West James St., Lancaster Theol. Sem., Lancaster, PA, 17603-2812
Evangelical and Reformed Historical Society Newsletter, 1,063

FFC
711 Chautauqua Ct, Pittsburgh, PA, 15214-3537
National Ferret Fancier's Club, 50

•**F.J. Mclaughlin Newsletter Network**
1346 Joan Dr, Southampton, PA, 18966-4341

FMC Corp.
PO Box 904, Chalfont, PA, 18914-0904
MH Systems Scene, 589

FMS Foundation
3401 Market Street, Suite #130, Philadelphia, PA, 19104
FMS Foundation, 1,117

Famlee Talk
136 S 10th St, Quakertown, PA, 18951-1504
Famlee Talk, 412

Ferraro & Associates
Rr 1 Box 62a, Adamsville, PA, 16110-8706
Orchid Hunter, 442

Ferret Fanciers Club
711 Chautauqua Ct, Pittsburgh, PA, 15214-3537
International Ferret Review, 49

Fine Arts Philatelists
7234 River Rd., Conestoga, PA, 17516-9761
Fine & Performing Arts Philately Journal, 971

Firestone Tire
PO Box 699, Pottstown, PA, 19464-0699
News, 592

Foreign Policy Research Institute
3615 Chestnut St., Philadelphia, PA, 19104-2671
Backchannel, 986

• See **MULTI-PUBLISHER INDEX** for list of publications.

Foundation for Jewish Studies
1531 S Negley Ave, Pittsburgh, PA, 15217-1419
Straighttalk, 1,071

Foundation for Philosophy of Creativity
Publ. Adm. Dept., Slippery Rock Univ., Slippery Rock, PA, 16057
Foundation for Philosophy of Creativity Newsletter, 973

Franklin & Marshall College
PO Box 3003, Lancaster, PA, 17604-3003
Pennsylvania Classical Association Bulletin, 824

Freedoms Foundation At Valley Forge
PO Box 706, Valley Forge, PA, 19482-0706
Focus, 310

Friends of the Springer Homestead
22 Hortense St, Uniontown, PA, 15401-3025
Friends of the Springer Homestead, 454

Future Skinnies of America
Rr 2 Box 423, Claysville, PA, 15323-9418
Future Skinnies of America, 507

G&W Recruiting Service
PO Box 2021, Sanatoga, PA, 19464-0902
G&W Recruiting Service, 434

George Kamm Paperweights
24 Townsend Ct, Lancaster, PA, 17603-6797
George Kamm Paperweights, 184

Glass, Pottery, Plastics
608 E Baltimore Pike # 607, Media, PA, 19063-1735
GPPAW Horizons, 708

Golf Collectors Society
600 E Cathedral Rd Apt G307, Philadelphia, PA, 19128-1929
Golf Collectors Society Bulletin, 480

Green Circle Program
1300 Spruce St, Philadelphia, PA, 19107-5812
Our Widening Circle, 815

HRB Systems
Box 60, Science Pk., State College, PA, 16804-0060
Networker, 591

Hahnemann Medical College, Hospital
235 N 15th St, Philadelphia, PA, 19102-1122
Medical Staff News, 568

Hank Roll Co.
2419 Greensburg Pike, Pittsburgh, PA, 15221-3665
WRITE!, 420

Hanover Investment Management Corp.
853 Second St Pike, Suite A-2, Richboro, PA, 18954
Sentinel Investment Letter, 685

Hanover Shoe Co., Inc.
240 Kindig Lane, Hanover, PA, 17331
Hanover Shoe News, 585

Hawk Mountain Sanctuary Assn.
Rt. 2, Kempton, PA, 19529-9802
Hawk Mountain News, 942

Heinz USA
PO Box 57, Pittsburgh, PA, 15230-0057
Heinz Line, 585

Henry Roll
2419 Greensburg Pike, Pittsburgh, PA, 15221-3665
Absurd Inquirer, 604

High-Tech Communications
103 Buckskin Ct, Sewickley, PA, 15143-9508
Advanced Technology for Developers, 212

•**ICON Information Concepts, Inc.**
211 S. 45th St., Philadelphia, PA, 19104-2995

•**IMS America**
660 W. Germantown Pike #905, Plymouth Meeting, PA, 19462-1048

•**Idea Group Publishing**
Olde Liberty Square, Suite 230, 4811 Jonestown Road, Harrisburg, PA, 17109

Immigration History Society
18 S 7th St, Philadelphia, PA, 19106-2314
Immigration History Newsletter, 542

Immortal News
1027 69th Ave, Philadelphia, PA, 19126-2911
Immortal News, 974

Independent Regulatory Review Commission
333 Market St Fl 14, Harrisburg, PA, 17101-2210
IRRC Mediator, 486

Institute for Psychosocial Studies
Bldg. G, Executive Quarters, 2300 Computer Road, Willow Grove, PA, 19090-9872
Interchange, The, 1,015

•**Institute for Scientific Information**
3501 Market St., Philadelphia, PA, 19104-3302

Insurance Institute of America
720 Providence Rd, Malvern, PA, 19355-3443
Professional Development Tips, 623

Intelligencer Printing
330 Eden Rd # 1768, Lancaster, PA, 17601-4218
Intellectual, The, 1,005

Intensive Caring Unlimited
910 Bent Ln., Philadelphia, PA, 19118-1008
Intensive Caring Unlimited, 413

International Camaro Club
2001 Pittston Ave, Scranton, PA, 18505-3233
In the Fast Lane, 73

•**Intl. Correspondence Schools**
Oak & Pawnee St., Scranton, PA, 18515-0001

International Missions, Inc.
PO Box 14866, Reading, PA, 19612-4866
Eastern Challenge, 1,063

International Precious Metals Inst.
4905 W Tilghman St Ste 160, Allentown, PA, 18104-9133
IPMI News and Reviews, 891

International Sled Dog Racing Association
C/o Team & Trail Printers, RR#4, Box 381, Tyrone, PA, 16686
Info, 280

International Society for Animal Rights, Inc.
421 S. State St., Clarks Summit, PA, 18411-1540
International Society for Animal Rights Report, 386

Intl. Society for Contemporary Legend Research
Penn State Univ., Hazleton, PA, 18201
FOAFtale News, 260

International Union of Mine, Mill
Five Gateway Ctr., Pittsburgh, PA, 15222-1209
Mine-Mill Union, 709

J.B. Lippincott Co.
227 E. Washington Sq., Philadelphia, PA, 19106
ASA Refresher Courses in Anesthesiology, 865

JDI, Inc.
PO Box 1003, North Wales, PA, 19454-0003
Raising Your Child's Self-Esteem, 170

Jaw Travers Publishing
2177 Carol Drive, Harrisburg, PA, 17110
Court Awareness, 1,130

Jim Smith Society, Inc.
2016 Milltown Rd, Camp Hill, PA, 17011-7433
Jim Smith Society-Newsletter, 178

John Baer's Sons
PO Box 328, Lancaster, PA, 17608-0328
Baer's Garden Newsletter, 440

John Benjamins North America
PO Box 27519, Philadelphia, PA, 19118-0519
Book Gazette, 820

John J. Nesbitt Inc.
State Rd. & Rhawn St., Philadelphia, PA, 19136
Nesbitt Newsbits, 591

John R. Scarano Jr
3024 Duckworth Dr, Santoga, PA, 19464
Slur, 917

John Rob
P.O. Box 1407, Chambersburg, PA, 17201
Budg'y, 889

KL Publications
4003 Forest Dr, Aliquippa, PA, 15001-4743
Home Office Connection, 938

•**Kerner Group**
3231 Forks St, Easton, PA, 18045-5970

Keystone Trails Association
PO Box 251, Cogan Station, PA, 17728-0251
Keystone Trails Association Newsletter, 943

Kitchen & Collectible News
4645 Laurel Ridge Dr, Harrisburg, PA, 17110-3446
Kitchen & Collectible News, 56

Kittochtinny Historical Society
175 E King St # 733, Chambersburg, PA, 17201-1806
Kittochtinny Newsletter, 543

Kutish Publications
PO Box 113, Wayne, PA, 19087-0113
Software Taxation Letter, 776

•**LRP Publications**
747 Dresher Rd., P.O. Box 980, Horsham, PA, 19044-0980

Ladies Pennsylvania Slovak Catholic Union
Northeastern Bank Bldg. , #9, Wilkes Barre, PA, 18701-2598
Zorniska (Morning Star), 1,060

Lafayette College Library
Skillman Library, Easton, PA, 18042
American Friends of Lafayette, 536

Lancaster Automobile Club
34 N Prince St, Lancaster, PA, 17603-3866
Lancaster Motorist, 1,186

Lancaster Mennonite Historical Society
2215 Millstream Rd, Lancaster, PA, 17602-1499
Mirror, 906

Latin American Studies Assn.
William Pitt Union, #946, Univ. of Pittsburgh, Pittsburgh, PA, 15260-0001
LASA Forum, 1,043

Le Hit Parade Co.
509 Penn Ayr Rd., Camp Hill, PA, 17011-2056
Le Hit Parade, 913

Learning Disabilities Association of America
4156 Library Rd., Pittsburgh, PA, 15234-1349
LDA Newsbriefs, 278

Legacy Books
PO Box 494, Hatboro, PA, 19040-0494
Come-All-Ye, 425

Lehigh-Northampton Counties Joint Planning Comm.
961 Marcon Blvd #310, Allentown, PA, 18103-9397
JPC Newsletter, 1,021

Lehigh Valley Section, American Chemical Society
45 Charles Ave, Nazareth, PA, 18064-1702
Octagon, The, 165

Lewis B. Weisfeld
1 Franklin Town Blvd Apt 1204, Philadelphia, PA, 19103-1246
Regulatory Update, 981

Liberty Bell Matchcover Club
6048 N Water St, Philadelphia, PA, 19120-2015
Liberty Bell Crier, 554

Library Educational Institute
Rr 1 Box 219, New Albany, PA, 18833-9799
Library PR News, 802

Lida Ltd.
504 W Mermaid Ln, Philadelphia, PA, 19118-4206
Discerning Traveler, 1,183

•**Lincoln Univ.**
Office of PR & Publications, Lincoln, PA, 19352

•**Lippincott-Raven Press Publishers**
227 E. Washington Square, Philadelphia, PA, 19106

•**Litigation Reporting Service**
PO Box 248, Chalfont, PA, 18914-0248

Little League Baseball
PO Box 3485, Williamsport, PA, 17701-0485
President's Newsletter, 1,134

Local 285, Rubber Workers
202 W Liberty St, Lancaster, PA, 17603-2714
Spotlight, 710

Lutheran Theological Seminary
61 N.W. Conferderate Ave., Gettysburg, PA, 17325-8421
Gettysburg Seminary Bulletin, 205

Lycoming College
Publications, Williamsport, PA, 17701
Lycourier, The, 205

MCC Office on Crime Justice
PO Box 500, Akron, PA, 17501-0500
Crime & Justice Network Newsletter, 989

MLP Enterprises
4202 Chestnut St # 1, Philadelphia, PA, 19104-3015
Community Service Business, 835

MLR Publishing Co.
229 S 18th St, Philadelphia, PA, 19103-6192
Corporate Restructuring, 134

•**Mack Printing Co.**
1991 Northampton St, Easton, PA, 18042-3189

•**Marcus Schneck & Associates**
1328 Chestnut St., #393, Emmaus, PA, 18049

Marigold Society of America
National Headquarters, P.O. Box 5112, New Britain, PA, 18901
Amerigold Newsletter, 440

Mark Hagenbuch
821 W Siddonsburg Rd, Dillsburg, PA, 17019-9320
Beech Grove, 448

Marlin Owners Club
Box 187, RD 5, Coatesville, PA, 19320-4142
Fish Facts, 72

Martin Bormann's Cranial Splints
PO Box 8166, Philadelphia, PA, 19101-8166
The Temptation of Saint Anthony, 984

•**Mealey Publications, Inc.**
PO Box 446, Wayne, PA, 19087-0446

Mechanical Contractors Association of Eastern PA, Inc.
1601 Market St Fl 550, Philadelphia, PA, 19103-2337
Spotlight on Service & Maintenance, 535

* See **MULTI-PUBLISHER INDEX** for list of publications.

Medical Publishing Co., Inc.
PO Box 24622h, Philadelphia, PA, 19111-0622
Parkinson's Disease Update, 883

Medrad Inc.
566 Alpha Dr, Pittsburgh, PA, 15238-2912
Injections from Medrad, 586

•Mennonite Central Committee
PO Box 500, 21 South 12th St., Akron, PA, 17501-0500

Mennonite Historians of Eastern PA
PO Box 82, Harleysville, PA, 19438-0082
Mennonite Historians of Eastern PA, 461

Merchants Bank
702 Hamilton Mall, Allentown, PA, 18101-2419
Bank Lines, 577

Merck & Co., Inc.
PO Box 4, West Point, PA, 19486-0004
Daily, The, 581

Mercyhurst College
501 E 38th St, Erie, PA, 16546-0001
Judean Sand, 205

Metropolitan Edison Co., General Public Utilities Corp.
PO Box 542, Reading, PA, 19603-0542
Met-Ed System, 590

Middle States Assn. of Colleges & Schools
3624 Market St., Philadelphia, PA, 19104-2614
CHE Letter, 302

Mifflin County Historical Society
1 W Market St # 1, Lewistown, PA, 17044-2128
Mifflin County Historical News, 544

Militarism Resource Project
318 S 49th St, Philadelphia, PA, 19143-1704
Militarism Resource Project News, 897

Military Order of the Loyal Legion of the U.S.
1805 Pine St., Philadelphia, PA, 19103-6601
Loyal Legion Historical Journal, 179

Millennium Watch Institute
PO Box 34021, Philadelphia, PA, 19101-4021
Millennial Prophecy Report, 1,048

Miniature Figure Collectors of America
102 Saint Pauls Rd., Ardmore, PA, 19003-2811
Guidon, 178

Mitchell & Assoc.
5654 Willow Terrace Dr, Bethel Park, PA, 15102-3528
Living Healthy, 516

•Mobile Air Conditioning Society, Inc.
PO Box 97, East Greenville, PA, 18041-0097

Moneytalk, Inc.
334 Highlark Dr., Box 1677, Larksville, PA, 18704-1699
Moneytalk, 254

Montgomery Bar Assn.
100 W. Airy St., Norristown, PA, 19401-4724
Montgomery County Law Reporter, 757

•Moore College of Art & Design
College Relations, The Parkway at 20th Street, Philadelphia, PA, 19103

NCCLS
940 West Valley Rd. Suite#14, Wayne, PA, 19087
National Committee for Clinical Laboratory Standards-Update, 881

NRCA
1900 Arch St, Philadelphia, PA, 19103-1404
Refrigeration News, 535

Natl. Adoption Center
1500 Walnut St Ste 701, Philadelphia, PA, 19102-3507
Adoption Update, 410

Natl. Assn. of Container Distributors
1900 Arch St, Philadelphia, PA, 19103-1404
Exchange Packet, 945

Natl. Board of Medical Examiners
3930 Chestnut St, Philadelphia, PA, 19104-3190
National Board Examiner, 881

National Federation of Abstracting & Information Services
1518 Walnut St., Suite 307, Philadelphia, PA, 19102-3403
NFAIS Newsletter, 805

Natl. Fed. of Independent Unions, Midwest Independent Union
1166 S 11th St, Philadelphia, PA, 19147-4627
News for Independent Unions, 704

National Flag Foundation
Flag Plaza, Pittsburgh, PA, 15219
Standard Bearer, 549

Natl. Institute of Diaper Services
2017 Walnut St, Philadelphia, PA, 19103-4403
National Institute of Diaper Services Newsletter, 1,119

•National Software Testing Laboratories
PO Box 1000, Plymouth Meeting, PA, 19462-0800

Nay Aug Park
Museum, Scranton, PA, 18510
Everhart Museum, 904

New Society Publishers
4527 Springfield Avenue, Philadelphia, PA, 19143-3708
Books to Build a New Society, 116

NewsNet, Inc.
945 Haverford Rd., Bryn Mawr, PA, 19010-3814
NewsNet Action Letter, 1,161

North American Association of Christians in Social Work
PO Box 7090, Saint Davids, PA, 19087-7090
Catalyst, 1,115

•North American Publishing Co.
401 N. Broad St., Philadelphia, PA, 19108

North American Shortwave Association
45 Wild Flower Road, Levittown, PA, 19057
Journal, The, 124

North American Society for Sports History
101 White Bldg., Penn State University, University Park, PA, 16802-3903
North American Society for Sports History Newsletter, 1,133

Northern Nut Growers Association
654 Beinhower Rd, Etters, PA, 17319-9774
Nutshell The, 44

One Spirit
Circulation, Camp Hill, PA, 17012-0001
One Spirit, 974

Open Doors for the Handicapped
601 Pressley st., Pittsburgh, PA, 15212-5654
Open Doors for the Handicapped Newsletter, 1,120

Original Traveling Chef
31 Ridge St, Pittston, PA, 18640-9526
Viands In Verse, 434

Orthodox Herald
Rr 3 Box A15, Hunlock Creek, PA, 18621-9547
Orthodox Herald, 1,074

Outdoor Power Equipment Distributors Assn.
1900 Arch St, Philadelphia, PA, 19103-1404
OPEDA Outlook, 850

Outdoor Writers Association of America, Inc.
2017 Cato Ave Ste 101, State College, PA, 16801-2765
Outdoors Unlimited, 944

Overbrook School for the Blind
6333 Malvern Ave, Philadelphia, PA, 19151-2529
Towers, 112

PNC Bank
5th Ave. and Wood St., 28th fl, Pittsburgh, PA, 15265
PNC Banknews, 594

P'Nai Or Religious Fellowship
7318 Germantown Ave., Philadelphia, PA, 19119-1793
NewMenorah, 1,070

PSBC
221 W. Germantown Pike, Plymouth Meeting, PA, 19462-1444
Small Business Chronicle, 152

PS Inc.
1651 Dublin Rd, Dresher, PA, 19025-1243
Hard n' Fast, 912

•Packaging Strategies
122 S Church St, West Chester, PA, 19382-3223

The Palomino Horse Association
Star Route Box 24, Dornsife, PA, 17823
Palomino Parade, 560

Peirce Junior College
Communications Dept., 1420 Pine Street, Philadelphia, PA, 19102-4699
Today, 192

Penn. Dept. of Labor & Industry/Bureau of Research & Statist
625 Cherry St, Reading, PA, 19602-1152
Reading Labor Market News Release, 492

Pennsylvania AFL-CIO
230 State St, Harrisburg, PA, 17101-1138
Pennsylvania AFL-CIO News, 710

Pennsylvania Assn. of Elementary School Principals
801 N. Second St., Harrisburg, PA, 17102
Perspective, 1,093

Pennsylvania Baker Assn.
47 W Main St, Mechanicsburg, PA, 17055-6262
Pennsylvania Baker, 79

Pennsylvania Bureau of Employment Security
Lancaster Job Center, 48-50 W. Chestnut St., Lancaster, PA, 17603-3582
Lancaster Area Labor Market Letter, 709

Pennsylvania Civil Service Commission
PO Box 569, Harrisburg, PA, 17108-0569
Pennsylvania Civil Service Commission Observations, 491

Pennsylvania Council of Teachers of English
Williamsport Area Community Co, Williamsport, PA, 17701
PCTE Bulletin, 324

Pennsylvania Dept. of Agriculture
2301 N Cameron St, Harrisburg, PA, 17110-9405
Agriculture News Bulletin, 37

Pennsylvania Department of Education
333 Market St Fl 10, Harrisburg, PA, 17126-0333
Pennsylvania Education, 325

Pennsylvania Dutch Folk Culture Society, Inc.
Lenhartsville, PA, 19534
Pennsylvania Dutch News and Views, 425

Pennsylvania Economy League, Inc.
1211 Chestnut St Ste 600, Philadelphia, PA, 19107-4116
Citizens Business, 1,019

Pennsylvania Electric Co.
1001 Broad St, Johnstown, PA, 15907-2437
Bulletin, 1,025

Pennsylvania Ethnic Heritage Studies Center
405 Bellfield Hall, 315 Bell-f, ield Ave. Univ. of Pittsburgh, Pittsburgh, PA, 15260
Pennsylvania Ethnic Heritage Newsletter, 399

Pennsylvania Guild of Craftsmen
Tyler Craft, Richboro, PA, 18954
Pennsylvania Crafts, 555

Pennsylvania Home Schoolers Newsletter
Rr 2 Box 117, Kittanning, PA, 16201-9311
Pennsylvania Home Schoolers Newsletter, 325

Pennsylvania Library Association
1919 N Front St, Harrisburg, PA, 17102-2214
Pennsylvania Library Association Bulletin, 807

Pennsylvania Newspaper Publishers' Association
2717 N Front St, Harrisburg, PA, 17110-1221
PNPA Press, 924

Pennsylvania Nurses Assn.
2578 Interstate Dr., PO Box 68525, Harrisburg, PA, 17110-9601
Pennsylvania Nurse, 931

Pennsylvania Nut Growers Assn.
654 Beinhower Rd, Etters, PA, 17319-9774
Nut Kernel, The, 1,009

Pennsylvania PTA
PO Box 4384, Harrisburg, PA, 17111-0384
PTA in Pennsylvania Bulletin, 324

Pennsylvania Partnerships for Children
931 N. Front St., Ste. 101, Harrisburg, PA, 17102-3422
Pennsylvania Partnerships for Children, 170

Pennsylvania Pharmacists Assn
508 N 3rd St, Harrisburg, PA, 17101-1112
Pharmacy News and Review, 287

Pennsylvania Police Criminal Law Bulletin
2579 Warren Rd, Indiana, PA, 15701-3219
Pennsylvania Police Criminal Law Bulletin, 789

Pennsylvania SPCA
350 E Erie Ave, Philadelphia, PA, 19134-1013
Animaldom, 48

Pennsylvania School Boards Assn., Inc.
774 Limekiln Rd., New Cumberland, PA, 17070-2398
Pennsylvania School Boards Association, Information Legislative Service, 1,093

•Pennsylvania State Employment Service
420 Wood St., PO Box 724, Clarion, PA, 16214-1336

Pennsylvania State Grange
1604 N 2nd St, Harrisburg, PA, 17102-2447
Grange Advocate, 41

Pennsylvania State Office of Employment
135 Franklin Ave, Scranton, PA, 18503-1935
Labor Market Letter, 702

Pennsylvania State Univ, Agriculture, Economics & Rural Dev.
201 Armsby Building, ., University Park, PA, 16802
Farm Economics, 40

Pennsylvania State Univ., Altoona Campus
3000 Ivyside Park, Altoona, PA, 16601-3760
Ivy Leaf, 192

Pennsylvania State Univ, College of Engineering
227 Hammond Bldg, University Park, PA, 16802-1401
Better Building Report, 244

Pennsylvania Traveler-Post
PO Box 776, Newtown, PA, 18940-0776
Pennsylvania Traveler-Post, 464

• See **MULTI-PUBLISHER INDEX** for list of publications.

Pennsylvania Veterinary Medical Assoc.
PO Box 403, Harrisburg, PA, 17108-0403
PVMA Newsletter, 1,201

People Concerned for the Unborn Child
3050 Pioneer Ave, Pittsburgh, PA, 15226-1739
People Concerned for the Unborn Child-Newsletter, 1,120

People's Medical Society
462 W Walnut St, Allentown, PA, 18102-5488
People's Medical Society Newsletter, 883

Peoples Music Network for Songs of Freedom & Struggle
1539 Pine St, Philadelphia, PA, 19102-4623
Sassafras, 1,122

Perceptive Marketers Agency, Ltd.
1100 E Hector St Ste 301, Conshohocken, PA, 19428-2374
Perceptive Report, 594

Phi Kappa Sigma Fraternity
PO Box 947, Valley Forge, PA, 19482-0947
Phi Kappa Sigma News Letter, 181

Phi Psi
Philadelphia College of Textil, Philadelphia, PA, 19144
Phi Psi Quarterly, 181

Philadelphia Advertising Club
PO Box 12923, Philadelphia, PA, 19108-0923
Ad News, 9

Philadelphia Art Alliance
251 S 18th St, Philadelphia, PA, 19103-6118
Art Alliance Bulletin, 62

Philadelphia Chamber of Commerce
8601 Roosevelt Blvd, Philadelphia, PA, 19152-2001
Northeast Business, 161

Philadelphia Clef Club of the Performing Arts
1231 N. Broad Street, Suite 209, Philadelphia, PA, 19122
Treble Clef, 918

Philadelphia Independent Film/Video Assn.
3701 Chestnut St., Philadelphia, PA, 19104-3104
Express Exchange, 419

Philadelphia Museum of Art
PO Box 7646, Philadelphia, PA, 19101-7646
PMA Members Newsletter, 907

Philip and Muriel Berman Center for Jewish Studies
Lehigh Univ., Maginnes Hall, Bethlehem, PA, 18015
Philip and Muriel Berman Center for Jewish Studies Newsletter, 1,070

Phoenix Society for Burn Survivors, Inc., The
11 Rust Hill Rd, Levittown, PA, 19056-2311
Icarus File, The, 567

Photo Review, The
301 Hill Ave, Langhorne, PA, 19047-2819
Photo Review Newsletter, The, 977

Pine Row Pubs.
PO Box 428, Washington Crossing, PA, 18977-0428
Potpourri from Herbal Acres, 555

Pittsburgh Theological Seminary
616 N Highland Ave, Pittsburgh, PA, 15206-2525
Panorama, 1,049

Prepress Business Observer
234 Benjamin West Ave, Swarthmore, PA, 19081-1421
Prepress Business Observer, 1,006

Presbyterian Medical Ctr. of Philadelphia-Univ. of PA
Public Relations, 39th St. & Market, Philadelphia, PA, 19104
Center Post, 502

Print Club
1614 Latimer St # 115, Philadelphia, PA, 19103-6308
Newsprint, 1,005

Privacy Newsletter
Dept. OXO1, PO Box 8206, Philadelphia, PA, 19101-8206
Privacy Newsletter, 255

Procrastinators' Club of America
PO Box 712, Bryn Athyn, PA, 19009-0712
Last Month's Newsletter, 179

•**Progressive Business Publications**
370 Technology Dr., #3019, Malverne, PA, 19355-9863

Promotional Pubs., Inc.
4232 Brownsville Rd., Ste. 137, Pittsburgh, PA, 15227
Office Machine Times, 939

RBMU Intl.
1431 Stuckert Rd., Warrington, PA, 18976-1526
Prayer Fellowship Bulletin, 1,065

RRP Publishers
PO Box 8, Easton, PA, 18044-0008
Applied Orgonometry, 258

Ranck/Rank Clan
300 Valleybrook Dr, Lancaster, PA, 17601-4633
Ranck Reporter, 465

Real Estate Entrepreneur
PO Box 13246, Reading, PA, 19612-3246
Real Estate Entrepreneur, The, 1,037

Refractories Institute, The
500 Wood St Ste 326, Pittsburgh, PA, 15222-2414
Refractory News, 479

Religious Public Relations Council
PO Box 296, Wernersville, PA, 19565-0296
Counselor, 1,046

Remington Rand
PO Box 500, Blue Bell, PA, 19422-0500
Univac News, 602

Richie Cunningham
227 Hampshire Drive, Chalfont, PA, 18914
70's Re-Visited, The, 985

Rising Sun
PO Box 627, Milesburg, PA, 16853-0627
Body Renaissance, 499

Robert Morris Associates
1 Liberty Pl., 1650 Market St., Suite 2300, Philadelphia, PA, 19103-7398
Commercial Lending Newsletter, 85

•**Rodale Press**
33 East Minor St., Emmaus, PA, 18098-0001

•**Rohm & Haas Co.**
Independence Mall West, Philadelphia, PA, 19105

Roofing Metal
167 W Walnut Pk Dr, Philadelphia, PA, 19120-1010
Trade Association News, 535

Round Table Press
PO Box 475, Southeastern, PA, 19399-0475
Round Table Review, 1,017

SPS Technologies
Highland Avenue, Jenkintown, PA, 19046
SPS News, 597

S. Todd Spare & Assoc.
P.O. Box 344, Leola, PA, 17540
Spare on Sales and Marketing, 22

•**Sacred Heart Hospital**
421 Chew St., Allentown, PA, 18102-3490

Satin Sheets
PO Box 427, Whitehall, PA, 18052-0427
Satin Sheets, 1,078

School Science & Mathematics Association, Inc.
400 East 2nd Street, Bloomsburg University, Bloomsburg, PA, 17815-1301
School Science and Mathematics, 329

Scleroderma Intl. Foundation
704 Gardner Center Rd, New Castle, PA, 16101-6018
Scleroderma Intl. Foundation-The Connector, 887

Scott Paper Co.
Scott Plaza 1, Philadelphia, PA, 19113
Scott World, 597

Scottish Historic & Research Society of Delaware Valley
102 Saint Pauls Rd, Ardmore, PA, 19003-2811
Rampant Lion, 408

Scranton Public Library
N. Washington Ave. & Vine St., Scranton, PA, 18503
District Note, 797

Sermatech International, Inc.
155 S Limerick Rd, Limerick, PA, 19468-1603
Sermatech Review, 1,002

Seven Mountains Scientific, Inc.
Box 650, Boalsburg, PA, 16804-0651
Advanced Battery Technology, 337

Seybold Publications, Inc.
428 East Baltimore Pike, Media, PA, 19063
Seybold Report on Publishing Systems, 1,007

Sheldon P. Catz
P.O. Box 1703, Pittsburgh, PA, 15230
The Columbo Newsletter, 817

Shopper Pubs., Inc.
1400 Easton Rd, Roslyn, PA, 19001-1606
Service Dealer's Newsletter, 845

Shore-Train Riders Club
5503 Moreland Ct Apt 4, Mechanicsburg, PA, 17055-5435
Shore-Train Rider, 1,180

Sierra Club, Pennsylvania Chapter
305 Christopher Street, Export, PA, 15632
Sylvanian, 394

Skynote Publishing
32510 Old Frankstown Road, Pittsburgh, PA, 15239-2909
Pittsburgh Musician Magazine, 916

Slippery Rock Univ.
201 Old Main, Slippery Rock, PA, 16057
Greensheet, 205

SmithKline Beecham
One Franklin Plaza, PO Box 7929, Philadelphia, PA, 19101-7929
SB News, 288

Society of Automotive Engineers, Inc.
400 Commonwealth Dr., Warrendale, PA, 15096-0001
SAE Update, 76

Society for Business Ethics
American College, 270 Bryn Mawr Ave., Bryn Mawr, PA, 19010-2196
Society for Business Ethics Newsletter, 975

Society of Catholic Medical Missionaries, Inc.
8400 Pine Rd, Philadelphia, PA, 19111-1312
Medical Mission Sisters News, 517

Society for Phenomenology and Existential Philosophy
Villanova University, Dept. of Philosophy, Villanova, PA, 19085
SPEP Newsletter, 975

Songwriter's Monthly
322 Eastwood Avenue, Feasterville, PA, 19053
Songwriter's Monthly, 918

Southeastern Pennsylvania Theological Library Assn.
Moravian College, Reeves Library, Bethlehem, PA, 18018-6650
Teamwork, 811

Special Library Association
1014 Manoa Rd, Wynnewood, PA, 19096-4032
Advertising Marketing Bulletin, 10

Spiritual Frontiers Fellowship Intl.
PO Box 7868, Philadelphia, PA, 19101-7868
Spiritual Frontiers Fellowship International Newsletter, 949

Sports Management News, Inc.
442 Featherbed Ln., Glen Mills, PA, 19342-1512
Sporting Goods Intelligence, 1,135

Stackpole Carbon Co.
Stackpole St., St. Marys, PA, 15857
Stackpole News, 599

State Health Watch
704 Stony Hill Road, Ste. 154, Yardley, PA, 19067
State Health Watch, 529

Steel Structures Painting Council
2100 Wharton St Ste 310, Pittsburgh, PA, 15203-1942
Steel Structures Painting Bulletin, 946

Sterling Drug Inc.
Pharmaceutical Production Grou, Myerstown, PA, 17067
Conveyor, 581

Stroudsburg Area Teachers Assn.
11 S 8th St, Stroudsburg, PA, 18360-1612
Stroudsburg Area Teachers Association News, 331

Suitainable Society Action Project, Inc
525 Midvale road, Upper Darby, PA, 19082-3607
SSAP Newsletter, 393

Sun Shipbuilding
Morton Ave., Chester, PA, 19013
Our Yard, 594

Swarthmore College
Publications, Swarthmore, PA, 19081
Common Speaking, 205

Swedenborg Foundation
PO Box 549, West Chester, PA, 19381-0549
Logos, 974

Symphonium
1349 N Sheridan Ave, Pittsburgh, PA, 15206-1759
Symphonium, 918

Synergic Resources Corporation
111 Presidential Blvd., Bala Cynwyd, PA, 19004
Energy Services Marketing Letter, 1,026

T.R. Report
1512 Spruce St., Philadelphia, PA, 19102-4524
Travelore Report, 1,191

Techni Research Associates, Inc.
PO Box T, Willow Grove, PA, 19090
World Technology/Patent Licensing Gazette, 952

•**Technomic Publishing Co., Inc.**
851 New Holland Ave. #3535, Lancaster, PA, 17601-5644

•**Temple University**
Anderson Hall #921, Philadelphia, PA, 19122

Temple Univ. Medical Center
Publications, Philadelphia, PA, 19122
Temple University Medical Alumni Bulletin, 888

•**Temple University School of Pharmacy**
3307 N Broad St, Philadelphia, PA, 19140-5193

* See **MULTI-PUBLISHER INDEX** for list of publications.

Thomas Jefferson University Hospital
11th and Chestnut Streets, Philadelphia, PA, 19107
Dining with Heart, 872

Three Mile Island Alert Inc.
315 Peffer St, Harrisburg, PA, 17102-1834
Alert, 1,025

To the Point
RD #1, Box 199, Chester Springs, PA, 19425-9801
To the Point, 241

Triangle Printing Co.
PO Box 1782, York, PA, 17405-1782
Triangle Times, 601

UGI Corp.
PO Box 858, Valley Forge, PA, 19482-0858
UGI Horizons, 601

Union of Latvian Baptists in America
832 Gettysburg Dr, Lansdale, PA, 19446-3104
Kristiga Baiss, 1,053

United Assn. of Christian Counselors Intl.
41 Short St, Harrisburg, PA, 17109-3731
Professional Christian Counselor, 1,065

United Humanitarians
PO Box 14587, Philadelphia, PA, 19115-0587
National Humanitarian, 1,119

U.S. Committee Sports for Israel, Inc.
1926 Arch St Ste 3f, Philadelphia, PA, 19103-1444
U.S. Committee Sports for Israel-Newsletter, 1,137

U.S. Space Education Assn.
Global Operations Center, 231 School Lane, Box 249, Rheems, PA, 17570-0249
Space Age Times, 32

United Steelworkers of America
PO Box 112730, Pittsburgh, PA, 15241-0330
Steelworkers Oldtimer, 1,109

Univ. of Pennsylvania
9414 Meadowbrook Ave, Philadelphia, PA, 19118-2624
Morris Arboretum Newsletter, 121

Univ. of Pittsburgh
135 N Bellefield Ave, Pittsburgh, PA, 15213-2609
Linkage, 803

University of Pittsburgh-Dept. Hispanic Languages
1309 Cathedral Of Learning, Pittsburgh, PA, 15260-6299
NAOS, 823

Upholsterers' Intl. Union
PO Box 660, Feasterville, PA, 19053-0660
U.I.U. Journal, 711

Valley Forge Military Academy & Junior College
1001 Eagle Rd, Wayne, PA, 19087-3694
Forge, The, 896

•**Vertex Systems, Inc.**
1041 Old Cassatt Rd., Berwyn, PA, 19312-1151

Vintage Volkswagen Club of America
818 Main St, Portage, PA, 15946-1717
VVWCA Newsletter, 77

Vivicon Productions Inc.
1000 Whitetail Court, Duncansville, PA, 16635
Watergardening News, 443

•**W.B. Saunders Co.**
Curtis Ctr., Independence Square West, Philadelphia, PA, 19106

Warren Library Assn
Warren, PA, 16365
Seneca District Newsletter, 810

Water Resources Assn. of the Delaware River Basin
Box 867, Davis Rd., Valley Forge, PA, 19482-0867
Newsletter, 1,204

Welsh Terrier Club of America
139 Hood School Rd, Indiana, PA, 15701-9208
Welsh Wag, 280

•**Wentworth Worldwide Media**
1866 Colonial Village Lane, PO Box 10488, Lancaster, PA, 17605-0488

•**Western Pennsylvania Conservancy**
316 4th Ave., Pittsburgh, PA, 15222-2075

Western Pennsylvania Genealogical Society
4400 Forbes Ave., Pittsburgh, PA, 15213-4080
Jots from the Point, 458

Western Pennsylvania Hospital
4800 Friendship Ave, Pittsburgh, PA, 15224-1722
WPH Medical Bulletin, 889

Western Pennsylvania School for Blind Children
201 N Bellefield Ave, Pittsburgh, PA, 15213-1458
Insights, 111

Wharton School, Univ. of Pennsylvania
Executive Education Division, 255 S. 38th St., Philadelphia, PA, 19104-6359
Executive Issues, 837

Wildlife Preservation Trust International
3400 W Girard Ave, Philadelphia, PA, 19104-1139
On the Edge, 390

Wohl Assocs.
915 Montgomery Ave., Ste. 309, Marberth, PA, 19072
Amy Wohl's Trendsletter, 212

Women for Sobriety, Inc.
PO Box 618, Quakertown, PA, 18951-0618
Sobering Thoughts, 1,211

Women's International League for Peace and Freedom
1213 Race St., Philadelphia, PA, 19107-1691
Program and Legislative Action, 997

Woodworking Machinery Distributors Association
Adams Bldg., No. 109, 251 DeKalb Pike, King of Prussia, PA, 19406
Vital Link, The, 250

Working Class Hero Beatles Club, The
3311 Niagara St, Pittsburgh, PA, 15213-4223
Working Class Hero Beatles Club, The, 418

Working Wine Guide, The
414 South Craig Street, Suite #263, Pittsburgh, PA, 15213
Working Wine Guide, The, 106

Worldwide Evangelization Crusade
709 Pennsylvania Ave # A, Fort Washington, PA, 19034-2910
Worldwide Thrust, 1,066

Puerto Rico

Caribbean Hotel Assn.
18 Marseilles St., Suite 2-B, Santurce, PR, 00907
CHAdvance, 1,183

EBA Inc./Publishing Division
33 Bolivia St., 4th Floor, San Juan, PR, 00917
Money Master, 94

•**Father & Son Publishing**
1959 Loiza St., #912, Santurce, PR, 00911-1850

Fundacion Educativa Ana G. Mendey
Apartado AE, Rio Piedras, PR, 00928
Carta del Presidente, 579

Sailaway Cruising Club
PO Box 473, Puerto Real, PR, 00740-0473
Tropical American Cruising, 115

Rhode Island

Alan Feinstein Associates
37 Alhambra Cir., Cranston, RI, 02905-3416
International Insiders Report, 670

American French Genealogical Society
PO Box 2113, Pawtucket, RI, 02861-0113
AFG News, 446

American Power Conversion
132 Fairgrounds Rd., P.O. Box 278, West Kingston, RI, 02892-9920
APC Currents, 337

American Sail Training Association
PO Box 1459, Newport, RI, 02840-0996
Running Free, 114

•**Audubon Society of Rhode Island**
12 Sanderson Rd, Smithfield, RI, 02917-2606

Coalition of Essential Schools/Brown Unv.
PO Box 1969, Providence, RI, 02912
Horace, 1,091

•**Fire-Medic Services**
19 Joslin St., Providence, RI, 02909-2599

Greater Providence Chamber of Commerce
Commerce Center, 30 Exchange Terrace, Providence, RI, 02903
Progress Report, 161

IGM Enterprises Inc.
71 Hope St. #155, Providence, RI, 02906-2001
Pediatric Report's Child Health Newsletter, 883

Intl. Railroad & Transportation Postcard Collectors Club
PO Box 6782, Providence, RI, 02940-6782
Transport World, 557

Jewelers Board of Trade
70 Catamore Blvd, East Providence, RI, 02914-1289
Jewelers Board of Trade Service Bulletin, 693

Kessler Marketing Intelligence
America's Cup Ave., 31 Bridge St., Newport, RI, 02840
Fiberoptics Marketing/Intelligence, 138

Kwan Um of Zen
528 Pound Rd, Cumberland, RI, 02864-2712
Kwan Um School of Zen Newsletter, 1,054

•**Manisses Communications Group, Inc.**
PO Box 3357, Providence, RI, 02906-0757

Manufacturing Jewelers and Silversmiths of America
One State St., 6th Floor, Providence, RI, 02908-5035
Benchmark, 693

•**Medica Press Inc.**
10 Dorrance St. - Rm. 500, Providence, RI, 02903-2018

Metascience Foundation
PO Box 32, Kingston, RI, 02881
Unlimited Horizons, 531

Modern Greek Society
Modern Greek Studies Ass., Box 9411, Providence, RI, 02940-9411
Modern Greek Society: A Social Science Newsletter, 634

N. American Assn. for the Diaconate
Centre for the Diaconate, 271 N. Main St., Providence, RI, 02903
Diakoneo, 1,063

Necronomicon Press
101 Lockwood St, West Warwick, RI, 02893-7622
New Lovecraft Collector, 920

New England City & Town
19 Joslin St., Providence, RI, 02909-2599
New England City & Town, 1,022

PLAN International USA
155 Plan Way, Warwick, RI, 02886-1099
Global Talk!, 631

Parkinsonian Speak-Out
55 Merrick St, Rumford, RI, 02916-2520
Parkinsonian Speak-Out, 523

Privacy Journal
PO Box 28577, Providence, RI, 02908-0577
Privacy Journal, 969

Promotion Idea File
19 Joslin Street, Providence, RI, 02909-2599
Promotion Idea File, 21

Rhode Island Dept. of Employment Security
101 Friendship St, Providence, RI, 02903-3716
Rhode Island Department of Employment Security, Employment Bulletin, 348

Rhode Island Dept. of State Library Services
300 Richmond St., Providence, RI, 02903-4222
Rhode Island Department of State Library Services Newsletter, 809

Rhode Island Division of Motor Vehicles
286 Main St, Pawtucket, RI, 02860-2908
Rhode Island Traffic Safety Reporter, 1,083

Rhode Island Hospital
593 Eddy St, Providence, RI, 02903-4923
Nite Lite, 569

Smoke Signals
500 Waterman Ave., Ste. 193, East Providence, RI, 02914
Smoke Signals: A Monthly Newsletter Devoted to the Smoking Fetish, 1,110

State of RI & Providence Plantations, Div. of Planning
265 Melrose St Rm 203, Providence, RI, 02907-2102
Rhode Island Monthly Progress Report, 1,024

Survivor Connections, Inc.
52 Lyndon Rd, Cranston, RI, 02905-1121
Survivor Activist, The, 1,018

Technic, Inc.
1 Spectacle St, Cranston, RI, 02910-1058
Technicnews, 154

•**Thomas Lopatosky**
19 Joslin Street, Providence, RI, 02909-2599

Twins Foundation
PO Box 6043, Providence, RI, 02940-6043
Twins Letter, 1,101

U.S. Environmental Protection Agency
South Ferry Rd., Narragansett, RI, 02882
Marine Ecology Research Highlights, 387

Univ. of Rhode Island Library
Promenade St., Kingston, RI, 02881
CRIARL Newsletter, 795

Univ. of Rhode Island Library Friends of the Library
Kingston, RI, 02881-0803
Library Link, 802

South Carolina

ALM International (American Leprosy Missions)
1 Alm Way, Greenville, SC, 29601-3060
Word & Deed, 889

AWS
2215 Devine St, Columbia, SC, 29205-2401
Alston Wilkes Society Newsletter, 784

• See **MULTI-PUBLISHER INDEX** for list of publications.

Advanced Materials
PO Box 6249, Hilton Head Island, SC, 29938-6249
Advanced Materials, 847

Alpha Epsilon Rho
Univ. of S. Carolina, Journali, Columbia, SC, 29208
Signals, 181

American Society of Photographers
PO Box 3191, Spartanburg, SC, 29304-3191
ASP Newsletter, 976

Anderson Chamber of Commerce
Box 1568, Sta. A, Anderson, SC, 29622-1568
New Horizons, 161

Association for Continuing Higher Education
P.O Box 118067, CE-P, Charleston, SC, 29423-8067
Five Minutes with ACHE, 310

Assn. for Educ. in Journalism & Mass Communication
1621 College St, Univ. of South Carolina, Columbia, SC, 29208-0251
AEJMC News, 694

Baptist Evangel
PO Box 59, Union, SC, 29379-0059
Baptist Evangel, 1,053

Belle W. Baruch Inst. for Marine Biology & Coastal Research
Univ. of South Carolina, Columbia, SC, 29208-0001
Tidings, 937

Blue Cross
20 At Alpine Rd., Columbia, SC, 29219-0001
Kaleidoscope, 588

Broach, Mijeski & Assoc.
PO Box 12074, Rock Hill, SC, 29731-2074
Carolina Report, 482

•Charleston Chapter SCGS
PO Box 20266, Charleston, SC, 29413-0266

Christian Writers Fellowship International
Rr 3 Box 1635, Clinton, SC, 29325-9542
Cross & Quill, the Christian Writers Newsletter, 306

Citadel Military College of SC, The
Association of Citadel Men, 97 Hagood Avenue, Charleston, SC, 29409-0001
Through the Sally Port, 192

Clemson University
104 Holtzendorff Hall, Clemson, SC, 29634-0001
Division of Computing & Information Technology Update, 220

Coffee Pot Press
PO Box 3906, Greenville, SC, 29608-3906
Low Fat for Life, 431

Cooking Contest Newsletter
PO Box 339, Summerville, SC, 29484-0339
Cooking Contest Newsletter, 427

Eastern Digital Resources
438 Malone Avenue North, Augusta, SC, 29841
Just Classified Catalog, 275

•Greater Columbia Chamber of Commerce
930 Richland St, Columbia, SC, 29201-2329

•Guidera Publishing Corp.
3 Myrtle Bank Rd, Hilton Head Island, SC, 29926-1809

•Imagine, Inc.
398 Avenue, PO Box 101, Clemson, SC, 29633-0101

International Association for Ecology
Savannah River Ecology Lab., Drawer E, Aiken, SC, 29802
INTECOL Newsletter, 384

Intl. Organization of Wooden Money Collectors
PO Box 395, Goose Creek, SC, 29445-0395
Bunyan's Chips, 927

John Williams
PO Box 970, Taylors, SC, 29687-0970
Williams' Family Bulletin, 470

Lee Resources
PO Box 16711, Greenville, SC, 29606-7711
People & Profits, 249

Magnesium Monthly Review
106 Spring Forest Rd, Greenville, SC, 29615-2241
Magnesium Monthly Review, 891

Nathaniel Hawthorne Society
Clemson Univ. Dept. Of English, Clemson, SC, 29634-0001
Nathaniel Hawthorne Society-Newsletter, 983

National Association for Continence
PO Box 8310, Spartanburg, SC, 29305-8310
NAFC Quarterly Newsletter, 519

National Association of Independent Patriot Club
PO Box 2368, Anderson, SC, 29622-2368
Patriot Cannon, 995

National Beta Club
151 West Lee Street, Spartanburg, SC, 29306-3012
Beta Parents, 301

National Collegiate Association for Secretaries
Univ. of SC, College of Business, Columbia, SC, 29208-0001
National Collegiate Association for Secretaries; Newsletter, 939

Natl. Council of Examiners for Engineering & Surveying
PO Box 1686, Clemson, SC, 29633-1686
NCEES Registration Bulletin, 362

Orangeburgh German Swiss Genealogical Society
PO Box 974, Orangeburg, SC, 29116-0974
Orangeburgh German-Swiss Newsletter, 463

Piedmont Historical Soc.
PO Box 8096, Spartanburg, SC, 29305-8096
Upper South Carolina Genealogy & History, 469

Preservation Society of Charleston
PO Box 521, Charleston, SC, 29402-0521
Preservation Progress, 61

•R.W. Livingston, Publishing
PO Box 60008, North Charleston, SC, 29419-0008

Reid Family Newsletter & Data
PO Box 488, Due West, SC, 29639-0488
Reid Family Newsletter & Data, 465

SPRUILL
27 Oak Forest Dr, Charleston, SC, 29407-7078
South Carolina Committee Against Hunger, 935

St. Francis Xavier Hospital
135 Rutledge Ave, Charleston, SC, 29401-1338
News, 569

Senior Golf of America
3013 Church St, Myrtle Beach, SC, 29577-5820
Senior Golf, 480

Sherman College of Straight Chiropractic
2020 Springfield Rd., PO Box 1452, Spartanburg, SC, 29304
Straight from Sherman, 529

Shoe Tester's Association
660 Spartan Blvd Ste 9, Spartanburg, SC, 29301-1300
STA Newsletter, 56

South Carolina Aeronautics Commission
PO Box 280068, Columbia, SC, 29228-0068
Palmetto Aviation, 32

South Carolina Arts Commission Media Arts Center
1800 Gervais St, Columbia, SC, 29201-3504
Independent Spirit, 857

South Carolina Dental Bulletin
120 Stonemark Ln, Columbia, SC, 29210-3841
South Carolina Dental Bulletin, 271

South Carolina Industrial Commission
PO Box 1715, Columbia, SC, 29202-1715
Safety News, 1,084

South Carolina State College
Publications, Orangeburg, SC, 29112
SCSC Review, 192

•South Carolina State Library
1500 Senate St. #11469, Columbia, SC, 29211-3815

South Carolina Vocational Rehabilitation Dept.
PO Box 15, West Columbia, SC, 29171-0015
New Horizons, 1,119

United Serpents
PO Box 8915, Columbia, SC, 29202-8915
Newsletter for Us, 915

University of South Carolina
1728 College St, Columbia, SC, 29201-3918
Freshman Year Experience Newsletter, 209

Univ. of South Carolina
Library, Columbia, SC, 29208
Thomas Cooper Library Reflections, 811

Univ. of South Carolina, College of Business Adm.
Division of Research, Columbia, SC, 29208
South Carolina Economic Indicators, 152

Univ. of South Carolina, College of Education
Publications, Wardlaw 301, Columbia, SC, 29208-0001
University of South Carolina Education Report, 334

Voluntaryists
PO Box 1275, Gramling, SC, 29348-0275
Voluntaryist, The, 999

WBR Pubs.
PO Box 71, Clemson, SC, 29633-0071
World Beer Review, 106

Winthrop College
200 Tillman, Rock Hill, SC, 29733
Winthrop Update, 192

South Dakota

American Legion, Dept. of South Dakota
PO Box 67, Watertown, SD, 57201-0067
South Dakota Legion News, 182

Associated School Boards of South Dakota
PO Box 1211, Pierre, SD, 57501-1211
ASBSD Bulletin, 1,089

Association on American Indian Affairs
PO Box 268, Sisseton, SD, 57262
Indian Affairs, 405

•Business Research Bureau
414 E. Clark, U of SD, Vermillion, SD, 57069

Carol Peterson
PO Box 536, Freeman, SD, 57029-0536
Shelby Exchange, 467

Dacotah Prairie Museum
PO Box 395, Aberdeen, SD, 57402-0395
Dacotah Prairie Times, 903

Dakota Wesleyan Univ.
1200 W University Ave, Mitchell, SD, 57301-4398
DWU World, 193

Disbrow Family Newsletter
435 N Franklin Ave, Sioux Falls, SD, 57103-0825
Disbrow Family Newsletter, 452

East River Electric Power Co-Op
PO Box E, Madison, SD, 57042-0227
East River Electric Power Guardian, 1,026

Enterprise Publishing Co Inc
107 West 2nd Street, Flandreau, SD, 57028
Small Business Tax Saver, 1,151

Gateway 2000
610 Gateway Dr., Box 2000, North Sioux City, SD, 57049-2000
Gateway Monitor, 223

Governmental Research Bureau
Univ. of S.D., Vermillion, SD, 57069
Public Affairs, 491

•Growth Fund Research, Inc.
PO Box 6600, Rapid City, SD, 57709-6600

Huron College
Publications, Huron, SD, 57350
Smoke Signals, 206

Institute of American Indian Studies
Univ. of South Dakota, Vermillion, SD, 57069
University of South Dakota Bulletin, 52

International Builders Exchange Executives
PO Box 2274, Rapid City, SD, 57709
Construction Executive Report, 245

Kilian Community College
224 N Phillips Ave, Sioux Falls, SD, 57102-0316
Kilian Community College, 206

Mt. Plains Library Association
I.D. Weeks Library, University of South Dakota, Vermillion, SD, 57069-2390
MPLA Newsletter, 804

Natl. Buffalo Assn.
10 Main St., Box 580, Ft. Pierre, SD, 57532
Buffalo!, 49

National Hereford Hog Record Association
Rr 1 Box 37, Flandreau, SD, 57028-9724
National Hereford Hog ASGN, 828

•North American Baptist Seminary
1321 W 22nd St, Sioux Falls, SD, 57105-1502

Presentation College
1500 N Main St, Aberdeen, SD, 57401-1280
Outline, 193

Randolph-Sheppard Vendors of America
1527 Royal Rd, Aberdeen, SD, 57401-7646
Vendorscope, 112

Red Cloud Indian School, Inc.
Holy Rosary Mission, Pine Ridge, SD, 57770
Red Cloud Country, 406

SDSU Census Data Center
PO Box 504, Brookings, SD, 57006-0504
SDSU Census Data Center Newsletter, 1,043

Salveson Co.
PO Box 602, Huron, SD, 57350-0602
Coin Machine Trader, 1,199

Shirley Baughman-O'Leary
PO Box 641, Belle Fourche, SD, 57717-0641
C.T.C. Cousin-To-Cousin Coast to Coast Courier, 450

South Dakota Assn. of County Commissioners
207 E. Capitol, #203, Pierre, SD, 57501-3161
SDACC County Comment, 492

South Dakota Dental Assn.
PO Box 1194, Pierre, SD, 57501-1194
South Dakota Dental Assn. Newsletter, 271

* See ***MULTI-PUBLISHER INDEX*** for list of publications.

South Dakota Dept. of Labor
420 S Roosevelt St, Aberdeen, SD, 57401-5131
South Dakota Labor Bulletin, 705

Susan Braunstein
610 Quincy St, Rapid City, SD, 57701-3630
Book Marks, 794

Tri-State Genealogical Society
905 5th Ave, Belle Fourche, SD, 57717-1702
WyMonDak Messenger, 470

Wheat Quality Council
PO Box 966, Pierre, SD, 57501-0966
Wheat Briefs, 48

Wicozanni Wowapi Good Health Newsletter
PO Box 572, Lake Andes, SD, 57356-0572
Wicozanni Wowapi Good Health Newsletter, 531

Tennessee

ACME Boot Company, Inc.
PO Box 749, Clarksville, TN, 37041-0749
Roundup, 597

American Assn. for State & Local History
530 Church St Ste 600, Nashville, TN, 37219-2325
History News Dispatch, 541

American Baptist Theological Seminary
1800 Baptist World Ctr. Dr., Nashville, TN, 37207
Lamplighter, 206

American General Life & Accident
2110 American Gen. Center, Nashville, TN, 37250-0001
InGeneral, 586

The Andy Griffith Show Rerun Watchers Club
9 Music Sq S Ste 146, Nashville, TN, 37203-3203
Bullet, The, 1,165

Association for the Development of Religious Information Syt
P.O Box 210735, Nashville, TN, 37221-0735
ADRIS Newsletter, 211

Association for Private Enterprise Education
Univ. Of Tenn., Martin, Martin, TN, 38238-0001
APEE Newsletter, 126

•**Astute Investor**
135 Beechwood Lane, Kingston, TN, 37763-4708

•**Baptist Sunday School Board**
127 9th Ave N, Nashville, TN, 37234-0002

Baroness Erlanger Hospital
975 E. Third St., Chattanooga, TN, 37403
Baroness, 561

Blue Cross-Blue Shield Communications Div.
801 Pine St, Chattanooga, TN, 37402-2520
Reflections, 596

Borod & Huggins Educational Services, Inc.
245 Wagner Pl Ste 200, Memphis, TN, 38103-3815
Borod & Huggins Educational Services-Newsletter, 301

Bridgestone-Firestone Tire
PO Box 3000, Lavergne, TN, 37086-3000
Transcom, 601

Broyles Printing
Rr 3 Box 178, Clinton, TN, 37716-9803
Broyles Family Newsletter, 449

Bureau of Business & Economic Research
Memphis State Univ., Memphis, TN, 38152-0001
Memphis Economy, 145

Busy Woman's Newsletter
PO Box 757, Cordova, TN, 38088-0757
Busy Woman's Newsletter, 1,207

Ceco Industries, Inc.
750 Old Hicory Blvd., #150, Brentwood, TN, 37027-4502
Ceco Scope, 245

Center for Health Services
Vanderbilt Medical Ctr., #17, Nashville, TN, 37232-0001
Center for Health Services Newsletter, 502

Chattanooga Audubon Society
900 N Sanctuary Rd, Chattanooga, TN, 37421-4105
Audubon Happenings, 941

Cheekwood
Forrest Park Dr., Nashville, TN, 37205
Cheekwood Calendar, 903

Christian Businessmen's Committee of USA
1800 Mccallie Ave # 3308, Chattanooga, TN, 37404-3025
CB, 1,061

Clan Sutherland Society of N. America, Inc.
2922 Primrose Cir, Nashville, TN, 37212-6016
Dunrobin Piper, 452

College Legal Information, Inc.
PO Box 150541, Nashville, TN, 37215-0541
Lex Collegii, 751

College Media Advisers, Inc.
Mj-300 Memphis State Univ., Memphis, TN, 38152-0001
CMA Newsletter, 694

Commission on Religion in Appalachia (CORA)
PO Box 52910, Knoxville, TN, 37950-2910
CORAspondent, 1,045

Contemporary Christian Communications
107 Kenner Ave, Nashville, TN, 37205-2207
CCM Update, 910

Cumberland County Playhouse
PO Box 484, Crossville, TN, 38557-0484
Spotlight Newsletter, 1,174

•**EAR Foundation**
2000 Church St # 111, Nashville, TN, 37236-0001

E.F. Williams
751 E Brookhaven Cir, Memphis, TN, 38117-4501
Environmental Control News for Southern Industry, 380

East Tennessee Development District
5616 Kingston Pike, Box 19806, Knoxville, TN, 37919-6325
ETDD Newsletter, 1,020

East Tennessee Historical Society
500 W Church Ave, Knoxville, TN, 37902-2505
Newsline, 545

Electric League of Chattanooga
PO Box 182255, Chattanooga, TN, 37422-7255
Electric Leaguer, 583

Elvis Worldwide Fan Club
3081 Sunrise St, Memphis, TN, 38127-1437
Elvis Worldwide Fan Club, 417

Equicor
1801 W End Ave Fl 3, Nashville, TN, 37203-2526
About Your Health, 575

•**Federal Express Corp.**
2837 Sprankel Ave., AMF Box 30, Memphis, TN, 38118-1587

Federation of Motion Picture Council
142 N Tucker St, Memphis, TN, 38104-2656
News Reel, 420

Food Industries Suppliers Assn.
401 Brokenwood Lane, Farifield Glade, TN, 38558
FISA Distributor News, 428

Franklin County Historical Society
PO Box 130, Winchester, TN, 37398-0130
Historical Tidings, 456

Free Will Baptist Bible College
3606 W End Ave, Nashville, TN, 37205-2498
Bulletin, 206

General Board of Discipleship of the United Methodist Church
PO Box 840, Nashville, TN, 37202-0840
Covenant Discipleship Quarterly, 1,062

George Robert Martin
Rr 2, Corryton, TN, 37721-9802
Ballcard Collector, 551

George Southerland
PO Box 4254, Chattanooga, TN, 37405-0254
Special Investment Situations, 686

Greater Knoxville Chamber of Commerce
301 E Church Ave, Knoxville, TN, 37915-2502
Greater Knoxville Chamber of Commerce Membership Newsletter, 159

Gulf Life Insurance Co.
Mc0204 American Gen Ctr., Nashville, TN, 37250-0001
Life in General, 588

Harding Graduate School of Religion
1000 Cherry Rd, Memphis, TN, 38117-5424
HGSR News, 206

Highlander Research & Education Center, Inc.
1959 Highlander Way, New Market, TN, 37820
Highlander Reports, 1,117

Historical Commission, Southern Baptist Conv.
901 Commerce St., Nashville, TN, 37203-3630
Baptist Heritage Update, 1,053

Hunter Museum of Art
10 Bluff View St, Chattanooga, TN, 37403-1111
Hunter Museum of Art Bulletin, 904

International Horn Society
P O Box 1083, Hixson, TN, 37343-1083
International Horn Society-Newsletter, 913

Kano Labs.
1000 Thompson Ln, Nashville, TN, 37211-2658
Genius At Work, 584

•**King Publishing Corp.**
6914 Office Park Cir # 52210, Knoxville, TN, 37909-1161

Knoxville Bar Assn.
PO Box 2027, Knoxville, TN, 37901-2027
Dicta Monthly, 731

Knoxville College
901 College St, Knoxville, TN, 37921-4799
Inside Knoxville College, 193

Leader Fedl. Savings
158 Madison Ave, Memphis, TN, 38103-2630
Leader Digest, 588

Lebanon
149 Public Sq, Lebanon, TN, 37087-2736
Lebanon and Wilson County Chamber of Commerce Letter, 160

•**Lewis L. Laska**
901 Church St, Nashville, TN, 37203-3411

•**M. Lee Smith Publishers & Printers ,LCC**
P.O. Box 198867, 162 Fourth Avenue North, Nashville, TN, 37219-8867

M Street Corp.
PO Box 1479, Madison, TN, 37116-5312
M Street Journal, 124

Mastering Life Ministries
P.O. box 110072, Nashville, TN, 37222
Mastering Life, 1,110

Memphis Brooks Museum of Art
Overton Park, Memphis, TN, 38104
Memphis Brooks Museum of Art Newsletter, 65

Memphis/Shelby County Staff Organization
1850 Peabody Ave, Memphis, TN, 38104-4021
Undercurrent: Memphis/Shelby County Public Library and Information Center Staff Newsletter, 812

Moneychanger
PO Box 1753, Memphis, TN, 38101-1753
Moneychanger, The, 677

Moonbeam Press
1725 B Madison #3, Memphis, TN, 38104
Shake Rattle & Roll, 917

Mountain Women's Exchange
205 5th St, Jellico, TN, 37762-2107
Mountain Women's Exchange-Newsletter, 1,119

Nashville Electric Service
1214 Church St, Nashville, TN, 37246-0002
N.E.S. News, 591

Nashville Songwriters Assn. Intl.
15 Music Sq W, Nashville, TN, 37203-3203
Leadsheet, The, 913

Natl. Assn. of Temple Educators
707 Summerly Dr, Nashville, TN, 37209-4218
NATE News, 1,070

National Caves Association
4138 Dark Hollow Road, McMinnville, TN, 37110-8629
NCA Cave Talk, 476

National Cotton Council of America
PO Box 12285, Memphis, TN, 38182-0285
Cotton's Week, 1,171

National Cottonseed Products Association
PO Box 172267, Memphis, TN, 38187-2267
NCPA Newsletter, 43

Natl. Democratic Front
PO Box 30505, Knoxville, TN, 37930-0505
Nationalist, 994

National Fund for Medical Education
8905 Kingston Pike, #12-483, Knoxville, TN, 37923-5011
NFME News, 320

Natl. Hardwood Lumber Assn.
PO Box 34518, Memphis, TN, 38184-0518
NHLA Export Directory, 830

Natl. Marine Representatives Assn.
PO Box 660, Camden, TN, 38320-0660
Tidings, 114

Natl. Model Railroad Assn.
4121 Cromwell Rd, Chattanooga, TN, 37421-2119
National Model Railroad Association Bulletin, 555

Natural Rights Center
PO Box 90, Summertown, TN, 38483-0090
Natural Rights, 994

Oak Ridge Boys Intl. Fan Club
329 Rockland Rd, Hendersonville, TN, 37075-3423
Oak Ridge Boys Intl. Team Spirit, 915

Oak Ridge National Library
PO Box 2008, Oak Ridge, TN, 37831-2008
RSIC Newsletter, 927

Parkridge Hospital
2333 Mccallie Ave, Chattanooga, TN, 37404-3258
Parkridge Probe, 594

Phlander Company
PO Box 5385, Cleveland, TN, 37320-5385
WorldWide Business Exchange, 156

* See ***MULTI-PUBLISHER INDEX*** for list of publications.

Plenty USA
PO Box 394, Summertown, TN, 38483-0394
Plenty Bulletin, 996

Psi Chi, the National Honor Society in Psychology
407 E 5th St # B, Chattanooga, TN, 37403-1823
Psi Chi Newsletter, 1,017

Rhea County Publishing Co, Inc
3687 Rhea County Highway, P.O. Box 286, Dayton, TN, 37321-0286
Rhea County Shopper, 25

Richards Manufacturing Co. Inc.
1450 E Brooks Rd, Memphis, TN, 38116-1804
Richards Reporter, 596

St. Jude Children's Research Hospital
501 St. Jude Place, Memphis, TN, 38105
LSAC News, 567

Scholl, Inc.
3030 Jackson Ave., 150 E. Huron St., Memphis, TN, 38112-2020
Dr. Scholl's Foot Health Forum, 504

School Age Notes
PO Box 40205, Nashville, TN, 37204-0205
School Age Notes, 1,093

Seventh House
Box OX-171263, Memphis, TN, 38187-1263
Seventh House, The, 816

Southern Bean Assn.
Mary Kirk-McCrary, 209 Kinwood Dr., Murfreesboro, TN, 37130
Bean Stalk, 448

Southern College of Optometry
1245 Madison Ave, Memphis, TN, 38104-2222
Visions Newsletter, 193

Southern Health Assn.
c/o Metro Health Dept., 311 23rd Avenue N, Nashville, TN, 37203
Southern Health Update, 528

State of Tennessee Department of Revenue
500 Deaderick St, Nashville, TN, 37242-0001
Tennessee Tax Quarterly, 1,155

Sunday School Board Southern Baptist Convention
127 9th Avenue, North, Nashville, TN, 37234-0001
Special Education Leadership, 331

Tau Beta Pi Assn., Inc.
Box 8840, Univ. Station, Knoxville, TN, 37996-0001
Bulletin of Tau Beta Pi, 359

•**Tennessee Arts Commission**
404 James Robertson Parkway, Suite 160, Nashville, TN, 37243-0780

Tennessee Congress of Parents
1905 Acklen Ave., Nashville, TN, 37212-3713
Tennessee Parent-Teacher Bulletin, 333

Tennessee Dental Assn.
2104 Sunset Place, PO Box 120188, Nashville, TN, 37212
Tennessee Dental Association News, 272

Tennessee Environmental Council
1700 Hayes St Ste 101, Nashville, TN, 37203-3014
ProTECt, 391

Tennessee Historical Commission
701 Broadway, Nashville, TN, 37243-0442
Courier, 539

Tennessee Hunger Coalition
PO Box 120961, Nashville, TN, 37212-0961
Tennessee Hunger Coalition News, 1,122

Tennessee Library Association
PO Box 158417, Nashville, TN, 37215-8417
TSLA Newsletter, 811

Tennessee Ornithological Society
Rr 7 Box 338, Elizabethton, TN, 37643-9145
Migrant, 942

Tennessee School Boards Assn.
500 13th Ave. , N., Nashville, TN, 37203-2808
Tennessee School Board Bulletin, 333

Tennessee School for the Deaf
2725 Island Home Blvd., Knoxville, TN, 37920-2700
Tennessee Observer, 534

Tennessee Technological Univ., University Archives
Box 5066, Cookeville, TN, 38505
Tennessee Archivists Newsletter, 811

•**Tennessee Valley Public Power Assn.**
1201 Chestnut St, Chattanooga, TN, 37402-5021

Travelin' Talk Network
PO Box 3534, Clarksville, TN, 37043-3534
Travelin' Talk, 1,191

Trevecca Nazarene College
333 Murfreesboro Rd, Nashville, TN, 37210-2834
Treveccan, 193

Tri-Son, Inc.
PO Box 40328, Nashville, TN, 37204-0328
Tri-Son, News, 918

•**Union Planters Corp.**
7130 Goodlett Farm Parkway, Cordova, TN, 38018

United Methodist Communications
810 12th Ave S, Nashville, TN, 37203-4704
UMCommunity, 601

•**United Methodist Publishing House**
201 Eighth Avenue South, Nashville, TN, 37203-0801

•**United South & Eastern Tribes, Inc.**
711 Stewarts Ferry Pike # 10, Nashville, TN, 37214-2634

•**University of Tennessee Agricultural Extensions**
PO Box 1071, Knoxville, TN, 37901-1071

University of Tennessee Department of Anthropology
Publications, 252 South Stadium Hall, Knoxville, TN, 37996-0720
Tennessee Anthropological Assn. Newsletter, 52

Univ. of Tennessee for Health Sciences
800 Madison Ave, Memphis, TN, 38103-3400
Allied Health Update, 193

Univ. of Tennessee Library
1015 Volunteer Blvd., Knoxville, TN, 37996-1000
UTK Librarian, 812

Westnash Resources
PO Box 90665, Nashville, TN, 37209-0665
Western Industry Report International, 156

Texas

•**AHA Stroke Connections**
7272 Greenville Ave, Dallas, TX, 75231-5129

AM&A Meakin/Art
402 West Taylor Avenue, Suite A-367, Round Rock, TX, 78664-4237
Newsletter, 146

ANJO Enterprises
5602 Glenlivet Pl, Greenville, TX, 75402-4205
ANJO Insight, 256

Abbey Publications
7105 Geneva Dr, Austin, TX, 78723-1510
Abbey Newsletter, 115

Aerobics Center
12200 Preston Rd, Dallas, TX, 75230-2223
Aerobics, 550

Alamo Area Council of Governments
118 Broadway St Ste 400, San Antonio, TX, 78205-1999
AACOG Region, 1,043

Allee's All Around
PO Box 347, Friendswood, TX, 77546-0347
Allee's All Around, 446

Alvin Community College
3110 Mustang Rd, Alvin, TX, 77511-4895
Intouch, 206

American Agricultural Editors Assn.
612 W 22nd St, Austin, TX, 78705-5116
Byline, 694

American Assn. of Housing Educators
Texas A&M Univ., College of Architecture, College Station, TX, 77843-0001
AAHE Newsletter, 59

American College of Emergency Physicians
1125 Executive Cir., Irving, TX, 75038-2530
ACEP News, 863

American Ex-Prisoners of War
3201 E Pioneer Pky Ste 40, Arlington, TX, 76010-5324
Ex-P O W Bulletin, 896

American Gay Atheists, Inc.
PO Box 66711, Houston, TX, 77266-6711
American Gay & Lesbian Atheist, 443

American Heart Association
7272 Greenville Ave, Dallas, TX, 75231-4596
HeartStyle, 875

American Porphyria Foundation
PO Box 22712, Houston, TX, 77227-2712
Porphyria News, 884

•**American Productivity & Quality Center**
123 N. Post Oak Ln., Ste. 300, Houston, TX, 77024-7718

American Society for the Study of Religion
Smu Dept. Of Religious Studies, Dallas, TX, 75275-0001
American Society for the Study of Religion Newsletter, 1,044

American Transfer
4204 Lindberg Dr, Dallas, TX, 75244-2401
ATSCO News, 575

Amon Carter Museum
3501 Camp Bowie Blvd, Fort Worth, TX, 76107-2365
Museum Archivist, 906

Animal Transportation Association
5521 Greenville Ave., Suite 104-310, Dallas, TX, 75206
Animal Transportation Association Newsletter, 48

•**Annie's Attic, Inc.**
222 Las Colinas Blvd W, Suite 1750, Irving, TX, 75039-5437

Annuity Board/Southern Baptist Convention
PO Box 2190, Dallas, TX, 75221-2190
Years Ahead, 1,054

Apache Corporation
2000 Post Oak Blvd., Ste. 100, Houston, TX, 77056-4400
Apache Arrows, 576

Apostolate of the Little Flower
906 Kentucky Ave, San Antonio, TX, 78201-6016
Apostolate of the Little Flower, 1,055

Aquarian Publications
1101 Post Oak Blvd Ste 312, Houston, TX, 77056-3105
Indigo Sun, 922

Ashtray Collectors' Club
PO Box 11652, Houston, TX, 77293-1652
Ashtray Journal, 1,175

Asian Pacific Travel Facts
6414 Kelly Elliott Rd, Arlington, TX, 76017-5130
Asian Pacific Travel Facts, 1,182

Asian/Pacific Travel Facts
6414 Kelly Elliott Rd Ste 220, Arlington, TX, 76017-5130
Asian/Pacific Travel Facts, 1,182

Assocs. Corp. of North America
250 Carpenter Frwy., Dallas, TX, 75222
Associates, 576

Association for Arid Land Studies
Texas Tech. University, Box 41036, Lubbock, TX, 79409-1036
AALS Newsletter, 35

Assn. of Health Facility Licensure & Certification Directors
1100 W 49th St # 309, Austin, TX, 78756-3101
Association of Health Facility Licensure & Certification Newsletter, 867

Association for Retarded Citizens/Texas
PO Box 5368, Austin, TX, 78763-5368
Texas Talk, 171

•**Assn. for the Study of Play**
Box 6375, Southwestern Univ., Georgetown, TX, 78626

Assn of Traditional Hooking Artists
3209 Erwin Drive, Plano, TX, 75074
ATHA Newsletter, 550

Aunt Caroline, Inc.
3806 Alisa Ann Dr, Corpus Christi, TX, 78418-3002
Aunt Caroline's Almanac, 48

Austin College
900 N Grand Ave # 6h, Sherman, TX, 75090-4440
Acknowledge, 193

Austin Tenth District Dental Society
3303 Northland Dr Ste 313, Austin, TX, 78731-4956
Tenth Times, 272

BR(E)ASHE(A)R(S) Family Branches
817 Stratford Dr., Bedford, TX, 76021-5321
BR(E)ASHE(A)R(S) Family Branches, 447

Baugh Center for Entrepreneurship
Baylor University, BU Box 8011, Waco, TX, 76798-8011
Academy of Management News, 833

Baylor College of Medicine
1 Baylor Plz Rm 176b, Houston, TX, 77030-3411
Baylor Medicine, 206

•**Baylor Univ.**
P.O. Box 98011, Waco, TX, 76798

Bell Helicopter Textron, Inc.
600 E Hurst St, Hurst, TX, 76053
Rotor Breeze, 32

Bell-Northern Research
2221 Lakeside Blvd, Richardson, TX, 75082-4305
One Vision, 593

Blaisdell Family Nat'l. Assn.
PO Box 707, Amarillo, TX, 79105-0707
Blaisdell Papers, 448

Blue Ridge Ostrich Ranch
PO Box 339, Blue Ridge, TX, 75424-0339
Ostriches, 828

Bogus
14227 Eventide, Cypress, TX, 77429
Bogus, 924

Bold Productions
PO Box 152281, Arlington, TX, 76015-8281
Really, a Free Newsletter, 119

•**Boy Scouts of America**
1325 W Walnut Hill Ln, Irving, TX, 75038-3096

* See *MULTI-PUBLISHER INDEX* for list of publications.

Building Officials Assn. of Texas
1601 Rio Grande St Ste 440, Austin, TX, 78701-1149
Bulletin, The, 481

•**Bureau of Business Research**
University of Texas, 21st St. & Speedway, Austin, TX, 78712-1104

Burwell Enterprises, Inc.
3724 Fm 1960 Rd W Ste 214, Houston, TX, 77068-3527
Information Broker, 858

Bushong Bulletin
1504 E. 52nd St., Odessa, TX, 79762-4457
Bushong Bulletin, 449

C Systems Ltd.
Box 708, 1006 Plume St., Winnsboro, TX, 75494
Admetrics, 9

Camp Horsemanship Assn.
5318 Old Bullard Rd, Tyler, TX, 75703-3612
CHA Newsletter, 559

Cass County Genealogical Society
PO Box 880, Atlanta, TX, 75551-0880
Cass County Connections, 450

Catholic Women's Fraternal of Texas-The K.J.Z.T.
PO Box 1884, Austin, TX, 78767-1884
K.J.Z.T. News, 1,057

Center for Asian Studies
Univ. of Texas at Austin, SSB Rm.4-126, Austin, TX, 78712
Center for Asian Studies Newsletter, 628

Center for Dredging Studies
Texas A & M Univ., Civil Engineering Dept., College Station, TX, 77843-3136
Center for Dredging Studies Newsletter, 364

Center for Neo-Hellenic Studies
1010 W 22nd St, Austin, TX, 78705-5306
Neo-Hellenika, 402

Central America Resource Center
PO Box 2327, Austin, TX, 78768-2327
Central America NewsPak, 628

Central Power & Light Co.
120 N Chaparral St # 2121, Corpus Christi, TX, 78401-2802
CPL Hot Line, 579

Central Texas College
PO Box 1800, Killeen, TX, 76540-1800
Memogram, 206

Chaparral Genealogical Soc.
PO Box 606, Tomball, TX, 77377-0606
Roadrunner, 466

•**Chihuahuan Desert Research Institute**
PO Box 1334, Alpine, TX, 79831-1334

Christ for the Nations
3404 Conway St, Dallas, TX, 75224-4092
Prayer & Share Newsletter, 1,065

Chuck Thompson and Associates
P.O. Box 11652, Houston, TX, 77293
St. Patrick Notes, 185

•**City of Richardson Texas**
411 West Arataho, Richardson, TX, 75080

City of San Antonio, Texas
PO Box 839966, San Antonio, TX, 78283-3966
City Beat, 482

Clan Gillean U.S.A.
PO Box 4061, Alvin, TX, 77512-4061
Pipings, The, 464

Clarke Printing
PO Box 460, San Antonio, TX, 78292-0460
Printer's Impressions, 595

Clinical Sociology Assn., Dept. of Sociology
Box 13408, N. Texas State Univ., Denton, TX, 76203-3408
Clinical Sociology Newsletter, 1,125

Clovis Herring
Rr 1 Box 123a, Buffalo, TX, 75831-9717
Pate Pioneers, 464

Coastal Bend Council of Governments
Box 9909, Corpus Christi, TX, 78469-9909
State of the Region, 493

College Sports Information Directors of America
Texas A&I Univ., Box 114, Kingsville, TX, 78363
College Sports Information Directors Digest, 1,130

Committee in Solidarity with Latin American Nonviolent Movem
1114 Noble St, Houston, TX, 77009-8438
Solidarity/Solidaridad, 638

Committee on South Asian Women
Texas A & M Univ., Pschology Dept., College Station, TX, 77843-0001
Committee on South Asian Women Bulletin, 403

Computer Aided Manufacturing Intl.
1250 E Copeland Rd Ste 500, Arlington, TX, 76011-4913
CAM-I News Alert, 213

Conference of Latin Americanist Geographers
P.O. Box 7819, Univ. of Texas Press, Austin, TX, 78713
CLAG Communication, 474

Cooling Tower Institute
530 Wells Fargo Dr Ste 107, Houston, TX, 77090-4026
Bibliography of Technical Papers Presented At OTI Meetings, 106

Cooper Airmotive
7555 Lemon Ave., P.O. Box 7086, Dallas, TX, 75209-0086
Aeroviews, 576

Corporate Jobs Outlook!
PO Box 670466, Dallas, TX, 75367-0466
Corporate Jobs Outlook!, 342

Cravens Dargan
PO Box 1660, Houston, TX, 77251-1660
Cravens Dargan, 581

Credit Card Collector
PO Box 460247, Houston, TX, 77056-8247
Credit Card Collector, 257

Crustacean Society
C/O Denton Belk, 840 E. Mulberry, San Antonio, TX, 78212
Ecdipiast, The, 109

•**Cypress Publishing**
PO Box 777, Cypress, TX, 77429-0777

DPA International
PO Box 440817, Houston, TX, 77244-0817
Boletin de Divulgacion Martiana, 402

Daily Commercial Record
706 Main St, Dallas, TX, 75202-3699
Daily Commercial Record, 730

Dallas Area Rapid Transit
PO Box 660163, Dallas, TX, 75266-9299
Connections, 581

Dallas County Dental Assistants Assn.
2217 E. Biscayne, Irving, TX, 75060-7214
Dallas Dental News, 269

Dallas Institute of Humanities and Culture
2719 Routh St, Dallas, TX, 75201-1975
Dallas Institute Newsletter, The, 1,020

Dallas Memorial Center for Holocaust Studies
7900 Northaven Rd, Dallas, TX, 75230-3352
Dallas Memorial Center for Holocaust Studies Newsletter, 539

Dallas Tenants Assn.
2906 Swiss Ave, Dallas, TX, 75204-5962
Dallas Tenants' News, 790

David Lee Riley
Voice For Animals, P.O. Box 120095, San Antonio, TX, 78212
Voice (for the animals), The, 50

Delta Kappa Gamma Society International
416 W 12th St, Austin, TX, 78701-1817
Delta Kappa Gamma News, 177

Dental Group Management Assn.
2425 Ashdale Dr Apt 35, Austin, TX, 78757-8152
Communicator-Dental, 268

Distribution Contractors Assn.
101 W Renner Rd Ste 250, Richardson, TX, 75082-2002
DCA News, 246

Don Caruth Associates
519 I-30, Suite 242, Rockwell, TX, 75087
CQSS Reporter, 835

Doron & Associates
1213 Ridgecrest Cir, Denton, TX, 76205-5421
DeskTop Presentations & Publishing, 307

DreamTrips!
PO Box 670466, Dallas, TX, 75367-0466
DreamTrips!, 1,183

•**Dresser Industries Inc.**
PO Box 718, Dallas, TX, 75221-0718

Eastfield College
3737 Motley Dr, Mesquite, TX, 75150-2099
Eastfield Era, 206

Educational Research Analysts
PO Box 7518, Longview, TX, 75607-7518
Mel Gabler's Newsletter, 317

Ellis Cousins Nationwide
1201 Maple Ave, Friona, TX, 79035-1405
Ellis Cousins Newsletter, 453

Eric Davidson
2183 Buckingham, #132, Richardson, TX, 75081
Chaotic Apochrypha, 922

Estep Family Assn.
12206 Brisbane Ave, Dallas, TX, 75234-6528
Estep Family Journal, 453

Eupsychian Press
PO Box 3090, Austin, TX, 78764-3090
Transformers Notebook, 975

•**Exxon Co., U.S.A.**
800 Bell St., Houston, TX, 77002

Exxon Co. USA
PO Box 4697, Houston, TX, 77210-4697
South Texan, 599

Exxon Co., U.S.A.
800 Bell St., Houston, TX, 77002
Energy, 956

FANS of Women's Sports
PO Box 49648, Austin, TX, 78765-9648
FANS of Women's Sports, 1,131

Fare Share Co.
4709 Weyhill Dr, Arlington, TX, 76013-5450
Fare Share-The Food Letter, 428

•**Federal Reserve Bank of Dallas**
Station K, Dallas, TX, 75222

Fed. of State Medical Boards of the U.S., Inc.
400 Fuller Wiser Road, Suite #300, Euless, TX, 76039-3855
FSMBNewsLine, 873

Fine Print Distributors
500 Pampa Drive, Austin, TX, 78752
Bam! Bam!, 952

Firestone Tire
Firestone Syn Rubber, Latex Co, Box 1269, Orange, TX, 77630
Petro-Chem, 594

Flippin Family Assn.
12206 Brisbane Ave, Dallas, TX, 75234-6528
Flipping Flippins, 453

Fort Concho National Historic Landmark
213 E Avenue D, San Angelo, TX, 76903-7020
Fort Concho Guidon, 904

Fort Worth Star Telegram
400 W 7th St, Fort Worth, TX, 76102-4793
Weekly Chaser, 603

Fossil Rim Wildlife Ctr.
Rr 1 Box 210, Glen Rose, TX, 76043-9729
Views from the Rim, 396

Foundation for the Advancement of Compassion & Truth
PO Box 90140, Arlington, TX, 76004-3140
International Healthwatch Report, 515

Fred Maia
P.O. Box 565101, Dallas, TX, 75356-5101
W5YI Report, 999

Gainesville Area Chamber of Commerce
101 S Culberson St, Gainesville, TX, 76240-4756
C of C Newsletter, 158

General Motors Corp.
Arlington Plant-GMC, Arlington, TX, 76010
Information Letter, 586

The Glove Collector
14057 Rolling Hills Ln, Dallas, TX, 75240-3807
Glove Collector Newsletter, The, 553

•**Good Communications, Inc.**
PO Box 10069, Austin, TX, 78766

Goodwill Industries of Houston Inc.
PO Box 21185, Houston, TX, 77226-1185
Goodwill News, 277

Gordon Jewelry Corp.
PO Box 152777, Irving, TX, 75015-2777
Gem, 584

Government Management Information Sciences
PO Box 926, Wichita Falls, TX, 76307-0926
GEM, 485

Gray House Publishing
2201 Wayne St, Copperas Cove, TX, 76522-4185
Stamp Pals International Newsletter, 972

Greater San Antonio Chamber of Commerce
602 E Commerce St, San Antonio, TX, 78205-2620
Chamber Today, The, 159

Greyhound Lines, Inc.
PO Box 660606, Dallas, TX, 75266-0606
Connections, 581

Groundwater Management Districts Assn.
PO Box 795, Dumas, TX, 79029-0795
Groundwater Management Districts Assn. Newsletter, 1,202

Harbison-Fischer Mfg. Co.
901 N Crowley Rd, Crowley, TX, 76036-3739
Pump Patter, 596

* See **MULTI-PUBLISHER INDEX** for list of publications.

Harbour-Witt Family Assn., Inc.
7904 Joliet Ave, Lubbock, TX, 79423-1720
Harbour-Witt Family Association Bulletin, 455

Harry Browne's Special Reports, Inc.
207 Jefferson Sq, Austin, TX, 78731-6211
Harry Browne's Special Reports, 667

Hart Information Systems
8030 Shoal Creek Blvd, Austin, TX, 78757-8039
Texas Administration Code, 493

Hart Publications. Inc.
4545 Post Oak Place Drive, Suite 210, Houston, TX, 77027-3105
Hart's Pipeline Digest Update Newsletter, 957

Henke
PO Box 1309, Houston, TX, 77251-1309
Round-Up, 597

•**Hoisager & Laird, Inc.**
101 S Jennings Ave Ste 204, Fort Worth, TX, 76104-1149

Hood County Genealogical Society
PO Box 1623, Granbury, TX, 76048-8623
Hood County Genealogical Society Newsletter, 456

Hood's Texas Brigade Association
PO Box 619, Hillsboro, TX, 76645-0619
Hood's Texas Brigade Association-Newsletter, 1,138

Houston Chronicle
PO Box 4260, Houston, TX, 77210-4260
Copy, 581

Houston Education Assn.
1415 Southmore Blvd, Houston, TX, 77004-5845
HEA Advocate, 311

Houston Lighting & Power Co.
611 Walker St, Houston, TX, 77002-4917
Transmissions, 601

Human Side Press Ltd.
1800 Bering Dr Ste 690, Houston, TX, 77057-3129
On the Human Side, 842

Hymn Society in the United States & Canada
Texas Christian Univ., PO Box 30854, Fort Worth, TX, 76129-0001
Stanza, 918

Information Technology, Information Services
University Of Houston, Houston, TX, 77204-0001
Open Channel, 233

Inside Publishing
2351 W. Northwest Hwy., Ste. 2115, Dallas, TX, 75220-4434
Insider, The, 434

Institute for Fusion Studies
Univ. of Texas at Austin, RLM 11 234, Austin, TX, 78712-1060
Institute for Fusion Studies Newsletter, 979

Institute for the Study of Earth & Moon
Southern Methodist Univ. Box, 274, Dallas, TX, 75275-0001
ISEM Newsletter, 476

Inter-Americas Consulting Group
PO Box 42184, Houston, TX, 77242-2184
Inter-Americas Business Newsletter, 647

Intercultural Development Research Assn.
5835 Callaghan Rd Ste 350, San Antonio, TX, 78228-1125
IDRA Newsletter, 312

Intl. Academy of Behavioral Medicine/Counseling & Psychology
13140 Coit Rd., Ste. 307, Dallas, TX, 75240
IABM Newsletter, 876

International Center for Arid Lands
PO Box 41036, Lubbock, TX, 79409-1036
ICASALS Newletter, 42

International Communication Associaton
PO Box 9589, Austin, TX, 78766-9589
ICA Newsletter, 696

Intl. Council of Psychologists
SW Texas State Univ., Psychology Dept., San Marcos, TX, 78666-4601
International Psychologist, 1,015

International Facility Management Association
1 E Greenway Plz Ste 1100, Houston, TX, 77046-0104
IFMA News, 247

Intl. Furnishings & Design Assn.
107 World Trade Ctr., Box 58045, Dallas, TX, 75258
IFTA Network, 625

•**International Risk Management Institute**
12222 Merit Dr Ste 1660, Dallas, TX, 75251-3207

International Society of Certified Electronics Technicians
2708 W. Berry, Ft. Worth, TX, 76109-2356
ISCET Update, 366

International Society of Worldwide Stamp Collectors, The
Rr 1 Box 69a/2505 Second St, Caddo Mills, TX, 75135-9704
Circuit, The, 970

International Television Assn.
6311 N. O'Connor Rd., Ste. 230, Irving, TX, 75039-3511
ITVA News, 1,167

J.E. Sparks & Associates
1404 N. Floyd Rd., Richardson, TX, 75080-4138
HealthCare Systems NewsLetter, 511

John K. Strecker Museum
Baylor University, Box 97154, Waco, TX, 76798
Strecker Museum News, 908

•**Julian Associates**
6831 Spencer Hwy. Suite 203, Pasadena, TX, 77505-1772

•**Justex Systems**
PO Box 6224, Huntsville, TX, 77342-6224

KIB Communications
PO Box 1676, Humble, TX, 77347-1676
Bare Texan, 1,124

Last Chance Forever
506 Avenue A, San Antonio, TX, 78215-1221
Feather in the Wind, 382

Library Managemental Services
5914 Highland Hills Dr, Austin, TX, 78731-4057
Practical Law Books Review, 119

Lighword Publishing Company
National Bank Building, 525 S. Main St., Suite 308, Del Rio, TX, 78840
Mind Quest, 607

Linguistics Research Center
Univ. of Texas, P.O. Box 74247, Austin, TX, 78713
Linguistics Research Quarterly Report, 823

Literary Sketches
PO Box 810571, Dallas, TX, 75381-0571
Literary Sketches, 818

Little People of America, Inc.
7238 Piedmont Dr, Dallas, TX, 75227-9324
LPA News, 179

Living Truth Ministries
1708 Patterson Rd, Austin, TX, 78733-6507
Flashpoint, 1,057

Lone Star Bring Co.
600 Lone Star Blvd, San Antonio, TX, 78204-1707
Bru-It, 578

Lone Star Publications of Humor
Ste. 103, Box 29000, San Antonio, TX, 78229
Lone Star Comedy Monthly, 605

Lorensen International Communications
PO Box 380022, San Antonio, TX, 78280-0022
International Cooking Contest Newsletter, 430

Lubbock Chamber of Commerce
PO Box 561, Lubbock, TX, 79408-0561
Greater Lubbock, 159

•**Lunar & Planetary Institute**
3600 Bay Area Blvd, Houston, TX, 77058-1113

Mailing List Systems
711 Directors Dr, Arlington, TX, 76011-5103
Canadian Direct Marketing Notes, 11

Mason West Co.
610 A E Battlefield, Suite #246, Springfield, TX, 65807-4865
Capital West, 723

McKone & Co.
1900 Westridge Dr, Irving, TX, 75038-2901
McKone, 590

Mended Hearts, Inc.
7320 Greenville Rd, Dallas, TX, 75231-4502
Mended Hearts Newsletter, 518

Mid-Continent Supply Co.
2240 Morriss Rd Ste 110, Flower Mound, TX, 75028-3587
Mid-Continent News, 590

Mid-Valley Pipeline Co.
PO Box 2388, Longview, TX, 75606-2388
Mid-Valley Impeller, 590

Miller Freeman, Inc.
13760 Noel Rd., Ste. 500, Dallas, TX, 75240-4332
Eliot Sharp's Financing News, 88

Mind Science Foundation
7979 Broadway St Ste 100, San Antonio, TX, 78209-2657
Mind Science Foundation News, 1,015

Missionary Assn. of Mary Immaculate
PO Box 96, San Antonio, TX, 78291-0096
Mission News, 1,058

Model A Ford Cabriolet Club
PO Box 515, Porter, TX, 77365-0515
Cabrioletter, The, 71

Monitor Communication Group
15995 N Barkers Landing Rd Ste, 320, Houston, TX, 77079-2461
Asbestos Monitor, 244

Mothers Without Custody
PO Box 27418, Houston, TX, 77227-7418
Mother-To-Mother, 413

Mountain Home Publishing
PO Box 829, Ingram, TX, 78025-0829
Alternatives for the Health Conscious Individual, 498

Natl. Assn. of Left-Handed Golfers
PO Box 801223, Houston, TX, 77280-1223
Southpaw Activities, 480

National Association for the Self-Employed, Inc.
2121 Precinct Line Rd, Hurst, TX, 76054-3136
Self-Employed America, 151

National Business Association
PO Box 700728, Dallas, TX, 75370
National Business News, 146

Natl. Catholic Committee on Scouting
1325 W Walnut Hill Ln # 6103, Irving, TX, 75038-3008
National Catholic Committee on Scouting Newsletter, 180

Natl. Character Laboratory
4635 Leeds Ave, El Paso, TX, 79903-1211
National Character Laboratory-Newsletter, 881

Natl. Electronics Service Dealers Assn.
2708 W. Berry St., Ft. Worth, TX, 76109-2397
NESDA Update, 339

Natl. Interagency Council on Smoking
7320 Greenville Ave, Dallas, TX, 75231-4502
Smoking and Health Newsletter, 528

Natl. Jewish Committee on Scouting
1325 W Walnut Hill Ln, Irving, TX, 75038-3008
Hatsofe, 178

Natl Swimming Pool Owner's Assoc.
1213 Ridgecrest Cir, Denton, TX, 76205-5421
Swimming Pool Today, 557

Natural Resources Information System
PO Box 13231, Austin, TX, 78711-3231
Texas, Natural Resources Information System, Newsletter, 395

Net Results
5001 Ave N, Lubbock, TX, 79412-2993
Net Results, 1,065

New Orleans Jazz Club of California
PO Box 1225, Kerrville, TX, 78029-1225
Jazz Newsletter, 913

•**Newsletters International**
2600 South Gessner Rd., Houston, TX, 77063-3297

Nondestructive Testing Info Analysis Center
415 Crystal Creek Dr, Austin, TX, 78746-4725
NTIAC Newsletter, 362

North American Assn. of Jewish Homes & Housing for the Aged
2525 Centerville Rd, Dallas, TX, 75228-2634
North American Association of Jewish Home & Housing for the Aged-Perspectives, 1,107

North Central Texas Council of Governments
Drawer COG, Arlington, TX, 76011
Your Region, 1,025

North Texas Amputee Support Group
3714 Lisa Ln, Mesquite, TX, 75150-2659
North Texas Amputee Support Group News, 278

Nu-Tec Publishing, Inc.
4715 Strack Rd., Ste. 211, Houston, TX, 77069-1617
Boycott Law Bulletin, 642

Oblate School of Theology
285 Oblate Dr, San Antonio, TX, 78216-6631
Newsletter (Oblate School of Theology) OST News, 193

Odd Fellows News of Texas
3324 W. 2nd Ave., Corsicana, TX, 75110
Odd Fellows News of Texas, 180

•**Offshore Data Services, Inc.**
PO Box 19909, Houston, TX, 77224-1909

Ogden Newsletter
1801 Ardath Ave, Wichita Falls, TX, 76301-6001
Ogden Newsletter, 463

Ontra, Inc.
816 Congress Ave., Austin, TX, 78701
Ontra Update, 1,036

Oral History Assn.
Baylor Universtiy, Po Box 97234, Waco, TX, 76798-7234
Oral History Association Newsletter, 546

* See ***MULTI-PUBLISHER INDEX*** for list of publications.

Organization for Research on Women & Communication
Dept. of Speech Communication, SW Texas State Univ., San Marcos, TX, 78666
Organization for Research on Women & Communication-Newsletter, 860

Outsiders Association
3934 Bryce Ave, Fort Worth, TX, 76107-4419
Outside View, 1,134

Pace Foods, Ltd.
PO Box 12636, San Antonio, TX, 78212-0636
Keeping Pace, 431

Panhandle Eastern Pipeline Co.
PO Box 2521, Houston, TX, 77252-2521
Houston Lines, 585

Panhandle-Plains Historical Society
WTAMU Box 967, 2401 Fourth Ave , Canyon, TX, 79016-0001
Corral Dust, 539

Parental Discretion
PO Box 758, Colleyville, TX, 76034-0758
Parental Discretion, 415

Peace Farm
Hc 2 Box 25, Panhandle, TX, 79068-9603
Advocate, 985

Peat, Marwick, Main & Co.
Thanksgiving Tower, 200 Crescent Court St. #300, Dallas, TX, 75201-1885
Research Notes, 432

Petroconsultants, Inc.
6600 Sands Point Dr # 740619, Houston, TX, 77074-3726
Petroconsultants International Oil Letter, 963

Philatex
PO Box 1197, San Antonio, TX, 78294-1197
Philatex, 972

Pier 1 Imports Inc.
2520 W. Freeway, Fort Worth, TX, 76119-4608
Helm, 585

Plains Cotton Growers, Inc.
4510 Englewood Ave, Lubbock, TX, 79414-1227
Cotton Talks, 39

Practical Perspectives Inc.
PO Box 202108, Austin, TX, 78720-2108
Library Currents, 802

Practitioners Publishing Co.
3221 Collinsworth St, Fort Worth, TX, 76107-6582
CPA Financial Planner Newsletter, 83

Printers Shareware News
5019 W Lovers Ln # 5021, Dallas, TX, 75209-3141
Printers Shareware News, 1,006

Printing Productions Systems
PO Box 5306, Austin, TX, 78763-5306
Texas Weekly, 999

•**Professional Training Assocs., Inc.**
210 Commerce Blvd, Round Rock, TX, 78664-2116

R&D Associates
16607 Blanco Rd Ste 501, San Antonio, TX, 78232-1940
Link, The, 431

•**RJM Communications**
PO Box 6645, Lubbock, TX, 79493-6645

RSR Corp.
2777 N Stemmons Fwy #1800, Dallas, TX, 75207-2277
RSR Lead Press, 596

Ralph Wilson Plastics Co.
Box 6110, Temple, TX, 76503-6110
Laminator, 588

Rathkamp Matchcover Society
25 Huntsmans Horn Cir Dept Dn, The Woodlands, TX, 77380-0938
Rathkamp Matchcover Society-Bulletin, 555

Recognition Equipment Inc.
PO Box 660204, Dallas, TX, 75266-0204
Letter of Recognition, 588

Reed Tool Co.
PO Box 998, Sherman, TX, 75091-0998
Quarterly, 596

•**Report Publications, Inc.**
PO Box 12368, Austin, TX, 78711-2368

Rice University/Fondren Library
6100 Main St Stop 44, Houston, TX, 77005-1827
News from Fondren, 805

Richard Scherer & Assocs.
PO Box 201676, Austin, TX, 78720-1676
Satellite Television Newsletter, 1,169

Ron Paul Investment Letter
PO Box 602, Lake Jackson, TX, 77566-0602
Ron Paul Survival Report, 684

SCOR Report
PO Box 781992, Dallas, TX, 75378-1992
SCOR Report, 98

S.L.A. Marshall Military History Collection
University Library, University, Of Texas At El Paso, El Paso, TX, 79968-0852
S.L.A. Marshall Military History Collection-Newsletter, 898

SSCC
PO Box 821143, Dallas, TX, 75382-1143
SSCC Newsletter, 210

STICS Inc.
9714 S Rice Ave, Houston, TX, 77096-4138
Nanotechnology & Microengineering Progress, 362

Saber Software Corp.
PO Box 9088, Dallas, TX, 75209-9088
Saber Point, 237

Sam Houston State Univ. Criminal Justice Dept.
Criminal Justice Ctr., Huntsville, TX, 77341
Criminal Justice Research Bulletin, 786

•**San Angelo Genealogical & Historical Soc.**
PO Box 3453, San Angelo, TX, 76902-3453

San Antonio Area Library System
203 St. Marys St., San Antonio, TX, 78205
SAALS Newsletter, 809

Sarco Management & Pubs.
2900 Wilcrest Dr Ste 122, Houston, TX, 77042-3355
Body Language, 71

Schlumberger Well Services
PO Box 2175, Houston, TX, 77252-2175
Schlumberger Sonde Off, 1,204

•**School Health Alert**
PO Box 13716, San Antonio, TX, 78213-0716

School Law Newsletter
PO Box 199, Ranger, TX, 76470-0199
School Law Newsletter, 209

Scott Campbell
PO Box 2678, San Angelo, TX, 76902-2678
Boer Trader & Meat Goat News, 827

Scott Publishing Co.
Rr 14 Box 394-A, Tyler, TX, 75707-9814
National Amateur Astronomy News, 69

Sea Grant College Program
PO Box 1675, Galveston, TX, 77553-1675
Marine Education, 317

Sears Roebuck
13319 Montfort Drive, Dallas, TX, 75240-5116
Southwesterner, 599

Seton Medical Center
1201 W 38th St, Austin, TX, 78705-1056
Quarterly, 571

•**Shannon Publications, Inc.**
9441 L.B.J. Fwy, Ste. #510 Box #2, Dallas, TX, 75243-4541

Shell Oil Co.
PO Box 2463, Houston, TX, 77252-2463
Shell Alumni News, 598

Sheshunoff Information Services, Inc.
P.O. Box 13203, Capitol Sta., Austin, TX, 78711-3203
Bank & S&L Quarterly Rating Service, 81

Shop Talk Inc.
5737 64th St, Lubbock, TX, 79424-1261
Shop Talk (Lubbock), 415

Silent Partners
8727 Shoal Creek Blvd., Austin, TX, 78757-6815
NHF Headlines, 519

Simpson Pasenda Paper Co.
PO Box 872, Pasadena, TX, 77501-0872
San Jacinto Spirit, 597

Single Life Institute
PO Box 2832, Abilene, TX, 79604-2832
News & Views/Single Life Inst., 815

Snap-On Tools Corp.
1405 Avenue T, Grand Prairie, TX, 75050-1234
Snap-On Field Manager News, 598

Society of Independent Professional Earth Scientists
4925 Greenville Ave Ste 170, Dallas, TX, 75206-4008
Society of Independent Professional Earth Scientists, Newsletter, 476

Source Strategies, Inc.
PO Box 120055, San Antonio, TX, 78212-9255
MarketShare, 574

Southern Methodist Univ, Inst for the Study of Earth and Man
Heroy Science Hall, 3225 D, Dallas, TX, 75203
Institute for the Study of Earth and Man Newsletter, 51

Southland Corp.
2828 N Haskell Ave, Dallas, TX, 75204-2990
Flash, 584

Southwest Airlines
PO Box 36662, Southwest Company Club, Dallas, TX, 75235-1662
Plane Talk, 32

Southwest Assn of Affiliated Agencies
1601 Rio Grande St Ste 440, Austin, TX, 78701-1149
SWAAA Newsletter, 624

Southwest Bluegrass Club
2704 Haley Ave, Fort Worth, TX, 76117-4147
Bluegrass Reflections, 910

Southwest Texas Genealogical Society
PO Box 295, Uvalde, TX, 78802-0295
Branches & Acorns, 449

•**Southwest Texas Methodist Hospital**
7700 Floyd Curl Dr, San Antonio, TX, 78229-3902

Southwestern Baptist Theological Seminary
Box 22000-3e, Fort Worth, TX, 76122-0001
Southwestern News, 193

Southwestern Ice Assn.
1601 Rio Grande St Ste 440, Austin, TX, 78701-1149
Southwestern Ice Association Newsletter, 851

Southwestern Life Insurance Co.
PO Box 2699, Dallas, TX, 75221-2699
Southwester, 599

•**State Bar of Texas**
PO Box 12487 Capitol Station, Austin, TX, 78711-2487

•**Stevens Publishing Corp.**
3630 J.H. Kultgen Frwy., Waco, TX, 76706

Stovall Group, The
310 E. I-30, Suite M102a, Garland, TX, 75043
Customer Service Report, 836

Success Concepts International
PO Box 3840, Humble, TX, 77347-3840
Success Ads, 23

Sullivan Company
PO Box 841002, Houston, TX, 77284-1002
Radio Promotion Bulletin, 125

Sunbelt
PO Box 796575, Dallas, TX, 75379-6575
Southwest Cleaning, 625

•**TCMR Communications**
PO Box 1179, Grapevine, TX, 76099-1179

TPN The Peoples Network
2420 Courtland Dr., Arlington, TX, 76017
Healthy, Wealthy & Wise, 140

Tabor Publishing
200 East Bethany Drive, Allen, TX, 75002
In The Meantime, 1,057

•**Tarrant County Hospital District**
1500 S Main St, Fort Worth, TX, 76104-4917

•**Taylor Publishing Co.**
1550 W Mockingbird Ln, Dallas, TX, 75235-5007

•**Ted Slanker**
RR 2, Box 175, Powderly, TX, 75473-9740

Texas A&M Univ., Ctr. for Energy & Mineral Resources
College Station, TX, 77843-1243
Texas Energy, 358

Texas Aeronautics Commission
125 E. 11th St., Austin, TX, 78701-2409
Texas Aeronautics Commission Newsletter, 33

The Texas Alliance for Human Needs
2520 Longview St Apt 311, Austin, TX, 78705-4235
Texas Alliance for Human Needs, The, 1,122

Texas Analyst
PO Box 8, Austin, TX, 78767-0008
Quorum Report, 492

Texas Assn. of Real Estate Inspectors
1601 Rio Grande St Ste 440, Austin, TX, 78701-1149
TAREI Times, 1,039

•**Texas Automotive Dismantlers & Recyclers Assn.**
823 Congress Ave. #1300, Austin, TX, 78701-2429

Texas Burglar & Fire Alarm Assn.
1601 Rio Grande St Ste 440, Austin, TX, 78701-1149
Lone Star Transmitter, 1,104

Texas Catholic Historical Society
Box 704, St. Edward's Univ., Austin, TX, 78767-0704
Texas Catholic Historical Society Newsletter, 549

Texas Chiropractic College
5912 Spencer Hwy, Pasadena, TX, 77505-1699
Back Page, 206

Texas Christian Univ.
Box 32929, Fort Worth, TX, 76129
Composition Studies/ Freshman English News, 305

* See **MULTI-PUBLISHER INDEX** for list of publications.

INDEX TO PUBLISHERS BY STATE

Utah

Texas College of Osteopathic Medicine
PO Box 9526, Fort Worth, TX, 76147-2526
Alumni Newsletter, 193

Texas Commerce Bank
PO Box 2558, Houston, TX, 77252-8050
Banker's Hours, 577

Texas Council of Painting & Decorating Contractors of Americ
1601 Rio Grande St Ste 440, Austin, TX, 78701-1149
Drop Cloth, The, 246

Texas Credit Union League
4455 LBJ Frwy., Box 225147, Dallas, TX, 75244-5992
Texas Leaguer, 99

Texas Date Nail Collectors Assn.
501 W. Horton, Brenham, TX, 77833
Nailer News, 185

Texas Dept. on Aging
Box 12786, Capitol Station, Austin, TX, 78711-2786
Aging Digest, 1,105

Texas Dept. of Agriculture
Box 12847 Cap. Station, Austin, TX, 78711-2847
Texas Livestock Market News, 829

Texas Dept. of Commerce
PO Box 12728, Austin, TX, 78711-2728
Results News Report, 161

Texas Dept. of Health
1100 W 49th St, Austin, TX, 78756-3199
Texas Health Bulletin, 530

Texas Eastern Transmission Corp.
PO Box 2521, Houston, TX, 77252-2521
Texas Eastern News, 600

•Texas Economic Publishers, Inc.
510 N. Valley Mills Dr., Ste. 300, Waco, TX, 76710-6076

Texas Energy Research Assoc.
5926 Balcones Dr Ste 220, Austin, TX, 78731-4263
Texas Energy Reporter, 358

Texas Gulf Historical Soc.
PO Box 1621, Beaumont, TX, 77704-1621
Texas Gulf Historical & Biographical Records, 468

Texas Higher Education Coordinating Board
PO Box 12788, Austin, TX, 78711-2788
CB Report, 302

Texas Historical Commission
PO Box 12276, Austin, TX, 78711-2276
Medallion, 544

Texas Hotel & Motel Assn.
900 Congress Ave Ste 310, Austin, TX, 78701-2432
Industry Update, 574

•Texas Instruments
PO Box 149149, Austin, TX, 78714-9149

Texas Lutheran College
1000 W Court St, Seguin, TX, 78155-5999
Carta Abierta, 405

Texas Medical Association
401 W. 15th St., Austin, TX, 78701-1680
Action-Texas Medical Association, 865

Texas Memorial Museum
2400 Trinity St., Univ. of Texas at Austin, Austin, TX, 78705
Texas Memorial Museum Bulletin, 908

Texas Motor Transportation Assn
PO Box 1669, Austin, TX, 78767-1669
TMTA Newsletter, 1,180

Texas Motorcycle Dealers Assn.
1601 Rio Grande St Ste 440, Austin, TX, 78701-1149
TMDA Newsletter, 76

Texas Petroleum Retailer
PO Box 9445, Austin, TX, 78766-9445
Texas Petroleum Retailer, 965

Texas Poultry
7915 Braes Meadow Dr, Houston, TX, 77071-1302
Texas Poultry, 1,001

•Texas Power
Box 6331, 1511 Bryan St., Dallas, TX, 75201

Texas Research Institute of Mental Sciences
1300 Moursund St, Houston, TX, 77030-3406
TRIMS Therapy Notes, 1,018

Texas State Directory Press
1800 Nueces St, Austin, TX, 78701-1120
Capitol Update, 482

Texas State Library
PO Box 12927, Austin, TX, 78711-2927
Library Developments, 802

Texas State Teachers Assn.
316 W 12th St, Austin, TX, 78701-1892
Texas Standard, 333

Texas State Technical College-Amarillo
PO Box 11197, Amarillo, TX, 79111-0197
Technoscope, 206

Texas Storytellers Association
PO Box 2806, Denton, TX, 76202-2806
Texas Teller Quarterly Newsletter, 825

Texas Transportation Institute
101 Tti/Ce Texas A&m, University System, College Station, TX, 77843-0001
Texas Transportation Researcher, 1,180

Texas Veterans Affairs Commission
Austin, TX, 78711
Texas Veterans Affairs Commission, Bulletin, 1,199

Texas Water Quality Assn.
1601 Rio Grande St Ste 440, Austin, TX, 78701-1149
H2O Quality Newsletter, 1,203

Texas Wesleyan University
PO Box 50010, Fort Worth, TX, 76105-0010
Texas Wesleyan Today, 193

Thermodynamics Rsrch. Ctr., Texas Engineering Exprmt Station
Texas A&m University, College Station, TX, 77843-0001
Thermodynamics At Texas A&M, 367

Thomas Nash Descendants Assn.
c/o D. Roberts, 2733 Running B, Dallas, TX, 75228
Family Treebune, 453

Tiger Publications
PO Box 8759, Amarillo, TX, 79114-8759
For Your Eyes Only, 896

Tom Hendricks
4000 Hawthorne #5, Dallas, TX, 75219
Musea, 65

Tom V. Murphy Enter.
PO Box 740875, Dallas, TX, 75374-0875
TVM Report, 420

Tracks to Adventure
2811 Jackson Ave Ste K, El Paso, TX, 79930-3937
Tracks RV News, 902

•Trendex Research Corp.
6006 Forest Bnd, San Antonio, TX, 78240-3330

Trident Syndicate, Inc.
PO Box 19909, Houston, TX, 77224-1909
Donald R. Morris Newsletter, 923

Trinity River Authority
5300 S Collins St, Arlington, TX, 76018-1710
Intra, 1,203

Turbine Support Div.
Chromalloy American Corp., Box 20148, San Antonio, TX, 78220
T-Blade, 600

USAA Federal Savings Bank
Marketing Programs Usaa, Building, San Antonio, TX, 78288-0001
At Your Command, 470

Uncommon Lodgings
12124 Midlake Dr, Dallas, TX, 75218-1354
Uncommon Lodgings, 575

United Ministries in Education
C/o Rev. Turecky, 14214 Edgecrest Dr., Dallas, TX, 75240
UME Letter, 1,066

United Services Automobile Assn.
Usaa Bldg., San Antonio, TX, 78288-0001
Highlights, 585

United We Stand America
PO Box 6, Dallas, TX, 75221
United We Stand America, 999

Univ. Film & Video Assn.
Univ. of N. Texas, Dept of RTVF, Box 13108, Denton, TX, 76203-3108
Digest of the Univ. Film & Video Assn., 419

Univ. of Houston, Center for Research in Bus.
Cullen Blvd., Houston, TX, 77004
University of Houston, Center for Research in Business and Economics, Bulletins, 155

University of North Texas Computing Center
NT Box 13495, Denton, TX, 76203
Benchmarks, 213

University of Texas
1100 Holcombe Blvd., Houston, TX, 77030-3907
Lifetime Health Letter, 516

Univ. of Texas Ex-Students Association
PO Box 7278, Austin, TX, 78713-7278
Texas Alcalde, 193

University of Texas General Libraries
Publications, Austin, TX, 78712
Library Bulletin, 801

University of Texas Health Science Center
7000 Fannin, Houston, TX, 77030-3907
University of Texas Lifetime Health Letter, 531

University of Texas-Health Science Center at San Antonio
7703 Floyd Curl Dr, San Antonio, TX, 78284-6200
News, The, 206

Univ. of Texas, Medical Branch
301 University Blvd., Galveston, TX, 77555-1311
Aging and the Human Spirit Newsletter, 1,106

University of Texas at Austin
Dept. of English Literature, PAR 108, Austin, TX, 78712-1164
William Carlos Williams Review, 826

Univ. of Texas at Austin Asian Studies Dept.
Ctr. for Asian Studies, SSB, 4.126, Austin, TX, 78712
Univ. of Texas At Austin Ctr. for Asian Studies Newsletter, 639

Univ. of Texas at Austin Libraries
PO Box P, Austin, TX, 78713-8916
General Libraries Newsletter, 798

University of Texas at El Paso
1101 N. Campbell St. News And, Publication Office, El Paso, TX, 79968-0001
Newsletter, 206

Victoria Chamber
PO Box 2465, Victoria, TX, 77902-2465
Victoria Chamber of Commerce Newsletter, 162

Vintage Radio & Phonograph Society, Inc.
PO Box 165345, Irving, TX, 75016-5345
Sound Waves, 556

Wharton Chamber of Commerce
PO Box 868, Wharton, TX, 77488-0868
Your Wharton Chamber of Commerce Newsletter, 162

Whitfields Utility Letter
2472 Bolsover St Ste 240, Houston, TX, 77005-2537
Whitfields Utility Letter, 692

William Horn
7038 Northaven Rd, Dallas, TX, 75230-3505
Silent Wings, 898

•William Spencer Educational Foundation
6701 Blanco Rd Apt 712, San Antonio, TX, 78216-6161

Windmillers' Gazette
PO Box 507, Rio Vista, TX, 76093-0507
Windmillers' Gazette, 48

Workover/Well Servicing Publications, Inc.
6060 N Central Expy Ste 428, Dallas, TX, 75206-5205
Field Reports, 138

Wyandotte Bantam Club of America
PO Box 408, Cleburne, TX, 76033-0408
Wyandotte Bantam Club of America Newsletter, 1,002

Zero1 Company
5114 Balcones Woods Dr., #307-389, Austin, TX, 78759
Digital Expo Update, 220

•Zeus Development Corporation
P.O. Box 272505, Houston, TX, 77277-2505

Utah

AGLL
P.O. Box 329, Bountiful, UT, 84011
Genealogy Bulletin, 454

Allen Communication, Inc.
5 Triad Ctr., 5th Fl., Salt Lake City, UT, 84180-1102
Promptlines, 234

Amaryllis Press
535 Parkview Dr, Park City, UT, 84060-5204
Amaryllis Review, 819

American Comparative Literature Assn.
3010 JKHB, Brigham Young University, Provo, UT, 84602
American Comparative Literature Assn. Newsletter, 819

American Society for Eighteenth-Century Studies
Utah State Univ. USU CC108, Logan, UT, 84322-3730
News Circular, 261

Ancestry, Inc.
PO Box 476, Salt Lake City, UT, 84110-0476
Ancestry Newsletter, 447

Biz Law Association, Inc.
PO Box 247, Springdale, UT, 84767-0247
Biz Law Update, 719

Business Law Update
PO Box 247, Springdale, UT, 84767-0247
Business Law Update, 720

Citizens Call
PO Box 1722, Cedar City, UT, 84721-1722
Citizen's Voice, 172

* See **MULTI-PUBLISHER INDEX** for list of publications.

1376

©**1996, Oxbridge Communications, Inc.**

* See ***MULTI-PUBLISHER INDEX*** for list of publications.

Phillip Camp Assocs.
Cox Rd., Woodstock, VT, 05091
Directions, 1,183

St. Michael's College
Winooski Pk., Colchester, VT, 05439-0001
Founders Hall, 193

Sands, Taylor & Wood Co.
PO Box 876, Norwich, VT, 05055-0876
Baking Sheet, The, 79

Seventh Generation
Colchester, VT, 05446-1672
Earth Impact, 377

Teachers' Laboratory Inc.
28 Birge St., PO Box 6480, Brattleboro, VT, 05302-6480
Connect, 305

Toward Freedom Inc.
209 College St # 202a, Burlington, VT, 05401-8306
Toward Freedom, 638

Vermont Academy of Arts
2 Buxton Ave, Middletown Springs, VT, 05757-4231
Vermont Academy of Arts & Sciences, 473

Vermont Archaeological Society, Inc.
C/O Victor R. Rolando, RR 1 Box 1521-3, Manchester Center, VT, 05255
VAS Newsletter, 59

Vermont Cancer Center
Univ. Of Vermont 1 S. Prospect, St., Burlington, VT, 05405-0001
VCC Newsletter, 889

Vermont Council on World Affairs
Trinity College, Burlington, VT, 05401-1496
Point of View, 636

Vermont Dept. of Agriculture, Food & Markets
116 State St. Drawer 20, Montpelier, VT, 05620-2901
Agriview, 37

Vermont Dept. of Employment & Training
PO Box 488, Montpelier, VT, 05601-0488
Vermont Labor Market, 706

Vermont Dept. of Libraries
Pavillion Office Bldg. 109, State. St., Montpelier, VT, 05609-0001
Vermont Department of Libraries News, 812

Vermont ETV
88 Ethan Allen Ave, Colchester, VT, 05446-3335
Vermont ETV Program Guide, 1,170

Vermont Institute of Natural Science
Church Hill Rd., Woodstock, VT, 05091
Natural Science Newsletter, 921

Vermont Philatelic Society
18 Fuller St, Montpelier, VT, 05602-2405
Vermont Philatelist, 972

Vermont Real Estate Commission
7 E State St, Montpelier, VT, 05602-3008
Vermont Real Estate Newsletter, 1,039

Vermont Right to Life
73 Main St Rm 30, Montpelier, VT, 05602-2944
Vermont Right to Life Newsletter, 176

Vermont School Boards Assn.
2 Prospect St, Montpelier, VT, 05602-3555
VSBA Newsletter, 335

Vermont State Department of Education
120 State St, Montpelier, VT, 05602-2703
Report to the Board, 327

Vermont State Medical Society
136 Main St, Montpelier, VT, 05602-2913
Medical Society Newsletter, 879

Volunteers for Peace
Tiffany Rd., Belmont, VT, 05730
International Workcamper, 632

Washington Electric Co-Op
Box 8, Rte. 14, E. Montpelier, VT, 05651-0008
Co-Op Currents, 337

Words, Ink
Emerson Falls Business Park, St. Johnsbury, VT, 05819
Executive Speechwriter Newsletter, 856

Zone VI Studios, Inc.
22 High St, Brattleboro, VT, 05301-3001
Zone VI Newsletter, 978

Virgin Islands

VTLS inc.,
100 Kraft Drive, Blacksburg, VI, 24060
VTLS EXPRESS A Publication of VTLS Inc., 242

Virginia

APPA: The Assn. of Higher Education Facilities Officers
1446 Duke St, Alexandria, VA, 22314-3492
Inside APPA, 1,091

A.R.E. Press
PO Box 595, Virginia Beach, VA, 23451-0595
Perspective on Consciousness Bulletin, 922

•**A.S. Pratt & Sons**
1911 Fort Myer Dr., Ste 308, Arlington, VA, 22209-1603

Academy for Implants and Transplants
PO Box 223, Springfield, VA, 22150-0223
Implant Update, 270

•**Access Reports, Inc.**
1624 Dogwood Lane, Lynchburg, VA, 24503

Accreditation Council for Accountancy & Taxation
1010 N Fairfax St, Alexandria, VA, 22314-1504
Accreditation Council for Accountancy & Taxation-Action Letter, 2

Ada Information Clearinghouse
PO Box 1866, Falls Church, VA, 22041
ADAIC News, 211

Aeronautical Repair Station Association
121 N Henry St, Alexandria, VA, 22314-2903
Hotline, 29

•**Air-Conditioning & Refrigeration Institute (ARI)**
4301 Fairfax Dr Ste 425, Arlington, VA, 22203-1627

•**Al-Anon Family Group Headquarters, Inc.**
1600 Corporate Landing Pkwy., Virginia Beach, VA, 23456

Altizer, Fisher, & Assoc.
PO Box 250, Richlands, VA, 24641-0250
National Coal Leader, 356

Ambulatory Pediatric Assn.
6728 Old Mclean Village Dr, Mc Lean, VA, 22101-3906
Ambulatory Pediatric Association Newsletter, 866

American Academy of Physician Assistants
950 N. Washington St., Alexandria, VA, 22314-1552
AAPA News, 863

American Advertising Distributors of Northern VA
708 Pendleton St, Alexandria, VA, 22314-1819
Clinical Connection, 532

•**American Alliance for Health, Physical Education, Recreation**
1900 Association Dr, Reston, VA, 22091-1599

•**American Anthropological Assn.**
4350 N. Fairfax Drive, Suite 640, Arlington, VA, 22203-1621

•**American Apparel Manufacturers Assn.**
2500 Wilson Blvd Ste 301, Arlington, VA, 22201-3834

American Assn. of Airport Executives
4212 King St, Alexandria, VA, 22302-1507
Airport Report, 26

American Assn. for Budget & Program Analysis
PO Box 1157, Falls Church, VA, 22041-0157
AABPA Newsletter, 1,018

American Association of Children's Residential Centers
1021 Prince Street, Alexandria, VA, 22314
Children's Residential Treatment News, 1,013

American Assn. of Colleges of Pharmacy
1426 Prince St, Alexandria, VA, 22314-2815
AACP News, 280

American Association of Family & Consumer Sciences
1555 King St., Alexandria, VA, 22314-2738
AACF Action, 557

American Assn. for Leisure and Recreation
1900 Association Dr, Reston, VA, 22091-1502
AALR Reporter, 949

American Assn. of Motor Vehicle Administrators
4301 Wilson Blvd Ste 400, Arlington, VA, 22203-1800
AAMVA Bulletin, 69

American Assn. of Pastoral Counselors
9504 A Lee Hwy., Fairfax, VA, 22031-2303
American Association of Pastoral Counselors Newsletter, 1,044

American Association of Professional Hypnotherapists
PO Box 29, Boones Mill, VA, 24065-0029
Hypnotherapy Today, 607

American Association of Public Health Dentistry
10619 Jousting Ln, Richmond, VA, 23235-3838
Communique, 268

American Assn. of Tissue Banks
1350 Beverly Rd Ste 220a, Mc Lean, VA, 22101-3924
American Association of Tissue Banks-Newsletter, 866

American Assn. of Travel Agents
1101 King St., Alexandria, VA, 22314-2944
ASTA Notes, 1,181

American Bed & Breakfast Association
PO Box 1387, Midlothian, VA, 23113-8387
Bed & Breakfast Shoptalk, 574

American Blind Bowling Assn.
3500 Terry Dr, Norfolk, VA, 23518-5731
Blind Bowler, The, 111

•**American College of Apothecaries**
205 Daingerfield Rd, Alexandria, VA, 22314-2833

American College of Health Care Administrators
325 S. Patrick St., Alexandria, VA, 22314-3571
Long-Term Care Administrator, 568

American College of Radiology
1891 Preston White Dr, Reston, VA, 22091-4397
American College of Radiology Bulletin, 866

American Council for Judaism
PO Box 9009, Alexandria, VA, 22304-0009
Special Interest Report, 1,071

American Counseling Assn.
5999 Stevenson Ave., Alexandria, VA, 22304-3300
ASCA Counselor, 298

American Dental Trade Assn.
4222 King St, Alexandria, VA, 22302-1597
American Dental Trade Association Update, 268

American Diabetes Association
1660 Duke St, Alexandria, VA, 22314-3447
Clinical Diabetes, 871

•**American Feed Industry Assn.**
1501 Wilson Blvd # 1100, Arlington, VA, 22209-2403

American Fern Society
326 West St., NW, Vienna, VA, 221814151, a
Fiddlehead Forum, 441

American Frozen Food Inst
2000 Corporate Ridge, Mc Lean, VA, 22102-4399
AFFI Letter, 426

•**American Gas Association**
1515 Wilson Blvd., Arlington, VA, 22209-2469

American Gear Manufacturers
1500 King St Ste 201, Alexandria, VA, 22314-2730
American Gear Manufacturers Association News Digest, 847

American Group Practice Association
1422 Duke St., Alexandria, VA, 22314-3430
Executive News Service, 1,196

American Helicopter Society, Inc.
217 N Washington St, Alexandria, VA, 22314-2538
Membergram, 31

American Horticultural Society
7931 E Boulevard Dr, Alexandria, VA, 22308-1300
American Horticultural Society Newsletter, 440

American Humor Studies Assn.
James Madison Unversity, English Dept., Harrisonburg, VA, 22807-0001
To Wit, 605

American Indian Society
22226 Cool Water Dr, Ruther Glen, VA, 22546-3309
American Indian Society Newsletter, 405

American Industrial Arts Students Assn.
1908 Association Dr., Reston, VA, 22091
School Scene, 329

American Industrial Hygiene Association
2700 Prosperity Ave # 250, Fairfax, VA, 22031-4320
American Industrial Hygiene Assn. Newsletter, 498

American Intellectual Property Law Assn.
2001 Jefferson Davis Hwy Ste, 203, Arlington, VA, 22202-3603
AIPLA Bulletin, 713

American Judges Assn.
300 Newport Ave., PO Box 8798, Williamsburg, VA, 23185-8798
AJA Benchmark, 713

American Meat Institute
1700 N Moore St Ste 1600, Arlington, VA, 22209-1903
American Meat Institute, Newsletter, 426

American Medical Women's Association, Inc.
801 N. Fairfax St., Ste. 400, Alexandria, VA, 22314-1757
What's Happening in AMWA, 889

American Mental Health Counselors Assn.
5999 Stevenson Ave., Alexandria, VA, 22304-3302
AMHCA News, 1,011

* See **MULTI-PUBLISHER INDEX** for list of publications.

American Political Network
3129 Mt. Vernon Ave., Alexandria, VA, 22305-2640
Abortion Report, 985

American Production and Inventory Control Society
500 W Annandale Rd, Falls Church, VA, 22046-4205
APICS News, 847

American Society of Consultant Pharmacists
1321 Duke St., 4 Floor, Alexandria, VA, 22204-2320
Clinical Consult, 282

American Society of Electroplated Plastics
1767 Business Center Dr., Reston, VA, 22090-5332
ASEP News and Views, 980

American Society for Industrial Security
1655 N. Fort Myer Dr., Ste. 1200, Arlington, VA, 22209-3108
ASIS Dynamics, 126

American Society of Newspaper Editors
PO Box 4090, Reston, VA, 22090-1700
Editors' Exchange, The, 923

American Society of Pension Actuaries
4350 Fairfax Dr Ste 820, Arlington, VA, 22203-1621
Pension Actuary, The, 623

American Sport Fishing Institute
1033 N. Fairfax St., Ste. 200, Alexandria, VA, 22314-1540
ASFI Bulletin, 371

American Statistical Assn.
1429 Duke St., Alexandria, VA, 22314-3415
AmStat News, 852

•**American Traffic Safety Services Assn.**
5440 Jefferson Davis Hwy, Fredericksburg, VA, 22407-2627

•**American Trucking Assn., Inc.**
Statistics Dept., 2200 Mill Rd., Alexandria, VA, 22314-4686

American Water Resources Assn.
950 Herndon Pky., Ste. 300, Herndon, VA, 22070-5528
Hydata News and Views, 1,203

American Waterways Operators
1600 Wilson Blvd Ste 1000, Arlington, VA, 22209-2597
AWO Letter, 1,176

American Women in Radio
1650 Tysons Blvd Ste 200, Mc Lean, VA, 22102-3915
AWRT News and Views, 122

American Wood Preservers Inst
1945 Old Gallows Rd Ste 550, Vienna, VA, 22182-3931
AWPI Newsletter, 829

Americans Against Union Control of Government
527 MAple Avenue, East, 3rd Fl., Vienna, VA, 22180-4713
Forewarned, 707

Ample Shopper
1150 E Market St, Charlottesville, VA, 22902-5351
Ample Shopper, 251

Amward Publications, Inc.
2030 Clarendon Blvd., Ste. 401, Arlington, VA, 22201-2911
Political Finance & Lobby Reporter, 996

Animal Health Institute
Box 1417, #D50, Alexandria, VA, 22313-1480
AHI Quarterly, 1,200

Arlin J. Brown Information Center Inc.
PO Box 251, Fort Belvoir, VA, 22060-0251
Health Victory Bulletin, 510

Ashoka: Innovators for the Public
1700 N. Moore St., Suite 1920, Arlington, VA, 22209-3644
Changemakers, 1,115

Assn. for the Advancement of Health Education
1900 Association Dr, Reston, VA, 22091-1502
HE-XTRA, 508

Assn. for the Advancement of Medical Instrumentation
3330 Washington Blvd., Ste 400, Arlington, VA, 22201-4502
AAMI News, 616

Assn. for Education & Rehabilatation of the Blind & Visually
206 N Washington St Ste 320, Alexandria, VA, 22314-2528
AER Report, 110

Assn. of Former Intelligence Officers
6723 Whittier Ave Ste 303a, Mc Lean, VA, 22101-4533
Periscope, 636

Association for Healthcare Philanthropy
313 Park Ave Ste 400, Falls Church, VA, 22046-3303
AHP Connect, 561

Association for Information Management
1700 Diagonal Rd Ste 300, Alexandria, VA, 22314-2866
Career Exchange Clearinghouse, 214

•**Association for Investment Management and Research**
AIMR, Box 3668, Charlottesville, VA, 22903-0668

Assn. of Part-Time Professionals
7700 Leesburg Pike Ste 216, Falls Church, VA, 22043-2615
Working Options, 350

Association of Physician Assistant Programs
950 N Washington St, Alexandria, VA, 22314-1534
APAP Update, 865

Association for Preservation Technology
PO Box 3511, Williamsburg, VA, 23187-3511
Association for Preservation Technology International Communique, 59

Association for the Preservation of Virginia Antiquities
2300 E Grace St, Richmond, VA, 23223-7152
APVA Newsletter, 59

Association for Science, Technology & Innovation
PO Box 1242, Arlington, VA, 22210-0542
ASTI Newsletter, 1,095

Association for Supervision & Curriculum Development
1250 N Pitt St, Alexandria, VA, 22314-1457
ASCD Update, 298

Audit/Watch, Inc.
PO Box 1181, Annandale, VA, 22003-9181
Efficient Auditor, 1,014

Auto Polish
PO Box 9505, Mc Lean, VA, 22102-0505
Dealership Management Review, 72

Automotive Information Council
13505 Dulles Technology Dr, Herndon, VA, 22071-3413
Cars & Comments, 71

Bank of Virginia Co.
PO Box 25970, Richmond, VA, 23260-5970
Signetwork, 598

Bankcard Holders of America
524 Branch Dr., Salem, VA, 24153-4119
Bankcard Consumer News, 257

Baptist World Alliance
6733 Curran St, Mc Lean, VA, 22101-6005
BWA News, 1,053

Bergerac International, Ltd.
Rr 1 Box 309, Gainesville, VA, 22065-2501
Atlantic Trade Report & Global Defense Industry, 641

Beta Kappa Chi Scientific Honor Society
Hampton Univ. , Box 6409, Hampton, VA, 23668
Beta Kappa Chi Bulletin, 1,095

Bistro Bistro Bits
4021 28th St S, Arlington, VA, 22206-2201
Bistro Bistro Bits, 426

Blue Reports Inc.
7325 Steele Mill Dr, Springfield, VA, 22150-3608
Blue Reports, 244

Bluefield College
3000 College Dr., Bluefield, VA, 24605-1799
Bluefield College News, 194

Boat Owners Association of the U.S.
800 S Pickett St, Alexandria, VA, 22304-4606
BOAT/U.S. Reports, 113

Books for All Times, Inc.
PO Box 2, Alexandria, VA, 22313-0002
Education in Focus, 308

Bowser Report
PO Box 6278, Newport News, VA, 23606-0278
Bowser Report, 656

Boyd E. Quate & Associates
Box 7065, Holland Station, Suffolk, VA, 23437
Q-Weather Forecast & Commodities Outlook, 683

Business Products Industry Assn., The
301 N. Fairfax St., Alexandria, VA, 22314-2696
BPIA Business Products Industry Report, 937

Business Scribe Inc.
105 Randolphs Grn, Williamsburg, VA, 23185-6554
How to Succeed in Rotten Times, 344

CAMCO
124 E Carolina Ave, Crewe, VA, 23930-1802
Mouser Report, The, 19

COPRED
George Mason University, 4400 University Drive, Fairfax, VA, 22030
Peace Chronical, 325

Cadmus Communications
1974 E Parham Rd, Richmond, VA, 23228-2206
Tuff Stuff's Baseball Bulletin, 102

•**Callahan Pubs.**
PO Box 1173, McLean, VA, 22101-1173

Cantrell Corp.
PO Box 3030, Oakton, VA, 22124-9030
International Employment Hotline, 345

•**Capitol Publications, Inc.**
1101 King St., Ste. 444, Alexandria, VA, 22314-2968

Casualty Actuarial Society
1100 N Glebe Rd Ste 600, Arlington, VA, 22201-4798
Actuarial Review, The, 617

Center for Earth Resource Management Applications
5528 Hempstead Way, Springfield, VA, 22151-4009
Recycled Paper News, 392

•**Center for Foreign Journalists**
11690-A Sunrise Valley Drive, Reston, VA, 22091

Center for Public Service, UVA
918 Emmet Street N., #300, Charlottesville, VA, 22903-4832
University of Virginia News Letter, 493

Charles Felix Assocs.
PO Box 1581, Leesburg, VA, 22075-1581
Food Protection Report, 429

•**Charlottesville-Albemarle County Chamber of Commerce**
PO Box 1564, Charlottesville, VA, 22902-1564

Chemical Manufacturers Association
1300 Wilson Blvd., Arlington, VA, 22209
ChemEcology, 163

Chihuahua Club of America
11530 Second Branch Rd., Chesterville, VA, 23832
Chi-Chatter Newsletter, 279

Children's Hospital of the King's Daughters
601 Children's Lane, Norfolk, VA, 23507
KIDStuff, 567

Christian Action Council
109 Carpenter Dr., Ste. 100, Sterling, VA, 20164-4467
Action Line, 1,113

Christian Legal Society
4208 Evergreen Ln Ste 222, Annandale, VA, 22003-3264
Briefly, 719

Citizen's Clearinghouse for Hazardous Wastes
PO Box 6806, Falls Church, VA, 22040-6806
Everyone's Backyard, 382

Club Managers Assn. of America
1733 King St, Alexandria, VA, 22314-2720
Outlook, 842

Coal Employment Project
16221 Sunnyknoll Ct, Dumfries, VA, 22026-1739
Coal Mining Women's Support Team-News!, 900

The Coastal Society
PO Box 25408, Alexandria, VA, 22313-5408
Coastal Society Bulletin, The, 375

Cole Publishing, Inc.
8659 Rio Grande Rd., Richmond, VA, 23229-7822
Scott Letter: Closed End Fund Report, The, 685

College of William & Mary
Publications, Williamsburg, VA, 23185
Virginia Business Report, 155

Commerce Publishing International
4001 9th St N Suite 904, Arlington, VA, 22203-1962
Russia Desk, 32

Commission on Accreditation for Law Enforcement Agencies, I.
10306 Eaton Pl Ste 320, Fairfax, VA, 22030-2201
Commission Update, 726

Commonwealth Alliance for Drug Rehab & Ed
Off. of Att. Genl., 101 N. 8th, Richmond, VA, 23219
Cadre, 501

Communications Concepts, Inc.
7481 Huntsman Blvd., Ste. 720, Springfield, VA, 22153-1648
Writing Concepts: The Business Communications Report, 698

Community Antenna Television Assn.
PO Box 1005, Fairfax, VA, 22030-1005
Community Antenna Television Assn., Inc., 123

•**Community Associations Institute**
1630 Duke Street, Alexandria, VA, 22314

Compass Publications, Inc.
1117 19th St N Ste 1000, Arlington, VA, 22209-1790
Washington Letter of Oceanography, 937

Compressed Gas Assn.
1725 Jefferson Davis Hwy Ste, 1004, Arlington, VA, 22202-4102
Compressions, 164

•**Computer Age-Millin Publishing Group**
714 Church Street, Alexandria, VA, 22314-4202

Concern for Helping Animals in Israel
PO Box 3341, Alexandria, VA, 22302-0341
CHAI Lights, 49

* See ***MULTI-PUBLISHER INDEX*** for list of publications.

Concerned Educators Against Forced Unionism
8001 Braddock Rd., #500, Springfield, VA, 22160-0001
Insiders Report, 708

Conference on Issues & Media
635 Slaters Ln Ste 102, Alexandria, VA, 22314-1177
Issues Management Letter, 858

•**Congressional Information Bureau, Inc.**
3030 Clarendon Blvd., Ste. 202, Arlington, VA, 22201-2845

Connie Gibson Wehrman Connor
PO Box 9, Oakton, VA, 22124-0009
Military Travel News, 897

Consortium on Peace Research, Education & Development
George Mason Univ., 4400 University Dr., Fairfax, VA, 22030-4444
COPRED Peace Chronicle, 987

Construction Specifications Institute
601 Madison St., Alexandria, VA, 22314-1741
SPEC-DATA Program, 250

Consumer Bankers Assn.
1000 Wilson Blvd., 30th Fl., Arlington, VA, 22209-3908
CBA Reports, 83

Contest Partners
PO Box 25227, Arlington, VA, 22202-9227
Contest News-Letter, 552

Conveyor Equipment Manufacturers Assn.
9384D Forestwood Ln., Manassas, VA, 22110-4702
CEMA Bulletin, 832

Cookies
9610 Greenview Lane, Manassas, VA, 22110
Cookies, 79

Corporate Information Svces., Inc.
PO Box 965, Midlothian, VA, 23113-0965
Theatre Information Bulletin, 1,174

Council for the Advancement of Citizenship
44 Canal Center Plz., Alexandria, VA, 22314-1593
Citizenship Education News, 988

•**Council of Better Business Bureaus**
4200 Wilson Blvd Ste 800, Arlington, VA, 22203-1800

•**Council for Exceptional Children**
1920 Association Dr., Reston, VA, 22091-1589

Counsellor Pubs.
PO Box 19070, Alexandria, VA, 22320-0070
Bankruptcy Counsellor, 718

•**Creative Communications, Inc.**
Box 1519-OX, Herndon, VA, 22070-1524

Crowl Family Association
9603 Bel Glade St, Fairfax, VA, 22031-1105
Crowl Connections, 451

•**DP Pubs.**
PO Box 7188, Fairfax Station, VA, 22039-7188

•**Dairy & Food Industries Supply Assn., Inc.**
1451 Dolley Madison Blvd., McLean, VA, 22101-3811

Dance Week
PO Box 55, Mc Lean, VA, 22101-0055
Dance Week, 265

•**DataTrends Pubs., Inc.**
895 B Harrison Street SE, PO Box 4460, Leesburg, VA, 22075

Decorative Laminate Products Assn.
13924 Braddock Rd # 100, Centreville, VA, 22020-1910
DLPA News, 980

Dept. of the Army, Military Traffic Mgt. Command
5611 Columbia Pike, Falls Church, VA, 22041-5000
Expediter, 896

Derwent Information Ltd
1420 Spring Hill Road, Suite 525, Maclean, VA, 22102
Gene Therapy Newsletter, 473

Direct Marketing Association of Washington
8229 Boone Blvd Ste 740, Vienna, VA, 22182-2623
DMAW Marketing Advents, 13

Directory Publishing Resources
Box 19107, George Mason Sta., Alexandria, VA, 22320
Directory Strategies, 117

•**Donley Technology**
PO Box 152, 220 Garfield Avenue, Colonial Beach, VA, 22443-0152

Douglas Publications
9609 Gayton Rd., Ste. 100, Richmond, VA, 23233-4904
Flooring Fax News, 437

•**Drug Policy Research Institute**
PO Box 3423, Arlington, VA, 22203-0423

Dulles Intl. Airport
2203 Burgee Ct, Reston, VA, 22091-4705
Fairfax Newsletter, 29

Dyna Moe
6703 Tennyson Drive, McLean, VA, 22101
Mystery Science Manifesto 3000, 696

EEI
66 Canal Center Plz Ste 200, Alexandria, VA, 22314-5507
Editorial Eye, 695

EPN Inc.
669 S. Washington St., Alexandria, VA, 22314-4109
European Packaging Newsletter and World Report, 945

Eastern Virginia Medical School
PO Box 1980, Norfolk, VA, 23501-1980
Class Newsletter, 207

Ed Helvey Productions
PO Box 1357, Winchester, VA, 22604-7857
Successtrax, 816

Edelman Communications, Inc.
12450 Fair Lakes Circle, Ste. 200, Fairfax, VA, 22033
Best of Your Money Matters with Ric Edelman, The, 655

Educated Traveler, Inc., The
PO Box 220822, Chantilly, VA, 22022-6822
Educated Traveler, The, 1,184

Education Funding Research Council
4301 Fairfax Dr Ste 875, Arlington, VA, 22203-1627
Education Funding News, 308

Educational Research Service
2000 Clarendon Blvd., Arlington, VA, 22201-2900
ERS Bulletin, 1,090

Electric Vehicle News
PO Box 148, Arlington, VA, 22210-0148
Electric Vehicle News, 1,177

Elisabeth Kubler-Ross Center
South Rt. 616, Head Waters, VA, 24442
Elisabeth Kubler-Ross Center Newsletter, 505

Ellen Glasgow Society
Randolph-Macon College, Ashland, VA, 23005
Ellen Glasgow Newsletter, 821

Encoders, Inc.
1101 King St., Ste. 110, Alexandria, VA, 22314
Communication Briefings, 855

Enterprise Publishing
6069 Crown Royal Cir, Alexandria, VA, 22310-1744
Small Business Wealth Builder, 152

EuroScope, Inc.
46679 Winchester Dr, Sterling, VA, 20164-3553
EuroScope, 630

Fairfax County Economic Development Authority
8300 Boone Blvd Ste 450, Vienna, VA, 22182-2626
Fairfax Prospectus, 138

Federal Employees' News Digest, Inc.
1850 Centennial Park Dr Ste, 520, Reston, VA, 22091-1517
Federal Employees News Digest, 1,196

Federal Research Service, Inc.
243 Church Street, N.W., Vienna, VA, 22180-4434
Federal Career Opportunities, 344

Federation of Egalitarian Communities
Acorn - RT. 3 Box 486A, Mineral, VA, 23117
Soundings, 816

Feingold Association of the U.S.
PO Box 6550, Alexandria, VA, 22306-0550
Pure Facts, 525

Financial Programs, Inc.
8621 Silver Oak Ct., Springfield, VA, 22153-2129
Federal Physicians, The, 874

•**Financial Service Associates, L.P.**
1101 King St., Ste 400, Alexandria, VA, 22314-2944

Financial Women International
200 N. Glebe Rd., Ste. 814, Arlington, VA, 22203-3728
Financial Woman Today, 1,208

Finvestor Report
7322 Pinewood St, Falls Church, VA, 22046-2726
Finvestor Report: Stocks Around Five Dollars, 664

Fleet Reserve Association
125 N West St, Alexandria, VA, 22314-2754
On Watch, 767

•**Flight Safety Foundation**
2200 Wilson Blvd Ste 500, Arlington, VA, 22201-3369

Folk Art Society of America
PO Box 17041, Richmond, VA, 23226-7041
Folk Art Messenger, 64

Food Processing Machinery & Supplies Assn.
200 Daingerfield Rd., Alexandria, VA, 22314-2884
FPM & SA Focus, 428

Foodservice & Packaging Institute Inc.
1901 N Moore St Ste 1111, Arlington, VA, 22209-1706
Environment News Digest (END), 428

Friends of Deanna Lund
545 Howard Dr, Salem, VA, 24153-2167
Deanna Gram, 1,167

Future Systems Incorporated
PO Box 26, Falls Church, VA, 22040-0026
Multimedia Monitor, 231

GIS Law and Policy Institute
370-R Neff Ave., Harrisonburg, VA, 22801
GIS Law, 475

GTE Telenet
12490 Sunrise Valley Dr, Reston, VA, 22091-3470
GTE Telenet Packet, 1,159

Gamewardens of Vietnam Assn.
PO Box 5523, Virginia Beach, VA, 23455-0523
Gamewarden Newsletter, 896

Gas Appliance Manufacturers Assn
1901 N. Moore St., #1100, Arlington, VA, 22209
Patent Digest, 952

George C. Marshall Foundation
Box 1600, VMI Parade Grounds, Lexington, VA, 24450-1600
George C. Marshall Foundation Topics, 540

George Wells, Publisher
2942 S Columbus St Apt A2, Arlington, VA, 22206-1444
Washington Beverage Insight, 105

Geoscience Information Society
4220 King St, Alexandria, VA, 22302-1507
GIS Newsletter, 476

Goodwill Communications
9829 Summerday Dr., Burke, VA, 22015-4026
Public Service Report, 861

•**Government Information Services, Inc.**
4301 Fairfax Dr., Ste. 875, Arlington, VA, 22203-1627

The Grant Advisor
PO Box 520, Linden, VA, 22642-0520
Grant Advisor, 311

HR Communication Services
PO Box 671, Richmond, VA, 23218-1671
Benefits Communicator, 834

Hampton Roads Chamber of Commerce
420 Bank St, Norfolk, VA, 23510-2401
Hampton Roads Chamber of Commerce, Newsletter, 160

•**Hardwood Plywood and Veneer Association**
1825 Michael Faraday Dr, P.O. Box 2759, Reston, VA, 22090-5304

Harrisonburg Rockingham Chamber of Commerce
800 Country Club Rd, Harrisonburg, VA, 22801-5033
HR Report, 160

Hawk Migration Assn. of North America
PO Box 3482 Rivermont Stn., Lynchburg, VA, 24503
Hawk Migration Assn. of North America-Newsletter, 942

Hayfield Citizens Association
5807 Ashfield Rd., c\o Robin Moyer, Alexandria, VA, 22310
Hayfield Citizens Association Newsletter, 1,043

•**Health Industry Distributors Assn.**
225 Reinekers Ln Ste 650, Alexandria, VA, 22314-2875

Health Sciences Communications Association
6728 Old Mclean Village Dr, Mc Lean, VA, 22101-3906
HESCA Feedback, 508

Higdon Family Assn., Inc.
PO Box 26008, Alexandria, VA, 22313-6008
Higdon Family Newsletter, 456

•**Highway Lost Data Institute**
1005 N Glebe Rd Ste 800, Arlington, VA, 22201-4751

Home Rental Publishing
PO Box 64442, Virginia Beach, VA, 23467-4442
Mr. Landlord, 1,036

Household Goods Forwarders Association of America
2320 Mill Rd. #102, Alexandria, VA, 22314-4691
Portal, 1,179

•**Hulbert Financial Digest**
316 Commerce St, Alexandria, VA, 22314-2802

Independent Lubricant Manufacturers Association
651 S Washington St, Alexandria, VA, 22314-4109
ILMA Compoundings, 957

Industrial Designers Society of America
142 Walker Rd, Great Falls, VA, 22066-1836
Design Perspectives, 607

Industrial Safety Equipment Assn.
1901 N. Moore St., Arlington, VA, 22209-1706
Safety Signals, 1,084

•**Information Technology Association of America**
1616 Fort Myer Dr Ste 1300, Arlington, VA, 22209-3103

* See *MULTI-PUBLISHER INDEX* for list of publications.

Institute of Early American History
PO Box 8781, Williamsburg, VA, 23187-8781
Uncommon Sense, 549

Institute for International Health and Development
1141 Custis Street, Alexandria, VA, 22308
Asia Stock Sourcebook, 654

Insulation Contractors Assn. of America
PO Box 26237, Alexandria, VA, 22313-6237
ICAA News, 247

International Apple Inst.
PO Box 1137, Mc Lean, VA, 22101-1137
IAI Apple News, 1,009

Intl. Assn. of Addictions & Offender Counseling
5999 Stevenson Ave., Alexandria, VA, 22304-3300
IAAOC Report, 787

•**International Association of Chiefs of Police**
515 N Washington St Ste 400, Alexandria, VA, 22314-2340

International Assn Counterterrorism & Security Professionals
PO Box 10265, Arlington, VA, 22210-1265
International Counterterrorism & Security Report, 1,104

International Association of Fire Chiefs, Inc.
4025 Fair Ridge Drive, Fairfax, VA, 22033-2868
IAFC On Scene, 421

•**International Bottled Water Association**
113 N Henry St, Alexandria, VA, 22314-2903

•**International Chiropractors Assn.**
1110 N. Glebe Rd., Ste. 1000, Arlington, VA, 22201-4795

International Communications Industries Assn.
3150 Spring St, Fairfax, VA, 22031-2399
Communications Industries Report, 855

Intl. Dental Health Foundation
11484 Washington Plz., W., Reston, VA, 22090-4312
Annotations, 268

Intl. Estimate, Inc.
3030 S Abingdon St, Arlington, VA, 22206-1605
Estimate, 630

International Federation for Family Life Promotion
2009 14th St N Ste 512, Arlington, VA, 22201-2514
IFFLP Bulletin, 514

Intl. Hardwood Products Assn.
4214 King St. West, Alexandria, VA, 22302
IHPA Newsletter, 830

Intl. Institute for Economic Research
PO Box 624, Gloucester, VA, 23061-0624
Intermarket Review, 670

Intl. Law & Trade Perspective
604 S. King St., Ste. 100B, Leesburg, VA, 22075-3911
International Law & Trade Perspective, 745

International Magnesium Association
1303 Vincent Pl Ste 1, McLean, VA, 22101-3615
Magnesium, 891

International Newspaper Advertising Executives
11600 Sunrise Valley Dr, Reston, VA, 22091-1412
Sales and Idea Book, 924

International Personnel Management Association
1617 Duke St., Alexandria, VA, 22314-3406
I.P.M.A. News, 839

International Publications
P.O. Box 19529, Alexandria, VA, 22320
Development Bank Business Report, 644

•**International Sign Association**
801 N Fairfax St Ste 205, Alexandria, VA, 22314-1757

International Society for Hybrid Microelectronics
1850 Centennial Park Drive, #105, Reston, VA, 22091
International Society for Hybrid Microelectronics Newsletter, 366

International Visual Literacy Association, Inc.
Virginia Tech., Old Security Bldg., #LRC, Blacksburg, VA, 24061-0232
Visual Literacy Review & Newsletter, 335

Interstate Truckload Carriers Conference
2200 Mill Rd, Alexandria, VA, 22314-4686
ITCC Truckload Carrier Report, 1,192

Investment & Speculation SIG, MENSA
11160 Glade Dr, Reston, VA, 22091-4709
Good News, 667

•**Issue Action Pubs. Inc.**
207 Loudoun St. SE, Leesburg, VA, 22075-3115

Izaak Walton League of America
1401 Wilson Blvd., Level B, Arlington, VA, 22209-2318
League Leader, 386

•**J.R. Publishing, Inc.**
PO Box 6654, Mc Lean, VA, 22106-6654

Jenkins Hill Publishing Co.
12340 B Minsummer Lane #302, Lake Ridge, VA, 22192
Majority Rules, 1,209

Jennifer Miller
3554 Chain Bridge Rd Ste 200, Fairfax, VA, 22030-2709
Monthly Newsletter for Mothers of Asthmatics, 519

Jewelry Price Report
PO Box 35, Rockville, VA, 23146-0035
JPR, 693

Jim Warren Communications
2030 Clarendon Ave., Suite #201, Arlington, VA, 22201
Transplant News, 888

Junior Engineering Technical Society
1420 King St Ste 405, Alexandria, VA, 22314-2750
JETS Report, 361

•**KCI Communications, Inc.**
1101 King St., Ste. 400, Alexandria, VA, 22314-2980

•**Kelly Communications**
Rr 13 Box 28, Charlottesville, VA, 22901-7927

Kevin J. Tankersley
524 E Luray Ave, Alexandria, VA, 22301-1606
Yurek Herald, 470

LIC International, Inc
PO Box 10265, Arlington, VA, 22210-1265
LIC International, 488

La Cuisine Kitchenware
323 Cameron St, Alexandria, VA, 22314-3219
A La Carte, 425

Le Soleil Francais
1633 Monument Avenue, Richmond, VA, 23220-2906
Le Soleil Francais, 1,186

•**Legal Publication Svces.**
2008 N Emerson St., Arlington, VA, 22207-1948

Legalize? SIG
PO Box 3240, Charlottesville, VA, 22903-0240
Legal-eyes, 285

Leni Reed Associates, Inc.
PO Box 666, Herndon, VA, 22070-0666
Supermarket Savvy Information Resource Service, 433

Library of Virginia
11th St. at Capitol Sq., Richmond, VA, 23219-3491
Library of Virginia News, 803

Life Extension Society
990 Powhatan St., Arlington, VA, 22205
Life Extension Society News, 515

Marketing Works! Publishing
1031 Sterling Rd Ste 204, Herndon, VA, 22070-3834
Marketing Shorts, 18

Mayan Crafts
1035 N Edgewood St, Arlington, VA, 22201-2119
New Creation News, 1,049

Media Management
PO Box 21433, Roanoke, VA, 24018-0145
Servant Life, 1,051

Media Research Ctr.
113 S West St., 2nd Floor, Alexandria, VA, 22314-2824
MediaWatch, 859

Medical Devices Report
PO Box 1062, Manassas, VA, 22110-1062
Medical Devices Report, 878

Michaelsen's Micro Magic, Inc.
PO Box 7332, Fredericksburg, VA, 22404-7332
Natural Resources Computer Newsletter, 388

•**Michie Law Publishing co.**
701 East Water Street, Charlottesville, VA, 22902-5389

Michigan Univ. Hospital, Dept. of Physical Medicine
c/o Nathan D. Zasler,MD, 11654 Rutgers Drive, Richmond, VA, 73233
Newsletter of the National Task Force on Sexuality and Disability., 1,110

Mid-Atlantic Assn. of Forensic Sciences
PO Box 196, Mc Lean, VA, 22101-0196
Scientific Sleuthing Newsletter, 790

Mid-Atlantic Council of Shopping Cntr. Mgrs.
22560 Glenn Dr Ste 118, Sterling, VA, 20164-4440
Mac News, 1,035

Mid-Atlantic Regional Archives Conference
c/o Marsha Trimble, Univ. of Virginia Law Library, Charlottesville, VA, 22901
Mid-Atlantic Archivist, 804

Military Marketing Services, Inc.
PO Box 2347, Falls Church, VA, 22042-0347
Military Living's R & R Report, 897

Monroe Institute
Rr 1 Box 175, Faber, VA, 22938-9751
TMI Focus, 949

Mothers of Asthmatics, Inc.
3554 Chain Bridge Rd Ste 200, Fairfax, VA, 22030-2709
MA Report, 516

Mountain Empire Community College
PO Box 700, Big Stone Gap, VA, 24219-0700
News Briefs, 207

Mountain Empire Genealogical Soc.
PO Box 628, Pound, VA, 24279-0628
Mountain Empire Genealogical Quarterly, 461

Muller Associates, Inc.
PO Box 75, Fairfax Station, VA, 22039-0075
Foreign Markets Advisory, 665

NP Publishing, Inc.
7936 Bressingham Dr., Fairfax Station, VA, 22039-3157
Employee Benefits for Non-Profits, 342

•**National Accounting & Finance Council**
2200 Mill Rd, Alexandria, VA, 22314-4686

Natl. Accrediting Commission of Cosmetology Arts & Sciences
901 N Stuart St., Ste 900, Arlington, VA, 22203-1854
NACCAS Review, 319

National Aeronautic Assn.
1815 Fort Myer Dr Ste 700, Arlington, VA, 22209-1805
For the Record, 29

Natl. Agricultural Marketing Officials
VA Dept. Ag. & Consumer Svcs., Box 1163, Richmond, VA, 23209
National Agricultural Marketing Officials-Newsletter, 43

Natl. Art Education Assn.
1916 Association Dr., Reston, VA, 22091-1590
NAEA News, 319

Natl. Assn. of Acred. Cosmetology Schls.
901 N Washington St Ste 206, Alexandria, VA, 22314-1535
NAACS Washington Update, 256

National Association of Biology Teachers
11250 Roger Bacon Dr Ste 19, Reston, VA, 22090-5202
News & Views, 322

National Association of Black Journalists
11600 Sunrise Valley Dr, Reston, VA, 22091-1412
National Association of Black Journalists Newsletter, 696

Natl. Assn. of Chain Drug Stores
Box 1417-D49, Alexandria, VA, 22313
NACDS Executive Newsletter, 285

Natl. Assn. of Children's Hospitals
401 Wythe St., Alexandria, VA, 22314-1926
NACHRI Newsletter, 569

National Association of College Admission Counselors
1631 Prince St., Alexandria, VA, 22314-2818
NACAC Bulletin, 319

National Assn. of College Auxiliary Services
PO Box 870, Staunton, VA, 24402-0870
N.A.C.A.S. Newsletter, 1,022

Natl. Assn. of Convenience Stores
1605 King St., Alexandria, VA, 22314-2726
NACS SCAN, 850

National Association of Dental Assistants
900 S Washington St Ste G13, Falls Church, VA, 22046-4041
Explorer, 269

National Association of Elementary School Principals
1615 Duke St, Alexandria, VA, 22314-3406
Communicator, 1,090

National Association of Executive Secretaries
900 S Washington St Ste G13, Falls Church, VA, 22046-4020
Exec-U-Tary, 938

National Association of Government Archives and Records
11th St. at Capitol Square, Richmond, VA, 23219
NAGARA Clearinghouse, 805

National Association of Housing Cooperatives
1614 King St, Alexandria, VA, 22314-2719
Cooperative Housing Bulletin, 1,032

Natl. Assn. of Marine Surveyors, Inc.
PO Box 9306, Chesapeake, VA, 23321-9306
NAMS News, 936

Natl. Assn. of Partners in Education
601 Wythe St Ste 200, Alexandria, VA, 22314-1937
Partners in Education, 325

National Association of Personnel Services
3133 Mount Vernon Ave, Alexandria, VA, 22305-2640
Inside NAPS, 345

* See ***MULTI-PUBLISHER INDEX*** for list of publications.

National Association of Physicians' Nurses
900 S Washington St Ste G13, Falls Church, VA, 22046-4020
Nightingale, 931

National Association of Postal Supervisors
1727 King St # 400, Alexandria, VA, 22314-2753
NAPS Letter, 971

National Association of RV Parks & Campgrounds
8605 Westwood Center Dr Ste, 201, Vienna, VA, 22182-2231
RV Park & Campground Report, 950

Natl. Assn. of Rehabilitation Facilities
1910 Association Dr Fl 2, Reston, VA, 22091-1502
Rehabilitation Review, 1,121

Natl. Assn. of the Remodeling Industry
4301 North Fairfax Dr Ste 310, Arlington, VA, 22203-1627
Nari Focus, 248

•**National Association of Secondary School Principals**
1904 Association Dr., Reston, VA, 22091-1537

National Association of Small Business Investment Companies
1199 N Fairfax St Ste 200, Alexandria, VA, 22314-1437
NASBIC News, 145

•**National Association for Sport & Physical Education**
1900 Association Dr., Reston, VA, 22091

National Association of State Boards of Education, Inc.
1012 Cameron St, Alexandria, VA, 22314-2427
Connection, 305

National Association of State Directors of Special Education
1800 Diagonal Rd Ste 320, Alexandria, VA, 22314-2840
Liaison Bulletin, 316

National Association of State Judicial Educators
300 Newport Ave, Williamsburg, VA, 23185-4147
NASJE News, 758

•**National Assn. of State Mental Retardation Prgm Directors**
113 Oronoco St, Alexandria, VA, 22314-2015

Natl. Assn. for Trade & Industrial Education
PO Box 1665, Leesburg, VA, 22075-1665
NATIE News Notes, 320

National Association of VA Physicians & Dentists
101 N. Alfred St., Ste. 200, Alexandria, VA, 22314-4005
NAVAPD News, 880

Natl. Assn. for Vietnamese & American Education
3206 Wynford Dr, Fairfax, VA, 22031-2831
National Association for Vietnamese & American Education-Newsletter, 321

Natl. Assn. of Women Judges, c/o Natl. Ctr. for State Courts
300 Newport Ave, Williamsburg, VA, 23185-4147
NAWJ Counterbalance, 758

National Automated Clearing House Association
607 Herndon Pky Ste 200, Herndon, VA, 22070-5477
Automated Payments Update, 80

National Aviation Club
PO Box 2717, Arlington, VA, 22202-0717
Aerolog, 25

Natl. Beer Wholesalers Assn.
1100 S Washington St, Falls Church, VA, 22046-4023
Legislative & Regulatory Issues Alert, 104

National Business Education Association
1914 Association Dr., Reston, VA, 22091-1596
Keying In, 142

National Cartographic Information Ctr., USGS
509 National Ctr., Reston, VA, 22092-0001
Newsletter, 476

Natl. Center for Homeopathy
801 N Fairfax St Ste 306, Alexandria, VA, 22314-1757
Homeopathy Today, 875

•**National Center for State Courts**
300 Newport Ave, Williamsburg, VA, 23185-4147

•**National Coalition for the Homeless**
PO Box 2410, Merrifield, VA, 22116-2410

National Coalition for Marine Conservation
3 W. Market St., #100, Leesburg, VA, 22075-2901
Marine Bulletin, 387

National Coffee Service Association
4000 Williamsburg Ct, Fairfax, VA, 22032-1139
What's Brewing, 105

Natl. Confectioners Assn.
7900 Westpark Dr Ste A320, Mc Lean, VA, 22102-4203
National Confectioners Assn. of the U.S. News Bulletin, 243

Natl. Conference of Appellate Court Clerks
300 Newport Ave, Williamsburg, VA, 23185-4147
National Conference of Appellate Court Clerks Newsletter, 760

Natl. Conference on Ministry to the Armed Forces
4141 N Henderson Rd Ste 13, Arlington, VA, 22203-2452
National Conference on Ministry to the Armed Forces Newsletter, 1,049

Natl. Conference of States on Building Codes & Standards
505 Huntmar Park Dr Ste 210, Herndon, VA, 22070-5100
NCSBCS News, 248

National Coordinating Council on Emergency Management
7297 Lee Hwy Ste N, Falls Church, VA, 22042-1707
NCCEM Bulletin, 1,022

Natl. Corvette Owner's Assn.
Box 777-A, Falls Church, VA, 22046-9860
For Vettes Only, 73

Natl. Early American Glass Club
PO Box 57, Fishers Hill, VA, 22626-0057
Glass Shards Newsletter, 479

•**Natl. Electrical Manufacturers Assn.**
1300 N. 17th St., Ste. 1847, Arlington, VA, 22209-3801

•**Natl. Erectors Assn.**
1501 Lee Hwy Ste 202, Arlington, VA, 22209-1109

•**National FFA Organization**
PO Box 15160, 5632 Mt. Vernon Memorial Hwy., Alexandria, VA, 22309-0160

National Genealogical Society
4527 17th St. N, Arlington, VA, 22207-2399
NGS Newsletter, 461

National Hospice Organization
1901 N. Moore St., Ste. 901, Arlington, VA, 22209-1714
NHO Newsline, 881

National Industries for the Blind
1901 N. Beauregard St., Ste. 200, Alexandria, VA, 22311-1727
Opportunity, 112

•**National Information Corp.**
1101 King Street, Alexandria, VA, 22314

National Institute for Automotive Service Excellence
13505 Dulles Technology Dr, Herndon, VA, 22071-3413
Blue Seal, 71

•**National Institute of Business Management**
1101 King St Ste 411, Alexandria, VA, 22314-2966

National Inst. for Certification in Engineering Technology
1420 King St., Alexandria, VA, 22314-2794
NICET Newsletter, 362

Natl. Institute of Governmental Purchasing
11800 Sunrise Valley Dr., Ste. 1050, Reston, VA, 22091-5302
NIGP Technical Bulletin, 1,028

National Investor Relations Institute
8045 Leesburg Pike., Ste. 600, Vienna, VA, 22182-2737
Investor Relations Update, 858

National Legal Research Group
2421 Ivy Road, P.O. Box 7187, Charlottesville, VA, 22903
South Carolina Appellate Digest, 776

•**National Mental Health Association**
1021 Prince St., Alexandria, VA, 22314-2971

Natl. Milk Producers Fed.
1840 Wilson Blvd., Arlington, VA, 22201-3086
News for Dairy Co-Ops, 265

Natl. Newspaper Assn.
1525 Wilson Blvd Ste 550, Arlington, VA, 22209-2411
Publishers Auxiliary, 772

National Nurses Association
1765 Business Center Dr, Reston, VA, 22090-5300
Vital Signs, 932

National Officers Assn.
PO Box 4975, Reston, VA, 22090-1464
Officers Call, 898

National Organization of Episcopolians for Life
10523 Main St., Fairfax, VA, 22030-3310
NOEL News, 1,067

National Paperbox Association
1201 E. Abingdon Dr., Ste. 203, Alexandria, VA, 22314-1420
Packet, The, 946

National Pasta Association
2101 Wilson Blvd., Ste. 920, Arlington, VA, 22201-3055
Positively Pasta!, 432

Natl. Patent Council
c/o Schellin, 2121 Crystal Dr., Arlington, VA, 22202-3706
Patent Trends, 952

•**National Private Truck Council**
66 Canal Center Plz., Ste. 600, Alexandria, VA, 22314-1591

•**Natl. Recreation & Park Assn.**
2775 S. Quincy St., Ste. 300, Arlington, VA, 22206-2236

Natl. Rehabilitation Assn.
633 S Washington St, Alexandria, VA, 22314-4109
NRA Newsletter, 1,119

National Rehabilitation Counseling Assn.
1910 Association Dr # 206, Reston, VA, 22091-1502
Professional Report, 525

National Resource Center for Consumers of Legal Services
6596 Main St., PO Box 340, Gloucester, VA, 23061
Legal Plan Letter, 751

National Right to Work Committee
8001 Braddock Rd. #500, Springfield, VA, 22160-0001
National Right to Work Newsletter, 710

Natl. SIDS Resourec Center
2070 Chain Bridge Rd., Ste. 450, Vienna, VA, 22182-2536
Information Exchange, 876

•**National School Boards Assn.**
1680 Duke St., Alexandria, VA, 22314-3493

•**National School Public Relations Assn.**
1501 Lee Hwy Ste 201, Arlington, VA, 22209-1109

Natl. School Transportation Assn.
PO Box 2639, Springfield, VA, 22152-0639
National School Transportation Assn. -Newsletter, 1,179

Natl. Science Foundation
4201 Wilson Boulevard, Arlington, VA, 22230
NSF Bulletin, 1,098

Natl. Senior Sports Assn.
PO Box 882, Fairfax, VA, 22030-0882
Senior Sports News, 1,109

Natl. Society of Fund Raising Executives
1101 King St Ste 700, Alexandria, VA, 22314-2944
NSFRE News, 969

Natl. Soc. of Public Accountants
1010 N Fairfax St, Alexandria, VA, 22314-1504
NSPA Washington Reporter, 6

•**National Taxpayers Union/NTU Foundation**
108 N. Alfred St., Alexandria, VA, 22314

•**National Technical Information Service U.S.**
5285 Port Royal Rd., Springfield, VA, 22161-0001

Natl. Water Data Exchange Program Office
Us Geological Survey 421 Natl., Ctr., 12201 Sunrise, Reston, VA, 22092-0001
NAWDEX Newsletter, 1,203

Natl. Water Resources Assn.
3800 Fairfax Dr, Ste 4, Arlington, VA, 22203-1703
National Water Line, 1,203

Natl. Wholesale Druggists' Assn.
1821 Michael Faraday Dr., Ste. 400, Reston, VA, 22090-5348
NWDA Executive Newsletter, 286

•**National Wildlife Federation**
8925 Leesburg Pike, Vienna, VA, 22184-0001

National Woodland Owners Association
374 Maple Ave E., Ste 210, Vienna, VA, 22180-4718
Woodland Report, 436

New American View
PO Box 999, Herndon, VA, 22070-0999
New American View, 489

New Party
8319 Fulham Ct, Richmond, VA, 23227-1712
New Party, 994

Newsletter Publishers Association
1401 Wilson Blvd., Suite 207, Arlington, VA, 22209-2341
Hotline, 953

Norfolk Botanical Garden Society
Azalea Garden Rd., Norfolk, VA, 23518
Norfolk Botanical Garden Society Bulletin, 442

Norfolk Foundation
1410 NationsBank Center, Norfolk, VA, 23510-2113
Norfolk Foundation, 1,043

North-South Skirmish Assn. Inc.
9700 Royerton Dr, Richmond, VA, 23228-1218
North-South Skirmish Association Newsletter, 495

Nubian Exchange
154 Patrick St. #175, Vienna, VA, 22182
Nubian Exchange News, 34

Office of the Attorney Genl.
101 N 8th St, Richmond, VA, 23219-2305
Law Digest, 748

* See **MULTI-PUBLISHER INDEX** for list of publications.

Office of Civil Defense
310 Turner Rd., Richmond, VA, 23225-6400
Emergency Planning Bulletin, 1,138

Old Dominion Press, Inc.
310 Tarrytown Dr, Richmond, VA, 23229-7323
Norwich and Norfolk Terrier News, 280

Option Weekly
4838 Randolph Dr, Annandale, VA, 22003-6222
Option Weekly, 681

Organization Management Inc.
13231 Pleasantview Ln, Fairfax, VA, 22033-3015
Non-Profit Legal & Tax Letter, 1,149

PAI
9520 Bent Creek Ln, Vienna, VA, 22182-1407
Issues & Strategy Bulletin, 992

PBS Video
1320 Braddock Pl., Alexandria, VA, 22314-1698
PBS Video News, 1,168

PV Energy Systems, Inc.
PO Box 290, Casanova, VA, 22017-0290
PV News, 357

Packaging Education Foundation
481 Carlisle Dr., Herndon, VA, 22070-4819
Briefs, 301

•**Painting**
3913 Old Lee Hwy., #33B, Fairfax, VA, 22030-2401

•**Parent Institute, The**
PO Box 7474, Fairfax Station, VA, 22039-7474

Parents Music Resource Center
1500 Arlington Blvd, Arlington, VA, 22209-3501
Video-Rising to the Challenge, 171

•**Pasha Publications, Inc**
1616 N. Fort Myer Dr., #1000, Arlington, VA, 22209-3103

Passenger Vessel Association
1600 Wilson Blvd., Ste. 1000-A, Arlington, VA, 22209
Foghorn, 1,184

Penny Resistance
8319 Fulham Ct, Richmond, VA, 23227-1712
Penny Resistance, 996

People-To-People Health Foundation/Project Hope
Millwood, VA, 22646-9999
Hope News, 513

Pepper Bird Publications
P.O. Box 1071, Williamsburg, VA, 23187-5604
Pepper Bird Pathways, 1,187

Permanent Intl. Assn. of Navigation Congresses
Water Resources Ctr., Ft. Belvoir, VA, 22060-5586
Newsletter, 1,112

Pinkerton Risk Assessment Services
1600 Wilson Blvd Ste 901, Arlington, VA, 22209-2505
Pinkerton World Status Map, 1,187

Plowshare Peace Center
PO Box 1623, Roanoke, VA, 24008-1623
Plowshare News, 996

Poet Band Co.
PO Box 2648, Newport News, VA, 23609-0648
Poetry Explosion Newsletter (PEN), 983

Portfolios Investment Advisory
PO Box 997, Lynchburg, VA, 24505-0997
Portfolios Investment Advisory, 682

Presbyterian School of Christian Education
1205 Palmyra Ave, Richmond, VA, 23227-4417
Source/Resource, 207

PresentFutures Group
101 Park Washington Ct #100, Falls Church, VA, 22046
PresentFutures Report, 148

Preservation Reports, Inc.
PO Box 569, Fairfax, VA, 22030-0569
Urban Conservation Report, 1,025

•**Printing Industries of America**
100 Daingerfield Rd., Alexandria, VA, 22314-2888

Propeller Club of the U. S.
3927 Old Lee Hwy Ste 101a, Fairfax, VA, 22030-2422
Proceedings of the American Merchant Marine Conference, 1,112

Public Risk Management Assn.
1815 Ft. Myer Drive, 10th Floor, Arlington, VA, 22209
Riskwatch, 624

Public Service Research Council
527 Maple Ave. East, 3rd Floor, Vienna, VA, 22180-4713
Government Union Critique, 708

Public Utilities Reports, Inc.
8229 Boone Blvd., Suite #401, Vienna, VA, 22182
P.U.R. Utility Weekly, 1,027

Publishers & Producers
P.O. Box 36, Annandale, VA, 22003
Manufacturing News, 850

Quate Assocs.
PO Box 7065, Suffolk, VA, 23437-0065
Quate's Grain/Weather Forecast, 45

Questel Publishing
8000 Westpark Dr., McLean, VA, 22102
Inside the PTO, 951

•**RESNA Technical Assistance Project**
1700 N. Moore St., Ste. 1540, Arlington, VA, 22209

Radio Business Report
3208B Old Franconia Rd, Alexandria, VA, 22310
Radio Business Report, 125

Railway Progress Institute
700 N. Fairfax St., Suite 661, Alexandria, VA, 22314-2098
Railway Progress News, 1,180

Randolph-Macon College
Publications, Ashland, VA, 23005
Bulletin of Randolph-Macon College, 194

Ray Olszewski
8080 Counselor Rd, Manassas, VA, 22111-4752
Magnifier, The, 65

Recreation Vehicle Dealers Association
3930 University Drive #500, Fairfax, VA, 22030-2515
RVDA News, 944

Recreational Vehicle Industry Assn.
1896 Preston White Dr, Reston, VA, 22090
Go Camping America!, 901

Regular Common Carrier Conference
5205 Leesburg Pike Ste 1110, Falls Church, VA, 22041-3802
Highway Common Carrier News Letter, 1,192

Religion Today
PO Box 21505, Roanoke, VA, 24018-0560
National & International Religion Report, 1,065

•**Research Institute of America**
1340 Braddock Pl., Ste. 400, Alexandria, VA, 22314-1651

•**Resources For Educators**
1717 Commonwealth Drive, Front Royal, VA, 22630

Restivo Communications
201 Elden St Ste 167, Herndon, VA, 22070-4812
Television & Radio Newsletter, 125

Review Publishing Co., Inc.
2601 W Cary St, Richmond, VA, 23220-5118
Virginia Municipal Review, 494

•**Roanoke Valley Chamber of Commerce**
212 S. Jefferson, Roanoke, VA, 24011

Robert Ciraulo
Taste of Elegance, 141 Algonquin Rd, Hampton, VA, 23661
Taste of Elegance, 433

Rockingham Memorial Hospital
235 Cantrell Ave, Harrisonburg, VA, 22801-3248
Bedside Banner, 561

•**Rouge et Noir Inc.**
PO Box 1146, Midlothian, VA, 23113-8146

Rural Virginia, Inc.
PO Box 105, Richmond, VA, 23201-0105
Rural Virginia Voice, 1,043

Ruritan Natl. Inc.
Ruritan Rd., PO Box 487, Dublin, VA, 24084
Ruritan, 181

SC & RA Newsletter
2750 Prospetity Ave., Suite #260, FairFax, VA, 22031-4312
SC & RA Newsletter, 1,180

S.C.R.O.O.G.E.
1447 Westwood Rd, Charlottesville, VA, 22903-5151
SCROOGE Newsletter, 605

•**SNL Securities**
410 E. Main St., P.O. Box 2124, Charlottesville, VA, 22902

Sail Assistance Intl. Liason Associates
1553 Bayville St, Norfolk, VA, 23503-1060
Sail Assistance News, 1,112

•**St. Anthony Consulting Group**
11410 Isaac Newton Sq., N., Ste. 200, Alexandria, VA, 22090-5012

St. Paul's College
406 Windsor Ave, Lawrenceville, VA, 23868-1299
Saint Paulite, 207

•**Salt Institute**
700 N Fairfax St Ste 600, Alexandria, VA, 22314-2040

Satellite Broadcasting & Communications Assn.
225 Reinekers Ln Ste 500, Alexandria, VA, 22314-2875
SBCA Report, 1,169

Scale Manufacturers Assn.
9384D Forestwood Ln., Manassas, VA, 22110-4702
SMA Weighlog, 832

Screen Printing Assn. Intl.
10015 Main St, Fairfax, VA, 22031-3403
Imagemaker, 1,005

Select Publishing Society
6756 Towne Lane Road, PO Box 1231A, McLean, VA, 22101-1231
Inside Out, 471

Service Civil Intl. USA
Rr 2 Box 506, Crozet, VA, 22932-9510
Workcamp News, 350

Shandler Enterprises Co.
PO Box 20503, Roanoke, VA, 24018
Baseball Forecaster, 101

Sharline
586 Truslow Road, Fredericksburg, VA, 22406
Virginia Wine Line, 434

Shelburne Securities Forecast
PO Box 5566, Arlington, VA, 22205-0066
Shelburne Securities Forecast, 685

Shellfish Institute of North America
1525 Wilson Blvd Ste 500, Arlington, VA, 22209-2411
Shellfish Soundings, 424

Sherwood Anderson Society
Univ. of Richmond, Richmond, VA, 23173
Winesburg Eagle, 826

Shipbuilders Council of America
4301 N. Fairfax Drive, Arlington, VA, 22203-1627
Shipyard Chronicle, 1,112

Ski Tripper
PO Box 20305, Roanoke, VA, 24018-0031
Ski Tripper, 1,113

Sleeper Co., The
PO Box 10570, Alexandria, VA, 22310-0570
Sleeper News, 1,043

Small Business Press
2000 14th St N Ste 450, Arlington, VA, 22201-2573
Set-Aside Alert, 151

Society for Advancement of Management
126 E Lee Ave Ste 11, Vinton, VA, 24179-2518
SAM Focus on Management, 844

Society of Cardiavascular Anesthesiologists
1910 Byrd Avenue, #100, PO Box 11086, Richmond, VA, 23230-1086
Society of Cardiovascular Anesthesiologists-Newsletter, 887

Society for Clinical & Experimental Hypnosis
8335 Allison Pointe Trail, Ste. 250, Indianapolis, VA, 46250-1686
International Society of Hypnosis Newsletter, 607

Society for Historical Archaeology
Dept. Anthropology, Box 8795, College of William & Mary, Williamsburg, VA, 23187-8795
Society for Historical Archaeology-Newsletter, 58

Society of National Association Pubs.
1735 N Lynn St Ste 950, Arlington, VA, 22209-2019
Snapshot, 152

Society of Satellite Professionals
2200 Wilson Blvd., No. 102-258, Arlington, VA, 22201
Orbiter, 1,161

Society for Service Professionals in Printing
PO Box 25768, Alexandria, VA, 22313-5768
Signature Service, 1,007

Society for Technical Communication
901 N Stuart St Ste 904, Arlington, VA, 22203-1854
Intercom, 858

Sophia Circle
8319 Fulham Ct, Richmond, VA, 23227-1712
Sophia Circle, 262

Sourceletter, Inc.
PO Box 7282, Arlington, VA, 22207-0282
Sourceletter, 99

•**Southern States Cooperative**
PO Box 26234, Richmond, VA, 23260-6234

SpEds
PO Box 68578, Virginia Beach, VA, 23455
Special Education Support Newsletter, 331

•**Sparks Companies Inc.**
6708 Whittier Ave, Mc Lean, VA, 22101-4529

Special Libraries Assn., Social Science Div.
2000 15th St N Ste 701, Arlington, VA, 22201-2627
Special Libraries Assn., Social Science Division Bulletin, 810

Speech Communication Association
5105 Backlick Rd Bldg E, Annandale, VA, 22003-6005
Spectra, 534

Standing Committee on Law & Natl. Security, ABA
1501 Trombone Ct, Vienna, VA, 22182-1646
National Security Law Report, 1,104

• See ***MULTI-PUBLISHER INDEX*** for list of publications.

Statistical Reporting Service
PO Box 1659, Richmond, VA, 23213-1659
Broiler Report, 1,000

•**Strategic Direction Publishers**
5352 Ashley Rd., Fairfax, VA, 22030

Strayer College
3045 Columbia Pike, Arlington, VA, 22204-4300
Strayer College Military Outreach, 207

Sumi-E Society of America, c/o Nippon Club
4200 Kings Mill Ln, Annandale, VA, 22003-2033
Sumi-E Notes, 67

SwingLetter, The
306 N Irving St, Arlington, VA, 22201-1242
SwingLetter, The, 266

T.O.G. Music Enterprises
2107 S Oakland St, Arlington, VA, 22204-5413
Insider, The, 912

Taurus Corp.
133 W Boscawen St # 767, Winchester, VA, 22601-4115
Taurus, 688

•**Tax Analysts**
6830 N. Fairfax Dr., Arlington, VA, 22213-1098

Teaching Co., The
7405 Alban Court, Ste. A107, Springfield, VA, 22150
Newsletter of The Teaching Company (Update), 323

•**Telecom Publishing Group**
1101 King St Ste 444, Alexandria, VA, 22314-2944

Telecommunications Industry Association
2500 Wilson Blvd., Ste. 300, Arlington, VA, 22201-3834
Industry Pulse, 1,159

Terrell Society of American, Inc.
Rr 5 Box 211, Bassett, VA, 24055-8964
Terrell Trails, 468

This Week in Richmond
117 Matoaka Rd, Richmond, VA, 23226-2214
This Week in Richmond, 1,189

Tidewater Nicaragua Project Foundation
3916 Shell Rd, Hampton, VA, 23669-4228
Tidewater Nicaragua Project Fdn. Newsletter, 638

Tiger on Spreads
PO Box 1414, Mc Lean, VA, 22101-1414
Tiger on Spreads, 689

Towing & Recovery Association of America
2200 Mill Rd, Alexandria, VA, 22314-4686
Towing News, 1,193

•**Travel Guide Inc.**
PO Box 3485, Charlottesville, VA, 22903-0485

Trout Unlimited
1500 Wilson Blvd., Arlington, VA, 22209-2404
Lines to Leaders, 423

Truck Renting & Leasing Assn.
1725 Duke Street, #600, Alexandria, VA, 22314-3457
Truck Renting & Leasing Assn. -News Digest, 155

Turn Back the Clock
12020 Sunrise Valley Drive, Reston, VA, 22090
Turn Back the Clock, 530

Type Reporter
11314 Chapel Rd, Fairfax, VA, 22039-1523
Type Reporter, 1,018

Uniformed Services Academy of Family Physicians
PO Box 11086, Richmond, VA, 23230-1086
Uniformed Services Academy of Family Physicians-Newsletter, 888

•**United Fresh Fruit & Vegetable Assn.**
727 N Washington St, Alexandria, VA, 22314-1924

•**United Olympic Life Insurance**
4601 Fairfax Dr., Arlington, VA, 22203-1500

U.S. Business Council for Southeastern Europe
PO Box 3635, Warrenton, VA, 22186-8235
Business News, 642

U.S. Dept. of Agriculture, Food & Nutrition Service
Alexandria, VA, 22302
Food & Nutrition, 428

U.S. Naturalized Citizen Assn.
399 Pendleton St., Alexandria, VA, 22314-2049
Interdependent Voice, 991

United Virginia Bankshares Inc.
PO Box 26665, Richmond, VA, 23261-6665
Spectrum, 599

Univ. of Richmond History of Economics Society
Economics Dept., Richmond, VA, 23173
History of Economics Soc. Bulletin, The, 292

Univ. of Virginia
402 Cabell Hall, Charlottesville, VA, 22903
Comparative Romance Linguistics Newsletter, 820

Valentine Museum
1015 E Clay St, Richmond, VA, 23219-1590
Valentine News, 908

Valley UniServ
620 Hawkins St, Harrisonburg, VA, 22801-4312
Together We Can, 333

Vedanta Society of Greater Washington
7430 Tower St, Falls Church, VA, 22046-1935
Vedanta Society of Greater Washington Bulletin, 1,067

Virginia Commission on Bicentennial of the US Constitution
Univ. of Virginia, 207 Minor Hall, Charlottesville, VA, 22903
Virginia Independent, 550

Virginia Commonwealth Univ. Judaic Studies
Judaic Studies Program, Richmond, VA, 23284
Menorah, 1,069

Virginia Cooperative Extension Svce.
Dept. of Agri. & Applied Econ, Blacksburg, VA, 24061
Horizons, 42

Virginia Credit Union League
PO Box 11469, Lynchburg, VA, 24506-1469
Virginian, 602

•**Virginia Department of Agriculture and Consumer Services**
1100 Bank St Ste 805, Richmond, VA, 23219-3638

Virginia Dept. of Alcoholic Beverage Control
2901 Hermitage Rd, Richmond, VA, 23220-1010
Inside Spirit, 104

Virginia Food Dealers Assn., Inc.
517 W. Grace St., Richmond, VA, 23220-4928
VFDA Update, 433

Virginia Genealogical Society
5001 W Broad St Ste 115, Richmond, VA, 23230-3023
Virginia Genealogical Society Newsletter, 469

Virginia Historical Society
PO Box 7311, Richmond, VA, 23221-0311
Virginia Historical Society History Notes, 550

Virginia Horse Council
PO Box 72, Riner, VA, 24149-0072
Virginia Horse Council News, 560

Virginia Library Assn.
669 S. Washington St., Alexandria, VA, 22314
Virginia Librarian Newsletter, 812

Virginia Marine Science Museum
717 General Booth Blvd, Virginia Beach, VA, 23451-4811
Lookdown, The, 905

Virginia Museum of Fine Arts
2800 Grove Ave, Richmond, VA, 23221-2466
Virginia Museum Bulletin, 908

Virginia Polytechnic Institute & State Univ.
101 Deitrick Hall, Blacksburg, VA, 24061
Techgram, 207

Virginia Polytechnic Inst. Virginia Cntr. for Coal & Energy
617 N Main St, Blacksburg, VA, 24060-3348
Energy Outlook, 353

Virginia School Boards Assn.
Peabody Hall, Univ. of Va., Charlottesville, VA, 22903
Virginia School Boards Association Newsletter, 1,094

Virginia State Bar
707 E Main St Ste 1500, Richmond, VA, 23219-2803
Docket Call, 732

Virginia State Dept. of Labor
Box 1358, 7000 Federal Bldg., Richmond, VA, 23211-1358
Labor Market Trends, A News Letter, Richmond Metropolitan Area, 702

Virginia State Health Dept.
109 Governor St # 515, Richmond, VA, 23219-3623
Virginia's Health, 531

Virginia Thoroughbred Assn.
38 Garrett St, Warrenton, VA, 22186-3107
Virginia Thoroughbred News, 560

Vocational Industrial Clubs of America
PO Box 3000, Leesburg, VA, 22075-0300
VICA Professional: VP Newsletter, 335

W.J. Chandler Assocs.
7410 Recard Ln, Alexandria, VA, 22307-1846
Land Letter, 386

•**Wakeman/Walworth**
300 N. Washington St., Alexandria, VA, 22314-2530

•**Washington Business Information, Inc.**
1117 19th St N Ste 200, Arlington, VA, 22209-1708

Washington Capital News Reports
3918 Prosperity Ave Ste 318, Fairfax, VA, 22031-3333
Fire Control Digest, 421

•**Washington Crime News Services**
3918 Prosperity Ave Ste 318, Fairfax, VA, 22031-3333

Washington National News Reports
3918 Prosperity Ave Ste 318, Fairfax, VA, 22031-3333
Electronic Warfare Digest, 895

Washington Pacific Pubs. Inc.
PO Box 26142, Alexandria, VA, 22313-6142
Washington Pacific Report , The, 640

•**Washington Regulatory Reporting Group**
PO Box 356, Basye, VA, 22810-0356

•**Water Environment Federation**
601 Wythe St, Alexandria, VA, 22314-1994

Weadon Printing Services, Inc.
6430 General Green Way, Alexandria, VA, 22312-2446
Weadon Printing Services-Newsletter, 1,008

Web Offset Association/PIA
100 Daingerfield Road, Alexandria, VA, 22314
WEB IMPRESSIONS, 1,164

•**Webster Communications Corp.**
1530 Key Blvd., PH 2, Arlington, VA, 22209-1532

Welsh Pony & Cob Soc. of Amer., Inc.
PO Box 2977, Winchester, VA, 22604-2177
Welsh Pony & Cob Society of America Newsletter, 560

Whitehall-Robins
PO Box 26609, Richmond, VA, 23261-6609
Counterpoint, 581

William Barney
7361 Silver Pine Dr, Springfield, VA, 22153-1819
Barney Family News, 448

Winchester-Frederick County Chamber of Commerce, Inc.
1360 S Pleasant Valley Rd, Winchester, VA, 22601-4447
Winchester, 162

Wine & Spirits Shippers Assn.
1180 Sunrise Valley Dr., Reston, VA, 22091
WSSA Grapevine, 105

Women in Community Service, Inc.
1900 N Beauregard St Ste 103, Alexandria, VA, 22311-1716
This Is WICS, 1,123

World Federation for Mental Health
1021 Prince St., Alexandria, VA, 22314-2971
World Federation for Mental Health Newsletter, 1,018

Worldwide Assurance for Employees of Public Agencies
7651 Leesburg Pike, Falls Church, VA, 22043-2520
WAEPA Record, 625

Wright Publishing Co.
1800 Diagonal Rd Ste 600, Alexandria, VA, 22314-2840
Deficit Letter, The, 1,196

Y.S. Publications, Inc.
4736 Lee Highway, Ste. 202, Arlington, VA, 22207
Equal Employer, The, 344

Zines!
221 North Blvd., Richmond, VA, 23220
Zines!, 955

Washington

AG Pilot International
PO Box 1607, Mount Vernon, WA, 98273-1607
IAAF Newsletter, 30

APA - The Engineered Wood Assoc.
PO Box 11700, Tacoma, WA, 98411-0700
APA-The Engineered Wood Assoc., 829

ARNOVA
Washington State University, Rt 2, Box 696 - Barbara Long, Pullman, WA, 99163
ARNOVA News, 1,113

Abundant Life Seed Foundation
Box 772, Pt. Townsend, WA, 98368-0772
Abundant Life Seed Foundation Newsletter, 439

All Source Systems
PO Box 596, Morton, WA, 98356-0596
All Source Digest, 1,002

American Brahms Society
Univ. Of Washington School Of, Music, P.O Box 353450, Seattle, WA, 98195-3450
American Brahms Society Newsletter, 909

American Civil Liberties Union of Washington
705 2nd Ave Ste 300, Seattle, WA, 98104-1799
Civil Liberties, 172

American Red Cross
1900 25th Ave S, Seattle, WA, 98144-4708
Crossroads, 1,116

American Society of Indexers
PO Box 48267, Seattle, WA, 98148-0267
Keywords, 801

* See **MULTI-PUBLISHER INDEX** for list of publications.

Andover Printing
837 Industry Dr, Seattle, WA, 98188-3411
Harvey's Cat, 1,005

Asian Foodbookery
PO Box 15947, Seattle, WA, 98115-0947
Asian Foodbookery, 426

Association for Social Anthropology in Oceania
Department of Anthropology, University Of Washingto,
Seattle, WA, 98195-0001
Association for Social Anthropology in Oceania Newsletter, 300

Association of Washington Business
1414 Cherry St SE # 658, Olympia, WA, 98501-2341
Washington Business, 156

Aviation Maintenance Foundation Intl.
PO Box 2826, Redmond, WA, 98073-2826
Industry News, 30

Ballard Printing
11732 1st Ave NE, Seattle, WA, 98125-4714
Washington Plumbing and Heating Contractor, 535

•**Bell Enterprises**
PO Box 10328, Spokane, WA, 99209-1328

•**Bette Butcher Topp**
1304 W. Cliffwood Ct., Spokane, WA, 99218-2917

Billington Publications, inc
PO Box 184, Point Roberts, WA, 98281-0184
Billington's Stock Focus II, 655

Brief Case
PO Box 98234, Tacoma, WA, 98498-0234
Brief Case, 449

Bruce Gould Pubs.
PO Box 16, Seattle, WA, 98111-0016
Bruce Gould on Commodities, 656

Budinger & Assoc.
3820 E Broadway Ave, Spokane, WA, 99202-4525
Subsurface, 476

Buses Intl. Assn.
PO Box 1472, Spokane, WA, 99210-1472
Buses Intl. Assn. Newsletter, 1,176

CEBIS
100 S. King St., Ste. 410, Seattle, WA, 98104
Central European Business Guide, 643

Career Management Consultants, Inc.
37628 Swede Heaven Rd, Arlington, WA, 98223-5217
Career Outplacement, 608

Caretaker Gazette, The
1845 NW Dean Stay, Pullman, WA, 99163-3509
Caretaker Gazette, The, 342

Cartoonist Northwest
PO Box 31122, Seattle, WA, 98103
Penstuff, 210

Cavda Pavonis, Dept. of English
Washington State Univ., Pullman, WA, 99164-0001
Cavda Pavonis: Hermetic Text Society Newsletter, 820

Center for the Prevention of Sexual & Domestic Violence
936 N. 34th St. #200, Seattle, WA, 98103-8869
Working Together, 1,124

Centralia College
600 W Locust St, Centralia, WA, 98531-4035
Banner, The, 207

Childhaven
316 Broadway, Seattle, WA, 98122-5325
Happenings, 169

Children's Hospital & Medical Center, CG-07
P.O Box 5371, Seattle, WA, 98105
Sudden Infant Death Syndrome Foundation of Washington Newsletter, 529

•**Citizens Committee for the Right to Keep & Bear Arms**
12500 NE 10th Pl, Bellevue, WA, 98005-2538

Clark Humphrey
2510 Western Box, Seattle, WA, 98121
Misc., 261

Colored Pencil Society of America
17006 106th Ave. SE, Renton, WA, 98055-5431
To The Point, 67

Communication Architects
PO Box 300, Lynnwood, WA, 98046-0300
National Keyword Forum, 231

Computhink Inc.
15127NE 24th St. #344, Redmond, WA, 98052-5547
Windows Watcher, 242

Connaught Education Services
Box 34069, Dept. 349, Seattle, WA, 98124
Free Materials for Schools & Libraries, 310

Conscience and Military Tax Campaign
4554 12th Ave. NE, Seattle, WA, 98105-4524
Conscience and Military Tax Campaign, 1,142

Copyright Information Services
PO Box 9728, Yakima, WA, 98909-0728
Miller's Copyright Newsletter, 756

•**Cosmic Awareness Communications**
PO Box 115, Olympia, WA, 98507-0115

Cougar Club of America
5810 142nd Place SE, Bellevue, WA, 98006-4318
Sign of the Cat, 76

DRS Geriatric Pub. Co.
4210 95th Ave SE, Mercer Island, WA, 98040-4230
Geriatric Care News, 507

•**Delta Society**
289 Perimeter Rd. E., Renton, WA, 98055-1329

Denali Group, Inc.
2815 NW Pine Cone Dr # 100, Issaquah, WA, 98027-8698
Sales Automation Success, 1,087

•**Editorial Resources, Inc.**
PO Box 20754, Seattle, WA, 98102

Europe Through the Back Door
109 4th Ave N # 2009, Edmonds, WA, 98020-3115
Europe Through the Back Door Travel Newsletter, 1,184

Everett Community College
801 Wetmore Ave, Everett, WA, 98201-1390
Trojan, 207

First Interstate Bank
PO Box 160, Seattle, WA, 98111-0160
Bank Wire, 577

Fisher Families
3960 German Rd., Kettle Falls, WA, 99141-9402
Fisher Families, 453

Ford Galaxie Club of America
PO Box 360, Salkum, WA, 98582-0360
Galaxie Gazette, 73

Frank Haulgren
P.O. Box 3038, Bellingham, WA, 98227
Radio Resistors Bulletin, 472

Frank Parsons
10235 SE 13th Pl, Bellevue, WA, 98004-6728
Frontiers of Freedom, 485

Fred W. Holder
950 S Falcon Rd, Camano Island, WA, 98292-8411
Blacksmith Gazette, 890

Freighter Travel Club of America
3524 Harts Lake Rd., Roy, WA, 98580-9125
Freighter Travel News, 1,184

Friends of Youth, Inc.
16225 NE 87th St Ste A6, Redmond, WA, 98052-3536
Friends of Youth Newsletter, 1,215

GNP Publications
PO Box 8642, Spokane, WA, 99203-8642
Modern Agnostic Journal, The, 1,049

Ginger's Rag
117 E. Louisa St #348, Seattle, WA, 98102
Ginger's Rag, 696

Giraffe Project
197 2nd Street, P O Box 759, Langley, WA, 98260-0759
Giraffe News, 968

Gluten Intolerance Group
PO Box 23053, Seattle, WA, 98102-0353
Gluten Intolerance Group's Newsletter, 933

Golden Companions Club
PO Box 754, Pullman, WA, 99163-0754
Golden Gateway, 1,184

Goodloe Report
PO Box 25736, Seattle, WA, 98125-1236
Goodloe Report, 740

Greater Seattle Chamber of Commerce
1301 Fifth Ste 2400, Seattle, WA, 98101
Perspective, 850

Green River Community College Students
12401 SE 320th St, Auburn, WA, 98092-3622
Knonahi, 207

Greenmoney Journal
W.608 Glass Ave., Spokane, WA, 99205
GreenMoney Journal, 667

HUB Publishing
PO Box 45025, Seattle, WA, 98145-0025
Cheap Leisure Thrills, 411

Haskins-Haskins Annals
2635 153rd Ave SE, Bellevue, WA, 98007-6513
Haskins-Haskins Annals, 455

Hearing, Speech
1620 18th Ave, Seattle, WA, 98122-2739
Speech & Deafness Newsletter, 267

Historical Gardener
1910 N 35th Pl, Mount Vernon, WA, 98273-8981
Historical Gardener, The, 441

History of Science Society, Inc., The
Univ. of Washington, 351330, Seattle, WA, 98195-1330
History of Science Society-Newsletter, 542

Hogrefe & Huber Publishers
P.O. 2487, Kirkland, WA, 98083
Allergy & Clinical Immunology News, 866

Hollywood Stuntmen's Hall of Fame, Inc.
8305 Lewis River Rd., Ariel, WA, 98603-9736
Hollywood Stuntmen's Hall of Fame News, 419

Holyearth Foundation
Box 10697, Winslow, WA, 98110-0697
Earthstewards Network News, 377

Hop Growers of America
PO Box 9218, Yakima, WA, 98909-0218
Hops USA, 103

International Association for the Study of Pain
909 NE 43rd St Ste 306, Seattle, WA, 98105-6020
Intl. Assn. for the Study of Pain-Newsletter, 876

International Bicycle Fund
4887 Columbia Drive S, Seattle, WA, 98108
IBF News, 923

International Society of Appraisers
16040 Christensen Rd., Suite #320, Seattle, WA, 98188-2929
ISA Newsletter, 438

Interstate Professional Applicators Assn.
PO Box 1420, Milton, WA, 98354
Pest Control Progress, 442

Island Grown Publications
1063 Alford Place, Bainbridge Island, WA, 98110
Globalist, The, 666

JSI
P.O. Box 95707, Seattle, WA, 98145-2707
JSI, 913

Jarvis Investment Corp.
PO Box 1031, Kent, WA, 98035-1031
Real Estate Investment, Trends & Opportunities, 1,037

Jerry Buchanan Advertising Agency
PO Box 2038, Vancouver, WA, 98668-2038
War Letter, 899

Judkins Family Assn.
1538 NW 60th St, Seattle, WA, 98107-2328
Judkins Journal, 458

KFH Pubs., Inc.
3530 Bagley Ave. N., Seattle, WA, 98103-9113
Cybernautics Digest, 856

Larry Yoshida
1919 Evergreen Park Dr. SW, Apt 79, Olympia, WA, 98502
Shemp, 262

League of Women Voters of Washington
1406 18th Ave, Seattle, WA, 98122-4126
Washington State Voter, 1,000

Legacy Communications
Unit 271, Box 8110, Blaine, WA, 98230-9966
Profit Letter, The, 683

Lesbian Mothers Natl. Defense Fund
PO Box 21567, Seattle, WA, 98111-3567
Mom's Apple Pie, 445

Lewis County Senior Svcs.
PO Box 297, Chehalis, WA, 98532-0297
Senior Dynamics, 1,109

Life Enthusiast Co-Op
PO Box 4415, Federal Way, WA, 98063-4415
Life Enthusiast Newsletter, 431

•**London Northwest**
929 S Bay Rd NE, Olympia, WA, 98506-4808

Lutheran Bible Institute
Providence Heights, 4221 228 Ave S.E., Issaquah, WA, 98027-9988
Advance, 194

Lutheran Peace Fellowship
1710 11th Ave, Seattle, WA, 98122-2420
PeaceNotes, 996

Marthe Arends
PO Box 1571, Snohomish, WA, 98291-1571
Pioneers- A Computer Genealogy Newslettter, 464

Mathanna Publications
PO Box 5351, Bellingham, WA, 98227-5351
Daycare Health, 503

Medina Children's Services
123 16th Ave, Seattle, WA, 98122-5684
Medina Connection, 1,118

* See **MULTI-PUBLISHER INDEX** for list of publications.

•**Microsoft Press**
One Microsoft Way, Redmond, WA, 98052-6399

Miller's
P.O. Box 8722, Spokane, WA, 99203-0722
Miller's Market Report, 477

Molly Stamos
7621 Aurora Avenue, North Seattle, WA, 98103
The Iron Lung, 1,132

Mountain Rescue Council
PO Box 67, Seattle, WA, 98111-0067
Bertrage, 1,078

Municipal League Foundation
810 3rd Ave., Seattle, WA, 98104
Municipal News, 1,043

Museum of Flight
9404 E Marginal Way S, Seattle, WA, 98108-4097
Museum of Flight News, 906

Mutual Fund Analyst
16212 Bothell-Everett Highway, #F147, Mill Creek, WA, 98012
Mutual Fund Analyst, 678

Myers Finance & Energy
S. 104 Freya St., #214-A, Spokane, WA, 99202
Myers Finance & Energy, 95

N. American Society of Teachers of the Alexander Technique
826 S. Dakes Street, Tacoma, WA, 98405-2726
NASTAT News, 319

N.R. Trading Co.
HCR 77 Box 382, Cosmopolis, WA, 98537-9600
North River Trading Post, 406

Nation Wide Sports Publications
2316 216th Pl NE, Redmond, WA, 98053-6324
Gold Sheet, 434

Natl. Lawyer's Guild-P&D Subcommittee
1205 Smith Tower, Seattle, WA, 98104
Peace & Disarmament News, 995

•**NewsData Corp.**
P.O. Box 900928, Seattle, WA, 98119-9228

Newsletter Publishing Corp.
117 W Mercer St Ste 200, Seattle, WA, 98119-3953
Marple's Business Newsletter, 144

Noble Group
PO Box 491, Bellevue, WA, 98009-0491
Perspective, 20

Noevir Consultant
6817 Rainier Ave. #1742, Gig Harbor, WA, 98335-1920
Small Business & Direct Response=Success, 22

Northeast Washington Genealogical Society
S. 195 Oak, C/O Colville Public Library, Colville, WA, 99114
Pioneer Branches, 464

•**Northwest College**
PO Box 579, Kirkland, WA, 98083-0579

Northwest Indian Fisheries Commission
6730, Dept. DB, Martin Way E., Olympia, WA, 98506
Northwest Indian Fisheries Commission News, 423

Northwest Mining Assn.
10 N Post St Ste 414, Spokane, WA, 99201-0705
Northwest Mining Assn.-Bulletin, 765

Nuclear Waste Program
P.O. Box 47600, Olympia, WA, 98504-7600
Hanford Update Newsletter, 1,203

•**Nuxoll Newsletters**
E. 1419 Marietta Ave., Spokane, WA, 99207

Over 50 and Fit
1202 E. Pike Street Suite #7, P.O. Box 22050, Seattle, WA, 98122
Over 50 and Fit, 523

Pacific First Fedl. Savings
PO Box 91029, Seattle, WA, 98111-9129
Spirit!, 599

Pacific Seabird Group
15 Central Way # 197, Kirkland, WA, 98033-6116
Pacific Seabird Group Bulletin, 942

Pacioli Society
Albers School of Business, Seattle University, Seattle, WA, 98122
Pacioli Society News, 7

•**Palouse Publications**
SE 310 Camino, Pullman, WA, 99163-2206

Paul A. Merriman & Assocs.
1200 Westlake Ave N, Seattle, WA, 98109-3500
Fund Exchange, 665

Peninsula College
Publications, Port Angeles, WA, 98362
Treasure Chest, 207

Penninsula College
Publications, Port Angeles, WA, 98362
Tidepools, 984

Physio Control Corp.
11811 Willows Rd NE, Redmond, WA, 98052-2015
Physio Control Monitor, 595

Piact/Path
4 Nickerson St., Seattle, WA, 98109-1699
Outlook, 523

Pierce County Medical Society
223 Tacoma Ave S, Tacoma, WA, 98402-2513
Pierce County Medical Society Newsletter, 884

Pike Market Senior Center
1931 1st Ave, Seattle, WA, 98101-1092
Parsley, Sage & Time, 1,108

•**Pinnacle Publishing, Inc.**
PO Box 888, 1800 72nd Ave. Ste. 217, Kent, WA, 98035-0888

•**Pioneer Publications**
PO Box 1179, Tum Tum, WA, 99034-1179

Planned Parenthood of Seattle-King County
2211 E Madison St, Seattle, WA, 98112-5336
Planned Parenthood of Seattle-King County, 415

Port of Seattle, Aviation Communications
PO Box 68727, Seattle, WA, 98168-0727
Sea-Tac Forum, 1,180

Premiere Publishing Ltd.
145 NW 85th St Ste 104, Seattle, WA, 98117-3148
Webb Report, The, 156

Prison Mission Assn.
PO Box 1587, Port Orchard, WA, 98366-0146
Mission Newsletter, 1,064

Puget Sound Regional Council
1011 Western Avenue, #500, Seattle, WA, 98104-1035
Regional View, 1,043

Quicksoft
219 1st Ave. N., #224, Seattle, WA, 98109
Quick Notes, 234

R.W. Beck
2101 4th Ave Ste 600, Seattle, WA, 98121-2375
Update, 364

Reading Reform Foundation
PO Box 98785, Tacoma, WA, 98498-0785
Sounds of Reading, 330

Real Estate Div.
Box 247, Olympia, WA, 98504-0001
Washington, 1,039

Redmond Communications
2661 Bel-Red Road Ste201, Bellevue, WA, 98008-5544
Microsoft Directions, 230

Renton Historical Society
235 Mill Ave. S, Renton, WA, 98055-2133
Renton Historical Society Newsletter, 547

Russian Far East Update
PO Box 22126, Seattle, WA, 98122
Russian Far East Update, 651

Ruth Dykeman Center
1033 SW 152nd St, Seattle, WA, 98166-1845
Ruth Dykeman Center Community Report, 1,121

•**SPIE International Society for Optical Engineering**
1000 20th St., Bellingham, WA, 98225-6705

St. Nicholas School
13510 1st Ave NE, Seattle, WA, 98125-3021
St. Nicholas News, 597

Saving Energy
5411 117th Ave SE, Bellevue, WA, 98006-3324
Saving Energy, 358

Seafood Trend Assoc.
8227 Ashworth Ave N, Seattle, WA, 98103-4434
Seafood Trend Newsletter, 432

Seattle Arts Commission
312 1st Ave. N, 2nd Floor, Seattle, WA, 98109-4501
Seattle Arts Newsletter, 262

Seattle Buddhist Church
1427 S Main St, Seattle, WA, 98144-2034
Seattle Betsuin, 1,054

Seattle City Light
1015 3rd Ave # 809, Seattle, WA, 98104-1198
Network, 591

Seattle Design
2601 Elliott Ave Ste 4119, Seattle, WA, 98121-1326
Newsletter Seattle Design, 625

Seattle Folklore Society
PO Box 30141, Seattle, WA, 98103-0141
S.F.S. Flyer, 425

Seattle Professional Engineering Employees Association
15205 52nd Ave S, Seattle, WA, 98188-2336
SPEEA Spotlite, 710

Seattle Public Library
1000 4th Ave, Seattle, WA, 98104-1193
Bookmark, 794

Seattle Public Schools
815 4th Ave. N., Seattle, WA, 98109-3902
Focus on Seattle Public Schools, 310

Seattle Teachers Assn.
720 Nob Hill Ave N, Seattle, WA, 98109-4195
STA News, 329

Seattle Univ.
12th & E. Columbia, Seattle, WA, 98122
Fragments, 207

•**Securities Sources**
Box 85600, Univ. Station, Seattle, WA, 98145-1600

Simpson Investment Information Services
1301 5th Ave. #1200, Seattle, WA, 98101-2613
Simpson Timber Company-Newsletter, 598

Single Father Advocate
PO Box 55443, Seattle, WA, 98155-0443
Father Rights News, 814

Sister of Providence Hospital
Public Relations, Everett, WA, 98206
Pacesetter, 570

Society for the Protection of Old Fishes, Inc.
School Of Fisheries Wh-10, Univ. Of Washington, Seattle, WA, 98195-0001
Spoof Newsletter, 937

Spectrum of Rainbows
372 Kcahhane Rd., Sequim, WA, 98382-1958
Illustrator Collector's News, The, 184

Spokane Chamber of Commerce
W. 1020 Riverside, Spokane, WA, 99201
Spokane Affairs, 162

Spokane Microcomputer Users Group
Box 10562, Spokane, WA, 99209-0562
SMUG Notes, 237

Starbucks Coffee Co.
2203 Airport Way South, P.O. Box 34510, Seattle, WA, 98124-1510
Coffee Matters, 103

State of Washington
1111 Washington St. South E, P.O. Box 47001, Olympia, WA, 98504-0001
Totem, 395

State of Washington, Dept. of Licensing
Box 9012, Olympia, WA, 98504-0001
Real Estate News, 1,038

Staveley NDT Technologies, Inc.
421 N Quay St, Kennewick, WA, 99336-7735
Staveley NDTech News, 851

T.I.C.N.
PO Box 1958, Sequim, WA, 98382-1958
Illustrator Magazine & Paper Collector's News, 184

Tacoma Dept. Public Utilities
PO Box 11007, Tacoma, WA, 98411-0007
Utilbits, 602

Tacoma-Pierce County Humane Society
2608 S Center St, Tacoma, WA, 98409-7602
Brief Paws, 49

Tacoma Public Library
1102 Tacoma Ave S, Tacoma, WA, 98402-2098
Offline, 593

Tea Times
PO Box 841, Langley, WA, 98260-0841
Tea Times, 105

Ted Rosen
P.O. Box 4257, Bellingham, WA, 98227
Smelly Hampster, 998

The Tenants Union
3902 S Ferdinand St, Seattle, WA, 98118-1740
Renter's Rag, 791

TidBITS
27541 SE 154th Pl., Issaquah, WA, 98027-7340
TidBITS, 241

Tim Paul
5208 18 NE, Seattle, WA, 98105
Subway Surfer, 556

Towers Club Press, Inc.
9107 NW 11th Ave, Vancouver, WA, 98665-6801
Towers Club Information Marketing Report, 23

Transafety, Inc.
PO Box 3100, Sequim, WA, 98382-5006
Transafety Reporter, 1,085

* See **MULTI-PUBLISHER INDEX** for list of publications.

Twin Peaks Press
PO Box 129, Vancouver, WA, 98666-0129
Helen Hecker's Hotline - Marketing Strategies for Publishers & Entrepreneur's, 118

Unique
6716 Eastside Dr. N.E., Suite 12-M, Brown's Point, WA, 98422-1114
Unique & Exotic Travel Reporter, 1,191

United Research
1020 108th Ave NE Ste 102, Bellevue, WA, 98004-4310
Peak Performance, 524

U.S. Dept. of Agriculture
2015 S 1st St Rm 4, Yakima, WA, 98903-2231
National Honey Market News, 44

U.S. Energy Research
Rockwell Intl., Atomics Intl., Richland, WA, 99352
Hanford News, 354

U.S. Navy, Code 165.4
Puget Sound Naval Shipyard, Bremerton, WA, 98314-0001
Salute, 1,112

University Friends Meeting
4001 9th Ave NE, Seattle, WA, 98105-6410
Gleamings, 1,074

Univ. of Washington
Engineering Annex, Fm-12, Seattle, WA, 98195-0001
Environmental Outlook, 381

Univ. of Washington Inst. for Public Policy
324 Parrington Hall, Dc-14, Seattle, WA, 98195-0001
Washington Policy Choices, 1,025

Univ. of Washington, School of Public Health
Dept. Of Environmental Health, Seattle, WA, 98195-0001
Environmental Health News, 380

University of Washington, School of Social Work
4101 15th Ave. NE, Seattle, WA, 98185-6299
University of Washington Forum, 1,123

Wagons of Steel
PO Box 1435, Vashon, WA, 98070-1435
Wagons of Steel, 77

•**Warren Publishing House, Inc.**
PO Box 2250, Everett, WA, 98203-0250

Washington Education Association
33434 8th Ave S, Auburn, WA, 98003-6323
WEA Action, 336

Washington Physicians for Social Responsibility
4554 12th Ave. NE, Seattle, WA, 98105-4524
Remedy, 998

Washington Research Council
1301 5th Ave Ste 2810, Seattle, WA, 98101-2603
WRC Notebook, 1,025

Washington State Dental Assn
2033 6th Ave Ste 333, Seattle, WA, 98121-2514
WSDA News, 272

Washington State Dental Hygienists' Assn.
PO Box 389, Lynnwood, WA, 98046-0389
WSDHA Newsletter, 272

Washington State Dept. of Emergency Mgt.
4220 E. Martin Way, Olympia, WA, 98504-0001
Washington Emergency Management News, 1,139

Washington State Dept. of Social & Health
Mail Stop Ob-46, Olympia, WA, 98504-0001
Connections, 1,116

Washington State Employment Security Dept.
PO Box 29, Kelso, WA, 98626-0002
Local Labor Market Developments; Longview Office, 703

Washington State Energy Office
809 Legion Way, SE, Olympia, WA, 98504-0001
WSEO Dispatch, 358

Washington State Insurance Commissioner's Office
Insurance Bldg., Aq-21, Olympia, WA, 98504-0001
Insurance Action Review, 620

Washington State Library
Aj-11, Olympia, WA, 98504-0001
Washington State Publications, 107

Washington State Lottery
Box 43000, Olympia, WA, 98504-0001
Lottery Retailer, 439

Washington State School Directors' Assn
221 College St NE, Olympia, WA, 98516-5313
Signal, 1,094

Washington State University English Dept.
Publications, Pullman, WA, 99164-0001
Cauda Pavonis: Studies in Hermeticism, 820

Washington State Univ. Libraries
Holland 221, Pullman, WA, 99163-5610
Record, 808

• See **MULTI-PUBLISHER INDEX** for list of publications.

Washington State Univ.-Long Beach
Research & Extension Unit, Rt. 1, Box 570, Long Beach, WA, 98631
Cranberry Vine, 39

Water Supply & Waste Section
Mail Stop Ld-11, Olympia, WA, 98504-0001
Water Tap, 1,205

•**Weidner Words**
2206 W Borden Rd, Spokane, WA, 99204-9668

Western Washington DX Club, Inc.
PO Box 224, Mercer Island, WA, 98040-0224
Totem Tabloid, 182

Wright Group, The
19201 120th Ave NE, Bothell, WA, 98011-9507
Whole Idea, The, 336

Writers Information Network
PO Box 11337, Bainbridge Island, WA, 98110-5337
Writers Information Network, 984

Yakima Valley Community College
PO Box 1647, Yakima, WA, 98907-1647
Hubcaps, 207

West Virginia

Alderson Hospitality House
PO Box 579, Alderson, WV, 25904-0579
Trumpet, The, 780

American Assn. for Correctional Psychology
WV Graduate College, 100 Angus E. Peyton Drive, South Charleston, WV, 25303-1600
Correctional Psychologist, The, 1,013

American Typecasting Fellowship
PO Box 263, Terra Alta, WV, 26764-0263
American Typecasting Fellowship Newsletter, 1,003

Ancient Mystic Order of Samaritans
974 Willey St, Morgantown, WV, 26505-5149
AMOS Realm, 1,061

Appalachia Educational Laboratory, Inc.
PO Box 1348, Charleston, WV, 25325-1348
Link, 316

Appalachian Bible College
Student Services, PO Box ABC, Bradley, WV, 25818
Introspect, 194

Assn. of Medical Rehabilitation Administrators
1733 Forest Hills Dr, Vienna, WV, 26105-3313
Newsletter of Medical Rehabilitation Administrators, 521

Automobile License Plate Collectors Assn.
Box 77, Horner, WV, 26372
ALPCA Newsletter, 550

Boone County Genealogical Society
PO Box 306, Madison, WV, 25130-0306
Boone Genealogical Quarterly, 448

Brooks Bird Club
707 Warwood Ave, Wheeling, WV, 26003-6958
Mail Bag, 942

CNG Transmission Corp.
PO Box 2450, Clarksburg, WV, 26302-2450
Main line, 589

Catholic Committee of Appalachia
PO Box 662, Webster Springs, WV, 26288-0662
Patchquilt, 1,059

ERIC Clearinghouse on Rural Education
PO Box 1348, Charleston, WV, 25325-1348
ERIC/CRESS Bulletin, 307

Fenton Art Glass Collectors of America, Inc.
PO Box 384, Williamstown, WV, 26187-0384
Butterfly Net, 52

Fostoria Glass Society of America
PO Box 826, Moundsville, WV, 26041-0826
Facets of Fostoria, 479

General Motors Corp.
1000 Warm Springs Ave, Martinsburg, WV, 25401-3800
Martinsburg Monitor, 590

Goodenow Family Association
Rt. 2 Box 718, Shepherdstown, WV, 25443
Goodenow's Ghosts, 455

Home Economics Education Assn.
122 Broadview Ave, Fairmont, WV, 26554-1422
Home Economics Educator, 558

Marshall Univ.
Publications, Huntington, WV, 25705
Parthenon, 207

Morgantown Area Chamber of Commerce
PO Box 658, Morgantown, WV, 26507-0658
Morgantown Area Chamber of Commerce Newsletter, 160

Mountain State Mended Hearts
PO Box 4665, Star City, WV, 26504
Heart Net, 512

•**Natl. Institute for Urban Wildlife**
P.O. Box 3015, Shepherdstown, WV, 25443-3015

Old West Shop Publishing
Box 5232-19, Vienna, WV, 26105
Westerner, The, 473

Pumbedissa
PO Box 117, Seneca Rocks, WV, 26884-0117
Pumbedissa, 1,070

Quest for Knowledge
5289 Preston St., Clarksburg, WV, 26301-3748
Showers of Blessings, 1,051

Ritchie Co. Historical Society
200 S Church St, Harrisville, WV, 26362-1246
Ritchie County Historical Society Newsletter, 465

Software Strategies & Tactics Inc.
Rr 2 Box 713, Harpers Ferry, WV, 25425-9416
Ada Strategies, 211

South Charleston Chamber of Commerce
411 1/2 D St, South Charleston, WV, 25303-3107
South Charleston Chamber of Commerce Newsletter, 162

Tri-County Researcher
PO Box 196, Proctor, WV, 26055-0196
Tri-County Researcher, 468

•**West Virginia Bureau of Employment Programs**
112 California Ave., Charleston, WV, 25305-0112

West Virginia Chamber of Commerce
PO Box 2789, Charleston, WV, 25330-2789
West Virginia Business Index, 156

West Virginia Institute of Technology
Publications, Montgomery, WV, 25136
Current Library Acquisitions, 106

West Virginia Legionnaire
PO Box 3191, Charleston, WV, 25332-3191
West Virginia Legionnaire, 1,199

•**West Virginia Library Commission**
Cultural Center, Charleston, WV, 25305

West Virginia Music Educators Assn., Inc. Hall of Fine Arts
West Liberty State College, West Liberty, WV, 26074-0335
Notes A Tempo, 915

West Virginia Scenic Trails Assn.
633 West Virginia Ave, Morgantown, WV, 26505-6764
Whoop 'N' Holler, 944

West Virginia School Boards Assn.
PO Box 1008, Charleston, WV, 25324-1008
On Board, 1,092

West Virginia State Dept. of Agriculture
1900 Kanawha Blvd E, Charleston, WV, 25305-0002
West Virginia Department of Agriculture Market Bulletin, 47

West Virginia State Dept. of Ed. & The Arts
Cultural Ctr., 1900 Kanawha Blvd. E., Charleston, WV, 25305-0300
Patterns, 261

West Virginia University Libraries
Box 6069, Morgantown, WV, 26506-6069
West Virginia & Regional History Collection-Newsletter, 550

West Virginia Univ. Printing Services
112 Communications Bldg., Evansville, WV, 26690
Agricultural & Forestry Experiment Station Bulletin, 36

•**West Virginia Univ. School of Journalism**
Box 6010, Morgantown, WV, 26506-6010

Wisconsin

9 to 5 Natl. Assn. of Working Women
238 W Wisconsin Ave Ste 700, Milwaukee, WI, 53203-2308
9 to 5 Newsletter, 1,205

ASCU
PO Box 5488, Madison, WI, 53705-0488
First Friday, 90

Airdance Inc
PO Box 708, Brookfield, WI, 53008-0708
B.C Contact!, 27

Altus Inc
PO Box 17869, Milwaukee, WI, 53217-0869
Anderson Report, 212

American Academy of Allergy & Immunology
611 E. Wells St., Milwaukee, WI, 53202-3889
Asthma & Allergy Advocate, 867

American College of Legal Medicine
611 East Wells Street, Milwaukee, WI, 53202
American College of Legal Medicine, Notes from the President, 866

American Communications Exchange
312 E Wisconsin Ave Ste 601, Milwaukee, WI, 53202-4305
Wireline, 272

American Institute of the History of Pharmacy
425 N. Charter Street, Madison, WI, 53706
AIHP Notes, 535

American Soc. of Agronomy
677 S Segoe Rd, Madison, WI, 53711-1048
Agronomy News, 37

•**Antique Outboard Motor Club, Inc.**
PO Box 09293, Milwaukee, WI, 53209-0293

Antique Snowmobile Club of America
217 W Alta Loma Cir, Thiensville, WI, 53092-1719
Iron Dog Tracks, 1,112

Arnold Investment Counsel, Inc.
700 N. Water St., Milwaukee, WI, 53202-4255
Primary Trend, 682

Arnold Jeffcoat
PO Box 25, Iola, WI, 54945-0025
Arnold Jeffcoat's Money Matters, 654

Art Factory, The
1025 West Seminary, Richland Center, WI, 53581
Scrollsaw Chatter, 256

ArthritiSource
2045 Kassner Drive, Green Bay, WI, 54304
Arthritis News, 498

•**Assets Protection Publishing**
P.O. Box 5323, Madison, WI, 53705-0323

Association of Family and Conciliation Courts
329 W Wilson St Rm 241, Madison, WI, 53703-3612
Association of Family and Conciliation Courts Newsletter, 716

August Derleth Society
PO Box 481, Sauk City, WI, 53583
August Derleth Society Newletter, 536

Badger Assocs. of the Blind
912 N. Hawley Rd., Milwaukee, WI, 53213-3298
Badger Informer, 110

Banta Company
PO Box 60, Menasha, WI, 54952-0060
Ecology Notes, 1,004

•**Beacon Health Corp.**
1001 W. Glen Oaks Ln., Suite 104, Mequon, WI, 53092-3366

Best Power Technology
PO Box 280, Necedah, WI, 54646-0280
Horizons, 338

Black Hawk Council of Girl Scouts
2710 Ski Ln, Madison, WI, 53713-3267
Semaphore, 598

•**Blue Cross Blue Shield United of Wisconsin**
401 W Michigan St, Milwaukee, WI, 53203-2804

Burrus Research Assoc., Inc.
PO Box 26413, Milwaukee, WI, 53226-0413
Technotrends Newsletter, 1,101

C.H. Raine
1320 Wisconsin Ave, Racine, WI, 53403-1978
Contemporary Health Journal, 503

C.P. Gauger & Co.
8450 W Forest Home Ave, Milwaukee, WI, 53228-3416
DB Publisher, 1,004

•**Carolyn Habelman**
RR 3, Box 253, Black River Falls, WI, 54615-9405

Casa Maria Catholic Worker
1131 N 21st St # 5206, Milwaukee, WI, 53233-1110
Casa Cry, 1,115

Center for Public Representation
121 S. Pinckney St., Madison, WI, 53703-3338
Public Eye, 771

Circle
PO Box 219, Mount Horeb, WI, 53572-0219
Pagan Spirit Alliance Newsletter, 1,074

Coalition of Women's Art Organizations
123 E. Beutel Rd., Port Washington, WI, 53074-1103
CWAO News, 64

Colombia Support Network
PO Box 1505, Madison, WI, 53701
Action on Colombia, 171

•**Committee Against Registration & Draft**
PO Box 262, Madison, WI, 53701-0262

Concerned Consumers League
436 West Wisconsin Avenue, Milwaukee, WI, 53203-2105
Consumer Forum, 252

Cornish American Heritage Society
Chy An Eglos, 2405 N. Brookfield Rd., Brookfield, WI, 53045
Tam Kernewek, 400

Correctional Service Federation-U.S.A.
436 W. Wisconsin Ave., Milwaukee, WI, 53203-2105
Correctional Service Federation-U.S.A. Newsletter, 785

•**Credit Union National Association, Inc.**
5710 Mineral Point, Madison, WI, 53705

Cutler-Hammer Inc.
4201 N 27th St, Milwaukee, WI, 53216-1807
Cutler-Hammer Record, 581

Dairyland Power Cooperative
PO Box 817, La Crosse, WI, 54602-0817
Short Circuits, 598

Dajja Enterprises
PO Box 24, Cambridge, WI, 53523-0024
AM Journal, 122

Dancers' Dateline
PO Box 346, Random Lake, WI, 53075-0346
Dancers' Dateline, 266

Danielle Consultants
PO Box 27688, Milwaukee, WI, 53227-0688
RTW Review, 55

Dodgeville Reminder
108 E. Merrimac St., Dodgeville, WI, 53533
Dodgeville Reminder, 25

Dr. Paul Dettloff
Rt #3, Arcadia, WI, 54612-9803
Cream Separator and Dairy Newsletter, 264

Dykes, Disability & Stuff
PO Box 8773, Madison, WI, 53708-8773
Dykes, Disability & Stuff, 277

EAA
PO Box 3086, Oshkosh, WI, 54903-3086
Technical Counselor Newsletters, 182

Easter Seal Soc. of Wis. Inc.
101 Nob Hill Rd Rm 301, Madison, WI, 53713-3969
Easter Seal Network News, 582

•**Edgewood College**
855 Woodrow St, Madison, WI, 53711-1997

Education Forward
PO Box 7841, Madison, WI, 53707-7841
Education Forward, 308

Einhorn Assocs., Inc.
2323 N Mayfair Rd Ste 490, Milwaukee, WI, 53226-1507
Einhorn Newsletter, 164

Engineers & Scientists of Milwaukee, Inc.
PO Box 644, Milwaukee, WI, 53201-0644
Milwaukee Engineering, 362

Environmental Information Services, Ltd.
PO Box 391, Brookfield, WI, 53008-0391
Wisconsin Environmental Law and Regulation Report, 397

Equitable Reserve Association
116 S. Commercial St., Box 448, Neenah, WI, 54956-3080
Equitable Reserve Guide, 178

•**Experimental Aircraft Association, Inc.**
EAA Aviation Center, 3000 Poberezny Rd., Oshkosh, WI, 54903-3086

•**FINL-Financial Independent Network Ltd., Inc.**
310 Second St., Boscobel, WI, 53805-1164

Families International
11700 W Lake Park Dr, Milwaukee, WI, 53224-3044
Newswire, 414

The Father, The Son
P.O. Box 561, Milwaukee, WI, 53007
The Father, The Son, 283

Festive Occasions
1205 Cliffwood Ln, La Crosse, WI, 54601-6084
Festivities, 369

First Natl. Bank
I S. Pinckney St., Madison, WI, 53701
Newsbriefs, 592

Fishing Hot Spots
1999 River St, Rhinelander, WI, 54501-2457
Fishing Hot Spots 'Newsline', 606

•**Forest Products Society**
2801 Marshall Ct., Madison, WI, 53705-2257

Fox Co., The
1100 W. Beecher., W. Allis, WI, 53227
Greater Milwaukee Dental Bulletin, 269

G. Wentworth Smith
PO Box 71, Columbus, WI, 53925-0071
Commercial Carpet Digest, 437

Gavarti Assocs. Ltd.
9240 N Sleepy Hollow Rd, Milwaukee, WI, 53217-1240
Tribology News, 851

General Motors Corp.
PO Box 629, Janesville, WI, 53547-0629
Daily Newsline, 581

Giddings & Lewis, Inc.
142 Doty St., PO Box 590, Fond Du Lac, WI, 54935-0590
Reaching Out, 596

Golda Meir Library
University of Wisconsin, Box 604, Milwaukee, WI, 53201-0604
Golda Meir Library Newsletter, 798

Greater LaCrosse Area C of C
PO Box 219, La Crosse, WI, 54602-0219
Update, 162

Harnischfeger Corp.
PO Box 554, Milwaukee, WI, 53201-0554
Noon News, 593

Hawkhill Assocs., Inc.
125 E. Gilman St., PO Box 1029, Madison, WI, 53701-1029
Hawkhill Science Newsletter, 1,097

Her Own Words
PO Box 5264, Madison, WI, 53705
Her Own Words, 925

Industrial Relations Research Association
University of Wisconsin, 1180 Observatory Dr., Madison, WI, 53706-1393
IRRA Newsletter, 612

Institute for Research on Poverty
1800 Observatory Dr.,, 3412 Soc. Sci., Madison, WI, 53706
Focus, 292

•**InterVarsity Christian Fellowship**
PO Box 7895, Madison, WI, 53707-7895

Intl. Council for Bird Preservation
Dept. of Wildlife Ecology, Uni, Madison, WI, 53706
International Council for Bird Preservation U.S. Section Newsletter, 942

International Crane Foundation
E11376 Shady Lane Rd, Baraboo, WI, 53913-9778
ICF Bugle, 942

International Endometriosis Assn.
8585 N 76th Pl, Milwaukee, WI, 53223-2633
Endometriosis Assn. International Newsletter, 505

•**International Foundation of Employee Benefit Plans**
18700 W Bluemound Rd #69, P O Box 69, Brookfield, WI, 53008-0069

Intl. Society of Certified Employee Benefit Specialists
18700 W. Bluemound Road, PO Box 209, Brookfield, WI, 53008-0209
Newsbriefs, 613

•**J.J. Keller & Assoc., Inc.**
PO Box 368, Neenah, WI, 54957-0368

•**JK Publishing Inc.**
PO Box 71020, Milwaukee, WI, 53211-7120

James Rhem & Associates, Inc.
213 Potter Street, Madison, WI, 53715
National Teaching & Learning Forum, 321

John C. Stauber
3318 Gregory St, Madison, WI, 53711
PR Watch, 20

Johnson Hill Press, Inc.
1233 Janesville Ave., PO Box 803, Ft. Atkinson, WI, 53538-0803
Ag Industry Watch, 36

Johnson Wax
1525 Howe St, Racine, WI, 53403-2236
Johnson Wax Weekly, 588

•**Jones Publishing Inc.**
N7450 Aanstad Rd., PO Box 5000, Iola, WI, 54945-5000

Journal/Sentinel Inc.
333 W State St, Milwaukee, WI, 53203-1305
Journal/Sentinel Ink, 588

•**Krause Publications, Inc.**
700 E. State St., Iola, WI, 54990-0001

Lac Courte Oreilles Ojibwa Community College
Rr 2 Box 2357, Hayward, WI, 54843-9419
Lac Courte Oreilles Ojibwa Community College News, 207

Leader, The
116 E Main St, Evansville, WI, 53536-1124
Leader, The, 25

* See **MULTI-PUBLISHER INDEX** for list of publications.

·Lessiter Publications
PO Box 624, Brookfield, WI, 53008-0624

Lincoln Fellowship of Wisconsin
1923 Grange Ave, Racine, WI, 53403-2328
Lincoln Ledger, 543

·Liturgical Pubs., Inc.
2875 S James Dr, New Berlin, WI, 53151-3662

MacWhyte Wire Rope Co.
2906 14th Ave, Kenosha, WI, 53140-5028
Macwhyte Whyte Line, 589

Madison Astrological Society
302 S Brooks St, Madison, WI, 53715-1502
Four Elements, 68

Madison Public Library Staff Assn.
201 W Mifflin St, Madison, WI, 53703-2511
Listening Post, 803

·Magna Publications, Inc.
611 N Sherman Ave, Madison, WI, 53704-4410

Mail Order Spice House
PO Box 1633, Milwaukee, WI, 53201-1633
Mail Order Spice House, 431

Major Trends
250 W. Coventry Court, Milwaukee, WI, 53217-3963
Major Trends, 675

Manitowoc County Historical Society
PO Box 574, Manitowoc, WI, 54221-0574
Manitowoc County Historical Society Pinecrest Spirit Newsletter, 543

Maranatha Baptist Bible College
745 W Main St, Watertown, WI, 53094-7638
Messenger, The, 208

Marinette Area C of C
PO Box 512, Marinette, WI, 54143-0512
Chamber of Commerce Memo, 158

·Marklin, Inc.
16988 W Victor Rd # 51319, New Berlin, WI, 53151-4135

Marquette Univ.
1212 W. Wisconsin Ave., Rm 315, PO Box 1881, Milwaukee, WI, 53201-1881
News & Views, 208

Master Brewers Assn of America
2421 N. Mayfair Rd., #310, Wauwatosa, WI, 53226-1407
Master Brewers Association of America Communications, 104

Medical Society of Milwaukee County
1126 S 70th St Ste S-507, Milwaukee, WI, 53214-3151
Membership Newsletter, 880

Metropolitan Milwaukee Association of Commerce
756 N. Milwaukee St., Milwaukee, WI, 53202-3719
Milwaukee Commerce Hot-Line, 160

Miller Brewing Co.
3939 W Highland Blvd, Milwaukee, WI, 53208-2866
Miller Management Briefing, 104

Milwaukee Adv. Club
231 W Wisconsin Ave Ste 701, Milwaukee, WI, 53203-2306
Torch, 23

Milwaukee Fire Dept.
711 W Wells St, Milwaukee, WI, 53233-1479
M.F.D. Register, 589

Milwaukee Grain Exchange
1900 S Harbor Dr, Milwaukee, WI, 53207-1027
Milwaukee Grain Exchange, Market Report, 418

Milwaukee Institute of Art & Design
273 E Erie St, Milwaukee, WI, 53202-6003
Ideas, Information & People, 194

Milwaukee Public Library
814 W Wisconsin Ave, Milwaukee, WI, 53233-2309
Milwaukee Reader, 804

Milwaukee Repertory Theater
108 E Wells St, Milwaukee, WI, 53202-3525
Prologue, 1,174

Milwaukee School of Engineering
1025 N Milwaukee St # 644, Milwaukee, WI, 53202-3118
President's Forum, 363

Mirro Aluminum Co.
1512 Washington St, Manitowoc, WI, 54220-5046
Mixing Bowl, 590

Modine Mfg. Co.
1500 De Koven Ave, Racine, WI, 53403-2540
ShopTalk, 76

Monroe City Hist. Soc.
PO Box 422, Sparta, WI, 54656-0422
Historical Time Capsules of Monroe County, 541

Moon Star Enterprises
PO Box 1718, Milwaukee, WI, 53201-1718
Winged Chariot, The, 68

Moose Ear Press
2722 County Park Road, P.O. Box 335, Chete, WI, 54728
Bridging The Gap, 973

NFDA Publications Inc.
11121 W Oklahoma Ave, P.O. Box 27641, Milwaukee, WI, 53227-0641
State Officers Bulletin, 437

Natl. Assn. for the Advancement of Aardvarks in America
947 Perkins Ave, Waukesha, WI, 53186-5247
Aardvarks in the News, 48

Natl. Assn. of Professors of Hebrew
1220 Linden Dr, Madison, WI, 53706-1525
Iggeret, 822

National Association for Retired Credit Union People
5910 Mineral Point Rd, Madison, WI, 53705-4456
Prime Line Bulletin, 816

Natl. Assn of Rocketry
1311 Edgewood Dr, Altoona, WI, 54720-2528
Sport Marketry, 33

National Butterfly Association
C/o Barnett Boat Company, 534 Commercial Avenue, Green Lake, WI, 54941
Butterflyer, The, 113

National Coalition for Campus Child Care, Inc.
PO Box 258, Cascade, WI, 53011-0258
NCCCC Newsletter, 170

National Federation of Catholic Physicians Guilds
850 Elm Grove Rd., Elm Grove, WI, 53122-2527
National Federation of Catholic Physicians Guilds Newsletter, 881

·Natl. Fluid Power Assn.
3333 N Mayfair Rd Ste 311, Milwaukee, WI, 53222-3219

Natl. Registration Center for Study Abroad
PO Box 1393, Milwaukee, WI, 53201-1393
New Horizons, 322

·National Sports Law Institute
Marquette Univ. Law School, P.O Box 1881, Milwaukee, WI, 53201-1881

National Telemedia Council
120 E Wilson St, Madison, WI, 53703-3423
Telemedium, 862

National Time Equipment Association
PO Box 13848, Milwaukee, WI, 53213-0848
Times, 241

·Ne-Naiah-Kaha-Kok
PO Box 1055, Keshena, WI, 54135-1055

Neuroelectric Soc., Inc.
Med. Col. of Wisconsin,, 8700 W. Wisconsin Ave., Milwaukee, WI, 53226
Neuroelectric News, 881

New Frontiers Center. Inc.
Rr 1, Oregon, WI, 53575-9801
New Frontiers, 922

Nicolet Federated Library System
515 Pine St, Green Bay, WI, 54301-5194
Nicolet Compass, 806

Norwegian Tracks
4909 Sherwood Rd, Madison, WI, 53711-1343
Norwegian Tracks, 463

Order of the Upright Ostrich
2824 N Stowell Ave, Milwaukee, WI, 53211-3774
Upright Ostrich, 999

Organization Development Corporation
PO Box 312, Mukwonago, WI, 53149
Re-Designing Customer Service, 149

Paragon Electric Co., Inc.
PO Box 28, Two Rivers, WI, 54241-0028
Parascope, 594

Parke Society, Inc.
P O Box 590, Milwaukee, WI, 53201
Parke Society Newsletter, 464

Per Adams
PO Box 376, Cameron, WI, 54822-0376
Male Call, 890

Pharmacy Week
PO Box 552, Madison, WI, 53701
Pharmacy Week, 348

·PhotoSource Intl.
Pine Lake Farm, 1910 35th Rd., Osceola, WI, 54020-5602

Polish Festivals, Inc.
7128 W Rawson Ave, Franklin, WI, 53132-9280
Dom Polski, 407

Priests of the Sacred Heart
Hales Corners, WI, 53130
Reign of the Sacred Heart, 1,059

Professional Reactor Operator Society
PO Box 181, Mishicot, WI, 54228-0181
Professional Reactor Operator Society-The Communicator, 927

Project Equality of Wisconsin, Inc.
1442 N Farwell Ave Ste 210, Milwaukee, WI, 53202-2913
Project Equality of Wisconsin-Newsletter & Buyers' Guide, 704

Rawski & Associates
PO Box 815, Minocqua, WI, 54568
Employment Trends, 343

Reply Coupon Collector
PO Box 165, Somers, WI, 53171-0165
Reply Coupon Collector, 555

Ronald Sadoff's Major Trends
250 W. Coventry, Milwaukee, WI, 53217-3961
Ronald Sadoff's Major Trends, 684

Royal R. LeMier & Co.
S7720 State Rd. 37, Eau Claire, WI, 54701-9075
Mutual Fund Specialist, 679

·Runzheimer Intl.
Runzheimer Park, Rochester, WI, 53167

Rural Network, Inc.
6236 Borden Rd, Boscobel, WI, 53805-9715
Rural Network Advocate, 816

Saint Francis Seminary
3257 S Lake Dr, Saint Francis, WI, 53235-3795
Salt of the Earth, 208

St. Joseph's Hospital
5000 W Chambers St, Milwaukee, WI, 53210-1688
Perspective, 570

Science for the Handicapped Assn.
C/O Ben Thompson, SHA/UWEC Brewer 271, Eau Claire, WI, 54701
Science for the Handicapped Good Newsletter, 329

Scouter's Digest
PO Box 1052, Marinette, WI, 54143-6052
Scouter's Digest, 1,215

Secura Insurance
2401 S Memorial Dr, Appleton, WI, 54915-1429
Viewpoint, 602

Sentry Insurance
1800 N Point Dr, Stevens Point, WI, 54482-0001
Sentry News, 598

Sheboygan Chamber of Commerce
712 Riverfront Dr., #101, Sheboygan, WI, 53081-4665
Sheboygan Chamber of Commerce, Monthly Newsletter, 161

Shenadoah Newsletter Co.
736 W Oklahoma St, Appleton, WI, 54914-3733
Shenandoah Newsletter, 406

Simplicity Manufacturing Co.
500 N. Spring St., Port Washington, WI, 53074-1752
Power News, The, 595

Society of the Divine Savior
Salvatorian Center, New Holstein, WI, 53062-0001
Hope, A Salvatorian Newsletter, 1,057

Southeastern Wisconsin Regional Planning Commission
916 N East Ave # 1607, Waukesha, WI, 53186-4808
SEWRPC Newsletter, 1,024

·State Historical Society of Wisconsin
816 State St., Madison, WI, 53706-1488

Swiss Connection, The
2845 N 72nd St, Milwaukee, WI, 53210-1106
Swiss Connection, The, 468

Technimet Corp.
2345 S 170th St, New Berlin, WI, 53151-2701
Technimet Topics, 363

Trees for Tomorrow Inc.
611 Sheridan St., Eagle River, WI, 54521
Northbound, 436

Truth, Inc.
10100 W. Blue Mound Rd., Wauwatosa, WI, 53226
Vatican Voices, 1,060

U.S. Curling Assn.
C/O Elgie Noble, Box 428, Poynette, WI, 53955
North American Curling News, 1,133

·Univ. of Wisconsin
1207 Seminole Hwy, Madison, WI, 53711-3726

Univ. of Wisconsin, Dept. of Plant Pathology
1630 Linden Dr, Madison, WI, 53706-1520
Phytophthora Newsletter, 121

Univ. of Wisconsin, Extension Services in Pharmacy
Pharmacy Bldg. Rm. 2308, Madison, WI, 53706
Wisconsin Pharmacy Extension Bulletin, 289

·Univ. of Wisconsin Hospitals
1300 University Ave, Madison, WI, 53706-1510

---

* See **MULTI-PUBLISHER INDEX** for list of publications.

©1996, Oxbridge Communications, Inc.

Univ. of Wisconsin, Industrial Relations Research Inst.
1180 Observatory Dr, Madison, WI, 53706-1320
WIRRA News, 194

Univ. Wisconsin-Madison
New Student Services, 905 University Ave., Ste.1, Madison, WI, 53715-1005
Information/the WAFLT Bulletin, 822

Univ. of Wisconsin Sea Grant Institute
1800 University Ave, Madison, WI, 53705-4090
Littoral Drift, 386

Univ. of Wisconsin, South Asian Area Ctr.
1242 Van Hise, 1220 Linden Dr., Madison, WI, 53706
News Report, 635

Valuation Research Corp.
411 E. Wisconsin Ave., Milwaukee, WI, 53202-4495
Valuation Researcher, 155

W. A. Krueger Co.
12821 W Bluemound Rd, Brookfield, WI, 53005-8038
Wak-Facts, 602

W. H. Brady Co.
727 W Glendale Ave, Milwaukee, WI, 53209-6509
Blue Streak Release, 578

WMC Service Corp.
501 E Washington Ave # 352, Madison, WI, 53703-2914
Wisconsin Safety & Health, 1,085

Wargo & Co., Inc.
100 E. Wisconsin Ave., Suite #350, Milwaukee, WI, 53202
HR Planning Newsletter, 611

West Bend Co.
400 E Washington St, West Bend, WI, 53095-2584
Craftsman, II, 581

Westfield Comics
8608 University Green, Box 620470, Middleton, WI, 53562-2510
Westfield Newsletter, 210

Willem Mengelberg Society
1408A Marshall St, Manitowoc, WI, 54220-5140
Willem Mengelberg Society Newsletter, 919

Winston J. Brill & Associates
4134 Cherokee Dr., Madison, WI, 53711-3031
R & D Innovator, 1,161

Wisconsin Academy of Sciences, Arts & Letters
1922 University Ave, Madison, WI, 53705-4013
Inside the Academy, 260

•**Wisconsin Bell, Inc.**
722 N Broadway, Milwaukee, WI, 53202-4303

Wisconsin Center for Education Research
1025 W. Johnston St. #785, Madison, WI, 53706-1706
WCER Highlights, 335

Wisconsin Commissioner of Securities
PO Box 1768, Madison, WI, 53701-1768
Wisconsin Securities Bulletin, 692

Wisconsin Dept. of Public Instruction
PO Box 7841, Madison, WI, 53707-7841
Channel, 795

Wisconsin Energy Bureau
PO Box 7868, Madison, WI, 53707-7868
Wisconsin Energy News, 358

Wisconsin Fathers for Equal Justice, Inc.
4406 Evergreen Rd, Wausau, WI, 54403-9447
Today's Dads, 416

Wisconsin Geological & National History Survey
3817 Mineral Point Rd, Madison, WI, 53705-5121
Surview, 477

Wisconsin Grocers Association
2601 Crossroads Dr Ste 185, Madison, WI, 53704-7923
WGA Update, 434

Wisconsin Library Assn., Inc.
4785 Hayes Rd., Madison, WI, 53704-7364
WLA Newsletter, 812

Wisconsin Motor Carriers Assn.
PO Box 44849, Madison, WI, 53744-4849
Wisconsin Motor Carrier, 1,194

Wisconsin Newspaper Assn.
702 N. Midvale Blvd., Madison, WI, 53705-3261
WNA Buletin, 924

Wisconsin Nuclear Weapons Freeze Campaign
2122 Luann Lane, Madison, WI, 53713-4526
In Our Hands, 991

Wisconsin Nurses Assn.
6117 Monona Dr., Madison, WI, 53716-3995
Stat, 932

Wisconsin PTA
4797 Hayes Rd. #2, Madison, WI, 53704-7333
Wisconsin Parent Teacher, 336

Wisconsin Painters
323 E Allouez Ave, Green Bay, WI, 54301-2105
Art in Wisconsin, 62

Wisconsin Regional Primate Research Center
1220 Capitol Ct, Madison, WI, 53715-1237
Primate Library Report: Audio-Visual Acquisitions, 1,217

Wisconsin School of Electronics
1227 N Sherman Ave, Madison, WI, 53704-4257
Orbit, The, 207

Wisconsin School for the Visually Handicapped-American Print
1700 W State St, Janesville, WI, 53546-5344
Free Press, 111

•**Wisconsin Taxpayers Alliance**
335 W Wilson St, Madison, WI, 53703-3612

Wisconsin Vocational Association
44 E Mifflin St Ste 104, Madison, WI, 53703-2800
Views and Visions, 335

Wisconsin Women's Network
122 State St Ste 406, Madison, WI, 53703-2500
Stateswoman, 1,212

Women's Health America, Inc.
PO Box 9690, Madison, WI, 53715
Women's Health Access Newsletter, 889

Wood Truss Council of America
5937 Meadowood Dr., Ste. 14, Madison, WI, 53711-4125
Woodwords, 852

Young American Bowling Alliance
5301 S 76th St, Greendale, WI, 53129-1192
YABA Framework, 1,138

•**Zimmerman & Associates, Inc.**
5307 South 92nd St., Hales Corners, WI, 53130-1677

Wyoming

AFC c/o Wyoming Film Office
1-25 At College Dr., Cheyenne, WY, 82002-0001
Association of Film Commissioners Newsletter, 419

FMC Corp., Industrial Chemical Div.
PO Box 872, Green River, WY, 82935-0872
Trona Times, 601

Foundation of the Twelve Apostles
PO Box 1231, Cheyenne, WY, 82003-1231
National Retreat Center Newsletter, 1,065

Fremont County Genealogical Society
Riverton Branch Library, 1330 W. Park, Riverton, WY, 82501
Fremont County Nostalgia News, 454

Mountain Plains Adult Education Association
Box 3374, University of Wyoming, Laramie, WY, 82071
MPAEA Newsletter, 316

National Education Service Center
PO Box 1279, Riverton, WY, 82501-1279
Education Jobs, 308

Sheridan College
PO Box 1500, Sheridan, WY, 82801-1500
Associate, The, 208

Sierra Club, Northern Plains Region
1427 Desmet Dr., Sheridan, WY, 82801
Wyoming Sierran, 398

Vore Buffalo Jump Foundation
PO Box 369, Sundance, WY, 82729-0369
Over the Edge, 546

Wyoming Congress of Parents & Teachers
5030 E 17th St, Casper, WY, 82609-3726
WYO Network, 336

Wyoming Dental Association
330 S Center St Ste 322, Casper, WY, 82601-2875
Wyoming Dental Association Newsletter, 272

Wyoming Department of Transportation
Aeronautics Division Box 1708, Cheyenne, WY, 82002-0001
Wyoming Aviation News, 34

•**Wyoming Geological Association**
PO Box 545, Casper, WY, 82602-0545

Wyoming Historical Society-Dept. of Commerce
Third Floor, Barrett Building, 2301 Central Avenue, Cheyenne, WY, 82002-0001
Wyoming History News, 550

Wyoming Nurses' Association
1603 Capitol Ave., Ste. 305, Cheyenne, WY, 82001-4561
Wyoming Nurse, 932

Wyoming State Department of Fire Prevention
Herschler Bldg., 1 West, Cheyenne, WY, 82002
Wyoming Fire News, 422

Wyoming State Library
Supreme Court & State Library, Cheyenne, WY, 82002-0001
Outrider, 807

Wyoming Taxpayers Association
2410 Pioneer Ave., Cheyenne, WY, 82001-3021
WTA Newsletter, 1,156

Wyoming Transportation Dept.
PO Box 1708, Cheyenne, WY, 82003-1708
Transportation Topics, 1,077

•**Wyoming Wool Grower's Association**
811 N Glenn Rd # 115, Casper, WY, 82601-1625

CANADA

Alberta

Alberta Association of Registered Nurses
11620-168 St., Edmonton, AB, T5M 4A6, Canada
AARN Newsletter, 928

Alberta Assn. of Social Workers
#52, 9912 106th Street, Edmonton, AB, T5K 1C5, Canada
Advocate, The, 1,113

Alberta Bicycle Assn.
11759 Broat, Edmonton, AB, T5M 3K6, Canada
Alberta Bicycle Assn., Newsletter, 262

Alberta Dept. of Energy
9945 108th St., 7th Floor, Edmonton, AB, T5K 2G6, Canada
Energy Savers, 353

•**Alberta Environmental Protection**
Resource Planning Branch, 9820 106th St., 9th Fl., Edmonton, AB, T5K 2J5, Canada

Alberta Environmental Protection, Operations Branch
Main Floor North Tower, Petroleum Plaza, 9945 108 St., Edmonton, AB, P5K 2G6, Canada
Hunter Training and Conservation, Instructor Newsletter, 606

•**Alberta Genealogical Society**
Box 12015, Edmonton, AB, T5J 3L2, Canada

Alberta Gymnastics Fed.
#207, 5800 2nd Street SW, Calgary, AB, T2H 0H2, Canada
Alberta Gymnast, 1,128

Alberta Health Records Association
Box 1752, Edmonton, AB, T5J 2P1, Canada
Record, The, 526

Alberta Historical Resources Foundation
8820-112 St., Edmonton, AB, T6G 2P8, Canada
Cornerstone, 538

Alberta Horticultural Assn., A.H.A. Secretary
c/o Adamson, Box 1 of 3, Lacombe, AB, T0C 1S0, Canada
Alberta Horticulturist, 439

Alberta Hospital Association
10009 108th St., Edmonton, AB, T5J 3C5, Canada
Healthcare Advocate, 564

Alberta Institute of Agrologists
8506 104th St., Edmonton, AB, T6E 4G4, Canada
Alberta Agrologist, 37

Alberta Land Surveyors Assn
14403 115th Ave., Edmonton, AB, T5M 3B8, Canada
ALS News, 364

Alberta School Boards Assn.
12310 105 Ave., Edmonton, AB, T5N 0Y4, Canada
Spectrum, 1,094

•**Alberta Teachers' Association**
11010-142 St., Edmonton, AB, T5N 2R1, Canada

Alberta Trucking Association
Box 5520, Station A, Calgary, AB, T2H 1X9, Canada
Truxfax Bulletin, 1,194

Alpine Club of Canada, Edmonton Section
PO Box 2040, Canmore, AB, T0L 0M0, Canada
Breeze, 943

Aquarian Print
Box 1657, Edmonton, AB, T5J 2N9, Canada
Our Green Emerald, 472

Archives Society of Alberta
P.O. Box 21080, Dominion Postal Outlet, Lelgary, AB, T2P 4H5, Canada
Archivists Society of Alberta Newsletter, 259

Arctic Institute of North America
2500 University Dr. N.W., Calgary, AB, T2N 1N4, Canada
Information North, 1,097

Association
12121 Jasper Ave., Ste. 605, Edmonton, AB, T5N 3X8, Canada
Association, The, 251

* See **MULTI-PUBLISHER INDEX** for list of publications.

Boreal Institute for Northern Studies
CW 401 Bio. Sci. Bldg., Univ. of Alberta, Edmonton, AB, T6G 2E9, Canada
Library Bulletin, 106

•**C.O. Nickle Pubs.**
999 8 St. SW, #300, Calgary, AB, T2R 1N7, Canada

Calgary Chamber of Commerce
517 Center St., S., Calary, AB, T2G 2C4, Canada
Commerce Comments, 159

Calgary Co-Operative Memorial Society Ltd.
28 Norseman Pl., N.W., Calgary, AB, T2K 5M6, Canada
Calgary Co-Operative Memorial Society Ltd. Newsletter, 437

Canada Society of Petroleum Geologists
505, 206-7 Ave. SW, Calgary, AB, T2P 0W7, Canada
CSPG Reservoir, 475

Canadian Assn. for Lab. Animal Science
M524 Biol. Sci. Bldg., Univ. Alberta, Edmonton, AB, T6G 2E9, Canada
Canadian Association for Laboratory Animal Science Newsletter, 109

Canadian Assn. of Oilwell Drilling Contractors
#800-540 5th Ave., SW, Calgary, AB, T2P 0M2, Canada
Inside CAODC, 958

Canadian Assn. of Pathologists
Royal Alexandra Hosp., Edmonton, AB, T5H 3V9, Canada
Canadian Association of Pathologists, Newsletter, 869

•**Canadian Assn. of Petroleum Producers**
2100-350 Seventh Ave., SW, Calgary, AB, T2P 3N9, Canada

Canadian Association of Slavists
Dept. Comparative Literature, 347 Arts Bldg.-Univ.of Alberta, Edmonton, AB, T6G 2E6, Canada
CAS Newsletter, 409

Canadian Astronomical Society
Mount Royal College, 4825 Richard Road S.W, Calgary, AB, T3E 6K6, Canada
Cassiopeia, 68

Canadian Cultural Society of the Deaf, Inc.
11337 61st Ave., House 144, Edmonton, AB, T6H 1M3, Canada
Canadian Cultural Society of the Deaf, CCSD Newsletter, 266

Canadian Figure Skating Assn. Alberta Sect.
11759 Groat Rd., Edmonton, AB, T5M 3K6, Canada
Skaters Edge, 1,135

Canadian Health Care Guild
#200 William Gray Building, 17410-107 Avenue, Edmonton, AB, T5S 1E9, Canada
CHCG Pulse, 929

Canadian Institute of Ukrainian Studies
352 Athabasca Hall, Univ. of Alberta, Edmonton, AB, T6G 2E8, Canada
Canadian Institute of Ukrainian Studies, Newsletter, 303

Canadian Murray Grey Assn.
Box 605, Red Deer, AB, T4N 5G6, Canada
Canadian Murray Grey News, 559

Canadian Native Friendship Centre
11205 101 Street, Edmonton, AB, T5G 2A4, Canada
Edmonton Native News, 1,044

Canadian Pensioners Concerned-Alberta Div.
11113 113th St., Edmonton, AB, T5G 2V1, Canada
Canadian Pensioners Concerned Alberta Div. Newsletter, 1,106

Canadian Society of Exploration Geophysicists
206 7th Ave. S.W., Rm. 406, Calgary, AB, T2P 0W7, Canada
Recorder, 477

Canadian Thoroughbred Horse Society
255 17th Ave. SW, Ste. 401, Calgary, AB, T2S 2T8, Canada
Horse Cents, 559

Cellular Neetworking Perspectives
2636 Toronto Crown, Calgary, AB, T2N 3WI, C
Cellular Networking Perspectives, 1,157

Certified General Accountants' Assn. of Alberta
555 Fourth Ave., S.W., #1410, Calgary, AB, T2P 3E7, Canada
Insight, 5

Coal Assn. of Canada
205 9th Ave. SE, #502, Calgary, AB, T2G 0R3, Canada
Coal Focus, 351

Confederation of Alberta Faculty Assn.
11043 90th Ave., Univ. of Alberta, Edmonton, AB, T6G 2E1, Canada
CAFA Report, 301

Economic Development Edmonton
9797 Jasper Ave., Edmonton Convention Centre, Edmonton, AB, T5J 1N9, Canada
Edmonton Report on Economic Development, 137

Edmonton Public Library
7 Sir Winston Churchill Sq., Edmonton, AB, T5J 2V4, Canada
Library Calendar, 802

Farm Equipment Dealers Assn. of Alberta-BC
#2921, 15th St., NE, Calgary, AB, T2E 7L8, Canada
Widespread, 35

Ian M. Doig & Assoc. Ltd.
1512 Evergreen Hill SW, Calgary, AB, T2Y 2V8, Canada
Doig's Digest, 956

Institute of Chartered Accountants of Alberta
Manu Life Place, Suite 580, 10180 101st Street, Edmonton, AB, T5J 4R2, Canada
Institute of Chartered Accountants of Alberta, Monthly Statement, 6

Insurance Institute of Southern Alberta
1015 4th St. SW, #801, Calgary, AB, T2R 1J4, Canada
Insurance Institute of Southern Alberta, Newsletter, 621

International Ombudsman Institute
University of Alberta, Faculty of Law, Edmonton, AB, T6G 2H5, Canada
International Ombudsman Institute Newsletter, 746

John Howard Society of Alberta
10136 100th St., #706, Edmonton, AB, T5J 0P1, Canada
John Howard Society of Alberta, Reporter, 787

Law Society of Alberta
919 11th Ave., SW Ste 600, Calgary, AB, T2R 1P3, Canada
Bencher's Advisory, 718

Le Conseil Francais/Alberta Teachers Assn.
11010-142nd St., Edmonton, AB, T5N 2R1, Canada
Chuchoteries, 305

Lethbridge Historical Society
Box 974, Lethbridge, AB, T1J 4A2, Canada
Lethbridge Historical Society Newsletter, 543

Motel Assn. of Alberta
10335 178th St., Ste. 202, Edmonton, AB, T5S 1R5, Canada
Checking-In, 574

Operation Eyesight Universal
4 Parkdale Crest N.W., Calgary, AB, T2N 3T8, Canada
Gift of Sight, 940

Parent Finders
Box 12031, Edmonton, AB, T5J 3L2, Canada
Parent Finders-Edmonton, 415

•**Petroleum Information Canada Ltd.**
Suite 500 Bow Valley Sq. III, 255 5th Ave., S.W., Calgary, AB, T2P 3G6, Canada

Population Research Laboratory
U. of Alberta-Sociology, 1-62 HM Tory Bldg., Edmonton, AB, T6G 2H4, Canada
PRL in Summary, 1,126

Programme in Religious Studies
Univ. of Calgary, Calgary, AB, T2N 1N4, Canada
Newsletter for Ugaritic Studies, 1,049

Progressive Conservative Assn. of Alberta
9912-106th St., Edmonton, AB, T5K 1C5, Canada
Progressive Conservative Association of Alberta Progress Bulletin, 997

Red Deer River Naturalists Society
Box 785, Red Deer, AB, T4N 5H2, Canada
Central Alberta Naturalist, 374

Regional Range Manager/Public Lands Branch
Box 3014 2 Fl. Sun Center, 530 8th St., S., Lethbridge, AB, T1J 4C7, Canada
Range Notes, 829

Rehabilitation Society of Calgary
#7, 11 St. SE, Calgary, AB, T2E 4Z2, Canada
Rehab Tab, 279

Sagitawa Friendship Centre
Box 5083, Peace River, AB, T8S 1R7, Canada
Achimowin, 405

Saint John's Edmonton Report
17327-106A Ave., Edmonton, AB, T5M 1T9, Canada
Saint John's Edmonton Report, 161

St-Paul Herald
C.P. 339, Saint Paul, AB, T0A 3A0, Canada
Heraut de Saint Paul, 1,057

Society of Management Accountants of Alberta
1800-125 Ninth Ave., S.E., Calgary, AB, T2G 0P6, Canada
Management Accounter, 6

•**Southam Information & Technology Group**
999 8th St. SW, #300, Calgary, AB, T2R 1N7, Canada

Sovereign Life Insurance Co.
500 4th Ave. SW, #800, Calgary, AB, T2P 2V6, Canada
Network, 591

Speech & Hearing Assn. of Alberta
10060 Jafper Ave., Suite 2210, Edmonton, AB, T5J 3R8, Canada
SHAA Newsletter, 534

Trail Riders of the Canadian Rockies Newsletter
P.O. Box 6742, Postal St. D, Calgary, AB, T2P 2E6, Canada
Trail Riders of the Canadian Rockies Newsletter, 1,189

Univ. of Alberta
89 Ave. & 113th St., Edmonton, AB, T6G 2J4, Canada
Library Editions, 802

Univ. of Alberta General Services
352 General Svcs. Bldg., Edmonton, AB, T6G 2H1, Canada
UCS Dispatch, 241

University of Calgary, Computer Services
2500 University Dr., NW, Calgary, AB, T2N 1N4, Canada
Big Byte, The, 213

Western Barley Growers Assn.
2116 27th Ave., NE, Ste. 232, Calgary, AB, T2E 7A6, Canada
Western Barley Growers Assn. Newsletter, 47

Western Canada Water & Wastewater Association
Box 6168, Sta. A, Calgary, AB, T2H 2L4, Canada
Western Canada Water, 616

Western Stock Growers Assn.
2116 27th Ave., NE, Ste. 101, Calgary, AB, T2E 7A6, Canada
Western Stock Growers Newsletter, 48

Writers Guild of Alberta
10523 100th Ave., Edmonton, AB, T5J OA8, Canada
West Word, 826

British Columbia

21st Century Media Communications
548 Cardero St., Vancouver, BC, V6G 2W6, Canada
Robotronics Age Newsletter, 235

Abbotsford Intl. Airshow Society
Box 361, Abbotsford, BC, V2S 4N9, Canada
Abbotsford International Airshow Newsletter, 25

Alpine Club of Canada
1815 St. Denis Rd., West Vancouver, BC, V7V 3W4, Canada
Avalanche Echoes, 1,112

Andrea Fernandez
624 E. 15th Street, North Vancouver, BC, V7L 2S2, Canada
Residential Garbage, 984

Archives Association of British Columbia
Box 78530, Univ. Post Office, Vancouver, BC, V6T 1Z4, Canada
AABC Newsletter, 791

•**Assn. of British Columbia Foresters**
1130 W. Pendes Street, Ste 1201, Vancouver, BC, V6E 4A4, Canada

Association for the Protection of Fur-Bearing Animals
2235 Commercial Dr., Vancouver, BC, V5N 4B6, Canada
Fur-Bearers Newsletter, 1,216

B.C. Fisheries Survival Coalition
Box 147-401 West Georgia St., Vancouver, BC, V6B - 5A1, Canada
Survival Coalition, 424

B.C. Safety Council
8589 Baxter Place, Burnaby, BC, V5A 4V7, Canada
Safety First, 1,084

B.C. School Trustees Assn.
1155 W. 8th Ave., Vancouver, BC, V6H 1C5, Canada
Education Leader, 308

BC Transit
1200 W. 73rd Ave., #400, Vancouver, BC, V6P 6M2, Canada
Buzzer, 579

Banana Productions
Box 2480, Sechelt, BC, V0N 3AC, Canada
Artistamp News, 63

Beale's Industry Letter
Box 48651, Bentall Ctr. 111, Vancouver, BC, V7X 1A3, Canada
Beale's Industry Letter, 37

Bicycling Assn. of British Columbia
1367 W. Broadway, #332, Vancouver, BC, V6H 4A9, Canada
Bicycling: BC, 263

* See **MULTI-PUBLISHER INDEX** for list of publications.

Bldg. Inspectors' Assn. of British Columbia
1158 21st St., W. Vancouver, BC, V7V 4B1, Canada
Building Inspectors' Assn. of British Columbia, News & Report, 244

Boys' & Girls' Clubs of Greater Vancouver
2875 St. George St., Vancouver, BC, V5T 3R8, Canada
Boys' and Girls' Clubs of Greater Vancouver, Bulletin, 1,214

British Columbia Artificial Insemination Centre
Box 40, Milner, BC, V0X 1T0, Canada
B.C.A.I. Newsletter, 264

British Columbia Assn. of Teachers of Classics
2235 Burrard St., Vancouver, BC, V6J 3H9, Canada
Vexillum, 335

British Columbia Camping Assn.
3302 Senkler Road, Belcarra, BC, V3H 4S3, Canada
British Columbia Camping Association, Newsletter, 943

British Columbia Chamber of Commerce
700 W. Pender St., Ste. 1607, Vancouver, BC, V6C 1G8, Canada
Chamber Comments, 158

British Columbia Chiropractic Assn.
532 W. Broadway, Vancouver, BC, V5Z 1E9, Canada
Newsletter, 521

British Columbia Civil Liberties Assn.
815 W. Hastings St., #425, Vancouver, BC, V6C 1B4, Canada
Democratic Commitment, 989

British Columbia Health Assn.
1333 W. Broadway, Suite 600, Vancouver, BC, V6H 4C7, Canada
BCHA News, 499

British Columbia Heart Foundation
1212 West Broadway, Vancouver, BC, V6H 3V2, Canada
Heart to Heart, 512

British Columbia Library Association
#110 - 6545 Bonsor Avenue, Burnaby, BC, V5H 1H3, Canada
BCLA Reporter, 793

British Columbia, Ministry of Environment, Lands and Parks
810 Blanshard, 1st Fl., Victoria, BC, V8V 1X4, Canada
Snow Survey Bulletin, 1,204

British Columbia Ministry of Transportation
940 Blanshard St., Victoria, BC, V8W 3E6, Canada
British Columbia Ferries, Fleet Bulletin, 578

British Columbia Pharmacy Assn.
3751 Shell Rd., Ste. 150, Richmond, BC, V6X 2W2, Canada
Tablet, The, 288

•**British Columbia Teachers' Federation**
100-550 West 6th Avenue, Vancouver, BC, V5Z 4P2, Canada

British Columbia Trucking Assn.
1-1610 Kebet Way, Port Coquitlam, BC, V3C 5W1, Canada
British Columbia Motor Transport Assn., News & Views, 1,176

Canadian Assn. of Univ. Teachers of German
Univ. of Victoria, PO Box 3045, Dept. of Germanic Studies, Victoria, BC, V8W 3P4, Canada
Canadian Assn. of Univ. Teachers of German, Newsletter, 303

•**Canadian Cancer Society-B.C. Div.**
565 W. 10th Ave., Vancouver, BC, V5Z 4J4, Canada

Canadian Indian Voice Society
429 E. 6th St., N. Vancouver, BC, V7L 1P8, Canada
Indian Voice, 405

•**Canadian Museum of Flight and Transportation**
13527 Crescent Rd, Surrey, BC, V4A 1S5, Canada

Canadian Music Research Council
Simon Fraser University, Faculty of Education, Burnaby, BC, V5A 1S6, Canada
Music Research News, 914

Canadian Paraplegic Assn, British Columbia Div.
780 SW Marine Dr., Vancouver, BC, V6P 5Y7, Canada
Paragraphic, 278

Canadian Wheelchair Sports Assn.
1200 Hornby St., #224, 1367 W. Broadway, Vancouver, BC, V6H 4A9, Canada
Newswheel, 1,133

Cerebral Palsy Association of B.C.
4423 Boundry Rd., Vancouver, BC, V5R 2N3, Canada
Round Table, 526

Certified General Accountants' Assn. of B.C.
1555 W. 8th Ave., Vancouver, BC, V6J 1T5, Canada
Certified General Accountants' Assn. of British Columbia, Newsletter, 4

College of Pharmacists of British Columbia
1765 W. 8th Ave., #200, Vancouver, BC, V6J 1V8, Canada
College of Pharmacists of British Columbia, the Bulletin, 282

Community Arts Council of Vancouver
837 Davey St., Vancouver, BC, V6Z 1B7, Canada
Arts Vancouver, 368

Computer Services Training Centre
City Hall, 453 12th Ave., Vancouver, BC, V5Y 1V4, Canada
Access, 211

Consulting Engineers of British Columbia
#514, 409 Granville St., Vancouver, BC, V6C 1T2, Canada
Commentary, 359

Danish Lutheran Church
6010 Kincaid St., Burnaby, BC, V5G 4N3, Canada
Kirkebaldet Church Newsletter, 1,072

Development Press
5096 Catalina Terrace, Victoria, BC, V8Y 2A5, Canada
Constructive Citizen Participation, 1,125

•**Education Students' Assn.**
Univ. of British Columbia, Vancouver, BC, Canada

Federation of British Columbia Nauturalists
321-1367 West Broadway, Vancouver, BC, V6H 4A9, Canada
B.C. Naturalist, 920

Finning Ltd.
555 Great Northern Way, Vancouver, BC, V5T 1E2, Canada
Bulldozer, 578

Forestry Canada Pacific & Yukon
506 W. Burnside Road, Victoria, BC, V8Z 1M5, Canada
Information Forestry, 436

Fran Kay & Associates
RR#2, Chase, BC, Canada
Hivelights, 430

Fraser Valley Real Estate Board
Box 99, 15463- 104th Ave., Surrey, BC, V3T 4W4, Canada
NewsReal, 592

•**George Cross News Letter Ltd.**
1710-609 Granville St., Vancouver, BC, V7Y 1G5, Canada

Greater Vancouver Libertarian Assn.
922 Cloverley St., North Vancouver, BC, V7L 1N3, Canada
West Coast Libertarian, 1,000

Green Party of British Columbia
505-620 View Street, Vancouver, BC, V8W 1J6, Canada
Green Party News, 383

Health Libraries Association of British Columbia
1383 W. 8th Ave., Vancouver, BC, V6H 4C4, Canada
HLABC Forum, 508

•**Independent Survey Co.**
Box 6000, Vancouver, BC, V6B 4B9, Canada

Institute of Certified Management Consultants of B.C.
1501-650 W. Georgia St., Vancouver, BC, V6B 4N9, Canada
CMC Report, 131

International Association for Social Science Information Svc
Data Library, Simon Fraser University, Burnaby, BC, V5A 1S6, Canada
IASSIST Quarterly, 799

Kanada Esperanto-Asocio
Box 2159, Sidney, BC, V8L 3S6, Canada
Alumeto, 819

Langara Faculty Association
Langara College, 100 W. 49th Ave., Vancouver, BC, V5Y 2Z6, Canada
Faculty Affairs, 310

Madison's Canadian Lumber Reporter
PO Box 2486, Vancouver, BC, V6B 3W7, Canada
Madison's Canadian Lumber Reporter, 830

Mechanical Contractors Assn. of B.C.
3210 Lake City Way, Burnaby, BC, V5A 3A4, Canada
Mechanical Contractor, 248

Min. of Municipal Affairs, Recreation & Culture
c/o Crown Publications, 546 Yates St., Victoria, BC, V8W 1K8, Canada
Electrical Safety Bulletin, 338

Ministry of Energy, Mines & Petroleum Resources
Mineral Resources Division, Parliament Bldgs., Victoria, BC, V8V 1X4, Canada
Oil Gas Production Report, 681

Mnemonic Box 115
#105-10277 35th Street, Surrey, BC, V3T 4C3, Canada
ACK!, 909

Moore/Parry Ltd.
3390 W. 41st Ave., Vancouver, BC, V6N 3E4, Canada
Legal Support Staff Newsletter, 751

•**National Media Archive**
626 Bute St., Vancouver, BC, V6E 3M1, Canada

Nicola Valley Museum Archives Assn.
2202 Jackson Ave., Box 1262, Merritt, BC, V0K 2B0, Canada
Nicola Valley Archives-Quarterly, 462

North Pacific Women Writers Association
3091 West 15th Avenue, Vancouver, BC, V6K 3A5, Canada
North Pacific Women Writers Retreat, 1,210

Open Space Art Society
5100 Fort Street, Victoria, BC, V8W 1E6, Canada
Open Space, 977

Outdoor Recreation Council of B.C.
334-1367 W. Broadway, Vancouver, BC, V6H 4A9, Canada
Outdoor Report, 944

Pacific Trollers' Assn.
5960 #6 Rd. #625, Richmond, BC, V6V 1Z1, Canada
Pacific Trollers Association Newsletter, 423

Petroleum Resources Div., Ministry of Energy Mines & Petrole
Parliament Bldg., Victoria, BC, V8V 1X4, Canada
Drilling & Land Report, 352

Potters Guild of British Columbia
1359 Cartwright St., Vancouver, BC, V6H 3R7, Canada
Newsletter, 479

Professional Employees Assn.
#201, 1001 Wharf St., Victoria, BC, V8W 1T6, Canada
Professional, The, 710

Prospector Publications
B101-325 Howe Street, Vancouver, BC, V6C 1Z7, Canada
Street Noises, 688

Provincial Judges Assn. of B.C.
350 Barlow Ave., Quesnel, BC, V2J 2C1, Canada
Provincial Judges Assn. of B. C. Newsletter, 771

Ralph
PO Box 505, 1288 Broughton Street, Vancouver, BC, V6G 2B5, Canada
Ralph: Coffee, Jazz, & Poetry, 984

Recreation and Parks Association
10551 Shellenbridge Way, #30, Richmond, BC, V6X 2W9, Canada
Rec BC, 944

Restaurant & Foodservices Assn. of B.C.
4190 Lougheed Hwy., #204, Burnaby, BC, V5C 6A8, Canada
Restaurant & Foodservices Assn. of British Columbia Newsletter, 1,076

Royal Life Saving Society Canada
1235 W. Pender, Vancouver, BC, V6E 2V6, Canada
West Coast Lifeliner, 531

Royal United Services Inst. of Vancouver Island
Bay St. Armory, 715 Bay St., Victoria, BC, V8T 1R1, Canada
R.U.S.I. Newsletter, 898

SRC Software Research Corp.
PO Box 6519, Depot 1, Victoria, BC, V8P 5M4, Canada
Personal Career Directions, 325

S & S Press Co., Ltd.
13964 Tallon Pl., Surrey, BC, V3V 5X8, Canada
Canada Letter, 131

St. John Ambulance
British Columbia Council, 6111 Cambie St., Vancouver, BC, V5Z 3B2, Canada
St. John Ambulance, Instructor's Digest, 527

Satellite Video Exchange Society
1965 Main St., Vancouver, BC, V5T 3C1, Canada
Video Inn/Mailer/Newsletter, 1,170

School of Community & Regional Planning
Univ. of B.C., 6333 Memorial Rd., Vancouver, BC, V6T 1W5, Canada
U.B.C Planning Papers, 1,024

Slovak Heritage and Cultural Society of British Columbia
3804 Yale Street, Burnaby, BC, V5C 1P6, Canada
Slovak Heritage Live, 409

Small Press Action Network
#19-155 W. 12th St., Box 47068, Vancouver, BC, V5Z 4L6, Canada
SPANzine, 954

* See **MULTI-PUBLISHER INDEX** for list of publications.

Society for Canadian Women in Science & Technology
140-515 W. Hastings St., Vancouver, BC, V6B 5K3, Canada
SCWIST News, 1,211

Society of Management Accountants of B.C.
1575-650 W. Georgia St., Box 11548, Vancouver, BC, V6B 4W7, Canada
CMA Update, 3

Spina Bifida Assn. of British Columbia
9460 140th St., Surrey, BC, V3V 5Z4, Canada
Spina Bifida Assn. of British Columbia Newsletter, 528

Survivor Update
Sutie 380, 401 W Georgia St., Box 147, Vancouver, BC, V4N4J6, Canada
Survival Update, 424

Trans Mountain Pipeline Co., Ltd.
Suite 900, 1333 W. Broadway, Vancouver, BC, V6H 4C2, Canada
FYI, 956

Univ. of British Columbia
6251 Cecil Green Park Rd., Vancouver, BC, V6K 1W5, Canada
UBC Gazette, 208

Univ. of British Columbia Forest Club
McMillan Bldg., Vancouver, BC, Canada
UBC Forester, 436

Univ. of British Columbia Library
1956 Main Mall, Vancouver, BC, V6T 1Y3, Canada
UBC Library News, 811

Univ. of British Columbia, Univ. Computing Svces.
6356 Agricultural Rd., Vancouver, BC, V6T 1W5, Canada
Campus Computing and Communications, 214

Uptrend Investment Services
Box 49333, Bentall Four, Vancouver, BC, V7X 1L4, Canada
Uptrend, the Canadian Penny Market Newsletter, 690

Vancouver Board of Trade
999 Canada Pl., #400, Vancouver, BC, V6C 3C1, Canada
Facts & Trends, 138

Vancouver Historical Society
Box 3071, Vancouver, BC, V6B 3X6, Canada
Vancouver Historical Society, Newsletter, 549

Vancouver Museums
1100 Chestnut St., Vancouver, BC, V6H 2L5, Canada
Muse News, 906

Vancouver Public Aquarium Assn.
Box 3232, Vancouver, BC, V6B 3X8, Canada
Vancouver Aquascene Aquarium Newsletter, 921

West Coast Environmental Law Research Foundation
207 W. Hastings St., Ste. 1001, Vancouver, BC, V6B 1H7, Canada
West Coast Environmental Law Research Foundation Newsletter, 397

West Coast Railway Assn.
Box 2790, Vancouver, BC, V6B 3X2, Canada
West Coast Railway Assn. Newsletter, 1,030

Westbridge Publications, Ltd.
2339 Granville St., Vancouver, BC, V6H 3G4, Canada
Westbridge Art Market Report, 67

Western Canada Fertilizer Assn.
12202G 86th Ave., Surrey, BC, V3W 3H7, Canada
Western Canada Fertilizer Assn. Newsletter, 47

Western Institute for the Deaf
2125 W. 7th Ave., Vancouver, BC, V6K 1X9, Canada
WID News, 534

•**Western Legal Publications**
301-1 Alexander St., Vancouver, BC, V6A 1B2, Canada

William Palmer Consultant Regd.
PO Box 8158, Victoria, BC, V8W 3R8, Canada
Bill Palmer's Word Watching, 854

Workers' Compensation Board of BC
6951 Westminster Hwy., Richmond, BC, V7C 1C6, Canada
Prevention at Work, 770

Y.M.C.A.
955 Burrard St., Vancouver, BC, V6Z 1Y2, Canada
YMCA, Weekly News, 1,138

Manitoba

Alliance Action, Inc.
B1-90 Garry St., Winnipeg, MB, R3C 4H1, Canada
Pro-Life News, 175

Appraisal Inst. of Canada
1111 Porpege Ave., Winnipeg, MB, R3G OS8, Canada
Appraisal Institute Digest, 1,031

Associated Manitoba Arts Festivals, Inc.
424-100 Arthur St., Winnipeg, MB, R3B 1H3, Canada
Focus on Festivals, 912

Assn. of Employees Supporting Education Services
405 - 275 Broadway, Winnipeg, MB, R3C 4M6, Canada
Inside AESES, 313

Assn. of Manitoba Archivists
Provincial Archives Manitoba, 200 Vaughan St., Winnipeg, MB, R3C 1T5, Canada
AMA Newsletter, 792

BBB of Winnipeg & Manitoba Inc.
365 Hargrave St., Suite 301, Winnipeg, MB, R3B 2K3, Canada
Dateline Winnipeg, 135

Brandon Univ.
Brandon Campus, Brandon, MB, R7A 6A9, Canada
Peace Research, 996

CARFAC Manitoba
221-100 Arthur St., Winnipeg, MB, R3B 1H3, Canada
Arterra, 63

Canadian Paraplegic Assn., Manitoba
825 Sherbrook Street, Winnipeg, MB, R3A 1M5, Canada
Paratracks, 523

Canadian Red Cross Society, Manitoba Div.
226 Osborne St. N., Winnipeg, MB, R3C 1V4, Canada
Canadian Red Cross Society News and Views, 1,115

Canadian Society of Cytology
Health Sciences Ctre., Winnipeg, MB, R3A 1A9, Canada
Canadian Society of Cytology Bulletin, 562

Canadian Society for Immunology
Univ. of Manitoba, Immunology Dept, 730 Wm. Ave., Winnipeg, MB, R3E 0W3, Canada
Canadian Society for Immunology, Bulletin, 870

Canadian Wheat Board
PO Box 816, Station Main, Winnipeg, MB, R3C 2P5, Canada
Grain Matters, 418

Canola Council of Canada
400-167 Lombard Ave., Winnipeg, MB, R3B OT6, Canada
Canola Digest, 418

Century Publishing Co.
167 Lombard Ave., Ste. 143, Winnipeg, MB, R3B 0T4, Canada
Agriweek, 37

Certified General Accountants Assn. of Manitoba
4 Donald St. S., Winnipeg, MB, R3L 2T7, Canada
Certified General Accountants Assn. of Manitoba Newsletter, 4

Entomological Society of Manitoba
c/o Agriculture Canada, 195 Dafoe Rd., Winnipeg, MB, R3T 2M9, Canada
Entomological Society of Manitoba, Newsletter, 370

Fellowship for Print Witness Inc.
300-228 Nortre Dame Avenue, Winnipeg, MB, R3B 1N7, Canada
ChristianWeek, 1,062

Grand Lodge of Manitoba. Indep. Order of Odd Fellows
381 Parkway Blvd., Flin Flon, MB, R8A 0K5, Canada
Golden Links, 178

Home & School Parent Teacher Fed. of Manitoba
1 Sir John Franklin Rd., Winnipeg, MB, R3N 1Z9, Canada
Home & School News, 312

•**Manitoba Action Committee on the Status of Women**
702-70 Arthur St., Winnipeg, MB, R3B 1G7, Canada

Manitoba Assn. of Library Technicians
Box 1872, Winnipeg, MB, R3C 3R1, Canada
MALT Newsletter, 803

Manitoba Assn. of Med. Radiation Technologists, Inc.
294 Duffield St., Winnipeg, MB, R3J 2J9, Canada
K.V.P. News, 877

Manitoba Assn. of School Trustees
191 Provencher Blvd., Winnipeg, MB, R2H 0G4, Canada
Manitoba Association of School Trustees Newsletter, 317

Manitoba Assn. for Schooling At Home
98 Baltimore Rd., Winnipeg, MB, R3L 1H1, Canada
Manitoba Assn. for Schooling At Home, Newsletter, 317

Manitoba Beef Cattle Performances Assn.
Box 232, Douglas, MB, R0K 0R0, Canada
Weight Report, 829

Manitoba Gymnastic Assn., Inc.
200 Main Street, Winnipeg, MB, R3C 4M2, Canada
Keeping in Touch with Manitoba Gymnastic Assn., 1,132

Manitoba Historical Society
The Grain Exchange, 470-167 Lombard Avenue, Winnipeg, MB, R3B 0T6, Canada
Manitoba Historical Society, Newsletter, 543

Manitoba Hydro
Box 815, Winnipeg, MB, R3C 2P4, Canada
Hydrogram, 585

Manitoba Intl. Folk Dance Assn.
Box 292, Winnipeg, MB, R3M 3S7, Canada
Manitoba Intl. Folk Dance Assn., Newsletter, 266

Manitoba League of the Physically Handicapped, Inc.
294 Portage Ave., #200, Winnipeg, MB, R3C 0B9, Canada
Manitoba League of the Physically Handicapped, Update, 517

Manitoba Medical Assn.
125 Sherbrook St., Winnipeg, MB, R3C 2B5, Canada
MMA Inter-Com, 878

Manitoba Museum of Man & Nature
190 Rupert Ave., Winnipeg, MB, R3B 0N2, Canada
Happenings Newsletter, 904

Manitoba Naturalists Society
63 Albert St. Rm. 401, Winnipeg, MB, R3B 1G4, Canada
Manitoba Naturalists Society, Bulletin, 387

Manitoba Organization of Nurses Assns.
502-275 Broadway, Winnipeg, MB, R3C 4M6, Canada
M.O.N.A. Pulse, 930

Manitoba Pharmaceutical Assn.
187 St Mary's Rd., Winnipeg, MB, R2H 1J2, Canada
Manitoba Pharmaceutical Assn., News Bulletin, 285

Manitoba Real Estate Assn.
1240 Portage Ave., 2nd fl., Winnipeg, MB, R3G 0T6, Canada
Real Estate Manitoba, 1,038

Manitoba School Library-Audio-Visual Assn.
191 Harcourt St., Winnipeg, MB, R3J 3H2, Canada
MSLAVA Journal/MSLAVA Newsletter, 804

Manitoba Underwater Council Inc.
Box 711, Winnipeg, MB, R3C 2K3, Canada
Man Underwater, 1,132

Manitoba Veterinary Medical Assn.
2989 Pembina Highway #203, Winnipeg, MB, R3T 2H5, Canada
Manitoba Veterinary Medical Assn. Newsletter, 1,201

Manitoba Writers' Guild
100 Arthur St., Rm. 206, Winnipeg, MB, R38 1H3, Canada
Manitoba Writers' Guild Newsletter, 823

North West Commercial Travellers' Assn. of Canada
291 Garry St., Box 336, Winnipeg, MB, R3C 2H6, Canada
National Executive/Commercial Traveller, 19

North Winnipeg Credit Union Ltd.
544 Selkirk Ave., Winnipeg, MB, R2W 2M9, Canada
Kredytova Kooperatyva Pivnichnoho Vinnipegu Biuleten North Winnipeg Credit Union Ltd. Bull, 410

Public Library Services
1525 First St., Brandon, MB, R7A 7A1, Canada
Public Library Services Newsletter, 808

Red River Community College
2055 Notre Dame Ave., Rm. D102, Winnipeg, MB, R3H 0J9, Canada
Projector, 208

Registered Psychiatric Nurses Assn. of Manitoba (R.P.N.A.M.)
1854 Portage Ave., Winnipeg, MB, R3J 0G9, Canada
RPNAM Update, 1,017

S.W. Branch, Manitoba Genealogical Soc.
53 Almond Cres., Brandon, MB, R7B 1A2, Canada
Leaf of the Branch, 459

Science Teachers' Assn. of Manitoba
295 Sutton Ave., Winnipeg, MB, R2G 0T1, Canada
Manitoba Science Teacher, 1,098

Society for Manitobans with Disabilities
825 Sherbrook St., Winnipeg, MB, R3A 1M5, Canada
Communique, 276

Square Dance Federation of Manitoba
195 Enfield, Winnipeg, MB, R2H 1B2, Canada
Manisquare, 266

Tourism Industry Assn. of Manitoba
375 York Ave., Ste. 232, Winnipeg, MB, R3C 3J3, Canada
Tourism Update, 1,189

Ukrainian Canadian Congress
456 Main St., Winnipeg, MB, R3B 1B6, Canada
Ukrainian Canadian Committee Bulletin, 410

Ukrainian Professional & Business Club of Winnipeg, Inc.
Box 1144, Winnipeg, MB, R3C 2Y1, Canada
Ukrainian Professional & Business Club Bulletin, 182

* See **MULTI-PUBLISHER INDEX** for list of publications.

University of Manitoba Libraries
University of Manitoba, Winnipeg, MB, R3T 2N2, Canada
Library Directions, 802

Univ. of Winnipeg
230 Lockhart Hall, Winnipeg, MB, R3B 2E9, Canada
Mandala, 208

Westarc Group, Inc.
Brandon University, Brandon, MB, R7A 6A9, Canada
Prairie Progress Newsletter, 148

Winnipeg Latvian Society
C/o O. Radovskias, 97 Lennox Ave., Winnipeg, MB, R2M
1B1, Canada
Vinipegas Latviesu Biedribas Izdevums Informators, 404

Zoological Society of Manitoba
Box 21059 Charleswood P.O., Winnipeg, MB, R3R
3R2, Canada
Zoolog, 1,217

New Brunswick

AEFNB
CP 712, Fredericton, NB, E3B 5B4, Canada
Nouvelles, 323

Association of Museums in New Brunswick
503 Queen St., Box 116 Station A, Fredericton, NB, E3B
4Y2, Canada
Bulletin, 903

Atlantic Bldg. Supply Dealers Assn.
95 Foundry St., #203, Moncton, NB, E1C 5H7, Canada
Atlantic Building Supply News, 244

Atlantic Provinces Transportation Commission
#330 1133 St. George Blvd., Moncton, NB, E1E 4E1,
Canada
Tips and Topics, 1,180

Beaverbrook Art Gallery
Box 605, Fredericton, NB, E3B 5A6, Canada
Beaverbrook Art Gallery, 63

CCNB
180 St. John St., Fredericton, NB, E3B 4A9, Canada
ECOAlert, 377

Canadian Paraplegic Assn. -New Brunswick
65 Brunswick St., Fredericton, NB, E3B 1G5, Canada
Paraelite, 523

College of Psychologists of New Brunswick
Box 1194, Sta. A, Fredericton, NB, E3B 5C8, Canada
College of Psychologists of New Brunswick, Bulletin, 1,013

Council of Archives of New Brunswick
Box 6000, Fredericton, NB, E3B 5H1, Canada
CANB Gazette, 794

Huntsman Marine Science Centre
Brandy Cove Rd., St. Andrews, NB, E0G 2X0, Canada
Huntsman Marine Science News, 423

Kings County Historical Society
c/o W. Harvey Dalling, Sec., Hampton, NB, E0G 1Z0,
Canada
Kings County Historical Society Newsletter, 542

•**Maritime Law Book Co.**
Box 302, Fredericton, NB, E3B 4Y9, Canada

•**New Brunswick Dept. of Agriculture**
Box 6000, Fredericton, NB, E3B 5H1, Canada

New Brunswick Genealogical Soc.
Box 3235, Sta. A, Fredericton, NB, E3A 5G9, Canada
Generations, 454

New Brunswick Health Records Assn.
1750 Sunset Drive, Bathurst, NB, E2A 4A4, Canada
New Brunswick Health Records Assn. Newsbreak, 520

New Brunswick Medical Society
176 York St., Fredericton, NB, E3B 3N8, Canada
New Brunswick Medical Society Newsletter, 882

New Brunswick Museum
277 Douglas Ave., Saint John, NB, E2K 1E5, Canada
NBM News, 907

New Brunswick Nurses' Union
750 Brunswick St., Fredericton, NB, E3B 1H9, Canada
Parasol, 931

New Brunswick Provincial Council Boy Scouts of Canada
55 Rothesay Ave., St. John, NB, E2J 2B2, Canada
Scouting News, 1,216

New Brunswick Public Employees Assn.
P. O. Box 95, Fredericton, NB, E3B 4Y2, Canada
Newsline, 710

New Brunswick School Trustees' Assn.
Box 501, Fredericton, NB, E3B 4Z9, Canada
Bulletin, 301

•**New Brunswick Teachers' Assn.**
Box 752, Fredericton, NB, E3B 5R6, Canada

New Brunswick Women's Institute
65 Brunswick St., #251, Fredericton, NB, E3B 1G5,
Canada
Home & Country, 1,209

Recreation & Park Assn. of New Brunswick
440 Wilsey Rd., Ste. 105, Frederickton, NB, E3B 7C5,
Canada
RECorder, 944

Saint John Board of Trade
40 King Street, Box 6037, Saint John, NB, E2L 4R5,
Canada
Saint John Business Today, 151

University of New Brunswick
Students Representative, PO Box 5050, St. John, NB,
E2L 4L5, Canada
Baron, The, 208

Westmorland Historical Society
RR 1, College Bridge, NB, E0A 1L0, Canada
Westmorland Historical Society, Newsletter, 550

Newfoundland

Assn. Newfoundland & Labrador Archivists
Colonial Bldg., Military Rd., St. Johns, NF, A1C 2C9,
Canada
Association of Newfoundland & Labrador Archivists Newsletter, 793

Assn. of Registered Nurses of Newfoundland
PO Box 6116, 55 Military Rd., St. John's, NF, A1C
5X8, Canada
ARNN Access, 928

Atlantic Provinces Council on the Sciences
Memorial Univ. of NF, Box 4200, St. John's, NF, A1C
5S7, Canada
Atlantic Science, 1,095

The Canadian Paraplegic Assn.-Newfoundland & Labrador Inc.
The Roberts Bldg. Ste. 202, 95 LeMarchant Rd., St.
Johns, NF, A1C 2H1, Canada
Rampart, 278

Centre for Cold Ocean Resources Engineering
Memorial Univ. of Newfoundland, St. John's, NF, A1B
3X5, Canada
C-CORE News, 935

Geological Assn. of Canada, Dept. of Earth Sciences
Dept.of Earth Sciences, Memorial University of NF, St.
John's, NF, A1B 3X5, Canada
Geolog, 476

Government of Newfoundland
Box 8700, St. John's, NF, A1B 4J6, Canada
Department of Education Newsletter, 307

Hang Gliding Assn. of Newfoundland
16 Woodbine Avenue, Corner Brook, NF, A2H 3N8,
Canada
Atlantic Inflight, 551

NRCAN - Canadian Forest Service
PO Box 6028, St. John's, NF, A1C 5X8, Canada
Woody Points, 436

Newfoundland Assn. of Architects
Box 5204, St. Johns, NF, A1C 5V5, Canada
Newfoundland Assn. of Architects Newsletter, 60

Newfoundland Assn. of Optometrists
Box 2284, Station C, St. John's, NF, A1C 6E6, Canada
Newfoundland Assn. of Optometrists Newsletter, 941

Newfoundland Assn. of Public Employees
Box 8100, St. John's, NF, A1B 3M9, Canada
Communicator, 707

•**Newfoundland Labrador Teachers Association**
3 Kenmount Rd., St. John's, NF, A1B 1W1, Canada

Newfoundland & Labrador Women's Inst.
Box 1854, St. John's, NF, A1C 5P9, Canada
Newfoundland and Labrador Women's Institute Newsletter, 1,210

Newfoundland Status of Women Council
Box 6072, St. John's, NF, A1C 5X8, Canada
Newfoundland Status of Women Council Newsletter, 1,210

Northwest Territories

Northwest Territories Assn. of Municipalities
Box 1529, Yellowknife, NT, X1A 2P2, Canada
Northwest Territories Assn. of Municipalities Newsletter, 490

Northwest Territories Registered Nurses Assn.
Box 2757, Yellowknife, NT, X1A 2R1, Canada
NWTRNA Newsletter, 930

Northwest Territories Teachers Assn.
Box 2340, Yellowknife, NT, X1A 2P7, Canada
Communicate, 305

Nunavut Teachers Association
40 Box 761, Iqaluit, NT, X0A-0H0, Canada
Uqaqta, 335

Nova Scotia

APSEA-RCHI
Box 308, Amherst, NS, B4H 3Z6, Canada
Martimer, 533

Acadia Divinity College
Publications, Wolfville, NS, B0P 1X0, Canada
Acadia Divinity College News, 194

Atlantic Provinces Economic Council
5121 Sackville St., #500, Halifax, NS, B3J 1K1, Canada
Atlantic Provinces Economic Council, Newsletter, 289

Better Business Bureau of Nova Scotia
Box 2124, Halifax, NS, B3J 3B7, Canada
Protector, 149

Bicycle Nova Scotia
Box 3010 S., Halifax, NS, B3J 3G6, Canada
Bicycle Nova Scotia Newsletter, 1,129

Camping Assn. of Nova Scotia
Box 3243, S. Halifax, NS, B3J 3H5, Canada
Camping Assn. of Nova Scotia, Newsletter, 943

Clan Donald Assn. of Nova Scotia
c/o St. Francis Xavier Univers, P.O. Box 5000, Antigonish,
NS, B2G 2W5, Canada
Clan Donald Bulletin, 450

Coordinating Council on Deafness of Nova Scotia
1660 Hollis, Ste. 803, Halifax, NS, B3J 1V7, Canada
Coordinating Council on Deafness of Nova Scotia News, 266

Council of Nova Scotia Archives
6016 University Archives, Halifax, NS, B3H 1W4, Canada
Council of Nova Scotia Archives, Newsletter, 796

Dalhousie University, Computer Centre
Publications, Halifax, NS, B3H 4H8, Canada
University Computer Centre Newsletter, 241

Fed. of Nova Scotian Heritage
1809 Barrington Street, #901, Halifax, NS, B3J 3K8,
Canada
Federation News, 904

Fundy Group Pubs.
Box 128, 2 Second St., Yarmouth, NS, B5A 4B1, Canada
Le Traveller, 1,186

Maritime Telegraph & Telephone
Public Affairs Dept., PO Box Box 880, Halifax, NS, B3J
2W3, Canada
Bulletin, 1,156

Metals Economics Group
1718 Argle St., Suite 300, Halifax, NS, B3J 3N6, Canada
Metals Economics Group Strategic Report, 901

•**NS Department of Natural Resources**
Box 68, Truro, NS, B2N 5B8, Canada

Nova Scotia Assn. of Architects
1361 Barrington St., Halifax, NS, B3J 1Y9, Canada
Nova Scotia Assn. of Architects Newsletter, 60

•**Nova Scotia Association of Health Organizations**
2 Dartmouth Rd., Bedford, NS, B4A 2K7, Canada

Nova Scotia Barrister's Society
1645 Granville Street, Suite 1101, Halifax, NS, B3J
1X3, Canada
Nova Scotia Current Law, 765

Nova Scotia Department of Agriculture
Box 550, Truro, NS, B2N 2E3, Canada
4-H Club News, 35

Nova Scotia Designer Crafts Council
1809 Barrington Street, Suite 901, Halifax, NS, B3J
3K8, Canada
Nova Scotia Designer Crafts Council Newsletter, 555

Nova Scotia Government Employees Union
100 Eileen Stubbs Ave., Dartmouth, NS, B3B 1Y6,
Canada
Nova Scotia Government Employees Union Newsletter, 704

Nova Scotia Institute of Agrologists
Box 550, Truro, NS, B2N 5E3, Canada
Nova Scotia Institute of Agrologists Newsletter, 44

Nova Scotia Liberal Assn.
Box 723, Halifax, NS, B3J 2T3, Canada
Liberalink, 993

Nova Scotia Library Assn.
c/o Glenda Roacne, 32 Glendale Ave., Lower Sackville,
NS, B4C 3M1, Canada
Nova Scotia Library Assn. News, 806

• See **MULTI-PUBLISHER INDEX** for list of publications.

Nova Scotia New Democratic Party
1657 Barrington St., Ste. 533, Halifax, NS, B3J 2A1, Canada
New Democrat, 994

Nova Scotia Nurses Union
65 Queen St., Dartmouth, NS, B2Y 1G4, Canada
Your Union Matters, 932

Nova Scotia Retired Teachers Assn.
3106 Dutch Village Road, Halifax, NS, B3L 4L7, Canada
Retired Teacher, 328

Nova Scotia School Boards Association
Box 605 Station M, Halifax, NS, B3J 2R7, Canada
NSSBA Newsletter, 1,092

Nova Scotia School Library Assn.
C/O Gatez Brook Junior High, RR #1, Head of Chezzetcook, NS, B0J 1N0, Canada
Nova Scotia School Library Assn. Bulletin, 806

Nova Scotia Special Olympics
Box 3010 South, Halifax, NS, B3J 3G6, Canada
Nova Scotia Special Olympics Newsletter, 1,133

•**Nova Scotia Teachers Union**
3106 Dutch Village Rd., Halifax, NS, B3L 4L7, Canada

Planned Parenthood Assn. of Halifax & Dartmouth
3115 Veith St., 3rd Fl., Halifax, NS, B3K 3G9, Canada
Communications in Family Planning, 411

Plant Industry Branch, Horticultural Crops
N.S. Dept. of Agriculture, Box 550, Truro, NS, B2N 5E3, Canada
Beekeeping Notes, 440

Pork Nova Scotia
Box 1341, Truro, NS, B2N 5N2, Canada
Porkfolio, 829

Recreation Assn. of NS
Box 3010 South, Halifax, NS, B3J 3G6, Canada
Recreation Assn. of Nova Scotia Tidings, 944

Royal Arch Masons of Nova Scotia
C/O L.C. Armstrong, RR #4, Shubenacadie, NS, B0N 2H0, Canada
Royal Craftsman, 181

Speech & Hearing Assn. of Nova Scotia
Box 775 Sta M, 5919 South St., Halifax, NS, B3J 2V2, Canada
Reverberations, 534

Squash Nova Scotia
Box 3010 South, Halifax, NS, B3J 3G6, Canada
Tell Tale, 1,136

•**Technical Univ. of Nova Scotia**
1360 Barrington St., Halifax, NS, B3L 4J1, Canada

Technology Associations Secretariat
Technology Innovation Centre, 1 Research Dr., Dartmouth, NS, B2Y 4M9, Canada
Network, 842

Union of Nova Scotia Municipalities
Suite 1106, 1809 Barrington Street, Halifax, NS, B3J 3K8, Canada
Municipal Open Line, 489

Universities Art Association of Canada
c/o D. Burnett, 5163 Duke St., Halifax, NS, B3J 3J6, Canada
Universities Art Association of Canada Journal, 67

Ontario

A.C.A.A.
Box 25, 197 Hunter St W, Peterborough, ON, K9H 2L1, Canada
Operation Mind Fuck, 472

ACCIS - The Graduate Workforce Professionals
1209 King St. W., #205, Toronto, ON, M6K 1G2, Canada
Resume, 328

Academy of Canadian Cinema and Television
158 Pearl St., Toronto, ON, M5H 1L3, Canada
Infocus, 420

Addiction Research Foundation
33 Russell St., Toronto, ON, M5S 2S1, Canada
Projection, 525

Advertising & Sales Club of Toronto
Box 237, Sta. K, Toronto, ON, M4P 2G5, Canada
ASCOT News, 9

Aerospace Industries Assn. of Canada
60 Queens St., #1200, Ottawa, ON, K1P 5Y7, Canada
Aerospace News, 25

Alcohol & Drug Concerns
4500 Sheppard Ave., E., Ste. 112H, Scarborough, ON, M1F 3R6, Canada
Concerns, 305

Anglican Church of Canada, Diocese of the Arctic
1055 Avenue Road, Toronto, ON, M5N 2C8, Canada
Arctic News, 1,052

Anglican Church of Canada, Diocese of Ottawa
71 Bronson Ave., Ottawa, ON, K1R 6O6, Canada
Anglican Church Women, News Bulletin, 1,052

Angus Telemanagement Group, Inc.
8 Old Kingston Road, Ajax, ON, L1T 2Z7, Canada
Telemanagement, 1,163

Animal Defence League of Canada
Box 3880, STN C, Ottawa, ON, K1Y 4M5, Canada
Animal Defence League of Canada News Bulletin, 48

Anne Petite Associates Limited
160 Guildwood Parkway, West Hill, ON, M1E 1P4, Canada
Service Report, The, 845

Archives Association of Ontario
Box 46009, College Park P. O., 444 Yonge Street, Toronto, ON, M5B 2L8, Canada
Off the Record, 806

•**Ariad Custom Publishing**
119 Spadina Ave., #1005, Toronto, ON, M5V 2L1, Canada

Armenian Evangelical Church
34 Glenforest Rd., Toronto, ON, M4N 1Z8, Canada
Canada Armenian Press Newsletter, 1,061

Art Gallery of Ontario
317 Dundas St., W., Toronto, ON, M5T 1G4, Canada
Journal, 905

Assn. for Bright Children of Ontario
2 Bloor St. W., #100-156, Toronto, ON, M4W 2G7, Canada
Association for Bright Children Newsmagazine, 167

Association of Canadian Archivists
Box 2596, Station D, Ottawa, ON, K1P 5W6, Canada
ACA Bulletin, 535

Assn. of Canadian Faculties of Dentistry
1815 Alta Vista Dr., #109, Ottawa, ON, K1G 3Y6, Canada
ACFD/AFDC's Forum, 267

Assn. of Canadian Industrial Designers
C/O Humber College, 205 Humber College Blvd., Rexdale, ON, M9W 5L7, Canada
Association of Canadian Industrial Designers, Newsletter, 607

Association of Canadian Map Libraries and Archives
National Archives of Canada., 344 Wellington St., Ottawa, ON, K1A 0N3, Canada
Association of Canadian Map Libraries & Archives Bulletin, 793

Assn. of Canadian Medical Colleges
774 Echo Drive, Ottawa, ON, K1S 5P2, Canada
ACMC Forum, 863

Assn. of Canadian Orchestras
56 the Esplanade, #311, Toronto, ON, M5E 1A7, Canada
Orchestra Canada/Orchestres Canada, 916

Assn. Canadienne des Detaillants en Quincaillerie
6800 Campobello Rd., Mississagua, ON, L5N 2L8, Canada
ACDQ Journaliste, 495

Association Canadienne d'Education
252 Bloor St. W, #8-200, Toronto, ON, M5S 1V5, Canada
Le Bulletin de l'ACE, 315

•**Assn. of Consulting Engineers of Canada**
130 Albert Street, Suite 616, Ottawa, ON, K1P 5G4, Canada

Assn. of Cultural Executives
133 Barton Ave., Toronto, ON, M6G 1R1, Canada
ACE News, 258

Assn. for the Export of Canadian Books
1 Nicholas St., #504, Ottawa, ON, K1N 7B7, Canada
BiblioExport, 115

Assn. Francaise des Conseils Scolaires de l'Ontario
435 Blvd Saint Laurent, Ottawa, ON, K1K 2Z8, Canada
l'Infoscolaire, 316

Assn. of Iroquois and Allied Indians
R.R. 2, Southwold, ON, N0L 2G0, Canada
Unity, 406

•**Assn for Media & Technology in Education in Canada**
3-1750 the Queensway, Ste. 1318, Etobicoke, ON, M9C 5H5, Canada

Assn. of Parliamentary Librarians in Canada
Library of Parliament, Parliament Bldgs., Ottawa, ON, K1A 0A9, Canada
Assn. of Parliamentary Librarians in Canada, Bulletin, 793

Association of Polish Engineers in Canada
206 Beverley, Toronto, ON, Canada
Association of Polish Engineers in Canada, Bulletin, 359

Australian High Commission
50 O'Connor St., Ottawa, ON, K1P 6L2, Canada
Australia Report, 626

•**Automobile Industries Assn.**
1272 Wellington St., Ottawa, ON, K1Y 3A7, Canada

Bank of Canada
Public Distribution, 234 Wellington St, Ottawa, ON, K1A 0G9, Canada
Weekly Financial Statistics, 100

Bank of Nova Scotia, Public & Corporate Affairs
44 King St. W., 8th Fl., Scotia Plz., Toronto, ON, M5H 1H1, Canada
Global Economic Outlook, 91

Baxter Publishing Co.
310 Dupont St., Toronto, ON, M5R 1V9, Canada
Canadian Defense Update, 894

•**Bedford House**
1800 Ironstone Mnr.Pickering, Toronto, ON, L1W 3T9, Canada

Best Bottles Inc.
PO Box 21011, Stratford, ON, N5A 7V4, Canada
Best Bottles Wineletter, 102

Birthright Intl.
777 Coxwell Ave., Toronto, ON, M4C 3C6, Canada
Birthright Life-Guardian, 1,114

Blendon Information Services
68 Longmore Street, Willowdale, ON, M2N 6T8, Canada
Industrial Specialties News, 900

Boiler Inspection
8 King St., E., Toronto, ON, M5C 1B5, Canada
Power Protection, 595

Boy Scouts of Canada, Toronto
9 Jackes Ave., Toronto, ON, M4T 1E2, Canada
Provincial Notes, 1,215

Brazil-Canada Chamber of Commerce
6-2400 Dundas St., W., Box 355, Mississauga, ON, L5K 2R8, Canada
Brazil-Canada Newsletter, 642

Burlington Fine Arts Association
425 Brock Ave., Burlington, ON, L7S 1M8, Canada
Burlington Fine Arts Association Newsletter, 63

•**Business Law Reporting Service**
Box 1762, Kingston, ON, K7L 5J6, Canada

Businesstek Publishing, Inc.
Box 250, Carleton Place, ON, K7C 3P4, Canada
Marketing Law Reporting Service, 18

•**Butterworths**
75 Clegg Rd., Markham, ON, L6G 1A1, Canada

CAMMAC
283 Bogert Ave., Toronto, ON, M2N 1L4, Canada
CAMMAC Newsletter, Southern Ontario Region, 910

•**CCH Canadian Ltd.**
6 Garamond Ct., North York, ON, M3C 1Z5, Canada

CDN Business Aircraft Association
1317-50 O'Connor St., Ottawa, ON, K1P 6L2, Canada
CBAA NEWS BRIEF, 28

CIRPA
214 King Street W., Suite 614, Toronto, ON, M5H 3S6, Canada
CIRPA Newsletter, 910

C.S.T. Consultants, Inc.
200-240 Duncan Mill Road, Don Mills, ON, M3B 3P1, Canada
C.S.T. Connection, 131

CUSO
2255 Carling Ave, Ste 400, Ottawa, ON, K2B 1A6, Canada
CUSO Forum, 303

Camford Information Services
801 York Mills Road, Suite 201, Don Mills, ON, M3B 1X7, Canada
Camford Chemical Report, 163

Canada Communication Group Operation
Ottawa, ON, K1A 0S9, Canada
Canada Corporations Bulletin, 131

Canada Dept. of Agriculture
930 Carling Ave., Ottawa, ON, K1A 0C7, Canada
Forage Notes, 418

Canada Institute for Scientific & Technical Information
Natl. Research Council, Canada, Bldg. M55, Montreal Rd., Ottawa, ON, K1A 0S2, Canada
CISTI News, 795

Canada Israel Committee
980 Yonge St., #402, Toronto, ON, M4W 2J5, Canada
Middle East Insider, 634

* See **MULTI-PUBLISHER INDEX** for list of publications.

* See *MULTI-PUBLISHER INDEX* for list of publications.

•**Canadian Institute of Chartered Accountants**
277 Wellington Street West, Toronto, ON, M5V 3H2, Canada

Canadian Institutes of Travel Counsellors
55 Eglinton Ave. East, Suite #209, Toronto, ON, M4P 1G8, Canada
Canadian Institutes of Travel Counsellors, Update, 1,183

Canadian Intramural Recreation Association
1600 James Naismith Drive, Suite 601, Gloucester, ON, K1B 5N4, Canada
CIRA Bulletin, 302

Canadian Jesuit Mission
1190 Danforth Ave., Toronto, ON, M4J 1M6, Canada
Canadian Jesuit Missions, 1,055

Canadian Lesbian & Gay Archives
P.O Box 639, Station A, Toronto, ON, M5W 1G2, Canada
Lesbian and Gay Archivist, 445

Canadian Magazine Publishers Assn.
2 Stewart St., Toronto, ON, M5V 1H6, Canada
Canadian Magazine Publishers Assn., 953

•**Canadian Masonry Contractors' Association**
360 Superior Blvd.,, Mississauga, ON, L5T-2N7, Canada

Canadian Mathematical Society
577 King Edward, Ste. 109, Box 450, Station A, Ottawa, ON, K1N 6N5, Canada
C.M.S. Notes, 852

Canadian Medical & Biological Engineering Society
Natl. Research Council, Montreal Rd., Bldg.M55, Rm393, Ottawa, ON, K1A 0R8, Canada
Canadian Medical and Biological Engineering Society Newsletter, 870

Canadian Merchant Service Guild
1150 Morrison Dr., Ottawa, ON, K2H 8S9, Canada
Guild News, 253

Canadian Motorcycle Assn., Inc.
500 James St. N., #201, Hamilton, ON, L8L 1J3, Canada
Canadian Motorcycle Assn., The Link, 1,176

Canadian Museums Assn
280 Metcalfe St., #400, Ottawa, ON, K2P 1R7, Canada
Museogramme, 906

Canadian Music Educators Association
16 Royaleigh Ave., Etobicoke, ON, M9P 2J5, Canada
CMEA Newsletter, 910

Canadian Musical Heritage Society
Box 53161, Ottawa, ON, K1N 1C5, Canada
News-Can. Musical Heritage Soc./Nouvelles de la Soc. pour le Patrimoine Musical Can., 915

Canadian Nuclear Assn. (CNA)
144 Front Street West Ste. 725, Toronto, ON, M5J 2L7, Canada
CNS Bulletin, 926

Canadian Nursery Trades Assn.
7856 Fifth Line S., RR 4 Stn. Main, Milton, ON, L9T 2X8, Canada
Canadian Nursery Trades Association Newsbrief, 38

Canadian Opera Co.
227 Front St. , E., Toronto, ON, M5A 1E8, Canada
Canadian Opera Company News, 911

Canadian Organization for Development through Education
321 Chapel St., Ottawa, ON, K1N 7Z2, Canada
Ngoma: The Talking Drum, 1,120

Canadian Parents for French
309 Cooper St., Suite 210, Ottawa, ON, K2P 0G5, Canada
CPF National News, 303

Canadian Payroll Assn.
1867 Yonge St., Ste. 801, toronto, ON, M4S 1Y5, Canada
Dialogue: The Canadian Payroll Assn., 609

Canadian Physiological Society
University of Western Ontario, Department of Physiology, London, ON, N6A 5C1, Canada
Physiology Canada, 980

Canadian Physiotherapy Assn.
890 Yonge St., 9th Fl., Toronto, ON, M4W 3P4, Canada
Contact, 979

Canadian Polish Congress
288 Roncesvalles Ave., Toronto, ON, M6R 2M4, Canada
Canadian Polish Congress. Information Bulletin, 407

Canadian Political Science Association
1 Stewart St. #205, Ottawa, ON, K1N 6H7, Canada
Canadian Political Science Association Bulletin, 987

Canadian Poultry & Egg Processors Council
2 Gurdwara Rd. Ste. 406, Ottawa, ON, K2E 1A2, Canada
Poultry Stocks & Supplies, 1,001

Canadian Printing Industries Assn.
75 Albert St., #906, Ottawa, ON, K1P 5E7, Canada
CBFA Newsletter, 1,003

Canadian Professional Golfers' Assn.
13450 Dublin Line, RR #1, Acton, ON, L7S 2W7, Canada
Canadian Professional Golfers' Assn., Bulletin, 480

Canadian Professional Sales Association
145 Wellington St. W., #310, Toronto, ON, M5J 1H8, Canada
Contact, 1,086

Canadian Progress Club
2395 Bayview Ave., North York, ON, M2L 1A2, Canada
Progression, 181

•**Canadian Public Health Assn.**
1565 Carling Ave., #400, Ottawa, ON, K1Z 8R1, Canada

•**Canadian Red Cross, Ontario Div.**
5700 Cancross Ct., Mississauga, ON, L5R 3E9, Canada

Canadian Rehabilitation Council for the Disabled
45 Sheppard Ave. E., #801, Toronto, ON, M2N 5W9, Canada
Access, 497

Canadian Religious Conference
324 Laurier Ave. E., Ottawa, ON, K1N 6P6, Canada
Canadian Religious Conference. CRC Bulletin, 1,045

•**Canadian Research Institute for the Advancement of Women**
151 Slater St., #408, Ottawa, ON, K1P 5H3, Canada

Canadian Restaurant & Foodservices Assn.
316 Bloor St., W., Toronto, ON, M5S 1W5, Canada
National Hospitality News, 1,076

Canadian Retail Hardware Assn.
6800 Campobello Rd., Mississauga, ON, L5N 2L8, Canada
CRHA Reporter, 496

Canadian Rose Society
10 Fairfax Cres., Scarborough, ON, M1L 1Z8, Canada
Rosarian, 443

Canadian Scene
73 Simcoe St., 3rd Fl., Toronto, ON, M5J 1W9, Canada
Canadian Scene, 1,044

Canadian Schizophrenia Foundation
16 Florence Ave., North York, ON, M2N 1E9, Canada
Health & Nutrition Update, 509

Canadian School Libraries Assn.
602-200 Elgin St., Ottawa, ON, K2P 1L5, Canada
School Libraries in Canada, 810

Canadian Seed Growers Assn
CPO Box 8455, Ottawa, ON, K1G 3T1, Canada
Seed Scoop, 46

Canadian Ski Council
7035 Fir Tee Dr., Mississauga, ON, L5S 1V6, Canada
Ski Focus, 1,135

Canadian Society of Club Managers
41 Shilton Rd., Agincourt, ON, M1S 2J8, Canada
Communique, 835

Canadian Society for Education Through Art
1487 Parish Ln., Oakville, ON, L6M 2Z6, Canada
Viewpoints, 67

Canadian Society of Environmental Biologists
Box 962, Station F, Toronto, ON, M4Y 2N9, Canada
Canadian Society of Environmental Biologists Newsletter, 374

Canadian Society for International Health
170 Laurier Ave. W, Suite #902, Ottawa, ON, K1P 5V5, Canada
Synergy, 529

Canadian Society of Laboratory Technologists
Box 2830, LCD 1, Hamilton, ON, L8N 3N8, Canada
Canadian Society of Laboratory Technologists, Bulletin, 1,095

Canadian Society of Military Medals & Insignia
1531 Bayview Ave, P.O Box 43536, Toronto, ON, M4G 4G8, Canada
Canadian Military Medals & Insignia Journal, 551

Canadian Special Olympics
40 St. Clair Ave. W., #209, Toronto, ON, M4V 1M2, Canada
Canadian Special Olympics, Bulletin, 1,130

Canadian Standards Association
178 Rexdale Boulevard, Rexdale, ON, M9W 1R3, Canada
CSA and the Consumer, 251

Canadian Table Tennis Association
1600 James Naismith Dr., Gloucester, ON, K1B 5N4, Canada
20/20, 1,128

Canadian Tax Foundation
One Queen St. E., Suite 1800, Toronto, ON, M5C 2Y2, Canada
Canadian Tax Highlights, 1,141

Canadian Tax Planners Ltd.
Box 6489, London, ON, N5W 3S5, Canada
Canadian Tax Planner's Newsletter, 1,141

Canadian Teachers' Fed.
110 Argyle Ave., Ottawa, ON, K2P 1B4, Canada
CTF Link, 303

Canadian Unitarian Council
188 Eglinton Ave. E. #706, Toronto, ON, M4P 2X7, Canada
Canadian Unitarian, 1,061

Canadian Urban Transit Assn.
55 York St., Suite 901, Toronto, ON, M5J 1R7, Canada
CUTA Forum, 1,176

Canadian Voice of Women for Peace
736 Bathurst St., Ste. 215, Toronto, ON, M5S 2R4, Canada
Voices, 1,212

Canadian Water Polo Assn.
1600 James Naismith Dr., Gloucester, ON, K1B 5N4, Canada
Newsletter of Water Polo Canada, 1,133

Canadian Water Ski Assn.
1600 James Naismith Dr., Gloucester, ON, K1B 5N4, Canada
Ski Nautique News, 1,113

Canadian Wood Council
1730 St. Laurent Blvd., Suite 350, Ottawa, ON, K1P 6L5, Canada
Wood Leader, 831

Canadian Wood Pallet & Container Assn.
Box 640, Pickering, ON, L1V 3T3, Canada
Canadian Wood Pallet & Container Assn., Newsletter, 830

Canoe Ontario
1220 Sheppard Ave. E., Willowdale, ON, M2K 2X1, Canada
Canews, 113

Carleton University Research Services
Dunton Tower, Rm. 1501, 1125 Colonel By Dr., Ottawa, ON, K1S 5B6, Canada
Challenge Fund Journal, 194

•**Carswell**
2075 Kennedy Road, One Corporate Plaza, Scarborough, ON, M1T 3V4, Canada

Casino Tourism Assn. Review
225 Ferris Rd., Toronto, ON, M4B 1H2, Canada
Casino News & Entertainment Review, 368

Catholic Health Association of Canada
1247 Kilborn Pl., Ottawa, ON, K1H 6K9, Canada
CHAC Info/Info ACCS, 500

Catholic Information Center
830 Bathurst St., Toronto, ON, M5R 3G1, Canada
Centre News, 1,056

Center for Resource Studies
Queens University, Kingston, ON, K7L 3N6, Canada
CRS Perspectives, 899

Centre for Professional Writing
200 University Ave. W, Waterloo, ON, N2L 3G1, Canada
Upon Further Muse, 862

Children's Aid Society of Ottawa-Carleton
1602 Telesat Ct., Gloucester, ON, K1B 1B1, Canada
Communique, 1,116

Children's Book Center
35 Spadina Rd., Toronto, ON, M5R 2S9, Canada
Children's Book News, 168

Christian Children's Fund of Canada
1027 McNicoll Ave. E., Scarborough, ON, M1W 3X2, Canada
Canadaid: A News Report to Sponsors and Friends, 1,115

Christian Horizons Newsletter
384 Arthur St., S., Elmira, ON, N3B 2P4, Canada
Christian Horizons Newsletter, 276

Christian Labour Assn. of Canada
5920 Atlantic Dr., Mississauga, ON, L4W 1N6, Canada
Guide, 1,208

Church Council on Justice & Corrections
507 Bank St., 2nd Fl., Ottawa, ON, K2P 1Z5, Canada
Church Council on Justice & Corrections, Update, 1,046

Church of Jesus Christ of Latter Day Saints
888 Byron Avenue, Ottawa, ON, K2A 0J1, Canada
Eastern Canada Church News, 1,073

Church Library Assn. of Ontario
1202 York Mills Rd., #1104, Don Mills, ON, M3A 1Y2, Canada
Library Lines, 802

•**Citizens for Safe Cycling (Ottawa-Carleton)**
PO Box 248, Station B, Ottawa, ON, K1P 6C4, Canada

---

* See **MULTI-PUBLISHER INDEX** for list of publications.

Clan Fraser Society of N.A., Canadian Region
71 Charles St. E., #1101, Toronto, ON, M4Y 2T3, Canada
Clan Fraser Society of N. America, Canadian Region Newsletter, 408

Clans & Scottish Societies of Canada
St. Andrew's Church, 73 Simcoe St., Toronto, ON, M5J 1W9, Canada
An Drochaid, 408

Coaching Assn. of Canada
1600 James Naismith Dr., Gloucester, ON, K1B 5N4, Canada
Science Periodical on Research & Technology in Sport, 1,135

Coalition for Lesbian & Gay Rights in Ontario
Box 822, Station A, Toronto, ON, M5W 1G3, Canada
CLGRO Newsletter, 444

College of Nurses of Ontario
101 Davenport Rd., Toronto, ON, M5R 3P1, Canada
College of Nurses of Ontario College Communique, 929

The College of Psychology of Ontario
1246 Yonge Street, Suite 201, Toronto, ON, M4T 1W5, Canada
Bulletin of the Ontario Bd. of Examiners in Psychology, 1,012

College of Veterinarians of Ontario
2106 Gordon St., Guelph, ON, N1L 1G6, Canada
Update, 1,202

Comite Canadien d'Action sur le Statut de la Femme
234 Eglinton Ave. E., Ste. 203, Toronto, ON, M4P 1K5, Canada
Act Now, 1,206

Committee on Monetary and Economic Reform
3284 Yonge St., Ste. 500, Toronto, ON, M4N 3M7, Canada
Economic Reform, 291

Compassion Canada
99 Enterprise Dr., S., London, ON, N6N 1B9, Canada
Compassion Today, 168

Concerned Friends of Ontario Citizens in Care Facilities
170 Merton Street, Toronto, ON, M4S 1A1, Canada
Concerned Friends, 502

Concord Publishing Ltd.
14 Prince Arthur Avenue, Toronto, ON, M5R 1A9, Canada
Employment Law Report, The, 343

Confederation of Canadian Unions
1331 1/2A St. Clair Ave., W, Toronto, ON, M6E 1C3, Canada
Confederation of Canadian Unions, Bulletin, 699

Conference Religieuse Canadienne
324 E. Laurier Ave., Ottawa, ON, K1N 6P6, Canada
Conference Religieuse Canadienne, Bulletin, 1,056

Conrad Grebel College
Publications, Waterloo, ON, N2L 3G6, Canada
Grebel Now, 208

Conservation Council of Ontario
489 College St., #506, Toronto, ON, M6G 1A5, Canada
Ontario Conservation News, 390

Consumer Health Organization of Canada
250 Sheppard Ave. E. #205, Box 248, Willowdale, ON, M2N 5S9, Canada
Consumer Health Newsletter, 503

Coop. Housing Fed. of Canada
225 Metcalfe Street, #311, Ottawa, ON, K2P 1P9, Canada
From the Rooftops, 584

Czechoslovak Assn. of Canada
740 Spadina Ave., Toronto, ON, M5S 2J2, Canada
Vestnik, 401

Dadswell Family Bulletin
1310 Brydges St., London, ON, N5W 2C4, Canada
Dadswell Family Bulletin, 451

David Dunlap Observatory
Box 360, Richmond Hill, ON, L4C 4Y6, Canada
David Dunlap Doings, 68

DeGroote School of Business
McMaster University, Hamilton, ON, L8S 4C7, Canada
Comparative Industrial Relations Newsletter, 608

DePutter Publishing Ltd.
190 Wortley Road Suite #200, London, ON, N6C 4Y7, Canada
Broadwater Market Letter, 38

Del Property Management, Inc.
4800 Dufferin St., Downsview, ON, M3H 5S9, Canada
Delogram, 1,033

Deliberations Research Inc.
Box 182, Adelaide St. Sta., Toronto, ON, M5C 2J1, Canada
Deliberations: The Ian McAvity Market Letter, 661

Dellcrest Children's Centre, Community Relations
1645 Sheppard Avenue W., Downsview, ON, M3M 2X4, Canada
Dellcrest News, 168

Design & Tech. Teachers Assn. of ON
38 Patina Dr., c/o Keith McLaren, Willowdale, ON, M2H 1R1, Canada
Design & Technology Education Bulletin, 307

Diversey Corp.
1 Roberts Beck Parkway, Mississauga, ON, L4Z 3S9, Canada
Conductor, 580

ECC Financial Group
67 Yonge St., #1200, Toronto, ON, M5E 1J8, Canada
Personal Financial Planning Letter, 96

Easter Seal Society
250 Ferrand Dr., Ste. 200, Don Mills, ON, M3C 3P2, Canada
Update, 1,123

•Electro Federation
10 Carlson Court, #210, Rexdale, ON, M9W 6L7, Canada

Empire Financial Group
259 King St. East, Kingston, ON, K7L 3A8, Canada
LifeLine / Vitalite, 622

Employment Equity Update
44 Laird Drive, Ste. 300, Toronto, ON, M4G 3T2, Canada
Employment Equity Update, 343

Energy Probe
225 Brunswick Ave., Toronto, ON, M5S 2M6, Canada
Energy Futures, 353

Entomological Society of Canada
393 Winston Ave., Ottawa, ON, K2A 1Y8, Canada
Entomological Society of Canada, Bulletin, 370

Eritrean Relief Assn. in Canada, Inc.
29 Prince Arthur Ave., Toronto, ON, M5R 1B2, Canada
Eritrean Newsletter, 583

•Evans Research Corp. of Canada
1 Eva Rd. #309, Etobicoke, ON, M9C 4Z5, Canada

Evasona Co.
Box 541, Thornhill, ON, L3T 2C0, Canada
Market Insider Bulletin, 676

•Evert Communications Ltd.
1296 Carling Ave., Ottawa, ON, K1Z 7K8, Canada

Excalibur Publications
420 Student Center, York Univ., North York, ON, M3J 1P3, Canada
York Gazette, 208

Excise/Cest News
9th Floor, Place Vanier 'C', 25 McArthur Avenue, Ottawa, ON, K1A 0L5, Canada
Revenue Canada, Excise/Cest News, 1,151

•Faculty of Arts and Science /Public Relations Dept.
University of Toronto, 100 St. George Street, Toronto, ON, M5S 1A1, Canada

Family Service Canada
220 Laurier Ave. W., Ste. 600, Ottawa, ON, K1P 5Z9, Canada
Let's Talk Families, 413

Farm Safety Assn., Inc.
340 Woodlawn Rd. W., #22, Guelph, ON, N1H 7K6, Canada
Farmsafe, 506

Federated Women's Institutes of Canada
251 Bank St. #606, Ottawa, ON, K2P 1X3, Canada
Federated News, 1,208

Fed. of Canadian Archers, Inc.
1600 James Naismith Dr., Gloucester, ON, K1B 5N4, Canada
Canadian Archer, 1,130

Federation of Cath. Parent/Teacher Assn. of Ontario
80 Sheppard Ave., Toronto, ON, M2N 6E8, Canada
Federation of C.P.T.A.s of Ontario Newsletter, 310

Fed. of Medical Women of Canada
106, 1815 Alta Vista Dr., Ottawa, ON, K1G 3Y6, Canada
Fed. of Medical Women of Canada, Newsletter, 874

Figure and Face
24 Bellair St., Toronto, ON, M5R 2C7, Canada
Figure and Face, 1,208

Figure Skating Coaches of Canada
Box 93, Agincourt, ON, M1S 3B4, Canada
Circle, 1,130

Financial Executive Institute Canada
141 Adelaide St. West, Ste. 1701, Toronto, ON, M5H 3L5, Canada
FEI Canada Newsletter, 88

Fink & Bornstein
466 DuPont Street, Toronto, ON, M5R 1W6, Canada
Fink and Bornstein Workers' Compensation Newsletter, 738

First Portuguese Canadian Club, Inc.
722 College St., Toronto, ON, M6G 1C4, Canada
First Portugese Canadian News (Noticias), 407

Floorcovering Institute of Ontario
25 Clairville Dr., Rexdale, ON, M9W 5Z7, Canada
FIO Covering Ontario, 625

Foreign Service Community Assn.
L.B. Pearson Bldg., Sussex Dr., Ottawa, ON, K1A 0G2, Canada
FSCA Bulletin, 583

•Friedberg Commodity Management Inc.
BCE Place, 181 Bay Street, Suite 250, P.O. Box 866, Toronto, ON, M5J 2T3, Canada

Gallup Canada, Inc.
180 Bloor St. W., 10th Fl., Toronto, ON, M5S 2V6, Canada
Gallup Poll, The, 990

Gardenesque
14 Gertrude Place, Toronto, ON, M4J 1R3, Canada
Gardenesque, 441

George Bonavia
3295 Southgate Road, Ottawa, ON, KIV 7Y3, Canada
From My Bookshelf: Books Noted For You, 798

Goodwill Industries of Toronto
234 Adelaide St., E., Toronto, ON, M5A 1M9, Canada
Goodwill Dimensions, 1,117

Goodyear Canada, Inc.
10 Four Seasons Pl., Islington, ON, M9B 6G2, Canada
Business Briefly, 578

Greater Welland Chamber of Commerce
55 Main St. E., Welland, ON, L3B 3W3, Canada
Welland Alive, 156

Guelph Historical Society
Box 1502, Guelph, ON, N1H 6N9, Canada
Guelph Historical Society Newsletter, 540

Haiku Canada Newsletter
Apt. 2609A, 500 Laurier W., Ap, Ottawa, ON, K1R 5E1, Canada
Haiku Canada Newsletter, 982

Halfyard Heritage
R. R. Halfyard, St. Catharines, ON, L2M 2E1, Canada
Halfyard Heritage, 455

Hamilton Automobile Club
393 Main St. E., Hamilton, ON, L8N 3T7, Canada
H.A.C. News, 73

Hamilton Naturalists Club
Box 89052, Hamilton, ON, L8S 4R5, Canada
Wood Duck, 921

Harold Taylor Time Consultants
2175 Sheppard Ave., E. #310, Willowdale, ON, M2J 1W8, Canada
Time Management Report, 846

Hartley Gibson Company, Ltd.
2533 Gerrard Street East, Scarborough, ON, M1N 1W9, Canada
Communicate 2000, 133

Heating, Refrigerating & Air Conditioning Inst. of Canada
5045 Orbitor Drive, Building 11, Suite 300, Mississauga, ON, L4W 4Y4, Canada
HRAI News, 534

•Hilborn Group Ltd., The
109 Vanderhoof Ave., Ste. 200, Toronto, ON, M4G 2H7, Canada

Horizons of Friendship
50 Covert Street, Cobourg, ON, K9A 4L1, Canada
Horizons Newsletter, 173

•Hospital Auxiliaries Assn. of Ontario
150 Ferrand Dr., Don Mills, ON, M3C 1H6, Canada

The Huguenot Society of Canada
10 Adelaide St. E., Toronto, ON, M5C 1J3, Canada
Huguenot Trails, 1,067

Human-Animal Bond Association of Canada
P.O. Box 71012, Maplehurst Postal Outlet, Burlington, ON, L7T 4J8, Canada
Animals & Us, 48

Human Rights Internet c/o Human Rights Centre
8 York Street, Suite 202, Ottawa, ON, K1N 5S6, Canada
Human Rights Research and Education Bulletin, 173

•Hume Publishing Company Ltd.
Suite 515, 4100 Yonge St., Willowdale, ON, M2P 2B9, Canada

Huntington Society of Canada
13 Water St. N., #3, Box 1269, Cambridge, ON, N1R 7G6, Canada
Horizon, 513

Huron County Historical Society
RR1 Box 16, Bayfield, ON, N0M 1G0, Canada
Huron Historical Notes, 542

* See **MULTI-PUBLISHER INDEX** for list of publications.

Hybrid Press Ltd.
Box 589, Orleans, ON, K1C 1S9, Canada
Pension Tax Reports, 1,150

Indexing & Abstracting Society of Canada
Box 744, Station F, Toronto, ON, M4Y 2N6, Canada
Indexing & Abstracting Society of Canada, Bulletin, 953

Industrial Accident Prevention Assn.
250 Yonge Street, Suite 2800, Toronto, ON, M5B 2N4, Canada
Accident Prevention Bi-Monthly, 1,078

•Informetrica Limited
Box 828, Station B, Ottawa, ON, K1P 5P9, Canada

Inner City Books
Box 1271, Station Q, Toronto, ON, M4T 2P4, Canada
Jung at Heart, 1,015

•Insight Press
55 University Avenue, Suite 1700, Toronto, ON, M5J 2V6, Canada

Institut Canadien des Assureurs-Vie Agrees et des Conseill
41 Lesmill Rd., Don Mills, ON, M3B 2T3, Canada
Commentaires, 619

Inst. of Chartered Life Underwriters & Financial Consultants
41 Lesmill Rd., Don Mills, ON, M3B 2T3, Canada
CLU Comment, 619

Institute for Christian Studies
229 College St., Toronto, ON, M5T 1R4, Canada
Perspective, 325

Institute of Corporate Directors in Canada
55 St. Claire Avenue, Suite 255, Toronto, ON, M4V 2Y7, Canada
Institute of Corporate Directors in Canada, Newsletter, 142

Institute of Public Administration
150 Eglinton Ave. East, Suite #305, Toronto, ON, M4P 1E8, Canada
Public Sector Management/ Management et Secteur Public, 1,024

Insurance Brokers Assn. of Ontario
90 Eglinton Ave. E., 2nd fl., Toronto, ON, M4P 2Y3, Canada
IBAO News, 620

Inter-Church Committee on Human Rights in Latin America
129 St. Clair Ave. W., Toronto, ON, M4V 1N5, Canada
ALERTA, 641

Inter-Varsity Christian Fellowship of Canada
Unit 17, 40 Vogell Rd., Richmond Hill, ON, L4B 3N6, Canada
Intercessor, 1,064

Intergovernmental Committee on Urban & Regional Research
150 Eglinton Ave. E., #301, Toronto, ON, M4P 1E8, Canada
Liaison, 488

Intl Commn for Coordination of Solidarity Among Sugar Worker
2084 Danforth Ave., Suite 3, Toronto, ON, M4C1J9, Canada
Sugar World, 705

International Council for Adult Education
720 Bathurst St., #500, Toronto, ON, M5S 2R4, Canada
ICAE News, 312

Intl. Gaming, Inc.
Box 73, Thornhill, ON, L3T 3N1, Canada
International Gamblers' Club Newsletter, 439

The International Save The Pun Foundation
Box 5040, Station A, Toronto, ON, M5W 1N4, Canada
Pundit, The, 605

Investment Canada
C.P. 2800, Succursale D, Ottawa, ON, K1P 6A5, Canada
Investing in Canada, 671

Investment Dealers Assn. of Canada
121 King St. W, Ste. 1600, Toronto, ON, M5H 3T9, Canada
IDA Report, 91

Jauna Gaita
636 Iroquuois Ave., Ancaster, ON, L9G 3B4, Canada
Jauna Gaita, 404

Jesuit Farm Project
Box 1238, 5 Douglas St., Guelph, ON, N1H 6N6, Canada
Foodland Alert, 41

Jewish Community Council of Ottawa
151 Chapel St., Ottawa, ON, K1N 7Y2, Canada
Ottawa Jewish Bulletin, 1,070

Jewish Genealogical Society of Canada (Toronto)
Box 446, Sta. A, Willowdale, ON, M2N 5T1, Canada
Shem Tov, 467

Jubilee Centre for Agricultural Research
115 Woolwich St., 2nd Floor, Guelph, ON, N1H 3V1, Canada
Earthkeeping Ontario, 39

Judo Ontario
1185 Eglinton Ave. East, North Nork, ON, M3C 3C6, Canada
Ontario Judoka, 1,133

Juvenile Diabetes Foundation
49 The Donway West, Suite 320, Don Mills, ON, M3C 3M9, Canada
In Search, 514

K. Clements Executive Dir. Assn. of Universities
350 Albert St., Ottawa, ON, K1R 1B1, Canada
Canadian Association for University Continuing Education Bulletin, 303

Ken Campbell Evangelistic Assn.
Box 100, Milton, ON, L9T 2Y3, Canada
Liberation, 1,064

Kingston Branch, Ontario Genealogical Soc.
Box 1394, Kingston, ON, K7L 5C6, Canada
Kingston Relations, 458

Lakehead University
Oliver Rd., Thunder Bay, ON, P7B 5E1, Canada
Agora, 299

Lambton County Historical Society, c/o Edward Phelps
1777 Lakeshore Rd., Sarnia, ON, Canada
Lambton County Historical Society, Bulletin, 543

•Latin American Working Group
603 1/2 Parliament St., Toronto, ON, M4X 1P9, Canada

Latvian Canadian Cultural Centre
4 Credit Union Dr., Toronto, ON, M4A 2N8, Canada
Toronto Centra, 404

Laurentian Univ.
Ramsey Lake Rd., Sudbury, ON, P3E 2C6, Canada
Laurentian Gazette, 208

Law Society of Upper Canada
Osgoode Hall, Toronto, ON, M5H 2N6, Canada
Law Society of Upper Canada Communique, 749

Le Centre Cor Jesu d'Ottawa
328 rue Chapel, Ottawa, ON, K1N 7Z3, Canada
Philippines, 1,059

Leading Natl. Advertisers
1200 Bay St., #405, Toronto, ON, M5R 2A5, Canada
Monthly Magazine Advertising Summary, 19

Leads
Box 9333, Ottawa, ON, K1G 3V1, Canada
Leads, 143

•League of Canadian Poets
54 Wolseley St., 3rd Floor, Toronto, ON, M5T 1A5, Canada

Learning Disabilities Assn. of Canada
Kildare House, 323 Chapel, Ottawa, ON, K1N 7Z2, Canada
National, 321

Leprosy Mission Canada
40 Wynford Dr., #216, Don MIlls, ON, M3C 1J5, Canada
In Action, 514

Libertarian Socialist Collective
Box 171, Station D, Toronto, ON, M6P 3J8, Canada
Red Menace, 997

Life Insurance Managers Association of Canada
1 Queen St. E., Suite 1700, Toronto, ON, M5C 2X9, Canada
LIMAC Newsletter, 621

Lloydmedia
1200 Markham Rd., Suite 301, Scarborough, ON, M1H 3C3, Canada
Database Marketing Newsletter, 13

Lonergan Research Institute
10 St. Mary, #500, Toronto, ON, M4Y 1P9, Canada
Lonergan Studies Newsletter, 974

Lung Association -Metro Toronto & York Region
573 King Street East, Suite 201, Toronto, ON, M5A 4L3, Canada
Take a Breather..., 529

•MPL Communications, Inc.
133 Richmond St. W., Ste. 700, Toronto, ON, M5H 3M8, Canada

MRG
Box 158, Station D, Toronto, ON, M6P 3J8, Canada
Medical Reform, 879

•Maclean Hunter Publishing Ltd.
Maclean Hunter Building, 777 Bay St., Toronto, ON, M5W 1A7, Canada

Marine Museum of the Great Lakes-Kingston
55 Ontario St., Kingston, ON, K7L 2Y2, Canada
Jib Gems, 905

Massage Therapy Focus on Health Care
324 OakDale Avenue, Ottawa, ON, Canada
Massage Therapy Focus on Health Care, 517

Match Int'l. Centre
200 Elgin St., #1102, Ottawa, ON, K2P 1L5, Canada
Bulletin Match, 627

McMaster Univ.
1280 Main St., W., Hamilton, ON, L8S 4L8, Canada
Records of Early English Drama Newsletter, 824

McMaster University Library Press
Mills Memorial Library, Hamilton, ON, L8S 4L6, Canada
McMaster University Library Research News, 804

•Medical Research Council of Canada
Holland Cross, 5th fl. Tower B, 1600 Scott St., Ottawa, ON, K1A 0W9, Canada

Microscopical Society of Canada
1712 Avenue Rd., Box 54560, Toronto, ON, M5M 4N5, Canada
Microscopial Society of Canada. Bulletin, 941

Ministry of Revenue
33 King Street West, Sixth Floor, Box 627, Oshawa, ON, L1H 8H5, Canada
Revenews, 150

Multiple Sclerosis Society of Canada
250 Bloor St. E., #820, Toronto, ON, M4W 3P9, Canada
MS Canada, 516

Municipal Electric Assn.
20 Eglinton Ave. W., #500, Box 2004, Toronto, ON, M4R 1K8, Canada
Circuit Breaker, 337

Municipal Engineers Assn.
530 Otto Road, Unit #2, Mississauga, ON, L5T 2L5, Canada
Municipal Engineers Assn. Newsletter, 362

Mutual of Omaha
500 Univ. Ave., Toronto, ON, M5G 1V8, Canada
MUO News, 589

Nabisco Canada
10 Park Lawn Rd., Etobicoke, ON, M84 3H8, Canada
Nabisco (year), 591

Natl. Anti-Poverty Org.
256 King Edward Ave., 3rd Fl., Ottawa, ON, K1N 7M1, Canada
NAPO News, 1,119

Natl. Assn. for Photographic Art
23 Latham Ave., Scarborough, ON, M1H 1Y3, Canada
Foto Flash, 976

Natl. Ballet of Canada
157 King Street East, Toronto, Ont., ON, M5C 1G9, Canada
Performer, 266

National CGIT Association
40 St. Clair Ave., Rm. 200, Toronto, ON, M4T 1M9, Canada
Torch, 1,052

Natl. Council of Women of Canada
Room 20, 270 MacLaren St., Ottawa, ON, K2P 0M3, Canada
Flashsheet & Newsletter, 1,208

Natl. Council of YMCA's of Canada
2160 Yonge St., Toronto, ON, M4S 2A9, Canada
Y-Canada, 1,216

Natl. Dairy Council of Canada
221 Laurier Ave., E., Ottawa, ON, K1N 6P1, Canada
National Dairy Council of Canada Direction, 264

National Health & Welfare Union
233 Gilmour St., Ste. 904, Ottawa, ON, K2P 0P1, Canada
National Health & Welfare Union Information Bulletin, 703

National Library of Canada
395 Wellington Street, Ottawa, ON, K1A 0N4, Canada
UDT Newsletter, 811

•National Research Council of Canada, Research Journals
1200 Montreal Rd., Bldg. M-55, Ottawa, ON, K1A 0R6, Canada

Naylor Communications
920 Yonge St 6th flr, Toronto, ON, M4W 3C7, Canada
OSCA Reports, 324

•Niagara Construction Assn.
34 Scott St., St. Catharines, ON, L2R 1C9, Canada

•Norfolk Historical Society
109 Norfolk St., S., Simcoe, ON, N3Y 2W3, Canada

North-South Institute
55 Murray, #200, Ottawa, ON, K1N 5M3, Canada
Review, 637

* See ***MULTI-PUBLISHER INDEX*** for list of publications.

North York Public Library
5120 Yonge Street, North York, ON, M2N 5N9, Canada
New Notes, 591

Northern Ontario Tourist Outfitters Assn.
Box 1140, North Bay, ON, P1B 8K4, Canada
Tourist Outfitter, 56

Older Adult Centres Assn. of Ontario
1220 Sheppard Ave. E. 350, Ste. 409A, Willowdale, ON, M2K 2X1, Canada
Older Adult Centres Assn. of Ontario Newsletter, 1,108

Ontario Alliance of Christian Schools
777 Hwy 53 East, Ancaster, ON, L9K 1J4, Canada
Communicator, 305

Ontario Amateur Wrestling Assn.
1185 Eglinton Ave. East, N. York, ON, M3C 3C6, Canada
Ontario Wrestler, 1,134

Ontario Archaeological Society
126 Willowdale Ave., #4, North York, ON, M2N 4Y2, Canada
Arch Notes, 57

Ontario Association of Applied Kinesiology
6519B Mississauga Rd., Mississauga, ON, L5N 1A6, Canada
Kinnection, 980

Ontario Assn. of Archers
1220 Sheppard Ave., E., Willowdale, ON, M2K 2X1, Canada
4 for 20, 1,128

Ontario Assn. of Committees of Adjustment
4 Egan Circle, 1 Huron St., Stratford, ON, N4Z 1C7, Canada
Ontario Assn. of Committees of Adjustment Newsletter, 490

Ontario Assn. of the Deaf
2395 Bayview Ave., North York, ON, M2L 1A2, Canada
Ontario Assn. of the Deaf Newsletter, 267

Ontario Assn. of Landscape Architects
75 The Donway W., Ste. 302, Don Mills, ON, M3C 2E9, Canada
OALA News, 60

Ontario Assn. of Medical Clinics
2045 Dufferin St., Toronto, ON, M6E 3R4, Canada
Group Practice, 874

Ontario Assn. of Optometrists
290 Lawrence Ave.,W., Toronto, ON, M5M 1B3, Canada
Ontario Assn. of Optometrists News, 941

Ontario Badminton Assn.
1220 Sheppard Ave., E., Willowdale, ON, M2K 2X1, Canada
Badminton Today, 1,129

Ontario Camping Assn.
1810 Avenue Rd., # 302, Toronto, ON, M5M 3Z1, Canada
OCAsional News, 950

Ontario Choral Fed.
100 Richmond St. E., Suite 200, Toronto, ON, M5C 2P9, Canada
Choirs Ontario, 911

Ontario Council for Leadership in Eucational Admin.
Ste. 12-115, Toronto, ON, M5S 1V5, Canada
Ontario Council for Leadership in Educational Admin., 1,092

•**Ontario Crafts Council**
35 McCaul St., Toronto, ON, M5T 1V7, Canada

Ontario Cycling Assn.
1185 Eglington Ave. E. #408, North York, ON, M3C 3C6, Canada
Cycle Ontario, 263

Ontario Dairy Council
6533 Mississauga Rd., #D, Mississauga, ON, L5N 1A6, Canada
Ontario Dairy Council, News & Views, 265

Ontario Dental Association
4 New Street, Toronto, ON, M5R 1P6, Canada
ODA News, 271

Ontario Electrical League
2 Lansing Square, Suite 1000, North York, ON, M2J 4P8, Canada
Dialogue, 337

Ontario Federation of Agriculture
491 W. Eglinton, #500, Toronto, ON, M5N 3A2, Canada
OFA Members' Digest, 44

Ontario Federation for the Cerebral Palsied
1630 Lawrence Ave. W., #104, Toronto, ON, M6L 1C5, Canada
Participaper, 523

Ontario Federation of Home & School Association
252 Bloor St. West, Suite 12-200, Toronto, ON, M5S 1V5, Canada
Ontario Federation of Home & School Association Bulletin, 1,092

Ontario Forestry Association
150 Consumers Rd., Suite 502, Willowdale, ON, M2J 1P9, Canada
Forest People, 435

•**Ontario Genealogical Society**
40 Orchard View Blvd., #251, Toronto, ON, M4R 1B9, Canada

Ontario Genealogical Society, Ottawa Branch
Box 8346, Ottawa, ON, K1G 3H8, Canada
Ottawa Branch News, 463

Ontario Genealogical Society: Whitby-Oshawa Branch
Box 174, Whitby, ON, L1N 5S1, Canada
Kindred Spirits, 458

Ontario General Contractors Association
6303 Airport Rd., Suite 308, Mississauga, ON, L4V 1R8, Canada
Ontario General Contractors Association - The Generals, 249

Ontario Goat Breeders' Assn.
Box 2776, Sta. A., Sudbury, ON, P3A 5J3, Canada
Browse, 38

Ontario Good Roads Assn.
530 Otto Rd., Unit 2, Mississauga, ON, L5T 2L5, Canada
Municipal Routes, 1,077

Ontario Government Libraries Council
C/o Legislative Library, Toronto, ON, M7A 1A2, Canada
OGLC Exchange, 490

Ontario Grape Growers Marketing Bd.
215 Ontario St., St. Catharines, ON, L2R 6Y3, Canada
Le Producteur de Raisin d'Ontario, Ontario Grape Grower, 1,009

Ontario Historical Society
34 Parkview Ave., Willowdale, ON, M2N 3Y2, Canada
OHS Bulletin, 546

Ontario Hospital Association
150 Ferrand Dr., Don Mills, ON, M3C 1H6, Canada
Ontario Hosptials Today, 570

Ontario Hydro Employees Union
244 Eglinton Avenue East, Toronto, ON, M4P 1K9, Canada
OHEU News, 710

Ontario Inst. of Agrologists
173 Wollwich Street, Suite 203, Guelph, ON, N1H 3V4, Canada
OIA Newsletter, 44

Ontario Libertarian Party
1 St Johns Rd, Toronto, ON, M4S 2A3, Canada
Libertarian Bulletin, 993

Ontario Library Assn.
100 Lombard St., Ste. 303, Toronto, ON, M5C 1M3, Canada
Inside OLA, 800

Ontario Municipal Social Services Assn.
5780 Timberlea Blvd., #108, Mississauga, ON, L4W 4W8, Canada
OMSSA Newsletter, 490

Ontario Natural Resources Safety Assn.
PO Box 2050, Stn. Main, 690 McKeonwn Ave., North Bay, ON, P1B 9P1, Canada
Health and Safety Resource, 435

Ontario Nurses Assn.
85 Granville St., #600, Toronto, ON, M5S 3A2, Canada
Ontario Nurses Association Newsletter, 931

Ontario Petroleum Institute, Inc.
555 Southdale Road East, Suite 104, London, ON, N6E 1A2, Canada
OPI Newsletter, 961

Ontario Pharmacist
23 Les Mill Rd., Ste. 301, Don Mill, ON, M3B 3P6, Canada
Ontario Pharmacist, 286

Ontario Physiotherapy Assn.
55 Eglinton Avenue East, Suite #210, Toronto, ON, M4P 1G8, Canada
Physiotherapy Today, 524

Ontario Public Buyers Assn.
Box 608, Maple, ON, L6A 1S5, Canada
Caveat Emptor, 1,028

Ontario Public School Teachers' Federation
5160 Orbitor Drive, Mississauga, ON, L4W 5H2, Canada
News, 1,092

Ontario Puppetry Assn.
Box 180, 65 Front St. W., Suite 0116, Toronto, ON, M2J 1E6, Canada
Ontario Puppetry Association Letter, 1,174

Ontario Reporters' Assn.
Simcoe, ON, N3Y 4L2, Canada
Journalist, 588

Ontario Rifle Assn.
31 Marchington Cir., 1207 Albion Rd., Scarborough, ON, M1R 3M6, Canada
Ontario Rifle Assn. Newsletter, 495

Ontario Secondary School Teachers' Federation
60 Mobile Dr., Toronto, ON, M4A 2P3, Canada
Federation Update, 310

Ontario Securities Commission
20 Queen St. W., #1800, Toronto, ON, M5H 3S8, Canada
OSC Bulletin, 680

Ontario Society of Occupational Therapists
55 Eglinton Ave. E., #210, Toronto, ON, M4P 1G8, Canada
Link, 878

Ontario Teachers Federation
1260 Bay St., Suite 700, Toronto, ON, M5R 2B5, Canada
Interaction (Ontario Teachers Federation), 313

Ontario Traffic Conference
20 Carlton St., Ste. 121, Toronto, ON, M5B 2H5, Canada
Ontario Traffic, 1,077

Ontario Vacation Farms Association
c/o S. Putzel, RR #2, Alma, ON, N0B 1A0, Canada
Ontario Vacation Farms, 1,187

Ontario Veterinary College
Univ. of Guelph, Dean's Office, Guelph, ON, N1G 2W1, Canada
Crest, 1,201

Ottawa Public Library
120 Metcalfe Street, Ottawa, ON, K1P 5M2, Canada
Ottawa Public Library Bulletin, 807

Parents of Multiple Births Assn. of Canada, Inc.
4981 Hwy. #7 E., Unit 12A #161, Markham, ON, L3R 1N1, Canada
Double Feature, 412

Parkinson Foundation of Canada
55 Bloor St. West, Ste. 230, Toronto, ON, M4W 1A5, Canada
Network, 520

Patients' Rights Assn.
40 Homewood Ave., Ste. 315, Toronto, ON, M4Y 2K2, Canada
Patients' Rights Assn. Newsletter, 175

Peace Latvian Lutheran Church
83 Main St., Ottawa, ON, K1S 1B5, Canada
Draudzes Vestis, 1,072

Periodical Writers Association of Canada
24 Ryerson Ave., Toronto, ON, M5T 2P3, Canada
PWAContact, 697

Peterborough Historical Society
Hutchison House, 270 Brock St., Peterborough, ON, K9H 2P9, Canada
Peterborough Historical Society, Bulletin, 546

Pharmaceutical Manufacturers Assn. of Canada
1111 Prince of Wales Dr., #3, Ottawa, ON, K2C 3T2, Canada
Pharmaceutical Manufacturers Assn. of Canada Newsletter, 286

Phoenix Counsel Inc.
1 Springbank Dr., St. Catharines, ON, L2S 2K1, Canada
It's Okay, 1,110

Pioneer Clubs Canada
Box 5447, 2320 Fairview Ave., Burlington, ON, L7R 4L2, Canada
In Touch, 586

•**Plan International Canada**
95 St. Clair Ave. W., Suite 1001, Toronto, ON, M4V 3B5, Canada

•**Playwrights Union of Canada**
54 Wolseley Street, Second Floor, Toronto, ON, M5T 1A5, Canada
Canplay, 1,172

Portside Publications
19 Stanwick Avenue, Toronto, ON, M4E 1Z2, Canada
English Resource, The, 821

•**Prentice-Hall Canada**
1870 Birchmont Rd., Scarborough, ON, M1P 2T1, Canada

Presbyterian Comment
P3-120 Edinburgh Rd., S., Guelph, ON, N1H 5P7, Canada
Presbyterian Comment, 1,074

* See ***MULTI-PUBLISHER INDEX*** for list of publications.

Professional Assn. of Canadian Theatres
Communications Centre, 64 Charles St. E., 2nd fl., Toronto, ON, M4Y 1T1, Canada
Impact!, 1,173

•**Professional Institute of the Public Service of Canada**
53 Auriga Dr., Nepean, ON, K2E 8C3, Canada

Professional Publishing Associates
269 Richmond St. W., Toronto, ON, M5V 1X1, Canada
Canadian Childbirth Educator, 501

Public Service Alliance of Canada
233 Gilmour, Ottawa, ON, K2P 0P1, Canada
PSAC Union Update, 704

Purchasing Management Assn of Canada
2 Carlton St., #1414, Toronto, ON, M5B 1J3, Canada
Progressive Purchasing, 1,028

Quaker Committee on Jails & Justice
60 Lowther Ave., Toronto, ON, M5R 1C7, Canada
Quaker Committee on Jails & Justice Newsletter, 772

The Ram's Horn
125 Highfield Rd., Toronto, ON, M4L 2T9, Canada
Ram's Horn, 45

Recycling Council of Ontario
489 College St., #504, Toronto, ON, M6G 1A5, Canada
Ontario Recycling Update, 390

Ringette Canada Publications
1600 James Nassmith Dr., Gloucester, ON, K1B 5N4, Canada
Annual Ringette Review, 1,129

Ringontario
1220 Shepard Ave E, Willowdale, ON, M0K 2X1, Canada
Ringontario, 1,134

Roaming Roots
75 Pitt Ave., Scarborough, ON, M1L 2R5, Canada
Roaming Roots: A Kent Family History, 466

Rolland, Inc.
140 McLevin, Unit 7, Scarborough, ON, M1B 3V1, Canada
Confidential. . . Newsletter, 946

Roman Catholic School Bd.
140 Cumberland, Ottawa, ON, K1N 7G9, Canada
Link, 1,215

Roslin Publishing, Inc.
24 Follis Avenue, Toronto, ON, M6G 1S3, Canada
Micro Alert: The Canadian Microcomputer Reference Guide, 229

Royal Architectural Institute of Canada
55 Murray - Suite 330, Ottawa, ON, M5W 1A7, Canada
Royal Architectural Institute of Canada Update, 61

•**Royal Bank of Canada**
9th fl., South Tower, Royal Bank Plaza, Toronto, ON, M5J 2J5, Canada

•**Royal Canadian Mounted Police**
1200 Vanien Parkway, Ottawa, ON, K1A 0R2, Canada

Royal College of Dentists of Canada
67 Berkeley St., Toronto, ON, M5A 2W5, Canada
Royal College of Dentists of Canada, 271

Royal Ontario Museum
100 Queen's Park, Toronto, ON, M5S 2C6, Canada
Archaeological Newsletter, 57

Royal Regiment of Canada
Fort York Armoury, 660 Fleet St. West, Toronto, ON, M5V 1A9, Canada
Royal Regiment of Canada Newsletter, 898

St. Catharines Chamber of Commerce
11 King St., Box 940, St. Catharines, ON, L2R 6Z4, Canada
St. Catharines News and Views, 161

St. Clair Group, The
30 St Clair Ave W #805, Toronto, ON, M4V 3A1, Canada
Performance, 370

St. John Ambulance
312 Laurier Ave. East, Box 388, Station A, Ottawa, ON, K1N 8V4, Canada
St. John News, 527

St. Patrick's German Congregation
131 McCarl St., Toronto, ON, M5T 1W3, Canada
Der Deutsche Katholik in Kanada, 1,056

Saint Paul Society
223 Main St., Ottawa, ON, K1S 1C4, Canada
Christian Communications, 1,056

Serbian Chetniks War Vets Assn.
Box 70, Fruitland, ON, L0R 1L0, Canada
Serbia, 408

Serbian League of Canada
335 Britannia Avenue, Hamilton, ON, L3H 1Y4, Canada
Kanadski Srbobran, 408

Service Employees Intl. Union
1 Credit Union Dr., Toronto, ON, M4A 2S6, Canada
204 Reporter, 706

Shaver Poultry Breeding Farms Ltd.
Box 400, Cambridge, ON, N1R 5V9, Canada
Shaver Focus, 1,001

Show Festival Theatre Foundation
Box 774, Niagara, ON, L0S 1J0, Canada
Pshaw, 1,174

Social Planning Council of Hamilton
255 West Ave., N, Hamilton, ON, L8L 5C8, Canada
Community, 1,019

Society of Ontario Nut Growers
C/o G.R. Hambleton, RR2, 1540 Concession 6 Rd., Niagara on the Lake, ON, L0S 1J0, Canada
Song News, 46

Software User, The
8 Vine Crescent, Barrie, ON, L4N 2B3, Canada
The Software User Newsletter, 239

•**Southam Business Communications, Inc.**
1450 Don Mills Rd., Don Mills, ON, M3B 2X7, Canada

Southwestern Ontario Square & Round Dance Assn.
C/O John & Irene Bullock, 690 Santa Monica Rd., London, ON, N6H 3W1, Canada
S.W.O.S.D.A. Bugle, 266

Special Libraries Assn., Toronto Chapter
740 Huron St., Toronto, ON, M4V 2W3, Canada
Courier, 796

Spina Bifida & Hydrocephalus Assn. of Ontario
35 McCaul Street, Suite 310, Toronto, ON, M5T 1V7, Canada
SB Current, 527

Sponsorship Report, The
555 Richmond street West, Suite 504, Toronto, ON, M5V 3B1, Canada
Sponsorship Report, The, 250

•**Statistics Canada**
Holland Ave/RH Coats, Holland Ave/Tunney's Pasture, Ottawa, ON, K1A O26, Canada

Statistics Canada, Agriculture Div., Farm Income & Prices Se
Tunney's Pasture, Ottawa, ON, K1A 0T6, Canada
Livestock Statistics Binder & Updates, 828

Steen Publishing Co.
RR #1, Cheltenham, ON, L0P 1C0, Canada
Fitness Bulletin, 506

Stephen Leacock Assn.
Box 854, Orillia, ON, L3V 6K8, Canada
Newspacket, 818

•**Sterling Communications**
1920 Ellesmere Road, Suite 104, Scarborough, ON, M1H 2WY, Canada

Stone & Cox Ltd.
111 Peter St., #202, Toronto, ON, M5V 2H1, Canada
Canadian Insurance Law Service, 723

Stratford Shakespearean Festival Foundation of Canada
Box 520, Stratford, ON, N5A 6V2, Canada
Fanfares, 1,173

Sudeten Club Forward, Toronto
179 Durant Avenue, Toronto, ON, M4J 4W5, Canada
Vorwarts, Forward, 182

Superannuated Teachers of Ontario
1260 Bay St., Toronto, ON, M5R 2B5, Canada
Superannuated Teachers of Ontario Newsletter, 1,094

Swiss Canadian News
25 Aylesbury Road, Islington, ON, M9A 2M3, Canada
Swiss Canadian News, 182

•**Sydenham Publishing**
344 23rd Street West, Owen Sound, ON, N4K 4G7, Canada

T.B.L. Communications, Inc.
75 Clegg Rd., Ste. #200, Markham, ON, L6G 1A9, Canada
Bottom Line's Canadian Internal Auditing Letter, 2

Tea & Coffee Assn. of Canada
885 Don Mills Rd., Ste. 301, Don Mills, ON, M3C 1V9, Canada
Coffee News Break, 68

Thyroid Foundation of Canada
1040 Gardiners Rd., Kingston, ON, K7P 1R7, Canada
Thyrobulletin, 530

Today's Parent Magazine Group
269 Richmond St., W., Toronto, ON, M5V 1X1, Canada
Your Baby, 78

Toronto Centre for Gay and Lesbian Studies
2 Bloor Street West, Suite 100-129, Toronto, ON, M4W 3E2, Canada
Centre/Fold, 444

Toronto Children's Chorus
931 College St., Toronto, ON, M6H 1A1, Canada
Toronto Children's Chorus, 918

•**Toronto-Dominion Bank**
Toronto Dominion Center, Box 1, Toronto, ON, M5K 1A2, Canada

Toronto Field Naturalists
20 College St., #11, Toronto, ON, M5G 1K2, Canada
Toronto Field Naturalist, 921

Toronto Public Library
281 Front St., E., Toronto, ON, M5A 4L2, Canada
T.P.L. News, 811

Toronto Sportsmen's Association
17 Mill St., Willowdale, ON, M2P 1B3, Canada
Outdoor Crest, 944

Traffic Injury Research Foundation
171 Nepean St., 6th Fl., Ottawa, ON, K2P 0B4, Canada
Impact, 1,080

Transport Canada
200 Kent St., Ottawa, ON, K1A 0N8, Canada
Aviation Safety, Ultralight and Balloon, 27

•**Transportation Assn. of Canada**
2323 St. Laurent Blvd., Ottawa, ON, K1G 4K6, Canada

Travel Scoop
1110 Yonge St., Suite 200, Toronto, ON, M4V 2L6, Canada
Travel Scoop Consumer Newsletter, 1,190

Turner's Syndrome Society
7777 Keele St. Fl. 2, Concord, ON, L4K 1Y7, Canada
Turner's Syndrome News, 530

•**UNICEF Canada**
443 Mt. Pleasant Rd., Toronto, ON, M4S 2L8, Canada

Ukrainian Youth Assn.
133 Fairview Ave., Toronto, ON, M6P 3A6, Canada
Maloda Ukraina, 410

United Senior Citizens of Ontario Inc.
3033 Lakeshore Blvd., W., Toronto, ON, M8V 1K5, Canada
Voice of United Senior Citizens of Ontario Inc., 1,109

University of Alberta Language Dept.
c/o Dept. of Modern Languages, McMaster Univ., Hamilton, ON, L8S 4M2, Canada
Comparative Literature in Canada/Litterature Comparee au Canada, 820

University of Guelph
Dept. of Univ. Communications, Guelph, ON, N1G 2W1, Canada
University of Guelph News Bulletin, 208

University of Guelph Department of Fine Art
Publications, Guelph, ON, N1G 2W1, Canada
Journal, 65

•**University of Guelph Educational Practice**
Publications, Guelph, ON, N1G 2W1, Canada

Univ. of Guelph English Dept.
Publications, Guelph, ON, N1G 2W1, Canada
Sidney Newsletter, 825

University of Guelph School of Engineering
Publications, Guelph, ON, N1G 2W1, Canada
Ontario Agricultural College Alumni News, 194

Univ. of Toronto, Faculty of Applied Science
35 St. George St., Toronto, ON, M5S 1A4, Canada
Engineering Forum, 360

University of Toronto Faculty of Library & Information Sci.
140 St. George St., Toronto, ON, M5S 1A1, Canada
Library and Information Science UPDATE, 802

University of Toronto Faculty of Medicine
Medical Sciences Building, 1 King's College Circ Rm 2388A, Toronto, ON, M5S 1A8, Canada
Med Ed News, 317

V.A. Biro and Associates
92 Beverley Street, Toronto, ON, M5T 1Y1, Canada
Weekly Terrorism Profile, 1,105

Varsity Publications, University of Toronto
44 St. George St., Toronto, ON, M5S 2E4, Canada
Forestry Alumni Newsletter, 194

Veterans Affairs Canada
P.O Box 7700, Charlottetown, ON, C1A 8M9, Canada
Carillon, 925

Vietnamese Assn., Toronto
1364 Dundas St., W., Toronto, ON, M6J 1Y2, Canada
Vietnamese Association's Newsletter, 410

Wayne Patterson
PO Box 130, Grimsby, ON, LSM 4G3, Canada
Developers and Chains, 1,033

Welland Historical Museum
65 Hooker, Welland, ON, L3C 5G9, Canada
Welland Historical Museum Newsletter, 908

• See **MULTI-PUBLISHER INDEX** for list of publications.

Westminster Word Processing
64 Smith St., Welland, ON, L3C 4H4, Canada
Ontario Industrial Arts Bulletin, 147

William M. Mercer, Limited
161 Bay Street, Toronto, ON, M5J 2S5, Canada
Mercer Bulletin, The, 613

Willow Beach Field Naturalists
Box 421, Port Hope, ON, L1A 3W4, Canada
Curlew, 941

Windsor Association of Mold Makers
220 Eastland Blvd., Windsor, ON, N8S 3G9, Canada
Windsor Association of Mold Makers, News, 981

Windsor District Chamber of Commerce
2575 Owellette Place, Windsor, ON, N8X 1L9, Canada
Business Briefs, 157

Women's College Hospital
76 Grenville Street, Toronto, ON, M6S 1B2, Canada
Women's Health Matters, 532

Women's Inter-Church Council of Canada
815 Danforth Ave., Suite 402, Toronto, ON, M4J 1L2, Canada
WICC Newsletter, 1,052

Women's Legal Education and Action Fund
415 Yonge Street, Suite 1800, Toronto, ON, M5B 2E7, Canada
LEAF Lines, 747

Work of Infinite Love of Sacred Heart
511 Durie St., Toronto, ON, M6S 3G8, Canada
Work of Infinite Love of Sacred Heart Newsletter, 1,060

World Federalist of Canada & World Federalist Foundation
207-145 Spruce St., Ottawa, ON, K1R 6P1, Canada
Canadian World Federalist, 987

World Literary of Canada
59 Front St. E., Toronto, ON, M5E 1B3, Canada
Worldlit, 336

Writer's Lifeline
Box 1641, Cornwall, ON, K6H 5V6, Canada
Writer's Lifeline, 984

Writers' Union of Canada
24 Ryerson Ave., Toronto, ON, M5T 2P3, Canada
Writers' Union of Canada Newsletter, 826

York University Institute for Social Research
4700 Keele St., North York, ON, M3J 1P3, Canada
York University Institute for Social Research Newsletter, 1,127

Young Women's Christian Assn. of Canada
80 Gerrard St. East, Toronto, ON, M5B 1G6, Canada
Young Women's Christian Assn. of Canada Newsletter, 183

Youth Society of Management Accountants
70 University Ave., Ste. 300, Toronto, ON, M5J 2M4, Canada
Directions, 4

Prince Edward Island

Canadian Society for Colour
C/O Dr. T. Nilsson, Prince Edward Isl., Charlottetown, PE, C1A 4P3, Canada
Canadian Society for Colour, Newsletter, 579

Construction Assn. of Prince Edward Island
Box 728, Charlottetown, PE, C1A 7L3, Canada
Construction News Bulletin, 246

Harry Fraser, Publisher
R.R. 1, Charlottetown, PE, C1A 7J6, Canada
Fraser's Potato Newsletter, 1,008

Natural History Society of Prince Edward Island
Box 2346, Charlottetown, PE, C1A 8C1, Canada
Island Naturalist, 921

Prince Edward Island Museum & Heritage Foundation
2 Kent St., Charlottetown, PE, C1A 1M6, Canada
Newsletter, 907

Prince Edward Island Public Service Assn.
Box 1116, 51 Univ. Ave., Charlottetown, PE, C1A 7M8, Canada
Prince Edward Island Public Service Assn. News, 1,023

Prince Edward Island School Trustees Assn.
3 Queen St., Box 2000, Charlottetown, PE, C1A 7N8, Canada
In Touch, 312

Prince Edward Island Teachers' Federation
24 Glen Stewart Drive, PO Box 6000, Charlottetown, PE, C1A 8B4, Canada
Prince Edward Island Teachers' Federation Newsletter, 1,093

Prince Edward Island Union of Public Sector Employees
Box 1116, Charlottetown, PE, C1A 7M8, Canada
Advocate, 698

•**Prince Edward Island Women's Institute**
P.E.I. Dept. of Agriculture, Fisheries & Forestry, POB 2000, Charlottetown, PE, C1A 7N8, Canada

Softball Prince Edward Island
Bonshaw, PE, C0A 1C0, Canada
Softball Prince Edward Island Newsletter, 1,135

Quebec

•**A Friend Indeed Publications, Inc.**
3575 Boul. Saint-Laurent, Ste. 402, Montreal, PQ, H2X 2T7, Canada

APES
50 Cremazie O, Montreal, PQ, H2P 2T2, Canada
Association des Pharmaciens des Etablissements de Sante du Quebec. Bulletin d'information., 281

Advertising & Sales Executives Club of Montreal
Suite 369, Queen Elizabeth Hot, Montreal, PQ, H3B 4A5, Canada
Communique, 12

Association des Archivistes du Quebec
C.P. 423, Sillery, PQ, G1T 2R8, Canada
La Chronique, 801

Association for Canadian Studies
Box 8888, Station Centre-Ville, Montreal, PQ, H3C 3P8, Canada
ACS Bulletin AEC, 297

Assn. des Conseils des Medecins et Dentistes du Quebec Bulle
308 est, boul. St. Joseph, Montreal, PQ, H2T 1J2, Canada
A.C.M.D.P.Q. Bulletin, 863

Assn. de la Construction du Quebec-Region de Montreal
470 Place Savoie, 3rd Fl., Montreal, PQ, H4P 1Z6, Canada
L'Entrepreneurship, 248

Assn. des Medecins de Langue Francaise du Canada
8355 St. Laurent Blvd., Montreal, PQ, H2P 2Z6, Canada
A.M.L.F.C. Bulletin, 864

Assn. Provinciale des Constructeurs d'Habitations du Quebec
5800 Boul. L.H. Lafontaine, Anjou, PQ, H1M 1S7, Canada
Information-Construction, 247

Assn. Pulmonaire du Quebec
4837 Rue Boyer, Suite 100, Montreal, PQ, H2J 3E6, Canada
Bulletin, 869

Association Quebecoise des Techniques de l'Eau
407 St-Laurent, Bureau 500, Montreal, PQ, H2Y 2Y5, Canada
Effluent, 1,202

•**Association pour la Sante Publique de Quebec**
3958 Rue Dandurand, Montreal, PQ, H1X 1P7, Canada

•**BCA Publications Ltd.**
1002 Sherbrook St. W., Montreal, PQ, H3A 3L6, Canada

Beauchemin-Beaton-LaPointe, Inc.
2045 Stanley St., Montreal, PQ, H3A 2V4, Canada
Chez BBL, 580

CEGEP de Trois Rivieres
3500, rue de Courval, Trois Rivieres, PQ, G9A 5E6, Canada
La Depeche, 209

Canada Communication Group/Depository Services Program
45 Sacre-Coeur Blvd., Room A2411E Natl. Printing Bur, Hull, PQ, K1A 0S9, Canada
Whats Up Doc?, 889

Canadian Amateur Musicians
1751 Richardson St., Ste. 2509, Montreal, PQ, H3K 1G6, Canada
Amateur Musician/Musicien Amateur Cammac, 909

Canadian Asian Stud. Assn-Centre D'etudes De L'asie De L'est
Universite De Montreal, C.P. 6128, Succ. Centre Ville, Montreal, PQ, H3C 3J7, Canada
Contact, 629

Canadian Electrical Assn.
1 Westmount Sq., Montreal, PQ, H3Z 2P9, Canada
Connections, 337

Canadian Hemophilia Society
1450 City Councillors, #840, Montreal, PQ, H3A 2E6, Canada
Hemophilia Today, 875

•**Canadian Jewish Congress**
1590 Ave. Dr. Penfield, Montreal, PQ, H3G 1C5, Canada

Canadian Marine Publications, Ltd.
1434 St. Catherine W., Ste 512, 5th Fl., Montreal, PQ, H3G 1R4, Canada
Great Lakes Navigation, 1,111

Canadian Music Centre
430 rue St. Pierre, #300, Montreal, PQ, H2Y 2M5, Canada
Alternance, 909

Canadian ORT Reporter
5165 Sherbrooke St., Ste. 208, Montreal, PQ, H4A 1T6, Canada
Canadian ORT Reporter, 870

Canadian Pension Conference
800 Rene Levesque W., #1100, Montreal, PQ, H3B 1X9, Canada
Canadian Pension Conference, Newsletter, 579

Canadian Psychological Assn.
6 Vincent Rd., Old Chelsea, PQ, J0X 1N0, Canada
Highlights, 1,014

Canadian Pulp & Paper Association
1155 Metcalfe St., Suite 1900, Montreal, PQ, H3B 4T6, Canada
Monthly Newsprint Report, 947

Canadian Railway Club
Box 162, Montreal, PQ, H3C 1C5, Canada
Canadian Railway Club Newsletter, 1,029

Canadian Wholesale Drug Assn.
1110 Sherbrooke St. W., #220, Montreal, PQ, H3A 1G8, Canada
Canadian Wholesale Drug Assn., Bulletin, 281

Canadian Zionist Fed.
5250 Decarie Blvd., Ste. 550, Montreal, PQ, H3X 2H9, Canada
Canadian Zionist, 987

Cegep de Rosemont
6400 16th Ave., Montreal, PQ, H1X 2S9, Canada
Quartier Libre, 208

Centre for Endangered Reptiles
347 Rue Bourget, Granby, PQ, J2G 1E8, Canada
Scales and Tales, 1,217

Centre Missionnaire Ste-Therese
4387 Esplanade, Montreal, PQ, H2W 1T3, Canada
Missionaries Together, 1,058

Cercles Jeunes Naturalistes
4101 rue Sherbrooke est, #12, Montreal, PQ, H1X 2B2, Canada
Feuillets du Naturaliste, 920

•**Commission des Ecoles Catholiques de Montreal**
3737 Sherbrooke St., E., Montreal, PQ, Canada

Council for Canadian Unity
2055 Peel St., Ste. 475, Montreal, PQ, H3A 1V4, Canada
Political Analysis Newsletter, 996

•**Dir Des Entreprise**
C.P. 1153, Quebec, PQ, G1K 7C3, Canada

Entretiens d'oraison: Message Spirituel
4120, ave. de Verdome, Montreal, PQ, H4A 3N1, Canada
Entretiens d'oraison: Message Spirituel, 1,056

Fed. des Associations de Professeurs des Universites du Queb
2715 Ch. de la Cote Ste-Cath., Montreal, PQ, H3T 1B6, Canada
Nouvelles Universitaires, 324

Fed. of Medical Specialists of Quebec
CP 216 Succ. Desjardins, Montreal, PQ, H5B 1G8, Canada
Fed. of Medical Specialists of Quebec, Bulletin, 874

GMFI
P.O. Box 25,, Station H, Montreal, PQ, H3G-2K5, Canada
Impartial Global Mutual Fund Investor, 669

Girl Guides of Canada
1939 deMaisonneuve Blvd. West, Montreal, PQ, H3H 1K3, Canada
Trumpet, The, 1,216

Greek Canadian Reportage
7438 Durocher St., Montreal, PQ, H3N 2A3, Canada
Greek Canadian Reportage, 402

Groupe Constructo
1500 Bd. Jules Poitras, St. Laurent, PQ, H4N 1X7, Canada
Quebec Construction, 249

Groupe Marxiste Revolutionnaire
342 est, rue Ontario, Montreal, PQ, Canada
La Taupe Rouge, 992

Imprimerie Drovin Inc.
815, rue Beaumont, Montreal, PQ, H2N 1W1, Canada
Le Feuillet Paroissial, 1,057

Institut d'Histoire de l'Amerique Francaise
261 Avenue Bloomfield, Montreal, PQ, H2V 3R6, Canada
Revue d'Histoire de l'Amerique Francaise, 547

* See **MULTI-PUBLISHER INDEX** for list of publications.

La Ligue de Securite du Quebec
2536 rue La Pierre, La Salle, PQ, H8N 2W9, Canada
Surveillant, 1,085

Les Cooperants, Societe Mutuelle d'Assurance-Vie
600, boul. de Maisonneuve Ques, Montreal, PQ, H3A
3J9, Canada
Sur le Champ, 625

Les Peres Blancs D' Afrique
180 Chemin Ste-foy, Quebec, PQ, G1R 4R2, Canada
Missions d' Afrique, 1,058

•Maxiplan Financial Club
Box 5255 Stn. C, 12687 52nd Ave., Montreal, PQ, H1E
2H6, Canada

McGill Univ. Dept. of Classics
855 Sherbrooke St. W., Montreal, PQ, H3A 2T7, Canada
Teiresias, 549

McGill University, Osler Library
3655 Drummond St., Montreal, PQ, H3G 1Y6, Canada
Osler Library Newsletter, 807

Missionary Sisters of the Immaculate Conception
100 Place J. Desnoyers, Laval, PQ, H7G 1A4, Canada
MIC Mission News, 1,058

Missionnaire Oblats de Marie Immaculee
460-1ere rue, Richelieu, PQ, J3L 4B5, Canada
Semeuse de Joie, 1,060

Montreal Board of Trade
5 Place Rue Marie, Plaza Level, Montreal, PQ, H3P
4Y2, Canada
Montreal Plus, 650

Montreal Catholic School Commission
3737 Sherbrooke St. E., Montreal, PQ, H1X 3B3, Canada
Public School, 1,093

Montreal Exchange
800 Victoria Sq., Stock Exchange Tower, Montreal, PQ,
H4Z 1A9, Canada
Futures and Options News, 666

Montreal General Hospital
1650 Cedar Ave., Rm. E 6-227, Montreal, PQ, H3G
1A4, Canada
Generally Speaking, 563

•Northern Telecom Ltd.
150 Montreal Toronto Blvd., Lachine, PQ, H8S 1B6,
Canada

Office des Communications Sociales
1340 E. Blvd. Saint Joseph, Montreal, PQ, H2J 1M3,
Canada
OCS Video, 860

Oratoire St. Joseph du Mont-Royal
3800 Queen Mary Rd., Montreal, PQ, H3V 1H6, Canada
*L'Ami du Frere Andre/The Friend of Brother Andre,
1,057*

•Ordre des Architectes du Quebec
1825 Blvd. Rene-Levesque Ouest, Montreal, PQ, H3H
1R4, Canada

Protestant School Bd of Greater Montreal
6000 Fielding Ave., Montreal, PQ, H3X 1T4, Canada
P.S.B.G.M. Communique, 1,092

Pubs. Alerte
25 av. Royale, Ste-Petronille, PQ, G0A 4C0, Canada
Alerte au Quebec, 1,044

Quebec Canada Foreign Mission Society
160 Plage Juge-Desnoyers, C.P. 69, L.D.R., Laval, PQ,
H7G 1A5, Canada
Missions-Etrangeres, 1,058

Quebec Forest Industries Assn.
1200 Germain-Des-Pres, #102, Ste-Foy, PQ, G1V
3M7, Canada
Papetier, 947

Quebec Homeschooling Advisory
4650 Acadia, Lachine, PQ, H8T 1N5, Canada
Quebec Homeschooling Advisory Newsletter, 327

Quebec Young Farmers Federation
Box 80, S.A. de Bellevue, PQ, H9X 3L4, Canada
News Spreader, 44

Regie de l'Assurance-Maladie du Quebec
1125, chemin Saint-Louis, Quebec, PQ, G1K 7T3,
Canada
Bulletin de l'Assurance, 618

Regroupement Quebecois des Sciences Sociales
INRS, 3465 Durocher, Montreal, PQ, H2X 2C6, Canada
Rezo, 1,127

Royal Victoria Hospital
687 Pine Ave. W., Montreal, PQ, H3A 1A1, Canada
Vic News, 573

Societe de Criminologie du Quebec
3 Place Laval, Unit 210, Laval, PQ, H7N 1A2, Canada
Societe de Criminologie du Quebec, 790

Societe de Genealogie de Quebec
C.P. 9066, Ste. Foy, PQ, G1V 4A8, Canada
L'Ancetre, 459

Societe Quebecoise d'Esperanto
6358-A rue de Bordeaux, Montreal, PQ, H2G 2R8,
Canada
La Riverego, 822

**•Societe Quebecoise de l'Autisme/Quebec Society
for Autism**
2300 Blvd. Rene Levesque Quest, Montreal, PQ, H3H
2R5, Canada

Societe des Traducteurs du Quebec
1140 de Maisonneuve, Suite 1060, Montreal, PQ, H3A
1M8, Canada
Antenne, 819

•Society of Toxicology of Canada
Box 517, Beaconsfield, PQ, H9W 5V1, Canada

**Syndicat du Personnel Non-Enseignant de l'Univ. du
Quebec/Ri**
300 Allee des Ursulines, Rimouski, PQ, J5L 3A1, Canada
L'Abordage, 709

**Syndicat des Professeurs du College de
Maisonneuve**
3800 est, rue Sherbrooke, Montreal, PQ, J4B 3P8,
Canada
Le V'La, 709

Teleglobe Canada
680 Sherbrooke St., W., Montreal, PQ, H3A 2S4, Canada
Spargo, 1,162

Travel Security Intelligencer
437 Grosvenor, Suite 12, Westmount, PQ, H3Y 2S5,
Canada
Travel Security Intelligencer, 1,190

Universite Laval Dept. Linguistiques
Comite de Terminologie, Ste. Foy, PQ, G1K 1P4, Canada
Bulletin de Terminologie, 820

Universite de Montreal
Box 6128, Station A, Montreal, PQ, H3C 3J7, Canada
*Chercheurs: Bulletin des Activites de Recherche de
l'Universite de Montreal, 1,096*

VDR Publications
Box 300, Victoria Station, Westmount, PQ, H37 2U5,
Canada
Canadian Paper Analyst, 946

Videazimut
3680 rue Jeanne Mance #430, Montreal, PQ, H2X
2K5, Canada
Clips, 1,166

Saskatchewan

Assn. Jeunesse Fransaskoise, Inc.
440 2e Ave. Nord, #203, Saskatoon, SK, S7K 2C3,
Canada
La Fransasque, 822

Assn. of Professional Engineers of Saskatchewan
2255 13th Ave., Regina, SK, S4P 0V6, Canada
Professional Edge, The, 363

Bureau of Statistics
2350 Albert St., 5th fl., Regina, SK, S4P 4A6, Canada
Saskatchewan Monthly Statistical Review, 295

Canadian Plains Research Center
University of Regina, Regina, SK, S4S 0A2, Canada
Canadian Plains Bulletin, 374

Catholic Health Assn. of Saskatchewan
1702 20th St., W., Saskatoon, SK, S7M 0Z9, Canada
CHAS Communique, 500

College of Dental Surgeons of Saskatchewan
202-728 Spadina Crescent E., Saskatoon, SK, S7K
4H7, Canada
*College of Dental Surgeons of Saskatchewan,
Newsletters, 268*

Community Health Services Association
455-2nd Ave., N., Saskatoon, SK, S7K 2C2, Canada
Focus: Social and Preventive Medicine, 506

**Community Planning Assn. of Canada. SK Div.
Newsletter**
2837 Dewdney Ave., Regina, SK, S4T 0X8, Canada
*Community Planning Association of Canada.
Saskatchewan Division Newsletter, 1,020*

Crown Life Ins. Co.
1901 Scarth St., Regina, SK, S4P 4L4, Canada
Contact, 581

Gaia Group
2108 Reynolds St., Regina, SK, S4N 3N1, Canada
Whisper in the Woods, 397

Greenwich Press
516 K South, Saskatoon, SK, S7M 2E2, Canada
Crosscurrents, 911

Institute of Chartered Accountants of Saskatchewan
1867 Hamilton St., #530, Regina, SK, S4P 2C2, Canada
Horizons, 5

Kiwanis, Western Canada
Box 581, Regina, SK, S4P 3A3, Canada
Kiwanis News, 179

Lakeland Library Region
10023 Thatcher Ave., Box 813, North Battleford, SK, S9A
2Z3, Canada
Reflections, 808

Lutheran Collegiate Bible Inst
Box 459, Outlook, SK, S0L 2N0, Canada
Beacon, 1,071

MacKenzie Art Gallery
3475 Albert St., Regina, SK, S4S 6X6, Canada
Vista, 67

Mcintosh Publishing Co.
1219 100 St., Box 430, North Battleford, SK, S9A 2Y5,
Canada
North-West Farmer-Rancher, 44

Museums Assn. of Saskatchewan
1808 Smith St., Regina, SK, S4P 2N3, Canada
Bulletin, 903

National Farmers Union/Canada
250-C 2nd Ave., S., Saskatoon, SK, S7K 2M1, Canada
National Farmers Union Newsletter, 43

Nature Saskatchewan
206 - 1860 Lorne Street, Regina, SK, S4P 2L7, Canada
Nature Views, 921

Prairie Agricultural Machinery Institute
Box 1900, Humboldt, SK, S0K 2A0, Canada
*Prairie Agricultural Machinery Institute, Evaluation
Report, 35*

Public Legal Education Assn. of Saskatchewan
220 3rd Ave. South, Rm. 210, Saskatoon, SK, S7K
1M1, Canada
PLEA, 767

Richard W. Unger Publications
610 4th St. E., Box 212, Spiritwood, SK, S0J 2M0, Canada
Lefty's Letter, 471

SPI Marketing Group
502 45th W., 2nd Fl., Saskatoon, SK, S7L 6H2, Canada
Saskatchewan, 829

Saskatchewan Abilities Council
2310 Louise Ave., Saskatoon, SK, S7J 2C7, Canada
Bulletin, 500

Saskatchewan Action Committee
2343 Cornwall St., Regina, SK, S4P 2L4, Canada
Network of Saskatchewan Women, 1,210

Saskatchewan Agricultural Graduates Assn., Inc.
Box 320, Sub. PO 6, Saskatoon, SK, S7N 0W0, Canada
SAGA, 46

Saskatchewan Alfalfa Seed Producers Assn.
107 Science Crescent, Saskatoon, SK, S7N 0X2, Canada
*Saskatchewan Alfalfa Seed Producers Assn.
Newsletter, 46*

Saskatchewan Archaeological Society
#5-816 1st Ave., N., Saskatoon, SK, S7K 1Y3, Canada
Saskatchewan Archaeological Society Newsletter, 58

Saskatchewan Archivists Society
Box 399, Substation 6, Saskatoon, SK, S7N 0W0,
Canada
Checklist, 795

Saskatchewan Assn. of Architects
200-642 Broadway Avenue, Saskatoon, SK, S7N 1A9,
Canada
Columns, 59

Saskatchewan Assn. of Certified Nursing Assistants
2310 Smith St., Regina, SK, S4P 2P6, Canada
*Saskatchewan Assn. of Certified Nursing Assistants
Newsletter, 932*

•Saskatchewan Assn of Health Organizations
1445 Park St., Regina, SK, S4N 4C5, Canada

Saskatchewan Assn. of Library Technicians
Box 9388, Saskatoon, SK, S7K 7E9, Canada
*Saskatchewan Assn. of Library Technicians
Newsletter, 809*

•Saskatchewan Association of Teachers of French
Box 1108, 2317 Arlington Ave., Saskatoon, SK, S7K
3N3, Canada

Saskatchewan Assn. of Teachers of German
Dept. of German & Slavic Langs, University of Regina,
Regina, SK, S4S 0A2, Canada
SPEA Newsletter, 1,134

•Saskatchewan Badminton Assn.
2205 Victoria Ave., Reginia, SK, S4P 0S4, Canada

Saskatchewan Band Assn.
1840 McIntyre St., Regina, SK, S4P 2P9, Canada
Saskatchewan Band Assn. Newsletter, 917

---

* See **MULTI-PUBLISHER INDEX** for list of publications.

Saskatchewan Canoe Assn.
Box 6064, Saskatoon, SK, S7K 4E5, Canada
Stern Words, 1,136

Saskatchewan Chamber of Commerce
1920 Broad St., #1630, Regina, SK, S4P 3V2, Canada
Legislative Report, 160

Saskatchewan Choral Federation
1870 Lorne St., Regina, SK, S4P 2L7, Canada
Saskatchewan Choral Federation Bulletin, 917

Saskatchewan Dept. of Agriculture & Food
Box 3003, Prince Albert, SK, S6V 6G1, Canada
Forage Seed News, 41

Saskatchewan Dietetic Assn.
BOX 3894, Regina, SK, S4P 3R8, Canada
Saskatchewan Dietetic Assn. Newsletter, 527

Saskatchewan Drama Association
2135 Albert St., #203, Regina, SK, S4P 2V1, Canada
SDA Newsletter, 1,174

Saskatchewan Energy & Mines, Petroleum & Natural Gas
1914 Hamilton St., Regina, SK, S4P 4V4, Canada
Drilling Activity Report, 956

•**Saskatchewan English Teachers' Assn.**
Box 1108, Saskatoon, SK, S7K 3N3, Canada

Saskatchewan Fed. of Labour
2709 12th Ave., #103, Regina, SK, S4T 1J3, Canada
Labour Reporter, 702

Saskatchewan Government Employees Union
1440 Broadway Ave., Regina, SK, S4P 1E2, Canada
Union Matters, 711

Saskatchewan Guidance & Counselling Assn.
Box 1108, Saskatoon, SK, S7K 3N3, Canada
SGCA Newsletter, 1,121

Saskatchewan Home Economics Teachers' Association
Box 1108, Saskatchewan, SK, S7K 3N3, Canada
SHETA Newsletter, 328

Saskatchewan Institute of Agrologists
#7-3012 Louise St., Saskatoon, SK, S7J 3L8, Canada
Saskatchewan Institute of Agrologists Newsletter, 46

•**Saskatchewan Library Assn.**
Box 3388, Regina, SK, S4P 3H1, Canada

Saskatchewan Middle Years Association
Box 1108, Saskatoon, SK, S7K 3N3, Canada
President's Newsletter, 326

Saskatchewan Music Educators Association
Box 519, Cudworth, SK, S0K 1B0, Canada
SMEA Newsletter, 328

Saskatchewan Pharmaceutical Assn.
2631 28th Ave., Ste. 301, Regina, SK, S4S 6X3, Canada
Saskatchewan Pharmaceutical Assn. Newsletter, 288

Saskatchewan Psychiatric Assn.
Saskatchewan Provincial Hosp., Box 39, N. Battleford, SK, S9A 2X8, Canada
Saskatchewan Psychiatric Assn. Newsletter, 1,011

Saskatchewan Pulse Crop Growers' Development Bd.
101-2515 Victoria Ave., Regina, SK, S4P 0T2, Canada
Pulse Crop Newsletter, 45

Saskatchewan Registered Music Teachers' Assn.
94 Green Meadow Rd., Regina, SK, S4V 0A8, Canada
Opus, 916

Saskatchewan Research Council - Technology Transfer Branch
15 Innovation Blvd., Saskatoon, SK, S7N 2X8, Canada
Saskatchewan Research Council, 845

Saskatchewan Safety Council
445 Hoffer Drive, Regina, SK, S4N 6E2, Canada
Saskatchewan Safety Council Link, 1,085

Saskatchewan School Trustees Assn.
400-2222-13th Ave., Regina, SK, S4P 3M7, Canada
SSTA Newsletter, 1,093

•**Saskatchewan Science Teachers' Society**
Box 1108, 2317 Arlington Ave., Saskatoon, SK, S7K 3N3, Canada

Saskatchewan Society for Autistic Children
3510 25th Ave., Regina, SK, S4S 1L8, Canada
Saskatchewan Society for Autistic Children Newsletter, 1,017

Saskatchewan Society for Education Through Art
Box 1108, 2317 Arlington Ave., Saskatoon, SK, S7K 3N3, Canada
S.S.E.A. Newsletter, 328

Saskatchewan Soc. for Prevention of Cruelty to Animals
Box 37, Saskatoon, SK, S7N 3K1, Canada
Saskatchewan Humanitarian, 50

Saskatchewan Special Olympics Society
1870 Lorne St., Regina, SK, S4P 2L7, Canada
Saskatchewan Special Olympics Society Newsletter, 1,135

•**Saskatchewan Teachers' Federation**
Box 1108, Saskatoon, SK, S7K 3N3, Canada

Saskatchewan Urban Municipalities Assn.
200-1819 Cornwall St., Regina, SK, S4P 2K4, Canada
New Urban Voice, 489

Saskatchewan Volleyball Assn.
1870 Lorne St., Regina, SK, S4P 2L7, Canada
Scoop, 1,135

•**Saskatchewan Wheat Pool**
2625 Victoria Ave., Regina, SK, S4T 7T9, Canada

Saskatchewan Women's Inst
Univ. of Saskatchewan, 137 Kirk Hall, Saskatoon, SK, S7N 0W0, Canada
Second Penny, 181

Saskatoon Public Library
311 23rd Street E., Saskatoon, SK, S7K 0J6, Canada
Preface, Your Guide to Library Programs and Services, 807

Scharf and Associates
1137 Elliott St., Saskatoon, SK, S7N 0V4, Canada
Creative Leap International, 135

Scrutiny
Box 1, Sub Post Off. 6, Saskatoon, SK, S7N 0W0, Canada
Scrutiny, 330

Softball Saskatchewan
2205 Victoria Ave., Regina, SK, S4P 0S4, Canada
Eighth Inning, 1,131

Teachers of Religion & Christian Ethics
Box 1108, Saskatoon, SK, S7K 3N3, Canada
TRACE Newsletter, 1,051

University of Saskatchewan - Ethnic Studies Assoc.
Publications, Saskatoon, SK, S7N 0W0, Canada
Canadian Ethnic Studies Association Bulletin, 398

Western Tract Mission Inc.
401-33rd St. W., Saskatoon, SK, S7L 0V5, Canada
Western Tract News, 1,066

Yukon Territory

Yukon Historical & Museums Assn.
Box 4357, Whitehorse, YK, Y1A 3T5, Canada
Yukon Historical & Museums Association Newsletter, 550

* See **MULTI-PUBLISHER INDEX** for list of publications.

Online Index

- Lists titles in alphabetical order. Includes name of online vendor carrying the publication and page number.

Title/ISSN Index

- Lists titles in alphabetical sequence. Includes ISSN designation and page number.

Administration & Management Special Interest Section Newsletter, 8756-629X , 532
Administrative Assistant Adviser, 126
Administrative Assistant's Update, 340
Administrative Focus, 0149-2322 , 1,089
Administrative Information Report, 299
Administrative Law News, 0567-9494 , 713
Administrator: The Source for Practical Ideas and Key Issues in Higher Education, 0744-7078 , 1,089
Adolescent Medicine, 0044-6335 , 865
Adoptalk, 1,113
Adoption Law and Practice, 713
Adoption Today Newsletter, 410
Adoption Update, 410
Adrian Day's Investment Analyst, 654
Adult Bible Study, 0162-4156 , 1,053
Adult & Continuing Education Today, 0001-8473 , 299
Adult Day Care Letter, 0885-4572 , 561
Adult Students Newsletter, 200
Adult Study Guide, 1,061
Advance — Colorado Springs, 1,012
Advance — Issaquah, 194
Advance Notice, 446
Advance Planning Letter, 654
Advanced Battery Technology, 0001-8627 , 337
Advanced Bible Study, 0162-4148 , 1,053
Advanced Ceramics Report, 0268-9847 , 847
Advanced Coatings & Surface Technology, 0896-422X , 162
Advanced Composites Bulletin, 0951-953X , 847
Advanced Composites Monthly, 1058-899X , 25
Advanced Construction Information Service, 243
Advanced Fuel Technologies, 955
Advanced Intelligent Network News, 1072-0030 , 211
Advanced Manufacturing Technology, 0885-5684 , 847
Advanced Materials, 0734-7146 , 847
Advanced Office Technologies Report, 1054-1462 , 211
Advanced Selling Power, 1,086
Advanced Technology for Developers, 212
Advanced Transportation Technology News, 1077-6877 , 1,176
Advanced Underwriting Service, 617
Advanced Wireless Communications, 1,156
Advances in Computer Archaelogy, 57
Advances in Small Animal Medicine and Surgery, 1041-7826 , 1,200
Adventure, 0001-8783 , 1,053
Adventures for Kids-Newsletter, 167
Adventures in Movement, 1,113
Advertised Retail Prices of Down & Down-&-Feather Filled Pillows, 1,171
Advertising Age Daily Fax Edition, 10
Advertising Compliance Service, 713
Advertising Creativity Newsletter, 10
Advertising Manager's Handbook, 25
Advertising Marketing Bulletin, 10
Advertising Topics, 10
Advertising Via Telemarketing Script Presentations Newsletter, 126
Advertising Wildfire, 10
Adviser Update, 832
Advisor, 1044-8152 , 299
Advocacy Update, 251
Advocate, The, 0161-7982 , 299
Advocate, 698
Advocate, The, 0847-2890 , 1,113
Advocate — Panhandle, 985
Advocate — San Pablo, 197
Adweek Special Report, 10
Aeltus Weekly, 617
Aero-Gramme, 1067-9219 , 299
Aerobics, 550
Aerolog, 25
Aerospace Daily, 25
Aerospace Facts, 576
Aerospace Industries Assn. Newsletter, 25
Aerospace News, 25
Aerospace Newsletter, 1,078
Aerospace Propulsion, 25
Aerostatical Notes, 26
Aeroviews, 576
Aesthetic Surgery, 865
Aetna-Izer, 576
AetnaSphere, 576
Affiliate, 0360-5485 , 713
Affiliate & Instructor News, 112
Affiliated Advertising Agencies Intl. News, 10
Affiliated Warehouse Companies Newsletter, 1,192
Affiliates in Training, 865
Affirmative Action Compliance Manual for Federal Contractors, 0148-8147 , 171
Affirmative Action/EEO Update, 1071-7390 , 171
Affordable Caribbean, The, 1,181
Afraid, 919
Africa Fund, 171
African Alternatives, 497
African-American Family History Assn. Newsletter, 446

African-American and Third World Archivists Roundtable Newsletter, 792
African-American Traveler, 1,182
African Insider, 626
African Studies Center Newsletter, 299
Africana Libraries Newsletter, 0148-7868 , 792
After the Fact, 340
Aftermarket Distribution, 69
Aftermarket Update, 69
Aftermarket Watch, 69
AgBioTech Stock Letter, 1066-0569 , 36
Ag Executive, 1053-2692 , 36
Ag Focus, 0899-7535 , 36
Ag Industry Watch, 36
Ag/Innovator, 36
Agency Briefs Newsletter, 617
Agency Law Quarterly Real Estate Intelligence Report, 1,030
Agency News Items, 576
Agenda, 1047-0727 — Ann Arbor, 985
Agenda — Washington, 171
Agenda in Brief, 1,068
Agenda Newsletter, The, 1,041
Agents News, 576
Aggressive Hockey Report, 1,128
Aging America Resources, 0892-0818 , 1,105
Aging Digest, 1,105
Aging and the Human Spirit Newsletter, 1,106
Aging News, 1,106
Aging News Alert, 1050-3196 , 1,106
Aging Research & Training News, 0197-4017 , 1,106
Agora, 299
Agora, Inc., 80
Agrarian Advocate, 371
AgriBioScan, 1079-9060 , 35
Agri-Mark Monthly, 264
Agri-Naturalist, 36
Agri-News, 36
Agricultural Chemical Newsletter, 36
Agricultural Credit Conditions Survey, 0737-948X , 36
Agricultural Digest, 36
Agricultural Estate, Tax & Business Planning, 1,139
Agricultural & Forestry Experiment Station Bulletin, 36
Agricultural Genetics Report, 0278-9736 , 36
Agricultural Law Update, 714
Agricultural Letter, 0002-1512 , 36
Agricultural Libraries Information Notes, 0095-2699 , 792
Agricultural Market Review, 36
Agriculture Council of America, 37
Agriculture & Food, 0364-7994 , 37
Agriculture News Bulletin, 37
Agriview, 37
Agriweek, 37
Agronomy News, 37
Agrotechnology Transfer, 0883-8631 , 37
Agrow World Crop Protection News, 37
Aid & Analysis, 654
Aid Bulletin - Addiction Intervention with the Disabled, 1,010
Aid for Education Report, 1058-1324 , 299
Aim, 171
Air Currents, 0400-8510 , 371
AirDaily, 371
Air Pollution Control, 371
Air Pollution Monitoring & Sampling, 371
Air Power Museum Bulletin, 0048-2358 , 902
Air Quality Data Management Software Report, 1084-9394 , 371
Air Quality Week, 371
Air Safety Week, 0893-1003 , 1,078
AirTECH News, 1066-193X , 372
Air Transport Newsletter, 1,078
Air & Water Pollution Control, 0890-0396 , 371
Air/Water Pollution Report's Environment Week, 372
Airborne Electronics Forecast, 26
Airborne R&M Systems Forecast, 26
Aircraft Engine Inventory Database License, 26
Aircraft Forecast, 26
Aircraft Value Newsletter, 1071-0655 , 26
Airline Financial News, 1040-5410 , 26
Airline Marketing News, 1071-1325 , 26
Airliners Monthly News, 26
Airport Highlights, 26
Airport Operation Bulletin, 1057-5537 , 26
Airport Report, 26
Airports, 26
Airspeed, 853
Aka Cord, 1,067
Akro Agate Gem, 478
Akron Daily Digest, 576
Akwa Letter, 497
Al-Anon in Institutions, 1054-142X , 1,114
Al-Anon Speaks Out, 1054-1446 , 1,114
Al Hanson's Economic Newsletter, 126
Al Owen's Newsletter Digest, 654
Alabama Business, 0002-4163 , 126
Alabama Development News, 0889-7468 , 126
Alabama Employment Law Letter, 1049-9369 , 714

Alabama Environmental Compliance Update, 1066-1131 , 714
Alabama Genealogical Society Newsletter, 446
Alabama Prison Project Newsletter, 784
Alabama Today, 127
Alaska Branching Out, 434
Alaska Employment Law Letter, 714
Alaska Forest Perspective, 576
Alaska Forest Products Newsletter, 434
Alaska Geology, 899
Alaska Legislative Digest, 985
Alaska Metaphysical Council Newsletter, 973
Alaska Nurse, 928
Alaska Report, 955
Alaska State Council on the Arts Bulletin, 62
Alaskan Malamute Club of America Newsletter, 279
Alateen Talk, 1054-1411 , 1,114
Albany Report, 985
Albert Advisor, 617
Albert Einstein College of Medicine Faculty News, 866
Alberta Agrologist, 37
Alberta Bicycle Assn., Newsletter, 262
Alberta Corporations Law Guide, 714
Alberta Counselletter, 0381-5951 , 299
Alberta Decisions Civil & Criminal Cases, 0313-7980 , 714
Alberta Genealogical Society Newsletter, 446
Alberta Gymnast, 1,128
Alberta Horticulturist, 439
Alberta, N.W.T. and Yukon Tax Reports, 1,139
Alberta Teachers' Association-Learning Resources Council-Newsletter, 0380-8491 , 299
Album Page, 970
Albuquerque Archaeological Society-Newsletter, 0002-4953 , 57
Alcohol & Drugs: Dot Compliance Manual, 1,192
Alcohol Issues Insights, 102
Alcohol Week, 955
Alcoholic Beverage Control/State Capitals, 0734-0842 , 102
Alcoholic Beverage Executive's Newsletter, 102
Alcoholism Briefs, 1076-2507 , 498
Alcoholism & Drug Abuse Weekly, 1042-1394 , 497
Alcyone Journal, 813
Alert — Harrisburg, 1,025
Alert — Hartford, 209
Alert — Los Angeles, 498
Alert, 0882-0929 — Sacramento, 127
Alert — Washington, 127
Alert — Washington, 1,206
Alert, National Service Dog Center Newsletter, 1069-0743 , 279
Alerte au Quebec, 1,044
Aleutian Current, 576
Alexander Agenda, 0890-9482 , 446
Alexander Paris Report, 654
Alexian Pulse, 561
Alexigram, 561
Alfred Adler Institute Newsletter, 1,012
Alhfam Bulletin, 0047-4851 , 902
Alimony, Child Support and Counsel Fees--Award, Modification and Enforcement, 714
All Points Bulletin Newsletter, 784
All Source Digest, 1,002
All States Tax Guide, 1,139
Allan Fine's Trends in Integrated Health Care, 1061-7620 , 561
Alldata News, 212
Allee's All Around, 0883-5926 , 446
Allegheny County Pharmacist, 281
Allegheny Lawyer, 714
Allen Ancestors, 446
Allen County Historical Society, Newsletter, 536
Allen Family Circle, 0865-3215 , 447
Allergy and Asthma Industry News, 1084-2721 , 866
Allergy & Clinical Immunology News, 0838-1925 , 866
Allergy Edge, 866
Allergy Hotline, 866
Alles' Around the World Knitting Machine News & Views, 551
Alliance, 1,030
Alliance Report, 273
Allied Health Update, 193
Alloy Digest, 890
Alone, 694
Along the Track, 576
Alpha, 561
Alpha Tau Delta President's Letter, 176
Alston Wilkes Society Newsletter, 784
Alternance, 909
Alternate Roots, 1,172
Alternative Agriculture News, 37
Alternative Aquaculture Network, 8755-7894 , 422
Alternative Currents, 80
Alternative Delivery Today, 970
Alternative Energy Trends & Forecasts, 350
Alternative Health Therapies Newsletter, 0899-5974 , 498
Alternative Models Newsletter, 1,044

©1996, Oxbridge Communications, Inc.

Eyepiece, 0146-7662 , *68*

F

FACS Forum, *1,111*
FACS Newsletter, *178*
FACTA Newsletter, 0014-5556 , *309*
FAIR-Immigration Report, 1067-3337 , *736*
FANS of Women's Sports, *1,131*
FAO Plant Protection Bulletin, *40*
FASEB Newsletter, *109*
FCC Daily Release Service, *736*
FCC Report, 0748-5714 , *1,158*
FCG Report, *138*
FCIA News, *620*
FCIB Intl. Bulletin, *88*
FCL Newsletter, 0532-7091 , *173*
F.C.M. Market Bulletin, *1,008*
FCNL Washington Newsletter, *1,196*
FDA Advertising and Promotion Manual, *736*
FDA Enforcement Manual, *736*
FDA Newsletter, *72*
FDA Outline, *484*
F-D-C Report -- 'The Tan Sheet', 1068-5316 , *283*
FDIC Consumer News, *88*
FDU Alumni News, *190*
F.E.A.R. Chronicles, *173*
FEDLINK Technical Notes, 0737-4178 , *797*
FEI Briefing, *88*
FEI Canada Newsletter, *88*
FELA Reporter and Railroad Liability Monitor, *1,029*
FERC Daily Release Service, *353*
FERC Practice & Procedure Manual, *354*
FERC Report, *89*
FFA Update, *40*
FFL Newsletter, *736*
FGD & DeNOx, *382*
FGS, 0894-3265 , *453*
FIAE Association Spotlight, *1,075*
FIA Executive Digest, *55*
FIERF Newsletter, *309*
FIO Covering Ontario, *625*
F-IR Update, *979*
FISA Distributor News, *428*
FLARR Foreign Language Assoc. of the Red River, *821*
FLEOA Newsletter, *786*
FLGC Newsletter, *444*
FLICC Newsletter, 0882-908X , *797*
FMA Bulletin, *837*
FMA News, *848*
FMCA Newsletter, *620*
FMRA News, *40*
FMS Foundation, 1069-0484 , *1,117*
FMedia!, 0890-6718 , *124*
FOAFtale News, *260*
FPDA News, *848*
FPM & SA Focus, *428*
FPRS Member Newsletter, *435*
FPRS Technical Newsletter Series: Timber Harvesting and Merchandising, *830*
FRBSF Weekly Letter, us/08090- , *89*
FRI Monthly Portfolio, 0014-6137 , *967*
FRM Weekly, *967*
FSCA Bulletin, *583*
FSC Monthly Bulletin, *253*
FSMBNewsLine, 1062-5380 , *873*
FTC FOIA Log, 0161-7036 , *138*
FTC WATCH, 0196-0016 , *138*
FT Systems, 0740-4980 , *222*
FWANY/News, *89*
FXC Investors Corp., *663*
FX Week, 1050-0782 , *89*
FYI — New York, *583*
FYI — Vancouver, *956*
FYI International, *583*
Fabian Domestic Investment Resource, *663*
Fabric Filter, *382*
Facets of Fostoria, *479*
Facets of Freshwater, *382*
Facial Plastic Times, *873*
Facilitator, *506*
Facilities Forum, *848*
Facility Manager's Alert, *246*
Facing History & Ourselves News, *309*
FactSheet, *138*
Factory Outlet Newsletter, *253*
Factory Sales of Electric Storage Batteries, 0380-7061 , *338*
Facts, *620*
Facts for Action, *989*
Facts on File World News Digest, 0014-6641 , *630*
Facts on the Funds, *664*
Facts & Trends, 0429-9949 , *138*
Faculty Affairs, *310*
Faculty Newsletter IUB Libraries, *797*
Fair Employment Compliance, 0885-7172 , *700*

Fair Employment Practices, 0149-2683 , *736*
Fair Employment Practices Guidelines, 1069-921X , *344*
Fair Employment Practices Summary of Latest Developments, 0525-2156 , *736*
Fair Employment Report, 0014-6919 , *344*
Fair Labor Standards Handbook, *484*
Fair Witness Focus, 1054-4208 , *1,199*
Fairfax Newsletter, *29*
Fairfax Prospectus, *138*
Fairs & Expositions, *368*
Faith and Fellowship, *1,072*
Faithful Steward, *664*
Fakes and Forgeries, *971*
Falcon, *201*
Falconer Facets, 0884-867X , *453*
Families in Crisis Funding Report, 1075-3184 , *412*
Family in America, 0892-2691 , *412*
Family Connection of the Cothren-Cochrane Surname, 0896-9302 , *453*
Family Connection of the O'Neil-Neil-O'Neill Surname, *453*
Family Health, *506*
Family Incomes, 0703-7368 , *291*
Family Investor, *664*
Family, Law and Democracy Report, *484*
Family Law Handbook, *412*
Family Law Reporter, 0148-7922 , *412*
Family Law: Texas Practice and Procedure, *736*
Family and Medical Leave Handbook, *736*
Family Policy, *412*
Family Relations/State Capitals, 0741-3505 , *736*
Family Research Report, *412*
Family Resource Coalition Report, 1041-8660 , *412*
Family Tax Planning, *1,143*
Family Travel Times, *1,184*
Family Treebune, *453*
Famlee Talk, *412*
Fan Club Monitor, 1081-5538 , *417*
Fancy Feathers, *1,001*
Fanfare, *453*
Fanfares, *1,173*
Fannie Mae Investor/Analyst Report, *89*
Fare Box, *927*
Fare Share-The Food Letter, 1052-3898 , *428*
Farm Broadcasters Letter, 0364-5444 , *40*
Farm City Week Newsletter, *40*
Farm Economics — University Park, *40*
Farm Economics — University Park, *40*
Farm Economics Facts & Opinions, *40*
Farm Publications Blue Books, *953*
Farm and Ranch Tax Letter, *40*
Farm Tax Saver, *40*
Farmers Federal Tax Alert, *1,143*
Farmers Grain & Livestock Corp. -Viewpoint, *40*
Farming for Profit, *40*
Farmsafe, *506*
Farr Footnotes, 0897-778X , *453*
FasTone, *222*
Fashion Calendar, *55*
Fashion International, *272*
Fashion Jewelry Review, *693*
Fashion Newsletter, *55*
Fashion Poetry Patterns, *982*
Fashion Reports, *437*
Fashion Retail Intelligence Newsletter, *55*
Fast Break, *1,131*
Fast Break Alert, *1,131*
Fast Foreward, *419*
Fast Track News - Automotive Sales & Production, *72*
Fast Tracks, *1,184*
Father Flood Lectionary Series, *1,047*
Father Rights News, *814*
Father Solanus Guild News, *1,056*
The Father, The Son, *283*
Fathers Brothers Sons, *890*
Fathom, *936*
Fatima Findings, 0014-8830 , *1,056*
Faucet Facts, *1,202*
Faulkner Newsletter, 0733-6357 , *821*
Favorably Positioned Stocks, 8756-4769 , *664*
Fax Reporter, *1,158*
Fax-Stat on Drugs, 1064-5055 , *283*
Faxfacts, *1,159*
Faxletter, 0882-231X , *797*
Feasting Fancies, *428*
The Feat Sheet, *471*
Feather in the Wind, *382*
Fed/Direct, *14*
Federal Action Affecting the States/State Capitals, 0734-1202 , *1,196*
Federal Administrative Law Judges Conference Newsletter, *736*
Federal Air Surgeon's Medical Bulletin, *29*
Federal Assistance Monitor, 1050-3242 , *968*
Federal Audit Guides, *5*
Federal Auditing Information Service for Higher Education, *5*
Federal Banking Law Reports, *736*

Federal Banking Law Service of A.S. Pratt, 0744-8791 , *736*
Federal Bankruptcy Handbook, *737*
Federal Budget Report, *484*
Federal Career Opportunities, 0279-2230 , *344*
Federal Carriers Reports, *1,177*
Federal Case News, *737*
Federal Civil Procedure Handbook, *737*
Federal Computer Market Report, 0163-1489 , *222*
Federal Consumer Protection: Laws, Rules, & Regulations, *737*
Federal Contract Disputes, 0747-9700 , *737*
Federal Contracts Report, 0014-9063 , *138*
Federal Court of Appeal Decisions, 0227-0390 , *737*
Federal Court of Canada Service, *737*
Federal Court Procurement Decisions, *484*
Federal Criminal Law Handbook, *737*
Federal Election Campaign Financing Guide, *989*
Federal Election Commission Record, *989*
Federal Employees News Digest, 1065-0970 , *1,196*
Federal Energy Regulatory Commission Reports, *354*
Federal Estate and Gift Tax Reports, *1,143*
Federal Estate & Gift Taxes, *1,143*
Federal Ethics Report, *484*
Federal Evidence Practice Guide, *737*
Federal Excise Tax, *1,143*
Federal Excise Tax Guide, *1,192*
Federal Excise Tax Reports, *1,144*
Federal Express International Newsletter, *646*
Federal Grants & Contracts Weekly, 0194-2247 , *968*
Federal Grants Management Handbook, 0195-2617 , *1,196*
Federal Guide, 0190-4558 , *89*
Federal Human Resources Week, *611*
Federal Income, Gift and Estate Taxation, *737*
Federal Income Tax Regulations, *1,144*
Federal Income Taxation of Banks and Financial Institutions, *1,144*
Federal Income Taxation of Corporations Filing Consolidated Returns, *1,144*
Federal Income Taxation of Corporations and Shareholders, *1,144*
Federal Income Taxation of Inventories, *1,144*
Federal Income Taxation of Real Estate, *1,033*
Federal Income Taxation of Real Estate: Forms & Analysis, *1,033*
Federal Labor-Management & Employee Relations Consultant, 0046-3418 , *1,196*
Federal Legislative Bulletin, *1,091*
Federal Librarian, 0273-1061 , *797*
Federal Litigation Guide, *737*
Federal Litigator, *737*
Federal Maritime Commission Digest Service, *1,111*
Federal Parks and Recreation, *950*
Federal Physicians, The, 1070-9029 , *874*
Federal Procurement Update, *484*
Federal Quality News, *484*
Federal Register Abstracts-Business Edition, *1,196*
Federal Register Abstracts-Master Edition, *1,196*
Federal Register Report, *1,196*
Federal Research Report, 0148-4109 , *310*
Federal Reserve Bulletin, *89*
Federal Reserve Notes, *89*
Federal Revenue Forms, *1,144*
Federal Rules of Evidence, *737*
Federal Rules of Evidence News, *737*
Federal Securities Act of 1933-Treatise and Primary Source Manual, *89*
Federal Securities Exchange Act of 1934, *89*
Federal Securities Law Reports, *737*
Federal Sentencing Manual, *737*
Federal & State Insurance Week, *620*
Federal Tax Articles, *1,144*
Federal Tax Coordinator 2d, *1,144*
Federal Tax Expeditor, *1,144*
Federal Tax Forms, *1,144*
Federal Tax Guide, *1,144*
Federal Tax Guide Reports, *1,144*
Federal Tax Manual With Monthly Reports, *1,197*
Federal Taxation of Life Insurance Companies, *1,144*
Federal Taxation of Oil and Gas Transactions, *956*
Federal Taxation of Partnerships and Partners, *1,144*
Federal Taxation of Trusts, Grantors and Beneficiaries, *738*
Federal Taxes, *1,145*
Federal Taxes Citator, *1,145*
Federal Technology Report, *485*
Federal Tort Claims Act News, *738*
Federal Update, *485*
Federal Veterinarian, 0164-6257 , *1,201*
Federated News, 0046-3485 , *1,208*
Federation of American Health Systems Hotline, *874*
Federation of C.P.T.A.s of Ontario Newsletter, 0700-9070 , *310*
Federation Highlights, 0049-6987 , *382*
Fed Letter, 0739-5299 , *89*
Fed. of Medical Specialists of Quebec, Bulletin, *874*
Fed. of Medical Women of Canada, Newsletter, *874*

G

GAG Recap, 604
GA-SK Newsletter, 267
GCS Users' Group Newsletter, 223
GED Items, 311
GEI Newsletter, 1,014
GEM, 485
GEM Notes, 1,202
GE News, 584
GF News, 584
GFOA Newsletter, 1,020
GFP Notes, 507
GHAA News, 507
G.H.S. Foot-Notes, 540
G.I. Joe Collectors Club, 184
GIS Law, 1064-2027 , 475
GIS Newsletter, 0046-5801 , 476
GLAAD Newsletter, 444
GLCA Faculty Newsletter, 311
GLTF Newsletter, 1045-2893 , 444
GMP Letter, The, 0196-626X , 507
G-Map, the Geographic Information, Mapping & Publishing Newsletter, 475
GOAL Gazette, 444
GPPAW Horizons, 708
GRA Reporter, 0016-3619 , 1,020
GRID, 354
GST & Commodity Tax, 0847-3528 , 1,145
GTE Telenet Packet, 1,159
GUI Program News, 223
G&W Recruiting Service, 434
Gaea, 476
Gage Family Newsletter, 454
Galaxie Gazette, 73
Gallatin Today, 191
Gallaudet Alumni Newsletter, 187
Gallup Poll, The, 1197-4303 , 990
Game Manager, 1066-0577 , 606
Game Researcher's Notes, 1050-6608 , 184
Game Times, 1050-6594 , 184
Gamewarden Newsletter, 896
Gaming Confidential, 439
Gander, The, 403
Ganymedia, 1,047
Garden Club of America Newsletter, 441
Garden Newsletter, 441
Garden Sampler, 441
Garden Views, 1,208
Gardenesque, 441
Garlic Times, 933
Garside Forecast, 666
Gary Galyean's Golf Letter, 480
Gary Halbert Letter, 15
Gas Buyer's Guide, 0742-3055 , 956
Gas Daily, 0885-5935 , 354
Gas Energy Review, 354
Gas Markets Week, 957
Gas Storage Report, 957
Gas Transactions Report, 957
Gas Transportation Marketing Service, 957
Gas Transportation Report, 957
Gas Turbine Engines/Markets, 832
Gas Turbine Forecast, 354
Gas Utilities Industry - Worldwide, 1,026
Gaslight Review, 584
Gate-Keeper, 540
Gated Wye, 421
Gates Gazette, 0897-7798 , 454
Gateway, 646
Gateway Monitor, 223
Gateways, 1,047
Gathered View, The, 277
Gaucher's Disease Registry Newsletter, 507
Gauge, The, 857
Gay Airline & Travel Club Newsletter, The, 1,184
Gay Center Voice, 0894-8984 , 444
Gebhart Society of America Newsletter, 454
Gem, 584
Gem & Jewelry Fact Sheets Quarterly Supplement, 693
Gene Lees Jazzletter, 912
Gene Perret's Round Table, 604
Gene Therapy Newsletter, 1354-8662 , 473
GeneWATCH, 0740-9737 , 474
Genealogical Society of Flemish Americans Newsletter, 398
Genealogical Society of Okeechobee Newsletter, 454
Genealogija, 454
Genealogy Bulletin, 1049-9571 , 454
Genealogy Workshop Bulletin, 454
General Aviation/Helicopter Accident Report, 0887-7823 , 740
General Contractors Association, Bulletin of The, 365
General Ledger, The, 5
General Libraries Newsletter, 0362-854X , 798
General Orders, 896
Generally Speaking, 0027-0709 , 563
Generation, 1,057

Generation After, 540
Generations, 0821-5359 — Fredericton, 454
Generations — Wayzata, 507
Generic Line, 1076-884X , 284
Genesis, 657710 , 507
Genetic Engineering Letter, 0276-1882 , 474
Genetic Technology News, 0272-9032 , 474
Genetically Speaking, 474
Genetics in Practice, 474
Genetics Society of Canada Bulletin, 0316-4357 , 474
Genius At Work, 584
Genre Press Digest, 1,102
Gentlestrength Times, 260
Genuine Article, The, 890
Geo-Monitor, 1057-4492 , 476
Geography Education Program UPDATE, 475
Geolog, 0227-3713 , 476
Geological Newsletter, 0270-5451 , 476
George C. Marshall Foundation Topics, 540
George Cross News Letter, 891
George Kamm Paperweights, 184
George Whalin's Retail Management Letter, 15
Georgeson Report, 0041-2406 , 139
Georgia Conservation Law Handbook, 787
Georgia Contrarian, The, 666
Georgia Courts Journal, 740
Georgia Criminal Law and Motor Vehicle Handbook, 740
Georgia Employment Law Letter, 1040-4813 , 740
Georgia Environmental Law Letter, 1044-2324 , 740
Georgia Extension Veterinary News, 1,201
Georgia Health Law Update, 1073-0559 , 507
Georgia Labor Market Trends, 700
Georgia Real Estate Law Letter, 1040-4805 , 740
Georgian Newsletter, 948
Gerald R. Ford Foundation Newsletter, 485
Geri-Source, 1,106
Geriatric Care, 929
Geriatric Care News, 0745-5070 , 507
Geriatric Medicine Alerts, 874
Geriatric Psychiatry News, 1,014
German American Business Council, 646
German American Commerce, 159
German-American World, 311
German Press Review, 695
German Tax & Business Law Guide, 1,145
Germinations, 441
Gerofiles, 1,107
Gerontology News, 874
Gesher, 1,068
Get Organized! News, The, 471
Get Ready Sheet, 0148-7566 , 1,167
Getting Along, 611
Getting and Spending, 311
Gettysburg Seminary Bulletin, 0362-0581 , 205
Geyser Geothermal Energy Newsletter, 354
Ghost Trackers Newsletter, 948
Gift Basket Idea Newsletter, 477
Gift of Sight — Calgary, 940
Gift of Sight — Oneonta, 940
Giftbeat, 272
Gifts, 1,057
Gilbert Criminal Law and Procedure of New York, 740
Gildea Resource Newsletter, 382
Gileland/Gilliland Newsletter, 454
Gillet, Gillette, Gillett Pride 'n' Joy, 0890-4022 , 455
Gilligan's Island News, 178
Ginger's Rag, 696
Giraffe News, 968
Girl Groups ('60's Rock N' Roll) Gazette, 417
Girls' Rodeo Association News, 559
Girth Shaking News/Midwest, 178
Giving USA Update, 0899-3793 , 968
Glass Reflections, 479
Glass Shards Newsletter, 479
Gleamings, 1,074
Gleams, 1072-7906 , 874
Global Business Technology Report, 139
Global Economic Outlook, 91
Global Electronics, 0739-0416 , 338
Global Environmental Change Report, 1049-9083 , 383
Global Financial Institutions Weekly, 91
Global Glimpses, 646
Global Investing, 666
Global Investment in Canada, 647
Global Investment Technology, 1058-3920 , 91
Global Issues, 188
Global Link, 0715-7320 , 1,117
Global Mail, 923
Global Market Perspective, 666
Global Missions, 1,117
Global Money Management, 666
Global Packaging & Brand Identity, 1078-5922 , 945
Global Positioning & Navigation News, 1072-3080 , 113
Global Private Banking - International Investment Outlook, 91
Global Report, 0730-9112 , 631
Global Statesmanship Ratings of the U.S. House, 485

Global Statesmanship Ratings of the U.S. Senate, 631
Global Survey, 1075-4644 , 896
Global Talk!, 631
Global Vision Investor Newletter Monthly, 666
Globalist, The, 666
Globe — Long Beach, 584
Globe — Rockville, 269
Globe Corner Bookstore, 1,184
GloboFax, 400
Gloria Pitzer's Secret Recipes Publications, 430
Glove Collector Newsletter, The, 553
Gluten Free Pantry, 430
Gluten Intolerance Group's Newsletter, 0890-507X , 933
Go Camping America!, 901
Goddard Newsletter, 455
Goethe News & Notes, 821
Going Public: The IPO Reporter, 0735-9950 , 666
Going Solo, 1,184
Gold Coast News, 1,040
Gold Coaster, 584
Gold Mining Stock Report, 666
Gold News/Nouvelles de l'Or, 891
Gold Newsletter, 666
Gold Pages, The, 1,117
Gold Sheet, 434
Gold Sheet: Quality Control Reports, 0163-2418 , 284
Gold and Silver Newsletter, 666
Gold Standard Review, 91
Gold Star Mother, 178
Gold Stock Alert, 666
Golda Meir Library Newsletter, 798
Goldberg Bulletin, 584
Golden Gateway, 1,184
Golden Links, 178
Golden Pen, 584
Golden Retriever Club of America News, 280
Golden Taffy, 311
Goldstock Letter, 666
Golf Clubmaker, 480
Golf Collectors Society Bulletin, 480
Golf Travel: The Guide for Discriminating Golfers, 480
Golf Update Newsletter, 480
Golf Writers Association of America Newsletter, 696
Golob's Oil Pollution Bulletin, 1051-6255 , 383
Gomberg-Fredrikson Report, 103
Goob, The, 822
Good Earth Times, 904
Good Guys, The, 73
Good Money: The Newsletter for Socially Concerned Investors, 0742-4515 , 667
Good News, 0890-4375 — Boston, 1,074
Good News — Miami, 631
Good News — New Berlin, 1,047
Good News — Reston, 667
Good News Letter, 1,047
Good-News-Letter, 933
GoodNewsletter, 184
Good Night News, 574
Good Samaritan Today, 563
Good Stuff, 798
Good and Welfare, 178
Good Word, 584
Goodall News, 584
Goodenow's Ghosts, 455
Goodkin Report, 990
Goodloe Report, 740
Goods & Services Bulletin, 139
Goods in Transit, 1,177
Goodtimers Newsletter, 585
Goodwill Dimensions, 1,117
Goodwill News, 277
Goodwin News, 0892-1423 , 455
Gordon Office Market Report, 1,034
Goren Bridge Letter, 553
Gospel Truth, 1,063
Gourd, 0888-5672 , 441
Government Accounting and Auditing Update, 5
Government Business Worldwide Reports, 0017-2588 , 485
Government Contract Compliance Guide, 485
Government Contract Costs Pricing & Accounting Report, 741
Government Contract Litigation Reporter, 1047-1758 , 741
Government Contractor, 741
Government Contracts Citator, 485
Government Contracts: Law, Administration and Procedure, 741
Government Contracts Reports, 1,197
Government Contracts Service, 1,028
Government Employee Relations Report, 0017-260X , 485
Government Inventions for Licensing, 0364-6491 , 139
Government Microcomputer Letter (GML), 0882-6587 , 485
Government Prime Contracts Monthly, 1,197
Government Pubs. News, 0897-5728 , 486

Jerome Riker Intl. Study of Organized Persecution of Children Newsletter
Knightline

TITLE/ISSN INDEX

Microlink, 230
Microporous Materials Technology News, 1077-6869, 165
Microprocessor Report, 0899-9341, 230
Microscopial Society of Canada. Bulletin, 0383-1825, 941
Microsoft Developer Network News, 230
Microsoft Directions, 230
Microsoft Press Window, 230
Microsoft Quarterly, 230
Microsoft Works in Education, 1046-1981, 230
Microwave News, 0275-6595, 518
Microwaves and Food Newsletter, 339
Mid-America Senior Tennis, 1,170
Mid American Outlook, 145
Mid-Atlantic Archivist, 0738-9396, 804
Mid-Atlantic Queries & Reviews, 1044-6915, 461
Mid-Continent News, 590
Mid-Continent Newsletter, 959
Mid-Continent Region Report, 959
Mid-Continent Region Rotary Report, 959
Mid-Continent States Petroleum Industry, 959
Mid Life Woman, 1061-348X, 1,209
Mid Net News, 590
Mid-Valley Impeller, 590
Middle East Business Intelligence, 0731-6305, 145
Middle East Insider, 634
Middle East Insight, 634
Middle East Labor Bulletin, 634
Middle East Policy Survey, 634
Middle East Trade Letter, 650
Middle/Fixed Income Letter, 677
Middle School Companion, The, 318
Middletown Bulletin, 471
Midland Report, 959
Midland Report New Locations, 959
Midrange Systems Advisory Service, 230
Midwest Chesterton News, 818
Midwest Energy Newsletter, 356
Midwest and Northeast Region Report, 960
Midwest Political Consultant, 993
Midwest Sociologist, 1,126
Midwest Transaction Guide, 756
Mifflin County Historical News, 544
Mighty Mopars, 74
Migrant, 942
Migration Today, 1,048
Mike Segal's Commodity Advisory, 677
Milacron Review, 590
Mile Post, 554
Mileposts, 1,187
Miles Alkalizer, 590
Miles College News, 195
Miles Review, The, 186
Milestones and Memories, 101
Milgrim on Licensing, 951
Milgrim on Trade Secrets, 951
Militarism Resource Project News, 897
Military Aircraft Forecast, 897
Military Aircraft Inventory Database License, 897
Military Force Structures of the World, 897
Military Living's R & R Report, 897
Military & Police Uniform Association Newsletter, 179
Military Robotics, 0896-0348, 897
Military Space, 0743-7897, 897
Military Travel News, 897
Military Vehicles Forecast, 897
Milk Market Bulletin, 264
Mill, 590
Millennial Prophecy Report, 1083-4761, 1,048
Millennium Pop, 914
Miller Management Briefing, 104
Miller Notes, 914
Miller's Copyright Newsletter, 756
Miller's Market Report, 477
Millipore Process News, 362
Milton Bradley News, 590
Milton Society of America, Bulletin, 823
Milwaukee Commerce Hot-Line, 0026-4342, 160
Milwaukee Engineering, 362
Milwaukee Grain Exchange, Market Report, 418
Milwaukee Reader, 804
Mime Times, 1,173
Mimi Sheraton's Taste, 1,075
Mind/Body Medicine Newsletter, The, 518
Mind-Expander, 974
Mind Garden Newsletter, The, 413
Mind Play, 145
Mind Quest, 607
Mind Science Foundation News, 1,015
Mindell Letter, The, 518
Mindszenty Report, 993
Mine-Mill Union, 709
Mine Regulation Reporter, 0192-4745, 901
Mine Safety and Health News, 901
Mineral Law Newsletter, 756
Minerals Research Laboratory Newsletter, 901
Minfax, 1,035

Mini' App'les, 230
Mini Examiner Newsletter, 1,015
Mini Headliner, 569
Mini Lab Focus, 977
Mini License Plate & Key Chain Tag Newsletter, 480
Mini Manager, 841
Mini-Thistle, 554
Miniature Book News, 118
Minicomputer/LAN Applications Analyzer, 230
Minicomputer Reports, 230
Mining Newsletter, 1,082
Ministerial Formation, 1,048
Minnesota Agricultural Economist, 43
Minnesota Bulletin, 111
Minnesota Center for Book Arts, 118
Minnesota Chemist, 0026-5411, 165
Minnesota Composers Forum, 914
Minnesota Department of Education, Public Library Newsletter, 804
Minnesota Division of Game and Fish, Technical Bulletin, 387
Minnesota Education Update, 318
Minnesota Employment Law Letter, 1054-6367, 756
Minnesota English Newsletter, 0544-3520, 318
Minnesota Environmental Compliance Update, 1072-916X, 756
Minnesota Genealogical Society Newsletter, 461
Minnesota Government Report, 488
Minnesota International Center, 634
Minnesota Labor Market Review, 703
Minnesota Landscape Arboretum News, 442
Minnesota Legal Register, 788
Minnesota Library Assn. Newsletter, 804
Minnesota Literature, 823
Minnesota Management Review, 145
Minnesota Nursing Accent, 930
Minnesota Pest Report, 43
Minnesota State Florists' Bulletin, 424
Minnesota Views, 160
Minolta Contact Sheet, 977
Minor News, 74
Minorities in Business Insider, 1050-3463, 145
Minority Contract Opportunities, 925
Minority Funding Report, 1047-3300, 1,119
Minority Markets Alert, 1041-7524, 19
Minsk Business News, 634
Minuteman, 535
Mirror — Jefferson City, 590
Mirror, 0738-7237 — Lancaster, 906
Misc., 261
Mishpochah Message, 1,069
Mision a las Americas Hoy, 1,053
Missilani, 590
Missile Forecast, 31
Mission News, 1,058
Mission Newsletter, 1,064
Mission Update, 1,058
Missionaries Together, 1,058
Missions-Etrangeres, 1,058
Missions Update, 1,064
Missions d' Afrique, 1,058
Mississippi Employment Law Letter, 1074-0430, 757
Mississippi History Newsletter, 544
Missouri Archeological Society Quarterly, 0743-7641, 57
Missouri Bar Bulletin, 757
Missouri Business, 160
Missouri Employment Law Letter, 1054-6375, 757
Missouri Enterprise, 0279-3261, 293
Missouri Environmental Compliance Update, 1075-959X, 757
Missouri Libraries, 0899-6458, 804
Missouri Monthly Vital Statistics, 518
Missouri Official, 1,022
Missouri Parent-Teacher, 318
Missouri River Report, 0733-8112, 1,203
Missouri Schools, 0745-1237, 318
Missouri State Emergency Management Agency Newsletter, 0197-6672, 1,138
Missouri Workers' Compensation Law Reporter, 757
Mistletoe Leaves, 544
Misuse of Medications, 1,107
Mitchell Report, The, 677
Mitzymitzy Ennui, 471
Mixed Media, 65
Mixin', 104
Mixing Bowl, 590
Mobile Data Report, 1040-7022, 230
Mobile Home Living, 902
Mobile and Industrial Catering, 1,076
Mobile Letter, 230
Mobile Phone News, 0737-5077, 1,160
Mobile Public Library Today, 805
Mobile Satellite News, 1046-5286, 1,160
Mobilehome Parks Report, 0273-2726, 902
Mobilia, 74
Model Laws, Regulations and Guidelines, 622
Model Mugging News, 1,082

The Modeler's Resource, 554
Modem User News, 230
Modern Accounting and Auditing Checklists, 6
Modern Agnostic Journal, The, 1,049
Modern Blacksmith, 892
Modern Construction and Development Forms, 248
Modern Divorce, 815
Modern Drafting Practices & Standards Manual & Updating Service, 367
Modern Federal Jury Instructions, 757
Modern Greek Society: A Social Science Newsletter, 0147-0779, 634
Modern Greek Studies Association Bulletin, 0047-7702, 544
Modern Job Safety & Health, 1,082
Modern Languages Newsletter, 318
Modern Merchant, 590
Modern Nutrition News, 934
Modern Real Estate Acquisition & Disposition Forms, 1,035
Modern Real Estate & Mortgage Forms: Checklists, 1,035
Modern Trust Forms Checklists, 94
Modern UCC Litigation Forms, 757
Mohonk Preserve Newsletter, 387
Moila Temple Bulletin, 179
Molasses Market News, 0145-0662, 1,138
Mom to Mom, 1,210
Momentum — Torrance, 590
Momentum — Washington, 445
Mom's Apple Pie, 445
Monday Memo, 318
Monday Morning Message, 438
Monday Morning Report, 519
Monday Report on Retailers, 273
Monday: a weekly newsletter on refugee and immigration issues, 399
Monetary Digest — Longwood, 94
Monetary Digest — Phoenix, 677
Monetary & Economic Review, 677
Monetary Outlook, The, 677
Money Engineer, 591
Money and Family Law, 0832-7653, 6
Money Laundering Alert, 1046-3070, 757
Money Laundering, Asset Forfeiture & Intl. Financial Crimes Newsletter, 1070-1486, 757
Money Laundering Law Report, 757
MoneyLetter, The, 0703-7613, 677
Money Maker Report, 1,035
Money Management Letter, 677
Money Manager's Compliance Advisor, 677
Money Master, 94
Money Paper, The, 677
Money Pro 'The Steve Crowley Report', 94
Money Reporter, 0709-0579, 677
Money Talks, 94
Money Watch Bulletin, 94
MoneyWorks for Women, 1,210
Moneychanger, The, 677
Moneytalk, 254
Mongolia Survey, 0895-6523, 261
Mongoose, 199
Monitor — Atlanta, 174
Monitor, 0260-6666 — Medford, 860
Monitor!, 993
Monitor, We the People & Our Two Cents Worth, 471
Mono Lake Newsletter, 0275-6633, 1,203
Monoclonal Antibody News, 0272-4588, 880
Monroe County Heritage, 544
Monroe County of Wisconsin Historical Society Time Capsules, 544
Monroe Juneau Jackson Counties Genealogy Newsletter, 461
Montana Employment Law Letter, 757
Montana League of Cities, 1,022
Montana Parent-Teacher, 318
Montana Post, 0047-7958, 544
Montana Schools, 318
Montana and the Sky, 31
Montana State Library News Update, 805
Montana State Univ. Mathematics Univ., 852
Montefiore Medicine, 569
Montessori Observer, 0889-5643, 318
Montgomery County Law Reporter, 757
Montgomery Village News, 1,041
Monthly Brewing Industry Commentary Including State Beer Statistics, 104
Monthly. . . Bulletin, 605
Monthly Bulletin (Quebec), 1,044
Monthly Bulletin of Utility Gas Sales, 1,026
Monthly Business Failure, 293
Monthly Completion Report, 960
Monthly Exports of Ducks & Geese, 1,001
Monthly Gram, 31
Monthly Guide, 1,054
Monthly Guide of Brooklyn Academy of Music, 914
Monthly Imports of Down Filled Outerwear, 55
Monthly Imports & Exports of Feathers & Down, 1,171

Monthly Imports & Exports of Finished Products by Firm, 1,171
Monthly Imports & Exports of Pillows & Comforters, 1,171
Monthly Imports & Exports of Sleeping Bags, 1,172
Monthly Letter About Evangelism, 1,064
Monthly Magazine Advertising Summary, 19
Monthly Newsletter for Mothers of Asthmatics, 519
Monthly Newsprint Report, 947
Monthly Price Review, 0566-3628 , 431
Monthly Product Announcement, 145
Monthly Report for Hairstylists & Salon Owners, 0277-0334 , 100
Monthly Statistics of Foreign Trade -Series A, 0474-5388 , 650
Monthly Statistics/Open-End Investment Companies Trends, 678
Monthly Stock Charts Canadian Companies, 678
Monthly Summary, 1,001
Monthly Truck Tonnage Report, 1,193
Montreal Plus, 650
Montserrat Progressive Society of New York Newsletter, 400
Moody Street Irregulars: A Jack Kerouac Newsletter, 0196-2604 , 823
Moody's Global Short-Term Market Record, 0888-5915 , 678
Moody's Monthly Short-Term Market Record, 678
Moore Family Register, 461
Moore News, 205
Moore's Federal Practice, 757
Moore's Manual-Federal Practice and Procedure, 757
Moore's Manual--Forms, 757
Morality in Media Newsletter, 0027-1004 , 758
Moravian Music Foundation Newsletter, 914
More Light Update, 0889-3985 , 445
Morehead Statement, 189
Morehouse Update, 199
More than a Paycheck, 994
Morfogen Assocs. Newsletter, 145
Morgan Link, 461
Morgantown Area Chamber of Commerce Newsletter, 160
Moriarty Clan, 461
Morim Bulletin, 318
Morningstar Closed-End Funds, 1059-1419 , 678
Morningstar Investor, 1065-3414 , 678
Morningstar Japan, 1061-1886 , 634
Morningstar Mutual Funds, 0890-7153 , 678
Morris Arboretum Newsletter, 121
Mortarboard — Americus, 209
Mortarboard — Convent Station, 318
Mortgage-Backed Securities Letter, 678
Mortgage Bank Weekly, 95
Mortgage Bankers Assn. of America-Washington Report, 95
Mortgage Marketplace, 95
Mortgage and Real Estate Executives Report, 0047-813X , 1,036
Morton Heritage, 0894-3974 , 461
Mortuary Science Monitor, 437
Mosaic-News from the Museum of Fine Arts, 906
Moskowitz Jacobs Inc., 19
Motel News, 575
Mother Cabrini Messenger, 1,058
Mother & Co., 1,210
Mother-To-Mother, 413
Motif, 53
Motion Picture Investor, 0742-8839 , 420
Motor Carrier-Freight Forwarder Service, 1,178
Motor Carrier Safety Report, 1,082
Motor Fleet Safety Supervision, 1,082
Motor News Analysis, 0027-1942 , 74
Motor Vator, 591
Motor Vehicle Regulation/State Capitals, 0016-1810 , 74
Motor Vehicle & Traffic Laws of New Jersey, 74
Motorcycle Business Newsletter, 263
Motorcycle Consumer News, 263
Motorist's Advocate, The, 74
Motorsports Marketing Sponsorship News, 19
Moultrie County Heritage, 544
Mount Angel Letter, 1,058
Mt. Holyoke College Art Museum-Newsletter, 906
Mount Savior Chronicle, 1,058
Mountain Empire Genealogical Quarterly, 461
Mountain Light, 544
Mountain Women's Exchange-Newsletter, 1,119
Mouser Report, The, 19
Mouthpiece, 270
Movement Support Network News, 758
Mr. Landlord, 1,036
Multicultural Messenger, 1,041
Multicultural Publishing and Education Council Newsletter, 1049-5428 , 119
Multimedia Business Report, 1051-953X , 231
Multimedia Daily, 1079-4212 , 231
Multimedia Monitor, 0739-7089 , 231
Multimedia Networking Newsletter, 231
Multimedia Publisher, 954

Multimedia Strategist, 758
Multimedia & Technology, 231
Multimedia Telecommunication News, 1,160
Multimedia Week, 1064-6639 , 860
Multinational Corporations Law: Mexico, Cntrl.America, Panama, Cntrl. American Common Mkt., 758
Multinational PR Report, 19
Multiple Linear Regression Viewpoints, 1,016
Multistate Corporate Income Tax Guide, 1,148
Multistate Sales Tax Guide, 1,148
Muncie Transmitter, 591
Muni Bond Fund Report, 678
Municipal Art Society Newsletter, 65
Municipal Attorney, 1,022
Municipal Engineers Assn. Newsletter, 362
Municipal Immunity Law Bulletin, 758
Municipal Law Docket, 1,022
Municipal Litigation Reporter, 0278-1501 , 758
Municipal News, 1,043
Municipal Open Line, 489
Municipal Routes, 1,077
Municipalities in the U.S. Supreme Court, 174
Munson-Williams-Proctor Institute Bulletin, 906
Munsters & the Addams Family Reunion, 417
Murder is Academic, 318
Murphy's Will Clauses, 758
Murray Hill News, 1,042
Murray Tube Bulletin, 591
MuseLetter, 914
Muse News, 906
Musea, 65
Museletter, The, 519
Museletter — Santa Rosa, 1,098
Museletter — Toronto, 983
Museogramme, 0380-4623 , 906
Museum Archivist, 906
Museum of Flight News, 906
Museum of the Great Plains Newsletter, 906
Museum Insights, 906
Museum Matters, 906
Museum Monthly, 906
Museum Newsletter, 0820-8336 , 907
Museum of Science Magazine, 907
Museum of Staten Island News, 907
MusiCopyright Intelligence, 7067-876X , 914
Music Box, 914
Music Business Insight, 914
Music Cataloging Bulletin, 0027-4283 , 805
Music Connoisseur, The, 914
Music Critics Association Newsletter, 914
Music From China, 914
Music Industry News, 914
Music Library Association Newsletter, 805
Music for the Love of It, 0898-8757 , 914
Music Notes, 0899-7292 , 202
Music Research News, 0700-3838 , 914
Music-Theatre Group Newsletter, 591
Music Time, 1,053
Musical News, 709
Musical Show, 1,173
Musu Zinios, 404
Mutual Fund Advisor, 1050-656X , 678
Mutual Fund Analyst, 678
Mutual Fund Buyer's Guide, 1067-1358 , 678
Mutual Fund Forecaster, 8755-9889 , 678
Mutual Fund Investing, 8756-5161 , 678
Mutual Fund Letter, 678
Mutual Fund Performance and Review, 679
Mutual Fund Specialist, 679
Mutual Fund Strategist, 679
Mutual Fund Trends, 679
Mutual Funds Guide, 679
Mutual Funds Scoreboard, 679
Mutual Piper, The, 622
My Pen Pal, 815
Myasthenia Gravis Foundation Newsletter, 880
Mycological Society of America Newsletter, 0541-4938 , 110
Myers Finance & Energy, 95
Mylan Messenger, 461
Mystery Collectors' Bookline, 920
Mystery Notebook, 0740-8870 , 920
Mystery Science Manifesto 3000, 696
Mystic Light of the Aladdin Knights, 555
Mythprint, 0146-9347 , 818

N

NAACLS News, 318
NAACS Washington Update, 256
NAAFA Newsletter, 174
NAAM Letter, 1,069
NAAP News — New York, 1,016
NAAP News — Washington, 569
NAA Reporter, 436
NAASR Newsletter, 0890-3794 , 400

NAATS Bulletin, 1,178
NAAWP News, 994
NABCA Bulletin, 6
NABE News — Washington, 293
NABE News — Washington, 319
NABE Outlook, Industry Survey & Policy Survey, 294
NABP Newsletter, 285
NABS Newsletter, 95
NABS Weekly, 100
NACAC Bulletin, 319
N.A.C.A.S. Newsletter, 1,022
NACCAS Review, 319
NACDS Executive Newsletter, 285
NACHRI Newsletter, 569
NACLites, 65
NACS SCAN, 850
NACUFS News Wave, 431
NADAP News/Report, 346
NAD Broadcaster, 533
NADO News, 248
NAEA News, 0160-6395 , 319
NAEB Bulletin, 1,028
NAEIR Advantage, 319
NAEN Bulletin, 1,091
NAFA Fleet Focus, 74
NAFC Quarterly Newsletter, 519
NAFE Member News, 1,210
NAFI Newsletter, 421
NAFSA Newsletter, 0027-5824 , 319
NAF Update, 519
NAGARA Clearinghouse, 805
NAHB Remodelor, The, 248
N.A.H.C. Report, 519
NAHRO Monitor, 0194-9268 , 1,022
NAHWW Newsletter, 557
NAIC Investor Advisory Service, 679
NAIC News, The, 622
NAIEC Newsletter, 319
NAIMA Museum News, 907
N.A.I.R. News, 1,132
NALP Bulletin, 346
NAMSB News, 55
NAMS News, 936
NAMTA News & Views, 65
NAN Bulletin, 1,022
NAOS, 823
NAOSMM Newsline, 1,098
NAPA News, 74
NAPBC Newsletter, 124
NAPET News, 977
NAP Forum, 145
NAPH National Newsletter, 0741-1405 , 278
NAPIA Bulletin, 622
NAPM News Bulletin, 285
NAPNSC Newsletter: Current Events & Comments, 319
NAPO News, 0820-7364 , 1,119
NAPSAC News, 0192-1223 , 413
NAPSEC News, 319
NAPSLO Newsletter, 622
NAPS Letter, 971
NAQP News, 1,005
NAQP Quick Bytes, 231
NARAL News, 0195-2862 , 519
NAREB Report, 1,036
NARF Legal Review, 758
NARHA News, 1067-5876 , 1,132
NARI Stethoscope, 880
NARM Sounding Board, 915
NASAA Reports, 679
NASACT Newsletter, 95
NASA STI Bulletin, 31
NASBIC News, 145
NASCA Inside Report, 1,110
NASCAR News, 0027-5999 , 1,133
NASCO Newsbriefs, 254
NASDAQ, 679
NASD Manual, 95
NASD Regulatory & Compliance Alert, 679
NASEA News, 703
NASFAA Newsletter, 0882-4630 , 319
NASFM NEWs, 850
NASJE News, 758
NAS Newsletter, 930
NASNewsletter, 930
NASOH Newsletter, 897
NASPA Forum, 0271-1672 , 319
NASPE News, 319
NASSP Curriculum Report, 0547-4205 , 1,092
NASSP Legal Memorandum, 0192-6152 , 1,092
NASSP NewsLeader, 0278-0569 , 1,092
NASTAT News, 319
NASWHP Information and Exchange Service, 1,119
NASW News, 1,119
NATAS News, 1062-9637 , 1,168
NATAT Washington Report, 0735-9691 , 1,022
NATE News, 1,070
NATIE News Notes, 320

Profiles in PDM, 844
Profit-The Bottom Line in Greater New Haven Business, 161
Profit Builder, 595
Profit-Building Strategies for Business Owners, 149
Profit Letter, The, 683
Profit-Sharing and Pension Forms, 614
Profit Strategies, 234
Profitable Investing, 1048-3667 , 683
Profits, 149
Program on Information Resources Policy-Review, 1,161
Program and Legislative Action, 997
Program Plans/Nursing Basic, 0734-1431 , 326
Progress, 326
Progress Against Cancer, 885
Progress in Dermatology, 885
Progress -GWU Medical Center, 571
Progress Notes — Iowa City, 1,017
Progress Notes — Louisville, 885
Progress in Public Health, 525
Progress Report — Providence, 161
Progress Report — Washington, 927
Progression, 181
Progressive Conservative Association of Alberta Progress Bulletin, 997
Progressive Purchasing, 1,028
Progressive Review, 0889-2202 , 997
Progressive Teacher, The, 0033-0825 , 326
Project Equality-Update, 175
Project Equality of Wisconsin-Newsletter & Buyers' Guide, 704
Project Management, 249
Project Profile, 595
Project Salvador Crafts, 256
Projection, 0229-2947 , 525
Projections, 112
Projector, 208
Projects Communique, 1,121
Projects with Industry Forum, 278
Prologue — Medford, 1,174
Prologue — Milwaukee, 1,174
Prometheus Report: Journal of Firesafety, 422
Promises, Pro-Mss, 1,102
Promotion Idea File, 21
Promotional Links, 21
Promotional Programming, 124
Promotional Test Questions, 771
Promotions of Member Tracks, 560
Promptlines, 234
Proof, 861
Prop 65 Litigation Reporter, 771
Prop 65 News, 391
Pro$perity Alert, 295
Property Insurance Report, 771
Property Tax Alert, 1,150
Property Taxes, 1,150
Prophetic Newsletter, 1,050
Proposed Consolidated Plan, 491
Propwash, 1,134
Prosecution and Defense of Criminal Conspiracy Cases, 771
Prosecution and Defense of Forfeiture Cases, 771
Prosecution and Defense of Sex Crimes, 1,110
Prospect Review, 357
Prospective Payment Guide, 525
Prospects Report, 101
Prosperous Living, 1,050
Protection of Assets Bulletin/Protection of Assets Manual, 0740-137X , 1,104
Protector, 149
Protestant Teachers Association Newsletter, 1,065
Prove it Pretzel Boy, 697
Provider, The, 596
Provincial - Industry Economic Services, 295
Provincial Judges Assn. of B. C. Newsletter, 771
Provincial Legislative Record, 491
Provincial Notes, 1,215
Provincial Tax Reorts, 1,150
Proving Medical Diagnosis and Prognosis, 885
Pru-Echo, 596
Prudent Speculator, The, 0743-0809 , 683
Prune Report, Daily, 1,009
Pryor Report, 149
Pshaw, 1,174
Psi Chi Newsletter, 0033-2569 , 1,017
PsycINFO, 1,017
Psych Discourse, 1,017
Psychiatric Topics, 1,011
Psychiatry Drug Alerts, 287
Psychic Guide Psychic Fair Network News, 922
Psychogram, 571
Psychologists for Social Responsibility Newsletter, 997
Psychopharmacology Update, 1068-5308 , 1,017
Psychosocial Nursing & Mental Health Service, 931
Psychotherapy Finances, 0163-1543 , 844
Psychotherapy Letter, The, 1047-9848 , 1,017
Public Accounting Report, 0161-309X , 7

Public Affairs, 491
Public Affairs Analyst, 1,023
Public Affairs Newsletter, 637
Public Affairs Report, 0033-3417 , 997
Public Assistance & Welfare Trends/State Capitals, 0734-1601 , 1,121
Public Bridge, 808
Public Broadcasting Report, 0193-3663 , 1,169
Public Citizen Health Letter, 0882-598X , 525
Public Contract Law News, 0569-3314 , 771
Public Domain Report, 1070-2555 , 66
Public Education Alert, 326
Public Employee Dismissals Bulletin, 1,023
Public Employee Newsletter, 1,083
Public Employer's Guide to Payroll Administration, 1,150
Public Employment Law Notes, 0809-9789 , 771
Public Employment Law Report, 1043-8211 , 771
Public Employment Reports, 0889-9789 , 491
Public Eye — Madison, 771
Public Eye, 0275-9322 — Somerville, 997
Public Health Letter, 525
Public Health/State Capitals, 0734-1156 , 525
Public History News, 547
Public Innovation Abroad, 1,023
Public Interest Briefs, 772
Public Interest Report, 1,099
Public Investment, 1,023
Public Investor, 683
Public Justice Report, 0742-5325 , 997
Public Lands Council-Washington Highlight Report, 391
Public Lands News, 1,024
Public Library Services Newsletter, 0706-7798 , 808
Public Policy Quarterly, 287
Public Power Weekly Newsletter, 1,027
Public Pulse, The, 1,126
Public Relations News, 0033-3697 , 861
Public Relations Officer, 196
Public Safety, 1,083
Public Safety and Justice Policies/State Capitals, 1061-9704 , 789
Public Safety Management, 0748-9927 , 422
Public Safety Personnel Updance, 1071-7412 , 789
Public School, 1,093
Public Sector, 0700-2092 , 997
Public Sector Arbitration Awards, 710
Public Sector Job Bulletin, 1072-3773 , 348
Public Sector Management/ Management et Secteur Public, 1183-1081 , 1,024
Public Service Report, 861
Public Utilities Newsletter, 1,083
Public Utilities/State Capitals, 0016-1888 , 1,027
Public Works History, 547
Public Works News, 0176-5473 , 1,024
Publicity & Marketing Ideas, 21
Publishers Auxiliary, 772
Publishers Information Bureau-Reports, 21
Publishers' Monthly Domestic Sales, 119
Publisher's Multinational Direct, 21
Publisher's Report, 0884-3090 , 119
Publishing Poynters, 119
Pubs. of the IRS, 1,150
Pubwatch Update, 119
Puerto Rico Tax Reports, 1,150
Puerto Rico Taxes, 1,151
Pull Together, 898
Pulp & Paper Forecaster, 946
Pulp & Paper Project Report, 947
Pulp & Paper Week, 947
Pulp & Paper Wood Report, 830
Pulpwood Highlights, 831
Pulse — Birmingham, 885
Pulse — Kent, 525
Pulse — New York, 571
Pulse, 0747-8631 — Wheaton, 1,065
Pulse Crop Newsletter, 45
Pulsebeat, 571
Pulsette, 571
Pumbedissa, 1,070
Pump Patter, 596
Pumplines, 596
Pun American Newsletter, 605
Punch Lines, 596
Punch List, 249
Pundit, The, 0712-1318 , 605
Purchaser's Legal Adviser, 0898-994X , 1,028
Purchasing Executive's Bulletin, 1,028
Purchasing Professional Newsletter, 0192-9607 , 1,028
Purdue University, Pharmacy, Nursing & Health Sciences Library Notes, 808
Pure Facts, 525
Pursuit, 192
Putnam County Heritage, 547

Q

Q, 596

QRC Advisor, 0747-7384 , 885
Q-Weather Forecast & Commodities Outlook, 683
Quad Report, The, 1072-3179 , 357
Quad Special Reports, The, 1072-3137 , 357
Quadrille, 193
Quagmire, 605
Quaker Committee on Jails & Justice Newsletter, 0824-6521 , 772
Quaker Concern, 0229-1916 , 1,121
Quaker Yeomen, 0737-8246 , 465
Qualelibet, 824
Qualified Plan Reference Service, 97
Quality 1st., 615
Quality Action Planner, 844
Quality of Care, 278
Quality Care Advocate, 525
Quality Customer Service, 97
Quality Executive, 844
Quality Improvement Quarterly, 1,007
Quality Letter for Healthcare Leaders, The, 844
Quality Management, 1040-0664 , 850
Quality Teaching, 326
Quantum Advantage Investment & Technology Report, 1,099
Quantum PC Report for CPAs, 234
Quarterdeck, The, 0891-2661 , 907
Quarterly — Austin, 571
Quarterly — Great Bend, 465
Quarterly — New Rochelle, 191
Quarterly — New York, 907
Quarterly — Sherman, 596
Quarterly Business Failures Report, 149
Quarterly Byte, The, 1052-5521 , 1,037
Quarterly CERCular Information Bulletin, 937
Quarterly Community Health Center News, 525
Quarterly Counselor, 772
Quarterly Domestic & Global Forecasts of Key Economic Indicators, 0888-787X , 149
Quarterly Labour Force Statistics, 0255-3627 , 295
Quarterly Performance Report, 683
Quarterly Report, 21
Quarterly Review of Doublespeak, 0735-5920 — Urbana, 326
Quarterly Studies/Review, 2756-4769 , 683
Quartier Libre, 208
Quate's Grain/Weather Forecast, 45
Quebec Construction, 0829-5263 , 249
Quebec Homeschooling Advisory Newsletter, 327
Quebec Tax Reports, 1,151
Queens Botanical Garden News, 443
Queen's Connection, 571
Queens County Bar Association, Queens Bar Bulletin, 772
Queen's Vision, 571
Query, 0033-6270 — Bryn Mawr, 623
Query, 1065-206X — Sunnyvale, 1,093
Questing, 1,188
Questing Heirs Genealogical Society, 465
Questionable Cartoons, 997
Quick, Easy, Cheap and Simple..the Newsletter, 558
Quick Notes, 234
Quick Topics, 243
Quickfill Application Notes, 234
Quicktrips Travel Letter, 1064-0339 , 1,188
Quill, 1,007
The Quill Pen Pal, 472
Quilt Peddler, 922
Quilter's Newsletter Magazine, 0274-712X , 555
Quincy Business News, 149
Quinnehtukqut, 391
Quintcentennial Quarterly, The, 409
Quodlibet, 0885-9442 , 916
Quorum Report, 492
Quote Quad, 234
Quote. . . Unquote, 1044-0518 , 1,059

R

RAB Instant Background, 125
RAC Journal, 363
RADAR, 75
RAP Session, 348
RASD Update, 0198-8344 , 808
RBA Insight, 432
RBI Newsletter, 0829-6782 , 101
RBMS Newsletter, 808
RBOC Update, 1,161
RBRVS Fee Schedule : A Plain-English Guide, 525
RCRA Corrective Action, 391
RCRA Corrective Action Manual, 392
RCRA Land Disposal Restrictions-A Guide to Compliance, 166
R & D Focus, 892
R & D Focus Drug News, 287
R & D Innovator, 1061-1894 , 1,161
REACH, 1,050
REC News Exchange, 0033-6904 , 1,050

Title Change Index

- Lists old title of publication, it's current name and page number.

G

GAF News - World of GAF, *603*
GEO Report, The - Eco-Profiteer, The, *662*
GMAC Newsletter - Inside GMAC, *313*
Gallery, AGO News - Journal, *905*
Gallup Report, The - Gallup Poll, The, *990*
Ganymede - Way Fourth, *1,067*
Gas Research Institute Digest - GRID, *354*
Gas Supply Review - Gas Energy Review, *354*
Gas Utilities Worldwide - Gas Utilities Industry - Worldwide, *1,026*
Gateway; Insights - Insights Today, *587*
Gay Airline Club Newsletter - Gay Airline & Travel Club Newsletter, The, *1,184*
Gay Archivist - Lesbian and Gay Archivist, *445*
Gay & Lesbian Franchise News, The - Franchise Wise (Quarterly newsletter of the intl gay & lesbian franchise assoc.), *444*
Gear/Excelsior - Blue Seal, *71*
General Aviation Accident Report - General Aviation/ Helicopter Accident Report, *740*
Genesee Valley Buyer - Purchasing Professional Newsletter, *1,028*
Genz Newsletter - Henkel Newsletter, *456*
Georgia Health Alert - Georgia Health Law Update, *507*
Georgia Peace & Justice Report - News-N-Notes, *994*
German Business Weekly - German American Commerce, *159*
Getty Conservation Institue Newsletter - Conservation: The Getty Conservation Institute Newsletter, *903*
Girl Groups Gazette - Girl Groups ('60's Rock N' Roll) Gazette, *417*
Global Electronics Information Newsletter - Global Electronics, *338*
Global Telecom Report - Wireless Business & Finance, *1,164*
Go-Getter - Foxtales, *584*
Goebel Miniatures Newsletter - Magnifier, The, *65*
Gold and Monetary Report - McAlvany Intelligence Advisor, *676*
Gold & Silver Update - Moneychanger, The, *677*
Golden Traveler - Golden Gateway, *1,184*
Gomberg Report, The - Gomberg-Fredrikson Report, *103*
Good Impressions - Magnet Marketing, *17*
Good News! - Prosperous Living, *1,050*
Good News - Goodwill Dimensions, *1,117*
Goodenough's Ghosts - Goodenow's Ghosts, *455*
Goodwill Quarterly - Working Times, *603*
Gopher Tortoise Council - Tortoise Burrow Bulletin, *395*
Gorman's New Product News - New Product News, *495*
Gourd Seed - Gourd, *441*
Government Report - Capitol Connection, *501*
Governor's Weekly Bulletin - Governors' Bulletin, *486*
Govt. Bus. Worldwide Report - International Observer, *632*
Graduate School of Library Science Newsletter - Graduate School of Library and Information Science Newsletter, *799*
Grain Market News - Calfornia Grain & Feeders Report, *418*
Gramercy Neighborhood News - Gramercy, *1,042*
The Grapevine - Good Night News, *574*
Graphic Artists Guild Newsletter - Guild News, *1,005*
Graphic Arts Industries Assn. - CBFA Newsletter, *1,003*
Graphiti - In Brief, *64*
Grawunder Connection, The - Grawunder and Graffunder Connection, The, *455*
Great Basin Mx Alliance Newsletter - Citizen Alert Newsletter, *375*
Greater Europe Report; Europe Report - Europe Today, *1,063*
Greater Knoxville - Greater Knoxville Chamber of Commerce Membership Newsletter, *159*
Greater Washington Area Labor Summary - Metropolitan Washington D.C. Area Labor Summary, *703*
Greener Pastures Gazatte - Rural Property Investor, *1,039*
Greenpeace Examiner - Greenpeace, *383*
Grist Mill - Columns, *538*
Grito del Sol - TQS News, *825*
Group Health Journal - GHAA Journal, *507*
Group Health News - GHAA News, *507*
Grower Forecast - Premium Grower, *105*
Growth Index - Chamber Forum, *158*
Growth Industry News - Industries in Transition, *141*
Guarantor, The; Global Guaranty; Global Asset Backed Monitor - Asset Sales Report, *80*
Guatemala - Report on Guatemala, *637*
Guide to Employment Law & Regulation - Employment Law Manual, *734*
Guilds - Spectra, *693*
Gulf of Mexico Rotary Service - Gulf of Mexico Rotary Report, *957*
Gulf Reconstruction Report - Gulf Business Report, *647*

H

HEALTHsports Bulletin - Ski for Light Bulletin, *528*
HIAS Reporter; HIAS Bulletin - HIAS Headlines & Highlights, *631*
HIP Report - NAFC Quarterly Newsletter, *519*
HKI Report - Insight, *111*
HPO Notes - Transit Postmark Collector, *972*
HRCC/CCRH - CFH Bulletin FCEH, *820*
Hadashot - Newsletter, *1,070*
Handicap News - Caring Connection, *1,115*
Handicapped Requirements Handbook - Section 504 Compliance Guide, *774*
Handicapped Rights & Regulations; Handicapped Americans Rept - Report on Disability Programs, *279*
Handicaptions - Connector, *1,116*
Happenings - ASI Posten, *409*
Happiness - Sons, *1,060*
Harambee - Alumni Line, *202*
Harriman Institute Forum - The Harriman Review, *631*
Harry S. Truman Library Institute Newsletter - Whistle Stop, *813*
Harvard Medical School Health Letter - Harvard Health Letter, *508*
Harvard University Art Museums Newsletter - Harvard University Art Museums Review, *64*
Hastings College Bulletin - Hastings College Today, *203*
Hawaii Swine Newsletter - Animal Sciences Newsletter, *827*
HazMatTranspt.Matls; ToxicMatls.Transpt; Asbestos Contrl Rpt - HazMat Transport News, *1,192*
Hazardous Materials Guide - Hazardous Regulation Guide, *164*
Hazardous Substances Advisor - Environmental Regulatory Advisor, *164*
Hazardous Waste Mangement Guide - Hazardous Waste Guide, *164*
Hazardous Waste Report - Hazardous Waste News, *384*
Hazardous Waste & Toxic Torts Law & Strategy - Environmental Compliance Litigation & Strategy, *734*
Hazelden News and Professional Update - Hazelden Voice, *1,117*
Headlines - Independent Grocer, *494*
Health Care Competition Week - Healthcare Systems Strategy Report, *565*
Health Commerce Line - Generic Line, *284*
Health for Life - Health & Longevity, *509*
Health Matters - Health Exchange, *509*
Health Planning - Health Care, *564*
Health Policy Week - Health Care Reform Week, *509*
Healthcare Association of New York State News - HANYS News, *508*
Healthcare Financial Ventures Relationships - Healthcare Business & Legal Strategies, *838*
Healthcare PR News - Healthcare PR & Marketing News, *511*
Healthcare Productivity Report - Strategies for Healthcare Excellence, *572*
Healthwise - Dr. Alexander Grant's Health Gazette, *504*
Heat Transfer - Heat Transfer/Fluid Flow Data Books, *367*
Heather News - Heather Notes, *121*
Hellenic-American Chamber of Commerce Bulletin - Hellenic-American Chamber of Commerce Newsletter, *160*
Heller Report on Educational Technology & Telecommunications - Internet Strategies for Education, *314*
Hemlock Quarterly - Hemlock Timelines, *875*
Hemophilia Newsnotes - Community Alert, *871*
Hepatitis B Coalition News - Hepatitis B Coalition News, *512*
Heritage Quarterly - Heritage, The, *541*
Hiawathian - Report, *947*
Higher Commission Letter - CHE Letter, *302*
Highlights - Newswire, *414*
Highway Financing & Contruction from the State Capitals - Highway Financing & Construction/State Capitals, *1,077*
Highway Highlights - Inside KDOT/Translines, *1,077*
Highway News - Transporation News, *1,077*
Highway Safety Highlights - Highway Safety Directions, *1,080*
Hispanic Arts News - AHA! Hispanic Arts News, *61*
Historians of Early Modern Europe - Scholars of Early Modern Studies, *548*
Historic Kansas City News - Historic Kansas City Foundation Gazette, *541*
History Trails & Tales Old & New - Portland Poynts, *547*
Hobo News - Hobo Times, *814*
Holistic Dental Digest - Holistic Dental Digest Plus, *512*
Hollywood Scriptletter - Hollywood Scriptwriter, *982*
Holyearth Network News - Earthstewards Network News, *377*
Home Business News; Work at Home Report - Home Income Reporter, *140*
Homeless Child - Messenger of St. Joseph's Union, *1,058*
Horizon - Covert Intelligence Letter, *895*
Horizons; Alerte - Bulletin, *903*
Horsefeathers - Directions for Utah Libraries, *796*
Hospi-Tales - JH News, *588*

Hospital Capital Formation Management Letter - Healthcare System Reform Alert, *511*
Hospital Cost Accounting Advisor - Hospital Cost Management & Accounting, *565*
Hospital Fund Raising Newsletter - Healthcare Fund Raising Newsletter, *564*
Hospital Highlights - Ontario Hosptials Today, *570*
Hospital Managed Care and Direct Contracting - Allan Fine's Trends in Integrated Health Care, *561*
Hospital Management Review - Healthcare Leadership Review, *564*
Hospital Marketing and Public Relations - Health Care Marketing and Public Relations, *564*
Hospital Patient Relations Report - RPT on Healthcare Mgnt. & Solutions, *931*
Hospital Personnel Administration - Human Resources Administrator, *567*
Hospital Pharmacy, - White Sheet, *289*
Hospital Purchasing Management - Hospital Materials Management, *566*
Hospital Strategy Report - Russ Coile's Health Trends, *572*
Hospitalta - Healthcare Advocate, *564*
Hostile Actions Against Civil Aviation - Select Hostile Actions Against Civil Aviation, *790*
Hot Buttoneer - Creative Selling, *1,086*
Hotline - Connections, *581*
House Cochlear Implant Assn. Newsletter - Review, The, *886*
Housing America - Building Systems Review, *373*
Housing World - HDA World, *1,021*
Hoverclub of America-Newsletter - Hovernews, *30*
Howard L. Shenson Report - Professional Consultant & Information Marketing Report, *843*
Hubergram - Uptrend, the Canadian Penny Market Newsletter, *690*
Hudson Viewer - Beacon Bulletin, *577*
Hughes Report - Management Report for Nonunion Organizations, *703*
Human Factors Bulletin - Human Factors and Aviation Medicine, *30*
Human Values & Aging Newsletter - Aging and the Human Spirit Newsletter, *1,106*
Humanitas - New Jersey Humanities, *261*
Hummernews - Harley Hummer, *263*
Huna Vistas - Huna Work, *1,067*
Hunting Report for Birdshooters & Waterfowlers, The - Bird Hunting Report, The, *606*
Hutchinson National I Newsletter - Emprise Investment Newsletter, *663*

I

IAC News - Online News, *233*
IAPNH Newsletter - IAHP Newsletter, *876*
IAQC Circle Report - AQP Report, *833*
IBC/Donoghue's Money Fund Report - IBC's Money Fund Report, *668*
IBIS Importers Newsletter - IBIS International Traders Newsletter, *647*
ICA Newsletter - ICA Today, *514*
ICA's Newsletter - Consumer Trends, *86*
ICC Newsletter - CCM Communicator, *131*
ICET Newsletter - NICET Newsletter, *362*
ICID Newsletter - USCID Newsletter, *395*
ICS Reporter - IQ Quarterly, *224*
ICTA News - ICTA Update, *1,185*
IDEA: Center City Report - IDA: Center City Report, *247*
IDP Report - Electronic Information Report, *856*
IE News: Aerospace - IE News: Aerospace & Defense, *30*
IE News: Energy Management - IE News: Energy, Environment & Plant Engineering, *355*
IE News: Management - Systems, *363*
IFFLP Newsletter - IFFLP Bulletin, *514*
I.G.A.B. Newsletter - Bureau Talk, *854*
IIABO News - IBAO News, *620*
IIHS Report - Highway Loss Reduction States Report, *1,080*
IMIS Council Newsletter - Exsports, *1,131*
IMS Weekly Marketeer - IMMS Weekly Marketeer, *620*
INN Newsletter; Assn. of Independent TV Stations Newsletter - INTV Capitol Newsletter, *1,167*
I.Q. Trends - Investment Quality Trends, *672*
IRA Bulletin - Retirement Plans Bulletin, *1,108*
IRAC Bulletin - Interfraternity Bulletin, *313*
IRA-Keogh Retirement Fund Report - Blue Book of Mutual Fund Reports, *656*
IRS Letter Rulings, Full Text - Letter Ruling Service, *1,148*
IRT: Issues, Review, & Tracking - Energy Newsbrief, *353*
ISAM Newsletter - Newsletter, Institute for Studies in American Music, *915*
ISDN Report - Bandwidth Report, *1,156*
ISIS Report - ISRI Report, *891*
ISS Letter - TAISSA Letter, *1,189*
ITIC Newsletter - Tsunami Newsletter, *937*
I.T.M. News - Tracks, *549*
IWY/TP Newsletter - Tribune, *1,212*
Idaho Aviation Report - Rudder Flutter, *32*

S

At Martin/Arnold everything we do is Big...

Big sizes

Big service

Big quality

Big smile

CACTUS Color Prints
UP TO
54"x44"

TYPE 'C' Color Prints & DURA TRANSparencies
UP TO
72"x120"

B&W MURALS
UP TO
50"x96"

IRIS Prints
UP TO
30"x40"

only our prices are little.

MARTIN/ARNOLD COLOR SYSTEMS, INC.
CREATIVE COMPUTER GRAPHICS
150 FIFTH AVENUE, NEW YORK, NY 10011
PHONE 212 • 675 • 7270
FAX/MODEM 212 • 633 • 1020

ODN 96

BUSINESS REPLY MAIL
FIRST CLASS PERMIT NO. 07644 NEW YORK, NY

POSTAGE WILL BE PAID BY ADDRESSEE

OXBRIDGE COMMUNICATIONS, INC.
150 Fifth Avenue
New York, NY 10114-0235

ODN 96

BUSINESS REPLY MAIL
FIRST CLASS PERMIT NO. 07644 NEW YORK, NY

POSTAGE WILL BE PAID BY ADDRESSEE

OXBRIDGE COMMUNICATIONS, INC.
150 Fifth Avenue
New York, NY 10114-0235

ODN 96

BUSINESS REPLY MAIL
FIRST CLASS PERMIT NO. 07644 NEW YORK, NY

POSTAGE WILL BE PAID BY ADDRESSEE

OXBRIDGE COMMUNICATIONS, INC.
150 Fifth Avenue
New York, NY 10114-0235